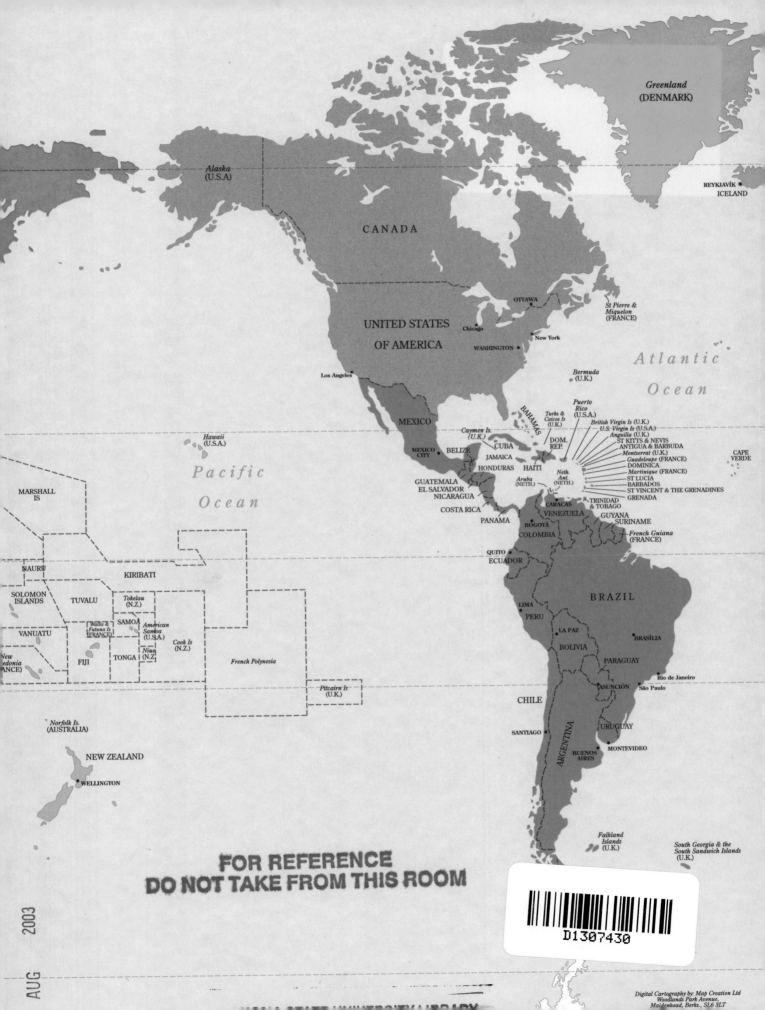

South America
Central America
and the
Caribbean
2002

South America Central America and the Caribbean 2002

10th Edition

EUROPA PUBLICATIONS · Taylor & Francis Group ·

First published 1985

© **Europa Publications 2001**
11 New Fetter Lane, London EC4P 4EE, United Kingdom
(A member of the Taylor & Francis Group)

ISBN 1-85743-121-9
ISSN 0258-0661

Editor: Jacqueline West
Regional Organizations Editors: Catriona Appeatu Holman,
Helen Canton
Statistics Editor: Andrew Thomas
Assistant Editors: Driss Fatih, Lauren Johnston, Colette Milward,
Tiara Misquitta, Alison Neale, Daniel Ward
Contributing Editor (Commodities): Simon Chapman
Editorial Co-ordinator: Mary Hill
Editorial Clerical Assistant: Fiona Vas

Imageset by MPG Dataworld and printed by Unwin Brothers Limited,
The Gresham Press
Old Woking, Surrey

FOREWORD

This 10th edition of SOUTH AMERICA, CENTRAL AMERICA AND THE CARIBBEAN provides a survey of the political and economic life both of the region and of the 48 countries and territories within it. The region, as suggested by the title, contains three distinct geopolitical areas. The South American sub-continent is divided into the territories of Argentina, Bolivia, Brazil, Chile, Colombia, Ecuador, the Falkland Islands, French Guiana, Guyana, Paraguay, Peru, Suriname, Uruguay and Venezuela, although French Guiana, Guyana and Suriname are often regarded as part of the Caribbean.

Five countries of the Central American isthmus (Costa Rica, El Salvador, Guatemala, Honduras and Nicaragua) have many shared historical traditions and have been affected by events within each other's boundaries. At the south of the isthmus, Panama has had a different historical development, and became independent from Colombia only in 1903. At the north-eastern extremity of the isthmus, Belize gained its independence from the United Kingdom in 1981 and, again, is usually considered as a Caribbean country. Mexico, though clearly culturally a 'Latin' American country, is geographically and, increasingly, economically part of North America.

The Caribbean is generally thought of as an island grouping, although frequently it also includes the mainland territories mentioned above. The political statuses of the Caribbean territories range from fully independent countries (e.g. Cuba, the Dominican Republic and Haiti), including independent members of the Commonwealth (e.g. Jamaica and Trinidad and Tobago), to dependencies of France (French Guiana, Guadeloupe and Martinique), the Netherlands (Aruba and the Netherlands Antilles), the United Kingdom (e.g. the Cayman Islands and Montserrat) and the USA (the US Virgin Islands), and finally to Puerto Rico in its 'commonwealth' association with the USA. Although Bermuda is geographically part of North America, it is also included in this book.

Part One consists of nine introductory articles, covering a variety of subjects of regional significance, be it the emergence of trade blocs and the proposed establishment of the Free Trade Area of the Americas in 2005 or an analysis of the implementation of the 'Plan Colombia' as part of the ongoing international effort against drugs in the region. Also included in this edition is an analysis of the banana trade dispute affecting the region, and its resolution. In Part Two, the chapters on major countries in the region include a facts-in-brief page, historical and economic articles written by experts on the countries, a statistical survey, directory and bibliography, while smaller countries are covered in summary accounts, with, for the first time, comprehensive statistical and directory sections. Part Three contains information on the region's major primary commodities and sections on international organizations, research institutes, periodicals and books that are relevant to the region.

August 2001

ACKNOWLEDGEMENTS

The editors gratefully acknowledge the co-operation, interest and enthusiasm for this 10th edition of SOUTH AMERICA, CENTRAL AMERICA AND THE CARIBBEAN which has been shown by the authors who have contributed to the volume. We are also indebted to the many organizations, embassies, high commissions and national statistical and information offices whose kind assistance in providing up-to-date information is greatly appreciated.

We are particularly grateful for permission to make extensive use of material from the following sources: the UN's *Demographic Yearbook, Statistical Yearbook, Industrial Commodity Statistics Yearbook* and *Monthly Bulletin of Statistics*; UNESCO's *Statistical Yearbook*; the FAO's *Production Yearbook, Yearbook of Forest Products* and *Yearbook of Fishery Statistics*; the ILO's *Yearbook of Labour Statistics*; the World Bank's *World Bank Atlas, Global Development Finance, World Development Report* and *World Development Indicators*; the World Tourism Organization's *Yearbook of Tourism Statistics*; and the IMF's monthly *International Financial Statistics,* figures from which have been used in the compilation of the Basic Economic Indicators tables. We are also grateful to the International Institute for Strategic Studies, Arundel House, 13–15 Arundel Street, London WC2R 3DX, for the use of defence statistics from *The Military Balance 2000–2001.*

EXPLANATORY NOTE ON THE DIRECTORY SECTION

The Directory section of each chapter covering a major country is arranged under the following, or similar, headings, where they apply:

THE CONSTITUTION

THE GOVERNMENT
HEAD OF STATE
CABINET/COUNCIL OF MINISTERS
MINISTRIES

LEGISLATURE

POLITICAL ORGANIZATIONS

DIPLOMATIC REPRESENTATION

JUDICIAL SYSTEM

RELIGION

THE PRESS

PUBLISHERS

BROADCASTING AND COMMUNICATIONS
TELECOMMUNICATIONS
RADIO
TELEVISION

FINANCE
CENTRAL BANK
STATE BANKS
DEVELOPMENT BANKS
COMMERCIAL BANKS
FOREIGN BANKS
BANKING ASSOCIATIONS
STOCK EXCHANGES
INSURANCE

TRADE AND INDUSTRY
GOVERNMENT AGENCIES
DEVELOPMENT ORGANIZATIONS
CHAMBERS OF COMMERCE
INDUSTRIAL AND TRADE ASSOCIATIONS
EMPLOYERS' ASSOCIATIONS
MAJOR COMPANIES
UTILITIES
TRADE UNIONS

TRANSPORT
RAILWAYS
ROADS
SHIPPING
CIVIL AVIATION

TOURISM

DEFENCE

EDUCATION

CONTENTS

CONTENTS

CONTENTS

PART THREE
Regional Information

THE CONTRIBUTORS

Dr Edmund Amann. Lecturer in Development Studies, University of Manchester.

Luciano Baracco. Researcher on Central America at the University of Bradford.

David Battman. Writer specializing in Latin American affairs.

Andrew Bounds. Central America correspondent of the *Financial Times*.

Dr David Browning. Fellow of St Cross College, University of Oxford, and Registrar, Oxford Centre for Islamic Studies.

Dr Julia Buxton. Lecturer in Politics at Kingston University and consultant in Venezuelan affairs.

Prof. Peter A. R. Calvert. Professor of Comparative and International Politics at the University of Southampton.

Prof. Paul Cammack. Professor in the Department of Government, University of Manchester.

Greg Chamberlain. Journalist specializing in Caribbean affairs and Editor of *Haiti-Hebdo* newsletter.

Dr David Corkill. Formerly Senior Lecturer in Spanish and Portuguese, University of Leeds.

James Ferguson. Writer specializing in Caribbean affairs.

Dr M. H. J. Finch. Lecturer in Economic History, University of Liverpool.

Lila Haines. Economic historian and business journalist specializing in the Cuban economy.

Canute James. Caribbean correspondent of the *Financial Times*.

Melanie Jones. Writer and researcher specializing in Cuban affairs.

Michael Kuczynski. Fellow and Director of Studies in Economics, Pembroke College, University of Cambridge.

Prof. Adrian McDonald. Professor of Environmental Management, University of Leeds.

James McDonough. Editor and Publisher at EPIN Publishing, including *The Puerto Rico Report* newsletter.

Sandy Markwick. Writer and researcher specializing in Latin American affairs.

Prof. Kenneth N. Medhurst. Professor Associate, University of Sheffield, Senior Research Associate, the Von Hugel Institute, St Edmund's College, University of Cambridge, and Canon Theologian, Anglican Diocese of Bradford.

Sir Keith Morris. Former British Ambassador to Colombia.

Philip J. O'Brien. Senior Lecturer in the Department of Sociology, University of Glasgow.

Dr Gabriel Palma. Lecturer in Economics, University of Cambridge.

Prof. A. J. Payne. Professor of Politics, University of Sheffield.

Prof. Jenny Pearce. Professor of Latin American Politics at the University of Bradford.

Dr George Philip. Lecturer in the Government Department, London School of Economics and Political Science.

Rod Prince. Journalist specializing in Caribbean affairs and Editor of *Caribbean Insight*.

Helen Schooley. Writer specializing in Latin American affairs.

Prof. Clifford T. Smith. Former Director of the Centre of Latin American Studies, University of Liverpool.

Prof. A. E. Thorndike. Formerly Senior Lecturer at the Graduate School of International Studies at the University of Birmingham.

Jo Tuckman. Freelance journalist specializing in Mexican and Central American affairs.

René van Dongen. Geographer and Vice-Principal of the School of the Nations, Georgetown, Guyana.

Phillip Wearne. Writer and researcher specializing in Latin American affairs.

Mark Wilson. Writer and researcher specializing in Caribbean affairs.

ABBREVIATIONS

Abog.	Abogado
AC	Acre
Acad.	Academician; Academy
Adm.	Admiral
admin.	administration
AG	Aktiengesellschaft (Joint Stock Company)
Ags	Aguascalientes
a.i.	ad interim
AID	(US) Agency for International Development
AIDS	acquired immunodeficiency syndrome
AK	Alaska
AL	Alabama, Alagoas
ALADI	Asociación Latino-Americana de Integración
Alt.	Alternate
AM	Amazonas; Amplitude Modulation
amalg.	amalgamated
AP	Amapá
Apdo	Apartado (Post Box)
approx.	approximately
Apt	Apartment
Apto	Apartamento
AR	Arkansas
asscn	association
assoc.	associate
asst	assistant
Aug.	August
auth.	authorized
Ave	Avenue
Av., Avda	Avenida (Avenue)
AZ	Arizona
BA	Bahia
BCN	Baja California Norte
BCS	Baja California Sur
Bd	Board
Blvd	Boulevard
b/d	barrels per day
Bldg	Building
BP	Boîte Postale (Post Box)
br.(s)	branch(es)
Brig.	Brigadier
BTN	Brussels Tariff Nomenclature
C	Centigrade
c.	*circa*; cuadra(s) (block(s))
CA	California; Compañía Anónima
CACM	Central American Common Market
Camp.	Campeche
cap.	capital
Capt.	Captain
CARICOM	Caribbean Community and Common Market
CCL	Caribbean Congress of Labour
Cdre	Commodore
CE	Ceará
Cen.	Central
CEO	Chief Executive Officer
cf.	confer (compare)
Chair.	Chairman
Chih.	Chihuahua
Chis	Chiapas
Cia, Cía	Companhia, Compañía
Cie	Compagnie
c.i.f.	cost, insurance and freight
C-in-C	Commander-in-Chief
circ.	circulation
CIS	Commonwealth of Independent States
cm	centimetre(s)
CMEA	Council for Mutual Economic Assistance
Cnr	Corner
CO	Colorado
Co	Company
Coah.	Coahuila
Col	Colonel
Col.	Colima, Colonia
Comecon	Council for Mutual Economic Assistance (CMEA)
Comm.	Commission
Commdr	Commander

Commdt	Commandant
Commr	Commissioner
Confed.	Confederation
Cont.	Contador
Corpn	Corporation
CP	Case Postale; Caixa Postal (Post Box)
Cres.	Crescent
CSTAL	Confederación Sindical de los Trabajadores de América Latina
CT	Connecticut
CTCA	Confederación de Trabajadores Centro-americanos
Cttee	Committee
cu	cubic
cwt	hundredweight
DC	District of Columbia, Distrito Central
DE	Delaware, Departamento Estatal
Dec.	December
Del.	Delegación
Dem.	Democratic; Democrat
Dep.	Deputy
dep.	deposits
Dept	Department
devt	development
DF	Distrito Federal
Dgo	Durango
Diag.	Diagonal
Dir	Director
Div.	Division
DN	Distrito Nacional
Dr(a)	Doctor(a)
Dr.	Drive
dpto	departamento
dwt	dead weight tons
E	East, Eastern
EC	Eastern Caribbean; European Community
ECCB	Eastern Caribbean Central Bank
ECLAC	(United Nations) Economic Commission for Latin America and the Caribbean
Econ.	Economist
ECOSOC	(United Nations) Economic and Social Council
ECU	European Currency Unit
Ed.(s)	Editor(s)
Edif.	Edificio (building)
edn	edition
EEC	European Economic Community
EFTA	European Free Trade Association
e.g.	exempli gratia (for example)
eKv	electron kilovolt
eMv	electron megavolt
Eng.	Engineer; Engineering
ES	Espírito Santo
Esc.	Escuela; Escudos; Escritorio
esq.	esquina (corner)
est.	established; estimate, estimated
etc.	et cetera
eV	eingetragener Verein
EU	European Union
excl.	excluding
exec.	executive
Ext.	Extension
F	Fahrenheit
f.	founded
FAO	Food and Agriculture Organization
Feb.	February
Fed.	Federation; Federal
FL	Florida
FM	frequency modulation
Fri.	Friday
fmrly	formerly
f.o.b.	free on board
Fr	Father
Fr.	Franc
ft	foot (feet)
g	gram(s)

ABBREVIATIONS

GA	Georgia		Man.	Manager; managing
GATT	General Agreement on Tariffs and Trade		MD	Maryland
GDP	gross domestic product		ME	Maine
Gen.	General		mem.	member
GM	genetically modified		MEV	mega electron volt
GmbH	Gesellschaft mit beschränkter Haftung (Limited Liability Company)		Méx.	México
			mfrs	manufacturers
GMT	Greenwich Mean Time		MG	Minas Gerais
GNP	gross national product		Mgr	Monseigneur; Monsignor
GO	Goiás		MHz	megahertz
Gov.	Governor		MI	Michigan
Govt	Government		Mich.	Michoacán
Gro	Guerrero		Mlle	Mademoiselle
grt	gross registered tons		mm	millimetre(s)
GSP	Global Social Product		Mme	Madame
Gto	Guanajuato		MN	Minnesota
gWh	gigawatt hours		MO	Missouri
			Mon.	Monday
ha	hectares		Mor.	Morelos
HE	His (or Her) Eminence; His (or Her) Excellency		MP	Member of Parliament
			MS	Mato Grosso do Sul; Mississippi
Hgo	Hidalgo		MSS	Manuscripts
HGV	Heavy goods vehicle		MT	Montana
HI	Hawaii		MW	megawatt(s); medium wave
HIPC	heavily indebted poor country		MWh	megawatt hour(s)
HIV	human immunodeficiency virus			
hl	hectolitre(s)		N	North, Northern
HM	His (or Her) Majesty		n.a.	not available
Hon.	Honorary (or Honourable)		NAFTA	North American Free Trade Agreement
HQ	Headquarters		Nat.	National
HRH	His (or Her) Royal Highness		NATO	North Atlantic Treaty Organisation
			Nay.	Nayarit
IA	Iowa		NC	North Carolina
ibid.	ibidem (in the same place)		NCO	Non-Commissioned Officer
IBRD	International Bank for Reconstruction and Development (World Bank)		ND	North Dakota
			NE	Nebraska
ICC	International Chamber of Commerce		NGO	Non-governmental organization
ICFTU	International Confederation of Free Trade Unions		NH	New Hampshire
			NJ	New Jersey
ID	Idaho		NL	Nuevo León
IDA	International Development Association		NM	New Mexico
IDB	Inter-American Development Bank		NMP	net material product
i.e.	id est (that is to say)		No(.)	number, número
IGAD	Intergovernmental Authority on Development		Nov.	November
IL	Illinois		nr	near
ILO	International Labour Organisation		nrt	net registered tons
IMF	International Monetary Fund		NV	Naamloze Vennootschap (Limited Company); Nevada
IN	Indiana			
in (ins)	inch (inches)		NY	New York
Inc.	Incorporated			
incl.	including		OAS	Organization of American States
Ind.	Independent		Oax.	Oaxaca
Ing.	Engineer		Oct.	October
Insp.	Inspector		OECD	Organization for Economic Co-operation and Development
Inst.	Institute, Instituto			
Int.	International		OECS	Organization of East Caribbean States
IRF	International Road Federation		Of.	Oficina
irreg.	irregular		OH	Ohio
Is	Islands		OK	Oklahoma
ISIC	International Standard Industrial Classification		OPEC	Organization of Petroleum Exporting Countries
			op. cit.	opere citato (in the work quoted)
Jal.	Jalisco		opp.	opposite
Jan.	January		OR	Oregon
Jr	Junior		Org.	Organization
Jt	Joint		ORIT	Organización Regional Interamericana de Trabajadores
kg	kilogram(s)			
kHz	Kilohertz		oz	troy ounces
km	kilometre(s)			
KS	Kansas		p.	page
kW	kilowatt(s)		PA	Pará, Pennsylvania
kWh	kilowatt hours		p.a.	per annum
KY	Kentucky		Parl.	Parliament(ary)
			PB	Paraíbo
LA	Louisiana		PC	Privy Counsellor
lb	pound(s)		PE	Pernambuco
LIBOR	London Inter-Bank Offered Rate		Perm. Rep.	Permanent Representative
Lic.	Licenciado		PI	Pianí
Licda	Licenciada		pl.	place
LNG	liquefied natural gas		PLC	Public Limited Company
LPG	liquefied petroleum gas		PMB	Private Mail Bag
Lt, Lieut	Lieutenant		POB	Post Office Box
Ltd, Ltda	Limited, Limitada		pp.	pages
			PR	Paraná
m	metre(s)		PREF	Poverty Reduction and Growth Facility
m.	million		Pres.	President
MA	Maranhão; Massachusetts		Prin.	Principal
Maj.	Major		Prof.	Professor
			Propr	Proprietor

ABBREVIATIONS

Prov.	Province; Provincial
Pte	Private
Pty	Proprietary
p.u.	paid up
publ.	publication; published
Publr(s)	Publisher(s)
Pue.	Puebla
Pvt.	Private
Q. Roo	Quintaya Roo
QC	Queen's Counsel
q.v.	quod vide (to which refer)
Qro	Querétaro
Rd	Road
reg., regd	register; registered
reorg.	reorganized
Rep.	Republic; Republican; Representative
Repub.	Republic
res	reserve(s)
retd	retired
Rev.	Reverend
RI	Rhode Island
RJ	Rio de Janeiro
Rm	Room
RN	Rio Grande do Norte
RO	Rondônia
RR	Roraima
RS	Rio Grande do Sul
Rt	Right
S	South; Southern; San
SA	Société Anonyme, Sociedad Anónima (limited company)
SARL	Sociedade Anônima de Responsabilidade Limitada (Joint Stock Company of Limited Liability)
Sat.	Saturday
SC	Santa Catarina, South Carolina
SD	South Dakota
SDR(s)	Special Drawing Right(s)
Sec.	Secretary
Sen.	Senior; Senator
Sept.	September
Sgt	Sergeant
Sin.	Sinaloa
SITC	Standard International Trade Classification
SJ	Society of Jesus
SLP	San Luis Potosí
s/n	sin número (no number)
Soc.	Society
Son.	Sonora
SP	São Paulo
Sq.	Square
sq	square (in measurements)
Sr	Senior; Señor
Sra	Señora
St(s)	Saint(s); Street(s)
Sta	Santa
Ste	Sainte
subs.	subscriptions; subscribed

Suc.	Sucursal
Sun.	Sunday
Supt	Superintendent
Tab.	Tabasco
Tamps	Tamaulipas
Tce	Terrace
tech., techn.	technical
tel.	telephone
Thurs.	Thursday
TJ	tetrajoule
Tlax.	Tlaxcala
TN	Tennessee
TO	Tocatins
Treas.	Treasurer
Tue.	Tuesday
TV	television
TX	Texas
u/a	unit of account
UEE	Unidade Ecónomica Estatal
UK	United Kingdom
UN	United Nations
UNCED	United Nations Conference on Environment and Development
UNCTAD	United Nations Conference on Trade and Development
UNDP	United Nations Development Programme
UNESCO	United Nations Educational, Scientific and Cultural Organization
UNHCR	United Nations High Commissioner for Refugees
Univ.	University
USA (US)	United States of America (United States)
USAID	United States Agency for International Development
USSR	Union of Soviet Socialist Republics
Urb.	Urbanización (urban district)
UT	Utah
VA	Virginia
VAT	Value-Added Tax
v-CJD	variant Creutzfeldt-Jakob disease
Ver.	Veracruz
VHF	Very High Frequency
VI	(US) Virgin Islands
viz.	videlicet (namely)
vol.(s)	volume(s)
W	West; Western
WA	Washington
WCL	World Confederation of Labour
Wed.	Wednesday
WFTU	World Federation of Trade Unions
WHO	World Health Organization
WI	Wisconsin
WTO	World Trade Organization
WV	West Virginia
WY	Wyoming
yr	year
Yuc.	Yucatán

INTERNATIONAL TELEPHONE CODES

These codes must be added to the relevant telephone and fax numbers listed in the directory sections. The code and number must be preceded by the International Dialling Code of the country from which you are calling.

Anguilla	1264
Antigua and Barbuda	1268
Argentina	54
Aruba	297
The Bahamas	1242
Barbados	1246
Belize	501
Bermuda	1441
Bolivia	591
Brazil	55
British Virgin Islands	1284
Cayman Islands	1345
Chile	56
Colombia	57
Costa Rica	506
Cuba	53
Dominica	1767
Dominican Republic	1809
Ecuador	593
El Salvador	503
Falkland Islands	500
French Guiana	594
Grenada	1473
Guadeloupe	590
Guatemala	502
Guyana	592
Haiti	509
Honduras	504
Jamaica	1876
Martinique	596
Mexico	52
Montserrat	1664
Netherlands Antilles	599
Nicaragua	505
Panama	507
Paraguay	595
Peru	51
Puerto Rico	1787
Saint Christopher and Nevis	1869
Saint Lucia	1758
Saint Vincent and the Grenadines	1784
Suriname	597
Trinidad and Tobago	1868
Turks and Caicos Islands	1649
US Virgin Islands	1340
Uruguay	598
Venezuela	58

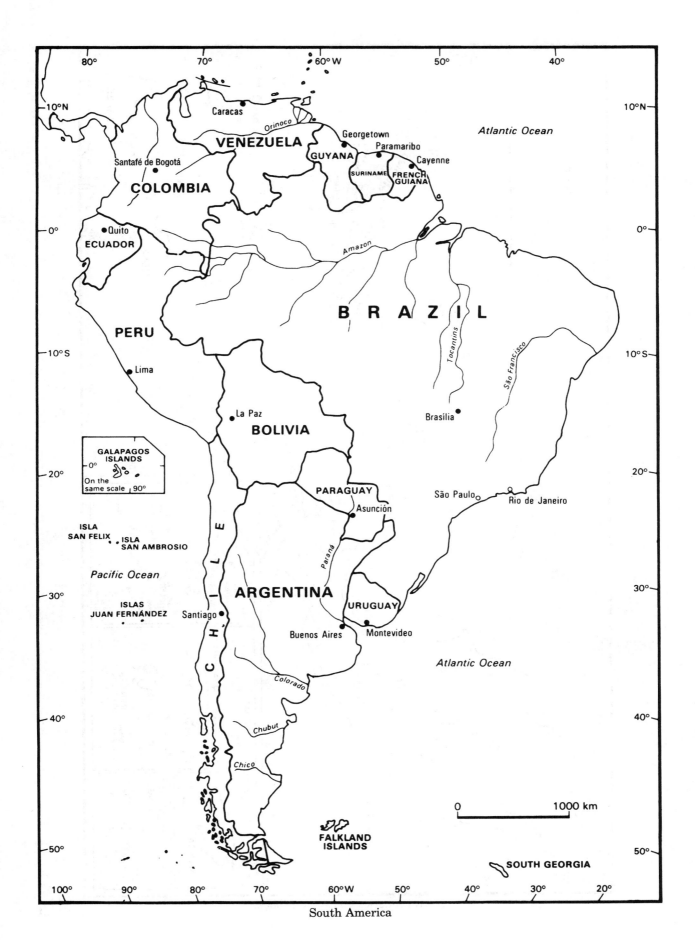

South America

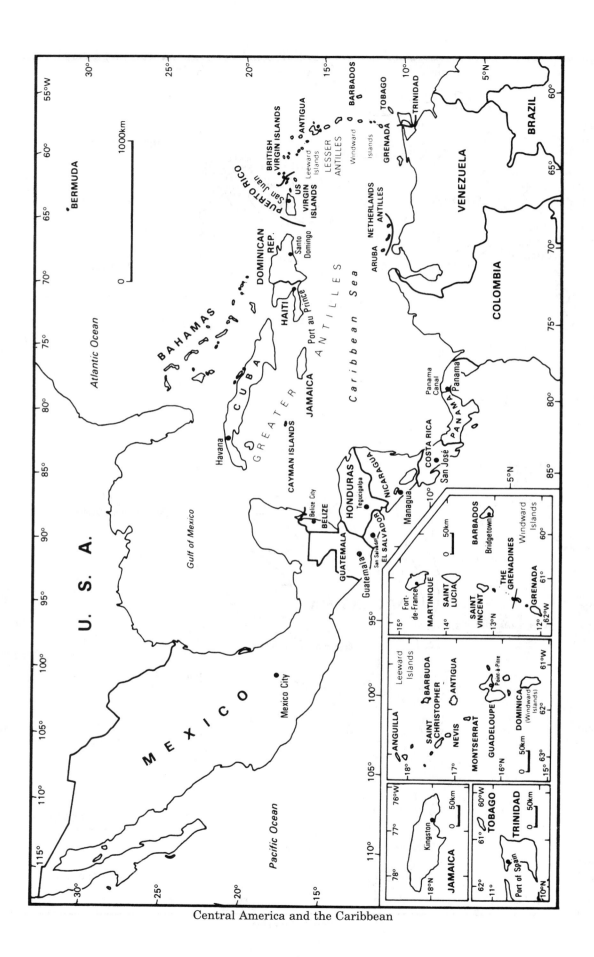

Central America and the Caribbean

xvi

PART ONE
General Survey

LATIN AMERICA: AN INTRODUCTION

Prof. PETER CALVERT

FORCES FOR CHANGE

For Latin America, the 20th century was a century of early promise unfulfilled. The century began well with the gradual consolidation of relatively democratic government and the acceptance of the major states as equal partners in the emerging world community. However, the onset of the Great Depression in 1930 was followed by decades of dictatorship. The promise of the Atlantic Charter soon gave way to the fear of revolutionary change following the onset of the 'Cold War'. Yet the revolutionary model advocated by Cuba and widely imitated by left-wing movements throughout the region failed, in turn, to justify expectations. Instead, the 1970s and 1980s saw the imposition of a military rule unchecked by democratic control or even sentiments of common humanity.

Military rule was justified by some on the grounds of efficiency. A strong, authoritarian government, it was argued, could do what divided civilian governments had allegedly failed to do, that is, to bring about the effective modernization of their country. However, lacking the discipline of public opinion, military government proved both inefficient and grossly corrupt. Even in the few countries with a civilian government expectations had outrun capacity, and in 1982 Mexico's failure to keep up national-debt repayments gave the world a new term: the debt crisis. For Latin America, the 1980s were a lost decade as inward investment almost ceased. One by one, the armed forces abdicated control, leaving civilian governments to attempt to resolve the complex of problems that their indebtedness entailed, without causing irreparable damage to the delicate fabric of democracy.

The Latin America of the 21st century, however, is going to be noticeably different from what has gone before. Three main forces are shaping it: globalization, integration and democratization.

GLOBALIZATION

The integration of Latin America into the world system began with the arrival in 1492 of the Spanish expedition led by Christopher Columbus. This, in turn, was followed by the conquest and settlement of the Caribbean islands and the coastal regions of the mainland. It took a long time. Peru was not effectively subdued for 80 years, Tayasal in Guatemala did not fall to the Spaniards until 1697 and the areas south of Buenos Aires in what is now Argentina and the River Bío-Bío in Chile were not conquered until well after independence.

For four centuries the Spanish Empire formed a single trading bloc dedicated to the principles of mercantilism. Between 1582 and 1640 the King of Spain was also King of Portugal and the two Empires were united under one ruler, though economic integration was never complete. With independence, however, came a long period of hostility between the former colonies and Spain. At the same time, the new states defined their own identity in relation to one another by emphasizing their differences rather than their similarities. The rising tide of nationalism soon fragmented the former Spanish Empire beyond repair. By contrast, Portuguese America—Brazil—remained unified, first as an Empire and then as a Republic (1889).

The newly independent states therefore each sought to establish their own links with other major powers. Several of these already had been able to establish a significant colonial presence in the Caribbean. Throughout the 19th century European intervention in the region therefore remained a possibility, though in practice British naval power made it unlikely. The rise of the USA, and its insistence on the separateness of the Western hemisphere (the Monroe Doctrine), helped to prolong the isolation of Latin America. However, the expansionism of the USA (Manifest Destiny), if briefly checked by the American Civil War, led to war with Spain in 1898. It was this war that signalled the emergence of the USA as the hegemonic power in the region.

After 1945 the victorious powers of the Second World War, led by the USA, created a new set of world institutions, both political and financial. The effectiveness of the United Nations (UN) as a political force for stability was repeatedly frustrated by the Cold War and the rivalry between the superpowers. Latin America and the Caribbean were no longer on the periphery. In 1961 Soviet influence was successfully consolidated in Cuba and, in the following year, the resolution of the Cuban missile crisis left the island the only country in the world with the armed forces of both superpowers on its national territory. Meanwhile, the struggle for influence in the region took on both a military and an economic form, aimed both at civil war and at the causes of civil war.

Globalization took many forms. The new world financial institutions increasingly came to impose a set of common standards against which success was to be measured. In practice, countries could no longer 'shop around' for foreign investment. The International Monetary Fund (IMF) set the terms ('conditionality') on which it would lend and private banks were not prepared to compete with it. As communications rapidly improved, Latin American leaders sought safety in numbers, so projects for regional and subregional integration multiplied.

INTEGRATION

After independence the dream of unity had persisted, and it was not confined to the Spanish-speaking territories. Simón Bolívar, the Liberator, summoned a meeting of other American states to meet at Panama in 1826. However, only four countries, including the USA, sent delegates to the Congress of Panama and not all arrived in time. Other Congresses of Latin American states later in the century helped lay the foundations of what was later to become known as the Inter-American System. Under the leadership of the USA these Congresses were formalized as an organization known, from 1910, as the Pan-American Union, based in the US capital, Washington, DC. In 1948 this grouping was converted into a regional organization, the Organization of American States (OAS).

Integration in Latin America, therefore, whether economic or political, is not a new idea. However, it first became really effective at subregional level. Following the end of the Cold War and the collapse of the USSR, there were important new developments on a subregional level. For the new century the leaders of the American states have set themselves an even more ambitious target, that of achieving free trade throughout the Western hemisphere by 2005. How realistic is this, and how is it to be achieved?

ECONOMIC INTEGRATION

The idea of economic integration can be traced back to the imperial dream of a single trading bloc for the entire region. However, its modern equivalent is very much a product of the modern, post-Second World War world. Creation of a Latin American Free Trade Area (LAFTA, or Área Latinoamericana de Libre Cambio—ALALC) was envisaged by the UN Economic Commission for Latin America (ECLA or Comisión Económica por América Latina—CEPAL) as early as 1955. ECLA itself was established as part of the UN Organization in 1948, to co-ordinate policies for economic development in Latin America. The Latin American states had wanted a Marshall Plan (European Reconstruction Program, proposed by George C. Marshall, the US Secretary of State) for the region; the USA wanted agreement on a defence treaty, the Rio Pact (for further details see below, under Political Integration). The compromise result was ECLA, which adopted its present title, Economic Commission for Latin America and the Caribbean (ECLAC or the Comisión Económica por América Latina y el Caribe—CEPALC) in 1984. All independent Latin American and Caribbean states are members of it, as are Canada, France, Italy, the Netherlands, Portugal, Spain, the United Kingdom and the USA. Its funds come from two sources: the UN budget and additional voluntary contributions.

ECLAC has two stated purposes: to further the economic growth of Latin America; and to strengthen the economic relations of the region with the rest of the world. This is achieved through studies, the preparation of reports and the annual publication of the *Economic Survey of Latin America*. From the beginning its work and that of its adherents (termed *cepalistas* from the initials of its original title in Spanish) was characterized by a distinctive viewpoint. This was first outlined by the economist Raúl Prebisch in his *Economic Development of Latin America and its Principal Problems* (1949). It took as given the need for state-led economic development, but emphasized the need for the distribution of the fruits of development and the consequent need to plan for the social aspects of development, such as employment and income distribution. In 1962 it established the Latin American Institute for Social and Economic Planning (Instituto Latinoamericano para Planificación Económica y Social—ILPES) at Santiago (Chile) to provide training and advisory services for governments and their officials. Though it was not one of its original purposes, ECLA formed a powerful stimulus for further moves towards regional and subregional integration.

LAFTA, consisting of Mexico and all the states of South America except for Panama, was created by the Treaty of Montevideo of 1960 that came into effect on 1 June 1961. However, because of the very different levels of economic growth of the member states, it failed to achieve its objective of promoting intra-regional trade and, by 1980, only 3% of all trade concessions had been made since the Treaty came into effect. Therefore, by the second Treaty of Montevideo, on 12 August 1980, LAFTA was reconstituted as the Latin American Integration Association (LAIA or the Asociación Latinoamericana de Integración—ALADI). The new organization had the more limited purpose of protecting existing trade arrangements. Its 11 members—10 South American states and Mexico—were divided into three tiers: most developed (Argentina, Brazil, Mexico); intermediate (Chile, Colombia, Peru, Uruguay, Venezuela); and least developed (Bolivia, Ecuador, Paraguay). Even in its new form the success of the organization was disappointing and much greater progress was made towards integration at a subregional level.

The US administrations of President Bill Clinton (1993–2001) revived hopes for pan-American economic integration. Leaders of 34 countries of the Americas convened in Miami (Florida, USA) in December 1994, at Clinton's invitation, to discuss a draft hemispheric free-trade agreement. They agreed to accept in principle a programme of biennial summit meetings that would lead to a convergence of existing trade blocs and to the establishment of a Free Trade Area of the Americas (FTAA) by 2005. In the following year, the 12 presidents of the Rio Group (the permanent organization established in 1987, which succeeded the *ad hoc* Contadora Group), reaffirming their commitment to democracy and the elimination of corruption, asserted their support for the proposal. Elsewhere there was some concern that successful subregional co-operation might be prejudiced. Hence formal negotiations did not begin until the Second Summit of the Americas at Santiago in March 1998. No agreement on the order of negotiations was reached. Nevertheless, the Third Summit of the Americas, held in Québec (Canada), in April 2001 reaffirmed the target date of 2005.

SUBREGIONAL ORGANIZATIONS

The first major subregional organization to emerge was the Andean Pact or Andean Group (Grupo Andino or Acuerdo de Cartagena), originally known as the Andean Subregional Integration Agreement. The Group took its Spanish name from the Treaty of Cartagena, signed at Cartagena de Indias (Colombia) by the Governments of Bolivia, Chile, Colombia, Ecuador and Peru on 26 May 1969. In February 1973 Venezuela joined the organization, but Chile withdrew from it on 21 January 1977, officially because of its hostility to foreign capital. However, in reality, it was because of the other members' criticism of, and unwillingness to work with, the dictatorial regime of Gen. Augusto Pinochet Ugarte. Even after the Mandate of Cartagena of May 1979, which advocated greater political and economic co-operation, local disputes continued to disrupt the working of the Group.

The purpose of the Andean Group was to promote economic integration between the member states, by progressive elimination of tariff barriers and the co-ordination of industrial development. Intra-Group trade grew significantly after its formation. The supreme authority of the Group was the Commission, made up of one ambassador from each member state. Foreign ministers met annually or as required to formulate external policy. The Andean Parliament (Parlamento Andino) of five members from each state had a purely advisory role, but the Court of Justice, established in 1984, settled disputes arising under the Treaty.

The Andean Pact led to the reduction of many tariffs and to some increase in intra-regional trade. Dissatisfaction with the rate of progress towards integration, however, led to the decision, taken at a summit meeting held in Cuzco (Peru) on 22–23 May 1990, to achieve free trade in goods by 1995. At a summit meeting in Venezuela in May 1991 heads of government approved the Declaration of Caracas, committing the five states to a free-trade zone by January 1992 and reaffirming the goal of a fully integrated common market by 1995. A military-backed coup in Peru by President Alberto Fujimori Keinya in April 1992, however, threatened to bring the whole process of integration to a halt when Peru withdrew temporarily from the Pact. Nevertheless, in March 1993 the other four of the five member states agreed to establish a customs union. In October tariffs were abolished altogether between three of the member states, Bolivia, Colombia and Ecuador. Peru subsequently rejoined the Pact, though it did not take part in negotiations leading to the creation of the unified market on 1 January 1995, and was not due to participate in the free-trade zone until mid-1996. In March 1996 an agreement was signed, in Trujillo (Peru), to restructure the Pact into an Andean Community of Nations (Comunidad Andina de Naciones—CAN), thus strengthening regional integration. However, after the recurrence of border conflict with Ecuador, in April 1997 Peru announced its intention to withdraw from the Community and failed to be represented at the summit meeting held in Sucre (Ecuador) that month. In the late 1990s, with Venezuela in economic crisis and Colombia affected by civil war, the Andean Community lost momentum. Two of its members, Chile and Bolivia, began to seek other ties and, in May 1999, the decision by the new Venezuelan Government of Lt-Col Hugo Chávez Frías to close its frontier to Colombian long-haul lorries for one year was a clear breach of community rules.

Nevertheless, the Andean Pact inspired, in turn, the Amazon Co-operation Treaty (Amazon Pact), signed in 1978, which was intended to promote the harmonious development of the Amazonian territories of Bolivia, Brazil, Colombia, Ecuador, Guyana, Peru, Suriname and Venezuela. Owing to the vast size of the region and the mutual suspicions of the countries involved, the agreement has had very little effect, although by entering into closer ties with Guyana, Brazil effectively checked Venezuela's ambitions to annex the Essequibo region and began the process of opening up direct road links to the Guyanan capital of Georgetown. In December 1995 the foreign ministers of the member states agreed to establish a regional secretariat in Brasília (Brazil) and signed the Lima Declaration on sustainable development.

Integration in the Southern Cone has been much more successful. On 26 March 1991 the Presidents of Argentina, Brazil, Paraguay and Uruguay, meeting at Asunción (Paraguay), signed an agreement, the Treaty of Asunción, to create a new common market in the Southern Cone, with its headquarters in Montevideo (Uruguay). This was followed by a 47% reduction in tariffs in June of the same year and the signature of a framework free-trade agreement with the USA. The new grouping, the Southern Common Market (Mercado Común del Sur—Mercosur or, in Portuguese, Mercado Comum do Sul—Mercosul), formed a natural development in view of the geographical unity of the Paraguay-Paraná Basin and a long series of bilateral accords, but its targets were exceptionally ambitious. With an estimated population in 1991 of over 190m. and a combined gross national product (GNP) of some US $550,000m., from the beginning it aimed to achieve free movement of goods and services by 31 December 1994. Despite all difficulties, agreement was reached on the twin problems of the common external tariff and trade imbalances. The customs union was formally inaugurated on 1 January 1995, on schedule, and, from the beginning, there was a marked increase in intra-regional trade. In March 2000 Argentina and Brazil reached agreement on their major point of dispute, trade in motor vehicles, and agreed to defer long-standing disputes on footwear, pigs, poultry, steel, sugar and textiles, thus opening the way for enlargement.

From the beginning both Bolivia and Chile made it clear that they did not want to be excluded from Mercosur. None the less, the eighth summit, held at Asunción on 5 August 1995, attended by the Presidents of Bolivia and Chile, resolved to admit neither country for the time being. However, at the ninth summit at Punta del Este (Uruguay) on 7 December, it was agreed to establish a free-trade zone with Bolivia and extend current bilateral agreements with Chile until March 1996. Following expiry of this deadline, agreement was reached on both Chile's physical integration (to provide a number of specified points of access) and its initial tariff regime, under which it could enter into associate status. At the 10th summit meeting, held in San Luís (Argentina) on 25 June 1996, Chile was admitted as an associate member with effect from 1 October. A framework free-trade agreement was also approved for Bolivia which would provide it with guaranteed access to both Atlantic and Pacific ports from 1997, and in June 2000 Chile announced its decision to seek full membership of Mercosur.

The other major issue facing Mercosur was relations with other groups and with the USA. In January 1995 foreign ministers of the Andean Pact countries, meeting at Santa Cruz de la Sierra (Bolivia), agreed to seek a free-trade agreement with Mercosur by 30 June. At the Seventh Ibero-American Summit, held on 8–9 November 1997 in Venezuela, and attended by 23 heads of state and government, representatives of the Andean Community and Mercosur agreed in principle to form a single trading bloc. In September 1996, at a meeting in Montevideo (Uruguay), the Mercosur countries concluded a co-operation agreement with the European Union (EU), signed in Madrid on 20 December, which envisaged a future free-trade zone incorporating both blocs. Furthermore, in 1999 the EU and Mercosur agreed to initiate discussions with a view to forming an integrated trading bloc some time after 2001.

Meanwhile, as noted above, there were important developments also in North America. In January 1988 the USA and Canada signed a Free Trade Agreement. Soon after the accession of Carlos Salinas de Gortari to the presidency of Mexico, in December of the same year, negotiations were opened for Mexico to join the Agreement. Negotiations were held between Canada, Mexico and the USA in February 1992, at which the US and Mexican delegations announced an Integrated Border Plan, by which the two Governments would work to clear environmental damage along their common frontier. These negotiations resulted in the completion of a draft treaty for a North American Free Trade Agreement (NAFTA). Mexico initialled the pact on 12 August 1993 and it was signed on 17 December, coming into effect on 1 January 1994.

By the beginning of the 21st century subregional projects had demonstrated considerable promise. On the other hand, their very success called into question the more ambitious plans for the FTAA, though technically they remained on course.

POLITICAL INTEGRATION

The Organization of American States (OAS or Organización de los Estados Americanos—OEA) is a multi-functional organization. Although it originated in a series of meetings to discuss commerce and trade, its purpose is to further peace, security, mutual understanding and co-operation among the states of the western hemisphere. With the belated accession of Canada in 1990 and Belize and Guyana in 1992, it had 35 member states (although Cuba's membership has remained in suspension since 1962). Established by Charter at the Ninth Inter-American Conference held at Bogotá (now Santafé de Bogotá, Colombia) in 1948, in 1970 the organization was reconstituted on its present basis by the Protocol of Buenos Aires. The General Assembly, which met for its first regular session at San José (Costa Rica) in 1971, replaced the Inter-American Conferences and various councils for specific purposes. The annual meeting of the General Assembly, a full-scale conference of foreign minis-

ters, is held in different capitals in rotation, but the headquarters, where the Permanent Council sits and Meetings of Consultation of Ministers of Foreign Affairs are normally held, is in Washington, DC. The Permanent Council consists of representatives of each of the member states with the rank of Ambassador, the chair rotating among the representatives in alphabetical order, three months at a time. Although the OAS Charter does allow for a role in international peace-keeping in certain circumstances, the countries of the region were also linked by a separate defence treaty, the Inter-American Treaty for Reciprocal Assistance, commonly known as the Rio Pact, concluded in 1947 as a continuation of wartime co-operation against the Axis Powers and inevitably dominated by the USA.

For many years the OAS fulfilled a useful role in airing current political issues and, through the work of its related agencies, achieving important, though less spectacular, gains for Latin American co-operation. Although derided in some quarters at the time, the pressure by the administration of US President Jimmy Carter (1977–81) for the improvement of human rights had a dramatic effect. It was ultimately to contribute significantly to the restoration of democracy throughout the hemisphere. In 1979 the Inter-American Court of Human Rights was established, with its seat in San José. Then, after the Falklands hostilities of 1982, open conflict between the USA and the majority of the Latin American states, both over this issue and over US policy towards Central America, effectively stultified the political work of the OAS.

After the collapse of the USSR and the end of the Cold War, there was a noticeable *rapprochement* between Latin America and the USA, which was increasingly seen as a model both of democratic government and economic liberalism. This was accompanied by dramatic moves towards closer economic integration in the region. Upon taking office in September 1994, the newly-elected Secretary-General of the OAS, former President César Gaviria Trujillo of Colombia (who was re-elected for a second term in 1999), immediately announced his support for the creation of a single free-trade zone in the Americas. However, the Organization's special role in regional peace-keeping remained primary and, from the end of the 1980s, the notion of collective intervention to maintain democracy was slowly, if reluctantly, accepted.

In a Special Meeting of Consultation held in Washington, DC, on 23 April 1996 foreign ministers successfully resolved to support the elected President of Paraguay against the threat of a 'technical' coup by his Army Commander, Gen. Lino Oviedo. The 26th General Assembly was held in Panama City in June 1996. It was dominated by opposition to the US 'Helms-Burton' legislation, which reinforced the economic blockade of Cuba. A resolution condemning the act was voted against only by the USA. Despite the tensions that remained between the USA and the other states, it was clear that in practice there was a very high level of political co-operation between them, though Cuba's position remained anomalous. At the 20th General Assembly, held in Windsor (Canada) in June 2000, the OAS failed to take effective action against Peru following the disputed re-election of President Fujimori.

DEMOCRATIZATION

The old image of the region as a collection of states ruled by corpulent dictators in comic-opera uniforms is so well established that it is likely to persist for some time yet. However, it is now an anachronism.

After 1930 the greatest threat to democracy came from the dominance of the armed forces. Several major states which had democratic governments by the mid-1990s—countries such as Argentina, Brazil and Chile—had had, until very recently, regimes which seized power by force, and maintained it by force or fraud. In most of them there was a long tradition of seizures of power. Latin American military *coups d'état* were proverbial. Such coups reflected very real problems. They typically tended to occur in adverse economic circumstances, against a background of growing popular discontent for both political and economic reasons.

What is often not realized about Latin America is that there is also a very strong tradition of democracy in the region, a tradition that goes back for over 150 years. The makers of the new nations of the early 19th century were strongly influenced by the liberal ideals of the French Revolution of 1789, and their claim to legitimacy rested upon the support of the people. By 1920 Argentina, Chile, Costa Rica and Uruguay, together with Brazil and Colombia, appeared to have achieved stable government. Accession to power was determined at the ballot box, though still, in most cases, by restricted electorates. In the next few decades these electorates were vastly extended. Despite the crises of the 1930s and the 1960s few governments thereafter failed to gain the endorsement of the people at a poll of some kind.

However, elections are a necessary, but not a sufficient condition of democracy. A working constitution, freedom of speech and of assembly, secret ballots, a fair count and constitutional remedies against infringement of civil rights are all needed as well. Only through the slow acceptance of good standards and the clear determination of the people to obtain them (as in Argentina in 1987, Brazil in 1992 or Mexico in 1997) can democracy be ensured. In short, there has to be some idea of 'civil society' within which citizens can exercise their democratic rights.

Undoubtedly, the main threat to democracy in the region in the 21st century was the international drugs trade and the corruption it brought in its trail. It affected not only the major producers, Colombia, Bolivia and Peru, but also Ecuador and, to a lesser extent, Cuba, Mexico, Panama and Venezuela. Another continuing problem throughout Latin America was that government retrenchment acted to widen the gap between rich and poor, with serious consequences for disadvantaged, particularly indigenous, groups. The persistence of corruption, moreover, inflamed their bitterness.

Though Colombia experienced left-wing guerrilla movements longer than any other country in the region, they never threatened the well-established competitive party system. Indeed, between 1982 and 1986 the Conservative President Dr Belisario Betancur Cuartas had some success in persuading the guerrillas to lay down their arms and re-enter competitive politics. Yet, under Betancur's Liberal successor, Dr Virgilio Barco Vargas (1986–90), political violence erupted again. It was contained, though at a heavy cost in terms of human rights, while rivalry between the two giant illegal drugs syndicates (the larger based in Medellín and a smaller one based in Cali) emerged instead as the most serious threat facing civil society. The creation of a new Constitution in 1991 offered the chance for many of the former armed opposition to find a place in democratic politics. Despite a series of political assassinations within their ranks, some did so and this did not incline the armed forces to intervene openly.

The Government of President Ernesto Samper Pizano (1994–98) represented an all-time low in the credibility of civil government in Colombia. His own reputation never recovered from the arrest, on 27 July 1995, of his election-campaign treasurer, Santiago Medina, on charges of using drugs money in the 1994 campaign. He, in turn, implicated the Minister of Defence, Fernando Botero, who was forced to resign. In September President Samper appeared before a congressional committee to deny any personal association with the drugs cartels, and in December 1995 the committee concluded that there was insufficient evidence to impeach him. Under his successor, Andrés Pastrana Arango, elected in August 1998, Colombia's problems of lawlessness, civil unrest and poverty intensified, despite successive rounds of peace talks with guerrilla groups.

In Venezuela, after a century of dictatorship, the process of transferring power through the ballot box was established only in 1958, largely thanks to the leadership of Rómulo Betancourt and the judicious use of Venezuela's petroleum wealth. Until 1994 Betancourt's Democratic Action (Acción Democrática) and the rival Social Christian Party (Partido Social Cristiano, or Comité de Organización Política Electoral Independiente—COPEI) alternated in power through free elections. As elsewhere, however, the world recession of the early 1980s had an adverse effect and, with the large debt accumulated in the years of prosperity, recovery was painful. In 1993 the incumbent President, Carlos Andrés Pérez (also President 1974–79), was successfully impeached on corruption charges and later imprisoned for two years. He had already become extremely unpopular on account of high unemployment and reductions in public expenditure and two abortive military coups showed the extent of the threat to democracy.

However, Venezuela's political system survived this severe crisis and, in 1994, Dr Rafael Caldera Rodríguez (formerly President 1969–74), though disowned by his party, was returned to the presidency at the head of an independent coalition. In 1998 voters again rejected both the historical political parties which had shared power since 1958. Instead, the nationalist Hugo Chávez Frías was elected President. Chávez had been implicated in two abortive coups against the civilian government in 1992 and had spent time in jail before being pardoned in 1994. Fighting a skilful electoral campaign, Chávez avoided making many political commitments. However, after taking office he successfully rallied support for the election of a new Constituent Assembly and the dissolution of the existing legislature. He even offered to mediate between the Government and rebels in neighbouring Colombia. He won re-election to the presidency in July 2000 and since then has taken vigorous steps to address Venezuela's persistent economic problems.

CONCLUSION

There has certainly been concern about the survival of democracy in other countries also. In Chile, the arrest in the United Kingdom in October 1998 of former President Gen. Augusto Pinochet disclosed the still formidable strength of the authoritarian right and mobilized the armed forces in his defence. However, in January 2000 Chileans peacefully elected Ricardo Lagos Escobar, the first Socialist President to take office since the fall of Dr Salvador Allende in 1973. Furthermore, although in July 2001 Chile's Supreme Court ruled that Pinochet was unfit to stand trial on health grounds, that the due legal processes were observed underlined how far Chilean democracy had come. In March 1999 the President of Paraguay, Raúl Cubas Grau, was forced to resign in the face of dismissal proceedings against him, following the assassination of his Vice-President; and in May 2000 a coup attempt in support of Gen. Oviedo failed (Oviedo was subsequently arrested in Brazil). Serious unrest in Bolivia led to the proclamation of a state of emergency in April 2000. Significantly, in all these cases the Constitution was respected and the political process continued to function.

Even where the constitutional order has clearly been breached, the power of the popular will has been felt. In Ecuador, the verdict of the electorate was set aside when President Abdalá Bucaram Ortiz was successfully impeached in 1997, but in January 2000 a civil-military coup deposed President Jamil Mahuad Witt, because of opposition to the neo-liberal economic measures that he had proposed. In the case of Peru, the re-election of Alberto Fujimori to the presidency in May 2000 was clearly in breach of the constitutional provision against re-election. Discontent was so great that in September he offered to hold fresh elections in which he would not be a candidate, but public disclosure of the corrupt dealings that had kept him in office precipitated his flight from the country and subsequent resignation in November. Results of elections held in Haiti in mid-2000 were also fiercely disputed and international observers refused to monitor the November presidential elections which returned Jean-Bertrand Aristide to the presidency with some 91% of the votes cast.

In the majority of countries, though, power has now been transferred peacefully through competition between civilian parties at democratic elections. The most recent and surprising example was that of Mexico, where the Partido Revolucionario Institucional (PRI—Institutional Revolutionary Party), in power since 1929, was voted out of office in July 2000. Military influence undoubtedly persisted in some places, but the biggest threat to democracy, real or imaginary, came from elected officials or their parties. Latin American states, therefore, have generally proved both willing and able to adapt to the challenges of the 'new world order'. Though prosperity continues to be very unevenly distributed, civil society has been strengthened by the growth and spread of grassroots organizations and the contest for power takes place, broadly speaking, within a constitutional framework.

THE CARIBBEAN: AN OVERVIEW

CANUTE JAMES

INTRODUCTION

The Caribbean began the new millennium preoccupied with many of the concerns that troubled it throughout the 1990s. The region was uncertain about the chances of progress, and even survival, of its small economies in a rapidly changing international economic environment. The strengthening of the bloc created by the partners in the North American Free Trade Agreement (NAFTA) and the end to the existing trade treaty with the European Union (EU) in 2000 made regional governments more aware of the increasing vulnerability of their small economies and of the need for economic co-operation. The region was also being driven towards a more co-operative approach to its economic future through the commitment given by all governments of the Americas (except Cuba, which was not invited to do so) to create a hemispheric free-trade agreement by 2005. Caribbean governments were being forced into increased fiscal constraints, which had adverse effects on living standards. Social infrastructure, such as health and education, were being reduced in the interest of fiscal discipline.

Admitting that there was a need for the region to co-operate and to find strength in numbers, Caribbean leaders indicated a commitment to creating the region's common market by the end of 2002. Previously, economic integration, which was the subject of frequent hyperbole among leaders, was slow and unsteady. The region was in danger of being forgotten in the gathering maelstrom of global economic change. Compared to NAFTA and the emerging Southern Common Market (Mercado Común del Sur—Mercosur, or, in Portuguese, Mercado Comum do Sul—Mercosul), which were set to become the cornerstones of the proposed Free Trade Area of the Americas in 2005, the Caribbean was contemplating changes that endangered future economic stability. Preferential European commodity markets that had supported the region's export sectors, began to be dismantled, as governments moved to meet the terms of their membership of the World Trade Organization (WTO, the successor to the General Agreement on Tariffs and Trade) in the rapid liberalization of trade.

In 2000 the region suffered from continued uncertainty about commodity markets and indications of a slowdown in the US economy. While high petroleum and gas prices assisted producers of these commodities, agricultural, or so-called 'soft', commodity markets remained mainly weak. The ease of the region's passage into the new millennium was being determined by the speed at which it adjusted to economic developments, particularly any downturn in the major industrial economies. After a period of weak prices, some sectors fared better in 2000. Jamaica, for example, increased its bauxite exports to the highest in 15 years. Trinidad and Tobago's energy-based economy, which had slowed down because of low petroleum prices, gathered momentum following petroleum price increases and growing demand for its natural gas, which attracted significant foreign investment. The increasingly hostile trade war between the USA and the countries of the EU over the banana market cost the region's exporters, particularly those islands whose economies were dependent on the fruit. The uncertainty over the market in 2000 led to a decline in banana production in that year. However, prospects for exports of the fruit improved significantly in April 2001 when the USA, the EU and Ecuador, the world's biggest exporter, agreed terms that ended the protracted dispute over access to the EU market. Caribbean exporters were heartened by the pact. The region's sugar exporters were largely unaffected by weak prices, as most had guaranteed markets and rates, far above those of the world market, for their exports under quota to EU member countries and the USA.

By 2000 the region appeared to have overcome the negative effects of the financial crises in Asia in late 1997 and 1998. However, another threat, which had appeared two years earlier, seemed, in 2000, to be causing damage to several small economies. In 1998 the Organisation for Economic Co-operation and Development (OECD), based in Paris (France), included several Caribbean states in a list of countries said to have harmful tax regimes. It demanded a review of the taxation regimes of jurisdictions which appeared to offer an unfair advantage, and which might be open to international financial criminal activity. Many Caribbean offshore financial centres felt threatened by the OECD's plan to list, in 2000, the jurisdictions that it felt were unfairly allowing non-residents to avoid paying tax in their country of residence. After charges from the Caribbean jurisdictions that it was acting unilaterally, the OECD agreed to postpone publication of the list until mid-2001. In April 2001 the Caribbean jurisdictions, described by the OECD as 'tax havens', were encouraged by the decision of the new administration of the USA, which is a member of the OECD, not to support the move to force the jurisdictions to change their tax laws.

With the progressive dismantling of preferential markets for commodities, several Caribbean countries were forced to contemplate fundamental economic restructuring. Most, however, were impeded by an inability to create economies of scale that would allow them to be internationally competitive. High production costs that sometimes exceeded market prices for commodities led some countries to look increasingly at competing in services. Having already established itself in the international tourism market, the region continued to expand other sectors of the service industry, such as information processing and offshore financing.

REGIONAL CO-OPERATION

In the 1990s the Caribbean Community and Common Market (CARICOM) intensified its efforts to improve the region's economic competitiveness through increased co-operation. The organisation was established in 1973, but had made slow progress towards its target of a regional common market. However, these increased efforts were frustrated by concerns that the differing levels of development within the community would put the smaller countries at a disadvantage. CARICOM achieved a major objective in July 1997 with acceptance of Haiti as a full member. Haiti's full membership was formalized in July 1999, bringing CARICOM membership to 15 (the English-speaking countries and territories, including Belize and Guyana, together with Suriname) countries and almost tripling its market to 14m. people. However, as the poorest country in the hemisphere, Haiti's productive resources and buying power were weak, so its effective contribution to CARICOM was limited. The Community also had difficulty in acting collectively on the evolution of a customs union, which had been created in 1984, with the implementation on common tariffs on imports from third countries. Here, also, there were derogations in order to satisfy the concerns of some countries, and signs that some governments were still hesitant in their move towards a common market by 1998. Following CARICOM's failure to achieve this goal, a new target for a common market was set for the end of 2002. At their annual summit in Barbados in July 2001, members agreed that, despite the delays, all of the main elements of the single market would be in place by the end of 2002. This would enable the organization to participate fully in the hemispheric free-trade agreement and to cope with the changes expected in trade relations with EU and NAFTA member countries. In addition to the customs union, in the late 1990s a nascent regional capital market was encouraging cross-listing of stocks on the Barbadian, Jamaican and Trinidadian exchanges. Increasing capital market activity was expected in late 2001 with the creation of a stock exchange in the Leeward and Windward Islands. An exchange is also planned in Guyana.

By the 1990s it had become evident that the Treaty of Chaguaramas, by which CARICOM had been created in 1973, was ill-suited for the demands of the 21st century. The Treaty limited the movement of capital, skills and business in the region and, therefore, was a barrier to greater regional integration. In 1997 a revision of the terms of the Treaty was formally adopted, by means of nine Protocols, in order to incorporate clauses on bilateral investment treaties, intellectual property rights and trade in services. Negotiations on new policies for trade and transportation, agriculture and industry were protracted and sometimes acrimonious. Member countries faced two major obstacles in the establishment of a single market. The first was the different levels of development among members. Gross national product (GNP) per head of about US $7,000 in Barbados in the mid-1990s was more than three times that of Jamaica and almost 25 times that of Haiti. Such disparities were not conducive to agreement on common policies, leading CARICOM to a series of derogations for less endowed economies, and threatening to complicate the establishment of the single market and economy.

The second obstacle was the creation of a common currency, which the region's leaders considered the most difficult challenge in the creation of the single market. Earlier efforts at making the region's currencies freely convertible were impeded by the mix of fixed and floating exchange rates. Although there was some progress in the late 1990s, a delay in the introduction of a common currency until after all other elements of the common market were in place, was the one issue on which the Community agreed. Such a matter demanded the harmonization of complex aspects such as interest rates, which in 2000 varied between 9% in Barbados and 20% in Jamaica. Debt-service ratios would also have to decrease, and there would have to be a certain degree of exchange-rate stability. A further complication was the combination of fixed currencies (the Barbados, Belize and the East Caribbean dollar were all linked to the US dollar) and floating currencies (those of Guyana, Jamaica and Trinidad and Tobago) in operation. A common currency was expected to increase trading on the nascent regional stock exchange. Cross listing of stocks on the exchanges would allow access to the markets from all parts of the Caribbean Community. However, substantial trading would be possible only after the exchanges' technology had improved and a method for early settlement of transactions had been agreed. In early 2001 Trinidad and Tobago followed Barbados and Jamaica in creating a modern securities depository.

The creation of a Caribbean customs union moved closer with the end of licensing requirements for imports from within CARICOM. The deregulation of regional trade proved a difficult issue to resolve. In addition to concerns about likely damage to local industry, governments were concerned that reduced tariffs and more open markets would result in a fall in income from trade taxes, such as customs duties, which were important to the public finances of many countries. Other aspects of potential common market remained controversial. CARICOM leaders were concerned about the highly contentious issue of the free movement of people. Some of the more affluent states feared an influx of unskilled people from poorer countries. It was unlikely that there would be any early agreement on this question. A cautious start was made in 1995, with an agreement that CARICOM nationals who were graduates of recognized universities would not require work permits in any member state. This was intended to allow free movement of skilled professionals. Journalists, entertainers, artists and athletes would also be allowed free movement.

CARICOM also moved towards closer co-operation in transport, with the deregulation of air transport. The 1995 heads of government meeting adopted an air-services agreement that liberalized inter-regional air transport links for all member countries' airlines. This was of benefit to international carriers such as BWIA West Indian Airways of Trinidad and Tobago, Air Jamaica and Suriname Airways (SLM), as well as commuter airlines such as Leeward Islands Air Transport (LIAT-based in Antigua and Barbuda), BWIA Express, Caribbean Star and Helen Air.

THE DECLINE IN FOREIGN AID

While there was some progress in aspects of economic and functional co-operation, at the beginning of the 21st century there continued to be general uncertainty about the region's immediate economic future. Aid levels fell significantly following the end of the Cold War. In 1994 US aid to the CARICOM region was US $24m., 10% of the figure one decade earlier,

according to the Community's Secretariat. It remained at this level thereafter. CARICOM leaders argued, however, that industrialized countries erred in believing that foreign aid represented only assistance to developing countries. There was a mutual benefit, it was suggested, as the developing countries were the major importers of the developed world's products, and the money given as aid effectively returned to the donor's economy.

The Caribbean was also unhappy with aid flows from the EU, the region's other main donor. The Caribbean members of the African, Caribbean and Pacific (ACP) group, which had a trade and aid treaty with the EU, received 90m. European Currency Units (ECU, which was replaced by the euro from 1 January 1999) in aid in 1995–2000, from a total of ECU 13,300m. for the 70 members of the whole ACP group. Regional governments claimed the EU was not fully accounting for the recent expansion of the Caribbean membership of the ACP. Regional officials claimed that although aid from the EU increased, this was more than offset by the expansion in the Caribbean group's population, from 6m. to 20m. with the inclusion of the Dominican Republic and Haiti in 1989.

THE MARKETS FOR CARIBBEAN COMMODITIES

The dilemma facing Caribbean banana exporters indicated the economic dangers that the region faced. Although supporting open markets and deregulated trade, the region attempted to retain its preferred access for bananas to the European market, in the face of persistent attacks by the USA and several Latin American producers. At the centre of the dispute was the new banana import regime of the EU (then still known as the European Community—EC) introduced in July 1993. It favoured imports from the former European colonies, which constituted the ACP group, and established a quota of 2m. metric tons of bananas per year on imports from Latin American countries. This followed the EU's import of 2.6m. metric tons from nine Latin American countries in 1992. US companies operating in Latin America complained to their Government that the EU preferences were discriminatory and unfairly favoured Europe's traditional suppliers. The US Special Trade Representative, in turn, complained to the WTO. Caribbean producers claimed that the USA had reneged on agreements to seek a negotiated solution before taking the matter to the WTO. The WTO upheld the US complaint in 1997 and the EU was given until 1 January 1999 to amend its import regime. Following the EU's failure to satisfy the WTO that its revised import regime complied with international trade regulations, in March 1999 the USA imposed certain trade sanctions against member countries.

In mid-1999 the region's banana producers (mainly the four Windward Island countries, which produced most of the bananas consumed in the United Kingdom) made a fundamental change in their efforts to maintain their EU market. Conceding that the WTO rulings had severely reduced their chances of retaining their preferences, the producers began to seek alterations in the tariff rate quotas used to allocate the EU market. Political leaders and exporters travelled to the USA and EU countries to discuss a new approach to protecting their market. The Caribbean exporters urged the USA and the EU to retain the tariff quota system in whatever amended form the banana-import regime would take. Non-traditional suppliers to the EU, such as those in Latin America, paid a punitive tariff if they exported above their quota to the EU. The Caribbean producers were attempting to obtain a special allotment within the tariff rate. The allotments were 2.5m. metric tons per year for non-traditional suppliers and 857,000 tons per year for the Caribbean and other exporters in the ACP group.

Caribbean producers and Latin American exporters met several times in late 1999 in an attempt to resolve their differences. It appeared, however, that the concessions that were being demanded of the Caribbean states were considered by them to be too severe. In addition, a waiver from the WTO would be required in order for the preferences to continue, and this could only be achieved with help from the US Special Trade Representative. Furthermore, Ecuador, the world's largest banana producer and, therefore, a powerful force in the sector, advocated the deregulation of trade in the fruit. One possibility was a reduction in the island producers' annual allotment and an increase in that of the non-traditional suppliers. Another option was to allow a lower tariff for bananas from non-traditional suppliers (ACP countries would continue to enjoy tariff-free access to the European market) and to abolish quotas. Regional officials suggested that there might also be changes that could favour companies that sold both Caribbean and Latin American bananas.

Nevertheless, Caribbean producers maintained that their product could not compete against cheaper fruit from Latin America. The cost of producing bananas in the islands was about three times that of Latin America. This was the result of the natural handicaps of steep terrain, the limited size of the islands, the small size of farms, poor soils and climatic hazards such as hurricanes. Farm workers on the islands were also paid more than their counterparts in Central and South America. The Windward Islands-Dominica, Grenada, Saint Lucia and Saint Vincent and the Grenadines depended on bananas for about 60% of total export earnings, and the industry was important to the stability of the East Caribbean dollar, the strongest currency in the region.

In 2000 the ACP states agreed to a successor to the trade pact with the EU. This was to run for eight years, allowing the developing countries a period of transition during which they would attempt to reduce their dependence on Europe's preferential markets. However, this agreement also needed a waiver from the WTO, a prospect that worried Caribbean exporters, given the WTO's firm stand against the EU preferences. Nevertheless, the dispute appeared to have been resolved in early 2001 to the satisfaction of all the parties, when the USA agreed to suspend punitive duties it had imposed on imports from the EU. The EU agreed to issue import licences to banana producers based on the history of the volumes of their exports between 1994 and 1996.

The Caribbean's sugar exporters were also uncertain about the future of their lucrative market. There was an acceptance that although the arrangement for marketing sugar would continue following the expiry of the Lomé Convention, the trade treaty between the EU and the ACP, there would be changes. The producers, however, were uncertain how extensive these would be, and they feared that alterations would irreparably damage their market. The producers received about 30 US cents per pound in weight for sugar supplied under quota to the EU. With world market prices at about one-third of this in the 1990s, the EU market kept afloat the sugar industries with high production costs. At the same time, several producers could find it increasingly difficult to retain their valuable US quotas, as Mexico's quota under NAFTA was to increase 30-fold, to 250,000 metric tons, in 2001.

The region's rum market was also anticipating a downturn following changes to the EU market. Caribbean producers asked the EU and the USA to delay the planned liberalization of the market for spirits, to allow the region's industry to adjust to what it claimed would be 'unfair' competition from other producers who benefited from subsidies. In 1996 the USA and the EU agreed to open up the market for white spirits, including rum, by 2003. However, Caribbean producers contended that they needed more time to prevent damage to their industry which supplied Europe, and which employed 10,000 people, with exports of about US $250m. per year. They were particularly concerned about the 'zero for zero' pact between the EU and the USA, which would lead to a reduction in tariffs on spirits and telecommunications. The market for white spirits, including rum, was to be opened up to all producers with the removal of barriers that allowed preferences for the Caribbean producers. The region's producers (which included Barbados, the Dominican Republic, Guyana, Haiti, Jamaica, Trinidad and Tobago, as well as the US possessions of Puerto Rico and the US Virgin Islands) maintained their markets in the USA and Europe would be over-supplied by more competitive products from other countries, mainly in South America and South East Asia.

Caribbean and Central American countries had preferential access to the US market on a range of products under the Caribbean Basin Initiative (CBI), a one-way, duty-free facility initiated in 1984. However, the CBI excluded a range of goods, including apparel, owing to fears in the US textile industry that the market could be flooded by cheap Caribbean imports. Caribbean Basin countries were given apparel export quotas under bilateral treaties with the USA, with set quantities for specified categories of apparel. Most of the region's apparel exports to the USA were produced under an offshore programme, in which garments were assembled from fabric made and cut in the USA, and re-exported to the USA with duty paid on the value added in assembly. An attempt to provide the region with parity with Mexico was repeatedly frustrated in the late 1990s, when legislators in the US capital, Washington, DC, removed the proposals from pending legislation. However, in mid-1999 Caribbean exporters were encouraged by the unanimous approval, by the US Senate's finance committee, of legislation on textile parity, proposed by D. Robert Graham, a Florida senator. Producers hoped that if the proposal were to be made law, it would give the apparel industry a stimulus, thereby preserving jobs and encouraging new investments. However, this proposal encountered some difficulty in 2000. Despite support for the CBI-parity proposal from the out-going US President Bill Clinton, the legislation was linked to a trade facilitation law for African countries, and was subject to contentious debate among legislators, some of whom made the issue of 'free trade' an element in the 2000 US presidential election campaign.

FREE TRADE AND THE ASSOCIATION OF CARIBBEAN STATES

While seeking improved access to traditional markets, the Caribbean continued to strengthen its links with neighbours that hitherto it had ignored as likely economic partners. In the 1990s CARICOM had sought bilateral free-trade agreements with several Latin American states, describing these as 'building blocks' for the proposed hemispheric free-trade pact in 2005. The agreements were to be similar, in many respects, to the free-trade agreements that CARICOM concluded with Venezuela (in 1991) and Colombia (in 1994), but would be based on immediate reciprocity.

In early 2000 CARICOM made an important advance in the expansion of trade in the region. After four years of negotiations the Dominican Republic signed a free trade agreement with CARICOM, which would give the country access to an expanded market of 47m. people, and allow it to be a trade bridge between the region and Central America. Signing of the agreement had been delayed following objections from Dominican soft-drink bottlers, who claimed that liberalization of trade would adversely affect them. As a consequence of these objections, soft drinks were among some 50 items excluded from the duty-free trade list. This list was to be the subject of continuing negotiations with CARICOM. Earlier in the same year the Dominican Republic reached free trade agreements with various Central American states. Consequently, the country would become a channel for future economic integration in Central America and the Caribbean.

Relations between Cuba and its neighbours continued to improve. The leaders of Barbados, Grenada, Jamaica and Saint Vincent and the Grenadines made official visits to Cuba in 1998 and 1999, where they advocated closer economic relations and criticized the US economic embargo of the island. The Cuban leader, Fidel Castro, repaid several of these visits. Caribbean leaders claimed success in changing aspects of US policy towards Cuba. Madeleine Albright, then the US Secretary of State, stated in 1998 that it was the responsibility of Cuba's neighbours to decide whether the island became a member of CARICOM. She claimed that the USA would not try to influence the organization's decision about whether to admit Cuba, although, according to CARICOM officials, Cuba had not applied for membership.

In early 2001 CARICOM leaders agreed to create the Caribbean Court of Justice that would replace the United Kingdom's Privy Council as the final appellate court for several former British colonies. The Court was intended to adjudicate on trade disputes that are expected from the planned common market. However the Court's other major function as a final appellate court in civil and criminal matters caused controversy. Several Caribbean governments were accused of planning to use the regional court to expedite capital punishment. Faced with increasingly violent crime and a high rate of murder, some governments were clearly frustrated by recent rulings of the British Privy Council that they claimed hindered them from executing convicted murderers.

CONCLUSION

The economic outlook for the region in the new millennium would be influenced by the efforts of the leaders of several eastern Caribbean islands to create a political union. The move towards such a confederation followed the election to office between 1996 and 2001 of several new, young leaders who appeared to have a more pragmatic and open approach to government. They argued that strength in numbers as a confederation would better allow them to deal with an increasingly hostile international economy. They believed that the islands— Antigua and Barbuda, Barbados, Dominica, Grenada, Montserrat, Saint Kitts and Nevis, Saint Lucia and Saint Vincent and the Grenadines—would be better able within a confederation to deal with the many problems they faced as small individual nations. The group, which would have a combined population of 700,000, planned to begin with co-operation in judicial matters with the establishment of the court of justice, civil aviation, maritime affairs, telecommunications, diplomatic representation, joint economic planning, management of exclusive economic zones, education, health, the environment and response to disasters. The proposal was given a fillip in early 1998 when Owen Arthur, the Prime Minister of Barbados, which was not involved in the original plans, said his country wanted to be part of the political union.

All the governments involved in the group have a common ideological position and all, with the exception of Barbados, which intended to join, were members of the Organisation of East Caribbean States (OECS), a sub-group of CARICOM. The islands had a long history of co-operation and met most of the conditions considered by the leaders as necessary for political union. The economic structure of the islands was similar, based on the production and export of agricultural commodities, with a growing dependency on tourism. The countries had a common language and, except for Barbados, a common currency, a common central bank and a common judicial system. Inter-island migration was heavy, as was trade. The countries also had common concerns: their commodity-based economies were threatened by attacks on their preferential markets in Europe and the emergence of powerful trade blocs; and aid from industrialized countries was being gradually reduced, while economic development caused several islands to lose their status as poor states with access to cheap multilateral funds. A previous attempt at political union in the Windward and Leeward Islands, the Federation of the West Indies, had collapsed in 1962, owing to strong nationalist opposition. Although leaders were not expecting any attempt at political unification in the early 21st century to be derailed for the same reason, the ghost of the collapsed Federation often haunted efforts at wider economic co-operation within the Caribbean region. Attempts at further regional integration often fell victim to parochial concerns and the need to respect national sovereignty.

LATIN AMERICAN AND CARIBBEAN ECONOMIES: AN INTRODUCTION

Prof. PETER CALVERT

BACKGROUND

In April 2001 a Summit of the Americas at Québec, Canada, resolved to create a Free Trade Area of the Americas (FTAA) covering all the Western Hemisphere (Cuba excepted) by 2005. The fanfare of publicity was itself considerable and was amplified by anti-capitalist public protest. Hence few outside the hemisphere would have noticed that this was in fact the third occasion on which this momentous decision had been taken and that negotiations since the previous summit in 1998, held in Santiago, (Chile) had not gone well. Collectively, Latin American and Caribbean states cover 20,461,000 sq km with a population of 508m. people (1999). To unify them into a single market with the advanced industrialized countries of the USA and Canada would indeed be a great political achievement. However, its economic value is much less certain. According to World Bank figures, GDP growth in the Latin American and Caribbean countries in 1998–99 was zero; in fact owing to the above-average growth in population, per head economic growth actually declined by 1.5%.

The problem is not new. Since 1945 Latin America has given the rest of the world in turn developmentalism, dependency theory and the debt crisis. In the 1990s the larger economies adopted the currently fashionable neoliberalism in various degrees. At the beginning of the 21st century, however, there is still no country in Latin America or the Caribbean about whose economy there is not repeated and well-justified concern. Some of the larger and many of the smaller states, moreover, face serious problems as a result of their continuing dependence on the export of one or two primary products.

The vast majority of Latin American states were in 1999 rated by the World Bank as upper-middle income economies. It was still true, however, that the richest country in Latin America, Argentina, with a per head GDP of $7,750, was less well off in 1999 than the poorest country in the European Union (EU), Portugal, per head GDP $11,030. This sense of grievance was a key factor behind the initially successful policy of Venezuelan President, Hugo Chávez Frías (1999–), to revitalize the Organization of Petroleum Exporting Countries (OPEC). In early 1998 Mexico and Venezuela agreed with Saudi Arabia that OPEC should be reinvigorated and crude production reduced. Between 1999 and mid-2000 this had the effect of increasing the price of crude petroleum on the world market from under US $10 per barrel to over $30 per barrel, causing consumer unrest and demonstrations by farmers and lorry drivers across Europe. However, even though Venezuela has negotiated preferential oil deals for selected Caribbean countries, including Cuba, other non-petroleum producing countries have suffered.

NATIONAL ECONOMIC STRATEGIES

Many believe that the insertion of Latin America into the world economy is responsible for many, if not all, of its modern economic problems. There are two problems, however: determining just at what point Latin American economies can be said to have become part of the world economy, and saying just what significance should be attached to it, so long after the event. Certainly, the process began with the Encounter of 1492 and the Spanish conquest of the 'Indies'. Conquest established a new pattern of land-ownership, and settlement accidentally introduced European diseases. Within 80 years the population of Mexico had fallen by 90% and the indigenous population of Cuba and Santo Domingo had virtually died out. The resulting labour shortage led to the systematic introduction of African slaves and the creation of a new plantation economy, which was to be replicated in Portuguese Brazil and in the British and French Caribbean islands.

Spain, driven by the theory of mercantilism, created a trans-atlantic closed market, in which production of primary goods for Spain was the main objective and purchase of goods in the Indies limited to Spanish industrial products. By the end of the colonial period, however, smuggling was widespread and determined efforts were being made by British traders to penetrate the colonial market. With independence in the early 19th century the Latin American states had to import capital from Europe and establish trading relations with the European colonial powers.

Traditionally in Latin America the state was seen as managing its national economy exactly as a good landlord would manage his estate: keeping it tidy and allowing nature to take its course. Improvements in productivity would take place only slowly and over a long period. The notion of economic development in the modern sense was a product of the industrial revolution in Europe, but Latin America lost some 50 years as a result of the turbulence following independence, which led to persistent capital flight. Industrialization, based on the technology of iron and steel, was impeded by the irregular distribution of these minerals both between, and within, states. Even today, Colombia exports most of its coal and Venezuela almost all its iron ore.

In the late 1940s, in a belated response to Latin American pressures first put forward at the Chapultepec (Mexico) conference in 1945, the UN Economic Commission for Latin America (ECLA, which adopted its present title, Economic Commission for Latin America and the Caribbean—ECLAC, or, in Spanish, the Comisión Económica por América Latina y el Caribe—CEPALC, in 1984) was created to promote economic growth. The results were disappointing. In Argentina, the Government of Arturo Frondizi (1958–62), was marked by a stagnating economy with relatively slow growth. In Brazil Juscelino Kubitschek (1956–61) had promised 50 years of development in five, but delivered 40 years' inflation in four.

With the intensification of the Cold War, the armed forces assumed control in the region. They blamed the civilians for economic failure and corruption, and justified their continued rule by promising real economic development. Military developmentalism had the advantage that the armed forces could use their control to break trade unions and impose a form of political stability intended to appeal to foreign investors. In order to enhance their control in a world of industrialized warfare, they gave priority to strategically important industries and major structural developments such as roads and dams. In the case of Brazil, at least, they achieved spectacular rates of economic growth, though not in fact ones much greater than their civilian predecessors. However, as inflation spiralled into three figures, much of the investment was wasted and the gap between rich and poor widened.

The dependency thesis was developed, especially in the Southern Cone countries, as a critique of military developmentalism. It argued that because the economies of Latin America were on the periphery of the world capitalist system, they had become dependent on the advanced industrialized countries and so could not undergo the same form of development. The 'core', the advanced industrialized countries, set the terms on which the international capitalist system operated, and hence the terms of trade were unfavorable and the capital tended to flow from the periphery towards the core. Latin American states could develop import-substitution strategies, therefore, but being unable to generate the necessary capital, were unable to go on to develop autonomous economic growth. These ideas spread rapidly in the early 1970s, just as the plantation economies of the Caribbean were having to cope with the challenge of independence. Led by Michael Manley of Jamaica they added their voices to those of Carlos Andrés Pérez of Venezuela and Luis Echeverría of Mexico, calling for a revision of the terms of trade, a Charter of Rights and Duties of States (CERDS) and a New International Economic Order (NIEO).

After 1945 there were in fact two substantial periods of investment in Latin America generally. The first was in the period 1950–65, when the developmentalists were in power in many Latin American states and the US economy was strong. The second came after the first so-called 'oil shock' of 1973, when the price of crude petroleum multiplied fivefold in one year, sending shock-waves through the world markets. The huge increase in the flow of 'petrodollars' to petroleum-producing states created the need for new places to invest the revenue, and Brazil and Mexico were high up the list of places that looked attractive. Banks both in Europe and in the USA competed fiercely to offer loans at competitive rates. The flow of inward investment was welcomed in the belief that it represented a real and permanent change in the world economy. However, the second 'oil shock' of 1979 precipitated a recession in the advanced industrialized countries. The result was what soon became known as 'the debt crisis'.

The crisis first became evident when, in August 1983, Mexico announced that it would be unable to meet the repayments on its national external debt. Confident that it would be able to pay for an ambitious programme of investment on increased revenues for petroleum, it had suffered because it was unable to increase production quickly enough to realize increased revenue before the North Sea and Alaskan North Slope discoveries drove down the price again. Worse still, by the beginning of the 1980s rising inflation in the USA had led to a sharp rise in world interest rates. These were to remain at historically very high levels throughout the decade. The result was that the very rapid accumulation of interest consistently outpaced the effects of stabilization programmes, while governments constantly faced the problem that the savage reductions in their national budgets that economic theory demanded were politically unacceptable to their supporters. Moreover, the debts of the 1970s and 1980s had been incurred in haste from a variety of private lenders. Faced by irate shareholders who had become habituated to the absurd idea that dividend payments would continue to rise indefinitely, US and European banks could not admit that any part of their outstanding loans might not be repaid, for fear of creating a panic. Ultimately, it was only the sensible decision of the major US player, Citicorp, to cut its exposure and mark down the book value of its debt in 1987 that paved the way for the safer disengagement of other banks.

In that one year, by a variety of methods, Brazil reduced its indebtedness by some US $6,000m., while Mexico retired $5,000m. of public-sector debt and more than $10,000m. of private-sector debt. However, like some of the other larger economies, these two countries (especially, for political reasons, Mexico), received more generous treatment than was always the case. Costa Rica was told simply to pay up, and the complaints of the smaller Caribbean countries were ignored, though fortunately for them, the favoured treatment of their exports to the European Community (known as the EU from 1993) under the Lomé Agreements helped give them some stability. In 2000 these agreements were replaced by the Cotonou Agreement, which would enter into force only after it had been ratified by the European Parliament and the national legislatures of the ACP (African, Caribbean and Pacific) states. (see Part Three, Regional Organizations, European Union).

Yet the 'muddling through' which was general in the 1980s, while imposing some restraint on the growth of the debt, did nothing to reduce it. The first real move to do so came only in the early 1990s in the form of the Brady Plan, so-called because it was originally put forward by Nicholas Brady, US President George Bush's (1989–93) Secretary of the Treasury. The Plan enabled Latin American countries, with the backing of the US Treasury, to implement, by agreement, more ambitious plans, not just of debt management, but also of debt reduction. Several countries—Mexico, Brazil, Venezuela—have taken advantage of these schemes to reduce their capital debt by converting it into various forms of equity. These schemes were apparently so successful that, following the crises that affected several East Asian economies in late 1997 and early 1998, officials from the International Monetary Fund (IMF), the World Bank and other international agencies advised Asian policy-makers to follow the Latin American example.

This inversion of economic roles in relation to previous decades did not last, and by 2000 there was considerably less optimism in Latin America. It was true that things had changed in the region since the 1980s. Macroeconomic and microeconomic policies had become more focused, the region's economies were increasingly open to international trade and foreign investment, and markets were being liberalized and state enterprises privatized. Servicing the external debt had become a lighter burden and the rate of inflation seemed to be under control everywhere. However, as Latin America was belatedly feeling the after-effects of the Asian crisis, it was necessary to recognize the limitations of the situation.

REGIONAL DIVERSITY

Brazil, the eighth largest economy in the world, and Mexico, the 12th largest, have impressive economic potential. However, such is the diversity within the region that earlier attempts to create a regional organization covering the whole of the hemisphere were frustrated by two facts. First, the USA dominates the hemisphere and no other economy has anywhere near its strength. Second, the remaining countries themselves fall into four groups, each with rather different problems. Most developed are Argentina, Brazil and Mexico. Intermediate among the South American states are Chile, Colombia, Peru, Uruguay and Venezuela, and comparable in the Caribbean region are the economies of Trinidad and Tobago, with its oil wealth, Panama, with the Canal, and Jamaica. Least developed areas include Bolivia, the Dominican Republic, Ecuador, Haiti, Paraguay and the remainder of Central America. Other states in the Caribbean region are small island developing states with very small economies dependent on tourism and the export of primary products that are highly sensitive to changes in the world economic climate.

Brazil stands out not only because of its sheer size but also for other reasons. On the positive side, it has immense natural resources, many of which have yet to be exploited. Its geographical position makes it attractive for foreign-owned companies to base their South American operations there. In the automobile industry, for example, Brazilian operations form an essential part of the world strategy of companies such as General Motors of the USA and Mercedes Benz of Germany (the latter also had a presence in Argentina). Moreover, with a population of about 164m. in 1999, the domestic market was large enough to sustain economic growth. Certainly income distribution in Brazil has long been very uneven and the imbalance has worsened since 1980: the bottom 20% of the population receive only about 2% of GDP while the top 10% of the Brazilian income-distribution pyramid, which is marginally larger than the whole population of Chile, has many times its purchasing power. This has had significant implications, not only for foreign investment, but also for social harmony and political stability. Assuming that they could remain in power, the rich and the middle sectors in Brazil were a tempting prospect for any potential investor. Hence no matter how incompetently the country's economy was managed, largely as a result of the continual battle for the control of policy between a President bent on stabilization and a Congress determined to protect local and corporate economic interests, the economy continued to grow.

This was just as well, since on the negative side, the Brazilian population also continued to grow rapidly. With more than half the population under the age of 16, and a high proportion either unemployed or underemployed, the capacity to tax was limited and the demand for education and social services high. Until the introduction of the Real Plan in 1994, pegging the new currency to the US dollar, the country had suffered from a particularly acute form of the general South American malaise of inflation. However, attempts by the Government of Fernando Henrique Cardoso (1995–) to restrain expenditure and to reform taxation and administration met with strong and often successful opposition from the legislature, the state bureaucracy and the judiciary. Although President Cardoso was re-elected for a second term in October 1998, by the end of that year Brazil was in recession and in January 1999 the Government was forced to abandon the exchange-rate peg of the 1994 Real Plan.

Within South America, Brazil has inevitably assumed the role of a regional leader, and, though suspected of 'imperialist' pretensions towards the rest of the region, this role has generally been constructive. Intellectuals have long been busy developing explanations for Brazil's failure to become as successful as the USA. Academic artefacts such as dependency theory, inertial inflation or the 'theory of large countries' might all fall into this category. Brazil did pressure its neighbours to support its candidate to head the newly created World Trade Organization (WTO) in 1995. It also launched the idea of a South American Free Trade Agreement, to compete with the North American Free Trade Agreement (NAFTA). However, despite periodic disputes, the Brazilian Government made significant concessions to keep Argentina as a satisfied partner in the existing regional grouping, the Southern Common Market (Mercado Común del Sur—Mercosur, or, in Portuguese, Mercado Comum do Sul—Mercosul), though, in any event, Argentina had strong incentives to stay with Mercosur. When, in the late 1990s, Argentina introduced temporary import controls, Brazil responded and showed itself prepared to import extra Argentine petroleum to redress the trade balance.

Mexico is also a special case. It is the only Latin American country that shares a frontier with the USA. Bilateral trade with the USA constitutes 90% of Mexico's exports and 90% of its imports. However, considering the history of the relationship between the two countries, the decision taken by the administration of Carlos Salinas de Gortari (1988-94) to seek to join the USA and Canada in NAFTA was a particularly bold one, even though it promised immense economic returns for Mexican economic interests.

MINING

Although the gold and silver of the colonial period are no longer of much interest, countries in the region are still heavily dependent on mining for export revenue, and there are vigorous attempts in all areas to locate new sources of revenue. The main interest focuses on the mainstays of the traditional economy, iron ore, non-ferrous metals such as copper, tin and nickel, and bauxite.

Mexico and Brazil were the first two states in the region to develop an indigenous steel industry based on local ores. Today, however, mining accounts for only a small fraction of Mexico's economy and only 6.9m. metric tons of iron ore were mined in 1999, compared with about 21m. in Venezuela. In contrast, of the 114m.. tonnes mined in Brazil in 1999, more than 80% was exported and Brazil's Companhia Vale do Rio Doce (CVRD) in Amazônia is the largest iron-ore producing and exporting company in the world.

The Bolivian deep-mined tin industry collapsed in the 1980s as a result of a combination of high production costs compared with alluvial tin from Malaysia and Indonesia, and the collapse of the producers' cartel, the International Tin Corporation (ITC). In both Chile and Peru, however, copper is still a mainstay of the economy. Chile has 22% of the world's copper reserves and strenuous efforts have been made to increase investment and raise production. Since 10% of the production of the state corporation Corporación Nacional del Cobre de Chile (COD-ELCO) was pledged to the armed forces, the company was not privatized, but foreign investment was encouraged and since 1995 the bulk of production has been in the hands of the private sector. In 1997 Chile produced over 3m. metric tons of copper, accounting for some 40% of the country's exports and production was still rising (and stood at almost 4.5m. tons in 1999). Unfortunately, as a result of the East Asian crisis, world prices fell by 24% in 1998 and have continued to fall. In 1992 Peru's severely undercapitalized mining sector was similarly opened up to foreign investment. However, by 1997 many of the smaller companies had closed and two-thirds of the country's production came from the long-established, US-owned Southern Peru Copper Corporation (SPCC) whose open-cast mines, Cuajone and Toquepala, were among the largest in the world. In contrast, the world's 12th largest copper deposit, Cerro Colorado, in Panama, remained undeveloped owing to low world prices, which resulted in the suspension of the first stage of development in 1997.

Part of Cuba's strategy for economic recovery in the 1990s involved a joint-venture agreement with a Canadian company to develop its large resources of nickel. Nickel production is second only to agriculture in the economy of the Dominican Republic. Bauxite is widely distributed on the world's surface

and the main resource available to Caribbean island states. Jamaica is the world's fourth largest exporter of bauxite, which, together with its derivative, alumina, accounted for some 43% of exports in 1998/99. On the mainland, with substantial hydroelectric power resources available, more than 80% of Suriname's export earnings were derived from bauxite and alumina products in 1998, but falling prices again curtailed revenue.

Although gold and silver are no longer of great interest, investment in gold-mining in Peru has proved extremely profitable and Peru is now the largest producer in Latin America. With a minimal initial investment of only US $37m., Yanacocha in Cajamarca, a joint leaching project of Newmont of Denver (Colorado, USA), Peru's Buenaventura and France's BRGM (Bureau de recherches géologiques et minières), recouped its investment after only seven months.

ENERGY

There are two major oil exporting countries in the region, Mexico and Venezuela, three significant exporters, Colombia, Ecuador and Trinidad and Tobago, while Argentina and Bolivia can meet all their domestic needs from their own resources.

Mexico had proven oil reserves of some 58,204m. barrels in 1999, when it produced 3.34m. barrels per day (b/d). However, between 1990 and 1998 petroleum exports had ceased to be a major contributor to the Mexican economy, accounting in 1998 for only 5.9% of export earnings. The petroleum industry was nationalized in 1938, and thereafter production had been stable for several decades until, in the early 1970s, the discovery of vast new oilfields in the Gulf region revitalized the industry. However, the price of Mexico's entry to NAFTA, achieved in 1994, was to open up the industry to foreign investment. The Mexican petroleum company PEMEX (Petróleos Mexicanos) was to remain state-owned, but all the respective 'downstream' activities were to be opened to foreign bidders. Foreign companies, especially in the other two NAFTA member countries, Canada and the USA, therefore adapted their strategies accordingly. The revenue prospects from the privatization of the Mexican petrochemicals industry suffered in 1996, when, as a result of the Government yielding to nationalist trade-union pressure, foreign interests were not allowed to participate in the process. The industry as a whole suffered even more from the fall in the world petroleum price, which in 1998 decreased to less than US $10 per barrel for benchmark crude, its lowest level in real terms since the first 'oil shock' of 1973.

The rise in the world price since that time has been partly as a result of the efforts of President Hugo Chávez of Venezuela to revitalize OPEC. Venezuela nationalized its oil industry in 1975, though its state petroleum company, Petróleos de Venezuela, SA (PDVSA), continued to collaborate closely with the petroleum majors. Excluding the Orinoco heavy petroleum belt, Venezuela has proven oil reserves of 75,000m. barrels, the largest of any country outside the Middle East and exports nearly 90% of its production, half of it to the USA. In addition, it has the world's fifth largest reserves of natural gas.

The oilfields discovered in the 1980s in Colombia have been developed, among others, by the British concerns Lasmo and British Petroleum, and despite sporadic terrorist attacks on the pipelines, have proved very profitable. Ecuador's industry, on the other hand, has not justified expectations, owing to high costs of production, its position on the Pacific coast of the Panama Canal and the insistence by the former military government on renegotiating the terms of business with the oil companies before they could commence production.

The construction of a natural-gas pipeline between Argentina and Chile, completed in 1997, was expected further to encourage competition and reduce costs in the Chilean domestic market. Two more gas pipelines between Argentina and Chile were being built, in Atacama in the north and Concepción in the south. However, the development of Argentina's gas fields meant a loss of market for Bolivia, which turned instead to Brazil.

TRANSPORT AND COMMUNICATIONS

An inadequate infrastructure continued to impede economic growth in Latin America at the beginning of the 21st century. Supply problems persisted in the key sectors of transport and telecommunications. Historically, transport in Latin America had been handicapped by four factors. Sheer distance and the mountainous topography were in themselves intimidating obstacles, coupled with a sparse population and hence the lack of an internal market. Whereas in the United Kingdom coal and iron ore could be found close together, even in Mexico, where both were found, they lay on opposite sides of the Sierra Madre. In the 1980s and 1990s, as Latin American countries abandoned their old styles of development to move towards more open economies, the need for a satisfactory transport system became imperative. A new demand for roads, railways, ports and airports appeared, resulting from the expansion of both traditional and non-traditional exports.

Historically, the need for a transport infrastructure had for many years been met by state-led investment funded by taxation. Early railway development in Latin America had been funded by private investment, but even in Argentina the extension of the narrow-gauge network to the more remote regions had depended on the state. Privatization of rail services in Argentina in the early 1990s cut state costs drastically and was followed by a significant increase in passenger and freight usage.

The Menem administration in Argentina in the 1990s saw in the construction of toll roads an obvious method of dealing with both traffic congestion and the construction of a road network in the interior of which less than 30% was paved. However, toll roads proved to be politically unpopular. Chile was the first country to introduce a fully operational system of tendering for the construction and running of private toll roads. Road projects with different forms of private-sector participation were also being carried out in Costa Rica, Mexico and Venezuela, while an ambitious plan had been developed to link Buenos Aires (Argentina) and São Paulo (Brazil) by motorway by way of a new bridge at Colonia in Uruguay., The overall cost was initially estimated at some US $2,500m.

From the beginning Latin Americans took a key interest in the possibilities offered by air transport. Colombia was the second country in the world to establish a state airline, now called AVIANCA, in 1940. By 1980 virtually every Latin American state had its own flag-carrier. However, owing to lack of demand, many operated at a loss or were heavily subsidized, and in Brazil and Peru services in the interior had to be maintained by the armed forces. The Argentine Government sold a majority stake in Aerolíneas Argentinas in 1991. However, 85% of it was bought by the Spanish state airline Iberia, which sold off its assets and left the Argentine company with huge debts. The Government was forced to buy part of its stake back in order to prevent bankruptcy. Iberia also bought Viasa, the Venezuelan state airline, which ceased to operate in 1997, leaving all 25 of its international routes in Iberia's hands.

The modernization of financial systems required good telecommunications networks, with the paradox that in many states customers abandoned fixed wire systems in favour of radio links and mobile telephones, which were cheaper to install if not to operate. The initial result was for new companies to establish themselves in the profitable business sector while leaving the task of providing communications for the masses to the unreconstructed state companies. Privatization and market liberalizaton, therefore, were not a sufficient guarantee that satisfactory services would follow. In the areas of market deregulation and the regulation of natural monopolies, considerable progress was made by the end of the 1990s, but suppliers could still engage in monopolistic practices. US and European telecommunications companies were active throughout Central America, even though the long-standing Cable & Wireless monopoly of services on the smaller Caribbean islands was much resented. The decision of the Organization of Eastern Caribbean States (OECS) in April 2001 to liberalize the sector was expected to lead to increased competition in the region's telecommunications market.

SOCIAL INFRASTRUCTURE

State-led investment had also become the norm for the provision of energy, clean water and sewage-disposal systems. However, installed capacity in Latin American infrastructure tended to be wasted, badly used or poorly maintained. There were several reasons why this was so. Political prestige attached to large, so-called 'white elephant' projects gave them priority in the corporate culture of international lending agencies. Inefficient administration by state bureaucrats however, led to corruption

and waste and a state of perpetual economic crisis led to long delays and consequent cost-overruns. The joint Argentine-Paraguayan Yaciretá hydroelectric project was delayed for years owing to the weak state of the Argentine economy and did not go on stream until 1997.

Local government in much of Latin America is weak and underfunded. In rural water-supply projects, for example, if participation by the local population was high, the quality of maintenance and the effectiveness of a project reaching its goals increased from as little as 8% to over 80%. Rural education remains a perpetual problem. As a share of their respective GDPs, Venezuela spent more on education than Singapore, but 80% of it went into administration, planning and higher education, leaving a large share of the population either without basic schooling or in schools of appalling quality. When the rate of capacity utilization was higher, this was usually because prices were kept artificially low by large subsidies, which often benefited the rich and the middle classes, but not the poor.

Given the prevailing climate of privatization and market liberalization in the 1990s, there was plenty of scope for participation by the local private sectors and for foreign investment. Despite ideological reservations, by 2001 British and French companies had invested in Mexico's water sector, building treatment plants and modernizing municipal systems. The market was immense, but also highly competitive, especially in comparison with other markets in the region such as Venezuela's. Not only European, but also Mexican, companies entered the competition. Water-treatment plants in Mexico were estimated to represent a market of about US $5,000m. and it was expected that Mexico City's water sector would be fully privatized.

INVESTMENT AND FINANCE

Latin America has historically suffered because its wealthier citizens have been unwilling to invest in their own countries. By the end of 1997 total net direct foreign investment in Latin America had reached US $44,000m., with $14,500m. going to Brazil, $12,000m. to Mexico, $4,500m. to Argentina, $4,000m. to Venezuela, $2,500m. each to Chile and Colombia, and $2,000m. to Peru. Economic reforms made some of these countries attractive, while Mexico was favoured by its membership of NAFTA and Brazil by its large domestic market.

During the six-year administration of President Carlos Salinas de Gortari (1988–94) total foreign investment in Mexico was US $48,000m., exactly twice the target set by his Government at the start of its term. This positive trend was sharply reversed in December 1994, when a poorly managed devaluation of the Mexican peso provoked a massive flight of capital. A sharp fall in inward investment followed in 1995 and 1996, not only to Mexico, but also to Argentina and to a lesser extent, to Brazil.

Mexico itself was rescued by a US $50,000m. credit facility extended by the US Government, the IMF, the Bank for International Settlements (BIS) and other organizations. Despite justifiable concern at whether the world financial community could afford to raise such sums in the event of another crisis in the region or elsewhere, the confidence of international investors recovered quite rapidly. By mid-1996 the flow of foreign investment to Latin America had resumed, although the Mexican crisis and the so-called 'tequila effect' in the rest of the region did demonstrate how fragile confidence was and the urgent need for political, institutional and policy reform in Mexico.

The East Asian crisis of 1997 and the failure of the Japanese economy to resume growth renewed interest among US investors in the possibilities of Latin America. Latin American companies seeking to raise money on Wall Street could do so by issuing American Depositary Receipts (ADRs), which were preferred because they were essentially non-voting shares. US investors were in any case likely to be less interested than local shareholders in the day-to-day running of businesses, many of which are still often family-controlled.

The capital flows were by no means in only one direction. Many Latin American firms invested abroad, just as US firms had done in the 19th century. Cemex, SA de CV, the Mexican cement firm, bought production facilities in Spain, the USA and Venezuela, and it was looking for further possibilities in Central America, Cuba, Peru and Asia. At least eight Chilean privately-run pension funds (Administradoras de Fondos Previsionales— AFPs) sold their expertise and invested directly in similar ventures in Argentina, Colombia and Peru. The Argentine petroleum company, Yacimientos Petrolíferos Fiscales (YPF—privatized in 1993), carried out exploration projects in Chile and Peru, while Brazil's Petroleos Brasilieiros (Petrobrás) was drilling even further afield from its main theatre of operations on Brazil's Continental Shelf, in the North Sea and the Persian Gulf.

Concern was expressed over both long-term and short-term aspects of the increase in foreign investment. This 'boom' would not last forever. It was temporary, even if some of its effects would not be. Indeed, as interest rates in the USA improved marginally in mid-1999, more short-term capital began to flow back there. A decline in the foreign-investment boom might generate political problems for some Latin American governments. If political uncertainty, elections, riots and (as in Colombia) local civil wars followed, inward foreign-investment flows would worsen and might even dry up altogether. In some cases, not enough new exports were being generated in order to pay for the returns on this investment. In some countries foreign investment relied for a return purely on the appreciation of the local currencies. The debt-to-exports ratios of Argentina, Brazil and Venezuela have not improved very much since the early 1980s (over 400%, about 300% and about 200%, respectively). There was also a problem with the 'quality' of foreign investment. Investment in 'bricks and mortar' was better than short-term capital inflows, because it did not generate instability.

Despite this huge inflow of foreign investment reaching Latin America, by 1997 the share of GDP which went into gross fixed capital formation had not recovered the peak levels shown before the debt crisis in 1982. For the aggregate of non-industrialized countries in the Western hemisphere (excluding Canada and the USA), investment as a share of GDP reached its highest in 1977 and 1978, at 25%, but declined thereafter. In 1990 it was only 18%. Among the medium-sized and large countries, investment had fully recovered only in Chile, from a pre-crisis peak of 23% in 1981 to a record low of 10% in 1983 and then to 29% by 1997. In Colombia, from a peak of 21% in 1981, the investment share recovered to 22% in 1988, but then it fell again, to 15% in 1991. In Costa Rica the pre-crisis peak was 29% in 1981, which recovered after the crisis to reach 28% in 1992. There was no information for Brazil before the debt crisis, but the investment share was 25% in 1989.

PRIVATIZATION

Privatization, deregulation and market liberalization were world-wide trends in the 1990s. In Latin America, privatizations were welcomed by domestic and foreign investors. The pioneer was Chile in the mid-1970s. A major problem was, however, the weakness of the local equity markets so that most privatizations were carried out by competitive tender, enabling large corporate purchasers to gain control of valuable resources at very low cost. From the government point of view, privatization offered a one-off opportunity to reduce the burden of debt. Hence Chile was also the first country to use debt-for-equity 'swaps': that is, the remission of debt in exchange for shares in state-owned companies. By mid-1999 Spanish investors held majority stakes in the three largest companies in the Chilean stock exchange (utilities holding company ENERSIS, energy generator Empresa Nacional de Electricidad—ENDESA, and telecommunications leader Telefónica Chile).

Argentina and Mexico followed suit much later. The sale of the Mexican telephone utility, Teléfonos de México (Telmex), was completed in May 1994 for some US $6,730m. The Argentine Government sold 45% of the national petroleum company, YPF, in June 1993, for $3,040m. By 1998 Argentina and Mexico had already privatized their most attractive assets and had little left to privatize, with the notable exceptions of Mexico's PEMEX and Argentina's nuclear-power industry. The trend also spread to the Caribbean, where in 1994 the Jamaican Government sold 70% of Air Jamaica for $26.5m. to Canadian and other investors.

For political or ideological reasons some countries were slower to privatize, Brazil and Peru among them. The first Peruvian privatization was in February 1994—two telecommunications companies, Compañía Peruana de Teléfonos (CPT) and ENTEL (Empresa Nacional de Telecomunicaciones del Perú). They were bought by Telefónica of Spain, which paid over US $2,000m. The privatization of Brazil's mining conglomerate CVRD, with interests in iron ore, iron, steel, gold, aluminium, cellulose and

railways, finally went ahead in April 1997. It was the largest privatization in Latin America. The initial sale, of 45% of the stock, brought the Government about $4,500m. The buyers were large Brazilian companies, with support from Japanese and South African groups. In May 1996 the Brazilian Government sold LIGHT, the Rio de Janeiro electricity-distribution company. A controlling stake was bought by a consortium headed by Electricité de France, one of several instances in the region where European state corporations bought into privatizations. Another noteworthy trend showed up when in 1994, Ecuador's Government sold its 20% share of Cemento Nacional to institutional investors in the United Kingdom and the USA, the investment bank Morgan Grenfell acted as an intermediary. Many international banks were increasingly making their profits in fees as intermediaries, rather than lending directly, as before the 1982 crisis.

Despite the reluctance of the Brazilian Government to privatize, by early 1994 it had raised about US $6,600m. from the practice, though little if any of this went to pay off the national debt. A system of cross subsidies complicated investment decisions. For example, Companhia Energética de Minas Gerais (CEMIG), the energy company of the State of Minas Gerais, was forced by the federal authorities to buy electricity from the Itaipú hydroelectrical plant on the border with Paraguay and to sell it to industrial users at a low price. Additionally, it charged an even lower price to some energy-intensive industries, such as aluminium production. CEMIG made losses every year between 1991 and 1993. However, it managed to sell US $200m. in Eurobonds at the beginning of 1994 and was privatized in 1997.

Some privatizations failed. The Peruvian process experienced a temporary reverse in May 1994 with the mining and smelting complex, Centromín, for which there were no bidders. Either the price was too high, or potential buyers were deterred by the fact that Centromín activities were notorious for the environmental damage they caused. However, fishmeal plants, electricity generation, banks, cement companies and zinc smelting and refining were successfully offered for sale in 1994–96. Venezuela's first attempt at privatizing the airline Línea Aéropostal Venezolana (Aeropostal), in May 1994, also failed because there were no tenders. The Mexican Government, more ruthlessly, simply allowed one of its two airlines to go bankrupt, thus successfully eliminating it as a state liability at no cost to itself.

Some activities and firms would not be privatized. However, possibilities of production complementation, partnerships or market sharing all offered scope for private and foreign investors. In 1994 Colombia's state-owned telephone utility, Empresa Nacional de Telecomunicaciones (TELECOM), entered into a partnership with Canada's Northern Telecom and the Miami-based (Florida, USA) investment bank, Vestcor Partners, in a new cellular telephone-network deal worth US $350m.

Foreign investment in Cuba, which had been progressing steadily, suffered a reverse in 1996 when the US Congress enforced more vigorously the embargo on trade and investment it had tried to impose on that country. In 1994 Cuba had sold one-half of its telephone company, EMTELCUBA (Empresa de Telecomunicaciones Internacionales), to Mexico's Grupo Domos. For the Cuban Government, selling one-half of EMTELCUBA was only the first step in what was expected to become, eventually, a substantial privatization programme. Among others, Canada's Sherritt formed a joint venture with a Cuban company to produce nickel and cobalt. Meanwhile a diplomatic effort in 1997–98 by Cuba among Western countries successfully reinforced opposition to US legislation, known as the Helms-Burton Act, which penalized trade and investment by foreign companies in Cuba, and encouraged US President Bill Clinton (1993–2001) to suspend the relevant provisions of the Act. At the same time, Cuba made strenuous and successful attempts at increasing tourism and, therefore, its convertible-currency earnings.

FOREIGN TRADE AND BALANCE OF PAYMENTS

Possibly the most striking characteristic of the response by Latin American and Caribbean nations to the onset of the debt crisis in 1982 was their attempts at opening their respective economies to international trade, although export performance was highly uneven from country to country. Between 1980 and

1997 exports increased by 17% in Bolivia, 66% in Guatemala, 71% in Peru, 72% in Honduras and 121% in El Salvador. The most successful exporter in this period was Mexico. Exports increased from an index value of 100 in 1980 to 780 in 1998. The pace of Mexican export expansion seemed to be continually improving, from 12% growth in 1993, to 17% in 1994 and to 33% in 1995. At that point a peak was reached, but, even then, Mexico's exports grew by a further 48% in the period 1995–98.

Many countries in the region engaged in deliberate and persistent efforts to improve their export performance, increasing export volumes and diversifying export structures. In the Chilean case 'non-traditional' exports meant other minerals, fruit, forestry products, fishmeal and manufactures. The export expansion was helped by a decline in maritime transport costs, containerization, limitations to trade-union power in ports and economies of scale. Chilean wine-makers claimed that by the 1990s it was cheaper to send wine to New York (USA) from Valparaíso in Chile than from California, on the other side of the USA. By 1999 exports represented about 10% of GDP in Argentina and Brazil, about 15% in Peru, almost 20% in Colombia, 30% in Chile, and over 30% in Ecuador, Mexico and Venezuela.

These export successes were especially remarkable since the international recession in the late 1980s and early 1990s depressed the prices of many of the region's commodity exports. Moreover, the inflows of foreign capital reaching Latin America in the same period combined with the new determination of most governments in the region to keep inflation under control to appreciate the local currencies. Between 1989 and 1996 the Chilean currency appreciated by about 5% annually in relation to the US dollar, although a real depreciation, which by mid-1999 amounted to about 10%, was provoked by the East Asian crisis in 1997–98. The Peruvian currency appreciated by 14% between mid-1993 and mid-1994. Both Argentina and Mexico used exchange-rate policy to lower inflationary expectations. Since the Argentine peso was made convertible at par with the dollar in 1991 (the so-called 'convertibility plan'), the dramatic growth in foreign capital inflows in the early 1990s led to a 'price inflation in dollars', representing a severe blow to the international competitiveness of Argentine goods. This arrangement increased the instability of the Argentine economy, as the 'tequila crisis' of January 1995 made apparent. The Colombian peso also appreciated, as production from new petroleum discoveries came on to the market during the second half of the 1990s. The exception was Venezuela, where the local currency (the bolívar) fell by 47% during the first half of 1994, followed by devaluations of more than 70% each in December 1995 and April 1996. Non-traditional exports, such as Chilean fruit or Peruvian high-quality cotton, were particularly sensitive to a high exchange rate.

The completion of the Uruguay Round of negotiations under the General Agreement on Tariffs and Trade (GATT), and the formation of its successor, the WTO in January 1995, was expected to add $270,000m. to world output by 2002. However though the impact of the agreement was expected to be very unequal, South America was expected to benefit to the tune of US $8,000m., of which Brazil alone would gain $3,400m. This was because the agreement contributed to an improvement in the prices for Latin America's manufactured exports and temperate-zone agricultural exports (dairy products, flowers, fruit, grains, meat, poultry, soya beans), but not its tropical ones (bananas, cocoa, coffee, cotton, sugar, tea). Most countries in the region stood to gain. Pressure from GATT had already convinced the EU of the advantages of granting better terms of import for Chilean apples and pears, for example. However, exports of Chilean copper to Japan could be replaced by US supplies, which had lower transport costs. Where this was possible, primary producers were taking a more active interest in schemes to sustain or stabilize international prices. Brazil was willing to play this role in the aluminium market and Venezuela in both aluminium and petroleum.

However, in the Caribbean, things were very different, as the administrations of US President Clinton, for political reasons, supported the large US banana corporations in using the new mechanism of the WTO to end EU support for the smaller, island Caribbean states. If successful, this would have devastated their economies, and it remains to be seen whether the agreement

reached in April 2001 between the EU and the administration of Clinton's successor, George W. Bush, would prove successful.

While the future of the FTAA remained undetermined, there was no doubt about the success of the five sub-regional integration schemes, which were at different stages of development at the beginning of the 21st century. The largest, and the only one in the world involving the world's leading economy, was NAFTA, comprising Canada, Mexico and the USA. In the south of South America Mercosur had already generated a 25% increase in trade between its full members, Argentina, Brazil, Paraguay and Uruguay, with Bolivia and Chile as associate members. The Andean Pact (renamed the Andean Community of Nations in March 1996 and comprising Bolivia, Colombia, Ecuador, Peru and Venezuela) had languished since 1982, but was already seeking to link up with Mercosur and create a unified trade zone for the whole of South America. Similarly in the Caribbean Basin the Central American Common Market (CACM) and the predominantly Commonwealth Caribbean's Caribbean Community and Common Market (CARICOM) saw in a common front with the Group of Three (G3—Colombia, Mexico and Venezuela) their best hope of negotiating satisfactory trade terms from the USA.

Of these subregional groupings, the most attractive in terms of population size and purchasing power was clearly NAFTA (which took effect on 1 January 1994). However, access to new member countries was to be strictly controlled, as candidates were monitored on workers' rights, the freedom to join trade unions, the elimination of forced labour and child exploitation, and the protection of the environment, of foreign investment and of intellectual property (for example, on pharmaceutical patents—Argentine unwillingness to respect US pharmaceutical patents could cost between US $500m.–$900m. per year, in a market of about $3,000m.) Chile indicated its willingness to join. However, President Clinton was unable to obtain 'fast track' authority from the US Congress to negotiate Chile's admission to NAFTA before the Summit of the Americas in Santiago, the Chilean capital, in April 1998. Also, the smaller Caribbean countries had to petition forcefully to be put on an equal standing with Mexican competition in face of US tariffs and quotas on Caribbean exports such as garments.

Another success was Mercosur/Mercosul, where trade between Argentina and Brazil continued to expand rapidly. However, despite its promise, it seemed Mercosur had failed to realize its full potential, because of Brazil's protectionist attitudes and its political and constitutional uncertainties. In both the Andean Community of Nations and Mercosur, complicated systems of rules of origin were proposed as an alternative to a common external tariff, given the difficulties for agreement on the latter. Unfortunately, rules of origin needed to be negotiated product by product, which made them highly inefficient and potentially corrupt. Chile became an 'associate member' of Mercosur in 1996 under an arrangement that would guarantee trade access in both directions, but would not require Chile to adopt Mercosur's common external tariff. Chile also negotiated several bilateral agreements with other Latin American countries. In 1994, it became a member of the Asia-Pacific Economic Co-operation (APEC) forum and, more improbably, became the first South American country to apply for membership of NAFTA. The Chileans clearly would have preferred—whether wisely or not—universal free trade, but they feared becoming isolated if the trend to form regional economic blocs became more pronounced and in 2000 finally decided to seek full membership of Mercosur.

EXTERNAL DEBT

Latin America's external debt was one of the economic issues which in the late 1980s would have been described by most observers as 'critical'. However, with few exceptions, by the end of the 1990s the external debt was not as serious a problem as it had been 10 years earlier. The conventional way of measuring the burden of debt was the debt-service ratio, defined as the sum of interest and repayments of all external debt, as a share of exports. This fell between 1986 and 1992 from 76% to 37% in Argentina, from 47% to 26% in Brazil, from 41% to 19% in Chile, from 43% to 28% in Ecuador, from 55% to 21% in Mexico and from 45% to 16% in Venezuela. However, in Peru it increased from 21% to 25% and in Colombia it rose from 34% in 1986 to reach 49% in 1989, before falling to 35% in 1992.

Another indicator of improvement in the external-debt issue was the ratio between the total external debt and total exports. In percentage terms, this ratio had fallen from 362 in 1984–88, to 221 in 1995, for the whole of Latin America and the Caribbean. With few exceptions, every country had seen substantial reductions in their external-debt burdens: Argentina, from 557 to 346; Brazil, from 383 to 322; Chile, from 352 to 108; Mexico, from 365 to 168; Venezuela, from 244 to 178. However, Nicaragua's and Peru's debt burdens had remained approximately the same (Peru's fell from 402 to 392 and Nicaragua's fell from 1,689 to 1,664) and Haiti's had worsened, from 222 to 600. Between 1995 and 1997 the situation worsened marginally for Argentina and Chile, but it improved further for most countries, and for Latin America as a whole. In 1997 the debt-to-exports ratios were 372 for Argentina, 319 for Brazil, 129 for Chile, 127 for Mexico and 198 for Latin America. In general, it was unlikely that any Latin American country would experience difficulties servicing its debt when the debt-to-exports ratio was 200 or less.

Debt-for-equity swaps and their variations were instrumental in reducing the debt burden. With support from the UN Children's Fund (UNICEF), Jamaica was involved in a 'debt-for-children' swap, by which a particular amount of debt was bought and then cancelled. In exchange, the Jamaican Government committed itself to investing resources in projects such as child immunization or the education of street children. The amount invested by the debtor government in these child programmes was usually lower than the face value of the debt being cancelled, the exact amount of the proposed investment being related to the price of Jamaican debt in the secondary market. 'Debt-for-environment' schemes were also used, involving several countries in the region. When reschedulings were due, these took place almost as a matter of course, although in some cases with fewer problems (Ecuador in the mid-1990s) than others (Brazil).

In the late 1990s only occasionally did debtor countries need to be reminded of their policy commitments by international agencies or official creditors (Guatemala was one example). The Brady Plan debt-rescheduling agreement reached by Peru and its creditors in 1996 was intended to be the last in the region. In mid-1996 Mexico swapped about US $1,750m. in old Brady bonds for new, 30-year bonds with no collateral. The Mexican intended target was $2,500m., but still this was a remarkable demonstration of confidence by international investors in the Mexican economy, coming as it did only 18 months after the peso crisis of December 1994 and the ensuing tequila effect. However, in September 1999 Ecuador defaulted on $44m. in interest payments due on its Brady bonds, the first country to do so, precipitating a demand by its creditors for accelerated repayment of capital. The Ecuadorean Government responded with a letter of intent to the IMF requesting a stand-by loan of $400m., to enable restructuring of the whole outstanding debt of $16,000m. This represented 110% of GDP and debt servicing accounted for a staggering 54% of the budget for 2000, approved by Congress on 25 November 1999. In April 2001 the Argentine Government, too, finally reached agreement with the IMF on a major restructuring package.

SAVINGS

According to most theorists of development economics, insufficient domestic savings are a typical barrier to economic growth in developing countries and Latin American economies have been no exception. Factors contributing to this situation included political instability (including military intervention), confiscatory measures (such as were originally tried by Carlos Menem in Argentina in the early 1990s) and persistent inflation. By the 1990s the rate of savings as a proportion of GDP in Latin America was about 19%, as compared with East Asia's 29%, and the old 'pay-as-you-go' state pension systems were bankrupt everywhere in the region, leading to angry protests by pensioners.

Chile's saving rate of 27% could be largely accounted for by the introduction of private pension companies (Administradoras de Fondos Previsionales—AFPs), which managed individual retirement accounts. The demographic conditions being favourable and the AFPs being carefully monitored by a regulatory agency, this experiment was a great success. The funds held by savers in Chilean AFPs amounted to over US $30,000m. (about 40% of the country's GDP) at mid-1999. The AFPs had accrued so much money that the Government was forced to allow them to invest abroad, in order to prevent them from forcing up share prices of well-established, profitable companies on the Santiago stock exchange. Such investment opportunities were in short supply, following substantial purchases of shares in such enterprises by large Spanish companies.

In Argentina the potential market for AFPs was even larger. The number of workers eligible was some 5m., and the contribution of AFPs to the capital market could be US $200m. per month. However, the introduction of AFPs suffered from a number of problems, among them disagreements in connection with the provision of state guarantees to savers, and with the nature and extent of the regulation of the pension companies. In early 1994 unrest within the ruling Partido Justicialista forced the Argentine Government to withdraw a proposal to make the state-owned Banco de la Nación Argentina offer dollar-linked pension funds, in direct competition with the privately-run AFPs. In Peru the introduction of AFPs was smoother, with two-thirds of the initial target of 1.2m. members achieved by the end of their first year of operation (in mid-1994). All eight Peruvian AFPs had international support. By the end of the century the total funds deposited in AFPs were expected to reach $4,000m.

Eventually the AFPs were bound to become a central institution in most of the region's financial markets and, together with the opening of the domestic economies to foreign financial operators, were likely to play a key role in the complete modernization of these markets. The authorization under NAFTA for foreign financial institutions to operate fully in Mexico was encouraging the rationalization of the domestic financial sector. This process was briefly interrupted by the fall in the value of the peso in December 1994, but it began again with renewed emphasis shortly afterwards.

ENVIRONMENTAL ISSUES

Almost by definition, development means changing the environment. Often, but not always, it also means damaging it, perhaps to the extent that the damage becomes irreversible. In the late 1980s and 1990s the Latin American rush to increase traditional and non-traditional exports created pressures upon the environment which had not been experienced previously. The rapid expansion of shrimp farming in Ecuador, for example, is believed to have damaged seriously many coastal species. The ongoing destruction of the Amazonian rain forest was encouraged by tax benefits and other legal means, in some cases with successive Brazilian administrations deliberately supporting colonization and export agriculture. In Chile, 100-year old trees were used to make woodchips, which were then exported to Japan. Exports of vegetables were important for the trade balances of a number of countries in the region, including Brazil, Chile, Colombia, Mexico and some Caribbean and Central American economies, and the demand for these was met by intensive farming with the generous use of fertilizers and pesticides. However, consumers in North America and Western Europe were becoming increasingly demanding in terms of the standards of environmental protection which they required from developing countries supplying them. It was feared that excessive pesticide use might not only poison consumers, but it might also encourage genetic change and the development of pesticide-resistant pests.

According to the Economist Intelligence Unit, of the eight largest countries in the region, environmental protection was lax both in theory and in practice in Argentina, Peru and Venezuela. In Brazil, protection was haphazard both legally and in practice. Only in Chile and Mexico was environmental protection becoming more strictly regulated and also enforced more in practice. Certainly a system of fines, payable in domestic currency, was in operation in Brazil. However, given that long time delays were allowed between the imposition of the fine and its payment, and the immensely high rates of Brazilian inflation before 1994, the system was meaningless until the inflation rate was brought under control in 1995.

Mexican law and practice were carefully scrutinized before the approval of NAFTA. The amount of lubricating oil being dumped into sewers every month there was estimated to be equivalent to the amount of pollution in the spill from the 1989 wreck of the oil-tanker Exxon Valdez. Between 1989 and 1994 the number of environmental government inspectors increased from less than 100 to 500, and the number of companies inspected grew from 1,380 in 1989 to 22,000 between August 1992 and March 1994. During this latter period 1,577 companies were closed down for contaminating the environment. The Mexican subsidiary of Chemical Waste Management increased its revenue by 40% during 1993. Grupo Sidek, which intended to raise US $200m. in ADSs, chose to appear on record stating that it sold its waste to a neighbouring cement company which used it to fire its kilns. Still, many regulations were not clear and many small and medium-sized companies could not afford to pay for those which were. Costs to individual firms would decline, should the Government decide to invest in the required environmental protection infrastructure.

Moreover, there was legitimate fear in Mexico that any Mexican abuses of the environment, real or imagined, were being attacked by US and Canadian politicians, companies and trade unions less out of a genuine concern for the environment than for protectionist reasons. A long-running irritant was a US ban on imports of Mexican tuna, imposed in the first instance because the drift nets also killed dolphins and threatened depletion of fishing stocks. Though all sides recognised the importance of conservation, there was a suspicion on the Mexican side that it was competition and not conservation that was the main issue in the USA.

CONCLUSION

By the beginning of the 21st century, there was still optimism about the general prospects for most Latin American economies. Recovery from the 1994 Mexican peso crisis and the subsequent tequila effect had been swift. Brazil and Venezuela were no longer the 'notorious exceptions' that they had been earlier in the decade. In the case of Brazil, inflation seemed to be finally under control, and the large size of its domestic market seemed to be able to allow the country to escape the worst consequences of any reverses. On the debit side, however, Argentina was in recession and the economic consequences of Colombia's political problems were increasingly apparent.

Investment in human capital was improving almost everywhere in the region. Many Latin American and Caribbean countries occupied high positions in the Human Development Index of the UN Development Programme (UNDP). There was also progress in the fight against corruption. In 1993 the Presidents of Brazil and Venezuela were impeached on charges of corruption. In June 1994 the Bolivian Congress impeached the Supreme Court's President after finding him guilty of soliciting bribes. In 2000 President Fujimori of Peru was forced to resign when a videotape was broadcast showing his most trusted subordinate, Vladimiro Montesinos, handing over cash to an opposition member of Congress.

There were opportunities as well as risks in the region for foreign investors, and there were dangers to the region from excessively volatile foreign-capital flows. Potentially there were high gains, but also high variances in the yields of Latin America's 'emerging markets'. This wide range in yields could be observed between individual stocks, between different countries, between different investment funds and between different periods. Despite dramatic increases in the value of shares on the stock markets of Argentina, Chile, Colombia, Mexico, Venezuela and others, during most of the 1990s, in general, the region's stock markets remained thinly traded, poorly regulated and exposed to wild, short-term cyclical fluctuations. In any case, increasingly the trend was for investors to look at individual companies, rather than at countries.

The varying performances of Latin America's economies demonstrated that the quality of policy-making was important. While it was dangerous to rely too much on foreign capital and on international trade, it was impossible to progress without them. Nevertheless, despite the Brazilian currency devaluation of early 1999, some general trends were apparent as the new century arrived. The Mexican Government would not leave NAFTA, and could not afford to return to interventionist and isolationist policies. Brazil would continue to make progress in expanding and opening its economy, controlling inflation, investing in human capital and physical infrastructure, reducing poverty and improving health and educational standards. The rest of the countries in the region would be likely to follow these examples and, in some cases, to improve on them. The popularity of regional economic integration was growing. One of the most favourable aspects was that few people any more seemed to expect miracles; realistic attitudes and approaches were the rule rather than the exception, among both ordinary voters and policy-makers.

THE CHURCH AND POLITICS IN LATIN AMERICA
Prof. KENNETH N. MEDHURST

THE WIDER SIGNIFICANCE OF THE LATIN AMERICAN CHURCH

From the 1960s the Roman Catholic Church of Latin America experienced major changes, the significance of which extended far beyond the region itself. From being a relatively unified body, committed to theologically and politically conservative positions, the Church became a divided and, in many instances, radicalized institution. On the outcome of debates within its ranks depended not only the future of Roman Catholicism in Latin America but also, in substantial measure, the immediate future of the Universal Church. Given that Latin America contained the largest number of baptized Roman Catholics in the world and was the one major 'Third World' region which was officially Christian, it seemed that the global impact of the Church at large might be much affected by developments within this particular area. Certainly radical Latin American Catholicism served as something of a model of inspiration in such diverse countries as the Philippines and South Africa. Equally, conservative Roman Catholic leaders within the world-wide Church attached particular importance to countering radical tendencies within the Latin American Church.

THE HISTORICAL BACKGROUND[1]

The roots of difficulties in the 1990s could, ultimately, be traced back to the Church's part in the region's colonization. Virtually from the outset, Church representatives established themselves in the region as allies of the Spanish or (in the case of Brazil) Portuguese authorities and in close association with colonial society's leaders. There were Church–state conflicts, but ecclesiastical institutions generally upheld the existing social hierarchy and their spokesmen endorsed imperial authority. A significant exception was the Dominican priest, Bartolomé de las Casas, who protested against the mistreatment of the indigenous population by early settlers and who can consequently be seen as a forerunner of modern Latin American Roman Catholic protest movements. Normally, and by virtue of special papal dispensations, the imperial power exercised a high degree of direct control over the Church. In exchange, the Church was officially protected against possible competitors, had a guaranteed place in the educational realm and was able to acquire major economic assets.

Political independence only partially changed this situation. The new republics tried to assert the same controls over the Church as had been exercised by their imperial predecessors. Similarly, independence brought no major social changes, and the Church therefore remained wedded to a hierarchical, largely rural society characterized by great inequalities. However, the new ruling élites contained liberal elements which sought to curtail the institution's cultural, social and political influence. Church leaders, by way of defence, strengthened their links with those conservative landowners and other groups which continued to regard Roman Catholicism as a useful instrument of social control or a valuable pillar of the established social order. Thus the 19th century witnessed a series of Church–state conflicts, and intra-élite political battles, over the Church's proper social role.

Such disputes had varying outcomes. At one end of the scale was Colombia, where a concordat guaranteed to the Roman Catholic Church a constantly privileged position. By sharp contrast was Mexico, where the Church was briefly proscribed, and where, more permanently, and despite continuing cultural significance, it tended to become politically marginalized. Also noteworthy was the case of Uruguay, which developed an unusually secularized society in which the Church lacked both political and social influence. Generally the situation settled at points between such extremes. The net effect was to confirm the Church as a socially conservative, if economically diminished, institution, the leaders of which tended to regard challenges to the established social order as inimical to the interests of the Roman Catholic religion.

THE CHALLENGE OF URBAN SOCIETY

This history tended to render the Church somewhat complacent about its hold on popular affections. Despite anticlerical elements among educated social élites, it was assumed that the majority of the population had some loyalty to Roman Catholic institutions. Processes of change revealed, however, that the Church's missionary task was far from complete. It became evident that orthodox and regular religious practice was predominantly a middle- or, more especially, upper-class phenomenon. The espousing of Roman Catholic practices or symbols frequently signified a 'popular' folk religion operating largely at the margins of the official Church.[2] For many indigenous Indians (Amerindians) or mestizos such religion was of a syncretic variety, incorporating pre-Christian beliefs or practices. In the case of descendants of transported slaves, African cults and Christianity mingled with one another. In other words, the Church's apparently secure position depended on alliances with economically and politically dominant groups, which masked the institution's vulnerability within society at large.

These underlying realities were exposed in the wake of 20th century processes of urbanization and industrialization. Throughout Latin America, and notably in Chile, newly urbanized groups gravitated towards secularized left-wing political or Protestant religious groups engaged in ideological competition with the Roman Catholic Church. Amid rapid change, such groups had an apparent relevance that the Church seemed to lack. The latter was consequently thrown onto the defensive, and, commencing in Chile, it implemented strategies designed to check the new perceived threats.[3] Groups were organized, under clerical auspices, with the aim of mobilizing middle-sector, working-class, and even peasant support for the Roman Catholic cause. A further intention was to promote a measure of social reform, but within the framework of inherited structures, which the Church continued to regard as normative.

ROMAN CATHOLIC REFORMISM

In Chile such currents of socially 'progressive' Roman Catholic thought eventually led to the establishment of a reformist Partido Demócrata Cristiano (PDC—Christian Democratic Party), which claimed to offer a middle way between revolutionary Marxism and right-wing authoritarianism.[4] This was not a confessional party (non-Roman Catholics could join), and it was not subordinate to the Catholic hierarchy. However, it did signify a serious attempt, by a substantial segment of Roman Catholic opinion, to establish more just or participatory economic, social and political institutions. It also testified to the impact on Latin America of progressive European Roman Catholic thought. This was of a reformist, and certainly not of a revolutionary kind, but, through the medium of European-trained leaders, and among some sections of local élite Catholic opinion, the ground was prepared for ultimately more radical approaches.

THE EMERGENCE OF CATHOLIC RADICALISM

The emergence of Roman Catholic radicalism can be traced back to the early 1960s and, particularly, to Brazil.[5] Amid a general, if limited, process of radicalization within the Brazilian polity, a section of the country's hierarchy, particularly inspired by Archbishop Helder Pessõa Câmara of Olinda and Recife, presided over attempts to commit the Church to radical reform programmes. For example, Catholic activists sought to promote a new political consciousness among peasant groups. There was a growing perception that the Church's long-term institutional interests might be best served by drawing closer to subordinate but majority social groups who were then attaining political awareness. More positively, social change promoted a re-evaluation of the ethical demands of the Christian Gospel and a heightened sensitivity to the demands of underprivileged sectors.

Naturally such changes did not command universal Roman Catholic assent. Thus, in Chile, the PDC (which came to power in 1964) owed much of its electoral advance to conservative interests more concerned with checking the progress of the Marxist left than with promoting structural changes. Similarly, there were leading Roman Catholic spokesmen who echoed the fears of those middle-class, business and agrarian interests that felt threatened by moves towards reform. In Chile's case, attempts to promote reform precipitated a process of polarization, which initially produced the election of Salvador Allende Gossen's Marxist Government and then, in 1973, the coup which established Gen. Augusto Pinochet Ugarte's military-based dictatorship. In the case of Brazil, attempts to promote substantial change were halted by the coup of 1964, which heralded almost 20 years of military government. Both coups, at least initially, elicited significant official Roman Catholic support and the approval of many of the Church's more influential lay constituents.

THE INTERNATIONAL CONTEXT

Such dramas had their origins within Latin America, but they were also enacted within a wider international context. Thus, the ferment of the early 1960s not only coincided with such great political upheavals as the Cuban revolution of 1959–60, but also occurred against the background of major changes in the international Roman Catholic community, associated with the Second Vatican Council ('Vatican II', 1962–65). Indeed, within Latin America, the Council's reassessment of the Roman Catholic Church's priorities and attitudes to secular society had particularly significant repercussions. On the one hand, this gathering legitimized what had previously been minority Latin American positions. On the other hand, many of the region's Church leaders had their attention drawn to new and potentially far-reaching possibilities. The result was a quickening of liturgical and theological debates, which pointed towards a somewhat less hierarchical and a more communally based Church. Similarly, the idea of reliance on state protection yielded to the concept of a Church more dependent upon its own clergy and reinvigorated laity. As part of the same picture, static and triumphalist understandings of the Church gave way, in some quarters, to such dynamic or open-ended notions of the Church as a 'Pilgrim People' or 'Servant Community'. Official blessing was even given to the idea of dialogue with secular left-wing groups, and to a shared quest for more just national and international economic structures.

The Second Vatican Council's impact was especially evident in the findings of the (Second) Latin American Episcopal Council (Consejo Episcopal Latinoamericano—CELAM), held in Medellín, Colombia, in 1968.[6] In part, this assembly could be viewed as an attempt to apply the general conclusions of Vatican II within a specific regional context. However, it could also be seen as an attempt to push Vatican II debates in new and unexpectedly radical directions. Thus, the Medellín gathering endorsed interpretations of Latin American problems which stressed the obstacles to justice and human development presented by the structures of the international capitalist order— an order seen to be systematically working to the disadvantage of the world's poorer regions and peoples. A political project, aimed at transforming the relevant national and international structures, was presented as a necessary expression of Christian concern for human welfare. It was suggested that traditional Roman Catholic understandings of sin had to go beyond personal misconduct to embrace the idea of sinful structures, the transformation of which, through collective action, could be regarded as an indispensable Christian commitment.

Initially, these changes of official position owed much to the initiative of Brazilian churchmen, who, having been divided or thrown on the defensive by the 1964 coup, were driven by the military regime's economic and internal security policies to adopt a more critical stance. Despite continuing divisions in the Brazilian Church, there was a certain solidarity against political repression, the abuse of human rights and economic policies which heaped the costs of development on society's most disadvantaged groups. Church-sponsored programmes, undertaken in defence of workers, shanty-town dwellers, peasants and Amerindians, indicated the new priorities of a substantial portion of the leadership of the Brazilian Church. In mobilizing widespread support for similar priorities, at the Medellín gathering, Brazilian churchmen took over the 'vanguard' role which had once belonged to their Chilean colleagues.

'LIBERATION THEOLOGY'[7]

The most striking post-Medellín development was the spread of 'liberation theology'. It was the approach to Latin America's problems signified by this term, which became the region's most celebrated contribution to international ecclesiastical debate. Liberation theology's spokesmen were not unanimous in their analyses and prescriptions, but they shared broadly similar understandings of Latin American realities, responded to them in generally agreed ways, and jointly left their imprint on the terms of international theological discussion. A major pioneer of liberation theology was the Peruvian priest, Gustavo Gutiérrez, who was, significantly, educated at the University of Louvain (Belgium); he served at Medellín as an expert adviser and was followed by others from different national Churches who, despite varying emphases, shared many of the same underlying preoccupations.

One generally agreed point of departure is that Christianity implies 'a preferential option for the poor', which must find some expression in a radical political commitment. Those concerned embrace a conflictual model of politics emphasizing the salience of class. Indeed, one of the chief objections levelled against liberation theology by its critics is that it not only represents an undue politicization of faith, but also tended indiscriminately to import Marxist categories into theological discourse. Certainly, official Church leaders, including some radicals, were concerned that liberation theology might involve the Church in the denial of traditional claims to be available to all social sectors. Equally, there was a fear that traditional clericalism could yield to a new clericalism of the left which, in an inappropriately utopian fashion, could equate the creation of a classless society with the advent of God's Kingdom. On the other hand, even some critics agree that liberation theology facilitated a badly needed rediscovery of the historical and socially critical dimensions of Christian faith. For example, the Exodus was adopted as a paradigm of a divine involvement in human affairs, pointing to the possibility of liberation from structural, as well as personal, obstacles to human fulfilment. Moreover, the same model is used to underline the need to involve the victims of oppression in the process of their own liberation.

One aspect of the relevant debates concerned the extent to which violence might be legitimately employed in the quest for justice. Prior to the Medellín conference, the celebrated Colombian priest, Camilo Torres, so despaired of reformism that he came to see membership of a Marxist rural guerrilla movement, Ejército de Liberación Nacional (ELN—National Liberation Army), as the most credible expression of his continuing Christian commitment. Moreover, Torres' death, in a confrontation with the Colombian military, provided the revolutionary left with a martyr who subsequently became a model for other Christian activists.

Following the Medellín assembly, Torres' example gained in currency, for that gathering's strictures on the institutionalized violence of Latin American regimes suggested, to some, the legitimization of armed struggle against oppressive governments. By contrast, many socially radical Roman Catholics, backed by Pope Paul VI (1963–78), identified with Archbishop Câmara's repudiation of violence and placed the emphasis on mobilization for peaceful change. The brutal crushing of left-wing movements during the 1970s, in such countries as Argentina, Chile and Uruguay, tended to add weight to the latter view. It was in the special circumstances of Nicaragua and El Salvador that the possible legitimacy of violent action remained an especially influential option. In Nicaragua significant segments of radicalized Catholic opinion shared in the revolutionary process which overthrew the Somoza regime, and some of their spokesmen, including priests, subsequently participated in the post-revolutionary, Sandinista order. In El Salvador it was local Roman Catholic communities, organized particularly by Jesuits, which, in significant measure, provided the seed-beds of later left-wing insurrectionary movements. The latter subsequently escaped from Church control, but, to a substantial extent, owed their initial impetus to radical Catholic activists.

'ECCLESIASTICAL BASE COMMUNITIES'[8]

At the local level liberation theology was commonly associated with the proliferation of 'ecclesiastical base communities'. These constituted a novel form of sub-parochial Church organization, providing unprecedented opportunities for lay participation. Their exact form varied from country to country, according to different cultural or political circumstances. In Colombia (atypically) they tended to serve as additional instruments of clerical control, but, elsewhere, they frequently enjoyed considerable autonomy.[9] Although sometimes led by clergy, or the members of religious orders, 'base communities' frequently operated under lay auspices. In this way, they nurtured a new stratum of locally rooted, lay, Roman Catholic leaders able, in part, to compensate for shortages of clergy. They also enabled socially underprivileged groups to worship, study the Bible, and interpret their own social or political situations in the light of biblical teaching. Thus, they revealed some capacity to bridge the gap between reflection and action, a feature often described as being characteristic of liberation theology. Indeed, such entities sometimes became instruments for articulating popular grievances, raising radical political consciousness, mobilizing support for political protest movements and training activists able to assume leadership positions within broader-based peasant, labour or political movements.

The nature of these activities varied along with changing political circumstances. Especially in Brazil, base communities acquired particular significance as instruments of popular resistance to authoritarian military rule. They provided an otherwise largely absent protective framework within which the critics or victims of official policies could sustain a measure of concerted opposition to the state. In the last years of Brazil's military rule they played a significant part in supporting unofficial trade unionism and in launching the radical opposition Partido dos Trabalhadores (Workers' Party). Significantly enough, the left's chief standard-bearer in Brazil's first popular presidential election of the post-military era emerged from this background. In Nicaragua and El Salvador such bodies provided the means for radical Roman Catholic involvement in revolutionary politics. In Nicaragua they also served as bases for those Catholics wishing to co-operate with the Sandinista regime in its attempt to establish a new post-revolutionary society.

CATHOLIC HIERARCHIES AND THEIR RESPONSES TO THEOLOGICAL AND POLITICAL CHANGE

Official Roman Catholic responses to such developments were mixed. Local hierarchies, in the main, welcomed and even positively encouraged attempts to broaden the Church's social base. Moreover, their own values and institutional interests sometimes disposed them to offer support to the political causes espoused by otherwise more radical activists. For example, a significant portion of the Brazilian hierarchy extended its patronage to working-class, peasant, human-rights and other movements working for an end to military rule.[10] The Chilean hierarchy similarly provided a shield under cover of which harassed opponents of Gen. Pinochet's regime could find opportunities for helping the victims of oppression, and for aiding the impoverished or jobless lower strata victims of the dictatorship's 'neo-liberal' economic policies.[11] The Paraguayan hierarchy provides another example of Church leaders finding themselves at the centre of opposition to apparently well-entrenched dictatorships. From an initial position of support for Gen. Alfredo Stroessner's regime (1954–89) the Paraguayan Church leadership moved towards a more critical stance, characterized by efforts to promote a dialogue between Government and opposition and, when these failed, towards the support or legitimization of outright dissent.[12] In all these instances, in fact, such officially promoted Catholic resistance was a significant factor in undermining the legitimacy of dictatorships, and hence in paving the way for alternative forms of rule. The Church above all became a focus for dissenters, who found it to be the one credible focus for mass resistance and, in the medium term, the one viable instrument for the articulation of their complaints. Thus, in the Chilean case, it seems as if the Church and

ecclesiastical agencies played a significant role in encouraging and organizing an anti-Pinochet vote in the plebiscite of 1988, which precipitated the dictator's departure from the office of President, and so allowed the restoration of democracy. In more obviously revolutionary or violent circumstances the Church may not play quite such a central role, but may, nevertheless, significantly contribute to the unfolding of events. Thus, in Nicaragua, members of the ecclesiastical hierarchy voiced opposition to the Somoza regime, and in El Salvador Archbishop Oscar Romero y Galdames was, albeit temporarily, a courageous critic of official practices and, as a consequence of pastoral experiences, a radicalized focus of political opposition.[13]

On the other hand, new forms of radical Roman Catholic activism provided official Church spokesmen with novel dilemmas which could lead them to adopt hostile or, much more commonly, ambivalent attitudes to recent changes. Particularly in the case of Argentina, the local hierarchy remained wedded to such conservative positions that, during the years of military rule (1976–83), few Church leaders were to be found speaking out against human-rights abuses, and most sought to marginalize the institution's more radical spokesmen. In other instances Church leaders might have identified themselves with particular acts of protest, and even with sustained opposition to authoritarian rule, while retaining long-term doubts about that 'popular Catholicism' especially associated with base communities, which characterized significant portions of the Latin American Church in the last decades of the 20th century. Thus, base communities could signify a challenge to traditional conceptions of clerical authority which bishops, concerned for ecclesiastical unity, might come to regard with suspicion. Such communities tend to assume or foster democratic, pluralistic or decentralized understandings of the Church, which the institution's official guardians might come to perceive as a challenge to their own authority. In addition, the same guardians had to cope with criticisms, and even withdrawal of support, from those traditionally important middle- or upper-class Roman Catholic groups most likely to be alienated by the newer radical trends. The latter's financial contribution to the Church, and their access to established political or economic élites, could make this an especially acute problem.

The examples of Brazil, Chile and Nicaragua suggested that as long as the Church felt compelled to attack violations of human rights by military-backed authoritarian regimes, internal tensions of this type could be restrained. Thus, in Chile, under Pinochet, the hierarchy found some basis for co-operating with left-wing Roman Catholic elements who had previously elicited official Church censure when they had offered support to Allende's Marxist coalition.

THE RETURN TO DEMOCRACY

In Chile, in particular, the experience of shared opposition to military rule might have so modified mutual perceptions as to facilitate some measure of continuing co-operation. Nevertheless, the restoration of democratic politics could also result in Church leaders seeking to reassert firm ecclesiastical controls or to distance themselves from their radical co-religionists. The re-emergence of parties and other forms of conventional political activity diminished the Church's perceived need or capacity to act as a major focus of dissent. This liberated Church leaders from some of the pressures that had led them, at least provisionally, to accept significant ecclesiastical experiments. Equally, there were instances, following the return to democracy, of base communities returning to more traditional forms of religious activity, which were less likely to be perceived as threatening to the established Church leaders.

The outcome of such initiatives is likely to depend on the general social or political context and the particular balance of forces within any given national Church. In Brazil, for example, moves back to liberal-democracy were accompanied by measured ecclesiastical attempts to put some distance between the Church and the conventional political arena. There was a perception that the Church need no longer be so embroiled in potentially divisive political controversies and should unite in support of more conventional pastoral strategies. In Argentina, by contrast, there remained a substantial degree of continuity, in that most politically active Church leaders remained wedded to the strategy that had long characterized the nation's hierarchy.

They continued to rely on private, intra-élite understandings with political leaders and largely to eschew open, popular forms of political engagement.

In Brazil and elsewhere two main factors were to ensure that the retreat from the political arena remained far from complete. Firstly, the policies of post-military administrations frequently seemed so reminiscent of their predecessors' that ecclesiastical leaders felt constrained to return to the political fray. The effects of neo-liberal economic policies, corruption and the failure to implement land-reform programmes were criticized. Secondly, Roman Catholic radicals, committed to 'a preferential option for the poor' were so entrenched and scattered throughout Brazil's ecclesiastical structures, that their demands for action could not readily be ignored. In the Chilean case, the advent of a centrist Christian Democratic-led administration and the existence of a rather more uniformly moderate episcopate produced a relatively orderly retreat from habitual political involvement. Radical grass-roots elements remained too numerous and too entrenched to be totally ignored. Nevertheless, it seemed they lacked the bargaining power needed to exert the pressure associated with their Brazilian counterparts. Certainly in the late 1990s the Chilean hierarchy was generally more inclined to be supportive of government and less likely to sustain a critical commentary on governmental activities.

Another variant on the same theme arose in the more obviously polarized situation of post-Somoza Nicaragua. Shared opposition to a personalized dictatorship there yielded to a public split between official leaders (notably Cardinal Obanda) opposed to the Sandinista regime and those Catholic activists who, despite the electoral reverses of 1990, when Sandinista President Daniel Ortega was succeeded by Violeta Barrios de Chamorro of the Unión Nacional Opositora (UNO—National Opposition Union), continued to support the Sandinista cause. Such conflicts graphically illustrated the possible extent of divisions within the Roman Catholic community.

THE CONSERVATIVE REACTION

In conflicts of this sort the more cautious or conservative forces could generally depend on the support of those making Vatican policy. Pope John Paul II (1978–) consistently indicated his support for those seeking to present less overtly politicized expressions of the Gospel and to rehabilitate traditional hierarchical understandings of ecclesiastical authority. Immediately after the Medellín conference, such conservative elements were put on the defensive. Subsequently, however, they regrouped and, led by the Colombian hierarchy, they sought to regain the initiative. They secured a major victory when they gained control over the permanent bureaucracy of CELAM. Those who had set the Medellín agenda yielded to more traditional elements who, at the next continent-wide episcopal gathering, held at Puebla (Mexico) in 1979, were resolved to win approval for a reordering of Church priorities.[14]

In practice, the Puebla findings represented a compromise between different tendencies. There was a new stress on evangelism, as conventionally understood, but there was also a renewal of the Church's commitment to social justice. Relatively radical elements clearly remained in place and able to argue their case. Puebla, therefore, did not represent a definitive settling of accounts, but a significant stage in a continuing debate. The debate continued at the further CELAM assembly held in the Dominican Republic during 1992.

From the early 1980s the Vatican generally strove to reinforce the Latin American Church's more conservative forces. Liberation theologians, such as the Brazilian Leonardo Boff, were the subject of Vatican inquiries or bans. More generally, in 1984 Cardinal Joseph Ratzinger, a close papal colleague and head of the Congregation for the Doctrine of the Faith, published a contentious and condemnatory critique of liberation theology. Also, an appointments policy was pursued throughout the region, whereby vacant episcopal sees were generally filled by relatively conservative figures known to support the 're-Romanization' of the local Church. The archdiocese of São Paulo (Brazil), which had been the progressive Church's most important centre, was divided into five dioceses in 1989. This move was widely perceived to be an attempt to weaken the influence of the local Cardinal Archbishop, Evaristo Arns, a potent patron of radical causes. In this instance, and elsewhere, the effect was

an alteration in the balance of senior ecclesiastical forces. In a country like Chile progressive bishops privately regarded themselves as a beleaguered minority. Nevertheless, the Pope continued publicly to press the claims of social justice and human rights. The human-rights records of the Chilean and Paraguayan dictatorships were openly attacked on a 1988 papal tour. Equally, pleas were made on behalf of the victims of, for example, Bolivian economic policies. There were subsequent papal attacks on the socially destructive consequences of prevailing neo-liberal free-market orthodoxies. In January 1998, during an unprecedented visit to Cuba, Pope John Paul II even went so far as to make some criticism of the USA's economic blockade of the island. More politicized and radicalized Roman Catholics consequently maintained a certain legitimacy. Even some Argentine Church leaders reacted against the social costs attached to President Carlos Menem's economic programme.[15]

THE PROTESTANT CHALLENGE[16]

These debates persisted against the background of continuing competition not only from secular political forces but also from sometimes dramatically expanding Protestant groups. The latter quite frequently had links outside the region and especially with US-based Christian organizations or churches. More liberal Protestant groups, principally drawn from the 'historic' reformed churches, on occasion forged ecumenical links with progressive Roman Catholics in joint support of radical social causes. Many Protestant groups, however, were of the strongly evangelical, fundamentalist or Pentecostal types which tended to stress the personal dimensions of faith and to occupy militantly anti-Roman Catholic positions. In the public domain they were liable to adopt ostensibly apolitical but effectively conservative postures sometimes coloured by fierce anti-Marxist responses.

The spread of Protestantism concerned Roman Catholics of all tendencies. For conservatives it represented a significant challenge to the Church's traditional dominance in the area. Radicals perceived obstacles to socio-economic and political change. They could cite the example of the former Guatemalan military dictator, Gen. Efraín Ríos Montt, who combined membership of a US-based Protestant sect with ruthless political repression. They could also point to the defection of as many as 14% of Chilean army officers from Roman Catholicism to evangelical Protestant groups.

In the 1980s and early 1990s the spread of militant Protestant groups was widely perceived in Latin America as having disturbing political implications. Such groups had become so identified with doctrinaire anti-Marxism that they were commonly regarded as instruments of US foreign policy. The links of the USA's 'new religious right' with Republican administrations, and with religious bodies active in Latin America, lent weight to this view. Especially in the strategically sensitive Central American region there was a tendency to view proselytizing campaigns supported by the USA as part of an attempt to neutralize radical Catholicism.

In the mid- and late 1990s, however, the situation seemed less clear and could more obviously be explained in various forms. In some cases the rapid growth of Protestantism was regarded as a critical comment upon the Roman Catholic Church's continuing difficulty in effectively communicating with less advantaged social groups and in providing a sense of community for many, especially urban dwellers caught up in rapid and disruptive socio-economic change. Thus, in Brazil there were considerably more Protestant converts than there were members of base communities. Some have seen the individualistic and sometimes otherworldly emphasis of Protestant groups as having greater appeal and apparent relevance for people overwhelmed by devastating socio-economic changes with which politicized expressions of faith seem unable to cope. Equally, there are observers who view such emphases as both an expression of, and a facilitator of, a limited upward social mobility on the part of hitherto socially marginalized groups. In other cases Protestant growth was not seen as the product of a direct competition in which the Roman Catholic Church was the loser, but as an important expression of a general and dynamic resurgence of Latin American religious life, positively affecting all the region's major religious institutions or traditions. Viewed in this way, socio-economic change, both in urban and rural settings, was a catalyst for widespread cultural transformations and changes in relationships between religious practice and the surrounding society. In this context, the emergence of novel forms of 'popular Catholicism' and of an increasingly popular Protestantism were seen as two parallel and complementary expressions of general, far-reaching upheaval.

Nevertheless, the danger of competition from Protestant evangelicals frequently constituted a rallying call around which Roman Catholic radicals and conservatives might at least provisionally come together. Not least, the relatively recent growth of Protestantism among middle sector and professional groups was seen to represent an incursion into a constituency once viewed as a peculiarly Catholic stronghold. Equally, the ability of former President Alberto Fujimori of Peru to mobilize Protestants in his successful electoral bids suggested a Protestant potential for influence in the political arena that Catholic leaders were likely to view as a substantial challenge.

CONCLUSION[17]

As the new millennium began, the ultimate outcome of the debates alluded to above remained uncertain. The Roman Catholic Church's internal life continued to be characterized by conflicts that arose from differences concerning the Church's nature, the exercise of ecclesiastical authority and the most appropriate forms of Christian cultural, social and political engagement. The very existence of such differences testified to the scope of the changes that overcame the Church in the latter half of the 20th century. The same differences also reflected changes within the Church's environment. Such transformations, most notably global capitalism's apparently irresistible triumph, the re-establishment of ostensibly democratic politics and Protestantism's dramatic growth, provided the context within which the debate continued.

Despite great changes there were some Catholic bishops, limited numbers of clergy and small, if vocal, lay groups (of mainly middle- or upper-middle class backgrounds), who remained firmly wedded to pre-Vatican II theological and political positions. Some supported right-wing authoritarian political solutions. Others, at least conditionally, accepted democracy, whilst continuing to see private engagement with traditional élites as the appropriate way of exercising political influence. There was a particular link between those with such outlooks and the influential, international Roman Catholic organization, Opus Dei. The Archbishop of Lima, Juan Luis Cipriani Thorne, was an example of a very senior churchman linked to this body. In 2001 he became the first self-proclaimed Opus Dei member to become a cardinal.

These groups increasingly found themselves in the minority. Only in Argentina did they constitute a large section of senior ecclesiastical opinion and even in that country the situation was changing. In 2001 Argentina's bishops publicly asked pardon for the Church's frequent silence during the years of military rule. Equally, they took their Government to task over the socially divisive and impoverishing consequences of neo-liberal economic policies. By adopting such positions they underlined just how far (and despite a general Vatican-inspired conservative reaction) the overall terms of modern theological debate had shifted. Thus, at the third millennium's outset Catholic leaders either tended to favour strict ecclesiastical conservatism combined with some general commitment to social justice, or moderate ecclesiastical conservatism combined with some commitment to social and political activism. Moreover, these leaders remained sometimes subject to pressure from more radical elements entrenched within base communities or even at more obviously senior ecclesiastical levels. They testified to a certain institutionalism of an ecclesiastically and politically radical Catholicism that, having outlived recent conservative reactions, continued to uphold communitarian and decentralized understandings of the Church, as well as challenging attitudes towards established secular institutions. That radicalism's durability partly reflected the extent to which ecclesiastical change mirrored irreversible socio-economic and political changes. Amid fast-growing urban areas where traditional social hierarchies were decaying and economic arrangements collapsing there was sometimes a quest for alternative structures. Part of Protestantism's appeal might be that its congregations, amid such flux, provided some sense of security, identity and certainty. Roman Catholic base com-

munities might represent corresponding responses to the same fast-changing environment.

The latter did not just reflect, but also helped to catalyse, social changes. Just as Protestantism's growth might facilitate some upward mobility, so Catholic base communities supplied some of Latin America's lower social strata with opportunities for developing political skills deployable within the wider society. This was especially evident during the period of military rule when many such communities first emerged. Liberal-democracy's restoration and the advent of less overtly adversarial politics tended to diminish the salience of such entities and simultaneously enhanced the will or capacity of ecclesiastical leaders to enforce hierarchical controls. The net result was some demobilization of local radical activists. Moreover, that demobilization's scale suggested that the extent of local cultural change might have been exaggerated. Nevertheless, Brazil's experience, and that of other countries, indicated that even within democratic contexts, conflicts might arise that limit the ability of clerical leaders to ignore locally engendered pressures and to pursue the path of political disengagement. Equally, the years 1999 and 2000 supplied evidence from several Latin American countries that the Church retained enough of the social salience, prestige and popular support needed for publicly exercising significant moral leadership of a sort that was generally in short supply, yet was perceived to be necessary for nurturing Latin America's fragile democracies.

Thus, members of the Venezuelan hierarchy, traditionally known for a relatively low public profile, questioned aspects of President Hugo Chávez Frías's (1999–) constitutional reform, designed to concentrate power in presidential hands. Their stress on the importance of the voluntary principle in public life was obviously inspired by a concern to protect ecclesiastical interests in, for example, the educational sphere. However, they were also reacting against the possible long-term threats to democracy posed by an elected and, for the time being, widely supported populist (and military) leader, of a familiar Latin American kind, offering ostensibly attractive, but quasi-authoritarian, solutions to perennial problems; apparent solutions that included attempts to marginalize the Church. Similarly, Paraguayan Church leaders spoke out in 2001 against military and political leaders responsible for corrupt, dubiously constitutional or overtly illegal behaviour. One campaign resulted in the imprisonment of a senior official. In Peru, a prominent churchman was proposed as chairman of a commission intended to oversee the controversial and constitutionally questionable election in 2000 that gave President Fujimori an additional term in office. Church leaders were divided over this issue. Moreover, the commission's chairman resigned before the election in the face of official pressure, which underlined the flawed nature of the electoral process. It was, nevertheless, striking that opposition groups should have seen at least sections of the Church as a morally credible force worthy of trust. That situation clearly persisted into the scandal-ridden post-Fujimori period. Bolivian churchmen also demonstrated that they, too, could command similar trust. Ecclesiastical spokesmen helped to broker an agreement between the Bolivian Government and striking workers engaged in a struggle that, initially, seemed to be without a peaceful solution. In 2000 Brazilian churchmen, for their part, helped to organize an unofficial referendum on the question of international debt, which demonstrated considerable popular opposition to the terms of Brazilian arrangements with international financial institutions. Church leaders were not united on this issue, but their institution's role in registering powerful dissenting undercurrents suggested that it retained a significant degree of credibility. Even in Colombia, where the markedly conservative hierarchy generally was close to the country's traditional élites, church leaders sought to mediate in the country's violent internal conflicts. Officially expressed fears for the personal safety of both the Archbishop of Cali and of Medellín indicate the seriousness of that engagement. Mexico provided further examples of ecclesiastical involvement in conflicts. Prior to the long-ruling and anti-clerical Partido Revolucionario Institucional's (PRI—Institutional Revolutionary Party) loss of power, the Church, in the state of Chiapas, offered some encouragement to allies of the insurgent Zapatista movement. The advent in 2000 of President Vicente Fox, at the head of the more obviously pro-Catholic Partido Acción Nacional

(PAN—National Action Party) significantly modified, though not entirely changed, the situation, with Church leaders tending to work alongside the new Government in attempts to resolve domestic conflict. The outstanding question was whether or not the apparently transformed nature of Mexican Church-state relations would incline the Church to adopt less socially critical attitudes.

The Mexican case, and other similar situations, drew particular attention to the dilemmas and challenges characterizing Latin American Catholicism at the beginning of the 21st century. Ecclesiastical involvement in conflict situations pointed to the limited yet significant opportunities that the Church created to participate in the construction of a civil society ultimately capable of effectively constraining state institutions and powerful economic interests—a civil society able to give the region's restored democracies additional substance and durability. However, the sometimes ambivalent responses of Church leaders raised the question of whether they had enough of the will and imagination needed fully to seize such opportunities. There was perhaps a prevailing tendency to underestimate the importance of grounding restored democracies in societies that facilitated popular participation and nurtured widespread debate. There was a corresponding tendency to see the re-establishment of formal democratic institutions as in itself sufficient and as an occasion for reining in those who perceived a need for a continuing mass and critical Catholic presence within the public arena. It was this which helped to explain why, in Brazil, following Dom Câmara's retirement as Archbishop of Olinda and Recife in 1995, his successor undid much of his pioneering work. It equally helps to explain the curtailing of the authority of the Cardinal Archbishop Arns. Arns' retirement in May 1998 and Câmara's death in August 1999 seemed to symbolize the extent to which advocates of the more radical approach had lost ground.

Neo-liberalism's apparently definitive triumph seemed, at least in the medium term, to provide a relatively congenial environment for the politically more conservative. Churchmen were concerned to focus more on evangelism as conventionally understood, and less on the Gospel's possible social and political implications. They confronted the relatively weak or disorganized civil societies within which the political left, including left-wing groups of Roman Catholic provenance, were on the defensive. Not least, events in Nicaragua and Cuba's post-Cold War isolation removed any credible revolutionary threat. The result might be the absence of obviously pressing incentives seriously to query prevailing priorities. However, even now, and certainly in the long term, political questions were likely to force themselves onto the ecclesiastical agenda that would jeopardize attempts to put some distance between the Church and the political arena. In Brazil, most notably, Catholic spokespeople were prompted to denounce the growing inequalities, the persisting corruption, the environmental depredation and the absence of serious land or other structural reforms that, in practice, characterized the new era of free-market capitalism and liberal-democracy. Certainly the Church appeared well, if not uniquely, placed to offer an authoritatively critical commentary upon the socially isolating, economically impoverishing, politically corrupting, culturally destructive and environmentally damaging consequences of the capitalism experienced by growing numbers of Latin Americans at the beginning of the 21st century. The extent to which Pope John Paul II turned the papacy itself into a global level critic of capitalism added credibility to this view. Despite ecclesiastically centralizing and other conservative tendencies within the Church its official international leadership emerged as one of the few powerful voices able to raise otherwise overlooked questions concerning an apparently triumphant global capitalist order. To provide just one illustration, John Paul II's visit to Cuba in January 1998 was used to urge political change within the island, but also to attack the externally exposed economic sanctions directed against Fidel Castro's embattled regime.

Sometimes internal divisions blunt the impact of otherwise authoritative prophetic pronouncements. This was not least true in the notoriously sensitive matter of human rights. As Central American developments indicated, Church leaders sometimes contributed powerfully to advancements of this cause, even in uncompromising contexts. During 1999, 2000 and 2001 churchmen in El Salvador and Guatemala played a significant part in bringing to justice some of those members of the local security forces allegedly responsible for grave abuses during earlier decades of violent internal conflict. On the other hand, Gen. Pinochet's detention in the United Kingdom in October 1998 prompted a pastorally inspired Vatican intervention on the general's behalf, designed to secure his return to Chile, rather than his extradition to Spain to answer criminal charges. This apparently represented a short-term success on the part of the ultra-conservative Roman Catholic pressure groups, which strikingly illustrates the complex and sometimes ambivalent nature of Roman Catholic political involvement in Latin America.

The Pinochet case indicated how Catholic activists, outflanked at one level of the ecclesiastical system, could hope to rally support at other levels, including the Vatican. In the long run, however, the same case tended to reinforce the perception of a church which, despite unresolved controversies, organizational complexity and a certain moral ambivalence, significantly and irreversibly shifted its ground. Following Pinochet's arrest and subsequent return home, senior churchmen within Chile were prominent among those social actors who engaged with Chilean military and political leaders in ways designed to strengthen their country's still fragile institutions. By helping to build domestic support for the idea of Chilean prosecution of the general, they helped to vindicate the Church's claim to have become a serious champion of human rights, liberal democracy and social justice. During 2001 some senior Chilean churchmen upset human-rights activists by stressing that the quest for justice should be accompanied by clemency towards military personnel implicated in past crimes. Nevertheless, it was widely acknowledged that the Church had positively contributed to changes in the terms of Chilean political debate and in the character of Chilean political culture. Not least, Chile's abolition of the death penalty, in 2001, was attributed, in significant measure, to Church influence.

In the last resort, the significance of such changes in Latin America's religious life had to be placed in a global context. The outcome of that region's internal church debate was likely, over coming decades, powerfully to affect the global Roman Catholic community's agenda. One possibly crude measure of this was that, following appointments made in 2001, of the 135 cardinals qualified to vote in the next papal elections, some 27 were Latin American. They would remain outnumbered by Europeans, but for the first time the latter would be in an overall minority—a fact of major significance pointing to great long-term changes within the Roman Catholic Church world-wide. Moreover, Latin American and other non-European church leaders were likely to be increasingly immersed in long-running and still unfolding debates concerning such fundamental issues as the nature of ecclesiastical authority and the character of the Roman Catholic Church's relationship with other Christians, other faiths and the world at large. As John Paul II's papacy perhaps drew towards its conclusion, the outcome of such debates was uncertain. Despite the generally conservative tenor of his reign, some appointments in 2001 to the college of cardinals suggested that advocates of a decentralized Church, open to serious dialogue with non-Catholics, remained a vital force still able to argue their case. Long-term, though sometimes contested, changes in the Latin American Church significantly contributed to this outcome. Not least, Latin America provided the setting for an especially important, still developing and historically novel encounter between Latin American Catholics and Protestants. It was an encounter that seemed likely to add a theologically, ecclesiastically and sociologically very important chapter to the entire post-Reformation history of Roman Catholic–Protestant relations. It was possible that parallel developments within each of these communities might have common roots in deep-seated processes of cultural, socio-economic and political change at regional and even global level. It was equally possible that the meeting between Roman Catholicism and Protestantism unfolding in Latin America at the beginning of the 21st century, would, in coming decades, significantly affect the nature of Christianity's overall global impact.

FOOTNOTES

1. For an important historical study of the Latin American Church, see Mecham, J. L. *Church and State in Latin America*. Revised Edn, Chapel Hill, NC, University of North Carolina Press, 1966.
2. On the subject of 'popular religion', see Levine D. H. (Ed.). *Religion and Political Conflict in Latin America*. Chapel Hill, NC, University of North Carolina Press, 1986. See also Bruneau, T. C. *et al* (Eds). *The Catholic Church and Religion in Latin America*. Centre for Developing Area Studies, Montreal, 1985.
3. On the Chilean Church, see Smith, B. H. *The Church and Politics in Chile: Challenge to Modern Catholicism*. Princeton, NJ, Princeton University Press, 1982.
4. For the subject of Christian Democracy, see Williams, E. J. *Democratic Parties*. Knoxville, TN, University of Tennessee Press, 1967. See also Fleet, M. *The Rise and Fall of Chilean Christian Democracy*. Princeton, NJ, Princeton University Press, 1985.
5. On the Brazilian Church, see Bruneau, T. C. *The Political Transformation of the Brazilian Catholic Church*. London, Cambridge University Press, 1984, and the same author's *The Church in Brazil: The Politics of Religion*. Austin, TX, University of Texas Press, 1982. See also Mainwaring, S. *The Catholic Church and Politics in Brazil*. London, Oxford University Press, 1986.
6. On the Medellín Conference, see Poblate, R. 'From Medellín to Puebla: Notes for Reflection' in Levine, D. H. (Ed.). *Churches and Politics in Latin America*. London, Sage, 1979.
7. Much has been written on the subject of 'Liberation Theology'. For an introduction to the subject, see Kee, A. *Domination or Liberation*. London, SCM, 1986, especially Chapter 3. Also Gutiérrez, G. *A Theology of Liberation, History, Politics and Salvation*. Mary Knoll Orbis Books, 1973. Gibellini, G. *Frontiers of Theology in Latin America*. London, SCM, 1975. Smith, C. *The Emergence of Liberation Theology: Radical Religion and Social Movement Theory*. Chicago, IL, Chicago University Press, 1991. Finally, Levine, D. H. *Popular Voices in Latin American Catholicism*. Princeton, NJ, Princeton University Press, 1992.
8. On 'Base Communities', see Levine, D. H. (Ed.). *Religion and Political Conflict in Latin America*, op. cit. For a recent account, see Vasquez, M. A. *The Brazilian Popular Church and the Crisis of Modernity*. Cambridge, Cambridge University Press, 1998.
9. On the Colombian Church, see Levine, D. H. *Religion and Politics in Latin America: The Catholic Church in Venezuela and Colombia*. Princeton, Princeton University Press. See also Medhurst, K. N. *The Church and Labour in Colombia*. Manchester, Manchester University Press, 1984.
10. cf. Mews, S. (Ed.). *Religion in Politics*. London, Longman, 1989. pp. 25–29.
11. Ibid. pp. 39–43.
12. Ibid. pp. 211–214.
13. On the Central American situation, see Berryman, P. *The Religious Roots of Rebellion*. London, SCM, 1984.
14. On the Puebla Conference, see Berryman, P. 'What happened at Puebla' in Levine, D. H. (Ed.). *Churches and Politics in Latin America*, op. cit.
15. Compare Medhurst, K. N., and Gutierrez, M. C. 'The Roman Catholic Church in Argentina', a paper presented to the congress of the International Political Science Association in Berlin (Germany) in 1994.
16. On Protestantism, see Martin, D. *Tongues of Fire. The Explosion of Protestantism in Latin America*. Oxford, Basil Blackwell, 1990. Also, Stoll, D. *Is Latin America Turning Protestant?* Berkeley, CA, University of California Press, 1990.
17. For general surveys of recent debates and dilemmas, compare the following two books: Keogh, D. (Ed.). *Church and Politics in Latin America*. London, Macmillan, 1990. And, Cleary, E. L., and Stewart-Gambino, H. *Conflict and Competition: The Latin American Church in a Changing Environment*. London, Lynne Reinner Publishers, 1992.

COMMODITIES IN LATIN AMERICA

Dr GEORGE PHILIP

Latin America is more generously endowed with commodity wealth than virtually any other major region of the world. This natural endowment is reflected in the fact that, excluding Mexico, over one-half of the region's total exports are primary products. However, while Latin America is far from being the world's poorest area, there is a general sense of unfulfilled opportunity. Commodity wealth has not brought about successful economic development. The old saying about a beggar sitting on a throne of gold (applied alternatively to Peru, Bolivia or to the region generally) still has resonance. Nor has the situation become any easier in recent years. Over the past generation Latin America's growth performance has actually worsened. We therefore need to consider both the factual question of which commodity policies have been adopted in the region as well as the more judgmental question of why resource-based development has not been more successful. The short answer is that the task of turning commodity wealth into real wealth is much more difficult than it appears, and that over-dependence on raw material exports has some real drawbacks.

THE POLITICS OF RESOURCE OWNERSHIP

Until the 1970s at least, most scholars tended to focus on the fact that relatively few people benefited from the region's commodity abundance. This was largely the consequence of ownership structures. Traditional ownership patterns were mainly of two kinds. Most of the region's mineral and petroleum resources were initially developed by foreigners. By the early part of the 20th century US-owned transnational corporations had become the most important foreign influence, although European investors were important too. Conversely, most agricultural commodities—with the important exception of bananas—were developed principally by Latin Americans. Here the concentrated pattern of land-ownership ensured that the greatest share of agricultural wealth remained in the hands of a small élite. In both cases, the broad mass of the people were excluded from ownership.

The capital, technology and marketing information required by mining and petroleum ventures (as well as bananas) tended to make it inevitable that these would be developed by transnational corporations. The transnational corporation was invented in the USA in the latter part of the 19th century in order to facilitate large-scale commercial and industrial organization. Direct foreign investment into Latin America expanded rapidly thereafter. Nationalist historians have sometimes blamed local capitalists for selling out too easily to foreign transnationals, but this criticism is mostly unfair. In cases where domestic ownership was possible, notably in the cases of Bolivia's tin mines and much of the medium-sized and smaller mining industry in Peru, local capital remained important. The Peruvian mining industry even today is to be distinguished from that of Chile by the greater role played by private domestic capital. However, the most important ventures, and the largest ones, were foreign-owned, owing to inherent problems of scale and organization. These larger projects included most of the petroleum industry and the largest mining ventures.

Latin American agriculture was largely developed via concentrated landholdings. Foreign influence mattered in sectors such as banking and transportation. However, land ownership defined a political élite as well as a commercial business class. In general, agriculture in even the most developed parts of the region (such as the Argentine Pampas—*pampa*) was not as productive as in the USA. Historians have tended to blame this on the greater overlap between land ownership and possession of political power than was typical in North America. It was also the case that agricultural workers were poorly paid and sometimes recruited under semi-servile conditions. This encouraged landowners to use labour-intensive techniques and to postpone or limit mechanization. It also limited the size of the domestic market. Productivity suffered while control over

human beings—an important consideration in political terms—was maximized.

In both cases, the resulting structure of ownership eventually became a political issue. As the 20th century wore on, urbanization led to a change in the balance of political power within the region. Urban-based reformers started to demand radical redistribution of landholdings and there were major land reforms in Mexico in the 1930s, Bolivia in the 1950s, Cuba and Chile in the 1960s, Peru in the early 1970s, and Nicaragua and El Salvador in the early 1980s. In Brazil and Argentina populist governments did not seek to alter the ownership of land as such, but they did institute policies calculated to reduce the profitability of agriculture and the power of the landlords. Food prices were sometimes controlled, and complicated exchange-rate policies were introduced in order to subsidize urban areas at the expense of the countryside. Effects upon agricultural productivity were mixed. Genuine land redistribution in favour of smaller-scale landholdings seemed to have had a positive effect in Chile and, to some degree, Mexico, where such policies were seriously attempted, while the Cuban and Peruvian patterns of land nationalization essentially failed. Fiscal discrimination against agriculture led to a reduction in investment and to the stagnation of agricultural production, though it may have helped somewhat with domestic industrialization.

In the petroleum and mining sectors, Latin American governments began to press for tax increases almost as soon as the foreign companies started to produce. They soon took the view that they were entitled to a significant share of any wealth created by private investment because this was based upon the exploitation of subsoil wealth, a view which was often resisted by the large petroleum and mining companies. Tax increases were soon followed by demands for full-scale state control. These demands were initially resisted and there were a number of important early battles, such as the nationalization of the Mexican petroleum sector in 1938. The pace of nationalization accelerated after the mid-1960s and by the late 1970s most of the original strongholds of foreign investment were state-controlled.

Little by little, therefore, it became increasingly implausible to argue—at any rate across the region as a whole—that the rewards from commodity production were going disproportionately to foreigners or to a small and privileged domestic élite. Reforms occurred at a very different pace across the region. In Mexico there had been comprehensive land reform and a petroleum nationalization by 1940, whereas in some Central American countries the landed élite still held real power as recently as the mid-1980s. There were also occasionally reactionary interludes in which agrarian reforms were bloodily (and mostly unsuccessfully) reversed. One of the most notorious cases was in Guatemala after 1954 when a *coup d'état*, aided and abetted by the United Fruit Company of Boston (USA), led to the reversal of a land-reform programme which many regarded as necessary and desirable. However, the general historical trend was towards the replacement of foreign by domestic control over petroleum and mineral wealth and, more hesitantly, by policies of distribution of agrarian wealth that reduced the political power of the landed élite. It is true that changes in agricultural technology in the 1970s led to a greater appreciation of the importance of larger economic units, but, at the end of the 1990s, this was much less of a political question than was once the case. The excessive power of a landed élite was no longer a problem holding back either democracy or development in the region as a whole.

It would be harsh to describe these agrarian reforms as having failed. Nevertheless, there were only a few cases in which agricultural productivity seriously increased as a result of reform. Mexico between 1940 and 1965 (although not after) and Chile over the past generation are unusual in this respect. In most of the region, the agricultural sector tended to stagnate from the early 1970s. By the same token, the result of petroleum and mining nationalizations were generally less positive than had once been expected. In order to understand why, we need to look beyond the issue of ownership to bring in questions of relative prices and trends in international trade.

RAÚL PREBISCH AND THE TERMS OF TRADE PROBLEM

Any discussion of the difficulties associated with the problem of turning the production of primary products into lasting development will be associated with the name of Raúl Prebisch. In a seminal article published in 1950 Prebisch argued that the terms of trade would always tend to move against the producers and exporters of raw materials. The producers of these materials would always tend to have less bargaining power than purchasers. This thesis proved controversial, and gave rise to an enormous academic literature. However, most indicators demonstrate that the average price of commodities has been on a downward trend from the beginning of the 1980s. This downturn followed a period when they were, in many cases, rather buoyant, and there was no doubt that this tendency damaged economic prospects in Latin America. What made matters worse was that Latin America also faced positive real interest rates after around 1980, so that a significant portion of commodity export revenue was taken up by debt-servicing costs. It was also clear that commodity prices could be subject to enormous fluctuations and that these, quite apart from any long-term trend or tendency, could cause real problems for exporter countries.

It is not easy to say what should be done in the face of such problems. Prebisch came to be associated with a school of economic thinking which eventually took positions that went far beyond what he had actually advocated. Essentially, however, Prebisch was associated with the idea of import-substituting industrialization (ISI). The point was that commodity exporters should diversify their economies by using the foreign exchange earned by their exports to finance industrialization. There was some merit in this policy, but some difficulties as well. A full discussion of the impact of ISI upon Latin America is impossible here. Briefly, there was much to be said for a considered policy of industrial promotion but the arguments in favour of an indiscriminate policy of tariff protection were much weaker. One often overlooked problem was that economies that adopted policies of tariff protection and other incentives to industrialization continued to be dependent upon the foreign currency earned by primary products until such time as their manufacturing sectors earned sufficient foreign exchange. That might, under ISI policies, be never. Moreover, to the extent that economies come to depend for their capital goods and industrial inputs upon foreign exchange earned by commodities, their economic dependency might actually be increased by ISI.

The impact of ISI upon commodity exports themselves was generally discouraging. Industrial promotion tended to lead to various forms of discrimination against traditional exports. Indeed, between 1945 and the beginning of the 1980s there was a general trend in the region for governments to de-emphasize any policy of increasing export volumes in favour of the twin objectives of replacing imports and seeking higher value from existing export volumes. This trend led to a sustained decline in Latin America's share of world trade. This occurred at a time when increases in world trade were highly dynamic and there was a close correlation between the growth of export volumes and economic growth in general. While more successful Asian economies tended to emphasize export growth after 1945, most Latin American economies became increasingly closed. Latin America largely missed out on the opportunities provided by the post-1945 boom in international trade.

An alternative policy sometimes adopted in addition to ISI was to seek to influence commodity markets directly, in some cases by the development of cartel arrangements. The most obvious example of a successful cartel was the Organization of Petroleum Exporting Countries (OPEC), which was formed in 1960. OPEC's most dramatic assertion of power occurred in the 1970s when the price of a barrel of petroleum rose from around US $1.20 at the beginning of the decade to as much as $40 at the end. The majority of these price increases occurred as a result of two supply shocks. One of these was the deliberate

Saudi Arabian decision to decrease petroleum production in October 1973 in order to pressure the USA to change its Middle Eastern policy. The other was the interruption of output from Iran, owing to the revolution that occurred in that country in 1979. As a result of the resulting price increases, Latin American petroleum-exporting countries, most notably Venezuela and Mexico, enjoyed enormous growths in their export income. A number of Latin American exporters of other commodities, such as bananas and copper, sought to follow suit, although they met with rather less success.

However, the subsequent history of petroleum production and prices was tumultuous. In retrospect, it could be seen that OPEC overplayed its hand and allowed the international petroleum price to rise too high at the end of the 1970s. This stimulated the growth of non-OPEC output, slower world-wide growth and substitution by other sources of energy. By the mid-1980s the position of the largest OPEC exporters was becoming untenable and prices had to fall. Despite considerable political turbulence in the Middle East, there was no sustained rise in prices until 1999. By the end of the decade, OPEC had finally been able to regain its position as the world's 'swing producer', as well as its production discipline. In the meantime, the main petroleum-exporting countries might have learned that a moderate but stable price was more in their interest than a high but unsustainable one. Certainly after the end of 1998, when the low point of the present oil price cycle was reached, there were encouraging signs that OPEC had learned from experience. The aim of maintaining a price level of around $25 per barrel was not seriously opposed by importing countries, while being high enough to allow for some economic reactivation in the petroleum-exporting countries.

During the last three decades of the 20th century the world's demand for petroleum increased very slowly, on balance by no more than the growth of population. However, a consistent decline in petroleum production in the USA and, during the past decade, Russia allowed OPEC to recover market share after 1986. Non-OPEC countries still had considerable hitherto unexploited potential for increased petroleum production, but many of the most promising geological areas were to be found in politically difficult countries where large-scale foreign investment was not easy to attract. This gave OPEC countries some possibility of influence in the future, provided they were not overly ambitious in their price increases.

THE PROBLEMS OF COMMODITY BOOMS: OIL AS AN EXAMPLE

An important consideration for any commodity-exporting country is that commodity booms can have serious negative consequences within the producing countries themselves. Here, again, the petroleum boom of the 1970s provides a perfect example of the hazards. There are several factors involved. One is the sheer difficulty of sensible planning in the absence of price stability. In principle it is difficult for any individual, company or country to plan a budget if they do not have any real idea of what their long-term income is likely to be. There is always a tendency to adjust to change too slowly. This is not such a problem when the price is increasing, but is serious indeed when it is falling. What made this problem particularly difficult for the 1970s petroleum exporters, apart from the price fluctuations themselves, was the ready availability of international credit at variable rates of interest. Bankers, like the petroleum exporters themselves, tended to be optimists. When revenue estimates fell back, it was not only the exporter governments that needed to conduct a reassessment, but also their creditors. The result of this reassessment was higher real interest rates, just at the time when the exporter government could least afford to pay them and when (at the beginning of the 1980s) there was a trend towards higher real interest rates world-wide, largely to counter the inflationary impact of higher international petroleum prices upon the importing countries.

There is also a macroeconomic argument that commodity-exporting countries that experience sudden growth typically suffer from exchange-rate overvaluation. This makes it difficult for them to develop other export sectors. Latin American countries that were spectacularly successful commodity exporters—Argentina and Uruguay with their agricultural wealth early in the 20th century, Chile with its copper industry in the 1940s,

Venezuela with its petroleum—tended to become dependent upon a limited range of products or even a single product. Petroleum drove out coffee in Venezuela during the 1930s, and the high real exchange rate in Venezuela compared to Colombia and Brazil disadvantaged coffee production in the late 1990s. In Mexico during the 1970s as well, there was real evidence that growing petroleum exports were adversely affecting non-petroleum exports.

Finally, there was a whole range of issues associated with the notion of 'rent seeking'. Adam Smith pointed out in the *Wealth of Nations* that a predictable moderate income was more likely to be a spur to further material progress than an abundant but fluctuating one. The perception that wealth comes largely from good luck is a psychological incentive to speculative, rather than productive, activity. This argument, while valid, needs to be made more precise and a little more complex. The key point has to do with the character of returned value provided by the commodity. Commodity exports return value to economies in several different ways. There is direct payment to labour. Early in the 20th century, labour was an important factor in the cost of commodity production, including petroleum production, and labour relations were often difficult. During the latter half of the 20th century, however, there was a vast increase in the capital intensity of virtually every kind of commodity production, again including petroleum. Labour still mattered somewhat, but it was no longer the force that it was. Another kind of returned value comes in the form of orders to local businesses for everything from offices to food. This can be important, particularly in remote areas where there are few competing forms of economic activity. Mining companies, much more than petroleum companies, sometimes generate quite significant amounts of value via local purchases. This is less true of petroleum producers where the most important form of returned value is typically taxation. As a result, high commodity prices are likely to be associated with an increase in tax or royalty revenue paid to the state. This was precisely the most striking characteristic of the 1970s petroleum boom.

The main effect of the boom was to transfer money to the governments of petroleum-exporting countries. This changed the whole character of the political system in the countries involved. In circumstances where taxes are mainly paid by individuals or local companies, there will be a powerful constituency of taxpayers who will want to be sure that their money is not wasted by governments or misappropriated via corruption. Where commodity prices are high, this constituency will weaken. Except where domestic political institutions are highly developed and effective, the degree of scrutiny of government may prove insufficient to cope with the additional temptations stemming from a flood of unexpected revenue. The normal desire of politicians to be seen to help their electorates or their friends will then take over and be subject to insufficient control. In consequence, a lot of money may be wasted. This would be bad enough even when the extra income earned from the export boom was permanent. However, the combination of government waste, economic fluctuations, over-borrowing and the inadvertent discouraging of alternative exports proved to be an extremely damaging combination.

THE ADOPTION OF FREE-MARKET REFORMS

From around 1982 a very different kind of economic policy was adopted in many countries of the region. A combination of economic crisis, extremely serious debt burdens and the declining prestige of economic nationalism following the ending of the Cold War, induced governments to move in the direction of market-orientated reforms. In terms of commodity policy, three consequences of this became evident.

Firstly, there were extensive privatizations, especially in the petroleum and mining sectors. Highlights included the sale of the major Brazilian mining company, CVRD (Companhia Vale do Rio Doce, SA), in 1997 and the total privatization of the Argentine state petroleum company, Yacimientos Petrolíferos Fiscales (YPF), finally completed in 1999. Of local significance were the privatization of the Bolivian petroleum industry, the Mexican copper industry and the extensive sales within the Peruvian mining and energy sectors. The financial consequences

of these ownership changes were significant, and led to some reduction in foreign indebtedness. There was also significant new private investment in various privatized companies, as well as, it must be said, some noticeable reductions in the size of the labour force.

Secondly, there was a far more determined effort to encourage non-traditional exports, including exports of primary products. In this respect, Chile led the way. Successive governments actively encouraged primary-product exporters, without following the Asian 'tiger' policy of encouraging vertical integration into manufacturing as well. The Chilean policy was very successful. Rapid growth of commodity exports, notably fruit, fish and forestry, underpinned rapid growth in the overall economy. At the turn of the 21st century Chile and Uruguay were the only Latin American economies to have a serious claim to be considered part of the developed world. However, other Latin American governments were impressed with the Chilean example and sought in their different ways to promote exports. In Peru there were attempts to link privatization to promises of enhanced investment. State companies were not sold purely on price, but on a mixture of price and a promise to invest in the future. Even Venezuela, considered to be one of the more reluctant adherents to policies of market-orientated reform, made real efforts to develop new mining sectors.

Finally, and most interesting of all, there was a marked change in the diplomatic posture of many Latin American governments. In the past many Latin American politicians and intellectuals were extremely distrustful of the USA, which they saw as promoting exploitative commercial relationships and interventionist political ones. However, by the late 1990s policy-makers in some countries were inclined to see US pressure as a means of opening world markets and combating protection directed against Latin American commodity exports, though other countries, notably Brazil, remained rather suspicious of the USA. Argentina and Chile became important members of the Cairns Group, which pressed for increased liberalization of agricultural products in the Uruguay Round of negotiations of the GATT (General Agreement on Tariffs and Trade—known as the World Trade Organization, WTO, from 1995), concluded in 1993. Furthermore, in the late 1990s there was a major trade conflict between the USA and the European Union (EU) over the protectionist policies which European countries extended towards the banana producers of the Caribbean. The Central American countries most affected were careful not to become too involved in this affair in order to avoid jeopardizing the aid received from Europe. However, the dispute demonstrated the way in which some Latin American governments have come to share with the USA a belief in the advantages of free markets in commodities—a stance which gives rise to potential disagreement with EU member states, which have always been much more protectionist where agriculture is concerned. (The banana trade dispute was finally resolved in early 2001.)

THE SIGNIFICANCE OF COMMODITY WEALTH IN THE 1990s

By the turn of the 21st century around one-half of the region's exports took the form of primary products. Excluding Mexico, the proportion was much higher. Of the other major countries of the region, only Brazil was a significant exporter of industrial goods. Many of these took the form of processed raw materials. Within the aggregate figure for raw materials, petroleum and mining were more important than agricultural products. Venezuela and, to a lesser extent, Ecuador and Mexico relied upon petroleum exports, while Argentina, Uruguay and Colombia depended largely upon agricultural exports.

It is clearly necessary to accept that there can be disadvantages in being dependent upon the export of a limited range of primary products. World demand for services is growing faster than it is for manufactures, and for manufactures faster than it is for primary commodities. Enhanced global wealth may not translate into greater demand for primary products. After all, people can only eat so much. Furthermore, there has been a dramatic increase in the productivity of agriculture in the developed countries since 1945 and this has exerted downward pressure on world prices. Diversification can help somewhat, as can a successful policy of discouraging protectionism against raw-material exports on the part of other regions of the world. Nevertheless, the need to achieve competitive prices for exports tends to run counter to any policy of redistributing returned value from the export product across society as a whole. Non-traditional commodity exports can certainly help particular groups within Latin America, but there are fewer resulting effects for the rest of society than is the case with, for example, petroleum.

Nevertheless, there were some advantages to commodity abundance. Latin American countries were able to attract international capital on relatively favourable terms for potential new, successful ventures. Moreover, the effect of some privatizations in the late 1990s was to help develop local capital markets. Privatized resource companies did, in some cases, become considerably more efficient and able to make unexpected economic contributions by seizing new opportunities. More generally, enhanced commodity production generated effective demand

which, provided that the right institutional underpinnings existed, might succeed in stimulating other kinds of economic activity.

If there is a general lesson to be learned from a considerable diversity of separate experiences it is that commodity development needs somehow to be integrated into a coherent development strategy. It is not that there is a single key to turning commodity abundance into development. Chile has succeeded in relative terms by emphasizing non-traditional commodity-based exports. Mexico has de-emphasized petroleum in favour of manufacturing exports. Venezuela, after failing to follow a coherent strategy for many years, is now committed to a pro-cartel policy that will work if an efficient state can somehow be developed to organize the recycling of oil revenues. However, commodity-based development strategies are always at best problematic and may continue to fall victim to negative unforeseen circumstances.

PLAN COLOMBIA AND THE WAR AGAINST DRUGS

PHILIP J. O'BRIEN

INTRODUCTION

In a major escalation in the war against illegal drugs in Latin America, at the end of 1998 President Bill Clinton of the USA (1993–2001) and the new Colombian President, Andrés Pastrana Arango, signed a Counter-Narcotics Alliance. It was an admission that the war against illegal drugs, at least in Colombia, was being lost. In September 1999 President Pastrana presented an ambitious 'plan for peace, prosperity and the strengthening of the state', subsequently known as the 'Plan Colombia', which involved spending some US $7,500m., including some $4,000m. from Colombia itself, over three years. The Plan's initial aim was to help solve Colombia's interlocking problems of illegal drugs, guerrilla insurgencies, a weak state apparatus, a weak rule of law, and a growing economic crisis. However, the emphasis, particularly as seen by the USA, was placed on combating the illegal drugs trade and guerrilla insurgencies, which were seen as almost indistinguishable from each other.

In January 2000 the Clinton administration introduced a package worth US $1,300m., the largest ever aid package to Latin America, for Colombia, and its neighbours. The package was signed into law on 13 July. The funding was presented as an emergency appropriation, but it soon became clear that additional money would be requested. Although Peru, Ecuador and Bolivia were included as aid beneficiaries, the package became known as the Plan Colombia and immediately became highly controversial, both within Colombia and internationally. The main portion of the aid was some $860m. to Colombia, three-quarters of which was allocated to the security forces. Most of that military allocation, about $417m., was designated to create three new battalions to 'push into southern Colombia', officially to create secure conditions for police anti-drug actions, including fumigation, in the departments of Putumayo and Caqueta. However, both these departments are coca-growing areas dominated by Colombia's largest guerrilla group, the Fuerzas Armadas Revolucionarias de Colombia (FARC). In practice, the distinction between anti-guerrilla actions and anti-drugs actions have become blurred. The funding was seen as a dramatic escalation in the war against illegal narcotics, and was a recognition that the bulk of coca production was now concentrated in Colombia itself.

However, the sheer size of the aid programme, and the participation of the US military and former US army personnel (working for private companies contracted to the US Department of State as part of a new policy of 'out-sourcing' low intensity conflicts) signalled that the USA was becoming involved in Colombia's internal struggles to a greater extent than hitherto. Colombia was deteriorating into what the Department of State termed a 'failed state', and as such could also endanger its already increasingly unstable neighbours, which, in turn, could threaten US interests in the whole Andean region. The Colombia problem reflected a much wider problem. Success in reducing coca production in countries such as Bolivia and Peru only seemed to produce the 'balloon effect': production just moved elsewhere, in this case to Colombia itself, the main producer of cocaine. For the anti-drugs warriors in the USA, this meant that the war against drugs had to be greatly intensified in Colombia, even at the cost of becoming involved in Colombia's internal problems.

None the less, despite 30 years and some US $30,000m. spent on anti-drugs policies, there was no sign that supply to the USA had been significantly curtailed or that demand in the USA had been significantly reduced. According to the 1997 World Drug Report for the UN Drug Control Programme (UNDCP), the value of the illegal drugs trade was estimated to be US $400,000m. per year. In comparison, in the same year, official development aid totalled $69,000m. Other reports have put the value of illegal drugs from Latin America alone at $350,000m. for that year. The latest figures suggest that neither the overall value nor the

quantity of illegal drugs had declined by 2001. Whatever the exact figure, it was clear that trade in illegal narcotics was one of the biggest businesses in the world, generating enormous profits.

Since the 1970s Latin America has been both the major producer and exporter of cocaine, and, by the 1990s, was becoming increasingly involved in the production of heroin. The region also continued to export a less dangerous drug, marijuana, and had become both a major producer and exporter of so-called 'designer drugs'. The impact of the production and export of these drugs in Latin America is far-reaching. In the four major drugs-producing and -exporting countries—Colombia, Bolivia, Mexico and Peru—drugs issues continue to dominate both domestic and international politics. Ecuador is now increasingly involved. The Caribbean and Central America are major transit routes for drugs, causing widespread corruption and violence. Brazil is thought to be the major exporter of illegal narcotics to Europe, as well as having part of its Amazon region used for the transporting and processing of drugs. Argentina, Chile and Venezuela have all become new transit routes for drugs. Drugs-related scandals at the highest levels of government and public life were common throughout the continent in the 1990s, and continued to plague the continent at the beginning of the new century. The problem of illegal drugs was clearly one of the major issues facing Latin America as it entered the 21st century, especially as it threatened to escalate into a military conflict.

COCA AND COCAINE PRODUCTION IN HISTORICAL PERSPECTIVE

The coca bush is native to the jungle areas of the Andean foothills. The chewing of the coca leaf, which South American Indians have been taking for over 1,000 years, is deeply embedded in the medicinal, religious and social traditions of the native societies of Bolivia, Colombia and Peru. The derivative of coca, cocaine, is a product of Western science. Pure cocaine, or cocaine base, is dissolved in dilute acids to form salts which are used as a recreational drug, the most common being cocaine hydrochloride, which is usually ground into a white powder base for use. By the end of the 19th century cocaine was widely used as a recreational drug by the more 'bohemian' sectors of European and American society. However, when its use spread, these countries declared the drug to be illegal, along with heroin and other substances. Between 1930 and the 1960s the use of illegal drugs, and even medical interest in them, declined. However, by the late 1960s illegal drugs began to be fashionable again, with cocaine becoming the most popular recreational drug after alcohol and tobacco (legal drugs) and marijuana (illegal drug).

CONSUMPTION OF COCAINE

In the 1980s the general attitude to cocaine and other illegal drugs began to change, as their dangerous effects became more widely known. Cocaine and heroin in particular are highly addictive, producing physiological and psychological disturbances and, in the case of acute intoxication, death. These drugs were becoming a serious health and social problem and, as at the beginning of the 20th century, were increasingly associated with crime. In particular, the consumption of 'crack', a cheap and extremely addictive mix of cocaine and other substances, reached almost epidemic proportions in some poor communities. In 2001 it was estimated that about 20% of cocaine users were seriously addicted, and that they accounted for around two-thirds of total consumption.

Official statistics showed that, in the USA, the number using any drugs fell after 1985. The US National Household Survey on Drug Abuse in 1998 showed that, in the previous year, 140m. people had used alcohol, 66m. cigarettes, 18.7m. marijuana, 3.8m. cocaine, 900,000 crack and 250,000 heroin. However, there is no evidence that the increasing expenditures on anti-drugs policies have been really effective. Deaths and the death rate from drug abuse doubled between 1979 and 1998, while prices have fallen dramatically and the purity of drugs has increased. The evidence from Europe and Japan seems similar. Estimates of the value of the illegal drugs market in the USA in 1998 ranged from US $80,000m. per year to $200,000m.—more than the annual profits of the top 500 US companies combined. It is estimated that between $40,000m. and $50,000m. per year is spent on illegal drugs in the USA.

THE PRODUCTION OF ILLEGAL DRUGS

Unlike marijuana production, which is produced largely within the USA by small-scale producers, the production of cocaine and heroin is organized like a multinational business, from outside the USA. The production of cocaine, the main illegal drug produced and exported from Latin America, was, until the 1990s, mainly organized by Colombian cartels. These cartels effectively monopolized the US and other markets. Statistics on cocaine are notoriously unreliable as they often respond to the different interests of the authorities and institutions in charge of dealing with the problem. Estimates of annual coca production are usually based on local government aerial photographs and US satellite photographs. More than 200,000 ha of land is thought to be occupied by coca plantations in Latin America, primarily in Bolivia, Colombia, Mexico and in Peru, with smaller quantities in Brazil, Ecuador and Paraguay. In 1993 US statistics claimed that Peru was responsible for the cultivation of about 60% of world coca, Bolivia 21% and Colombia 18%. However, the latest estimates in 2001 put Colombia ahead of Bolivia and Peru in terms of cultivation, producing over 60% of the coca used for cocaine. Estimates of cocaine yields are even more difficult to make than estimates of coca-leaf cultivation, as the content of the drug in the leaf varies from between 0.23% to as high as 0.85%, and how much leaf is actually processed is unknown.

In the 1990s there was a dramatic increase in the cultivation of opium poppies, particularly in Colombia, Guatemala and Mexico, and in the processing of the poppies into heroin. The USA's Drug Enforcement Agency (DEA) estimated that, in the late 1990s, over 35% of the world's heroin supply came from Latin America, whereas, at the beginning of the decade, almost the entire supply originated in Asia.

Drugs seizures improved dramatically from the late 1980s and eradication efforts by Latin American governments have had an effect. Nevertheless, the 1999 Report of the International Narcotics Control Board claimed that, in spite of the exceptional coca bush eradication programme in Bolivia and significant reduction in Peru, the area under illicit coca bush cultivation, the availability of coca leaf for the production of cocaine and the supply of cocaine to illicit markets from the region did not seem to have been significantly reduced. The prices from cocaine do fluctuate. In 1997 UN figures suggested that a South American peasant received about US $610 per kg of coca leaves; cocaine base was $860 per kg and cocaine hydrochloride was about $1,500 per kg. Cocaine could then be sold wholesale in the USA at about $25,250 per kg, and to the consumer, as cocaine powder, at as much as $110,000. The large return is clearly made at the retail stage. The latest figures indicate that the price of both cocaine and heroin has fallen dramatically: between 1991 and 1998 the price of one gram of pure cocaine fell from $379 to $169 and that of heroin from $3,115 to $1,800.

IMPACT ON PRODUCER COUNTRIES

In the short term it would seem that the production of coca and cocaine might bring a number of beneficial effects to the producer economies. Thousands of peasant families and rural workers earn higher wages than they could obtain from any other crop. Although there are problems of price fluctuations and government attempts to destroy the crop, not to mention the risk of violence from drugs traffickers or guerrillas, coca is a good perennial crop. It grows quickly, can be harvested frequently, can be planted with other crops, and is also relatively pest-free and can even be grown on fairly poor, marginal land. Local towns, too, experience a dramatic growth in construction and service industries. However, in the medium-term, drugs-led development creates problems. Such a large 'underground' economic system undermines any attempt at government regulation of the economy. The existence of a substantial amount of unregulated dollars in the economy encourages contraband activity, making it difficult for local industry to compete and undermining local financial institutions. Local food crops can be disrupted, land markets distorted and there is a growth in speculative activities. Government is perhaps the institution most adversely affected by illegal drugs: it finds it difficult to control the economy; loses revenue, as the tax base dwindles; and has extra costs attempting to control the illegal market.

The overall impact on society is more serious. Cocaine creates a state within a state and, moreover, a violent and lawless one: Colombia has the highest murder rate in the world. Guerrilla groups try to enter the cocaine market and the drugs barons themselves virtually control private armies. Furthermore, although the Latin American countries first saw cocaine addiction as the rich countries' problem, addiction in Latin American countries has also developed into a serious problem, especially among the young. Bribery, corruption and murder become endemic. Such are the sums of money involved that no sector is immune—from peasant to urban poor, from petty official to industrialist, from the police and army to the judiciary, and from the politician to the presidential office. The power of cocaine is all pervading, reaching all sectors of society.

COLOMBIA

Illegal drugs have probably had the most dramatic impact in Colombia where the production of cocaine is almost entirely concentrated. It was the Colombian drugs barons who effectively controlled the international cocaine trade. In the 1960s Colombian drugs traffickers began to export, in large quantities, the marijuana (cannabis) grown by some 40,000 peasants along the Atlantic coast of the country before the USA persuaded the Colombian Government to destroy the marijuana plantations. However, by 1985 the drugs traders were exploiting a much more profitable drug and, moreover, one much more difficult to detect, cocaine. For many drugs dealers the experience acquired in marketing marijuana in the USA proved invaluable for establishing the distribution network for cocaine. The largest drugs cartel was established by Carlos Lehder Rivas and Jorge Luís Ochoa in the mid-1970s. These two, together with Rodríguez Gacha ('the Mexican') and Pablo Escobar, formed the 'Medellín cartel', a drugs syndicate which operated from the mountain city of Medellín, and which was assumed to control about 70% of the cocaine trade until the early 1990s. It was led by Escobar, despite his imprisonment in 1991 (he escaped in July 1992), until his death in 1993. The other main Colombian drugs cartel was built around Gilberto Rodríguez Orejuela's Cali group, originally much smaller than the Medellín cartel, but which largely replaced it by the mid-1990s.

The Colombian drugs barons ran the cocaine trade like a vertically integrated multinational company. They controlled the farmers growing the coca leaf, the transport of the coca base into Colombia, the refining of coca base into cocaine hydrochloride, the transport of the cocaine into the USA and, from the 1980s, into Europe and Japan, and the distribution and sale of cocaine. Finally, it was the Colombian cartels that imposed a 'quality' control on the finished product. It is not known how much cocaine was produced in Colombia each year. In the early 1990s a study by a Colombian policy research group estimated the annual drugs revenue at US $4,000m., more than one-half the recorded value of legal exports. A recent UNDCP-financed study on the Colombian drugs trade between 1982 and 1998 claimed that drugs exports as a percentage of Colombia's gross domestic product (GDP) declined in this period, with all coca plantations taking up about 3% of agricultural land and 2% of total farm employment. However, the same study pointed out that drugs traffickers owned about 4.4m. ha of land, worth about $2,400m., and that about $550m. of which went to guerrillas in the form of 'protection tax'.

For a long period the Colombian Government ignored the activities of the cocaine barons. As a consequence, these were able to establish themselves openly in Medellín and Cali and to gain supporters of their interests in both the upper and lower chambers of Congress. They infiltrated the army, police and judiciary and set up many businesses. In 1981 the Government established a special anti-drugs police to co-ordinate drugs-control operations throughout the country. However, it was only in 1984 that a serious drive to combat the drugs barons began. The then Minister of Justice, Rodrigo Lara Bonilla, named the leading traffickers, forcing them to go underground. In April 1984, because of these initiatives, Lara Bonilla was assassinated, provoking the start of a war between the Government and the drugs barons. For some time it seemed that the drugs barons would win this war: judges investigating the trade were frequently murdered or investigated for taking bribes from the drugs cartels. The Government did have some success, managing to extradite to the USA, Carlos Lehder, who was reportedly betrayed by rivals within the cartels, in 1988. This success, however, was offset by the release of other leading drugs traffickers on dubious legal technicalities.

The situation worsened at the end of the decade with a spate of killings of magistrates, editors of newspapers, left-wing politicians, the Attorney-General, police chiefs and, finally, Luis Carlos Galán Sarmiento, a leading presidential candidate. The murder of Galán aroused the active indignation of the Colombian people, enabling President Virgilio Barco Vargas (1986–90) to declare 'total' war against the drugs barons. The Government re-established an extradition policy with the USA and sent more than a dozen middle-ranking traffickers there. The drugs barons, the so-called Extraditables, responded viciously: an AVIANCA aeroplane, on an internal flight, was blown up, killing 107 people, and a bomb was exploded outside the headquarters of the secret police, killing 52 people and wounding 653. Nevertheless, events had turned against the drugs-cartel leaders. Over 1,500 properties were seized, including some of the largest estates in Colombia. In December 1989 Gonzalo Rodríguez Gacha, 'the Mexican', generally considered the most violent of the Medellín cartel, was shot and killed by the police. As a result, in 1990 Escobar offered to negotiate with the Government, an offer that, particularly in an election year, was welcomed. Many Colombians seemed to favour an end to the drugs war. Moreover, while attention had been focused on the leaders of the Medellín cartel, smaller groups, such as those in Cali, replaced them. By the end of 1991 the Cali cartel had increased its share of the US cocaine market from 30% at the beginning of 1990, to some 70%, as well as being in control of 90% of the smaller European market. For a while at least, Cali and other cartels avoided the political assassinations and controversies surrounding the Medellín group.

In 1991 the new President of Colombia, César Gaviria Trujillo (1990–94), announced his 'Integral Pacification Plan'. The Plan controversially proposed to end the extradition of drugs traffickers who surrendered and to commute, by up to one-third, any sentences which might be imposed by the Colombian courts. The proposals yielded immediate results. Firstly, the Ochoa brothers, among the highest-ranking in the Medellín cartel, surrendered, followed by their leader, Pablo Escobar. Escobar and the Ochoas were considered the wealthiest people in Latin America, the former having an estimated fortune of US $2,500m. in 1990. Escobar secured his incarceration at an army-guarded prison, lived in some comfort and was still able to operate his business from captivity. He escaped in July 1992 by walking out of the prison, but was finally shot and killed in December 1993. The collapse of the Medellín cartel was a major victory for the Government. Nevertheless, drugs-related violence did not end in Colombia, nor did the overall supply of drugs from Latin America to North America and Europe.

The death of Escobar and the dissolution of the Medellín cartel turned attention to the Cali cartel, which was operated by a much more sophisticated group. The problems inherited by the new Colombian President, Ernesto Samper Pizano (1994–98), who assumed office in August 1994, were immediately compounded by accusations that he had received a contribution of between US $6m. and $16m. from the Cali cartel towards his electoral campaign. The accusations led to the arrests of his campaign treasurer and his campaign manager. The critical accusation, however, was against President Samper himself. The USA, in particular, remained unconvinced of his innocence. In spite of, or perhaps because of, the accusations, President Samper vigorously pursued a strict anti-drugs policy. The anti-narcotics police achieved a number of successes, notably the killing or detainment of the entire leadership of the Cali cartel by mid-1996. President Samper did achieve some success in combating the drugs trade: there was an increase in the amount of narcotics seized, as well as in the eradication of both coca and opium-poppy bushes, the destruction of drugs-processing laboratories and the capture of drugs traffickers. However, by concentrating so much on anti-drugs policies, he allowed the guerrillas to expand their operations, and in spite of his anti-drugs actions, relations between Colombia and the USA deteriorated. During President Samper's term of office the USA's approach became increasingly interventionist, rather than co-operative.

PLAN COLOMBIA AND ITS CONSEQUENCES

Andrés Pastrana Arango, elected as Colombian President in 1998, made his most immediate priorities the opening of peace talks with the FARC, and the improvement of relations with the USA. The second priority required a bold new initiative on the anti-drugs front, although closer ties with the USA would make any domestic settlement with the guerrillas more difficult. The dismantling of both the Cali and Medellín cartels had led to a fragmentation of the control of the drugs business in Colombia. The leaders of the large cartels were replaced by numerous, small businessmen, without criminal records, operating in gangs of 10–20 members. The arrest, in October 1999, of 30 of Colombia's leading drugs dealers in what was known as 'Operation Millennium', including former leading members of the Medellín cartel, offered some insights into the new organization of illegal drugs in Colombia. Illegal drugs seem to be organized now in loose networks of small drug dealers rather than large cartels. However, these networks seemed to be part of link organizations, which were in turn, some of the biggest multinational drugs-marketing operations in the world, with a daily income of over US $1m.

The break-up of the cartels, and the success in reducing coca-growing in Peru and Bolivia also led to the guerrilla groups playing a more direct role in the drugs business. The USA's Central Intelligence Agency (CIA) estimated that in 1999 Colombia's cocaine output increased by 20%, and with 136,200 ha under leaf in 2000 (compared to 50,900 ha in 1995), Colombia had become the biggest coca grower in the world, in spite of a successful herbicide eradication programme. The bulk of this increased production was thought to be mainly concentrated in the south of Colombia, in an area traditionally under guerrilla control, though that control is frequently contested by paramilitary groups, themselves major actors in the cocaine trade. Even before the US Congress approved the aid for Plan Colombia, the CIA had already trained and equipped one of the three proposed anti-narcotics battalions. However, the military push into southern Colombia was postponed in order to prevent major clashes with the guerrillas that would risk high causalities, and could finally end the intermittent peace negotiations with the guerrillas. In 2001 the new US President, George W. Bush (2001–), inherited a major dilemma. Various US reports showed that the entry of cocaine into the USA had increased in 2000 compared to the previous year, that in 2000 Colombia produced 583,000 metric tons of coca, compared to 521,400 tons in 1999. It was also reported that fumigation was not working as well as expected because although the amount of hectares destroyed using dangerous herbicides and agro-chemicals had increased dramatically in 2000, to 56,975 ha, the amount of area planted for coca had also grown. President Bush's advisers had initially openly advocated ending the false distinction between counter-insurgency and counter-narcotics efforts. As one adviser put it 'the narco-traffickers and the guerrillas compose one dangerous network'. However, Bush's overall policy towards Colombia remained the same as that of the previous administration: to force drugs-financed rebels into peace negotiations on the Government's terms. At the same time, the new US administration was anxious to improve its 'ugly American' image and to allay criticism of Plan Colombia, particularly from Colombia's neighbours and its European allies (who, by June 2001 had only offered US $280m. instead of the hoped-for $2,000m.). European countries criticized the large military component of the Plan and there were fears that its implementation would lead to instability spreading throughout the Andean region. Governors in southern Colombia also protested at the use of aerial crop destruction programme, which they claimed had an adverse environmental impact. The Bush administration, therefore, proposed the Andean Regional Initiative. This represented a modification of Plan Colombia: an additional $882m. was to be spent in 2001–02, mainly on attempting to improve social and economic conditions in neighbouring Andean countries. Particular attention was to be paid to alternative income-generating crops and regional education programmes. The EU was to monitor the crop-spraying programme. Nevertheless, the basic principles of the Initiative remained the same as that of Plan Colombia: to reduce significantly the flow of drugs from the Andean region into the USA. In 2001 Colombia continued to slide further into the quagmire. Paramilitary massacres and army and paramilitary clashes with the guerrillas continued to result in increasing numbers of refugees fleeing across the borders or into other parts of the country. Paramilitary forces grew, usually with the tacit support of the army, six-fold in the last eight years, and in 2001 constituted a powerful military force. They too are now major actors in the drugs trade. In the first six months of 2000, according to the Government's ombudsman, 512 unarmed civilians were killed by the paramilitary group, the Autodefensas Unidas de Colombia (AUC), compared with 120 killed by guerrilla groups. By 2001 paramilitary activity was thought to be responsible for about 240 non-combat deaths per month, compared to 50 by the guerrillas. In 2001 the Colombian Government finally realized the threat paramilitary organizations posed, and arrested several high-ranking AUC members. The arrests led to changes in the higher echelons of the AUC, but resulted only in a re-enforcement of the organization's more extremist elements. The situation in Colombia has also resulted in a massive 'brain drain' from the country: some 800,000 professionals have left in 1997–2001. As the death toll, the number of refugees, the economic costs and the production of coca and cocaine all continued to rise, the future for Colombia looked bleak.

BOLIVIA

Coca production in Bolivia traditionally took place in the Yungas region, to the east of La Paz. However, beginning in the 1960s, coca production moved to the agricultural colonization zone, Chaparé, in the department of Cochabamba. About 90% of coca was grown there in the 1980s, largely on family farms. Consequently, coca production in Chaparé increased dramatically, from about 6,000 metric tons before 1970 to 122,000 tons by 1985. To obtain more value added, many peasant farmers entered the first stage of processing the coca leaf into coca paste, thus making it easier to transport.

In Bolivia government figures estimated that the gross value of illegal drugs in 1986 was between US $2,000m. and $2,500m., some 53%–60% of the GDP of the formal economy, or three to four times the value of legal exports. In 1990 the Bolivian President, Jaime Paz Zamora (1989–93), claimed that 70% of his country's real GDP was cocaine-related. In 1997 the UN claimed that more than 50% of Bolivia's export earnings came from drugs and a US report suggested that, in spite of an eradication programme of 6,000 ha per year, the area under coca cultivation increased by 27% in the early 1990s.

In the 1980s the problem of drugs in Bolivia was compounded by the collapse of the formal economy. Drugs offered a lifeline for thousands of the rural and urban poor and unemployed tin miners: an estimated 300,000 people were employed in the growing, processing and transport of drugs. If those providing goods and services to this sector were included, then as many as one in six (some claim one in three) Bolivians might be connected to the cocaine economy. The benefits of coca production were unevenly spread throughout Bolivian society. Basic needs, such as clean water, health care and education, and even rural electrification, were still to be met. At the same time, a 'nouveau riche', involved in the distribution and 'laundering' (the processing of illicitly obtained funds into legitimate holdings) of profits from coca, had a whole service industry of night-clubs, boutiques and luxury consumer goods built around them.

At the end of the 1980s the Government targeted well-known drugs traffickers and many leading figures were arrested and extradited. In 1992 the Government of President Zamora introduced a Colombian-style policy of leniency towards drugs traffickers who surrendered to the authorities. This clemency included a promise that they would not be extradited to the USA nor would they receive more than five years in prison. The

policy met with some success, and major figures in the Bolivian cocaine industry surrendered. An informer's evidence led to the arrest of over 60 members of the Chavarria and Mariposa drugs rings in 1994. In the same year, however, allegations that former President Zamora was involved in drugs trafficking led to his retirement from politics.

This scandal overshadowed an optimistic report from the US Agency for International Development, which revealed a fall in the value of drugs in Bolivia, from 8% of GDP in 1989, to 3% in 1992. Bolivia had met its US-set drugs-eradication targets and in 1995 signed an extradition treaty with the USA as part of a deal to obtain US and UN aid. However, politically, attempts at eradication in Bolivia were problematic: coca growers were well organized and willing to enter into confrontation with the Government. Violent conflicts were frequent. In 1997 coca growers even succeeded in having four representatives elected to the National Congress. Thus, until recently, government eradication policies in Bolivia were only moderately successful, and frequently led to violent protests. Growers who voluntarily replaced coca with another crop received a single payment of US $2,500 per ha of coca. However, in spite of the success of eradicating some 40,000 ha of coca in the 1990s, the area in production actually increased, with 50,000 ha of new plantings. Furthermore, as the Colombian cartels encountered problems, Bolivian drugs traffickers began to produce their own supply of cocaine.

The US Government has invested some US $130m. in alternative development programmes. However, as long as there was a huge differential in price between coca and other crops, it seemed that some Bolivian growers reverted to coca cultivation after participating in alternative programmes. As a result, in 1998, the US Government decided to reduce its compensation and alternative development budget to Bolivia to $1,650 per ha, shifting the emphasis of the programme to interdiction. It also increased Bolivia's eradication target to 7,000 ha per year. The Chaparé coca growers regarded this move almost as a declaration of war. In the same year, President Hugo Bánzer Suárez, who had taken office in the previous year, outlined his plan to eliminate illegal coca production by 2002. The proposals, known as 'Plan Dignidad', which were supported by the USA, met with much opposition. The combined policy of repression, as well as compensation for alternative development crops, albeit on a declining scale the longer peasant farmers delayed, together with financial and technical support from the USA seems to have met with some success. By 2001 more than 40,000 ha had been eliminated by hand over four years: coca growing in Chaparé, was virtually eliminated, and the objective to eliminate illegal coca by 2002 was on schedule. However, a new series of protests over the eradication programmes led President Bánzer to postpone the elimination of the last illegal coca plantations in the Yungas.

The success of the coca eradication programme in Bolivia, attributed by many to a mixture of compensation to grow alternative crops, tough policies, the ability to withstand massive and often violent protests, and a determined government, were seen as lessons which could be applied elsewhere. The main problem, however, was to see if the 'balloon' effect would lead to resurgence again of coca growing, particularly if the price differential between coca and alternative crops grew.

PERU

Production of coca in Peru followed a similar pattern to that of Bolivia. Most of the legal production was concentrated around the Cuzco area, especially in the valleys of La Convención and Lares. The sudden increase in coca production occurred in Alto Huallaga, a remote region in Peru's central Andean chain, comprising the departments of Huánuco and San Martín, where 60% of all illegal coca production was grown. In the late 1980s at least 250,000 people were involved in the production of coca, with up to 40% of the rural workers in Alto Huallaga involved in the harvesting of coca. The daily wage for a rural worker in illegal coca was about four times that of rural workers in other crops. In the 1990s, as the Peruvian authorities intensified their operations against the coca growing in Alto Huallaga and with the 1992 fungus destroying many crops, coca production moved into new regions. Many peasants, therefore, moved to areas outside Alto Huallaga, such as the Marañón and Quillabamba

Valleys, where they continued to make new coca plantations. Estimates for annual Peruvian coca production varied from 155,500 metric tons of leaves to 365,542 tons with the annual value of coca production estimated at US $1,500m.–$2,500m., with some $600m.–$800m. of this figure remaining in Peru.

The impact of coca in Peru was complicated by its association with the guerrilla insurgents. Some estimated that 50%–80% of the finance for the Sendero Luminoso's popular war derived from revenue from coca sales. For a period, the influence of Sendero Luminoso appeared to be growing throughout the Amazon, creating the possibility of a general war of resistance if the Peruvian Government, under pressure from the USA, attempted to eradicate the production of coca. However, in the early 1990s the Peruvian army claimed major successes against Sendero Luminoso in Alto Huallaga, principally by taking on the task of defending coca planters. The capture of the leader of Sendero Luminoso, Abimael Guzmán Reynoso (known as the 'Chairman' or 'Commander' Gonzalo), in September 1992 eased this problem. Then, in 1994, the Government began a major offensive in Alto Huallaga to end the final vestiges of Sendero Luminoso resistance.

Following the election of Alberto Fujimori to the presidency of Peru in 1990, the interdiction of drugs and the arrest of major Peruvian drugs traffickers improved noticeably. Nevertheless, accusations of alleged links between the Peruvian military and the cocaine traffickers were common. In 1996 the President began an anti-drugs strategy, passing a law declaring a state of emergency in coca-producing areas and establishing an anti-drugs commission to conduct policy. According to UN figures Peru reduced its coca production from 115,000 ha in 1995 to 34,100 ha in 2000. Peasant families growing coca, originally about 346,000, fell by almost 40% in 1995–99. This was partly owing to the fall in coca price compared to viable alternatives, particularly coffee, but also because of tough policies.

It is estimated that cocaine produced fell from 606 metric tons in 1992 to a projected 192 tons by 2000. However, after the fall of Fujimori in 2000, evidence surfaced that proved that the disgraced former President's head of secret police, Vladimiro Montesinos, and former commanders of the armed forces were involved in military 'protection rackets'. Some 220 senior military officers were discharged and others placed under house arrest. There is also evidence that drugs gangs are regrouping, and, with the steep fall in the price of coffee, coca is once again a very attractive crop to peasant farmers. The target eradication programme for 2001 has been suspended and the onus is now on incoming President, Alejandro Toledo (elected in June 2001), to prevent the 340,000 peasant farmers once involved in coca production from returning to that crop.

MEXICO

By the end of the 1990s, as Mexican drug dealers moved quickly to replace the Colombian cartels, it was thought that Mexico produced as much cocaine as Colombia. Mexico was a major producer and exporter of cocaine, heroin and marijuana as well as 'designer drugs'. Five major cartels, those of Juárez, Tijuana, Sonora, Sinaloa and Golfo, operated a drugs business worth an estimated US $30,000m. per year. As in Colombia, corruption was endemic: there were numerous allegations of involvement in the drugs cartels levelled at high-ranking officials and those in public life. In February 1997 the head of the Government's counter-narcotics agency, Gen. Jesús Gutiérrez Rebollo, was dismissed from his post and charged with receiving money from the Juárez cartel. He was eventually sentenced to more than 30 years' imprisonment for storing and transporting weapons and for abuse of authority. In late 1998 Raúl Salinas de Gortari, the brother of Carlos Salinas de Gortari (President in 1988–94), was accused of laundering profits from the trafficking of illicit drugs. Furthermore, in the same year, the former Governor of Quintana Roo, Mario Ernesto Villanueva Madrid, went into hiding following the issuing of a warrant for his arrest on charges of drugs trafficking. Under his rule the popular holiday resort, Cancún, had become a major transhipment point for cocaine into the USA.

Many key drug dealers were killed, often in internecine disputes with other drugs dealers such as the notorious 'Lord of the Skies', or arrested. However, as in Colombia, the problem of corruption was endemic with accusations that leading politic-

ians from the ruling Partido Revolucionario Institucional (PRI) were involved with the illegal trade. However, unlike with Colombia, the USA adopted a much more cautious interventionist role in Mexico, for example, always granting the country drug certification approval. The new President of Mexico, Vicente Fox Quesada, elected in 2000, ended the long PRI monopoly on power and quickly established good relations with the USA. Fox opted for a quieter, less ostentatious offensive against the drugs traffickers, a policy that quickly had some success with the arrest, in June 2001, of Ramón Alcides Magana, one of the leading figures in the Juárez cartel, and, in the same month, the extradition to the USA of another alleged leading drugs trafficker, Francisco Rafael Camarena Macías.

INTERNATIONAL INTERVENTION

Drugs-related abuse and violence remain serious problems and, with the exceptions of Bolivia and Peru, there is little evidence of success in the USA's international narcotics-control policies in terms of halting the supply of illegal drugs into the USA.

Initially, the USA hoped to form an anti-drugs regional alliance through a series of presidential summits, the first of which was held in Cartagena de Indias (Colombia) in 1990. These 'drugs summits' were a clear indication that cocaine had become an international issue. For the USA, the war on drugs had become an integral part of the country's national security doctrine. This war became part of the low-intensity conflict strategy and involved linking drugs to guerrilla activity, although the relationship between the guerrillas and the drugs barons was always an uneasy one.

Following the US invasion of Panama in December 1989 and the subsequent surrender of the Head of Government, Gen. Manuel Noriega Morena, the USA developed a more direct military strategy to combat the drugs trade. There was widespread concern throughout Latin America that the USA was over-emphasizing the military aspect in the fight against drugs. At the Cartagena and other summits the US strategy was to encourage specific eradication targets and comprehensive drugs strategies, as well as persuading the local armed forces to attempt 'permanent disruption' of the drugs supply chain. The Latin American response was to urge more aid to encourage coca farmers to change to alternative crops, to have greater co-operation on money laundering and to begin multilateral training of the Latin American police and military. The summits led to a number of co-operative agreements. However, such measures, while of some use, were not considered sufficient by the USA.

Although periodic summits continued, the USA decided that bilateral diplomatic pressure was more likely to produce favourable results. Colombia, in particular, was singled out as needing more direct pressure. The USA did not conceal its belief that President Samper did have connections with the drugs barons, and was clearly in favour of his resignation. The USA introduced a system of annual certification for drugs-producing countries' efforts in combating trafficking in 1986: failure to receive a certificate could result in the imposition of trade and aid sanctions. In 1996–98 Colombia failed to get the certificate, but trade sanctions were waived. In contrast, Mexico was 'certified' in 1997 and 1998, at a time when there was a huge increase in illegal drugs in Mexico. By exerting such bilateral pressure, the USA hoped to obtain extradition treaties and to increase sentences on convicted drugs dealers in Latin America. The policy met with some success in Colombia: prison sentences were increased for drugs-related offences and legislation on extradition passed. However, it became clear that the annual certification process was creating severe diplomatic problems and was widely seen as unfair. In 1999 the USA adopted a less aggressive stance and awarded certificates to Mexico, Peru and Bolivia, and even gave a conditional certificate to Colombia. In 2001 the US Senate Foreign Relations Committee proposed that the certification process be replaced with a more co-operative, multilateral approach. However, from 2000 the main focus was on the success or failure of Plan Colombia. Neighbouring countries, particularly Venezuela, expressed concerns over the Plan and it now remains an open question whether the recent successes against illegal drugs in Bolivia and Peru can be maintained, and extended to Colombia.

THE FIGHT AGAINST ILLICIT DRUGS

There are a number of issues in the fight to contain the illegal drugs trade: eradication, interdiction, creating an effective anti-narcotics police, reducing corruption, pressuring and persuading local governments to take effective action, attacking profits and reducing demand. Officially, all the cocaine-producing countries support eradication programmes. However, manual eradication is costly and time consuming, while the alternative, crop spraying, encounters serious environmental and health objections: only Colombia, despite internal opposition, has agreed to use crop spraying. However, although eradication programmes in Peru and Bolivia met with some success, they usually resulted in coca-growing peasants just moving to other areas. Persuading the rural poor to grow another crop is another alternative. However, crop substitution is both slow and expensive and no other crop is as profitable as coca. As seen to a certain extent in Peru and Bolivia, technical assistance and good prices for viable alternative crops are essential. Eradication, compensation and alternative crops play an important part in the efforts to control cocaine production. In all countries the creation of an effective, relatively uncorrupt, specialist anti-narcotics police has made a difference in destroying some of the most notorious drugs cartels. In this battle an effective, relatively uncorrupt, government and judicial system make an important difference.

Interdiction, which involves seizing the drugs at any time between the laboratory stage and distribution, remains the favoured method of attempting to control the drugs trade. There is improved co-ordination between the USA and the supplier countries, but the problem is that production and distribution of cocaine in particular are fairly mobile: as long as such large profits can be made, there are enough remote areas in Latin America where it will be profitable to produce drugs. Interdiction by capturing the drugs in transit is also difficult. The transport of cocaine (and the laundering of money from cocaine) is a complex business: as one route and method was closed, another appeared. For example, from the late 1980s interdiction deterred the formerly favoured routes of the Caribbean islands into Florida (USA). Instead, by the mid-1990s some 60% of cocaine passed through Mexico. Surveillance for interdiction was made more difficult when in 1999 Panama ended the use of surveillance flights from the Howard Base in the Panama Canal Zone, forcing the USA to look for alternative locations, such as the islands of Aruba and the Netherlands Antilles, off the coast of Venezuela, and Ecuador. However, Venezuela refused permission for such planes to fly over its territory. Given the complexity of transport routes and operations, the US military still estimated that only about 10%–15% of shipments of drugs are seized. Furthermore, as interception increased, Latin America's drugs trade began to diversify, with new production centres, products and trade routes opening up. For example, Guatemala and, from the late 1990s, Colombia and Mexico, increased production of opium poppies and heroin.

From the late 1980s the USA and some European countries made their financial laws stricter and improved information exchange, to prevent the laundering of drugs profits. In 1989, following a long investigation, US officials arrested managers and closed down the Bank of Credit and Commerce International (BCCI), accusing it of processing thousands of millions of 'drugs dollars'. In spite of some significant success against banks involved in the laundering of drugs money, most banks still maintained their 'secrecy'. Some US $100,000m.–$200,000m. of drugs money may be laundered in the USA annually, with many household name companies inadvertently involved in the process. It is clear that there is still a need for effective legislation to control this profitable business.

Drugs strategies hitherto have tended to emphasize the law-and-order aspect over any other considerations. This meant that one solution, which has proponents in Latin America and some in the USA and Europe, has still not been considered—namely the legalization, control and discouragement of drugs, in an attempt to at least remove the criminals from the drugs trade. All the evidence points to the fact that demand brings forth supply. Furthermore, until demand is significantly reduced in the rich countries, there was every chance that poor countries would produce to meet that demand. Certainly, in spite of local successes, the war against drugs was not being won and the international community was still looking for a new drugs policy that would work.

THE ENVIRONMENT IN LATIN AMERICA
Prof. ADRIAN MCDONALD

INTRODUCTION

There are many definitions of Latin America. These are based primarily on linguistic or geographic boundaries. In its widest interpretation Latin America consists of South and Central America, the Caribbean and those parts of the southern USA that have a substantial Spanish-speaking population. Such a very large part of the world will clearly encompass a very diverse range of environments, environmental institutions and environmental pressures. This article can thus address only key issues and brief case studies. However, these case studies in particular can represent either typical cases or specific extremes.

Environment too has many definitions. These range from 'something that surrounds' to 'the aggregate of circumstances surrounding an organism...specifically...combination of external physical factors that affect and influence growth and development and the complex social and cultural conditions ...affecting the nature of...a community'. These two definitions illustrate the way in which the definition of environment has changed substantially in the last 30 years, from an essentially natural concept of the physical geographical milieu in which people of a region exist, to a recognition of ecology and sustainability which emphasizes complexity and connectivity. That connectivity could be either between physical elements of the landscape, for example between land and rivers, between economic, social and environmental issue, or between a temporal inter-relation between this generation and future generations and their rights to inherit a sustainable environment. It is the latter definitions that we lean towards in this account.

ECONOMY AND ENVIRONMENT

Economy cannot easily be separated from environment. Economic resources are drawn from the environment and 'waste' products from economic activity are returned to the environment. High quality or unique environments are economic products in their own right. Nor is the relationship simple. The relation between environment and economy is often portrayed as an 'inverted U'. The basis to the relationship is as follows. Low income equates to low pollution at an early stage in economic development. Thereafter, the growth in environmental burden relates to the economic growth but reaches a threshold, after which environmental burden declines as the wealthy population becomes more vociferous and aware of environmental well-being and value. While this common paradigm is particularly seductive in the potentially high growth of Latin America, it is not well supported in empirical evidence and is founded on a very limited information base. The relation between economy and environment is as much a consequence of history, institutional arrangements and political commitment as it is a process-based determination.

BIODIVERSITY AND CONSERVATION

There are major international agreements to conserve the world's biological diversity. Biodiversity encompasses more than a simple range of species (diversity) but recognizes specialization as well as speciation. Many groups argue that to achieve conservation of biodiversity, the focus should not be diluted by attempts at world coverage but should focus on prime sites for conservation. These prime sites are mainly in the tropics and between 17 and 25 so-called 'hot spots' have been identified by the international pressure group Conservation International Foundation,[1] based in Washington, DC (USA). Conservation International estimate that the proposed priority areas occupy less than 2% of the Earth's land surface but contain roughly 40% of the planet's known plant life and more than 25% of its animal species.

The global position of Latin America, spanning the tropics, and the presence of a significant altitudinal profile across almost all these latitudes makes Latin American environments vital to such conservation. Indeed, of the 25 hot spots identified by Conservation International, no less than seven are in Latin America. Furthermore, one of the three tropical wilderness areas of global significance is in Latin America (the Upper Amazon and Guyana shield) and contains over 60% of the world total tropical wilderness area.

The seven biodiversity hotspots of global significance in Latin America are: the tropical Andes; Mesoamerica; the Caribbean; the Atlantic forest region; Choco, Darien and Western Ecuador; the Brazilian Cerrado; Central Chile. Each of these sites presents complex management problems, at the heart of which is preservation and conservation. However, effective management is made immensely more complex by the tourist interest in such rare and special places, an interest that threatens in some ways but could provide the alternative income and political will to help conservation. This form of tourism is called ecotourism.

Ecotourism means many things to many people. It certainly covers the viewing of rare and beautiful animals and habitats and may validly involve the archaeological wonders that are hard to separate in Latin America from their natural environment milieu. Thus, Dominica has a water-rich forest environment and Costa Rica a diverse set of environments worthy of tourist interest in their own right. In contrast, in Peru Machu Picchu and particularly the Nazca Lines have an environmental component to their grandeur, but both are the focus of a major tourist operation, centred on the cultural history but not without consequent environmental (erosion, noise, etc.) problems.

EXPLOITATION OF PRIMARY RESOURCES

Latin America is rich in biological, land, water and mineral resources. With high population growth rates and with a political imperative to promote development, the exploitation of natural resources is high on the agenda. However, such exploitation is not without environmental ramifications.

Consider then the case of gold mining on the Madre de Dios River in Bolivia and Peru. This has several environmental impacts associated with the winning of the gold-bearing rocks and the extraction of the gold from the rocks and sediment on the riverbed. To achieve this, boats have systematically destroyed the riverbanks and bed of the Madre de Dios for many miles. A riverbed is a delicate habitat, a biosurface that supports complex microscopic life that supports an aquatic food chain. In addition to the direct destruction, the resulting sediment has choked the spawning grounds of fish for many more miles downstream. A Western perspective might question why people would do this to their environment. The answer, of course, is economic survival. The crew members in the boats exist on a daily fixed wage of US $8 and to retain their jobs they have to produce 120g of gold per day. These then are the economic impetuses not dissimilar to those that drove coal and steel related impacts in the USA, the United Kingdom and elsewhere only a generation ago.

However, perhaps the most dangerous part of the work on the Madre de Dios River is the use of highly toxic mercury to extract the gold from the silt. An amalgam of mercury and gold is heated on a small open stove from which the mercury evaporates as white smoke leaving behind the almost pure gold. It is technically possible to trap the mercury in a chimney and recycle it, but this is almost never done. Instead, the mercury escapes into the air where the heavy daily rains wash it into the river. Recycling is pointless given the relative price of gold and mercury. Recycling would only take place under a strict regulatory regime. While Latin America has a growing body of environmental regulation it does not, as yet, have the fiscal strength to enforce the regulations.

These impacts affect real people living in the area. This is not simply a matter of academic debate, but the well-being of people and of the habitats on which they depend. There are almost no fish left in the river and those that remain are affected by mercury contamination. Worst affected are the indigenous peoples, including the Harakmbut, who live in the forests near the river. Not only have they gradually lost land to the colonists, but they consume the remaining mercury-contaminated fish. Studies have shown that over time, mercury may cause people to lose sensation in their limbs as the toxin destroys their nervous systems. Eyesight eventually deteriorates, and they may suffer convulsions, paralysis and, eventually, death.

POPULATION, URBANIZATION AND RURAL DEPOPULATION

Population characteristics and environmental pressures are closely linked. Resource availability can only realistically be assessed on a per head basis. Such an assessment for Latin America is considered below. There are two key elements in the assessment of population. The first is the growth rate and the absolute population total for a region and the second is the concentration of that population. In a human context, and certainly in the case of Latin America, this is interpreted as the degree of urbanization.

One generation ago Latin America had, with Africa, the highest regional growth rate. In 2000 access to contraception and changed attitudes and knowledge, particularly among women, has helped fertility rates to fall by more than 50% in the generation. It is argued by the US-based Population Action International (whose analysis is acknowledged here as one of the underpinnings of this account[2]) that the slowing of population growth will occur through better reproductive health and guidance. So while Latin America has not reached the developed Western world total fertility rates (of 2.1 or fewer births per woman), the change is strongly in that direction. Only in Guatemala and Honduras does the fertility rate exceed five. Elsewhere it is below five and the dominant rate (found in nine of the mainland countries) lies between 2.2 and 3 children per woman. The largest absolute populations in Latin America (above 20m. in 2000) are summarized in Table 1 below. Brazil, the largest population in Latin America, is the fifth most populous country in the world; Mexico, the second-largest population in Latin America, was the 11th-largest country, in population terms, in the world in 2000.

POPULATION
(millions)

	2000	2025*
Brazil	170.12	217.93
Mexico	98.88	130.20
Colombia	42.32	59.76
Argentina	37.03	47.16
Peru	25.66	35.52
Venezuela	24.17	34.78

* Medium projection.
Table 1.

In resource and environmental planning, time horizons of 25 years, as used in the table above and in subsequent tables, are common. It is therefore important to appreciate that there is a considerable degree of uncertainty in the projections of population. In the table above a medium projection is provided but, for example, in the case of Brazil there also exists a high projection (238m.) and a low projection (198m.). All are correct depending on which set of assumptions is deemed reasonable. However, as time passes it is possible to assess the past predictions and, in general, the lower projections have proven closer to reality.

The second element in the growth pattern is that of urbanization and consequential rural depopulation. Let us take Colombia as an example. Demographically, Colombia reached stability at the beginning of the 1990s. There was a moderate annual growth rate of 1.9% in 1990–97 and in mid-1999 population was estimated at 41.6m. However, until the early 1990s population grew at inconceivable speed. The population of the country's capital, Santafé de Bogotá, increased from barely 100,000 inhabitants at the start of the century (when the total population was just over 3m.) to more than 6m. by mid-1997 (during independence, being capital city of one of four Viceroys, it did not reach 30,000). The second-largest city, Cali, had an estimated population of about 2m., as did Medellín and its metropolitan area, and there are half a dozen more cities nearing 1m. inhabitants. Rural population in the mid-20th century was 75% of the total figure, but by 2000 it was less than 32% of the population as a whole. This is a picture of an urban Colombia, multipolar, that is, with several urban areas being the focus of regions. In South America as a whole the urban population is approaching 80% of the total population. This rapid growth in the urban population is probably the most important immediate driver of environmental degradation. The speed of expansion was owing to the migration-derived growth, rather than to a pure demographic dynamic. Inevitably, the urban infrastructure did not expand at the same speed and, in the case of water and sewerage in particular, major inadequacies are evident. These will be examined below.

RESOURCE SCARCITY AND ENVIRONMENTAL PRESSURE

The population estimates discussed above can be used to provide an estimate of the per head availability and pressure on resources. Four crucial attributes are considered below: water resources, forest resources, arable land and carbon loading.

Table 2 gives the water resource availability per head in 2000 and 2025. The Latin American countries listed are those that are included in the 100 most water-poor countries. Two measures can be used to interpret or give meaning to these figures. Water stress occurs when the annual availability of renewable fresh water is less than 1,667 cu m per head and water scarcity occurs when this figure falls below 1,000 cu m per head. Thus, no Latin American country was deemed water scarce in 2000 and only two, Haiti and Peru, were water stressed. By 2025, however, Haiti will be water scarce.

RENEWABLE WATER RESOURCE*
(cu m per head)

	2000	2025
Haiti	1,338	918
Peru	1,559	1,126
Dominican Republic	2,354	1,791
El Salvador	3,019	2,091
Cuba	3,080	2,924
Jamaica	3,214	2,558
Mexico	3,614	2,745
Trinidad and Tobago	3,938	3,415
Honduras	1,338	918
Guatemala	10,189	5,854

Table 2: Water resource availability in Latin America.

* These are gross figures and do not reflect access constraints, quality, spatial or temporal distributions which affect availability in reality (McDonald and Kay, 1988, see Bibliography).

Table 3 identifies the availability of arable land per head again in the most resource-scarce Latin American countries. A per head figure of 0.07 ha per head has been used as the threshold amount of land needed to move from scarcity to relative sufficiency. This is a minimum figure and a rather simplistic threshold. There is some disagreement as to whether land for fuel needs should be added to that figure. Although no Latin American country reaches that threshold in 2000 and only one is on the threshold in 2025, it would only require a reassessment of 0.1 ha per head to place all these countries on, or near, the threshold. Furthermore, as many of these countries have land held in large quantities by a very small élite these per head estimates can be misleading. Large numbers of people are landless peasants or people with land resources already below, or very near to, the threshold. Such an imbalance provides the basis of considerable unrest and political instability.

ARABLE LAND AVAILABILITY IN LATIN AMERICA
(ha per head)

	2000	2025
Trinidad and Tobago	0.09	0.08
Colombia	0.10	0.07
Jamaica	0.11	0.08
Haiti	0.11	0.08
Grenada	0.12	0.11
Costa Rica	0.13	0.09
El Salvador	0.13	0.09
Venezuela	0.14	0.10
Chile	0.15	0.12
Suriname	0.16	0.13
Peru	0.16	0.12
Guatemala	0.17	0.10

Table 3: Arable land availability in Latin America in 2000 and 2025.

Forests are probably the common perception of the dominant land cover in Latin America. Nevertheless, before considering the forests it is important to recall that there are large areas of mid-latitude and altitudinal grasslands, scrubland and desert. These are important habitats in their own right and are the resource base for many people, but are not considered in these examples. Table 4 gives the per-head forest resource in the most forest-limited Latin American countries. Again, the identification of a threshold is somewhat arbitrary. A per head forest area of 0.1 ha has been used by some analysts and, set at that level, Haiti, El Salvador and Jamaica have very limited forest resource availability. By 2025 Trinidad and Tobago and the Dominican Republic will be added to that list. However, given the strict interpretation of other resource thresholds already discussed it could be argued that a forest resource per head of 0.25 hectares per person is more appropriate. At that level the majority of the countries tabulated would face low levels of forest cover, although perhaps not reaching the criticality implicit in a 0.1 ha threshold. Some countries, such as Brazil, have a much greater forest resource, some 10 times the threshold.

FOREST COVER IN LATIN AMERICA
(ha per head)

	2000	2025
Haiti	0.00	0.00
El Salvador	0.01	0.00
Jamaica	0.05	0.01
Trinidad and Tobago	0.12	0.07
Dominican Republic	0.17	0.09
Uruguay	0.24	0.21
Costa Rica	0.27	0.08
Guatemala	0.30	0.11
Chile	0.51	0.36
Mexico	0.54	0.33
Honduras	0.56	0.33

Table 4: The forest resource per head for most forest-stressed countries in Latin America.

The pressure on the natural environment through the decline in resource and the increase in population will lead directly to further environmental problems such as land loss through erosion, sedimentation and damage to river systems, etc. In addition, however, there are direct environmental pressures. One measure of such pressure is the carbon-dioxide load. This is an important global-warming compound. Table 5 identifies the Latin American countries contributing the largest absolute loads in 1996 and 2025. Per head load is less significant in this case, but growth in population is equated to increase in load through the index given.

RAIN FOREST CASE STUDY

Colombia's Amazon region is considered one of the greatest areas of biodiversity in the world, serving as home to over 22,000 plants and animal species. This biodiversity has great practical value (for example, raw materials for new drugs development) as well as aesthetic value. This region is also the home

of a number of indigenous peoples who depend on plant and animal abundance for their survival. This region, like many other tropical rain-forest regions, is considered threatened. Economic and social pressures have led to the deforestation of 200m. ha of the world's tropical rain forests from 1990. These pressures are global and widely documented. They are logging, clearance for farming, urban and infrastructure development, and mining.

CO_2 Emissions

	'000 metric tons of carbon		Per Head Emissions
	1996	2025	
Trinidad and Tobago	6,069	7,135	4.78
Venezuela	31,235	48,685	1.40
Suriname	573	734	1.40
Jamaica	2,743	3,568	1.10
Mexico	95,007	133,410	1.02
Argentina	35,440	47,456	1.01
Chile	13,313	18,046	0.92
Cuba	8,507	9,109	0.77
Panama	1,823	2,573	0.68
Ecuador	6,683	10,166	0.57

Table 5: Carbon yields in Latin America. The information relates to the greatest per head yields.

In 1991 a consortium of foreign petroleum companies, led by the US concern Conoco Incorporated, proposed to develop several oilfields in Colombia's Amazon region, in an area known as Block 16. Conoco had already spent US $90m. on exploration of the area. It has identified over 200m. barrels of petroleum reserves, a huge figure that would amount to 20% of Colombia's total reserves. The debate over the future of Colombia's rain forests sets two compelling perspectives against each another. Conoco and the Colombian Government believe that the oilfields can be developed in an environmentally sensitive way, while environmental organizations, indigenous people's representatives and multilateral lending institutions all question the consortium's intent and the appropriate development strategy for the region. In this respect then, the perspectives are little different from those in the case of large tropical dams. It should be noted that Latin America has developed less than 35% of its hydropower potential.

Conoco, recognizing the complexity of its plan to proceed with petroleum exploration, presented a proposed environmental-protection plan and requested that major stakeholders meet and discuss its proposal. Conoco's proposed development plan would require an investment of US $600m. for drilling and production equipment, two parallel 160 km pipelines and a new 140 km road. Approximately 10% of the total expected investment is intended for environmental-protection initiatives. Conoco submitted this plan for approval to the Colombian state oil company, Empresa Colombiana de Petróleos (ECOPETROL), which manages petroleum exploration and production. The development proposal was questioned in some quarters, as past development efforts by ECOPETROL and foreign petroleum companies have damaged forest and water resources and resulted in the colonization of rain-forest areas. By 2001 the Colombian Government had yet to establish comprehensive environmental guidelines on petroleum exploration and extraction activities.

Block 16 bisects two national parks, Los Katios in Colombia and Darien in Panama. These two areas are claimed by numerous ecologists as two of the most biologically diverse regions in the world. The Block also is located within the traditional territory of the Orewa, Guambianos and Paez indigenous tribes. Environmental and indigenous peoples' groups are pressuring the Colombian and Panamanian Governments to halt future development in the region. In order to meet its financial obligations to Conoco, ECOPETROL solicited the World Bank (International Bank for Reconstruction and Development) for a US $100m. loan. In response, indigenous and environmental groups demanded that the loan be reconsidered and that no further development in rain forests be allowed until various demands were met.

INSTITUTIONAL REFORM

This review of some of the environmental issues facing Latin America is necessarily negative, for the region faces great challenges. However, there are many examples of success and enterprise. Institutional reform has been a significant feature, particularly in the water sector, in many countries of the region, including Argentina, Mexico and Chile. In the 1980s in Mexico the large irrigation districts under federal control had insufficient funding for maintenance and were in severe decline. The Government created the National Water Commission (Comisión Nacional de Agua—CNA), which brought about the transfer of irrigation management to the owners of the land, in effect to co-operatives. The first transfer was in 1990 and by 1995 316 irrigation associations had been formed, controlling 70% of Mexico's 3.2m. ha of irrigated land. The best, and most commercially astute with the most potential for financial autonomy, were the first farmers to lead the new associations. The advantage was management autonomy and a *de facto* ownership of the resource, albeit on a 20-year lease. The threat was the simple admission by the Government that it could not afford to operate the system and that it would therefore decline and eventually cease operation. The Mexican privatization, although perhaps mutualization is a more accurate description, has been held up as a successful example of institutional reform.

Institutional reform has also been fundamental in the improvement of urban water supply. Rapid urban development, far outstripping development of infrastructure, has been identified as one of the processes through which environmental pressures have increased. As much as 70% of waters supplied by utilities in Latin America are lost as leakage. In the Brazilian state of São Paulo, a staggering 93% of the population are urban dwellers. After the democratization process, which took place in 1983, non-governmental organizations (NGOs) and professional organizations in particular, promoted a new form of management and a political awareness of environment and resource issues. This resulted in the adoption of a new Federal Constitution in which water and environmental issues are explicitly recognized. A National Water Resources Policy and a National Water Resources Management System was created within the Federal Constitution (section 21). These recognize the inseparability of water quality and quantity issues, of the rights and responsibilities of upstream and downstream users and of the effects and influence on its neighbours of what is claimed to be the largest population and biggest industrial complex in Latin America.[3] This satisfies the first three stages in the framework for sustainable environmental management at the basin or regional scale, namely assessment of national policy needs, co-operation (if international resources are involved) and the development of a management plan. Implementation and evaluation, the last two stages in such planning, are as yet incomplete in the case of São Paulo. (For further information see Braga, 1999, and the Ministry of Housing, Planning and Environment, 2000, in Bibliography.)

Institutional infrastructure alone is not always sufficient to provide environmental protection even for 'signature' regions having special environmental significance. The 21 islands of the Galapagos are protected by the Ecuadorean Government through the granting of National Park status (to 90% of the land mass, 693,700 ha) in 1959. This was enhanced, in 1967, by the provision of a permanent Park Superintendent, as well as regulations and accredited guides. Furthermore, the surrounding seas are designated a Marine Park. Nevertheless, all this was insufficient to prevent a potentially devastating oil spill on the Islands. On 16 January 2001 the tanker Jessica, owned by the Ecuadorean company, Acotramar, ran aground on the island of San Cristóbal. Despite efforts to avert a major oil spill, about one million litres of fuel oil are claimed to have leaked into the sea (there are widely differing reports), reaching some 80 km from the spill site and causing marine fauna deaths. That the damage was not more severe was owing to good fortune and favourable sea conditions (rather like the potentially much worse spill from the Braer tanker off the Shetland Islands in 1993), and the prompt response of the Galapagos National Park Service and the Ecuadorean Navy. Nevertheless, the resultant lawsuit filed by the National Park Service against Acotramar

and the fuel company, Petrochemical, suggests that US $14m. was the minimum figure being sought in damages. If such an environmental disaster could occur on such special isolated islands far from main tanker routes, the prospects for the crowded Caribbean archipelago were poor.

CONCLUSION

Any attempt to summarize the most critical environmental concerns in Latin America is made more complex by the immense diversity of the region. To simplify, the island Latin American nations of the Caribbean are considered separately.

All small, tropical-island nations have particular environmental problems, local in nature. Typically, they have water-quantity problems owing to the rapidity of runoff and the limited storage potentials. Water-quality issues arise from the trapping of pollution in coral reef supported lagoons. Tourist pressures exacerbate these water problems. The reefs themselves are sensitive[4], yet attract both ecotourism and adventure tourism. Furthermore, the tropical-island tourist trade flourishes on a stereotype of golden beaches, resulting in an inevitable pressure to reduce the area of mangrove swamp in favour of the much less erosion-resistant sandy beach. Finally, development focuses on the sea front and the seasonal pressures affect sensitive sand dunes and place pressure on infrastructure capacity. The Barbados Declaration of 1994 noted that Small Island Developing States, of which the nations and islands of the Caribbean are prime examples, are 'particularly vulnerable to natural as well as environmental disasters and have a limited capacity to respond to and recover from such disasters'. Despite the aspirations of this Declaration, the Seventh Commission on Sustainable Development, held in 1999, saw little progress in implementation.

The mainland Latin American countries have different concerns. All have ratified, at different times, the main international environmental treaties on biodiversity, traffic in endangered species, climate change and ozone depletion. At the Ministerial Conference held in The Hague (Netherlands) in October 1999, most Latin American countries reported the following key environmental concerns at national level: soil degradation, desertification, urban air pollution, urban water pollution, agricultural runoff, deforestation, biodiversity/habitat loss, water supply and mining. Uruguay made particular mention of cross-boundary pollution.[5]

So in Latin America, one of the most diverse environments on earth, covering mesa, deserts, glaciers, rain forest, rivers and mountains, three essential environmental concerns remained: deforestation and soil degradation; loss of habitat and biodiversity; and the impacts of rapid urbanization.

FOOTNOTES

1. The author acknowledges Conservation International Foundation. Errors in interpretation remain with the author.
2. The author has abstracted from the tables, added, and in some cases corrected, statistics, but the indebtedness to Population Action International remains. See Englemann et al in Bibliography.
3. This is contentious. If Mexico were considered part of Latin America, Mexico City would have some claim to this title. However, Mexico is often classed as part of North America and, thus, not strictly Latin America.
4. The vulnerability of different islands is classified through SIDS (Small Island Developing States within the United Nations Environment Programme—UNEP). Details can be found in UNEP's Islands Directory.
5. As reported in country profiles produced for the Ministerial Conference in The Hague, Netherlands, in October 1999 (see Bibliography) and by the World Resources Institute, based in Washington, DC (USA).

BIBLIOGRAPHY

Braga, B. 'The Management of Urban Water Conflicts in the Metropolitan Region of Urban São Paulo: Towards Upstream/Downstream Hydrosolidarity', pp. 89–96 of *Proceedings of International Water Resources Association Seminar*. Stockholm, 14 August 1999.

Englemann, R., Cincotta, R., Dye, B., Gardner-Outlaw, T., and Wisnewski, J. *People in the Balance*. Population Action International, Washington, DC, 2000.

McDonald, A., and Kay, D. *Water Resources Issues and Strategies*. London, Longman, 1988.

Ministry of Housing, Planning and Environment. 'Framework for Sustainable River Management. Recommendations of an Expert Workshop held at The Hague in October 1999.' Second World Water Forum and Ministerial Conference, The Hague, 2000.

Soussan, J., McDonald, A., Mitchell, G., Smout, I., and Chadwick, M. (Eds). *Second World Water Forum and Ministerial Conference: Final Report*. World Water Council, The Hague, 2000.

CENTRAL AMERICA AFTER HURRICANE MITCH

Prof. JENNY PEARCE

NATURAL AND UNNATURAL DISASTERS IN LATIN AMERICA

The volcanic isthmus of Central America is one of the most disaster-prone regions of the world. It is situated on highly active tectonic faults, has over 27 active volcanoes and is located at the western extreme of the Caribbean hurricane belt.[1] Among the natural disasters in recent history were the earthquakes in Nicaragua in 1972, Guatemala in 1976 and El Salvador in 1986. Furthermore, there are regular lesser catastrophes in the region, especially in the hurricane season, such as tidal waves, floods and landslides, which destroy crops and forests. There is also the impact of the warm current which periodically appears along the Pacific coast, known as El Niño, as well as other climatic factors which mean that, rather than torrential rains, it is sometimes drought that destroys vulnerable livelihoods. 'Hurricane Mitch', which wreaked devastation across Central America in October–November 1998 was thus only the most recent of the region's plagues. However, it was acknowledged to have been the 20th century's worst.

Moreover, man-made disaster, in the form of prolonged civil war in the region in the 1980s cost 300,000 lives and caused huge economic losses and physical destruction. The region was still far from completing its post-war political and economic reconstruction process when Hurricane Mitch struck.

A feature of all of the region's major natural disasters is that they tended to have considerable impact on the 'unnatural', political ones. The Nicaraguan earthquake of 1972 resulted in at least 10,000 dead, 20,000 injured and 300,000 homeless. It also destroyed 75% of Managua's buildings: Managua has never been rebuilt.[2] Politically, it provoked widespread opposition to the presidency of Anastasio Somoza Dabayle (1967–79) after the dictator had made a personal fortune from aid money and reconstruction contracts and his National Guard had pillaged and resold emergency supplies. Traditional business allies denied a share of the spoils began to turn against him, while the opposition Sandinista National Liberation Front (Frente Sandinista de Liberación Nacional—FSLN) was able to rally greater popular support.

The 1976 earthquake in Guatemala cost 22,000 lives, injured 77,000 and left homeless more than 1m. people.[3] The President, Gen. Kjell Laugerud García (1974–78), tried to avoid the corrupt misuse of international aid witnessed in Nicaragua, but his moves to exert control over aid flows antagonized his far right allies, while death squads were reactivated to deal with left-wing opposition. One of the most notable legacies of this earthquake was the formation of several non-governmental organizations (NGOs) to direct aid from international bodies. Many NGOs were to become important channels for humanitarian assistance to the indigenous highland communities targeted by the army in their counter-insurgency campaigns in the early 1980s. A number of these groups re-emerged from hiding in the late 1980s and 1990s to mobilize support for the Agreement for a Firm and Lasting Peace, signed in 1996, which formally ended the 36-year civil war in Guatemala.

Finally, the administratively incompetent response of President José Napoleón Duarte (1980–89) to the 1986 earthquake in El Salvador further discredited a head of state widely regarded as US President Ronald Reagan's (1981–89) civilian figurehead, legitimizing the arming and training of El Salvador's armed forces by the US Congress. The earthquake, which killed 12,000 and left 150,000 homeless[4], contributed to Duarte's ultimate demise and to the return of the extreme right to the presidency in 1989, with the election of the Nationalist Republican Alliance's (Alianza Republicana Nacionalista—ARENA) candidate, Alfredo Cristiani Burkard.

This interplay between natural and unnatural disasters demonstrates much about the nature of regimes in Central America in the 1970s and 1980s. Of the five Central American republics (Costa Rica, El Salvador, Guatemala, Honduras and Nicaragua) only Costa Rica could seriously claim to operate a democratic and civilian political system. Costa Rica's pattern of landownership lacked the extreme inequality of resource distribution characteristic of the other republics (except perhaps Honduras, where there had been some agrarian reform). The natural disasters impacted most severely on the poorest sector of a generally impoverished population. It was the people from this sector whose houses were built from the most fragile materials and were located at the edge of ravines or on unstable land, and who lacked the resources to help them survive the destruction of their homes and crops. The earthquakes dramatically highlighted the social inequalities and corrupt, repressive regimes which encouraged people to rally to armed insurgent groups.

For these reasons, Hurricane Mitch cannot be analysed purely in terms of its macro- and micro-level economic impact. Many observers are equally interested in its political impact, particularly in the worst affected countries of Nicaragua and Honduras. Has the response to Hurricane Mitch demonstrated that post-war Central America can not only respond economically to its natural disasters, but also that the political systems have become resilient and legitimate enough not to be shaken by them?

THE IMMEDIATE HUMAN COST

Atlantic Tropical Storm Mitch was upgraded to a Class Five hurricane (only four hurricanes in the region have ever reached Class Five) in the early morning of 24 October 1998. At its height, on 26 and 27 October, winds reached speeds of 180 mph. It produced torrential rains that caused extensive flooding and landslides. In total, 9,975 people died and 12,532 people were injured, with a further 9,062 people missing, presumed dead. Almost 2.5m. Central Americans were left homeless and some 2.3m. were evacuated. Honduras bore the brunt of its impact. The hurricane hovered over the country for two days with devastating consequences for the northern seaboard area. It then changed course and began to move slowly southwest across central and southern Honduras and as far as El Salvador. It created downpours that lasted five days.

Choluteca in Honduras registered 914 mm of rainfall between October 25 and 31, 42 times the normal level for that time of year.[5] At least 6,600 Hondurans were known to have died, with a further 8,052 missing, presumed dead. There were 11,998 severely injured people and almost 1.4m. people were left homeless. Nearly 500,000 houses were destroyed and, as of February 1999, 80,000 people were living in refuges in the capital, Tegucigalpa. One-third of the country's road network was damaged, 169 bridges destroyed and six entire villages disappeared. Tegucigalpa itself was particularly badly affected and was cut in two by the Choluteca river. Among the damage was the destruction of the Ministry of Education building and all documentation on the country's students.

Nicaragua was also badly affected by the hurricane, with 2,863 dead and 867,752 people homeless, almost 20% of the population. The northern and western regions were worst affected, in particular, the municipalities of Chinandega and León. The village of Posoltego was buried under a mudslide, with huge loss of life. Forty-two bridges were destroyed and 29 damaged, and 8,000 km of highway were affected. In addition, 343 schools were destroyed. El Salvador and Guatemala suffered less fatalities (240 and 268 deaths, respectively). However, both countries experienced substantial damage to infrastructure and to agricultural production. In El Salvador almost 10,000 homes were destroyed or damaged and in Guatemala the figure was double that. The impact of Hurricane Mitch was least in Costa Rica; nevertheless, eight people died and 96 houses and three bridges were damaged or destroyed in the area along the Parrita river in the Pacific Central region of the country.

THE ECONOMIC COST

A preliminary study by the Costa Rican research institute, Consejeros Económicos y Financieros (CEFSA), at the beginning of 1999, estimated that total hurricane damage in the region was US $6,500m.[6] This represented 13% of the overall regional gross domestic product (GDP). Regional growth in 1998 had been estimated at 5.1%. As a result of Hurricane Mitch, this figure was revised to 4.2%. However, the impact of the economic loss and physical damage varied between countries.

The two weakest and most heavily indebted economies in Central America, Honduras and Nicaragua, bore the brunt of the hurricane's damage. In 1998 the Honduran economy grew by 2.9%, compared to 5.1% in the previous year and to the pre-hurricane estimate of 5.0%. Initial estimates put the cost of Mitch for Honduras at more than US $3,300m., 62% of the country's GDP in 1998; the Inter-American Development Bank (IDB) increased this estimate to $5,000m. in March 1999, equivalent to Honduras's total GDP in 1997.[7] According to the UN Economic Commission for Latin America and the Caribbean, 45% of total losses were in agriculture and important export sectors were affected as well as peasant production of maize and beans. Agricultural production decreased by 2.9% in 1998 and by an estimated 8.7% in 1999. One-half of the expected cereal and bean crop, around 262,000 metric tons, was destroyed. The banana plantations of the northern Atlantic coast were particularly severely affected. The US company Chiquita, which owned 17,000 of the 46,000 acres (18,616 ha) planted with bananas in Honduras, estimated damage of $850m. and that it would take nine months to restore production levels. In the meantime, it laid off 7,782 workers. Jobs were also lost owing to the decrease in the palm-oil, shrimp and melon production on the north coast. Around 30% of the 1998 coffee crop was lost, but this sector would take longer to recover than banana output. Furthermore, some $100m.-worth of livestock perished.

The impact of Hurricane Mitch on President Carlos Roberto Flores Facussé's strategy for macroeconomic stabilization and poverty alleviation was therefore considerable. The President had been in office for less than a year and Honduras had a history of macroeconomic instability and corruption: President Flores had been seeking to negotiate an agreement with the International Monetary Fund (IMF) which would require credit restraint and reductions in public expenditure. However, instead of an estimated fiscal deficit of less than 1% in 1998, it reached 3% of GDP at the end of the year. Furthermore, credit restraint would seriously undermine the support farmers needed in order to replace their lost seeds and animals. International assistance and debt relief were considered fundamental to the reconstruction effort. Foreign debt-service payments absorbed about 38% of the Honduran budget in 1998, over 30% of the country's exports of goods and services: around 61% of this debt was to multilateral institutions.

Nicaragua sustained US $1,400m.-worth of damage as a result of Hurricane Mitch, equivalent to 70% of its GDP. The country's peasant agriculture sector was the worst affected.[8] Nitlapán, Central America University's research institute, estimated that 270,000 ha of land was affected, with 180,000 head of cattle killed and a loss of US $80m. in agricultural production. Nicaragua's macroeconomic stability was already heavily dependent on foreign assistance. In early 1998 the Government of President Arnoldo Alemán Lacayo had negotiated a second Enhanced Structural-Adjustment Facility (ESAF) with the IMF and before the hurricane struck was expected to meet IMF conditionality, in spite of previous government failure to do so. UN representatives in Managua had expressed their deep concern at the likely social impact of ESAF II. However, the IMF's concern was with the improved macroeconomic indicators that made the ESAF agreement possible. Hurricane Mitch came at a time when there was some optimism about renewed economic growth in Nicaragua. In the end, the growth rate for 1998 was 4.1%, compared to 5.2% in the previous year. All sectors were affected. Agricultural production increased by 4.8% in 1999, compared with 7% in 1998 and 10% in 1997. Nicaragua was forced into even greater reliance on external financing and external-policy regulation. The country's debt-servicing ratio was 33% of the budget, or some 25% of total exports. Unlike Honduras, 67% of Nicaragua's external debt was bilateral. In September 1999 Nicaragua was declared eligible for inclusion in the IMF–World Bank 'Highly Indebted Poor Countries' (HIPC) debt-relief initiative, which made the cancellation of 80%–90% of the country's foreign debt possible.

Hurricane Mitch cost El Salvador an estimated US $17,600m., or about 8% of its GDP: reconstruction costs were estimated at $2,000m.[9] Guatemala lost only an estimated $17,200m., or 4% of its GDP: some $747.9m.-worth of damage was caused.[10] Costa Rica's losses were an insignificant percentage of its GDP, but an estimated $47.8m. in agricultural production was lost.[11]

These figures represented the immediate impact of Hurricane Mitch on the region's economy. The cost of reconstruction, the loss of export revenue and pressure on balance of payments would be felt more strongly in 1999. In 1999 Honduran GDP decreased by 1.9%: banana exports, which contributed an estimated US $212m. in export earnings in 1997, had almost ceased, following the destruction of more than 70% of the total crop. In 1999 banana exports earned just $38m., compared with $176m. in 1998. The international community was called upon not just to respond to the emergency, but to support a process of long-term reconstruction.

THE INTERNATIONAL RESPONSE

The World Bank and IMF were already deeply involved in the economic processes in the Central American region, particularly in the post-war reconstruction of El Salvador, Guatemala and Nicaragua. At an IDB Consultative Group meeting of bilateral donors in Washington, DC (USA), in December 1998, some debt relief was agreed. However, only France and Cuba offered to cancel debts. The 'Paris Club' of government creditors agreed a three-year suspension of payments on remaining loans owed by Honduras and Nicaragua, although interest on the outstanding debt would continue to accumulate. This was the least that could be done, as neither country was in any position to service its debt in the aftermath of Hurricane Mitch. In addition to the debt relief, the international community promised significant amounts of emergency support. The USA increased its initial contribution to US $300m., the World Bank announced US $1,000m. in new, interest-free 40-year loans, in addition to the $200m. already promised, and the European Union (EU) committed $423m.[12] Altogether, the Consultative Group of bilateral donors and multilateral agencies pledged a total of $6,300m. in aid and loans to the region. To qualify for this assistance governments had to present their reconstruction programmes at a further meeting in Stockholm (Sweden) on 18–25 May 1999.

The international community was keen to ensure that the reconstruction aid was put to good effect in the region, unlike in the past. Creditor nations were keen to oversee both macroeconomic policy-making and the strategic use and disbursement of funds. The IDB announced that the Stockholm meeting was to include a workshop on 'Transparency and Governance'. This aimed to improve probity in government and to ensure that efforts to rebuild Central America were not impeded by corruption.[13] The title of the Consultative Group meeting—The Reconstruction and Transformation of Central America—made it apparent that the international community intended the reconstruction effort to do more than return Central America to its pre-Mitch condition. The objective was to make governments confront unfinished tasks of economic and political modernization. The weeks before the conference saw increasing debate and conflict around each country's proposed reconstruction programmes.

At the Stockholm meeting, which brought together Central American governments, Central American NGOs and civil society organizations and international donor governments, a series of principles were agreed upon. These were then enshrined in the so-called 'Stockholm Declaration'. This called for international donors and the beneficiary countries to work together to reduce poverty and promote sustainable growth within a framework of democracy, respect for human rights, the rule of law, good governance and transparency, decentralization and the reduction of ecological vulnerability. At the meeting the international donor community pledged a further US $9,000m. in humanitarian aid, long-term concessional loans and debt relief. A so-called 'Follow-Up Group' to the Stockholm meeting was established later in the year. This was initially composed of Canada, Germany, Spain, Sweden and the USA; however, it was later expanded to include Japan, the IDB and the UN Development Programme (UNDP).

THE PEASANT ECONOMY

In order to understand the scale of the losses and their differing social impact, it is important to distinguish between the impact on the region's macroeconomic performance and on its fragile peasant economy. Hurricane Mitch had a particularly devastating impact on the economy of poor peasants in the region. Even in El Salvador, where fewer people died and the macroeconomic impact was relatively small, the impact on the rural economy of the impoverished eastern regions of San Miguel, La Unión, La Paz and Usulatán was severe. Levels of poverty in rural areas in Central America were up to 30% higher than in the urban areas.

At the Consultative Group meeting in Washington, DC, in December 1998, the Swedish development minister, Pierre Schori, acknowledged that there was a connection between the devastation caused by Hurricane Mitch and the development model prevailing within Central America: 'We are now seeing the effects of unsustainable development and lack of urban planning and of an unequal distribution of land, deforestation, population pressure and poverty'.[14] Like so many disasters in the Central American region, Mitch highlighted the inability of prevailing development policies to meet the needs of the poor and to improve their living standards.

The vulnerability of poor peasant households was made apparent by the hurricane in a number of ways. The first was the location of peasant farms, in the ecologically damaged marginal lands of the Central American isthmus. The growth of cash-crop agriculture in Central America was accompanied by expulsion of peasants to these marginal areas where the absence of any planned land and natural-resource management made them particularly exposed to the impact of natural disasters such as landslides. Hurricane Mitch drew attention to the environmental catastrophe in Central America and to the severity of the consequences for the rural poor. In March 1999, at a conference entitled 'Environmental Management and Reducing Vulnerability to Natural Disasters', the IDB's regional operations manager stated that 'Central America was sitting on a time bomb caused by environmental abuse. Uncontrolled deforestation, poor watershed management and inappropriate agricultural practices have severely degraded the water absorption and retention capacity of vast areas of Central America. This multiplied the destructive effect of Hurricane Mitch by increasing the volume of flooding and the number of landslides, and will do so again unless preventive measures are taken'.[15]

A second issue was the vulnerability of the peasant household economy and the question of food security. In the region of Honduras most severely affected by the hurricane, most incomes would only meet up to one-half of a family's basic food needs in a normal year. For the rest, households would rely on temporary contracts on the larger farms and plantations. This type of employment ceased as a result of the hurricane. Peasants were responsible for most domestic grain production, which did not, in any case, meet the country's food needs. Family food production was decimated because Hurricane Mitch struck at the end of October 1998, just before the harvesting of the *postrera*, the second and main crop of the year, which accounted for 80% of annual output. The UN Food and Agriculture Organization and the World Food Programme estimated that over 800,000 Hondurans in rural areas would qualify for emergency food supplies until September 1999. A similar situation resulted in Nicaragua, where 40% of the area planted with beans and 32% of the area planted with corn was devastated.[16] The peasant economy was responsible for 70% of Nicaragua's food consumption, so the effect on food security was very great indeed.

A third factor was the highly unequal pattern of land distribution, which encouraged the settlement of ever more marginal lands. Most peasants lived on tiny plots: in Honduras, two-thirds of farms were less than 5 ha in size. Also, an estimated 20% of households in the rural areas of Honduras were headed by women, who had to cope with both production and childcare. Land-ownership patterns had serious consequences for the reconstruction process. Shortage of land to rebuild destroyed homes became a major problem in Honduras. In Nicaragua, the mayor of Posoltega, which was buried in a mudslide, announced that over 3,600 acres (1,457 ha) were needed before planting time in the following year. Nevertheless, the country's Agrarian Reform Institute's main task remained the processing of indemnification claims by those affected by the progressive agrarian reform of the Sandinista Government, in other words, a reversal of the aims of that reform. Access to credit for reconstruction was also problematic. In Nicaragua, many peasants whose farms survived nevertheless required considerable credit to repair damage and restart production. Poor peasants always found it difficult to gain credit in Central America. In Nicaragua, the National Development Bank, which had been charged with the task of apportioning funds to peasants, had been replaced by the Rural Credit Fund, which had not begun to function by late 1998. Most peasants depended on alternative rural credit funds administered by NGOs, which were unable to meet the large demand, even before Hurricane Mitch.

The peasant economy in Central America was in crisis long before October 1998. This crisis lay behind the rise of guerrilla insurgencies throughout the region in the 1980s. However, the peace processes that ended the region's civil wars did not impact on the structure of socio-economic power in Central America. The effects of Hurricane Mitch exacerbated this ongoing crisis. One consequence of the continuing situation was a population exodus from rural areas. During the civil wars of the 1980s many emigrated for political, as well as economic, reasons. In 1980–90 there was a threefold increase in the number of Central American emigrants: 87% of these emigrants went to the USA. In the 1990s the impact of the war, the critical situation of peasant agriculture and the lack of employment opportunities led to further migration. Many of these migrants were illegal: according to the US Immigration and Naturalization Service, an estimated 13% of the 5m. illegal migrants in the USA in 1996 were from Central America.[17] Many poor families in the region depended on the remittances sent back by relatives in the USA. A home survey in El Salvador in 1997 found that just over 40% of all households living under the poverty line received remittances from migrants in that year. The USA expels the illegal migrants where possible and there is often the threat of mass expulsions. In the wake of Hurricane Mitch, the impact of such expulsions would be particularly harsh on families dependent on remittances. Hurricane Mitch, in its turn, fuelled fears in the USA of even greater influxes of immigrants. On his visit to the region in March 1999, US President Bill Clinton (1993–2001) offered more reconstruction aid but little to those seeking a more flexible immigration policy. While deportations were suspended immediately after Mitch[18], by March 1999 they had been resumed for Salvadoreans and Guatemalans. The problem was not only confined to extra-regional migration: nearly 500,000 Nicaraguans worked in Costa Rica, for example, and many sought refuge there after the hurricane.

Given the depth of the crisis in Central America, many activists in social organizations and popular movements saw Hurricane Mitch as an opportunity to reconstruct and reassess the region's rural economy. Moreover, immediately before the Consultative Group meeting in Stockholm in May 1999 Pierre Schori argued that the disaster offered a chance to 'construct something new'. In order to do this, he called for the involvement of the people in the region, insisting that local and popular support for the reconstruction effort was vital.[19] Schori was aware of the profound criticism voiced by Central American development organizations of their governments' response to the disaster. However, the dual conditions for reconstruction advocated by the Special Consultative Group on Central America, a body mainly composed of EU donor countries, faced many obstacles. Donors attempted to encourage both a regional focus and the inclusion of 'civil society' in the discussion on the reconstruction. The regional focus failed because of the varying degrees in which the hurricane affected the region, which meant that, ultimately, governments presented their own separate plans. The second issue confronted the tradition of authoritarian, centralized and élitist rule in the region.

THE POLITICS OF HURRICANE MITCH

As with all Central America's disasters, reconstruction aid played its role in the political battles in the region. In El Salvador, Hurricane Mitch was widely felt to have worked in favour of the ruling ARENA party. The party's ability to channel international aid to disaster victims contributed to its victory in the presidential election of March 1999, although the ARENA Government's medium-term efforts to improve the economic situation exacerbated by the hurricane resulted in defeat for the party in the legislative elections of March 2000.

In Honduras, under pressure from a much more cautious international aid community, President Flores attempted to ensure that aid was not misused. The Comptroller-General was called upon to closely control the financial assistance. Political tension in Honduras resulted from disagreement over long-term reconstruction plans rather than over the disbursement of emergency aid. Social organizations and NGOs criticized what they saw as the President's authoritarian response to the disaster and his establishment of a small Reconstruction Cabinet, consisting of only his close party supporters. This Cabinet was to effectively prepare and then control the national reconstruction plan, to be presented at the Stockholm donors' conference. In January 1999 the Citizens' Forum issued a statement in which it strongly criticized the President's increased authoritarianism and his exclusion of civil sectors of society in the preparation of a reconstruction and transformation plan acceptable to the Honduran people and to the international donors.[20]

In early 1999, as disagreements with the Honduran Government increased, a number of NGOs and religious and development forums, including the Citizens' Forum, established a new co-ordinating body, INTERFOROS. This new grouping drew up its own reconstruction proposal, in which it suggested linking international aid to institutional reconstruction, as well as further political and judicial reform and democratization. It raised some of the real difficulties concerning gaining access to land for rebuilding, as land prices had risen in the wake of Hurricane Mitch. It recommended that land be valued at its pre-hurricane appraised value. In addition, it proposed measures that would protect women and would ensure community participation in, and control over, reconstruction. The plan called for property deeds to be put in the name of the woman rather than the couple and that if the house was subsequently sold agreement would be required from the person responsible for looking after the youngest children. It proposed that community work groups be established to construct houses and that a revolving fund be created through the repayment of loans, to be managed by the communities themselves. Unsurprisingly, this plan was at first rejected by the Government. In December 1999 there were widespread protests in north-west Honduras to demand an acceleration in the rebuilding programme. However, INTERFOROS was ultimately effective in bringing about co-ordination and articulation among different social sectors, as well as demonstrating a capacity to make proposals on a national scale. By 2001 it had achieved domestic and international credibility and had succeeded in establishing a good, constant working relationship with the Honduran Government.

In Nicaragua the political impact of Hurricane Mitch similarly highlighted the profound differences in policy between the Government of President Alemán and the NGOs in the country, many of which had their roots in the Sandinista Government of the 1980s. Many of these development organizations were, however, deeply suspicious of the pact between the opposition FSLN leadership and President Alemán's Government, discussion about which had taken place throughout 1998. An alliance was agreed in principle in November. The willingness of the FSLN to support a Government whose economic policies adversely affected the poorest sectors of the population was considered a betrayal of Sandinista values and deeply divided the movement. In addition, President Alemán's response in the immediate aftermath of the hurricane was considered extremely cynical: he refused assistance from a Cuban medical team, for instance, and attempted (unsuccessfully) to impose a tax on aid channelled through Nicaraguan NGOs. The Government was also accused of attempting to use reconstruction aid to create a more modern infrastructure to attract foreign investment. At the Consultative Group meeting in Washington, DC, President Alemán submitted a proposal to extend the Managua to Masaya road from a two-lane to a four-lane highway. This road had suffered no damage from Hurricane Mitch but was the country's main commercial highway. The use of reconstruction aid became a major political issue in the negotiations between the Government and the FSLN opposition. Nicaragua's construction industry was owned by many political associates of President Alemán, as well as by a new class of Sandinista businessman. Construction contracts would be a lucrative business opportunity.

Charges of corruption had been levelled against the Government of President Alemán from its inception. Many grassroots Sandinistas felt their leadership was failing to make the Government accountable for its actions and that the FSLN was not a serious opposition force. As the donors' Stockholm meeting drew near, international bodies began to pressure President Alemán to address issues of governability and governance. The international community was concerned that reconstruction aid was not being used to encourage greater transparency in public administration and decentralization, and that the participation of 'civil society' in the relief effort was not being encouraged. In November 1999 Oxfam International and the EU publicly criticized the Nicaraguan Government in its allocation of reconstruction aid, and, in late 1999, a number of international aid programmes were suspended.

As in Honduras, one of the most significant political developments arising from the disaster in Nicaragua was the way NGOs responded to emergency needs and used the opportunity to raise fundamental issues over democratic governance in the region. The emphasis placed by the international donor community on such issues helped to legitimize their role. It did not mean, however, that the Government took the NGOs' views into account. Immediately after the hurricane, some 350 organizations began to co-ordinate their efforts and established the Non-Governmental Emergency Relief and Reconstruction Coalition. Like INTERFOROS in Honduras, the Coalition took a broader look at Nicaraguan society and institutions. It took its conclusion to the Washington meeting in a document entitled 'Turning the Mitch Tragedy into an Opportunity for the Human and Sustainable Development of Nicaragua', in which it argued that the hurricane highlighted the fact that so-called development in the region was 'increasingly less sustainable and more inhuman'.[21] It called for a consensual National Emergency and Reconstruction Programme, which would include government institutions, civil organizations and business groups. However, unlike INTERFOROS in Honduras, the Coalition's relations with the Nicaraguan Government continued to be strained. In early 1999 the Coalition proposed that it and the Government present a joint consensual document to donors at the meeting in Stockholm. This proposition was rejected by the Government. In February a survey by the Coalition of over 10,000 households in the 80 municipalities affected by Hurricane Mitch showed that a majority of people were still awaiting the help that would enable them to rebuild their lives. In early 2000 President Alemán threatened to deport Ana Quiros, the Coalition's co-ordinator, on the grounds that her immigration papers were not in order. Furthermore, in February, the Government announced that it would enforce legislation establishing regulations for NGOs, in addition to announcing that the Nicaraguan Institute for Statistics and Census would conduct an investigation into the expenditure of all NGOs in the country.

PROGRESS AND PREOCCUPATIONS

In 2000 further Consultative Group meetings were held in order to review the progress made by the individual Governments of Honduras and Nicaragua in implementing their respective national plans.

A Consultative Group meeting took place in Tegucigalpa on 6–8 February 2000, chaired by the IDB. More than 200 delegates participated, including representatives of the Honduran Government and civil society organizations, as well as representatives from over 400 donor countries and international organizations. Issues covered at the meeting included: macro-economic stability; support of the Honduran Government's efforts to gain debt relief under the HIPC initiative, to which the country had been admitted in December 1999, as well as its development of a comprehensive poverty reduction strategy; progress made in the area of good governance, transparency and accountability, including the establishment of an independent Comptroller-General's Office; advances in the Government's decentralization plans, which were linked to efforts to strengthen democracy and citizen participation; the expansion of the fiscal and administrative capacity of municipalities, especially for poor communities; government initiatives in developing measures to mitigate the impact of natural disasters with early warning systems, and disaster response capacities involving local community participation. The Honduran Government reported to the meeting that, of the US $2,800m. pledged for Honduras in May 1999, agreements signed as of February 2000 amounted to $1,400m., or about 50% of the amounts pledged, with total disbursements amounting to $492m. In 1999 donor assistance contributed to the large volume of reconstruction investments and balance of payments, which significantly facilitated the recovery of the Honduran economy. As a result of the progress made by the Honduran Government, in July 2000 the IMF and the World Bank agreed to support a comprehensive debt reduction package for Honduras under the enhanced HIPC initiative. The country's debt service payments would be reduced by $900m over 20 years.

The Consultative Group meeting for Nicaragua was held in Washington, DC, on 23–24 May 2000 and was attended by over 45 delegations representing bilateral donors, multilateral lending organizations, UN agencies, the Nicaraguan Government and Nicaraguan NGO and civil society organizations. There was unanimous agreement at the meeting that poverty reduction was the overriding development goal and challenge confronting Nicaragua. However, the Consultative Group acknowledged that some progress had been achieved. Such progress included: the design of a comprehensive anti-poverty programme with civil society participation; the creation of a legal and institutional framework that guaranteed public-sector honesty and accountability; the approval of the law for the creation of a National System for Preventing, Mitigating, and Responding to Natural Disasters in addition to efforts underway for a National Strategy for Sustainable Development; the introduction of an Administrative Career law and a Civil Servants' law as part of the project for the Strengthening and Development of Municipalities. Moreover, in 1998–99 the Nicaraguan economy grew with reduced levels of inflation. A further positive indication was that a wide range of civil society organizations had participated in preparing the country document for the meeting.

However, the Consultative Group agreed that many tasks remained outstanding. Nicaragua's National Council for Economic and Social Planning needed to contribute to the effective monitoring of implementation of national projects, and the Government had to continue its implementation of policies and measures designed to comply with prior IMF agreements. It was also proposed that the Government should define and implement a specific strategy aimed at rural development and the increase of production and income of small farmers. Further transparency and accountability was called for in public administration and government, and the administration of President Alemán was urged to promote an electoral process that was not discriminatory and would guarantee equal opportunities for candidates and political parties. The development of an overall strategy for reducing poverty and preventing natural disasters was necessary, as was the development of a clear and coherent strategy of municipal development with a regulatory framework and access to financial resources as well as municipal-level human-resources training. There was also some concern that authorities involved in cases of corruption in the post-Hurricane Mitch period had not been brought to justice.

Donors at the meeting called on the Nicaraguan Government to 'maintain economic stability, increase the battle on poverty, strengthen transparency and accountability—especially in the fight against corruption, strengthen democratic governance and promote a broader level of participations in the elections'. While César Gaviria Trujillo, the Secretary-General of the Organization of American States (OAS), praised Nicaragua's economic recuperation over the past decade, not all donors shared the same enthusiasm. The Swedish Government criticized the Alemán Government for mismanagement of international funds intended for post-Hurricane Mitch reconstruction. At the beginning of 2000 Sweden and Germany had cancelled aid projects, owing to charges of corruption levelled against the administration in Nicaragua. According to the Nicaraguan Central Bank, the country received US $665m. in reconstruction funding, of which $340m. were donations and $310m. were credits, principally from the IDB, the World Bank and the IMF. The World

Bank and the IMF indicated that if the Alemán administration failed to improve its relief effort, Nicaragua's inclusion in the HIPC programme would be jeopardized.

A further general Consultative Group meeting was scheduled to be held in Madrid (Spain) on 18–19 January 2001. By October 2000 no agenda had been produced by the IDB for this meeting. INTERFOROS and the Non-Governmental Emergency Relief and Reconstruction Coalition claimed that the meeting was intended more as an event for international investors interested in Central America rather than an opportunity for international donors and Central American governmental and civil society organizations to analyse jointly the implementation of the principles of the Stockholm Declaration.

A regional Central American civil society co-ordinator, Centro America Solidaria (CAS), which brings together similar bodies from the other Central American countries, was established. CAS proposed that the Madrid meeting prioritize poverty-reduction strategies from a social perspective, as well as government transparency and accountability, good governance, environmental issues and disaster preparedness. CAS also proposed that its members be incorporated into the official delegations from each of the Central American countries.

By the end of 2000 there was a growing feeling among international and local NGOs and social organizations, or 'civil society organisations' (CSOs) as they called themselves, that the international community was reneging on the commitments made at the Stockholm meeting. There was very slow progress by donors in converting pledges of aid into actual reconstruction funds. Donors were concerned by the weak institutional capacity of Central American governments and by the problem of corruption. The CSOs welcomed donor emphasis on transparency, but did not feel that donors were taking their legitimate concerns to their logical conclusion, and channelling funds in a decentralized way through local municipalities and NGOs. Despite the discourse on decentralization by donors throughout the 1990s, local government was seriously under-funded and lacking basic and human material resources. The Nicaraguan Government discriminated against the opposition Sandinista-led councils which controlled the areas most damaged by Mitch, and withheld aid. International and local NGOs bore the burden of serious reconstruction work, but there was a large divide between the international NGOs that knew and respected the organizational capacity within the region, and those who swept in to the region as experts in emergency aid and failed to co-ordinate locally. This lack of co-ordination has been a huge problem in the reconstruction process. On the other hand, areas where there was no previous history of NGO presence have failed to access any reconstruction aid at all. By the end of 2000, many international NGOs were supporting the CAS and calling upon the donor countries to use the forthcoming Madrid meeting to re-emphasize the Stockholm Declaration and to develop a new, inclusive human development paradigm for the transformation of the Central American region.

2001: EARTHQUAKE IN EL SALVADOR

Expectations were dashed and anxieties rekindled when an earthquake in El Salvador in January 2001 led to the postponement of the Madrid conference to 8–9 March, with an agenda that fell far short of the expectations of the CSOs in the region and their international allies. The earthquake, which measured 7.6 on the Richter scale, struck off the Pacific coast on 13 January and devastated El Salvador's Pacific departments (Usulatán, La Paz and La Libertad in particular). The official death toll was 827. Over one million people were severely affected, with nearly 150,000 houses destroyed or damaged. The middle class neighbourhood of Las Colinas in San Salvador reported the greatest number of deaths when a landslide buried hundreds of houses. Over the next six weeks there were daily tremors and aftershocks; one which measured 5.6 on the Richter scale had its epicentre in San Salvador itself. On 28 February hundreds of people, mostly women, children and the elderly, staged a demonstration to protest the lack of aid.

Against this background, the Madrid Consultative Group meeting was felt by the CSOs to represent a turn away from the principles of the Stockholm meeting. They issued a declaration that the 'Madrid meeting has been a lost opportunity to reaffirm the commitment to the Stockholm principles, the transformation of the region and struggle against poverty.'[22] The emphasis in Madrid had been on investment, liberalization, market opening and infrastructural development, which they feared would contribute to greater inequalities and social and environmental vulnerability in the Central American region.

CONCLUSION

Economically, Hurricane Mitch had a devastating impact on Central America, particularly Honduras and Nicaragua. The lives and livelihoods of the poorest sectors of the region's population bore the brunt of this devastation. Even before the disaster, this population lived a precarious existence: Hurricane Mitch dramatically revealed the extent to which governments in the region neglected or ignored the majority of the population. Many saw the hurricane as an opportunity to challenge the prevailing development imperatives. The international community, meanwhile, was divided. Some gave priority still to economic adjustment and macroeconomic reform. Others argued that without debt forgiveness, a real change of economic direction and agrarian reform, the poor would neither recover from Mitch nor aspire to the sustainable livelihoods to which the UNDP, among others, argued all human beings had a right. By 2001 local and international NGOs feared that the international community had opted to follow the former route and were downplaying their initial commitment to promote transformative processes and poverty eradication.

Politically, Hurricane Mitch revealed that most of Central America's governments still clung to past practices of authoritarianism, clientelism and corruption. It was clear that the struggle for democracy and social justice that had inspired armed uprisings in the 1980s had won only minor changes. One difference from the past did make itself apparent in the aftermath of Mitch, however. Social organization was more vibrant and dynamic than ever before in the region's history. The hurricane stimulated greater activity and purpose amongst NGOs and the grass roots organizations. Another notable difference was the beginning of a change in attitude of the international community towards government in the region. While some welcomed the embrace by ruling élites of the neo-liberal economic strategies they advocated, donors could no longer ignore the failure of those élites to demonstrate equal enthusiasm for political liberalization and modernization. While few Western governments had openly condemned the state repression that followed the earthquakes of the 1970s, the international community made it clear that it would not tolerate such action in the 1990s. However, the response of Central American governments to the Stockholm meeting of bilateral donors disappointed many: in particular, their failure to coordinate a regional response and to submit a joint proposal on reconstruction. Instead, there was a series of individual presentations, with minimal or no serious consultation with development organizations. Central American governments seemed content to allow international co-operation to pay the cost of reconstruction. International donors appeared to shift gear between the Stockholm and Madrid meetings. Owing to frustration at corruption and ineffective governmental responses, aid disbursements were very slow. However, they were unwilling to take action that would force governments to work with local municipalities and NGOs or to shift their policies towards the poor.

As a result, the March 2001 Madrid meeting's emphasis on private sector development and competitiveness seemed to many to miss the fundamental challenge facing the region. An increasing number of studies suggested that natural forces were not the heart of the problems facing Central America. Social and environmental trends were responsible for the fragmentation and shrinkage of forested area: at the beginning of the 21st century only 10% of the original forests survived in the region and 80% of these were threatened. The main cause of deforestation is the expansion of the agricultural frontier owing to pressure of population growth, unequal distribution of land, and weak land tenure systems. Demographic pressure and the failure of rural livelihoods increased migration to urban areas where illegal, uncontrolled and unplanned expansion created serious environmental, as well as social, problems. Hurricane Mitch itself caused severe changes in the geodynamics of watersheds and hydrographical systems. At the Stockholm meeting the IDB's Regional Operations Department reported on the environmental management problems of the region and reported that the capacity to absorb high levels of water and run-off has been drastically reduced in the Choluteca, Ulúa and Cangrejal rivers in Honduras, the Lempa river in El Salvador, and the Montagua river and the Lake Amatitlán watershed in Guatemala. Such a development enhanced the risks of floods and landslides.[23] Many would argue that without a development model that prioritized the environmental and social problems of the region, Central America would remain exposed to ongoing lesser and major disasters. Such a development model would have to be supported by an international community prepared to work seriously with those social sectors and organizations within the region committed to such an aim. Many observers did not see such a commitment at the Madrid meeting.

BIBLIOGRAPHICAL REFERENCES

1. Inter-American Development Bank, Regional Operations Department 2: Reducing Vulnerability to Natural Hazards: Lessons Learned from Hurricane Mitch: A Strategy Paper on Environmental Management. Stockholm, Sweden, 25–28 May 1999, mimeo: 3.
2. James Dunkerley, *Power in the Isthmus: A Political History of Modern Central America*. London, Verso, 1988. p. 235.
3. Ibid. p. 469.
4. Ibid. p. 411.
5. *Envio*. March 1999.
6. *Oxford Analytica*, Economic and Political Prospects for 1999. 7 January 1999.
7. 'Country Report: Honduras'. Inter-American Development Bank, March 1999.
8. The hurricane directly affected about 900 acres (364 ha) of coffee, but the country has over 45,000 acres (18,212 ha) planted; only about 10% of the 34,000 acres (13,760 ha) of sugar cane grown in the country was affected. *Envio*, December 1998.
9. Inforpress, 7 May 1999.
10. Ibid.
11. Inforpress, 13 November 1998.
12. In April 1999 a mission by the World Bank finally agreed to include Honduras and Nicaragua in the Highly Indebted Poor Countries Initiatives. This would involve a partial pardon of debt and further renegotiation. In anticipation, Honduras signed an agreement with the IMF in March of that year.
13. For further information, see 'Transparency and Governance', Inter-American Development Bank: Consultative Group Meeting for the Reconstruction and Transformation of Central America. Stockholm, May 25–28 1999.
14. Press release, Swedish Ministry of Foreign Affairs, 11 December 1998.
15. Newsletter, Consultative Group Meeting for the Reconstruction and Transformation of Central America, No 2, May 1999.
16. *Envio*, December 1998.
17. *Envio*, March 1999.
18. *Inforpress*, 12 March 1999.
19. Press release, Swedish Ministry for Foreign Affairs, 25 May 1999.
20. For more information, see Ricardo Falla in *Envio*, January–February 1999.
21. *Envio*, December 1998.
22. Visión de País, Publicación 4, Marzo/Abril 2001.
23. Inter-American Development Bank, Regional Operations Department 2: op. cit., mimeo: 4.

THE BANANA TRADE DISPUTE

MICHAEL KUCZYNSKI

INTRODUCTION

On 19 April 1999 the Dispute Settlement Body of the World Trade Organization (WTO) allowed the USA to penalize, through the imposition of tariffs (under the notorious Section 301 of the US Trade Act of 1974), some US $191m.-worth of imports from the European Union (EU). A roster of 17 miscellaneous products, ranging from handbags to coffee-making machines, was drawn up, intended to be used as bargaining power. Each item targeted a vocal group of national producers in the EU, particularly French producers. After four months the USA applied a punitive tariff of 100% to a first selection of nine products. Soon afterwards pressure was increased through the introduction of a US congressional requirement that the selection among this roster of targets be rotated at six-monthly intervals. In the event, however, further rotation of these so-called 'carousel' sanctions did not occur. Instead, on 11 April 2001 the new US administration of President George W. Bush reached an understanding with the EU as a result of which on 1 July the punitive duties on items of EU origin were lifted. The final outcome of the dispute is still contingent on further steps yet to be taken by the EU (by 1 January 2002). Yet this particular trade dispute now appears to be resolved, and the process of adjustment to its solution begins for the activity at the centre of the dispute, the banana trade from Latin America and the Caribbean.

At issue in the dispute had been the regime for the importation and distribution of bananas, mainly from Latin America and the Caribbean, introduced by the EU (then still known as the European Community—EC) in July 1993 as part of its Single Market programme.[1] The regime was known as the Common-Market Organization, or Regulation 404. It favoured imports from the former European colonies which constitute the African, Caribbean and Pacific (ACP) grouping, limiting to a quota of 2m. metric tons per year the EU's imports of bananas from Latin American countries. Formally, the US interest in the issue had arisen, not from its own banana production in Florida, but from injury to the trio of US companies which dominate international marketing of bananas. The adverse effects that such oligopolistic dominance might itself cause to producers and consumers at large, although widely debated in other circles, have not been at issue in the dispute. The USA has held that as a result of Regulation 404 its firms had lost nearly 50 % of their EU market share.

In Latin America and the Caribbean interests in the dispute were divided, as they have been in Europe itself. Island producers with post-colonial links to their former metropolitan centres happen to have substantially higher costs of production, and they have benefited from continued protected access to the EU market. Others in the Caribbean and, mainly in Central and South America, achieve generally lower costs of production, and they have been adversely affected by the diversion of trade implicit in the EU's preferential treatment of former colonies. Within Europe the largest consumer, Germany, has no relevant colonial ties and has thus been opposed to preferential treatment of less efficient producers—the more so as the German public, accustomed to cheap bananas for decades prior to the 1993 EU regime, are the world's highest per-head consumers of the product.

PRODUCT AND MARKET

Originating most probably in South East Asia, 'the ripe banana from the mellow hill' as Byron termed it (*The Island*, 1823) appears to have reached Latin America and the Caribbean in the 16th century, perhaps earlier. Its commercial cultivation began in the 18th century, typically as plantain to feed slave labour. However, it was with the opening of the Panama Canal and modern methods of refrigerated transportation at the beginning of the 20th century—the famous white-painted banana boats of the United Fruit Company—that the product acquired its importance in international trade. Two varieties of banana dominate the modern production for export of a plant requiring a hot and humid tropical climate: the larger *Gros Michel*, which thrives close to the equator, and the smaller, thinner-skinned *Cavendish* better suited to the somewhat more temperate conditions of the Caribbean or southern Brazil.

As a tropical product in international trade, bananas are second only to coffee in importance, and the Western Hemisphere has long since overtaken Africa and Asia as the world's source of export production. Even so, at around US $3,000m. per year, exports scarcely amount to 0.7% of total world trade in food products, and coffee exports total at least three times that figure. As in the case of coffee, however, production for export is often disproportionately important in the local producers' economic and social life. For the Windward Islands, for example, the cultivation of bananas provides in excess of four-fifths of total output, one-half of exports, and one-third of total employment. The main local alternative as a cash crop is sugar cane. However, as the price of bananas has long been far more stable than that of sugar cane (or coffee, for that matter), there has been a persistent incentive to switch investment into banana production. (This is so despite banana trees being particularly susceptible to destruction by tropical storms, as well as the blight called Panama disease.) The importance of the crop to small Caribbean islands thus became much greater after the particularly sharp fluctuations in the price of sugar in the 1960s, and this disincentive to sugar-cane was increased by the incentives to sugar-beet production in the EU under its Common Agricultural Policy (CAP).

Even so, the Caribbean islands remain relatively small suppliers in the aggregate of the world market, all together accounting for scarcely one-eighth of total world exports, with Martinique taking one-third of that small share. Ecuador, the biggest producer, supplies one-fifth of world imports, and the next three largest Central and South American producers (Colombia, Costa Rica, and Honduras) supply a further two-fifths. The balance of world imports, approximately one-quarter, is divided among other Latin American exporters, the Philippines, and Florida (USA), alongside other occasional supplies. African exports, although important on individual European markets (France and Italy), on average amount to barely 3% of world imports. It is worth noting, however, that the greater part of the world's banana crop does not in fact enter into international trade. Latin America and the Caribbean account for some 80%–85% of world exports, but only for some 30% of world production.

The stability of the international price of bananas is mainly explained, not by the relatively short lead-time involved from re-planting to fruition (six to eight months), but by two other features. Firstly, there are numerous small producers—mainly in Africa and in Asia—whose production does not regularly enter into international trade yet who, by exporting their small surpluses intermittently as world shortages appear or disappear, serve to stabilize international supply. Secondly, and equally important, there is the influence of the structure of costs and the related structure of production and distribution. The fruit are picked grown but not yet ripe, and the transportation, control of ripening, and distribution of a highly perishable product, constitute much the biggest part of the total cost of production. Of that total cost of production it is reckoned that as much as 88% is generated after the crop has been loaded on to the banana boat; the corresponding figure for coffee is 60%, an estimate that includes substantial manufacturing downstream. (The proportion of non-local costs for 'non-dollar' bananas reaching the countries of the EU is somewhat lower because of higher local labour costs of production. This is discussed further below.)

In their structure of costs, bananas are quite unusual among products in international trade. On the one hand, labour is cheap at the point of original production, which depresses local costs (particularly in the case of so-called 'dollar' producers, through a combination of greater efficiency and lesser worker protection). On the other hand, the high fixed costs involved in transportation and thereafter downstream into retail, mean that the structure of production is powerfully oligopolistic: a small number of operators control the bulk of world trade. Naturally, this raises margins above true competitive cost, from the point of loading the banana boat onwards. It also tends to keep those margins fairly stable.

Specifically, three US-based international companies (Chiquita, Dole and Del Monte) exercise integrated vertical control, in all but final retailing, on upwards of 65%–70% of the world export market.[2] In the EU those same three firms have accounted for 66% of the market; with one of them (Chiquita) controlling over 40% by itself. Individual segments of the EU market are even more concentrated. In the United Kingdom three firms alone supply 95% of the market. (The trio in this case includes Fyffes) The French and German markets are, it is true, somewhat less concentrated; in the latter the largest four suppliers account for just over 80% of the national market; in the former for just less than 60%. However, in France this apparently lower degree of concentration conceals the fact that the additional suppliers are quasi-monopolies handling production from formerly colonial Caribbean islands (French Guiana, Guadeloupe and Martinique) under protected access to the metropolitan market.[3] Thus, it remains broadly true to say that in the main consuming markets of advanced countries, bananas reach retailers under conditions which are quite imperfectly competitive.

INTERNATIONAL TRADING ARRANGEMENTS

After the collapse in world trade in the Great Depression of 1929–34, the USA took the lead in establishing a new international trading system. From 1948 onwards, while remaining an extension of US policy, the trading system was formalized as a succession of multilateral arrangements under the General Agreement on Tariffs and Trade (GATT). Until the late 1980s the logic of these arrangements, known as reciprocal free trade, excluded primary products.

In minerals such as petroleum, bauxite, or iron ore, the combination of heavy capital costs and geopolitics tended to place production and the articulation of international trade in the hands of a relatively small number of specialist international companies—an arrangement which often began to unravel in the 1970s. In temperate agricultural products most of the advanced countries belonging to what became known as the Organisation for Economic Co-operation and Development (OECD) practised a policy of protection. They departed from this practice only to make limited quota concessions to imports from their own client-states in the developing world. In tropical products arrangements varied. Where there was competing domestic production in the OECD countries, as in the case of cotton, or sugar-beet for sugar-cane, quota concessions to sphere-of-influence clients prevailed. Where competing domestic interests were absent, arrangements ranged instead from completely free importation, through excises imposed for the sake of tax revenue, to efforts at market control (whether to stabilize prices or to control producer cartels).

In the case of bananas a mottled trading regime developed. The heavy capital costs involved in the refrigerated transportation of perishables continued to assign, as in minerals, the small number of existing international firms, the dominant marketing role—a role, which, by 1930, had been consolidated. At the same time, where they existed, former colonial links—together with the national banana-marketing companies which had thus arisen in the corresponding metropolitan centres—also generated preferential concessions, through a mixture of quotas in favour of the former colony and tariffs or excises against bananas from other provenances. In other cases, tariffs or excises could popularly be justified as revenue-raising, by taxing items which older generations still viewed as exotic luxuries.

So, for example in Europe, France, Italy, Spain and the United Kingdom settled for quotas-cum-tariffs and distribution favouring former colonies (or, in the French case, départements d'outre-mer) and their own banana companies. Most of the rest of the continent, except for Germany, opted for some revenue-raising tariffs. Germany, in an apparently Bismarckian policy of enhancing balanced nutrition for children, adopted a regime of practically free importation which gave the three banana 'majors' market freedom, but, nonetheless, kept prices substantially lower there than elsewhere.

This mixed pattern was slightly modified, but not essentially changed, under the EC's Common Agricultural Policy (CAP). Through a series of agreements beginning in 1963 and later known as the Lomé Conventions, individual preference schemes were replaced by a common package of EU assistance to former colonial (ACP) producers, including the French départements d'outre-mer. In many cases, this involved both free-market access and financial assistance related to commodity production. In the case of bananas, however, at the insistence of Germany, common arrangements were not fully established. Germany kept its free trade; the revenue-raising importing countries exempted ACP imports from their 20% tariff on bananas; and the former colonial powers formalized their preferential quotas under these uncommon common-market arrangements. As it happened, however, ACP production proved inelastic, and the preferential quota arrangements resulted in more expensive, rather than more plentiful, supplies. It is worth noting, though, that bananas were not the only item in which preferences for former colonies produced disparities vis à vis third parties: for various reasons, sugar and beef production also remained anomalous.

As a result, in the early 1990s as before, the EU market for bananas was segmented between those admitting 'dollar' bananas more or less readily from Central and South America, and those reserving a preferential quota for ACP producers. The segmentation was, of course, helped by the concentration of distribution on individual national markets. (The appellation 'dollar banana' comes from the handling of the non-preferential trade by the trio of US oligopolists.).

Two developments, both in the early 1990s, then set the stage for the banana dispute of the late 1990s. On the one hand, in response to various pressures of internal malperformance, sometimes referred to as 'Eurosclerosis', the EU introduced its programme of completion of the Single Market, or '1992'. On the other hand, in order to include important third parties in other aspects of the negotiation, the Uruguay Round of GATT multilateral trade negotiations, which began in the late 1980s, broke with the earlier tradition of excluding primary products (and services) from reciprocal free-trade negotiations. This conjunction forced a reconsideration of EC arrangements in a number of areas, in particular bananas.

FROM REGULATION 404 TO SECTION 407

In May 1993, in the spirit of the then recently concluded Uruguay Round, a GATT panel of experts, to which the existing regime had been referred, objected to the EC's arrangements for importation and distribution of bananas. Given that the Single Market programme was in progress, the panel's finding was put in abeyance, rather than endorsed by the GATT Council. Instead, on 1 July 1993 the EC adopted a new version of the arrangements, in the form of a Common Market Organization (CMO) for bananas. The relevant instrument was Regulation 404 of the EU Council of Ministers. It introduced a mixture of quotas and tariffs for overall imports into the EC: a tariff-free quota of 1.7m. metric tons for the hitherto favoured 'non-dollar' suppliers, and a tariff-laden quota of 2m. tons for the dollar suppliers. Capacity constraints—some might instead say inefficiency—meant that non-dollar, former colonial suppliers were unlikely to exceed their quota (should they do so they would pay a penalty of a little over US $750 per ton).[4] The specific tariff on 'dollar' bananas was set at a little over $100 per ton within the quota, with a punitive $850 for excesses over quota. The regime was to be administered through import licences, the distribution of which, instead of being on a 'first come, first served' basis, favoured the banana companies associated with départements d'outre-mer and ACP producers. Such a system seemingly limited the market share of the major US companies, since a licence was required to access a quota. Chiquita, the US importer with the largest historical share of the EU market and the best US political connections, objected particularly to 'first come, first served'. It is this feature which gave particular prominence to the USA as a party to the subsequent dispute.

In 1994, following the conclusion of the Uruguay Round of trade negotiations, five Latin American producers (excluding Ecuador) objected to CMO, both in its retention of preferential access and in the level of the implied tariff. Their objection was upheld. The EU proposed various adjustments, including an upward revision of the 'dollar' quota and a downward revision of the tariff. Notably, also, the distribution of import licences was modified to accommodate a few Latin American co-operative exporting entities (in particular from Colombia), a move which failed to mollify the USA.

Meanwhile, on 1 January 1995, in the wake of the Uruguay Round, GATT had been superseded by the WTO. To the protocols of GATT were added those of a General Agreement on Trade in Services (GATS) which, among other things, covered the marketing activities of international companies. The forum for complaints about international trade arrangements thus moved from the GATT Council to the WTO's Dispute Settlement Body (DSB) and, in effect, this meant prosecution of complaints through somewhat more formal procedures than hitherto.

Under GATT a member's trading practices had been open to challenge under consultative procedures and, in order to prevent formal findings, a defendant could proceed to temporize through adjustments. Under WTO procedures, however, a member can block a consultative challenge without engaging in temporizing adjustments. If so, however, depending on the strategy of its adversaries, it becomes exposed to the risk of formal proceedings before the DSB. If a complaint is upheld by that body, the plaintiff might be awarded the right punitively to suspend trading concessions against the defendant, up to a value of imports (of goods, services, or intellectual property) commensurate with the damage adjudged to have been sustained. That right of punitive treatment can then either be exercised by the plaintiff, or held in reserve as a threat, in order to induce the desired adjustment to trading practices.

In May 1996 four Latin American producers, this time including Ecuador, were persuaded by the USA to instigate formal proceedings before the DSB against the EU's banana CMO. The producers were doing so largely under post-Uruguay Round provisions for trade in goods, and the USA largely under GATS on behalf of its three banana majors. In May 1997 the DSB ruled that the EU arrangements were indeed inconsistent with those two sets of principles, post-Uruguay GATT and GATS, *inter alia* owing to the way in which ('first come, first served') quota licences were distributed. The ruling was appealed by the EU, but upheld a couple of months later at the DSB's appellate level. A deadline of 1 January 1 1999 was set for compliance. The EU thereupon introduced adjustments and claimed compliance just in time. Those adjustments aimed, as in 1994, to mollify the producing countries through quota and tariff changes, rather than to accommodate the US majors through changes to licence access.

From that point onwards divisions began to appear between the Latin American producing countries and the USA, in terms both of speed and bargaining posture. (Notably divisions also appeared among the US majors, with second-ranking Dole willing to chance the 'first come, first served' regime while Chiquita, the leading distributor, continued its strenuous opposition.) Ecuador mounted a relatively leisurely and courteous challenge to the compliance of the revised EU procedures, which, it claimed, remained inconsistent with WTO criteria in their discrimination between ACP and Latin American suppliers. This challenge was at length upheld, and in May 2000, after various procedural rounds, Ecuador was granted the right to suspend concessions to the EU—in manufactured goods, services, and the treatment of intellectual property—on a trading total of US $202m.-worth of imports. In the event, however, this right remained unexercised by the time the dispute had effectively been settled in July 2001.

Pressed by its banana majors and by its Congress, the USA moved instead relatively swiftly and aggressively. Action against the EU's banana regime was taken in tandem with equally aggressive moves over hormone-treated beef, another skirmish in the EU–US trade war. As soon as the CMO compliance deadline of 1 January 1999 had passed the USA sought DSB authority to apply penalties totalling US $520m. to EU

imports (this being the US estimate of injury through denial of business to US companies). Following arbitration the DSB reduced the injury to $191.4m. In April 1999, under what is known as Section 301 of the 1974 trade act, the USA proceeded to impose 100% *ad valorem* duties on a list of 9 out of 17 carefully selected imports from the EU. Further, to mark its dissatisfaction with EU progress in the interim, the US Congress approved the inclusion of Section 407 in the Trade and Development Act of May 2000. This is the notorious 'carousel' provision, requiring that the list of targeted imports be subject to rotation, initially after four months, and then at six-monthly intervals.

Over the two years that followed the initial imposition of the carousel sanctions the USA and EU negotiators continued to skirmish. The US Trade Representative, Charlene Barshefksy, used the threat of the rotation of sanctions as a bargaining tool. Meanwhile, the EU Council of Ministers attempted adjustments to its system of quota-distribution which would mollify US distributors and meet WTO requirements, while balancing the interests of those with a post-colonial clientele against those with a taste for cheaper bananas. In late 2000, shortly before the US presidential election EU negotiators proposed a regime for banana importation and distribution that would abandon all quotas by 2006; but in the interim, would maintain the present quota-cum-tariff system in conjunction with a 'first come, first served' procedure for access to the requisite licences. While Ecuador expressed its inclination to accept this proposal, the other main Latin American producers demurred. The second-largest US company, Dole, gave its support to the revised EU scheme, but the largest (Chiquita) rejected it, combining its politically-influential rejection with the threat of filing for bankruptcy by citing cash-flow difficulties linked to the EU banana regime. Once the new US administration had been inaugurated in January 2001, a resolution was quite quickly reached in Chiquita's favour.

In the understanding reached on 11 April 2001 with the new US Trade Representative, Robert B. Zoellick, the EU conceded a phased but decisive move away from quotas protecting 'non-dollar' shipments. As in the earlier offer, by January 2006 quotas were to be eliminated completely and replaced by a tariff uniformly applicable to all imports. In the interim, the 'dollar' quota was to be increased by 100,000 metric tons and, most importantly, licences to existing quotas were to be offered on the basis of historic market share, rather than 'first come, first served', a victory for Chiquita. When the first deadline (referring to determination of historic market-shares for licences) was met on 1 July 2001, the USA lifted its carousel sanctions. In its understanding with the EU the USA has retained the right to reimpose those sanctions at a higher rate, if the promised 'dollar' quota increase was not implemented by 1 January 2002. However, such a revival of the dispute seemed unlikely as licensing by historic market-share was the key concession.[5]

RIGHTS AND WRONGS

Central and South American bananas for export are generally produced at a substantially lower cost than in the Caribbean. Estimates suggest local costs of around two-thirds of those in the islands. Likewise, although the three major companies which handle the bulk of the Latin American supplies enjoy oligopolistic advantages over their smaller rivals handling the island trade, they also enjoy greater economies of scale. While they may inflate their margins, their costs are lower. Moreover, there is evidence that the capacity to expand production is, in the long term, greater in Central and South America than in the Caribbean. Therefore, it is plausible to suppose that an unrestricted trading environment would indeed deliver cheaper bananas to the consumer. In Europe, that indeed as been the clear experience of Germany, where the equivalent retail price has habitually been less than three-quarters of the price in France or the United Kingdom, and, accordingly, consumption is much higher. The conclusion that the favouring of the Caribbean producers by successive EU regimes has been costly to consumers is inescapable.

What, however, of the conditions of production and distribution? It is difficult to establish clearly how much of the lower costs of Central and South America derive from efficiency, and how much from lesser worker-protection and environmental concern. Needless to say, the 'dollar' side has argued efficiency, while the EU side has argued working conditions and ecological wastage. This debate, like the merits of marketing through giant or smaller companies, is difficult to resolve, though, certainly, in themselves the large banana companies need no favours, whatever the cash-flow difficulties experienced by Chiquita in 2000–01 may have been. Indeed, some may find it distasteful that a dispute in international trade should have been driven by the interests of an oligopoly, where at the producers' end there are very poor people on both sides of the argument.

EU protection of Caribbean producers was, at times, defended by reference to the scarcity of attractive alternatives to banana production in small states where, diminutive as its output may be on the world market, that activity, even if it is relatively inefficient, is decisive for local income and employment. The case has been made, for instance, that narcotics processing and smuggling could easily become the dominant economic activity in some areas once preferential treatment of bananas is withdrawn. Apart from the fact that the entire region, Caribbean and Latin America, is afflicted with surplus urban labour, so that (regarding employment) narcotics production can, and probably does, happily co-exist with bananas output, the difficulty with this argument is twofold. On the one hand, some of the small Central American states (Honduras, for example) are just as dependent as the Caribbean micro-states on banana production, and they are more efficient. On the other hand, much of the excessive dependence on somewhat inefficient banana production in parts of the Caribbean has in fact been promoted, if not created, by the EU's CAP, which has given protective preference to domestic sugar-beet over post-colonial sugar-cane.

The lesson of this sorry episode is that righting wrongs through trade restrictions does as much harm as good. It has long been clear that, whatever the tactical vicissitudes of EU–US trade warfare, the Caribbean banana producers would ultimately lose their preferential treatment—as it now appears they will by 2006. Means other than protection need to be found to sustain income and employment. One possibility is purposefully to increase efficiency in the banana sector itself, rather than sacrifice working conditions and environmental concerns. Organic bananas, still at less than 1% of total global exports, offer some scope for island producers, though prices have been falling and consolidation is needed if small-scale production is to cover costs.

FOOTNOTES

1. The term EU was adopted only in 1994 to designate what was known at the time as the European Communities, The latter name is, however, formally still in use to designate in international trade negotiations the negotiating arm of what has become the EU. For simplicity the term EU is used here throughout, both for the institutions before 1994, and the negotiating arm afterwards.
2. In the 1990s each company adopted its main brand name as its corporate title: Chiquita (formerly United Brands and, before that, United Fruit Co.); Dole (formerly Castle & Cooke and, before that, Standard Fruit); and Del Monte (formerly California Packers, then variously bought and sold until its current independence).
3. Strictly speaking, the main such former colonies are, as *départements d'outre-mer*, administratively part of France.
4. The relevant tariffs were expressed in European Currency Units (ECUs), each worth around US $1.10 at the time.
5. The other dispute leading to US imposition of 'carousel' sanctions (over the EU's ban on hormone-treated beef) remained unresolved in July 2001.

PART TWO
Country Surveys

ANGUILLA

Area: 96 sq km (37.4 sq miles); Anguilla 91 sq km, Sombrero 5.

Population (official estimate, July 2000): 11,407.

Capital: The Valley (population 595 at 1992 census).

Language: English.

Religion: Several Christian denominations and sects are represented.

Climate: Subtropical; average temperature 27°C (80°F); mean annual rainfall 914 mm (36 in.).

Time: GMT –4 hours.

Public Holidays: 2002: 1 January (New Year's Day), 29 March (Good Friday), 1 April (Easter Monday), 1 May (Labour Day), 20 May (Whit Monday), 31 May (Anguilla Day), 17 June (Queen's Official Birthday), 5 August (August Monday), 8 August (August Thursday), 9 August (Constitution Day), 19 December (Separation Day), 25–26 December (Christmas). **2003:** 1 January (New Year's Day), 18 April (Good Friday), 21 April (Easter Monday), 1 May (Labour Day), 30 May (Anguilla Day), 9 June (Whit Monday), 16 June (Queen's Official Birthday), 4 August (August Monday), 7 August (August Thursday), 8 August (Constitution Day), 19 December (Separation Day), 25–26 December (Christmas).

Currency: Eastern Caribbean dollar; US $1 = EC $2.70 (fixed rate since July 1976); EC $100 = £25.87 = US $37.04 = €41.73 (30 April 2001).

Weights and Measures: Metric, but some imperial weights and measures are still used.

History

Anguilla is a United Kingdom Overseas Territory and the British monarch is represented locally by a Governor. From February 1998 the British Dependent Territories were referred to as the United Kingdom Overseas Territories, following the announcement of the interim findings of a British government review of the United Kingdom's relations with the Overseas Territories.

Anguilla was a British colony from 1650 until 1967, when St Christopher (St Kitts)-Nevis-Anguilla became a State in Association with the United Kingdom and gained internal independence. In 1967, led by Ronald Webster of the People's Progressive Party (PPP), Anguilla repudiated government from St Kitts. In 1969, after the failure of negotiations, British forces occupied the island to install a British Commissioner. In 1980 Anguilla formally separated from St Kitts-Nevis, at which point the island became a British Dependent Territory. In 1977 Emile Gumbs (also of the PPP) replaced Webster as Chief Minister. Webster returned to power in 1980, as leader of the Anguilla Alliance (ANA). In 1981 Webster founded the Anguilla People's Party (APP), which in the same year won five of the seven seats in the House of Assembly. The ANA won the 1984 election and Emile Gumbs became Chief Minister; Webster resigned from the leadership of the APP, which then renamed itself the Anguilla Democratic Party (ADP).

Following a general election in February 1989, Gumbs remained Chief Minister, though the ANA secured an overall majority in the House of Assembly. In March 1991 capital punishment was abolished in the British Caribbean territories. In the general election of March 1994 the ANA, the ADP and the AUP each won two seats, with, respectively, 35.7%, 31.2% and 11.4% of the total votes cast. An independent member, Osbourne Fleming, held the remaining seat. A coalition was formed between the ADP and the AUP and the AUP leader, Hubert Hughes, became Chief Minister. Controversy surrounding the appointment of one of the nominated Members of Parliament, David Carty, resulted in a dispute between Hughes and the Governor, Alan Shave. Despite a ruling by the Constitutional Court that Carty's appointment was legal, in December 1995 the Speaker refused to swear him into the House of Assembly, which provoked protests from other legislators, particularly Fleming.

In October 1995 the island suffered severe damage from 'Hurricane Luis'. Destruction of buildings and infrastructure, as well as damage to the agricultural sector, was estimated to be worth some EC $72m. Chief Minister Hughes criticized the response of the British Government to the hurricane. In September 1997 he was also critical of the Governor, Robert Harris, accusing him of being oblivious to his country's needs. In 1998 Hughes criticized the current Constitution for vesting executive authority in the Governor rather than in locally-elected ministers. In September of this year the British Government announced that its Overseas Dependencies were to be renamed United Kingdom Overseas Territories. In March 1999 it issued a policy document confirming the change of name, and guaranteeing citizens of Overseas Dependencies the right to British citizenship. The British Government also required that the Anguillan Constitution be revised in order to conform to British and international standards.

In Anguilla's legislative elections, held on 4 March 1999, the AUP and the ADP both retained their two seats, gaining 1,579 and 704 of the total votes cast, respectively. The opposition ANA, now with Osbourne Fleming as a member, increased its share to three seats, securing 2,053 votes. The AUP–ADP coalition, which campaigned on its record of encouraging the development of the tourist and offshore financial services sectors, therefore maintained control of the House of Assembly and Hughes was reappointed Chief Minister.

In June 1999 the resignation from the Government of the ADP leader, Victor Banks, deprived the coalition of its majority. Hughes, however, refused to resign, provoking Banks and the three ANA deputies to withdraw from the House, demanding that fresh elections be held. Lacking the necessary quorum in the legislature, the Government was unable to implement policy or to introduce a budget for 1999/2000.

The political crisis continued until January 2000, when Hughes agreed to hold further elections, on 3 March. At the elections, the ANA won three seats, the AUP two, and the ADP one, while Edison Baird was elected as an independent. Osbourne Fleming, by now ANA leader, was subsequently appointed the Chief Minister of an Executive Council which included two other ANA ministers, while Banks was reappointed Minister of Finance, Economic Development, Investment and Commerce. In February 2000 Peter Johnstone replaced Robert Harris as Governor.

Following Anguilla's inclusion on an Organisation for Economic Co-operation and Development blacklist of tax havens in 2000, the Government introduced a number of articles of legislation to combat money-laundering on the island, including the establishment of a 'Money Laundering Reporting Authority'.

In January 2001 Anguilla was to commence a series of town hall meetings about rewriting its constitution and its relationship with the United Kingdom. In the same month, following the United Kingdom's incorporation of the European Union's Convention on Human Rights, homosexuality was legalized in Anguilla.

Economy

In 1999 the real gross domestic product (GDP) of Anguilla increased by an estimated 7.5%. GDP per head was estimated at EC $18,096 in 1999. Between 1992 and 1999 real GDP increased by an annual average of 5.1%. Real GDP grew by an estimated 1.0% in 2000. This decrease in growth was partly attributable to the effects of 'Hurricane Lenny', which struck the island in November 1999.

In an effort to diversify the economy, the Government encouraged the development of tourism and the 'offshore' banking sector from the 1980s. In 1990, however, more stringent regulations governing banking operations were introduced. The 'offshore' sector was reported to have expanded by 23% in 1995, following the introduction of new legislation aimed to encourage increased investment. The sector contributed some 12% of gross domestic product (GDP) in 1999. Moreover, in 1999 the registration of international businesses increased by some 36% on the previous year.

By the 1990s tourism was the dominant sector of the economy, providing some 35.4% of GDP in 1995. The sector was badly affected by 'Hurricane Luis' which devastated the island in October 1995. However, tourist levels soon recovered and in 1999 the hotel and restaurant sector remained the largest contributor to GDP (27.3%). The contribution to GDP from the hotel and restaurant sector increased by 1.6% in 1998 and by 6.6% in 1999. In the latter year services as a whole accounted for 76.2% of GDP. In 1999 tourist expenditure totalled EC \$154.23m., despite the impact of 'Hurricane Lenny', which forced the temporary closure of the island's two largest tourist resorts.The USA provides most stay-over visitors to Anguilla: 59.9% of the total in 1998. GDP in services increased by 3.3% in 1998 and by 7.3% in 1999.

Agriculture also expanded from the late 1980s, helped by changes in crops and favourable rainfall. In 1999 agriculture (including fishing) contributed 2.7% of GDP. According to the Eastern Caribbean Central Bank (ECCB), agricultural GDP increased by an annual average of 0.2% during 1993–99. GDP in the sector increased by 7.2% in 1998. Production, however, fell by 11.0% in 1999, mainly as a result of Hurricane Lenny. Livestock-rearing traditionally supplies significant export earnings, but the principal productive sector is the fishing industry (which is also a major employer).

The industrial sector (including mining, manufacturing, construction and power) increased by 8.5% in 1998, according to the ECCB. This was primarily owing to increased construction activities. Industry accounted for 21.1% of GDP in 1999. Most industry is traditionally based on salt production and shipbuilding. Some of the island's income is provided in the form of workers' remittances from the several thousand Anguillans living abroad, principally in the USA, the United Kingdom and the US Virgin Islands.

The new Government in 2000 committed itself to increased state investment in tourism, financial services and fisheries. The Government also hoped to establish the island as a centre for information technology and electronic commerce, and to raise revenue from the sale and leasing of internet domain names. In June the Government launched an internet service which would facilitate the incorporation of off-shore companies in the Anguilla tax regime. Anguilla also hoped to benefit from an agreement with a US company, Beal Aerospace, who were to build a commercial rocket launch pad on land on Sombrero Island leased from the Government at an annual fee of some US \$6m. In March 2001 the Government committed itself to increased capital and current expenditure. A fiscal surplus of some EC \$2.1m. was forecast for 2001, compared to an estimated deficit of EC \$5.8m. in 2000.

In 1998 the Organisation of Economic Co-operation and Development (OECD) included Anguilla in a list of countries it considered to operate harmful tax regimes. It postponed publication of the list, but requested that legislative changes be made and greater legal and administrative transparency be introduced in those countries. Following publication of the list in 2000, the Government introduced a number of pieces of legislation to combat money-laundering on the island, including the establishment of a 'Money Laundering Reporting Authority'.

Statistical Survey

Source: Government of Anguilla, The Secretariat, The Valley; tel. 497-2451; fax 497-3389; e-mail stats@gov.ai; internet www.gov.ai.

AREA AND POPULATION

Area (sq km): 96 (Anguilla 91, Sombrero 5).

Population: 8,960 (males 4,473; females 4,487) at census of 14 April 1992; 11,407 (official estimate) in July 2000.

Density (July 1998): 116.1 per sq km.

Principal Town (population at 1992 census): The Valley (capital) 595.

Births, Marriages and Deaths (1998): Birth rate 17.04 per 1,000; Marriage rate 21.8 per 1,000 (1993); Death rate 5.47 per 1,000.

Expectation of Life (official estimates, years at birth, 1998): males 74.39; females 80.43.

Economically Active Population (persons aged 14 years and over, 1992 census): Agriculture, hunting, forestry and fishing 175; Mining and quarrying 7; Manufacturing 131; Electricity, gas and water 86; Construction 754; Trade, restaurants and hotels 1,441; Transport, storage and communications 326; Financing, insurance, real estate and business services 214; Community, social and personal services 969; Activities not adequately defined 19; *Total employed* 4,122 (males 2,397, females 1,725); Unemployed 324 (males 156, females 168); *Total labour force* 4,446 (males 2,553, females 1,893). Source: ILO, *Yearbook of Labour Statistics.*

AGRICULTURE, ETC.

Fishing (metric tons, live weight, 1998): Finfishes 240, Caribbean spiny lobster 100, Stromboid conchs 20; Total catch 360. Source: FAO, *Yearbook of Fishery Statistics.*

FINANCE

Currency and Exchange Rates: 100 cents = 1 Eastern Caribbean dollar (EC \$). *Sterling, US Dollar and Euro Equivalents* (30 April 2001): £1 sterling = EC \$3.866; US \$1 = EC \$2.700; €1 = EC \$2.397; EC \$100 = £25.87 = US \$37.04 = €41.73. *Exchange Rate:* Fixed at US \$1 = EC \$2.70 since July 1976.

Budget (provisional figures, EC \$ million, 1999): *Current revenue* Tax revenue 55.4 (Taxes on international trade and transactions 38.8); Non-tax revenue 12.3; Capital grants 3.7; Total 71.4. *Current expenditure* Wages and salaries 33.9, Other goods and services 25.0, Transfers and subsidies 2.6, Interest payments 0.5; Capital expenditure 11.8; Total 73.8. Source: Eastern Caribbean Central Bank, *Report and Statement of Accounts.*

Cost of Living (Consumer Price Index; 12 months ending 30 November; base: 1990 = 100): 122.1 in 1997; 125.2 in 1998; 126.0 in 1999. Source: ILO, *Yearbook of Labour Statistics.*

Gross Domestic Product by Economic Activity (EC \$ million at current prices, 1999): Agriculture, hunting, forestry and fishing 7.0; Mining and quarrying 2.4; Manufacturing 3.2; Electricity, gas and water 9.8; Construction 39.5; Wholesale and retail 17.8; Hotels and restaurants 70.8; Transport 13.8; Communications 19.8; Banks and insurance 28.0; Real estate and housing 7.9; Other services 4.1; Government services 35.1; *Sub-total* 259.0; *Less* Imputed bank service charge 26.1; *GDP at factor cost* 232.9. Source: Eastern Caribbean Central Bank, *National Accounts.*

Balance of Payments (EC \$ million, 1999): Export of goods f.o.b. 7.84; Imports of goods f.o.b. –218.31; *Trade balance* –210.47; Exports of services 183.32; Imports of services –103.43; *Balance on goods and services* –130.58; Other income received 9.92; Other income paid –18.74; *Balance on goods, services and income* –139.4; Current transfers received 18.47; Current transfers paid –19.45; *Current balance* –140.38; Capital account (net) 7.16; Direct investment (net) 108.39; Other investment (net) 56.57; Net errors and omissions –26.98; *Overall balance* 4.76. Source: Eastern Caribbean Central Bank, *Balance of Payments.*

EXTERNAL TRADE

2000: (US \$ million) Total imports c.i.f. 99.2; Total exports f.o.b. 3.3. Source: ILO.

TRANSPORT

Road Traffic (1992): 4,620 registered motor vehicles.

Shipping: *Merchant Fleet* (registered at 31 December 2000): 4; Total displacement 993 grt. Source: Lloyd's Register of Shipping, *World Fleet Statistics.*

TOURISM

Visitor arrivals: 113,865 (Stop-overs 43,181, Excursionists 70,684) in 1997; 113,796 (Stop-overs 43,874; Excursionists 69,922) in 1998; 106,729 (Stop-overs 46,782, Excursionists 59,947) in 1999.

Tourist receipts (EC \$m.): 162.99 in 1997; 166.53 in 1998; 154.23 in 1999.

COMMUNICATIONS MEDIA

Radio Receivers (1997): 3,000 in use.

Television Receivers (1997) 1,000 in use.

Telephones (1995): 4,000 main lines in use.

Telefax Stations (1993): 190 in use.

Sources: UN, *Statistical Yearbook*; UNESCO, *Statistical Yearbook.*

EDUCATION

Pre-primary (1996/97): 10 schools, 26 teachers, 417 pupils.

Primary (1996/97): 7 schools, 80 teachers, 1,557 pupils.

General Secondary (1996/97): 75 teachers, 1,062 pupils.
Source: UNESCO, *Statistical Yearbook*.

Directory

The Constitution

The Constitution, established in 1976, accorded Anguilla the status of a British Dependent Territory. It formally became a separate dependency on 19 December 1980, and is administered under the Anguilla Constitution Orders of 1982 and 1990. British Dependent Territories were referred to as United Kingdom Overseas Territories from February 1998 and draft legislation confirming this change and granting citizens rights to full British citizenship and residence in the United Kingdom was published in March 1999. The UK Government proposals also included the requirement that the Constitutions of Overseas Territories should be revised in order to conform to British and international standards. The process of revision of the Anguillan Constitution began in September 1999.

The British monarch is represented locally by a Governor, who presides over the Executive Council and the House of Assembly. The Governor is responsible for defence, external affairs (including international financial affairs), internal security (including the police), the public service, the judiciary and the audit. The Governor appoints a Deputy Governor. On matters relating to internal security, the public service and the appointment of an acting governor or deputy governor, the Governor is required to consult the Chief Minister. The Executive Council consists of the Chief Minister and not more than three other ministers (appointed by the Governor from the elected members of the legislative House of Assembly) and two *ex-officio* members (the Deputy Governor and the Attorney-General). The House of Assembly is elected for a maximum term of five years by universal adult suffrage and consists of seven elected members, two *ex-officio* members (the Deputy Governor and the Attorney-General) and two nominated members who are appointed by the Governor, one upon the advice of the Chief Minister, and one after consultations with the Chief Minister and the Leader of the Opposition. The House elects a Speaker and a Deputy Speaker.

The Governor may order the dissolution of the House of Assembly if a resolution of 'no confidence' is passed in the Government, and elections must be held within two months of the dissolution.

The Constitution provides for an Anguilla Belonger Commission, which determines cases of whether a person can be 'regarded as belonging to Anguilla' (i.e. having 'belonger' status). A belonger is someone of Anguillan birth or parentage, someone who has married a belonger, or someone who is a citizen of the United Kingdom Overseas Territories from Anguilla (by birth, parentage, adoption or naturalization). The Commission may grant belonger status to those who have been domiciled and ordinarily resident in Anguilla for not less than 15 years.

The Government

Governor: PETER JOHNSTONE (appointed February 2000).

EXECUTIVE COUNCIL
(August 2001)

Chief Minister and Minister of Home Affairs, Tourism, Agriculture, Fisheries and Environment: OSBOURNE FLEMING (ANA).

Minister of Finance, Economic Development, Investment and Commerce: VICTOR BANKS (ADP).

Minister of Education, Health, Social Development and Lands: ERIC REID (ANA).

Minister of Infrastructure, Communications, Public Utilities, Transportation and Housing: KENNETH HARRIGAN (ANA).

Attorney-General: KURT DEFREITAS.

Deputy Governor: HENRY MCCRORY.

MINISTRIES

Office of the Governor: Government House, POB 60, The Valley; tel. 497-2622; fax 497-3151.

Office of the Chief Minister: The Secretariat, The Valley; tel. 497-2518; fax 497-3389; e-mail chief-minister@gov.ai.

All ministries are based in The Valley, mostly at the Secretariat (tel. 497-2451; internet www.gov.ai).

Legislature

HOUSE OF ASSEMBLY

Speaker: LEROY ROGERS.

Clerk to House of Assembly: Rev. JOHN A. GUMBS.

Election, 3 March 2000

Party	% of votes	Seats
Anguilla National Alliance (ANA)* . . .	34.1	3
Independents	30.8	1
Anguilla United Party (AUP)	12.1	2
Anguilla Democratic Party (ADP)* . . .	10.8	1
Anguilla Patriotic Movement (APM) . . .	3.9	—
Movement for Grassroots Democracy (MFGR) .	3.6	—
Total (incl. others)	100.0	7

* The ANA and the ADP formed an electoral alliance, the United Front.

There are also two *ex-officio* members and two nominated members.

Political Organizations

Anguilla Democratic Party (ADP): The Valley; f. 1981 as Anguilla People's Party; name changed 1984; Leader VICTOR BANKS.

Anguilla National Alliance (ANA): The Valley; f. 1980 by reconstitution of People's Progressive Party; Leader OSBOURNE FLEMING.

Anguilla Patriotic Movement (APM): The Valley, f. 2000; Leaders QUINCEY GUMBS, FRANKLIN RICHARDSON.

Anguilla United Party (AUP): The Valley; f. 1979, revived 1984; Leader HUBERT HUGHES.

Movement for Grassroots Democracy (MFGR): The Valley; f. 2000; Leaders JOHN BENJAMIN, JOYCE KENTISH.

Judicial System

Justice is administered by the High Court, Court of Appeal and Magistrates' Courts. During the High Court sitting, the Eastern Caribbean Supreme Court provides Anguilla with a judge.

Religion

CHRISTIANITY

The Anglican Communion

Anglicans in Anguilla are adherents of the Church in the Province of the West Indies, comprising nine dioceses. Anguilla forms part of the diocese of the North Eastern Caribbean and Aruba.

Bishop of the North Eastern Caribbean and Aruba: Rt Revd LEROY ERROL BROOKS; St Mary's Rectory, POB 180, The Valley; fax 497-3012; e-mail diocesnesca@candw.ag.

The Roman Catholic Church

The diocese of St John's-Basseterre, suffragan to the archdiocese of Castries (Saint Lucia), includes Anguilla, Antigua and Barbuda, the British Virgin Islands, Montserrat and Saint Christopher and Nevis. The Bishop resides in St John's, Antigua.

Roman Catholic Church: St Gerard's, POB 47, The Valley; tel. 497-2405.

Protestant Churches

Methodist Church: South Hill; Minister (vacant).

The Seventh-day Adventist, Baptist, Church of God, Pentecostal, Apostolic Faith and Jehovah's Witnesses Churches and sects are also represented.

The Press

Anguilla Life Magazine: Caribbean Commercial Centre, POB 109, The Valley; tel. 497-3080; fax 497-2501; 3 a year; circ. 10,000.

The Light: POB 1373, The Valley; tel. 497-5058; fax 497-5795; e-mail thelight@anguillanet.com; internet www.thelight-anguilla.com; f. 1993; weekly; newsletter; Editor GEORGE HODGE.

Official Gazette: The Valley; tel. 497-5081; monthly; government news-sheet.

What We Do in Anguilla: POB 1373, The Valley; annual; official tourism guide; tel. 497-5641; fax 497-5795; e-mail thelight@anguilland.com; internet www.anguillatourguide.com; f. 1991; Editor MARY STEEL; circ. 50,000.

Broadcasting and Communications

TELECOMMUNICATIONS

Cable and Wireless Anguilla: POB 77, The Valley: tel. 497-3100; fax 497-2501; internet www.anguillanet.com.

Eastern Caribbean Cellular: POB 1000, George Hill, tel. 497-2100.

BROADCASTING
Radio

Caribbean Beacon Radio: POB 690, Long Road, The Valley; tel. 497-4340; fax 497-4311; (Head Office: POB 7008, Columbus, Ga 31908, USA); f. 1981; privately owned and operated; religious and commercial; broadcasts 24 hours daily; Pres. Dr GENE SCOTT; CEO B. MONSELL HAZELL.

Radio Anguilla: Department of Information and Broadcasting, The Valley; tel. 497-2218; fax 497-5432; f. 1969; owned and operated by the Govt of Anguilla since 1976; 250,000 listeners throughout the north-eastern Caribbean; broadcasts 17 hours daily; Dir of Information and Broadcasting NAT HODGE; News Editor WYCLIFFE RICHARDSON.

ZJF FM: The Valley; tel. 497-3157; f. 1989; commercial.

Television

All Island Cable Television Service Ltd: POB 336, George Hill, The Valley; tel. 497-3600; fax 497-3602.

Network Community Television Ltd: POB 333, Sachasses; tel. 497-3919; fax 497-3909.

Finance

(cap. = capital; dep. = deposits; res = reserves; m. = million; amounts in EC dollars)

CENTRAL BANK

Eastern Caribbean Central Bank: Fairplay Commercial Complex, The Valley; tel. 497-5050; fax 497-5150; HQ in Basseterre, Saint Christopher and Nevis; bank of issue and central monetary authority for Anguilla, Antigua and Barbuda, Dominica, Grenada, Montserrat, Saint Christopher and Nevis, Saint Lucia and Saint Vincent and the Grenadines; Governor K. DWIGHT VENNER.

COMMERCIAL BANKS

Barclays Bank PLC (United Kingdom): POB 140, The Valley; tel. 497-2301; fax 497-2980; Man. DEREK PINARD.

Caribbean Commercial Bank (Anguilla) Ltd: POB 23, The Valley; tel. 497-2571; fax 497-3570; e-mail ccbaxa@anguillanet.com; Man. PRESTON BRYAN.

National Bank of Anguilla Ltd: POB 44, The Valley; tel. 497-2101; fax 497-3310; e-mail nbabankl@anguillanet.com; internet www.nba.ai; f. 1985; cap. 5.4m., res 10.5m., dep. 145.1m. (Mar. 1998); Chair. E. VALENTINE BANKS; Gen. Man. SELWYN F. HORSFORD.

Scotiabank Anguilla Ltd: POB 250, Fairplay Commercial Centre, The Valley; tel. 497-3333; fax 497-3344; e-mail anguillatork15@bnsdial.com; Man. WALTER MACCALMAN.

There are 'offshore', foreign banks based on the island, but most are not authorized to operate in Anguilla. There is a financial complex known as the Caribbean Commercial Centre in The Valley.

Anguilla Offshore Financial Centre: POB 60, The Valley; tel. 497-5881; fax 497-5872; internet www.anguillaoffshore.com.

TRUST COMPANIES

Emerald Trust International Ltd: POB 645, The Valley; tel. 497-5342; fax 497-5812; e-mail emerald@offshore.com.ai; Man. THOMAS PEACOCK.

Financial Services Co Ltd: POB 58, The Valley; tel. 497-3777; fax 497-5377; e-mail firstanguilla@anguillalaw.com.

First Anguilla Trust Co Ltd: Victoria House, POB 58, The Valley; tel. 497-8800; fax 497-8880; e-mail websterdyrud@anguillanet.com; Mans JOHN DYRUD, PALMAVON WEBSTER.

Hansa Bank and Trust Co Ltd: POB 213, The Valley; tel. 497-3802; fax 497-3801; e-mail hansa@ibm.net; internet www.hansa.net.

INSURANCE

Anguilla Mutual Assurance Co Ltd: Stony Ground, The Valley; tel. 497-2246.

Anguilla National Insurance Co Ltd: Airport Rd, POB 44, The Valley; tel. 497-5280; fax 497-3870.

British American Insurance Co Ltd: Herbert's Commercial Centre, POB 148; tel. 497-2653; fax 497-5933.

D-3 Enterprises Ltd: Herbert's Commercial Centre, POB 1377, The Valley; tel. 497-3525; fax 497-3526; Man. CLEMENT RUAN.

Gulf Insurance Ltd: Blowing Point; tel. 497-6613.

Malliouhana Insurance Co Ltd: Herbert's Commercial Centre, POB 492, The Valley; tel. 497-3710; fax 497-3712; Man. MONICA HODGE.

Nagico Insurance: POB 79, The Valley; tel. 497-2976; fax 497-3303.

National Caribbean Insurance Co Ltd: Herbert's Commercial Centre, POB 323, The Valley; tel. 497-2865; fax 497-3783.

Trade and Industry
DEVELOPMENT ORGANIZATION

Anguilla Development Board: POB 285, Wallblake Rd, The Valley; tel. 497-3690; fax 497-2959.

CHAMBER OF COMMERCE

Anguilla Chamber of Commerce: POB 321, The Valley; tel. 497-2701; fax 497-5858; Exec. Dir PAULA MACK; Pres. SUTCLIFFE HODGE.

INDUSTRIAL AND TRADE ASSOCIATION

Anguilla Financial Services Association: POB 1071, The Valley: e-mail arichardson@anguillanet.com; Pres. ALEX RICHARDSON; Vice-Pres. JOSEPH BRICE.

UTILITIES
Electricity

Anguilla Electricity Co Ltd: POB 400, The Valley; tel. 497-5200; fax 497-5440; operates a power station and generators.

Transport
ROADS

Anguilla has 140 km (87 miles) of roads, of which 100 km (62 miles) are tarred.

SHIPPING

The principal port of entry is Sandy Ground on Road Bay. There is a daily ferry service between Blowing Point and Marigot (St Martin).

Link Ferries: Little Harbour; tel. 497-2231; fax 497-3290; e-mail fbconnor@anguillanet.com; internet link.ai; f. 1992; daily services to Julianna International Airport (St Martin) and charter services; Owner FRANKLYN CONNOR.

CIVIL AVIATION

Wallblake Airport, 3.2 km (2 miles) from The Valley, has a bitumen-surfaced runway with a length of 1,100m (3,600 ft). In February 1996 Anguilla signed an agreement with the Government of Aruba providing for the construction of a new jet airport on the north coast of the island, with finance of some US $30m. from the Aruba Investment Bank. In mid-1997 it was announced that Wallblake Airport was to be replaced by a new airport with a 1,833m.-long (6,000 ft) runway. The US $25m. construction, which began in 1998 was due for completion in 2000.

Air Anguilla: POB 110, Wallblake; tel. 497-2643; fax 497-2982; scheduled services to St Thomas, St Maarten/St Martin, Saint Christopher and Beef Island (British Virgin Islands); Pres. RESTORMEL FRANKLIN.

American Eagle: POB 659, Wallblake Airport; tel. 497-3131; fax 497-3502; operates scheduled flights from Puerto Rico three times a day (December to April) and once daily (May to November).

Tyden Air: POB 107, Wallblake Airport; tel. 497-2719; fax 497-3079; charter company servicing whole Caribbean.

Tourism

Anguilla's sandy beaches and unspoilt natural beauty attract tourists and also day visitors from neighbouring St Maarten/St Martin. The tourist sector was damaged by the effects of Hurricane Luis in

1995, but had recovered to pre-hurricane levels by 1997. In November 1999 'Hurricane Lenny' badly affected Anguilla, forcing the temporary closure of the island's two largest hotels. In 1998 tourist arrivals totalled 106,729. In 1998 59.9% of stop-over tourists were from the USA, 10.9% were from other Caribbean countries, while most of the remainder were from the United Kingdom, Canada, Italy and Germany. There were some 1,200 hotel rooms on the island in 1994. Earnings from the tourist industry totalled EC $154.23m. in 1999.

Anguilla Tourist Board: POB 1388, The Valley; tel. 497-2759; fax 497-2710; e-mail atbtour@anguillanet.com; internet www.anguilla-vacation.com.

Anguilla Hotel and Tourism Association: POB 1388, Old Factory Plaza, The Valley; tel. 497-2944; fax 497-3091; e-mail ahta@anguillanet.com; f. 1981; Exec. Dir MIMI GRATTON.

Defence

The United Kingdom is responsible for the defence of Anguilla.

Education

Education is free and compulsory between the ages of five and 16 years. Primary education begins at five years of age and lasts for six years. Secondary education, beginning at 11 years of age, lasts for a further six years. There are six government primary schools and one government secondary school. A 'comprehensive' secondary school education system was introduced in September 1986. Post-secondary education is undertaken abroad. Government expenditure on education in the budget for 1991 was EC $4.8m., equivalent to 17% of total expenditure. According to official sources, about 5% of the adult population are illiterate.

ANTIGUA AND BARBUDA

Area: 441.6 sq km (170.5 sq miles); Antigua 280 sq km, Barbuda 161 sq km, Redonda 1.6 sq km.

Population (official estimate, mid-2000): 66,422.

Capital: St John's (population 22,342 at 1991 census).

Language: English (official); an English patois is widely used.

Religion: Mainly Anglican, but several other Christian denominations are represented.

Climate: Tropical; average temperature 27°C (81°F); average rainfall 1,000 mm.

Time: GMT −4 hours.

Public Holidays: 2002: 1 January (New Year's Day), 29 March (Good Friday), 31 March (Easter Monday), 6 May (Labour Day), 20 May (Whit Monday), 8 June (Queen's Official Birthday), 1 July (Vere Cornwall Bird, Sr Day), 5–6 August (Carnival), 7 October, 1 November (Independence Day), 25–26 December (Christmas). **2003:** 1 January (New Year's Day), 18 April (Good Friday), 21 April (Easter Monday), 5 May (Labour Day), 9 June (Whit Monday), 14 June (Queen's Official Birthday), 7 July (Vere Cornwall Bird, Sr Day),4–5 August (Carnival), 7 October, 1 November (Independence Day), 25–26 December (Christmas).

Currency: Eastern Caribbean dollar; US $1 = EC $2.700 (fixed rate since July 1976); EC $100 = £24.82 = US $37.04 = €39.80 (30 April 2001).

Weights and Measures: Imperial; metric system being introduced.

History

Antigua and Barbuda is a constitutional monarchy within the Commonwealth. Queen Elizabeth II is the Head of State and is represented in Antigua and Barbuda by a Governor-General. There is a bicameral legislature, Parliament, with an elected chamber.

The territory was administered as part of the Leeward Islands until 1959. It attained associated status, with full internal self-government, in 1967. On 1 November 1981 Antigua and Barbuda became independent, as a unitary state, despite a strong campaign for separate independence by the inhabitants (about 1,000) of Barbuda. Vere C. Bird, Sr, of the Antigua Labour Party (ALP), which, except between 1971 and 1976, has held power since 1946, became the islands' first Prime Minister. In March 1992 three opposition parties merged, to form the United Progressive Party (UPP), led by Baldwin Spencer. In Barbuda opposition was expressed in a campaign for greater autonomy, led by the Barbuda People's Movement (BPM), which controlled all nine seats on the Barbuda Council from 1989.

In September 1993, following a series of financial and political scandals, Lester Bird, son of Vere C. Bird, succeeded his father as leader of the ALP. He became Prime Minister after the general election of 1994, in which the ALP won 11 out of 17 seats. Allegations and scandals involving ALP members continued during Lester Bird's administration: in May 1995 the premier's brother, Ivor Bird, was arrested on drugs charges and in June 1996 the opposition newspaper, *Outlet*, accused the former Prime Minister, Vere C. Bird, of having profited from transactions involving government land. In September 1995 'Hurricane Luis' inflicted an estimated US $300m.-worth of damage on the territory.

In March 1997 the BPM defeated the ALP's ally, the New Barbuda Development Movement, in elections to the Barbuda Council, winning all five of the contested seats and thus gaining control of all the seats in the nine-member Council. In late May and early June sittings in the House of Representatives were boycotted by the UPP during a parliamentary debate on a proposed US $300m.–tourism development on Guiana Island. The opposition claimed that the Prime Minister had failed to publish the proposals for public discussion prior to the parliamentary debate and that the project would have adverse effects on the island's ecology. The project was, none the less, endorsed

by the legislature and in August *Outlet* published further allegations regarding government-supported drugs-trafficking. In December 1997 Vere Bird, Jr, the eldest son of Vere C. Bird, was wounded in a shooting incident on the same day as the Government agreed terms for the compulsory resettlement of Guiana Island's only occupants, Cyril 'Taffy' Bufton and his wife. Bufton was subsequently charged with attempted murder, but was acquitted in October 1998. The UPP denied government allegations of its involvement in the attack.

In February 1997 the Government announced that four Russian and one Ukrainian 'offshore' banks were to be closed down, owing to 'irregularities' in their operations (they were suspected of 'laundering' money for the Russian mafia). In April Wrenford Ferrance, the government Special Adviser, was appointed to the post of superintendent of 'offshore' banks and insurance companies and director of international business corporations. Following the collapse, under suspicious circumstances, of the Antigua-based European Union Bank in August, the 51 remaining 'offshore' banks in Antigua and Barbuda were requested to submit full details of their operations in an attempt to combat further fraud. However, in May 1998 two more 'offshore' banks were implicated in a money-laundering case. In October the Government introduced legislation aimed at preventing such irregularities, while simultaneously promoting the development of the 'offshore' financial sector. However, in March 1999 the US Government published a report which claimed that the recent Antiguan legislation had weakened regulations concerning money-laundering and increased the secrecy surrounding 'offshore' banks. It also advised US banks to scrutinize all financial dealings with Antigua and Barbuda, which was described as a potential 'haven for money-laundering activities'. In April the United Kingdom issued a similar financial advisory to its banks. In response, in July Antigua became the first Eastern Caribbean country to bring into force a treaty with the USA on extradition and mutual legal assistance. Furthermore, in September the Government announced the establishment of an independent body to regulate 'offshore' banking, and promised to make existing controls more stringent. Nevertheless, in 2000 Antigua and Barbuda's financial system was criticized by the Organisation for Economic Co-operation and Development (OECD) and the Financial Action Task Force on Money Laundering (FATF, based at the OECD). However, by July 2001 the country had satisfied the United Kingdom that its financial institutions no longer needed special attention and had conformed to the FATF rules on harmful tax practices.

In August 1998 the House of Representatives approved an amendment to voting regulations, allowing all citizens who had been born abroad (including non-Commonwealth citizens) but who had been resident in Antigua and Barbuda for more than three years to vote. Elections to the House of Representatives took place on 9 March 1999. The ALP increased its representation in the 17-seat legislature to 12, at the expense of the UPP, who secured four seats. The BPM retained its single seat. The UPP protested the results, although independent observers declared the election to have been free, although they expressed reservations concerning its fairness, owing to the ALP's large-scale expenditure and use of the media during its electoral campaign. Lester Bird was reappointed premier. The new Cabinet controversially included Vere Bird, Jr, as Minister of Agriculture, Lands and Fisheries (despite a 1990 ruling declaring him unfit to hold public office). In June Vere C. Bird, Sr, died, aged 88. In November Vincent Derrick was re-elected Chairman of the UPP.

In January 2000 the Government established a commission, chaired by Sir Fred Philips, a former Governor of Saint Christopher and Nevis, to review the Constitution. The commission was to examine the role of the Government, political parties and non-governmental organizations, and was to focus on the maintenance of democracy and accountability. In addition, increased tensions between Antigua and Barbuda, and the latter's demands for autonomy, meant that constitutional change was a much discussed issue throughout 2001.

In November 2000 the Government introduced a controversial 2% turnover tax. In the same month Prime Minister Bird requested that the IMF send a team of tax specialists to the islands to consult with the Government, the private sector and trade unions on the development of a 'new, efficient and modern' tax system. The Government forecast that the review and adoption of the new arrangements could take between 18 months and two years.

Antigua and Barbuda is a member of CARICOM and of the Organisation of Eastern Caribbean States (OECS—see Regional Organizations in Part Three). It is a leading opponent of closer political integration in both groups.

Economy

Tourism is the main economic activity, accounting, directly and indirectly, for some 60% of gross domestic product (GDP) in the 1990s and about 35% of employment in 1991. The industry was severely affected by Hurricane Luis in 1995, but showed signs of recovery from 1996, when tourist arrivals increased to 528,172, an increase of 12.5% on the previous year. Visitor arrivals increased to 540,773 in 1997, to 577,024 in 1998 and to 588,866 in 1999. Total expenditure from tourism amounted to EC $782.9m. in this latest year. Most tourists are from the USA (31% in 1998), the United Kingdom (27%), Canada (7%) and other Caribbean countries (11%).

Compared with tourism, the agricultural sector is far less significant to Antigua and Barbuda's economy. However, agricultural output began to increase significantly after 1985, following the introduction of new crops, although adverse weather conditions continued to affect production levels. Agricultural GDP increased, in real terms, between 1990 and 1998 at an average rate of 1.1% per year. It rose by 4.8% in 1997, by 4.2% in 1998 and by 3.2% in 1999. In 1999 agriculture contributed 3.6% of GDP. In 2000 the Ministry of Agriculture, Lands and Fisheries announced a programme to encourage farmers to increase production.

Industry (comprising mining, manufacturing, construction and utilities) provided 17.7% of GDP in 1999. The principal industrial activity is construction, which accounted for 11.3% of

GDP in the same year. In 1996 the construction sector grew by 12.0%, mainly owing to ongoing rehabilitation projects necessitated by 'Hurricane Luis'. In 1997 growth in the sector slowed to 8.0%. In 1998 construction growth was 10.0%. Industrial GDP increased, in real terms, at an average rate of 3.4% per year during 1990–98. It rose by 8.3% in 1997, by 3.1% in 1998 and by 8.5% in 1999. Mining and quarrying contributed 1.6% of GDP in 1999. The real GDP of the mining sector increased at an average rate of 2.7% per year during 1990–98, and by an estimated 8.0% in 1998. The manufacturing sector consists of some light industries producing garments, paper, paint, furniture, food and beverage products, and the assembly of household appliances and electrical components for export. Manufacturing contributed 2.1% of GDP in 1999. In real terms, the manufacturing sector declined at an average rate of 0.6% per year during 1990–98, but increased by an estimated 5.5% in 1998.

During the 1980s and 1990s the Government endeavoured to diversify the economy, in order to reduce the dependence on tourism. In 1993 legislation was approved allowing the establishment of a free-trade zone, to encourage the manufacture of goods for export, in the north-east of Antigua. The territory's main economic problems included its high debt-servicing commitments: total external debt at the end of 1998 amounted to US $357.0m.; and in 1998/99 debt-servicing costs were expected to account for EC $83.9m., 20.2% of total expenditure. A government economic austerity programme was initiated in 1996, which included a two-year 'freeze' of the salaries of public-sector employees and a reduction of 10% in government ministers' earnings. However, by 1997 the country was experiencing a degree of economic recovery; according to the Eastern Caribbean Central Bank the economy expanded by an estimated 5.6% in 1997, and by 3.9% in 1998. The economic expansion was projected to be 4.6% in 1999. In the same year GDP, measured at current prices, was EC $1,497.1m., equivalent to EC $22,539 per head. In July 1998 Antigua joined fellow members of the OECS in applying for group membership of the Inter-American Development Bank. In September 1999 plans to privatize the state broadcasting service were announced. In the following month it was reported that all but two of the country's external debts had been rescheduled and in August 2000 the United Kingdom agreed to cancel US $9m. in debt and to reschedule a further $6m. over 10 years.

Statistical Survey

Source (unless otherwise stated): Ministry of Finance, High St, St John's; tel. 462-4860; fax 462-1622.

AREA AND POPULATION

Area: 441.6 sq km (170.5 sq miles).

Population: 65,525 (males 31,054, females 34,471) at census of 7 April 1970; 62,922 (provisional result) at census of 28 May 1991; 66,422 (official estimate) at mid-2000.

Density (estimate, mid-1998): 158.1 per sq km.

Principal Town: St John's (capital), population 22,342 at 1991 census.

Births, Marriages and Deaths (registrations): Live births (provisional, 1997) 1,448 (birth rate 21.6 per 1,000); Marriages (1987) 343 (marriage rate 5.4 per 1,000); Deaths (1995) 434 (death rate 6.4 per 1,000). Source: UN, *Demographic Yearbook*.

Expectation of Life (World Bank estimate, years at birth, 1998): 75.

Employment (persons aged 15 years and over, census of 28 May 1991): Agriculture, forestry and fishing 1,040; Mining and quarrying 64; Manufacturing 1,444; Electricity, gas and water 435; Construction 3,109; Trade, restaurants and hotels 8,524; Transport, storage and communications 2,395; Finance, insurance, real estate and business services 1,454; Community, social and personal services 6,406; Activities not adequately defined 1,882; Total employed 26,753 (males 14,564, females 12,189). Source: ILO, *Yearbook of Labour Statistics*.

1998: Total active labour force (estimate) 30,000. Source: IMF *Antigua and Barbuda: Statistical Annex* (December 1999).

AGRICULTURE, ETC.

Principal Crops (FAO estimates, '000 metric tons, 2000): Vegetables 1.6; Melons 0.7; Mangoes 1.3; Other fruits 7.0. Source: FAO.

Livestock (FAO estimates, '000 head, year ending September 1999): Asses 1; Cattle 16; Pigs 2; Sheep 12; Goats 12; Poultry 90. Source: FAO.

Livestock Products (FAO estimates, '000 metric tons, 2000): Beef and veal 1; Cows' milk 6. Source: FAO.

Fishing (FAO estimates, metric tons, live weight, 1998): Total catch 500 (Marine fishes 380, Caribbean spiny lobster 65, Stromboid conchs 55). Source: FAO, *Yearbook of Fishery Statistics*.

INDUSTRY

Production (estimates, 1988): Rum 4,000 hectolitres; Wines and vodka 2,000 hectolitres; Electric energy (1995) 98m. kWh. Source: UN, *Industrial Commodity Statistics Yearbook*.

FINANCE

Currency and Exchange Rates: 100 cents = 1 Eastern Caribbean dollar (EC $). *Sterling, US Dollar and Euro Equivalents* (29 December 2000): £1 sterling = EC $4.029; US $1 = EC $2.700; €1 = EC $2.512; EC $100 = £24.82 = US $37.04 = €39.80. *Exchange rate:* Fixed at US $1 = EC $2.700 since July 1976.

Budget (EC $ million, preliminary, 1999): *Revenue:* Tax revenue 302.4 (Taxes on income and profits 35.1, Taxes on domestic goods and services 63.3, Taxes on international transactions 199.8); Other current revenue 44.7; Capital revenue 4.0; Total 351.1, excluding grants received (6.8). *Expenditure:* Current expenditure 388.6 (Personal emoluments 220.0, Other goods and services 98.5, Interest payments 31.8, Transfers and subsidies 38.4); Capital expenditure 47.5; Total 436.1. Source: Eastern Caribbean Central Bank, *Report and Statement of Accounts.*

International Reserves (US $ million at 31 December 2000): IMF special drawing rights 0.01; Foreign exchange 63.55; Total 63.56. Source: IMF, *International Financial Statistics.*

Money Supply (EC $ million at 31 December 2000): Currency outside banks 84.63; Demand deposits at deposit money banks 225.05; Total money (incl. others) 309.69. Source: IMF, *International Financial Statistics.*

Cost of Living (Consumer Price Index; base: 1997 = 100): 100.0 in 1997; 103.4 in 1998; 104.6 in 1999. Source: ILO, *Yearbook of Labour Statistics.*

Expenditure on the Gross Domestic Product (EC $ million at current prices, 1999): Government final consumption expenditure 401.4; Private final consumption expenditure 897.3; Gross capital formation 807.1; *Total domestic expenditure* 2,105.8; Exports of goods and services 1,159.5; *Less* Imports of goods and services 1,506.3; *GDP in purchasers' values* 1,759.0. Source: IMF, *International Financial Statistics.*

Gross Domestic Product by Economic Activity (EC $ million at current prices, 1999): Agriculture, hunting, forestry and fishing 59.12; Mining and quarrying 25.74; Manufacturing 33.64; Electricity and water 44.71; Construction 183.38; Trade 162.36; Restaurants and hotels 179.64; Transport and communications 310.69; Finance, insurance, real estate and business services 254.83; Government services 260.85; Other community, social and personal services 110.75; *Sub-total* 1,625.70; *Less* Imputed bank service charges 128.59; *GDP at factor cost* 1,497.11. Source: Eastern Caribbean Central Bank, *National Accounts.*

Balance of Payments (EC $ million, 1999): Exports of goods f.o.b. 96.89; Imports of goods f.o.b. –915.86; *Trade balance* –818.97; Exports of services 1,162.91; Imports of services –487.40; *Balance on goods and services* –143.46; Other income received 9.73; Other income paid –90.48; *Balance on goods, services and income* –224.21; Current transfers received 66.19; Current transfers paid –10.47; *Current balance* –168.49; Capital account (net) 22.78; Direct investment (net) 71.63; Portfolio investment (net) 7.25; Other investment (net) 32.28; Net errors and omissions 62.53; *Overall balance* 27.98. Source: Eastern Caribbean Central Bank, *Balance of Payments.*

EXTERNAL TRADE

Total Trade (EC $ million): *Imports c.i.f.:* 999.7 in 1997; 1,056.5 in 1998; 1,040.8 in 1999. *Exports f.o.b.:* 104.8 in 1997; 100.9 in 1998; 96.9 in 1999. Source: Eastern Caribbean Central Bank, *Balance of Payments.*

Principal Commodities (EC $ million, estimates 1998): *Imports:* Food and live animals 89.2; Beverages and tobacco 27.1; Mineral fuels, lubricants, etc. 72.1; Chemicals and related products 50.0; Basic manufactures 252.1; Machinery and transport equipment 232.8; Miscellaneous manufactured articles 113.6. Total (incl. others) 854.6. *Exports:* Food and live animals 2.4; Mineral fuels, lubricants, etc. 13.7; Chemicals and related products 6.2; Basic

manufactures 6.6; Machinery and transport equipment 22.6; Miscellaneous manufactured articles 25.1; Total (incl. others) 78.3. Source: OECS, *External Merchandise Trade Annual Report.*

Principal Trading Partners (EC $ million, estimates, 1998): *Imports:* Barbados 14.7; Canada 26.0; Trinidad and Tobago 26.6; United Kingdom 86.3; USA 227.5; Total (incl. others) 854.6. *Exports:* Barbados 7.4; Canada 1.4; French West Indies 1.3; Italy 1.8; Jamaica 1.6; Montserrat 2.5; Saint Christopher and Nevis 3.6; Saint Lucia 5.7; Trinidad and Tobago 5.7; United Kingdom 4.8, USA 1.4; Total (incl. others) 78.3. Source: OECS, *Digest of Trade Statistics.*

TRANSPORT

Road Traffic (registered vehicles, 1995): Passenger motor cars 15,100; Commercial vehicles 4,800. Source: UN, *Statistical Yearbook.*

Shipping (international freight traffic, '000 metric tons, 1990): Goods loaded 28; Goods unloaded 113 (Source: UN, *Monthly Bulletin of Statistics*). *Arrivals* (vessels, 1987): 3,940. *Merchant Fleet* (registered at 31 December): 759 vessels (total displacement 4,224,380 grt) in 2000. (Source: Lloyd's Register of Shipping, *World Fleet Statistics*).

Civil Aviation (traffic on scheduled services, 1997): Kilometres flown (million) 12; Passengers carried ('000) 1,250; Passenger-km (million) 250; Total ton-km (million) 23. Source: UN, *Statistical Yearbook.*

TOURISM

Visitor Arrivals: 540,773 in 1997; 577,024 in 1998; 588,866 (231,714 stop-overs, 328,038 cruise-ship passengers, 17,358 yacht passengers, 11,756 excursionists) in 1999.

Tourism Receipts (EC $ million): 749.3 in 1997; 759.6 in 1998; 782.9 in 1999.

Source: Eastern Caribbean Central Bank, *Statistical Digest, Balance of Payments* and *Report and Statement of Accounts.*

COMMUNICATIONS MEDIA

Daily Newspaper (1996): 1 (estimated circulation 6,000)*.

Non-Daily Newspapers (1996): 4*.

Radio Receivers (1997): 36,000 in use*.

Television Receivers (1997): 31,000 in use*.

Telephones (1996): 27,556 in use.

Telefax Stations (year ending 31 March 1997): 850 in use†.

Mobile Telephones (year ending 31 March 1997): 1,300 subscribers†.

* Source: UNESCO, *Statistical Yearbook.*
† Source: UN, *Statistical Yearbook.*

EDUCATION

Pre-primary (1983): 21 schools; 23 teachers; 677 pupils.

Primary (1987/88): 43 schools; 446 teachers; 9,298 students (1991/92).

Secondary (1991/92): 15 schools (1987/88); 400 teachers (estimate); 5,845 students.

Tertiary (1986): 2 colleges; 631 students.

Directory

The Constitution

The Constitution, which came into force at the independence of Antigua and Barbuda on 1 November 1981, states that Antigua and Barbuda is a 'unitary sovereign democratic state'. The main provisions of the Constitution are summarized below:

FUNDAMENTAL RIGHTS AND FREEDOMS

Regardless of race, place of origin, political opinion, colour, creed or sex, but subject to respect for the rights and freedoms of others and for the public interest, every person in Antigua and Barbuda is entitled to the rights of life, liberty, security of the person, the enjoyment of property and the protection of the law. Freedom of movement, of conscience, of expression (including freedom of the press), of peaceful assembly and association is guaranteed and the inviolability of family life, personal privacy, home and other property is maintained. Protection is afforded from discrimination on the grounds of race, sex, etc., and from slavery, forced labour, torture and inhuman treatment.

THE GOVERNOR-GENERAL

The British sovereign, as Monarch of Antigua and Barbuda, is the Head of State and is represented by a Governor-General of local citizenship.

PARLIAMENT

Parliament consists of the Monarch, a 17-member Senate and the House of Representatives composed of 17 elected members. Senators are appointed by the Governor-General: 11 on the advice of the Prime Minister (one of whom must be an inhabitant of Barbuda), four on the advice of the Leader of the Opposition, one at his own discretion and one on the advice of the Barbuda Council. The Barbuda Council is the principal organ of local government in that island, whose membership and functions are determined by Parliament. The life of Parliament is five years.

Each constituency returns one Representative to the House who is directly elected in accordance with the Constitution.

The Attorney-General, if not otherwise a member of the House, is an ex-officio member but does not have the right to vote.

Every citizen over the age of 18 is eligible to vote.

Parliament may alter any of the provisions of the Constitution.

THE EXECUTIVE

Executive authority is vested in the Monarch and exercisable by the Governor-General. The Governor-General appoints as Prime Minister that member of the House who, in the Governor-General's view, is best able to command the support of the majority of the members of the House, and other ministers on the advice of the Prime Minister. The Governor-General may remove the Prime Minister from office if a resolution of no confidence is passed by the House and the Prime Minister does not either resign or advise the Governor-General to dissolve Parliament within seven days.

The Cabinet consists of the Prime Minister and other ministers and the Attorney-General.

The Leader of the Opposition is appointed by the Governor-General as that member of the House who, in the Governor-General's view, is best able to command the support of a majority of members of the House who do not support the Government.

CITIZENSHIP

All persons born in Antigua and Barbuda before independence who, immediately prior to independence, were citizens of the United Kingdom and Colonies automatically become citizens of Antigua and Barbuda. All persons born outside the country with a parent or grandparent possessing citizenship of Antigua and Barbuda automatically acquire citizenship as do those born in the country after independence. Provision is made for the acquisition of citizenship by those to whom it would not automatically be granted.

The Government

Head of State: HM Queen ELIZABETH II (succeeded to the throne 6 February 1952).

Governor-General: Sir JAMES CARLISLE (took office 10 June 1993).

CABINET
(August 2001)

Prime Minister and Minister of Foreign Affairs, Caribbean Community Affairs, Defence and Security, Finance and Merchant Shipping: LESTER BIRD.

Minister of Justice and Legal Affairs, and Attorney-General: Dr ERROL CORT.

Minister of Public Utilities, Aviation, Transport and Housing: ROBIN YEARWOOD.

Minister of Home Affairs, Urban Development and Renewal and Social Improvement: JOHN ST LUCE.

Minister of Tourism and the Environment: MOLWYN JOSEPH.

Minister of Health: (vacant).

Minister of Education, Culture and Technology: Dr RODNEY WILLIAMS.

Minister of Agriculture, Lands and Fisheries: VERE BIRD, Jr.

Minister of Trade, Industry and Business Development: HILROY HUMPHREYS.

Minister of Labour, Co-operatives and Public Safety: STEADROY BENJAMIN.

Minister of Planning, Implementation and Public Service Affairs: GASTON BROWN.

Minister of Youth Affairs and Sports: Sen. GUY YEARWOOD.

Minister of State in the Office of the Prime Minister with responsibility for Finance: Sen. ASOT MICHAEL.

Minister of State in the Ministry of Trade with responsibility for Industrial Development and Manufacturing: JEREMY LONGFORD.

Minister of State in the Ministry of Public Works, Communications and Insurance with responsibility for Development Control Authority and Youth Empowerment: Sen. BERNARD GEORGE WALKER.

Minister of State in the Office of the Prime Minister with responsibility for Information and Broadcasting: Sen. GUY YEARWOOD.

MINISTRIES

Office of the Prime Minister: Queen Elizabeth Highway, St John's; tel. 462-4956; fax 462-3225; e-mail pmo@candw.ag; internet www.antiguabarbuda.net/pmo.

Ministry of Agriculture, Lands and Fisheries: Queen Elizabeth Highway, St John's; tel. 462-1543; fax 462-6104.

Ministry of Education, Culture and Technology: Church St, St John's; tel. 462-4959; fax 462-4970.

Ministry of Finance: High St, St John's; tel. 462-4860; fax 462-1622.

Ministry of Foreign Affairs: Queen Elizabeth Highway, St John's; tel. 462-1052; fax 462-2482; e-mail minforeign@candw.ag; internet www.antiguabarbuda.net/external.

Ministry of Health: St John's St, St John's; tel. 462-1600; fax 462-5003.

Ministry of Home Affairs, Urban Development and Renewal and Social Improvement: St John's.

Ministry of Justice and Legal Affairs, and Office of the Attorney-General: Hadeed Bldg, Redcliffe St, St John's; tel. 462-6037; fax 562-1879; e-mail legalaffairs@candw.ag; internet www.antiguabarbuda.net/ag.

Ministry of Labour, Co-operatives and Public Safety: Redcliffe St, St John's; tel. 462-0011; fax 462-1595.

Ministry of Planning, Implementation and Public Service Affairs: St John's.

Ministry of Public Safety: St John's.

Ministry of Public Utilities, Aviation, Transport and Housing: St John's St, St John's; tel. 462-0894; fax 462-1529.

Ministry of Public Works, Communications and Insurance: St John's.

Ministry of Tourism and the Environment: Queen Elizabeth Highway, St John's; tel. 462-4625; fax 462-2836; e-mail mintourenv@candw.ag.

Ministry of Trade, Industry and Business Development: Redcliffe St, St John's; tel. 462-1543; fax 462-5003.

Ministry of Youth Affairs and Sports: St John's.

Legislature

PARLIAMENT
Senate

President: MILLICENT PERCIVAL.

There are 17 nominated members.

House of Representatives

Speaker: BRIDGETTE HARRIS.

Ex-Officio Member: The Attorney-General.

Clerk: L. DOWE.

General Election, 9 March 1999

Party		Votes cast	%	Seats
Antigua Labour Party	. .	17,417	52.6	12
United Progressive Party	.	14,817	44.8	4
Barbuda People's Movement	.	418	1.3	1
Independents and others	. .	439	1.3	—
Total	. . . . .	33,091	100.0	17

Political Organizations

Antigua Labour Party (ALP): St Mary's St, POB 948, St John's; tel. 462-2235; f. 1968; Leader LESTER BIRD; Chair. VERE BIRD, Jr.

Barbuda Independence Movement: Codrington; f. 1983 as Organisation for National Reconstruction, re-formed 1988; advocates self-government for Barbuda; Pres. ARTHUR SHABAZZ-NIBBS.

Barbuda National Party: Codrington; Leader ERIC BURTON.

Barbuda People's Movement (BPM): Codrington; campaigns for separate status for Barbuda; Parliamentary Leader THOMAS HILBOURNE FRANK; Chair. FABIAN JONES.

National Reform Movement (NRM): POB 1318, St John's.

New Barbuda Development Movement: Codrington; linked with the Antigua Labour Party.

United Progressive Party (UPP): Nevis Street, St John's; tel. 462-1818; fax 462-5937; e-mail upp@candw.ag; f. 1992 by merger of the Antigua Caribbean Liberation Movement (f. 1979), the Progressive Labour Movement (f. 1970) and the United National Democratic Party (f. 1986); Leader BALDWIN SPENCER; Dep. Leader CHARLESWORTH SAMUEL; Chair. VINCENT DERRICK.

Diplomatic Representation

EMBASSIES AND HIGH COMMISSION IN ANTIGUA AND BARBUDA

China, People's Republic: Cedar Valley, POB 1446, St John's; tel. 462-1125; (Ambassador resident in Barbados).

United Kingdom: British High Commission, Price Waterhouse Centre, 11 Old Parham Rd, POB 483, St John's; tel. 562-2124; fax 462-2806; e-mail britishh@candw.ag; (High Commissioner resident in Barbados).

Venezuela: Cross and Redcliffe Sts, POB 1201, St John's; tel. 462-1574; fax 462-1570; e-mail venezuela@mail.candw.ag; Ambassador: ALBERTO GARANTÓN.

Judicial System

Justice is administered by the Eastern Caribbean Supreme Court, based in Saint Lucia, which consists of a High Court of Justice and a Court of Appeal. One of the Court's Puisne Judges is resident in and responsible for Antigua and Barbuda, and presides over the Court of Summary Jurisdiction on the islands. There are also Magistrates' Courts for lesser cases.

Chief Justice: DENNIS BYRON.

Solicitor-General: LEBRECHT HESSE.

Attorney-General: Dr ERROL CORT.

Religion

The majority of the inhabitants profess Christianity, and the largest denomination is the Church in the Province of the West Indies (Anglican Communion).

CHRISTIANITY

Antigua Christian Council: POB 863, St John's; tel. 462-0261; f. 1964; five mem. churches; Pres. Rt Rev. DONALD J. REECE (Roman Catholic Bishop of St John's—Basseterre); Exec. Sec. EDRIS ROBERTS.

The Anglican Communion

Anglicans in Antigua and Barbuda are adherents of the Church in the Province of the West Indies. The diocese of the North Eastern Caribbean and Aruba comprises 12 islands: Antigua, Saint Christopher (St Kitts), Nevis, Anguilla, Barbuda, Montserrat, Dominica, Saba, St Maarten/St Martin, Aruba, St Bartholomew and St Eustatius; the total number of Anglicans is about 60,000. The See City is St John's, Antigua.

Bishop of the North Eastern Caribbean and Aruba: Rt Rev. LEROY ERROL BROOKS, Bishop's Lodge, POB 23, St John's; tel. 462-0151; fax 462-2090; e-mail dioceseneca@candw.ag.

The Roman Catholic Church

The diocese of St John's-Basseterre, suffragan to the archdiocese of Castries (Saint Lucia), includes Anguilla, Antigua and Barbuda, the British Virgin Islands, Montserrat and Saint Christopher and Nevis. At 31 December 1998 there were an estimated 14,313 adherents in the diocese. The Bishop participates in the Antilles Episcopal Conference (whose Secretariat is based in Port of Spain, Trinidad).

Bishop of St John's-Basseterre: Rt Rev. DONALD JAMES REECE, Chancery Offices, POB 836, St John's; tel. 461-1135; fax 462-2383; e-mail djr@candw.ag.

Other Christian Churches

Antigua Baptist Association: POB 277, St John's; tel. 462-1254; Pres. IVOR CHARLES.

Methodist Church: c/o POB 863, St John's; Superintendent Rev. ELOY CHRISTOPHER.

St John's Evangelical Lutheran Church: Woods Centre, POB W77, St John's; tel. 462-2896; e-mail lutheran@candw.ag; Pastors M. HENRICH, J. STERNHAGEN, T. SATORIUS.

There are also Pentecostal, Seventh-day Adventist, Moravian, Nazarene, Salvation Army and Wesleyan Holiness places of worship.

The Press

Antigua Sun: Woods Mall, POB W263, Friar's Hill Rd, St John's; tel. 480-5960; fax 480-5968; e-mail antiguasun@stanfordeagle.com; internet www.antiguanice.com/thesun; twice weekly; Publr ALLEN STANFORD.

Business Expressions: POB 774, St John's; tel. 462-0743; fax 462-4575; e-mail chamcom@candw.ag; monthly; organ of the Antigua and Barbuda Chamber of Commerce and Industry.

Daily Observer: Fort Rd, POB 1318, St John's; fax 462-5561; internet www.antiguaobserver.com; Publr SAMUEL DERRICK; Editor WINSTON A. DERRICK.

The Nation's Voice: Public Information Division, Church St and Independence Ave, POB 590, St John's; tel. 462-0090; weekly.

National Informer: St John's; weekly.

The Outlet: Marble Hill Rd, McKinnons, POB 493, St John's; tel. 462-4410; fax 462-0438; e-mail outletpub@candw.ag; f. 1975; weekly; publ. by the Antigua Caribbean Liberation Movement (founder member of the United Progressive Party in 1992); Editor TIM HECTOR; circ. 5,000.

The Worker's Voice: Emancipation Hall, 46 North St, POB 3, St John's; tel. 462-0090; f. 1943; twice weekly; official organ of the Antigua Labour Party and the Antigua Trades and Labour Union; Editor NOEL THOMAS; circ. 6,000.

FOREIGN NEWS AGENCY

Inter Press Service (IPS) (Italy): Old Parham Rd, St John's; tel. 462-3602; Correspondent LOUIS DANIEL.

Publishers

Antigua Printing and Publishing Ltd: POB 670, St John's; tel. 462-1265; fax 462-6200.

Wadadli Productions Ltd: POB 571, St John's; tel. 462-4489.

Broadcasting and Communications

TELECOMMUNICATIONS

Most telephone services are provided by the Antigua Public Utilities Authority (see Trade and Industry).

Cable & Wireless (Antigua and Barbuda) Ltd: 42–44 St Mary's St, St John's; internet www.cwantigua.com; owned by Cable & Wireless PLC (United Kingdom).

RADIO

ABS Radio: POB 590, St John's; tel. 462-3602; internet www.cmattcomm.com/abs.htm; f. 1956; subsidiary of Antigua and Barbuda Broadcasting Service (see Television, below); Programme Man. D. L. PAYNE.

Caribbean Radio Lighthouse: POB 1057, St John's; tel. 462-1454; e-mail cradiolight@candw.ag; internet www.mannelli.com/lighthouse; f. 1975; religious broadcasts; operated by Baptist Int. Mission Inc. (USA); Dir CURTIS L. WAITE.

Caribbean Relay Co Ltd: POB 1203, St John's; tel. 462-0994; fax 462-0487; e-mail cm-crc@candw.ag; jtly-operated by British Broadcasting Corpn and Deutsche Welle.

Radio ZDK: Grenville Radio Ltd, POB 1100, St John's; tel. 462-1100; f. 1970; commercial; Programme Dir IVOR BIRD; CEO E. PHILIP.

Sun FM Radio: St John's; commercial.

TELEVISION

Antigua and Barbuda Broadcasting Service (ABS): Directorate of Broadcasting and Public Information, POB 590, St John's; tel. 462-0010; fax 462-4442; scheduled for privatization; Dir-Gen. HOLLIS HENRY; CEO DENIS LEANDRO; subsidiary:

  ABS Television: POB 1280, St John's; tel. 462-0010; fax 462-1622; f. 1964; Programme Man. JAMES TANNY ROSE.

CTV Entertainment Systems: 25 Long St, St John's; tel. 462-0346; fax 462-4211; cable television co; transmits 13 channels of US television 24 hours per day to subscribers; Programme Dir J. COX.

Finance

(cap. = capital; res = reserves; dep. = deposits; brs = branches)

BANKING

The Eastern Caribbean Central Bank (see Part Three), based in Saint Christopher, is the central issuing and monetary authority for Antigua and Barbuda.

Antigua Barbuda Investment Bank Ltd: High St and Corn Alley, POB 1679, St John's; tel. 480-2700; fax 480-2750; e-mail aob@candw.ag; f. 1990; cap. EC $6.3m., res EC $2.3m., dep. EC $107.5m. (Sept. 1997); three subsidiaries: Antigua Overseas Bank Ltd, ABI Trust Ltd and AOB Holdings Ltd; Chair. EUSTACE FRANCIS; Man. Dir McALISTER ABBOTT; 2 brs.

Antigua Commercial Bank: St Mary's and Thames Sts, POB 95, St John's; tel. 462-1217; fax 462-1220; internet www.actionline.com; f. 1955; auth. cap. EC $5m.; Man. JOHN BENJAMIN; 2 brs.

Antigua and Barbuda Development Bank: 27 St Mary's St, POB 1279, St John's; tel. 462-0838; fax 462-0839; f. 1974; Man. S. ALEX OSBORNE.

Bank of Antigua: 1000 Airport Blvd, Coolidge, POB 315, St John's; tel. 462-4282; fax 462-4718; internet www.bankofantigua.com; Chair. ALLEN STANFORD; 1 br.

Foreign Banks

Bank of Nova Scotia (Canada): High St, POB 342, St John's; tel. 480-1500; fax 480-1554; Man. LEN WRIGHT.

Barclays Bank PLC (United Kingdom): High St, POB 225, St John's; tel. 480-5000; fax 462-4910; Man. WINSTON ST AGATHE.

Canadian Imperial Bank of Commerce: High St and Corn Alley, POB 28, St John's; tel. 462-0836; fax 462-4439; Man. G. R. HILTS.

Caribbean Banking Corporation Ltd (Trinidad and Tobago): 45 High St, POB 1324, St John's; tel. 462-4217; fax 462-5040; Man. B. P. DE CASTRO.

Royal Bank of Canada: High and Market Sts, POB 252, St John's; tel. 480-1151; offers a trustee service.

Swiss American National Bank of Antigua Ltd: High St, POB 1302, St John's; tel. 462-4460; fax 462-0274; f. 1983; cap. US $1.0m., res US $2.1m., dep. US $31.9m. (Dec. 1993); Gen. Man. JOHN GREAVES; 3 brs.

In mid-1997 there were 51 registered 'offshore' banks in Antigua and Barbuda.

INSURANCE

Several foreign companies have offices in Antigua. Local insurance companies include the following:

General Insurance Co Ltd: Upper Redcliffe St, POB 340, St John's; tel. 462-2346; fax 462-4482.

Sentinel Insurance Co Ltd: Coolidge, POB 207, St John's; tel. 462-4603.

State Insurance Corpn: Redcliffe St, POB 290, St John's; tel. 462-0110; fax 462-2649; f. 1977; Chair. Dr VINCENT RICHARDS; Gen. Man. ROLSTON BARTHLEY.

Trade and Industry

DEVELOPMENT ORGANIZATIONS

Barbuda Development Agency: St John's; economic development projects for Barbuda.

Development Control Authority: St John's; internet www.antiguagov.com/dca.

Industrial Development Board: Newgate St, St John's; tel. 462-1038; fax 462-1033; f. 1984 to stimulate investment in local industries.

St John's Development Corporation: Heritage Quay, POB 1473, St John's; tel. 462-2776; fax 462-3931; e-mail stjohnsdevcorp@candw.ag; internet www.firstyellow.com/stjohnsdev; f. 1986; manages the Heritage Quay Duty Free Shopping Complex, Vendors' Mall, Public Market and Cultural and Exhibition Complex.

CHAMBER OF COMMERCE

Antigua and Barbuda Chamber of Commerce and Industry Ltd: Redcliffe St, POB 774, St John's; tel. 462-0743; fax 462-4575; e-mail chamcom@candw.ag; f. 1944 as Antigua Chamber of Commerce Ltd; name changed as above in 1991, following the collapse of the Antigua and Barbuda Manufacturers' Asscn; Pres. CLARVIS JOSEPH.

INDUSTRIAL AND TRADE ASSOCIATIONS

Antigua Cotton Growers' Association: Dunbars, St John's; tel. 462-4962; Chair. FRANCIS HENRY; Sec. PETER BLANCHETTE.

Antigua Fisheries Corpn: St John's; e-mail fisheries@candw.ag; partly funded by the Antigua and Barbuda Development Bank; aims to help local fishermen.

Antigua Sugar Industry Corpn: Gunthorpes, POB 899, St George's; tel. 462-0653.

Private Sector Organization of Antigua and Barbuda: St John's.

EMPLOYERS' ORGANIZATION

Antigua Employers' Federation: Upper High Street, POB 298, St John's; tel. 462-0449; fax 462-0449; e-mail aempfed@candw.ag; f. 1950; 120 mems; Chair. JOAN UNDERWOOD; Exec. Sec. HENDERSON BASS.

UTILITIES

Antigua Public Utilities Authority (APUA): St Mary's St, POB 416, St John's ; tel. 480-7000; fax 462-2782; generation, transmission and distribution of electricity; internal telecommunications; collec-

tion, treatment, storage and distribution of water; Gen. Man. PETER BENJAMIN.

TRADE UNIONS

Antigua and Barbuda Meteorological Officers Association: c/o V. C. Bird International Airport, Gabatco, POB 1051, St John's; tel. and fax 462-4606; Pres. LEONARD JOSIAH.

Antigua and Barbuda Public Service Association (ABPSA): POB 1285, St John's; tel. 463-6427; fax 461-5821; e-mail abpsa@candw.ag; Pres. JAMES SPENCER; Gen. Sec. ELLOY DE FREITAS; 550 mems.

Antigua and Barbuda Union of Teachers: c/o Ministry of Education, Culture and Technology, Church St, St John's; tel. 462-2692; Pres. COLIN GREENE; Sec. FOSTER ROBERTS.

Antigua Trades and Labour Union (ATLU): 46 North St, POB 3, St John's; tel. 462-0090; fax 462-4056; e-mail atandlu@candw.ag; f. 1939; affiliated to the Antigua Labour Party; Pres. WIGLEY GEORGE; Gen. Sec. NATALIE PAYNE; about 10,000 mems.

Antigua Workers' Union (AWU): Freedom Hall, Newgate St, POB 940, St John's; tel. 462-2005; fax 462-5220; e-mail awu@candw.ag; f. 1967 following split with ATLU; not affiliated to any party; Pres. MAURICE CHRISTIAN; Gen. Sec. KEITHLYN SMITH; 10,000 mems.

Transport

ROADS

There are 384 km (239 miles) of main roads and 781 km (485 miles) of secondary dry-weather roads.

SHIPPING

The main harbour is the St John's Deep Water Harbour. It is used by cruise ships and a number of foreign shipping lines. There are regular cargo and passenger services internationally and regionally. At Falmouth, on the south side of Antigua, is a former Royal Navy dockyard in English Harbour. The harbour is now used by yachts and private pleasure craft.

Antigua and Barbuda Port Authority: Deep Water Harbour, POB 1052, St John's; tel. 462-4243; fax 462-2510; f. 1968; responsible to Ministry of Finance; Chair. LLEWELLYN SMITH; Port Man. LEROY ADAMS.

Joseph, Vernon, Toy Contractors Ltd: Nut Grove St, St John's.

Parenzio Shipping Co Ltd: Nevis St, St John's.

Vernon Edwards Shipping Co: Thames St, POB 82, St John's; tel. 462-2034; fax 462-2035; e-mail vedwards@candw.ag; cargo service to and from San Juan, Puerto Rico.

The West Indies Oil Co Ltd: Friars Hill Rd, POB 230, St John's; tel. 462-0140; fax 462-0543.

CIVIL AVIATION

Antigua's V.C. Bird (formerly Coolidge) International Airport, 9 km (5.6 miles) north-east of St John's, is modern and accommodates jet-engined aircraft. There is a small airstrip at Codrington on Barbuda. Antigua and Barbuda Airlines, a nominal company, controls international routes, but services to Europe and North America are operated by American Airlines (USA), Continental Airlines (USA), Lufthansa (Germany) and Air Canada. Antigua and Barbuda is a shareholder in, and the headquarters of, the regional airline, LIAT. Other regional services are operated by BWIA (Trinidad and Tobago) and Air BVI (British Virgin Islands).

LIAT (1974) Ltd: POB 819, V.C. Bird Int. Airport, St John's; tel. 480-5600; fax 480-5625; e-mail li.sales.mrkting@candw.ag; internet www.liatairline.com; f. 1956 as Leeward Islands Air Transport Services, jointly-owned by 11 regional Govts; privatized in 1995; shares are held by the Govts of Antigua and Barbuda, Montserrat, Grenada, Barbados, Trinidad and Tobago, Jamaica, Guyana, Dominica, Saint Lucia, Saint Vincent and the Grenadines and Saint Christopher and Nevis (30.8%), BWIA (29.2%), LIAT employees (13.3%) and private investors (26.7%); scheduled passenger and cargo services to 19 destinations in the Caribbean; charter flights are also undertaken; Chair. AZIZ HADEED; Exec. Dir DAVID JARDINE.

Carib Aviation Ltd: V.C. Bird Int. Airport; tel. 462-3147; fax 462-3125; e-mail caribav@candw.ag; charter co; operates regional services.

Tourism

Tourism is the country's main industry. Antigua offers a reputed 365 beaches, an annual international sailing regatta and Carnival week, and the historic Nelson's Dockyard in English Harbour (a national park since 1985). Barbuda is less developed but is noted for its beauty, wildlife and beaches of pink sand. In 1986 the

Government established the St John's Development Corporation to oversee the redevelopment of the capital as a commercial duty-free centre, with extra cruise-ship facilities. In 1999 there were 588,866 tourist arrivals, including 328,038 cruise-ship passengers. In 1998 some 31% of stop-over visitors came from the USA, 27% from the United Kingdom, 19% from other Caribbean countries and 7% from Canada. There were an estimated 3,225 hotel rooms in 1996.

Antigua and Barbuda Department of Tourism: Nevis St and Friendly Alley, POB 363, St John's; tel. 462-0029; fax 462-2483; e-mail info@antigua-barbuda.org; internet www.antigua-barbuda.org; Dir-Gen. SHIRLENE NIBBS; Asst Man. IRMA TOMLINSON.

Antigua Hotels and Tourist Association (AHTA): Island House, Newgate St, POB 454, St John's; tel. 462-3703; fax 462-3702; e-mail ahta@candw.ag; internet www.antiguahotels.org; Chair. ROBERT S. SHERMAN; Exec. Dir CYNTHIA G. SIMON.

Defence

There is a small defence force of 150 men (army 125, navy 25). The US Government leases two military bases on Antigua. Antigua and Barbuda participates in the US-sponsored Regional Security System. The defence budget in 2000 was estimated at EC $12.0m.

Education

Education is compulsory for 11 years between five and 16 years of age. Primary education begins at the age of five and normally lasts for seven years. Secondary education, beginning at 12 years of age, lasts for five years, comprising a first cycle of three years and a second cycle of two years. In 1987/88 there were 43 primary and 15 secondary schools; the majority of schools are administered by the Government. In 1991/92 some 9,298 primary school pupils and 5,845 secondary school pupils were enrolled. Teacher-training and technical training are available at the Antigua State College in St John's. An extra-mural department of the University of the West Indies offers several foundation courses leading to higher study at branches elsewhere. The adult literacy rate in Antigua and Barbuda is more than 90%, one of the highest rates in the Eastern Caribbean. Current government expenditure on education in 1993/94 was projected at EC $37.1m., equivalent to 12.8% of total budgetary expenditure.

ARGENTINA

Area: 2,780,400 sq km (1,073,518 sq miles).

Population (official estimate, mid-2000): 37,031,802.

Capital: Buenos Aires, provisional population 2,960,976 at 1991 census (metropolitan area 10,686,163).

Language: Spanish (official).

Religion: mainly Christianity (90% Roman Catholic, 2% Protestant).

Climate: ranges from subtropical in the north to subantarctic in the south; generally moderate summer rainfall.

Time: GMT –3 hours.

Public Holidays

2002: 1 January (New Year's Day), 29 April (Good Friday), 1 May (Labour Day), 25 May (Anniversary of the 1810 Revolution), 10 June (Occupation of the Islas Malvinas), 17 June (for Flag Day), 9 July (Independence Day), 19 August (for Death of Gen. José de San Martín), 14 October (for Columbus Day), 25 December (Christmas Day).

2003: 1 January (New Year's Day), 18 April (Good Friday), 1 May (Labour Day), 25 May (Anniversary of the 1810 Revolution), 9 June (for Occupation of the Islas Malvinas), 23 June (for Flag Day), 9 July (Independence Day), 18 August (for Death of Gen. José de San Martín), 13 October (for Columbus Day), 25 December (Christmas).

Currency: New peso argentino; 100 pesos = £69.88 = US $100.05 = €112.72 (30 April 2001).

Weights and Measures: The metric system is in force.

Basic Economic Indicators

	1998	1999	2000
Gross domestic product (million pesos at 1993 prices)	288,123	278,320	276,948
GDP per head ('000 pesos at 1993 prices)	7,976	7,609	7,479
GDP (million pesos at current prices)	298,948	283,260	285,045
GDP per head ('000 pesos at current prices)	8,275.4	7,743.9	7,697.3
Annual growth of real GDP (%)	3.9	–3.4	0.5
Annual growth of real GDP per head (%)	2.5	–4.6	–1.7
Government budget (million pesos at current prices):			
Revenue	42,921.1	49,257.5	n.a.
Expenditure (incl. lending minus repayments)	47,069.4	49,214.2	n.a.
Consumer price index (base: 1995 = 100)	101.6	100.4	99.5
Rate of inflation (annual average, %)	0.9	–1.2	–0.9
Foreign exchange reserves (US $ million at 31 December)	24,488	26,114	24,414
Imports c.i.f. (US $ million)	31,404	25,508	25,149
Exports f.o.b. (US $ million)	26,441	23,333	26,298
Balance of payments (current account, US $ million)	–14,704	–12,446	–9,358

Gross national product per head measured at purchasing power parity (PPP) (GNP converted to US dollars by the PPP exchange rate, 1999): 11,940.

Total labour force (estimate at mid-1999): 14,692,000.

Unemployment (May 2000): 15.4%.

Total external debt (1999): US $154,362m.

Infant mortality rate (per 1,000 live births, 1998): 19.1.

Life expectancy (years at birth, 1999): 73 (males 69, females 77).

Adult population with HIV/AIDS (15–49 years, 1999): 0.69%.

School enrolment ratio (6–17 years, 1996): 98%.

Adult literacy rate (15 years and over, 2000): 96.9% (males 96.9; females 96.8).

Energy consumption per head (kg of oil equivalent, 1998): 1,726.

Carbon dioxide emissions per head (metric tons, 1997): 3.9.

Passenger motor cars in use (per 1,000 of population, 1998): 139.7.

Television receivers in use (per 1,000 of population, 1997): 223.

Personal computers in use (per 1,000 of population, 1999): 49.2.

History

Prof. PETER CALVERT

In colonial times Argentina lay on the furthest edges of the Spanish Empire. The first Spanish settlers in what is now Argentina came from Peru. Buenos Aires, though founded in 1580 and a fine natural port, stagnated while all trade had to be channelled through Lima and, until 1776 (when the Viceroyalty of the River Plate—Río de la Plata was established), the region remained backward and neglected. Direct trade between Buenos Aires and Spain, in hides and in silver from what is now Bolivia, stimulated the growth of the town. After 1776 it began to grow rapidly. In 1807 the bold attempt of Sir Home Popham to seize the city for the British Empire taught its inhabitants that they could defend themselves—the names of the battles, Reconquista and Defensa, are still commemorated throughout the country. With Spain itself in the hands of the French Emperor Napoleon Bonaparte's forces, the city freed itself from Spanish rule in 1810 and its Cabildo (town council) governed on behalf of the Spanish king, Ferdinand VII, even though he was, at the time, a captive of Napoleon. It was only in 1816, when the Spanish moved to recapture Buenos Aires, that the independence of the United Provinces of South America was declared at Tucumán.

Buenos Aires in 1810 was already bigger by far than the other main towns scattered along the River Plate and in the west and north-west, in the lee of the Andes. The colony was underpopulated for its size, although the vast and largely treeless plains, the hinterland of Buenos Aires known as the Pampas (*pampa*), still contained a substantial Indian (Amerindian) population. In the vast, flat, rural plain of the Province (as opposed to the City) of Buenos Aires, roamed the Argentine cowboy, the *gaucho*, whose distinctive culture blended Spanish and Indian elements.

Much of Argentine history in the 19th century focused on the problem of constitutional organization, owing to the rivalry between Buenos Aires and the other Provinces. The former favoured a centralized structure, with Buenos Aires dominant, while the latter wanted a federal structure with provincial autonomy. Buenos Aires derived its revenues from the port, while the prices of provincial manufactures, such as textiles, were undercut by cheaper foreign imports. Buenos Aires did not share its wealth with the other Provinces and, moreover, grew more European in its outlook and amenities, while the Provinces remained backward, dominated by autocratic, often savage, rulers (caudillos). The struggle between federalists and centralists was halted after 1835 by the dictatorship of Juan Manuel de Rosas, caudillo of Buenos Aires. He ignored the national problem, giving the provincial rulers complete freedom of action in return for their recognition of him as national leader. Paradoxically, this helped create the national unity he opposed. In 1852 he was deposed by a coalition of his political opponents and died in exile in Southampton (United Kingdom) in 1877.

In 1853 a federal Constitution was created for the new Argentine Republic. Buenos Aires seceded from the federation, but in 1859 was defeated in a military confrontation with the other Provinces. Then in 1861 it joined the union in order to dominate it, and, with its economic strength, finally triumphed in 1880, when the city of Buenos Aires replaced Rosario as the national capital. A new capital for the old Province of Buenos Aires was built at La Plata. The provincial caudillos made the transition to being more conventional politicians, though it was the great landowners, the estancieros, who dominated national life.

The next four decades were years of economic transformation as the combined impact of British investment, European immigration, the expansion of the railways and exploitation of corn and grain of the Pampas made Argentina by far the most advanced of the Latin American states. These developments initially benefited the landowners (cattle barons and commercial agriculturists) who dominated politics, but new classes of professionals (bankers, brokers and lawyers) and an urban working class emerged with the rapid growth of cities and began to challenge the hold of the ruling classes.

The first challenge came in the 1890s with the foundation of the Radical and Socialist parties, but fraudulent elections kept the oligarchy of landowners, merchants and bankers in power. In 1912, however, President Roque Sáenz Peña, though a conservative, insisted on the adoption of a law introducing secret ballots, to reduce electoral corruption. As a result, in 1916 Hipólito Yrigoyen, nephew of the founder of the Radical party, the Unión Cívica Radical (UCR—Radical Civic Union), became Argentina's first popularly elected President and began a six-year term of office. The economy was still growing strongly and manufacturing industry developed under Yrigoyen's Radical successor, Marcelo T. de Alvear. The Radicals now dominated government and in 1928 Yrigoyen was elected to a second term, causing a split in the party. Before the effects of the 1929 depression were felt, Yrigoyen's reclusiveness made it possible for a small band of armed cadets to seize power in 1930, led by a retired general, José E. Uriburu.

From 1932 to 1943, a period known as the 'Infamous Decade', the oligarchy resumed power in the form of a loose coalition (the Concordancia) of Conservatives and anti-personalist Radicals, supported by the Armed Forces. It was their friends and supporters who benefited from the economic recovery. The Second World War divided Argentine society further. Some leaders were strongly pro-Allied, but others, not least in the Armed Forces, pro-Axis.

THE PERONATO

The turning point in modern Argentine history came in 1943, when it seemed that the civilian politicians would install a pro-Allied president, and the army intervened again. Col Juan Domingo Perón, secretary of the army lodge that planned and executed the coup, became Minister of War and Secretary for Labour and Social Welfare in the military Government. He promoted labour reforms and encouraged unionization, becoming immensely popular with the masses, though not with the oligarchy. In 1946, in a free election, he won the presidency decisively. In 1949 he amended the Constitution to permit his immediate re-election and held power until 1955.

The regime had many of the marks of a dictatorship—control of the media, suppression of dissent, interference in universities. However, it rested on an alliance with trade unions and the popular support of the urban underprivileged, the *descamisados* (shirtless ones). Large welfare programmes brought real benefits to the poor and were dramatized by Perón's charismatic wife, Eva Duarte de Perón ('Evita'), who came to be regarded virtually as a saint.

A staunch nationalist, Perón bought out the British-owned railways and other public utilities, greatly accelerated industrialization under strong government control, and increased the role of the state in the economy. In his foreign policy he sought a 'Third Position', later to be termed non-alignment, and the leadership of South America. However, he neglected the agricultural sector, formerly the basis of Argentina's export trade. Rural migration increased and serious economic imbalances developed. As inflation rose and agricultural output fell, the economy's growth slowed down. Eva Perón died in July 1952, depriving her husband of his strongest ally with the masses. However, though the military had been alienated by her prominence, and some officers were already tired of Perón himself, support for the regime remained strong.

During his second term, from 1951, after surviving an attempted military coup, Perón tempered his policies. He resisted workers' wage demands, supported the farmers and, from 1954, encouraged foreign capital in the petroleum industry. Such changes alienated many former supporters. Discontent grew with both the repressive nature of the regime and with the large and over-zealous bureaucracy. Attacks by his supporters on the Roman Catholic Church compounded Perón's problems. Finally, in September 1955, the Armed Forces intervened and Perón went into exile in Spain. However, his legacy and his political movement survived, to form the fundamental divide in Argentine politics for the next three decades. The critical factor was the antagonism between the Armed Forces and the Peronists, the former trying for 18 years to exclude both Perón and his supporters from national politics.

THE MILITARY INTERVENE, 1955–83

Between 1955 and 1983 Argentina's political history was very turbulent. The leader of the coup of 1955, Gen. Lonardi, who was prepared to work with the Peronists, was soon deposed by the more uncompromising Gen. Pedro Aramburu. For three years (1955–58) he attempted to suppress all vestiges of Peronism. Elections from which the Peronists were barred returned a left-wing Radical, Arturo Frondizi (1958–62), under whom economic development accelerated and inflation became an endemic problem. When Frondizi proposed to allow the Peronists (though not Perón himself) to stand for election, he was deposed by the army. New elections were held in 1963 and Dr Arturo Illia, another Radical, was elected. However, in 1966 the military ousted him also, claiming that he had been ineffective. The new military Government headed by Juan Carlos Onganía (1966–70) made it clear that it intended to stay in power as long as was 'necessary' to revive the economy. Supported by authoritarian controls, his Minister of Economy and Labour, Adalberto Krieger Vasena, produced a viable, but austere, recovery plan. However, Vasena was forced to resign in May 1969 in the wake of a mass demonstration in the city of Córdoba (the 'Cordobazo'). Further strikes and protests followed.

Meanwhile, under the influence of the Cuban Revolution and its aftermath, younger Peronists had adopted revolutionary tactics. Two main urban guerrilla movements emerged, a pro-Cuban organization called the Revolutionary Army of the People (Ejército Revolucionario del Pueblo—ERP) and a Peronist group known as the Montoneros. The Montoneros kidnapped and murdered former President Aramburu, thereby undermining Onganía, whose colleagues deposed him in June 1970. An unknown general, Roberto Levingston, was appointed to head the Government, but was replaced in March 1971 by Gen. Alejandro Lanusse, the organizer of the 1970 coup, who took over the presidency himself.

The Peróns, 1973–76

Lanusse inherited an impossible situation. With guerrilla violence growing and with the economy suffering from such frequent political changes that long-term, consistent policies could not be implemented, he took the ultimate gamble of holding fresh elections in March 1973 and allowing the Peronists to take part for the first time in 20 years. Perón's candidacy was disallowed (he had now been in exile for 18 years) but his proxy, Héctor Cámpora, was allowed to stand, and was duly elected. However, Cámpora's presidency was short; having offered freedom to captured guerrillas, he resigned in order to force Perón's return. The military, internally divided, yielded to the demand for new elections. Perón's return to the country in June 1973 was marred by a gun-battle at Ezeiza Airport in which many died. In September, nevertheless, he was returned to the presidency, with his third wife, María Estela ('Isabelita') Martínez de Perón, as Vice-President. Inevitably, the conflicting hopes of his supporters were disappointed. Perón, now a sick man of 78, was unable to meet the many conflicting demands made on him during his short third term as President, though much was said and planned along the social democratic lines which he had seen working well in Europe. He tried to distance himself from the leftist fringe that had infiltrated the movement during the last years of military proscription, only to find that political violence originating from both the left- and right-wing increased.

At his death on 1 July 1974, his widow Isabelita assumed the presidency in a situation of increasing chaos, becoming, by an irony of history, Latin America's (and indeed the world's) first woman executive president. The Peronist movement was now not only divided, its extreme wings were, in fact, at war, and rightist 'death-squads' appeared, controlled by Isabelita Perón's chief confidant and Minister of Social Welfare, José López Rega.

The country slid towards anarchy; inflation rose to 364% in 1976, violence spread and the Government did little to stop it. In March 1976 the Armed Forces again seized power.

The Military Junta, 1976–83

The governing junta of service chiefs chose the commander of the Army, Gen. Jorge Videla, as the new President. Under their leadership there began what the Government termed euphemistically the 'Process of National Reorganization'. The period has since become better known abroad as the 'dirty war', *la guerra sucia*.

The Process was a concerted attempt to eradicate terrorism by the use of terror. Tens of thousands of 'suspects' were arrested and, it was alleged, tortured and murdered. There were reports that people were arrested simply to fulfil the quotas imposed on government agencies. The most conservative estimates put the number of people killed, or who 'disappeared', at between 10,000 and 15,000. Such a wholesale purge inevitably included some genuine terrorists and by 1978 the capacity for disruption by the Montoneros and the ERP had been drastically reduced by the death, exile or imprisonment of their known leaders.

Meanwhile, massive borrowing and the over-valuation of the currency led to a rapid growth in consumer spending, giving the middle classes a false sense of prosperity. Videla, who had retired from the Army and junta in August 1978, was succeeded as President, in a quasi-constitutional fashion, by Gen. Roberto Viola in March 1981, just at the start of economic recession. Ill-health and the opposition of military conservatives to his relatively conciliatory policies forced Viola out of office in November. A right-wing nationalist, Gen. Leopoldo Fortunato Galtieri, took over in December as President and head of the junta.

At the beginning of 1982 there was a series of labour demonstrations and strikes, culminating, on 30 March, in a violent confrontation between demonstrators and government forces in Buenos Aires. From the moment of his seizure of power, however, Galtieri had prepared a plan which, he believed, would guarantee his position. On 2 April Argentine forces seized the British-ruled Falkland Islands (Islas Malvinas) in the South Atlantic, title to which had been disputed by Argentina since British occupation in 1833. The tiny British garrison was rapidly overwhelmed by 10,000 Argentine soldiers and repossession of sovereignty was declared. Initially, the seizure was a resounding success for the Government—even the Peronists supported it. However, the final defeat of the Argentine forces by British troops on 14 June was a catastrophe and a national humiliation. The military Government of Galtieri, inept politically and economically, had failed in its own professional field. Galtieri was abruptly replaced, and a retired general, Reynaldo Bignone, selected to head an interim government under cover of which the military could retreat from power.

THE RETURN TO DEMOCRACY

Bignone, having established a dialogue with the political parties, called elections for 30 October 1983, in an atmosphere of deep economic crisis and national confusion, fuelled by growing civilian demands for the investigation of human-rights abuses committed by the services. The UCR (Radicals) and the Partido Justicialista (Peronists), the two main parties, chose, as their respective presidential candidates, Raúl Alfonsín and Italo Luder. The former, a 57-year-old lawyer, who had courageously opposed the war and had had a record of defence of human rights, obtained a massive victory over Luder, who lacked charisma and whose party was deeply divided.

The Presidency of Raúl Alfonsín, 1983–1989

Inaugurated as President in December 1983, Alfonsín faced massive problems. Of a foreign debt of US $40,000m. left by the military government, one-quarter at least had been wasted and another quarter was never traced. Meanwhile, 'hyperinflation' and economic stagnation combined to disappoint the hopes that Alfonsín's victory had aroused. The trade unions, still largely in Peronist hands, reacted to the new Government's imposition of austerity measures by staging a one-day general strike in May 1985, while the military carefully watched the progress of trials of former leaders of the Armed Forces. During the first year of Alfonsín's presidency, after protracted negotiations, he managed to renegotiate the foreign debt, maintain political stability, and reach some accord with the Peronists. Equally significantly, he finalized with Chile a long-standing dispute over possession of three islets in the Beagle Channel, the settlement of which had almost brought the two countries to war in 1978.

Two issues dominated Alfonsín's government: relations with the military and the resuscitation of the economy. In theory committed to eradicating the military from Argentine politics and to establishing a working democratic system, Alfonsín soon had to temper his policies with reality. The Falklands-Malvinas débâcle provided the opportunity to restructure the military High Command; Alfonsín removed anti-democratic senior officers and replaced them with more co-operative ones. The defence budget was drastically reduced, for economic as well as for political reasons, and in the 1986 defence budget a start was made on reducing the traditional significance of the Armed Forces in the nation's economic life.

The 'Dirty War' and Relations with the Military

Complicating the issue was the popular demand for the trial of service personnel for gross abuses of human rights during the 'dirty war'. Ostensibly an asset to Alfonsín, public pressure on this issue was, in fact, a two-edged weapon. National revulsion at evidence of military atrocities came up against the claims of the military that 'the dirty war' was a 'just war', and that a general amnesty should be enacted. Alfonsín attempted to resolve this conflict in December 1986, when Congress approved a law, known popularly as the 'Punto Final' (Full Stop) Law, which established a 60-day deadline for new indictments. The Government had expected that only some 70 such cases might be presented. However, by March 1987, owing to the zeal of the civil courts, over 250 indictments had been accepted, and, for the first time, serving officers, as well as retired ones, were accused.

In April 1987 military rebellions broke out in Córdoba and later at the Campo de Mayo itself. Although there were popular demonstrations in support of democracy, concessions were made to the military, despite the ensuing controversy. A new army Chief of Staff was appointed and Alfonsín submitted to Congress legislative proposals, which came to be known as the 'Obediencia Debida' (Due Obedience) Law, whereby most military officers accused of human-rights violations were to be absolved of their crimes on the grounds that they had simply obeyed orders. Out of some 370 members of the Armed Forces due to be tried for human-rights offences, only between 30 and 50 were now left to face charges. Even this number was too many for some sectors of the military and there were further insurrections in January and December 1988. These were outwardly firmly suppressed by the Government, although again there were accusations that Alfonsín subsequently made concessions to the military which resembled some of the rebels' demands. A doomed attempt to resuscitate the guerrilla conflict, led by Enrique Gorriarán Merlo, which led to the deaths of 39 left-wing guerrillas in an attack in January 1989 on a military base at La Tablada, 25 km west of Buenos Aires, brought public congratulations by Alfonsín for the army's swift suppression of the uprising.

Economic Crisis

The second major imponderable for Alfonsín was the Argentine economy. After pursuing gradualist policies to reactivate the economy in 1984 and the first half of 1985, the Government turned instead to the fashionable doctrine of the 'heterodox shock' in June 1985. This involved the introduction of austerity measures, under the 'Austral Plan', named after the new currency which was to end inflation, then running at an estimated annual rate of 1,129%. The Government's action led to labour unrest, with the Peronist-dominated trade unions holding a series of one-day strikes. Hence, despite its initial promise, the Plan was effectively abandoned while the mid-term elections took place.

With the elections out of the way and inflation again soaring, in February 1987 a new economic programme, the second Austral Plan (the 'Australito') was implemented. Again the Government's attempts at achieving economic stabilization were unsuccessful; the deficit on the public-sector account worsened and inflation continued to spiral upwards. In early 1989 the World Bank, which until that time had, like most other multilateral lending agencies, supported Alfonsín, suspended all its

financing in Argentina. Negotiations with international creditors were deferred indefinitely. Despite the efforts of two new finance ministers in as many months, no credible economic strategy emerged and control over inflation was abandoned while the elections of May 1989 were held.

President Menem's First Term, 1989–1995

Victory went to the Peronist candidate, Carlos Saúl Menem, the flamboyant former Governor of the inland Province of La Rioja. In his campaign Menem captured the popular vote and a Peronist majority in the Senate with the promise of a 'production revolution' based on wage increases and significant aid to industry. Yet long before he was scheduled to take office, the seriousness of the economic crisis led Alfonsín to try to reach an agreement with the Peronists on economic strategy. This Menem wisely declined, and all attempts at accommodation between the in-coming and out-going Governments resulted in failure. Instead, food riots, looting and bombings in several Argentine cities forced Alfonsín to impose a state of siege and to hand over presidential power to Menem five months early, on 8 July, in order to avoid a total breakdown of public authority.

When Menem succeeded Alfonsín it was the first time since 1928 that an elected President had handed over to his successor without military pressure. Democracy, even in the midst of the greatest economic crisis of the century, was immensely popular. It was immediately clear, moreover, that Menem's economic strategy, to turn Argentina into what he called a 'popular market-capitalist country', was much closer to that of the Radicals than the campaign had suggested. The intention was not to revolutionize the system but to bring together a corporate capitalist coalition, containing businessmen, foreign creditors, the unions, the Armed Forces and the Church. This policy marked an immediate departure from the interventionist approach associated with early Peronism, though it was closer to the many pragmatist elements in Perón's thought and policies. President Menem first entrusted the conduct of his anti-inflationary policies to economists of Argentina's only native multinational company, Bunge and Born. The attempt failed and the association with Bunge and Born ended in December 1989, after only five months. Meanwhile, a widespread lack of confidence was reflected in the collapse of the currency and a second hyperinflationary wave.

Menem's relaxed use of presidential authority, divisions in the Cabinet and reluctant support for policies so different to traditional Peronism increased the difficulty in reducing state expenditure and in selling state-owned enterprises. With regard to the military, President Menem, who had spent the entire period of the military regime under house arrest, from the outset advocated conciliation, despite strong resistance from among his own supporters. After weeks of rumour a series of pardons affecting 277 individuals, some of them guerrillas, and including members of the military junta responsible for the Falklands débâcle, was issued in October 1989. In other ways President Menem was firmer; the leaders of the rebellions against Alfonsín were dismissed by Menem's Chief of Staff, Gen. Isidro Cáceres, and when some supporters of Col Mohammed Ali Seneildín, leader of the December 1988 revolt, rebelled on 3 December and seized the military headquarters, with the loss of at least three lives, any question of negotiation was speedily rejected, the headquarters stormed and the leaders charged with insurrection. They were sentenced to indefinite imprisonment and discharged from the service. The price was President Menem's irreversible decision to issue, on 29 December, his long-heralded pardon of Gen. Jorge Videla and others convicted for human-rights crimes during the 'dirty war'. At the same time the relative strength of the Armed Forces continued to decline. In February 1990 the President took the personal decision to resume diplomatic relations with the United Kingdom, while postponing discussion of the sovereignty of the disputed islands.

Transforming the Economy

Meanwhile, in January 1991 Domingo Cavallo was appointed economy minister and proceeded to implement a far-reaching programme of economic stabilization. This had three main aims. The first was the so-called 'dollarization' of the economy, whereby the Argentine economy was linked to the US economy by the establishment of a new currency, the peso, worth 10,000 australes, at parity with the US $. The second was an ambitious programme of privatization, reversing 40 years of Peronist policy. The third aim was to improve government finances by raising revenue and eliminating tax evasion, by means such as the 'fiscal pact' with an agricultural development association, the Argentina Rural Society (Sociedad Rural Argentina—SRA). By the time of President Menem's state visit to the USA in November, he was celebrated as Latin America's leading free market reformer and US ally. As a result, in March 1992 the President secured a promise of debt reduction under the Brady Initiative (a plan for debt relief originally proposed by Nicholas Brady, the US Secretary of the Treasury, in 1989).

At the same time, support for the ruling Peronist party strengthened. In the provincial elections the Peronists won 15 of the 21 governorships at stake, including that of the Province of Buenos Aires, where Vice-President Eduardo Duhalde gained 47% of the votes cast. Although their opponents were in disarray, the Peronists were not free of problems, of which the two main ones were the persistent accusations of corruption levelled against them and their inability to agree on a successor to President Menem. Thus, in February 1993 a campaign was begun among the executive of the Partido Justicialista for an amendment to the Constitution to permit Menem, like Perón before him, to be re-elected for a consecutive term. The project was supported by declarations from 14 provincial governors and, conditionally, by the Peronist wing of the General Confederation of Labour (Confederación General del Trabajo—CGT).

The Peronists consolidated their control of the Chamber of Deputies in partial legislative elections of 3 October 1993. In the same month they also gained Senate approval for the reform proposal and announced their intention to conduct a national referendum on constitutional reform. In December President Menem declared his intention to seek re-election in 1995.

Elections to a 305-seat constituent assembly, which was to draft and approve the proposed constitution, took place on 10 April 1994. The Peronists failed to gain the majority that would guarantee the passing of the constitutional amendments. On 22 August the assembly approved the new Constitution which allowed for the possibility of presidential re-election for a second term. It came into force on the following day. Other constitutional amendments included the reduction of the presidential mandate from six years to four; delegation of some presidential powers to a Chief of Cabinet; a run-off election for presidential and vice-presidential candidates when neither obtained 45% of the votes cast, or 40% when the nearest candidate gained less than 30% of the ballot; the establishment of an autonomous government in the city of Buenos Aires with a directly elected mayor; the extension of congressional sessions to nine months; an increase in the number of senators from each province from two to three; the creation of a Council of Magistrates and other judicial reforms.

Presidential elections were scheduled for 14 May 1995. In January Menem named Carlos Ruckauf, the Minister of the Interior, as his candidate for the new post of Vice-President. The UCR presidential candidate was Horacio Massaccesi, Governor of Río Negro. Menem also faced a strong challenge from José Octavio Bordón, of the Frente por un País en Solidaridad (Frepaso—the name chosen in December 1994 for the Frente Grande), which gained fresh support from dissident Peronists and some Radicals. In the event, however, the election was overshadowed by the impact on the economy of the Mexican economic crisis (the 'tequila effect'), caused by the dramatic fall in the value of the Mexican peso in December 1994. In March 1995 the Government undertook an economic consolidation programme, with the aid of US $7,000m. in international and domestic credits. Public spending was drastically reduced and the unemployment rate increased from 12.5% to 18.6% of the economically active population in April–July. An employment initiative costing $1,500m. was announced by President Menem in August, but there was still widespread social unrest in major cities throughout the year.

In spite of the worsening economic situation and the Government's continuing austerity programme, however, in May 1995 President Menem became only the third Argentine president to win re-election, gaining 49.9% of the votes cast in the first round of voting and thereby avoiding a second ballot.

Bordón came second, while Massaccesi obtained only 17.1%, the worst result for the UCR since 1916. At concurrent provincial and legislative elections the ruling Peronists won nine of the 14 gubernatorial elections and increased their representation in the enlarged 257-seat Chamber of Deputies to an overall majority. Frepaso, however, won the largest share of the 130 legislative seats contested, largely at the expense of the UCR, with almost 35% of the votes cast.

President Menem's Second Term, 1995–99

The second term, almost inevitably, was an anticlimax. Following his victory, President Menem announced the composition of a largely unaltered Cabinet, led by Eduardo Bauzá, in the new post of Cabinet Chief. However, tensions within the new Government soon became evident. President Menem showed increasing irritation at the power of Domingo Cavallo, who had been reappointed to the economy ministry, and who complained publicly of resistance to reform among entrenched interests in government. In March 1996 Bauzá resigned as Cabinet Chief on health grounds and was replaced by Jorge Rodríguez, hitherto Minister of Education and Culture. At the same time, President Menem established an Economic and Social Council, consisting of trade-union and business leaders, which was to assist in determining economic policy. The move was opposed by Cavallo, who accused the President of attempting to employ interventionist policies. On 26 July, soon after Menem had accepted the resignation of both the justice and defence ministers, Rodolfo Barra and Oscar Camilión, respectively, Cavallo was dismissed from the Cabinet. He was replaced as economy minister by Roque Fernández, hitherto President of the Central Bank. Fernández, an ally of Cavallo, continued his predecessor's policies and the financial position of the country was unaffected.

Nevertheless, the effects on the political situation were marked. In March 1997 Cavallo formed his own party, Acción por la República (AR—Action for the Republic), and in July he and Gustavo Béliz, the former Minister of the Interior and leader of the political grouping Nueva Dirigencia (ND—New Democracy), announced their electoral alliance. They immediately launched a mordant attack on alleged governmental corruption. Meanwhile, throughout 1997 the Government's popularity was further undermined by widespread and sometimes violent social and industrial unrest, caused by discontent with the Government's economic austerity measures and reports of corruption, and in the mid-term elections of October 1997 the PJ lost their overall majority in the Chamber of Deputies. The popularity of the Peronists remained low in 1998 as unemployment persisted and President Menem and Governor Duhalde battled publicly for control of their party. The President launched an unsuccessful campaign to amend the Constitution again, in order that he might stand for a third term, but, as expected, Governor Duhalde won the Peronist nomination.

At the same time, hopes intensified of holding senior military officers to account for their role in the 'dirty war'. In 1997 Judge Alfredo Bagnasco began an investigation into the alleged systematic theft of as many as 300 infants from jailed political opponents of the junta. Most of these children had then been adopted by military couples and details of their true parentage remained obscure. Though many 'dirty war' criminals had been convicted and jailed for other crimes in 1985, and subsequently pardoned by President Menem, Judge Bagnasco argued that the pardons did not cover crimes against children, that these crimes were ongoing in effect and that, therefore, the investigation was legitimate and relevant. Former junta Presidents, Gens Videla and Bignone, were arrested in June 1998 and January 1999, respectively, and others summoned to give evidence included Gen. Galtieri and the former head of the navy, Adm. Emilio Massera. Vice Adm. Rubén Oscar Franco and Gen. Guillermo Suárez Mason were arrested in 1999, after former naval captain Jorge Acosta had surrendered voluntarily.

On 30 December 1999 the Spanish magistrate Baltasar Garzón issued international arrest warrants for 49 people alleged to be complicit in genocide, terrorism and torture, including former military presidents Videla and Galtieri, effectively confining them to Argentine territory. Although, in January 2000, a federal judge refused their extradition, arrests of Franco and Suárez Mason, as well as the discovery in Lomas de Zamora of some bodies of the 'disappeared', proved that the issue was still very much an important one in Argentina.

The Presidency of Fernando de la Rúa, 1999–

Elections to the presidency were held on 24 October 1999. Fernando de la Rúa of the UCR, the conservative, 62-year-old Mayor of the Federal District of Buenos Aires, was the candidate of the unified opposition ATJE. His two main opponents were Eduardo Duhalde, whose nomination by the Partido Justicial-ista was endorsed by Menem, and Domingo Cavallo of the AR. De la Rúa won a decisive victory, gaining 48.5% of the votes cast, compared to Duhalde, who secured 38.1% of the ballot, and Cavallo, who came third with 10.1% of the votes. Carlos Ruckauf, the out-going Vice-President, was elected to succeed Duhalde as Governor of the Province of Buenos Aires, the nation's second most powerful political position in concurrently held gubernatorial elections. The ATJE were also successful in partial elections to the Chamber of Deputies, also held on the same day, winning 63 of the 130 seats to be renewed, and thereby increasing the party's total number to 127, just two short of an absolute majority. In contrast, the Peronists won 50 seats, reducing their legislative representation to 101. Cavallo's AR secured nine seats.

The new President was sworn in on 10 December 1999, and immediately faced a serious economic crisis. He appointed Rodolfo Terragno as his head of Cabinet and José Luis Machinea as Minister of the Economy. Later that month the new Congress approved an austerity budget which reduced public expenditure by US $1,400m., as well as a major tax-reform programme and a federal revenue-sharing scheme. In April 2000 the Senate approved a major revision of employment law. The legislation met with public criticism and led to mass demonstrations by public-sector workers and, subsequently, to two 24-hour national strikes organized by the CGT. In May the ruling ATJE confirmed its position when its candidate, Aníbal Ibarra, was elected Mayor of the Federal District of Buenos Aires. However, later that year the Government came under intense pressure after it was alleged that some senators had received bribes from government officials to approve the controversial employment law. In September Congress voted to end the immunity that protected law-makers, judges and government ministers from prosecution, and thus allow an investigation into the corruption allegations. However, in October the Government was further weakened after the resignation of the Vice-President and leader of Frepaso, Carlos 'Chacho' Alvarez. A cabinet reshuffle, in which Terragno was replaced by Chrystian Colombo as cabinet chief, precipitated the resignation, as Alvarez was angered by the President's refusal to replace ministers implicated in corruption allegations.

In September 2000 the Government proposed to reduce the fiscal deficit in 2001 from US $5,300m. to $4,100m., by cutting government expenditure by $700m. The Alliance in Congress then declared an economic emergency and passed an anti-evasion law and a law to reduce corporate taxes. On 14 November, in a televised address, the President announced that the country faced 'a veritable catastrophe'. The IMF did agree to emergency aid, amounting to more than $7,000m., and an agreement to this effect was signed in January 2001; however, there were severe conditions attached. These included abolition of the existing state pension scheme and the freezing of federal transfers to the provinces. In March 2001 President de la Rúa was forced to reappoint Domingo Cavallo (who, in May 2000, had unsuccessfully run for the mayoralty of the capital), as Minister of the Economy, following the resignation of two economy ministers in the same month. In late March the Senate approved a request by the President for special executive powers to implement reforms, such as deregulation of the financial markets and the restructuring of government agencies, in order to improve the economic situation.

In March 2001 a federal judge, Gabriel Cavallo, in a landmark ruling, revoked two amnesty laws (Full Stop and Due Obedience acts) on the grounds that they were incompatible with the American Convention on Human Rights. Human-rights campaigners were hopeful that the ruling could be applied to other investigations of abuses during the 'dirty war'. In early June former President Carlos Menem was arrested for illegal arms

trafficking during his terms in office. Although he strongly denied the allegations, in July he was formally charged with selling arms to Croatia and Ecuador, in violation of international embargoes in the early 1990s.

Foreign Policy

In the 1990s Argentina emerged as a close ally of the USA and an active participant in multi-national peace-keeping operations, signalling the country's intention to adopt a more prominent role in international affairs, despite economic constraints which forced reductions in the military budget and the strength of the Armed Forces. During an official visit in 1997 US President Bill Clinton commended Argentina's participation in more than 12 UN missions of the preceding decade, including those in Bosnia and Herzegovina, Cyprus and Haiti, and announced that he would seek non-NATO (North Atlantic Treaty Organization) ally status for the country. This would allow Argentina access to certain military funding and to a wider range of surplus US and NATO weaponry. The announcement drew protests from neighbours, particularly Brazil and Chile, who claimed that it could lead to a regional imbalance.

Although Argentina restored full diplomatic relations with the United Kingdom in February 1990, and agreements were subsequently concluded on the protection of fish stocks and the reduction of military restrictions in the South Atlantic region, the question of the Falkland Islands' disputed sovereignty was not resolved. The new Constitution of August 1994 reiterated Argentina's claim to sovereignty over the Islands and, following his re-election in May 1995, President Menem reaffirmed his goal of recovering the Malvinas by 2000 by peaceful negotiation. Nevertheless, discussion of the issue was suspended while tense, long-running negotiations on lucrative fishing rights in the region continued. In September 1995 Argentina and the United Kingdom signed a comprehensive agreement on joint oil explora-tion in the region following the discovery of petroleum deposits in 1993. In August 2001 Tony Blair became the first serving British Prime Minister to visit Argentina. However, the issue of the Falklands Islands' sovereignty was not discussed.

In January 1997 President Menem, in a communiqué marking the 164th anniversary of Britain's resumption of sovereignty over the Falkland Islands/Malvinas, reasserted both Argentina's claim to the Islands and his policy of seeking a peaceful resolu-tion to the dispute. Nevertheless, relations between the two countries continued to improve and, following the installation of a new British government in May 1997, this *rapprochement* was demonstrated by an official visit by President Menem to the United Kingdom in October 1998. During that conciliatory visit the President paid tribute to the British servicemen who had died during the 1982 conflict and disavowed the use of force to resolve the sovereignty issue. Two months later the United Kingdom announced the relaxation of its arms embargo against Argentina. However, the strain put on bilateral relations by the presentation to Congress, in early 1998, of draft legislation on sanctions to be imposed on petroleum companies and fishing vessels operating in Falkland Island waters without Argentine authorization, and the hostile Argentine reaction to apparent assertions of the Islanders' right to self-determination made by the Prince of Wales, the heir to the British throne, during an official visit in March 1999, were reminders of the continuing political sensitivity of the issue. In July 1999, however, Argen-tina and the United Kingdom agreed to end the ban on Argentine citizens visiting the Falkland Islands and to re-establish direct flights there from October. Furthermore, one of de la Rúa's first statements after his election confirmed his intention to maintain existing policy on the Islands.

Following treaties, signed in 1985 and 1991, respectively, which resolved sovereignty disputes involving the Beagle Channel islands and territory in the Antarctic region, relations with Chile were further stabilized in November 1996 when an Arbitration Court settled the last remaining mainland boundary question (the 'southern glaciers' issue). During a state visit to Argentina in April 1997, the main purpose of which was to confirm Chile's desire to enter the Southern Common Market (Mercado Común del Sur—Mercosur), the President of Chile, Eduardo Frei Ruíz-Tagle, also affirmed his support for Argentina's claim to the Falkland Islands. In August 1998 the two countries held joint naval exercises for the first time and in December the two countries' heads of state signed a further

agreement on the southern glaciers question, which was ratified by the Argentine Senate in June 1999, thus ending a century of border disputes in the Southern Andes.

Economy
Prof. PETER CALVERT

Argentina, with a land area of 2,780,400 sq km (excluding Antarctica), is the eighth-largest country in the world by area, and one immensely rich in natural resources. Moreover, though in population it ranks fourth in Latin America, in the world it ranks only 29th, with an estimated 37m. inhabitants at mid-2000. Population density was low, only 13.3 per sq km, yet one-third of the population lived in Greater Buenos Aires (population some 14m. in mid-2000) and 89.6% of the country was regarded as urban. The country's average annual rate of population growth in 1999 was 1.2%. In the same year the crude birth rate was 18.6 per thousand, the crude death rate 7.6 per thousand and infant mortality 18.3 per thousand. In 1999 expectation of life at birth was 73 years (77 for females and 69 for males). According to World Bank figures, gross national product (GNP) per head in 1999 was US $7,600 making Argentina an upper middle-income country. On the Human Development Index (HDI) of the United Nations Development Programme (UNDP) it ranked 39th in the world, four places below its 1998 position. Of those over 15 years of age, over 96% were literate.

Geographically, Argentina comprises four very diverse regions. The Andean area adjoins the entire western boundary with Chile, and with Bolivia in the north-west. In the north the forested flat lands of the Chaco and the flood plains of Mesopotamia (between the Paraná and Uruguay rivers) border Paraguay and Brazil. The Pampas (*pampa*), the vast plain which is the heart of the country, stretches from Buenos Aires on the Atlantic to the Andes and, north to south, from the Chaco to the Río (River) Colorado. This is the heartland of the country, the location of both its rich agricultural resources and its industry. To the south of the Río Colorado lies the fourth region, Patagonia, characterized by windswept plateaux pastured by sheep. The climate varies from subtropical in the north to subantarctic in the far south. Ushuaia, in Tierra del Fuego, is the most southerly town in the world. Argentina also claims as its national territory a substantial sector of Antarctica and several groups of islands in the South Atlantic (notably the Falkland Islands, or Islas Malvinas as they are known in Argentina, the subject of dispute with the United Kingdom).

HISTORY
The modern economic history of Argentina began with unification of most of the country under constitutional rule in 1853. In 1860 Argentina had a population of some 2m. and no more than 80 km of railway track. However, stable government, good communications and good economic opportunities attracted foreign migrants, capital and enterprise. Between 1857 and 1930 more than 6m. immigrants, mostly from Italy and other Southern European countries, entered Argentina. By 1914 the railway network, much of it built by British capital and engineering but much of it also by the state, had grown to 32,000 km, centred on Buenos Aires and Rosario. The key to this growth lay in the exploitation of the rich soil of the Pampas, as a small landowning élite and their employees, with improved breeds of cattle and sheep, turned Argentina into the world's greatest grazing ground and one of its principal granaries. The exploitation of the refrigerator ship from 1876 made possible an export trade in chilled and frozen meat. By 1914 Argentina was responsible for one-half of the world's beef exports, one-sixth of its mutton exports and one-10th of its wool exports, as well as providing vast exports of wheat, maize and linseed to growing consumer markets in Europe and North America.

The Federal Capital, Buenos Aires, mirrored that growth. Its population grew fivefold between 1880 and 1914, to 1.5m. As well as being the hub of the railway network, it was the major port for burgeoning exports and increasing imports of manufac-

tured goods. Foreign capital, skills and personnel were crucial in transforming country and capital alike, with British enterprise being predominant.

After the world depression that followed the First World War, the economy resumed its growth, with manufacturing industry developing from the 1920s. However, the financial crisis of 1929 severely damaged the economy of Argentina. Recovery in the 1930s was based on import substitution for manufactured goods, and by the 1940s the contribution of industry to the gross domestic product (GDP) was higher than that of the agrarian sector, which had benefited from Argentina's neutrality in the Second World War. With the advent to power of Col Juan Domingo Perón in 1946, the trend towards industrialization was accentuated and the growth of a powerful trade-union movement under his leadership allowed the masses a larger share of the national wealth. However, later governments found this labour movement unmanageable, while the neglect of agriculture, the traditional basis of export earnings, diminished its competitiveness in world markets, though for a long time this fact was concealed by the enormous fertility of the Pampas.

The military governments of 1976–83 adopted free-market policies. In theory they were seeking to introduce domestic efficiency by allowing liberal external competition, encouraging foreign investment and reducing the state's role in economic management. In practice, however, the overvaluation of the currency created an illusion of prosperity among their middle-class supporters (the *plata dulce*), encouraged imports and accelerated inflation. Furthermore, military authoritarianism actually extended the role of the state and, with it, the powers and numbers of the bureaucracy. Foreign borrowing covered the huge budget deficits, so that debt servicing grew enormously. With the return to civilian government in 1983, successive finance ministers struggled to overcome the legacy of their predecessors but without notable success until the early 1990s, when Argentina's GDP began to show respectable annual growth, after almost two decades of stagnation or decline.

AGRICULTURE, FORESTRY AND FISHING
It was the Pampas which created modern Argentina and its products—agricultural and pastoral—remain vital to the economy. It comprises only one-fifth of the total national territory, but contains two-thirds of the population, including that of the capital, Buenos Aires. In 1999 agriculture (including forestry and fishing) employed only 1,466,000 people, some 10.0% of the work-force, and accounted for just 4.4% of GDP. The main cash crops are wheat, maize, sorghum and soya beans. The country is completely self-sufficient in basic foodstuffs, and the majority of most agricultural products are available for export. Food and live animals accounted for some 35.7% of exports by value in 1998. In 1990–99 agricultural GDP increased by an annual average of 3.1%.

In 1996/97 the cereal and oilseed crop reached a record 52m. metric tons but totalled only some 44m. tons in 2000. According to the UN Food and Agriculture Organization (FAO), in 2000 Argentina produced 16.5m. metric tons of wheat, 16.2m. tons of maize, 3.4m. tons of sorghum, 2.1m. tons of other grains and just under 6.3m. tons of oilcrops. Grain exports had long been crucial to the Argentine economy but these increased further after 1979, because of the imposition of a US embargo on grain exports to the USSR. As a result, the USSR agreed to import a minimum of 4.5m. metric tons of Argentine grain annually until 1985 and, in 1986, to continue such imports, albeit at a substantially reduced level, for a further five years. Hence, the economic collapse and subsequent dissolution of the USSR had a serious effect on Argentina's economy. Exports subsequently recovered strongly, aided by Argentina's favoured position in the southern hemisphere. In 1999 exports of wheat and flour totalled 9.3m. metric tons, valued at $1,071.9m.

Other crops and fruits include sugar cane, rice, linseed, potatoes, tomatoes, cotton, tea and grapes. In 2000 an estimated 16m. metric tons of sugar cane was harvested. Most of Argentina's internationally known wines are grown in the Province of Mendoza and some at Cafayate, south of Salta. Although only about 2% of the average production of over 22m. hectolitres (hl) per year was exported in the early 1990s, quality increased sharply thereafter and successful efforts were made to expand traditional export markets and to find new ones, with such success that in 1999 Argentina exported 1.408m. metric tons of wine, with a value of $141.0m.

Although Argentina is no longer the world's principal exporter of beef, livestock production and meat sales abroad remained highly significant in both the internal and external economy. The cattle population fell from some 56m. head in 1980 to about 50m. in 1993, rising to 55m. in 2000. In 1999 316,530 metric tons of meat and meat preparations were exported, with a value of US $817m. Russia succeeded the USSR as Argentina's chief recipient of beef exports. Despite improved internal control of foot-and-mouth disease, the USA and Japan still imposed a ban on imports of Argentine fresh and frozen meat. In August 2000 an estimated 3,200 cattle were destroyed on suspicion that they had been infected with foot-and-mouth antibodies from Paraguayan cattle. In March 2001 there was a confirmed outbreak and by June some 1,100 cases of foot-and-mouth disease were found in Argentina. Domestic consumption accounted for as much as 90% of total beef production.

The sheep population fell sharply during the 20th century—from about 66m. head in 1900 to 14.5m. in 2000. Wool (greasy) output in this year was an estimated 68,000 tons. Pig and poultry products are not significant export items, although the home markets have expanded with the rising cost of living. In 2000 the FAO recorded 4.2m. pigs and 65m. chickens, along with an estimated 3.6m. horses, reflecting both their use for transport in the more remote areas and Argentina's world-wide pre-eminence on the polo field.

Forestry was comparatively neglected, although forests covered 18.6% of the land area in 1995 (according to the FAO). By the early 1990s woodland was being lost at an average rate of about 0.2% per year. Roundwood production in 1999 amounted to 5.7m. cubic metres. Most was consumed by the domestic market. Fishing, too, was under-exploited, although offshore resources were large and the vessels of many other nations were active in the South Atlantic. However, in the late 1980s and early 1990s the value of fishing exports rose considerably, from US $86.2m. in 1985, to $861.8m. by 1998. In that year the total catch was estimated at 1,130,163 metric tons, more than four times the 1984 figure of 315,170 tons.

MINING AND POWER

The chief metallic ore used is iron, with 4.21m. metric tons of crude steel being produced in 1998. Aluminium production stood at 187,158 metric tons in the previous year. Official figures for the extraction of other minerals in 1998 were: 35,560 metric tons of zinc; 15,004 tons of lead; 35,768 kg of silver; and 20,400 kg of gold. In 1997 coal reserves were estimated at 143m. short tons and production was 350,000 short tons. Uranium reserves were estimated at some 25,000 metric tons in the early 1990s but production, almost entirely for domestic use, fell from 123 metric tons in 1992 to only 9 tons in 1998. In 1997 the Bajo de la Alumbrera open-pit gold and copper mine, the country's largest, became fully operational, increasing substantially total mineral output.

Argentina was fully self-sufficient in energy and likely to continue to be so. Total commercial energy production in 1996 was 55.9m. metric tons of oil equivalent and in 1998 oil and gas accounted for 75% of all energy consumed. The major oilfield, Golfo San Jorge, discovered in 1907, is at Comodoro Rivadavia in Patagonia. It provides over 30% of national output. The other major onshore fields are Neuquén-Río/Negro-La Pampa, with 28% of total production, and the Cuyana field near Mendoza, in the foothills of the Andes west of Buenos Aires, providing some 25%. Proven reserves of petroleum amounted to 2,600m. barrels in 1999 and production rose steeply, from under 500,000 b/d in

1991, to more than 902,000 b/d in 1998. The depletion of land-based reserves has encouraged interest in increased offshore exploration, notably on the continental shelf which stretches to the Falkland Islands. Agreement with the United Kingdom on the joint development of the petroleum deposits of the Malvinas Basin around the Falkland Islands was reached in September 1995, but the initial results of exploration proved disappointing.

A state petroleum company, Yacimientos Petrolíferos Fiscales (YPF), was established in 1922 and, by the 1980s, controlled almost two-thirds of the country's refining capacity. However, a decline in petroleum production in 1987 prompted Argentina to import petroleum for the first time in 25 years. YPF's operating losses and huge overseas debt led to the Government allowing private-sector companies, including Esso Standard Oil Company and Royal Dutch/Shell Group, to operate in Argentine oilfields. In 1990 the Government offered 39 state oilfields and four of the biggest petroleum reserves for sale as part of the ongoing privatization programme, and in 1991 the industry was deregulated. The sale of the main tranche of a streamlined YPF was finalized in 1993. In 1998 YPF still controlled 50% of Argentine oil production, 40% of natural gas production and 60% of natural gas marketing. Its total revenues were US $5,500m. and its net profit $580m. In January 1999 the Government sold a 15% stake in YPF to Repsol of Spain. In June Repsol completed its purchase of the remaining 85% of the company (of which the Government itself still owned 5.3%, valued at over $800m.), to form the world's 10th largest oil and gas corporation, controlling 4,100m. barrels of petroleum reserves.

Natural gas reserves were estimated at 686,586m. cu m in 1999, when production was an estimated 42,425m. cu m. The discovery of extensive gas and oilfields off the coast of Tierra del Fuego made Argentina the second-largest producer in Latin America and would eventually, it was hoped, eliminate the need to import gas from Bolivia. Other deposits were at Neuquén in the far south of Patagonia. Several thousand kilometres of pipelines linked these fields, those of Mendoza and the southern Bolivian gas field with Buenos Aires and other main urban centres. Production nearly doubled between 1993 and 1998, from 19,420m. cu m to 38,631m. cu m. At present rates of consumption Argentina's known gas reserves will last some 20 years; however, production is planned to expand at an annual rate of 3.6% in the coming decade.

Total installed electrical generating capacity in 1998 was 21,758 MW. Electricity production in 1999 was an estimated 78,793m. kWh and average electricity consumption per head in 1998 was 1,891.4 kWh. Of this, 47.6% was provided by hydroelectric power, 42.7% from conventional thermal generation, 9.5% nuclear and 0.3% imported. The hydroelectric potential of Argentina was estimated at some 30,000 MW and has been increasingly exploited since the 1970s, when Argentina increased its hydroelectric output 10-fold Concerns about the long-term effects of silting spurred work on the Yacyretá dam, a joint project with Paraguay on the River Paraná, with an installed generating capacity of 2,700 MW (scaled down from the planned 4,050 MW). Construction was delayed by financial shortages and the plant was not fully operational until 1998, when cracks in the walls led to three of the plants 20 turbines being taken out of production. Given the huge debt which the project now carries it is not expected to operate above 60% of capacity in the foreseeable future. A hydroelectric complex, with an expected capacity of 2,000 MW, which was under construction on the Limay river, was expected to provide a further 9% of the country's energy requirements. However, the joint Argentine-Paraguayan Corpus project on the River Paraná, with an anticipated generating capacity of 6,900 MW, was delayed following public opposition. An interconnection project with the Brazilian grid, between Paraná and São Paulo (Brazil), which began construction in 2000, offered more hope of early completion.

Nuclear power was more important to Argentina's energy plans in the 1980s and the country is still the leading nuclear-power producer in Latin America. The Atucha I heavy-water reactor, with a capacity of 640 MW, began operating in 1973, and the 600-MW Embalse Río Tercero, in Córdoba, started production in 1984. However, development of the Atucha II heavy-water reactor (capacity 690 MW) was halted in 1990 for financial and environmental reasons and remains incomplete.

MANUFACTURING

Argentine industrialization proceeded apace from the 1930s, stimulated by import-substitution policies. As early as the 1940s the value of industrial production exceeded that of the agricultural and pastoral sectors combined. However, the 'free-market' policies of the military regimes of 1966–73 and 1976–83 allowed foreign competition to increase and reduced industrial output. For the rest of the 1980s the manufacturing sector remained in decline, as did the economy as a whole, principally owing to weak domestic demand and the restricted availability of credit caused by high levels of inflation. Manufacturing accounted for 18.2% of GDP in 1999.

The key industrial and manufacturing sectors are the motor industry, consumer goods (especially 'white' goods such as refrigerators, washing machines and television receivers), pharmaceuticals, cosmetics, electronic equipment, fibres, cement, rubber and paper and other wood products. Argentina is self-sufficient in basic manufactures, producing 7.1m. metric tons of cement and 1.1m. tons of paper in 1999. Argentina is bound to depend essentially on its primary exports in the foreseeable future, but world markets are weak, and only a continued restructuring of the industrial sector to increase manufactured exports is likely to compensate for this. The country has comparative advantages in such fields as petrochemicals and agro-industries, but has long lacked a stable economic climate in which they could prosper. However, 260,750 tons of polyethylene and 96,761 tons of polyvinylchloride were produced in 1999.

In the same year, Argentine factories produced 224,733 cars, 66,544 commercial motor vehicles and 8.0m. car tyres, and in the consumer-goods sector, 413,105 washing machines, 1,335,000 television sets, 402,818 domestic refrigerators and 83,723 home freezers.

President Menem's decree of October 1991 proved to be only the first step in the liberalization of the economy. The decree ordered the removal of almost all of the remaining bureaucratic apparatus of state control. The promised new round of privatizations occurred in July 1992 with the sale of the municipal electricity enterprise, Servicios Eléctricos del Gran Buenos Aires (SEGBA), as two networks, for US $900m. At the same time, almost 80% of the steel company, Sociedad Mixta Siderúrgia Argentina (SOMISA), and 70% of the natural-gas company, Gas del Estado, the main-route networks and the eight regional distributors, were offered for tender. Privatization of a wide range of other activities followed.

The Government claimed that liberalization resulted in the creation of many new jobs. However, between 1980 and 1993 the proportion of those employed in manufacturing fell from 40% to 30%, while there, as elsewhere, part-time labour increased, especially for women. In July 1995 the monthly rate of unemployment, according to official estimates reached 18.6%, owing to the effects of the Mexican peso crisis. Thereafter, the unemployment rate fell only slowly and stood at 15.4% in May 2000.

TRANSPORT AND COMMUNICATIONS

Argentina long had the most developed communications system in Latin America, stemming from its earlier economic development and the establishment of a rail network from the mid-19th century. Privatization of the rail sector began in 1991 with the franchising of the Rosario–Bahía Blanca grain line to a Techint–Iowa State Railroad consortium. The franchising strategy was complicated by protests from the provincial governments over payments introduced to subsidize loss-making passenger services. Furthermore, in March 1993 12 Provinces lost their passenger-train services, although Córdoba's service later won a reprieve. Following privatization, railway use increased significantly. In 1998 there were approximately 33,000 km of track carrying 480m. passengers (an increase of about 30% in two years) and 18.8m. metric tons of freight.

In 2000 there were 215,434 km of roads, of which 63,553 km (29.4%) were paved. National bus services are good. More than 4.9m. passenger cars and almost 1.4m. commercial vehicles were in use in 1997. The leasing of highways proved to be the most controversial, problematic and politically unpopular part of the Menem Government's privatization programme. Nevertheless, in 1998 the network carried 87m. vehicles, which paid US $366.8m. in tolls.

In the Federal Capital, metropolitan bus services, which were deregulated in the 1960s, were complemented by an efficient and spacious underground network. The Subterráneo (Subte), the oldest system in South America, was privatized in 1993. Shipping is not well developed, considering Argentina's large export trade and access to 10.950 km of navigable waterways. There are 13 major ports, of which Buenos Aires is the largest and most significant. The major shipping firm is Empresas Líneas Marítimas Argentinas. In 2000 there were 493vessels, amounting to 464,326 gross registered tons, under the national flag.

The sale of the national airline, Aerolíneas Argentinas, to a consortium led by Spain's Iberia Airlines, was agreed in 1990. However, the deal was not completed until March 1992 and, even then, involved a substantial loss to the Government. The airline operated an international service, with direct flights to and from Europe, North America, and other Latin American countries; it was also the principal internal airline. The major international airport at Buenos Aires is at Ezeiza. The smaller Aeroparque Jorge Newbery lies at the heart of the city and, though it operates essentially as an internal entrepôt, also caters for a limited number of flights to neighbouring Latin American countries. There are eight other international airports in the country and some 1,359 provincial airports. In 1998 they handled 6,342,000 international and 6,996,000 domestic air passengers. In the same year Argentina's two postal services handled 868m. items. There were 7,095,000 telephone lines in use in 1998 (19.6 per 1,000 inhabitants).

Tourism is still comparatively underdeveloped, partly because of the distance from Europe and the USA and partly because of the considerable distances between the major centres of tourist interest. However, the Dirección General de Turismo promoted better amenities, including hotels and national parks, in places of outstanding historic and natural interest, and income from this source increased considerably from the late 1980s. Tourist arrivals in 1998 totalled almost 3.0m. and receipts amounted to US $5.36m.

INVESTMENT AND FINANCE

The policies pursued by the successive military governments from 1976 to 1983 emphasized international competitiveness and a reduction in the rate of inflation. Devaluation and obstruction of external trade, caused by the Falklands conflict, created a fall of 45% in the value of goods purchased abroad in 1982, compared with 1981. Although this resulted in a surplus of US $2,764m. in the balance of trade in 1982, the balance of payments deteriorated seriously. By the end of that year the interim military Government of General Bignone could not meet its debt-servicing obligations, and emergency help was sought from the International Monetary Fund (IMF) and creditor banks. A new currency, the peso argentino, was introduced, worth 1,000 old pesos (the peso ley). However, real GDP in 1983 was still below the level of 1974 and GDP per head fell by 13.5% in the period 1974–83.

The initial response of the Alfonsín Government to this crisis was to try to stimulate economic growth while increasing taxation and reducing public expenditure broadly in line with the IMF's austerity proposals. However, investment remained depressed and inflation reached 434% in the year to December 1983. The Austral Plan, introduced in June 1985, was the first example in Latin America of the so-called 'heterodox shock'. It sought to eliminate inflation at once by a complete wage and price 'freeze' for 90 days, while at the same time breaking the inflationary spiral by instituting a new currency, the austral (A), worth 1,000 pesos argentinos. Initially, it appeared to have been reasonably successful. However, inflation continued to rise and the wages and prices freeze, which was a necessary part of the Plan, was breached by the Government itself. The basic structural problems of the economy and difficulties over wage policy worsened as the 1989 presidential election approached. In order to prevent further economic instability, President Alfonsín handed over power early to the President-elect, Carlos Menem.

The incoming economic team of President Menem introduced a new plan in July 1989. This was a conventional stabilization programme, comprising a 54% devaluation, increases in public-utility rates and reductions in trade tariffs. The rate of inflation quickly fell to under 10% per month, allowing Menem to agree on a US $1,400m. stand-by loan from the IMF in October. However, the recovery was short-lived.

Effective stabilization of the currency only came as a result of the measures introduced in January 1991, by the new economy minister, Domingo Cavallo. The key to his 'Convertibility Plan' was the so-called 'dollarization' of the economy, linking the Argentine currency to the US dollar, with a fixed exchange rate of ₳10,000 to the US $, supported by foreign exchange or gold reserves at the Central Bank. This had the immediate effect of restraining the rise in consumer prices, although inflation to the year end was still 84%. On 1 January 1992 another currency, the nuevo peso argentino, equal to US $1, replaced the austral as a visible symbol of the change.

In July 1993 industrial output reached record levels. The rate of inflation for the year to September 1993 fell to 8.9% and (average deposit) interest rates fell from 17,236% in 1989 to 17% in 1992. In January 1994 the monthly rate of interest was 8%. Total reserves, excluding gold, were US $11,960m. in November 1993, when the peso was rated the third-strongest currency in the world, after the Japanese yen and the Singapore dollar. At the end of the year the fiscal surplus stood at $5,100m., well ahead of the IMF target of $4,400m. The economy, as measured by GDP at constant prices, grew by 8.9% in 1991, 8.7% in 1992, 6.0% in 1993 and 7.4% in 1994.

Argentina's recovery suffered a sharp reverse from the effects of the Mexican peso crisis of December 1994 (the 'tequila effect'). Revenues in December 1995, when adjusted for uncollected taxes, stood at US $3,760m., 1.9% below the corresponding figure for December 1994. Following the Mexican devaluation, in early 1995 severe restrictions were placed on public spending, in an attempt to support the Argentine peso. Widespread tax evasion continued to limit the capacity of the Government to raise revenue and to lower the value-added tax rate from 21% to 18%, as had been hoped. In 1995 the fiscal deficit was $2,400m., a figure nominally supposed to be covered by privatization revenues. After initial predictions of economic growth in 1995 of 3%, the economy actually contracted by 4%. Thereafter, however, the economy resumed its growth, with GDP increasing by 5.5% in 1996 and 8.1% in 1997. At the same time, inflation remained under control, with average increases in consumer prices of just 0.2% and 0.5% in 1996 and 1997, respectively. The economy continued to expand strongly in the first six months of 1998 but was then restrained by economic crisis in Brazil. The annual inflation rate increased slightly, to 0.9%, but, economic growth slowed to 3.9%. In 1999 the economic situation worsened, with a contraction in GDP of 3.4% and a negative inflation rate of 1.2%.

In 1996 the fiscal deficit widened to US $6,600m., $4,500m. more than the IMF target, and the structural-adjustment plan announced in August was so unpopular that President Menem abandoned his earlier pledge to have it approved by Congress and instead proposed to implement it by decree. In 1997 the IMF target for the fiscal deficit of $4,500m. was only narrowly bettered, as was the target of $3,500m. for 1998. In January 1997 the economy minister, Roque Fernández, gave international investors a promise that there would be no devaluation of the currency for at least 10 years, and the Government remained fully committed to maintaining the dollar parity. Although the currency has long been significantly overvalued, the Argentine peso was not significantly affected, contrary to expectations, by Brazilian devaluation in April 1999. Nevertheless, the risk of devaluation, and the burdensome interest rate premium that Argentina pays to investors in mitigation, led the Government to consider the politically sensitive issue of a wholesale replacement of the peso with the US dollar.

In December 1999, therefore, incoming President Fernando de la Rua inherited an economy already in crisis. GDP had fallen by 3.4% during 1999 while the fiscal deficit had widened to some 2.5% of GDP. The new Government arranged a US $7,400m. stand-by facility with the IMF. Throughout 2000 the Government struggled with Congress to implement an austerity programme. The situation continued, however, to worsen and in December a further $14,000m. loan agreement was negotiated. GDP growth in this year was 0.5%. In spite of the loan agreement, in March 2001 the first quarter fiscal target was missed because of falling tax revenues. At this point Domingo Cavallo was again appointed Minister of the Economy and in

May he successfully negotiated a supplementary agreement with the IMF that would give the country continued access to a $40,000m. package of financial aid, even though the fiscal deficit at the year end was still expected to be $6,500m. However, with confidence already eroded, there were continuing fears that he would not be able to avoid both devaluation and default. In June the Senate approved the introduction of a new exchange-rate regime which would fix the peso at midpoint between the US dollar and the euro as soon as the euro reached parity with the dollar. The new regime was widely interpreted as a *de facto* partial devaluation of the currency.

FOREIGN TRADE, BALANCE OF PAYMENTS AND DEBT

In the 1980s Argentina generally had a favourable balance of trade but an unfavourable balance of payments. However, by 1993 the trade balance turned to deficit, owing to a continued rise in the value of imports. By 1998 the trade deficit was $3,117m., which decreased to $770m. in the following year. In 2000 there was a trade surplus of $2,541m. The deficit on current account was $14,704m. in 1998, before decreasing slightly, to $12,446m., in 1999 and to $9,358m. in 2000.

Exports were valued at $26,441m. in 1998 and $23,000m. in 1999. Pastoral and agricultural products and food, drink and tobacco remained the major export items. By the 1990s the European Union (EU, known as the European Community until November 1993) was established as Argentina's largest trading partner. However, in the late 1990s trade with the USA again increased and the global figure disguised interesting variations. Provisional figures for 1999 confirmed Brazil to be Argentina's largest export market, the destination for 24% of exports by value in that year, followed by the EU (21%) and the USA (11%). In 1998 Argentina's imports had originated from a much broader range of sources, with Asia assuming an increased importance, but in 1999 the EU still accounted for 28% of imports, Brazil for 22% and the USA for 20%. There was steady progress in the 1990s in extending intra-regional trade. In August 1986 Argentina and Brazil signed a trade pact and agreed on the formation of a customs union. From July 1990 Argentina was actively participating in the creation of a Southern Common Market (Mercado Común del Sur—Mercosur or, in Portuguese, Mercado Comum do Sul—Mercosul), covering Argentina, Brazil, Paraguay and Uruguay. The 25 agreements which were signed at the initial meeting included provisions either to abolish or to reduce import duties and quotas on a wide range of goods. However, with President Menem's vigorous partisanship, on 1 January 1995 the common external tariff was established, as well as an open frontier between Argentina and its partners. Mercosur became the only major trading bloc with which Argentina ran a trade surplus, which amounted to US $1,483m. in 1998. A major trade dispute with Brazil over creating a balanced regime for trade in motor vehicles was ended by agreement in March 2000, at which a number of minor points of dispute were also shelved.

Apart from the vertiginous rise and fall of inflation (Argentina is the only country in the world to have experienced continuous triple-digit inflation for more than 15 years), the most dramatic feature of the economy in the 1980s and 1990s was the massive increase in foreign debt. This grew from US $35,700m. in 1981, to $74,473m. in 1993. After 1983 rescheduling negotiations between Argentina, the IMF and creditor banks were a permanent feature of financial policy and, on occasions, were difficult. The country consistently failed to meet its targets and in mid-1989 World Bank financing was suspended.

Following President Menem's inauguration in July 1989, the implementation of the Bunge and Born Plan enabled agreement to be reached with the IMF for a US $1,400m. stand-by loan. The first part of the privatization programme, begun in mid-1990, recovered more than $5,000m. in foreign debt, as payment was made largely by debt-for-equity 'swaps'. A further substantial reduction followed in 1991 and in 1992 agreement was reached with foreign private creditor banks to consolidate $30,000m.-worth of debt and so reduce the country's capital obligation to some $48,000m. Under the principles of the US Brady Initiative (an initiative on debt relief originally proposed by Nicholas Brady, the US Secretary of the Treasury, in 1989), the agreement included a substantial debt write-off, by conversion either to par bonds at low fixed interest rates or to discount bonds. Arrears of interest would be cleared by a single payment of $700m. lent by the international banks.

However, although Argentina was able to withstand the effects of the Mexican financial crisis and maintain convertibility, the Government, as a consequence, was forced to resume borrowing. In 1995 alone external debt increased from US $77,388m. to $89,679m. This figure gave a debt-to-GNP ratio of 27.8%, debt as a proportion to exports of goods and services of 320.2%, and debt-service as 34.7% of exports. In 1996 the Government was able to secure further loans and in February 1998 signed a new three-year accord with the IMF under the Extended Finance Facility, for $2,800m. At the end of 1999 Argentina's total external debt stood at $154,362m. This figure gave a debt-to-GDP ratio of 48.3% and debt service as 69.3% of exports of goods and services. Total debt service in 1999 was $25,723.2m., when the World Bank classified Argentina as a severely indebted middle-income country. In May 2001 the new administration was faced with the unpalatable prospect of negotiating a voluntary restructuring of the national debt at a time when it was unlikely to have any access to international capital markets for months to come.

In 1999 central government expenditure amounted to US $51,040m. Of this, $22,465m. (44.0%) was spent on social services, $8,681m. (17.0%) on debt servicing, $5,375m. (10.5%) on government and administration, $3,573m. (7.0%) on defence and public order, and $2,496m. (4.9%) on economic services.

CONCLUSION

Argentina's resources—material and human—are large, and the country made good progress in surmounting the economic problems of the 1980s. President Menem's Government, after first repeating the mistakes of its predecessors, showed itself ready to recognize economic reality and deal with the country's deep-seated problems. The disastrous cycle of military intervention, economic crisis and ineffective civilian government which, in the period 1930–90, took Argentina from being the seventh-richest country in the world to being the 77th, was ended. The 'dollarization' of the economy virtually eliminated inflation and brought financial stability and the repatriation of capital for productive investment. However, the trade and fiscal deficits, high levels of unemployment and an overvalued currency remained problems for the Government of President de la Rúa, as did the high and increasing level of public debt.

Statistical Survey

Sources (unless otherwise stated): Instituto Nacional de Estadística y Censos, Avda Julio A. Roca 609, 1067 Buenos Aires; tel. (11) 4349-9613; fax (11) 4349-9601; e-mail okace@indec.mecon.ar; internet www.indec.mecon.ar; and Banco Central de la República Argentina, Reconquista 266, 1003 Buenos Aires; tel. (11) 4394-8111; fax (11) 4334-5712.

Area and Population

AREA, POPULATION AND DENSITY

Area (sq km)	2,780,400*
Population (census results)†	
22 October 1980	27,949,480
15 May 1991	
Males	15,937,980
Females	16,677,548
Total	32,615,528
Population (official estimates at mid-year)	
1998	36,124,933
1999	36,578,358
2000	37,031,802
Density (per sq km) at mid-2000	13.3

* 1,073,518 sq miles. The figure excludes the Falkland Islands (Islas Malvinas) and Antarctic territory claimed by Argentina.

† Figures exclude adjustment for underenumeration, estimated to have been 1% at the 1980 census and 0.9% at the 1991 census.

PROVINCES (mid-2000)

	Area (sq km)	Estimated population*	Density (per sq km)	Capital
Buenos Aires— Federal District .	200	3,046,663	15,233.3	
Buenos Aires— Province . . .	307,571	14,214,701	46.2	La Plata
Catamarca . .	102,602	318,147	3.1	San Fernando del Valle de Catamarca
Chaco . . .	99,633	951,795	9.6	Resistencia
Chubut . .	224,686	448,028	2.0	Rawson
Córdoba . .	165,321	3,090,803	18.7	Córdoba
Corrientes . .	88,199	921,933	10.5	Corrientes
Entre Ríos .	78,781	1,113,438	14.1	Paraná
Formosa . .	72,066	504,185	7.0	Formosa
Jujuy . . .	53,219	604,002	11.3	San Salvador de Jujuy
La Pampa . .	143,440	306,113	2.1	Santa Rosa
La Rioja . .	89,680	280,198	3.1	La Rioja
Mendoza . .	148,827	1,607,618	10.8	Mendoza
Misiones . .	29,801	995,326	33.4	Posadas
Neuquén . .	94,078	560,726	6.0	Neuquén
Río Negro . .	203,013	618,486	3.0	Viedma
Salta . . .	155,488	1,067,347	6.9	Salta
San Juan . .	89,651	578,504	6.5	San Juan
San Luis . .	76,748	363,345	4.7	San Luis
Santa Cruz . .	243,943	206,897	0.8	Río Gallegos
Santa Fe . .	133,007	3,098,661	23.3	Santa Fe
Santiago del Estero	136,351	725,993	5.3	Santiago del Estero
Tucumán . .	22,524	1,293,349	57.4	San Miguel de Tucumán
Territory				
Tierra del Fuego .	21,571	115,538	5.4	Ushuaia
Total . . .	2,780,400	37,031,802	13.3	Buenos Aires

* Figures have been estimated independently, so the total may not be the sum of the component parts.

PRINCIPAL TOWNS (population at 1991 census)*

Buenos Aires			San Isidro	299,023
(capital)	2,965,403		Vicente López	289,505
Córdoba	1,157,507		Moreno	287,715
San Justo			Esteban Echeverría	275,793
(La Matanza)	1,121,298		Bahía Blanca	260,096
Rosario	907,718		Corrientes	258,103
General Sarmiento	652,969		Tigre	257,922
Morón	643,553		Florencio Varela	254,997
Lomas de			Berazategui	244,929
Zamora	574,330		Resistencia	229,212
La Plata	521,936		Paraná	207,041
Mar del Plata	512,880		Posadas	201,273
Quilmes	511,234		Villa Nueva	
San Miguel de			(Guaymallén)	200,595
Tucumán	470,809		Santiago del Estero	189,947
Lanús	468,561		Godoy Cruz	179,588
Almirante Brown	450,698		San Salvador de	
General San			Jujuy	178,748
Martín	406,809		Neuquén	167,296
Merlo	390,858		Formosa	147,636
Salta	367,550		Las Heras	145,823
Santa Fe	353,063		San Fernando	141,063
Caseros	349,376		Río Cuarto	134,355
Avellaneda	344,991			

* In each case the figures refer to the city proper. At the 1991 census the population of the Buenos Aires agglomeration was 11,298,030.

BIRTHS AND DEATHS

	Registered live births		Registered deaths	
	Number	Rate (per 1,000)	Number	Rate (per 1,000)
1991	694,776	21.1	255,609	7.8
1992	678,761	20.3	262,287	7.9
1993	667,518	19.8	267,286	7.9
1994	707,869	20.7	260,245	7.6
1995	658,735	18.9	268,997	7.7
1996	675,437	19.2	268,715	7.6
1997	692,357	19.4	270,910	7.6
1998	683,301	18.9	280,180	7.8

Marriages: 158,805 (marriage rate 4.6 per 1,000) in 1995; 148,721 (4.2 per 1,000) in 1996.

Source: mainly UN, *Demographic Yearbook* and *Population and Vital Statistics Report*.

Expectation of life (UN estimates, years at birth, 1990–95): 71.9 (males 68.6; females 75.7). Source: UN, *World Population Prospects: The 1998 Revision*.

ECONOMICALLY ACTIVE POPULATION
(persons aged 14 years and over, census of 15 May 1991)

	Males	Females	Total
Agriculture, hunting, forestry and fishing	1,142,674	222,196	1,364,870
Mining and quarrying	43,905	3,525	47,430
Manufacturing	1,590,713	546,090	2,136,803
Electricity, gas and water	92,469	11,318	103,787
Construction	818,831	17,617	836,448
Wholesale and retail trade, restaurants and hotels	1,730,600	808,702	2,539,302
Transport, storage and communication	583,938	54,024	637,962
Finance, insurance, real estate and business services	432,264	222,757	655,021
Community, social and personal services	1,459,492	2,464,552	3,924,044
Activities not adequately described	81,013	41,648	122,661
Total employed	7,975,899	4,392,429	12,368,328
Unemployed	447,488	386,384	833,872
Total labour force	8,423,387	4,778,813	13,202,200

1995 (provisional figures, sample survey, persons aged 15 years and over): Total active population 14,345,171 (males 9,087,075; females 5,258,096) (Source: ILO, *Yearbook of Labour Statistics*).

Mid-1999 (estimates in '000): Agriculture, etc. 1,466; Total labour force 14,692 (Source: FAO).

Agriculture

PRINCIPAL CROPS ('000 metric tons)

	1998	1999	2000
Wheat	12,400	14,200	16,500*
Rice (paddy)	1,036	1,658	858
Barley	539	400	450†
Maize	19,360	13,500	16,200
Rye	66	104	115†
Oats	383	507	555†
Millet	47	45	47
Sorghum	3,762	3,222	3,350
Potatoes	3,412	3,450†	3,500†
Sweet potatoes	312	315†	320†
Cassava (Manioc)†	160	170	170
Dry beans	303	340	297
Other pulses	58	60	61
Soybeans	18,732	20,000	20,200
Groundnuts (in shell)	896	486	600
Sunflower seed	5,600	7,100	5,750*
Linseed	75	85	47
Olives†	88	85	95
Tomatoes	647	650†	660†
Pumpkins, squash and gourds†	289	430	450†
Onions (dry)	798	800†	820†
Carrots†	245*	240†	245
Watermelons†	130	125	125
Grapes	2,002	2,425	2,201†
Sugar cane†	19,400	16,700*	16,000*
Apples	1,034	1,116	1,117†
Pears	537	390	395†
Peaches and nectarines	257	240	245†
Oranges	984	660	685*
Tangerines, mandarins, clementines and satsumas	394	340*	340*
Lemons and limes	1,021	1,043	1,050*
Grapefruit and pomelos	216	178	165*
Bananas	170†	175†	175
Tea (made)	57	56	58†
Tobacco (leaves)	117	111†	111*
Cotton (lint)	316	196*	121†

* Unofficial figure   † FAO estimate(s)..
Source: FAO.

LIVESTOCK ('000 head, year ending September)

	1998	1999	2000*
Horses*	3,300	3,600	3,600
Mules*	175	180	180
Asses*	95	95	95
Cattle	54,600	55,000*	55,000
Pigs*	3,500	4,200	4,200
Sheep	15,232†	14,000†	14,500
Goats†	4,450	4,500	4,500
Chickens*	60,000	60,000	65,000
Ducks*	2,200	2,300	2,300
Geese*	120	130	130
Turkeys	2,700	2,800	2,800

* FAO estimate(s).   † Unofficial figures.
Source: FAO.

LIVESTOCK PRODUCTS ('000 metric tons)

	1998	1999	2000
Beef and veal	2,452	2,653	2,900*
Mutton and lamb	48*	45*	50†
Goat meat	9	9	9
Pig meat	156	181	190†
Horse meat†	50	55	55
Poultry meat	896	953	937
Cows' milk	9,833	10,632	9,800*
Butter	52*	55†	55†
Cheese	420	425*	432*
Hen eggs	278	286	286†
Wool (greasy)	62	65	68†
Cattle hides (fresh)	338	364	399

* Unofficial figure(s).   †FAO estimate(s).
Source: FAO.

Forestry

ROUNDWOOD REMOVALS ('000 cubic metres, excl. bark)

	1997	1998	1999
Sawlogs, veneer logs and logs for sleepers	1,958	735	735
Pulpwood	3,577	3,784	3,784
Other industrial wood . . .	197	119	119
Fuel wood	1,157	1,103	1,103
Total	6,889	5,741	5,741

Source: FAO, *Yearbook of Forest Products.*

SAWNWOOD PRODUCTION
('000 cubic metres, incl. railway sleepers)

	1996	1997	1998
Coniferous (softwood) . .	594	594	594
Broadleaved (hardwood) . . .	1,117	1,117	1,117
Total	1,711	1,711	1,711

Source: FAO, *Yearbook of Forest Products.*

Fishing

('000 metric tons, live weight)

	1996	1997	1998
Capture	1,248.7	1,351.1	1,128.8
Southern blue whiting . . .	85.0	79.9	71.6
Argentine hake . . .	597.6	584.0	458.4
Patagonian grenadier . . .	44.1	41.8	96.2
Argentine shortfin squid . .	292.6	412.0	291.2
Aquaculture	1.3	1.3	1.3*
Total catch	1,250.1	1,352.4	1,130.2

*FAO estimate.

Note: The data exclude aquatic plants (FAO estimates, '000 metric tons, capture only): 2.3 in 1996; 2.3 in 1997; 2.3 in 1998. Also excluded are aquatic mammals, recorded by number rather than by weight. The number of toothed whales caught was 15 in 1998.

Source: FAO, *Yearbook of Fishery Statistics.*

Mining

('000 metric tons, unless otherwise indicated)

	1996	1997	1998
Crude petroleum ('000 cu metres) .	45,570	48,403	49,147*
Natural gas (million cu metres) .	34,650	37,073	38,631*
Lead ore†	11.3	13.8	15.0
Zinc ore†	31.1	33.4	35.6
Silver ore (metric tons) . .	50.4	52.6	35.8
Uranium ore (metric tons)† . .	27	41	9
Gold ore (kilograms)† . . .	723	2,289	20,400

* Estimate.
† Figures refer to the metal content of ores and concentrates.

1999 (estimates): Crude petroleum 46,508,000 cu m; Natural gas 42,425m. cu m.

Industry

SELECTED PRODUCTS ('000 metric tons, unless otherwise indicated)

	1997	1998	1999
Wheat flour*	3,640	3,739	3,563
Beer (sales,'000 hectolitres) . .	12,687	12,395*	12,503†
Cigarettes (million units) . . .	1,940	1,967	1,996
Paper and paper products . .	1,143	1,159	1,130
Rubber tyres for motor vehicles ('000)	8,138	9,190	8,085
Portland cement	6,769	7,092	7,187*
Distillate fuel oils . . .	10,490	10,709	11,070
Residual fuel oils . . .	1,702	1,740	1,817
Motor spirit (petrol)('000 cu metres)	7,094	7,736	7,864
Kerosene ('000 cu metres) . .	203	181	171
Passenger motor vehicles ('000 units)	366	353	225
Refrigerators ('000 units) . .	410	424	403
Washing machines ('000 units)	603*	624	413
Television receivers ('000) . .	1,630	1,592	1,335
Electric energy (million kWh) . .	73,240	76,200	78,493*

* Provisional figure(s).
† Estimate.

Finance

CURRENCY AND EXCHANGE RATES

Monetary Units:
  100 centavos = 1 nuevo peso argentino (new Argentine peso).

Sterling, Dollar and Euro Equivalents (30 April 2001)
  £1 sterling = 1.4311 nuevos pesos;
  US $1 = 99.95 centavos;
  €1 = 88.72 centavos;
  100 nuevos pesos = £69.88 = $100.05 = €112.72.

Note: The nuevo peso argentino was introduced on 1 January 1992, replacing the austral at a rate of 1 nuevo peso = 10,000 australes. The austral had been introduced on 15 June 1985, replacing the peso argentino at the rate of 1 austral = 1,000 pesos argentinos. The peso argentino, equal to 10,000 former pesos, had itself been introduced on 1 June 1983. The official exchange rate has been fixed at US $1 = 99.95 centavos since April 1996.

BUDGET (million new pesos)*

Revenue	1998	1999
Taxation	50,785.5	51,200.7
Taxes on income, profits, etc.	9,654.0	9,401.0
Social security contributions	10,857.0	9,910.0
Domestic taxes on goods and services . .	27,390.0	26,038.0
Value-added tax	20,857.0	18,771.0
Excises	1,942.0	1,830.0
Taxes on international trade and transactions	2,875.0	2,364.0
Import duties	2,694.0	2,227.0
Export duties	28.0	25.0
Other current revenue	3,530.5	4,422.2
Capital revenue	428.6	998.4
Total revenue	54,744.6	56,621.3

Expenditure	1998	1999
General public services	4,602.7	5,375.3
Defence	1,994.3	2,076.5
Public order and safety	1,414.8	1,496.4
Education and culture	2,847.3	3,192. 8
Health	3,109.5	3,180.0
Social security and welfare	22,525.9	22,464.5
Housing and community amenities	1,079.7	878.0
Other social services	1,180.4	1,086.2
Economic affairs and services	2,867.7	2,495.5
Agriculture	386.1	361.4
Fuel, energy and mining	348.7	373.1
Transportation and communication	1,914.8	1,587.3
Industry	98.4	99.2
Other purposes	162.0	114.0
Interest payments	6,991.7	8,680.9
Sub-total	48,776.0	51,040.0
Adjustment to cash basis	11,236.9	12,622.0
Total expenditure	60,012.9	63,662.0
Current	55,975.0	59,548.1
Capital	4,037.9	4,113.9

2000 (forecasts, million new pesos): *Revenue:* Taxation 52,023.2; Other current revenue 3,730.8; Capital revenue 878.6; Total 56,632.6; *Expenditure:* Current expenditure 57,712.8; Capital expenditure 3,388.1; Total 61,100.9.

* Budget figures refer to the consolidated accounts of the public sector, comprising the central Government, provincial and municipal governments, and publicly-owned enterprises.

INTERNATIONAL RESERVES (US $ million at 31 December)

	1998	1999	2000
Gold*	124	121	7
IMF special drawing rights	264	138	733
Foreign exchange	24,488	26,114	24,414
Total	24,876	26,373	25,154

* National valuation.

Source: IMF, *International Financial Statistics.*

MONEY SUPPLY (million new pesos at 31 December)

	1998	1999	2000
Currency outside banks	13,503	13,736	12,572
Demand deposits at commercial banks	7,986	8,099	7,281
Total money	21,489	21,836	19,853

Source: IMF, *International Financial Statistics.*

COST OF LIVING (Consumer Price Index for Buenos Aires metropolitan area; annual averages; base: 1988 = 100)

	1997	1998	1999
Food	274,621	279,216	268,980
Clothing	176,184	171,767	165,508
Housing	323,543	320,884	325,006
All items (incl. others)	323,668	326,661	322,849

NATIONAL ACCOUNTS (million new pesos at current prices)
Expenditure on the Gross Domestic Product

	1998	1999	2000
Government final consumption expenditure	37,353	38,918	39,298
Private final consumption expenditure	206,434	197,204	197,497
Gross fixed capital formation	59,595	50,629	45,620
Total domestic expenditure*	306,394	288,059	286,935
Exports of goods and services	31,122	27,759	30,686
Less Imports of goods and services	38,568	32,558	32,576
GDP in purchasers' values	298,948	283,260	285,045
GDP at constant 1993 prices	288,123	278,320	276,948

*Including adjustment.

Source: IMF, *International Financial Statistics.*

Gross Domestic Product by Economic Activity

	1997	1998*	1999*
Agriculture, hunting and forestry	14,625	15,275	11,636
Fishing	668	647	693
Mining and quarrying	5,633	4,291	4,821
Manufacturing	53,382	53,266	48,471
Electricity, gas and water supply	5,502	5,749	6,041
Construction	15,080	16,635	15,970
Wholesale and retail trade	41,477	42,385	37,849
Hotels and restaurants	7,644	8,110	7,957
Transport, storage and communications	22,952	23,952	22,614
Financial intermediation	10,116	10,393	10,955
Real estate, renting and business activities	44,567	45,522	45,511
Public administration and defence†	15,860	15,463	16,820
Education, health and social work	21,366	22,155	22,730
Other community, social and personal service activities‡	14,221	14,111	14,059
Sub-total	273,093	278,632	266,127
Value-added tax	20,474	20,857	18,771
Import duties	2,827	2,741	2,278
Less Imputed bank service charge	3,534	4,099	4,406
GDP in purchasers' values	292,859	298,131	282,769

*Provisional figures.
† Including extra-territorial organizations and bodies.
‡ Including private households with employed persons.

BALANCE OF PAYMENTS (US $ million)

	1998	1999	2000
Exports of goods f.o.b.	26,441	23,333	26,298
Imports of goods f.o.b.	−29,558	−24,103	−23,757
Trade balance	−3,117	−770	2,541
Exports of services	4,650	4,434	4,536
Imports of services	−9,106	−8,531	−8,840
Balance on goods and services	−7,573	−4,867	−1,763
Other income received	6,142	6,097	7,440
Other income paid	−13,570	−13,949	−15,213
Balance on goods, services and income	−15,001	−12,719	−9,536
Current transfers received	600	565	506
Current transfers paid	−303	−292	−328
Current balance	−14,704	−12,446	−9,358
Direct investment abroad	−2,324	−1,250	−912
Direct investment from abroad	7,280	24,148	11,154
Portfolio investment assets	−2,065	−2,037	−1,456
Portfolio investment liabilities	10,829	−4,418	−94
Other investment assets	−4	−2,837	−2,357
Other investment liabilities	5,188	1,828	1,408
Net errors and omissions	−110	−975	439
Overall balance	4,090	2,013	−1,176

Source: IMF, *International Financial Statistics.*

External Trade

PRINCIPAL COMMODITIES (distribution by SITC, US $ million)

Imports c.i.f.	1996	1997	1998
Food and live animals . . .	1,025.7	1,212.0	1,221.3
Crude materials (inedible) except fuels	787.4	1,023.4	912.8
Mineral fuels, lubricants, etc. .	885.8	927.1	818.0
Petroleum, petroleum products, etc.	616.7	617.7	490.4
Chemicals and related products	4,264.1	4,724.3	4,799.5
Organic chemicals . . .	1,226.9	1,397.6	1,362.6
Medicinal and pharmaceutical products . . .	582.6	663.6	781.1
Artificial resins, plastic materials, etc. . .	770.9	961.2	941.5
Products of polymerization, etc.	479.6	632.8	591.5
Basic manufactures . .	3,544.8	4,615.4	4,686.5
Paper, paperboard and manufactures . . .	721.8	865.8	916.0
Paper and paperboard (not cut to size or shape) . . .	583.1	693.3	761.4
Textile yarn, fabrics, etc. . .	609.7	792.5	794.7
Iron and steel	525.0	845.0	797.4
Machinery and transport equipment	10,902.0	14,794.2	15,449.0
Power-generating machinery and equipment	887.5	1,115.4	1,494.8
Internal combustion piston engines and parts . .	506.9	719.8	654.0
Machinery specialized for particular industries . . .	1,091.0	1,435.0	1,354.3
General industrial machinery, equipment and parts . .	1,867.0	2,247.4	2,179.8
Office machines and automatic data-processing equipment . .	815.3	1,125.0	1,249.4
Automatic data-processing machines, etc. . . .	543.1	746.2	806.3
Telecommunications and sound equipment . . .	1,083.1	1,720.7	1,685.2
Television and radio-broadcasting transmitters, etc.	281.4	653.4	682.3
Other electrical machinery, apparatus, etc. . .	1,604.3	2,112.6	2,074.8
Road vehicles and parts* . .	2,983.7	4,383.9	4,874.4
Passenger motor cars (excl. buses)	1,198.4	1,561.3	1,623.1
Motor vehicles for goods transport, etc. . .	532.9	866.5	1,169.9
Goods vehicles (lorries and trucks)	509.4	839.8	1,129.8
Parts and accessories for cars, buses, lorries, etc.* . .	1,061.4	1,620.3	1,686.0
Miscellaneous manufactured articles	2,209.7	2,779.2	2,883.2
Total (incl. others) . . .	23,761.6	30,349.5	31,029.7

Exports f.o.b.	1996	1997	1998
Food and live animals . . .	9,241.6	9,899.2	9,042.4
Meat and meat preparations . .	1,073.9	1,024.3	817.4
Fresh, chilled or frozen meat .	781.0	763.5	590.7
Meat of bovine animals .	627.1	622.8	474.1
Fish, crustaceans, molluscs and preparations . . .	1,003.9	1,028.4	861.8
Fish, fresh (live or dead), chilled or frozen	494.9	535.9	452.0
Cereals and cereal preparations .	2,802.9	3,293.6	3,254.5
Wheat (including spelt) and meslin, unmilled . .	1,065.7	1,343.1	1,298.4
Maize (corn), unmilled . . .	1,239.4	1,346.8	1,335.2
Vegetables and fruit . . .	1,180.5	1,273.8	1,264.6
Fresh or dried fruit and nuts (excl. oil nuts) . .	508.7	534.7	512.8
Feeding-stuff for animals (excl. unmilled cereals) . . .	2,367.0	2,399.3	1,945.9
Oilcake and other residues . .	2,293.4	2,313.6	1,867.5
Cake, etc., of soya beans .	1,984.1	2,039.7	1,691.7
Crude materials (inedible) except fuels	1,869.2	1,137.0	1,987.2
Oil seeds and oleaginous fruit .	955.1	326.8	1,030.9
Soya beans	588.2	144.4	643.1
Textile fibres and waste . . .	625.5	451.7	296.0
Cotton	500.8	335.9	226.3
Mineral fuels, lubricants, etc. .	3,096.2	3,073.8	1,937.7
Petroleum, petroleum products, etc.	2,973.3	2,933.5	1,790.4
Crude petroleum oils, etc. .	2,320.0	2,176.0	1,227.9
Refined petroleum products .	584.9	701.0	514.0
Animal and vegetable oils, fats and waxes	1,882.6	2,203.5	2,580.2
Fixed vegetable oils and fats .	1,857.2	2,179.0	2,556.8
Soya bean oil	900.8	1,043.0	1,383.6
Sunflower seed oil . . .	832.1	1,000.1	1,029.5
Chemicals and related products	1,320.1	1,499.5	1,679.3
Basic manufactures . . .	2,852.0	3,172.6	2,806.1
Leather, leather manufactures and dressed furskins . .	926.5	1,016.1	835.0
Leather	823.8	932.3	767.3
Iron and steel	797.8	865.3	827.2
Tubes, pipes and fittings . .	457.9	530.1	515.7
Machinery and transport equipment	2,592.5	3,944.5	4,060.0
Road vehicles and parts* . .	1,514.6	2,620.4	2,943.7
Passenger motor cars (excl. buses)	803.9	1,509.1	1,605.4
Motor vehicles for goods transport, etc. . .	253.1	606.5	793.0
Goods vehicles (lorries and trucks)	250.6	597.9	775.2
Miscellaneous manufactured articles	667.0	702.1	647.3
Total (incl. others) . . .	23,809.7	26,264.4	25,322.6

* Excluding tyres, engines and electrical parts.

Source: UN, *International Trade Statistics Yearbook*.

1999 (US $ million): Imports c.i.f. 25,508; Exports f.o.b. 23,333.

PRINCIPAL TRADING PARTNERS (US $ million)

Imports c.i.f.	1997	1998	1999*
Belgium	291	289	259
Brazil	6,914	7,005	5,596
Canada	450	385	290
Chile	688	708	639
China, People's Republic . .	1,006	1,167	992
France (incl. Monaco) . .	1,375	1,584	1,504
Germany	1,655	1,876	1,409
Italy	1,747	1,605	1,355
Japan	1,150	1,453	1,608
Mexico	610	603	491
Paraguay	320	348	304
Spain	1,256	1,285	1,000
United Kingdom	802	797	543
USA	6,095	6,227	4,996
Uruguay	371	528	389
Total (incl. others)	30,450	31,378	25,508

Exports f.o.b.	1997	1998	1999*
Belgium	304	278	310
Bolivia	464	431	321
Brazil	8,133	7,949	5,690
Canada	135	227	239
Chile	1,932	1,857	1,869
China, People's Republic . .	871	682	508
France (incl. Monaco) . .	310	315	349
Germany	503	564	629
Iran	659	476	155
Italy	730	753	689
Japan	554	657	528
Mexico	216	261	282
Netherlands	880	1,100	1,013
Paraguay	624	622	563
Peru	306	326	213
South Africa	304	253	308
Spain	623	842	962
United Kingdom	320	256	263
USA	2,204	2,212	2,653
Uruguay	840	843	812
Venezuela	315	364	247
Total (incl. others)	26,431	26,434	23,333

* Provisional.

Transport

RAILWAYS (traffic)

	1997	1998	1999
Passengers carried (million) . .	459	480	481
Freight carried ('000 tons) . .	18,904	18,828	17,489
Passenger-km (million) . .	9,324	9,652	9,102
Freight ton-km (million) . .	9,835	9,824	9,102

ROAD TRAFFIC (motor vehicles in use)

	1996	1997	1998
Passenger cars	4,783,908	4,901,265	5,047,630
Buses and coaches . . .	38,434	40,191	43,232
Lorries and vans	1,248,527	1,332,344	1,453,335
Motorcycles and mopeds . . .	35,640	n.a.	n.a.

Source: International Road Federation, *World Road Statistics*.

SHIPPING
Merchant Fleet (registered at 31 December)

	1998	1999	2000
Number of vessels . . .	501	493	493
Total displacement ('000 grt) . .	498.7	477.3	464.3

Source: Lloyd's Register of Shipping, *World Fleet Statistics*.

International Sea-borne Freight Traffic ('000 metric tons)

	1996	1997	1998
Goods loaded	52,068	58,512	69,372
Goods unloaded	16,728	19,116	19,536

Source: UN, *Monthly Bulletin of Statistics*.

CIVIL AVIATION (traffic on scheduled services)

	1995	1996	1997
Kilometres flown (million) . .	108	133	155
Passengers carried ('000) . .	6,642	7,193	8,600
Passenger-km (million) . .	11,892	13,360	14,338
Total ton-km (million) . .	1,338	1,447	1,600

Source: UN, *Statistical Yearbook*.

Tourism

TOURISM ARRIVALS BY REGION ('000)

	1996	1997	1998
Europe	298.9	317.8	341.4
North America	221.3	242.2	263.9
South America:			
Bolivia	119.8	142.9	145.2
Brazil	412.1	445.3	466.1
Chile	482.6	481.6	527.6
Paraguay	506.6	442.7	478.3
Uruguay	397.1	504.4	544.9
Total (incl. others*) . . .	2,613.9	2,764.2	2,969.8

* Excluding nationals residing abroad.

Source: World Tourism Organization, *Yearbook of Tourism Statistics*.

Tourism receipts (US $ million): 4,572 in 1996; 4,069 in 1997; 5,363 in 1998.

Communications Media

	1995	1996	1997
Radio receivers ('000 in use) . .	23,500	23,850	24,300
Television receivers ('000 in use)	7,600	7,800	7,950
Telephones* ('000 main lines in use)	5,532	6,120	6,824
Telefax stations*† ('000 in use)	50	60	70
Mobile cellular telephones* ('000 subscribers)	340.7	667.0	2,009.1
Daily newspapers	190†	181	n.a
Books (number of titles) . . .	9,113	9,850	11,919

* Year ending September.

† Estimate(s).

1998: Telephones ('000 main lines in use) 7,095; Books (number of titles) 13,156

Sources: mainly UNESCO, *Statistical Yearbook*, and UN, *Statistical Yearbook*.

Education

(1999)

	Institutions	Students	Teachers
Pre-primary	15,946	1,180,733	77,103
Primary	22,283	4,609,077	307,874
Secondary	21,492	3,281,512	127,718
Universities*	36	945,790	113,797
Colleges of higher education . .	1,708	391,010	12,427

* 1998 figures for state universities only.

Source: Ministerio de Cultura y Educación.

Directory

The Constitution

The return to civilian rule in 1983 represented a return to the principles of the 1853 Constitution, with some changes in electoral details. In August 1994 a new Constitution was approved, which contained 19 new articles, 40 amendments to existing articles and the addition of a chapter on New Rights and Guarantees. The Constitution is summarized below:

DECLARATIONS, RIGHTS AND GUARANTEES

Each province has the right to exercise its own administration of justice, municipal system and primary education. The Roman Catholic religion, being the faith of the majority of the nation, shall enjoy state protection; freedom of religious belief is guaranteed to all other denominations. The prior ethnical existence of indigenous peoples and their rights, as well as the common ownership of lands they traditionally occupy, are recognized. All inhabitants of the country have the right to work and exercise any legal trade; to petition the authorities; to leave or enter the Argentine territory; to use or dispose of their properties; to associate for a peaceable or useful purpose; to teach and acquire education, and to express freely their opinion in the press without censorship. The State does not admit any prerogative of blood, birth, privilege or titles of nobility. Equality is the basis of all duties and public offices. No citizens may be detained, except for reasons and in the manner prescribed by the law; or sentenced other than by virtue of a law existing prior to the offence and by decision of the competent tribunal after the hearing and defence of the person concerned. Private residence, property and correspondence are inviolable. No one may enter the home of a citizen or carry out any search in it without his consent, unless by a warrant from the competent authority; no one may suffer expropriation, except in case of public necessity and provided that the appropriate compensation has been paid in accordance with the provisions of the laws. In no case may the penalty of confiscation of property be imposed.

LEGISLATIVE POWER

Legislative power is vested in the bicameral Congreso (Congress), comprising the Cámara de Diputados (Chamber of Deputies) and the Senado (Senate). The Chamber of Deputies has 257 directly-elected members, chosen for four years and eligible for re-election; approximately one-half of the membership of the Chamber shall be renewed every two years. Until October 1995 the Senate had 48 members, chosen by provincial legislatures for a nine-year term, with one-third of the seats renewable every three years. Since October 1995 elections have provided for a third senator, elected by provincial legislatures. From 2001 the members of the expanded Senate will serve a six-year term.

The powers of Congress include regulating foreign trade; fixing import and export duties; levying taxes for a specified time whenever the defence, common safety or general welfare of the State so requires; contracting loans on the nation's credit; regulating the internal and external debt and the currency system of the country; fixing the budget and facilitating the prosperity and welfare of the nation. Congress must approve required and urgent decrees and delegated legislation. Congress also approves or rejects treaties, authorizes the Executive to declare war or make peace, and establishes the strength of the Armed Forces in peace and war.

EXECUTIVE POWER

Executive power is vested in the President, who is the supreme head of the nation and controls the general administration of the country. The President issues the instructions and rulings necessary for the execution of the laws of the country, and himself takes part in drawing up and promulgating those laws. The President appoints, with the approval of the Senate, the judges of the Supreme Court and all other competent tribunals, ambassadors, civil servants, members of the judiciary and senior officers of the Armed Forces and bishops. The President may also appoint and remove, without reference to another body, his cabinet ministers. The President is Commander-in-Chief of all the Armed Forces. The President and Vice-President are elected directly for a four-year term, renewable only once.

JUDICIAL POWER

Judicial power is exercised by the Supreme Court and all other competent tribunals. The Supreme Court is responsible for the internal administration of all tribunals. In April 1990 the number of Supreme Court judges was increased from five to nine.

PROVINCIAL GOVERNMENT

The 22 provinces, the Federal District of Buenos Aires and the National Territory of Tierra del Fuego retain all the power not delegated to the Federal Government. They are governed by their own institutions and elect their own governors, legislators and officials.

The Government

HEAD OF STATE

President of the Republic: FERNANDO DE LA RÚA (took office 10 December 1999).

Vice-President of the Republic: (vacant).

CABINET
(August 2001)

Cabinet Chief: CHRYSTIAN COLOMBO.

Minister of the Interior: RAMÓN MESTRE.

Minister of Foreign Affairs, International Trade and Worship: ADALBERTO RODRÍGUEZ GIAVARINI.

Minister of Education: ANDRÉS DELICH.

Minister of Defence: HORACIO JAUNARENA.

Minister of the Economy: DOMINGO CAVALLO.

Minister of Infrastructure and Housing: CARLOS BASTOS.

Minister of Labour: PATRICIA BULLRICH.

Minister of Health: HÉCTOR LOMBARDO.

Minister of Justice and Human Rights: JORGE DE LA RÚA.

Minister of Social Development and the Environment: JUAN PABLO CAFIERO.

MINISTRIES

General Secretariat to the Presidency: Balcarce 50, 1064 Buenos Aires; tel. (11) 4344-3662; fax (11) 4344-3789; e-mail secgral-@presidencia.net.ar.

Ministry of Defence: Azopardo 250, 1328 Buenos Aires; tel. (11) 4346-8800; e-mail mindef@mindef.gov.ar; internet www.mindef.-gov.ar.

Ministry of the Economy: Hipólito Yrigoyen 250, 1310 Buenos Aires; tel. (11) 4349-5000; e-mail edinfpub@mecon.gov.ar; internet www.mecon.gov.ar.

Ministry of Education: Pizzurno 935, 1020 Buenos Aires; tel. (11) 4129-1000; e-mail info@me.gov.ar; internet www.me.gov.ar/index1.html.

Ministry of Foreign Affairs, International Trade and Worship: Esmeralda 1212, 1007 Buenos Aires; tel. (11) 4819-7000; e-mail web@mrecic.gov.ar; internet www.mrecic.gov.ar.

Ministry of Health: 9 de Julio 1925, 1332 Buenos Aires; tel. (11) 4381-8911; fax (11) 4381-2182; internet www.msal.gov.ar.

Ministry of Infrastructure and Housing: Avda Paseo Colón 171, 1063 Buenos Aires; tel. (11) 4349-5000.

Ministry of the Interior: Balcarce 50, 1064 Buenos Aires; tel. (11) 446-9841; fax (11) 4331-6376; internet www.mininterior.gov.ar.

Ministry of Justice and Human Rights: Sarmiento 329, 1041 Buenos Aires; tel. (11) 4328-3015; internet www.jus.gov.ar.

Ministry of Labour: Leandro N. Alem 650, 1001 Buenos Aires; tel. (11) 4311-2913; fax (11) 4312-7860; internet www.trabajo.gov.ar.

Ministry of Social Development and the Environment: Avda 9 de Julio 1925, 14°, 1332 Buenos Aires; tel. (11) 4379-3600; e-mail desarrollosocial@desarrollosocial.gov.ar; internet www.desarrollo-social.gov.ar.

President and Legislature

PRESIDENT

Election, 24 October 1999

Candidates	Votes	% votes cast
FERNANDO DE LA RÚA (ATJE)	9,039,892	48.50
EDUARDO DUHALDE (PJ)	7,100,678	38.09
DOMINGO CAVALLO (AR)	1,881,417	10.09
Others	618,846	3.32
Total	18,640,833	100.00

CONGRESO
Cámara de Diputados
(Chamber of Deputies)

President: RAFAEL MANUEL PASCUAL.

The Chamber has 257 members, who hold office for a four-year term, with approximately one-half of the seats renewable every two years.

Legislative Elections, 24 October 1999*

	Seats
Alianza para el Trabajo, la Justicia y la Educación (ATJE)†	127
Partido Justicialista (PJ)	101
Acción por la República (AR)	12
Others	17
Total	257

* The table indicates the distribution of the total number of seats, following the elections for 130 seats.
† Alliance comprising Frente del País Solidario and the Unión Cívica Radical.

Senado
(Senate)

President: MARIO LOSADA.

Distribution of Seats, November 1997*

	Seats
Partido Justicialista (PJ)	36
Unión Cívica Radical (UCR)	15
Frente del País Solidario (Frepaso)	2
Provincial parties	10
Total	63

* Until October 1995 the Senate comprised 48 members, who were nominated by the legislative bodies of the Federal District, the National Territory, and each province (two Senators for each), with the exception of Buenos Aires, which elected its Senators by means of a special Electoral College. The Senate's term of office was nine years, with one-third of the seats renewable every three years. Since October 1995 elections have provided for an expanded Senate (three members from each region) with a six-year term of office (one-third of the seats being renewable every three years).

PROVINCIAL ADMINISTRATORS
(August 2001)

Mayor of the Federal District of Buenos Aires: ANÍBAL IBARRA.

Governor of the Province of Buenos Aires: CARLOS RUCKAUF.

Governor of the Province of Catamarca: OSCAR CASTILLO.

Governor of the Province of Chaco: ANGEL ROZAS.

Governor of the Province of Chubut: JOSÉ LUIS LIZURUME.

Governor of the Province of Córdoba: JOSÉ MANUEL DE LA SOTA.

Governor of the Province of Corrientes: (vacant)*.

Governor of the Province of Entre Ríos: SERGIO MONTIEL.

Governor of the Province of Formosa: GILDO INSFRÁN.

Governor of the Province of Jujuy: EDUARDO FELLNER.

Governor of the Province of La Pampa: RUBÉN HUGO MARÍN.

Governor of the Province of La Rioja: ANGEL EDUARDO MAZA.

Governor of the Province of Mendoza: ROBERTO IGLESIAS.

Governor of the Province of Misiones: CARLOS ROVIRA.

Governor of the Province of Neuquén: JORGE SOBISCH.

Governor of the Province of Río Negro: PABLO VERANI.

Governor of the Province of Salta: JUAN CARLOS ROMERO.

Governor of the Province of San Juan: ALFREDO AVELÍN.

Governor of the Province of San Luis: ADOLFO RODRÍGUEZ SAA.

Governor of the Province of Santa Cruz: NÉSTOR KIRSCHNER.

Governor of the Province of Santa Fe: CARLOS REUTEMANN.

Governor of the Province of Santiago del Estero: CARLOS JUÁREZ.

Governor of the Province of Tucumán: JULIO MIRANDA.

Governor of the Territory of Tierra del Fuego: CARLOS MANFREDOTTI.

* Ramón Mestre was appointed as mediator of Corrientes in December 1999.

Political Organizations

Acción por la República—Nueva Dirigencia (AR—ND): Buenos Aires; f. 1997; electoral alliance; Leaders CARO FIGUEROA.

Acción por la República (AR): Buenos Aires; e-mailaccionrepu blic@geocities.com; f. 1997; right-wing; Leader CARO FIGUEROA.

Nueva Dirigencia (ND): Buenos Aires; f. 1996; centre-right; Leader GUSTAVO BÉLIZ.

Alianza para el Trabajo, la Justicia y la Educación (ATJE): Buenos Aires; f. 1997; electoral alliance comprising the UCR and Frepaso.

Frente del País Solidario (Frepaso): Buenos Aires; internet www.visit-ar.com/nuevoespacio/frepaso.htm; f. 1994; centre-left coalition of socialist, communist and Christian Democrat groups; Leader CARLOS ALVAREZ.

Unión Cívica Radical (UCR): Alsina 1786, 1088 Buenos Aires; tel. and fax (11) 4375-2000; e-mail info@ucr.org.ar; internet www.uc r.org.ar; moderate; f. 1890; Pres. RAÚL ALFONSÍN; 2,920,650 mems.

Movimiento por la Dignidad y la Independencia (Modin): Buenos Aires; f. 1991; right-wing; Leader Col ALDO RICO.

Movimiento de Integración y Desarrollo (MID): Buenos Aires; f. 1963; Leader ARTURO FRONDIZI; 145,000 mems.

Movimiento al Socialismo (MAS): Chile 1362, 1098 Buenos Aires; tel. (11) 4381-2718; fax (11) 4381-2976; e-mail mas@giga.com.ar; internet www.wp.com/mas; Leaders RUBÉN VISCONTI, LUIS ZAMORA; 55,000 mems.

Partido Comunista de Argentina: Buenos Aires; f. 1918; Leader PATRICIO ECHEGARAY; Sec.-Gen. ATHOS FAVA; 76,000 mems.

Partido Demócrata Cristiano (PDC): Combate de los Pozos 1055, 1222 Buenos Aires; fax (11) 426-3413; f. 1954; Leader ESIO ARIEL SILVEIRA; 85,000 mems.

Partido Demócrata Progresista (PDP): Chile 1934, 1227 Buenos Aires; Leader RAFAEL MARTÍNEZ RAYMONDA; 97,000 mems.

Partido Intransigente: Buenos Aires; f. 1957; left-wing; Leaders Dr OSCAR ALENDE, LISANDRO VIALE; Sec. MARIANO LORENCES; 90,000 mems.

Partido Justicialista (PJ): Buenos Aires; Peronist party; f. 1945; Pres. CARLOS SAÚL MENEM; 3m. mems; three factions within party:

Frente Renovador, Justicia, Democracia y Participación— Frejudepa: f. 1985; reformist wing; Leaders CARLOS SAÚL MENEM, ANTONIO CAFIERO, CARLOS GROSSO.

Movimiento Nacional 17 de Octubre: Leader HERMINIO IGLESIAS.

Oficialistas: Leaders JOSÉ MARÍA VERNET, LORENZO MIGUEL.

Partido Nacional de Centro: Buenos Aires; f. 1980; conservative; Leader RAÚL RIVANERA CARLES.

Partido Nacionalista de los Trabajadores (PNT): Buenos Aires; f. 1990; extreme right-wing; Leader ALEJANDRO BIONDINI.

Partido Obrero: Ayacucho 444, Buenos Aires; tel. (11) 4953-3824; fax (11) 4953-7164; internet www.po.org.ar; f. 1982; Trotskyist; Leaders JORGE ALTAMIRA, CHRISTIAN RATH; 61,000 mems.

Partido Popular Cristiano: Leader JOSÉ ANTONIO ALLENDE.

Partido Socialista Democrático: Rivadavia 2307, 1034 Buenos Aires; Leader AMÉRICO GHIOLDI; 39,000 mems.

Partido Socialista Popular: f. 1982; Leaders GUILLERMO ESTÉVEZ BOERO, EDGARDO ROSSI; 60,500 mems.

Política Abierta para la Integridad Social (PAIS): Buenos Aires; f. 1994 following split with the PJ.

Unión del Centro Democrático (UCeDé): Buenos Aires; f. 1980 as coalition of eight minor political organizations to challenge the 'domestic monopoly' of the populist movements; Leader ÁLVARO ALSOGARAY.

Unión para la Nueva Mayoría: Buenos Aires; f. 1986; centre-right; Leader JOSÉ ANTONIO ROMERO FERIS.

The following political parties and groupings contested the 1999 presidential elections: Alianza Cristiana Social, Frente para la Resistencia Social, Izquierda Unida, Partido Humanista, Partido Obrero, Partido Socialista Auténtico and the Partido de Trabajadores Socialistas.

Other parties and groupings include: Afirmación Peronista, Alianza Socialista, Confederación Socialista Argentina, Cruzada Renovadora (San Juan), Frente Cívica y Socialista (Catamarca), Fuerza Republicana (Tucumán), Movimiento Línea Popular, Movimiento Patriótico de Liberación, Movimiento Peronista, Movimiento Popular Neuquino, Movimiento Popular (Tierra del Fuego), Partido Autonomista (Corrientes), Partido Bloquista de San Juan, Partido Conservador Popular, Partido Izquierda Nacional, Partido Liberal (Corrientes), Partido Obrero Comunista Marxista-Leninista, Partido Socialista Unificado and Renovador de Salta.

The following political parties and guerrilla groups are illegal:

Intransigencia y Movilización Peronista: Peronist faction; Leader NILDA GARRES.

Movimiento Todos por la Patria (MTP): left-wing movement.

Partido Peronista Auténtico (PPA): f. 1975; Peronist faction; Leaders MARIO FIRMENICH, OSCAR BIDEGAIN, RICARDO OBREGÓN CANO.

Partido Revolucionario de Trabajadores: political wing of the **Ejército Revolucionario del Pueblo (ERP);** Leader LUIS MATTINI.

Triple A—Alianza Anticomunista Argentina: extreme right-wing; Leader ANÍBAL GORDON (in prison).

Diplomatic Representation

EMBASSIES IN ARGENTINA

Albania: Avda del Libertador 946, 4°, 1001 Buenos Aires; tel. (11) 4812-8366; fax (11) 4815-2512; e-mail ambasada.bue@netsat.com.ar; Ambassador: EDMOND TRAKO.

Algeria: Montevideo 1889, 1021 Buenos Aires; tel. (11) 4815-1271; fax (11) 4815-8837; e-mail argelia@peoples.com.ar; Ambassador: NOURREDINE AYADI.

Armenia: Avda Roque S. Peña 570, 3°, 1035 Buenos Aires; tel. (11) 4345-2051; fax (11) 4343-2467; e-mail armenia@teletel.com.ar; Ambassador: ARA AIVASYAN.

Australia: Villanueva 1400, 1426 Buenos Aires; tel. (11) 4777-6580; fax (11) 4776-3349; e-mail dima-buenos_aires@dfait.gov.au; internet www.australia.org.ar; Ambassador: SHARYN MINAHAN.

Austria: French 3671, 1425 Buenos Aires; tel. (11) 4802-7195; fax (11) 4805-4016; Ambassador: YURI STANDENAT.

Belarus: Cazadores 2166, 1428 Buenos Aires; tel. (11) 4788-9394; fax (11) 4788-2322; Ambassador: VADIM LAZERKO.

Belgium: Defensa 113, 8°, 1065 Buenos Aires; tel. (11) 4331-0066; fax (11) 4311-0814; e-mail buenosaires@diplobel.org; internet www.diplobel.org/argentina/default.htm; Ambassador: RONALD DE LANGHE.

Bolivia: Avda Corrientes 545, 2°, 1043 Buenos Aires; tel. (11) 4394-6042; Ambassador: FERNANDO B. BALLIVIAN.

Bosnia and Herzegovina: Miñones 2445, Buenos Aires; tel. (11) 4896-0284; fax (11) 4896-0351; Ambassador: DUSKO LADAN.

Brazil: Arroyo 1142, 1007 Buenos Aires; tel. (11) 444-0035; fax (11) 4814-4085; e-mail embras@embrasil.org.ar; internet www.brasil .org.ar; Ambassador: SEBASTIÃO DO REGO BARROS NETTO.

Bulgaria: Mariscal A. J. de Sucre 1568, 1428 Buenos Aires; tel. (11) 4781-8644; fax (11) 4786-6273; e-mail embular@sinectis.com.ar; internet www.sinectis.com.ar/u/embular; Ambassador: ATRANAS I. BUDEV.

Canada: Tagle 2828, 1425 Buenos Aires; tel. (11) 4805-3032; fax (11) 4806-1209; internet www.dfait-maeci.gc.ca/bairs; Ambassador: JEAN-PAUL HUBERT.

Chile: Tagle 2762, 1425 Buenos Aires; tel. (11) 4802-7020; fax (11) 4804-5927; Ambassador: JORGE ARRATE MACNIVEN.

China, People's Republic: Avda Crisólogo Larralde 5349, 1431 Buenos Aires; tel. (11) 4543-8862; fax (11) 4545-1141; Ambassador: ZHANG SHAYING.

Colombia: Carlos Pellegrini 1363, 3°, 1010 Buenos Aires; tel. (11) 4325-0494; fax (11) 4322-9370; e-mail emargent@internet.siscot el.com; Ambassador: NELSON P. HERNÁNDEZ.

Congo, Democratic Republic: Callao 322, 2°, Buenos Aires; tel. (11) 4373-7565; fax (11) 4374-9865; Chargé d'affaires a.i.: YEMBA LOHAKA.

Costa Rica: Avda Callao 1103, 9°I, 1023 Buenos Aires; tel. (11) 4815-8160; fax (11) 4815-8159; e-mail embarica@infovia.com.ar; Ambassador: EDUARDO F. OTOYA BOULANGER.

Croatia: Gorostiaga 2104, 1426 Buenos Aires; tel. (11) 4777-6409; fax (11) 4777-9159; e-mail vrbsas@infovia.com.ar; Chargé d'affaires a.i. GORDANA MESTROVIC.

Cuba: Virrey del Pino 1810, 1426 Buenos Aires; tel. (11) 4782-9049; fax (11) 4786-7713; e-mail embcuba@teletel.com.ar; Ambassador: ALEJANDRO J. GONZÁLEZ.

Czech Republic: Villanueva 1356, 2° Buenos Aires; tel. (11) 4777-0435; fax (11) 4771-0075; e-mail buenosaires@embassy.mzv.cz; Ambassador: EDITA HRDA.

Denmark: Avda Leandro N. Alem 1074, 9°, 1001 Buenos Aires; tel. (11) 4312-6901; fax (11) 4312-7857; e-mail ambadane@ambad ane.org.ar; Ambassador: JENS PETER LARSEN.

Dominican Republic: Avda Santa Fe 1206, 2°c, 1059 Buenos Aires; tel. (11) 4811-4669; fax (11) 4804-3902; Ambassador: CIRILO J. CASTELLANOS ARAÚJO.

Ecuador: Quintana 585, 9° y 10°, 1129 Buenos Aires; tel. (11) 4804-0073; fax (11) 4804-0074; Ambassador: HARRY KLEIN MANN.

Egypt: Olleros 2140, 1425 Buenos Aires; tel. (11) 4899-0300; fax (11) 4899-0803; Ambassador: MOHAMED DAGHASH.

El Salvador: Esmeralda 1066, 7°, 1059 Buenos Aires; tel. (11) 4311-1864; fax (11) 4314-7628; Ambassador: ALFONSO QUIÑÓNEZ MEZA.

Finland: Avda Santa Fe 846, 5°, 1059 Buenos Aires; tel. (11) 4312-0600; fax (11) 4312-0670; e-mail finembue@sinectis.com.ar; internet www.finlandia.org.ar; Ambassador: RISTO KAARLO VELTHEIM.

France: Cerrito 1399, 1010 Buenos Aires; tel. (11) 4819-2930; fax (11) 4393-1235; e-mail ambafr@impsat1.com.ar; internet www.embafrancia-argentina.org; Ambassador: PAUL DIJOUD.

Germany: Villanueva 1055, 1426 Buenos Aires; tel. (11) 4778-2500; fax (11) 4778-2550; e-mail embalem@infovia.com.ar; internet www.embalemana.com.ar; Ambassador: HANS ULRICH D. SPOHN.

Greece: Avda Roque S. Peña 547, 4°, 1035 Buenos Aires; tel. (11) 4342-4598; fax (11) 4342-2838; Ambassador: GEORGES GEORGIOU.

Guatemala: Avda Santa Fe 830, 5°, 1059 Buenos Aires; tel. (11) 4313-9160; fax (11) 4313-9181; e-mail embagua@peoples.com.ar; Ambassador: ERNESTO GÁLVEZ CORONADO.

Haiti: Avda Figueroa Alcorta 3297, 1425 Buenos Aires; tel. (11) 4802-0211; fax (11) 4802-3984; e-mail embahaiti@interar.com.ar; Ambassador: EDRIS SAINT-AMAND.

Holy See: Avda Alvear 1605, 1014 Buenos Aires; tel. (11) 4813-9697; fax (11) 4815-4097; Apostolic Nuncio: Most Rev. SANTOS ABRIL Y CASTELLÓ, Titular Archbishop of Tamada.

Honduras: Avda Libertador 1146, 1112 Buenos Aires; tel. (11) 4804-6181; fax (11) 4804-3222; e-mail honduras@ciudad.com.ar; Ambassador: NAPOLEÓN ALVAREZ ALVARADO.

Hungary: Coronel Díaz 1874, 1425 Buenos Aires; tel. (11) 4822-0767; fax (11) 4805-3918; e-mail hungria@escape.com.ar; Ambassador: BELA BARDOCZ.

India: Córdoba 950, 4°, 1054 Buenos Aires; tel. (11) 4393-4001; fax (11) 4393-4063; e-mail indembarg@infomatic.com.ar; internet www.indembarg.org.ar; Ambassador: NIGAM PRAKASH.

Indonesia: Mariscal Ramón Castilla 2901, 1425 Buenos Aires; tel. (11) 4807-2211; fax (11) 4802-4448; e-mail emindo@tournet.com.ar; Ambassador: ACHMAD SURYADI.

Iran: Avda Figueroa Alcorta 3229, 1425 Buenos Aires; tel. (11) 4802-1470; fax (11) 4805-4409; Chargé d'affaires a.i.: ABDOLRAHIM SADATIFAR.

Ireland: Suipacha 1380, 2°, 1011 Buenos Aires; tel. (11) 4325-8588; fax (11) 4325-7572; e-mail embirl@tournet.com.ar; internet irlgov.ie/iveagh; Ambassador: PAULA SLATTERY.

Israel: Avda. de Mayo 701, 10°, 1084 Buenos Aires; tel. (11) 4338-2500; internet www.israel-embassy.org.ar/embajada.html; Ambassador: BENJAMIN ORON.

Italy: Billinghurst 2577, 1425 Buenos Aires; tel. (11) 4802-0071;fax (11) 4804-4914; e-mail stampa@ambitalia-bsas.org.ar; internet www.ambitalia-bsas.org.ar; Ambassador: GIOVANNI JANNUZZI.

Japan: Bouchard 547, 17°, Buenos Aires; tel. (11) 4318-8200; fax (11) 4318-8210; Ambassador: TERUO KIJIMA.

Korea, Republic: Avda del Libertador 2395, 1425 Buenos Aires; tel. (11) 4802-8062; fax (11) 4803-6993; e-mail embcorea@cscom.com.ar; internet www.mofat.go.kr/argentina.htm; Ambassador: SEUNG-YOUNG KIM.

Kuwait: Uruguay 739, 1015 Buenos Aires; tel. (11) 4374-7202; fax (11) 4374-8718; e-mail kuwait@microstar.com.ar; internet www.kuwait.com.ar; Ambassador: SALEM G. AZ-ZAMANAN.

Lebanon: Avda del Libertador 2354, 1425 Buenos Aires; tel. (11) 4802-4492; fax (11) 4802-2909; Ambassador: HICHAM SALIM HAMDAN.

Libya: 3 de Febrero 1358, 1426 Buenos Aires; tel. (11) 4788-3760; fax (11) 4788-9394; Chargé d'affaires a.i.: MOHAMED M. ELHABESHI.

Malaysia: Villanueva 1040-1048, 1062 Buenos Aires; tel. (11) 4776-0504; e-mail malasia@fibertel.com.ar; Ambassador: Dato M. SANTHANANABAN.

Mexico: Larrea 1230, 1117 Buenos Aires; tel. (11) 4821-7172; fax (11) 4821-7251; e-mail embamexarg@intlink.com.ar; Ambassador: MARIA GREEN MACIAS.

Morocco: Mariscal Ramón Castilla 2952, 1425 Buenos Aires; tel. (11) 4801-8154; fax (11) 4802-0136; e-mail sifamabueno@tournet.com.ar; internet www.embajadamarruecos.org.ar; Ambassador: MOHAMED MAA EL-AININ.

Netherlands: Avda de Mayo 701, 19°, 1084 Buenos Aires; tel. (11) 4334-4000; fax (11) 4334-2717; e-mail nlgovbue@informatic.com.ar; Ambassador: J. E. CRAANEN.

New Zealand: Carlos Pellegrine 1427, 5°, 1010; Buenos Aires; tel. (11) 4328-0747; fax (11) 4328-0757; Ambassador: CAROLINE FORSYTH.

Nicaragua: Avda Corrientes 2548, 4°I, 1426 Buenos Aires; tel. (11) 4951-3463; fax (11) 4952-7557; e-mail embanic@overnet.com.ar; Ambassador: EMILIO J. SOLIS BERMUDEZ.

Nigeria: Rosales 2674, 1636 Olivos, Buenos Aires; tel. (11) 4771-6541; fax (11) 4790-7564; Ambassador: MOHAMMAD A. WALI.

Norway: Esmeralda 909, 3°B, 1007 Buenos Aires; tel. (11) 4312-2204; fax (11) 4315-2831; e-mail embajada.noruega@way.net.ar; Ambassador: SISSEL BREIE.

Pakistan: Gorostiaga 2176, 1426 Buenos Aires; tel. (11) 4782-7663; fax (11) 4776-1186; e-mail parepbaires@sinectis.com.ar; Ambassador: SAEED KHALID.

Panama: Avda Santa Fe 1461, 5°, 1060 Buenos Aires; tel. (11) 4811-1254; fax (11) 4814-0450; e-mail epar@ba.net; Ambassador: MERCEDES ALFARO DE LÓPEZ.

Paraguay: Avda Las Heras 2545, 1425 Buenos Aires; tel. (11) 4802-3826; fax (11) 4801-0657; Ambassador: CARLOS ALBERTO GONZÁLEZ GARABELLI.

Peru: Avda del Libertador 1720, 1425 Buenos Aires; tel. (11) 4802-2000; fax (11) 4802-5887; Ambassador: HUGO DE ZELA MARTÍNEZ.

Philippines: Juramento 1945, 1428 Buenos Aires; tel. (11) 4781-4173; fax (11) 4783-8171; e-mail phba@peoples.com.ar; Ambassador: CARLOS A. VILLA ABRILLE.

Poland: Alejandro M. de Aguado 2870, 1425 Buenos Aires; tel. (11) 4802-9681; fax (11) 4802-9683; e-mail polemb@datamarkets.com.ar; Ambassador: EUGENIUSZ NOWORYTA.

Portugal: Córdoba 315, 3°, 1054 Buenos Aires; tel. (11) 4311-2586; fax (11) 4311-2586; Ambassador: JOSÉ A. BAPTISTA LÓPEZ E SEABRA.

Romania: Arroyo 962-970, 1007 Buenos Aires; tel. and fax (11) 4322-2600; e-mail embarombue@fibertel.com.ar; Ambassador: CRISTIAN LAZARESCU.

Russia: Rodríguez Peña 1741, 1021 Buenos Aires; tel. (11) 4813-1552; fax (11) 4812-1794; Ambassador: EVGENY M. ASTAKHOV.

Saudi Arabia: Alejandro M. de Aguado 2881, 1425 Buenos Aires; tel. (11) 4802-4735; Ambassador: ADNAN B. BAGHDADI.

Slovakia: Avda Figueroa Alcorta 3240, 1425 Buenos Aires; tel. (11) 4786-0692; fax (11) 4786-0938; Ambassador: JAN JURISTA.

Slovenia: Suipacha 1380, 3°, 1001 Buenos Aires; tel. (11) 4393-2067; fax (11) 4326-0829; Chargé d'affaires a.i.: TOMAZ KUNSTELJ.

South Africa: Marcelo T. de Alvear 590, 8°, 1058 Buenos Aires; tel. (11) 4317-2900; fax (11) 4317-2951; e-mail saemba@sicoar.com; Ambassador: AUBREY X. NKOMO.

Spain: Mariscal Ramón Castilla 2720, 1425 Buenos Aires; tel. (11) 4802-6031; fax (11) 4802-0719; Ambassador: MANUEL ALABART.

Sweden: Casilla 3599, Correo Central 1000, Buenos Aires; tel. (11) 4311-3088; fax (11) 4311-8052; e-mail swedemb@infovia.com.ar; Ambassador: PETER LANDELIUS.

Switzerland: Avda Santa Fe 846, 10°, 1059 Buenos Aires; tel. (11) 4311-6491; fax (11) 4313-2998; e-mail vertretung@bue.rep.admin.ch; Ambassador: ARMIN RITZ.

Syria: Calloa 956, 1023 Buenos Aires; tel. (11) 4813-2113; fax (11) 4814-3211; Ambassador: MASSOUN KASSAWAT.

Thailand: Virrey del Pino 2458, 6°, 1426 Buenos Aires; tel. (11) 4785-6504; fax (11) 4785-6548; e-mail thbsemb@tournet.com.ar; Ambassador: PONGSAK DISYATAT.

Tunisia: Ciudad de la Paz 3086, 1429 Buenos Aires; tel. (11) 4544-2618; fax (11) 4545-6369; e-mail embtun@peoples.com.ar; Ambassador: GHAZI JOMAA.

Turkey: 11 de Setiembre 1382, 1426 Buenos Aires; tel. (11) 4788-3239; fax (11) 4784-9179; e-mail iyihava@ba.net; Ambassador: ERHAN YIGITBASIOGLU.

Ukraine: Lafinur 3057, 1425 Buenos Aires; tel. (11) 4802-7316; fax (11) 4802-3864; Ambassador: OLEKSANDR MAIDANNYK.

United Kingdom: Dr Luis Agote 2412/52, 1425 Buenos Aires; tel. (11) 4803-7070; fax (11) 4806-5713; e-mail ukembarg@starnet.net.ar; internet www.britain.org.ar; Ambassador: Sir ROBIN CHRISTOPHER.

USA: Avda Colombia 4300, 1425 Buenos Aires; tel. (11) 4774-7611; fax (11) 4775-4205; internet usembassy.state.gov/baires_embassy; Ambassador: JAMES D. WALSH.

Uruguay: Avda Las Heras 1907, 1127 Buenos Aires; tel. (11) 4803-6030; fax (11) 4807-3050; e-mail embarou@impsat1.com.ar; Ambassador: ALBERTO C. VOLONTÉ BERRO.

Venezuela: Virrey Loreto 2035, 1428 Buenos Aires; tel. (11) 4788-4944; fax (11) 4784-4311; e-mail venargs@peoples.com.ar; internet www.la-embajada.com.ar; Ambassador: EDMUNDO GONZÁLEZ URRUTIA.

Viet Nam: 11 de Septiembre 1442, 1426 Buenos Aires; tel. (11) 4783-1802; fax (11) 4782-0078; e-mail sqvnartn@teletel.com.ar; Ambassador: HOAN TRAN-QUANG.

Yugoslavia: Marcelo T. de Alvear 1705, 1060 Buenos Aires; tel. (11) 4811-2860; fax (11) 4812-1070; e-mail snovak@ipm.net; Ambassador: GOJKO CELEBIC.

Judicial System

SUPREME COURT

Corte Suprema: Talcahuano 550, 4°, 1013 Buenos Aires; tel. (11) 440-0837; fax (11) 440-2270; internet www.pjn.gov.ar/corte.htm.

The nine members of the Supreme Court are appointed by the President, with the agreement of at least two-thirds of the Senate. Members are dismissed by impeachment.

President: JULIO SALVADOR NAZARENO.

Vice-President: EDUARDO MOLINÉ O'CONNOR.

Justices: CARLOS SANTIAGO FAYT, AUGUSTO CÉSAR BELLUSCIO, ENRIQUE SANTIAGO PETRACCHI, ADOLFO VÁZQUEZ, ANTONIO BOGGIANO, GUILLERMO A. F. LÓPEZ, GUSTAVO A. BOSSERT.

OTHER COURTS

Judges of the lower, national or further lower courts are appointed by the President, with the agreement of the Senate, and are dismissed by impeachment. From 1999, however, judges were to retire on reaching 75 years of age.

The Federal Court of Appeal in Buenos Aires has three courts: civil and commercial, criminal, and administrative. There are six other courts of appeal in Buenos Aires: civil, commercial, criminal, peace, labour, and penal-economic. There are also federal appeal courts in: La Plata, Bahía Blanca, Paraná, Rosario, Córdoba, Mendoza, Tucumán and Resistencia. In August 1994, following constitutional amendments, the Office of the Attorney-General was established as an independent entity and a Council of Magistrates was envisaged. In December 1997 the Senate adopted legislation to create the Council.

The provincial courts each have their own Supreme Court and a system of subsidiary courts. They deal with cases originating within and confined to the provinces.

Attorney-General: OSCAR LUJÁN FAPPIANO.

Religion

CHRISTIANITY

More than 90% of the population are Roman Catholics and about 2% are Protestants.

Federación Argentina de Iglesias Evangélicas (Argentine Federation of Evangelical Churches): José María Moreno 873, 1424 Buenos Aires; tel. and fax (11) 4922-5356; e-mail faie@faie.com.ar; f. 1938; 29 mem. churches; Pres. Rev. RODOLFO B. REINICH (Río de la Plata Evangelical Church); Exec. Sec. Rev. FLORENCIA HIMITIAN.

The Roman Catholic Church

Argentina comprises 14 archdioceses, 50 dioceses (including one each for Uniate Catholics of the Ukrainian rite, of the Maronite rite and of the Armenian rite) and three territorial prelatures. The Archbishop of Buenos Aires is also the Ordinary for Catholics of Oriental rites, and the Bishop of San Gregorio de Narek en Buenos Aires is also the Apostolic Exarch of Latin America and Mexico for Catholics of the Armenian rite.

Bishops' Conference: Conferencia Episcopal Argentina, Suipacha 1034, 1008 Buenos Aires; tel. (11) 4328-0993; fax (11) 4328-9570; e-mail seccea@satlink.com.ar; f. 1959; Pres. Mgr ESTANISLAO ESTEBAN KARLIC, Archbishop of Paraná.

Armenian Rite

Bishop of San Gregorio de Narek en Buenos Aires: VARTAN WALDIR BOGHOSSIAN, Charcas 3529, 1425 Buenos Aires; tel. (11) 4824-1613; fax (11) 4827-1975; e-mail exarmal@usa.net; internet www.fast.to/exarcado.

Latin Rite

Archbishop of Bahía Blanca: RÓMULO GARCÍA, Avda Colón 164, 8000 Bahía Blanca; tel. (291) 455-0707; fax (291) 452-2070; e-mail arzobispado@bblanca.com.ar.

Archbishop of Buenos Aires: Cardinal JORGE BERGOGLIO, Arzobispado, Rivadavia 415, 1002 Buenos Aires; tel. (11) 4343-3925; fax (11) 4334-8373; e-mail arzobispado@arzbaires.org.ar.

Archbishop of Córdoba: CARLOS JOSÉ NÁÑEZ, Hipólito Yrigoyen 98, 5000 Córdoba; tel. (351) 422-1015; fax (351) 425-5082.

Archbishop of Corrientes: DOMINGO SALVADOR CASTAGNA, 9 de Julio 1543, 3400 Corrientes; tel. and fax (3783) 422436; e-mail arzctes@arnet.com.ar.

Archbishop of La Plata: HÉCTOR RUBÉN AGUER, Arzobispado, Calle 14, 1009, 1900 La Plata; tel. (221) 425-1656; fax (221) 425-8269; e-mail arzolap@satlink.com.

Archbishop of Mendoza: JOSÉ MARÍA ARANCIBIA, Catamarca 98, 5500 Mendoza; tel. (261) 423-3862; fax (261) 429-5415; e-mailarzo bispadomza@supernet.com.ar.

Archbishop of Mercedes-Luján: RUBÉN HÉCTOR DI MONTE, Calle 22, No 745, 6600 Mercedes, Buenos Aires; tel. (2324) 432-412; fax (2324) 432-104; e-mail arzomerce@yahoo.com.

Archbishop of Paraná: Mgr ESTANISLAO ESTEBAN KARLIC, Monte Caseros 77, 3100 Paraná; tel. (343) 431-1440; fax (343) 423-0372; e-mail arzparan@satlink.com.ar.

Archbishop of Resistencia: CARMELO JUAN GIAQUINTA, Bartolomé Mitre 363, Casilla 35, 3500 Resistencia; tel. and fax (3722) 434573; e-mail arzobrcia@lared.com.ar.

Archbishop of Rosario: EDUARDO VICENTE MIRÁS, Córdoba 1677, 2000 Rosario; tel. (341) 425-1298; fax (341) 425-1207; e-mail arzo bros@lidernet.co.ar; internet www.lidernet.com.ar/arzobros.

Archbishop of Salta: MARIO ANTONIO CARGNELLO, España 596, 4400 Salta; tel. (387) 421-4306; fax (387) 421-3101; e-mail arzobisposal ta@infovia.com.ar

Archbishop of San Juan de Cuyo: ALFONSO DELGADO EVERS, Bartolomé Mitre 250 Oeste, 5400 San Juan de Cuyo; tel. (264) 422-2578; fax (264) 427-3530.

Archbishop of Santa Fe de la Vera Cruz: EDGARDO GABRIEL STORNI, Avda General López 2720, 3000 Santa Fe; tel. (342) 459-5791; fax (342) 459-4491; e-mail arzobsfe@infovia.com.ar.

Archbishop of Tucumán: LUIS HÉCTOR VILLALBA, Avda Sarmiento 895, 4000 San Miguel de Tucumán; tel. (381) 422-6345; fax (381) 431-0617; e-mail arztuc@arnet.com.ar.

Maronite Rite

Bishop of San Charbel en Buenos Aires: CHARBEL MERHI, Eparquía Maronita, Paraguay 834, 1057 Buenos Aires; tel. (11) 4311-7299; fax (11) 4312-8348; e-mail mcharbel@hotmail.com.

Ukrainian Rite

Bishop of Santa María del Patrocinio en Buenos Aires: (vacant); **A**postolic Administrator: Rt Rev. MIGUEL MYKYCEJ (Titular Bishop of Nazianzus), Ramón L. Falcón 3950, Casilla 28, 1407 Buenos Aires; tel. (11) 4671-4192; fax (11) 4671-7265; e-mail pekrov @ciudad.com.ar.

The Anglican Communion

The Iglesia Anglicana del Cono Sur de América (Anglican Church of the Southern Cone of America) was formally inaugurated in Buenos Aires in April 1983. The Church comprises seven dioceses: Argentina, Northern Argentina, Chile, Paraguay, Peru, Bolivia and Uruguay. The Primate is the Bishop of Northern Argentina.

Bishop of Argentina: Rt Rev. DAVID LEAKE, 25 de Mayo 282, 1002 Buenos Aires; Casilla 4293, Correo Central 1000, Buenos Aires; tel. (11) 4342-4618; fax (11) 4331-0234; e-mail diocesisanglibue@arnet .com.ar.

Bishop of Northern Argentina: Rt Rev. MAURICE SINCLAIR, Casilla 187, 4400 Salta; jurisdiction extends to Jujuy, Salta, Tucumán, Catamarca, Santiago del Estero, Formosa and Chaco; tel. (387) 431-1718; fax (387) 431-2622; e-mail sinclair@salnet.com.ar.

Protestant Churches

Convención Evangélica Bautista Argentina (Baptist Evangelical Convention): Virrey Liniers 42, 1174 Buenos Aires; tel. and fax (11) 4864-2711; e-mail ceba@sion.com; f. 1909; Pres. CARLOS A. CARAMUTTI.

Iglesia Evangélica Congregacionalista (Evangelical Congregational Church): Perón 525, 3100 Paraná; tel. (43) 21-6172; f. 1924; 100 congregations, 8,000 mems, 24,000 adherents; Supt Rev. REYNOLDO HORSTT.

Iglesia Evangélica Luterana Argentina (Evangelical Lutheran Church of Argentina): Ing. Silveyra 1639-41, 1607 Villa Adelina, Buenos Aires; tel. (11) 4766-7948; fax (11) 4766-7948; f. 1905; 30,000 mems; Pres. WALDOMIRO MAILI.

Iglesia Evangélica del Río de la Plata (Evangelical Church of the River Plate): Mariscal Sucre 2855, 1428 Buenos Aires; tel. (11) 4787-0436; fax (11) 4787-0335; e-mail ierp@ierp.org.ar; f. 1899; 40,000 mems; Pres. JUAN PEDRO SCHAAD.

Iglesia Evangélica Metodista Argentina (Methodist Church of Argentina): Rivadavia 4044, 3°, 1205 Buenos Aires; tel. (11) 4982-3712; fax (11) 4981-0885; e-mail iema@iema.com.ar; internet www.iema.com.ar; f. 1836; 6,040 mems, 9,000 adherents, seven regional superintendents; Bishop ALDO M. ETCHEGOYEN; Exec. Sec.-Gen. Bd DANIEL A. FAVARO.

JUDAISM

Delegación de Asociaciones Israelitas Argentinas—DAIA (Delegation of Argentine Jewish Associations): Pasteur 633, 7°, 1028 Buenos Aires; tel. and fax (11) 4953-1785; e-mail daia@info via.com.ar; f. 1935; there are about 250,000 Jews in Argentina, mostly in Buenos Aires; Pres. Dr RUBÉN E. BERAJA; Sec.-Gen. Dr JOSÉ KESTELMAN.

The Press

PRINCIPAL DAILIES
Buenos Aires

Ambito Financiero: Avda Paseo Colón 1196, 1063 Buenos Aires; tel. (11) 4349-1500; fax (11) 4349-1505; e-mail correo@afinanciero .com; internet www.afinanciero.com; f. 1976; morning (Mon.–Fri.); business; Dir JULIO A. RAMOS; circ. 115,000.

Buenos Aires Herald: Azopardo 455, 1107 Buenos Aires; tel. (11) 4342-1535; fax (11) 4334-7917; e-mail info@buenosairesherald.com; internet www.buenosairesherald.com; f. 1876; English; morning; independent; Editor-in-Chief ANDREW GRAHAM YOOLL; circ. 20,000.

Boletín Oficial de la República Argentina: Suipacha 767, 1008 Buenos Aires; tel. (11) 4322-3982; fax (11) 4322-3982; f. 1893; morning (Mon.–Fri.); official records publication; Dir RUBÉN ANTONIO SOSA; circ. 15,000.

Clarín: Piedras 1743, 1140 Buenos Aires; tel. (11) 4309-7500; fax (11) 4309-7559; e-mail lectores@www.clarin.com; internet www.clar in.com; f. 1945; morning; independent; Dir ERNESTINA L. HERRERA DE NOBLE; circ. 616,000 (daily), 1.0m. (Sunday).

Crónica: Avda Juan de Garay 40, 1063 Buenos Aires; tel. (11) 4361-1001; fax (11) 4361-4237; f. 1963; morning and evening; Dir MARIO ALBERTO FERNÁNDEZ (morning), RICARDO GANGEME (evening); circ. 330,000 (morning), 190,000 (evening), 450,000 (Sunday).

El Cronista: Honduras 5663, 1414 Buenos Aires; tel. (11) 4778-6789; fax (11) 4778-6727; e-mail cronista@sadei.org.ar; f. 1908; morning; Dir NÉSTOR SCIBONA; circ. 65,000.

Diario Popular: Beguiristain 142, 1872 Sarandí, Avellaneda, Buenos Aires; tel. (11) 4204-2778; fax (11) 4205-2376; e-mail redac pop@inea.net.ar; f. 1974; morning; Dir ALBERTO ALBERTENGO; circ. 145,000.

La Gaceta: Beguiristain 182, 1870 Avellaneda, Buenos Aires; Dir RICARDO WEST OCAMPO; circ. 35,000.

La Nación: Bouchard 551, 1106 Buenos Aires; tel. (11) 4319-1600; fax (11) 4319-1969; e-mail cescribano@lanacion.com.ar; internet www.lanacion.com.ar; f. 1870; morning; independent; Dir BARTOLOMÉ MITRE; circ. 184,000.

Página 12: Avda Belgrano 671, 1092 Buenos Aires; tel. (11) 4334-2334; fax (11) 4334-2335; e-mail lectores@pagina12.com.ar; internet www.pagina12.com.ar; f. 1987; morning; independent; Dir ERNESTO TIFFEMBERG; Editor FERNANDO SOKOLOWICZ; circ. 280,000.

La Prensa: Azopardo 715, 1107 Buenos Aires; tel. (11) 4349-1000; fax (11) 4349-1025; e-mail laprensa@interlink.com; internet www.in terlink.com.ar/laprensa; f. 1869; morning; independent; Dir FLO-RENCIO ALDREY IGLESIAS; circ. 100,000.

La Razón: Río Cuarto 1242, 1168 Buenos Aires; tel. and fax (11) 4309-6000; e-mail larazon@arnet.com.ar; internet www.larazon .com.ar; f. 1992; evening; Dir OSCAR MAGDALENA; circ. 62,000.

El Sol: Hipólito Yrigoyen 122, Quilmes, 1878 Buenos Aires; tel. and fax (11) 4257-6325; e-mail elsol@elsolquilmes.com.ar; internet www.elsolquilmes.com.ar; f. 1927; Dir RODRIGO GHISANI; circ. 25,000.

Tiempo Argentino: Buenos Aires; tel. (11) 428-1929; Editor Dr TOMÁS LEONA; circ. 75,000.

PRINCIPAL PROVINCIAL DAILIES
Catamarca

El Ancasti: Sarmiento 526, 1°, 4700 Catamarca; tel. and fax (3833) 431385; e-mail ancasti@satlink.com; f. 1988; morning; Dir ROQUE EDUARDO MOLAS; circ. 8,000.

Chaco

Norte: Carlos Pellegrini 744, 3500 Resistencia; tel. (3722) 428204; fax (3722) 426047; e-mail prensanorte@diarionorte.com.ar; f. 1968; Dir MIGUEL A. FERNÁNDEZ; circ. 14,000.

Chubut

Crónica: Impresora Patagónica, Namuncurá 122, 9000 Comodoro Rivadavia; tel. (297) 447-1200; fax (297) 447-1780; e-mail cronica@ arnet.com.ar; f. 1962; morning; Dir Dr DIEGO JOAQUÍN ZAMIT; circ. 15,000.

Córdoba

Comercio y Justicia: Mariano Moreno 378, 5000 Córdoba; tel. and fax (351) 422-0202; e-mail sistemas@powernet.com.ar; internet www.powernet.com.ar/cyj; f. 1939; morning; economic and legal news; Editor PABLO EGUÍA; circ. 5,800.

La Voz del Interior: Avellaneda 1661, 5000 Córdoba; tel. (351) 4757200; fax (351) 4757201; e-mail lavoz@satlink.com; internet www.intervoz.com.ar; f. 1904; morning; independent; Dir Dr CARLOS HUGO JORNET; circ. 68,000.

Corrientes

El Litoral: Hipólito Yrigoyen 990, 3400 Corrientes; tel. and fax (3783) 422227; e-mail el-litoral@compunort.com.ar; internet www.corrientes.com.ar/el-litoral; f. 1960; morning; Dir CARLOS A. ROMERO FERIS; circ. 25,000.

El Territorio: Avda Quaranta 4307, 3300 Posadas; tel. and fax (3752) 452100; e-mail elterritorio@elterritorio.com.ar; internet www.elterritorio.com.ar; f. 1925; Dir GONZALO PELTZER; circ. 22,000 (Mon.–Fri.), 28,000 (Sunday).

Entre Ríos

El Diario: Buenos Aires y Urquiza, 3100 Paraná; tel. (343) 423-1000; fax (343) 431-9104; e-mail saer@satlink.com; internet www.el diario.com.ar; f. 1914; morning; democratic; Dir Dr LUIS F.ET-CHEVEHERE; circ. 25,000.

El Heraldo: Quintana 42, 3200 Concordia; tel. (345) 421-5304; fax (345) 421-1397; e-mail heraldo@infovia.com.ar; internet www.elher aldo.com.ar; f. 1915; evening; Editor Dr CARLOS LIEBERMANN; circ. 10,000.

Mendoza

Los Andes: Avda San Martín 1049, 5500 Mendoza; tel. (261) 4491200; fax (261) 4202011; e-mail amartinez@losandes.com.ar; internet www.losandes.net; f. 1982; morning; Dir JORGE ENRIQUE OVIEDO; circ. 107,000.

Provincia de Buenos Aires

El Atlántico: Bolívar 2975, 7600 Mar del Plata; tel. (223) 435462; f. 1938; morning; Dir OSCAR ALBERTO GASTIARENA; circ. 20,000.

La Capital: Avda Champagnat 2551, 7600 Mar del Plata; tel. (223) 478-8490; fax (223) 478-1038; e-mail diario@lacapitalnet.com.ar; internet www.lacapitalnet.com.ar; f. 1905; Dir FLORENCIO ALDREY IGLESIAS; circ. 32,000.

El Día: Avda A. Diagonal 80, 817-21, 1900 La Plata; tel. (221) 425-0101; fax (221) 423-2996; e-mail redaccion@eldia.com; f. 1884; morning; independent; Dir RAÚL E. KRAISELBURD; circ. 54,868.

Ecos Diarios: Calle 62, No 2486, 7630 Necochea; tel. (2262) 430754; fax (2262) 420485; e-mail ecosdiar@satlink.com; internet www.ecos diarios.com.ar; f. 1921; morning; independent; Dir GUILLERMO IGNACIO; circ. 6,000.

La Nueva Provincia: Sarmiento 54–64, 8000 Bahía Blanca; tel. (291) 459-0000; fax (291) 459-0001; e-mail nprovin@relay.startel; internet www.lanueva.com.ar; f. 1898; morning; independent; Dir DIANA JULIO DE MASSOT; circ. 36,000 (Mon.–Fri.), 55,000 (Sunday).

La Voz del Pueblo: Avda San Martín 991, 7500 Tres Arroyos; tel. (2983) 430680; fax (2938) 430682; e-mail redaccion@lavozdelpueblo .com.ar; f. 1902; morning; independent; Dir ALBERTO JORGE MACIEL; circ. 8,500.

Río Negro

Río Negro: 9 de Julio 733, 8332, Gen. Roca, Río Negro; tel. (2941) 439300; fax (2941) 430517; e-mail rnredaccion@rionet.rionegro .com.ar; internet www.rionegro.com.ar; f. 1912; morning; Editor NÉLIDA RAJNERI DE GAMBA.

Salta

El Tribuno: Avda Ex Combatientes de Malvinas 3890, 4400 Salta; tel. (387) 424-0000; fax (387) 424-1382; e-mail tribuno@salnet .com.ar; internet www.eltribuno.com.ar; f. 1949; morning; Dir RO-BERTO EDUARDO ROMERO; circ. 25,000.

San Juan

Diario de Cuyo: Mendoza 380 Sur, 5400 San Juan; tel. (264) 429-0016; fax (264) 429-0004; e-mail diarcuyo@esternet.net.ar; f. 1947; morning; independent; Dir Francisco Montes; circ. 25,000.

San Luis

El Diario de La República: Junín 741, 5700 San Luis; tel. (2623) 422037; fax (2623) 428770; e-mail paynesa@infovia.com.ar; f. 1966; Dir Zulema A. Rodríguez Saa de Divizia; circ. 12,000.

Santa Fe

La Capital: Sarmiento 763, 2000 Rosario; tel. (341) 420-1100; fax (341) 420-1114; e-mail elagos@lacapital.com.ar; f. 1867; morning; independent; Dir Carlos María Lagos; circ. 65,000.

El Litoral: Avda 25 de Mayo 3536, 3000 Santa Fe; tel. (342) 450-2500; fax (342) 450-2530; e-mail litoral@litoral.com.ar; internet www.litoral.com.ar; f. 1918; morning; independent; Dir Gustavo Víttori; circ. 37,000.

Santiago del Estero

El Liberal: Libertad 263, 4200 Santiago del Estero; tel. (385) 422-4400; fax (385) 422-4538; e-mail liberal@teletrel.com.ar; internet www.sdnet.com.ar; f. 1898; morning; Exec. Dir José Luis Castiglione; Editorial Dir Dr Julio César Castiglione; circ. 20,000.

Tucumán

La Gaceta: Mendoza 654, 4000 San Miguel de Tucumán; tel. (381) 431-1111; fax (381) 431-1597; e-mail redaccion@lagaceta.com.ar; internet www.lagaceta.com.ar; f. 1912; morning; independent; Dir Alberto García Hamilton; circ. 70,000.

WEEKLY NEWSPAPER

El Informador Público: Uruguay 252, 3°F, 1015 Buenos Aires; tel. (11) 4476-3551; fax (11) 4342-2628; f. 1986.

PERIODICALS

Aeroespacio: Casilla 37, Sucursal 12B, 1412 Buenos Aires; tel. and fax (11) 4514-1562; e-mail info@aeroespacio.com.ar; internet www.aeroespacio.com.ar; f. 1940; every 2 months, aeronautics; Dir Jorge A. Cuadros; circ. 24,000.

Billiken: Azopardo 579, 1307 Buenos Aires; tel. (11) 4342-7071; fax (11) 4343-7040; e-mail artebilliken@atlantida.com.ar; f. 1919; weekly; children's magazine; Dir Juan Carlos Porras. circ. 240,000.

Casas y Jardines: Sarmiento 643, 1382 Buenos Aires; tel. (11) 445-1793; f. 1932; every 2 months; houses and gardens; publ. by Editorial Contémpora SRL; Dir Norberto M. Muzio.

Chacra y Campo Moderno: Editorial Atlántida, SA, Azopardo 579, 1307 Buenos Aires; tel. (11) 4331-4591; fax (11) 4331-3272; f. 1930; monthly; farm and country magazine; Dir Constancio C. Vigil; circ. 35,000.

Claudia: Avda Córdoba 1345, 12°, Buenos Aires; tel. (11) 442-3275; fax (11) 4814-3948; f. 1957; monthly; women's magazine; Dir Ana Torrejón; circ. 150,000.

El Economista: Avda Córdoba 632, 2°, 1054 Buenos Aires; tel. (11) 4322-7360; fax (11) 4322-8157; f. 1951; weekly; financial; Dir Dr D. Radonjic; circ. 37,800.

Fotografía Universal: Buenos Aires; monthly; circ. 39,500.

Gente: Azopardo 579, 3°, 1307 Buenos Aires; tel. (11) 433-4591; f. 1965; weekly; general; Dir Jorge de Luján Gutiérrez; circ. 133,000.

El Gráfico: Paseo Colón 505, 2°, 1063 Buenos Aires; tel. (11) 4341-5100; fax (11) 4341-5137; f. 1919; weekly; sport; Dir Aldo Proietto; circ. 127,000.

Guía Latinoamericana de Transportes: Florida 8287 esq. Portinari, 1669 Del Viso (Ptdo de Pilar), Provincia de Buenos Aires; tel. (11) 4320-7004; fax (11) 4307-1956; f. 1968; every 2 months; travel information and timetables; Editor Dr Armando Schlecker Hirsch; circ. 7,500.

Humor: Venezuela 842, 1095 Buenos Aires; tel. (11) 4334-5400; fax (11) 411-2700; f. 1978; every 2 weeks; satirical revue; Editor Andrés Cascioli; circ. 180,000.

Legislación Argentina: Talcahuano 650, 1013 Buenos Aires; tel. (11) 4371-0528; e-mail jurispru@lvd.com.ar; f. 1958; weekly; law; Dir Ricardo Estévez Boero; circ. 15,000.

Mercado: Rivadavia 877, 2°, 1002 Buenos Aires; tel. (11) 4346-9400; fax (11) 4343-7880; e-mail mdiez@mercado.com.ar; internet www.mercado.com.ar; f. 1969; monthly; business; Dir Miguel Angel Diez; circ. 28,000.

Mundo Israelita: Pueyrredón 538, 1°B, 1032 Buenos Aires; tel. (11) 4961-7999; fax (11) 4961-0763; f. 1923; weekly; Editor Dr José Kestelman; circ. 15,000.

Nuestra Arquitectura: Sarmiento 643, 5°, 1382 Buenos Aires; tel. (11) 445-1793; f. 1929; every 2 months; architecture; publ. by Editorial Contémpora SRL; Dir Norberto M. Muzio.

Para Ti: Azopardo 579, 1307 Buenos Aires; tel. (11) 4331-4591; fax (11) 4331-3272; f. 1922; weekly; women's interest; Dir Aníbal C. Vigil; circ. 104,000.

Pensamiento Económico: Avda Leandro N. Alem 36, 1003 Buenos Aires; tel. (11) 4331-8051; fax (11) 4331-8055; e-mail cac@cac.com.ar; internet www.cac.com.ar; f. 1925; quarterly; review of Cámara Argentina de Comercio; Dir Dr Carlos L. P. Antonucci.

La Prensa Médica Argentina: Junín 845, 1113 Buenos Aires; tel. (11) 4961-9793; fax (11) 4961-9494; e-mail presmedarg@hotmail.com; f. 1914; monthly; medical; Editor Dr P. A. López; circ. 8,000.

Prensa Obrera: Ayacucho 444, Buenos Aires; tel. (11) 4953-3824; fax (11) 4953-7164; f. 1982; weekly; publication of Partido Obrero; circ. 16,000.

La Semana: Sarmiento 1113, 1041 Buenos Aires; tel. (11) 435-2552; general; Editor Daniel Pliner.

La Semana Médica: Arenales 3574, 1425 Buenos Aires; tel. (11) 4824-5673; f. 1894; monthly; Dir Dr Eduardo F. Mele; circ. 7,000.

Siete Días Ilustrados: Avda Leandro N. Alem 896, 1001 Buenos Aires; tel. (11) 432-6010; f. 1967; weekly; general; Dir Ricardo Cámara; circ. 110,000.

Técnica e Industria: Buenos Aires; tel. (11) 446-3193; f. 1922; monthly; technology and industry; Dir E. R. Fedele; circ. 5,000.

Visión: French 2820, 2°A, 1425 Buenos Aires; tel. (11) 4825-1258; fax (11) 4827-1004; e-mail edlatin@visionmag.com.ar; f. 1950; fortnightly; Latin American affairs, politics; Editor Luis Vidal Rucabado.

Vosotras: Avda Leandro N. Alem 896, 3°, 1001 Buenos Aires; tel. (11) 432-6010; f. 1935; women's weekly; Dir Abel Zanotto; circ. 33,000. Monthly supplements: **Labores:** circ. 130,000; **Modas:** circ. 70,000.

NEWS AGENCIES

Agencia TELAM, SA: Bolívar 531, 1066 Buenos Aires; tel. (11) 4339-0315; fax (11) 4339-0316; e-mail telam@sinectis.com.ar; internet www.telam.com.ar; Dir Rodolfo Pousá.

Diarios y Noticias (DYN): Avda Julio A. Roca 636, 8°, 1067 Buenos Aires; tel. (11) 4342-3040; fax (11) 4342-3043; e-mail info@dyn.com.ar; internet www.dyn.com.ar; Editor Santiago González.

Noticias Argentinas, SA (NA): Suipacha 570, 3°B, 1008 Buenos Aires; tel. (11) 4394-7522; fax (11) 4394-7648; f. 1973; Dir Luis Fernando Torres.

Foreign Bureaux

Agence France-Presse (AFP): Avda Corrientes 456, 3°, Of. 34/37, 1366 Buenos Aires; tel. (11) 4394-8169; fax (11) 4393-9912; e-mail afp-baires@tournet.com.ar; internet www.afp.com; Bureau Chief Jean Virebayre.

Agencia EFE (Spain): Guido 1770, 1016 Buenos Aires; tel. (11) 4812-9596; fax (11) 4815-8691; Bureau Chief Agustín de Gracia.

Agenzia Nazionale Stampa Associata (ANSA) (Italy): San Martín 320, 6°, 1004 Buenos Aires; tel. (11) 4394-7568; fax (11) 4394-5214; e-mail ansabairestec@infovia.com.ar; Bureau Chief Antonio Cavallari.

Associated Press (AP) (USA): Bouchard 551, 5°, Casilla 1296, 1106 Buenos Aires; tel. (11) 4311-0081; fax (11) 4311-0082; Bureau Chief William H. Heath.

Deutsche Presse-Agentur (dpa) (Germany): Buenos Aires; tel. (11) 4311-5311; e-mail msvgroth@ba.net; Bureau Chief Dr Hendrik Groth.

Informatsionnoye Telegrafnoye Agentstvo Rossii-Telegrafnoye Agentstvo Suverennykh Stran (ITAR-TASS) (Russia): Avda Córdoba 652, 11°E, 1054 Buenos Aires; tel. (11) 4392-2044; Dir Isidoro Gilbert.

Inter Press Service (IPS) (Italy): Buenos Aires; tel. (11) 4394-0829; Bureau Chief Ramón M. Gorriarán; Correspondent Gustavo Capdevilla.

Magyar Távirati Iroda (MTI) (Hungary): Marcelo T. de Alvear 624, 3° 16, 1058 Buenos Aires; tel. (11) 4312-9596; Correspondent Endre Simó.

Prensa Latina (Cuba): Buenos Aires; tel. (11) 4394-0565; Correspondent Mario Hernández del Llano.

Reuters (United Kingdom): Avda Eduardo Madero 940, 25°, 1106 Buenos Aires; tel. (11) 4318-0600; fax (11) 4318-0698; Dir CARLOS PÍA MANGIONE.

United Press International (UPI) (USA): Avda Belgrano 271, Casilla 796, Correo Central 1000, 1092 Buenos Aires; tel. (11) 434-5501; fax (11) 4334-1818; Dir ALBERTO J. SCHAZÍN.

Xinhua (New China) News Agency (People's Republic of China): Tucumán 540, 14°, Apto D, 1049 Buenos Aires; tel. (11) 4313-9755; Bureau Chief JU QINGDONG.

The following are also represented: Central News Agency (Taiwan), Interpress (Poland), Jiji Press (Japan).

PRESS ASSOCIATION

Asociación de Entidades Periodísticas Argentinas (ADEPA): Chacabuco 314, 3°, 1069 Buenos Aires; tel. and fax (11) 4331-1500; e-mail adepa@ciudad.com.ar; internet www.adepa.com.ar; f. 1962; Pres. GUILLERMO IGNACIO.

Publishers

Editorial Abril, SA: Suipacha 664, 1093 Buenos Aires; tel. (11) 4331-0112; f. 1961; fiction, non-fiction, children's books, textbooks; Dir ROBERTO M. ARES.

Editorial Acme, SA: Santa Magdalena 635, 1277 Buenos Aires; tel. (11) 428-2014; f. 1949; general fiction, children's books, agriculture, textbooks; Man. Dir EMILIO I. GONZÁLEZ.

Aguilar, Altea, Taurus, Alfaguara, SA de Ediciones: Beazley 3860, 1437 Buenos Aires; tel. (11) 4912-7220; fax (11) 4912-7440; internet www.santillana.com.ar; f. 1946; general, literature, children's books; Gen. Man. CARLOS CALVO.

Editorial Albatros, SACI: Hipólito Yrigoyen 3920, 1208 Buenos Aires; tel. (11) 4982-5439; fax (11) 4981-1161; f. 1967; technical, non-fiction, social sciences, sport, children's books, medicine and agriculture; Pres. ANDREA INÉS CANEVARO.

Amorrortu Editores, SA: Paraguay 1225, 7°, 1057 Buenos Aires; tel. (11) 4393-8812; fax (11) 4325-6307; f. 1967; anthropology, religion, economics, sociology, philosophy, psychology, psychoanalysis, current affairs; Man. Dir HORACIO DE AMORRORTU.

Angel Estrada y Cía, SA: Bolívar 462-66, 1066 Buenos Aires; tel. (11) 4331-6521; fax (11) 4331-6527; f. 1869; textbooks, children's books; Gen. Man. OSCAR DOMECQ.

Editorial El Ateneo, Librerías Yenny, SA: Patagones 2463, 1282 Buenos Aires; tel. (11) 4942-9002; fax (11) 4942-9162; e-mail librerías@yenny.com.ar; f. 1912; medicine, engineering, economics and general; Pres. EDUARDO CARLOS GRUNEISEN; Commercial Dir JORGE GONZÁLEZ.

Editorial Atlántida, SA: Azopardo 579, 1307 Buenos Aires; tel. (11) 4346-0100; fax (11) 4331-3272; internet www.atlantida.com; f. 1918; fiction and non-fiction, children's books; Chair. JORGE CONSTANCIO TERRA.

Ediciones La Aurora: Buenos Aires; tel. and fax (11) 4941-8940; f. 1925; general, religion, spirituality, theology, philosophy, psychology, history, semiology, linguistics; Dir Dr HUGO O. ORTEGA.

Az Editora, SA: Paraguay 2351, 1121 Buenos Aires; tel. (11) 961-4036; fax (11) 961-0089; f. 1976; social sciences and medicine; Pres. DANTE OMAR VILLALBA.

Biblioteca Nacional de Maestros: c/o Ministry of Education, Pizzurno 935, planta baja, 1020 Buenos Aires; tel. (11) 4811-0275; e-mail gperrone@me.gov.ar; internet www.bnm.me.gov.ar; f. 1884; Dir GRACIELA PERRONE.

Centro Editor de América Latina, SA: Salta 38, 3°, 1074 Buenos Aires; tel. (11) 435-9449; f. 1967; literature, history; Man. Dir JOSÉ B. SPIVACOW.

Editorial Claretiana: Lima 1360, 1138 Buenos Aires; tel. (11) 427-9250; fax (11) 427-4015; e-mail editorial@editorialclaretiana.com.ar; internet www.editorialclaretiana.com.ar; f. 1956; Catholicism; Dir GUSTAVO LARRAZÁBAL.

Editorial Claridad, SA: Viamonte 1730, 1°, 1055 Buenos Aires; tel. (11) 4371-6402; fax (11) 4375-1659; e-mail editorial@heliasta.com.ar; internet www.heliasta.com.ar; f. 1922; literature, biographies, social science, politics, reference, dictionaries; Pres. Dra ANA MARÍA CABANELLAS.

Club de Lectores: Avda de Mayo 624, 1084 Buenos Aires; tel. (11) 434-6251; f. 1938; non-fiction; Dir JUAN MANUEL FONTENLA.

Club de Poetas: Casilla 189, 1401 Buenos Aires; f. 1975; poetry and literature; Exec. Dir JUAN MANUEL FONTENLA.

Editorial Columba: Sarmiento 1889, 5°, 1044 Buenos Aires; tel. (11) 445-4297; f. 1953; classics in translation, 20th century; Man. Dir CLAUDIO A. COLUMBA.

Editorial Contémpora, SRL: Sarmiento 643, 5°, 1382 Buenos Aires; tel. (11) 445-1793; architecture, town-planning, interior decoration and gardening; Dir NORBERTO C. MUZIO.

Cosmopolita, SRL: Piedras 744, 1070 Buenos Aires; tel. and fax (11) 4361-8049; f. 1940; science and technology; Man. Dir RUTH F. DE RAPP.

Depalma, SA: Talcahuano 494, 1013 Buenos Aires; tel. (11) 4371-7306; fax (11) 4371-6913; e-mail info@ed-depalma.com; internet www.ed-depalma.com; f. 1944; periodicals and books covering law, politics, sociology, philosophy, history and economics; CEO ALBERTO O. ERMILIO; Dir NICOLAS VON DER PAHLEN.

Editorial Difusión, SA: Sarandi 1065–67, Buenos Aires; tel. (11) 4941-0088; f. 1937; literature, philosophy, religion, education, textbooks, children's books; Dir DOMINGO PALOMBELLA.

Edicial, SA: Rivadavia 739, 1002 Buenos Aires; tel. (11) 4342-8481; fax (11) 4343-1151; e-mail edicial@ssdnet.com.ar; internet www.ssdnet.com.ar/edicial; f. 1931; education; Man. Dir J. A. MUSSET.

Emecé Editores, SA: Alsina 2062, 1090 Buenos Aires; tel. (11) 4954-0105; fax (11) 4953-4200; e-mail editorial@emece.com.ar; internet www.emece.com.ar; f. 1939; fiction, non-fiction, biographies, history, art, essays; Pres. ALFREDO DEL CARRIL.

Espasa Calpe Argentina, SA: Buenos Aires; tel. (11) 4342-0073; fax (11) 4345-1776; f. 1937; literature, science, dictionaries; publ. *Colección Austral*; Dir GUILLERMO SCHAUELZON.

Angel Estrada y Cía, SA: Bolívar 462-466, 1066 Buenos Aires; tel. (11) 331-6521; f. 1869; education; Gen. Man. ZSOLT ARÁRDY.

EUDEBA—Editorial Universitaria de Buenos Aires: Rivadavia 1573, 1033 Buenos Aires; tel. (11) 4383-8025; fax (11) 4383-2202; e-mail eudeba@eudeba.com.ar; internet www.eudeba.com.ar; f. 1958; university text books and general interest publications; Pres. Dr LUIS YANES.

Fabril Editora, SA: Buenos Aires; tel. (11) 421-3601; f. 1958; non-fiction, science, arts, education and reference; Editorial Man. ANDRÉS ALFONSO BRAVO; Business Man. RÓMULO AYERZA.

Editorial Glem, SACIF: Avda Caseros 2056, 1264 Buenos Aires; tel. (11) 426-6641; f. 1933; psychology, technology; Pres. JOSÉ ALFREDO TUCCI.

Editorial Guadalupe: Mansilla 3865, 1425 Buenos Aires; tel. (11) 4826-8587; fax (11) 4805-4112; e-mail ventas@editorialguadalupe.com.ar; f. 1895; social sciences, religion, anthropology, children's books, and pedagogy; Dir P. LORENZO GOYENECHE.

Editorial Heliasta, SRL: Viamonte 1730, 1°, 1055 Buenos Aires; tel. (11) 4371-6402; fax (11) 4375-1659; e-mail editorial@heliasta.com.ar; internet www.heliasta.com.ar; f. 1944; literature, biography, dictionaries, legal; Pres. Dra ANA MARÍA CABANELLAS.

Editorial Hemisferio Sur, SA: Pasteur 743, 1028 Buenos Aires; tel. (11) 4952-9825; fax (11) 4952-8454; e-mail informe@hemisferiosur.com.ar; internet www.hemisferiosur.com.ar; f.1966; agriculture, veterinary and food science; Man. Dir ADOLFO JULIÁN PEÑA.

Editorial Hispano-Americana, SA (HASA): Alsina 731, 1087 Buenos Aires; tel. (11) 4331-5051; f. 1934; science and technology; Pres. Prof. HÉCTOR OSCAR ALGARRA.

Editorial Inter-Médica, SAICI: Junín 917, 1°, Casilla 4625, 1113 Buenos Aires; tel. (11) 4961-9234; fax (11) 4961-5572; e-mail info@inter-medica.com.ar; internet www.inter-medica.com.ar; f. 1959; medicine, dentistry, psychology, psychiatry, veterinary; Pres. JORGE MODYEIEVSKY.

Editorial Inter-Vet, SA: Avda de los Constituyentes 3141, Buenos Aires; tel. (11) 451-2382; f. 1987; veterinary; Pres. JORGE MODYEIEVSKY.

Kapelusz Editora, SA: San José 831, 1076 Buenos Aires; tel. (11) 4342-7400; fax (11) 4331-8020; e-mail pedidos@kapelusz.com.ar; internet www.kapelusz.com.ar; f. 1905; textbooks, psychology, pedagogy, children's books; Gen. Man. TOMÁS CASTILLO.

Editorial Kier, SACIFI: Avda Santa Fe 1260, 1059 Buenos Aires; tel. (11) 4811-0507; fax (11) 4811-3395; e-mail info@kier.com.ar; internet www.kier.com.ar; f. 1907; Eastern doctrines and religions, astrology, parapsychology, tarot, I Ching, occultism, cabbala, freemasonry and natural medicine; Pres. HÉCTOR S. PIBERNUS; Mans SERGIO PIBERNUS, OSVALDO PIBERNUS, CRISTÍNA GRIGNA.

Ediciones Librerías Fausto: Avda Corrientes 1316, 1043 Buenos Aires; tel. (11) 4476-4919; fax (11) 4476-3914; f. 1943; fiction and non-fiction; Man. RAFAEL ZORRILLA.

Carlos Lohlé, SA: Tacuarí 1516, 1139 Buenos Aires; tel. (11) 427-9969; f. 1953; philosophy, religion, belles-lettres; Dir FRANCISCO M. LOHLÉ.

Editorial Losada, SA: Moreno 3362/64, 1209 Buenos Aires; tel. (11) 4863-8608; fax (11) 4864-0434; f. 1938; general; Pres. JOSÉ JUAN FERNÁNDEZ REGUERA.

Ediciones Macchi, SA: Alsina 1535/37, 1088 Buenos Aires; tel. (11) 446-2506; fax (11) 446-0594; f. 1947; economic sciences; Pres. Raúl Luis Macchi; Dir Julio Alberto Mendonça.

Editorial Médica Panamericana, SA: Marcelo T. de Alvear 2145, 1122 Buenos Aires; tel. (11) 4821-5520; fax (11) 4825-5006; e-mail info@medicapanamericana.com.ar; internet www.medicapanamericana.com.ar; f. 1962; medicine and health sciences; Pres. Hugo Brik.

Ediciones Nueva Visión, SAIC: Tucumán 3748, 1189 Buenos Aires; tel. (11) 4864-5050; fax (11) 4863-5980; e-mail ednuevavision @ciudad.com.ar; f. 1954; psychology, education, social sciences, linguistics; Man. Dir Haydée P. de Giacone.

Editorial Paidós: Defensa 599, 1°, 1065 Buenos Aires; tel. (11) 4331-2275; fax (11) 4345-6769; f. 1945; social sciences, medicine, philosophy, religion, history, literature, textbooks; Man. Dir Marita Gottheil.

Plaza y Janés, SA: Buenos Aires; tel. (11) 486-6769; popular fiction and non-fiction; Man. Dir Jorge Pérez.

Editorial Plus Ultra, SA: Callao 575, 1022 Buenos Aires; tel. (11) 4374-2953; f. 1964; literature, history, textbooks, law, economics, politics, sociology, pedagogy, children's books; Man. Editors Rafael Román, Lorenzo Marengo.

Editorial Santillana: Buenos Aires; f. 1960; education; Pres. Jesús de Polanco Gutiérrez.

Schapire Editor, SRL: Uruguay 1249, 1016 Buenos Aires; tel. (11) 4812-0765; fax (11) 4815-0369; f. 1941; music, art, theatre, sociology, history, fiction; Dir Miguel Schapire Dalmat.

Editorial Sigmar, SACI: Belgrano 1580, 7°, 1093 Buenos Aires; tel. (11) 4383-3045; fax (11) 4383-5633; e-mail editorial@sigmar .com.ar; f. 1941; children's books; Man. Dir Roberto Chwat.

Editorial Sopena Argentina, SACI e I: Buenos Aires; tel. (11) 438-7182; f. 1918; dictionaries, classics, chess, health, politics, history, children's books; Exec. Pres. Daniel Carlos Olsen.

Editorial Stella: Viamonte 1984, 1056 Buenos Aires; tel. (11) 446-0346; general non-fiction and textbooks; owned by Asociación Educacionista Argentina.

Editorial Sudamericana, SA: Humberto 545, 1°, 1103 Buenos Aires; tel. (11) 4300-5400; fax (11) 4362-7364; e-mail edsudame@sat link.com; f. 1939; general fiction and non-fiction; Gen. Man. Olaf Hantel.

Editorial Troquel, SA: Dr E. Finochietto 473, 1143 Buenos Aires; tel. (11) 427-1116; fax (11) 423-9350; f. 1954; general literature, and textbooks; Pres. Gustavo A. Ressia.

PUBLISHERS' ASSOCIATION

Cámara Argentina de Publicaciones: Reconquista 1011, 6°, 1003 Buenos Aires; tel. (11) 4311-6855; f. 1970; Pres. Agustín dos Santos; Man. Luis Francisco Houlin.

Broadcasting and Communications

Secretaría de Comunicaciones: Sarmiento 151, 4°, 1000 Buenos Aires; tel. (11) 4318-9410; fax (11) 4318-9432; co-ordinates 30 stations and the international service; Sec. Dr Germán Kammerath.

Subsecretaría de Planificación y Gestión Tecnológica: Sarmiento 151, 4°, 1000 Buenos Aires; tel. (11) 4311-5909; Under-Sec. Ing. Leonardo José Leibson.

Subsecretaría de Radiocomunicaciones: Sarmiento 151, 4°, 1000 Buenos Aires; tel. (11) 4311-5909; Under-Sec. Ing. Alfredo R. Parodi.

Subsecretaría de Telecomunicaciones: Sarmiento 151, 4°, 1000 Buenos Aires; tel. (11) 4311-5909; Under-Sec. Julio I. Guillán.

Comité Federal de Radiodifusión (COMFER): Suipacha 765, 9°, 1008 Buenos Aires; tel. (11) 4320-4900; fax (11) 4394-6866; e-mail mlagier@comfer.gov.ar; f. 1972; controls various technical aspects of broadcasting and transmission of programmes; Head Gustavo López.

TELECOMMUNICATIONS

Cámara de Informática y Comunicaciones de la República Argentina (CICOMRA): Avda Córdoba 744, 2°, 1054 Buenos Aires; tel. (11) 4325-8839; fax (11) 4325-9604; e-mail cicomra@starnet .net.ar.

Comisión Nacional de Comunicaciones (CNC): Perú 103, 9°, 1067 Buenos Aires; tel. (11) 4347-9242; fax (11) 4347-9244; Pres. Dr Roberto Catalán.

Cía Ericsson SACI: Avda Madero, 1020 Buenos Aires; tel. (11) 4319-5500; fax (11) 4315-0629; Dir-Gen. Ing. Rolando Zubirán.

Cía de Radiocomunicaciones Móviles SA: Tucumán 744, 9°, 1049 Buenos Aires; tel. (11) 4325-5006; fax (11) 4325-5334; mobile telecommunications co; Pres. Lic. Mauricio E. Wior.

Movicom: Tucumán 744, 2°, 1049 Buenos Aires; tel. (11) 4978-4773; fax (11) 4978-7373; e-mail rree@movi.com.ar; internet www.movi.com.ar; telecommunications services, including cellular phones, trunking, paging and wireless access to the internet; Pres. Lic. Mauricio Wior.

Telecom Argentina: Alicia Moreau de Justo 50, 1107 Buenos Aires; tel. (11) 4968-4000; fax (11) 4968-1420; e-mail inversores@in tersrv.telecom.com.ar; internet www.telecom.com.ar; provision of telecommunication services in the north of Argentina; Pres. Juan Carlos Masjoan.

Telecomunicaciones Internacionales de Argentina, SA (TELINTAR): 25 de Mayo 457, 7°, 1002 Buenos Aires; tel. (11) 4318-0500; fax (11) 4313-4924; e-mail mlamas@telintar.com.ar; internet www.telintar.com.ar; Sec.-Gen. Dr Marcelo Miguel Lamas.

Telefónica de Argentina, SA (TASA): Tucumán 1, 17°, 1049 Buenos Aires; tel. (11) 4345-5772; fax (11) 4345-5771; e-mail gabello @telefonica.com.ar; internet www.telefonica.com.ar; provision of telecommunication services in the south of Argentina; Pres. Carlos Fernández Prida.

RADIO

There are three privately-owned stations in Buenos Aires and 72 in the interior. There are also 37 state-controlled stations, four provincial, three municipal and three university stations. The principal ones are Radio Antártida, Radio Argentina, Radio Belgrano, Radio Ciudad de Buenos Aires, Radio Excelsior, Radio Mitre, Radio El Mundo, Radio Nacional, Radio del Plata, Radio Rivadavia and Radio Splendid, all in Buenos Aires.

Radio Nacional: Maipú 555, 1006 Buenos Aires; tel. (11) 4325-4590; fax (11) 4325-4313; e-mail secretariansor@sion.com; Dir Mario Andrés Cella; controls:

Cadena Argentina de Radiodifusión (CAR): Avda Entre Ríos 149, 3°, 1079 Buenos Aires; tel. (11) 4325-9100; fax (11) 4325-9433; groups all national state-owned commercial stations which are operated directly by the Subsecretaría Operativa.

LRA Radio Nacional de Buenos Aires: Maipú 555, 1006 Buenos Aires; tel. and fax (11) 4325-9433; e-mail rna@mecon.ar; f. 1937; Dir Patricia Ivone Barral.

Radiodifusión Argentina al Exterior (RAE): Maipú 555, 1006 Buenos Aires; tel. (11) 4325-6368; fax (11) 4325-9433; e-mail rna@mecon.ar; f. 1958; broadcasts in eight languages to all areas of the world; Dir-Gen. Perla Damuri.

Asociación de Radiodifusoras Privadas Argentinas (ARPA): Juan D. Perón 1561, 8°, 1037 Buenos Aires; tel. (11) 4382-4412; f. 1958; an association of all but three of the privately-owned commercial stations; Pres. Domingo F. L. Elías.

TELEVISION

There are 44 television channels, of which 29 are privately-owned and 15 are owned by provincial and national authorities. The national television network is regulated by the Comité Federal de Radiodifusión (see above).

The following are some of the more important television stations in Argentina: Argentina Televisora Color LS82 Canal 7, LS83 (Canal 9 Libertad), LS84 (Canal 11 Telefé), LS85 Canal 13 ArTeAr SA, LV80 Telenueva, LU81 Teledifusora Bahiense SA, LV81 Canal 12 Telecor SACI, Dicor Difusión Córdoba, LV80 TV Canal 10 Universidad Nacional Córdoba, and LU82 TV Mar del Plata SA.

Asociación de Teleradiodifusoras Argentinas (ATA): Avda Córdoba 323, 6°, 1054 Buenos Aires; tel. (11) 4312-4208; fax (11) 4315-4681; e-mail info@ata.org.ar; internet www.ata.org.ar; f. 1959; asscn of 22 private television channels; Pres. Carlos Fontan Balestra.

ATC—Argentina Televisora Color LS82 TV Canal 7: Avda Figueroa Alcorta 2977, 1425 Buenos Aires; tel. (11) 4802-6001; fax (11) 4802-9878; e-mail presidencia@canal7argentina.com.ar; internet www.canal7argentina.com.ar; state-controlled channel; Dir Mario Andrés Cella.

Azul Televisión—LS83 (Canal 9 Libertad): Dorrego 1708, Buenos Aires; tel. (11) 777-2321; fax (11) 777-9620; e-mail noticias@ azultv.com; internet www.azultv.com; private channel; Dir Alejandro Ramay.

LS84 (Canal 11 Telefé): Pavón 2444, 1248 Buenos Aires; tel. (11) 4941-9549; fax (11) 4942-6773; leased to a private concession in 1992; Pres. Pedro Simoncini.

LS85: Canal 13 (ArTeAr SA): Avda San Juan 1170, 1147 Buenos Aires; tel. (11) 4305-0013; fax (11) 4307-0315; e-mail webmas ter@webtv.artear.com; internet www.webtv.artear.com.ar; f. 1989; leased to a private concession in 1992; Dir-Gen. Lucio Pagliaro.

Finance

(cap. = capital; res = reserves; dep. = deposits; m. = million;
amounts in nuevos pesos argentinos—$, unless otherwise stated)

BANKING

At the end of 1998 there were three public banks, 14 municipal banks, 44 domestic private banks, 39 foreign private banks and four co-operative banks.

Central Bank

Banco Central de la República Argentina: Reconquista 266, 1003 Buenos Aires; tel. (11) 4348-3500; fax (11) 4348-3955; e-mail sistema@bcra.gov.ar; internet www.bcra.gov.ar; f. 1935 as a central reserve bank; it has the right of note issue; all capital is held by the State; cap. $1,921m., res $1,074m., dep. $1,477m. (Dec. 1998); Pres. ROQUE MACCARONE.

Government-owned Commercial Banks

Banco de la Ciudad de Buenos Aires: Florida 302, 1313 Buenos Aires; tel. (11) 4329-8600; fax (11) 4112-098; e-mail bciudad5@banco ciudad.com.ar; internet www.bancociudad.com.ar; municipal bank; f. 1878; cap. and res $200.0m. (Oct. 1998); Chair. HORACIO CHIGHIZOLA; 31 brs.

Banco de Inversión y Commercio Exterior, SA (BICE): 25 de Mayo 526, 1002 Buenos Aires; tel. (11) 4317-6900; fax (11) 4311-5596; e-mail presidencia@bice.com.ar; internet www.bice.com.ar; f. 1991; dep. $237.1m. (Dec. 1998); Pres. DIEGO YOFRE.

Banco de la Nación Argentina: Bartolomé Mitre 326, 1036 Buenos Aires; tel. (11) 4347-6000; fax (11) 4347-8078; e-mail eoliver a@bna.com.ar; internet www.bna.com.ar; f. 1891; national bank; cap. $381.0m., res $1,717.5m., dep. $15,422.7m. (Dec. 1998); Pres. ENRIQUE OLIVERA; 541 brs.

Banco de la Pampa: Carlos Pellegrini 255, 6300 Santa Rosa; tel. (2954) 433008; fax (2954) 433196; f. 1958; cap. $6.9m., res $136.2m., dep. $873.6m. (June 1999); Pres. LUIS E. ROLDÁN; 112 brs.

Banco de la Provincia de Buenos Aires: Avda San Martín 137, 1004 Buenos Aires; tel. (11) 4331-2561; fax (11) 4331-5154; e-mail baprocri@internet.siscotel.com; internet www.bpba.com; f. 1822; provincial bank; cap. $750.0m., res $472.4m., dep. $12,452.9m. (Dec. 1998); Pres. RICARDO GUTIÉRREZ; 313 brs.

Banco de la Provincia del Chubut: Rivadavia 615, 9103 Rawson; tel. (2965) 482506; dep. $170.0m., total assets $456.8m. (May 1995); Principal Officer FREDERICO G. POLAK.

Banco de la Provincia de Córdoba: San Jerónimo 166, 5000 Córdoba; tel. (351) 420-7200; fax (351) 422-9718; e-mailgcomex terior@bancocordoba.com; internet www.bancocordoba.com; f. 1873; provincial bank; cap. $47.6m., res $142.8m., dep. $1,036.1 (Dec. 1994); Pres. JUAN A. OMEDO GUERRA; 152 brs.

Banco de la Provincia de Jujuy: Alvear 999, 4600 San Salvador de Jujuy; tel. (3882) 423003; f. 1933; dep. $87.9m., total assets $134.8m. (May 1995); Pres. Dr ARMANDO EDUARDO FERNÁNDEZ.

Banco de la Provincia del Neuquén: Avda Argentina 41/45, 8300 Neuquén; tel. (299) 434221; fax (299) 4480439; internet www.bpn.com.ar; f. 1960; dep. $232.8m., total assets $388.6m. (March 1995); Pres. OMAR SANTIAGO NEGRETTI; 22 brs.

Banco de la Provincia de San Luis: Rivadavia 602, 5700 San Luis; tel. (2623) 425013; fax (2623) 424943; dep. $88.8m., total assets $107.8m. (May 1995); Principal Officer SALVADOR OMAR CAMPO.

Banco de la Provincia de Santa Cruz: Avda General Roca 802, 9400 Río Gallegos; tel. (2966) 420845; dep. $211.7m., total assets $382.1m. (June 1995); Govt Admin. EDUARDO LABOLIDA.

Banco de la Provincia de Santiago del Estero: Avda Belgrano 529 Sur, 4200 Santiago del Estero; tel. (385) 422-2300; dep. $69.9m., total assets $101.6m. (Jan. 1995); Pres. AMÉRICO DAHER.

Banco de la Provincia de Tucumán: San Martín 362, 4000 San Miguel de Tucumán; tel. (381) 431-1709; dep. $164.7m., total assets $359.5m. (March 1995); Govt Admin. EMILIO APAZA.

Banco Provincial de Salta: España 550, 4400 Salta; tel.(387) 422-1300; fax (387) 431-0020; f. 1887; dep. $40.7m., total assets $125.0m. (June 1995); Pres. Dr REYNALDO ALFREDO NOGUEIRA; 19 brs.

Banco Social de Córdoba: 27 de Abril 185, 1°, 5000 Córdoba; tel. (351) 422-3367; dep. $187.3m., total assets $677.3m. (June 1995); Pres. Dr JAIME POMPAS.

Banco del Territorio Nacional de Tierra del Fuego, Antártida e Islas del Atlántico Sur: San Martín, esq. Roca, 9410 Ushuaia; tel. (2901) 424087; national bank; cap. and res $21.8m., dep. $54.2m. (June 1992); Pres. OSVALDO MANUEL RODRÍGUEZ.

Nuevo Banco de Santa Fé, SA: Tucumán 2545, 2°, 3000 Santa Fe; tel. (341) 452-2225; fax (341) 452-1037; e-mail nbsdirsf@infovia .com.ar; f. 1847 as Banco Provincial de Santa Fe, adopted current name in 1998; provincial bank; cap. $60.0m., res $31.1m., dep. $643.5m.; Chair. JOSÉ ENRIQUE ROHM; 105 brs.

Private Commercial Banks

Banco BI Creditanstalt, SA: Bouchard 547, 24°, 1106 Buenos Aires; tel. (11) 4319-8400; fax (11) 4319-8230; e-mail bi_credit@ impsat1.com.ar; f. 1971; fmrly Banco Interfinanzas; cap. $38.3m., res $8.0m., dep. $367.8m. (Dec. 1999); Pres. Dr MIGUEL ANGEL ANGELINO.

Banco Baires, SA: Buenos Aires; tel. (11) 4394-5851; fax (11) 4325-8548; f. 1956 as Baires Exchange House, adopted current name in 1992 following merger with Banco Mediterráneo, SA; cap. $11.6m., res $1.3m., dep. $56.5m. (Dec. 1994); Pres. G. ANÍBAL MENÉNDEZ.

Banco Bansud, SA: Sarmiento 447, 1041 Buenos Aires; tel. (11) 4348-6500; fax (11) 4325-5641; internet www.bansud.com; f. 1995 after merger of Banesto Banco Shaw, SA and Banco del Sud, SA; cap. $44.4m., res $302.2m., dep. $1,432.7m. (June 1997); Pres. LEONARDO ANIDJAR; 39 brs.

Banco Caja de Ahorro, SA: Avda Corrientes 629, 1324 Buenos Aires; tel. (11) 4323-5000; fax (11) 4323-5073; internet www.lacaja .com.ar; f. 1923 as Banco Mercantil Argentino, SA, adopted current name in 1999 following merger with Banco Caja de Ahorro, SA; cap. $0.1m., res $61.5m., dep. $587.3m. (Dec. 1997); Pres. NOEL WERTHEIN.

Banco CMF, SA: Macacha Güemes 555, Puerto Madero, 1107 Buenos Aires; tel. (11) 4318-6800; fax (11) 4318-6859; f. 1978 as Corporación Metropolitana de Finanzas, SA, adopted current name in 1999; cap. $41.0m., res $4.7m., dep. $433.7m. (Dec. 1998); Pres. JOSÉ P. BENEGAS LYNCH.

Banco Comercial Israelita, SA: Bartolomé Mitre 702, 2000 Rosario; tel. (341) 420-0557; fax (341) 420-0517; f. 1921; cap. $4.3m., res $20.5m., dep. $232.0m. (June 1998); Pres. Ing. DAVID ZCARNY; 4 brs.

Banco de Corrientes: 9 de Julio 1099, esq. San Juan, 3400 Corrientes; tel. (3783) 479200; fax (3783) 479283; f. 1951 as Banco de la República de Corrientes; adopted current name in 1993, after transfer to private ownership; cap. and res $38.5m., dep. $126.7m. (June 1995); Pres. JUAN RAMÓN BRANCHI; 33 brs.

Banco Crédito Provincial SA: Calle 7, esq. 50, Casilla 54, 1900 La Plata; tel. and fax (221) 429-2000; f. 1911; cap. $2.5m., res $40.5m., dep. $160.5m. (June 1995); Pres. ANTONIO R. FALABELLA; 47 brs.

Banco de Entre Ríos SA: Monte Caseros 128, 3100 Paraná; tel. (343) 423-1200; fax (343) 421-1221; e-mail bersaext@satlink.com; f. 1935; provincial bank; transferred to private ownership in 1995; cap. $55.2m., res $3.2m., dep. $715.5m. (June 1999); Pres. CARLOS ALBERTO CELAÁ; 29 brs.

Banco Florencia, SA: Reconquista 353, 1003 Buenos Aires; tel. (11) 4325-5949; fax (11) 4325-5849; f. 1984; cap. and res $8.8m., dep. $11.8m. (Dec. 1993); Chair. ALBERTO BRUNET; Vice-Chair. JORGE GONZÁLEZ.

Banco Francés, SA: Reconquista 199, 1003 Buenos Aires; tel. (11) 4346-4000; fax (11) 4346-4320; internet www.bancofrances.com; f. 1886 as Banco Francés del Río de la Plata, SA; adopted current name in 1998 following merger with Banco de Crédito Argentino; dep. US $5,883.6m., total assets US $9,447.4m. (March 1999); Chair. GERVÁSIO COLLAR ZAVALETA; 75 brs.

Banco de Galicia y Buenos Aires SA: Juan D. Perón 407, Casilla 86, 1038 Buenos Aires; tel. (11) 4394-7080; fax (11) 4393-1603; internet www.bancogalicia.com.ar; f. 1905; cap. $405.4m., res $516.0m., dep. $11,640.3m. (June 1999); Chair. EDUARDO J. ESCASANY; 165 brs.

Banco General de Negocios, SA: Esmeralda 120/38, 1035 Buenos Aires; tel. (11) 4320-6100; fax (11) 4334-6422; f. 1978; dep. $591.2m. (Dec. 1998); Chair. JOSÉ E. ROHM.

Banco Israelita de Córdoba, SA: Ituzaingó 60, 5000 Córdoba; tel. (351) 420-3200; fax (351) 424-3616; f. 1942; cap. $9.0m., res $18.3m., dep. $160.5m. (June 1995); Pres. JUAN MACHTEY; 20 brs.

Banco Macro, SA: Sarmiento 735, 1041 Buenos Aires; tel. (11) 4323-6300; fax (11) 4325-6935; e-mail bmmholding@inea.com.ar; f. 1997 by merger of Banco Macro, SA (f. 1988) and Banco de Misiones, SA; adopted current name in 1991 following merger with Banco de Salta; cap. and res $96.7m., dep. $668.8m. (Dec. 1999); Pres. JORGE HORACIO BRITO.

Banco Mariva, SA: Sarmiento 500, 1041 Buenos Aires; tel. (11) 4331-7571; fax (11) 4321-2222; f. 1980; cap. $30.0m., res $10.0m., dep. $206.3m. (Dec.1994); Pres. RICARDO MAY.

Banco Popular Financiero: Sobremonte 801, Casilla 5800, Río Cuarto, Córdoba; tel. (3586) 430001; f. 1964; cap. and res $8.8m., dep. \$41.2m. (June 1992); Pres. José Osvaldo Travaglia; Vice-Pres. Hugo Ricardo Lardone.

Banco Río de la Plata, SA: Bartolomé Mitre 480, 1036 Buenos Aires; tel. (11) 4341-1000; fax (11) 4341-1554; internet www.bancorio .com.ar; f. 1908; cap. \$150.0m., res \$269.1m., dep. \$5,372.6m. (Dec. 1996); Pres. Jorge Gregorio Pérez Compaño; 169 brs.

Banco Suquía, SA: 25 de Mayo 160, 5000 Córdoba; tel. (351) 420-0200; fax (351) 420-0443; internet www.bancosuquia.com.ar; f. 1961 as Banco del Suquía, SA; adopted current name in 1998; cap. \$80.6m., res \$66.1m., dep. \$1,481.5m. (June 1998); Pres. Aldo Benito Roggio; Gen. Man. Raúl Fernández; 98 brs.

Banco de Valores, SA: Sarmiento 310, 1041 Buenos Aires; tel. (11) 4323-6900; fax (11) 4334-1731; e-mail bcoval@internet.siscotel.com; internet www.bancodevalores.com; f. 1978; cap. \$10.0m., res \$5.9m., dep. \$201.8m. (Dec. 1998); Pres. Miguel A. Amoretti; 1 br.

Banco Velox, SA: San Martín 298, 1004 Buenos Aires; tel. (11) 4320-0200; fax (11) 4393-7672; f. 1983; cap. and res \$97.4m., dep. \$261.0m. (June 1999); Pres. Juan Peirano; 8 brs.

Banex: San Martín 136, 1004 Buenos Aires; tel. (11) 4340-3000; fax (11) 4334-4402; internet www.banex.com.ar; f. 1998 by merger of Exprinter Banco with Banco San Luis, SA; cap. \$29.1m., res \$15.8m., dep. \$188.4m. (Dec. 1998); Pres. María del Carmen Algorta de Supervielle.

HSBC Banco Roberts, SA: 25 de Mayo 701, 26°, 1084 Buenos Aires; tel. (11) 4344-3333; fax (11) 4334-6404; f. 1978 as Banco Roberts, SA; adopted current name in 1998; cap. \$219.7m., res \$100.2m., dep. \$4,473.8m. (June 1999); Chair. and CEO Michael Smith; 68 brs.

Nuevo Banco del Chaco, SA: Güemes 40, 3500 Resistencia; tel. (3722) 424888; f. 1958 as Banco del Chaco; transferred to private ownership and adopted current name in 1994; cap. \$10.5m., dep. \$45.4m. (June 1995); 28 brs.

Nuevo Banco de Formosa: 25 de Mayo 102, 3600 Formosa; tel. (3717) 426030; transferred to private ownership in 1995; dep. \$145.3m., total assets \$235.7m. (May 1995); Pres. José Manuel Pablo Viudes.

Co-operative Banks

Banco Almafuerte Cooperativo Ltdo: Corrales Viejos 64, 1437 Buenos Aires; tel. (11) 4911-5153; fax (11) 4911-6887; f. 1978; cap. \$18.3m., res \$38.1m., dep. \$378.4m. (Dec. 1997); Pres. Dr Elías Farah; 27 brs.

Banco Credicoop Cooperativo Ltdo: Reconquista 484, 1003 Buenos Aires; tel. (11) 4320-5000; fax (11) 4324-5891; e-mail cred icoop@rcc.com.ar; internet www.credicoop.com.ar; f. 1979; cap. \$0.4m., res \$210.5m., dep. \$1,870.1m. (June 1999); Pres. Raúl Guelman.

Banco Mayo Cooperativo Ltdo: Sarmiento 706, 1041 Buenos Aires; tel. (11) 4329-2400; fax (11) 4326-8080; f. 1978; cap. \$83.4m., res \$32.4m., dep. \$904.2m. (June 1997); Chair. Rubén E. Beraja; 106 brs.

Banco Patricios: Florida 101, 1005 Buenos Aires; tel. (11) 4331-1786; fax (11) 4331-6887; f. 1927; cap. and res \$19.1m., dep. \$144.0m. (Dec. 1993); Pres. Dr Alberto Spolski.

Banco Roco Cooperativo Ltdo: 25 de Mayo 122, 1002 Buenos Aires; tel. (11) 4342-0051; fax (11) 4331-6596; f. 1961; cap. and res \$10.8m., dep. \$58.1m. (Dec. 1992); Pres. Alfredo B. Arregui.

Other National Bank

Banco Hipotecario Nacional: Reconquista 151, 5°, 1003 Buenos Aires; tel. (11) 4347-5470; fax (11) 4347-5416; e-mail info@hipotecario .com.ar; internet www.hipotecario.com.ar; f. 1886; partially privat-ized in Jan. 1999; mortgage bank; cap. and res \$322.4m., dep. \$83.6m. (April 1992); Pres. Miguel Kiguel; 23 brs.

Foreign Banks

ABN Amro Bank N.V. (Netherlands): Florida 361, Casilla 171, 1005 Buenos Aires; tel. (11) 4320-0600; fax (11) 4322-0839; f. 1914; cap. and res \$37.7m., dep. \$94.5m. (June 1992); Gen. Man. César A. Deymonnaz.

Banca Nazionale del Lavoro, SA—BNL (Italy): Florida 40, 1005 Buenos Aires; tel. (11) 4323-4400; fax (11) 4323-4689; internet www.bnl.com.ar; cap. \$272m., dep. \$2,306m. (June 1999); took over Banco de Italia y Río de la Plata in 1987; Pres. Ademaro Lanzara; Gen. Man. Niccolo Pandolfiu; 136 brs.

Banco do Brasil, SA (Brazil): Sarmiento 487, Casilla 2684, 1041 Buenos Aires; tel. (11) 4394-0939; fax (11) 4394-9577; f. 1960; cap. and res \$33.9m., dep. \$2.0m. (June 1992); Gen. Man. Hélio Testoni.

Banco do Estado de São Paulo (Brazil): Tucumán 821, Casilla 2177, 1049 Buenos Aires; tel. (11) 4325-9533; fax (11) 4325-9527; cap. and res \$11.7m., dep. \$6.7m. (June 1992); Gen. Man. Carlos Alberto Bergamasco.

Banco Europeo para América Latina (BEAL), SA: Juan D. Perón 338, 1038 Buenos Aires; tel. (11) 4331-6544; fax (11) 4331-2010; e-mail bealbsa@inter.prov.com; f. 1914; cap. and res \$60m., dep. \$121m. (Nov. 1996); Gen. Mans Jean Pierre Smerd, Klaus Krsger.

Banco Itaú Buen Ayre, SA (Brazil): 25 de Mayo 476, 2°, 1002 Buenos Aires; tel. (11) 4325-6698; fax (11) 4394-1057; internet www.itau.com.ar; fmrly Banco Itaú Argentina, SA, renamed as above following purchase of Banco del Buen Ayre, SA, in May 1998; cap. and res \$20.2m., dep. \$1.2m. (June 1992); Dir-Gen. Antonio Carlos B. de Oliveira; 94 brs.

Banco Sudameris Argentina, SA: Juan D. Perón 500, 1038 Buenos Aires; tel. (11) 4329-5200; fax (11) 4331-2793; e-mail market ing@sudameris.com.ar; internet www.sudameris.com.ar; f. 1912; cap. \$89.0m., res \$11.5m., dep. \$977.2m. (Dec. 1998); Exec. Dir Carlos González Taboada.

Banco Supervielle-Société Générale, SA: Reconquista 330, 1003 Buenos Aires; tel. (11) 4329-8000; fax (11) 4329-8080; e-mail info@ar .socgen.com; internet www.supervielle.com.ar; f. 1887 as Banco Sup-ervielle de Buenos Aires, SA, adopted current name in 1979; cap. \$50.5m., res \$25.7m., dep. \$649.7m. (Dec. 1997); Chair. and Gen. Man. Marc-Emmanuel Vives; 40 brs.

Bank of Tokyo-Mitsubishi, Ltd (Japan): Avda Corrientes 420, 1043 Buenos Aires; tel. (11) 4348-2001; fax (11) 4322-6607; f. 1956; cap. and res \$20m., dep. \$81m. (Sept. 1994); Gen. Man. Kazuo Omi.

BankBoston NA (USA): Florida 99, 1005 Buenos Aires; tel. (11) 4346-2000; fax (11) 4346-3200; f. 1784; cap. \$456.8m., dep. \$4,012m.; total assets \$8,677m. (Sept. 1998); Pres. Ing. Manuel Sacerdote; 139 brs.

Banque Nationale de Paris, SA (France): 25 de Mayo 471, 1002 Buenos Aires; tel. (11) 4318-0318; fax (11) 4311-1368; f. 1981; cap. and res \$29.4m., dep. \$86.7m. (June 1992); Gen. Man. Chislain de Beaucé.

Chase Manhattan Bank (USA): Arenales 707, 5°, 1061 Buenos Aires; tel. (11) 4319-2400; fax (11) 4319-2416; f. 1904; cap. and res \$46.3m., dep. \$12,387m. (Sept. 1992); Gen. Man. Marcelo Podestá.

Citibank, NA (USA): Colón 58, Bahía Blanca, 8000 Buenos Aires; tel. (11) 4331-8281; f. 1914; cap. and res \$172.8m., dep. \$660.8m. (June 1992); Pres. Ricardo Angles; Vice-Pres. Guillermo Stanley; 16 brs.

Deutsche Bank Argentina, SA (Germany): Bartolomé Mitre 401, Casilla 995, 1036 Buenos Aires; tel. (11) 4343-2510; fax (11) 4343-3536; f. 1960; cap. and res \$123.6m., dep. \$801.0m. (June 1994); Gen. Man. Gerardo Greiser; 47 brs.

Lloyds Bank (Bank of London and South America) Ltd (United Kingdom): Tronador 4890, 13°, Casilla 128, 1003 Buenos Aires; tel. (11) 4335-3551; fax (11) 4342-7487; f. 1862; subsidiary of Lloyds Bank TSB Group; cap. and res \$108.1m., dep. \$583.4m. (Sept. 1997); Gen. Man. for Argentina Colin J. Mitchell; 31 brs.

Morgan Guaranty Trust Co of New York (USA): Avda Corri-entes 411, 1043 Buenos Aires; tel. and fax (11) 4325-8046; cap. and res \$29.1m., dep. \$11.6m. (June 1992); Gen. Man. José McLoughlin.

Republic National Bank of New York (USA): Bartolomé Mitre 343, 1036 Buenos Aires; tel. (11) 4343-0161; fax (11) 4331-6064; cap. and res \$17.2m., dep. \$13.6m. (March 1994); Gen. Man. Alberto Muchnick.

Scotiabank Quilmes, SA (Canada): Juan D. Perón 564, 1038 Buenos Aires; tel. (11) 1338-8000; fax (11) 4338-8511; e-mail bqcorp @infovia.com; internet www.scotiabankquilmes.co.ar; f. 1907 as Banco Popular de Quilmes, SA, adopted current name in 1999 following merger with the Bank of Nova Scotia; cap. \$133.0m., res \$5.0m., dep. \$2,107.2m.; Pres. William Peter Sutton; 88 brs.

Bankers' Associations

Asociación de Bancos de la Argentina (ABA): San Martín 229, 10°, 1004 Buenos Aires; tel. (11) 4394-1430; fax (11) 4394-6340; e-mail webmaster@aba-argentina.com; internet www.aba-argentina .com; f. 1999 by merger of Asociación de Bancos de la República Argentina (f. 1919) and Asociación de Bancos Argentinos (f. 1972); Pres. Lic. Eduardo J. Escasany; Exec. Dir Dr Norberto Carlos Peruzzotti.

Asociación de Bancos del Interior de la República Argentina (ABIRA): Avda Corrientes 538, 4°, 1043 Buenos Aires; tel. (11) 4394-3439; fax (11) 4394-5682; f. 1956; Pres. Dr Jorge Federico Christensen; Dir Raúl Passano; 30 mems.

Asociación de Bancos Públicos y Privados de la República Argentina (ABAPPRA): Florida 470, 1°, 1005 Buenos Aires; tel. (11) 4322-6321; fax (11) 4322-6721; e-mail info@abappra.com.ar; internet www.abappra.com; f. 1959; Pres. ENRIQUE OLIVERA; Man. LUIS B. BUCAFUSCO; 31 mems.

Federación de Bancos Cooperativos de la República Argentina (FEBANCOOP): Maipú 374, 9°/10°, 1006 Buenos Aires; tel. (11) 4394-9949; f. 1973; Pres. OMAR C. TRILLO; Exec. Sec. JUAN CARLOS ROMANO; 32 mems.

STOCK EXCHANGES

Mercado de Valores de Buenos Aires, SA: 25 de Mayo 367, 8°–10°, 1002 Buenos Aires; tel. (11) 4313-6021; fax (11) 4313-4472; internet www.merval.sba.com.ar; Pres. EUGENIO DE BARY.

There are also stock exchanges at Córdoba, Rosario, Mendoza and La Plata.

Supervisory Authority

Comisión Nacional de Valores (CNV): 25 de Mayo 175, 1002Buenos Aires; tel. (11) 4342-4607; fax (11) 4331-0639; e-mail gharte@mecon.ar; internet www.cnv.gob.ar; monitors capital markets; Pres. GUILLERMO HARTENECK.

INSURANCE

Superintendencia de Seguros de la Nación: Avda Julio A. Roca 721, 5°, 1067 Buenos Aires; tel. (11) 4331-8733; fax (11) 4331-9821; f. 1938; Superintendent Dr IGNACIO WARNES.

In December 1993 there were 249 insurance companies operating in Argentina, of which 11 were foreign. The following is a list of those offering all classes or a specialized service.

La Agrícola, SA: Buenos Aires; tel. (11) 4394-5031; f. 1905; associated co La Regional; all classes; Pres. LUIS R. MARCO; First Vice-Pres. JUSTO J. DE CORRAL.

Aseguradora de Créditos y Garantías, SA: Avda Corrientes 415, 4°, 1043 Buenos Aires; tel. (11) 4394-4037; fax (11) 4394-0320; e-mail acgtias@infovia.com.ar; internet www.acg.com.ar; f. 1965; Pres. Lic. HORACIO SCAPPARONE; Exec. Vice-Pres. Dr ANÍBAL E. LÓPEZ.

Aseguradora de Río Negro y Neuquén: Avda Alem 503, Cipolletti, Río Negro; tel. (299) 477-2725; fax (299) 477-0321; f. 1960; all classes; Gen. Man. ERNESTO LÓPEZ.

Aseguradores de Cauciones, SA: Paraguay 580, 1057 Buenos Aires; tel. (11) 4318-3700; fax (11) 4318-3799; e-mail directorio@caucion.com.ar; internet www.caucion.com.ar; f. 1968; all classes; Pres. JOSÉ DE VEDIA.

Aseguradores Industriales, SA: Juan D. Perón 650, 6°, 1038 Buenos Aires; tel. (11) 4326-8881; fax (11) 4326-3742; f. 1961; all classes; Exec. Pres. Dir LUIS ESTEBAN LOFORTE.

La Austral: Buenos Aires; tel. (11) 442-9881; fax (11) 4953-4459; f. 1942; all classes; Pres. RODOLFO H. TAYLOR.

Colón, Cía de Seguros Generales, SA: San Martín 548–550, 1004 Buenos Aires; tel. (11) 4320-3800; fax (11) 4320-3802; f. 1962; all classes; Gen. Man. L. D. STSCK.

Columbia, SA de Seguros: Juan D. Perón 690, 1038 Buenos Aires; tel. (11) 4325-0208; fax (11) 4326-1392; f. 1918; all classes; Pres. MARTA BLANCO; Gen. Man. HORACIO H. PETRILLO.

El Comercio, Cía de Seguros a Prima Fija, SA: Avda Corrientes 415, 3° y 5°, 1043 Buenos Aires; tel. (11) 4394-9111; fax (11) 4393-1207; f. 1889; all classes; Pres. DONALD JOSÉ SMITH BALMACEDA; Man. PABLO DOMINGO F. LONGO.

Cía Argentina de Seguros de Créditos a la Exportación, SA: Corrientes 345, 7°, 1043 Buenos Aires; tel. (11) 4313-3048; fax (11) 4313-2919; f. 1967; covers credit and extraordinary and political risks for Argentine exports; Pres. LUIS ORCOYEN; Gen. Man. Dr MARIANO A. GARCÍA GALISTEO.

Cía Aseguradora Argentina, SA: Avda Roque S. Peña 555, 1035 Buenos Aires; tel. (11) 430-1571; fax (11) 430-5973; f. 1918; all classes; Man. GUIDO LUTTINI; Vice-Pres. ALBERTO FRAGUIO.

La Continental, Cía de Seguros Generales SA: Avda Corrientes 655, 1043 Buenos Aires; tel. (11) 4393-8051; fax (11) 4325-7101; f. 1912; all classes; Pres. RAÚL MASCARENHAS.

La Franco-Argentina, SA: Buenos Aires; tel. (11) 430-3091; f. 1896; all classes; Pres. Dr GUILLERMO MORENO HUEYO; Gen. Man. Dra HAYDÉE GUZIAN DE RAMÍREZ.

Hermes, SA: Edif. Hermes, Bartolomé Mitre 754/60, 1036 Buenos Aires; tel. (11) 4331-4506; fax (11) 4343-5552; e-mail hermes@mbox.servicenet.com.ar; f. 1926; all classes; Pres. DIONISIO KATOPODIS; Gen. Man. FRANCISCO MARTÍN ZABALO.

India, Cía de Seguros Generales SA: Avda Roque S. Peña 728/36, 1035 Buenos Aires; tel. (11) 4328-6001; fax (11) 4328-5602; f. 1950; all classes; Pres. ALFREDO JUAN PRIESSE; Vice-Pres. Dr RAÚL ALBERTO GUARDIA.

Instituto Italo-Argentino de Seguros Generales, SA: Avda Roque S. Peña 890, 1035 Buenos Aires; tel. (11) 4320-9200; fax (11) 4320-9229; f. 1920; all classes; Pres. ALEJANDRO A. SOLDATI.

La Meridional, Cía Argentina de Seguros SA: Juan D. Perón 646, 1038 Buenos Aires; tel. (11) 4909-7000; fax (11) 4909-7274; e-mail meridi@starnet.net.ar; f. 1949; life and general; Pres. GUILLERMO V. LASCANO QUINTANA; Gen. Man. PETER HAMMER.

Plus Ultra, Cía Argentina de Seguros, SA: San Martín 548–50, 1004 Buenos Aires; tel. (11) 4393-5069; f. 1956; all classes; Gen. Man. L. D. STSCK.

La Primera, SA: Blvd Villegas y Oro, Trenque Lauquén, Prov. Buenos Aires; tel. (11) 4393-8125; all classes; Pres. ENRIQUE RAÚL U. BOTTINI; Man. Dr RODOLFO RAÚL D'ONOFRIO.

La Rectora, SA: Avda Corrientes 848, 1043 Buenos Aires; tel. (11) 4394-6081; fax (11) 4394-3251; f. 1951; all classes; Pres. PEDRO PASCUAL MEGNA; Gen. Man. ANTONIO LÓPEZ BUENO.

La República Cía Argentina de Seguros Generales, SA: San Martín 627/29, 1374 Buenos Aires; tel. (11) 4314-1000; fax (11) 4318-8778; e-mail ccastell@republica.com.ar; f. 1928; group life and general; Pres. JOSÉ T. GUZMAN DUMAS; Gen. Man. EDUARDO ESCRIÑA.

Sud América Terrestre y Marítima Cía de Seguros Generales, SA: Florida 15, 2°, Galería Florida 1, 1005 Buenos Aires; tel. (11) 4340-5100; fax (11) 4340-5380; f. 1919; all classes; Pres. EMA SÁNCHEZ DE LARRAGOITI; Vice-Pres. ALAIN HOMBREUX.

La Unión Gremial, SA: Mitre 665/99, 2000 Rosario, Santa Fe; tel. (341) 426-2900; fax (341) 425-9802; f. 1908; general; Gen. Man. EDUARDO IGNACIO LLOBET.

La Universal: Buenos Aires; tel. (11) 442-9881; fax (11) 4953-4459; f. 1905; all classes; Pres. RODOLFO H. TAYLOR.

Zurich-Iguazú Cía de Seguros, SA: San Martín 442, 1004 Buenos Aires; tel. (11) 4329-0400; fax (11) 4322-4688; f. 1947; all classes; Pres. RAMÓN SANTAMARINA.

Reinsurance

Instituto Nacional de Reaseguros: Avda Julio A. Roca 694, 1067 Buenos Aires; tel. (11) 4334-0084; fax (11) 4334-5588; f. 1947; reinsurance in all branches; Pres. and Man. REINALDO A. CASTRO.

Insurance Associations

Asociación Argentina de Cías de Seguros (AACS): 25 de Mayo 565, 2°, 1002 Buenos Aires; tel. (11) 4312-7790; fax (11) 4312-6300; e-mail secret@aacsra.org.ar; f. 1894; 60 mems; Pres. ROBERTO F. E. SOLLITTO.

Asociación de Entidades Aseguradoras Privadas de la República Argentina (EAPRA): Esmeralda 684, 4°, 1007 Buenos Aires; tel. (11) 4393-2268; fax (11) 4393-2283; f. 1875; asscn of 12 foreign insurance cos operating in Argentina; Pres. Dr PIERO ZUPPELLI; Sec. BERNARDO VON DER GOLTZ.

Trade and Industry

GOVERNMENT AGENCIES

Cámara de Exportadores de la República Argentina: Avda Roque S. Peña 740, 1°, 1035 Buenos Aires; tel. (11) 4394-4351; fax (11) 4328-1003; e-mail contacto@cera.org.ar; internet www.cera.org.ar; f. 1943 to promote exports; 700 mems.

Consejo Federal de Inversiones: San Martín 871, 1004 Buenos Aires; tel. (11) 4313-5557; fax (11) 4313-4486; federal board to co-ordinate domestic and foreign investment and provide technological aid for the provinces; Sec.-Gen. Ing. JUAN JOSÉ CIÁCERA.

Dirección de Forestación (DF): Avda Paseo Colón 982, anexo jardin, 1063 Buenos Aires; tel. (11) 4349-2124; fax (11) 4349-2102; e-mail fsanti@sagyp.mecon.ar; assumed the responsibilities of the national forestry commission (Instituto Forestal Nacional—IFONA) in 1991, following its dissolution; supervised by the Secretaría de Agricultura, Ganadería y Pesca; maintains the Centro de Documentación e Información Forestal; Library Man. NILDA E. FERNÁNDEZ.

Instituto de Desarrollo Económico y Social (IDES): Araoz 2838, 1425 Buenos Aires; tel. (11) 4804-4949; fax (11) 4804-5856; e-mail ides@clasco.edu.ar; internet www.clacso.edu.ar/~ides; f. 1960; investigation into social sciences and promotion of social and economic devt; 700 mems; Pres. BERNARDO KOSACOFF; Sec. ADRIANA MARSHALL.

Junta Nacional de Granos: Avda Paseo Colón 359, 1063 Buenos Aires; tel. (11) 430-0641; national grain board; supervises commercial practices and organizes the construction of farm silos and port elevators; Pres. JORGE CORT.

Secretaría de Agricultura, Ganadería, Pesca y Alimentación: Avda Paseo Colón 922/982, 1°, Of. 146, 1063 Buenos Aires; tel. (11) 4349-2291; fax (11) 4349-2292; e-mail mpelle@sagyp.mecon.ar; internet www.siiap.sagyp.mecon.ar; f. 1871; undertakes regulatory, promotional, advisory and administrative responsibilities on behalf of the meat, livestock and fisheries industries; Sec. FELIPE C. SOLA.

Sindicatura General de Empresas Públicas: Lavalle 1429, 1048 Buenos Aires; tel. (11) 449-5415; fax (11) 4476-4054; f. 1978; to exercise external control over wholly- or partly-owned public enterprises; Pres. ALBERTO R. ABAD.

DEVELOPMENT ORGANIZATIONS

Instituto Argentino del Petróleo y Gas: Maipú 645, 3°, 1006 Buenos Aires; tel. (11) 4325-8008; fax (11) 4393-5494; e-mail informa@iapg.org.ar; internet www.iapg.org.ar; f. 1958; established to promote the devt of petroleum exploration and exploitation; Pres. Ing. E. J. ROCCHI.

Secretario de Programación Económica: Hipólito Yrigoyen 250, 8°, Of. 819, Buenos Aires; tel. (11) 4349-5710; fax (11) 4349-5714; f. 1961 to formulate national long-term devt plans; Sec. Dr JUAN JOSÉ LACH.

Sociedad Rural Argentina: Florida 460, 1005 Buenos Aires; tel. (11) 4324-4700; fax (11) 4324-4774; f. 1866; private org. to promote the devt of agriculture; Pres. ENRIQUE C. CROTTO; 9,400 mems.

CHAMBERS OF COMMERCE

Cámara Argentina de Comercio: Avda Leandro N. Alem 36, 1003 Buenos Aires; tel. (11) 4331-8051; fax (11) 4331-8055; e-mail gerencia@cac.com.ar; f. 1924; Pres. JORGE LUIS DI FIORI.

Cámara de Comercio, Industria y Producción de la República Argentina: Florida 1, 4°, 1005 Buenos Aires; tel. (11) 4331-0813; fax (11) 4331-9116; f. 1913; Pres. JOSÉ CHEDIEK; Vice-Pres. Dr FAUSTINO S. DIÉGUEZ, Dr JORGE M. MAZALAN; 1,500 mems.

Cámara de Comercio Exterior de Rosario: Avda Córdoba 1868, 2000 Rosario, Santa Fe; tel. and fax (341) 425-7147; e-mail ccer@commerce.com.ar; internet www.commerce.com.ar; f. 1958; deals with imports and exports; Pres. JUAN CARLOS RETAMERO; Vice-Pres. EDUARDO C. SALVATIERRA; 150 mems.

Similar chambers are located in most of the larger centres and there are many foreign chambers of commerce.

INDUSTRIAL AND TRADE ASSOCIATIONS

Asociación de Importadores y Exportadores de la República Argentina: Avda Belgrano 124, 1°, 1092 Buenos Aires; tel. (11) 4342-0010; fax (11) 4342-1312; e-mail aiera@aiera.org.ar; internet www.aiera.org.ar; f. 1966; Pres. HÉCTOR MARCELLO VIDAL; Man. ADRIANO DE FINA.

Asociación de Industriales Textiles Argentinos: Buenos Aires; tel. (11) 4373-2256; fax (11) 4373-2351; f. 1945; textile industry; Pres. BERNARDO ABRAMOVICH; 250 mems.

Asociación de Industrias Argentinas de Carnes: Buenos Aires; tel. (11) 4322-5244; meat industry; refrigerated and canned beef and mutton; Pres. JORGE BORSELLA.

Asociación Vitivinícola Argentina: Güemes 4464, 1425 Buenos Aires; tel. (11) 4774-3370; f. 1904; wine industry; Pres. LUCIANO COTUMACCIO; Man. Lic. MARIO J. GIORDANO.

Cámara de Sociedades Anónimas: Florida 1, 3°, 1005 Buenos Aires; tel. (11) 4342-9013; fax (11) 4342-9225; Pres. Dr ALFONSO DE LA FERRERE; Man. CARLOS ALBERTO PERRONE.

Centro de Exportadores de Cereales: Bouchard 454, 7°, 1106 Buenos Aires; tel. (11) 4311-1697; fax (11) 4312-6924; f. 1943; grain exporters; Pres. RAUL S. LOEH.

Confederaciones Rurales Argentinas: México 628, 2°, 1097 Buenos Aires; tel. (11) 4261-1501; Pres. ARTURO J. NAVARRO.

Coordinadora de Actividades Mercantiles Empresarias: Buenos Aires; Pres. OSVALDO CORNIDE.

Federación Lanera Argentina: Avda Paseo Colón 823, 5°, 1063 Buenos Aires; tel. (11) 4300-7661; fax (11) 4361-6517; f. 1929; wool industry; Pres. JULIO AISENSTEIN; Sec. RICHARD VON GERSTENBERG; 80 mems.

EMPLOYERS' ORGANIZATION

Unión Industrial Argentina (UIA): Avda Leandro N. Alem 1067, 11°, 1001 Buenos Aires; tel. (11) 4313-4474; fax (11) 4313-2413; e-mail uia01@act.net.ar; f. 1887; re-established in 1974 with the fusion of the Confederación Industrial Argentina (CINA) and the Confederación General de la Industria; following the dissolution of the CINA in 1977, the UIA was formed in 1979; asscn of manufacturers, representing industrial corpns; Pres. OSVALDO RIAL; Sec.-Gen. Dr JOSÉ I. DE MENDIGUREN.

MAJOR COMPANIES

Aceros Bragado, SACIF: Bernardo de Yrigoyen 190, 1072 Buenos Aires; tel. (11) 4385-952; fax (11) 4112-068; f. 1969; foundry, mill rolls, bearing trucks, laminating; Pres. BERNARDO ABEL COLL; 1,670 employees.

Acindar Industria Argentina de Aceros, SA: Estanislao Zeballos 2739, Beccar, Buenos Aires; tel. (11) 4719-8500; fax (11) 4719-8501; e-mail webmaster@acindar.com.ar; internet www.acindar.com.ar; f. 1942; production of iron and steel; Pres. ARTURO ACEVEDO; 3,922 employees.

Alpargatas, SAIC: Avda Regimento de Los Patricios 1142, 1266 Buenos Aires; tel. (11) 4303-0041; fax (11) 4303-2401; internet www.moda.com.ar; f. 1885; textile and footwear manufacturers; Pres. PATRICIO ZAVALIA LAGOS; 8,000 employees.

ALUAR—Aluminio Argentino, SAIC: Pasteur 4600, Victoria, 1644 Buenos Aires; tel. (11) 4725-8000; fax (11) 4725-8091; internet www.aluar.com.ar; f. 1970; aluminium production; Pres. DOLORES QUINTANILLA DE MADANES; 1,790 employees.

Astra, Compañía Argentina de Petróleo, SA: Tucumán 744, 1049 Buenos Aires; tel. (11) 4329-0293; fax (11) 4329-0019; internet www.astra-capsa.com; f. 1912; petroleum services and products; Pres. Dr RICARDO GRÜNEISEN; 725 employees.

Atanor, SA: Pte Gral J. D. Perón 646, 3°, 1038 Buenos Aires; tel. (11) 4327-2330; fax (11) 4393-6427; e-mail dircomex@atanorsa.com.ar; internet www.atanorsa.com.ar; f. 1943; producers of chemicals and petrochemicals; Pres. MIGUEL ANGEL GONZÁLEZ; 857 employees.

BAESA—Buenos Aires Embotelladora, SA: Roque Saenz Peña 308, San Isidro Buenos Aires; tel. (11) 4747-8317; fax (11) 4747-3846; f. 1989; makers of canned and bottled soft drinks; Chair., Pres. and CEO OSVALDO H BAÑOS; 5,500 employees.

Bagley, SA: Avda Montes de Oca 169, 1270 Buenos Aires; tel. (11) 4300-0202; fax (11) 4341-4013; f. 1887; manufacturers of crackers, snacks, biscuits, chocolate products and wines and spirits; Pres. ERNESTO O'FARRELL; 5,011 employees.

Bayer Argentina, SA: Ricardo Gutiérrez 3652, 1605 Buenos Aires; tel. (11) 4762-7000; fax (11) 4762-7100; f. 1958; production of chemicals, agrochemicals and pharmaceuticals; parent co Bayer AG, Germany; Pres. and Gen. Man. HELMUT FLETCHNER; 1,176 employees.

Bunge y Born, SA: 25 de Mayo 501, 1°, 1002 Buenos Aires; tel. (11) 4311-5201; fax (11) 4318-6629; f. 1919; vegetable-oil mills; CEO Dr SALVADOR CARBÓ; 4,567 employees.

CANALE, SA: Avda Martín García 320, 1165 Buenos Aires; tel. (11) 4307-4000; fax (11) 4307-1090; f. 1975; manufacturers of biscuits; Pres. FELIX DEVOTO; 1,688 employees.

Celulosa Argentina, SA: Avda Pomilio s/n, Capitan Bermudez, 2154 Santa Fe; tel. (41) 911-402; fax (41) 911-401; f. 1929; manufacturers of paper and paper products; Pres. JORGE SANGUINETTI; 1,000 employees.

Central Costanera, SA (CECCO): Avda España 3301, 1107 Buenos Aires; tel. (11) 4307-3041; fax (11) 4307-1705; f. 1992; electricity production and distribution; CEO MIGUEL ORTIZ; Chair. JAIME BAUZÁ BAUZÁ; 600 employees.

Cervecería Malteria Quilmes, SAICA: 12 de Octubre y Gran Canaria s/n, 1878 Quilmes, Buenos Aires; tel. (11) 4349-1700; fax (11) 4326-0026; f. 1890; beer and malt producers; Pres. CARLOS MIGUENS; 1,601 employees.

Compañía Azucarera Concepción, SA: San Martín 662, 1004 Buenos Aires; tel. (11) 4311-3444; fax (11) 4312-0418; manufacturers of sugar cane and alcohol; Pres. HORACIO GARCÍA GONZÁLEZ; 3,289 employees.

Compañía Continental, SACIMFA: Avda Córdoba 883, 11°, 1054 Buenos Aires; tel. (11) 4319-2300; fax (11) 319-2383; grain merchants; Pres. CARLOS A. ORIS DE ROA; 235 employees.

Disco, SA: Larrea 847, 1°, 1117 Buenos Aires; tel. (11) 4964-8000; fax (11) 4964-8039; internet www.disco.com.ar; f. 1969; supermarket chain; Chair. LEITZIA VEJO DE PEIRANO; 5,100 employees.

Duperial, SAIC: Paseo Colón 285, 1330 Buenos Aires; tel. (11) 4322-011. 1937; manufacturers of plastic and chemical products; subsidiary of Imperial Chemical Industries, United Kingdom; Pres. PEDRO GRUNWALD; 2,200 employees.

Electroclor, SA: Paseo Colón 221, Planta Baja, Buenos Aires: tel. (11) 4331-7969; fax (11) 4334-0168; f. 1936; industrial chemical manufacturers; 565 employees.

Esso SA Petrolera Argentina: Carlos María Della Paolera 297, 1101 Buenos Aires; tel. (11) 4319-1400; fax (11) 4319-1227; f. 1911; active in all spheres of the petroleum industry; subsidiary of Exxon Corpn, USA; Pres. CARLOS DE JESÚS; 1,800 employees.

Ferrum, SA: España 496, Avellaneda, 1870 Buenos Aires; tel. (11) 4222-1500; fax (11) 4222-3464; e-mail info@ferrum.com; internet www.ferrum.com; f. 1911; building material manufacturers; Pres. RODOLFO J. VEIGENER; Vice-Pres. JOAQUÍN C. VEIGENER; 1,200 employees.

Fiplasto, SACI: Alsina 756, 1087 Buenos Aires; tel. (11) 4331-2518; fax (11) 4331-2518; e-mail info@fiplasto.com.ar; internet www.fiplasto.com; f. 1946; hardwood and veneer manufacturers; Pres. MAXIMO FEDERICO LELOIR; 316 employees.

Ford Argentina, SA: Henry Ford/Ruta Panamericana s/n, General Pacheco, 1617 Buenos Aires; tel. (11) 4756-9000; fax (11) 4756-9001; f. 1913; manufacture of motor vehicles; owned by Ford Motor Co, USA; Pres. JORGE TOMAS MOSTANY; 5,200 employees.

GATIC, SAICFIA: Eva Perón 2535, San Martín, 1650 Buenos Aires; tel. (11) 4753-9040; fax (11) 4752-5536; f. 1953; rubber footwear makers; Pres. EDUARDO IEVART BAKCHELLIAN; 4,666 employees.

General Electric Technical Services Co, Inc.: Avda Leandro N. Alem 619, 9°, 1001 Buenos Aires; tel. (11) 4313-2880; fax (11) 4111-794; f. 1920; sales of industrial equipment; engineering services; subsidiary of International General Electric Co, USA; 900 employees.

Grafex, SAGCIF: Calle Larralde 3419, 1273 Buenos Aires; tel. (11) 4207-2506; fax (11) 4207-4720; e-mail ventas@grafex.com.ar; internet www.grafex.com.ar; f. 1894; manufacturers and distributors of photographic equipment; Pres. Dr JORGE F. BERGER; 500 employees.

IBM Argentina, SA: Ing. Enrique Butti 275, 1300 Buenos Aires; tel. (11) 4313-0014; fax (11) 4313-2360; internet www.ibm.com.ar; f. 1923; computer hardware and software; owned by IBM Corpn, USA; Pres. ENRIQUE BACEÑO; 1,200 employees.

INDUPA, SAIC: Viamonte 1494, 1055 Buenos Aires; tel. (11) 4316-2300; fax (11) 4316-2390; f. 1948; manufacturers of chemicals; Pres. JEAN PIERRE LAPAGE; 480 employees.

Ingenio y Refinería San Martín del Tabacal, SA: El Tabacal, Oran, 4453 Provincia de Salta; tel. (387) 842-1800; fax (387) 842-1941; e-mail tabacal@salnet.com.ar; f. 1943; sugar cane and citrus fruit cultivation; Man. Dir RANDOLPH I. FLEMING; 1,200 employees.

IPAKO Industrias Petroquímicas Argentinas, SA: Céspedes 3857, 1427 Buenos Aires; tel. (11) 4555-6000; fax (11) 4555-1434; f. 1960; petrochemical manufacturers; Pres. FEDERICO J. L. ZORRA-QUÍN; 600 employees.

Kraft-Suchard, SA Argentina: Avda Int Francisco Rabanal 3220, 1437 Buenos Aires; tel. (11) 4630-8000; fax (11) 4924-3003; f. 1933; chocolate, sweets and frozen confectionery; Chair. and CEO JUAN PEDRO MUNRO; 600 employees.

Laboratorios Bagó, SA: Bernardo de Yrigoyen 248, 1072 Buenos Aires; tel. (11) 4334-9081; fax (11) 4334-5813; e-mail marketing @lab_bago.datamar.com.ar; f. 1934; pharmaceuticals; Pres. Dr JUAN CARLOS BAGÓ; 936 employees.

Ledesma, SAAI: Avda Corrientes 415, 8°, 1043 Buenos Aires; tel. (11) 4326-5101; fax (11) 4325-7666; f. 1914; sugar producers; Pres. Dr CARLOS PEDRO BLAQUIER; 3,970 employees.

Loma Negra, SA: Avda Roque Saénz Peña 640, 1035 Buenos Aires; tel. (11) 4331-1533; fax (11) 4331-3024; internet www.lomanegra.com.ar; f. 1926; cement and building materials manufacturing; Pres. MARÍA AMALIA SARA LACROZE DE FFORTABAT; 2,200 employees.

Massalin Particulares, SA: Avda Leandro N. Alem 466, 9°, 1003 Buenos Aires; tel. (11) 4319-4100; fax (11) 4319-4150; f. 1980; cigarette and tobacco producers; Pres. RAFAEL ARGUELLES; 2,500 employees.

Mercedes Benz Argentina, SACIFIM: Avda del Libertador 2424, 1425 Buenos Aires; tel. (11) 4801-6355; fax (11) 4808-8705; f. 1952; manufacturers of trucks, buses and engines; subsidiary of Daimler Benz AG, Germany; Pres. KARL HEINZ HARTMANN; 1,600 employees.

Juan Minetti, SA: Ituzaingo 87, 5000 Córdoba; tel. (51) 267-500; fax (51) 267-551; e-mail jmgg@satlink.com; internet www.juanminetti.com; f. 1932; manufacturers of hydraulic cement; Chair. ENRIQUE S. PALACIO MINETTI; 830 employees.

Molinos Río de la Plata, SA: Paseo Colón 746, 1323 Buenos Aires; tel. (11) 4331-7977; fax (11) 4331-5718; internet www.molinos.com.ar; f. 1931; manufacturers of flour and grain products; Pres. and CEO JORGE ABERTO CASTRO GOLPE; 4,200 employees.

Nestlé de Productos Alimenticios: Carlos Pelegrino 887, 1009 Buenos Aires; tel. (11) 4329-8100; fax (11) 4329-8200; manufacturers of condensed milk, instant coffee, milk powder and confectionary; subsidiary of Nestlé, SA, Switzerland; Dir-Gen. CLAUDIO BARTOLINI; 3,400 employees.

Nobleza-Piccardo, SAICF: 25 de Mayo 555, 1002 Buenos Aires; tel. (11) 4311-4516; fax (11) 4313-2499; f. 1898; cigarette and tobacco manufacturers; Pres. and Gen. Man. MARK M. COBBEN; 1,700 employees.

Philips Argentina, SA: Vedía 3892, 1430 Buenos Aires; tel. (11) 4541-4106; fax (11) 4542-0066; internet www.philips.com.ar; f. 1935; manufacturers of electrical equipment; subsidiary of Philips Golampenfabrieken NV, Netherlands; Pres. Ing ANTON MOLENAR; 1,780 employees.

Pirelli Cables, SAIC: Avda Argentina 6784, 1439 Buenos Aires; tel. (11) 4630-2000; fax (11) 4630-2100; Pres. ELVIO BALDINELLI; 1,900 employees.

Pluspetrol Exploración y Producción, SA: Edif. Pluspetrol Lima 339, 1073 Buenos Aires; tel. (11) 4340-2222; fax (11) 4340-2215; f. 1977; oil and gas exploration and production; Chair. and Pres. LUIS ALBERTO REY; 363 employees.

Química Estrella, SACII: Avda de los Constituyentes 2995, 1427 Buenos Aires; tel. (11) 4521-2891; fax (11) 4522-3022; f. 1906; pharmaceutical manufacturers; Pres. JOSÉ A. MARTÍNEZ; 600 employees.

Renault Argentina, SA: Fray Justo María de Oro 1744, 1414 Buenos Aires; tel. (11) 4778-2000; fax (11) 4778-2023; internet www.renaultarg.com; f. 1955 as Ciadea, SA; motor vehicle manufacturers; Pres. MANUEL FERNANDO ANTELO; 4,200 employees.

Rigolleau, SA: Carlos Pelegrini 450, 1884 Buenos Aires: tel. (11) 4256-2011; fax (11) 4256-2544; e-mail info@rigolleau.com.ar; internet www.rigolleau.com.ar; f. 1906; makers of glass and glass products; Pres. ENRIQUE CATTORINI; 1,485 employees.

Roggio e Hijos Benito, SA: Blvd Las Herreras 402, 5000 Córdoba; tel. (51) 20-094; fax (51) 243-696; f. 1955; holding co in field of construction; Pres. VITO REMO ROGGIO; 2,156 employees.

Sevel Argentina, SA: Juan Domingo Perón 1001, Villa Bosch, 1682 Provincia de Buenos Aires; tel. (11) 4734-3005; fax (11) 4734-3007; internet www.sevel.com.ar; f. 1965; automobile manufacturers; Chair. MAURICIO NACRI; 7,500 employees.

Siderca, SAIC: Dr Jorge A. Simini 250, 2804 Campana, Buenos Aires; tel. (11) 4318-2100; fax (11) 4310-1000; e-mail infodst@siderca.com; internet www.dstpipes.com; f. 1954; seamless steel pipe manufacturers; Pres. ROBERTO ROCCA; 3,916 employees.

SOMISA—Sociedad Mixta Siderúrgia Argentina: Belgrano 737, 1092 Buenos Aires; tel. (11) 4331-951; fax (11) 4344-061; f. 1947; manufacturers of steel; Pres. CARLOS AMANCIO MAGLIANO; 12,300 employees.

Xerox Argentina, ICSA: Jaramillo 1595, Casilla 1664, 1429 Buenos Aires; tel. (11) 4326-7265; fax (11) 4703-7701; internet www.xerox.com.ar; f. 1967; document processing; subsidiary of Xerox Corpn, USA; Pres. EDUARDO GABRIEL LIJTMAER; 500 employees.

Yacimientos Petrolíferos Fiscales, SA (YPF): Avda Roque Saénz Peña 777, 1364 Buenos Aires; tel. (11) 4326-7265; fax (11) 4329-2113; internet www.ypf.com.ar; f. 1922; petroleum and gas exploration and production; state-owned until 1992; Pres. MIGUEL MADANES; 9,750 employees.

UTILITIES
Regulatory Authorities

Ente Nacional Regulador de la Electricidad (ENRE): Avda Eduardo Madero 1020, 10°, 1106 Buenos Aires; tel. (11) 4314-5805; fax (11) 4314-5416; internet www.enre.gov.ar.

Ente Nacional Regulador del Gas (ENARGAS): Suipacha 636, 10°, 1008 Buenos Aires; tel. (11) 4325-9292; fax (11) 4348-0550; internet www.enargas.gov.ar.

Electricity

Central Costanera, SA (CECCO): Avda España 3301, 1107 Buenos Aires; tel. (11) 4307-3040; fax (11) 4307-1706; generation, transmission, distribution and sale of thermal electric energy; Chair. JAIME BAUZÁ BAUZÁ.

Central Puerto, SA (CEPU): Avda Tomás Edison 2701, 1104 Buenos Aires; tel. (11) 4317-5000; fax (11) 4317-5099; electricity generating co; CEO ANTONIO BÜCHI BUC.

Comisión Nacional de Energía Atómica (CNEA): Avda del Libertador 8250, 1429 Buenos Aires; tel. (11) 4704-1384; fax (11) 4704-1176; e-mail freijo@cnea.edu.ar; internet www.cnea.gov.ar;

f. 1950; scheduled for transfer to private ownership; nuclear energy science and technology; Pres. JACOBO DAN BENINSON.

Comisión Técnica Mixta de Salto Grande (CTMSG): Avda Leandro N. Alem 449, 1003 Buenos Aires; operates Salto Grande hydroelectric station, which has an installed capacity of 650 MW; joint Argentine-Uruguayan project.

Dirección de Energía de la Provincia de Buenos Aires: Calle 55, No. 570, La Reja, 1900 Buenos Aires; tel. (11) 4415-000; fax (11) 4216-124; f. 1957; electricity co for province of Buenos Aires; Dir AGUSTÍN NÚÑEZ.

Empresa Distribuidora y Comercializadora Norte, SA (EDENOR): Azopardo 1025, 1107 Buenos Aires; tel. (11) 4348-2121; fax (11) 4334-0805; e-mail ofitel@edenor.com.ar; internet www .edenor.com.ar; distribution of electricity.

Empresa Distribuidora Sur, SA (EDESUR): San José, 140, 1076 Buenos Aires; tel. (11) 4381-8981; fax (11) 4383-3699; internet www.edesur.com.ar; f. 1992; distribution of electricity; Gen. Man. Ing. JOSÉ MARÍA ROVIRA.

Entidad Binacional Yacyretá: Avda Eduardo Madero 942, 21°–22°, 1106 Buenos Aires; tel. (11) 4510-7500; e-mail rrpp@ eby.org.ar; internet www.yacyreta.org.ar; operates the hydroelectic dam at Yacyretá on the Paraná river, owned jointly by Argentina and Paraguay. Completed in 1998, it is one of the world's largest hydroelectric complexes, consisting of 20 generators with a total generating capacity of 2,700 MW.

Hidronor Ingeniería y Servicios, SA (HISSA): Hipólito Yrigoyen 1530, 6°, 1089 Buenos Aires; tel. and fax (11) 4382-6316; e-mail info@hidronor.com; formerly HIDRONOR, SA, the largest producer of electricity in Argentina; responsible for developing the hydroelectric potential of the Limay and neighbouring rivers; transferred to private ownership in 1992 and divided into the following companies:

Central Hidroeléctrica Alicurá, SA: Avda Leandro N. Alem 712, 7°, 1001 Buenos Aires.

Central Hidroeléctrica Cerros Colorados, SA: Avda Leandro N. Alem 690, 12°, 1001 Buenos Aires.

Central Hidroeléctrica El Chocón, SA: Suipacha 268, 9°, Of. A, Buenos Aires.

Hidroeléctrica Piedra del Aguila, SA: Avda Tomás Edison 1251, 1104 Buenos Aires; tel. (11) 4315-2586; fax (11) 4317-5174; Pres. Dr URIEL FEDERICO O'FARRELL; Gen. Man. IGNACIO J. ROSNER.

Transener, SA: Avda Paseo Colón 728, 6°, 1063 Buenos Aires; tel. (11) 4342-6925; fax (11) 4342-7147; energy transmission co.

Pérez Companc, SA: Maipú 1, 1084 Buenos Aires; tel. (11) 4331-8393; fax (11) 4331-8369; internet www.pecom.com.ar; operates the hydroelectric dam at Pichi Picún Leufu; Chair. JORGE GREGORIO PÉREZ COMPANC.

Servicios Eléctricos del Gran Buenos Aires, SA (SEGBA): Balcarce 184, 1002 Buenos Aires; tel. (11) 4331-1901; Principal Officer CARLOS A. MATTAUSCH.

Gas

Distribuidora de Gas del Centro, SA: Avda Hipólito Yrigoyen 475, 5000 Córdoba; tel. (351) 4688-100; fax (351) 4681-568; state-owned co, distributes natural gas.

Metrogás, SA: Avda Montes de Oca 1120, 1271 Buenos Aires; tel. (11) 4309-1000; fax (11) 4309-1366; internet www.metrogas.com; gas distribution; Dir-Gen. WILLIAM ADAMSON.

Transportadora de Gas del Norte, SA: Don Bosco 3672, 3°, 1206 Buenos Aires; tel. (11) 4959-2000; fax (11) 4959-2253; state-owned co, distributes natural gas; Gen. Man. FREDDY CAMEO.

Transportadora de Gas del Sur, SA (TGS): Don Bosco 3672, 5°, 1206 Buenos Aires; tel. (11) 4865-9050; fax (11) 4865-9059; e-mail totgs@tgs.com.ar; internet www.tgs.com.ar; processing and transport of natural gas; Gen. Dir EDUARDO OJEA QUINTANA

Water

Aguas Argentinas: Buenos Aires; distribution of water in Buenos Aires; privatized in 1993; Dir-Gen. JEAN-LOUIS CHAUSSADE.

TRADE UNIONS

Congreso de los Trabajadores Argentinos (CTA): Buenos Aires; dissident trade union confederation; Leader VÍCTOR DE GENARO.

Confederación General del Trabajo—CGT (General Confederation of Labour): Buenos Aires; f. 1984; Peronist; represents approx. 90% of Argentina's 1,100 trade unions; Sec.-Gen. HUGO MOYANO.

Movimiento de Trabajadores Argentinos (MTA): Buenos Aires; dissident trade union confederation.

Transport

Comisión Nacional de Regulación del Transporte (CNRT): Maipú 88, 1084, Buenos Aires; tel. (11) 4819-3000; e-mail msenet@ mecon.gov.ar; internet www.cnrt.gov.ar; regulates domestic and international transport services; part of Ministry of Infrastructure and Housing.

Secretaría de Obras Públicas y Transporte: Hipólito Yrigoyen 250, 12°, 1310 Buenos Aires; tel. (11) 4349-7254; fax (11) 4349-7201; Sec. Ing. ARMANDO GUIBERT.

Secretaría de Transporte Metropolitano y de Larga Distancia: Hipólito Yrigoyen 250, 12°, 1310 Buenos Aires; tel. (11) 4349-7162; fax (11) 4349-7146; Under-Sec. Dr ARMANDO CANOSA.

Secretaría de Transporte Aero-Comercial: Hipólito Yrigoyen 250, 12°, 1310 Buenos Aires; tel. (11) 4349-7203; fax (11) 4349-7206; Under-Sec. Arq. FERMÍN ALARCIA.

Dirección de Estudios y Proyectos: Hipólito Yrigoyen 250, 12°, 1310 Buenos Aires; tel. (11) 4349-7127; fax (11) 4349-7128; Dir Ing. JOSÉ LUIS JAGODNIK.

RAILWAYS

Lines: General Belgrano (narrow-gauge), General Roca, General Bartolomé Mitre, General San Martín, Domingo Faustino Sarmiento (all wide-gauge), General Urquiza (medium-gauge) and Línea Metropolitana, which controls the railways of Buenos Aires and its suburbs. There are direct rail links with the Bolivian Railways network to Santa Cruz de la Sierra and La Paz; with Chile, through the Las Cuevas–Caracoles tunnel (across the Andes) and between Salta and Antofagasta; with Brazil, across the Paso de los Libres and Uruguayana bridge; with Paraguay (between Posadas and Encarnación by ferry-boat); and with Uruguay (between Concordia and Salto). In 1995 there were 33,000 km of tracks. In the Buenos Aires commuter area 270.4 km of wide-gauge track and 52 km of medium gauge track are electrified.

Plans for the eventual total privatization of Ferrocarriles Argentinos (FA) were initiated in 1991, with the transfer to private ownership of the Rosario–Bahía Blanca grain line and with the reallocation of responsibility for services in Buenos Aires to the newly-created Ferrocarriles Metropolitanos, prior to its privatization.

In early 1993 central government funding for the FA was suspended and responsibility for existing inter-city passenger routes was devolved to respective provincial governments. However, owing to lack of resources, few provinces have successfully assumed the operation of services, and many trains have been suspended. At the same time, long-distance freight services were sold as six separate 30-year concessions (including lines and rolling stock) to private operators. By late 1996 all freight services had been transferred to private management, with the exception of Ferrocarril Belgrano, SA, which was in the process of undergoing privatization. The Buenos Aires commuter system was divided into eight concerns (one of which incorporates the underground railway system) and was offered for sale to private operators as 10- or 20-year (subsidized) concessions. The railway network is currently regulated by the National Commission for Transport Regulation (CNRT—see above).

Ferrocarriles Argentinos (FA): Salta 1929, 1137 Buenos Aires; tel. (11) 4304-1557; fax (11) 4313-3129; f. 1948 with the nationalization of all foreign property; autonomous body but policies established by the Secretaría de Obras Públicas y Transporte; dismantled and responsibilities transferred in 1993 (see above); Trustee DANIEL OSCAR HALPERIN; Gen. Man. P. SUÁREZ.

Ferrocarriles Metropolitanos, SA (FEMESA): Bartolomé Mitre 2815, Buenos Aires; tel. (11) 4865-4135; fax (11) 4861-8757; f. 1991 to assume responsibility for services in the capital; 820 km of track; Pres. MATÍAS ORDÓÑEZ; concessions to operate services have been awarded to:

Ferrovías.

Metropolitano: f. 1993; operates three commuter lines.

Metrovías: Bartolomé Mitre 3342, 1201 Buenos Aires; tel. (11) 4959-6800; fax (11) 4866-3037; e-mail info@metrovias.com.ar; internet www.metrovias.com; f. 1994; operates subway (Subterráneos de Buenos Aires—see below) and two commuter lines.

Trainmet.

Trenes de Buenos Aires: took over operations of two commuter lines from state in 1995.

Cámara de Industriales Ferroviarios: Alsina 1609, 1°, Buenos Aires; tel. (11) 4371-5571; private org. to promote the devt of Argentine railway industries; Pres. Ing. ANA MARÍA GUIBAUDI.

The following consortia were awarded 30-year concessions to operate rail services, during 1991–94:

Consorcio Nuevo Central Argentino (CNCA): Buenos Aires; operates freight services on the Bartolomé Mitre lines; 5,011 km of track; Pres. H. URQUIA.

Ferrocarril Buenos Aires al Pacífico/San Martín (BAP): Avda Santa Fe 4636, 3°, Buenos Aires; tel. (11) 4778-2486; fax (11) 4778-2493; operates services on much of the San Martín line, and on 706 km of the Sarmiento line; 6,106 km of track; Pres. and Gen. Man. E. GLEZER.

Ferrocarril General Belgrano, SA (FGB): Maipú 88, 1084 Buenos Aires; tel. and fax (11) 4343-7220; fax (11) 4343-7229; f. 1993; operates freight services; Pres. Dr IGNACIO A. LUDVEÑA.

Ferrocarril Mesopotámico General Urquiza (FMGU): Avda Santa Fe 4636, 3°, 1425 Buenos Aires; tel. (11) 4778-2425; fax (11) 4778-2493; operates freight services on the Urquiza lines; 2,272 km of track; Pres. and Gen. Man. E. GLEZER.

Ferroexpreso Pampeano (FEPSA): Bouchard 680, 9°, 1106 Buenos Aires; tel. (11) 4318-4900; fax (11) 4510-4945; operates services on the Rosario–Bahía Blanca grain lines; 5,193 km of track; Pres. H. MASOERO.

Ferrosur Roca (FR): Bouchard 680, 8°, 1106 Buenos Aires; tel. (11) 4319-3900; fax (11) 4319-3901; e-mail ferrosur@impsat1.com.ar; operator of freight services on the Roca lines since 1993; 3,000 km of track; Pres. AMELIA LACROZE DE FORTABAT; Gen. Man. SERGIO DO REGO.

Buenos Aires also has an underground railway system:

Subterráneos de Buenos Aires: Bartolomé Mitre 3342, 1201 Buenos Aires; tel. (11) 4862-6844; fax (11) 4864-0633; f. 1913; became completely state-owned in 1951; fmrly controlled by the Municipalidad de la Ciudad de Buenos Aires; responsibility for operations was transferred, in 1993, to a private consortium (Metrovías) with a 20-year concession; five underground lines totalling 36.5 km, 63 stations, and a 7.4 km light rail line with 13 stations, which was inaugurated in 1987; Pres. A.VERRA.

ROADS

In 1999 there were 215,471 km of roads, of which 29.4% were paved. Four branches of the Pan-American highway run from Buenos Aires to the borders of Chile, Bolivia, Paraguay and Brazil. In 1996 9,932 km of main roads were under private management. Construction work on a 41-km bridge across the River Plate (linking Punta Lara in Argentina with Colonia del Sacramento in Uruguay) was scheduled to begin in the late 1990s.

Dirección Nacional de Vialidad: Avda Julio A. Roca 378, Buenos Aires; tel. (11) 4343-2838; fax (11) 4343-7292; controlled by the Secretaría de Transportes; Gen. Man. Ing. ELIO VERGARA.

Asociación Argentina de Empresarios Transporte Automotor (AAETA): Bernardo de Irigoyen 330, 6°, 1072 Buenos Aires; e-mail aaeta@sei.com.ar; internet www.aaeta.org.ar; Gen. Man. Ing. MARCELO GONZÁLEZ.

Federación Argentina de Entidades Empresarias de Autotransporte de Cargas (FADEAC): Avda 25 de Mayo 1370, 3°, 1372 Buenos Aires; tel. (11) 4383-3635; Pres. ROGELIO CAVALIERI IRIBARNE.

There are several international passenger and freight services including:

Autobuses Sudamericanos, SA: Buenos Aires; tel. (11) 4307-1956; fax (11) 4307-1956; f. 1928; international bus services; car and bus rentals; charter bus services; Pres. ARMANDO SCHLECKER HIRSCH; Gen. Man. MIGUEL ANGEL RUGGIERO.

INLAND WATERWAYS

There is considerable traffic in coastal and river shipping, mainly carrying petroleum and its derivatives.

Dirección Nacional de Construcciones Portuarias y Vías Navegables: Avda España 221, 4°, Buenos Aires; tel. (11) 4361-5964; responsible for the maintenance and improvement of waterways and dredging operations; Dir Ing. ENRIQUE CASALS DE ALBA.

SHIPPING

There are more than 100 ports, of which the most important are Buenos Aires, Quequén and Bahía Blanca. There are specialized terminals at Ensenada, Comodoro Rivadavia, San Lorenzo and Campana (petroleum); Bahía Blanca, Rosario, Santa Fe, Villa Concepción, Mar del Plata and Quequén (cereals); and San Nicolas and San Fernando (raw and construction materials). In 1998 Argentina's merchant fleet totalled 501 vessels amounting to 498,715 grt.

Administración General de Puertos: Avda Ing. Huergo 431, 1°, Buenos Aires; tel. (11) 4343-2425; fax (11) 4331-0298; e-mail comercial@bairesport.gov.ar; internet www.bairesport.gov.ar; f. 1956; state enterprise for direction, administration and exploitation of all national sea- and river-ports; scheduled for transfer to private ownership; Pres. LUIS A. ROURA.

Capitanía General del Puerto: Avda Julio A. Roca 734, 2°, 1067 Buenos Aires; tel. (11) 434-9784; f. 1967; co-ordination of port operations; Port Captain Capt. PEDRO TARAMASCO.

Administración General de Puertos (Santa Fe): Duque 1 Cabacera, Santa Fe; tel. (42) 41732.

Consorcio de Gestión del Puerto de Bahía Blanca: Avda Dr Mario M. Guido s/n, 8103 Provincia de Buenos Aires; tel. (91) 57-3213; Pres. JOSÉ E. CONTE; Sec.-Gen. CLAUDIO MARCELO CONTE.

Terminales Portuarias Argentinas: Buenos Aires; operates one of five recently privatized cargo and container terminals in the port of Buenos Aires.

Terminales Río de la Plata: Buenos Aires; operates one of five recently privatized cargo and container terminals in the port of Buenos Aires.

Empresa Líneas Marítimas Argentinas, SA (ELMA): Avda Corrientes 389, 1327 Buenos Aires; tel. (11) 4312-9245; fax (11) 4311-7954; f. 1941 as state-owned org.; transferred to private ownership in 1994; operates vessels to northern Europe, the Mediterranean, west and east coasts of Canada and the USA, Gulf of Mexico, Caribbean ports, Brazil, Pacific ports of Central and South America, Far East, northern and southern Africa and the Near East; Pres. PABLO DOMINGO DE ZORZI.

Other private shipping companies operating on coastal and overseas routes include:

Antártida Pesquera Industrial: Moreno 1270, 5°, 1091 Buenos Aires; tel. (11) 4381-0167; fax (11) 4381-0519; Pres. J. M. S. MIRANDA; Man. Dir J. R. S. MIRANDA.

Astramar Cía Argentina de Navegación, SAC: Buenos Aires; tel. (11) 4311-3678; fax (11) 4311-7534; Pres. ENRIQUE W. REDDIG.

Bottacchi SA de Navegación: Maipú 509, 2°, 1006 Buenos Aires; tel. (11) 4392-7411; fax (11) 411-1280; Pres. ANGEL L. M. BOTTACCHI.

Maruba S. en C. por Argentina: Maipú 535, 7°, 1006 Buenos Aires; tel. (11) 4322-7173; fax (11) 4322-3353; Chartering Man. R. J. DICKIN.

Yacimientos Petrolíferos Fiscales (YPF): Avda Roque S. Peña 777, 1364 Buenos Aires; tel. (11) 446-7271; privatization finalized in 1993; Pres. NELLS LEÓN.

CIVIL AVIATION

Argentina has 10 international airports (Aeroparque Jorge Newbery, Córdoba, Corrientes, El Plumerillo, Ezeiza, Jujuy, Resistencia, Río Gallegos, Salta and San Carlos de Bariloche). Ezeiza, 35 km from Buenos Aires, is one of the most important air terminals in Latin America. More than 30 airports were scheduled for transfer to private ownership in the late 1990s.

Aerolíneas Argentinas: Bouchard 547, 9°, 1106 Buenos Aires; tel. (11) 4317-3000; fax (11) 4320-2116; internet www.aerolineas.com.ar; f. 1950; transfer to private ownership initiated in 1990; services to North and Central America, Europe, the Far East, New Zealand, South Africa and destinations throughout South America; the internal network covers the whole country; passengers, mail and freight are carried; CEO Emilio Cabrera.

Austral Líneas Aéreas (ALA): Corrientes 485, 9°, 1398, Buenos Aires; tel. (11) 4317-3600; fax (11) 4317-3777; internet www.austral.com.ar; f. 1971; domestic flights linking 27 cities in Argentina; Pres. MANUEL CASERO.

CATA Líneas Aéreas S.A.C.I.F.I.: Cerrito 1320, 3°, 1010 Buenos Aires; tel. (11) 4812-3390; fax (11) 4811-2966; e-mail cataaer@satlink.com; internet www.webs.satlink.com/usuarios/c/cataaer/; f. 1978; domestic passenger flights; Pres. ROQUE PUGLIESE.

Líneas Aéreas Entre Ríos: Salvador Caputo, Paraná , Entre Ríos; tel. (343) 436-2013; fax (343) 436-2177; e-mail contable@laer.com.ar; internet www.laer.com.ar; f. 1988; scheduled domestic passenger services; Gen. Man. LUIS VARISCO.

Líneas Aéreas del Estado (LADE): Perú 710, 1068 Buenos Aires; tel. (11) 4362-1853; fax (11) 4300-0031; e-mail director@lade.com.ar; Dir GUILLERMO JOSÉ TESTONI.

Líneas Aéreas Privadas Argentinas (LAPA): Avda Santa Fe 1970, 2°, 1123 Buenos Aires; tel. (11) 4812-0953; fax (11) 4814-2100; e-mail gcaputi@lapa.com.ar; f. 1976; domestic scheduled passenger services, and international routes to Uruguay; Pres. GUSTAVO ANDRÉS DEUTSCH.

Transporte Aéreo Costa Atlántica (TACA): Bernardo de Yrigoyen 1370, 1°, Ofs 25–26, 1138 Buenos Aires; tel. (11) 4307-1956; fax (11) 4307-8899; f. 1956; domestic and international passenger and freight services between Argentina and Bolivia, Brazil and the USA; Pres. Dr ARMANDO SCHLECKER HIRSCH.

Transportes Aéreos Neuquén: Diagonal 25 de Mayo 180, 8300 Neuquén; tel. (299) 4423076; fax (299) 4488926; e-mail tancentr@satlink.com.ar; domestic routes; Pres. JOSÉ CHALÉN; Gen. Man. PATROCINIO VALVERDE MORAIS.

Valls Líneas Aéreas: Río Grande, Tierra del Fuego; f. 1995; operates three routes between destinations in southern Argentina, Chile and the South Atlantic islands.

Tourism

Argentina's superb tourist attractions include the Andes mountains, the lake district centred on Bariloche (where there is a National Park), Patagonia, the Atlantic beaches and Mar del Plata, the Iguazú falls, the Pampas and Tierra del Fuego. Tourist arrivals in Argentina in 1998 totalled 4,859,867. In the same year tourist receipts were US $5,363m.

Secretaría de Turismo de la Nación: Suipacha 1111, 20°, 1368 Buenos Aires; tel. (11) 4312-5611; fax (11) 4313-6834; e-mail unisec@turismo.gov.ar; internet www.turismo.gov.ar; Sec. HERNÁN SANTIAGO LOMBARDI.

Asociación Argentina de Agencias de Viajes y Turismo (AAAVYT): Viamonte 640, 10°, 1053 Buenos Aires; tel. (11) 4325-4691; fax (11) 4322-9641; e-mail secretaria@aaavyt.org.ar; f. 1951; Pres. MARCOS A. PALACIOS; Gen. Man. GERARDO BELO.

Defence

In August 2000 Argentina's Armed Forces numbered an estimated 71,100: Army 41,400, Navy 17,200 (including Naval Air Force), Air Force 12,500. There were also 375,000 trained reservists and paramilitary forces numbering 31,240. In April 1995 conscription was ended and a professional (voluntary) military service was created in its place.

Defence Expenditure: An estimated 3,800m. new pesos in 2000.

Chief of Staff (Army): Lt-Gen. RICARDO BRINZONI.

Chief of Staff (Navy): Adm. JOAQUÍN STELLA.

Chief of Staff (Air Force): Brig.-Gen. WALTER BARBERO.

Education

Education from pre-school to university level is available free of charge. Education is officially compulsory for all children at primary level, between the ages of six and 14 years. Secondary education lasts for between five and seven years, depending on the type of course: the normal certificate of education (bachillerato) takes five years, whereas a course leading to a commercial bachillerato lasts five years, and one leading to a technical or agricultural bachillerato takes six years. Technical education is supervised by the Consejo Nacional de Educación Técnica. Non-university higher education, usually leading to a teaching qualification, is for three or four years, while university courses last for four years or more. There are 36 state universities and some 48 private universities. According to census results, the average rate of adult illiteracy declined from 7.4% in 1970 to only 3.8% in 1995. The total enrolment at primary and secondary schools in 1996 was estimated at 99.4% and 67.2% of the school-age population, respectively. Central Government expenditure on education for 1997 was 2,561.0m. new pesos, 5.7% of total public expenditure.

Bibliography

For works on South America generally, see Select Bibliography (Books).

Alonso, P. *Between Revolution and the Ballot Box: The Origins of the Argentine Radical Party.* Cambridge, Cambridge University Press, 2000.

Auyero, J. *Poor People's Politics: Peronist Survival Networks and the Legacy of Evita.* Durham, NC, Duke University Press, 2001.

Bergquist, C. *Labor in Latin America: Comparative Essays on Chile, Argentina, Venezuela and Colombia.* Stanford, CA, Stanford University Press, 1986.

Burns, J. *The Land that Lost its Heroes: The Falklands, the Post-War and Alfonsín.* London, Bloomsbury, 1987.

Calvert, S. and P. *Argentina: Political Culture and Instability.* London, Macmillan, 1989.

Cardoso, O. R., Kirschbaum, R., and van der Kooy, E. *Malvinas: La Trama Secreta.* Buenos Aires, Sudamericana/Planeta, 1983.

Corradi, J. E. *The Fitful Republic: Economy, Society and Politics in Argentina.* Boulder, CO, Westview Press, 1985.

Crawley, E. *A House Divided: Argentina, 1880–1980.* London, C. Hurst & Co, 1984.

Dallas, R. 'The President versus the Generals in Argentina', in *The World Today*, Vol. 40. 1984.

Dávila Villiers, D. R. 'Competition and Co-operation in the River Plate: The Democratic Transition and Mercosur', in *Bulletin of Latin American Research*, Vol. 11, No 3 (September), pp. 261–77. 1992.

Escude, C. *Foreign Policy Theory in Menem's Argentina.* Gainesville, FL, University Press of Florida, 1997.

Gibson, E. *Class and Conservative Parties: Argentina in Comparative Perspective.* Baltimore, MD, Johns Hopkins University Press, 1996.

Graham-Yooll, A. *The Forgotten Colony: A History of the English Speaking Communities in Argentina.* London, Hutchinson, 1981.

Greenup, L. and R. *Revolution Before Breakfast: Argentina 1941–46.* Westport, CT, Greenwood Press, 1974.

Gustafson, L. S. *The Sovereignty Dispute over the Falkland (Malvinas) Islands.* New York, NY, Oxford University Press, 1988.

Horowitz, J. 'The Impact of pre-1943 Labor Union Traditions on Peronism', in *Journal of Latin American Studies*, Vol. 15, Part 1 (May). 1983.

Leventhal, P. L., and Tanzer, S. (Eds). *Averting a Latin American Nuclear Arms Race: New Prospects and Challenges for Argentine–Brazilian Co-operation.* London, Macmillan, 1992.

Lewis, C. M., and Torrents, N. (Eds). *Argentina in the Crisis Years (1983–1990): From Alfonsín to Menem.* London, Institute of Latin American Studies, 1993.

Lewis, P. *The Crisis of Argentine Capitalism.* Chapel Hill, NC, University of North Carolina Press, 1990.

Makin, G. 'The Military in Argentine Politics, 1880-1982', in *Journal of International Studies*, Vol. 12. 1983.

Munck, R., Falcón, R. and Galitelli, B. *Argentina: From Anarchism to Peronism, Workers, Unions and Politics, 1855–1985.* London, Zed Books Ltd, 1987.

Peralta Ramos, M., and Waisman, C. H. (Eds). *From Military Rule to Liberal Democracy in Argentina.* Boulder, CO, Westview Press, 1987.

Philip, G. 'The Fall of the Argentine Military', in *Third World Quarterly*, Vol. 6, No 3 (July), pp. 634–37. 1984.

'Military-Authoritarianism in South America: Brazil, Chile, Uruguay and Argentina', in *Political Studies*, No 32. 1984.

Powers, N. *Grassroots Expectations of Democracy and Economy: Argentina in Comparative Perspective.* Pittsburgh, PA, University of Pittsburgh Press, 2001.

Rock, D. *Argentina, 1515–1987: From Spanish Colonization to the Falklands War and Alfonsín.* London, I. B. Tauris & Co, 1987.

Authoritarian Argentina: The Nationalist Movement, Its History and Its Impact. Berkeley, CA, University of California Press, 1995.

Sawers, L. *The Other Argentina: The Interior and National Development.* Boulder, CO, Westview Press, 1998.

Tedesco, L. *Democracy in Argentina.* Ilford, Essex, Frank Cass & Co Ltd, 1999.

Di Tella, G. *Argentina under Perón, 1973–76: The Nation's experience with a Labour-based Government.* London, Macmillan, 1983.

Di Tella, G. and Dornbusch, R. (Eds). *The Political Economy of Argentina, 1946–83.* London, Macmillan, 1989.

Di Tella, T. S. 'Working Class Organisation and Politics in Argentina', in *Latin American Research Review*, Vol. 16. 1981.

Terragno, R. H. *Argentina in the Twenty-First Century*. London, Lynne Rienner Publishers, 1988.

Tiano, S. 'Authoritarianism and Political Culture in Argentina and Chile in the mid-l960s', in *Latin American Research Review*, Vol. 31. 1986.

Timerman, J. *Prisoner without a Name; Cell without a Number*. Harmondsworth, Penguin, 1981.

Turner, F. C., and Miguens, J. E. (Eds). *Juan Perón and the Reshaping of Argentina*. Pittsburgh, PA, University of Pittsburgh Press, 1983.

Vacs, A. C. *Discreet Partners: Argentina and the USSR since 1917* (trans. Michael Joyce). Pittsburgh, PA, University of Pittsburgh Press, 1984.

Vanucci, A. P. 'The Influence of Latin American Governments on the Shaping of United States Foreign Policy: The Case of US–Argentine Relations, 1943–1948', in *Journal of Latin American Studies*, Vol. 18, Part 2 (November). 1986.

ARUBA

Area: 193 sq km (74.5 sq miles).

Population (1999): 95,201.

Capital: Oranjestad, estimated population 17,000 in 1992.

Language: Dutch (official); Papiamento and English are both widely spoken; Spanish.

Religion: Predominantly Christianity (mainly Roman Catholicism).

Climate: Tropical; average annual temperature 28°C (82°F); average annual rainfall 426 mm.

Time: GMT–4 hours.

Public Holidays

2002: 1 January (New Year's Day), 25 January (Gilberto F. (Betico) Croes' Birthday), 11 February (Lenten Carnival), 18 March (Flag Day), 29 March–1 April (Easter), 30 April (Queen's Day), 1 May (Labour Day), 9 May (Ascension Day), 25–26 December (Christmas).

2003: 1 January (New Year's Day), 27 January (for Gilberto F. (Betico) Croes' Birthday), 3 March (Lenten Carnival), 18 March (Flag Day), 18–21 April (Easter), 30 April (Queen's Day), 1 May (Labour Day), 29 May (Ascension Day), 25–26 December (Christmas).

Currency: Gulden (guilder) or florin; 100 guilders = £39.02= US $55.87 = €62.94 (30 April 2001).

Weights and Measures: The metric system is in force.

Basic Economic Indicators

	1997	1998	1999
Gross domestic product (US $ million at current prices)	1,651.4	1,728.5	1,821.8
GDP per head (US $ at current prices)	18,075	n.a.	19,136
Annual growth of real GDP (%)	3.0	2.8	3.0
Consumer price index (annual average; base: 1995 = 100)*	106	108	111
Rate of inflation (annual average, %)†	3.0	1.9	2.3
Foreign exchange reserves (US $ million, at 31 December)‡	172.3	222.2	219.9
Exports (US $ million).	24.1	29.1	29.2
Balance of payments (current account, US $ million)§	–195.8	–18.8	–333.2

Note: Some of the above figures are supplied by the Central Bank of Aruba.
* 98 in 2000.
† –11.6% in 2000.
‡ US $208.0m. in 2000.
§ US $282.3m. in 2000.

Gross domestic product per head measured at purchasing power parity (PPP) (GDP converted to US dollars by the PPP exchange rate, estimate, 1996): 21,000.

Total labour force (1997): 44,840.

Unemployment (1997): 7.4%.

Life expectancy (years at birth, estimate, 1998): 77.

Infant mortality rate (per 1,000 live births, estimate, 1998): 8.0.

Adult literacy rate (estimate, 15 years and over, 1995): 97%.

Energy consumption per head (kg of coal equivalent, 1990): 3,917.

Passenger motor cars in use (per 1,000 of population, 1994): 396.

Television receivers in use (per 1,000 of population, estimate, 1997): 219.

History

Geographically, Aruba was one of the group of dry and flat limestone islands situated just off the coast of Venezuela and known as the 'Leeward Islands' (*Benedenwindse Eilands*), or the 'ABC islands' (the other two members of the group being Bonaire and Curaçao). Some 800 km (500 miles) to the north were the 'Windward Islands' (*Bovenwindse Eilands*), consisting of Sint (St) Maarten, St Eustacius ('Statia') and Saba. The six islands of the Netherlands Dependencies—comprising Aruba and the Netherlands Antilles (the 'Antilles of the Five', see separate chapter)—formed part of the once-powerful Dutch trading empire, and still fulfil that role. The two island groups were administered as Curaçao and Dependencies between 1845 and 1948. Having been promised independence by Queen Wilhelmina of the Netherlands during the Second World War, in 1954 Aruba and the Antilles of the Five were granted autonomous federation status, and, along with the metropolitan Netherlands, declared an integral part of the Kingdom of the Netherlands.

Although Aruba was claimed by the Spanish in 1499, and settled by them, the Spanish claim to the island was successfully challenged by the Dutch, who seized it in a series of raids between 1630 and 1640, mostly through the entrepreneurial activity of the Dutch West India Company. The Treaty of Munster eventually recognized Dutch claims in 1648. The trading importance of the island was emphasized by the fact that the Dutch West India Company ruled it until 1828. Before being established as entrepôt trading centres, the Leeward Islands had been smuggling havens, serving Terra Firma (now Venezuela). In addition, salt pans were developed, which were of great commercial importance to the Dutch, owing to Spain's monopoly on supplies from its South American possessions. However, by the time the Dutch Crown assumed control of the island, Aruba's commercial value had lessened considerably. Slavery was abolished in 1863 and the island suffered an economic decline that lasted until the discovery of significant petroleum deposits in and around Lake Maracaibo, in Venezuela, at the beginning of the 20th century. As a result, in 1929 the Lago Oil and Transport Company (a subsidiary of the Standard Oil Company of the USA, now the Exxon Corporation) established a petroleum refinery at San Nicolas. The economy expanded rapidly thereafter.

In 1954 Aruba became a member of the autonomous federation of the Netherlands Antilles. However, many islanders came to resent what they regarded as the excessive demands made upon Aruban wealth and resources by the other islands in the federation. Aruba's principal political party, the People's Electoral Movement (Movimentu Electoral di Pueblo—MEP), led by Gilberto (Betico) Croes, campaigned for Aruban independence from its foundation in 1971. In a referendum held in March 1977 82% of participants were in favour of Aruba's withdrawal from the Antillean federation. Although the other islands were opposed to proposed independence, the Netherlands itself had begun, from the early 1960s, to encourage secession. The Dutch Government was responsible for providing extensive administrative and financial aid to its dependencies. In May 1969 high levels of unemployment provoked serious riots and looting in Willemstad, which were only quelled by the deployment of troops from the Netherlands. The incident reinforced the view that the Netherlands had responsibility without power.

The MEP used its position in the coalition Government of the Netherlands Antilles, formed in 1979, to press for concessions from the other islands towards early independence for Aruba. As a result, there were frequent clashes with other members of the Government and on two occasions the MEP withdrew from the coalition. A major issue was the distribution of offshore petroleum revenue. Whereas the Federal Government wanted it to be shared among the islands, the MEP insisted that it should accrue to the island concerned. The Dutch opened negotiations on the issue in late 1981 and in March 1983 it was agreed that Aruba would leave the federation on 1 January 1986

and assume *status aparte*. It would proceed to independence 10 years later. The only stipulation was that Aruba would form a co-operative union with the Antilles of the Five in economic and monetary affairs.

The MEP increased its representation in the Aruban Staten in the April 1983 local elections, and Croes remained as leader of the island's Government. However, following the closure of the Exxon refinery in April 1985, with the loss of 1,500 jobs and US $140m. in foreign-exchange earnings, the party was forced to introduce unpopular emergency measures. In November the MEP lost power in Aruba, to a four-party coalition led by the Aruban People's Party (Arubaanse Volkspartij—AVP). Aruba gained, as planned, its *status aparte*, and the AVP leader, Jan Hendrik Albert (Henny) Eman, became its first Prime Minister.

At first the Aruban Government and people were confident that the Dutch would yield on the question of independence, which few islanders now actually wanted. However, by 1989, following an upturn in the economy, the popular mood was less certain. Extensive tourist development and associated construction work was reinforced by the development of an 'offshore' finance facility, a resurgence in the petroleum storage and transhipment industry and plans to reopen parts of the Lago refinery in 1991. The pro-independence MEP, by then led by Nelson Oduber, was returned to power in the January 1989 election. The AVP, now in opposition, remained highly critical of the new Government's plans on independence and proposed a referendum on the issue. Eventually, the Netherlands Government proposed a new constitutional settlement between the three 'Kingdoms' and, in 1990, ceased to demand Aruban secession by 1996.

In March 1994, at a meeting in The Hague, the Governments of Aruba, the Netherlands and the Netherlands Antilles decided to abandon plans for Aruba's transition to full independence. The possibility of a passage to full independence at a later date was not excluded, but was not considered a priority, and would require the approval of the Aruban people, by referendum, as well as the support of a two-thirds majority in the Staten. Instead, the aim came to be an increase in autonomy, or *separashon*, in the federation, which would bind Aruba more closely to the Antilles of the Five, with whom relations had improved after 1986. Moreover, in the general election in July the AVP won the greatest number of seats in the parliament and formed a coalition Government with the Liberal Aruban Organization (Organisacion Liberal Arubano—OLA). This coalition lasted until September 1997, when the OLA withdrew from government and the Staten was dissolved. A general election was held on 12 December, in which all political groupings retained their number of parliamentary seats. Following protracted negotiations, the AVP and the OLA renewed their coalition in mid-1998, and a new Council of Ministers, headed by Eman, was appointed. In 2001 OLA again withdrew its support from the coalition following a dispute over the planned privatization of the Aruba Tourism Authority. Legislative elections were expected to take place in September 2001.

From 1988 Aruba's relations with the 'metropolitan' Netherlands were dominated by the latter's pressure for more control to be exercised over the large amount of aid that it gave to Aruba, the issue of independence. Perhaps the key issue was the future arrangements for the island's security, since Aruba's geographical proximity to the South American mainland was considered to make it particularly susceptible to use as a drugs-trafficking base. In September 1990 Aruba announced that it was to adopt the 1988 UN Convention on measures to combat trade in illegal drugs; a joint Dutch and Aruban team was formed to conduct investigations. The Staten also ratified the Council of Europe Convention of 1990, in an attempt to demonstrate the island's commitment to combating money 'laundering' (the processing of illicitly obtained funds into legitimate holdings). In December 1996, however, the USA included Aruba on its list of major drugs-producing or transit countries. As a result, new legislation was introduced in October 1997 to facilitate the extradition of suspected drugs traffickers and money launderers.

In May 1999 the US navy and air force began patrols from a base in Aruba in an effort to counter the transport of illicit drugs.

Economy

As part of the Kingdom of the Netherlands, Aruba is classed as an Overseas Territory in association with the European Union. It forms a co-operative union with the Antilles of the Five in monetary and economic affairs. Aruba also has observer status with the Caribbean Community and Common Market (CARICOM).

The secession of Aruba in 1986 from the Netherlands Antilles federation was marked by political rancour and economic disruption. Although the island's economy showed remarkable resilience in the late 1980s and 1990s, neither Aruba nor the 'Antilles of the Five' anticipated the extent of 'capital flight' (withdrawal of funds and investments) that occurred, mostly by local citizens. In spite of this, at the end of the 1990s Aruba still enjoyed a relatively prosperous economy, substantially based on tourism and commerce. Compared to other islands in the Dutch Caribbean, Aruba was able to capitalize on its remarkable beaches and offshore attractions to develop a mass tourist industry very rapidly (and maintain nil unemployment even once the period of rapid construction activity was over). Another alleviating factor was the generous levels of aid, both official and unofficial, through welfare payments and remittances, from the metropolitan Netherlands. Aruba's new administration, led by Jan Hendrik Albert (Henny) Eman of the Aruban People's Party's (Arubaanse Volkspartij—AVP), demanded the establishment and acceptance by the Antilles (and of Curaçao in particular) of the Aruban guilder, on a par with the Antillean guilder. There was also much argument over the division of the former federation's assets between the Antilles of the Five and Aruba, at the agreed ratio of 70:30. Gold and foreign reserves were allocated on the ratio of 63:27, with 10% to be held in a reserve fund.

Between 1987 and 1993 the Aruban economy grew at an average annual rate of 10% per year. Entirely attributed to unexpectedly high levels of investment in tourism, growth eased to an average 5.1% in 1994–96, as hotel accommodation reached saturation point and construction eased. Tourist receipts fell because of excessive discounting, causing the Government to ease monetary restrictions in March 1995. Money supply and consumer demand increased, prompting the International Monetary Fund (IMF) to warn of the risk of higher rates of inflation. In late 1995 strict credit restrictions were imposed and average inflation for 1995 was 3.4%, down from 6.3% the year before. Thereafter, the increase in consumer prices continued to fall, with recorded inflation at 3.2% in 1996, 3.0% in 1997, 1.9% in 1998 and 2.3% in 1999. In 2000 consumer prices actually decreased by 11.6%. An estimated 7.4% of the work-force was unemployed in 1997.

In 1997, according to estimates by the World Bank, Aruba's gross national product (GNP), measured at average 1995–97 prices, was estimated to be US $1,181m. Gross domestic product (GDP) in current prices, according to estimates by the Central Bank, was US $1,821.8m., equivalent to US $19,136 per head, in 1999. In real terms GDP increased by an estimated 3.0% in 1997, 2.8% in 1998 and 3.0% in 1999. Between 1990 and 1996 the population was estimated to have increased by an annual average of 2.7%.

There is little agricultural activity in Aruba, owing to the poor quality of the soil, combined with water shortages (large desalination plants provide most of the water used, although the cost of this process is high). The major crop is aloes (used in the manufacture of cosmetics and pharmaceuticals). There is a small fishing industry and some livestock is raised.

For most of the 20th century the refining and transhipment of imported petroleum and petroleum products formed the basis of Aruba's relative economic prosperity. The Lago Oil and Transport Company (a subsidiary of the Standard Oil Company of the USA, now the Exxon Corporation) established a petroleum

refinery at San Nicolas in 1929. Most of the crude petroleum for the refineries came from the nearby Venezuelan fields, and the refined products were mainly shipped to the USA. At its peak, in the mid-1950s, the Lago plant was processing up to 600,000 barrels per day (b/d). In the 1970s the industry diversified into petroleum storage. A huge terminal was built to handle supertankers carrying African and Middle Eastern petroleum and petroleum products. Since US ports on the eastern seaboard could not handle tankers over 60,000 dwt, the deep-water facilities of the island were ideal. However, in the early 1980s the sector suffered a sudden, dramatic decline following the US authorities' decision to allow construction of large offshore terminals on the US Gulf of Mexico and eastern coast. Furthermore, these new US terminals fed into US refineries.

As a consequence of this and of the reduction in supplies from Venezuela, owing to the imposition of production quotas by the Organization of Petroleum Exporting Countries (OPEC), the Lago plant ceased operations in 1985. The Government lost nearly US $80m. per year in tax revenues, or about 60% of the island's income. Following riots in protest at the closure, the Dutch Government agreed to emergency aid, on the condition that emergency financial austerity measures were put into effect. Aruba's budget deficit increased to $56m. in 1985, but Dutch and IMF aid halved that figure by the following year. In late 1990 the refinery was partially reopened, following $110m.-worth of renovation. By 1993 production was an estimated 140,000 b/d and it was envisaged that, following a further renovation, production would rise to 278,000 b/d in 2000. There was a large petrochemical transhipment terminal on Aruba and a small petrochemicals industry. In 1995 a $100m. advanced-technology coker plant opened, to supply liquefied petroleum gas, largely for export to the USA. This plant increased refining capacity to 200,000 b/d.

From the mid-1980s service industries, particularly the financial and tourist sectors, became Aruba's principal economic activity. The financial sector was well established and attempts were made to encourage the growth of a data-processing industry, aimed at US companies in particular. Aruba also established an 'offshore' company facility, aimed particularly at the Latin American market. In June 2000, however, the Organisation for Economic Co-operation and Development (OECD) urged the Government to improve further the accountability and transparency of the financial services it provided, or face economic sanctions. In June 2001 Aruba agreed to conform to the OECD's guide-lines on the elimination of harmful tax practices.

Aruba's main source of income was tourism. This sector was responsible for Aruba's dramatic economic recovery following the closure of the Lago refinery. By 1988 the growth rate in the sector was one of the highest in the Caribbean, strengthened by high inflows of foreign investment. Liberal, but closely monitored casino laws were promoted, as well as the exceptionally good beaches, clear waters and reefs. The number of hotel rooms increased from 2,078 in 1986 to 6,619 in 1998. Aggressive marketing and new air services resulted in stop-over arrivals increasing to 688,437 in 1999, from 181,200 in 1986. Cruise-ship passengers totalled 289,100 in 1999 and receipts from tourism amounted to A Fl. 1,392.0m. Successive Governments attempted to reduce dependency on tourism by encouraging investment in diversification. In 1992, following six consecutive years of growth, during which time there was a threefold increase in hotel capacity, a moratorium was imposed on construction in the sector, both in order to allow for infrastructural development and in recognition of the adverse environmental impact involved. Despite this, a US $56m. expansion of Aruba's airport terminal was completed in 2000.

In 1999 it was estimated that the budget deficit would be A Fl. 24.1m. In 1999 Aruba recorded a visible trade deficit of $591.7m. and there was a deficit on the current account of the balance of payments of $333.2m. In 2000 these deficits decreased to $28.3m. and $282.3m., respectively. Despite this fall, Aruba is obliged to import most of its requirements, particularly machinery and transport equipment, basic manufactures and foodstuffs. In 2000 the principal source of imports, excluding the petroleum sector and the 'free zone', was the USA (59.4% of the total), followed by the Netherlands and the Netherlands Antilles. The USA, as well as Colombia, was also the principal market for exports (25.6% of the total); other important markets were Venezuela, the Netherlands and the Netherlands Antilles. At the end of 1999 total government debt was A Fl. 1,109.1m., equivalent to 34% of GDP, of which 29.8% was owed to external creditors, primarily the Government of the Netherlands (20.8%). In spite of Aruba's economic prosperity, it seemed clear that dependence on the Dutch would continue into the 21st century.

Statistical Survey

Sources (unless otherwise stated): Department of Economic Affairs, Commerce and Industry (Direktie Economische Zaken, Handel en Industrie), Sun Plaza Bldg, L. G. Smith Blvd 160, Oranjestad; tel. (8) 21181; fax (8) 34494; e-mail deaci@setarnet.aw; internet www.arubastatistics.com; Centrale Bank van Aruba, Havenstraat 2, Oranjestad; tel. (8) 22509; fax (8) 32251; e-mail cbaua@setarnet.aw.

AREA AND POPULATION

Area: 193 sq km (74.5 sq miles).

Population: 66,687 (males 32,821, females 33,866) at census of 6 October 1991; 95,201 at 31 December 1999.

Density (December 1999): 493.3 per sq km.

Births and Deaths (1997): Registered live births 1,452 (birth rate 16.9 per 1,000); Registered deaths 469 (death rate 5.5 per 1,000). Source: UN, *Population and Vital Statistics Report*.

Expectation of Life (years at birth, 1991): Males 71.1; Females 77.1. Source: UN, *Demographic Yearbook*.

Economically Active Population (persons aged 15 years and over, 1997): Agriculture, hunting and forestry 196; Manufacturing 2,585; Electricity, gas and water 776; Construction 3,409; Wholesale and retail trade, repairs 7,238; Hotels and restaurants 7,019; Transport, storage and communications 3,375; Financial intermediation 1,507; Real estate, renting and business activities 3,222; Public administration, defence and social security 4,338; Education 1,298; Health and social work 2,061; Other community, social and personal services 3,032; Private households with employed persons 1,302; Extra-territorial organizations and bodies 10; Other 133; Total employed 41,501 (males 23,486, females 18,015); Unemployed 3,339 (males 1,693, females 1,646); Total labour force 44,840 (males 25,179, females 19,661). Source: ILO.

FISHING

Total catch (metric tons, live weight, 1998): 182 (Groupers 22, Snappers and jobfishes 50, Wahoo 70, Other marine fishes 40). Source: FAO, *Yearbook of Fishery Statistics*.

INDUSTRY

Electric Energy (million kWh, 1999): 614.9.

FINANCE

Currency and Exchange Rates: 100 cents = 1 Aruban gulden (guilder) or florin (A Fl.). *Sterling, Dollar and Euro Equivalents* (30 April 2001): £1 sterling = A Fl. 2.563; US $1 = A Fl. 1.790; €1 = A Fl. 1.589; A Fl. 100 = £39.02 = $55.87 = €62.94. Note: The Aruban florin was introduced in January 1986, replacing (at par) the Netherlands Antilles guilder or florin (NA Fl.). Since its introduction, the currency has had a fixed exchange rate of US $1 = A Fl. 1.79.

Budget (A Fl. million, 1999): *Revenue:* Tax revenue 608.5 (Taxes on income and profits 309.0, Taxes on commodities 198.0, Taxes on property 35.2, Taxes on services 44.8, Foreign exchange commission 21.6); Other current revenue 102.9; Total 711.4 (excl. grants received 1.4). *Expenditure:* Wages 222.3; Employers' contributions 45.6; Wage subsidies 85.6; Goods and services 197.7; Interest payments 32.9; Subsidies 28.2; Transfers 54.2; Direct investment 37.0; Other expenditure 33.4; Total 736.9.

International Reserves (US $ million at 31 December 2000): Gold 22.90; Foreign exchange 208.01; Total 230.91. Source: IMF, *International Financial Statistics*.

Money Supply (A Fl. million at 31 December 2000): Currency outside banks 122.49; Demand deposits at commercial banks 471.23; Total money (incl. others) 597.52. Source: IMF, *International Financial Statistics*.

Cost of Living (Consumer Price Index; base: 1995 = 100): 108 in 1998; 111 in 1999; 98 in 2000. Source: IMF, *International Financial Statistics*.

Gross Domestic Product (US $ million at current prices): 1,651.4 in 1997; 1,728.5 in 1998; 1,821.8 in 1999.

Balance of Payments (US $ million, 2000): Exports of goods f.o.b. 2,582.1; Imports of goods f.o.b. −2,610.4 *Trade balance* −28.3; Exports of services 1,032.0; Imports of services −678.7; *Balance on goods and services* 325.0; Other income received 46.8; Other income paid −53.5; *Balance on goods, services and income* 318.3; Current transfers received 46.2; Current transfers paid −82.2; *Current balance* 282.3; Capital account (net) 9.9; Direct investment abroad −11.7; Direct investment from abroad −227.5; Portfolio investment assets −42.9; Portfolio investment liabilities 2.1; Other investment assets −97.7; Other investment liabilities 63.1; Net errors and omissions 6.5; *Overall balance* −15.9. Source: IMF, *International Financial Statistics*.

EXTERNAL TRADE

Principal Commodities (US $ million, preliminary figures, 2000): *Imports c.i.f.:* Live animals and animal products 55.8; Vegetable products 26.4; Prepared foodstuffs; beverages, spirits and vinegar; tobacco and manufactured substitutes 79.3; Products of chemical or allied industries 90.5; Plastics, rubber and articles thereof 23.8; Paper-making material; paper and paperboard and articles thereof 23.3; Textiles and textile articles 44.4; Articles of stone, plaster, cement, asbestos, mica, etc; ceramic products; glass and glassware 19.3; Natural or cultured pearls, precious or semi-precious stones, precious metals, metals clad with precious metal, and articles thereof; imitation jewellery; coin 34.3; Base metals and articles thereof 50.7; Machinery and mechanical appliances; electrical equipment; sound and television apparatus 105.7; Vehicles, aircraft, vessels and associated transport equipment 65.7; Optical, photographic, cinematographic, measuring, checking, precision, medical or surgical instruments and apparatus; clocks and watches; musical instruments, parts and accessories thereof 30.9; Total (incl. others) 721.8. *Exports f.o.b.:* Live animals and animal products 10.3; Natural or cultured pearls, precious or semi-precious stones, precious metals, metals clad with precious metal, and articles thereof; imitation jewellery; coin 1.9; Base metals and articles thereof 2.8; Machinery and mechanical appliances; electrical equipment; sound and television apparatus 2.2; Vehicles, aircraft, vessels and associated transport equipment 1.3; Works of art, collector's pieces, and antiques 4.6; Total (incl. others) 27.3. Note: Figures exclude transactions of the petroleum sector and those of the Free Zone of Aruba. The value of total trade (in US $ million) on an f.o.b. basis in 1999 was: Imports 2,005.2; Exports 1,413.5.

Principal Trading Partners (US $ million, preliminary figures, 2000): *Imports c.i.f.:* Mexico 12.8; Netherlands 90.2; Netherlands Antilles 28.5; Panama 15.2; USA 428.5; Venezuela 26.4; Total (incl. others) 721.8. *Exports f.o.b.:* Colombia 7.0; Netherlands 2.4; Netherlands Antilles 2.9; USA 7.0; Venezuela 3.4; Total (incl. others) 27.3. Note: All figures exclude transactions of the petroleum sector and those of the Free Trade Zone of Aruba.

TRANSPORT

Road Traffic (motor vehicles in use, December 1998): Passenger cars 37,569; Lorries 734; Buses 339; Taxis 400; Rental cars 3,067; Other cars 428; Motor cycles 604; Total 43,141.

Shipping (1999): *Arrivals:* Oil tankers 452; Cruise ships 230.

Civil Aviation: *Aircraft landings:* 16,518 in 1997; 16,343 in 1998; 16,690 in 1999. *Passenger numbers:* 1,785,039 in 1997; 1,785,747 in 1998; 1,872,230 in 1999.

TOURISM

Tourist Arrivals ('000): 943.7 (646.0 stop-over visitors, 297.7 cruise-ship passengers) in 1997; 905.2 (647.4 stop-over visitors, 257.8 cruise-ship passengers) in 1998; 977.5 (688.4 stop-over visitors, 289.1 cruise-ship passengers) in 1999.

Tourism Receipts: A Fl. 1,392.0m. in 1999.

COMMUNICATIONS MEDIA

Radio Receivers (1997): 50,000 in use.

Television Receivers (1997): 20,000 in use.

Telephones (1999): 36,557 in use.

Telefax Stations (1996): 3,600 in use.

Mobile Cellular Telephones (1999): 11,300 subscribers.

Daily Newspapers (1996): 13 titles (estimated circulation 73,000 copies per issue).

Sources: mainly UNESCO, *Statistical Yearbook,* and UN, *Statistical Yearbook.*

EDUCATION

Pre-primary (1999/2000): 23 schools; 2,708 pupils; 100 teachers.

Primary (1999/2000): 33 schools; 8,633 pupils; 404 teachers.

General Secondary (1999/2000): 10 schools; 4,210 pupils; 236 teachers.

Technical-Vocational Secondary (1999/2000): 1 school; 1,869 pupils; 145 teachers.

Community College (1999/2000): 1 school; 1,187 pupils; 106 teachers.

University (1999/2000): 1 university; 208 students; 24 tutors.

Teacher Training (1999/2000): 1 institution; 204 students; 30 teachers.

Special Education (1999/2000): 4 schools; 277 pupils; 54 teachers.

Private, non-aided (1999/2000): 4 schools; 553 pupils; 58 teachers.

Directory

The Constitution

On 1 January 1986 Aruba acquired separate status (*status aparte*) within the Kingdom of the Netherlands. The form of government is similar to that for the Netherlands Antilles, which is embodied in the Charter of the Kingdom of the Netherlands (operational from 20 December 1954). The Netherlands, the Netherlands Antilles (Antilles of the Five) and Aruba each enjoy full autonomy in domestic and internal affairs, and are united on a basis of equality for the protection of their common interests and the granting of mutual assistance. In economic and monetary affairs there is a co-operative union between Aruba and the Antilles of the Five, known as the 'Union of the Netherlands Antilles and Aruba'.

The monarch of the Netherlands is represented in Aruba by the Governor, who is appointed by the Dutch Crown for a term of six years. The Government of Aruba appoints a minister plenipotentiary to represent it in the Government of the Kingdom. Whenever the Netherlands Council of Ministers is dealing with matters coming under the heading of joint affairs of the realm (in practice mainly foreign affairs and defence), the Council assumes the status of Council of Ministers of the Kingdom. In that event, Aruba's Minister Plenipotentiary takes part, with full voting powers, in the deliberations.

A legislative proposal regarding affairs of the realm and applying to Aruba as well as to the 'metropolitan' Netherlands is sent, simultaneously with its submission, to the Staten Generaal (the Netherlands parliament) and to the Staten (parliament) of Aruba. The latter body can report in writing to the Staten Generaal on the draft Kingdom Statute and designate one or more special delegates to attend the debates and furnish information in the meetings of the Chambers of the Staten Generaal. Before the final vote on a draft the Minister Plenipotentiary has the right to express an opinion on it. If he disapproves of the draft, and if in the Second Chamber a three-fifths' majority of the votes cast is not obtained, the discussions on the draft are suspended and further deliberations take place in the Council of Ministers of the Kingdom. When special delegates attend the meetings of the Chambers this right devolves upon the delegates of the parliamentary body designated for this purpose.

The Governor has executive power in external affairs, which he exercises in co-operation with the Council of Ministers. He is assisted by an advisory council which consists of at least five members appointed by him.

Executive power in internal affairs is vested in a nominated Council of Ministers, responsible to the Staten. The Aruban Staten consists of 21 members, who are elected by universal adult suffrage for four years (subject to dissolution), on the basis of proportional representation. Inhabitants have the right to vote if they have Dutch nationality and have reached 18 years of age. Voting is not compulsory.

The Government

HEAD OF STATE

Head of State: HM Queen BEATRIX of the Netherlands.

Governor: OLINDO KOOLMAN (took office in 1992).

COUNCIL OF MINISTERS

A coalition of the Arubaanse Volkspartij (AVP) and the Organisacion Liberal Arubano (OLA).

(August 2001)

Prime Minister and Minister of General Affairs: JAN HENDRIK ALBERT (HENNY) EMAN (AVP).

Deputy Prime Minister and Minister of Transport, Communications and Utilities: GLENBERT F. CROES (OLA).

Minister of Economic Affairs and Tourism: LILIA G. BEKEMARTÍNEZ (OLA).

Minister of Education and Labour: MARY WEVER-LACLE (AVP).

Minister of Finance and Public Works: ROBERTICO R. CROES (AVP).

Minister of Public Health, Sports and Social Affairs: Dr ISRAEL POSNER (OLA).

Minister of Justice: EDDY CROES.

Minister Plenipotentiary and Member of the Council of Ministers of the Realm for Aruba in the Netherlands: ANTONIO G. CROES (AVP).

Minister Plenipotentiary of the Realm for Aruba in Washington, DC (USA): F. P. CORONEL.

MINISTRIES

Office of the Governor: Plaza Henny Eman 3, Oranjestad.

Office of the Prime Minister: Government Offices, L. G. Smith Blvd 76, Oranjestad; tel. (8) 39022; fax (8) 38958.

Ministry of Economic Affairs and Tourism: L. G. Smith Blvd 76, Oranjestad; tel. (8) 39035; fax (8) 35084; internet www.arubaeconomicaffairs.com.

Ministry of Education and Labour: L. G. Smith Blvd 76, Oranjestad; tel. (8) 30937; fax (8) 28328.

Ministry of Finance and Public Works: L. G. Smith Blvd 76, Oranjestad; tel. (8) 39148; fax (8) 39147.

Ministry of General Affairs: L. G. Smith Blvd 76, Oranjestad; tel. (8) 39022; fax (8) 38958.

Ministry of Public Health, Sports and Social Affairs: L. G. Smith Blvd 76, Oranjestad; tel. 834966; fax 835082.

Ministry of Justice: L. G. Smith Blvd 76, Oranjestad; tel. (8) 39131; fax (8) 25388.

Ministry of Transport, Communications and Utilities: L. G. Smith Blvd 76, Oranjestad; tel. (8) 39695; fax (8) 35985.

Office of the Minister Plenipotentiary for Aruba: Schimmelpennicklaan 1, 2517 JN The Hague, the Netherlands; tel. (70) 356-6200; fax (70) 345-1446.

Legislature

STATEN

President: EDDY CROES, Staten, L. G. Smith Blvd 72, Oranjestad.

General Election, 12 December 1997

Party	% of votes	Seats
Arubaanse Volkspartij	41.3	10
Movimentu Electoral di Pueblo . . .	38.8	9
Organisacion Liberal Arubano . . .	8.9	2
Partido Patriótico Arubano . . .	4.6	—
Accion Democratico Nacional . . .	2.4	—
Others	4.0	—
Total	100.0	21

Political Organizations

Accion Democratico Nacional (ADN) (National Democratic Action): Oranjestad; f. 1985; Leader PEDRO CHARRO KELLY.

Arubaanse Volkspartij (AVP) (Aruba People's Party): Oranjestad; tel. (8) 33500; fax (8) 37870; f. 1942; advocates Aruba's separate status; Leader JAN HENDRIK ALBERT (HENNY) EMAN.

Movimentu Electoral di Pueblo (MEP) (People's Electoral Movement): Santa Cruz 74d, Oranjestad; tel. (8) 54495; fax (8) 50768; e-mail mep@setarnet.aw; internet www.setarnet.aw/organisationpage/mep; f. 1971; socialist; 1,200 mems; Pres. and Leader NELSON ORLANDO ODUBER.

Movimiento Aruba Solidario (MAS) (Aruba Solidarity Movement): Oranjestad; f. 1997.

Organisacion Liberal Arubano (OLA) (Aruban Liberal Organization): Oranjestad; f. 1991; Leader GLENBERT F. CROES.

Partido pa un Aruba Restructura Awor (PARA) (Aruba Reform Party): Oranjestad; f. 1997; Leader URBANO LOBEZ.

Partido Patriótico Arubano (PPA) (Patriotic Party of Aruba): Oranjestad; internet www.visitaruba.com/ppa/jrpeterson; f. 1949; social democratic; opposed to complete independence for Aruba; Leader BENEDICT J. M. (BENNY) NISBETT.

Judicial System

Legal authority is exercised by the Court of First Instance. Appeals are heard by the Joint High Court of Justice of the Netherlands Antilles and Aruba.

Attorney-General of Aruba: JAN H. M. ZWINKELS.

Courts of Justice: J. G. Emanstraat 51, Oranjestad.

Religion

Roman Catholics form the largest religious community, numbering more than 80% of the population. The Anglicans and the Methodist, Dutch Protestant and other Protestant churches have a total membership of about 6,500. There are approximately 130 Jews.

CHRISTIANITY

The Roman Catholic Church

Aruba forms part of the diocese of Willemstad, comprising the Netherlands Antilles and Aruba. The Bishop resides in Willemstad (Curaçao, Netherlands Antilles).

Roman Catholic Church: J. Yrausquin Plein 3, POB 702, Oranjestad; tel. (8) 21434; fax (8) 21409.

The Anglican Communion

Within the Church in the Province of the West Indies, Aruba forms part of the diocese of the North Eastern Caribbean and Aruba. The Bishop is resident in The Valley, Anguilla.

Anglican Church: Holy Cross, Weg Seroe Pretoe 31, Sint Nicolaas; tel. (8) 45142; fax (8) 43394.

Protestant Churches

Baptist Church: Aruba Baptist Mission, SBC, Paradera 98-C; tel. (8) 83893.

Church of Christ: Pastoor Hendrikstraat 107, Sint Nicolaas; tel. (8) 48172.

Dutch Protestant Church: Wilhelminastraat 1, Oranjestad; tel. (8) 21435.

Evangelical Church: C. Huygenstraat 17, POB 272, Oranjestad; tel. (8) 22058.

Faith Revival Center: Rooi Afo 10, Paradera; tel. (8) 31010.

Iglesia Evangelica Pentecostal: Asamblea di Dios, Reamurstraat 2, Oranjestad; tel. (8) 31940.

Jehovah's Witnesses: Guyabastraat 3, Oranjestad; tel. (8) 28963.

Methodist Church: Longfellowstraat, Oranjestad; tel. (8) 45243.

New Apostolic Church: Goletstraat SA, Oranjestad; tel. (8) 33762.

Pentacostal Apostolic Assembly: Bernhardstraat 185; tel. (8) 48710.

Seventh-day Adventist: Weststraat, Oranjestad; tel. (8) 45896.

JUDAISM

Beth Israel Synagogue: Adriaan Laclé Blvd, Oranjestad; tel. (8) 23272; fax (8) 23534.

BAHÁ'Í FAITH

Spiritual Assembly: Bucutiweg 19, Oranjestad; tel. (8) 23104.

The Press

DAILIES

Amigoe di Aruba: Caya G. F. (Betico) Croes 110, POB 323, Oranjestad; tel. (8) 24333; fax (8) 22368; internet amigoe.com; f. 1884; Dutch; Gen. Man. and Editor-in-Chief MICHAEL O. WILLEMSE; circ. 12,000 (in Aruba and Netherlands Antilles).

Aruba Today: Weststraat 22, Oranjestad; tel. (8) 27800; fax (8) 27093; Editor-in-Chief VANJA ODUBER.

Beurs- en Nieuwsberichten: Bachstraat 6, Oranjestad; tel. (8) 21465; f. 1935; Dutch.

Bon Dia Aruba: Weststraat 22, Oranjestad; tel. (8) 27800; fax (8) 27044; e-mail comment@bondia.com; internet www.bondia.com; Dir VICTOR WINKLAAR.

Corant: Newtonstraat 14, Oranjestad; tel. (8) 28628; fax (8) 34834; f.1986; Papiamento; Dir STANLEY ARENDS.

Dagblad voor Aruba: Oranjestad; tel. (8) 30705; fax (8) 20587; Dir JOSSY M. MANSUR.

Diario: Engelandstraat 29, POB 577, Oranjestad; tel. (8) 826747; fax (8) 828551; e-mail diario@setanet.aw; internet www.diarioaruba.com; f. 1980; Papiamento; morning; Editor/Man. JOSSY M. MANSUR; circ. 15,000.

Extra: Dominicanessenstraat 17, Oranjestad; tel. (8) 834034; fax (8) 21639; Papiamento; Dir C. FRANKEN.

The News: Italiestraat 5, POB 300, Oranjestad; tel. (8) 24725; fax (8) 26125; f. 1951; English; Publr GERARDUS J. SCHOUTEN; Editor BEN BENNET; circ. 6,900.

Nobo: Dominicanessenstraat 17, Oranjestad; tel. (8) 34034; fax (8) 27272; Dir ADRIAAN ARENDS.

La Prensa: Bachstraat 6, POB 566 Oranjestad; tel. (8) 21199; fax (8) 28634; f. 1929; Papiamento; Editor THOMAS C. PIETERSZ.

NEWS AGENCIES

Algemeen Nederlands Persbureau (ANP) (The Netherlands): Caya G. F. (Betico) Croes 110, POB 323, Oranjestad; tel. (8) 24333; fax (8) 22368.

Aruba News Agencies: Bachstraat 6, Oranjestad; tel. (8) 21243.

Foreign Bureau

United Press International (UPI) (USA): Italiestraat 5, Oranjestad; tel. (8) 24725.

Publishers

Aruba Experience Publications NV: L. G. Smith Blvd 58, Oranjestad; tel. (8) 34467.

Caribbean Publishing Co (CPC) Ltd: L. G. Smith Blvd 116, Oranjestad; tel. (8) 20485; fax (8) 20484.

De Wit Stores NV: L. G. Smith Blvd 110, POB 386, Oranjestad; tel. (8) 23500; fax (8) 21575; e-mail dewitstores@setarnet.aw; f. 1948; Man. Dir R. DE ZWART.

Gold Book Publishing: L. G. Smith Blvd 116, Oranjestad; tel. (8) 20485; fax (8) 20484.

Oranjestad Printing NV: Italiestraat 5, POB 300, Oranjestad; Man. Dir GERARDUS J. SCHOUTEN.

Publicidad Aruba NV: Wilhelminastraat 101, Oranjestad; tel. (8) 25132.

Publicidad Exito Aruba SA: Domenicanessenstraat 17, POB 142, Oranjestad; tel. (8) 22020; fax (8) 24242; f. 1958.

Rozenstand Publishing Co: Cuquisastraat 1, Oranjestad; tel. (8) 24482.

VAD Printers Inc.: L. G. Smith Blvd 110, POB 201, Oranjestad; tel. (8) 24550; fax (8) 33072; e-mail vadprinting@setarnet.aw; fmrly Verenigde Antilliaanse Drukkerijen NV.

Van Dorp Aruba NV: Caya G.F. (Betico) Croes 77, POB 596, Oranjestad; tel. (8) 23076; fax (8) 23573.

Broadcasting and Communications

TELECOMMUNICATIONS

Intervoice Aruba NV: L. G. Smith Blvd 17, Oranjestad; tel. (8) 30756.

SITA Aruba: Kon Beatrix Luchthaven, Oranjestad; tel. (8) 31980.

Servicio di Telecomunicacion di Aruba (SETAR): Seroe Blanco, POB 13, Oranjestad; tel. (8) 25151; fax (8) 33593.

BROADCASTING
Radio

Canal 90 FM Stereo: Van Leeuwenhoekstraat 26, Oranjestad; tel. (8) 24134.

Cristal Sound 1-01 7 FM: J. G. Emanstraat 124A, Oranjestad; tel. (8) 27726; fax (8) 20144.

Radio 1270: Bernardstraat 138, POB 28, Sint Nicolaas; tel. (8) 45602; fax (8) 27753; commercial station; programmes in Dutch, English, Spanish and Papiamento; Dir F. A. LEAUER; Station Man. J. A. C. ALDERS.

Radio Carina FM: Datustraat 10A, Oranjestad; tel. (8) 21450; fax (8) 31955; commercial station; programmes in Dutch, English, Spanish and Papiamento; Dir-Gen. ALBERT R. DIEFFENTHALER.

Radio Caruso Booy FM: G. M. De Bruynewijk 49, Savaneta; tel. (8) 47752; fax (8) 43351; commercial station; broadcasts for 24 hrs a day; programmes in Dutch, English, Spanish and Papiamento; Pres. HUBERT E. A. BOOY; Gen. Man. SIRA BOOY.

Radio Galactica FM: J. G. Emanstraat 120, Oranjestad; tel. (8) 20999; fax (8) 38999; f. 1990; Dir MODESTO J. ODUBER; Station Man. MAIKEL J. ODUBER.

Radio Kelkboom: Bloemond 14, POB 146, Oranjestad; tel. (8) 21899; fax (8) 34825; e-mail RadioKelkboom@setarnet.aw; f. 1954; commercial radio station; programmes in Dutch, English, Spanish and Papiamento; Owners CARLOS A. KELKBOOM and E. A. M. KELKBOOM; Dir EMILE A. M. KELKBOOM.

Radio Victoria: Washington 23, POB 5291, Oranjestad; tel. (8) 73444; fax (8) 73444; f. 1958; religious and cultural FM radio station owned by the Radio Victoria Foundation; programmes in Dutch, English, Spanish and Papiamento; Pres. N. J. F. ARTS.

Voz di Aruba (Voice of Aruba): Van Leeuwenhoekstraat 26, POB 219, Oranjestad; tel. (8) 24134; commercial radio station; programmes in Dutch, English, Spanish and Papiamento; also operates Canal 90 on FM; Dir A. M. ARENDS, Jr.

Television

Tele-Aruba NV: Pos Chiquito 1A, POB 392, Oranjestad; tel. (8) 57302; fax (8) 51683; f. 1963; formerly operated by Netherlands Antilles Television Co; commercial; govt-owned; Gen. Man. M. MARCHENA.

Finance

(cap. = capital; res = reserves; dep. = deposits; m. = million; brs = branches; amounts in Aruban guilders).

BANKING
Central Bank

Centrale Bank van Aruba: Havenstraat 2, Oranjestad; tel. (8) 22509; fax (8) 32251; e-mail cbawa@setarnet.aw; internet www .cbaruba.org; f. 1986; cap. 10.0m., res 56.0m., dep. 250.4m. (Dec. 1999); Pres. A. R. CARAM (acting); Exec. Dir K. A. H. POLVLIET.

Commercial Banks

ABN AMRO Bank NV: Caya G. F. (Betico) Croes 89, Oranjestad; tel. (8) 21515; fax (8) 21856; Man. J. W. VAN DEN BOSCH; 3 brs.

Aruba Bank NV: Caya G. F. (Betico) Croes 41, POB 192, Oranjestad; tel. (8) 21550; fax (8) 29152; e-mail abank@setsrnet.aw; f. 1925; cap. and res 21m., dep. 300m. (1996); Man. Dir I. A. DURAND; 8 brs.

Banco di Caribe NV: Caya G. F. (Betico) Croes 90–92, Oranjestad; tel. (8) 32168; fax (8) 32422; f. 1987; Gen. Man. E. A. DE KORT; 1 br.

Caribbean Mercantile Bank NV: Caya G. F. (Betico) Croes 53, POB 28, Oranjestad; tel. (8) 23118; fax (8) 24373; e-mail executive_office@cmbnv.com; internet www.cmbnv.com; f. 1963; cap. 4.0m., res 35.3m., dep. 650.4m. (Dec. 1999); Man. Dir L. CAPRILES; 6 brs.

First National Bank of Aruba NV: Caya G. F. (Betico) Croes 67, Oranjestad; tel. (8) 33221; fax (8) 21756; e-mail firstcr@setarnet.aw; f. 1987; acquired by Royal Bank of Trinidad and Tobago Ltd in 1998; Man. Dir EDWIN L. TROMP; Gen. Man. CHARLES RUND; 1 br.

Inarco International Bank NV: Arulex Bldg, Punta Bravo z/n, POB 650, Oranjestad; tel. (8) 22138; fax (8) 32363.

Interbank Aruba NV: Caya G. F. (Betico) Croes 38, POB 96,Oranjestad; tel. (8) 31080; fax (8) 24058; e-mail info@interbankaruba.com; f. 1987; Man. Dir I. A. DURAND; 3 brs.

OHRA Hypotheek & Postspaarbank NK: L. G. Smith Blvd 60, Oranjestad; tel. (8) 39666; fax (8) 39498; e-mail pmuijres@ohrabank .aua.com.

Volkskredietbank: L. G. Smith Blvd 68, Oranjestad; tel. (8) 22380; fax (8) 36618; internet www.volkskredietbankaruba.com; state-owned.

Investment Bank

Aruban Investment Bank NV: Wilhelminastraat 32–36, POB 1011, Oranjestad; tel. (8) 27327; fax (8) 27461; e-mail aib@setarnet .aw; f. 1987; Pres. P. J. ALBRECHT.

'Offshore' Bank

Citibank NA: Caya G.F. (Betico) Croes 85, Oranjestad.

INSURANCE

There were 10 life insurance companies active in Aruba in mid-1999.

Trade and Industry

DEVELOPMENT ORGANIZATION

Department of Economic Affairs, Commerce and Industry (Direktie Economische Zaken, Handel en Industrie): Sun Plaza Bldg, L. G. Smith Blvd 160, Oranjestad; tel. (8) 21181; fax (8) 34494; e-mail deaci@setarnet.aw; internet www.arubaeconomic affairs.com; Dir HUMPHREY O. VAN TRIKT.

CHAMBER OF COMMERCE AND INDUSTRY

Aruba Chamber of Commerce and Industry: Zoutmanstraat 21, POB 140, Oranjestad; tel. (8) 21566; fax (8) 33962; e-mail auachamber@setarnet.aw; internet www.arubachamber.org; f. 1930; Pres. ROLAND W. PETERSON; Exec. Dir L. C. DE SOUZA.

TRADE ASSOCIATION

Aruba Trade and Industry Association: ATTA Bldg, Pedro Gallegostraat 6, POB 562, Oranjestad; tel. (8) 27593; fax (8) 33068; e-mail atiaruba@setarnet.aw; f. 1945; Pres. JOSSY M. LACLE.

MAJOR COMPANIES

The following are some of the leading industrial and commercial companies currently operating in Aruba:

ACM & Industries NV: Barcadera 5B, POB 2197, cultured marble/onyx products; Dir JAN SJAUW KOEN FA.

AIISCO NV: Barcadera 5A, POB 503, Oranjestad; tel. (8) 55912; fax (8) 55120; manufactures industrial detergents; Dir SAMUEL JONKHOUT.

Antilles Industrial Gases NV: Balashi, POB 387, Oranjestad: tel. (8) 22173; fax (8) 22823; f. 1963; industrial-gas producers; Man. Dir STANLEY DE MARCHENA; 15 employees.

Antilliaanse Handel Maatschappij NV: Fergusonstraat 7, Oranjestad; tel. (8) 24040; construction materials; Man. Dir HERMAN STEENHUIZEN; 81 employees.

Aruba Aloe Balm NV: Sabana Blanco 41, Oranjestad; tel. (8) 32188; fax (8) 26081; aloe-based skin-care products; Dir JACOBUS VEEL.

Arubaanse Verffabriek NV: L. G. Smith Blvd 144, POB 297, Oranjestad; tel. (8) 22519; fax (8) 27225; manufactures paints; Dir HANS HENRÍQUEZ.

Aruba Candle Co: Franlinstraat z/n, POB 240, Oranjestad; tel. and fax (8) 21958; candles, disinfectants; Dir MICHAEL SALADIN.

Aruba Handelmaatschappij NV: Nassaustraat 14, Oranjestad; groceries; Man. Dir RAOUL C. HENRÍQUEZ; 120 employees.

Aruba Trading Company: POB 156, Oranjestad; tel. (8) 22602; fax (8) 35757; f. 1928; distribution of general goods, incl. food and drink, clothing and household items; Man. Dir ANDREW L. BARBER; 80 employees.

Barcadera Cement Aruba: c/o J. G. Emanstraat 118A, POB 614, Oranjestad; tel. (8) 37286; fax (8) 31545; Dir CANDELARIO THIEL.

Carex Paper Products NV: Belgiëstraat 5, Oranjestad; tel. (8) 21404; fax (8) 31114; manufactures toilet paper, kitchen towels; Man. MARLON JACOBS.

Caribbean Paint Factory NV: Fergusonstraat 57D, POB 273, Oranjestad; tel. (8) 25339; fax (8) 37063; manufactures paint; Dir ANTON KAMERMANS.

Coastal Aruba Refinery Co NV: Seroe Colorado, POB 2150, Sint Nicholas; tel. (8) 94904; fax (8) 49087; f. 1989; petroleum refinery; Man. Dir MICHAEL RENFORD; 500 employees.

Hoori NV: Balashi 70, POB 1176, Oranjestad; tel. (8) 56400; fax (8) 51466; Dir MOON CHIU CHAN.

R. J. van der Sar NV: Barcadera 9, POB 299, Oranjestad; tel. (8) 50631; fax (8) 50645; manufactures disinfectants, soaps, detergents; Dir ROBERT NIEUW.

West India Mercantile Co (Aruba) NV: Nassaustraat 62, Oranjestad; subsidiary of West India Mercantile Co NV, Curaçao; electrical appliances; Man. RUBÉN J. FYNJE.

UTILITIES

Electricity and Water

Water en Energiebedrijf Aruba (WEB) NV: Balashi 76, POB 575, Oranjestad; tel. (8) 54600; fax (8) 57681; e-mail webaruba@setarnet.aw; internet www.webaruba.com.

Gas

Aruba Gas Supply Company Ltd (ARUGAS): Oranjestad.

BOC Gases Aruba: Balashi 21N, POB 190, Oranjestad; tel. (8) 52624; fax (8) 52823.

TRADE UNIONS

Federashon di Trahadonan Arubano—FTA (Aruban Workers' Federation): Bernardstraat 23, Sint Nicolaas; tel. (8) 45448; fax (8) 45504; f. 1964; independent; affiliated to World Confederation of Labour; Sec.-Gen. ANSELMO PONTILIUS.

There are also several unions for government and semi-government workers and employees.

Transport

There are no railways, but Aruba has a network of all-weather roads.

Arubus NV: Sabana Blanco 67, Oranjestad; tel. (8) 27089; fax (8) 28633; state-owned company providing public transport services.

SHIPPING

The island's principal seaport is Oranjestad, whose harbour can accommodate ocean-going vessels. There are also ports at Barcadera and Sint Nicolaas.

Aruba Ports Authority NV: L. G. Smith Blvd 23, Oranjestad; tel. (8) 26633; fax (8) 32896; f. 1981; Dir M. H. HENRÍQUEZ.

Officina Maritima de Aruba: Oranjestad; tel. (8) 21622.

Principal Shipping Companies

Beng Lian Shipping S. de R. L. A. V. V.: Dominicanessenstraat 22, Oranjestad.

Magna Shipping Co: Koningstraat 52, Oranjestad; tel. (8) 24349.

Rodoca Shipping and Trading SA: Parkietenbos 30, Barcadera Harbour; tel. (8) 50096; fax (8) 23371; formerly Aruba Shipping and Chartering Co NV.

Windward Island Agencies: Heyligerweg, POB 66, Oranjestad.

CIVIL AVIATION

The Queen Beatrix International Airport, about 2.5 km from Oranjestad, is served by numerous airlines, linking the island with destinations in the Caribbean, Europe, the USA and Central and South America. A project to upgrade and expand the airport was completed in mid-2000. In November 2000 the national carrier, Air Aruba, was declared bankrupt. A new airline was expected to begin operations in mid- to late 2001.

Tourism

Aruba's white sandy beaches, particularly along the southern coast, are an attraction for foreign visitors, and tourism is a major industry. The number of hotel rooms increased from 2,078 in 1986 to 6,789 in 1999. In 1998 most stop-over visitors came from the USA (57.5%), Venezuela (15.3%), the Netherlands (4.8%), Brazil (2.5%) and Canada (3.8%). In 1999 there were 683,300 stop-over visitors. In the same year 289,100 cruise-ship passengers visited Aruba. Receipts from tourism visitors totalled A Fl. 1,392.0m. in 1999.

Aruba Tourism Authority: L. G. Smith Blvd 172, Oranjestad; tel. (8) 23777; fax (8) 37403; e-mail ata.aruba@toaruba.com; internet www.aruba.com; Man. Dir MYRNA JANSEN-FELICIANO.

Aruba Hotel and Tourism Association: L. G. Smith Blvd 174, POB 542, Oranjestad; tel. (8) 22607; fax (8) 24202; e-mail ahata@setarnet.aw; internet www.aruba.com; CEO RORY ARENDS.

Cruise Tourism Authority—Aruba: POB 5254, Suite 227, Royal Plaza Mall, L. G. Smith Blvd 94, Oranjestad; tel. (8) 33648; fax (8) 35088; e-mail int1721@setarnet.aw; internet www.cruisearuba.com.

Defence

The Netherlands is responsible for Aruba's defence, and military service is compulsory. The Dutch-appointed Governor is Commander-in-Chief of the armed forces on the island. A Dutch naval contingent is stationed in the Netherlands Antilles and Aruba.

Education

A Compulsory Education Act was introduced in 1999 for those aged between four and 16. Kindergarten begins at four years of age. Primary education begins at six years of age and lasts for six years. Secondary education, beginning at the age of 12, lasts for up to six years. The main language of instruction is Dutch, but Papiamento (using a different spelling system from the Netherlands Antilles) is used in kindergarten and primary education and in the lower levels of technical and vocational education. Papiamento is also being introduced onto the curriculum in all schools. Aruba has two institutes of higher education: the University of Aruba, comprising the School of Law and the School of Business Administration, which had 214 students in 1998/99; and the Teachers' College, which had 180 students in the same period. There is also a community college. The majority of students, however, continue their studies abroad, generally in the Netherlands. Government expenditure in education in 1999 was planned at A Fl.113.8m., 12.6% of total spending and equivalent to an estimated 3.4% of GDP.

THE BAHAMAS

Area: 13,939 sq km (5,382 sq miles).

Population (official estimate at mid-1999): 298,300.

Capital: Nassau (on the island of New Providence), estimated population 172,000 in 1997.

Language: English.

Religion: Predominantly Christianity, with the Anglican, Baptist, Roman Catholic and Methodist Churches the principal denominations.

Climate: Mild and sub-tropical; average temperature is 30°C (86°F) in summer and 20°C (68°F) in winter; mean annual rainfall is about 1,000 mm (39 in).

Time: GMT –5 hours.

Public Holidays

2002: 1 January (New Year's Day), 29 March (Good Friday), 1 April (Easter Monday), 20 May (Whit Monday), 7 June (Labour Day), 10 July (Independence Day), 5 August (Emancipation Day), 12 October (Discovery Day/Columbus Day), 25–26 December (Christmas).

2003: 1 January (New Year's Day), 18 April (Good Friday), 21 April (Easter Monday), 1 June (Labour Day), 9 June (Whit Monday), 10 July (Independence Day), 2 August (Emancipation Day), 12 October (Discovery Day/Columbus Day), 25–26 December (Christmas).

Currency: Bahamian dollar; B $100 = £69.84 = US $100 = € 112.66 (30 April 2001).

Weights and Measures: The imperial system is used.

Basic Economic Indicators

	1997	1998	1999
Annual growth of real GDP (%)	3.3	3.0	n.a.
Government budget (million B $ at current prices):			
Revenue	728.1	760.9	868.7
Expenditure	829.3	807.2	884.5
Consumer price index (annual average; base: 1995 = 100)*	101.9	103.3	104.6
Rate of inflation (annual average, %)†	0.5	1.3	1.3
Foreign exchange reserves (US $ million at 31 December)‡	218.6	337.7	401.9
Imports c.i.f. (US $ million)§	1,666	1,873	1,911
Exports f.o.b. (US $ million)‖	181	300	450
Balance of payments (current account, US $ million)	–472.1	–995.4	–671.9

* 106.3 in 2000.
† 1.6% in 2000.
‡ US $341.4m. in 2000.
§ US $1,421m. in 2000.
‖ US $400m. in 2000.

Gross national product per head measured at purchasing power parity (PPP) (GNP converted to US dollars by the PPP exchange rate, 1998): 10,460.

Total labour force (1999): 157,640.

Unemployment (1999): 7.8%.

Total external debt (31 December 1998): B $85.0m.

Life expectancy (years at birth, 1999): 74.0.

Infant mortality rate (provisional, per 1,000 live births, 1996): 18.4.

Adult population with HIV/AIDS (15–49 years, 1999): 4.3%

School enrolment ratio (5–16 years, 1996): 93%.

Adult literacy rate (15 years and over, 2000): 96.1% (males 95.4%; females 96.8%).

Carbon dioxide emissions per head (metric tons, 1997): 6.0.

Passenger motor cars in use (estimate, per 1,000 of population, 1996): 161.4.

Television receivers in use (per 1,000 of population, 1997): 230.

History

MARK WILSON

Based on an earlier text by Prof. A. E. THORNDIKE

INTRODUCTION

The nearly 700 islands and 2,000 uninhabited cays that make up the Bahamian archipelago stretch in a 1,220-km arc towards the northern edge of the Caribbean from a point some 80 km off the coast of Florida (USA). One of the islands, San Salvador or Watling Island, is widely believed to have been the navigator Christopher Columbus's first landfall in the New World, in October 1492. The Spanish are thought to have deported and enslaved the original Lucayan inhabitants, but otherwise took little interest in the dry and somewhat barren islands. The British also found little to attract them to the islands, although a royal charter permitting their exploitation was granted to Sir Robert Heath in 1629. The first British settlers were Puritans from Bermuda, who arrived on Eleuthera in 1647. Other migrants from Bermuda also came, to seek salt. New Providence became the site of the capital, Nassau, from 1666. The other islands became collectively known as the Out Islands and, more recently, as the Family Islands. The soil and climate were not suitable for commercial agriculture and piracy became the basis of the economy, until its eradication from 1719 by the British Governor, Capt. Woodes Rogers.

Population growth was slow. As recently as 1782 there were only 4,000 inhabitants, of whom some 43% were white. However, with the ending of the American War of Independence at this time, loyalist settlers who had been expelled from the former British colonies on the mainland arrived. New Englanders settled some of the smaller islands as fishermen, while southerners brought slaves and established cotton plantations on some of the larger islands. Within four years, the population had grown to 8,950, of whom 67% were black. However, the cotton plantations were soon abandoned, owing to insect pests and soil exhaustion. In total, fewer than 10,000 slaves were landed in the colony and many were freed from bondage long before emancipation in 1834, when the population was an estimated 21,000. Then, as now, whites formed a significant minority. A further minority group originated directly from Africa, without any experience of New World slavery: several Bahamian villages were constructed on land granted to Africans freed by the British navy from captured Spanish vessels, which were intercepted *en route* to Cuba, following the abolition of the slave trade. Poor soil and a dry climate continued to prevent the development of plantation agriculture. The economy was based successively on plundering wrecks, gun-running during the American Civil War (1861–65), the cultivation of citrus and pineapples, sponge fishing and the smuggling of rum and whisky during the US 'Prohibition' of alcoholic liquors in 1919–33.

Although there was some miscegenation, a rigid colour bar prevented black advancement. Accordingly, when a representative House of Assembly was established in 1729, it was an exclusive preserve of the white settlers and merchants. Despite being briefly suspended in 1776, when the colony was captured by the rebel American colonists, and again in 1782 when it surrendered to the Spanish, the House of Assembly remained a permanent feature of Bahamian politics.

Although free black property owners were able to vote from 1807, and the Assembly had four non-white members by as early as 1834, political and economic life was controlled, to all intents and purposes, by a white merchant élite, the so-called 'Bay Street Boys' (named after Nassau's main commercial street). This oligarchy practised blatant electoral bribery in small Out Island constituencies, where the secret ballot was not introduced until 1949. The élite's electoral power was challenged by just a small number of black and mixed-race members and by Sir Etienne Dupuch's 'Nassau Tribune'.

POLITICAL AWAKENING

Black political awakening can be traced to the so-called Burma Road riots in 1942. By this time, after centuries of extreme variations in the island's fortunes, the economy was beginning to expand, with tourism growing steadily from the 1920s and the construction of US military bases required by the Second World War. The riots erupted over the issue of differential wages paid during the construction of a US Air Force base, to foreign and white workers on the one hand and to black Bahamians on the other. Two people were killed and 25 injured in the riots, which were followed by significant pay increases for black workers. The colony's first political party, the Progressive Liberal Party (PLP) was founded by a group of mixed-race professionals in 1953. In 1956 Sir Etienne Dupuch successfully advocated legislation to outlaw racial discrimination in public places. The 'Bay Street Boys' responded to the formation of the PLP by creating the United Bahamian Party (UBP). Lynden (later Sir Lynden) Pindling, a newly qualified black lawyer, later took over the leadership of the PLP, breaking with an older generation of mainly mixed-race PLP politicians. A tourist industry strike in 1958 was followed by universal male suffrage and the creation of four seats in New Providence, to reduce under-representation of the most densely populated island. The UBP benefited from the continuing over-representation of the less populous islands and won a majority of seats in the 1962 election, with only 36% of the popular vote. Less than the 45% polled by the PLP. However, reports of the privately owned Grand Bahama Port Authority, which had recently been granted a casino licence, paying large consultancy fees to cabinet ministers, severely damaged the reputation of the oligarchy.

INDEPENDENCE

In the historic January 1967 general election vigorous PLP campaigning resulted in each party winning 18 seats in the 38-seat House of Assembly. The sole representative of the Labour Party held the balance of power, and pledged his support for the PLP, which was therefore able to form a Government; Pindling, hailed as the 'Black Moses', became premier. The racial strife and economic collapse confidently predicted by the UBP never materialized and a series of constitutional reforms was soon introduced. Because of the insistence by the PLP on black advancement, local control over immigration was regarded as especially important, and the import of mainly white, expatriate labour became progressively restricted.

The PLP won the 1968 election, securing 29 legislative seats; and, after further endorsement at a general election in 1972, the PLP led the country to independence in 1973. There was, however, growing middle-class resentment at Pindling's dictatorial style of leadership, while allegations of corruption became widespread. Dissident members resigned from the PLP and in 1972 merged with the remnants of the UBP to form a new opposition party, the Free National Movement (FNM).

By the mid-1970s drugs trafficking and the laundering of illegal funds into legitimate holdings had become significant activities in the Bahamas. In 1984 the total value of the illegal drugs trade passing through the islands was conservatively estimated at some US $800m. Worse still was a virtual epidemic in the local use of drugs. Violent crime increased dramatically as addiction began to affect members of all social classes across the Bahamas. Initially, Pindling resisted pressure from the US administration, notably the Drug Enforcement Agency (DEA). However, in 1983 he was publicly accused by a US television network of personal involvement and was forced to establish a Royal Commission to investigate the issue.

The Commission reported in December 1984. Although no evidence was published implicating Pindling, the same could not be said of several other ministers. However, a minority report noted a prominent Bahamian businessman, Everette Bannister, had made substantial payments to Pindling, enabling the Prime Minister to spend more than eight times his official salary (in early 1989 Bannister was indicted in the USA, on charges of conspiring with the Colombian Medellín cartel to transport drugs through the Bahamas). However, few dismissals followed and Pindling was re-endorsed as party leader at the October 1985 PLP convention. Two cabinet ministers, Hubert Ingraham and Perry Christie, who also shared a legal practice, resigned in protest. These two were later to become Prime Minister and leader of the opposition, respectively.

The damage caused to Bahamian–US relations was serious. The US administration's concern went beyond trafficking: the strict banking secrecy laws, under which US and other offshore banks in the islands operated, were also criticized because of their misuse by criminals. Moreover, US companies and individuals who used Bahamian banks deprived the US Internal Revenue Service (IRS) of tax income. Consequently, the Bahamas were excluded from the US Caribbean Basin Initiative and tax concessions were not granted to US insurance companies wishing to exploit Bahamian offshore facilities, nor to US corporations holding conventions in the islands. The Bahamas Government denounced US demands that the DEA and IRS be allowed access to bank records and be permitted to search for drugs as an 'imperialist' infringement of sovereignty.

Aware of increasing public concern and international pressure, Pindling realized that co-operation with the USA was essential. A compromise was reached: drugs searches in the Bahamas could be made by the US Coastguard and the DEA, but only with the Bahamian police involved. The first such joint operation took place as early as April 1985, in Bimini, when the authorities seized 34,000 metric tons of marijuana, 2,500 kg of processed cocaine and US $1.4m.-worth of aircraft and ships. Expenditure on coastguard and defence forces was increased and several notable Colombian smugglers were arrested, including Carlos Lehder Rivas. Other measures followed: free passage and diplomatic immunity were granted to DEA agents; a joint drugs-interdiction force was formed; and in 1989 both countries signed a Mutual Legal Assistance Treaty (M-LAT), providing for collaboration in the investigation of criminal allegations within the offshore industry. A similar agreement was also signed with Canada. However, drugs trafficking continued to pose a problem, even though anti-smuggling measures had achieved some success.

At the end of the 1980s Pindling's confidence was such that he was dismissive of accusations (made by Lehder at his trial in Miami, USA) that he had been given US $400,000 by Lehder himself. In 1991 elected representatives were required to state their assets for the first time; 10 of the 13 cabinet ministers and 25 members of the Assembly declared more than $1m. Local opinion was, if anything, surprised at the modesty of the amounts reported. One PLP minister, Kendal Nottage, who was dismissed in 1985, but reappointed after the 1987 elections, reported assets of more than $11m. He was indicted in the USA in 1989 on charges of conspiring to conceal the illegal profits of a major Colombian drugs dealer.

DOMESTIC POLITICS AND THE RISE OF THE FNM

The PLP remained the dominant political force in the 1980s, accusing the FNM of subservience to the USA and to local white Bahamian interests. However, the party lost some ground in the 1987 election, winning 31 seats to the FNM's 16 in an enlarged 49-seat House of Assembly. Christie and Ingraham were elected as independents. The FNM leader, Kendal Isaacs, subsequently resigned and was succeeded by his deputy, Cecil Wallace-Whitfield, who, however, died in 1990. Hubert Ingraham, who had joined the FNM one month earlier, became leader of the party. Perry Christie soon afterwards rejoined the PLP.

Prospects for the FNM improved as the economy worsened. Measures taken under US pressure against cocaine smuggling and money laundering reduced the free flow of funds into the economy from the mid-1980s. A consequent fall in consumer demand induced a recession in the formal sector of the economy.

This was followed by an 11% decline in tourist arrivals in 1989–92. As a result, some hotels closed, while others placed staff on a reduced working week. Pindling was forced to introduce three successive austerity budgets and restraints on credit, which affected all sectors of society. The Government was also damaged by new scandals, over widespread corruption involving several state-owned businesses. A vigorous campaign by the FNM resulted in the defeat of the PLP in the general election of 19 August 1992. Ingraham became Prime Minister and the extent of economic mismanagement and of corrupt practices in several public corporations under the PLP regime only then began to become apparent. A Commission of Inquiry was established, to investigate the affairs of three corporations: Bahamasair (which had lost US $35m. in 1992 alone); the Hotel Corporation; and the Bahamas Telecommunications Company (BaTelCo). The report on Bahamasair, published in late 1995, revealed an astonishing record of corruption, involving two members of the PLP, and serious mismanagement, resulting in substantial losses. The inquiry into the BaTelCo, the results of which were published at the same time, reported extensive nepotism and managerial incompetence. The report on the Hotel Corporation was delayed owing to legal obstacles in obtaining Pindling's bank records.

The FNM's confident campaign prior to the March 1997 general election culminated in a clear victory, with the party winning 34 of the 40 seats in a reduced House of Assembly. Sir Lynden Pindling, diminished by a series of scandals and suffering from the effects of treatment for cancer, resigned as PLP leader in April, and later announced his retirement from Parliament, after 41 years (he died in August 2000). He was succeeded as party leader by Perry Christie. In September the PLP's parliamentary strength was reduced to only five seats when the Government won a by-election in Pindling's old seat, South Andros. Although the party retained 42% of the popular vote in the 1997 general election, with loyal support from low-income voters in Nassau, it did little subsequently to re-establish its fortunes. The PLP was further damaged in January 2000 by the resignation of its deputy leader, Bernard Nottage, who subsequently formed a rival party, the Coalition for Democratic Reform. However, the PLP could not be dismissed as a force in Bahamian politics.

Following its victory in the 1997 general election, the FNM suggested establishing a commission to give detailed consideration to constitutional reforms, including a proposed limit of two terms of office for the Prime Minister, which would thus prevent Hubert Ingraham from leading a government after the next election. Other possible reforms included the assignation of independent status to the Elections Commission, the Boundaries Commission and the Office of the Director of Public Prosecutions; and changes to the structure and appointment of the Senate. However, with new elections due by July 2002 and expected earlier, by mid-2001 no real progress had been made on these proposals. A cabinet reshuffle in February 2001 promoted some younger ministers, while others were given new portfolios; this was widely interpreted as a move to prepare a new generation for a change of leadership. Indeed, in July Ingraham announced his intention to retire from politics in the next 12 months, irrespective of his party winning a third term in power.

INTO THE 21ST CENTURY

In the late 1990s there was a resurgence in drugs trafficking, as the Mexican route for Colombian cocaine became more difficult and Haiti, just south of the Bahamas, increased its importance as a transhipment point, as did Jamaica. A report published in 2001 for the Caribbean office of the UN Drug Control Programme suggested that around 41 metric tons of cocaine passed through the Bahamas annually, equivalent to around 6% of South American production. An analysis of balance of payment statistics by the US embassy in Nassau suggested that cocaine and marijuana smuggling resulted in foreign exchange inflows of US $200-300m. dollars annually, a sum which would be equivalent to 11%–17% of formal sector merchandise imports, or 4%–7% of gross domestic product (GDP). On this basis, the report suggested drugs transhipment might rival, or even surpass, the Bahamian banking industry in economic impact. The USA includes the Bahamas on a list of 26 major drugs source or transhipment countries, but acknowledges the progress that the Bahamian Government has made in reducing narcotics activity. Local cocaine seizures in 2000 totalled an encouraging 2.75 metric tons, while a major transhipment ring was reportedly broken in February 2001.

The resurgence of drugs trafficking, in turn, led to an increase in violent crime, with a sharp growth in gun-related offences in 1999–2000. The number of armed robberies rose to three per day in late 1999, while there were 72 murders in 2000. The murder rate of 24.0 for every 100,000 persons was comparable with that of Jamaica. There were indications that many of these killings were connected to organized criminal activity. The prosperity of the mass market tourism industry was not affected by increased criminal activity. However, from the late 1990s, expansion and reconstruction of large hotels such as Sun International's Atlantis resort on Paradise Island gave rise to local concerns over the loss of beach access. This provoked fears in some quarters that Bahamians were losing control of their country to foreigners. The Government attempted to show that it was sensitive to these concerns, stressing its awareness of environmental issues. Nevertheless, doubts remained and fears over increasing foreign interest in the islands were demonstrated in 2000 by vigorous opposition to the impending privatization of the national telecommunications company, BaTelCo. The sale was subject to repeated delays and remained incomplete in mid-2001.

There was increasing international concern in from 1999 over the standard of regulation of international financial centres. In May 2000 the Bahamas was listed by the Financial Action Task Force on Money Laundering (FATF, based at the OECD's headquarters) as a non-co-operative jurisdiction. In the second half of 2000 the Government devoted considerable political attention to reform of the 'offshore' financial sector. New legislation established a Financial Intelligence Unit in October, improved the mechanism for international co-operation in criminal proceedings and required international business companies to keep records showing their beneficial ownership. A further law was passed increasing the regulatory capacity of the Central Bank. As a result of the measures, in June 2001 the FATF removed the Bahamas from its list of non-co-operative countries.

Economy

MARK WILSON

The economy of the Bahamas is one of the most prosperous of the Caribbean and Latin American nations, with an estimated per-head gross domestic product (GDP) of US $16,185 in 2000, a higher figure than any independent country in Latin America and the Caribbean (the Bahamian dollar is at par with the US dollar). The Bahamas' rating with the Moody's investor agency was also the highest in the region. The country was also rated 33rd in the United Nations Development Programme's Human Development Index, second in the region only to Barbados, which was placed 30th.

Following a recession which lasted from 1988 to 1993, from 1993 there was continuous economic growth. Positive economic growth of 1.7% was recorded in 1993. There has been positive growth in every year since then, initially at a slow rate (0.9% in 1994, 0.3% in 1995), but higher than 3% in every year thereafter, with Central Bank estimates of 6% growth in 1999 and 5% in 2000. Foreign direct investment was very high throughout the late 1990s and was equivalent to an estimated 4.8% of GDP in 2000. Recovery was prompted largely by new hotel investment, much of it stimulated by the sale to new investors of the dilapidated properties of the Government's hotel corporation, and by the increased hotel occupancy of stop-over visitors. In 2000 the annual rate of unemployment was close to 7%, compared with 14.8% in 1992.

There is no personal or corporate income tax in the Bahamas. Duties on imports made up 58.8% of the Government's recurrent revenue in 1999/2000. As a result, retail prices were relatively high, although the inflation rate declined from an annual average of 4.4% in 1985–95, to an average annual rate of 1.2% in 1995–2000. Consumer prices rose by an annual average of 1.6% in 2000. Taxes directly related to tourism (hotel occupancy tax, departure tax and gaming tax) made up a further 11.2% of government revenue in 1999/2000. However, the small tax base posed problems. In spite of successive tax increases, government revenue was equivalent to only 19.3% of GDP in 1999/2000, much lower than the proportion prevailing in other Caribbean islands, such as Barbados, where government revenue was equivalent to 32.2% of GDP in the same year. The Bahamas is likely to join the World Trade Organization within the next few years, a move which will necessitate a reduction in import duties. To protect the tax base while avoiding the need for an income tax, it is thought that a sales tax will be introduced within the next few years.

The fiscal deficit increased sharply in the late 1980s, reaching 4.2% of GDP in 1989. It decreased to 0.3% by 1993/94, and remained low thereafter, with the exception of 1996/97, when the deficit increased sharply to reach 3.6% of GDP, partly as a result of spending commitments made before the 1997 general election. The fiscal deficit fell back to 1.6% of GDP in 1997/98 and was reduced further in each of the succeeding years. With the recurrent fiscal account in surplus, the Government aimed to eliminate its overall deficit in 2000/01, an objective which, shortly before the (30 June) end of the financial year, it appeared to have missed by only the narrowest of margins. Foreign-currency debt servicing cost US $68.0m. in 2000, equivalent to 7.4% of the recurrent revenue of US $918.2m. The debt-service ratio, however, was a respectable 2.6% of the estimated value of exports of goods and services in the same year, down from 5.4% in 1997. Salaries accounted for 51.4% of total recurrent expenditure in 1993/94, but only 44.2% of that figure in 1999/2000, marking a gradual decrease in public-sector employment. Most government-owned hotels were sold in 1993–97 and privatization was expected to continue in 2001, with the long-delayed divestment of the Bahamas Telecommunications Company (BaTelCo) expected to be followed, after the next election, by the Bahamas Electricity Corporation (BEC). In both cases, a significant proportion of shares were to be reserved for employees and for other local investors.

In 1955 an area of 603 sq km (233 sq miles), approximately one-third of the island of Grand Bahama, was granted to the privately owned Grand Bahama Port Authority (GBPA), with important tax concessions under the Hawksbill Creek Agreement. Freeport, which owed its existence entirely to that Agreement, developed considerably. The GBPA aimed originally to construct a manufacturing centre. The focus then shifted to tourism and residential development. Within Freeport, the operation of the port and airport, land development and the management of the water and electricity supply were private-sector activities. Under the PLP Government, Grand Bahama was regarded as an opposition stronghold, and was consequently neglected by the central administration. The petroleum refinery and cement plant were closed, and tourism stagnated. In 1993 the Hawksbill Creek Agreement was extended to 2054, with tax exemptions running to 2015. This contributed to renewed economic development, with a Hong Kong-owned company, Hutchison Whampoa, the principal investor.

The Out Islands, or Family Islands, varied enormously in the degree of economic development achieved. In the northern Bahamas, activities such as tourism and fishing brought prosperity to a number of islands, including Abaco, Spanish Wells, Eleuthera and Bimini. In contrast, some islands in the southern Bahamas, such as Mayaguana, Acklins and Crooked Island had small populations and a very limited range of economic activity.

TOURISM

Tourism was the basis of prosperity in the Bahamas, and remained by far the most important sector of the economy. It employed some 30% of the labour force. The islands are closer to the USA than are most other Caribbean destinations. For this reason, commercial tourism developed comparatively early, with the construction of the Royal Victoria Hotel in Nassau commencing just before the US Civil War of the 1860s. Luxury winter tourism developed further between 1920 and 1940, and from the 1950s jet travel opened the islands as a mass-market destination. The number of visitors (including cruise-ship passengers, who accounted for some 60% of tourist arrivals in 1999) increased from 32,000 in 1949 to 1.1m. in 1979 and to 4.2m. in 2000. Such a marked increase led to rapid growth in commercial activity and a significant increase in living standards.

Following a fall in tourist arrivals in the late 1980s and early 1990s, a vast increase in tourism-related investment prompted a recovery in the sector. This investment totalled US $1,500m.–$2,000m. over five years and involved hotel construction and refurbishment, an extension to Nassau International Airport and new air links. As a result, room occupancy in Nassau increased from 52% in 1992 to 72.8% in 2000, in spite of a greatly increased room stock, and tourist receipts rose to US $1,814m. The opening of 'private island' facilities by cruise lines and a refurbished cruise port facility in Nassau contributed to an increase in cruise-passenger arrivals, which totalled 2,512,000 in 2000. The Bahamas received more cruise-ship passengers than any other Caribbean destination, although with much lower per head spending than stop-over tourists.

The increase in tourism investment in the late 1990s involved the reconstruction of most of the existing hotels in Nassau followed, in 1999–2001, by the major properties on Grand Bahama. This activity involved the extensive development of the Sun International Atlantis resort on Paradise Island, which completed the second stage of its US $450m. expansion project in December 1998. The completed project included 2,355 rooms, a marina, a casino and a conference facility, with 5,600 staff, equivalent to 4% of national employment. Further expansion was expected: construction of a US $100m. condominium-marina project began in 2001. Nassau's hotel properties were large, and many belonged to international chains, a great asset for US marketing, which relied heavily on branding. On Grand Bahama, much of the available accommodation was previously owned by the Hotel Corporation and had, by the 1990s, become rather dilapidated. In 1997 the largest properties were sold to Hutchison Whampoa, which undertook a full redevelopment and reopened with 1,350 rooms in late 2000. The 965-room Princess Resort and Casino was sold in May 2000, with renovation in progress in mid-2001. In spite of their excellent beaches and wildlife resources, the Family Islands remained relatively undeveloped. There were few air links to the north-eastern USA, and travel via Nassau could be inconvenient. Large-scale developments were, however, built or planned on several islands, including Eleuthera and Exuma.

Agriculture and manufacturing were poorly developed, and tourist operators purchased little locally. Food, furnishings, even souvenirs, were generally shipped in from Miami; some construction projects imported pre-assembled and pre-fitted hotel rooms, thus minimizing the need for local labour. For this reason, retained earnings were poor. In addition, many major hotel projects were given important tax concessions.

In 1997 there were 1.62m. stop-over tourist arrivals and 1.74m. cruise passengers. Detailed tourist statistics were not available from 1998, for technical reasons. However, there was a slight decrease in arrivals in 1998, with much of the room-stock out of service for reconstruction. This was followed by an increase in room capacity at the end of this year and in 1999–2000. Stop-over arrivals in 1999 increased by an estimated 8.3% above 1997 levels and cruise passenger numbers up by 43.4%. In 1998 the tourism sector directly contributed 15% of GDP, while in 2000 travel receipts covered 96% of the cost of goods imported. Owing to the proximity of the USA, the European market was less important to the Bahamian tourist industry than it was to that of the rest of the Caribbean. In 1997 some 81% of stop-over arrivals came from the USA. In the same year some 8% of visitors came from Europe and 6% came from Canada.

'OFFSHORE' FINANCE AND REGISTRATION

Nassau is a major international financial centre. In 1998 international banks operating in the Bahamas managed US $250,000m. in assets, with a further US $90,000m. in 900 locally-managed mutual funds. The financial sector was estimated to have generated a gross US $260m., or some 7% of GDP, in 1996. However, by the 1990s the Bahamas had lost its former dominant position as an offshore financial centre. From being one of the world's best known offshore centres, dating from the 1920s, the financial services industry in the Bahamas declined almost every year from the early 1980s until 1991. Whereas in 1976 some 49% of Organisation for Economic Co-operation and Development (OECD) offshore assets in developing countries were administered from Nassau, by 1998 its market share was only 10%, with the Cayman Islands taking 31% and Hong Kong 25%. In the world-wide ranking of the financial centres of metropolitan and developing countries, Nassau declined from third place in 1976 to 15th by 1998. Nassau, however, lost market share partly because there was no longer a tax advantage in booking large international loans offshore, leading to loss of business which had in any event accounted for relatively little value added. However, in the more economically significant business of private banking and trust management, the reputation of the Bahamas was severely damaged by extensive money-laundering activity in the early 1980s. Suffering from the country's image of sleaze and corruption and with many financial institutions having to defend themselves against the persistent enquiries of overseas law-enforcement and tax authorities (mainly from the USA), a number of institutions reduced their operations or chose alternative centres, notably the Cayman Islands. Aggressive marketing of company registration and other services by newer financial centres, such as the British Virgin Islands, also allowed them to capture a share of the market which they did not thereafter relinquish.

Resolute action was taken to cleanse the industry of illegal funds and to remove the minority damaging the industry's reputation. The reforms began in 1989, with more rapid progress being made after the 1992 elections and the change of government. There was much on which to base a recovery: the accumulation of expertise was probably unrivalled in the Caribbean and, in spite of the Mutual Legal Assistance Treaty signed with the USA in 1989, under most conditions, legal protection for banking secrecy remained. By 1991 the industry was once more expanding. Legislation was updated on international business companies and mutual funds in 1995, on money laundering in 1996 and on trusts in 1998.

Overseas marketing of financial services was, from April 1998, handled by the Financial Services Promotion Board. However, the captive insurance sector was less developed than in Bermuda, Barbados and other jurisdictions which, unlike the Bahamas, enjoyed tax concessions granted by the US or Canadian authorities. Money-laundering controls were evaluated by the Caribbean Financial Action Task Force in 1997. The Bahamas remained classified in the 2000 US International Narcotics Control Strategy Report as a 'Country of Primary Concern' with regard to money laundering, partly because of its banking secrecy laws and the size and complexity of its offshore financial sector.

In May 2000 the Bahamas was included by the OECD on a list of 35 'tax havens'. OECD members threatened to impose counter-measures if plans were not announced to bring Bahamian tax and secrecy regulations in line with their requirements by June 2001. In the same month, the intergovernmental Financial Action Task Force (FATF, based at the OECD Secretariat) included the Bahamas in a list of 15 non-co-operative jurisdictions. The FATF report criticized the practice of issuing bearer shares, which make beneficial ownership of financial assets impossible to trace; long delays and restricted responses to requests for judicial assistance; and rules which allow intermediaries to avoid revealing the names of their clients. Along with the other jurisdictions, in June the Bahamas was the subject of an advisory statement from the US Treasury, which asked US financial institutions to apply 'enhanced scrutiny' to transactions with the country. The Bahamian authorities made it clear that they would accelerate their efforts to bring the jurisdiction into line with international requirements, and 11 new financial reform measures were passed by Parliament by the end of the year. The Bahamas was removed from the FATF blacklist in June 2001, while the OECD appeared likely to drop its threat to introduce counter-measures against tax havens.

The Bahamas International Securities Exchange opened in May 2000 and by June 2001 was trading the shares of 17 local companies with total market capitalization of US $1,800m. Mutual funds were also listed, but not traded; and there were plans to trade public- and private-sector debt.

Local expenditure by offshore companies was US $94.8m. in 2000, down from $117.5m. in 1995, but still equivalent to 7.0% of the visible trade deficit. Total employment in the offshore finance sector was approximately 3,600, equivalent to 2.5% of the employed labour force. Although expatriates continued to play an important role, by the start of the 21st century a high proportion of professional positions were held by Bahamian nationals.

During the 1990s company registration, in particular, witnessed spectacular growth, following the International Business Company Act of 1990. Owing to simplified automated procedures and tax concessions there were 102,200 registered International Business Companies at the end of 1999. However, income from this source fell in the early months of 2001 as a result of stricter financial regulation. The other area of offshore activity to continue to perform well into the 1990s was that of ship registration. The Bahamas ship registry, relaunched after the adoption of the Bahamas Maritime Authority Act in 1995, was the world's third in terms of gross registered tonnage, behind Panama and Liberia. It was managed by the Bahamas Maritime Authority, which had offices in London, Nassau and New York (USA). Registered displacement was some 26.8m. gross registered tons (grt) by 1998. In 1997 Hutchison Whampoa opened a US $78m. international container-transhipment terminal at Freeport, Grand Bahama; after completion of a US $71m. expansion in 1999 it was capable of handling 950,000 container units per year and was to act as an intercontinental hub port serving North America, the Caribbean and South America. Further expansion was planned in 2000–01.

INDUSTRY

Industrial development was a relatively late arrival in the Bahamas, dating from 1960 and the formation of the Grand Bahama Development Company, based in the free-trade zone in Freeport, itself only established by the 1955 Hawksbill Creek Agreement. Freeport was at first dominated by ship bunkering and petroleum refining. However, proposals to develop Grand Bahama as a major industrial centre did not come to fruition; refining operations at the Bahamas Oil Refining Company ceased in 1985 and a cement plant built to serve the US market also closed. There remained some interest in petroleum and natural-gas exploration; drilling by a US company, on Grand Bahama Bank, continued from 1986, but with no positive results.

In the 1990s, however, high labour and utilities costs, and the small size of the local market, combined to severely limit the development of industrial activity, although a number of manufacturers produced for the local market, among them a brewery, soft-drinks companies, paper converters and printers. Bacardi operated a rum refinery in Nassau, which made use of imported molasses to produce light rums for export to Europe, under the Lomé Convention (which expired in February 2000 and was replaced by the Cotonou Agreement—see Part Three, Regional Organizations, European Union). Rum exports fell from US $33.4m. or 27% of domestic export earnings in 1991 to

only $2.9m. (3.1% of domestic earnings) in 1995, before recovering to $12.2m., or 8.8%, in 1998.

Of greater significance were a number of enclave industries located on Grand Bahama, which benefited from the island's tax concessions and port facilities. A Freeport company had facilities for the repair of containers, fabrication of steel structures and instrumentation system maintenance. There is also a plant producing expandable polystyrene. Exports of chemicals and hormones totalled US $26.5m. in 1998; however, two chemicals plants which were operating in that year closed in late 2000 and in early 2001. A $75m. cruise-ship repair-facility on Grand Bahama was established in 2000 and was expected to be fully operational by 2004 with total employment of 470. Also in Grand Bahama, in 2001 the US company Enron put forward a proposal for a US $400m Liquefied Natural Gas (LNG) regasification terminal and handling facility to serve Florida (USA), to which it would be connected by a 145-km underwater pipeline. In 1998 a 13.5 MW electricity generating plant, constructed at a cost of $17.5m., opened in Freeport. On the remote island of Inagua in the southern Bahamas, the main employer was the US-owned Morton Salt Company, which produced salt through the evaporation of sea water. Exports in 1998 were worth $12.9m.

Industry (including construction and utilities) provided 10.8% of GDP in 1992 and employed 14.6% of the working population in 1997 (construction accounted for 9.2%). Manufacturing and mining contributed 4.2% of GDP in 1995. However, high wages and costs continued to be serious disadvantages.

AGRICULTURE AND FISHING

Agriculture never played a leading role in the Bahamian economy and at the turn of the 21st century it was estimated to account for less than 3% of GDP. More than 80% of food was imported. Agricultural resources are severely limited since rainfall is low, few areas have groundwater for irrigation and much of the land consists of bare limestone rock with only scattered patches of soil.

In 1997 agricultural production accounted for only 1% of total land area. There were small-scale farmers on many of the Family Islands, who produced livestock, fruit and vegetables in limited quantities for local markets. Larger commercial farms on New Providence, the most populous island, produced eggs and poultry, constituting one-half of agricultural production. Feed and other supplies were imported. Ornamental plants and flowers accounted for another 12.7% of agricultural production. In 1992 the Government made 15,000 acres (6,000 ha) of land available to local and foreign investors for fruit and vegetable farming. By 1995 over 20,000 acres (8,000 ha) were devoted to citrus-fruit cultivation. To protect local producers, imports of some crops, such as bananas, were restricted. A number of sizeable agro-businesses in the larger islands of the northern Bahamas operated as enclave industries, growing citrus and other fruit and vegetable crops for export. Some farms used crushed limestone rock as a growing medium and nutrients were sometimes added to groundwater used for irrigation. Total exports of fruit and vegetables amounted to US $1.2m. in 1998.

Commercial fishing remained an important economic activity on some of the smaller islands, such as Spanish Wells, and supplied more than one-half of domestic exports in the late 1990s. Exports of crawfish (spiny lobster) amounted to US $57.5m. in 1998, with another US $12.9m. from other fisheries exports. Such primary economic activities, however, remained peripheral in their contribution to the national wealth of the Bahamas.

Statistical Survey

Source (unless otherwise stated): Central Bank of the Bahamas, Frederick St, POB N-4868, Nassau;
tel. 322-2193; fax 322-4321.

AREA AND POPULATION

Area: 13,939 sq km (5,382 sq miles).

Population: 209,505 at census of 12 May 1980; 255,095 (males 124,992, females 130,103) at census of 2 May 1990; 298,300 (official estimate) in 1999. *By island* (1990): New Providence 172,196 (including the capital, Nassau); Grand Bahama 40,898; Andros 8,187; Eleuthera 10,586.

Density (1999): 21.4 per sq km.

Principal Town: Nassau (capital), population 172,000 (1997).

Births, Marriages and Deaths (1996): Registered live births 5,873 (birth rate 20.7 per 1,000); Registered marriages 2,628 (marriage rate 9.3 per 1,000); Registered deaths 1,537 (death rate 5.4 per 1,000). Source: UN, *Demographic Yearbook* and *Population and Vital Statistics Report*.

Expectation of Life (World Bank estimate, years at birth, 1999): 74.

Economically Active Population (sample survey, persons aged 15 years and over, excl. armed forces, April 1999): Agriculture, hunting, forestry and fishing 5,835; Mining, quarrying, electricity, gas and water 1,745; Manufacturing 5,910; Construction 16,540; Wholesale and retail trade 19,955; Hotels and restaurants 23,300; Transport, storage and communications 10,305; Finance, insurance, real estate and business services 13,350; Community, social and personal services 47,780; Activities not adequately defined 630; *Total employed* 145,350 (males 77,245, females 68,105); *Unemployed* 12,290 (males 4,955, females 7,335); *Total labour force* 157,640 (males, 82,200, females 75,440). Source: ILO Caribbean Office.

AGRICULTURE, ETC.

Principal Crops ('000 metric tons, 2000): Roots and tubers 1; Sugar cane 45*; Tomatoes 3; Other vegetables 18*; Lemons and limes 8; Grapefruit and pomelos 12; Bananas 2; Other fruits 4. *FAO estimate. Source: FAO.

Livestock (FAO estimates, '000 head, year ending September 2000): Cattle 0.7; Pigs 5.9; Sheep 5.7; Goats 14.5; Poultry 5,000. Source: FAO.

Livestock Products ('000 metric tons, 2000): Poultry meat 9.7; Cows' milk 0.6*; Goats' milk 1.1*; Hen eggs 1.1*. *FAO estimate. Source: FAO.

Forestry ('000 cu m, 1999): Roundwood removals: Sawlogs and veneer logs 17; Sawnwood production: Coniferous (softwood) 1. Source: FAO, *Yearbook of Forest Products*.

Fishing ('000 metric tons, live weight, 1998): Capture 10.1 (Groupers 0.7, Snappers 0.8, Caribbean spiny lobster 7.6, Stromboid conchs 0.7); Aquaculture 0.0 (FAO estimate); Total catch 10.1. Figures exclude marine shells (39 metric tons) and sponges (60 tons). Source: FAO, *Yearbook of Fishery Statistics*.

MINING

Production (estimates, '000 metric tons): Unrefined salt 900 in 1999; Aragonite 1,200 in 1997. Source: US Geological Survey.

INDUSTRY

Production (estimate, million kWh, 1998): Electric energy 1,227.

FINANCE

Currency and Exchange Rates: 100 cents = 1 Bahamian dollar (B $). *Sterling, US Dollar and Euro Equivalents* (30 April 2001): £1 sterling = B $1.4318; US $1 = B $1.0000; €1 = 88.76 cents; B $100 = £69.84 = US $100.00 = €112.66. *Exchange Rate:* Since February 1970 the official exchange rate, applicable to most transactions, has been US $1 = B $1, i.e., the Bahamian dollar has been at par with the US dollar. There is also an investment currency rate, applicable to certain capital transactions between residents and non-residents and to direct investments outside the Bahamas. Since 1987 this exchange rate has been fixed at US $1 = B $1.225.

General Budget (estimates, B $ million, year ending 30 June 1999): *Revenue:* Total 839.1. *Expenditure:* Education 164.7; Uniformed services 90.6; Health 134.3; Tourism 57.3; Public works 55.7; Social services 47.5; Public debt interest 106.6; Total (incl. other) 862.6 (current 767.1; capital 95.5).

1999/2000 (forecasts, B $ million): Recurrent revenue 895.6; Recurrent expenditure 838.7; Capital expenditure 95.8.

2000/01 (forecasts, B $ million): Total revenue 998; Recurrent expenditure 949; Capital expenditure 128.

International Reserves (US $ million at 31 December 2000): Reserve position in IMF 8.1; Foreign exchange 341.4; Total 349.6. Source: IMF, *International Financial Statistics*.

Money Supply (B $ million at 31 December 2000): Currency outside banks 152.1; Demand deposits at deposit money banks 629.9; Total money (incl. others) 797.9. Source: IMF, *International Financial Statistics*.

Cost of Living (consumer price index; base: 1995 = 100): 103.3 in 1998; 104.6 in 1999; 106.3 in 2000. Source: IMF, *International Financial Statistics*.

Gross Domestic Product (US $ million at current prices): 3,201 in 1995; 3,621 in 1996; 3,795 in 1997. Source: UN, *Statistical Yearbook*.

Expenditure on the Gross Domestic Product (B $ million at current prices, 1995): Government final consumption expenditure 483.9; Private final consumption expenditure 2,077.4; Increase in stocks 13.8; Gross fixed capital formation 698.5; *Total domestic expenditure* 3,273.6; Exports of goods and services 1,680.1; *Less* Imports of goods and services 1,819.6; Statistical discrepancy –64.7; *GDP in purchasers' values* 3,069.4. Source: IMF, *International Financial Statistics*.

Gross Domestic Product by Economic Activity (B $ million at current prices, 1992): Agriculture, hunting, forestry and fishing 89; Manufacturing (incl. mining and quarrying) 105; Electricity, gas and water 88; Construction 91; Trade, restaurants and hotels 705; Transport, storage and communications 227; Finance, insurance, real estate and business services 610; Government services 336; Other community, social and personal services 310; Other services 55; Statistical discrepancy 13; *Sub-total* 2,629; Import duties 268; Other indirect taxes 162; *GDP in purchasers' values* 3,059. Source: UN, *National Accounts Statistics*.

Balance of Payments* (US $ million, 1999): Exports of goods f.o.b. 379.9; Imports of goods f.o.b. –1,808.1; *Trade balance* –1,428.2; Exports of services 1,811.2; Imports of services –953.8; *Balance on goods and services* –570.8; Other income received 229.6; Other income paid –367.2; *Balance on goods, services and income* –708.4; Current transfers received 49.0; Current transfers paid –12.5; *Current balance* –671.9; Capital account (net) –14.5; Direct investment abroad –0.2; Direct investment from abroad 144.6; Other investment assets –12,487.1; Other investment liabilities 12,954.1; Net errors and omissions 140.2; *Overall balance* 65.2. Source: IMF, *International Financial Statistics*.

* The figures for merchandise imports and exports exclude petroleum and petroleum products, except imports for local consumption.

EXTERNAL TRADE*

Principal Commodities (US $ million, 1998): *Imports c.i.f.:* Food and live animals 260.1; Crude materials (inedible) except fuels 45.3; Mineral fuels, lubricants etc. 112.7; Chemicals 160.5; Basic manufactures 358.7; Machinery and transport equipment 555.8; Miscellaneous manufactured articles 257.7; Total (incl. others) 1,816.4. *Exports f.o.b.:* Food and live animals 75.3; Beverages and tobacco 12.8; Crude materials (inedible) except fuels 28.4; Chemicals 67.0; Basic manufactures 26.1; Machinery and transport equipment 78.2; Miscellaneous manufactured articles 12.4; Total (incl. others) 300.3.

1999 (US $ million): Total imports c.i.f. 1,911; Total exports f.o.b. 450.

2000 (US $ million): Total imports c.i.f. 1,421; Total exports f.o.b. 400. Source: IMF, International Financial Statistics.

Principal Trading Partners (US $ million, 1991): *Imports c.i.f.:* Aruba 52.2; Canada 21.2; Denmark 23.7; France 20.8; Nigeria 23.9; USA 866.0; Total (incl. others) 1,091.2. *Exports f.o.b.:* Canada 6.7; France 14.5; Germany 6.2; Mexico 4.0; United Kingdom 27.2; USA 142.5; Total (incl. others) 225.1. Source: UN, *International Trade Statistics Yearbook*.

1995 (US $ million): *Imports c.i.f.* (excl. mineral fuels): Canada 11.3; USA 1,008.7; Total (incl. others) 1,243.1. *Exports f.o.b.:* Canada 3.4; United Kingdom 4.0; USA 142.6; Total (incl. others) 175.9.

* The data exclude imports and exports of crude petroleum and residual fuel oils that are brought into the Bahamas for storage on behalf of foreign companies abroad. Also excluded is trade in certain chemical products.

TRANSPORT

Road Traffic (vehicles in use, 1995): 67,100 passenger cars; 13,700 commercial vehicles. Source: UN, *Statistical Yearbook*.

Shipping: *Merchant fleet* (displacement, '000 grt at 31 December): 24,409 in 1996; 25,523 in 1997; 27,716 in 1998. (Source: Lloyd's Register of Shipping, *World Fleet Statistics*). *International sea-borne freight traffic* (estimates, '000 metric tons, 1990): Goods loaded 5,920; Goods unloaded 5,705. Source: UN, *Monthly Bulletin of Statistics*.

Civil Aviation (1997): Kilometres flown (million) 2; Passengers carried ('000) 704; Passenger-km (million) 140; Total ton-km (million) 13. Source: UN, *Statistical Yearbook*.

TOURISM

Tourist Arrivals: 3,453,769 in 1997; 3,346,329 in 1998; 3,655,839 (1,436,952 by air, 2,281,887 by sea) in 1999.

Tourism Receipts (estimates, B $ million): 1,398 in 1996; 1,416 in 1997; 1,408 in 1998.

COMMUNICATIONS MEDIA

Radio Receivers (1997): 215,000 in use.
Television Receivers (1997): 67,000 in use.
Telephones (estimate, 1997): 96,000 main lines in use.
Telefax Stations (1996): 500 in use.
Mobile Cellular Telephones (1997): 6,152 subscribers.
Daily Newspapers (1996): 3 titles (total circulation 28,000 copies).
Sources: UN, *Statistical Yearbook*; UNESCO, *Statistical Yearbook*.

EDUCATION

Pre-primary (1996/97): 20 schools; 76 teachers; 1,094 pupils.
Primary (1996/97): 113 schools; 1,540 teachers (estimate); 34,199 students.
Secondary (1996/97): 37 junior/senior high schools (1990); 1,352 teachers (public education only); 27,970 students (public education only).
Tertiary (1987): 249 teachers; 5,305 students.
In 1993 there were 3,201 students registered at the College of the Bahamas.
Source: mainly UNESCO, *Statistical Yearbook*.

Directory

The Constitution

A representative House of Assembly was first established in 1729, although universal adult suffrage was not introduced until 1962. A new Constitution for the Commonwealth of the Bahamas came into force at independence, on 10 July 1973. The main provisions of the Constitution are summarized below:

Parliament consists of a Governor-General (representing the British monarch, who is Head of State), a nominated Senate and an elected House of Assembly. The Governor-General appoints the Prime Minister and, on the latter's recommendation, the remainder of the Cabinet. Apart from the Prime Minister, the Cabinet has no fewer than eight other ministers, of whom one is the Attorney-General. The Governor-General also appoints a Leader of the Opposition.

The Senate (upper house) consists of 16 members, of whom nine are appointed by the Governor-General on the advice of the Prime Minister, four on the advice of the Leader of the Opposition and three on the Prime Minister's advice after consultation with the Leader of the Opposition. The House of Assembly (lower house) has 40 members. A Constituencies Commission reviews numbers and boundaries at intervals of not more than five years and can recommend alterations for approval of the House. The life of Parliament is limited to a maximum of five years.

The Constitution provides for a Supreme Court and a Court of Appeal.

The Government

Head of State: HM Queen ELIZABETH II (succeeded to the throne 6 February 1952).
Governor-General: Sir ORVILLE TURNQUEST (appointed 22 February 1995).

THE CABINET
(August 2001)

Prime Minister: HUBERT ALEXANDER INGRAHAM.
Deputy Prime Minister and Minister of National Security: FRANK HOWARD WATSON.
Minister of Foreign Affairs: JANET GWENNET BOSTWICK.
Minister of Tourism: ORVILLE ALTON THOMPSON (TOMMY) TURNQUEST.
Minister of Finance: WILLIAM C. ALLEN.
Minister of Education, Youth and Sports: Sen. DION ALEXANDER FOULKES.
Minister of Housing and Social Development: ALGERNON SIDNEY PATRICK BENEDICT ALLEN.
Minister of Agriculture and Fisheries: JAMES FRANKLIN KNOWLES.
Minister of Public Works: KENNETH RUSSELL.
Minister of Transport, Aviation and Local Government: CORNELIUS ALVIN SMITH.
Minister of Health: Sen. Dr RONALD L. KNOWLES.
Minister of Public Service and Cultural Affairs: THERESA MOXEY-INGRAHAM.

Minister of Labour and Immigration: EARL DEVAUX.
Minister of Justice and Attorney-General: CARL WILSHIRE BETHEL.
Minister of Economic Development: ZHIVARGO S. LAING.

MINISTRIES

Attorney-General's Office and Ministry of Justice: Post Office Bldg, East Hill St, POB N-3007, Nassau; tel. 322-1141; fax 356-4179.
Office of the Prime Minister: Sir Cecil V. Wallace-Whitfield Centre, POB CB-10980, Nassau; tel. 327-5826; fax 327-5806.
Office of the Deputy Prime Minister: Churchill Bldg, Bay St, POB N-3217, Nassau; tel. 356-6792; fax 356-6087.
Ministry of Agriculture and Fisheries: Levy Bldg, East Bay St, POB N-3028, Nassau; tel. 325-7502; fax 322-1767.
Ministry of Economic Development: Manx Bldg, West Bay St, POB N-4849, Nassau; tel. 328-2700; fax 328-1324.
Ministry of Education, Youth and Sports: Collins House, Shirley St, POB N-3913, Nassau; tel. 322-8140; fax 322-8491.
Ministry of Finance: Cecil V. Wallace Whitfield Centre, West Bay St, POB N-3017, Nassau; tel. 327-1530; fax 327-1618.
Ministry of Foreign Affairs: East Hill St, POB N-3746, Nassau; tel. 322-7624; fax 328-8212; e-mail mfabahamas@batelnet.bs.
Ministry of Health: Royal Victoria Gardens, East Hill St, POB N-3730, Nassau; tel. 322-7425; fax 322-7788.
Ministry of Housing and Social Development: Frederick House, Frederick St, POB N13206, Nassau; tel. 356-0765; fax 323-3883.
Ministry of Labour and Immigration: Post Office Bldg, East Hill St, POB N-3008, Nassau; tel. 323-7814; fax 325-1920.
Ministry of National Security: Churchill Bldg, Bay St, POB N-3217, Nassau; tel. 356-6792; fax 356-6087.
Ministry of Public Service and Cultural Affairs: Post Office Bldg, East Hill St, POB N-4891, Nassau; tel. 322-6250; fax 322-6546.
Ministry of Public Works: John F. Kennedy Drive, POB N-8156, Nassau; tel. 322-4830; fax 326-7344.
Ministry of Tourism: Market Plaza, Bay St, POB N-3701, Nassau; tel. 322-7500; fax 328-0945; internet www.bahamas.com.
Ministry of Transport, Aviation and Local Government: Pilot House Complex, POB N-10114, Nassau; tel. 394-0445; fax 394-5920.

Legislature

PARLIAMENT

Houses of Parliament: Parliament Sq., Nassau.

Senate

President: J. Henry Bostwick.
There are 16 nominated members.

House of Assembly

Speaker: Rome Italia Johnson.
The House has 40 members.

General Election, 14 March 1997

Party	Seats*
Free National Movement (FNM)	34
Progressive Liberal Party (PLP)	6
Total	40

* In a by-election in September 1997 an FNM member replaced the former PLP leader, Sir Lynden Pindling, who announced his retirement from parliamentary politics in July (he died in August 2000). Furthermore, in 2000 a PLP deputy left the party and formed the Coalition for Democratic Reform.

Political Organizations

Coalition for Democratic Reform (CDR): Nassau; f. 2000; centrist; Leader BERNARD NOTTAGE.

Free National Movement (FNM): POB N-10713, Nassau; tel. 393-7863; fax 393-7914; f. 1972; Leader HUBERT A. INGRAHAM.

Progressive Liberal Party (PLP): Nassau; tel. 325-2900; f. 1953; centrist party; Leader PERRY CHRISTIE; Chair. OBIE WILCHCOMBE.

Diplomatic Representation

EMBASSIES AND HIGH COMMISSION
IN THE BAHAMAS

China, People's Republic: 17 Clipper Island, Sandyport, POB CB-13500, Nassau; tel. 327-5206; Ambassador: MA SHUXVE.

United Kingdom: Ansbacher Bldg, 3rd Floor, East St, POB N-7516, Nassau; tel. 325-7471; fax 323-3871; High Commissioner: PETER HEIGL.

USA: Mosmar Bldg, Queen St, POB N-8197, Nassau; tel. 322-1181; fax 328-7838; Ambassador: (vacant).

Judicial System

The Judicial Committee of the Privy Council (based in the United Kingdom), the Bahamas Court of Appeal, the Supreme Court and the Magistrates' Courts are the main courts of the Bahamian judicial system.

All courts have both a criminal and civil jurisdiction. The Magistrates' Courts are presided over by professionally qualified Stipendiary and Circuit Magistrates in New Providence and Grand Bahama, and by Island Administrators sitting as Magistrates in the Family Islands.

Whereas all magistrates are empowered to try offences that may be tried summarily, a Stipendiary and Circuit Magistrate may, with the consent of the accused, also try certain less serious indictable offences. The jurisdiction of magistrates is, however, limited by law.

The Supreme Court consists of the Chief Justice, two Senior Justices and six Justices. The Supreme Court also sits in Freeport, with two Justices.

Appeals in almost all matters lie from the Supreme Court to the Court of Appeal, with further appeal in certain instances to the Judicial Committee of the Privy Council.

Supreme Court of the Bahamas: Parliament Sq., POB N-8167, Nassau; tel. 322-3315; fax 323-6895; Chief Justice JOAN SAWYER.

Court of Appeal: POB N-8167, Nassau; tel. 322-3315; fax 325-6895; Pres. JOHAQUIM C. GONZALES-SABOLA.

Magistrates' Courts: POB N-421, Nassau; tel. 325-4573; fax 323-1446; 15 magistrates and a circuit magistrate.

Registrar of the Supreme Court: ESTELLE EVANS; POB N-167, Nassau; tel. 322-4348; fax 325-6895.

Attorney-General: CARL WILSHIRE BETHEL.

Office of the Attorney-General: Post Office Bldg, East Hill St, POB N-3007, Nassau; tel. 322-1141; fax 356-4179; Dir of Legal Affairs RHONDA BAIN; Dir of Public Prosecutions BERNARD TURNER (acting).

Registrar-General: STERLING QUANT, 50 Shirley St, POB N-532, Nassau; tel. 322-3316; fax 322 553.

Religion

Most of the population profess Christianity, but there are also small communities of Jews and Muslims.

CHRISTIANITY

According to the census of 1990, there were 79,465 Baptists (31.2% of the population), 40,894 Roman Catholics (16.0%) and 40,881 Anglicans (16.0%). Other important denominations include the Pentecostal Church (5.5%), the Church of Christ (5.0%) and the Methodists (4.8%).

Bahamas Christian Council: 97 Wulff Rd, POB SS-4394, Nassau; tel. 356-3588; fax 394-4677; f. 1948; 27 mem. churches; Pres. Rev. SIMEON B. HALL.

The Roman Catholic Church

The Bahamas comprises the single diocese of Nassau, suffragan to the archdiocese of Kingston in Jamaica. At 31 December 1999 there were an estimated 47,626 adherents in the Bahamas. The Bishop participates in the Antilles Episcopal Conference (whose Secretariat is based in Port of Spain, Trinidad). The Turks and Caicos Islands are also under the jurisdiction of the Bishop of Nassau.

Bishop of Nassau: Rt Rev. LAWRENCE A. BURKE, The Hermitage, West St, POB N-8187, Nassau; tel. 322-8919; fax 322-2599; e-mail rcchancery@grouper.batelnet.bs.

The Anglican Communion

Anglicans in the Bahamas are adherents of the Church in the Province of the West Indies. The diocese also includes the Turks and Caicos Islands.

Archbishop of the West Indies, and Bishop of the Bahamas and the Turks and Caicos Islands: Most Rev. DREXEL GOMEZ, Bishop's Lodge, POB N-7107, Nassau; tel. 322-3015; fax 322-7943.

Other Christian Churches

Bahamas Conference of The Methodist Church: POB SS-5103, Nassau; tel. 393-3726; fax 393-8135; e-mail bcmc@bahamas.net; Pres. Rev. CHARLES SWEETING.

Bahamas Conference of Seventh-day Adventists: Harrold Rd, POB N-356, Nassau; tel. 341-4021; fax 341-4088; internet www.bahamasconference.org.

Bahamas Evangelical Church Association: Carmichael Rd, POB N-1224, Nassau; tel. 362-1024.

Greek Orthodox Church: Church of the Annunciation, West St, POB N-823, Nassau; tel. 322-4382; f. 1928; part of the Archdiocese of North and South America, based in New York (USA); Priest Rev. THEOPHANIS KULYVAS.

Methodist Church Conference in the Bahamas (MCCA): POB N-3702, Nassau; tel. 373-1888; Conference Pres. Rev. LIVINGSTON MALCOLM.

Other denominations include African Methodist Episcopal, the Assemblies of Brethren, Christian Science, the Jehovah's Witnesses, the Salvation Army, Pentecostal, Presbyterian, Seventh Day Adventist, Baptist, Lutheran and Assembly of God churches.

BAHÀ'Í FAITH

Bahá'í National Spiritual Assembly: Shirley St, POB N-7105, Nassau; tel. 326-0607; e-mail nsabaha@hotmail.com.

OTHER RELIGIONS

Islam

There is a small community of Muslims in the Bahamas.

Islaamic Centre: Carmichael Road, POB N-10711, Nassau; tel. 341-6612.

Islaamic Centre Jamaat Ul-Islam: 13 Davies St, Oakes Field, POB N-10711, Nassau; tel. 325-0413.

Judaism

Most of the Bahamian Jewish community are based on Grand Bahama. There were 126 Jews, according to the 1990 census.

Bahamas Jewish Congregation Synagogue: POB CB-11003, Cable Beach Shopping Centre, Nassau; tel. 327-2064.

The Press

NEWSPAPERS

Bahama Journal: Media House, POB N-8610, Nassau; tel. 325-3082; fax 356-7256; internet www.love97fm.com/journal.htm; daily; circ. 5,000.

Freeport News: Cedar St, POB F-40007, Freeport; tel. 352-8321; fax 352-3449; f. 1961; daily; Gen. Man. DORLAN COLLIE; Editor ROBYN ADDERLEY; circ. 6,000.

The Nassau Guardian: 4 Carter St, Oakes Field, POB N-3011, Nassau; tel. 323-5654; fax 363-3783; internet www.thenassauguardian.com; f. 1844; daily; Gen. Man. PATRICK WALKES; Editor (vacant); circ. 12,277.

The Punch: POB N-4081, Nassau; tel. 322-7112; fax 323-5268; twice weekly; Editor IVAN JOHNSON; circ. 25,000.

The Tribune: Shirley St, POB N-3207, Nassau; tel. 322-1986; fax 328-2398; e-mail tribune@100jamz.com; f. 1903; daily; Publr and Editor EILEEN DUPUCH CARRON; circ. 13,500.

PERIODICALS

The Bahamas Financial Digest: Miramar House, Bay and Christie Sts, POB N-4271, Nassau; tel. 356-2981; fax 356-7118; e-mail michael.symonette@batelnet.bs; f. 1973; 4 a year; business and investment; Publr and Editor MICHAEL A. SYMONETTE; circ. 15,890.

Bahamas Tourist News: Bayparl Bldg, Parliament St, POB N-4855, Nassau; tel. 322-4528; fax 322-4527; f. 1962; monthly; Editor BOBBY BOWER; circ. 360,000 (annually).

Nassau City Magazine: Miramar House, Bay and Christie Sts, POB N-4824, Nassau; tel. 356-2981; fax 326-2849.

Official Gazette: c/o Cabinet Office, POB N-7147, Nassau; tel. 322-2805; weekly; publ. by the Cabinet Office.

What's On Magazine: Woodes Rogers Wharf, POB CB-11713, Nassau; tel. 323-2323; fax 322-3428; e-mail info@whatsonbahamas.com; internet www.whatsonbahamas.com; monthly; Publr NEIL ABERLE.

Publishers

Bahamas Free Press Ltd: POB CB-13309, Nassau; tel. 323-8961.

Etienne Dupuch Jr Publications Ltd: 51 Hawthorne Rd, POB N-7513, Nassau; tel. 323-5665; fax 323-5728; e-mail dupuch@bahamasnet.com; internet www.dupuch.com; publishes *Bahamas Handbook*, *Trailblazer* maps, *What To Do* magazines, *Welcome Bahamas*, *Tadpole* (educational colouring book) series and *Dining and Entertainment Guide*; Dirs ETIENNE DUPUCH, Jr, S. P. DUPUCH.

Media Enterprises Ltd: 31 Shirley Park Ave, POB N-9240, Nassau; tel. 325-8210; fax 325-8065; e-mail info@bahamasmedia.com; internet www.bahamasmedia.com; Publishing Dir NEIL E. SEALEY.

Printing Tours and Publishing: Miramar House, Bay and Christie Sts, POB N-4846, Nassau; tel. 356-2981; fax 356-7118.

Sacha de Frisching Publishing: POB N-7776, Nassau; tel. 362-6230; fax 362-6274; children's books.

Star Publishers Ltd: POB N-4855, Nassau; tel. 322-3724; fax 322-4537; e-mail starpub@bahamas.net.bs; internet www.supermaps.com.

Broadcasting and Communications

TELECOMMUNICATIONS

Bahamas Telecommunications Co (BaTelCo): POB N-3048, John F. Kennedy Drive, Nassau; tel. 302-7000; fax 326-7474; e-mail info@batelnet.bs; internet www.batelnet.bs; state-owned; scheduled for partial privatization in late 2001.

BROADCASTING

Radio

Broadcasting Corporation of the Bahamas: POB N-1347, Centreville, New Providence; tel. 322-4623; fax 322-3924; internet www.znsbahamas.com; f. 1936; govt-owned; commercial; Chair. MICHAEL D. SMITH; Gen. Man. EDWIN LIGHTBOURNE.

Radio Bahamas: internet www.univox.com/radio/zns.html; f. 1936; broadcasts 24 hours per day on four stations: the main Radio Bahamas (ZNS1), Radio New Providence (ZNS2), which are both based in Nassau, Radio Power 104.5 FM, and the Northern Service (ZNS3—Freeport; f. 1973; Station Man. ANTHONY FORSTER); Programme Man. TANYA PINDER.

Cool 96 FM: POB F-40773, Freeport, Grand Bahama; tel. 353-7440; fax 352-8709.

Love 97 FM: Bahamas Media House, East St North, POB N-3909, Nassau; tel. 356-2555; e-mail twilliams@jonescommunications.com; internet www.love97fm.com.

More 95.9 FM: POB CR-54245, Nassau; tel. 361-2447; e-mail more fm94.9@batelnet.bs.

Tribune Radio Ltd (One Hundred JAMZ): Shirley and Deveaux St, POB N-3207, Nassau; tel. 328-4771; fax 356-5343; e-mail michelle@100jamz.com; internet www2.100jamz.com; Programming Dir ERIC WARD.

Television

Broadcasting Corporation of the Bahamas: (see Radio).

Bahamas Television: f. 1977; broadcasts for Nassau, New Providence and the Central Bahamas; transmitting power of 50,000 watts; full colour; Programme Man. CARL BETHEL.

US television programmes and some satellite programmes can be received. Most islands have a cable-television service.

Finance

In recent years the Bahamas has developed into one of the world's foremost financial centres (there are no corporation, income, capital gains or withholding taxes or estate duty), and finance has become a significant feature of the economy. At June 1999 there were 416 banks and trust companies operating in the Bahamas, of which 199 had a physical presence in the islands.

BANKING

(cap. = capital; dep. = deposits; res = reserves; m. = million;

brs = branches)

Central Bank

The Central Bank of the Bahamas: Frederick St, POB N-4868, Nassau; tel. 322-2193; fax 322-4321; e-mail CBOB@batelnet.bs; f. 1973; bank of issue; cap. B \$3.0m., res B \$79.7m., dep. B \$146.9m. (Dec. 1998); Gov. JULIAN W. FRANCIS; Dep. Gov. WENDY CRAIGG.

Development Bank

The Bahamas Development Bank: Cable Beach, West Bay St, POB N-3034, Nassau; tel. 327-5780; fax 327-5047; f. 1978 to fund approved projects and channel funds into appropriate investments; Chair. FREDERICK GOTTLIEB.

Principal Bahamian-based Banks

Bank of the Bahamas Ltd: Shirley St, POB N-7118, Nassau; tel. 326-2560; fax 325-2762; f. 1970, name changed as above in 1988, when Bank of Montreal Bahamas Ltd became jointly owned by Govt and Euro Canadian Bank; 50% owned by Govt, 50% owned by c. 4,000 Bahamian shareholders; cap. B \$10.0m., res B \$1.0m., dep. B \$172.3m. (June 1999); Chair. HUGH G. SANDS; Man. Dir P. M. ALLEN-DEAN; 8 brs.

Commonwealth Bank Ltd: 610 Bay St, POB SS-5541, Nassau; tel. 394-7373; f. 1960; Pres. WILLIAM SANDS; 8 brs.

Private Investment Bank and Trust (Bahamas) Ltd: Devonshire House, Queen St, POB N-3918, Nassau; tel. 302-5950; fax 302-5970; f. 1984 as Bank Worms and Co International Ltd; renamed in 1990, 1996 and 1998; cap. US \$3.0m., res US \$1.8m., dep. US \$247.7m. (Dec. 1997); Chair. and Dir FRANÇOIS ROUGE.

Principal Foreign Banks

Banco Internacional de Costa Rica Ltd: Bank Lane, POB N-7768, Nassau; fax 326-5020; e-mail bicsacr@sol.racsa.co.cr; internet www.bisca.com; f. 1976; 55% owned by Banco Nacional de Costa Rica, 20% owned by Banco de Costa Rica, 10% owned by Banco Crédito de Agrícola de Cartago; Chair. ALFONSO GUARDIA M.; CEO THELMO VARGAS M.

Bank of Nova Scotia International Ltd (Canada): Scotiabank Bldg, Rawson Sq., POB N-7545, Nassau; tel. 365-1517; fax 328-8473; Vice-Pres. and Man. A. C. ALLEN; 13 brs.

Barclays Bank PLC (United Kingdom): Charlotte House, Shirley St, POB N-3221, Nassau; tel. 325-7384; fax 322-8267; internet www.bahamas.barclays.com; Dir SHARON BROWN.

BNP Paribas (Bahamas) Ltd: Beaumont House, 3rd Floor, Bay St, POB N-4883, Nassau; tel. 326-5935; fax 3265871; internet www.bnpgroup.com; Man. Dir ANDRÉ LAMOTHE.

BSI Overseas (Bahamas) Ltd (Italy): UBS House, East Bay St, POB N-7130, Nassau; tel. 394-9200; fax 394-9220; f. 1990; wholly-owned subsid. of Banca della Svizzera Italiana; cap. US \$10.0m., res US \$44.1m., dep. US \$1,121.9m. (Dec. 1998); Chair. Dr A. GYSI; Man. IVOR J. HERRINGTON.

Canadian Imperial Bank of Commerce (CIBC) (Canada): 4th Floor, 308 East Bay St, POB N-8329, Nassau; tel. 393-4710; fax 393-4280; internet www.cibc.com; Area Man. TERRY HILTS; 9 brs.

Citibank NA (USA): Citibank Bldg, Thompson Blvd, Oakes Field, POB N-8158, Nassau; tel. 322-8510; fax 302-8555; internet www.citibank.com; Gen. Man. ALISON JOHNSTON; 2 brs.

Credit Suisse (Bahamas) Ltd (Switzerland): Bahamas Financial Centre, Shirley and Charlotte Sts, POB N-4928, Nassau; tel. 356-8100; fax 326-6589; f. 1968; subsidiary of Credit Suisse Zurich; portfolio and asset management, offshore company management, trustee services; cap. US \$12.0m., res US \$20.0m., dep. US \$500.7m. (Dec. 1997); Man. Dir GREGOR MAISSEN.

Handelsfinanz-CCF Bank International Ltd (Switzerland): Third Floor, Maritime House, Frederick St, POB N-10441, Nassau; tel. 328-8644; fax 328-8600; f. 1971; cap. US \$5.0m., res US \$11.5m., dep. US $544.8m. (Dec. 1998); Pres. and Gen. Man. FERDINANDO M. MENCONI.

Lloyds TSB Bank International (Bahamas) Ltd (United Kingdom): Bolam House, King and George Sts, POB N-4843, Nassau; tel. 302-3000; fax 322-8719; f. 1977; cap. US $15.0m., dep. US $305.1 (Dec. 1998); Principal Man. and Dir DAVID G. NICOLL.

National Bank of Canada (International) Ltd: Charlotte House, Charlotte St, POB N-3015, Nassau; tel. 322-4024; fax 323-8086; e-mail nabkint@batelnet.bs; f. 1978; 100% owned by Natcan Holdings International Ltd; Gen. Man. JACQUES LATENDRESSE.

Overseas Union Bank and Trust (Bahamas) Ltd (Switzerland): 250 Bay St, POB N-8184, Nassau; tel. 322-2476; fax 323-8771; f. 1980; cap. US $5.0m., res US $6.2m., dep. US $97.9m. (Dec. 1997); Chair. Dr CARLO SGANZINI; Gen. Man. URS FREI.

Pictet Bank and Trust Ltd (Switzerland): Charlotte House, Charlotte St, POB N-4837, Nassau; tel. 322-3938; fax 323-7986; e-mail pbtbah@bahamas.net.bs; internet www.pictet.com/nassau.htm; f. 1978; cap. US $1.0m., res US $10.0m., dep. US $126.2m. (Dec. 1995); Chair. and Dir CLAUDE DEMOLE.

Royal Bank of Canada Ltd (Canada): 323 Bay St, POB N-7537, Nassau; tel. 322-8700; fax 323-6381; internet www.royalbank.com; Vice-Pres. MICHAEL F. PHELAN; 16 brs.

Royal Bank of Scotland (Nassau) Ltd (United Kingdom): 3rd Floor, Bahamas Financial Centre, Shirley and Charlotte Sts, POB N-3045, Nassau; tel. 322-4643; fax 326-7559; e-mail info@rbsint.bs; f. 1951 as E. D. Sassoon Bank and Trust Ltd, name changed 1978, 1986 and 1989; cap. US $2.0m., res US $7.3m., dep. US 289.5m. (Sept. 1998); Chair. JAMES D. PATON; CEO DAVID BARRON.

UBS (Bahamas) Ltd (Switzerland): Swiss Bank House, East Bay St, POB N-7757, Nassau; tel. 394-9300; fax 394-9333; f. 1968 as Swiss Bank Corpn (Overseas) Ltd, name changed as above 1998; cap. US $4.0m., dep. US $420.2m. (Dec. 1997); Chair. ERNST BALSIGER; Exec. Dir and Pres. PHILIP WHITE.

Principal Bahamian Trust Companies

Ansbacher (Bahamas) Ltd: Ansbacher House, Bank Lane, POB N-7768, Nassau; tel. 322-1161; fax 326-5020; e-mail ansbbah@batelnet.bs; incorporated 1957 as Bahamas International Trust Co Ltd, name changed 1994; cap. B $1.0m., res B $9.7m., dep. B $190.3m. (Sept. 1998); Man. Dir DAVID L. E. FAWKES.

Bank of Nova Scotia Trust Company (Bahamas) Ltd: POB N-3016, Nassau; tel. 356-1500; fax 326-0991; e-mail scotiatr@100jamz.com; wholly owned by the Bank of Nova Scotia International Ltd.

Chase Manhattan Trust Corpn: Shirley and Charlotte Sts, POB N-3708, Nassau; tel. 356-1305; fax 325-1706; Gen. Man. KEN BROWN; 4 brs.

Leadenhall Bank and Trust Co Ltd: IBM Bldg, Bay St at Church St, POB N-1965, Nassau; tel. 325-5508; fax 328-7030; e-mail drounce@leadentrust.com; f. 1976; Man. Dir DAVID J. ROUNCE.

MeesPierson (Bahamas) Ltd: POB SS-5539, Nassau; tel. 393-8777; fax 393-0582; internet www.mpbahamas.com; f. 1987; subsidiary of MeesPierson International AG of Zug, Switzerland; Chair. IAN D. FAIR; Gen. Man. RONALD J. A. DE GRAAF.

Oceanic Bank and Trust: Euro Canadian Centre, POB N-8327, Nassau; tel. 322-7461; fax 326-6177; f. 1969.

Winterbotham Trust Co Ltd: Bolam House, King and George Sts, POB N-3026, Nassau; tel. 356-5454; fax 356-9432; e-mail nassau@winterbotham.com; internet www.winterbotham.com; cap. US $3.8m.; CEO GEOFFREY HOOPER; 2 brs.

Bankers' Organizations

Association of International Banks and Trust Companies in the Bahamas: POB N-7880, Nassau; tel. 394-6755; Chair. BRUCE BELL.

Bahamas Institute of Bankers: Royal Palm Mall, Mackey St, POB N-3202, Nassau; tel. 393-0456; fax 394-3503; Pres. KIM BODIE.

INSURANCE

The leading British and a number of US, Canadian and Caribbean companies have agents in Nassau and Freeport. Local insurance companies include the following:

Allied Bahamas Insurance Co Ltd: 93 Collins Ave, POB N-121, Nassau; tel. 326-3537; fax 356-2192; general, aviation and marine.

Bahamas First General Insurance Co Ltd: 93 Collins Ave, POB N-1216, Nassau; tel. 326-5439; fax 326-5472.

Colina Insurance Co Ltd: 12 Village Rd, POB N-4728, Nassau; tel. 393-2224; fax 393-1710.

The Family Guardian Insurance Co Ltd: East Bay St, POB SS-6232, Nassau; tel. 393-1023; f. 1965.

Association

Bahamas General Insurance Association: POB N-860, Nassau; tel. 323-2596; fax 328-4354; Acting Co-ordinator DAVID KLEAN.

Trade and Industry

DEVELOPMENT ORGANIZATIONS

Bahamas Agricultural and Industrial Corpn (BAIC): BAIC Bldg, East Bay St, POB N-4940, Nassau; tel. 322-3740; fax 322-2123; f. 1981 as an amalgamation of Bahamas Development Corpn and Bahamas Agricultural Corpn for the promotion of greater co-operation between tourism and other sectors of the economy through the development of small- and medium-sized enterprises; Exec. Chair. ALVIN SMITH.

Bahamas Financial Service Board: 4th Floor, Euro-Canadian Centre, POB N-1764; tel. 356-2985; fax 326-7007; e-mail bfsb@bahamas.net.bs; internet www.bfsbbahamas.com; Chair. Ian Fair.

Bahamas Investment Authority: Cecil V. Wallace-Whitfield Centre, POB CB-10980, Nassau; tel. 327-5970; fax 327-5907; Exec. Dir BASIL H. ALBURY.

Bahamas Light Industries Development Council: POB SS-5599, Nassau; tel. 394-1907; Pres. LESLIE MILLER.

Nassau Paradise Island Promotion Board: Dean's Lane, Fort Charlotte, POB N-7799, Nassau; tel. 322-8381; fax 325-8998; f. 1970; Chair. GEORGE R. MYERS; Sec. MICHAEL C. RECKLEY; 30 mems.

CHAMBER OF COMMERCE

Bahamas Chamber of Commerce: Shirley St, POB N-665, Nassau; tel. 322-2145; fax 322-4649; f. 1935 to promote, foster and protect trade, industry and commerce; Pres. A. BISMARK COAKLEY; Exec. Dir RUBY L. SWEETING; 450 mems.

EMPLOYERS' ASSOCIATIONS

Bahamas Association of Land Surveyors: POB N-10147, Nassau; tel. 322-4569; Pres. DONALD THOMPSON; Vice-Pres. GODFREY HUMES; 30 mems.

Bahamas Boatmen's Association: POB ES-5212, Nassau; f. 1974; Pres. and Sec. FREDERICK GOMEZ.

Bahamas Contractors' Association: POB N-8049, Nassau; Pres. BRENDON C. WATSON; Sec. EMMANUEL ALEXIOU.

Bahamas Employers' Confederation: POB N-166, Nassau; tel. 393-5613; fax 322-4649; f. 1963; Pres. REGINALD LOBOSKY.

Bahamas Hotel Employers' Association: Dean's Lane, Fort Charlotte, POB N-7799, Nassau; tel. 322-2262; fax 325-8998; f. 1958; Pres. J. BARRIE FARRINGTON; Exec. Dir MICHAEL C. RECKLEY; 26 mems.

Bahamas Institute of Chartered Accountants: Star Plaza, Mackey St, POB N-7037, Nassau; tel. 394-3439; fax 394-3629; f. 1971; Pres. L. EDGAR MOXEY.

Bahamas Institute of Professional Engineers: Nassau; tel. 322-3356; fax 323-8503; Pres. ANTHONY DEAN.

Bahamas Motor Dealers' Association: POB N-3919, Nassau; tel. 328-7671; fax 328-1922; Pres. HARRY ROBERTS.

Bahamas Real Estate Association: Bahamas Chamber Bldg, POB N-8860, Nassau; tel. 325-4942; fax 322-4649; Pres. PATRICK STRACHAN.

MAJOR COMPANIES
Construction

Bahamas Marine Construction Co Ltd: Bay and Victoria Sts, POB N-7512, Nassau; tel. and fax 322-2571; focuses on the construction of ports, docks and marinas; Chair. GEORGE MOSKO; Man. Dir JAMES GEORGE MOSKO; 111 employees.

Balfour Beatty Construction (Bahamas) Ltd: Cable Beach, POB N-4892, Nassau; tel. 327-6312; fax 327-6977; f. 1986; subsidiary of Balfour Beatty Ltd, UK; civil engineering and construction; Chair. ROBERT BIGGAN; Man. Dir DUNCAN HEMINGWAY; 2,000 employees.

Bovis Bahamas Ltd: International Bldg, First Floor, POB F-40025, Freeport; tel. 352-6711; fax 352-8310; construction and project management; Pres. KEITH PERRY.

Freeport Concrete: ready-mix concrete manufacturers.

Guarantee Builders Ltd: Bernard Rd, POB N-1754, Nassau; tel. 393-2931; fax 393-2984; f. 1960; residential and heavy construction; Pres. HUBERT FOWLER; 400 employees.

Maura Lumber Co (Holdings) Ltd: East Shirley and Church St, POB SS-6330, Nassau; tel. 325-8412; fax 322-1516; f. 1943; construction supplies; Pres. MICHAEL J. MAURA; Vice-Pres. H. GARLAND EVANS; 155 employees.

Mosko's United Construction Ltd: Bay St and Victoria Ave, POB N-641, Nassau; tel 322-2825; fax 325-2571; f. 1958; Pres. GEORGE MOSKO; 567 employees.

Food and Beverages

Aquapure Water: POB SS-6244, Nassau; tel. 393-1904; fax 393-1936; produces purified and deionized bottled water.

Bacardi and Co Ltd: Millar Rd, POB N-838, Nassau; tel. 362-1412; fax 362-1918; f. 1960; distilling and rum manufacture; Pres. MANUELA J. CUTILLAS JUSTIZ; 120 employees.

Bahama Palm Groves Ltd: Don Mackely Blvd, POB 20096, Marsh Harbour; tel. 367-3086; fax 367-2223; f. 1986; fruit sellers; Man. Dir RANDY KEY; 287 employees.

Bahamas Supermarkets Ltd: East West Highway, POB N-3738, Nassau; tel. 393-2830; fax 393-1232; f. 1968; Pres. C. WINGE; Chair. JAMES KUFELDT; 700 employees.

Butler and Sands Co Ltd: John F. Kennedy Drive, POB N-51, Nassau; tel. 322-7586; fax 326-6655; e-mail mail@butlersands.com; internet www.butlersands.com; f. 1949; alcoholic-drink distribution; Pres. EVERETTE SANDS.

Gladstone Farms Ltd: POB CB-13019, Nassau; tel. 361-4359; fax 361-6472; e-mail rchernos@bahamas.net; f. 1959; chicken farming; CEO R. J. CHERNOS; 240 employees.

Grand Bahamas Food Co: Grand Bahama Highway, POB F-2540, Freeport; tel 352-9801; fax 352-8870; f. 1968; food wholesalers and retailers; Pres. MINAS VARDAOULIS; 245 employees.

Pepsi Cola (Bahamas) Bottling Co Ltd: Soldier Rd, POB N-3004, Nassau; tel. 364-5640; fax 393-5744; f. 1991; soft-drinks manufacturer; Man. MARCIO RAMOS; 21 employees.

Super Value Food Stores Ltd: Golden Gates Shopping Centre, POB N-3039, Nassau; tel. 361-5220; fax 361-5583; f. 1965; Pres. RUPERT WINER ROBERTS, Jr; Vice-Pres M. A. ROBERTS, CANDY KELLY; 567 employees.

Pharmaceuticals

Syntex Pharmaceuticals International Ltd: West Sunrise Highway, POB F-42430, Freeport; tel. 352-8171; fax 352-6950; f. 1967; manufacturer of pharmaceutical products; Pres. JAMES WILSON; Chair. PAUL FREIMAN; 10,000 employees.

Miscellaneous

Bahamas International Trust Co Ltd: Bitco Bldg, Bank Lane, Nassau; tel. 322-11; security brokers and dealers; Man. Dir J. M. KNOTT.

Bahamas Realty: POB N-1132, Nassau; tel. 393-8168; fax 393-0326; e-mail brealty@bahamasrealty.bs; internet www.bahamasrealty.bs; f. 1978 as Caribbean Management and Sales Ltd; real estate; Pres. ROBIN B. BROWNING.

BORCO (Bahamas Oil Refining Co): POB F-2435; West Sunrise Highway, Freeport; tel. 352-9811; fax 352-4029; f. 1964; petroleum distribution; owned by Petróleos de Venezuela (PDVSA); Pres. ESTEBAN LEÓN.

Grand Bahama Development Co Ltd: Pioneer Way, POB F-2666; Nassau; tel. 352-6711; fax 352-9864; f. 1961; holding co; Chair. JACK HAYWOOD; 300 employees.

H. G. Christie Ltd: Millar's Court, POB N-8164, Nassau; tel. 322-1041; fax 326-5642; e-mail sales@christie.com; real estate service; f. 1922.

Hutchison Port Holdings (HPH): POB F-42465, Freeport; tel. 352-9651; fax 352-6888; internet www.hph.com.hk; port holding co; owned by Hutchison Whampoa of Hong Kong; subsidiaries include Grand Bahama Airport Co, Freeport Container Port and Freeport Harbour Co; Man. Dir JOHN E. MEREDITH; Exec. Dirs RICHARD PEARSON, JAMES S. TSIEN.

J. S. R. Real Estate Ltd: POB F-93, Freeport; tel. 352-7201; fax 352-7203; real estate, developments, condominiums, residency and investing.

Polymers International Ltd: POB F-42684; tel. 352-3506; fax 352-2779; f. 1997; manufacturer of polystyrene products.

The Resort at Bahamia: Mall St Sunrise, POB F-40207, Freeport; tel. 350-7000; fax 350-7003; f. 1973; management of hotels; Man. TYRONE THURSTON; 500 employees.

Resorts Int. (Bahamas) Ltd: POB N-4777, Nassau; tel. 363-3703; fax 363-3703; f. 1967; holding co involved in management and operation of hotels; Man. Dir GABRIEL SASTRE; 2,900 employees.

Sun and Sea Estates Ltd: Freeport; owns the Clarion Atlantic Beach Hotel and the Flamingo Beach Resort; Vice-Pres. PAUL MATTENBERGER.

Sun International Hotels Ltd: c/o Holiday Inn, POB N-4777, Paradise Island; tel. 363-3000; South African co, owns the Atlantis Resort, under expansion in 1998, and the Holiday Inn on Paradise Island; Chair. and CEO SOL KERZNER.

Taylor Industries Ltd: Shirley St, POB N-4806, Nassau; tel. 322-8941; fax 328-0453; f. 1945; electrical appliances and supplies; Pres. and Gen. Man. DEREK TAYLOR; 87 employees.

Templeton Global Advisers Ltd: POB N-7759, Lyford Cay, Nassau; tel. 362-4600; fax 361-4308; f. 1986; investment consultants and security brokers; Chair. CHARLES JOHNSON; 400 employees.

UTILITIES
Electricity

The Bahamas Electricity Corpn (BEC): Pond and Tucker Rd, POB N-7509, Nassau; tel. 325-4101; fax 323-6852; state-owned; scheduled for privatization; provides 70% of the islands' power-generating capacity.

Freeport Power and Light Co Ltd: Mercantile Bldg, Cedar St, POB F-888, Freeport; f. 1962; tel. 352-6611; privately-owned; Pres. ALBERT J. MILLER.

Gas

Caribbean Gas Storage and Terminal Ltd: POB N-9665, Nassau; tel. 327-5587; fax 362-5006; e-mail info@caribbeangas.com; internet www.caribbeangas.com; f. 1992.

Tropigas: Nassau; **tel.** 322-2404.

Water

Bahamas Water and Sewerage Corpn: 87 Thompson Blvd, POB N-3905, Nassau; tel. 302-5500; fax 356-7152; e-mail wcexcoff@batel net.bs; internet www.wsc.com.bs; Chair. MICHAEL L. BARNETT.

TRADE UNIONS

All Bahamian unions are members of one of the following:

National Congress of Trade Unions: Horseshoe Drive, POB GT-2887, Nassau; tel. 356-7457; Pres. LEROY HANNA; 20,000 mems.

Trade Union Congress: Warwick St, Nassau; tel. 394-6301; fax 394-7401; Pres. OBIE FERGUSON; 12,500 mems.

The main unions are as follows:

Bahamas Airport and Allied Workers' Union: Workers House, Harrold Rd, POB N-3364, Nassau; tel. 323-5030; f. 1958; Pres. FRANKLYN CARTER; Gen. Sec. PATRICE TYNES-RODGERS; 550 mems.

Bahamas Brewery, Distillers and Allied Workers' Union: Nassau; **f.** 1968; Pres. BRADICK CLEARE; Gen. Sec. DAVID KEMP; 140 mems.

Bahamas Communications and Public Officers' Union: Farrington Rd, POB N-3190, Nassau; tel. 322-1537; fax 323-8719; e-mail prebcpou@batelnet.bs; f. 1973; Pres. D. SHANE GIBSON; Sec.-Gen. ROBERT A. FARQUHARSON; 2,100 mems.

Bahamas Doctors' Union: Nassau; Pres. Dr EUGENE NEWERY; Gen. Sec. GEORGE SHERMAN.

Bahamas Electrical Workers' Union: East West Highway, POB GT-2535, Nassau; tel. 393-1431; Pres. SAMUEL MITCHELL; Gen. Sec. JONATHAN CAMBRIDGE.

Bahamas Hotel Catering and Allied Workers' Union: POB GT-2514, Nassau; tel. 323-5933; fax 325-6546; f. 1958; Pres. THOMAS BASTIAN; Gen. Sec. LEO DOUGLAS; 6,500 mems.

Bahamas Maritime Port and Allied Workers' Union: POB SS-6501, Nassau; tel. 328-7502; Pres. ANTHONY WILLIAMS; Sec.-Gen. FREDERICK N. RODGERS.

Bahamas Musicians' and Entertainers' Union: Horseshoe Drive, POB N-880, Nassau; tel. 322-3734; fax 323-3537; f. 1958; Pres. LEROY (DUKE) HANNA; Gen. Sec. PORTIA NOTTAGE; 410 mems.

Bahamas Public Services Union: Wulff Rd, POB N-4692, Nassau; tel. 325-0038; fax 323-5287; f. 1959; Pres. WILLIAM MCDONALD; Sec.-Gen. SYNIDA DORSETT; 4,247 mems.

Bahamas Taxi-Cab Union: POB N-1077, Nassau; tel. 323-5952; Pres. FELIX ROLLE (acting); Gen. Sec. ROSCOE WEECH.

Bahamas Union of Teachers: 104 Bethel Ave, Stapledon Gardens, POB N-3482, Nassau; tel. 323-7085; fax 323-7086; f. 1945; Pres. KINGSLEY BLACK; Gen. Sec. HELENA CARTWRIGHT; 2,600 mems.

Eastside Stevedores' Union: POB N-1176, Nassau; f. 1972; Pres. SALATHIEL MACKEY; Gen. Sec. CURTIS TURNQUEST.

Grand Bahama Construction, Refinery and Maintenance Workers' Union: 33A Kipling Bldg, POB F-839, Freeport; tel. 352-7438; f. 1971; Pres. JAMES TAYLOR; Gen. Sec. EPHRAIM BLACK.

United Brotherhood of Longshoremen's Union: Wulff Rd, POB N-7317, Nassau; f. 1959; Pres. J. MCKINNEY; Gen. Sec. W. SWANN; 157 mems.

Transport

ROADS

There are about 966 km (600 miles) of roads in New Providence and 1,368 km (850 miles) in the Family Islands, mainly on Grand Bahama, Cat Island, Eleuthera, Exuma and Long Island. In 2001 the Inter-American Development Bank approved a B $42.2m. loan to improve transport infrastructure and services. Some 23 km of roads will be improved and 15 km built.

SHIPPING

The principal seaport is at Nassau (New Providence), which can accommodate the very largest cruise ships. Passenger arrivals exceed two million annually. The other main ports are at Freeport (Grand Bahama), where a container terminal opened in 1997, and Matthew Town (Inagua). There are also modern berthing facilities for cruise ships at Potters Cay (New Providence), Governor's Harbour (Eleuthera), Morgan's Bluff (North Andros) and George Town (Exuma).

The Bahamas converted to free-flag status in 1976, and by 1983 possessed the world's third-largest open-registry fleet. The fleet's displacement was 27,715,783 grt in December 1998 (the third-largest national fleet in the world).

There is a weekly cargo and passenger service to all the Family Islands.

Bahamas Maritime Authority: POB N-4679, Nassau; tel. 394-5022; fax 394-5023; f. 1995; promotes ship registration and co-ordinates maritime administration.

Freeport Harbour Co Ltd: POB F-42465, Freeport; tel. 352-9651; fax 352-6888; e-mail fhcol@batelnet.bs; Gen. Man. MICHAEL J. POWER.

Nassau Port Authority: Prince George Wharf, POB N-8175, Nassau; tel. 356-7354; fax 322-5545; regulates principal port of the Bahamas; Port Dir ANTHONY ALLENS.

Principal Shipping Companies

Cavalier Shipping: Arawak Cay, POB N-8170, New Providence; tel. 328-3035.

Dockendale Shipping Co Ltd: Dockendale House, West Bay St, POB N-10455, Nassau; tel. 325-0448; fax 328-1542; e-mail dockship @dockendale.com; f. 1973; ship management; Man. Dir L. J. FERNANDES; Tech. Dir K. VALLURI.

Eleuthera Express Shipping Co: POB N-4201, Nassau.

Grand Master Shipping Co: POB N-4208, Nassau.

Grenville Ventures Ltd: 43 Elizabeth Ave, POB CB-13022, Nassau.

HJH Trading Co Ltd: POB N-4402, Nassau; tel. 392-3939; fax 392-1828.

Gladstone Patton: POB SS-5178, Nassau.

Pioneer Shipping Ltd: Union Wharf, POB N-3044, Nassau; tel. 325-7889; fax 325-2214.

Teekay Shipping Corporation: TK House, Bayside Executive Park, West Bay St & Blake Rd, POB AP-59213, Nassau; tel. 502-8820; fax 502-8840; internet www.teekay.com; Pres. and CEO BJORN MOLLER.

Tropical Shipping Co Ltd: POB N-8183, Nassau; tel. 322-1012; fax 323-7566.

United Shipping Co Ltd: POB F-42552, Freeport; tel. 352-9315; fax 352-4034; e-mail info@unitedship.com; internet www.unitedship.com.

CIVIL AVIATION

Nassau International Airport (15 km (9 miles) outside the capital) and Freeport International Airport (5 km (3 miles) outside the city, on Grand Bahama) are the main terminals for international and internal services. There are also important airports at West End (Grand Bahama) and Rock Sound (Eleuthera) and some 50 smaller airports and landing strips throughout the islands.

Bahamasair Holdings Ltd: Coral Harbour Rd, POB N-4881, Nassau; tel. 377-8451; fax 377-8550; e-mail astuart@bahamasair.com; internet www.bahamasair.com; f. 1973; scheduled services between Nassau, Freeport, destinations within the USA and 20 locations within the Family Islands; Chair. ANTHONY MILLER; Man. Dir PAT ROLLE (acting).

Tourism

The mild climate and beautiful beaches attract many tourists. In 1998 tourist arrivals decreased by 9.3%, compared with the previous year, to 3,655,839 (including 2,281,887 by sea) in 1999. The majority of stop-over arrivals (81% in 1997) were from the USA. Receipts from the tourist industry decreased by 0.6% in 1998, compared with the previous year, to B $1,408m. In September 1999 there were 223 hotels in the country, with a total of 14,080 rooms.

Ministry of Tourism: Bay St, POB N-3701, Nassau; tel. 322-7500; fax 328-0945; internet www.bahamas.com; Dir-Gen. VINCENT VANDERPOOL-WALLACE.

Bahamas Hotel Association: Dean's Lane, Fort Charlotte, POB N-7799, Nassau; tel. 322-8381; fax 326-5346; e-mail bhainfo@batel net.bs; Exec. Vice-Pres. BASIL H. SMITH.

Bahamas Tourism and Development Authority: POB SS-5256, Nassau; tel. 394-3575; Exec. Dir DIANE PHILLIPS.

Hotel Corporation of the Bahamas: West Bay St, POB N-9520, Nassau; tel. 327-8395; fax 327-6978; Chair. GEOFFREY JOHNSTONE; Chief Exec. WARREN ROLLE.

Defence

The Royal Bahamian Defence Force, a paramilitary coastguard, is the only security force in the Bahamas, and numbered 860 (including 70 women) in August 2000. The defence budget includes expenditure on the 2,300-strong police force and is mostly used to finance the campaign against drugs trafficking.

Defence Budget (2000): B $26m.

Commodore: DAVID ROLLE.

Education

Education is compulsory between the ages of five and 16 years, and is provided free of charge in government schools. There are several private and denominational schools. Primary education begins at five years of age and lasts for six years. Secondary education, beginning at the age of 11, also lasts for six years and is divided into two equal cycles. In 1995 100% of children in the relevant age-group were enrolled at primary level. In the same year 86% of children in the relevant age-group were enrolled at secondary level. The University of the West Indies has an extra-mural department in Nassau, offering degree courses in hotel management and tourism. The Bahamas Hotel Training College was established in 1992. The Bahamas Law School, part of the University of the West Indies, opened in 1998. Technical, teacher-training and professional qualifications can be obtained at the two campuses of the College of the Bahamas. Government expenditure on education in 1998/99 was B $164.7m., or 19.1% of total government spending. The 2001/02 budget included some US $190.2m. on education.

Bibliography

For works on the Caribbean generally, see Select Bibliography (Books).

Block, A. A. *Masters of Paradise: Organized Crime and the Internal Revenue Service in the Bahamas.* Somerset, NJ, Transaction Publishers, 1997.

Craton, M., and Saunders, G. *Islanders in the Stream: A History of the Bahamian People: From the Ending of Slavery to the Twenty-First Century.* Athens, GA, University of Georgia Press, 1998.

Eneas, G. Agriculture in the Bahamas: *Historical Development 1492-1992.* Media Publishing Ltd, 1998.

Kelly, R. C., Ewing, D., Doyle, S., and Youngblood, D. *Country Review, Bahamas, 1998/1999.* Commercial Data International, 1998.

BARBADOS

Area: 430 sq km (166 sq miles).

Population (official estimate, December 1999): 267,900.

Capital: Bridgetown, population 5,928 in 1990.

Language: English.

Religion: Predominantly Christianity, with the Anglican Church the principal denomination; about 90 other Christian denominations are also represented. There are small groups of Hindus, Muslims and Jews.

Climate: There is a rainy season from July to November, and the climate is cool during the rest of the year. The mean annual temperature is about 26°C (78°F).

Time: GMT –4 hours.

Public Holidays

2002: 1 January (New Year's Day), 21 January (Errol Barrow Memorial Day), 29 March (Good Friday), 1 April (Easter Monday), 28 April (National Heroes' Day), 1 May (Labour Day), 20 May (Whit Monday), 1 August (Emancipation Day), 6 August (Kadooment Day), 30 November (Independence Day), 25–26 December (Christmas).

2003: 1 January (New Year's Day), 21 January (Errol Barrow Memorial Day), 18 April (Good Friday), 21 April (Easter Monday), 28 April (National Heroes' Day), 1 May (Labour Day), 9 June (Whit Monday), 1 August (Emancipation Day), 4 August (Kadooment Day), 30 November (Independence Day), 25–26 December (Christmas).

Currency: Barbadian dollar; Bds $100 = £34.92 = US $50.00 = €56.33 (30 April 2001).

Weights and measures: The metric system is used.

Basic Economic Indicators

	1997	1998	1999
Gross domestic product (million Bds $ at 1974 prices)	889.7	928.6	951.9
GDP per head (Bds $ at 1974 prices)	3,344	3,474	3,553
GDP (million Bds $ at current prices)	4,410	4,756	4,980
Annual growth of real GDP (%)	2.9	4.4	2.5
Annual growth of real GDP per head (%)	2.2	3.9	2.3
Government budget (million Bds $ at current prices):			
Revenue	1,424.5	1,526.8	1,545.6
Expenditure	1,458.0	1,573.7	1,660.8
Consumer price index (annual average; base: 1995 = 100)*	110.3	108.9	110.6
Rate of inflation (annual average, %)†	7.7	–1.3	1.6
Foreign exchange reserves (US $ million at 31 December)‡	264.9	365.9	295.5
Imports c.i.f. (US $ million) §	996	1,010	1,108
Exports f.o.b. (US $ million)‖	283	252	264
Balance of payments (current account, US $ million)	–50.0	–56.5	–125.8

* 113.3 in 2000.
† 2.4% in 2000.
‡ Bds $466.6m. in 2000.
§ US $1,156m. in 2000.
‖ US $272m. in 2000.

Gross national product per head measured at purchasing power parity (PPP) (GNP converted to US dollars by the PPP exchange rate, 1998): 12,260.

Total labour force (labour force sample survey, 1999): 136,600.

Unemployment (1999): 10.4%.

Total external debt (1999): US $589m.

Life expectancy (years at birth, 1998): 75.3.

Infant mortality rate (per 1,000 live births, 1998): 13.6.

Adult population with HIV/AIDS (15-49 years, 1999): 1.17%

School enrolment ratio: (1998) 5–12 years 97%; 11–16 years 69%.

Adult literacy rate (15 years and over, 1999): 97.0%.

Carbon dioxide emissions per head (metric tons, 1997): 3.7.

Passenger motor cars in use (estimate, per 1,000 of population, 1996): 136.4.

Television receivers in use (per 1,000 of population, 1997): 285.

Personal computers in use (per 1,000 of population, 1999): 78.1.

History

MARK WILSON

Based on an earlier article by PROF. A. E. THORNDIKE

The Amerindians who settled Barbados from around AD 350 left the island during the 16th century, so that the first British settlers, who arrived in 1627, found no indigenous inhabitants. Barbados remained under British sovereignty until political independence in 1966, thereby earning itself the sobriquet 'Little England', and Barbadians played an important role in the settlement and administration of Britain's other Caribbean possessions. The first British settlers were smallholders growing tobacco and other crops, using the labour of indentured servants. However, fundamental change came with the introduction in the 1640s of sugar cane, by Dutch merchants, who brought plants from the Dutch settlements in Brazil. Sugar production required considerable labour and capital for the manufacturing process, a large work-force and extensive acreage, so large estate-owners supplanted the smallholders and, increasingly, slaves (of African origin) replaced the European servants. Although the first slaves arrived in 1627, they were few in number until the 1640s. By 1655 slaves formed 47% of a population of 43,000 and by 1712 they formed 77% of a total population of some 54,500. Many whites moved on to other British settlements in the Caribbean or on to the American mainland. Those who stayed, unless they were landowners, became craftsmen, overseers or merchants, or in some cases led a marginal and socially isolated existence as 'poor whites'. The black slave population was harshly treated and there were attempted slave revolts in 1675, 1692, 1702 and 1816. Slavery was eventually abolished in 1834, but its legacy was a highly stratified class-based society, still based, to some extent, on gradations of colour.

The British settlers established a House of Assembly in 1639 to represent their interests. Based on the 'representational system', the franchise was strictly limited by a property qualification. *De facto* power was exercised by the House of Assembly through its control of the public purse; hence it was able to hinder any attempt at reform by successive Governors. In 1876 the British Governor, John Pope Hennessey, proposed the establishment of a confederation to link Barbados and the Windward Islands. This suggestion was resisted by the Assembly, but was seen by many blacks as a partial solution to their difficulties. Eight people were killed in the ensuing Confederation Riots, and Pope Hennessey was subsequently transferred to Hong Kong. The first mixed-race member of the Assembly, Samuel Jackman Prescod, was elected in 1843, and the franchise was significantly widened in 1884. But even the reformed property qualification continued to exclude the majority of blacks from the franchise. In 1856 the Assembly introduced district medical officers, and a Board of Education was formed in 1878, under the influence of the Anglican bishop, John Mitchinson. A non-white professional middle-class emerged during the 19th century; Sir Conrad Reeves, a mixed-race politician and lawyer, was Chief Justice from 1886 to 1902. However, further political and social advance was to wait until the rise of the labour movement in the 1930s.

Charles Duncan O'Neal founded the Democratic League, influenced by Fabian principles, in 1924. Its first member, Chrissie Brathwaite, was elected to the Assembly in the same year, and the Workingmen's Association was founded in 1926. The poor economic climate and the impoverished condition of most Barbadians (Bajans) led, as was also the case in most of the other British West Indian territories, to labour disturbances. In July 1937 14 people were killed and 47 injured in island-wide riots. A later commission of inquiry expressed no surprise at the disturbances, once the inequalities in Barbadian society at the time were revealed. The Barbados Progressive League was founded in 1938, its leaders including Grantley (later Sir Grantley) Adams. It gained five seats in the House of Assembly in 1940 and was strengthened considerably by an alliance with the Barbados Workers' Union (BWU), founded by Adams and Hugh Springer. In 1943 the League successfully campaigned for an extension of the franchise. In the 1944 general election the League won seven seats, with eight won by Wynter Crawford's more radical West Indian National Congress party and eight by the traditionalist Electors' Association, established by the landowning and merchant élite. Adams and other elected members subsequently joined the Executive Committee, the principal policy-making instrument. The League was renamed the Barbados Labour Party in 1946, and made gains at the expense of both other parties in the elections held in 1946 and 1948.

Universal adult suffrage was introduced in 1950 and in the general election held in 1951 the BLP won 16 of the 24 seats. Ministerial government was introduced in 1954 and Adams was appointed Premier. He subsequently became Prime Minister of the West Indies Federation, from January 1958 until its dissolution in 1962, and was succeeded as Premier of Barbados by Dr Hugh Cummins.

Following the 1951 election victory, those who favoured a more socialist approach, such as Errol Barrow, became disenchanted with those, like Adams, who favoured gradualist policies. In 1955 a small group, later named the Democratic Labour Party (DLP), led by Barrow, split from the BLP and joined forces with former members of the Congress Party. The BLP won 15 seats in the subsequent 1956 election, with the DLP and the Progressive Conservative Party each obtaining four. In October 1961 full internal self-government was granted and, in the ensuing general election, the DLP won 16 seats to the BLP's five, with one Independent seat and four for the traditionalist Barbados National Party. Britain tried to promote an association of Barbados and the neighbouring Leeward and Windward Islands, following the collapse of the West Indies Federation in 1962. However, this attempt was not successful, and Barrow led Barbados to separate independence in November 1966, and became its first Prime Minister. Thereafter, a two-party system, based on the two Labour parties, prevailed.

The DLP was ousted from power in 1976 and the BLP leader, J. M. G. M. 'Tom' Adams, son of Sir Grantley Adams, became Prime Minister. The BLP also won the 1981 election, winning 17 of the 27 seats in the newly enlarged House of Assembly. Adams played a leading role in support of the US military intervention in Grenada in 1983. He died suddenly in 1985 and was succeeded by Bernard St John, under whose leadership the BLP was heavily defeated by the DLP in the May 1986 election, when the BLP won only three seats. St John lost his seat and a former Minister of Foreign Affairs, Henry Forde, assumed the BLP leadership. Errol Barrow once again became Prime Minister. The underlying reason for the Government's defeat lay in the country's past history. The issue of racism and 'white power' was never far from the surface; the BLP had become too closely identified, in many people's view, with the light-coloured business élite, from which it received substantial funds. Barrow, on the other hand, appealed to the black population and promised tax reforms to aid the black middle class. There was also dissatisfaction with the BLP's strong identification with US policy in the region, which offended nationalist sensibilities. Barrow's stand on this and other regional issues made him an imposing political force. His sudden death in June 1987 was, however, not entirely unexpected, given his refusal of medical advice pertaining to his strenuous work schedule. He was succeeded by his one-time deputy, Erskine Sandiford.

Sandiford's first political test was the resignation, in September 1987, of the Minister of Finance, Dr Richard (Richie)

Haynes, who saw himself as a possible future Prime Minister. At the same time, the economic situation began to deteriorate, partly as result of Haynes' tax measures and partly as a result of the closure in 1986 of the island's main manufacturing operation, a semi-conductor plant. In February 1989 Haynes formed the National Democratic Party (NDP), with three other DLP parliamentarians, thus displacing Forde as the official leader of the Opposition. In the general election of January 1991 the BLP gained 10 seats to the DLP's 18. The fortunes of the BLP were restored with those of the two-party system; all four NDP members lost their seats. Support for the Sandiford regime declined rapidly thereafter, as austerity measures were introduced as a condition of International Monetary Fund assistance to the economy, made necessary by a serious economic crisis. This situation was exploited to great effect by a rejuvenated BLP, led by a dynamic new leader, Owen Arthur. At the general election of 6 September 1994 the BLP won 19 of the 28 seats, while the DLP retained only eight and the NDP regained one, although the DLP and the NDP together secured more votes than the BLP. Arthur became Prime Minister.

Arthur, a former professional economist, promoted economic recovery and international competitiveness in order to reduce the high levels of unemployment in the country, and economic growth resumed from 1993. He proved himself capable of populist gestures, passing a constitutional amendment forbidding future reductions in pay for public employees. He also significantly broadened the BLP's support base, retaining its links with the business community while at the same time attracting a considerable number of nationalist intellectuals and trade unionists. In 1997 a public holiday to mark Emancipation Day was declared, and a National Heroes' Day was introduced on the anniversary of the birth of Sir Grantley Adams. The anniversary of the 1937 Confederation Riots was declared a 'day of national significance', and a pilot project was commenced towards the teaching of black studies in primary and secondary schools. In September 1998 Owen Arthur, exercising his 'politics of inclusion', offered the position of consultant on matters of poverty alleviation to Hamilton Lashley, a prominent DLP member of the House of Assembly. In October Lashley transferred his support to the BLP.

In May 1995 Arthur announced the formation of a commission, chaired by Henry (later Sir Henry) Forde, to advise the Government on reforms to the country's Constitution. In July 1996 the commission was charged with considering, in particular, the continuing role of the British monarch as head of state. The commission reported in December 1998 and, as expected, recommended the replacement of the British monarch with a ceremonial President. It also proposed changes in the composition of the Senate, provision for peoples' initiatives to introduce new legislation and stronger constitutional backing for the Auditor General and the Public Accounts Committee. Replacement of the Privy Council, the highest judicial body, with a Caribbean Court of Appeal, to be jointly established with other Caribbean islands, was also expected.

Support from across the political spectrum and a rapidly growing economy helped the BLP to gain an unprecedented victory in the general election of 20 January 1999, receiving 64.8% of the total votes cast and winning 26 of the 28 seats in the House of Assembly. The opposition DLP emerged from the election severely weakened, gaining 35.1% of the votes cast and only two seats.

In keeping with growing nationalist sentiment, in April 1999 Trafalgar Square, in the centre of Bridgetown, was renamed National Heroes' Square, and the decision was made to replace the statue of Admiral Lord Horatio Nelson which stood there, with one of Errol Barrow. In August 2000 Arthur announced that a referendum would be held on the replacement of the monarch with a republic, a proposal which had the clear support of all political parties and which was widely expected to be approved. However, a constitutional stand-off between President and Prime Minster in neighbouring Trinidad and Tobago in late 2000 and early 2001 led to a wider appreciation of the need for careful consideration of the relations between an elected government and a ceremonial president; and no further move towards the establishment of a republic had been made by mid-2001.

Barbados played a leading role in late 2000 and early 2001 in moves by offshore financial centres to head off initiatives by the Organisation for Economic Co-operation and Development (OECD) against tax havens, and by the intergovernmental Financial Action Task Force (FATF, based at the OECD headquarters) against money laundering. The country co-chaired a joint working group on money laundering, established as a result of an initiative at the Commonwealth Finance Ministers' meeting in Malta in September 2000. This was a considerable diplomatic success for Barbados both regionally and internationally.

Economy
MARK WILSON

Barbados is more economically and socially developed than most of the English-speaking Caribbean, with a per-head gross domestic product (GDP) of US $9,187 in 1999, among the highest in the region. The island functions as an air transport hub for the eastern Caribbean and is the site of the headquarters of several regional organizations. With high standards of education, infrastructure and health care, in 2000 the island was ranked higher than any other economy in Latin America and the Caribbean by the Human Development Index, produced by the UN Development Programme. Barbados ranked 30th worldwide, behind the economies of the Organisation for Economic Co-operation and Development (OECD) members, but ahead of the Bahamas (33rd) and Argentina (35th). This was all the more remarkable because the country had one of the largest population densities in the world (some 621.6 per sq km in December 2000). A US $390m. programme for curriculum reform and the introduction of technology into education, known as Edutech 2000, was scheduled for completion by 2007.

On mid-year projections 2001 was expected to be the ninth successive year of economic growth, with GDP expected to grow by close to 2.0%, after growth of 3.7% in 2000 and an average economic increase of 3.1% in 1994–99. Several hotel construction projects were planned or in progress, as well as major investments in the port and airport. A sewage system to serve the south coast was also under construction. The Government has partially privatized a number of public-sector companies, including the Barbados National Bank, the Caribbean Broadcasting Corporation (CBC) and further privatizations were expected.

In December 2000 the unemployment rate was 9.3%, 16.9% below the March 1993 figure of 26.2%, and the lowest figure recorded since the regular publication of employment data began in 1975. Although some consumer prices are high by international standards, the underlying rate of inflation was modest from 1992. Prices rose sharply at the start of 1997, when the introduction of a value-added tax (VAT) increased the annual inflation rate to 7.7%. However, this was followed by a 1.3% reduction in the retail price index in 1998. Prices increased by 1.6% in 1999. An increase in international energy costs was mainly responsible for a 2.4% inflation rate in 2001.

In the 1990s successive Governments took a reasonably cautious approach to budgeting and overall fiscal deficits remained under control, with the current account largely in surplus. A 1996 deficit equivalent to 3.2% of GDP was reduced in 1997 to 0.9% with the introduction of the VAT. The deficit remained at 0.8% in 1998, but rose to 2.3% in 1999, before falling back to 1.4% in 2000. This reduction was achieved in spite of one-off expenditure in compensation for a 1991–93 civil service pay cut.

The balance of payments current account was in surplus from 1992 to 1996, with high and rising earnings from tourism and other services compensating for a permanent negative balance on merchandise trade. Continuing economic growth from 1997, however, brought about a rapid increase in imports of consumer and capital goods, resulting in a current-account deficit, which rose from US $50.0m. in 1997 to US $56.5m. in 1998 and US $125.8m. in 1999, before falling back to US $108.4m. in 2000. The current-account deficit was in part covered by a capital-account surplus, which rose from US $24.1m. in 1998 to US $141.7m. in 1999 and a record US $271.1m. in 2000. Investment in tourism-related construction projects, electricity generation and other areas brought about strong capital inflows For 2000, net private sector long-term capital and financial inflows totalled US $136.6m., with reserves also boosted by government borrowing of US $100m and project funds of US $36.6m.

Throughout the 1990s net international reserves increased strongly. From a low point of Bds $38.9m. in 1991, reserves reached an all-time high of Bds $1,096.5m. in March 2001. The healthy growth was helped by tourism receipts and some precautionary borrowing on international financial markets in mid-2000.

The period of positive economic growth that began in 1993 had been preceded by economic stagnation from the mid-1980s, which had forced the Government to seek the assistance of the International Monetary Fund (IMF). This downturn had followed two decades of political stability and economic prosperity in the 1960s and 1970s. In 1991, as a precondition of an IMF agreement (finally reached in February 1992), the Government was forced to introduce a severe austerity programme, including a stabilization tax and an 8% reduction in pay for public-service workers. This coincided with a period of severe difficulties for the sugar industry (until the 1970s the principal foreign-exchange earner), which recorded low production. A downturn in tourism (which from the 1970s had replaced the sugar industry as the principal economic sector) was also experienced, associated with a recession in North America. With stricter macroeconomic policies, there were sharp increases in interest rates and in unemployment. GDP fell by a cumulative total of 12.9% during 1989–92.

The IMF loan agreement consisted of a US $33.68m. stand-by credit, and a US $31.25m. compensatory and contingency financing facility, to be drawn on over a period of 15 months. Other assistance for the country's structural-adjustment measures was obtained from foreign commercial banks and the Inter-American Development Bank. While the stabilization programme provided immediate relief to the economy, recovery began only in 1993, when economic conditions improved in Barbados' main tourist and export markets. A national wage 'freeze', imposed in April 1993, was removed in April 1995 and public-sector pay agreements were restored. At the same time, the Government, the private sector and the trade unions agreed a tripartite two-year protocol covering wages, prices and conditions of employment, which reflected a high degree of consensus regarding social and economic goals. New protocols were agreed in 1995 and 1998 and had considerable symbolic importance in cementing the national traditions of consensus and compromise.

TOURISM

Barbados had a well-established tourist industry, employing 10% of the working population in 1999. The industry grew rapidly in the 1960s and 1970s and again in 1986–89. However, in the early 1990s poor market conditions, a fall in charter-plane services and an increasingly poor reputation for value for money resulted in a 16% decline in arrivals. Recovery began in 1993; stop-over tourist arrivals increased by 34.3% between 1992 and 2000, to reach 545,027 in the later year, the highest number ever recorded. Tourism accounted for 11.2% of GDP in 1999 and produced 55.2% of foreign exchange earnings. The number of cruise-ship passengers rose from 99,168 in 1984 to 533,278 in 2000.

Labour costs in Barbados were much higher than in some competing destinations and the landscape less immediately striking. However, the island enjoyed a high percentage of repeat visitors. All-inclusive holiday packages accounted for a relatively small market share, thus encouraging spending out-side hotel premises. The closure of the Barbados Hilton for reconstruction in 1999 (it was expected to reopen by 2003) meant that no major international chains were represented on the island, and there were no properties with more than 300 rooms. As a result of this and other refurbishment projects there was, from mid-1999, a temporary fall in the rate of growth of tourism earnings, compensated for by an increase in the long term. The United Kingdom, in 1999, accounted for some 41.1% of stop-over arrivals. However, the lack of large brand-name hotels was partly responsible for Barbados' poor performance in North America from 1986, and also impeded the development of conference and incentive tourism.

Tourist accommodation was, from the 1950s, concentrated on the sheltered south and west coasts, which were highly urbanized. By the 1990s further expansion depended on the development of inland or east coast sites, with the use of sports facilities to compensate for the distance from the sea, or on the redevelopment of sites which were already used for tourism or other urban purposes, such as the reconstruction of the Barbados Hilton on the south coast, along with the redevelopment of the adjacent Mobil petroleum refinery site for tourism. Attempts were made to attract a major international chain for this project. However, the Sandals chain encountered problems in finalizing its separate proposals for a 600-room west-coast property on the site of the former Cunard Paradise Beach. In 1999 it offered this important hotel site for sale, but, by mid-2001, had yet to find a buyer.

FINANCIAL AND INFORMATION SERVICES

Barbados had a well-developed local banking and insurance industry. CIBC West Indies Holdings, a regional bank whose operations extended to Jamaica and the Bahamas, was head-quartered in Barbados. The main local insurance companies were also active in other Caribbean markets and in 2001 jointly agreed to purchase a majority stake in Jamaica's largest life insurance company. There was a small local securities exchange, on which locally-based companies had a market capitalization of Bds $3,427m. in April 2001. In addition, some Trinidadian and Jamaican companies had cross-listings on the Barbados exchange, bringing total capitalization to Bds $6,101m.

The 'offshore' financial sector, mainly specializing in insurance, was a sector of some promise. The growth of offshore financial facilities was encouraged by the negotiation of double taxation agreements with other countries, although the sector did not operate on the same scale as that of the Bahamas, Bermuda or the Cayman Islands. However, it was a significant employer and foreign-exchange earner. Earnings were estimated at Bds $122m. in 1995, equivalent to 17.8% of the island's imports. Barbados has an extensive network of double taxation and tax-information exchange treaties, and a fairly high standard of financial regulation. There is an active anti-money laundering (the transfer of illegally-earned funds into legitimate accounts) regime, which was further strengthened by new legislation in 1998, although Barbados remained classified by the USA as a 'country of concern' with regard to money laundering. Active regulation discouraged more dubious clients, but attracted businesses such as captive insurance companies and US foreign sales corporations (FSCs). An International Business Companies Act, passed in 1991, resulted in the registration of 3,828 international business companies by the end of 2000, in addition to 2,981 FSCs, 441 exempt insurance and insurance management companies and 55 offshore banks. The offshore sector contributed an estimated US $150m. in foreign earnings in 1995.

International developments in 1999 and 2000 placed all offshore financial services sectors under increasing pressure. In July 1999 a World Trade Organization dispute panel ruled in favour of a complaint by the European Union (EU) that tax exemptions for US FSCs amounted to an export subsidy worth US $2,000m. per year. The USA was instructed to reform its regulations by October 2000. This was of particular concern to Barbados, which is one of a very small number of offshore centres approved by the USA for FSC registration. In May 2000 the OECD placed Barbados on a list of tax 'havens' which were threatened with counter-measures from June 2001 if they failed to modify tax regimes in line with OECD requirements. The island escaped inclusion on a Financial Action Task Force on

Money Laundering (FATF, based at the OECD Secretariat) list of non-co-operating jurisdictions in the same month, and was given relatively high rating in a Financial Stability Forum report on bank supervision capability, but these international initiatives received a hostile reaction from the Barbadian Government, which played a leading role in international lobbying by offshore centres against the FATF and OECD initiatives. With the new US administration of George W. Bush adopting a more flexible policy on tax matters, the threat of serious international action against offshore tax havens appeared to have receded by mid-2001.

The informatics industry originated in the early 1980s with data-entry operations. Employment in the sector reached 2,972 in December 1997, but fell subsequently, to 1,808 by December 1999. By the mid-1990s routine work was handled by scanning systems, and work that was still done manually could be sourced more cheaply from countries with lower labour costs. However, Barbados retained a comparative advantage in high-end work. Informatics costs in Barbados in 1997 amounted to some 13 US cents per unit, far lower than the cost of 30 cents per unit in the USA. Furthermore, Barbados has a higher standard of education and a more adaptable English-speaking labour force than many of its competitors and is also in the same time zone as the eastern USA. The island specializes in semi-skilled 'back-office' operations, such as the processing of insurance claims or database management. Software development was another area of activity, with telemarketing seen in 2001 as a promising area for future growth The sector's foreign-exchange earnings totalled US $35m. in 1998.

MANUFACTURING

The manufacturing sector was in a depressed state from the mid-1980s and the restraints on credit and consumer spending, imposed progressively from 1991, resulted in bankruptcies and factory closures. Economic recovery in the late 1990s failed to benefit most manufacturing industries, because of the gradual erosion of protective barriers against imports. The main manufacturing industries employed over 15,000 people in 1986, but only 9,900 or 8.4% of total employment in 1999. However, Barbados had a surprisingly wide range of manufacturing industries, producing consumer products for the local and regional market, although labour costs were higher than in most Caribbean islands and power costs much higher than in Trinidad and Tobago. The closure of the small oil refinery in 1998 was a gain for the economy, as refinery products could be imported more cheaply from Trinidad and Tobago, and a valuable site was released for tourist development.

The removal of trade barriers caused difficulties for some manufacturers in the 1990s. The clothing and wooden furniture industries, which had been in decline since the mid-1980s, virtually disappeared. However, the more efficient producers in other branches of manufacturing managed to survive and in some cases to expand their export sales. In 1999 manufactured exports (excluding the traditional products of sugar and rum) earned US $135.8m.

The remaining heavy industrial plant was the Arawak cement plant in the north of the island, owned by a Trinidadian company, which used local limestone and low-cost orimulsion fuel from Venezuela. After having been closed for some years, the kiln reopened in 1997 and, owing to the activity of the construction industry in Barbados and throughout the eastern Caribbean, worked close to full capacity.

Petroleum production was another major industrial activity. Crude petroleum production began in 1973, and rose to 679,000 barrels in 1985 before declining to 328,000 barrels in 1997 as wells were depleted. However, an onshore drilling programme begun in that year increased production dramatically from 1998. Total extraction increased to 576,636 barrels in 1998 and reached 708,500 barrels in 1999, equivalent to one-third of local consumption; however, with a reduced drilling programme, output fell to 559,675 barrels in 2000. Natural-gas production stood at 46.9m. cu m in 1999. There is a piped supply to most urban and suburban areas, while some electric generation capacity transferred to natural gas from 1999. A US-based company, Conoco Inc., operated an offshore petroleum and gas exploration programme in partnership with the French concern Elf Aquitaine; initial seismic surveys showed promising geolog-

ical prospects, but exploratory drilling was not expected to start until 2002 at the earliest.

SUGAR AND AGRICULTURE

Sugar was the mainstay of the economy until the rise of the tourist industry in the 1950s and 1960s. In 1946 the industry accounted for 37.8% of GDP and 55% of foreign-exchange earnings, employing some 25,100 people. By the late 1990s sugar cane was still the main agricultural crop; however, in 1999 the industry accounted for only 1.3% of GDP, 2.2% of foreign-exchange earnings and 2.5% of total employment.

In spite of a guaranteed price for exports to Europe, under the Lomé Convention (which expired in February 2000 and was replaced by the Cotonou Agreement in June—see Part Three, Regional Organizations, European Union), the sugar industry suffered from severe economic problems from the 1980s. These related mainly to high production costs and inefficiencies associated with the traditional management system. Farmers left many sugar farms uncultivated, in order to capitalize upon the high prices which could sometimes be obtained for land set aside for urban development. By 1992 a high proportion of estates had borrowed heavily from the state-owned Barbados National Bank and had accumulated debts greater than the value of their assets. Barbados Sugar Industries Ltd (BSIL), which owned and operated the factories, owed nearly Bds $100m. by early 1992. The IMF indicated it could not continue to tolerate the situation and, soon after final agreement was reached with the Fund, in February 1992, it was announced that BSIL would go into receivership. The factories and the most heavily-indebted estates were placed under the management of the Barbados Agricultural Management Company, which from 1994 was run on a management contract by a British company, Booker-Tate. Amid considerable political controversy, Booker-Tate insisted on a restructuring of the entire sugar industry, with one-third of the debt to be cancelled, one-third to be converted into equity in a new company and the remaining one-third to be serviced as an active loan. The Government also guaranteed a loan of US $11.5m. from the Caribbean Development Bank. In return, a plan to increase production to 75,000 metric tons of raw sugar within five years was put into operation. In early 1993 the IMF approved the plan. The initial contract expired in June 1998 and was subsequently extended. However, by June 2001, no long-term decision had been made about the future management of the industry.

The valuable EU quota of 54,000 metric tons of sugar (worth some US $34m. in foreign exchange) was not fulfilled from 1991 to 1995. The US quota of 14,239 tons was not fulfilled and was reduced to 5,000 tons in 1995. From 1990 the rum industry was forced to import over one-half of its annual requirement of 20,000 tons of molasses. Production reached a low point of 38,500 tons in 1995, partly as a consequence of a severe drought in the previous year. Thereafter output varied between a high of 64,600 metric tons in 1997 and a low of 48,000 tons in the following year, with the 2001 crop producing a disappointing 49,796 tons. Earnings meanwhile have suffered from the declining value of the euro against the US dollar. The export price fell from Bds $1,362 in 1995 to Bds $1,123 in 1999, with the final figure for 2001 expected to be close to Bds $900. With production costs estimated at Bds $1,493 per ton, sugar subsidies, which totalled Bds $100m. in the 1990s, threatened to spiral out of control. Proposals for safeguarding the future of the industry include a new sugar factory, which would cost around Bds $200m., but would produce 40% more sugar from the same volume of cane and would incorporate a 64 MW electricity generation plant.

The soil held nutrients well, but was thin. Rainfall was generally adequate, but there were occasional severe droughts. Groundwater supplies were not sufficient for large-scale irrigation. These problems impeded the development of other agricultural activities. There was some commercial production of vegetables and root crops. The island was virtually self-sufficient in poultry products and in fresh milk, activities which depended to a significant extent on imported inputs. There was some pig farming and lamb was produced from the local Black Belly short-haired sheep. More than 90% of the fishing catch (which stood at 3,594 metric tons in 1998) was landed at complexes which were built at Oistins and Bridgetown in the 1980s.

However, despite some self-sufficiency, agricultural production (including forestry) and fishing contributed only an estimated 4.9% of GDP in 1999, and employed 4.2% of the economically active population.

Statistical Survey

Sources (unless otherwise stated): Barbados Statistical Service, National Insurance Bldg, 3rd Floor, Fairchild St, Bridgetown; tel. 427-7841; fax 435-2198; e-mail barstats@caribsurf.com; internet www.bgis.gov.bb/stats. Central Bank of Barbados, Spry St, POB 1016, Bridgetown; tel. 436-6870; fax 427-1431; e-mail cbb.libr@caribsurf.com; internet www .centralbank.org.bb.

AREA AND POPULATION

Area: 430 sq km (166 sq miles).

Population: 252,029 (males 119,665, females 132,364) at census of 12 May 1980; 257,082 (provisional) at census of 2 May 1990; 267,900 (official estimate) at mid-1999.

Density (mid-1999): 623.0 per sq km.

Ethnic Groups (*de jure* population, excl. persons resident in institutions, 1990 census): Black 228,683; White 8,022; Mixed race 5,886; Total (incl. others) 247,288.

Principal Town: Bridgetown (capital), population 5,928 at 1990 census.

Births, Marriages and Deaths (provisional registrations, 1998): Live births 3,612 (birth rate 13.6 per 1,000); Marriages (1997) 3,377 (marriage rate 12.7 per 1,000); Deaths 2,471 (death rate 9.3 per 1,000).

Expectation of Life (UN estimates, years at birth, 1990–95): 75.3 (males 72.9; females 77.9). Source: UN, *World Population Prospects: The 1998 Revision.*

Economically Active Population (labour force sample survey, '000 persons aged 15 years and over, excl. armed forces, 1999): Agriculture, forestry and fishing 5.2; Manufacturing 10.3; Electricity, gas and water 2.0; Construction and quarrying 14.0; Wholesale and retail trade 17.2; Tourism 12.3; Transport, storage and communications 4.5; Financing, insurance, real estate and business services 7.0; Community, social and personal services 49.7; Activities not adequately defined 0.2; Total employed 122.4 (males 65.5, females 56.9); Unemployed 14.2 (males 5.5, females 8.7); Total labour force 136.6 (males 71.0, females 65.6). Source: ILO Caribbean Office.

AGRICULTURE, ETC.

Principal Crops (FAO estimates, '000 metric tons, 2000): Maize 2; Sweet potatoes 5; Cassava 1; Yams 1; Pulses 1; Coconuts 2; Cabbages 1; Tomatoes 1; Pumpkins 1; Cucumbers 1; Chillies and peppers 1; String beans 1; Carrots 1; Other vegetables 5; Sugar cane 500; Bananas 1; Other fruits 2. Source: FAO.

Livestock (FAO estimates, '000 head, year ending September 2000): Horses 1; Mules 2; Asses 2; Cattle 23; Pigs 33; Sheep 41; Goats 5; Poultry 3,600. Source: FAO.

Livestock Products ('000 metric tons, 2000): Beef and veal 1*; Pig meat 4; Poultry meat 12; Cows' milk 8; Hen eggs 1*. *FAO estimate Source: FAO.

Forestry ('000 cubic metres): Roundwood removals 5 in 1997; 5 in 1998; 5 in 1999. Source: FAO, *Yearbook of Forest Products.*

Fishing (metric tons, live weight, 1998): Total catch 3,594 (Flying-fishes 2,680, Common dolphinfish 482, Yellowfin tuna 146, Marlins, sailfishes, etc. 109). Source: FAO, *Yearbook of Fishery Statistics.*

MINING

Production: Natural gas 24.2 million cu m in 1998; Crude petroleum 708,500 barrels in 1999.

INDUSTRY

Selected Products (official estimates, 1998): Raw sugar (1999) 53,196 metric tons; Rum 8,830,000 litres; Beer (1995) 7,429,000 litres; Cigarettes (1995) 65 metric tons; Batteries 17,165; Electric energy 715m. kWh.

FINANCE

Currency and Exchange Rates: 100 cents = 1 Barbados dollar (Bds $). *Sterling, US Dollar and Euro Equivalents* (30 April 2001): £1 sterling = Bds $2.864; US $1 = Bds $2.000; €1 = Bds $1.775; Bds $100 = £34.92 = US $50.00 = €56.33. *Exchange Rate*: Fixed at US $1 = Bds $2.000 since 1986.

Budget (estimates, Bds $ million, year ending 31 March 2000): *Revenue*: Tax revenue 1,562.0 (Taxes on income and profits 512.9,

Levies 75.2, Taxes on property 98.2, Domestic taxes on goods and services 727.8, Taxes on international trade 134.6); Other current revenue 49.6; Total 1,611.6. *Expenditure:* Current 1,409.9 (Wages and salaries 565.2, Other goods and services 163.4, Interest payments 230.7, Transfers and subsidies 413.4); Capital (incl. net lending 4.5) 266.7; Total 1,676.6.

2000/01 (projections, Bds $ million): Total revenue and grants 1,724.7; Total expenditure 1,781.9 (Capital expenditure and net lending 291.9).

Note: Budgetary data refer to current and capital budgets only and exclude operations of the National Insurance Fund and other central government units with their own budgets.

International Reserves (US $ million at 31 December 2000): IMF special drawing rights 0.02; Reserve position in IMF 6.09; Foreign exchange 466.58; Total 472.69. Source: IMF, *International Financial Statistics.*

Money Supply (Bds $ million at 31 December 2000): Currency outside banks 310.7; Demand deposits at commercial banks 825.7; Total money (incl. others) 1,140.4. Source: IMF, *International Financial Statistics.*

Cost of Living (Index of Retail Prices; base: 1995 = 100): 108.9 in 1998; 110.6 in 1999; 113.3 in 2000. Source: IMF, *International Financial Statistics.*

Expenditure on the Gross Domestic Product (provisional, Bds $ million at current prices, 1999): Government final consumption expenditure 1,128.3; Private final consumption expenditure 3,134.1; Increase in stocks 10.5; Gross fixed capital formation 957.8; *Total domestic expenditure* 5,230.7; Exports of goods and services 2,509.2; *Less* Imports of goods and services 2,759.8; *GDP in purchasers' values* 4,980.1. Source: IMF, *Barbados: Statistical Appendix* (December 2000).

Gross Domestic Product by Economic Activity (Bds $ million at current prices, 1998): Agriculture, hunting, forestry and fishing 158.1; Mining and quarrying 20.1; Manufacturing 243.5; Electricity, gas and water 126.4; Construction 240.6; Wholesale and retail trade 702.2; Tourism 482.2; Transport, storage and communications 381.7; Finance, insurance, real estate and business services 715.7; Government services 674.5; Other community, social and personal services 179.8; *GDP at factor cost* 3,924.8; Indirect taxes, *less* subsidies 852.1; *GDP in purchasers' values* 4,776.9.

Balance of Payments (US $ million, 1999): Exports of goods f.o.b. 262.0; Imports of goods f.o.b. –953.7; *Trade balance* –691.7; Exports of services 1,025.4; Imports of services –454.2; *Balance on goods and services* –120.6; Other income received 66.7; Other income paid –138.1; *Balance on goods, services and income* –192.0; Current transfers received 94.0; Current transfers paid –27.7; *Current balance* –125.8; Capital account (net) 3.8; Direct investment abroad –1.3; Direct investment from abroad 17.4; Portfolio investment assets –18.6; Portfolio investment liabilities 44.9; Other investment assets –93.1; Other investment liabilities 170.2; Net errors and omissions –38.9; *Overall balance* –36.3. Source: IMF, *International Financial Statistics.*

EXTERNAL TRADE

Principal Commodities (US $ million, 1998): *Imports c.i.f.:* Food and live animals 137.3 (Cereals and cereal preparations 29.8, Vegetables and fruit 27.8); Beverages and tobacco 21.8; Crude materials (inedible) except fuels 38.3 (Cork and wood 24.2); Mineral fuels, lubricants, etc. 81.7 (Refined petroleum products 76.4); Chemicals and related products 104.5 (Medicinal and pharmaceutical products 29.8); Basic manufactures 171.8 (Paper, paperboard and manufactures 29.8, Textile yarn, fabrics, etc. 22.7, Non-metallic mineral manufactures 25.7, Iron and steel 22.3); Machinery and transport equipment 305.5 (Machinery specialized for particular industries 26.7, General industrial machinery and equipment 44.4, Office machines and automatic data-processing equipment 33.2, Telecommunications and sound equipment 31.4, Other electrical machinery, apparatus, etc. 54.8, Road vehicles and parts 101.5); Miscellaneous manufactured articles 152.6; Total (incl. others) 1,022.1. *Exports f.o.b.:* Food and live animals 61.2 (Cereals and cereal preparations 8.8, Raw sugar 27.6, Margarine and shortening 5.4); Beverages and tobacco 17.3 (Alcoholic beverages 15.2); Mineral fuels, lubricants, etc. 40.5 (Petroleum, petroleum products, etc. 40.5); Chemicals and related products 34.9 (Medicinal and pharmaceutical products 11.0, Essential oils, perfume materials and cleansing preparations 7.1, Disinfectants, insecticides, fungicides, etc. 10.4); Basic manufactures 40.1 (Paper, paperboards and manufactures 11.9, Non-metallic mineral manufactures 10.2, Metal containers for storage and transport 5.2); Machinery and transport equipment 34.0 (Electrical machinery, apparatus, etc. 24.5); Miscellaneous manufactured articles 27.9 (Unused stamps, banknotes, share certificates, etc. 6.7); Total (incl. others) 258.7. Source: UN, *International Trade Statistics Yearbook.*

Principal Trading Partners (US $ million, preliminary, 1999): *Imports:* Canada 46.2; Jamaica 11.4; Trinidad and Tobago 123.9; United Kingdom 89.3; USA 442.6; Total (incl. others) 1,067.9. *Exports:* Antigua and Barbuda 6.2; Canada 6.8; Dominica 4.6; Grenada 5.9; Guyana 5.9; Jamaica 16.8; Saint Lucia 11.0; Saint Vincent and the Grenadines 7.8; Trinidad and Tobago 27.7; United Kingdom 36.0; USA 42.5; Total (incl. others) 250.4. Source: IMF, *Barbados: Statistical Appendix* (December 2000).

TRANSPORT

Road Traffic (motor vehicles in use, 1999): Private cars 60,826; Buses and coaches 1,262; Lorries and vans 8,316; Motorcycles and mopeds 1,410; Road tractors 748.

Shipping (estimated freight traffic, '000 metric tons, 1990): Goods loaded 206; Goods unloaded 538. Source: UN, *Monthly Bulletin of Statistics. Total goods handled* ('000 metric tons, 1997): 1,095. Source: Barbados Port Authority. *Merchant Fleet* (vessels registered at 31 December 2000): Number of vessels 79; Total displacement 733,319 grt. Source: Lloyd's Register of Shipping, *World Fleet Statistics.*

Civil Aviation (1994): Aircraft movements 36,100; Freight loaded 5,052.3 metric tons; Freight unloaded 8,548.3 metric tons.

TOURISM

Tourist Arrivals: *Stop-overs:* 512,397 in 1998; 517,869 in 1999; 545,027 in 2000. *Cruise-ship passengers:* 506,610 in 1998; 445,821 in 1999; 533,278 in 2000.

Tourist arrivals by country ('000 persons, 1998): Canada 60.0; Germany 12.1; Trinidad and Tobago 19.3; United Kingdom 186.7; USA 106.3; Total (incl. others) 512.4. Source: Ministry of Labour, Sports and Public Sector Reform.

Tourism Receipts (US $ million): 663.4 in 1997; 711.9 in 1998; 681.1 (provisional) in 1999. Source: IMF, *Barbados: Statistical Appendix* (December 2000).

COMMUNICATIONS MEDIA

Radio Receivers (1997): 237,000 in use.

Television Receivers (1997): 76,000 in use.

Telephones (year ending 31 March 1997): 108,000 in use.

Telefax Stations (year ending 31 March 1997): 1,800 in use.

Mobile Cellular Telephones (year ending 31 March 1997): 8,013 subscribers.

Book Production (1983): 87 titles (18 books, 69 pamphlets).

Newspapers: *Daily* (1996): 2 (circulation 53,000). *Non-daily* (1990): 4 (estimated circulation 95,000).

Sources: partly UNESCO, *Statistical Yearbook*, and UN, *Statistical Yearbook.*

EDUCATION

Pre-primary (1995/96): 84 schools; 529 teachers; 4,689 pupils.
Primary (1995/96): 79 schools; 944 teachers; 18,513 pupils.
Secondary (1995/96): 21 schools; 1,263 teachers; 21,455 pupils.
Tertiary (1995/96): 4 schools; 544 teachers (1984); 6,622 students.

Directory

The Constitution

The parliamentary system has been established since the 17th century, when the first Assembly sat, in 1639, and the Charter of Barbados was granted, in 1652. A new Constitution came into force on 30 November 1966, when Barbados became independent. Under its terms, protection is afforded to individuals from slavery and forced labour, from inhuman treatment, deprivation of property, arbitrary search and entry, and racial discrimination; freedom of conscience, of expression, assembly, and movement are guaranteed.

Executive power is nominally vested in the British monarch, as Head of State, represented in Barbados by a Governor-General, who appoints the Prime Minister and, on the advice of the Prime Minister, appoints other ministers and some senators.

The Cabinet consists of the Prime Minister, appointed by the Governor-General as being the person best able to command a majority in the House of Assembly, and not fewer than five other ministers. Provision is also made for a Privy Council, presided over by the Governor-General.

Parliament consists of the Governor-General and a bicameral legislature, comprising the Senate and the House of Assembly. The Senate has 21 members: 12 appointed by the Governor-General on the advice of the Prime Minister, two on the advice of the Leader of the Opposition and seven as representatives of such interests as the Governor-General considers appropriate. The House of Assembly has (since January 1991) 28 members, elected by universal adult suffrage for a term of five years (subject to dissolution). The minimum voting age is 18 years.

The Constitution also provides for the establishment of Service Commissions for the Judicial and Legal Service, the Public Service, the Police Service and the Statutory Boards Service. These Commissions are exempt from legal investigation; they have executive powers relating to appointments, dismissals and disciplinary control of the services for which they are responsible.

The Government

Head of State: HM Queen ELIZABETH II (succeeded to the throne 6 February 1952).

Governor-General: Sir CLIFFORD HUSBANDS (appointed 1 June 1996).

THE CABINET
(August 2001)

Prime Minister and Minister of Finance and Economic Affairs, of Defence and Security and for the Civil Service: OWEN S. ARTHUR.

Deputy Prime Minister and Minister of Foreign Affairs and Foreign Trade: BILLIE A. MILLER.

Attorney-General and Minister of Home Affairs: DAVID A. C. SIMMONS.

Minister of Education, Youth Affairs and Culture: MIA A. MOTTLEY.

Minister of Health: Sen. PHILLIP GODDARD.

Minister of the Environment, Energy and Natural Resources: RAWLE C. EASTMOND.

Minister of Agriculture and Rural Development: ANTHONY P. WOOD.

Minister of Social Transformation: HAMILTON F. LASHLEY.

Minister of Tourism and of International Transport: NOEL A. LYNCH.

Minister of Housing and Lands: GLINE A. CLARKE.

Minister of Commerce, Consumer Affairs and Business Development: RONALD TOPPIN.

Minister of Industry and International Business: REGINALD R. FARLEY.

Minister of Labour, Sports and Public-Sector Reform: RUDOLPH N. GREENIDGE.

Minister of Public Works and Transport: ROMMEL MARSHALL.

Minister of State in the Office of the Prime Minister and the Ministry for the Civil Service (with responsibility for Information): GLYNE S. H. MURRAY.

MINISTRIES

Office of the Prime Minister: Government Headquarters, Bay St, St Michael; tel. 436-6435; fax 436-9280; e-mail info@primeminister.gov.bb; internet www.primeminister.gov.bb.

Ministry of Agriculture and Rural Development: Graeme Hall, POB 505, Christ Church; tel. 428-4150; fax 420-8444; internet www.barbados.gov.bb/minagri.

Ministry for the Civil Service: Roebuck Plaza, 20–23 Roebuck St, Bridgetown; tel. 426-2390; fax 228-0093.

Ministry of Commerce, Consumer Affairs and Business Development: Government Headquarters, Bay St, St Michael; tel. 427-5270.

Ministry of Defence and Security: Government Headquarters, Bay St, St Michael; tel. 436-1970.

Ministry of Education, Youth Affairs and Culture: Elsie Payne Complex, Constitution Rd, Bridgetown; tel. 430-2700; fax 436-2411.

Minister of the Environment, Energy and Natural Resources: Frank Walcott Bldg, Culloden Rd, St Michael; tel. 431-7692.

Ministry of Finance and Economic Affairs: Government Headquarters, Bay St, St Michael; tel. 436-6435; fax 429-4032.

Ministry of Foreign Affairs and Foreign Trade: 1 Culloden Rd, St Michael; tel. 436-2990; fax 429-6652; e-mail barbados@foreign.gov.bb; internet www.foreign.barbadosgov.org.

Ministry of Health: Jemmott's Lane, St Michael; tel. 426-5080; fax 426-5570.

Ministry of Home Affairs: General Post Office Bldg, Level 5, Cheapside, Bridgetown; tel. 228-8961; fax 437-3794; e-mail mha@caribsurf.com.

Ministry of Housing and Lands: Culloden Rd, St Michael; tel. 431-7600; fax 435-0174; e-mail psmhl@caribsurf.com.

Ministry of Industry and International Business: The Business Centre, Upton, St Michael; tel. 430-2200; fax 429-6849; e-mail mtbbar@caribsurf.com.

Ministry of International Transport: Port Authority Bldg, University Row, Bridgetown; tel. 426-9144; fax 429-3809.

Ministry of Labour, Sports and Public-Sector Reform: National Insurance Bldg, 5th Floor, Fairchild St, Bridgetown; tel. 436-6320; fax 426-8959; internet www.labour.gov.bb.

Ministry of Public Works and Transport: The Pine, St Michael; tel. 429-2191; fax 437-8133; internet www.publicworks.gov.bb.

Ministry of Social Transformation: Nicholas House, Broad St, Bridgetown; tel. 228-5878.

Ministry of Tourism: Sherbourne Conference Centre, Two Mile Hill, St Michael; tel. 430-7500; fax 436-4828.

Office of the Attorney-General: Sir Frank Walcott Bldg, Culloden Rd, St Michael; tel. 431-7707; fax 435-9533; e-mail attygen@caribsurf.com.bb.

Legislature

PARLIAMENT
Senate
President: FRED GOLLOP.

There are 21 members.

House of Assembly
Speaker: ISHMAEL ROETT.

Clerk of Parliament: GEORGE BRANCKER.

General Election, 20 January 1999

Party	Votes	%	Seats
Barbados Labour Party (BLP)	83,085	64.85	26
Democratic Labour Party (DLP)	44,974	35.10	2
Others	64	0.05	—
Total	128,123	100.00	28

Political Organizations

Barbados Labour Party: Grantley Adams House, 111 Roebuck St, Bridgetown; tel. 429-1990; e-mail hq@blp.org.bb; internet www.blp.org.bb; f. 1938; moderate social democrat; Leader OWEN ARTHUR; Chair. REGINALD FARLEY; Gen. Sec. MIA A. MOTTLEY.

Democratic Labour Party: George St, Belleville, St Michael; tel. 429-3104; fax 429-3007; e-mail dlp@dlpbarbados.bb; internet www.dlpbarbados.org; f. 1955; Leader DAVID THOMPSON.

National Democratic Party: 'Sueños', 3 Sixth Ave, Belleville; tel. 429-6882; f. 1989 by split from Democratic Labour Party; Leader Dr RICHARD (RICHIE) HAYNES.

Diplomatic Representation

EMBASSIES AND HIGH COMMISSIONS IN BARBADOS

Australia: Bishops Court Hill, Pine Rd, St Michael; tel. 435-2834; High Commissioner: P. M. SMITH.

Brazil: Sunjet House, 3rd Floor, Fairchild St, Bridgetown; tel. 427-1735; fax 427-1744; Ambassador: CARLOS ALFREDO PINTO DA SILVA.

Canada: Bishops Court Hill, Pine Rd, POB 404, St Michael; tel. 429-3550; fax 429-3780; High Commissioner: DUANE VAN BESELAERE.

China, People's Republic: 17 Golf View Terrace, Rockley, Christ Church; tel. 435-6890; fax 435-8300; Ambassador: ZHAN DAODE.

Colombia: 'Rosemary', Dayrells Rd, Rockley, POB 37W, Christ Church; tel. 429-6821; fax 429-6830; e-mail colombiaembassy@sunbeach.net; Ambassador: JOSÉ JOAQUÍN GORI.

Costa Rica: Trident House, 2nd Floor, Broad St, Bridgetown; tel. 431-0250; fax 431-0261; e-mail embcr@sunbeach.net; Ambassador: SOL VILLAMICHEL MORALES.

Cuba: Cuba Erin Court, Collymore Rock, St Michael; tel. 435-2769; Ambassador: JOSÉ DE J. CONEJO.

Guatemala: Bridgetown; tel. 435-3542; fax 435-2638; Ambassador: JULIO ROBERTO PALOMO.

United Kingdom: Lower Collymore Rock, POB 676, St Michael; tel. 430-7800; fax 430-7826; e-mail britishhc@sunbeach.net; internet www.britishhc.org; High Commissioner: GORDON M. BAKER.

USA: Canadian Imperial Bank of Commerce Bldg, Broad St, POB 302, Bridgetown; tel. 436-4950; fax 429-5246; Ambassador: JAMES A. DALEY.

Venezuela: Hastings, Main Rd, Christ Church; tel. 435-7619; fax 435-7830; e-mail embaven@sunbeach.net; Ambassador: ANGEL BRITO VILLARROEL.

Judicial System

Justice is administered by the Supreme Court of Judicature, which consists of a High Court and a Court of Appeal. Final appeal lies with the Judicial Committee of the Privy Council, in the United Kingdom. There are Magistrates' Courts for lesser offences, with appeal to the Court of Appeal.

Supreme Court: Judiciary Office, Coleridge St, Bridgetown; tel. 426-3461; fax 246-2405.

Chief Justice: Sir DENYS WILLIAMS.

Justices of Appeal: G. C. R. MOE, ERROL DA COSTA CHASE, COLIN A. WILLIAMS.

Judges of the High Court: FREDERICK A. WATERMAN, MARIE A. MACCORMACK, E. GARVEY HUSBANDS, CARLISLE PAYNE, SHERMAN MOORE, LIONEL DACOSTA GREENIDGE.

Registrar of the Supreme Court: SANDRA MASON.

Office of the Attorney-General: Sir Frank Walcott Bldg, Culloden Rd, St Michael; tel. 431-7707; fax 435-9533; e-mail attygen@caribsurf.com.bb; Dir of Public Prosecutions CHARLES LEACOCK; e-mail cbleacock@inaccs.com.bb.

Religion

More than 100 religious denominations and sects are represented in Barbados, but the vast majority of the population profess Christianity. According to the 1980 census, there were 96,894 Anglicans (or some 40% of the total population), while the Pentecostal (8%) and Methodist (7%) churches were next in importance. The regional Caribbean Conference of Churches is based in Barbados. There are also small groups of Hindus, Muslims and Jews.

Caribbean Conference of Churches: POB 616, Bridgetown; tel. 427-2681; fax 429-2075; e-mail cccbdos@cariaccess.com; internet www.cariblife.com/pub/ccc.

CHRISTIANITY
The Anglican Communion

Anglicans in Barbados are adherents of the Church in the Province of the West Indies, comprising eight dioceses. The Archbishop of the Province is the Bishop of the Bahamas and the Turks and Caicos Islands, resident in Nassau, the Bahamas. In Barbados there is a Provincial Office (St George's Church, St George) and an Anglican Theological College (Codrington College, St John).

Bishop of Barbados: Rt Rev. Dr JOHN DUNLOP HOLDER, Diocesan Office, Mandeville House, Bridgetown; tel. 426-2761; fax 427-5867.

Barbados Christian Council: Caribbean Conference of Churches Bldg, George St and Collymore Rock, St Michael; tel. 426-6014.

The Roman Catholic Church

Barbados comprises a single diocese (formed in January 1990, when the diocese of Bridgetown-Kingstown was divided), which is suffragan to the archdiocese of Port of Spain (Trinidad and Tobago). At 31 December 1999 there were an estimated 10,000 adherents in the diocese. The Bishop participates in the Antilles Episcopal Conference (currently based in Port of Spain, Trinidad and Tobago).

Bishop of Bridgetown: Rt Rev. MALCOLM GALT, St Patrick's Presbytery, Jemmott's Lane, POB 1223, Bridgetown; tel. 426-3510; fax 429-6198.

Protestant Churches

Baptist Churches of Barbados: National Baptist Convention, President Kennedy Dr., Bridgetown; tel. 429-2697.

Church of God (Caribbean Atlantic Assembly): St Michael's Plaza, St Michael's Row, POB 1, Bridgetown; tel. 427-5770; Pres. Rev. VICTOR BABB.

Church of Jesus Christ of Latter-day Saints (Mormons)— West Indies Mission: Bridgetown; tel. 435-8595; fax 435-8278.

Church of the Nazarene: District Office, Eagle Hall, Bridgetown; tel. 425-1067.

Methodist Church: Bethel Church Office, Bay St, Bridgetown; tel. 426-2223.

Moravian Church: Roebuck St, Bridgetown; tel. 426-2337; Superintendent Rev. ERROL CONNOR.

Seventh-day Adventists (East Caribbean Conference): Brydens Ave, Brittons Hill, POB 223, St Michael; tel. 429-7234; fax 429-8055.

Wesleyan Holiness Church: General Headquarters, Bank Hall; tel. 429-4864.

Other denominations include the Abundant Life Assembly, the African Orthodox Church, the Apostolic Church, the Assemblies of Brethren, the Berean Bible Brethren, the Bethel Evangelical Church, Christ is the Answer Family Church, the Church of God the Prophecy, the Ethiopian Orthodox Church, the Full Gospel Assembly, Love Gospel Assembly, the New Testament Church of God, the Pentecostal Assemblies of the West Indies, the People's Cathedral, the Salvation Army, Presbyterian congregations, the African Methodist Episcopal Church, the Mt Olive United Holy Church of America and Jehovah's Witnesses.

ISLAM

In 1996 there were an estimated 2,000 Muslims in Barbados.

Islamic Teaching Centre: Harts Gap, Hastings; tel. 427-0120.

JUDAISM

Jewish Community: Nidhe Israel and Shaara Tzedek Synagogue, Rockley New Rd, POB 651, Bridgetown; tel. 437-1290; fax 437-1303; there were 60 Jews in Barbados in 1997; Pres. RACHELLE ALTMAN; Sec. SHARON ORAN.

Caribbean Jewish Congress: POB 1331, Bridgetown; tel. 436-8163; fax 437-4992; e-mail waw@sunbeach.net; f. 1994; aims to foster closer relations between Jewish communities in the region and to promote greater understanding of the Jewish faith; Dir-Gen. W. A. WINSTON BEN ZEBEDEE.

HINDUISM

Hindu Community: Hindu Temple, Roberts Complex. Government Hill, St Michael; tel. 434-4638; there were 411 Hindus at the census of 1980.

The Press

Barbados Advocate: POB 230, St Michael; tel. 434-2000; fax 434-2020; e-mail advocate@sunbeach.net; f. 1895; daily; Pres. and CEO HUMPHREY METZGEN; Editor REUDON EVERSLEY; circ. 11,413.

The Beacon: 111 Roebuck St, Bridgetown; organ of the Barbados Labour Party; weekly; circ. 15,000.

The Broad Street Journal: Letchworth Complex, Garrison, St Michael; tel. 437-8770; fax 437-8772; e-mail bsj@sunbeach.net; internet www.broadstreetjournal.com; f. 1993; weekly; business; Editor PATRICK HOYOS.

Caribbean Week: Lefferts Place, River Rd, St Michael; tel. 436-1906; fax 436-1904; e-mail cweek@sunbeach.net; internet www.cweek.com; f. 1989; fortnightly; Editor-in-Chief JOHN E. LOVELL; Publr TIMOTHY C. FORSYTH; circ. 56,200.

The Nation: Nation House, Fontabelle, St Michael; tel. 430-5400; fax 427-6968; e-mail nationnews@sunbeach.net; internet www.nationnews.com; f. 1973; daily; Pres. and Editor-in-Chief HAROLD HOYTE; circ. 23,144 (weekday), 33,084 (weekend).

Official Gazette: Government Printing Office, Bay St, St Michael; tel. 436-6776; Mon. and Thur.

Sunday Advocate: POB 230, St Michael; tel. 434-2000; fax 434-2020; e-mail advocate@sunbeach.net; f. 1895; CEO HUMPHREY METZGEN; Editor REUDON EVERSLEY; circ. 17,490.

The Sunday Sun: Fontabelle, St Michael; tel. 436-6240; fax 427-6968; e-mail subs@sunbeach.net; f. 1977; Dir HAROLD HOYTE; circ. 42,286.

Weekend Investigator: POB 230, St Michael; tel. 434-2000; circ. 14,305.

NEWS AGENCIES

Caribbean News Agency (CANA): Culloden View, Beckles Rd, St Michael; tel. 429-2903; fax 429-4355; f. 1976; internet www.cananews.com; public and private shareholders from English-speaking Caribbean; Chair. COLIN D. MURRAY; Gen. Man. TREVOR SIMPSON.

Foreign Bureaux

Inter Press Service (IPS) (Italy): POB 697, Bridgetown; tel. 426-4474; Correspondent MARVA COSSY.

United Press International (UPI) (USA): Bridgetown; tel. 436-0465; internet www.upi.com; Correspondent RICKEY SINGH.

Xinhua (New China) News Agency (People's Republic of China): Christ Church; Chief Correspondent DING BAOZHONG.

Agence France-Presse (AFP) is also represented.

Publishers

The Advocate Publishing Co Ltd: POB 230, St Michael; tel. 434-2000; fax 434-2020.

Business Tutors: POB 800E St Michael; tel. 428-5664; fax 429-4854; e-mail pchad@caribsurf.com; business, management, computers.

Carib Research and Publications Inc: POB 556, Bridgetown; tel. 438-0580; f. 1986; regional interests; CEO Dr FARLEY BRAITHWAITE.

Nation Publishing Co Ltd: Nation House, Fontabelle, St Michael; tel. 436-6240; fax 427-6968.

Broadcasting and Communications

TELECOMMUNICATIONS

Cable & Wireless BET Ltd: POB 32, Wildey, St Michael; tel. 292-6000; fax 427-5808; e-mail bdsinfo@caribsurf.com; internet www.candwbet.com.bb; fmrly Barbados External Telecommunications Ltd; provides international telecommunications services; owned by Cable & Wireless PLC (United Kingdom).

Barbados Telephone Co Ltd (Bartel): The Windsor Lodge, Government Hill, St Michael; tel. 429-5050; fax 436-5036; provides domestic telecommunications services; subsidiary of Cable & Wireless BET Ltd, reported to have merged with parent co in March 2001.

BROADCASTING

Regulatory Authority

Caribbean Broadcasting Corporation (CBC): The Pine, POB 900, Bridgetown; tel. 429-2041; fax 429-4795; f. 1963; Chair. F. BREWSTER.

Radio

Barbados Broadcasting Service Ltd: Astoria St George, Bridgetown; tel. 437-9550; fax 437-9554; f. 1981; FM station.

Faith 102 FM; religious broadcasting.

Barbados Rediffusion Service Ltd: River Rd, Bridgetown; tel. 430-7300; fax 429-8093; f. 1935; public company; Gen. Man. VIC FERNANDES.

HOTT FM, at River Rd, Bridgetown (f. 1998), is a commercial station.

Voice of Barbados, at River Rd, Bridgetown (f. 1981), is a commercial station covering Barbados and the eastern Caribbean.

YESS Ten-Four FM, at River Rd, Bridgetown (f. 1988), is a commercial station.

CBC Radio: POB 900, Bridgetown; tel. 429-2041; fax 429-4795; e-mail CBC.@.CaribNet.Net; f. 1963; commercial; Programme Man. W. CALLENDER.

CBC Radio 900, f. 1963, broadcasts 21 hours daily.

Radio Liberty FM, f. 1984, broadcasts 24 hours daily.

Television

CBC TV: POB 900, Bridgetown; tel. 429-2041; fax 429-4795; f. 1964; Channel Eight is the main national service, broadcasting 24 hours daily; a maximum of 30 subscription channels are available through Multi Choice; Gen. Man. MELBA SMITH; Programme Man. HILDA COX.

Finance

In December 1999 there were 3,399 international business companies, 2,867 foreign sales corporations, 47 offshore banks licensees and 401 captive insurance and insurance-management companies registered in Barbados.

BANKING

(cap. = capital; auth. = authorized; dep. = deposits;res = reserves; brs = branches; m. = million;amounts in Barbados dollars)

Central Bank

Central Bank of Barbados: Tom Adams Financial Centre, POB 1016, Spry St, Bridgetown; tel. 436-6870; fax 427-9559; e-mail cbb.libr@centralbank.com; internet www.centralbank.org.bb; f. 1972; bank of issue; cap. 2.0m., res 10.0m., dep. 250.9m. (Dec. 1998); Gov. MARION WILLIAMS; Deputy Gov. CARLOS HOLDER.

Commercial Banks

Caribbean Commercial Bank Ltd: Lower Broad St, POB 1007c, Bridgetown; tel. 431-2500; fax 431-2530; f. 1984; cap. 25.0m., res 3.8m., dep. 146.9m. (Dec. 1998); Pres. and CEO MARIANO R. BROWNE; 4 brs.

CIBC West Indies Holdings: CIBC Centre, POB 405, Warren, St Michael; tel. 367-2500; fax 424-8923; internet www.westindies.cibc.com; operates banking network throughout Caribbean; parent co of CIBC Caribbean Ltd; Chair. JOHN HUNKIN; 9 brs.

Mutual Bank of the Caribbean Inc.: Trident House, Lower Broad St c, Bridgetown; tel. 436-8335; fax 429-5734; 4 brs.

Regional Development Bank

Caribbean Development Bank: Wildey, POB 408, St Michael; tel. 431-1600; fax 426-7269; e-mail info@caribank.org; internet www.caribank.org; f. 1970; cap. 152.1m., res 6.3m. (Dec. 1999); Pres. Sir NEVILLE V. NICHOLLS.

National Bank

Barbados National Bank (BNB): 2 Broad St, POB 1002, Bridgetown; tel. 431-5739; fax 426-5037; f. 1978 by merger; cap 47.5m., res 26.0m., dep. 595.4m., total assets 747.2m. (Dec. 1998); scheduled for privatization in 2001; Chair. GRENVILLE PHILLIPS; CEO and Man. Dir LOUIS GREENIDGE; 6 brs.

Foreign Banks

Bank of Nova Scotia (Canada): Broad St, POB 202, Bridgetown; tel. 431-3000; fax 228-8574; Man. PETER F. VAN SCHIE; 6 brs.

Barclays Bank PLC (United Kingdom): Broad Street, POB 301, Bridgetown; tel. 431-5262; fax 429-4785; f. 1837; 4 brs.

Royal Bank of Canada: Trident House, Broad St, POB 68, Bridgetown; tel. 431-6700; fax 431-4271; e-mail roycorp@caribsurf.com; f. 1911; 1 br.

Victoria Bank (Canada): f. 1873; openedApril 2001.

Trust Companies

Bank of Nova Scotia Trust Co (Caribbean) Ltd: Bank of Nova Scotia Bldg, Broad St, POB 1003b, Bridgetown; tel. 431-3120; fax 426-0969.

Barbados International Bank and Trust Co: The Financial Services Centre, Bishop's Court Hill, POB 111, St Michael; tel. 436-7000; fax 436-7057.

Barclays Bank PLC Trustee Branch: Broad St, Bridgetown; tel. 431-5296.

CIBC Trust and Merchant Bank (Barbados) Ltd: CIBC Centre, POB 405, Warren, St Michael; tel. 367-2324; fax 421-7178.

Clico Mortgage & Finance Corporation: C L Duprey Financial Centre, Walrond St, Bridgetown; tel. 431-4719; fax 426-6168; e-mail cmfc@sunbeach.net.

Ernst & Young Trust Corporation: Bush Hill, Garrison, St Michael; tel. 430-3900.

Royal Bank of Canada Financial Corporation: Bldg 2, Chelston Park, Collymore Rock, St Michael; tel. 431-6580; fax 429-3800; e-mail roycorp@caribsurf.com; Man. N. L. SMITH.

St Michael Trust: The Financial Services Centre, Bishop's Court Hill, St Michael; tel. 436-7000; fax 436-7057; e-mail bb@fiscglobal.com; internet www.fiscglobal.com; f. 1987.

STOCK EXCHANGE

Securities Exchange of Barbados (SEB): Tom Adams Financial Centre, 5th Floor, Church Village, Bridgetown; tel. 436-9871; fax 429-8942; e-mail sebd@caribsurf.com; f. 1987; in 1989 the Govts of Barbados, Trinidad and Tobago and Jamaica agreed to link exchanges; cross-trading began in April 1991; Chair. NEVILLE LEROY SMITH; Gen. Man. VIRGINIA MAPP.

INSURANCE

The leading British and a number of US and Canadian companies have agents in Barbados. At the end of 1995 230 captive insurance companies were registered in the country. Local insurance companies include the following:

Barbados Fire & Commercial Insurance Co: Beckwith Place, Broad St, POB 150, Bridgetown; tel. 431-2800; fax 426-0752; e-mail bf&c@caribsurf.com; f. 1996, following merger of Barbados Commercial Insurance Co. Ltd and Barbados Fire and General Insurance Co (f. 1880).

Barbados Mutual Life Assurance Society: Collymore Rock, St Michael; tel. 431-7000; fax 436-8829; f. 1840; Chair. COLIN G. GODDARD; Pres. J. ARTHUR L. BETHELL.

Insurance Corporation of Barbados: Roebuck St, Bridgetown; tel. 427-5590; fax 426-3393; f. 1978; cap. Bds $3m.; Man. Dir WISMAR GREAVES; Gen. Man. MONICA SKINNER.

Life of Barbados Ltd: Wildey, POB 69, St Michael; tel. 426-1060; fax 436-8835; f. 1971; Pres. and CEO STEPHEN ALLEYNE.

United Insurance Co Ltd: United Insurance Centre, Lower Broad St, POB 1215, Bridgetown; tel. 430-1900; fax 436-7573; e-mail united@caribsurf.com; f. 1976; Man. Dir DAVE A. BLACKMAN.

Insurance Association

Insurance Association of the Caribbean: IAC Bldg, St Michael; Collymore Rock, St Michael; tel. 427-5608; fax 427-7277; regional asscn.

Trade and Industry

GOVERNMENT AGENCY

Barbados Agricultural Management Co Ltd: Warrens, POB 719c, St Michael; tel. 425-0010; fax 425-0007; e-mail bamc@cariaccess.com; Chair. R. CARL SYLVESTER; Gen. Man. E. LeROY ROACH.

DEVELOPMENT ORGANIZATIONS

Barbados Agriculture Development and Marketing Corpn: Fairy Valley, Christ Church; tel. 428-0250; fax 428-0152; f. 1993 by merger; programme of diversification and land reforms; Chair. TYRONE POWER; CEO E. LeROY ROACH.

Barbados Investment and Development Corpn: Pelican House, Princess Alice Highway, Bridgetown; tel. 427-5350; fax 426-7802; e-mail bidc@bidc.org; internet www.bidc.com; f. 1992 by merger; facilitates the devt of the industrial sector, especially in the areas of manufacturing, information technology and financial services; offers free consultancy to investors; provides factory space for lease or rent; administers the Fiscal Incentives Legislation; Chair. TREVOR CLARKE; CEO ERROL HUMPHREY.

Department for International Development in the Caribbean: Collymore Rock, POB 167, St Michael; tel. 436-9873; fax 426-2194; Head BRIAN THOMSON.

CHAMBER OF COMMERCE

Barbados Chamber of Commerce and Industry: Nemwil House, 1st Floor, Lower Collymore Rock, POB 189, St Michael; tel. 426-2056; fax 429-2907; e-mail bdscham@caribsurf.com; internet www.bdscham.com; f. 1825; 176 mem. firms, 276 reps; Pres. HALLAM EDWARDS; Exec. Dir ROLPH JORDAN.

INDUSTRIAL AND TRADE ASSOCIATIONS

Barbados Agricultural Society: The Grotto, Beckles Rd, St Michael; tel. 436-6683; fax 435-0651; e-mail heshimu@sunbeach.net; Pres. TYRONE POWER.

Barbados Association of Medical Practitioners: BAMP Complex, Spring Garden, St Michael; tel. 429-7569; fax 435-2328; e-mail bamp@infinetworx.com; Pres. JEROME WALCOTT.

Barbados Association of Professional Engineers: POB 666, Bridgetown; tel. 425-6105; fax 425-6673; f. 1964; Pres. GLYNE BARKER; Sec. PATRICK CLARKE.

Barbados Hotel and Tourism Association: Fourth Ave, Belleville, St Michael; tel. 426-5041; fax 429-2845; e-mail bhta@maccs.com.bb; internet www.funbarbados.com/bhta; Pres. ALAN BANFIELD; Exec. Vice-Pres. SUSAN SPRINGER.

Barbados Manufacturers' Association: Bldg 1, Pelican Industrial Park, St Michael; tel. 426-4474; fax 436-5182; e-mail bmexproducts@sunbeach.net; internet www.bma.org.bb; f. 1964; Pres. DERECK FOSTER; Exec. Dir CLIFTON E. MAYNARD; 100 mem. firms.

West Indian Sea Island Cotton Association (Inc): c/o Barbados Agricultural Development and Marketing Corpn, Fairy Valley, Christ Church; tel. 428-0250; Pres. E. LeRoy Roach; Sec. Michael I. Edghill; 11 mem. asscns.

EMPLOYERS' ORGANIZATION

Barbados Employers' Confederation: Nemwil House, 1st Floor, Collymore Rock, St Michael; tel. 426-1574; fax 429-2907; e-mail bcon@sunbeach.net; internet www.barbadosemployers.com; f. 1956; Pres. Harcourt Sandiford; 235 mems (incl. associate mems).

MAJOR COMPANIES
Construction and Cement

Arawak Cement Co Ltd: Checker Hall, St Lucy; tel. 439-9880; fax 439-7976; f. 1981; manufacture and marketing of cement; state-owned; Chair. Lawrence Nurse; Gen. Man. Trevor King; 76 employees.

C. O. Williams Construction Ltd: Lears, St Michael; tel. 436-3910.

Edghill Associates Ltd: Websters Industrial Park, Wildey, St Michael; heavy construction; Dir Richard Edghill; 300 employees.

Manning, Wilkinson and Challoner Ltd: The Pierhead, POB 176, Bridgetown; tel. 426-2731; fax 426-5510; f. 1969; trade in building materials, furniture and hardware products; Man. Dir Wayne Kirton; 276 employees.

Food and Beverages

A. S. Bryden and Sons (Barbados) Ltd: Barbados Hill, St Michael; tel. 431-2600; fax 426-0755; f. 1898; manufacturing of oils and fats; retail, import and export business; insurance agency; Chair. and Man. Dir John G. Bellamy; 350 employees.

Banks Barbados Breweries Ltd: Wildey, St Michael; tel. 429-2113; brewery.

Barbados Agricultural Management Co Ltd: POB 719, Bridgetown, St Michael; tel. 425-2211; fax 425-3505; f. 1993; growing and processing of sugar cane; Chair. David Seale; Exec. Chair. Attlee Brathwaite; 2,500 employees; CEO Leroy Roach.

Barbados Bottling Co Ltd: POB 226, Bridgetown; tel. 420-8881; fax 428-4095; manufacturer of soft drinks; f. 1944; Chair. Alan Field; Man. Dir Richard Scozier; 113 employees.

Barbados Dairy Industries Ltd: Pine Hill Dairy, POB 56B, Bridgetown; tel. 430-4100; fax 429-3514; e-mail mp108@sunbeach.net; f. 1966; manufacturer of dairy and related products; Chair. Allan Fields; Pres. Carl Sylvester; Gen. Man. Stephen Goodridge; 200 employees.

Barbados Mills Ltd: Spring Garden Highway, POB 260, St Michael; tel. 427-8880; fax 427-8886; f. 1977; manufacturer of flour and other grain-derived products; Gen. Man. Carlos Belgrave; 93 employees.

BICO Ltd: Harbour Industrial Park, Bridgetown; tel. 430-2100; fax 426-2198; e-mail bicoltd@sunbeach.net; f. 1901; manufacturer of desserts and ice cream; sales Bds $13.4m. (1996); Chair. Sir John Goddard; Man. Dir C. A. St John; 123 employees.

Hanschell and Inniss Ltd: POB 143, Bridgetown; tel. 426-2415; fax 427-6938; manufacture and distribution of food and soft drinks; Chair. Patrick Mayers; 145 employees.

Mount Gay Distilleries Ltd: POB 208, Brandon's Gap, Deaco's Rd, POB 208, Bridgetown; tel. 425-9897; fax 425-8770; f. 1955; subsidiary of McKesson Corpn, USA; rum distilling; Man. Dir Patrick Dussossoy Marshall; 104 employees.

R. L. Seale and Co Ltd: Clarence House, Tudor Bridge, POB 864, St Michael; tel. 426-0334; fax 436-6003; e-mail rseale@caribsurf.com; f. 1926; manufacture and distribution of rum, sale of food; Chair and Man. Dir David Seale; 245 employees.

Miscellaneous

Barbados Shipping and Trading Co Ltd: Musson Bldg, Hincks St, POB 1227c, Bridgetown; tel. 426-3844; fax 427-4719; e-mail richard_marshall@bsandtco.com; f. 1920; Chair. C. D. Bynoe; Man. Dir A. C. Fields.

Booth Steamship Company (Barbados) Ltd: Cockspur House, 1st Floor, Nile St, POB 263, Bridgetown; tel. 427-5131; fax 426-0484.

BRC West Indies Ltd: Cane Garden, St Thomas; tel. 425-0687; fax 425-2941; e-mail brc@ribsurf.com; internet www.construction-caribbean.com; f. 1979; manufacturer of wire mesh and steel products; sales Bds $20m. (1996); Chair. R. S. Williams; Man. Dir Peter Gooding; 42 employees.

Collins Ltd: Warrens Industrial Park, POB 203, Bridgetown, St Michael; tel. 425-4550; fax 424-9182; e-mail colcar@caribsurf.com; distributor of pharmaceuticals, hospital supplies, toiletries, confec-

tionery, canned and snack foods throughout the Caribbean; Man. Dir Peter F. Bourne; 155 employees.

Courts (Barbados) Ltd: St George St, POB 699, Bridgetown; tel. 431-6851; fax 429-5445; f. 1969; subsidiary of Courts (Furnishers) PLC, UK; retail of furniture and domestic appliances; sales Bd $44.1m. (1995/96); Chair. Edmund G. Cohen; Man. Dir Steve Marshall; 190 employees.

Goddard Enterprises Ltd: Mutual Bldg, 2nd Floor, Lower Broad St, Bridgetown; tel. 430-5700; fax 436-8934; e-mail gelinfo@goddent.bb; f. 1921; rum production, meat processing, bakery production, in-flight and airport-terminal catering, duty-free sales, lumber and building supplies, air conditioning and electrical contracting, insurance and financial services, shipping agent, automotive agency; sales Bds $354m. (1997/8); Chair. C. G. Goddard; Man. Dir Joseph N. Goddard; 2,000 employees.

International Resistive Co (Barbados) Ltd: Newton Industrial Park, Newton, Christchurch; tel. 428-9957; fax 428-9966; f. 1986; manufacturer of electrical resistors; Man. Salim Juman; 344 employees.

Juman's Garment Factory (Barbados) Ltd: Grazette's Industrial Park, POB 1206, Bridgetown, St Michael; tel. 425-1330; fax 424-3023; f. 1966; manufacturing of garments; Man. Dir Harvey Khan Juman; 134 employees.

Knowledge Development Institute: Bridgetown; tel. 435-2997; Barbadian–US joint venture; software development company; Jt Heads Tyrone Mowatt, Basil Springer; 40 employees.

Mico Garment Factory Ltd: Harbour Industrial Park, POB 621, Bridgetown; tel. 426-2941; fax 429-7267; f. 1964; manufacture of clothing; Chair. Mohammed Ibrahim Juman; Man. Dir Aphzal Juman; 143 employees.

Roberts Manufacturing Co Ltd: POB 1275, Lower Estate, Bridgetown, St Michael; tel. 429-2131; fax 426-5604; e-mail m.clarke@rmco.com; f. 1944; subsidiary of Barbados Shipping and Trading Co Ltd (see under Shipping); manufacturers of shortening, margarine, edible oils and animal feeds; sales Bds $62m. (1998); Chair. Alan C. Fields; Gen. Man. M. A. Clarke; 160 employees.

St James Beach Hotels PLC: Warrens, St Michael; tel. 438-4690; fax 438-4696; f. 1969; holding company in the hotel industry; Chair. Ray Horney; 720 employees.

UTILITIES
Electricity

Barbados Light and Power Co (BL & P): POB 142, Garrison Hill, St Michael; tel. 436-1800; fax 436-9933; electricity generator and distributor; operates two stations with a combined capacity of 152,500 kW.

Public Utilities Board: cnr Pine Plantation Rd, Collymore Rock, St Michael; tel. 427-5693; fax 437-3542; e-mail ftchq@caribsurf.com; f. 1955; utility regulator.

Gas

Barbados National Oil Co Ltd (BNOCL): POB 175, Woodbourne, St Philip; tel. 423-0918; fax 423-0166; internet www.bnocl.com; f. 1979; extraction of petroleum and natural gas; state-owned, scheduled for privatization; Chair. Harcourt Lewis; 166 employees.

National Petroleum Corporation: Wildey; tel. 430-4000; gas production and distribution.

Water

Barbados Water Authority: The Pine, St Michael; tel. 427-3990.

TRADE UNIONS

Principal unions include:

Barbados Secondary Teachers' Union: Ryeburn, Eighth Ave, Belleville, St Michael; tel. 429-7676; e-mail bstumail@caribsurf.com; f. 1949; Pres. Phil Perry; Gen. Sec. Patrick Frost; 382 mems.

Barbados Union of Teachers: Welches, POB 58, St Michael; tel. 436-6139; f. 1974; Pres. Ronald Da C. Jones; Gen. Sec. Harry Husbands; 2,000 mems.

Barbados Workers' Union: Solidarity House, Harmony Hall, POB 172, St Michael; tel. 426-3492; fax 436-6496; e-mail bwu@caribsurf.com; internet www.bwu-bb.org; f. 1941; operates a Labour College; Sec.-Gen. Leroy Trotman; 20,000 mems.

Caribbean Association of Media Workers (Camwork): Bridgetown; f. 1986; regional; Pres. Rickey Singh.

National Union of Public Workers: Dalkeith Rd, POB 174, Bridgetown; tel. 426-1764; fax 436-1795; e-mail nupwbarbados@sunbeach.net; f. 1944; Pres. Millicent M. B. Small; Gen. Sec. Joseph E. Goddard; 6,000 mems.

Transport

ROADS

Ministry of Public Works and Transport: The Pine, St Michael; tel. 429-2191; fax 437-8133; internet www.publicworks.gov.bb; maintains a network of 1,573 km (977 miles) of roads, of which 1,496 km (930 miles) are paved; Chief Tech. Officer C. H. ARCHER.

SHIPPING

Bridgetown harbour has berths for eight ships and simultaneous bunkering facilities for five. A four-year project to extend the harbour, providing increased capacity for cruise ships, was due to begin in 1997 at a cost of Bds $120m.

Barbados Port Authority: University Row, Bridgetown Harbour; tel. 430-4700; fax 429-5348; internet www.barbadosport.com; Gen. Man. EVERTON WALTERS; Port Dir Capt. H. L. VAN SLUYTMAN.

Shipping Association of Barbados: Trident House, 2nd Floor, Broad St, Bridgetown; tel. 427-9860; fax 426-8392; e-mail shasba@caribsurf.com.

Principal Shipping Companies

Barbados Shipping and Trading Co Ltd: Musson Bldg, Hincks St, POB 1227C, Bridgetown; tel. 426-3844; fax 427-4719; e-mail richard_marshall@bsandtco.com; f. 1920; Chair. C. D. BYNOE; Man. Dir A. C. FIELDS.

Bernuth Agencies: White Park Rd, Bridgetown; tel. 431-3343.

Carlisle Shipping Ltd: Carlisle House, Bridgetown; tel. 430-4803.

DaCosta Ltd: Carlisle House, Hincks St, POB 103, Bridgetown; tel. 431-8700; fax 431-0051; shipping company; Man. Dir JOHN WILKINSON.

T. Geddes Grant Bros: White Park Rd, Bridgetown; tel. 431-3300.

Hassell, Eric and Son Ltd: Carlisle House, Hincks St, Bridgetown; tel. 436-6102; fax 429-3416; e-mail info@erichassell.com; internet www.erichassell.com; shipping agent, stevedoring contractor and cargo fowarder.

Maersk: James Fort Bldg, Hincks St, Bridgetown; tel. 430-4816.

Tec Marine: Carlisle House, Hincks St, Bridgetown; tel. 430-4816.

Tropical Shipping Kensington: Fontabelle Rd, St Michael; tel. 426-9990; fax 426-7750; internet www.tropical.com.

Windward Lines Ltd: Brighton Warehouse Complex, Black Rock, St Michael; tel. 425-7402.

CIVIL AVIATION

The principal airport is Grantley Adams International Airport, at Seawell, 18 km (11 miles) from Bridgetown.

Tourism

The natural attractions of the island consist chiefly of the warm climate and varied scenery. In addition, there are many facilities for outdoor sports of all kinds. Revenue from tourism increased from Bds $13m. in 1960 to some Bds $1,500m. in 1998. The number of stop-over tourist arrivals was 517,869 in 1999, while the number of visiting cruise-ship passengers was 445,821. There were some 6,000 hotel rooms on the island in 1999.

Barbados Tourism Authority: Harbour Rd, POB 242, Bridgetown; tel. 427-2623; fax 426-4080; e-mail btainfo@barbados.org; internet www.barbados.org; f. 1993 to replace Barbados Board of Tourism; offices in London, New York, Los Angeles, Miami, Toronto, Frankfurt, Milan, The Hague, Paris and Stockholm; Chair. HUDSON HUSBANDS; Pres. and CEO OLIVER JORDAN.

Defence

The Barbados Defence Force was established in April 1978. It is divided into regular defence units and a coastguard service with armed patrol boats. The total strength of the armed forces at August 2000 was an estimated 610, comprising an army of 500 members and a navy of 110. There was also a reserve force of 430 members.

Defence Budget (1999): Bds $23.0m. (US $12m.).

Chief of Staff: Brig. RUDYARD LEWIS.

Education

Education is compulsory for 12 years, between five and 16 years of age. Primary education begins at the age of five and lasts for seven years. Secondary education, beginning at 12 years of age, lasts for six years. In 1998 enrolment of children in the primary age-group was 97% (males 99%, females 95%), and in the secondary-school age-group enrolment was 69% (males 67%, females 71%). Tuition at all government schools is free. In the same year enrolment at tertiary level was 33.7% of the relevant age-group (males 22.2%; females 34.2%). Degree courses in a variety of subjects are offered at the Cave Hill campus of the University of the West Indies. A two-year clinical-training programme for medical students is conducted by the School of Clinic Medicine and Research of the University, while an in-service training programme for teachers is provided by the School of Education. Government expenditure on education in 1998/99 was Bds $289.7m., representing 18.8% of total budget spending.

Bibliography

For works on the Caribbean generally, see Select Bibliography (Books).

Beckles, H. A History of Barbados from Amerindian Settlement to Nation State. Cambridge, Cambridge University Press, 1990.

Drummond, I., and Marsden, T. The Condition of Sustainability. London, Routledge, 1999.

Fraser, H., et al. A–Z of Barbadian Heritage. Heinemann Caribbean, Kingston, 1990.

Girvan, N. (Ed.). Poverty, Empowerment and Social Development in the Caribbean. Barbados, Canoe Press, 1997.

Hoyos, F. A. Grantley Adams and the Social Revolution. London, Macmillan, 1974.

Barbados: A History from the Amerindians to Independence. London, Macmillan, 1986.

Potter, R. B. *Barbados*, World Bibliographical Series. Oxford, Clio, 1987.

BELIZE

Area: 22,965 sq km (8,867 sq miles).

Population (census of 12 May 2000): 240,204.

Capital: Belmopan, population 8,130 at census of 12 May 2000.

Language: English (official); Spanish is the mother tongue of about one-half of the population, and there are small communities of Garifuna and Maya speakers in the south. An English 'creole' is almost universally understood.

Religion: Predominantly Christianity; the largest denomination is the Roman Catholic Church.

Climate: Subtropical, tempered by trade winds; average temperature is 24°C (75°F) from November to January and 27°C (81°F) from May to September; mean annual rainfall in Belize City is 1,650 mm (65 ins).

Time: GMT –6 hours.

Public Holidays

2002: 1 January (New Year's Day), 11 March (for Baron Bliss Day), 29 March–1 April (Easter), 1 May (Labour Day), 24 May (Commonwealth Day), 10 September (St George's Caye Day), 23 September (for Independence Day), 14 October (for Columbus Day), 19 November (Garifuna Settlement Day), 25–26 December (Christmas).

2003: 1 January (New Year's Day), 10 March (for Baron Bliss Day), 18–21 April (Easter), 1 May (Labour Day), 26 May (for Commonwealth Day), 10 September (St George's Caye Day), 22 September (for Independence Day), 13 October (for Columbus Day), 19 November (Garifuna Settlement Day), 25–26 December (Christmas).

Currency: Belizean dollar; BZ $100 = £34.92 = US $50.00 = €56.33 (30 April 2001).

Weights and Measures: The imperial system is used, but petrol and paraffin are measured in terms of the US gallon (3.785 litres).

Basic Economic Indicators

	1998	1999	2000
Gross domestic product (BZ $ million at 1984 prices)	912.6	965.0	1,036.2
GDP per head (BZ $ at 1984 prices)	3,968	4,106	4,300
GDP (BZ $ million at current prices)	1,262.6	1,401.9	1,472.8
GDP per head (BZ $ at current prices)	5,490	5,966	6,111
Annual growth of real GDP (%)	2.9	5.7	7.4
Annual growth of real GDP per head (%)	0.2	3.5	4.7
Government budget ('000 BZ $, year beginning 1 April):			
Revenue	296.9	n.a.	n.a.
Expenditure	260.0	n.a.	1.0
Consumer price index (base: 1995 = 100)	106.6	105.3	105.9
Rate of inflation (annual average, %)	–0.9	–1.2	0.6
Foreign exchange reserves (US $ million at 31 December)	38.8	64.1	115.8
Imports c.i.f. (US $ million)	325	366	450
Exports f.o.b. (US $ million)	155	166	194
Balance of payments (current account, US $ million)	–59.8	–77.4	n.a.

Gross national product per head measured at purchasing power parity (PPP) (US dollars, converted by the PPP exchange rate, 1999): 4,492.

Total labour force: (1999): 89,210.

Unemployment (estimate,1999): 12.8%.

Total external debt (1999): US $273m.

Life expectancy (years at birth, 1998): 74.9.

Infant mortality rate (per 1,000 live births, 1998, UN estimate): 29.1.

Adult population with HIV/AIDS (15–49 years, 1999): 2.01%.

School enrolment ratio (5–16 years, 1998): 73%.

Adult literacy rate (2000): 93.25% (males 93.3 females 93.2).

Carbon dioxide emissions per head (metric tons, 1997): 1.7.

Passenger motor cars in use (per 1,000 of population, 1998): 42.

Television receivers in use (per 1,000 of population, 1997): 18.

Personal computers in use (per 1,000 of population, 1999): 106.4.

History

HELEN SCHOOLEY

INTRODUCTION

Belize lies on the Caribbean coast of the Central American isthmus. It was the centre of the Mayan empire, which flourished between AD 300 and 600, but by the time the Spanish arrived in the 16th century there were very few Mayans left, and the Mayan buildings were already in ruins. As Spanish colonial rule there was only tenuous, the earliest European settlers were British buccaneers, who began arriving in the mid-17th century and made use of the many sheltered anchorage points along the coast for raids on Spanish shipping. Spain mounted repeated attacks against the British settlers, but in 1763 granted them rights to fell logwood, and recognized British sovereignty in the Treaty of Amiens of 1802. Under the name British Honduras, the area was governed by British administrators from 1786. It became subject to British law in 1840 and was designated a crown colony in 1862. The significance of the colony to the United Kingdom (which had trading interests all along the Caribbean coast) was primarily economic; it had the best deep-water port facilities in the region and, in the early 19th century, up to 95% of Central American trade passed through the settlement.

The country's ethnic structure reflects successive waves of immigration, encouraged in view of the country's underpopulation. There were relatively few original Amerindian (chiefly Mayan) inhabitants, and few British settlers stayed permanently. From the early 17th century many Africans came as slaves (slavery in the British colonies was abolished progressively between 1833 and 1838), and many early immigrants came from the West Indies. According to the 1980 census, Creoles (of mainly African descent) accounted for 40% of the population, Mestizos (of mixed Mayan and European descent) for 33%, Garifuna or 'Black Caribs' (of mixed Amerindian and African blood, deported from Saint Vincent in 1797) for 8% and Amerindians, the ethnic descendants of the original inhabitants, for 7%. However, the arrival in the 1980s of an estimated 30,000 Central American refugees into a population of around 200,000, caused a major change in the country's ethnography, and by the 1991 census, Spanish speakers outnumbered English speakers, causing some resentment. By 1995 Mestizos accounted for 44% of the population, Creoles for 38%, Amerindians for 11% and Garifuna for 7%. In addition, during the 1990s the Government actively encouraged immigration from Asia and the Middle East.

After gaining independence from Spain in 1821, Guatemala began to lay claim to the area (as did Mexico for a limited period). In 1859 Guatemala recognized the colony's boundaries in exchange for a British undertaking to construct a road from Guatemala City to the Caribbean coast. However, the road was never built, as the commercial importance of British Honduras declined markedly with the completion of the Panama railway in 1855, moving the focus of Central American trade to the Pacific seaboard. Guatemala did not actively pursue the matter of the unbuilt road until it abrogated the treaty in 1945, claiming that the United Kingdom had failed to fulfil its obligations.

THE RISE OF THE PUP

In 1949 the colony's first major internal political issue arose, when a scandal occurred over a substantial devaluation of the British Honduras dollar. The controversy led to the formation of the People's United Party (PUP) in 1950, led by George Price, which assumed an anti-British stance and demanded independence. In 1954, under a new Constitution, a general election, with universal adult suffrage, was held. Of the nine seats in the new Legislative Assembly, eight were won by the PUP. The party won all nine seats at the 1957 election and all 18 seats in the enlarged House of 1961, elected under a new Constitution that established ministerial government with a bicameral legislature. The post of First Minister was assumed by Price.

The colony was granted self-government in 1964 and, after the 1965 elections, George Price became Premier, with the PUP holding 16 seats in the House of Representatives and the National Independence Party (NIP) two. The PUP extended its majority to 17 seats in 1969, although this was reduced to 12 in 1974, and 13 in 1979, when the remaining five seats were won by the United Democratic Party (UDP). In January 1972 the city of Belmopan, built to replace Belize City, which had been devastated by a hurricane in 1961, was declared the new capital, and in June 1973 British Honduras was officially renamed Belize.

INDEPENDENCE

As a result of the proposal to grant the colony self-government, Guatemala renewed its claim to the territory. Bilateral negotiations between Guatemala and the United Kingdom opened in 1962, but in the following year Guatemala claimed that the constitutional conference on self-government was prejudicial to its interests and suspended diplomatic relations with the United Kingdom. At the request of both countries a US commission was formed to study the issue. Its report, issued in 1968, recommended independence for British Honduras and its incorporation into the Central American community, while urging the territory to collaborate with Guatemala on foreign policy and grant it transit rights to the Caribbean Sea. Informal British–Guatemalan negotiations, held in 1972, collapsed, when Guatemala objected to a British military exercise in the colony, and the subsequent British decision to station a permanent military garrison there. Negotiations were resumed in February 1975, but ended in July after the United Kingdom rejected a proposal involving the cession of the southern sector of Belize (comprising about one-quarter of its territory).

In 1975 the PUP, prompted by the impasse in the negotiations, began campaigning for international support for independence. The Caribbean Community and Common Market (CARICOM), which Belize had joined in 1974, and the Non-aligned Movement both declared their support for Belizean independence. From 1975 repeated UN General Assembly resolutions were passed, which urged the settlement of the dispute, and eventually, in 1980, the independence of Belize. In 1976 Panama became the first of the Central American states to oppose Guatemala's claim to the territory and by 1980 only Honduras and El Salvador still voted in Guatemala's favour.

Following the signature by British, Guatemalan and Belizean delegations of 'Heads of Agreement' in March 1981, the UDP (an advocate of a more gradualist approach to independence) announced its opposition and organized anti-government demonstrations. The Heads of Agreement incorporated a broad commitment to Belizean independence and respect for its territorial integrity, while providing Guatemala with access to the Caribbean Sea. They were intended to be a preparation for a formal treaty, to be concluded before the constitutional conference on independence held in April. When the constitutional conference was held first instead, Guatemala protested and suspended consular relations with the United Kingdom.

Belize attained full independence, within the Commonwealth, on 21 September 1981, and George Price assumed the office of Prime Minister. The UDP, however, boycotted the celebrations and Guatemala refused to recognize the state's sovereignty. Meanwhile, the United Kingdom agreed to continue its defence commitment to Belize for 'an appropriate period'. During the next decade a series of attempts was made to hold negotiations. These foundered, until 1984, on Guatemala's refusal to recognize any delegate from Belize, and it was another seven years before a compromise was reached. In August 1991 the Guatemalan Government declared that it would recognize 'the right of the people of Belize to self-determination'. In return for this concession, Belize agreed to a redefinition of its maritime boundaries, allowing Guatemala access to ports on its Caribbean coast.

The 30-year domination by Price and the PUP of national politics ended in December 1984, with an overwhelming victory for the UDP in legislative elections. The party won 21 of the 28 seats in the enlarged House of Representatives and the UDP leader since 1982, Manuel Esquivel, became Prime Minister. The PUP returned to power, however, in September 1989, when five UDP ministers lost their seats. It was during this term of office that Price negotiated the accord under which Guatemala would recognize Belizean independence. After a decade of uncertainty and interrupted negotiations, Guatemala established diplomatic relations with Belize in September 1991. Under the terms of the accord Belize was to legislate to reduce its maritime boundaries and to allow Guatemala access to the Caribbean Sea and use of its port facilities. The Maritime Areas Bill, approved in January 1992, caused divisions within the UDP and led to the formation of the Patriotic Alliance for Territorial Integrity (PATI) in December 1991, by some members of the UDP wanting to co-ordinate opposition to the Bill. In January 1992 disagreement between UDP leaders and PATI activists led to the expulsion or resignation of five UDP members. These members formed the National Alliance for Belizean Rights (NABR) in February, led by Robert Aikman, the former UDP Deputy Leader and Minister of Transport.

In April 1993 Belize and Guatemala signed a non-aggression pact. However, relations between the two countries were jeopardized by the ousting of the Guatemalan President, Jorge Serrano Elías, on 1 June and by the surprise defeat of the PUP in early legislative elections held later in the same month. On 13 May 1993 the British Government announced the withdrawal of the British garrison in Belize, on the grounds that it would no longer be needed, given Belize's improved relations with Guatemala and the ending of civil wars in Nicaragua and El Salvador. Although the base continued to be used for regular British military exercises, the gradual reduction of British military personnel, from 1,350 to 180, had pronounced effects on the national economy and in June 2000 led to an unsuccessful appeal by Belize for a return to the pre-1993 level of military aid.

The departure of the British garrison, criticism of the accord with Guatemala and economic issues, in particular the fear of devaluation in order to meet election-campaign tax promises, resulted in the PUP's poor performance in the June 1993 general election. Although the PUP won more than 51% of the votes, the UDP gained 16 seats in the 29-seat House of Representatives, and Esquivel became Prime Minister. The new Government suspended ratification of the agreement with Guatemala, although the new Guatemalan President, Ramiro de León Carpio, announced that Guatemala would continue to respect Belize's independence. In March 1994 Guatemala formally reaffirmed its territorial claim to Belize. In mid-1994 Esquivel accused Guatemala of employing destabilizing tactics against Belize by encouraging Guatemalans to occupy and settle in areas of Belizean forest. In November 1998 Belize and Guatemala agreed to establish a joint commission to deal with immigration and cross-border traffic. However, bilateral negotiations scheduled for February 2000 were overshadowed by renewed tension. In January the Guatemalan Government announced that it was increasing its military presence near to the disputed territory, precipitating a series of border and diplomatic incidents. Bilateral talks resumed in May, when a panel of negotiators was installed at the headquarters of the Organization of American States (OAS), in Washington, DC (USA). There were further border incidents in late 2000, despite an agreement in November designed to stabilize diplomatic and trade relations and to increase communications between the Belizean and Guatemalan armed forces. In January 2001 the Pan-American Institute of Geography and History, in Mexico City (Mexico), was asked to determine the location of the 'adjacency line' between Belize and Guatemala. In February the Institute issued a report defining the border, which was accepted by both countries, without prejudice on the sovereignty issue. Subsequent negotiations, under the auspices of the OAS, focused on the issue of some 45 Guatemalan families living in the disputed territory. Belize accused Guatemala of using the families, 89% of whom had moved to the area in the past year, to assert sovereignty

over the territory, and an agreement was reached to relocate the families.

DOMESTIC POLITICS

Like its PUP predecessor, the UDP Government faced economic recession and drugs-related crime. In January 1995 the Government announced the latest in a series of controversial 'economic citizenship' programmes, under which foreign nationals could apply for Belizean citizenship in return for an application fee of US $50,000 per family unit. The scheme was designed to attract wealthy Hong Kong citizens, and in a similar form had first been introduced by the PUP Government of 1979–84. Information offices on the programme were opened in many countries world-wide, although the scheme came under scrutiny in mid-1995, with reports that Belize was being used as a channel for illegal immigration, particularly from the People's Republic of China and the Republic of China (Taiwan), to the USA. In January 1999 a 14-member Political Reform Commission was established in order to review the system of governance in Belize. In March 2000 this Commission suggested that the policy of economic citizenship be abolished. The rise in crime during the 1990s prompted increased demands for the use of the death penalty, which, although passed on 20 occasions between 1990 and 1998, was in every case overturned by the British Privy Council.

Increasing dissatisfaction with the UDP Government resulted in an overwhelming victory for the PUP in the general election of August 1998. The PUP won more than 59% of the votes cast, gaining 26 seats in the 29-seat House of Representatives and its leader, Said Musa, became Prime Minister. The PUP victory focused media attention on Michael Ashcroft, a businessman with dual Belizean and British citizenship, who held extensive financial interests in Belize (see below, in Economy). He was widely reputed to have lent major financial support to the PUP election campaign, and after the PUP took office he was controversially appointed the country's ambassador to the UN. (He resigned the post in March 2000, when he received a life peerage in the British House of Lords.) Ashcroft was chairman and CEO of the Belize Holdings (BHI) Corporation (known as Carlisle Holdings Ltd from 1999), which in 1990 (under the previous PUP administration) had been granted a 30-year tax exemption, which the Esquivel Government had attempted unsuccessfully to overturn.

In 1999 the British Government commissioned an investigation, by KPMG accountants, into Belize's financial set up, including the regulation of the 'offshore' sector and the impact of tax concessions on the level of poverty. The British Government had previously suspended debt relief to Belize, pending the completion of the audit. However, following the conclusion of the investigation in late 2000, it requested that the inquiry be expanded to investigate public investment companies operating from Belize, including Ashcroft's Carlisle Holdings. Ashcroft became the focus of media attention again in late 2000 and early 2001, following a series of high-profile arguments with the British High Commissioner, Tim David, allegedly regarding the investigation into Ashcroft's offshore interests. On 24 June 2001 Ashcroft served a writ on two British cabinet ministers for an alleged breach of his privacy, regarding the leak of government documents revealing these arguments to the press. In January 1998 the UDP Government introduced a programme to improve living conditions in the south of the country. A government survey carried out in 1996 indicated that one-third of the population were living at or below the poverty line, and that one-quarter of all homes in rural areas lacked a safe and adequate water supply, resulting in the spread of water-borne diseases, especially cholera and malaria. Furthermore, it was reported in February 1998 that Belize, in common with other Caribbean and Central American countries, was facing a substantial increase in the mosquito-transmitted dengue fever. The south was home to many of the Honduran and Guatemalan refugees of the 1980s, and also to about one-half of the country's Mayan population, who opposed a number of regional development projects, notably challenging the Government's right to grant concessions to fell logwood on their ancestral land.

REGIONAL RELATIONS

Although Belize traditionally identified itself as a Caribbean country, independence from the United Kingdom and accession to the OAS in 1991 heralded an increasing involvement in Latin American affairs. The influx during the 1980s of thousands of Central American refugees and settlers caused major changes in the population, with racial, political and social implications. By the 1991 census, Spanish speakers outnumbered English speakers. In February 1996 the Government ratified an agreement with Guatemala, El Salvador and Honduras to co-operate in the conservation and tourism promotion of Mayan archaeological sites. In 1997 the USA accused Belize of failing to address money laundering through its financial sector, and placed the country on its list of nations deemed to be not 'fully co-operating' with the USA in its counter-narcotics efforts. Belize was, however, removed from the list in March 2000. The first major deployment of US troops in Belize occurred under the 'New Horizon' joint military exercise held between February and May 2000. The exercise involved 3,500 US troops, working in relays of small teams, on social infrastructure projects, including the establishment of a programme of basic medical services. In March the Inter-American Investment Corporation, part of the Inter-American Development Bank (IDB), announced the allocation of funds for development projects in Belize. On 1 December 2000, following nine years of Observer status, Belize was given full membership of the Sistema de la Integración Centroamericana (SICA—Central American Integration System). In May 2001 Belize formally applied for membership of the organization's Banco Centroamericano de Integración Económica (BCIE—Central American Bank for Economic Integration).

In early October 2000 'Hurricane Keith' destroyed power and telecommunications lines, damaged buildings and created flash floods in Belize, causing an estimated US $200m. of damage. Emergency funds for reconstruction were provided by the IDB, the Red Cross and the British Government, among others. Later in that month the IDB approved a US $9.8m. loan to improve the infrastructure and service of the health sector; further funding was to be provided by the Caribbean Development Bank and the European Commission.

Economy

HELEN SCHOOLEY

British settlers were originally attracted to Belize by its forests, for dyes and timber. Following the country's decline as a trading base in the mid-19th century, forestry became the chief economic activity until it was overtaken by agriculture in the 1960s. In the late 1950s some 40% of the land was held in large estates (one-third by the Belize Estates and Produce Co) and only 3% was under cultivation; by 1981 some 15% of cultivable land had been brought into production, although this represented only one-half the possible acreage. Sugar became the main crop, especially after the arrival of the British company, Tate and Lyle, in 1963. In order to address the shortage of manpower, successive Governments encouraged immigration, and, increasingly, migrant workers from Central America settled in the country.

The economy expanded rapidly in the late 1980s, chiefly as a result of programmes of diversification and privatization. In the early 1990s the rate of gross domestic product (GDP) growth contracted sharply, from 10.3% in 1990 to 1.5% in 1994, but recovered to reach 3.9% in 1995. The strength of agricultural exports and tourism compensated for problems in the timber industry and sluggish performance in construction and garment-assembly. The country's growth in 1995 was set against a background of regional decline, with Belize one of only three Caribbean countries not experiencing decelerated or negative growth that year. In 1996, however, the increase in GDP, in real terms, was 1.4%. This figure rose to 2.9% in 1998, increasing to 5.7% in 1999. In 2000 the economy expanded by 7.4%, the highest of the decade.

AGRICULTURE

Agriculture, forestry and fishing contributed 18.1% of GDP and 75% of export earnings in 1999, and employed 29.9% of the working population in 1997. The main crops were sugar cane, bananas and citrus fruits (notably oranges and grapefruit), and sugar cane was the country's leading export commodity, contributing almost one-quarter of total revenue in 1999 and employing some 13% of the labour force. On 8 June 2001 the Government approved a Sugar Industry Bill intended to reform the sector, reducing the State's role, while encouraging outside investment. Other significant crops were maize, red kidney beans, rice, tobacco and marine products. From the early 1980s there were initiatives to diversify the agricultural sector, including the cultivation of papaya, mangoes, peanuts and pineapples, and also to revitalize timber production. Dependence on agriculture made the economy vulnerable to the fluctuations of international markets, disease and the country's location on a hurricane belt. (In 1931 a hurricane almost totally destroyed Belize City and, after 'Hurricane Hattie' struck in October 1961,

it was decided to build a new capital city at Belmopan, at a cost of over £4m., most of which was provided by the United Kingdom.) As a member of the Commonwealth, Belize benefited from low tariffs on its exports to the European Union (EU) under the Lomé Convention (which expired in February 2000 and was replaced by the Cotonou Agreement in June—see Part Three, Regional Organizations), and tariff-free access to the USA under the Caribbean Basin Initiative.

In the late 1980s new areas were planted with citrus trees, resulting in increased yields from 1992, and in the early 1990s the amount of land under rice cultivation was also extended, with a 55% increase in rice production in 1994/95. In the banana industry, which expanded markedly after its privatization in 1985, the adoption of a new variety was expected to raise the annual crop by between 20% and 50% in the early 2000s. Bananas contributed US $27.3m. in export earnings in 1999. However, on 11 April 2001, following an EU–USA agreement regarding banana imports, the EU preferential market for Caribbean bananas was to end. From 1 July a transitional system, issuing licences according to historical trade patterns, was to be implemented, while the definitive tariff-only system was to be in place for 1 January 2006. This was expected to adversely affect banana revenue. On a much smaller scale, growth of papaya for export expanded in the late 1990s, although the production of dried papaya, potentially much more lucrative, was delayed by the high cost of installing the necessary machinery. Another new and expanding crop in the 1990s was peppers, in which production rose from 70,000 lbs in 1995 to 357,000 lbs in 1999. Coffee was first planted on a commercial scale in 1989, producing the first crop in 1994; by 1999 coffee crops covered some 100 acres.

Encouragement of cultivation of new land and development of the timber industry brought the agricultural sector into conflict with environmental concerns. A 1996 plan to redistribute land and increase the country's profitable citrus fruit production resulted in the destruction of some of the country's rainforest. One of the most prized Belizean timber products was mahogany, which in November 1995 was listed internationally as an endangered species. Between 1973 and 1997 the Government granted 17 logging concessions in the Toledo district, in the south of the country, to foreign companies (a number of which were from South East Asia) requiring mahogany. In late 1996 controversy arose over the Government's proposals to upgrade the road through the mountains to Punta Gorda on the coast, linking it to the Central American Highway through Guatemala. A Mayan delegation successfully appealed to the Inter-American Development Bank (IDB) to base funding on greater consideration of the project's cultural and environmental impact. The finance was eventually approved in January 1998.

Belize has rich fishing grounds, yielding both white fish and shellfish, and in 1999 seafood products contributed an estimated 16.7% (US \$27.8m.) of total export earnings The fishing sector expanded markedly during the 1990s; shrimp production grew from 450,000 lbs in 1990 to around 4.7m. lbs in 1999, and in that year raised US \$19.5m. in export revenue. Initially the majority of the fish exported went to the USA, but further development of the shrimp industry, financed by the USA, was directed at the European market. Another important contributor to shrimp production was lobster, worth over US \$8m. in 1999; other areas included conchs, sharks and aquarium fish.

The early 1980s saw a rapid development in the illegal cultivation of marijuana. A crop-spraying programme reduced the crop by an estimated 90% by the end of the decade, but the legacy of this trade was the establishment of transit routes through Belize of Colombian cocaine (and, later, heroin) destined for the US market, and a consequent rise in drugs-related crime. The country's terrain and underdeveloped infrastructure made the detection and prevention of trafficking exceedingly difficult for Belize's limited security forces. More positively, the growth of marijuana opened up the possibility of the legal cultivation of hemp for export.

MANUFACTURING

Two significant areas of manufacturing to emerge were food processing and garment assembly. Successive Governments offered (often controversial) tax concessions for foreign agribusiness investors, including Tate and Lyle and the US chocolate concern, Hershey. In 1990 the United Democratic Party (UDP) protested against concessions made by the People's United Party (PUP) Government in 1990 to the Belize Holdings (BHI) Corporation (known as Carlisle Holding Ltd from 1999— see above, in History), the banking and finance concern, which also had stakes in fruit-processing, broadcasting, electricity, and tourism ventures. BHI sold off its fruit-processing interests in 1999.

In addition to sugar, the prime processed-food export was orange and grapefruit concentrate (making up 16.5% of export revenue in 1999), which in 2000 had duty-free access to the US and EU markets and to the Caribbean Community and Common Market (CARICOM). New ventures included the manufacture of hot pepper sauces, worth US \$206,000 in 1998, and coffee, grown organically and hand-picked for a niche market, mostly in the USA and Singapore. Investment was being sought for expanding meat processing and dried fruit production. A small-scale industry existed for the production of items in wood and conch shell for the tourist market. The garment sector accounted for around 11.8% of export revenue in 1999 and faced competition from Mexican assembly plants favoured by the launch of the North American Free Trade Agreement (NAFTA). Belizean investment promotion focused on the country's proximity to Mexico and the favourable trade agreements with Canada, Europe and the USA. The establishment of NAFTA prompted Belize to build a series of in-bond manufacturing plants under joint ventures with Mexico, in free-trade zones situated along the northern border with Mexico. These plants concentrated on light manufacturing and telecommunications equipment. Manufacturing, particularly of clothing, accounted for 12.4% of GDP in 1999 and employed 11.3% of the working population in 1997.

MINING AND ENERGY

A number of mineral deposits were located in Belize, including bauxite and gold, but none proved to be commercially viable, with the exception of limestone quarrying. In 1999 mining accounted for 0.6% of GDP and only 0.1% of employment in 1997. In 1988 a Mines and Minerals Law was passed, designed chiefly for petroleum production, awarding all mineral rights to the Government. Exploration had begun in 1938, concentrated on shore, in the north of the country, and off shore in the south, in the Bay of Campeche. During the 1980s Belize became particularly attractive to foreign petroleum companies for investment, in comparison with its more turbulent Central American neighbours. The first well was drilled in 1955, and the largest deposit discovered had an estimated yield of between

10 and 20 barrels per day, while national requirements ran to around 600,000 barrels per year. In 1996 a consortium of four foreign companies started exploratory drilling for deposits a few miles off Glover's Reef. In 1999 mineral fuel imports accounted for 15.3% of Belize's total import costs.

The Government also encouraged the development of other forms of energy, and the 1991/92 budget removed all duties on solar- and wind-energy devices. In 1993 a US company began construction of the Mollejón hydroelectric station, on the Macal River, and the project was financed by the International Finance Corporation and the Caribbean Development Bank. Despite criticism by the UDP of the cost and efficiency of the project, construction continued and the plant came into operation under Belize Electricity Ltd. Further infrastructure projects announced in 1998 included the development of facilities at Belmopan's Fort Point port and the installation of the country's second underground fibre-optic telecommunications link.

TOURISM AND ENVIRONMENT

In the 1980s efforts were made to establish a tourist industry; by the late 1990s the sector had become the country's second largest foreign exchange earner, worth nearly US \$100m. per year. The chief attractions were the Caribbean coast, the country's Mayan heritage, and the country's natural environment, particularly its rain forests and the barrier reef, the second largest in the world. A major hotel construction programme began in 1990, and by 1995 over 60 hotels had been built. The majority of visitors came from the USA, and in 1999 tourist arrivals totalled an estimated 326,642. In 1999 the Government passed the Gaming Control Act regulating new gambling ventures, designed chiefly for the tourist market. The sector employed about 20% of the working population and in 1999 accounted for some 17.5% of GDP. Expansion of the sector concentrated on diving, low-impact tourism, conservation of the country's varied flora and fauna, and sustainable development projects. In 1995 Belize boasted the largest proportion of territory dedicated to national parks of any country in the world.

The development of tourism highlighted the importance of the country's environment. During the 1990s legislation was introduced to protect the nation's forestry reserves and the mangrove belts along the coast, which formed a natural filtration system for the coastal fisheries, especially the shellfish beds. However, reports suggested that the legislation was rarely enforced. Another major environmental concern was the effect of chemical products used in the production of sugar cane, which ran off the fields into the water system, affecting the fisheries. In addition, the chemicals curbed the rat population, thereby reducing the number of snakes available for export, either live, or dead and dried for medicinal use.

In 2000 scientists at the Smithsonian Institution in Washington, DC (USA), expressed concern regarding the destruction of the central barrier reef off the coast of Belize. The destruction, by 'bleaching' of the coral, was a result of rising sea temperatures caused by global warming.

BANKING AND INVESTMENT

From the early 1990s the Government promoted Belize as an 'offshore' financial centre, stressing its political stability. The first offshore banks opened in 1996 and by 2000 there were over 10,000 offshore companies registered in Belize. The Financial Institutions Act of January 1996 tightened the regulations on the country's banking system and aligned them with those of other CARICOM member countries. In 1998 the Organisation for Economic Co-operation and Development (OECD) investigated tax havens and business secrecy, culminating in a report 'Harmful Tax Competition: An Emerging Global Issue', regarding those jurisdictions considered harmful tax regimes, which included Belize. In response the Government established an International Financial Commission in 1999 to regulate the sector, and in July 2000, in order to increase transparency, the Commission ended the practice of dealing in bearer shares. The banking and finance sector was dominated by Michael Ashcroft (now Lord Ashcroft, see above, in History), whose interests were re-grouped into Carlisle Holdings in 1999. The Carlisle Holdings company also owned the Belize Bank, operated the sale of passports under the 1995 'economic citizenship' programme, had a stake in the company running the international shipping register established in 1989, and took over the telecommunications monopoly, Belize Telecommunications, in October 2000. In order to stimulate new enterprises and investment, legislation had been introduced in 1990 granting incentives and tax exemptions to companies operating in the country's Export Processing Zones (EPZ). Internet banking was introduced in the late 1990s, and in 1999 incentive programmes were launched to promote data processing ventures, through foreign investment in the EPZs.

FINANCES

As a result of the economic downturn in 1994, Belize recorded a deficit on the current budget of BZ $5.5m. in 1994/95, the first such deficit since 1985/86. Austerity measures implemented in 1995 and the renewal of the controversial 'economic-citizenship' programme helped to reduce the budget deficit, which stood at a projected BZ $32.6m. in the financial year ending March 1998 (equivalent to 2.3% of GDP). The incoming PUP Government inherited a budget deficit of BZ $50.2m. in 1998/99, equivalent to 4% of GDP. However, in the financial year 1999/2000 the deficit was partially offset by the privatization of the state electricity utility and the sale of mortgages on the secondary market.

In 1996 Belize recorded a trade deficit of US $58.2m. The deficit on the current account of the balance of payments was US $6.6m. The 1996/97 budget included a considerable proportion of 'extraordinary receipts'. Value-added tax (VAT) at 15% was introduced with effect from the beginning of April 1996, to replace a gross receipts tax in operation since 1994. The tax was unpopular and the PUP Government, elected in August 1998, fulfilled its election pledge to abolish it, introducing an 8% sales tax in its place in April 1999, despite claims that the removal of VAT would place pressure on fiscal targets, given the prevailing depression in world trade. In 1997 the deficit on the current account of the balance of payments increased to US $31.9m., while the trade deficit increased to US $89.5m. The trade deficit increased further in 1998, to US $104.7m., and to US $128.8m. in 1999, owing to an increase in imports. The current-account deficit stood at US $77.4m. in 1999.

A central concern of the Government's monetary policy was the pegging of the currency to the US dollar from 1976, at the rate of US $1.00 equal to BZ $2.00. The average annual rate of inflation stood at 2.9% in 1995, before increasing to 6.4% in 1996. In 1997, however, this figure decreased to 1.0% and in 1998 consumer prices decreased, by 0.9%. This deflationary trend continued in 1999, when consumer prices decreased by a further 1.2%; however, in 2000 consumer prices increased by 0.6%. Total external debt stood at US $273.0m. at the end of 1999 (equivalent to 37.4% of GDP); the country's bilateral debt was owed mainly to the USA and the United Kingdom, and much of it was held on concessionary terms. In October 1998 Belize agreed to restructure its substantial debt to the Republic of China (Taiwan) and Taiwan agreed to provide Belize with an additional BZ $100m., over a period of five years, for housing construction. The Government anticipated that the restructuring agreement would help to control the level of debt-servicing and would reduce the external debt to 30% of GDP within three years.

CONCLUSION

The scaling down of the British garrison from 1994 resulted in a loss of income in Belize. The presence of the garrison was estimated to have contributed 15%–20% of the country's GDP. The country faced competition from the implementation of NAFTA and from the gradual cessation of the EU preferential market for Caribbean bananas from July 2001. The PUP's electoral pledge of 15,000 new jobs proved a powerful contribution to its electoral victory in 1998, given that the rate of unemployment was an estimated 12.8% in mid-1999.

The country's two foremost foreign-exchange earners, agricultural products and tourism, were adversely affected by 'Hurricane Mitch', which struck in October 1998, and, to a lesser extent, by 'Hurricane Keith' in October 2000. Although these sectors have proved their ability to recover relatively quickly between seasons, the damage highlighted the limited nature of the country's infrastructure. A World Bank (International Bank for Reconstruction and Development—IBRD) loan of US $13m., approved in September 2000, was intended to bring the country's total of paved roads to over 500 km, including a bypass for Belize City, and also to provide improved drainage and flood protection in five areas. Government agencies identified the considerable potential for international investment in many sectors. In a report produced in 1998, the Belize Development Trust advocated the establishment of a Belize Stock Exchange, while recognizing that the domestic economic climate might not yet support one. The size of the country made it sensitive to relatively small-scale developments; for example, the 'New Horizon' US military exercise held in early 2000 (see above, in History), brought an estimated US $12m. to the Belizean economy. In May 2001 the Central American countries, including Belize, reached an agreement with Mexico for the integration of the region through the Puebla-Panamá Plan, a series of joint transport, industry and tourism projects.

Statistical Survey

Source (unless otherwise stated): Central Statistical Office, Ministry of Finance, 2nd Floor, New Administration Bldg, Belmopan; tel. (8) 22207; fax (8) 23206; e-mail csogob@blt.net.

AREA AND POPULATION

Area: 22,965 sq km (8,867 sq miles).

Population: 144,857 at census of 12 May 1980; 189,774 (males 96,289, females 93,485) at census of 12 May 1991; 240,204 (males 121,278, females 118,926) at census of 12 May 2000.

Density (May 2000): 10.5 per sq km.

Districts (population at census of 12 May 2000): Belize 68,197; Cayo 52,564; Orange Walk 38,890; Corozal 32,708; Stann Creek 24,548; Toledo 23,297.

Principal Towns (population at census of 12 May 2000): Belmopan (capital) 8,130; Belize City (former capital) 49,050; Orange Walk 13,483; San Ignacio/Santa Elena 13,260; Dangriga (formerly Stann Creek) 8,814; Corozal 7,888; Benque Viejo 5,088; San Pedro 4,499; Punta Gorda 4,329.

Births, Marriages and Deaths (1997): Registered live births 5,738 (birth rate 24.9 per 1,000); Registered marriages 1,515 (marriage rate 6.6 per 1,000); Registered deaths 1,173 (death rate 5.1 per 1,000). Source: UN, *Demographic Yearbook*.

Expectation of Life (years at birth, 1998): Males 73.5; Females 76.3. Source: UNDP, *Human Development Report*.

Economically Active Population (sample survey, April 1997): Agriculture, hunting, forestry and fishing 21,140; Mining and quarrying 95; Manufacturing 7,980; Electricity, gas and water 985; Construction 3,835; Trade, restaurants and hotels 15,155; Transport, storage and communications 3,655; Financing, insurance, real estate and business services 2,360; Community, social and personal services 12,225; Private households 2,915; Other 335; Total employed 70,680.

AGRICULTURE, ETC.

Principal Crops (FAO estimates, '000 metric tons unless otherwise stated, 2000): Sugar cane 1,181; Maize 38; Rice (paddy) 11; Roots and tubers 4; Pulses (dry beans) 5; Coconuts 3; Other vegetables 5; Oranges 190; Grapefruit and Pomelos 42; Bananas 75; Other fruit 3. Source: FAO.

Livestock (FAO estimates, '000 head, 2000): Horses 5; Mules 4; Cattle 59; Pigs 24; Sheep 3; Goats 1; Chickens 1,400. Source: FAO.

Livestock Products ('000 metric tons, 2000): Meat 10; Cows' milk 7*; Hen eggs 2*. *FAO estimate. Source: FAO.

Forestry ('000 cu m): *Roundwood removals* (1999): Industrial wood (Sawlogs) 62, Fuel wood 126, Total 188. *Sawnwood* (1999): Coniferous (softwood) 5, Broadleaved (hardwood) 30, Total 35. Source: FAO, *Yearbook of Forest Products*.

Fishing (metric tons, live weight, 1998): Capture 2,206 (Porgies, seabreams 183, European pilchard 126, Other marine fishes 485, Caribbean spiny lobster 502, Penaeus shrimps 40, Stromboid conchs 252, Cuttlefish, bobtail squids 406, Octopuses, etc. 185); Aquaculture 1,809* (Tilapias 136*, Whiteleg shrimp 1,642); Total catch 4,015. *FAO estimate. Source: FAO, *Yearbook of Fishery Statistics*.

INDUSTRY

Production (preliminary figures, 1999): Raw sugar 115,205 long tons; Molasses 40,285 long tons; Cigarettes 92 million; Beer 1,455,000 gallons; Batteries 7,440; Flour 17,780,000 lb; Fertilizers 22,894 metric tons; Garments 2,134,000 items; Citrus concentrate 3,719,000 gallons; Soft drinks 1,728,000 cases. Source: IMF, *Belize: Statistical Appendix* (June 2000).

FINANCE

Currency and Exchange Rates: 100 cents = 1 Belizean dollar (BZ $). *Sterling, US Dollar and Euro Equivalents* (30 April 2001): £1 sterling = BZ $2.864; US $1 = BZ $2.000; €1 = BZ $1.775; BZ $100 = £34.92 = US $50.00 = €56.33. *Exchange rate:* Fixed at US $1 = BZ $2.000 since May 1976.

Budget (BZ $ million, year ending 31 March): *1997/98* (projections): *Revenue:* Taxation 251.3 (Taxes on income, profits, etc. 52.3, Domestic taxes on goods and services 101.3, Import duties 83.6); Other current revenue 29.8 (Entrepreneurial and property income 10.2, Administrative fees, etc. 14.9); Capital revenue 2.2; Total 283.4, excl. grants (41.2). *Expenditure:* General public services 41.3; Defence 19.7; Public order and safety 25.7; Education 74.2; Health 29.6; Social security and welfare 21.4; Housing and community amenities 9.3; Recreational, cultural and religious affairs 4.8; Economic services 101.9 (Agriculture, forestry, fishing and hunting 22.5, Transport and communications 60.8); Other purposes 34.3 (Interest payments 29.0); Total 362.3 (Current 244.8, Capital 117.4), excl. lending minus repayments (−5.1). Source: IMF, *Government Finance Statistics Yearbook*.

International Reserves (US $ million at 31 December 2000): IMF special drawing rights 1.56; Reserve position in the IMF 5.52; Foreign exchange 115.82; Total 122.9. Source: IMF, *International Financial Statistics*.

Money Supply (BZ $ million at 31 December 2000): Currency outside banks 95.96; Demand deposits at commercial banks 185.99; Total money (incl. others) 287.32. Source: IMF, *International Financial Statistics*.

Cost of Living (Consumer Price Index; base: 1995 = 100): 106.6 in 1998; 105.3 in 1999; 105.9 in 2000. Source: IMF, *International Financial Statistics*.

Expenditure on the Gross Domestic Product (BZ $ million at current prices, 2000): Government final consumption expenditure 224.5; Private final consumption expenditure 994.6; Increase in stocks 41.8; Gross fixed capital formation 476.7; *Total domestic expenditure* 1,737.6; Exports of goods and services 739.1; *Less* Imports of goods and services 1,010.3; *GDP in purchasers' values* 1,472.8. Source: IMF, *International Financial Statistics*.

Gross Domestic Product by Economic Activity (BZ $ million at current prices, 1999: Agriculture, hunting, forestry and fishing 216.6; Mining and quarrying 7.2; Manufacturing 148.6; Electricity, gas and water 31.4; Construction 73.1; Wholesale and retail trade, restaurants and hotels 243.5; Transport, storage and communications 121.9; Finance, insurance, real estate and business services 149.3; Community, social and personal services 207.8; *Sub-total* 1,199.0; *Less* Imputed bank service charges 45.5; *GDP at factor cost* 1,154.0; *GDP at constant 1984 prices* 806.3. Source: UN Economic Commission for Latin America and the Caribbean, *Statistical Yearbook*.

Balance of Payments (US $ million, 1999): Exports of goods f.o.b. 201.5; Imports of goods c.i.f. −330.3; *Trade balance* −128.8; Exports of services 154.1; Imports of services −105.1; *Balance on goods and services* −79.8; Other income received 7.3; Other income paid −41.5; *Balance on goods, services and income* −114.0; Current transfers received 40.0; Current transfers paid −3.5; *Current balance* −77.4; Capital account (net) −2.0; Direct investment abroad 48.9; Direct investment from abroad 3.5; Portfolio investment assets −0.7; Portfolio investment liabilities 33.6; Other investment assets −8.9; Other investment liabilities −9.5; Net errors and omissions 4.3; *Overall balance* −8.3. Source: IMF, *International Financial Statistics*.

EXTERNAL TRADE

Principal Commodities (preliminary figures, US $ million, 1999): *Imports c.i.f.:* Food and live animals 45.2; Beverages and tobacco 4.6; Mineral fuels, lubricants, etc. 47.2; Chemicals 30.9; Basic manufactures 47.7; Machinery and transport equipment 84.6; Miscellaneous manufactured articles 36.5; Total (incl. others) 309.2. *Exports f.o.b.:* Food and live animals 143.3 (Sugar 41.0, Seafood products 27.8, Bananas 27.3, Citrus concentrates 27.4, Single strength juices 9.5); Miscellaneous manufactured articles 19.6 (Garments 19.6); Total (incl. others) 166.1. Note: Figures refer to retained imports and domestic exports. The data exclude re-exports. Source: IMF, *Belize: Statistical Appendix* (June 2000).

Principal Trading Partners (preliminary figures, US $ million, 1999): *Imports c.i.f.:* Mexico 45.8; United Kingdom 17.6; USA 192.9; Total (incl. others) 366.3. *Exports f.o.b.* (excl. re-exports): United Kingdom 47.4; USA 62.7; Total (incl. others) 166.1. Source: IMF, *Belize: Statistical Appendix* (June 2000).

TRANSPORT

Road Traffic (motor vehicles licensed, 1998): 21,684. Source: IRF, *World Road Statistics*.

Shipping (sea-borne freight traffic, '000 metric tons, 1996): Goods loaded 255.4; Goods unloaded 277.1. *Merchant Fleet* (vessels registered at 31 December 1998): Number of vessels 1,308; Total displacement 2,382,478 grt. Source: Lloyd's Register of Shipping, *World Fleet Statistics*.

Civil Aviation (preliminary, 1997): Passenger arrivals 95,337.

TOURISM

Tourist Arrivals: 304,562 (cruise-ship passengers 2,678) in 1997; 288,098 (cruise-ship passengers 14,183) in 1998; 326,642 (cruise-ship passengers 34,130) in 1999.

Tourist Receipts (US $ million): 88.0 in 1997; 108.3 in 1998; 111.5 in 1999.

Hotels: 383 in 1997; 408 in 1998; 390 in 1999.

Source: Belize Tourist Board.

COMMUNICATIONS MEDIA

Radio Receivers (1997): 133,000 in use*.

Television Receivers (1997): 41,000 in use*.

Telephones (1997): 31,000 main lines in use†.

Telefax Stations (1996): 500 in use†.

Mobile Cellular Telephones (1997): 3,023 subscribers†.

Book Production (1996): 107 titles*.

Newspapers: *Non-daily* (1996): 6 (circulation 80,000)*.

* Source: UNESCO, *Statistical Yearbook*.

† Source: UN, *Statistical Yearbook*.

EDUCATION

Pre-primary* (1994/95): 90 schools, 190 teachers, 3,311 students.

Primary (1996/97): 280 schools, 1,966 teachers (1995/96), 53,110 students.

Secondary (1996/97): 30 schools, 697 teachers (1995/96), 10,912 students.

Higher (1996/97): 11 institutions, 254 teachers (1995/96), 2,500 students.

* Source: UNESCO, *Statistical Yearbook*.

Directory

The Constitution

The Constitution came into effect at the independence of Belize on 21 September 1981. Its main provisions are summarized below:

FUNDAMENTAL RIGHTS AND FREEDOMS

Regardless of race, place of origin, political opinions, colour, creed or sex, but subject to respect for the rights and freedoms of others and for the public interest, every person in Belize is entitled to the rights of life, liberty, security of the person, and the protection of the law. Freedom of movement, of conscience, of expression, of assembly and association and the right to work are guaranteed and the inviolability of family life, personal privacy, home and other property and of human dignity is upheld. Protection is afforded from discrimination on the grounds of race, sex, etc., and from slavery, forced labour and inhuman treatment.

CITIZENSHIP

All persons born in Belize before independence who, immediately prior to independence, were citizens of the United Kingdom and Colonies automatically become citizens of Belize. All persons born outside the country having a husband, parent or grandparent in possession of Belizean citizenship automatically acquire citizenship, as do those born in the country after independence. Provision is made which permits persons who do not automatically become citizens of Belize to be registered as such. (Belizean citizenship was also offered, under the Belize Loans Act 1986, in exchange for interest-free loans of US $25,000 with a 10-year maturity. The scheme was officially ended in June 1994, following sustained criticism of alleged corruption on the part of officials. However, a revised economic citizenship programme, offering citizenship in return for a minimum investment of US $75,000, received government approval in early 1995.)

THE GOVERNOR-GENERAL

The British monarch, as Head of State, is represented in Belize by a Governor-General, a Belizean national.

Belize Advisory Council

The Council consists of not less than six people 'of integrity and high national standing', appointed by the Governor-General for up to 10 years upon the advice of the Prime Minister. The Leader of the Opposition must concur with the appointment of two members and be consulted about the remainder. The Council exists to advise the Governor-General, particularly in the exercise of the prerogative of mercy, and to convene as a tribunal to consider the removal from office of certain senior public servants and judges.

THE EXECUTIVE

Executive authority is vested in the British monarch and exercised by the Governor-General. The Governor-General appoints as Prime Minister that member of the House of Representatives who, in the Governor-General's view, is best able to command the support of the majority of the members of the House, and appoints a Deputy Prime Minister and other Ministers on the advice of the Prime Minister. The Governor-General may remove the Prime Minister from office if a resolution of 'no confidence' is passed by the House and the Prime Minister does not, within seven days, either resign or advise the Governor-General to dissolve the National Assembly. The Cabinet consists of the Prime Minister and other Ministers.

The Leader of the Opposition is appointed by the Governor-General as that member of the House who, in the Governor-General's view, is best able to command the support of a majority of the members of the House who do not support the Government.

THE LEGISLATURE

The Legislature consists of a National Assembly comprising two chambers: the Senate, with eight nominated members; and the House of Representatives, with 29 elected members. The Assembly's normal term is five years. Senators are appointed by the Governor-General: five on the advice of the Prime Minister; two on the advice of the Leader of the Opposition or on the advice of persons selected by the Governor-General; and one after consultation with the Belize Advisory Council. If any person who is not a Senator is elected to be President of the Senate, he or she shall be an ex-officio Senator in addition to the eight nominees.

Each constituency returns one Representative to the House, who is directly elected in accordance with the Constitution.

If a person who is not a member of the House is elected to be Speaker of the House, he or she shall be an ex-officio member in addition to the 29 members directly elected. Every citizen older than 18 years is eligible to vote. The National Assembly may alter any of the provisions of the Constitution.

The Government

Head of State: HM Queen ELIZABETH II (succeeded to the throne 6 February 1952).

Governor-General: Sir COLVILLE YOUNG (appointed 17 November 1993).

THE CABINET
(August 2001)

Prime Minister and Minister of Finance and of Foreign Affairs: SAID MUSA.

Deputy Prime Minister and Minister of Natural Resources and the Environment and of Industry: JOHN BRICEÑO.

Senior Minister: GEORGE CADLE PRICE.

Minister of National Security and of Economic Development: JORGE ESPAT.

Minister of Public Utilities, Energy, Communications and Immigration: MAXWELL SAMUELS.

Minister of Budget Management, Investment and Trade and Head of the Central Bank: RALPH FONSECA.

Minister of Health and Public Services: JOSE COYE.

Minister of the Sugar Industry, Labour and Local Government: VALDEMAR CASTILLO.

Minister of Human Development, Civil Society and Women: DOLORES BALDERAMOS GARCIA.

Minister of Agriculture, Fisheries and Co-operatives: DANIEL SILVA, Jr.

Minister of Public Works, Transport and of the Citrus and Banana Industries: HENRY CANTON.

Minister of Education and Sports: CORDEL HYDE.

Minister of Youth and Tourism: MARK ESPAT.

Minister of Rural Development and Culture: MARCIAL MES.

Minister of Housing, Urban Renewal and Home Affairs: RICHARD BRADLEY.

Attorney-General and Minister of Information: GODFREY SMITH.

Minister of State in the Ministry of Natural Resources and the Environment: SERVULO BEAZA.

Minister of State in the Ministry of Industry: PATRICIA ARCEO.

MINISTRIES

Office of the Prime Minister: New Administrative Bldg, Belmopan; tel. (8) 22346; fax (8) 20071; e-mail prime-minister@belize.gov.bz.

Ministry of Agriculture, Fisheries and Co-operatives: 2nd Floor, West Block Bldg, Belmopan; tel. (8) 22241; fax (8) 22409; e-mail mafpaeu@btl.net.

Ministry of the Attorney-General: Belmopan; tel. (8) 22504; fax (8) 23390; e-mail atgenmin@btl.net.

Ministry of Budget Management, Investment and Trade: New Administration Bldg, Belmopan; tel. (8) 22345; fax (8) 22195.

Ministry of Economic Development: New Administration Bldg, Belmopan; tel. (8) 22526.

Ministry of Education and Sports: West Block Bldg, Belmopan; tel. (8) 23380; fax (8) 23389; e-mail educate@btl.net.

Ministry of Finance: New Administration Bldg, Belmopan; tel. (8) 22169; fax (8) 23317; e-mail finsecmof@btl.net.

Ministry of Foreign and Latin American Affairs: POB 174, New Administration Bldg, Belmopan; tel. (8) 22167; fax (8) 22854; e-mail belizemfa@btl.net.

Ministry of Health and Public Services: New Administration Bldg, Belmopan; tel. (8) 22325; fax (8) 22942.

Ministry of Housing, Urban Renewal and Home Affairs: East Block Bldg, Belmopan; tel. (1) 22016; fax (8) 23337.

Ministry of Human Development, Civil Society and Women: West Block, Independence Hill, Belmopan; tel. (8) 22161; fax (8) 23175.

Ministry of Industry: East Block Bldg, Belmopan; tel. (8) 22153.

Ministry of Information and Broadcasting: East Block Bldg, Belmopan; tel. (8) 20094.

Ministry of National Security: Curl Osmond Thompson Bldg, Belmopan; tel. (8) 22225; fax (8) 22615; e-mail mnsi@btl.net.

Ministry of Natural Resources and the Environment: Market Sq., Belmopan; tel. (8) 22249; fax (8) 22333; e-mail lincenbze@btl.net.

Ministry of Public Utilities, Energy, Communications and Immigration: Power Lane, Belmopan; tel. (8) 22817; fax (8) 23317.

Ministry of Public Works, Transport and of the Citrus and Banana Industries: Power Lane, Belmopan; tel. (8) 22136; fax (8) 23282; e-mail peumow@btl.net.

Ministry of Rural Development and Culture: East Block, Belmopan; tel. (8) 22444; fax (8) 20317; e-mail ruraldev@btl.net.

Ministry of the Sugar Industry, Labour and Local Government: 3rd Floor, Diamond Bldg, Constitution Drive, Belmopan; tel. (8) 23990; fax (8) 23365; e-mail msillg@belize.gov.bz.

Ministry of Youth and Tourism: Constitution Drive, Belmopan; tel. (8) 23393; fax (8) 23815; e-mail tourismmdpt@btl.net.

Legislature

NATIONAL ASSEMBLY
The Senate

President: Elizabeth Zabaneh.

There are eight nominated members.

House of Representatives

Speaker: Sylvia Flores.

Clerk: Jesus Ken.

General Election, 27 August 1998

	Votes cast	% of total	Seats
People's United Party (PUP) .	50,330	59.30	26
United Democratic Party (UDP)	33,237	39.16	3
Others	1,309	1.54	—
Total	84,876	100.00	29

Political Organizations

National Alliance for Belizean Rights (NABR): Belize City; f. 1992 by UDP members opposed to compromise over territorial dispute with Guatemala; Chair. (vacant); Co-ordinator Philip S. W. Goldson.

People's United Party (PUP): Belize City; tel. (2) 45886; fax (2) 31940; f. 1950; based on organized labour; merged with Christian Democratic Party in 1988; Leader Said Musa; Chair. Jorge Espat; Deputy Leaders Max Samuels, John Briceño.

United Democratic Party (UDP): South End Bel-China Bridge, POB 1898, Belize City; tel. (2) 76441; fax (2) 31004; e-mail info@udp.org.bz; internet www.udp.org.bz; f. 1974 by merger of People's Development Movement, Liberal Party and National Independence Party; conservative; Leader Dean Barrow; Chair. Elodio Aragon.

Diplomatic Representation

EMBASSIES AND HIGH COMMISSION
IN BELIZE

China (Taiwan): 3rd Floor, Blake's Bldg, cnr Hutson and Eyre Sts, POB 1020, Belize City; tel. (2) 78744; fax (2) 33082; e-mail embroc@btl.net; Ambassador: Tasi Erh-Huang.

Colombia: 12 St Matthew St, POB 1805, Belize City; tel. (2) 35623; fax (2) 31972; e-mail colombia@btl.net; Ambassador: Hector Caceres Florez.

Costa Rica: 38 Princess Margaret Drive, POB 2235, Belize City; tel. (2) 32878; fax (2) 32818; e-mail cremb@btl.net; Ambassador: Marco Vinicio Vargas P.

Cuba: 6048 Manatee Drive, Buttonwood Bay, POB 1775, Belize City; tel. (2) 35345.

El Salvador: 49 Nanche St, POB 215, Belmopan; tel. (8) 23404; fax (8) 23569; Ambassador: Manuel Antonio Vásquez Mena.

Guatemala: 8 'A' St, POB 1771, Belize City; tel. (2) 33314; fax (2) 35140; e-mail guatemb.bz@btl.net; Ambassador: Jorge Skinner-Klee.

Honduras: 22 Gabourel Lane, POB 285, Belize City; tel. (2) 45889; fax (2) 30562; Chargé d'affaires: Carlos Augusto Matuté Rivera.

Mexico: 20 North Park St, POB 754, Belize City; tel. (2) 30193; fax (2) 78742; Ambassador: Federico Uruchua.

United Kingdom: Embassy Sq., POB 91, Belmopan; tel. (8) 22146; fax (8) 22761; e-mail brithicom@btl.net; internet www.bhcbelize.org; High Commissioner: Timothy J. David.

USA: 29 Gabourel Lane, POB 286, Belize City; tel. (2) 77161; fax (2) 30802; e-mail brithicom@btl.net; internet www.usemb-belize.gov; Ambassador: Carolyn Curiel.

Venezuela: 18–20 Unity Blvd, POB 49, Belmopan; tel. (8) 22384; fax (8) 22022; e-mail embaven@btl.net; Ambassador: Christiaan van der Ree.

Judicial System

Summary Jurisdiction Courts (criminal jurisdiction) and District Courts (civil jurisdiction), presided over by magistrates, are established in each of the six judicial districts. Summary Jurisdiction Courts have a wide jurisdiction in summary offences and a limited jurisdiction in indictable matters. Appeals lie to the Supreme Court, which has jurisdiction corresponding to the English High Court of Justice and where a jury system is in operation. From the Supreme Court further appeals lie to a Court of Appeal, established in 1967, which holds an average of four sessions per year. Final appeals are made to the Judicial Committee of the Privy Council in the United Kingdom.

Court of Appeal: Kenneth George, Dr Nicholas Liverpool, Manuel Sosa.

Chief Justice: Abdulai Osmar Conteh (acting).

Supreme Court: Supreme Court Bldg, Belize City; tel. (2) 77256; fax (2) 70181; internet www.supremecourt.com; Registrar Raymond A. Usher.

Chief Magistrate: Herbert Lord, Paslow Bldg, Belize City; tel. (2) 77164.

Religion

CHRISTIANITY

Most of the population are Christian, the largest denomination being the Roman Catholic Church (62% of the population, according to the census of 1980). The other main groups were the Anglican (12% in 1980), Methodist (6%), Mennonite (4%), Seventh-day Adventist (3%) and Pentecostal (2%) churches.

Belize Council of Churches: 149 Allenby St, POB 508, Belize City; tel. (2) 77077; f. 1957 as Church World Service Committee, present name adopted 1984; eight mem. Churches, four assoc. bodies; Pres. Maj. Errol Robateau (Salvation Army); Gen. Sec. Sadie Vernon.

The Roman Catholic Church

Belize comprises the single diocese of Belize City-Belmopan, suffragan to the archdiocese of Kingston in Jamaica. In December 1999 it was estimated that there were 132,940 adherents in the diocese. The Bishop participates in the Antilles Episcopal Conference (whose secretariat is based in Port of Spain, Trinidad and Tobago).

Bishop of Belize City-Belmopan: Osmond Peter Martin, Bishop's House, 144 North Front St, POB 616, Belize City; tel. (2) 72122; fax (2) 31922.

The Anglican Communion

Anglicans in Belize belong to the Church in the Province of the West Indies, comprising eight dioceses. The Archbishop of the Province is the Bishop of North Eastern Caribbean and Aruba, resident in St John's, Antigua.

Bishop of Belize: Rt Rev. Sylvestre Donato Romero-Palma, Bishopthorpe, 25 Southern Foreshore, POB 535, Belize City; tel. (2) 73029; fax (2) 76898; e-mail bzediocese@btl.net.

Protestant Churches

Methodist Church (Belize/Honduras District Conference): 88 Regent St, POB 212, Belize City; tel. (2) 77173; fax (2) 75870; f. 1824; c. 2,620 mems; District Pres. Rev. Dr Lesley G. Anderson.

Mennonite Congregations in Belize: POB 427, Belize City; tel. (8) 30137; fax (8) 30101; f. 1958; four main Mennonite settlements: at Spanish Lookout, Shipyard, Little Belize and Blue Creek; Bishops J. B. LOEWEN, J. K. BARKMAN, P. THIESSEN, H. R. PENNER, CORNELIUS ENNS.

Other denominations active in the country include the Seventh-day Adventists, Pentecostals, Presbyterians, Baptists, Moravians, Jehovah's Witnesses, the Church of God, the Assemblies of Brethren and the Salvation Army.

OTHER RELIGIONS

There are also small communities of Hindus (106, according to the census of 1980), Muslims (110 in 1980), Jews (92 in 1980) and Bahá'ís.

The Press

Amandala: Amandala Press, 3304 Partridge St, POB 15, Belize City; tel. (2) 24476; fax (2) 24702; internet www.belizemall.com/amandala/; f. 1969; weekly; independent; Editor EVAN X. HYDE; circ. 45,000.

The Belize Observer: e-mail belizeobserver@excite.com; internet www.belizeobserver.com.

The Belize Times: 3 Queen St, POB 506, Belize City; tel. (2) 45757; fax (2) 31940; e-mail editor@belizetimes.com; internet www.belizetimes.com; f. 1956; weekly; party political paper of PUP; Editor ANDREW STEINHAUER; circ. 6,000.

Belize Today: Belize Information Service, East Block, POB 60, Belmopan; tel. (8) 22159; fax (8) 23242; monthly; official; Editor MIGUEL H. HERNÁNDEZ Jr; circ. 17,000.

Government Gazette: Government Printery, 1 Power Lane, Belmopan; tel. (8) 22127; fax (8) 23367; e-mail info@gazette.gov.bz; internet www.gazette.gov.br; official; weekly; Editor L. J. NICHOLAS.

The Reporter: 147 cnr Allenby and West Sts, POB 707, Belize City; tel. (2) 72503; f. 1968; weekly; Editor HARRY LAWRENCE; circ. 6,500.

The San Pedro Sun: POB 35, San Pedro Town, Ambergris Caye; fax (26) 2905; e-mail sanpedrosun@btl.net; internet www.ambergriscaye.com; weekly; Editors DAN JAMISON, EILEEN JAMISON.

NEWS AGENCY

Agencia EFE (Spain): c/o POB 506, Belize City; tel. (2) 45757; Correspondent AMALIA MAI.

Publisher

Government Printery: 1 Power Lane, Belmopan; tel. (8) 22293; f. 1871; responsible for printing, binding and engraving requirements of all govt depts and ministries; publications include annual govt estimates, govt magazines and the official *Government Gazette*.

Broadcasting and Communications

TELECOMMUNICATIONS

Belize Telecommunications Ltd: Esquivel Telecom Centre, St Thomas St, POB 603, Belize City; tel. (2) 32868; fax (2) 32096; e-mail educ@btl.net; internet www.btl.net; f. 1987; owned by Carlisle Group; Chair. MICHAEL A. ASHCROFT; CEO EDBERTO TESECUM.

Office of Telecommunications: Administration Complex, Mahogany St Extension, Belize City; tel. (2) 24938; fax (2) 24939; Dir CLIFFORD SLUSHER.

RADIO

Broadcasting Corporation of Belize (BCB): Albert Cattouse Bldg, Regent St, POB 89, Belize City; tel. (2) 72468; fax (2) 75040; e-mail rbgold@btl.net; f. 1937; privatized in 1998; broadcasts in English (75%) and Spanish; also transmits programmes in Garifuna and Maya; Gen. Man. RUTH STAINE-DAWSON.

Love FM: Belize City; e-mail lovefm@btl.net; internet www.lovefm.com; f. 1992; purchased Friends FM in 1998; Man. Dir RENE VILLANUEVA.

Radio Krem Ltd: 3304 Partridge St, POB 15, Belize City; tel. (2) 75929; fax (2) 74079; commercial; purchased Radio Belize in 1998; Man. EVA S. HYDE.

Other private radio stations broadcasting in Belize include: Estereo Amor, My Refuge Christian Radio, Radio 2000 and Voice of America.

TELEVISION

In August 1986 the Belize Broadcasting Authority issued licences to eight television operators for 14 channels, which mainly retransmit US satellite programmes, thus placing television in Belize on a fully legal basis for the first time.

Baymen Broadcasting Network (Channel 9): 27 Baymen Ave, Belize City; tel. (2) 44400; fax (2) 31242; commercial; Man. MARIE HOARE.

BCB Teleproductions: POB 89, Belize City; govt-owned; video production unit; local programmes for broadcasting.

Channel 5 Belize: POB 679, Belize City; tel. (2) 73146; fax (2) 74936; e-mail gbtv@btl.com; internet www.channel5belize.com; f. 1991.

Tropical Vision (Channels 7 and 11): 73 Albert St, Belize City; tel. (2) 77246; fax (2) 75040; commercial; Man. NESTOR VASQUEZ.

Finance

(cap. = capital; res = reserves; dep. = deposits; brs = branches)

BANKING
Central Bank

Central Bank of Belize: Gabourel Lane, POB 852, Belize City; tel. (2) 36194; fax (2) 36226; e-mail governor@cenbank.gov.bz; f. 1982; cap. BZ \$10m., res 11.6m., dep. 70.4m. (1999); Head RALPH FONSECA; Gov. KEITH A. ARNOLD.

Development Bank

Development Finance Corporation: Bliss Parade, Belmopan; tel. (8) 23360; fax (8) 23096; e-mail dfc@btl.net; internet www.dfcbelize.org; f. 1972; issued cap. BZ \$10m.; Chair. GLENN GODFREY; Gen. Man. ROBERTO BAUTISTA; 5 brs.

Other Banks

Atlantic Bank Ltd: Cnr Freetown Rd and Cleghorn St, POB 481, Belize City; tel. (2) 34123; fax (2) 33907; e-mail atlantic@btl.net; internet www.atlabank.com; f. 1971; total assets BZ \$163.7m.; Chair. Dr GUILLERMO BUESO.

Barclays Bank PLC (United Kingdom): 21 Albert St, POB 363, Belize City; tel. (2) 77211; fax (2) 78572; Man. TILVAN KING; 3 brs.

Belize Bank Ltd: 60 Market Sq., POB 364, Belize City; tel. (2) 77132; fax (2) 72712; e-mail bblbz@belizebank.com; cap. BZ \$4.3m., res BZ \$4.3m., dep. BZ \$280.1m. (April 1997); Chair. Sir EDNEY CAIN; Senior Vice-Pres. and Gen. Man. LOUIS ANTHONY SWASEY; 9 brs.

Provident Bank and Trust of Belize: 35 Barrack Rd and Craig St, POB 1867, Belize City; tel. (2) 35698; fax (2) 30368; e-mail services@providentbank.bz; internet www.providentbelize.com; f. 1998; cap. BZ \$2.6m., dep. BZ \$56.1m. (2000); Chair. RICARDO ESCALANTE; Man. LEOPOLDO WAIGHT.

Scotiabank (Canada): Albert St, POB 708, Belize City; tel. (2) 77027; fax 77416; e-mail cmobel@btl.net; Gen. Man. C. E. MARCEL; 6 brs.

There is also a government savings bank.

INSURANCE

General insurance is provided by local companies, and British, US and Jamaican companies are also represented.

Trade and Industry

STATUTORY BODIES

Banana Control Board: c/o Dept of Agriculture, West Block, Belmopan; management of banana industry; in 1989 it was decided to make it responsible to growers, not an independent executive; Head LALO GARCIA.

Belize Beef Corporation: c/o Dept of Agriculture, West Block, Belmopan; f. 1978; semi-governmental organization to aid development of cattle-rearing industry; Dir DEEDIE RUNKEL.

Belize Marketing Board: 117 North Front St, POB 633, Belize City; tel. (2) 77402; fax (2) 77656; f. 1948 to encourage the growing of staple food crops; purchases crops at guaranteed prices, supervises processing, storing and marketing intelligence; Chair. SILAS C. CAYETANO.

Belize Sugar Board: 7, 2nd St South, Corozal Town; tel. (4) 22005; fax (4) 22672; f. 1960 to control the sugar industry and cane production; includes representatives of the Government, sugar manufacturers, cane farmers and the public sector; Chair. ORLANDO PUGA; Exec. Sec. MARIA PUERTO.

Citrus Control Board: c/o Dept of Agriculture, West Block, Belmopan; tel. (8) 22199; f. 1966; determines basic quota for each producer, fixes annual price of citrus; Chair. C. SOSA.

DEVELOPMENT ORGANIZATIONS

Belize Reconstruction and Development Corporation: 36 Trinity Blvd, POB 1, Belmopan; tel. (8) 22271; fax (8) 23992; e-mail recondev@btl.net; Gen. Man. ALOYSIUS PALACIO.

Belize Trade and Investment Development Service: 14 Orchid Garden St, Belmopan; tel. (8) 23737; fax (8) 20595; e-mail beltraide@belize.gov.bz; internet www.belizeinvest.org.bz; f. 1986 as a joint government and private-sector institution to encourage export and investment; Gen. Man. PETER USHER.

Department of Economic Development: Ministry of Budget Planning, Economic Development, Investment and Trade, New Administrative Bldg, Belmopan; tel. (8) 22526; fax (8) 23111; administration of public and private-sector investment and planning; statistics agency; Head HUMBERTO PAREDES.

CHAMBER OF COMMERCE

Belize Chamber of Commerce and Industry: 63 Regent St, POB 291, Belize City; tel. (2) 73148; fax (2) 74984; e-mail bcci@btl.net; internet www.belize.org; f. 1920; Pres. Dr. GILBERT CANTON; Gen. Man. KEVIN HERRERA; 300 mems.

EMPLOYERS' ASSOCIATIONS

Banana Growers' Association: Big Creek, Independence Village, Stann Creek District; tel. (6) 22001; fax (6) 22112; e-mail banana@btl.net.

Belize Cane Farmers' Association: 34 San Antonio Rd, Orange Walk; tel. (3) 22005; fax (3) 23171; f. 1959 to assist cane farmers and negotiate with the Sugar Board and manufacturers on their behalf; Chair. PABLO TUN; 16 district brs.

Belize Livestock Producers' Association: 47.5 miles Western Highway, POB 183, Belmopan; tel. (8) 23202; fax (8) 23886; e-mail blpa@btl.net; Chair. PETE LIZARRAGA.

Citrus Growers' Association: 9 miles Stann Creek Valley Rd, POB 7, Stann Creek District; tel. (5) 23585; fax (5) 22686; e-mail cga@btl.net; f. 1966; CEO BRIDGET COLLERTON.

MAJOR COMPANIES

Belize Brewing Co Ltd: 1 King St, POB 1068, Belize City; tel. (2) 77031; fax (2) 72399; f. 1968; subsidiary of Bowen & Bowen Ltd; producers of malt liquors; Pres. BARRY BOWEN; 120 employees.

Belize Estate Co Ltd: Slaughterhouse Rd, POB 151, Belize City; tel. (2) 30641; fax (2) 31367; e-mail bec@bowen.com.bz; internet www.kiarental.com; f. 1875; subsidiary of Bowen & Bowen Ltd; importers and dealers of alcoholic drinks, shipping agents, main Ford dealers, operation of tourist enterprises; Pres. BARRY M. BOWEN; Man. Dir WILLIAM R. J. AYRES; 94 employees.

Belize Sugar Industries Ltd: Tower Hill, POB 29, Orange Walk Town; tel. (3) 22150; fax (3) 23247; e-mail bsiltd@btl.net; f. 1963; public co; raw sugar manufacturers; CEO L. M. BROWN; 350 employees.

Carlisle Holdings Ltd: 60 Market Sq, POB 1764, Belize City; tel. (2) 72660; fax (2) 75854; holding co with banking and financial services operations in Belize; investments in infrastructure development and agro-processing and distribution in Central America and the Caribbean region; Chair. and CEO MICHAEL A. ASHCROFT; Deputy Chair. DAVID B. HAMMOND; 62,000 employees (world-wide).

Esso Standard Oil SA Ltd: Caesar Rodge Rd, POB 238, Belize City; tel. (2) 77323; fax (2) 77726; e-mail ecgss@btl.net; petroleum exploration and distribution; Man. RUFINO LIN.

Hofius Ltd: 19 Albert St, POB 226, Belize City; tel. (2) 77231; fax (2) 74751; e-mail hofiusace@btl.net; f. 1892; hardware and home products, real estate sales, boats and marine fittings, food distribution; CEO JOHN CRUMP; 50 employees.

Mark C. Hulse: 25 Regent St, Belize City; tel (2) 73227; fax (2) 77037; accountancy and management consultancy services; Sr Partner MARK C. HULSE.

Prosser Agrotec and Fertilizer Co: 7.5 miles Western Highway, POB 566, Belize City; tel. (2) 35392; fax (2) 25548; e-mail prosser@btl.net; manufacture of industrial chemicals and fertilizers; CEO SALVADOR ESPAT.

Shell Belize Ltd: 2 miles Northern Highway, POB 608, Belize City; tel (2) 30406; fax (2) 30704; e-mail shellbze@btl.net; f. 1938; subsidiary of Shell Petroleum Co, United Kingdom; marketing and distribution of petroleum, petroleum products and chemical products; Chair. PAUL TRIMMER; 20 employees.

Texaco Belize Ltd: 4.5 miles Western Highway, Belize City; tel. (2) 24340; fax (2) 24355; subsidiary of Texaco Inc, USA; exploration and production of petroleum and gas, refining and distribution of petroleum and gas products; Man. HECTOR LÓPEZ.

UTILITIES
Electricity

Office of Electricity Supply: Mahogany St, POB 1846, Belize City; tel. (2) 24995; fax (2) 24994; f. 1992; Dir-Gen. HERMAN CHARLESWORTH.

Belize Electricity Co Ltd (BECOL): 115 Barrack Rd, POB 327, Belize City; tel. (2) 70954; fax (2) 30891; e-mail bel@btl.net; 95% owned by Fortis Inc. (Canada); operates Mollejon hydroelectric plant; Chair. NESTOR VASQUEZ; CEO LUIS LUE.

Belize Electricity Ltd (BEL): 2.5 miles Northern Highway, POB 327, Belize City; tel. (2) 70954; fax (2) 30891; e-mail pr@bel.com.bz; internet www.bel.com.bz; fmrly Belize Electricity Board, changed name upon privatization in 1999; Chair. ROBERT USHER.

Water

Belize Water Services Ltd: 44 Regent St, Belize City; tel. (2) 77097; fax (2) 77092; f. 1971 as Water and Sewer Authority (WASA); changed name upon privatization in March 2001; 82.7% owned by Cascal, BV (United Kingdom/Netherlands); CEO PETER WRENCH.

TRADE UNIONS

National Trades Union Congress of Belize (NTUCB): POB 2359, Belize City; tel. (2) 71596; fax (2) 72864; Pres. RAY DAVIS; Gen. Sec. DORENE QUIROS.

Principal Unions

United General Workers' Union: 1259 Lakeland City, Dangriga; tel. (5) 22105; f. 1979 by amalgamation of the Belize General Development Workers' Union and the Southern Christian Union; three branch unions affiliated to the central body; affiliated to ICFTU; Pres. FRANCIS SABAL; Gen. Sec. CONRAD SAMBULA.

Belize National Teachers' Union: POB 382, Belize City; tel. (2) 72857; Pres. HELEN STUART; Sec. MIGUEL WONG; 1,000 mems.

Christian Workers' Union: 107B Cemetery Rd, Belize City; tel. (2) 72150; f. 1962; general; Pres. JAMES McFOY; Gen. Sec. ANTONIO GONZÁLEZ; 1,000 mems.

Democratic Independent Union: Belize City; Pres. CYRIL DAVIS; 1,250 mems.

Public Service Union of Belize: Hilltop, POB 458, Belmopan; tel. (8) 23885; fax (8) 20283; e-mail belizepsu@btl.net; f. 1922; public workers; Pres. MARGARET VENTURA; Sec.-Gen. HUBERT ENRIQUEZ; 1,582 mems.

United Banners Banana Workers' Union: Dangriga; f. 1995; Pres. MARCIANA FUNEZ.

Transport

Department of Transport: Forest Drive, Belmopan; tel. (8) 22417; fax (8) 23379; Commissioner PHILLIP BRACKETT.

RAILWAYS

There are no railways in Belize.

ROADS

There are 1,419 km (882 miles) of all-weather main and feeder roads and 651 km (405 miles) of cart roads and bush trails. About 805 km (500 miles) of logging and forest tracks are usable by heavy-duty vehicles in the dry season. In 2000 the World Bank (International Bank for Reconstruction and Development—IBRD) approved a loan of US $13m. for road construction.

SHIPPING

There is a deep-water port at Belize City and a second port at Commerce Bight, near Dangriga (formerly Stann Creek), to the south of Belize City. There is a port for the export of bananas at Big Creek. Nine major shipping lines operate vessels calling at Belize City, including the Carol Line (consisting of Harrison, Hapag-Lloyd, Nedlloyd and CGM).

Belize Port Authority: Caesar Ridge Rd, POB 633, Belize City; tel. (2) 72439; fax (2) 73571; e-mail portbz@btl.net; f. 1980; Chair. KAY MENZIES; Ports Commr ALFRED B. COYE.

Belize Lines Ltd: 37 Regent St, Belize City.

CIVIL AVIATION

Phillip S. W. Goldson International Airport, 14 km (9 miles) from Belize City, can accommodate medium-sized jet-engined aircraft. A new terminal was completed in 1990. There are airstrips for light aircraft on internal flights near the major towns and offshore islands. The runway was extended in 2000.

Department of Civil Aviation: POB 367, Belize City; e-mail aviation@btl.net; Dir EFRAIN GOMEZ.

Maya Island Air: Municipal Airport, POB 458, Belize City; tel. (2) 35795; fax (2) 30585; e-mail mayair@btl.net; internet www.ambergriscaye.com/islandair; f. 1997 as merger between Maya Airways Ltd and Island Air; operated by Belize Air Group; internal services, centred on Belize City, and charter flights to neighbouring countries; Exec. Dir TREVOR ROE; Gen. Man. PABLO ESPAT.

Tropical Air Services (Tropic Air): San Pedro, POB 20, Ambergris Caye; tel. (2) 62012; fax (2) 62338; e-mail djonsson@btl.net; f. 1979; operates internal services and services to Mexico and Guatemala; Chair. CELI MCCORKLE; Man. Dir JOHN GREIF.

Tourism

The main tourist attractions are the beaches and the barrier reef, diving, fishing and the Mayan archaeological sites. There are nine major wildlife reserves (including the world's only reserves for the jaguar and for the red-footed booby), and government policy is to develop 'eco-tourism', based on the attractions of an unspoilt environment and Belize's natural history. The country's wildlife also includes howler monkeys and 500 species of birds, and its barrier reef is the second largest in the world. However, in May 2000 scientists reported that the high sea temperatures recorded in 1998, caused by the El Niño phenomenon and global warming, had resulted in extensive damage to the coral population. There were some 390 hotels in Belize in 1999. In the same year there were an estimated 157,000 tourist arrivals and tourist receipts totalled an estimated US $99m. In February 1996 the Mundo Maya Agreement was ratified, according to which Belize, El Salvador, Guatemala, Honduras and Mexico would co-operate in the management of Mayan archaeological remains. In February 2000 the Belize Tourist Board announced that all tour operators and guides needed to obtain a licence. In June the Inter-American Development Bank approved a loan of US $11m. towards the Government's tourism development plan. A hotel development in Belize City was to open in 2001.

Belize Tourist Board: Level 2, Central Bank Bldg, POB 325, Gabourel Lane, Belize City; tel. (2) 31913; fax (2) 31943; e-mail info@travelbelize.org; internet www.travelbelize.org; f. 1964; fmrly Belize Tourist Bureau; eight mems; Chair. PATTY ARCEO; Dir TRACY TAEGAR.

Belize Tourism Industry Association (BTIA): 10 North Park St, POB 62, Belize City; tel. (2) 75717; fax (2) 78710; e-mail btia@btl.net; internet www.btia.org; Pres. WADE BEVIER (acting).

Defence

The Belize Defence Force was formed in 1978 and was based on a combination of the existing Police Special Force and the Belize Volunteer Guard. Military service is voluntary, but provision has been made for the establishment of National Service, if necessary to supplement normal recruitment. In August 2000 the regular Armed Forces totalled approximately 1,050 and there were some 700 militia reserves. In 1994 all British forces were withdrawn from Belize, with the exception of about 180 troops who remained to organize jungle-warfare training.

Defence Budget (2000): an estimated BZ $17m.

Belize Defence Force Commander: Brig.-Gen. CEDRIC BORLAND.

Education

Education is compulsory for all children between the ages of five and 14 years. Primary education, beginning at five years of age and lasting for eight years, is provided free of charge, principally through subsidized denominational schools under government control. In 1996/97 there were 53,110 pupils enrolled at 280 primary schools. Secondary education, beginning at the age of 13, lasts for four years. There were 10,912 students enrolled in 30 general secondary schools in 1996/97. In 1997 primary enrolment included an estimated 99.9% of children in the relevant age-group (males 99.9%; females 99.9%), while secondary enrolment in that year was equivalent to 63.6% (males 64.6%; females 62.6%).

In 1996/97 there were 2,500 students enrolled in 11 other educational institutions, which included technical, vocational and teacher-training colleges. The University College of Belize was established in 1986 and there is also an extra-mural branch of the University of the West Indies in Belize. In early 2000 it was announced that a new University of Belize was to be formed through the amalgamation of five higher education institutions, including the University College of Belize and Belize Technical College. In the financial year 1997/98, budget expenditure on education was envisaged at BZ $74.2m., representing 20.5% of total spending by the central Government. In 1998 the average rate of adult illiteracy was 7.3% (males 7.1%; females 7.5%).

Bibliography

For works on the Caribbean generally, see Select Bibliography (Books).

Bethell, L. (Ed.). *The Cambridge History of Latin America*. Cambridge, Cambridge University Press, 1985.

British Honduras: The Guatemalan Claim. London, Central Information Office, 1960.

Collier, S., Blakemore, H., and Skidmore, T. E. (Eds). *The Cambridge Encyclopedia of Latin America and the Caribbean*. Cambridge, Cambridge University Press, 1985.

Cutlack, M. *Belize, Ecotourism in Action*. London, Macmillan, 1993.

Fernandez, J. A. *Belize: Case Study for Democracy in Central America*. Avebury, Gower Publishing Co Ltd, 1989.

Humphreys, R. A. *The Diplomatic History of British Honduras*. Oxford, Oxford University Press, 1961.

Moberg, M. *Myths of Ethnicity and Nation: Immigration, Work and Identity in the Belize Banana Industry*. Knoxville, TN, University of Tennessee Press, 1997.

Norton, N. *Belize*. London, Cadogan Press, 1997.

Simmons, D. C. *Confederate Settlements in British Honduras*. Jefferson, NC, McFarland & Co, 2001.

Turner, B. L., and Harrison, P. D. (Eds). *Pulltrouser Swamp: Ancient Maya Habitat, Agriculture and Settlement in Northern Belize*. Salt Lake City, UT, University of Utah Press, 2000.

BERMUDA

Area: 53 sq km (20.59 sq miles); the Bermudas or Somers Islands comprise about 150 islands.

Population (World Bank estimate, 1999): 64,000.

Capital: Hamilton (population 1,100 at 1991 census).

Language: English.

Religion: Predominantly Christian; the Anglican Communion is the main denomination, but several others are represented.

Climate: Mild and humid; average temperature range 18°–30°C (64°–86°F) May–Oct., 16°–20°C (61°–68°F) Dec.–Feb.; average rainfall 1,470 mm (58.0 in).

Time: GMT −4 hours.

Public Holidays: 2002: 1 January (New Year's Day), 29 March (Good Friday), 24 May (Bermuda Day), 17 June (Queen's Official Birthday), 1 August (Cup Match), 2 August (Somers' Day), 2 September (Labour Day), 11 November (Remembrance Day), 25–26 December (Christmas). **2003:** 1 January (New Year's Day), 18 April (Good Friday), 24 May (Bermuda Day), 16 June (Queen's Official Birthday), 31 July (Cup Match), 1 August (Somers' Day), 1 September (Labour Day), 11 November (Remembrance Day), 25–26 December (Christmas).

Currency: Bermuda dollar; US $1 = B $1.00 (at par since February 1970); B $100 = £69.84 = US $100.00 = €112.66 (30 April 2001).

Weights and Measures: Metric; imperial and US systems still used in certain fields.

History

Bermuda is a Crown Colony of the United Kingdom. The British monarch is represented in the islands by a Governor.

The 1968 Constitution gave Bermuda (the oldest British colony, established in 1684) internal self-government. The 1968 elections were won by the moderate, multiracial United Bermuda Party (UBP). However, Bermudian society was riven by racial tensions and in the early 1970s there were considerable levels of violence, including the assassination of the Governor of the Colony. At the 1976 election the UBP remained in power. However, it lost seats to the mainly black, pro-independence, left-wing Progressive Labour Party (PLP), which gained 46% of the vote, but only 14 of the 40 seats in the House of Assembly. It narrowly retained power in 1980, but regained the seats it had lost in the following election, in 1983. Meanwhile, in 1982, John W. Swan (later knighted) became party leader and Premier. The UBP won a decisive victory in the 1985 elections, but in 1989 it lost seats, although it maintained its majority. The UBP remained in government after the general election of October 1993 (the first to be held since the voting age was lowered from 21 to 18 years), having won 22 seats (compared to 18 seats secured by the PLP).

On 16 August 1995 a referendum was held on independence from the United Kingdom, despite the strenuous opposition of the PLP, which stated that the issue ought to be decided in a general election and urged its supporters to boycott the poll. In the referendum, which had a relatively low turn-out for Bermuda of 58.8%, some 73.6% of participants registered their opposition to independence. The debate had polarized opinion within the ruling party and Swan subsequently resigned as premier and as leader of the UBP. He was succeeded in both posts by the erstwhile finance minister, Dr David Saul, under whose leadership the divisions within the UBP deepened. Saul remained neutral on the independence issue. A motion of censure against him was approved in the House of Assembly in June 1996, with the support of five UBP members, prompted by Saul's decision to authorize the establishment of a foreign-owned franchise restaurant in Bermuda, in contravention of a ruling by the Bermuda Monetary Authority. Having failed to restore party unity, Saul resigned as Premier and UBP leader in March 1997. He was replaced by Pamela Gordon.

In August 1996 the Leader of the Opposition, Frederick Wade, died. At a by-election in October Wade's former seat was retained by the PLP, and in the following month the party's Deputy Leader, Jennifer Smith, was elected to the leadership of the organization.

In June 1998 the Court of Appeal upheld the constitutionality of the Prohibited Restaurants Act, which had been passed by the House of Assembly to prevent a further attempt by a consortium of investors, which included Sir John Swan, to bring fast-food franchises to Bermuda. The deep divisions within the UBP were exposed once again by the acrimonious debate over the legislation and overshadowed the party's campaign for the parliamentary elections of 9 November 1998. At these elections, the PLP received 54.2% of the votes cast, winning 26 seats and its first ever majority in the House of Assembly. The UBP obtained 44.1% of the ballot and 14 seats. On 10 November Jennifer Smith was sworn in as Bermuda's first PLP Premier. She declared that no immediate moves towards independence were planned, although it remained a stated aim of the party. She also reassured the international business community that her Government would seek to enhance Bermuda's attraction as an international business center, and that she would resist any attempts to alter the island's tax status. In February 1999, nevertheless, the premier reassured members of the Organisation for Economic Co-operation and Development (OECD) that Bermuda would make efforts to improve regulation of the 'off-shore' financial services sector.

In April 1999 Smith appointed L. Milton Scott as Minister of Education. In March the British Government published draft legislation confirming that its Dependencies were to be referred to as United Kingdom Overseas Territories; the document stated that all such territories would be required to comply with European standards on human rights and financial regulation. In October it was announced that in accordance with these reforms, corporal and capital punishment were to be abolished in Bermuda.

In July 1999 the Judicial Committee of the Privy Council again upheld the constitutionality of the Prohibited Restaurants Act and subsequently rejected a final appeal by the investor consortium. On 20 July 2000 the Government passed legislation, intended to promote equal opportunities, requiring companies to monitor the racial composition of their work-force. Following the OECD's Financial Action Task Force's investigation into tax 'havens', in 1998, in June 2000 Bermuda pledged to conform to international standards before the end of 2005. This was likely to include the abolition of the 60/40 rule, by which all businesses aimed at the local market had to be 60%-owned by a Bermudian individual or entity. The Government had, however, pledged to maintain its existing tax system, which included no income tax. In December the members of the House of Assembly agreed, for the first time, to declare their assets and financial interests. On 2 November 2000, in an internal PLP election, Jennifer Smith was re-elected leader of the party, with 81 of the 116 votes cast.

Aside from the worrying decline in the tourism industry and the increase in the value of drugs seizures by Bermudian customs, the most important issue the Government faced during the first six months of 2001 was that of constitutional change. The Government and the opposition UBP fundamentally disagreed about proposed changes to the voting system and electoral boundaries. Racial issues were at the heart of the conflict, with the ruling PLP claiming the present system favoured the traditionally 'white' UBP. In December 2000 the House of Assembly approved a motion requesting the British Government to approve the establishment of a boundaries commission, which would recommend the size of the island's constituencies. Any changes would be subject to ratification by the United Kingdom's Foreign and Commonwealth Office. In January 2001 the UBP submitted a 8,500-signature petition to the British Government, demanding a constitutional conference or referendum before any changes were made. Gordon also claimed that some Bermudians had refused to sign the petition fearing recriminations. The British Foreign and Commonwealth Office, however, stated that a constitutional conference was unnecessary, and in April it began consultations over the proposed changes1.

Economy

Despite the growth of financial services, in 1996 it was estimated that tourism still accounted for almost one-half of foreign exchange earnings and, directly and indirectly, 65% of employment. Visitor expenditure accounted for 19.1% of GDP in 1999/2000. In 2000 an estimated 13.8% of the employed labour force worked in restaurants and hotels. The sector earned an estimated B \$479m. in 1999. The majority of visitors come from the USA (some 78% of total arrivals by air in 1998), Canada and the United Kingdom. In 2000 537,577 tourists visited Bermuda. Plans were approved in early 1999 for an eco-tourism development, the first major hotel development for more than 25 years. Despite the decline in the tourist industry in the late 1990s, international tourism receipts in 1998 were B \$480m., a slight increase on the previous year. In June 2000 the Minister of Tourism, David H. Allen, announced that Bermuda would join the Caribbean Tourism Organization. Nevertheless, although the number of cruise ship passengers increased in both 1999 and 2000, the number of air arrivals fell. In 2000 Bermuda had suffered its worst year for tourism since 1979. In May 2001 the Bermuda Alliance for Tourism announced plans to rebrand Bermuda as a luxury destination. The ongoing decline in the tourist sector was likely to also affect the retail sector, and to lead to an overall increase in unemployment.

'Offshore' commercial and financial services were estimated to earn more than one-third of foreign exchange in 1995. Some 18.7% of the employed work-force were engaged directly in the financial, insurance, real-estate and business sectors in 2000. At the end of 1998 there were 10,960 registered exempt companies. The Bermudian insurance industry was estimated to have doubled during the last decade of the 20th century and by 2000 was the world's third largest.

Bermuda is very dependent upon food and energy imports, mainly from the USA, and has few export commodities. Therefore, it consistently records a large visible trade deficit (B \$661m. in 1999). Receipts from the service industries normally ensure a surplus on the current account of the balance of payments; however, the decline in the tourism sector led to a deficit in the net current account in 2000, of B \$40m. The USA is the principal source of imports (76.0% of total imports in 1997) and the principal market for exports. Manufacturing and construction accounted for some 10% of GDP in 1996 and employed less than 5% of the work-force. Smaller industry includes ship repair, small boat building and manufacture of paint, perfume, pharmaceuticals, mineral-water extracts and handicrafts.

In 1999/2000 Bermuda's gross domestic product at market prices (GDP) was US \$2,623.9m. In 1997/98 GDP per head was estimated to be equivalent to some US \$34,600, one of the highest levels in the world. In the financial year ending 31 March 1998 Bermuda recorded a budgetary surplus of some B \$65.7m. A budgetary deficit of B \$24.8m. was projected for the 1998/99 financial year. The average annual rate of inflation was 2.6% in 1990–99. The rate decreased to 2.0% in 1998, but increased to 2.4% in 1999. Some 1.5% of the labour force were registered unemployed in 1995, although unofficial sources estimated that the rate might be as high as 15%. However, in February 2001 the government figures indicated that unemployment had fallen for the first time since 1993.

Statistics Survey

Source: Department of Information Services, Global House, 43 Church St, Hamilton HM 12; tel. 292-6384; fax 295-5267.

AREA AND POPULATION

Area: 53 sq km (20.59 sq miles).

Population (excluding visitors): 58,460 (males 28,345; females 30,115) at census of 20 May 1991; 60,144 (official estimate) at 31 December 1996; 64,000 (World Bank estimate) in 1999; *Principal towns* (population at 1991 census): Hamilton 1,100; St George's 1,648.

Density (1999, estimate): 1,207.5 per sq km.

Births, Marriages and Deaths (1998): Birth rate 13.2 per 1,000; Marriage rate 16.6 per 1,000; Death rate 7.8 per 1,000.

Expectation of Life (years at birth, official estimates, 1996): Males 70.0; Females 78.0.

Employment (excluding unpaid family workers, 2000): Agriculture, fishing and quarrying 561; Manufacturing 1,211; Electricity, gas and water 447; Construction 2,601; Wholesale and retail trade 5,090; Restaurants and hotels 5,175; Transport and communications 2,918; Financial intermediation and real estate 3,423; Business activities 3,568; Public administration 4,259; Education, health and social services 2,796; Other community, social and personnel services 2,207; International business activity 3,216; Total 37,472.

AGRICULTURE, ETC.

Principal Crops (FAO estimates, metric tons, 2000): Potatoes 1,000; Vegetables and melons 3,000. Source: FAO.

Livestock ('000 head, FAO estimates, 2000): Cattle 1; Horses 1; Pigs 1. Source: FAO.

Livestock Products (metric tons, 2000): Cows' milk 1,000 (FAO estimate). Source: FAO.

Fishing (metric tons, live weight, 1998): Groupers 43, Snappers 29, Carangids 48, Wahoo 108, Yellowfin tuna 53, Caribbean spiny lobster 30; Total catch 460. Source: FAO, *Yearbook of Fishery Statistics*.

INDUSTRY

Electric Energy (production, million kWh): 518 in 1993; 527 in 1994; 521 in 1995. Source: UN, *Industrial Commodity Statistics Yearbook*.

FINANCE

Currency and Exchange Rates: 100 cents = 1 Bermuda dollar (B \$). *Sterling, US Dollar and Euro Equivalents* (30 April 2001): £1 sterling = B \$1.4318; US \$1 = B \$1.000; €1 = 88.76 cents; B \$100 = £69.84 = US \$100.00 = €112.66. *Exchange Rate:* The Bermuda dollar is at par with the US dollar. Note: US and Canadian currencies are also accepted.

Budget (B \$ million, 1997/98): *Total revenue* 517.5 (Customs duties 150.5; Payroll tax 137.8; Hotel occupancy tax 13.1; Passenger tax 21.3; Land tax 25.9; International company tax 34.7; Stamp duties 21.2). *Total expenditure* 451.8 (Salaries and wages 224.8; Other goods and services 136.7; Grants and contributions 90.3; Capital expenditure 72.3).

Cost of Living (Consumer Price Index; base: 1990 = 100): 120.6 in 1997; 123.0 in 1998; 126.0 in 1999.

Expenditure on the Gross Domestic Product (B \$ million at current prices, year ending 31 March 2000): Government final consumption expenditure 325.4; Private final consumption expenditure 1,654.3; Gross fixed capital formation 413.2; *Total domestic expenditure* 2,392.9; Exports of goods and services 1,549.2; *Less* Imports of goods and services 1,318.2; GDP in purchasers' values 2,623.9.

Balance of Payments (B \$ million, 2000): Payments (gross) 1,613 (Imports 719); Receipts (gross) 1,810 (Tourism 434, Professional services 930); *Current balance* (net) –40. Source: Bermuda Monetary Authority.

EXTERNAL TRADE

Principal Commodities (US \$ million, 1997): *Imports* Food and live animals 98.0; Beverages and tobacco 26.4; Crude materials (inedible) except fuels 9.0; Mineral fuels and lubricants 45.3; Chemicals 49.0; Basic manufactures 98.5; Machinery and transport equipment 151.0; Miscellaneous manufactured articles 131.4; Total (incl. others) 632.0. *Exports:* Total 23.0.

1998 (B \$ million): Total imports 629.18; Total exports 44.94.

Principal Trading Partners (US \$ million): *Imports* (1997): Canada 34.5; France 7.5; Japan 20.0; United Kingdom 30.8; USA 480.0; Total (incl. others) 631.9. *Exports* (1995): France 7.5; United Kingdom 3.9; USA 31.3; Total (incl. others) 62.9.

Source: UN, *International Trade Statistics Yearbook*.

TRANSPORT

Road Traffic (vehicles in use, 1998): Private cars 22,000; Motorcycles 24,250; Buses, taxis and limousines 725; Trucks and tank wagons 3,513; Other 770; Total 51,258.

Shipping: *Ship arrivals* (1998): Cruise ships 151; Cargo ships 189; Oil and gas tankers 23. *Merchant Fleet** (registered at 31 December 2000): 129; Total displacement 5,751,816 grt. *International freight traffic†* ('000 metric tons, 1990): Goods loaded 130; Goods unloaded 470.

* Source: Lloyd's Register of Shipping, *World Fleet Statistics*.

† Source: UN, *Monthly Bulletin of Statistics*.

Civil Aviation (1996): Aircraft arrivals 5,322; passengers 368,756 (1998); air cargo 5,908,624 kg; air mail 191,239 kg.

TOURISM

Visitor Arrivals: 557,087 (arrivals by air 368,756; cruise ship passengers 188,331) in 1998; 548,467 (arrivals by air 354,026; cruise ship passengers 194,441) in 1999; 537,577 (arrivals by air 328,305; cruise ship passengers 209,272) in 2000. Source: Bermuda Department of Tourism.

COMMUNICATIONS MEDIA

Radio Receivers (1997): 82,000 in use.
Television Receivers (1997): 66,000 in use.
Telephones (1996): 49,000 main lines in use.
Mobile Cellular Telephones (1996): 7,980 subscribers.
Daily Newspapers (1996): 1 (estimated circulation 17,000).
Non-Daily Newspapers (1996): 2 (estimated circulation 13,000).
Sources: UNESCO, *Statistical Yearbook*; UN, *Statistical Yearbook*.

EDUCATION

Pre-primary (1996/97): 12 schools; 51 teachers; 452 pupils.
Primary (1996/97): 26 schools; 478 teachers; 5,883 pupils.
General Secondary (1996/97): 14 schools (incl. 2 denominational, 1 USAF and 3 other private schools, 1992); 355 teachers; 3,726 pupils.
Higher (1998): 1 institution; 677 students.
Source: mainly UNESCO, *Statistical Yearbook*.

Directory
The Constitution

The Constitution, introduced on 8 June 1968 and amended in 1973 and 1979, contains provisions relating to the protection of fundamental rights and freedoms of the individual; the powers and duties of the Governor; the composition, powers and procedure of the Legislature; the Cabinet; the judiciary; the public service and finance.

The British monarch is represented by an appointed Governor, who retains responsibility for external affairs, defence, internal security and the police.

The Legislature consists of the monarch, the Senate and the House of Assembly. Three members of the Senate are appointed at the Governor's discretion, five on the advice of the Government leader and three on the advice of the Opposition leader. The Senate elects a President and Vice-President. The House of Assembly, consisting of 40 members elected under universal adult franchise from 20 constituencies, elects a Speaker and a Deputy Speaker, and sits for a five-year term.

The Cabinet consists of the Premier and at least six other members of the Legislature. The Governor appoints the majority leader in the House of Assembly as Premier, who in turn nominates the other members of the Cabinet. They are assigned responsibilities for government departments and other business and, in some cases, are assisted by Permanent Cabinet Secretaries.

The Cabinet is presided over by the Premier. The Governor's Council enables the Governor to consult with the Premier and two other members of the Cabinet nominated by the Premier on matters for which the Governor has responsibility. The Secretary to the Cabinet, who heads the public service, acts as secretary to the Governor's Council.

Voters must be British subjects aged 18 years or over (lowered from 21 years in 1990), and, if not possessing Bermudian status, must have been registered as electors on 1 May 1976. Candidates for election must qualify as electors, and must possess Bermudian status.

Under draft legislation published by the British Government in March 1999, Bermudian citizens have the right to United Kingdom citizenship and the right of abode in the United Kingdom. British citizens do not enjoy reciprocal rights.

The Government

Governor and Commander-in-Chief: JOHN THOROLD MASEFIELD (took office 4 June 1997).
Deputy Governor: TIM GURNEY.

CABINET
(August 2001)

Premier: JENNIFER M. SMITH.
Deputy Premier, Minister of Finance: C. EUGENE COX.

Minister of Legislative Affairs and Attorney-General: Dame LOIS BROWNE-EVANS.
Minister of Development and Opportunity and of the Environment: TERRY E. LISTER.
Minister of Education: L. MILTON SCOTT.
Minister of Health and Family Services: NELSON B. A. BASCOMBE.
Minister of Labour, Home Affairs and Public Safety: PAULA A. COX.
Minister of Telecommunications and E-Commerce: MAURINE (RENEE) WEBB.
Minister of Tourism: DAVID H. ALLEN.
Minister of Transport: Dr EWART F. BROWN.
Minister of Works and Engineering: W. ALEX SCOTT.
Minister of Youth, Sports and Recreation: DENNIS P. LISTER.
Minister without Portfolio: RANDY HORTON.

MINISTRIES

Office of the Governor: Government House, 11 Langton Hill, Pembroke HM 13; tel. 292-3600; fax 292-6831.
Office of the Premier: Cabinet Office, Cabinet Bldg, 105 Front St, Hamilton HM 12; tel. 292-5502; fax 292-8397; e-mail premier@bdagov.bm.
Ministry of Development and Opportunity: Global House, 43 Church St, Hamilton HM 12; tel. 292-5998; fax 295-5267.
Ministry of Education: Second Floor, 7 Point Finger Rd, Paget DV 04, POB HM 1185, Hamilton HM EX; tel. 236-6904; fax 236-4006.
Ministry of the Environment, Development and Opportunity: Government Administration Bldg, 30 Parliament St, Hamilton HM 12; tel. 295-5151; fax 292-2349; e-mail environment@northrock.bm.
Ministry of Finance: Government Administration Bldg, 30 Parliament St, Hamilton HM 12; tel. 295-5151; fax 295-5727.
Ministry of Health and Family Services: 7 Point Finger Rd, Paget DV 04, POB HM 380, Hamilton HM BX; tel. 236-0224; fax 236-3937.
Ministry of Labour, Home Affairs and Public Safety: Government Administration Bldg, 30 Parliament St, POB HM 1364, Hamilton HM 12; tel. 295-5151; fax 295-4780.
Ministry of Legislative Affairs, Attorney-General's Chambers: Global House, 43 Church St, Hamilton HM 12; tel. 293-2463; fax 292-3608; email govtlaur@ibl.bm.
Ministry of Telecommunications and E-Commerce: Golinsky Bldg, 60 Reid St, POB HM 101, Hamilton HM 13; tel. 295-5151; fax 296-9444; internet www.mtec.bm.
Ministry of Tourism and Marine Services: Global House, 43 Church St, Hamilton HM 12; tel. 292-0023; fax 292-7537.
Ministry of Transport: Global House, 43 Church St, Hamilton HM 12; tel. 295-3130; fax 295-1013.
Ministry of Works and Engineering: Post Office Bldg, 56 Church St, POB HM 525, Hamilton HM 12; tel. 295-5151; fax 295-0170.
Ministry of Youth, Sport and Recreation: Old Fire Station Bldg, 81 Court St, Hamilton HM 12; tel. 295-0855; fax 295-6292.

Legislature
SENATE

President: ALFRED OUGHTON.
Vice-President: Dr IDWAL WYN (WALWYN) HUGHES.
There are 11 nominated members.

HOUSE OF ASSEMBLY

Speaker: STANLEY W. LOWE.
Deputy Speaker: W. M. LISTER.

There are 40 elected members. Two candidates are elected by each constituency. The House of Assembly meets on Fridays when in session, and on Mondays, Wednesdays and Fridays during the period that the annual budget is debated.

Clerk to the Legislature: Y. MURIEL ROACH, The Legislature, Hamilton; tel. 292-7408; fax 292-2006; e-mail mroach@bda.gov.bm.

General Election, 9 November 1998

Party					% of votes	Seats
Progressive Labour Party	.	.	.	.	54.2	26
United Bermuda Party	.	.	.	.	44.1	14
National Liberal Party	.	.	.	.	0.8	—
Independents	.	.	.	.	.	0.8	—
Total	.	.	.	.	.	100.0	40

Political Organizations

National Liberal Party (NLP): 53 Church St, Hamilton HM 12, POB HM 1794, Hamilton HM FX; tel. 292-8587; f. 1985; Leader D. WALDRON; Chair. GRAEME OUTERBRIDGE.

Progressive Labour Party (PLP): Alaska Hall, 16 Court St, POB 1367, Hamilton HM 12; tel. 292-2264; fax 295-7890; e-mail plp@plp.bm; internet www.plp.bm; f. 1963; advocates the 'Bermudianization' of the economy, more equitable taxation, a more developed system of welfare and preparation for independence; Leader JENNIFER M. SMITH; Deputy Leader C. EUGENE COX; Chair. VICTOR FISHINGTON.

United Bermuda Party (UBP): Central Office, 87 John F. Burrows Bldg, Chancery Lane, Hamilton HM 12, POB HM 715, Hamilton HM CX; tel. 295-0729; fax 292-7195; e-mail info@ubp.bm; internet www.ubp.bm; f. 1964; policy of participatory democracy, supporting system of free enterprise; Leader PAMELA F. GORDON; Chair. AUSTIN B. WOODS.

Judicial System

Chief Justice: AUSTIN WARD.

President of the Court of Appeal: Sir JAMES ASTWOOD.

Registrar of Supreme Court and Court of Appeal: CHARLENE SCOTT (acting).

Attorney-General: Dame LOIS BROWNE-EVANS.

Director of Public Prosecutions: KHAMISI TOKUMBO.

Solicitor-General: WILLIAM PEARCE.

The Court of Appeal was established in 1964, with powers and jurisdiction of equivalent courts in other parts of the Commonwealth. The Supreme Court has jurisdiction over all serious criminal matters and has unlimited civil jurisdiction. The Court also hears civil and criminal appeals from the Magistrates' Courts. The three Magistrates' Courts have jurisdiction over all petty offences, and have a limited civil jurisdiction.

Religion

CHRISTIANITY

In 1991 it was estimated that 28% of the population were members of the Anglican Communion, 15% were Roman Catholics, 12% were African Methodist Episcopalians, 6% were Seventh-day Adventists and 5% were Wesleyan Methodists. The Presbyterian Church, the Baptist Church and the Pentecostal Church are also active in Bermuda.

The Anglican Communion

The Anglican Church of Bermuda consists of a single, extra-provincial diocese, directly under the metropolitan jurisdiction of the Archbishop of Canterbury, the Primate of All England. There are about 23,000 Anglicans and Episcopalians in Bermuda.

Bishop of Bermuda: Rt Rev. EWEN RATTERAY, Bishop's Lodge, 18 Ferrar's Lane, Pembroke HM 08, POB HM 769, Hamilton HM CX; tel. 292-6987; fax 292-5421; e-mail bishopratteray@ibl.bm; internet www.anglican.bm.

The Roman Catholic Church

Bermuda forms a single diocese, suffragan to the archdiocese of Kingston in Jamaica. At 31 December 1999 there were an estimated 8,712 adherents in the Territory. The Bishop participates in the Antilles Episcopal Conference (currently based in Port of Spain, Trinidad and Tobago).

Bishop of Hamilton in Bermuda: ROBERT JOSEPH KURTZ, St Theresa's Cathedral, 13 Elliott St, POB HM 1191, Hamilton HM EX; tel. 292-0607; fax 292-2477.

Protestant Churches

Baptist Church: Emmanuel Baptist Church, 35 Dundonald St, Hamilton HM 10; tel. 295-6555; Minister DANIEL STANLEY.

Wesley Methodist Church: 41 Church St, POB HM 346, Hamilton HM BX; tel. 292-0418; fax 295-9460.

The Press

Bermuda Magazine: POB HM 2032, Hamilton HM HX; tel. 292-7279; e-mail cbarclay@ibl.bm; f. 1990; quarterly; Editor-in-Chief CHARLES BARCLAY.

The Bermuda Sun: 41 Victoria St, POB HM 1241, Hamilton HM FX; tel. 295-3902; fax 292-5597; e-mail bdasun@ibl.bm; internet www.bermudasun.bm; f. 1964; two a week; official government gazette; Editor TONY McWILLIAM; circ. 12,500.

The Bermuda Times: Hamilton; tel. 292-2596; fax 295-8771.

Bermuda Weekly: 19 Elliot St, Hamilton; tel. 295-3902.

The Bermudian: 13 Addendum Lane, Pitt's Bay Rd, Pembroke HM07; POB HM 283, Hamilton HM AX; tel. 295-0695; fax 295-8616; e-mail berpub@ibl.bm; f. 1930; monthly; pictorial and resort magazine; Editor MEREDITH EBBIN; circ. 7,500.

Cable TV Guide: 41 Victoria St, Hamilton HM 12; tel. 295-3902; fax 295-5597.

The Mid-Ocean News: 2 Par-la-Ville Rd, POB HM 1025, Hamilton HM DX; tel. 295-5881; f. 1911; weekly with *TV Guide*; Editor TIM HODGSON; Gen. Man. KEITH JENSEN; circ. 14,500.

The Royal Gazette: Par-la-Ville Rd, POB HM 1025, Hamilton HM DX; tel. 295-5881; e-mail editorial@gazette.newsmedia.bm; internet www.accessbda.bm/gazette.htm; f. 1828; morning daily; Editor WILLIAM J. ZUILL; Gen. Man. KEITH JENSEN; circ. 17,500.

TV Week: 2 Par-la-Ville Rd, Hamilton HM 08; tel. 295-5881.

The Worker's Voice: 49 Union Sq., Hamilton HM 12; tel. 292-0044; fax 295-7992; e-mail biu@ibl.bm; fortnightly; organ of the Bermuda Industrial Union; Editor Dr B. B. BALL.

Publisher

Bermudian Publishing Co: POB HM 283, Hamilton HM AX; tel. 295-0695; fax 295-8616; social sciences, sociology, sports; Editor KEVIN STEVENSON.

Broadcasting and Communications

TELECOMMUNICATIONS

Bermuda Telephone Co (BTC): 30 Victoria St, POB 1021, Hamilton HM DX; tel. 295-1001; fax 295-1192; internet www.btc.bm.

Bermuda Digital Communications: Hamilton; tel. 296-4010; e-mail info@bdc.bm; internet www.bdc.bm; mobile cellular telephone operator; Chair. and CEO KURT EVE.

Cable and Wireless (Bermuda) Ltd: 1 Middle Rd, Smith's FL 03, POB HM 151, Hamilton HM AX; tel. 297-7000; fax 295-7909; e-mail helpdesk@bda.cwplc.com; internet www.cwbda.net.bm.

Tele-Bermuda International (TBI): Hamilton; f. 1997; provides an international service; owns a fibre-optic network connecting Bermuda and the USA; Gen. Man. JAMES FITZGERALD.

BROADCASTING

Radio

Bermuda Broadcasting Company: POB HM 452, Hamilton HM BX; tel. 295-2828; fax 295-4282; e-mail zbmzfb@bermuda broadcasting.com; internet www.bermudabroadcasting.com; f. 1982 as merger of ZBM (f. 1943) and ZFB (f. 1962); operates 4 radio stations; CEO ULRIC P. RICHARDSON; Operations Man. E. DELANO INGHAM.

DeFontes Broadcasting Co Ltd—VSB: POB HM 1450, Hamilton HM FX; tel. 295-1450; fax 295-1658; e-mail vsbnews@ibl.bm; f. 1981 as St George's Broadcasting Co; commercial; 4 radio stations; Pres. KENNETH DEFONTES; Station Man. MIKE BISHOP.

Television

Bermuda Broadcasting Company: (see Radio); operates 2 TV stations (Channels 7 and 9).

Bermuda Cablevision Ltd: 19 Laffan St, Hamilton; tel. 292-5544; fax 296-3157; e-mail cablegod@ibl.bm; f. 1988; 57 channels; Pres. DAVID LINES; Gen. Man. CARL MUSSON.

DeFontes Broadcasting Co Ltd—VSB: (see Radio); operates 1 TV station.

Finance

(cap. = capital; dep. = deposits; res = reserves; m. = million;
br. = branch; amounts in Bermuda dollars)

BANKING
Central Bank

Bermuda Monetary Authority: Burnaby House, 26 Burnaby St,
POB HM 2447, Hamilton HM 11; tel. 295-5278; fax 292-7471;
e-mail info@bma.bm; internet www.bma.bm; f. 1969; central issuing
and monetary authority; cap. 9.0m., res 12.3m., total assets 92.4m.
(Dec. 1998); Chair. CHERYL-ANN LISTER; Gen. Man. MUNRO SUTHER-
LAND.

Commercial Banks

Bank of Bermuda Ltd: 6 Front St, POB HM 1020 Hamilton HM 11;
tel. 295-4000; fax 295-7093; e-mail smithpw@bankofbermuda.com;
internet www.bankofbermuda.com; f. 1889; cap. 20.2m., res 171.5m.,
dep. 8,731.5m. (June 1999); Chair. ELDON H. TRIMINGHAM; Pres. and
CEO HENRY B. SMITH; 6 domestic brs, 3 overseas brs.

Bank of N. T. Butterfield & Son Ltd: 65 Front St, POB HM 195,
Hamilton HM AX; tel. 295-1111; fax 292-4365; e-mail bntb@ibl.bm;
internet www.bankofbutterfield.com; f. 1858; inc. 1904; cap. 20.1m.,
dep. 4,108.7m., total assets 4,512.5m. (June 1999); Chair. Dr JAMES
A. C. KING; Pres. and CEO M. CALUM JOHNSTON; 4 domestic brs, 3
overseas brs.

Bermuda Commercial Bank Ltd: Bermuda Commercial Bank
Bldg, 44 Church St, POB HM 1748, Hamilton HM GX; tel. 295-
5678; fax 295-8091; f. 1969; 32%-owned by First Curaçao International Bank NV; cap. 10.3m., res 12.7m., dep. 428.2m. (Sept. 1999);
Pres. JOHN DEUSS; Man. Dir BARRY MULHOLLAND (acting).

STOCK EXCHANGE

Bermuda Stock Exchange: 3rd Floor, Washington Mall, Church
St, Hamilton HM FX; tel. 292-7212; fax 292-7619; e-mail
info@bsx.com; internet bsx.com; Chief Exec. WILLIAM WOODS.

INSURANCE

Bermuda had a total of 1,947 registered insurance companies in
1994, the majority of which are subsidiaries of foreign insurance
companies, or owned by foreign industrial or financial concerns.
Many of them have offices on the island.

Insurance Information Office: Cedarpark Centre, 48 Cedar Ave,
POB HM 2911, Hamilton HM LX; tel. 292-9829; fax 295-3532;
e-mail biminfo@ibl.bm; internet www.bermuda-insurance.org.

Major Companies

ACE Bermuda: ACE Bldg, 30 Woodbourne Ave, POB HM 1015,
Hamilton HM DX; tel. 295-5200; fax 295-5221; e-mail info@
acelimited.com; internet www.acelimited.com; Chair. BRIAN DUPER-
REAULT.

Argus Insurance Co Ltd: Argus Insurance Bldg, 12 Wesley St,
POB HM 1064, Hamilton HM EX; tel. 295-2021; fax 292-6763;
e-mail insurance@argus.bm; internet www.argus.bm.

Bermuda Insurance Management Association (BIMA): POB
HM 1752, Hamilton HM GX; tel. 295-4864; fax 292-7375.

Paumanock Insurance Co Ltd: POB HM 2267, Hamilton HM
JX; tel. 292-2404; fax 292-2648.

X. L. Insurance Co Ltd: Cumberland House, 1 Victoria St, Hamilton; tel. 292-8515; fax 292-7524; e-mail info@xl.bm; Pres. ROBERT
J. COONEY; Chief Exec. BRAIN O'HARA.

Trade and Industry

GOVERNMENT AGENCY

Bermuda Registrar of Companies: Government Administration
Bldg, 30 Parliament St, Hamilton HM 12; tel. 295-5151; fax 292-
6640.

DEVELOPMENT ORGANIZATION

Bermuda Small Business Development Corpn: POB HM 637,
Hamilton HM CX; tel. 292-5570; fax 295-1600; e-mail bsbdc@ibl.bm;
internet www.bsbdc.bm; f. 1980; funded jointly by the Government
and private banks; guarantees loans to small businesses; assets
$500,000; Gen. Man. WILLIAM SPRIGGS.

CHAMBER OF COMMERCE

Bermuda Chamber of Commerce: 1 Point Pleasant Rd, POB
HM 655, Hamilton HM CX; tel. 295-4201; fax 292-5779; e-mail
bcc@ibm.bm; internet www.bermudacommerce.com; f. 1905; Pres.
CHARLES GOSLING; Exec. Vice-Pres. DIANE GORDON; 750 mems.

INDUSTRIAL AND TRADE ASSOCIATION

Bermuda International Business Association (BIBA): 1 Washington Mall, Hamilton HM 11; tel. 292-0632; fax 292-1797; Chair.
RAYMOND MEDEIROS.

EMPLOYERS' ASSOCIATIONS

Bermuda Employers' Council: 304 Bermuda Mechanics Bldg,
Hamilton; tel. 295-5070; fax 295-1966; e-mail mdixon@bec.bm;
f. 1960; advisory body on labour relations; Pres. GERALD SIMONS;
Exec. Dir MALCOLM DIXON; 347 mems.

Construction Association of Bermuda: POB HM 238, Hamilton
HM AX; tel. 292-5920; fax 292-5864; f. 1968; Pres. D. EXELL; Hon.
Sec. L. MARSHALL; 33 mems.

Hotel Employers of Bermuda: c/o Bermuda Hotel Association,
'Carmel', 61 King St, Hamilton HM 19; tel. 295-2127; fax 292-6671;
e-mail johnh@ibl.bm; internet www.bermudahotels.com; f. 1968;
Pres. NORMAN MASTALIR; Exec. Dir JOHN HARVEY; 7 mems.

UTILITY
Electricity

Bermuda Electric Light Co Ltd: Serpentine Rd, Pembroke; tel.
295-5111.

TRADE UNIONS

In 1997 trade union membership was estimated at 8,859. There are
nine registered trade unions, the principal ones being:

Bermuda Federation of Musicians and Variety Artists: Reid
St, POB HM 6, Hamilton HM AX; tel. 291-0138; Sec.-Gen. LLOYD H.
L. SIMMONS; 318 mems.

Bermuda Industrial Union: 49 Union Sq., Hamilton HM 12; tel.
292-0044; fax 295-7992; e-mail biu@ibl.bm; f. 1946; Pres. DERRICK
BURGESS; Gen. Sec. HELENA BURGESS; 5,202 mems.

Bermuda Public Services Association: POB HM 763, Hamilton
HM CX; tel. 292-6985; fax 292-1149; e-mail beepsa@ibl.bm; re-
formed 1961; Pres. BETTY CHRISTOPHER; Gen. Sec. EDWARD G. BALL,
JR; 2,500 mems.

Bermuda Union of Teachers: POB HM 726, Hamilton HM CX;
tel. 292-6515; fax 292-0697; e-mail butunion@ibl.bm; f. 1919; Pres.
ANTHONY E. WOLFFE; Gen. Sec. MICHAEL A. CHARLES; 700 mems.

Transport

ROADS

There are some 240 km (150 miles) of well-surfaced roads, with
almost 6 km (4 miles) reserved for cyclists and pedestrians. Each
Bermudian household is permitted only one passenger vehicle, and
visitors may only hire mopeds, to limit traffic congestion.

SHIPPING

The chief port of Bermuda is Hamilton, with a secondary port at St
George's. Both are used by freight and cruise ships. There is also a
'free' port, Freeport, on Ireland Island. In 2000 it was proposed to
enlarge Hamilton docks in order to accommodate larger cruise ships.
There remained, however, fears that such an enlargement would
place excessive strain on the island's environment and infrastructure. Bermuda is a free-flag nation, and, at December 1996, the
shipping register comprised 91 vessels totalling 3,462,210 grt (the
fifth-largest free-flag merchant fleet in the world).

Department of Marine and Ports Services: POB HM 180,
Hamilton HM AX; tel. 295-6575; fax 295-5523; e-mail marineports@
bolagov.bm; Dir of Marine and Ports Services RONALD D. ROSS;
Deputy Dir and Habour Master MICHAEL DOLDING.

Bermuda Registry of Shipping: POB HM 1628, Hamilton HM
GX; tel. 295-7251; fax 295-3718.

Principal Shipping Companies

A. M. Services Ltd: 10 Queen St, Hamilton HM 11; tel. 295-0850;
fax 292-3704.

Atlantic Marine Limited Partnership: Richmond House, 12 Par-
la-Ville Rd, POB HM 2089, Hamilton HM HX; tel. 295-0614; fax
292-1549; e-mail amlp@amlp.bm; internet www.amlp.bm; f. 1970;
Pres. JENS ALERS.

B + H Ocean Carriers Ltd: 3rd Floor, Par-la-Ville Place, 14 Par-
la-Ville Rd, POB HM 2257 HM JX, Hamilton; tel. 295-6875; fax
295-6796; Chair. M. S. HUDNER.

Benor Tankers Ltd: Cedar House, 41 Cedar Ave, HM 12 Hamilton;
Pres. CARL-ERIK HAAVALDSEN; Chair. HARRY RUTTEN.

Bermuda International Shipping Ltd: POB GE 4, St George's
GE BX; tel. 297-2303; fax 292-1583; Dir J. HENRY HAYWARD.

Container Ship Management Ltd: 14 Par-la-Ville Rd, Hamilton HM 08; tel. 295-1624; fax 295-3781.

Gearbulk Holding Ltd: Par-la-Ville Place, 14 Par-la-Ville Rd, HM JX Hamilton; tel. 295-2184; fax 295-2234.

Globe Forwarding Co: 32 Parliament St, Hamilton; tel. 292-3218; fax 295-3502.

Golden Ocean Management: Clarendon House, 2 Church St West, POB 1022, Hamilton; Man. Dir ROBERT J. KNUTZEN.

Norwegian Cruise Line: 3rd Floor, Reid House, Church St, POB 1564, Hamilton; Chair. EINAR KLOSTER.

Red Rose Ltd: Clarendon House, Church St, Hamilton; Pres. FRANK MUTCH; Sec. ALAN L. BROWN.

Shell Bermuda (Overseas) Ltd: Shell House, Ferry Reach, POB 2, St George's 1.

Unicool Ltd: POB HM 1179, HM EX Hamilton; tel. 295-2244; fax 292-8666; Pres. MATS JANSSON.

Worldwide Shipping Managers Ltd: Suite 402, 7 Reid St, POB HM 1862, HM 11 Hamilton; tel. 295-3770; fax 295-3801.

CIVIL AVIATION

The former US Naval Air Station (the only airfield) was returned to the Government of Bermuda in September 1995, following the closure of the base and the withdrawal of US forces from the islands.

Bermuda International Airport: 3 Cahow Way, St George's GE CX; e-mail dao@bdagov.bm; internet www.bermudaairport.com; Gen. Man. (vacant).

Department of Civil Aviation: Channel House, Longfield Rd, Southside, St David's; tel. 293-1640; fax 293-2417; e-mail imacintyre@bdagov.bm; internet www.dca.gov.bm; responsible for all civil aviation matters; Dir of Civil Aviation IAN MACINTYRE.

Delta Airlines: Kindley Field; tel. 293-2050; passenger and air cargo service.

Tourism

Tourism is the principal industry of Bermuda and is government-sponsored. The great attractions of the islands are the climate, scenery, and facilities for outdoor entertainment of all types. In 1999 a total of 537,577 tourists (including 209,272 cruise-ship passengers) visited Bermuda. In 1998 the industry earned B $487m. In 2000 there were 3,400 hotel rooms. The majority of visitors are from the USA.

Department of Tourism: Global House, 43 Church St, Hamilton HM 12; tel. 292-0023; fax 292-7537; internet www.bermudatourism .org; Dir of Tourism RICHARD CALDERON.

Bermuda Hotel Association: 'Carmel', 61 King St, Hamilton HM 19; tel. 295-2127; fax 292-6671; e-mail johnh@ibl.bm; internet www.bermudahotels.com; Chair. J. CHRISTOPHER ASTWOOD; Exec. Dir JOHN HARVEY; Pres. MURIEL RICHARDSON; 35 mem. hotels.

Defence

The local defence force is the Bermuda Regiment, with a strength of some 700 men and women in 1993. The Regiment employs selective conscription.

Education

There is free compulsory education in government schools between the ages of five and 16 years, and a number of scholarships are awarded for higher education and teacher training. There are also seven private secondary schools which charge fees. The Bermuda College, founded in 1972, accepts students over the age of 16, and is the only post-secondary educational institution. Extramural degree courses are available through Queen's University, Canada, and Indiana and Maryland Universities, USA. A major programme to upgrade the education system, involving the establishment of five new primary and two secondary schools, was to be implemented between 1996 and 2002. In 1991/92 government expenditure on education (some B $60m.) accounted for 14.2% of total expenditure.

BOLIVIA

Area: 1,098,581 sq km (424,164 sq miles).

Population (official estimate, mid-2000):8,328,700.

Capital (administrative): La Paz, population 1,004,440, estimate at mid-2000).

Languages: The official languages are Spanish, Quechua and Aymará.

Religion: mainly Christianity (estimated 6.9m. Roman Catholics at 31 December 1998).

Climate: ranges from humid and tropical in the northern and eastern lowlands to cool and cold in the Andes mountains above 3,500 m; most rain falls between November and March.

Time: GMT −4 hours.

Public Holidays

2002: 1 January (New Year), 10 February (Oruro only), 29 March (Good Friday), 15 April (Tarija only), 1 May (Labour Day), 25 May (Sucre only), 30 May (Corpus Christi), 16 July (La Paz only), 6 August (Independence Day), 14 September (Cochabamba only), 24 September (Santa Cruz only), 1 October (Pando only), 1 November (All Saints' Day and Potosí), 10 November (Oruro only), 18 November (Beni only), 25 December (Christmas).

2003: 1 January (New Year), 10 February (Oruro only), 18 April (Good Friday), 15 April (Tarija only), 1 May (Labour Day), 25 May (Sucre only), 19 June (Corpus Christi), 16 July (La Paz only), 6 August (Independence Day), 14 September (Cochabamba only), 24 September (Santa Cruz only), 1 October (Pando only), 1 November (All Saints' Day and Potosí), 10 November (Oruro only), 18 November (Beni only), 25 December (Christmas).

Currency: Boliviano; 1,000 bolivianos = £107.28 = US $153.61 = €173.06 (30 April 2001).

Weights and measures: Metric system officially in force, but various old Spanish measures also used.

Basic Economic Indicators

	1998	1999	2000
Gross domestic product (million bolivianos at 1990 prices).	21,759	21,854	22,372*
GDP per head (bolivianos at 1990 prices)*.	2,737.0	2,685.7	2,686.1
GDP (million bolivianos at current prices)	47,042	48,588	52,511*
GDP per head (bolivianos at current prices)	5,917.3	5,971.2	6,304.8*
Annual growth of real GDP (%)	5.2	0.4	2.4*
Annual growth of real GDP per head (%)	2.8	−1.9	0.1*
Government budget (million bolivianos at current prices)			
Revenue.	11,699	12,131	n.a.
Expenditure.	13,615	14,100	n.a.
Consumer price index (base: 1995 = 100)	126.8	129.5	135.5
Rate of inflation (annual average, %)	7.7	2.2	4.6
Foreign exchange reserves (US $ million at 31 December).	834.4	866.9	777.1
Imports c.i.f. (US $ million)	1,850.9	1,983.0	1,755.1
Exports f.o.b. (US $ million)	1,103.9	1,051.2	1,214.5
Balance of payments (current account, US $ million)	−678.1	−555.8	n.a.

* Estimates.

Gross national product (US dollars, converted by the PPP exchange rate, 1999): 2,300.

Total labour force (estimate, mid-1999): 3,307,000.

Unemployment (estimate, November 1997): 2.1%.

Total external debt (1999): US $6,157m.

Life expectancy (years at birth, 2000): 62.5 (males 60.8, females 64.3).

Infant mortality rate (per 1,000 live births, 2000): 67.

Adult population with HIV/AIDS (15–49 years, 1999): 0.10%.

School enrolment ratio (6–17 years, 1991): 79%.

Adult literacy rate (15 years and over, 2000): 85.75% (males 92.1, females 79.4).

Commercial energy consumption per head (kg of oil equivalent, 1997): 548.

Carbon dioxide emissions (per head metric tons, 1997): 1.4.

Passenger motor cars in use (per 1,000 of population, 1996): 32.1.

Television receivers in use (per 1,000 of population, 1997): 116.

Personal computers in use (per 1,000 of population, 1999): 12.3.

History

Prof. PETER CALVERT

Bolivia was the seat of advanced Indian (Amerindian) cultures long before the arrival of Europeans and between 56% and 70% of its population are estimated to be of indigenous descent. The decisive factor in its modern history has been the location of its seat of power on the highlands of the Andes. From this base, its rulers have tried to maintain its unity, whilst striving on the one hand to maintain its communications with the outside world and on the other to expand down into the tropical lowlands of the Oriente.

The impressive monuments of Tiwanaku, Samaipata, Incallajta and Iskanwaya are evidence of the skills of Bolivia's early inhabitants. The Tiwanakan culture emerged south of Lake Titicaca *c*. 200 BC. It disappeared around AD 1200 and in around 1450 highland Bolivia was incorporated into the Inca empire of Tahuantinsuyo, with its base at Cuzco, in what is now Peru.

The Spanish conquistadores, driven by the relentless desire for gold and silver, reached Bolivia, which they termed Upper Peru, from the sea coast. In 1538 Pizarro defeated the Inca forces in the Titicaca region and his brothers penetrated further south, along the Inca roads, to establish the town of Chuquisaca (now Sucre). La Paz was founded in 1549, Cochabamba in 1571 and Tarija in 1574. Within a few decades, the mines of Upper Peru were being exploited directly to fund the imperial ambitions of Spain. Labour was obtained by forcing the local inhabitants to work in the mines and the discovery of mercury at Huancavelica (now in Peru) ended the initial dependence on Spain itself for the means by which the metal could be separated from the ore. At its height Potosí, with a population of more than 100,000, was the largest urban area in the Western Hemisphere. Socially, however, it remained a distant dependency of the Viceregal Court at Lima, while in 1776 the Charcas Valley in the south was separated from Peru when it became part of the new Viceroyalty of the Río de la Plata.

INDEPENDENCE

The province of Charcas was represented at Tucumán in 1816 where independence was proclaimed by the United Provinces (now Argentina). The highlands of Upper Peru had to wait for the arrival of the Liberator, Simón Bolívar, in the early 1820s to throw off its allegiance both to Spain and to Peru. In 1825 its leader Gen. Antonio Sucre offered to name the country after Bolívar if he would recognize its independence and give a Constitution to what was initially to become one of the largest independent states in the Americas.

However, from the beginning Bolivia's lack of unity condemned it both to internal political turbulence and to constant involvement in regional conflict. A short-lived attempt at confederation with Peru was successfully frustrated by Chile in 1841. In the 1850s silver mining revived, but the workers from Chile were needed to develop a new source of wealth in the nitrate fields of Antofagasta. Fearing Chile's ambitions, Bolivia signed a secret defence treaty with Peru. However, in the War of the Pacific (1879–83) Chile won a decisive victory over both Bolivia and Peru, gaining control of the valuable nitrate fields and depriving Bolivia of its coastal territory, a loss which ever since has remained a source of friction between the two countries. It was not until 1904 that a peace treaty obliged Chile to build a railway from La Paz to Arica (Chile), which became Bolivia's main outlet to the outside world.

Towards the end of the 19th century silver production reached a peak. However, with the general adoption of the gold standard, prices collapsed. Nevertheless, Bolivia was also rich in tin, often found associated with silver, but largely ignored until the rise of demand from the canning industry. It was tin, not silver, that drew Bolivia into the modern world economy. The industry came to be dominated by three business empires, the Patiño, Aramayo and Hochschild interests. Labour was recruited from the Indian population of the altiplano and railways were built, linking the mines to the Chilean ports of Antofagasta and Mollendo. However, travel within Bolivia was to remain exceptionally difficult until the age of air travel.

Political instability was replaced, between 1884 and 1920, by stable government under a two-party system of Conservatives and Liberals. Essentially, these represented the rural land-owning oligarchy and the powerful mining interests, an élite often known as the Rosca (circle). However, from 1920 to 1932 consensus government began to break down, with the emergence of the Republican party, the growth of trade unions among miners and railwaymen and the increasing discontent among the peasantry, traders and artisans of the cities, especially in La Paz. The expansion of Bolivian forces eastwards into the sparsely populated territory of the Chaco Boreal was checked by Paraguay in 1929. In the Chaco War (1932–35) Bolivian forces suffered a disastrous defeat and Paraguayan forces came within sight of the southern Bolivian oilfield before peace could be secured.

THE 'BOLIVIAN REVOLUTION'

Military governments dominated the years between 1938 and 1952, as former commanders sought to justify their existence. However, new political parties competed for the support of the powerful miners' union, the urban workers and the new middle class. The most important of these parties was the Movimiento Nacionalista Revolucionario (MNR—Nationalist Revolutionary Movement), founded in 1942. After a presidential election in May 1951 had given him the largest share of the popular vote, a military coup prevented the MNR's candidate, Víctor Paz Estenssoro, from assuming power. However, in April 1952 the miners fought their way into La Paz and brought about a true, if limited, social revolution.

The MNR took power under the presidency of Paz Estenssoro, with Hernán Siles Zuazo as Vice-President. The new Government introduced universal adult suffrage, nationalized the mining sector, implemented a land-reform programme and, for a time, dismantled the power of the Army. Trade unions were organized into a confederation (Central Obrera Boliviana—COB). Emphasis was given to economic development, with US aid. The national petroleum company, Yacimientos Petrolíferos Fiscales Bolivianos (YPFB), was reorganized. A new petroleum code invited exploration and development by foreign companies. Roads were built and encouragement was given to colonization in the region of Santa Cruz. The MNR remained in power until 1964, with Paz Estenssoro and Siles Zuazo alternating as President. This period saw the MNR gradually retreating from its earlier policies of radical reform and introducing measures of monetary stabilization, but also slowly alienating both miners and peasants.

MILITARY GOVERNMENTS OF 1964–1982

The military coup which toppled Paz Estenssoro and ended the MNR regime in 1964 heralded the start of one of the most turbulent and complex periods in Bolivia's history. After two years of joint rule with Gen. Alfredo Ovando Candía, elections in 1966 returned Gen. René Barrientos Ortuño as sole President, the first in Bolivia's history to speak Quechua. It was during his term that the Argentine-born Cuban revolutionary, Ernesto ('Che') Guevara, led his ill-fated expedition to Bolivia. Distrustful peasants failed to support his small group. It was quickly rounded up, and Guevara himself was shot at Vallegrande on 9 October 1967. In April 1969, however, Gen. Barrientos Ortuño was killed in an air crash. Gen. Ovando Candía deposed his civilian successor, Luis Adolfo Siles Salinas, in September 1969, and reassumed the presidency. A power struggle ensued between right- and left-wing army officers. In 1970 Gen. Juan José Torres González, supported by the leftist military faction, was installed as President and sought to implement a programme of radical reforms, including worker participation in management and agrarian reform. However, in August 1971 Col (later Gen.) Hugo Bánzer Suárez deposed the Torres Government in a brief battle, supported by right-wing members of the Army, the right-wing Falange Socialista Boliviana and a section of the MNR.

The Bánzer dictatorship (1971–78) was the longest period of continuous rule in the country's history and proved to be a period of growth and relative stability. The price was a ban on all political and trade-union activity. Bánzer Suárez's coup had been supported by the Brazilian military regime in return for a promise to upgrade communications links to Brazil and allow Brazil access to the iron-ore deposits of the Oriente. Bolivia had joined the Andean Pact (Acuerdo de Cartagena—known as the Andean Community of Nations from March 1996) in May 1969, but Bánzer was keen to develop a direct link to the Atlantic. At the same time he also sought to fulfil the old dream of Bolivian politicians and persuade Chile to cede a land corridor to the Pacific, though without success. Moreover, the issue provoked the Bolivian military again to intervene in politics. In 1978 Gen. Juan Pereda Asbún led a successful coup against President Bánzer, although he himself was then ousted, in November of the same year, by Gen. David Padilla Aranciba, with the assistance of national left-wing groups.

Presidential and legislative elections were held in July 1979. The presidential contest resulted in almost equal support for two former presidents, Siles Zuazo and Paz Estenssoro, each leading a rival faction of the MNR. Congress, in turn, failed to give a majority to either candidate and an interim Government was formed under Walter Guevara Arce, President of the Senate. In November 1979 the temporary administration was overthrown by a right-wing army officer, Col Alberto Natusch Busch. He resigned 15 days later, after failing to gain the support of Congress. Lidia Gueiler Tejada, President of the Chamber of Deputies, became Bolivia's first woman Head of State, with presidential and legislative elections planned for June 1980.

The García Meza 'Narco-Regime', 1980–81

In the 1980 presidential election Siles Zuazo and Paz Estenssoro were again the main protagonists. Neither candidate obtained a clear majority. Before Congress could resolve the issue a military junta seized power, led by Gen. Luis García Meza Tejada. The regime of Gen. García Meza, characterized by corruption and oppression, was sponsored by the Argentine military Government and supported by Argentine special forces. Their aim was to pre-empt any return to democracy and secure a reliable ally in the event of war between Argentina and Chile. The dictatorship was supported by a section of the military leadership deeply involved in the illegal drugs trade. With the country in economic crisis, farmers readily turned to growing coca. The USA refused to recognize the new Government. International aid to Bolivia was suspended and Bolivia withdrew temporarily from the Andean Pact.

In August 1981 Gen. García Meza was ousted from power by a military junta. Elections were planned for April 1983 but by September 1982 Bolivia's economic situation had deteriorated to such an extent that the military regime had no option but to bring forward the transfer of power to a civilian government to enable the country to negotiate successfully with foreign governments and the international lending agencies. In October 1982 Siles Zuazo was installed as President for a four-year term, on the basis of the 1980 election results. Over the next 12 years a determined effort was made to bring García Meza to account for his abuses of power. In March 1994 he was finally arrested in São Paulo (Brazil) on charges of drugs trafficking. In October of that year the Brazilian Supreme Court approved his extradition. He was returned to Bolivia on 14 March 1995, to serve a 30-year prison term to which he had been sentenced *in absentia* in 1993.

The armed forces had been a factor in politics since independence, except between 1880 and 1920 and in a brief period of the MNR regime. From 1964, and especially during the Bánzer regime, military government increasingly involved the appointment of officers to the heads of ministries and state corporations, in place of civilians. The Army itself became influential in

economic development, organizing settlement projects, irrigation schemes and agro-industrial enterprises. However, once it had yielded power in 1982, as elsewhere in Latin America, the military gradually withdrew from politics, eschewing participation in political activity and, both in public and in private, supporting the Constitution and its democratic institutions.

THE RETURN TO ELECTED GOVERNMENT

Siles Zuazo's electoral alliance of his own Movimiento Nacionalista Revolucionario de Izquierda (MNR-I—Left-Wing Nationalist Revolutionary Movement), the Movimiento de la Izquierda Revolucionaria (MIR—Movement of the Revolutionary Left) and the Partido Comunista de Bolivia (Communist Party of Bolivia) was reflected in his first Cabinet. However, consensus within the alliance was often elusive and resulted in a series of government reorganizations. Other characteristics of Siles Zuazo's second period of government were persistent coup rumours and industrial unrest. In November 1984, following a general strike, President Siles Zuazo announced he would bring the general elections forward by one year.

The elections of 14 July 1985 gave a narrow lead to the Acción Democrática Nacionalista (ADN—Nationalist Democratic Action), under Bánzer, over Paz Estenssoro's Movimiento Nacionalista Revolucionario Histórico (MNR-H—Historic Nationalist Revolutionary Movement). In the absence of an overall majority, the issue was resolved by the National Congress. Paz Estenssoro, with the support of the left, narrowly defeated Bánzer and again took office as President.

The new Government focused its attention on rescuing the country's economy from collapse. At the end of August 1985 President Paz Estenssoro announced his New Economic Policy, which introduced a series of austere domestic measures. The new economic stabilization programme exposed Bolivia to local and international free-market forces, imposed a wage 'freeze' in the public sector, removed subsidies, supported strict monetary control and committed the Government to reducing expenditure and decentralizing state enterprises. The severity of the measures was a great shock to the Bolivian people and brought the Government into direct confrontation with the COB, prompting a state of siege to be declared in September. Within months, however, inflation had fallen from a record 16,000% per year to double figures.

The effect of the measures was greatly increased by the sudden collapse of the world tin market in late 1985, which precipitated the long-standing crisis in the country's mining economy and turned its leaders away from traditional mineral production towards new economic sectors and new regions of the country. By this time President Paz Estenssoro had secured majority support for his policies in Congress, by formally agreeing to an alliance with Bánzer and the ADN, entitled the Pacto para la Democracia (Pact for Democracy). In January 1986 cabinet changes strengthened the Government's resolve to maintain austerity. By early 1987 favourable results were emerging: inflation had been further reduced; debts had been rescheduled; and the International Monetary Fund (IMF) had resumed the allocation of stand-by credits. There was much discontent with the Government's austerity measures but the Pact for Democracy remained in force.

The results of the presidential elections of May 1989 gave Gonzalo Sánchez de Lozada, the MNR candidate, 23.07% of the votes cast, Bánzer, the ADN candidate, 22.70% and Jaime Paz Zamora of the MIR 19.64%. As in 1985 no candidate obtained a majority, leaving responsibility for the choice of President with Congress. In an unexpected move, Bánzer chose to support his former rival, Paz Zamora, who secured the presidency on 6 August 1989. In return for its support, the ADN was given important positions in the coalition Government of 'national unity', under the Acuerdo Patriótico (Patriotic Accord).

Austerity measures maintained by the new Government caused unrest and provoked the reimposition of a state of siege in November 1989. President Paz Zamora's privatization programme proceeded slowly and, in an attempt to attract foreign investment, legislation was enacted which allowed foreign participation in Bolivian mining and petroleum industries. A major success was the signing of an agreement with Peru, in January 1992, granting Bolivia free-port status at the Peruvian port of Ilo. This gave Bolivia a new outlet to the Pacific and made it potentially less dependent on its road and rail links to Chile. In June a shift towards a new alignment was signalled when Paz Zamora attended a presidential summit of the Southern Common Market (Mercado Común del Sur—Mercosur), the new economic grouping of Argentina, Brazil, Paraguay and Uruguay. The burden of the external debt lessened under President Paz Zamora, but the cost to the Bolivian people was high. The standard of living, already one of the lowest in South America, declined precipitously.

In January 1992 a pact, signed between the COB and the Government, gave miners' unions consultative rights in the proposed mines-privatization programme. However, the COB's power was in decline. Urban and industrial expansion had seen the articulation of other workers' interests besides those of the miners. The peasantry found an effective voice only as a result of land reform, when many peasant unions were hastily formed. Peasant leaders (*caciques*) became an important pressure group, while indigenous Indian groups united to form their own party. At the same time a new agro-commercial élite emerged to eclipse the old rural oligarchy. The private mining sector grew in importance in the 1970s, and the expansion of the public sector and industrial growth created a new class of professionals, white-collar workers and business entrepreneurs. Meanwhile, a wealthy society emerged in the Oriente of eastern Bolivia, largely dependent on illicit funds. This new grouping had sufficient power, in terms of both patronage and force, to be a significant challenge to the Government. Now under pressure from the USA, the Government initiated a series of operations against the traffickers and their processing plants. Political opponents claimed that Bolivia's national sovereignty was being undermined. However, the inflow of illegal revenue from the drugs trade helped to stabilize the exchange rate and moderate the money supply, both essential contributory factors in a return to the international economic system. President Paz Zamora had estimated that 70% of Bolivia's real gross domestic product (GDP) was drugs-related and that more than 50% of its exports were financed by the illegal trade. Hence, the balance of power and advantage was a delicate one.

In June 1993 Gonzalo 'Goni' Sánchez de Lozada, the architect of President Paz Estensorro's lauded New Economic Policy, was elected President. His candidate for the vice-presidency was Víctor Hugo Cárdenas, the Aymaran leader of the Movimiento Revolucionario Túpaj Katarí de Liberación (MRTKL—Túpaj Katarí Revolutionary Liberation Movement). The latter's appeal to peasant and Indian voters was crucial, as no candidate secured the requisite absolute majority on the first ballot, a congressional vote was scheduled for 4 August. On 9 June, however, Bánzer withdrew from the contest, leaving Sánchez de Lozada's candidacy unopposed. Cabinet portfolios in his government were allocated to members of the UCS and MBL, sealing an alliance which gave the Government 97 of the 157 seats in Congress, an alliance which lasted until September 1994.

Industrial action by teachers, supported by the COB, culminated in early 1995 in an indefinite strike. In response, the Government declared a state of siege for 90 days. Military units were deployed throughout the country and 370 union leaders (including the Secretary-General of the COB, Oscar Salas) were arrested and banished to remote areas. Meanwhile, however, more senior public officials were implicated in the illegal drugs trade. In September four members of the Special Force for the Fight Against Drugs (Fuerza Especial para la Lucha Contra los Narcóticos—FELCN), including the second-in-command, Col Fernando Tarifa, were dismissed after an investigation into their involvement with drugs traffickers. Moreover, there was intense civil unrest in the Chaparé valley, where, despite a voluntary coca-eradication programme, forces of the Mobile Rural Patrol Unit (Unidad Móvil de Patrullaje Rural—UMOPAR) had begun to occupy villages and to destroy coca plantations. Violent clashes between peasant farmers and UMOPAR personnel resulted in the deaths of several peasants and the arrest of almost 1,000 coca growers. As a consequence, negotiations between coca growers and the Government broke down. In 1996 there were protests from women coca growers against the US-sponsored scheme of compulsory eradication and the denial of basic human rights. A series of strikes in early 2001, in protest at the sale to a Chilean corporation of the

Eastern Railway and the 'capitalization' of the state petroleum corporation, YPFB, culminated in a general strike on 25 March and clashes with police in which one demonstrator died. However, the Government negotiated directly with individual unions and, on 21 April, the COB was forced to accept the original public-sector pay agreement with no concessions on the privatization programme.

THE RETURN OF BÁNZER SUÁREZ, 1997–2001

The acrimonious campaign for the presidential election of 1 June 1997 was marked by expressions of increasing discontent with the Government's economic-reform programme. Despite outspoken criticism of his human-rights record while in power, the populist campaign of former dictator Hugo Bánzer Suárez secured the largest share of the votes cast (22.3%). Next were Juan Carlos Durán of the ruling MNR and Jaime Paz Zamora, with 17.7% and 16.7% of the ballot, respectively. At legislative elections held concurrently the ADN won 46 congressional seats, the MIR won 31 and the MNR secured 29 seats. The UCS and Conciencia de Patria (Condepa—Conscience of the Fatherland) finished with 23 and 20 seats, respectively. Subsequently, the ADN concluded a pact with the MIR, the UCS and Condepa, thus securing a congressional majority. As a result, on 5 August Bánzer was elected to the presidency, with the support of 118 of the 157 deputies, becoming the first former dictator in South America since 1952 to return as a democratically elected President.

President Bánzer undertook to continue the work of the previous Government, enthusiastically adopting as his own both the 'Washington Consensus' on free-market economic-reform and the US-supported campaign to combat illicit coca production. In August 1997 the new Government signed a co-operation agreement with the USA which provided funds for the continuation of compensation payments to coca growers who agreed to the destruction of their crops. This policy had been widely criticized for its emphasis on the suppression of coca cultivation rather than on the development of alternative crops and, moreover, for its apparent lack of impact on levels of coca production in Bolivia, as farmers were encouraged to plant extra crops, solely to be surrendered, or used the payments to replant their crops in more remote areas. Nevertheless, in early 1998 the Government announced that the scheme would be extended, with the aim of eradicating all illegal coca cultivation by 2002. In April and May there were violent clashes between farmers in the Cochabamba region and security forces engaged in crop eradication and in August more than 1,000 coca growers marched 800 km from Chaparé to La Paz to demand an end to land confiscation, the incarceration of coca growers and reductions in compensation payments to farmers. President Bánzer rejected their demands, however, and the announcement, in late 1998, that the headquarters of the armed forces were to be moved to Cochabamba from La Paz during 1999 seemed to confirm the Government's determination to curtail the activities of the coca farmers.

President Bánzer remained a controversial figure, as domestic and international attention focused increasingly on the human-rights abuses committed during his dictatorship in the 1970s, and his coalition Government experienced instability and embarrassment. In July 1998 divisions within Condepa, which caused the resignation of Freddy Conde, the agriculture minister, prompted the President to expel that party from the governing coalition. The resignations, in May 1999, of labour minister Leopoldo López and of senior police commander Ivar Narváez, a confidant of President Bánzer, amid allegations of corruption, tainted the administration further. However, it was hoped that the announcement, in mid-1999, of reforms to the judicial system would reduce corruption and increase the accountability of the police force though there was little evidence of this. Bolivia's economic position remained critical. Nevertheless, in recognition of a decade of progress in economic stabilization, in 1998 Bolivia became the first country in Latin America to be designated eligible for debt-service relief under the World Bank-led Heavily Indebted Poor Countries (HIPC) initiative and from 1999 onwards became a pilot country for the Comprehensive Development Framework, co-sponsored by the IMF and the World Bank.

In November 1999 the Argentine Government agreed to pay US $224,000 compensation to the widow of former President Juan José Torres, murdered in Buenos Aires in 1976 as part of Operation Condor. In the previous month Congress approved a new penal code, incorporating, for the first time, customary Quechua and Aymará law. As Bolivia's standing improved with foreign governments and multilateral lending institutions, it was hoped that the country would be enabled to sustain long-term economic growth and a greater measure of political stability. However, in the meanwhile a sharp increase in water charges in Cochabamba in early 2000 ignited violent demonstrations, which spread to other areas. In April a brief strike by the police forced the Government to withdraw the measure, which had been intended to help the newly privatized water authority fund improvements in supply. This precipitated a cabinet reshuffle, which increased the representation of the ADN by one post at the expense of the MIR, while the UCS retained its two ministerial posts.

The Government was put under further pressure in September 2000 when demonstrations by striking teachers demanding higher salaries, and farmers protesting against the Government's plans to restrict the cultivation of the coca leaf, brought the country to a standstill. Violence between the protesters and riot police resulted in at least 10 fatalities. The protests ended in October when the Government agreed to offer the teachers bonus payments and, as a concession to the farmers, to stop the construction of three military bases in the Chaparé region. However, at the same time, the Government made it clear that the coca eradication programme was not negotiable, and claimed, though it was yet to be substantiated, that in 2000 the area cultivated for coca had been successfully reduced by some 45%. As a result, Bolivia faced a deepening economic crisis under the management of a most unpopular Government.

In July 2001 it was confirmed that President Bánzer was undergoing chemotherapy for cancer of the lung and liver in Washington, DC (USA). At the end of the month he confirmed his intention to resign as President on 6 August. The Vice-President, Jorge Quiroga Ramírez, assumed the presidency, and immediately replaced 12 of the 16 cabinet members.

Economy

Prof. PETER CALVERT

Bolivia is a country of great natural diversity in the heart of South America. It has an area of 1,098,581 sq km (424,164 sq miles) but had an officially estimated population of only 8,328,700 at mid-2000, giving a population density of just 7.6 people per sq km. Population growth per year averaged 2.35% in 1990–99 and was 2.35% in 2000. In the same year the crude birth rate was 31.9 per 1,000 and death rate 8.6 per 1,000; infant mortality was estimated to have fallen from 92.0 per 1000 in 1991 to 67 in 2000. Life expectancy at birth in 2000, at 62.5 (male 60.8; female 64.3) years, remained among the lowest in Latin America. Some 67% of the population were below the national poverty line. Gross national product (GNP) per head in 1999 was only US $990 (or by purchasing power parity $2,300), placing Bolivia at the lower end of the World Bank's lower-middle-income countries.

Bolivia has substantial natural resources but is hindered economically by its land-locked position and the high altitude of much of the country. Some 70% of the population live on the high plateau known as the altiplano, which occupies approximately one-half of the national territory. The altiplano, at between 3,660 m and 3,800 m above sea-level, is flanked by Andean ranges: to the west by the Cordillera Occidental, and to the east by the Cordillera Real, which is rich in mineral deposits. The northern altiplano has a more moist climate, receiving a mean annual rainfall of 600–700 mm, concentrated in the months from October to March. Temperatures are adequate for arable farming, though temperatures fall sharply at night (by up to 20° C or more). Occasional frosts, hail and droughts can threaten agricultural production. The more sparsely populated south-western altiplano is dry and cold.

To the east and north-east of the high plateau lie the valles, foothills which form a geologically dissected and diverse region fringing the Cordillera Real. At intermediate altitudes they enjoy mild climates suitable for temperate-zone crops such as wheat and soya beans. The semi-tropical Yungas region to the north-east of, and in close proximity to, the capital La Paz supports the commercial cultivation of coffee, maize, cassava, bananas and oranges. The eastern plains of the Oriente can be subdivided into the rain forests, savannah grasslands and swamps of the Amazonian north-east, and the seasonally dry and hot scrublands and grasslands of the Gran Chaco in the east. Population growth in the low-lying Oriente, in particular in and around Santa Cruz, fuelled by the discovery of significant petroleum and natural-gas deposits, resulted in the region accounting for more than one-quarter of the population by the late 1980s. In 1999 62% of the population lived in urban areas.

AGRICULTURE

In 1998 only 2.0m. ha (1.8%), of Bolivia's total land area of 109.4m. ha were classified as arable. A further 229,000 ha (0.2%) were given over to permanent crops and 33.8m. ha (31%) to permanent pasture. Some 53% was classified as forest and woodland and 21% as other terrain (mostly mountain). Agriculture, forestry and fishing accounted for some 28.5% of Bolivia's gross domestic product (GDP) in 1986. By 2000, however, the sector's contribution had fallen to 15.5%, despite employing an estimated 44.5% of the economically active population. Of the 1,498,000 people estimated to be employed in the agricultural sector in 2000, some two-thirds were engaged in subsistence agriculture, predominantly in the central highlands, accounting for many of the 67% of the population who, in 1998, lived below the national poverty line. The fertile tropical lowlands of the Oriente are dominated by more capital-intensive commercial farms, many of which attract significant foreign investment.

The performance of the agricultural sector is prone to marked fluctuations, dictated, largely, by weather conditions. The importance of the sector in terms of national subsistence as well as GDP makes these fluctuations significant for Bolivia's economic well-being. Regular floods in the north-east of the country in March or April are compounded by the torrential rains and lowland flooding typically brought by the climatic phenomenon known as El Niño (a warm current that periodically appears along the Pacific coast of South America). Agricultural GDP increased at an annual average rate of 13.7% in 1990–97. Overall agricultural output increased by an estimated 1.1% in 1998/99, but had still not reached its pre-1997 level.

Maize, wheat, rice and potatoes are the principal foodstuffs grown for domestic consumption. However, grain imports had to supplement low domestic production from the late 1980s onwards. In 1998 Bolivia imported some 223,491 metric tons of cereals, at a cost of US $72.5m. According to the UN Food and Agriculture Organization (FAO), total cereal production in 2000 1.3m. tons. In this year wheat production, which fluctuated considerably in the 1990s, fell back to 104,262 tons, from 140,594 tons in 1999. Maize production was 653,271 tons and output of rice (paddy) was 310,099 tons in 2000, an 18% increase on the 1994 figure. Cassava (manioc) production in 2000 was 514,794 tons, mainly for domestic consumption. Production of oilcrops in 2000 was 271,105 tons.

In the 1990s, in response to an increase in overseas demand, there was a substantial increase in the growth of soya (soybeans), cultivated chiefly in the Santa Cruz area, where the climate allows for two harvests each year. In 2000 the area under soya-bean cultivation was 618,000 ha, compared with just 175,000 ha in 1991, but production fell from 1,071,000 tons in

1998 to 762,200 tons in 1999, before rising to 1,231,555 tons in 2000. By the late 1990s soya was Bolivia's most important legal agricultural export, although cotton, coffee and sugar were also grown. In 1999 Bolivia exported 169,000 tons of soya, with a value of US $35m. Cotton lint exports of 13,000 tons had a value of $18m. and exports of coffee (7,501 tons) were valued at $14.1m. By the early 1990s sugar production had fallen by some 30% in a decade. In 2000 83,838 ha of land were used to cultivate sugar cane and 3.6m. tons were produced; but in the previous year only 17,070 tons of sugar had been produced for export, with a value of $17m. Forestry was an important export earner, but had also been adversely affected by recession: in 1998 Bolivia exported 218,000 cu m of sawnwood with a value of US $50.8m., but in 1999 only 44,200 cu m, worth US $22.7m., was exported.

However, Bolivia's most valuable agricultural exports were coca and its derivatives. Coca was grown from pre-Colombian times, although its modern economic significance dated only from the 1960s. Bolivia is the third-largest cultivator of coca in the world and in recent years has produced approximately one-third of the world's cocaine, predominantly in the departments of El Chaparé and Yungas. Official sources estimated that around 80,000 peasant farmers were engaged directly in its production; however, a far greater number of Bolivians depended on the industry for their livelihood. Cultivation for non-traditional use was made illegal in 1988 and was supposed to be confined to some 12,000 ha. However, an estimated US $350m. was generated for the local economy through legal coca cultivation in 1988 and 1989, increasing to $216m. in 1990 alone. A far greater sum of money, generated by illegal coca production and the increased production of coca paste, was banked offshore. In 1990 government sources estimated that around $600m. were absorbed annually into the economy as a result of the illegal trade in coca and its derivatives.

The importance of Bolivian coca leaf in the international cocaine trade prompted considerable official US interest in the restriction of coca cultivation. US military and economic assistance was made dependent upon meeting eradication targets of 5,000–8,000 ha each year and programmes were instituted to compensate farmers for the destruction of their coca and to encourage the development of alternative crops. However, by 1997 many observers believed this approach to be ineffective, as, despite the provision of US finance worth some US $500m. since 1990, there had been no net reduction in coca production. In 1990 50,300 metric tons of coca leaf were produced on 58,400 ha. In 1994 the cultivation of 49,200 ha yielded 48,100 tons of coca and the US Central Intelligence Agency (CIA) estimated that 73,000 tons of coca leaf were grown on 46,900 ha in 1997. In 1998, despite the Bolivian Government's introduction of an aggressive coca-eradication programme, consequent rural unrest and the decision of the US administration to redirect its alternative development budget to interdiction, the FAO estimated that production increased again, with 50,300 ha yielding 116,000 tons. In 2000 it was claimed that the area cultivated had been reduced by some 45%. Whether or not this was true, and the past record suggested it was unlikely, with large sections of the rural community dependent upon lucrative coca cultivation for their survival, and without the realistic prospect of substituting other crops, the Government's eradication efforts had brought disaster to rural communities and cost it some $500m. per year in lost revenues.

Cattle stocks were estimated at 6.7m. head in 2000. There were a total of 8.8m. sheep and 1.9m. camelids (including llama, used as beasts of burden, and alpaca, valued for their wool). Some 74m. chickens and 420,000 cavies and other rodents were also kept, largely for domestic consumption. In 1998 the total fish catch was 6,440 metric tons.

MINING

The importance of the mining sector for the Bolivian economy was belied by its relatively modest contribution to the country's GDP. In 2000 mining and quarrying contributed an estimated 11.7% of GDP and, in 1997, employed only about 1.8% of the working population. However, it was in Bolivia's trade balance that the sector's significance became clear. In 1997 the mining industry generated US $519m. in export revenue, accounting for 43% of total export earnings.

Rich reserves of high-content ores made Bolivia the world's second-largest tin producer, after Malaysia, for much of the 20th century. The state-owned mining corporation, Corporación Minera de Bolivia (COMIBOL), was founded in 1952, following President Paz Estenssoro's nationalization of Bolivia's larger mines, and produced 27% of Bolivian non-ferrous metal output. However, by the early 1980s Bolivia's share of the world tin market was already in decline, as richer seams neared exhaustion and production inefficiencies limited competitiveness. Then, in October 1985, the world price of tin decreased dramatically, following the withdrawal of the International Tin Council (see section on Tin in Major Commodities of Latin America, Part Three) from the market. COMIBOL was severely affected, as a result of its size, its relative inefficiency and its vulnerability to both external pressures and direct state intervention. Tin production fell to 8,128 metric tons in 1987, barely one-fifth of 1970s' production levels.

In the 1990s Bolivian deep-mined tin remained uncompetitive compared with the low-cost alluvial tin produced by Malaysia, Indonesia and Thailand. Bolivia was also surpassed by neighbours Brazil and Peru in terms of the volume of tin-concentrate production. By 1993 the Bolivian tin industry was running at a loss, prompting a focus on the best, and therefore the cheapest, seams. Small-mine owners were demanding government subsidies in order to increase prices which, along with subsidized inputs, would, they claimed, allow their mines to stay operative. However, while prices remained roughly constant, production again declined, from 18,634 metric tons in 1993 to an estimated 12,503 tons in 2000.

The mining industry diversified towards the end of the 20th century, however, and increased production of gold, silver and zinc, in particular, offset the decline in tin mining. Gold production increased from just 0.5 metric tons in 1990 to 12.0 tons in 2000 and output of silver rose from 310 tons to 434 tons in the same period. The value of zinc production increased from US $29.6m. in 1985 to $172.0m. in 1992, in which year 143,936 metric tons of zinc were mined; in 2000 output of zinc was an estimated 149,134 tons. Production of other industrial metals in that year included 9,523 metric tons of lead, 1,907 tons of antimony and 495 tons of tungsten. The discovery of huge deposits of silver, zinc and lead in the depressed San Cristobal region of southern Bolivia in 1996 further reinvigorated the mining sector. Apex Silver (USA) planned to invest $300m. to bring the mine into production in 2001, when it was expected to yield an average annual output of 132,700 metric tons of zinc, 39,500 tons of lead and 435 tons of silver, making it the world's fourth-largest silver mine, but low world prices continued to discourage development.

Other potentially viable concessions, such as the huge deposits of iron ore at Mutún, near Puerto Suárez, remained under-exploited, owing to the combination of an adverse political climate, the need for high levels of new investment and poor infrastructure. In 1990 the Government liberalized investment regulations, affording foreign companies the same treatment as Bolivian companies, and in April 1991 legislation was passed which allowed foreign companies to mine within the 50-km frontier zone and to forge joint ventures with COMIBOL for the first time. In October 1991 the Government awarded the concession for the previously unexploited lithium deposits in the Salar de Uyuni, the world's largest salt pan, to the multinational mining concern, Lithco. By that time 11 foreign companies had expressed interest in the joint-ventures programme and the first such deal was agreed in February 1992 with Compañía de Minerales Especializados (a subsidiary of a US-owned corporation) to develop deposits at Tasna. However, under pressure from the mineworkers' union, Federación Sindical de Trabajadores Mineros de Bolivia (FSTMB), the Government halted the joint-ventures programme in late 1992. The programme was then declared unconstitutional by the Supreme Court in February 1993, on the grounds that public companies were public property and therefore ineligible for foreign involvement. COMIBOL was not a candidate for privatization at that time.

After a lengthy legal battle, however, in mid-1995 COMIBOL was designated for capitalization, a variant of privatization in which private-sector companies would bid for 50% of the shares and full management control of the state company, the funds to be invested directly into the company's operations. Five bidders presented themselves for participation in joint mining ventures, including Silver Standard Resources of Vancouver (Canada), which bid for a joint share of El Asiento, a 2,000-ha silver and gold deposit in the Potosí region. In the same year COMIBOL planned to capitalize properties grouped under its subsidiary company, Vinto; this included deposits and mines, as well as the tin and antimony smelters and a lead-silver refinery. However, the Vinto capitalization suffered lengthy delays, principally owing to industrial unrest from miners opposed to the private development of the sector, and this was typical of the faltering progress of the initiative. Workers at the Huanuni and Colquiri mines began the protests in early 1996 and work at the Huanuni mine was suspended once again in March 1999, in support of 200 miners who were threatened with redundancy if they refused voluntary retirement in preparation for the mine's privatization.

ENERGY

Bolivia is effectively self-sufficient in energy. Domestic energy consumption remained reasonably low (548 kg oil equivalent per head in 1997). In 1999 petroleum accounted for 61% of energy consumed and gas for 25.6%, with the balance being supplied by traditional combustibles, and electricity production satisfying only a limited proportion of demand. Hydrocarbons represented 2.5% of GDP in 1997.

In January 2000 total proven crude petroleum reserves were estimated to be equivalent to 131.9m. barrels and were concentrated in the east and south-east of the country. Camiri had remained an important production site since it began production in 1927, and the oilfields in the departments of Chuquisica, Santa Cruz and Tarija continued to produce crude petroleum in significant quantities. Production peaked at 49,000 b/d (barrels per day) in 1973 but had declined to about 19,000 b/d by 1987. Production and exports expanded in the 1990s, however, with petroleum and its products earning US $40.1m. in export revenues in 1998, more than double the figure for 1993. In 1998 output stood at 12.6m. barrels, but decreased thereafter, reaching 10.1m. barrels in 2000.

In 1937, the year in which YPFB was created, petroleum companies were nationalized. However, the sector suffered from a lack of capital input as successive Governments failed to reinvest profits. From the 1930s foreign exploration companies also operated intermittently in Bolivia and in 1991 the US companies Tesoro and Occidental Petroleum produced more than one-sixth of Bolivia's crude petroleum output. At the end of 1992 exploration licences were held by 12 major oil companies, following the relaxation of exploration and production legislation which introduced a profit-sharing scheme with YPFB in 1991. YPFB was one of the first companies listed for the new Government's capitalization programme, begun in early 1995. The process suffered delays, partly owing to confrontations between the Government and the trade-union confederation, Central Obrera Boliviana (COB). However, YPFB was privatized in 1996.

At the end of 2000 reserves of natural gas were estimated at 7,010,000m. cu ft, with the main fields to be found in the south and south-east of the country. The export of natural gas was an important source of foreign currency; in 1985 natural-gas revenues of US $373m. accounted for 60% of total export earnings. However, this figure had declined to 26.1% by 1991, the time of the expiry of Bolivia's 20-year supply contract with the Argentine Government and, although the value of natural-gas exports remained fairly stable in the 1990s, the sector's share of total export earnings had fallen to just 4.3% by 1998, when natural-gas production totalled 92,232m. cu ft. In September 1996 work began on a 3,150 km natural-gas pipeline from Río Grande, near Santa Cruz, to São Paulo State, in Brazil, the largest project of its kind in South America. The section from Santa Cruz to Guararema (Brazil), to connect with the existing Rio–São Paulo pipeline, was completed in December 1998. It came onstream in July 1999 but so far has been operating well short of its 1,060m. cu ft of gas per day (cu ft/d) capacity. Under the terms of its supply contract, Bolivia was scheduled to increase its exports to Brazil from about 180m. cu ft/d to 320m. cu ft/d by 2000, and then to more than 1,000m. cu ft/d by 2005, with that level to be maintained until 2019. A contract

signed in the early 1990s with Paraguay ensured sales of a further 20m.–60m. cu ft/d.

Initially, there were concerns whether sufficient gas reserves were available to service the supply contract with Brazil. However, in 1998 a major new gas deposit was found near Santa Cruz, with reserves estimated at 1,700,000m. cu ft, and in June 1999 came the discovery of a potentially huge field in Tarija, with reserves in the region of 10,000,000m. cu ft. These deposits were expected to guarantee existing contracts and ensure high levels of investment in Bolivia's gas sector in the future. Throughout 2000 gas production continued to rise steeply, reaching 127,044m. cu ft. During an official visit to Brazil in March 2000 the President signed a new gas supply agreement. Though Bolivia was supplying Brazil with some 310m cu ft/d, the contract for 2000 was for 740m cu ft/d and the target for 2004 was set at 3,000m cu ft/d.

In 1998 installed electricity capacity was 971 MW, 54% of which was thermal and 43% hydroelectric. Electricity production was 2,580m. kWh in 1998 and consumption of electricity was a modest 370 kWh per head. The state-owned Empresa Nacional de Electricidad (ENDE) had formerly administered some 62% of installed capacity and the private-sector Compañía Boliviana de Energía Eléctrica a further 36%. However, ENDE was privatized in 1995, under the Government's capitalization programme, and the new law divided the company into three distinct enterprises (now largely US-owned), requiring a strict separation between generation, transmission and distribution. Bolivia has enormous unexploited hydroelectric potential, estimated at 38,857 MW, with some 34,200 MW on the Amazonian margins of the Andes, which the Government remained keen to exploit.

MANUFACTURING

In the first half of the 1990s manufacturing industry was utilizing little more than one-half of its installed capacity and non-durable consumer goods accounted for approximately 60% of the sector's output. The manufacture of durable consumer goods was modest. Processing of agricultural output and the manufacture of construction materials were potential growth areas. Demand for beer, aerated drinks, conserved beef, cement and tiles was high; growth was also strong in the frozen meat, textiles, flour-milling and baking sectors. The mining and energy sectors supported a number of ancillary operations. The state-owned Empresa Nacional de Fundiciones (ENAF), the fourth-largest smelting operation in the world, was capitalized in 1996. Bolivia also undertook some petroleum refining and had a small petrochemical industry. Measured by their contribution to the sector's GDP, in 1995 the principal branches of manufacturing were food products (30.9%—including meat preparations 10.5%, and beverages 9.1%), petroleum refineries (20.7%), jewellery and related articles (5.7%) and cement (3.8%). The manufacturing sector grew at an annual average rate of 4.2% in 1990–97 and accounted for some 17.8% of Bolivia's GDP in 2000.

In 1992 about one-half of the manufacturing work-force was self-employed or worked in a family enterprise. Accurate assessment of this sector was difficult, as many small enterprises lay outside the formal sector. These were frequently engaged in the production of textiles, handicrafts and food processing. Historically, the manufacturing sector was adversely affected by expensive credit, the high cost of imported inputs, foreign competition and contraband; demand was subdued by wage controls. Structurally, Bolivia's poor transport network further limited the efficiency of the domestic manufacturing sector, and the size and low purchasing power of the population restricted the potential market. In 2000 industry (including manufacturing) accounted for 33.2% of GDP and the services sector for 51.3%.

TRANSPORT AND COMMUNICATIONS

Bolivia's trade regime was dependent on its access to seaports, which, historically, was limited and subject to disruption. Bolivia lost its coastal territory of Antofagasta (now Atacama) to Chile in the War of the Pacific (1879–83) and thereafter was dependent on Chile for its main access to the sea at Arica. The Treaty of Ilo, signed in January 1992, granted Bolivia use of that Pacific seaport in Peru and Bolivia also has free port privileges in ports in Argentina, Brazil and Paraguay. In addition, an extensive and reliable transport system, essential for the successful exploitation of Bolivia's mineral and energy reserves, for the operation of the commercial farming sector, for national integration and for the effective delivery of social services, still did not exist at the end of the 20th century.

Bolivia's national rail network consisted of two distinct systems, both of which were owned and managed by the formerly state-owned railway company, Empresa Nacional de Ferrocarriles (ENFE), which was capitalized in 1995. The eastern system ran in the Santa Cruz lowlands and, with 1,423 km of track in 1994, linked Bolivia with Argentina at La Quiaca and with Brazil at Corumbá, with connections to the Atlantic coast at São Paulo. The western, or Andean, system had 2,274 km of track. Plans to lay track between Santa Cruz and Cochabamba, which would complete an Atlantic–Pacific rail connection, took a step forward with a feasibility study into a Santa Cruz–Arquile link. In 1995 the two systems carried a total of 646,814 passengers (a steep decline from 1,361,376 in 1991) and 1.3m. metric tons of freight.

The road system in 1999 covered 52,216 km, of which an estimated 2,872 km (5.5%) were paved. The country's major road artery links La Paz with Santa Cruz via Oruro and Cochabamba. The Pan-American Highway links Bolivia directly with Argentina and Peru. A paved road link to the Pacific coast at Arica (Chile) was completed in 1996. Mining operations in the east and south-east of the country were impeded by a poor road network, while seasonal rains in the Amazonian north-east periodically severed overland communications. There were 223,829 passenger vehicles in 1996. In late 1997 the Government announced plans to construct 1,844 km of new roads, in order to improve Bolivia's links with neighbouring countries.

Despite the aridity of much of its territory, Bolivia has some 14,000 km of navigable waterways in the east of the country, along the Rivers Chaparé, Guaporé and Mamoré, in the Amazonian north-east and on the River Paraguay. In November 1994 plans were finalized to widen and deepen the River Paraguay, thus providing a waterway linking Bolivia with the Atlantic coast in Uruguay. The project was expected to take three years to complete and cost some US $7,000m., but in 2001 work had still not begun, principally owing to environmental concerns.

Bolivia had approximately 1,109 airports of which 13 had paved runways, including international terminals at La Paz (El Alto) and Santa Cruz. The national air carrier, Lloyd Aéreo Boliviano (LAB), was privatized in 1995, when a Brazilian airline, VASP (Viação Aérea de São Paulo), paid US $47.5m. for a 49% stake, becoming the principal shareholder.

The state telecommunications company, Empresa Nacional de Telecomunicaciones (ENTEL), was privatized in 1995. In 1997 there were 535,000 main telephone lines in use (69.0 per thousand). There were 129 MW/LW radio stations (all AM) and 68 short-wave stations, and 48 television stations broadcasting to some 900,000 receivers. In 1999 there were five internet service providers.

TOURISM

Despite financial assistance from, among others, the Inter-American Development Bank (IDB), and an increased interest from European travellers, tourism in the early 1990s was suppressed by fears of cholera and terrorist activity in neighbouring Peru. Nevertheless, figures indicated a steady increase in both numbers of tourist arrivals and receipts. In 1998 420,491 foreign visitors arrived at Bolivian hotels. Between 1990 and 1997 revenue from tourism increased from US $93m. to $170m.

GOVERNMENT FINANCE AND INVESTMENT

Inflation began to rise after 1978, accompanied by frequent devaluations of the currency against the US dollar. Governments tried to cope with the effects by indexation of minimum wages, fixing of exchange rates and price controls. In 1984 public revenue was equivalent to only 5% of GDP, with widespread tax evasion, while government expenditure was equal to 33% of GDP. In the absence of foreign credits, the deficit had to be covered domestically. This resulted in rapid monetary growth and 'hyperinflation'. In August 1985, amid growing budget deficits, goods shortages and devaluations, Bolivia's annualized inflation rate reached 16,000%.

In that month President Víctor Paz Estenssoro introduced the New Economic Policy (NEP), an economic austerity programme which caused considerable social hardship and unrest but reduced inflation to double figures within a few months. In 1987 a new currency was adopted, the boliviano, equivalent to one million pesos. Average annual inflation in 1985–95 was 18.4%. The NEP reduced the wages and salaries and the number of public-sector employees; it also ended many trade restrictions, price controls and subsidies, thus further reducing state-sector expenditure. Successive Governments maintained these austerity measures. Since a large proportion of public revenue came from taxes and royalties from the mining and energy sectors, sectors which were vulnerable to demand and price fluctuations, efforts were also made to broaden the tax base. Value-added tax (VAT) on consumer goods was introduced in 1986. Tax revenue represented 11.8% of GDP in 1995, against 17.5% in 1989. However, the fiscal deficit rose to 3% in 1997, largely as a result of the introduction of a new pension scheme.

Bolivia's GDP increased, in real terms, by an annual average of 4.2% in 1990–99; GDP increased by 5.0% in 1997, by 5.2% in 1998 but by only 0.4% in 1999, as a result of the ending of gas sales to Argentina. The economy expanded by 2.4% in 2000. Public-sector investment, which declined sharply during the late 1970s and throughout the 1980s, recovered in the 1990s. Gross domestic investment was 19.6% of GDP in 1998 (compared with 5.6% in 1986 and 16.6% of GDP in 1996). In 2000 the annual rate of inflation was 4.6% (compared with 2.2% in 1999 and 7.7% in 1998).

BANKING AND CREDIT

In 1993 a new banking law permitted banks to hold deposits and to make loans in foreign currencies. Deposits in commercial banks increased from US $50m. in 1985 to just under $2,400m. at the end of 1995. By 1999 an estimated 85% of all deposits in Bolivian banks were held in US dollars.

Financial-sector activity grew consistently in the early 1990s, as the privatization programme progressed, despite strong resistance from opposition parties and trade unions. The initial response was unenthusiastic; by the end of 1993 only 15 of the 100 public enterprises offered for privatization had been sold, generating just US $4.5m. However, a public-sector capitalization programme, initiated in 1995, which aimed to generate funds for investment by offering private-sector concerns the opportunity to purchase a 50% controlling interest in several of the principal state-owned companies, was considerably more successful. In 1995 alone, the capitalization of public-sector concerns in the electricity, telecommunications, railway and airline industries generated revenues of some $836m., which, under the terms of the Government's programme, were invested directly in their operations; almost all of this new investment came from foreign investors.

FOREIGN TRADE AND BALANCE OF PAYMENTS

Export markets diversified in the late 1980s and 1990s: in 1986 53.2% of exports went to Argentina, much of it natural gas, payment for which was often well in arrears. In 2000 the total value of exports was US $1,442m. The principal exports in 2000 were metals (34.6%), soya beans (15.2%), natural gas (9.9%), jewellery (2.5%) and cork and wood (2.3%) and their main destinations were the USA (24%), Colombia (13%), the United Kingdom (12%), Brazil (11%), and Switzerland (11%). In the same year total imports were valued at $1,977m., 22% of which came from the USA, 15% from Argentina, 14% from Brazil and 8% from Chile. In 1999 capital goods, notably machinery and transport equipment, accounted for 48% of imports by value, chemicals for 11%, petroleum for 5% and food for a further 5%.

Exports to the European Community (EC—known as the European Union from November 1993) increased significantly from the 1980s and 1990s, although trade was hindered by distance and high transportation costs. Bolivian products (clothes and leather excepted) entered the USA free of duty, on a concessionary basis, under the Andean Trade Preference Act (ATPA). Bolivia was a member of the Andean Community of Nations from its foundation in 1969 (when it was known as the Andean Pact): in 1992 exports to member countries totalled US $90m. and imports $30m. However, during the mid-1990s Bolivia favoured closer links with the Southern Common Market

(Mercado Común del Sur—Mercosur), which consisted of Argentina, Brazil, Paraguay and Uruguay. Bolivia became an associate member in December 1996, committed to the phasing out of trade tariffs with the Mercosur countries within eight years, and in 2000 Bolivia declared its intention further to strengthen links with Mercosur, with the aim of eventually becoming a full member.

Bolivia's persistent trade deficit improved to $488.0m. in 1999, from US $655.4m. in 1998, nevertheless a substantial increase from figures recorded in the early 1990s. This problem was caused by a fall in the value of hydrocarbon exports and increases in imports of fuel and of capital goods. In 1999 the current-account deficit was $555.8m. down from $678.1m. in the previous year. From 1995 to 1998 the long-term overall balance-of-payments deficit was reversed (a surplus of $100.9m. was achieved in 1998). However, in 1999 a deficit of $41.8m. was recorded.

After 1980 servicing of the debt accumulated during the latter half of the 1970s became difficult, and interest payments were suspended in 1984. The Government's austerity programme incorporated the basic features of an International Monetary Fund (IMF) structural-adjustment plan, in return for which official donors financed the 'buy-back' of Bolivia's commercial debt by agreement with the 'Paris Club' of Western creditor governments. Debt was exchanged on favourable terms with Argentina and Brazil and, under the Enterprise for the Americas Initiative, the USA cancelled government-held debt. By May 1993 Bolivia had all but cleared its debt with the international commercial banks, notwithstanding that the success of the initiative largely depended on the recycling of US dollars illegally earned by the narcotics trade and at the Paris Club meeting in December 1995 its debt stock was reduced by 67%.

However, at the end of 1999 Bolivia's total external debt outstanding and disbursed was US $6,157m. The cost of debt-servicing in the this year was equivalent to 32.1% of the total value of exports of goods and services, compared to 30.2% in 1998. Bolivia's debt burden was widely acknowledged to be a major factor inhibiting economic growth and, in recognition of the progress made over a decade in macroeconomic stabilization,

in September 1998 the World Bank and the IMF approved a debt-relief package worth some $760m. Bolivia became the first country in Latin America to receive debt-service relief under the terms of the World Bank-led Heavily-Indebted Poor Countries (HIPC) programme. It has since qualified for HIPC II and since 1999 has been regarded as a pilot country for the World Bank and IMF-sponsored Comprehensive Development Framework, a programme which is intended, in part, to complement debt reduction plans. At the end of 2000 reserves, including gold, totalled $1,058.9m.

OUTLOOK

In mid-2001 the Government faced increasing resistance to its economic programme from trade unions and indigenous groups. It was expected to continue to encourage private-sector investment and to stimulate private-sector capital inflows, and further efforts would undoubtedly be made to encourage non-traditional exports. There was still significant need for expansion and improvement of the country's infrastructure. The outlook for metals was not encouraging but the prospects for hydrocarbons had improved markedly, even though it was estimated that some 50% of the country's gas production was still going to waste. Moreover, the US-funded coca-eradication programme had sharply reduced the national income while, at the same time, encountering determined resistance from rural interests which threatened to escalate into outright insurrection. Although there was consistent economic growth in the 1990s, it was still insufficient to make a significant impact on poverty, which continued to present the major challenge to the Government. Unemployment was officially 11.4% at the end of the decade, but this figure clearly understated the extent of underemployment. Malnutrition affected 9% of children under the age of five and 40% of the population did not have access to a safe water supply. In 1999 Bolivia ranked 114th on the UN Development Programme's Human Development Index. The sustained austerity measures, wage controls and taxation increases of the late 1980s and early 1990s stabilized the economy but reinforced the position of Bolivia's population as mainland Latin America's poorest country.

Statistical Survey

Sources (unless otherwise indicated): Instituto Nacional de Estadística, Plaza Mario Guzmán Aspiazu No. 1, Casilla 6129, La Paz; tel. (2) 36-7443; internet www.ine.gov.bo; Banco Central de Bolivia, Ayacucho esq. Mercado, Casilla 3118, La Paz; tel. (2) 37-4151; fax (2) 39-2398; internet www.bcb.gov.bo.

Area and Population

AREA, POPULATION AND DENSITY

Area (sq km)	
Land	1,084,391
Inland water	14,190
Total	1,098,581*
Population (census results)†	
29 September 1976	4,613,486
3 June 1992	
Males	3,171,265
Females	3,249,527
Total	6,420,792
Population (official estimates at mid-year)	
1998	7,949,933
1999	8,137,113
2000	8,328,700
Density (per sq km) at mid-2000	7.6

* 424,164 sq miles.
† Figures exclude adjustment for underenumeration. This was estimated at 6.99% in 1976 and at 6.92% in 1992.

DEPARTMENTS (official estimates at mid-2000)

	Area (sq km)	Population	Density (per sq km)	Capital
Beni . . .	213,564	366,047	1.7	Trinidad
Chuquisaca .	51,524	589,948	11.4	Sucre
Cochabamba .	55,631	1,524,724	27.4	Cochabamba
La Paz . .	133,985	2,406,377	18.0	La Paz
Oruro . .	53,588	393,991	7.4	Oruro
Pando . .	63,827	57,316	0.8	Cobija
Potosí . .	118,218	774,696	6.6	Potosí
Santa Cruz .	370,621	1,812,522	4.9	Santa Cruz de la Sierra
Tarija . .	37,623	403,079	10.7	Tarija
Total . .	1,098,581	8,328,700	7.6	

PRINCIPAL TOWNS (estimated population at mid-2000)

Santa Cruz de la Sierra	1,034,070	Sucre (legal capital) .	223,436
La Paz (administrative capital) . .	1,004,440	Tarija	162,973
		Potosí	162,212
Cochabamba. . .	616,022	Sacaba	108,377
El Alto . . .	568,919	Quillacollo . . .	102,138
Oruro . . .	248,273		

BIRTHS AND DEATHS (UN estimates, annual averages)

	1980–85	1985–90	1990–95
Birth rate (per 1,000). . .	38.2	36.6	35.7
Death rate (per 1,000) . .	13.5	11.5	10.2

Expectation of life (UN estimates, years at birth, 1990–95): 59.3 (males 57.7, females 61.0).

Source: UN, *World Population Prospects: The 1998 Revision.*

ECONOMICALLY ACTIVE POPULATION
(labour force surveys, '000 persons aged 10 years and over, at November)

	1996	1997
Agriculture	1,620.7	1,518.7
Forestry and fishing	14.6	23.1
Mining and quarrying	53.7	63.9
Manufacturing	403.6	393.5
Electricity, gas and water supply . .	9.9	11.0
Construction.	172.4	187.0
Wholesale and retail trade; repair of motor vehicles, motorcycles and personal and household goods	562.3	505.9
Hotels and restaurants . . .	135.2	126.5
Transport, storage and communications .	147.6	170.5
Financial intermediation	18.1	20.1
Real estate, renting and business activities .	51.9	58.8
Public administration and defence; compulsory social security	91.8	78.8
Education	137.9	158.8
Health and social work . . .	59.9	62.9
Other community, social and personal service activities	67.5	70.4
Private households with employed persons. .	127.0	117.8
Extra-territorial organizations and bodies . .	1.6	2.1
Total employed.	3,675.7	3,569.7
Unemployed	65.0	75.4
Total labour force	3,740.7	3,645.2
Males	2,008.7	2,048.8
Females	1,731.9	1,596.4

Mid-1999 (estimates in '000): Agriculture, etc. 1,470; Total labour force 3,307 (Source: FAO).

Agriculture

PRINCIPAL CROPS ('000 metric tons)

	1998	1999	2000
Wheat	164	141	104
Rice (paddy)	301	189	310
Barley	41	50	64
Maize	424	613	653
Sorghum	121	148	95
Potatoes.	495	783	927
Cassava (Manioc) . . .	357	400	515
Other roots and tubers* . . .	95	110	110
Pulses	26	34	32
Soya beans	1,071	762	1,232
Groundnuts (in shell). . .	12	13	14
Sunflower seeds	115	95	96
Tomatoes	80	84	137
Pumpkins, squash and gourds .	104	107	109
Onions (dry)	48	49	50*
Peas (green)	20	26	30
Carrots	33	36	36
Other vegetables	177	199	181
Watermelons	21	22	23
Sugar cane	4,241	4,160	3,602
Oranges.	101	106	115
Tangerines, mandarins, clementines and satsumas . .	55	60	69
Lemons and limes . . .	62	63	64
Grapefruit and pomelos . .	29	29	28
Pineapples	46	53	59
Papayas.	22	23	23
Peaches and nectarines . .	36	36*	37
Grapes	23	24	28
Bananas	403†	419†	695
Plantains*	173	180	187
Other fruits and berries* . . .	46	49	35
Chestnuts	32	34	34
Coffee (green)	24	23	25
Cotton (lint)	19	20*	20*
Natural rubber	11*	11*	11

* FAO estimate(s).   † Unofficial figure(s).

Source: FAO.

LIVESTOCK ('000 head, year ending September)

	1998	1999	2000
Horses*	322	322	322
Mules*	81	81	81
Asses*	631	631	631
Cattle	6,387	6,556	6,725
Pigs.	2,637	2,715	2,793
Sheep	8,409	8,575	8,752
Goats	1,496	1,500*	1,500*
Chickens	77,717	85,000	73,856†
Ducks*	270	280	280
Turkeys*	150	150	150

* FAO estimate(s).   † Unofficial figure.

Source: FAO.

LIVESTOCK PRODUCTS ('000 metric tons)

	1998	1999	2000
Beef and veal	151	155	160
Mutton and lamb . . .	15	15	16
Goat meat	6	6	6
Pig meat	72	74	76
Poultry meat	136	145	139
Cows' milk	193	202	231
Sheep's milk. . . .	29	29*	29*
Goats' milk	11	11	11*
Cheese	7	7	7
Hen eggs*	40	41	37
Wool: greasy* . . .	8	9	3
Cattle hides (fresh) . . .	18	18	19
Sheepskins (fresh) . . .	5	5	6

* FAO estimates.

Source: FAO.

Forestry

ROUNDWOOD REMOVALS ('000 cubic metres, excl. bark)

	1996	1997	1998
Sawlogs, veneer logs and logs for sleepers	491	489	233
Pulpwood	383	383	383
Other industrial wood	18	18	18
Fuel wood	1,293	1,323	1,355
Total	**2,185**	**2,213**	**1,989**

1999: Sawlogs, veneer logs and logs for sleepers 502, other industrial wood 18, Fuel wood 1,386.

Source: FAO, *Yearbook of Forest Products.*

SAWNWOOD PRODUCTION ('000 cubic metres, incl. railway sleepers)

	1997	1998	1999
Coniferous (softwood)*	15	15	15
Broadleaved (hardwood)	165	203	244
Total	**180**	**218**	**259**

* FAO estimates.

Source: FAO, *Yearbook of Forest Products.*

Fishing

(metric tons, live weight)

	1996	1997	1998
Capture	5,988	6,038	6,055
Freshwater fishes	4,800	4,850	4,865
Rainbow trout	338	338	340
Silversides (sand smelts)	850	850	850
Aquaculture	380	387	385
Rainbow trout	300	312	320
Total catch	**6,368**	**6,425**	**6,440**

Note: Figures exclude crocodiles and alligators, recorded by number rather than by weight. The number of spectacled caimans caught was: 15,961 in 1997; 1,757 in 1998.

Source: FAO, *Yearbook of Fishery Statistics.*

Mining*

(metric tons, unless otherwise indicated)

	1998	1999	2000†
Crude petroleum ('000 barrels)	12,628	10,680	10,106
Natural gas (million cu feet)	109,673	92,232	127,044
Copper	48	250	110
Tin	11,308	12,417	12,503
Lead	13,848	10,153	9,523
Zinc	152,110	146,144	149,134
Tungsten (Wolfram)	627	421	495
Antimony	4,735	2,790	1,907
Silver	404	423	434
Gold (kg)	14,445	11,782	12,000

* Figures for metallic minerals refer to the metal content of ores.
† Provisional figures.

Source: partly IMF, *Bolivia: Statistical Annex* (June 2001).

Industry

SELECTED PRODUCTS ('000 metric tons, unless otherwise indicated)

	1997	1998	1999*
Flour	465	549	576
Cement	970	1,095	1,163
Refined sugar	332	285	294
Carbonated drinks ('000 hectolitres)	1,867	2,368	2,281
Beer ('000 hectolitres)	1,702	1,922	1,840
Cigarettes (packets)	73,166	69,949	67,332
Alcohol ('000 litres)	27,678	31,154	26,412
Diesel oil ('000 barrels)	2,866	3,034	3,063
Motor spirit (petrol) ('000 barrels)	3,941	4,003	4,176
Electric energy (million kWh)	3,528	2,580	n.a.

* Provisional figures.

Tin (primary metal, metric tons): 16,853 in 1997; 11,102 in 1998; 11,000 (estimate) in 1999 (Source: US Geological Survey).

Finance

CURRENCY AND EXCHANGE RATES

Monetary Units

100 centavos = 1 boliviano (B).

Sterling, Dollar and Euro Equivalents (30 April 2001)

£1 sterling = 9.321 bolivianos;
US $1 = 6.510 bolivianos;
€1 = 5.778 bolivianos;
1,000 bolivianos = £107.28 = $153.61 = €173.06.

Average Exchange Rate (bolivianos per US $)

1998   5.5101
1999   5.8124
2000   6.1835

BUDGET (million bolivianos)

Revenue	1998	1999	2000
Tax revenue	8,824	8,417	9,048
Domestic taxes	8,104	7,784	8,395
Customs duties	720	633	654
Non-tax revenue	562	1,320	1,022
Capital revenue	326	217	316
Foreign grants	450	420	664
Other revenue	155	189	223
Total	**10,317**	**10,562**	**11,274**

Expenditure	1998	1999	2000
Current expenditure	10,274	10,426	11,378
Wages and salaries	3,513	4,313	4,551
Goods and services	774	914	923
Interest	540	473	628
Transfers	4,637	4,395	4,964
Rest of general government	1,730	1,567	1,835
Public enterprises	159	304	219
Private sector	2,747	2,524	2,911
Other current expenditure	811	331	311
Capital expenditure	1,295	1,753	1,961
Fixed capital formation	959	1,375	1,607
Transfers	288	349	336
Total	**11,570**	**12,179**	**13,338**

Source: IMF, *Bolivia: Statistical Annex* (June 2001).

INTERNATIONAL RESERVES (US $ million at 31 December)

	1998	1999	2000
Gold*	234.9	235.7	234.7
IMF special drawing rights . .	37.7	37.4	35.6
Reserve position in IMF . . .	12.5	12.2	11.6
Foreign exchange . . .	834.4	866.9	777.1
Total	1,119.5	1,152.2	1,058.9

* National valuation (US $ 250 per troy oz each year).

Source: IMF, *International Financial Statistics*.

MONEY SUPPLY (million bolivianos at 31 December)

	1998	1999	2000
Currency outside banks . .	2,193	2,173	2,189
Demand deposits at commercial banks.	1,124	1,031	1,150
Total money	3,895	3,670	3,995

Source: IMF, *International Financial Statistics*.

COST OF LIVING
(Consumer Price Index for urban areas; base: 1991 = 100)

	1998	1999	2000
Food and beverages . . .	185.94	183.89	186.89
Fuel and light	192.12	210.02	238.90
Clothing and footwear . . .	161.76	168.44	177.45
Rent	130.52	138.09	145.32
All items (incl. others) . .	184.71	188.70	197.39

NATIONAL ACCOUNTS
Expenditure on the Gross Domestic Product
(million bolivianos at current prices)

	1998	1999	2000*
Government final consumption expenditure . . .	6,624	7,088	7,566
Private final consumption expenditure . . .	34,154	36,137	38,752
Increase in stocks . . .	143	−278	167
Gross fixed capital formation . .	10,762	9,435	9,702
Total domestic expenditure .	51,684	52,382	56,187
Exports of goods and services .	7,434	7,904	9,325
Less Imports of goods and services .	12,076	11,698	13,001
GDP in purchasers' values .	47,042	48,588	52,511
GDP at constant 1990 prices	21,759	21,854	22,372

* Preliminary.

Source: IMF, *Bolivia: Statistical Annex* (June 2001).

Gross Domestic Product by Economic Activity
(million bolivianos at constant 1990 prices)

	1998	1999	2000*
Agriculture, hunting, forestry and fishing	2,994	3,080	3,172
Mining and quarrying . . .	2,123	2,018	2,414
Manufacturing	3,504	3,588	3,647
Construction.	986	807	731
Trade	1,820	1,816	1,871
Transport, storage and communications . . .	2,394	2,392	2,456
Finance, insurance, real estate and business services . . .	2,795	3,155	2,903
Government services . . .	1,948	1,978	1,996
Other community, social and personal services . . .	1,214	1,209	1,270
Sub-total	19,777	20,043	20,459
Adjustments.	1,982	1,811	1,913
GDP in purchasers' values .	21,759	21,854	22,372

* Preliminary figures.

Source: IMF, *Bolivia: Statistical Annex* (June 2001).

BALANCE OF PAYMENTS (US $ million)

	1997	1998	1999
Exports of goods f.o.b. . . .	1,166.6	1,104.0	1,051.1
Imports of goods f.o.b. . . .	−1,643.6	−1,759.4	−1,539.1
Trade balance . . .	−477.0	−655.4	−488.0
Exports of services . . .	247.2	251.0	259.5
Imports of services . . .	−418.7	−441.3	−449.5
Balance on goods and services .	−648.5	−845.7	−678.1
Other income received . .	98.2	127.0	157.1
Other income paid . . .	−294.7	−289.3	−358.4
Balance on goods, services and income . .	−845.0	−1,008.0	−879.4
Current transfers received . .	300.3	341.6	352.2
Current transfers paid . . .	−8.8	−11.7	−28.6
Current balance . . .	−553.5	−678.1	−555.8
Capital account (net). . . .	25.3	9.9	—
Direct investment abroad. . .	−2.5	−2.5	−2.5
Direct investment from abroad .	730.6	957.3	1,016.4
Portfolio investment assets . .	−53.2	−74.5	−44.4
Portfolio investment liabilities .	—	—	−16.9
Other investment assets . .	−19.9	−111.4	−170.1
Other investment liabilities . .	234.8	314.4	−31.8
Net errors and omissions . .	−260.6	−314.2	−236.7
Overall balance . . .	101.0	100.9	−41.8

Source: IMF, *International Financial Statistics*.

External Trade

PRINCIPAL COMMODITIES (distribution by SITC, US $ million)

Imports c.i.f.	1996	1997	1998
Food and live animals . . .	156.6	142.2	162.2
Cereals and cereal preparations .	86.3	65.9	72.5
Wheat (including spelt) and meslin, unmilled. . .	60.2	38.4	32.2
Crude materials (inedible) except fuels	52.0	52.4	38.1
Mineral fuels, lubricants, etc. .	48.0	144.2	110.9
Petroleum, petroleum products, etc.	47.9	144.2	110.8
Refined petroleum products .	39.8	136.5	104.1
Gas oils (distillate fuels) . .	30.9	109.4	78.8
Chemicals and related products	202.7	232.2	253.3
Essential oils, perfume materials and cleansing preparations .	31.3	35.9	36.1
Artificial resins, plastic materials, etc.	42.6	48.3	46.1
Products of polymerization, etc.	34.2	39.6	36.3
Basic manufactures . .	230.0	251.0	421.7
Paper, paperboard and manufactures	35.8	45.2	45.7
Iron and steel	68.9	78.8	225.3
Tubes, pipes and fittings .	18.3	26.7	163.5
'Seamless' tubes and pipes	8.4	16.7	149.6
Machinery and transport equipment	788.8	931.0	1,170.4
Power-generating machinery and equipment	47.2	22.6	32.7
Machinery specialized for particular industries . .	101.4	122.4	187.7
Civil engineering and contractors' plant and equipment	35.2	56.1	111.6
Construction and mining machinery . . .	24.4	30.0	49.1
General industrial machinery, equipment and parts . .	67.9	92.5	122.9
Telecommunications and sound equipment . . .	117.2	180.9	117.4
Electrical line telephonic and telegraphic apparatus .	49.6	86.5	55.4
Other electrical machinery, apparatus, etc. . .	49.7	66.5	63.9
Road vehicles and parts* . .	233.3	352.4	524.9
Passenger motor cars (excl. buses)	107.3	148.7	238.8

PRINCIPAL COMMODITIES (distribution by SITC, US $ million)

Imports c.i.f. — *continued*	1996	1997	1998
Motor vehicles for the transport of goods, etc.	75.7	126.9	189.2
Goods vehicles	69.6	118.9	177.8
Other road motor vehicles . .	32.1	56.2	73.7
Public-service vehicles (e.g. buses)	27.6	47.7	52.0
Other transport equipment and parts*	150.4	61.7	91.6
Aircraft, associated equipment and parts*	150.0	60.0	86.6
Miscellaneous manufactured articles	113.1	103.8	147.0
Non-monetary gold (excl. ores and concentrates) . . .	42.0	43.7	36.5
Total (incl. others)	1,643.1	1,909.2	2,350.2

* Excluding tyres, engines and electrical parts.

Exports f.o.b.	1996	1997	1998
Food and live animals . . .	179.1	230.7	216.8
Vegetables and fruit	42.3	53.0	48.9
Fresh or dried fruit and nuts (excl. oil nuts)	29.3	31.5	31.4
Edible nuts	28.4	31.1	30.9
Brazil nuts	27.6	30.8	28.3
Sugar, sugar preparations and honey	28.1	22.3	23.8
Sugar and honey	27.9	22.1	23.6
Coffee, tea, cocoa and spices . .	17.1	27.0	15.9
Feeding-stuff for animals (excl. unmilled cereals) . . .	81.7	117.7	106.0
Oil-cake and other residues from the extraction of vegetable oils	81.1	117.7	105.9
Oil-cake and residues from soya beans	78.2	112.2	100.8
Crude materials (inedible) except fuels	428.7	468.5	379.1
Oil seeds and oleaginous fruit. .	84.6	75.8	64.6
Soya beans	64.8	61.6	47.3
Cork and wood	68.9	67.2	50.5
Simply worked wood and railway sleepers	68.9	67.1	50.4
Sawn non-coniferous wood .	64.6	61.8	45.1
Textile fibres (excl. wool tops) and waste	32.4	40.5	16.5
Cotton	31.3	39.3	15.5
Raw cotton (excl. linters) . .	31.3	39.3	15.5
Metalliferous ores and metal scrap	235.0	275.3	238.1
Base metal ores and concentrates	182.5	226.8	178.7
Zinc ores and concentrates .	151.7	200.1	157.8
Precious metal ores and concentrates	52.2	48.0	58.8
Mineral fuels, lubricants etc. .	142.1	107.1	96.4
Petroleum, petroleum products, etc.	47.4	37.0	40.1
Crude petroleum oils, etc. . .	38.5	28.2	30.3
Gas (natural and manufactured)	94.5	70.1	56.3
Petroleum gases and other gaseous hydrocarbons . .	94.5	69.9	55.5
Animal and vegetable oils, fats and waxes	40.5	59.3	72.6
Fixed vegetable oils and fats . .	40.5	59.3	72.5
Soya bean oil	39.5	55.1	68.7
Basic manufactures	146.0	142.9	115.5
Non-ferrous metals . . .	113.9	102.1	74.1
Tin and tin alloys	101.2	90.4	58.3
Unwrought tin and alloys. .	100.2	90.0	57.8
Machinery and transport equipment	76.7	14.8	189.0

Exports f.o.b. — *continued*	1996	1997	1998
Transport equipment and parts*	62.2	5.6	156.1
Aircraft, associated equipment and parts*	59.4	4.0	148.7
Miscellaneous manufactured articles	49.6	115.1	115.6
Clothing and accessories (excl. footwear)	28.5	26.6	27.2
Jewellery, goldsmiths' and silversmiths' wares, etc. . .	11.4	74.6	61.6
Non-monetary gold (excl. ores and concentrates)	n.a.	110.6	112.7
Total (incl. others)	1,087.0	1,272.1	1,323.3

* Excluding tyres, engines and electrical parts.

Source: UN, *International Trade Statistics Yearbook.*

PRINCIPAL TRADING PARTNERS (US $ million)*

Imports c.i.f.	1998	1999	2000
Argentina	232.4	243.8	302.7
Brazil	256.8	269.0	278.8
Canada	27.7	15.3	14.0
Chile	141.9	129.9	163.1
Colombia	46.2	40.2	47.0
Denmark	25.7	n.a.	n.a.
Germany	57.9	48.9	39.5
Italy	37.8	31.1	42.7
Japan	463.0	155.5	103.2
Korea, Republic	29.0	n.a.	n.a.
Mexico	38.8	43.2	45.7
Peru	94.9	87.4	98.8
Spain	36.9	n.a.	n.a.
Sweden	108.0	37.4	22.7
United Kingdom	18.0	15.6	10.4
USA	550.7	438.0	430.6
Venezuela	23.5	19.8	14.3
Total (incl. others)	2,350.2	1,854.5	1,976.7

Exports f.o.b.	1998	1999	2000
Argentina	141.3	76.6	48.5
Belgium-Luxembourg . . .	64.0	n.a.	n.a.
Brazil	30.1	40.9	164.1
Chile	34.2	27.7	29.2
Colombia	86.5	126.9	192.7
Ecuador	80.2	71.4	5.2
Germany	21.4	14.9	13.3
Mexico	6.6	7.7	6.5
Peru	140.5	75.3	59.9
Switzerland-Liechtenstein . .	83.8	69.3	163.2
United Kingdom	198.9	180.0	167.6
USA	303.2	464.7	349.3
Uruguay	50.1	78.0	69.3
Total (incl. others)	1,323.3	1,401.9	1,441.7

* Imports by country of provenance; exports by country of last consignment.

Source: partly UN, *International Trade Statistics Yearbook.*

Transport

RAILWAYS (traffic)

	1996	1997	1998
Passenger-kilometres (million) .	197	225	270
Freight ton-kilometres (million) .	780	839	908

Source: UN, *Statistical Yearbook.*

ROAD TRAFFIC (motor vehicles in use at 31 December)

	1994	1995	1996
Passenger cars	198,734	213,666	223,829
Buses	18,884	19,627	20,322
Lorries and vans	108,214	114,357	118,214
Tractors	9	9	10
Motorcycles	62,725	64,936	66,113

Source: IRF, *World Road Statistics*.

1997: Passenger cars ('000 in use) 234.1; Commercial vehicles ('000 in use) 124.8.
1998: Passenger cars ('000 in use) 235.7; Commercial vehicles ('000 in use) 122.2. (Source: UN, *Statistical Yearbook*).

CIVIL AVIATION (traffic on scheduled services)

	1995	1996	1997
Kilometres flown (million) . .	16	24	28
Passengers carried ('000) . .	1,224	1,783	2,251
Passenger-km (million) . .	1,234	1,634	2,143
Freight ton-km (million) . .	187	223	274

Source: UN, *Statistical Yearbook*.

Tourism

ARRIVALS AT HOTELS (regional capitals only, '000)

Country of origin	1996	1997	1998
Argentina	41.0	51.0	53.7
Brazil	34.8	36.8	36.1
Chile	23.4	28.6	28.9
France	20.2	19.6	21.9
Germany	23.8	22.8	22.9
Israel	12.7	9.6	10.6
Italy	8.4	7.8	8.4
Japan	7.7	6.8	6.3
Netherlands	10.9	10.8	11.5
Peru	56.2	62.5	66.2
Spain	11.4	10.2	11.2
Switzerland	10.8	9.7	9.3
United Kingdom . . .	12.2	12.0	13.2
USA	39.6	40.4	45.0
Total (incl. others) . . .	376.9	397.5	420.5

Total tourism receipts (US $ million): 159 in 1996; 170 in 1997.
Source: World Tourism Organization, *Yearbook of Tourism Statistics*.

Communications Media

	1995	1996	1997
Radio receivers ('000 in use) .	4,980	5,100	5,250
Television receivers ('000 in use) .	850	875	900
Telephones ('000 main lines in use)	295*	425	535
Mobile cellular telephones (subscribers)	10,000	20,300	116,000
Daily newspapers:			
Number	17	18	n.a.
Average circulation ('000 copies)	410	420	n.a.

* Installed lines.

Sources: UNESCO, *Statistical Yearbook*; UN, *Statistical Yearbook*.

Education

(1998)

	Institutions	Teachers	Students
Pre-primary	2,294*	4,168	188,145
Primary	12,639†	63,056	1,547,203
Secondary	n.a.	15,132	320,736
Higher			
Universities and equivalent	n.a.	4,261‡	184,169§
Other	n.a.	1,302‖	34,889‖

* 1988.   † 1987.   ‡ 1991.   § 1997.   ‖ 1989.
Source: partly UNESCO, *Statistical Yearbook*.

Directory

The Constitution

Bolivia became an independent republic in 1825 and received its first Constitution in November 1826. Since that date a number of new Constitutions have been promulgated. Following the *coup d'état* of November 1964, the Constitution of 1947 was revived. Under its provisions, executive power is vested in the President, who chairs the Cabinet. According to the revised Constitution, the President is elected by direct suffrage for a five-year term (extended from four years in 1997) and is not eligible for immediate re-election. In the event of the President's death or failure to assume office, the Vice-President or, failing the Vice-President, the President of the Senate becomes interim Head of State.

The President has power to appoint members of the Cabinet and diplomatic representatives from a panel proposed by the Senate. The President is responsible for the conduct of foreign affairs and is also empowered to issue decrees, and initiate legislation by special messages to Congress.

Congress consists of a Senate (27 members) and a Chamber of Deputies (130 members). Congress meets annually and its ordinary sessions last only 90 working days, which may be extended to 120. Each of the nine departments (La Paz, Chuquisaca, Oruro, Beni, Santa Cruz, Potosí, Tarija, Cochabamba and Pando), into which the country is divided for administrative purposes, elects three senators. Members of both houses are elected for five years.

The supreme administrative, political and military authority in each department is vested in a prefect appointed by the President. The sub-divisions of each department, known as provinces, are administered by sub-prefects. The provinces are further divided into cantons. There are 94 provinces and some 1,000 cantons. The capital of each department has its autonomous municipal council and controls its own revenue and expenditure.

Public order, education and roads are under national control.

A decree issued in July 1952 conferred the franchise on all persons who had reached the age of 21 years, whether literate or illiterate. Previously the franchise had been restricted to literate persons. (The voting age for married persons was lowered to 18 years at the 1989 elections.)

The Government

HEAD OF STATE

President: JORGE FERNANDO QUIROGA RAMÍREZ (ADN) (took office 6 August 2001, following the resignation of HUGO BÁNZER SUÁREZ, elected 5 August 1997).

Vice-President: (vacant).

THE CABINET
(August 2001)

Minister of Foreign Affairs and Worship: GUSTAVO FERNÁNDEZ.

Minister of the Interior: LEOPOLDO FERNÁNDEZ FERREIRA.

Minister of National Defence: OSCAR GUILARTE LUJAN.

Minister of Finance: JACQUES TRIGO.

Minister of Sustainable Development and Planning: RAMIRO CAVERO URIONA.

Minister of Justice and Human Rights: MARIO SERRATE RUIZ.

Minister of the Presidency: JOSÉ LUIS LUPO FLORES (ADN).

Minister of Health and Social Welfare: ENRIQUE PAZ ARGANDONA.

Minister of Labour and Small Enterprises: JORGE PACHECO FRANCO.

Minister of Education, Culture and Sport: AMALIA ANAYA JALDIN.

Minister of Agriculture, Livestock and Rural Development: WALTER NUÑEZ RODRÍGUEZ.

Minister of Foreign Trade and Investment: CLAUDIO MANSILLA PEÑA.

Minister for Economic Development: CARLOS KEMPFF BRUNO.

Minister of Housing and Basic Services: JAVIER NOGALES ITURRI.

Minister of Peasants', Indigenous Peoples' and Ethnic Affairs: WIGBERTO RIVERO PINTOREMAIN.

Minister for Government Information: MAURO BERTERO GUTIERREZ.

MINISTRIES

Ministry of Agriculture, Livestock and Rural Development: Avda Camacho 1471, La Paz.

Ministry of Economic Development: Edif. Palacio de Comunicaciones, Avda Mariscal Santa Cruz, La Paz; tel. (2) 37-7234; fax (2) 35-9955; e-mail contactos@desarrollo.gov.bo; internet www.desarrollo.gov.bo.

Ministry of Education, Culture and Sport: Casilla 6500, La Paz.

Ministry of Finance: Edif. Palacio de Comunicaciones, Avda Mariscal Santa Cruz, La Paz; tel. (2) 37-7234; fax (2) 35-9955.

Ministry of Foreign Affairs and Worship: Calle Ingavi, esq. Junin, La Paz; tel. (2) 37-1150; fax (2) 37-1155; e-mail mreuno@rree.gov.bo; internet www.rree.gov.bo.

Ministry of Foreign Trade and Investment: Edif. Palacio de las Comunicaciones, Avda Mariscal Santa Cruz, La Paz; tel. (2) 37-7222; fax (2) 37-7451; e-mail despacho@mcei-bolivia.com; internet www.mcei-bolivia.com.

Ministry of Government Information: Edif. La Urbana, 5°, Avda Camacho 1485, La Paz; tel. (2) 33-9027; fax (2) 39-1607; internet www.comunica.gov.bo.

Ministry of Health and Social Welfare: Plaza del Estudiante, La Paz; tel. (2) 37-1373; fax (2) 39-1590; e-mail minsalud@ceibo.entelnet.bo; internet www.sns.gov.bo.

Ministry of Housing and Basic Services: Avda Edif. Ex-Conavi, 20 de Octubre 2230, La Paz; tel. (2) 36-0469; fax (2) 37-1335; e-mail minviv@ceibo.entelnet.bo.

Ministry of the Interior: Avda Arce 2409, esq. Belisario Salinas, La Paz; tel. (2) 37-0460; fax (2) 37-1334.

Ministry of Justice and Human Rights: Casilla 6966, La Paz; tel. (2) 36-1083; fax (2) 36-530; e-mail minjust@caoba.entelnet.bo.

Ministry of Labour and Small Enterprises: Calle Yanacocha, esq. Mercado, La Paz; tel. (2) 36-4164; fax (2) 37-1387; e-mail mintrabajo@unete.com.

Ministry of National Defence: Plaza Avaroa, esq. 20 de Octubre, La Paz; tel. (2) 37-7130; fax (2) 35-3156; e-mail mindef2@ceiboentelnet.bo.

Ministry of Peasants', Indigenous Peoples' and Ethnic Affairs: La Paz.

Ministry of the Presidency: Palacio de Gobierno, Plaza Murillo, La Paz; tel. (2) 37-1082; fax (2) 37-1388.

Ministry of Sustainable Development and Planning: Avda Mariscal Santa Cruz, Edif. De la Ex-Comibol, 8°, Casilla 12814, La Paz; tel. and fax (2) 31-0860; e-mail sdnp@coord.rds.org.bo; internet www.rds.org.bo.

President and Legislature

PRESIDENT

At the presidential election that took place on 1 June 1997 the majority of votes were spread between five of the 10 candidates. Gen. (retd) Hugo Bánzer Suárez of the Acción Democrática Nacionalista (ADN) obtained 22.3% of the votes cast, Juan Carlos Durán of the Movimiento Nacionalista Revolucionario (MNR) won 17.7%, Jaime Paz Zamora of the Movimiento de la Izquierda Revolucionaria (MIR) won 16.7%, Ivo Kuljis of the Unión Cívica Solidaridad (UCS) secured 15.9% and Remedios Loza of Conciencia de Patria (Condepa) won 15.8%. As no candidate obtained the requisite absolute majority, responsibility for the selection of the President passed to the new National Congress. As a result of the formation of a coalition between the ADN, the MIR, the UCS, the NFR, Condepa and an Independent, Bánzer was elected President with 118 votes on 5 August and took office the following day. Condepa was removed from the governing coalition in mid-1998.

CONGRESO NACIONAL

President of the Senate: LEOPOLDO FERNÁNDEZ.

President of the Chamber of Deputies: JALIL MELGAR.

General Election, 1 June 1997

| | Seats | |
Party	Chamber of Deputies	Senate
Acción Democrática Nacionalista (ADN)	33	13
Movimiento Nacionalista Revolucionario (Histórico) (MNR) .	26	3
Movimiento de la Izquierda Revolucionaria (MIR) . . .	25	6
Unión Cívica Solidaridad (UCS) . .	21	2
Conciencia de Patria (Condepa) . .	17	3
Movimiento Bolivia Libre (MBL) . .	4	—
Izquierda Unida	4	—
Total	**130**	**27**

Political Organizations

Acción Democrática Nacionalista (ADN): La Paz; internet www.bolivian.com/adn; f. 1979; right-wing; Leader HUGO BÁNZER SUÁREZ; Nat. Exec. Sec. JORGE LANDÍVAR.

Alianza de Renovación Boliviana (ARBOL): La Paz; f. 1993; conservative; Leader CASIANO ACALLE CHOQUE.

Bolivia Insurgente: La Paz; f. 1996; populist party; Leader MÓNICA MEDINA.

Conciencia de Patria (Condepa): La Paz; f. 1988; populist party; Leader REMEDIOS LOZA.

Frente Revolucionario de Izquierda (FRI): La Paz; left-wing; Leader OSCAR ZAMORA.

Movimiento Bolivariano: La Paz; f. 1999; Leader CRISTINA CORRALES.

Movimiento Bolivia Libre (MBL): Edif. Camiri, Of. 601, Calle Comercio 972 esq. Yanacocha, Casilla 10382, La Paz; tel. (2) 34-0257; fax (2) 39-2242; f. 1985; left-wing; breakaway faction of MIR; Pres. MIGUEL URIOSTE.

Movimiento Hacia el Socialismo (MAS): La Paz; left-wing.

Movimiento de la Izquierda Revolucionaria (MIR): Avda América 119, 2°, La Paz; e-mail mir@ceibo.entelnet.bo; internet www.cibergallo.com; f. 1971; split into several factions in 1985; left-wing; Leader JAIME PAZ ZAMORA; Sec.-Gen. OSCAR EID FRANCO.

Movimiento sin Miedo: La Paz; f. 1999; left-wing; Leader JUAN DEL GRANADO.

Movimiento Nacionalista Revolucionario (Histórico)—MNR: Calle Nicolás Acosta 574, tel. (2) 49-0748; fax (2) 49-0009; e-mail mnr2002@ceibo.entelnet.bo; La Paz, formerly part of the Movimiento Nacionalista Revolucionario (MNR, f. 1942); centre-right; Leader GONZALO SÁNCHEZ DE LOZADA; Sec.-Gen. CARLOS SÁNCHEZ BERZAIN; 360,000 mems.

Movimiento Revolucionario Túpac Katarí de Liberación (MRTKL): Avda Baptista 939, Casilla 9133, La Paz; tel. 35-4784; f. 1978; peasant party; Leader VÍCTOR HUGO CÁRDENAS CONDE; Sec.-Gen. NORBERTO PÉREZ HIDALGO; 80,000 mems.

Nueva Fuerza Republicana (NFR): Cochabamba; Leader MANFRED REYES VILLA.

Partido Comunista de Bolivia (PCB): La Paz; f. 1950; Leader MARCOS DOMIC; First Sec. SIMÓN REYES RIVERA.

Partido Demócrata Cristiano (PDC): Casilla 4345, La Paz; f. 1954; Pres. BENJAMÍN MIGUEL HARB; Sec. ANTONIO CANELAS-GALATOIRE; 50,000 mems.

Partido Obrero Revolucionario (POR): Correo Central, La Paz; f. 1935; Trotskyist; Leader GUILLERMO LORA.

Partido Revolucionario de la Izquierda Nacionalista (PRIN): Calle Colón 693, La Paz; f. 1964; left-wing; Leader JUAN LECHIN OQUENDO.

Partido Socialista-Uno (PS-1): La Paz; Leader JERJES JUSTINIANO.

Partido de Vanguardia Obrera: Plaza Venezuela 1452, La Paz; Leader FILEMÓN ESCOBAR.

Unión Cívica Solidaridad (UCS): Calle Mercado 1064, 6°, La Paz; tel. (2) 36-0297; fax (2) 37-2200; f. 1989; populist; Leader JOHNNY FERNÁNDEZ.

Vanguardia Revolucionaria 9 de Abril: Avda 6 de Agosto 2170, Casilla 5810, La Paz; tel. (2) 32-0311; fax 39-1439; Leader Dr CARLOS SERRATE REICH.

Other parties include the Alianza de Renovación Boliviana, the Alianza Democrática Socialista and the Eje Patriótica.

Diplomatic Representation

EMBASSIES IN BOLIVIA

Argentina: Calle Aspiazu 497, La Paz; tel. (2) 35-3233; fax (2) 39-1083; Ambassador: ARTURO E. OSSORIO ARANA.

Belgium: Avda Hernando Siles 5290, Casilla 2433, La Paz; tel. (2) 78-4925; fax (2) 78-6764; e-mail amblapaz@entelnet.bo; Ambassador: ALAIN KUNDYCKI.

Brazil: Edif. Metrobol, Calle Capitán Ravelo 2334, Casilla 429, La Paz; tel. (2) 44-0202; fax (2) 44-0043; internet www.embajadabrasil.org.bo; Ambassador: STELIO MARCOS AMARANTE.

China, People's Republic: Los Pinos 8532, Casilla 10005, La Paz; tel. (2) 79-3851; fax (2) 79-7121; e-mail emb-china@kolla.net; Ambassador: WONG YONGZHAN.

Colombia: Calle 20 de Octubre 2427, Casilla 1418, La Paz; tel. (2) 78-4491; fax 78-6510; e-mail emcol@caoba.entelnet.bo; Ambassador: LAURA OCHOA DE ARDILA.

Costa Rica: Avda 14 de Septiembre 4850, Casilla 2780, La Paz; tel. and fax (2) 79-3201; Ambassador: ISABEL CARAZO SABORÍA DE SAENZ.

Cuba: Avda Arequipa 8037, Calacoto, La Paz; tel. (2) 72-1157; fax (2) 72-3419; e-mail embacuba@ceibo.entelnet.bo; Ambassador: RAÚL BARZAGA NAVAS.

Denmark: Edif. Fortaleza, Avda Arce 2799 esq. Cordero, 9°, Casilla 9860, La Paz; tel. (2) 43-2070; fax (2) 43-3150; e-mail ambdklp@ceibo.entelnet.bo; Chargé d'affaires: MICHAEL HJORTS.

Ecuador: Edif. Herrman, 14°, Plaza Venezuela, Casilla 406, La Paz; tel. (2) 33-1588; fax (2) 39-1932; e-mail mecuabol@caoba.entelnet.bo; Ambassador: LUIS MORENO GUERRA.

Egypt: Avda Ballivián 599, Casilla 2956, La Paz; tel. (2) 78-6511; fax (2) 78-4325; Ambassador: Dr MAHMOUD AMIN HASSANEIN.

France: Avda Hernando Silés 5390, esq. Calle 8, Obrajes, Casilla 717, La Paz; tel. (2) 78-6114; fax (2) 78-6746; e-mail amfrabo@ceibo.entelnet.bo; internet www.ambafrance-bo.org.bo; Ambassador: GÉRARD DUMONT.

Germany: Avda Arce 2395, Casilla 5265, La Paz; tel. (2) 44-0066; fax (2) 44-1441, e-mail germany@ceibo.entelnet.bo; Ambassador: JOACHIM KAUSCH.

Holy See: Avda Arce 2990, Casilla 136, La Paz; tel. (2) 43-1007; fax (2) 43-2120; e-mail nunzibol@caoba.entelnet.bo; Apostolic Nuncio: Most Rev. JÓZEF WESOŁOWSKI, Titular Archbishop of Slebte (Slebty).

Israel: Edif. Esperanza, 10°, Avda Mariscal Santa Cruz, Casilla 1309, La Paz; tel. (2) 39-1126; fax 39-1712; email emisrabo@ceibo.entelnet.bo; Ambassador: ISAAC LAVIE BACHMAN.

Italy: Avda 6 de Agosto 2575, Casilla 626, La Paz; tel. (2) 43-4929; fax 43-4975; e-mail ambitlap@ceibo.entelnet.bo; Ambassador: Dr EUGENIO CAMPO.

Japan: Calle Rosendo Gutiérrez 497, Casilla 2725, La Paz; tel. (2) 37-3151; fax (2) 39-1052; Ambassador: HIROYUKI KIMOTO.

Korea, Democratic People's Republic: La Paz; Ambassador: KIM CHAN SIK.

Mexico: Sánchez Bustamente 509, Casilla 430, La Paz; tel. (2) 77-2212; fax (2) 77-1855; e-mail embamex@kolla.net; internet www.embamex-bolivia.org; Ambassador: Lic. MARGARITA DIEGUEZ ARMA.

Panama: Avda Ballivián 1110, Casilla 678, La Paz; tel. (2) 79-2036; fax (2) 79-7290; e-mail empanbol@ceibo.entelnet.bo; Ambassador: CARMEN G. MENÉNDEZ.

Paraguay: Edif. Illimani II, Avda 6 de Agosto y Pedro Salazar, Casilla 882, La Paz; tel. (2) 43-3176; fax (2) 43-2201; e-mail empara bo@ceibo.entelnet.bo; Ambassador: EMILIO LORENZO G. FRANCO.

Peru: Calle F. Guachalla 300, Casilla 668, La Paz; tel. (2) 44-1250; fax (2) 44-1240; e-mail embbol@caoba.entelnet.bo; Ambassador: Dr HARRY BELEVAN-McBRIDE.

Russia: Avda Walter Guevara Arce 8129, Casilla 5494, La Paz; tel. (2) 78-6419; fax (2) 78-6531; e-mail embrusia@ceibo.entelnet.bo; Ambassador: GUENNADI VASILIEVICH SIZOV.

Spain: Avda 6 de Agosto 2860, Casilla 282, La Paz; tel. (2) 43-3518; fax (2) 43-2752; e-mail riolui@ceibo.entelnet.bo; Ambassador: MANUEL VITURRO DE LA TORRE.

Switzerland: Edif. Petrolero, Avda 16 de Julio 1616, Casilla 657, La Paz; tel. (2) 31-5471; fax (2) 39-1462; e-mail swiembol@ceibo.entelnet.bo; Ambassador: ERIC MARTIN.

United Kingdom: Avda Arce 2732–2754, Casilla 694, La Paz; tel. (2) 43-3424; fax (2) 43-1073; e-mail ppa@mail.rds.org.bo; Ambassador: GRAHAM MINTER.

USA: Avda Arce 2780, Casilla 425, La Paz; tel. (2) 43-0251; fax (2) 43-3900; internet www.megalink.com/usemblapaz; Ambassador: MANUEL ROCHA.

Uruguay: Avda 6 de Agosto 2577, Casilla 441, La Paz; tel. (2) 43-0080; fax 43-0087; e-mail urulivia@datacom-bo.net; Ambassador: JUAN A. PACHECO RAMÍREZ.

Venezuela: Edif. Illimani, 4°, Avda Arce esq. Campos, Casilla 960, La Paz; tel. (2) 43-1365; fax (2) 43-2348; e-mail hecmaldo@ceibo.entelnet.bo; Ambassador: OTTO R. VEITIA MATOS.

Judicial System

SUPREME COURT

Corte Suprema: Calle Pilinco 352, Sucre; tel. (64) 21883; fax (64) 32696.

Judicial power is vested in the Supreme Court. There are 12 members, appointed by Congress for a term of 10 years. The court is divided into four chambers of three justices each. Two chambers deal with civil cases, the third deals with criminal cases and the fourth deals with administrative, social and mining cases. The President of the Supreme Court presides over joint sessions of the courts and attends the joint sessions for cassation cases.

President of the Supreme Court: Dr GUILLERMO ARANCIBIA.

DISTRICT COURTS

There is a District Court sitting in each Department, and additional provincial and local courts to try minor cases.

ATTORNEY-GENERAL

In addition to the Attorney-General at Sucre (appointed by the President on the proposal of the Senate), there is a District Attorney in each Department as well as circuit judges.

Attorney-General: OSCAR CRESPO.

Religion

The majority of the population are Roman Catholics; there were an estimated 7.0m. adherents at 31 December 1999, equivalent to 82.3% of the population. Religious freedom is guaranteed. There is a small Jewish community, as well as various Protestant denominations, in Bolivia.

CHRISTIANITY

The Roman Catholic Church

Bolivia comprises four archdioceses, six dioceses, two Territorial Prelatures and five Apostolic Vicariates.

Bishops' Conference: Conferencia Episcopal Boliviana, Calle Potosí 814, Casilla 2309, La Paz; tel. (2) 40-6855; fax (2) 40-6798; e-mail comceb@ceibo.entelnet.bo; f. 1972; Pres. Cardinal JULIO TERRAZAS SANDOVAL, Archbishop of Santa Cruz de la Sierra.

Archbishop of Cochabamba: Most Rev. TITO SOLARI, Avda Heroínas esq. Zenteno Anaya, Casilla 129, Cochabamba; tel. (42) 56562; fax (42) 50522; e-mail arz.cbba@supernet.com.bo.

Archbishop of La Paz: Most Rev. EDMUNDO LUIS FLAVIO ABASTOFLOR MONTERO, Calle Ballivián 1277, Casilla 259, La Paz; tel. (2) 34-1920; fax (2) 39-1244; e-mail arzonslp@ceibo.entelnet.bo.

Archbishop of Santa Cruz de la Sierra: Cardinal JULIO TERRAZAS SANDOVAL, Calle Ingavi 49, Casilla 25, Santa Cruz; tel. (3) 32-4286; fax (3) 33-0181; e-mail asc@scbbs-bo.com.

Archbishop of Sucre: Most Rev. JESÚS GERVASIO PÉREZ RODRÍGUEZ, Calle Bolívar 702, Casilla 205, Sucre; tel. (64) 51587; fax (64) 60336.

The Anglican Communion

Within the Iglesia Anglicana del Cono Sur de América (Anglican Church of the Southern Cone of America), Bolivia forms part of the diocese of Peru. The Bishop is resident in Lima, Peru.

Protestant Churches

Baptist Union of Bolivia: Casilla 2199; tel. (2) 22-9538, La Paz; Pres. Rev. AUGUSTO CHULJO.

Convención Bautista Boliviana (Baptist Convention of Bolivia): Casilla 3147, Santa Cruz; tel. (3) 340717; fax (3) 340717; f. 1947; Pres. EIRA SORUCO DE FLORES.

Iglesia Evangélica Metodista en Bolivia (Evangelical Methodist Church in Bolivia): Casillas 356 y 8347, La Paz; tel. (2) 34-2702; fax (2) 35-7046; autonomous since 1969; 10,000 mems; Bishop Rev. EFRAÍN YANAPA.

BAHÁ'Í FAITH

National Spiritual Assembly of the Bahá'ís of Bolivia: Casilla 1613, La Paz; tel. (2) 78-5058; fax (2) 78-2387; e-mail aebahais@caoba.entelnet.bo; mems resident in 6,229 localities.

The Press

DAILY NEWSPAPERS

Cochabamba

Opinión: General Acha 0252, Casilla 287, Cochabamba; tel. (42) 54402; fax (42) 15121; f. 1985; Dir EDWIN TAPIA FRONTANILLA; Man. Editor JAIME BUITRAGO.

Los Tiempos: Plaza Quintanilla-Norte, Casilla 525, Cochabamba; tel. (42) 54561; fax (42) 54577; e-mail lostiempos@lostiempos.bo.net; internet www.lostiempos.com; f. 1943; morning; independent; Dir FERNANDO CANELAS; Man. Editor MIGUEL LORA; circ. 19,000.

La Paz

El Diario: Calle Loayza 118, Casilla 5, La Paz; tel. (2) 39-0900; fax (2) 36-3846; e-mail contacto@eldiario.net; internet www.eldiario.net; f. 1904; morning; conservative; Dir JORGE CARRASCO JAHNSEN; Man. Editor MAURICIO CARRASCO; circ. 55,000.

Hoy: Pasaje Carrasco 1718, Casilla 477, La Paz; tel. (2) 24-4154; fax (2) 24-4147; e-mail hoy@wara.bolnet.bo; f. 1968; morning and midday editions; independent; Pres. SAMUEL DORIA MEDINA; Dir HERNÁN PAREDES MUÑOZ; circ. 12,000.

Jornada: Edif. Almirante Grau 672, Casilla 1628, La Paz; tel. (2) 35-3844; fax (2) 35-6213; e-mail jornada@ceibo.entelnet.bo; f. 1964; evening; independent; Dir JAIME RÍOS CHACÓN; circ. 11,500.

Presencia: Avda Mariscal Santa Cruz 2150, Casilla 3276, La Paz; tel. (2) 37-2340; fax (2) 39-1040; e-mail prsencia@caoba.entelnet.bo; f. 1952; morning and evening; Catholic; Pres. JESÚS LÓPEZ DE LAMA; Dir Lic. JUAN CRISTÓBAL SORUCO; Man. Lic. MARÍA LUISA URDAY; circ. 20,000.

La Razón: Jorge Sáenz 1330, Casilla 13100, La Paz; tel. (2) 22-2727; fax (2) 22-2049; internet www.la-razon.com; f. 1990; Pres. RAÚL GARAFULIC GUTIÉRREZ; Dir JORGE CANELAS SÁENZ; circ. 27,000.

Ultima Hora: Avda Camacho 1372, Casilla 5920, La Paz; tel. (2) 39-2115; fax (2) 39-2139; e-mail uhora@wara.bolnet.bo; f. 1939; evening; independent; Propr LUIS MERCADO ROCABADO; Pres. MAURO BERTERO; Dir MARIANO BAPTISTA GUMUCIO; circ. 15,000.

Oruro

El Expreso: Potosí 4921 esq. Villarroel, Oruro; f. 1973; morning; independent; right-wing; Dir ALBERTO FRONTANILLA MORALES; circ. 1,000.

La Patria: Avda Camacho 1892, Casilla 48, Oruro; tel. (52) 50761; fax (52) 50781; f. 1919; morning; independent; Pres. MARCELO MIRRALLES BOVÁ; Dir ENRIQUE MIRALLES BONNECARRERE; circ. 6,000.

Potosí

El Siglo: Calle Linares 99, Casilla 389, Potosí; f. 1975; morning; Dir WILSON MENDIETA PACHECO; circ. 1,500.

Santa Cruz

El Deber: Avda El Trompillo 1144, Casilla 2144, Santa Cruz; tel. (3) 53-8000; fax (3) 53-9053; e-mail info.eldeber@eldeber.com; internet www.eldeber.com; f. 1955; morning; independent; Dir PEDRO RIVERO MERCADO; Man. Editor GUILLERMO RIVERO JORDÁN; circ. 35,000.

La Estrella del Oriente: Calle Sucre 558, Casilla 736, Santa Cruz; tel. (3) 37-0707; fax (3) 37-0557; e-mail estrella@mitai.nrs.bolnet.bo; internet www.laestrella.com; f. 1864; Pres. JORGE LANDÍVAR ROCA; Man. Editor TUFFI ARÉ.

El Mundo: Parque Industrial PI-7, Casilla 1984, Santa Cruz; tel. (3) 46-4646; fax (3) 46-5057; e-mail elmundo@mitai.nrs.bolnet.bo; f. 1979; morning; owned by Santa Cruz Industrialists' Association; Pres. WALTER PAREJAS MORENO; Dir JUAN JAVIER ZEBALLOS GUTIÉRREZ; circ. 15,000.

El Nuevo Día: Calle Independencia 470, Casilla 5344, Santa Cruz; tel. (3) 33-7474; fax (3) 36-0303; f. 1987; Dir NANCY EKLUND VDA DE GUTIÉRREZ; Man. Editor JORGE ORÍAS HERRERA.

Trinidad

La Razón: Avda Bolívar 295, Casilla 166, Trinidad; tel. (46) 21377; f. 1972; Dir CARLOS VÉLEZ.

PERIODICALS

Actualidad Boliviana Confidencial (ABC): Fernando Guachalla 969, Casilla 648, La Paz; f. 1966; weekly; Dir HUGO GONZÁLEZ RIOJA; circ. 6,000.

Aquí: Casilla 10937, La Paz; tel. (2) 34-3524; fax (2) 35-2455; f. 1979; weekly; circ. 10,000.

Bolivia Libre: Edif. Esperanza, 5°, Avda Mariscal Santa Cruz 2150, Casilla 6500, La Paz; fortnightly; govt organ.

Carta Cruceña de Integración: Casilla 3531, Santa Cruz de la Sierra; weekly; Dirs HERNÁN LLANOVARCED A., JOHNNY LAZARTE J.

Comentarios Económicos de Actualidad (CEA): Casilla 312097, La Paz; tel. (2) 43-0122; fax (2) 43-2554; e-mail veceba@caoba.entelnet.bo; f. 1983; fortnightly; articles and economic analyses; Editor GUIDO CESPEDES.

Información Política y Económica (IPE): Calle Comercio, Casilla 2484, La Paz; weekly; Dir GONZALO LÓPEZ MUÑOZ.

Informe R: La Paz; weekly; Editor SARA MONROY.

Notas: Casilla 5782, La Paz; tel. (2) 37-3773; fax (2) 36-5153; weekly; political and economic analysis; Editor JOSÉ GRAMUNT DE MORAGAS.

El Noticiero: Sucre; weekly; Dir DAVID CABEZAS; circ. 1,500.

Prensa Libre: Sucre; tel. (64) 41293; fax (64) 32768; f. 1989; weekly; Dir JORGE ENCERAS DIAZ.

Servicio de Información Confidencial (SIC): Elías Sagárnaga 274, Casilla 5035, La Paz; weekly; publ. by Asociación Nacional de Prensa; Dir JOSÉ CARRANZA.

Siglo XXI: La Paz; weekly.

Unión: Sucre; weekly; Dir JAIME MERILES.

Visión Boliviana: Calle Loayza 420, Casilla 2870, La Paz; 6 a year.

PRESS ASSOCIATIONS

Asociación Nacional de la Prensa: Avda 6 de Agosto 2170, Casilla 477, La Paz; tel. (2) 36-9916; Pres. Dr CARLOS SERRATE REICH.

Asociación de Periodistas de La Paz: Avda 6 de Agosto 2170, Casilla 477, La Paz; tel. (2) 36-9916; fax (2) 32-3701; f. 1929; Pres. MARIO MALDONADO VISCARRA; Vice-Pres. MARÍA EUGENIA VERASTEGUI A.

NEWS AGENCIES

Agencia de Noticias Fides (ANF): Edif. Mariscal de Ayacucho, 5°, Of. 501, Calle Loayza, Casilla 5782, La Paz; tel. (2) 36-5152; fax (2) 36-5153; owned by Roman Catholic Church; Dir JOSÉ GRAMUNT DE MORAGAS.

Foreign Bureaux

Agencia EFE (Spain): Edif. Esperanza, Avda Mariscal Santa Cruz 2150, Casilla 7403, La Paz; tel. (2) 36-7205; fax (2) 39-1441; e-mail fvv@caoba.entelnet.bo; Bureau Chief FERNANDO DE VALENZUELA.

Agenzia Nazionale Stampa Associata (ANSA) (Italy): La Paz; tel. (2) 35-5521; fax (2) 36-8221; Correspondent RAÚL PENARANDA UNDURRAGA.

Associated Press (AP) (USA): Edif. Mariscal de Ayacucho, Of. 1209, Calle Loayza, Casilla 9569, La Paz; tel. (2) 37-0128; Correspondent PETER J. MCFARREN.

Deutsche Presse-Agentur (dpa) (Germany): Edif. Esperanza, 9°, Of. 3, Av. Mariscal Santa Cruz 2150, Casilla 13885, La Paz; tel. (2) 35-2684; fax (2) 39-2488; Correspondent ROBERT BROCKMANN.

Informatsionnoye Telegrafnoye Agentstvo Rossii-Telegrafnoye Agentstvo Suverennykh Stran (ITARTASS) (Russia): Casilla 6839, San Miguel, Bloque 0–33, Casa 958, La Paz; tel. (2) 79-2108; Correspondent ELDAR ABDULLAEV.

Inter Press Service (IPS) (Italy): Edif. Esperanza, 6°, Of. 6, Casilla 4313, La Paz; tel. (2) 36-1227; Correspondent RONALD GREBE LÓPEZ.

Prensa Latina (Cuba): La Paz; tel. (2) 32-3479; Correspondent MANUEL ROBLES SOSA.

Reuters (United Kingdom): Edif. Loayza, 3°, Of. 301, Calle Loayza 349, Casilla 4057, La Paz; tel. (2) 35-1106; fax (2) 39-1366; Correspondent RENÉ VILLEGAS MONJE.

Rossiyskoye Informatsionnoye Agentstvo—Novosti (RIA—Novosti) (Russia): La Paz; tel. (2) 37-3857; Correspondent VLADIMIR RAMÍREZ.

United Press International (UPI) (USA): Plaza Venezuela 1479, 7°, Of. 702, Casilla 1219, La Paz; tel. (2) 78-4172; fax (2) 78-4066; Correspondent ALBERTO ZUAZO NATHES.

Agence France-Presse and Telam (Argentina) are also represented.

Publishers

Editora Khana Cruz SRL: Avda Camacho 1372, Casilla 5920, La Paz; tel. (2) 37-0263; Dir GLADIS ANDRADE.

Editora Lux: Edif. Esperanza, Avda Mariscal Santa Cruz, Casilla 1566, La Paz; tel. (2) 32-9102; fax (2) 34-3968; f. 1952; Dir FELICISIMO TARILONTE PÉREZ.

Editorial los Amigos del Libro: Avda Heroínas E-0311, Casilla 450, Cochabamba; tel. (42) 51140; fax (41) 15128; e-mail amigol@amigol.bo.net; f. 1945; general; Man. Dir WERNER GUTTENTAG.

Editorial Bruño: Loayza 167, Casilla 4809, La Paz; tel. (2) 33-1254; fax (2) 33-5043; f. 1964; Dir IGNACIO LOMAS.

Editorial Don Bosco: Calle Tihuanacu 116, Casilla 4458, La Paz; tel. (2) 37-1757; fax (2) 36-2822; f. 1896; social sciences and literature; Dir GIAMPAOLO MARIO MAZZON.

Editorial Icthus: La Paz; **tel.** (2) 35-4007; f. 1967; general and textbooks; Man. Dir DANIEL AQUIZE.

Editorial Popular: Plaza Pérez Velasco 787, Casilla 4171, La Paz; tel. (2) 35-0701; f. 1935; textbooks, postcards, tourist guides, etc; Man. Dir GERMÁN VILLAMOR.

Editorial Puerta del Sol: Edif. Litoral Sub Suelo, Avda Mariscal Santa Cruz, La Paz; tel. (2) 36-0746; f. 1965; Man. Dir OSCAR CRESPO.

Empresa Editora Proinsa: Avda Saavedra 2055, Casilla 7181, La Paz; tel. (2) 22-7781; fax (2) 22-6671; f. 1974; school books; Dirs FLOREN SANABRIA G., CARLOS SANABRIA C.

Gisbert y Cía, SA: Calle Comercio 1270, Casilla 195, La Paz; tel. (2) 20-2626; fax (2) 20-2911; e-mail libgis@ceibo.entelnet.bo; f. 1907; textbooks, history, law and general; Pres. JAVIER GISBERT; Dirs MARÍA DEL CARMEN SCHULCZEWSKI, ANTONIO SCHULCZEWSKI.

Ivar American: Calle Potosí 1375, Casilla 6016, La Paz; tel. (2) 36-1519; Man. Dir HÉCTOR IBÁÑEZ.

Librería Editorial Juventud: Plaza Murillo 519, Casilla 1489, La Paz; tel. (2) 40-6248; fax (2) 40-7033; f. 1946; textbooks and general; Dir GUSTAVO URQUIZO MENDOZA.

Librería El Ateneo SRL: Calle Ballivián 1275, Casilla 7917, La Paz; tel. (2) 36-9925; fax (2) 39-1513; Dirs JUAN CHIRVECHES D., MIRIAN C. DE CHIRVECHES.

Librería Dismo Ltda: Calle Comercio 806, Casilla 988, La Paz; tel. (2) 35-3119; fax (2) 31-6545; Dir TERESA GONZÁLEZ DE ALVAREZ.

Librería La Paz: Calle Campos y Villegas, Edif. Artemis, Casilla 539, La Paz; tel. (2) 43-4927; fax (2) 43-5004; e-mail liblapaz@ceibo.entelnet.bo; f. 1900; Dirs EDUARDO BURGOS R., CARLOS BURGOS M.

Librería La Universal SRL: Calle Genaro Sanjines 538, Casilla 2888, La Paz; tel. (2) 34-2961; f. 1958; Man. Dir ROLANDO CONDORI.

Librería San Pablo: Calle Colón 627, Casilla 3152, La Paz; tel. (2) 32-6084; f. 1967; Man. Dir MARÍA DE JESÚS VALERIANO.

PUBLISHERS' ASSOCIATION

Cámara Boliviana del Libro: Calle Capitán Ravelo 2116, Casilla 682, La Paz; tel. (2) 44-4239; fax (2) 44-1523; e-mail cabolib@ceibo.entelnet.bo; f. 1947; Pres. CARMEN TEJERINA DE TERRAZAS; Gen. Man. VERONICA FLORES BEDREGAL.

Broadcasting and Communications

TELECOMMUNICATIONS

Cámara Nacional de Medios de Comunicación: Casilla 2431, La Paz.

Empresa Nacional de Telecomunicaciones (ENTEL): Edif. Palacio de Comunicaciones, Federico Zuazo 1771, Casilla 4450, La Paz; tel. (2) 31-3030; fax (2) 39-1789; internet www.entelnet.bo; f. 1965; privatized under the Govt's capitalization programme in 1995; Exec. Pres. FRANCO BERTONI; Gen. Man. MICHAEL ANGELO ORDÓÑEZ.

Superintendencia de Telecomunicaciones: Edif. M. Cristina, Plaza España, Casilla 6692, La Paz; tel. (2) 41-6641; fax (2) 41-8183; e-mail supertel@ceibo.entelnet.bo; f. 1995; govt-controlled broadcasting authority; Superintendent Ing. GUIDO LOAYZA.

BROADCASTING

Radio

There were 145 radio stations in 1990, the majority of which were commercial. Broadcasts are in Spanish, Aymará and Quechua.

Asociación Boliviana de Radiodifusoras (ASBORA): Edif. Jazmin, 10°, Avda 20 de Octubre 2019, Casilla 5324, La Paz; tel. (2) 36-5154; fax (2) 35-3069; broadcasting authority; Pres. TERESA SANJINÉS L.; Vice-Pres. LUIS ANTONIO SERRANO.

Educación Radiofónica de Bolivia (ERBOL): Calle Ballivian 1323, 4°, Casilla 5946, La Paz; tel. (2) 35-4142; fax (2) 39-1985;

asscn of 28 educational radio stations in Bolivia; Gen. Sec. RONALD GREBE LÓPEZ.

Television

Corporación Boliviana de Televisión Canal 30: Calle Obispo Cárdenas 1475, Casilla 8980, La Paz; tel. (2) 31-5031; fax (2) 31-9563; f. 1996; Pres. RICARDO CLAURE; Dir ALEX MEJÍA.

Empresa Nacional de Televisión Boliviana Canal 7: Edif. La Urbana, 6° y 7°, Avda Camacho 1486, Casilla 900, La Paz; tel. (2) 37-6356; fax (2) 35-9753; f. 1969; govt network operating stations in La Paz, Oruro, Cochabamba, Potosí, Chuquisaca, Pando, Beni, Tarija and Santa Cruz; Gen. Man. MIGUEL N. MONTERO VACA.

Televisión Boliviano Canal 2: Casilla 4837, La Paz.

Televisión Universitaria Canal 13: Edif. 'Hoy', 12°–13°, Avda 6 de Agosto 2170, Casilla 13383, La Paz; tel. (2) 35-9297; fax (2) 35-9298; f. 1980; educational programmes; stations in Oruro, Cochabamba, Potosí, Sucre, Tarija, Beni and Santa Cruz; Dir Lic. ROBERTO CUEVAS RAMÍREZ.

Finance

(cap. = capital; p.u. = paid up; res = reserves;dep. = deposits; m. = million; brs = branches; amounts are inbolivianos unless otherwise stated)

BANKING

Supervisory Authority

Superintendencia de Bancos y Entidades Financieras: Plaza Isabel la Católica 2507, Casilla 447, La Paz; tel. (2) 43-1919; fax (2) 43-0028; e-mail supban@lp.superbancos.gov.bo; internet www.superbancos.gov.bo; f. 1928; Supt Lic. LUIS FERNANDO CALVO UNZUETA.

State Bank

Banco Central de Bolivia: Avda Ayacucho esq. Mercado, Casilla 3118, La Paz; tel. (2) 37-4151; fax (2) 39-2398; e-mail vmarquez@mail.bcb.gov.bo; internet www.bcb.gov.bo; f. 1911 as Banco de la Nación Boliviana, name changed as above 1928; bank of issue; cap. 96.6m., res 215.6m. (Dec. 1996); Pres. Dr JUAN ANTONIO MORALES ANAYA; Gen. Man. Lic. MARCELA NOGALES.

Commercial Banks

Banco Bisa SA: Avda 16 de Julio 1628, Casilla 1290, La Paz; tel. (2) 35-9471; fax (2) 39-1735; e-mail mcastellanos@grupobisa.com; internet www.grupobisa.com; f. 1963; cap. 285m., res 34m., dep. 2,800m. (Dec. 1998); Pres. Ing. JULIÓ LEÓN PRADO; Gen. Man. JOSÉ LUIS ARANGUREN AGUIRRE.

Banco de Crédito de Bolivia, SA: Calle Colón esq. Mercado 1308, Casilla 907, La Paz; tel. (2) 36-0025; fax (2) 39-1044; e-mail bancnalp@acaoba.entelnet.bo; f. 1993 as Banco Popular, SA, name changed as above 1994; 61% owned by Banco de Crédito del Perú; cap. US $26.1m., res US $1.9m., dep. US $511.3m. (Dec. 1998); Chair. DIONISIO ROMERO SEMINARIO; Gen. JAVIER SANCHEZ GRIÑÁN CABALLERO; 6 brs.

Banco Económico SA-SCZ: Calle Ayacucho 166, Casilla 5603, Santa Cruz; tel. (3) 36-1177; fax (3) 36-1184; e-mail bcneco@roble.scz.entelnet.bo; f. 1990; dep. US $290.4m., total assets US $328.1m. (Dec. 1998); Pres. LUIS PERROGÓN TOLEDO; Gen. Man. Ing. JUSTO YEPEZ KAKUDA; 14 brs.

Banco Ganadero SA-Santa Cruz: Calle Bolivar 99, Casilla 4492, Santa Cruz; tel. (3) 36-1616; fax (3) 36-1617; e-mail hkrutzfeldt@bancoganadero.co.bo; internet www.bancoganadero.com; f. 1994; cap. and res 108.1m.; dep. 1,078.1m. (Dec. 2000); Pres. FERNANDO MONASTERIO NIEME; Gen. Man. HERMANN KRUTZFELDT.

Banco Mercantil, SA: Calle Ayacucho esq. Mercado 295, Casilla 423, La Paz; tel. (2) 31-5131; fax (2) 39-1735; e-mail bercant@caoba.entelnet.bo; internet www.mercantil.com.bo; f. 1905; cap. and res 38.5m., dep. 379m. (Sept. 1997); Pres. EDUARDO QUINTANILLA; Gen. Man. MARCELO DÍEZ DE MEDINA; 39 brs.

Banco Nacional de Bolivia: Avda Camacho esq. Colón, Casilla 360, La Paz; tel. (2) 35-4616; fax (2) 37-1279; e-mail info@bnb.com.bo; internet www.bnb.bolivia.com; f. 1871; cap. 189.3m., res 46.1m., dep. 3,108.9m. (Dec. 1998); Pres. JUAN CARIAGA O.; Gen. Man. EDUARDO ALVAREZ LEMAITRE; 10 brs.

Banco Santa Cruz, SA: Calle Junín 154, Casilla 865, Santa Cruz; tel. (3) 36-9911; fax (3) 35-0114; e-mail bancruz@mailbsc.com.bo; internet www.bsc.com.bo; f. 1965; 90% owned by Banco Central Hispanoamericano (Spain); cap. and res 44.2m., dep. 315.4m. (June 1990); Pres. ANTONIO ESCÁMEZ TORRES; Gen. Man. LUIS YAGÜE JIMENO; 44 brs.

Banco Solidario, SA: Calle Nicolás Acosta esq. Cañada Strongest 289, Casilla 13176, La Paz; tel. (2) 48-4242; fax (2) 48-6468; e-mail info@bancosol.com.bo; f. 1992; Pres. ROBERTO CAPRILES; Gen. Man. KURT KOENIGSFEST; 43 brs.

Banco Unión, SA: Calle Libertad 165, Casilla 4057, Santa Cruz; tel. (3) 36-6869; fax (3) 34-0684; e-mail info@bancounion.com.bo; f. 1982; cap. 48.8m., res 7.6m., dep. 1,056.5m. (Dec. 1994); Pres. Ing. ANDRÉS PETRICEVIC; Gen. Man. Ing. LUIS SAAVEDRA BRUNO; 31 brs.

Foreign Banks

Banco ABN AMRO Real, SA (USA): Avda 16 de Julio 1642, Casilla 10008, La Paz; tel. (2) 33-4477; fax (2) 33-5588; e-mail real@caoba.entelnet.bo; f. 1978 as Banco Real, name changed as above 2000; dep. US $8.3m.; total assets US $17.5m. (Dec. 1997); Operations Man. JOSÉ PORFIRIO VASCONCELOS.

Banco do Brasil, SA: Avda Camacho 1468, Planta Baja, Casilla 1650, La Paz; tel. (2) 37-7272; fax (2) 39-1036; e-mail bblapaz@caoba .entelnet.bo; f. 1961; Gen. Man. LEO SCHNEIDERS; 1 br.

Banco de la Nación Argentina: Avda 16 de Julio 1486, Casilla 2745-4312, La Paz; tel. (2) 35-9218; fax (2) 39-1392; e-mail bancnalp @caoba.entelnet.bo; internet www.bna.com.ar; f. 1891; Man. EDUARDO CASADO; 2 brs.

Citibank NA (USA): Edif. Multicentro Torre B, Calle Rosendo Gutiérrez esq. Arce 146, La Paz; tel. (2) 43-0099; fax (2) 44-0433; e-mail juan.leyes@citicorp.com; f. 1966; Vice-Pres. MARIO BEDOYA GARLAND; Gen. Man. AGUSTÍN DÁVALOS; 2 brs.

Dresdner Bank Lateinamerika AG: Calle Rosendo Gutiérrez esq. Arce 136, Edif. Multicentro Torre B, La Paz; tel. (2) 43-4114; fax (2) 43-4115; fmrly Deutsch-Südamerikanische Bank AG and Dresdner Bank AG; Gen. Man. NILS HUPKA.

Banking Association

Asociación de Bancos Privados de Bolivia (ASOBAN): Edif. Cámara Nacional de Comercio, 15°, Avda Mariscal Santa Cruz esq. Colombia 1392, Casilla 5822, La Paz; tel. (2) 36-1308; fax (2) 39-1093; e-mail asoban@wara.bdnet.bo; f. 1957; Pres. EMILIO UNZUETA; Exec. Sec. CARLOS ITURRALDE B.; 18 mems.

STOCK EXCHANGE
Supervisory Authority

Superintendencia de Pensiones, Valores y Seguros: Calle Reyes Ortiz esq. Federico Zuazo, Torres Gundlach, 3°, Casilla 6118, La Paz; tel. (2) 33-1212; fax (2) 33-0001; e-mail spvs@caoba.entel net.bo; Superintendent Dr PABLO GOTTRET VALDÉS; Intendent FRANCISCO GÓMEZ.

Bolsa Boliviana de Valores SA: Edif. Zambrana P.B., Calle Montevideo 142, Casilla 12521, La Paz; tel (2) 39-2911; fax (2) 35-2308; e-mail info@bolsa-valores-bolivia.com; internet www.bolsa-valores bolivia.com; f. 1989; Pres. Lic. LUIS FELIPE RIVERO MENDOZA; Gen. Man. Lic. ARMANDO ALVAREZ ARNAL.

INSURANCE
Supervisory Authority

Superintendencia de Pensiones, Valores y Seguros: (see above).

National Companies

Adriatica Seguros y Reaseguros, SA: Avda Cristóbal de Mendoza 250, Santa Cruz; tel. (3) 36-6667; fax (3) 36-0600; e-mail adriatica@ cotas.com.bo; Pres. ANTONIO OLEA BAUDOIN; Gen. Man. EDUARDO LANDÍVAR ROCA.

Alianza, Cía de Seguros y Reaseguros, SA: Avda 20 de Octubre 2680, esq. Campos Zona San Jorge, Casilla 11873, La Paz; tel. (2) 43-2121; fax (2) 43-2511; e-mail alianza@ceibo.entelnet.bo; Pres. JUAN MANUEL PEÑA ROCA; Gen. Man. CÉSAR EYZAGUIRRE ANGELES.

Alianza Vida Seguros y Reaseguros, SA: Avda Viedma 19, Casilla 1043, Santa Cruz; tel. (3) 37-5656; fax (3) 37-5666; e-mail alejandro@sc.alianzaseguros.com; Pres. RAÚL ADLER K.; Gen. Man. ALEJANDRO YBARRA C.

Aseguranza Internacional, SA: Avda San Martín 1000-B esq. Calle Pablo Sanz, Casilla 1188, Santa Cruz; tel. (3) 43-7443; fax (3) 43-7439; Pres. DAVIDA GUTIÉRREZ.

Bisa Seguros y Reaseguros, SA: Edif. San Pablo, 13°, Avda 16 de Julio 1479, Casilla 3669, La Paz; tel. (2) 35-2123; fax (2) 39-2500; e-mail bisaseguros@grupobisa.com; Pres. JULIO LEÓN PRADO; Exec. Vice-Pres. ALEJANDRO MACLEAN C.

Bolívar de Seguros, SA: Edif. Bolívar, Avda Mariscal Santa Cruz 1287, Casilla 1459, La Paz; tel. (2) 36-3688; fax (2) 32-2158; Pres. FREDDY OPORTO MÉNDEZ.

La Boliviana Ciacruz de Seguros y Reaseguros, SA: Calle Colón, esq. Mercado 288, Casilla 5959, La Paz; tel. (2) 20-3131; fax (2) 20-4087; e-mail bolseg@caoba.entelnet.bo; f. 1946; all classes; Pres. GONZALO BEDOYA HERRERA.

Compañía de Seguros y Reaseguros Cruceño, SA: Calle René Moreno esq. Lemoyne 607, Santa Cruz; tel. (3) 33-8985; fax (3) 33-8984; e-mail seg.crycena@mail.cotas.com.bo; Pres. Lic. GUIDO HINOJOSA; Gen. Man. NELSON HINOJOSA.

Credinform International SA de Seguros: Edif. Credinform, Calle Potosí esq. Ayacucho 1220, Casilla 1724, La Paz; tel. (2) 31-5566; fax (2) 39-1225; e-mail credinfo@caoba.entelnet.bo; f. 1954; all classes; Pres. Dr ROBÍN BARRAGÁN PELÁEZ; Gen. Man. MIGUEL ANGEL BARRAGÁN IBARGUEN.

Delta Insurance Co, SA: Calle España, Casilla 920, Cochabamba; tel. (42) 25-7765; fax (42) 22-0451; f. 1965; all classes except life; Pres. CARLOS CHRISTIE JUSTINIANO.

La Fenix Boliviana, SA de Seguros y Reaseguros: Calle Potosí, Edif. Naira Mezzanine Of 5, Casilla 4409, La Paz; tel. (2) 35-3708; fax (2) 37-0187; Pres. ORLANDO NOGALES.

Nacional de Seguros y Reaseguros, SA: Calle Libertad esq. Cañoto 879, Casilla 6794, Santa Cruz; tel. (3) 34-6969; fax (3) 34-2415; e-mail nalseg@bibosi.scz.entelnet.bo; f. 1977; fmrly known as Condor, SA de Seguros y Reaseguros; Pres. TONCHI ETEROVIC NIEGOVIC; Gen. Man. LUIS ALBERTO FLOR CORTEZ.

Seguros Illimani, SA: Edif. Mariscal de Ayacucho, 10°, Calle Loayza, Casilla 133, La Paz; tel. (2) 20-3040; fax (2) 39-1149; e-mail sisalp@ceibo.entelnet.bo; f. 1979; all classes; Pres. FERNANDO ARCE GRANDCHANT; Gen. Man. LUIS ARCE OSTRIA.

Unicruz Cía de Seguros de Vida, SA: Zona El Trompillo 76 Perimetral y Río Grande, Santa Cruz; tel. (3) 54-0707; fax (3) 53-9549; e-mail unicruz@bibosi.scz.entelnet.bo; Pres. FRANCISCO NALDA MUJICA.

Unión de Seguros, SA: Edif. El Cóndor, 16°, Calle Batallón Colorados, Casilla 2922, La Paz; tel. (2) 35-8155; fax (2) 39-2049; all classes; Pres. Dr JORGE RENGEL SILLERICO; Man. VÍCTOR ROSAS.

La Vitalicia Seguros y Reaseguros de Vida, SA: Avda 6 de Agosto 2170, Edif. Hoy Mezzanine, La Paz; tel. (2) 33-4303; fax (2) 33-3792; e-mail vitalseg@ceibo.entelnet.bo; Pres. JULIO CÉSAR L. PRADO.

There are also four foreign-owned insurance companies operating in Bolivia: American Life Insurance Co, American Home Assurance Co, United States Fire Insurance Co and International Health Insurance Danmarck.

Insurance Association

Asociación Boliviana de Aseguradores: Edif. Castilla, 5°, Of. 506, Calle Loayza esq. Mercado 250, Casilla 4804, La Paz; tel. (2) 31-0056; fax (2) 20-1088; e-mail abasegu@ceibo.entelnet.bo; f. 1962; Pres. ALFONSO IBÁÑEZ; Gen. Man. CARLOS BAUDOIN D.

Trade and Industry
GOVERNMENT AGENCIES

Cámara Nacional de Exportadores (CAMEX): Avda Arce 2017, esq. Goitia, Casilla 12145, La Paz; tel. (2) 34-1220; fax (2) 36-1491; e-mail camex@caoba.entelnet.bo; internet www.camex-lpb.com; f. 1970; Pres. LUIS NEMTALA YAMIN; Gen. Man. JORGE ADRIAZOLA REIMERS.

Centro de Promoción Bolivia (CEPROBOL): Calle Mercado 1328, 18°, Casilla 10871, La Paz; tel. (2) 33-6886; fax (2) 33-6996; e-mail ceprobol@ceprobol.gov.bo; internet www.ceprobol.gov.bo; f. 1998 as a successor to the Instituto Nacional de Promoción de Exportaciones (INPEX).

Instituto Nacional de Inversiones (INI): Edif. Cristal, 10°, Calle Yanacocha, Casilla 4393, La Paz; tel. (2) 37-5730; fax (2) 36-7297; e-mail abeseg@kolla.net.bo; f. 1971; state institution for the promotion of new investments and the application of the Investment Law; Exec. Dir Ing. JOSÉ MARIO FERNÁNDEZ IRAHOLA.

Sistema de Regulación Sectorial (SIRESE): Edif. Capitán Ravelo, 8°, Casilla 9647, La Paz; tel. (2) 44-4545; fax (2) 44-4017; e-mail sg@sirese.gov.bo; internet www.sirese.gov.bo; f. 1994; regulatory body for the formerly state-owned companies and utilities; oversees the general co-ordination and growth of the regulatory system and the work of its Superintendencies of Electricity, Hydrocarbons, Telecommunications, Transport and Water; Superintendent Gen. CLAUDE BESSE ARZE.

DEVELOPMENT ORGANIZATIONS

Consejo Nacional de Acreditación y Medición de la Calidad Educativa (CONAMED): La Paz; f. 1994; education quality board.

Consejo Nacional de Planificación (CONEPLAN): Edif. Banco Central de Bolivia, 26°, Calle Mercado esq. Ayacucho, Casilla 3118, La Paz; tel. (2) 37-4151; fax (2) 35-3840; e-mail claves@ mail.bcb.gov.bo; internet www.bcb.gov.bo; f. 1985.

Corporación de las Fuerzas Armadas para el Desarrollo Nacional (COFADENA): Avda 6 de Agosto 2649, Casilla 1015, La Paz; tel. (2) 37-7305; fax (2) 36-0900; f. 1972; industrial, agricultural and mining holding company and development organization owned by the Bolivian armed forces; Gen. Man. Col JUAN MANUEL ROSALES.

Corporación Regional de Desarrollo de La Paz (CORDEPAZ): Avda Arce 2529, Edif. Santa Isabel, Casilla 6102, La Paz; tel. (2) 43-0313; fax (2) 43-2152; f. 1972; decentralized government institution to foster the development of the La Paz area; Pres. Lic. RICARDO PAZ BALLIVIÁN; Gen. Man. Ing. JUAN G. CARRASCO R.

Instituto para el Desarrollo de la Pequeña Unidad Productiva: La Paz.

CHAMBERS OF COMMERCE

Cámara Nacional de Comercio: Edif. Cámara Nacional de Comercio, Avda Mariscal Santa Cruz 1392, 1°, Casilla 7, La Paz; tel. (2) 35-0042; fax (2) 39-1004; e-mail cnc@boliviacomercio.org.bo; internet www.boliviacomercio.org.bo; f. 1890; 30 brs and special brs; Pres. ALEJANDRO YAFFAR DE LA BARRA; Gen. Man. JOSÉ KUHN POPPE.

Cámara de Comercio de Oruro: Pasaje Guachalla s/n, Casilla 148, Oruro; tel. and fax (52) 50606; f. 1895; e-mail camacor@coteor .net.bo; Pres. ALVARO CORNEJO GAZCÓN; Gen. Man. LUIS CAMACHO VARGAS.

Cámara Departamental de Industria y Comercio de Santa Cruz: Calle Suárez de Figueroa 127, 3°, Casilla 180, Santa Cruz; tel. (3) 33-4555; fax (3) 34-2353; e-mail cainco@cainco.org.bo; internet www.cainco.org.bo; f. 1915; Pres. ZVONKO MATKOVIC FLEIG; Gen. Man. Lic. OSCAR ORTIZ ANTELO.

Cámara Departamental de Comercio de Cochabamba: Calle Sucre E-0336, Casilla 493, Cochabamba; tel. (42) 57715; fax (42) 57717; e-mail camcom@pino.cbb.entelnet.bo; internet www .camind.com/cadeco; f. 1922; Pres. Ing. CARLOS OLMEDO Z.; Gen. Man. Lic. JUAN CARLOS AVILA S.

Cámara Departamental de Comercio e Industria de Potosí: Calle Matos 12, Casilla 149, Potosí; tel. (62) 22641; fax (62) 22641; Pres. JAVIER FLORES CASTRO; Gen. Man. WALTER ZABALA AYLLON.

Cámara Departamental de Industria y Comercio de Chuquisaca: Calle España 64, Casilla 33, Sucre; tel. (64) 51194; fax (64) 51850; e-mail cicch@camara.scr.entelnet.bo; f. 1923; Pres. MARCO MIHAIC; Gen. Man. Lic. ALFREDO YÁNEZ MERCADO.

Cámara Departamental de Comercio e Industria de Cobija—Pando: Plaza Germán Busch, Casilla 110, Cobija; tel. (842) 3139; fax (842) 2291; Pres. NEMESIO RAMÍREZ.

Cámara Departamental de Industria y Comercio de Tarija: Avda Bolívar 0413, 1°, Casilla 74, Tarija; tel. (66) 22737; fax (66) 24053; e-mail metfess@olivo.tja.entelnet.bo; Pres. RENE SILBERMANN U.; Gen. Man. VÍCTOR ARAMAYO.

Cámara Departamental de Comercio de Trinidad—Beni: Casilla 96, Trinidad; tel. (46) 22365; fax (46) 21400; Pres. EDUARDO AVILA ALVERDI.

INDUSTRIAL AND TRADE ASSOCIATIONS

Cámara Agropecuaria del Oriente: 3 anillo interno zona Oeste, Casilla 116, Santa Cruz; tel. (3) 52-2200; fax (3) 52-2621; e-mail caosrz@bibosi.scz.entelnet.bo; f. 1964; agriculture and livestock association for eastern Bolivia; Pres. RICARDO FRERKING ORTIZ; Gen. Man. WALTER NÚÑEZ RODRÍGUEZ.

Cámara Agropecuaria de La Paz: Avda 16 de Julio 1525, Casilla 12521, La Paz; tel. (2) 39-2911; fax (2) 35-2308; Pres. ALBERTO DE OLIVA MAYA; Gen. Man. JUAN CARLOS ZAMORANO.

Cámara Forestal de Bolivia: Prolongación Manuel Ignacio Salvatierra 1055, Casilla 346, Santa Cruz; tel. (3) 33-2699; fax (3) 33-1456; e-mail foresbol@cotas.com.bo; internet www.cadex.org/camara forestal; f. 1969; represents the interests of the Bolivian timber industry; Pres. MARIO BARBERY SCIARONI; Gen. Man. Lic. ARTURO BOWLES OLHAGARAY.

Cámara Nacional de Industrias: Edif. Cámara Nacional de Comercio, 14°, Avda Mariscal Santa Cruz 1392, Casilla 611, La Paz; tel. (2) 37-4476; fax (2) 36-2766; e-mail cni@mail.megalink.com; internet www.bolivia-industry.com; f. 1931; Pres. ROBERTO MUSTAFÁ; Man. GERARDO VELASCO T.

Cámara Nacional de Minería: Pasaje Bernardo Trigo 429, Casilla 2022, La Paz; tel. (2) 35-0623; f. 1953; mining institute; Pres. Ing. LUIS PRADO BARRIENTOS; Sec.-Gen. GERMÁN GORDILLO S.

Comité Boliviano de Productores de Antimonio: Pasajes Bernardo Trigo 429, Casilla 14451, La Paz; tel. (2) 44-2140; fax (2) 44-1653; f. 1978; controls the marketing, pricing and promotion policies of the antimony industry; Pres. ALBERTO BARRIOS MORALES; Sec.-Gen. Dr ALCIDES RODRÍGUEZ J.

Comité Boliviano del Café (COBOLCA): Calle Nicaragua 1638, Casilla 9770, La Paz; tel. (2) 22-3883; fax (2) 24-4591; e-mail cobolca @ceibo.entelnet.bo; controls the export, quality, marketing and growing policies of the coffee industry; Gen. Man. MAURICIO VILLAR-ROEL.

EMPLOYERS' ASSOCIATIONS

Asociación Nacional de Mineros Medianos: Calle Pedro Salazar 600 esq. Presbítero Medina, Casilla 6190, La Paz; tel. (2) 41-7522; fax (2) 41-4123; e-mail anmm@caoba.entelnet.bo; f. 1939; association of the 14 private medium-sized mining companies; Pres. RAÚL ESPAÑA-SMITH; Sec.-Gen. ROLANDO JORDÁN.

Confederación de Empresarios Privados de Bolivia (CEPB): Edif. Cámara Nacional de Comercio, 7°, Avda Mariscal Santa Cruz 1392, Casilla 20439, La Paz; tel. (2) 35-6831; e-mail cepbol@ceibo .entelnet.bo; internet www.cepb.org; largest national employers' organization; Pres. Lic. CARLOS CALVO GALINDO; Exec. Sec. Lic. JOHNNY NOGALES VIRUEZ.

There are also employers' federations in Santa Cruz, Cochabamba, Oruro, Potosí, Beni and Tarija.

MAJOR COMPANIES

ADM-SAO, SA: Parque Industrial Pesado, Casilla 1295, Santa Cruz; tel. (3) 46-0888; fax (3) 46-3941; e-mail saogc@admsao.com; internet www.admsao.com; f. 1975; edible vegetable oils and soya-bean products; Pres. ANDRÉS PETRICEVIC; Gen. Man. CARLOS E. KEMPFF; 560 employees.

Cervecería Boliviana Nacional, SA: Calle Chuquisaca 121, La Paz; tel. (2) 45-5455; fax (2) 45-5375; e-mail cbn@pacena.com; internet www.pacena.com; f. 1886; brewing; Pres. JOHNNY FERNÁNDEZ SAUCEDO; Gen. Man. Lic. ANTONIO CAMBEROS; 275 employees.

Cervecería Santa Cruz, SA: Avda Busch, 3er Anillo Interno, Santa Cruz; tel. (3) 53-5000; fax (3) 53-7070; f. 1952; brewing; Pres. HERMANN WILLE; Dir-Gen. VICTOR KELLEMBERGER; 250 employees.

Cervecería Taquiña, SA: Avda Centenario Final, Zona Taquiña, La Paz; tel. (2) 28-7500; fax (2) 29-6403; f. 1895; brewing; Pres. ERNESTO ASBUN GIZAUI; Gen. Man. FAUSTINO ARIAS REY; 345 employees.

Corporación Automotriz Boliviana, SA (CABSA): Avda 6 de Agosto 2860, San Jorge, La Paz; tel. (2) 43-0183; fax (2) 43-3166; e-mail cabsamgt@datacom-bo.net; f. 1986; sale of new and used cars; Pres. RAMIRO CABEZAS; 55 employees.

Compañía Industrial Azucarera San Aurelio, SA: Avda San Aurelio esq. 4 anillo, Zona Sud, Casilla 94, Santa Cruz; tel. (3) 352-2882; fax (3) 334-1182; e-mail ciasa@unete.com; sugar refining; Pres. EDUARDO GUTIÉRREZ SOSA; 800 employees.

Compañía Industrial Maderera Ltda: Parque Industrial Pesado 10, Santa Cruz; tel. (3) 33-9405; fax (3) 46-1502; f. 1974; sawmill operations; Pres. CRISTÓBAL RODA DAZA; 265 employees.

Compañía Industrial de Tabacos, SA: Avda Montes 515, Casilla 210, La Paz; tel. (2) 32-2265; fax (2) 35-0104; e-mail citsa@ceibo.en-telnet.bo; f. 1934; cigarette manufacturers; Pres. RODOLFO KAVLIN; Gen. Man. JORGE PAREJA; 200 employees.

Compañía Minera del Sur (COMSUR): Edif. Petrolero, Avda 16 de Julio 1616, La Paz; tel. (2) 36-1018; fax (2) 39-1016; e-mail comsur@caoba.entelnet.bo; f. 1965; mining and processing of lead and zinc ores; Pres. JAIME URJEL; 1,456 employees.

Cooperativa Boliviana de Cemento (COBOCE): Avda San Martín 558, Cochabamba; tel. (2) 32-5366; fax (42) 22485; internet www.coboce.com; f. 1966; manufacture and distribution of cement; Gen. Man. JAIME MENDEZ QUIROGA; 455 employees.

Corporación Minera de Bolivia (COMIBOL): Avda Camacho esq. Loayza, La Paz; tel. (2) 36-7681; fax (2) 36-7483; e-mail uccbm1@caoba.entelnet.bo; internet www.comibol.com; f. 1952; state mining corpn; taken over by FSTMB (miners' union) in April 1983; owns both mines and processing plants; Pres. Dr ALBERTO ALANDIA BARRÓN; Gen. Man. LUIS ARNAL; 26,000 employees.

Drogueria Inti, SA; Calle Socobaya 242, Casilla 1421, La Paz; tel. (2) 36-6170; fax (2) 39-1005; e-mail droginti@caoba.entelnet.bo; internet www.inti.com.bo; f. 1936; manufacture and distribution of pharmaceuticals; Pres. FRIEDRICH OHNES TANZER; Man. Dieter SCHILLING; 400 employees.

Empresa Metalúrgica Vinto (EMV): Avda Villazón 1966, La Paz; tel. (2) 35-9270; fax (2) 36-3722; f. 1966; state co for the smelting of non-ferrous minerals and special alloys; expected to be privatized under the Govt's capitalization programme; Exec. Pres. FERNANDO FREUDENTHAL; Gen. Man. RENÉ CANDIA; 950 employees.

Empresa Minera Inti Raymi, SA: Corneta Mamani 1989, La Paz; tel. (2) 35-8111; fax (2) 32-5322; f. 1982; mining; 435 employees.

Empresa Minera Unificada, SA (EMUSA): Avda 20 de Octubre 1968, La Paz; tel. (2) 32-2407; fax (2) 35-8462; f. 1946; mining and processing of metal ores; Pres. LUIS MERCADO; 416 employees.

Fábrica Nacional de Cemento, SA (FANCESA): Pasaje Armando Alba 80, Casilla 887, Sucre; tel. (64) 53882; fax (64) 41221; f. 1959; manufacturers of cement; Pres. Ing. ANTONIO MOSTAJO FERNÁNDEZ; Gen. Man. Ing. EDDY DECORMICK CARVAJAL; 300 employees.

Ferrari Ghezzi Ltda: Avda 6 de Octubre y Lira 171, Oruro; tel. (52) 41065; fax (52) 40110; e-mail arzabe1@nogal.oru.entelnet.bo; f. 1935; food production and processing; Gen. Man. CARLOS FERRARI; 500 employees.

Gravetal Bolivia, SA: Edif. Banco Nacional de Bolivia, 6°, René Moreno, Santa Cruz; tel. and fax (3) 36-3601; e-mail gravetal@gravetal.com; internet www.gravetal.com; f. 1992; production of soya-bean oil and soya-bean meal; Pres. HERNÁN OSORNO CARDENAS; Gen. Man. JORGE ARIAS LAZANO.

Industrias de Aceite, SA: Carretera al Norte Km 6.5; Casilla 1759, Santa Cruz; tel. (3) 44-3000; fax (3) 443-010; e-mail fino@fino.com.bo; f 1954; manufacture of edible vegetable oils; Pres. RONALD CAMPBELL GARCÍA; employees 1,080.

Ingenio Azucarero Guabira, SA: Guabira, Montero, Santa Cruz; tel. (92) 20225; fax (92) 20633; f. 1956; processing and refining of sugar cane and alcohol distillation; Pres. Ing. MARIANO AGUILERA; Dir-Gen. Ing. RUDIGER TREPP; 800 employees.

La Papelera, SA: Calle Loayza 178, Casilla 4601, La Paz; tel. (2) 35-2983; fax (2) 32-5323; e-mail lapapelera@lapapelera.com; internet www.lapapelera.com; f. 1941; paper and plastics manufacturers; Pres. EMILIO VON BERGEN; Gen. Man. CONRAD VON BERGEN; 780 employees.

Manufactura Boliviana, SA (MANACO): Avda Busch 2005, La Paz; tel. (2) 32-4778; fax (2) 35-4007; f. 1940; manufacturers of footwear; Pres. PABLO DERMIZAKY PEREDO; Gen. Man. CARLOS BUSTAMENTE MORALES; 771 employees.

Manufacturas Textiles Forno, SA: Avda Chacaltaya 789, Casilla 881, La Paz; tel. (2) 35-2520; fax (2) 35-1600; production of textiles; Pres. Lic. JAVIER GISBERT; Gen. Man. CARLOS FORNO H.; 465 employees.

Orbol, SA: Avda Tarapaca, El Alto, La Paz; tel. (2) 81-5540; fax (2) 81-5595; e-mail bolgold@ceibo.entelnet.bo; f. 1988; manufacturer and exporter of gold and sterling silver jewellery to the Americas and Europe; Dir AUGUSTO MILLARES; 387 employees.

Sagic, SA: Avda Andrés Julio Batani 425, La Paz; tel. (2) 79-4344; fax (2) 79-4347; e-mail sagic@wara.bolnet.bo; f. 1925; producer and exporter of alcoholic beverages and fresh fruit; Gen. Mans CARLOS CALVO GALINDO, ERNESTO REINAGA.

Servicio Nacional de Caminos (SNC): Avda Mariscal Santa Cruz, La Paz; tel. (2) 357-2200; fax (2) 39-1764; f. 1961; state co responsible for road construction and maintenance; Exec. Dir Ing. CÉSAR LÓPEZ CÓRTEZ; 2,100 employees.

Sociedad Boliviana de Cementos, SA (SOBOCE): Calle Mercado 1075, 1°, Casilla 557, La Paz; tel. (2) 35-3544; fax (2) 35-0416; e-mail soboce@utama.bolnet.bo; internet www.soboce.com; f. 1925; manufacturers of cement; Pres. SAMUEL DORIA MEDINA; Gen. Man. SUSANA DORIA MEDINA AUZA; 235 employees.

Sociedad Comercial e Industrial Hansa Ltda (HANSA): Edif. Hansa, Calle Yanacocha esq. Mercado 1004, La Paz; tel. (2) 31-4445; fax (2) 37-0397; f. 1954; import and trading of telecommunications equipment, hardware, industrial machinery, motor vehicles and mining equipment; Gen. Man. GERARDO KYLLMANN DIECKELMANN; 370 employees.

Yacimientos Petrolíferos Fiscales Bolivianos (YPFB): Calle Bueno 185, Casilla 401, La Paz; tel. (2) 35-6540; fax (2) 39-2596; f. 1936; exploration, drilling, production, refining, transportation and distribution of petroleum; privatized in 1996; Exec. Pres. Dr ARTURO CASTAÑOS ICHAZO; Vice-Pres. for Operations Ing. FREDDY ESCOBAR ROSAS; 4,900 employees.

UTILITIES
Electricity

Superintendencia de Electricidad: Avda 16 de Julio 1571, La Paz; tel. (2) 31-2401; fax (2) 31-2393; e-mail superele@superele.gov.bo; internet www.superele.gov.bo; f. 1996; regulates the electricity sector; Superintendent ALEJANDRO NOWOTNY VERA;Gen. Sec. ROLANDO LÓPEZ.

Compañía Boliviana de Energía Eléctrica, SA (COBEE): Avda Hernando Siles 5635, Casilla 353, La Paz; tel. (2) 78-2474; fax (2) 78-5920; e-mail cobee@cobee.com; f. 1925; second largest private producer and distributor of electricity serving the areas of La Paz and Oruro; in 1998 the company generated 25.9% of all electricity produced in Bolivia; Chair. D. H. BUSWELL.

Electropaz: Avda Illimani 1987, La Paz; tel. (2) 22-2200; fax (2) 22-3756; Gen. Man. Ing. ANGEL GÓMEZ.

Empresa Nacional de Electricidad, SA (ENDE): Colombia 655, esq. Falsuri, Casilla 565, Cochabamba; tel. (4) 25-9500; fax (4) 25-9509; f. 1962; former state electricity company; privatized under the Govt's capitalization programme in 1995 and divided into three arms concerned with generation, transmission and distribution, respectively; Pres. Ing. Dr ENRIQUE GÓMEZ DE ANGELO; Gen. Man. Ing. JORGE DE LA VEGA BARNECHEA.

Gas

Numerous distributors of natural gas exist throughout the country, many of which are owned by the petroleum distributor, Yacimientos Petrolíferos Fiscales Bolivianos (YPFB).

CO-OPERATIVE

Instituto Nacional de Co-operativas (INALCO): Edif. Lotería Nacional, 4°, Avda Mariscal Santa Cruz y Cochabamba, La Paz; tel. (2) 37-4366; fax (2) 37-2104; e-mail inalcolp@ceibo.entelnet.bo; f. 1974; Pres. DAVID AYAVIRI.

TRADE UNIONS

Central Obrera Boliviana (COB): Edif. COB, Calle Pisagua 618, Casilla 6552, La Paz; tel. (2) 28-3220; fax (2) 28-0420; f. 1952; main union confederation; 800,000 mems; Exec. Sec. ALBERTO CAMACHO PARDO; Sec.-Gen. OSCAR SALAS MOYA.

Affiliated unions:

Central Obrera Departamental de La Paz: Estación Central 284, La Paz; tel. (2) 35-2898; Exec. Sec. GENARO TORRICO.

Confederación Sindical Unica de los Trabajadores Campesinos de Bolivia (CSUTCB): Calle Sucre, esq. Yanacocha, La Paz; tel. (2) 36-9433; f. 1979; peasant farmers' union; Exec. Sec. JUAN DE LA CRUZ VILLCA.

Federación de Empleados de Industria Fabril: Edif. Fabril, 5°, Plaza de San Francisco, La Paz; tel. (2) 40-6799; fax (2) 40-7044; Exec. Sec. ALEX GÁLVEZ.

Federación Sindical de Trabajadores Mineros de Bolivia (FSTMB): Plaza Venezuela 1470, Casilla 14565, La Paz; tel. (2) 35-9656; fax (2) 48-4948; f. 1944; mineworkers' union; Exec. Sec. MILTON GONZÁLEZ; Gen. Sec. EDGAR RAMÍREZ SANTIESTÉBAN; 27,000 mems.

Federación Sindical de Trabajadores Petroleros de Bolivia: Calle México 1504, La Paz; tel. (2) 35-1748; Exec. Sec. NEFTALY-MENDOZA DURÁN.

Confederación General de Trabajadores Fabriles de Bolivia (CGTFB): Avda Armentia 452, Casilla 21590, La Paz; tel. (2) 37-1603; fax (2) 32-4302; e-mail dirabc@bo.net; f. 1951; manufacturing workers' union; Exec. Sec. ANGEL ASTURIZAGA; Gen. Sec. ROBERTO ENCINAS.

Transport
RAILWAYS

Empresa Nacional de Ferrocarriles (ENFE): Estación Central de Ferrocarriles, Plaza Zalles, Casilla 428, La Paz; tel. (2) 35-9935; fax (2) 39-2106; f. 1964; administers most of the railways in Bolivia; privatized under the Government's capitalization programme in 1995. Total networks: 3,698 km (1995); Andina network: 2,274 km; Eastern network: 1,424 km; Gen. Man. RAFAEL ECHAZU BROWN.

A former private railway, Machacamarca–Uncia, owned by Corporación Minera de Bolivia (105 km), merged with the Andina network of ENFE in 1987. There are plans to construct a railway line with Brazilian assistance, to link Cochabamba and Santa Cruz. There were also plans for the construction of a rail link between Santa Cruz and Mutún on the border with Brazil.

ROADS

In 1999 Bolivia had some 52,216 km of roads, of which an estimated 5.5% were paved. Almost the entire road network is concentrated in the altiplano region and the Andes valleys. A 560-km highway runs from Santa Cruz to Cochabamba, serving a colonization scheme on virgin lands around Santa Cruz. The Pan-American Highway, linking Argentina and Peru, crosses Bolivia from south to north-west. In late 1997 the Government announced the construction of

1,844 km of new roads in the hope of improving Bolivia's connections with neighbouring countries.

INLAND WATERWAYS

By agreement with Paraguay in 1938 (confirmed in 1939), Bolivia has an outlet on the River Paraguay. This arrangement, together with navigation rights on the Paraná, gives Bolivia access to the River Plate and the sea. The River Paraguay is navigable for vessels of 12-ft draught for 288 km beyond Asunción, in Paraguay, and for smaller boats another 960 km to Corumbá in Brazil. In late 1994 plans were finalized to widen and deepen the River Paraguay, providing a waterway from Bolivia to the Atlantic coast in Uruguay. However, in 2000 work on the project had still not begun, owing largely to environmental concerns.

In 1974 Bolivia was granted free duty access to the Brazilian coastal ports of Belém and Santos and the inland ports of Corumbá and Port Velho. In 1976 Argentina granted Bolivia free port facilities at Rosario on the River Paraná. In 1992 an agreement was signed with Peru, granting Bolivia access to (and the use, without customs formalities, of) the Pacific port of Ilo. Most of Bolivia's foreign trade is handled through the ports of Matarani (Peru), Antofagasta and Arica (Chile), Rosario and Buenos Aires (Argentina) and Santos (Brazil). An agreement between Bolivia and Chile to reform Bolivia's access arrangements to the port of Arica came into effect in January 1996.

Bolivia has over 14,000 km of navigable rivers, which connect most of Bolivia with the Amazon basin.

Bolivian River Navigation Company: f. 1958; services from Puerto Suárez to Buenos Aires (Argentina).

OCEAN SHIPPING

Líneas Navieras Bolivianas (LINABOL): Edif. Hansa, 16°, Avda Mariscal Santa Cruz, Apdo 11160, La Paz; tel. (2) 37-9459; fax (2) 39-1079; Pres. Vice-Adm. LUIS AZURDUY ZAMBRANA; Vice-Pres. WOLFGANG APT.

CIVIL AVIATION

Bolivia has 30 airports including the two international airports at La Paz (El Alto) and Santa Cruz (Viru-Viru).

Dirección General de Aeronaútica Civil: Avda Mariscal Santa Cruz 1278, Casilla 9360; La Paz; tel. (2) 37-4142; e-mail dgacbol@ceibo-entelnet.bo; internet www.dgac.gov.bo; f. 1947; Dir-Gen. ORLANDO MONTOYA KOËSTER.

AeroSur: Calle Colón y Avda Irala, Casilla 3104, Santa Cruz; tel. (3) 36-4446; fax (3) 33-0666; e-mail javiedr.gonzalez@aerosur.com; f. 1992 by the merger of existing charter cos following deregulation; privately-owned; Pres. OSCAR ALCOCER; Gen. Man. FERNANDO PRUDENCIO.

Lloyd Aéreo Boliviano, SAM (LAB): Casilla 132, Aeropuerto 'Jorge Wilstermann', Cochabamba; tel. (4) 25-1270; fax (4) 25-0766; e-mail lider@labairlines.bo.net; internet www.labairlines.bo.net; f. 1925; privatized under the Government's capitalization programme in 1995; owned by Bolivian Govt (48.3%), VASP-Brazil (49%), private interests (2.7%); operates a network of scheduled services to 12 cities within Bolivia and to 21 international destinations in South America, Central America and the USA; Pres. ULISSES CANHEDO AZEVEDO; Gen. Man. ANTONIO SANCHES.

Transportes Aéreos Bolivianos (TAB): Casilla 12237, La Paz; tel. (42) 37-8325; fax (42) 35-9660; f. 1977; regional scheduled and charter cargo services; Gen. Man. LUIS GUERECA PADILLA; Chair. CARLO APARICIO.

Transportes Aéreos Militares: Avda Montes 738, La Paz; tel. (2) 37-9286; internal passenger and cargo services; Dir-Gen. REMBERTO DURÁN.

Tourism

Bolivia's tourist attractions include Lake Titicaca, at 3,810 m (12,500 ft) above sea-level, pre-Incan ruins at Tiwanaku, Chacaltaya in the Andes mountains, which has the highest ski-run in the world, and the UNESCO World Cultural Heritage Sites of Potosí and Sucre. In 1998 420,491 foreign visitors arrived at hotels in Bolivian regional capitals. In 1996 receipts from tourism totalled US $161m. Tourists come mainly from South American countries, the USA and Europe.

Asociación Boliviana de Agencias de Viajes y Turismo: Edif. Litoral, Avda Mariscal Santa Cruz 1351, Casilla 3967, La Paz; f. 1984; Pres. EUGENIO MONROY VÉLEZ.

Viceministerio de Turismo: Avda Mariscal Santa Cruz, 16°, Casilla 1868, La Paz; tel. (2) 35-8312; fax (2) 37-4630; e-mail etorres@mcei-gov.bo; internet www.bolivia-travel.gov.bo; Vice-Minister of Tourism EDGAR TORRES SARAVIA.

Defence

In August 2000 Bolivia's Armed Forces numbered 32,500: Army 25,000 (including 18,000 conscripts), Navy 4,500, Air Force 3,000. There were plans to increase this number to 35,000. Military service, lasting one year, is selective. There were also 31,100 National Police paramilitaries and some 6,000 anti-drugs police.

Defence Expenditure: The budget allocation for 2000 was 796m. bolivianos.

Commander-in-Chief of the Armed Forces: Gen. CARLOS BEJAR MOLINA.

Commander-General of the Army: Gen. ALFONSO SAAVEDRA.

Commander-General of the Navy: Adm. JORGE ZABALA.

Commander-General of the Air Force: Gen. OSCAR GUILARTE.

Education

Education in Bolivia is free and, where possible, compulsory between the ages of six and 14 years. In 1990 the total enrolment at primary and secondary schools was equivalent to 77% of the school-age population (81% of boys; 73% of girls). In that year an estimated 95% of children in the relevant age-group attended primary schools (99% of boys; 90% of girls), while the comparable ratio for secondary enrolment was only 37% (40% of boys; 34% of girls). In 1991 the total enrolment at primary and secondary schools was equivalent to 79% of the school-age population. There are eight state universities and two private universities. Expenditure on education by the central Government in 1998 amounted to 19.6% of government expenditure, some 2,023.4m. bolivianos.

Bibliography

For works on South America generally, see Select Bibliography (Books).

Alexander, R. J. *Bolivia: Past, Present and Future of its Politics.* New York, NY, Praeger Publrs, 1982.

Crabtree, J., Duffy, G., and Pearce, J. *The Great Tin Crash: Bolivia and the World Tin Market.* London, Latin American Bureau, 1987.

Dunkerley, J. *Rebellion in the Veins: Political Struggle in Bolivia, 1952–82.* London, Verso, 1984.

Farcau, B. *The Chaco War: Boliva and Paraguay, 1932–1935.* New York, NY, Praeger Publrs, 1996.

Greaves, T., and Culver, W. (Eds). *Miners and Mining in the Americas.* Manchester, Manchester University Press, 1986.

Healy, K. *Llamas, Weavings and Organic Chocolate: Multilateral Grassroots Development in the Andes and Amazon of Bolivia.* Notre Dame, IN, University of Notre Dame Press, 2000.

James, D. (Ed.). *The Complete Bolivian Diaries of Che Guevara.* New York, NY, Cooper Square Press, 2000.

Jemio, L. C. *Debt, Crisis and Reform in Bolivia: Biting the Bullet.* The Hague, Institute of Social Studies, 2001.

Kelley, J., and Klein, H. S. *Revolution and the Rebirth of Inequality: A Theory Applied to the National Revolution in Bolivia.* Berkeley and Los Angeles, CA, University of California Press, 1981.

Klein, H. S. *Bolivia: The Evolution of a Multi-Ethnic Society.* New York, NY, Oxford University Press, 1982.

Lehman, K. D. *Bolivia and the United States: A Limited Partnership*. Athens, GA, University of Georgia Press, 1999.

Lora, G. *A History of the Bolivian Labour Movement, 1848–1971*. Cambridge, Cambridge University Press, 1977.

Menzel, S. H. *Fire in the Andes: US Foreign Policy and Cocaine Politics in Bolivia and Peru*. Lanham, MD, University Press of America, 1996.

Painter, J. *Bolivia and Coca: A Study in Dependency*. London, Lynne Rienner Publrs, 1994.

Rhyne, E. *Mainstreaming Microfinance: How Lending to the Poor Began, Grew and Came of Age in Bolivia*. Bloomfield, CT, Kumarian Press, 2001.

Stephnson, M. *Gender and Modernity in Andean Bolivia*. Austin, TX, University of Texas Press, 1999.

Villegas, H. *Pombo, a Man of Che's Guerilla: With Che Guevara in Bolivia 1966–68*. London, Pathfinder Press, 1997.

BRAZIL

Area: 8,547,404 sq km (3,300,171 sq miles).

Population: 169,543,612 (provisional), at census of 1 August 2000.

Capital: Brasília, population 2,043,169(provisional, at census of 1 August 2000).

Language: Portuguese (official).

Religion: Predominantly Christian (89% Roman Catholic).

Climate: ranges from tropical in the Amazon basin to temperate in the central and southern uplands.

Time: GMT −3 hours (standard time), GMT −4 hours (western Brazil).

Public Holidays

2002: 1 January (New Year's Day—Universal Confraternization Day), 11–13 February (Carnival), 29 March (Good Friday), 21 April (Tiradentes Day—Discovery of Brazil), 1 May (Labour Day), 9 May (Ascension Day), 30 May (Corpus Christi), 7 September (Independence Day), 12 October (Our Lady Aparecida, Patron Saint of Brazil), 2 November (All Souls' Day), 15 November (Proclamation of the Republic), 25 December (Christmas Day).

2003: 1 January (New Year's Day—Universal Confraternization Day), 3–5 March (Carnival), 18 April (Good Friday), 21 April (Tiradentes Day—Discovery of Brazil), 1 May (Labour Day), 29 May (Ascension Day), 19 June (Corpus Christi), 7 September (Independence Day), 12 October (Our Lady Aparecida, Patron Saint of Brazil), 2 November (All Souls' Day), 15 November (Proclamation of the Republic), 25 December (Christmas Day).

States and municipalities also celebrate other holidays locally, such as 20 January (Foundation of Rio de Janeiro) and 25 January (Foundation of São Paulo).

Currency: Real; 100 reais = £31.97 = US $45.77 = €51.57 (30 April 2001).

Weights and Measures: The metric system is in force.

Basic Economic Indicators

	1998	1999	2000
Gross domestic product (million R $ at 2000 prices)	1,034,989	1,043,161	1,089,688
GDP per head ('000 R $ at 2000 prices)	6,397	6,363	6,560
Annual growth of real GDP (%)	0.2	0.8	4.5
Annual growth of real GDP per head (%)	−1.1	−0.5	3.1
Consumer price index (annual average, Rio de Janeiro; base: 1995 = 100)	127.7	133.9	143.4
Rate of inflation (annual average, %)	3.2	4.9	7.0
Foreign exchange reserves (US $ million at 31 December)	42,578	34,786	32,488
Imports c.i.f. (US $ million)	60,618	51,675	58,532
Exports f.o.b. (US $ million);	51,120	48,011	55,086
Balance of payments (current account, US $ million)	−33,829	−25,400	−24,632

Gross national product per head measured at purchasing power parity (PPP) (US dollars, converted by the PPP exchange rate, 1999): 6,317.

Total labour force (excl. aborigines, northern rural population, non-resident foreigners, etc., 1999): 79,315.3.

Unemployment (excl. aborigines, northern rural population, non-resident foreigners, etc., 1999): 9.6%.

Total external debt (1999): US $244,673m.

Life expectancy (years at birth, estimate, mid-1999): 67 (male 63.4, female 70.8).

Infant mortality rate (per 1,000 live births, 1998): 33.

Adult population with HIV/AIDS (15–49 years, 1999): 0.57%

School enrolment ratio (7–17 years, 1997): 107%.

Adult literacy rate (15 years and over, 2000): 85.3% (males 85.1%, females 85.4%).

Carbon dioxide emissions per head (metric tons, 1997): 1.9.

Passenger motor cars in use (estimate, per 1,000 of population, 1997): 76.7.

Television receivers in use (per 1,000 of population, 1997): 223.

Personal computers in use (per 1,000 of population, 1999): 36.3.

History

Dr EDMUND AMMAN

Based on an earlier text by Dr Paul Cammack

Brazil was Portugal's only American colony, and survived as a single unit after independence to become Latin America's only Portuguese-speaking nation. During the period of Portuguese colonial rule, thousands of Africans were forcibly transported to Brazil to work as slaves. As a result of the flight of the Portuguese royal family to the colony in 1807, Brazil attained independence in 1822 under Prince Pedro, who became Emperor Pedro I of Brazil. The country remained a monarchy until 1889, when a republic was declared, one year after the abolition of slavery. A federalist constitution was adopted in 1891. The regime that it instituted endured until it was overthrown in 1930, in a revolution which brought Dr Getúlio Vargas to power. Vargas oversaw the introduction of a new and more centralized Constitution in 1934, but established a military-backed dictatorship in 1937 rather than retire from the presidency in 1938. The new regime (the Estado Novo) lasted until 1945, when the military itself withdrew its support and forced Vargas from power.

THE RESTORATION OF DEMOCRACY

The restoration of democracy with the new Constitution of 1946 gave most Brazilians their first experience of political involvement and inaugurated nearly two decades of continuous but unstable party competition. The period was dominated by Vargas, now presenting himself, with some success, as a champion of the masses, and his heirs. They were grouped in the broadly conservative Partido Social Democrático (PSD—Social Democratic Party) and the leftist and increasingly influential Partido Trabalhista Brasileiro (PTB—Brazilian Workers' Party), and opposed by the liberal União Democrática Nacional (UDN—National Democratic Union) and by the Partido Social Progressivo (Social Progress Party). Vargas was elected to the presidency in 1951, but committed suicide in 1954, when the military demanded his resignation. Over the next 10 years Brazil gradually declined into a state of acute political crisis. Industrialization proceeded rapidly under the presidency of Juscelino Kubitschek (1956–61), but the economic strains which were created, and the political tensions arising out of urbanization and swift social change, proved too great for the fragile political system. As pressure mounted for social and structural reform, the UDN secured the presidency for the first time, through a recently recruited independent, Jânio Quadros, at elections in October 1960. Within months of taking power in January 1961, Quadros resigned, alleging lack of support from the National Congress, and the country was plunged into crisis. He was succeeded by the Vice-President, PTB leader João Goulart, after the military had forced a change from a presidential to a parliamentary system, with Tancredo de Almeida Neves as Prime Minister.

Under pressure from the left to adopt a radical programme, including a major land reform, Goulart at first hesitated, but, after regaining presidential powers in a January 1963 referendum, he moved to respond to such demands. Before the ensuing radicalization was far advanced, the military intervened, seizing power on 1 April 1964. The military coup brought an end to two decades of fragile democracy, marked by a refusal on the part of the privileged élites to countenance any degree of social reform, and a general failure on the part of political parties to establish themselves as independent actors, rather than as clientelistic groupings reliant upon the patronage powers of the state.

MILITARY RULE AFTER 1964

The 21-year military regime was a curious hybrid. The armed forces concentrated power in their own hands, but kept the National Congress in session (except for an extended period in 1968–69 and a brief time in 1977) while denying it autonomy. Successive purges removed all but the most moderate opponents of the regime. The military executive was vested with power to govern by decree, and the parties existing in 1964 were replaced by a two-party system, with pro-government forces congregating in the majority Aliança Renovadora Nacional (ARENA—National Renewal Alliance) and the remaining opposition members grouped in the Movimento Democrático Brasileiro (MDB—Brazilian Democratic Movement). The dictatorship was at its most harsh between 1968 and 1974, particularly under Gen. Emílio Garrastazú Médici. The already highly authoritarian Constitution approved in 1967 was heavily amended in 1969 to strengthen further the power of the military executive, and the elections of 1966 and 1970, held in conditions which made meaningful competition impossible, gave emphatic majorities to the government party. Throughout this period, the retention of a system of political parties combined with a concentration of powers of decision in the military executive pushed to extremes the tendency for the governing party to act as a clientelistic machine. In 1974 Gen. Ernesto Geisel (President, 1974–79), relying on the appeal of limited liberalization and Brazil's burst of economic growth after recession had come to an end in 1967, allowed more open elections. The electoral system protected the government majority, but the unexpected gains that were made by the MDB, particularly in the elections for one-third of the Senate, may be seen in retrospect as marking the beginning of the long retreat of the military from power.

From 1974 onwards the military lacked a natural majority in the country, but persisted in holding elections on schedule, seeking to maintain their hold on power by a series of expedient measures such as the indirect election (to all intents and purposes the appointment) of one-third of the Senate. This failed to conceal either their unpopularity or their waning self-confidence. Geisel's successor, Gen. João Baptista de Figueiredo (1979–85), was the beneficiary of a decision to prolong the presidential mandate by one year, but it fell to him to oversee the departure of the military from power. An attempt to regain the initiative by dissolving the two-party system in 1979, in a bid to divide the opposition and to halt the advance of the reorganized and increasingly effective MDB, failed in its objective. ARENA was reconstituted, shorn of some of its elements, as the Partido Democrático Social (PDS—Social Democratic Party), while a number of opposition parties appeared, led by the renamed Partido do Movimento Democrático Brasileiro (PMDB—Party of the Brazilian Democratic Movement). Among the new parties the most prominent were the Partido dos Trabalhadores (PT—Workers' Party), led by Luiz Inácio 'Lula' da Silva, an independent labour-union organizer from São Paulo, and the Partido Democrático Trabalhista (PDT—Democratic Workers' Party), a reincarnation of the old PTB led by Leonel de Moura Brizola, Goulart's brother-in-law. A centrist Partido Popular (PP—People's Party) also briefly appeared, led by veteran politician Tancredo Neves, formerly of the pre-coup PSD. When the Government introduced legislation to prevent cross-party voting in the 1982 elections, in a further attempt to stem the tide of opposition gains, the PP dissolved itself and the great majority of its members joined the PMDB.

THE WANE OF MILITARY AUTHORITY

By 1982 five years of social mobilization and protest, focused primarily on the factories and working-class communities of São Paulo and co-ordinated as much by the Roman Catholic Church as by the parties and unions, had pushed the military on to the defensive. The 1982 elections gave the governorships of the leading states to the opposition (with direct gubernatorial elections for the first time since 1966) and gave the combined opposition forces a majority in the Chamber of Deputies. In June 1984 a substantial Chamber vote in favour of direct elections failed to gain the required two-thirds majority, but the military executive lost control of its own party, and saw the official nomination for its presidential candidate go to civilian banker and financier Paulo Salim Maluf, former Governor of São Paulo. His aggressive style provoked a division of the government party and led to the formation of a separate Liberal Alliance, which subsequently became the Partido do Frente Liberal (PFL—Liberal Front Party). This grouping gave its support to PMDB candidate Tancredo Neves, and secured the vice-presidential candidacy for José Sarney, until recently leader of the pro-government PDS. As a result, the college that was to elect the President changed from government to opposition control. Lacking other options, the military acquiesced in Neves's victory, achieved by a massive 300-vote majority in the 686-member college when voting took place on 15 January 1985. The transfer of power took place as scheduled on 15 March, but Neves, then 74 years old, required emergency surgical treatment on the eve of his accession. As a result, José Sarney was sworn in as Acting President. He assumed full presidential powers after Neves's death in April.

THE RETURN TO DEMOCRACY, 1985

Brazil returned to competitive liberal democracy in challenging circumstances. Economic growth was faltering as inflation spiralled far beyond the levels it had reached when the military intervened in 1964. Socially, the strains of rapid industrialization and urbanization over previous decades had been exacerbated by the sharp worsening of income distribution over the period of military rule, leading to growing malnutrition and absolute poverty in urban and rural areas alike. Amid a general recognition of the need for political and social reform and economic redistribution on a substantial scale, civilian politicians were under pressure to address a range of issues which had been neglected during the period of military rule. Initial suspicion arising from Sarney's recent links with the armed forces limited his popular appeal, and his relations with the dominant PMDB proved to be difficult. However, he pledged himself to implement the programme which Neves had proposed and reached a peak of popularity in 1986, as a consequence of the temporary success of the Cruzado Plan, an anti-inflation programme announced in February. The election, in November, of the National Congress as a Constituent Assembly marked the first stage in the transition to the adoption of a new constitution and a full return to democracy. The November election also marked a zenith for the PMDB, which won 22 of the 23 state governorships and majorities in both Houses of Congress.

However, the apparent economic and political success of the transition to democracy proved short-lived. The key measures of the Cruzado Plan were abandoned immediately after the congressional elections, and it collapsed altogether in early 1987. Debates over the new constitution were dominated by rivalry between the President and Congress, and conflict over the extent to which commitments to social reform should be written into the document. Part of the problem lay in the changed character of the once reformist PMDB. Over the period since its establishment as the leading opposition force in the 1970s, it had attracted the support of successive groups of conservatives abandoning the military as their prospects faded, and it was no longer a party committed to genuine reform. A new Constitution was finally passed on 6 October 1988. It provided for a five-year presidential term and adopted a conservative stance with regard to land reform in particular. The PMDB split in late 1989, with many of its founders moving into a new social democratic party, the Partido da Social Democracia Brasileira (PSDB—Brazilian Social Democracy Party), including former professor of sociology, political exile and São Paulo senator Fernando Henrique Cardoso. Signs of a serious challenge from the left emerged in the municipal elections of November 1988, in which Lula da Silva's hitherto small PT won control of São Paulo and 35 other major towns and cities across the country, while Brizola's PDT was successful in Rio de Janeiro.

THE RISE AND FALL OF COLLOR DE MELLO

With the first direct presidential election for three decades only a year away, and the Government in disarray, the Governor of the small north-eastern State of Alagoas, Fernando Collor de Mello, announced his candidacy for the presidency at the head of the tiny Partido de Reconstrução Nacional (PRN—Party of National Reconstruction). Presenting himself as a reforming outsider and strongly backed by the media, he emerged late in the campaign as the most credible challenger to the more radical trio of da Silva, Brizola and Mário Covas (candidate for the PSDB). In the first round of voting, held on 15 November 1989, Collor de Mello took 29% of the votes cast to Lula's 16%, with Brizola (only a fraction behind da Silva) and all other candidates eliminated. In the second round of the elections, just over one month later, Collor de Mello defeated da Silva's late challenge to win the presidency with 53% of the valid votes cast.

President Collor de Mello soon introduced a radical reform programme aimed at reducing public employment, lowering government expenditure and liberalizing the economy. Among the more dramatic measures that emerged in this period were a programme of radical trade liberalization, the temporary suspension of bank accounts, intensified privatization and a reduction in public investment. At the same time, Brazil, in conjunction with Argentina, Paraguay and Uruguay, began to establish the free-trade zone known as Mercosul (Mercado Comum do Sul or, in Spanish, Mercado Común del Sur—Mercosur), the completion of which was scheduled for the beginning of 1995. However, the initial results of these reforms were disappointing, with a sharp recession in 1990 followed by a resumption of inflation in 1991. Collor de Mello replaced the whole of his economic team as a result, but found his popularity and congressional support dwindling, even after the poor performance of the left in the legislative elections of October 1990.

President Collor de Mello's position deteriorated further in 1992 as he failed to persuade the PSDB and other congressional parties to support a new reform programme. Then, the National Congress voted to bring forward a referendum (originally scheduled for September 1993) on changing to a parliamentary system of government. Most seriously, after a series of corruption scandals affecting his Government and causing ministerial resignations, in May his own brother, Pedro Collor de Mello, began a national campaign against the President's campaign manager and confidant, Paulo César Farias. The ensuing succession of corruption scandals soon involved the President himself and ultimately led to his downfall. After being suspended from office in September, after a senate inquiry into the charges of corruption against him, Collor de Mello resigned the presidency in December of the same year. The Vice-President, a relatively unknown politician from Minas Gerais, Itamar Augusto Cantiero Franco, became Acting President in September and was confirmed as President on 29 December.

THE TRANSITION TO DEMOCRACY IN CRISIS, 1993–94

With the coming of Itamar Franco to power, the crisis surrounding the attempted transition to democracy deepened further. A number of serious problems, some with deep historical roots, made decisive action imperative, but Franco lacked both the necessary political experience and the organized political support which would have made effective government possible. Inflation was continuing to worsen and was threatening to spiral entirely out of control. Economic growth, too, continued to falter, while levels of foreign investment dwindled as international confidence in the Brazilian economy fell further. On the political side, pressure was already mounting for reform of the indecisive 1988 Constitution, while public discontent with politicians in general, fuelled by the diet of scandal and corruption from the Collor de Mello presidency, brought the future of the transition into question. Most seriously, Brazil's party political system, chronically weak and prone to fragmentation throughout the republican period, appeared once again to be in terminal decline. No party was able to elect a President, to provide majority support in the National Congress for the resulting administration and to exert sufficient authority over powerful élites to achieve either economic stability or social reform. In addition, the successive failure of Sarney and Collor de Mello, and the numerous political and economic stabilization programmes which they had started and abandoned, had created intense scepticism among Brazilian citizens. With the fund of goodwill with which the Sarney Government had embarked upon the transition now entirely exhausted, the new Government found it far harder to establish its credibility than its predecessors had done. These difficulties combined to make the situation of the Franco Government and the political system as a whole extremely precarious by the beginning of 1994.

Economic affairs were dominated by the effort to introduce a credible programme of economic adjustment backed by fiscal reforms. There was an urgent need to dramatically reduce inflation, restore growth, balance the budget and address the pressing problem of the steadily worsening distribution of income. Fernando Henrique Cardoso (Minister of Finance, May 1993–March 1994), therefore, sought repeatedly but largely unsuccessfully to introduce a series of wide-ranging structural reforms to the fiscal system. By early 1994 he had succeeded in introducing a limited fiscal reform package incorporating selected expenditure reductions and the introduction of a Social Emergency Fund. The latter removed from state and local governments resources which had previously represented valuable political patronage, and instead put them under the control of the federal Government for designated social spending. In this way at least a degree of progress was made in addressing some of the structural problems underlying the federal Government's ongoing fiscal crisis. However, the compulsory transfer of large resources from the federal to the state and local governments remained a serious, and constitutionally embedded, obstacle to the achievement of a balanced budget. At the same time, the introduction of a new transitional accounting unit (Unidade Real da Valor—URV), at parity with the US dollar, from 1 March 1994, alongside the existing currency, prepared the way for the introduction of a new currency in July.

THE PRESIDENTIAL ELECTION AND THE REAL PLAN, 1994

With the Government weak and the National Congress discredited, the immediate beneficiaries were da Silva and the PT. During the first part of 1994 da Silva himself soon emerged as the leading contender of the left in the approaching presidential elections. A consensus eventually emerged in government, business and army circles in favour of the centrist Minister of Finance, Cardoso. He was untainted by any suggestion of corruption and was perceived to be sincerely committed to economic stability and social reform. He resigned as Minister of Finance some six months before the elections, in order to be eligible, and duly announced his candidacy shortly thereafter, although he continued to trail behind da Silva in the opinion polls.

The final stages of the Franco presidency were dominated by the long-awaited and much-postponed programme of economic reform, the centrepiece of which was the introduction, on 1 July 1994, of a new currency, the real, pegged to the US dollar. The reform measures, known as the Real Plan, immediately became the object of the hostility of the PT, which argued that it would lead to the impoverishment of workers already suffering the consequences of high inflation and failing public services. However, the initial impact of the Real Plan appeared broadly positive as inflation was dramatically reduced, the real incomes of poorer groups rose and consumer purchasing power increased. In association with these developments, real economic growth reached a relatively healthy 6.0% in 1994. The continuing restraint of inflation meant that by August Cardoso was the leading candidate, according to opinion polls.

By the time of the election on 3 October 1994, Cardoso's popularity was such that he won the presidency without the need to proceed to a second ballot, gaining 54.3% of the valid votes cast. Da Silva only gained 27.0% of the valid votes cast. The election of Cardoso appeared to demonstrate that Brazilian voters had opted for a path of moderate reform rather than radical change or conservative reaction. However, as the first term of the Cardoso presidency was to prove, even moderate reform appeared, at times, to be beyond the reach of the new administration.

CARDOSO'S FIRST TERM, 1995–98

When President Cardoso assumed office on 1 January 1995 he had committed himself to a series of key constitutional reforms, aimed at accelerating the modernization of the economic and social fabric and overcoming the federal Government's fiscal crisis. The principal reforms envisaged were: an end to state monopolies in petroleum and telecommunications; the allowance of foreign investment in mining and hydroelectric projects; a reform of the civil service, encompassing reorganization and changes in pay and conditions of service; a major overhaul of the social-security system involving the setting of an upper limit on benefits, an end to early retirement for certain groups and the unification of previously disparate pension schemes; fundamental alterations to the federal Government's taxation and budgetary regimes involving a broadening of the tax base and a reduction in transfers to state and municipal governments; an increased emphasis on achieving a more even pattern of landholding in rural areas.

The newly elected President achieved some initial success with his proposed reforms with the approval, in February–March 1995, of constitutional changes terminating state monopolies and permitting foreign investment in the industries mentioned above. In addition, the programme of economic liberalization was given impetus by the full implementation of the Mercosul free-trade area on 1 January 1995. However, the momentum established at the beginning of 1995 did not continue as the reform programme encountered a number of obstacles during 1996 and 1997. In particular, as had long been the case, the Government found it very difficult to exercise control over the budget deficit. The constitutionally mandated transfers of funds between the federal Government and the state and municipal governments led to a weakening of the federal Government's fiscal position as expenditures expanded. Slow progress on the reform of the civil service and the social-security system meant that other major items of expenditure could not be reduced in compensation. Other important structural-reform programmes also ran into difficulties as opposition mounted in the National Congress. In particular, much-needed reforms of the landholding system encountered difficulties as factions within the governing coalition exercised opposition. The lack of progress in this area resulted in a growing number of confrontations between landless farmers and landowners. Many of these confrontations became very violent, resulting in the loss of life.

The impasse in the reform programme was exacerbated by the existence of an ideological divide between the two main parties of the coalition: President Cardoso's social democratic PSDB and the conservative PFL. Even within the parties themselves, there was little internal cohesion, discipline or ideological coherence. The PSDB, for example, was, and continued to be, characterized by considerable divisions between its left wing, which tended to favour more radical social reform, and its centre, the approach of which was far more cautious. Frequently, these features produced a political culture in which party loyalty, ideology and co-operation with the presidency often tended to be subsumed by regional advocacy and the demands of special interest groups.

The first major test of the popularity of President Cardoso's Government came in October 1996 with the holding of municipal elections. Despite the efforts of the administration to renew its popular mandate, the performance of candidates from the government coalition parties was decidedly mixed. Although the parties gained some new mayors, the results of the elections hardly constituted a clear endorsement of the new Government. Perhaps the most disappointing outcome of the polls for the Government was the defeat of the PSDB candidate, José Serra, in the contest for the mayoralty of São Paulo. The winner of this key election, Celso Pitta, was heavily supported by the populist opposition politician, Paulo Salim Maluf of the Partido Progressista Brasileiro (PPB—Brazilian Progressive Party). At the time, Maluf's political victory appeared to strengthen his chances of standing for election to the presidency in 1998.

Despite the relatively slow pace of progress of the reform programme, the Government secured an important political victory in July 1997 with the approval of a constitutional amendment allowing the President, as well as state governors and mayors, to run for a second term in office. This important achievement was secured at a price, however, namely the increased power awarded to the non-PSDB members of the governing coalition. In order to pass the amendment, President Cardoso was forced to support Antônio Carlos Margalhães of the PFL and Michel Temer of the PMDB in their successful candidacies for the presidencies of the Federal Senate and Chamber of Deputies, respectively. The implications of this for the wider reform programme were not necessarily favourable, as PMDB and PFL politicians had tended to be among those most effective in delaying the passage of important legislation.

Although fiscal, social-security and administrative reforms remained delayed by the National Congress throughout 1996 and most of 1997, considerably more progress was made with the privatization and economic liberalization programmes. In May 1996 steps were taken towards the sale of the Brazilian electricity network, Centrais Elétricas Brasileiras, SA (ELETROBRAS).The privatization of the federal rail network, Rede Ferroviária Federal, SA (RFFSA), also began in 1996 and was completed the following year. Following a series of delays, the huge mining group, Companhia Vale do Rio Doce, SA (CVRD), was privatized in May 1997.

From 1997 onwards a series of other major privatizations occurred, many in the energy sector. By far the most significant privatization to date, however, was implemented in the telecommunications sector with the sale of the subsidiaries of Telecomunicaçoães Brasileiras, SA (Telebrás) in July 1998. The privatization of Telebrás was followed by a rapid liberalization of the sector, most notably the auctioning of concessions to operate mobile cellular telephone services. The Government also accelerated its attempts to privatize the state banking sector in the late 1990s, with the sale of Banco do Estado do Rio de Janeiro, SA (Banerj) in June 1997. More significantly, after substantial delays, the Government succeeded in privatizing the country's largest state bank, Banespa (Banco do Estado de São Paulo, SA), in November 2000. The sale of Banespa, to Banco Santander of Spain raised just over R $7,000m., far more than had been expected.

After a series of delays, in August 1997 legislation enabling the liberalization of the petroleum sector became law. In a radical departure, the new regulatory framework for the sector allowed the participation of foreign enterprises in the exploration for petroleum within Brazil. This clearly eroded the monopoly status which the state-owned Petróleo Brasileiro, SA (PETROBRAS), had enjoyed since its foundation in 1953. With the new legislation in place, a series of exploration concessions were auctioned off to both domestic and foreign bidders between 1998 and 2001.

Despite the achievements in economic policy described above, lack of progress on constitutional reform left unaddressed a series of lingering macroeconomic problems. In particular, the Brazilian economy remained unable to escape from its tendency to accumulate heavy internal and external deficits. In early 1995 the authorities were forced to raise tariffs and impose a stricter monetary policy, in an attempt to reduce the increasing trade deficit. As a consequence, economic growth declined. Following a relaxation in monetary policy, the economy continued to expand in 1996 and 1997 and the average annual rate of inflation declined significantly. However, despite an increasingly protectionist trade policy, the trade deficit continued to expand and the public-sector deficit remained constant.

The persistence of these deficits became an increasing source of concern to international investors in the first half of 1997. Following a series of financial and economic crises in several Asian economies in late 1997, international attention began to focus on the Brazilian economy, which, like its Asian counterparts, had accumulated a substantial current-account deficit. By October, serious doubts were being expressed in international financial markets as to the ability of the Brazilian Government to avoid a rapid, unplanned devaluation of the real. In order to maintain the valuation of the currency and avoid a resurgence of inflation, President Cardoso introduced a series of emergency measures intended to lower the budget deficit in November. At the same time, interest rates were rapidly raised and attempts were made to exercise control over the increasing trade deficit.

As a result of these measures the rate of economic expansion was much reduced in the early half of 1998. The atmosphere of urgency surrounding the implementation of the measures, did, however, have some favourable political effects. In underlining

the need for further progress on structural reform, the crisis induced notable advances in the passage of important legislation through the Chamber of Deputies. After an extraordinary session of the National Congress during January and February 1998, crucial social-security reforms were successfully enacted, while the Government's civil-service reforms were finally approved in March. By the beginning of August, a second term in office for Cardoso's Government appeared to be a foregone conclusion. However, international financial events during that month caused the Government considerable unease and demonstrated once again the vulnerability of Brazil's economy. The severe devaluation of the Russian rouble in mid-August destabilized international financial markets and prompted renewed concern amongst investors over the scale of Brazil's high external and fiscal deficits. As financial disruption increased world-wide, investors began to withdraw resources from Brazil in ever larger quantities, causing a sharp decline in international reserves and testing the Government's ability to defend the value of the real. In response to such pressure the Government was forced to raise interest rates, a politically unpopular step, particularly in light of the decline in economic activity.

By September 1998 Brazil was experiencing a period of economic crisis in which the sustainability of the Real Plan seemed increasingly in doubt. The political effects of this crisis, however, ultimately proved far from unfavourable for the Government. Emphasizing the technical competence of his economic-policy team and underlining the inexperience of the main opposition candidates, President Cardoso undertook an effective last-minute election campaign. In the presidential election held on 4 October Cardoso became the first President to be re-elected for a consecutive term in office, securing 53.1% of the valid votes cast, compared with 31.7% for his closest rival, Lula da Silva. The results of the legislative and gubernatorial elections, however, were not as favourable for Cardoso's PSDB. Although the governing coalition in the Chamber of Deputies secured 377 of the Chamber's 513 seats, the PSDB's 99 seats did not constitute a significant increase in the party's overall representation within the National Congress. In addition the elections did little to alter the fractious nature of congressional politics and the weak discipline within and between the pro-government parties. Moreover, the election of the populist anti-Cardoso state governors, Itamar Franco in Minas Gerais, Anthony Garotinho in Rio de Janeiro and Olívio Dutra in Rio Grande do Sul, provided focal points for increasingly vocal regional opposition to the federal government.

CARDOSO'S SECOND TERM, 1998–

Despite the generally favourable domestic and international reaction to President Cardoso's re-election, Brazil's economic situation continued to deteriorate in late 1998. The Government's problems worsened in late November following the resignation of Luís Carlos Mendonça de Barros, the Minister of Communications; his brother, José Roberto Mendonça de Barros, the Foreign Trade Secretary; and the President of the National Development Bank (Banco Nacional do Desenvolvimento Econômico e Social—BNDES), André Lara Resende. The resignation of these senior figures, who were close allies of the President, resulted from the exposure of a scandal involving illegal tape recordings of telephone conversations detailing their alleged attempts to influence the sale, to the private sector, of Telebrás in July 1998.

On 2 December 1998 the Chamber of Deputies voted to reject a significant government fiscal reform measure affecting public-employee pension contributions. The failure of this legislation increased concerns over the Government's ability to meet targets laid down by the International Monetary Fund (IMF) and led to further outflows of foreign capital. By January 1999 it became apparent that the exchange-rate policy pursued by the Government was becoming untenable. Moreover, in the same month former President Itamar Franco, the newly-elected Governor of Minas Gerais, declared that the state was defaulting on its debt to the federal Government, thus indirectly precipitating the devaluation of the real. The proposed reforms to Brazil's pension scheme, however, were finally endorsed in January, somewhat enhancing the prospects of President Cardoso's fiscal austerity programme. However, this achievement proved to be short-lived with the Supreme Court ruling key elements of the reforms unconstitutional in September 1999.

By the second week of January 1999, the drain of foreign exchange reserves had become significant. Faced with the imminent prospect of a complete depletion of reserves, on 13 January the Central Bank announced that the real was to float freely against the US dollar. Following the flotation, the real swiftly depreciated against the dollar and other major currencies. With the Real Plan apparently in ruins, one of its key architects, the Governor of the Central Bank, Gustavo Franco, resigned, to be replaced by Francisco Lopes. The crisis at the core of the Government's economic policy-making team intensified several days later when Lopes also resigned. Moreover, in May allegations emerged that Lopes had improperly assisted two troubled financial institutions whose balance sheets had been severely affected by the devaluation. However, the subsequent congressional investigation into his conduct in May and June only uncovered limited evidence of wrongdoing and exacted little damage on the Government. In an attempt to strengthen his administration against any further allegations of financial impropriety, President Cardoso undertook a reallocation of cabinet portfolios in July, appointing Clóvis Carvalho to the post of Minister for Development, Industry and Trade. However, Carvalho was replaced by Alcides Tápias, a former banker, in late 1999.

While the devaluation of the real did not affect the economy as severely as had been predicted, it did have the effect of galvanizing congressional opinion in favour of accelerating the fiscal and structural reform programme. In an important measure designed to reduce the recurrent deficits of the social security system, the National Congress finally approved the *Fator Previdenciário* in November 1999; this created a greater correspondence between social security contributions and payments. Furthermore, in April 2000 a Law of Fiscal Responsibility was approved by the Senate, establishing stricter regulations for the setting of state and municipal budgets. The introduction of legislation in this area was essential if the burden of fiscal adjustment was to be more evenly shared between all levels of government. Moreover, both the budgets for 2000 and 2001 were approved by the National Congress with minimal amendments. However, the Government has remained frustrated in its attempts to introduce comprehensive taxation reform.

Accelerated progress in the area of fiscal reform coincided with a number of political developments in early 2000. In January the Minister of Defence, Elcio Alvares, was dismissed by President Cardoso, allegedly as a result of a disagreement between himself and several other cabinet members; Alvares was replaced by the former Attorney-General, Geraldo Magela Quintão. In April the Minister of Justice, José Carlos Dias, resigned following a disagreement over a joint drugs-control programme with Bolivia. He was replaced by the former national secretary for human rights, José Gregori; and the following month the Minister for Sports and Tourism, Rafael Greca, was dismissed and replaced by PFL member, Carlos Melles. In mid-February, Cardoso's PSDB announced a new congressional alliance with the centrist PTB. This alliance further increased the divisions between the PSDB and its leading coalition partner in the National Congress, the centre-right PFL. Tensions between the two parties' worsened following accusations by a senior member of the PFL, Antônio Carlos Margalhães, that Cardoso was not taking a strong enough stand on corruption. In August the PTB announced that it was to dissolve its alliance with PSDB, thus re-establishing the PFL as the largest party in the Chamber of Deputies.

In late March 2000 the Mayor of São Paulo, Celso Pitta, was accused by his wife of bribing members of the city council to reject a move for his dismissal, proposed in 1997. (Pitta had been involved in a senate investigation into alleged fraudulent bond issues; he was subsequently found guilty of fraud, but remained in office pending an appeal.) It was later alleged that Pitta had received a substantial loan from a businessman in return for favourable treatment from his administration and Pitta was dismissed as Mayor. However, he was permitted to remain in office, pending a further appeal and, following a ruling in mid-June by the federal court of appeal, he was reinstated.

Municipal elections, held in October 2000, took place in all 26 states bar the Federal District, and represented a crucial test of the Government's popularity prior to the presidential election scheduled for October 2002. In 11 of Brazil's 62 most important municipalities, the governing coalition ceded control to opposition parties. In line with expectations, the opposition PT (Workers') Party performed relatively well, taking control of 17 cities, an increase on the five they already held. The PT secured its most significant gain in São Paulo, where its mayoral candidate, Marta Suplicy, was victorious. Overall, the PSDB obtained 15.9% of votes cast, the PMDB 15.7% of votes and the PT 14.1%.

The results of the municipal elections indicated a strong showing for the left-wing opposition. However, whether this would translate into a favourable performance in the presidential contest in 2002 remained uncertain. Two factors underpin this conclusion. Firstly, municipal elections, naturally enough, are generally fought on local issues, whereas in presidential contests national and international issues figure more strongly. Secondly, despite their recent gains, the left-wing parties are yet to produce a candidate with a sufficiently broad-based popularity to seriously threaten the putative candidates of the centre and centre-right, notably the PSDB's José Serra. However, in challenging the governing coalition, the left will be able to draw on a lingering popular dissatisfaction with standards in public life.

Throughout 2000 and 2001 the Government has been embroiled in an extensive scandal involving allegations of embezzlement and corruption at a senior levels. According to allegations which emerged in early 2000, a former presidential adviser, Eduardo Jorge Caldas Pereira, a prominent senator, Luiz Estevão, and a federal judge, Nicolau dos Santos Neto, were among the participants in a scheme to divert some R $170m. in public funds destined for the construction of a courthouse in São Paulo. Immediately following the accusations, Estevão was expelled from the National Congress while dos Santos Neto went into hiding. Following dos Santos Neto's arrest in early 2001, it was feared that his impending trial could cause the Government further embarrassment. In particular, there fears were expressed that further formal investigation could substantiate suggestions that a culture tolerant of corruption had embedded itself at senior levels of government. Indeed, further evidence of high-level corruption emerged in November 2000 following the publication of a report on organized drugs-trafficking and crime in Brazil, implicating a number of state deputies and mayors, as well as individuals in the National Congress, the judiciary and the armed forces.

Among its other effects, the eruption of the São Paulo courthouse scandal added fresh impetus to Margalhães' long-running campaign against sleaze in government. Throughout the second half of 2000, Margalhães attempted unsuccessfully to force the Government into undertaking a broad congressional investigation into corruption. Having, thus far, failed in that endeavour, in February 2001 Margalhães turned his attention to the election of the Presidents of the Senate and the Chamber of Deputies, alleging that his possible successor as senate leader, the President of the PMDB, Jader Barbalho, was involved in corrupt activities. Following Barbalho's election ion 14 February, Margalhães increased his attacks on the Government, provoking President Cardoso to dismiss, nine days later, two PFL ministers, Rodolpho Tourinho (Minister for Mines and Energy) and Waldeck Ornélas (Minister for Social Security and Assistance), on the grounds that they had not defended the Government against Margalhães' allegations. They were replaced, in March, by José Jorge and Roberto Brant, respectively. The President of the PSDB, Aécio Neves, was elected President of the Chamber of Deputies. In April the release of telephone transcripts secretly recorded by the police investigating the disappearance of some US $830m. from an Amazonian development company, Sudam, caused further embarrassment to the ruling coalition (particularly to Barbalho, who was personally connected to the development company). Despite his attempts to expose corruption in government, Margalhães himself became involved in allegations of impropriety. Following a congressional investigation it emerged that Margalhães may have improperly instigated the disclosure of confidential computerized voting records relating to the Senate's expulsion of Luiz Estevão. Initially denying the claims of investigators, Margalhães resigned his seat in the Senate in May. In the same month the Minister for National Integration, Fernando Bezerra, resigned following allegations of bribery; it was believed that he had received funds from a development agency, Sudene, in return for favours. (Sudene was dissolved in early May, by President Cardoso, along with Sudam, on grounds of corruption.)

The controversy surrounding allegations of high-level sleaze and the departure of Margalhães both acted to stall the Government's ambitious legislative programme. In mid-2001 legislation aimed at reforming the tax and social security systems remained stalled in congressional committees. Moreover, the Government's hard-won reputation for competent economic management appeared to be coming under increasing strain. Between the end of 2000 and July 2001, the real significantly weakened against the US dollar and other major currencies, as a consequence of the economic crisis in Argentina, as well as the political disarray in Brazil. The resignation, in July, of the Minister of Development, Industry and Trade, Alcides Tápias, did little to help economic confidence. By mid-2001 signs had emerged that the weakening of the real had led to an increase in inflation, prompting the authorities to increase interest rates and lower growth forecasts. To add to the Government's difficulties, unusually low levels of rainfall had led to water levels in hydroelectric reservoirs falling to critically low levels. To prevent this problem from worsening, the authorities were forced to implement an emergency programme of energy conservation, which threatened to further reduce economic growth as well as adversely affect the Government's popularity. Thus, as Brazil entered the second half of 2001, the Government faced the serious challenge of trying to consolidate its considerable achievements against a background of political infighting and a deteriorating economy.

Economy

Dr GABRIEL PALMA

In the colonial period and in the first century of independence, Brazil experienced three successive export cycles. The first based on sugar, in the north-east around Recife and Salvador; the second based on gold and diamond mining, in what is now the central state of Minas Gerais; and the third, from the early 19th century onwards, based on coffee. Initially grown with the help of slave labour in the state of Rio de Janeiro, coffee production achieved its most dynamic expansion in the state of São Paulo after 1890, as European migrants, predominantly Italians, moved into the region in large numbers. It was only in the 1980s that coffee lost its place to soya beans as Brazil's leading agricultural export. Although there was spectacular expansion of rubber production in the Amazon region between 1890 and 1920 (brought to an abrupt halt by the establishment of plantations in South East Asia, from Brazilian stock), it did not prevent the shift in the centre of the Brazilian economy, from the northeast to the centre-south of the country. This was marked by the transfer of the capital from Bahia (now Salvador) to Rio de Janeiro in 1761, and by the emergence in the 20th century of São Paulo as the country's dominant industrial, financial and commercial centre.

The country's economy was dominated by the 'industrial triangle' of São Paulo–Rio de Janeiro–Belo Horizonte. This was in spite of the establishment of nuclei of development in the northeast and in the south, and increasing flows of investment into Amazonia. The cities and rural areas of the centre-south attracted a persistent flow of migrants from the impoverished and over-populated north-east, partly offset by a counter-flow from the south into Amazonia.

Although the country already had a significant manufacturing sector before the depression of the 1930s, the latter was a determining factor in the political élite finally abandoning the coffee-based export sector and turning decisively towards industrialization. For six decades thereafter, governments pursued a fairly successful state-led industrial development through often-unorthodox interventionist policies. As a result, Brazil emerged as a major industrial power in the developing world, and by the late 1980s it had become the 10th largest economy in the world.

Despite bouts of selective economic nationalism, foreign capital was generally welcomed into the manufacturing sector, beginning in particular in the 1950s. However, the state frequently insisted upon stringent requirements relating to the source of capital, the transfer of technology, and joint ventures (often with state, rather than private, capital). One of the key aims of reforms in the 1990s was to reverse this pattern of state-led development in favour of deregulation of the economy, financial and trade liberalization, and the integration with Argentina, Paraguay and Uruguay into a regional common market, Mercosul (Mercado Comum do Sul or, more familiarly, in Spanish, Mercosur—Southern Common Market).

A striking feature of state-led development was a massive building of productive capacity, particularly in the areas of energy, heavy industry and capital goods. As a consequence of this, and of Brazil's large internal market and abundant and extraordinarily varied natural resources, the country experienced rapid (though markedly cyclical) growth after the Second World War. Between 1947 and 1980, an average compound real rate of growth of output of 7% per year was achieved, placing Brazil in the East Asian, rather than in the Latin American 'growth league', during this period. As a result, domestic output increased nearly 10-fold in this 33-year period. However, the 1982 debt crisis not only brought this long period of rapid growth to an abrupt end, but also marked the permanent return of Brazil to the Latin American 'growth league', characterized by low and highly volatile economic performance.

After the 1982 crisis, Brazil experienced a severe recession, made more acute by rising inflation and heavy debt burden. Thus, between 1981 and 1983, Brazil's real gross domestic product (GDP) declined by some 6%; thereafter until the implementation of the Real Plan in 1994 (see below) it fluctuated between small increases and contractions. During the first months of the Plan, GDP accelerated rapidly, reaching a high of 10.4% in the first quarter of 1995 (all quarterly growth figures refer to rates *vis-à-vis* the same quarter in the previous year). The main growth stimulus was the expansionary effect of both the sudden disappearance of the 'inflationary tax', and the massive increase in foreign inflows.

This rapid expansion of aggregate demand soon proved unsustainable, owing to both external and internal constraints. The external factor was the so-called 'tequila effect', which followed the Mexican financial crisis of December 1994; this made the whole issue of Brazil's future access to international financial markets (the cornerstone of the new economic policies) much more uncertain. Internal constraints were, principally, the fact that the balance of payments and the public sector deficit had begun to deteriorate rapidly. The former was the result of increased expenditure and trade liberalization bringing about a rapid growth of imports; the latter was a result of the implementation of the Plan being characterized by a dramatic increase in public debt (especially that of the federal Government and Central Bank), mainly as a consequence of rigidities in public finances and high interest rates, which not only became a permanent feature of the Plan, but were also to remain higher than the growth of public revenues; this meant that the Government continuously was forced to 'capitalize' part of its interest payments (or borrow in order to be able to pay for its existing obligations). Furthermore, the Real Plan added indirectly to the stock of public debt, as a result of its association with a series of banking crises both in the private and public sectors, the first of which occurred in 1995. With mounting internal and external problems, the Government took a series of drastic measures in 1995 to ensure a sharp decline in the rate of growth of private expenditure, notably, a further increase in interest rates. These measures proved effective in the short term; between the first quarters of 1995 and 1996 GDP fell by some 12 percentage points. However, as a result of the effectiveness of these measures, the Government was deluded into believing that fiscal reforms were no longer urgent. Such an omission resulted thereafter in increased financial fragility, particularly in the banking system and the public sector.

Following such a decline in output growth (the economy entered into recession in the first quarter of 1996, with a quarterly figure of -1.4%), the Government began to ease monetary and fiscal conditions and the economy began to recover again, reaching a growth rate of 4.5% by the last quarter of 1996, to continue growing at nearly 4% during the first half of 1997. However the economy was then adversely affected by the East Asian financial crisis in July 1997 and by the devaluation of the Russian rouble in August 1998. As a result, the economy returned to recession in the second half of 1998. The Brazilian economy was more vulnerable to the Russian crisis than other economies owing to the financial fragility in both public and private sectors. The Government responded to the crisis by introducing further strict economic measures. The recession, and the general uncertainties prevailing both in the country and in international financial markets with regard to the Brazilian economy (in particular, the Government's ability to manage its finances, banking-sector fragility and the growing deficit in the balance of payments) were exacerbated by the declaration, in early 1999, by the Governor of Minas Gerais, former President Itamar Franco, that the state was defaulting on its debt to the federal Government. Although the amounts involved were low, it was feared that other State Governors (many of them belonging to opposition parties and with large central government debts) would follow suit. Such fears led to a massive withdrawal of funds from the Central Bank (about one-half of its total reserves) and the Government was forced to float the real on 13 January.

Most observers expected that, as a result of this devaluation and financial collapse, Brazil would enter into a period of acute recession, increased inflation and exchange-rate volatility. However, GDP increased by 0.8% in 1999 and this recovery continued in 2000, with the economy growing at 4.5% for the year as a whole. Furthermore, consumer prices increased by just 4.9% in 1999 and 7.0% in 2000. The real stabilized at a rate just under two reales per US dollar for the rest of the latter year, a relative stability that continued into 2000. The low inflationary effect of the devaluation was owing to several factors, not least the fact that the country was in recession in January 1999. Also, the speed at which Brazil recovered from the crisis was aided by the fact that the country's imports represented only 10% of GDP. Furthermore, the International Monetary Fund (IMF) had already agreed a rescue package for the country and, having learnt from the East Asia crisis, was prepared to be much more flexible in its terms. Finally, international financial markets did not panic as much as was initially feared.

With the exception of the 1994 Real Plan, attempts to halt periodically rampant inflation since the 1982 debt crisis experienced only brief success. With the rate of increase in consumer prices at over 200% per year when the military left power in 1985, it was then held at close to zero for nine months in 1986, following the implementation of President José Sarney's Cruzado Plan. Under this Plan the cruzeiro was replaced by a new currency, the cruzado, which was equivalent to 1,000 units of the old currency. Owing to balance of payment problems, by the late 1980s inflation accelerated rapidly again, reaching 1,900% in 1989. In March 1990, with an annual rate of inflation threatening to reach 5,000%, the new President, Fernando Collor de Mello, introduced the New Brazil programme or 'Collor Plan', which restored the cruzeiro as the national currency and implemented a set of measures that succeeded in reducing inflation to just under 3,000% for the year as a whole, and to 473% in 1991. However, following the collapse of the Collor Government in late 1992, inflation rose again, reaching some 2,500% in 1993. Following the successful implementation of the Real Plan in mid-1994, the annual rate of inflation decreased sharply, reaching 3.2% in 1998.

Despite the difficult economic problems left by the long period of military rule, this phase saw the completion of a process, which was already well under way before the 1964 coup. This was the emergence of Brazil as a major industrial world power. However, the legacy left by the military regimes to their civilian successors was a very complex one, and not only because of the high rates of inflation and levels of foreign debt. When the military departed from government it also left what proved to be a weak and ineffective institutional setting, a culture of political and economic corruption, and an extraordinary level of inequality—if Brazil's economy had significantly improved during the military rule, the lot of the majority of its people certainly had not. All these, as well as the legacy of the debt crisis, rendered Cardoso's attempt at reform and economic liberalization, at best, a particularly difficult process.

DEREGULATION, PRIVATIZATION AND REGIONAL INTEGRATION

The post-1982 debt crisis and recession placed the model of state-led development under considerable strain, not just in Brazil but throughout Latin America. In Brazil, this was compounded by the economic and political difficulties of the transition to democracy. This was characterized by a profound move towards trade and financial liberalization, wholesale privatization and market deregulation. Brazil's economic reforms actually began in March 1990, before the Real Plan, when the incoming President, Collor de Mello, announced the removal of subsidies for exports, and phased reductions in tariffs, as part of his Collor Plan. This was followed in 1991 by a large-scale privatization programme, the deregulation of the fuel market, and the announcement of the dissolution of the coffee and sugar trading boards. Despite the political weakness of Collor de Mello's short presidency and its unsure handling of macroeconomic policy, the initiatives it launched permanently changed the direction of Brazilian economic development. Tariffs were set to halve in three years, with no tariff exceeding 35% by the end of that period. Of equal moment was the commitment to remove the cumbersome system of import licensing.

The programme of privatization was initially intended to raise US $18,000m. from the disposal of 27 state companies. Privatization eventually began in October, with the sale of the USIMINAS (Usinas Siderúrgicas de Minas Gerais, SA) steel mill. Although the sale raised $1,200m., this was an unusual privatization in that other state companies bought large stakes in it (especially CVRD—Companhia Vale do Rio Doce, SA, and the pension fund of the state-owned Banco do Brasil) and only 6% of the shares on offer were bought by foreign investors. Also, the sale allowed SIDERBRÁS (Siderúrgia Brasileira, SA), a holding company that previously owned a large share of USIMINAS, to redeem a significant proportion of its public debt. Over the following months further privatizations took place in smaller concerns, but receipts tended to fall far short of the target. Privatization receipts totalled $1,600m. in 1991, reached $2,600m. in 1993 and fell thereafter to a mere $910m. in 1995. From that year onwards the Government of President Fernando Henrique Cardoso gave a further impetus to the privatization process, which resulted in receipts reaching $3,700m. In the first half of 1997 two privatizations doubled the receipts from 1996: these were the sale of 40% of CVRD for $3,200m. and the sale of concessions for cellular telephones for about $4,000m. This process increased rapidly in 1998, particularly owing to the sale of about 20% of the state telecommunications company, Telebrás (Telecommuincações Brasileiras, SA) for $19,000m.

A related policy initiative of the Collor Government was the creation in March 1991 of Mercosul. Trade between Brazil and Argentina grew by 45% in the first year alone; in all, exports to Argentina grew more than four-fold between 1991 and 1998, and imports from Argentina five-fold. In 1998 17% of exports (and about one-quarter of manufactured exports) and 16% of imports were with Mercosul countries. However, the economic problems of Brazil and Argentina raised doubts as to whether the harmonization of tariffs and economic integration could be sustained. In fact, intra-Mercosul trade, after having grown by 20% in 1997, fell by 3% with the worsening economic situation of 1998, and by 24% in 1999; although this trade recovered in 2000 (by about 16%.), it fell again in the first half of 2001.

In 1992 escalating corruption charges and a series of private scandals led to the resignation of President Collor de Mello. His deputy, Itamar Franco, became President in December. Economic policy continued very much unchanged during the first year of President Franco's Government, with its principal objectives being the liberalization of most prices, control over public expenditure and a strict monetary policy through high interest rates (the average real lending interest rate for the year reached 197%). In May 1993, after several changes of finance minister, President Franco appointed Senator Fernando Henrique Cardoso to the position. Together with a group of highly skilled economists, including Edgar Bacha and Pedro Malan, Cardoso devised the all-encompassing Real Plan, which began operations on 1 July 1994 (named after the new currency, which it introduced, the real). The main characteristic of this new Plan was that, as opposed to most of its predecessors, it intended to avoid 'shock treatments', price freezes or surprise announcements. It attempted to reduce prices by three interconnected means: firstly, by reducing inflationary expectations, principally through the fixing of the real to the US dollar, at a rate of one real to the dollar (but, crucially, not rigidly 'pegged' to the dollar, as in Argentina); secondly, by reducing inflationary 'inertia' by dismantling a complex system of indexation; and, thirdly, through the progressive achievement of an internal and external macroeconomic equilibrium. The Plan acquired an overwhelming degree of consensus and public support. Its initial successes in mid-1994 helped Cardoso's campaign for the presidency, to which he was elected in October of that year.

AGRICULTURE

Agriculture (including hunting, forestry and fishing) employed 21.9% of the total labour force in 1999, compared to more than 30% in 1980. The sector accounted for 7.9% of GDP and 27% of exports (including processed foods, like orange juice) in 1999 (compared to 71% of exports in 1970). Sectoral growth was highly volatile through the 1980s and early 1990s, but expanded consistently at the end of the decade: in 1997 it expanded by 2.7%, by 0.2% in 1998, by 7.5% in 1999 and by 1.9% in 2000. Nevertheless, so far the sector has failed to respond to the challenge of generating foreign exchange following the economic crisis and devaluation of January 1999.

The new pattern of growth was supposed to recover the role of agriculture as a substantial source of foreign exchange. Emphasis was given to large-scale commercial farming and to export crops. However, not only did these exports perform badly, but also food production for the internal market suffered, with many thousands of peasants and small farmers being forced from their land. Annual coffee production fluctuated widely in the late 1980s, between 2m. and 4.4m. metric tons (in dry cherries, of which about one-half is actual green coffee beans); from 1989 to 1991 the crop levelled to some 3m. tons per year, and then declined by some 17% between 1991 and 1994. Output fell again in 1995, to just 1.9m. tons, increased in 1996 to 2.6m. tons, fell to 2.4m. tons in 1997, expanded significantly in to 3.4m. tons in 1998, and stayed at this level in 1999 and 2000 (3.3m. tons and 3.6m. tons, respectively). In 1998 exports of coffee beans amounted to US $2,400m., $2,230m. in 1999 and $1,560m. in 2000 (less than 3% of total exports).

In the mid-1980s soya beans (soybeans) rivalled coffee as Brazil's leading agricultural export. By 1990, partly as a result of dramatically decreasing coffee prices, soya earnings were more than double those from coffee. The harvest rose from 15m. metric tons in 1980, to 24m. tons in 1989. Thereafter, however, the crop fell as low as 15m. tons in 1991, before recovering in the mid-1990s. Soya-bean production stood at 32.7m. in 2000. The harvested area in 2000 was more than 10 times larger than that in 1970. There were also spectacular increases in sugar-cane harvests during the 1980s, with production increasing from 103m. metric tons in 1976, when the alcohol programme (see Petroleum and Ethanol, below) was introduced, rising fairly steadily to reach 345.3m. tons in 1998, before falling slightly to 337.2m. tons in 1999, and to 24.7m. tons in 2000. The harvested area in 2000 was almost twice that of 1976.

Orange juice established itself as Brazil's third most important agricultural export in 1984, as a result of increased production (which had doubled since 1979) and rising prices (as a consequence of frosts in Florida, USA). Output of oranges increased from 17m. metric tons in 1994 to 23m. tons in 1999 and 2000. Banana production grew steadily in the 1980s and more erratically in the 1990s, from 4.5m. metric tons in 1990 to 6.1m. tons in 1997; output fell to 5.6m. tons in 1998, but increased again to over 6m. tons in 1999.

The bias towards exports had adverse effects on domestic food supplies, as areas hitherto devoted to food crops diverted production, and many trade restrictions over food imports remained in place. Between 1965 and 1985 the area under cultivation for basic grains increased by 30%, while that for sugar cane, oranges and soya beans tripled. According to some estimates, food output per head actually declined in the period 1965–85, and stagnated thereafter. Production of paddy rice reached a peak of 9.6m. metric tons in 1976, a figure not surpassed until the mid-1980s; production decreased again in the late mid-1990s, but increased to 11.8m. tons in 1999 and 11.2m. tons in 2000. In 2000 the harvested area of rice was just under one-half that of 1980, but output was about one-third greater. Production of beans (the other staple crop) had increased only slightly from the levels of the early 1970s, but decreased from the mid-1990s, reaching 3.0m. tons in 2000. Production of maize (corn) remained fairly stable for most of the 1980s, at around 20m. metric tons per year, before rising sharply to 26.6m. tons in 1989. Production fluctuated in the 1990s, and stood at 32m. metric tons in 1999 and 2000. Wheat, once heavily subsidized, recovered from a poor harvest of less than 2m. metric tons in 1984, but declined subsequently to a low of 1.5m. tons in 1995, obviously finding it difficult to compete with new Argentine Mercosul imports. However, output then doubled in 1996, to 3.4m. tons, before falling again thereafter: in 2000 wheat output was 1.9m. tons. The area harvested in 2000 was less than one-half that of 1980.

MINING

Although mining (including quarrying) accounted overall for only a small proportion of Brazil's GDP (1.6% in 1999), it was important to exports and to industrial production. In 1996–1998 it was the most dynamic sector of the Brazilian economy, growing by 6%, 4.8%, and 8%, respectively. In 1999 Brazil produced iron ore with 114m. metric tons of iron content and was by far the world's largest exporter. Exports of iron ore averaged 80m. tons per year in the early 1980s and passed the 100m. tons mark in 1986. In 1997 exports of iron ore and concentrates reached US $2,2,846m. Exports increased by 14.3% in 1998, but decreased by 15.6% in 1999. The bulk of iron-ore exports traditionally came from the 'iron quadrangle', in Minas Gerais, from the Brazilian mining groups Mineracões Brasileiras Reunidas, SA (MBR) and CVRD, the latter being the largest iron-ore producing and exporting company in the world. By the 1990s deposits in the hitherto inaccessible Amazon State of Pará, were reached by road and rail and were supplied with electricity from the Tucuruí hydroelectric power-station (see Power, below). By 1999 they provided about one-quarter of national production.

Brazil is also a significant producer of manganese, with output of 770,000 metric tons in 1999, and of tin, where rapid expansion took total output from 20,000 tons in 1984 to a peak of some 50,000 tons in 1989, before decreasing again to 13,202 tons in 1999. In addition, the country is a large exporter of gold, although production is difficult to estimate, as about two-thirds comes from independent prospectors (*garimpeiros*) in frontier areas, where conflict with native Indian (Amerindian) inhabitants is frequent and violent. Official estimates put output at 40,943 kg in 1999. Brazil has 1,600m. tons of bauxite reserves, of between 40% and 50% purity, largely in Minas Gerais and the Amazon region. Annual output rose to around 10m. tons in the 1980s, but stagnated around that level in the 1990s (reaching 12.9m. tons in 1999).

POWER

In the mid-1990s Brazil exploited only about one-quarter of its potential for the generation of hydroelectric power. Even so, power from this source met about 95% of the country's total electricity needs. The major increase in total capacity from the late 1980s stemmed from two significant developments in 1984: the entry into operation of the first turbines at the Itaipú hydroelectricity complex on the Paraguayan border (expected to produce as much as 35% of Brazil's total electricity requirements when fully operational); and the opening of the Tucuruí plant, on the Tocantins river, in the Amazon region. The former plant provided additional generating capacity of about 12,000 MW to the national grid by the early 1990s, to the benefit, primarily, of the centre-south of the country; the latter, capable of supplying some 2,000 MW, served the mining and processing operations centred on the Carajás region. In all, the production of electricity by hydroelectric generation in 1999 was well over 50 times that of 1980. Moreover, it was announced in late 2000 that plans were underway to further expand the hydroelectric power-station at Itaipú, increasing its generating capacity to 14,000 MW. However, a recent drought and lack of new investment has threatened substantially to reduce the production of this type of electricity in 2001; to compensate for this, and avoid rolling blackouts, in June 2001 the Government implemented a six-month rationing system in an attempt to reduced consumption by 20%. Initial reports indicated that the energy-saving measures were successful; however, the Government warned that planned power cuts could occur throughout the remainder of the year, depending on levels of rainfall, as well as on the continued successful implementation of the rationing system.

The nuclear-power industry in Brazil has a troubled history and has been an extraordinarily expensive and unsuccessful experiment. The nuclear plant Angra I, which began production in 1985 after a series of technical problems and delays, had to be closed down almost immediately after for safety reasons. It was again closed for several months in 1987, because of generating difficulties, and has operated only intermittently thereafter, and at very low capacity (often below 10%). Financial constraints hindered the completion of Angra II, which became operational in mid-2000. However, as a result of the recent problems in the hydroelectric sector, and following the decision in May 2001 by the new US administration of George W. Bush to build the first nuclear plants in the USA since the 1970s, the Cardoso Government gave strong indications in mid-2001 that it was planning to invest in a further plant, Angra III. In 1988 the supervisory Higher Council for Nuclear Policy, the Conselho Superior de Política Nuclear, was created and Nucleares Brasileiras (NUCLEBRÁS) was dissolved; the management and development of nuclear-power plants was transferred to the electricity sector, principally to the state electricity concern, ELETROBRÁS (Centrais Elétricas Brasileiras, SA).

PETROLEUM AND ETHANOL

In the early 1980s Brazil's petroleum sector underwent a transformation of momentous consequence. The first advance was a doubling of domestic production, as a result of the discovery and development of the Campos oilfield, off shore from the state of Rio de Janeiro. The second factor was a massive programme to reduce oil imports via its substitution by alcohol, through the production of ethanol derived from sugar cane. The combination of these two factors, as well as falling petroleum prices, during a period in which demand was stable or even declining, resulted in a decrease in the share of imports accounted for by petroleum (and lubricants), from over 50% in 1979 to 20% in 1986, and just 7% in 1998. In 1999 its share increased marginally to nearly 9% and was expected to continue this slight expansion in 2000. As Brazil met about 80% of its domestic petroleum requirements, the dramatic oil price increase in early 2000 had little effect on imports.

After years in which PETROBRÁS (Petróleo Brasileiro, SA) had invested heavily in a largely fruitless search for petroleum, in 1974 the first strike was made in the Campos field. At that time domestic production was about 175,000 barrels per day (b/d). In 1981 production was 220,000 b/d and, in the following year, the Campos field came 'on stream'. As a consequence, production averaged 593,000 b/d by 1986 and rose further in the rest of the decade. In the early 1990s record levels of production, of over 700,000 b/d, were achieved, placing Brazil third among regional producers, after Mexico and Venezuela. Production continued to increase thereafter and in 1999, as part of plans to reorganize and modernize the company, it was announced that PETROBRÁS would be transformed into a regional, rather than just a national, entity, with a new mixed-ownership structure (although the state would permanently retain a clear dominant control). One of the first components of

the modernization project was a US $1,000m. scheme to improve safety following two major oil spills. As such, the Government's plans for the petroleum industry seemed to differ from those for other industries where there was previous state involvement, and one in which outright privatization was explicitly ruled out. In addition to petroleum, Brazil produced 11,855m. cu m. of natural gas in 1999.

The controversial ethanol programme dated from the founding of PROALCOOL in 1976. From that time thousands of hectares were planted with sugar cane, more than 400 processing plants were constructed and a capacity of 160m. hectolitres of ethanol production per year were achieved. The macroeconomic and environmental benefits of this programme have always been disputed. Soon after the beginning of the programme a 20% ethanol content in fuel oil was mandatory and, in the mid-1980s, the automobile and truck industries in Brazil changed the bulk of their production to engines that burnt either 'gasahol' or 100% ethanol. By 1986 more than 50% of fuel oil consumption was of ethanol and production was approaching 120m. hectolitres but, as a result of rapidly falling petroleum prices, the production cost of hydrated alcohol reached a level twice that of imported petroleum. The removal of most subsidies and price controls in 1990 was followed in 1991 by the closure of 67 of the units producing ethanol. Thereafter, production continued to decline as demand fell away, placing the future of the whole programme in doubt. However, the sharp increase in the price of petroleum at the end of the 1990s brought a new lease of life to this industry.

MANUFACTURING

According to official figures, in 1999 manufacturing employed 10.4% of the labour force, compared to 18% in 1980. In terms of output, this sector was responsible for 20.4% of GDP in 1999, compared to 25% in 1990 and 31% in 1982. Despite this rapid 'de-industrialization' process, the industrial structure of the country was still remarkably diverse, and this was fully reflected in the breadth of the manufacturing sector. A particular feature was the depth of the manufacturing capacity ancillary to primary commodities, mining and power sectors. As noted above, a substantial proportion of sugar cane was utilized for the production of ethanol. In the mining sector, a significant proportion of iron ore was processed before export. Steel production reached a temporary high in 1988 of 25m. metric tons (when Brazil was responsible for nearly 60% of all steel produced in Latin America), with more than one-half of it being exported. World over-supply, falling prices and US restrictions to Brazilian steel imports led to a decrease in production and exports. Steel production recovered in the mid-1990s, and by 1999 remained at the same level as in 1988. Moreover, the country was largely self-sufficient in the areas of hydroelectricity and transmission systems, producing many of its own turbines, generators, transformers and reactors. Increasing competitiveness in deep-sea petroleum exploration and extraction won PETROBRÁS substantial contracts to provide drilling platforms and other equipment for Middle Eastern and other oilfields. Industrialized inputs into agriculture came increasingly from the domestic chemicals sector. The vehicle industry supplied tractors for the extensive internal market. Links with the primary sector thus played an important part in Brazil's advanced manufacturing base.

A second source of stimulus to the sector was the demand coming from a large internal market. Here, the vehicle and components industry played a key role. Rapid expansion of the passenger motor vehicle sector in the 1960s and 1970s, following the entry of European and then US manufacturers, resulted in production levels in Brazil of about 1m. vehicles per year by the end of the 1970s. The recession that began in 1982 adversely affected this sector, reducing domestic demand by 40%. Production recovered to 1.3m. units in 1994, and increased to 1.7m. in 1997, before falling sharply to 1.1m. in 1999. However, some of the large foreign investments in the country in the 1990s were intended to modernize and enlarge this sector; therefore, it is expected that output would increase again in the future.

Partial trade liberalization had a double-edged effect on the vehicle industry. On the one hand, imports increased very rapidly, from 26,000 units in 1992, to 300,000 units in the first six months of 1995. As a result, imports, which represented only 3% of apparent car consumption in 1991, increased to well over one-third in 1995. In terms of value, imports of passenger motor cars grew nearly nine-fold in only six years, from US $358m. in 1989 to over $3,000m. in 1995; however, there was a sharp decrease in this figure in 1996, to $1,600m., following an increase in tariffs for non-Mercosul imports and the introduction of stricter monetary policy. This figure increased again in 1997 and 1998, to about $2,500m., but then fell again in 1999, to just $1,200m. On the other hand, exports also increased very rapidly, albeit erratically, mainly owing to the depressed state of the internal market, increased foreign investment, the development of Mercosul, and some improvement in output quality (a long-standing problem for Brazilian exports). Exports of passenger vehicles increased by 41% in 1996, by 136% in 1997 and by 11% in 1998. However, these exports declined by nearly 33% in 1999 before recovering in 2000, when they reached US $1,450m. between January and October.

The rising proportion of exports from the manufacturing sector was an indicator of the strength and some degree of sophistication of industrial production. In addition to the exports of cars, trucks and buses, Brazil exported passenger jet aircraft (particularly the quiet and economical Bandeirante) and military aircraft (such as the trainer aeroplane, the Tucano). The state-owned EMBRAER (Empresa Brasileira de Aeronáutica, SA) developed a range of models for export and engaged in joint ventures, in the civilian and military fields, with a number of foreign governments and corporations. Exports of these products reached US $2,535m. between January and October 2000.

The recession experienced by Brazil in the early 1980s severely affected the industrial sector. The crisis was exacerbated by sharp reductions in state investment, historically important in all areas and central to the development of the capital-goods industry. However, overall manufacturing production recovered strongly in the middle years of the decade, as exports increased significantly, and then faltered and declined at the end of the 1980s. President Collor de Mello's reforms in March 1990 provoked a further sharp recession. In such periods the capital-goods sector was the most troubled, partly as a consequence of the energetic creation of forward capacity throughout the 1970s, often as a deliberately counter-cyclical policy on the part of the military authorities. In 1991 the depth of the crisis was indicated by a fall of 17% in the value of the average industrial wage. In 1992 manufacturing production fell again by 4.2%; by this time output was 8.3% lower than in 1980. Output recovered in each year between 1993 and 1997, but difficult conditions in 1998 and 1999 led to a contraction in the sector of 3.3% and 1.3%, respectively. Output recovered in 2000, with production in the third quarter reaching a level 5.2% higher than the same period in 1999.

However, this cyclical output performance in manufacturing was the average of very different dynamics within the sector; for example, while production of consumer durables grew by 32% between 1995 and 1997, production of capital goods decreased by 8%. These roles were reversed between 1997 and 1999, when the former not only declined, but did so at a much higher rate than the latter (27% and 9%, respectively). Partial trade liberalization, in a context of financial deregulation in an unstable environment, proved to be a major challenge for Brazil's manufacturing industry, the outcome of which still remained uncertain.

TRANSPORT INFRASTRUCTURE

One of the key characteristics of industrial policy in Brazil from the 1960s was its emphasis on road construction, as a stimulus to the domestic car and truck industry. This was the case even with regard to the opening up of the Amazon region and the agricultural frontier. In December 1999 Brazil had some 22.7m. road vehicles (excluding goods vehicles, motor cycles and mopeds) and there were about 1.7m. km of roads, just 9.5% of which were paved. In addition, there were some 28,056 km of railway line, much of which served the mining areas of Minas Gerais and Carajás. Rail projects for lines between the mining areas and the ports of Tubarao and São Luis accounted for the bulk of investment in the railways from the mid-1980s.

There are more than 40 deep-water ports, the largest being Santos, Rio de Janeiro, Paranguá, Recife and Vitória. Santos handles some 30m. metric tons of cargo per year, and important

new facilities have been developed for 'roll on-roll off' containers there. Brazil has the largest merchant fleet in Latin America. The River Amazon is navigable for 3,700 km, as far as Iquitos, in Peru; and ocean-going ships can reach as far as Manaus, 1,600 km upstream. On account of Brazil's size and the obstacles presented to other means of transport, by jungles, rivers and mountains, air travel is very important. There are about 1,500 airports and airstrips, of which 21 handle international flights, although the bulk of international traffic goes through São Paulo and Rio de Janeiro (each having two airports).

TOURISM

Tourism had the potential to become an important net source of foreign exchange for Brazil; however, earnings were not only tiny with respect to the extraordinary potential of a country such as Brazil, but were only a fraction of the expenditure in tourism by Brazilians abroad. It was obvious that with improved security for tourists (the rapidly growing crime rate in Brazil proved to be the main obstacle for the tourism industry), more investment in infrastructure, and better promotion, Brazil could significantly improve its tourist industry. In 1999 5.1m. tourists visited Brazil, but more than one-half came from other Mercosul countries and Chile. Receipts from tourism stood at US $3,994m. in the same year. Further development of the industry seemed to be one of the most obvious foreign-exchange targets of government policy, in view both of the attractions of the country, and the structural changes taking place in the world market for tourism, with emphasis being placed upon more 'exotic' locations. However, it seemed inevitable that unless the authorities made substantial improvements in law and order it was unlikely that tourist numbers would increase significantly in the near future.

ENVIRONMENTAL ISSUES

The environmental damage and ecological destruction in Brazil was a growing feature of Brazilian development in the 20th century, and of extreme significance from the 1970s. After 1964 the military obsession with 'occupying Amazonia' meshed with their 'developmentalism at any cost' mentality, hospitality to foreign capital and enthusiasm for large-scale projects. This resulted in a series of ill-advised road-building, farming and mining ventures, whose impact on the environment was severe and destructive. The worst of these were the Transamazonian Highway, the highly corrupt, heavily subsidized and economically unproductive ranching projects of the 1970s, the controversial project of the Tucuruí dam, and the promotion of energy-intensive aluminium production. By the end of the 1980s much of the ranching had been abandoned, but mining expanded considerably.

It was estimated at the beginning of the 1990s that on average as much as 200,000 sq. km of the Amazon rainforest were destroyed every year. In spite of the decline in large-scale ventures, the burning of rainforest for land clearance continued apace into the 1990s. This figure reached record levels at the beginning of 1998, owing to deliberate large-scale fires near the border with Venezuela (close to the Yanomani reserves) that became uncontrollable. Extensive logging for export and charcoal production, without which the Carajás iron-ore project would have been uneconomical, also continued into the 1990s. Furthermore, the conflict between an estimated 50,000 gold prospectors and 9,000 Yanomani Indians (the latter groups ravaged by new diseases brought by the miners) was accompanied by the equally insidious effects of the introduction into the Amazon river system of as many as 200 metric tons of mercury every year, from the process of gold production. These developments, along with the well-publicized conflicts between rubber-tappers and local warlords in the far north of the country, culminating in the death of union activist Chico Mendes in December 1988, led to the emergence of powerful local and international opposition movements. Following President Sarney's Government indecisive policies, alternately limiting Yanomani reserves and rejecting international pressure on nationalist-populistic grounds, then taking nominal measures to remove gold prospectors and to increase regulation of activities in the Amazon area, President Collor de Mello's administration adopted a more environmentalist outlook, appointing a renowned campaigner on ecological issues, José Lutzemberger, as Minister of the Environment. This was followed by the commencement of 'Operation Amazonia' in 1990, and Brazil's hosting of the UN Conference on Environment and Development, or 'Earth Summit', in 1992.

In spite of such spectacular initiatives and the related discussions on linking debt reduction to the creation of forest reserves, it remained the case that the Brazilian Government lacked the capacity and the will to monitor and control the activities of the hundreds of thousands of individuals pushed into the Amazon by poverty and the expansion of commercial farming elsewhere in Brazil. Moreover, Collor de Mello soon dismissed Lutzemberger from the Cabinet, following his attempt to introduce a comprehensive environmental development plan, opposed by the Government. Neither President Franco's nor President Cardoso's Governments proved any better in this respect. In the immediate future the ecological impact of Amazonian development probably depended more on international pressure on foreign investors and funding institutions, and the overall rhythm of economic activity, rather than on the efforts of future Brazilian Governments themselves.

INVESTMENT AND FINANCE

Throughout the period of Brazil's rapid industrial expansion, public-sector investment consistently surpassed private investment. Therefore, the reductions in state investment from the mid-1980s had a significant effect on the rate of expansion of productive capacity and the economy as a whole. In the second half of the 1980s public-sector companies were expected to be self-financing and, with foreign borrowing almost impossible, levels of investment inevitably fell substantially. Gross fixed capital formation in machinery and equipment (measured in constant 1990 prices) fell by 47% between 1980 and 1992. Total investment, in turn, decreased by one-third in that period. In terms of percentages of GDP, gross domestic investment fell from over 32% of GDP in 1980 to 21% in 1995, 20% in 1996 and 1997, 19.9% in 1998, and 18.9% in 1999.

The make up of this investment between the public and private sector changed sharply, with public investment all but disappearing. According to official figures for 1997 and 1998, while current expenditure by the public sector reached 20% of GDP, public expenditure by the federal Government in capital formation represented just above 1% of GDP. The corresponding figure for the various states and municipalities was 15% and 1.6%, respectively. As public expenditure in education and health also fell as a percentage of GDP, total public expenditure in physical and human capital fell from (the already low levels of) 11.4% in 1993 to just 7% in 1998. In 1999 these figures fell even more as a result of the urgent need to increase the primary surplus following the January devaluation and related financial crisis. This policy is bound to have a significant negative impact on Brazil's potential for long-term growth.

The finance of investment also changed significantly after 1980. In that year gross national savings financed 88% of investment, while foreign savings financed the remaining 12%. However, as foreign savings became more difficult to obtain following the 1982 debt crisis, until 1994 investment had to be fully financed with national savings. This picture changed abruptly with financial liberalization: the inflow of foreign savings increased from 0.3% of GDP in 1994 to 9% in 1997. This figure increased in the first half of 1988, but collapsed following the devaluation of the Russian currency. Useful as these foreign savings could be, in Brazil, as in the rest of Latin America, increased foreign savings became a substitute for, instead of a complement to, national savings. In Brazil these decreased sharply, from over 21% of GDP in 1993 to 16% in 1998; in 1999 there was a continuation of this downward trend.

The federal deficit averaged over 4% of GDP between 1985 and 1988 and increased sharply to over 8% in 1989 at the time of the Cruzado Plan. With the failure of the Plan, economic policy-making became paralysed until the inauguration of a new President in 1990. One of the main aims of President Collor's New Brazil programme was to transform the increasing deficit into a surplus of 2% through a mixture of tax increases, expenditure reductions and privatization receipts. Although a budget surplus was achieved in 1990 (equivalent to 1.4% of GDP), the Government was not able to sustain this achievement, and small deficits were recorded in 1991 and 1992. Following a

change of economy minister, the original aims of the plan remained in place, but more orthodox policies, centred on high real interest rates, were implemented. However, these also failed to eliminate the public-sector deficit, to reduce inflation, or to prompt a sustained resumption of growth. One of the obvious reasons why Collor could not balance the budget was that his own policy of high interest rates trebled the servicing of public debt in just one year (to 4.4% of GDP).

The economic situation did not change much until the implementation of the Real Plan in 1994. In December 1993 the then Minister of Finance, Fernando Henrique Cardoso, proposed a new stabilization plan which, unlike its predecessors, aimed to attack the root causes of inflation, while at the same time attempting to achieve financial balance in the public sector. This Plan was implemented in three stages between March and July 1994. In so far as monetary policy was concerned, instruments and rules were devised to guarantee price stability. Quarterly quantitative goals were established for the monetary base to indicate the Government's intention of not utilizing inflationary financing. To keep consumption to levels compatible with price stability, special attention was to be given to credit expansion. New reserve requirements were imposed on the banking system, including an increase to 100% to additional demand deposit. A relatively fixed exchange-rate system was introduced, in which the Central Bank would intervene to avoid destabilizing speculation with the new currency. Several measures were adopted which were aimed at attaining fiscal balance, such as the Federal Securities Debt Amortization Fund. Furthermore, the system of guarantees and endorsements granted by the national treasury was discontinued.

Following full implementation of the Real Plan, the monthly rate of inflation, which had reached a record of nearly 50% in June 1994, fell immediately to approximately 2% in three months. However, the Plan was not equally successful as far as the public-sector deficit was concerned. Even though an initial surplus was achieved in 1994 (equivalent to 1.4% of GDP), by 1995 this had already turned into a substantial deficit of 4.9% of GDP. This deficit was reduced in 1996, but increased to 4.3% in 1997, as a result of the increase in interest rates that followed the East Asian financial crisis. Again, mainly as a result of the further increase in interest rates that followed the Russian devaluation in mid-August and further absorption of 'bad' debt from the private sector and state governments (debt that was extremely unlikely to be recovered), the 1998 deficit reached almost 8% of GDP. As a result, net public debt (that is, total public debt minus international reserves and public financial assets) increased at a very rapid pace in the mid-1990s, from US $215,000m. in December 1995 to $320,000m. at the end of 1998. This figure, although not excessively large as a share of GDP compared to other countries (42.3%), became unmanageable owing to continuous high levels of interest rates. Over 80% of this net debt was domestic. The federal Government and Central Bank component of the gross internal debt almost trebled in 1995–98, from about $80,000m. to $226,000m.

As the 'primary' accounts of the federal Government and Central Bank were either in surplus or roughly in balance throughout the period of the Plan, the large increase in debt was caused by a number of factors. The first of these was the large and continuous absorption of bad financial debt from the private sector and state governments. The key problem of the banking sector arose mainly because financial liberalization created a disparity between the requirements of its assets and liabilities—the former were domestic and required low interest rates to perform, the latter had a substantial foreign-exchange exposure and required high interest rates not to dramatically increase. As interest rates could not be both low and high at the same time, continuous high interest rates made the banking sector increasingly fragile on its assets side and more vulnerable on its liability side, because if the government high-interest rate policy failed, the resulting devaluation was likely to be significant. The second factor was that public-sector debt also increased because of high interest rates and lack of fiscal reforms, which led to a situation in which the interest rate paid on public debt was continuously larger than both the growth of public revenues and the returns on foreign exchange reserves.

As a result of the fiscal adjustment agreed with the IMF following the January 1999 devaluation, the public sector deficit decreased to 6.8% of GDP in that year; this trend continued in 2000, with the accumulated deficit to October totalling 4.0% of GDP. However, these reduced deficits still added to the net public debt, which by November 2000 had reached 48.5% of GDP.

Brazil's long-term failure to generate a trade surplus to pay for its existing foreign obligations, and the long periods it enjoyed of easy access to international finance, led to a rapid increase in its foreign debt since the late 1960s. Rising international interest rates and increased short-term borrowing forced Brazil's foreign debt inexorably higher. This was a direct consequence of Brazil having made the same mistake as most Latin American countries in the 1970s—it opened the capital account of the balance of payments at a time of high international liquidity and borrowed heavily at variable interest rates, without having had a clear programme of export expansion able to generate the foreign exchange required to service the resulting growing foreign debt. In 1987 the country declared a moratorium on payments on its medium- and long-term debt, by then worth some US $120,000m. Foreign debt continued to increase, reaching $244,673m. in 1999 (equivalent to nearly five times the level of Brazil's exports of goods and services). The structure of this debt between the share owed by the public and private sectors also changed substantially after the implementation of the Real Plan: in the early 1990s about 80% of the external debt was public; by 1998 only 40% remained public and the share of the private sector had increased to 60%.

Following the international financial crisis of 1982 Brazil was involved in virtually continuous negotiations with the IMF, commercial banks and the 'Paris Club' of creditor nations. The exception was the announcement during the Cruzado Plan, in February 1987, of a unilateral moratorium on most of Brazil's medium- and long-term debt. An agreement for a stand-by loan of US $1,400m. was reached with the IMF in August 1988, leading to the lifting of the moratorium. In 1989, however, increased arrears and failure to meet IMF conditions led to the withholding of a $600m. tranche of the stand-by loan. President Collor de Mello's new programme was generally well received in financial circles, and helped in reaching a new agreement with the IMF for a $2,000m. loan in 1990. In 1992 the IMF agreed a new stand-by credit of $2,100m.

The reduction of international interest rates and the resumption of voluntary international capital movement into the country in the early 1990s were enormously helpful to Brazil in coping with its foreign-debt problem in the short-term. Private capital inflows into Brazil (in the form of direct foreign investment, bonds and portfolio equity) recorded a significant increase. Direct foreign investment flows from European countries into Brazil reached a total of US $3,300m. in 1987–90 (about one-half of the Latin American total), while those from the USA reached $5,400m. However, the increases of US interest rates and the high volatility of international financial markets at the beginning of 1994 again brought into doubt Brazil's future capacity for both servicing its growing foreign debt and for achieving external macroeconomic equilibrium. This was compounded by the requirements of the Real Plan. However, in 1995 the net inflow of foreign capital increased dramatically, to $29,400m., twice as much as in the previous year. In 1996 these inflows increased even further, totalling an unprecedented $34,300m. (or 72% of exports). In 1997, mainly as a result of the East Asian crisis, these net inflows were reduced to $26,000m., and in 1998 there was a further decrease (to US $20,000m.), owing to the Russian devaluation. Following the January 1999 crisis these inflows fell even more during this year (to US $13,925m.), to end up at just US $7,579m. between January and September 2000. In January 2001 the World Bank approved a US $758m. loan to enable Brazil to meet its foreign debt repayments.

Thus, the Real Plan was implemented during a period in which Brazil had three major external shocks that had severe implications for its external finances. Firstly, the devaluation of the Mexican peso in 1994 (resulting in the so-called 'tequila effect'), the East Asian crisis in 1997, and the Russian devaluation and default in 1998. The tequila effect led to a reduction in the inflow of foreign capital into Brazil during the first quarter of 1995. Foreign reserves also fell by US $7,000m. in the same period. However, these problems did not persist, and there was a rapid return to the country of private foreign capital.

In 1997 the upheaval in international financial markets reduced the net inflow into Brazil from $10,400m. to only $700m. in just one quarter. Nevertheless, the foreign direct investment component of these inflows continued to increase. Again, the sharp fall in net inflows at the end of 1997 was reversed by the first quarter of 1998. However, the impact of events in Russia in August 1998, and later in January 1999 in Brazil resulted in further massive outflows.

FOREIGN TRADE AND THE BALANCE OF PAYMENTS

Until 1980 Brazil suffered persistent deficits on its balance of trade, largely attributable to imports of petroleum and capital goods. After the 1982 debt crisis this deficit had to be changed into a surplus in order to generate the foreign exchange needed for the financial requirements of the current account. This was achieved mainly through weak domestic demand, the domestic production of and substitution for petroleum, growing capital-goods self-sufficiency, and a policy of export promotion. Imports in 1984–86 were at practically the same level as in 1975–78, whereas exports more than doubled over the same period. The trade surpluses continued until the implementation of the Real Plan in 1994, when the rapid increase in imports (50% in one year) brought about a significant deterioration in the trade surplus, which turned to a deficit of US $3,157m. in 1995, a figure that increased to $5,453m. in 1996. Following the East Asian crisis in mid-1997 the Government introduced strict policies to reduce the mounting deficit. Nevertheless, the trade deficit increased to $6,652m. in 1997, before decreasing slightly to $6,603m. in 1998. This was the result of a rapid increase in the value of merchandise imports that followed the process of import liberalization and the overvaluation of the currency. Exports also increased in the same period but not at the same rate. As a result of the January 1999 crisis, additional policies were implemented in an attempt to turn the deficit into a surplus that would help finance the large obligations of the current account and to comply with the conditions of the IMF rescue package. Consequently, the trade deficit for 1999 decreased to some $1,261m., and fell to just $696m. in 2000.

Despite important trade surpluses between 1983 and 1994, heavy debt obligations still produced deficits in the current account of the balance of payments in seven years of this period. The Real Plan started in 1994 with a small current-account deficit of US $1,153m.; however, by 1995 this deficit had risen dramatically to $18,136m. The deterioration in the current account continued thereafter, with the deficit reaching $33,829m. in 1998 (equivalent to 4.5% of GDP and 70% of merchandise exports). In spite of the January 1999 devaluation and the improvement in the trade deficit, the current-account deficit decreased only slightly in that year, to $25,400m.; the current account deficit was estimated at $24,632m. in 2000.

Substantial as these deficits were, for most of the time in the 1990s capital inflows into the country were even larger, massively increasing the level of foreign reserves. These increased from US $36,069m. in December 1994 to $58,322m. in 1996. This led to a significant amount of complacency on the part of the Government. However, by December 1998 these reserves had decreased to $42,578m., leading to the devaluation of the real in January 1999. At December 200 foreign-exchange reserves stood at $32,488m., a decrease on the previous year's figure of $34,786m.

As in the aftermath of the Mexican peso crisis in 1995, most analysts were surprised by the speed of the return of foreign capital to Brazil following the 1997 East Asian crisis. This was clearly helped by the rapid reaction from the Brazilian authorities, which swiftly increased deposit interest rates to an annualized level of 43%, raised some import tariffs significantly, and took measures to facilitate these inflows. However, this short-term success carried with it the danger of complacency, and by mid-1998, particularly owing to the massive inflow of foreign capital in the first half of the year, the East Asian crisis appeared to have been totally forgotten. As it was, by then, and before the Russian devaluation, Brazil already needed to borrow abroad at a premium, pay a higher price for its huge debt, sell some of its export products at a discount, and cope with reduced demand for its exports from Asia and Argentina. Added to this was the urgent problem of the public accounts. However, in a year of presidential, gubernatorial and municipal elections little was done. This might have helped Cardoso's re-election to the presidency, but did little to strengthen the Brazilian economy. As a result, the Russian crisis of mid-1998 affected the Brazilian economy much more adversely than either of the two previous crises and by January 1999 the Central Bank had little option but to devalue. To contain the subsequent crisis, the Government not only had to increase deposit interest rates yet again, this time to 45%, but also had to be more serious about its determination to decrease the public-sector deficit. The IMF made the latter a condition of its financial rescue programme.

The initial recovery from the crisis was impressive, but many of the problems that led to the crisis still persisted in mid-2001. Both the internal and external debts continued to heavily tax both the public finance and the balance of payments. In 1999 the Government still had to use about 30% of its revenues in debt service and pay US $9,000m. in interest on its foreign debt, and an additional $27,000m. for the amortization of this debt in the first six months of 2000 alone. In all, in 1999 the public sector had to make interest payments equivalent to 6.8% of GDP (only fractionally lower than the 7.6% figure for 1998), and the figure for the first two quarters of 2000 (4% of GDP) indicates that interest payments for the whole year would be similar to those in 1999. By mid-2001 no plans for serious fiscal reform had yet been agreed upon between the Government and the National Congress. Initial indicators for the level of economic activity in the first half of 2001 showed a relatively strong performance in the first quarter. The 2001 budget, approved in January, projected a growth of 4.5% for the economy; expenditure was forecast at 950,000m. reais and a fiscal surplus of 28,100m. reais was projected. However, a significant slowdown of this post-crisis recovery occurred during the second quarter of the year. Events in the USA and Argentina, and the high price of oil adversely affected the situation. Furthermore, it was expected that this trend would be accentuated in the second half of the year as a result of the impact of electricity rationing. The consumer price index in April 2001 showed an increasing inflationary pressure (6.6% for the last 12 months, higher than the 4% target), and this rate was expected to increase further as a result of the surcharges in electricity prices and the devaluation of the exchange rate. As a result, the Central Bank increased interest rates, which reached 16.8% in June. Moreover, imports were growing faster than exports, placing added pressure on the balance of payments and the exchange rate.

CONCLUSION

The legacy left by the military regimes to their civilian successors was a complex one. The Brazil of 1985 was very different from that of 1964. However, if Brazil's economy had improved significantly during this period, extreme inequality meant that the lot of its people certainly did not. The Sarney Government proved unable either to alleviate even the worst of the social problems afflicting rural and urban areas or to deal with the pressing problems of debt, inflation and volatility in economic growth. President Collor de Mello's attempt to bring about a significant shift in the character of the economy and its external relations, and to put an end to over 50 years of state-led development failed, as short-term economic problems and the emergence of massive corruption revealed the fragility of his political base. His successor, Itamar Franco, also proved unable to deal with Brazil's major political and economic problems, but achieved some success with the appointment of Fernando Henrique Cardoso as Minister of Finance. President Franco

allowed Cardoso and his team to devise and implement what at the time seemed to be the best planned and most ambitious stabilization programme in Latin America since the 1982 debt crisis. The Real Plan succeeded in dramatically reducing inflation and resulted in the election of Cardoso to the presidency. However, the Plan's successes were at a high cost.

One of the strengths of the Brazilian economy in the past was that its economic authorities (of different political persuasions) did not allow its domestic inflation, exchange rate and external balance to become a constraint on economic growth. As this policy ended in the late 1980s in 'hyper-stagflation' (extremely high rates of inflation combined with economic stagnation), by the late 1990s the economic authorities had reversed these priorities almost completely by not allowing the exchange rate, the external and internal balances, or economic growth to become a constraint in their fight against inflation. Although inflation was controlled very successfully—even more impressively after the January 1999 devaluation—this created major economic problems, exacerbated by the fact that the Real Plan was being implemented simultaneously with trade and financial liberalization in a highly volatile international environment, and an unsuccessful attempt at fiscal reform, pension reform and a general restructuring of the public sector.

A domestic deregulated but badly supervised financial market, closely linked to a highly liquid but unstable international financial market, coupled with a domestic economy characterized by large imbalances, made a sudden collapse of confidence and withdrawal of funds a real possibility. Such a possibility seemed not to have been fully realized by Brazilian policy-makers, even after the Mexican and East Asian crises. The important issue, as the experience of almost all Latin American countries demonstrated, was that using the nominal rate of exchange as the main anti-inflationary 'anchor', coupled with allowing volatile foreign finance to dominate the balance of payments and monetary policy, could all too easily lead to economic crisis. After the initial successful stabilization, a controlled increased devaluation, a decrease in interest rates and an increase in public revenues as part of a major fiscal reform that would also rationalize public expenditure, were the only sensible options. However, when in 1998 the time came for the Government to stop prevaricating over fiscal reform, this coincided with presidential and legislative elections, and, therefore, such a controversial initiative was not implemented.

Finally, and crucially, the Cardoso Government had the unique advantage of assuming power at a time when the Brazilian people were disillusioned with previous economic policies and were desperate for an end to hyperinflation; however, President Cardoso appeared to believe that this was political capital that he could endlessly exploit. The price paid so far for this complacency appeared to be extremely high.

In summary, by mid-2001 the Brazilian economy was facing a set of adverse shocks and President Cardoso's room for manoeuvre was decreasing dramatically. The government coalition was weak and likely to face further internal conflict in the period preceding the 2002 elections. However, both the President of the Central Bank, Armínio Fraga Neto, and the long-serving Minister of Finance, Pedro Sampaio Malan, still commanded high respect in domestic and international financial markets. Furthermore, their day-to-day running of the economy, although not devoid of controversy, has so far ensured that the growing economic problems facing Brazil could be contained without resulting in an economic crisis similar to that affecting Argentina in mid-2001.

Statistical Survey

Sources (unless otherwise stated): Economic Research Department, Banco Central do Brasil, SBS, Q 03, Bloco B, Brasília, DF; tel. (61) 414-1074; fax (61) 414-2036; e-mail coace.depec.@bcb.gov.br; internet www.bcb.gov.br/; Instituto Brasileiro de Geografia e Estatística (IBGE), Centro de Documentação e Disseminação de Informações (CDDI), Rua Gen. Canabarro 706, 4° andar, 20271-201 Maracanã, Rio de Janeiro, RJ; tel. (21) 569-2901; fax (21) 284-1959; internet www.ibge.gov.br.

Area and Population

AREA, POPULATION AND DENSITY

Area (sq km)	8,547,403.5*
Population (census results)†	
1 August 1996	
Males	77,442,865
Females	79,628,298
Total	157,070,163
1 August 2000, provisional	169,543,612
Population (official estimates at mid-year)†	
1997	159,636,400
1998	161,790,300
1999	163,947,600
Density (per sq km) at 2000	19.8

* 3,300,170.9 sq miles.
† Excluding Indian jungle population, numbering 45,429 in 1950.

ADMINISTRATIVE DIVISIONS
(population at census of 1 August 2000, provisional)

State	Population	Capital
Acre (AC)	557,337	Rio Branco
Alagoas (AL)	2,817,903	Maceió
Amapá (AP)	475,843	Macapá
Amazonas (AM)	2,840,889	Manaus
Bahia (BA)	13,066,764	Salvador
Ceará (CE)	7,417,402	Fortaleza
Espírito Santo (ES) . . .	3,093,171	Vitória
Goiás (GO)	4,994,897	Goiânia
Maranhão (MA)	5,638,381	São Luís
Mato Grosso (MT) . . .	2,498,150	Cuiabá
Mato Grosso do Sul (MS) . .	2,075,275	Campo Grande
Minas Gerais (MG) . . .	17,835,488	Belo Horizonte
Pará (PA)	6,188,685	Belém
Paraíba (PB)	3,436,718	João Pessoa
Paraná (PR)	9,558,126	Curitiba
Pernambuco (PE)	7,910,992	Recife
Piauí (PI)	2,840,969	Teresina
Rio de Janeiro (RJ) . . .	14,367,225	Rio de Janeiro
Rio Grande do Norte (RN) . .	2,770,730	Natal
Rio Grande do Sul (RS) . .	10,178,970	Porto Alegre
Rondônia (RO)	1,377,792	Porto Velho
Roraima (RR)	324,152	Boa Vista
Santa Catarina (SC) . . .	5,333,284	Florianópolis
São Paulo (SP)	36,966,527	São Paulo
Sergipe (SE)	1,779,522	Aracaju
Tocantins (TO)	1,155,251	Palmas
Distrito Federal (DF) . . .	2,043,169	Brasília
Total	169,543,612	—

PRINCIPAL TOWNS (population at census of 1 August 2000, provisional)*

São Paulo . . .	9,785,640	João Pessoa	. .	594,922
Rio de Janeiro . .	5,850,544	Jaboatão	. .	567,319
Salvador . . .	2,439,881	São José dos		
Belo Horizonte . .	2,229,697	Campos .	. .	532,403
Fortaleza . . .	2,138,234	Contagem	. .	531,715
Brasília (capital) .	2,043,169	Ribeirão Preto .		502,333
Curitiba . . .	1,586,898	Sorocaba	. .	487,907
Recife	1,421,947	Uberlândia	. .	487,887
Manaus . . .	1,394,724	Cuiabá	. .	475,632
Porto Alegre . .	1,320,069	Aracaju	. .	460,898
Belém	1,271,615	Niterói	. .	458,465
Goiânia . . .	1,083,396	São João de		
Guarulhos . . .	1,048,280	Meriti	. .	449,562
Campinas . . .	951,824	Juíz de Fora	. .	443,359
Nova Iguaçu . .	915,364	Londrina	. .	433,264
São Gonçalo . .	889,828	Feira de Santana	.	431,458
São Luís . . .	834,968	Santos	. .	415,543
Maceió . . .	794,894	Joinville	. .	414,350
Duque de Caxias .	767,724	Ananindeua	. .	391,994
Natal	709,422	Campos dos		
São Bernardo do		Goytacazes	. .	363,489
Campo . . .	688,161	Maná . .	. .	363,112
Teresina . . .	676,596	Olinda	. .	361,300
Campo Grande . .	654,832	Diadema	. .	356,389
Osasco . . .	650,993	Carapicuíba	. .	343,668
Santo André . .	648,443	Vila Velha .	. .	343,567

* Figures refer to *municípios*, which may contain rural districts.

BIRTHS AND DEATHS (official estimates)

	Birth rate (per 1,000)	Death rate (per 1,000)
1992	22.09	7.04
1993	21.37	6.98
1994	20.75	6.92
1995	20.14	6.87
1996	19.69	6.82
1997	19.25	6.78
1998	20.30	6.75
1999	20.10	6.72

Expectation of life (official estimates, years at birth, mid-1999): 66.97 (males 63.35; females 70.76).

ECONOMICALLY ACTIVE POPULATION (household surveys, September each year, '000 persons aged 10 years and over)*

	1997	1998	1999
Agriculture, hunting, forestry and fishing	16,770.7	16,338.1	17,372.1
Manufacturing	8,507.0	8,230.6	8,278.1
Mining and quarrying . . }	774.3	861.6	783.1
Electricity, gas and water . . }			
Construction	4,583.5	4,980.0	4,743.1
Wholesale and retail trade . .	9,222.8	9,417.0	9,618.4
Transport and communications .	2,759.0	2,786.6	2,815.2
Community, social and personal services (incl. restaurants and hotels)	25,436.4	26,040.5	26,721.3
Financing, insurance, real estate and business services . . }	1,277.9	1,308.7	1,344.3
Activities not adequately defined }			
Total employed . . .	69,331.5	69,963.1	71,676.2
Unemployed	5,881.8	6,922.6	7,639.1
Total labour force . . .	75,213.3	76,885.7	79,315.3
Males	44,832.2	45,614.0	46,480.9
Females	30,381.1	31,271.7	32,834.4

* Figures exclude the rural population of the States of Rondônia, Acre, Amazonas, Roraima, Pará and Amapá.

Agriculture

PRINCIPAL CROPS ('000 metric tons)

	1998	1999	2000
Wheat	2,270	2,438	1,895
Rice (paddy)	7,716	11,783	11,168
Barley	300	315	370
Maize	29,602	32,038	32,038
Oats	207	288	225
Sorghum	590	574	842
Potatoes	2,784	2,843	2,582
Sweet potatoes . . .	445	480	500*
Cassava (Manioc) . .	19,503	20,892	22,960
Yams*	225	230	230
Dry beans	2,191	2,817	3,037
Soybeans (Soya beans) . .	31,307	30,901	32,687
Groundnuts (in shell) . .	193	173	188
Castor beans	17	31	108
Cottonseed†	742	892	n.a.
Coconuts	1,540	1,723	1,822
Babassu kernels . . .	752	n.a.	n.a.
Tomatoes	2,784	3,251	3,043
Onions (dry)	838	990	1,078
Other vegetables and melons . .	2,418	2,414	2,417
Water-melons	599	600	600*
Sugar cane	345,255	337,165	324,668
Grapes	774	895	978
Apples	791	944	1,160
Peaches and nectarines . . .	140	155*	155*
Oranges	20,851	22,768	22,745
Tangerines, mandarins, clementines and satsumas . .	781	760†	770*

— *continued*	1998	1999	2000
Lemons and limes	519	520	520*
Avocados	84	85	85*
Mangoes	469	500	500*
Pineapples	1,113	1,175	1,353
Bananas§	532,220	552,778	633,935
Papayas	3,243	3,300	3,300*
Cashew nuts	54	131	154
Coffee beans (green)‖ . . .	1,689	1,634	1,824
Cocoa beans	281	205	210
Tobacco (leaves)	505	626	594
Jute and allied fibres . . .	8	8	7
Sisal	116	194	195
Cotton (lint)†	387	467	632
Other fibre crops . . .	99	99*	99*
Natural rubber	66†	70†	70*

* FAO estimate(s).
† Unofficial figure(s).
‡ In '000 fruit.
§ In '000 bunches.
‖ Official figures, reported in terms of dry cherries, have been converted into green coffee beans at 50%.

Source: FAO.

LIVESTOCK ('000 head, year ending September)

	1998	1999	2000
Cattle	163,154	163,470	167,471
Buffaloes	1,017	1,100*	1,150*
Horses	5,867	5,900*	3,900*
Asses	1,233	1,250*	1,250*
Mules	1,292	1,400*	1,400*
Pigs	30,007	27,425	27,320
Sheep	14,268	15,000*	15,000*
Goats	8,164	8,500*	8,500*
Chickens	765,222	943,000*	1,006,000*
Ducks*	4,000	3,750	3,400
Turkeys*	8,200	8,700	8,700

* FAO estimates.
Source: FAO.

LIVESTOCK PRODUCTS ('000 metric tons)

	1998	1999	2000
Beef and veal	5,794	6,182	6,460
Mutton and lamb* . . .	68	71	71
Goat meat*	34	38	39
Pig meat	1,652	1,752	1,804
Horse meat*	14	15	15
Poultry meat	4,969	5,647	6,020
Cows' milk	19,273	21,700†	22,134†
Goats' milk	141	141	141
Butter and ghee† . . .	68	69	72
Cheese	39	39	39
Dried milk†	240	244	256
Hen eggs	1,390†	1,400*	1,400*
Other poultry eggs* . . .	45	44	44
Honey	18	18	18
Wool:			
greasy	15	15*	15*
scoured*	16	16	n.a.
Cattle hides (fresh) . . .	637†	667†	667*

* FAO estimate(s).   † Unofficial figure(s).

Source: FAO.

Forestry

ROUNDWOOD REMOVALS
('000 cubic metres, excl. bark)

	1997	1998	1999
Sawlogs, veneer logs and logs for sleepers	47,779	46,779	46,779
Pulpwood	30,701	30,701	30,701
Other industrial wood	6,204	6,284	6,365
Fuel wood	114,052	114,052	114,052
Total	198,736	197,816	197,897

Source: FAO, *Yearbook of Forest Products.*

SAWNWOOD PRODUCTION
(FAO estimates, '000 cubic metres, incl. railway sleepers)

	1997	1998	1999
Coniferous (softwood)	8,591	8,591	8,591
Broadleaved (hardwood)	10,500	10,000	10,000
Total	19,091	18,591	18,591

Source: FAO, *Yearbook of Forest Products.*

Fishing

('000 metric tons, live weight)

	1996	1997	1998
Capture	715.5	744.6	760.0
Characins	84.9	68.1	68.5
Freshwater siluroids	47.3	52.6	52.9
Weakfishes	26.5	26.0	29.1
Whitemouth croaker	23.4	23.3	26.2
Brazilian sardinella	97.1	117.6	82.3
Skipjack tuna	22.5	26.6	23.8
Penaeus shrimps	23.8	25.3	28.3
Aquaculture	77.7*	87.7	95.0*
Common carp	23.9*	35.5	38.5*
Total catch	793.2*	832.3	855.0*

* FAO estimate.

Note: Figures exclude aquatic mammals, recorded by number rather than by weight. The number of baleen whales caught was: 1 in 1997; 1 in 1998. The number of toothed whales caught was: 513 in 1996; 171 in 1997; 136 in 1998. Also excluded are crocodiles. The number of spectacled caimans caught was: 659 in 1996; 7,307 in 1997; 242 in 1998.

Source: FAO, *Yearbook of Fishery Statistics.*

Mining

('000 metric tons, unless otherwise indicated)

	1997	1998	1999
Hard coal	5,632	5,571	5,720
Crude petroleum ('000 cubic metres)	50,446	58,279	65,451
Natural gas (million cubic metres)	9,865	10,833	11,855
Iron ore:			
gross weight[1]	185,128	207,017	190,345
metal content[1]	122,184	124,210	114,207
Copper concentrates (metric tons)[2]	39,952	34,446	31,371
Nickel ore (metric tons)[2]	31,936	36,764	43,784
Bauxite	11,671	11,961	12,880
Lead concentrates (metric tons)[2]	8,729	7,567	10,281
Zinc concentrates (metric tons)[2]	152,634	87,475	98,590
Tin concentrates (metric tons)[2]	18,291	14,238	13,202
Manganese ore[2]	977	988	770
Chromium ore (metric tons)[3]	112,274	160,742	190,000
Tungsten concentrates (metric tons)[2]	40	—	—
Ilmenite (metric tons)	97,174	103,000	96,000
Rutile (metric tons)	1,742	1,800	4,300
Zirconium concentrates (metric tons)[4]	19,252	20,132	29,448
Silver (kilograms)[5]	26,598	34,000	42,000
Gold (kilograms)[6]	58,488	49,567	40,943
Bentonite (beneficiated)	230.0	220.0	274.6
Kaolin (beneficiated)	1,165.0	1,373.9	1,516.7
Magnesite (beneficiated)	294.6	308.3	259.8
Phosphate rock[7]	4,275.6	4,421.4	4,300.6
Potash salts[8]	280.2	326.5	348.2
Fluorspar (Fluorite) (metric tons)[9,10]	78,032	72,082	44,926
Barite (Barytes) (beneficiated) (metric tons)	51,961	46,632	44,906
Salt (unrefined):			
marine	5,064	5,353	4,528
rock	1,452	1,484	1,430
Gypsum and anhydrite (crude)	1,507.1	1,632.0	1,456.3
Graphite (natural) (metric tons)[1,9]	40,587	61,369	n.a.
Asbestos (fibre)[1,9,11]	170	170	170
Mica (metric tons)	4,000	4,000	5,000
Talc and pyrophyllite (crude)	444.3	452.2	460.0
Diamonds ('000 carats):			
gem[1,11]	300	300	300
industrial[1,11]	600	600	600

[1] Data from the US Geological Survey.
[2] Figures refer to the metal content of ores and concentrates.
[3] Figures refer to the chromic oxide (Cr_2O_3) content.
[4] Including production of baddeleyite-caldasite.
[5] Figures refer to primary production only. The production of secondary silver (in kilograms) was: 32,000 in 1997; 40,000 in 1998; 50,000 in 1999.
[6] Including production by independent miners (garimpeiros): 17,426 kg in 1997; 11,780 kg in 1998; 2,556 kg in 1999.
[7] Figures refer to the gross weight of concentrates. The phosphoric acid (P_2O_5) content (in '000 metric tons) was: 1,510 in 1997; 1,561 in 1998; 1,528 in 1999.
[8] Figures refer to the potassium oxide (K_2O) content.
[9] Figures refer to marketable products.
[10] Acid-grade and metallurgical-grade concentrates.
[11] Estimated production.

Source (unless otherwise indicated): Departamento Nacional de Producão Mineral, Ministério de Minas e Energia.

Industry

SELECTED PRODUCTS ('000 metric tons, unless otherwise indicated)

	1997	1998	1999
Asphalt	1,572	2,060	n.a.
Electric power (million kWh) . .	330,358	341,880	n.a.
Pig-iron	25,013	25,111	25,549
Crude steel	26,153	25,760	24,996
Cement*	38,096	39,942	40,270
Passenger cars ('000 units) . .	1,678	1,254	1,102
Commercial vehicles (units) . .	390,800	331,614	248,367
Tractors (units)	24,494	25,167	22,157
Newsprint	265	273	n.a.

* Portland cement only.

Finance

CURRENCY AND EXCHANGE RATES

Monetary Units

100 centavos = 1 real (plural: reais).

Sterling, Dollar and Euro Equivalents (30 April 2001)

£1 sterling = 3.1281 reais;
US $1 = 2.1847;
€1 = 1.9391 reais;
100 reais = £31.97 = $45.77 = €51.57.

Average Exchange Rates (reais per US $)

1998	1.161
1999	1.815
2000	1.830

Note: In March 1986 the cruzeiro (CR $) was replaced by a new currency unit, the cruzado (CZ $), equivalent to 1,000 cruzeiros. In January 1989 the cruzado was, in turn, replaced by the new cruzado (NCZ $), equivalent to CZ $1,000 and initially at par with the US dollar (US $). In March 1990 the new cruzado was replaced by the cruzeiro (CR $), at an exchange rate of one new cruzado for one cruzeiro. In August 1993 the cruzeiro was replaced by the cruzeiro real, equivalent to CR $1,000. On 1 March 1994, in preparation for the introduction of a new currency, a transitional accounting unit, the Unidade Real de Valor (at par with the US $), came into operation, alongside the cruzeiro real. On 1 July 1994 the cruzeiro real was replaced by the real (R $), also at par with the US $ and thus equivalent to 2,750 cruzeiros reais.

BUDGET (R $ million)*

Revenue	1997	1998	1999
Tax revenue	108,731	130,681	147,366
Income tax	32,244	41,675	46,471
Value-added tax on industrial products	16,551	16,092	16,084
Tax on financial operations . .	3,769	3,514	4,843
Import duty	5,103	6,490	7,806
Tax on financial and share transactions	6,908	8,113	7,948
Social security contributions	18,405	17,732	30,935
Tax on profits of legal entities	7,241	7,183	9,477
Contributions to Social Integration Programme and Financial Reserve Fund for Public Employees . . .	7,228	6,783	6,776
Repayment of loans . . .	7,200	8,278	11,386
Transfer of profits from Banco do Brasil	103	127	29
Total	116,034	139,086	158,781

Expenditure	1997	1998	1999
Earmarked expenditures . . .	32,193	38,468	40,062
Transfers to state and local governments†	25,042	29,166	33,432
Other expenditures . . .	86,965	107,471	121,233
Wages and social contributions	42,848	47,296	50,169
Interest payments	17,975	27,706	35,439
Funding and investment . .	24,252	32,469	35,625
Lending	2,522	2,394	2,414
Total	121,680	148,333	163,709

* Figures refer to cash operations of the National Treasury, including the collection and transfer of earmarked revenues for social expenditure purposes. The data exclude the transactions of other funds and accounts controlled by the Federal Government.
† Constitutionally mandated participation funds.

CENTRAL BANK RESERVES (US $ million at 31 December)

	1998	1999	2000
Gold*	1,358	929	523
IMF special drawing rights . .	2	10	—
Foreign exchange . . .	42,578	34,786	32,488
Total	43,938	35,725	33,011

* Valued at market-related prices.

Source: IMF, *International Financial Statistics*.

MONEY SUPPLY (R $ million at 31 December)

	1998	1999	2000
Currency outside banks . . .	21,185	25,978	28,642
Demand deposits at deposit money banks	29,059	36,251	45,002
Total money (incl. others) . .	54,819	62,287	74,024

Source: IMF, *International Financial Statistics*.

COST OF LIVING

(Consumer Price Index at December; base: December 1995 = 100)

	1998	1999	2000
All items	127.7	133.9	143.4

Source: IMF, *International Financial Statistics*.

NATIONAL ACCOUNTS (R $ '000 at current prices)

Composition of the Gross National Product

	1997	1998	1999
Compensation of employees	318,785,117	328,210,516	360,096,000
Operating surplus . . } Consumption of fixed capital }	419,503,163	445,594,317	446,596,000
Gross domestic product (GDP) at factor cost .	738,288,280	773,804,833	806,692,000
Indirect taxes . . .	129,541,930	129,464,334	157,273,000
Less Subsidies . . .	3,719,184	3,455,035	3,106,000
GDP in purchasers' values	864,111,026	899,814,132	960,859,000
Factor income received from abroad	5,579,926	5,396,135	7,353,000
Less Factor income paid abroad	22,690,178	27,758,308	42,176,000
Gross national product .	847,000,774	877,451,959	926,036,000

Expenditure on the Gross Domestic Product

	1997	1998	1999
Government final consumption expenditure	154,238,952	159,920,518	181,160,000
Private final consumption expenditure . . .	545,113,309	572,390,773	593,938,000
Increase in stocks . .	15,342,520	12,271,254	14,639,000
Gross fixed capital formation .	172,212,039	179,202,590	181,813,000
Total domestic expenditure.	886,906,820	923,785,135	971,550,000
Exports of goods and services .	65,490,952	66,862,010	101,809,000
Less Imports of goods and services	88,286,746	90,833,013	112,501,000
GDP in purchasers' values .	864,111,026	899,814,132	960,858,000
GDP at constant 1999 prices	951,234,004	953,326,719	960,858,000

Gross Domestic Product by Economic Activity (at factor cost)

	1997	1998	1999
Agriculture, hunting, forestry and fishing .	68,005,538	75,764,350	79,405,305
Mining and quarrying . .	7,776,999	5,758,810	15,950,243
Manufacturing . . .	183,882,826	182,662,269	206,238,561
Electricity, gas and water .	22,898,942	24,744,889	27,480,539
Construction . . .	86,411,103	92,320,930	91,185,424
Trade, restaurants and hotels	66,363,727	65,236,525	73,793,894
Transport, storage and communications . .	43,724,018	50,389,591	52,366,761
Finance, insurance, real estate and business services	56,858,506	58,847,844	61,206,655
Government services . .	131,863,343	139,291,228	155,082,481
Rents	131,344,876	138,031,488	138,267,466
Other community, social and personal services .	109,310,045	113,286,599	106,174,809
Sub-total	908,439,922	946,334,523	1,007,075,270
Less Imputed bank service charge	44,328,896	46,520,391	46,217,270
Total	864,111,026	899,814,132	960,858,000

BALANCE OF PAYMENTS (US $ million)

	1998	1999	2000
Exports of goods f.o.b. . .	51,136	48,011	55,087
Imports of goods f.o.b. . .	−57,739	−49,272	−55,783
Trade balance	−6,603	−1,261	−696
Exports of services . .	7,631	7,189	9,382
Imports of services . .	−16,676	−14,172	−16,956
Balance on goods and services	−15,648	−8,244	−8,270
Other income received . .	4,914	3,936	3,620
Other income paid . . .	−24,531	−22,780	−21,504
Balance on goods, services and income	−35,265	−27,088	−26,154
Current transfers received .	1,795	1,969	1,828
Current transfers paid . .	−359	−281	−306
Current balance . . .	−33,829	−25,400	−24,632
Capital account (net) . .	375	339	272
Direct investment abroad .	−2,721	−1,690	−2,280
Direct investment from abroad .	31,913	28,576	32,779
Portfolio investment assets .	−594	258	−1,697
Portfolio investment liabilities .	19,013	3,542	8,646
Financial derivatives assets .	n.a.	642	386
Financial derivatives liabilities	n.a.	−729	−583
Other investment assets . .	−5,992	−4,399	−2,992
Other investment liabilities .	−21,556	−18,144	−4,890
Net errors and omissions . .	−2,911	240	2,971
Overall balance . . .	−16,302	−16,765	7,980

Source: IMF, *International Financial Statistics.*

External Trade

PRINCIPAL COMMODITIES
(distribution by SITC, US $ million, excl. military goods)

Imports f.o.b.	1997	1998	1999
Food and live animals . . .	4,226.2	4,626.7	3.280
Cereals and cereal preparations .	1,569.3	1,939.8	1,440
Crude materials (inedible) except fuels	2,364.8	1,925.8	1,569
Mineral fuels, lubricants, etc. .	6,783.1	5,110.0	5,433
Petroleum, petroleum products, etc.	5,549.2	3,925.0	4,336
Chemicals and related products	9,255.7	9,554.0	9,274
Organic chemicals . . .	3,289.8	3,158.5	2,942
Medicinal and pharmaceutical products	1,410.6	1,582.0	1,916
Plastics in primary forms . .	1,091.0	1,117.1	1,009
Basic manufactures . .	6,257.8	6,171.4	4,776
Machinery and transport equipment . . .	26,021.3	25,777.0	21,450
Power-generating machinery and equipment	1,979.8	2,331.0	2,290
Machinery specialized for particular industries . .	3,355.9	2,976.0	2,322
General industrial machinery, equipment and parts . .	3,582.5	3,624.0	2,748
Office machines and automatic data-processing machines .	1,718.3	1,733.0	1,541
Telecommunications and sound equipment	3,277.4	2,773.0	2,575
Other electrical machinery, apparatus, etc. . . .	4,877.0	4,745.5	4,452
Road vehicles and parts* . .	5,319.7	5,607.3	3,409
Other transport equipment* . .	1,018.9	1,125.1	1,210
Miscellaneous manufactured articles	4,238.8	3,903.2	3,020
Professional, scientific and controlling instruments, etc. .	1,212.3	1,258.5	1,117
Total (incl. others) . . .	59,757.7	57,734.0	49,224

* Excluding tyres, engines and electrical parts.

Exports f.o.b.	1997	1998	1999
Food and live animals . . .	11,438.8	10,363.3	10,386.0
Meat and meat preparations .	1,556.3	1,591.5	1,928.6
Vegetables and fruit . . .	1,428.5	1,667.6	1,691.4
Sugar, sugar preparations and honey	1,863.6	2,030.7	2,011.3
Coffee, tea, cocoa and spices . .	3,426.3	2,939.3	2,761.0
Feeding-stuff for animals (excl. unmilled cereals) . . .	2,841.9	1,800.7	1,586.9
Beverages and tobacco . .	1,755.4	1,624.6	1,017.8
Tobacco and tobacco manufactures	1,664.8	1,559.0	961.2
Crude materials (inedible) except fuels	7,700.8	7,949.0	7,163.5
Oil seeds and oleaginous fruit .	2,453.6	2,180.4	1,595.1
Pulp and waste paper . . .	1,024.2	1,049.4	1,243.6
Metalliferous ores and metal scrap .	3,190.5	3,661.6	3,168.2
Chemicals and related products	3,402.7	3,195.6	3,019.8
Organic chemicals . . .	1,155.1	1,054.7	1,016.2
Basic manufactures . .	11,223.0	10,184.4	9,776.3
Textile yarn, fabrics, etc. . .	1,021.9	891.0	819.9
Iron and steel	3,889.2	3,671.1	3,103.1
Non-ferrous metals . . .	1,668.0	1,276.0	1,499.3
Machinery and transport equipment . . .	11,992.6	12,600.5	11,386.7
Power-generating machinery and equipment	1,488.6	1,550.2	1,384.3
Machinery specialized for particular industries . .	1,289.0	1,163.1	854.7

Exports f.o.b. — *continued*	1997	1998	1999
General industrial machinery, equipment and parts . . .	1,595.3	1,508.4	1,411.8
Electrical machinery, apparatus, etc.	1,640.5	1,534.5	1,682.1
Road vehicles and parts* . . .	4,453.3	4,827.8	3,499.6
Other transport equipment* . .	1,000.1	1,481.3	1,937.7
Miscellaneous manufactured articles	3,084.1	2,869.0	2,888.9
Footwear	1,594.5	1,387.1	1,342.3
Total (incl. others) . . .	52,994.3	51,139.9	48,011.4

* Excluding tyres, engines and electrical parts.

PRINCIPAL TRADING PARTNERS (US $ million)*

Imports f.o.b.	1997	1998	1999
Algeria	766	624	988
Argentina	7,941	8,031	5,814
Belgium-Luxembourg . . .	638	718	493
Canada	1,416	1,338	973
Chile	974	817	718
China, People's Republic . .	1,166	1,034	865
France	1,641	1,977	1,989
Germany	4,959	5,239	4,714
Italy	3,407	3,232	2,598
Japan	3,534	3,277	2,576
Korea, Republic	1,355	988	1,019
Mexico	1,173	983	618
Netherlands	576	697	594
Nigeria	520	612	738
Paraguay	518	350	260
Saudi Arabia	1,100	727	615
Spain	1,141	1,195	1,179
Sweden	857	1,104	924
Switzerland	854	902	773
Taiwan	801	699	540
United Kingdom	1,451	1,489	1,222
USA	13,706	13,512	11,730
Uruguay	967	1,042	647
Venezuela	1,006	756	974
Total (incl. others) . . .	59,746	57,734	49,843

Exports f.o.b.	1997	1998	1999
Argentina	6,770	6,748	5,364
Belgium-Luxembourg . . .	1,483	2,195	1,817
Canada	584	544	513
Chile	1,197	1,024	896
China, People's Republic . . .	1,088	905	676
France	1,113	1,231	1,200
Germany	2,608	3,006	2,544
Iran	245	493	495
Italy	1,709	1,931	1,845
Japan	3,068	2,205	2,193
Korea, Republic	737	467	628
Mexico	828	1,002	1,068
Netherlands	3,998	2,745	2,594
Paraguay	1,407	1,249	744
Russia	761	647	746
Spain	1,057	1,056	1,169
United Kingdom	1,259	1,339	1,437
USA	9,276	9,747	10,675
Uruguay	870	881	670
Venezuela	768	706	537
Total (incl. others) . . .	52,994	51,140	48,011

* Imports by country of purchase; exports by country of last consignment.

Source: Ministério do Desenvolvimento, Indústria e Comércio Exterior, Brasília, DF.

Transport

RAILWAYS*

	1997	1998	1999
Passengers (million) . . .	1,221	1,255	n.a.
Passenger-km (million) . . .	12,688	12,667	n.a.
Freight ('000 metric tons) . .	267,795	271,829	271,799
Freight ton-km (million) . .	138,724	142,446	140,817

* Including suburban and metro services.

Source: Empresa Brasileira de Planejamento de Transportes (GEIPOT), Brasília, DF.

ROAD TRAFFIC (motor vehicles in use at 31 December)

	1997	1998	1999
Passenger cars	20,194,882	21,313,351	22,347,423
Buses and coaches . . .	348,168	430,062	400,048
Light goods vehicles . . .	3,158,695	3,313,774	3,193,058
Heavy goods vehicles . . .	1,699,338	1,755,877	1,778,084
Motorcycles and mopeds . .	3,365,121	3,854,646	4,222,705

Source: Empresa Brasileira de Planejamento de Transportes (GEIPOT).

SHIPPING
Merchant Fleet (registered at 31 December)

	1998	1999	2000
Number of vessels . . .	504	503	505
Total displacement ('000 grt) . .	4,171	3,933	3,809

Source: Lloyd's Register of Shipping, *World Fleet Statistics*.

International Sea-borne Freight Traffic ('000 metric tons)

	1997	1998	1999
Goods loaded	259,238	269,935	269,863
Goods unloaded	155,002	173,070	165,847

Source: Empresa Brasileira de Planejamento de Transportes (GEIPOT).

CIVIL AVIATION (embarked passengers, mail and cargo)

	1997	1998	1999
Number of passengers ('000) . .	25,149	32,179	30,678
Passenger-km (million) . .	44,930	49,291	44,158
Freight ton-km ('000)* . .	5,657,255	6,023,161	5,380,194

* Including mail.

Source: Empresa Brasileira de Planejamento de Transportes (GEIPOT), Brasília, DF.

Tourism

FOREIGN TOURIST ARRIVALS

Country of origin	1997	1998	1999
Argentina	938,973	1,467,922	1,548,571
Bolivia	n.a.	150,242	145,070
Chile	92,233	159,673	170,564
France	84,552	121,272	131,978
Germany	140,578	262,740	282,846
Italy	123,114	169,566	177,589
Paraguay	146,581	451,693	501,425
Portugal	63,315	105,593	115,088
Spain	63,809	91,968	99,677
United Kingdom	62,308	117,518	125,607
USA	402,200	524,093	559,367
Uruguay	206,468	359,186	383,741
Total (incl. others) . . .	n.a.	4,818,084	5,107,169

Receipts from tourism (US $ million): 2,594.9 in 1997; 3,678 in 1998; 3,994 in 1999.

Source: Instituto Brasileiro de Turismo—EMBRATUR, Brasília, DF.

Communications Media

	1995	1996	1997
Radio receivers ('000 in use)* . .	63,500	70,000	71,000
Television receivers ('000 in use)* .	35,000	36,000	36,500
Daily newspapers*			
Number	352	380	n.a.
Average circulation ('000 copies)	6,551	6,472	n.a.
Non-daily newspapers*			
Number	703	938	n.a.
Telephones in use ('000 main lines)†	14,875	17,729	n.a.
Telefax stations‡	270,000§	350,000§	500,000
Mobile cellular telephones			
(subscribers)‡	1,285,533	2,498,154	4,400,000

* Source: UNESCO, *Statistical Yearbook*.
† Source: Fundação Instituto Brasileiro de Geografia e Estatística (IBGE).
‡ Source: UN, *Statistical Yearbook*.
§ Provisional figure.

1998 ('000): Fixed telephone lines 22,599.9; Mobile cellular telephones 9,099.9 (Source: ANATEL, Ministério das Comunicações, Brasília, DF).

Education

(1998)

	Institutions	Teachers	Students
Pre-primary . . .	78,107	219,594	4,111,153
Literacy classes (Classe			
de Alfabetização) . .	34,064	46,126	806,288
Primary	187,497	1,460,469	35,845,742
Secondary	17,602	380,222	6,968,531
Higher*	900	173,705	1,948,200

* 1997 figures (preliminary).

Source: Ministério da Educação, Brasília, DF.

Directory

The Constitution

A new Constitution was promulgated on 5 October 1988. The following is a summary of the main provisions:

The Federative Republic of Brazil, formed by the indissoluble union of the States, the Municipalities and the Federal District, is constituted as a democratic state. All power emanates from the people. The Federative Republic of Brazil seeks the economic, political, social and cultural integration of the peoples of Latin America.

All are equal before the law. The inviolability of the right to life, freedom, equality, security and property is guaranteed. No one shall be subjected to torture. Freedom of thought, conscience, religious belief and expression are guaranteed, as is privacy. The principles of habeas corpus and 'habeas data' (the latter giving citizens access to personal information held in government data banks) are granted. There is freedom of association, and the right to strike is guaranteed.

There is universal suffrage by direct secret ballot. Voting is compulsory for literate persons between 18 and 69 years of age, and optional for those who are illiterate, those over 70 years of age and those aged 16 and 17.

Brasília is the federal capital. The Union's competence includes maintaining relations with foreign states, and taking part in international organizations; declaring war and making peace; guaranteeing national defence; decreeing a state of siege; issuing currency; supervising credits, etc.; formulating and implementing plans for economic and social development; maintaining national services, including communications, energy, the judiciary and the police; legislating on civil, commercial, penal, procedural, electoral, agrarian, maritime, aeronautical, spatial and labour law, etc. The Union, States, Federal District and Municipalities must protect the Constitution, laws and democratic institutions, and preserve national heritage.

The States are responsible for electing their Governors by universal suffrage and direct secret ballot for a four-year term. The organization of the Municipalities, the Federal District and the Territories is regulated by law.

The Union may intervene in the States and in the Federal District only in certain circumstances, such as a threat to national security or public order, and then only after reference to the National Congress.

LEGISLATIVE POWER

The legislative power is exercised by the Congresso Nacional (National Congress), which is composed of the Câmara dos Deputados (Chamber of Deputies) and the Senado Federal (Federal Senate). Elections for deputies and senators take place simultaneously throughout the country; candidates for the Congresso must be Brazilian by birth and have full exercise of their political rights. They must be at least 21 years of age in the case of deputies and at least 35 years of age in the case of senators. The Congresso meets twice a year in ordinary sessions, and extraordinary sessions may be convened by the President of the Republic, the Presidents of the Câmara and the Senado, or at the request of the majority of the members of either house.

The Câmara is made up of representatives of the people, elected by a system of proportional representation in each State, Territory and the Federal District for a period of four years. The total number of deputies representing the States and the Federal District will be established in proportion to the population; each Territory will elect four deputies.

The Senado is composed of representatives of the States and the Federal District, elected according to the principle of majority. Each State and the Federal District will elect three senators with a mandate of eight years, with elections after four years for one-third of the members and after another four years for the remaining two-thirds. Each Senator is elected with two substitutes. The Senado approves, by secret ballot, the choice of Magistrates, when required by the Constitution; of the Attorney-General of the Republic, of the Ministers of the Accounts Tribunal, of the Territorial Governors, of the president and directors of the central bank and of the permanent heads of diplomatic missions.

The Congreso is responsible for deciding on all matters within the competence of the Union, especially fiscal and budgetary arrangements, national, regional and local plans and programmes, the strength of the armed forces and territorial limits. It is also responsible for making definitive resolutions on international treaties, and for authorizing the President to declare war.

The powers of the Câmara include authorizing the instigation of legal proceedings against the President and Vice-President of the Republic and Ministers of State. The Senado may indict and impose sentence on the President and Vice-President of the Republic and Ministers of State.

Constitutional amendments may be proposed by at least one-third of the members of either house, by the President or by more than one-half of the legislative assemblies of the units of the Federation. Amendments must be ratified by three-fifths of the members of each house. The Constitution may not be amended during times of national emergency, such as a state of siege.

EXECUTIVE POWER

Executive power is exercised by the President of the Republic, aided by the Ministers of State. Candidates for the Presidency and Vice-Presidency must be Brazilian-born, be in full exercise of their political rights and be over 35 years of age. The candidate who obtains an absolute majority of votes will be elected President. If no candidate attains an absolute majority, the two candidates who have received the most votes proceed to a second round of voting, at which the candidate obtaining the majority of valid votes will be elected President. The President holds office for a term of four years and (under an amendment adopted in 1997) is eligible for re-election.

The Ministers of State are chosen by the President and their duties include countersigning acts and decrees signed by the President, expediting instructions for the enactment of laws, decrees and regulations, and presentation to the President of an annual report of their activities.

The Council of the Republic is the higher consultative organ of the President of the Republic. It comprises the Vice-President of the Republic, the Presidents of the Câmara and Senado, the leaders of the majority and of the minority in each house, the Minister of Justice, two members appointed by the President of the Republic, two elected by the Senado and two elected by the Câmara, the latter six having a mandate of three years.

The National Defence Council advises the President on matters relating to national sovereignty and defence. It comprises the Vice-President of the Republic, the Presidents of the Câmara and Senado, the Minister of Justice, military Ministers and the Ministers of Foreign Affairs and of Planning.

JUDICIAL POWER

Judicial power in the Union is exercised by the Supreme Federal Tribunal; the Higher Tribunal of Justice; the Regional Federal Tribunals and federal judges; Labour Tribunals and judges; Electoral Tribunals and judges; Military Tribunals and judges; and the States' Tribunals and judges. Judges are appointed for life; they may not undertake any other employment. The Tribunals elect their own controlling organs and organize their own internal structure.

The Supreme Federal Tribunal, situated in the Union capital, has jurisdiction over the whole national territory and is composed of 11 ministers. The ministers are nominated by the President after approval by the Senado, from Brazilian-born citizens, between the ages of 35 and 65 years, of proved judicial knowledge and experience.

The Government

HEAD OF STATE

President: FERNANDO HENRIQUE CARDOSO (took office 1 January 1995, re-elected 4 October 1998).

Vice-President: MARCO ANTÔNIO DE O. MACIEL.

THE CABINET
(August 2001)

Minister of Foreign Affairs: CELSO LAFER.

Minister of Justice: JOSÉ GREGORI.

Minister of Finance: PEDRO SAMPAIO MALAN.

Minister of Defence: GERALDO MAGELA DA CRUZ QUINTÃO.

Minister of Agriculture and Food Supply: MARCUS VINICIUS PRATINI DE MORÃES.

Minister of Agrarian Reform: RAÚL BELENS JUNGMANN PINTO.

Minister of Labour and Employment: PAULO JOBÍM, Filho (acting).

Minister of Transport: ELISEU LEMOS PADILHA.

Minister of Planning, Budget and Administration: MARTUS ANTÔNIO RODRIGUES TAVARES.

Minister of Mines and Energy: JOSÉ JORGE DE VASCONCELOS LIMA.

Minister of Culture: FRANCISCO CORRÊA WEFFORT.

Minister of the Environment: JOSÉ SARNEY, Filho.

Minister of Development, Industry and Trade: SERGIO AMARAL.

Minister of Education: PAULO RENATO DE SOUZA.

Minister of Health: JOSÉ SERRA.

Minister of National Integration: RAMEZ TEBET.

Minister of Social Security and Assistance: ROBERTO LÚCIO ROCHA BRANT.

Minister of Communications: JOÃO PIMENTA DA VEIGA, Filho.

Minister of Science and Technology: RONALDO SARDENBERG.

Minister of Sport and Tourism: CARLOS MELLES.

MINISTRIES

Office of the President: Palácio do Planalto, 4° andar, 70150-900 Brasília, DF; tel. (61) 411-1573; fax (61) 323-1461; e-mail casacivil@planalto.gov.br; internet www.planalto.gov.br.

Office of the Civilian Cabinet: Palácio do Planalto, 4° andar, Praça dos Três Poderes, 70150 Brasílila, DF; tel. (61) 211-1034; fax (61) 321-5804.

Ministry of Agrarian Reform: Edif. Palacio do Desenvolvimento, 70057 Brasília, DF; tel. (61) 223-8852; fax (61) 226-3855; internet www.incra.gov.br.

Ministry of Agriculture and Food Supply: Esplanada dos Ministérios, Bloco D, 8° andar, 70043 Brasília, DF; tel. (61) 226-5161; fax (61) 218-2586; internet www.agricultura.gov.br.

Ministry of Communications: Esplanada dos Ministérios, Bloco R, 8° andar, 70044 Brasília, DF; tel. (61) 311-6000; fax (61) 226-3980; internet www.mc.gov.br.

Ministry of Culture: Esplanada dos Ministérios, Bloco B, 3° andar, 70068-900 Brasília, DF; tel. (61) 316-2172; fax (61) 225-9162; internet www.minc.gov.br.

Ministry of Defence: Esplanada dos Ministérios, Bloco Q, 70049-900 Brasília, DF; tel. (61) 223-5356; fax (61) 321-2477; e-mail faleconosco@defesa.gov.br; internet www.defesa.gov.br.

Ministry of Development, Industry and Trade: Esplanada dos Ministérios, Bloco J, 7° andar, Sala 700, 70056-900 Brasília, DF; tel. (61) 325-2056; fax (61) 325-2063; internet www.mdic.gov.br.

Ministry of Education: Esplanada dos Ministérios, Bloco L, 8° andar, 70047-900 Brasília, DF; tel. (61) 225-6515; fax (61) 223-0564; e-mail acordabr@acb.mec.gov.br; internet www.mec.gov.br.

Ministry of the Environment: SAIN, Av. L4 Norte, Edif. Sede Terreo, 70800 Brasília, DF; tel. (61) 226-8221; fax (61) 322-1058; internet www.mma.gov.br.

Ministry of Finance: Esplanada dos Ministérios, Bloco P, 5° andar, 70048 Brasília, DF; tel. (61) 412-2548; fax (61) 226-9084; internet www.fazenda.gov.br.

Ministry of Foreign Affairs: Palácio do Itamaraty, Esplanada dos Ministérios, Bloco H, 70170-900 Brasília, DF; tel. (61) 411-6161; fax (61) 225-1272; internet www.mre.gov.br.

Ministry of Health: Esplanada dos Ministérios, Bloco G, 5° andar, 70058 Brasília, DF; tel. (61) 223-3169; fax (61) 224-8747; internet www.saude.gov.br.

Ministry of Justice: Esplanada dos Ministérios, Bloco T, 4° andar, 70064-900 Brasília, DF; tel. (61) 226-4404; fax (61) 322-6817; internet www.mj.gov.br.

Ministry of Labour and Employment: Esplanada dos Ministérios, Bloco F, 5° andar, 70059-900 Brasília, DF; tel. (61) 225-0041; fax (61) 226-3577; e-mail internacional@mtb.gov.br; internet www.mtb.gov.br.

Ministry of Mines and Energy: Esplanada dos Ministérios, Bloco U, 7° andar, 70000 Brasília, DF; tel. (61) 225-8106; fax (61) 225-5407; internet www.mme.gov.br.

Ministry of National Integration: Esplanada dos Ministérios, 70000 Brasília, DF; internet www.integracao.gov.br.

Ministry of Planning, Budget and Administration: Esplanada dos Ministérios, Bloco K, 70040-602 Brasília, DF; tel. (61) 215-4100; fax (61) 321-5292; internet www.planejamento.gov.br.

Ministry of Science and Technology: Esplanada dos Ministérios, Bloco E, 4° andar, 70062-900 Brasília, DF; tel. (61) 224-4364; fax (61) 225-7496; internet www.mct.gov.br.

Ministry of Social Security and Assistance: Esplanada dos Ministérios, Bloco A, 6° andar, 70054-900 Brasília, DF; tel. (61) 224-7300; fax (61) 226-3861; internet www.previdenciasocial.gov.br.

Ministry of Sport and Tourism: Esplanada dos Ministérios, Brasília, DF; internet www.met.gov.br.

Ministry of Transport: Esplanada dos Ministérios, Bloco R, 70000 Brasília, DF; tel. (61) 218-6335; fax (61) 218-6315; internet www.transportes.gov.br.

President and Legislature

PRESIDENT

Election, 4 October 1998

Candidate	Valid votes cast	% valid votes cast
FERNANDO HENRIQUE CARDOSO (PSDB) . .	35,936,916	53.06
LUIZ INÁCIO 'LULA' DA SILVA (PT) . . .	21,475,348	31.71
CIRO GOMES (PPS)	7,426,235	10.97
Others	2,884,528	4.26
Total	**67,723,027**	**100.00**

CONGRESSO NACIONAL
(National Congress)

Câmara dos Deputados
(Chamber of Deputies)

President: AÉCIO NEVES (PSDB).

The Chamber has 513 members who hold office for a four-year term.

General Election, 4 October 1998

Party	Seats
Partido da Frente Liberal (PFL)	106
Partido da Social Democracia Brasileira (PSDB)	99
Partido do Movimento Democrático Brasileiro (PMDB)	82
Partido Progressista Brasileiro (PPB)	60
Partido dos Trabalhadores (PT)	58
Partido Trabalhista Brasileiro (PTB)	31
Partido Democrático Trabalhista (PDT)	25
Partido Socialista Brasileiro (PSB)	19
Partido Liberal (PL)	12
Partido Comunista do Brasil (PC do B)	7
Partido Popular Socialista (PPS)	3
Others	11
Total	**513**

Senado Federal

(Federal Senate)

President: JADER BARBALHO (PMDB).

The 81 members of the Senate are elected by the 26 States and the Federal District (three Senators for each) according to the principle of majority. The Senate's term of office is eight years, with elections after four years for one-third of the members and after another four years for the remaining two-thirds.

Following the elections of 4 October 1998, the PMDB was represented by 27 senators, the PFL by 19, the PSDB by 16, the PT by 7 and the PPB by 5. The PSB, the PDT, the PTB and the PPS were also represented.

Governors

STATES

Acre: JORGE NEY VIANA (PT).

Alagoas: RONALDO AUGUSTO LESSA (PSB).

Amapá: JOÃO ALBERTO RODRIGUES CAPIBERIBE (PSB).

Amazonas: AMAZONINO ARMANDO MENDES (PFL).

Bahia: CÉSAR AUGUSTO RABELO BORGES (PFL).

Ceará: TASSO RIBEIRO JEREISSATI (PSDB).

Espírito Santo: JOSÉ IGNÁCIO FERREIRA (PSDB).

Goiás: MARCONI FERREIRA PERILLO (PSDB).

Maranhão: ROSEANA SARNEY MURAD (PFL).

Mato Grosso: DANTE MARTINS DE OLIVEIRA (PSDB).

Mato Grosso do Sul: ANTÔNIO ZECA (PT).

Minas Gerais: ITAMAR AUGUSTO CAUTIERO FRANCO (PMDB).

Pará: ALMIR DE OLIVEIRA GABRIEL (PSDB).

Paraíba: JOSÉ TARGINO MARANHÃO (PMDB).

Paraná: JAIME LERNER (PFL).

Pernambuco: JARBAS DE ANDRADE VASCONCELOS (PMDB).

Piauí: MÃO SANTA (PMDB).

Rio de Janeiro: ANTHONY WILLIAM GAROTINHO MATHEUS DE OLIVEIRA (PDT).

Rio Grande do Norte: GARIBALDI ALVES, Filho (PMDB).

Rio Grande do Sul: OLÍVIO DUTRA (PT).

Rondônia: JOSÉ DE ABREU BIANCO (PFL).

Roraima: NEUDO RIBEIRO CAMPOS (PTB).

Santa Catarina: ESPERIDIÃO AMIN HELOU, Filho (PPB).

São Paulo: GERALDO ALCKMIN.

Sergipe: ALBANO DO PRADO PIMENTEL FRANCO (PSDB).

Tocantins: JOSÉ WILSON SIQUEIRA CAMPOS (PFL).

FEDERAL DISTRICT

Brasília: JOAQUIM DOMINGOS RORIZ (PMDB).

Political Organizations

In May 1985 the National Congress approved a constitutional amendment providing for the free formation of political parties.

Partido Comunista do Brasil (PC do B): Rua Major Diogo 834, Bela Vista, 01324-000 São Paulo, SP; tel. (11) 232-1622; fax (11) 3106-4104; e-mail pcdobcc@uol.com.br; internet www.pcdob.org.br; f. 1922; Leader ALDO REBELO; Sec.-Gen. JOÃO AMAZONAS; 185,000 mems.

Partido Democrático Trabalhista (PDT): Rua Marechal Câmara 160, 4°, 20050 Rio de Janeiro, RJ; fax (21) 262-8834; e-mail pdtnac@ domain.com.br; internet www.pdt.org.br; f. 1980; formerly the PTB (Partido Trabalhista Brasileiro), renamed 1980 when that name was awarded to a dissident group following controversial judicial proceedings; member of Socialist International; Pres. LEONEL BRIZOLA; Gen. Sec. MANOEL DIAS.

Partido da Frente Liberal (PFL): Câmara dos Deputados, 70160-900 Brasília, DF; internet www.pfl.org.br; f. 1984 by moderate members of the PDS and PMDB; Pres. JORGE BORNHAUSEN; Gen. Sec. JOSÉ CARLOS ALELUIA.

Partido Liberal (PL): Câmara dos Deputados, 70160-900 Brasília, DF; Tel. (61) 318-5899; internet www.pl.org.br; Pres. VALDEMAR COSTA NETO.

Partido do Movimento Democrático Brasileiro (PMDB): Câmara dos Deputados, Edif. Principal, 70160-900 Brasília, DF; tel. (61) 318-5120; e-mail pmdb@tba.com.br; internet www.pmdb.org.br; f. 1980; moderate elements of former MDB; merged with Partido Popular February 1982; Pres. JADER BARBALHO; Sec.-Gen. SARANA FELIPE; factions include: the **Históricos** and the **Movimento da Unidade Progressiva (MUP)**.

Partido Popular Socialista (PPS): Rua Coronel Lisboa 260, Vila Mariana, 04020-040, São Paulo, SP; tel. (11) 570-2182; fax (11) 549-9841; internet www.pps.com.br; f. 1922; Pres. ROBERTO FREIRE.

Partido Progressista Brasileiro (PPB): Senado Federal, Anexo 1, 17° andar, 70165-900 Brasília, DF; tel. (61) 311-3041; fax (61) 226-8192; internet www.ppb.org.br; f. 1995 by merger of Partido Progressista Reformador (PPR), Partido Progressista (PP) and the Partido Republicano Progressista (PRP); right-wing; Pres. PAULO SALIM MALUF; Sec.-Gen. BENEDITO DOMINGOS.

Partido de Reconstrução Nacional (PRN): Brasília, DF; f. 1988; right-wing; Leader FERNANDO COLLOR DE MELLO.

Partido da Social Democracia Brasileira (PSDB): SCN, Quadro 04, Bloco B, Torre C, Sala 303/B, Centro Empresarial Varig, 70710-500 Brasília, DF; tel. (61) 328-0045; fax (61) 328-2120; e-mail tucano@psdb.org.br; internet www.psdb.org.br; f. 1988; centre-left; formed by dissident members of the PMDB (incl. Históricos), PFL, PDS, PDT, PSB and PTB; Pres. TEOTONIO VILELA, Filho; Sec.-Gen. MÁRCIO FORTES.

Partido Socialista Brasileiro (PSB): Brasília, DF; tel. (61) 318-6951; fax (61) 318-2104; internet www.psb.org.br; f. 1947; Pres. MIGUEL ARRAES; Sec.-Gen. RENATO SOARES.

Partido dos Trabalhadores (PT): Congresso Nacional, 70160, Brasília, DF; tel. (61) 224-1699; internet www.pt.org.br; f. 1980; first independent labour party; associated with the *autêntico* branch of the trade union movement; 350,000 mems; Pres. JOSÉ DIRCEU DE OLIVEIRA E SILVA; Vice-Pres. JACÓ BITTAR.

Partido Trabalhista Brasileiro (PTB): SCLN 303, Bloco C, Sala 105, Asa Norte, 70735-530 Brasília, DF; tel. (61) 226-0477; fax (61) 225-4757; e-mail ptb@ptb.org.br; internet www.ptb.org.br; f. 1980; Pres. JOSÉ EDUARDO ANDRADE VIEIRA; Sec.-Gen. RODRIGUES PALMA.

Other political parties represented in the Congresso Nacional include the Partido Social Cristão (PSC; internet www.psc.org.br), the Partido Social-Democrático (PSD), the Partido Verde (PV; internet www.pv.org.br) and the Partido da Mobilização Nacional (PMN; internet www.pmn.org.br).

Diplomatic Representation

EMBASSIES IN BRAZIL

Algeria: SHIS, QI 09, Conj. 13, Casa 01, Lago Sul, 70472-900 Brasília, DF; tel. (61) 248-4039; fax (61) 248-4691; Ambassador: LAHCÈNE MOUSSAOUI.

Angola: SHIS, QI 07, Conj. 11, Casa 9, 71625-160 Brasília, DF; tel. (61) 248-4489; fax (61) 248-1567; Ambassador: ALBERTO CORREIA NETO.

Argentina: SHIS, QL 02, Conj. 1, Casa 19, Lago Sul, 70442-900 Brasília, DF; tel. (61) 356-3000; fax (61) 365-2109; Ambassador: JUAN JOSÉ URANGA.

Australia: SHIS, QI 09, Conj. 16, Casa 01, Lago Sul, 70469-900 Brasília, DF; tel. (61) 248-5569; fax (61) 248-1066; e-mail embaustr@nutecnet.com.br; Ambassador: GARY ALFRED CONROY.

Austria: SES, Quadra 811, Av. das Nações, Lote 40, 70426-900 Brasília, DF; tel. (61) 443-3111; fax (61) 443-5233; e-mail emb .austria@zaz.com.br; Ambassador: DANIEL KRUMHOLZ.

Bangladesh: SHIS, QI 07, Conj. 03, Casa 04, 71615-230 Brasília, DF; tel. (61) 248-4905; fax (61) 248-4609; e-mail bdoot.bz@nutecnet .com.br; Ambassador: SYED NOOR HOSSAIN.

Belgium: SES, Av. das Nações, Lote 32, 70422-900 Brasília, DF; tel. (61) 443-1133; fax (61) 443-1219; Ambassador: JEAN-MIGUEL VERANNEMAN DE WATERVLIET.

Bolivia: SHIS, QI 19, Conj. 13, Casa 19, Lago Sul, Brasília, DF; tel. (61) 366-3432; fax (61) 366-3136; e-mail embol@vol.com.br; Ambassador: GONZALO MONTENEGRO IRIGOYEN.

Bulgaria: SEN, Av. das Nações, Lote 8, 70432-900 Brasília, DF; tel. (61) 223-6193; fax (61) 323-3285; e-mail tchavo@tba.com.br; Ambassador: VENTZISLAV ANGUELOV IVANOV.

Cameroon: SHIS, QI 11, Conj. 10, Casa 06, Lago Sul, 71600-900 Brasília, DF; tel. (61) 248-5403; fax (61) 248-0443; Ambassador: MARTIN NGUELE MBARGA.

Canada: SES, Av. das Nações, Quadra 803, Lote 16, 70410-900 Brasília, DF; CP 00961, 70359-970 Brasília, DF; tel. (61) 321-2171; fax (61) 321-4529; e-mail brsla@dfait-maeci.gc.ca; Ambassador: JEAN-PIERRE JUNEAU.

Cape Verde: SHIS, QL 07, Conj. 01, Casa 06, 71615-210 Brasília, DF; tel. (61) 248-1210; fax (61) 248-1210; e-mail embcaboverde@rudah.com.br; Ambassador: MANUEL AUGUSTO AMANTE DE ROSA.

Chile: SES, Av. das Nações, Quadra 803, Lote 11, 70407-900 Brasília, DF; tel. (61) 322-5151; fax (61) 322-2966; e-mail embchile@terra.com.br; Ambassador: CARLOS EDUARDO MENA KEYMER.

China, People's Republic: SES, Av. das Nações, Lote 51, 70443-900 Brasília, DF; tel. (61) 346-4436; fax (61) 346-3299; Ambassador: WAN YONGXIANG.

Colombia: SES, Av. das Nações, Quadra 803, Lote 10, 70444-900 Brasília, DF; tel. (61) 226-8997; fax (61) 224-4732; e-mail embcol@tba.com.br; Ambassador: SAMUEL NAVAS PINZÓN.

Congo, Democratic Republic: SMPW, Quadra 11, Conj. 2, Lote 06, Lago Sul, CP 07-041, 71600 Brasília, DF; tel. (61) 338-7386; Chargé d'affaires a.i. : LUMBA MFULUNKATU.

Costa Rica: SRTVN 701, Conj. C, Ala A, Salas 308/310, Edifício Centro Empresarial Norte, 70710-200, Brasília, DF; tel. (61) 328-2219; fax (61) 328-2243; e-mail embrica@solar.com.br; Ambassador: (vacant).

Côte d'Ivoire: SEN. Av. das Nações, Lote 9, 70473-900, Brasília, DF; tel. (61) 321-4656; fax (61) 321-1306; Ambassador: COLETTE GALLIE LAMBIN.

Croatia: SHIS QI 9, Conj. 11, Casa 3, 71625-110 Brasília, DF; tel. (61) 248-0610; fax (61) 248-1708; Ambassador: ZELIMIR URBAN.

Cuba: SHIS, QI 15, Conj. 18, Casa 01, Lago Sul, 70481-900 Brasília, DF; tel. (61) 248-4710; fax (61) 248-6778; Ambassador: JORGE LEZCANO PÉREZ.

Czech Republic: Av. das Nações, Quadra 805, Lote 21, 70414-900, CP 970 Brasília, DF; tel. (61) 242-7785; fax (61) 242-7833; e-mail czech@brnet.com.br; Ambassador: LADISLAV SKERIK.

Denmark: SES, Av. das Nações, Lote 26, 70416-900 Brasília, DF; tel. (61) 443-8188; fax (61) 443-5232; e-mail danmark@tba.com.br; Ambassador: ANITA HUGAU.

Dominican Republic: SHIS, QL 8, Conj. 5, Casa 14, Lago Sul, 70460-900 Brasília, DF; tel. and fax (61) 248-1405; e-mail embjdargan@nutcnet.com.br; Ambassador: CIRO AMAURY DARGAM CRUZ.

Ecuador: SHIS, QI 11, Conj. 9, Casa 24, 71625-290 Brasília, DF; tel. (61) 248-5560; fax (61) 248-1290; e-mail embec@solar.com.br; Ambassador: DIEGO RIBADENEIRA ESPINOSA.

Egypt: SEN, Av. das Nações, Lote 12, Asa Norte, 70435-900 Brasília, DF; tel. (61) 323-8800; fax (61) 323-1039; e-mail embegypt@tba.com.br; internet www.tba.com.br/pages/embegypt; Ambassador: HATEM AZIZ SEIF EN-NASR.

El Salvador: SHIS, QI 07, Conj. 6, Casa 14, 71615-260 Brasília, DF; tel. (61) 364-4141; fax (61) 364-2459; e-mail embelsalvador@tba.com.br; Ambassador: MARTÍN ALBERTO RIVERA GÓMEZ.

Finland: SES, Av. das Nações, Lote 27, 70417-900 Brasília, DF; tel. (61) 443-7151; fax (61) 443-3315; e-mail suomi@tba.com.br/finlandia; Ambassador: ASKO HENRIK NUMMINEN.

France: SES, Av. das Nações, Lote 4, 70404-900 Brasília, DF; tel. (61) 312-9100; fax (61) 312-9108; Ambassador: ALAIN ROUQUIÉ.

Gabon: SHIS QI 9, Conj. 11, Casa 24, 71615-300, Brasília, DF; tel. (61) 248-3536; fax (61) 248-2241; e-mail mgabao@nutecnet.com.br; Ambassador: MARCEL ODONGUI-BONNARD.

Germany: SES, Av. das Nações, Lote 25, 70415-900 Brasília, DF; tel. (61) 443-7330; fax (61) 443-7508; Ambassador: HANS-BODO BERTRAM.

Ghana: SHIS, QL 10, Conj. 8, Casa 2, CP 07-0456, 70466-900 Brasília, DF; tel. (61) 248-6047; fax (61) 248-7913; Chargé d'affaires a.i.: SAMMIE PESKY EDDICO .

Greece: SES, Av. das Nações, Quadra 805, Lote 22, 70480-900 Brasília, DF; tel. (61) 443-6573; fax (61) 443-6902; e-mail emb grecia@zaz.com.br; internet www.emb-grecia.org; Ambassador: STRATOS DOUKAS.

Guatemala: SHIS, QI 09, Conj. 2, Casa 08, 71625-020 Brasília, DF; tel. (61) 248-3318; fax (61) 248-4383; Ambassador: GLORIA VICTORIA PENSABENE DE TROCHE.

Guyana: SBN, Quadra 2, Bloco J, Edif. Paulo Maurício, 13° andar, salas 1310–1315, 70438-900 Brasília, DF; tel. (61) 326-9728; fax (61) 326-3022; e-mail embguyana@apis.com.br; Ambassador: MARILYN CHERYL MILES.

Haiti: SHIS, QI 17, Conj. 4, Casa 19, Lago Sul, 70465-900 Brasília, DF; tel. (61) 248-6860; fax (61) 248-7472; Chargé d'affaires: JEAN-VICTOR HARVEL JEAN-BAPTISTE.

Holy See: SES, Av. das Nações, Lote 1, CP 153, 70359-970 Brasília, DF (Apostolic Nunciature); tel. (61) 223-0794; fax (61) 224-9365; e-mail nunapost@sdar.com.br; Apostolic Nuncio: Most Rev. ALFIO RAPISARDA, Titular Archbishop of Cannae.

Honduras: SBN, Edif. Engenheiro Paulo Maurício, Salas 712–716, 70040-905 Brasília, DF; tel. (61) 248-1200; fax (61) 248-1425; Ambassador: GERARDO MARTÍNEZ BLANCO.

Hungary: SES, Av. das Nações, Quadra 805, Lote 19, 70413-900 Brasília, DF; tel. (61) 443-0836; fax (61) 443-3434; e-mail huembbrz@uninet.com.br; internet www.hungria.org.br; Ambassador: TAMÁS RÓZSA.

India: SHIS, QL 08, Conj. 8, Casa 01, 71625-285 Brasília, DF; tel. (61) 248-4006; fax (61) 248-7849; Ambassador: MUTHAL PUREDATH M. MENON.

Indonesia: SES, Av. das Nações, Quadra 805, Lote 20, 70479-900 Brasília, DF; tel. (61) 443-1788; fax (61) 443-8020; Ambassador: SUTADI DJAJAKUSUMA.

Iran: SES, Av. das Nações, Lote 31, 70421-900 Brasília, DF; tel. (61) 242-5733; fax (61) 224-9640; Ambassador: MANSOUR MOAZAMI.

Iraq: SES, Av. das Nações, Quadra 815, Lote 64, 70430-900 Brasília, DF; tel. (61) 346-2822; fax (61) 346-7034; Ambassador: AHMED IBRAHIM AL-AZZAWI.

Israel: SES, Av. das Nações, Lote 38, 70424-900 Brasília, DF; tel. (61) 244-7675; fax (61) 244-6129; e-mail embisrae@solar.com.br; Ambassador: DANIEL GAZIT.

Italy: SES, Av. das Nações, Lote 30, 70420 Brasília, DF; tel. (61) 443-0044; fax (61)443-1231; e-mail embitalia@zaz.com.br; internet www.embitalia.org.br; Ambassador: VINCENZO PETRONE.

Japan: SES, Av. das Nações, Lote 39, 70425-900 Brasília, DF; tel. (61) 242-6866; fax (61) 242-0738; Ambassador: KATSUNARI SUZUKI.

Jordan: SHIS, QI 9, Conj. 18, Casa 14, 70483-900 Brasília, DF; tel. (61) 248-5407; fax (61) 248-1698; Ambassador: FARIS SHAWKAT MUFTI.

Korea, Republic: SEN, Av. das Nações, Lote 14, 70436-900 Brasília, DF; tel. (61) 321-2500; fax (61) 321-2508; Ambassador: KIM MYONG-BAI.

Kuwait: SHIS, QI 05, Chácara 30, 71600-750 Brasília, DF; tel. (61) 248-2323; fax (61) 248-0969; Ambassador: NASSER SABEEH B. AS-SABEEH.

Lebanon: SES, Av. das Nações, Quadra 805, Lote 17, 70411-900 Brasília, DF; tel. (61) 443-9837; fax (61) 443-8574; e-mail emblibano @uol.com.br; Ambassador: ISHAYA EL-KHOURY.

Libya: SHIS, QI 15, Chácara 26, CP 3505, 70462-900 Brasília, DF; tel. (61) 248-6710; fax (61) 248-0598; Chargé d'affaires a.i.: MOHAMED HEIMEDA SAAD MATRI.

Malaysia: SHIS, QI 05, Chácara 62, Lago Sul, 70477-900 Brasília, DF; tel. (61) 248-5008; fax (61) 248-6307; e-mail mwbrasilia@persocom.com.br; Ambassador: S. THANARAJASINGAM.

Malta: Av. W3 Norte, Quadra 507, Bloco C, 70740-535 Brasília, DF; tel. (61) 272-0402; fax (61) 347-4940; Ambassador: WOLFGANG FRANZ JOSEF SAUER.

Mexico: SES, Av. das Nações, Lote 18, 70412-900 Brasília, DF; tel. (61) 244-1011; fax (61) 443-6275; e-mail embamexbra@brnet.com.br; Ambassador: CECILIA SOTO GONZÁLEZ.

Morocco: SEN, Av. das Nações, Lote 2, 70432-900 Brasília, DF; tel. (61) 321-4487; fax (61) 321-0745; e-mail sifamabr@tba.com.br; internet www.mincom.gov.ma; Ambassador: ABDELMALEK CHARKAOUI GHAZOUANI.

Mozambique: SHIS, QL 12, Conj. 7, Casa 9, 71630-275 Brasília, DF; tel. (61) 248-4222; fax (61) 248-3917; Ambassador: FELIZARDA ISAURA MONTEIRO.

Myanmar: SHIS, QL 8, Conj. 4, Casa 5, 71620-245 Brasília, DF; tel. (61) 248-3747; fax (61) 248-1922; e-mail mebrsl@brnet.com.br; Ambassador: U. KYAW MIYNT.

Netherlands: SES, Av. das Nações, Quadra 801, Lote 05, 7045-900 Brasília, DF; tel. (61) 321-4769; fax (61) 321-1518; e-mail nlgovbra@pepz.brnet.com.br; Ambassador: FRANCISCUS BENEDICTUS ANTONIUS MARIA VAN HAREN.

New Zealand: SHIS, QL 10, Conj. 08, Casa 10, Lago Sul, 71630-085; tel. (61) 924-8034; fax (61) 364-0278; e-mail jeff_langley@mfat.gov.nz; Ambassador: JEFFERY PATRICK LANGLEY.

Nicaragua: SHIS, QI 03, Conj. 01, Casa 06, Lago Sul, 71605-210 Brasília, DF; tel. (61) 365-2555; fax (61) 365-2562; Ambassador: EDGARD SOLÍS MARTÍNEZ.

Nigeria: SEN, Av. das Nações, Lote 05, CP 03-710, 70459-900 Brasília, DF; tel. (61) 226-1717; fax (61) 224-0320; Ambassador: JOSEF SOOKORE EGBUSON.

Norway: SES, Av. das Nações, Lote 28, CP 07-0670, 70418-900 Brasília, DF; tel. (61) 443-8720; fax (61) 443-2942; e-mail embno@tba.com.br; Ambassador: LIV AGNES KERR.

Pakistan: SHIS, QL 12, Conj. 02, Casa 19, 71615-140 Brasília, DF; tel. (61) 364-1632; fax (61) 248-0246; Ambassador: MUHAMMAD NASSER MIAN.

Panama: SHIS, QL 6, Conj. 11, Casa 18, 71625-260 Brasília, DF; tel. (61) 248-7309; fax (61) 248-2834; e-mail empanama@nettur.com.br; Ambassador: OLIMPO ANÍBAL SAEZ MARCUCCI.

Paraguay: SES, Av. das Nações, Quadra 811, Lote 42, CP 14-2314, 70427-900 Brasília, DF; tel. (61) 242-3742; fax (61) 242-4605; Ambassador: LUÍS GONZALEZ ARIAS.

Peru: SES, Av. das Nações, Lote 43, 70428-900 Brasília, DF; tel. (61) 242-9933; fax (61) 244-9344; e-mail emb_peru@nutecnet.com.br; Ambassador: EDUARDO PONCE VIVANCO.

Philippines: SEN, Av. das Nações, Lote 1, 70431 Brasília, DF; tel. (61) 223-5143; fax (61) 226-7411; e-mail pr@pop.persocom.com.br; Ambassador: OSCAR G. VALENZUELA.

Poland: SES, Av. das Nações, Lote 33, 70423-900 Brasília, DF; tel. (61) 443-3438; fax (61) 242-8543; Ambassador: JACEK HINZ.

Portugal: SES, Av. das Nações, Lote 2, 70402-900 Brasília, DF; tel. (61) 321-3434; fax (61) 224-7347; e-mail embporbr@abordo.com.br; Ambassador: ANTÓNIO MANUEL CANASTREIRO FRANCO.

Romania: SEN, Av. das Nações, Lote 6, 70456 Brasília, DF; tel. (61) 226-0746; fax (61) 226-6629; e-mail romenia@tba.com.br; Ambassador: ION FLOROIU.

Russia: SES, Av. das Nações, Quadra 801, Lote A, 70476-900 Brasília, DF; tel. (61) 223-3094; fax (61) 223-5094; e-mail embrus@brnet.com.br; internet www.brnet.com.br/pages/embrus; Ambassador: VASSILII PETROVICH GROMOV.

Saudi Arabia: SHIS, QL 10, Conj. 9, Casa 20, 70471-900 Brasília, DF; tel. (61) 248-3523; fax (61) 284-2905; Ambassador: ANWAR ABD RABBUH.

Slovakia: Av. das Nações, Quadra 805, Lote 21, 70414-900 Brasília, DF; tel. (61) 443-1263; fax (61) 443-1267; Ambassador: JOZEF ADAMEC.

South Africa: SES, Av. das Nações, Lote 6, CP 11-1170, 70406 Brasília, DF; tel. (61) 312-9500; fax (61) 322-8491; e-mail saemb@brnet.com.br; Ambassador: MBULELO RAKWENA.

Spain: SES, Av. das Nações, Lote 44, 70429-900 Brasília, DF; tel. (61) 244-2121; fax (61) 242-1781; Ambassador: JOSÉ CODERCH PLANAS.

Suriname: SHIS, QI 09, Conj. 8, Casa 24, 70457-900 Brasília, DF; tel. (61) 248-6706; fax (61) 248-3791; e-mail sur.emb@persocom.com.br; Chargé d'affaires a.i.: ROBBY D. RAMLAKHAN.

Sweden: SES, Av. das Nações, Lote 29, 70419-900 Brasília, DF; tel. (61) 443-1444; fax (61) 443-1187; e-mail swebra@tba.com.br; Ambassador: CHRISTER MANHUSEN.

Switzerland: SES, Av. das Nações, Lote 41, 70448-900 Brasília, DF; CP 08671, 70312-970 Brasília, DF; tel. (61) 443-5500; fax (61) 443-5711; e-mail swissembra@brasilia.com.br; Ambassador: JÜRG LEUTERT.

Syria: SEN, Av. das Nações, Lote 11, 70434-900 Brasília, DF; tel. (61) 226-0970; fax (61) 223-2595; Ambassador: CHAHINE FARAH.

Thailand: SEN, Av. das Nações Norte, Lote 10, 70433-900 Brasília, DF; tel. (61) 224-6943; fax (61) 321-2994; Ambassador: SAMROENG LAKSANASUT.

Trinidad and Tobago: SHIS, QL 02, Conj. 02, Casa 01, 71665-028 Brasília, DF; tel. (61) 365-1132; fax (61) 365-1733; e-mail trinbago@tba.com.br; Ambassador: ROBERT M. TORRY.

Tunisia: SHIS, QI 9, Conj. 16, Casa 20, 71625-160 Brasília, DF; tel. (61) 248-3725; fax (61) 248-7355; Ambassador: HASSINE BOUZID.

Turkey: SES, Av. das Nações, Lote 23, 70452-900 Brasília, DF; tel. (61) 242-1850; fax (61) 242-1448; e-mail emb.turquia@conectanet.com.br; Ambassador: SEVINÇ DALYANOĞLU.

Ukraine: SHIS, QL 6, Conj. 2, Casa 17, 71620-025 Brasília, DF; tel. (61) 365-3889; fax (61) 365-3898; e-mail brucremb@zaz.com.br; Chargé d'Affaires: ROSTYSLAV TRONENKO.

United Arab Emirates: SHIS, QI 5, Chácara 18, 70486-901 Brasília, DF; tel. (61) 248-0717; fax (61) 248-7543; Ambassador: SAEED HAMED AL-JUNAIBI.

United Kingdom: SES, Quadra 801, Conj. K, Lote 8, CP 07-0586, 70408-900 Brasília, DF; tel. (61) 225-2710; fax (61) 225-1777; e-mail britemb@nutecnet.com.br; Ambassador: ROGER BRIDGELAND BONE.

USA: SES, Av. das Nações, Quadra 801, Lote 3, 70403-900 Brasília, DF; tel. (61) 321-7272; fax (61) 225-9136; Ambassador: ANTHONY STEPHEN HARRINGTON.

Uruguay: SES, Av. das Nações, Lote 14, 70450-900 Brasília, DF; tel. (61) 322-1200; fax (61) 322-6534; e-mail urubras@tba.com.br; Ambassador: AUGUSTIN ESPINOSA LLOVERAS.

Venezuela: SES, Av. das Nações, Quadra 803, Lote 13, 70451-900 Brasília, DF; tel. (61) 322-1011; fax (61) 226-5633; e-mail embvenbr@nutecnet.com.br; Ambassador: MILOS ALCALAY.

Viet Nam: SHIS, QI 05, Conj. 07, Casa 21, 71615-070 Brasília, DF; tel. and fax (61) 364-5587; Ambassador: (vacant)

Yugoslavia: SES, Av. das Nações, Quadra 803, Lote 15, 70409-900 Brasília, DF; tel. (61) 223-7272; fax (61) 223-8462; e-mail embiugos@nutecnet.com.br; Chargé d'affaires a.i.: RADIVOJE LAZAREVIĆ.

Judicial System

The judiciary powers of the State are held by the following: the Supreme Federal Tribunal, the Higher Tribunal of Justice, the five Regional Federal Tribunals and Federal Judges, the Higher Labour Tribunal, the 24 Regional Labour Tribunals, the Conciliation and Judgment Councils and Labour Judges, the Higher Electoral Tribunal, the 27 Regional Electoral Tribunals, the Electoral Judges and Electoral Councils, the Higher Military Tribunal, the Military Tribunals and Military Judges, the Tribunals of the States and Judges of the States, the Tribunal of the Federal District and of the Territories and Judges of the Federal District and of the Territories.

The Supreme Federal Tribunal comprises 11 ministers, nominated by the President and approved by the Senate. Its most important role is to rule on the final interpretation of the Constitution. The Supreme Federal Tribunal has the power to declare an act of Congress void if it is unconstitutional. It judges offences committed by persons such as the President, the Vice-President, members of the Congresso Nacional, Ministers of State, its own members, the Attorney General, judges of other higher courts, and heads of permanent diplomatic missions. It also judges cases of litigation between the Union and the States, between the States, or between foreign nations and the Union or the States; disputes as to jurisdiction between higher Tribunals, or between the latter and any other court, in cases involving the extradition of criminals, and others related to the writs of habeas corpus and habeas data, and in other cases.

The Higher Tribunal of Justice comprises at least 33 members, appointed by the President and approved by the Senado. Its jurisdiction includes the judgment of offences committed by State Governors. The Regional Federal Tribunals comprise at least seven judges, recruited when possible in the respective region and appointed by the President of the Republic. The Higher Labour Tribunal comprises 27 members, appointed by the President and approved by the Senado. The judges of the Regional Labour Tribunals are also appointed by the President. The Higher Electoral Tribunal comprises at least seven members: three judges from among those of the Supreme Federal Tribunal, two from the Higher Tribunal of Justice (elected by secret ballot) and two lawyers appointed by the President. The Regional Electoral Tribunals are also composed of seven members. The Higher Military Tribunal comprises 15 life members, appointed by the President and approved by the Senate; three from the navy, four from the army, three from the air force and five civilian members. The States are responsible for the administration of their own justice, according to the principles established by the Constitution.

SUPREME FEDERAL TRIBUNAL

Supreme Federal Tribunal: Praça dos Três Poderes, 70175-900 Brasília, DF; tel. (61) 316-5000; fax (61) 316-5483; internet www.stf.gov.br.

President: MARCO AURÉLIO MENDES DE FARIAS MELLO.

Vice-President: ILMAR NASCIMENTO GALVÃO.

Justices: JOSÉ CARLOS MOREIRA ALVES, JOSÉ NÉRI DA SILVEIRA, SYDNEY SANCHES, LUIZ OCTAVIO PIRES E ALBUQUERQUE GALLOTTI, JOSÉ PAULO SEPÚLVEDA PERTENCE, JOSÉ CELSO DE MELLO, Filho, MAURÍCIO JOSÉ CORRÊA, NELSON DE AZEVEDO JOBIM.

Attorney-General: GERALDO BRINDEIRO.

Director-General (Secretariat): JOSÉ GERALDO DE LANA TÔRRES.

Religion

CHRISTIANITY

Conselho Nacional de Igrejas Cristãs do Brasil—CONIC (National Council of Christian Churches in Brazil): SCS, Quadra 01, Bloco E, Edif. Ceará, Sala 713, 70303-900 Brasília, DF; tel. (61) 321-8341; fax (61) 321-3034; f. 1982; seven mem. churches; Pres. P. JOAQUIM BEATO; Exec. Sec. P. ERVINO SCHMIDT.

The Roman Catholic Church

Brazil comprises 38 archdioceses, 210 dioceses (including one each for Catholics of the Maronite, Melkite and Ukrainian Rites), 14 territorial prelatures and two territorial abbacies. The Archbishop of São Sebastião do Rio de Janeiro is also the Ordinary for Catholics of other Oriental Rites in Brazil (estimated at 10,000 in 1994). The great majority of Brazil's population are adherents of the Roman Catholic Church (around 106m. at the time of the 1980 census), although a report published by the Brazilian weekly, *Veja*, in July 1989 concluded that since 1950 the membership of non-Catholic Christian Churches had risen from 3% to 6% of the total population, while membership of the Roman Catholic Church had fallen from 93% to 89% of Brazilians.

Bishops' Conference: Conferência Nacional dos Bispos do Brasil, SE/Sul Q 801, Conj. B, CP 02067, 70259-970 Brasília, DF; tel. (61) 313-8300; fax (61) 313-8303; e-mail cnbb@cnbb.org.br; f. 1980 (statutes approved 1986); Pres. JAYME HENRIQUE CHEMELLO, Bishop of Pelotas, RS; Sec.-Gen. RAYMUNDO DAMASCENO ASSIS.

Latin Rite

Archbishop of São Salvador da Bahia, BA: Cardinal GERALDO MAJELLA AGNELO, Primate of Brazil, Rua Martin Afonso de Souza 270, 40100-050 Salvador, BA; tel. and fax (71) 328-6699.

Archbishop of Aparecida, SP: Cardinal ALOÍSIO LORSCHEIDER.

Archbishop of Aracajú, SE: JOSÉ PALMEIRA LESSA.

Archbishop of Belém do Pará, PA: VICENTE JOAQUIM ZICO.

Archbishop of Belo Horizonte, MG: Cardinal SERAFIM FERNANDES DE ARAÚJO.

Archbishop of Botucatú, SP: ALOYSIO JOSÉ LEAL PENNA.

Archbishop of Brasília, DF: Cardinal JOSÉ FREIRE FALCÃO.

Archbishop of Campinas, SP: GILBERTO PEREIRA LOPES.

Archbishop of Campo Grande, MS: VITÓRIO PAVANELLO.

Archbishop of Cascavel, PR: LÚCIO IGNÁCIO BAUMGAERTNER.

Archbishop of Cuiabá, MT: BONIFÁCIO PICCININI.

Archbishop of Curitiba, PR: PEDRO ANTÔNIO MARCHETTI FEDALTO.

Archbishop of Diamantina, MG: PAULO LOPES DE FARIA.

Archbishop of Florianópolis, SC: EUSÉBIO OSCAR SCHEID.

Archbishop of Fortaleza, CE: JOSÉ ANTÔNIO APARECIDO TOSI MARQUES.

Archbishop of Goiânia, GO: ANTÔNIO RIBEIRO DE OLIVEIRA.

Archbishop of Juiz de Fora, MG: CLÓVIS FRAINER.

Archbishop of Londrina, PR: ALBANO BORTOLETTO CAVALLIN.

Archbishop of Maceió, AL: EDVALDO GONÇALVES AMARAL.

Archbishop of Manaus, AM: LUIZ SOARES VIEIRA.

Archbishop of Mariana, MG: LUCIANO PEDRO MENDES DE ALMEIDA.

Archbishop of Maringá, PR: MURILO SEBASTIÃO RAMOS KRIEGER.

Archbishop of Natal, RN: HEITOR DE ARAÚJO SALES.

Archbishop of Niterói, RJ: CARLOS ALBERTO ETCHANDY GIMENONAVARRO.

Archbishop of Olinda e Recife, PE: JOSÉ CARDOSO SOBRINHO.

Archbishop of Palmas, PR: ALBERTO TAVEIRA CORRÊA.

Archbishop of Paraíba, PB: MARCELO PINTO CARVALHEIRA.

Archbishop of Porto Alegre, RS: DADEUS GRINGS.

Archbishop of Porto Velho, RO: MOACYR GRECHI.

Archbishop of Pouso Alegre, MG: RICARDO PEDRO CHAVES PINTO, Filho.

Archbishop of Ribeirão Prêto, SP: ARNALDO RIBEIRO.

Archbishop of São Luís do Maranhão, MA: PAULO EDUARDO DE ANDRADE PONTE.

Archbishop of São Paulo, SP: Cardinal CLAUDIO HUMMES.

Archbishop of São Sebastião do Rio de Janeiro, RJ: Cardinal EUGÊNIO DE ARAÚJO SALES.

Archbishop of Sorocaba, SP: JOSÉ LAMBERT.

Archbishop of Teresina, PI: CELSO JOSÉ PINTO DA SILVA.

Archbishop of Uberaba, MG: ALOÍSIO ROQUE OPPERMANN.

Archbishop of Vitória, ES: SILVESTRE LUÍS SCANDIAN.

Maronite Rite

Bishop of Nossa Senhora do Líbano em São Paulo, SP: JOSEPH MAHFOUZ.

Melkite Rite

Bishop of Nossa Senhora do Paraíso em São Paulo, SP: FARES MAAKAROUN.

Ukrainian Rite

Bishop of São João Batista em Curitiba, PR: EFRAIM BASÍLIO KREVEY.

The Anglican Communion

Anglicans form the Episcopal Anglican Church of Brazil (Igreja Episcopal Anglicana do Brasil), comprising seven dioceses.

Igreja Episcopal Anglicana do Brasil: CP 11-510, 90841-970 Porto Alegre, RS; tel. and fax (51) 318-6200; f. 1890; 103,021 mems (1997); Primate Most Rev. GLAUCO SOARES DE LIMA, Bishop of São Paulo-Brazil; Gen. Sec. Rev. MAURICIO J. A. DE ANDRADE; e-mail m_andrade@ieab.org.br.

Protestant Churches

Igreja Cristã Reformada do Brasil: CP 2808, 01000 São Paulo, SP; Pres. Rev. JANOS APOSTOL.

Igreja Evangélica de Confissão Luterana no Brasil (IECLB): Rua Senhor dos Passos 202, 2° andar, CP 2876, 90020-180 Porto Alegre, RS; tel. (51) 221-3433; fax (51) 225-7244; e-mailsecretaria geral@ieclb.org.br; internet www.iedb.org.br; f. 1949; 714,000 mems; Pres. Pastor HUBERTO KIRCHHEIM.

Igreja Evangélica Congregacional do Brasil: CP 414, 98700 Ijuí, RS; tel. (55) 332-4656; f. 1942; 41,000 mems, 310 congregations; Pres. Rev. H. HARTMUT W. HACHTMANN.

Igreja Evangélica Luterana do Brasil: Rua Cel. Lucas de Oliveira 894, 90440-010 Porto Alegre, RS; tel. (51) 332-2111; fax (51) 332-8145; e-mail ielb@ielb.org.br; internet www.ielb.org.br; f. 1904; 218,600 mems; Pres. Rev. CARLOS WALTER WINTERLE.

Igreja Metodista do Brasil: General Communication Secretariat, Rua Artur Azevedo 1192, Apdo 81, Pinheiros, 05404 São Paulo, SP; Exec. Sec. Dr ONÉSIMO DE OLIVEIRA CARDOSO.

Igreja Presbiteriana Unida do Brasil (IPU): CP 01-212, 29001-970 Vitória, ES; tel. (27) 222-8024; f. 1978; Sec. PAULO RÜCKERT.

BAHÁ'Í FAITH

Bahá'í Community of Brazil: SHIS, QL 08, Conj. 2, Casa 15, 71620-285, Brasília, DF; CP 7035, 71620-225 Brasília, DF; tel. (61) 364-3594; fax (61) 364-3470; e-mail secext@bahai.org.br; f. 1921; Sec. IRADJ ROBERTO EGHRARI.

BUDDHISM

Federação das Seitas Budistas do Brasil: Av. Paulo Ferreira 1133, 02915-100, São Paulo, SP; tel. (11) 876-5771; fax (11) 877-8687.

Sociedade Budista do Brasil (Rio Buddhist Vihara): Dom Joaquim Mamede 45, Lagoinha, Santa Tereza, 20241-390 Rio de Janeiro, RJ; tel. (21) 205-4400; f. 1972; Principal Dr PUHULWELLE VIPASSI.

The Press

The most striking feature of the Brazilian press is the relatively small circulation of newspapers in comparison with the size of the population. The newspapers with the largest circulations are *O Día* (250,000), *O Globo* (350,000), *Fôlha de São Paulo* (560,000), and *O Estado de São Paulo* (242,000). The low circulation is mainly owing to high costs resulting from distribution difficulties. In consequence there are no national newspapers. In 1996 a total of 380 daily newspaper titles were published in Brazil.

DAILY NEWSPAPERS

Belém, PA

O Liberal: Rua Gaspar Viana 253, 66020 Belém, PA; tel. (91) 222-3000; fax (91) 224-1906; f. 1946; Pres. LUCIDEA MAIORANA; circ. 20,000.

Belo Horizonte, MG

Diário da Tarde: Rua Goiás 36, 30190 Belo Horizonte, MG; tel. (31) 273-2322; fax (31) 273-4400; f. 1931; evening; Dir-Gen. PAULO C. DE ARAÚJO; total circ. 150,000.

Diário de Minas: Rua Francisco Salles 540, 30150-220 Belo Horizonte, MG; tel. (31) 222-5622; f. 1949; Pres. MARCO AURÍLIO F. CARONE; circ. 50,000.

Diário do Comércio: Av. Américo Vespúcio 1660, 31.230 Belo Horizonte, MG; tel. (31) 469-1011; fax (31) 469-1080; f. 1932; Pres. JOSÉ COSTA.

Estado de Minas: Rua Goiás 36, 30190 Belo Horizonte, MG; tel. (31) 273-2322; fax (31) 273-4400; f. 1928; morning; independent; Pres. PAULO C. DE ARAÚJO; circ. 65,000.

Blumenau, SC

Jornal de Santa Catarina: Rua São Paulo 1120, 89010-000 Blumenau, SC; tel. (2147) 340-1400; e-mail redacao@santa.com.br; f. 1971; Dir ALVARO IAHNIG; circ. 25,000.

Brasília, DF

Correio Brasiliense: SIG, Q2, Lotes 300/340, 70610-901 Brasília, DF; tel. (61) 321-1314; fax (61) 321-2856; f. 1960; Dir-Gen. PAULO C. DE ARAÚJO; circ. 30,000.

Jornal de Brasília: SIG, Trecho 1, Lotes 585/645, 70610-400 Brasília, DF; tel. (61) 225-2515; f. 1972; Dir-Gen. FERNANDO CÔMA; circ. 25,000.

Campinas, SP

Correio Popular: Rua Conceição 124, 13010-902 Campinas, SP; tel. (192) 32-8588; fax (192) 31-8152; f. 1927; Pres. SYLVINO DE GODOY NETO; circ. 40,000.

Curitiba, PR

O Estado do Paraná: Rua João Tschannerl 800, 80820-000 Curitiba, PR; tel. (41) 335-8811; fax (41) 335-2838; f. 1951; Pres. PAULO CRUZ PIMENTEL; circ. 15,000.

Gazeta do Povo: Praça Carlos Gomes 4, 80010 Curitiba, PR; tel. (41) 224-0522; fax (41) 225-6848; f. 1919; Pres. FRANCISCO CUNHA PEREIRA; circ. 40,000.

Tribuna do Paraná: Rua João Tschannerl 800, 80820-010 Curitiba PR; tel. (41) 335-8811; fax (41) 335-2838; f. 1956; Pres. PAULO CRUZ PIMENTEL; circ. 15,000.

Florianópolis, SC

O Estado: Rodovia SC-401, Km 3, 88030 Florianópolis, SC; tel. (482) 388-8888; fax (482) 380-0711; f. 1915; Pres. JOSÉ MATUSALÉM COMELLI; circ. 20,000.

Fortaleza, CE

Jornal O Povo: Av. Aguanambi 282, 60055 Fortaleza, CE; tel. (85) 211-9666; fax (85) 231-5792; f. 1928; evening; Pres. DEMÓCRITO ROCHA DUMMAR; circ. 20,000.

Tribuna do Ceará: Av. Desemb. Moreira 2900, 60170 Fortaleza, CE; tel. (85) 247-3066; fax (85) 272-2799; f. 1957; Dir JOSÉ A. SANCHO; circ. 12,000.

Goiânia, GO

Diário da Manhã: Av. Anhanguera 2833, Setor Leste Universitário, 74000 Goiânia, GO; tel. (62) 261-7371; f. 1980; Pres. JULIO NASSER CUSTÓDIO DOS SANTOS; circ. 16,000.

Jornal O Popular: Rua Thómas Edson Q7, Setor Serrinha, 74835-130 Goiânia, GO; tel. (62) 250-1000; fax (62) 241-1018; f. 1938; Pres. JAIME CÂMARA JÚNIOR; circ. 65,000.

Londrina, PR

Fôlha de Londrina: Rua Piauí 241, 86010 Londrina, PR; tel. (432) 24-2020; fax (432) 21-1051; f. 1948; Pres. JOÃO MILANEZ; circ. 40,000.

Manaus, AM

A Crítica: Av. André Araújo, Km 3, 69060 Manaus; tel. (92) 642-2000; fax (92) 642-1501; f. 1949; Dir UMBERTO CADERARO; circ. 19,000.

Niterói, RJ

O Fluminense: Rua Visconde de Itaboraí 184, 24030 Niterói, RJ; tel. (21) 719-3311; fax (21) 719-6344; f. 1978; Dir ALBERTO FRANCISCO TORRES; circ. 80,000.

Jornal de Icarai: Rua Barão de Amazonas 31, 24030111 Niterói, RJ; tel. (21) 719-1886; e-mail icarai@urbi.com.br; f. 1926; daily.

A Tribuna: Rua Barão do Amazonas 31, 24030111 Niterói, RJ; tel. (21) 719-1886; e-mail icarai@urbi.com.br; f. 1926; daily; Dir-Gen. JOURDAN AMÓRA; circ. 10,000.

Porto Alegre, RS

Zero Hora: Av. Ipiranga 1075, 90169-900 Porto Alegre, RS; tel. (51) 218-4101; fax (51) 218-4405; internet www.rbs.com.br; f. 1964; Pres. NELSON SIROTSKY; circ. 165,000 (Mon.), 170,000 weekdays, 240,000 Sunday.

Recife, PE

Diário de Pernambuco: Praça da Independência 12, 2° andar, 50010-300 Recife, PE; tel. (81) 424-3666; fax (81) 424-2527; f. 1825; morning; independent; Pres. ANTÔNIO C. DA COSTA; circ. 31,000.

Ribeirão Preto, SP

Diário da Manhã: Rua Duque de Caxias 179, 14015 Ribeirão Preto, SP; tel. (16) 634-0909; f. 1898; Dir PAULO M. SANT'ANNA; circ. 17,000.

Rio de Janeiro, RJ

O Dia: Rua Riachuelo 359, 20235 Rio de Janeiro, RJ; tel. (21) 272-8000; fax (21) 507-1038; f. 1951; morning; centrist labour; Pres. ANTÔNIO ARY DE CARVALHO; circ. 250,000 weekdays, 500,000 Sundays.

O Globo: Rua Irineu Marinho 35, CP 1090, 20233-900 Rio de Janeiro, RJ; tel. (21) 534-5000; fax (21) 534-5510; f. 1925; morning; Dir FRANCISCO GRAELL; circ. 350,000 weekdays, 600,000 Sundays.

Jornal do Brasil: Av. Brasil 500, 6° andar, São Cristovão, 20949-900 Rio de Janeiro, RJ; tel. (21) 585-4422; f. 1891; morning; Catholic, liberal; Pres. M. F. DO NASCIMENTO BRITO; circ. 200,000 weekdays, 325,000 Sundays.

Jornal do Comércio: Rua do Livramento 189, 20221 Rio de Janeiro, RJ; tel. (21) 253-6675; f. 1827; morning; Pres. AUSTREGÉSILO DE ATHAYDE; circ. 31,000 weekdays.

Jornal dos Sports: Rua Tenente Possolo 15/25, 20230-160 Rio de Janeiro, RJ; tel. (21) 232-8010; e-mail esportes@vol.com.br; f. 1931; morning; sporting daily; Dir MILTON COELHO DA GRAÇA; circ. 39,000.

Ultima Hora: Rua Equador 702, 20220 Rio de Janeiro, RJ; tel. (21) 223-2444; fax (21) 223-2444; f. 1951; evening; Dir K. NUNES; circ. 56,000.

Salvador, BA

Jornal da Bahia: Rua Peruvia Carneiro 220, 41100 Salvador, BA; tel. (71) 384-2919; fax (71) 384-5726; f. 1958; Pres. MÁRIO KERTÉSZ; circ. 20,000.

Jornal Correio da Bahia: Av. Luis Viana Filho s/n, 41100 Salvador, BA; tel. (71) 371-2811; fax (71) 231-3944; f. 1979; Pres. ARMANDO GONÇALVES.

Jornal da Tarde: Av. Tancredo Neves 1092, 41820-020 Salvador, BA; tel. (71) 231-9683; fax (71) 231-1064; f. 1912; evening; Pres. REGINA SIMÕES DE MELLO LEITÃO; circ. 54,000.

Santo André, SP

Diário do Grande ABC: Rua Catequese 562, 09090-900 Santo André, SP; tel. (11) 715-8112; fax (11) 715-8257; e-mail MauryDotto @dgabc.com.br; internet www.dgabc.com.br; f. 1958; Pres. MAURY DE CAMPOS DOTTO; circ. 78,500.

Santos, SP

A Tribuna: Rua General Câmara 90/94, 11010-903 Santos, SP; tel. (13) 211-7000; fax (13) 219-6783; f. 1984; Dir ROBERTO M. SANTINI; circ. 40,000.

São Luís, MA

O Imparcial: Rua Afonso Pena 46, 65000 São Luís, MA; tel. (98) 222-5120; fax (98) 222-5120; f. 1926; Dir-Gen. PEDRO BATISTA FREIRE.

São Paulo, SP

Diário Comércio e Indústria: Rua Alvaro de Carvalho 354, 01050-020 São Paulo, SP; tel. (11) 256-5011; fax (11) 258-1989; f. 1933; morning; Pres. HAMILTON LUCAS DE OLIVEIRA; circ. 50,000.

Diário Popular: Rua Major Quedinho 28, 1°-6° andares, 01050 São Paulo, SP; tel. (11) 258-2133; fax (11) 256-1627; f. 1884; evening; independent; Dir RICARDO GURAL DE SABEYA; circ. 90,000.

O Estado de São Paulo: Av. Eng. Caetano Álvares 55, 02550 São Paulo, SP; tel. (11) 856-2122; fax (11) 266-2206; f. 1875; morning; independent; Dir FRANCISCO MESQUITA NETO; circ. 242,000 weekdays, 460,000 Sundays.

Fôlha de São Paulo: Alameda Barão de Limeira 425, Campos Elíseos, 01202-900 São Paulo, SP; tel. (11) 224-3222; fax (11) 223-1644; f. 1921; morning; Editorial Dir OCTAVIO FRIAS, Filho; circ. 557,650 weekdays, 1,401,178 Sundays.

Gazeta Mercantil: Rua Major Quedinho 90, 5° andar, 01050 São Paulo, SP; tel. (11) 256-3133; fax (11) 258-5864; f. 1920; business paper; Pres. LUIZ FERREIRA LEVY; circ. 80,000.

Jornal da Tarde: Rua Peixoto Gomidi 671, 01409 São Paulo, SP; tel. (11) 284-1944; fax (11) 289-3548; f. 1966; evening; independent; Dir R. MESQUITA; circ. 120,000, 180,000 Mondays.

Notícias Populares: Alameda Barão de Limeira 425, 01202 São Paulo, SP; tel. (11) 874-2222; fax (11) 223-1644; f. 1963; Dir RENATO CASTANHARI; circ. 150,000.

Vitória, ES

A Gazeta: Rua Charic Murad 902, 29050 Vitória, ES; tel. (27) 222-8333; fax (27) 223-1525; f. 1928; Pres. MARIO LINDENBERG; circ. 19,000.

PERIODICALS

Rio de Janeiro, RJ

Amiga: Rua do Russel 766/804, 22214 Rio de Janeiro, RJ; tel. (21) 285-0033; fax (21) 205-9998; weekly; women's interest; Pres. ADOLPHO BLOCH; circ. 83,000.

Antenna-Eletrônica Popular: Av. Marechal Floriano 143, CP 151, 20080-005 Rio de Janeiro, RJ; tel. (21) 223-2442; fax (21) 263-8840; e-mail antenna@unisys.com.br; internet www.anep.com.br; f. 1926; monthly; telecommunications and electronics, radio, TV, hi-fi, amateur and CB radio; Dir GILBERTO AFFONSO PENNA, Filho; circ. 15,000.

Carinho: Rua do Russel 766/804, 22214 Rio de Janeiro, RJ; tel. (21) 285-0033; fax (21) 205-9998; monthly; women's interest; Pres. ADOLPHO BLOCH; circ. 65,000.

Conjuntura Econômica: Praia de Botafogo 190, Sala 923, 22253-900 Rio de Janeiro, RJ; tel. (21) 536-9267; fax (21) 551-2799; f. 1947; monthly; economics and finance; published by Fundação Getúlio Vargas; Pres. JORGE OSCAR DE MELLO FLÓRES; Editor LAURO VIEIRA DE FARIA; circ. 20,000.

Desfile: Rua do Russel 766/804, 22214 Rio de Janeiro, RJ; tel. (21) 285-0033; fax (21) 205-9998; f. 1969; monthly; women's interest; Dir ADOLPHO BLOCH; circ. 120,000.

Ele Ela: Rua do Russel 766/804, 22214 Rio de Janeiro RJ; tel. (21) 285-0033; fax (21) 205-9998; f. 1969; monthly; men's interest; Dir ADOLPHO BLOCH; circ. 150,000.

Manchete: Rua do Russel 766/804, 20214 Rio de Janeiro, RJ; tel. (21) 285-0033; fax (21) 205-9998; f. 1952; weekly; general; Dir ADOLPHO BLOCH; circ. 110,000.

São Paulo, SP

Capricho: Rua Geraldo Flausino Gomes 61, 6°, 04573-900 São Paulo, SP; tel. (11) 534-5231; monthly; youth interest; Dir ROBERTO CIVITA; circ. 250,000.

Carícia: Av. das Nações Unidas 5777, 05479-900 São Paulo, SP; tel. (11) 211-7866; fax (11) 813-9115; monthly; women's interest; Dir ANGELO ROSSI; circ. 210,000.

Casa e Jardim: B. Machado 82, 01230-010 São Paulo, SP; fax (11) 824-9079; f. 1953; monthly; homes and gardens, illustrated; Pres. LUCIANA JALONETSKY; circ. 120,000.

Claudia: Rua Geraldo Flausino Gomes 61, CP 2371, 04573-900 São Paulo, SP; tel. (11) 534-5130; fax (11) 534-5638; f. 1962; monthly; women's magazine; Dir ROBERTO CIVITA; circ. 460,000.

Criativa: Rua do Centúria 655, 05065-001, São Paulo, SP; tel. (11) 874-6003; fax (11) 864-0271; monthly; women's interest; Dir-Gen. RICARDO A. SÁNCHEZ; circ. 121,000.

Digesto Econômico: Associação Comercial de São Paulo, Rua Boa Vista 51, 01014-911 São Paulo, SP; tel. (11) 234-3322; fax (11) 239-0067; every 2 months; Pres. ELVIO ALIPRANDI; Chief Editor JOÃO DE SCANTIMBURGO.

Disney Especial: Av. das Nações Unidas 7221, 05477-000 São Paulo, SP; tel. (11) 3037-2000; fax (11) 3037-4124; every 2 months; children's magazine; Dir ROBERTO CIVITA; circ. 211,600.

Elle: Av. das Nações Unidas 7221, 05425-902 São Paulo; tel. (11) 3037-5197; fax (11) 3037-5451; f. 1988; internet www.uol.com.br/elle; monthly; women's magazine; Editor CARLOS COSTA; circ. 100,000.

Exame: Av. Octaviano Alves de Lima, 4400, 02909-900 São Paulo, SP; tel. (11) 877-1421; fax (11) 877-1437; f. 1967; e-mail publicidade .exame@email.abril.com.br; 2 a week; business; Dir JOSÉ ROBERTO GUZZO; circ. 168,300.

Iris, A Revista da Imagem: Rua Brito Peixoto 322, Brooklin, 04582-020 São Paulo, SP; tel. (11) 531-1299; fax (11) 531-1627; e-mail irisfoto@totalnet.com.br; internet www.totalnet.com.br/irisfoto; f. 1947; monthly; photography and general pictures; Dirs BEATRIZ AZEVEDO MARQUES, HÉLIO M. VALENTONI; circ. 50,000.

Manequim: Rua Geraldo Flausino Gomes 61, 04573-900 São Paulo, SP; tel. (11) 534-5668; fax (11) 534-5632; monthly; fashion; Dir ROBERTO CIVITA; circ. 300,000.

Máquinas e Metais: Alameda Olga 315, 01155-900, São Paulo, SP; tel. (11) 3824-5300; fax (11) 3662-0103; e-mail info@arandanet .com.br; internet www.arandanet.com.br; f. 1964; monthly; machine and metal industries; Editor JOSÉ ROBERTO GONÇALVES; circ. 15,000.

Marie Claire: Rua Dr Renato Paes Barros 613, 04530-000 São Paulo, SP; tel. (11) 866-3373; monthly; women's magazine; Publr REGINA LEMUS; circ. 273,000.

Mickey: Av. das Nações Unidas 7221, 05477-000 São Paulo, SP; tel. (11) 3037-2000; fax (11) 3037-4124; monthly; children's magazine; Dir ROBERTO CIVITA; circ. 76,000.

Micromundo-Computerworld do Brasil: Rua Caçapava 79, 01408 São Paulo, SP; tel. (11) 289-1767; monthly; computers; Gen. Dir ERIC HIPPEAU; circ. 38,000.

Nova: Rua Geraldo Flausino Gomes 61, 04573-900 São Paulo, SP; tel. (11) 534-5712; fax (11) 534-5187; f. 1973; monthly; women's interest; Dir ROBERTO CIVITA; circ. 300,000.

Pato Donald: Av. das Nações Unidas 7221, 05477-000 São Paulo, SP; tel. (11) 3037-2000; fax (11) 3037-4124; every 2 weeks; children's magazine; Dir ROBERTO CIVITA; circ. 120,000.

Placar: Av. das Nações Unidas 7221, 14° andar, 05477-000 São Paulo, SP; tel. (11) 3037-5816; fax (11) 3037-5597; e-mail placar .leitor@email.abril.com.br; f. 1970; monthly; soccer magazine; Dir MARCELO DURATE; circ. 127,000.

Quatro Rodas: Rua Geraldo Flausino Gomes 61, Brooklin, 04573-900 São Paulo, SP; tel. (11) 534-5491; fax (11) 530-8549; f. 1960; monthly; motoring; Pres. ROBERTO CIVITA; circ. 250,000.

Revista O Carreteiro: Rua Palacete das Aguias 239, 04035-021 São Paulo, SP; tel. (11) 542-9311; monthly; transport; Dirs JOÃO ALBERTO ANTUNES DE FIGUEIREDO, EDSON PEREIRA COELHO; circ. 80,000.

Saúde: Av. das Nações Unidas 5777, 05479-900 São Paulo, SP; tel. (11) 211-7675; fax (11) 813-9115; monthly; health; Dir ANGELO ROSSI; circ. 180,000.

Veja: Rua do Copturno 571, 6°, São Paulo, SP; tel. (11) 877-1322; fax (11) 877-1640; internet www.veja.com.br; f. 1968; news weekly; Dirs JOSÉ ROBERTO GUZZO, TALES ALVARENGA, MÁRIO SERGIO CONTI; circ. 800,000.

Visão: São Paulo, SP; tel. (11) 549-4344. 1952; weekly; news magazine; Editor HENRY MAKSOUD; circ. 148,822.

NEWS AGENCIES

Editora Abril, SA: Av. Otaviano Alves de Lima 4400, CP 2372, 02909-970 São Paulo, SP; tel. (11) 877-1322; fax (11) 877-1640; f. 1950; Pres. ROBERTO CIVITA.

Agência ANDA: Edif. Correio Brasiliense, Setor das Indústrias Gráficas 300/350, Brasília, DF; Dir EDILSON VARELA.

Agência o Estado de São Paulo: Av. Eng. Caetano Alvares 55, 02588-900 São Paulo, SP; tel. (11) 856-2122; Rep. SAMUEL DIRCEU F. BUENO.

Agência Fôlha de São Paulo: Alameda Barão de Limeira 425, 4° andar, 01290-900 São Paulo; tel. (11) 224-3790; fax (11) 221-0675; Dir MARION STRECKER.

Agência Globo: Rua Irineu Marinho 35, 2° andar, Centro, 20233-900 Rio de Janeiro, RJ; tel. (21) 292-2000; fax (21) 292-2000; Dir CARLOS LEMOS.

Agência Jornal do Brasil: Av. Brasil 500, 6° andar, São Cristóvão, 20949-900 Rio de Janeiro, RJ; tel. (21) 585-4453; fax (21) 580-9944; f. 1966; Exec. Dir. EDGAR LISBOA.

Foreign Bureaux

Agence France-Presse (AFP) (France): CP 2575-ZC-00, Rua México 21, 7° andar, 20031-144 Rio de Janeiro, RJ; tel. (21) 533-4555; fax (21) 262-7933; e-mail afprio@unisys.com.br; Bureau Chief (Brazil) ALAIN BOEBION.

Agencia EFE (Spain): Praia de Botafogo 228, Bloco B, Gr. 1106, 22359-900 Rio de Janeiro, RJ; tel. (21) 553-6355; fax (21) 553-8823; e-mail redario@efebrasil.com.br; Bureau Chief FRANCISCO R. FIGUÉROA.

Agenzia Nazionale Stampa Associata (ANSA) (Italy): Av. São Luís 258, 23° andar, Of. 1302, São Paulo, SP; tel. (11) 256-5835; Bureau Chief RICCARDO CARUCCI.

Associated Press (AP) (USA): Av. Brasil 500, sala 847, CP 72-ZC-00, 20001 Rio de Janeiro, RJ; tel. (21) 580-4422; Bureau Chief BRUCE HANDLER; Rua Major Quedinho Sala 707, CP 3815, 01050 São Paulo, SP; tel. (11) 256-0520; fax (11) 256-4135; Correspondent STAN LEHMAN; a/c Sucursal Fôlha de São Paulo, CLS 104 Bloco C Loja 41, CP 14-2260, 70343 Brasília, DF; tel. (61) 223-9492; Correspondent JORGE MEDEROS.

Deutsche Presse-Agentur (dpa) (Germany): Rua Abade Ramos 65, 22461-90 Rio de Janeiro, RJ; tel. (21) 266-5937; fax (21) 537-8273; Bureau Chief ESTEBAN ENGEL.

Inter Press Service (IPS) (Italy): Rua Vicente de Souza 29, 2° andar, 22251-070 Rio de Janeiro, RJ; tel. (21) 286-5605; fax (21) 286-5324; Correspondent MARIO CHIZUO OSAVA.

Jiji Tsushin-Sha (Jiji Press) (Japan): Av. Paulista 854, 13° andar, Conj. 133, Bela Vista, 01310-913 São Paulo, SP; tel. (11) 285-0025; fax (11) 285-3816; e-mail jijisp@nethall.com.br; f. 1958; Chief Correspondent MUTSUHIRO TAKABAYASHI.

Kyodo Tsushin (Japan): Praia do Flamengo 168-701, Flamengo, 22210 Rio de Janeiro, RJ; tel. (21) 285-2412; fax (21) 285-2270; Bureau Chief TAKAYOSHI MAKITA.

Prensa Latina (Cuba): Marechal Mascarenhas de Moraís 121, Apto 602, Copacabana, 22030-040 Rio de Janeiro, RJ; tel. and fax (21) 237-1766; Correspondent FRANCISCO FORTEZA.

Reuters (United Kingdom): Av. Nações Unidas 17891, 8° andar, 04795-100 São Paulo, SP; tel. (11) 232-4411; fax (11) 604-6538; Rua Sete de Setembro 99, 4° andar, sala 401, 20050-005 Rio de Janeiro, RJ; tel. (21) 507-4151; fax (21) 507-2120; Bureau Chief (News and Television): ADRIAN DICKSON.

United Press International (UPI) (USA): Rua Uruguaiana 94, 18°, Centro, 20050 Rio de Janeiro, RJ; tel. (21) 224-4194; fax (21)

232-8293; Rua Sete de Abril 230, Bloco A, 816/817, 01044 São Paulo, SP; tel. (11) 258-6869; Edif. Gilberto Salamão, Sala 805/806, 70305 Brasília, DF; tel. (61) 224-6413. Man. ANTÓNIO PRAXEDES; Chief Correspondent H. E. COYA HONORES.

Xinhua (New China) News Agency (People's Republic of China): SHIS QI 15, Conj. 16, Casa 14, CP 7089, 71.600 Brasília, DF; tel. (61) 248-5489; Chief Correspondent WANG ZHIGEN.

Central News Agency (Taiwan) and Rossiyskoye Informatsionnoye Agentstvo—Novosti (Russia) are also represented in Brazil.

PRESS ASSOCIATIONS

Associação Brasileira de Imprensa: Rua Araújo Porto Alegre 71, Castelo, 20030 Rio de Janeiro, RJ; f. 1908; 4,000 mems; Pres. (vacant); Sec. JOSUÉ ALMEIDA.

Associação Nacional de Editores de Revistas: SCS, Edif. Bandeirantes 201/204, 70300-910 Brasília, DF; tel. (61) 322-5511; fax (61) 321-8348; e-mail arkoadvice@arkoadvice.com.br; Pres. JOSÉ CARLOS SALLES NETO; Exec. Vice-Pres. Dr MURILLO DE ARAGÃO.

Federação Nacional dos Jornalistas—FENAJ: Higs 707, Bloco R, Casa 54, 70351-718 Brasília, DF; tel. (61) 244-0650; fax (61) 242-6616; f. 1946; represents 31 regional unions; Pres. AMÉRICO CÉSAR ANTUNES.

Publishers

Rio de Janeiro, RJ

Ao Livro Técnico Indústria e Comércio Ltda: Rua Sá Freire 36/40, São Cristóvão, 20930-430 Rio de Janeiro, RJ; tel. (21) 580-1168; fax (21) 580-9955; internet www.editoraaolivrotécnico.com.br; f. 1933; textbooks, children's and teenagers' fiction and non-fiction, art books, dictionaries; Man. Dir REYNALDO MAX PAUL BLUHM.

Bloch Editores, SA: Rua do Russell 766/804, Glória, 22214 Rio de Janeiro, RJ; tel. (21) 265-2012; fax (21) 205-9998; f. 1966; general; Pres. ADOLPHO BLOCH.

Distribuidora Record de Serviços de Imprensa, SA: Rua Argentina 171, São Cristóvão, CP 884, 20921 Rio de Janeiro, RJ; tel. (21) 585-2000; fax (21) 580-4911; e-mail sacm@record.com.br; internet www.record.com.br; f. 1941; general fiction and non-fiction, education, textbooks, fine arts; Pres. SÉRGIO MACHADO.

Ediouro Publicações, SA: Rua Nova Jerusalém 345, CP 1880, Bonsucesso, 21042-230 Rio de Janeiro, RJ; tel. (21) 260-6122; fax (21) 280-2438; e-mail editoriallivros@ediouro.com.br; internet www.ediouro.com.br; f. 1939; general; Pres. JORGE CARNEIRO.

Editora Artenova, SA: Rua Pref. Olímpio de Mello 1774, Benfica, 20000 Rio de Janeiro, RJ; tel. (21) 264-9198; f. 1971; sociology, psychology, occultism, cinema, literature, politics and history; Man. Dir ALVARO PACHECO.

Editora Brasil-América (EBAL), SA: Rua Gen. Almério de Moura 302/320, São Cristóvão, 20921-060 Rio de Janeiro, RJ; tel. (21) 580-0303; fax (21) 580-1637; f. 1945; children's books; Dir PAULO ADOLFO AIZEN.

Editora Campus: Rua Sete de Setembro 111, 16° andar, 20050-002 Rio de Janeiro; tel. (21) 509-5340; fax (21) 507-1991; e-mail c.rothmuller@campus.com.br; internet www.campus.com.br; business, computing, non-fiction; Man. Dir CLAUDIO ROTHMULLER.

Editora Delta, SA: Av. Almirante Barroso 63, 26° andar, CP 2226, 20031 Rio de Janeiro, RJ; tel. (21) 240-0072; f. 1958; reference books.

Editora Expressão e Cultura—Exped Ltda: Estrada dos Bandeirantes 1700, Bloco E, 22710-113, Rio de Janeiro, RJ; tel. (21) 444-0676; fax (21) 444-0700; e-mail exped@ggh.com.br; f. 1967; textbooks, literature, reference; Gen. Man. RICARDO AUGUSTO PAMPLONA VAZ.

Editora e Gráfica Miguel Couto, SA: Rua da Passagem 78, Loja A, Botafogo, 22290-030 Rio de Janeiro, RJ; tel. (21) 541-5145; f. 1969; engineering; Dir PAULO KOBLER PINTO LOPES SAMPAIO.

Editora Nova Fronteira, SA: Rua Bambina 25, Botafogo, 22251-050 Rio de Janeiro, RJ; tel. (21) 537-8770; fax (21) 286-6755; e-mail nova2@embratel.net.br; f. 1965; fiction, psychology, history, politics, science fiction, poetry, leisure, reference; Pres. CARLOS ÁUGUSTO LACERDA.

Editora Vozes, Ltda: Rua Frei Luís 100, CP 90023, 25689-900 Petrópolis, RJ; tel. (242) 43-5112; fax (242) 31-4676; e-mail editorial @vozes.com.br; f. 1901; Catholic publishers; management, theology, anthropology, fine arts, history, linguistics, science, fiction, education, data processing, etc.; Dir STEPHEN OTTENBREIT.

Livraria Francisco Alves Editora, SA: Rua Uruguaiana 94/13°, 20050-002 Rio de Janeiro, RJ; tel. (21) 221-3198; fax (21) 242-3438; f. 1854; textbooks, fiction, non-fiction; Pres. CARLOS LEAL.

Livraria José Olympio Editora, SA: Rua da Glória 344, 4° andar, Glória, 20241-180 Rio de Janeiro, RJ; tel. (21) 509-6939; fax (21)

242-0802; f. 1931; juvenile, science, history, philosophy, psychology, sociology, fiction; Dir MANOEL ROBERTO DOMINGUES.

São Paulo, SP

Atual Editora, Ltda: Av. Gen. Valdomiro de Lima 833, Pq. Jaba-quara, 04344-070 São Paulo, SP; tel. (11) 5071-2288; fax (11) 5071-3099; e-mail www.atualeditora.com.br; f. 1973; school and children's books, literature; Dirs GELSON IEZZI, OSVALDO DOLCE.

Cia Editora Nacional: Rua Joli 294, Brás, CP 5312, 03016 São Paulo, SP; tel. (11) 291-2355; fax (11) 291-8614; f. 1925; textbooks, history, science, social sciences, philosophy, fiction, juvenile; Dirs JORGE YUNES, PAULO C.MARTI.

Cia Melhoramentos de São Paulo: Rua Tito 479, 05051-000 São Paulo, SP; tel. (11) 3874-0854; fax (11) 3874-0855; f. 1890; general non-fiction; e-mail blerner@melhoramentos.com.br; internet www.melhoramentos.com.br; Dir BRENO LERNER.

Ebid-Editora Páginas Amarelas Ltda: Av. Liberdade 956, 5° andar, 01502-001 São Paulo, SP; tel. (11) 278-6622; fax (11) 279-8723; e-mail mail@guiaspaginasamarelas.com.br; f. 1947; commercial directories.

Editora Abril, SA: Av. da Nações Unidas 7221, 05425-902 São Paulo, SP; tel. (11) 3037-2000; fax (11) 3037-5638; f. 1950; Pres. ROBERTO CIVITA.

Editora Atica, SA: Rua Barão de Iguape 110, 01507-900 São Paulo, SP; tel. (11) 3346-3000; fax (11) 3277-4146; e-mail editora@atica .com.br; f. 1965; textbooks, Brazilian and African literature; Pres. VICENTE PAZ FERNANDEZ.

Editora Atlas, SA: Rua Conselheiro Nébias 1384, Campos Elíseos, 01203-904 São Paulo, SP; tel. 221-9144; fax (11) 220-7830; e-mail edatlas@editora-atlas.com.br; f. 1944; business administration, data-processing, economics, accounting, law, education, social sciences; Pres. LUIZ HERRMANN.

Editora Brasiliense, SA: Mariano de Sousa 664, 03411-090 São Paulo, SP; tel. (11) 6942-0545; fax (11) 6942-0813; e-mail brasilse@ uol.com.br; f. 1943; education, racism, gender studies, human rights, ecology, history, literature, social sciences; Man. YOLANDA C. DA SILVA PRADO.

Editora do Brasil, SA: Rua Conselheiro Nébias 887, Campos Elíseos, CP 4986, 01203-001 São Paulo, SP; tel. (11) 222-0211; fax (11) 222-9655; e-mail editora@editoradobrasil.com.be; internet www.editoradobrasil.com.br; f. 1943; education; Pres. Dr CARLOS COSTA.

Editora FTD, SA: Rua Manoel Dutra 225, 01328-010 São Paulo, SP; tel. (11) 253-5011; fax (11) 288-0132; e-mail ftd@dial&ta.com.br; f. 1897; textbooks; Pres. JOÃO TISSI.

Editora Globo, SA: Av. Jaguare 1485/1487, 05346-902 São Paulo, SP; tel. (11) 874-6000; fax (11) 836-7098; e-mail dflmkt@edglobo .com.br; f. 1957; fiction, engineering, agriculture, cookery, environmental studies; Gen. Man. RICARDO A. FISCHER.

Editora Luzeiro Ltda: Rua Almirante Barroso 730, Brás, 03025-001 São Paulo, SP; tel. (11) 292-3188; f. 1973; folklore and literature.

Editora Michalany Ltda: Rua Biobedas 321, Saúde, 04302-010 São Paulo, SP; tel. (11) 585-2012; fax (11) 276-8775; e-mail edit ora@editoramichalany.com.br; internet www.editoramichalany .com.br; f. 1965; biographies, economics, textbooks, geography,history, religion, maps; Dir DOUGLAS MICHALANY.

Editora Moderna, Ltda: Rua Padre Adelino 758, Belenzinho, 03303-904, São Paulo, SP; tel. (11) 6090-1316; fax (11) 6090-1369; e-mail moderna@moderna.com.br; internet www.moderna.com.br; Pres. RICARDO ARISSA FELTRE.

Editora Pioneira: Praça Dirceu de Lima 313, Casa Verde, 02515-050 São Paulo, SP; tel. (11) 858-3199; fax (11) 858-0443; e-mail pioneira@virtual-net.com.br; f. 1960; architecture, computers, political and social sciences, business studies, languages, children's books; Dirs ROBERTO GUAZZELLI, LILIANA GUAZZELLI.

Editora Revista dos Tribunais Ltda: Rua Conde do Pinhal 78, CP 8153, 01501 São Paulo, SP; tel. (11) 37-8689; f. 1955; law and jurisprudence, administration, economics and social sciences; Man. Dir NELSON PALMA TRAVASSOS.

Editora Rideel Ltda: Alameda Afonso Schmidt 879, Santa Terezinha, 02450-001 São Paulo, SP; tel. (11) 6977-8344; fax (11) 6976-7415; e-mail sac@rideel.com.br; internet www.rideel.com.br; f. 1971; general; Dir ITALO AMADIO.

Editora Scipione Ltda: Praça Carlos Gomes 46, 01501-040 São Paulo, SP; tel. (11) 239-2255; fax (11) 239-1700; e-mail scipione@ scipione.com.br; internet www.scipione.com.br; f. 1983; schoolbooks, literature, reference; Dir LUIZ ESTEVES SALLUM.

Encyclopaedia Britannica do Brasil Publicações Ltda: Rua Rego Freitas 192, Vila Buarque, CP 299, 01059-970 São Paulo, SP; tel. (11) 250-1900; fax (11) 250-1960; e-mail vicepresidencia@barsa .com.br; f. 1951; reference books.

Instituto Brasileiro de Edições Pedagógicas, Ltda: Rua Joli 294, 03016-020 São Paulo, SP; tel. (11) 6099-7799; fax (11) 6694-5338; e-mail editoras@ibep-nacional.com.br; internet www.ibep nacional.com.br; f. 1965; textbooks, foreign languages and reference books.

Lex Editora, SA: Rua Machado de Assis 47/57, Vila Mariana, 04106-900 São Paulo, SP; tel. (11) 5549-0122; fax (11) 5575-9138; e-mail adm@lexli.com.br; internet www.lexli.com.br; f. 1937; legislation and jurisprudence; Dir MILTON NICOLAU VITALE PATARA.

Saraiva SA Livreiros Editores: Av. Marquês de São Vicente 1697, CP 2362, 01139-904 São Paulo, SP; tel. (11) 861-3344; fax (11) 861-3308; f. 1914; education, textbooks, law, economics; Pres. JORGE EDUARDO SARAIVA.

Belo Horizonte, MG

Editora Lê, SA: Av. D. Pedro II, 4550 Jardin Montanhês, CP 2585, 30730 Belo Horizonte, MG; tel. (31) 34131720. 1967; textbooks.

Editora Lemi, SA: Av. Nossa Senhora de Fátima 1945, CP 1890, 30000 Belo Horizonte, MG; tel. (31) 201-8044; f. 1967; administration, accounting, law, ecology, economics, textbooks, children's books and reference books.

Editora Vigília, Ltda: Rua Felipe dos Santos 508, Bairro de Lourdes, CP 1068, 30180-160 Belo Horizonte, MG; e-mail lerg@ planetarium.com.br; tel. (31) 337-2744; fax (31) 337-2834; f. 1960; general.

Curitiba, PR

Editora Educacional Brasileira, SA: Rua XV de Novembro 178, salas 101/04, CP 7498, 80000 Curitiba, PR; tel. (41) 223-5012; f. 1963; biology, textbooks and reference books.

PUBLISHERS' ASSOCIATIONS

Associação Brasileira do Livro: Av. 13 de Maio 23, 16°, 20031-000 Rio de Janeiro, RJ; tel. (21) 240-9115; fax (21) 532-6678; e-mail abralivro@uol.com.br; Pres. MARCOS DAVID GOMES.

Câmara Brasileira do Livro: Av. Ipiranga 1267, 10° andar, 01039-907 São Paulo, SP; tel. (11) 3315-8277; fax (11) 229-7463; e-mail cbl@cbl.org.br; internet www.cbl.org.br; f. 1946; Pres. RAUL WASSERMANN.

Sindicato Nacional dos Editores de Livros—SNEL: Av. Rio Branco 37, 1503/6 and 1510/12, 20090-003 Rio de Janeiro, RJ; tel. (21) 233-6481; fax (21) 253-8502; e-mail snel@snel.org.br; internet www.snel.org.br; 200 mems; Pres. PAULO ROBERTO ROCCO; Man. ANTÔNIO LASKOS.

There are also regional publishers' associations.

Broadcasting and Communications

TELECOMMUNICATIONS

BCP Telecomunicações: São Paulo; internet www.bcp.com.br; f. 1997; mobile services in São Paulo area; Pres. ROBERTO PEÓN.

Empresa Brasileira de Telecomunicações, SA (EMBRATEL): Av. Pres. Vargas 1012, CP 2363, 20179-900 Rio de Janeiro, RJ; tel. (21) 519-8182; e-mail cmsocial@embratel.net.br; internet www .embratel.com.br; f. 1965; operates national and international telecommunications system; controlled by MCI WorldCom of USA; Chair. DANIEL CRAWFORD.

Empresa Brasileira de Comunicação, SA (Radiobrás): CP 04-0340, 70710 Brasília, DF; tel. (61) 321-3949; fax (61) 321-7602; internet www.radiobras.gov.br; f. 1988 following merger of Empresa Brasileira de Radiodifusão and Empresa Brasileira de Notícias; Pres. MARCELO AMORIM NETTO.

Telecomunicações Brasileiras, SA (Telebrás): SAS Quadra 6, Conjunto Sede, Brasília, DF; tel. (61) 215-2120; fax (61) 322-1213; internet www.telebras.com.br; f. 1972; transferred to the private sector in July 1998; 28 divisions.

Telecomunicações de Rio de Janeiro (Telerj): Rio de Janeiro; internet www.telerj.com.br.

Telecomunicações de São Paulo, SA (Telesp): Rua Martiniano de Carvalho 851, 01321-001 São Paulo; tel. (11) 285-8011; fax (11) 253-3050; e-mail webmaster@telesp.com.br; internet www.telesp.com.br; services operated by Telefónica, SA, of Spain; Pres. FERNANDO XAVIER FERREIRA; Chief Exec. SAMPAIO DORIA.

Regulatory Authority

Agência Nacional de Telecomunicações (ANATEL): SAS Quadra 06, Bloco H, 3° andar, 70313-900, Brasília, DF; tel. (61) 312-2336; fax (61) 312-2211; e-mail biblioteca@anatel.gov.br; internet www.anatel.gov.br/default.htm; f. 1998; Pres. RENATO GUERREIRO.

RADIO

In April 1992 there were 2,917 radio stations in Brazil, including 20 in Brasília, 38 in Rio de Janeiro, 32 in São Paulo, 24 in Curitiba, 24 in Porto Alegre and 23 in Belo Horizonte.

The main broadcasting stations in Rio de Janeiro are: Rádio Nacional, Rádio Globo, Rádio Eldorado, Rádio Jornal do Brasil, Rádio Tupi and Rádio Mundial. In São Paulo the main stations are Rádio Bandeirantes, Rádio Mulher, Rádio Eldorado, Rádio Gazeta and Rádio Excelsior; and in Brasília: Rádio Nacional, Rádio Alvorada, Rádio Planalto and Rádio Capital.

Rádio Nacional do Brásil (RADIOBRÁSIL): CP 070747, 70359-970 Brasília; tel. 321-3949; fax 321-7602; e-mail maurilio@radiobras .gov.br; internet www.radiobras.gov.br; Pres. MAURÍLIO FERREIRA LIMA.

TELEVISION

In April 1992 there were 256 television stations in Brazil, of which 118 were in the state capitals and six in Brasília.

The main television networks are:

TV Bandeirantes—Canal 13: Rádio e Televisão Bandeirantes Ltda, Rua Radiantes 13, 05699 São Paulo, SP; tel. (11) 842-3011; fax (11) 842-3067; 65 TV stations and repeaters throughout Brazil; Pres. JOÃO JORGE SAAD.

RBS TV-TV Gaúcha, SA: Rua Rádio y TV Gaúcha 189, 90850-080 Porto Alegre, RS; tel. (51) 218-5002; fax (51) 218-5005; Vice-Pres WALMOR BERGESCH.

TV Globo—Canal 4: Rua Lopes Quintas 303, Jardim Botânico, 22460-010 Rio de Janeiro, RJ; tel. (21) 511-1711; fax (21) 511-4305; e-mail apm@domain.com.br; internet www.redeglobo.com.br; f. 1965; 8 stations; national network; Dir ADILSON PONTES MALTA.

TV Manchete-Canal 6: Rua do Russel 766, 20000 Rio de Janeiro, RJ; tel. (21) 265-2012; Dir-Gen. R. FURTADO.

TV Record—Rede Record de Televisão—Radio Record, SA: Rua de Várzea 240, Barra Funda, 01140-080 São Paulo, SP; tel. (11) 824-7000; Pres. JOÃO BATISTA R. SILVA; Exec. Vice-Pres. H. GONÇALVES.

TVSBT—Canal 4 de São Paulo, SA: Rua Dona Santa Veloso 535, Vila Guilherme, 02050 São Paulo, SP; tel. (11) 292-9044; fax (11) 264-6004; Vice-Pres. GUILHERME STOLIAR.

BROADCASTING ASSOCIATIONS

Associação Brasileira de Emissoras de Rádio e Televisão (ABERT): Centro Empresarial Varig, SCN Quadra 04, Bloco B, Conjunto 501, Pétala A, 70710-500 Brasília, DF; tel. (61) 327-4600; fax (61) 327-3660; e-mail abert@abert.org.br; internet www.abert .org.br; f. 1962; mems: 32 shortwave, 1,275 FM, 1,574 medium-wave and 80 tropical-wave radio stations and 258 television stations (1997); Pres. PAULO MACHADO DE CARVALHO NETO; Exec. Dir OSCAR PICONEZ.

There are regional associations for Bahia, Ceará, Goiás, Minas Gerais, Grande do Sul, Santa Catarina, São Paulo, Amazonas, Distrito Federal, Mato Grosso and Mato Grosso do Sul (combined) and Sergipe.

Finance

(cap. = capital; dep. = deposits; res = reserves; m. = million; brs = branches; amounts in reais, unless otherwise stated)

BANKING

Conselho Monetário Nacional: SBS, Q.03, Bloco B, Edif. Sede do Banco do Brasil, 21° andar, 70074-900 Brasília, DF; tel. (61) 414-1945; fax (61) 414-2528; f. 1964 to formulate monetary policy and to supervise the banking system; Pres. Minister of Finance.

Central Bank

Banco Central do Brasil: SBS, Q 03, Bloco B, CP 04-0170, 70074-900 Brasília, DF; tel. (61) 414-1000; fax (61) 223-1033; e-mail secre .surel@bcb.gov.br; internet www.bcb.gov.br; f. 1965 to execute the decisions of the Conselho Monetário Nacional; bank of issue; Pres. ARMÍNIO FRAGA NETO; 10 brs.

State Commercial Banks

Banco do Brasil, SA: Setor Bancário Sul, SBS, Quadra 4, Bloco C, Lote 32, 70089-900 Brasília, DF; tel. (61) 310-3400; fax (61) 310-2563; internet www.bancobrasil.com.br; f. 1808; cap. 6,629.9m., dep. 78,743.8m. (Dec. 1998); Pres. PAOLO CESAR XIMENES ALVES FERREIRA; 2,778 brs.

Banco do Estado do Rio Grande do Sul, SA: Rua Capitão Montanha 177, CP 505, 90010-040 Porto Alegre, RS; tel. (51) 215-2501; fax (51) 215-1715; e-mail banrisul@banrisul.com.br; internet www.banrisul.com.br; f. 1928; cap. 1,667.2m., res −1,190.3m., dep. 13,214.9 (Dec. 1998); Pres. João Alcir Verle; 303 brs.

Banco do Estado de Santa Catarina SA: Rua Padre Miguelinho 80, CEP 88010-550, Florianópolis, SC; tel. (48) 224-2100; fax (48) 223-4962; e-mail decam/dinte@besc.com.br; internet www.besc.com.br; f. 1962; cap. 158.1m., res 104.3m., dep. 1,329.6m. (Dec. 1997); Pres. Vitor Fontana.

Banco do Estado de São Paulo, SA (Banespa): Praça Antônio Prado 6, 01010-010 São Paulo, SP; tel. (11) 259-7722; fax (11) 239-2409; e-mail presidencia@banespa.com; f. 1926; cap. 2,409.3m., res 1,733.9m., dep. 12,650.7m. (Dec. 1998); sold in Nov. 2000 to Banco Santander (Spain); Chair. Eduardo Agusto de Almeida Guimarães; 1,404 brs.

Banco do Nordeste do Brasil, SA: Av. Paranjana 5700, Passaré, 60740-000 Fortaleza, CE; tel. (85) 299-3022; fax (85) 299-3585; e-mail info@banconordeste.gov.br; internet www.banconordeste.gov.br; f. 1954; cap. 831.0m., res 124.7m., dep. 1,474.9m. (Dec. 1999); Pres. and CEO Byron Costa de Queiroz; 186 brs.

Private Banks

Banco ABN AMRO SA: Av. Paulista 1374, 3° andar, 01310-916 São Paulo, SP; tel. (11) 525-6000; fax (11) 525-6387.

Banco da Amazônia, SA: Av. Presidente Vargas 800, 66017-000 Belém, PA; tel. (91) 216-3000; fax (91) 223-5403; internet www.bancoamazonia.com.br; f. 1942; cap. 88,211m., res 78,957m., dep. 638,953m. (Dec. 1998); Pres. Anivaldo Juvenil Vale; 109 brs.

Banco América do Sul, SA: Av. Brigadeiro Luís Antônio 2020, 01318-911 São Paulo, SP; tel. (11) 3170-9899; fax (11) 3170-9564; e-mail bas@bas.com.br; internet www.bas.com.br; f. 1940; cap. 214.6m., dep. 2,832.8m. (Dec. 1997); CEO Yves L. J. Lejeune; 139 brs.

Banco Barclays e Galicia, SA: Av. Paulista 1842, Edif. Cetenco Plaza, Torre Norte 24°–25° andares, 01310-200 São Paulo, SP; tel. (11) 269-2700; fax (11) 283-3168; e-mail barclays@barclays.com.br; internet www.barclays.com; f. 1967 as Banco de Investimento; cap. 170.1m., res 22.9m., dep. 197.8m. (Dec. 1999); Pres. Peter Anderson.

Banco BBA-Creditanstalt, SA: Av. Paulista 37, 20°, 01311-902 São Paulo, SP; tel. (11) 281-8000; fax (11) 284-2158; e-mailbancob ba@bba.com.br; internet www.bba.com.br; f. 1988; cap. 161.6m., res 747.7m., dep. 5,019.9m. (Dec. 1999); Pres. Fernão Carlos Botelho Bracher; 5 brs.

Banco BMC, SA: Av. das Nações Unidas 12.995, 24° andar, 04578-000 São Paulo, SP; tel. (11) 5503-7807; fax (11) 5503-7676; e-mail bancobmc@bmc.com.br; internet www.bmc.com.br; f. 1939, adopted current name in 1990; cap. 159.8m., res 13.5m., dep. 1,134.8m. (Dec. 1999); Chair. Francisco Jaime Nogueira Pinheiro; 9 brs.

Banco BMG, SA: Av. Alvares Cabral 1707, Santo Agostinho, 30170-001 Belo Horizonte, MG; tel. (31) 290-3000; fax (31) 290-3315; f. 1988; cap. 89.8m., res 50.9m., dep. 305.0m. (Dec. 1996); Pres. Flávio Pentagna Guimarães; 4 brs.

Banco Bandeirantes, SA: Rua Boa Vista 162, 01014-902 São Paulo, SP; tel. (11) 233-7155; fax (11) 233-7329; e-mail band@bandei rantes.com.br; f. 1944; cap. 546.4m., res U225.8m., dep. 3,534.7m. (Dec. 1998); acquired by Unibanco in 2000; Pres. Dr Carlos Traguelho; 167 brs.

Banco Bilbao Vizcaya Argentaria Brasil, SA: Av. Antônio Carlos Magalhães 2728, 41840-000 Salvador, BA; tel. (71) 354-7000; fax (71) 354-7106; internet www.exceleconomico.com.br; f. 1996 as a result of merger of Excel Banco and Banco Econômico; name changed in 2000; cap. 1,000.0m., res 353.6m., dep. 4,868.3m. (Dec. 1999); Pres. Ezequiel Nasser; 232 brs.

Banco Boavista Interatlântico, SA: Praça Pio X 118, 20091-040 Rio de Janeiro, RJ; tel. (21) 849-1661; fax (21) 253-1579; e-mail boavista@ibm.net; internet www.boavista.com.br; f. 1997; cap. 627.9m., res U111.8m., dep. 4,050.6m. (Dec. 1998); acquired by Banco Bradesco in 2000; Pres. and Gen. Man. José Luiz Silveira Miranda.

Banco Bozano, Simonsen, SA: Av. Rio Branco 138-Centro, 20057-900 Rio de Janeiro, RJ; tel. (21) 508-4711; fax (21) 508-4479; e-mail info@bozano.com.br; f. 1967; cap. 248.2m., res 266.4m., dep. 5,103.1m. (Dec. 1998); Pres. Paulo Veiga Ferraz Pereira; 4 brs.

Banco Bradesco, SA: Cidade de Deus, Vila Yara, 06029-900 Osasco, SP; tel. (11) 708-14011; fax (11) 708-44630; internet www.bradesco.com.br; f. 1943; fmrly Banco Brasileiro de Descontos; cap. 3,800.0m., res 2,969.2m., dep. 49,974.3m. (Dec. 1999); Chair. Lázaro de Mello Brandão; Vice-Chair. Antônio Bornia; 2,106 brs.

Banco CCF Brasil SA: Av. Brigadeiro Faria Lima 3064, 1°–4° andares, Itaim Bibi, 01451-000 São Paulo, SP; tel. (11) 827-5000; fax (11) 827-5299; internet www.ccfbrasil.com.br; f. 1980; cap. 409.2m., res 189.4m., dep. 537.8m. (Dec. 1999); Pres. Bernard Mencier.

Banco Chase Manhattan, SA: Rua Verbo Divino, 04719-002 São Paulo, SP; tel. (11) 546-4433; fax (11) 546-4624; f. 1925; fmrly Banco Lar Brasileiro, SA; Chair. Peter Anderson.

Banco Cidade, SA: Praça Dom José Gaspar 106, 01047-010 São Paulo, SP; tel. (11) 3150-5000; fax (11) 255-4176; e-mail cambio .comercial@bancocidade.com.br; internet www.bancocidade.com.br; f. 1965; cap. 75.0m., res 99.5m., dep. 1,278.1m. (Dec. 1998); Pres. Edmundo Safdié; 25 brs.

Banco Credibanco, SA: Av Paulista 1294, 21° andar, 01310-915 São Paulo, SP; tel. (11) 3150-5000; fax (11) 285-3431; e-mail crediban@credibanco.com.br; internet www.credibanco.com.br; f. 1967; cap. 120.0m., res 63.6m., dep. 458.1m. (Dec. 1998); CEO Peter Anderson; 2 brs.

Banco de Crédito Nacional, SA (BCN): Av. das Nações Unidas 12901, CENU-Torre Oeste, 04578-000 Vila Cordeiro, SP; tel. (11) 5509-2801; fax (11) 5509-2802; internet www.bcn.com.br; f. 1924; acquired by Banco Bradesco in 1997; cap. 580.0m., res 327.3m., dep. 7,713.5m. (Dec. 1999); Pres. José Luiz Acar Pedro; 122 brs.

Banco Dibens, SA: Alameda Santos 200, Cerqueira Cesar, 01418-000 São Paulo, SP; tel. (11) 253-2177; fax (11) 284-3132; f. 1989; cap. 81.7m., res 84.0m., dep. 760.9m. (Dec. 1996); Pres. Mauro Saddi; 23 brs.

Banco do Estado de Minas Gerais, SA: Rua Rio de Janeiro 471, Centro Belo Horizonte, 30160-910 Belo Horizonte, MG; tel. (31) 239-1211; fax (31) 239-1859; f. 1967; acquired by Banco de Crédito Nacional in 1997; cap. 240.8m., res −157.6m., dep. 2,450.3m. (Dec. 1997); Pres. José Afonso B. Beltrão da Silva; 755 brs.

Banco do Estado do Paraná, SA (Banestado): Rua Máximo João Kopp 274, Santa Cândida, 82630-900 Curitiba, PR; tel. (41) 351-8745; fax (41) 351-7252; e-mail helphb@email.banestado.com.br; internet www.banestado.com.br; f. 1928; cap. 3,988.9m., resU3,555.3m., dep. 4,203.5m. (Dec. 1999); acquired by Banco Itaú in 2000; Pres. Reinhold Stephanes; 389 brs.

Banco Fibra: Av. Brigadeiro Faria Lima 3064, 7° andar, Itaim Bibi, 01451-000, São Paulo, SP; tel. (11) 3827-6700; fax (11) 3827-6620; e-mail internacional@bancofibra.com.br; f. 1988; cap. 106.1m., res 111.4m., dep. 1,334.0m. (Dec. 1998); Pres. Benjamin Steinbruch; CEO João Ayres Rabello, Filho.

Banco Francês e Brasileiro, SA: Av. Paulista 1294, 01310-915 São Paulo, SP; tel. (11) 238-8216; fax (11) 238-8622; e-mail bfb.inter national@itau.com.br; internet www.bfb.com.br; f. 1948; affiliated with Crédit Lyonnais; cap. 472.3m., res 29.5m., dep. 1,152.0m. (Dec. 1997); Pres. Roberto Egydio Setúbal; 32 brs.

Banco Industrial e Comercial, SA: Rua Boa Vista 192, 01014-030 São Paulo, SP; tel. (11) 237-6904; fax (11) 3107-5290; e-mail bicbanco.dinte@uol.com.br; internet www.bicbanco.com.br; f. 1938; cap. 191.7m., res 62.9m., dep. 725.6m. (June 2000); Pres. José Bezerra de Menezes; 38 brs.

Banco Itaú, SA: Rua Boa Vista 176, CP 30341, 01014-919 São Paulo, SP; tel. (11) 237-3000; fax (11) 277-1044; e-mail info@itau .com.br; internet www.itau.com.br; f. 1944; cap. 2,500.0m., res 3,406.7m., dep. 28,288.8m. (Dec. 1999); Chair. Olavo Egydio Setúbal; Pres. and CEO Roberto Egydio Setúbal; 1,070 brs.

Banco Mercantil de São Paulo: CP 4077, Av. Paulista 1450, 01310-917 São Paulo; tel. (11) 252-2121; fax (11) 284-3312; e-mail finasa@finasa.com.br; internet www.finasa.com.br; f. 1938; name changed 2000; cap. 817.4m., res 189.6m., dep. 3,832.6m. (Dec. 1999); Pres. Dr Gastão Eduardo de Bueno Vidigal.

Banco Pactual: Av. República do Chile 230, 28° e 29° andares, 20031-170 Rio de Janeiro, RJ; tel. (21) 272-1100; fax (21) 533-1661; e-mail webmaster@pactual.com.br; internet www.pactual.com.br; f. 1983; cap. 175.9m., res 92.5m., dep. 1,767.0m. (Dec. 1998); Pres. Luís Cezar Fernandes.

Banco Safra, SA: Av. Paulista 2100, 16° andar, 01310-930 São Paulo, SP; tel. (11) 3175-7575; fax (11) 3175-8605; f. 1940; e-mail safrapact@uol.com.br; internet www.safra.com.br; cap. 314.5m., res 706.9m., dep. 10,808.4m. (Dec. 1999); Pres. Carlos Alberto Vieira; 68 brs.

Banco Santander Brasil, SA: Rua Funchal 160, 04551-903 São Paulo, SP; tel. (11) 828-7322; fax (11) 828-7208; f. 1940; Banco Geral do Comercio; Pres. Luiz Roberto Ortiz Nascimento; 41 brs.

Banco Santander Meridional, SA: Rua General Câmara 156, Centro, 90010-230 Porto Alegre, RS; tel. (51) 287-5700; fax (51) 508-5769; internet www.meridional.com.br; f. 1985, formerly Banco Sulbrasileiro, SA; taken over by the Government in Aug. 1985; acquired by Banco Bozano, Simonsen in 1997; name changed 2000; cap. 1,200.5m., res −121.1m., dep. 5,782.5m. (Dec. 1998); Pres. Paulo Veiga Ferraz Pereira; 227 brs.

Banco Sogeral, SA: Rua Verbo Divino 1207, 3° e 4° andares, CP 8785, 04719-002 São Paulo, SP; tel. (11) 5180-5052; fax (11) 5180-5258; f. 1981; internet www.sogeral.com.br; cap. 83.0m., res 18.7m., dep. 457.2m. (Dec. 1998); Pres. Eric Dhoste; 1 br.

Banco Sudameris Brasil, SA: Av. Paulista 1000, 2°, 10°–16°andares, 01310-100 São Paulo, SP; tel. (11) 3170-9899; fax (11) 289-1239; internet www.sudameris.com.br; f. 1910; cap.

742.6m., res 93.6m., dep. 4,803.3m. (Dec. 1998); Exec. Dirs YVES L. J. LEJEUNE, SEBASTIÃO G. T. CUNHA; 153 brs.

BankBoston SA: Rua Líbero Badaró 487-3°, 01009-000 São Paulo, SP; tel. (11) 3118-5622; fax (11) 3118-4438; internet www.bankbos ton.com.br; Pres. GERALDO JOSÉ CARBONE; 31 brs.

HSBC Bank Brasil, SA, Banco Multiplo: Travessa Oliveira Belo 34, Centro, 80020-030 Curitiba, PR; tel. (41) 321-6161; fax (41) 321-6081; internet www.hsbc.com.br; f. 1997; cap. 874.5m., res 106.6m., dep. 7,633.8m. (Dec. 1998); Pres. M. F. GEOGHEGAN; 1,214 brs.

UNIBANCO—União de Bancos Brasileiros, SA: Av. Eusébio Matoso 891, 22° andar, CP 8185, 05423-901 São Paulo, SP; tel. (11) 867-4461; fax (11) 814-0528; e-mail investor.relations@unibanco .com.br; internet www.unibanco.com.br; f. 1924; cap.2,324.1m., res 1,677.6m., dep. 13,476.2m. (Dec. 1999); Chair. PEDRO MOREIRA SALLES; 639 brs.

Development Banks

Banco de Desenvolvimento de Minas Gerais, SA—BDMG: Rua da Bahia 1600, CP 1026, 30160-011 Belo Horizonte, MG; tel. (31) 226-3292; fax (31) 273-5084; f. 1962; long-term credit operations; cap. 250.5m., res –124.6m., dep. 3.3m. (Dec. 1997); Pres. MARCOS RAYMUNDO PESSÒA DUARTE.

Banco de Desenvolvimento do Espírito Santo, SA: Av. Princesa Isabel 54, Edif. Caparão, 12° andar, CP 1168, 29010-906 Vitória, ES; tel. (27) 223-8333; fax (27) 223-6307; total assets US $12.5m. (Dec. 1993); Pres. SÉRGIO MANOEL NADER BORGES.

Banco Nacional de Crédito Cooperativo, SA: Brasília, DF; tel. (61) 224-5575; established in association with the Ministry of Agriculture and guaranteed by the Federal Government to provide co-operative credit; cap. 4.7m. (cruzeiros, July 1990); Pres. ESUP-ÉRIO S. DE CAMPOS AGUILAR (acting); 41 brs.

Banco Nacional do Desenvolvimento Econômico e Social (BNDES): Av. República do Chile 100, 20139-900 Rio de Janeiro, RJ; tel. (21) 277-7447; fax (21) 533-1665; internet www.bndes.gov.br; f. 1952 to act as main instrument for financing of development schemes sponsored by the Government and to support programmes for the development of the national economy; charged with supervision of privatization programme of the 1990s; Pres. FRANCISCO GROS; 2 brs.

Banco Regional de Desenvolvimento do Extremo Sul (BRDE): Rua Uruguai 155, 3°–4° andares, CP 139, 90010-140 Porto Alegre, RS; tel. (51) 121-9200. 1961; cap. 15m. (Dec. 1993); development bank for the states of Paraná, Rio Grande do Sul and Santa Catarina; finances small- and medium-sized enterprises; Dir-Pres. NELSON WEDEKIN; 3 brs.

Investment Bank

Banco de Investimentos CSFB Garantia, SA: Av. Brigadeiro Faria Lima 3064, 13° andar, Itaim Bibi, 01451-020 São Paulo, SP; tel. (11) 821-6000; fax (11) 821-6900; f. 1971; fmrly Banco de Investimentos Gerais; cap. 956.6m., res 107.2m., dep. 1,794.7m. (Dec. 1996); Dir LUIS ALBERTO MENDES RODRIGUES; 1 br.

State-owned Savings Bank

Caixa Econômica Federal: SBS, Q 04, Lote 3/4, Edif. Sede de Caixa Econômica, 70070-000 Brasília, DF; tel. (61) 321-9209; fax (61) 225-0215; f. 1860; cap. 60,247,000m. (cruzeiros, May 1993); dep. 796,113,000m. (April 1993); Pres. EMÍLIO CARRAZAI; 1,752 brs.

Foreign Banks

Banco de la Nación Argentina: Av. Paulista 2319, Sobreloja, 01310 São Paulo, SP; tel. (11) 883-1555; fax (11) 881-4630; e-mail bnaspbb@dialdata.com.br; f. 1891; Dir-Gen. GERARDO LUIS PONCE; 2 brs.

Banco Unión (Venezuela): Av. Paulista 1708, 01310 São Paulo, SP; tel. (11) 283-3722; fax (11) 283-2434; f.1892; Dir-Gen. DONALDISON MARQUES DA SILVA.

The Chase Manhattan Bank (USA): Rua Verbo Divino 1400, São Paulo, SP; tel. (11) 546-4433; fax (11) 546-44624.

Dresdner Bank Lateinamerika AG (Germany): Rua Verbo Divino 1488, Centro Empresarial Transatlântico, CP 3641, 01064-970 São Paulo, SP; e-mail brazil.rep-office@dresdner-bank.com; fmrly Deutsch-Sudamerikanische Bank; tel. (11) 5188-6700; fax (11) 5188-6900; f. 1969; Chair. WALTER U. HAAGEN; 3 brs.

Lloyds TSB Bank PLC (United Kingdom): Av. Brig. Faria Lima 2020, 01452 São Paulo, SP; tel. (11) 818-8311; fax (11) 818-8403; e-mail lloyds.dmkt@lloyds.com.br; Gen. Man. DAVID V. THOMAS; 11 brs.

Banking Associations

Federação Brasileira das Associações de Bancos: Rua Líbero Badaró 425, 17° andar, 01069-900 São Paulo, SP; tel. (11) 239-

3000; fax (11) 607-8486; f. 1966; Pres. MAURÍCIO SCHULMAN; Vice-Pres ROBERTO EGYDIO SETÚBAL, JOSÉ AFONSO SANCHO.

Sindicato dos Bancos dos Estados do Rio de Janeiro e Espírito Santo: Av. Rio Branco 81, 19° andar, Rio de Janeiro, RJ; Pres. THEÓPHILO DE AZEREDO SANTOS; Vice-Pres. Dr NELSON MUFARREJ.

Sindicato dos Bancos dos Estados de São Paulo, Paraná, Mato Grosso e Mato Grosso do Sul: Rua Líbero Badaró 293, 13° andar, 01905 São Paulo, SP; f. 1924; Pres. PAULO DE QUEIROZ.

There are other banking associations in Maceió, Salvador, Fortaleza, Belo Horizonte, João Pessoa, Recife and Porto Alegre.

STOCK EXCHANGES

Comissão de Valores Mobiliários CVM: Rua Sete de Setembro 111, 32° andar, 20159-900 Rio de Janeiro, RJ; tel. (21) 212-0200; fax (21) 212-0524; e-mail pte@cvm.gov.br; f. 1977 to supervise the operations of the stock exchanges and develop the Brazilian securities market; Chair. JOSÉ LUIZ OSORIO DE ALMEIDA, Filho.

Bolsa de Valores do Rio de Janeiro: Praça XV de Novembro 20, 20010-010 Rio de Janeiro, RJ; tel. (21) 514-1010; fax (21) 242-8066; e-mail info@bvrj.com.br; internet www.bvrj.com.br; f. 1845; focuses on the trading of fixed income government bonds and foreign exchange; Chair. SERGIO LUIZ BERARDI.

Bolsa de Valores de São Paulo (BOVESPA): Rua XV de Novembro 275, 01013-001 São Paulo, SP; tel. (11) 233-2000; fax (11) 233-2099; e-mail bovespa@bovespa.com.br; internet www.bovespa .com.br; f. 1890; 550 companies listed in 1997; CEO GILBERTO MIFANO.

There are commodity exchanges at Porto Alegre, Vitória, Recife, Santos and São Paulo.

INSURANCE
Supervisory Authorities

Superintendência de Seguros Privados (SUSEP): Rua Buenos Aires 256, 4° andar, 20061-000 Rio de Janeiro, RJ; tel. (21) 297-4415; fax (21) 221-6664; f. 1966; within Ministry of Finance; Superintendent HELIO PORTOCARRERO.

Conselho Nacional de Seguros Privados (CNSP): Rua Buenos Aires 256, 20061-000 Rio de Janeiro, RJ; tel. (21) 297-4415; fax (21) 221-6664; f. 1966; Sec. THERESA CHRISTINA CUNHA MARTINS.

Federação Nacional dos Corretores de Seguros e de Capitalização (FENACOR): Av. Rio Branco 147, 6° andar, 20040-006 Rio de Janeiro, RJ; tel. (21) 507-0033; fax (21) 507-0041; e-mail leoncio@fenacor.com.br; Pres. LEÔNCIO DE ARRUDA.

Federação Nacional das Empresas de Seguros Privados e de Capitalização (FENASEG): Rua Senador Dantas 74, 20031-200 Rio de Janeiro, RJ; tel. (21) 524-1204; fax (21) 220-0046; e-mail fenaseg@fenaseg.org.br; Pres. JOÃO ELISIO FERRAZ DE CAMPOS.

IRBBrasil Resseguros: Av. Marechal Câmara 171, Castelo, 20020-900 Rio de Janeiro, RJ; tel. (21) 272-0200; fax (21) 240-6261; e-mail info@irb-brasilre.com.br; internet www.irb-brasilre.com.br; f. 1939; fmrly Instituto de Resseguros do Brasil; reinsurance; Pres. DEMÓS-THENES MADUREIRA DE PINHO, Filho.

Principal Companies

The following is a list of the principal national insurance companies, selected on the basis of assets.

AGF Brasil Seguros, SA: Rua Luís Coelho 26, 01309-000 São Paulo; tel. (11) 281-5572; fax (11) 283-1401; internet www.agf.com.br; Dir EUGÉNIO DE OLIVEIRA MELLO.

Cia de Seguros Aliança da Bahia: Rua Pinto Martins 11, 2° andar, 40015-020 Salvador, BA; tel. (71) 242-1055; fax (71) 242-8998; f. 1870; general; Pres. PAULO SÉRGIO FREIRE DE CARVALHO GONÇALVES TOURINHO.

Cia de Seguros Aliança do Brasil: Rua Senador Dantas 105, 32° andar, 20031-201 Rio de Janeiro; tel. (21) 533-1080; fax (21) 220-2105; Pres. KHALID MOHAMMED RAOUF.

Allianz-Bradesco Seguros, SA: Rua Barão de Itapagipe 225, 20269-900 Rio de Janeiro; tel. (21) 563-1101; fax (21) 293-9489.

BCN Seguradora, SA: Alameda Santos 1940, 9° andar, 01418-100 São Paulo; tel. (11) 283-2244; fax (11) 284-3415; internet www.bcn.com.br/seguro.htm; f. 1946; Pres. ANTÓNIO GRISI, Filho.

Bradesco Previdência e Seguros, SA: Av. Deputado Emílio Carlos 970, 06028-000 São Paulo; tel. (11) 704-4466; fax (11) 703-3063; internet www.bradesco.com.br/prodserv/bradprev.html; f. 1989; Pres. ANTÓNIO LOPES CRISTÓVÃO.

Bradesco Seguros, SA: Rua Barão de Itapagipe 225, 20269-900 Rio de Janeiro, RJ; tel. (21) 563-1199; fax (21) 503-1466; internet www.bradesco.com.br/prodserv/bradseg.html; f. 1935; general; Pres. EDUARDO VIANNA.

CGU Cia de Seguros: Av. Almirante Barroso 52, 23° e 24° andares, 20031-000 Rio de Janeiro; tel. (21) 292-1125; fax (21) 262-0291;

internet www.york.com.br/york0700.html; Pres. ROBERT CHARLES WHEELER.

Finasa Seguradora, SA: Alameda Santos 1827, 6° andar, CJS 61, 01419-002 São Paulo; tel. (11) 253-8181; fax (11) 285-1994; internet www.finasa.com.br/ficoli02.html; f. 1939; Pres. MARCELLO DE CAMARGO VIDIGAL.

Golden Cross Seguradora, SA: Rua Maestro Cardim 1164, 013200-301 Rio de Janeiro, RJ; tel. (21) 283-4922; fax (21) 289-4624; e-mail comunica@goldencross.com.br; internet www.golden.com.br; f. 1971; Pres. ALBERT BULLUS.

HSBC Seguros (Brasil), SA: Travessa Oliveira Belo 11-B, 2° andar, 80020-030 Curitiba, PR; tel. (41) 321-6162; fax (41) 321-8800; f. 1938; all classes; Pres. SIMON LLOYD BRETT.

Itaú Seguros, SA: Praça Alfredo Egydio de Souza Aranha 100, Bloco A, 04344-920 São Paulo, SP; tel. (11) 5019-3322; fax (11) 5019-3530; e-mail itauseguros@itauseguros.com.br; internet www.itau seguros.com.br; f. 1921; all classes; Pres. LUIZ DE CAMPOS SALLES.

Cia de Seguros Minas-Brasil: Rua dos Caetés 745, 5° andar, 30120-080 Belo Horizonte, MG; tel. (31) 219-3882; fax (31) 219-3820; f. 1938; life and risk; Pres. JOSÉ CARNEIRO DE ARAÚJO.

Cia Paulista de Seguros: Rua Dr Geraldo Campos Moreira 110, 04571-020 São Paulo, SP; tel. (11) 5505-2010; fax (11) 5505-2122; internet www.pauliseg.com.br; f. 1906; general; Pres. PHILLIP NORTON MOORE.

Porto Seguro Cia de Seguros Gerais: Rua Guaianazes 1238, 01204-001 São Paulo, SP; tel. (11) 224-6129; fax (11) 222-6213; internet www.porto-seguro.com.br; f. 1945; life and risk; Pres. ROSA GARFINKEL.

Sasse, Cia Nacional de Seguros Gerais: SCN Qd. 01, Bl. A, 15°–17° andares, 70710-500 Brasília, DF; tel. (61) 329-2400; fax (61) 321-0600; internet www.sasse.com.br; f. 1967; general; Pres. PEDRO PEREIRA DE FREITAS.

Sul América Aetna Seguros e Previdência, SA: Rua Anchieta 35, 9° andar, 01016-030 São Paulo; tel. (11) 232-6131; fax (11) 606-8141; internet www.sulaamerica.com.br; f. 1996; Pres. RONY CASTRO DE OLIVEIRA LYRIO.

Sul América, Cia Nacional de Seguros: Rua da Quitanda 86, 20091-000 Rio de Janeiro, RJ; tel. (21) 276-8585; fax (21) 276-8317; f. 1895; life and risk; Pres. RONY CASTRO DE OLIVEIRA LYRIO.

Sul América Santa Cruz Seguros, SA: Tv. Franc. Leonardo Truda 98, 6° andar, 90010-050 Porto Alegre; tel. (51) 211-5455; fax (51) 225-5894; f. 1943; Pres. RONY CASTRO DE OLIVEIRA LYRIO.

Unibanco Seguros, SA: Av. Eusébio Matoso 1375, 13° andar, 05423-180 São Paulo, SP; tel. (11) 819-8000; fax (11) 3039-4005; internet www.unibancoseguros.com.br; f. 1946; life and risk; Pres. JOSÉ CASTRO ARAÚJO RUDGE.

Vera Cruz Seguradora, SA: Av. Maria Coelho Aguiar 215, Bloco D, 3° andar, 05804-906 São Paulo, SP; tel. (11) 3741-3815; fax (11) 3741-3827; internet www.veracruz.com.br; f. 1955; general; Pres. ALFREDO FERNANDEZ DE L. ORTIZ DE ZARATE.

Trade and Industry

GOVERNMENT AGENCIES

Agência Nacional de Petróleo (ANP): Brasília, DF; internet www.anp.gov.br; f. 1998; regulatory body of the petroleum industry; Chair. DAVID ZYLBERSTAJN.

Comissão de Fusão e Incorporação de Empresa (COFIE): Ministério da Fazenda, Edif. Sede, Ala B, 1° andar, Esplanada dos Ministérios, Brasília, DF; tel. (61) 225-3405; mergers commission; Pres. SEBASTIÃO MARCOS VITAL; Exec. Sec. EDGAR BEZERRA LEITE, Filho.

Conselho de Desenvolvimento Comercial (CDC): Bloco R, Esplanada dos Ministérios, 70044 Brasília, DF; tel. (61) 223-0308; commercial development council; Exec. Sec. Dr RUY COUTINHO DO NASCIMENTO.

Conselho de Desenvolvimento Econômico (CDE): Bloco K, 7° andar, Esplanada dos Ministérios, 70063 Brasília, DF; tel. (61) 215-4100; f. 1974; economic development council; Gen. Sec. JOÃO BATISTA DE ABREU.

Conselho de Desenvolvimento Social (CDS): Bloco K, 3° andar, 382, Esplanada dos Ministérios, 70063 Brasília, DF; tel. (61) 215-4477; social development council; Exec. Sec. JOÃO A. TELES.

Conselho Nacional do Comércio Exterior (CONCEX): Fazenda, 5° andar, Gabinete do Ministro, Bloco 6, Esplanada dos Ministérios, 70048 Brasília, DF; tel. (61) 223-4856; f. 1966; responsible for foreign exchange and trade policies and for the control of export activities; Exec. Sec. NAMIR SALEK.

Conselho Nacional de Desenvolvimento Científico e Tecnológico (CNPq): Brasília, DF; tel. (61) 348-9401; fax (61) 273-2955; f. 1951; scientific and technological development council; Pres. JOSÉ GALIZIA TUNDISI.

Conselho Nacional de Desenvolvimento Pecuário (CONDEPE): to promote livestock development.

Conselho de Não-Ferrosos e de Siderurgia (CONSIDER): Ministério da Indústria e Comércio, Esplanada dos Ministérios, Bloco 7, 7° andar, 70056-900 Brasília, DF; tel. (61) 224-6039; f. 1973; exercises a supervisory role over development policy in the non-ferrous and iron and steel industries; Exec. Sec. WILLIAM ROCHA CANTAL.

Fundação Instituto Brasileiro de Geografia e Estatística (IBGE): Centro de Documentação e Disseminação de Informações (CDDI), Rua Gen. Canabarro 706, 2° andar, Maracanã, 20271-201 Rio de Janeiro, RJ; tel. (21) 569-5997; fax (21) 569-1103; e-mail webmaster@ibge.gov.br; internet www.ibge.gov.br; f. 1936; produces and analyses statistical, geographical, cartographic, geodetic, demographic and socio-economic information; Pres. (IBGE) SÉRGIO BESSERMAN VIANNA; Superintendent (CDDI) DAVID WU TAI.

Instituto Nacional de Metrologia, Normalização e Qualidade Industrial (INMETRO): Rua Santa Alexandrina 416, Rio Comprido, 20261-232 Rio de Janeiro, RJ; tel. (21) 273-9002; fax (21) 293-0954; e-mail pusi@inmetro.gov.br; in 1981 INMETRO absorbed the Instituto Nacional de Pesos e Medidas (INPM), the weights and measures institute; Pres. Dr JÚLIO CESAR CARMO BUENO.

Instituto de Planejamento Econômico e Social (IPEA): SBS, Edif. BNDE, 6° andar, 70076 Brasília, DF; tel. (61) 225-4350; planning institute; Pres. RICARDO SANTIAGO.

Secretaria Especial de Desenvolvimento Industrial: Brasília, DF; tel. (61) 225-7556; fax (61) 224-5629; f. 1969; industrial development council; offers fiscal incentives for selected industries and for producers of manufactured goods under the Special Export Programme; Exec. Sec. Dr ERNESTO CARRARA.

REGIONAL DEVELOPMENT ORGANIZATIONS

Companhia de Desenvolvimento dos Vales do São Francisco e do Parnaíba (CODEVASF): SGAN, Q 601, Lote 1, Edif. Manoel Novaes, 70830-901 Brasília, DF; tel. (61) 312-4758; fax (61) 226-8819; e-mail divulgacao@codevasf.gov.br; internet www.codevasf .gov.br/indice.html; f. 1974; promotes integrated development of resources of São Francisco and Parnaíba Valley.

Superintendência do Desenvolvimento da Amazônia (SUDAM): Av. Almirante Barroso 426, Bairro do Marco, 66000 Belém, PA; tel. (91) 226-0044; f. 1966 to develop the Amazon regions of Brazil; supervises industrial, cattle breeding and basic services projects; Superintendent Eng. HENRY CHECRALLA KAYATH.

Superintendência do Desenvolvimento do Nordeste (SUDENE): Edif. SUDENE s/n, Praça Ministro João Gonçalves de Souza, Cidade Universitária, 50670-900 Recife, PE; tel. (81) 416-2880; fax (81) 453-1277; f. 1959; attached to the Ministry of Planning, Budget and Co-ordination; assists development of north-east Brazil; Superintendent NILTON MOREIRA RODRIGUES.

Superintendência do Desenvolvimento da Região Centro Oeste (SUDECO): SAS, Quadra 1, Bloco A, Lotes 9/10, 70070 Brasília, DF; tel. (61) 225-6111; f. 1967 to co-ordinate development projects in the states of Goiás, Mato Grosso, Mato Grosso do Sul, Rondônia and Distrito Federal; Superintendent RAMEZ TEBET.

Superintendência da Zona Franca de Manaus (SUFRAMA): Rua Ministro João Gonçalves de Souza s/n, Distrito Industrial, 69075-770 Manaus, AM; tel. (92) 237-1691; fax (92) 237-6549; e-mail 15dinf@internet.com.br; to assist in the development of the Manaus Free Zone; Superintendent MAURO RICARDO MACHADO COSTA.

AGRICULTURAL, INDUSTRIAL AND TRADE ORGANIZATIONS

ABRASSUCOS: São Paulo, SP; association of orange juice industry; Pres. MÁRIO BRANCO PERES.

Associação do Comércio Exterior do Brasil (AEB): Av. General Justo 335, 4° andar, Rio de Janeiro, RJ; tel. (21) 240-5048; fax (21) 240-5463; e-mail aebbras@embratel.net.br; internet www.probrazil .com/aeb.html; exporters' association.

Companhia de Pesquisa de Recursos Minerais (CPRM): Esplanada dos Ministérios, Bloco U, 7° andar, 70055-900 Brasília, DF; mining research, attached to the Ministry of Mining and Energy; Pres. CARLOS BERBERT.

Confederação das Associações Comerciais do Brasil: Brasília, DF; confederation of chambers of commerce in each state; Pres. AMAURY TEMPORAL.

Confederação Nacional da Agricultura (CNA): Brasília, DF; tel. (61) 225-3150; national agricultural confederation; Pres. ALYSSON PAULINELLI.

Confederação Nacional do Comércio (CNC): SCS, Edif. Presidente Dutra, 4° andar, Quadra 11, 70327 Brasília, DF; tel. (61) 223-0578; national confederation comprising 35 affiliated federations of commerce; Pres. ANTÔNIO JOSÉ DOMINGUES DE OLIVEIRA SANTOS.

Confederação Nacional da Indústria (CNI): Av. Nilo Peçanha 50, 34° andar, 20044 Rio de Janeiro, RJ; tel. (21) 292-7766; fax (21) 262-1495; f. 1938; national confederation of industry comprising 26 state industrial federations; Pres. Dr ALBANO DO PRADO FRANCO; Vice-Pres. MÁRIO AMATO.

Conselho dos Exportadores de Café Verde do Brasil (CECAFE): internet www.coffee.com.br/cecafe/; in process of formation in 1999/2000 through merger of Federação Brasileira dos Exportadores de Café and Associação Brasileira dos Exportadores de Café; council of green coffee exporters.

Departamento Nacional da Produção Mineral (DNPM): SAN, Quadra 1, Bloco B, 3° andar, 70040-200 Brasília, DF; tel. (61) 224-7097; fax (61) 225-8274; e-mail webmaster@dnpm.gov.br; internet www.dnpm.gov.br; f. 1934; responsible for geological studies and control of exploration of mineral resources; Dir-Gen. JOÃO R. PIMENTEL.

Empresa Brasileira de Pesquisa Agropecuária (EMBRAPA): SAIN, Parque Rural, W/3 Norte, CP 040315, 70770-901 Brasília, DF; tel. (61) 348-4433; fax (61) 347-1041; f. 1973; attached to the Ministry of Agriculture; agricultural research; Pres. ALBERTO DUQUE PORTUGAL.

Federação das Indústrias do Estado de São Paulo (FIESP): Av. Paulista 1313, 01311-923 São Paulo, SP; tel. (11) 252-4200; fax (11) 284-3611; regional manufacturers' association; Pres. CARLOS EDUARDO MOREIRA FERREIRA.

Instituto Brasileiro do Meio Ambiente e Recursos Naturais Renováveis (IBAMA): Ed. Sede IBAMA, Av. SAIN, L4 Norte, Bloco C, Subsolo, 70800-200 Brasília, DF; tel. (61) 316-1205; fax (61) 226-5094; e-mail cnia@sede.ibama.gov.br; internet www.ibama.gov.br; f. 1967; responsible for the annual formulation of national environmental plans; merged with SEMA (National Environmental Agency) in 1988 and replaced the IBDF in 1989; Pres. EDUARDO MAILIUS.

Instituto Brasileiro do Mineração (IBRAM): Brasília, DF; Pres. JOÃO SÉRGIO MARINHO NUNES.

Instituto Nacional da Propriedade Industrial (INPI): Praça Mauá 7, 18° andar, 20081-240 Rio de Janeiro, RJ; tel. (21) 223-4182; fax (21) 263-2539; e-mail inpipres@inpi.gov.br; internet www.inpi.gov.br; f. 1970; intellectual property, etc.; Pres. JORGE MACHADO.

Instituto Nacional de Tecnologia (INT): Av. Venezuela 82, 8° andar, 20081-310 Rio de Janeiro, RJ; tel. (21) 206-1100; fax (21) 263-6552; e-mail int@ riosoft.softex.br; internet www.int.gov.br; f. 1921; co-operates in national industrial development; Dir JOÃO LUIZ HANRIOT SELASCO.

MAJOR COMPANIES
Metals and Chemicals

Aço Minas Gerais SA (AÇOMINAS): Rod Minas Gerais 443 Km 0.7, Fazenda do Cadete, 36406 Ouro Branco, MG; tel. (31) 749-2749; fax (31) 749-2233; internet www. acominas.com.br; f. 1963; manufacturers of iron and steel products; Pres. LUIZ ANDRÉ RICO VICENTE; 3,423 employees.

Aços Villares, SA: Av. Interlagos 4455, 04669-900 São Paulo, SP; tel. (11) 525-3322; fax (11) 548-2212; f. 1944; steel producers; Pres. PAULO DIEDERICHSEN VILLARES; Vice-Pres. WILSON NÉLIO BRUMER; 4,307 employees.

Alcoa Aluminio, SA: aluminium producers; Pres. ADJARMA AZEVEDO.

Companhia Aços Especiais Itabira (ACESITA): Av. João Pinheiro 580, Centro, Belo Horizonte, MG 30130-180; tel. (31) 235-4200; fax (31) 273-7218; tel. (31) 235-4200; fax (31) 273-7218; e-mail invest@acesita.com.br; internet www.acesita.com.br; f. 1944; iron and steel producers; Pres. JOSÉ RONALDO FIDELIS; 5,545 employees.

Companhia Petroquímica do Sul (COPESUL): Rod BR 386 Km 419, Pólo Petroquímico, 95853-000 Triunfo, RS; tel. (51) 457-1100; fax (51) 457-1135; f. 1976; manufacturers of industrial chemicals and petrochemicals; Pres. EDUARDO EUGÉNIO GOUVÊA VIEIRA; 743 employees.

Companhia Siderúrgica Belgo-Mineira: Av. Carandaí 1115, 25° andar, 30130-915 Belo Horizonte, MG; tel. (31) 219-1122; fax (31) 273-2927; internet www.belgomineira.com.br; f. 1921; steel mill; Pres. FRANÇOIS MOYEN; 4,292 employees.

Companhia Siderúrgica da Guanabara (COSIGUA): Av. João XXIII 6777, 23568-900 Rio de Janeiro, RJ; tel. (51) 330-2777; fax (51) 330-2695; f. 1961; steel manufacturers; Pres. JORGE GERDAU JOHANNPETER; 4,234 employees.

Companhia Siderúrgica de Tubarão: Av. Brigadeiro Eduardo Gomes s/n, Jardim Limoeira, 29160 Serra, ES; tel. (27) 348-1004; fax (27) 348-1485; f. 1976; manufacturers of steel slabs; Pres. WILSON NÉLLO BRUMER; 3,610 employees.

Copene Petroquímica do Nordeste, SA: Rua Eteno 1561, Polo Petroquímica, 42800 Camaçari, BA; tel. (71) 832-5606; fax (71) 832-1733; internet www.copene.com.br; f. 1972; manufacturers of petrochemicals; Chair. CARLOS MARIANI BITTENCOURT; 1,000 employees.

Empresa Brasileira de Aeronáutica, SA (EMBRAER): Av. Brig. Faria Lima 2170, 12227-901 São José dos Campos, SP; tel. (12) 345-1106; fax (12) 321-1884; f. 1969; aeronautics industry; Pres. MAURICIO NOVIS BOTELHO; 5,931 employees.

Mannesman, SA: Av. Olinto Meireles 65, 30161-970 Belo Horizonte, MG; tel. (31) 328-2121; fax (31) 333-4471; internet www.mannesman.com.br; f. 1952; production of welded pipes and hot rolled bars; Pres. HANS-PETER AUGUST HUSS; 5,267 employees.

Usinas Siderúrgicas de Minas Gerais, SA (USIMINAS): Rua Prof. José Vieira de Mendonça 3011, 31310-260 Belo Horizonte, MG; tel. (31) 499-8000; fax (31) 499-8899; e-mail pgn@usiminas.com.br; internet www.usiminas.com.br; f. 1956; steel mill; privatized in 1991; Pres. ADEMAR DE CARVALHO BARBOSA; 7,794 employees.

White Martins: Rua Mayrink Veiga 9, 20090-050 Rio de Janeiro, RJ; tel. (21) 588-6232; fax (21) 588-6794; f. 1912; manufacturers and distributors of industrial gases, welding equipment and seamless cylinders; CEO IVAN FERREIRA GARCÍA; 10,000 employees.

Mining

Caemi Mineração e Metalurgia, SA: Praia de Botafogo 300, 8°, 22259-900 Rio de Janeiro, RJ; tel. (21) 536-4100; fax (21) 552-2745; internet www.caemi.com.br; f. 1987; mining and processing of iron ore, bauxite, kaolin and chromite; Pres. WANDERLEI VIÇOSO FAGUNDES; 2,400 employees.

Companhia Brasileira de Petróleo Ipiranga, SA: Rua Francisco Eugênio 329, 20948-900 Rio de Janeiro, RJ; tel. (21) 574-5858; fax (21) 569-8796; internet www.ipiranga.com.br; f. 1959; petroleum and petroleum products; Pres. JOÃO PEDRO GOUVÊA VIEIRA; Vice-Pres. SÉRGIO SILVEIRA SARAIVA; 1,812 employees.

   Distribuidora de Productos de Petróleo Ipiranga SA: Rua Dolores Alcaraz Caldas 90, Praia das Belas, 90110-180 Porto Alegre, RS; tel. (51) 216-4411; fax (51) 224-0403; internet www.ipiranga.com.br; f. 1957; distribution of petroleum derivatives; Pres. SÉRGIO SILVEIRA SARAIVA; Vice-Pres. CARLOS ALBERTO MARTINS BASTOS; 369 employees.

Companhia Vale do Rio Doce, SA (CVRD): Av. Graça Aranha 26, 6° andar, Bairro Castelo, 20005-900 Rio de Janeiro, RJ; tel. (21) 272-4477; fax (21) 272-4324; internet www.cvrd.com.br; f. 1942; fmr state-owned mining co, privatized in 1997; owns and operates two systems: in the north, the Carajás iron-ore mine and railway, and port of Ponta da Madeira; in the south, the Itabira iron-ore mine, the Vitória–Minas railway and the port of Tubarão; largest gold producer in Latin America; also involved in forestry and pulp production, aluminium and other minerals; Chair. JOSÉ LUIZ PÉREZ GARRIDO; 15,500 employees.

Minerações Brasileiras Reunidas, SA (MBR): Praia de Botafogo 300, 8° andar, Rio de Janeiro, RJ 22259-900; tel. (21) 536-4314; fax (21) 552-2346; e-mail nsa@mbr.com.br; internet www.mbr.com.br; f. 1964; mining of iron ores; Chair. OSCAR AUGUSTO DE CAMARGO, Filho; 1,800 employees.

Petróleo Brasileiro, SA (PETROBRÁS): Av. República do Chile 65, 20035-900 Rio de Janeiro, RJ; tel. (21) 534-4477; fax (21) 220-5052; internet www.petrobras.com; f. 1953; production of petroleum and petroleum products; Pres. HENRI PHILIPPE REICHSTUL; 46,226 employees.

   Petrobrás Distribuidora, SA: Rua General Canabarro 500, Maracanã, 20271-201 Rio de Janeiro, RJ; tel. (21) 876-4045; fax (21) 876-4977; e-mail rel.invest@br-petrobras.com.br; internet www.br-petrobras.com.br; f. 1971; distribution of all petroleum by-products; Pres. LUIS ANTÔNIO VIANA; 3,536 employees.

   Petrobrás Fertilizantes, SA (PETROFÉRTIL): Av. República do Chile 65, Sala 907, 20035-900 Rio de Janeiro, RJ; tel. (21) 534-4951; fax (21) 220-0460; f. 1976; Pres. JOSÉ MACHADO SOBRINHO; 145 employees..

   Petrobrás Internacional, SA (BRASPETRO): Rua General Canabarro 500, 20271-900 Rio de Janeiro, RJ; tel. (21) 876-3001; fax (21) 876-3400; e-mail office@braspetro.petrobras.com.br; internet www.petrobras.com.br; f. 1972; international division with operations in Algeria, Angola, People's Republic of China, Colombia, the Congo, Ghana, Guatemala, Libya, Norway, Trinidad and Tobago, Uruguay and Yemen; Chair. JORGE MARQUES DE TOLEDO CAMARGO; 234 employees.

   Petrobrás Química, SA (PETROQUISA): Rua Buenos Aires 40, 2° andar, 20070-020 Rio de Janeiro, RJ; tel. (21) 297-3778; fax (21) 262-4294; f. 1968; petrochemicals industry; controls 27 affiliated companies and four subsidiaries; Pres. RUY ALUIZO ALBERGARIA.

Motor Vehicles

Brasmotor, SA: Av. Brigadeiro Faria Lima 1478, 18°, 01452-001 São Paulo, SP; tel. (11) 3039-5533; fax (11) 3039-5566; e-mail merca do@brasmotor.com.br; internet www.brasmotor.com.br; f. 1945; distributes motor vehicles and household appliances; Pres. HUGO MIGUEL ETCHENIQUE; 10 employees.

Companhia Fabricadora de Peças (COFAP): Av. Alexandre de Gusamão 1395, 09110-901 Santo André, SP; tel. (11) 411-8211; fax (11) 411-4677; f. 1951; manufacturers of motor-vehicle components; Pres. CLEDORVINO BELINI; 7,100 employees.

Ford Brasil, Ltda: Av. Taboão 899, 09870-900 São Bernardo do Campo; tel. (11) 848-9209; fax (11) 848-9057; internet www.ford .com.br; f. 1987; subsidiary of Ford Motor Co of the USA; motor vehicles; Pres. JAMES PADILLA; 3,700 employees.

Iochpe-Maxion, SA: Rua Luigi Galvani 146, 13° andar, 04795-900 São Paulo, SP; tel. (11) 5506-8883; fax (11) 5514-7717; internet www.iochpe-maxion.com.br; f. 1918; motor-vehicle manufacturers; Pres. IVONCY BROCHMANN IOSCHPE; Vice-Pres. DANIEL IOSCHPE; 6,820 employees.

Mercedes Benz do Brasil, SA: Av. Alfred Jurzykowski 562, Vila Pauliceia, 09880-900 São Bernardo do Campo, SP; tel. (11) 758-6611; fax (11) 758-7667; internet www.mercedes-benz.com.br; subsidiary of Mercedes Daimler AG of Germany; motor-car, truck and bus-chassis production; Pres. BEN VAN SCHAIK; 12,000 employees.

Volkswagen do Brasil, SA: Rua Volkswagen 291, POB 8890, 04344-900 São Paulo, SP; tel. (11) 5582-5030; fax (11) 578-0947; internet www.volkswagen.com.br; f. 1953; subsidiary of Volkswagen AG of Germany; manufacture of trucks and passenger commercial vehicles; Pres. HERBERT DEMEL; 47,000 employees.

Rubber, Textiles and Paper

Aracruz Celulose, SA: Rua Lauro Müller 116, 21/22° andar, 22999-900 Rio de Janeiro, RJ; tel. (21) 545-8111; fax (21) 295-7943; e-mail info@aracruz.infonet.com; internet www.aracruz.com.br; f. 1972; wood and bleached eucalyptus pulp; Chair. ERLING SVEN LORENTZEN; Pres. and CEO CARLOS AUGUSTO LIRA AGUIRA; 2,303 employees.

Companhia Suzano de Papel e Celulose: Av. Brigadeiro Faria Lima 1355, 5° ao 10° andares, 01452-919 São Paulo, SP; tel. (11) 3037-9326; fax (11) 3037-9313; e-mail suzano@suzano.com.br; internet www.suzano.com.br; f. 1923; makes and distributes eucalyptus pulp and paper products; Pres. MAX FEFFER; 3,562 employees.

Indústrias Klabin de Papel e Celulose, SA (IKPC): Rua Formosa 367, 18° andar, 01049-000 São Paulo, SP; tel. (11) 250-4000; fax (11) 250-4067; e-mail klabin@klabin.com.br; internet www.klabin.com.br; f. 1934; manufacturers of paper and paper products;. Chair. DANIEL MIGUEL KLABIN; CEO JOSMAR VERILLO; 9,568 employees.

Pirelli Pneus, SA: Av. Giovanni Battista Pirelli 871, Vila Homero Thon, 09111-340 Santo André, SP; tel. (11) 252-8751; fax (11) 252-8777; e-mail webpneus@pirelli.com.br; internet www.pirelli.com; f. 1988; owned by Pirelli of Italy; makers of rubber inner tubes and tyres; Pres. GIORGIO DELLA SETA FERRARI CORBELLI GRECO; 4,864 employees.

Ripasa SA Celulose e Papel: Largo São Bento 64, 4° andar, 01029-010 São Paulo, SP; tel. (11) 225-5000; fax (11) 228-5622; f. 1959; production of pulp, paper and paper products; Pres. WALTER ZARZUR DERANI; 3,500 employees.

Tecelagem Kuehnrich, SA (TEKA): Rua Paulo Kuehnrich 68, 89052-900 Blumenau, SC; tel. (47) 321-5000; fax (47) 321-5050; f. 1935; textile manufacturers; Pres. ROLF KUEHNRICH; 6,500 employees.

Construction

Construções e Comércio Camargo Correa, SA: Rua Funchal 160, Vila Olímpia, 04551-903 São Paulo, SP; tel. (11) 821-5511; fax (11) 820-3532; f. 1946; heavy construction; Pres. RAPHAEL ANTONIO NOGUEIRA DE FREITAS; 6,470 employees.

Construtora Andrade Gutierrez, SA: Rua dos Pampas 484, Prado, 30410-900 Belo Horizonte, MG; tel. (31) 290-6933; fax (31) 295-2955; internet www.andradegutierrez.com.br; f. 1948; civil engineering; Pres. ROBERTO GUTIERREZ; 14,200 employees.

Construtora Queiroz Galvão, SA: Av. Rio Branco 156, 20043-900 Rio de Janeiro, RJ; tel. (21) 292-3993; fax (21) 240-9367; e-mail suporte@ggalvao.com.br; f. 1983; civil-engineering and construction projects; Pres. ANTÔNIO DE QUEIROZ GALVÃO; Man. Dir JOÃO ANTÔNIO DE QUEIROZ GALVÃO ; 6,853 employees.

Montreal Engenharia, SA: Rua Pinheiro Machado 22, 22231 Rio de Janeiro, RJ; tel. (21) 205-5252; fax (21) 270-6750; f. 1954; civil engineering, industrial construction and petroleum exploration; Pres. DEREK LOVELL-PARKER; 5,500 employees.

Odebrecht, SA: Av. Tancredo Neves 450, 41827-900 Salvador, BA; tel. (71) 340-1111; fax (71) 341-9129; e-mail info@odebrecht.com.br; internet www.odebrecht.com.br; holding company; Pres. EMÍLIO ODEBRECHT.

Food Products and Processing

Bompreço Supermercados do Nordeste, SA: Av. Caxangá 3841, Iputinga, 50670-902 Recife, PE; tel. (81) 271-7339; fax (81) 271-7337;

e-mail ccollier@bompreco.com.br; internet www.bompreco.com.br; f. 1935; retail trade: 78 supermarkets and 14 hypermarkets; Pres. JOÃO CARLOS PAES MENDONÇA; 17,633 employees.

Ceval Alimentos, SA: Rodovia Jorge Lacerda Km 20, CP 45, 89110 Gaspar, SC; tel. (47) 331-2222; fax (47) 331-2005; e-mail investor@bnu.nutecnet.com.br; internet www.ceval.com.br; f. 1972; manufacturers of edible oils and agro-industrial products; Pres. ALBERTO WEISSER; 13,828 employees.

Companhia Antarctica Paulista: Av. Presidente Wilson 274, Mooca, 03107-900 São Paulo, SP; tel. (11) 3273-1000; fax (11) 3273-1900; e-mail doriswh@ibm.net; internet www.antarctica.com.br; brewery and soft-drink makers; Chair. JOSÉ HEITOR ATTÍLIO GRACIOSO; 5,600 employees.

Companhia Cervejaria Brahma: Rua Marquês de Sapucai 200, 20215-900 Rio de Janeiro, RJ; tel. (21) 503-9393; internet www .brahma.com.br; f. 1888; beer and soft-drink makers; Pres. MARCEL HERMANN TELLES; 13,660 employees.

Perdigão Agroindustrial, SA: Av. Escola Politécnica 760, 05350-000 São Paulo, SP; tel. (11) 868-5300; fax (11) 869-4436; e-mail perdigao@perdigao.com.br; internet www.perdigao.com.br; f. 1934; meat processing and packaging; Pres. EGGON JOÃO DA SILVA; 15,078 employees.

Sadia, SA: Alameda Tocantins 525, 06455-921 Barueri, SP; tel. (11) 7296-4432; fax (11) 7296-4510; internet www.sadia.com.br; f. 1944; refrigeration, meat packing, animal feeds; Pres. WALTER FONTANA, Filho; 22,331 employees.

Other

Companhia Vidraria Santa Marina: Av. Santa Marina 482, Agua Blanca, 05036-900 São Paulo, SP; tel. (11) 3874-7988; fax (11) 3874-1941; f. 1896; glass manufacturers; Chair. JEAN JACQUES FAUST; 2,700 employees.

Duratex, SA: Av. Paulista 1938, Paraíso, 01310-942 São Paulo, SP; tel. (11) 3179-7733; fax (11) 3179-7355; f. 1951; manufacturers of hardboard and plywood, ceramic products and bathroom fixtures; Chair. EUDORO VILLELA; Pres. PAULO SETUBAL; 6,288 employees.

Electrolux do Brasil, SA: Rua Verbo Divino 1488, 04719-904 São Paulo, SP; e-mail eluxfct@electrolux.com.br; internet www.electrolux.com.br; f. 1926; makers of refrigerators, freezers and vacuum cleaners; Pres. ROLAND FOLKE ASELL; 431 employees.

Empresa Brasileira de Correios e Telégrafos (ECT): SBN Lote 3, Edif. Sede, 17° andar, Conj. 3, Bloco A, 70002-900 Brasília, DF; tel. (61) 426-2450; fax (61) 426-2310; e-mail robervalcorrea@correios .com.br; internet www.correios.com.br; f. 1969; posts and telegraph; Pres. HASSAN GEBRIM; 82,253 employees.

Indústrias Villares, SA: Av. Interlagos 4455, 04669-900 São Paulo, SP; tel. (11) 525-3222; fax (11) 548-2212; f. 1918; produces and maintains lifts and escalators; Pres. PAULO DIEDERICHSEN VILLARES; Vice-Pres. WILSON NÉLIO BRUMER; 3,856 employees.

Lojas Americanas, SA: Rua Sacadura Cabral 102, Saúde, 20081-260 Rio de Janeiro, RJ; tel. (21) 271-6556; fax (21) 206-6687; e-mail gisomar.marinho@lasa.com.br; internet www.lasa.com.br; f. 1929; retail traders; sold to Comptoirs Modernes, SA, in November 1998; Pres. CARLOS ALBERTO DA VEIGA SICUPIRA; 11,669 employees.

Souza Cruz, SA: Rua Candelária 66, 20092-900 Rio de Janeiro, RJ; tel. (21) 279-9339; fax (21) 263-4343; f. 1903; manufacturers of cigarettes and tobacco; Pres. ANTÔNIO MONTEIRO DE CASTRO, Filho; 10,500 employees.

UTILITIES
Electricity

Centrais Elétricas Brasileiras, SA (ELETROBRÁS): Edif. Petrobrás, Rua Dois, Setor de Autarquias Norte, 70040-903 Brasília, DF; tel. (61) 223-5050; fax (61) 225-5502; e-mail maryann@eletrobras.gov.br; internet www.eletrobras.gov.br; f. 1962; government holding company responsible for planning, financing and managing Brazil's electrical energy programme; scheduled for division into eight generating cos and privatization; Pres. FIRMINO FERREIRA SAMPAIO NETO.

Centrais Elétricas do Norte do Brasil, SA (ELETRONORTE): SCN, Quadra 6, Conj. A, Blocos B/C, sala 602, Super Center Venâncio 3000, 70718-500 Brasília, DF; tel. (61) 429-5151; fax (61) 328-1566; e-mail elnweb@eln.gov.br; internet www.eln.gov.br; f. 1973; Pres. BENEDITO APARECIDO CARRARO.

Centrais Elétricas do Sul do Brasil, SA (ELETROSUL): Rua Deputado Antônio Edu Vieira 999, Pantanal, 88040-901 Florianópolis, SC; tel. (48) 231-7000; fax (48) 234-3434; Gerasul responsible for generating capacity; f. 1968; Pres. FIRMINO FERREIRA SAMPAIO NETO.

Companhia Hidro Elétrica do São Francisco (CHESF): 333 Edif. André Falcão, Bloco A, sala 313 Bongi, Rua Delmiro Golveia, 50761-901 Recife, PE; tel. (81) 229-2000; fax (81) 229-2390; e-mail chesf@chesf.com.br; internet www.chesf.com.br; f. 1948; Pres. MOZART DE SIQUEIRA CAMPOS ARAÚJO.

Furnas Centrais Elétricas, SA: Rua Real Grandeza 219, Bloco A, 16° andar, Botafogo, 22281-031 Rio de Janeiro, RJ; tel. (21) 528-3112; fax (21) 528-3438; internet www.furnas.com.br; f. 1957; Pres. LUIZ CARLOS SANTOS .

Associated companies include:

Espírito Santo Centrais Elétricas, SA (ESCELSA): Rua Sete de Setembro 362, Centro, CP 01-0452, 29015-000 Vitória, ES; tel. (27) 321-9000; fax (27) 322-0378; internet www.escelsa.com.br; f. 1968; Pres. JOSÉ GUSTAVO DE SOUZA.

Nuclebrás Engenharia, SA (NUCLEN): Rua Visconde de Ouro Preto 5, 12° andar, Botafogo, 22250-180 Rio de Janeiro, RJ; tel. (21) 552-2345; fax (21) 552-1745; f. 1975; nuclear-power generation/distribution; Pres. EVALDO CÉSARI DE OLIVEIRA.

Centrais Elétricas de Santa Catarina, SA (CELESC): Rodovia SC 404, Km 3, Itacorubi, 88034-900 Florianópolis, SC; tel. (48) 231-5000; fax (48) 231-6530; e-mail celesc@celesc.com.br; internet www.celesc.com.br; production and distribution of electricity throughout state of Santa Catarina; Pres. FRANCISCO DE ASSIS KÜSTER.

Comissão Nacional de Energia Nuclear (CNEN): Rua General Severiano 90, Botafogo, 22294-900 Rio de Janeiro, RJ; tel. (21) 295-2232; fax (21) 546-2442; e-mail corin@cnen.gov.br; internet www.cnen.gov.br; f. 1956; state organization responsible for management of nuclear power programme; Pres. MARCIO COSTA.

Companhia de Eletricidade do Estado da Bahia (COELBA): Av. Edgard Santos 300, Cabula IV, 41186-900 Salvador, BA; tel. (71) 370-5130; fax (71) 370-5132; Pres. EDUARDO LÓPEZ ARANGUREN MARCOS.

Companhia de Eletricidade do Estado do Rio de Janeiro (CERJ): Rua Visconde do Rio Branco 429, Centro, 24020-003 Niterói, RJ; tel. (21) 613-7120; fax (21) 613-7196; internet www.cerj.com.br; f. 1907; Pres. ALEJANDRO DANÚS CHIRIGHIN.

Companhia Energética Ceará (COELCE): Av. Barão de Studart 2917, 60120-002 Fortaleza, CE; tel. (85) 247-1444; fax (85) 272-4711; internet www.coelce.com.br; f. 1971; Pres. CARLOS EDUARDO CARVALHO ALVES.

Companhia Energética de Minas Gerais (CEMIG): Av. Barbacena 1200, 30123-970 Belo Horizonte; tel. (31) 349-2111; fax (31) 299-3700; e-mail mail@cemig.com.br; internet www.cemig.com.br; fmrly state-owned, sold to a Brazilian-US consortium in May 1997; Pres. JOSÉ DA COSTA CARVALGO NETO.

Companhia Energética de Pernambuco (CELPE): Av. João de Barros 111, Sala 301, 50050-902 Recife, PE; tel. (81) 3217-5168; e-mail celpe@celpe.com.br; internet www.celpe.com.br; state distributor of electricity; CEO JOÃO BOSCO DE ALMEIDA.

Companhia Energética de São Paulo (CESP): Al. Ministro Rocha Azevedo 25, 01410-900 São Paulo, SP; tel. (11) 234-6015; fax (11) 288-0338; e-mail presiden@cesp.com.br; internet www.cesp.com.br; f. 1966; Pres. GUILHERME AUGUSTO CIRNE DE TOLEDO.

Companhia Força e Luz Cataguazes-Leopoldina: Praça Rui Barbosa 80, 36770-000 Cataguases, MG; tel. (32) 429-6000; fax (32) 421-4240; internet www.cataguazes.com.br; f. 1905; Pres. MANOEL OTONI NEIVA.

Companhia Paranaense de Energia (COPEL): Rua Coronel Dulcídio 800, 80420-170 Curitiba, PR; tel. (41) 322-3535; fax (41) 331-4145; e-mail copel@mail.copel.com.br; internet www.copel.com.br; f. 1954; state distributor of electricity and gas; Pres. NEY AMINTHAS DE BARROS BRAGA.

Companhia Paulista de Força e Luz: Rodovia Campinas Mogi-Mirim Km 2.5, Campinas, SP; tel. (192) 253-8704; fax (192) 252-7644; provides electricity through govt concessions.

Eletricidade de São Paulo (ELETROPAULO): Av. Alfredo Egidio de Souza Aranha 100, 04791-900 São Paulo, SP; tel. (11) 546-1467; fax (11) 239-1387; e-mail administracao@eletropaulo.com.br; internet www.eletropaulo.com.br; f. 1899; state-owned, but partially privatized in 1998; Pres. MARC ANDRÉ PERREIRA.

Itaipú Binacional: Av. Tancredo Neves 6731, 85856-970 Foz de Iguaçu, PR; tel. (45) 520-5252; e-mail itaipu@itaipu.gov.br; internet www.itaipu.gov.br; f. 1974; 1,490 employees (Itaipú Brasil–1998); Dir-Gen. (Brazil) EUCLIDES SCALCO.

LIGHT – Serviços de Eletricidade, SA: Av. Marechal Floriano 168, CP 0571, 20080-002 Rio de Janeiro, RJ; tel. (21) 211-7171; fax (21) 233-1249; e-mail light@lightrio.com.br; internet www.lightrio.com.br; f. 1905; electricity generation and distribution in Rio de Janeiro; formerly state-owned, sold to a Brazilian-French-US consortium in 1996; Pres. LUIZ DAVID TRAVESSO.

Regulatory Agency

Agência Nacional de Energia Elétrica (ANEEL): SGAN 603, Módulo J, 70830-030 Brasília, DF; e-mail aneel@aneel.gov.br; internet www.aneel.gov.br; Dir JOSÉ MARIA ABDO.

Gas

Companhia Estadual de Gás do Rio de Janeiro (CEG): Av. Rio Vargas 1, 4° andar, 20090-003 Rio de Janeiro, RJ; tel. (21) 588-8600; fax (21) 588-8651; internet www.ceg.com.br; f. 1969; gas distribution in the Rio de Janeiro region; privatized in July 1997.

Companhia de Gás de São Paulo (COMGÁS): Rua Augusta 1600, 9° andar, 01304-901 São Paulo, SP; tel. (11) 3177-5000; fax (11) 3177-5042; email gaspla@comgas.com.br; internet www.comgas.com.br; f. 1978 distribution in São Paulo of gas; sold in April 1999 to consortium including British Gas PLC and Royal Dutch/Shell Group; Pres. JULIO CESAR LAMOUNIER NAPA.

Water

The first transfers to private ownership of state-owned water and sewerage companies were scheduled to commence in 2000.

Agua e Esgostos do Piauí (AGESPISA): Av. Mal Castelo Branco 101, Cabral, 64000 Teresina, PI; tel. (862) 239-300; f. 1962; state-owned; water and waste management; Pres. OLIVÃO GOMES DA SOUSA.

Companhia de Agua e Esgosto de Ceará (CAGECE): Rua Lauro Vieira Chaves 1030, Fortaleza; tel. (85) 247-2422; internet www.cagece.com.br; state-owned; water and sewerage services; Gen. Man. JOSÉ DE RIBAMAR DA SILVA.

Companhia Algoas Industrial (CINAL): Rodovia Divaldo Suruagy, Km 12, 57160-000 Marechal Deodoro, AL; tel. (82) 269-1100; fax (82) 269-1199; internet www.cinal.com.br; f. 1982; management of steam and treated water; Dir PAULO ALBERQUERQUE MARANHÃO.

Companhia Espírito Santense de Saneamento (CESAN): Av. Governador Bley, 186, Edif. BEMGE, 29010-150 Vitória ES; tel. (27) 322-8399; fax (27) 322-4551; internet www. cesan.com.br; f. 1968; state-owned; construction, maintenance and operation of water supply and sewerage systems; Pres. CLÁUDIO DE MORAES MACHADO.

Companhia Estadual de Aguas e Esgostos (CEDAE): Rua Sacadura Cabral 103, 9° andar, 20081-260 Rio de Janeiro, RJ; tel. (21) 296-0025; fax (21) 296-0416; state-owned; water supply and sewerage treatment; Pres. ALBERTO JOSÉ MENDES GOMES.

Companhia Pernambucana Saneamento (COMPESA): Av. Cruz Cabugá 1387, Bairro Santo Amaro, 50040-905 Recife, PE; tel. (81) 421-1711; fax (81) 421-2712; state-owned; management and operation of regional water supply in the state of Pernambuco; Pres. GUSTAVO DE MATTO PONTUAL SAMPAIO.

Companhia Riograndense de Saneamento (CORSAN): Rua Caldas Júnior 120, 18° andar, 90010-260 Porto Alegre, RS; tel. (51) 228-5622; fax (51) 215-5700; e-mail ascon@corsan.com.br; internet www.corsan.com.br; f. 1965; state-owned; management and operation of regional water supply and sanitation programmes; Dir. DIETER WARTCHOW.

Companhia de Saneamento Básico do Estado de São Paulo (SABESP): Rua Costa Carvalho 300, 05429-000 São Paulo, SP; tel. (11) 3030-4000; internet www.sabesp.com.br; f. 1973; state-owned; supplies basic sanitation services for the state of São Paulo, including water treatment and supply; Pres. ARIOVALDO CARMIGNANI.

TRADE UNIONS

Central Unica dos Trabalhadores (CUT): Rua São Bento 405, Edif. Martinelli, 7° andar, 01011 São Paulo, SP; tel. (11) 255-7500; fax (11) 37-5626; f. 1983; central union confederation; left-wing; Pres. VINCENTE PAULO DA SILVA; Gen. Sec. GILMAR CARNEIRO.

Confederação General dos Trabalhadores (CGT): São Paulo, SP; f. 1986; fmrly Coordenação Nacional das Classes Trabalhadoras; represents 1,258 labour organizations linked to PMDB; Pres. LUÍS ANTÔNIO MEDEIROS.

Confederação Nacional dos Metalúrgicos (Metal Workers): f. 1985; Pres. JOAQUIM DOS SANTOS ANDRADE.

Confederação Nacional das Profissões Liberais (CNPL) (Liberal Professions): SAU/SUL, Edif. Belvedere Gr. 202, 70070-000 Brasília, DF; tel. (61) 223-1683; fax (61) 223-1944; e-mail cnpliber@nutecnet.com.br; internet www.bsb.nutecut.com.br/web/cnpl; f. 1953; confederation of liberal professions; Pres. LUÍS EDUARDO GAUTÉRIO GALLO; Exec. Sec. JOSÉ ANTÔNIO BRITO ANDRADE.

Confederação Nacional dos Trabalhadores na Indústria (CNTI) (Industrial Workers): Av. W/3 Norte, Quadra 505, Lote 01, 70730-517 Brasília, DF; tel. (61) 274-4150; fax (61) 274-7001; f. 1946; Pres. JOSÉ CALIXTO RAMOS.

Confederação Nacional dos Trabalhadores no Comércio (CNTC) (Commercial Workers): Av. W/5 Sul, Quadra 902, Bloco C, 70390 Brasília, DF; tel. (61) 224-3511; f. 1946; Pres. ANTÔNIO DE OLIVEIRA SANTOS.

Confederação Nacional dos Trabalhadores em Transportes Marítimos, Fluviais e Aéreos (CONTTMAF) (Maritime, River and Air Transport Workers): Av. Pres. Vargas 446, gr. 2205,

20071 Rio de Janeiro, RJ; tel. (21) 233-8329; f. 1957; Pres. MAURÍCIO MONTEIRO SANT'ANNA.

Confederação Nacional dos Trabalhadores em Comunicações e Publicidade (CONTCOP) (Communications and Advertising Workers): SCS, Edif. Serra Dourada, 7° andar, gr. 705/709, Q 11, 70315 Brasília, DF; tel. (61) 224-7926; fax (61) 224-5686; f. 1964; 350,000 mems; Pres. ANTÔNIO MARIA THAUMATURGO CORTIZO.

Confederação Nacional dos Trabalhadores nas Empresas de Crédito (CONTEC) (Workers in Credit Institutions): SEP-SUL, Av. W4, EQ 707/907 Lote E, 70351 Brasília, DF; tel. (61) 244-5833; f. 1958; 814,532 mems (1988); Pres. LOURENÇO FERREIRA DO PRADO.

Confederação Nacional dos Trabalhadores em Estabelecimentos de Educação e Cultura (CNTEEC) (Workers in Education and Culture): SAS, Quadra 4, Bloco B, 70302 Brasília, DF; tel. (61) 226-2988; f. 1967; Pres. MIGUEL ABRAHÃO.

Confederação Nacional dos Trabalhadores na Agricultura (CONTAG) (Agricultural Workers): SDS, Ed Venâncio VI, 1° andar, 70393-900 Brasília, DF; tel. (61) 321-2288; fax (61) 321-3229; f. 1964; Pres. FRANCISCO URBANO ARAÚJO, Filho.

Força Sindical (FS): São Paulo, SP; f. 1991; 6m. mems (1991); Pres. LUÍS ANTÔNIO MEDEIROS.

Transport

Ministério dos Transportes: see section on the Government (Ministries).

Empresa Brasileira de Planejamento de Transportes (GEIPOT): SAN, Quadra 3, Blocos N/O, Edif. Núcleo dos Transportes, 70040-902 Brasília, DF; tel. (61) 315-4890; fax (61) 315-4895; e-mail deind@geipot.gov.br; internet www.geipot.gov.br; f. 1973; agency for the promotion of an integrated modern transport system; advises the Minister of Transport on transport policy; Pres. CARLOS ALBERTO WANDERLEY NÓBREGA.

RAILWAYS

Rede Ferroviária Federal, SA (RFFSA) (Federal Railway Corporation): Praça Procópio Ferreira 86, 20221-030 Rio de Janeiro, RJ; tel. (21) 516-1890; fax (21) 516-1390; internet www.rffsa.gov.br; f. 1957; holding company for 18 railways grouped into regional networks, with total track length of 20,500 km in 1998; privatization of federal railways was completed in 1997; freight services; Pres. ISAAC POPOUTCHI.

Companhia Brasileira de Trens Urbanos (CBTU): Estrada Velha da Tijuca 77, Usina, 20531-080 Rio de Janeiro, RJ; tel. (21) 575-3399; fax (21) 571-6149; fmrly responsible for surburban networks and metro systems throughout Brazil; 252 km in 1998; the transfer of each city network to its respective local government is currently under way; Pres. LUIZ OTAVIO MOTA VALADARES.

Belo Horizonte Metro (CBTU/STU/BH-Demetrô): Av. Afonso Pena 1500, 11° andar, 30130-921 Belo Horizonte, MG; tel. (31) 250-4002; fax (31) 250-4004; e-mail metrobh@gold.horizontes.com.br; f. 1986; 21.2 km open in 1997; Gen. Man. M. L. L. SIQUEIRA.

Trem Metropolitano de Recife: Rua José Natário 478, Areias, 50900-000 Recife, PE; tel. (81) 455-4655; fax (81) 455-4422; f. 1985; 53 km open in 1997; Supt FERNANDO ANTÔNIO C. DUEIRE.

There are also railways owned by state governments and several privately-owned railways:

Companhia Fluminense de Trens Urbanos (Flumitrens): Praça Cristiano Otoni, sala 445, 20221 Rio de Janeiro, RJ; tel. (21) 233-8594; fax (21) 253-3089; f. 1975 as operating division of RFFSA, current name adopted following takeover by state government in 1994; suburban services in Rio de Janeiro and its environs; 293 km open in 1998; Supt MURILO JUNQUEIRA.

Companhia do Metropolitano do Rio de Janeiro: Av. Nossa Senhora de Copacabana 493, 22021-031 Rio de Janeiro, RJ; tel. (21) 235-4041; fax (21) 235-4546; 2-line metro system, 42 km open in 1997; Pres. ALVARO J. M. SANTOS.

Companhia do Metropolitano de São Paulo: Rua Augusta 1626, 03310-200 São Paulo, SP; tel. (11) 283-7411; fax (11) 283-5228; f. 1974; 3-line metro system, 56 km open in 1998; Pres. PAULO CLARINDO GOLDSCHMIDT.

Companhia Paulista de Trens Metropolitanos (CPTM): Av. Paulista 402, 5° andar, 01310-903 São Paulo, SP; tel. (11) 281-6101; fax (11) 288-2224; f. 1993 to incorporate suburban lines fmrly operated by the CBTU and FEPASA; 286 km; Pres. Eng. OLIVER HOSSEPIAN SALLES DE LIMA.

Departamento Metropolitano de Transportes Urbanos: SES, Quadra 4, Lote 6, Brasília, DF; tel. (61) 317-4090; fax (61) 226-9546; the first section of the Brasília metro, linking the capital with the western suburb of Samambaia, was inaugurated in 1994; 38.5 km open in 1997; Dir LEONARDO DE FARIA E SILVA.

Empresa de Trens Urbanos de Porto Alegre, SA: Av. Ernesto Neugebauer 1985, 90250-140 Porto Alegre, RS; tel. (51) 371-5000; fax (51) 371-1219; e-mail secos@trensurb.com.br; internet www.tren surb.com.br; f. 1985; 31 km open in 1998; Pres. PEDRO BISCH NETO.

Estrada de Ferro do Amapá: Praia de Botafogo 300, 11° andar, ala A, 22250-050 Rio de Janeiro, RJ; tel. (21) 552-4422; f. 1957; operated by Indústria e Comércio de Minérios, SA; 194 km open in 1998; Pres. OSVALDO LUIZ SENRA PESSOA.

Estrada de Ferro Campos do Jordão: Rua Martin Cabral 87, CP 11, 12400-000 Pindamonhangaba, SP; tel. (22) 242-4233; fax (22) 242-2499; operated by the Tourism Secretariat of the State of São Paulo; 47 km open in 1998; Dir ARTHUR FERREIRA DOS SANTOS.

Estrada de Ferro Carajás: Av. dos Portugueses s/n, 65085-580 São Luís, MA; tel. (98) 218-4000; fax (98) 218-4530; f. 1985 for movement of minerals from the Serra do Carajás to the new port at Ponta da Madeira; operated by the Companhia Vale do Rio Doce; 955 km open in 1998; Supt JUARES SALIBRA.

Estrada de Ferro do Jari: Monte Dourado, 68230-000 Pará, PA; tel. (91) 735-1155; fax (91) 735-1475; transportation of timber and bauxite; 68 km open; Dir ARMINDO LUIZ BARETTA.

Estrada de Ferro Mineração Rio do Norte, SA: Praia do Flamengo 200, 5° e 6° andares, 22210-030 Rio de Janeiro, RJ; tel. (21) 205-9112; fax (21) 545-5717; 35 km open in 1998; Pres. ANTÔNIO JOÃO TORRES.

Estrada de Ferro Paraná-Oeste, SA (Ferroeste): Av. Iguaçu 420-7°, 80230-902 Curitiba, PR; tel. (41) 322-1811; fax (41) 233-2147; f. 1988 to serve the grain-producing regions in Paraná and Mato Grosso do Sul; 248 km inaugurated in 1995; privatized in late 1996, Brazilian company, Ferropar, appointed as administrator; Pres. JOSÉ HERALDO CARNEIRO LOBO.

Estrada de Ferro Vitória-Minas: Av. Dante Michelini 5.500, 29090-900 Vitória, ES; tel. (27) 335-3666; fax (27) 226-0093; f. 1942; operated by Companhia Vale de Rio Doce; transport of iron ore, general cargo and passengers; 898 km open in 1998; Dir THIER BARSOTTI MANZANO.

Ferrovia Bandeirante, SA (Ferroban): Rua Mauá 51, 01018-900 São Paulo, SP; tel. (11) 222-3392; fax (11) 220-8852; f. 1971 by merger of five railways operated by São Paulo State; transferred to private ownership, Nov. 1998; fmrly Ferrovia Paulista; 4,235 km open in 1998.

ROADS

In 1999 there were an estimated 1,700,000 km of roads in Brazil, of which 161,500 km were paved. Brasília has been a focal point for inter-regional development, and paved roads link the capital with every region of Brazil. The building of completely new roads has taken place predominantly in the north. Roads are the principal mode of transport, accounting for 63% of freight and 96% of passenger traffic, including long-distance bus services, in 1998. Major projects include the 5,000-km Trans-Amazonian Highway, running from Recife and Cabedelo to the Peruvian border, the 4,138-km Cuibá–Santarém highway, which will run in a north–south direction, and the 3,555-km Trans-Brasiliana project, which will link Marabá, on the Trans-Amazonian highway, with Aceguá, on the Uruguayan frontier. A 20-year plan to construct a highway linking São Paulo with the Argentine and Chilean capitals was endorsed in 1992 within the context of the development of the Southern Cone Common Market (Mercosul).

Departamento Nacional de Estradas de Rodagem (DNER) (National Roads Development): SAN, Quadra 3, Blocos N/O, 4° andar, Edif. Núcleo dos Transportes, 70040-902 Brasília, DF; tel. (61) 315-4100; fax (61) 315-4050; f. 1945 to plan and execute federal road policy and to supervise state and municipal roads with the aim of integrating them into the national network; Dir GENÉSIO B. SOUZA.

INLAND WATERWAYS

River transport plays only a minor part in the movement of goods. There are three major river systems, the Amazon, Paraná and the São Francisco. The Amazon is navigable for 3,680 km, as far as Iquitos in Peru, and ocean-going ships can reach Manaus, 1,600 km upstream. Plans have been drawn up to improve the inland waterway system and one plan is to link the Amazon and Upper Paraná to provide a navigable waterway across the centre of the country. In October 1993 the member governments of Mercosul, together with Bolivia, reaffirmed their commitment to a 10-year development programme (initiated in 1992) for the extension of the Tietê Paraná river network along the Paraguay and Paraná Rivers as far as Buenos Aires, improving access to Atlantic ports and creating a 3,442 km waterway system, navigable throughout the year.

Secretaria de Transportes Aquaviários: Ministério dos Transportes, SAN, Quadra 3, Blocos N/O, 70040-902 Brasília, DF; tel. (61) 315-8102; Sec. WILDJAN DA FONSECA MAGNO.

Administração da Hidrovia do Paraguai (AHIPAR): Rua Treze de Junho 960, Corumbá, MS; tel. (67) 231-2841; fax (67) 231-2661; Supt. PAULO CÉSAR C. GOMES DA SILVA.

Administração da Hidrovia do Paraná (AHRANA): Rua Vinte e Quatro de Maio 55, 9° andar, Conj. B, 01041-001 São Paulo, SP; tel. (11) 221-3230; fax (11) 220-8689; Supt LUIZ EDUARDO GARCIA.

Administração da Hidrovia do São Francisco (AHSFRA): Praça do Porto 70, Distrito Industrial, 39270-000 Pirapora, MG; tel. (38) 741-2555; fax (38) 741-2510; Supt JOSÉ H. BORATO JABUR JÚNIOR.

Administração das Hidrovias do Sul (AHSUL): Praça Oswaldo Cruz 15, 3° andar, 90030-160 Porto Alegre, RS; tel. (51) 228-3677; fax (51) 226-9068; Supt JOSÉ LUIZ F. DE AZAMBUJA.

Empresa de Navegação da Amazônia, SA (ENASA): Av. Pres. Vargas 41, 66000-000 Belém, PA; tel. (91) 223-3878; fax (91) 224-0528; f. 1967; cargo and passenger services on the Amazon river and its principal tributaries, connecting the port of Belém with all major river ports; Pres. ANTÔNIO DE SOUZA MENDONÇA; 48 vessels.

SHIPPING

There are more than 40 deep-water ports in Brazil, all but two of which (Luis Correia and Imbituba) are directly or indirectly administered by the Government. The majority of ports are operated by eight state-owned concerns (Cia Docas do Pará, Maranhão, Ceará, Rio Grande do Norte, Bahia, Espírito Santo, Rio de Janeiro and Estado de São Paulo), while a smaller number (including Suape, Cabedelo, Barra dos Coqueiros, São Sebastião, Paranaguá, Antonina, São Francisco do Sul, Porto Alegre, Pelotas and Rio Grande) are administered by state governments. In late 1996 the Government announced plans to privatize 31 ports (including Santos and Rio de Janeiro).

The ports of Santos, Rio de Janeiro and Rio Grande have specialized container terminals handling more than 1,200,000 TEUs (20-ft equivalent units of containerized cargo) per year. Santos is the major container port in Brazil, accounting for 800,000 TEUs annually. The ports of Paranaguá, Itajaí, São Francisco do Sul, Salvador, Vitória and Imbituba cater for containerized cargo to a lesser extent.

Total cargo handled by Brazilian ports in 1999 amounted to 436m. tons, compared with 443m. tons in 1998 (of which 250m. was bulk cargo, 148m. was liquid cargo and 45m. was general cargo). Some 43,000 vessels used Brazil's ports in 1998.

Brazil's merchant fleet comprised 505 vessels totalling 3,808,762 grt in December 2000.

Departamento de Marinha Mercante: Coordenação Geral de Transporte Maritimo, Av. Rio Branco 103, 6° e 8° andar, 20040-004 Rio de Janeiro, RJ; tel. (21) 221-4014; fax (21) 221-5929; Dir PAULO OCTÁVIO DE PAIVA ALMEIDA.

Port Authorities

Departamento de Portos: SAN, Quadra 3, Blocos N/O, CEP 70040-902, Brasília, DF; Dir PAULO ROBERTO K. TANNFNBAUM.

Paranaguá: Administração dos Portos de Paranaguá e Antonina (APPA), BR-277, km 0, 83206-380 Paranaguá, PR; tel. (41) 420-1102; fax (41) 423-4252; Port Admin. Eng. OSIRIS STENGHEL GUIMARÃES.

Recife: Administração do Porto do Recife, Praça Artur Oscar, 50030-370 Recife, PE; tel. (81) 424-4044; fax (81) 224-2848; Port Dir CARLOS DO REGO VILAR.

Rio de Janeiro: Companhia Docas do Rio de Janeiro (CDRJ), Rua do Acre 21, 20081-000 Rio de Janeiro, RJ; tel. (21) 296-5151; fax (21) 253-0528; CDRJ also administers the ports of Forno, Niterói, Sepetiba and Angra dos Reis; Pres. MAURO OROFINO CAMPOS.

Rio Grande: Administração do Porto de Rio Grande, Av. Honório Bicalho, CP 198, 96201-020 Rio Grande do Sul, RS; tel. (532) 31-1996; fax (532) 31-1857; Port Dir LUIZ FRANCISCO SPOTORNO.

Santos: Companhia Docas do Estado de São Paulo (CODESP), Av. Conselheiro Rodrigues Alves s/n, 11015-900 Santos, SP; tel. (13) 222-5485; fax (13) 222-3068; e-mail codesp@carrier.com.br; internet www.portodesantos.com; CODESP also administers the ports of Charqueadas, Estrela, Cáceres, Corumbá/Ladário, and the waterways of Paraná (AHRANA), Paraguai (AHIPAR) and the South (AHSUL); Pres. WAGNER GONÇALVES ROSSI.

São Francisco do Sul: Administração do Porto de São Francisco do Sul, Av. Eng. Leite Ribeiro 782, CP 71, 89240-000 São Francisco do Sul, SC; tel. (474) 44-0200; fax (474) 44-0115; Dir-Gen. ARNALDO S. THIAGO.

Tubarão: Companhia Vale do Rio Doce, Porto de Tubarão, Vitória, ES; tel. (27) 335-5727; fax (27) 228-0612; Port Dir CANDIDO COTTA PACHECO.

Vitória: Companhia Docas do Espírito Santo (CODESA), Av. Getúlio Vargas 556, Centro, 29020-030 Vitória, ES; tel. (27) 321-1311; fax (27) 222-7360; e-mail codesa@codesa.com.br; internet www.codesa.com.br; f. 1983; Pres. FÁBIO NUNES FALCE.

Other ports are served by the following state-owned companies:

Companhia Docas do Estado de Bahia: Av. da França 1551, 40010-000 Salvador, BA; tel. (71) 243-5066; fax (71) 241-6712; administers the ports of Aracaju, Salvador, Aratu, Ilhéus and Pirapora, and the São Francisco waterway (AHSFRA); Pres. JORGE FRANCISCO MEDAUAR.

Companhia Docas do Estado de Ceará (CDC): Praça Amigos da Marinha s/n, 60180-640 Fortaleza, CE; tel. (85) 263-1551; fax (85) 263-2433; administers the port of Fortaleza; Dir MARCELO MOTA TEIXEIRA.

Companhia Docas de Maranhão (CODOMAR): Porto do Itaquí, Rua de Paz 561, 65085-370 São Luís, MA; tel. (98) 222-2412; fax (98) 221-1394; administers ports of Itaquí and Manaus, and waterways of the Western Amazon (AHIMOC) and the North-East (AHINOR); Dir WASHINGTON DE OLIVEIRA VIEGAS.

Companhia Docas do Pará (CDP): Av. Pres. Vargas 41, 2° andar, 66010-000 Belém, PA; tel. (91) 216-2011; fax (91) 241-1741; f. 1967; administers the ports of Belém, Macapá, Porto Velho, Santarém and Vila do Conde, and the waterways of the Eastern Amazon (AHIMOR) and Tocantins and Araguaia (AHITAR); Dir-Pres. CARLOS ACATAUSSÚ NUNES.

Companhia Docas do Estado do Rio Grande do Norte (CODERN): Av. Hildebrando de Góis 2220, Ribeira, 59010-700 Natal, RN; tel. (84) 211-5311; fax (84) 221-6072; administers the ports of Areia Branca, Natal, Recife and Maceió; Dir EMILSON MEDEIROS DOS SANTOS.

Other State-owned Companies

Companhia de Navegação do Estado de Rio de Janeiro: Praça 15 de Novembro 21, 20010-010 Rio de Janeiro, RJ; tel (21) 533-6661; fax (21) 252-0524; Pres. MARCOS TEIXEIRA.

Frota Nacional de Petroleiros—Fronape: Rua Carlos Seidl 188, CP 51015, 20931, Rio de Janeiro, RJ; tel. (21) 585-3355; f. 1953; fleet of tankers operated by the state petroleum company, PETROBRÁS, and the Ministry of Transport; Chair. ALBANO DE SOUZA GONÇALVES.

Private Companies

Companhia Docas de Imbituba (CDI): Porto de Imbituba, Av. Presidente Vargas s/n, 88780-000 Imbituba, SC; tel. (482) 55-0080; fax (482) 55-0701; administers the port of Imbituba; Exec. Dir. MANUEL ALVES DO VALE.

Companhia de Navegação do Norte (CONAN): Av. Rio Branco 23, 25° andar, 20090-003 Rio de Janeiro, RJ; tel. (21) 223-4155; fax (21) 253-7128; f. 1965; services to Brazil, Argentina, Uruguay and inland waterways; Chair. J. R. RIBEIRO SALOMÃO.

Empresa de Navegação Aliança, SA: Av. Pasteur 110, Botafogo, 22290-240 Rio de Janeiro, RJ; tel. (21) 546-1112; fax (21) 546-1161; f. 1950; cargo services to Argentina, Uruguay, Europe, Baltic, Atlantic and North Sea ports; Pres. CARLOS G. E. FISCHER.

Companhia de Navegação do São Francisco: Av. São Francisco 1517, 39270-000 Pirapora, MG; tel. (38) 741-1444; fax (38) 741-1164; Pres. JOSÉ HUMBERTO BARATA JABUR.

Frota Oceânica Brasileira, SA: Av. Venezuela 110, CP 21-020, 20081-310 Rio de Janeiro, RJ; tel. (21) 291-5153; fax (21) 263-1439; f. 1947; Pres. JOSÉ CARLOS FRAGOSO PIRES; Vice-Pres. LUIZ J. C. ALHANATI.

Serviço de Navegação Bacia Prata: Av. 14 de Março 1700, 79370-000 Ladário, MS; tel. (67) 231-4354; Dir LUIZ CARLOS DA SILVA ALEXANDRE.

Vale do Rio Doce Navegação, SA (DOCENAVE): Rua Voluntários da Pátria 143, Botafogo, 22279-900 Rio de Janeiro, RJ; tel. (21) 536-8002; fax (21) 536-8276; bulk carrier to Japan, Arabian Gulf, Europe, North America and Argentina; Pres. AKIRA KATSUGARI.

CIVIL AVIATION

There are about 1,500 airports and airstrips. Of the 67 principal airports 22 are international, although most international traffic is handled by the two airports at Rio de Janeiro and two at São Paulo.

Empresa Brasileira de Infra-Estrutura Aeroportuária (INFRAERO): SCS, Q 04, NR 58, Edif. Infraero, 6° andar, 70304-902 Brasília, DF; tel. (61) 312-3170; fax (61) 312-3105; e-mail fernandalima@infraero.gov.br; internet www.infraero.gov.br; Pres. EDUARDO BOGALHO PETTENGILL.

Principal Airlines

Lider Taxi Aéreo, SA: Av. Santa Rosa 123, 31270-750 Belo Horizonte, MG; tel. (31) 490-4500; fax (31) 490-4600; internet www.lidertaxiaereo.com.br; f. 1958; Pres. JOSÉ AFONSO ASSUMPÇÃO.

Nordeste Linhas Aéreas Regionais: Av. Tancredo Neves 1672, Edif. Catabas Empresarial, 1° andar, Pituba, 41820-020 Salvador, BA; tel. (71) 341-7533; fax (71) 341-0393; e-mail nordeste@provider

.com.br; internet www.nordeste.com.br; f. 1976; services to 26 destinations in north-east Brazil; Pres. PERCY LOURENÇO RODRIGUES.

Pantanal Linhas Aéreas Sul-Matogrossenses, SA: Av. das Nações Unidas 10989, 8° andar, São Paulo, SP; tel. (11) 3040-3900; fax (11) 866-3424; e-mail pantanal@uninet.com.br; internet www.pantanal-airlines.com.br; f. 1993; regional services; Pres. MARCOS FERREIRA SAMPAIO.

Rio-Sul Serviços Aéreos Regionais, SA: Av. Rio Branco 85, 11° andar, 20040-004 Rio de Janeiro, RJ; tel. (21) 263-4282; fax (21) 253-2044; internet www.rio-sul.com; f. 1976; subsidiary of VARIG; domestic passenger services to cities in southern Brazil; Pres. PAULO ENRIQUE MORÃES COCO.

TAM—Transportes Aéreos Regionais (TAM): Av. Pedro Bueno 1400, 04342-001 São Paulo, SP; tel. (11) 5582-8811; fax (11) 578-5946; e-mail tamimprensa@tam.com.br; internet www.tam-airlines.com.br; f. 1976; scheduled passenger and cargo services from São Paulo to destinations throughout Brazil; Pres. DANIEL MANDELLI MARTIN.

Transbrasil SA Linhas Aéreas: Zona C 01, Lotes 8/9, Aeroporto Internacional, 71608 Brasília, DF; tel. (61) 248-0900; fax (61) 242-5893; internet www.transbrasil.com.br; f. 1955 as Sadia, renamed 1972; scheduled passenger and cargo services to major Brazilian cities and Orlando; cargo charter flights to the USA; Pres. OMAR FONTANA.

Transportes Aéreos Regionais da Bacia Amazônica (TABA): Av. Governador José Malcher 883, 66055-260 Belém, PA; tel. (91) 223-6300; fax (91) 223-0471; f. 1976; domestic passenger services throughout north-west Brazil; Chair. MARCÍLIO JACQUES GIBSON.

VARIG, SA (Viação Aérea Rio Grandense): Rua 18 de Novembro 120, 90240-040 Porto Alegre, RS; tel. (51) 358-4233; fax (51) 358-7001; internet www.varig.com.br; f. 1927; international services throughout North, Central and South America, Africa, Western Europe and Japan; domestic services to major Brazilian cities; cargo services; Chair. and Pres. FERNANDO PINTO.

VASP, SA (Viação Aérea São Paulo): Praça Comte-Lineu Gomes s/n, Aeroporto Congonhas, 04626-910 São Paulo, SP; tel. (11) 532-3000; fax (11) 542-0880; internet www.vasp.com.br; f. 1933; privatized in Sept. 1990; domestic services throughout Brazil; international services to Argentina, Belgium, the Caribbean, South Korea and the USA; Pres. WAGNER CANHEDO.

Tourism

In 1999 some 5.1m. tourists visited Brazil. Receipts from tourism totalled US $3,994m. in that year. Rio de Janeiro, with its famous beaches, is the centre of the tourist trade. Like Salvador, Recife and other towns, it has excellent examples of Portuguese colonial and modern architecture. The modern capital, Brasília, incorporates a new concept of city planning and is the nation's show-piece. Other attractions are the Iguaçu Falls, the seventh largest (by volume) in the world, the tropical forests of the Amazon basin and the wildlife of the Pantanal.

Instituto Brasileiro de Turismo—EMBRATUR: SCN, Q 02, Bloco G, 3° andar, 70710-500 Brasília, DF; tel. (61) 224-9100; fax (61) 223-9889; internet www.embratur.gov.br; f. 1966; Pres. CAIO LUIZ DE CARVALHO.

Seção de Feiras e Turismo/Departamento de Promoção Comercial: Ministério das Relações Exteriores, Esplanada dos Ministérios, 5° andar, Sala 523, 70170-900 Brasília, DF; tel. (61) 411-6394; fax (61) 322-0833; e-mail docstt@mre.gov.br; internet www.braziltradenet.gov.br; f. 1977; organizes Brazil's participation in trade fairs and commercial exhibitions abroad; Principal Officer ANTÔNIO J. M. DE SOUZA E SILVA.

Defence

In August 2000 Brazil's Armed Forces numbered 287,000 men: Army 189,000 (including 40,000 conscripts); Navy 48,000 (3,200 are conscripts; also including 1,150 in the naval air force and 13,900 marines); and Air Force 50,000 (including 5,000 conscripts). Reserves number 1,115,000 and there were some 385,600 in the paramilitary Public Security Forces, state militias under Army control. Military service lasts for 12 months and is compulsory for men between 18 and 45 years of age.

Defence Budget: R $17.900m. (US $9,900m.) in 2000.

Chief of Staff of the Air Forces: Gen. BENEDITO ONOFRE BEZERRA LEONEL.

Chief of Staff of the Army: Gen. GLEUBER VIEIRA.

Chief of Staff of the Navy: Adm. SERGIO GITIRANA FLORENCIO CHAGASTELES.

Education

Education is free in Brazil in official schools at primary and secondary level. Primary education is compulsory between the ages of seven and 14 years and lasts for seven years. Secondary education begins at 15 years of age and lasts for three years. The Federal Government is responsible for higher education, and in 1997 there were 150 universities, of which 77 were state administered. In 1998 95.8% of children in the relevant age-group were enrolled at primary schools, but only 30.7% of those aged 15 to 17 were enrolled at secondary schools. In the same year, according to official figures, 35,845,742 children were enrolled at 187,497 primary schools, while 6,968,531 were enrolled at 17,602 secondary schools. There were 78,107 pre-primary schools with 4,111,153 pupils. There is a large number of private institutions at all levels of education. In 1997 central government expenditure on education and sport was forecast at R $10,376m., or 2.4% of total expenditure.

Bibliography

For works on South America generally, see Select Bibliography (Books).

Arruda, M. *External Debt (Brazil and the International Financial Crisis)*. London, Oluto Press Ltd, 2000.

Bacha, E.L., and Klein, H.S. (Eds). *Social Change in Brazil, 1945–1985: The Incomplete Transition*. Austin, TX, University of Texas Press, 1983.

Baer, W. *The Brazilian Economy (Growth and Development)*. Praeger Publrs, 2001.

Black, J. K. *US Penetration of Brazil*. Philadelphia, PA, University of Pennsylvania Press, 1977.

Branford, S., and Kucinski, B. *Brazil: Carnival of the Oppressed*. London, Latin American Bureau, 1995.

Bresser Pereira, L. *Development and Crisis in Brazil, 1930–1983*. Boulder, CO, Westview Press, 1984.

Cardoso, F. E., and Faletto, E. *Dependency and Development in Latin America*. Berkeley, CA, University of California Press, 1979.

Chilcote, R. H. *Power and the Ruling Classes in Northeast Brazil: Juazeiro and Petrolina in Transition*. Cambridge, Cambridge University Press, 1990.

Cockburn, A., and Hecht, S. B. *The Fate of the Forest: Developers, Destroyers and Defenders of the Amazon*. London, Verso, 1988.

Conniff, M. L., and McCann, F. D. *Modern Brazil: Elites and Masses in Historical Perspective*. Lincoln, NE, University of Nebraska Press.

Flynn, P. *Brazil: A Political Analysis*. London, Ernest Benn, 1978.

Freyre, G. *The Masters and the Slaves: a Study in the Development of Brazilian Civilization*. New York, NY, Alfred A. Knopf, 1946.

Frieden, J. A. 'The Brazilian Borrowing Experience' in *Latin American Research Review*, 22, 1, 1987, 95.

Furtado, C. 'Rescuing Brazil, Reversing Recession' in *Third World Quarterly*, Vol. 6, No. 3. 1984.

Goertzel, T. G. *Fernando Henrique Cardoso–Reinventing Democracy in Brazil*. Boulder, CO, Lynne Rienner Publrs, 1999.

Gonçalves, R. 'Brazil's search for stabilisation' in *Third World Quarterly*, Vol. 7, No. 2. 1985.

Hecht, S., and Cockburn, A. *The Fate of the Forest: Developers, Destroyers and Defenders of the Amazon*. London, Verso, 1989.

Hemming, J. *Amazon Frontier: The Defeat of the Brazilian Indians*. London, Macmillan, 1987.

Leff, N. H. *Underdevelopment and Development in Brazil* (Vol. 1: *Economic Structure and Change 1822–1947*; Vol. 2: *Reassessing the Obstacles to Economic Development*). London, George Allen & Unwin, 1982.

Lincoln, G. *Brazil's Second Chance (En Route Toward the First World)*. Washington, DC, The Brookings Institution, 2001.

Mendes, C. *Fight for the Forest: Chico Mendes in his own Words*. London, Latin American Bureau, 1989.

Moreira Alves, M. H. *State and Opposition in Military Brazil.* Austin, TX, University of Texas Press, 1985.

Navarro, Z. 'Democracy, citizenship and representation: rural social movements in southern Brazil, 1978–1990' in *Bulletin of Latin American Research*, Vol. 13, No. 2 (May), 129–154. 1994.

Payne, L.A. *Brazilian Industrialists and Democratic Change.* Baltimore, MD, Johns Hopkins University Press, 1994.

Ribeiro, D. *The Brazilian People (The Formation and Meaning of Brazil).* Gainesville, FL, University Press of Florida, 2000.

Rosenn, K. S., and Downes, R. *Corruption and Political Reform in Brazil (The Aftermath of Fernando Collor De Mello).* Boulder, CO, Lynne Rienner Publrs, 1999.

Schneider, R. M. *Brazil: Culture and Politics in a New Industrial Powerhouse.* Boulder, CO, Westview Press, 1996.

Skidmore, T. E. *The Politics of Military Rule in Brazil, 1964–85.* Oxford, Oxford University Press, 1990.

THE BRITISH VIRGIN ISLANDS

Area: 153 sq km (59 sq miles); consists of over 40 islands.

Population (estimate, 2000): 19,615.

Capital: Road Town (Tortola); population 5,989 in 1998.

Language: English.

Religion: Predominantly Christian; the largest denominations are the Methodist Church and the Church of God.

Climate: Subtropical; average annual rainfall 1,000 mm.

Time: GMT –4 hours.

Public Holidays: 2002: 1 January (New Year's Day), 7 March (Lavity Stoutt's Birthday), 11 March (Commonwealth Day), 29 March (Good Friday), 1 April (Easter Monday), 20 May (Whit Monday), 8 June (Queen's Official Birthday), 1 July (Territory Day), 5–7 August (Festival Monday, Tuesday and Wednesday), 21 October (Saint Ursula's Day), 25–26 December (Christmas). **2003:** 1 January (New Year's Day), 7 March (Lavity Stoutt's Birthday), 10 March (Commonwealth Day), 18 April (Good Friday), 21 April (Easter Monday), 9 June (Whit Monday), 14 June (Queen's Official Birthday), 1 July (for Territory Day), 4–6 August (Festival Monday, Tuesday and Wednesday), 21 October (for Saint Ursula's Day), 25–26 December (Christmas).

Currency: US dollar; US $100 = £69.84 = €112.66 (30 April 2001).

Weights and Measures: Imperial.

History

The islands are a United Kingdom Overseas Territory, and the British monarch is represented by the Governor.

Between 1872 and 1956 the islands were part of the Leeward Islands Federation (a British colony). In 1960 direct responsibility was assumed by an appointed Administrator (later redesignated Governor). Under the provisions of the 1967 Constitution, H. Lavity Stoutt of the Virgin Islands Party (VIP) became the first Chief Minister, but he was later replaced by an independent, Willard Wheatley. The Constitution was amended in 1977 to allow the islands greater internal self-government. After the 1979 election, Stoutt resumed the office of Chief Minister. In 1983 the United Party (UP) formed a coalition with the sole independent in the Legislative Council, Cyril Romney, who became Chief Minister. In the next general election, in September 1986, the VIP won five of the nine elective seats and Stoutt was appointed Chief Minister.

In March 1989 the Independent People's Movement (IPM) was founded, and it won one seat at the November 1990 general election. The VIP secured six seats and independents the remaining two. In early 1994 the Constitution was amended to provide for an enlarged Legislative Council of 13 seats. Elections to the legislature were held on 20 February 1995; the VIP won five seats, the UP and the Concerned Citizens' Movement (CCM—formerly IPM) two seats each and independent candidates three. With the support of an independent, the VIP was able to form a Government: Stoutt retained the premiership until his sudden death in May, when he was replaced by his deputy, Ralph O'Neal. At a by-election held in July for the vacant seat, the VIP candidate was successful.

In December 1997 the leader of the CCM, Walwyn Brewley, was appointed as Leader of the Opposition in the Legislative Council, replacing the leader of the United Party, Conrad Maduro.

In March 1999 the British Government published draft legislation confirming that its Dependencies were to be referred to as United Kingdom Overseas Territories; the document stated that all such territories would be required to comply with European standards on human rights and financial regulation. In the general election of 17 May 1999 the VIP won seven seats, retaining control of the Legislative Council. The National Democratic Party (NDP), formed the previous year, won five seats and the CCM retained one. O'Neal reappointed the members of the previous Executive Council.

In July 1999 a consultant was appointed to review the Constitution. Towards the end of the year several changes were proposed, including more frequent meetings of the Legislative Council and the removal of the Governor's power to veto legislation; the Governor would also be obliged to consult with the Executive Council before implementing policy in his areas of special responsibility. The main aim of the proposed legislation was to regulate the financial-services sector. The Governor, Frank Savage, who also announced the introduction of a comprehensive review of the education system, announced that the drafting of the proposed amendments to the Constitution would continue throughout the year. In October the Legislative Council approved a proposal to repeal the islands' controversial law denying entry to people with 'Rastafarian or hippy hairstyles'. Chief Minister O'Neal later announced that the public would be consulted before the proposal was referred to the Executive Council.

On 20 July 2000 the appointment of the Minister of Health, Education, Culture and Welfare, Eileene Parsons, was revoked, reportedly owing to difference of opinion within the VIP. O'Neal claimed that Parsons had been planning a coup against his administration because of his intention to replace Parsons as Minister for Education and Culture with Andrew Fahie (Parsons would have retained the health and welfare portfolios). Fahie's appointment was the result of the British Government's decision to allow the number of ministers to be increased to five. Parsons subsequently joined the NDP. Later in the month Ethlyn E. Smith was appointed Minister for Health and Welfare and Andrew Fahie was appointed Minister of Education and Culture. Smith's move to the VIP meant that the party retained its majority. The Minister for Communications, Works and Public Utilities, J. Alvin Christopher, was appointed Deputy Chief Minister, a position also previously held by Parsons.

On 26 August 2000 the Government passed legislation abolishing corporal punishment in keeping with the United Kingdom's acceptance of the European Convention of Human Rights. In February 2001 Mark Vanterpool, one of the NDP's founding members, defected to the governing VIP. He stated that he believed he could best serve his constituency by joining the current administration, which had also committed itself to sponsoring key infrastructure projects, for which he had long campaigned. Vanterpool's change of allegiance prompted speculation that further defections from the NDP were imminent.

Economy

In 1998 gross domestic product (GDP) was recorded as US $573.7m., in current prices. In that year real GDP grew by an estimated 6.8%.

Services, primarily tourism and financial services, constitute the principal economic sector of the British Virgin Islands, contributing 88.6% of GDP in 1997. About one-half of the islands' national income is provided by tourism. In 1998 tourism earned some US $215m. and in 1995 employed one-third of the working population, directly or indirectly. Some 60% of stop-over visitors stay aboard yachts. Nevertheless, in 1996 the hotels and restaurants sector directly contributed 12.8% of GDP. In the mid-1990s a National Tourism Plan was commissioned to develop the industry, while preventing environmental damage. However, the decline in tourist numbers towards the end of the decade led the Government to allocate greater resources to the sector in the 1999 budget. In 2001 the budget included $53m. expenditure on a new airport, in addition to further investment to the country's infrastructure

Financial services expanded rapidly as a result of legislative measures adopted in 1984, and in 1998 the 'offshore' sector contributed 51.1% of direct government revenue (some US $70.4m.). There were 350,000 international businesses registered in the islands in early 2000 (a substantial increase compared with the previous year). The islands have also recorded significant growth in the establishment of mutual funds and of insurance companies. However, in 2000 the British Virgin Islands was included in a group of harmful tax jurisdictions identified by the Organisation of Economic Co-operation and Development (OECD). Publication of a 'blacklist' was postponed until mid-2001 and the OECD requested legislative changes and the introduction of greater legal and administrative transparency. Nevertheless, revenues from annual licence fees paid by off-shore companies continued to grow in the 2000/01 period.

The main trading partners are the US territories of Puerto Rico and the neighbouring US Virgin Islands, as well as the United Kingdom and the USA. The principal exports are fruit and vegetables, fish, rum, gravel and sand. Light industrial products include concrete, stone and paint. Industry (including mining, manufacturing, construction and public utilities) contributed 9.9% of GDP in 1997 and engaged 21.3% of the employed labour force in 1996. The agricultural sector contributed 1.5% of GDP in 1997, and engaged 1.9% of those in paid employment in 1996. In November 1999 the Government announced that it intended to raise the level of agricultural production, through the revision of legislation and policy relating to the sector, in order to ensure self-sufficiency in agriculture and a limited level of exports. In 2001 the Government was looking to develop deep sea fishing commercially for domestic and export markets.

The Territory recorded a trade deficit of $127.5m. in 1990. The trade deficit is normally offset by receipts from tourism, development aid, remittances from islanders working abroad (many in the US Virgin Islands) and, increasingly, from the 'offshore' financial sector.

In the financial year ending 30 June 1998 there was an estimated recurrent budgetary surplus of US $15.0m. Projected recurrent expenditure for 1998 was US $123.0m. The budget for 2001 projected revenue of US $186.6m. against recurrent expenditure of US $145.3m., amounting to a projected surplus of US $41.3m. In 1995/96 there was a deficit of US $22m. on the current account of the balance of payments. British budgetary support ceased in 1977, but the United Kingdom grants assistance for capital development. The average annual rate of inflation was 4.3% in 1990–96; consumer prices increased by an average of 5.9% in 1997. Unemployment remained negligible.

Statistical Survey

Source: Development Planning Unit, Central Administrative Complex, Road Town, Tortola; tel. 494-3701; fax 494-3947; e-mail dpu@dpu.org; internet www.dpu.org.

AREA AND POPULATION

Area: 153 sq km (59 sq miles). *Principal islands* (sq km): Tortola 54.4; Anegada 38.8; Virgin Gorda 21.4; Jost Van Dyke 9.1.

Population: 16,644 (males 8,570; females 8,074) at census of 12 May 1991; 19,864 (males 10,234; females 9,630) in 1999; *By island* (1980): Tortola 9,119; Virgin Gorda 1,412; Anegada 164; Jost Van Dyke 134; Other islands 156; (1991) Tortola 13,568.

Density (1999): 129.8 per sq km.

Principal Town: Road Town (capital), population 2,500 (estimate, 1987).

Births, Marriages and Deaths (registrations, 1989): 244 live births (birth rate 19.5 per 1,000); (1988) 176 marriages (marriage rate 14.2 per 1,000); 77 deaths (death rate 6.1 per 1,000). Source: UN, *Demographic Yearbook.*

Employment (1996): Agriculture, hunting and forestry 110; Fishing 84; Mining and quarrying 26; Manufacturing 573; Electricity, gas and water supply 176; Construction 1,349; Wholesale and retail trade 1,270; Hotels and restaurants 2,118; Transport, storage and communications 734; Financial intermediation 377; Real estate, renting and business activities 704; Public administration and defence 945; Education 373; Health and social work 296; Other community, social and personal service activities 297; Private households with employed persons 458; Not classifiable by economic activity 59; Total 9,949 (males 5,635, females 4,314).

AGRICULTURE, ETC.

Livestock ('000 head, 2000, estimates) Cattle 2, Sheep 6, Goats 10, Pigs 2. Source: FAO.

Fishing (metric tons, live weight, 1998): Snappers 36, Yellow snapper 53, Jacks, crevalles 64, Wahoo 40, Stromboid conchs 33; Total catch 944. Source: FAO, *Yearbook of Fishery Statistics.*

INDUSTRY

Electric Energy (production, million kWh): 45 in 1993; 45 in 1994; 45 in 1995. Source: UN, *Industrial Commodity Statistics Yearbook.*

FINANCE

Currency and Exchange Rate: United States currency is used: 100 cents = 1 US dollar ($). *Sterling and Euro Equivalents* (30 April 2001): £1 sterling = US $1.4318; €1 = 88.76 US cents; US $100 = £69.84 = €112.66.

Budget (estimates, $ million, 1998/99): Recurrent revenue 143.0; Recurrent expenditure 116.1; Capital expenditure 54.8.

Cost of Living (Consumer Price Index for Road Town; base: March 1995 = 100): 111.5 in May 1997; 116.0 in May 1998.

Gross Domestic Product ($ million, at market prices): 413.6 in 1994; 456.6 in 1995; 504.1 in 1996.

Gross Domestic Product by Economic Activity (Current prices, $ million, 1997): Agriculture, hunting and forestry 3.5; Fishing 5.2; Mining and quarrying 3.5; Manufacturing 6.0; Electricity, gas and water 11.2; Construction 36.0; Wholesale and retail trade 110.0; Hotels and restaurants 87.8; Transport, storage and communications 47.0; Financial intermediation 151.7; Real estate, renting and business services 48.0; Public administration 30.1; Education 10.4; Health and social work 7.3; Other community, social and personal services 10.2; Private households with employed persons 3.8; Subtotal 571.7; Import duty 17.0; *Less* imputed service charges 15.0; GDP in purchasers' values 573.7.

EXTERNAL TRADE

Principal Commodities ($ '000): *Imports c.i.f.* (1997): Food and live animals 31,515; Beverages and tobacco 8,797; Crude materials (inedible) except fuels 1,168; Mineral fuels, lubricants, etc. 9,847; Chemicals 8,816; Basic manufactures 31,715; Machinery and transport equipment 47,019; Total (incl. others) 116,379. *Exports f.o.b.* (1996): Food and live animals 368; Beverages and tobacco 3,967; Crude materials (inedible) except fuels 1,334; Total (incl. others) 5,862.

Principal Trading Partners ($ '000): *Imports c.i.f.* (1997): Antigua and Barbuda 1,807; Trinidad and Tobago 2,555; United Kingdom 406; USA 94,651; Total (incl. others) 166,379. *Exports f.o.b.* (1996): USA and Puerto Rico 1,077; US Virgin Islands 2,001; Total (incl. others) 5,862.

1999 ($ '000): Imports 208,419; Exports 2,081.

Source: mainly UN, *International Trade Statistics Yearbook.*

TRANSPORT

Road Traffic (motor vehicles in use): 6,900 in 1992; 6,700 in 1993; 7,000 in 1994. Source: UN, *Statistical Yearbook.*

1997: (Motor vehicles registered and licenced) 7,944.

Shipping: *International Freight Traffic* ('000 metric tons, 1997): Goods unloaded 102.6. *Cargo Ship Arrivals* (1988): 1,139. *Merchant Fleet* (vessels registered, at 31 December 2000): 18; Total displacement 74,273 grt. Source: Lloyd's Register of Shipping, *World Fleet Statistics.*

Civil Aviation (aircraft arrivals): 8,972 in 1985; 9,854 in 1986.

TOURISM

Visitor Arrivals: 412,032 (stop-over visitors 243,683; excursionists 8,749; cruise ship passengers 159,600) in 1996; 365,668 (stop-over visitors 244,318; excursionists 16,486; cruise ship passengers 104,864) in 1997; 392,290 (stop-over visitors 279,097; excursionists 8,051; cruise ship passengers 105,142) in 1998. Source: British Virgin Islands Tourist Board.

1999 (preliminary) stop-over visitors 287,156; cruise ship passengers 174,551.

COMMUNICATIONS MEDIA

Radio Receivers (1997): 9,000 in use.

Television Receivers (1997): 4,000 in use.

Telephones (1995): 9,000 main lines in use.

Non-Daily Newspapers (1996): 2 (estimated circulation 4,000).

Sources: UNESCO, *Statistical Yearbook*; UN, *Statistical Yearbook.*

EDUCATION

Pre-primary (1997): 5 schools (1994/95); 52 teachers (1994/95); 206 pupils.

Primary (1997): 20 schools (1993/94); 169 teachers (1994/95); 2,760 pupils.

Secondary (1997): 4 schools (1988); 115 teachers (1994/95); 1,478 pupils.

Directory
The Constitution

The British Virgin Islands have had a representative assembly since 1774. The present Constitution took effect from June 1977. Under its terms, the Governor is responsible for defence and internal security, external affairs, terms and conditions of service of public officers, and the administration of the Courts. The Governor also possesses reserved legislative powers in respect of legislation necessary in the interests of his special responsibilities. There is an Executive Council, with the Governor as Chairman, one *ex-officio* member (the Attorney-General), the Chief Minister (appointed by the Governor from among the elected members of the Legislative Council) who has responsibility for finance, and three other ministers (appointed by the Governor on the advice of the Chief Minister); and a Legislative Council consisting of a Speaker, chosen from outside the Council, one *ex-officio* member (the Attorney-General) and 13 elected members (nine members from one-member electoral districts and four members representing the Territory 'at large').

The division of the islands into nine electoral districts, instead of seven, came into effect at the November 1979 general election. The four 'at large' seats were introduced at the February 1995 general election. The minimum voting age was lowered from 21 years to 18 years.

The Government

Governor: FRANK J. SAVAGE (assumed office May 1998).

Deputy Governor: ELTON GEORGES.

EXECUTIVE COUNCIL
(August 2001)

Chairman: The Governor.

Chief Minister and Minister for Finance: RALPH T. O'NEAL.

Minister for Natural Resources and Labour: JULIAN FRAZER.

Minister for Communications, Works and Public Utilities: J. ALVIN CHRISTOPHER.

Minister for Education and Culture: ANDREW FAHIE.

Minister for Health and Welfare: ETHLYN SMITH.

Attorney-General: (vacant).

MINISTRIES

Office of the Governor: Government House, Tortola; tel. 494-2345; fax 494-5790: e-mail bvigovernor@bvigovernment.com; internet www.bvigovernment.org/governor.

Office of the Deputy Governor: Central Administration Bldg, Road Town, Tortola; tel. 468-3701; fax 494-6481; e-mail egeorges@bvigovernment.org; internet www.bvigovernment.org.

Office of the Chief Minister: Road Town, Tortola; tel. 494-3701; fax 494-4435; e-mail pcsmo@bvigovernment.org.

Ministry of Communications and Works: Road Town, Tortola; tel. 494-3701; e-mail mcw@bvigovernment.org.

Ministry of Finance: Pasea Estate, Road Town, Tortola; tel. 494-3701; fax 494-6180; e-mail finance@mail.caribsurf.com.

Ministry of Health, Education, Culture and Welfare: Road Town, Tortola; tel. 494-3887.

Ministry of Natural Resources and Labour: Road Town, Tortola; tel. 494-3614.

All ministries are based in Road Town, Tortola, mainly at the Central Administration Building (fax 494-4435; e-mail tsm@bvigovernment.org; internet www.bvigovernment.org).

LEGISLATIVE COUNCIL

Speaker: REUBEN VANTERPOOL.

Clerk: JULIA LEONARD-MASSICOTT.

General Election, 17 May 1999

Party	% of vote	Seats
Virgin Islands Party	38.0	7
National Democratic Party	36.9	5
Concerned Citizens' Movement	4.0	1
United Party	7.7	—
Independent	13.4	—
Total	100.0	13

Political Organizations

Concerned Citizens' Movement (CCM): Road Town, Tortola; f. 1994 as successor to Independent People's Movement; Leader WALWYN BREWLEY.

National Democratic Party (NDP): Road Town, Tortola; f. 1998; Chair. RUSSELL HARRIGAN; Leader ORLANDO SMITH.

United Party (UP): Road Town, Tortola; Chair. ROY PICKERING; Leader CONRAD MADURO.

Virgin Islands Party (VIP): Road Town, Tortola; Leader RALPH T. O'NEAL.

Judicial System

Justice is administered by the Eastern Caribbean Supreme Court, based in Saint Lucia, which consists of two divisions: The High Court of Justice and the Court of Appeal. There are two resident High Court Judges, and a visiting Court of Appeal which is comprised of the Chief Justice and two Judges of Appeal and which sits twice a year in the British Virgin Islands. There is also a Magistrate's Court, which hears prescribed civil and criminal cases. The final Court of Appeal is the Privy Council in the United Kingdom.

Resident Judges: STANLEY MOORE, KENNETH BENJAMIN.

Magistrate: DORIEN TAYLOR.

Registrar: GAIL CHARLES.

Religion

CHRISTIANITY
The Roman Catholic Church

The diocese of St John's-Basseterre, suffragan to the archdiocese of Castries (Saint Lucia), includes Anguilla, Antigua and Barbuda, the British Virgin Islands, Montserrat and Saint Christopher and Nevis. The Bishop is resident in St John's, Antigua.

The Anglican Communion

The British and US Virgin Islands form a single, missionary diocese of the Episcopal Church of the United States of America. The Bishop of the Virgin Islands is resident on St Thomas in the US Virgin Islands.

Protestant Churches

Various Protestant denominations are represented, principally the Methodist Church. Others include the Seventh-day Adventist, Church of God and Baptist Churches.

The Press

The BVI Beacon: POB 3030, Road Town, Tortola; tel. 494-3767; fax 494-6267; e-mail bvibeacon@caribsurf.com; internet www.bvibeacon.com; f. 1984; weekly; Editor LINNELL M. ABBOTT; circ. 3,400.

BVI Pennysaver: POB 3892, Lower Estate, Road Town, Tortola; tel. 494-8106; fax 494-8647.

The Island Sun: POB 21, Road Town, Tortola; tel. 494-2476; fax 494-7789; e-mail issun@candwbvi.net; internet www.islandsun.com; f. 1962; weekly; Editor VERNON PICKERING; circ. 2,850.

The Welcome: POB 133, Road Town, Tortola; tel. 494-2413; fax 494-4413; e-mail paul@bviwelcome.com; internet www.bviwelcome.com; f. 1971; every 2 months; general, tourist information; Publr PAUL BACKSHALL; Editor CLAUDIA COLLI; annual circ. 165,000.

Publisher

Caribbean Publishing Co (BVI) Ltd: Alcedo Hodge Bldg, 1 Wickhams Cay, POB 266, Road Town, Tortola; tel. 494-2060; fax 494-3060.

Broadcasting and Communications

TELECOMMUNICATIONS

Telephone Services Management: Central Administration Building, Road Town, Tortola; tel. 494-4728; fax 494-6551; e-mail tsmu@caribsurf.com; internet www.bvigovernment.org/tsmu/index.htm; government agency.

Antelecom NV: POB 103, Schouburgweg 22; tel 631111; fax 631376.

Cable and Wireless (WI) Ltd: Cutlass Bldg, Wickhams Cay 1, POB 440, Road Town, Tortola; tel. 494-4444; fax 494-6967; e-mail c&wbvi@caribsurf.com.

CCT Boatphone Ltd: Town Office, Mill Mall, POB 267, Road Town, Tortola; tel. 494-3825; fax 494-4933; e-mail boatphon@caribsurf.com; internet www.britishvirginislands.com/boatphone; mobile cellular telephone operator.

BROADCASTING
Radio

Caribbean Broadcasting System: POB 3049, Road Town, Tortola; tel. 494-4990; commercial; Gen. Man. ALVIN KORNGOLD.

Virgin Islands Broadcasting Ltd—Radio ZBVI: Baughers Bay, POB 78, Road Town, Tortola; tel. 494-2430; fax 494-2010; e-mail zbvi@caribsurf.com; internet www.zbvi.com; f. 1965; commercial; Gen. Man. HARVEY HERBERT; CEO OLIN HESTER.

Television

BVI Cable TV: Fishlock Rd, POB 694, Road Town, Tortola; tel. 494-3205; fax 494-2952; programmes from US Virgin Islands and Puerto Rico; 12 stations; Man. Dir TODD KLINDWORTH.

Television West Indies Ltd—ZBTV: Broadcast Peak, Chawell, POB 34, Tortola; tel. 494-3332; commercial.

Finance
BANKING
Commercial Banks

Banco Popular de Puerto Rico: POB 67, Road Town, Tortola; tel. 494-2117; fax 494-5294; Man. SANDRA SCATLIFFE.

Bank of East Asia (BVI) Ltd: POB 901, Road Town, Tortola; tel. 495-5588; fax 494-4513; Man. ELIZABETH WILKINSON.

Bank of Nova Scotia (Canada): Wickhams Cay 1, POB 434, Road Town, Tortola; tel. 494-2526; fax 494-4657; f. 1967; Man. T. C. BELL.

Barclays Bank PLC (United Kingdom): Wickhams Cay 1, POB 70, Road Town, Tortola; tel. 494-2171; fax 494-4315; f. 1965; Man. CHARLES CRANE; br. on Virgin Gorda.

Chase Manhattan Bank: Wickhams Cay 1, POB 435, Road Town, Tortola; tel. 494-2662; fax 494-5106; f. 1968; Man. MARGUERITE D. HODGE.

Citco Bank (BVI) Ltd: POB 662, Road Town, Tortola; tel. 494-2217; fax 494-3917; Man. RENE ROMER.

Croreridge Bank Ltd: POB 71, Road Town, Tortola; tel. 494-2233; fax 494-3547; Man. RICHARD A. PETERS.

DISA Bank (BVI) Ltd: POB 985, Road Town, Tortola; tel. 494-6036; fax 494-4980; Man. ROSA RESTREPO.

HSBC Guyerzeller Bank (BVI) Ltd: POB 3162, Road Town, Tortola; tel. 494-5416; fax 494-5417; e-mail rhbvi@surfbvi.com; Dir KENNETH W. MORGAN.

Rathbone Bank (BVI) Ltd: POB 986, Road Town, Tortola; tel. 494-6544; fax 494-6532; Man. PETER POOLE.

VP Bank (BVI) Ltd: POB 3463, Road Town, Tortola; tel. 494-1100; fax 494-1194; internet www.vpbankbvi.com; Gen-Man. PETER REICHENSTEIN.

Development Bank

Development Bank of the British Virgin Islands: Wickhams Cay 1, POB 275, Road Town, Tortola; tel. 494-3737; fax 494-3119; state-owned.

INSURANCE

Caribbean Insurance Ltd: POB 129, Road Town, Tortola; tel. 494-2728; fax 494-4394; Man. JOHN WILLIAMS.

Marine Insurance Office (BVI) Ltd: POB 874, Road Town, Tortola; tel 494-3795; fax 494-4540; Man. WESLEY WOODHOUSE.

Several US and other foreign companies have agents in the British Virgin Islands.

Trade and Industry
GOVERNMENT AGENCY

Trade and Investment Promotion Department: Office of the Chief Minister, Road Town, Tortola; tel. 494-3701; fax 494-6413.

CHAMBER OF COMMERCE

British Virgin Islands Chamber of Commerce and Hotel Association: James Frett Bldg, POB 376, Road Town, Tortola; tel. 294-3514; fax 494-6179; e-mail bviccha@surfbvi.com; internet www.bvihotels.org; f. 1986; Chair. KEDRICK MALONE; Exec. Dir NADINE BATTLE.

UTILITIES
Electricity

British Virgin Islands Electricity Corpn: Long Bush, POB 268, Road Town, Tortola; tel. 494-3911; fax 494-4291; e-mail bviecce@caribsurf.com; state-owned.

Transport
ROADS

There are about 160 km (100 miles) of motorable roads, and in 1993 there were about 8,000 motor vehicles in use. In early 1996 work began on a dual carriageway road in the Road Town area, at a cost of US $4.8m.

SHIPPING

There are two direct steamship services, one from the United Kingdom and one from the USA. Motor launches maintain daily mail and passenger services with St Thomas and St John, US Virgin Islands. A new cruise-ship pier, built at a cost of US $6.9m. with assistance from the Caribbean Development Bank, was opened in Road Town in 1994 and work on its expansion was begun in 1998.

British Virgin Islands Port Authority: Port Purcell, POB 4, Road Town, Tortola; tel. 494-3435; fax 494-2642; e-mail infosysmanager@ports.bvigovernment.org; internet www.bviports.org; Man. Dir MARGARET A. PENN.

Tropical Shipping: POB 250, Pasea Estate, Road Town, Tortola; tel. 494-5288; fax 494-3505; e-mail vgonzalez@tropical.com; internet www.tropical.com; Man. VINCE GONZALEZ.

CIVIL AVIATION

Beef Island Airport, about 16 km (10 miles) from Road Town, has a runway with a length of 1,100m (3,700 ft). In February 2000 work began to lengthen the runway to 1,500m (4,700 ft) and to construct a new passenger terminal. Upon completion of the renovation, scheduled for July 2001, the airport was to be renamed Terrence B. Lettsome Airport. Captain Auguste George Airport on Anegada has been designated an international point of entry and was resurfaced in the late 1990s. The airport runway on Virgin Gorda was to be extended to 1,200m (4,000 ft) to allow larger aircraft to land.

Director of Civil Aviation: M. CREQUE; tel. 494-3701.

Tourism

The main attraction of the islands is their tranquillity and clear waters, which provide excellent facilities for sailing, fishing, diving and other water sports. In 1998 there 1,231 hotel rooms in the islands and 365 rooms in guest-houses and rented apartments. There are also many charter yachts offering overnight accommodation. There were an estimated 392,290 visitors in 1998, of whom 279,097 were stop-over tourists. The majority of tourists are from the United States (57.3% of stop-over tourists in 1998). Some 146 cruise ships called at the islands in 1998. Receipts from tourism were estimated at US $210.8m. in that year.

British Virgin Islands Tourist Board: Social Security Bldg, Waterfront Dr., POB 134, Road Town, Tortola; tel. 494-3134; fax 494-3866; e-mail bvitourb@caribsurf.com; internet www.bvitouristboard.com; Dir of Tourism ANNE LENNARD (acting).

British Virgin Islands Chamber of Commerce and Hotel Association: see Chamber of Commerce above.

Defence

The United Kingdom is responsible for the defence of the islands. In September 1999 it was announced that Royal Air Force patrols were to be undertaken from the islands in order to intercept drugs-traffickers. Central government expenditure on defence totalled US $0.4m. in 1997.

Education

Primary education is free, universal and compulsory between the ages of five and 11. Secondary education is also free and lasts from 12 to 16 years of age. In 1994 some 482 pupils were enrolled in pre-primary schools and 2,625 in primary schools. In 1993 some 1,309 were enrolled in secondary education. Higher education is available at the University of the Virgin Islands (St Thomas, US Virgin Islands) and elsewhere in the Caribbean, in North America and in the United Kingdom. In 1990 only 0.7% of the adult population had received no schooling; illiteracy rates amongst the adult population were estimated at 1.8% of the total population in 1991. Central government expenditure on education in 1997 was US $17.1m.

THE CAYMAN ISLANDS

Area: 259 sq km (100 sq miles).

Population (census of 10 October 1999): 39,410 (males 19,311; females 20,099).

Capital: George Town (Grand Cayman); population 20,626 at census of 10 October 1999.

Language: English.

Religion: Several Christian denominations are represented.

Climate: Mild; average temperature 21°C (70°F); low rainfall.

Time: GMT –5 hours.

Public Holidays: 2002: 1 January (New Year's Day), 13 February (Ash Wednesday), 29 March (Good Friday), 1 April (Easter Monday), 20 May (Discovery Day), 8 June (Queen's Official Birthday), 1 July (Constitution Day), 11 November (Remembrance Day), 25–26 December (Christmas). **2003:** 1 January (New Year's Day), 5 February (Ash Wednesday), 18 April (Good Friday), 21 April (Easter Monday), 19 May (Discovery Day), 16 June (Queen's Official Birthday), 7 July (Constitution Day), 11 November (Remembrance Day), 25–26 December (Christmas).

Currency: Cayman Islands dollar; US $1 = 83.3 CI cents (fixed rate); CI $100 = £83.81 = US $120.00 = €135.20 (30 April 2001).

Weights and Measures: Imperial.

History

The Cayman Islands constitute a United Kingdom Overseas Territory, with an Executive Council headed by the Governor, who is the representative of the British monarch.

Grand Cayman became a British colony in 1670, with the two smaller islands settled only in 1833. Until 1959 all three islands were a dependency of Jamaica. In 1962 a separate Administrator for the islands was appointed (redesignated Governor in 1971). The Constitution was revised in 1972, 1992 and 1994. The Governor is Chairman of the Executive Council (comprising three other official members and five members elected by the Legislative Assembly from among their own number). The Legislative Assembly comprises three members appointed by the Governor and 15 elected members.

In the absence of formal political parties, elections to the Assembly were contested every four years by independents and by individuals standing as 'teams'. In August 1991, however, the territory's first formal political organization since the 1960s was formed, the Progressive Democratic Party. It opposed various provisions of the proposed constitutional reforms. It developed into a broad coalition and was renamed the National Team, and then won 12 of the 15 elective seats at the general election of November 1992. The new Government did not seek the introduction of a post of chief minister. At a general election on 20 November 1996 the National Team remained in power, winning nine seats in the Legislative Assembly. Two new groupings, the Democratic Alliance and Team Cayman secured two seats and one seat, respectively.

A serious problem for the Cayman Islands in recent years was drugs-related crime. In the 1990s an estimated 75% of all thefts and burglaries in the islands were attributed, directly or indirectly, to the drugs trade. The Mutual Legal Assistance Treaty (signed in 1986, and ratified by the US Senate in 1990) between the Cayman Islands and the USA provides for the mutual exchange of information for use in combating crime (particularly drugs-trafficking and the diversion of funds gained illegally from the drugs trade). Further legislation relating to the abuse of the financial sector by criminal organizations was approved in November 1996.

In March 1999 the British Government published draft legislation confirming that its Dependencies were to be referred to as United Kingdom Overseas Territories; the document stated that all such territories would be required to comply with European standards on human rights and financial regulation. While the Cayman Islands were praised for legislative efforts to prevent the abuse of the 'offshore' banking industry by criminal organizations, notably drugs traffickers, proposed reforms of European Union legislation threatened to undermine the islands' financial-services sector.

In April 2000 the Government announced that it had employed a US company to carry out a survey of public opinion in order to determine public reactions to the United Kingdom Government's proposals to institute constitutional and legal reforms on the islands. The results of the survey were to be conveyed to the Select Committee of the British Parliament responsible for considering the implications of the proposed reforms.

On 8 November 2000 the governing National Team suffered a heavy defeat in the General Election. It lost six of its nine seats, including that held by Truman Bodden, the Leader of Government Business. The Minister of Agriculture, John McLean, lost his seat to his cousin, Arden McLean. The newly elected Legislative Assembly voted for Kurt Tibbetts of the Democratic Alliance as Leader of Government Business. Important issues in the election campaign included the islands' constitutional status, immigration, housing and environmental protection.

Economy

Since the introduction of secrecy laws in respect of bank accounts and other professional information in the late 1960s, and the easing of foreign-exchange regulations in the 1970s (finally abandoned entirely in 1980), the islands have developed as one of the world's major 'offshore' financial markets. In 1998 the sector contributed an estimated 30% of GDP and employed more than 10% of the labour force. In 1999 there were 570 banks and trust companies and 2,271 mutual funds on the islands, according to the Caribbean Development Bank. The absence of any form of direct taxation also made the islands well-known as a 'tax haven'.

In July 1986 a treaty of mutual assistance was signed with the USA, providing access for US law-enforcement agencies to the financial records of Cayman Islands banks, in cases where serious criminal activity is suspected. This agreement was confirmed by the US legislature in 1990. In November 1996 the powers of the authorities to investigate such cases was augmented. A newly established monetary authority responsible for managing the islands' currency and reserves and for regulating the financial sector began operations in early 1997. In June 1999 the Cayman Islands announced that in order to achieve certification under the UN's Offshore Initiative, a UN agency, the Global Programme Against Money Laundering, was to review the territory's financial systems and regulations. However, in early 2000 the Organisation of Economic Co-operation and Development (OECD) announced the forthcoming publication of a 'blacklist' of harmful tax regimes, which included the Cayman Islands. Following complaints from the Caribbean jurisdictions included in the list, however, publication was postponed until mid-2001. The Cayman Islands pledged to adopt international standards of legal and administrative transparency before the end of the 2005.

In March 2001 the Cayman Islands Monetary Authority (CIMA) took control of a 'shell bank' (a bank with no offices on the islands and no local accounts) following a US Senate report that the bank had been used to launder money for a Mexican drug cartel. The Government was already taking steps to eliminate shell banks. In February the Government threatened to withdraw the licences of some 62 private banks if they did not open and staff offices in the Caymans. Following these measures the OECD removed the Cayman Islands from its blacklist in June 2001.

In addition to offshore financial services, the tourism sector contributes strongly to the economy. Both of these sectors benefit from the Cayman Islands' political stability, good infrastructure and extensive development In 1991 tourism accounted for some 23% of gross domestic product and, directly or indirectly, 50%

of employment. It earned an estimated US $510m. in 1998. Most tourists are from the USA (74% of stop-over arrivals in 1996). The industry is marketed toward the wealthier visitor and, since 1987, the Government has limited the number of cruise-ship passengers. In the late 1990s the Government attempted to limit tourist numbers in order to minimize damage to the environment. There is also an active construction sector (contributing 8.9% of GDP in 1991). However, the agricultural and light industrial sectors are small; more than 90% of the islands' food needs are imported. In particular, agriculture is limited by infertile soil, low rainfall and high labour costs. Traditional fishing activities, chiefly of turtles, declined from 1970, particularly after the USA imposed an import ban on turtle products in 1979 (the islands possess the world's only commercial turtle farm). A stock exchange began operations in early 1997. In 1999 there were some 50,951 registered companies on the islands, according to the Caribbean Development Bank.

Statistical Survey

Source: Government Information Services, Cricket Square, Elgin Avenue, George Town, Grand Cayman; tel. 949-8092; fax 949-5936.

AREA AND POPULATION

Area: 262 sq km (102 sq miles). The main island of Grand Cayman is about 197 sq km (76 sq miles), about one-half of which is swamp; Cayman Brac is 39 sq km (15 sq miles); Little Cayman is 26 sq km (11 sq miles).

Population: 39,410 (males 19,311; females 20,099) at census of 10 October 1999: Grand Cayman 37,473; Cayman Brac 1,822; Little Cayman 115.

Density (1999): 150.4 per sq km.

Principal Towns (1999 census): George Town (capital) 20,626; West Bay 8,243; Bodden Town 5,764.

Births, Marriages and Deaths (2000): Birth rate 15 per 1,000; Marriage rate 9.7 per 1,000 (1995); Death rate 3.3 per 1,000.

Expectation of life (years at birth 1998): males 75.37; females 78.81.

Economically Active Population (sample survey, persons aged 15 years and over, October 1995): Agriculture, hunting, forestry and fishing 270; Manufacturing 320; Electricity, gas and water 245; Construction 1,805; Trade, restaurants and hotels 5,555; Transport, storage and communications 1,785; Financing, insurance, real estate and business services 3,570; Community, social and personal services 5,295; Total employment 18,845 (males 8,930, females 9,910). Figures exclude persons seeking work for the first time, totalling 100 (males 60, females 40), and other unemployed persons, totalling 900 (males 455, females 445).

1997: Total employment 20,725 (males 10,425, females 10,300); Total unemployment 895 (males 345, females 550). Source: ILO.

AGRICULTURE, ETC.

Livestock (2000): 1,550 head of cattle; 3,000 chickens; 950 goats; 300 pigs.

Fishing (metric tons, live weight, 1998): Marine fishes 125, Natantian decapods 150; Total catch 275. Source: FAO, *Yearbook of Fishery Statistics*.

INDUSTRY

Electric Energy (production, million kWh): 252 (provisional) in 1993; 285 (provisional) in 1994; 297 in 1995. Source: UN, *Industrial Commodity Statistics Yearbook*.

FINANCE

Currency and Exchange Rates: 100 cents = 1 Cayman Islands dollar (CI $). *Sterling, US Dollar and Euro Equivalents* (30 April 2001): £1 sterling = CI $1.1932; US $1 = 83.33 CI cents; €1 = 73.97 CI cents; CI $100 = £83.81 = US $120.00 = €135.20. *Exchange rate:* Fixed at CI $1 = US $1.20.

Budget (CI $ million, 1999): *Revenue:* Tax revenue 152.3 (Taxes on goods and services 65.6, Import duties 86.7); Other current revenue 19.4; Total 171.7. *Expenditure:* General public services 60.8; Protective services 20.0; Education 20.4; Health 15.1; Social welfare 10.8; Tourism 15.7; Agriculture 1.9; Housing, construction and planning 2.4; Transport and communications 16.7; Total 163.8.

1999 (estimates, US $ million): Total recurrent revenue 328. Total recurrent and statutory expenditure 270.

Cost of Living (Consumer Price Index; base: September 1994 = 100): 112.0 in 1998; 118.9 in 1999; 121.7 in 2000.

Gross Domestic Product (CI $ million in current prices): 952 in 1995; 892.4 in 1996; 971.9 in 1997.

Gross Domestic Product by Economic Activity (CI $ million in current prices, 1991): Primary industries 5; Manufacturing 9; Electricity, gas and water 19; Construction 54; Trade, restaurants and hotels 138; Transport, storage and communications 65; Finance, insurance, real estate and business services 210; Community, social and personal services 42; Government services 63; Statistical discrepancy 1; Sub-total 606; Import duties *less* imputed bank service charge 11; GDP in purchasers' values 617.

EXTERNAL TRADE

Principal Commodities (US $ million): *Imports c.i.f.* (1996): Food and live animals 70.3; Beverages and tobacco 15.2; Mineral fuels, lubricants, etc. 41.2 (Refined petroleum products 39.8); Chemicals 22.2; Basic manufactures 51.3; Machinery and transport equipment 98.4; Miscellaneous manufactured articles 69.9; Total (incl. others) 377.9. *Exports f.o.b.* (1994): Total 2.7.

Principal Trading Partners (US $ million): *Imports c.i.f.* (1996): Japan 8.2; Netherlands Antilles 40.1; United Kingdom 6.8; USA 289.7; Total (incl. others) 377.9. *Exports f.o.b.* (1994): USA 0.9; Total 2.6.

Source: UN, *International Trade Statistics Yearbook*.

TRANSPORT

Road Traffic (2000): Motor vehicles in use 24,791.

Shipping: *International Freight Traffic* ('000 metric tons, 1995): Goods loaded 735 (1990); Goods unloaded 239,138 (2000). *Cargo Vessels* (1995): Vessels 15, Calls at port 266. *Merchant Fleet* (vessels registered at 31 December 2000): 133; Total displacement 1,796,353 grt. Source: Lloyd's Register of Shipping, *World Fleet Statistics*.

TOURISM

Visitor Arrivals: 1,214,397 (arrivals by air 342,993, cruise ship passengers 871,404) in 1998; 1,358,217 (arrivals by air 322,695, cruise ship passengers 1,035,522) in 1999; 1,346,886 (arrivals by air 316,029, cruise ship passengers 1,030,857) in 2000.

COMMUNICATIONS MEDIA

Radio Receivers: 36,000 in use in 1997.

Television Receivers: 23,239 in use in 1999.

Telephones: 34,702 main lines in use in 2000.

Telefax stations: 116 in use in 1993.

Mobile Cellular Telephones (subscribers): 11,370 in 2000.

Daily Newspapers: 1 (circulation 10,500) in 2000.

EDUCATION

Institutions (2001): 10 state primary schools (with 2,246 pupils); 9 private primary and secondary schools (2,238 pupils); 3 state high schools (1,750 pupils); 1 community college; 1 private college (519 pupils).

Directory
The Constitution

The Constitution of 1959 was revised in 1972, 1992 and 1994. Under its terms, the Governor, who is appointed for four years, is responsible for defence and internal security, external affairs, and the public service. The Executive Council comprises the Chief Secretary, the Financial Secretary, the Attorney-General and five other Ministers elected by the Legislative Assembly from their own number. The Governor assigns ministerial portfolios to the elected members of the Executive Council. The office of Administrative Secretary was abolished in April 1992 and replaced by the re-established post of Chief Secretary. There are 15 elected members of the Legislative Assembly (elected by direct, universal adult suffrage for a term of four years) and three official members appointed by the Governor. The Speaker presides over the Assembly. The United Kingdom retains full control over foreign affairs.

The Government

Governor: PETER SMITH (assumed office 5 May 1999).

EXECUTIVE COUNCIL
(August 2001)

Chairman: The Governor.

Chief Secretary*: JAMES RYAN.

Attorney-General*: DAVID BALLANTYNE.

Financial Secretary*: GEORGE MCCARTHY.

Leader of Government Business: KURT TIBBETTS.

Deputy Leader of Government Business and Minister of Tourism, Environment and Transport: MCKEEVA BUSH.

Minister for Community Development, Women's Affairs, Youth and Sport: EDNA MOYLE.

Minister for Education, Human Resources and Culture: ROY BODDEN.

Minister for Health and Information Technology: LINFORD PIERSON.

* Appointed by the Governor.

A District Commissioner, Jenny Manderson, represents the Governor on Cayman Brac and Little Cayman.

LEGISLATIVE ASSEMBLY

Members: The Chief Secretary, the Financial Secretary, the Attorney-General, and 15 elected members. The most recent general election to the Assembly was on 8 November 2000. There are no formal political parties (apart from the National Team, formed in 1992 to oppose aspects of the draft constitution) and personalities tend to be more important. In February 1991 a Speaker was elected to preside over the Assembly (despite provision for such a post in the Constitution, the functions of the Speaker had hitherto been assumed by the Governor).

Speaker: Capt. MABRY S. KIRCONNELL.

Leader of Government Business: KURT TIBBETTS.

GOVERNMENT OFFICES

Office of the Governor: Government Administration Bldg, Elgin Ave, George Town, Grand Cayman; tel. 949-7900; fax 949-7544; e-mail staffoff@candw.ky.

All official Government offices and Ministries are located in the Government Administration Bldg, Elgin Ave, George Town, Grand Cayman.

Political Organization

There have been no formal political parties in the Cayman Islands since the 1960s. However, an organization was established in 1992 to express opposition to the constitutional amendments under review in that year:

National Team: Grand Cayman; f. 1992; Leader THOMAS C. JEFFERSON.

Judicial System

There is a Grand Court of the Islands (with Supreme Court status), a Summary Court, a Youth Court and a Coroner's Court. The Grand Court has jurisdiction in all civil matters, admiralty matters, and in trials on indictment. Appeals lie to the Court of Appeal of the Cayman Islands and beyond that to the Privy Council in the United Kingdom. The Summary Courts deal with criminal and civil matters (up to a certain limit defined by law) and appeals lie to the Grand Court.

Chief Justice: ANTHONY SMELLIE.

President of the Court of Appeal: EDWARD ZACCA.

Solicitor-General: SAMUEL BULGIN.

Registrar of the Grand Court of the Islands: DELENE M. BODDEN, Court's Office, George Town, Grand Cayman; tel. 949-4296; fax 949-9856.

Religion
CHRISTIANITY

The oldest-established denominations are (on Grand Cayman) the United Church of Jamaica and Grand Cayman (Presbyterian), and (on Cayman Brac) the Baptist Church. Anglicans are adherents of the Church in the Province of the West Indies (Grand Cayman forms part of the diocese of Jamaica). Within the Roman Catholic Church, the Cayman Islands forms part of the archdiocese of Kingston in Jamaica. Other denominations include the Church of God, Church of God (Full Gospel), Church of Christ, Seventh-day Adventist, Wesleyan Holiness, Jehovah's Witnesses, Church of the Latter Day Saints, Bahá'í and Church of God (Universal). In 1999 there were an estimated 90 churches in the Cayman Islands,

including seven churches on Cayman Brac, and a Baptist Church on Little Cayman.

The Press

Cayman Executive: POB 173, George Town, Grand Cayman; tel. 949-5111; fax 949-7033; quarterly; Publr BRIAN UZZELL.

Chamber of Commerce Newsletter: POB 1000, George Town, Grand Cayman; f. 1965; tel. 949-8090; fax 949-0220; e-mail chamber@candw.ky; internet www.cayman.com.ky/chamber; monthly; Man. WIL PINEAU; circ. 5,000.

The Daily Caymanian Compass: POB 1365, Grand Cayman; tel. 949-5111; fax 949-7033; f. 1965; 5 a week; Publr BRIAN UZZELL; circ. 9,500.

The New Caymanian: POB 1139, George Town, Grand Cayman; tel. 949-7414; fax 949-0036; weekly; Publr and Editor-in-Chief PETER JACKSON.

Publishers

Caribbean Publishing Co (Cayman) Ltd: Paddington Place, Suite 306, POB 688, George Town, Grand Cayman; tel. 949-7027; fax 949-8366; f. 1978.

Cayman Free Press Ltd: POB 1365, Crewe Rd, George Town, Grand Cayman; tel. 949-5111; fax 949-7033.

Cayman Publishing Co: POB 173, George Town, Grand Cayman; tel. 949-5111; fax 949-7033.

Progressive Publications Ltd: Economy Printers Bldg, POB 764, George Town, Grand Cayman; tel. 949-5780; fax 949-7674.

Broadcasting and Communications
TELECOMMUNICATIONS

Cable and Wireless (Cayman Islands) Ltd: Anderson Sq., POB 293, George Town, Grand Cayman; tel. 949-7800; fax 949-7962; internet www.candw.ky; f. 1966.

BROADCASTING
Radio

Radio Cayman: Elgin Ave, POB 1110, George Town, Grand Cayman; tel. 949-7799; fax 949-6536; e-mail radiocym@candw.ky; started full-time broadcasting 1976; govt-owned commercial radio station; service in English; Dir LOXLEY E. M. BANKS.

Radio Heaven 97 FM: POB 31481 SMB, Industrial Park, George Town, Grand Cayman; tel. 945-2797; fax 945-2707; e-mail heaven97@candw.ky; f. 1997; Christian broadcasting, music and news; commercial station.

Radio ICCI-FM: International College of the Cayman Islands, Newlands, Grand Cayman; tel. 947-1100; fax 947-1210; e-mail icci@candw.ky; f. 1973; educational and cultural; Pres. Dr ELSA M. CUMMINGS.

Radio Z99.9 FM: POB 30110, Grand Cayman; tel. 945-1166; fax 945-1006; internet www.z99.ky; Gen. Man. RANDY MERREN.

Reggae 97.3 FM: Grand Cayman; internet www.reggae973fm.com; commercial music station.

Television

Cayman Adventist Network (CATN/TV): George Town, Grand Cayman; tel. 949-2739; f. 1996; local and international programmes, mainly religious.

Cayman Christian TV Ltd: George Town, Grand Cayman; relays Christian broadcasting from the Trinity Broadcasting Network (USA).

Cayman International Television Network (CITN): POB 55G, Sound Way, George Town, Grand Cayman; tel. 945-2739; fax 945-1373; f. 1992; 24 hrs daily; local and international news and US entertainment; 10-channel cable service of international programmes by subscription; Mans COLIN WILSON, JOANNE WILSON.

Cayman Television Service (CTS): George Town, Grand Cayman; f. 1993; 24 hrs daily; local and international news from a regional perspective; Mans COLIN WILSON, JOANNE WILSON.

Finance

Banking facilities are provided by commercial banks. The islands have become an important centre for 'offshore' companies and trusts. At the end of 1999 there were 50,951 companies and 570 licensed banks (including 45 of the world's 50 largest banks) and trust companies registered in the Cayman Islands. At the end of 1997 30 banks were licensed to transact local business. The number of insurance companies registered increased from 65 in 1986 to 473 in

September 1998. Some 2,271 mutual funds were registered at the end of 1999. The islands are well-known as a tax haven because of the absence of any form of direct taxation. In 1997 assets held by banks registered in the Cayman Islands totalled some US $504,000m.

Cayman Islands Monetary Authority: POB 10052, Elizabethan Sq., George Town, Grand Cayman; tel. 949-7089; fax 949-2532; e-mail cima@cimoney.com.ky; f. 1997; responsible for managing the Territory's currency and reserves and for regulating the financial services sector; cap. CI $4.3m., res 6.8m., dep. 40.5m. (Dec. 1997); Man. Dir NEVILLE GRANT; Gen. Man. CINDY BUSH.

PRINCIPAL BANKS AND TRUST COMPANIES

AALL Trust and Banking Corpn Ltd: AALL Bldg, POB 1166, George Town, Grand Cayman; tel. 949-5588; fax 949-8265; Man. Dir KEVIN DOYLE.

Banco Português do Atlântico: POB 30124, Grand Cayman; tel. 949-8322; fax 949-7743; Gen. Man. HELENA SOARES CARNEIRO.

Bank of America National Trust and Savings Association: Fort St, POB 1078, Grand Cayman; tel. 949-8514; fax 949-5346; Man. Dir H. TERRY CUSH.

Bank America Trust and Banking Corpn Ltd: POB 1092, Anchorage Centre, Grand Cayman; tel. 949-7888; fax 949-7883; Man. Dir DANIEL R. HAASE.

Bank of Butterfield International (Cayman) Ltd: Butterfield House, 68 Fort St, POB 705, Grand Cayman; tel. 949-7055; fax 949-7004; e-mail info@bankofbutterfield.ky; internet www.bankofbutterfield.ky; f. 1967; subsidiary of N. T. Butterfield & Son Ltd, Bermuda; cap. US $16.5m., res 35.0m., dep. 786.8m. (June 1998); Man. Dir CONOR J. O'DEA; 3 brs.

Bank of Nova Scotia: Cardinall Ave, POB 689, George Town, Grand Cayman; tel. 949-7666; fax 949-0020; also runs trust company; Man. A. BRODIE.

Bank of Novia Scotia Trust Company (Cayman) Ltd: POB 501, George Town, Grand Cayman; tel. 949-2001; fax 949-7097; e-mail cayman@scotiatrust.com; internet www.scotiatrust.com.

Barclays Bank PLC: Edward St, POB 68 GT, Grand Cayman; tel. 949-7300; fax 949-7179; e-mail BBPLCcym@candw.ky; one sub-br. at Cayman Brac; Dir PETER S. HINSON.

Barclays Finance Corporation of the Cayman Islands Ltd: POB 1321, George Town, Grand Cayman; tel. 949-4310; fax 949-7179.

Barclays Private Bank and Trust (Cayman) Ltd: POB 487, George Town, Grand Cayman; tel. 949-7128; fax 949-7657; f. 1988.

Bermuda Trust (Cayman) Ltd: Floor 3, British American Tower, POB 513, George Town, Grand Cayman; tel. 949-9898; fax 949-7959; f. 1968 as Arawak Trust Co; became subsidiary of Bank of Bermuda in 1988; bank and trust services; Chair. ELDON TRIMINGHAM; Man. Dir STANLEY WRIGHT; Gen. Man. RICHARD RICH.

British American Bank Ltd: POB 914, George Town, Grand Cayman; tel. 949-7822; fax 949-6064; Pres. and CEO LEONARD EBANKS.

CIBC Bank and Trust Co (Cayman) Ltd: POB 694, George Town, Grand Cayman; tel. 949-8666; fax 949-7904; f. 1967; subsidiary of Canadian Imperial Bank of Commerce.

Caledonian Bank and Trust Ltd: POB 1043, George Town, Grand Cayman; tel. 949-0050; fax 949-8062; Man. Dir DAVID SARGISON.

Cayman National Bank Ltd: 200 Elgin Ave, POB 1097, George Town, Grand Cayman; tel. 949-4655; fax 949-7506; e-mail cnb@candw.ky; f. 1974; subsidiary of Cayman National Corporation; cap. CI $2.4m., res 41.2m., dep 448.0m. (Oct. 1999); Chair. ERIC J. CRUTCHLEY; Pres. DAVID MCCONNEY; 6 brs.

Coutts (Cayman) Ltd: POB 707, West Bay Rd, George Town, Grand Cayman; tel. 945-4777; fax 945-4799; internet www.coutts.com; fmrly NatWest International Trust Corpn (Cayman) Ltd; Man. Dir ANDREW GALLOWAY.

Deutsche Bank (Cayman) Ltd: 31 West 52nd St, 10019, George Town, Grand Cayman; tel. 949-8244; fax 949-8178; e-mail dmg cay@candw.ky; cap. US $5.0m., res 20.3m., dep. 129.3m. (Dec. 1998); Exec. Dir T. GODBER.

Fortis Bank (Cayman) Ltd: POB 2003, Grand Cayman; tel. 949-7942; fax 949-8340; f. 1984 as Pierson Heldring & Pierson (Cayman) Ltd; name changed to Mees Pierson (Cayman) Ltd in 1993; present name adopted in June 2000; Man. Dir ROGER HANSON.

HSBC Financial Services (Cayman) Ltd: POB 1109, Mary St, George Town, Grand Cayman; tel. 949-7755; fax 949-7634; e-mail midban@candw.ky; internet www.hsbc.ky; f. 1982; Dirs T. CLARK, D. A. WHITEFIELD.

IBJ Schroder Bank and Trust Co: West Wind Bldg, POB 1040, George Town, Grand Cayman; tel. 949-5566; Man. ROGER HEALY.

Lloyds Bank International (Cayman) Ltd: POB 857, George Town, Grand Cayman; tel. 949-7854; fax 949-0090; Man. ROGER C. BARKER.

Mercury Bank and Trust Ltd: POB 2424, George Town, Grand Cayman; tel. 949-0800; fax 949-0295; Man. VOLKER MERGENTHALER.

Merrill Lynch Bank and Trust Co (Cayman) Ltd: POB 1164, George Town, Grand Cayman; tel. 949-8206; fax 949-8895.

Royal Bank of Canada: POB 245, Grand Cayman; tel. 949-4600; fax 949-7396; Man. HARRY C. CHISHOLM.

Royal Bank of Canada Trust Co (Cayman) Ltd: POB 1586; tel. 949-9107; fax 949-5777.

UBS (Cayman Islands) Ltd: POB 852G, UBS House, 227 Elgin Ave, George Town, Grand Cayman; tel. 914-1000; fax 914-4000; Pres. and Exec. Dir JURG KAUFMAN.

Banking Association

Cayman Islands Bankers' Association: POB 676 GT, Macdonald Sq., Fort St, George Town, Grand Cayman; tel. 949-0330; fax 945-1448; Pres. EDUARDO D'ANGELO P. SILVA.

STOCK EXCHANGE

Cayman Islands Stock Exchange: POB 2408 GT, George Town, Grand Cayman; tel. 945-6060; fax 945-6061; e-mail csx@csx.com.ky; internet www.csx.com.ky; f. 1997; 227 companies registered (March 2000).

INSURANCE

Several foreign companies have agents in the islands. There were 26 domestic and 361 'offshore' companies registered at the end of 1994. A total of 473 companies were registered in September 1998. Local companies include the following:

British Caymanian Insurance Agency Ltd: Elizabethan Sq., POB 74, Grand Cayman; tel. 949-8699; fax 949-8411.

Capital Life Insurance: Capital Life Bldg, Eastern Ave, POB 1816 GT, George Town, Grand Cayman; tel. 949-7717; fax 949-8741.

Caribbean Home Insurance: POB 931 GT, Commerce House 7, Genesis Close, George Town, Grand Cayman; tel. 949-7788; fax 949-8422.

Cayman General Insurance Co Ltd: Cayman National Bank Bldg, 200 Elgin Ave, POB 2171, George Town, Grand Cayman; tel. 949-7028; fax 949-7457.

Global Life Assurance Co Ltd: Global House, POB 1087, North Church St, Grand Cayman; tel. 949-8211; fax 949-8262.

Trade and Industry
DEVELOPMENT ORGANIZATION

Agricultural and Industrial Development Board: 3rd Floor, Tower Bldg, POB 1271 GT, George Town, Grand Cayman; tel. 949-5277; fax 949-6168; e-mail aidb@gov.ky; development loans organization; Gen. Man. ANGELA MILLER.

CHAMBER OF COMMERCE

Cayman Islands Chamber of Commerce: Macdonald Sq, Fort St, POB 1000, George Town, Grand Cayman; tel. 949-8090; fax 949-0220; e-mail chamber@candw.ky; internet www.caymanchamber.ky; f. 1965; Pres. W. BURNS CONOLLY; Man. WIL PINEAU; 730 local mems.

EMPLOYERS' ORGANIZATION

Labour Office: Tower Bldg, 4th Floor; tel. 949-0941; fax 949-6057; Dir DALE M. BANKS.

The Cayman Islands have had a labour law since 1942, but only three trade unions have been registered.

UTILITIES
Electricity

Caribbean Utilities Co. Ltd (CUC): Corporate HQ & Plant, North Sound Road, POB 38, George Town, Grand Cayman; tel. 949-5200; fax 949-4621; e-mail sparky@cuc-cayman.com; internet www.cuc-cayman.com; Pres. and CEO PETER A. THOMSON.

Cayman Brac Power and Light Co. Ltd: Stake Bay Point, POB 95, Stake Bay, Cayman Brac; tel. 948-2224; fax 948-2204.

West Indies Power Corpn Ltd: CUC Corporate Centre, North Sound Road, POB 38, George Town, Grand Cayman; tel 949-2250.

Water

Cayman Islands Water Authority: 13G Red Gate Rd, POB 1104 GT, George Town, Grand Cayman; tel. 949-6352; fax 949-0094; e-mail wac@candw.ky.

Cayman Water Co. Ltd. (CWC): Trafalgar Place, West Bay Road, POB 1114, George Town, Grand Cayman; tel. 945-4277; fax 945-4191.

Transport

ROADS

There are some 406 km (252 miles) of motorable roads, of which 304 km (189 miles) are surfaced with tarmac. The road network connects all districts on Grand Cayman and Cayman Brac (which has 76 km (47 miles) of motorable road), and there are 27 miles of motorable road on Little Cayman (of which about 11 miles are paved). During 1996 work began on the construction of a major new road linking the important tourist area of West Bay with the airport industrial park area on Grand Cayman.

SHIPPING

George Town is the principal port and a new port facility was opened in July 1977. Cruise liners, container ships and smaller cargo vessels ply between the Cayman Islands, Florida, Jamaica and Costa Rica. There is no cruise ship dock in the Cayman Islands. Ships anchor off George Town and ferry passengers ashore to the North or South Dock Terminals in George Town. In 1993 the Government limited the number of cruise ship passengers to 6,000 per day. The port of Cayman Brac is Creek; there are limited facilities on Little Cayman.

Port Authority of the Cayman Islands: Harbour Drive, POB 1358 GT, George Town, Grand Cayman; tel. 949-2055; fax 949-5820; e-mail ebush@caymanport.com; Port Dir ERROL BUSH.

Cayman Islands Shipping Registry: Elizabeth Sq., POB 2256, George Town, Grand Cayman; tel. 949-8831; fax 949-8849; Dir PETER GIBBS.

Cayman Brac Shipping Corporation: Banksville Ave, Stake Bay, POB 25, Cayman Brac; tel. 948-2221; fax 948-2289.

Cayman Freight Shipping Ltd: POB 1372, George Town, Grand Cayman; tel. 949-4977; fax 949-8402; e-mail cfssi@candw.ky; internet www.seaboardmarine.com.

Thompson Shipping Co Ltd: POB 188, Terminal Eastern Ave, George Town, Grand Cayman; tel. 949-8044; fax 949-8349; f. 1977.

CIVIL AVIATION

There are two international airports in the Territory: Owen Roberts International Airport, 3.5 km (2 miles) from George Town, and Gerrard Smith Airport on Cayman Brac. Both are capable of handling jet-engined aircraft. Edward Bodden Airport on Little Cayman can cater for light aircraft. The islands are served by several scheduled carriers.

Civil Aviation Authority: Beacon House, POB 10277 APO, George Town, Grand Cayman; tel. 949-7811; fax 949-0761; e-mail rs_caa@candw.ky; f. 1987; Dir RICHARD SMITH.

Cayman Airways Ltd: POB 1101, George Town, Grand Cayman; tel. 949-8200; fax 949-7607; internet www.caymanairways.com; f. 1968; wholly govt-owned since 1977; operates local services and scheduled flights to Jamaica, Honduras and the USA; Chair. SHERIDAN BROOKS-HURST; Exec. Vice-Pres. MIKE ADAM.

Island Air: POB 2433 GT, Airport Rd, George Town, Grand Cayman; tel. 949-0241; fax 949-7044; operates daily scheduled services between Grand Cayman, Cayman Brac and Little Cayman.

Tourism

The Cayman Islands are a major tourist destination, the majority of visitors coming from North America. The beaches and opportunities for diving in the offshore reefs form the main attraction for most tourists. Major celebrations include Pirates' Week in October and the costume festivals on Grand Cayman (Batabano), at the end of April, and, one week later, on Cayman Brac (Brachanal). In 1995 there were an estimated 7,648 hotel beds. In 2000 there were 316,029 arrivals by air and 1,030,857 cruise visitors. In 1997 the tourist industry earned an estimated US $508m.

Cayman Islands Department of Tourism: Cricket Sq., POB 67, George Town, Grand Cayman; tel. 949-0623; fax 949-4053; internet www.divecayman.ky; f. 1965; Dir ANGELA MARTINS.

Cayman Islands Hotel and Condominium Association (CIHCA): West Bay Rd, POB 1367, George Town; tel. 947-4057; fax 947-4143; Pres. WILLI GIGER; Sec. L. EBANKS.

Sister Islands Tourism Association: Stake Bay, POB 187, Cayman Brac; tel. and fax 948-1345.

Defence

The United Kingdom is responsible for the defence of the Cayman Islands.

Education

Schooling is compulsory for children between the ages of five and 15 years. It is provided free in 10 government-run primary schools, and there are also three state secondary schools, as well as six church-sponsored schools (five of which offer secondary as well as primary education). Primary education, from five years of age, lasts for six years. Secondary education is for seven years. Government expenditure on education in 1994 was CI $31.5m. (20.9% of total spending). Some CI $17.7m. (9.9% of total expenditure) was allocated for education in 1995.

CHILE

Area: 756,626 sq km (292,135 sq miles).

Population (official estimate for mid-2000): 15,211,308.

Capital: Santiago, population (provisional, 30 June 1999): 4,731,946.

Language: Spanish (official).

Religion: Mainly Christianity (80% Roman Catholic).

Climate: ranges from extremely dry and hot in the north to cold and very wet in the south, with temperate regions in the centre.

Time: GMT –4 hours (GMT –3 hours in summer).

Public Holidays

2002: 1 January (New Year's Day), 29–30 March (Good Friday and Easter Saturday), 1 May (Labour Day), 21 May (Battle of Iquique), 29 June (St Peter and St Paul), 15 August (Assump-tion), 4 September (National Unity Day), 18 September (Independence Day), 19 September (Armed Forces Day), 12 October (Day of the Race, anniversary of the discovery of America), 1 November (All Saints' Day), 8 December (Immaculate Conception), 25 December (Christmas Day).

2003: 1 January (New Year's Day), 18–19 April (Good Friday and Easter Saturday), 1 May (Labour Day), 21 May (Battle of Iquique), 29 June (St Peter and St Paul), 15 August (Assumption), 4 September (National Unity Day), 18 September (Independence Day), 19 September (Armed Forces Day), 12 October (Day of the Race, anniversary of the discovery of America), 1 November (All Saints' Day), 8 December (Immaculate Conception), 25 December (Christmas Day).

Currency: Chilean peso; 1,000 Chilean pesos = £1.164 = US $1.667 = €1.878 (30 April 2001).

Weights and Measures: The metric system is in force.

Basic Economic Indicators

	1998	1999	2000
Gross domestic product ('000 million Chilean pesos at 1986 prices)	8,153.0	8,059.8	8,493.4
GDP per head ('000 Chilean pesos at 1986 prices)	550.0	537.0	558.4
GDP ('000 million Chilean pesos at current prices)	33,630.4	34,422.8	37,774.7
GDP per head(million Chilean pesos at current prices)	2,269.0	2,292.1	2,483.3
Annual growth of real GDP (%)	3.9	–1.1	5.4
Annual growth of real GDP per head (%)	2.5	–2.4	4.0
Government budget ('000 million Chilean pesos at current prices):			
Revenue	7,733.1	7,748.7	n.a.
Expenditure	7,576.3	8,237.0	n.a.
Consumer price index (base: 1995 = 100)	120	124	129
Rate of inflation (annual average, %)	5.1	3.3	3.8
Foreign exchange reserves (US $ million at 31 December)	15.049.4	13.977.3	14,380.5
Imports c.i.f. (US $ million)	18,779	15,137	18,070
Exports f.o.b. (US $ million)	14,830	15,616	18,158
Balance of payments (current account, US $ million)	–4,139	–80	n.a.

Gross national product per head measured at purchasing power parity (PPP) (US dollars, converted by the PPP exchange rate, 1999): 8,410.

Total labour force (sample survey, Oct.–Dec. 1999): 5,933,600.

Unemployment (2000): 9.2%.

Total external debt (1999): US $37,762m.

Life expectancy (years at birth, 1999): 75 (males 72, females 78).

Infant mortality rate (per 1,000 live births, 1999): 10.

Adult population with HIV/AIDS (15–49 years, 1999): 0.19%.

School enrolment ratio (6–17 years, 1996): 93%.

Adult literacy rate (15 years and over,2000): 95.7% (males 95.9 females 95.5)

Energy consumption per head (kg of oil equivalent, 1998): 1,594.

Carbon dioxide emissions per head (metric tons, 1997): 4.1.

Passenger motor cars in use (per 1,000 of population, 1999):88.2.

Television receivers in use (per 1,000 of population, 1997): 215.

Personal computers in use (per 1,000 of population, 1999): 66.6.

History

PHILIP J.O'BRIEN

From the foundation of its capital, Santiago, in 1541, to the achievement of independence in 1818, Chile was the most remote of Spain's American colonies. Throughout that period Chile was a geographically compact territory with 'natural' frontiers: the Pacific Ocean to the west, the mountain chain of the Andes to the east, the Atacama Desert to the north and the River Bío-Bío to the south. Chile was then one-third of its present size, some 1,000 km long and at no point more than 160 km wide. It was a rich, agricultural region with a Mediterranean climate and natural irrigation provided by rivers rising in the Andes and flowing to the Pacific.

Chile's expansion, to its present size, came only in the 1880s. Following Chile's victory over Bolivia and Peru, in the War of the Pacific (1879–83), the country gained the northern provinces of Antofagasta (from Bolivia) and Tarapacá (from Peru). Its territory further expanded with the subjugation of the Araucanian Indians (Amerindians) south of the Bío-Bío, which had been a military frontier throughout the colonial period.

The European minority dominated society and the economy as landowners, mine-owners and traders, while the largely illiterate mestizo masses obeyed them. Independence from Spain meant little change socially and economically. However, the compact nature of the colony and the solidarity of its upper class gave Chile an early sense of nationality and, after a short period of turbulence, constitutional and political stability. The Constitution of 1833 (which lasted until 1925) conferred extensive powers on the President; the military played little part in politics and a multi-party system emerged, in which power changed hands without recourse to arms. Only three attempts at revolution occurred in the 19th century, and only one of these, in 1891, succeeded. The habits of evolutionary progress were ingrained.

THE DEVELOPMENT OF PARTY POLITICS

However, the habits of evolutionary progress came under increasing strain. The population grew and cities expanded, while politics remained a largely aristocratic pursuit. This caused new social pressures from the lower classes which began to challenge the traditional order. Moreover, the benefits of economic growth in the 19th and 20th centuries, based primarily on exports of wheat, silver, copper and, between 1880 and 1920, nitrates, were unevenly distributed. Trade unions were established and new political parties emerged, alongside the older Conservative, Liberal and Radical parties. The first important left-wing party was founded in 1912, becoming the Communist Party in 1922. Government repression of strikes, particularly in the cities and the nitrate works of the north, by the 1920s created a divided nation, ruled by a political class which ignored reality.

In 1920 Arturo Alessandri Palma campaigned for the presidency, on a programme of economic and social reform, winning the election narrowly. However, his programme was obstructed by congressional opposition. The military, unpaid for months like all other public servants, intervened to break Chile's legalistic tradition in 1924. Alessandri left the country and a start was made to secure better administration, with Congress being forced to enact some reforms. A second military coup in 1925, organized by junior officers who suspected the high command of delaying the programme of reforms, resulted in Alessandri's return to power. His second period of government lasted only a few months, during which time, however, a new Constitution was introduced. Alessandri was ousted by the Minister of War, Col Carlos Ibáñez del Campo, who became President in 1927.

During Ibáñez's four years of government there was a sizeable expansion of public works, funded by foreign loans and administrative reform. However, the Great Depression of 1929–31 caused his downfall. Several short-lived, contrasting Governments, including a 'Socialist Republic', followed rapidly until in 1932 new elections returned Alessandri to the presidency.

This six-year term saw an austere but effective economic recovery and the return to the constitutional tradition.

The Great Depression, however, had created other parties, notably the Socialist Party in 1933 and a Falange Party, which later became the Christian Democratic Party (Partido Demócrata Cristiano—PDC). Therefore, an increasing number of parties competed for votes and rarely could one party rule alone, thereby necessitating compromise, but at times at the cost of efficiency. Moreover, fundamental social problems remained. The previous system had some achievements, particularly in education. However, as late as the 1940s, 80% of the arable land was owned by 3% of landholders and the agrarian population, which comprised about one-third of the total, remained unorganized until the late 1960s.

The middle-class radical Popular Front dominated government from 1938 to 1952, firstly in coalition with the left-wing parties and then with a variety of others. State intervention in the economy grew markedly in this period, though the shifting alliances or coalitions in government, culminating in the outlawing of the Communist Party in 1948, created public disillusion with politics. In 1952 Carlos Ibáñez del Campo was re-elected to the presidency. However, he failed to achieve political stability in government or to address the increasing economic problems. In 1958 Arturo Alessandri's son, Jorge, a prominent right-wing businessman, was elected President, beating the Marxist Salvador Allende Gossens by a narrow margin. Alessandri governed with a pragmatically formed series of Cabinets. Meanwhile, a new central political force had been growing, to challenge the dominance of the Radical party. The PDC, led by Eduardo Frei Montalva, had an extensive reform programme which held increasing appeal. In 1964 Frei won the presidency with over 50% of the votes cast, the first clear public mandate for decades. One year later, the Christian Democrats gained control of the lower house of the legislature, in congressional elections, the first single party to do so in over 100 years. However, they did not have a majority in the Senate which prevented much of Frei's reformist legislation. Nevertheless, in housing, health and education reform, much was achieved; an agrarian reform law was finally enacted and the Government secured a 50% stake in the largely US-owned major copper mines.

THE ELECTION OF THE ALLENDE GOVERNMENT

Obstructed in the Senate and hindered by a drought in the late 1960s, Frei's Government could not fulfil its electoral promises. On the left, the Socialist and Communist parties united with the Radicals in a coalition (the Popular Unity) with Salvador Allende as its Presidential candidate for the 1970 elections. The Christian Democrats chose Radomiro Tomic, on the left of the party, while the right-wing National Party backed Jorge Alessandri.

Allende won a close election, beating Alessandri into second place by only 39,000 of the votes cast, in an electorate of 3,539,000. Like Frei's 'revolution in liberty', Allende's 'Chilean road to socialism' was intended to preserve the constitutional, democratic system while executing a more radical programme of economic and social change than any hitherto attempted.

An extensive programme of nationalization of monopolies, such as the copper industry, the domestic banking system and other sectors, as well as exchange and commodity controls, was soon implemented. The Government extended its relations with socialist (Communist) states, inviting the Cuban leader, Fidel Castro Ruz, to visit Chile in November 1971. Using both a long-forgotten law of the 'Socialist Republic' of 1932, which gave the state power to take over industries deemed to have 'failed to supply the people', and the state development corporation's (Corporación de Fomento de la Producción—CORFO) buying up of private shares, many banks and other businesses passed into state control. In addition revolutionary groups pressured the Government to introduce more radical policies by inciting workers to seize factories and landed estates, thereby disrupting production. While Allende condemned such activities, the opposition accused the Government of doing nothing to stop them. Political polarization developed rapidly and violence on the streets increased.

The economy declined dramatically, primarily because of the internal conflicts, but also because of the reduction in foreign aid and the 'informal blockade' imposed by the USA. Inflation had increased rapidly, and there were widespread shortages. The economy was in crisis. Allende's attempt to pacify the opposition by bringing members of the military into his Government failed. The country moved towards a political crisis.

MILITARY DICTATORSHIP AND GEN. PINOCHET

Chile's internal disarray was resolved on 11 September 1973 by the intervention of the armed services, including the paramilitary police, in a combined operation to overthrow the Government. President Allende died in an attack on the presidential palace. Many of his supporters were killed, arrested or exiled. All political activity was suspended. In addition, Congress was dissolved and censorship introduced. The constitutional, democratic system of government, which had lasted for so long, was replaced by a military regime, dominated by the head of the Army, Gen. Augusto Pinochet Ugarte. His policy was to extirpate Marxism from Chile and to allow only a slow return to a competitive party system. He also aimed not only to repair the economy but, indeed, to reverse the patterns of the past, by severely reducing the role of the state in economic management.

The regime was authoritarian and brutal in its repression of discontent. It maintained a considerable measure of support from sectors of the population which preferred strict order to the threat of chaos. Restrictions on the non-Marxist parties meant that the most important, but cautious, critic of the Government, particularly in the area of human rights, became the Roman Catholic Church. Institutionally, Pinochet's plan was contained in the new Constitution of 1980, which was accepted by two-thirds of the electorate in a referendum and gave the President wide-reaching powers.

ECONOMIC RECESSION AND POLITICAL OPPOSITION

During the rest of the 1970s the military regime followed an economic stabilization plan, which, however, had substantial social costs, in terms of jobs and the living standards of the majority of the population. The plan reduced inflation and import tariffs, and diversified Chile's exports. By 1981 Chile was one of the most free-enterprise, open economies in the world. However, falling copper prices in a world recession, a heavy concentration of economic power with too little supervision, the massive growth of foreign debt and a policy of maintaining a fixed exchange rate led to a recession in Chile, in 1982 and 1983.

Internationally the Pinochet regime was always very isolated because of its record on human rights. However, in 1983 Chile did succeed, with the return of democracy to Argentina, in resolving a protracted territorial dispute over three islands in the Beagle Channel. The dispute, which had continued for a century, almost led the countries to war in 1978 but, with the assistance of papal mediation, an agreement was reached in October 1984.

The reduction in economic prosperity, coupled with social and political discontent, led to political protests. Under the leadership of the Federation of Copper Workers (Confederación de Trabajadores del Cobre), the trade unions formed the National Workers' Command (Comando Nacional de Trabajadores), and organized national protest days, with the aim of forcing Pinochet to resign. The initial protests, bringing together trade unions, students and shanty-town dwellers, as well as the opposition political parties, surpassed expectations. In the August 1983 protest, Pinochet declared a state of siege and put on to the streets of Santiago 18,000 troops, who killed 32 protesters and arrested 1,200. The protest forced Pinochet to appoint a civilian as Minister of the Interior to negotiate with the opposition forces. The opposition, however, was divided, with the centre parties in a new coalition, the Alianza Democrática

(Democratic Alliance), while the left-wing parties formed the Movimiento Democrático Popular (Popular Democratic Movement). The opposition failed to convert general public discontent into effective political support. Pinochet was determined to repress the protests and not concede to the opposition's demands for congressional elections to be held before 1989.

Despite the Government's attempts, allegedly including assassinations, to eradicate internal opposition, the campaign of public protests continued. In September 1986, after an attempt to assassinate Pinochet by the Frente Patriótico Manuel Rodríguez (FPMR), the guerrilla group of the banned Communist Party, a highly repressive state of siege was reimposed. However, in January 1987, in anticipation of a visit by the head of the Roman Catholic Church, Pope John Paul II, Pinochet ended the state of siege and began to allow some political exiles to return home.

THE DEFEAT OF PINOCHET

In March 1987 the Government promulgated a law whereby non-Marxist political parties were allowed to register officially to organise for the plebiscite to be held on 5 October 1988. The plebiscite gave voters a simple option: a 'yes' vote would confirm as President the sole candidate nominated by the Pinochet regime; a 'no' vote would oblige the regime to hold open elections within one year. Initially, 13 parties and political groups campaigned for a 'no' vote and in June 1988 the Communist Party joined this campaign. Following US pressure, the Government lifted the state of emergency, in preparation for the plebiscite. Despite internal disagreements over Pinochet's candidacy, the junta nominated him, in August, as the regime's candidate.

The plebiscite resulted in a defeat for Pinochet: 55% voted 'no', 43% 'yes'. Under the 1980 Constitution, Pinochet was obliged to hold elections for the presidency and for the two houses of the National Congress (though part of the Senate was nominated by the President). The elections were announced for December 1989, with the newly elected President taking office on 11 March 1990.

After negotiations with Co-ordination of the Parties for Democracy (CPD), a 17-party grouping of the opposition, and the right-wing National Renovation Pinochet agreed to fifty-four reforms to the 1980 Constitution which were approved in a further national plebiscite. These included the reduction of the next President's term to four years, the redrafting of Article Eight (which banned Marxist parties), the introduction of a military–civilian parity on a National Security Council with its veto powers curtailed, an increase in the number of senators from 26 to 38 and the ability to change the Constitution by a two-thirds' vote of the Senate and the Chamber of Deputies.

THE GOVERNMENT OF PRESIDENT AYLWIN

In the elections of 15 December 1989, Aylwin, the leader of the Christian democrats and head of the coalition, the CPD, polled 55.2% of the votes cast, Büchi, the right -wing candidate, 29.4% and Errázuriz, an independent, 15.4%. The PDC emerged as the main party, winning 13 of the 38 elected senatorial seats and 38 of the 120 seats in the lower chamber. The CPD alliance, dominated by the Christian Democrats and the Socialists, as a whole won a clear majority in the Chamber of Deputies (72 seats out of 120), but faced a potential opposition majority in the Senate, where it held 22 seats, as opposed to the right-wing's 16 seats, which could combine with the nine (later reduced to eight) non-elected senators.

The new Government faced three main problems. The first was what to do about past human-rights abuses. The second was how to deal with Pinochet and the Army. According to the 1980 Constitution, Gen. Pinochet was allowed to remain for eight years as Commander of the Armed Forces, after he relinquished the presidency in 1989. The third was how to consolidate democracy and maintain macroeconomic balances, while responding to the demands of the poorer sectors of society.

THE RETTIG REPORT

On April 24 1990 President Aylwin signed a decree creating the Commission for Truth and Reconciliation, (Comisión por la Verdad y la Reconciliación), chaired by former Senator Raul Rettig, to investigate the most serious allegations of human-rights violations between September 1973 and March 1990. The Rettig Report, on human-rights abuses during the Pinochet regime, was published on 5 March 1991. It documented the deaths of 2,279 people, nearly all caused by agents of the state. The Report concluded that the Pinochet regime had executed a 'systematic policy of extermination', that the responsibility reached as high as Gen. Pinochet and that the judiciary not only did not attempt to prevent human-rights abuses, but allowed military courts to pass death sentences. This added to pressure for Pinochet's resignation, although, following the military's declaration of loyalty to him, Pinochet rejected the Report's conclusions.

On 1 April 1991 Senator Jaime Guzmán, a leading supporter of the Pinochet regime, was murdered. Guzmán's assassination prevented any follow up to the Rettig Report. Aylwin declared that Chileans must not think about justice for those guilty of human-rights abuses, because that could destabilize democracy. Compensation was given to families of the victims, but little effort was made to bring the guilty to justice with the exception of those responsible for the murder in Washington, DC (USA), of the former Chilean ambassador to the USA, Orlando Letelier, and his US associate, Ronnie Moffat; and the sentencing of three police officers to life imprisonment for the murder of three teachers in 1985.

CONSOLIDATING DEMOCRACY

At the beginning of 1992 the Government declared its two main aims to be the 'consolidation of democracy' and 'growth with equity'. A fundamental step towards the achievement of the first objective was the municipal elections on 28 June, which represented the first opportunity for Chileans to vote for local authorities since 1971. The government parties won 53.4% of the votes cast, demonstrating a clear endorsement of the ruling coalition. However, constitutional amendments envisaged by President Aylwin (including plans to restore presidential power to remove Commanders-in-Chief of the Armed Forces, to counter right-wing bias in the electoral system, to balance politically the composition of the constitutional tribunal and to abolish government-appointed senators) failed to secure a majority in the Senate. In December 1993, after much deliberation, a proposal to extend the presidential mandate to a six-year, non-renewable term was approved by both houses.

THE GOVERNMENT OF PRESIDENT FREI

The presidential election of 11 December 1993 resulted in an overwhelming victory for the CPD candidate, Eduardo Frei Ruiz-Tagle, a Christian Democrat senator and son of the late Eduardo Frei Montalva, the former President, with 58% of the votes cast. Arturo Alessandri Besa (also the son of a former President), the candidate of the right-wing coalition, the Unión para el Progreso de Chile (Union for the Progress of Chile—UPC), came second with 24% of the votes cast. However, the ruling coalition failed to make significant gains at concurrently conducted congressional elections. Without a two-thirds majority in the National Congress President Frei was unable to amend what remained of Gen. Pinochet's 1980 Constitution, a task he had indicated would be one of his priorities.

This failure to change the Constitution bedevilled the Government. And there were a series of conflicts with the military over such matters as early retirements and imprisonments over human-rights issues. The spectacular escape from prison of the leaders of the guerrilla group, Frente Patriótico Manuel Rodríguez, strengthened the position of the military as President Frei was obliged to create a new intelligence system. Throughout the military remained highly resentful of any attempt either to accuse them of 'crimes' committed under Pinochet or any attempt to question their authority or budgets, said to be the largest in Latin America. When Pinochet retired as head of the Armed Forces in March 1998, he assumed his seat for life in the Senate, which gave him immunity from prosecution. A relatively young general, Ricardo Izurieta, then aged 54, was appointed to replace Pinochet. He promised a new era in military–civilian relations.

Congressional elections to renew all 120 seats in the lower house and 20 of the elective seats in the upper house were held on 11 December 1997. With about 40% of the potential electorate abstaining, the governing coalition won just over 50% of the

vote, while the right-wing opposition won 36.2% of the vote, an increase of 3% over 1993. This meant that the Government's majority was insufficient to vote through major constitutional changes, including the abolition of the 'designated' senators. With four retired Generals designated as senators, Gen. Pinochet, as senator for life, and two retired generals who won seats for the right-wing there was a sizeable 'military bloc' in the Senate, which together with the right-wing senators, constituted a majority in the upper house. Chile remained far being a proper democracy.

THE PINOCHET AFFAIR

In spite of these tensions, however, by late 1998 Chile's progress towards full democracy, although slow, looked secure. Then, on 16 October 1998, Gen. Pinochet was arrested during a visit to London in response to a preliminary extradition request issued by a Spanish judge, Baltasar Garzón, regarding charges of crimes of torture and murder committed against some 4,000 people, including Spanish nationals, by his administration during 1973–90. Pinochet had been visiting the United Kingdom both for health reasons and to discuss weapons procurements. The Chilean Government and Pinochet had both assumed he had diplomatic immunity, although neither took the precaution of securing accreditation with the British Government. The arrest led to lengthy legal wrangles in the United Kingdom and threatened to undermine Chile's delicate political and military balance.

The British Government attempted to present Pinochet's arrest as a strictly legal problem. On 25 November 1998 a panel of five senior law lords, sitting in the United Kingdom's House of Lords, overturned (by a 3–2 majority) an earlier high court ruling that Pinochet was entitled to 'sovereign immunity' as a former head of state. However, on 17 December the ruling was set aside on the grounds that one of the law lords had not declared a connection with the international human-rights campaign group, Amnesty International. In a new hearing in March 1999 a new seven-member appellate committee of law lords decided that Pinochet was not immune to prosecution as a former head of state, and therefore could be extradited to Spain, but that he could only be tried for crimes committed after 1988, when the United Kingdom had adhered fully to the international convention on torture. Three weeks later the British Secretary of State for the Home Department, Jack Straw, confirmed that he would allow extradition proceedings to continue and on 8 October it was decided that the extradition to Spain could proceed. Meanwhile the Chilean Government formally requested that Pinochet be allowed to return to Chile on the grounds of ill health. In January 2000 a group of independent medical specialists examined Pinochet, and, upon receiving their report that Pinochet was medically unfit to stand trial in Spain, Straw announced that he was inclined to order Pinochet's release. However, he did grant interested groups a further opportunity to make representations in support of Pinochet's extradition. Representations were received from legal authorities in Belgium, France, Spain and Switzerland, and from six human-rights organizations. Nevertheless, on 2 March Straw announced that Pinochet was to be released, and he returned to Chile on the following day. Within Chile the repercussions of Pinochet's detention in the United Kingdom were enormous. The Chilean Government consistently argued that Pinochet's arrest was an unwarranted interference in the country's internal affairs, and that Pinochet should be returned to Chile where he could be tried. Chilean society was divided over the affair. Although opinion polls indicated that over 60% believed there had been abuses of human rights for which Pinochet was responsible, a sizeable 30% still viewed him as one of Chile's greatest rulers. There were demonstrations and counter-demonstrations, and the Armed Forces expressed their disquiet. They became increasingly worried about the judicial proceedings against former generals in the wake of Pinochet's arrest. However, in spite of the tensions there was no real threat to democracy and the presidential elections of late 1999 and early 2000 proceeded peacefully, even though the Pinochet affair in the United Kingdom was at a crucial stage.

THE PRESIDENTIAL ELECTIONS OF 1999 AND 2000

The Pinochet affair, coupled with an economic downturn, accentuated the problems within the governing coalition. There was already tension within the coalition over the choice of its presidential candidate. Partido Socialista de Chile (PS), a member of the CPD alliance, believed that they were entitled to provide the presidential nominee, particularly as they had a popular candidate in Ricardo Lagos Escobar. This prospect led to a fierce dispute within the PDC. After a bitter primary campaign, Lagos achieved an overwhelming victory over his Christian Democrat rival, Andrés Zaldívar, leaving the PDC in some disarray. In contrast, the right-wing united around the populist Joaquin Lavín Infante of the Unión Demócrata Independiente (UDI). The Pinochet affair, together with the impact of Chile's most serious economic crisis since the return of democracy, made the presidential elections one of the most closely contested for some time. In the first round, held on 12 December 1999, Lagos received 47.96% of the total votes cast, with Lavín obtaining 47.52%. Four minor candidates, among whom only Gladys Marín Millie (the Communist Party candidate) received more than 3% of the poll, were eliminated. At the subsequent second round of voting, which took place on 16 January 2000, Lagos emerged victorious with 51.31% of the total votes, while Lavin received 48.69%. Lagos thus became the first Socialist President in Chile since the death of Salvador Allende in 1973.

The incoming President faced the same problem as his two predecessors: how to secure constitutional change that would remove 'the authoritarian enclaves' remaining from the Pinochet Constitution without having a sufficient majority in both houses of the National Congress. The CPD, headed by Lagos, held 70 out of the 120 seats in the lower chamber, and even had 20 of the 38 elected seats in the Senate. However, with nine designated senators, the majority of whom were still Pinochet supporters, and two senators for life, one of whom was Gen. Pinochet, Lagos could not muster the two-thirds majority needed to obtain constitutional change without the support of the right-wing. Moreover, even within the CPD, the PS had far fewer seats than the Christian Democrats in both the lower chamber and the Senate. In selecting his Cabinet, Lagos reflected his desire to keep the CPD united by carefully ensuring a balance between the constituent parties: seven ministers were from the PDC, 4 from the PS, three from the Popular Democrats, and two from the Radicals.

THE PRESIDENCY OF RICARDO LAGOS, 2000–

Three issues immediately confronted the new President: the continuing tensions over human-rights trials, including possibly that of Pinochet; Mapuche militancy against timber and other companies taking over and damaging the environment of their ancestral lands (see below); and the ongoing economic problems.

The return of Pinochet to Chile in March 2000, which included a public welcome by the heads of the Armed Forces, was a clear warning that any attempt to put Pinochet on trial in Chile would face obstacles. However, what was new, and would make an important difference, was the change in Chile's judiciary. Under President Frei a number of judges appointed by Pinochet had retired, and were replaced by more independent-minded appointees. One such judge was Juan Guzmán Tapia, who vigorously took up the legal case against Pinochet and others accused of human-rights infringements. In Chile, as in the United Kingdom, the law had to take its slow, and at times torturous, course. The first obstacle to overcome was the amnesty law passed by Pinochet in 1978. A flaw was found in the legislation, namely that it did not cover the crime of abduction. Abduction was therefore a crime until such time as the abductee was produced, either alive or dead. As there were no bodies for 'the disappeared', these were all technically abducted. The accusations against Pinochet were mainly for the crime of abduction. The second obstacle was Pinochet's immunity from prosecution, owing to his status as senator for life. To lift Pinochet's immunity Judge Guzmán, had to go through the due legal procedures. The first court, the Santiago Appeal Court, voted to lift Pinochet's political immunity. In August 2000 the case went, on appeal, to the Supreme Court which, in an historical judgement, voted 14 to six to confirm the Santiago Appeal Court's decision to lift Pinochet's political immunity. The third obstacle was how to prove Pinochet's 'direct responsibility'. A

key case was the alleged 'caravan of death' associated with Gen. Arrelano Stark, who toured Chile in 1973 and reportedly killed an estimated 72 prisoners; 19 of these prisoners remained legal abductions, as no bodies had been found. With a total of 240 lawsuits filed against Pinochet, in December 2000 Judge Guzmán indicted Pinochet on charges of aggravated kidnapping and murder in the 'caravan of death' case. However, in Chile everyone over 70 must be subject to medical examinations to determine whether they are mentally fit to stand trial. Pinochet's lawyers argued that it would be undignified for Pinochet to undergo medical examinations. Faced with the prospect of medical examinations, and possibly a trial, the supporters of Pinochet undertook a political campaign to put pressure on the Government. The head of the army, Gen. Irzueta, sent a representative to the unveiling of a plaque in honour of victims of left-wing terrorism at the Pinochet Foundation in Santiago. Pinochet issued a document justifying his record and claiming he was not guilty of the crimes of which he was accused. Demonstrations were held in his defence. The right-wing contingent in the National Congress offered to allow the Constitution to be changed if all human-rights trials were abandoned. During all of this President Lagos remained firm, saying that he would not interfere in the due process of law. However, he did accede to a request by the military to convene the National Security Council, which can be summoned when there is a supposed threat to institutional order, but before the meeting could take place, the Santiago Appeal Court overturned the house arrest order on Pinochet on the grounds that his case had been improperly handled (he was not questioned before being charged), a decision subsequently confirmed by the Supreme Court. However, the Supreme Court also ruled that Pinochet must undergo the medical tests. In early January 2001, after failing to appear for previously scheduled tests, Pinochet finally consented to the medical examination and was subsequently questioned. On 31 January Judge Guzmán issued an order for the arrest of Pinochet on charges of kidnap and murder.

After appeals and counter-appeals, in March 2001 the Santiago Appeal Court reduced the charges against Pinochet from being the intellectual author of murder and kidnappings to acting as an accessory after the fact by concealing evidence in the 'caravan of death' case. Pinochet was freed on bail from house arrest, and was ordered to undergo a battery of psychological tests to determine if he was fit to stand trial. The Supreme Court confirmed the Appeal Court decision. The psychological tests found that Pinochet was suffering from mild dementia following his strokes in the United Kingdom, and that he had speech difficulties, but he had not lost his memory. In July the Appeal Court ruled, by 2–1, that Pinochet was mentally unfit to stand trial. It was widely believed, as a result of the ruling, that Pinochet would never be prosecuted.

Meanwhile, in June 2000, the Mesa de Diálogo, a round-table discussion between human-rights lawyers and the military, came to an agreement whereby the anonymity of any military person offering information on the whereabouts of the disappeared would be guaranteed. The Relatives of the Disappeared organization condemned the agreement, as the discovery of bodies would mean the legal abduction charge would be replaced by that of homicide which was covered by the amnesty law. After much delay the military finally submitted a report, in January 2001, which had been drawn up without the co-operation of the Relatives of the Disappeared organization. The report documented the cases of 29 disappeared whose bodies were scattered in graves around central Chile and 151 whose bodies had been dumped at sea. However, only three of the bodies discovered in graves have been identified, and one body, supposedly dumped at sea, was found at an army barracks. The Relatives of the Disappeared accused the Armed Forces of covering -up the murders. Disputes over human-rights abuses during the Pinochet regime continued to dominate the passions and much of the politics of Chile.

ENVIRONMENTAL ISSUES

In the mid-1990s, in keeping with the rest of the world, a new political problem emerged in Chile: that of environmental degradation. Chile's rapid economic growth rates were dependent on the exploitation of the country's vast natural resources many of which showed signs of severe environmental stress.

For example, salmon and trout farming were causing serious damage to lakes and coastal waters in the south of Chile and more than 62% of Chilean territory was affected by creeping desertification. Furthermore, Chile was rapidly losing its native tree species. In addition mining, dam and forestry projects were causing violent protests particularly by the Mapuche (or Araucano) indigenous peoples, who increasingly began to campaign for the restitution of their ancestral lands. Following violent protests in Temuco, after a court decision to allow the national electricity company ENDESA to resume its controversial Ralco dam project, which left 30 people hurt, President Lagos announced a Historical Truth and New Deal Commission to consider the demands and needs of the Mapuche communities. However, the failure of the Government to halt work on the Ralco dam led to a resumption of violent demonstrations by Mapuche groups in 2001.

CONCLUSION

After a slight decline of 1.1% in Chile's GDP growth rate in 1999, the first since 1983, there was an economic recovery in 2000 and 2001, but the continuing high rate of unemployment remained a source of political tension. Nevertheless, with the Chilean right-wing unable to agree an electoral pact for the congressional elections, due to be held in December 2001, the Government hoped to be able to increase its congressional majority sufficiently to be able to carry out its constitutional reform proposals. These proposals, which were submitted by the congressional Constitutional Commission in March 2001, included the elimination of a clause prohibiting the dismissal of a Commander-in-Chief of the Armed Forces, the eradication of non-elected senators for life and a reduction in the presidential term of office from six to four years. Chilean politics continued to remain stable, if somewhat becalmed.

Economy

PHILIP J. O'BRIEN

With a length of some 4,200 km and an average width of 180 km, Chile has a wider variety of climate and topography than any other country of comparable area. This ranges from the desert north, rich in minerals, through the fertile central valley, the agricultural heart of the country, to the southern, wetter forest region, source of the country's wood products. Further south still are the open grasslands of Chilean Patagonia, the chief sheep-rearing region and, off shore, the country's major source of petroleum. Since Chile's entire western frontier is the Pacific shoreline, its resources of fish products are immense.

Like other Latin American countries, Chile's economic history was dominated by the export of primary products: wheat in the colonial period; copper and nitrates in the 19th and early 20th centuries; and, until recently, primarily copper. From 1880 to 1920 export taxes on nitrate accounted for roughly one-half of government income, until synthetics destroyed the world market in the natural product. Thereafter, with heavy foreign capital and technological investment, copper dominated the economy. Chile possessed an estimated one-quarter of the world's proven reserves of copper and, in 1982, became the world's leading producer. However, this dependence on primary exports, subject to fluctuations in world markets, proved disadvantageous at times. During the Great Depression Chile was affected more severely than any other country, since 80% of government revenue came from copper and nitrates.

The reaction to this Depression, in the 1930s and onwards, was to pursue import-substitution policies in industry, under the protection of high tariffs. Moreover, a tradition of state intervention in the economy was accentuated, notably by the establishment, in 1939, of the National Development Corporation (Corporación de Fomento de la Producción—CORFO), under the aegis of which a large number of state-owned enterprises prospered. By the end of the 1960s the results of increased state control were not impressive: per head economic growth rates were low; unemployment and inflation high. By 1970 copper accounted for 75% of exports by value, indicating an unbalanced economy.

The Socialist Government (1970–73), under Salvador Allende Gossens, accentuated state control, nationalized the copper industry, the banking sector and many private enterprises, and redistributed land to peasants. The economic upheaval which followed facilitated the military intervention of September 1973. The military regime, led by Gen. Augusto Pinochet Ugarte, initiated policies to reverse the trends of decades, with the assistance of successive economic teams. The Government's principal objectives were: to reduce inflation; to reduce over-staffing in highly protected, inefficient industries; to diversify the export pattern, thus reducing dependence on copper, and to expose Chilean industry to foreign competition by reducing import tariffs. In short, the aim was to enable Chile to realize better the potential of its enormous natural resources.

To achieve these aims public expenditure was reduced; tariff barriers fell to the lowest in the world (averaging 10%, apart from the automobile industry, where a more 'gradualist' policy was followed); denationalization of banks and credit was introduced; and foreign investment was encouraged, under liberal laws on taxation and remittance of profits. By 1980 Chile was one of the most free-market economies in the world. Although the social costs were high (unemployment reached over 20% in several years), the economic results were impressive. The annual average inflation was reduced from over 500% in 1973, to 9.9% in 1982. Dependence on copper for export revenue fell from 75% in 1970, to under 50% in 1980, as 'non-traditional' exports such as wine, fruit, wood and fish products were encouraged. Foreign capital, invested chiefly in mining, increased to over US $4,000m. by 1980.

These results were reflected in sustained economic growth from 1976 until 1981. However, both GDP and gross national product (GNP) were reduced substantially from 1981 as the economy went into recession. This was caused by a combination of circumstances. The impact of the growing world recession reduced copper prices; lax financial management leading to a banking crisis, the maintenance of a fixed exchange rate for years, which kept inflation down but at the same time encouraged imports and discouraged exports leading to a huge current-account deficit, and, in general, the too-drastic application of the free-market model were all to blame. Bankruptcies proliferated and unemployment increased dramatically, to 17.8% in mid-1983.

In 1983 the banking system in Chile virtually collapsed, and had to be rescued by massive state intervention. Foreign confidence disappeared, and the Chilean peso lost 90% of its value in 12 months. GDP decreased by 14.1% and urban unemployment became the highest in Latin America, resulting in considerable social unrest. Imports declined by almost one-half and the foreign debt reached $17,200m., or 71.1% of GNP. Almost 80% of export earnings were needed for debt servicing. Rescheduling the foreign debt, under the auspices of the International Monetary Fund (IMF), became imperative.

From 1984, however, a free-market, export-led, 'crawling-peg' exchange-rate policy was pursued, which initiated a period of sustained economic recovery, averaging over 5.5% annual GDP growth, for the rest of the 1980s. Chile's economic results from 1984 onwards stand out from those in other Latin American countries, registering the best growth rate in the region during the 1980s. Nevertheless, GDP per head only surpassed that of 1981 in 1989.

The Government of President Patricio Aylwin Azócar, which took office in March 1990, continued the expansionary export-led growth policies of its predecessor. In the four years of President Aylwin's administration Chile's GDP grew, on average, by 6.2% per year, by far the best growth under any

Chilean Government, and some three times faster than that of the rest of Latin America, and four times faster than the growth rate of major industrialized countries. Investment also expanded rapidly, almost doubling in the four years of Aylwin's Government.

Eduardo Frei Ruiz-Tagle, who assumed the presidency in March 1994, inherited a sound economy. He too continued to reaffirm Chile's commitment to low inflation and export-led growth. GDP continued to expand rapidly growing by 10.6% in 1995, and by 7.4% both 1996 and 1997. The Chilean economy's average GDP growth was 3% between 1981 and 1990 and 5.6% from 1990 to 1999. Not unsurprisingly, until 1998 the country's economic performance earned praise from foreign banks, attracting good rates of investment. With inflation under control, rapidly expanding exports, high levels of liquidity and sustained economic growth, Chile was even favourably compared to the successful 'tiger' economies of Asia. However, economic problems began to accumulate in 1998, with GDP growth falling to 3.9% in that year and the economy actually contracting by 1.1% in 1999. Nevertheless, in 2000 GDP growth recovered to stand at 5%, and was forecast to increase by 5.6% in 2001. Unemployment continued to decrease from 16.7% of the work-force in 1983 to 6.1% in 1997. However, with the economic recession the unemployment rate increased to 9.8% in 1999. In 2000 the unemployment rate was 9.2% and, in 2001, was likely to be higher, with unemployment heavily concentrated in some regions such Valparaíso (13.4%). The rate of unemployment among the young remained persistently high, at around 15%. In 2001 the Government allocated a special US $350m. to reduce unemployment.

Inflation remained well under control. From 30.7% in 1985, it fell as low as 14.7% in 1988, before increasing again, to 26.0% in 1991. Thereafter it decreased, and stood at 3.3% in 1999, before increasing slightly to 3.8% in 2000. The forecast for inflation in 2001 was around 4.6%. These favourable results were achieved by maintaining strict control over external accounts and finances, and encouraging investments, particularly in exports. The Pinochet Government promoted private investment, through a controversial policy of de-nationalizing state assets, and the encouragement of exports through selective tariffs, technical aid and supported prices. At the same time, encouraged by strict fiscal policy, in accordance with the IMF's requirements, foreign investment also increased, after the years of recession. Its role in the economy was enhanced by the Government's policy of capitalizing external debt. By aggressively using 'debt-swap' mechanisms, under which external creditors were able to sell or exchange their debt for Chilean assets, the country slightly decreased its overall debt, between 1985 and 1990, from US $20,400m. to $19,114m. Even though the foreign debt increased to $31,443m. in 1997, very little of this was short-term debt. By 1999 however foreign debt increased to $37,762m.

Crucially, during the mid-1990s Chile managed to maintain a steady flow of foreign capital inflows without being destabilized by them. It achieved this mainly by encouraging direct foreign investment rather than short-term speculative capital inflows, thus making the balance of payments less sensitive to interest-rate changes and financial-market perceptions. Furthermore, the private pension funds and private health-care schemes, established in the 1980s, contributed to the development of a local capital market, and played a key role in the high rates of savings and investment. However, in 2000 foreign investment fell to US $3,700m., the lowest level since 1995.

Declines in world petroleum prices (Chile imported some 50% of its domestic requirements), a prosperous export sector and reductions in international interest rates were also important factors in the country's rapid growth. Prices for exports improved fairly consistently from 1984 to 1998, and the value of merchandise exports grew from US $2,500m. in 1978 to $16,663m. in 1997. Following the Asian crisis, exports fell to $14,831 in 1998 and increased slightly to $15,616m.in 1999. In 2000 exports grew by 6.3% and are estimated to grow by 7.5% in 2001. The growth is mainly attributable to the increase in world copper prices. There was also a rapid diversification of export markets. By 1996 Chile had over 2,000 exporting companies, supplying over 2,700 products to 170 countries. Framework agreements signed with the European Union (EU), the agreement with the

Southern Common Market (Mercosur—comprising Argentina, Brazil, Paraguay and Uruguay), and the bilateral trade agreements with Canada and Mexico (which offset the failure to secure accession to the North American Free Trade Agreement (NAFTA), the free-trade zone between Canada, Mexico and the USA), helped secure Chile's high level of exports until 1998.

Such steady progress impressed the international financial community, both public and private. The reforms of the 1970s and 1980s resulted in an efficient economy, which was competitive in the international market. Macroeconomic policy, both fiscal and monetary, was carefully controlled, leading to manageable levels of inflation. In the early 1990s domestic savings and investment was at a high level, ensuring that Chile avoided the recessions which occurred elsewhere in the continent following the Mexican economic crisis of 1994.

However, although the economy grew, the social cost was high for a long time. The minimum monthly wage, earned by one-fifth of the country's 5m.-strong work-force, was considerably lower in 1990 than at the beginning of the 1980s. Moreover, although in 1993, for the first time, the real urban minimum wage was above that of 1980, wages' share of GDP fell from 34.8% in 1985/86 to 33.4% in 1992/93, while profits' share went up from 38.3% to 44.0% in the same period. Improvements have been made in decreasing poverty: official government statistics showed that in 1990 40% of the population were still classified as extremely poor; in 1997 the figure was 25% with 6.5% defined as 'hard-core' poor. This meant that some 3.2m. Chileans lived below the official poverty line with urban poverty accounting for over 80%. The recession, beginning in 1998, made the elimination of extreme poverty more difficult. By 2001, with unemployment remaining high, there was still a persistent, although declining, problem of a high level of poverty. However, the Government of Ricardo Lagos did seem to be addressing the problem, and the incidence of extreme poverty has been significantly reduced.

AGRICULTURE, FORESTRY AND FISHING

Agriculture was the mainstay of Chile's colonial economy, with wheat and cattle (primarily for hides and tallow) the main products. The country's central valley is very fertile and suitable for a wide variety of crops and fruit. Between 1970 and 1973 extensive disinvestment occurred, as a result of land seizures. However, the Pinochet Government returned land to the previous owners and provided incentives for increased exports. After the 1970s commercialization of the agrarian sector continued, with a consequent decrease in the rural population, from 27% of the total population in 1975, to 15% by 1999.

Agriculture, forestry and fishing, as a percentage of GDP, was consistently high during the 1980s, reaching 9.5% in 1988. Thereafter the sector's share fell to around 8.1% in 1999. The main food crops are wheat, maize, barley, oats, rice, rye, potatoes and other vegetables, with levels of production fluctuating, depending on areas sown and climatic factors. Traditional crops in the 1990s had such low profitability that many farmers were changing to the cultivation of forestry and fruit. Farmers held a series of mass protests to demand government action to improve the profitability of the sector, and to protest at the terms of the agreement for Chile's membership of Mercosur. The future for some of Chile's traditional food crops like wheat, rice and maize are increasingly bleak. Agriculture in general was badly affected by the effects of El Niño, the warm current which periodically appears along the Pacific coast, in 1997. Then, in 1998 and 1999, Chile experienced its worst drought for 50 years. All areas of agriculture had substantial losses, and although agricultural GDP increased by 3.0% in 1998, the sector declined by 0.6% in 1999.

Production of fruit increased greatly during the 1980s, becoming second only to copper as an export earner. By the end of the decade the fruit industry employed some 250,000 people, earning 12% of the country's export income. The rapid increases in fruit exports came from plums, apples, pears, grapes, berries and kiwi fruit (a variety of Chinese gooseberry). Total fruit exports earned US $1,066m. in 1998. In 1997 El Niño severely affected several fruit crops, and there were decreases in production of 60% for plums, 58% for apricots and 24% for peaches. The severe draught in 1998/1999 continued to affect adversely many fruit crops, though there were signs of a significant recovery in 2000 and 2001.

Wine was one of Chile's best-known products for decades, although until the 1980s relatively little was exported. In 1997 production was an estimated 382,000 metric tons and in 1999 exports accounted for US $510.5m. In 1996 Chile possessed vineyards covering an area of 53,000 ha, and its wines had earned popularity abroad, particularly among its main export markets of Canada, the United Kingdom and the USA. However, in 1999 production and sales were adversely affected by drought, though a major recovery was detected in 2000 and 2001.

Forestry products were one of the most dynamic areas in the Chilean economy in the 1980s, principally as a result of the superb growing conditions in the south, where pine grows faster than anywhere else in the world, and of the country's generous re-forestation laws. Chile has more than one-half of the world's temperate rain forests, although by the end of the 20th century this was fast disappearing. Up to 80% of Chile's natural forests were damaged, with 120,000 ha per year being lost. Over 60% of this loss can be attributed to the native trees being replaced by fast growing exotic varieties. Forestry employs some 60,000 workers directly and another 60,000 indirectly. Over 50 countries import Chilean pulp, sawn-wood, logs, newsprint and other forestry products. Some 72,900 ha of land were reforested in 1988, entirely by private companies. Forestry products accounted for only 2.8% of export revenues in 1973, but by 1993 this figure had increased to 13.1%, becoming Chile's second largest foreign exchange earner. This sector continued to expand, increasingly producing processed articles, rather than primary products. Export earnings from forestry increased from US $323m. in 1985 to $2,400m. in 1995. Owing to a fall in prices for forestry products, exports decreased to $1,030m. in 1997. Exports increased to $1,800m. in 1999, in spite of some of the worst forest fires in Chilean history in 1998, when over 91,000 ha of woodland was destroyed. In 2000 there was a dramatic increase in forestry exports, to some $2,100m., mainly owing to the high world prices for pulp.

Investments continued to be high in the forestry sector, even though a problem for many forestry projects was the clash with local Mapuche communities, who viewed some of the projects as encroachments on their ancestral lands.

Fishing in Chile also expanded rapidly from the late 1970s. Canning was carried out in plants, situated mostly in the north, with an installed capacity to process some 1,300 metric tons of raw material per day. The fishing catch, which stood at 2.9m. metric tons in 1980, increased to 3.6m. tons in 1998. Over 75% of the fishing catch was processed into fishmeal. Fishery exports, including processed products, increased from US $62m. in 1985 to $1,245m. in 1998. Frozen-fish exports also increased rapidly. A new development was the growth of fish farms, in the south of Chile. In 1995 Chile became the world's second largest salmon exporter after Norway, exporting about 145,000 tons of salmon, worth about $614m. in 1997. However, the swift and spectacular penetration of the US market (about 30% of Chilean salmon exports) led the USA to impose additional tariffs against two salmon-exporting firms on the grounds of dumping. Despite these obstacles, the value of exports of Chilean salmon reached $1,000m. in 2000, an increase of 10% on 1999. As in the rest of the continent, the sector was adversely affected by El Niño, and in 1999 total fish exports decreased by an estimated 13%, though there was a recovery in 2000. However, fishmeal failed to recover, and in 1999 was worth only $278m. in exports compared to $627m. in 1995.

MINING AND POWER

Mining was always of crucial importance to the Chilean economy. The country has an impressive share of world mining reserves: 22% of the world's copper reserves; 100% of nitrates; 23% of selenium; 20% of molybdenum; 12% of iodine; and 5% of gold. Although it employed only some 1.4% of the work-force in 1999, the sector was, as it had been historically, a critical export sector, contributing a provisional 11.1% of GDP in 1999. Mining exports increased from US $7,850m. in 1995 to $8,050m. in 1997.

In 1982 Chile became the world's leading copper producer, with production of 1.26m. metric tons (copper content of ores), and copper accounted for 45.5% of exports by value. Production continued to increase thereafter, and stood at 4.4m. metric tons

in 1999, an increase of almost 18% on the previous year's figure. Large investments were made in mining in 1996 and 1997, mainly in the development of new copper mines. Some experts, however, believed that Chile might be overproducing, which could lead to a fall in world copper prices. From 1987, the copper price rose steadily to reach its highest point of $1.34 per lb in 1995. However, the copper-trading scandal of mid-1996, involving a Japanese company, Sumitomo Corporation, reduced the price, causing both a fall in Chile's copper revenues and the postponement of some investment plans. Furthermore, partly as a result of the Asian financial crisis in 1998, copper prices decreased to their lowest value, in real terms, in the 20th century at $0.61 per lb in February 1999. Thus, although in 1998 copper sales increased by some 12%, their value declined by some 24%. However, after February 1999 copper prices began to increase steadily, reaching an estimated $0.93 per lb in 2001.

As a result of such price fluctuations, copper's share of total export revenue did not increase in line with output: in the 1970s export earnings from copper had been over 70% of total export earnings; by 1992 they accounted for 38.5% of total exports. Thereafter, however, mining increased in importance, and in 1998 accounted for almost one-half of all export earnings, 28% of which were from copper. This increased slightly by 2000. Exports were valued at US $4,162.8m. in 1999. Other minerals, such as molybdenum, iron ore, nitrate and other salts, zinc, lead and coal, gold and silver, are also important foreign-exchange earners.

In 2000 the Corporación Nacional del Cobre de Chile (CODELCO) earned profits of $952.6m., an increase of 31.4% compared with 1999. However, the long-term future of Chilean copper was far from secure: reserves could be exhausted within 60 years, with the large private sector developments, which began in 1988, surviving for just 20 years.

The large-scale copper industry, concentrated at Chuquicamata, Andina and Salvador, in the north, and at El Teniente, in the central valley, was nationalized by the Allende Government. Copper production was dominated by the CODELCO. In 1993 there were demands to privatize CODELCO, following the loss of over US $200m. in copper futures trading. The incident, usually attributed to trading errors (although there were allegations of fraud), led to a modernization of the corporation, including the decentralization of the four main mines. The Government also intended to curtail the transfer of 10% of CODELCO's earnings to the military, but this proved to be too unpopular with them. However, in 2000 President Lagos limited military expenditure to solely its statutory 10% of CODELCO's sales. In 1995 private copper output, amounting to 1.37m. metric tons, exceeded CODELCO's output of 1.14m. tons for the first time, although the corporation still represented about one-fifth of Chile's total export earnings. It was expected that CODELCO's share of total output would fall to about 35% by 2000 and that its future developments would be in association with foreign partners. In 2000 CODELCO opened negotiations to establish joint ventures in Brazil, Mexico and Peru.

The increasingly important role of foreign investment in mining was not without controversy. The La Escondida copper-mining project, which. in 1996, became the largest mine in the country, was entirely owned by foreign multinationals: Utah International owns 60%, Rio Tinto Zinc 30%, and Mitsubishi Corporation and Nippon Mining Co 10%. The La Escondida deal effectively ended the Chilean state's domination of copper production and, arguably, the country's direct benefits from the enterprise were thus reduced. Subsequently, major private mines were opened at La Disputada, La Candelaria, and Zaldivar. Other developments included the acquisition of a 12% stake in the Collahuasi copper project, expected to be one of the world's biggest and cheapest mines, by a Japanese consortium of Mitsui and Nippon Mining. The mine was controlled by Minorco, a subsidiary of Anglo-American Corporation of South Africa and Falconbridge of Canada.

Chile's energy resources are based on hydroelectric capacity and petroleum, both of which were expanded in the 1980s. Given the physical configuration of a large number of fast-flowing rivers, fed by the melting snows of the Andes and running east-to-west to the Pacific, Chile has the highest hydro-electric potential in the world. Total potential generating capacity was estimated at 18,700 MW. From the mid-1970s there was an ambitious expansion programme, assisted by the Inter-American Development Bank. The Colbún-Machicura station, on the River Maule, began operating in 1985, producing a further 3,060m. kWh per year, about 25% of Chile's total generating capacity. Six further plants also began operations in the late 1980s. In the early 1990s construction of the Pehuenche plant (capacity 500 MW) was completed, with the help of a World Bank loan of US $95m. The project met with much opposition from environmental and indigenous groups.

Following the privatization, at a very low price, of the state energy company, Empresa Nacional de Electricidad (ENDESA), in 1988, there was much criticism of the management of the energy sector. In 1997 ENDESA—España acquired virtual control of the Chilean power consortium, ENERSIS, and therefore about 40% control of Chilean energy. The deal aroused accusations of 'insider information' (benefiting from information not publicly known), and provoked government criticism. Disquiet with the privatization process reached a crisis in 1999 when, partly owing to the drought, there were severe energy shortages. The issue became highly political, particularly given the virtual monopoly of the Chilean electricity system by ENDESA. President Frei ordered the private utilities to increase their generating capacity or face severe fines. Legislation was introduced increasing potential penalties from US $26,800 to $6m., and making the utilities liable to pay compensation to users for non-compliance with the terms of their concessions. ENDESA recovered in 2000, when it made a profit of $189.8m., compared to the substantial losses of previous years.

In October 1993 British Gas and the US company, Tenneco Gas, won a contract to operate a US $1,650m. project to pipe natural gas from Argentina to Chile; there were plans for the construction of three gas-fired power-stations in Chile, with a total capacity in excess of 1,100 MW. Total investments in gas projects amounted to some $3,000m. By 2005 it was expected that natural gas would supply 25% of Chile's electricity needs.

Petroleum was exploited from the 1940s, when fields in Tierra del Fuego and Magallanes began operations. Following extensive exploration and exploitation in the early 1980s by the Empresa Nacional de Petróleo (ENAP), 45% of the country's requirements were met domestically. Foreign participation was significant, notably by US concerns such as Atlantic Richfield, Amerada Hess and Phillips Petroleum. At the end of the 1980s Chile was importing some 60,000 barrels per day (b/d) of petroleum, from Ecuador and Venezuela, to meet domestic demand. Production declined after 1982. In 1997 a plan to privatize up to 60% of ENAP was announced.

INDUSTRY

Industry was the sector that experienced the widest fluctuations in output after 1973. Chilean industry developed from the 1930s with a high degree of tariff protection in a policy of import substitution until 1973. The Pinochet Government's 'shock treatment' of dismantling tariff barriers, thus encouraging competitive foreign imports, was a shock to many industries, notably textiles. The effects of the free-market policy pursued from the mid-1970s to the early 1980s reduced the contribution to GDP of industry as a whole from 25% in 1975, to only 17.7% in 1992. However, industrial production began to recover thereafter. Industry contributed an estimated 35.1% of GDP in 1999, when it accounted for 23.4% of the employed labour force.

In 1999 the manufacturing accounted for an estimated 16.3% of GDP. The key sectors within manufacturing were textiles, motor cars, chemicals, rubber products, cement and consumer goods. Competition from abroad and low levels of domestic investment were one reason for the decline. Furthermore, the monetarist model adopted caused an increased concentration of wealth and economic power in fewer hands, notably banking and financial groups, rather than industrialists. Increasingly from 1981 industry suffered through the long-standing fixed exchange rate and, in depressed world conditions for exports, the sector declined. Industry lost a 3% share of GDP between 1981 and 1982. With policy changes, a slow recovery began in 1983, and industrial output increased by an annual average of 6.7%, between then and 1988. During 1990–99 industrial GDP increased by an annual average of 6.3%.Following growth of just 0.6% in 1998, in 1999 and 2000 the sector improved by 2.8% and 2.1%, respectively. The plastics and transport equipment

sectors, in particular, grew rapidly. However, manufacturing exports in 2000 increased by a less than expected 2%, mainly because of the slow growth in Mercosur, where sales fell by 8% compared with the previous year.

The steel industry, dating effectively from 1950 and based at Huachipato near Talcahuano, expanded during the late 1990s, following a decrease in exports and production from the late 1980s. Construction, too, was a sector much affected by fluctuations in the Chilean economy. In 1999 the sector's share of GDP stood at 5.2%.

For many years foreign investment in Chilean industry was low, despite the free-market policies of the Pinochet Government. However, having increased by 140% between 1986 and 1987, foreign investment continued to grow, owing to the 'debt-for-equity' conversions and the extensive privatization process. Although the majority of foreign capital was invested in mining, industry attracted an increasing share. US investments remained preponderant in Chile, although British interests were also traditionally strong. Chile's good economic performance encouraged foreign bankers and businessmen in general to invest in the country's stock market and to take advantage of the debt-conversion schemes. The Government of President Frei maintained the pace of privatization, selling the state's shares in a number of companies, including the airline carrier Línea Aérea Nacional de Chile (LAN-Chile), the electricity supplier Empresa Eléctrica del Norte (EDELNOR), the shipping company Empresa Marítima (Empremar Chile), and, in June 1999, Empresa Metropolitana de Obras Sanitarias (EMOS), Chile's biggest water company. The economic recession in 1998 and 1999 badly affected the manufacturing sector, particularly the capital goods sector, and both foreign and domestic investment declined.

TRANSPORT AND COMMUNICATIONS

Internal transport in Chile is well developed. Railway lines, which were being increasingly electrified, linked Iquique, in the desert north, to Puerto Montt, in the south, with feeder lines running laterally from this central line to important towns and cities. Four international railways extended to Argentina, Bolivia and Peru. The Frei Government began the process of privatizing the Chilean railways. Freight services were sold in 1995, and the rest of the rail service was to be privatized in stages. Overall the Government was said to be aiming to acquire investments of US $400m. in a privatized railway system.

The road network in Chile in 1999 covered 79,353 km, part of it (3,455 km) being Chile's section of the Pan-American Highway. In the same year about 18.9% of the total network was paved. In 1997 private investment in roads exceeded that of public investment. The national bus service, linking main towns from north to south of the central valley, is considered excellent, as is Santiago's underground railway system.

Shipping facilities are also well-developed, essential for a country with such a long coastline. In the late 1990s about a dozen companies were engaged in the coastal and international trade. The state controlled the port authority and roughly 40% of the merchant marine. The main ports are Valparaíso, Talcahuano, San Antonio and Antofagasta. Following a severe earthquake in March 1985, more than US $1,600m. was spent on the reconstruction of San Antonio, and its port was upgraded to handle 3m. metric tons of imports annually, compared with the previous 1m. tons. In 1999 President Frei announced that the ports of Valparaíso, San Antonio and San Vicente of Talcahuano were to be privatized.

Owing to its topography, Chile needs a large number of airports to facilitate communications. The international airport, Santiago, is served by some 18 international airlines and two national ones. Chile's other main airport is Chacalluta, 14 km north-east of Arica. The national carrier, LAN-Chile, serves major cities within the country and is also an international line. Internally, it is supplemented by Línea Aérea del Cobre (LADECO), the airline of CODELCO.

Chileans responded well to the new communication industries. Following its privatization in the late 1980s, the telecommunications industry grew rapidly. By 1995 some 500,000 households had cable television, and by 1998 there were some 1.5m. subscribers. In 2000 there were 3.4m. mobile phones in use. The Compañía de Teléfonos de Chile was privatized in

1988 and subsequently controlled by Telefónica of Spain, which secured a 63.1% share. Deregulation of the market produced fierce competition, resulting in a reduction in costs to the consumer, and a massive increase in usage.

TOURISM

In 1998 tourism earned $1,062m., representing the fifth largest source of foreign currency for Chile. This growth was attributed to Chile's wide range of scenic beauty as well as government efforts to promote tourism, both internally and externally, through the Servicio Nacional de Turismo. Much private investment went into tourist centres, such as Marbella, to enable Chile to compete with resorts in the region, such as Punta del Este in Uruguay. Efforts were made to enhance the attraction of major cities, notably Santiago, although the capital remained one of the most polluted cities in the world. In 1999 tourism receipts fell to $894m.

FINANCE

In 1982 the lack of financial regulation of the banking sector and the inter-relationship of financial groups and industries, to which excessive loans had been made, created a crisis in the Chilean banks. The inability of the private sector to pay its debts in the recession forced the Government to take over nine major banks in 1981 and 1983, and to liquidate two others at a cost of US $4,200m., owed to the Central Bank.

It took several years for the financial system to recover. In 1989, although Chilean private banks reported an operational surplus, there were no profits for common stockholders because of the requirement to repurchase bad loans previously assumed by the Central Bank. The newly elected Government indicated that it must continue to honour the debt assumed during the 1983 banking crisis, and the subsequent administration, under President Frei, set a 40-year time limit on the private banks' repayment of the $4,200m. debt. Chile's two largest banks, Banco de Chile and Banco de Santiago, each owed over $1,000m. In the 1990s bank profits, bank deposits and bank loans expanded rapidly by about 15% per year. Legislation passed in the late 1990s was to allow greater overseas activities, including lending to Chilean companies abroad.

FOREIGN TRADE, FOREIGN INVESTMENT AND REGIONAL BLOCS

From 1986 onwards exports, owing, in part, to favourable prices, increased steadily, from US $3,823m. in 1985 to $16,678m. in 1997. There was a decline in 1998 to $14,830m., but exports increased to $15,616m. in 1999 and to $18,158m. in 2000. In 1998 Chile had a trade deficit of $2,516m., but the deficit turned to a surplus of $1,664m. in 1999 and this increased to $1,690m. in 2000. After 1985 a period of sustained economic recovery, as well as sound fiscal management, restored international confidence in the Chilean economy, so Chile had few problems in re-financing its foreign debt. As a sign of confidence, the World Bank's Multilateral Investment Guarantee Agency (MIGA) chose Chile as the first Latin American country, and only the second world-wide, to receive a political risk insurance contract from the private-sector orientated agency since it began operating in 1988.

Chile was one of the first countries to explore the possibilities of establishing a free-trade zone with the USA, following US President George Bush's (1989–93) 'Initiative for the Americas'. The country was hoping to be able to participate in NAFTA, which formally came into effect at the beginning of 1994. However, Chile failed to secure 'fast-track' status for its bid to join NAFTA. In practice, however, this proved beneficial, as Chile decided actively to pursue other trade negotiations. It secured bilateral free trade agreements with Canada and Mexico. Furthermore, Chile and Mercosur agreed an association accord whereby Chile would become a member of the Mercosur free-trade zone but not the customs union, as Chile's flat-rate 11% external tariff was at variance with the differential common external tariff of the four Mercosur countries. Special agreements were made on sensitive items like Chilean wheat and some sectors, such as vehicle manufacturing and services, were excluded from the agreement altogether. Given that almost one-half of Chile's investments abroad were in Mercosur countries,

particularly Argentina, the agreement would significantly improve the country's foreign economic links.

Chile was admitted to Mercosur as a full associate member in October 1996, and the Government has stated that it intends to become a full member. Chile's shift towards Mercosur is profound. Officials have described it as moving beyond free trade agreements towards integration. Already plans to build 'bi-oceanic corridors' to facilitate movement between the Pacific and the Atlantic Oceans are going ahead. However, Brazil, in particular, was opposed to Chile's decision to re-open bilateral negotiations on a free trade agreement with the USA in 2001. The Brazilian Government wanted Mercosur countries to negotiate as a unified block with outside bodies, while within Chile, environmentalists and labour leaders argued that the USA was seeking a free trade agreement in order to weaken the South American trade grouping. In addition, Chile signed a new framework agreement with the EU, which would facilitate trade liberalization with this key trading partner. The country also joined the Asia–Pacific Economic Group (APEC) in 1994, emphasizing the importance of Pacific trade.

In 2000 Chile's international reserves stood at $15,047.6m., and, at the end of 1999, its external debt was $37,762m. Traditionally, owing to its scheme for taxes on short-term capital flows, Chile had little short-term capital debt. The tax ended in 1998, and in 2000 Chile abolished all capital controls to encourage investment. Chile hoped to become the international financial centre in South America, but critics feared that the decision to abolish capital controls would make it vulnerable to external volatility.

Chile has been one of the most successful Latin American countries in attracting direct foreign investment (FDI). In 1996 FDI was equivalent to about 2.8% of GDP, compared to 1.2% for Argentina and 0.8% for Brazil. FDI to Chile increased from US $2,700m. in 1993 to a record $9,800m., in 1999, one-third of which originated from Spain. In 2000 foreign private investment was $3,700m., the lowest since 1995, partly as a result of high US interest rates. With no major privatizations planned, FDI may remain low for some time, although it is hoped that the gas pipeline from Bolivia to the Pacific will lead to a substantial private foreign investment.

Chile has also emerged as a foreign investor in its own right with US $2,250m. of foreign investments ($1,200m. of this figure was invested in South America, almost one-half in Argentina). The total value of Chilean investments in the whole of Latin America was estimated at $14,900m. in 1990–96.

CONCLUSIONS

Chile's economic recovery in the mid-1980s was most impressive, especially when compared to the country's Latin American neighbours. However, recovery initially was achieved at a high social cost. At the beginning of the 1990s one-half of all Chileans lived below the official poverty line and one-quarter were in a situation of extreme poverty. Wealth distribution had worsened, with the richest 20% of the population taking 80% of income. Nevertheless, after 1997 income distribution to improved, and absolute poverty began to decrease.

Until 1998 wages continued to increase. By this year the average family income was 87% higher than in 1988. Unemployment too decreased, although concentration of high youth unemployment in the shanty towns around Santiago remained a source of strong social pressures. With unemployment rapidly increasing in 1998 and 1999 and not significantly falling in 2000 and 2001, social tensions were becoming more widespread.

The Pinochet regime did not preside over a constantly prosperous economy, but a fluctuating one. From 1990 until 1999 Chile achieved a remarkable annual average of 7.2% in GDP growth. It achieved sustained growth by having the most open, stable and liberalized economy in Latin America. Chile underwent a profound economic, social, and political change with productivity gains, high growth, strong external position, low single figure inflation and with improvements in nearly all social indicators including overall literacy, malnutrition, education standards, infant mortality and life expectancy. Chile is now ranked 34th in the United Nations Development Programme's Human Development Index, the highest in Latin America. However, after a period of long and stable economic growth, at the end of the 1990s Chile returned to its more familiar fluctuating economic cycle. The full opening of the Chilean economy to the international economy always made it vulnerable to significant changes. So it proved when a major crisis affected the East Asian economies at the end of 1997. Initially, the Chilean Government believed it could make adjustments to compensate for the fall in the demand for its exports in Asia. These adjustments were mainly designed to lessen the current-account deficit. In 1998 the Government introduced three fiscal adjustment packages, increasing interest rates, tightening monetary targets and reducing state expenditure. The result was a contraction in economic growth of 1.1% in 1999 and a large increase in unemployment. To counter the downturn, in mid-1999 Presi-dent Frei announced a cut in interest rates, to 5%, the disbursement of US $58m. of state investment, particularly in construction, and the granting of more export credits for small and medium-sized firms. In 2000 Chile's economy showed clear signs of a significant recovery (when it grew by 5.4%), but in 2001 fears that the Chilean economy was again slowing down led the Minister of Finance to cut interest rates again and to propose a 15-point plan, which included the abolition of capital gains tax and the removal of any restrictions on foreign investment. However, the success of these measures was dependent upon the state of the world economy in general, and the US economy in particular.

Statistical Survey

Sources (unless otherwise stated): Instituto Nacional de Estadísticas, Avda Bulnes 418, Casilla 498-3, Correo 3, Santiago; tel. (2) 366-7777; fax (2) 671-2169; e-mail inesdadm@reuna.cl; internet www.ine.cl; Banco Central de Chile, Agustinas 1180, Santiago; tel. (2) 696-2281; fax (2) 698-4847; e-mail bcch@bcentral.cl; internet www.bcentral.cl.

Area and Population

AREA, POPULATION AND DENSITY*

Area (sq km)	756,096†
Population (census results)‡	
21 April 1982	11,329,736
22 April 1992	
Males	6,553,254
Females	6,795,147
Total	13,348,401
Population (official estimates at mid-year)	
1998	14,821,714
1999	15,017,760
2000	15,211,308
Density (per sq km) at mid-2000	20.1

* Excluding Chilean Antarctic Territory (approximately 1,250,000 sq km).
† 291,930 sq miles.
‡ Excluding adjustment for underenumeration.

REGIONS (30 June 2000)

		Area (sq km)	Population ('000)	Capital
I	De Tarapacá . .	59,099.1	398.9	Iquique
II	De Antofagasta .	126,049.1	468.4	Antofagasta
III	De Atacama . .	75,176.2	273.6	Copiapó
IV	De Coquimbo . .	40,579.9	577.9	La Serena
V	De Valparaíso . .	16,396.1	1,561.4	Valparaíso
VI	Del Libertador Gen. Bernardo O'Higgins .	16,387.0	788.8	Rancagua
VII	Del Maule . .	30,296.1	915.2	Talca
VIII	Del Bíobío . .	37,062.6	1,936.3	Concepción
IX	De la Araucanía .	31,842.3	874.2	Temuco
X	De Los Lagos . .	67,013.1	1,061.5	Puerto Montt
XI	Aisén del Gen. Carlos Ibáñez del Campo .	108,494.4	95.0	Coihaique
XII	De Magallanes y Antártica Chilena .	132,297.2	157.8	Punta Arenas
	Metropolitan Region (Santiago) . .	15,403.2	6,102.2	—
	Total	756,096.3	15,211.3	—

PRINCIPAL TOWNS (provisional figures, population at 30 June 2000)

Gran Santiago (capital) . . .	5,493,062	Arica	185,622
Puente Alto . .	425,056	Talca	182,445
Concepción . .	379,860	Chillán . . .	171,207
Viña del Mar . .	342,715	Iquique . . .	169,997
Valparaíso . .	285,262	Puerto Montt . .	138,138
Talcahuano . .	280,941	Coquimbo . . .	135,622
Temuco . . .	273,223	Osorno . . .	131,666
Antofagasta . .	251,868	La Serena . . .	130,426
San Bernardo . .	246,491	Calama . . .	128,073
Rancagua . . .	213,735	Valdivia . . .	125,999
		Punta Arenas . .	124,246

BIRTHS, MARRIAGES AND DEATHS

	Registered live births		Registered marriages		Registered deaths	
	Number	Rate (per 1,000)	Number	Rate (per 1,000)	Number	Rate (per 1,000)
1991 . .	299,456	22.5	91,732	6.9	74,862	5.6
1992 . .	293,787	21.7	89,370	6.6	74,090	5.5
1993 . .	290,438	21.1	92,821	6.7	76,261	5.5
1994 . .	288,175	20.6	91,555	6.5	75,445	5.4
1995 . .	279,928	19.7	87,205	6.1	78,531	5.5
1996 . .	264,793	18.4	83,547	5.8	79,123	5.5
1997 . .	259,959	17.8	78,077	5.3	78,472	5.4
1998 . .	257,105	17.3	73,456	5.0	80,257	5.4

Expectation of Life (official estimates, years at birth, 1997): Males 72.13; Females 78.10.

Source: partly UN, *Demographic Yearbook*.

ECONOMICALLY ACTIVE POPULATION*
('000 persons aged 15 years and over, October–December)

	1997	1998	1999
Agriculture, hunting, forestry and fishing .	775.9	784.4	780.1
Mining and quarrying . .	87.9	81.8	73.3
Manufacturing . . .	860.8	818.6	775.5
Electricity, gas and water . .	31.1	37.6	28.5
Construction . . .	488.8	448.5	388.6
Trade, restaurants and hotels .	975.9	1,005.5	1,027.2
Transport, storage and communications . . .	401.0	432.7	403.2
Financing, insurance, real estate and business services .	376.5	405.7	390.4
Community, social and personal services . . .	1,382.4	1,417.7	1,537.7
Total employed . . .	**5,380.2**	**5,432.3**	**5,404.5**
Unemployed	303.6	419.2	529.1
Total labour force . . .	**5,683.8**	**5,851.5**	**5,933.6**
Males	3,812.5	3,895.9	3,926.5
Females	1,871.3	1,955.7	2,007.0

* Figures are based on sample surveys, covering 36,000 households, and exclude members of the armed forces. Estimates are made independently, therefore totals are not always the sum of the component parts.

Agriculture

PRINCIPAL CROPS ('000 metric tons)

	1998	1999	2000
Wheat	1,682	1,197	1,500
Rice (paddy)	104	61	113
Barley	115	81	75†
Oats	250	201	260
Maize	943	624	646
Dry beans	55	31	33†
Potatoes	792	995	992†
Sugar beet	3,085	3,100	3,350†
Rapeseed	52	72	50†
Tomatoes*	1,205	1,243	1,267
Pumpkins, etc. . . .	111	100†	100
Onions (dry)	219	263†	282
Watermelons . . .	60	60	63*
Melons†	60	60	62*
Grapes	1,642	1,575	1,650
Apples	1,000	1,165	750
Peaches and nectarines . .	269	310	310*

* FAO estimate(s).   † Unofficial figure.

Source: FAO.

LIVESTOCK ('000 head, year ending September)

	1998	1999	2000
Horses*	600	600	600*
Cattle	4,160	4,134	4,068
Pigs	1,962	2,221	2,465
Sheep	3,754	4,116	4,114
Goats	740*	740*	740*
Chickens*	70,000	70,000	70,000

* FAO estimate(s).

Source: FAO.

LIVESTOCK PRODUCTS ('000 metric tons)

	1998	1999	2000
Beef and veal	256	226	253
Mutton and lamb . . .	11	12	13*
Pig meat	235	244	269
Horse meat	11	11*	11*
Poultry meat	339	344	344
Cows' milk	2,080	2,050	2,160†
Goats' milk*	10	11	10*
Butter	11	12	11*
Cheese	53	53	53
Hen eggs*	95	95	95
Wool: greasy	15	17*	17*

* FAO estimate(s).   † Unofficial figure.

Source: FAO.

Forestry

ROUNDWOOD REMOVALS ('000 cubic metres, excluding bark)

	1996	1997	1998
Sawlogs, veneer logs and logs for sleepers	11,024	12,132	10,313
Pulpwood	7,765	7,063	10,738
Other industrial wood . .	593	375	263
Fuel wood	10,449	10,407	10,356
Total	**29,831**	**29,977**	**31,670**

1999: Annual production as in 1998 (FAO estimates).

Source: FAO, *Yearbook of Forest Products*.

SAWNWOOD PRODUCTION
('000 cubic metres, including railway sleepers)

	1996	1997	1998
Coniferous (softwood) . . .	3,744	4,274	4,222
Broadleaved (hardwood) . . .	396	387	329
Total	**4,140**	**4,661**	**4,551**

1999: Annual production as in 1998 (FAO estimates).

Source: FAO, *Yearbook of Forest Products*.

Fishing

('000 metric tons, live weight)

	1996	1997	1998
Capture	6,691.0	5,811.6	3,265.3
Patagonian grenadier . .	379.0	71.5	354.2
Chilean jack mackerel . .	3,883.3	2,917.1	1,612.9
Araucanian herring . .	446.7	441.2	317.6
Anchoveta (Peruvian anchovy) .	1,400.6	1,757.5	522.7
Chub mackerel . . .	146.6	211.6	71.8
Aquaculture	217.9	272.3	293.0
Atlantic salmon . . .	77.3	96.7	107.1
Total catch	**6,908.9**	**6,083.9**	**3,558.4**

Note: Figures exclude aquatic plants ('000 metric tons): 322.0 (capture 216.8, aquaculture 105.2) in 1996; 281.6 (capture 178.8, aquaculture 102.8) in 1997; 265.9 (capture 197.5, aquaculture 68.4) in 1998. Also excluded are aquatic mammals, recorded by number rather than by weight. The number of South American sea lions caught was: 96 in 1996; 16 in 1997.

Source: FAO, *Yearbook of Fishery Statistics*.

Mining

('000 metric tons, unless otherwise indicated)

	1997	1998	1999
Copper (metal content) . . .	3,511.5	3,757.8	4,421.6
Coal	1,387.2	319.0	513.8
Iron ore*	8,738	9,112	8,345
Calcium carbonate . . .	5,618	5,999	n.a.
Sodium sulphate (metric tons) .	1,335	1,298	n.a.
Zinc—metal content (metric tons) .	34,350	16,066	32,263
Molybdenum—metal content (kilograms)	21,337	25,297	27,269
Manganese (kilograms)† . .	62,750	48,931	40,507
Gold (kilograms) . . .	49,486	44,990	46,668
Silver (metric tons) . . .	1,091.5	1,340.6	1,380.4
Petroleum ('000 cubic metres) . .	489.0	468.7	446.0
Natural gas ('000 cubic metres) .	3,211	3,218	n.a.

* Gross weight. The estimated iron content is 61%.
† Gross weight. The estimated metal content is 32%.

Source: partly Servicio Nacional de Geología y Minería.

Industry

SELECTED PRODUCTS ('000 metric tons, unless otherwise indicated)

	1997	1998	1999
Refined sugar	470	470	434
Beer (million litres) . . .	364	367	333
Soft drinks (million litres) . .	1,195	1,197	1,154
Cigarettes (million) . . .	12,522	12,904	13,174
Non-rubber footwear ('000 pairs) .	7,638	6,777	5,940
Particle board ('000 cu metres) .	315	242	257
Mattresses ('000) . . .	1,131	1,100	1,082
Sulphuric acid	1,864	1,983	2,436
Motor spirit (petrol) . . .	1,972	2,078	2,153
Kerosene and jet fuel . .	814	753	831
Distillate fuel oils . . .	2,937	3,544	3,840
Residual fuel oils . . .	1,663	n.a.	n.a.
Cement	3,191	3,280	2,508
Tyres ('000)	2,509	2,350	2,551
Glass sheets ('000 sq metres) . .	21,075	21,313	21,523
Blister copper	181	165	177
Refined fire copper . . .	125	129	163
Electrolytic copper . . .	1,261	1,437	1,463

Electric Energy: (million kWh): 32,549 in 1997; 34,886 in 1998; 38,019 in 1999.

Finance

CURRENCY AND EXCHANGE RATES

Monetary Units

100 centavos = 1 Chilean peso.

Sterling, Dollar and Euro Equivalents (30 April 2001)

£1 sterling = 858.9 pesos;
US $1 = 599.9 pesos;
€1 = 532.5 pesos;
1,000 Chilean pesos = £1.164 = $1.667 = €1.878.

Average Exchange Rate (pesos per US $)

1998   460.29
1999   508.78
2000   535.47

BUDGET (million pesos)

Revenue	1997	1998	1999
Current revenue	7,342,126	7,713,838	7,741,513
Taxation	6,122,304	6,449,178	6,332,835
Taxes on income, profits and capital gains . . .	1,302,365	1,431,404	1,312,195
Social security contributions .	449,471	496,839	527,042
Domestic taxes on goods and services	3,395,782	3,585,474	3,629,354
Sales or turnover taxes .	2,726,764	2,845,357	2,811,585
Excises	669,018	740,117	817,769
Taxes on international trade and transactions . .	615,723	612,817	535,490
Other taxes	358,962	322,644	328,754
Administrative fees and charges, non-industrial and incidental sales . .	470,910	559,516	650,311
Other current revenue* . .	748,912	705,146	758,367
Capital revenue	24,516	19,223	7,139
Total revenue	7,366,642	7,733,061	7,748,652

Expenditure*	1997	1998	1999
General public services . .	269,235	309,805	340,902
Defence	564,636	633,496	679,392
Public order and safety . .	375,528	428,476	477,136
Education	1,069,653	1,252,143	1,384,085
Health	806,542	917,025	976,662
Social security and welfare .	2,311,247	2,574,210	2,913,285
Housing	351,387	376,728	432,779
Economic services . . .	1,020,972	1,056,790	1,099,923
Interest payments . . .	140,777	233,225	120,712
Sub-total	6,909,976	7,781,898	8,424,877
Less Lending included in expenditure . . .	214,631	205,590	187,890
Total expenditure . . .	6,695,345	7,576,308	8,236,987
Current	5,575,812	6,324,627	6,882,153
Capital	1,119,533	1,251,681	1,354,833

* Excluding net lending.

INTERNATIONAL RESERVES (US $ million at 31 December)

	1998	1999	2000
Gold*	321.9	316.9	318.3
IMF special drawing rights . .	8.3	18.5	24.6
Reserve position in IMF . . .	604.9	411.0	324.2
Foreign exchange . . .	15,049.4	13,977.3	14,380.5
Total	15,984.5	14,723.7	15,047.6

* National valuation.

Source: IMF, *International Financial Statistics.*

MONEY SUPPLY ('000 million pesos at 31 December)

	1998	1999	2000
Currency outside banks . . .	977.3	1,185.6	1,128.6
Demand deposits at commercial banks	1,821.9	2,533.0	2,776.6
Total money (incl. others) . .	2,799.4	3,718.9	3,905.4

Source: IMF, *International Financial Statistics.*

COST OF LIVING

(Consumer Price Index for Santiago; base: 1990 = 100)

	1997	1998	1999
Food (incl. beverages) . . .	222.3	230.6	231.2
Rent, fuel and light . . .	214.3	224.0	229.6
Clothing (incl. footwear) . . .	136.4	130.9	126.8
All items (incl. others) . .	217.8	228.9	236.5

2000: Food 234.4, All items 234.4.

Source: ILO, *Yearbook of Labour Statistics.*

NATIONAL ACCOUNTS

Expenditure on the Gross Domestic Product
('000 million pesos at current prices)

	1998	1999	2000
Government final consumption expenditure	3,770.1	4,126.5	4,601.9
Private final consumption expenditure	22,032.1	22,067.5	23,917.2
Increase in stocks	480.5	78.4	424.2
Gross fixed capital formation	8,744.1	7,521.7	8,429.9
Total domestic expenditure	35,026.8	29,794.1	37,373.2
Exports of goods and services	8,986.4	9,989.3	12,031.0
Less Imports of goods and services	10,382.9	9,360.5	11,629.4
GDP in purchasers' values	33,630.3	30,422.9	37,774.8
GDP at constant 1986 prices	8,153.0	8,059.8	8,493.4

Source: IMF, *International Financial Statistics*.

Gross Domestic Product by Economic Activity
('000 million pesos at constant 1986 prices)

	1997	1998*	1999*
Agriculture and forestry	452.1	465.5	460.0
Fishing	120.0	123.9	126.0
Mining and quarrying	659.3	686.0	801.9
Manufacturing	1,203.6	1,185.5	1,177.5
Electricity, gas and water	177.6	186.2	189.5
Construction	416.9	415.3	374.0
Trade, restaurants and hotels	1,356.4	1,425.9	1,375.4
Transport, storage and communications	644.5	716.7	735.8
Financial services	1,053.6	1,090.9	1,079.8
Real estate, renting and business activities†	253.5	261.6	269.2
Personal services	461.7	476.7	475.0
Public administration	167.4	169.7	172.0
Sub-total	6,966.8	7,203.9	7,236.3
Value-added tax	742.4	773.4	749.9
Import duties	647.3	658.8	551.3
Less Inputed bank service charge	511.3	526.7	516.8
GDP in purchasers' values	7,845.1	8,109.4	8,020.7

* Figures are provisional.
† Including imputed rents of owner-occupied dwellings.

BALANCE OF PAYMENTS (US $ million)

	1997	1998	1999
Exports of goods f.o.b.	16,663	14,831	15,616
Imports of goods f.o.b.	−18,221	−17,347	−13,951
Trade balance	−1,558	−2,516	1,664
Exports of services	4,109	4,122	3,790
Imports of services	−4,063	−4,236	−4,106
Balance on goods and services	−1,512	−2,630	1,348
Other income received	1,086	1,135	1,103
Other income paid	−3,823	−3,107	−2,983
Balance on goods, services and income	−4,249	−4,602	−532
Current transfers received	877	815	793
Current transfers paid	−356	−352	−341
Current balance	−3,728	−4,139	−80
Direct investment abroad	−1,865	−2,798	−4,855
Direct investment from abroad	5,219	4,638	9,221
Portfolio investment assets	−238	−1,420	−2,366
Portfolio investment liabilities	2,603	591	2,496
Other investment assets	−843	−2,546	−6,390
Other investment liabilities	2,479	4,716	1,065
Net errors and omissions	−443	−1,177	151
Overall balance	3,184	−2,135	−758

Source: IMF, *International Financial Statistics*.

External Trade

PRINCIPAL COMMODITIES (distribution by SITC, US $ million)

Imports c.i.f.	1996	1997	1998
Food and live animals	1,026.2	1,024.1	995.9
Mineral fuels, lubricants, etc.	1,847.5	1,818.3	1,506.3
Petroleum, petroleum products, etc.	1,536.1	1,504.5	1,140.4
Crude petroleum oils, etc.	1,158.8	1,131.2	845.2
Chemicals and related products	1,959.4	2,024.6	1,934.4
Artificial resins, plastic materials, etc.	443.4	498.9	439.3
Products of polymerization, etc.	345.0	390.5	333.6
Basic manufactures	2,471.9	2,740.2	2,739.8
Paper, paperboard and manufactures	337.4	387.4	381.2
Textile yarn, fabrics, etc.	500.2	500.8	461.0
Iron and steel	480.9	577.4	605.9
Machinery and transport equipment	7,147.5	7,875.1	7,362.5
Power-generating machinery and equipment	406.7	460.1	413.9
Machinery specialized for particular industries	1,174.2	1,228.8	1,152.1
General industrial machinery, equipment and parts	1,236.4	1,450.1	1,297.5
Office machines and automatic data-processing equipment	530.0	619.2	595.5
Automatic data-processing equipment	369.3	451.3	407.9
Telecommunications and sound equipment	699.2	865.1	1,023.0
Other electrical machinery, apparatus, etc.	710.4	836.7	801.8
Road vehicles and parts*	2,043.4	2,217.7	1,794.8
Passenger motor cars (excl. buses)	862.0	915.2	689.3
Lorries and trucks	663.5	717.0	617.6
Miscellaneous manufactured articles	1,663.2	1,891.5	1,875.6
Clothing and accessories (excl. footwear)	416.4	441.8	468.8
Total (incl. others)	16,810.0	18,110.9	17,082.5

* Data on parts exclude tyres, engines and electrical parts.

Exports f.o.b.	1996	1997	1998
Food and live animals	3,733.6	3,634.7	3,564.4
Fish, crustaceans and molluscs, and preparations thereof	1,042.9	1,216.3	1,244.7
Fish, fresh (live or dead), chilled or frozen	736.2	854.3	920.7
Fish, frozen (excl. fillets)	333.9	397.7	397.5
Vegetables and fruit	1,568.6	1,388.2	1,434.8
Fruit and nuts (excl. oil nuts), fresh or dried	1,083.5	1,006.5	1,066.0
Grapes, fresh or dried	463.8	455.6	440.7
Grapes, fresh	429.4	414.0	403.5
Feeding-stuff for animals (excl. unmilled cereals)	639.3	583.5	371.8
Flours and meals of fish, crustaceans or mulluscs, unfit for human consumption	612.6	555.4	348.9
Beverages and tobacco	319.9	452.1	567.2
Beverages	300.4	439.2	553.9
Alcoholic beverages	297.4	434.4	548.9
Wine of fresh grapes	293.8	424.0	510.5
Crude materials (inedible) except fuels	3,947.5	4,150.9	3,367.8
Cork and wood	619.6	700.3	525.6
Simply worked wood and railway sleepers	332.5	429.7	360.9
Coniferous wood, sawn, etc.	318.1	414.5	344.7
Pulp and waste paper	764.9	690.5	693.8
Chemical wood pulp, soda or sulphate	764.4	689.3	692.4
Metalliferous ores and metal scrap	2,278.2	2,473.9	1,859.4
Copper ores and concentrates (excl. matte)	1,879.5	2,017.7	1,399.5
Chemicals and related products	545.2	762.2	765.1
Inorganic chemicals	253.5	319.8	369.4

Exports f.o.b. — *continued*	1996	1997	1998
Basic manufactures . . .	5,339.3	6,111.9	5,085.3
Non-ferrous metals	4,563.2	5,277.3	4,307.1
Copper	4,401.0	5,142.5	4,162.8
Copper and copper alloys, refined or not, unwrought .	4,263.8	5,019.3	4,068.1
Unrefined copper (incl. blister copper but excl. cement copper) . . .	532.8	370.7	264.7
Refined copper (incl. copper alloys other than master alloys), unwrought . .	3,731.0	4,648.5	3,803.4
Machinery and transport equipment	372.2	428.6	492.0
Miscellaneous manufactured articles	344.8	378.3	371.2
Non-monetary gold (excl. ores and concentrates) . . .	427.6	382.1	275.3
Total (incl. others)	15,406.8	16,678.3	14,841.7

Source: UN, *International Trade Statistics Yearbook*.

1999 (US $ million): *Imports c.i.f.:* 15,137; *Exports f.o.b.:* 15,616. Source: IMF, *International Financial Statistics*.

PRINCIPAL TRADING PARTNERS (US $ million)*

Imports c.i.f.	1996	1997	1998
Argentina	1,634.2	1,837.2	1,900.5
Brazil	1,065.7	1,242.8	1,092.3
Canada	408.1	432.5	494.5
China, People's Republic . .	635.8	721.3	753.1
Colombia	222.4	201.2	176.0
Ecuador	224.9	258.6	149.6
France	582.0	502.1	680.5
Germany	729.9	842.7	811.7
Italy	550.8	699.7	680.3
Japan	949.7	1,054.7	994.6
Korea, Republic	556.8	558.8	545.2
Mexico	927.2	1,076.2	849.9
Spain	530.4	621.1	656.0
Sweden	271.3	352.0	246.7
Taiwan	220.9	225.1	200.2
United Kingdom	281.7	320.2	256.3
USA	4,109.5	4,332.6	4,025.8
Venezuela	313.2	273.4	236.1
Total (incl. others) . . .	16,975.0	18,330.7	17,277.5

Exports f.o.b.	1996	1997	1998
Argentina	699.9	780.9	735.1
Belgium-Luxembourg . . .	247.7	272.6	345.6
Bolivia	207.8	228.5	249.6
Brazil	934.5	957.2	781.2
China, People's Republic . .	467.2	598.1	459.7
Colombia	194.1	227.9	211.2
France	392.8	458.0	443.5
Germany	742.3	747.0	538.4
Italy	475.3	499.5	668.5
Japan	2,495.7	2,675.8	1,959.3
Korea, Republic	864.1	989.7	384.7
Mexico	146.2	376.3	488.5
Netherlands	393.6	423.2	432.6
Peru	321.3	347.8	352.9
Spain	281.8	345.2	275.1
Taiwan	629.1	785.6	525.0
United Kingdom	886.5	1,061.6	1,161.2
USA	2,559.1	2,710.5	2,609.7
Venezuela	141.2	158.3	176.8
Total (incl. others) . . .	15,396.2	17,024.8	14,757.1

* Imports by country of purchase; exports by country of sale.

Transport

PRINCIPAL RAILWAYS

	1997	1998	1999*
Passenger journeys ('000) . .	8,271	9,659	10,008
Passenger-kilometres ('000) . .	551,830	518,226	637,120
Freight ('000 metric tons) . .	18,012	20,634	21,250
Freight ton-kilometres (million) .	2,330	2,650	2,896

* Figures are provisional.

ROAD TRAFFIC (motor vehicles in use)

	1997	1998	1999
Passenger cars (excl. taxis) . .	1,061,122	1,121,262	1,206,986
Buses and coaches (incl. taxis) .	163,946	168,695	173,228
Lorries and vans	585,959	619,086	652,059
Specialized vehicles (incl. tractors)	14,475	14,310	13,714
Motor cycles and mopeds . .	34,051	30,893	31,419

SHIPPING
Merchant Fleet (registered at 31 December)

	1998	1999	2000
Number of vessels	472	472	471
Total displacement ('000 grt) . .	753.0	820.0	842.3

Source: Lloyd's Register of Shipping, *World Fleet Statistics*.

International Sea-borne Shipping (freight traffic, '000 metric tons)

	1997	1998	1999*
Goods loaded	30,126	28,178	31,208
Goods unloaded	18,487	19,193	19,455

* Figures are provisional.

CIVIL AVIATION (traffic on scheduled services)

	1997	1998	1999
Kilometres flown (million) . .	109	139	107
Passengers ('000) . . .	4,693	5,102	5,188
Passenger-km (million) . .	8,597	9,698	10,650
Freight (million ton-km) . . .	1,030	1,248	1,139

Source: Dirección de Aeronaútica Civil.

Tourism

ARRIVALS BY NATIONALITY

	1997	1998	1999
Argentina	754,001	815,601	801,660
Bolivia	127,470	150,895	118,676
Brazil	86,712	83,132	67,751
Germany	39,493	40,073	42,233
Peru	199,785	180,684	122,929
Spain	33,398	35,902	32,831
USA	108,542	127,652	124,044
Total (incl. others) . . .	1,643,640	1,759,279	1,622,252

Tourism receipts (US $ million): 1,019 in 1997; 1,062 in 1998; 894 in 1999.

Sources: World Tourism Organization, *Yearbook of Tourism Statistics*; Servicio Nacional de Turismo.

Communications Media

	1995	1996	1997
Radio receivers ('000 in use) . .	4,950	5,100	5,180
Television receivers ('000 in use) .	3,050	3,100	3,150
Telephones ('000 main lines in use)	1,885	2,248	2,630
Telefax stations (number in use) .	25,000	32,000	40,000
Mobile cellular telephones			
(subscribers)	197,314	335,430	410,000
Book production: titles . .	2,469	n.a.	n.a.
Daily newspapers . . .	56	52	n.a.

Source: mainly UNESCO, *Statistical Yearbook*.

Education*

(1998)

	Students		
	Males	Females	Total
Pre-primary	137,518	132,749	270,267
Primary	1,172,740	1,101,674	2,274,414
Special primary	24,616	15,888	40,504
Secondary	422,280	426,656	848,936
Higher (incl. universities) . .	217,152	185,791	402,943

* Figures are provisional.

Directory

The Constitution

The 1981 Constitution, described as a 'transition to democracy', separated the presidency from the Junta and provided for presidential elections and for the re-establishment of the bicameral legislature, consisting of an upper chamber (Senado) of both elected and appointed Senators, who are to serve an eight-year term, and a lower chamber (Cámara de Diputados) of 120 Deputies elected for a four-year term. All former Presidents are to be Senators for life. There is a National Security Council consisting of the President of the Republic, the heads of the armed forces and the police, and the Presidents of the Supreme Court and the Senado.

In July 1989 a national referendum approved 54 reforms to the Constitution, including 47 proposed by the Government and seven by the Military Junta. Among provisions made within the articles were an increase in the number of directly elected senators from 26 to 38, the abolition of the need for the approval of two successive Congresos for constitutional amendments (the support of two-thirds of the Cámara de Diputados and the Senado being sufficient), the reduction in term of office for the President to be elected in 1989 from eight to four years, with no immediate re-election possible, and the redrafting of the provision that outlawed Marxist groups so as to ensure 'true and responsible political pluralism'. The President's right to dismiss the Congreso and sentence to internal exile were eliminated.

In November 1991 the Congreso approved constitutional changes to local government. The amendments provided for the replacement of centrally appointed local officials with directly elected representatives.

In February 1994 an amendment to the Constitution was approved whereby the length of the presidential term was reduced from eight to six years.

The Government

HEAD OF STATE

President: RICARDO LAGOS ESCOBAR (took office 10 March 2000).

THE CABINET
(August 2001)

A coalition of parties represented in the Concertación de los Partidos de la Democracia (CPD), including the Partido Demócrata Cristiano (PDC), the Partido Socialista de Chile (PS), the Partido Por la Democracia (PPD) and the Partido Radical Socialdemócrata (PRSD).

Minister of the Interior: JOSÉ MIGUEL INSULZA SALINAS (PS).

Minister of Foreign Affairs: MARIA SOLEDAD ALVEAR VALENZUELA (PDC).

Minister of National Defence: MARIO FERNÁNDEZ BAEZA (PDC).

Minister of Finance: NICOLÁS EYZAGUIRRE GUZMÁN (PPD).

Minister, Secretary-General of the Presidency: ALAVARO GARCÍA HURTADO (PPD).

Minister, Secretary-General to the Government: CLAUDIO HUEPE GARCÍA (PDC).

Minister of Economy, Mining and Energy: JOSÉ DE GREGORIO REBECO (PDC).

Minister of Planning and Co-operation: ALEJANDRA KRAUSS VALLE (PDC).

Minister of Education: MARIANA AYLWIN ORYARZÚN (PDC).

Minister of Justice: JOSÉ ANTONIO GÓMEZ URRUTIA (PRSD).

Minister of Labour and Social Security: RICARDO SOLARI SAAVEDRA (PS).

Minister of Public Works, Transport and Telecommunications: CARLOS CRUZ LORENZEN.

Minister of Health: Dr MICHELLE BACHELET JERIA (PS).

Minister of Housing and Urban Planning: JAIME RAVINET DE LA FUENTE (PDC).

Minister of Agriculture: JAIME CAMPOS QUIROGA (PRSD).

Minister of the National Women's Service (Sernam): ADRIANA DELPIANO PUELMA (PS).

MINISTRIES

Ministry of Agriculture: Teatinos 40, Santiago; tel. (2) 696-5698; fax (2) 696-4496; e-mail prensa@minagri.gob.cl; internet www.minagri.gob.cl.

Ministry of Economy, Mining and Energy: Teatinos 120, 10°, Santiago; tel. (2) 672-5522; fax (2) 672-6040.

Ministry of Education: Alameda 1371, 7°, Santiago; tel. (2) 698-3351; fax (2) 688-2300.

Ministry of Finance: Teatinos 120, 12°, Santiago; tel. (2) 675-5800; fax (2) 671-6479.

Ministry of Foreign Affairs: Catedral 1158, Santiago; tel. (2) 679-4200; fax (2) 696-8796.

Ministry of Health: Enrique MacIver 541, 3°, Santiago; tel. (2) 639-4001; fax (2) 633-2405.

Ministry of Housing and Urban Development: Alameda 924, Santiago; tel. (2) 638-3366; fax (2) 633-3892.

Ministry of the Interior: Palacio de la Moneda, Santiago; tel. (2) 690-4000; fax (2) 699-2165.

Ministry of Justice: Morandé 107, Santiago; tel. (2) 674-3100; fax (2) 695-4558.

Ministry of Labour and Social Security: Huérfanos 1273, 6°, Santiago; tel. (2) 695-5133; fax (2) 698-8473; e-mail mintrab@mintrab.gob.cl; internet www.mintrab.gob.cl.

Ministry of National Defence: Villavicencio 364, 22°, Edif. Diego Portales, Santiago; tel. (2) 222-1202; fax (2) 634-5339.

Ministry of the National Women's Service (Sernam): Teatinos 950, 5°, Santiago; tel. (2) 549-6100; fax (2) 549-6248; e-mail clopez@sernam.cl; internet www.mujereschile.cl.

Ministry of Planning and Co-operation (MIDEPLAN): Ahumada 48, 7°, Santiago; tel. (2) 675-1400; fax (2) 672-1879; internet www.mideplan.cl.

Ministry of Public Works: Morandé 59, 2°, Santiago; tel. (2) 361-3000; fax (2) 672-5281.

Ministry of Transport and Telecommunications: Amunátegui 139, 3°, Santiago; tel. (2) 421-3000; fax (2) 672-2785; e-mail mtt@mtt.cl.

Office of the Minister Secretary-General of Government: Palacio de la Moneda, Santiago; tel. (2) 690-4160; fax (2) 697-1756; e-mail cmladini@segegob.cl; internet www.segegob.cl.

Office of the Minister Secretary-General of the Presidency: Palacio de la Moneda, Santiago; tel. (2) 690-4218; fax (2) 690-4329.

President and Legislature

PRESIDENT

Election, 12 December 1999 and 16 January 2000

	% of votes cast, 12 Dec. 1999	% of votes cast, 16 Jan. 2000
RICARDO LAGOS ESCOBAR (CPD) . .	48.0	51.3
JOAQUÍN LAVÍN INFANTE (Alianza por Chile)	47.5	48.7
GLADYS MARÍN MILLIE (PCCh) . .	3.2	—
TOMÁS HIRSCH GOLDSCHMIDT (PH) .	0.5	—
SARA LARRAÍN RUIZ-TAGLIE . .	0.4	—
ARTURO FREI BOLÍVAR (UCCP) . .	0.4	—
Total . . .	100.0	100.0

CONGRESO NACIONAL

Senado*
(Senate)

President: ANDRÉS ZALDÍVAR LARRAÍN (PDC).

General Election, 11 December 1997*

	Valid votes	% of valid votes	Seats
Partido Demócrata Cristiano (PDC)	1,223,495	29.24	10
Unión Demócrata Independiente (UDI)	717,919	17.16	3
Renovación Nacional (RN). . .	620,799	14.84	2
Partido Socialista de Chile (PS)	609,725	14.57	1
Partido Comunista de Chile (PCCh)	352,327	8.42	4
Independents . . .	293,429	7.02	—
Partido por la Democracia (PPD)	180,468	4.31	—
Partido Humanista (PH) . .	92,880	2.22	—
Partido Radical Socialdemócrata (PRSD)	75,680	1.81	—
Unión de Centro-Centro Progresista (UCCP)	17,725	0.42	—
Total	4,184,447	100.00	20

In addition, there were 220,945 blank and 632,538 spoiled votes.

* Results of elections to renew 20 of the 39 elective seats in the Senado. In addition, there are eight (originally nine) designated senators, and a constitutional provision for former Presidents to assume a seat for life, in an *ex-officio* capacity. In March 1998 former President Pinochet assumed a senatorial seat, bringing the total number of senators to 48.

Cámara de Diputados
(Chamber of Deputies)

President: CARLOS MONTES CISTERNA (PS).

General Election, 11 December 1997

	Valid votes	% of valid votes	Seats
Partido Demócrata Cristiano (PDC)	1,317,441	22.98	39
Renovación Nacional (RN). . .	962,247	16.78	23
Unión Demócrata Independiente (UDI)	827,324	14.43	17
Partido por la Democracia (PPD)	719,575	12.55	16
Partido Socialista de Chile (PS)	636,357	11.10	11
Independents . . .	433,210	7.56	8
Partido Comunista de Chile (PCCh)	393,523	6.86	—
Partido Radical Socialdemócrata (PRSD)	179,701	3.13	4
Partido Humanista (PH) . .	166,569	2.91	—
Unión de Centro-Centro Progresista (UCCP) . . .	68,185	1.19	1
Partido Democracia del Sur (PDS)	20,635	0.36	1
Nueva Alianza Popular (NAP). .	8,947	0.16	—
Total	5,733,714	100.00	120

In addition, there were 295,581 blank and 943,235 spoiled votes.

Political Organizations

The most prominent political organizations are:

Partido Comunista de Chile (PCCh): San Pablo 2271, Santiago; tel. (2) 695-4791; fax (2) 695-1150; achieved legal status in October 1990; Pres. GLADYS MARÍN MILLIE.

Partido Democracia Social: San Antonio 220, Of. 604, Santiago; tel. (2) 39-4244; democratic socialist party; Pres. LUIS ANGEL SANTIBÁÑEZ; Sec.-Gen. JAIME CARMONA DONOSO.

***Partido Demócrata Cristiano (PDC):** Alameda B. O'Higgins 1460, 2°, Santiago; tel. (2) 252-7408; fax (2) 697-3465; f. 1957; member of CPD; Pres. GUTENBERG MARTÍNEZ; Vice-Pres. MARÍA ROZAS.

***Partido Democrático de Izquierda ((PDI):** Londres 37, Of. 16, Santiago; tel. and fax (2) 632-144; Pres. LUIS GODOY GÓMEZ.

Partido Humanista (PH): Alameda B. O'Higgins 129, 4°, Santiago; tel. (2) 632-6787; fax (2) 223-9016; internet www.partidohumanista.cl; Pres. CARLOS DONOSO PACHECO; Sec.-Gen. WILFREDO ALFGEN.

Partido Izquierda Cristiana (PIC): Compañia 2404, Santiago; tel. (2) 671-8410; fax (2) 671-7837; e-mail naitun@entelchile.net; Pres. CARLOS DONOSO PACHECO; Sec.-Gen. PATRICIO VÉJAR MERCADO.

***Partido Liberal:** Huelén 102, 2°, Providencia, Santiago; liberal party; tel. (2) 235-3752; fax (2) 264-0792; f. 1998 by dissident centrist politicians; Pres. ADOLFO BALLA.

***Partido Mapu Obrero Campesino:** Eleuterio Ramírez 1463, Santiago; tel. and fax (2) 696-6342; Pres. SAMUEL BELLO SEPÚLVEDA; Sec.-Gen. HUMBERTO SOLAR DÁVILA.

***Partido por la Democracia (PPD):** Erasmo Escala 2154, Santiago; tel. and fax (2) 671-2320; internet www.ppd.cl; Pres. SERGIO BITAR CHACRA; Sec.-Gen. RICARDO BRODSKY BAUDET.

***Partido Radical Socialdemócrata (PRSD):** Miraflores 495, Santiago; tel. (2) 639-4769; fax (2) 639-1053; centre-left; allied to CPD; Pres. ANSELMO SULE CANDIA; Sec.-Gen. PATRICIO MORALES AGUIRRE.

†**Partido Renovación Nacional:** Antonio Varas 454, Providencia, Santiago; tel. (2) 235-2436; fax (2) 244-3966; e-mail rn@carn.cl; internet www.rn.cl; f. 1987; right-wing; Pres. SEBASTIÁN PIÑERA; Sec.-Gen. ALBERTO HAUDÓN DEL RÍO.

Partido Social Demócrata (PSD): París 815, Casilla 50.220, Correo Central, Santiago; tel. (2) 39-9064; f. 1973; Pres. ARTURO VENEGAS GUTIÉRREZ; Sec.-Gen. LEVIÁN MUÑOZ PELLICER.

***Partido Socialista de Chile (PS):** Concha y Toro 36, Santiago; tel. (2) 696-4106; fax (2) 699-5429; e-mail pschile@reuna.cl; f. 1933; left-wing; member of Socialist International; Pres. RICARDO NÚÑEZ MUÑOZ; Sec.-Gen. CAMILO ESCALONA MEDINA.

†**Partido Unión Demócrata Independiente (UDI):** Suecia 286, Santiago; tel. (2) 233-0037; fax (2) 233-6189; e-mail udi@caudi.cl; internet www.udi.cl; f. 1989; right-wing; Pres. PABLO LONGUEIRA MONTES; Sec.-Gen. JUAN ANTONIO COLOMA CORREA.

* **Members of the Concertación de Partidos por la Democracia (CPD):** Londres 57, Santiago; tel. and fax (2) 633-1691; e-mail concert@ctcreuna.cl; f. 1988 as the Comando por el No, an opposition front to campaign against the military regime in the plebiscite of 5 October 1988; name changed to above following plebiscite; Leader RICARDO LAGOS ESCOBAR.

† **Members of the Alianza por Chile:** Santiago; f. 1996 as the Unión por Chile; name changed to above in 1999; right-wing alliance; Leader JOAQUÍN LAVÍN.

Diplomatic Representation

EMBASSIES IN CHILE

Argentina: Miraflores 285, Santiago; tel. (2) 633-1076; fax (2) 639-3321; e-mail embajada.dearg001@chilnet.cl; Ambassador: JOSÉ MARÍA ALVAREZ DE TOLEDO.

Australia: Gertrudis Echeñique 420, Casilla 33, Correo 10, Las Condes, Santiago; tel. (2) 228-5065; fax (2) 208-1707; e-mail cancilau @bellsouth.cl; Ambassador: SUSAN TANNER.

Austria: Barros Errázuriz 1968, 3°, Santiago; tel. (2) 233-4281; fax (2) 204-9382; e-mail santiagodechile@bmaa.gv.at; Ambassador: PETER WILFLING.

Belgium: Providencia 2653, 11°, Of. 1104, Santiago; tel. (2) 232-1070; fax (2) 232-1073; e-mail santiago@diplobel.org; Ambassador: JOHAN BALLEGEER.

Brazil: Alonso Ovalle 1665, Santiago; tel. (2) 672-5000; fax (2) 698-1021; e-mail embrasil@brasembsantiago.cl; Ambassador: GUILHERME LEITE-RIBEIRO.

Bulgaria: Rodolfo Bentjerodt 4895, Santiago; tel. (2) 228-3110; fax (2) 208-0404; e-mail embajada.debul0001@chilnet.cl.

Canada: Nueva Tajamar 481, 12°, Santiago; tel. (2) 362-9660; fax (2) 362-9665; e-mail stago@dfait-maeci.gc.ca; internet www.dfait maeci.gc.ca/santiago; Ambassador: PAUL D. DURAND.

China, People's Republic: Pedro de Valdivia 550, Santiago; tel. (2) 233-9880; fax (2) 234-1129; e-mail em.na@ctcinternet.cl; Ambassador: ZHANG SHAYING.

Colombia: Presidente Errázuriz 3943, Santiago; tel. (2) 206-1314; fax (2) 208-0712; e-mail emcolchi@entelchile.net; Ambassador: RAFAEL PÉREZ M.

Costa Rica: Concepción 65, Of. 801, Santiago; tel. (2) 235-1869; fax (2) 235-1326; e-mail embajada.decas001@chilnet.cl; Ambassador: MARIO GARNIER BORELLA.

Croatia: Jorge VI 306, Santiago; tel. (2) 211-4518, fax (2) 212-4998; e-mail embajada@croatia.cl; Ambassador: IVE LIVLJANIĆ.

Cuba: Los Leones 1346, Providencia, Santiago; tel. (2) 274-5021; fax (2) 274-5708; Ambassador: ARAMÍS FUENTE HERNÁNDEZ.

Czech Republic: Avda El Golf 254, Santiago; tel. (2) 231-1910; fax (2) 232-0707; e-mail santiago@embassy.mzv.cz; Ambassador: JIRI JIRANEK.

Denmark: Jacques Cazotte 5531, Casilla 13430, Vitacura, Santiago; tel. (2) 218-5949; fax (2) 218-1736; e-mail santiago@danish-embassy.cl; Ambassador: BENT KIILERICH.

Dominican Republic: Augusto Leguia Norte 79, Santiago; tel. (2) 245-0667; fax (2) 245-1648; e-mail consulad.odere001@chilnet.cl; Ambassador: RAFAEL VÁLDEZ HICARIO.

Ecuador: Avda Providencia 1979, 5°, Santiago; tel. (2) 231-5073; fax (2) 232-5833; e-mail eecuador@ctc-mundo.cl; Ambassador: JAIME MARCHANT.

Egypt: Roberto del Río 1871, Providencia, Santiago; tel. (2) 274-8881; fax (2) 274-6334; e-mail embajada.deegi001@chilnet.cl; Ambassador: TALAAT SELMY.

El Salvador: Coronel 2330, Of. 51, Santiago; tel. (2) 233-8324; fax (2) 231-0960; e-mail embajada.deels001@chilnet.cl; Ambassador: HUGO CARRILLO CORLETO.

Finland: Alcántara 200, Of. 201, Las Condes, Santiago; tel. (2) 263-4917; fax (2) 263-4701; e-mail embfin@ctc-mundo.net; Ambassador: RISTO KAUPPI.

France: Condeu 65, Providencia, Santiago; tel. (2) 225-1030; fax (2) 274-1353; e-mail ambassade@ambafrance-cl.org; internet www.france.cl; Ambassador: JEAN-MICHEL GAUSSOT.

Germany: Agustinas 785, 7° y 8°, Casilla 9949, Santiago; tel. (2) 463-2500; fax (2) 463-2525; e-mail emb.alemana.stgo@bellsouth.cl; internet www.embajadadealemania.cl; Ambassador: GEORG CLEMENS DICK.

Greece: Isidora Goyenechea 3356, Of. 21; tel. (2) 231-1244; fax (2) 231-1246; e-mail embgrel@chilesat.net; Ambassador DIMITRIOS MANOLÓPOULOS.

Guatemala: Nuncio Sótero Sonz 55, 8°, Santiago; tel. (2) 335-1565; fax (2) 335-1285; e-mail embajada.degua001@chilnet.cl; Ambassador: JOSE MAURICIO RODRÍGUEZ W.

Haiti: Zurich 255, Of. 21, Los Condes, Santiago; tel. (2) 231-8233; fax (2) 231-0967; e-mail embajada.dehai001@chilnet.cl; Ambassador: GUY PIERRE ANDRÉ.

Holy See: Calle Nuncio Sótero Sanz 200, Casilla 16.836, Correo 9, Santiago (Apostolic Nunciature); tel. (2) 231-2020; fax (2) 231-0868; e-mail nunciatu@entelchile.net; Nuncio: Most Rev. LUIGI VENTURA, Titular Archbishop of Equilio.

Honduras: Rosario Sur 269, Santiago; tel. (2) 212-3682; fax (2) 224-1291; e-mail embajada.dehon001@chilnet.cl; Ambassador: ROBERTO MARTÍNEZ ORDÓÑEZ.

Hungary: Avda los Leones 2279, Providencia, Santiago; tel (2) 204-7977; fax (2) 234-1277; e-mail huembstg@entelchile-net; internet www.chilenet.net/huembstg; Ambassador: TAMÁS TÓTH.

India: Triana 871, Casilla 10433, Santiago; tel. (2) 235-2633; fax (2) 235-9607; e-mail embindia@entelchile.net; Ambassador: K. P. ERNEST.

Indonesia: Nueva Costanera 3318, Santiago; tel. (2) 207-6266; fax (2) 207-9901; e-mail embajada.delar003@chilnet.cl; Ambassador: NOOR HANDONO.

Iran: Luis Thayer Ojeda 1955, Santiago; tel. (2) 209-5373; fax (2) 209-5236; e-mail zagro@cmet.net; Chargé d'affaires: SAYED MUHAMMAD HASHEM CALISHEMI.

Israel: San Sebastián 2812, 5°, Casilla 1224, Santiago; tel. (2) 750-0500; fax (2) 750-0555; e-mail eisraelp@rdc.cl; Ambassador: ORI NOY.

Italy: Clemente Fabres 1050, Santiago; tel. (2) 225-9439; fax (2) 223-2467; e-mail italcom@entelchile.net; Ambassador: EMILIO BARBARANI.

Japan: Avda Ricardo Lyon 520, Santiago; tel. (2) 232-1807; fax (2) 232-1812; e-mail embajada.dejap001@chilnet.cl; Ambassador: SHUICHI NOMIYAMA.

Jordan: San Pascual 446, Santiago; tel. (2) 228-8989; fax (2) 228-8783; e-mail embajada.dejor001@chilnet.cl; Ambassador: ATEF HALASA.

Korea, Republic: Alcántara 74, Casilla 1301, Santiago; tel. (2) 228-4214; fax (2) 206-2355; e-mail embajada.decor001@chilnet.cl; Ambassador: CHO YOUNG-HA.

Lebanon: Alianza 1728, Santiago; tel. (2) 232-5027; fax (2) 219-3502; e-mail líbano@netline.cl; Ambassador: MASSOUD MALUF.

Malaysia: Tajamar 183, Of. 1002, Santiago; tel. (2) 233-6698; fax (2) 234-3853; e-mail embajada.demal001@chilnet.cl; Ambassador: LILY ZACHARIAH.

Mexico: Félix de Amesti 128, Santiago; tel. (2) 206-6133; fax (2) 206-6146; e-mail embamex@ia.cl; Ambassador: RAÚL VALDÉS AGUILAR.

Morocco: Los Leones 668, Providencia, Santiago; tel. (2) 366-1050; fax (2) 266-1052; e-mail ambmarch@entelchile.net; Ambassador: ABDELLATIF EL ALOUI.

Netherlands: Las Violetas 2368, Casilla 56-D, Santiago; tel. (2) 223-6825; fax (2) 225-2737; e-mail nlqoustq@holanda-paisesbajos.cl;Ambassador: JOHN C. F. VON MÜHLEN.

New Zealand: Avda Isidora Goyenechea 3516, Casilla 112, Las Condes, Santiago; tel. (2) 231-4204; fax (2) 231-9040; e-maile mbajada.denue001@chilnet.cl; Ambassador: DAVID G. MCKEE.

Nicaragua: El Bosque Norte 0140, Of. 33, Santiago; tel. (2) 231-2034; e-mail embajada.denic001@chilnet.cl; Chargé d'affaires a.i.: MARÍA JOSEFINA LAGOS DE CARDENAL.

Norway: San Sebastián 2839, Of. 509, Casilla 2431, Santiago; tel. (2) 234-2888; fax (2) 234-2201; e-mail ambassade-santiago@ud.dep.telemax.no; Ambassador: MARTIN TORE BJØRNDAL.

Panama: Lota 2257, Of. 203, Santiago; tel. (2) 231-1641; fax (2) 234-4086; e-mail embajada.depan001@chilnet.cl; Ambassador: RICARDO MORENO VILLALAZ.

Paraguay: Huérfanos 886, 5°, Ofs 514-515, Santiago; tel. (2) 639-4640; fax (2) 633-4426; e-mail embajada.delpa001@chilnet.cl; Ambassador: CARLOS VILLAGRA MARSAL.

Peru: Avda Andrés Bello 1751, Providencia, Santiago 9, Casilla 16277, Santiago; tel. (2) 235-2356; fax (2) 235-8139; e-mail embajada.peru@chilnet.cl; Ambassador: JORGE COLUNGE VILLACORTA.

Philippines: Félix de Amesti 367, Santiago; tel. (2) 208-1313; fax (2) 208-1400; e-mail embajada.defil001@chilnet.cl; Ambassador: HERMENEGILDO C. CRUZ.

Poland: Mar del Plata 2055, Santiago; tel. (2) 204-1213; fax (2) 204-9332; e-mail embchile@entelchile.net; Ambassador: DANIEL PASSENT.

Portugal: Nuncio Sótero Sanz 35, 5°, Santiago; tel. (2) 232-3034; fax (2) 231-8809; e-mail embajada.depor001@chilnet.cl; Ambassador: RUI FÉLIX-ALVES.

Romania: Benjamín 2955, Santiago; tel. (2) 231-1893; fax (2) 231-2325; e-mail embajada.derum001@chilnet.cl; Ambassador: VASILE DAN.

Russia: Cristobal Colón 4152, Las Condes, Santiago; tel. (2) 208-3413; fax (2) 206-1386; e-mail embrusia@mcl.cl; internet www.rucl.virtualave.net; Ambassador: ALEXEI G. KVASVOV.

South Africa: Avda 11 de Septiembre 2353, 16°, Torre San Ramón, Santiago; tel. (2) 231-2860; fax (2) 231-3185; e-mail embajada.desud 001@chilnet.cl; Ambassador: C. S. C. VENTER.

Spain: Avda Andrés Bello 1895, Casilla 16456, Providencia, Santiago; tel. (2) 235-2755; fax (2) 236-1547; e-mailembajada.deesp001@chilnet.cl; internet www.embajada-sudafrica.cl; Ambassador: JUAN MANUEL EGEA IBÁÑEZ.

Sweden: 11 de Septiembre 2353, 4°, Santiago; tel. (2) 231-2733; fax (2) 232-4188; e-mail ambassaden.santiago-de-chile@foreign.ministry.se; Ambassador: ARNE RODIN.

Switzerland: Avda Américo Vespucio Sur 100, 14°, Santiago; tel. (2) 263-4211; fax (2) 263-4094; e-mail vertretung@san.rep.admin.ch; Ambassador: HANS-PETER ERISMANN.

Syria: Carmencita 111, Casilla 12, Correo 10, Santiago; tel. (2) 232-7471; Ambassador: HISHAM HALLAJ.

Thailand: Avda Americo Vespucio 100, 15°, Las Condes, Santiago; tel. (2) 263-0710; fax (2) 263-0803; e-mail thaichil@ctcreuna.cl; internet www.rte-chile.thaiembdc.org; Ambassador: BUSBA BUNNAG.

Turkey: Calle Nuncio Sótero Sanz 136, Providencia, Santiago; tel. (2) 233-6066; fax (2) 206-6146; e-mail embajada.delar006@chilnet.cl; Ambassador: SADI CALISLAR.

Ukraine: Los Conquistadores 1700, 28°, Santiago; tel. (2) 334-5689; fax (2) 334-4556.

United Kingdom: Avda el Bosque Norte 0125, Casilla 72 D, Santiago; tel. (2) 370-4100; fax (2) 370-2140; e-mail consulate@santiago.mail.fco.gov.uk; internet www.britemb.cl; Ambassador: L. GREGORY FAULKNER.

USA: Andrés Bello 2800, Las Condes, Santiago; tel. (2) 232-2600; fax (2) 330-3710; internet www.usembassy.cl; Ambassador: JOHN O'LEARY.

Uruguay: Avda Pedro de Valdivia 711, Casilla 2636, Santiago; tel. (2) 204-7988; fax (2) 204-7772; e-mail urusgo@mailnet.rdl.cl; Ambassador: ALFREDO BIANCHI PALAZZO.

Venezuela: Bustos 2021, Santiago; tel. (2) 225-0021; fax (2) 209-9117; e-mail embajada.deven001@chilnet.cl; Ambassador: HÉCTOR VARGAS ACOSTA.

Yugoslavia: Exequías Allende 2370, Providencia, Casilla 16597, Santiago 9; tel. (2) 223-0510; fax (2) 233-9890; e-mail embajada.deyug001@chilnet.cl; Chargé d'affaires: SVETISLAV RAJEVIC.

Judicial System

The Supreme Courts consist of 21 members.

There are Courts of Appeal (in the cities or departments of Arica, Iquique, Antofagasta, Copiapó, La Serena, Valparaíso, Santiago, San Miguel, Rancagua, Talca, Chillán, Concepción, Temuco, Valdivia, Puerto Montt, Coyhaique and Punta Arenas) whose members are appointed from a list submitted to the President of the Republic by the Supreme Court. The number of members of each court varies. Judges of the lower courts are appointed in a similar manner from lists submitted by the Court of Appeal of the district in which the vacancy arises. Judges and Ministers of the Supreme Court do not continue in office beyond the age of 75 years.

In March 1998 a major reform of the judiciary was implemented, including an increase, from 17 to 21, in the number of Ministers of the Supreme Court.

Corte Suprema: Plaza Montt Varas, Santiago; tel. (2) 698-0561; fax (2) 695-2144.

President of the Supreme Court: HERNÁN ALVAREZ GARCÍA.

Ministers of the Supreme Court:

SERVANDO JORDÁN LÓPEZ, OSCAR CARRASCO ACUÑA, ENRIQUE TAPIA WITTING, ELEODORO ORTIZ SEPÚLVEDA, JORGE RODRÍGUEZ ARIZTÍA, LUIS CORREA BULO, GUILLERMO NAVAS BUSTAMANTE, ALBERTO CHAIGNEAU DEL CAMPO, ENRIQUE CURY URZÚA, JOSÉ LUIS PÉREZ ZAÑARTU, OSVALDO FAÚNDEZ VALLEJOS, HUMBERTO ESPEJO ZÚÑIGA, RICARDO GÁLVEZ BLANCO, ORLANDO ALVAREZ HERNÁNDEZ, DOMINGO YURAC SOTO, MARIO GARRIDO MONTT, MARCOS LIBEDINSKY TSCHORNE, URBANO MARÍN VALLEJO, JOSÉ BENQUIS CAMHI, JORGE MEDINA CUEVAS.

Attorney-General: GUILLERMO PIEDRABUENA.

Secretary of the Court: CARLOS A. MENESES PIZARRO.

Corporación Nacional de Reparación y Reconciliación: f. 1992 in order to co-ordinate and implement the recommendations of the **Comisión Nacional de Verdad y Reconciliación,** which was established in 1990 to investigate violations of human rights committed during the military dictatorship, and which delivered its report in 1991; Pres. ALEJANDRO GONZÁLEZ POBLETE; Exec. Sec. ANDRÉS DOMÍNGUEZ VIAL.

Religion

Some 75% of the population are Roman Catholics; there were an estimated 11.3m. adherents at 31 December 1999.

CHRISTIANITY

The Roman Catholic Church

Chile comprises five archdioceses, 17 dioceses, two territorial prelatures and two apostolic vicariates.

Bishops' Conference: Conferencia Episcopal de Chile, Cienfuegos 47, Casilla 517-V, Correo 21, Santiago; tel. (2) 671-7733; fax (2) 698-1416; e-mail sge@cechnet.cl; internet www.cechnet.cl; f. 1955; Pres. Cardinal FRANCISCO JAVIER ERRÁZURIZ OSSA, Archbishop of Santiago de Chile.

Archbishop of Antofagasta: PATRICIO INFANTE ALFONSO, San Martín 2628, Casilla E, Antofagasta; tel. (55) 26-8856; fax (55) 22-3021; e-mail arzoanto@cechnet.cl.

Archbishop of Concepción: ANTONIO MORENO CASAMITJANA, Calle Barros Arana 544, Casilla 65-C, Concepción; tel. (41) 22-8173; fax (41) 23-2844; e-mail arconcep@cechnet.cl.

Archbishop of La Serena: MANUEL DONOSO DONOSO, Los Carrera 450, Casilla 613, La Serena; tel. (51) 21-2325; fax (51) 22-5886; e-mail mdonoso@cechnet.cl.

Archbishop of Puerto Montt:CRISTÍAN CARO CORDERO, Calle Benavente 385, Casilla 17, Puerto Montt; tel. (65) 25-2215; fax (65) 27-1861; e-mail pmontt@cechnet.cl.

Archbishop of Santiago de Chile: Cardinal FRANCISCO JAVIER ERRÁZURIZ OSSA, Erasmo Escala 1884, Casilla 30-D, Santiago; tel. (2) 696-3275; fax (2) 698-9137.

The Anglican Communion

Anglicans in Chile come within the Diocese of Chile, which forms part of the Anglican Church of the Southern Cone of America, covering Argentina, Bolivia, Chile, Paraguay, Peru and Uruguay.

Bishop of Chile: Rt Rev. H. F. ZAVALA M., Iglesia Anglicana, Casilla 50675, Santiago; tel. (2) 639-1509; fax (2) 639-4581; e-mail fzavala@evangel.cl.

Other Christian Churches

Baptist Evangelical Convention: Casilla 41-22, Santiago; tel. (2) 222-4085; fax (2) 635-4104; f. 1908; Pres. MOISÉS PINTO; Gen. Sec. VÍCTOR OLIVARES.

Evangelical Lutheran Church: Pedro de Valdivia 3420-H, Depto 33, Nuñoa, Casilla 15167, Santiago; tel. (2) 225-0091; fax (2) 205-2193; f. 1937 as German Evangelical Church in Chile; present name adopted in 1959; Pres. MARTIN JUNGE; 2,500 mems.

Jehovah's Witnesses: Avda Concha y Toro 3456, Puente Alto; tel. (2) 288-1264; fax (2) 288-1257; Dir PEDRO J. LOVATO GROSSO.

Methodist Church: Sargento Aldea 1041, Casilla 67, Santiago; tel. (2) 556-6074; fax (2) 554-1763; autonomous since 1969; 7,317 mems; Bishop NEFTALÍ ARAVENA BRAVO.

Orthodox Chruch of the Patriarch of Antioch: Avda Perú 502, Recoleta, Santiago; tel. and fax (2) 737-4697; Archbishop Mons. SERGIO ABAD.

Pentecostal Church: Calle Pena 1103, Casilla de Correo 2, Curicó; tel. (75) 1035; f. 1945; 90,000 mems; Bishop ENRIQUE CHÁVEZ CAMPOS.

Pentecostal Church Mission: Calle Passy 032, Casilla 238, Santiago; tel. (2) 634-6785; fax (2) 634-6786; f. 1952; Sec. Rev. DANIEL GODOY FERNÁNDEZ; Pres. Rev. ERASMO FARFÁN FIGUEROA; 12,000 mems.

JUDAISM

Comité Representativo de las Entidades Judías en Chile (CREJ): Ricardo Lyon 812, Providencia, Santiago; tel. (2) 274-7101; fax (2) 269-7005; Pres. ELIMAT Y. JASON.

Comunidad Israelita Sefardi de Chile: Ricardo Lyon 812, Providencia, Santiago; tel. (2) 209-8086; fax (2) 204-7382; Pres. SALOMON CAMHI AVAYU; Rabbi IOSEF GABAY.

ISLAM

Sociedad Unión Musulmana: Mezquita As-Salam, Campoamor 2975, esq. Chile-España, Ñuñoa, Santiago; tel. (2) 343-1376; fax (2) 343-11378; Pres. OUSAMA ABUGHAZALÉ.

BAHÁ'Í FAITH

National Spiritual Assembly: Casilla 3731, Manuel de Salas 356, Ñuñoa, Santiago; tel. (2) 269-2005; fax (2) 225-8276; e-mail nsachile@chileat.net; internet www.bci.ord/nsachile; Co-ordinator ROBERTO JARA B.

The Press

Most newspapers of nation-wide circulation in Chile are published in Santiago.

DAILIES

Circulation figures listed below are supplied mainly by the Asociación Nacional de la Prensa. Other sources give much lower figures.

Santiago

La Cuarta: Diagonal Vicuña Mackenna 2004, Santiago; tel. (2) 555-0034; fax (2) 556-8727; morning; Gen. Man. JUAN CARLOS LARRAÍN WORMALD.

El Diario: San Crescente 81, 3°, Las Condes, Santiago; tel. (2) 339-1000; fax (2) 231-3340; e-mail buzon@eldiario; internet www.eldiario.cl; f. 1988; morning; Gen. Man. JOSÉ MIGUEL RESPALDIZA CHICHARNO; circ. 20,000.

Diario Oficial de la República de Chile: Agustinas 1269, Santiago; tel. (2) 695-5500; fax (2) 698-2222; internet www.diarioficial.cl; f. 1877; Dir FLORENCIO CEBALLOS B.; circ. 10,000.

Estrategia: Rafael Cañas 114, Providencia, Santiago; tel. (2) 252-4000; fax (2) 236-1114; e-mail estrategia@reuna.cl; internet www.reuna.estrategia.cl; f. 1978; morning; Dir VÍCTOR MAÑUEL O. MÉNDEZ.

El Mercurio: Avda Santa María 5542, Casilla 13-D, Santiago; tel. (2) 330-1111; fax (2) 228-9042; e-mail mercurio@mercurio.cl; internet www.emol.com; f. 1827; morning; conservative; Gen. Man. FERNANDO CISTERNAS BRAVO; circ. 120,000 (weekdays), 280,000 (Sun.).

La Nación: Agustinas 1269, Casilla 81-D, Santiago; tel. (2) 787-0100; fax (2) 698-1059; f. 1917 to replace govt-subsidized *El Cronista*; morning; financial; Propr Soc. Periodística La Nación; Dir GUILLERMO HORMAZÁBAL SALGADO; circ. 45,000.

La Segunda: Avda Santa María 5542, Casilla 13-D, Santiago; tel. (2) 330-1111; fax (2) 228-9289; internet www.lasegunda.com; f. 1931; evening; Dir CRISTIÁN ZEGERS ARIZTÍA; circ. 40,000.

La Tercera: Vicuña Mackenna 1870, Santiago; tel. (2) 551-7067; fax (2) 550-7999; e-mail latercera@copesa.cl; internet www.latercera.cl; f. 1950; morning; Dir FERNANDO PAULSEN; circ. 200,000.

Las Ultimas Noticias: Bellavista 0112, Providencia, Santiago; tel. (2) 730-3000; fax (2) 730-3331; f. 1902; morning; Gen. Man. JUAN ENRIQUE CANALES BESA; owned by the Proprs of *El Mercurio*; circ. 150,000 (except Sat. and Sun.).

Antofagasta

La Estrella del Norte: Manuel Antonio Matta 2112, Antofagasta; tel. (55) 26-4835; f. 1966; evening; Dir CAUPOLICÁN MÁRQUEZ VERGARA; circ. 5,000.

El Mercurio: Manuel Antonio Matta 2112, Antofagasta; tel. (55) 26-4815; fax (55) 25-1710; f. 1906; morning; conservative independent; Proprs Soc. Chilena de Publicaciones; Dir ROBERTO RETAMAL PACHECO; circ. 9,000.

Arica

La Estrella de Arica: San Marcos 580, Arica; tel. (58) 22-5024; fax (58) 25-2890; f. 1976; Dir REINALDO NEIRA RUIZ; circ. 10,000.

Atacama

Chañarcillo: Los Carrera 801, Chañaral, Atacama; tel. (52) 21-9044; f. 1992; morning; Dir LUIS CERPA HIDALGO.

Calama

El Mercurio: Sotomayor 2025, Calama; tel. (56) 25-1090; f. 1968; Propr Soc. Chilena de Publicaciones; Dir ROBERTO RETAMAL PACHECO; circ. 4,500 (weekdays), 7,000 (Sun.).

Chillán

La Discusión de Chillán, SA: Calle 18 de Septiembre 721, Casilla 479, Chillán; tel. (42) 21-2650; fax (42) 21-3578; e-mail ladiscu@ctcreuna.cl; f. 1870; morning; independent; Dir TITO CASTILLO PERALTA; circ. 5,000.

Concepción

El Sur: Calle Freire 799, Casilla 8-C, Concepción; tel. (41) 23-5825; f. 1882; morning; independent; Dir RAFAEL MAIRA LAMAS; circ. 28,000 (weekdays), 45,000 (Sun.).

Copiapó

Atacama: Manuel Rodríguez 740, Copiapó; tel. (52) 2255; morning; independent; Dir SAMUEL SALGADO; circ. 6,500.

Coyhaique

El Diario de Aisén: 21 de Mayo 410, Coyhaique; tel. (67) 234-850; fax (67) 232-318; Dir ALDO MARCHESSE COMPODÓNICO.

Curicó

La Prensa: Merced 373, Casilla 6-D, Curicó; tel. (75) 31-0453; fax (75) 31-1924; e-mail laprensa@entelchile.net; internetdiariolaprensa.cl; f. 1898; morning; right-wing; Man. Dir MANUEL MASSA MAUTINO; circ. 4,000.

Iquique

La Estrella de Iquique: Luis Uribe 452, Iquique; tel. (57) 42-2805; fax (57) 42-7975; f. 1966; evening; Dir ARCADIO CASTILLO ORTÍZ; circ. 10,000.

El Nortino: Baquedano 1470, Iquique; tel. (57) 41-6666; fax (57) 41-2997; e-mail nortino@entelchile.net; f. 1992; morning; Dir-Gen. REYNALDO BERRÍOS GONZÁLEZ.

La Serena

El Día: Brasil 431, La Serena; tel. (51) 22-2863; fax (51) 22-2844; f. 1944; morning; Dir ANTONIO PUGA RODRÍGUEZ; circ. 10,800.

Los Angeles

La Tribuna: Calle Colo Colo 464, Casilla 15-D, Los Angeles; tel. (43) 31-3315; fax (43) 31-1040; independent; Dir CIRILO GUZMÁN DE LA FUENTE; circ. 4,500.

Osorno

El Diario Austral: Avda B. O'Higgins 870, Osorno; tel. (64) 23-5191; fax (64) 23-5192; f. 1982; Dir CARLOS NOLI A.; circ. 6,500 (weekdays), 7,300 (Sun.).

Ovalle

El Ovallino: Victoria 323-B, Ovalle; tel. and fax (53) 627-557; Dir JORGE CONTADOR ARAYA.

Puerto Montt

El Llanquíhue: Antonio Varas 167, Puerto Montt; tel. (65) 25-5115; fax (65) 432-401; e-mail ellanquihue@123click.cl; f. 1885; Dir ERNESTO MONTALBA; circ. 4,800 (weekdays), 5,700 (Sun.).

Punta Arenas

La Prensa Austral: Waldo Seguel 636, Casilla 9-D, Punta Arenas; tel. (61) 24-3166; fax (61) 24-7406; e-mail prensa@webcom.com; internet www.prensaaustral.com; f. 1941; morning; independent; Dir MANUEL GONZÁLEZ ARAYA; circ. 10,000, Sunday (*El Magallanes*; f. 1894) 12,000.

Quillota

El Observador: La Concepción 277, Casilla 1-D, Quillota; tel. (33) 312-096; fax (33) 311-417; Dir ROBERTO SILVA BIJIT.

Rancagua

El Rancagüino: O'Carroll 518, Rancagua; tel. (72) 23-0345; fax (72) 22-1483; f. 1915; independent; Dirs HÉCTOR GONZÁLEZ, ALEJANDRO GONZÁLEZ; circ. 10,000.

Talca

El Centro: Tres Oriente 798, Talca; tel. (71) 22-0946; fax (71) 22-0924; f. 1989; Gen. Man. HUGO SAAVEDRA OTEIZA.

Temuco

El Diario Austral: Antonio Varas 945, Casilla 1-D, Temuco; tel. (45) 21-2575; fax (45) 23-9189; f. 1916; morning; commercial, industrial and agricultural interests; Dir MARCO ANTONIO PINTO ZEPEDA; Propr Soc. Periodística Araucanía, SA; circ. 15,100 (weekdays), 23,500 (Sun.).

Tocopilla

La Prensa de Tocopilla: Bolívar 1244, Tocopilla; tel. (83) 81-3036; f. 1924; morning; independent; Gen. Man. JORGE LEIVA CONCHA; circ. 3,000.

Valdivia

El Diario Austral: Yungay 499, Valdivia; tel. (63) 21-3353; fax (63) 21-2236; f. 1982; Dir GUSTAVO SERRANO COTAPOS; circ. 5,600.

Valparaíso

La Estrella: Esmeralda 1002, Casilla 57-V, Valparaíso; tel. (32) 26-4230; fax (32) 26-4241; e-mail estrell@entelchile.net; f. 1921; evening; independent; Dir ALFONSO CASTAGNETO; owned by the Proprs of *El Mercurio*; circ. 28,000 (weekdays), 35,000 (Sat.).

El Mercurio: Esmeralda 1002, Casilla 57-V, Valparaíso; tel. (32) 25-8011; fax (32) 21-8287; f. 1827; morning; Dir ENRIQUE SCHRÖDER VICUÑA; owned by the Proprs of *El Mercurio* in Santiago; circ. 65,000.

Viña del Mar

El Expreso: 3 Poniente 61, Casilla 617, Viñar del Mar; tel. (32) 972-020; fax (32) 972-217; e-mail editor@entelchile.net; internet www.imaginativa.cl/expreso; Man. Dir ENRIQUE ALVARADO AGUILERA.

PERIODICALS

Santiago

Apsi: Gen. Alberto Reyes 032, Providencia, Casilla 9896, Santiago; tel. (2) 77-5450; f. 1976; fortnightly; Dir MARCELO CONTRERAS NIETO; circ. 30,000.

La Bicicleta: José Fagnano 614, Santiago; tel. (2) 222-3969; satirical; Dir ANTONIO DE LA FUENTE.

CA (Ciudad/Arquitectura) Revista Oficial del Colegio de Arquitectos de Chile AG: Manuel Montt 515, Santiago; tel. (2) 235-3368; fax (2) 235-8403; f. 1964; 4 a year; architects' magazine; Editor Arq. JAIME MÁRQUEZ ROJAS; circ. 3,500.

Carola: San Francisco 116, Casilla 1858, Santiago; tel. (2) 33-6433; fortnightly; women's magazine; published by Editorial Antártica, SA; Dir ISABEL MARGARITA AGUIRRE DE MAINO.

Cauce: Huérfanos 713, Of. 604–60, Santiago; tel. (2) 38-2304; fortnightly; political, economic and cultural affairs; Dir ANGEL FLISFICH; circ. 10,000.

Chile Agrícola: Teresa Vial 1170, Casilla 2, Correo 13, Santiago; tel. and fax (2) 522-2627; e-mail chileagric@chile.com; f. 1975; 6 per year; farming; Dir Ing. Agr. RAÚL GONZÁLEZ VALENZUELA; circ. 10,000.

Chile Forestal: Avda Bulnes 259, Of. 406, Santiago; tel. (2) 671-1850; fax (2) 696-6724; f. 1974; monthly; technical information and features on forestry sector; Dir MARIELA ESPEJO SUAZO; circ. 4,000.

Cosas: Almirante Pastene 329, Providencia, Santiago; tel. (2) 364-5100; fax (2) 235-8331; f. 1976; fortnightly; international affairs; Dir MÓNICA COMANDARI KAISER; circ. 40,000.

Creces: Manuel Montt 1922, Santiago; tel. (2) 223-4337; monthly; science and technology; Dir SERGIO PRENAFETA; circ. 12,000.

Deporte Total: Santiago; tel. (2) 251-6236; fax (2) 204-7420; f. 1981; weekly; sport, illustrated; Dir JUAN IGNACIO OTO LARIOS; circ. 25,000.

Economía y Sociedad: MacIver 125, 10°, Santiago; tel. (2) 33-1034; Dir José Piñera; circ. 10,000.

Ercilla: Luis Thayer Ojeda 1626, Providencia, Santiago; tel. (2) 251-6236; f. 1936; weekly; general interest; Dir Joaquín González; circ. 28,000.

Gestión: Luis Carrera 1289, Vitacura, Santiago; tel. (2) 655-6100; fax (2) 655-6408; internet www.estrategia.cl/gestion.htm; f. 1975; monthly; business matters; Dir Víctor Manuel Ojeda Méndez; circ. 38,000.

Hoy: María Luisa Santander 0436, Clasificador 654, Correo Central, Santiago; tel. (2) 225-6926; fax (2) 225-4669; e-mail hoy@mail net.rdc.cl; internet www.reuna.cl/hoy; f. 1977; weekly; general interest; Dir Ascanio Cavallo Castro; circ. 30,000.

Internet: Avda Carlos Valdovinos 251; tel. (2) 552-5599; e-mail director@interra.cl; monthly; internet and new technology; Dir Florencio Uteras.

Jurídica del Trabajo: Avda Bulnes 180, Of. 80, Casilla 9447, Santiago; tel. (2) 696-7474; fax (2) 672-6320; f. 1930; 10 a year; Editor Iván K. Hernández; circ. 1,000.

Mensaje: Almirante Barroso 24, Casilla 10445, Santiago; tel. (2) 696-0653; fax (2) 698-0617; e-mail mensaje@interaccess.cl; internet www.mensaje.cl; f. 1951; monthly; national, church and international affairs; Dir Antonio Delfau; circ. 7,000.

Microbyte: Avda Condell 1879, Ñuñoa, Santiago; tel. (2) 341-7507; fax (2) 341-7504; f. 1984; monthly; computer science; Dir José Kaffman; circ. 6,000.

News Review: Casilla 151/9, Santiago; tel. (2) 236-9511; fax (2) 236-0887; e-mail newsrevi@netline.cl; f. 1991; weekly; English language news; Dir Graham A. Wigg.

Paula: Avda Santa María 0120, Providencia,, Santiago; tel. (2) 200-0585; fax (2) 200-0490; e-mail revpaula@paula.cl; 1967; monthly; women's interest; Dir Paula Recart; circ. 85,000.

Punto Final: San Diego 31, Of. 606, Casilla 13954, Correo 21, Santiago; tel. (2) 697-0615; e-mail punto@interaccess.cl; internet www.puntofinal.cl; f. 1965; fortnightly; politics; left-wing; Dir Manuel Cabieses; circ. 15,000.

¿Qué Pasa?: Vicuña Mackenna 1870, Ñuñoa, Santiago; tel. (2) 551-7067; fax (2) 550-7529; f. 1971; weekly; general interest; Dir Bernadita del Solar Vera; circ. 30,000.

El Siglo: Diagonal Paraguay 458, Casilla 13479, Santiago; tel.and fax (2) 633-0074; f. 1989; fortnightly; published by the Communist Party of Chile (PCCh); Dir Claudio Denegri Quintana.

Super Rock: Luis Thayer Ojeda 1626, Casilla 3092, Providencia, Santiago; tel. (2) 74-8231. 1985; weekly; Latin and European rock music, illustrated; Dir Darío Rojas Morales; circ. 40,000.

The Clinic: Las Claras 195, Providencia, Santiago; tel. (2) 343-5850; fax (2) 343-4088; e-mail theclinic@bigfoot.com; forthnightly; political and social satire; Dir Patricio Fernández.

Vea: Luis Thayer Ojeda 1626, Casilla 3092, Providencia, Santiago; tel. (2) 74-9421. 1939; weekly; general interest, illustrated; Dir Darío Rojas Morales; circ. 150,000.

PRESS ASSOCIATION

Asociación Nacional de la Prensa: Agustinas 1357, 12°, Santiago; tel. (2) 696-6431; fax (2) 698-7699; Pres. Carlos Paul Lamas; Sec. Fernando Silva Vargas.

NEWS AGENCIES

Agencia Chile Noticias (ACN): Dr Pedro Lautaro 2048, Providencia, Santiago; tel. (2) 209-2640; fax (2) 341-4336; e-mail chilenoti cias@entelchile.com; internet www.chilenoticias.cl; Dir Norberto Parra Hidalgo.

Chile Information Project (CHIP): Avda Santa María 227, Recoleta, Santiago; tel. (2) 777-5376; e-mail anderson@chip.mic.cl; internet www.santiagotimes.cl; English language; Dir Stephen J. Anderson.

Europa Press: Biarritz 1913, Providencia, Santiago; tel. and fax (2) 274-3552; e-mail europapress@rdc.cl; Dir José Ríos Vial.

Orbe Servicios Informativos, SA: Phillips 56, 6°, Of. 66, Santiago; tel. (2) 39-4774; Dir Sebastiano Bertolone Galletti.

Foreign Bureaux

Agence France-Presse (France): Avda B. O'Higgins 1316, 9°, Apt. 92, Santiago; tel. (2) 696-0559; Correspondent Humberto Zumarán Araya.

Agencia EFE (Spain): Coronel Santiago Bueras 188, Santiago; tel. (2) 638-0179; fax (2) 633-6130; e-mail direccion@agenciaefe.tie.cl; internet www.efe.es; f. 1966; Bureau Chief Mn Manuel Fuentes García.

Agenzia Nazionale Stampa Associata (ANSA) (Italy): Moneda 1040, Of. 702, Santiago; tel. (2) 698-5811; fax (2) 698-3447; f. 1945; Bureau Chief Giorgio Bagoni Bettollini.

Associated Press (AP) (USA): Tenderini 85, 10°, Of. 100, Casilla 2653, Santiago; tel. (2) 33-5015; Bureau Chief Kevin Noblet.

Bloomberg News (USA): Miraflores 222, Santiago; tel. (2) 638-6820; fax (2) 698-3447; Dir Mike Smith.

Deutsche Presse-Agentur (dpa) (Germany): San Antonio 427, Of. 306, Santiago; tel. (2) 639-3633; Correspondent Carlos Dorat.

Inter Press Service (IPS) (Italy): Santiago; tel. (2) 39-7091; Dir and Correspondent Gustavo González Rodríguez.

Prensa Latina (Cuba): Bombero Ossa 1010, Of. 1104, Santiago; tel. (2) 671-8222; fax (2) 695-8605; Correspondent Lidia Señaris Cejas.

Reuters (United Kingdom): Neuva York 33, 11°, Casilla 4248, Santiago; tel. (2) 672-8800; fax (2) 696-0161; Correspondent Roger Atwood.

United Press International (UPI) (USA): Nataniel 47, 9°, Casilla 71-D, Santiago; tel. (2) 696-0162; fax (2) 698-6605; Bureau Chief Fernando Lepé.

Xinhua (New China) News Agency (People's Republic of China): Biarritz 1981, Providencia, Santiago; tel. (2) 25-5033; Correspondent Sun Kuoguowein.

Association

Asociación de Corresponsales de la Prensa Extranjera en Chile: Coronel Santiago Bueras 188, Santiago; tel. (2) 632-1890; fax (2) 633-6130; Pres. Omar Ruz.

Publishers

Distribuidora Molino, SA: Abtao 574, Santiago; tel. (2) 776-2295; fax (2) 776-6425; e-mail distribuidoramolino@chilnet.cl; internet www.chilnet.cl/distmolino; Admin. Man. Jorge Vargas Araya.

Ediciones y Comunicaciones Ltda: Luis Thayer Ojeda 0115, Santiago; tel. (2) 232-1241; fax (2) 234-9467; e-mail edicom@chil net.cl; internet www.chilnet.cl/edicom/; publs include *Anuario Farmacológico*; Gen. Man. Mario Silva Martínez.

Ediciones San Pablo: Vicuña MacKenna 10777, Casilla 3746, Santiago; tel. (2) 288-2025; fax (2) 288-2026; e-mail dgraledi@ cnet.net; Catholic texts; Dir-Gen. P. Luis Neira Ramírez.

Ediciones Técnicas Ltda: Matilde Salamanca 736, 6°, Santiago; tel. (2) 209-8100; fax (2) 209-8101; e-mail editec@editec.cl; internet www.editec.cl; Pres. Ricardo Cortes Donoso; Gen. Man. Roly Solis Sepúlveda.

Ediciones Universidad Católica de Valparaíso: Universidad Católica de Valparaíso, 12 de Febrero 187, Casilla 1415, Valparaíso; tel. (32) 25-3087; fax (32) 27-3429; also Moneda 673, 8°, Santiago; tel. (2) 633-2230; f. 1970; general literature, social sciences, engineering, education, music, arts, textbooks; Gen. Man. Karlheinz Laage H.

Editora Nacional Gabriel Mistral Ltda: Santiago; tel. (2) 77-9522; literature, history, philosophy, religion, art, education; government-owned; Man. Dir José Harrison de la Barra.

Editorial Andrés Bello/Jurídica de Chile: Avda Ricardo Lyon 946, Casilla 4256, Providencia, Santiago; tel. (2) 204-9900; fax (2) 225-3600; e-mail mmallea@entelchile.net; internet www.juridicade chile.com; f. 1947; history, arts, literature, politics, economics, textbooks, law and social science; Gen. Man. Julio Serrano Lamas.

Editorial Antártica, SA: San Francisco 116, Santiago; tel. (2) 639-4650; fax (2) 633-4475; f. 1978; Gen. Man. Hernán Aguirre Mackay.

Editorial Cuatro Vientos Ltda: Errázuriz 3293, Nuñoa, Santiago; tel. (2) 225-5343; fax (2) 341-3107; e-mail 4vientos@netline.cl; internet www.cuatrovientos.net; Man. Editor Juan Francisco Huneeus Cox.

Editorial El Sembrador: Sargento Aldea 1041, Casilla 2037, Santiago; tel. (2) 556-9454; Dir Isaías Gutiérrez.

Editorial Evolución, SA: General del Canto 105, Of. 707, Santiago; tel. (2) 236-4789; fax (2) 236-4796; e-mail evoluc@entelchile.net; internet www.evolucion.cl.

Editorial Nascimento, SA: Chiloé 1433, Casilla 2298, Santiago; tel. (2) 555-0254; f. 1898; general; Man. Dir Carlos George Nascimento Márquez.

Editorial Renacimiento: Huérfanos 623, Santiago; tel. (2) 639-6621; fax (2) 633-9374; internet www.feriachilenodellibro.cl; Gen. Man. Alberto Aldea.

Editorial San Lucas Ltda: Guardia Vieja 293, Of. 201, Santiago; tel. (2) 334-1583; fax (2) 233-2457; e-mail sanlucas@chilesat.net; internet www.muyinteresante.com/; Gen. Man. Christian Middleton O.

Editorial Terra Chile: Ernesto Pinto Lagarrigue 156-H, Recoleta, Santiago; tel. (2) 737-4455; fax (2) 738-0445; Gen. Man. Orlando Milesi.

Editorial Texido: Manuel Antonio Tocornal 1487, Santiago; tel. (2) 555-5534; fax (2) 555-5466; Gen. Man. ELSA ZLATER.

Editorial Tiempo Presente Ltda: Almirante Pastene 329, Providencia, Santiago; tel. (2) 364-5100; fax (2) 235-8331; e-mail cosas@mailnet.rdc.cl; internet www.cosas.com; Gen. Man. JUAN LUIS SOMMERS.

Editorial Trineo, SA: Los Olmos 3685, Macul, Santiago; tel. (2) 272-5945; fax (2) 272-0212; e-mail triven@crnet.net; internet www.cmet.net/trineo/; Gen. Man. CARLOS JÉREZ HERNÁNDEZ.

Editorial Universitaria, SA: María Luisa Santander 0447, Casilla 10220, Providencia, Santiago; tel. (2) 223-4555; fax (2) 209-9455; e-mail edituniv@reuna.cl; f. 1947; general literature, social science, technical, textbooks; Man. Dir EDUARDO CASTRO.

Empresa Editora Zig-Zag SA: Los Conquistadores 1700, 17°-B, Providencia, Santiago; tel. (2) 335-7477; fax (2) 335-7445; e-mail zigzag@zigzag.cl; f. 1934; general publishers of literary works, reference books and magazines; Pres. GONZALO VIAL C.; Gen. Man. FRANCISCO PÉREZ FRUGONE.

McGraw-Hill/Interamericana de Chile Ltda: Avda Seminario 541, Santiago; tel;. (2) 222-9405; (2) 635-4467; e-mail mcgrawhill .int001@chilnet.cl; internet www.bookshop.co.uk.

Publicaciones Técnicas, SA (PUBLITECSA): Serrano 172, Santiago; tel. (2) 365-8000; fax (2) 365-8010; e-mail acliente@publitecsa.cl; internet www.publitecsa.cl/; Commercial Man. CARLOS MUNIZAGA.

Red Internacional del Libro Ltda: Avda Eliodoro Yáñez 1934, Of. 14, Santiago; tel. (2) 223-8100; fax (2) 225-4269; e-mail redil@interactiva.cl; internet www.riledutores.cl; Commercial Man. ELEONORA FINKELSTEIN.

PUBLISHERS' ASSOCIATION

Cámara Chilena del Libro AG: Avda B. O'Higgins 1370, Of. 502, Casilla 13526, Santiago; tel. (2) 672-0348; fax (2) 687-4271; e-mail camlibro@terra.cl; internet www.camilbro.cl; Pres. EDUARDO CASTILLO GARCÍA; Exec. Sec. RAQUEL TORNERO GÓMEZ.

Broadcasting and Communications

TELECOMMUNICATIONS

Regulatory Authority

Subsecretaría de Telecomunicaciones (Department of Telecommunications, Ministry of Public Works, Transport and Telecommunications): Amunátegui 139, 5°, Casilla 120, Correo 21, Santiago; tel. (2) 672-6502; fax (2) 421-3553; e-mail subtel@subtel.cl; Under-Sec. CHRISTIAN NICOLAI ORELLANA.

Major Operators

Alcatel de Chile: Monseñor Sótero Sanz 55, 3°, Providencia, Santiago; tel. (2) 230-3000; fax (2) 231-1862; internet www.alcatel.com; Pres. SERGE TCHURUK; Gen. Man. MARCEL MAFILLE.

AT Chile: Vitacura 2939, 8° y 9°, Vitacura, Santiago; tel. (2) 380-0171; fax (2) 382-5142; e-mail info@firstcom.cl; internet www.attla.cl; Pres. PATRICIO NORTHLAND; Gen. Man. CARLOS FERNÁNDEZ.

Chilesat: Rinconada El Salto 202, Huechuraba, Santiago; tel. (2) 380-0171; fax (2) 382-5142; e-mail tlchile@chilesat.net; internet www.chilesat.net; Pres. JUAN EDUARDO IBÁÑEZ; Gen. Man. RAMÓN VALDIVIESO.

CMET Compañía de Telefónos: Avda Los Leones 1412, Providencia, Santiago; tel. (2) 251-333; fax (2) 274-9573; Pres. JULIO YUBERO; Gen. Man. AGUSTIN CASTELLON.

Empresa Nacional de Telecomunicaciones, SA—ENTEL Chile, SA: Andrés Bello 2687, 14°, Casilla 4254, Santiago; tel. (2) 360-0123; fax (2) 661-7299; internet www.entel.cl; f. 1964; operates the Chilean land satellite stations of Longovilo, Punta Arenas and Coihaique, linked to INTELSAT system; 52% owned by Telecom Italia; Pres. JUAN HURTADO.

PTT Comunicaciones: Marín 0193, Providencia, Santiago; tel. (2) 665-1000; fax (2) 665-1004; e-mail pttsa@ctinternet.cl; internet wwww.pttsa.com; Gen. Man. JAVIER MOLINOS.

Telefónica Chile: Apoquindo 4499, 10°, Casilla 16-D, Santiago; tel. (2) 691-2020; fax (2) 691-2009; formerly Compañía de Telecomunicaicones de Chile, SA; Gen. Man. JACINTO DÍAZ SÁNCHEZ.

TELEX-CHILE, SA: Rinconada El Salto 202, Santiago; tel. (2) 380-0171; fax (2) 382-5142; internet www.telex.cl; Pres. JUAN EDUARDO IBÁÑEZ; Gen. Man. RAMÓN VALDIVIESO.

VTR Gobal Com: Reyes Lavalle 3340, 9°, Las Condes, Santiago; tel. (2) 310-1000; fax (2) 310-1560; internet www.aldea.com; Pres. BLAS TOMIC.

BROADCASTING

Regulatory Authority

Asociación de Radiodifusores de Chile (ARCHI): Pasaje Matte 956, Of. 801, Casilla 10476, Santiago; tel. (2) 639-8755; fax (2) 639-4205; f. 1936; 455 broadcasting stations; Pres. CÉSAR MOLFINO MENDOZA.

Radio

In 1999, according to official sources, there were 1,046 radio stations (867 FM and 179 AM) transmitting in Chile.

Agricultura (AM y FM): Avda Manuel Rodríguez 15, Santiago; tel. (2) 695-3088; fax (2) 672-2749; owned by Sociedad Nacional de Agricultura; Pres. MANUEL VALDÉS VALDÉS; Gen. Man. GUIDO ERRÁZURIZ MORENO.

Aurora FM (Iberoamerican Radio Chile): Phillips 40, 2°, Of. 26, Santiago; tel. (2) 632-4104; fax (2) 639-8868; f. 1982; Pres. ERNESTO CORONA BOZZO; Gen. Man. JUAN CARRASCO HERNÁNDEZ.

Beethoven FM: Garibaldi 1620, Ñuñoa, Santiago; tel. (2) 274-7951; fax (2) 274-3323; internet www.beethovenfm.cl; f. 1981; affiliate stations in Viña del Mar and Temuco; Dir ADOLFO FLORES SAYLER.

Belén AM: Benavente 385, 3°, Casilla 17, Puerto Montt; tel. (65) 25-8048; e-mail radiobel.en001@chilnet.cl; f. 1990; owned by Archbishopric of Puerto Montt; Dir NELSON GONZÁLEZ ANDRADE; Gen. Man. CARLOS WAGNER CATALÁN.

Bío Bío La Radio: Pedro de Valdivia 37, Santiago; tel. (2) 231-2757; fax (2) 233-7997; affiliate stations in Concepción, Los Angeles, Temuco, Ancud, Castro, Osorno, Puerto Montt and Valdivia.

Chilena Solonoticias (AM y FM): Phillips 40, 2°, Casilla 10277; tel. (2) 463-5000; fax (2) 463-5100; e-mail radio@radiochilena.cl; internet www.radiochilena.com; f. 1922; Dir DANIEL LESCOT.

Radio El Conquistador FM: El Conquistador del Monte 4644, Huechuraba, Santiago; tel. (2) 740-9090; fax (2) 740-4992; e-mail rconquis@entelchile.net; internet www.openbox.com/conquistador; f. 1962; affiliate stations in Santiago, Iquique, Antofagasta, La Serena, Viña del Mar, Rancagua, Talca, Chillán, Concepción, Talcahuano, Pucón, Temuco, Villarrica, Lago Llanquihue, Osorno, Puerto Montt, Puerto Varas, Valdivia and Punta Arenas; Gen. Man. URSULA BURKERT FALK.

Radio Cooperativa (AM y FM): Antonio Bellet 223, Casilla 16367, Correo 9, Santiago; tel. (2) 235-2695; fax (2) 235-2320; f. 1936; affiliate stations in Copiapó, Bahía Inglesa, Coquimbo, La Serena, Valparaíso, Concepción, Talcahuano, Temuco and Villarrica; Pres. LUIS AJENJO I.; Gen. Man. SERGIO PARRA G.

La Clave FM: Monjitas 454, Of. 406, Santiago; tel. (2) 633-1621; fax (2) 639-2914; f. 1980; Pres. MIGUEL NASUR ALLEL; Gen. Man. VÍCTOR IBARRA NEGRETE.

Duna FM: Dr Torres Boonen 136, Casilla 13962, Santiago; tel. (2) 225-5494; fax (2) 225-6901; e-mail dunafm@entelchile.net; affiliate stations in Viña del Mar and Concepción; Pres. FELIPE LAMARCA CLARO; Gen. Man. ANA HOLUIGUE BARROS.

Estrella del Mar AM: Ramírez 207, Ancud-Isla de Chiloé; tel. (65) 62-2095; fax (65) 62-2722; e-mail estrella@telsur.cl; f. 1982; affiliate stations in Castro and Quellón; Dir MIGUEL ANGEL MILLAR SILVA.

Festival AM: Paseo Cousiño 8, Casilla 337, Viña del Mar; tel. (32) 88-1229; fax (32) 68-0266; e-mail radiofes.tival002@chilnet.cl; f. 1976; Pres. LUIS MUÑOZ AHUMADA; Gen. Man. SANTIAGO CHIESA HOWARD.

Finísima FM: Luis Thayer Ojeda 1145, Casilla 67, Santiago; tel. (2) 233-5771; fax (2) 231-0611; affiliate stations in Santiago, Arica, Iquique, Calama, Copiapó, La Serena, Ovalle, Isla de Pascua, Quilpe, San Antonio, San Felipe, Villa Alemana, Viña del Mar, Rancagua, Talca, Chillán, Concepción, Los Angeles, Temuco, Puerto Montt, Coihayque, Puerto Aysen and Punto Arenas; Gen. Man. CRISTIÁN WAGNER MUÑOZ.

FM-Hit: Eliodoro Yáñez 1783, Providencia, Santiago; tel. (2) 274-6737; fax (2) 274-8928; internet www.concierto.cl; affiliate stations in Santiago, Iquique, Antofagasta, San Antonio, La Serena, Viña del Mar, Concepción, Temuco, Osorno and Puerto Montt; Gen. Man. JAIME VEGA DE KUYPER.

Horizonte: Avda Los Leones 1625, Providencia, Santiago; tel. (2) 274-6737; fax (2) 274-8900; internet www.concierto.cl/horizon.htm; f. 1985; affiliate stations in Iquique, La Serena, Viña del Mar, Concepción, Temuco and Osorno.

Infinita FM: Avda Los Leones 1285, Casilla Los Leones 1285, Providencia, Santiago; tel. (2) 204-2813; fax (2) 341-6737; f. 1977; affiliate stations in Santiago, Viña del Mar, Concepción and Valdivia; Gen. Man. CARLOS ALBERTO PEÑAFIEL GUARACHI.

Radio Nacional de Chile: Argomedo 369, Santiago; tel. (2) 638-1348; fax (2) 632-1065; affiliate stations in Arica and Punta Arenas; Gen. Man. SANTIAGO AGLIATI.

Para Ti FM: El Conquistador del Monte 4644, Huechuraba, Santiago; tel. (2) 740-9393; fax (2) 740-9051; internet www.openbox.com/

manquehue; affiliate stations in La Serena and Viña del Mar; Gen. Man. FELIPE MOLFINO BURKERT.

Radio Polar: Bories 871, 2°, Punta Arenas; tel. (61) 24-1417; fax (61) 22-8344; f. 1940; Pres. RENÉ VENEGAS OLMEDO.

Pudahuel FM: Eliodoro Yáñez 1783, Providencia, Santiago; tel. (2) 223-0704; fax (2) 223-7589; e-mail radio@pudahuel.cl; internet www.pudahuel.cl; f. 1966; affiliate stations in Arica, Iquique, Antofagasta, Calama, Copiapó, Coquimbo, La Serena, Ovalle, San Felipe, Valparaíso, Viña del Mar, Rancagua, Curico, Linares, Talca, Chillán, Concepción, Los Angeles, Talcahuano, Pucón, Temuco, Villarrica, Ancud-Castro, Osorno, Puerto Montt, Valdivia and Punta Arenas; Pres. SUSANA MUTINELLI ANCHUBIDART; Gen. Man. JOAQUÍN BLAYA BARRIOS.

Santa María de Guadalupe: Miguel Claro 161, Casilla 2626, Santiago; tel. (2) 235-7996; fax (2) 235-8527; affiliate stations in Arica, Iquique, Antofagasta, La Serena, Viña del Mar, Temuco, Puerto Varas, Coihayque and Punta Arenas; Dir ALFONSO CHADWICK.

Superandina FM: Santa Rosa 441, Of. 34, Casilla 401, Los Andes; tel. (34) 42-2515; fax (34) 42-4095; f. 1987; Dir JOSÉ ANDRÉS GÁLVEZ.

Universo FM: Félix de Amesti 124, 8°, Santiago; tel. (2) 206-6065; fax (2) 206-6049; affiliate stations in Iquique, Copiapó, La Serena, Ovalle, Concepción, Temuco, Puerto Montt, Coihayque and Punta Arenas; Pres. ALVARO LARRAÍN.

Television

Canal 2°Rock & Pop: Chucre Manzur 15, Providencia, Santiago; tel. (2) 73-7880; fax (2) 73-5845; Exec. Dir LUIS AJENJO ISAS.

Corporación de Televisión de la Universidad Católica de Chile—Canal 13: Inés Matte Urrejola 0848, Casilla 14600, Providencia, Santiago; tel. (2) 251-4000; fax (2) 630-2040; e-mail dasein@reuna.cl; internet www.reuna.cl/teletrece/corpora.html; f. 1959; non-commercial; Exec. Dir ELEODORO RODRÍGUEZ MATTE; Gen. Man. MANUEL VEGA RODRÍGUEZ.

La Red Televisión, S.A./TV Azteca Chile, S.A.: Manquehue Sur 1201, Las Condes, Santiago; tel. (2) 212-1111; fax (2) 246-5881; e-mail administracion@lared.cl; f. 1991; Pres. JUAN CARLOS LATORRE; Gen. Man. MARCELO PAMDOLFO.

Megavisión, S.A.—Canal 9: Avda Vicuña Mackenna 1348, Santiago; tel. (2) 555-5400; fax (2) 551-8916; e-mail mega@mcl.cl; internet www.mcl.cl/megavision; f. 1990; Pres. RICARDO CLARO VALDÉS; Gen. Man. JOSÉ DÍAZ DEL RÍO.

Red de Televisión S.A./Chilevisión—Canal 11: Inés Matte Urrejola 0825, Casilla 16547, Correo 9, Providencia, Santiago; tel. (2) 737-2227; fax (2) 737-7923; e-mail chu@cmet.net; internet www.chilevision.emet.net; News Dir FELIPE POZO.

Red de Televisión Universidad del Norte, SA: Carrera 1625, Casilla 1045, Antofagasta; tel. (83) 22-6725. 1981; operates Canal 11-Arica, Canal 12-Iquique, Canal 4-Antofagasta and Canal 5-La Serena; Dir SERGIO HERRERA.

Televisión Nacional de Chile—Canal 7: Bellavista 0990, Casilla 16104, Providencia, Santiago; tel. (2) 707-7777; fax (2) 707-7766; e-mail rrpp@tvn.cl; internet www.tvn.cl; government network of 145 stations and an international satellite signal; Chair. LUIS ORTIZ QUIROGA; Gen. Man. MARIO CONCA ROSENDE.

Corporación de Television de la Universidad Católica de Valparaíso: Agua Santa Alta 2455, Casilla 247; Viña del Mar; tel. (32) 616-000; fax (32) 610-505; e-mail tv@ucv.cl; f. 1957; Dir JORGE A. BORNSCHEUER.

Finance

(cap. = capital; p.u. = paid up; dep. = deposits; res = reserves;m. = million; amounts in pesos unless otherwise specified)

BANKING
Supervisory Authority

Superintendencia de Bancos e Instituciones Financieras: Moneda 1123, 6°, Casilla 15-D, Santiago; tel. (2) 442-6200; fax (2) 441-0914; e-mail superintendente@sbif.cl; internet www.sbif.cl; f. 1925; affiliated to Ministry of Finance; Superintendent ENRIQUE MARSHALL RIVERA.

Central Bank

Banco Central de Chile: Agustinas 1180, Santiago; tel. (2) 670-2000; fax (2) 698-4647; e-mail bcch@bcentral.cl; internet www.bcentral.cl; f. 1926; under Ministry of Finance until Dec. 1989, when autonomy was granted; bank of issue; cap. 717,470.3m., total assets 16,717,758.1m. (Dec. 2000); Pres. CARLOS MASSAD; Gen. Man. CAMILO CARRASCO.

State Bank

Banco del Estado de Chile: Avda B. O'Higgins 1111, Santiago; tel. (2) 670-7000; fax (2) 670-5094; e-mail mforno@bech.cl; internet www.bancoestado.cl; f. 1953; state bank; cap. 274,801.1m., res 2,086,100m., dep. 3,970,190.3m. (Dec. 1998); Pres. JAIME ESTÉVEZ; Gen. Man. JOSÉ MANUEL MENA; 214 brs.

Commercial Banks

Banco de A. Edwards: Huérfanos 740, Santiago; tel. (2) 388-3000; fax (2) 388-4428; internet www.banedwards.cl; f. 1851; cap. 73,649m., res 8,649m., dep. 994,221m. (Dec. 1995); Pres. ANDRONICO LUKSIC; Gen. Man. GUSTAVO FAVRE DOMÍNGUEZ; 61 brs.

Banco BICE: Teatinos 220, Santiago; tel. (2) 692-2000; fax (2) 696-5324; e-mail webmaster@bice.cl; internet www.bice.cl; f. 1979 as Banco Industrial y de Comercio Exterior; name changed as above in 1988; cap. and res 60,065.4m., dep. 851,465.4m. (Dec. 1998); Pres. and Chair. BERNARDO MATTE; Gen. Man. CRISTIAN EYZAGUIRRE; 13 brs.

Banco de Chile: Ahumada 251, Casilla 151-D, Santiago; tel. (2) 637-1111; fax (2) 637-3434; internet www.bancochile.cl; f. 1894; 55% owned by the Luksic group; cap. and res 302,272.3m., dep. 3,917,410.2m. (Dec. 1999); Chair. SEGISMUNDO SCHULIN-ZEUTHEN SERRANO; Gen. Man. RENÉ LEHUEDÉ; 102 brs.

Banco de Crédito e Inversiones: Huérfanos 1134, Casilla 136-D, Santiago; tel. (2) 692-7000; fax (2) 695-3777; e-mail webmaster@bci.cl; internet www.bci.cl; f. 1937; cap. and res 132,329.6m., dep. 2,619,703.0m. (Dec. 1998); Pres. LUIS ENRIQUE YARUR REY; Gen. Man. HUMBERTO BÉJARES; 112 brs.

Banco del Desarrollo: Avda B. O'Higgins 949, 3°, Casilla 320-V, Correo 21, Santiago; tel. (2) 674-5000; fax (2) 671-5547; e-mail bdd@bandes.cl; internet www. bdesarrollo.cl; f. 1983; cap. US \$119.7m., dep. US \$2,108.4m. (Dec. 1998); Pres. VICENTE CARUZ MIDDLETON; Gen. Man. HUGO TRIVELLI; 80 brs.

Banco Internacional: Moneda 818, Casilla 135-D, Santiago; tel. (2) 369-7000; fax (2) 369-7367; e-mail infor@binter.cl; f. 1944; placed under state control Jan. 1983 but returned to the private sector in May 1986; cap. 6,845.4m., res 5,870.7m., dep. 132,219.4m. (Dec. 1998); Pres. ALEJANDRO L. FURMAN SIHMAN; Gen. Man. ALVARO ACHONDO GONZÁLEZ; 11 brs.

Banco Santander-Chile: Bandera 140, Casilla 57-D, Santiago; tel. (2) 320-2000; fax (2) 330-8877; internet www.bsantander.cl; f. 1926; cap. 56,745.0m., res 11,015.1m., dep. 900,891.9m. (Dec. 1994); subsidiary of Banco de Santander (Spain); incorporated Banco Osorno y La Unión in 1996; Pres. EMILIO BOTÍN SANZ DE SAUTUOLA Y GARCÍA DE LOS RÍOS; Gen. Man. OSCAR VON CHRISMAR; 72 brs.

Banco Santiago: Bandera 201, 3°, Casilla 14437, Santiago; tel. (2) 647-4000; fax (2) 671-7152; e-mail comelec@bancosantiago.cl; internet www.bancosantiago.cl; f. 1997 by merger of Banco O'Higgins and Banco de Santiago; cap. 373,203.3m., res 11,940.5m., dep. 4,621,991m. (Dec. 1999); Chair. CARLOS OLIVOS MARCHANT; Gen. Man. FERNANDO CAÑAS; 163 brs.

Banco Security: Agustinas 621, Santiago; tel. (2) 270-4000; fax (2) 270-4001; e-mail banco@security.cl; internet www.security.cl; f. 1981; fmrly Banco Urquijo de Chile; cap. and res 54,300.6m., dep. 661,327.2m. (Dec. 1998); Pres. FRANCISCO SILVA S.; Gen. Man. RAMÓN ELUCHANS O.; 11 brs.

Banco Sud Americano: Morandé 226, Casilla 90-D, Santiago; tel. (2) 692-6000; fax (2) 698-6008; e-mail bsa@bsa.cl; internet www.bsa.cl; f. 1944; cap. 57,300.9m., res 35,035.8m., dep. 1,090,037.7m. (Dec. 1998); Chair. RICHARD E. WAUGH; CEO LUIS FERNANDO TOBÓN; 49 brs.

BBV Banco BHIF: Huérfanos 1234, Casilla 517, Santiago; tel. (2) 679-1000; fax (2) 698-5640; internet www.bhif.cl; f. 1883; was merged with Banco Nacional in 1989; acquired Banesto Chile Bank in Feb. 1995; controlling interest acquired by Banco Bilbao Vizcaya (Spain) in Sept. 1998; name changed as above in 1999; cap. 103,849.5m., res 44,387.2m., dep. 1,178,799.1m. (Dec. 1998); Pres. JOSÉ SAID SAFFIE; CEO CARLOS SENENT-SALES; 78 brs.

Corpbanca: Huérfanos 1072, Casilla 80-D, Santiago; tel. (2) 696-2741; fax (2) 696-0271; e-mail fburgos@corpbanca.cl; internet www.corpbanca.cl; f. 1871 as Banco de Concepción, current name adopted in March 1997; cap. and res 106,951.5m., dep. 1,144,161.2m. (Dec. 1999); Chair. CARLOS ABUMOHOR; Gen. Man. JORGE SELUME; 65 brs.

Dresdner Banque Nationale de Paris: Huérfanos 1219, Casilla 10492, Santiago; tel. (2) 731-4444; fax (2) 460-8177; e-mail info@dresbnp.cl; internet www.dresbnp.cl; f. 1958 as Banco Continental; bought by Crédit Lyonnais in Sept. 1987; current name adopted in 1996; cap. and res 23,319.8m., dep. 249,655.1m. (Dec. 1999); Pres. WALTER SIEBEL; Gen. Man. EWALD DOERNER; 1 br.

ING Bank (Chile), SA: Avda Nueva Tajamar 481, 17°, Of. 1701, Casilla 500-V, Las Condes, Santiago; tel. (2) 330-0600; fax (2) 699-1113; cap. and res 10.1m. (Oct. 1995); Pres. ALBERT JACOB STAAL; Gen. Man. GERMÁN TAGLE O'RYAN; 1 br.

Foreign Banks

Foreign banks with branches in Chile include the following:
ABN AMRO Bank (Netherlands), American Express Bank Ltd (USA), Banco do Brasil, Banco do Estado de São Paulo (Brazil), Banco de la Nación Argentina, Banco Real (Brazil), Banco Sudameris (France and Italy), Bank of America NT & SA (USA), Bank of Boston (USA), Bank of Tokyo-Mitsubishi Ltd (Japan), BBVA Banco BHIF (Spain), Chase Manhattan Bank NA, Citibank NA (USA), HSBC Bank (United Kingdom), Republic National Bank of New York (USA).

Finance Corporations

Financiera Atlas, SA: Nueva de Lyon 72, 7°, Santiago; tel. (2) 233-3151; fax (2) 233-3152; Gen. Man. NEIL A. DENTON FEILMANN.

Financiera Condell, SA: Ahumada 179, 9°, Santiago; tel. (2) 672-1222; fax (2) 699-2590; Gen. Man. ANTONIO S. UNDURRAGA OLIVOS.

Financiera Conosur: Avda B. O'Higgins 1980, 7°, Santiago; tel. (2) 697-1491; fax (2) 696-3133; internet www.financieraconosur.cl; Pres. JOSÉ LUIS DEL RÍO; Gen. Man. EDMUNDO HERMOSILLA.

Banking Association

Asociación de Bancos e Instituciones Financieras de Chile AG: Ahumada 179, 12°, Santiago; tel. (2) 699-3977; fax (2) 698-8945; internet www.abif.cl; f. 1945; Pres. HERNÁN SOMERVILLE SENN; Gen. Man. ALEJANDRO ALARCÓN PÉREZ.

Other Financial Supervisory Bodies

Superintendencia de Administradoras de Fondos de Pensiones (AFPs) (Superintendency of Pensions Fund Administrators): Huérfanos 1273, 9°, Casilla 3955, Santiago; tel. (2) 753-0122; fax (2) 753-0122; e-mail info@safp.cl; internet www.safp.cl; f. 1981; CEO ALEJANDRO FERREIRO Y.

Superintendencia de Previsión Social (Superintendency of Social Security): Huérfanos 1376, 5°, Santiago; tel. (2) 696-8092; fax (2) 696-4672; CEO LUIS ORLANDINI MOLINA.

STOCK EXCHANGES

Bolsa de Comercio de Santiago: La Bolsa 64, Casilla 123-D, Santiago; tel. (2) 698-2001; fax (2) 697-2236; e-mail fleder mann@comercio.bolsantiago; internet www.bolsantiago.cl; f. 1893; 44 mems; Pres. PABLO YRARRÁZAVAL VALDÉS; Gen. Man. JOSÉ ANTONIO MARTÍNEZ Z.

Bolsa de Corredores—Valores de Valparaíso: Prat 798, Casilla 218-V, Valparaíso; tel. (32) 25-0677; fax (32) 21-2764; e-mail bolsade c.orred001@chilnet.cl; f. 1905; Pres. CARLOS F. MARÍN ORREGO; Man. ARIE JOEL GELFENSTEIN FREUNDLICH.

Bolsa Electrónica de Chile: Huérfanos 770, 14°, Santiago; tel. (2) 639-4699; fax (2) 639-9015; e-mail info@bolchile.cl; internet www.bolchile.cl; Gen. Man. JUAN CARLOS SPENCER OSSA.

INSURANCE

In 1999 there were 60 general, life and reinsurance companies operating in Chile.

Supervisory Authority

Superintendencia de Valores y Seguros: Teatinos 120, 6°, Santiago; tel. (2) 549-5900; fax (2) 549-5965; e-mail svalseg@ibm.net; internet www.svs.cl; f. 1931; under Ministry of Finance; Supt ALVARO CLARK DE LA CERDA.

Principal Companies

Aetna Chile Seguros de Vida, SA: Suecia 211, 7°, Santiago; tel. (2) 364-2000; fax (2) 364-2010; e-mail jdupre@aetna.cl; internet www.aetna.cl; f. 1981; life; Pres. SERGIO BAEZA VALDÉS; Gen. Man. FERNANDO HASENBERG NATOLI.

Aseguradora Magallanes, SA: Agustinas 1022, Of. 722; tel. (2) 365-4800; fax (2) 365-4860; e-mail fvarela@magallanes.cl; internet www.magallanes.cl; f. 1957; general; Pres. SERGIO LARRAÍN; Gen. Man. FERNANDO VARELA.

Axa Seguros Generales, SA: Huérfanos 1189, 2°, 3° y 4°, Casilla 429-V, Santiago; tel. (2) 679-9200; fax (2) 679-9300; internet www.axa.cl; f. 1936; general; Gen. Man BARNARDO SERRANO LOPEZ.

Chubb de Chile, SA: Gertrudis Echeñique 30, 4°, Santiago; tel. (2) 206-2191; fax (2) 206-2735; internet www.chubb.com/chile; f. 1992; general; Gen. Man. CLAUDIO M. ROSSI.

Cía de Seguros de Crédito Continental, SA: Avda Isidora Goyenechea 3162, 6°, Edif. Parque 1 Golf, Santiago; tel. (2) 636-4000; fax (2) 636-4001; e-mail comer@continental.cl; f. 1990; general; Gen. Man. FRANCISCO ARTIGAS CELIS.

Cía de Seguros Generales Aetna Chile, SA: Suecia 211, Santiago; tel. (2) 364-2000; fax (2) 364-2060; internet www.aetna.cl; f.

1899; general; Pres. SERGIO BAEZA VALDÉS; Gen. Man. MAXIMO ERRÁZURIZ DE SOLMINIHAC.

Cía de Seguros Generales Consorcio Nacional de Seguros, SA: Apoquindo 3039, Casilla 28, Correo 10, Santiago; tel. (2) 250-2500; fax (2) 364-2525; f. 1992; general; Gen. Man. ARMANDO BRICEÑO NEFF.

Cía de Seguros Generales Cruz del Sur, SA: Paseo Puente 574, 7°, Casilla 2682, Santiago; tel. (2) 690-6000; fax (2) 698-9126; f. 1974; general; Pres. ROBERTO ANGELINI; Gen. Man. MIKEL URIARTE.

Cía de Seguros Generales Euroamérica, SA: Agustinas 1127, 2°, Casilla 180-D, Santiago; tel. (2) 672-7242; fax (2) 696-4086; internet www.euroamerica.cl; f. 1986; general; Gen. Man. JUAN ENRIQUE BUDINICH SANTANDER.

Cía de Seguros Generales La Chilena Consolidada, SA: Pedro de Valdivia 195, Casilla 16587, Correo 9, Providencia, Santiago; tel. (2) 200-7000; fax (2) 274-9933; f. 1905; general; Gen. Man. IGNACIO BARRIGA UGARTE.

Cía de Seguros de Vida Consorcio Nacional de Seguros, SA: Avda El Bosque Sur 180, 3°, Casilla 232, Correo 35, Providencia, Santiago; tel. (2) 230-4000; fax (2) 230-4050; e-mail guillermomarti nez@consorcio.cl; f. 1916; life; Pres. JUAN BILBAO HORMAECHE; Gen. Man. MARCOS BÜCHI BUC.

Cía de Seguros de Vida La Construcción, SA: Avda Providencia 1806, 11°–18°, Providencia, Santiago; tel. (2) 340-3000; fax (2) 340-3024; e-mail seguros@laconstruccion.sa.cl; f. 1985; life; Pres. VÍCTOR MANUEL JARPA RIVEROS; Gen. Man. MANUEL ZEGERS IRARRÁZAVAL.

Cía de Seguros de Vida Cruz del Sur, SA: Paseo Puente 574, 4°, Casilla 2682, Santiago; tel. (2) 690-6000; fax (2) 698-9126; internet www.cruzdelsur.cl; f. 1992; life; Pres. ROBERTO ANGELINI; Gen. Man. MIKEL URIARTE.

Cía de Seguros de Vida Euroamérica, SA: Agustinas 1127, 3°, Casilla 21-D, Santiago; tel. (2) 782-7000; fax (2) 699-0732; e-mail deptoservicio@eurovida.cl; internet www.eurovida.cl; f. 1962; life; Pres. BENJAMIN DAVIS CLARKE; Gen. Man. PATRICIA JAIME VÉLIZ.

Cía de Seguros de Vida Santander, SA: Bandera 150, Santiago; tel. (2) 640-1177; fax (2) 640-1377; e-mail servicio@santanderseg.cl; internet www.netra.santanderseg.cl/index; f. 1989; life; Pres. FRANCISCO MARTÍN LÓPEZ-QUESADA.

ING, Seguros de Vida, SA: Nueva Tajamar 555; 18°, Casilla 70, Correo 10, Santiago; tel. (2) 252-1500; fax (2) 252-1504; internet www.INGgrupo.com; f. 1989; life; Gen. Man. ANDRÉS TAGLE DOMINGUEZ.

La Interamericana Compañía de Seguros de Vida: Agustinas 640, 9°, Casilla 163, Correo Central, Santiago; tel. (2) 630-3000; fax (2) 633-3222; internet www.intervida.cl/interamerica; f. 1980; life; Pres. RICARDO PERALTA VALENZUELA; Gen. Man. ANDRÉS SAAVEDRA ECHEVERRÍA.

Le Mans—ISE Compañia Seguros Generales, SA: Encomenderos 113, Casilla 185-D, Centro 192, Las Condes, Santiago; tel. (2) 230-9000; fax (2) 232-8209; e-mail lemans@lemans.cl; internet www.lemans.cl; f. 1888; general; Pres. IGNACIO WALKER CONCHA; Gen. Man. MARC GARÇON.

Mapfre Garantas y Crédito, SA: Teatinos 280, 5°, Santiago; tel. (2) 870-1500; fax (2) 870-1501; e-mail mapfreg@entelchile.net; f. 1991; general; Gen. Man. RODRIGO CAMPERO PETERS.

Renta Nacional Compañía de Seguros de Vida, SA: Amunátegui 178, 1° y 2°, Santiago; tel. (2) 670-0200; fax (2) 670-0399; e-mail renta@rentanac.cl; f. 1982; life; Pres. JORGE SIMS SAN ROMÁN; Gen. Man. ROBERTO MORA.

Seguros Previsión Vida, SA: Hendaya 60, 7°, Casilla 134, Correo 34, Santiago; tel. (2) 750-2400; fax (2) 750-2440; e-mail seguro@pre vision.cl; internet www.prevision.cl; f. 1981; life; Pres. FRANCISCO SILVA; Gen. Man. CARLOS FERNÁNDEZ.

Reinsurance

American Re-Insurance Company (Chile), SA: Avda Nueva Tajamar 481, Torre Norte, Of. 505, Santiago; tel. (2) 339-7171; fax (2) 339-7117; f. 1981; general; Pres. MAHMOUD ABDALLAH; Gen. Man. MAURICIO RIESCO VALDÉS.

Caja Reaseguradora de Chile, SA (Generales): Apoquindo 4449, 8°, Casilla 2753, Santiago; tel. (2) 338-1200; fax (2) 206-4063; f. 1927; general; Pres. ANDRÉS JIMÉNES; Gen. Man. ANDRÉS CHAPARRO KAUFMAN.

Caja Reaseguradora de Chile, SA: Apoquindo 4449, 8°, Santiago; tel. (2) 228-6106; fax (2) 698-9730; f. 1980; life; Pres. ANDRÉS JIMÉNES.

Cía de Reaseguros de Vida Soince, SA: Bandera 150, Santiago; tel. (2) 640-1177; internet www.santanderseg.cl; f. 1990; life; Pres. FRANCISCO MARTÍN LÓPEZ-QUESADA.

Insurance Association

Asociación de Aseguradores de Chile, AG: La Concepción 322, Of. 501, Providencia, Santiago; tel. (2) 236-2596; fax (2) 235-1502;

e-mail seguros@aach.cl; internet www.aach.cl; f. 1931; Pres. MARCOS BÜCHI BUC; Gen. Man. JOAQUÍN ECHENIQUE RIVERA.

Trade and Industry

GOVERNMENT AGENCIES

Corporación de Fomento de la Producción—CORFO: Moneda 921, Casilla 3886, Santiago; tel. (2) 638-0521; fax (2) 671-1058; f. 1939; holding group of principal state enterprises; grants loans and guarantees to private sector; responsible for sale of non-strategic state enterprises; Gen. Man. EDUARDO BITRÁN COLODRO.

PROCHILE (Dirección General de Relaciones Económicas Internacionales): Avda B. O'Higgins 1315, 2°, Casilla 14087, Correo 21, Santiago; tel. (2) 565-9000; fax (2) 696-0639; e-mail info@prochile.cl; internet www.uxdirecon.prochile.cl; f. 1974; bureau of international economic affairs; Dir HÉCTOR CASANUEVA OJEDA.

Servicio Nacional de Capacitación y Empleo (National Training and Employment Service): Huérfanos 1273, 11°, Santiago; tel. (2) 696-8213; fax (2) 696-5039; internet www.sence.cl; attached to Ministry of Labour and Social Security; Dir IGNACIO LARRAECHEA LOESSER.

STATE CORPORATION

Corporación Nacional del Cobre de Chile (CODELCO—Chile): Huérfanos 1270, Casilla 150-D, Santiago; tel. (2) 690-3000; fax (2) 690-3059; internet www.codelcochile.com; f. 1976 as a state-owned enterprise with five copper-producing operational divisions at Chuquicamata, Radomiro Tomić, Salvador, Andina and El Teniente; attached to Ministry of Mines; Exec. Pres. JUAN VILLARZÚ RHODE; 17,403 employees.

DEVELOPMENT ORGANIZATIONS

Comisión Chilena de Energía Nuclear: Amunátegui 95, Casilla 188-D, Santiago; tel. (2) 699-0070; fax (2) 699-1618; e-mail gtorres@gopher.cchen.cl; internet www.cchen.cl; f. 1965; government body to develop peaceful uses of atomic energy; concentrates, regulates and controls all matters related to nuclear energy; Exec. Dir GONZALO TORRES OVIEDO.

Corporación Nacional de Desarrollo Indígena (Conadi): Manuel Mott 1070, Temuco; tel. (45) 324-111; fax (2) 234-323; internet www.conadi.cl; promote the economic and social development of indigenous communities.

Corporación Nacional Forestal—CONAF: Avda Bulnes 285, Of. 501, Santiago; tel. (2) 672-2724; fax (2) 671-5881; f. 1970 to promote forestry activities, to enforce forestry law, to promote afforestation, to administer subsidies for afforestation projects and to increase and preserve forest resources; manages 13.97m. ha designated as National Parks, Natural Monuments and National Reserves; under Ministry of Agriculture; Exec. Dir Ing. CRISTIÁN PALMA ARANCIBIA.

Empresa Nacional de Minería—ENAMI: MacIver 459, 2°, Casilla 100-D, Santiago; tel. (2) 637-5000; fax (2) 637-5436; promotes the development of the small- and medium-sized mines; attached to Ministry of Mines; partially privatized; Exec. Vice-Pres. PATRICIO ARTIAGOITIA ALTI.

CHAMBERS OF COMMERCE

Cámara de Comercio de Santiago de Chile, AG: Santa Lucía 302, 3°, Casilla 1297, Santiago; tel. (2) 360-7000; fax (2) 633-3395; f. 1919; 1,300 mems; Pres. PETER T. HILL; Man. CLAUDIO ORTIZ T.

Cámara de la Producción y del Comercio de Concepción: Cauplicán 567, 2°, Concepción; tel. (41) 241-440; fax (41) 227-903; e-mail bseguel@cpcc.cl; internet www.cpcc.cl; Pres. HERNÁN ASCUI; Gen. Man. LEONCIO TÍO.

Cámara Nacional de Comercio, Servicios y Turismo de Chile: Merced 230, Santiago; tel. (2) 365-4000; fax (2) 365-4001; internet www.cnc.cl; f. 1858; Pres. FERNANDO LIHN CONCHA; Gen. Sec. JOSÉ MANUEL MELERO ABAROA; 120 mems.

There are chambers of commerce in all major towns.

INDUSTRIAL AND TRADE ASSOCIATIONS

Servicio Agrícola y Ganadero (SAG): Avda Bulnes 140, Santiago; tel. (2) 698-2244; fax (2) 672-1812; e-mail sag@sag.minagri.gob.cl; internet www.sag.gob.cl; under Ministry of Agriculture; responsible for the protection and development of safe practice in the sector; Exec. Dir ANTONIO YAKSIC SOULÉ.

Sociedad Agrícola y Servicios Isla de Pascua: Alfredo Lecanne-lier 1940, Providencia, Santiago; tel. (2) 232-7497; fax (2) 232-7497; administers agriculture and public services on Easter Island; Gen. Man. GERARDO VELASCO.

Subsecretaría de Pesca: Bellavista 168, 16-18°, Valparaíso; tel. (32) 21-2187; fax (32) 21-2790; f. 1976; controls and promotes fishing industry; Sub-Sec. PATRICIO BERNAL PONCE.

EMPLOYERS' ORGANIZATIONS

Confederación de la Producción y del Comercio: Monseñor Sótero Sanz 182, Providencia, Santiago; tel. (2) 231-9764; fax (2) 231-9808; f. 1936; Pres. WALTER RIESCO SALVO; Gen. Man. CRISTIÁN PIZARRO ALLARD.

Affiliated organizations:

Asociación de Bancos e Instituciones Financieras de Chile (q.v.).

Cámara Chilena de la Construcción: Marchant Pereira 10, 3°, Providencia, Casilla Clasificador 679, Santiago; tel. (2) 233-1131; fax (2) 232-7600; f. 1951; Pres. VÍCTOR MANUEL JARPA RIVEROS; Gen. Man. BLAS BELLOLIO RODRÍGUEZ; 3,000 mems.

Sociedad de Fomento Fabril, FG: Avda Andrés Bello 2777, 3°, Casilla 37, Correo 35, Tobalaba, Santiago; tel. (2) 203-3100; fax (2) 203-3101; f. 1883; largest employers' organization; Pres. PEDRO LIZANA GREVE; Man. FREDERICO MONTES LIRA; 2,000 mems.

Sociedad Nacional de Agricultura—Federación Gremial (SNA): Tenderini 187, 2°, Casilla 40-D, Santiago; tel. (2) 639-6710; fax (2) 633-7771; f. 1838; landowners' association; controls Radio Stations CB 57 and XQB8 (FM) in Santiago, CB-97 in Valparaíso, CD-120 in Los Angeles, CA-144 in La Serena, CD-127 in Temuco; Pres. RICARDO ARIZTÍA DE CASTRO; Gen. Sec. LUIS QUIROZA ARRAU.

Sociedad Nacional de Minería—SONAMI: Teatinos 20, 3°, Of. 33, Casilla 1807, Santiago; tel. (2) 695-5626; fax (2) 697-1778; f. 1883; Pres. WALTER RIESCO SALVO; Man. MANUEL CERECEDA VIDAL.

Confederación de Asociaciones Gremiales y Federaciones de Agricultores de Chile: Lautaro 218, Los Angeles; registered with Ministry of Economic Affairs in 1981; Pres. DOMINGO DURÁN NEUMANN; Gen. Sec. ADOLFO LARRAÍN V.

Confederación del Comercio Detallista de Chile, AG: Merced 380, 8°, Of. 74, Santiago; tel. (2) 39-5719; fax (2) 38-0338; f. 1938; retail trade; registered with Ministry of Economic Affairs in 1980; Nat. Pres. RAFAEL CUMSILLE ZAPAPA; Sec.-Gen. JAIME PÉREZ RODRÍGUEZ.

Confederación Gremial Nacional Unida de la Mediana y Pequeña Industria, Servicios y Artesanado—CONUPIA: Santiago; registered with Ministry of Economic Affairs in 1980; small- and medium-sized industries and crafts; Pres. FÉLIX LUQUE PORTILLA.

There are many federations of private industrialists, organized by industry and region.

MAJOR COMPANIES
Mining

Compañía de Petróleos de Chile, SA—COPEC: Agustinas 1382, 1°–7°, Casilla 9391, Santiago; tel. (2) 698-1881; fax (2) 699-3794; internet www.copec.cl; f. 1934; manufacturers of petroleum products; Gen. Man. JORGE BUNSTER; 5,000 employees.

Empresa Minera de Mantos Blancos, SA: Avda Pedro de Valdivia 295, Correo 9, Santiago; tel. (2) 350-8600; fax (2) 274-5968; e-mail jbeams@mantos.cl; internet www.mantos.cl; f. 1955; copper-mining co; Pres. PATRICK ESNOUF; 818 employees.

Empresa Nacional de Petróleo—ENAP: Vitacura 2736, 10°, Las Condes, Santiago; tel. (2) 280-3000; fax (2) 280-3199; internet www.enap.cl; f. 1950; state-owned petroleum and gas exploration and production; plans to privatize up to 60% of the company were announced in 1997; Pres. SERGIO JIMÉNEZ; Gen. Man. ALVARO GARCÍA ALAMOS; 3,220 employees.

Minera Escondida Ltda: Avda Americo Vespucio 100, Santiago; tel. (2) 207-6868; fax (2) 330-5056; e-mail escondida@chilnet.cl; internet www.chilnet.cl/escondida; f. 1985; mining; Pres. BRUCE L. TURNER; 2,100 employees.

Sociedad Punta del Cobre, SA: Rancagua 200, Copiapó; tel. (52) 217-353; fax (52) 633-6259; e-mail letelier@entelchile.net; f. 1989; copper processing; Chair. FERNANDO HARAMBILLET A.; Gen. Man. GONZALO CASTILLO OLIVARES; 360 employees.

Sociedad Química y Minera de Chile, SA—SQM, SA: El Trovado 4285, Las Condes, Santiago; tel. (2) 425-2000; fax (2) 633-4223; e-mail webmaster@sqm.cl; internet www.sqm.cl; f. 1968; mining co; Pres. JULIO PONCE; Gen. Man. PATRICIO CONTESSE GONZÁLEZ; 2,745 employees.

Food Products and Processing

Compañía Cervecerías Unidas, SA—CCU: Bandera 84, 6°–11°, Casilla 1977, Santiago; tel. (2) 670-3000; fax (2) 670-3222; e-mail ccuir@ccu-sa.com; internet www.ccu-sa.com; f. 1902; beverages; Pres. GUILLERMO LUKSIC CRAIG; Gen. Man. PATRICIO JOTTAR; 4,776 employees.

Embotelladora Andina, SA: Carlos Valdovinos 560, San Joaquín, Casilla 488, Correo 3, Santiago; tel. (2) 550-9000; fax (2) 551-4130; internet www.andina.cl; f. 1946; beverages; Chair. ALBERTO HURTADO; Vice-Chair. JOSÉ SAID; 5,900 employees.

Empresa Pesquera Eperva, SA: Huérfanos 863, 3°, Casilla 4179, Santiago; tel. (2) 633-1155; fax (2) 639-3436; f. 1955; marine products; CEO FELIPE ZALDIVAR LARRAÍN; 600 employees.

Empresas Carozzi, SA: Camino Longitudinal Sur 5201, San Bernardo, Santiago; tel. (2) 697-1747; fax (2) 857-2579; e-mail ecarozzi@rdc.cl; f. 1898; food processing; Pres. GONZALO BOFILL DE CASO; Gen. Man. JORGE ASPILLAGA FUENZALIDA; 3,620 employees.

Industria Azucarera Nacional, SA—IANSA: Bustamente 26, Casilla 189, Correo 22, Santiago; tel. (2) 565-5500; fax (2) 565-5525; e-mail rsanhuez@iansa.cl; www.iansa.cl; f. 1953; sugar production; CEO CHRISTIAN CHADWICK; 2,300 employees.

Sociedad Pesquera Coloso, SA: Playa Los Gringos, Arica; tel. (58) 23-2490; fax (58) 25-4242; e-mail service@coloso.cl; internet www.coloso.cl; group of fishing enterprises; Gen. Man. DOMINGO JIMÉNEZ OLMO; 1,590 employees.

Viña Concha y Toro, SA: Nueva Tajamar 481, Las Condes, Santiago; tel. (2) 821-7300; fax (2) 203-6740; e-mail vcoir@conchaytoro; internet www.conchaytoro.cl; f. 1883; wine producers; Gen. Man. EDUARDO GUILISASTI; 1,400 employees.

Viña San Pedro, SA: La Concepción 351, Providencia, Santiago; tel. (2) 235-2600; fax (2) 235-2411; internet www.sanpedro.cl; f. 1865; wine producers; Gen. Man. MATIAS ELTON NECOCHEA; 347 employees.

Wood, Cement and Paper

Celulosa Arauco y Constitución, SA: Agustinas 1070, 6°, Casilla 880, Santiago; tel. (2) 677-7200; fax (2) 698-5967; internet www.arauco.cl; f. 1979; wood pulp manufacturers; forest and fishing activities through affiliated companies; Chair. JOSÉ TOMAS GUZMAN; CEO ALEJANDRO PÉREZ RODRÍGUEZ; 2,400 employees.

Empresas CMPC, SA: Agustinas 1343, 8°, Santiago; tel. (2) 441-2000; fax (2) 671-4119; internet www.cmpc.cl; f. 1920; paper and packaging manufacturers, cellulose and wood pulp; Chair. ERNESTO AYALA O.; CEO ARTURO MACKENNA I.; 7,994 employees.

Empresas Melón, SA: Miraflores 178, 4°, Casilla 14140, Santiago; tel. (2) 638-1005; fax (2) 639-4979; f. 1908; manufacturers of cement; Gen. Man. RICHARD J. CHENEY HAIG; 600 employees.

Maderas y Sintéticos, SA—MASISA: Los Conquistadores 1700, 12° y 13°, Santiago; tel. (2) 707-8800; fax (2) 234-2666; f. 1960; sawmill; CEO G. ZEGERS; 950 employees.

Metals and Chemicals

Compañía Electro Metalúrgica, SA—ELECMETAL: Vicuña MacKenna 1570, Santiago; tel. (2) 361-4000; fax (2) 361-4021; e-mail ventas@elecmetal.cl; internet www.elecmetal.cl; f. 1917; runs metal foundry, manufactures parts for heavy machinery; Gen. Man. JUAN PABLO ARMAS MACDONALD; 340 employees.

Compañía Industrial El Volcán, SA: Phillips 40, Of. 42, Santiago; tel. (2) 639-6038; fax (2) 633-1349; f. 1916; makers of insulation and gypsum products; Pres. PATRICIO GREZ; 287 employees.

Laboratorio Chile, SA: Avda Maratón 1315, Ñuñoa, Santiago; tel. (2) 365-5000; fax (2) 365-5100; e-mail pilar.rodriguez@labchile.cl; internet www.labchile.cl; f. 1896; pharmaceutical co; CEO PABLO LAMARCA CLAVO; 1,653 employees.

Madeco, SA: Ureta Cox 930, Casilla 116-D, Santiago; tel. (2) 520-1000; fax (2) 520-1030; e-mail cgt@madeco.cl; internet www.madeco.cl; f. 1944; metallurgy; Gen. Man. ALBERTO CUSSEN; 5,448 employees.

Others

CAP, SA: Huérfanos 669, 8°, Santiago; tel. (2) 520-2000; fax (2) 633-7082; internet www.cap.cl; f. 1991; security brokers; Pres. ROBERTO DE ANDRACA BARBAS; 4,746 employees.

Compañía Chilena de Fosforos, SA: Los Conquistadores 1700, 15°, Providencia, Santiago; tel. (2) 707-6200; fax (2) 231-5072; f. 1913; makers of matches; CEO JOSÉ LUIS VENDER; 1,600 employees.

Compañía Tecno Industrial, SA—CTI, SA: Alberto Llona 777, Maipú, Santiago; tel. (2) 531-2131; fax (2) 531-4103; e-mail gbengoa@cti.cl; internet www.cti.cl; f. 1905; makers of refrigerators and freezers; Gen. Man. GONZALO BENGOA; 1,100 employees.

Cristalerías de Chile, SA: Hendaya 60, Of. 201, Las Condes, Santiago; tel. (2) 246-8888; fax (2) 246-8800; e-mail cchile@mail net.rdc.cl; internet www.cristalchile.cl; f. 1904; glass-bottle makers; CEO CIRILO ELTON GONZÁLEZ; 696 employees.

Empresas CCT, SA: El Bosque Norte 0125, Las Condes, Santiago; tel. (2) 232-7566; fax (2) 232-0757; f. 1909; subsidiary of British American Tobacco Co Ltd, United Kingdom; tobacco co; Gen. Man. ROBERTO FREIRE; 115 employees.

Sodimac, SA: Avda Presidente Eduardo Frei 3092, Renca, Casilla 3110, Santiago; tel. (2) 738-1000; fax (2) 641-8650; internet www.sodimac.com; f. 1982; retail of home improvement products; Chair. JUAN PABLO DEL RIO GOUDIE; 4,100 employees.

TÉLEX CHILE, SA: Riconada El Salto 202; tel. (2) 380-0171; fax (2) 382-5180; e-mail tlchile@chilesat.net; internet www.chilesat.net/telex; f. 1982; telecommunications co; CEO JUAN EDUARDO IBÁÑEZ WALTER; 1,465 employees.

UTILITIES

Comisión Nacional de Energía: Teatinos 120, 7°, Santiago; tel. (2) 365-6842; fax (2) 365-6834; Pres. OSCAR LANDERRETCHE GACITÚA.

General

COLBUN: Avda 11 de Septiembre 2353, 9°, Santiago; tel. (2) 231-3414; fax (2) 231-6609; state power utility; scheduled for privatization once anti-monopoly legislation was in place.

Electricity

Arauco Generación: Vitacura 2771, 9°, Las Condes, Santiago; tel. (2) 560-6700; fax (2) 236-5090; e-mail gic@arauco.cl; Pres. ARMANDO LOLAS; Gen. Man. HERNÁN ARRIAGADA.

BMV Industrias Electricas: Avda Vicuña Mackenna 1540, Nuñoa, Santiago; tel. (2) 555-8806; fax (2) 555-8807; Gen. Man. ANGÉLICA PADOVANI.

Chilectra, SA: Santo Domingo 789, Casilla 1557, Santiago; tel. (2) 632-2000; fax (2) 639-3280; e-mail rrpp@chilectra.cl; internet www.chilectra.cl; f. 1921; transmission and distribution of electrical energy; supplies distribution companies including the Empresa Eléctrica Municipal de Lo Barnechea, Empresa Municipal de Til-Til, Empresa Eléctrica de Colina, SA and the Cía Eléctrica del Río Maipo, SA; holds overseas distribution concessions in Argentina, Peru and Brazil; Pres. JORGE ROSENBLUT; Gen. Man. JULIO VALENZUELA.

Chilquinta Energía, SA: General Cruz 222, Valparaíso; tel. (32) 502-000; fax (32) 210-723; f. 1995; Pres. HÉCTOR MADARIAGA; Gen. Man. CRISTIÁN ARNOLDS.

Compañía Eléctrica del Litoral, SA: San Sebastián 2952, Of. 202, Las Condes, Santiago; tel. (2) 362-1436; fax (2) 362-1437; e-mail litoral@litoral.cl.

Compañía General de Electricidad—CGE: Teatinos 280, Santiago; tel. (2) 680-7000; fax (2) 680-7104; e-mail cge@cge.cl; internet www.cge.cl; Pres. JOSÉ CLARO; Gen. Man. GUILLERMO MATTA FUENZALIDA.

EMELAT (Empresa Eléctrica Atacama, SA): Circunvalación Ignacio Carrera, Copiapó; tel. (52) 21-3551; fax (52) 21-3393; f. 1981; distribution company; Pres. DAURÓPEDIS GARCÍA DE LA PASTORA; Gen. Man. JUAN JAIME DÍAZ CARRASCO.

EMELSA (Empresa Eléctrica de Melpilla, Colchagua y Maule, SA): Alameda 886, 5° y 6°, Santiago; tel. (2) 633-3852; fax (2) 633-6944; Gen. Man. EDUARDO VALENZUELA.

Empresa Eléctrica de Antofagasta, SAELECDA: Orella 643, Antofagasta; tel. (55) 541-9209; Dir L. BITRAN.

Empresa Eléctrica de Arica, SA: Baquedano 731, Arica; tel. (58) 23-1880; fax (58) 23-1105; Dir DAURÓPEDIS GARCÍA DE LA PASTORA.

Empresa Eléctrica de Aysen, SA: Francisco Bilbao 412, Casilla 280, Coyhaique; tel. (67) 23-1293; fax (67) 23-1293; f. 1983; Gen. Man. JORGE BARRIENTOS TECA.

Empresa Eléctrica Emec, SA: Los Talleres 1831, Barrio Industrial, Coquimbo; tel. (51) 20-1000; fax (51) 24-0200; e-mail emecsa@entelchile.net; f. 1980; Pres. RAMÓN ABOITIZ M.; Gen. Man. PABLO GUARDA B.

Empresa Eléctrica de Iquique, SA: Zegeres 469, Iquique; tel. (57) 42-3053; fax (57) 42-7181; CEO ALEJANDRO BLANCO SCHULER.

Empresa Eléctrica del Norte Grande (EDELNOR): Avda Grecia 750, Antofagasta; tel. (55) 24-8500; fax (55) 28-8094; f. 1981; Dir J. W. HOLDEN, III.

Empresa Eléctrica Pehuenche, SA—EEP: Moneda 1025, Santiago; fax (2) 696-5568; f. 1986; Gen. Man. ERNESTO SILVA BAFALLUY.

Empresa Eléctrica Pilmaiquen, SA: Las Bellotas 199, Of. 104, Providencia, Santiago; tel. (2) 233-4072; fax (2) 231-9780; Dir A. C. RODRÍGUEZ.

Empresa Nacional de Electricidad, SA—ENDESA: Santa Rosa 76, Casilla 1392, Santiago; tel. (2) 630-9000; fax (2) 635-3938; e-mail comunicacion@endesa.cl; internet www.emdea.cl; f. 1943; installed capacity 2,428,310 MW; ENERSIS (see below) obtained majority control of ENDESA in April 1999; Gen. Man. HECTOR LÓPEZ.

ENERSIS, SA: Santo Domingo 789, Casilla 1557, Correo Central, Santiago; tel. (2) 638-0840; fax (2) 633-4661; e-mail enersis@chil net.cl; internet www.enersis.com; f. 1981; holding company generating and distributing electricity through its subsidiaries throughout South America, including ENDESA of Chile (see above); 32% interest acquired by ENDESA of Spain in 1997, a further 31.78% acquired in 1999; Gen. Man. PABLO IHNEN DE LA FUENTE.

Gener, SA: Miraflores 222, 4°, Casilla 3514, Santiago; tel. (2) 632-3909; fax (2) 633-4499; f. 1981 as Chilectra Generación, SA following the restructuring of Compañía Chilena de Electricidad, SA; privatized in 1988 and Chilgener, SA adopted in 1989; current name adopted in 1998; owned by AES Corp. (USA); responsible for operation of power plants Renca, Ventanas, Laguna Verde, El Indio, Altalfal, Maitenes, Queltehues and Volcán; total generating capacity 1,746.2 MW (Dec. 1997); Pres. NAVEED ISMAIL; Gen. Man. ANDRÉS GLUSKI.

Empresa Eléctrica Guacolda, SA: Agustinas 1022, Of. 1022, Santiago; tel. (2) 697-3212; fax (2) 671-5343; operates a thermoelectric power-station in Huasco; installed capacity of 304 MW.

Empresa Eléctrica Santiago: Miraflores 222, 4°, Santiago; tel. (2) 686-8664; fax (2) 686-8447; operates the Nueva Renca thermoelectric plant in Santiago; installed capacity of 370 MW.

Energía Verde: O'Higgins 940, Of. 90, Concepción; tel. (41) 25-3228; fax (41) 25-3227; operates two co-generation power stations at Constitución and Laja and a steam plant at Nacimiento; supplies the Cabrero industrial plant.

Norgener, SA: Miraflores 222, 5°, Santiago; tel. (2) 632-6291; fax (2) 696-8810; northern subsidiary supplying the mining industry; operates power plants with installed capacity of 274.4 MW.

SAESA (Sociedad Austral de Electricidad, SA): Manuel Bulnes 441, Osorno; tel. (64) 23-3531; fax (64) 23-6256; CEO FELIPE LAMARCA CLARO.

Gas

Abastecedora de Combustible: Vicuña Mackenna 55, Providencia, Santiago; tel. (2) 639-9251; fax (2) 693-9249; internet www.abastible.cl; Pres. FELIPE LAMARCA; Gen. Man. JOSÉ ODONE.

AGA Chili, SA: Juan Bautista Pistene 2344, Santiago; tel. (2) 232-8711; natural-gas utility.

Compañía de Consumidores de Gas de Santiago—GASCO, SA: Rosas 1062, Casilla 8-D, Santiago; tel. (2) 698-2121; fax (2) 695-2685; e-mail gasco@chilnet.cl; internet www.gasco.cl; natural-gas utility; supplies Santiago and Punta Arenas regions; Pres. GABRIEL DEL REAL; Gen. Man. CARLOS ROCCA.

Compañía de Gas de Concepción, SA: En Continuidad De Giro, Avda Artura Prat 175, Concepción; tel. (41) 235-133; natural-gas utility.

Electrogas: Apoquindo 3076, Of. 402, Las Condes, Santiago; tel. (2) 232-1839; fax (2) 233-4931; Gen. Man. CARLOS ANDREANI.

Gas Valpo: Valparaíso; tel. (32) 27-7000; fax (32) 21-3092; e-mail info@gasvalpo.cl.

GasAndes: Santiago; distributes gas transported from the Argentine province of Mendoza via a 463-km pipeline.

Industrias Codigas: Camino a Melipilla 11000, Maipú, Santiago; tel.(2) 557-8870; fax (92) 538-6647; Pes. EDUARDO CABELLO; Gen. Man. CHRISTIAN CORNEJO.

Lipigas: Avda Libertad 51, Viña del Mar; tel. (32) 689-668; fax (32) 656-595; e-mail info@lipigas.cl; internet www.lipigas.cl; Pres. JAIME SANTA CRUZ; Gen. Man. MARIO FERNÁNDEZ.

Metrogas: El Bosque Norte 0177, 11°, Las Condes, Santiago; tel. (2) 337-8000; fax (2) 332-0348; internet www.metrogas.cl; natural-gas utility; Pres. JUAN CLARO; Gen. Man. EDUARDO MORANDÉ.

Water

Desalari Ltda: Arturo Prat 391, Of. 73, Arica; tel. (58) 25-0179; fax (58) 25-6652; e-mail desalari.ltda001@chilnet.cl.

Empresa Metropolitana de Obras Sanitarias, SA (EMOS): Avda Presidente Balmaceda 1398, Santiago; tel. (2) 688-1000; fax (2) 698-5871; e-mail info@emos.cl; internet www.emos.cl; water supply and sanitation services to Santiago and the surrounding area; sold to a French-Spanish consortium in June 1999; Gen. Man. ANGEL SIMON.

Sigsig Ltda (Tecnagent): Presidente Errázuriz 3262, Santiago; tel. (2) 335-2001; fax (2) 334-8466; e-mail tecnagent@tecnagent.cl; internet www.tecnagent.cl; Pres. RAÚL SIGREN BINDHOFF; Gen. Man. RAÚL A. SIGREN O.

TRADE UNIONS

There are more than 50 national labour federations and unions.

Central Unions

Central Autónoma de Trabajadores (CAT): Sazié 1761, Casilla 6510480, Santiago; tel. and fax (2) 695-3388; e-mail catchile@entelchile.net; Pres. OSVALSO ERBACH ALVAREZ, Sec. Gen. PEDRO SAAVEDRA.

Central Unitaria de Trabajadores de Chile (CUT): Avda B. O'Higgins 1346, Santiago; tel. (2) 695-8053; fax (2) 695-8055; e-mail cutchile@chilesat.net; f. 1988; two associations, 27 confederations, 49 federations; 36 regional headquarters; Pres. ARTURO MARTÍNEZ MOLINA; 411,000 mems.

Movimiento Unitario Campesino y Etnias de Chile (MUCECH): Portugal 623, Of. 1-A, Santiago; tel. (2) 222-6572; fax 635-1518; e-mail mucech@ia.cl; Pres. EUGENIO LEÓN GAJARDO; Nat. Sec. RIGOBERTO TURRA PAREDES.

Union Confederations

There are 37 union confederations, of which the following are among the most important:

Agrupación Nacional de Empleados Fiscales (ANEF): Avda B. O'Higgins 1603, Santiago; tel. (2) 696-2957; fax 699-3806; affiliated to CUT; Pres. RAÚL DE LA PUENTE PEÑA; Sec.-Gen. FRESIA AROCS ALBARRACÍN.

Confederación Bancaria: Agustinas 1185, Of. 92, Santiago; tel. (2) 699-5597; affiliated to CUT; Pres. DIEGO OLIVARES ARAVENA; Sec.-Gen. RAÚL REQUENA MARTÍNEZ.

Confederación de Empleados Particulares de Chile (CEPCH): Teatinos 20, Of. 1, Casilla 1771, Santiago; tel. (2) 72-2093; trade union for workers in private sector; affiliated to CUT; Pres. ANGÉLICA CARVALLO PRENAFETA; Sec.-Gen. ANDRÉS BUSTOS GONZÁLEZ.

Confederación de Personal en Retiro y Montepío de las Fuerzas Armadas (CAPREDENA): Nataniel Cox 265, Casilla 14988, Santiago; tel. (2) 698-4657; fax (2) 671-5980; Pres. OSCAR HEILCALEO CHEUQUE; Sec. Gen. OSCAR SÁEZ TRONCOSO.

Confederación General de Trabajadores del Transporte Terrestre (CGTT): Almirante Latorre 355, 2°, Of. 3, Santiago; tel. and fax (2) 695-9551; affiliated to CUT; Pres. ULISES MARTÍNEZ SEPÚLVEDA; Sec.-Gen. RODOLFO DOSSETTO UGALDE.

Confederación National Campesina: Gorbea 1769, Santiago; tel. and fax (2) 695-2017; affiliated to CUT; Pres. EUGENIO LEÓN GAJARDO; Sec.-Gen. REÑE ASTUDILLO R.

Confederación Nacional de Federaciones y Sindicatos de Empresas e Interempresas de Trabajadores del Transporte Terrestre y Afines (CONATRACH): Concha y Toro 2-A, 2°, Santiago; tel. (2) 698-0810; fax (2) 698-0810; Pres. PEDRO MONSALVE FUENTES; Sec. Gen. PEDRO JARA ESPINOZA.

Confederación Nacional de Federaciones y Sindicatos de Trabajadores Textiles y Ramos Similares (CONTEXTIL): Nataniel Cox 152 B, 1°, Santiago; tel. and fax (2) 696-8098; affiliated to the CUT; Pres. PATRICIA C. CARRILLO; Sec.-Gen. MARIA FELISA GARAY ASTUDILLO.

Confederación Nacional de Gente de Mar, Marítimos, Portuarios y Pesqueros (CONGEMAR): Tomás Ramos 158-172, Casilla 2210, Valparaíso; tel. (32) 255-430; fax (32) 257-580; affiliated to CUT; Pres. WALTER ASTORGA LOBOS; Sec.-Gen. JUAN GUZMÁN CARRASCO.

Confederación Nacional de Sindicatos Agrícolas—Unidad Obrero Campesina (UOC): Eleuterio Ramírez 1463, Santiago; tel. and fax (2) 696-6342; affiliated to CUT; Pres. OSCAR VALLADARES GONZÁLEZ; Sec.-Gen. DANIEL SAN MARTÍN VALLEJOS.

Confederación Nacional de Sindicatos de Trabajadores de la Construcción, Maderas, Materiales de Edificación y Actividades Conexas: Almirante Hurtado 2069, Santiago; tel. (2) 695-3908; fax (2) 696-4536; affiliated to CUT; Pres. MIGUEL ANGEL SOLÍS VIERA; Sec.-Gen. ADRIAN FUENTES HERMOSILLA.

Confederación Nacional de Sindicatos y Federaciones de Trabajadores Metalúrgicos (CONSTRAMET): Avda Francia 1317, Independencia, Santiago; tel. (2) 737-6875; fax (2) 443-0039; e-mail contrame@mailnet.rdc.cl; affiliated to CUT; Pres. MIGUEL SOTO ROA; Sec.-Gen. MIGUEL CHÁVEZ SOAZO.

Confederación Nacional de Trabajadores de la Alimentación y Afines (CONTALCH): Lizt 3082, San Joaquín, Santiago; tel. and fax (2) 553-2193; affiliated to CUT; Pres. CIJIFREDO VERA VERA.

Confederación Nacional de Trabajadores de la Industria del Pan (CONAPAN): Tucapel Jiménez 32, 2°, Santiago; tel. and fax (2) 672-1622; affiliated to CUT; Pres. LUIS ALEGRÍA ALEGRÍA; Sec. LUIS PALACIOS CAMPOS.

Confederación Nacional de Trabajadores de la Industria Textil (CONTEVECH): Agustinas 2349, Santiago; tel. (2) 699-3442, fax (2) 687-3269; affiliated to CUT; Pres. MIGUEL VEGA FUENTES; Sec.-Gen. OSCAR CÁCERES YÁÑEZ.

Confederación Nacional de Trabajadores del Comercio (CONATRADECO): Londres 73, Santiago; tel. and fax (2) 638-6718; Pres. EDMUNDO LILLO ARAVENA; Sec.-Gen. FEDERICO MUJICA CANALES.

Confederación Nacional de Trabajadores del Comercio (CONSFECOVE): Monjitas 454, Of. 606, Santiago; tel. (2) 632-2950; fax (2) 632-2884; affiliated to CUT; Pres. CLAUDIO ARAVENA ALVAREZ; Sec.-Gen. SUSANA ROSAS VALDEBENITO.

Confederación Nacional de Trabajadores del Cuero y Calzado (FONACC): Arturo Prat 1490, Santiago; tel. (2) 556-9602; affiliated to CUT; Pres. MANUEL JIMÉNEZ TORRES; Sec.-Gen. VÍCTOR LABBÉ SILVA.

Confederación Nacional de Trabajadores Electrometalúrgicos, Mineros, Automotrices (CONSFETEMA): Vicuña Mackenna 3101, Casilla 1803, Correo Central, San Joaquín, Santiago; tel. (2) 238-1732; fax 553-6494; Pres. LUIS SEPÚLVEDA DEL RÍO.

Confederación Nacional de Trabajadores Forestales (CTF): Rengo 884, Casilla 2717, Concepción; tel. and fax (41) 220-0407; Pres. JORGE GONZÁLEZ CASTILLO; Sec.-Gen. GUSTAVO CARRASO SALAZAR.

Confederación Nacional de Trabajadores Independientes Suplementeros: Roberto Pretot 18, Santiago; tel. (2) 699-4390; Pres. IVAN ENCINA CARO; Sec. RAMÓN GONZÁLEZ.

Confederación Nacional de Trabajadores Molineros: Bascuñan Guerrero 1739, Casilla 703, Correo 21, Santiago; tel. and fax (2) 683-8882; Pres. JOSÉ VÁSQUEZ ALIAGA.

Confederación Nacional Minera: Príncipe de Gales 88, Casilla 10361, Correo Central, Santiago; tel. (2) 696-6945; fax (2) 696-6945; Pres. MOISÉS LABRAÑA MENA; Sec.-Gen. JOSÉ CARRILLO BERMEDO.

Confederación Nacional Sindical Campesina y del Agro 'El Surco': Chacabuco 625, Santiago; tel. and fax (2) 681-1032; e-mail asurco@entelchile.net; affiliated to CUT; Pres. FERNANDO VALÁSQUEZ SERRANO; Sec.-Gen. SERGIO DÍAZ TAPIA.

There are also 45 union federations and over 100 individual unions.

Transport

RAILWAYS

State Railways

Empresa de los Ferrocarriles del Estado: Avda B. O'Higgins 3170, Santiago; tel. (2) 779-0707; fax (2) 689-8434; f. 1851; 3,427 km of track (1997); the State Railways are divided between the Ferrocarril Regional de Arica (formerly Ferrocarril Arica–La Paz), Ferrocarriles del Pacífico (cargo division), Metro Regional de Valparaíso (passenger service only) and Ferrovía (formerly the Ferrocarril del Sur); several lines scheduled for privatization; Pres. H. TRIVELLI; Gen. Man. DANIEL F. KOPRICH.

Parastatal Railways

Ferrocarriles del Pacífico (FEPASA): Alfredo Barros Errázuriz 1960, 6°, Providencia, Santiago; tel. (2) 330-4900; fax (2) 330-4905; e-mail fepasa@chilnet.cl; f. 1993; freight services; scheduled for privatization; Gen. Man. F. LANGER.

Metro de Santiago: Empresa de Transporte de Pasajeros Metro, SA, Avda B. O'Higgins 1414, Santiago; tel. (2) 698-8218; fax (2) 252-6364; e-mail gerencia.marketing@metro-chile.cl; internet www.metro-chile.cl; started operations 1975; 40.4 km (2000); 3 lines; Pres. FERNANDO BUSTAMENTE HUENTA; Gen. Man. R. AZÓCAR HIDALGO.

Private Railways

Antofagasta (Chile) and Bolivia Railway PLC: Bolívar 255, Casillas ST, Antofagasta; tel. (55) 20-6700; fax (55) 20-6220; e-mail webmaster@fcab.cl; internet www.fcab.com; f. 1888; British-owned; operates an internat. railway to Bolivia and Argentina; cargo forwarding services; total track length 934 km; Chair. ANDRÓNICO LUKSIC ABAROA; Gen. Man. M. V. SEPÚLVEDA.

Empresa de Transporte Ferroviario, SA (Ferronor): Avda Alessandri 042, Coquimbo; tel. (51) 31-2442; fax (51) 31-3460; 2,200 km of track (1995); established as a public/private concern, following the transfer of the Ferrocarril Regional del Norte de Chile to the Ministry of Production Development (CORFO) as a *Sociedad Anónima* in 1989; controlling interest purchased by RailAmerica of the USA in 1997; operates cargo services only; Pres. G. MARINO; Gen. Man. P. ESPY.

Ferrocarril Codelco-Chile: Barquito, Region III, Atacama; tel. (52) 48-8521; fax (52) 48-8522; Gen. Man. B. BEHN THEUNE.

Diego de Almagro a Potrerillos: transport of forest products, minerals and manufactures; 99 km.

Ferrocarril Rancagua–Teniente: transport of forest products, livestock, minerals and manufactures; 68 km.

Ferrocarril Tocopilla–Toco: Calle Arturo Prat 1060, Casilla 2098, Tocopilla; tel. (55) 81-2139; fax (55) 81-2650; owned by Sociedad Química y Minera de Chile, SA; 117 km (1995); Gen. Man. SEGISFREDO HURTADO GUERRERO.

Association

Asociación Chilena de Conservación de Patrimonio Ferroviario (Chilean Railway SocietyACCPF): Casilla 179-D, Santiago; tel. (2) 210-2280; fax (2) 280-0252; Pres. H. VENEGAS.

ROADS

The total length of roads in Chile in 1999 was an estimated 79,353 km, of which some 15,062 km were highways and some 34,326 km were secondary roads. The road system includes the completely paved Pan American Highway extending 3,455 km from north to south. Toll gates exist on major motorways. The 1,200 km-Carretera Austral (Southern Highway), linking Puerto Montt and Puerto Yungay, was completed in March 1996, at an estimated total cost of US \$200m.

SHIPPING

As a consequence of Chile's difficult topography, maritime transport is of particular importance. In 1997 90% of the country's foreign trade was carried by sea (51m. metric tons). The principal ports are Valparaíso, Talcahuano, Antofagasta, San Antonio, Arica, Iquique, Coquimbo, San Vicente, Puerto Montt and Punta Arenas. Most port operations were privatized in the late 1990s.

Chile's merchant fleet amounted to 753,432 grt (comprising 472 vessels) at December 1998.

Supervisory Authorities

Asociación Nacional de Armadores: Blanco 869, 3°, Valparaíso; tel. (32) 21-2057; fax (32) 21-2017; e-mail armadore@entelchile.net; f. 1931; shipowners' association; Pres. JUAN FERNANDO WAIDELE; Gen. Man. ARTURO SIERRA MERINO.

Cámara Marítima y Portuaria de Chile, AG: Blanco 869, 3°, Valparaíso; tel. (32) 25-3443; fax (32) 25-0231; e-mail camport@entelchile.net; Pres. JAIME BARAHONA VARGAS; Vice-Pres. RODOLFO GARCÍA SÁNCHEZ.

Dirección General de Territorio Marítimo y Marina Mercante: Errázuriz 537, 4°, Valparaíso; tel. (32) 25-8061; fax (32) 25-2539; maritime admin. of the coast and national waters, control of the merchant navy; Dir Rear Adm. FERNANDO LAZCANO.

Empresa Portuaria Antofagasta: Grecia s/n, Antofagasta; tel. (55) 25-1737; fax (55) 22-3171; e-mail epa@puertoantofagasta.cl; Pres. BLAS ENRIQUE ESPINOZA SEPÚLVEDA; Dir EDUARDO SALVADOR ABEDRAPO BUSTOS.

Empresa Portuaria Arica: Máximo Lira 389, Arica; tel. (58) 25-5078; fax (58) 23-2284; e-mail puertoarica@entelchile.net; Pres. CARLOS EDUARDO MENA KEYMER; Dir RAÚL RICARDO BALBONTÍN FERNÁNDEZ.

Empresa Portuaria Austral: B. O'Higgins 1385, Punta Arenas; tel. (61) 24-1760; fax (61) 24-1822; e-mail portspug@ctc-mundo.net; Pres. LAUTARO HERNÁN POBLETE KNUDTZON-TRAMPE; Dir FERNANDO ARTURO JOFRÉ WEISS.

Empresa Portuaria Chacabuco: B. O'Higgins s/n, Puerto Chacabuco; tel. (67) 35-1198; fax (67) 35-1174; e-mail ptochb@entelchile.net; Pres. LUIS MUSALEM MUSALEM; Dir RAIMUNDO CRISTI SAAVEDRA.

Empresa Portuaria Coquimbo: Melgareja 676, Coquimbo; tel. (51) 31-3606; fax (51) 32-6146; e-mail ptoqq@entelchile.net; Pres. ARMANDO ARANCIBIA CALDERÓN; Gen. Man. MIGUEL ZUVIC MUJICA.

Empresa Portuaria Iquique: Jorge Barrera 62, Iquique; tel. (57) 40-0100; fax (57) 41-3176; e-mail epi@port-iquique.cl; internet www.port-iquique.cl; f. 1998; Pres. PATRICIO ARRAU PONS; Gen. Man. PEDRO DÁVILA PINO.

Empresa Portuaria Puerto Montt: Angelmó 1673, Puerto Montt; tel. (65) 25-2247; e-mail puertomont@telsur.cl; Pres. JOSÉ DANIEL BARRETA SÁEZ; Gen. Man. RICARDO GHIORZI CARCEY.

Empresa Portuaria San Antonio: Alan Macowan 0245, San Antonio; tel. (35) 21-2159; fax (35) 21-2114; e-mail correo@saiport.cl; internet www.saiport.cl; f. 1960; Pres. JOSÉ MANUEL MORALES TALLAR; Gen. Man. FERNANDO CRISÓSTOMO BURGOS.

Empresa Portuaria Talcahuano-San Vicente: Latorre 1590, Talcahuano; tel. (41) 54-1419; fax (41) 54-1807; e-mail eportuaria@ptotalsve.co.cl; Pres. JUAN ENRIQUE COEYMANS AVARIA; Gen. Man. PATRICIO CAMPAÑA CUELLO.

Empresa Portuaria Valparaíso: Errázuriz 25, 4°, Of. 1, Valparaíso; tel. (32) 44-8700; fax (32) 23-4427; e-mail hjaeger@portvalparaiso.cl; internet www.portvalparaiso.cl; Pres. GABRIEL ALDONEY V.; Gen. Man. HARALD JAEGER KARL.

Principal Shipping Companies
Santiago

Cía Chilena de Navegación Interoceánica, SA: Avda Andrés Bello 2687, 17°, Las Condes, Santiago; tel. (2) 339-1300; fax (2) 203-9060; e-mail info@ccni.cl; internet www.ccnl.cl; f. 1930; regular sailings to Japan, Republic of Korea, Taiwan, Hong Kong, USA, Mexico, South Pacific, South Africa and Europe; bulk and dry cargo services; Chair. BELTRAN F. URENDA; CEO ALEJANDRO PATTILLO.

Marítima Antares, SA: MacIver 225, Of. 2001, 2°, Santiago; tel. (2) 38-3036; Pres. ALFONSO GARCÍA-MIÑAUR G.; Gen. Man. LUIS BEDRIÑANA RODRÍGUEZ.

Naviera Magallanes, SA (NAVIMAG): Avda El Bosque, Norte 0440, 11°, Of. 1103/1104, Las Condes, Santiago; tel. (2) 203-5180;

fax (2) 203-5191; f. 1979; Chair. PEDRO LECAROS MENÉNDEZ; Gen. Man. EDUARDO SALAZAR RETAMALES.

Nisa Navegación, SA: Avda El Bosque Norte 0440, 11°, Casilla 2829, Santiago; tel.(2) 203-5180; fax (2) 203-5190; Chair. PEDRO LECAROS MENÉNDEZ; Gen. Man. SERGIO VIAL.

Valparaíso

A. J. Broom y Cía, SAC: Blanco 951, Casilla 910, Valparaíso and MacIver 225, 10°, Casilla 448, Santiago; e-mail genman ager@ajbroom.cl; f. 1920; Pres. GASTÓN ANRÍQUEZ; Man. Dir JAMES C. WELLS M.

Agencias Universales, SA (AGUNSA): Urriola 87, 3°, Valparaíso; tel. (32) 21-7333; fax (32) 25-4261; maritime transportation and shipping, port and docking services; Dir JOSÉ URENDA; Gen. Man. FRANCO MONTALBETTI.

Cía Sud-Americana de Vapores: Plaza Sotomayor 50, Casilla 49-V, Valparaíso; tel. (32) 20-3000; fax (32) 20-3333; also Hendaya 60, 12°, Santiago; tel. (2) 330-7000; fax (2) 330-7700; f. 1872; regular service between South America and US/Canadian ports, US Gulf ports, North European, Mediterranean, Scandinavian and Far East ports; bulk carriers, tramp and reefer services; Pres. RICARDO CLARO VALDÉS; Gen. Man. FRANCISCO SILVA DONOSO.

Empresa Marítima, SA (Empremar Chile): Almirante Gómez Carreño 49, Casilla 105-V, Valparaíso; tel. (32) 25-0563; fax (32) 21-3904; f. 1953; international and coastal services; Chair. LORENZO CAGLEVIC.

Naviera Chilena del Pacífico, SA: Almirante Señoret 70, 6°, Casilla 370, Valparaíso; tel. (32) 25-0563; fax (32) 25-3869; e-mail nachipav@entelchile.net; also Serrano 14, Of. 502, Casilla 2290, Santiago; tel. (2) 633-3063; fax (2) 639-2069; e-mail nachipa@entel chile.net; cargo; Pres. ARTURO FERNÁNDEZ ZEGERS; Gen. Man. PABLO SIMIAN ZAMORANO.

Sociedad Anónima de Navegación Petrolera (SONAP): Cochrane 813, 6°, Casilla 1870, Valparaíso; tel. (32) 25-9476; fax (32) 25-1325; e-mail valsonap@sonap.cl; f. 1954; tanker services; Chair. FELIPE VIAL C.; Gen. Man. JOSÉ THOMSEN Q.

Transmares Naviera Chilena Ltda: Moneda 970, 20°, Edif. Eurocentro, Casilla 193-D, Santiago; tel. (2) 630-1000; fax (2) 698-9205; e-mail transmares@transmares.cl; also Cochrane 813, 8°, Casilla 52-V, Valparaíso; tel. (32) 20-2000; fax (32) 25-6607; f. 1969; dry cargo service Chile–Uruguay–Brazil; Chair. WOLF VON APPEN; CEO RICARDO SCHLECHTER.

Several foreign shipping companies operate services to Valparaíso.

Punta Arenas

Cía Marítima de Punta Arenas, SA: Avda Independencia 830, Casilla 337, Punta Arenas; tel. (61) 24-1702; fax (61) 24-7514; also Casilla 2829, Santiago; tel. (2) 203-5180; fax (2) 203-5191; f. 1949; shipping agents and owners operating in the Magellan Straits; Pres. PEDRO LECAROS MENÉNDEZ; Gen. Man. ARTURO STORAKER MOLINA.

Puerto Montt

Transporte Marítimo Chiloé-Aysén, SA: Angelmo 2187, Puerto Monttjel. (65) 27-0419; Deputy Man. PEDRO HERNÁNDEZ LEHMAN.

San Antonio

Naviera Aysén Ltda: San Antonio; tel. (35) 32578; also Huérfanos 1147, Of. 542, Santiago; tel. (2) 698-8680; Man. RAÚL QUINTANA A.

CIVIL AVIATION

There are 325 airfields in the country, of which eight have long runways. Arturo Merino Benítez, 20 km north-east of Santiago, and Chacalluta, 14 km north-east of Arica, are the principal international airports.

Aero Continente: Marchant Pereira 357; tel. (2) 204-2424; fax (2) 209-2358; internet www.aerocontinente.com.

Aerocardal: José Arrieta 7808, Casilla 9630, La Reina, Santiago; tel. (2) 279-3535; fax (2) 279-4272; f. 1989; charter services; Chair. ALEX CASASEMPERE.

Aerovías DAP: Casilla 633, Punta Arenas; tel. (61) 22-3340; fax (61) 22-1693; f. 1980; domestic services; CEO ALEX PISCEVIC.

Avant Airlines: e-mail reservas@avant.cl; internet www.avant.cl; Gen. Man. ROLANDO UAUY.

Lineas Aéreas Chilenas: B. O'Higgins 107, 7°, Santiago; tel. (2) 290-5140; fax (2) 290-5144; Man. RICARDO MARDONES.

Línea Aérea Nacional de Chile (LAN-Chile): Américo Vespucio 901, Renca, Santiago; tel. (2) 565-2525; fax (2) 565-1729; internet www.lanchile.com; f. 1929; operates scheduled domestic passenger and cargo services, also Santiago–Easter Island; international services to French Polynesia, Spain, and throughout North and South America; under the Govt's privatization programme, 99% of LAN-Chile shares have been sold to private interests since 1989; Pres. JORGE AWAD MEHECH; CEO ENRIQUE CUETO.

Línea Aérea del Cobre SA–LADECO: Américo Vespucio 901, Renca, Santiago; tel. (2) 565-3131; fax (2) 639-9115; internet www.ladeco.cl; f. 1945; affiliated to LAN-Chile in 1996; internal passenger and cargo services; international passenger and cargo services to the USA and throughout South America; Chair. JOSÉ LUIZ IBÁÑEZ; CEO GASTÓN CUMMINS.

Tourism

Chile has a wide variety of attractions for the tourist, including fine beaches, ski resorts in the Andes, lakes, rivers and desert scenery. There are many opportunities for hunting and fishing in thesouthern archipelago, where there are plans to make an integrated tourist area with Argentina, requiring investment of US $120m. Isla de Pascua (Easter Island) may also be visited by tourists. In 1998 there were an estimated 1.76m. tourist arrivals, and receipts from tourism totalled US $1,062m.

Servicio Nacional de Turismo—SERNATUR: Avda Providencia 1550, Casilla 14082, Santiago; tel. (2) 731-8300; fax (2) 251-8469; e-mail info@sernatur.cl; internet www.senatur.cl; f. 1975; Pres. MARÍA EUGENIA CASTRO; Man. ISABEL BACHLER.

Asociación Chilena de Empresas de Turismo—ACHET: Moneda 973, Of. 647, Casilla 3402, Santiago; tel. (2) 696-5677; fax (2) 699-4245; f. 1945; 240 mems; Pres. IVONNE LAHAYE DE MONTES MARDONES; Man. CARLOS MESCHI MONTALDO.

Defence

At 1 August 2000 Chile's Armed Forces numbered 87,000, including 30,600 conscripts: the Army 51,000 (including 27,000 conscripts); the Navy 24,000 (including naval air force and marines); and the Air Force 12,000 (including 1,500 conscripts). There were also para-military forces of 29,500 carabineros. Military service in the Navy or the Air Force is compulsory for men at 19 years of age and lasts for 22 months. Military service in the Army lasts for 12 months.

Defence Expenditure: Expenditure was budgeted at 1,096,000m. pesos in 2000.

Commander-in-Chief of the Army: Gen. RICARDO IZURIETA.

Commander-in-Chief of the Navy: Adm. MIGUEL VERGARA.

Commander-in-Chief of the Air Force: Gen. PATRICIO RÍOS PONCE.

Education

Primary education in Chile is free and compulsory for eight years, beginning at six or seven years of age. It is divided into two cycles: the first lasts for four years and provides a general education; the second cycle offers a more specialized schooling. Secondary education is divided into the humanities–science programme (lasting four years), with the emphasis on general education and possible entrance to university, and the technical–professional programme (lasting for up to six years), designed to fulfil the requirements of specialist training. In 1997 280,302 pupils attended kindergarten, 2,254,786 pupils attended primary school and 823,003 attended secondary school. There are three types of higher-education institution: universities, professional institutes and centres of technical information. In 1997 there were 380,603 students in higher education. An intensive literacy campaign begun in 1980, reduced the rate of adult illiteracy from 11% in 1970, to an estimated 4.8% in 1997. Expenditure on education by all levels of government in 1997 was about 1,069,650m. pesos (15.5% of total public spending).

Bibliography

For works on South America generally, see Select Bibliography (Books)

Barr-Melej, P. *Reforming Chile: Cultural Politics, Nationalism and the Rise of the Middle Class*. Chapel Hill, NC, University of North Carolina Press, 2001.

Bergquist, C. *Labor in Latin America: Comparative Essays on Chile, Argentina, Venezuela and Colombia*. Stanford, CA, Stanford University Press, 1986.

Bethell, L. (Ed.). *Chile since Independence*. Cambridge, Cambridge University Press, 1993.

Blakemore, H. 'Back to the Barracks: The Chilean Case', in *Third World Quarterly*, Vol. 7, No. 1 (January). 1985.

Bouvier, V. *Alliance or Compliance, Implications of the Chilean Experience for the Catholic Church in Latin America*. Syracuse, NY, Syracuse University Press, 1983.

Collier, S., and Sater, W. *A History of Chile, 1808–1994*. 1996.

Drake, P. W., and Jaksić, I. (Eds). *The Struggle for Democracy in Chile*, revised edn. Lincoln, NE, University of Nebraska Press, 1995.

Falcoff, M. *Modern Chile 1970–1989*. New Brunswick, NJ, Transaction Publishers, 1989.

Faúndez, J. *Marxism and Democracy in Chile: From 1932 to the fall of Allende*. New Haven, CT, Yale University Press, 1989.

Fortín, C. 'The Failure of Repressive Monetarism: Chile, 1973–1983', in *Third World Quarterly*, Vol. 6, No. 2 (April). 1984.

Hite, K. *When the Romance Ended: Leaders of the Chilean Left, 1968–1998*. New York, NY, Columbia University Press, 2000.

Hojman, D. E. *Chile: The Political Economy of Development and Democracy in the 1990s*. Basingstoke, Macmillan, 1993.

Kaufman, E. *Crisis in Allende's Chile: New Perspectives*. New York, NY, Praeger Publrs, 1988.

Londregan, J. *Legislative Institutions and Ideology in Chile — Political Economy of Institutions and Decisions*. Cambridge, Cambridge University Press, 2000.

Mamalakis, M. J. *The Growth and Structure of the Chilean Economy*. New Haven, CT and London, Yale University Press, 1996.

Monteón, M. *Chile in the Nitrate Era: The Evolution of Economic Dependence, 1880–1930*. Madison, WI, University of Wisconsin Press, 1982.

Moreno, F. J. *Legitimacy and Stability in Latin America: A Study of Chilean Political Culture*. New York, NY, New York University Press, 1969.

O'Brien, P., and Roddick, J. *Chile, the Pinochet Decade*. London, Macmillan, 1983.

Oppenheim, L. H. *Politics in Chile: Democracy, Authoritarianism and the Search for Development*. Boulder, CO, Westview Press, 1999.

O'Shaughnessy, H. *Pinochet: the Politics of Torture*. London, Latin American Bureau, 1999.

Paley, J. *Marketing Democracy: Power and Social Movements in Post-Dictatorship Chile*. Los Angeles, CA, University of California Press, 2001.

Pollack, B., and Rosenkranz, H. *Revolutionary Social Democracy: The Chilean Socialist Party*. London, Frances Pinter, 1986.

Pollack, M. *The New Right in Chile 1973–1977*. Basingstoke, Macmillan, 2000.

Remmer, K. L. *Party Competition in Argentina and Chile; Political Recruitment and Public Policy, 1890–1930*. Lincoln, NE, University of Nebraska Press, 1984.

Rosemblatt, K. A. *Gendered Compromises: Political Cultures and the State in Chile, 1920–1950*. Chapel Hill, NC, University of North Carolina Press, 2000.

Siavelis, P. *The President and Congress in Post-Authoritarian Chile: Institutional Constraints to Democratic Consolidation*. Pennsylvania, PA, Penn State University Press, 1999.

Sigmund, P. E. *The United States and Democracy in Chile*. Baltimore, MD, Johns Hopkins for Twentieth Century Fund, 1993.

Smith, B. *The Church and Politics in Chile, Challenges to Modern Catholicism*. Princeton, NJ, Princeton University Press, 1982.

Spooner, M. H. *Soldiers in a Narrow Land: The Pinochet Regime in Chile*. Los Angeles, CA, University of California Press, 1999.

Valdés, J. G. *Pinochet's Economists*. Cambridge, Cambridge University Press, 1995.

Verdugo, P. *Chile, Pinochet and the Caravan of Death*. Boulder, CO, Lynne Rienner Publrs, 2001.

COLOMBIA

Area: 1,141,748 sq km (440,831 sq miles).

Population (official estimate at mid-1999): 41,589,018.

Capital: Santafé de Bogotá, population 6,260,862 (estimate at mid-1999).

Language: Spanish (official).

Religion: Predominantly Christianity (95% Roman Catholic).

Climate: Conditions vary with altitude, from tropical in coastal regions, temperate on the plateaux to cold in the Andes mountains.

Time: GMT –5 hours.

Public Holidays

2002: 1 January (New Year's Day), 7 January (for Epiphany), 19 March (for St Joseph's Day), 28 March (Maundy Thursday), 29 April (Good Friday), 1 May (Labour Day), 9 May (Ascension Day), 30 May (for Corpus Christi), 1 July (for SS Peter and Paul), 20 July (Independence), 7 August (Battle of Boyacá), 19 August (for Assumption), 14 October (for Columbus Day), 4 November (for All Saints' Day), 11 November (Independence of Cartagena), 8 December (Immaculate Conception), 25 December (Christmas Day).

2003: 1 January (New Year's Day), 6 January (Epiphany), 24 March (for St Joseph's Day), 17 April (Maundy Thursday), 18 April (Good Friday), 1 May (Labour Day), 2 June (for Ascension Day), 23 June (for Corpus Christi), 30 June (for SS Peter and Paul), 20 July (Independence), 7 August (Battle of Boyacá), 18 August (for Assumption), 13 October (for Columbus Day), 3 November (for All Saints' Day), 17 November (for Independence of Cartagena), 8 December (Immaculate Conception), 25 December (Christmas Day).

Currency: Colombian peso; 10,000 pesos = £2.976 = US $4.261 = €4.800 (30 April 2001).

Weights and Measures: The metric system is in force.

Basic Economic Indicators

	1998	1999	2000
Gross domestic product ('000 million Colombian pesos at 1994 prices)	75,412.4	72,208.7	74,230.2
GDP per head ('000 Colombian pesos at 1994 prices)	1,847.1	1,736.2	1,754.0
GDP ('000 million Colombian pesos at current prices)	140,953.2	152,358.9	172,996.0
GDP per head ('000 Colombian pesos at current prices)	3,037.8	3,663.4	4,087.7
Annual growth of real GDP (%)	0.6	–4.2	2.8
Annual growth of real GDP per head (%)	1.3	–6.0	1.0
Government budget ('000 million Colombian pesos at current prices):			
Revenue	16,880.2	20,144.0	23,285.3
Expenditure	23,492.0	28,152.8	34,444.4
Consumer price index (annual average; base: 1995 = 100)	172.0	191.3	209.4
Rate of inflation (annual average, %)	20.4	11.2	9.5
Foreign exchange reserves (US $ million at 31 December)	7,983	7,580	8,498
Imports c.i.f. (US $ million)	14,635	10,659	11,539
Exports f.o.b. (US $ million)	10,852	11,576	13,040
Balance of payments (current account, US $ million)	–5,209	–61	n.a.

Gross national product per head at purchasing power parity (PPP) (US dollars, converted by the PPP exchange rate, 1999): 5,709.

Total labour force (March 2000): 15,417,000.

Unemployment (1999): 19.4%.

Total external debt (1999): US $33,624m.

Life expectancy (years at birth, 1999, estimate): 70 (males 66, females 74).

Infant mortality rate (per 1,000 live births, 1999, estimate): 24.

Adult population with HIV/AIDS (15–49 years, 1999): 0.31%.

School enrolment ratio (6–16 years, 1996): 94%.

Adult literacy rate (15 years and over, 2000): 91.8% (male 8.2%; female 8.2%).

Commercial energy consumption per head (kg of oil equivalent, 1998): 753.

Carbon dioxide emissions per head (metric tons, 1997): 1.8.

Passenger motor cars in use (estimate, per 1,000 of population, 1999): 43.4.

Television receivers in use (per 1,000 of population, 1997): 115.

Personal computers in use (per 1,000 of population, 1999): 33.7.

History

Sir KEITH MORRIS

Colombia shares many characteristics with the other Latin American countries and particularly with its Andean neighbours. However, its geography, pre-Colombian and colonial history gave the country distinctive features that were accentuated following independence and became increasingly marked in the 20th century. The Andes mountain range divides into three *cordilleras* when it enters Colombia. The Pacific coast is largely jungle and mangrove swamps. The 60% of the country to the east of the Andes is divided between the llanos (savannah, much of which is flooded for nine months of the year) and Amazonian jungle. Many places are only accessible by air. With its capital at Santafé de Bogotá (500 miles from the Caribbean ports of entry and 8,600 ft high in the eastern *cordillera*) the country was inevitably inward looking and regional.

The regionalism was reinforced by the country's Indian heritage. Although Colombia had many different civilizations before the Spanish conquest in the 16th century (they reached a high level of sophistication, producing the finest gold work in the Americas), they were never united in a large state like the Inca or Aztec Empires. Few of them have survived as distinct groups and most were hispanicized, unlike those in Ecuador, Peru and Bolivia to the south. By the end of the colonial period the majority of Colombians were mestizos (of mixed European and Indian descent) with significant European and mulatto minorities—the latter descended from the African slaves imported to work in the gold mines. The resulting lack of communal identity added individualism to the regionalism and localism, which geography and pre-colonial history had encouraged.

INDEPENDENCE AND THE 19TH CENTURY

Nueva Granada became a Viceroyalty in 1739. Santafé de Bogotá inevitably had a great concentration of the region's lawyers and administrators. Simón Bolívar made it the target of his great independence campaign of 1819 and there established the capital of Gran Colombia, comprising present day Colombia, Venezuela, Ecuador and Panama. However, Gran Colombia broke up amid much bitterness in 1830, leaving the Colombians with a strong preference for civilian government after their experience with Bolívar and his largely Venezuelan generals. Bolívar's Vice-President, Gen. Francisco de Paula Santander, who returned from exile in London (United Kingdom) after the overthrow of Bolívar to assume the presidency was, in contrast, honoured as 'the man of laws.'

Following independence, Colombia's politics in the 19th century bore a great resemblance to those of its neighbours. It was a turbulent period with nine civil wars. These were essentially struggles for power between the two main currents of national political life that had, by the middle of the century, emerged as the Liberal and Conservative Parties. The only issue that consistently divided them was the greater or lesser role of the Roman Catholic Church; the Liberal Party contained anticlerical elements. There was little dispute over economic policy and both parties were at times federalist, at times centralist, though the Liberals inclined more towards the former. However, party allegiance was often decided as much by family and locality as by doctrine.

The collapse of Gran Colombia had other lasting effects. It left Colombia with the largest share of the Gran Colombian debt. The Colombian state therefore began in poor financial state. It remained poor for the rest of the century, firstly because of the lack of large commodity discoveries and, secondly, owing to a weak external sector (the only effective form of taxation in 19th century Latin America was customs duties, which depended on foreign trade). As a result, the state was chronically weak with an army of only 2,000–3,000 men, which was frequently incapable of maintaining public order. No Colombian President could exercise the sort of authority that later enabled the Venezuelan leader, Gen. Juan Vicente Gómez (1908–35), to

effectively disarm the Venezuelan population in the early 1900s. The Colombian Constitution alternated between extreme federalism (1863) and excessive centralism (1886). The latter was confirmed by the War of the Thousand Days (1899–1902), but the centralism was more policy than practice. Governments had to pay due respect to regional and local feeling.

EARLY 20TH CENTURY

Colombia's story in the 20th century was to diverge greatly from that of its neighbours. It was to have much greater constitutional stability (only one four-year military regime) and steadier economic development, but, paradoxically, more violence.

A consequence of the difficult geography and the poverty of the state, which was to plague Colombia throughout the 20th century, was the development of a frontier tradition. Colombia is a land of many internal frontiers as colonos (colonists) cleared the river valleys and advanced ever higher into the sierras, as well as opening up the llanos and the jungle. As the state was absent in most of these areas, traditions of private justice prevailed. The ability to defend oneself became much admired, which may explain some of the tolerance shown to guerrillas to this day. The rural conflicts that afflicted Colombia in the 1980s and 1990s led to many colonos taking their weapons and their frontier customs to the cities.

From the end of the 'War of the Thousand Days' (1899–1902) until the mid-1940s, Colombia enjoyed relative tranquillity. The Conservatives remained in power until 1930. The coffee and textile industries developed greatly, mainly in Medellín. In 1930 the Conservatives divided into factions, which allowed a moderate Liberal, Enrique Olaya Herrera, to govern in coalition with Conservatives. An attack by Peru on Colombia's Amazonian territories in 1931 ensured wide support for the new Government. President Alfonso López Pumarejo, who succeeded Olaya in 1934, introduced 'New Deal' type reforms, consolidating the Liberal's popular support. His successor, Eduardo Santos Montejo (1938–42), slowed the pace of reform. López was re-elected in 1942, but this time met increasing opposition and resigned in 1945.

Divisions within the Liberal Party led to a Conservative victory in 1946. However, by 1948 the Liberals had reunited behind the popular figure of Jorge Eliécer Gaitán, the dissident Liberal candidate in the 1946 elections. The assassination of Gaitán in Santafé de Bogotá (then known as Bogotá) on 9 April 1948 led to an outbreak of civil unrest, known as the *Bogotazo*, with days of rioting, leaving several thousand dead. Gaitán, whose fiery oratory had won him a strong personal following, had been not only expected to regain the presidency for the Liberals in the 1950 elections, but was seen as a radical leader who would introduce significant social change. The Government managed to restore order in the cities, but the conflict spread to the rural areas. 'La Violencia', as the period became known, continued until 1958 and may have claimed the lives of as many as 200,000 people.

FRENTE NACIONAL, 1958–74

The military, led by Gen. Gustavo Rojas Pinilla, took power in 1953. His coup, the only one in the 20th century, initially enjoyed popular support; this, however, waned as it became clear that he did not intend to restore constitutional government. A military junta removed Rojas in 1957 and, in the following year, power was transferred to a Frente Nacional. This power-sharing agreement between the two parties provided for them to alternate in the presidency for four terms and to have equal number of seats in the cabinet and Congress. This was less undemocratic than it sounds as under the Colombian system one claims party allegiance and the seats on both sides were strongly contested, with Communists winning some Liberal seats and Rojas's movement, the Alianza Nacional Popular (ANAPO) well represented.

Violence declined under the Frente Nacional as most of the remaining armed groups relinquished violence or were suppressed. However, the success of the Cuban revolution in 1959 gave fresh impetus to guerrilla activity. One of the surviving groups relaunched itself in the mid-1960s as the Fuerzas Armadas Revolucionarias de Colombia (FARC), the military wing of the pro-Soviet Communist Party, with strong support in some rural areas. The Ejército de Liberación Nacional (ELN), a Cuban-oriented movement, whose members were originally middle-class students and included several Roman Catholic priests, was founded at the same time. The Ejército Popular de Liberación (EPL), a smaller, Maoist guerrilla movement, followed in 1969.

Generally, the Frente Nacional's period of rule, which formally ended in 1974, was one of good economic growth and social progress, especially under Carlos Lleras Restrepo (1966–70), who gave much impetus to agrarian and administrative reform. In the 1970 presidential election, the narrow victory of the official Conservative candidate, Misael Pastrana, was challenged by the second-placed candidate, Gen. Rojas, representing ANAPO. When Pastrana's victory was confirmed there were mass protests, as the result reinforced the popularly-held view that the system was unfair and could not produce change peacefully. One consequence was the founding by some ANAPO supporters in 1974 of the Movimiento 19 de April (M-19), a non-Marxist guerrilla group, which, unlike others, was initially city-based.

RETURN TO LIBERAL GOVERNMENT, 1974–82

In the presidential elections of 1974 the Liberal candidate, Alfonso López Michelsen, won a decisive victory over the Conservative Alvaro Gómez and the ANAPO contender, Maria Eugenia Rojas de Moreno Díaz. Curiously, the fathers of all three were former Presidents. The expectations aroused by López's victory were great. He was the first Liberal to win a fully competitive election since his father, whose name still symbolized progressive liberalism. However, he was committed to continue to govern in coalition with the Conservatives and any attempt at constitutional reform faced formidable opposition in Congress and the Supreme Court. The world economy was also in recession following the 1973 petroleum crisis. In fact, López Michelson's administration's most lasting achievement was probably the introduction of association contracts for oil exploration, at a time when other Latin American countries were nationalizing their oil industries. This would lead to the great discoveries at Caño Limón in 1982 and at Cusiana in 1991.

President López Michelson's successor, Julio Cesar Turbay Ayala, who was elected in 1978, was the first Lebanese to be elected President outside the Lebanon. He had risen through party ranks and was chosen instead of former President Lleras. His Conservative opponent, Belisario Betancur Cuartas, came from a working-class family in Medellín. This suggested that Colombian politics was more open to the talents than the 1974 election had led people to believe. Turbay took a firm and unpopular stand against the Argentine invasion of the Falkland Islands (Islas Malvinas) in 1982. He also sought to solve the problems of urban terrorism and drugs trafficking. His efforts met with some success, although his counter-insurgency campaign against guerrillas in 1982 provoked many allegations of human-rights abuses by the armed forces.

THE DRUGS TRADE

The illegal drugs trade became the key factor in Colombia in the late 20th century. It began quietly in the 1970s with the cultivation and export of marijuana. Then, some Colombians saw the opportunity to gain a dominant role in the cocaine business. The coca paste was produced largely in Peru and Bolivia and flown to Colombia, which was strategically placed to process it into cocaine and ship it to the USA. By the early 1980s two groups in Medellín and Cali controlled most of the trade. Their activities were already on a large scale before the Government or society realized the extent of the threat. When challenged by the Government they retaliated and unleashed a cycle of violence that has continued to the present. In the case of the Medellín cartel under Pablo Escobar, violence escalated

into narcoterrorism (a direct assault on the State to force it to abandon the policy of extradition to USA). The traffickers also hired paramilitaries to defend their newly acquired ranches from attack by the guerrillas. These paramilitary groups, often originally formed by the Army, have gone increasingly on the offensive and have killed many civilians in their counter-guerrilla war. Ironically, the traffickers have often financed the very guerrillas that their paramilitaries have been fighting. Many cocaine laboratories and much of the coca cultivation were situated in the jungle in south-east Colombia where the FARC was strong. The drugs cartels paid the FARC 'protection' money, which rapidly made the FARC into the world's richest guerrilla group. The advent of opium poppy cultivation in the early 1990s and the increase in coca cultivation from 1995 made the FARC even richer.

The impact of the drugs trade on Colombia went much further than the direct effects described above. It diverted and weakened the judicial system and security forces, allowing common criminality greater impunity and creating a culture of violence and contempt for any legal or moral restraints.

REFORM, PEACE AND NARCOTERRORISM, 1982–90

In May 1982 the Conservative candidate, Betancur Cuartas, was elected to the presidency, mainly owing to divisions within the Liberal Party. Betancur had moved from the right of the party to its far left. However, with a Liberal majority in Congress he had to continue the tradition of coalition government. Like his predecessors, he followed a prudent economic policy and encouraged foreign investment. His innovations focused on foreign policy and peace issues. Under his leadership, Colombia, traditionally a loyal US ally, became a member of the Non-Aligned Movement as well as the Contadora Group, which assisted efforts to find a peaceful solution to the conflicts in Central America.

Domestically, Betancur attempted to resolve Colombia's internal conflict by agreement. He granted an amnesty to guerrilla prisoners and concluded cease-fires with the FARC, M-19 and the EPL. The FARC founded a political party, the Unión Patriótica (UP), which contested the 1986 elections. However, the cease-fires with both M-19 and EPL broke down and in November 1985 the M-19 seized the Palace of Justice. In the ensuing recapture of the building by the Army about 100 people were killed, including 11 judges, leading to strong public criticism of both the Government and the Army. Many observers concluded that the cease-fires had benefited the guerrillas, particularly the FARC, which had used the time to build up its forces. Betancur also faced the beginnings of narcoterrorism when, in 1984, drugs traffickers from Medellín assassinated the justice minister, Rodrigo Lara Bonilla, who had taken the first serious measures to combat their activities. Betancur concluded that extradition to the USA was the only effective means of tackling the problem.

The drugs-trafficking problem was to dominate the presidency of the Liberal Virgilio Barco Vargas, elected in 1986 by a decisive majority. His offer to the Conservatives of a limited participation in government was refused, which resulted in the first single-party Government since 1953. Barco shared Betancur's belief in extradition, but the Supreme Court twice ruled that such a treaty with the USA was unconstitutional. Barco, however, used emergency decrees to proceed with extraditions. The Medellín drugs cartel began a campaign of terror to force the Government to abandon this policy. In August 1989 it assassinated Luis Carlos Galán, the favourite to win the Liberal Party's presidential nomination in 1990. The M-19 and UP presidential candidates were also assassinated in early 1990. An AVIANCA aeroplane was blown up, as were government offices, and in the first seven months of 1990 over 200 policemen were killed in Medellín. Barco refused to be intimidated and called successfully for international support to counter the cartel's threat.

He also continued the peace process with the guerrillas. The cease-fire with the FARC broke down in 1987, but in 1989 a settlement was reached with the M-19. They regrouped as the Alianza Democrática—M-19 (AD—M-19) and participated in the 1990 elections. Their presidential candidate, Carlos Pizarro, was assassinated by the cartel, but his successor, Antonio Navarro Wolff, won 12% of the votes cast. Successful negotiations with the EPL, the Partido Revolucionario de Trabajadores (PRT) and the Comando Quintín Lame were also concluded in 1990. Sadly, hopes that the FARC and the ELN might also enter into peaceful dialogue were frustrated by the killing of over 2,000 members of the UP, largely by paramilitaries linked to the Medellín cartel. Many of the paramilitary groups had been set up by the Army, but as they fell increasingly under control of drug cartels, they had been declared illegal in 1989. The fact that the FARC had resumed its war against the Government in 1987 put the UP in an extremely difficult position.

The first step in decentralizing the political system, so long sought, came with the election of mayors in 1988. However, further efforts at constitutional reform failed in early 1990, when amendments to prohibit extradition were introduced. President Barco did however make some progress in liberalizing the highly protected economy. Prudent management by successive Governments ensured that Colombia avoided the debt rescheduling and hyperinflation that afflicted the rest of Latin America in the 1980s; however, by the beginning of the 1990s the rate of growth had slowed and the import-substitution model was beginning to look less attractive.

CÉSAR GAVIRIA TRUJILLO AND THE REFORM PROJECT, 1990–94

César Gaviria Trujillo, the Liberal candidate elected President in May 1990, was determined to accelerate political reform and the liberalization of the economy, a policy known as *apertura* (opening). After decades in which Congress and the Supreme Court had opposed almost all constitutional change, an informal referendum, held at the time of the presidential election in 1990, produced a huge majority in favour of the establishment of a Constituent Assembly. Elections to the Assembly were held in December and the AD—M-19 and the Liberals received the largest share of the vote (27% each). Seats were also allocated to the EPL, the PRT and the Comando Quintín Lame.

The Constituent Assembly drafted a new constitution in 1991. It guaranteed every conceivable human right, and took decentralization further through the election of governors and the transfer of functions and central funds to departments and municipalities. It weakened the presidency by limiting emergency powers and providing for censure of ministers. A Constitutional Court was created, as was a prosecution service. Citizens were given the right to challenge almost any measure through an injunction (tutela) and extradition was prohibited. The Medellín cartel had halted its mass terrorists attacks when Gaviria took office, but had kidnapped several prominent figures. Gaviria offered the cartel the possibility of avoiding extradition if they released their hostages and surrendered, an offer that several prominent cartel members, including its leader, Pablo Escobar, accepted. In the legislative elections of October 1991 the AD—M-19 received only 10% of the votes and the Liberals regained their traditional majority.

In his first year in office Gaviria liberalized labour markets, removed price controls and improved terms for foreign investment. He also abolished import licences and drastically reduced tariffs. In an attempt to ensure that Colombian industry benefited from the sudden advent of international competition, Gaviria promoted rapid integration within the Andean community, especially with Venezuela and Ecuador. Such success could not be sustained, however. The liberalization of the political system was not completed by a peace settlement with the FARC and the ELN. Negotiations with both groups failed in Caracas (Venezuela) in 1991 and in Tlaxcala (Mexico) in 1992. This was followed in April 1992 by a drought, which in a country that was 80% dependent on hydropower, resulted in 13 months of power cuts. In July the Government was humiliated when Pablo Escobar escaped from his luxurious prison outside Medellín and returned to narcoterrorism. However, his organization was gradually dismantled and he was killed by the police in Medellín in December 1993. The economy began to recover from the 1992 drought, and grew at over 5% in 1993 and 1994. Gaviria's determination to persist with his reforms, in spite of set-backs, was admired and he left office in 1994 the most popular President in recent history and was immediately elected Secretary-General of the Organization of American States.

ERNESTO SAMPER PIZANO: SOCIAL REFORM AND POLITICAL CRISIS

In June 1994 the Liberal Party's Ernesto Samper was elected by a narrow margin in Colombia's first two-round presidential election. Two days later his defeated Conservative opponent, Andrés Pastrana Arango, disclosed the existence of taped conversations suggesting that the Cali drugs cartel had partly financed Samper's campaign, an accusation that cast a shadow over his whole presidency. An initial investigation cleared Samper, but one year later the case was reopened when his treasurer, Santiago Medina, and then his campaign manager (at the time his Minister of Defence) accused him of personal involvement. This led to two successive congressional investigations, which dominated the second year of his presidency. The House of Representatives finally voted to clear him of any wrongdoing in June 1996 but this was perceived by many as a political, rather than a legal, verdict.

This long-running political crisis, which was exacerbated by US policy (see below), made it difficult for Samper to carry out the social-reform programme on which he had been elected. Always on the social-democratic wing of the Party, Samper had made clear his reservations about the rapid pace of *apertura* pursued by Gaviria (under whom he had served as Minister of Economic Development until late 1991). As President he aimed not to reverse this policy, but to moderate it. He also promised to increase social spending to alleviate poverty, a problem hitherto neglected.

Samper's domestic problems were exacerbated by the response of the USA. Initially, the US Government stated that Samper, despite the allegations, would be judged on the results of his anti-narcotics policy. This proved to be quite successful, with the leaders of the Cali cartel captured in 1995. However, when Medina made his accusations against Samper in mid-1995, US policy shifted and the administration of President Bill Clinton openly expressed its lack of confidence in Samper and demanded that further anti-narcotics legislation be passed (seizure of assets, stricter penalties and even the reintroduction of extradition). Samper eventually complied. Colombia was meanwhile refused certification for its anti-narcotic efforts in both 1996 and 1997 and only received a conditional certification in 1998. The consequences of decertification were severe: Colombia received no US export credits and the USA voted against loans to Colombia from multilateral banks. The confidence of both domestic and foreign investors inevitably declined. The fiscal deficit and foreign debt rose and economic growth slowed. The FARC and the ELN were correspondingly encouraged and saw no reason to negotiate with a President that the USA considered corrupt. US pressure, although it damaged his Government and the country, undoubtedly helped Samper to maintain a considerable level of popular support as many Colombians resented such blatant US interference.

ANDRÉS PASTRANA ARANGO: THE PEACE PROCESS AND THE 'PLAN COLOMBIA'

The 1998 presidential contest was the closest fought in Colombian history. In the first round the Liberal candidate, Horacio Serpa, was less than one percentage point ahead of Andrés Pastrana, the defeated 1994 Conservative candidate. Noemí Sanín Posada, a former foreign minister running as an independent, came a close third, a result that reflected the electorate's dissatisfaction with the traditional parties. In the second round, however, Pastrana won by 500,000 votes. The turn-out was 60%, unusually high for Colombia, suggesting that faith in the democratic process itself remained strong. Serpa, a popular and effective candidate, was seen by many as too close to Samper, whom he had strongly defended while serving as his Minister of Interior. Many leading Liberals had supported Pastrana, believing him better placed to end Colombia's isolation, restore confidence in the economy and restart the peace process.

Unfortunately, the means to achieving the last two goals were often in conflict. Restoring economic confidence meant reducing the fiscal deficit sharply by reducing public expenditure and raising taxes (See Economy, below). In the short term this worsened the recession Pastrana had inherited from the previous administration. It made it very difficult to ensure popular support for the peace process, which ideally required increased military spending to protect the population and to put pressure on the guerrillas and increased social spending to mitigate rising unemployment

President-elect Pastrana took the initiative on peace, by meeting Manuel Marulanda Vélez, leader of the FARC, in his jungle hideout. Such a dramatic step relaunched the peace process. The new President's cabinet appointments reassured the markets that Colombia was returning to its prudent tradition of orthodox financial management. US relations immediately improved. Pastrana made a state visit to the USA in October 1998, the first in 23 years. The USA granted Colombia full certification in March 1999 and in 2000 gave US $1,300m to help restore peace and stability and reduce the drugs trade. This funding formed the US portion of the so-called 'Plan Colombia' (see below).

However, President Pastrana encountered difficulties in sustaining the peace process. To persuade the rebels to negotiate he had to cede them, temporarily, 41,000 sq km. in south-east Colombia, from which all government troops were withdrawn. The FARC, having received this territory, successfully insisted on the removal of any restrictions before they would agree an agenda for the talks. Public support soon decreased sharply when it became clear the FARC was using the demilitarized zone as a safe haven and was keeping military prisoners and kidnapped civilians there. Public discontent increased when both FARC and ELN began to kidnap more indiscriminately, taking many middle-class and child victims. The slow progress of negotiations, halted several times by the FARC, added to the frustration. An agreement made at Los Pozos by Pastrana and Marulanda on 9 February 2001 that provided for international involvement and mechanisms for resolving disputes and tackling the paramilitary problem gave some hope that progress could eventually be made.

The existence of the demilitarized zone caused considerable concern in the Army, as did the measures that Pastrana took against officers suspected of involvement with the paramilitaries. However, the President's support for firmer military action against the FARC, while negotiating, and his success in winning substantially increased US aid for the Armed Forces ensured that military discontent was contained. In fact, from November 1998 at Mitu, the Armed Forces, whose combined operations and intelligence capacity have greatly improved, have won all major engagements against the FARC. This contrasted with the last two years of the Samper administration when the Army suffered several humiliating defeats. However, this shift in the military balance did not register with public opinion since guerrilla attacks continued closer to large cities and kidnapping increased. This led to increased support for the paramilitaries whose numbers rose faster than those of the FARC. The increase in popularity of the paramilitaries put the ELN under great pressure. The latter, which, in 2000–01, was engaged in proximity talks with the Government, in their turn exerted pressure with periodic mass kidnappings. Their demand for a demilitarized zone, albeit much smaller and with controls, was repeatedly frustrated by local protest, partly promoted by the paramilitaries.

In 2001 the Government's hopes rested largely on the Plan Colombia. Conceived originally by Pastrana as a contingency plan for Colombia's coca- and opium poppy-growing regions, it developed into an ambitious, US $7,500m. project to strengthen the Colombian state. It aims include increasing the efficiency of both the security forces and the judicial system, eliminating drugs production through both eradication and crop substitution, and reducing unemployment. The international community was to fund almost 50% of the Plan. The US contribution of $1,300m., approved by the US Congress in July 2000, included a military component of $1,000m., but also significant sums for judicial reform and human-rights education. In early 2001 the new administration of President George W. Bush committed itself to a further US $882m. under the new Andean Region Initiative, introduced following international criticism of the Plan. Under this new Initiative, the member states of the European Union (EU) agreed to provide US$300m. This was all to be devoted to non-military projects and the EU made clear that its aid was not linked to Plan Colombia. This reflected warnings by non-governmental organizations in the region that human-rights abuses could rise as a main component of aid went to the security forces, whose links to paramilitary groups

were, allegedly, yet to be severed. Colombia's Andean neighbours feared that an escalation in violence would force thousands of refugees on to their territories and subsequently strengthened their borders. Roughly one-half of the new Initiative's funding went to Colombia's neighbours. In March 2000 Pastrana was confronted with a widespread political corruption scandal in Congress. He proposed to hold a referendum on political reform and hold elections; however, the offer was withdrawn in May after legislators suggested that Pastrana himself should also face elections. His political problems were compounded when, at the same time, several ministers were forced to resign after being implicated in corruption scandals. A cabinet reshuffle swiftly followed, with an increase in the number of Liberals and independents represented in the Government. In local elections, held in October, independent candidates won mayoral races in four of Colombia's five largest cities (including Santafé de Bogotá). The results were interpreted as a sign of voters' frustration with the Government.

INTERNATIONAL POLICY

Given Colombia's association in the popular mind with violence it is worth stressing that Colombia has an impeccable record in international matters. Colombia has never attacked another country and lost Panama through US intervention in 1903. Colombia has been a consistent opponent of the use of force to settle disputes and voted to condemn the Argentine invasion of the Falkland Islands (Islas Malvinas) in 1982 despite the pressure of most other Latin American countries. The country has contributed to UN peace-keeping operations from the beginning.

A founder of the Andean Pact in 1969, Colombia under President Gaviria played a leading role in the 1990s in making economic integration a reality, initially with Venezuela and Ecuador. This was followed by the formation of a free-trade area with Venezuela and Mexico in 1994. Close economic integration with Venezuela reduced the risk that a long-running dispute over offshore rights in the Gulf of Maracaibo and frequent incursions by Colombian guerrillas might lead to a conflict. However, relations between the two countries deteriorated slightly following the election to the Venezuelan presidency in 1999 of Hugo Chávez Frías, as his attempts to mediate in Colombia's internal conflict were not always welcomed by the Colombian Government.

Traditionally, Colombia has been a loyal US ally, although its role in the Non-Aligned Movement from the 1980s has led to some more independent stands. Close collaboration with the USA on anti-narcotics policy was established under President Barco and continued thereafter, albeit with difficulties under President Samper (see above). Colombia has long ceased to be the introverted Andean republic, which President López Michelsen referred to as an 'Andean Tibet'. It has become an active and respected player but which, at the beginning of the 21st century needed international support to help cope with its internal problems.

OUTLOOK

Optimism was in short supply in 2001. The economy's export-led recovery, which had started in 2000, was continuing but it was erratic and was only beginning to have a positive impact on investment and employment. The public had lost faith in the peace process, although the Los Pozos agreement of February 2001 had established more coherent mechanisms for ensuring progress. A cease-fire seemed a remote possibility. Meanwhile, the high level of kidnapping and guerrilla and paramilitary attacks on small towns continued unabated, despite the improved performance of the Armed Forces in major confrontations with the FARC. Local opposition to a new demilitarized zone frustrated chances of a settlement with the ELN, which the latter seemed keen to conclude. (In February 2001 more than 10,000 people in Bolívar participated in a peaceful demonstration against the establishment of the zone.)

The medium-term prospects, however, looked markedly better. The commitment by both the USA and the EU in 2000 to provide significant financial aid under the Plan Colombia or outside it represented recognition of the international community's responsibility for Colombia's drugs-fuelled internal conflict. It seemed improbable that this commitment would lessen, especially in a country so strategically placed as Colombia. The peace process, so criticized by Colombians, had made it politically possible for the international community to pledge aid. Eventually, the FARC could well be faced with the choice of settling or seeing their position eroded by a steadily strengthened Colombian state. The Colombians' deep attachment to constitutional rule would once again prevail.

Economy

DAVID BATTMAN

Revised for this edition by Sir KEITH MORRIS

INTRODUCTION

The main economic activity of the viceroyalty of New Granada (including present-day Colombia) was gold mining, with production concentrated in Antioquia, Chocó and Cauca. However, most of the population was involved in agricultural production. The colony, and the independent republic which succeeded it in the first part of the 19th century, remained poor and isolated until the latter half of the 20th century. Poor communications between the interior of Colombia and the rest of the world impeded development and limited immigration. This, in turn, meant that the internal market was small and that early attempts at industrialization tended to fail. Furthermore, foreign investors were also deterred.

However, the same factors combined to place much of the economy in Colombian ownership. Despite early foreign involvement in the coffee sector, all aspects of coffee growing, processing and exporting became an exclusively Colombian concern. The capitalists of Antioquia, particularly those in Medellín, quickly secured a prominent position. During the 19th century they gained dominance in gold mining, acquired relatively superior commercial experience and enjoyed an advantageous position in the coffee industry. It was in Medellín that the most successful advances in manufacturing were also made, most notably through the development of a textile industry, which proved a model of import-substitution. Although there were also other centres of industrialization, for instance in Santafé de Bogotá and in the Caribbean area, Medellín's merchant class quickly secured a control of the country's economic development, which was only seriously challenged in the late 20th century.

Agriculture remained important to the economy in the 19th and early 20th centuries, with tobacco, coffee and bananas the most important agricultural products. The development of these crops prompted, and was in turn assisted by, the development of steam navigation on the Magdalena River and of a railway network. These developments opened new areas for colonization. However, Colombia's rail network was, for topographical reasons, not an extensive one, a problem that remained at the beginning of the 21st century. Nevertheless, Colombia had become the world's leading exporter of mild coffee by the 1920s, helping the country enter its first period of relative economic prosperity since the 1870s.

The period of economic well-being in the 1920s ended abruptly with the Great Depression of the 1930s. The Depression prompted austerity but also increased import-substituting industrialization, strengthening domestic producers' dominance in the economy. Exceptionally consistent growth of gross domestic product (GDP) was sustained thereafter until the late 1990s. Colombia became popular with multilateral and private banking organizations for its exemplary record of foreign-debt repayment at this time, in marked contrast to its neighbours. Increased growth in the early 1990s was encouraged by the economic liberalization programme of President César Gaviria Trujillo (1990–94). The economic programme reduced tariffs, virtually eliminated import restrictions, liberalized foreign investment regulations, privatized state enterprises, opened the communications sector to private competition and adopted a market-based exchange rate.

However, the economy weakened in the second half of the decade. Although the administration of Ernesto Samper Pizano (1994–98) largely maintained the free-market policies implemented by Gaviria, the economic downturn was triggered by a steep increase in central government spending. This spending was intended to bolster Samper's political support when he was under investigation by Congress for allegations that his election campaign had been partly funded by drugs-traffickers. It was further aggravated by a clause in the new Constitution of 1991 that stipulated an increase in the amount of central government funds be equalled in regional authority expenditure. The increasing cost of the civil conflict during Samper's presidency also undermined economic performance. The civil conflict and related violence cost an estimated 4% of GDP, equivalent to US $4,000m. per year. These factors combined to produce a sharp increase in the fiscal deficit, generating inflationary pressure, which led to interest- and exchange-rate instability, but failed to generate significant economic growth.

The Government of Andrés Pastrana Arango, which took office in August 1998, inherited an incipient recession. The downturn was exacerbated by a sharp decline in international commodity prices and prevailing instability in emerging markets. Economic growth of 3.4% in 1997 was followed by disappointing growth of 0.6% in 1998 and a 4.2% contraction in 1999, when the country registered its worst economic performance since records began at the start of the 20th century. The economic decline was in sharp contrast to the average 4% annual growth witnessed throughout the 1970s, 1980s and most of the 1990s. The depth of the recession in 1999 reduced inflation to a 30-year low of 11.2%, compared with 20.4% in 1998, but unemployment increased to 19.4%, the highest level since records began.

The Government's fiscally conservative, orthodox economic programme for recovery was based on a three-year US $3,000m. extended fund facility agreement approved by the International Monetary Fund (IMF) in December 1999. Conditions of the agreement included a reduction in the fiscal deficit to 3.6% of GDP from the unusually high 5.4% in 1999, growth of 3% and an inflation target of 10%. Austerity measures in 2000 included a strict budget with a sharp 30% reduction in social spending to $2,000m., plus an increase in taxes equal to 1.8% of GDP, to reduce the fiscal deficit. Proposed fiscal reforms included pension reform and the introduction of a limit on central government transfers to regional authorities. (In mid-2001 the latter was close to final approval but pension reform was still at an early stage.) The Government intended to complement this with an ambitious privatization programme, but progress on this was disappointingly slow. However, the credit-rating agency, Standard & Poor's, downgraded Colombia's sovereign debt rating in September 1999, partly owing to the debilitating economic impact of the civil conflict, and criticized the weakened capacity of the Pastrana Government to implement effective economic policies. In May 2000 the agency further downgraded the debt rating owing to concerns that political obstacles could delay legislative approval of IMF-prescribed economic measures.

Despite these negative signals the economy started to recover in 2000, when GDP growth of 2.8% was recorded. The IMF targets for the reductions in the public-sector deficit and inflation were both more than met at 3.4% and 9.5%, respectively. The current account also went into surplus, helped by an increase in exports of 13%. The Government hoped that growth would increase to 4% in 2001, but a 1.7% increase in the first quarter of the year suggested that this would be hard to achieve. However, industrial production grew by 3.48% in the first four months of 2001 and both building licences and capital goods imports in first two months gave signs of an upturn in private investment. A revival of construction, hitherto hindered by a constitutional court ruling of the on interest rates for subsidized housing, was critical to any significant reduction in unemployment, which stood at just under 18% in April 2001, down from a peak of 20% in 2000.

AGRICULTURE

Agriculture, including forestry, fishing and hunting, was always the mainstay of the economy. Colombia produces a wide array of products, owing to the great variety of climates and topography. The sector's contribution to GDP fell from 26% in 1976 to 19% in 1998. The main reasons for this decline were measures instituted from 1989 under Colombia's economic-liberalization plan, including a reduction in tariffs on imports that led to a fivefold increase in agricultural imports in the 1990s. Low productivity also played its part, while other contributory factors included diversification of the economy, low world prices for the country's main commodities, insecurity in rural areas, a lack of credit and a fall in exports caused by the appreciation of the peso. In 2000 agriculture (including forestry and fishing) employed 20.9% of the labour force (compared with 37.9% of the work-force in 1970 and 51.4% in 1960). Farmers and ranchers suffered the most under the economic liberalization of the Gaviria administration; the Sociedad de Agricultores de Colombia (SAC), the farmers' union, reported that over 100,000 people lost their jobs in the agricultural sector between 1990 and 1994. Pressure from the powerful agricultural lobby resulted in President Samper introducing special measures designed to protect the sector. These included a mixture of government credits to large and small producers, guaranteed markets for some crops, improved marketing of national crops and increased expenditure on rural infrastructure, mainly housing. The sector, however, remained bedevilled by the problems of rural violence, encouraged by guerrilla and drugs-traffickers' activities. In 1996–99 agricultural production was almost stagnant; a decrease of just over 1% in 1996 was balanced by rises of less than 1% in both 1997 and 1998. In 1999 agriculture performed better than the rest of the economy, falling only by an estimated 0.4%. In the first nine months of 2000 growth resumed, at over 4%, as the peso became more competitive and coffee production increased by some 15%.

Coffee

In 2001 coffee remained Colombia's leading legal cash and export crop, and Colombian coffee enjoyed an excellent reputation around the world. Colombia remained the world's second-largest producer after Brazil. However, coffee was overtaken by petroleum and its derivatives as the single most important export commodity. In 1980–86 coffee accounted for between 45% and 58% of total export earnings; this figure had fallen to 11.4% by 1999. Coffee accounted for one-third of employment in agriculture, with small and medium-sized holdings still responsible for a considerable percentage of the crop. There were about 400,000 coffee farms, which created a rural middle-class unusual in Latin America.

The coffee sector was well regulated. Policy was set by the semi-official National Federation of Coffee Growers (Federación Nacional de Cafeteros de Colombia—FNC), which accounted for 40% of total exports. The National Coffee Fund (Fondo Nacional de Café) was established to help producers overcome considerable variations in world prices. In the mid-1980s high world prices and the Government's policy of maintaining stable internal prices encouraged increased production and Colombia began to challenge Brazil's position as the leading coffee-producing nation, with a share of the world market in the region of 20% in the late 1980s and early 1990s. Maintenance of the National Coffee Fund meant that the sector was able to absorb the collapse of the International Coffee Agreement in July 1989, when world prices fell by 50%. However, by this time the crop was being sold at a serious loss and production, which had reached 1.1m. metric tons in 1992 (an increase of more than 50% on levels of the mid-1980s), began to decline. In 1993 a majority of the main producing countries agreed to form the Association of Coffee Producing Countries (Asociación Mundial de Productores de Café—see under Regional Organizations, in Part Three) to regulate world coffee production. This followed alarm at coffee prices that in real terms, were lower than at any other time in the 20th century. Since then both production

and prices have fluctuated widely. In 2001 the price reached its lowest level since 1993 (exports declined to $1,324m. in 1999 and to $1,068m in 2000, when production fell by an unofficial 17.9%, to 630,000 tons). Such a fall put Colombia's small-scale producers at a disadvantage against their large-scale Brazilian competitors and increasingly against the Vietnamese, recent entrants to the market with extremely low labour costs. Nevertheless, output recovered strongly in 2001, helped by the devaluations and measures taken by the FNC to improve quality further.

Bananas

While coffee was by far the most important crop, a policy of diversification was followed. Bananas, sugar, cut flowers and cotton steadily increased their share of the export market. Bananas became the second most important legal export crop, earning US $476m. in 1998 and accounting for 4.4% of total export earnings. Most of the crop was grown in the Uraba region in north-west Colombia; the region's coastal location facilitated shipment abroad. The success of the banana crop in the 1980s and early 1990s led to replanting in the Santa Marta area, further east along the coast. In 1994 Colombia, along with Costa Rica, Nicaragua and Venezuela, signed a framework agreement with the European Union (EU) that gave them 48% of the EU's 2.2m. metric-ton quota for Latin American bananas. In 1998, however, the European Court of Justice ruled against the framework agreement, which it declared to be discriminatory because it exempted banana producers from African, Caribbean and Pacific (ACP) countries and from EU dependencies from the export licence system set for bananas from other regions. The USA protested to the World Trade Organization regarding the EU's modified measures. In April 2001 the USA and the EU reached an agreement under which quotas would be phased out by 2006 after which a tariff-only regime would apply. This should finally put an end to the banana wars that have complicated trade relations for the last decade. (For details of the international 'banana war', see Part One, General Survey, and Part Three, Major Commodities of Latin America.)

Flowers

Colombia's cut-flower sector did not exist until the late 1960s, but by the 1990s the country was the world's second-largest exporter (after the Netherlands). Colombia was the leading supplier of imported fresh-cut flowers sold in the USA, with an 88% market share. Producers based predominantly in the Sabana plain, around the capital, took advantage of the year-round temperate climate and proximity to Santafé de Bogotá's international airport to establish this non-traditional export. In the early 1990s the sector suffered from the appreciation, in real terms, of the currency. Furthermore, this appreciation occurred at a time when rising production costs and increasing competition from new competitors in Kenya, Costa Rica and Ecuador were adversely affecting Colombian producers' share of the cut-flower market. However, the value of cut-flower exports still continued to rise, reaching US $556.5m. (5.1% of total exports) in 1998. Exports declined slightly in 1999, to $550m., but increased to $580m. in 2000. Producers who had survived the over-valuation of the peso by cutting costs were well placed when the peso fell at the end of the decade.

Palm Oil

Colombia was estimated to have more than 3.5m. ha of optimum land for palm cultivation, with one of the highest yields of palm oil per hectare in the world, and in the late 1990s the Government introduced a flexible credit system to encourage producers. By 1999 Colombia was the world's fourth-largest producer of palm oil, with output projected to reach 465,000 metric tons. However, owing principally to uncompetitive costs, only 150,000 ha were under cultivation and, while output had increased by 65% from 1992, only 20% of production was exported. Once again the devaluation of the peso at the end of the decade improved the industry's prospects greatly. There was also an increased focus on the cultivation, for export, of the more exotic fruits native to Colombia, such as star fruit and guanabana. Exports of these fruits, as well as of palm oil, were expected to continue to increase. However, their importance within the overall level of exports was small.

Staples

The 'traditional' domestic agricultural sector was still dominated by the production of potatoes, maize, beans, plantains, cassava, citrus and other fruits. Although dietary customs changed, these remained the staple foods for most Colombians. Generally, output of these staple crops decreased in the early 1990s, owing to the reduction of trade tariffs and the consequent increase in imports. Production levels then stabilized and, in some cases, increased. Potato output stood at about 2.7m. metric tons in 2000, an increase from 2.4m. tons in 1991. Rice remained an important crop; 2.1m. tons were produced in 2000. It was grown in the eastern plains, or llanos, and in the department of Tolima. Sugar-cane cultivation, which was based in the Cauca Valley near Cali on an area of some 150,000 ha, increased by more than 50% in the 1990s, with sugar production rising from 2.1m. metric tons in 1996 to 2.4m. in 2000.

Livestock

Government initiatives to promote the supply of meat and dairy products through the use of subsidies led to an expansion in the amount of arable land dedicated to livestock. Almost 80% of the cattle population was based in the llanos. Production of beef and veal rose from 3.52m. head slaughtered in 1995 to 3.83m in 1998. It fell slightly in 1999, to an estimated 3.62m., but recovered to an estimated 3.77m. in 2000. A problem facing many ranchers was endemic guerrilla violence in their cattle-raising areas. Wealthy ranch owners, particularly those with drugs connections, could afford to defend their landholdings, but for the increasingly impoverished peasant class the general level of insecurity was indicated by a fall of 600,000 ha in the area sown with arable crops between 1990 and 1995. In 2001 the threat of guerrilla and paramilitary violence continued to depress levels of rural investment and discourage foreign involvement in the sector.

Agrarian Reform

From 1982 successive Governments attempted to improve the economic and social infrastructure in rural areas. President Samper pledged to increase such expenditure but was impeded by the economic slowdown. Despite the introduction of the first agrarian-reform law in 1961, Colombia's record has been disappointing. The pattern of landholding varies greatly from region to region. The highlands of the eastern cordillera are largely farmed by smallholders, often subsistence farmers. The coffee zone in the central cordillera is farmed in family-size commercial farms. The Caribbean coast and the llanos are where the large cattle ranches are situated. A continuing problem was the question of legal title. Many settlers (colonos) occupied land on Colombia's many internal frontiers. Their legal position often remained obscure.

Drugs

The illicit drugs trade has undoubtedly both contributed to Colombia's economic growth and hindered it. Marijuana and coca have long been grown in the country. Moreover, in the 1990s there was an expansion, mainly in the south-west of the country, in the cultivation of the opium poppy, used to make heroin. The benefits or otherwise of this hidden input were disputed, as, by its nature, the trade resisted quantification. It was claimed in April 1994 that traffickers remitted some US \$5,000m. to the country every year, a figure representing roughly 10% of GDP and equal to a large proportion of legal exports. However, other government estimates put the figure at closer to \$1,000m. which seems much more likely since a high proportion of drugs money was kept outside the country for obvious reasons. The Government also regularly argued that the cost in terms of extra security expenditure and lost foreign investment was much higher than any gains. Certainly the extra drugs-related crime and violence in rural areas, along with associated environmental damage, had a major negative impact. Nevertheless, while some rural areas were effectively isolated from markets for legal agricultural produce, the attraction of growing illegal drugs crops, which would be collected by traffickers and which commanded a higher price, would remain. However, it is worth noting that many of the growers went to such areas specifically to grow such crops, often sent by the traffickers.

MINING AND ENERGY

At the beginning of the 1980s energy and mining accounted for no more than 1% of GDP. This was something of a surprise, as the country had important gold reserves, produced 95% of the world's emeralds and had high expectations of petroleum discoveries. Colombia's mighty rivers offered a source of hydroelectric power and it had large coal reserves. However, major investments by state and private corporations helped to accelerate development during the 1980s, and by 1992 the mining and quarrying sector had grown to account for 7.6% of GDP, with petroleum overtaking coffee as the main single legal export. Owing to the relative expansion of other sectors of the economy, mining and quarrying only contributed 5% in 1998, but, in the following year, hydrocarbon resources alone provided almost 40% of export earnings. This remarkable transformation was based largely on expanding petroleum production, but also reflected other important developments in the mining sector.

Oil and Gas

Although petroleum exploration occurred intermittently for most of the 20th century, unfavourable political conditions, a lack of incentives for foreign companies and geology combined to prevent significant discoveries. After reaching a peak of 79.6m. barrels in 1970, petroleum production declined to 44.9m. barrels in 1979, as exploration failed to keep pace with production. However, the administration of Alfonso López Michelsen (1974–78) introduced association contracts for oil exploration that kept Colombia open to foreign companies just when most other Latin American countries were nationalizing their oil industries. The policy led to important discoveries in Arauca, where development of the Caño Limón oilfield in the mid-1980s helped to ensure that national production increased from 64.4m. barrels in 1985 to 275.5m. barrels by 1998.

The discovery in Arauca encouraged the state-owned petroleum company, Empresa Colombiana de Petróleos (ECOPETROL) to undertake an ambitious five-year plan in 1987, which aimed to secure Colombia's self-sufficiency in petroleum after 1993. One priority was to discover new reserves of petroleum in order to allow exports, as well as meeting domestic demand. The other priority was to increase domestic refining capacity to ensure real self-sufficiency and to overcome the need to import refined petroleum and related products. In 1991 petroleum and its derivatives accounted for about 6.0% of the total value of imports. By 1999 this share was 2.8% of imports. The country's refineries produced a surplus of fuel oil and other heavy products, allowing exports of some 60,000 b/d (barrels per day) of these products. Most refining occurs at Barrancabermeja and Cartagena and ECOPETROL was planning to almost double capacity at the Cartagena refinery, in order to reduce further the requirement for petroleum imports.

By 1990 petroleum was also being produced along the length of the Magdalena valley, in Putumayo and in the eastern llanos. In 1991 a foreign consortium, led by British Petroleum (BP), discovered large petroleum and natural-gas reserves in Casanare, estimated to total 1,500m.–2,000m. barrels, the largest in Colombia to date. Exploration activity had taken place in this area in the foothills of the eastern cordillera since the 1920s, but without major success. Improved seismic capacity and drilling technology made it possible to discover and extract oil at depths of 15,000 ft and more. In partnership with ECOPETROL, the Cusiana/Cupiagua oilfield was declared commercial in 1993 and in the following two years national production increased by some 40%. By mid-1999 petroleum production had reached some 840,000 b/d, but by the end of 2000 output had declined to 685,000 b/d. Crude petroleum reserves were 2,600m. barrels in 2000.

Exploration activity had declined during the second half of the 1990s as a result of a combination of factors. Firstly, in 1989 Colombia had made stricter the terms of its association contracts, believing that the US company, Occidental Petroleum Corporation, had profited too greatly from Caño Limón. However, conditions in the Andean foothills for BP were more difficult and, although the Cusiana/Cupiagua oilfield was under the old contractual terms, it was only its vast scale that made it viable. BP's next contract, Piedemonte, was on the 1989 terms and looked much less attractive. Other explorers, especially those considering smaller fields, were discouraged. The second disincentive was the security situation as guerrilla groups followed the discoveries and pipelines south from Arauca to Casanare. The Government deployed more troops in the region from 1993, but could not eliminate the risks entirely. Thirdly, better alternatives emerged. Most of the world's petroleum provinces, which had excluded foreign companies from the mid-1970s, were, by the 1990s, competing to attract them. Venezuela, which had ambitious expansion plans, proved the toughest competitor.

The Samper administration improved the terms for foreign exploration, but without success. It also attempted to modify BP's terms for Piedemonte to make development viable but met with legal, legislative and trade-union opposition. In 1999 the Pastrana Government improved the terms significantly, helped by the realization that the reserve situation was becoming critical. As a result, 32 new contracts were signed in 2000 (compared with one in 1999), the most in 20 years, and 16 more in the first half of 2001. ECOPETROL also agreed improvements to BP and Occidental's Piedemonte and Samore contracts, respectively. There was a dramatic increase in exploration activity.

Colombia's gas potential tended to be overlooked because of the attention focused on the petroleum sector. However, there were large gas fields associated with major oilfields with reserves estimated at 6,900,000m. cu ft. In 1997 ECOPETROL's gas-distribution subsidiary, Empresa Colombiana de Gas (ECOGAS), was incorporated as a separate public entity with responsibility for the development of the distribution network. ECOGAS embarked on a US $1,000m. programme of investment in the network, part of the Government's strategy to increase the industry's customer base from 4m. in 1998 to 18m. by 2006. Both the building and operating of the pipelines and the distribution to consumers was transferred to the private sector.

Metals

Security problems also affected the mining industry, in particular gold mining. This was because most gold production was small-scale and primitive, and mines were likely to be situated in isolated regions, especially susceptible to guerrilla activity. Nevertheless, in the early 1990s Colombia was the world's eighth-largest producer of gold. In 1996 gold exports earned US $204m.; however, by 1998 this figure had decreased to $19.6m. There was considerable potential for expansion, which had yet to be realized by the early 2000s, mainly because many gold mines were situated in north-west Colombia where civil conflict was endemic. Conversely, the nickel industry, concentrated at the Cerro Matoso plant, continued to expand. Output reached 57,000 lbs. in 1999, with an export value of $154m. These figures improved further in 2000, to 61,000 lbs. and $211m., respectively. New investment would increase capacity to 80,000 lbs. By 1997 Colombia had become the world's fifth-largest nickel exporter.

Emeralds

Colombia claims to produce about 60% of the world's emeralds and hosted the first international emerald congress in November 1996. The state mining company, Minerales de Colombia (MINERALCO), was attempting to legitimize and increase control over a notoriously unregulated industry. The exact size of Colombia's emerald production was difficult to measure because many stones were smuggled abroad. Official figures for exports were US $452m. in 1995, making them Colombia's fourth most valuable export commodity. Thereafter, official exports declined to only $96m. in 2000.

Coal

It was coal which offered Colombia the greatest mining opportunities. In the 1990s it became apparent that Colombia had the largest coal reserves in Latin America, estimated at around 6,700m. metric tons, or around 200 years' supply at 1999 rates of extraction. Several large-scale projects greatly increased the contribution of this industry to GDP growth. The most important venture was the development in the 1980s of the El Cerrejón coal complex in La Guajira, the largest mining project in Colombian history. El Cerrejón was jointly developed by the state company, Carbones de Colombia (CARBOCOL) and International Resources Corporation (Intercor), a Colombian subsidiary of the US petroleum company, Exxon. It involved the construction of a railway to transport the coal for export from the mine to a new, purpose-built port, Puerto Bolívar. Coal from El Cerrejón was high quality steam coal, low in sulphur and minerals, and most was exported to Italy and the United Kingdom. By 1999 the mine was producing some 17m. tons of coal annually and it was hoped that the Government's decision to allow increased shipments through the Puerto Bolivar terminal would enable output to double within five years. Drummond Coal of the USA was also developing a major coal-mine and supporting infrastructure, south of El Cerrejón, in César. The planned production was 10m. tons per year.

Several other projects were also being developed, with foreign investment being actively encouraged by the reform of mining legislation. By the end of the 1990s Colombia had become the fourth-ranked producer and exporter world-wide and coal was Colombia's third most valuable export, with revenues increasing from US $595m. in 1995 to $935m. in 1998, before declining to $794m. in 2000 (7% of total exports). In 1999 the contract between CARBOCOL and Exxon to operate El Cerrejón, which had been scheduled to expire in 2008, was extended for 25 years. In October 2000 CARBOCOL was sold to an international consortium of Billiton (now BHP Billiton) PLC, Anglo-American PLC, and Glencore International AG for $453m.

Power

Electricity generation and distribution was the least successful area of the energy sector. Massive projects drawn up during the 1970s and mainly financed through borrowing proved more costly and overran completion dates. Bureaucratic inefficiency and corruption, a lack of co-ordination between those responsible, poor maintenance and power thefts all contributed to the problem. The situation was exacerbated in 1992 when a drought caused by El Niño (a warm current that periodically appears in the Pacific, disrupting normal weather patterns) resulted in extremely low water levels, reducing supplies to hydroelectric generators. In an energy-rich country, electricity was rationed for large parts of the day for over a year. A rapid expansion programme of thermal power-stations was begun in order to increase electricity output in line with demand, which grew at 4.5% per year in the 1990s and was projected to rise by more than 5% per year in 2000–10, and to end the reliance on hydroelectric power, which still accounted for over three-quarters of production.

The programme included an aggressive privatization policy, with the divestment of eight electricity companies between 1996 and 1998, realizing revenues of more than US $5,000m. In preparation for privatization the municipal electricity company, Empresa de Energía de Bogotá (EEB), was divided into two subsidiary companies; Codensa for electricity distribution, and Emgesa for electricity generation. In September 1997 a consortium led by ENDESA, the Spanish power group, and Enersis, a Chilean holding company for Latin America's largest electricity group, paid $1,200m. for a 49% stake and management control of Codensa. At the same time, ENDESA and Enersis paid $951m. for Emgesa. The sales were conducted according to the 'capitalization' model, with the funds going to the companies, in order to pay debts and finance new investment, rather than to the city; this made the prices, which were among the highest paid for Latin American electricity companies, look more reasonable. The Pastrana Government's plans to privatize the electrical transmission company, Interconexión Eléctrica (ISA), valued at in excess of $1,000m., as well as other smaller power companies, ran into both commercial and legal difficulties and were still pending in mid-2001.

MANUFACTURING

Manufacturing accounted for just less than one-fifth of GDP throughout most of the 1980s and 1990s (18.0% in 1998). Production was centred in Santafé de Bogotá, Medellín, Cali and Barranquilla, and was dominated by large private conglomerates. The manufacturing sector was protected by high tariffs and import controls until 1990, when President Gaviria sought to increase competition, efficiency and exports through the policy of *apertura* (opening). In August 1991 the Government completed at a stroke a planned four-year phased reduction of tariffs. This was painful for most Colombian producers, as until 1990 manufacturing developed with a focus on meeting local demand for most consumer goods and many intermediate goods.

Consequently, average annual growth in manufacturing GDP slowed from 5.0% in 1980–90 to 1.5% in 1990–97. As well as having to face foreign competition they had a currency which was overvalued. This limited the opportunities opened up to industry by regional integration during the Gaviria presidency, although exports to the Andean neighbours did increase greatly. Another significant problem was smuggling, which was often financed by drugs traffickers. The Pastrana administration increased efforts to resolve this problem. After 5.5% growth in 1995 manufacturing production remained stagnant until 1999, when the sector experienced a 12.8% contraction. In 2000 it increased by over 10% as demand began to recover and as a competitive peso led to export growth of manufactures of around 20%.

Food and beverages made up the largest element of manufacturing, of which a significant proportion was accounted for by coffee milling. Excluding coffee milling, the food sector did not fare well in the 1990s, owing to import penetration. The sector would account for a projected 3.8% of GDP in 1999. Other products, such as textiles and leather, chemicals, motor cars and electrical engineering, made a greater contribution to the manufacturing sector, helped by an increase in foreign investment from the mid-1980s. The chemicals industry was the beneficiary of considerable investment and was also stimulated by the lowering of trade barriers in the early 1990s, as this reduced the cost of imported inputs and created the conditions for greater transfer of technology. The industry, which was dominated by multinational companies, grew steadily, producing pharmaceuticals, fertilizers, insecticides, plastic resins, alkalis and acids, cosmetics, detergents and paints. The value of chemicals exports increased from US $235m. in 1990 to $1,359m. in 2000, which accounted for almost 10% of total export revenues.

Foreign companies also invested in car-assembly operations, with Renault of France and Toyota of Japan owning majority shares in the locally registered company, Sofasa Renault, and General Motors of the USA and Mazda of Japan involved in Fábrica Colombiana de Automotores (COLMOTORES) and Compañía Colombiana Automotriz (CCA), respectively. These three companies dominated what was, until 1992, a highly protected sector. In 1997 car manufacturers assembled a record 80,000 units, but the subsequent economic decline had a severe impact on the sector, with many jobs lost and production down to 32,000 in 1999. Production recovered to 50,000 in 2000.

The textiles industry, in contrast, dated from the beginning of the 20th century. Based mainly in Medellín, textile mills were the motor of Colombia's early industrialization. In 1992 exports of textiles and leather products generated an estimated US $905.3m. (12.5% of total export earnings). However, the industry was particularly adversely affected by the withdrawal of trade barriers and by the overvaluation of the peso in the mid-1990s, although the effect was not uniform. Some companies, in particular leather-goods and clothing manufacturers, became successful exporters. Others were simply unable to adjust to the changes. Local manufacturers claimed that foreign competitors took advantage of the situation to flood the Colombian market with imports and to engage in other unfair practices. The Government implemented some protective measures in 1993, but the pressure was on local textile manufacturers to reduce costs, improve design and become more competitive. In 1999 export revenue from the sector fell to $872.9m., but recovered to $939m. (just under 7% of total exports) in 2000. The recovery was clearly helped by the currency devaluation.

TELECOMMUNICATIONS

One of the most dynamic sectors of the economy in the 1990s was telecommunications. National telecommunications, formerly the exclusive monopoly of the state telecommunications company, Empresa Nacional de Telecomunicaciones (TELECOM), were deregulated in the 1990s. In 1994 licences to provide cellular telephone services, worth some US $1,200m., were awarded to six private companies. While the economic slowdown afflicted most sectors of the economy in 1998–99, the telecommunications industry continued to expand and by 1999 it accounted for 2.7% of GDP. The Government projected that growth would average 12% per year over the following decade and that the sector would account for 8% of GDP by 2007.

Colombia's telecommunications system was well developed compared with those of many other Latin American countries. With 13.7 lines per 100 inhabitants in 1999, Colombia ranked third in South America, behind Argentina and Chile, in terms of telephone coverage. By 1999 Colombia was also linked to the USA by a fibre-optic, submarine cable and, along with the other Andean nations, was part of an ambitious project to create a 7,500-km fibre-optic network.

FINANCIAL SERVICES

Colombia's financial-services sector was well developed by regional standards, particularly in banking. Banking supervision had been more rigorously enforced after a crisis in 1982, when the Government was forced to renationalize 70% of the banking sector. In the 1990s most of the sector returned to private ownership, with foreign investors, principally from Spain, a significant presence. The banking sector prospered in the early 1990s, owing in large part to the privatization and liberalization process. However, as elsewhere in Latin America the product range of banks was very limited and the banks were therefore over dependent on loan income. As a result, they were not always prudent in their lending and when the economy entered recession in 1998 many of the institutions were in grave difficulty with large bad debts. The problem was made more acute when interest rates were increased to record levels in late 1998 in order to reduce the public-sector deficit. In 1999 the Government was forced to carry out a major bank rescue using an estimated 7% of GDP. By mid-2001 most banks had returned to profitability and foreign banks accounted for 31% of the system's assets. The stock exchanges in Santafé de Bogotá, Cali and Medellín also grew rapidly as a result of the privatization and deregulation measures undertaken in the 1990s. None the less, market capitalization remained small by international standards.

CONSTRUCTION

The construction sector enjoyed a period of rapid expansion in the early 1990s. The area authorized for construction was increased by just over one-third in 1992, with construction activity concentrated in the three largest cities and around 80% of it directed towards housing. From 1996 this highly cyclical industry suffered seriously from the economic slowdown and then the recession. Construction declined by 13% in 1996, grew by 2% in 1997, but fell again by 12% and 24% in 1998 and 1999, respectively. A reduction in the amount of drugs money directed at speculative high-cost housing was one element in this decline, as was the increasingly rapid emigration of middle class professionals. The Government attempted to revive the sector and employment by increasing expenditure on low-cost housing, but was constrained in the short term by budgetary restrictions and an unhelpful constitutional court ruling on mortgage rates. Activity continued to fall in first half of 2000, but a modest recovery then began that showed signs of strengthening in 2001. The sector contributed about 3% of GDP in 1998.

PRIVATIZATION AND INFRASTRUCTURE

The administration of President Gaviria began a privatization programme intended to improve Colombia's dilapidated infrastructure. Ports, power-stations, railway concessions and waste-disposal services were transferred to the private sector. Concessions were also let for the construction (or modernization) of airports, roads and water utilities. Industrial assets were prepared for privatization by the Institute of Industrial Development (Instituto de Fomento Industrial—IFI). By early 1994 the IFI had disposed of holdings in the automotive, paper and chemical sectors. Several banks were also sold to the private sector, including to foreign banks. In its first year, the Samper administration sold only US $230m.-worth of state assets, compared to $1,700m. in 1994. In early 1996 ECOPETROL sold its $110m. stake in the natural-gas distributor, Promigas, to the US company, Enron. The pace of privatization accelerated in 1997 with the sales of Codensa and Emgesa, the distribution and generating subsidiaries of EEB, and by the end of the year investors had purchased nearly $4,000m.-worth of public-sector electricity assets, placing almost 45% of Colombia's electricity-generating capacity in foreign hands. More banks were also privatized. The Pastrana administration planned to privatize the remaining large, state-owned assets in the power sector, ISA, the transmission company, and Isagen, its generating counterpart. The sale was delayed several times in order to ensure a favourable outcome and then because of legal difficulties. Isagen, which has 1,600 MW of capacity and is valued at $450m., was scheduled to be privatized during 2001, as was the much larger ISA. Fourteen municipal electricity distributors were also to be sold in 2001. The sale of CARBOCOL, postponed by the previous administration, took place in late 2000 for $453m. The city of Bogotá telephone company, Empresa de Telecomunicaciones de Santafé de Bogotá (ETB), was also scheduled to be sold in 2001, following many delays. The privatization was expected to raise almost $1,500m.

FOREIGN TRADE AND BALANCE OF PAYMENTS

The economy's historical dependence on commodities, and especially on coffee, meant that the level of export earnings always fluctuated with world prices. By the early 1990s petroleum had overtaken coffee as the main export, but this was also a volatile commodity: guerrilla sabotage and falling world prices meant that the value of exports of petroleum and its derivatives decreased from US $1,460.5m. in 1991 to $1,312.7m. (15.5% of total exports) by 1994, though there was a rapid increase thereafter, primarily owing to the rise in production capacity. The price increase and greater production increased exports to $3,757m. in 1999 (32%) and, despite falling output, to $4,560m. in 2000. The mining sector was also increasingly important, with rapidly growing coal and nickel sales. Non-traditional exports, in particular cut flowers and bananas and manufactures, became more important, but suffered from a strengthening peso in the mid-1990s. This was in spite of privileged access for Colombian goods to the USA and the EU, assistance that was essentially provided in recognition and support of Colombia's anti-drugs efforts. However, non-traditional exports benefited from the devaluations at the end of the decade and increased by 17% in 2000.

Under the protectionist regime in force in Colombia until 1990/91, imports remained relatively modest. However, with *apertura* imports increased, reaching a record $14,635m. by 1998. This led to Colombia running increasingly large trade and current-account deficits in the second half of the decade. In 1998 the trade deficit was $2,452m. and the current-account deficit $5,209m. In 1999 total imports declined in value to $10,659m. and exports rose to $11,576m., resulting in a trade surplus of $1,776m. The current-account deficit declined to $61m. In 2000 exports rose by almost 13% (traditional by 8.9%; non-traditional by 17.1%), to $13,040m. and imports rose by 8.3% at $11,539m. The trade surplus was an estimated $1,505m. The current account returned to surplus.

INVESTMENT AND INDEBTEDNESS

Direct investment was a significant element in Colombia's economic growth, and an important support for the capital account, particularly in the 1990s. It increased considerably when the Andean Pact's rules limiting foreign holdings to 49% were abolished in 1990 and the Gaviria administration introduced equal treatment for foreign investors, except for several strategic sectors. Much European capital entered Colombia during the 1990s, firstly in the petroleum industry (particularly from France and the United Kingdom), and then with the privatization of banks and electricity (Spain). Foreign direct investment (FDI), which was always the great majority of foreign investment, increased gradually from 1990. Following important privatizations in 1996 and 1997, FDI reached $3,111m. and $5,639m. respectively, in these years. In 1998 it declined to $2,961m. and in 1999 was only $1,140m. There was a slight recovery in 2000. Renewed oil exploration was likely to lead to much higher figures in 2001. The USA remained by far the largest investor.

Colombia did not participate in the major foreign borrowing of the 1970s, and pursued policies that enabled it to maintain the most favourable debt profile of the major economies in Latin America. It was the only country in the region that avoided major debt rescheduling in the problematic 1980s. External debt grew very gradually from the mid-1980s (US $17,000m. in 1986) to the mid-1990s ($24,912m. in 1995). This meant a fall in terms of GDP from 46% to 27%. However, the debt increased more rapidly in the second half of the decade, largely owing to greater borrowing by the private sector. In 1999 it stood at $33,624m., or 38.9% of GDP. Of this figure, $19,751m. was public-sector debt, (22.8% of GDP) mostly long-term, and $13,873m. was private-sector debt (16.0% of GDP). Debt at the end of 2000 was projected to be $33,751m., or 40.6% of GDP.

OUTLOOK

In 2001 the economy was continuing the slow recovery that had started in 2000, but growth remained uneven and confidence was not yet fully restored. The traditional optimism of Colombia's dynamic entrepreneurial class had been dented by the first recession in almost 70 years. It was, of course, unlikely that Colombia would ever return to its traditional consistent growth. From 1990 the country had become increasingly integrated in the global economy with the risks as well as the advantages that that implied. There were concerns that the renewed growth in 20-01 would be difficult to maintain. It could be affected adversely by various factors; a breakdown in the peace process with the guerrillas, further government expenditure cuts, another bank failure, the high dollar indebtedness of the private sector, a sharp fall in the price of petroleum. Unemployment reached a record 20% in 2000 and from 1998 there was an unprecedented emigration of professionals.

There were, however, also grounds for the cautious optimism of the Government. Colombia was on course to restore international confidence. The IMF target for public-sector deficit reduction was more than met in 2000 when it was reduced to 3.4% (target 3.5%) from 5.4% in the previous year. The high oil price helped, but Congress passed tax increases equal to 1.8% of GDP in 2000. Legislation requiring local governments to reduce their running costs was also approved. A constitutional reform to limit the automatic transfer of funds to local government had made much progress in Congress by mid-2001 and the Government was preparing to reform the pensions sector. Expenditure in both these areas had become unsustainable. The deficit target of 2.8% for 2001 and 1.8% in 2002 looked difficult, but not impossible.

Colombia also had strong support from the international community. The support given in 2000 by both USA and the EU to President Pastrana's 'Plan Colombia', the $7,500m. package intended to ensure the success of the peace process by restoring economic stability, strengthening the country's institutions and reducing the drugs trade, was a striking confirmation of this. Implicitly, the international community was accepting its own share of the responsibility for the damage that the drugs trade has caused Colombia.

There were also favourable elements in the economic conjuncture. For most of the 1990s Colombian products were overvalued. The devaluations of 1998–2000 made Colombian industry and agriculture much more competitive in both export and domestic markets. This was reflected in the vigorous growth of non-traditional exports in 2000. The competitive edge was less likely than hitherto to be quickly eroded because inflation had decreased to single figures for the first time in a generation (9.5% in 2000). Interest rates were also at their lowest in 2000–01. Colombia, therefore, had a real possibility of an export-led return to rapid growth, which could be reinforced by the repatriation of Colombian capital and a revived interest on the part of foreign investors. The country's long tradition of growth and prudent economic management, together with its richness in natural and human resources could well make it again an attractive place for investment, provided that President Pastrana's return to sound finance was maintained by his successor in 2002 and that there was progress towards peace.

Statistical Survey

Sources (unless otherwise stated): Departamento Administrativo Nacional de Estadística (DANE), Centro Administrativo Nacional (CAN), Avda El Dorado, Apdo Aéreo 80043, Santafé de Bogotá, DC; tel. (1) 222-1100; fax (1) 222-2107; internet www.dane.gov.co; Banco de la República, Carrera 7, No 14-78, Apdo Aéreo 3531, Santafé de Bogotá, DC; tel. (1) 343-1090; fax (1) 286-1731; internet www.banrep.gov.co.

Area and Population

AREA, POPULATION AND DENSITY

Area (sq km)	
Total	1,141,748*
Population (census results)†	
15 October 1985	
Males	14,642,835
Females	14,838,160
Total	29,480,995
24 October 1993	37,664,711
Population (official estimates at mid-year)	
1997	40,064,092
1998	40,826,815
1999	41,589,018
Density (per sq km) at mid-1999	36.4

* 440,831 sq miles.
† Revised figures, including adjustment for underenumeration. The enumerated total was 27,853,436 (males 13,785,523; females 14,067,913) in 1985 and 33,109,840 (males 16,296,539; females 16,813,301) in 1993.

DEPARTMENTS (census of 24 October 1993)

Department	Area (sq km)	Population	Capital (with population)
Amazonas . . .	109,665	56,399	Leticia (30,045)
Antioquia . . .	63,612	4,919,619	Medellín (1,834,881)
Arauca . . .	23,818	185,882	Arauca (59,805)
Atlántico . . .	3,388	1,837,468	Barranquilla (1,090,618)
Bolívar . . .	25,978	1,702,188	Cartagena (747,390)
Boyacá . . .	23,189	1,315,579	Tunja (112,807)
Caldas . . .	7,888	1,055,577	Manizales (345,539)
Caquetá. . .	88,965	367,898	Florencia (107,620)
Casanare . . .	44,640	211,329	Yopal (57,279)
Cauca . . .	29,308	1,127,678	Popayán (207,700)
César . . .	22,905	827,219	Valledupar (278,216)
Chocó . . .	46,530	406,199	Quibdó (122,371)
Córdoba . . .	25,020	1,275,623	Montería (308,506)
Cundinamarca . .	22,623	1,875,337	Santafé de Bogotá*
Guainía . . .	72,238	28,478	Puerto Inírida (18,270)
La Guajira . . .	20,848	433,361	Riohacha (109,474)
Guaviare . . .	42,327	97,602	San José del Guaviare (48,237)
Huila . . .	19,890	843,798	Neiva (278,350)
Magdalena . . .	23,188	1,127,691	Santa Marta (313,072)
Meta . . .	85,635	618,427	Villavicencio (272,118)
Nariño . . .	33,268	1,443,671	Pasto (331,866)
Norte de Santander .	21,658	1,162,474	Cúcuta (538,126)
Putumayo . . .	24,885	264,291	Mocoa (25,910)
Quindío . . .	1,845	495,212	Armenia (258,990)
Risaralda . .	4,140	844,184	Pereira (401,909)
San Andrés y Providencia Islands	44	61,040	San Andrés (56,361)
Santander del Sur .	30,537	1,811,740	Bucaramanga (472,461)
Sucre . . .	10,917	701,105	Sincelejo (194,962)
Tolima . . .	23,562	1,286,078	Ibagué (399,838)
Valle del Cauca . .	22,140	3,736,090	Cali (1,847,176)
Vaupés . . .	65,268	24,671	Mitú (13,177)
Vichada . . .	100,242	62,073	Puerto Carreño (11,452)

Capital District

Santafé de Bogotá, DC	1,587	5,484,244	Bogotá*
Total	1,141,748	37,664,711	

* The capital city, Santafé de Bogotá, exists as the capital of a department as well as the Capital District. The city's population is included only in Santafé de Bogotá, DC.

PRINCIPAL TOWNS
(estimated population at mid-1999)

Santafé de Bogotá, DC (capital) . .	6,260,862	Neiva	300,052
Cali . . .	2,077,386	Soledad . . .	295,058
Medellín . .	1,861,265	Armenia . .	281,422
Barranquilla . .	1,223,260	Villavicencio .	273,140
Cartagena . .	805,757	Soacha . .	272,058
Cúcuta . . .	606,932	Valledupar .	263,247
Bucaramanga . .	515,555	Montería . .	248,245
Ibagué . . .	393,664	Itagüí . . .	228,985
Pereira . . .	381,725	Palmira . .	226,509
Santa Marta . .	359,147	Buenaventura .	224,336
Manizales . . .	337,580	Floridablanca .	221,913
Bello . . .	333,470	Sincelejo . .	220,704
Pasto . . .	332,396	Popayán . .	200,719

BIRTHS, MARRIAGES AND DEATHS*

	Registered live births	Registered deaths
1983	829,348	140,292
1984	825,842	137,189
1985	835,922	153,947
1986	931,956	146,346
1987	937,426	151,957

Registered live births: 989,071 in 1998; 989,117 in 1999.
Registered deaths: 173,506 in 1996; 167,172 in 1997; 171,210 in 1998.
Registered marriages: 102,448 in 1980; 95,845 in 1981; 70,350 in 1986.

* Data are tabulated by year of registration rather than by year of occurrence, although registration is incomplete. According to UN estimates, the average annual rates in 1985–90 were: births 27.8 per 1,000; deaths 6.5 per 1,000; and in 1990–95: births 27.0 per 1,000; deaths 6.4 per 1,000 (Source: UN, *World Population Prospects: The 1998 Revision*).

Expectation of life (UN estimates, years at birth, 1990–95): 68.2 (males 64.3; females 73.0) (Source: UN, *World Population Prospects: The 1998 Revision*).

ECONOMICALLY ACTIVE POPULATION
(household survey, '000 persons, March 2000)

	Males	Females	Total
Agriculture, hunting, forestry and fishing	2,822	400	3,221
Mining, electricity, gas and water	311	49	359
Manufacturing	1,145	806	1,951
Construction.	664	36	700
Trade, restaurants and hotels. .	1,742	1,727	3,469
Transport, storage and communications . . .	643	90	842
Finance, insurance, real estate and business services .	383	238	621
Community, social and personal services	1,729	2,510	4,239
Activities not adequately described	9	5	14
Total labour force	9,557	5,860	15,417

Agriculture

PRINCIPAL CROPS ('000 metric tons)

	1998	1999	2000
Wheat	39	36	36*
Rice (paddy)	1,898	2,059	2,100†
Barley	12	15	15*
Maize	755	975	1,010†
Sorghum	189	201	201*
Potatoes	2,547	2,705	2,705*
Cassava (Manioc)	1,597	1,956	1,956*
Soybeans	72	44	50*
Seed cotton	97	109	155*
Cabbages*	210	250	250*
Tomatoes*	347	390	390*
Onions (dry)*	200	248	248*
Carrots*	185	210	210*
Sugar cane*	34,000	36,900	37,000*
Oranges	470*	509	509*
Pineapples	360*	408	408*
Bananas	1,517	1,570	1,570*
Plantains	2,559	2,689	2,689*
Coffee (green)	767	648	630†
Cocoa beans	51	52	52*
Tobacco (blond and black)	30	33	33*

* FAO estimate(s).
† Unofficial figure.

Source: FAO.

LIVESTOCK ('000 head, year ending September)

	1998	1999	2000
Horses*	2,450	2,500	2,500
Mules*	590	595	595
Asses*	710	715	715
Cattle	25,764	25,614	26,000*
Pigs	2,452	2,765	2,800*
Sheep	1,994	2,196	2,200*
Goats	1,050	1,115	1,120*
Poultry*	95,000	98,000	100,000

* FAO estimates.

Source: FAO.

LIVESTOCK PRODUCTS ('000 metric tons)

	1998	1999	1999
Beef and veal	766	724*	754
Mutton and lamb†	9	10	10
Goat meat	6	6	6†
Pig meat†	135	150	152
Horse meat	5	5	5
Poultry meat	507	504	520†
Cows' milk	5,712	5,710†	5,740†
Cheese	51	51	51†
Butter and ghee	18	18	18
Poultry eggs	323	339	350†
Cattle hides	81	85	83

* Unofficial figure.
† FAO estimate(s).

Source: FAO.

Forestry

ROUNDWOOD REMOVALS ('000 cu metres, excl. bark)

	1997	1998	1999
Sawlogs, veneer logs and logs for sleepers*	1,706*	800	800
Pulpwood	589†	3	16
Other industrial wood	66	22	5
Fuel wood	16,401	16,712	17,024
Total	18,762	17,537	17,845

* Assumed to be unchanged from 1994.
† Assumed to be unchanged from 1986.

Source: FAO, *Yearbook of Forest Products*.

SAWNWOOD PRODUCTION ('000 cu metres, incl. railway sleepers)

	1997	1998	1999
Coniferous (softwood)	139	6	1
Broadleaved (hardwood)	946	154	179
Total	1,085	160	180

Source: FAO, *Yearbook of Forest Products*.

Fishing

('000 metric tons, live weight)

	1996	1997	1998
Capture*	131.1	149.4	167.5
Characins	5.5	3.7	6.4
Other freshwater fishes	17.6	16.9	15.2
Pacific anchoveta	26.3	28.7	28.5
Skipjack tuna	15.7	24.3	30.0
Yellowfin tuna	18.3	42.3	14.5
Other tuna-like fishes	26.3	12.1	59.5
Aquaculture	30.0	43.7	45.9
Tilapias and other cichlids	14.0	16.1	17.7
Cachama blanca	6.2	11.6	11.8
Rainbow trout	4.5	7.8	6.2
Whiteleg shrimp	5.2	6.9	7.5
Total catch	161.1	193.1	213.4

* Data refer to landings.

Note: Figures exclude crocodiles, recorded by number rather than by weight. The number of spectacled caimans caught was: 656,522 in 1996; 452,707 in 1997; 670,389 in 1998.

Source: FAO, *Yearbook of Fishery Statistics*.

Mining

('000 metric tons, unless otherwise indicated)

	1996	1997	1998
Gold ('000 troy oz)	690.1	521.8	598.0
Silver ('000 troy oz)	190.0	109.5	167.7
Salt (refined)	560.3	n.a.	n.a.
Hard coal*	30,065	n.a.	n.a.
Iron ore†	595.6	754.9	525.9
Crude petroleum ('000 barrels)	228,748	238,046	275,475

* Source: UN, *Industrial Commodity Statistics Yearbook*.

† Figures refer to the gross weight of ore. The estimated iron content is 46%.

Industry

SELECTED PRODUCTS ('000 metric tons, unless otherwise indicated)

	1996	1997	1998
Sugar	2,149.2	2,136.2	2,125.6
Cement	8,590.1	8,870.4	8,464.0
Steel ingots	298.4	344.9	264.5
Diesel oil ('000 barrels) . .	24,552	24,266	23,210
Fuel oil ('000 barrels) . .	19,453	19,700	18,758
Motor fuel ('000 barrels) . .	41,160	34,445	38,354

Finance

CURRENCY AND EXCHANGE RATES

Monetary Units

100 centavos = 1 Colombian peso.

Sterling, Dollar and Euro Equivalents (30 April 2001)

£1 sterling = 3,360.0 pesos;
US $1 = 2,346.7 pesos;
€1 = 2,083.0 pesos;
10,000 Colombian pesos = £2.976 = $4.261 = €4.801.

Average Exchange Rate (pesos per US $)

1998   1,426.04
1999   1,756.23
2000   2,087.90

CENTRAL GOVERNMENT BUDGET ('000 million pesos)

Revenue	1996	1997	1998
Direct taxation	4,804.9	5,038.7	7,280.7
Indirect taxation	7,720.1	8,247.9	8,285.5
Rates and fines	102.7	399.7	104.6
Revenue under contracts . .	290.8	30.3	—
Credit resources	5,380.2	8,721.9	10,527.9
Other	2,387.4	4,386.4	2,047.6
Total	20,686.1	26,824.9	28,246.3

Expenditure*	1996	1997	1998
Congress and comptrollership . .	186.4	238.9	281.0
General administration . .	879.7	856.0	742.0
Home office and foreign affairs .	123.2	127.7	147.8
Finance and public credit . .	3,184.6	3,509.1	3,263.7
Public works and transportation .	1,370.6	1,519.6	1,207.4
Defence	2,039.5	2,466.6	2,605.4
Police	973.0	1,237.4	1,471.4
Agriculture	811.8	622.3	425.0
Health	1,309.4	1,597.9	1,862.7
Education	2,950.3	3,656.9	4,706.9
Development, labour, mines and communications . .	1,411.4	1,674.5	1,765.3
Justice and legal affairs . .	947.7	1,118.2	1,234.8
Trade	31.1	26.2	21.2
Environment	139.0	167.5	138.7
Culture	—	12.4	64.3
Total	16,357.7	18,831.1	19,937.4

* Excluding public debt.

INTERNATIONAL RESERVES (US $ million at 31 December)

	1998	1999	2000
Gold*	103	95	89
IMF special drawing rights . .	196	131	135
Reserve position in IMF . .	575	392	372
Foreign exchange	7,983	7,580	8,498
Total	8,857	8,198	9,094

* Valued at market-related prices.

Source: IMF, *International Financial Statistics*.

MONEY SUPPLY ('000 million pesos at 31 December)

	1998	1999	2000
Currency outside banks . .	4,997.3	6,507.4	7,676.2
Demand deposits at commercial banks . .	5,673.3	6,533.1	8,845.0
Total money (incl. others) . .	10,785.7	13,404.5	16,859.7

Source: IMF, *International Financial Statistics*.

COST OF LIVING

(Consumer price index for low-income families; base: 1990 = 100)

	1997	1998	1999
Food and beverages . . .	379.4	465.5	491.1
Clothing and footwear . . .	295.0	320.2	336.6
Rent, fuel and light* . . .	525.4	617.3	680.7
All items (incl. others) . . .	432.1	520.2	578.5

* Including certain household equipment.

Source: ILO, *Yearbook of Labour Statistics*.

NATIONAL ACCOUNTS ('000 million pesos at current prices)

Composition of the Gross National Product

	1995	1996	1997
Compensation of employees . .	29,558.6	37,367.1	45,299.5
Operating surplus . . . } Consumption of fixed capital . . }	46,803.3	54,250.6	64,472.3
Gross domestic product (GDP) at factor cost	76,361.9	91,617.7	109,771.8
Indirect taxes	8,518.1	9,766.5	12,598.9
Less Subsidies	440.9	672.8	663.2
GDP in purchasers' values . .	84,439.1	100,711.4	121,707.5
Net factor income from abroad .	−1,441.7	−2,128.3	−2,705.7
Gross national product (GNP) .	82,997.4	98,583.1	119,001.8

Expenditure on the Gross Domestic Product

	1997	1998	1999
Government final consumption expenditure	24,245.7	28,887.2	36,634.4
Private final consumption expenditure	79,193.8	94,680.3	98,524.8
Increase in stocks	874.0	1,328.1	563.9
Gross fixed capital formation .	24,591.8	24,445.4	18,197.7
Total domestic expenditure .	128,905.3	149,341.0	153,920.8
Exports of goods and services .	18,063.3	21,331.5	27,500.4
Less Imports of goods and services	25,261.0	29,623.1	29,601.3
GDP in purchasers' values . .	121,707.5	141,295.2*	152,165.8*

* Including adjustment.

Source: IMF, *International Financial Statistics*.

Gross Domestic Product by Economic Activity

	1995	1996	1997
Agriculture, hunting and forestry	11,528.5	12,546.9	14,937.1
Fishing	308.2	312.7	405.9
Mining and quarrying	3,273.8	4,178.8	4,260.6
Manufacturing	12,464.5	14,511.7	16,782.0
Electricity, gas and water	2,623.6	3,419.7	4,190.6
Construction	6,318.7	6,611.7	7,723.5
Wholesale and retail trade; repair of motor vehicles, motorcycles and personal and household goods	7,960.4	9,277.3	11,153.4
Hotels and restaurants	2,233.0	2,637.9	2,706.7
Transport, storage and communications	6,067.2	6,957.7	8,539.8
Financial intermediation	5,125.0	6,625.8	8,172.2
Real estate, renting and business activities	9,850.8	12,135.9	14,939.1
Public administration and defence; compulsory social security	5,716.9	8,606.4	10,890.7
Education	3,626.9	5,365.8	7,300.9
Health and social work	3,103.2	3,790.1	4,717.1
Other community, social and personal service activities	1,433.4	1,732.0	2,082.0
Private households with employed persons	424.0	494.2	568.5
Sub-total	82,058.3	99,204.6	119,370.2
Less Imputed bank service charge	4,610.9	6,157.4	7,451.1
GDP in basic prices	77,447.4	93,047.2	111,919.1
Taxes on products	7,113.7	7,792.3	9,847.9
Less Subsidies on products	122.0	128.1	59.5
GDP in purchasers' values	84,439.1	100,711.4	121,707.5

BALANCE OF PAYMENTS (US $ million)

	1997	1998	1999
Exports of goods f.o.b.	12,064	11,480	12,030
Imports of goods f.o.b.	−14,705	−13,932	−10,254
Trade balance	−2,641	−2,452	1,776
Exports of services	2,135	1,925	1,835
Imports of services	−3,650	−3,394	−3,097
Balance on goods and services	−4,156	−3,921	514
Other income received	891	912	796
Other income paid	−3,213	−2,627	−2,217
Balance on goods, services and income	−6,478	−5,636	−907
Current transfers received	831	596	1,103
Current transfers paid	−217	−169	−257
Current balance	−5,864	−5,209	−61
Direct investment abroad	−810	−529	6
Direct investment from abroad	5,638	2,961	1,109
Portfolio investment assets	−762	801	−1,419
Portfolio investment liabilities	1,673	1,008	650
Other investment assets	−1,112	−326	−114
Financial derivatives liabilities	290	−39	100
Other investment liabilities	2,100	381	−428
Net errors and omissions	−876	−445	−155
Overall balance	277	−1,397	−312

Source: IMF, *International Financial Statistics*.

External Trade

PRINCIPAL COMMODITIES (US $ million)

Imports c.i.f.	1998	1999
Vegetables and vegetable products	849.2	652.3
Prepared foodstuffs, beverages and tobacco	953.8	788.3
Textiles and leather products	689.9	580.8
Paper and paper products	494.8	422.9
Chemical products	2,737.2	2,352.5
Petroleum and its derivatives	371.8	302.6
Metals	755.7	379.8
Mechanical, electrical and transport equipment	6,898.5	4,488.0
Total (incl. others)	14,634.7	10,659.1

Source: Dirección de Impuestos y Aduanas Nacionales.

Exports f.o.b.	1998	1999
Vegetables and vegetable products	1,157.6	1,187.8
Coffee	1,893.1	1,323.7
Coal	935.7	847.9
Petroleum and its derivatives	2,328.9	3,757.0
Prepared foodstuffs, beverages and tobacco	945.7	799.5
Textiles and leather products	932.8	872.9
Paper and publishing	272.8	259.3
Chemicals	1,021.5	1,103.0
Mechanical, electrical and transport equipment	601.5	477.6
Total (incl. others)	10,865.6	11,568.7

PRINCIPAL TRADING PARTNERS (US $ million)

Imports c.i.f.	1998	1999
Argentina	243.1	177.0
Belgium-Luxembourg	228.9	188.8
Brazil	520.0	428.5
Canada	406.4	212.2
Chile	238.8	272.7
Ecuador	318.5	262.4
France	376.9	273.3
Germany	749.3	452.7
Italy	357.9	213.0
Japan	844.7	417.3
Korea, Republic	273.9	159.6
Mexico	620.0	475.2
Netherlands	226.1	151.4
Panama	204.3	282.4
Peru	155.7	111.6
Spain	416.6	257.0
Sweden	153.8	82.1
United Kingdom	301.7	155.1
USA	5,092.3	4,099.9
Venezuela	1,399.4	888.1
Total (incl. others)	14,634.7	10,659.1

Source: Dirección de Impuestos y Aduanas Nacionales.

Exports f.o.b.	1998	1999
Belgium-Luxembourg	318.1	261.0
Brazil	101.6	166.2
Canada	136.9	120.1
Chile	159.3	152.2
Costa Rica	102.1	115.8
Ecuador	581.5	323.8
France	231.0	140.5
Germany	684.5	485.5
Italy	214.6	198.8
Japan	268.5	245.0
Mexico	128.5	201.6
Netherlands	288.7	169.5
Panama	106.1	144.0
Peru	370.1	357.3
Puerto Rico	101.7	167.3
Spain	151.0	149.3
United Kingdom	236.6	212.5
USA	4,048.5	5,615.4
Venezuela	1,154.6	915.6
Total (incl. others)	10,865.6	11,568.7

Transport

RAILWAYS (traffic)

	1996	1997	1998
Freight ('000 metric tons). . .	321	348	281
Freight ton-km ('000). . .	746,544	736,427	657,585

Source: Sociedad de Transporte Ferroviario, SA.

ROAD TRAFFIC (motor vehicles in use)

	1997	1998	1999
Passenger cars . . .	1,694,323	1,776,100	1,803,201
Buses	126,362	131,987	134,799
Goods vehicles . . .	179,530	183,335	184,495
Motorcycles	385,378	450,283	479,073

Source: IRF, *World Road Statistics*.

SHIPPING
Merchant Fleet (registered at 31 December)

	1998	1999	2000
Number of vessels . . .	112	113	111
Total displacement ('000 grt) . .	111.7	96.9	81.4

Source: Lloyd's Register of Shipping, *World Fleet Statistics*.

Domestic Sea-borne Freight Traffic ('000 metric tons)

	1987	1988	1989
Goods loaded and unloaded . .	772.1	944.8	464.6

International Sea-borne Freight Traffic ('000 metric tons)

	1996	1997	1998
Goods loaded . . .	38,053	47,567	40,965
Goods unloaded . . .	13,257	27,097	19,732

CIVIL AVIATION (traffic)

	1997	1998	1999
Domestic			
Passengers carried ('000) . .	8,027	7,947	7,545
Freight carried (metric tons) .	135,154	113,790	129,806
International			
Passengers ('000):			
arrivals . . .	1,311	1,373	1,337
departures . . .	1,355	1,407	1,480
Freight (metric tons):			
loaded	198,572	205,866	145,596
unloaded	226,875	232,979	233,015

Source: Departamento Administrativo de Aeronáutica Civil.

Tourism

TOURIST ARRIVALS ('000)

Country of origin	1995	1996	1997
Argentina . . .	32.0	29.9	20.2
Aruba . . .	38.5	30.3	24.8
Brazil . . .	24.3	22.0	16.8
Canada . . .	20.8	16.3	18.0
Chile . . .	22.1	19.5	13.4
Costa Rica . . .	33.6	25.2	12.9
Cuba . . .	18.7	24.6	17.1
Ecuador . . .	79.8	77.5	57.4
France . . .	34.0	31.2	23.3
Germany . . .	36.7	32.1	18.2
Mexico . . .	35.6	32.9	25.8
Panama . . .	146.6	137.7	105.0
Peru . . .	41.1	35.0	31.1
Spain . . .	63.9	61.9	54.1
United Kingdom . . .	21.8	18.8	18.2
USA . . .	537.4	477.4	386.5
Venezuela . . .	163.4	142.5	99.3
Total (incl. others) . . .	1,399.0	1,254.0	969.0

Tourism receipts (US $ million): 859 in 1995; 905 in 1996; 955 in 1997.
Source: World Tourism Organization, *Yearbook of Tourism Statistics*.

Communications Media

	1995	1996	1997
Telephones ('000 main lines in use)	3,873	4,645	5,334
Telefax stations ('000 in use) . .	100	141	173
Mobile cellular telephones ('000 subscribers) . .	275	523	1,265
Radio receivers ('000 in use) . .	20,200	20,600	21,000
Television receivers ('000 in use) .	4,200	4,500	4,590
Daily newspapers: number . .	34	37	n.a.

Book production: 1,481 titles in 1991.
Sources: UN, *Statistical Yearbook*; UNESCO, *Statistical Yearbook*.

Education

(1999)

	Institutions	Teachers	Pupils
Nursery	30,138	58,524	1,034,182
Primary	60,183	214,911	5,162,260
Secondary	13,421	200,337	3,594,083
Higher (incl. universities)* . .	266	75,568	673,353

* 1996 figures.

Source: partly Ministerio de Educación Nacional.

Directory

The Constitution

A new, 380-article Constitution, drafted by a 74-member National Constituent Assembly, took effect from 6 July 1991. The new Constitution retained the institutional framework of a directly-elected President with a non-renewable four-year term of office, together with a bicameral legislature composed of an upper house or Senate (with 102 directly-elected members) and a lower house or House of Representatives (with 161 members, to include at least two representatives of each national department). A Vice-President is elected at the same time as the President, and also holds office for a term of four years.

The new Constitution also contained comprehensive provisions for the recognition and protection of civil rights, and for the reform of the structures and procedures of political participation and of the judiciary.

The fundamental principles upon which the new Constitution is based are embodied in articles 1–10.

Article 1: Colombia is a lawful state, organized as a single Republic, decentralized, with autonomous territorial entities, democratic, participatory and pluralist, founded on respect for human dignity, on the labour and solidarity of its people and on the prevalence of the general interest.

Article 2: The essential aims of the State are: to serve the community, to promote general prosperity and to guarantee the effectiveness of the principles, rights and obligations embodied in the Constitution, to facilitate the participation of all in the decisions which affect them and in the economic, political, administrative and cultural life of the nation; to defend national independence, to maintain territorial integrity and to ensure peaceful coexistence and the validity of the law.

The authorities of the Republic are instituted to protect the residents of Colombia, in regard to their life, honour, goods, beliefs and other rights and liberties, and to ensure the fulfilment of the obligations of the State and of the individual.

Article 3: Sovereignty rests exclusively with the people, from whom public power emanates. The people exercise power directly or through their representatives in the manner established by the Constitution.

Article 4: The Constitution is the highest authority. In all cases of incompatability between the Constitution and the law or other juridical rules, constitutional dispositions will apply.

It is the duty of nationals and foreigners in Colombia to observe the Constitution and the law, and to respect and obey the authorities.

Article 5: The State recognizes, without discrimination, the primacy of the inalienable rights of the individual and protects the family as the basic institution of society.

Article 6: Individuals are solely responsible to the authorities for infringements of the Constitution and of the law. Public servants are equally accountable and are responsible to the authorities for failure to fulfil their function or abuse of their position.

Article 7: The State recognizes and protects the ethnic diversity of the Colombian nation.

Article 8: It is an obligation of the State and of the people to protect the cultural and natural riches of the nation.

Article 9: The foreign relations of the State are based on national sovereignty, with respect for self-determination of people and with recognition of the principles of international law accepted by Colombia.

Similarly, Colombia's external politics will be directed towards Caribbean and Latin American integration.

Article 10: Spanish (Castellano) is the official language of Colombia. The languages and dialects of ethnic groups are officially recognized within their territories. Education in communities with their own linguistic traditions will be bilingual.

The Government

HEAD OF STATE

President: ANDRÉS PASTRANA ARANGO (took office 7 August 1998).
Vice-President and Minister of National Defence: GUSTAVO BELL LEMUS.

CABINET
(August 2001)

A coalition of the Partido Conservador Colombiano (PCC), the Partido Liberal Colombiano (PL) and independents (Ind.).

Minister of the Interior: ARMANDO ESTRADA VILLA.
Minister of Foreign Affairs: GUILLERMO FERNÁNDEZ DE SOTO (PCC).
Minister of Justice and Law: RÓMULO GONZÁLEZ TRUJILLO (PCC).
Minister of Finance and Public Credit: JUAN MANUEL SANTOS CALDERÓN (PL).
Minister of Agriculture and Rural Development: RODRIGO VILLALBA MOSQUERA (PCC).
Minister of Labour and Social Security: ANGELINO GARZÓN (Ind.).
Minister of Foreign Trade: MARTA LUCÍA RAMÍREZ DE RINCÓN (Ind.).
Minister of Public Health: SARA ORDÓNEZ (PCC).
Minister of Economic Development: EDUARDO PIZANO (PCC).
Minister of Mines and Energy: LUIS RAMIRO VALENCIA COSSIO (PCC).
Minister of National Education: FRANCISCO JOSÉ LLOREDA MERA (PCC).
Minister of Communications: ANGELA MONTOYA HOLGUÍN (PCC).
Minister of Transport: GUSTAVO CANAL MORA (PCC).
Minister of the Environment: JUAN MAYR MALDONADO (Ind.).
Minister of Culture: ARACELY MORALES LÓPEZ (Ind.).

MINISTRIES

Office of the President: Palacio de Nariño, Carrera 8A, No 7-26, Santafé de Bogotá, DC; tel. (1) 562-9300; fax (1) 286-8063.

Ministry of Agriculture and Rural Development: Avda Jiménez, No 7-65, Santafé de Bogotá, DC; tel. (1) 334-1199; fax (1) 284-1775; e-mail minagric@colomsat.net.co; internet www.minagricultura.gov.co.

Ministry of Communications: Edif. Murillo Toro, Carrera 7 y 8, Calle 12 y 13, Apdo Aéreo 14515, Santafé de Bogotá, DC; tel. (1) 286-6911; fax (1) 344-3434; internet www.mincomunicaciones.gov.co.

Ministry of Culture: Calle 8, No 6-97, Santafé de Bogotá, DC; tel. (1) 342-4100; fax (1) 342-1721; e-mail fvasquez@mincultura.gov.co; internet www.mincultura.gov.co.

Ministry of Economic Development: Carrera 13, No 28-01, 5°–9°, Apdo Aéreo 99412, Santafé de Bogotá, DC; tel. (1) 320-0077; fax (1) 350-5791; internet www.mindesa.gov.co.

Ministry of the Environment: Calle 37, No 8-40, Santafé de Bogotá, DC; tel. (1) 288-6877; fax (1) 288-9788; internet www.minambiente.gov.co.

Ministry of Finance and Public Credit: Carrera 8A, No 6-64, Of. 308, Santafé de Bogotá, DC; tel. (1) 284-5400; fax (1) 286-3858; internet www.minhacienda.gov.co.

Ministry of Foreign Affairs: Palacio de San Carlos, Calle 10A, No 5-51, Santafé de Bogotá, DC; tel. (1) 282-7811; fax (1) 341-6777; internet www.minrelext.gov.co.

Ministry of Foreign Trade: Calle 28, No 13A-15, 5°, 7° y 9°, Santafé de Bogotá, DC; tel. (1) 286-9111; fax (1) 336-3690; internet www.mincomex.gov.co.

Ministry of the Interior: Palacio Echeverry, Carrera 8A, No 8-09, Santafé de Bogotá, DC; tel. (1) 334-0630; fax (1) 341-9583; internet www.presidencia.gov.co/mininterior.

Ministry of Justice and Law: Avda Jiménez, No 8-89, Santafé de Bogotá, DC; tel. (1) 286-0211; fax (1) 281-6384; internet www.minjusticia.gov.co.

Ministry of Labour and Social Security: Carrera 7A, No 34-50, Santafé de Bogotá, DC; tel. (1) 287-3434; fax (1) 285-7091; e-mail oaai@tutopia.com.

Ministry of Mines and Energy: Centro Administrativo Nacional (CAN), Avda El Dorado, Santafé de Bogotá, DC; tel. (1) 222-4555; fax (1) 222-3651; internet www.minminas.gov.co.

Ministry of National Defence: Centro Administrativo Nacional (CAN), 2°, Avda El Dorado, Santafé de Bogotá, DC; tel. (1) 220-4999; fax (1) 222-1874; internet www.mindefensa.gov.co.

Ministry of National Education: Centro Administrativo Nacional (CAN), Of. 501, Avda El Dorado, Santafé de Bogotá, DC; tel. (1) 222-2800; fax (1) 222-4578; internet www.icfes.gov.co/men.html.

Ministry of Public Health: Carrera 13, No 32-76, Santafé de Bogotá, DC; tel. (1) 336-5066; fax (1) 336-0296; internet www.minsalud.gov.co.

Ministry of Transport: Centro Administrativo Nacional (CAN), Of. 409, Avda El Dorado, Santafé de Bogotá, DC; tel. (1) 222-4411; fax (1) 222-1647; internet www.mintransporte.gov.co.

President and Legislature

PRESIDENT

Presidential Elections, 31 May and 21 June 1998

	Votes	
	First ballot (votes)	Second ballot %
ANDRÉS PASTRANA ARANGO (PCC) . . .	3,607,945	50.4
HORACIO SERPA URIBE (PL) . . .	3,634,823	46.5
NOEMÍ SANÍN POSADA . . .	2,824,735	—
Gen. (retd) HAROLD BEDOYA PIZARRO . .	191,981	—
Others	125,822	—

CONGRESO
Senado
(Senate)

President: MARIO URIBE ESCOBAR.

General Election, 8 March 1998

	Seats
Partido Liberal Colombiano (PL)	53
Partido Conservador Colombiano (PCC)	27
Independent groups	20
Indigenous groups*	2
Total	**102**

* Under the reforms of the Constitution in 1991, at least two Senate seats are reserved for indigenous groups.

Cámara de Representantes
(House of Representatives)

President: BASILIO VILLAMIZAR.

General Election, 8 March 1998

	Seats	% of votes cast
Partido Liberal Colombiano (PL) . . .	84	52.2
Independent groups	30	18.6
Partido Conservador Colombiano (PCC) .	28	17.4
Coalitions	16	9.9
Others	3	1.9
Total	**161**	**100.0**

Political Organizations

Alianza Democrática—M-19 (AD—M-19): Transversal 28, No 37-78, Santafé de Bogotá, DC; tel. (1) 368-9436; f. 1990; alliance of centre-left groups (including factions of Unión Patriótica, Colombia Unida, Frente Popular and Socialismo Democrático) which supported the M-19 campaign for elections to the National Constituent Assembly in December 1990; Leader DIEGO MONTAÑA CUÉLLAR.

Alianza Nacional Popular (ANAPO): Carrera 18, No 33-95, Santafé de Bogotá, DC; tel. (1) 287-7050; fax (1) 245-3138; f. 1971 by supporters of Gen. Gustavo Rojas Pinilla; populist party; Leader MARÍA EUGENIA ROJAS DE MORENO DÍAZ.

Democracia Cristiana: Avda 42, No 18-08, Apdo 25867, Santafé de Bogotá, DC; tel. (1) 285-6639; f. 1964; Christian Democrat party; 10,000 mems; Pres. JUAN A. POLO FIGUEROA; Sec.-Gen. DIEGO ARANGO OSORIO.

Frente Social y Político: left-wing; Presidential Candidate LUIS EDUARDO GARZÓN.

Frente por la Unidad del Pueblo (FUP): Santafé de Bogotá, DC; extreme left-wing front comprising socialists and Maoists.

Movimiento 19 de Abril (M-19): Calle 26, No 13B-09, Of. 1401, Santafé de Bogotá, DC; tel. (1) 282-7891; fax (1) 282-8129; f. 1970 by followers of Gen. Gustavo Rojas Pinilla and dissident factions from the FARC (see below); left-wing urban guerrilla group, until formally constituted as a political party in Oct. 1989; Leaders ANTONIO NAVARRO WOLFF, OTTY PATIÑO.

Movimiento Colombia Unida (CU): Santafé de Bogotá, DC; left-wing group allied to the UP; Leader ADALBERTO CARVAJAL.

Movimiento Nacional Conservador (MNC): Carrera 16, No 33-24, Santafé de Bogotá, DC; tel. (1) 245-4418; fax (1) 284-8529; Sec.-Gen. JUAN PABLO CEPERA MÁRQUEZ.

Movimiento Nacional Progresista (MNP): Carrera 10, No 19-45, Of. 708, Santafé de Bogotá, DC; tel. (1) 286-7517; fax (1) 341-9368; Sec.-Gen. EDUARDO AISAMAK LEÓN BELTRÁN.

Movimiento Obrero Independiente Revolucionario (MOIR): Calle 52A, No 20-09, Santafé de Bogotá, DC; tel. (1) 249-4312; e-mail moir@moir.org.co; internet www.moir.org.co; left-wing workers' movement; Maoist; Leader HÉCTOR VALENGA.

Movimiento de Salvación Nacional (MSN): Carrera 7A, No 58-00, Santafé de Bogotá, DC; tel. (1) 249-0209; fax (1) 310-1991; f. 1990; split from the Partido Conservador Colombiano.

Movimiento Unitario Metapolítico (MUM): Calle 13, No 68D-40, Santafé de Bogotá, DC; tel. (1) 292-1330; fax (1) 292-5502; f. 1985; populist-occultist party; Leader REGINA BETANCOURT DE LISKA.

Mujeres para la Democracia: Santafé de Bogotá, DC; f. 1991; women's party; Leader ANGELA CUEVAS DE DOLMETSCH.

Partido Conservador Colombiano (PCC): Avda 22, No 37-09, Santafé de Bogotá, DC; tel. (1) 369-0011; fax (1) 369-0187; f. 1849; 2.9m. mems; Pres. CARLOS HOLGUIN SARDI; Sec.-Gen. HUMBERTO ZULUAGA MONEDERO.

Partido Liberal Colombiano (PL): Avda Caracas, No 36-01, Santafé de Bogotá, DC; tel. (1) 287-9311; fax (1) 287-9540; f. 1815; divided into two factions, the official group (HERNANDO DURÁN LUSSÁN, MIGUEL PINEDO) and the independent group, Nuevo Liberalismo (New Liberalism, led by Dr ALBERTO SANTOFIMIO BOTERO, ERNESTO SAMPER PIZANO, EDUARDO MESTRE); Pres. LUIS FERNANDO JARAMILLO.

Partido Nacional Cristiano (PNC): Calle 22C, No 31-01, Santafé de Bogotá, DC; tel. (1) 337-9211; fax (1) 269-3621; e-mail mision2@latino.net.co; Pres. LIÑO LEAL COLLAZOS.

Unidad Democrática de la Izquierda (Democratic Unity of the Left): Santafé de Bogotá, DC; f. 1982; left-wing coalition incorporating the following parties:

Firmes: Santafé de Bogotá, DC; democratic party.

Partido Comunista Colombiano (PC): Calle 18A, No 14-56, Apdo Aéreo 2523, Santafé de Bogotá, DC; tel. (1) 334-1947; fax (1) 281-8259; f. 1930; Marxist-Leninist party; Sec.-Gen. ALVARO VÁSQUEZ DEL REAL.

Partido Socialista de los Trabajadores (PST): Santafé de Bogotá, DC; workers' socialist party; Leader MARÍA SOCORRO RAMÍREZ.

Unión Patriótica (UP): Carrera 13A, No 38-32, Of. 204, Santafé de Bogota, DC; fax (1) 570-4400; f. 1985; Marxist party formed by the FARC (see below); obtained legal status in 1986; Pres. ERNÁN PASTRANA; Exec. Sec. OVIDIO SALINAS.

The following guerrilla groups and illegal organizations were active in the late 1980s and in the 1990s:

Autodefensas Unidas de Colombia (AUC): right-wing paramilitary org.; 2,000 mems; Political Leader CARLOS CASTAÑO.

Comando Ricardo Franco-Frente Sur: f. 1984; common front formed by dissident factions from the FARC and M-19 (see below); Leader JAVIER DELGADO.

Ejército de Liberación Nacional (ELN): Castroite guerrilla movement; f. 1965; 930 mems; political status recognized by the Govt in 1998; Leaders NICOLÁS ROGRÍGUEZ BAUTISTA, VÁSQUEZ CASTAÑO; factions include:

Corriente de Renovación Socialista (CRS): (ceased hostilities in December 1993).

Frente Simón Bolívar: (ceased hostilities in December 1985).

Frente Antonio Nariño: (ceased hostilities in December 1985).

Frente Domingo Laín: formed splinter group in October 1993; armed wing.

Ejército Popular de Liberación (EPL): Maoist guerrilla movement; f. 1969; splinter group from Communist Party; abandoned armed struggle in March 1991; joined the political mainstream as the **Partido de Esperanza, Paz y Libertad (EPL)**; Leader FRANCISCO CARABALLO.

Frente Popular de Liberación Nacional (FPLN): f. 1994 by dissident members of the ELN and the EPL.

Fuerzas Armadas Revolucionarias de Colombia (FARC): fmrly military wing of the Communist Party; composed of 39 armed fronts; political status recognized by the Govt in 1998; Leader MANUEL MARULANDA VÉLEZ (alias TIROFIJO).

Movimiento de Autodefensa Obrera (MAO): workers' self-defence movement; Trotskyite; Leader ADELAIDA ABADIA REY.

Movimiento de Restauración Nacional (MORENA): right-wing; Leader ARMANDO VALENZUELA RUIZ.

Muerte a Secuestradores (MAS) (Death to Kidnappers): right-wing paramilitary org.; funded by drugs dealers.

Nuevo Frente Revolucionario del Pueblo: f. 1986; faction of M-19; active in Cundinamarca region.

Partido Revolucionario de Trabajadores (PRT): left-wing; abandoned its armed struggle in 1991 and announced its intention to join the political mainstream as part of the Alianza Democrática.

Patria Libre: f. 1985; left-wing guerrilla movement.

In late 1985 the M-19, the Comando Ricardo Franco-Frente Sur and the **Comando Quintín Lame** (an indigenous organization active in the department of Cauca) announced the formation of a united front, the **Coordinadora Guerrillera Nacional (CGN)**. In 1986 the CGN participated in joint campaigns with the Movimiento Revolucionario Tupac Amarú (Peru) and the Alfaro Vive ¡Carajo! (Ecuador). The alliance operated under the name of **Batallón América**. In late 1987 six guerrilla groups, including the ELN, the FARC and the M-19, formed a joint front, to be known as the **Coordinadora Guerrillera Simón Bolívar (CGSB)** and subsequently as the **Coordinadora Nacional Guerrillera Simón Bolívar (CNGSB)**.

Diplomatic Representation

EMBASSIES IN COLOMBIA

Argentina: Avda 40A, No 13-09, 16°, Santafé de Bogotá, DC; tel. (1) 288-0900; Ambassador: CARLOS CARRASCO.

Austria: Carrera 11, No 75-29, Santafé de Bogotá, DC; tel. (1) 235-6628; Ambassador: MARIANNE DA COSTA DE MORAES.

Belgium: Calle 26, No 4A-45, 7°, Santafé de Bogotá, DC; tel. (1) 282-8881; fax (1) 282-8862; Ambassador: FRANCOIS RONSE.

Bolivia: Carrera 9, No 114-96, Santafé de Bogotá, DC; tel. (1) 629-8237; fax (1) 612-9325; e-mail embolivia-bogota@rree.gov.bo; Ambassador: GUIDO RIVEROS FRANCK.

Bosnia and Herzegovina: Carrera 13A, No 89-38, Of. 607, Santafé de Bogotá, DC; tel. (1) 618-4869; fax (1) 618-4847; Chargé d'affaires: NARCISA ABDULAGIĆ.

Brazil: Calle 93, No 14-20, 8°, Santafé de Bogotá, DC; tel. (1) 218-0800; Ambassador: MARCOS CAMACHO DE VINCENZI.

Canada: Calle 7, No 115-33, Apdo Aéreo 53531, Santafé de Bogotá, DC; tel. (1) 657-9800; fax (1) 657-9912; internet www.dfait-maeci.gc.ca/bogota; Ambassador: C. GUILLERMO E. RISHCHYNSKI.

Chile: Calle 100, No 11B-44, Santafé de Bogotá, DC; tel. (1) 214-7926; Ambassador: OSCAR PIZARRO ROMERO.

China, People's Republic: Calle 16, No 98-30A-41, Santafé de Bogotá, DC; tel. (1) 622-3215; fax (1) 622-3114; e-mail embchina@andinet.com; Ambassador: JU YIJIE.

Costa Rica: Carrera 15, No 102-25, Santafé de Bogotá, DC; tel. (1) 622-8830; fax (1) 623-0205; Ambassador: Dr FERNANDO DEL CASTILLO RIGGIONI.

Cuba: Carrera 9, No 92-54, Santafé de Bogotá, DC; tel. (1) 257-3353; fax (1) 611-4382; Ambassador: LUIS HERNÁNDEZ OJEDA.

Czech Republic: Carrera 7, No 113-16, 4°, Santafé de Bogotá, DC; tel. (1) 215-0633; fax (1) 612-8205.

Dominican Republic: Carrera 16A, No 86A-33, Santafé de Bogotá, DC; tel. (1) 621-1925; fax (1) 236-2588; Ambassador: MIGUEL A. FERSOBE PICHARDO.

Ecuador: Calle 89, No 13-07, Santafé de Bogotá, DC; tel. (1) 257-0066; fax (1) 257-9799; Ambassador: Dr FERNANDO RIBADENEIRA.

Egypt: Carrera 19A, No 98-17, Santafé de Bogotá, DC; tel. (1) 236-4832; Ambassador: AHMED FATHI ABULKHEIR.

El Salvador: Carrera 9A, No 80-15, Of. 503, Edif. El Nogal, Santafé de Bogotá, DC; tel. (1) 211-0012; fax (1) 255-9482; Ambassador: GUILLERMO RUBIO FUNES.

France: Carrera 11, No 93-12, Santafé de Bogotá, DC; tel. (1) 285-4311; Ambassador: DANIEL PARFAIT.

Germany: Edif. Sisky, 6°, Carrera 4, No 72-35, Apdo Aéreo 91808, Santafé de Bogotá, DC; tel. (1) 348-4040; fax (1) 210-4256; Ambassador: PETER VON JAGOW.

Guatemala: Transversal 29A, No 139A-41, Santafé de Bogotá, DC; tel. (1) 259-1496; fax (1) 274-5365; e-mail emguacol@colomsat.net.co; Ambassador: DANTE MARINELLI GOLOM.

Haiti: Carrera 11A, No 96-63, Santafé de Bogotá, DC; tel. (1) 256-6236; fax (1) 218-0326; Chargé d'affaires: CARLO TOUSSAINT.

Holy See: Carrera 15, No 36-33, Apdo Aéreo 3740, Santafé de Bogotá, DC (Apostolic Nunciature); tel. (1) 320-0289; fax (1) 285-1817; e-mail nunciocol@col1.telecom.com.co; Apostolic Nuncio: Most Rev. BENIAMINO STELLA, Titular Archbishop of Midila.

Honduras: Carrera 16, No 85-15, Of. 302, Santafé de Bogotá, DC; tel. (1) 236-0357; fax (1) 616-0774; Ambassador: HERNÁN ANTONIO BERMÚDEZ.

Hungary: Carrera 6A, No 77-46, Santafé de Bogotá, DC; tel. (1) 347-1467; fax (1) 347-1469; e-mail huembog1@netsoft.net.co; Ambassador: JÓZSEF NAGY.

India: Calle 71A, No 6-30, Of. 501, Santafé de Bogotá, DC; tel. (1) 217-5143; fax (1) 212-7648; e-mail indembog@colomsat.net.co; Ambassador: PRAMATHESH RATH.

Iran: Calle 96, No 11A-16/20, Santafé de Bogotá, DC; tel. (1) 218-6205; fax (1) 610-2556; Ambassador: HOSSEIN SHEIKH ZEINEDDIN.

Indonesia: Carrera 9, No 76-27, Santafé de Bogotá, DC; tel. (1) 217-6738; fax (1) 210-3507.

Israel: Calle 35, No 7-25, 14°, Santafé de Bogotá, DC; tel. (1) 287-7808; fax (1) 287-7783; Ambassador: AVRAHAM HADAD.

Italy: Calle 93B, No 9-92, Apdo Aéreo 50901, Santafé de Bogotá, DC; tel. (1) 218-6680; fax (1) 610-5886; e-mail ambitbog@internet.com.co; internet www.ambitaliabogota.org; Ambassador: FELICE SCAUSO.

Japan: Carrera 9A, No 99-02, 6°, Edif. Latinoamericano de Seguros, Santafé de Bogotá, DC; tel. (1) 618-2800; fax (1) 618-2828; Ambassador: GUNKATSU KANO.

Korea, Democratic People's Republic: Santafé de Bogotá, DC; Ambassador: JI YONG HO.

Korea, Republic: Calle 94, No 9-39, Santafé de Bogotá, DC; tel. (1) 616-7200; fax (1) 610-0338; e-mail embcorea@cable.net.co; Ambassador: WON JONG-CHAN.

Lebanon: Calle 74, No 12-44, Santafé de Bogotá, DC; tel. (1) 212-8360; fax (1) 347-9106; Ambassador: MOUNIR KHREICH.

Mexico: Calle 99, No 12-08, Santafé de Bogotá, DC; tel. (1) 256-6121; internet www.sre.gob.mx/colombia; Ambassador: LUIS ORTIZ MONASTERIO.

Morocco: Carrera 13A, No 98-33, Santafé de Bogotá, DC; tel. (1) 218-7147; fax (1) 218-8068; Ambassador: MOHAMED AYACHI.

Netherlands: Carrera 13, No 93-40, 5°, Apdo Aéreo 43585, Santafé de Bogotá, DC; tel. (1) 611-5080; fax (1) 623-3020; e-mail nlgovbog@trauco.colomsat.net.co; Ambassador: TEUNIS KAMPER.

Nicaragua: Transversal 19A, No 108-77, Santafé de Bogotá, DC; tel. (1) 214-1445; fax (1) 215-9582; Ambassador: DONALD CASTILLO RIVAS.

Panama: Calle 92, No 7-70, Santafé de Bogotá, DC; tel. (1) 257-5068; Ambassador: ALFREDO ANTONIO MONTANER.

Paraguay: Calle 57, No 7-11, Of. 702, Apdo Aéreo 20085, Santafé de Bogotá, DC; tel. (1) 255-4160; Ambassador: GERARDO FOGEL.

Peru: Carrera 10, No 93-48, Santafé de Bogotá, DC; tel. (1) 257-6292; fax (1) 623-5102; Ambassador: ALEJANDRO GORDILLO FERNÁNDEZ.

Poland: Calle 104A, No 23-48, Santafé de Bogotá, DC; tel. (1) 214-0143; fax (1) 218-0854; e-mail epolonia@col1.telecom.com.co; Ambassador: PAWEL KULKA KULPIOWSKI.

Portugal: Calle 71, No 11-10, Of. 703, Santafé de Bogotá, DC; tel. (1) 212-4223; Ambassador: AUGUSTO MARTINS GONÇALVES P.

Romania: Carrera 7, No 92-58, Santafé de Bogotá, DC; tel. (1) 256-6438; Ambassador CRISTIAN LAZARESCU.

Russia: Carrera 4, No 75-00, Apdo Aéreo 90600, Santafé de Bogotá, DC; tel. (1) 212-1881; fax (1) 210-4694; e-mail embrusia@impsat.net.co; Ambassador: EDNAN AGAYEV.

Slovakia: Avda 13, No 104A-30, Santafé de Bogotá, DC; tel. (1) 214-2240.

Spain: Calle 92, No 12-68, Santafé de Bogotá, DC; tel. (1) 618-1888; fax (1) 616-6104; Ambassador: YAGO PICO DE COAÑA.

Sweden: Calle 72, No 5-83, 9°, Santafé de Bogotá, DC; tel. (1) 325-2165; fax (1) 325-2166; Ambassador: BJÖRN STERNBY.

Switzerland: Carrera 9, No 74-08/1101, 11°, Santafé de Bogotá, DC; tel. (1) 349-7230; fax (1) 349-7195; Ambassador: VIKTOR CHRISTEN.

United Kingdom: Carrera 9, No 76-49, 9°, Santafé de Bogotá, DC; tel. (1) 317-6690; fax (1) 317-6265; e-mail britain@cable.net.co; internet www.britain.gov.co; Ambassador: JEREMY W. THORP.

USA: Calle 22D-bis, No 47-51, Apdo Aéreo 3831, Santafé de Bogotá, DC; tel. (1) 315-0811; fax (1) 315-2197; internet usembassy.state.gov/posts/co1/wwwhmane.html; Ambassador: ANNE W. PATTERSON.

Uruguay: Carrera 9A, No 80-15, 11°, Apdo Aéreo 101466, Santafé de Bogotá, DC; tel. (1) 235-2748; fax (1) 248-3734; e-mail urucolom@impsat.com.co; Ambassador: DOMINGO SCHIPANI.

Venezuela: Carrera 11, No 87-51, 5°, Santafé de Bogotá, DC; tel. (1) 640-1213; fax (1) 640-1242; e-mail embajada@embaven.org.co; Ambassador: ROY CHADERTON.

Yugoslavia: Calle 93A, No 9A-22, Apdo Aéreo 91074, Santafé de Bogotá, DC; tel. (1) 257-0290; Ambassador: RADOMIR ZECEVIĆ.

Judicial System

The constitutional integrity of the State is ensured by the Constitutional Court. The Constitutional Court is composed of nine judges who are elected by the Senate for eight years. Judges of the Constitutional Court are not eligible for re-election.

President of the Constitutional Court: FABIO MORÓN DÍAZ.

Judges of the Constitutional Court: ALEJANDRO MARTÍNEZ CABALLERO, VLADIMIRO NARANJO MESA, ANTONIO BARRERO CARBONELL, CARLOS GAVIRIA DÍAZ, ALVARO TAFUR GALVIS, JOSÉ GREGORIO HERNÁNDEZ, EDUARDO CIFUENTES MUÑOZ, ALFREDO BELTRAN SIERRA.

The ordinary judicial integrity of the State is ensured by the Supreme Court of Justice. The Supreme Court of Justice is composed of the Courts of Civil and Agrarian, Penal and Laboral Cassation. Judges of the Supreme Court of Justice are selected from the nominees of the Higher Council of Justice and serve an eight-year term of office which is not renewable.

Prosecutor-General: ALFONSO GÓMEZ MÉNDEZ.

Attorney-General: EDGARDO JOSÉ MAYA VILLAZON.

SUPREME COURT OF JUSTICE

Supreme Court of Justice: Carrera 7A, No 27-18, Santafé de Bogotá, DC; fax (1) 334-8745; internet www.fij.edu.co.

President: Dr JORGE ANTONIO CASTILLO RUGECES.

Vice-President: FERNANDO ARBOLEDA RIPOLL.

Court of Civil and Agrarian Cassation (seven judges): President: JORGE ANTONIO CASTILLO RUGELES.

Court of Penal Cassation (nine judges): President: JORGE ANIBAL GÓMEZ GALLEGO.

Court of Laboral Cassation (seven judges): President: JOSÉ ROBERTO HERRERA VERGARA.

Religion

Roman Catholicism is the religion of 95% of the population.

CHRISTIANITY
The Roman Catholic Church

Colombia comprises 12 archdioceses, 48 dioceses and 10 Apostolic Vicariates.

Bishops' Conference: Conferencia Episcopal de Colombia, Carrera 47, No 84-87, Apdo Aéreo 7448, Santafé de Bogotá, DC; tel. (1) 311-4277; fax (1) 311-5575; e-mail colcec@net.co; f. 1978 (statutes approved 1996); Pres. ALBERTO GIRALDO JARAMILLO, Archbishop of Medellín.

Archbishop of Barranquilla: RUBÉN SALAZAR GÓMEZ, Carrera 45, No 53-122, Apdo Aéreo 1160, Barranquilla, Atlántico; tel. (5) 340-1648; fax (5) 340-6239; e-mail arquidio@arquidiocesibaq.org.co.

Archbishop of Bucaramanga: VÍCTOR MANUEL LÓPEZ FORERO, Calle 33, No 21-18, Bucaramanga, Santander; tel. (7) 642-4387; fax (7) 642-1361; e-mail prensacuria@latinmail.com.

Archbishop of Cali: ISAÍAS DUARTE CANCINO, Carrera 4, No 7-17, Apdo Aéreo 8924, Cali, Valle del Cauca; tel. (2) 889-0562; fax (2) 83-7980.

Archbishop of Cartagena: CARLOS JOSÉ RUISECO VIEIRA, Apdo Aéreo 400, Cartagena; tel. (5) 664-5308; fax (5) 664-4974; e-mail arzoctg@telecartagena.com.

Archbishop of Ibagué: JUAN FRANCISCO SARASTI JARAMILLO, Calle 10, No 2-58, Ibagué, Tolima; tel. (82) 61-1680; fax (82) 63-2681.

Archbishop of Manizales: FABIO BETANCUR TIRADO, Carrera 23, No 19-22, Manizales, Caldas; tel. (68) 84-0114; fax (68) 82-1853.

Archbishop of Medellín: ALBERTO GIRALDO JARAMILLO, Calle 57, No 49-44, 3°, Medellín; tel. (4) 251-7700; fax (4) 251-9395; e-mail arquidiomed@epm.net.co.

Archbishop of Nueva Pamplona: GUSTAVO MARTÍNEZ FRÍAS, Carrera 5, No 4-87, Nueva Pamplona; tel. (4) 68-2886; fax (4) 68-4540.

Archbishop of Popayán: IVÁN MARÍN-LÓPEZ, Calle 5, No 6-71, Apdo Aéreo 593, Popayán; tel. (928) 24-1710; fax (928) 24-0101.

Archbishop of Santa Fe de Antioquia: IGNACIO GÓMEZ ARISTIZÁBAL, Plazuela Martínez Pardo, No 12-11, Santa Fe de Antioquia; tel. (94) 853-1155; fax (94) 853-1596; e-mail arquistafe@edatel.net.co.

Archbishop of Santafé de Bogotá: Cardinal PEDRO RUBIANO SÁENZ, Carrera 7A, No 10-20, Santafé de Bogotá, DC; tel. (1) 350-5511; fax (1) 350-7290; e-mail cancilleria@arquidiocesisbogota.org.co.co.

Archbishop of Tunja: LUIS AUGUSTO CASTRO QUIROGA; Calle 17, No 9-85, Apdo Aéreo 1019, Tunja, Boyacá; tel. (987) 42-2094; fax (987) 42-2096; e-mail arquidio@telecom.com.co.

The Anglican Communion

Anglicans in Colombia are members of the Episcopal Church in the USA.

Bishop of Colombia: Rt Rev. BERNARDO MERINO BOTERO, Carrera 6, No 49-85, Apdo Aéreo 52964, Santafé de Bogotá, DC; tel. (1) 288-3167; fax (1) 288-3248; there are 3,500 baptized mems, 2,000 communicant mems, 29 parishes, missions and preaching stations; 5 schools and 1 orphanage; 8 clergy.

Protestant Churches

The Baptist Convention: Apdo Aéreo 51988, Medellín; tel. (4) 38-9623; Pres. RAMÓN MEDINA IBÁÑEZ; Exec. Sec. Rev. RAMIRO PÉREZ HOYOS.

Iglesia Evangélica Luterana de Colombia: Calle 75, No 20-54, Apdo Aéreo 51538, Santafé de Bogotá, DC; tel. (1) 212-5735; fax (1) 212-5714; e-mail ielco@yahoo.com; 3,000 mems; Pres. Bishop NEHEMÍAS PARADA.

BAHÁ'Í FAITH

National Spiritual Assembly: Apdo Aéreo 51387, Santafé de Bogotá, DC; tel. (1) 268-1658; fax (1) 268-1665; e-mail bahaicol@colombianet.net; adherents in 1,013 localities.

JUDAISM

There is a community of about 25,000 with 66 synagogues.

The Press

DAILIES

Santafé de Bogotá, DC

El Espacio: Carrera 61, No 45-35, Apdo Aéreo 80111, Avda El Dorado, Santafé de Bogotá, DC; tel. (1) 410-5066; fax (1) 410-4595; f. 1965; evening; Dir JAIME ARDILA CASAMITJANA; circ. 159,000.

El Espectador: Carrera 68, No 23-71, Apdo Aéreo 3441, Santafé de Bogotá, DC; tel. (1) 294-5555; fax (1) 260-2323; e-mail redactor@elespectador.com; internet www.elespectador.com; f. 1887; morning; Dir CARLOS LLERAS; Editor LUIS CAÑÓN; circ. 200,000.

El Nuevo Siglo: Calle 45A, No 102-02, Apdo Aéreo 5452, Santafé de Bogotá, DC; tel. (1) 413-9200; fax (1) 413-8547; f. 1925; Conservative; Dirs JUAN PABLO URIBE, JUAN GABRIEL URIBE; circ. 68,000.

La República: Calle 46, No 103-59, Santafé de Bogotá, DC; tel. (1) 413-5077; fax (1) 413-3725; f. 1953; morning; economics; Dir RODRIGO OSPINA HERNÁNDEZ; Editor JORGE EMILIO SIERRA M.; circ. 55,000.

El Tiempo: Avda El Dorado, No 59-70, Apdo Aéreo 3633, Santafé de Bogotá, DC; tel. (1) 294-0100; fax (1) 410-5088; internet www.eltiempo.com; f. 1911; morning; Liberal; Dir ENRIQUE SANTOS CALDERÓN; Editor FRANCISCO SANTOS: circ. 265,118 (weekdays), 536,377 (Sundays).

Barranquilla, Atlántico

El Heraldo: Calle 53B, No 46-25, Barranquilla, Atlántico; tel. (5) 41-1090; fax (5) 41-6918; e-mail elheraldo@metrotel.net.co; internet www.elheraldo.com.co; f. 1933; morning; Liberal; Dir JUAN B. FERNÁNDEZ; circ. 70,000.

La Libertad: Carrera 53, No 55-166, Barranquilla, Atlántico; tel. (5) 31-1517; Liberal; Dir ROBERTO ESPER REBAJE; circ. 25,000.

El Tiempo Caribe: Carrera 50B No 41-18, Barranquilla, Atlántico; tel. (5) 379-1510; fax (5) 341-7715; e-mail orlgam@eltiempo.com.co; internet www.eltiempo.com; f. 1956; daily; Liberal; Dir ORLANDA GAMBOA; circ. 45,000.

Bucaramanga, Santander del Sur

El Frente: Calle 35, No 12-22, Apdo Aéreo 665, Bucaramanga, Santander del Sur; tel. (7) 42-5369; fax (7) 33-4541; f. 1942; morning; Conservative; Dir RAFAEL SERRANO PRADA; circ. 10,000.

Vanguardia Liberal: Calle 34, No 13-42, Bucaramanga, Santander del Sur; tel. (7) 33-4000; fax (7) 30-2443; e-mail vanglibe@colomsat.net.co; f. 1919; morning; Liberal; Sunday illustrated literary supplement and women's supplement; Dir and Man. ALEJANDRO GALVIS RAMÍREZ; circ. 48,000.

Cali, Valle del Cauca

Occidente: Calle 12, No 5-22, Cali, Valle del Cauca; tel. (2) 895-9756; fax (2) 884-6572; e-mail occidente@cali.cercol.net.co; f. 1961; morning; Conservative; Dir ALVARO H. CAICEDO GONZÁLEZ; circ. 25,000.

El País: Carrera 2A, No 24-46, Apdo Aéreo 4766, Cali, Valle del Cauca; tel. (2) 883-5011; fax (2) 883-5014; e-mail diario@elpaiscali.com; internet www.elpais-cali.com; f. 1950; Conservative; Dir FRANCISCO JOSÉ LLOREDA MERA; circ. 60,000 (weekdays), 120,000 (Saturdays), 108,304 (Sundays).

El Pueblo: Avda 3A, Norte 35-N-10, Cali, Valle del Cauca; tel. (2) 68-8110; morning; Liberal; Dir LUIS FERNANDO LONDOÑO CAPURRO; circ. 50,000.

Cartagena, Bolívar

El Universal: Calle 30, No 17-36, Cartagena, Bolívar; fax (5) 666-1964; e-mail eluniversal@ctgred.net.co; internet www.eluniversal.com.co; f. 1948; daily; Liberal; Dir PEDRO LUIS MOGOLLÓN; Man. GERARDO ARAÚJO; circ. 30,000.

Cúcuta, Norte de Santander

Diario La Frontera: Calle 14, No 3-44, Cúcuta, Norte de Santander; tel. and fax (75) 71-0505; f. 1951; morning; Dir MARIO JAVIER PACHECO GARCÍA; circ. 25,000.

La Opinión: Avda 4, No 16-12, Cúcuta, Norte de Santander; tel. (75) 71-9999; fax (75) 71-7869; e-mail laopinion@coll.telecom.com.co; f. 1960; morning; Liberal; Dir Dr JOSÉ EUSTORGIO COLMENARES OSSA; circ. 26,000.

Manizales, Caldas

La Patria: Carrera 20, No 21-51, Apdo Aéreo 70, Manizales, Caldas; tel. (68) 84-2460; fax (68) 84-7158; e-mail lapatria@lapatria.com; f. 1921; morning; Independent; Dir Dr LUIS JOSÉ RESTREPO RESTREPO; circ. 22,000.

Medellín, Antioquia

El Colombiano: Carrera 48, No 30 sur-119, Apdo Aéreo 80636, Medellín, Antioquia; tel. (4) 331-5252; fax (4) 331-4858; e-mail elcolombiano@elcolombiano.com.co; internet www.elcolombiano.com; f. 1912; morning; Conservative; Dir ANA MERCEDES GÓMEZ MARTÍNEZ; circ. 90,000.

El Mundo: Calle 53, No 74-50, Apdo Aéreo 53874, Medellín, Antioquia; tel. (4) 264-2800; fax (4) 264-3729; e-mail elmundo@elmundo.com; internet www.elmundo.com; f. 1979; Dir GUILLERMO GAVIRIA; Man. ANÍBAL GAVIRIA CORREA; circ. 25,000.

Montería, Córdoba

El Meridiano de Córdoba: Avda Circunvalar, No 38-30, Montería, Córdoba; tel. (47) 82-6888; fax (47) 82-1981; e-mail meridiano@monteria.cetcol.net.co; internet www.elmeridianodecordoba.com; f. 1995; morning; Dir WILLIAM ENRIQUE SALLEG TABOADA; circ. 17,000.

Neiva

Diario del Huila: Calle 8A, No 6-30, Neiva; tel. (88) 71-2458; fax (88) 71-2446; f. 1966; Dir MARÍA M. RENGIFO DE D.; circ. 12,000.

Pasto, Nariño

El Derecho: Calle 20, No 26-20, Pasto, Nariño; tel. (277) 2170; f. 1928; Conservative; Pres. Dr JOSÉ ELÍAS DEL HIERRO; Dir EDUARDO F. MAZUERA; circ. 12,000.

Pereira, Risaralda

Diario del Otún: Carrera 8A, No 22-75, Apdo Aéreo 2533, Pereira, Risaralda; tel. (63) 51313; fax (1) 324-1900; e-mail eldiario@inter co.net.co; internet www.eldiario.com.co; f. 1982; Financial Dir JAVIER IGNACIO RAMÍREZ MÚNERA; circ. 30,000.

El Imparcial: km 11 vía Pereira-Armenia, El Jordán, Pereira, Risaralda; tel. (63) 25-9935; fax (63) 25-9934; f. 1948; morning; Dir ZAHUR KLEMATH ZAPATA; circ. 15,000.

La Tarde: Carrera 9A, No 20-54, Pereira, Risaralda; tel. (63) 35-7976; fax (63) 35-5187; f. 1975; evening; Man. LUIS FERNANDO BAENA MEJÍA; circ. 15,000.

Popayán, Cauca

El Liberal: Carrera 3, No 2-60, Apdo Aéreo 538, Popayán, Cauca; tel. (28) 24-2418; fax (28) 23-3888; f. 1938; Man. CARLOS ALBERTO CABAL JIMÉNEZ; circ. 6,500.

Santa Marta, Magdalena

El Informador: Calle 21, No 5-06, Santa Marta, Magdalena; f. 1921; Liberal; Dir JOSÉ B. VIVES; circ. 9,000.

Tunja, Boyacá

Diario de Boyacá: Tunja, Boyacá; Dir-Gen. Dr CARLOS H. MOJICA; circ. 3,000.

Villavicencio, Meta

Clarín del Llano: Villavicencio, Meta; tel. (866) 23207; Conservative; Dir ELÍAS MATUS TORRES; circ. 5,000.

PERIODICALS

Santafé de Bogotá, DC

Antena: Santafé de Bogotá, DC; television, cinema and show business; circ. 10,000.

Arco: Carrera 6, No 35-39, Apdo Aéreo 8624, Santafé de Bogotá, DC; tel. (1) 285-1500; f. 1959; monthly; history, philosophy, literature and humanities; Dir ALVARO VALENCIA TOVAR; circ. 10,000.

ART NEXUS/Arte en Colombia: Carrera 5, No 67-19, Apdo Aéreo 90193, Santafé de Bogotá, DC; tel. (1) 312-9435; fax (1) 312-9252; e-mail artnex@impsat.net.co; f. 1976; quarterly; Latin American art, architecture, films and photography; editions in English and Spanish; Dir CELIA SREDNI DE BIRBRAGHER; Exec. Editor IVONNE PINI; circ. 15,000.

El Campesino: Carrera 39A, No 15-11, Santafé de Bogotá, DC; f. 1958; weekly; cultural; Dir JOAQUÍN GUTIÉRREZ MACÍAS; circ. 70,000.

Consigna: Diagonal 34, No 5-11, Santafé de Bogotá, DC; tel. (1) 287-1157; fortnightly; Turbayista; Dir (vacant); circ. 10,000.

Coyuntura Económica: Calle 78, No 9-91, Apdo Aéreo 75074, Santafé de Bogotá, DC; tel. (1) 312-5300; fax (1) 212-6073; e-mail bibliote@fedesarrollo.org.co; f. 1970; quarterly; economics; published by Fundación para Educación Superior y el Desarrollo (FEDESARROLLO); Editor MARÍA ANGÉLICA ARBELAEZ; circ. 1,500.

Cromos Magazine: Calle 70A, No 7-81, Apdo Aéreo 59317, Santafé de Bogotá, DC; f. 1916; weekly; illustrated; general news; Dir ALBERTO ZALAMEA; circ. 102,000.

As Deportes: Calle 20, No 4-55, Santafé de Bogotá, DC; f. 1978; sports; circ. 25,000.

Economía Colombiana: Edif. de los Ministerios, Of. 126A, No 6-40, Santafé de Bogotá, DC; f. 1984; published by Contraloría General de la República; monthly; economics.

Escala: Calle 30, No 17-70, Santafé de Bogotá, DC; tel. (1) 287-8200; fax (1) 232-5148; e-mail escala@col-online.com; f. 1962; fortnightly; architecture; Dir DAVID SERNA CÁRDENAS; circ. 16,000.

Estrategia: Carrera 4A, 25A–12B, Santafé de Bogotá, DC; monthly; economics; Dir RODRIGO OTERO.

Guión: Carrera 16, No 36-89, Apdo Aéreo 19857; Santafé de Bogotá, DC; tel. (1) 232-2660; f. 1977; weekly; general; Conservative; Dir JUAN CARLOS PASTRANA; circ. 35,000.

Hit: Calle 20, No 4-55, Santafé de Bogotá, DC; cinema and show business; circ. 20,000.

Hoy Por Hoy: Santafé de Bogotá, DC; weekly; Dir DIANA TURBAY DE URIBE.

Menorah: Apdo Aéreo 9081, Santafé de Bogotá, DC; tel. (1) 611-2014; f. 1950; independent monthly review for the Jewish community; Dir ELIÉCER CELNIK; circ. 10,000.

Nueva Frontera: Carrera 7A, No 17-01, 5°, Santafé de Bogotá, DC; tel. (1) 334-3763; f. 1974; weekly; politics, society, arts and culture; Liberal; Dir CARLOS LLERAS RESTREPO; circ. 23,000.

Pluma: Apdo Aéreo 12190, Santafé de Bogotá, DC; monthly; art and literature; Dir (vacant); circ. 70,000.

Que Hubo: Santafé de Bogotá, DC; weekly; general; Editor CONSUELO MONTEJO; circ. 15,000.

Revista Diners: Calle 85, No 18-32, 6°, Santafé de Bogotá, DC; tel. (1) 636-0508; fax (1) 623-1762; e-mail diners@cable.net.co; f. 1963; monthly; Dir GERMÁN SANTAMARÍA; circ. 110,000.

Semana: Calle 93B, No 13-47, Santafé de Bogotá, DC; tel. (1) 622-2277; fax (1) 621-0475; general; Pres. FELIPE LÓPEZ CABALLERO.

Síntesis Económica: Calle 70A, No 10-52, Santafé de Bogotá, DC; tel. (1) 212-5121; fax (1) 212-8365; f. 1975; weekly; economics; Dir FÉLIX LAFAURIE RIVERA; circ. 16,000.

Teorema: Calle 70A, No 8-17, Santafé de Bogotá, DC; tel. (1) 217-2266; fax (1) 212-0639; f. 1983; computer technology; Dir DIONISIO IBÁÑEZ; circ. 5,000.

Tribuna Médica: Calle 8B, No 68A-41 y Calle 123, No 8-20, Santafé de Bogotá, DC; tel. (1) 262-6085; fax (1) 262-4459; f. 1961; monthly; medical and scientific; Editor JACK ALBERTO GRIMBERG; circ. 50,000.

Tribuna Roja: Apdo Aéreo 19042, Santafé de Bogotá, DC; tel. (1) 243-0371; f. 1971; quarterly; organ of the MOIR (pro-Maoist Communist party); Dir CARLOS NARANJO; circ. 300,000.

Vea: Calle 20, No 4-55, Santafé de Bogotá, DC; weekly; popular; circ. 90,000.

Voz La Verdad del Pueblo: Carrera 8, No 19-34, Of. 310–311, Santafé de Bogotá, DC; tel. (1) 284-5209; fax (1) 342-5041; weekly; left-wing; Dir CARLOS A. LOZANO G.; circ. 45,000.

NEWS AGENCIES

Ciep—El País: Carrera 16, No 36-35, Santafé de Bogotá, DC; tel. (1) 232-6816; fax (1) 288-0236; Dir JORGE TÉLLEZ.

Colprensa: Diagonal 34, No 5-63, Apdo Aéreo 20333, Santafé de Bogotá, DC; tel. (1) 287-2200; fax (1) 285-5915; e-mail colpre@el sitio.net.co; f. 1980; Dir ROBERTO VARGAS GALVIS.

Foreign Bureaux

Agence France-Presse (AFP): Carrera 5, No 16-14, Of. 807, Apdo Aéreo 4654, Santafé de Bogotá, DC; tel. (1) 281-8613; Dir MARIE SANZ.

Agencia EFE (Spain): Carrera 16, No 39A-69, Apdo Aéreo 16038, Santafé de Bogotá, DC; tel. (1) 285-1576; fax (1) 285-1598; Bureau Chief ANTONIO MARTÍNEZ MARTÍN.

Agenzia Nazionale Stampa Associata (ANSA) (Italy): Carrera 4, No 67-30, Apdo Aéreo 16077, Santafé de Bogotá, DC; tel. (1) 211-9617; fax (1) 212-5409; Bureau Chief ALBERTO ROJAS MORALES.

Associated Press (AP) (USA): Transversal 14, No 122-36, Apdo Aéreo 093643, Santafé de Bogotá, DC; tel. (1) 619-3487; fax (1) 213-8467; e-mail apbogota@bigfoot.com; Bureau Chief FRANK BAJAK.

Central News Agency Inc. (Taiwan): Carrera 13A, No 98-34, Santafé de Bogotá, DC; tel. (1) 25-6342; Correspondent CHRISTINA CHOW.

Deutsche Presse-Agentur (dpa) (Germany): Carrera 7A, No 17-01, Of. 909, Santafé de Bogotá, DC; tel. (1) 284-7481; fax (1) 281-8065; Correspondent RODRIGO RUIZ TOVAR.

Informatsionnoye Telegrafnoye Agentstvo Rossii—Telegrafnoye Agentstvo Suverennykh Stran (ITAR—TASS) (Russia): Calle 20, No 7-17, Of. 901, Santafé de Bogotá, DC; tel. (1) 243-6720; Correspondent GENNADII KOCHUK.

Inter Press Service (IPS) (Italy): Calle 19, No 3-50, Of. 602, Apdo Aéreo 7739, Santafé de Bogotá, DC; tel. (1) 341-8841; fax (1) 334-2249; Correspondent MARÍA ISABEL GARCÍA NAVARRETE.

Prensa Latina: Carrera 3, No 21-46, Apdo Aéreo 30372, Santafé de Bogotá, DC; tel. (1) 282-4527; fax (1) 281-7286; Bureau Chief FAUSTO TRIANA.

Reuters (United Kingdom): Calle 94A, No 13-34, 4°, Apdo Aéreo 29848, Santafé de Bogotá, DC; tel. (1) 610-7633; fax (1) 610-7733; Correspondent MICHAEL STOTT.

United Press International (UPI) (USA): Carrera 4A, No 67-30, 4°, Apdo Aéreo 57570, Santafé de Bogotá, DC; tel. (1) 211-9106; Correspondent FEDERICO FULLEDA.

Xinhua (New China) News Agency (People's Republic of China): Calle 74, No 4-26, Apdo Aéreo 501, Santafé de Bogotá, DC; tel (1) 211-5347; Dir HOU YAOQI.

PRESS ASSOCIATIONS

Asociación Colombiana de Periodistas: Avda Jiménez, No 8-74, Of. 510, Santafé de Bogotá, DC; tel. (1) 243-6056.

Asociación Nacional de Diarios Colombianos (ANDIARIOS): Calle 61, No 5-20, Apdo Aéreo 13663, Santafé de Bogotá, DC; tel. (1) 212-8694; fax (1) 212-7894; f. 1962; 30 affiliated newspapers; Pres. LUIS MIGUEL DE BEDOUT; Vice-Pres. LUIS FERNANDO BAENA.

Asociación de la Prensa Extranjera: Pedro Meléndez, No 87-93, Santafé de Bogotá, DC; tel. (1) 288-3011.

Círculo de Periodistas de Santafé de Bogotá, DC (CPB): Calle 26, No 13A-23, 23°, Santafé de Bogotá, DC; tel. (1) 282-4217; Pres. MARÍA TERESA HERRÁN.

Publishers

Santafé de Bogotá, DC

Comunicadores Técnicos Ltda: Carrera 18, No 46-58, Apdo Aéreo 28797, Santafé de Bogotá, DC; technical; Dir PEDRO P. MORCILLO.

Ediciones Cultural Colombiana Ltda: Calle 72, No 16-15 y 16-21, Apdo Aéreo 6307, Santafé de Bogotá, DC; tel. (1) 217-6529; fax (1) 217-6570; f. 1951; textbooks; Dir JOSÉ PORTO VÁSQUEZ.

Ediciones Lerner Ltda: Calle 8A, No 68A-41, Apdo Aéreo 8304, Santafé de Bogotá, DC; tel. (1) 420-0650; fax (1) 262-4459; f. 1959; general; Commercial Man. FABIO CAICEDO GÓMEZ.

Editora Cinco, SA: Calle 61, No 13-23, 7°, Apdo Aéreo 15188, Santafé de Bogotá, DC; tel. (1) 285-6200; recreation, culture, textbooks, general; Man. PEDRO VARGAS G.

Editorial El Globo, SA: Calle 16, No 4-96, Apdo Aéreo 6806, Santafé de Bogotá, DC.

Editorial Presencia, Ltda: Calle 23, No 24-20, Apdo Aéreo 41500, Santafé de Bogotá, DC; tel. (1) 269-2188; fax (1) 269-6830; textbooks, tradebooks; Gen. Man. MARÍA UMAÑA DE TANCO.

Editorial San Pablo: Carrera 46, No 22A–90, Quintaparedes, Apdo Aéreo 080152, Santafé de Bogotá, DC; tel. (1) 368-2099; fax (1) 244-4383; f. 1951; religion, culture, humanism; Editorial Dir JOHN FREDY ECHAVARRÍA A.

Editorial Temis SA: Calle 13, No 6-45, Apdo Aéreo 5941, Santafé de Bogotá, DC; tel. (1) 269-0713; fax (1) 292-5801; f. 1951; law, sociology, politics; Man. Dir JORGE GUERRERO.

Editorial Voluntad, SA: Carrera 7A, No 24-89, 24°, Santafé de Bogotá, DC; tel. (1) 286-0666; fax (1) 286-5540; e-mail voluntad@col omsat.net.co; f. 1930; school books; Pres. GASTÓN DE BEDOUT.

Fundación Centro de Investigación y Educación Popular (CINEP): Carrera 5A, No 33A-08, Apdo Aéreo 25916, Santafé de Bogotá, DC; tel. (1) 285-8977; fax (1) 287-9089; f. 1977; education and social sciences; Man. Dir FRANCISCO DE ROUX.

Instituto Caro y Cuervo: Carrera 11, No 64-37, Apdo Aéreo 51502, Santafé de Bogotá, DC; tel. (1) 255-8289; fax (1) 217-0243; e-mail carocuer@gaitana.interred.net.co; internet www.caroycuervo .edu.co; f. 1942; philology, general linguistics and reference; Man. Dir IGNACIO CHAVES CUEVAS; Gen. Sec. CARLOS JULIO LUQUE CAGUA.

Inversiones Cromos SA: Calle 70A, No 7-81, Apdo Aéreo 59317, Santafé de Bogotá, DC; tel. (1) 217-1754; fax (1) 211-2642; f. 1916; Dir ALBERTO ZALAMEA; Gen. Man. JORGE EDUARDO CORREA ROBLEDO.

Legis, SA: Avda El Dorado, No 81-10, Apdo Aéreo 98888, Santafé de Bogotá, DC; tel. (1) 263-4100; fax (1) 295-2650; f. 1952; economics, law, general; Man. MAURICIO SERNA MELÉNDEZ.

McGraw Hill Interamericana, SA: Avda Américas, No 46-41, Apdo Aéreo 81078, Santafé de Bogotá, DC; tel. (1) 337-7800; fax (1) 245-4786; e-mail cmarquez@mcgraw-hill.com; university textbooks; Dir-Gen. CARLOS G. MÁRQUEZ.

Publicar, SA: Avda 68, No 75A-50, 4°, Centro Comercial Metrópolis, Apdo Aéreo 8010, Santafé de Bogotá, DC; tel. (1) 225-5555; fax (1) 225-4015; e-mail m-navia@publicar.com; internet www.pub licar.com; f. 1954; directories; CEO MARÍA SOL NAVIA.

Siglo del Hombre Editores Ltda: Carrera 32, No 25-46, Santafé de Bogotá, DC; tel. (1) 337-7700; fax (1) 337-7665; e-mailsiglodelhom bre@sky.net.co; f. 1992; arts, politics, anthropology, history, fiction, etc.; Gen. Man. EMILIA FRANCO DE ARCILA.

Tercer Mundo Editores SA: Transversal 2A, No 67-27, Apdo Aéreo 4817, Santafé de Bogotá, DC; tel. (1) 255-1539; fax (1) 212-5976; e-mail tmundoed@polcola.com.co; f. 1963; social sciences; Pres. SANTIAGO POMBO VEJARANO.

ASSOCIATIONS

Cámara Colombiana del Libro: Carrera 17A, No 37-27, Apdo Aéreo 8998, Santafé de Bogotá, DC; tel. (1) 288-6188; fax (1) 287-3320; e-mail camlibro@camlibro.com.co; internet www.camlibro .com.co; f. 1951; Pres. GONZALO ARBOLEDA; Exec. Dir RICHARD URIBE SCHROEDER; 120 mems.

Colcultura: Calle 8, No 6-97, 2°, Santafé de Bogotá, DC; tel. (1) 282-8656; fax (1) 282-5104; Dir ISADORA DE NORDEN.

Fundalectura: Avda 40, No 16-46, Santafé de Bogotá, DC; tel. (1) 320-1511; fax (1) 287-7071; e-mail fundalec@cable.net.co; internet www.fundalectura.org.co; Exec. Dir SILVIA CASTRILLÓN.

Broadcasting and Communications

Ministerio de Comunicaciones, Dirección de Telecomunicaciones: Edif. Murillo Toro, Carreras 7A y 8A, Calle 12A y 13, Apdo Aéreo 14515, Santafé de Bogotá, DC; tel. (1) 286-6911; fax (1) 286-1185; broadcasting authority; Dir Minister of Communications.

Instituto Nacional de Radio y Televisión—INRAVISION: Centro Administrativo Nacional (CAN), Avda El Dorado, Santafé de Bogotá, DC; tel. (1) 222-0700; fax (1) 222-0080; e-mail inras@col1 .telecom.com.co; f. 1954; govt-run TV and radio broadcasting network; educational and commercial broadcasting; Dir GUSTAVO SAMPER RODRÍGUEZ.

TELECOMMUNICATIONS

Celumóvil SA: Calle 71A, No 6-30, 18°, Santafé de Bogotá, DC; tel. (1) 346-1666; fax (1) 211-2031; Sec.-Gen. CARLOS BERNARDO CARREÑO R.

Empresa Nacional de Telecomunicaciones (TELECOM): Calle 23, No 13-49, Santafé de Bogotá, DC; tel. (1) 286-0077; fax (1) 282-8768; e-mail jblackbu@bogota.telecom.net.co; internet www.tele com.com.co; f. 1947; national telecommunications enterprise; Pres. JULIO MOLANO GONZÁLEZ.

Empresa de Telecomunicaciones de Santafé de Bogotá (ETB): Carrera 7A, No 20–37, Santafé de Bogotá, DC; tel. (1) 341-4233; fax (1) 342-3550; e-mail sugeetb@axesnet.com; internet www.etb.com.co; Bogotá telephone co; scheduled for privatization in 2000; Pres. SERGIO REGUEROS.

BROADCASTING
Radio

In 1988 there were 516 radio stations officially registered with the Ministry of Communications. Most radio stations belong to ASOMEDIOS. The principal radio networks are as follows:

Cadena Radial Auténtica: Calle 32, No 16-12, Apdo Aéreo 18350, Santafé de Bogotá, DC; tel. (1) 285-3360; fax (1) 285-2505; f. 1983; stations include Radio Auténtica and Radio Mundial; Pres. JORGE ENRIQUE GÓMEZ MONTEALEGRE.

Cadena Radial La Libertad Ltda: Carrera 53, No 55-166, Apdo Aéreo 3143, Barranquilla; tel. (5) 31-1517; fax (5) 32-1279; news and music programmes for Barranquilla, Cartagena and Santa Marta; stations include Emisora Ondas del Caribe (youth programmes), Radio Libertad (classical music programmes) and Emisora Fuentes.

Cadena Super: Calle 16A, No 86A-78, Santafé de Bogotá, DC; tel. (1) 618-1371; fax (1) 618-1360; internet www.889.com.co; f. 1971; stations include Radio Super and Super Stereo FM; Pres. JAIME PAVA NAVARRO.

Cadena Melodía de Colombia: Calle 45, No 13-70, Santafé de Bogotá, DC; tel. (1) 323-1500; fax (1) 288-4020; Pres. EFRAÍN PÁEZ ESPITIA.

CARACOL, SA (Primera Cadena Radial Colombiana, SA): Carretera 39A, No 15-81, Apdo Aéreo 9291, Santafé de Bogotá, DC; tel. (1) 337-8866; fax (1) 337-7126; internet www.caracol.com.co; f. 1948; 126 stations; Pres. JOSÉ MANUEL RESTREPO FERNÁNDEZ DE SOTO.

Circuito Todelar de Colombia: Avda 13, No 84-42, Apdo Aéreo 27344, Santafé de Bogotá, DC; tel. (1) 616-1011; fax (1) 616-0056; f. 1953; 74 stations; Pres. BERNARDO TOBÓN DE LA ROCHE.

Colmundo Radio, SA ('La Cadena de la Paz'): Diagonal 58, 26A-29, Apdo Aéreo 36750, Santafé de Bogotá, DC; tel. (1) 217-8911; fax (1) 217-9358; f. 1989; Pres. Dr NÉSTOR CHAMORRO P.

Organización Radial Olímpica, SA (ORO, SA): Calle 72, No 48-37, 2°, Apdo Aéreo 51266, Barranquilla; tel. (5) 358-0500; fax (5) 345-9080; programmes for the Antioquia and Atlantic coast regions.

Radio Cadena Nacional, SA (RCN Radio): Carrera 13A, No 37-32, Santafé de Bogotá, DC; tel. (1) 288-2288; fax (1) 288-6130; e-mail rcn@impsat.net.co; internet www.rcn.com.co; 116 stations; official network; Pres. RICARDO LONDOÑO LONDOÑO.

Radiodifusora Nacional de Colombia: Centro Administrativo Nacional (CAN), Avda El Dorado, Santafé de Bogotá, DC; tel. (1) 222-0415; fax (1) 222-0409; e-mail radiodifusora@hotmail.com; f. 1940; national public radio; Dir ATHALA MORRIS.

Radiodifusores Unidos, SA (RAU): Carrera 13, No 85-51, Of. 705, Santafé de Bogotá, DC; tel. (1) 617-0584; commercial network of independent local and regional stations throughout the country.

Television

Television services began in 1954, and the NTSC colour television system was adopted in 1979. The government-run broadcasting network, INRAVISION, controls two national commercial stations and one national educational station. There are also three regional stations. Broadcasting time is distributed among competing programmers through a public tender. The first two privately-run stations began test transmissions in mid-1998.

Cadena Uno: Centro Administrativo Nacional (CAN), Avda El Dorado, Santafé de Bogotá, DC; tel. (1) 342-3777; fax (1) 341-6198; e-mail cadena1@latino.net.co; internet www.cadena1.com.co; f. 1992; Dir FERNANDO BARRERO CHÁVEZ.

Canal 3: Centro Administrativo Nacional (CAN), Avda El Dorado, Santafé de Bogotá, DC; tel. (1) 222-1640; fax (1) 222-1514; f. 1970; Exec. Dir RODRIGO ANTONIO DURÁN BUSTOS.

Canal A: Calle 35, No 7-51, CENPRO, Santafé de Bogotá, DC; tel. (1) 232-3196; fax (1) 245-7526; f. 1966; Gen. Man. ROCÍO FERNÁNDEZ DEL CASTILLO.

Caracol Televisión, SA: Calle 76, No 11-35, Apdo Aéreo 26484, Santafé de Bogotá, DC; tel. (1) 319-0860; fax (1) 321-1720; f. 1969; Pres. RICARDO ALARCÓN GAVIRIA.

Teleantioquia: Carrera 41, No 52-28, Edif. EDA, 3°, Apdo Aéreo 8183, Medellín, Antioquia; tel. (4) 262-0311; fax (4) 262-0832; f. 1985; Pres. ALVARO URIBE VÉLEZ.

Telecafé: Carrera 24, No 19-51, Apdo Aéreo 770, Manizales, Caldas; tel. (68) 84-5678; fax (68) 84-4623; e-mail telecafe@col2.telecom.com.co; f. 1986; Gen. Man. JUAN MANUEL LENIS LARA.

Telecaribe: Carrera 54, No 72-142, 11°, Barranquilla, Atlántico; tel. (5) 358-2297; fax (5) 356-0924; e-mail ealviz@canal.telecaribe.com.co; internet www.telecaribe.com.co; f. 1986; Gen. Man. IVÁN OVALLE POVEDA.

Telepacífico: Calle 5A, No 38A-14, 3°, esq. Centro Comercial Imbanaco, Cali, Valle del Cauca; tel. (2) 589-933; fax (2) 588-281; Gen. Man. LUIS GUILLERMO RESTREPO.

TV Cúcuta: Calle 4, No 11E-41, Quinta Oriental Cúcuta, Norte de Santander; tel. (75) 74-7874; fax (75) 75-2922; f. 1992; Pres. JOSÉ A. ARMELLA.

ASSOCIATIONS

Asociación Nacional de Medios de Comunicación (ASOMEDIOS): Carrera 22, No 85-72, Santafé de Bogotá, DC; tel. (1) 611-1300; fax (1) 621-6292; f. 1978 and merged with ANRADIO (Asociación Nacional de Radio, Televisión y Cine de Colombia) in 1980; Pres. Dr SERGIO ARBOLEDA CASAS.

Federación Nacional de Radio (FEDERADIO): Santafé de Bogotá, DC; Dir LIBARDO TABORDA BOLÍVAR.

Finance

(cap. = capital; res = reserves; dep. = deposits; m. = million; amounts in pesos, unless otherwise indicated)

Contraloría General de la República: Carrera 10, No 17-18, Torre Colseguros, 27°, Santafé de Bogotá, DC; tel. (1) 282-7905; fax (1) 282-3549; Controller-General Dr MANUEL FRANCISCO BECERRA.

BANKING

In August 1989 the Government authorized plans to return to private ownership 65% of the assets of all financial institutions nationalized after the financial crisis of 1982.

Supervisory Authority

Superintendencia Bancaria: Carrera 7A, No 4-49, 11°, Apdo Aéreo 3460, Santafé de Bogotá, DC; tel. (1) 350-8166; fax (1) 350-7999; e-mail superban@superbancaria.gov.co; internet www.superbancaria.gov.co; Banking Supt PATRICIA CORREA BONILLA.

Central Bank

Banco de la República: Carrera 7A, No 14-78, 5°, Apdo Aéreo 3531, Santafé de Bogotá, DC; tel. (1) 343-0190; fax (1) 286-1731; f. 1923; internet www.banrep.gov.co; sole bank of issue; cap. 12.7m.; res 11,238.6m.; dep. 4,570.0m. (Dec 1999) Gov. MIGUEL URRUTIA MONTOYA; 28 brs.

Commercial Banks

Santafé de Bogotá, DC

ABN AMRO Bank (Colombia), SA (fmrly Banco Real de Colombia): Carrera 7A, No 33-80, Apdo Aéreo 34262, Santafé de Bogotá, DC; tel. (1) 285-0763; fax (1) 285-5671; f. 1975; cap. 8,110.5m., res 6,217.7m., dep. 56,787.7m. (Dec. 1993); Pres. CARLOS EDUARDO ARRUDA PENTEADO; 17 brs.

Banco Agrario de Colombia: Carrera 6, No 14-98, Santafé de Bogotá, DC; tel. (1) 212-3404; fax (1) 345-2279; f. 1999; Pres. JUAN BAUTISTA PÉREZ RUBIANO.

Banco America Colombia (fmrly Banco Colombo-Americano): Carrera 7, No 71-52, Torre B, 4°, Apdo Aéreo 12327, Santafé de Bogotá, DC; tel. (1) 312-2020; fax (1) 312-1645; cap. 3,268m., res 6,205m., dep. 14,475m. (Dec. 1993); wholly-owned subsidiary of Bank of America; Pres. EDUARDO ROMERO JARAMILLO; 1 br.

Banco Andino Colombia, SA (fmrly Banco de Crédito y Comercio): Carrera 7A, No 71-52, Torre B, 1°, 18° y 19°, Apdo Aéreo 6826, Santafé de Bogotá, DC; tel. (1) 312-3666; fax (1) 312-3273; e-mail geraldo@latino.net.co; f. 1954; cap. 7,206.5m., res 10,705.9m., dep. 121,367.4m. (Dec. 1993); Pres. CARLOS CUEVAS; 21 brs.

Banco Anglo-Colombiano (Lloyds Bank): Carrera 7, No 71-21, 16°, Apdo Aéreo 3532, Santafé de Bogotá, DC; tel. (1) 334-5088; fax (1) 341-9433; e-mail anglomer@impsat.net.co; internet www.bancoanglocolombiano.com; f. 1976; cap. 14,990.7m., res 24,983.8m., dep. 229,629.3. (Dec. 1996); Pres. DAVID HUTCHINSON; 52 brs.

Banco de Bogotá: Calle 36, No 7-47, 15°, Apdo Aéreo 3436, Santafé de Bogotá, DC; tel. (1) 332-0032; fax (1) 338-3375; internet www.bancodebogota.com.co; f. 1870; acquired Banco del Comercio in 1992; cap. 876.6m.; res 572.4m.; dep. 3,103.0m. (June 2000); Pres. Dr ALEJANDRO FIGUEROA JARAMILLO; 274 brs.

Banco Cafetero (Bancafe): Calle 28, No 13A-15, Apdo Aéreo 240332, Santafé de Bogotá, DC; tel. (1) 341-1511; fax (1) 284-6516; f.1953; cap. US $45,288.4m., res 598,622.2m., dep. 3,330,281.8m. (Dec. 1999); Pres. GILBERTO GÓMEZ ARANGO; 301 brs.

Banco Caja Social: Carrera 7, No 77-65, 11°, Santafé de Bogotá, DC; tel. (1) 310-0099; fax (1) 313-0809; e-mail bancaj_vjurid ica@fundacion-social; f. 1911; savings bank; cap. 93,077m., res 13,543m., dep. 559,729m. (Dec. 1996); Pres. EULALIA ARBOLEDA DE MONTES; 135 brs.

Banco Central Hipotecario: Carrera 6, No 15-32, 11°, Apdo Aéreo 3637, Santafé de Bogotá, DC; tel. (1) 336-0055; fax (1) 282-2802; f. 1932; Pres. MARÍA JOSÉ GARCÍA JARAMILLO; 132 brs.

Banco Colpatria, SA: Carrera 7A, No 24-89, 12°, Apdo Aéreo 30241, Santafé de Bogotá, DC; tel. (1) 286-8277; fax (1) 334-0867; internet www.banco.colpatria.com; f. 1955; cap. 1,002m., res 15,575m., dep. 197,390m. (Dec. 1994); Pres. SANTIAGO PERDOMO MALDONADO; 26 brs.

Banco de Comercio Exterior de Colombia, SA—BANCOLDEX: Calle 28, No 13A-15, 38°, Apdo Aéreo 240092, Santafé de Bogotá, DC; tel. (1) 341-0677; fax (1) 284-5087; internet www.bancoldex.com; f. 1992; provides financing alternatives for Colombian exporters; affiliate trust company FIDUCOLDEX, SA manages PROEXPORT (Export Promotion Trust); Pres. MIGUEL GÓMEZ MARTÍNEZ.

Banco de Crédito: Carrera 7, No 27-18, Santafé de Bogotá, DC; tel. (1) 286-8400; fax (1) 286-7236; e-mail loginter@impsat.net.co; internet www.bancodecredito.com; f. 1963; cap. 60,000.0m., res 61,880.0m., dep. 870,537.5m. (Dec. 1998); Pres. JAMES P. FENTON; 24 brs.

Banco Mercantil de Colombia, SA (fmrly Banco de los Trabajadores): Avda 82, No 12-18, 8°, Santafé de Bogotá, DC; tel. (1) 635-0035; fax (1) 623-7669; e-mail bmjuridi@impsat.net.co; internet www.bancomercantil.com; f. 1974; wholly-owned subsidiary of Banco Mercantil (Venezuela); cap. 19,409.9m., res 24,459.5m., dep. 98,699.7m. (Dec. 1997); Pres. GUSTAVO SINTES ULLOA; 10 brs.

Banco del Pacífico, SA: Calle 100, 19-05, Santafé de Bogotá, DC; tel. (1) 416-5945; fax (1) 611-2339; e-mail cbernal@banpacifico.com.co; f. 1994; wholly-owned by Banco del Pacífico, SA, Guayaquil (Ecuador); cap. 12,000.0m., res 6,120.2m., dep. 196,873.3m. (Dec. 1996); Pres. JUAN CARLOS BERNAL 3 brs.

Banco Popular, SA: Calle 17, 7-43, 4°, Apdo Aéreo 6796, Santafé de Bogotá, DC; tel. (1) 283-3964; fax (1) 281-9448; e-mail upinter nacional@bancopopular.com.co; internet www.bancopopular.com.co; f. 1951; cap. 68,486m., res 331,363m., dep. 2,043,749m. (Dec. 1998); Pres. JOSÉ HERNÁN RINCÓN GÓMEZ; 158 brs.

Banco Santander: Carrera 10A, No 28-49, Edif. Bavaria, 9°, Santafé de Bogotá, DC; tel. (1) 282-5266; fax (1) 281-0311; internet www.bancosantander.com.co; f. 1961; Pres. MONICA IÑES MARÍA APARICIO; 30 brs.

Banco Standard Chartered: Calle 74, No 6-65, Santafé de Bogotá, DC; tel. (1) 217-7200; fax (1) 212-5786; f. 1982; cap. 10,312m., res 5,574m., dep. 84,200m. (Dec. 1996); Pres. HANS JUERGUEN HEILKUHL OCHOA; 11 brs.

Banco Sudameris Colombia (fmrly Banco Francés e Italiano): Carrera 11, No 94A-03, 5°, Apdo Aéreo 3440, Santafé de Bogotá, DC; tel. (1) 636-8729; fax (1) 636-7702; internet www.banco-sudameris.com.co; cap. 14,113.6m., res 60,949.3m., dep. 528,588.2m. (Dec. 1997); Pres. GIANCARLO PANICUCCI; 7 brs.

Banco Tequendama, SA: Diagonal 27, No 6-70, 2°, Santafé de Bogotá, DC; tel. (1) 320-2100; fax (1) 287-7020; f. 1976; wholly-owned subsidiary of Banco Construcción (Venezuela); cap. 12,049m., dep. 53,522m. (Dec. 1992); Pres. HÉCTOR MUÑOZ ARJUELA; 11 brs.

Banco Unión Colombiano (fmrly Banco Royal Colombiano): Torre Banco Unión Colombiano, Carrera 7A, No 71-52, 2°, Apdo Aéreo 3438, Santafé de Bogotá, DC; tel. (1) 312-0411; fax (1) 312-0843; e-mail bcounion@impsat.net.co; f. 1925; cap. 12,350.3m. res 27,667.2m., dep. 131,063.0m. (Dec. 1995); Pres. ALBERTO GUILLERMO VILLAVECES MEDINA; 26 brs.

BBV-Banco Ganadero: Carrera 9A, No 72-21, 11°, Apdo Aéreo 53859, Santafé de Bogotá, DC; tel. (1) 347-1600; fax (1) 235-1248; f. 1956 as Banco Ganadero; name changed as above 1998; cap. 879,467.8m., dep. 2,989,659.8m. (Dec. 1998); Exec. Pres. JOSÉ MARÍA AYALA VARGAS; 286 brs.

Citibank Colombia, SA: Carrera 9A, No 99-02, 3°, Santafé de Bogotá, DC; tel. (1) 618-4455; fax (1) 621-0259; internet www.citibank.com/colombia; wholly-owned subsidiary of Citibank (USA); cap. 483m., res 9,399m., dep. 152,139m. (Dec. 1992); Pres. ANTONIO URIBE; 23 brs.

Cali

Banco de Occidente: Carrera 4, No 7-61, 12°, Apdo Aéreo 4400, Cali, Valle del Cauca; tel. (2) 886-1117; fax (2) 886-1297; e-mail banoccdi@col2.telecom.com.co; internet www.bancooccidente.com.co; cap. 2,790,400m.; res 281,808m., dep. 1,795,245m. (Dec. 1998); Pres. EFRAIN OTERO ÁLVAREZ; 116 brs.

Medellín

Bancolombia, SA (fmrly Banco Industrial de Colombia): Carrera 52, No 50-20, Medellín, Antioquia; tel. (4) 251-5474; fax (4) 513-4827; e-mail mfranco@bancolombia.com.co; internet www.bancolombia.com.co; f. 1945; renamed 1998 following merger with Banco de Colombia; cap. 169,524m., res 768,382m., dep. 4,386,515m. (Dec. 1999); Pres. JORGE LONDOÑO SALDARRIAGA; 341 brs.

Banking Associations

Asociación Bancaria y de Entidades Financieras de Colombia: Carrera 9A, No 74-08, 9°, Santafé de Bogotá, DC; tel. (1) 249-6411; fax (1) 211-9915; e-mail info@asobancaria.com; internet www.asobancaria.com; f. 1936; 56 mem. banks; Pres. PATRICIA CÁRDENAS SANTA MARÍA.

Asociación Nacional de Instituciones Financieras (ANIF): Calle 70A, No 7-86, Santafé de Bogotá, DC; tel. (1) 310-1500; fax (1) 235-5947; Pres. ARMANDO MONTENEGRO TRUJILLO.

STOCK EXCHANGES

Superintendencia de Valores: Avda El Dorado, Calle 26, No 68-85, Torre Suramericana, 2° y 3°, Santafé de Bogotá, DC; tel. (1) 427-0222; fax (1) 427-0870; f. 1979 to regulate the securities market; Supt JORGE GABRIEL TABOADA HOYOS.

Bolsa de Bogotá: Carrera 8A, No 13-82, 4°-8°, Apdo Aéreo 3584, Santafé de Bogotá, DC; tel. (1) 243-6501; fax (1) 281-3170; f. 1928; Pres. AUGUSTO ACOSTA TORRES; Sec.-Gen. MARÍA FERNANDA TORRES.

Bolsa de Medellín, SA: Carrera 50, No 50-48, 2°, Apdo Aéreo 3535, Medellín, Antioquia; tel. (4) 260-3000; fax (4) 251-1981; e-mail info@medellin.impsat.net.co; f. 1961; Pres. CRISTIÁN TORO LUDEKE.

Bolsa de Occidente, SA: Calle 10, No 4-40, 13°, Apdo Aéreo 11718, Santiago de Cali; tel. (2) 889-8400; fax (2) 889-9435; e-mail bolsaocc@cali.cetcol.net.co; internet www.bolsadeoccidente.com.co; f. 1983; Pres. JOSÉ RICARDO CAICEDO PEÑA.

INSURANCE

Principal National Companies

ACE Seguros, SA: Calle 72, No 10-51, 6°, 7° y 8°, Apdo Aéreo 29782, Santafé de Bogotá, DC; tel. (1) 319-0300; fax (1) 319-0304; internet www.ace-ina.com; fmrly Cigna Seguros de Colombia, SA; Pres. ALVARO A. ROZO PALOU.

Aseguradora Colseguros, SA: Carrera 13A, No 29-24, Parque Central Bavaria, Apdo Aéreo 3537, Santafé de Bogotá, DC; tel. (1) 561-6392; fax (1) 561-6427; e-mail thiermoo@colseguros.com; internet www.colseguros.com; f. 1874; Pres. MAX THIERMANN.

Aseguradora El Libertador, SA: Carrera 13, No 26-45, 9°, Apdo Aéreo 10285, Santafé de Bogotá, DC; tel. (1) 281-2427; fax (1) 286-0662; e-mail aselib@impsat.net.co; Pres. FERNANDO ROJAS CÁRDENAS.

Aseguradora Solidaria de Colombia: Carrera 12, No 93-30, Apdo Aéreo 252030, Santafé de Bogotá, DC; tel. (1) 621-4330; fax (1) 621-4321; e-mail eguzman@solidaria.com.co; Pres. CARLOS GUZMÁN.

Chubb de Colombia Cía de Seguros, SA: Carrera 7A, No 71-52, Torre B, 10°, Apdo Aéreo 26931, Santafé de Bogotá, DC; tel. (1) 312-3700; fax (1) 312-2401; e-mail jvelandia@chubb.com.co; Pres. LUIS FERNANDO MATHIEU.

Cía Agrícola de Seguros, SA: Carrera 11, No 93-46, Apdo Aéreo 7212, Santafé de Bogotá, DC; tel. (1) 635-5827; fax (1) 635-5876; e-mail agricola@impsat.net.co; f. 1952; Pres. Dr JOSÉ F. JARAMILLO HOYOS.

Cía Aseguradora de Fianzas, SA (Confianza): Calle 82, No 11-37, 7°, Apdo Aéreo 056965, Santafé de Bogotá, DC; tel. (1) 617-0899; fax (1) 610-8866; e-mail rjaramillo@confianza.com; Pres. RODRIGO JARAMILLO ARANGO.

Cía Central de Seguros, SA: Carrera 7A, No 76-07, 9°, Apdo Aéreo 5764, Santafé de Bogotá, DC; tel. (1) 319-0700; fax (1) 640-5553; e-mail recursos@centralseguros.com.co; internet www.centralseguros.com.co; f. 1956; Pres. SYLVIA LUZ RINCÓN LEMA.

Cía de Seguros Atlas, SA: Calle 21, No 23-22, 3°-11°, Apdo Aéreo 413, Manizales, Caldas; tel. (68) 84-1500; fax (168) 84-1447; e-mail satlas@andi.org.co; internet www.andi.org.co/seguros_atlas.htm; Pres. JORGE HOYOS MAYA.

Cía de Seguros Bolívar, SA: Carrera 10A, No 16-39, Apdo Aéreo 4421, Santafé de Bogotá, DC; tel. (1) 341-0077; fax (1) 281-8262; e-mail maria.cristina.zuluga@bolnet.com.co; f. 1939; Pres. JORGE E. URIBE MONTAÑO.

Cía de Seguros Colmena, SA: Calle 72, No 10-07, 7° y 8°, Apdo Aéreo 6774, Santafé de Bogotá, DC; tel. (1) 211-9111; fax (1) 211-4952; e-mail juand@colmena-seguros.com.co; Pres. JUAN MANUEL DÍAZ-GRANADOS.

Cía de Seguros Generales Aurora, SA: Edif. Seguros Aurora, 1°, 2° y 3°, Carrera 7, No 74-21, Apdo Aéreo 8006, Santafé de Bogotá, DC; tel. (1) 212-2800; fax (1) 212-2138; e-mail aurosis@colomsat.net.co; Pres. GERMÁN ESPINOSA.

Cía Mundial de Seguros, SA: Calle 33, No 6-94, 2° y 3°, Santafé de Bogotá, DC; tel. (1) 285-5600; fax (1) 285-1220; e-mail mundial@impsat.net.co; Dir-Gen. CAMILO FERNÁNDEZ ESCOVAR.

Cía Suramericana de Seguros, SA: Centro Suramericana, Carrera 64B, No 49A-30, Apdo Aéreo 780, Medellín, Antioquia; tel. (4) 260-2100; fax (4) 260-3194; e-mail contactenos@suramericana.com.co; internet www.suramericana.com.co; f. 1944; Pres. Dr NICANOR RESTREPO SANTAMARÍA.

Condor SA, Cía de Seguros Generales: Calle 119, No 16-59, Apdo Aéreo 57018, Santafé de Bogotá, DC; tel. (1) 612-0666; fax (1) 215-6121; Pres. EUDORO CARVAJAL IBÁÑEZ.

Generali Colombia–Seguros Generales, SA: Carrera 7A, No 72-13, 1°, 7° y 8°, Apdo Aéreo 076478, Santafé de Bogotá, DC; tel. (1) 217-8411; fax (1) 255-1164; Pres. MARCO PAPINI.

La Ganadera Cía de Seguros, SA: Carrera 7, No 71-52, Torre B, 11°, Apdo Aéreo 052347, Santafé de Bogotá, DC; tel. (1) 312-2630; fax (1) 312-2599; e-mail ganadera@impsat.net.co; internet www.laganadera.com.co; Pres. CARLOS VERGARA GÓMEZ.

La Interamericana Cía de Seguros Generales, SA: Calle 78, No 9-57, 4° y 5°, Apdo Aéreo 92381, Santafé de Bogotá, DC; tel. (1) 210-2200; fax (1) 210-2021; e-mail interb1@ibm.net; Pres. DIDIER SERRANO.

La Previsora, SA, Cía de Seguros: Calle 57, No 8-93, Apdo Aéreo 52946, Santafé de Bogotá, DC; tel. (1) 211-2880; fax (1) 211-8717; e-mail previpr@andinet.com; Pres. ALVARO ESCALLÓN EMILIANI.

Liberty Seguros, SA: Calle 71A, No 6-30, 2°, 3°, 4° y 14°, Apdo Aéreo 100327, Santafé de Bogotá, DC; tel. (1) 212-4900; fax (1) 212-7706; e-mail lhernandez@impsat.net.co; f. 1954; fmrly Latinoamericana de Seguros, SA; Pres. MAURICIO GARCÍA ORTIZ.

Mapfre Seguros Generales de Colombia, SA: Carrera 7A, No 74-36, 2°, Apdo Aéreo 28525, Santafé de Bogotá, DC; tel. (1) 346-8702; fax (1) 346-8793; e-mail jmincha@mapfre.com.co; Pres. JOSÉ MANUEL INCHAUSTI.

Pan American de Colombia Cía de Seguros de Vida, SA: Carrera 7A, No 75-09, Apdo Aéreo 76000, Santafé de Bogotá, DC; tel. (1) 212-1300; fax (1) 217-8799; e-mail aponton@reymoreno.net.co; Pres. ALFONSO PONTÓN.

Real Seguros, SA: Carrera 7A, No 115-33, 10°, Apdo Aéreo 7412, Santafé de Bogotá, DC; tel. (1) 523-1400; fax (1) 523-4010; e-mail realseg@colomsat.net.co; Gen. Man. JOSÉ LUIZ TOMAZINI.

Royal and Sun Alliance Seguros (Colombia), SA: Carrera 7A, No 32-33, 6°, 7°, 11° y 12°, Santafé de Bogotá, DC; tel. (1) 561-0380; fax (1) 320-3726; e-mail meradeo@royal-sunalliance-col.com; internet www.royal-sunalliance-col.com; fmrly Seguros Fénix, SA; Pres. DINAND BLOM.

Segurexpo de Colombia, SA: Calle 72, No 6-44, 12°, Apdo Aéreo 75140, Santafé de Bogotá, DC; tel. (1) 217-0900; fax (1) 210-0218; e-mail segurexp@col1.telecom.co; Pres. JUAN PABLO LUQUE LUQUE.

Seguros Alfa, SA: Carrera 13, No 27-47, 22° y 23°, Apdo Aéreo 27718, Santafé de Bogotá, DC; tel. (1) 344-4720; fax (1) 344-6770; e-mail sistemas@andinet.lat.net; Pres. JESÚS HERNANDO GÓMEZ.

Seguros Colpatria, SA: Carrera 7A, No 24-89, 9°, Apdo Aéreo 7762, Santafé de Bogotá, DC; tel. (1) 616-6655; fax (1) 281-5053; e-mail capicolc@openway.com.co; Pres. Dr FERNANDO QUINTERO.

Seguros La Equidad, OC: Calle 19, No 6-68, 10°, 11° y 12°, Apdo Aéreo 30261, Santafé de Bogotá, DC; tel. (1) 284-1910; fax (1)

286-5124; e-mail equidad@colomsat.net.co; Pres. Dr JULIO ENRIQUE MEDRANO LEÓN.

Seguros del Estado, SA: Carrera 11, No 90-20, Apdo Aéreo 6810, Santafé de Bogotá, DC; tel. (1) 218-6977; fax (1) 218-0971; e-mail seguros2@latino.net.co; Pres. Dr JORGE MORA SÁNCHEZ.

Skandia Seguros de Vida, SA: Avda 19, No 113-30, Apdo Aéreo 100327, Santafé de Bogotá, DC; tel. (1) 214-1200; fax (1) 214-0038; Pres. RAFAEL JARAMILLO SAMPER.

Insurance Association

Federación de Aseguradores Colombianos—FASECOLDA: Carrera 7A, No 26-20, 11° y 12°, Apdo Aéreo 5233, Santafé de Bogotá, DC; tel. (1) 210-8080; fax (1) 210-7090; e-mail fasecolda@fasecold a.com; internet www.fasecolda.com; f. 1976; 33 mems; Pres. Dr WILLIAM R. FADUL VERGARA.

Trade and Industry

GOVERNMENT AGENCIES

Departamento Nacional de Planeación: Calle 26, No 13-19, 14°, Santafé de Bogotá, DC; tel. (1) 336-1600; fax (1) 281-3348; f. 1958; supervises and administers devt projects; approves foreign investments; Dir JOSÉ ANTONIO OCAMPO GAVIRIA.

Instituto Colombiano de Comercio Exterior—INCOMEX: Calle 28, No 13A-15, 5°, Apdo Aéreo 240193, Santafé de Bogotá, DC; tel. (1) 283-3284; fax (1) 281-2560; sets and executes foreign trade policy; Dir. MARÍA URIZA PARDO.

Instituto Colombiano de la Reforma Agraria—INCORA: Centro Administrativo Nacional (CAN), Avda El Dorado, Apdo Aéreo 151046, Santafé de Bogotá, DC; tel. (1) 222-0963; f. 1962; a public institution which, on behalf of the govt, administers public lands and those it acquires; reclaims land by irrigation and drainage facilities, roads, etc. to increase productivity in agriculture and stock-breeding; provides technical assistance and loans; supervises the distribution of land throughout the country; Dir GERMÁN BULA E.

Superintendencia de Industria y Comercio—SUPERINDUS-TRIA: Carrera 13, No 27-00, 5°, Santafé de Bogotá, DC; tel. (1) 234-2035; fax (1) 281-3125; supervises chambers of commerce; controls standards and prices; Supt MARCO AURELIO ZULUAGA GIRALDO.

Superintendencia de Sociedades—SUPERSOCIEDADES: Avda El Dorado, No 46-80, Apdo Aéreo 4188, Santafé de Bogotá, DC; tel. (1) 222-0566; fax (1) 221-1027; e-mail supersoc1@sinpro.gov.co; f. 1931; oversees activities of local and foreign corpns; Supt DARÍO LAGUADO MONSALVE.

DEVELOPMENT ORGANIZATIONS

Fondo Nacional de Proyectos de Desarrollo—FONADE: Calle 26, No 13-19, 19°-22°, Apdo Aéreo 24110, Santafé de Bogotá, DC; tel. (1) 594-0407; fax (1) 282-6018; e-mail fonade@colomsat.net.co; f. 1968; responsible for channelling loans towards economic devt projects; administered by a committee under the head of the Departamento Nacional de Planeación; FONADE works in close association with other official planning orgs; Gen. Man. Dr AGUSTÍN MEJÍA JARAMILLO.

Fundación para el Desarrollo Integral del Valle del Cauca—FDI: Calle 8, No 3-14, 17°, Apdo Aéreo 7482, Cali, Valle del Cauca; tel. (2) 80-6660; fax (2) 82-4627; f. 1969; industrial devt org.; Pres. GUNNAR LINDAHL HELLBERG; Exec. Pres. FABIO RODRÍGUEZ GONZÁLEZ.

CHAMBERS OF COMMERCE

Confederación Colombiana de Cámaras de Comercio—CON-FECAMARAS: Carrera 13, No 27-47, Of. 502, Apdo Aéreo 29750, Santafé de Bogotá, DC; tel. (1) 288-1200; fax (1) 288-4228; e-mail confecamaras@inter.net.co; internet www.confecamaras.org.co; f. 1969; 56 mems.; Exec. Pres. EUGENIO MARULANDA GÓMEZ.

Cámara de Comercio de Bogotá: Carrera 9A, No 16-21, Santafé de Bogotá, DC; tel. (1) 334-7900; fax (1) 284-8506; internet www.ccb.org.co; f. 1878; 3,650 mem. orgs; Dir ARIEL JARAMILLO JARA-MILLO; Exec.-Pres. GUILLERMO FERNÁNDEZ DE SOTO.

There are also local Chambers of Commerce in the capital towns of all the Departments and in many of the other trading centres.

INDUSTRIAL AND TRADE ASSOCIATIONS

Colombiana de Minería—COLMINAS: Santafé de Bogotá, DC; state mining concern; Man. ALFONSO RODRÍGUEZ KILBER.

Corporación de la Industria Aeronáutica Colombiana, SA (CIAC SA): Aeropuerto Internacional El Dorado, Entrada 1 y 2, Apdo Aéreo 14446, Santafé de Bogotá, DC; tel. (1) 413-9735; fax (1) 413-8673; Gen. Man. ALBERTO MELÉNDEZ.

Empresa Colombia de Niquel—ECONIQUEL: Santafé de Bogotá, DC; tel. (1) 232-3839; administers state nickel resources; Dir JAVIER RESTREPO TORO.

Empresa Colombiana de Uranio—COLURANIO: Centro Administrativo Nacional (CAN), 4°, Ministerio de Minas y Energía, Santafé de Bogotá, DC; tel. (1) 244-5440; f. 1977 to further the exploration, processing and marketing of radio-active minerals; initial cap. US $750,000; Dir JAIME GARCÍA.

Empresa de Comercialización de Productos Perecederos—EMCOPER: Santafé de Bogotá, DC; tel. (1) 235-5507; attached to Ministry of Agriculture; Dir LUIS FERNANDO LONDOÑO RUIZ.

Industria Militar—INDUMIL: Diagonal 40, No 47-75, Apdo Aéreo 7272, Santafé de Bogotá, DC; tel. (1) 222-3001; fax (1) 222-4889; attached to Ministry of National Defence; Man. Adm. (retd) MAN-UEL F. AVENDAÑO.

Instituto Colombiano Agropecuario (ICA): Calle 37, No 8-43, 4° y 5°, Apdo Aéreo 7984, Santafé de Bogotá, DC; tel. (1) 285-5520; fax (1) 285-4351; f. 1962; institute for promotion, co-ordination and implementation of research into and teaching and devt of agriculture and animal husbandry; Dir Dr HERNÁN MARIN GUTIÉRREZ.

Instituto de Crédito Territorial (ICT): Carrera 13, No 18-51, Apdo Aéreo 4037, Santafé de Bogotá, DC; tel. (1) 234-3560; Gen. Man. GABRIEL GIRALDO.

Instituto de Fomento Industrial (IFI): Calle 16, No 6-66, Edif. Avianca, 7°-15°, Apdo Aéreo 4222, Santafé de Bogotá, DC; tel. (1) 336-0377; fax (1) 286-4166; f. 1940; state finance corpn for enterprise devt; cap. 469,808m. pesos, total assets 2,246,480m. pesos (Dec. 1998); Pres. ENRIQUE CAMACHO MATAMOROS.

Instituto de Hidrología, Meteorología y Estudios Ambientales IDEAM: Diagonal 97, No 17-60, 1°, 2°, 3° y 7°, Santafé de Bogotá, DC; tel. (1) 283-6927; fax (1) 635-6218; f. 1995; responsible for irrigation, flood control, drainage, hydrology and meteorology; Dir PABLO LEYVA.

Instituto de Investigaciones en Geociencias, Minería y Química—INGEOMINAS: Diagonal 53, No 34-53, Apdo Aéreo 4865, Santafé de Bogotá, DC; tel. (1) 222-1811; fax (1) 222-3597; f. 1968; responsible for mineral research, geological mapping and research including hydrogeology, remote sensing, geochemistry and geophysics; Dir Dr ADOLFO ALARCÓN GUZMÁN.

Instituto de Mercadeo Agropecuario—IDEMA: Carrera 10A, No 16-82, Of. 1006, Santafé de Bogotá, DC; tel. (1) 342-2596; fax (1) 283-1838; state enterprise for the marketing of agricultural products; Dir-Gen. ENRIQUE CARLOS RUIZ RAAD.

Instituto Nacional de Fomento Municipal—INSFOPAL: Centro Administrativo Nacional (CAN), Avda El Dorado, Santafé de Bogotá, DC; tel. (1) 222-3177; Gen. Man. JAIME MARIO SALAZAR VELÁSQUEZ.

Instituto Nacional de los Recursos Naturales Renovables y del Ambiente—INDERENA: Diagonal 34, No 5-18, 3°, Santafé de Bogotá, DC; tel. (1) 285-4417. 1968; govt agency regulating the devt of natural resources.

Minerales de Colombia, SA (MINERALCO): Calle 32, No 13-07, Apdo Aéreo 17878, Santafé de Bogotá, DC; tel. (1) 287-7136; fax (1) 87-4606; administers state resources of emerald, copper, gold, sulphur, gypsum, phosphate rock and other minerals except coal, petroleum and uranium; Gen. Man. ORLANDO ALVAREZ PÉREZ.

Sociedad Minera del Guainía (SMG): Santafé de Bogotá, DC; f. 1987; state enterprise for exploration, mining and marketing of gold; Pres. Dr JORGE BENDECK OLIVELLA.

There are several other agricultural and regional development organizations.

EMPLOYERS' AND PRODUCERS' ORGANIZATIONS

Asociación Colombiana Popular de Industriales (ACOPI): Carrera 23, No 41-94, Apdo Aéreo 16451, Santafé de Bogotá, DC; tel. (1) 244-2741; fax (1) 268-8965; f. 1951; asscn of small industrialists; Pres. JUAN A. PINTO SAAVEDRA; Man. MIGUEL CARRILLO M.

Asociación de Cultivadores de Caña de Azúcar de Colombia (ASOCAÑA): Calle 58N, No 3N-15, Apdo Aéreo 4448, Cali, Valle del Cauca; tel. (2) 64-7902; fax (2) 64-5888; f. 1959; sugar planters' asscn; Pres. Dr RICARDO VILLAVECES PARDO.

Asociación Nacional de Exportadores (ANALDEX): Carrera 10, No 27, Int. 137, Of. 902, Apdo Aéreo 29812, Santafé de Bogotá, DC; tel. (1) 342-0788; fax (1) 284-6911; exporters' asscn; Pres. JORGE RAMÍREZ OCAMPO.

Asociación Nacional de Exportadores de Café de Colombia: Calle 72, No 10-07, Of. 1101, Santafé de Bogotá, DC; tel. (1) 347-8419; fax (1) 347-9523; f. 1938; private asscn of coffee exporters; Pres. JORGE E. LOZANO MANCERA.

Asociación Nacional de Industriales (ANDI) (National Asscn of Manufacturers): Calle 52, No 47-48, Apdo Aéreo 997, Medellín, Antioquia; tel. (4) 511-1177; fax (4) 251-8830; f. 1944; Pres. LUIS CARLOS VILLEGAS ECHEVERRI; 9 brs; 756 mems.

Expocafé Ltda: Edif. Seguros Caribe, Carrera 7A, No 74-36, 3°, Apdo Aéreo 41244, Santafé de Bogotá, DC; tel. (1) 217-8900; fax (1)

217-3554; f. 1985; coffee exporting org.; Gen. Man. Luis José Alvarez L.

Federación Colombiana de Ganaderos (FEDEGAN): Carrera 14, No 36-65, Apdo Aéreo 9709, Santafé de Bogotá, DC; tel. (1) 245-3041; fax (1) 232-7153; f. 1963; cattle raisers' asscn; about 350,000 affiliates; Pres. José Raimundo Sojo Zambrano.

Federación Nacional de Cacaoteros: Carrera 17, No 30-39, Apdo Aéreo 17736, Santafé de Bogotá, DC; tel. (1) 288-7188; fax (1) 288-4424; fed. of cocoa growers; Gen. Man. Dr Miguel Uribe.

Federación Nacional de Cafeteros de Colombia (National Federation of Coffee Growers): Calle 73, No 8-13, Apdo Aéreo 57534, Santafé de Bogotá, DC; tel. (1) 345-6600; fax (1) 217-1021; f. 1927; totally responsible for fostering and regulating the coffee economy; Gen. Man. Jorge Cárdenas Gutiérrez; 203,000 mems.

Federación Nacional de Cultivadores de Cereales (FEN-ALCE): Carrera 14, No 97-62, Apdo Aéreo 8694, Santafé de Bogotá, DC; tel. (1) 218-9366; fax (1) 218-9463; f. 1960; fed. of grain growers; Gen. Man. Adriano Quintana Silva; 12,000 mems.

Federación Nacional de Comerciantes (FENALCO): Carrera 4, No 19-85, 7°, Santafé de Bogotá, DC; tel. (1) 286-0600; fax (1) 282-7573; fed. of businessmen; Pres. Sabas Pretelt de la Vega.

Sociedad de Agricultores de Colombia (SAC) (Colombian Farmers' Society): Carrera 7A, No 24-89, 44°, Apdo Aéreo 3638, Santafé de Bogotá, DC; tel. (1) 281-0263; fax (1) 284-4572; e-mail socdeagr@impsat.net.co; f. 1871; Pres. Juan Manuel Ospina Restrepo; Sec.-Gen. Dr Gabriel Martínez Teláez.

There are several other organizations, including those for rice growers, engineers and financiers.

MAJOR COMPANIES

The following are some of the leading industrial and commercial companies operating in Colombia:

Acerías Paz del Río, SA: Carrera 8, No 13-31, 7°, Santafé de Bogotá, DC; tel. (1) 282-8111; fax (1) 282-3480; e-mail apdr@multi.net.co; f. 1948; mining and processing of iron ores; Pres. Rodrigo Mesa Cadavid; 2,450 employees.

Almacenes Exito, SA: Carrera 48, No 32B, Envigado; tel. (4) 335-9090; fax (4) 331-4792; internet www.exito.com.co; f. 1972; wholesaling and retailing; Pres. Gonzalo Restrepo López; 8,500 employees.

Alpina Productos Alimenticios, SA: Carrera 63, No 15–61, Santafé de Bogotá, DC; tel. (1) 414-0011; fax (1) 414-1480; e-mail alpina@alpina.com; internet www.alpina.com.co; f. 1984; food and food processing; Pres. Hernan Mendez; 2,800 employees.

Anglo-American PLC: internet www.angloamerican.co.uk; f. 1917; mining and natural resources; part of consortium that bought CARBOCOL (see below) in 2000, owns 50% of Cerrejón coal-mine; CEO Tony Trahar.

Bavaria, SA: Calle 94, No 7A-47, Santafé de Bogotá, DC; tel. (1) 610-0200; fax (1) 610-2364; e-mail bavaria@bavaria.com.co; internet www.bavaria.com.co; f. 1889; holding co with principal interests in brewing and the manufacture of soft drinks; also transport, telecommunications, construction, forestry and fishing; Pres. Augusto López Valencia; Sec.-Gen. Juan Manuel Arboleda Perdomo; 10,400 employees.

BHP Billiton: internet www.bhpbilliton.com; f. 2001 following merger of BHP of Australia and British–South African co Billiton; mining and natural resources; part of consortium that bought CARBOCOL (see below) in 2000.

BP Exploration Company (Colombia) Ltd: Carrera 9A, No 99-02, 4°, Santafé de Bogotá, DC; tel. (1) 222-8855; fax (1) 218-3108; f. 1972; subsidiary of British Petroleum; exploration for hydrocarbons reserves; Legal Rep. Alvaro Camargo Patiño; 1,020 employees.

Carbones de Colombia, SA (CARBOCOL): Carrera 7A, No 71-52, Torre B, 6°, Apdo Aéreo 29740, Santafé de Bogotá, DC; tel. (1) 312-2228; fax (1) 312-2205; internet www.carbocol.gov.co; f. 1976; exploration, mining, processing and marketing of coal; fmrly state-owned and privatized in late 2000; Pres. Dr Antonio Pretelt Emiliani; 445 employees.

Carvajal, SA: Calle 29 Norte, No 6A-40, Apdo Aéreo 46, Cali; tel. (2) 667-5011; fax (2) 661-6581; internet www.carvajal.com.co; f. 1941; holding co with principal interests in printing and publishing; also construction, electronic components, telecommunications, trade, personal credit and the manufacture of office furniture; Pres. Adolfo Carvajal Quelquejeu; 10,000 employees.

Cementos Diamante, SA: Autopista Medellín 66A-48, Santafé de Bogotá, DC; tel. (1) 434-4128; fax (1) 610-9181; f. 1927; manufacture of cement; Pres. Andrés Uribe Crane; Gen. Man. Jairo Echavarria B.; 1,000 employees.

Cerro Matoso, SA: Carrera 7A, No 26-20, 8°, Santafé de Bogotá, DC; tel. (1) 288-7066; fax (5) 285-7974; f. 1979; mining of ferrous ores; Pres. Enrique Andrade; 700 employees.

Cervecería Aguila, SA: Calle 10, No 38-56, Barranquilla; tel. (5) 341-1900; fax (5) 332-5366; f. 1967; brewery; parent co is Bavaria, SA; Pres. Alvaro Pupo Pupo; 980 employees.

Cervecería Leona, SA: Autopista Norte Tocancipa Km 37, Tocancipa; tel. (1) 857-4425; f. 1992; Legal Rep. Ricardo Humberto Restrepo; 400 employees.

Cervecería Unión, SA: Carrera 50A, No 38-39, Itaguï, Medellín; tel. (4) 372-2400; fax (4) 372-3488; f. 1931; brewery; parent company is Bavaria, SA; Pres. Luis Fernando Arango Arango; Dir Dr Juan Guillermo Abad Cock; 900 employees.

Compañía Colombiana de Tejidos, SA (COLTEJER): Calle 62, No 44-103, Apdo Aéreo 636, Medellín; tel. (4) 373-0370; fax (4) 281-6640; e-mail coltejer@coltejer.com.co; internet www.coltejer.com.co; f. 1907; textile manufacturers; Pres. Ricardo Mejía C.; 5,922 employees.

Compañía Colombiana Automotriz, SA (CCA): Carretera 11, No 94-02, Santafé de Bogotá, DC; tel. (1) 218-4111; fax (1) 257-2410; f. 1973; automobile manufacturers; majority of shares held by Mazda Ltd and Mitsubishi Corpn of Japan; 1,169 employees.

Comunicación Celular, SA (COMCEL): Calle 90, No 14-37, Santafé de Bogotá, DC; tel (1) 616-9797; fax (1) 623-1287; f. 1992; mobile telecommunications; Legal Rep. Peter Burrowes Gómez; 1,151 employees.

Cristalería Peldar, SA: Calle 39s, No 48-180, Apdo Aéreo 215, Envigado; tel. (4) 333-0548; fax (4) 270-4225; f. 1949; manufacture of glass products; Pres. Gilberto Restepo; 1,800 employees.

Empresa Colombiana de Petróleos (ECOPETROL): Edif. Ecopetrol, Carrera 13, No 36-24, Apdo Aéreo 5938, Santafé de Bogotá, DC; tel. (1) 234-4000; fax (1) 234-4743; e-mail webmaster@ecopetrol.com.co; internet www.ecopetrol.com.co; f. 1948; state-owned co for the exploration, production, refining and transportation of petroleum; Pres. Alberto Calderón Zuleta; 12,323 employees.

Enka de Colombia, SA: Carrera 63, No 49A-31, Medellín; tel. (4) 260-0900; fax (4) 260-5050; e-mail camacol@enka.com.co; internet www.enka.com.co; f. 1964; manufacture of synthetic fibres; Pres. Alvaro Concha Maldonado; 1,600 employees.

Esso Colombiana: Carretera 7, No 36-45, Santafé de Bogotá, DC; tel. (1) 285-2080; fax (1) 285-8404; f. 1951; petroleum and gas exploration and extraction; Pres. Alvaro Torres Peña; 568 employees.

Fábrica Colombiana de Automotores, SA (COLMOTORES): Avda Boyacá, No 36A-03 Sur, Santafé de Bogotá, DC; tel. (1) 710-1111; fax (1) 204-0826; subsidiary of General Motors Corpn, USA; producers of passenger and commercial vehicles, spare parts and accessories; Pres. Víctor Hugo Coello; 1,254 employees.

Fábrica de Aceitas Vegetales, SA: Calle 12, No 37-19, Santafé de Bogotá, DC; tel. (1) 237-8555. 1961; food production and processing including the manufacture of vegetable oils; Gen. Man. Iván Hoyos Robledo; 760 employees.

Fábrica de Hilados y Tejidos El Hato, SA (FABRICATO): Calle 51, No 49-11, 2°, Medellín; tel. (4) 511-5666; fax (4) 251-5905; e-mail fabrica1@antioq.grupopro.com.co; f. 1923; manufacture and export of cotton, textiles and synthetic fibre goods; Pres. Dr Jorge Restrepo Palacios; 4,325 employees.

Glencore International AG: e-mail info@glencore.com; internet www.glencore.com; Swiss-owned co, mining and natural resources; part of consortium that bought CARBOCOL (see above) in 2000.

Gran Cadena de Almacenes Colombianos, SA (CADENALCO): Calle 30A, No 65B-57, Medellín; tel. (4) 265-1515; fax (4) 253-6196; e-mail cadenal@antioq.grupopro.com.co; f. 1959; retailing; Pres. Germán Jaramillo Olano; 9,125 employees.

Industrias Alimenticias Noel, SA: Carrera 52, No 2-38, Apdo 897, Medellín; tel. (4) 285-1111; fax (4) 285-3553; e-mail webmaster @noel.com.co; internet www.noel.com.co; f. 1933; food production and processing including meat products, confectionery, powdered soft drinks and vegetable protein; Pres. Rafael Mario Villa Moreno; 2,000 employees.

Industrias Centrales de Acero, SA: Calle 13, No 39-10, Santafé de Bogotá, DC; tel. and fax (1) 268-6730. 1956; manufacture of household appliances; Pres. Pedro Mejía Mejía; 400 employees.

Ingenio del Cauca, SA: Carrera 9, No 28-103, Cali; tel. (2) 885-4545; fax (2) 443-3071; f. 1963; cultivation and processing of sugar cane; Pres. Bd of Dirs Carlos Ardila Lülle; 5,109 employees.

Ingenio Providencia, SA: Carrera 28, No 28-63, Palmira; tel. (2) 275-7171; fax (2) 438-4955; f. 1926; cultivation and wholesale of sugar cane; Pres. Alcardo Molina Abadia; 2,700 employees.

International Resources Corporation (Intercor): Carrera 54, No 72-80, Santafé de Bogotá, DC; tel. (1) 285-2080; f. 1975; mining; parent co is Exxon (USA); Pres. Ramon de la Torre; 2,200 employees.

Leonisa Internacional: Carrera 51, No 13-158, Medellín; tel. (4) 265-4000; fax (4) 265-0617; e-mail leonisa1@antioq.grupopro.com.co; internet www.colombiaexport.com/leonisa.htm; f. 1956; manufacturers of men's and women's clothing; Pres. OSCAR ECHEVERRI RESTREPO; 2,000 employees.

Mobil de Colombia, SA: Calle 70, No 7-30, 13°, Santafé de Bogotá, DC; tel. (1) 255-3100; fax (1) 217-8625; f. 1919; petroleum products; Pres. PETER J. CIAPPARELLI; 430 employees.

Occidental de Colombia, Inc: Calle 77A, No 11-32, Apdo 92171, Santafé de Bogotá, DC; tel. (1) 346-0111; fax (1) 211-6820; f. 1977; petroleum and gas exploration and production; 681 employees.

Pizano, SA: Carrera 9, No 74-08, 9°, Santafé de Bogotá, DC; tel. (1) 616-1088; fax (1) 255-1709; haulage and freight forwarding; Pres. BERNARDO PIZANO DE BRIGARD; 1,550 employees.

Productora de Papeles, SA (PROPAL): Carrera 16A, No 78-11, Of. 201, Santafé de Bogotá, DC; tel. (1) 635-9245; fax (1) 635-9297; internet www.propal.com.co; f. 1957; owners of two paper mills manufacturing paper products; Pres. JAIME GÓMEZ; 1,100 employees.

Promigas: Calle 66, No 67-123, Baranquilla; tel. (95) 344-0550; fax (95) 344-1421; internet www.promigas.com.co; f. 1974; natural-gas distributor, network covers 60% of the country; Pres. ANTONIO CELIA MARTÍNEZ.

Smurfit Cartón de Colombia, SA: Calle 15, No 18-109, Yumbo, Cali; tel. (2) 669-4000; fax (2) 442-5822; internet www.smurfit. com.co; cap. 488,000m. pesos; manufacturers of paper and packaging materials; subsidiary of Container Corpn of America Jefferson Smurfit Group PLC; Pres. ROBERTO SILVA; Vice-Pres. VICTOR GIRALDO; 2,376 employees.

Sociedad de Fabricación de Automotores, SA (Sofasa Renault): Calle 72, No 7-82, 16°, Santafé de Bogotá, DC; tel. (1) 210-0666; fax (1) 210-2184; internet www.sofasa.com.co; f. 1969; manufacture of motor vehicles and spare parts; Legal Rep. JUAN MANUEL CUNILL; 873 employees.

Supertiendas y Droguerías Olimpica, SA: Carrera 36, No 38-03, Barranquilla; tel. (53) 41-5912; fax (53) 41-1516; f. 1977; retailing; Pres. GUSTAVO ENRIQUE VISBAL GALOFRE; 4,600 employees.

Tecnoquímicas, SA: Calle 23, No 7-39, Cali; tel. (2) 882-5555; fax (2) 883-8859; f. 1983; manufacture of pharmaceuticals; Pres. FRANCISCO BARBERI ZAMORANO; 1,670 employees.

Tejidos El Condor, SA (TEJICONDOR): Carrera 65, No 45-23, Apdo 815, Medellín; tel. (4) 260-2600; fax (4) 260-3706; f. 1934; manufacture of textiles, incl. cotton weaving; Chair. L. M. SANIN ECHEVERRI; 1,515 employees.

Triton Colombia, Inc: Carrera 9A, No 99-02, Of. 407, Santafé de Bogotá, DC; tel. (1) 618-2411; fax (1) 618-2553; f. 1982; subsidiary of US co, Triton; petroleum exploration and production; Pres. MICHAEL MURPHY; 19 employees.

UTILITIES
Electricity

Corporación Eléctrica de la Costa Atlántica (Corelca): Calle 55, No 72-109, 9°, Barranquilla, Atlántico; tel. (5) 356-0200; fax (5) 356-2370; responsible for supplying electricity to the Atlantic departments; generates more than 2,000m. kWh annually from thermal power-stations; Man. Dir HERNÁN CORREA NOGUERA.

Empresa de Energía Eléctrica de Bogotá, SA (EEB): Avda El Dorado, No 55-51, Santafé de Bogotá, DC; tel. (1) 221-1665; fax (1) 221-6858; internet www.eeb.com.co; provides electricity for Bogotá area by generating capacity of 680 MW, mainly hydroelectric; Man. Dir PAULO OROZCO DÍAS.

Instituto Colombiano de Energía Eléctrica (ICEL): Carrera 13, No 27-00, 3°, Apdo Aéreo 16243, Santafé de Bogotá, DC; tel. (1) 342-0181; fax (1) 286-2934; formulates policy for the devt of electrical energy; constructs systems for the generation, transmission and distribution of electrical energy; Man. DOUGLAS VELÁSQUEZ JACOME; Sec.-Gen. PATRICIA OLIVEROS LAVERDE.

Interconexión Eléctrica, SA (ISA): Calle 12 Sur, No 18-168, Apdo Aéreo 8915, Medellín, Antioquia; tel. (4) 317-1331; fax (4) 823-970; e-mail isa@isa.com.co; internet www.isa.com.co; f. 1967; created by Colombia's principal electricity production and distribution cos to form a national network; installed capacity of 2,641m. kWh; operates major power-stations at Chivor and San Carlos; scheduled for privatization in 2001; Man. Dir JAVIER GUTIÉRREZ.

Isagen: Medellín, Antioquia; e-mail isagen@isagen.com.co; internet www.isagen.com.co; state-owned, scheduled for privatization in late 2000; generates electricity from three hydraulic and two thermal power plants.

Gas

Gas Natural ESP: Avda 40A, No 13-09, 9°, Santafé de Bogotá, DC; tel. (1) 338-1199; fax (1) 288-0807; f. 1987; private gas corpn; Pres. ANTONI PERIS MINGOT.

Gasoriente: distributes gas to 8 municipalities in north-easternColombia.

TRADE UNIONS

According to official figures, an estimated 900 of Colombia's 2,000 trade unions are independent.

Central Unitaria de Trabajadores (CUT): Calle 35, No 7-25, 9°, Apdo Aéreo 221, Santafé de Bogotá, DC; tel. (1) 288-8577; fax (1) 287-5769; f. 1986; comprises 50 feds and 80% of all trade union members; Pres. (vacant); Sec.-Gen. MIGUEL ANTONIO CARO.

Frente Sindical Democrática (FSD): f. 1984; centre-right trade union alliance; comprises:

> **Confederación de Trabajadores de Colombia (CTC) (Colombian Confederation of Workers):** Calle 39, No 26A-23, 5°, Apdo Aéreo 4780, Santafé de Bogotá, DC; tel. (1) 269-7119; f. 1934; mainly Liberal; 600 affiliates, including 6 national orgs and 20 regional feds; admitted to ICFTU; Pres. ALVIS FERNÁNDEZ; 400,000 mems.

> **Confederación de Trabajadores Democráticos de Colombia (CTDC):** Carrera 13, No 59-52, Of. 303, Santafé de Bogotá, DC; tel. (1) 255-3146; fax (1) 484-581; f. 1988; comprises 23 industrial feds and 22 national unions; Pres. MARIO DE J. VALDERRAMA.

> **Confederación General de Trabajadores Democráticos (CGTD):** Calle 39A, No 14-48, Apdo Aéreo 5415, Santafé de Bogotá, DC; tel. (1) 288-1560; fax (1) 288-1504; Christian Democrat; Sec.-Gen. JULIO ROBERTO GÓMEZ ESGUERRA.

Transport

Land transport in Colombia is rendered difficult by high mountains, so the principal means of long-distance transport is by air. As a result of the development of the El Cerrejón coal field, Colombia's first deep-water port was constructed at Bahía de Portete and a 150 km rail link between El Cerrejón and the port became operational in 1989.

Instituto Nacional del Transporte (INTRA): Edif. Minobras (CAN), 6°, Apdo Aéreo 24990, Santafé de Bogotá, DC; tel. (1) 222-4100; govt body; Dir Dr GUILLERMO ANZOLA LIZARAZO.

RAILWAYS

In 1989, following the entry into liquidation of the Ferrocarriles Nacionales de Colombia (FNC), the Government created three new companies, which assumed responsibility for the rail network in 1992. However, the new companies were beset by financial difficulties, and many rail services were subsequently suspended.

> **Empresa Colombiana de Vías Férreas (Ferrovías):** Calle 31, No 6-41, 20°, Santafé de Bogotá, DC; tel. (1) 636-9673; fax (1) 287-2515; responsible for the maintenance and devt of the national rail network; Dir JUAN GONZALO JARAMILLO.

> **Ferroviario Atlántico, SA:** Calle 72, No 13-23, 2°, Santafé de Bogotá, DC; tel. (1) 255-8684; fax (1) 255-8704; operated on a 30-year concession, awarded in 1998 to Asociación Futura Ferrocarriles de la Paz (Fepaz); 1,490 km (1993).

> **Fondo de Pasivo Social de Ferrocarriles Nacionales de Colombia:** Santafé de Bogotá, DC; administers welfare services for existing and former employees of the FNC.

El Cerrejón Mine Railway: International Colombia Resources Corpn, Carrera 54, No 72-80, Apdo Aéreo 52499, Barranquilla, Atlántico; tel. (5) 350-5389; fax (5) 350-2249; f. 1989 to link the mine and the port at Bahía de Portete; 150 km (1996); Supt M. MENDOZA.

Metro de Medellín Ltda: Calle 44, No 46-001, Apdo Aéreo 9128, Medellín, Antioquia; tel. (4) 452-6000; fax (4) 452-4450; e-mail emetro@col3.telecom.com.co; two-line metro with 25 stations opened in stages in 1995–96; 29 km; Gen. Man. LUIS GUILLERMO GÓMEZ A.

ROADS

In 1999 there were an estimated 112,988 km of roads, of which 16,575 km were highways and main roads and 70,483 km were secondary roads. About 14% of the total road network was paved in the same year. The country's main highways are the Caribbean Trunk Highway, the Eastern and Western Trunk Highways, the Central Trunk Highway and there are also roads into the interior. There are plans to construct a Jungle Edge highway to give access to the interior, a link road between Turbo, Bahía Solano and Medellín, a highway between Bogotá and Villavicencio and to complete the short section of the Pan-American highway between Panama and Colombia. In 1992 the World Bank granted a loan of US $266m. to Colombia for the construction of 400 km of new roads and the completion of 2,000 km of roads begun under an earlier programme.

There are a number of national bus companies and road haulage companies.

Instituto Nacional de Vías: Transversal 45, Entrada 2, Santafé de Bogotá, DC; tel. (1) 428-0400; fax (1) 315-6713; e-mail director@ latino.net.co; f. 1966, reorganized 1994; wholly state-owned; responsible to the Ministry of Transport; maintenance and construction of national road network; Gen. Man. LUIS E. TOBON CARDONA.

INLAND WATERWAYS

The Magdalena–Cauca river system is the centre of river traffic and is navigable for 1,500 km, while the Atrato is navigable for 687 km. The Orinoco system has more than five navigable rivers, which total more than 4,000 km of potential navigation (mainly through Venezuela); the Amazonas system has four main rivers, which total 3,000 navigable km (mainly through Brazil). There are plans to connect the Arauca with the Meta, and the Putamayo with the Amazon, and also to construct an Atrato–Truandó inter-oceanic canal.

Dirección de Navegación y Puertos: Edif. Minobras (CAN), Of. 562, Santafé de Bogotá, DC; tel. (1) 222-1248; responsible for river works and transport; the waterways system is divided into four sectors: Magdalena, Atrato, Orinoquia, and Amazonia; Dir ALBERTO RODRÍGUEZ ROJAS.

SHIPPING

The four most important ocean terminals are Buenaventura on the Pacific coast and Santa Marta, Barranquilla and Cartagena on the Atlantic coast. The port of Tumaco on the Pacific coast is gaining in importance and there are plans for construction of a deep-water port at Bahía Solano.

In 1998 Colombia's merchant fleet totalled 111,686 grt.

Port Authorities

Port of Barranquilla: Sociedad Portuaria Regional de Barranquilla, Carrera 38, Calle 1A, Barranquilla, Atlántico; tel. (5) 379-9555; fax (5) 379-9557; e-mail sprbbaq@latino.net.co; internet www.sprb.com.co; privatized in 1993; Port Man. ANÍBAL DAU.

Port of Buenaventura: Empresa Puertos de Colombia, Edif. El Café, Of. 1, Buenaventura; tel. (224) 22543; fax (224) 34447; Port Man. VÍCTOR GONZÁLEZ.

Port of Cartagena: Sociedad Portuaria Regional de Cartagena, SA, Manga, Terminal Marítimo, Cartagena, Bolívar; tel. (5) 660-7781; fax (5) 650-2239; e-mail comercial@sprc.com.co; internet www.sprc.com.co; f. 1959; Port Man. ALFONSO SALAS TRUJILLO; Harbour Master Capt. GONZALO PARRA.

Port of Santa Marta: Empresa Puertos de Colombia, Calle 15, No 3-25, 11°, Santa Marta, Magdalena; tel. (54) 210739; fax (54) 210711; Port Man. JULIÁN PALACIOS.

Principal Shipping Companies

Flota Mercante Grancolombiana, SA: Edif. Grancolombiana, Carrera 13, No 27-75, Apdo Aéreo 4482, Santafé de Bogotá, DC; tel. (1) 286-0200; fax (1) 286-9028; f. 1946; owned by the Colombian Coffee Growers' Federation (80%) and Ecuador Development Bank (20%); f. 1946; one of Latin America's leading cargo carriers serving 45 countries world-wide; Pres. LUIS FERNANDO ALARCÓN MANTILLA.

Colombiana Internacional de Vapores, Ltda (Colvapores): Avda Caracas, No 35-02, Apdo Aéreo 17227, Santafé de Bogotá, DC; cargo services mainly to the USA.

Líneas Agromar, Ltda: Calle 73, Vía 40-350, Apdo Aéreo 3256, Barranquilla, Atlántico; tel. (5) 345-1874; fax (5) 345-9634; Pres. MANUEL DEL DAGO FERNÁNDEZ.

Petromar Ltda: Bosque, Diagonal 23, No 56-152, Apdo Aéreo 505, Cartagena, Bolívar; tel. (5) 662-7208; fax (5) 662-7592; Chair. SAVERIO MINERVINI S.

Transportadora Colombiana de Graneles, SA (NAVESCO, SA): Avda 19, No 118-95, Of. 214-301, Santafé de Bogotá, DC; tel. (1) 620-9035; fax (1) 620-8801; e-mail navesco@colomsat.net.co; Gen. Man. GUILLERMO SOLANO VARELA.

Several foreign shipping lines call at Colombian ports.

CIVIL AVIATION

Colombia has more than 100 airports, including 11 international airports: Santafé de Bogotá, DC (El Dorado International Airport), Medellín, Cali, Barranquilla, Bucaramanga, Cartagena, Cúcuta, Leticia, Pereira, San Andrés and Santa Marta.

Airports Authority

Unidad Administrativa Especial de Aeronáutica Civil: Aeropuerto Internacional El Dorado, 4°, Santafé de Bogotá, DC; tel. (1) 413-9500; fax (1) 413-9878; f. 1967 as Departamento Administrativo de Aeronáutica Civil, reorganized 1993; wholly state-owned; Dir ERNESTO HUERTAS ESCACALLÓN.

National Airlines

Aerolíneas Centrales de Colombia, SA (ACES): Edif. del Café, Calle 49, No 50-21, 34°, Apdo Aéreo 6503, Medellín, Antioquia; tel.

(4) 251-7500; fax (4) 251-1677; e-mail gusuga@acescolombia.com.co; internet www.acescolombia.com; f. 1971; operates scheduled domestic passenger services throughout Colombia, and charter and scheduled flights to the USA and the Caribbean; Pres. JUAN E. POSADA.

Aerotaca, SA (Aerotransportes Casanare): Avda El Dorado, Entrada 1, Interior 20, Santafé de Bogotá, DC; tel. (1) 413-9884; fax (1) 413-5256; f. 1965; scheduled regional and domestic passenger services; Gen. Man. RAFAEL URDANETA.

AVIANCA (Aerovías Nacionales de Colombia, SA): Avda El Dorado, No 93-30, 5°, Santafé de Bogotá, DC; tel. (1) 413-9511; fax (1) 413-8716; internet www.avianca.com; f. 1940; operates domestic services to all cities in Colombia and international services to the USA, France, Spain and throughout Central and Southern America; Chair. ANDRÉS OBREGÓN SANTO DOMINGO; Pres. GUSTAVO A. LENIS.

Intercontinental de Aviación: Avda El Dorado, Entrada 2, Interior 6, Santafé de Bogotá, DC; tel. (1) 413-9700; fax (1) 413-8458; internet www.insite-network.com/inter; f. 1965 as Aeropesca Colombia (Aerovías de Pesca y Colonización del Suroeste Colombiano): operates scheduled domestic, regional and international passenger and cargo services; Pres. Capt. LUIS HERNÁNDEZ ZIA.

Servicio de Aeronavegación a Territorios Nacionales (Satena): Avda El Dorado, Entrada 1, Interior 11, Apdo Aéreo 11163, Santafé de Bogotá, DC; tel. (1) 413-8438; fax (1) 413-8178; f. 1962; commercial enterprise attached to the Ministry of National Defence; internal services; CEO and Gen. Man. Brig.-Gen. ALFREDO GARCÍA ROJAS.

Sociedad Aeronáutica de Medellín Consolidada, SA (SAM): Edif. SAM, Calle 53, No 45-211, 21°, Apdo Aéreo 1085, Medellín, Antioquia; tel. (4) 251-5544; fax (4) 251-0711; f. 1945; subsidiary of AVIANCA; internal services; and international cargo services to Central America and the Caribbean; Pres JULIO MARIO SANTODOMINGO, GUSTAVO LENIS.

Transportes Aéreos Mercantiles Panamericanos (Tampa): Carrera 76, No 34A-61, Apdo Aéreo 494, Medellín, Antioquia; tel. (4) 250-2939; fax (4) 250-5639; e-mail tampa@ticsanet.net; f. 1973; operates international cargo services to destinations throughout South America, also to Puerto Rico and the USA; Chair. GUSTAVO MORENO; Pres. FREDERICK JACOBSEN.

In addition, the following airlines operate international and domestic charter cargo services: Aerosucre Colombia, Aero Transcolombiana de Carga (ATC), Aerovías Colombianas (ARCA), Líneas Aéreas del Caribe (LAC Airlines Colombia), and Líneas Aéreas Suraméricanas (LAS).

Tourism

The principal tourist attractions are the Caribbean coast (including the island of San Andrés), the 16th-century walled city of Cartagena, the Amazonian town of Leticia, the Andes mountains rising to 5,700 m above sea-level, the extensive forests and jungles, pre-Columbian relics and monuments of colonial art. In 1997 there were 968,999 visitors (compared with 1,253,999 in 1996), most of whom came from Venezuela, Ecuador and the USA. Tourism receipts in 1997 were estimated to be US $955m.

Viceministerio de Turismo: Calle 28, No 13A-15, 17°, Edif. Centro de Comercio Internacional, Santafé de Bogotá, DC; tel. (1) 283-9558; fax (1) 286-4492; Vice-Minister of Tourism MARÍA PAULINA ESPINOSA DE LÓPEZ.

Asociación Colombiana de Agencias de Viajes y Turismo—ANATO: Carrera 21, No 83-63/71, Santafé de Bogotá, DC; tel. (1) 610-7099; fax (1) 218-7103; e-mail presidencia@anato.com.co; internet www.anato.com.co; f. 1949; Pres. Dr OSCAR RUEDA GARCÍA.

Defence

In August 2000 Colombia's Armed Forces numbered 153,000 (including some 74,700 conscripts): Army 130,000 (including 63,800 conscripts), Navy 15,000 (including 8,500 marines), Air Force 8,000 (including some 3,900 conscripts). There were also reserves of 60,700 and a paramilitary National Police Force numbering about 95,000. Military service is compulsory (except for students) and lasts for 12–18 months. In June 2001 President Pastrana announced the creation of a mobile brigade, comprising some 1,630 troops, to be deployed in the south-east of the country, a guerrilla stronghold. The unit was to begin operations by the end of 2001.

Defence Expenditure (estimate, 2000): 4,000,000m. pesos.

Chief of Staff of the Armed Forces: Gen. FERNANDO TAPIAS STAHELIN.

Commander of the Army: Gen. JORGE ENRIQUE MORA RANGEL.

Commander of the Navy: Adm. SERGIO GARCÍA TORRES.

Commander of the Air Force: Gen. HECTOR FABIO VELASCO.

Education

Education in Colombia commences at nursery level for children under six years of age. Primary education is free and compulsory for five years. Admission to secondary school is conditional upon the successful completion of these five years. Secondary education is for four years. Following completion of this period, pupils may pursue a further two years of vocational study, leading to the Bachiller examination. In 1995 the total enrolment at primary and secondary schools was equivalent to 85% and 50% of the school-age population, respectively. In 1996 there were an estimated 48,933 primary schools. In the same year there were an estimated 266 higher-education institutes (including universities) in Colombia. There are plans to construct an Open University to meet the increasing demand for higher education. Expenditure on education by the central Government in 1997 was 3,656,937m. pesos, representing 19.3% of total spending.

Bibliography

For works on South America generally, see Select Bibliography (Books).

Ardila Galvis, C. *The Heart of the War in Colombia*. London, Latin American Bureau, 2000.

Bagley, B. M. 'Dateline Drug Wars: Columbia—The Wrong Policy', in *Foreign Policy*, No. 77 (Winter). 1988/89.

Bergquist, C. W. *Coffee and Conflict in Colombia, 1886–1910*. Durham, NC, Duke University Press, 1978.

Labor in Latin America: Comparative Essays on Chile, Argentina, Venezuela and Colombia. Stanford, CA, Stanford University Press, 1986.

Berry, R. A., Hellman, R. G., and Solaún, M. (Eds). *Politics of Compromise: Coalition Government in Colombia*. New Brunswick, NJ, 1980.

Bushnell, D. *The Making of Modern Colombia: A Nation in Spite of Itself*. Berkeley, CA, University of California Press, 1993.

Drexler, R. W. *Colombia and the United States: Narcotics Traffic and a Failed Foreign Policy*. Jefferson, NC, McFarland & Company, 1997.

Galvis, C. A. *The Heart of the War in Colombia*. London, Latin American Bureau, 1999.

Giraldo, J. *Colombia: The Genocidal Democracy*. Monroe, ME, Common Courage Press, 1996.

Hartlyn, J. *The Politics of Coalition Rule in Colombia*. Cambridge, Cambridge University Press, 1988.

Henderson, J. *Modernization in Colombia: The Laureano Gómez Years, 1889–1965*. Florida, FL, University Press of Florida, 2001.

Kline, H. F. *Colombia: Portrait of Unity and Diversity*. Boulder, CO, Westview Press, 1983.

State Building and Conflict Resolution in Colombia, 1986–1994. Tuscaloosa, AL, University of Alabama Press, 1999.

Palacios, M. *Coffee in Colombia, 1850–1970: An Economic, Social and Political History*. Cambridge, Cambridge University Press, 1980.

Payne, J. *Patterns of Conflict in Colombia*. New Haven, CT, Yale University Press, 1968.

Pearce, J. *Columbia: Inside the Labyrinth*. London, Latin American Bureau, 1990.

Rausch, J. *Colombia: Territorial Rule and the Llanos Frontier*. Florida, FL, University Press of Florida, 1999.

Safford, F., and Palacios, M. *Colombia: Fragmented Land, Divided Society*. Oxford, Oxford University Press, 2001.

Sanchez, G., and Meertens, D. Bandits, *Peasants and Politics: The Case of 'La Violencia' in Colombia*. Austin, TX, University of Texas Press, 2001.

Wade, P. *Blackness and Race Mixture: The Dynamics of Racial Identity in Colombia*. Baltimore, MD, Johns Hopkins University Press, 1993.

COSTA RICA

Area: 51,100 sq km (19,730 sq miles).

Population (official estimate for mid-2000): 3,651,803.

Capital: San José, estimated population 345,599 in mid-2000.

Language: Spanish (official); an English creole is also spoken in the Atlantic coastal provinces.

Religion: Mainly Christianity: Roman Catholicism is the official religion and is professed by more than 80% of the population; other churches are also represented.

Climate: Tropical in the coastal lowlands, but temperate on the highland plateau.

Time: GMT –6 hours.

Public Holidays

2002: 1 January (New Year's Day), 19 March (Feast of St Joseph, San José only), 28 March (Maundy Thursday), 29 March (Good Friday), 11 April (Anniversary of the Battle of Rivas), 1 May (Labour Day), 30 May (Corpus Christi), 29 June (SS Peter and Paul), 25 July (Anniversary of the Annexation of Guana-

caste Province), 2 August (Our Lady of the Angels), 15 August (Assumption), 15 September (Independence Day), 12 October (Columbus Day), 1 December (Abolition of the Armed Forces Day), 8 December (Immaculate Conception), 25 December (Christmas Day), 28–31 December (San José only).

2003: 1 January (New Year's Day), 19 March (Feast of St Joseph, San José only), 11 April (Anniversary of the Battle of Rivas), 17 April (Maundy Thursday), 18 April (Good Friday), 1 May (Labour Day), 19 June (Corpus Christi), 29 June (SS Peter and Paul), 25 July (Anniversary of the Annexation of Guanacaste Province), 2 August (Our Lady of the Angels), 15 August (Assumption), 15 September (Independence Day), 12 October (Columbus Day), 1 December (Abolition of the Armed Forces Day), 8 December (Immaculate Conception), 25 December (Christmas Day), 28–31 December (San José only).

Currency: Costa Rican colón; 1,000 colones = £2.152 = US $3.081 = €3.471 (30 April 2001).

Weights and Measures: The metric system is in force.

Basic Economic Indicators

	1998	1999	2000
Gross domestic product (GDP) (million colones at 1991 prices).	1,285,243	1,391,827	1,415,869
GDP per head (colones at 1991 prices).	364,091	387,695	n.a.
GDP (million colones at current prices)	3,571,522	4,343,922	n.a.
GDP per head (colones at current prices)	1,011,762	1,210,006	n.a.
Annual growth of real GDP (%)	8.4	8.3	1.7
Annual growth of real GDP per head (%)	6.2	6.5	n.a.
Government budget (million colones at current prices):			
Revenue.	444,486	547,434	599,101
Expenditure.	533,921	646,425	739,274
Consumer price index (annual average for San José; base: 1995 = 100)	148.6	163.5	181.5
Rate of inflation (annual average, %)	11.7	10.0	11.0
Foreign exchange reserves (US $ million at 31 December)	1,051.0	1,432.1	1,291.2
Imports c.i.f. (US $ million)	6,230	6,320	6,372
Exports f.o.b. (US $ million)	5,511	6,577	5,685
Balance of payments (current account, US $ million)	–520.8	–649.5	n.a.

Gross national product per head measured at purchasing power parity (PPP) (US dollars, converted by the PPP exchange rate, 1999): 5,770.

Economically active population (household survey, July 1999): 1,300,150.

Unemployment (2000): 5.2%.

Total external debt (1999): US $4,182m.

Life expectancy (years at birth, 1998): 76.8 (males 74.4, females 79.1).

Infant mortality rate (per 1,000 live births, 2000): 10.8.

Adult population with HIV/AIDS (15–49 years, 1999): 0.54%.

School enrolment ratio (6–16 years, 1998): 66%.

Adult literacy rate (15 years and over, 2000): 95.7 (males 95.6; females 95.7).

Energy consumption per head (kg of oil equivalent, 1998): 789.

Carbon dioxide emissions per head (metric tons, 1997): 1.6.

Passenger motor cars in use (per 1,000 of population, 1996): 129.8.

Television receivers in use (per 1,000 of population, 1997): 140.

Personal computers in use (per 1,000 of population, 1999): 101.7.

History

Dr JENNY PEARCE

Revised for this edition by ANDREW BOUNDS

Rumours of gold and treasure led the navigator Christopher Columbus to bestow the name of Costa Rica (rich coast) on the country's Caribbean shore, where he landed in 1502. He was leading a Spanish expedition, during his final voyage from Europe to the New World. There was no gold and the indigenous Indian (Amerindian) inhabitants were hostile; the country was not settled until 1522, when the Spaniards moved south and colonized the central plateau, the Meseta Central. Costa Rica's Indian population was small and nomadic, except for a group of Mayas in the highlands; diseases which the Europeans brought to the area killed large numbers living in the Meseta Central. The Spanish settlers turned to agriculture and, for many years, remained poor subsistence farmers. Costa Rica differed from the other countries in the region, having much greater ethnic homogeneity, and its isolation from the colonial Government (the Captaincy-General of Guatemala) resulted in the development of an individualistic and agrarian society, with small landowners. Cartago was founded in 1563, but there was no expansion of settlement until the beginning of the 18th century, when small groups left the Meseta Central to establish other cities. San José, now the capital of Costa Rica, was founded in 1737.

INDEPENDENCE

Costa Rica joined the other countries of the region in their declaration of independence from Spain in 1821 (following the Spanish Revolution of 1820). It became part of the newly formed Mexican Empire, which lasted for a couple of violent years until 1823, when Costa Rica joined the United Provinces of Central America. Costa Rica became an independent republic in 1838, following the collapse of the Central American federation.

With independence came the search for economic expansion. Coffee, introduced from Cuba in 1808, became a major contributor to development. The Government offered free land to coffee growers, establishing a large landowning peasantry. Considerable quantities of coffee were being exported by 1850. The opening in 1890 of the railway between San José and Puerto Limón, along the Reventazón valley, further facilitated this lucrative trade. With prosperity, settlement spread and bananas were introduced in 1878. Jamaican labourers were brought to Costa Rica, to clear large areas of land along the Caribbean coast; when production reached its peak, in 1913, interest was then shown in the Pacific coast.

THE MOVE TOWARDS STABILITY

Politically, Costa Rica remained stable throughout the 20th century, with the exception of two short periods, 1917–19 and 1948. In January 1917 Federico Tinoco ousted the elected President, Alfredo González, who had been elected by a very narrow margin, and assumed the presidency under the new Constitution. The USA refused to recognize Tinoco's revolutionary Government, but a counter-revolution, resulting in victory at the presidential election for Julio Acosta, repaired relations between the two countries. There followed a period of democratic and orderly government in Costa Rica, which, in contrast to its neighbours, did not have a politically ambitious military. However, the presidential election campaign of 1948 was characterized by violent protests, including a 15-day general strike. When the opposition candidate, Otilio Ulate Blanco, won, the government candidate, Rafael Angel Calderón Fournier, and his party contested the result, which was nullified. In March 1948 José Figueres Ferrer led a revolt in support of Ulate. A month of fighting ensued until a truce was agreed, and Santos León Herrera was installed as the interim President. In May the Constitution was abrogated and Figueres and his junta took over government. A constitutional assembly convened in January 1949, formulating a new Constitution, which abolished the army. In November the junta resigned and the President-elect, Otilio Ulate, was inaugurated.

THE EMERGENCE OF THE PLN

Figueres, a socialist, found Ulate too moderate, and withdrew his support in 1952, forming the Partido de Liberación Nacional (PLN). He dominated Costa Rican politics for the next two decades, serving as President between 1953 and 1958 and, again, from 1970 to 1974. The Figueres Governments and that of his PLN successor between 1974 and 1978, Daniel Oduber Quirós, instituted policies of nationalization and social welfare, whereas the intervening conservative administrations reversed many of the PLN policies and encouraged private enterprise. Conservative government returned between 1978 and 1982, under Rodrigo Carazo Odio; in 1981, as instability in Central America mounted, he was criticized for his alleged involvement in the illegal flow of arms between Cuba and El Salvador.

Elections on 7 February 1982 resulted in a decisive victory for the PLN's presidential candidate, Luis Alberto Monge Alvarez, with 58% of the votes cast. The ruling conservative Coalición Unidad candidate came second, with 34%. The PLN won 33 of the 55 seats in the Asamblea Legislativa (Legislative Assembly), giving them a clear working majority. The Monge administration, which took office in May 1982, was confronted by two major issues: the domestic economic crisis and the external problem of conflict in the region, focusing on Costa Rica's northern neighbour, Nicaragua.

THE ARIAS PRESIDENCY

Although the Monge Government achieved only limited economic success, the PLN won a decisive, if surprising, victory at the presidential and legislative elections in February 1986. The PLN's victory was attributed to the dynamism and youth of their leader, Oscar Arias Sánchez, who, at the age of 44, was the youngest president in the country's history. He was regarded as a reaction against the extremism of his main opponent, the right-wing Calderón Fournier. On taking office, President Arias announced his desire for the country to pursue a more independent policy, while at the same time recognizing the necessity of maintaining good relations with the USA, in order to ensure a supply of foreign aid. In addition, the new Government made a commitment to the development of the 'welfare state' and the creation of 25,000 new jobs and 20,000 new dwellings each year.

However, the Government's economic policies were perceived by many as a capitulation to the International Monetary Fund (IMF). Strikes in the public sector in 1988 were followed by protests by farmers, who were aggrieved at the Government's 'Agriculture for Change' policy of promoting the cultivation of cash crops to appease the IMF. Labour unrest increased in 1989 as trade unions, professional bodies and civic groups united to demonstrate against the Government's policies of structural adjustment. However, in spite of these protests, during President Arias' term of office gross domestic product (GDP) grew by 4% each year, the annual inflation rate was reduced to below 10%, unemployment declined to under 4% of the total labour force and Costa Rica's debt to foreign banks was renegotiated.

In September 1989 a report by the Asamblea Legislativa's commission of inquiry into the extent of drugs-trafficking and related activities was published. This seriously affected the prospects for the ruling PLN in the approaching presidential and legislative elections. The report implicated many political and business figures of involvement in illegal activities, including the former PLN President, Daniel Oduber Quirós, and Leonel Villalobos, a PLN deputy, both of whom were forced to resign from all public positions. This scandal, combined with a general desire for a change of government, led to the victory of Calderón Fournier, of the Partido Unidad Social Cristiana (PUSC), in the presidential election of February 1990. Calderón obtained 51% of the votes, while the PLN candidate, Carlos Manuel Castillo, obtained 47%. The PUSC also secured a majority in the Asamblea Legislativa.

POLITICS IN THE 1990s: FROM CALDERÓN TO RODRÍGUEZ

Politics in the 1990s were dominated by debates over the future of Costa Rica's state welfare system and public-sector utilities. Costa Ricans were justifiably protective of the exceptional social harmony which the country enjoyed compared to others in the region. Nevertheless, economic adjustment measures adopted in order to qualify for further IMF credits and loans threatened the welfarism that underpinned that harmony.

The presidency of Calderón (1990–94) was dominated by this issue. The overall economic performance during his administration was good; real GDP growth in 1993 was 6.3%, official unemployment was an estimated 4.1% and the average annual increase in consumer prices was 9.8%, well below the Government's target of 12% for the year. However, the Government's privatization programme and reductions in expenditure in the education and public-health sectors created increasing social and political tensions. The opposition PLN prevented approval for the third phase of the structural-adjustment programme in 1993. A total of US $280m. in multilateral funding for this programme depended on congressional approval of legislation to modernize the economy, including the privatization of the telecommunications and health sectors and of the state petroleum company, Refinadora Costarricense de Petróleo (Recope). The PLN strongly opposed the privatization programme and proposals to reduce the public-sector work-force by 25,000. In 1994 José María Figueres Olsen, son of José Figueres Ferrer, the former President, stood as the PLN's presidential candidate. If elected, he pledged to eradicate poverty and to use multilateral funding to improve housing, education, health and other social programmes, rather than implement the public-sector reforms agreed by President Calderón with the World Bank (International Bank for Reconstruction and Development—IBRD). With this manifesto, Figueres secured 48.4% of the votes cast in the elections of 6 February, and thus obtained a narrow victory over Miguel Angel Rodríguez, the PUSC candidate, who gained 46.6% of the votes cast. In the simultaneous legislative elections, the PLN obtained 28 seats in the 57-seat Asamblea Legislativa, one short of an overall majority. The PUSC won 24 seats, with the remaining five seats being secured by independent candidates (most of whom would often vote with the PLN). Figueres assumed the presidency on 8 May 1994.

As President, however, Figueres rapidly converted to free-market economics: during 1995 he restored relations with the IMF and the World Bank by agreeing to a new structural-adjustment programme. In October the Government signed a letter of intent with the IMF, which led to the release of loans from both the Inter-American Development Bank (IDB) and the World Bank. These loans had been previously delayed by the Government's failure to meet economic performance targets in 1994. Tax reforms were a particular priority of the Figueres administration, owing to the ongoing fiscal deficit problem: in April the Government made an agreement with the opposition PUSC to ensure the implementation of tax increases and austerity measures agreed with the IMF. The PUSC was divided over this support for Figueres, while the President succeeded in consolidating his position within his own party, in spite of internal opposition to his shift to neo-liberal policies.

However, within the country as a whole social unrest increased, particularly among public-sector workers, who were threatened with redundancies and salary reductions. In 1996 protests and strikes led to the suspension of plans to privatize the energy and telecommunications sectors, in favour of a restructuring plan. Nevertheless, under its agreement with the IMF, the Government pledged to reduce the fiscal deficit from the equivalent of 8.3% of GDP in 1994 to 0.5% of GDP by 1996, a target that it failed to meet. President Figueres' popularity decreased dramatically in 1995–96 as living standards fell,

taxes increased, and the social spending which protected many Costa Ricans from poverty was drastically reduced.

Despite an improvement in economic conditions during 1997, President Figueres' popularity did not recover and, as the 1998 elections approached, there were deep divisions within the PLN. Lack of support from prominent party officials, including the former President, Oscar Arias Sánchez, damaged the chances of the PLN's presidential candidate, José Miguel Corrales. The election on 1 February 1998 resulted in victory for Miguel Angel Rodríguez Echeverría of the PUSC, with 46.9% of the votes cast, to Corrales' 44.4%. The PUSC obtained 27 seats in the 57-seat Asamblea Legislativa and the PLN won 23 seats, with the remaining seven seats being secured by independent candidates who together gained 8.8% of the votes. Costa Rica's electoral turn-out was historically around 80%; the 1998 elections, however, demonstrated the level of public disillusionment with the established parties: there was a 28% abstention rate, compared with 18.9% in 1994. The public found little to distinguish between the PLN and the PUSC and was uninspired by the record number of 13 presidential candidates. Thus, Rodríguez assumed office on 8 May without a clear mandate, announcing his intention to focus on policies relevant to women, the young and the poor.

THE RODRÍGUEZ ADMINISTRATION

Under President Rodríguez real GDP increased by 8.4% in 1998 and by 8.3% in 1999 before falling to 1.7% in 2000, while inflation fell. However, economic growth largely failed to translate into improved living conditions for ordinary Costa Ricans. A large part of the economic boom was in the tax-free export zones, which were not integrated into the economy as a whole. Moreover, Rodríguez suffered a serious reverse in April 2000, when the largest popular protests in 30 years forced the Government to withdraw legislation to open the energy and telecommunications industries to private investment. The Supreme Court subsequently rejected the proposed law on procedural grounds. A similar privatization attempt had been obstructed by the PLN in the previous year. A special commission, established in May, composed of representatives of government, the private sector and trade unions also failed to agree on the question.

This privatization debate encapsulated the difficulty in implementing unpopular economic reforms aimed at solving the state's fiscal crisis and reducing the level of state intervention in the economy. This was the most contentious issue in Costa Rican politics in the 1990s. By mid-2000 the public rejection of the energy legislation and the lack of tangible social benefits from economic growth had combined to make the Rodríguez Government one of the most unpopular in recent history. President Rodríguez continued his efforts to solve the Government's fiscal problems by announcing plans for the sale of Banco de Costa Rica and the country's ports, and by expanding attempts to attract private investors to improve transport infrastructure. However, his personal unpopularity and the likelihood that his chosen successor would not be selected as the PUSC's presidential candidate at the 2002 elections, increased the chances of political paralysis and an ineffectual administration. In March 2000 former President Arias campaigned for a constitutional amendment to enable him to stand in the 2002 presidential elections. When, in May, the ruling PUSC decided not to support the amendment, Arias appealed to the Constitutional Court. The Court ruled against him in September, ending his hopes of standing.

The Government also faced opposition from farmers, in the form of violent demonstrations, over its policy of increasing tariffs on food imports, and from industrial and agricultural workers over its apparent favouring of employers' interests and its perceived hostility to independent trade unions. In May 1999 the International Confederation of Free Trade Unions (ICFTU) filed a complaint at the International Labour Organization (ILO) over alleged mistreatment of trade-union members, and within the banana sector there were persistent reports of harassment and attacks on trade unionists.

In September 2000 President Rodríguez announced the establishment of a new Ministry of Foreign Commerce, to complement the Ministry of the Economy, Industry and Commerce. In June 2001, in an attempt to increase political participation in decisions and to prevent further political impasse, President

Rodríguez appointed a constitutional reform commission to re-commend the changes necessary to convert the current presidential governing system into a semi-parliamentary one.

FOREIGN POLICY: FROM REGIONAL CONFLICT TO TRADE CONFLICTS

Costa Rican foreign policy was dominated in the 1980s by the regional conflicts in Central America. In 1983 an official proclamation of neutrality was made, by which Costa Rica would not be used as a base for attack against its neighbours. However, in these years Costa Rica collaborated closely with US policy towards the region. In 1984 a Nicaraguan counter-revolutionary ('Contra') base was established in the north of the country. Moreover, the decision in 1985 to create an anti-guerrilla battalion, to be trained by US military advisers, fuelled public scepticism about the Government's commitment to Costa Rican neutrality.

Nevertheless, the Government of President Arias, which assumed office in May 1986, fully restored diplomatic relations with Nicaragua. Furthermore, a peace accord based on proposals by Arias was signed by the Presidents of the five Latin Central American countries (Costa Rica, El Salvador, Guatemala, Honduras and Nicaragua) at a meeting in Esquipulas, Guatemala, in August 1987. Acceptance, albeit provisionally, of the plan was regarded as a personal triumph for President Arias, who was awarded the Nobel Peace Prize in October. Despite continuing US pressure (which included the US administration's announcement, in 1986, of plans to reduce aid to Costa Rica), President Arias maintained his neutrality. In January 1988 he organized the first meeting between Nicaraguan government officials and Contra leaders, in order to discuss terms for a cease-fire. The Arias initiatives also led towards the UN-supervised peace settlement in El Salvador in 1992.

Following the defeat of the Sandinista Government in the Nicaraguan general election of 1990 and the signing of the El Salvadorean peace agreement two years later, relative peace was restored to the Central American region. Trade issues subsequently dominated Costa Rican foreign policy in the 1990s. In 1991 Costa Rica had become a member of the General Agreement on Tariffs and Trade (GATT, which was superseded by the World Trade Organization in 1995). The country also sought to join the North American Free Trade Agreement (NAFTA), indicating the priority of trade relations with the USA and Mexico over those with its neighbours in the Central American Common Market. Costa Rica signed a free-trade agreement with Mexico in March 1994, giving some 86% of Costa Rican exports duty-free access to the Mexican market. The free-trade agreement led to an increase in Mexican investment in Costa Rica, but only a small number of transnational corporations based in Costa Rica were able to take advantage of the new export opportunities.

In May 2000 the US President, Bill Clinton (1993–2001), passed legislation enhancing the Caribbean Basin Initiative, first introduced in 1983, granting NAFTA parity to products from Costa Rica and 23 other countries in the region. This was intended to rectify the perceived advantage gained by Mexico over its regional competitors as a result of the creation of NAFTA in 1995. In November 1999 Costa Rica signed a free-trade agreement with Chile, which was ratified in December 2000, and in April 2001 the country reached a similar accord with Canada. A deal with Panama, negotiated with the other four Central American countries, was expected by the end of the year.

In early 1995 relations with Nicaragua became strained when it was alleged that a group of illegal Nicaraguan immigrants had been expelled from Costa Rica in a violent manner. A tightening of immigration policy in Costa Rica resulted in further expulsions. (In 1998 the Costa Rican Government estimated that there were 400,000–500,000 Nicaraguan immigrants in the country, of whom some 250,000 were residing illegally.) On 1 February 1999 a six-month amnesty was declared for all illegal Nicaraguan immigrants who had entered Costa Rica before 9 November 1998. However, by the end of the amnesty only 160,000 immigrants had registered for the one-year renewable residence permits. In July 1998 further antagonism developed as Nicaragua reasserted its sovereignty over the San Juan river, which formed the border between the two countries, by prohibiting Costa Rican civil guards from carrying arms while navigating the river. In June 2000 this dispute appeared to be settled when both Governments agreed a procedure that would allow armed Costa Rican police officers to patrol the river; however, tensions continued as Nicaragua periodically raised the issue. In May 2001 a fresh dispute arose, following the implementation of a US $25 charge for Costa Ricans using the river. In October 2000 Costa Rica ratified a maritime boundaries treaty with Colombia, recognizing their control over 500,000 sq km of the Pacific Ocean, including the Isla del Coco. In July 2001 a dispute arose over the symbolism of a wall built on the frontier between Costa Rica and Nicaragua to control border traffic.

Economy

Dr JENNY PEARCE

Revised for this edition by ANDREW BOUNDS

According to the 2000 census, Costa Rica's population was 3.8m., of which over 90% were white, 3% black and 1% Indian (Amerindian); 49% lived in urban areas. Population growth per year averaged 2.3% in 1990–98. With a per head income of US $3,886 in 2000 Costa Rica was among the lower-middle income countries in the World Bank (International Bank for Reconstruction and Development—IBRD) ranking. However, owing to an historically extensive welfare state, Costa Rica's health and education indicators compared favourably with those of many industrialized countries. In 2000 life expectancy at birth was 76 years and infant mortality was just 10.8 per 1,000 live births. Also, Costa Rica had the highest adult literacy rate in Central America, at 95.3% of the population in 1998 (although there were rates of as low as 30% among the Indian population).

Strong economic growth in Costa Rica during the 1970s was followed by rapid decline in the early 1980s, caused by poor commodity prices, loss of export markets and general world recession. In 1982 real gross domestic product (GDP) fell by 7.5%, the average annual inflation rate was 120%, the public-sector deficit was equivalent to 14% of GDP and the current-account deficit on the balance of payments amounted to 16% of GDP. Thereafter, stabilization measures restored positive growth and, according to World Bank estimates, GDP expanded at an average annual rate of 4.8% between 1983 and 1988 and inflation was reduced to 15%–20% by the end of the decade. However, these austerity measures also placed at great risk Costa Rica's reputation for equity and social welfare. The UN's Economic Commission for Latin America and the Caribbean (ECLAC) estimated that the population living in 'poverty' increased from 27.2% in 1980 to 47.4% in 1988, while those living in 'extreme poverty' increased from 17.7% to 36.8% over the same period. Moreover, despite an expanding export sector and healthy investment rates, large fiscal and external deficits remained and had to be financed by internal and external borrowing. Costa Rica's external debt increased from US $1,700m. in 1980 to $4,530m. by 1988 and, unable to meet its debt-servicing commitments, the country sought help from the International Monetary Fund (IMF) and the World Bank.

In the 1990s successive Governments were caught between the demands of the IMF and World Bank, which required the implementation of structural reforms before credits would be allocated, and those of the electorate, which resisted strongly any attempts to scale back state intervention. Although progress was made in debt reduction, in 1991 the failure to fulfil target reductions in the fiscal deficit forced the Government to suspend the third phase of a structural-adjustment programme. The Government's fiscal problems worsened steadily in the second half of the 1990s, leading to a rise in domestic public debt from an average of 28% of GDP from 1991–97 to 34.8% in 2000. Rising interest rate payments on this debt only exacerbated the Government's problems and it began a series of bond issues on the international market in an effort to exchange some 38% of its domestic debt for external debt, carrying lower interest rates. Despite these pressures, the Government of Miguel Angel Rodríguez Echeverría, which came to power in May 1998, managed to maintain the downward pressure on the annual rate of inflation.

During the 1990s many significant reforms were introduced, including reductions in public-sector employment, changes to the pensions and tax systems, and measures to promote foreign investment and to facilitate private-sector participation in activities, such as banking and insurance, formerly confined to the state sector. Export and growth prospects were transformed by the establishment of two microprocessing plants of the US manufacturer, Intel, in March 1998, which added 3%–4% to GDP in 1999, although a decrease in microchip exports in the following year caused a decrease of 2.3%.

The economy grew by 8.4% in 1998. This figure increased by 8.3% in 1999, before falling back to 1.7% in 2000. Owing to this sharp increase at the end of the decade, growth averaged 4.1% from 1991–99, one of the highest rates in Latin America. However, this form of export-driven expansion created a form of advanced technology enclave economy, which failed to lead to social recovery. Private consumption grew by only 1% in 2000, unemployment stood at 5.2% in 2000 (compared to 6.0% in 1999), and underemployment at 6%.

AGRICULTURE

Along with forestry and fisheries, agriculture, contributed 9.3% of GDP and employed 20.4% of the economically active population in 2000. The major crops were coffee and bananas for export, and maize, rice and beans for domestic use. In the 1960s and early 1970s agricultural production increased by an average of 5% per year. Thereafter, the performance of the sector was disappointing, recording average annual growth of just 3.1% in 1980–90, and 2.5% in 1990–99. In 1998 agricultural growth recovered to 6.1% before falling back to 3.5% in 1999, largely in response to fluctuations in the prices of coffee and bananas. As a result of falling prices, total agricultural export earnings remained roughly constant from 1996–98, fell to US $1,422.2m. in 1999 and to $1,270.9m. in 2000. Successful attempts were made to improve yields and to diversify into non-traditional crops such as African palm and tropical fruit. In March 2000 farmers in Cartago protested over increased competition from imported vegetables.

Bananas

Apart from a brief period in the mid-1980s, bananas were Costa Rica's main export commodity. Between 1984 and 1986, however, output of bananas fell from 1.2m. metric tons to 1.0m. tons, according to UN Food and Agriculture Organization (FAO) estimates, and the crop's share of export earnings decreased from 25% to 20%. The principal factors in this decline were rising production costs and falling world prices, which led to a reduction in the area used for banana cultivation. In 1985 the closure of the Pacific-coast operations of Compañía Bananera de Costa Rica brought widespread economic depression to the region, since many of its towns were wholly dependent on the company's fortunes. Consequently, the Government purchased 1,700 hectares (ha) of the abandoned plantations (which totalled 2,300 ha), which were converted to the cultivation of cocoa. Elsewhere also, bananas were being replaced by more profitable crops, such as African palm, sugar cane and exotic fruits.

The Costa Rican banana industry recovered gradually, but then faced a new threat from the European Union (EU—known as the European Community until November 1993) quota system, which came into effect on 1 July 1993. The quota system, designed to protect banana production in the former European

colonies, placed an annual limit of 2.0m. metric tons on banana imports from Latin American countries (compared to actual imports of 2.6m. tons in 1992). This led to the flooding of non-EU markets and a significant decrease in banana prices in Costa Rica. Despite this, in 1995 total production was some 2.3m. tons and exports accounted for 25.7% of total export revenues. However, Costa Rican producers were then operating under severe pressure caused by falling prices, continuing market-access problems and climatic adversity, which in 1996 caused the loss of 1% of the country's total crop. In early 1999, following years of protests from the USA and Latin American countries and the EU's failure to satisfy the World Trade Organization (WTO) that its banana-import regime complied with international trade regulations, the USA was permitted to impose compensatory tariffs on specific imports from the EU. These tariffs were removed, following an EU–USA accord on 11 April 2001, under which the EU preferential market was to end. From 1 July a transitional system, issuing licences according to historical trade patterns, was to be implemented, with the definitive tariff-only system entering into force on 1 January 2006. However, a world surfeit continued, forcing down prices to producers from $5.60 per 40 lb box in June 1999 to $5.20 one year later. The situation became critical in late 2000, following the closure of four plantations, resulting in the loss of some 1,200 jobs, and the cancellation of contracts in Costa Rica by the three principal exporters, Chiquita Brands, the Banana Development Corporation and the Standard Fruits Company. Exports in bananas fell by $100m. in 2000 to $531.3m. (9% of total exports). Production in 2000 was an estimated 2.7m. tons. In April 2001, despite resistance from the multinationals, the Government fixed the price of a 40 lb box at $5.25. In July 2001 more than 1,000 ha of banana plantations were destroyed in an attempt to prevent the further spread of the 'sigatoka negra' blight.

Coffee

Coffee, grown in the volcanic soil of Costa Rica's central plateau, was the country's main export commodity in the mid-1980s. In 1986 coffee exports represented 34% of total export revenue. Most plantations were of relatively modest size (less than 10 ha). but the technical advancement of Costa Rican production, which achieved among the highest yields in the world, enabled output to expand steadily, to a peak of 168,000 tons by 1992. However, sharp falls in the international price of coffee, which caused bankruptcies and led many coffee growers to diversify into other crops, resulted in a decline in export earnings to just US $203m. in that year (12% of total export revenue), from a record $392m. in 1986. As part of an agreement with other producers, aimed at forcing increases in prices, Costa Rica held back about one-fifth of its 1993 coffee output from the world market. Prices improved in 1994 and 1995. However, the impact of 'Hurricane César' in August 1996 halted the recovery, but by 1998 output, at an estimated 171,000 tons, had regained its 1992 level. Production decreased slightly in 1999, to an estimated 163,900 tons and remained at this level (163,500 tons) in 2000. International prices reached a 30-year low in early 2001 and coffee production suffered. In 1999 and 2000 exports were around $280m., in contrast to the average of $404m. from 1995–98. The Government channelled $23m. from the national coffee stabilization fund to aid small farmers. Central American producers, along with Mexico, Colombia and Brazil, agreed to retain up to 10% of their stocks in order to allow the price to rise; however, the arrangement proved difficult to enforce. In February 2001 coffee crops were under threat from a plague. Despite precautionary measures, the plague was expected to affect the crop in the following year.

Sugar

By the mid-1980s the contribution of sugar to Costa Rican export revenues had fallen to about 1% (some US $11m.), owing to a decline in world sugar prices, and output had fallen similarly. However, sugar production began to increase once again, in spite of a reduction in the annual US sugar quota at the end of the 1990s. The rise in output was principally owing to a shift by wealthy farmers in Guanacaste away from sorghum and rice cultivation and into sugar cane, following the Government's reduction in support for the former two crops. In 1990 output of raw sugar was 246,000 metric tons and exports earned $25m., a 64% rise on the previous year, resulting from an increase in world prices. Production continued to increase until 1996, when it reached 348,790 tons; in 1997 output declined to 328,350 tons before increasing to 376,070 tons in 1998. This trend continued in 1999, when output reached an unofficial 379,000 tons. Production stood at an estimated 351,000 tons in 2000. In 1999 export earnings from sugar were an estimated $29m.

Crops

Crops for domestic consumption included maize, beans and rice, which were grown mainly on small farms with low yields, although advances were being made in rice cultivation, and the size of the units of production was also increasing. There was a 26% decline in cultivated land in the late 1980s, as small producers of domestically consumed foodstuffs did not receive the incentives offered to producers of exports. By this time Costa Rica was no longer self-sufficient in food. The US Agency for International Development (USAID) gave priority to non-traditional crops such as cocoa, African oil palm, cotton, vegetables, cut flowers, macadamia nuts, coconut and tropical fruit. Exports of these crops grew at an average rate of 11% per year in 1991–95. Oranges, in particular, flourished and orange juice exports rose by 50% in 2000, to US $54.5m.

Forestry and Fishing

Costa Rica had considerable forestry resources, but these were not exploited to the full. The Government was concerned about the deforestation caused by the extensive felling of trees without adequate replanting. A US $275m. programme to maintain and develop the forestry resource over the following 20 years was announced in 1990. There was also a growing fishing industry, mainly for shrimps, sardines and tuna. In 1998 the total catch was 29,300 metric tons (live weight), a decrease of 6.1% on the previous year's catch. Fisheries exports increased from US $216m. in 1996 to $259m. in 1997.

MINING AND POWER

Costa Rica had deposits of iron ore (400m. metric tons), bauxite (150m. tons), sulphur (11m. tons), manganese, mercury, gold and silver. However, by the end of the 21st century only the last two were mined. Production of gold was centred on the Tres Hermanos mine, owned by a subsidiary of Ariel Resources Ltd of Canada. Costa Rican gold production increased from 260 kg in 1993 to 500 kg in 1997.

There were substantial reserves of petroleum but they remained largely unexploited. The petroleum refinery at Puerto Limón, with a capacity of 15,000 barrels per day (b/d), was supplied with crude petroleum from Mexico and Venezuela, provided at preferential rates under the terms of the 1980 Treaty of San José. A 320 km pipeline was to be built, linking the Caribbean and Pacific coasts, with a capacity of 1m. b/d. There were plans, hitherto unrealized, to develop coal reserves in the Zent field, in order to reduce the dependence on imported petroleum. The state petroleum concern, Refinadora Costarricense de Petróleo (Recope), estimated the reserves at 16m. metric tons, of which 5.6m. tons were proven.

Energy consumption grew by an annual average of 5.7% in 1980–92. By the mid-1980s Costa Rica had virtually eliminated the need for petroleum products for electricity generation, through its development of hydroelectric power resources, the use of fuel wood, bagasse (vegetable waste) and sugar-cane alcohol. The use of geothermal energy from volcanoes was also developed. The Lake Arenal hydroelectric project, in Guanacaste, was opened in 1979 and, at its full capacity of 1,974 MW, was expected to supply all of Costa Rica's electricity needs. By 1990 Costa Rica had reduced its energy imports as a proportion of total merchandise imports to 5.0% and by 1997 had become a net exporter of electricity.

At the end of 1993 the Government authorized the state electricity company, Instituto Costarricense de Electricidad (ICE), to raise US $512m. in order to finance its third Electricity Development Programme. The Programme included a $300m. hydroelectric power project on the Río Reventazón, to be completed by June 2000, and the country's first wind-generated power plant, and envisaged the extension of electricity supplies to 93.9% of the population. By 1999 coverage was 94.7% and in 2000 99.5% of electricity was generated from renewable sources. In 2000 the ICE announced plans to build a 1,250 MW hydroelectric plant at Boruca, south of San José, by 2011. Depending on demand throughout Central America, the plan's potential capacity was 5,000 MW. In the 1990s repeated government attempts to pass the legislation necessary to privatize the ICE and Recope or, at least, to open the energy sector to private-sector investment were defeated by the Asamblea Legislativa (Legislative Assembly) or by the public-sector unions. In April 2000 President Rodríguez was forced to abandon these plans, following widespread street protests. Nevertheless, in 1999 private generators, that had entered the market in 1990, accounted for 12.5% of the electricity consumed.

MANUFACTURING

With the manufacturing sector generating 24.1% of GDP in 2000, Costa Rica was the most industrialized country in Central America. Fast growth in this sector during the 1960s (averaging some 11% per year) and 1970s (averaging 8% per year) resulted in a high level of diversification. Industry expanded under the protection of the Central American Common Market (CACM) and output remained mainly for the domestic and regional markets. In the 1980s a contraction in demand caused a manufacturing recession, but growth returned in the 1990s, with industrial GDP increasing by an average annual rate of 3.7% in 1990–99, by 11.4% in 1998 and by 24.5% in 1999. However, manufacturing GDP decreased in 2000 by an estimated 2.9%. In the mid-1990s over two-thirds of industry was involved in the manufacture of non-durable consumer goods, mainly food, beverages and tobacco, but chemicals, plastics and tyres were also produced.

In 1986 a privately owned 'free-trade zone' was established to assemble goods for export (mainly textiles and electronic products). Its success and subsequent expansion contributed to a doubling of manufacturing exports between 1987 and 1993, with the value of free-trade zone exports increasing from US $7m. in 1986 to $252m. in 1993. In 1998 Intel began production at an assembly plant in the free-trade zone at Rivera de Belén, west of San José, the first of four facilities in a projected $500m. investment programme. Although only employing some 2,200 people, Intel galvanized Costa Rica's export and growth figures. In 1998 electronic circuitry accounted for 40% of all exports, eclipsing traditional mainstays such as coffee and bananas, and total exports from free-trade zones increased from $2,000m. in 1998 to $3,318m. in 2000, accounting for 56% of all exports. In 1999 Costa Rica achieved a trade surplus for the first time in four decades, of $659.6m., although this reverted to a deficit of $475m. in 2000. A national software company exported programmes worth $50m. in 2000. In May 2001, following a brief closure for modernization and, consequently, a drop in production, the Intel plant re-opened.

TOURISM

Tourism became Costa Rica's largest single source of foreign-exchange earnings in the early and mid-1990s, with annual growth rates in the sector of over 20% between 1987 and 1994. During this period revenue increased from US $136.2m. to $679.2m., leading to significant investment in hotel and leisure facilities and turning Costa Rica into one of the world's fastest-growing tourist destinations. In 2000 Costa Rica received 1,100,400 visitors and revenues increased by 14% to some $$1,140m. In general, the country's history of political stability, as well as its fine beaches and extensive system of national parks and protected areas, provided a solid basis of appeal to tourists. In 2000–01 the Government was targeting tourists from Northern Europe and the Southern Cone to diversify away from its dependence on North American visitors. In the late 1990s, despite the microprocessing industry's contribution, tourism remained the single most important contributor to the Costa Rican economy, as some 48% of the money spent by tourists remained in the country.

TRANSPORT INFRASTRUCTURE

In 1997 there were 35,597 km of roads, of which about 17% were paved. The main road was the Pan-American Highway (fully paved). During the 1990s new roads were being built between San José and Caldera, between San José and Puerto Limón, and along the Pacific coast, linking Playas de Jacó with Quepos and Puerto Cortés. In 1997 the Government's offer of road improvement concessions to private contractors resulted in problems. A road-modernization project agreed with Mexican contractors was queried by the national audit office, which found irregularities in the contract and annulled it. Another consortium was unable to finance a project. In early 2001 the Government advertised contracts for road infrastructure improvements.

During the 1980s a new port on the Gulf of Nicoya, at Caldera, replaced Puntarenas as the principal Pacific port, although facilities at the latter were improved in 1990–96, as part of a general upgrading of the transport network. New facilities were installed at Puerto Limón, on the Caribbean coast, although there was considerable damage caused by an earthquake in April 1991. The Pacific ports were scheduled to be leased to a private operator by the end of 2001.

There were about 950 km of railway, of which a sizeable proportion were plantation lines. In 1995 the state railway company, Instituto Costarricense de Ferrocarriles (INCOFER), suspended operations to the public indefinitely, pending privatization, although the transport of cargo continued. In 2000 a feasibility study concluded that the railway could be run profitably; before its closure INCOFER transported some 750,000 metric tons of cargo per year. Privatization was scheduled for 2001.

The main airport, Juan Santamaría, at El Coco, near San José, was served by domestic and international airlines. In 2000 it was the busiest airport in Central America, transporting 1.5m. passengers per year. Its modernization was vital to the development of the tourist industry, not least because of safety concerns raised by the US Federal Aviation Administration. In the same year a consortium, led by Bechtel of the USA, was given a 20-year management contract of the airport. It pledged to invest US $161m., of which $120m. was given by the International Finance Corporation, part of the World Bank. There was a second international airport at Liberia.

FINANCE AND INVESTMENT

By 1982 adverse economic conditions and a lack of fiscal reform had precipitated a crisis in Costa Rica's public finances, with the budget deficit equal to 14% of GDP in that year. Following the implementation of a stabilization plan, by 1985 the budget deficit had been reduced to 2.5% of GDP and the recovery was further encouraged by an improvement in the country's trade performance. However, the terms of trade worsened subsequently and, owing to the failure to reach economic targets, proposed loans by the IMF and the World Bank were withdrawn. Despite further stabilization measures, including a 15% increase in the prices of electricity and petroleum, the budget deficit increased to 3.9% of GDP in 1989, and was estimated to have deteriorated further in 1990, to 5.2% of GDP. The Government of President Rafael Angel Calderón Fournier (1990–94) was frustrated in its tax-reform efforts by an uncooperative legislature and focused on reducing inflation through strict monetary control. In this aim it was largely successful, with annual inflation falling from 28.7% in 1991, to 21.8% in 1992, and to 9.8% in the following year. GDP growth produced higher tax revenues and the public-sector deficit declined to 1.1% of GDP in 1992, also helped by lower total interest payments. However, the budget deficit increased once again, to 1.9% in 1993 and 8.3% in 1994 and the average annual rate of inflation also increased, reaching 23.2% in 1995, before falling to 11.7% in 1998, 10.0% in 1999 and 11.0% in 2000.

Although the fiscal deficit continued to be a major preoccupation of successive Governments in the 1990s, budget reductions and tax measures were politically very difficult to pursue. President José María Figueres Olsen (1994–98) agreed to IMF demands that the budget deficit be reduced to 0.5% of GDP by the end of 1996, but forceful resistance from labour organizations and from within the legislature prevented significant progress in government-expenditure reductions, tax increases and the divestment of public assets. The deficit widened, in fact, reaching an estimated 5.2% in 1996, before decreasing to 4.2% in the following year. The new Government of President Rodríguez, elected in February 1998, attempted to overcome the political

obstacles to modernization by initiating a consensus-building approach. However, in April 1999 the legislature's unwillingness to approve a package of constitutional amendments, designed to end state monopolies in energy, telecommunications and insurance, signalled the failure of this effort. In the first six months of 1999 the creation of 3,000 public-sector jobs in the priority areas of education and the police, coupled with lower-than-expected tax revenues, led to renewed anxiety about the budget deficit, which reached an estimated 3.7% in 2000, owing to rising interest payments on the internal debt and lower tax receipts from exports. In July 2001 the Asamblea Legislativa approved a tax reform bill that would decrease tax on basic goods, while increasing tax on some luxury goods and services.

The 1990s saw an increase in foreign direct investment (FDI), as Costa Rica moved from being predominantly an exporter of coffee and bananas, to an advanced technology and *maquila* (parts assembly) exporter, with a successful tourist industry. Total annual FDI increased from US $172m. in 1991 to an estimated $600m. in 1999, principally owing to Intel. In 2000 total annual FDI was $420m., one-half of which came from tourism. Slow progress on privatization meant that most of this investment was in new facilities rather than the acquisition of state-owned enterprises. In 1999 US companies accounted for 58% of incoming investment; some 53% of investment was channelled into manufacturing and 16% went into tourism.

BALANCE OF PAYMENTS AND THE EXTERNAL DEBT

The economic growth of the mid-1980s stimulated demand for imported raw materials and capital goods, which more than offset rising exports, resulting in increasing trade deficits. In 1990 the trade deficit was US $442.5m. In the 1990s exports continued to perform well, but further strong economic growth, and the reduction of import tariffs in 1993 to a maximum of 20%, contributed to a dramatic increase in the trade deficit, to $760.8m. in 1993. While the trade deficits were partially offset by increased tourism revenues and the operations of the free-trade zones, they remained at a high level in the mid-1990s. Visible trade deficits of $249.2m., $234.4m. and $244.5m. were recorded in 1996, 1997 and 1998, respectively, necessitating high levels of external borrowing. However, export performance improved from 1998, owing mainly to output by Intel, and in 1999 the trade balance went into surplus for the first time in four decades. However, while there was a trade surplus, the impact on the balance of payments was much more limited, since a large part of that which entered the country in export receipts left as profit repatriation. Although free-trade zone income increased in 1998–2000, profits repatriation also increased over the same period. Moreover, the sharp growth in microprocessor exports masked a sluggish performance in traditional export sectors, which was revealed by the 2000 external trade figures.

The problem of external debt became increasingly severe in the late 1990s. By the end of 1988 the cost of servicing Costa Rica's total external debt of US $4,530m. was $715m., equivalent to 58.9% of export earnings, and interest arrears of more than $300m. had been accumulated. In 1989 the country's debt to the 'Paris Club' of Western creditor governments was rescheduled over 10 years and debt relief was secured on $1,150m. of the country's $1,800m. commercial-bank debt, under the terms of the US Brady Initiative. The external debt had fallen to $3,772m. by the end of 1990, but new long-term borrowing in 1990–91 meant that interest payments did not decrease significantly. By 1995, in which year the external debt totalled $3,800m., debt as a percentage of GDP had been reduced to 13.7%. A new agreement with the IMF was signed in October of that year, which led to the release of further credits from the World Bank and the Inter-American Development Bank (IDB). This enabled the country to pay its Paris Club debt in 1996, through the disbursement of the first instalment of an IDB loan. Costa Rica's total external debt at the end of 1999 was $4,182m., of which $3,186m. was long-term public debt. Owing to improved exports, the ratio of debt-servicing to exports fell in the late 1990s, reaching 6.4% in 1999. While external debt was the problem of the 1980s and 1990s, internal debt was that of the 2000s. Internal debt reached $5,354m. in 1999 and total debt was 54.6% of GDP. From 1998 the Government sought to exchange some of this internal debt for foreign debt at lower interest rates, by issuing bonds. In 2000 it sold $1,000m. and was to issue a further $950m. over the subsequent three years. Debt reduction was to remain a priority if resources were to be released for productive investment.

OUTLOOK

By the end of the 1990s relative political stability had emerged in Central America, allowing policy-makers to focus on economic and social issues. In Costa Rica the most important issue of that decade was the dilemma of balancing the structural economic change demanded by international financial agencies with the country's traditional commitment to social welfare and equity. The country's faltering progress towards economic liberalization in the 1990s ensured that the issue remained the Government priority at the beginning of the next decade.

President Rodríguez discovered within his first two years in office the political difficulties involved in attempting to execute a programme of market reforms. His Government, like its predecessors, was required to implement economic liberalization measures in such a way that the delicate balance between economic development and social justice was seen to be maintained. The boom in the microprocessor, *maquila* and tourist industries had created something of a two-track economy in Costa Rica, in which impressive overall growth and export figures masked a worrying degree of stagnation in traditional sectors of the economy, such as agriculture, which generated a large proportion of jobs. Further polarization, as well as the Government's persistent fiscal problems, could undermine the social stability and consensual politics, for which Costa Rica was renowned. By 2001 President Rodríguez was emphasizing the Government's achievements in health and education, which had helped to attract advanced-technology companies, rather than the economy. The task of liberalization would fall to his successor, following the elections that were due to take place in February 2002. However, the next President was unlikely to receive a strong mandate as widespread political apathy suggested another low turn-out. In May the Central American countries, including Costa Rica, agreed to establish, with Mexico, the 'Plan Puebla–Panamá': a series of joint transport, industry and tourism projects intended to integrate the region.

Statistical Survey

Sources (unless otherwise stated): Dirección General de Estadística y Censos, Ministry of the Economy, Industry and Commerce, Apdo 10.163, 1000 San José; tel. 221-0983; fax 223-0813; internet www.inec.go.cr; Banco Central de Costa Rica, Avdas Central y Primera, Calles 2 y 4, Apdo 10.058, 1000 San José; tel. 233-4233; fax 223-4658; internet www.bccr.fi.cr.

Area and Population

AREA, POPULATION AND DENSITY

Area (sq km)	
Land	51,060
Inland water	40
Total	51,100*
Population (census results)†	
14 May 1973	1,871,780
11 June 1984	
Males	1,208,216
Females	1,208,593
Total	2,416,809
Population (official estimates at mid-year)	
1998	3,525,701
1999	3,589,163
2000	3,651,803
Density (per sq km) at mid-2000	71.5

* 19,730 sq miles.
† Excluding adjustment for underenumeration.

Census of 28 June 2000 (provisional results): Total population 3,824,593 (males 1,913,910; females 1,910,683).

PROVINCES (mid-2000)

	Area (sq km)	Population (estimates)	Density (per sq km)	Capital (with population)
Alajuela .	9,757.5	655,944	67.2	Alajuela (189,981)
Cartago .	3,124.7	408,571	130.8	Cartago (129,910)
Guanacaste	10,140.7	285,388	28.1	Liberia (44,979)
Heredia .	2,657.0	293,939	110.6	Heredia (81,947)
Limón .	9,188.5	286,221	31.1	Limón (84,986)
Puntarenas	11,265.7	406,448	36.1	Puntarenas (110,190)
San José .	4,965.9	1,315,292	264.9	San José (345,599)
Total .	51,100.0	3,651,803	71.5	—

BIRTHS, MARRIAGES AND DEATHS

	Registered live births		Registered marriages		Registered deaths	
	Number	Rate (per 1,000)	Number	Rate (per 1,000)	Number	Rate (per 1,000)
1992 . .	80,164	25.6	20,888	6.7	12,253	3.9
1993 . .	79,714	24.6	21,715	6.7	12,543	3.8
1994 . .	80,391	24.6	21,520	6.5	13,313	4.0
1995 . .	80,306	24.1	24,274	7.3	14,061	4.2
1996 . .	79,203	23.3	23,574	6.9	13,993	4.1
1997 . .	78,018	22.5	n.a.	n.a.	14,260	4.1
1998 . .	76,982	21.8	24,831	7.0	14,708	4.2
1999 . .	78,526	21.9	25,613	7.1	15,052	4.2

Expectation of life (estimates, years at birth, 1998): 76.2 (males 74.4; females 79.1) (Source: UN Development Programme, *Human Development Report*).

ECONOMICALLY ACTIVE POPULATION*
(persons aged 12 years and over, household survey, '000 persons, July)

	1997	1998	1999
Agriculture, hunting and forestry	246.54	255.82	250.19
Fishing	6.18	5.77	6.27
Mining and quarrying	1.48	1.60	2.13
Manufacturing	190.97	203.50	204.00
Electricity, gas and water supply	13.65	13.10	13.25
Construction	84.02	81.18	82.62
Wholesale and retail trade	179.57	193.28	203.86
Hotels and restaurants	54.64	58.45	64.72
Transport, storage and communications	65.77	73.27	74.61
Financial intermediation	25.79	29.45	20.37
Real estate, renting and business activities	3.38	4.59	5.45
Education	68.26	71.76	65.39
Health and social work	52.96	59.40	55.80
Other community, social and personal service activities	150.77	157.79	158.86
Private households with employed persons	73.94	77.94	83.50
Extra-territorial organizations and bodies	1.29	2.87	2.21
Not classifiable by economic activity	8.13	10.24	6.93
Total employed	**1,227.33**	**1,300.01**	**1,300.15**
Unemployed	74.29	76.54	83.31
Total labour force	**1,301.62**	**1,376.55**	**1,383.45**

* Figures for activities are rounded to the nearest 10 persons.

Source: ILO, *Yearbook of Labour Statistics.*

2000 ('000 persons): Agriculture, etc. 269.21; Mining and quarrying 2.61; Manufacturing 190.26; Electricity, gas and water supply 10.88; Construction 89.72; Wholesale and retail trade 266.83; Transport, storage and communications 78.83; Finance 64.26; Services 337.09; Activities not adequately defined 8.95; Total employed 1,318.63; Unemployed 71.94; Total labour force 1,390.56 (males 943.70; females 446.86).

Agriculture

PRINCIPAL CROPS ('000 metric tons)

	1998	1999	2000
Rice (paddy)	286.0	284.7	264.2
Maize	27.5	27.4	23.3
Beans (dry)	13.5	16.9	15.9
Palm kernels	25.0	23.1	24.9
Palm oil	108.6	109.0	133.9
Sugar cane†	3,850.0	3,950.0	4,000.0
Bananas†	2,500.0	2,700.0	2,700.0
Coffee (green)	171.0	163.9	163.5
Cocoa beans	0.8	0.9	1.5

* Unofficial figure(s).   † FAO estimate(s).

Source: FAO.

LIVESTOCK ('000 head, year ending September)

	1998	1999	2000
Horses*	114.5	114.5	114.5
Mules*	5.0	5.0	5.0
Asses*	7.6	7.6	7.6
Cattle	1,527.0†	1,617.0†	1,715.4
Pigs*	360.0	390.0	390.0
Sheep*	2.5	2.5	2.5
Goats*	1.7	1.7	1.7

Poultry (million): 17,000* in 1998; 17,000* in 1999; 17,135 in 2000.

* FAO estimates.   † Unofficial figures.

Source: FAO.

LIVESTOCK PRODUCTS ('000 metric tons)

	1998	1999	2000
Beef and veal	82.0	75.4	83.2
Pig meat	24.8	26.6	16.5
Poultry meat	72.1	76.8	64.9
Cows' milk	584.0	671.0	707.1
Cheese	5.4	5.8	5.8*
Butter and ghee	3.5	3.5	3.5*
Hen eggs	27.2	27.2	27.2*
Cattle hides (fresh)*	10.7	11.7	11.7

* FAO estimate(s).

Source: FAO.

Forestry

ROUNDWOOD REMOVALS
('000 cubic metres, excluding bark)

	1997	1998	1999
Sawlogs, veneer logs and logs for sleepers	1,400	1,400	1,400
Other industrial wood	260	266	273
Fuel wood	3,548	3,637	3,724
Total	**5,216**	**5,303**	**5,397**

Source: FAO, *Yearbook of Forest Products.*

SAWNWOOD PRODUCTION (FAO estimates, '000 cubic metres)

	1997	1998	1999
Coniferous (softwood)	12	12	12
Broadleaved (hardwood)	768	768	768
Total	**780**	**780**	**780**

Source: FAO, *Yearbook of Forest Products.*

Fishing

('000 metric tons, live weight)

	1996	1997	1998
Capture	24.2	24.2	20.6
Freshwater fishes	1.9	0.8	0.8
Clupeoids	0.9	1.6	1.0
Tuna-like fishes	3.9	1.0	1.2
Sharks, rays, skates, etc.	2.5	2.8	3.3
Other marine fishes	10.1	14.1	11.1
Penaeus shrimps	2.3	2.0	1.4
Natantian decapods	1.4	1.0	0.7
Aquaculture	7.0	7.0	8.7
Tilapias	4.1	4.1	5.4
Whiteleg shrimp	2.4	2.4	2.3
Total catch	**31.2**	**31.2**	**29.3**

Source: FAO, *Yearbook of Fishery Statistics.*

Industry

SELECTED PRODUCTS
('000 metric tons, unless otherwise indicated)

	1995	1996	1997
Cigarettes (million units)	16	16	n.a.
Non-cellulosic continuous fibres	7.7	7.8	7.9
Jet fuels	37	30	35
Motor spirit (gasoline)	100	77	81
Naphthas	5	12	7
Kerosene	3	3	6
Distillate fuel oils	203	175	176
Residual fuel oils	369	310	325
Bitumen	25	23	26
Liquefied petroleum gas (refined)	2	2	2
Cement	990	n.a.	n.a.
Electric energy (million kWh)	4,840	4,894	5,589

Source: UN, *Industrial Commodity Statistics Yearbook*.

1999: Electric energy 6,198 million kWh.

Finance

CURRENCY AND EXCHANGE RATES
Monetary Units
100 céntimos =1 Costa Rican colón.

Sterling, Dollar and Euro Equivalents (30 April 2001)
£1 sterling = 464.8 colones;
US $1 = 324.6 colones;
€1 = 288.1 colones;
1,000 Costa Rican colones = £2.152 = $3.081 = €3.471.

Average Exchange Rate (colones per US $)
1998   257.23
1999   285.68
2000   308.19

GENERAL BUDGET (million colones)

Revenue	1997	1998	1999
Taxation	373,776	455,522	538,867
Income tax	66,268	88,588	131,932
Social security contributions	14,454	15,500	17,694
Taxes on property	2,705	2,619	2,422
Taxes on goods and services	237,596	291,473	339,891
Taxes on international trade	52,753	57,341	46,928
Other current revenue	2,356	3,152	1,866
Current transfers	1,368	1,031	2,237
Capital transfers	—	—	20,257
Total	377,500	459,704	563,227

Expenditure	1997	1998	1999
Current expenditure	416,329	498,236	603,110
Wages and salaries	128,256	155,541	191,193
Social security contributions	14,427	21,031	21,906
Other purchases of goods and services	16,944	21,121	21,883
Interest payments	113,579	116,026	164,226
Internal	103,024	103,577	142,840
External	10,555	12,449	21,386
Current transfers	143,124	184,517	203,901
Capital expenditure	49,153	50,701	59,968
Investment	20,339	20,491	24,457
Capital transfers	28,814	30,210	35,511
Total	465,482	548,936	663,078

INTERNATIONAL RESERVES (US $ million at 31 December)

	1998	1999	2000
Gold*	0.02	0.02	0.02
IMF special drawing rights	0.07	0.81	0.43
Reserve position in IMF	12.29	27.45	26.06
Foreign exchange	1,051.04	1,432.14	1,291.27
Total	1,063.41	1,460.42	1,317.78

* National valuation.

Source: IMF, *International Financial Statistics*.

MONEY SUPPLY ('000 million colones at 31 December)

	1998	1999	2000
Currency outside banks	124.2	154.9	143.0
Demand deposits at commercial banks	279.6	330.7	456.0
Total money (incl. others)	415.4	516.6	617.7

Source: IMF, *International Financial Statistics*.

COST OF LIVING
(Consumer Price Index; base: January 1995 = 100)

	1998	1999	2000
Food, beverages and tobacco	165.0	181.0	198.7
Clothing and footwear	135.8	145.2	152.4
Housing	138.2	153.8	173.9
All items (incl. others)	159.6	175.7	194.9

NATIONAL ACCOUNTS (million colones at current prices)
Expenditure on the Gross Domestic Product

	1998	1999*	2000*
Government final consumption expenditure	469,316	565,217	656,330
Private final consumption expenditure	2,540,540	2,890,647	3,247,697
Increase in stocks	−22,033	−8,762	−25,371
Gross fixed capital formation	731,353	788,938	835,571
Total domestic expenditure	3,719,176	4,236,040	4,714,228
Exports of goods and services	1,714,312	2,296,597	2,353,963
Less Imports of goods and services	1,809,169	2,065,454	2,276,170
GDP in purchasers' values	3,624,318	4,467,184	4,792,021
GDP at constant 1991 prices	1,285,243	1,391,827	1,411,882

* Figures are provisional.

Gross Domestic Product by Economic Activity

	1998	1999*	2000*
Agriculture, hunting, forestry and fishing	424,803	431,192	425,845
Mining and quarrying	4,796	6,172	6,505
Manufacturing	764,384	1,186,814	1,099,797
Electricity, gas and water	90,497	94,733	121,770
Construction	136,781	152,459	175,480
Trade, restaurants and hotels	667,778	765,956	869,717
Transport, storage and communications	285,962	315,207	358,053
Finance and insurance	145,662	178,810	212,802
Real estate	156,534	178,336	204,089
Other business services	85,828	105,229	122,644
Public administration	121,874	146,113	169,099
Other community, social and personal services	530,774	660,781	791,150
Sub-total	3,415,673	4,221,801	4,556,951
Less Imputed bank service charge	99,427	128,908	164,745
GDP at basic prices	3,316,246	4,092,893	4,392,206
Taxes, less subsidies, on products	308,073	374,291	472,255
GDP in purchasers' values	3,624,318	4,467,184	4,864,461

* Figures are provisional.

BALANCE OF PAYMENTS (US $ million)

	1997	1998	1999
Exports of goods f.o.b. . . .	4,220.6	5,538.3	6,667.7
Imports of goods f.o.b. . . .	−4,718.2	−5,937.4	−6,008.1
Trade balance	−497.6	−399.0	659.6
Exports of services . . .	1,128.6	1,343.4	1,525.6
Imports of services . . .	−988.4	−1,109.8	−1,173.7
Balance on goods and services	−357.4	−165.5	1,011.6
Other income received . .	185.4	182.7	198.2
Other income paid . . .	−434.4	−651.2	−1,961.4
Balance on goods, services and income	−606.4	−634.0	−751.6
Current transfers received . .	191.2	190.5	190.7
Current transfers paid . .	−65.7	−77.3	−88.6
Current balance . . .	−480.9	−520.8	−649.5
Direct investment abroad. . .	−4.4	−4.8	−5.0
Direct investment from abroad .	408.2	613.1	669.3
Portfolio investment assets .	−22.5	−33.9	−28.1
Portfolio investment liabilities .	−190.8	−296.0	−239.7
Other investment assets . .	−267.4	−95.6	106.8
Other investment liabilities .	206.7	16.2	73.3
Net errors and omissions . .	157.8	−182.6	224.2
Overall balance . . .	−193.3	−504.3	151.3

Source: IMF, *International Financial Statistics*.

External Trade

PRINCIPAL COMMODITIES (US $ million)

Imports c.i.f.	1998	1999	2000
Raw materials for industry and mining . . .	3,137.8	3,411.5	3,335.4
Raw materials for agriculture. .	156.9	151.7	141.7
Consumer non-durables . .	743.3	770.7	807.7
Consumer durables . . .	540.0	371.9	371.8
Capital goods for industry and mining . . .	963.9	900.7	851.2
Capital goods for transport . .	205.4	195.5	178.7
Building materials . . .	172.6	174.1	173.4
Fuels and lubricants . . .	260.8	320.2	472.1
Total (incl. others) . . .	6,238.4	6,350.7	6,379.8

Exports f.o.b.	1998	1999	2000
Livestock and fishing products .	350.8	168.5	159.7
Agricultural products (unprocessed)	1,588.9	1,422.2	1,270.9
Bananas	634.5	632.2	531.3
Coffee.	409.4	289.5	277.8
Pineapples . . .	112.4	133.1	121.1
Industrial products .	3,569.1	5,129.4	4,466.8
Textiles	812.1	804.4	772.6
Electrical components for microprocessors .	959.7	2,526.0	1,653.3
Products of food industry . .	378.4	387.3	382.3
Other products of Free Zone .	344.3	668.3	886.3
Infusion equipment . . .	64.8	79.6	169.3
Total	5,508.8	6,720.1	5,897.4

Source: Promotora del Comercio Exterior de Costa Rica.

PRINCIPAL TRADING PARTNERS (US $ million)

Imports c.i.f.	1998	1999	2000
Brazil	88.6	99.9	113.7
Canada	84.8	74.1	72.7
China, People's Republic . . .	58.1	60.5	78.4
Colombia	98.4	97.5	120.9
El Salvador	115.3	106.8	91.0
France	72.0	74.6	93.4
Germany	131.0	124.8	124.6
Guatemala	144.8	142.2	139.9
Italy	88.1	79.3	73.4
Japan	385.1	300.7	214.7
Korea, Republic	93.6	108.2	117.5
Mexico	328.2	345.6	392.7
Netherlands	53.4	45.0	96.0
Panama	92.7	86.0	91.1
Spain	100.2	89.1	143.9
Taiwan	71.0	68.7	65.4
USA	3,464.2	3,581.4	3,388.0
Venezuela	186.3	248.8	337.3
Total (incl. others) . . .	6,238.7	6,350.7	6,373.3

Exports f.o.b.	1998	1999	2000
Belgium-Luxembourg . . .	93.8	66.5	115.2
Canada	87.3	40.2	35.1
El Salvador	111.8	115.4	135.2
France	85.0	40.6	35.5
Germany	216.3	183.7	137.5
Guatemala	171.9	179.5	193.4
Honduras	90.5	102.4	115.8
Hong Kong	55.8	35.7	17.4
Italy	137.6	105.2	99.9
Japan	64.2	128.2	50.9
Malaysia	114.9	63.4	52.5
Mexico	82.6	144.2	98.2
Netherlands	204.2	452.3	394.9
Nicaragua	141.6	177.4	179.1
Panama	119.7	126.3	129.0
Puerto Rico	136.8	175.4	163.2
Singapore	40.1	75.0	43.7
Spain	98.7	68.6	24.2
United Kingdom	219.3	387.8	300.0
USA	2,551.3	3,452.1	3,056.7
Total (incl. others) . . .	5,478.5	6,719.0	5,897.3

Source: Ministry of Foreign Commerce.

Transport

RAILWAYS

	1992	1993	1994
Passenger journeys	11,580	367,803	335,276
Freight ton-km (million) . . .	845.2	833.2	729.3

Source: Ministry of Public Works and Transport.

ROAD TRAFFIC (motor vehicles in use at 31 December)

	1997	1998*	1999*
Private cars	294,083	316,844	326,524
Buses and coaches . . .	10,317	11,102	11,441
Goods vehicles	153,111	164,796	169,831
Motorcycles and mopeds . . .	n.a.	79,446	81,564

* Estimate(s).

Source: mainly IRF, *World Road Statistics*.

SHIPPING

Merchant Fleet (registered at 31 December)

	1996	1997	1998
Number of vessels	14	14	14
Total displacement ('000 grt) . .	5.9	5.9	5.6

Source: Lloyd's Register of Shipping, *World Fleet Statistics*.

International Sea-borne Freight Traffic ('000 metric tons)

	1996	1997	1998
Goods loaded	3,017	3,421	3,721
Goods unloaded	3,972	4,522	5,188

Source: Ministry of Public Works and Transport.

CIVIL AVIATION (traffic on scheduled services)

	1996	1997	1998
Passengers carried ('000) . . .	918	992	1,170
Air freight ton-km (million) . .	45	55	96

Sources: International Civil Aviation Organization; UN, *Statistical Yearbook*; World Bank, *World Development Indicators*.

Communications Media

	1995	1996	1997
Radio receivers ('000 in use) . .	900	950	980
Television receivers ('000 in use) .	490	510	525
Telephones ('000 main lines in use)	479	526	584
Telefax stations (number in use) .	6,600	7,500	8,500
Mobile cellular telephones (subscribers)	18,704	46,531	64,387
Daily newspapers:			
Number	5*	6	6
Circulation	300*	320	n.a.

Non-daily newspapers: 12 in 1991 (average circulation 106,000 copies).
Book production: 1,034 titles (excluding pamphlets) in 1995.

* Estimate.

Sources: UNESCO, *Statistical Yearbook*, and UN, *Statistical Yearbook*.

Education

(1999)

	Institu-tions	Tea-chers	Students		
			Males	Females	Total
Pre-primary . . .	1,821	3,604	40,015	37,952	77,967
Primary . . .	3,768	20,185	275,976	259,081	535,057
Secondary . . .	468	11,891	115,443	119,982	235,425
General . . .	386	8,908	92,202	96,895	189,097
Vocational . . .	82	2,983	23,241	23,087	46,328
Tertiary . . .	52	n.a.	n.a.	n.a.	59,947

Tourism

FOREIGN TOURIST ARRIVALS BY COUNTRY OF ORIGIN

	1997	1998	1999
Canada	37,032	42,097	43,662
Colombia	19,357	22,013	26,449
El Salvador	24,166	24,741	28,752
Germany	27,406	23,366	24,034
Guatemala	26,360	30,982	34,064
Honduras	18,319	19,380	26,762
Italy	18,878	17,079	16,827
Mexico	25,347	30,109	31,972
Nicaragua	129,333	170,059	166,511
Panama	48,861	48,648	53,249
Spain	20,461	24,453	27,833
USA	285,361	347,442	392,217
Total (incl. others) . . .	811,490	942,853	1,027,462

Tourism receipts (US $ million): 830 in 1998; 1,002 in 1999; 1,140 in 2000 (preliminary figure).

Directory

The Constitution

The present Constitution of Costa Rica was promulgated in November 1949. Its main provisions are summarized below:

GOVERNMENT

The government is unitary: provincial and local bodies derive their authority from the national Government. The country is divided into seven Provinces, each administered by a Governor who is appointed by the President. The Provinces are divided into Cantons, and each Canton into Districts. There is an elected Municipal Council in the chief city of each Canton, the number of its members being related to the population of the Canton. The Municipal Council supervises the affairs of the Canton. Municipal government is closely regulated by national law, particularly in matters of finance.

LEGISLATURE

The government consists of three branches: legislative, executive and judicial. Legislative power is vested in a single chamber, the

Legislative Assembly, which meets in regular session twice a year—from 1 May to 31 July, and from 1 September to 30 November. Special sessions may be convoked by the President to consider specified business. The Assembly is composed of 57 deputies elected for four years. The chief powers of the Assembly are to enact laws, levy taxes, authorize declarations of war and, by a two-thirds' majority, suspend, in cases of civil disorder, certain civil liberties guaranteed in the Constitution.

Bills may be initiated by the Assembly or by the Executive and must have three readings, in at least two different legislative periods, before they become law. The Assembly may override the presidential vote by a two-thirds' majority.

EXECUTIVE

The executive branch is headed by the President, who is assisted by the Cabinet. If the President should resign or be incapacitated, the executive power is entrusted to the First Vice-President; next in line to succeed to executive power are the Second Vice-President and the President of the Legislative Assembly.

The President sees that the laws and the provisions of the Constitution are carried out, and maintains order; has power to appoint and remove cabinet ministers and diplomatic representatives, and to negotiate treaties with foreign nations (which are, however, subject to ratification by the Legislative Assembly). The President is assisted in these duties by a Cabinet, each member of which is head of an executive department.

ELECTORATE

Suffrage is universal, compulsory and secret for persons over the age of 18 years.

DEFENCE

A novel feature of the Costa Rican Constitution is the clause outlawing a national army. Only by a continental convention or for the purpose of national defence may a military force be organized.

The Government

HEAD OF STATE

President: MIGUEL ANGEL RODRÍGUEZ ECHEVERRÍA (took office 8 May 1998).

First Vice-President and Minister of Culture: ASTRID FISCHEL VOLIO.

Second Vice-President and Minister of the Environment and Energy: ELIZABETH ODIO BENITO.

THE CABINET
(August 2001)

Minister of Agriculture and Livestock: Ing. ALBERTO DENT-ZELEDON.

Minister of the Economy, Industry and Commerce: GILBERTO BARRANTES RODRÍGUEZ.

Minister of the Environment and Energy: ELIZABETH ODIO BENITO.

Minister of Finance: LEONEL BARUCH GOLDBERG.

Minister of Foreign Commerce: TOMÁS DUEÑAS LEIVA.

Minister of Foreign Relations: Ing. ROBERTO ROJAS LÓPEZ.

Minister of Housing: DONALD MONROE.

Minister of Justice: MÓNICA NÁGEL BERGER.

Minister of Labour and Social Security: (vacant).

Minister of the Presidency and of Planning: DANILO CHAVERRI SOTO.

Minister of Public Education: CLAUDIO GUTIÉRREZ CARRANZA.

Minister of Public Health: Dr ROGELIO PARDO EVANS.

Minister of Public Security: ROGELIO RAMOS MARTÍNEZ.

Minister of Public Works and Transport: CARLOS CASTRO ARIAS.

Minister of Science and Technology: Dr GUY F. DE TÉRAMOND PERALTA.

Minister of Women's Affairs: YOLANDA INGIANNA.

MINISTRIES

Ministry of Agriculture and Livestock: Apdo 10.094, 1000 San José; tel. 290-5463; fax 231-2062; internet www.mag.go.cr.

Ministry of the Economy, Industry and Commerce: Edificio Antiguo CODESA, Calles 1 y 3, Avda Central, 1000 San José; tel. 222-1016; fax 222-2305; internet www.meic.go.cr.

Ministry of the Environment and Energy: Avdas 8 y 10, Calle 25, Apdo 10.104, 1000 San José; tel. 257-1417; fax 257-0697; e-mail root@ns.minae.go.cr; internet www.minae.go.cr.

Ministry of Finance: Apdo 5.016, San José; tel. 222-2481; fax 255-4874; internet www.hacienda.go.cr.

Ministry of Foreign Commerce: Montes de Oca, Apdo 96, 2050 San José; tel. 256-7111; fax 255-3281; e-mail info@comex.go.cr; internet www.comex.go.cr.

Ministry of Foreign Relations: Apdo 10.027, 1000 San José; tel. 223-7555; fax 223-9328; internet www.rree.go.cr.

Ministry of Housing: Paseo de los Estudiantes, Apdo 222, 1002 San José; tel. 257-9166; fax 255-1976.

Ministry of Justice: Apdo 5.685, 1000 San José; tel. 223-9739; fax 223-3879; e-mail mnagel@gobnet.go.cr.

Ministry of Labour and Social Security: Apdo 10.133, 1000 San José; tel. 221-0238.

Ministry of the Presidency and of Planning: Avdas 3 y 5, Calle 4, Apdo 10.127, 1000 San José; tel. 221-9524; fax 253-6243; internet www.mideplan.go.cr.

Ministry of Public Education: Apdo 10.087, 1000 San José; tel. 222-0229; fax 233-0390; internet www.mep.go.cr.

Ministry of Public Health: Apdo 10.123, 1000 San José; tel. 233-0683; fax 255-4997; internet www.netsalud.sa.cr.

Ministry of Public Security: Apdo 55, 4874 San José; tel. 226-0093; fax 226-6581; internet www.msp.go.cr.

Ministry of Public Works and Transport: Apdo 10.176, 1000 San José; tel. 226-7311; fax 227-1434.

Ministry of Science and Technology: San José; internet www.micit.go.cr.

Ministry of Women's Affairs: San José.

President and Legislature

PRESIDENT

Presidential Election, 1 February 1998

Candidate	Votes	% of votes cast
MIGUEL ANGEL RODRÍGUEZ ECHEVERRÍA (PUSC)	650,399	46.9
JOSÉ MIGUEL CORRALES BOLAÑOS (PLN) . .	616,600	44.4
VLADIMIR DE LA CRUZ DE LEMOS (FD) . . .	41,922	3.0
WÁLTER MUÑOZ CÉSPEDES (PIN)	20,226	1.5
SHERMAN THOMAS JACKSON (PRC) . . .	19,103	1.4
ALVARO GONZÁLEZ ESPINOZA (PD) . . .	13,559	1.0
Total (incl. others)*	1,387,287	100.0

* Excluding 6,080 blank ballots.

ASAMBLEA LEGISLATIVA

General Election, 1 February 1998

Party	Seats
Partido Unidad Social Cristiana (PUSC)	27
Partido de Liberación Nacional (PLN)	23
Fuerza Democrática (FD)	3
Partido Movimiento Libertario (PML)	2
Partido Integración Nacional (PIN)	1
Partido Acción Laborista Agrícola (PALA) . . .	1
Total	57

Political Organizations

Acción Agrícola Cartaginesa: Cartago; provincial party; Pres. JUAN BRENES CASTILLO; Sec. RODRIGO FALLAS BONILLA.

Alianza Nacional Cristiana (ANC): Calle Vargas Araya, Condominio UNI, 50m norte Bazar Tere, Apdo 353, 2050 San José; tel. 253-2772; f. 1981; national party; Pres. VÍCTOR HUGO GONZÁLEZ MONTERO; Sec. SALVADOR ESTABAN BEATRIZ PORRAS.

Cambio 2000: 200m al sur del Banco Popular de San José, Edif. esquinero, frente a la Sociedad de Seguros de Vida del Magisterio Nacional, San José; tel. 221-0694; f. 2000; national party; Pres. WALTER COTO MOLINA; Sec. ROSA MARÍA ARTAVIA RODRÍGUEZ. Coalition comprising:

    Acción Democrática Alajuelense: Alajuela; provincial party; Pres. FRANCISCO ALFARO FERNÁNDEZ; Sec. JUAN BAUTISTA CHACÓN SOTO.

Partido Pueblo Unido: 300m sur de la Iglesia de Zapote, Apdo 4.565, 1000 San José; tel. 224-2364; fax 224-2364; f. 1995; national party; Pres. Trino Barrantes Araya; Sec. Humberto Vargas Carbonell.

Independiente Obrero: Edif. Multifamiliares, Hatillo 5, Apdo 179, 1000 San José; tel. 254-5450; fax 252-1107; f. 1971; national party; Pres. José Alberto Cubero Carmona; Sec. Luis Fernando Salazar Villegas.

Nuevo Partido Democrático: Central Barrio Naciones Unidas, detrás del Centro Comercial del Sur, Apdo 528, 2100 San José; tel. 227-1422; fax 283-4857; f. 1996; national party; Pres. Rodrigo Gutiérrez Schwanhauser; Sec. Rosa María Zeledon Gómez.

Partido Acción Laborista Agrícola (PALA): San José; f. 1987.

Partido Alajuelita Nueva: Alajuelita Centro, 100W Escuela Abraham Lincoln, San José; tel. 254-3879; fax 254-6072; f. 1981; Pres. Annie Badilla Calderón; Sec. Carlos Retana Retana.

Partido Auténtico Limonense: Limón; provincial party; Pres. Marvin Wright Lindo; Sec. Guillermo Joseph Wignall.

Partido Demócrata (PD): Frente a las Oficinas del INVU, barrio Amón, contiguo a Restaurante La Criollita, Apdo 121, San José; tel. 256-4168; fax 256-0350; f. 1996; national party; Pres. Alvaro González Espinoza; Sec. Ana María Pérez Granados.

Partido Fuerza Democrática (FD): Calle 28, Paseo Colón y Avda 1a, San José; tel. 256-2947; fax 243-2850; f. 1992 as coalition; later became national party; Pes. Vladimir De La Cruz De Lemos; Sec. José Merino Del Río.

Partido Integración Nacional (PIN): Del ferrocarril del Atlántico 100m al sur, Edif. Nortesa 2°, Of. 4, San José; tel. 256-1836; fax 255-0834; e-mail wmunoz@congreso.aleg.go.cr; internet www.pin .freeservers.com; f. 1996; national party; Pres. Dr Walter Muñoz Céspedes; Sec.-Gen. Ana Lourdes Gólcher González.

Partido Liberación Nacional (PLN): Mata Redonda, 125m oeste del Ministerio de Agricultura y Ganadería, Casa Liberacionista José Figueres Ferrer, Apdo 10.051, 1000 San José; tel. 232-5033; fax 231-4097; e-mail palina@sol.racsa.co.cr; internet www.pln.org; f. 1952; national social democratic party; affiliated to the Socialist International; 500,000 mems; Pres. (vacant); Sec.-Gen. Rolando González Ulloa.

Partido Movimiento Libertario (PML): Oficina de Cabinas San Isidro, Barrio Los Yoses Sur, Apdo 4.674, 1000 San José; tel. 283-4545; fax 221-6822; e-mail otto@libertario.org; internet www.liber tario.org; f. 1994; national party; Pres. Otto Guevara Guth; Sec.-Gen. Raúl Costales Domínguez.

Partido Patriotico Nacional: Curridabat, Residencial Hacienda Vieja, de la entrada principal 200m al sur y 200m al este, Casa esquinera, Apdo 1.525, San José; tel. 272-0835; fax 253-5868; f. 1971; national party; Pres. Daniel Enrique Reynolds Vargas; Sec. Erick Delgado León.

Partido Renovación Costarricense (PRC): Centro Educativo Instituto de Desarrollo de Inteligencia, Hatillo 1, Avda Villanea, Apdo 31, 1300 San José; tel. 254-3651; fax 252-3270; f. 1995; national party; Pres. Gerardo Justo Orozco Alvarez; Sec. Carlos Avendaño Calvo.

Partido Rescate Nacional: De la Iglesia Católica de San Pedro de Montes de Oca 150m al oeste, contiguo al restaurante El Farolito, San José; tel. 234-9569; fax 225-0931; f. 1996; national party; Pres. Carlos Vargas Solano; Sec. Buenaventura Carlos Villalobos Brenes.

Partido Unidad Social Cristiana (PUSC): 100m norte y 25m este del costado este de Plaza de Sol, Apdo 10.095, 1000 San José; tel. 280-8615; fax 280-8607; internet www.pusc.or.cr; f. 1983; national party; Pres. Rina Contreras López; Sec. Carlos Palma Rodríguez.

Partido Unión General (PUGEN): 50m al sur de la Antigua Mercedez Benz del Paseo Colón, Edif. Wade Rent-a-Car, Apdo 440, San José; tel. 771-0524; fax 771-0737; e-mail pugen@apc.c.co.cr; f. 1980; national party; Pres. Dr Carlos A. Fernández Vega; Sec. María Lourdes Rodríguez Morales.

Diplomatic Representation

EMBASSIES IN COSTA RICA

Argentina: Curridabat, Apdo 1.963, 1000 San José; tel. 234-6520; fax 283-9983; e-mail embarg@sol.racsa.co.cr; Ambassador: Manuel Maria Pinto.

Belgium: Los Yoses, 4a entrada, 25m sur, Apdo 3.725, 1000 San José; tel. 225-6255; fax 225-0351; e-mail ambelsaj@sol.racsa.co.cr; Ambassador: Michel Delfosse.

Bolivia: Barrio Rohrmoser 669, Apdo 84.810, 1000 San José; tel. 288-1529; fax 232-7292; e-mail embocr@sol.racsa.co.cr; Ambassador: Jaime Soria Padro.

Brazil: Paseo Colón frente a Nissan Lachner y Sáenz, Apdo 10.132, 1000 San José; tel. 233-1544; fax 223-4325; e-mail embbsjo@sol.rac sa.co.cr; Ambassador: Joao Carlos de Souza de Gomes.

Canada: Oficentro Ejecutivo La Sabana, Edif. 5, 3°, detrás de la Contraloría, Centro Colón, Apdo 351, 1007 San José; tel. 296-4149; fax 296-4270; e-mail canadacr@sol.racsa.co.cr; Ambassador: Denis Thibault.

Chile: De la Pulpería La Luz 125m norte, Casa 116, Apdo 10.102, 1000 San José; tel. 224-4243; fax 253-7016; e-mail echilecr@sol.rac sa.co.cr; Ambassador: Edmundo Vargas Carreño.

China (Taiwan): 300m al norte y 150 al este de la Iglesia Sta Teresita, Barrio Escalante, Apdo 676, 2010 San José; tel. 224-8180; fax 253-8333; e-mail embajroc@sol.racsa.co.cr; internet www.cr .roetaiwan.org.pa; Ambassador: Kao-wen Mao.

Colombia: Apdo 3.154, 1000 San José; tel. 283-6871; fax 283-6818; e-mail emcosric@sol.racsa.co.cr; Ambassador: Julio Anibal Riaño Velandi.

Czech Republic: 75m oeste de la entrada principal del Colegio Humboldt, Apdo 12.041, 1000 San José; tel. 296-5671; fax 296-5595; e-mail sanjose@embassy.mzv.cz; Ambassador: Ing. Vít Korselt.

Dominican Republic: Lomas de Ayarco, Curridabat, de la Embajada de Rusia 100m oeste, 300m sur, 300m oeste y 150m norte, Apdo 4.746, 1000 San José; tel. 283-8103; fax 280-7604; e-mail teredom@sol.racsa.co.cr; Ambassador: Teresita Migdalia Torres - García.

Ecuador: Edif. de la esquina sureste del Museo Nacional, 125m al este, Avda 2, Calles 19 y 21, Apdo 1.374, 1000 San José; tel. 232-1503; fax 232-2086; e-mail embecuar@sol.racsa.co.cr; Ambassador: Lic. Francisco Proaño Arandi.

El Salvador: Paseo Colón, Calle 30, Avda 1, No 53, Apdo 1.378, 1000 San José; tel. 222-3648; fax 258-1234; e-mail embasacr@sol.rac sa.co.cr; Ambassador: Ernesto Ferreiro Rusconi.

France: Carretera a Curridabat, del Indoor Club 200m sur y 25m oeste, Apdo 10.177, 1000 San José; tel. 225-0733; fax 253-7027; e-mail sjfrance@sol.racsa.co.cr; Ambassador: Nicole Tramond.

Germany: Barrio Rohrmoser, de la Casa de Oscar Arias 200m norte, 75m este, Apdo 4.017, 1000 San José; tel. 232-5533; fax 231-6403; e-mail info@embajada-alemana.org; internet www.embajada alemana.org; Ambassador Dr Wilfried Rupprecht.

Guatemala: De Pops Curridabat 500m sur y 30m este, 2a Casa Izquierda, Apdo 328, 1000 San José; tel. 283-2290; fax 283-2556; e-mail embaguat@sol.racsa.co.cr; Ambassador: Guillermo Alfredo Argüeta Villagrán.

Holy See: Urbanización Rohrmoser, Sabana Oeste, Centro Colón, Apdo 992, 1007 San José (Apostolic Nunciature); tel. 232-2128; fax 231-2557; e-mail nuapcr@sol.racsa.co.cr; Apostolic Nuncio: Most Rev. Antonio Sozzo, Titular Archbishop of Concordia.

Honduras: Los Yoses sur, del ITAN hacia la Presidencia la primera entrada a la izquierda, 200m norte y 100m este, Apdo 2.239, 1000 San José; tel. 234-9502; fax 253-2209; e-mail emhondcr@sol.racsa .co.cr; Ambassador: Aristides Mejía Castro.

Israel: Edif. Centro Colón, 11°, Calle 2, Avdas 2 y 4, Apdo 5.147, 1000 San José; tel. 221-6444; fax 257-0867; e-mail embofisr@sol.rac sa.co.cr; Ambassador: Yaacov Brakha.

Italy: Los Yoses, 5a entrada, Apdo 1.729, 1000 San José; tel. 224-6574; fax 225-8200; e-mail ambiter@sol.racsa.co.cr; internet www.ambitcr.com; Ambassador: Franco Micieli de Biase.

Japan: Oficentro Ejecutivo La Sabana, Edif. 7, 3°, detrás de la Contraloría, Sabana Sur, Apdo 501, 1000 San José; tel. 232-1255; fax 231-3140; e-mail embjapon@sol.racsa.co.cr; Ambassador: Naotoshi Sugiuchi.

Korea, Republic: Oficentro Ejecutivo La Sabana, Edif. 2, 3°, Sabana Sur, Apdo 838, 1007 San José; tel. 220-3160; fax 220-3168; e-mail koreasec@sol.racsa.co.cr; Ambassador: Kim Young-sik.

Mexico: Avda 7, No 1371, Apdo 10.107, 1000 San José; tel. 257-0633; fax 222-6080; e-mail embamex@sol.racsa.co.cr; Ambassador: Enrique Berruga Filloy.

Netherlands: Los Yoses, Avda 8, Calles 35 y 37, Apdo 10.285, 1000 San José; tel. 296-1490; fax 296-2933; e-mail nethemb@sol.racsa .co.cr; Ambassador: Henricus Gajentaan.

Nicaragua: Edif. Trianón, Avda Central 250, Barrio la California, Apdo 1.382, 1000 San José; tel. 222-2373; fax 221-5481; e-mail embanic@sol.racsa.co.cr; Ambassador: Dr Enrique Paguaga Fernández.

Panama: Del Centro Colón 275m norte, Calle 38, Avda 5 y 7, Apdo 94, 1000 San José; tel. 257-3241; fax 257-4864; Ambassador: Virginia I. Burgoa.

Peru: Barrio Pops de Curridabat, del Indoor Club 100m sur y 50m oeste, Apdo 4.248, 1000 San José; tel. 225-9145; fax 253-0457; Ambassador: Alberto Varillas Montenegro.

Poland: De la Iglesia Santa Teresita 300m este, 3307, Barrio Escalante, Apdo 664, 2010 San José; tel. 225-1481; fax 225-1592; e-mail polonia@sol.racsa.co.cr; Ambassador: MIECZYSLAW BIERNACKI.

Romania: Urbanización Rohrmoser, al costado norte de la Nunciatura Apostólica, Sabana Oeste, Centro Colón, Apdo 10.321, 1000 San José; tel. 231-0741; fax 232-6461; e-mail embromsj@sol.racsa.co.cr; Ambassador: GHEORGHE UGLEAN.

Russia: Curridabat, Lomas de Ayarco Sur, de la carretera a Cartago, 1a entrada, 100m sur, Apdo 6.340, 1000 San José; tel. 272-1021; fax 272-0142; e-mail emrusa@sol.racsa.co.cr; Ambassador: VLADIMIR N. KAZIMIROV.

Spain: Calle 32, Paseo Colón, Avda 2, Apdo 10.150, 1000 San José; tel. 222-1933; fax 222-4180; e-mail embaes@racsa.co.cr; Ambassador: VICTOR IBÁÑEZ-MARTIN MELLADO.

Switzerland: Paseo Colón, Centro Colón, Apdo 895, 1007 San José; tel. 221-4829; fax 255-2831; e-mail swiemsj@sol.racsa.co.cr; Ambassador: Dr RODOLPHE S. IMHOOF.

United Kingdom: Edif. Centro Colón, 11°, Apdo 815, 1007 San José; tel. 258-2025; fax 233-9938; e-mail britemb@sol.racsa.co.cr; Ambassador: PETER J. SPICELEY.

Uruguay: Avda 14, Calles 35 y 37, Apdo 3.448, 1000 San José; tel. 253-2755; fax 234-9909; e-mail embajrou@sol.racsa.co.cr; Ambassador: ANTONIO RICARDO MORELL BORDOLI.

USA: Pavas, frente Centro Comercial, Apdo 920, 1200 San José; tel. 220-3939; fax 220-2305; e-mail hdssjo@usia.gov; internet usembassy.or.cr; Ambassador: THOMAS J. DODD.

Venezuela: Avda Central, Los Yoses, 5a entrada, Apdo 10.230, 1000 San José; tel. 225-5813; fax 253-1453; Ambassador: NOEL SIMÓN GARCÍA GÓMEZ.

Judicial System

Ultimate judicial power is vested in the Supreme Court, the 22 justices of which are elected by the Assembly for a term of eight years, and are automatically re-elected for an equal period, unless the Assembly decides to the contrary by a two-thirds vote. Judges of the lower courts are appointed by the Supreme Court's five-member Supreme Council.

The Supreme Court may also meet as the Corte Plena, with power to declare laws and decrees unconstitutional. There are, in addition, four appellate courts, criminal courts, civil courts and special courts. The jury system is not used.

La Corte Suprema: San José; tel. 295-3000; fax 257-0801.

President of the Supreme Court: EDGAR CERVANTES VILLALTA.

Religion

Under the Constitution, all forms of worship are tolerated. Roman Catholicism is the official religion of the country. Various Protestant Churches are represented. There are an estimated 7,000 members of the Methodist Church.

CHRISTIANITY
The Roman Catholic Church

Costa Rica comprises one archdiocese and six dioceses. At 31 December 1999 Roman Catholics represented some 87.1% of the total population.

Bishops' Conference: Conferencia Episcopal de Costa Rica, Arzobispado, Apdo 497, 1000 San José; tel. 221-3053; fax 221-6662; f. 1977; Pres. Most Rev. ROMÁN ARRIETA VILLALOBOS, Archbishop of San José de Costa Rica.

Archbishop of San José de Costa Rica: Most Rev. ROMÁN ARRIETA VILLALOBOS, Arzobispado, Apdo 497, 1000 San José; tel. 258-1015; fax 221-2427; e-mail curiam@sol.racsa.co.cr.

The Anglican Communion

Costa Rica comprises one of the five dioceses of the Iglesia Anglicana de la Región Central de América.

Bishop of Costa Rica: Rt Rev. CORNELIUS JOSHUA WILSON, Apdo 2.773, 1000 San José; tel. 225-0209; fax 253-8331; e-mail amiecr@sol.racsa.co.cr.

Other Churches

Federación de Asociaciones Bautistas de Costa Rica: Apdo 1.631, 2100 Guadalupe; tel. 253-5820; fax 253-4723; f. 1946; represents Baptist churches; Pres. CARLOS MANUEL UMAÑA ROJAS.

Iglesia Evangélica Luterana de Costa Rica (Evangelical Lutheran Church of Costa Rica): Apdo 1.512, 1200 San José; tel. 231-3345; fax 291-0986; e-mail evkirche@sol.racsa.co.cr; f. 1966; 600 mems; Pres. Rev. RENÉ LAMMER.

Iglesia Evangélica Metodista de Costa Rica (Evangelical Methodist Church of Costa Rica): Apdo 5.481, 1000 San José; tel. 236-2171; fax 236-5921; autonomous since 1973; 6,000 mems; Pres. Bishop LUIS F. PALOMO.

BAHÁ'Í FAITH

Bahá'í Information Centre: Apdo 553, 1150 San José; tel. 231-0647; fax 296-1033; adherents resident in 242 localities.

National Spiritual Assembly of the Bahá'ís of Costa Rica: Apdo 553, 1150 La Uruca; tel. 231-0647; fax 296-1033; e-mail bahaiscr@sol.racsa.co.cr.

The Press

DAILIES

Al Día: Llorente de Tibás, Apdo 70.270, San José; tel. 247-4647; fax 247-4665; e-mail aldia@nacion.co.cr; f. 1992; morning; independent; Dir ARMANDO M. GONZÁLEZ RODICIO; circ. 60,000.

Boletín Judicial: La Uruca, Apdo 5.024, San José; tel. 231-5222; f. 1878; journal of the judiciary; Dir ISAÍAS CASTRO VARGAS; circ. 2,500.

Diario Extra: Edif. Borrasé, 2°, Calle 4, Avda 4, Apdo 177, 1009 San José; tel. 223-9505; fax 223-5921; internet www.diarioextra.com; f. 1978; morning; independent; Dir WILLIAM GÓMEZ VARGAS; circ. 120,000.

La Gaceta: La Uruca, Apdo 5.024, San José; tel. 231-5222; internet www.imprenal.go.cr; f. 1878; official gazette; Dir ISAÍAS CASTRO VARGAS; circ. 5,300.

El Heraldo: 400m al este de las oficinas centrales, Apdo 1.500, San José; tel. 222-6665; fax 222-3039; e-mail info@elheraldo.net; internet www.elheraldo.net; f. 1994; morning; independent; Dir ERWIN KNOHR R.; circ. 30,000.

La Nación: Llorente de Tibás, Apdo 10.138, 1000 San José; tel. 247-4747; fax 247-5026; e-mail webmaster@nacion.co.cr; internet www.nacion.co.cr; f. 1946; morning; independent; Pres. MANUEL F. JIMÉNEZ ECHEVERRÍA; circ. 118,000.

La Prensa Libre: Calle 4, Avda 4, Apdo 10.121, San José; tel. 223-6666; fax 233-6831; e-mail plibre@prensalibre.co.cr; internet www.prensalibre.co.cr; f. 1889; evening; independent; Dir ANDRÉS BORRASÉ SANOU; circ. 56,000.

La República: Barrio Tournón, Guadalupe, Apdo 2.130, San José; tel. 223-0266; fax 255-3950; e-mail larazon@sol.racsa.co.cr; internet www.larepublica.net; f. 1950, reorganized 1967; morning; independent; Dir JULIO SUÑOL; circ. 60,000.

PERIODICALS

Abanico: Calle 4, esq. Avda 4, Apdo 10.121, San José; tel. 223-6666; fax 223-4671; weekly supplement of *La Prensa Libre*; women's interests; Editor MARÍA DEL CARMEN POZO C.; circ. 50,000.

Acta Médica: Sabana Sur, Apdo 548, San José; tel. 232-3433; f. 1954; organ of the Colegio de Médicos; 3 issues per year; Editor Dr BAUDILIO MORA MORA; circ. 2,000.

El Cafetalero: Calle 1, Avdas 18 y 20, Apdo 37, 1000 San José; tel. 222-6411; fax 223-6025; e-mail evilla@icafe.go.cr; f. 1964 as Noticiero del Café; changed name in 2000; bi-monthly; coffee journal; owned by the Instituto del Café de Costa Rica; Editor ERNESTO VILLALOBOS; circ. 10,000.

Contrapunto: La Uruca, Apdo 7, 1980 San José; tel. 231-3333; f. 1978; fortnightly; publication of Sistema Nacional de Radio y Televisión; Dir FABIO MUÑOZ CAMPOS; circ. 10,000.

Eco Católico: Calle 22, Avdas 3 y 5, Apdo 1.064, San José; tel. 222-6156; fax 256-0407; f. 1931; Catholic weekly; Dir ARMANDO ALFARO; circ. 20,000.

Mujer y Hogar: San José; f. 1943; weekly; women's journal; Editor and Gen. Man. CARMEN CORNEJO MÉNDEZ; circ. 15,000.

Perfil: Llorente de Tibás, Apdo 1.517, 1100 San José, 1000; tel. 247-4345; fax 247-5110; e-mail perfil@nacion.co.cr; f. 1984; fortnightly; women's interest; Dir CAROLINA CARAZO BARRANTES; circ. 16,000.

Polémica: Icadis, Paseo de los Estudiantes, Apdo 1.006, San José; tel. 233-3964; f. 1981; every 4 months; left-wing; Dir GABRIEL AGUILERA PERALTA.

Primera Plana: Sabana Este, San José; tel. 255-1590.

Rumbo: Llorente de Tibás, Apdo 10.138, 1000 San José; tel. 240-4848; fax 240-6480; f. 1984; weekly; general; Dir ROXANA ZÚÑIGA; circ. 15,000.

San José News: Apdo 7, 2730 San José; 2 a week; Dir CHRISTIAN RODRÍGUEZ.

Semanario Libertad: Calle 4, Avdas 8 y 10, Apdo 6.613, 1000 San José; tel. 225-5857; f. 1962; weekly; organ of the Partido del Pueblo Costarricense; Dir RODOLFO ULLOA B.; Editor JOSÉ A. ZÚÑIGA; circ. 10,000.

Semanario Universidad: Ciudad Universitaria Rodrigo Facio, San Pedro, Montes de Oca, Apdo 21, San José; tel. 207-5355; fax 207-4774; internet cariari.ucr.ac.cr; f. 1970; weekly; general; Dir CARLOS MORALES; circ. 15,000.

The Tico Times: Calle 15, Avda 8, Apdo 4.632, 1000 San José; tel. 258-1558; fax 223-6378; e-mail ttimes@sol.racsa.co.cr; internet www.ticotimes.net; weekly; in English; Dir DERY DYER; circ. 15,210.

Tiempos de Costa Rica: Casa 3372 Barrio Escalante, Avda 9, 480m este, San José; tel. 280-2332; fax 280-6840; internet www.tdm.com; f. 1996; Costa Rican edition of the international *Tiempos de Mundo*.

PRESS ASSOCIATIONS

Colegio de Periodistas de Costa Rica: Sabana Este, Calle 42, Avda 4, Apdo 5.416, San José; tel. 233-5850; fax 223-8669; f. 1969; 550 mems; Exec. Dir Licda ADRIANA NÚÑEZ.

Sindicato Nacional de Periodistas: Sabana Este, Calle 42, Avda 4, Apdo 5.416, San José; tel. 222-7589; f. 1970; 200 mems; Sec.-Gen. ADRIÁN ROJAS JAÉN.

FOREIGN NEWS BUREAUX

ACAN-EFE (Central America): Costado Sur, Casa Matute Gómez, Casa 1912, Apdo 84.930, San José; tel. 222-6785; Correspondent WILFREDO CHACÓN SERRANO.

Agence France-Presse (France): Calle 13, Avdas 9 y 11 bis, Apdo 5.276, San José; tel. 233-0757; Correspondent DOMINIQUE PETTIT.

Agencia EFE (Spain): Avda 10, Calles 19 y 21, No 1912, Apdo 84.930, San José; tel. 222-6785.

Agenzia Nazionale Stampa Associata (ANSA) (Italy): c/o Diario La República, Barrio Tournón, Guadalupe, Apdo 545, 1200 San José; tel. 231-1140; fax 231-1140; Correspondent LUIS CARTÍN S.

Associated Press (AP) (USA): San José; internet www.ap.org; Correspondent REID MILLER.

Deutsche Presse-Agentur (dpa) (Germany): Edif. 152, 3°, Calle 11, Avdas 1 y 3, Apdo 7.156, San José; tel. 233-0604; fax 233-0604; Correspondent ERNESTO RAMÍREZ.

Informatsionnoye Telegrafnoye Agentstvo Rossii—Telegrafnoye Agentstvo Suverennykh Stran (ITAR—TASS) (Russia): De la Casa Italia 1000m este, 50m norte, Casa 675, Apdo 1.011, San José; tel. 224-1560; Correspondent ENRIQUE MORA.

Inter Press Service (IPS) (Italy): Latin American Regional Center, Calle 11, Avdas 1 y 3, No 152, Paseo de los Estudiantes, Apdo 70, 1002 San José; tel. 255-3861; fax 233-8583; Regional Dir GONZALO ORTIZ-CRESPO.

Prensa Latina (Cuba): Avda 11, No 3185, Calles 31 y 33, Barrio Escalante (de la parrillada 25m oeste), San José; tel. 253-1457; Correspondent FRANCISCO A. URIZARRI TAMAYO.

Rossiyskoye Informatsionnoye Agentstvo—Novosti (RIA—Novosti) (Russia): De la Casa Italiana 100m este, 50m norte, San José; tel. 224-1560.

United Press International (UPI) (USA): Calle 15, Avda 2, Radioperiódicos Reloj, Apdo 4.334, San José; tel. 222-2644; Correspondent WILLIAM CESPEDES CHAVARRÍA.

Xinhua (New China) News Agency (People's Republic of China): Apdo 4.774, San José; tel. 231-3497; Correspondent XU BIHUA.

Publishers

Alfalit Internacional: Apdo 292, 4050 Alajuela; f. 1961; educational; Dirs GILBERTO BERNAL, OSMUNDO PONCE.

Antonio Lehmann Librería, Imprenta y Litografía, Ltda: Calles 1 y 3, Avda Central, Apdo 10.011, San José; tel. 223-1212; f. 1896; general fiction, educational, textbooks; Man. Dir ANTONIO LEHMANN STRUVE.

Editorial Caribe: Apdo 1.307, San José; tel. 222-7244; f. 1949; religious textbooks; Dir JOHN STROWEL.

Editorial Costa Rica: 100m sur y 50m este del Supermercado Periféricos en San Francisco de Dos Ríos, Apdo 10.010, San José; tel. 286-1817; f. 1959; government-owned; cultural; Gen. Man. SHEILA DI PALMA GAMBOA.

Editorial Fernández Arce: Apdo 6.523, 1000 San José; tel. 224-5201; fax 225-6109; f. 1967; textbooks for primary, secondary and university education; Dir Dr MARIO FERNÁNDEZ LOBO.

Editorial de la Universidad Autónoma de Centroamérica (UACA): Apdo 7.637, 1000 San José; tel. 234-0701; fax 224-0391; e-mail lauaca@sol.racsa.co.cr; f. 1981; Editor ALBERTO DI MARE.

Editorial de la Universidad Estatal a Distancia (EUNED): Paseo de los Estudiantes, Apdo 597, 1002 San José; tel. 223-5430; fax 257-5042; f. 1979; Dir AUXILIADORA PROTTI QUESADA.

Editorial Universitaria Centroamericana (EDUCA): Ciudad Universitaria Rodrigo Facio, San Pedro, Montes de Oca, Apdo 64, 2060 San José; tel. 224-3727; fax 253-9141; e-mail educacr@sol.racsa.co.cr; f. 1969; organ of the CSUCA; science, literature, philosophy; Dir ANITA DE FORMOSO.

Mesén Editores: Urbanización El Cedral, 52, Cedros de Montes de Oca, Apdo 6.306, 1000 San José; tel. 253-5203; fax 283-0681; f. 1978; general; Dir DENNIS MESÉN SEGURA.

Trejos Hermanos Sucs, SA: Curridabat, Apdo 10.096, San José; tel. 224-2411; f. 1912; general and reference; Man. ALVARO TREJOS.

PUBLISHING ASSOCIATION

Cámara Costarricense del Libro: San José; e-mail ccl@libroscr.com; internet www.libroscr.com; f. 1978; Pres. MARIO CASTILLO MÉNDEZ.

Broadcasting and Communications

TELECOMMUNICATIONS

Cámara Costarricense de Telecomunicaciones: Edif. Centro Colón, Apdo 591, 1007 San José; tel. and fax 255-3422; Pres. EVITA ARGUEDAS MAKLOUF.

Cámara Nacional de Medios de Comunicación Colectiva (CANAMECC): Apdo 6.574, 1000 San José; tel. 222-4820; f. 1954; Pres. ANDRÉS QUINTANA CAVALLINI.

Instituto Costarricense de Electricidad (ICE): govt agency for power and telecommunications (see Trade and Industry: Utilities, below).

Radiográfica Costarricense, SA (RACSA): Avda 5, Calle 1, Frente al Edif. Numar, Apdo 54, 1000 San José; tel. 287-0087; fax 287-0379; e-mail mcruz@sol.sacsa.co.cr; f. 1921; state telecommunications co.; Dir-Gen. MARCO A. CRUZ MIRANDA.

RADIO

Asociación Costarricense de Información y Cultura (ACIC): Apdo 365, 1009 San José; f. 1983; independent body; controls private radio stations; Pres. JUAN FCO. MONTEALEGRE MARTÍN.

Cámara Nacional de Radio (CANARA): Paseo de los Estudiantes, Apdo 1.583, 1002 San José; tel. 233-1845; fax 255-4483; e-mail canara@sol.racsa.co.cr; internet www.canara.org; f. 1947; Exec. Dir LUZMILDA VARGAS GONZÁLEZ.

Control Nacional de Radio (CNR): Dirección Nacional de Comunicaciones, Ministerio de Gobernación y Policia, Apdo 10.006, 1000 San José; tel. 221-0992; fax 283-0741; f. 1954; governmental supervisory department; Dir MELVIN MURILLO ALVAREZ.

Non-commercial

Faro del Caribe: Apdo 2.710, 1000 San José; tel. 226-2573; fax 227-1725; f. 1948; religious and cultural programmes in Spanish and English; Man. CARLOS ROZOTTO PIEDRASANTA.

Radio Costa Rica: De Autos Bohío, en barrio Córdoba, 100m sur y 100m este, Apdo 6.462, 1000 San José; tel. 227-4690; fax 231-3408; e-mail canalcr@sol.racsa.co.cr; f. 1988; broadcasts Voice of America news bulletins (in Spanish) and locally-produced educational and entertainment programmes; Gen. Man. ANTONIO ALEXANDRE GARCÍA.

Radio Fides: Avda 4, Curia Metropolitana, Apdo 5.079, 1000 San José; tel. 233-4546; fax 233-2387; f. 1952; Roman Catholic station; Dir Rev. ROMÁN ARRIETA VILLALOBOS.

Radio Nacional: 1 km oeste del Parque Nacional de Diversiones, La Uruca, Apdo 7, 1980 San José; tel. 231-7983; fax 220-0070; e-mail sinart@sol.racsa.co.cr; f. 1978; Dir RODOLFO RODRÍGUEZ.

Radio Santa Clara: Santa Clara, San Carlos, Apdo 221, Ciudad Quesada, Alajuela; tel. 479-1264; f. 1986; Roman Catholic station; Dir Rev. MARCO A. SOLÍS V.

Radio Universidad: Ciudad Universitaria Rodrigo Facio, San Pedro, Montes de Oca, Apdo 2.060, 1000 San José; tel. 207-5356; fax 207-5459; f. 1949; classical music; Dir CARLOS MORALES.

Commercial

There are about 40 commercial radio stations, including:

89 Ya!: Costado sur del Parque Desamparados, Apdo 301, San José; tel. 259-3657; fax 250-2376; f. 1995; Dir ALEXANDER RAMOS RODRÍGUEZ.

Cadena de Emisoras Columbia: San José; tel. 234-0355; fax 225-9275; operates Radio Columbia, Radio Uno, Radio Sabrosa, Radio Puntarenas; Dir C. ARNOLDO ALFARO CHAVARRA.

Cadena Musical: Apdo 854, 1000, San José; tel. 257-2789; fax 233-9975; f. 1954; operates Radio Musical, Radio Emperador; Gen. Man. JORGE JAVIER CASTRO.

Grupo Centro: Apdo 6.133, San José; tel. 240-7591; fax 236-3672; operates Radio Centro 96.3 FM, Radio 820 AM, Televisora Guanacasteca Channels 16 and 28; Dir ROBERTO HERNÁNDEZ RAMÍREZ.

Radio Chorotega: Apdo 92, 5175 Santa Cruz de Guanacaste; tel. 663-2757; fax 663-0183; f. 1983; Roman Catholic station; Dir Rev. EMILIO MONTES DE OCA CORDERO.

Radio Emaus: San Vito de Coto Brus; tel. and fax 773-3101; f. 1962; Roman Catholic station; Dir Rev. LUIS PAULINO CABRERA SOTO.

Radio Monumental: Avda Central y 2, Calle 2, Apdo 800, 1000 San José; tel. 222-0000; fax 222-8237; e-mail monument@sol.racsa.co.cr; internet www.novanet.co.cr/monumental; f. 1929; all news station; Gen. Man. TERESA MARÍA CHÁVES ZAMORA.

Radio Sinaí: Apdo 262, 8000 San Isidro de El General; tel. 771-0367; f. 1957; Roman Catholic station; Dir Mgr ALVARO COTO OROZCO.

Sistema Radiofónico: Edif. Galería La Paz, 3°, Avda 2, Calles 2 y 4, Apdo 341, 1000 San José; tel. 222-4344; fax 255-0587; operates Radio Reloj; Dir Dr HERNÁN BARQUERO MONTES DE OCA.

TELEVISION
Government-owned

Sistema Nacional de Radio y Televisión Cultural (SINART): 1 km al oeste del Parque Nacional de Diversiones La Uruca, Apdo 7, 1980 San José; tel. 231-0839; fax 231-6604; e-mail sinart@racsa.co.cr; f. 1977; cultural; Dir-Gen. GUIDO SÁENZ GONZÁLEZ.

Commercial

Alphavisión (Canal 19): Detrás Iglesia de Santa María y Griega, Carretera a Desamparados, Apdo 1490, San José; tel. 226-9333; fax 226-9095; f. 1987; Gen. Man. CECILIA RAMÍREZ.

Canal 2: Del Hospital México 300m oeste, Antiguo Hotel Cristal, Apdo 2.860, San José; tel. 231-2222; fax 231-0791; f. 1983; Pres. RAMÓN COLL MONTERO.

Canal 54: De Plaza Mayot, en Rohrmoser, 50m oeste, 50m sur, Apdo 640, San José; tel. 232-6337; fax 231-3408; e-mail canalcr@sol.racsa.co.cr; f. 1996; Pres. ANTONIO ALEXANDRE GARCÍA.

Corporación Costarricense de Televisión, SA (Canal 6): Apdo 2.860, 1000 San José; tel. 232-9255; fax 232-6087; Gen. Man. MARIO SOTELA BLEN.

Multivisión de Costa Rica, Ltda (Canales 4 y 9): 150m oeste del Centro Comercial de Guadelupe, Apdo 4.666, 1000 San José; tel. 233-4444; fax 221-1734; f. 1961; operates Radio Sistema Universal A.M. (f. 1956), Channel 9 (f. 1962) and Channel 4 (f. 1964) and FM (f. 1980); Gen. Man. ARNOLD VARGAS V.

Televisora de Costa Rica (Canal 7), SA (Teletica): Costado oeste Estadio Nacional, Apdo 3.876, San José; tel. 232-2222; fax 231-6258; f. 1960; operates Channel 7; Pres. OLGA COZZA DE PICADO; Gen. Man. RENÉ PICADO COZZA.

Televisora Sur y Norte (Canal 11): Apdo 99, 1000 San José; tel. 233-4988; Gen. Man. FEDERICO ZAMORA.

Finance

(cap. = capital; p.u. = paid up; res = reserves; dep. = deposits; m. = million; brs = branches; amounts in colones, unless otherwise indicated)

BANKING

Banco Central de Costa Rica: Avdas Central y Primera, Calles 2 y 4, Apdo 10.058, 1000 San José; tel. 233-4233; fax 233-5930; internet www.bccr.fi.cr; f. 1950; cap. 5.0m., res 120,750.4m., total resources 1,404,932.1m. (1999); scheduled for privatization in 2001; Pres. EDUARDO LIZANO FAIT; Man. JOSÉ RAFAEL BRENES.

State-owned Banks

Banco de Costa Rica: Avdas Central y 2, Calles 4 y 6, Apdo 10.035, 1000 San José; tel. 255-1100; fax 255-0911; internet www.bancosta.fi.cr; f. 1877; responsible for industry; total assets 10,353m. (1999); Pres. MARIANO GUARDIA CAÑAS; Gen. Man. MARIO BARRENECHEA; 44 brs and agencies.

Banco Nacional de Costa Rica: Calles 2 y 4, Avda Primera, Apdo 10.015, 1000 San José; tel. 221-2223; fax 233-3875; internet www.bncr.fi.cr; f. 1914; responsible for the agricultural sector; cap. 18,444.4m., res 8,367.1m., dep. 657,306.4m. (1999); Gen. Man. Lic. OMAR GARRO V.; 125 brs and agencies.

Banco Popular y de Desarrollo Comunal: Calle 1, Avdas 2 y 4, Apdo 10.190, San José; tel. 257-5797; fax 255-1966; f. 1969; total assets 29,450m. (1999); Pres. Ing. RODOLFO NAVAS ALVARADO; Gen. Man. ALVARO UREÑA ALVAREZ.

Private Banks

Banco Bancrecen, SA: Sabana sur, Mata Redonda, Apdo 1.289, 1200 San José; tel. 296-5301; fax 296-5305; e-mail bancrecen@sol.racsa.co.cr; internet www.bancrecen.fi.cr; Pres. ROBERTO ALCANTARA ROJAS.

Banco BANEX, SA: Barrio Tournón, Diagonal a Ulacit, Apdo 8.983, 1000 San José; tel. 257-0522; fax 257-5967; e-mail interna@banex.co.cr; internet www.banex.co.cr; f. 1981 as Banco Agroindustrial y de Exportaciones, SA; adopted present name 1987; cap. 9,590.9m., res. 1,250.2m., dep. 111,441.1m. (Dec. 2000); Pres. ALBERTO VALLARINO; Gen. Man. JAVIER LEJÁRRAGA; 9 brs.

Banco Bantec, SA: Frente antigua Canada Dry, La Uruca, Apdo 1.164, 1000 San José; tel. 290-8585; fax 290-2939.

Banco BCT, SA: Calle Central No. 160, Apdo 7.698, San José; tel. 257-0544; fax 233-6833; e-mail banco@bct.fi.cr; f. 1984; total assets 13,794m. (1999); merged with Banco del Comercio, SA in 2000; Pres. ANTONIO BURGUÉS; Gen. Man. Lic. LEONEL BARUCH.

Banco de Crédito Centroamericano, SA (Bancentro): Calles 26 y 38, Paseo Colón, de la Mercedes Benz 200m norte y 150m oeste, Apdo 5.099, 1000 San José; tel. 280-5555; fax 280-5090; f. 1974; cap. 492m. (1996); Pres. ROBERTO J. ZAMORA LLANES; Gen. Man GILBERTO SERRANO GUTIÉRREZ.

Banco Cuscatlan de Costa Rica, SA: Del Puente Juan Pablo II, 150m norte, Canton Central, La Uruca, Apdo 6.531, 1000 San José; tel. 299-0299; fax 232-7476; e-mail cuscatlan@cuscatlancr.com; f. 1984 as Banco de Fomento Agrícola; changed name to Banco BFA in 1994; changed name to above in 2000; Pres. ERNESTO ROHRMOSER; Gen. Man. and CEO MANUEL PÉREZ LARA.

Banco Elca, SA: Del Centro Colón, 200m norte, Paseo Colón, Apdo 1.112, 1000 San José; tel. 258-3355; fax 233-8383; e-mail banelca@sol.racsa.co.cr; f. 1985 as Banco de la Industria; changed name to above in 2000; Pres. Lic. ALBÁN BRENES IBARRA; Gen. Man. Dr ABELARDO BRENES IBARRA.

Banco Finadesa, SA: Paseo Colón, Carmen, Apdo 5.336, 1000 San José; tel. 243-8900; fax 257-0051; e-mail finadesa@finadesa.com.

Banco Improsa, SA: 2985 Calle 29 y 31, Avda 5, Carmen, San José; tel. 257-0689; fax 223-7319; e-mail banimpro@sol.racsa.co.cr.

Banco Interfin, SA: Calle 3, Avdas 2 y 4, Apdo 6.899, San José; tel. 287-4000; fax 233-4823; f. 1982; total assets 11,139m. (1999); Pres. Ing. LUIS LUKOWIECKI; Gen. Man. Dr LUIS LIBERMAN.

Banco Internacional de Costa Rica, SA: Edif. Inmobiliaria BICSA, Barrio Tournón, Apdo 6.116, San José; tel. 243-1000; fax 257-2378; f. 1987; cap. and res 1,625m. (Nov. 1994); Pres. Lic. FERNANDO SUÑOL PREGO; Gen. Man. MARCO ALFARO CHAVARRÍA.

Banco Metropolitano, SA: Calle Central, Avda 2, Apdo 6.714, 1000 San José; tel. 290-6900; fax 296-9665; f. 1985; cap. 386.0m., res 610.1m., dep. 3,828.9m. (Dec. 1996); Pres. ABRAHAM MELTZER SPIGEL; Gen. Man. FRANCISCO LAY SOLANO; 1 br.

Banco Promérica, SA: Edif. Promérica, Sabana oeste canal 7, Mata Redonda, Apdo 1.289, 1200 San José; tel. 296-4848; fax 232-5727; e-mail promeric@sol.racsa.co.cr.

Banco de San José, SA: Calle Central, Avdas 3 y 5, Apdo 5.445, 1000 San José; tel. 256-9911; fax 223-3063; f. 1968; fmrly Bank of America, SA; total assets 10,616m. (1999); Pres. ERNESTO CASTEGNARO ODIO; Gen. Man. MARIO MONTEALEGRE-SABORÍO.

Banco Uno, SA: Calle 28, Paseo Colón, Merced, Apdo 5.884, 1000 San José; tel. 257-1344; fax 257-2215; e-mail pacifico@cos.pibnet.com.

Citibank (Costa Rica), SA: Oficentro ejecutivo la Sabana, distrito Mata Redonda, Apdo 10.277, San José; tel. 296-1494; fax 296-2458.

Scotiabank Costa Rica: Avda Primera, Calles Central y 2, Apdo 5.395, 1000, San José; tel. 287-8700; fax 255-3076; f. 1995; Gen. Man. BRIAN W. BRADY; 11 brs.

Credit Co-operatives

Federación Nacional de Cooperativas de Ahorro y Crédito (Fedecrédito, RL): Calle 20, Avdas 8 y 10, Apdo 4.748, 1000 San José; tel. 233-5666; fax 257-1724; f. 1963; 55 co-operatives, with 150,000 mems; combined cap. US $82m.; Pres. Lic. CARLOS BONILLA AYUB; Gen. Man. Lic. MARIO VARGAS ALVARADO.

Banking Association

Asociación Bancaria Costarricense: San José; tel. 253-2889; fax 225-0987; e-mail abc@abc.fi.cr; internet www.abc.fi.cr; Pres. Dr LUIS LIBERMAN.

STOCK EXCHANGE

Bolsa Nacional de Valores, SA: Edif. Cartagena, 4°, Calle Central, Avda Primera, Santa Ana, Apdo 6155, 1000 San José; tel. 204-4848; fax 204-4802; e-mail bnv@bnv.co.cr; f. 1976; Chair. RODRIGO ARIAS SÁNCHEZ; CEO FEDERICO CARRILLO ZÜRCHER.

INSURANCE

In mid-1998 the Legislative Assembly approved legislative reform effectively terminating the state monopoly of all insurance activities.

Instituto Nacional de Seguros: Calles 9 y 9 bis, Avda 7, Apdo 10.061, 1000 San José; tel. 223-5800; fax 255-3381; internet www.ins.go.cr; f. 1924; administers the state monopoly of insurance; services of foreign insurance companies may be used only by authorization of the Ministry of the Economy, Industry and Commerce, and only after the Instituto has certified that it will not accept the risk; Exec. Pres. JORGE A. HERNÁNDEZ CASTAÑEDA; Gen. Man. ANA ROSS SALAZAR.

Trade and Industry

GOVERNMENT AGENCIES

Instituto Nacional de Vivienda y Urbanismo (INVU): Apdo 2.534, San José; tel. 221-5266; fax 223-4006; housing and town planning institute; Exec. Pres. Ing. Lic. VICTOR EVELIO CASTRO; Gen. Man. Lic. PEDRO HERNÁNDEZ RUIZ.

Ministry of Planning: Avdas 3 y 5, Calle 4, Apdo 10.127, 1000 San José; tel. 221-9524; fax 253-6243; f. 1963; formulates and supervises execution of the National Development Plan; main aims: to increase national productivity; to improve distribution of income and social services; to increase citizen participation in solution of socio-economic problems; Pres. Dr LEONARDO GARNIER.

Promotora del Comercio Exterior de Costa Rica (PROC-OMER): Calle 40, Avdas Central y 3, Centro Colón, Apdo 1.278, 1007 San José; tel. 256-7111; fax 233-5755; e-mail info@procomer.com; internet www.procomer.com; f. 1968 to improve international competitiveness by providing services aimed at increasing, diversifying and expediting international trade.

DEVELOPMENT ORGANIZATIONS

Cámara de Azucareros: Calle 3, Avda Fernández Güell, Apdo 1.577, 1000 San José; tel. 221-2103; fax 222-1358; f. 1949; sugar growers; Pres. RODRIGO ARIAS SÁNCHEZ.

Cámara Nacional de Bananeros: Edif. Urcha, 3°, Calle 11, Avda 6, Apdo 10.273, 1000 San José; tel. 222-7891; fax 233-1268; f. 1967; banana growers; Pres. Lic. JOSÉ ALVARO SANDOVAL; Exec. Dir Lic. JORGE MADRIGAL.

Cámara Nacional de Cafetaleros: Calle 3, Avdas 6 y 8, No. 652, Apdo 1.310, San José; tel. 221-8207; fax 257-5381; f. 1948; 70 mems; coffee millers and growers; Pres. CARLOS R. AUBERT Z.; Exec. Dir JOAQUÍN VALVERDE B.

Cámara Nacional de Ganaderos: Edif. Ilifilán, 4°, Calles 4 y 6, Avda Central, Apdo 5.539, 1000 San José; tel. 222-1652; cattle farmers; Pres. Ing. ALBERTO JOSÉ AMADOR ZAMORA.

Cámara Nacional de Artesanía y Pequeña Industria de Costa Rica (CANAPI): Calle 17, Avda 10, detrás estatua de San Martín, Apdo 1.783 Goicoechea, 2100 San José; tel. 223-2763; fax 255-4873; e-mail canapi@sol.racsa.co.cr; f. 1963; development, marketing and export of small-scale industries and handicrafts; Pres. and Exec. Dir RODRIGO GONZÁLEZ.

Costa Rican Investment and Development Board (CINDE): Apdo 7.170, 1000 San José; tel. 220-0366; fax 220-4750; e-mail cindes.m@sol.racsa.co.cr; internet www.cinde.co.cr; f. 1983; coalition for development of initiatives to attract foreign investment for production and export of new products; Chair. EMILIO BRUCE; CEO ENRIQUE EGLOFF.

Instituto del Café de Costa Rica: Calle 1, Avdas 18 y 20, Apdo 37, San José; tel. 222-6411; fax 222-2838; www.icafe.go.cr/home page.nsf; f. 1948 to develop the coffee industry, to control production and to regulate marketing; Pres. Lic. LUIS DIEGO ESCALANTE; Exec. Dir GUILLERMO CANET.

CHAMBERS OF COMMERCE

Cámara de Comercio de Costa Rica: Urbanización Tournón, 150m noroeste del parqueo del Centro Comercial El Pueblo, Apdo 1.114, 1000 San José; tel. 221-0005; fax 233-7091; e-mail biofair@sol .racsa.co.cr; f. 1915; 900 mems; Pres. EMILIO BRUCE JIMÉNEZ; Exec. Dir Lic. EUGENIO PIGNATARO PACHECO.

Cámara de Industrias de Costa Rica: 350m sur de la Fuente de la Hispanidad, San Pedro de Montes de Oca, Apdo 10.003, San José; tel. 281-0006; fax 234-6163; e-mail cicr@cicr.com; internet www.cicr.com; Pres. Ing. MARCO VINICIO RUIZ; Exec. Dir MAYI ANTILLON GUERRERO.

Unión Costarricense de Cámaras y Asociaciones de la Empresa Privada (UCCAEP): 1002 Paseo de los Estudiantes, Apdo 539, San José; tel. 290-5595; fax 290-5596; f. 1974; business federation; Pres. Ing. SAMUEL YANKELEWITZ BERGER; Exec. Dir ALVARO RAMÍREZ BOGANTES.

INDUSTRIAL AND TRADE ASSOCIATIONS

Cámara Nacional de Agricultura y Agroindustria: Avda 10-10 bis, Cv. 23, Apdo 1.671, 1000 San José; tel. 221-6864; fax 233-8658;

e-mail cnacr@sol.racsa.co.cr; f. 1947; Pres. Ing. LEONEL PERALTA; Exec. Dir Lic. JOSÉ CARLOS BARQUERO ARCE.

Consejo Nacional de Producción: Calle 36 a 12, Apdo 2.205, San José; tel. 223-6033; fax 233-9660; f. 1948 to encourage agricultural and fish production and to regulate production and distribution of basic commodities; Pres. Ing. JAVIER FLORES GALAGARZA; Man. Lic. VIRGINIA VALVERDE DE MOLINA.

Instituto de Desarrollo Agrícola (IDA): Apdo 5.054, 1000 San José; tel. 224-6066; Exec. Pres. Ing. ROBERTO SOLÓRZANO SANABRIA; Gen. Man. Ing. JORGE ANGEL JIMÉNEZ CALDERÓN.

Instituto Mixto de Ayuda Social (IMAS): Calle 29, Avdas 2 y 4, Apdo 6.213, San José; tel. 225-5555; fax 224-8783; Pres. CLOTILDE FONSECA QUESADA.

Instituto Nacional de Fomento Cooperativo: Apdo 10.103, 1000 San José; tel. 223-4355; fax 255-3835; f. 1973; to encourage the establishment of co-operatives and to provide technical assistance and credit facilities; Pres. Lic. RAFAEL ANGEL ROJAS JIMÉNEZ; Exec. Dir Lic. LUIS ANTONIO MONGE ROMÁN.

MAJOR COMPANIES

The following are some of the major industrial and commercial companies operating in Costa Rica:

Atlas Eléctrica, SA: Carretera a Heredia, Apdo 2.166, 1000 San José; tel. 260-3737; fax 260-3930; e-mail atlasele@sol.racsa.co.cr; f. 1961; manufacturers of domestic cooking and refrigeration appliances; Chair. WALTER KISSLING; Man. Dir JORGE RODRÍGUEZ ULLOA; 750 employees.

Central Azucarera Tempisque, SA: De la Pops en la Savana, 300m oeste 100m sur, San José; tel. 231-5405; fax 688-8185; f. 1988; cultivation and processing of sugar cane; Pres. RICARDO CAMPOLLO; 870 employees.

Cooperativa Agrícola Industrial Victoria, RL: Apdo 176, 3 km del centro de Grecia, 41000 Grecia; tel. 494-1866; fax 444-6346; e-mail caivicto@sol.racsa.co.cr; f. 1949; local coffee and sugar growers and processors; Pres. FRANCISCO MURILLO CARVAJAL; Gen. Man. DAGOBERTO RODRÍGUEZ; 345 employees.

Cooperativa de Productores de Leche, RL (COPROLE): Calles 21–23, Avdas 10–12, Apdo 605, 1000 San José; tel. 223-8822; fax 223-2302; f. 1948; manufacturers of dairy products and fruit juices; Pres. CARLOS VARGAS ALFARO; 2,526 employees.

Corporación Bananera Nacional, SA (CORBANA): Zapote frente casa Presidencial, Apdo 6.504, 1000 San José; tel. 283-4114; fax 253-9117; e-mail corbana@sol.racsa.co.cr; internet www.corban a.com; f. 1973; cultivation and wholesale of agricultural produce, incl. bananas; Pres. VICTOR E. HERRERA ARAUZ; 1,700 employees.

Corporación de Desarrollo Pinero de Costa Rica, SA (PIN-DECO): Apdo 4.084, 1000 San José; tel. 222-9211; fax 233-7808; f. 1978; cultivation and wholesale of agricultural products; Dir-Gen. RODRIGO JIMÉNEZ; 1,700 employees.

Corporación Pipasa, SA: 1.5 km al oeste de la Firestone, La Ribera de Belén, Apdo 22, 4005 San Antonio Belén; tel. 293-4801; fax 293-3492; e-mail pipasa@sol.racsa.co.cr; f. 1969; breeding and wholesale of poultry products; Pres. CALIXTO CHAVES ZAMORA; 1,670 employees.

Corrugados Belén, SA (CORBEL): San Antonio de Belén, Apdo 100, 40005 Belén; tel. 239-0122; fax 239-1023; e-mail corbel@racsa .co.cr; manufacturers of corrugated cardboard boxes; Pres. ALVARO ESQUIVEL; 2,131 employees.

Derivados de Maiz Alimenticios, SA (DEMASA): San Gabriel de Calle Blancos, Apdo 7.299, 1000 San José; tel. 232-9744; fax 231-1935; e-mail demasa@sol.racsa.co.cr; internet www.demasa.co.cr; f. 1986; food processing; Pres. HANS J. BUCHER; 2,500 employees.

Fertilizantes de Centroamérica, SA (FERTICA): Edif. Santiago-millas, Barrio Dent, Apdo 5.350, 1000 San José; tel. 224-3344; fax 224-9147; e-mail fertica@sol.racsa.co.cr; f. 1961; manufacturers of chemical fertilizers; Pres. JAIME CAREY TAGLE; 360 employees.

Florida Ice and Farm Company, SA: Calles 12 y 14, Avda 4, Apdo 10.021, 1000 San José; tel. 221-3722; fax 223-7830; e-mail editavar@ccr.co.cr; f. 1966; Pres. RODOLFO JIMÉNEZ; 1,465 employees.

Hules Técnicos, SA: 150m norte de La Cañada, Apdo 84.140, 1000 San José; tel. 231-2911; fax 220-4502; f. 1976; manufacturers of rubber and rubber products; Pres. SAMUEL GUZOSKI ROSE; 673 employees.

INCSA, Corporación: Barrio Tournón, Frente Periódico La República, Apdo 4.009, 1000 San José; tel. 287-8686; fax 255-2962; e-mail cemincsa@sol.racsa.co.cr; f. 1960 as Industria Nacional de Cemento; name changed to above in 2000; manufacturers of cement; Pres. HARRY J. ZÜRCHER BLEN; 1,500 employees.

Industria de Cerámica Costarricense, SA: La Uruca, 400m norte de Almeda, Apdo 4.120, 1000 San José; tel.232-5266; fax 220-0044; f. 1957; manufacture of ceramic plumbing fixtures; Pres. CARLOS ARAYA LIZANO; 876 employees.

Instituto Costarricense de Acueductos y Alcantarillados: Calle 5, Avda Central, Apdo 5.120, 1000 San José; tel. 255-1125; fax 256-5642; e-mail aya@netsalud.sa.cr; f. 1961; construction and operation of water and sewerage services; Pres. MARIO FERNÁNDEZ ORTIZ; 2,975 employees.

Refinadora Costarricense de Petróleo (Recope): San Guadalupe de Iglesia 200, Apdo 4.351, 1000 San José; tel. 257-6544; fax 255-4993; f. 1961; state petroleum co; Pres. MANUEL ENRIQUE GÓMEZ C.; 1,100 employees.

Standard Fruit Company: Calle 5–7, 1° Avda, Fte Escorial, 1000 San José; tel. 223-8522; fax 255-2466; Dir JERRY VRIESENGA; 3,250 employees.

Textiles Industriales de Centroamerica, SA (TICATEX): Apdo 10.293, 1000 San José; tel. 239-0011; fax 239-0355; e-mail ticagg@intercentro.com; f. 1965; subsidiary of Toyobo Co Ltd, Japan; manufacturers of textiles; Pres. NOBUYA ISHII; 400 employees.

Vidrieria Centroamericana, SA: San Nicolás de Cartago, Apdo 355, 7050 Cartago; tel. 551-2684; fax 551-4473; f. 1973; manufacturers of glass; Pres. WILLHELM STEINVORTH HERRERA; 500 employees.

UTILITIES
Electricity

Cía Nacional de Fuerza y Luz, SA: Calle Central y Primera, Avda 5, Apdo 10.026, 1000 San José; tel. 296-4608; fax 296-3950; internet www.cnfl.go.cr; f. 1941; electricity company; Pres. RAFAEL SEQUEIRA R.; Gen. Man. PABLO COB SABORIO.

Instituto Costarricense de Electricidad—ICE (Costa Rican Electricity Institute): Apdo 10.032, 1000 San José; tel. 220-7720; fax 220-1555; internet www.ice.co.cr; f. 1949; govt agency for power and telecommunications; Exec. Pres. Ing. RAFAEL SEQUEIRA RAMÍREZ; Gen. Man. INGRID HERRMAN.

Servicio Nacional de Electricidad: Apdo 936, 1000 San José; tel. 220-0102; fax 220-0374; co-ordinates the development of the electricity industry; Chair. LEONEL FONSECA.

Water

Instituto Costarricense de Acueductos y Alcantarillados: Avda Central, Calle 5, Apdo 5.120, 1000 San José; tel. 233-2155; fax 222-2259; water and sewerage; Pres. MARIO FERNÁNDEZ ORTIZ.

TRADE UNIONS

Central del Movimiento de Trabajadores Costarricenses—CMTC (Costa Rican Workers' Union): Calle 20, Avdas 3 y 5, Apdo 4.137, 1000 San José; tel. 221-7701; fax 221-3353; e-mail cmtccr@solracsa.co.cr; Pres. DENNIS CABEZAS BADILLA.

Confederación Auténtica de Trabajadores Democráticos (Democratic Workers' Union): Calle 13, Avdas 10 y 12, Solera; tel. 253-2971; Pres. LUIS ARMANDO GUTIÉRREZ; Sec.-Gen. Prof. CARLOS VARGAS.

Confederación Costarricense de Trabajadores Democráticos (Costa Rican Confederation of Democratic Workers): Calles 3 y 5, Avda 12, Apdo 2.167, San José; tel. 222-1981; f. 1966; mem. ICFTU and ORIT; Sec.-Gen. LUIS ARMANDO GUTIÉRREZ R.; 50,000 mems.

Confederación Unitaria de Trabajadores—CUT: Calles 1 y 3, Avda 12, Casa 142, Apdo 186, 1009 San José; tel. 233-4188; f. 1980 from a merger of the Federación Nacional de Trabajadores Públicos and the Confederación General de Trabajadores; 53 affiliated unions; Sec.-Gen. GILBER BERMÚDEZ UMAÑA; c. 75,000 mems.

Federación Sindical Agraria Nacional—FESIAN (National Agrarian Confederation): Apdo 2.167, 1000 San José; tel. 233-5897; 20,000 member families; Sec.-Gen. JUAN MEJÍA VILLALOBOS.

The **Consejo Permanente de los Trabajadores,** formed in 1986, comprises six union organizations and two teachers' unions.

Transport

Ministry of Public Works and Transport: Apdo 10.176, 1000 San José; tel. 226-7311; fax 227-1434; the Ministry is responsible for setting tariffs, allocating funds, maintaining existing systems and constructing new ones.

Cámara Nacional de Transportes: San José; national chamber of transport.

RAILWAYS

In 1998 there were 581.0 km of railway track.

Instituto Costarricense de Ferrocarriles (INCOFER): Calle 2, Avda 20, Apdo 1, 1009 San José; tel. 221-0777; fax 257-7220; e-mail incofer@sol.racsa.co.cr; f. 1985; government-owned; 471 km, of which 388 km are electrified.

INCOFER comprised:

División I: Atlantic sector running between Limón, Río Frío, Valle la Estrella and Siquirres. Main line of 109 km, with additional 120 km of branch lines, almost exclusively for transport of bananas; services resumed in 1999.

División II: Pacific sector running from San José to Puntarenas and Caldera; 116 km of track, principally for transport of cargo.

Note: In 1995 INCOFER suspended most operations, pending privatization; in 2000 plans were proposed to re-open INCOFER for cargo transport only.

ROADS

In 1997 there were 35,597 km of roads, of which 7,405 km were main roads and 28,192 km were secondary roads. An estimated 21% of the total road network was paved in 1998.

SHIPPING

Local services operate between the Costa Rican ports of Puntarenas and Limón and those of Colón and Cristóbal in Panama and other Central American ports. The multi-million dollar project at Caldera on the Gulf of Nicoya is now in operation as the main Pacific port; Puntarenas is being used as the second port. The Caribbean coast is served by the port complex of Limón/Moín. International services are operated by various foreign shipping lines. In 2000 plans were announced to open up the ports to private investment and operation from 2002.

Junta de Administración Portuaria y de Desarrollo Económico de la Vertiente Atlántica (JAPDEVA): Calle 17, Avda 7, Apdo 5.330, 1000 San José; tel. 233-5301; state agency for the development of Atlantic ports; Exec. Pres. Ing. JORGE ARTURO CASTRO HERRERA.

Instituto Costarricense de Puertos del Pacífico (INCOP): Calle 36, Avda 3, Apdo 543, 1000 San José; tel. 223-7111; fax 223-9527; f. 1972; state agency for the development of Pacific ports; Exec. Pres. GERARDO MEDINA MADRIZ.

CIVIL AVIATION

Costa Rica's main international airport is the Juan Santamaría Airport, 16 km from San José at El Coco. Following a report by the US Federal Aviation Administration, the Government began negotiating a contract of expansion and modernization, to begin in 2001. There is a second international airport, the Daniel Oduber Quirós Airport, at Liberia and there are regional airports at Limón and Pavas (Tobías Bolaños Airport).

Aero Costa Rica: San José; regional carrier; Chair. CALIXTO CHAVEL; Gen. Man. JUAN FERNÁNDEZ.

Líneas Aéreas Costarricenses, SA—LACSA (Costa Rican Airlines): Edif. Lacsa, La Uruca, Apdo 1.531, San José; tel. 290-2727; fax 232-4178; internet www.flylatinamerica.com; f. 1945; operates international services within Latin America and to North America; Chair. ALONSO LARA; Pres. JOSÉ G. ROJAS.

Servicios Aéreos Nacionales, SA (SANSA): Paseo Colón, Centro Colón, Apdo 999, 1.007 San José; tel. 233-2714; fax 255-2176; subsidiary of LACSA; international, regional and domestic scheduled passenger and cargo services; Man. Dir CARLOS MANUEL DELGADO AGUILAR.

Servicios de Carga Aérea (SERCA): Aeropuerto Internacional Juan Santamaría, Apdo 6.855, San José; f. 1982; operates cargo service from San José.

Tourism

Costa Rica boasts a system of nature reserves and national parks unique in the world, which cover one-third of the country. The main tourist features are the Irazú and Poás volcanoes, the Orosí valley and the ruins of the colonial church at Ujarras. Tourists also visit San José, the capital, the Pacific beaches of Guanacaste and Puntarenas, and the Caribbean beaches of Limón. In 2001 there were numerous hotel and resort construction projects underway in the Guanacaste province. The project was being undertaken by the Instituto Costarricense de Turismo. In May 2001 one of the country's principal tourist sites, La Casona de Santa Rosa, was almost completely destroyed by fire. Some 942,853 tourists visited Costa Rica in 1998, when tourism receipts totalled an estimated US $830m. In this year most visitors came from the USA (36.9% of the total) and Nicaragua (18.0%). There were 27,103 hotel rooms in Costa Rica in 1998.

Cámara Nacional de Turismo (Canatur): tel. 234-6222; fax 253-8102; e-mail info@tourism.co.cr; internet www.costarica.tourism.co.cr.

Instituto Costarricense de Turismo: Edif. Genaro Valverde, Calles 5 y 7, Avda 4, Apdo 777, 1000 San José; tel. 223-1733; fax

223-5107; internet www.tourism-costarica.com; f. 1955; Exec. Pres. Ing. CARLOS ROESCH CARRANZA.

Defence

Costa Rica has had no armed forces since 1948. In August 2000 Rural and Civil Guards totalled 2,000 and 4,400 men, respectively. In addition, there were 2,000 Border Security Police. In 1985 an anti-terrorist battalion was formed, composed of 750 Civil Guards; in 1994 it was superseded by the Immediate Action Unit.

Defence Expenditure: Spending on the security forces and on border and maritime patrols was 25,600m. colones (US $86m.) in 2000.

Minister of Public Security: ROGELIO RAMOS MARTÍNEZ.

Education

Education in Costa Rica is free, and is compulsory between six and 15 years of age. Primary education begins at the age of six and lasts for six years. Official secondary education consists of a three-year basic course, followed by a more highly specialized course of two years. In 1997 an estimated 91.8% (males 91.1%; females 92.5%) of children aged six to 11 were enrolled at primary schools, while 55.8% (males 54.7%; females 56.9%) of those aged 12 to 16 received secondary education. In 1998 there were 3,711 primary schools and in 1996 there were 358 secondary schools. In 2000 there were 39 universities, including one 'open university'. In 1998, according to estimates by the UN Development Programme, Costa Rica's adult illiteracy rate was 4.7% (males 4.7%; females 4.6%). In 1996 government expenditure on the education system was about 22.8% of total spending.

Bibliography

For works on Central America generally, see Select Bibliography (Books).

Ameringer, C. *Don Pepe: A Political Biography of José Figueres of Costa Rica*. Albuquerque, NM, University of New Mexico Press.

Arias Sánchez, O. R. 'Costa Rica: At the Centre of the Storm', in *Socialist Affairs*, No. 2. 1986.

Bell, J. P. *Crisis in Costa Rica: The 1948 Revolution*. Austin, TX, University of Texas Press.

Biesanz, M., et al. *The Ticos: Culture and Social Change in Costa Rica*. Boulder, CO, Lynne Rienner, 1998.

Booth, J. A. *Costa Rica: Quest for Democracy*. Boulder, CO, Westview Press, 1999.

Costa Rica Research Group. *Executive Report on Strategies in Costa Rica (Strategic Planning Series)*. San Diego, CA, Icon Group International, 2000.

Creedman, T. S. *Historical Dictionary of Costa Rica*. Metuchen, NJ, Scarecrow Press, 1978.

Evans, S. *The Green Republic: A Conservation History of Costa Rica*. Austin, TX, University of Texas Press, 1999.

Helmuth, C. *Culture and Customs of Costa Rica*. Westport, CT, Greenwood Publishing Group, 2000.

Longley, K. *The Sparrow and the Hawk: Costa Rica and the United States During the Rise of José Figueres*. Tuscaloosa, AL, University of Alabama Press, 1997.

Ramírez, M. *Costa Rica's Refugee Program and the Prospects for Repatriation of Nicaraguan Refugees*. Austin, TX, Central America Resource Center, 1988.

Williams, P. J. *The Catholic Church and Politics in Nicaragua and Costa Rica*. Basingstoke, Macmillan, 1989.

CUBA

Area: 110,860 sq km (42,803 sq miles).

Population (official estimate at mid-2001): 11,229,688.

Capital: Havana (La Habana), estimated population 2,189,716 on 31 December 1999.

Language: Spanish.

Religion: Mainly Christianity (Roman Catholicism predominates).

Climate: Tropical, but tempered by sea breezes; annual average temperature is 25°C (77°F); hurricanes are frequent.

Time: GMT –5 hours (GMT –4 hours in summer).

Public Holidays

2002: 1 January (Liberation Day), 1 May (Labour Day), 25–27 July (Anniversary of the 1953 Revolution), 10 October (Wars of Independence Day), 25 December (Christmas Day).

2003: 1 January (Liberation Day), 1 May (Labour Day), 25–27 July (Anniversary of the 1953 Revolution), 10 October (Wars of Independence Day), 25 December (Christmas Day).

Currency: Cuban peso; 100 pesos = £69.84 = US $100.00 = €112.66 (30 April 2001).

Weights and Measures: The metric system is in force.

Basic Economic Indicators

	1998	1999	2000
Gross domestic product (million pesos at constant 1981 prices)	14,754.1	15,674.4	16,556.4
GDP per head (pesos at constant 1981 prices)	1,324.4	1,404.5	1,478.4
GDP (million pesos at current prices)	23,900.8	25,503.6	27,634.7
GDP per head (pesos at current prices)	2,145.5	2,281.2	2,463.3
Annual growth of real GDP (%)	1.2	6.2	5.6
Annual growth of real GDP per head (%)	0.6	6.0	5.3
Government budget (million pesos at current prices):			
Revenue	12,502.0	13,419.2	14,505.0
Expenditure	13,061.7	14,030.9	15,243.0
Merchandise imports f.o.b. (million pesos)	3,987.3	4,181.2	4,323.2
Merchandise exports f.o.b. (million pesos)	1,819.1	1,512.2	1,456.1
Balance of payments (current account, US $ million)	–392.4	–456.1	n.a.

Economically active population (1998): 3,753,600.

Unemployment (official estimate, 2000): 5.5%.

Total foreign debt (estimate, December 1999): US $12,000m.

Life expectancy (years at birth, 1990–95): 75 (males 74; female 77).

Infant mortality rate (per 1,000 live births, 1993): 9.4.

Adult population with HIV/AIDS (15–49 years, 1999): 0.03%.

School enrolment ratio (6–17 years, 1996): 93%.

Adult literacy rate (15 years and over, estimate, 2000): 96.4% (males 96.4%; females 96.5%).

Energy consumption per head (kg of coal equivalent, 1998): 1,066.

Carbon dioxide emissions per head (metric tons, 1997): 2.3.

Passenger motor cars in use (per 1,000 of population, estimate, 1997): 15.6.

Television receivers in use (per 1,000 of population, 1997): 239.

Personal computers in use (per 1,000 of population, 1999): 9.9.

History

MELANIE JONES

Cuban archaeological and anthropological studies identified a number of ethnic groups that lived on the island prior to the Spanish invasion of 1511. Christopher Columbus, the Genoese navigator in the service of the Spanish Crown, who landed on Cuba in 1492, made reports of a relatively sophisticated agricultural society in parts of the island. Researchers identified this group as the Taínos. There were Siboneys and Guanahuatabeys also in evidence prior to the Conquest. The indigenous population is calculated to have reached a peak of some 100,000 by 1511, before falling drastically to a mere 4,000 by 1550.

In 1500 a Spanish cartographer, Juan de la Cosa, drew a map of Cuba very similar to the one used to this day, in spite of Columbus' insistence that the island formed part of the continental mainland. However, Cuba was largely forgotten by Spain until the early 16th century. It was only in 1508 that another Spaniard, Sebastian de Ocampo, completed a circumnavigation of Cuba, thereby conclusively establishing its insular nature. The information gathered on this expedition was later to be used in the Spanish occupation of the island.

The Spanish conquest of Cuba took from 1511 until 1515. Indigenous resistance was destroyed, and with the execution of the political leader, Hatuey, Spanish dominance was secured. The first seven townships were founded during this period: Baracoa (1512); Bayamo (1513); Trinidad, Sancti Spíritus and Havana (1514); and Puerto Príncipe and Santiago de Cuba (1515). The last became the first capital of Cuba, remaining so for some decades.

COLONIAL RULE AND THE INDEPENDENCE WARS

The colonial administrative apparatus was installed in the 16th century: *cabildos* (municipal councils) had authority over the townships, with a governor representing the Spanish Crown. The trade department, based in Seville, controlled colonial commerce, the other major power being the Roman Catholic Church. Efforts were at first focused on developing the mining industry. However, as deposits were exhausted and the indigenous population exterminated, attention was turned to agriculture, and a new, enslaved labour force was introduced from Africa. The first sugar mills appeared in the late 16th century and tobacco cultivation spread throughout the 17th century. However, the threat of piracy grew ever greater. When a French privateer, Jacques de Sores, occupied Havana (by now the capital) in 1555, causing the governor to flee, the Spanish authorities were forced to reconsider the country's strategic importance. Fortifications were built around the port, which had become a port of call for fleets *en route* to Spain with cargoes of gold and silver from the Americas.

The early centuries of poor economic development were also characterized by totalitarian domination on the part of Spain and the population of the island frequently resorted to dependence on contraband. Spain itself was weakened by constant wars with other European Powers, and although the reign of Philip V (1700–1746) resulted in some economic progress, the central government's over-zealous control of the tobacco industry led to a number of protests which were violently crushed.

The British occupied Havana for a period of 11 months during 1762–63, eventually returning it to Spain in exchange for Florida. However, this short period created a number of trading possibilities for Cuba, and a certain divergence between the native Creoles and the Spanish emerged. The rapid expansion of the sugar trade defined the development of the Cuban economy at the end of the 18th century. Cuba was to become the world leader in sugar production, a situation that was to have a profound influence on political events even into the 20th century.

At a time when the slave trade was experiencing a general decline, Cuba saw the influx of some 500,000 slaves over a period of 50 years. Owing to the violent slave rebellion in the nearby French territory of Santo Domingo (now Haiti) in 1791, and the fear inspired by the growing numbers of blacks, the Creoles delayed any thoughts of pursuing independence from Spain. The slave trade was made illegal in 1817, but 'trafficking' was widespread. Rebellions were dealt with swiftly and brutally, and slave resistance tended to be manifested in the form of 'runaways' (*cimarrones*), who established communities in remote mountain areas known as *palenques*. The effective abolition of slavery did not take place until 1886.

Cuba was the last Spanish colony in the Americas, and only broke free from Spanish rule after three wars of independence. The first, known as the Ten-Year War or Yara Revolution, commenced in October 1868, when a landowner, Carlos Manuel de Céspedes (known as the 'Father of the Nation'), freed his slaves from the Demajagua sugar mill. Weaknesses were evident on both sides, the Spanish impeded by the chaos that followed the fall of their monarch, Isabella II, and the Cuban forces divided by an internal struggle between the reformists, those seeking independence and those who saw their future in annexation by the USA. The war finally ended in 1878, when the Zanjón Pact was signed, introducing freedom for rebel slaves and the extension of political rights to Cuba. However, attempts at reconciliation in the country were frustrated by the Baraguá protest, in which a new, mixed-race leader, Antonio Maceo, called for the full abolition of slavery and complete independence. Thus began the second conflict, known as the Little War, which lasted for only two years. Then, in 1894 Spain terminated the existing trade agreement between Cuba and the USA, causing an economic crisis. The final campaign began in February 1895, after the radical and popular elements had gained widespread support. José Martí, the ideologue of the independence forces, who had long warned of the dangers of US interference, was killed in an early skirmish. The war was long and bloody, eventually prompting the USA to intervene.

US INTERVENTION AND THE 'PUPPET' REPUBLIC

From as early as 1805 US agents were instructed to monitor events in Cuba. On more than one occasion the USA attempted to enter into negotiations with Spain over Cuba, and prior to the US Civil War (1861–65) many slave owners harboured the hope that annexation would protect their interests. However, the USA never officially recognized the struggle of the *mambises*, as the independence forces were known, for both commercial and strategic reasons. With an end to the Cuban war for independence approaching, the mysterious explosion in February 1898 of the USS *Maine*, anchored in Havana port to provide protection for US citizens, presented the USA with the pretext to intervene against Spain. In a brief campaign US forces captured Cuba, Puerto Rico and the Philippines, so bringing an end to the war and to much of what remained of the Spanish colonial empire.

The Treaty of Paris, signed by the USA and Spain in December 1898, marked an official end to the hostilities and a formal renunciation of Spanish sovereignty in Cuba. There followed three years of US military occupation until, on 20 May 1902, Cuba was granted independence. Tomás Estrada Palma, a pragmatic proponent of annexation to the USA, became the first President of the new Republic. Estrada Palma had signed the Platt Amendment in the previous year, by virtue of which the USA reserved the right to intervene in Cuba and to maintain a military installation on the island. Indeed, a second period of US intervention lasted from 1906 to 1909, following a rebellion by disgruntled liberals who disputed the re-election of Estrada Palma to the presidency. Thereafter the country suffered successive political and economic crises, a situation compounded by widespread corruption.

In 1924–33 Gerardo Machado occupied the presidency in what was known as the 'bloody decade'. This period was characterized by a succession of scandals concerning political corruption, by an incipient trade-union movement and by the first signs of organized crime. A number of student and worker groups emerged, including the Federation of University Students (FEU), the Anti-Imperialist League and the José Martí People's University for Workers. The Communist Party was formed in 1925 by Carlos Baliño, a close collaborator of Martí, and Julio Antonio Mella, who was assassinated in Mexico in 1929. The parties were illegal and their leaders persecuted. In 1929 the Great Depression began and sugar prices plummeted, causing student and labour opposition groups to join forces in an attempt to bring about change. In March 1930 the country experienced an abortive general strike and in September a student radical was assassinated, unleashing a wave of public protest. By 1933 the country was in the midst of violent unrest, and in July the USA sent a diplomat, Sumner Welles, to mediate. The following month a general strike led the army to abandon support for Machado and he was overthrown by a military coup. Carlos Manuel de Céspedes (the younger) was installed as President. Machado fled to the Bahamas and later took up residence in the USA. In September the Sergeants' Revolt, led by Sgt (later Gen.) Fulgencio Batista Zaldivar, in turn overthrew Céspedes, who was replaced by Ramón Grau San Martín, a professor from the University of Havana.

Grau's 100-day Government comprised representatives from the entire political spectrum, with student leader Antonio Guiteras appointed Minister of the Interior. The Government introduced a number of social benefits, improving working conditions and land distribution, and gave women the right to vote. The USA, however, refused to recognize the Government and Grau resigned in 1934, leaving the way clear for Batista, who was to dominate Cuban politics for the next 25 years. Batista was the guiding force behind a series of 'puppet' presidents. In 1934 the Platt Amendment was abrogated, and a new Reciprocity Treaty enacted in its place. The workers' movement evolved with the establishment of the Confederation of Cuban Workers (CTC). In 1940 a new Constitution, aspiring to democracy and social justice, was completed, and Batista was proclaimed the constitutionally elected President, with the support of US investors.

Grau assumed the presidency once again in 1944 at the head of the Authentic Party, but this was a shadow of the Government of 1933. Carlos Prío Socarrás succeeded him in 1948, but his term was brought to an end in 1952 when Batista seized power in a bloodless coup. Eduardo Chibás left the Authentic Party in 1947 to form the more radical Orthodox Party. A strong candidate for the presidency, Chibás publicly committed suicide during a radio broadcast in 1951.

On assuming power Batista revoked the Constitution of 1940, annulling the legislative functions of government and any semblance of democracy. In the following year, the first signs of the pending revolution were manifested. On 26 July 1953 a radical opposition group, led by Fidel Castro Ruz, staged an assault on the Moncada garrison in Santiago de Cuba. The attack failed, and Castro was imprisoned with those companions who were not killed in the attempt. The speech made by Castro in his own defence, recorded under the title of 'History Will Absolve Me', became the doctrine of the new revolutionary forces. Castro was sentenced to 15 years' imprisonment. In 1954, unopposed, Batista was elected to another four-year term in government. In an effort to court public opinion, President Batista released Castro into exile in 1955 under a general amnesty. He departed for Mexico as the leader of the newly formed '26 July Movement' to organize resistance forces against Batista. The future guerrillas, among them a young Argentine doctor, Ernesto ('Che') Guevara, followed a rigorous theoretical-military training programme.

FIDEL CASTRO'S REVOLUTION

In December 1956 Castro and 81 followers landed in Cuba aboard the yacht *Granma*, miles from the planned location and missing the pre-arranged date of 30 November. The expedition was widely believed to have been a failure, since all but 12 revolutionaries were soon captured or killed. This nucleus, however, was sufficient to initiate a new guerrilla movement in the Sierra Maestra mountains of south-eastern Cuba. In March 1957 the University Directorate (Directorio Universitario), a group of intellectuals organized by José Antonio Echeverría,

attacked the presidential palace in an attempt to assassinate Batista. The attack failed and Echeverría was killed, after having announced Batista's demise on a radio broadcast. However, as a result of the attempt President Batista was seen to be vulnerable, and his sporadic acts of retaliation further eroded his popularity.

The guerrilla movement expanded throughout the countryside and was paralleled by growing insurgency in the cities, which combined acts of sabotage against economic targets with an increasing number of political assassinations and kidnappings. An attempt to overthrow President Batista by means of a general strike in April 1958 failed. The Government planned a retaliatory offensive, but this was thwarted when Raúl Castro Ruz, Fidel Castro's brother, took several prominent foreigners, mostly North Americans, as hostages, thus provoking diplomatic pressure on Batista by the US Government, which imposed an arms embargo, tantamount to a withdrawal of support. This had a devastating effect on the morale of the armed forces, and the election, later that year, of the official candidate provoked further consternation among those who still hoped for a political solution. Meanwhile, revolutionary activity was gaining momentum. In Santa Clara, Guevara's forces received ample assistance from the local population and widespread support for the revolutionary forces was evident. On 1 January 1959 the army seized power. With Batista's subsequent flight from Cuba and the collapse of his regime, Castro's rebel forces occupied Havana.

Castro first unified all the remaining military groups under his control, incorporating the remnants of the University Directorate in order to avoid a repetition of the divisions in leadership that had brought an end to the revolution of 1933. In January 1959 a new Constitution, the Fundamental Law, was introduced. Manuel Urrutia Lléo was appointed President and in March Fidel Castro took the post of Prime Minister, with his brother, Raúl, as his deputy. Once established, the first government policies were swiftly effected, with the expropriation and nationalization of all major enterprises, including foreign sugar estates, and agrarian reform. Internal conflict and opposition from certain sectors of the population led Castro to consider resignation, but public opinion generally seemed to support the guerrilla leader, and so it was Urrutia who resigned. Osvaldo Dorticós Torrado was named President in his place. As measures grew more radical, acts of violence, conspiracy and desertion escalated. Approximately 700,000 mainly white, middle-class Cubans emigrated, their places, notably in the administration, filled by Communist militants. Prominent among them was Che Guevara, who was, for a time, the ideological guiding force of the revolution.

In April and May 1959 Castro visited the US cities of New York and Washington, DC. He was well received, in spite of adverse publicity over the execution of Batista supporters, but he failed to establish the desired links with the US Government. By May 1960, as Cuba and the USSR re-established diplomatic relations, those with the USA were steadily deteriorating. In July the sugar quota was suspended and in October all US business interests in Cuba were expropriated, without compensation. A full economic embargo was imposed by the USA in the same month. In January 1961 the USA severed its diplomatic links with Cuba, and pressurized other Latin American countries to do likewise. In 1962 Cuba was suspended from the Organization of American States (OAS), Mexico alone maintaining its traditional links with the country. Cuba became an essential part of the US external and internal political agenda, the Cuban exile community having become a powerful political lobby within the USA. In April 1961, with the support of the US administration, the exiled forces launched an unsuccessful attack on the Bay of Pigs (Bahía de Cochinos). The failure of the invasion led Castro to proclaim Cuba a Socialist state 'of the poor, by the poor and for the poor' and all remaining internal dissent was suppressed. Some 120,000 exiles were taken prisoner and their trials broadcast throughout the country.

The new Government favoured the Soviet model of economic planning, 'democratic socialism'. Collectivization and industrialization were the main ingredients of the Cuban experiment, with a brief incursion into the Marxist policies of the Chinese Revolution (favouring agriculture) in the late 1960s. However, the attempt at industrialization was, to a large extent, unsuccessful, since although the country had mineral deposits, it had no known petroleum reserves. In addition, Cuba had no history of industrialization, the economy having been dominated by sugar production, and Soviet planning and techniques were inadequate for Cuba's needs. However, in July 1972 Cuba's links with the USSR were increased when the country joined the Council for Mutual Economic Assistance (CMEA), an organization linking the USSR and other Communist states. As a result of its membership, Cuba received preferential trading rights and technical advice from the USSR and other Eastern European countries. Between 1959 and 1984, in spite of Cuba's continued status as an underdeveloped country, substantial advances were made in the sectors of education and health, and a thriving cultural programme emerged. Illiteracy was virtually eradicated and infant mortality brought in line with developed countries.

At the political level, in 1961 the numerous pro-government groups which had evolved were merged under one overarching group, the Organizaciones Revolucionarias Integradas (ORI—Integrated Revolutionary Organizations). Highly criticized for its incompetence, the ORI was renamed the Partido Unido de la Revolución Socialista Cubana (PURSC—United Party of the Cuban Socialist Revolution) in 1962, Castro having declared himself a Marxist-Leninist, and in 1965 this in turn became the Partido Comunista de Cuba (PCC—Communist Party of Cuba).

In October 1962 the friction between Cuba and the USA ignited into an international incident known as the Cuban Missile Crisis, after US reconnaissance aircraft detected the presence of Soviet nuclear warheads on the island. As the USA established a naval blockade, the possibility of a superpower confrontation over Cuba seemed imminent. The crisis was eventually resolved between the USSR and the USA, and the missile bases were dismantled, but Cuba's position was, humiliatingly, ignored.

In 1965 Guevara left Cuba to continue the revolutionary struggle abroad. The abject failure of the Cuban style of guerrilla warfare (*foquismo*) and Guevara's subsequent death in Bolivia in 1967 dealt a bitter blow to Cuba's internationalist aspirations. Nevertheless, Che Guevara was seen as a martyr of the revolution, widely respected in Cuba and a revolutionary icon worldwide. The return of his body from Bolivia in July 1997, for burial in Cuba, was a national event.

In 1970 Cuba suffered another reverse in its highly publicized campaign to produce a sugar harvest of 10m. metric tons, by means of which the country aspired to emerge from its condition of economic underdevelopment. This was to be the decisive test for the revolution and vast amounts of resources were diverted from other sectors. The failure, ultimately, to reach this target only served to emphasize the country's economic dependence on sugar and tobacco. So began a period of gentle liberalization, described as a 'retreat into socialism'. The 1971–85 period introduced decentralization and material incentives, but was accompanied by the expansion of the 'black' (parallel, illegal) market.

In June 1974 Cuba's first elections since the Revolution were held for municipal offices in Matanzas province. The following year marked the beginning of Cuban participation in the independence struggles of African nations such as Angola and Ethiopia, which lasted until the early 1990s. It was also the year of the First Congress of the PCC and the proclamation of a new, Socialist Constitution, under which Fidel Castro added Head of State to his former title of Head of Government in 1976. In October elections to municipal assemblies were held. The assemblies subsequently elected delegates to provincial assemblies and deputies to the Asamblea Nacional del Poder Popular (National Assembly of People's Power), inaugurated as 'the supreme organ of state' in December 1976. The Asamblea Nacional in turn selected the members of a new Council of State, with Castro as President. The second Congress of the PCC was held in April 1980.

In April 1980 restrictions on emigration were temporarily lifted after 10,000 people occupied the grounds of the Peruvian embassy. The result was the emigration of some 125,000 Cubans to the USA (agreement was later reached on the return of some 2,500 emigrants deemed 'excludable', after they had served sentences in US prisons). In April 1982 tourism and investment in Cuba by US nationals was prohibited by the US authorities,

although there was a trend towards improved links between Cuba and other Latin American countries at this time. A brief clash between US troops and Cuban construction workers during the 1983 US invasion of Grenada resulted in a renewed deterioration in relations between the two countries. In December 1984 agreement was reached on the resumption of Cuban immigration into the USA. However, when the Voice of America broadcasting network founded Radio Martí, a station transmitting news and other programmes from Florida (USA) to Cuba, relations became further strained, and the immigration accord was suspended until October 1997.

The Third Congress of the PCC, held in February 1986, resulted in the retirement of many veterans of the Revolution, and the promotion of women and blacks. In the same year Mother Teresa of Calcutta, the Nobel Peace Prize laureate, visited the island and contact with the Roman Catholic Church was restored. In a renewed effort to increase diplomatic links, Cuba honoured an agreement to withdraw all troops from Angola within a period of 30 months; this withdrawal was completed by May 1991. In September 1988 Cuba established diplomatic links with the European Community (from 1993 known as the European Union—EU).

From 1986 there was a shift away from the liberal policies of previous years, which were replaced by a process of 'rectification of errors and correction of deviant trends'. In June 1989 the conviction and subsequent execution of Gen. Arnaldo Ochoa, one of only five Heroes of the Revolution, signalled a serious political crisis in Cuba. Ochoa, who had commanded Cuban troops in Angola and Ethiopia, was accused of drugs-trafficking with the Colombian Medellín cartel and of involvement with illegal ivory and diamond sales in Angola. Important government figures were implicated, and both the Minister of the Interior and the Minister of Transport were imprisoned as a consequence of the affair. It remained unclear whether the accused had been acting for themselves in extending officially endorsed black-market operations to evade the US trade embargo, or whether the Cuban leadership itself was implicated. However, the publicity received by the scandal seriously undermined the credibility of the regime.

THE SPECIAL PERIOD FROM 1990

Until the advent of the Soviet reformist concept of *perestroika* (restructuring) in the mid-1980s and the subsequent demise of the USSR, Cuba had received critical economic and military assistance from the Communist superpower. However, with the final dissolution of the Soviet Federation in December 1991, Cuba saw this special relationship evaporate. In 1991 the CMEA was dissolved, leaving Cuba effectively isolated on both economic and ideological fronts. With the 1990 electoral defeat of the Sandinista regime in Nicaragua, Cuba lost the last of its allies in the region.

The declaration of a 'special period in time of peace' in late 1990 was marked by increasing shortages; Cuba's petroleum supplies having been severely curtailed, ox-carts and Chinese bicycles became the chief modes of transport. The crisis reached its peak in 1993. Many state enterprises were closed owing to a lack of fuel and raw materials, and key sectors, such as education and public health, were seriously affected. The adoption by the USA of the Cuban Democracy Act, also known as the Torricelli Act, in October 1992, tightened the embargo, further compounding the country's economic problems.

A meeting of the Asamblea Nacional, convened in July 1992, granted Castro, as Head of State, new emergency powers, introduced direct elections to the Asamblea Nacional, outlawed discrimination on the grounds of religious beliefs, and permitted foreign investment. Member of the 'old guard' were replaced by new figures. In the same year Castro offered his abdication in exchange for the suspension of the US trade embargo by the US President-elect, Bill Clinton.

While indicating his distaste for economic reform, Castro acknowledged its necessity. The reforms introduced were designed to allow space for the functioning of market mechanisms, under extensive state regulation, while safeguarding the standards of social welfare. In July 1993 a 30-year ban on the possession of foreign currency was lifted in an attempt to recoup the 'hard' or convertible currency, principally US dollars, circulating in the black market, and to increase remittances from

Cuban exiles. This move introduced, in effect, a two-tier economy in which pesos would buy basic foodstuffs and US dollars would purchase most other goods. State farms were decentralized, with the formation of the semi-autonomous Unidades Básicas de Producción Cooperativa (UBPCs—Units of Basic Co-operative Production). Other reforms included the growing list of enterprises open to self-employment, such as the *paladares* (restaurants in private homes).

In April 1994 four new government ministries (Economic Co-operation, Economy and Planning, Finance and Prices, and Foreign Investment) were created, reflecting a significant change in the country's economic management. However, the economic restructuring came too late for some, and in July and August local ferries were hijacked and disturbances broke out throughout Havana. Castro made a television appearance announcing that if the US Government failed to halt illegal emigration, Cuba would suspend its own travel restrictions. Thousands of Cubans put out to sea in makeshift craft in the 'rafters' exodus, only to be returned to Cuba and held at the US naval base at Guantánamo, as President Clinton revoked the 1966 Cuban Adjustment Act, which conferred automatic refugee status on Cubans, until then one of the most firmly entrenched parts of US policy. Border restrictions were eventually reinstated in September, as part of a bilateral immigration accord, in which the USA resolved to admit a minimum of 20,000 Cubans to the USA each year. Negotiations continued until May 1995, when the USA made a commitment to repatriate all Cubans reaching the US coasts illegally.

US–Cuban relations were once again strained in February 1996 when two light aircraft belonging to the US-based exile group, Brothers to the Rescue, were shot down after having allegedly entered Cuban airspace. As a direct response, in March 1996 President Clinton signed the punitive legislation, known as the Cuban Liberty and Solidarity Act (commonly referred to as the Helms-Burton Act, after its instigators), which threatened to impose sanctions on countries trading with or investing in Cuba. Canada and Mexico sought to dispute the extraterritorial nature of the Act under the provisions of the North American Free Trade Agreement (NAFTA) and the EU requested a disputes panel with the World Trade Organization (WTO). The complaint was subsequently dropped in return for a US commitment to waive sanctions against member countries doing business in Cuba.

In January 1998 Cuba received world-wide publicity because of the official visit of Pope John Paul II to the island. Although the Pope openly questioned certain aspects of official policy, he also condemned the US trade embargo. In February the Cuban authorities responded to papal intercessions for clemency towards political prisoners, releasing almost 200 of some 270 prisoners listed by the Vatican.

An increasing number of religious, humanitarian and business organizations became involved in the dispute over trade sanctions. In January 1999 the US Government announced the introduction of measures to broaden remittances and humanitarian flights from the USA to Cuba, to increase co-operation in areas of mutual interest, such as drugs-trafficking and migration issues, and to encourage people-to-people contacts. US sources stressed that the aim of the measures was to facilitate a peaceful transition of power without providing any direct assistance to the Cuban Government.

In November 2000 the UN General Assembly passed a resolution by an overwhelming majority condemning the US trade embargo on Cuba for the ninth time; only Israel and the Marshall Islands supported the US vote in favour of continuing the sanctions. In late 2000 the US Congress requested a detailed study from the International Trade Administration on the economic impact of the sanctions. A report from an independent 'think tank' in the USA, the Council of Foreign Relations, advocated an easing of restrictions in relations with Cuba, while stopping short of an end to all sanctions. It emphasized that current policy served to alienate sectors of Cuban society that were important to the US Government, such as the Roman Catholic Church and certain dissident groups. In 2000 the Cuban economy, with increased foreign investment and a series of modernization reforms, was showing some signs of recovery. A Ministry of Auditing and Control was established in May 2001 in an effort to expose corruption and to improve economic efficiency.

INTERNATIONAL RELATIONS

Cuba continued to strengthen its links throughout Latin America and the Caribbean and was admitted as a full member of the Latin American Integration Association (LAIA, known as the Asociación Latinoamericana de Integración—ALADI, in Spanish) in November 1998. While Cuba's normally solid relations with Mexico deteriorated in 2000 upon the election to the presidency of Vicente Fox, who secured Cuba's exclusion from the San José Agreement, in November 2000 Castro's friend and ally, Venezuelan President Lt-Col (retd) Hugo Chávez Frías, agreed to supply one-third of the country's petroleum requirements, on preferential terms. In exchange, Cuba was to send medical and sports services to Venezuela. In November 1999 Cuba's hosting of the Annual Ibero-American Summit was proclaimed 'a diplomatic triumph'. Efforts from Cuban exiles in Miami (USA) to encourage a boycott of the event were, to a large extent, thwarted, with just three Presidents (Costa Rica, El Salvador and Nicaragua) staying away. At the following year's Summit, held in Panama, Castro clashed with heads of state from El Salvador, Mexico and Spain after refusing to sign a special declaration condemning terrorism by the Basque separatist organization in Spain, Euskadi ta Askatasuna (ETA).

Prior to the 2000 Summit anti-Castro activist, Luis Posada Carriles, along with three others, was arrested for an alleged plot to assassinate Castro. Posada Carriles had escaped from custody in Venezuela, where he was indicted for the bombing of a Cuban aeroplane near Barbados in 1976 and was also implicated in a series of hotel bombings in Havana in 1997. The Cuban Government requested Posada Carriles' extradition, which was refused.

In April 2000 the Office of the UN High Commissioner for Human Rights denounced the Cuba for repressing religious groups and political dissent. This judgement proved a great disappointment for the Government and led to demonstrations in Havana. Cuba subsequently withdrew its earlier request to join the African, Caribbean and Pacific (ACP) states–EU Joint Assembly, in the belief that the EU would impose selective and discriminatory conditions. However, a number of accords with individual countries and conciliatory moves by both parties in 2000–01 indicated progress towards an agreement.

A motion, sponsored by the Czech Republic, to censure Cuba for human rights violations approved at the UN's Human Rights Commission in April 2001, however, was described as a 'moral victory' by the Cuban foreign ministry, after what they described as an unprecedented campaign of pressure against the countries on the Commission. In response to the motion, Castro accused a number of Latin American countries of servility to the USA: the Argentine ambassador to Cuba was recalled by his Government as a result of the remarks. This motion followed the detention, in January 2001, of two prominent Czech citizens, charge with acting against Cuban national security and inciting a rebellion, having met with dissident groups. The two, former finance minister and current member of the Czech parliament, Ivan Pilip, and a political activist and former student leader, Jan Bubenik, were released in February after making a formal apology. In May the USA, believed by Cuba to be the principal force behind the motion, lost its seat on the Commission for the first time since its establishment in 1947. In the previous month Cuba announced that three men connected to Cuban–American exile groups and in the possession of arms, had been arrested by border guards on an offshore island. In May an Amnesty International report condemned the serious increase in human rights abuses in Cuba.

In December 2000 the first visit by a Russian head of state since the collapse of the USSR effectively ruptured relations took place. Russian President Vladimir Putin and Castro signed a number of accords aimed at increasing bilateral ties, and discussed a possible reduction in Cuba's Soviet era debt, which included work on unfinished projects, including a nuclear power plant begun in the early 1980s. Putin recognized Cuba as Russia's most important partner in Latin America, but emphasized that future relations would be on a sound economic footing. Co-operation agreements totalling some US $400m. were also signed with the President of the People's Republic of China,

Jiang Zemin, while a tour of the Middle East in early 2001 included an official visit to Iran, where Castro issued a joint statement with President Mohammad Khatami condemning terrorism and US sanctions. Both leaders were listed by the USA as sponsors of state terrorism.

Throughout the 1990s there were indications of a tendency among the Cuban exile community, mainly in the USA, to seek contact with Cuba and to eschew violence as an option. Although those favouring a hard-line stance remained a potent force, with strong financial backing, many became disaffected with recent US policy and a generational gap has emerged. In 2001 Cuba celebrated the 40th anniversary of its victory at the Bay of Pigs. Senior officials in the administration of US President John F. Kennedy (1961–63), former US Central Intelligence Agency leaders and Cuban officials, including Castro himself, gathered to commemorate the event that had set the tone of Cuban–US relations in the following decades, and members of the invading 2506 Brigade shook hands with the Cuban soldiers they had fought in 1961.

THE CUBAN DIASPORA

The case of Elián González, the five-year-old boy found floating on an inner tube in the Atlantic Ocean three miles from Fort Lauderdale (Florida, USA) in November 1999, highlighted the growing divisions within the Cuban emigrant community in the USA. Elián was one of just three survivors of a shipwreck in which his mother and 10 others died. The Cuban exile community, with strong links to the Cuban-American National Foundation (CANF), attempted to initiate legislation to have him granted US citizenship as a political refugee, although he was a minor. The bitterly fought custody battle between Miami-based relatives and his father, who wished to return with him to Cuba, involved the US Attorney-General, the media and even President Clinton himself. In April 2000 armed Federal Bureau of Investigation agents seized Elián from his Miami relatives. The US Supreme Court declined to hear further appeals from Elián's US-based family and he finally returned to Cuba on 28 June 2000.

In Cuba the case was presented as an abduction by the USA, provoking public demonstrations and daily televised 'tribunas abiertas' (open courts), which condemned the boy's detention in the USA. The case rallied popular support, cementing a sense of national unity among Cubans disaffected by isolation and deprivation, while, for once, Fidel Castro found himself on the same side as the US administration and public opinion. The Government afterwards endeavoured to maintain the momentum of popular participation and mobilization with the tribunas abiertas formalized to discuss concerns such as US sanctions, the attempt on Castro's life and the discriminatory migration policies of the USA, which were seen to stimulate dangerous illegal immigration bids. One such incident occurred in September 2000, when a crop-dusting aeroplane was stolen and crashed at sea. The Cuban passengers were allowed to

stay in the USA, while the Cuban Government, aware of the sensitivity of this issue in the wake of the Elián affair, chose not to pursue the matter.

On 23 October 2000 Cuba imposed a 10% tax on all telephone calls between Cuba and the USA, in response to the USA's decision to use Cuban funds frozen in US bank accounts belonging to Cuban telephone company to compensate the families of the Cuban-American pilots shot down in 1996. In December Cuba suspended telephone links with the USA, following the refusal of US telecommunications companies to pay the levy. On 16 May 2001 controversial legislation was introduced to the US Senate for a Cuban Solidarity Pact, offering material support to dissidents working for change inside Cuba. In June five Cubans were convicted in a court in Miami, in Florida (USA) for activities endangering US national security. Their conviction was accompanied by demonstrations in Cuba demanding their release.

CONCLUSION

In a characteristically defiant gesture, Fidel Castro insisted that the 2000 millennium festivities were one year early and Cuba marked the occasion on the eve of 2001. The Government took the opportunity to celebrate the number of US Presidents that Castro has outlasted; the tally has now reached nine. Events in 2000 seemed to indicate an improvement in US–Cuban relations, culminating in the passing of legislation in October 2000 ending restrictions on the sale of food and medicines. However, in the weeks preceding the US presidential election in November the Cuban–American lobby was successful in neutralizing the effects of this measure; there would be no access to US credit to make such purchases, the travel ban on US citizens would be written into law and sales of Cuban goods in the USA would still be prohibited. A subsequent visit from the sponsors of the legislation failed to convince Castro that the measures would have any practical application. The deadline to enact the law expired in February 2001. The votes of the Cuban–American exiles in Florida (USA) were considered instrumental in the election of George W. Bush as President of the USA. As a result, this powerful interest group expected to have its support repaid by the adoption of a tougher position on Cuba. President Bush's gave assurances that normal relations with Cuba would not be resumed in the absence of democratic elections and appointed to important positions in his administration personnel known for their support of the embargo against Cuba. Nevertheless, in 2001 there were signs of a softening in attitudes. US Secretary of State, Colin Powell, when questioned by a congressional sub-committee on the matter, spoke in muted praise of Castro, acknowledging that he had done 'some good for his people'; however, he expressed the opinion that there would be no end to the embargo while Castro remained in power. While President Bush was likely to continue courting the support of the Cuban–American community, further challenges to the embargo were expected in the near future.

Economy

LILA HAINES

ECONOMIC POLICY

For most of the period after the 1959 Revolution economic policy in Cuba was guided by a commitment to collective ownership of the means of production and, in particular following full membership (in 1972) of the Council for Mutual Economic Assistance (CMEA), to central planning. The recession in Cuba's economy in the late 1980s and early 1990s, after the collapse of the Eastern European socialist (Communist) bloc, led to a reassessment of economic policy. The new approach initially had a mainly external focus: seeking inward investment and developing tourism to obtain convertible ('hard') currency, while attempting to alleviate the social effects of a precipitous drop in foreign trade, including the loss of vital food and fuel imports from the socialist bloc, and remain faithful to the basic principles

of socialism. The Government reduced domestic spending and non-essential imports and declared a 'special period in time of peace', an austerity programme which was marked by food shortages, less expenditure on power and public transport, and attempts to improve the efficiency of state enterprises. By 1993, however, the system was clearly in danger of collapse: the money supply was increasing rapidly; subsidies to loss-making industries were soaring; and the 'black market' (parallel, illegal economy) was expanding, with the state often unable to supply even basic rations.

ECONOMIC REFORMS

In July 1993 President Fidel Castro Ruz announced the legalization of the use of hard currency by Cubans, one of several cautious, although significant, economic reforms arising from policy decisions taken at the Fourth Congress of the Cuban Communist Party (PCC), held in October 1991. Constitutional amendments passed in July 1992 liberalized the concept of property and the state's economic role, promised protection to foreign investors and granted limited recognition to private enterprise, thus preparing for new legislation and the use of new policy instruments from 1993.

Thereafter, a shift away from direct control of production was discernible and state enterprises were given greater operational freedom. However, the state retained ownership of the resource base and the Government continued to set economic priorities, to control the flow of essential commodities and carefully to monitor the use of hard-currency finance. A law passed in 1998 aimed to raise managerial standards and to make enterprises self-financing. It also reaffirmed the state enterprise as the basic business unit in the national economy and suggested that central government and enterprise decisions be harmonized. This period also saw slow but clear changes in social attitudes and the business culture, resulting from overseas investment, a greater Western presence in foreign trade and the opening of new employment opportunities (mainly in tourism).

In 1994 the Government also began to use monetary and fiscal instruments of economic policy, which subsequently gained in importance. As part of this policy the Government introduced new taxes aimed at eradicating surplus liquidity, and reintroduced taxation on income from self-employment and hard-currency earnings in 1995 and 1996, respectively. It also reduced subsidies to state enterprises and began to implement a system of profit taxation. These measures fulfilled the aims of increasing government revenues and curbing inflation and the money supply, although the exact result was difficult to measure owing to a number of factors, including the existence of several markets and currencies. However, government data showed cash in circulation and recorded regular savings contracting in 1994 and 1995, but returning to a rising trend in succeeding years. Although no index of consumer prices was published, official estimates also showed negative consumer price inflation during 1995 and 1996 (−11.5% and −4.9%, respectively), but judged that inflation was approximately 1.9% in 1997, 2.9% in 1998 and 2.9% in 1999.

For over three decades the state controlled the prices of all officially traded goods and provided a heavily subsidized 'basket' of essential products to all citizens. In 1994, when it became clear that it could no longer directly ensure minimum consumer supplies, the Government authorized the opening of non-regulated farm-produce markets and other retail outlets where prices responded to supply and demand. Together with the division of most state farms into smaller workers' co-operatives called Unidades Básicas de Producción Cooperativa (UBPC— Units of Basic Co-operative Production) from 1993, and the leasing of smallholdings to individuals, this measure helped to ease food shortages. However, agricultural output did not increase as much as had been hoped (see Agriculture, Forestry and Fishing below). Moreover, the reforms caused the alternative economy to evolve a trade pattern similar to that found elsewhere in Latin America. Black-market activity had increased dramatically in the early 1990s, absorbing a high proportion of household disposable income. This tendency was propagated by factors such as the partial legalization of private retailing, the spread of legitimate hard-currency shops and the payment of bonuses in convertible pesos or scarce goods to workers in important sectors (see Human Resources and Employment below). However, Cuba's economy remained heavily regulated, with state-controlled prices artificially low and those in much of the informal sector over-inflated.

THE FINANCIAL SECTOR

In 1994, in a radical policy departure, foreign banks were authorized to open representative offices, but not branches, in Cuba. This move signalled the start of a programme that reformed and modernized the domestic financial system. Banking had become a state monopoly in 1960 and, until the 1990s, the Banco Nacional de Cuba (BNC) and Banco Popular de Ahorro, the national savings bank, were the only domestic banking institutions. In 1995 a chain of exchange bureaux began to operate, buying US dollars and selling both convertible and old pesos (see below). New banks were also established to provide commercial and private banking services and development financing. In 1997 the BNC's central banking functions passed to a new central bank, the Banco Central de Cuba (BCC). Banking operations were also modernized. The insurance sector also expanded and began to form joint ventures with overseas insurance companies. A number of overseas-based investment funds opened offices in Havana. In 1999 a monetary policy committee was established, which met weekly to set domestic interest rates.

In the immediate aftermath of hard-currency liberalization in 1993, as the economy became more unbalanced and political tensions rose, the Cuban peso continued to fall rapidly in value against the US dollar. The peso recovered, however, from its lowest rate of 120 pesos per dollar in mid-1994 to an average of 19.18 pesos per dollar two years later and remained around 21–23 pesos per dollar in subsequent years. A convertible peso, at par with the US dollar, was introduced in December 1994 and by the late 1990s the US dollar circulated freely alongside the traditional and the convertible peso. However, these rates were available for personal transactions only and the official exchange rate remained at one peso to one US dollar. Full currency convertibility remained unlikely while Cuba's foreign-debt problem persisted. The budget deficit was reduced from an estimated 6.7% of gross domestic product (GDP) at current prices in 1994, to an estimated 2% of GDP in 1997, thereafter rising slightly but remaining under 3% of GDP in succeeding years.

US POLICY AND REFORM

Overall, US policy (notably the trade embargo) negatively affected the Cuban economy, mainly through higher import costs, the loss of potential tourism and other services revenue, and a high-risk investment and trade climate. However, US trade sanctions, retained mainly as the result of pressure from a powerful Cuban exiles' lobby, failed to achieve their aim of bringing down the Castro Government. They were implemented with varying degrees of severity, in response to political events. In March 1998 and January 1999 the US President, Bill Clinton, announced his intention to ease aspects of the trade embargo. In October 2000, following an acrimonious passage through the US Congress, legislation was approved that allowed US food and medicine sales, but attached conditions (see below) that left most parties dissatisfied, including President Clinton, who saw his power to ease or tighten travel restrictions removed.

INFRASTRUCTURE

About one-half of Cuba's estimated 60,858-km road system was built after 1960. A central highway links Pinar del Río in the west with Santiago de Cuba in the east. Causeways join the mainland to keys off the north coast, which, since 1990, have been developed as tourist resorts. During the 1990s much of the road surface deteriorated, but from 1996 some maintenance and infrastructure work was recommenced. More than one-half of the 12,000-km rail network serves the sugar industry while the rest offers passenger and other freight services. This too suffered seriously from neglect during the 1990s, and usage decreased in line with the decline of the sugar industry. Railways serving tourist resorts attracted some investment in the late 1990s. At the start of the new millennium the principal mode of public transport in Cuba remained the bus, although services were severely curtailed after 1990, owing to a lack of hard currency to buy fuel, spare parts or new stock.

Havana handled more than one-half of the country's maritime cargo, making it by far the most important of 16 commercial seaports and 23 minor ports. A cruise-ship terminal was added to Havana's facilities in 1995, and ports at Santiago and Nipe Bay were also upgraded to take cruise liners. A supertanker base at Matanzas on the north coast could accommodate petroleum tankers of up to 150,000 metric tons in capacity. The petroleum industry operated 11 sea terminals and 17 land storage facilities designed for domestic trade. New pipelines and tanker bases were constructed to support the growing nickel sector.

Civil aviation enjoyed a dramatic, tourism-led expansion during the 1990s. The main carrier was the national airline, Empresa Consolidada Cubana de Aviación (Cubana), which flew to over 40 countries. Cubana, the smaller local air companies and the national air services enterprise were brought under the umbrella of the newly formed Corporación de la Aviación Cubana in 1997. State and overseas investment modernized and expanded the island's airports, which number 20, the newest of which opened in mid-2001 on Cayo Coco, the most dynamic of the recently developed offshore tourist resorts.

With just 3.4 telephones per 100 inhabitants in 1997, Cuba had one of the lowest penetration rates in the Western hemisphere and most of the system was obsolete. Modernization began after June 1994, when the Government sanctioned the sale of 49% of the state telecommunications enterprise to a Mexican company, Grupo Domos. The 55-year agreement granted the resulting joint venture, Empresa de Telecomunicaciones de Cuba (Etecsa), the exclusive right to provide the main telephone services for 12 years. The Mexican investors later withdrew, and almost 30% of the venture was owned by an Italian company by 1997. By December 2000 300,000 digital lines had been installed, funded largely by growth in revenue from international calls. However, periodic political disputes between the USA and Cuba caused interruptions to services and to the transfer of payments to Cuba.

HUMAN RESOURCES AND EMPLOYMENT

The economic reforms of the 1990s began a shift away from the state domination of employment that had resulted from the nationalization programmes of the 1960s. The state sector accounted for 75.0% of civilian employment at the end of 1998, compared with 95.4% in 1989. The remainder were mainly private or co-operative farmers or self-employed, and some 106,000 worked in the new foreign sector. Unemployment in Cuba at the end of 2000 was officially 5.5%, compared with 6.0% in 1999. However, the UN Economic Commission for Latin America and the Caribbean estimated that underemployment might have increased to about 34% in 1996, although work in the 'black' market absorbed much of the surplus labour. Underemployment, long endemic in state enterprises, was being addressed: government ministries and other agencies and state enterprises made large-scale staff reductions, while rising urban youth unemployment led to a reassessment of educational priorities.

In a major departure from the moral stimulus approach which characterized the Ernesto ('Che') Guevara era of 'socialist economics', workers were offered material incentives to stimulate greater labour productivity. Another departure from established practice was the decision to introduce social-security deductions from employees' salaries. A pay-scale was agreed which, beginning at 130 pesos per month and rising to 700 pesos, covered a much wider range than had been standard in officially remunerated businesses for several decades. Average annual pay increased from 2,256 pesos in 1989 to 2,568 pesos in 1997. Salaries in joint ventures were 15%–30% above sectoral averages. In 1999 employees in the education and public-health sectors received an average 30% pay rise. This was the first such pay settlement for workers other than those in productive or hard-currency earning sectors.

In 1995 agriculture (including forestry and fishing) employed around 23% of the economically active population and industry 22%, compared with 40% and 13%, respectively, in 1960. The service sector employed about 50% of the work-force. Women formed 37.6% of the labour force, rising to 42.0% in the state sector and to 73.2% in health, a sector employing over 328,500 people. Investment in universal education after 1959 produced a well-educated work-force, which was perceived as an asset in attracting foreign investment.

FOREIGN TRADE

Prior to 1959 Cuba's main trading partner was the USA, which had consolidated its dominance after Cuban independence from Spain in 1898. In 1958, the year preceding the overthrow of Fulgencio Batista Zaldivar by the Castro-led revolutionaries, 68% of foreign trade was with the USA and Cuban sugar enjoyed preferential entry to the US market. This position changed radically in the early 1960s, when the new Government tried to implement a programme that it believed reflected its commitment to social justice.

After the Cuban Government had nationalized assets belonging to US companies, valued at over US \$1,000m., the USA severed diplomatic relations in January 1961, supported

the unsuccessful Bay of Pigs invasion by anti-Castro exiles in April and, in March 1962, extended to all goods the partial trade embargo it had imposed on Cuba in 1960. The so-called Cuban Missile Crisis of October 1962, following the deployment by the Soviet Government of nuclear warheads near Havana, demonstrated Cuba's peripheral status in relation to the Cold War 'superpowers' of the USA and the USSR. The country was left with little choice but to depend on the USSR for its trade revenue, as well as for aid to implement an ambitious social and economic development programme.

After 1962 foreign trade was conducted increasingly with the Communist bloc, although the People's Republic of China, Japan and some countries of Western Europe each took a small, but significant, share at various times. In 1989 over 80% of foreign trade was with Eastern Europe. As a result of the collapse of trade with the Soviet bloc from 1990, the value of merchandise trade plummeted from US \$13,500m. in 1989 to less than \$3,170m. in 1993. Recovery was slow and included a diversification of trading partners and greater integration with the world market. In 1998 exports of goods were less than one-third of their 1989 level. The European Union (EU) accounted for 30% of Cuba's foreign trade in 1998, the Americas (excluding the USA owing to that country's ban on trade with Cuba) accounted for nearly 35% and Asia for 15%. Nevertheless, Russia had succeeded to the Soviet role of Cuba's leading trade partner, taking more than 20% of exports.

Of greater significance was the change in the composition of export earnings. Services comprised a growing share of overall foreign trade, mainly owing to increases in the tourism sector. In 1998 merchandise exports were valued at approximately US \$1,721m., whereas tourism receipts totalled \$1,626m., while sugar brought in just \$600m. This underlined the significant shift away from sugar as the leading sector, both in terms of export revenue and weight in the economy.

By the late 1990s Cuba was no longer the world's leading sugar exporter, following a precipitous drop in harvest yields (see Agriculture, Forestry and Fishing below). Nevertheless, it remained an important export earner. The other main exports were nickel and tobacco products. Seafood exports, which increased in line with the development of deep-sea and in-shore fishing after 1959, declined after 1990 but began to recover in 1995. Exports of health products, though still small, were growing, particularly to Latin America and the People's Republic of China. In 1997 exports from this sector accounted for an estimated 2.4% of the value of total exports.

Total spending on imports of goods and services decreased to US \$2,320m. in 1993 but increased thereafter. The composition of merchandise imports changed considerably from the 1980s. Food and fuel together accounted for around 60% of imports in 1993, but little more than 10% in 1998. Under 1996 legislation the Government opened four free-trade zones to promote exports of goods and services and to help resuscitate dormant domestic industry by attracting more foreign investment and spreading its benefits to new geographic and economic areas. However, they did not figure noticeably in exports, although it was considered that they might have attracted smaller companies which would not have invested where there was greater risk of claims for future compensation from US-based individuals or corporations.

THE US TRADE EMBARGO

The US trade embargo, implemented with varying degrees of severity since first imposed by President John F. Kennedy in 1960, was strengthened in 1992, when the Cuban Democracy Act, or Torricelli Act, banned trade with Cuba by overseas subsidiaries of US companies. A further dimension was added in March 1996 when President Clinton signed into law the Cuban Liberty and Solidarity Act (commonly known as the Helms-Burton Act), which aimed to halt foreign investment in Cuba. It provoked exceptionally strong protests by other Western Governments concerned by its attempted extraterritorial reach.

Contrary to international norms, this legislation potentially opened the US courts to claimants who had obtained US citizenship after their property in Cuba was nationalized. However, President Clinton repeatedly exercised his right to postpone the implementation of Title IV, the section of the Act allowing US nationals to claim damages in US federal courts from overseas companies believed to be 'trafficking' in confiscated Cuban property. (Claims by former owners of such property resident in countries other than the USA had been settled.) In July 2001 Clinton's successor, George W. Bush, suspended the implementation of Title IV for a further six months. Title III, which made executives of companies investing in Cuba (and their dependents) liable to exclusion from the USA, was implemented selectively.

In March 1998 and again in January 1999 President Clinton announced plans to ease restrictions relating to travel by Cuban Americans for family visits, cash remittances and the export of food and medicines to Cuba. As a result, additional flights were authorized. In July 1999 Western Union was allowed to begin cash transfers to Cuba, in partnership with a Cuban enterprise, and the US Department of the Treasury licensed the pharmaceuticals company SmithKline Beecham (later Glaxo SmithKline) to market a Cuban meningitis vaccine. In October 2000 legislation was passed that allowed US food and medicine sales to Cuba. However, the potential for such trade was restricted by the conditions attached, such as a ban on financing by US banks or official credits. Other conditions also made the expansion of US–Cuban trade difficult. Imports of most Cuban goods remained illegal. Other sanctions legislation such as the Torricelli and Helms-Burton Acts and the 'Trading with the Enemy' Act remained operational. These included a clause of the Torricelli Act that forbade ships to enter US ports within six months of entering a Cuban port for the purpose of trade. However, in February 2001 the USA granted the first licence to run a scheduled route to Cuba to the shipping company, Crowley Liner Services. In July the US Department of Commerce announced new regulations regarding the US sales to Cuba covered in the October 2000 legislation, although public and private financing to fund the sales remained prohibited. However, the Cuban Government refused to trade with the USA under what it considered 'discriminatory and humiliating terms'. Also in July, the US House of Representatives approved a proposal, by 240 votes to 186, to lift restrictions on most travel to Cuba.

In mid-2000 the EU called for a World Trade Organization disputes panel to rule on Section 211 of the 1998 US Omnibus Appropriations Act, under which trademarks used in connection with assets confiscated by the Cuban Government could not be registered without permission from the original owner. This followed a 1999 US court ruling against Havana Club International, a joint venture between Pernod Ricard of France and Cuba's Havana Rum and Liquors, concerning the use of the Havana Club rum brand name in the USA (the ruling was upheld by the US Supreme Court in October 2000). In response to the ruling, Cuba announced a new Bacardí brand, initiating a further dispute, this time with the Bacardí company in Bermuda.

FOREIGN INVESTMENT

Legal from 1982, foreign investment only became a priority for the Cuban Government following the collapse of the Communist bloc at the end of the 1980s. In September 1995 foreign investment (up to 100%) was legalized in all sectors of the economy except defence, public health and education, and in 1996 a law was passed allowing the establishment of free-trade zones and industrial parks. US companies were prevented by their own laws from investing in Cuba and the US Helms-Burton Act made negotiations with companies from third countries more difficult, although it did not halt the flow of overseas investment. At the end of 2000 cumulative investments and commitments totalled US $5,000m., and 394 joint ventures and other forms of economic association with overseas companies were operating, with an estimated annual turnover of US $1,200m. Many such partnerships were with the new type of nominally autonomous limited company (Sociedad Anónima), usually with the state (or its nominee) as the major or only shareholder.

A combination of political concerns and evolving official priorities caused changes to the investment pattern to emerge during 2000. The Government halted foreign investment in real estate, one of the most sough-after investment opportunities, and the Cuban partners in property ventures bought back the units that had already been built. This was unsurprising, as political opposition had prevented a planned real estate law from being enacted. There was also a growing preference for larger projects in important areas, such as energy and infrastructure, and for partners who could offer loan finance. The purchase in 2000 of 50% of the state citrus marketing company by a French–Spanish company, Altadis, brought in US $500m. and might have signalled another trend.

THE FOREIGN DEBT

At the end of 1999, according to the Banco Central de Cuba, the hard-currency foreign debt was US $11,078m. The total was an estimated $12m. if the debt to Russia were included at a conversion rate similar to that used by Nicaragua for repayment of its Russian debt. Debt servicing was over $1.1m. in 1998 and 1999. Talks with the 'Paris Club' of Western creditors took place in 2000, but progress was prevented, in part, by indecision regarding the inclusion of the debt to Russia. The debt to the USSR was 15,000m. roubles ($27,000m.) in 1991, when the Soviet Government granted Cuba a moratorium. The Russian Federation, the main successor state as far as Cuba's suspended Soviet obligations were concerned, initially decided not to press for repayment. Bilateral discussions with Russia took place in 2000–01 and included the possible conversion of debt to equity through joint-venture contracts. In 1998 agreement was reached on rescheduling approximately $750m. of the island's commercial debt to Japan, which held over 15% of total Cuban convertible-currency debt. In 2000 Japan also agreed to the rescheduling of $114m. in official trade credits and restored export credit guarantees worth $120m. Germany also agreed to the repayment, over 21 years, of $108m. of debt, equivalent to the amount of outstanding hard-currency debt. The inflow of new finance such as that from the Habanos deal (see Foreign Investment) was also expected to ease the situation by allowing Cuban enterprises access to longer-term borrowing on better terms instead of relying on expensive short term credits.

AGRICULTURE, FORESTRY AND FISHING

Agriculture and fisheries accounted for 6.3% of GDP in 1998 and employed some 14.9% of the labour force in 1998. The fall in the sector's contribution to national income reflected the effects of the post-Soviet economic crisis and endemic problems, some of which were broached, though not fully tackled, in the mid-1990s. Foreign financing helped to overcome input shortages in sugar cane, tobacco and citrus fruits, although relief was short-lived in the case of sugar. The 1994 law legalizing free-market sales of agricultural produce (with some exclusions) increased food availability, but production was still below national needs. Although legal, there was little foreign investment in agriculture—the sale of land was not allowed.

A 1993 law divided most sugar and non-sugar state farms into over 4,000 UBPCs. Small areas of land were leased to individuals for private cultivation, especially of coffee and tobacco, which helped stimulate output, although the number returning to the land was not significant. This reduced the land owned directly by the state from over 82% in 1989 to 26% in 1996. The rest was held by private farmers, traditional co-operative farms and the UBPCs. However, most UBPCs were unprofitable. They claimed to be penalized by the low prices paid by the state, to which they were obliged to sell 80% of their produce, as well as by overpriced inputs and services available only from state enterprises and by onerous repayment terms on the capital stock bought from state farms on formation. Indeed, in practice, according to some observers, many UBPCs were little more than subsidiaries of the enterprises from which they were formed, particularly in the sugar industry. By 1998 central government subsidies were being phased out and UBPCs were required to take up bank loans instead.

Sugar, which accounted for an estimated US $900m. of export earnings in 1997 (down from $4,333m. in 1990), was grown on 28% of the 6.7m. ha classified as agricultural land. The sugar industry was organized on the basis of agro-industrial complexes, with 156 sugar mills, 17 refineries, 13 alcohol distilleries and 21 other installations manufacturing products from sugarcane derivatives. The cumulative effect of shortages of inputs, spare parts and fuel caused sugar production to fall significantly, to 3.2m. metric tons, raw value, in the 1997/98 harvest, from an annual average of 7.6m. tons in 1985–89. The implementation of the USA's Helms-Burton Act in early 1996 led overseas banks and traders who had financed the industry to review their commitments. The military Chief of Staff, Gen. Ulises Rosales del Toro, appointed as Minister for Sugar in 1997, attempted to achieve greater efficiency and discipline, closed the least efficient sugar mills and ended the practice of cutting young cane. Although such measures did not prevent the harvest from falling to a 50-year low in 1997/98, recovery began in 1998/99, when the harvest reached 3.8m. tons, and continued in 1999/2000 when a harvest of just over 4m. tons was recorded. However, drought damaged the following year's crop and harvests were not expected to return to pre-crisis levels. Export earnings were adversely affected by low sugar prices.

From an annual average of 43,000 metric tons in 1986–90, tobacco production fell rapidly, to 17,000 tons in 1993, before recovering to 37,000 tons in 1998, owing to pre-financing obtained from the main French and Spanish buyers and incentive schemes for producers. Output was further expanded by allocating more land to private farmers, who formed 80% of producers. This allowed significant expansion in the production of cigars, to respond to growing demand on the world market. The sector opted for a high-quality image with premium prices on the international market. This approach was reinforced when a French–Spanish company, Altadis, purchased 50% of the state marketing board in 2000. In 2000 tobacco production stood at an estimated 30,600 tons.

From just over 1m. metric tons in 1990, citrus-fruit output, by some estimates, halved to 505,000 tons in 1994. However, in this sector also, yields recovered somewhat where foreign partners were involved, providing inputs for a modern foreign-financed juicing industry on the island as well as earning export income. In 2000 output was an estimated 703,741 tons. Other crops showed an erratic production pattern, though the trend was mainly towards recovery.

The dairy industry, which with poultry was one of the agricultural successes of the revolutionary period, was severely affected by the collapse of foreign trade relations with the Soviet bloc. The national herd was bred to produce high yields from a feedlot system (according to which cattle were kept indoors and fed automatically) and adapted badly to grazing when cheap Soviet feed imports were curtailed. Milk production in 1996 was less than one-third of its 1990 level of just over 1m. metric tons, but recovered slightly thereafter and stood at an estimated 617,000 tons in 2000. Overall, private farmers recorded the most notable increases, a fact attributed largely to the incentive offered by the opening of deregulated farmers' markets. Irregularity characterized most food sectors throughout the 1990s.

Investment in both deep-sea and in-shore fishing after the 1959 Revolution raised the average annual catch from 178m. metric tons in 1961–65 to 1,078m. tons in 1986–90. Fish farming was developed, and was the main source of fish for domestic consumers in the 1990s. Lobster, prawns and shrimp were exported, as was the catch from Cuba's deep-sea fishing fleet. An ageing fleet combined with fuel and other shortages produced a 1994 catch of less than one-half that of 1989, although increases were recorded from 1995 onwards. Lobster processing plants were modernized to respond to demand from exports and tourism. A scheme introduced in 1998, whereby fishing boats were leased as co-operative businesses to their crews, was reported to have raised the in-shore catch.

Following a reforestation programme, by the mid-1990s forestry covered 21% of Cuban territory, up from 18% in 1987. However, like most of the economy, the sector suffered from resource shortages in the 1990s and by the end of the decade was seeking foreign investment, although there were no reports of such investment by 2001.

MINING AND ENERGY

Gold was the first economic resource developed by the Spaniards in Cuba, in 1515–38. Copper was mined from 1530 onwards. However, mining was thereafter of little economic importance in Cuba, accounting for just 1% of national income in 1953. One study valued mining output at US $467m. between 1902 and 1950, approximately equivalent to a single post-Second World War sugar harvest.

The island developed production of industrial minerals such as zeolite and in the 1990s copper, gold, silver and other metals received attention from foreign prospectors. However, deposits of such minerals were insignificant compared with Cuba's proven and estimated reserves of nickel and cobalt, which were among the world's largest. Between 1965 and 1990 the sector was dominated by Soviet technology, with its attendant inefficiencies, and dependence on Eastern European trade. Nickel output increased from 26,900 metric tons in 1994 to 72,000 tons in 2000, and was expected to surpass 75,000 tons in 2001. The recovery was mainly owing to significant joint-venture agreements, particularly with a Canadian corporation, which included a 50% Cuban share in a Canadian refinery. In the early 2000s there was renewed Russian interest in the sector, possibly as part of a debt for equity deal.

Energy was one of the Cuban economy's weakest sectors, depending on imported petroleum to generate over 80% of its electricity. Some 13m. metric tons of petroleum were formerly imported annually from the USSR, on a barter basis, with around 2m. tons being re-exported. When Russian trade was established on a market-prices basis, Cuban petroleum imports decreased sharply. Cuba held international bidding rounds for petroleum exploration blocks in 1993, 1996 and 2000, the latter for blocks in the Gulf of Mexico. Canadian and European companies began prospecting onshore and offshore. While there were no major petroleum discoveries and some foreign companies withdrew from the project, small but significant discoveries were made. As a result, domestic crude extraction rose from 0.7m. tons in 1990 to some 2.7m. tons in 2000. Additionally, Canadian investment allowed natural gas to be harnessed for energy generation, bringing the total generated from domestic sources to over 50% in 2000. In the same year the country generated 70% of their electricity requirement from domestic oil. Cuba expected to generate 90% in 2001, and to be self-sufficient in oil production by 2005, when output was to reach some 6m. tons. In 2000 two oil-processing plants were planned for Santiago de Cuba and Cienfuegos and two power-generation plants were being built by Sherritt Power of Canada. In December Cuba announced that construction of the Juragua nuclear power plant, which had never been completed, was to be abandoned. However, in February 2001 the engineering company, SES Tlmace (Slovakia), won a contract to reconstruct the oil-burning power-station in Santa Cruz.

INDUSTRY

From 1962 Cuba invested heavily in developing and diversifying an industrial base that had previously been dominated by sugar. In 1965–72 the main focus was on rehabilitating sugar mills (which were nationalized with most existing industry in the early 1960s) and building up the production of spare parts, agricultural equipment, cement and fertilizers. Investment spending accelerated in 1976–90, so that by the end of the 1980s Cuba had developed a varied industrial base, ranging from food processing and light industry to construction materials, chemicals, machine tools, paper and glass. However, there were several major weaknesses, which became more pronounced as industry came to a near standstill after Cuba's Communist bloc markets disappeared. A steep fall in crucial petroleum imports led to the closure of most plants. This was exacerbated by the fuel inefficiency of many factories constructed with Soviet or other Eastern European aid, and which were often too large for Cuba's needs. Other by-products of the close integration with the CMEA included the unsuitability of many Cuban products for Western markets. There was also heavy dependence on imported raw materials for many sectors, perhaps most marked in the chemicals industry which, according to one leading Cuban analyst, was at least 20 years behind its counterparts in most large and medium-sized Latin American countries.

In the 1990s the Government attempted to make industry more efficient through measures such as dividing large enterprises into smaller and more manageable entities, using only the most efficient lines and reducing staff. Such measures were believed to be essential for attracting inward investment to manufacturing and some sectors recorded higher output after 1994. This was often linked to tourism, in cases such as construction materials and furniture, or to foreign investment, as in nickel processing. It seemed, however, that most plants were still producing at a fraction of installed capacity, although official data showed that manufacturing output was 20% higher in 2000 than it had been in 1995. Manufacturing in general, like that of the overall economy, was restrained by the sugar industry's disappointing results and by low levels of finance availability. Subsidies were cut and finance from the new banking sector was both relatively expensive and dependent on acceptable projections of future returns.

PHARMACEUTICALS AND HEALTH CARE

One area that continued to receive significant support from the Government despite the 1990s crisis was the indigenous pharmaceuticals and medical-goods sector which, it was claimed, was capable of producing 80% of national requirements. The Government justified its policy decision by the need to protect the national health-care service, and to recover the state's earlier spending on training and infrastructure. Between 1989 and 1995 over US $345m. in hard currency was invested in the medical-pharmaceutical industry. Existing laboratories and production lines were improved and the biotechnology sector's production capacity expanded. A network of science parks was established to organize the contribution of some 200 life-science institutions to the national economy and leading research and development centres began to form joint-venture agreements. Exports of medical products, valued at $8.7m. in 1986, reached an estimated $135m. in 1997. These included new vaccines, interferons, monoclonal antibodies and technologically advanced products developed by leading institutions such as the biotechnology and genetic-engineering centre in Havana. The sector received a potential boost in July 1999 when a joint venture was formed with the pharmaceutical manufacturer SmithKline Beecham to market the Cuban meningitis vaccine, raising hopes that Cuban medical products might finally start to penetrate more lucrative Western markets.

TOURISM

In the 1990s the international tourism sector in Cuba experienced rapid growth, having virtually disappeared after the USA, in 1961, banned travel to the island by its citizens. Arrivals, mainly from Europe and Canada, rose from some 340,300 in 1990 to an estimated 1.6m. in 1999. Gross tourism revenue increased from US $243.4m. to an estimated $1,714m. in the same period. However, arrivals in 2000, at 1.8m., were below the Ministry of Tourism target of 2m. visitors. In 2000 tourism employed some 100,000 people directly and a further 2,000 people indirectly.

Having been orientated primarily towards domestic tourism for nearly 30 years, in the 1980s the tourism industry was identified as a potentially rich source of convertible currency. Overseas investment to help develop the industry was sought, and the first agreement to build a joint-venture hotel was signed in 1989 with a leading Spanish hotel group. Expansion plans for the period to 2000 required US $1,334m. in convertible currency, which Cuba sought from domestic and foreign sources, including joint ventures with foreign partners, conventional loans, mortgage-backed securities and offshore public companies. By mid-1997 21 tourism joint ventures had committed over $600m. in capital. However, official sources claimed that foreign capital remained of less importance than that from national sources and, although the number and origin of foreign participants in the industry increased, most overseas companies managed, rather than owned, the hotels they operated. It proved difficult, however, to develop the cruise-ship circuit, despite attempts by several cruise-ship operators. The importance of US ports and visitors in the sector, the US ban on travel to Cuba and the uncertainty aroused by the shipping clause of the Torricelli Act (see above) were among the negative factors limiting the potential for further expansion. In the context of the global fall in tourism to Latin America, tourism was likely to grow at a more modest, but still significant pace, and remain the principal source of export income.

ECONOMIC OUTLOOK

In the early 2000s there were indications that Cuba was beginning to recover from possibly the worst decline suffered by any Communist bloc economy. Real GDP, which had suffered a cumulative fall of almost 35% in 1989–94, rose by 0.7% in 1994 and continued to record positive growth. However, it fluctuated considerably, from 1.2% in 1998 to 6.2% in 1999, reflecting both some recovery in important sectors and the growth of tourism, but also unstable factors such as the poor performance of the sugar industry. This emphasized the significant domestic and external obstacles the still-fragile and sugar-dependent economy faced. Despite steady recovery in some sectors, the economy was operating considerably below capacity. Agricultural output was depressed in sectors crucial to the domestic food supply, such as dairying. The sugar industry required thorough restructuring. Analysts expected growth in the range of 4%–5.5% over the early 2000s, following official estimates of 5.6% GDP growth in 2000. In 1999 Cuba recorded a trade deficit of US $600m., and a deficit of $456m. on the current account of the balance of payments. In 2000 there was an estimated budget deficit of 738m. pesos.

Although pressure for an easing of sanctions increased within the USA in 1999–2000, the legislation introduced was not sufficient to result in a significant improvement in US–Cuban trade. There were moves to introduce further legislation easing the sanctions, but US President Bush was not expected to support them. An early and definitive solution to the problem of the US $12,000m. hard-currency foreign debt was not expected, although the rescheduling of debt to Japan and Germany and the commencement of talks with the Paris Club were likely to have a helpful influence on the commercial climate. Negotiations with Russia on possible debt-for-equity deals might help to resolve the debt impasse and ease international financing, but could equally be difficult to implement, owing to resistance by existing Western investors reluctant to see Russia re-entering sectors such as nickel. Cuba was not a member of the World Bank or the International Monetary Fund and had little hope of an agreement that would give it access to cheaper new credits. Nevertheless, the sale of 50% of the state cigar distributor was expected to ease the financial situation in the short term. The inflow of overseas investment was expected to continue to increase, although some negative impact was expected from the suspension of inward investment in real estate.

In 2001 the Government appeared to be convinced that it was pursuing the correct methods of achieving fiscal targets. It was expected to continue with the same cautious approach to economic reform, including the restructuring of domestic production and gradual price liberalization, while remaining committed to a planned economy. This was likely to be confirmed by the five-yearly congress of the Partido Comunista de Cuba (PCC—Communist Party of Cuba), scheduled for 2002. Tourism appeared likely to continue its expansion, although at a slower pace. Mining and several smaller sectors were also expected to expand, but growing revenue from these sources was likely to be at least partially offset by low sugar prices and high-cost imports. The net effect was thought likely to be slow but steady growth, very gradual improvement in living standards, some minor adjustment of policy instruments and, in the medium term, a revaluation of economic policy leading to less dependence on sugar, and additional operational freedom for state enterprises, with a trend towards a reduction in size, and some growth in private, principally foreign-financed enterprises.

Statistical Survey

Source (unless otherwise stated): Cámara de Comercio de la República de Cuba, Calle 21, No 661/701, esq. Calle A, Apdo 4237, Vedado, Havana; tel. (7) 30-3356; fax (7) 33-3042; internet www.camaracuba.cubaweb.cu; Oficina Nacional de Estadísticas, Calle Paseo 60, entre 3 y 5, Vedado, Havana; tel. (7) 30-0005; fax (7) 33-3083; internet www.cubagov.cu/otras_info/estadisticas.htm.

Area and Population

AREA, POPULATION AND DENSITY

Area (sq km)	110,860*
Population (census results)	
6 September 1970	8,569,121
11 September 1981	
Males	4,914,873
Females	4,808,732
Total	9,723,605
Population (official estimates at mid-year)	
1999	11,142,691
2000	11,187,673
2001	11,229,688
Density (per sq km) at mid-2001	101.3

* 42,803 sq miles.

PROVINCES (31 December 1999)

	Population (estimates)	Principal towns (with population)
Camagüey . . .	785,800	Camagüey (306,049)
Ciego de Avila . .	407,400	
Cienfuegos . .	395,100	Cienfuegos (137,513)
Granma . . .	830,000	Bayamo (143,600)
Guantánamo . .	512,300	Guantánamo (208,030)
La Habana . .	2,891,500	La Habana (Havana, the capital) (2,189,716)
Holguín . . .	1,029,700	Holguín (259,300)
Isla de la Juventud .	79,500	
Matanzas . .	658,100	Matanzas (124,754)
Pinar del Rio . .	734,900	Pinar del Rio (148,500)
Sancti Spíritus . .	460,600	
Santiago de Cuba .	1,032,500	Santiago de Cuba (441,524)
Las Tunas . . .	527,900	Las Tunas (137,331)
Villa Clara . .	834,900	Santa Clara (210,100)
Total . . .	11,180,200	

BIRTHS, MARRIAGES AND DEATHS*

	Registered live births†		Registered marriages‡		Registered deaths	
	Number	Rate (per 1,000)	Number	Rate (per 1,000)	Number	Rate (per 1,000)
1993 . .	152,233	14.0	135,138	12.4	78,531	7.2
1994 . .	147,265	13.4	116,935	10.7	78,648	7.2
1995 . .	147,170	13.4	70,413	6.4	77,937	7.1
1996 . .	140,276	12.7	65,009	5.9	79,662	7.2
1997 . .	152,681	13.8	60,900§	5.5	77,316	7.0
1998 . .	151,080	13.6	64,900	5.8	77,565	7.0
1999 . .	150,785	13.5	57,300	5.1	79,499	7.1
2000§ . .	143,528	12.8	57,000	5.1	76,448	6.8

* Data are tabulated by year of registration rather than by year of occurrence.
† Births registered in the National Consumers Register, established on 31 December 1964.
‡ Including consensual unions formalized in response to special legislation.
§ Provisional.

Expectation of life (UNDP estimates, years at birth, 1998): 76.3 (males 74.3; females 78.2). Source: UN Development Programme, *Human Development Report*.

ECONOMICALLY ACTIVE POPULATION (1981 census)

	Males	Females	Total
Agriculture, hunting, forestry and fishing	677,565	113,304	790,869
Mining and quarrying . . .			
Manufacturing	472,399	195,941	668,340
Electricity, gas and water . .			
Construction	279,327	33,913	313,240
Trade, restaurants and hotels .	170,192	135,438	305,630
Transport, storage and communications	205,421	43,223	248,644
Financing, insurance, real estate and business services . . .			
Community, social and personal services	541,387	544,665	1,086,052
Activities not adequately defined .	87,778	40,139	127,917
Total labour force	2,434,069	1,106,623	3,540,692

Source: ILO, *Yearbook of Labour Statistics*.

1998 (persons aged 15 years and over): Total employed 3,753,600; Unemployment rate 6.6%.

CIVILIAN EMPLOYMENT IN THE STATE SECTOR
(annual averages, '000 persons)

	1987	1988	1989
Industry*	726.9	742.8	767.5
Construction	314.1	339.4	344.3
Agriculture	602.7	653.2	690.3
Forestry	30.1	26.8	30.8
Transport	196.9	199.9	204.4
Communications	28.4	30.1	31.5
Trade	376.2	387.3	395.3
Social services	116.5	121.5	124.5
Science and technology . . .	28.7	27.5	27.4
Education	383.0	388.2	396.4
Arts and culture	42.2	42.1	43.9
Public health	222.4	232.5	243.5
Finance and insurance . . .	20.6	20.9	21.7
Administration	161.4	155.1	151.7
Total (incl. others)	3,299.2	3,408.4	3,526.6

* Fishing, mining, manufacturing, electricity, gas and water.

Agriculture

PRINCIPAL CROPS ('000 metric tons)

	1998	1999	2000
Rice (paddy) .	280.4	368.8	368.8*
Maize .	110.8	185.3	185.3*
Potatoes .	206.2	344.2	344.2*
Sweet potatoes .	157.5	195.1	195.1*
Cassava (Manioc) .	205.8	210.0*	210.0*
Dry beans .	18.5	17.3	17.3*
Groundnuts (in shell)* .	15.0	15.0	15.0
Coconuts* .	26.0	26.0	26.0
Cabbages* .	28.0	30.0	30.0
Tomatoes .	112.2	129.2	129.2*
Pumpkins, squash and gourds* .	47.0	50.0	50.0
Cucumbers and gherkins* .	37.0	40.0	40.0
Other vegetables* .	68.0	80.0	80.0
Sugar cane .	32,800.0	34,000.0	36,000.0*
Oranges .	358.7	440.6	440.6*
Tangerines, mandarins, clementines and satsumas* .	6.5	6.5	6.5
Lemons and limes .	17.3	21.1	21.1
Grapefruit and pomelos .	324.1	232.9	232.9*
Mangoes .	43.0	64.2	64.2*
Pineapples* .	19.0	19.0	19.0
Bananas .	153.5	133.3	133.3*
Plantains .	308.7	329.0†	329.0*
Coffee (green)† .	13.5	22.0†	16.5†
Tobacco (leaves) .	37.9	30.6	30.6*

* FAO estimate(s).   † Unofficial figure(s).

Source: FAO.

LIVESTOCK ('000 head, year ending September)

	1998	1999	2000
Cattle .	4,643.7	4,405.8	4,700.0*
Horses .	433.6	450.0	450.0*
Mules .	24.3	24.5	24.5*
Pigs* .	2,400.0	2,500.0	2,800.0
Sheep* .	310.0	310.0	310.0
Goats .	162.1	207.5	140.0*

Poultry (million): 13,118 in 1998; 13,151 in 1999; 15,000* in 2000.

* FAO estimate(s).

Source: FAO.

LIVESTOCK PRODUCTS ('000 metric tons)

	1998	1999	2000
Beef and veal .	69.4	72.7	75.0*
Pig meat .	97.8	103.4	110.0*
Poultry meat .	59.6	60.1	65.0*
Cows' milk .	655.3	617.8	617.8*
Butter and ghee* .	7.5	7.5	7.5
Cheese* .	14.5	14.5	14.5
Hen eggs .	59.3	74.4	74.4*

* FAO estimate(s).

Source: FAO.

Forestry

ROUNDWOOD REMOVALS ('000 cubic metres, excl. bark)

	1997	1998	1999
Sawlogs, veneer logs and logs for sleepers .	193	193	128
Other industrial wood .	418	418	278
Fuel wood .	1,177	1,182	1,187
Total .	1,788	1,793	1,593

Source: FAO, *Yearbook of Forest Products*.

SAWNWOOD PRODUCTION
('000 cubic metres, incl. railway sleepers)

	1997	1998	1999
Coniferous (softwood) .	59	59	66
Broadleaved (hardwood) .	72	72	80
Total .	130	130	146

Source: FAO, *Yearbook of Forest Products*.

Fishing

('000 metric tons, live weight)

	1996	1997	1998
Capture .	75.8	77.3	62.2
Silver hake .	22.3	12.7	6.3
Caribbean spiny lobster .	9.4	9.0	9.4
Aquaculture .	33.9	46.2	38.0
Silver carp .	15.5	22.6	25.2
Blue tilapia .	11.9	11.1	5.8
Total catch .	109.7	123.6	100.2

Note: Figures exclude crocodiles, recorded by number rather than by weight. The number of spectacled caimans caught was: 302 in 1996; 506 in 1997; 5 in 1998. Also excluded are sponges (metric tons): 56.8 in 1996; 81.5 in 1997; 72.1 in 1998.

Source: FAO, *Yearbook of Fishery Statistics*.

Mining

('000 metric tons, unless otherwise indicated)

	1996	1997	1998
Crude petroleum .	1,275.9	1,461.5	1,678.2
Natural gas (million cu metres) .	19.3	37.2	124.1
Copper concentrates (metric tons) .	2,362.3	2,208.2	1,351.4
Nickel and cobalt (metal content) .	53.7	61.6	67.7
Refractory chromium .	37.3	44.1	46.0
Salt (unrefined) .	159.8	163.6	134.6
Silica and sand ('000 cu metres) .	1,828.2	1,949.1	1,861.2
Crushed stone ('000 cu metres) .	2,899.9	2,919.6	2,860.0

1999: Crude petroleum ('000 metric tons) 2,104.3; Natural gas (million cubic metres) 460.0; Nickel and cobalt ('000 metric tons, metal content) 66.5.

Industry

SELECTED PRODUCTS
('000 metric tons, unless otherwise indicated)

	1998	1999	2000
Crude steel .	278.0	302.7	327.3
Grey cement .	1,713.4	1,784.6	1,632.7
Detergent .	12.2	12.9	13.1
Fertilizers .	156.7	138.3	118.2
Tyres ('000) .	164.7	156.6	160.5
Woven textile fabrics (million sq metres) .	54.0	51.0	47.5
Cotton yarn .	4.5	3.2	2.2
Cigarettes ('000 million) .	11.7	12.3	12.1
Cigars (million) .	263.5	284.0	240.3
Raw sugar .	3,100.0	3,700.0	3,900.0
Beer ('000 hectolitres) .	1,759.4	2,008.5	2,136.1
Soft drinks ('000 hectolitres) .	2,536.8	2,743.0	2,842.0
Electric energy (million kWh) .	14,145.1	14,487.5	15,028.8

Finance

CURRENCY AND EXCHANGE RATES

Monetary Units:
100 centavos = 1 Cuban peso.

Sterling, Dollar and Euro Equivalents (30 April 2001)
£1 sterling = 1.4318 pesos;
US $1 = 1.0000 pesos;
€1 = 88.76 centavos;
100 Cuban pesos = £69.84 = $100.00 = €112.66.

Note: The foregoing information relates to official exchange rates. For the purposes of foreign trade, the peso was at par with the US dollar during each of the 10 years 1987–96. A 'convertible peso' was introduced in December 1994. The free market rate of exchange in September 1998 was US $1 = 23 Cuban pesos.

STATE BUDGET (million pesos)

	1998	1999	2000
Total revenue	12,502.0	13,419.0	14,505.0
Total expenditure . . .	13,061.7	14,030.9	15,243.0
Productive sector . .	2,588.4	2,669.8	2,728.0
Housing and community services	1,705.1	1,785.7	1,786.0
Education	1,509.7	1,829.6	2,125.0
Public health . . .	1,344.9	1,553.1	1,726.0
Government administration and judicial bodies . . .	437.8	457.4	537.0
Defence and public order . .	537.1	752.3	935.0

Source: Ministry of Finance and Prices.

INTERNATIONAL RESERVES (million pesos at 31 December)

	1987	1988
Gold and other precious metals	17.5	19.5
Cash and deposits in foreign banks (convertible currency)	36.5	78.0
Sub-total	54.0	97.5
Deposits in foreign banks (in transferable roubles)	142.5	137.0
Total	196.5	234.5

NATIONAL ACCOUNTS

Composition of Gross National Product
(million pesos at current prices)

	1996	1997	1998
Compensation of employees . .	10,181.9	10,291.9	10,328.3
Operating surplus . . . }			
Consumption of fixed capital . . }	5,671.2	6,085.4	6,631.8
Gross domestic product (GDP) at factor cost	15,853.1	16,377.3	16,960.1
Indirect taxes *less* subsidies . .	6,961.6	6,574.5	6,940.7
GDP in purchasers' values .	22,814.7	22,951.8	23,900.8
Less Factor income from abroad (net)	492.6	482.9	599.2
Gross national product . .	22,322.1	22,468.9	23,301.6

Source: UN Economic Commission for Latin America and the Caribbean, *Statistical Yearbook*.

1999 (million pesos at current prices): GDP in purchasers' values 25,503.6.

Expenditure on the Gross Domestic Product
(million pesos at current prices)

	1996	1997	1998
Government final consumption expenditure	5,521.8	5,513.8	5,642.3
Private final consumption expenditure	16,281.7	16,347.0	17,109.0
Increase in stocks	−637.4	−513.6	−544.2
Gross fixed capital formation . .	2,258.2	2,274.7	2,431.4
Total domestic expenditure .	23,424.3	23,621.9	24,638.5
Exports of goods and services . .	3,563.6	3,785.5	3,872.3
Less Imports of goods and services	4,173.2	4,455.6	4,610.0
GDP in purchasers' values .	22,814.7	22,951.8	23,900.8
GDP at constant 1981 prices .	14,218.0	14,572.4	14,754.0

Source: UN Economic Commission for Latin America and the Caribbean, *Statistical Yearbook*.

Gross Domestic Product by Economic Activity
(million pesos at current prices)

	1996	1997	1998
Agriculture, hunting, forestry and fishing	1,548.1	1,531.9	1,473.2
Mining and quarrying . . .	332.2	349.5	360.5
Manufacturing	8,367.1	8,401.8	8,923.2
Electricity, gas and water . .	483.6	487.6	471.8
Construction	1,176.5	1,217.2	1,282.5
Wholesale and retail trade, restaurants and hotels . .	4,774.3	4,832.5	5,023.4
Transport, storage and communications . . .	1,000.3	1,018.5	1,061.1
Finance, insurance, real estate and business services . .	488.4	498.3	546.6
Community, social and personal services	4,221.0	4,263.3	4,372.9
Sub total	22,391.5	22,600.6	23,515.0
Import duties	423.2	351.2	385.6
Total	22,814.7	22,951.8	23,900.8

Source: UN Economic Commission for Latin America and the Caribbean, *Statistical Yearbook*.

BALANCE OF PAYMENTS (million pesos)

	1996	1997	1998
Exports of goods	1,866.2	1,823.1	1,444.4
Imports of goods . . .	−3,656.5	−4,087.6	−4,229.7
Trade balance	−1,790.3	−2,264.5	−2,785.3
Services (net)	1,372.4	1,519.0	2,168.2
Balance on goods and services .	−417.9	−745.5	−617.1
Other income (net) . . .	−492.6	−482.9	−599.2
Balance on goods, services and income	−910.5	−1,228.4	−1,216.3
Current transfers (net) . . .	743.7	791.7	820.0
Current balance . . .	−166.8	−436.7	−396.3
Direct investment (net) . . .	82.1	442.0	206.6
Other long-term capital (net) . .	225.8	344.9	426.1
Other capital (net) . .	−133.5	−329.5	−219.4
Overall balance . . .	7.6	20.7	17.0

External Trade

PRINCIPAL COMMODITIES (US $ million)

Imports c.i.f.	1994	1995	1996
Food and live animals . . .	467.4	610.9	689.2
Dairy products and birds' eggs .	72.1	90.4	84.9
Cereals and cereal preparations	237.1	331.6	396.9
Wheat and meslin (unmilled) .	119.7	132.8	158.4
Rice	72.5	107.3	126.5
Vegetables and fruit . . .	60.6	57.2	61.1
Dried beans, peas, lentils, etc. (shelled)	56.0	49.8	49.3
Bran sharps, etc. . . .	49.1	49.9	60.6
Crude materials (inedible) except fuels	79.9	113.7	98.3
Mineral fuels, lubricants, etc.. .	766.7	871.9	971.6
Petroleum and petroleum products	742.6	849.6	953.1
Crude petroleum oils, etc. .	170.3	156.2	250.2
Kerosene and other medium oils	245.1	330.7	333.1
Gas oils	216.4	256.9	299.4
Chemicals and related products .	172.9	309.2	302.6
Disinfectants, insecticides, fungicides, weed-killers, etc. .	44.6	64.7	55.7
Basic manufactures . . .	198.4	374.6	520.1
Rubber manufactures . .	42.5	74.4	54.2
Iron and steel . . .	43.9	90.5	125.1
Machinery and transport equipment	196.3	426.7	561.6
Power-generating machinery and equipment	96.7	197.5	256.1
Miscellaneous manufactured articles	32.1	93.0	177.2
Total (incl. others)	2,016.9	2,882.6	3,480.7

Exports f.o.b.	1994	1995	1996
Food and live animals . .	914.6	899.6	1,159.5
Fish, crustaceans, molluscs and preparations . . .	99.3	121.8	125.0
Fresh, chilled or frozen fish .	98.2	120.6	124.6
Vegetables and fruit . .	30.3	31.3	38.5
Sugar, sugar preparations and honey	763.3	718.1	976.5
Raw beet and cane sugars (solid)	748.1	704.5	951.7
Beverages and tobacco . .	78.8	112.1	120.0
Tobacco and tobacco manufactures . . .	71.4	102.1	108.4
Manufactured tobacco . .	55.2	75.5	79.4
Crude materials (inedible) except fuels	208.9	351.8	437.6
Metalliferous ores and metal scrap	206.6	347.8	433.9
Nickel ores, concentrates, etc..	196.1	323.7	417.1
Chemicals and related products .	77.6	53.2	57.7
Medicaments	76.3	48.3	51.7
Basic manufactures . . .	42.5	60.3	57.0
Iron and steel	21.4	30.5	32.7
Total (incl. others) . . .	1,330.8	1,491.7	1,848.9

Source: UN, *International Trade Statistics Yearbook*.

PRINCIPAL TRADING PARTNERS (US $ million)

Imports c.i.f.	1996	1997	1998
Argentina	137	131	78
Brazil	47	55	66
Canada	187	266	263
China, People's Republic . .	111	172	140
France	217	233	285
Germany	77	66	83
Italy	124	134	213
Mexico	350	n.a.	n.a.
Netherlands Antilles . . .	40	44	50
Spain	513	522	584
Russia	508	314	77
United Kingdom . . .	42	34	61
Venezuela	126	140	145
Total (incl. others) . . .	3,007	2,846	2,613

Source: IMF, *Direction of Trade Statistics Yearbook*.

Exports f.o.b.	1996	1997	1998
Algeria	35	41	44
Belarus	25	77	25
Canada	294	255	227
China, People's Republic . .	125	91	85
Colombia	19	25	29
Egypt	15	69	79
France	48	50	55
Germany	24	28	26
Japan	61	99	56
Netherlands	204	240	230
Russia	369	320	374
Spain	119	112	130
United Kingdom . . .	27	22	24
Total (incl. others) . . .	1,855	1,755	1,721

Source: IMF, *Direction of Trade Statistics Yearbook*.

Transport

RAILWAYS

	1996	1997	1998
Passenger-kilometres (million) . . .	2,159.5	1,962.2	–
Freight ton-kilometres (million) .	1,054.5	1,074.8	1,017.8

Source: UN Economic Commission for Latin America and the Caribbean, *Statistical Yearbook*.

Passengers ('000): 16,000 in 1998; 16,000 in 1999.
Freight carried ('000 metric tons): 6,037.8 in 1999.

ROAD TRAFFIC (motor vehicles in use at 31 December)

	1996	1997
Passenger cars	216,575	172,574
Buses and coaches	28,089	28,861
Lorries and vans	246,105	156,634

Source: IRF, *World Road Statistics*.

SHIPPING
Merchant Fleet (registered at 31 December)

	1996	1997	1998
Number of vessels	324	148	105
Total displacement ('000 grt) . .	291	203	158

Source: Lloyd's Register of Shipping, *World Fleet Statistics*.

International Sea-borne Freight Traffic ('000 metric tons)

	1988	1989	1990
Goods loaded	8,600	8,517	8,092
Goods unloaded	15,500	15,595	15,440

Source: UN, *Monthly Bulletin of Statistics.*

CIVIL AVIATION (traffic on scheduled services)

	1995	1996	1997
Kilometres flown (million) . .	16	20	26
Passengers carried ('000) . .	824	929	1,117
Passenger- kilometres (million) . .	2,006	2,649	3,543
Total ton-kilometres (million) .	219	292	388

Source: UN, *Statistical Yearbook.*

Tourism

ARRIVALS BY NATIONALITY*

	1996	1997	1998
Argentina	31,331	41,511	47,579
Canada	162,766	169,686	215,644
Colombia	25,251	28,745	20,702
France	62,742	93,897	101,604
Germany	80,185	86,509	148,987
Italy	192,297	200,238	186,688
Mexico	37,229	52,712	61,589
Spain	117,957	116,606	140,435
United Kingdom	28,077	46,215	64,276
USA	27,113	34,956	46,778
Total (incl. others) . . .	1,004,336	1,170,083	1,415,832

* Figures include same-day visitors (excursionists).

Sources: World Tourism Organization, *Yearbook of Tourism Statistics*; World Bank, *World Development Indicators.*

Tourism arrivals ('000): 1,561 in 1999; 1,774 in 2000.

Tourism receipts (US $ million): 1,338 in 1997; 1,626 in 1998; 1,714 in 1999 .

Communications Media

	1995	1996	1997
Radio receivers ('000 in use) . .	3,850	3,870	3,900
Television receivers ('000 in use) .	2,500	2,600	2,640
Telephones ('000 main lines in use)	353	356	371
Mobile cellular telephones (subscribers)	1,939	2,427	2,994
Book production (titles) . . .	698	679	625

Telefax stations (number in use): 392 in 1992.

Sources: mainly UNESCO, *Statistical Yearbook,* and UN, *Statistical Yearbook.*

Book production (titles): 621 in 1998; 708 in 1999.

Education

(1999/2000)

	Institutions	Teachers	Students
Pre-primary	1,114	19,600	149,100
Primary	9,375	76,300	987,900
Secondary	2,018	70,900	857,700
Universities	37	23,500	106,800

Directory

The Constitution

Following the assumption of power by the Castro regime, on 1 January 1959, the Constitution was suspended and a Fundamental Law of the Republic was instituted, with effect from 7 February 1959. In February 1976 Cuba's first socialist Constitution came into force after being submitted to the first Congress of the Communist Party of Cuba, in December 1975, and to popular referendum, in February 1976; it was amended in July 1992. The main provisions of the Constitution, as amended, are summarized below:

POLITICAL, SOCIAL AND ECONOMIC PRINCIPLES

The Republic of Cuba is a socialist, independent, and sovereign state, organized with all and for the sake of all as a unitary and democratic republic for the enjoyment of political freedom, social justice, collective and individual well-being and human solidarity. Sovereignty rests with the people, from whom originates the power of the State. The Communist Party of Cuba is the leading force of society and the State. The State recognizes, respects and guarantees freedom of religion. Religious institutions are separate from the State. The socialist State carries out the will of the working people and guarantees work, medical care, education, food, clothing and housing. The Republic of Cuba bases its relations with other socialist countries on socialist internationalism, friendship, co-operation and

mutual assistance. It reaffirms its willingness to integrate with and co-operate with the countries of Latin America and the Caribbean.

The State organizes and directs the economic life of the nation in accordance with a central social and economic development plan. The State directs and controls foreign trade. The State recognizes the right of small farmers to own their lands and other means of production and to sell that land. The State guarantees the right of citizens to ownership of personal property in the form of earnings, savings, place of residence and other possessions and objects which serve to satisfy their material and cultural needs. The State also guarantees the right of inheritance.

Cuban citizenship is acquired by birth or through naturalization. The State protects the family, motherhood and matrimony.

The State directs and encourages all aspects of education, culture and science.

All citizens have equal rights and are subject to equal duties.

The State guarantees the right to medical care, education, freedom of speech and press, assembly, demonstration, association and privacy. In the socialist society work is the right and duty, and a source of pride for every citizen.

GOVERNMENT

National Assembly of People's Power

The National Assembly of People's Power (Asamblea Nacional del Poder Popular) is the supreme organ of the State and is the only organ with constituent and legislative authority. It is composed of deputies, over the age of 18, elected by free, direct and secret ballot, for a period of five years. All Cuban citizens aged 16 years or more, except those who are mentally incapacitated or who have committed a crime, are eligible to vote. The National Assembly of People's Power holds two ordinary sessions a year and a special session when requested by one-third of the deputies or by the Council of State. More than one-half of the total number of deputies must be present for a session to be held.

All decisions made by the Assembly, except those relating to constitutional reforms, are adopted by a simple majority of votes. The deputies may be recalled by their electors at any time.

The National Assembly of People's Power has the following functions:

to reform the Constitution;

to approve, modify and annul laws;

to supervise all organs of the State and government;

to decide on the constitutionality of laws and decrees;

to revoke decree-laws issued by the Council of State and the Council of Ministers;

to discuss and approve economic and social development plans, the state budget, monetary and credit systems;

to approve the general outlines of foreign and domestic policy, to ratify and annul international treaties, to declare war and approve peace treaties;

to approve the administrative division of the country;

to elect the President, First Vice-President, the Vice-Presidents and other members of the Council of State;

to elect the President, Vice-President and Secretary of the National Assembly;

to appoint the members of the Council of Ministers on the proposal of the President of the Council of State;

to elect the President, Vice-President and other judges of the People's Supreme Court;

to elect the Attorney-General and the Deputy Attorney-Generals;

to grant amnesty;

to call referendums.

The President of the National Assembly presides over sessions of the Assembly, calls ordinary sessions, proposes the draft agenda, signs the Official Gazette, organizes the work of the commissions appointed by the Assembly and attends the meetings of the Council of State.

Council of State

The Council of State is elected from the members of the National Assembly and represents that Assembly in the period between sessions. It comprises a President, one First Vice-President, five Vice-Presidents, one Secretary and 23 other members. Its mandate ends when a new Assembly meets. All decisions are adopted by a simple majority of votes. It is accountable for its actions to the National Assembly.

The Council of State has the following functions:

to call special sessions of the National Assembly;

to set the date for the election of a new Assembly;

to issue decree-laws in the period between the sessions of the National Assembly;

to decree mobilization in the event of war and to approve peace treaties when the Assembly is in recess;

to issue instructions to the courts and the Office of the Attorney-General of the Republic;

to appoint and remove ambassadors of Cuba abroad on the proposal of its President, to grant or refuse recognition to diplomatic representatives of other countries to Cuba;

to suspend those provisions of the Council of Ministers that are not in accordance with the Constitution;

to revoke the resolutions of the Executive Committee of the local organs of People's Power which are contrary to the Constitution or laws and decrees formulated by other higher organs.

The President of the Council of State is Head of State and Head of Government and for all purposes the Council of State is the highest representative of the Cuban state.

Head of State

The President of the Council of State is the Head of State and the Head of Government and has the following powers:

to represent the State and Government and conduct general policy;

to convene and preside over the sessions of the Council of State and the Council of Ministers;

to supervise the ministries and other administrative bodies;

to propose the members of the Council of Ministers to the National Assembly of People's Power;

to receive the credentials of the heads of foreign diplomatic missions;

to sign the decree-laws and other resolutions of the Council of State;

to exercise the Supreme Command of all armed institutions and determine their general organization;

to preside over the National Defence Council;

to declare a state of emergency in the cases outlined in the Constitution.

In the case of absence, illness or death of the President of the Council of State, the First Vice-President assumes the President's duties.

The Council of Ministers

The Council of Ministers is the highest-ranking executive and administrative organ. It is composed of the Head of State and Government, as its President, the First Vice-President, the Vice-Presidents, the Ministers, the Secretary and other members determined by law. Its Executive Committee is composed of the President, the First Vice-President, the Vice-Presidents and other members of the Council of Ministers determined by the President.

The Council of Ministers has the following powers:

to conduct political, economic, cultural, scientific, social and defence policy as outlined by the National Assembly;

to approve international treaties;

to propose projects for the general development plan and, if they are approved by the National Assembly, to supervise their implementation;

to conduct foreign policy and trade;

to draw up bills and submit them to the National Assembly;

to draw up the draft state budget;

to conduct general administration, implement laws, issue decrees and supervise defence and national security.

The Council of Ministers is accountable to the National Assembly of People's Power.

LOCAL GOVERNMENT

The country is divided into 14 provinces and 169 municipalities. The provinces are: Pinar del Río, Habana, Ciudad de la Habana, Matanzas, Villa Clara, Cienfuegos, Sancti Spíritus, Ciego de Avila, Camagüey, Las Tunas, Holguín, Granma, Santiago de Cuba and Guantánamo.

Voting for delegates to the municipal assemblies is direct, secret and voluntary. All citizens over 16 years of age are eligible to vote. The number of delegates to each assembly is proportionate to the number of people living in that area. A delegate must obtain more than one-half of the total number of votes cast in the constituency in order to be elected. The Municipal and Provincial Assemblies of People's Power are elected by free, direct and secret ballot. Nominations for Municipal and Provincial Executive Committees of People's Power are submitted to the relevant assembly by a commission presided over by a representative of the Communist Party's leading organ and consisting of representatives of youth, workers', farmers', revolutionary and women's organizations. The President and Secretary of each of the regional and the provincial assemblies are the only full-time members, the other delegates carrying out their functions in addition to their normal employment.

The regular and extraordinary sessions of the local Assemblies of People's Power are public. More than one-half of the total number of members must be present in order for agreements made to be valid. Agreements are adopted by simple majority.

JUDICIARY

Judicial power is exercised by the People's Supreme Court and all other competent tribunals and courts. The People's Supreme Court is the supreme judicial authority and is accountable only to the National Assembly of People's Power. It can propose laws and issue regulations through its Council of Government. Judges are independent but the courts must inform the electorate of their activities at least once a year. Every accused person has the right to a defence and can be tried only by a tribunal.

The Office of the Attorney-General is subordinate only to the National Assembly and the Council of State and is responsible for ensuring that the law is properly obeyed.

The Constitution may be totally or partially modified only by a two-thirds majority vote in the National Assembly of People's Power. If the modification is total, or if it concerns the composition and powers of the National Assembly of People's Power or the Council of State, or the rights and duties contained in the Constitution, it also requires a positive vote by referendum.

The Government

(August 2001)

Head of State: Dr FIDEL CASTRO RUZ (took office 2 December 1976; re-elected December 1981, December 1986, March 1993 and February 1998).

COUNCIL OF STATE

President: Dr FIDEL CASTRO RUZ.

First Vice-President: Gen. RAÚL CASTRO RUZ.

Vice-Presidents:

JUAN ALMEIDA BOSQUE.

Gen. ABELARDO COLOMÉ IBARRA.

CARLOS LAGE DÁVILA.

JUAN ESTEBAN LAZO HERNÁNDEZ.

JOSÉ RAMÓN MACHADO VENTURA.

Secretary: Dr JOSÉ M. MIYAR BARRUECOS.

Members:

JOSÉ RAMÓN BALAGUER CABRERA.

VILMA ESPÍN GUILLOIS DE CASTRO.

Dr ARMANDO HART DÁVALOS.

ORLANDO LUGO FONTE.

REGLA MARTÍNEZ HERRERA.

MAÍA CARIDAD ABREUS RUIZ.

CONRADO MARTÍNEZ CORONA.

Gen. JULIO CASAS REGUEIRO.

MARCOS RAÚL AGUILERA GUETÓN.

JOSÉ LUIS RODRÍGUEZ GARCÍA.

SALVADOR VALDÉS MESA.

PEDRO MIRET PRIETO.

ROBERTO T. DÍAZ SOTOLONGO.

SERGIO CORRIERI HERNÁNDEZ.

ROBERTO FERNÁNDEZ RETAMAR.

FELIPE RAMÓN PÉREZ ROQUE.

MARCOS J. PORTAL LEÓN.

CARIDAD DIEGO BELLO.

JUAN CONTINO ASLÁN.

PEDRO ROSS LEAL.

OTTO RIVERO TORRES.

CARLOS MANUEL VALENCIAGA DÍAZ.

Dra ROSA ELENA SIMEÓN NEGRÍN.

COUNCIL OF MINISTERS

President: Dr FIDEL CASTRO RUZ.

First Vice-President: Gen. RAÚL CASTRO RUZ.

Secretary: CARLOS LAGE DÁVILA.

Vice-Presidents:

OSMANY CIENFUEGOS GORRIARÁN.

OSMANY CIENFUEGOS GORRIARÁN.

PEDRO MIRET PRIETO.

JOSÉ LUIS RODRÍGUEZ GARCÍA.

Minister of Agriculture: ALFREDO JORDÁN MORALES.

Minister of Foreign Trade: RAÚL DE LA NUEZ RAMÍREZ.

Minister of Internal Trade: BARBARA CASTILLO CUESTA.

Minister of Information and Communications: Gen. ROBERTO IGNACIO GONZÁLEZ PLANAS.

Minister of Construction: JUAN MARIO JUNCO DEL PINO.

Minister of Culture: ABEL ENRIQUE PRIETO JIMÉNEZ.

Minister of Economy and Planning: JOSÉ LUIS RODRÍGUEZ GARCÍA.

Minister of Education: LUIS IGNACIO GÓMEZ GUTIÉRREZ.

Minister of Higher Education: FERNANDO VECINO ALEGRET.

Minister of the Revolutionary Armed Forces: Gen. RAÚL CASTRO RUZ.

Minister of Finance and Prices: JOSÉ MANUEL MILLARES RODRÍGUEZ.

Minister of the Food Industry: ALEJANDRO ROCA IGLESIAS.

Minister of Foreign Investment and Economic Co-operation: MARTHA LOMAS MORALES.

Minister of Sugar: Gen. ULISES ROSALES DEL TORO.

Minister of the Construction Materials Industry: (vacant).

Minister of Light Industry: JESÚS D. PÉREZ OTHÓN.

Minister of the Fishing Industry: ALFREDO LÓPEZ VALDÉS.

Minister of the Iron and Steel, Metallurgical and Electronic Industries: FERNANDO ACOSTA SANTANA.

Minister of Basic Industries: MARCOS J. PORTAL LEÓN.

Minister of the Interior: Gen. ABELARDO COLOMÉ IBARRA.

Minister of Justice: ROBERTO T. DÍAZ SOTOLONGO.

Minister of Foreign Affairs: FELIPE RAMÓN PÉREZ ROQUE.

Minister of Labour and Social Security: ALFREDO MORALES CARTAYA.

Minister of Public Health: CARLOS DOTRES MARTÍNEZ.

Minister of Science, Technology and the Environment: Dra ROSA ELENA SIMEÓN NEGRÍN.

Minister of Transport: ALVARO PÉREZ MORALES.

Minister of Tourism: IBRAHÍM FERRADAZ GARCÍA.

Minister of Auditing and Control: LINA OLINDA PEDRAZA RODRÍGUEZ.

Minister, President of the Banco Central de Cuba: FRANCISCO SOBERÓN VALDÉS.

Ministers without Portfolio: RICARDO CABRISAS RUIZ, WILFREDO LÓPEZ RODRÍGUEZ.

MINISTRIES

Ministry of Agriculture: Avda Independencia, entre Conill y Sta Ana, Havana; tel. (7) 84-5770; fax (7) 33-5086.

Ministry of Auditing and Control: Havana; replaced the National Auditing Office in 2001.

Ministry of Basic Industries: Avda Salvador Allende 666, Havana; tel. (7) 70-7711.

Ministry of Construction: Avda Carlos M. de Céspedes y Calle 35, Havana; tel. (7) 81-8385; fax (7) 33-5585; e-mail dirinter@ceniai.inf.cu.

Ministry of the Construction Materials Industry: Calle 17, esq. O, Vedado, Havana; tel. (7) 32-2541; fax (7) 33-3176.

Ministry of Culture: Calle 2, No 258, entre 11 y 13, Vedado, Havana; tel. (7) 55-2228; fax (7) 66-2053; e-mail rinter@min.cult.cu; internet www.cubarte.cult.cu.

Ministry of Economy and Planning: 20 de Mayo y Ayestarán, Plaza de la Revolución, Havana; fax (7) 33-3387.

Ministry of Education: Obispo 160, Havana; tel. (7) 61-4888.

Ministry of Finance and Prices: Obispo 211, esq. Cuba, Havana; tel. (7) 57-3280; fax (7) 33-8050; internet www2.cuba.cu/economia/finanzas.

Ministry of the Fishing Industry: Avda 5 y 248 Jaimanitas, Santa Fé, Havana; tel. (7) 29-7034; fax (7) 24-9168; e-mail alvarez@fishery.inf.cu.

Ministry of the Food Industry: Avda 41, No 4455, Playa, Havana; tel. (7) 23-6801; fax (7) 23-4052; e-mail minalvm1@ceniai.inf.cu.

Ministry of Foreign Affairs: Calzada 360, esq. G, Vedado, Havana; tel. (7) 55-3537; fax (7) 33-3460; e-mail cubaminrex@minrex.gov.cu; internet www.cubaminrex.cu.

Ministry of Foreign Investment and Economic Co-operation: Primera No 2203, entre 22 y 24, Miramar, Havana; tel. (7) 22-3873; fax (7) 24-2105; e-mail epinv@minuce.cu.

Ministry of Foreign Trade: Infanta 16, esquina 23, Vedado, Havana; tel. (7) 55-0428; fax (7) 55-0376; e-mail cepecdir@infocex.cu; internet www.infocex.cu/cepec/.

Ministry of Higher Education: Calle 23, No 565, esq. a F, Vedado, Havana; tel. (7) 3-6655; fax (7) 33-3090; e-mail dri@reduniv.edu.cu.

Ministry of Information and Communications: Plaza de la Revolución 'José Martí', Apdo 10600, Havana; tel. (7) 81-7654.

Ministry of the Interior: Plaza de la Revolución, Havana.

Ministry of Internal Trade: Calle Habana 258, Havana; tel. (7) 62-5790.

Ministry of the Iron and Steel, Metallurgical and Electronic Industries: Avda Rancho Boyeros y Calle 100, Havana; tel. (7) 20-4861.

Ministry of Justice: Calle 0, No 216, entre 23 y Humboldt, Vedado, Apdo 10400, Havana 4; tel. (7) 32-6319.

Ministry of Labour and Social Security: Calle 23, esq. Calles O y P, Vedado, Havana; tel. (7) 55-0071; fax (7) 33-5816; e-mail mtssmin@ceniai.inf.cu.

Ministry of Light Industry: Empedrado 302, Havana; tel. (7) 67-0387; fax (7) 67-0329; e-mail ministro@minil.org.cu; internet www.ligera.cu.

Ministry of Public Health: Calle 23, No 301, Vedado, Havana; tel. (7) 32-2561.

Ministry of the Revolutionary Armed Forces: Plaza de la Revolución, Havana.

Ministry of Science, Technology and the Environment: Havana.

Ministry of Sugar: Calle 23, No 171, Vedado, Havana; tel. (7) 30-5061.

Ministry of Tourism: Havana; internet www.cubatravel.cu.

Ministry of Transport: Avda Independencia y Tulipán, Havana; tel. (7) 81-2076.

Legislature

ASAMBLEA NACIONAL DEL PODER POPULAR

The National Assembly of People's Power was constituted on 2 December 1976. In July 1992 the National Assembly adopted a constitutional amendment providing for legislative elections by direct vote. Only candidates nominated by the PCC were permitted to contest the elections. At elections to the National Assembly conducted on 11 January 1998 all 601 candidates were elected. Of the 7.8m. registered voters, 98.35% participated in the elections. Only 5% of votes cast were blank or spoilt.

President: RICARDO ALARCÓN DE QUESADA.

Vice-President: JAIME CROMBET HERNÁNDEZ MAURELL.

Secretary: Dr ERNESTO SUÁREZ MÉNDEZ.

Political Organizations

Partido Comunista de Cuba (PCC) (Communist Party of Cuba): Havana; internet www2.cuba.cu/politica/webpcc; f. 1961 as the Organizaciones Revolucionarias Integradas (ORI) from a fusion of the Partido Socialista Popular (Communist), Fidel Castro's Movimiento 26 de Julio and the Directorio Revolucionario 13 de Marzo; became the Partido Unido de la Revolución Socialista Cubana (PURSC) in 1962; renamed as the Partido Comunista de Cuba in 1965; 150-member Central Committee, Political Bureau (24 mems in 1997), and five Commissions; 706,132 mems (1994).

Political Bureau: Dr FIDEL CASTRO RUZ, Gen. RAÚL CASTRO RUZ, JUAN ALMEIDA BOSQUE, JOSÉ RAMÓN MACHADO VENTURA, JUAN ESTEBAN LAZO HERNÁNDEZ, Gen. ABELARDO COLOMÉ IBARRA, PEDRO ROSS LEAL, CARLOS LAGE DÁVILA, ROBERTO ROBAÍNA GONZÁLEZ, ALFREDO JORDÁN MORALES, Gen. ULISES ROSALES DEL TORO, CONCEPCIÓN CAMPA HUERGO, YADIRA GARCÍA VERA, ABEL ENRIQUE PRIETO JIMÉNEZ, Gen. JULIO CASAS REGUEIRO, Gen. LEOPOLDO CINTRA FRÍAS, RICARDO ALARCÓN DE QUESADA, JOSÉ RAMÓN BALAGUER CABRERA, MISAEL ENAMORADO DAGER, Gen. RAMÓN ESPINOSA MARTÍN, MARCOS J. PORTAL LEÓN, JUAN CARLOS ROBINSON AGRAMONTE, PEDRO SÁEZ MONTEJO, JORGE LUIS SIERRA CRUZ.

There are a number of dissident groups operating in Cuba. These include:

Concertación Democrática Cubana—CDC: f. 1991; alliance of 11 dissident organizations campaigning for political pluralism and economic reform; Leader ELIZARDO SÁNCHEZ SANTA CRUZ.

Cuban Democratic Platform: f. 1990; alliance comprising three dissident organizations:

Coordinadora Social Demócrata.

Partido Demócrata Cristiano de Cuba—PDC: POB 558987, Miami, FL 33155, USA; tel. (305) 264-9411; fax (954) 489-1572; e-mail amayawarry@aol.com; internet www.pdc-cuba.org.

Unión Liberal Cubana: Menéndez y Pelayo 83, 28007 Madrid, Spain; fax (91) 5011342; e-mail cubaliberal@mercuryin.es; internet www.cubaliberal.org; mem. of Liberal International; Founder and Chair. CARLOS ALBERTO MONTANER.

Partido Cubano Ortodoxo: f. 1999; Leader NELSON AGUIAR.

Partido Liberal Democrático de Cuba: Chair. OSVALDO ALFONSO VALDÉS.

Partido pro-Derechos Humanos: f. 1988 to defend human rights in Cuba; Pres. HIRAM ABI COBAS; Sec.-Gen. TANIA DÍAZ.

Partido Social Revolucionario Democrático de Cuba: POB 351081, Miami, FL 33135, USA; tel. and fax (305) 649-2886; e-mail soreb123@aol.com; Pres. JORGE VALLS.

Partido Solidaridad Democrática—PSD: POB 310063, Miami, FL 33131, USA; tel. (305) 408-2659; e-mail gladyperez@aol.com; internet www.ccsi.com/~ams/psd; Pres. FERNANDO SÁNCHEZ LÓPEZ.

Solidaridad Cubana: Leader FERNANDO SÁNCHEZ LÓPEZ.

Diplomatic Representation

EMBASSIES IN CUBA

Algeria: Avda 5, No 2802, esq. 28, Miramar, Havana; tel. (7) 24-2835; fax (7) 24-2702; Ambassador: RABAH KEROUAZ.

Angola: Avda 5, No 1012, entre 10 y 12, Miramar, Havana; tel. (7) 29-2205; fax (7) 24-2117; Ambassador: JOAO MANUEL BERNARDO.

Austria: Calle 4, No 101, entre 1 y 3, Miramar, Havana; tel. (7) 24-2824; fax (7) 24-1235; Ambassador: Dra HELGA KONRAD.

Belarus: Avda 5, No 3802, entre 38 y 40, Miramar, Havana; tel. (7) 33-0341; fax (7) 33-0340; Chargé d'affaires a.i.: VLADIMIR PISCHACO.

Belgium: Avda 5, No 7408, esq. 76, Miramar, Havana; tel. (7) 24-2410; fax (7) 24-1318; Ambassador: PATRICK DE BEYTER.

Belize: Avda 5, No 3608, entre 36 y 36A, Miramar, Havana; tel. (7) 24-3504; fax (7) 24-3506; e-mail belize.embassy@tip.etecsa.cu; Ambassador: AMALIA MAI-RANCHARAN.

Benin: Calle 20, No 119, entre 1 y 3, Miramar, Havana; tel. (7) 24-2179; fax (7) 24-2334; Ambassador: SIMPLICE GNANGUESSY.

Bolivia: Calle 26, No 113, entre 1 y 3, Miramar, Havana; tel. (7) 24-2426; fax (7) 24-2127; Ambassador: MARIA EUGENIA SALINAS INARRA.

Brazil: Calle Lamparilla, No 2, 4°K, Miramar, Havana; tel. (7) 66-9052; fax (7) 66-2912; Ambassador: LUCIANO MARTINS DE ALMEIDA.

Bulgaria: Calle B, No 252, entre 11 y 13, Vedado, Havana; tel. (7) 33-3125; fax (7) 33-3297; Chargé d'affaires a.i.: EMILIA STEFANOVA.

Burkina Faso: Calle 40, No 516, entre 5 y 7A, Miramar, Havana; tel. (7) 24-2217; fax (7) 24-1942; e-mail ambfaso@cenia.inf.cu; Ambassador: SALIF NÉBIÉ.

Cambodia: Avda 5, No 7001, esq. 70, Miramar, Havana; tel. (7) 24-1496; fax (7) 24-6400; Ambassador: CHIM PRORNG.

Canada: Calle 30, No 518, entre 5 y 7, Miramar, Havana; tel. (7) 24-2516; fax (7) 24-2044; e-mail havan@dfait-maeci.gc.ca; Chargé d'affaires a.i.: JENNIFER IRISH.

Cape Verde: Calle 20, No 2001, esq. 7, Miramar, Havana; tel. (7) 24-2979; fax (7) 24-1072; e-mail ecvc@ceniai.inf.cu; Ambassador: FATIMA LIMA VEIGA.

Chile: Avda 33, No 1423, entre 16 y 18, Mitamar, Havana; tel. (7) 24-1222; fax (7) 24-1694; Ambassador: GERMÁN GUERRERO PAVEZ.

China, People's Republic: Calle 13, No 551, Vedado, Havana; tel. (7) 33-3005; fax (7) 33-3092; Ambassador: WANG CHENGJIA.

Colombia: Calle 14, No 515, entre 5 y 7, Miramar, Havana; tel. (7) 24-1246; fax (7) 24-1249; Ambassador: JULIO LONDOÑO PAREDES.

Congo, Republic: Avda 5, No 1003, Miramar, Havana; tel. and fax 24-9055; Ambassador: PASCAL ONGUEMBY.

Czech Republic: Avda Kohly 259, entre 41 y 43, Nuevo Vedado, Havana; tel. (7) 33-3201; fax (7) 33-3596; Chargé d'affaires a.i.: JOSEF MARSICEK.

Dominican Republic: Avda 5, No 9202, entre 92 y 94, Miramar, Havana; tel. (7) 24-8429; fax (7) 24-8431; Ambassador: Dr DANIEL GUERRERO TAVERAS.

Ecuador: Avda 5A, No 4407, entre 44 y 46, Miramar, Havana; tel. (7) 24-2034; fax (7) 24-2868; Ambassador: JOSÉ EDUARDO TOBAR FIERRO.

Egypt: Avda 5, No 1801, esq. 18, Miramar, Havana; tel. (7) 24-2441; fax (7) 24-0905; Ambassador: HAZEM MUHAMMAD TAHER.

Ethiopia: Calle 6, No 318, Miramar, Havana; tel. (7) 22-1260; Ambassador: ABEBE BELAYNEH.

Finland: Havana; tel. (7) 33-2698; Ambassador: HEIKKI PUURUNEN.

France: Calle 14, No 312, entre 3 y 5, Miramar, Havana; tel. (7) 24-2132; fax (7) 24-1439; Ambassador: JEAN DÉVY.

Germany: Calle B, No 652, esq. 13, Vedado, Havana; tel. (7) 33-2539; fax (7) 33-1586; Ambassador: Dr REINHOLD HUBER.

Ghana: Avda 5, No 1808, esq. 20, Miramar, Havana; tel. (7) 24-2153; fax (7) 24-2317; Ambassador: Dr KWAKU DANSO-BOAFO.

Greece: Avda 5, No 7802, entre 78, Miramar, Havana; tel. (7) 24-2995; fax (7) 24-1784; Ambassador: GEORGE COSTOULAS.

Guatemala: Calle 16, No 505, entre 3 y 5, Miramar, Havana; tel. 24-3417; fax 24-3200; Ambassador: HUGO RENÉ GUZMÁN MALDONADO.

Guinea: Calle 20, No 504, entre 5 y 7, Miramar, Havana; tel. (7) 24-2003; fax (7) 24-2380; Ambassador: CHEICK ALIOUNE CONDÉ.

Guinea-Bissau: Calle 14, No 313, entre 3 y 5, Miramar, Havana; tel. (7) 24-2689; fax (7) 24-2794; Chargé d'affaires a.i.: LIBERATO GOMES.

Guyana: Calle 18, No 506, entre 5 y 7, Miramar, Havana; tel. (7) 24-2094; fax (7) 24-2867; Chargé d'affaires: TIMOTHY N. CRICHLOW.

Haiti: No 6804, entre 68 y 70, Miramar, Havana; tel. (7) 24-5421; fax (7) 24-5423; Chargé d'affaires a.i.: JEAN WILLIAM EXANTUS.

Holy See: Calle 12, No 514, entre 5 y 7, Miramar, Havana (Apostolic Nunciature); tel. (7) 24-2700; fax (7) 24-2257; e-mail csa@pcn.net); Apostolic Nuncio: Most Rev. LUIS ROBLES DÍAZ, Titular Archbishop of Stefaniaco.

Hungary: Calle G, No 458, entre 19 y 21, Vedado, Havana; tel. (7) 33-3365; fax (7) 33-3286; e-mail embhuncu@ceniai.inf.cu; Ambassador: VILMOS KOPÁNYI.

India: Calle 21, No 202, esq. a K, Vedado, Havana; tel. (7) 33-3777; fax (7) 33-3287; e-mail eoihav@ceniai.inf.cu; Ambassador: RAMIAH RAJAGOPALAN.

Indonesia: Avda 5, No 1607, esq. 18, Miramar, Havana; tel. (7) 24-9618; fax (7) 24-9617; Ambassador: Dr R. HARIDADI SUDJONO.

Iran: Avda 5, No 3002, esq. 30, Miramar, Havana; tel. (7) 24-2675; fax (7) 24-2770; Ambassador: SEYED DAVOOD MOHSENI SALEHI MONFARED.

Iraq: Avda 5, No 8201, entre 82 y 84, Miramar, Havana; tel. (7) 24-1607; fax (7) 24-2157; Ambassador: MUHAMMED MAHMOUD K. H. AL-AMILI.

Italy: Paseo 606, No 54, entre 25 y 27, Vedado, Havana; tel. (7) 33-3334; fax (7) 33-3416; e-mail ambitcub@ip.etecsa.cu; Ambassador: GIUSEPPE MOSCATO.

Jamaica: Avda 5, No 3608, entre 36 y 36A, Miramar, Havana; tel. (7) 24-2908; fax (7) 24-2531; e-mail embjmcub@mail.infocom.etecsa.cu; Ambassador: CARLYLE DUNKLEY.

Japan: Centro de Negocios Miramar, Avda 3, No 1, 5°, esq. 80, Miramar, Havana; tel. (7) 24-3508; fax (7) 24-8902; Ambassador: MUTSUO MABUCHI.

Korea, Democratic People's Republic: Calle 17, No 752, Vedado, Havana; tel. (7) 66-2313; fax (7) 33-3073; Ambassador: PAK TONG-CHUN.

Laos: Avda 5, No 2808, esq. 30, Miramar, Havana; tel. (7) 24-1056; fax (7) 24-9622; Ambassador: CHANPHENG SIHAPHOM.

Lebanon: Calle 17A, No 16403, entre 164 y 174, Siboney, Havana; tel. (7) 28-6220; fax (7) 28-6432; e-mail lbcunet@ceniai.inf.cu; Ambassador: SLEIMAN C. RASSI.

Libya: Avda 7, No 1402, esq. 14, Miramar, Havana; tel. (7) 24-2192; fax (7) 24-2991; Chargé d'affaires a.i.: ABDULLATIF H. EL-KHAZMI.

Mexico: Calle 12, No 518, Miramar, Playa, Havana; tel. (7) 24-2553; fax (7) 24-2717; Ambassador: RICARDO PASCOE.

Mongolia: Calle 66, No 505, esq. 5, Miramar, Havana; tel. (7) 24-2763; fax (7) 24-0639; Ambassador: BALJIN NYAMAA.

Mozambique: Avda 7, No 2203, entre 22 y 24, Miramar, Havana; tel. (7) 24-2443; fax (7) 24-2232; Ambassador: JULIO GONCALO BRAGA.

Namibia: Avda 5, No 4406, entre 44 y 46, Miramar, Havana; tel. (7) 24-1430; fax (7) 24-1431; e-mail embnamib@ceniai.inf.cu; Ambassador: ELÍA AKWAAKE.

Netherlands: Calle 8, No 307, entre 3 y 5, Miramar, Havana; tel. (7) 24-2511; fax (7) 24-2059; Ambassador: CORNELIA MINDERHOUD.

Nicaragua: Calle 20, No 709, entre 7 y 9, Miramar, Havana; tel. (7) 24-1025; fax (7) 24-6323; Chargé d'affaires a.i.: Dr LUIS NAPOLEÓN GADEA ARÓSTEGUI.

Nigeria: Avda 5, No 1401, entre 14 y 16, Miramar, Havana; tel. (7) 24-2898; fax (7) 24-2202; Ambassador: NGAM NWACHUKWU.

Panama: Calle 26, No 109, entre 1 y 3, Miramar, Havana; tel. (7) 24-1673; fax (7) 24-1674; Ambassador: MARCO ANTONIO ALARCÓN PALOMINO.

Paraguay: Calle 34, No 503, entre 5 y 7, Miramar, Havana; tel. (7) 24-0884; fax (7) 24-0883; Chargé d'affaires a.i.: ANASTACIO MEDINA ARMOA.

Peru: Calle 30, No 107, entre 1 y 3, Miramar, Havana; tel. (7) 24-2477; fax (7) 24-2636; Ambassador: JUAN CASTILLA MEZA.

Philippines: Avda 5, No 2207, esq. 24, Miramar, Havana; tel. (7) 24-1372; fax (7) 24-2915; e-mail philhav@ip.etecsa.cu; Ambassador: WENCESLAO JOSÉ O. QUIROLGICO.

Poland: Cale G, No 452, esq. 19, Vedado, Havana; tel. (7) 66-2439; fax (7) 66-2442; Ambassador: JAN JANISZEWSKI.

Portugal: Avda 5, No 6604, entre 66 y 68, Miramar, Havana; tel. (7) 24-2871; fax (7) 24-2593; Ambassador: MANUEL SILVA DUARTE COSTA.

Romania: Calle 21, No 307, Vedado, Havana; tel. (7) 33-3325; fax (7) 33-3324; e-mail erumania@ceniai.inf.cu; Ambassador: GHEORGHE UGLEAN.

Russia: Avda 5, No 6402, entre 62 y 66, Miramar, Havana; tel. (7) 24-2686; fax (7) 24-1038; Ambassador: ANDREI VICTOROVICH DIMITRIEV.

Slovakia: Calle 66, No 521, entre 5B y 7, Miramar, Havana; tel. (7) 24-1884; fax (7) 24-1883; Chargé d'affaires a.i.: JÁN GÁBOR.

South Africa: Avda 5, No 4201, esq. 42, Miramar, Havana; tel. (7) 24-9658; fax (7) 24-1101; Ambassador: NOEL MAKHAYA NDLOU JOHN MOSIA.

Spain: Cárcel No 51, esq. Zulueta, Havana; tel. (7) 33-8025; fax (7) 33-8006; Ambassador: JESÚS GRACIA ALDEZ.

Sri Lanka: Calle 32, No 307, entre 3 y 5, Miramar, Havana; tel. (7) 24-2562; fax (7) 24-2183; e-mail sri.lanka@ip.etecsa.cu; Chargé d'affaires a.i. JAYANTHA DISSANAYAKE.

Sweden: Calle 34, No 510, entre 5 y 7, Miramar, Havana; tel. (7) 24-2831; fax (7) 24-1194; e-mail ambassaden.havanna@foreign.ministry.se; Ambassador: EIVOR HALKJAER.

Switzerland: Avda 5, No 2005, entre 20 y 22, Miramar, Havana; tel. (7) 24-2611; fax (7) 24-1148; e-mail swissem@ip.etecsa.cu; Ambassador: JEAN-CAUDE RICHARD.

Syria: Avda 5, No 7402, entre 74 y 76, Miramar, Havana; tel. (7) 24-2266; fax (7) 24-2829; Chargé d'affaires: Dr CHAHIN FARAH.

Turkey: Avda 5, No 3805, entre 36 y 40, Miramar, Havana; tel. (7) 24-1205; fax (7) 24-2899; e-mail turkemb@ip.etecsa.cu; Ambassador: ATAMAN YALGIN.

Uganda: Calle 20, No 713, entre 7 y 9, Miramar, Havana; tel. (7) 24-0469; fax (7) 33-6668; Ambassador: ELIZABETH PAULA NAPEYOK.

Ukraine: Avda 5, No 4405, entre 44 y 46, Miramar, Havana; tel. (7) 24-2586; fax (7) 24-2341; Ambassador: EVGEN G. SVINARCHUK.

United Kingdom: Calle 34, No 702/4, esq. 7, Miramar, Havana; tel. (7) 24-1771; fax (7) 24-8104; e-mail embrit@ceniai.inf.cu; Ambassador: PAUL HARE.

USA (Relations broken off in 1961): Interests Section: Calzada, entre L y M, Vedado, Havana; tel. (7) 33-3543; fax (7) 66-2095; Principal Officer: VICKY HUDDLESTON.

Uruguay: Calle 14, No 506, entre 5 y 7, Miramar, Havana; tel. (7) 24-2311; fax (7) 24-2246; e-mail urucub@ceniai.inf.cu; Ambassador: ENRIQUE ESTRÁZULAS.

Venezuela: Calle 36A, No 704, entre 7 y 42, Miramar, Havana; tel. (7) 24-2662; fax (7) 24-2773; e-mail vencuba@ceniai.cu; Chargé d'affaires a.i.: ROCÍO MANEIRO.

Viet Nam: Avda 5, No 1802, Miramar, Havana; tel. (7) 24-1502; fax (7) 24-1041; Ambassador: THAI VAN LUNG.

Yemen: Calle 16, No 503, entre 5 y 7, Miramar, Havana; tel. (7) 24-1506; fax (7) 24-1131; Ambassador: Dr AHMED ABDULLA ABDUL ELAH.

Yugoslavia: Calle 42, No 115, entre 1 y 3, Miramar, Havana; tel. (7) 24-2488; fax (7) 24-2982; Ambassador: LJILJANA KADIC.

Zimbabwe: Avda 3, No 1001, esq. a 10, Miramar, Havana; tel. (7) 24-2857; fax (7) 24-2720; Ambassador: JEVANA BEN MASEKO.

Judicial System

The judicial system comprises the People's Supreme Court, the People's Provincial Courts and the People's Municipal Courts. The People's Supreme Court exercises the highest judicial authority.

PEOPLE'S SUPREME COURT

The People's Supreme Court comprises the Plenum, the six Courts of Justice in joint session and the Council of Government. When the Courts of Justice are in joint session they comprise all the professional and lay judges, the Attorney-General and the Minister of Justice. The Council of Government comprises the President and Vice-President of the People's Supreme Court, the Presidents of each Court of Justice and the Attorney-General of the Republic. The Minister of Justice may participate in its meetings.

President: Dr RUBÉN REMIGIO FERRO.

Vice-Presidents: Dr MANUEL DE JESÚS PÉREZ PÉREZ, Dra GRACIELA PRIETO MARTÍN.

Criminal Court:
President: Dr JORGE L. BODES TORRES.

Civil and Administrative Court:
President: ANDRÉS BOLAÑOS GASSÓ.

Labour Court:
President: Dr ANTONIO R. MARTÍN SÁNCHEZ.

Court for State Security:
President: Dr GUILLERMO HERNÁNDEZ INFANTE.

Economic Court:
President: Dr ELPIDIO PÉREZ SUÁREZ.

Military Court:
President: Col JUAN MARINO FUENTES CALZADO.

Attorney-General: JUAN ESCALONA REGUERA.

Religion

There is no established Church, and all religions are permitted, though Roman Catholicism predominates. The Afro-Cuban religions of Regla de Ocha (Santéria) and Regla Conga (Palo Monte) also have numerous adherents.

CHRISTIANITY

Consejo Ecuménico de Cuba (Ecumenical Council of Cuba): Calle 14, No 304, entre 3 y 5, Miramar, Playa, Havana; tel. (7) 33-1792; fax (7) 33-178820; f. 1941; 11 mem. churches; Pres. Rev. ORESTES GONZÁLEZ; Exec. Sec. Rev. JOSÉ LÓPEZ.

The Roman Catholic Church

Cuba comprises three archdioceses and eight dioceses. At 31 December 1999 there were 5,258,722 adherents, representing 46.7% of the total population.

Conferencia de Obispos Católicos de Cuba—COCC (Bishops' Conference): Calle 26, No 314, entre 3 y 5, Miramar, Apdo 594, Havana; tel. (7) 29-2395; fax (7) 24-2168; e-mail dei@cocc.co.cu; f. 1983; Pres. ADOLFO RODRÍGUEZ HERRERA, Archbishop of Camagüey.

Archbishop of Camagüey: ADOLFO RODRÍGUEZ HERRERA, Calle Luaces, No 55, Apdo 105, Camagüey 70100; tel. (322) 92268; fax (322) 87143.

Archbishop of San Cristóbal de la Habana: Cardinal JAIME LUCAS ORTEGA Y ALAMINO, Calle Habana No 152, esq. a Chacón, Apdo 594, Havana 10100; tel. (7) 62-4000; fax (7) 33-8109; e-mail cocc@brigadoo.com.

Archbishop of Santiago de Cuba: PEDRO CLARO MEURICE ESTÍU, Sánchez Hechevarría No 607, Apdo 26, Santiago de Cuba 90100; tel. (226) 25480; fax (226) 86186.

The Anglican Communion

Anglicans are adherents of the Iglesia Episcopal de Cuba (Episcopal Church of Cuba).

Bishop of Cuba: Rt Rev. JORGE PERERA HURTADO, Calle 6, No 273, Vedado, Havana 10400; fax (7) 33-3293.

Protestant Churches

Convención Bautista de Cuba Oriental (Baptist Convention of Eastern Cuba): San Jerónimo, No 467, entre Calvario y Carnicería, Santiago; tel. 2-0173; f. 1905; Pres. Rev. Dr ROY ACOSTA; Sec. RAFAEL MUSTELIER.

Iglesia Metodista en Cuba (Methodist Church in Cuba): Calle K, No 502, 25 y 27, Vedado, Apdo 10400, Havana; tel. (7) 32-2991; fax (7) 33-3135; e-mail imecu@ip.etecsa.cu; autonomous since 1968; 6,000 mems; Bishop RICARDO PEREIRA DÍAZ.

Iglesia Presbiteriana-Reformada en Cuba (Presbyterian-Reformed Church in Cuba): Apdo 154, Matanzas; autonomous since 1967; 8,000 mems; Gen. Sec. Rev. Dr SERGIO ARCE.

Other denominations active in Cuba include the Apostolic Church of Jesus Christ, the Bethel Evangelical Church, the Christian Pentecostal Church, the Church of God, the Church of the Nazarene, the Free Baptist Convention, the Holy Pentecost Church, the Pentecostal Congregational Church and the Salvation Army.

The Press

DAILY

In October 1990 President Castro announced that, in accordance with other wide-ranging economic austerity measures, only one newspaper, *Granma*, would henceforth be published as a nation-wide daily. The other national dailies were to become weeklies or were to cease publication.

Granma: Avda Gen. Suárez y Territorial, Plaza de la Revolución, Apdo 6187, Havana; tel. (7) 81-3333; fax (7) 33-5176; e-mail redac@granmai.get.cma.net; internet www.granma.cubaweb.cu; f. 1965 to replace *Hoy* and *Revolución*; official Communist Party organ; Dir FRANK AGÜERO GÓMEZ; circ. 400,000.

PERIODICALS

Adelante: Avda A, Rpto Jayamá, Camagüey; f. 1959; morning; Dir EVARISTO SARDIÑAS VERA; circ. 42,000.

Ahora: Salida a San Germán y Circunvalación, Holguín; f. 1962; Dir RADOBALDO MARTÍNEZ PÉREZ; circ. 50,000.

ANAP: Línea 206, entre H e I, Vedado, Havana; f. 1961; monthly; information for small farmers; Dir LEONEL VÁLDEZ ALONSO; circ. 30,000.

Bastión: Territorial esq. a Gen. Suárez, Plaza de la Revolución, Havana; tel. (7) 79-3361; organ of the Revolutionary Armed Forces; Dir FRANK AGÜERO GÓMEZ; circ. 65,000.

Bohemia: Avda Independencia y San Pedro, Apdo 6000, Havana; tel. (7) 81-9213; fax (7) 33-5511; e-mail bohemia@bohemia.get.tor.cu; f. 1908; weekly; politics; Dir JOSÉ FERNÁNDEZ VEGA; circ. 100,000.

Boletín Alimentaria de Cuba: Amargura 103, 10100 Havana; tel. (7) 62-9245; f. 1996; quarterly; food industry; Dir ANTONIO CAMPOS; circ. 10,000.

El Caimán Barbudo: Paseo 613, Vedado, Havana; f. 1966; monthly; cultural; Dir ALEX PAUSIDES; circ. 47,000.

Cinco de Septiembre: Calle 35, No 5609, entre 56 y 58, Cienfuegos; f. 1980; Dir FRANCISCO VALDÉS PETITÓN; circ. 18,000.

Cómicos: Calle 28, No 112, entre 1 y 3, Miramar, Havana; tel. (7) 22-5892; monthly; humorous; circ. 70,000.

Con la Guardia en Alto: Havana; **f.** 1961; monthly; for mems of the Committees for the Defence of the Revolution; Dir OMELIA GUERRA PÉREZ; circ. 60,000.

Cuba Internacional: Calle 21, No 406, Vedado, Havana 4, Apdo 3603 Havana 3; tel. (7) 32-3578; fax (7) 32-3268; f. 1959; monthly; political; Dir FÉLIX ALBISÚ; circ. 30,000.

Dedeté: Territorial y Gen. Suárez, Plaza de la Revolución, Apdo 6344, Havana; tel. (7) 82-0134; fax (7) 81-8621; e-mail jrebelde@tele da.get.cma.net; f. 1969; monthly; Dir ALEN LAUZÁN; circ. 70,000.

La Demajagua: Amado Estévez, esq. Calle 10, Rpto R. Reyes, Bayamo; f. 1977; Dir PEDRO MORA ESTRADA; circ. 21,000.

El Deporte, Derecho del Pueblo: Vía Blanca y Boyeros, Havana; tel. (7) 40-6838; f. 1968; monthly; sport; Dir MANUEL VAILLANT CARPENTE; circ. 15,000.

Escambray: Adolfo del Castillo 10, Sancti Spíritus; tel. (41) 23003; e-mail escambray@esiss.colombus.cu; internet www.escambray.isla grande.cu; f. 1979; Dir JUAN ANTONIO BORREGO DÍAZ; circ. 21,000.

Girón: Avda Camilo Cienfuegos No 10505, P. Nuero, Matanzas; f. 1960; Dir OTHONIEL GONZÁLEZ QUEVEDO; circ. 25,000.

Guerrillero: Colón esq. Delicias y Adela Azcuy, Pinar del Río; f. 1969; Dir RONALD SUÁREZ; circ. 33,000.

El Habanero: Gen. Suárez y Territorial, Plaza de la Revolución, Apdo 6269, Havana; tel. (7) 6160; f. 1987; Dir TUBAL PÁEZ HERNÁNDEZ; circ. 21,000.

Invasor: Marcial Gómez 401, esq. Estrada Palma, Ciego de Avila; f. 1979; Dir MIGDALIA UTRERA PEÑA; circ. 10,500.

Juventud Rebelde: Territorial esq. Gen. Suárez, Plaza de la Revolución, Apdo 6344, Havana; tel. (7) 82-0155; fax (7) 33-8959; e-mail cida@jrebelde.cip.cu; internet www.jrebelde.cubaweb.cu; f. 1965; organ of the Young Communist League; Dir ROGELIO POLANCO FUENTES; circ. 250,000.

Juventud Técnica: Prado 553, esq. Teniente Rey, Habana Vieja, Havana; tel. (7) 62-4330; e-mail eabril@jcce.org.cu; internet www .juventudtecnica.cu; f. 1965; every 2 months; scientific-technical; Dir MIRIAM ZITO VALDÉS; circ. 20,000.

Mar y Pesca: San Ignacio 303, Havana; tel. (7) 61-5518; fax 33-8438; f. 1965; quarterly; fishing; Dir GUSTAVO LÓPEZ; circ. 20,000.

El Militante Comunista: Calle 11, No 160, Vedado, Havana; tel. (7) 32-7581; f. 1967; monthly; Communist Party publication; Dir MANUEL MENÉNDEZ; circ. 200,000.

Moncada: Havana; f. 1966; monthly; Dir RICARDO MARTÍNEZ; circ. 70,000.

Muchacha: Galiano 264, esq. Neptuno, Havana; tel. (7) 61-5919; f. 1980; monthly; young women's magazine; Dir SILVIA MARTÍNEZ; circ. 120,000.

Mujeres: Galiano 264, esq. Neptuno, Havana; tel. (7) 61-5919; f. 1961; monthly; women's magazine; Dir REGLA ZULUETA; circ. 270,000.

El Muñe: Calle 28, No 112, entre 1 y 3, Mirimar, Havana; tel. (7) 22-5892; weekly; circ. 50,000.

Opciones: Territorial esq. Gen. Suárez, Plaza de la Revolucíon, Havana; e-mail jrebelde@teleda.get.cma.net; internet www.cuba web.cu/jrebelde/index.html; weekly; finance, commerce and tourism.

Opina: Edif. Focsa, M entre 17 y 19, Havana; f. 1979; 2 a month; consumer-orientated; published by Institute of Internal Demand; Dir EUGENIO RODRÍGUEZ BALARI; circ. 250,000.

Pablo: Calle 28, No 112, entre 1 y 3, Mirimar, Havana; tel. (7) 22-5892; 16 a year; circ. 53,000.

Palante: Calle 21, No 954, entre 8 y 10, Vedado, Havana; tel. (7) 3-5098; f. 1961; weekly; humorous; Dir ROSENDO GUTIÉRREZ ROMÁN; circ. 235,000.

Pionero: Calle 17, No 354, Havana 4; tel. (7) 32-4571; f. 1961; weekly; children's magazine; Dir PEDRO GONZÁLEZ (PÉGLEZ); circ. 210,000.

Prisma: Calle 21 y Avda G, No 406, Vedado, Havana; tel. (7) 8-7995; f. 1979; bimonthly; international news; Man. Dir LUIS MANUEL ARCE; circ. 15,000 (Spanish), 10,000 (English).

RIL: O'Reilly 358, Havana; tel. (7) 62-0777; f. 1972; 2 a month; technical; Dir Exec. Council of Publicity Dept, Ministry of Light Industry; Chief Officer MIREYA CRESPO; circ. 8,000.

Sierra Maestra: Avda de Los Desfiles, Santiago de Cuba; tel. (7) 2-2813; f. 1957; weekly; Dir ARNALDO CLAVEL CARMENATY; circ. 45,000.

Sol de Cuba: Calle 19, No 60, entre M y N, Vedado, Havana 4; tel. (7) 32-9881; f. 1983; every 3 months; Spanish, English and French editions; Gen. Dir ALCIDES GIRO MITJANS; Editorial Dir DORIS VÉLEZ; circ. 200,000.

Somos Jóvenes: Calle 17, No 354, esq. H, Vedado, Havana; tel. (7) 32-4571; f. 1977; monthly; Dir GUILLERMO CABRERA; circ. 200,000.

Trabajadores: Territorial esq. Gen. Suárez, Plaza de la Revolución, Havana; tel. (7) 79-0819; f. 1970; organ of the trade-union movement; Dir JORGE LUIS CANELA CIURANA; circ. 150,000.

Tribuna de la Habana: Territorial esq. Gen. Suárez, Plaza de la Revolución, Havana; tel. (7) 81-5932; f. 1980; weekly; Dir ANGEL ZÚÑIGA SUÁREZ; circ. 90,000.

Vanguardia: Céspedes 5 (altos), Santa Clara, Matanzas; f. 1962; Dir PEDRO HERNÁNDEZ SOTO; circ. 24,000.

Venceremos: Carretera Jamaica, Km 1½, Guantánamo; tel. (7) 35980; f. 1962; Dir HAYDÉE LEÓN MOYA; circ. 28,000.

Ventiseis: Avda Carlos J. Finley, Las Tunas; f. 1977; Dir JOSÉ INFANTES REYES; circ. 21,000.

Verde Olivo: Avda de Rancho Boyeros y San Pedro, Havana; tel. (7) 79-8373; f. 1959; monthly; organ of the Revolutionary Armed Forces; Dir EUGENIO SUÁREZ PÉREZ; circ. 100,000.

Victoria: Carretera de la Fe, Km 1½, Plaza de la Revolución, Nueva Gerona, Isla de la Juventud; f. 1967; Dir NIEVE VARONA PUENTE; circ. 9,200.

PRESS ASSOCIATIONS

Unión de Periodistas de Cuba: Calle 23, No 452, esq. I, Vedado, 10400 Havana; tel. (7) 32-7098; fax (7) 33-3079; e-mail upec@jcce.org.cu; f. 1963; Pres. TUBAL PÁEZ HERNÁNDEZ.

Unión de Escritores y Artistas de Cuba: Calle 17, No 351, Vedado, Havana; tel. (7) 32-4571; fax (7) 33-3158; Pres. ABEL E. PRIETO JIMÉNEZ; Exec. Vice-Pres. LISANDRO OTERO.

NEWS AGENCIES

Agencia de Información Nacional (AIN): Calle 23, No 358, esq. a J, Vedado, Havana; tel. (7) 32-5541; fax (7) 66-2049; e-mail RPT@ain.sld.cu; national news agency; Dir ROBERTO PAVÓN TAMAYO.

Prensa Latina (Agencia Informativa Latinoamericana, SA): Calle 23, No 201, esq. a N, Vedado, Havana; tel. (7) 32-5561; fax (7) 33-3069; e-mail dirdifu@prensa-latina.cu; internet www.prensa latina.cu; f. 1959; Dir PEDRO MARGOLLES VILLANUEVA.

Foreign Bureaux

Agence France-Presse (AFP): Calle 17, No 4, 13°, entre N y O, Vedado, Havana; tel. (7) 33-3503; fax (7) 33-3034; e-mail mlsanz@ip .etecsa.cu; Bureau Chief MARIE SANZ.

Agencia EFE (Spain): Calle 36, No 110, entre 1 y 3, Miramar, Apdo 5, Havana; tel. (7) 33-2293; fax (7) 33-2272; Bureau Chief SOLEDAD MARÍN MARTÍN.

Agenzia Nazionale Stampa Associata (ANSA) (Italy): Edif. Fomeillán, Línea 5, Dpt 12, Vedado, Havana; tel. (7) 33-3542; Correspondent KATTY SALERNO.

Associated Press (AP) (USA): Havana.

Bulgarska Telegrafna Agentsia (BTA) (Bulgaria): Edif. Focsa, Calle 17, esq. M, Vedado, Apdo 22E, Havana; tel. (7) 32-4779; Bureau Chief VASIL MIKOULACH.

Česká tisková kancelář (ČTK) (Czech Republic): Edif. Fajardo, Calle 17 y M, Vedado, Apdo 3A, Vedado, Havana; tel. (7) 32-6101; Bureau Chief PAVEL ZOVADIL.

Deutsche Presse-Agentur (dpa) (Germany): Edif. Focsa, Calle 17 y M, Vedado, Apdo 2K, Havana; tel. (7) 33-3501; Bureau Chief VICTORIO COPA.

Informatsionnoye Telegrafnoye Agentstvo Rossii –Telegrafnoye Agentstvo Suverennykh Stran (ITAR—TASS)(Russia): Calle 96, No 317, entre 3 y 5, Miramar, Havana 4; tel. (7) 29-2528; Bureau Chief ALEKSANDR KANICHEV.

Inter Press Service (IPS) (Italy): Calle 36A, No 121 Bajos, esq. a 3, Miramar, Apdo 1, Havana; tel. (7) 22-1981; Bureau Chief CLAUDE JOSEPH HACKIN; Correspondent CARLOS BASTISTA MORENO.

Korean Central News Agency (Democratic People's Republic of Korea): Calle 10, No 613, esq. 25, Vedado, Apdo 6, Havana; tel. (7) 31-4201; Bureau Chief CHANG YON CHOL.

Magyar Távirati Iroda (MTI) (Hungary): Edif. Fajardo, Calle 17 y M, Apdo 2C, Havana; tel. (7) 32-8353; Bureau Chief: ZOLTÁN TAKACS; Correspondent TIBOR CSÁSZÁR.

Novinska Agencija Tanjug (Yugoslavia): Calle 5F, No 9801, esq. 98, Miramar, Havana; tel. (7) 22-7671; Bureau Chief DUŠAN DAKOVIĆ.

Polska Agencja Prasowa (PAP) (Poland): Calle 6, No 702, Apdo 5, entre 7 y 9, Miramar; Havana; tel. (7) 20-7067; Bureau Chief PIOTR SOMMERFED.

Reuters (United Kingdom): Edif. Someillán, Linea 5, 9°, Vedado, Havana 4; tel. (7) 33-3145; Bureau Chief FRANCES KERRY.

Rossiyskoye Informatsionnoye Agentstvo—Novosti (RIA—Novosti) (Russia): Calle 28, No 510, entre 5 y 7, Miramar, Havana; tel. (7) 22-4129; Bureau Chief YURII GOLOVIATENKO.

Viet Nam Agency (VNA): Calle 16, No 514, 1°, entre 5 y 7, Miramar, Havana; tel. (7) 2-4455; Bureau Chief PHAM DINH LOI.

Xinhua (New China) News Agency (People's Republic of China): Calle G, No 259, esq. 13, Vedado, Havana; tel. (7) 32-4616; Bureau Chief GAO YONGHUA.

Publishers

Casa de las Américas: Calle 3 y Avda G, Vedado, Havana; tel. (7) 32-3587; fax (7) 32-7272; e-mail casa@arsoft.cult.cu; f. 1960; Latin American literature and social sciences; Dir ROBERTO FERNÁNDEZ RETAMAR.

Ediciones Unión: Calle 17, No 354 esq. a H, Vedado, Havana; tel. (7) 55-3112; fax (7) 33-3158; e-mail uneac@artsoft.cult.cu; f.1962; publishing arm of the Unión de Escritores y Artistas de Cuba; Cuban literature, art; Dir MERCY RUIZ.

Editora Abril: Prado 553, esq. Teniente Rey, Habana Vieja, Havana; tel. (7) 62-7871; fax (7) 62-7871; e-mail eabril@tinored.cu; f. 1980; attached to the Union of Young Communists; children's literature; Dir IROEL SÁNCHEZ ESPINOSA.

Editora Política: Belascoaín No 864, esq. a Desagüe y Peñalver, Havana; tel. (7) 79-8553; fax (7) 81-1081; e-mail editors@epol .cipcc.get.cma.net; f. 1963; publishing institution of the Communist Party of Cuba; Dir SANTIAGO DÓRQUEZ PÉREZ.

Editorial Academia: Industria No 452, esq. a San José, Habana Vieja, Havana; tel. (7) 62-9501; f. 1963; attached to the Ministry of Science, Technology and the Environment; scientific and technical; Dir MIRIAM RAYA HERNÁNDEZ.

Editorial de Ciencias Médicas y Centro Nacional de Información de Ciencias Médicas: Calle E, No 452, entre 19 y 21, Vedado, Apdo 6520, Havana 10400; tel. (7) 32-4519; fax (7) 32-5008; attached to the Ministry of Public Health; books and magazines specializing in the medical sciences; Dir AUGUSTO HERNÁNDEZ BATISTA.

Editorial Ciencias Sociales: Calle 14, No 4104, entre 41 y 43, Miramar, Playa, Havana; tel. (7) 23-3959; f. 1967; attached to the Cuban Book Institute; social and political literature, history, philosophy, juridical sciences and economics; Dir RICARDO GARCÍA PAMPÍN.

Editorial Científico-Técnica: Calle 2, No 58, entre 3 y 5, Vedado, Havana; tel. (7) 3-9417; f. 1967; attached to the Ministry of Culture; technical and scientific literature; Dir ISIDRO FERNÁNDEZ RODRÍGUEZ.

Editorial Gente Nueva: Palacio del Segundo Cabo, Calle O'Reilly, No 4, esq. a Tacón, Havana; tel. (7) 62-4753; f. 1967; books for children; Dir RUBÉN DEL VALLE LANTARÓN.

Editorial José Martí/Arte y Literatura: Calzada 259, entre I y J, Apdo 4208, Havana; tel. (7) 33-3541; fax (7) 33-8187; f. 1983; attached to the Ministry of Culture; foreign-language publishing; Dir CECILIA INFANTE GUERRERO.

Editorial Letras Cubanas: Calle O'Reilly, No 4, esq. Tacón, Habana Vieja, Havana; tel. (7) 62-4378; fax (7) 33-8187; e-mail elc@icl.cult.cu; f. 1977; attached to the Ministry of Culture; general, particularly classic and contemporary Cuban literature and arts; Dir DANIEL GARCÍA SANTOS.

Editorial Oriente: Santa Lucía 356, Santiago de Cuba; tel. (226) 22496; fax (226) 23715; e-mail edoriente@cultstgo.cult.cu; f. 1971; publishes works from the Eastern provinces; literature, art and culture and practical books (cookery, house and home, crafts and games); Dir AIDA BAHR.

Editorial Pueblo y Educación: Avda 3A, No 4601, entre 46 y 60, Playa, Havana; tel. (7) 22-1490; fax (7) 24-0844; e-mail epe@ceniai .inf.cu; f. 1971; textbooks and educational publications; publishes Revista Educación three times a year (circ. 2,200); Dir CATALINA LAJUD HERRERO.

Government Publishing Houses

Instituto Cubano del Libro: Palacio del Segundo Cabo, Calle O'Reilly, No 4, esq. a Tacón, Havana; tel. (7) 62-4789; fax (7) 33-8187; e-mail cclfilh@artsoft.cult.cu; printing and publishing organization attached to the Ministry of Culture which combines several publishing houses and has direct links with others; presides over the National Editorial Council (CEN); Pres. OMAR GONZÁLEZ JIMÉNEZ.

Oficina de Publicaciones: Calle 17, No 552, esq. a D, Vedado, Havana; tel. (7) 32-1883; fax (7) 33-5106; attached to the Council of State; books, pamphlets and other printed media on historical and political matters; Dir PEDRO ALVAREZ TABÍO.

Broadcasting and Communications

TELECOMMUNICATIONS

Empresa de Telecomunicaciones de Cuba, SA (ETECSA): Calle Egido, No 610, entre Gloria y Apodaca, Habana Vieja, Havana; tel. (7) 33-4848; fax (7) 33-5144; Exec. Pres. RAFAEL MARRERO GÓMEZ.

Empresa de Telecomunicaciones Internacionales (EMTEL-CUBA): Zanja, No 855, 6°, Havana; tel. (7) 70-8794; fax (7) 78-

3722; 50% sold to Mexico's Grupo Domor in 1994; Dir REGINO GONZÁLEZ TOLEDO.

Instituto de Investigación y Desarrollo de las Telecomunicaciones (LACETEL): Rancho Boyeros, Km 14½, Santiago de las Vegas, Rancho Boyeros, Havana; tel. (7) 20-2929; fax (7) 33-5812; Dir EDUARDO TRUFFÍN TRIANA.

Ministerio de Comunicaciones (Dirección General de Telecomunicaciones): Plaza de la Revolución, Havana: Dir CARLOS MARTÍNEZ ALBUERNE.

Teléfonos Celulares de Cuba, SA (CUBACEL): Calle 28, No 10, entre 5 y 7, Playa, Havana; tel. (7) 33-2222; fax (7) 33-1737; Dir-Gen. RAFAEL GALINDO MIER.

BROADCASTING

Ministerio de la Informática y las Comunicaciones (Dirección de Frecuencias Radioeléctricas): Plaza de la Revolución, Apdo 10600, Havana; tel. (7) 70-6932; Dir CARLOS MARTÍNEZ ALBUERNE.

Empresa Cubana de Radio y Televisión (INTERTV): Avda 23, No 156, entre N y O, Vedado, Havana; tel. (7) 32-7571; fax (7) 33-3939; Dir ANDRÉS SALCEDO GANCEDO.

Instituto Cubano de Radio y Televisión (ICRT): Edif. Radiocentro, Avda 23, No 258, entre L y M, Vedado, Havana 4; tel. (7) 32-1568; fax (7) 33-3107; e-mail icrt@cecm.get.tur.cu; f. 1962; Pres. ERNESTO LÓPEZ DOMÍNGUEZ.

Radio

In 1997 there were 5 national networks and 1 international network, 14 provincial radio stations and 31 municipal radio stations, with a total of some 170 transmitters.

Radio Enciclopedia: Calle N, No 266, entre 21 y 23, Vedado, Havana; tel. (7) 81-2809; national network; instrumental music programmes; 24 hours daily; Dir EDELSA PALACIOS GORDO.

Radio Habana Cuba: Infanta 105 esq. a 25, 6°, Apdo 6240, Havana; tel. (7) 57-6533; fax (7) 79-5810; e-mail cartas@radiohc.org; f. 1961; shortwave station; broadcasts in Spanish, English, French, Portuguese, Arabic, Esperanto, Quechua, Guaraní and Creole; Dir MILAGRO HERNÁNDEZ CUBA.

CMBF—Radio Musical Nacional: Edif. ENE, Calle N, entre 23 y 21, Vedado, Havana; tel. (7) 57-5527; f. 1948; national network; classical music programmes; 17 hours daily; Dir LUIZ LÓPEZ-QUINTANA.

Radio Progreso: Infanta 105, Apdo 3042, Havana; tel. (7) 70-4561; f. 1929; national network; mainly entertainment and music; 24 hours daily; Dir MANUEL E. ANDRÉS MAZORRA.

Radio Rebelde: Edif. ICRT, Avda 23, No 258, entre L y M, Vedado, Apdo 6277, Havana; tel. (7) 31-3514; fax (7) 33-4270; e-mail rebelde @ceniai.inf.cu; internet www.cuba.cu/RRebelde; f. 1958 (merged with Radio Liberación in 1984); national network; 24-hour news programmes, music and sports; Dir Gen. PEDRO P. FIGUEREDO RODRÍGUEZ.

Radio Reloj: Edif. Radiocentro, Avda 23, No 258, entre L y M, Vedado, Havana; tel. (7) 32-9689; f. 1947; national network; 24-hour news service; Dir OSVALDO RODRÍGUEZ MARTÍNEZ.

Television

Instituto Cubano de Radiodifusión (Televisión Nacional): Calle M, No 313, entre 21 y 23, Vedado, Havana; tel. (7) 32-5000; broadcasts in colour on channel 2 and channel 6; Vice-Pres. JOSEFA BRACERO TORRES, OVIDIO CABRERA, ERNESTO LÓPEZ.

Cubavisión: Calle M, No 313, Vedado, Havana.

Tele Rebelde: Mazón, No 52, Vedado, Havana; tel. (7) 32-3369; Vice-Pres. GARY GONZÁLEZ.

CHTV: Habana Libre Hotel, Havana; f. 1990; subsidiary station of Tele-Rebelde.

Finance

(cap. = capital; p.u. = paid up; res = reserves; dep. = deposits; m. = million; brs = branches)

BANKING

All banks were nationalized in 1960. Legislation establishing the national banking system was approved by the Council of State in 1984. A restructuring of the banking system, initiated in 1995, to accommodate Cuba's transformation to a more market-orientated economy was proceeding in 2001. A new central bank, the Banco Central de Cuba (BCC), was created in 1997 to supersede the Banco Nacional de Cuba (BNC). The BCC was to be responsible for issuing currency, proposing and implementing monetary policy and the regulation of financial institutions. The BNC was to continue functioning as a commercial bank and servicing the country's foreign

debt. Also envisaged in the restructuring of the banking system was the creation of an investment bank, the Banco de Inversiones, to provide medium- and long-term financing for investment, and the Banco Financiero Internacional, SA, to offer short-term financing. A new agro-industrial and commercial bank was also to be created to provide services for farmers and co-operatives. The new banking system is under the control of Grupo Nueva Banca, which holds a majority share in each institution.

Central Bank

Banco Central de Cuba (BCC): Havana; f. 1997; sole bank of issue; Pres. FRANCISCO SOBERÓN VALDEZ.

Commercial Banks

Banco Financiero Internacional, SA: Edif. Someillán, Calle Línea y O, Vedado, Havana; tel. (7) 32-1518; fax (7) 33-3006; f. 1984; autonomous; cap. US $10m. (1985); finances Cuba's foreign trade; Chair. EDUARDO BENCOMO ZURDOS; Gen. Man. ARNALDO ALAYÓN.

Banco Internacional de Comercio, SA: 20 de Mayo y Ayestarán, Apdo 6113, Havana; tel. (7) 55-5482; fax (7) 33-5112; e-mail bicsa@ bicsa.colombus.cu; f. 1993; cap. and res US $45.5m., dep. $212.7m. (Dec. 1997); Chair. ERNESTO MEDINA.

Banco Metropolitano: Avda 5 y Calle 112, Playa, Havana; tel. (7)24-3869; fax (7) 24-9193; e-mail banmetcm@nbbcm.colombus.cu; internet www.banco-metropolitano.com; f. 1996; offers foreign currency and deposit account facilities; Pres. IVANIOSKY MATOS TORRES; Dir PEDRO DE LA ROSA GONZALEZ.

Banco Nacional de Cuba (BNC): Aguiar 456, entre Amargura y Lamparillla, Havana; tel. (7) 62-8896; fax (7) 66-9514; e-mail postmaster@bnc.cu; f. 1950, reorganized 1997; Chair. DIANA AMELIA FERNÁNDEZ VILA.

Foreign Banks

There are 13 foreign banks represented in Cuba, including Banco Bilbao Vizcaya (Spain), Banco de Comercio Exterior de México, Banco Exterior de España, Banco Sabadell (Spain), ING Bank (Netherlands) and Société General de France.

Savings Bank

Banco Popular del Ahorro: Calle 16, No 306, entre 3 y 5, Playa, Havana; tel. (7) 22-2545; f. 1983; savings bank; cap. 30m. pesos; dep. 5,363.7m. pesos; Pres. MARISELA FERREYRA DE LA GÁNDARA; 520 brs.

INSURANCE
State Organizations

Empresa del Seguro Estatal Nacional (ESEN): Obispo No 211, 3°, Apdo 109, 10100 Havana; tel. (7) 60-4111; f. 1978; motor and agricultural insurance; Man. Dir PEDRO MANUEL ROCHE ALVAREZ.

Seguros Internacionales de Cuba, SA—Esicuba: Cuba No 314, Apdo 79, Havana; tel. (7) 62-5051; fax (7) 33-8038; f. 1963; reorganized 1986; all classes of insurance except life; Pres. RAMÓN MARTÍNEZ CARRERA.

Trade and Industry

GOVERNMENT AGENCIES

Ministry of Foreign Investment and Economic Co-operation: Primera No 1404, entre 14 y 16, Miramar, Havana; tel. (7) 22-3873; fax (7) 24-0797; e-mail cecupi@ceniai.cu.

Free-Trade Zones National Office: Calie 22, No 528, entre 3 y 5, Miramar, Havana; tel. (7) 24-7636; fax (7) 24-7637.

CHAMBER OF COMMERCE

Cámara de Comercio de la República de Cuba: Calle 21, No 661, esq. Calle A, Apdo 4237, Vedado, Havana; tel. (7) 30-4436; fax (7) 33-3042; e-mail adm@camaracuba.com.cu; internet www.cam aracuba.com.cu; f. 1963; mems include all Cuban foreign trade enterprises and the most important agricultural and industrial enterprises; Pres. ANTONIO L. CARRICARTE CORONA; Sec.-Gen. SARA MARTA DÍAZ.

AGRICULTURAL ORGANIZATION

Asociación Nacional de Agricultores Pequeños—ANAP (National Association of Small Farmers): Calle I, No 206, entre Linea y 13, Vedado, Havana; tel. (7) 32-4541; fax (7) 33-4244; f. 1961; 220,000 mems; Pres. ORLANDO LUGO FONTE; Vice-Pres. EVELIO PAUSA BELLO.

STATE IMPORT-EXPORT BOARDS

Alimport (Empresa Cubana Importadora de Alimentos): Infanta 16, 3°, Apdo 7006, Havana; tel. (7) 54-2501; fax (7) 33-3151;

e-mail precios@alimport.com.cu; controls import of foodstuffs and liquors; Man. Dir PEDRO ALVAREZ BORREGO.

Autoimport (Empresa Central de Abastecimiento y Venta de Equipos de Transporte Ligero): Galiano 213, entre Concordia y Virtudes, Havana; tel. (7) 62-8180; imports cars, light vehicles, motor cycles and spare parts; Man. Dir ÉDELIO VERA RODRÍGUEZ.

Aviaimport (Empresa Cubana Importadora y Exportadora de Aviación): Calle 182, No 126, entre 1 y 5, Reparto Flores, Playa, Havana; tel. (7) 21-7687; fax (7) 33-6234; import and export of aircraft and components; Man. Dir MARCOS LAGO MARTÍNEZ.

Caribex (Empresa Exportadora del Caribe): Aparthotel Las Brisas, Apdo 3c 41, Villa Panamericana, Havana; tel. (7) 95-1140; fax (7) 95-1142; e-mail acepex@fishnavy.inf.cu; import and export of seafood and marine products; Dir PEDRO SUÁREZ GAMBE.

Construimport (Empresa Central de Abastecimiento y Venta de Equipos de Construcción y sus Piezas): Carretera de Varona, Km 1½, Capdevila, Havana; tel. (7) 45-2567; fax (7) 66-6180; e-mail construimport@colombus.cu; f. 1969; controls the import and export of construction machinery and equipment; Man. Dir JESÚS SERRANO RODRÍGUEZ.

Consumimport (Empresa Cubana Importadora de Artículos de Consumo General): Calle 23, No 55, 9°, Apdo 6427, Vedado, Havana; tel. (7) 54-3110; fax (7) 54-2142; e-mail comer@consumim port.infocex.cu; f. 1962; imports and exports general consumer goods; Dir MERCEDES REY HECHAVARRÍA.

Copextel (Corporación Productora y Exportadora de Tecnología Electrónica): Calle 194 y 7A, Siboney, Havana; tel. (7) 21-8400; fax (7) 33-1414; f. 1986; exports LTEL personal computers and micro-computer software; Man. Dir LUIS J. CARRASCO.

Coprefil (Empresa Comercial y de Producciones Filatélicas): Zanja No 855, 2°, esq. San Francisco e Infanta, Havana 1; tel. (7) 7-8812; fax (7) 33-5077; imports and exports postage stamps, postcards, calendars, handicrafts, communications equipment, electronics, watches, etc.; Dir NELSON IGLESIAS FERNÁNDEZ.

Cubaelectrónica (Empresa Importadora y Exportadora de Productos de la Electrónica): Calle 22, No 510, entre 5 y 7, Miramar, Havana; tel. (7) 22-7316; fax (7) 33-1233; f. 1986; imports and exports electronic equipment and devices; Man. LUIS BLANCA.

Cubaexport (Empresa Cubana Exportadora de Alimentos y Productos Varios): Calle 23, No 55, entre Infanta y P, 8°, Vedado, Apdo 6719, Havana; tel. (7) 54-3130; fax (7) 33-3587; e-mail cexport-@infocex.cu; export of foodstuffs and industrial products; Man. Dir MILDA PICOS RIVERS.

Cubafrutas (Empresa Cubana Exportadora de Frutas Tropicales): Calle 23, No 55, Apdo 6683, Vedado, Havana; tel. and fax (7) 79-5653; f. 1979; controls export of fruits, vegetables and canned foodstuffs; Dir JORGE AMARO MOREJÓN.

Cubalse (Empresa para Prestación de Servicios al Cuerpo Diplomático): Avda 3 y Final, Miramar, Havana; tel. (7) 24-2284; fax (7) 24-2282; e-mail cubalse@ceniai.inf.cu; f. 1974; imports consumer goods for the diplomatic corps and foreign technicians residing in Cuba; exports beverages and tobacco, leather goods and foodstuffs; other operations include real estate, retail trade, restaurants, clubs, automobile business, state-of-the-art equipment and household appliances, construction, investments, wholesale, road transport, freight transit, shipping, publicity, photography and video, financing, legal matters; Pres. REIDAL RONCOURT FONT.

Cubametales (Empresa Cubana Importadora de Metales, Combustibles y Lubricantes): Infanta 16, 4°, Apdo 6917, Vedado, Havana; tel. (7) 70-4225; fax (7) 33-3477; controls import of metals (ferrous and non-ferrous), crude petroleum and petroleum products; also engaged in the export of petroleum products and ferrous and non-ferrous scrap; Dir RAFAEL PRIEDE GONZÁLEZ.

Cubaniquel (Empresa Cubana Exportadora de Minerales y Metales): Calle 23, No 55, 8°, Apdo 6128, Havana; tel. (7) 33-5334; fax (7) 33-3332; f. 1961; sole exporter of minerals and metals; Man. Dir ARIEL MASÓ MARZAL.

Cubatabaco (Empresa Cubana del Tabaco): Calle O'Reilly, No 104, Apdo 6557, Havana; tel. (7) 61-5759; fax (7) 33-8214; f. 1962; controls export of leaf tobacco, cigars and cigarettes to France; Dir JUAN MANUEL DÍAZ TENORIO.

Cubatécnica (Empresa de Contratación de Asistencia Técnica): Calle 12, No 513, entre 5 y 7, Miramar, Havana; tel. (7) 22-3270; fax (7) 24-0923; e-mail cubatec@ceniai.inf.cu; f. 1976; controls export and import of technical assistance; Dir FÉLIX GONZÁLEZ NAVERÁN.

Cubatex (Empresa Cubana Importadora de Fibras, Tejidos, Cueros y sus Productos): Calle 23, No 55, Apdo 7115, Vedado, Havana; tel. (7) 70-3269; fax (7) 33-3321; controls import of fibres, textiles, hides and by-products and export of fabric and clothing; Dir LUISA AMPARO SESÍN VIDAL.

Cubazúcar (Empresa Cubana Exportadora de Azúcar y sus Derivados): Calle 23, No 55, 7°, Vedado, Apdo 6647, Havana;

tel. (7) 54-2175; fax (7) 33-3482; e-mail cubazucar@cbz.infocex.cu; f. 1962; controls export of sugar, molasses and alcohol; Dir ALEJANDRO GUTIÉRREZ MAIRIGAL.

Ecimact (Empresa Comercial de Industrias de Materiales, Construcción y Turismo): Calle 1c, entre 152 y 154, Miramar, Havana; tel. (7) 21-9783; controls import and export of engineering services and plant for industrial construction and tourist complexes; Dir OCTAVIO CASTILLA CANGAS.

Ecimetal (Empresa Importadora y Exportadora de Objetivos Industriales): Calle 23, No 55, esq. Plaza, Vedado, Havana; tel. (7) 55-0548; fax (7) 33-4737; e-mail ecimetal@infocex.cu; f. 1977; controls import and export of plant, equipment and raw materials for all major industrial sectors; Dir ADALBERTO DUMÉNIGO CABRERA.

Ediciones Cubanas (Empresa de Comercio Exterior de Publicaciones): Obispo 527, Apdo 43, Havana; tel. (7) 63-1989; fax (7) 33-8943; e-mail edicuba@artsoft.cult.cu; controls import and export of books and periodicals; Dir ADALBERTO DUMÉNIGO CABRERA.

Egrem (Estudios de Grabaciones y Ediciones Musicales): San Miguel 410, Havana; tel. (7) 62-9762; fax (7) 33-8043; f. 1964; controls the import and export of records, tapes, printed music and musical instruments; Dir Gen. JULIO BALLESTER GUZMÁN.

Emexcon (Empresa Importadora y Exportadora de la Construcción): Calle 25, No 2602, Miramar, Havana; tel. (7) 22-3694; f. 1978; consulting engineer services, contracting, import and export of building materials and equipment; Dir ELEODORO PÉREZ.

Emiat (Empresa Importadora y Exportadora de Suministros Técnicos): Calle 20, No 519, entre 5 y 7, Miramar, Havana; tel. (7) 22-1163; fax (7) 22-5176; f. 1983; imports technical materials, equipment and special products; exports furniture, kitchen utensils and accessories; Dir MARTA ALFONSO SÁNCHEZ.

Emidict (Empresa Especializada Importadora, Exportadora y Distribuidora para la Ciencia y la Técnica): Calle 16, No 102, esq. Avda 1, Miramar, Playa, 13000 Havana; tel. (7) 22-8452; fax (7) 24-1768; e-mail emidict@ceniai.inf.cu; f. 1982; controls import and export of scientific and technical products and equipment, live animals; scientific information; Dir MIGUEL JULIO PÉREZ FLEITAS.

Energoimport (Empresa Importadora de Objetivos Electroenergéticos): Calle 7, No 2602, esq. a 26, Miramar, Havana; tel. (7) 23-8156; fax (7) 33-0147; f. 1977; controls import of equipment for electricity generation; Man. LÁZARO HERNÁNDEZ.

Eprob (Empresa de Proyectos para las Industrias de la Básica): Avda 31A, entre 18 y 20, Miramar, Playa, Apdo 12100, Havana; tel. (7) 33-2146; fax (7) 33-2146; f. 1967; exports consulting services and processing of engineering construction projects, consulting services and supplies of complete industrial plants and turnkey projects; Man. Dir RAÚL RIVERO MARTÍNEZ.

Eproyiv (Empresa de Proyectos para Industrias Varias): Calle 33, No 1815, entre 18 y 20, Playa, Havana; tel. (7) 24-2149; e-mail eproyiv@ceniai.inf.cu; f. 1967; consulting services, feasibility studies, development of basic and detailed engineering models, project management and turn-key projects; Dir MARTA ELENA HERNÁNDEZ DÍAZ.

Esi (Empresa de Suministros Industriales): Calle Aguiar, No 556, entre Teniente Rey y Muralla, Havana; tel. (7) 62-0696; fax (7) 33-8951; f. 1985; imports machinery, equipment and components for industrial plants; Dir-Gen. FRANCISCO DÍAZ CABRERA.

Fecuimport (Empresa Cubana Importadora y Exportadora de Ferrocarriles): Avda 7, No 6209, entre 62 y 66, Miramar, Apdo 6003, Havana; tel. (7) 79-7678; f. 1968; imports and exports railway equipment; Pres. DOMINGO HERRERA.

Ferrimport (Empresa Cubana Importadora de Artículos de Ferretería): Calle 23, No 55, 2°, Vedado, Apdo 6258, Havana; tel. (7) 70-6678; fax (7) 79-4417; importers of industrial hardware; Dir.-Gen. ALEJANDRO MUSTELIER.

Fondo Cubano de Bienes Culturales: Calle 36, esq. 47, Reparto Kohly, Playa, Havana; tel. (7) 23-6523; fax (7) 24-0391; f. 1978; controls export of fine handicraft and works of art; Dir ANGEL ARCOS.

Habanos, S.A.: Mercaderes 21, Havana; tel. 33-8998; fax 33-8946; e-mail habanos@infocex.cu; f. 1994; controls export of leaf tobacco, cigars and cigarettes (except to France—see Cubatabaco).

ICAIC (Instituto Cubano del Arte y Industria Cinematográficos): Calle 23, No 1155, Vedado, Havana 4; tel. (7) 55-3128; fax (7) 33-3032; f. 1959; production, import and export of films and newsreel; Dir ANTONIO RODRÍGUEZ RODRÍGUEZ.

Imexin (Empresa Importadora y Exportadora de Infraestructura): Avda 5, No 1007, esq. a 12, Miramar, Havana; tel. (7) 23-9293; f. 1977; controls import and export of infrastructure; Man. Dir RAÚL BENCE VIJANDE.

Imexpal (Empresa Importadora y Exportadora de Plantas Alimentarias, sus Complementos y Derivados): Calle 22, No 313, entre 3 y 5, Miramar, Havana; tel. (7) 29-1671; controls import and export of food-processing plants and related items; Man. Dir Ing. CONCEPCIÓN BUENO CAMPOS.

Maprinter (Empresa Cubana Importadora y Exportadora de Materias Primas y Productos Intermedios): Infanta 16, 2A, Apdo 2110, Havana; tel. (7) 74-2971; fax (7) 33-3535; f. 1962; controls import and export of raw materials and intermediate products; Dir ENRIQUE DÍAZ DE VILLEGAS OTERO.

Maquimport (Empresa Cubana Importadora de Maquinarias y Equipos): Calle 23, No 55, 6°, Vedado, Apdo 6052, Havana; tel. (7) 55-0639; fax (7) 33-5443; e-mail maquimport@infocex-cu; imports industrial goods and equipment; Dir JORGE MIGUEL HERNÁNDEZ.

Marpesca (Empresa Cubana Importadora y Exportadora de Buques Mercantes y de Pesca): Conill No 580, esq. Avda 26, Nuevo Vedado, Havana; tel. (7) 81-1300; f. 1978; imports and exports ships and port and fishing equipment; Dir JOSÉ CEREIJO CASAS.

Medicuba (Empresa Cubana Importadora y Exportadora de Productos Médicos): Máximo Gómez 1, esq. a Egido, Havana; tel. (7) 62-3983; fax (7) 61-7995; e-mail medicuba@infomed.sld.cu; enterprise for the export and import of medical and pharmaceutical products; Dir ALFONSO SÁNCHEZ DÍAZ.

Produimport (Empresa Central de Abastecimiento y Venta de Productos Químicos y de la Goma): Calle Consulado 262, entre Animas y Virtudes, Havana; tel. (7) 62-0581; fax (7) 62-9588; f. 1977; imports and exports spare parts for motor vehicles; Dir JOSÉ GUERRA MATOS.

Quimimport (Empresa Cubana Importadora y Exportadora de Productos Químicos): Calle 23, No 55, Apdo 6088, Vedado, Havana; tel. (7) 33-3394; fax (7) 33-3190; controls import and export of chemical products; Dir ARMANDO BARRERA MARTÍNEZ.

Suchel (Empresa de Jabonería y Perfumería): Calzada de Buenos Aires 353, esq. a Durege, Apdo 6359, Havana; tel. (7) 33-8008; fax (7) 33-5311; f. 1985; exports and imports materials for the detergent, perfumery and cosmetics industry, exports cosmetics, perfumes, hotel amenities and household products; Dir JOSÉ GARCÍA DÍAZ.

Tecnoazúcar (Empresa de Servicios Técnicos e Ingeniería para la Agro-industria Azucarera): Calle 12, No 310, entre 3 y 5, Miramar, Playa, Havana; tel. (7) 29-5441; fax (7) 33-1218; imports machinery and equipment for the sugar industry, provides technical and engineering assistance for the sugar industry; exports sugar-machinery equipment and spare parts; provides engineering and technical assistance services for sugar-cane by-product industry; Gen. Man. VICTOR R. HERNÁNDEZ MARTÍNEZ.

Tecnoimport (Empresa Importadora y Exportadora de Productos Técnicos): Edif. La Marina, Avda del Puerto 102, entre Justiz y Obrapía, Habana Vieja, Havana; tel. (7) 61-5552; fax (7) 66-9777; f. 1968; imports technical products; Dir ADEL IZQUIERDO RODRÍGUEZ.

Tecnotex (Empresa Cubana Exportadora e Importadora de Servicios, Artículos y Productos Técnicos Especializados): Avda 47, No 3419, Playa, Havana; tel. (7) 81-3989; fax (7) 33-1682; f. 1983; imports specialized technical and radiocommunications equipment, exports outdoor equipment and geodetic networks; Dir ADEL IZQUIERDO RODRÍGUEZ.

Tractoimport (Empresa Central de Abastecimiento y Venta de Maquinaria Agrícola y sus Piezas de Repuesto): Avda Rancho Boyeros y Calle 100, Apdo 7007, Havana; tel. (7) 45-2166; fax (7) 267-0786; e-mail direccion@tractoimport.colombus.cu; f. 1960 for the import of tractors and agricultural equipment; also exports pumps and agricultural implements; Dir ABDEL GARCÍA GONZÁLEZ.

Transimport (Empresa Central de Abastecimiento y Venta de Equipos de Transporte Pesados y sus Piezas): Calle 102 y Avda 63, Marianao, Apdo 6665, 11500 Havana; tel. (7) 20-0325; fax (7) 33-5338; f. 1962; controls import and export of vehicles and transportation equipment; Dir JESÚS DINIS RIVERO.

OTHER MAJOR COMPANIES

CariFin (Caribbean Finance Investments Ltd): Calle 22, Nos 311 y 313, entre 3 y 5, Miramar, Havana; tel. (7) 24-4468; fax (7) 24-4140; e-mail havana@cdc.com.cu; f. 1996 in the British Virgin Islands; started lending operations in Cuba in 1997; subsidiary of the Commonwealth Devt Corpn and Grupo Nueva Banca, SA; financial services such as loans to businesses, international money transfers and leasing of equipment and machinery; Dir WILLIAM WHITE; Gen. Man. STEVEN MACQUEEN; 23 employees.

Corporación Habanos SA: Calle O'Reilly, No 104, Apdo 6657, Havana; tel. (7) 33-9509; fax (7) 33-8946; manufacturer of tobacco products; Pres. OSCAR BASUALTO.

Electrocimex, SA: Apdo B1, Miramar, Havana 00290; tel. (7) 33-2938; fax (7) 33-2100; f. 1968; distribution of electrical and electronic products; Man. LUIS LERA; 98 employees.

Grupo Refrigeración y Calderas: Calle Municipio 401, Guasaboba, Havana; tel. (7) 33-8090; fax (7) 33-8501; f. 1985; manufacturer of refrigerators and air-conditioning appliances; Man. Dir EMILIO MARILL; 2,200 employees.

Holmer Gold Mines Ltd: Calle A, No 506, entre 21 y 23, Vedado, Apdo 5 Interior, Havana; tel. (7) 33-3966; fax (7) 66-2074; e-mail holmer@ceniai.inf.cu; internet www.holmergold.com; f. 1993; Canadian exploration and prospecting mining co; responsible for the opening of Cuba's first silver mine in 1999; Pres. and CEO Dr K. SETHU RAMAN; Vice-Pres. DOUG LEWIS; 8 employees.

Unión de Empresas Constructoras Caribe (Corporación Uneca): Avda 9A, No 614, entre 6 y 10, Miramar, Havana; tel. (7) 29-4576; fax (7) 33-1637; f. 1984; construction work, particularly within the tourist industry; sales of US $135m. (1995); Pres. FRANCISCO HERNÁNDEZ.

UTILITIES
Electricity
Empresa Consolidada de Electricidad: Avda Salvador Allende 666, Havana; public utility.

TRADE UNIONS

All workers have the right to become members of a national trade union according to their industry and economic branch.

The following industries and labour branches have their own unions: Agriculture, Chemistry and Energetics, Civil Workers of the Revolutionary Armed Forces, Commerce and Gastronomy, Communications, Construction, Culture, Defence, Education and Science, Food, Forestry, Health, Light Industry, Merchant Marine, Mining and Metallurgy, Ports and Fishing, Public Administration, Sugar, Tobacco and Transport.

Central de Tradajadores de Cuba—CTC (Confederation of Cuban Workers): Palacio de los Trabajadores, San Carlos y Peñalver, Havana; tel. (7) 78-4901; f. 1939; affiliated to WFTU and CPUSTAL; 19 national trade unions affiliated; Gen. Sec. PEDRO ROSS LEAL; 2,767,806 mems (1996).

Transport

The Ministry of Transport controls all public transport.

RAILWAYS

The total length of railways in 1998 was 14,331 km, of which 9,638 km were used by the sugar industry. The remaining 4,520 km were public service railways operated by Ferrocarriles de Cuba. All railways were nationalized in 1960.

Ferrocarriles de Cuba: Edif. Estación Central, Egido y Arsenal, Havana; tel. (7) 70-1076; fax (7) 33-1489; f. 1960; operates public services; Dir-Gen. FERNANDO PÉREZ LÓPEZ; divided as follows:

División Occidente: serves Pinar del Río, Ciudad de la Habana, Havana Province and Matanzas.

División Centro: serves Villa Clara, Cienfuegos and Sancti Spíritus.

División Centro-Este: serves Camagüey, Ciego de Avila and Tunas.

División Oriente: serves Santiago de Cuba, Granma, Guantánamo and Holguín.

División Camilo Cienfuegos: serves part of Havana Province and Matanzas.

ROADS

In 1997 there were an estimated 60,858 km of roads, of which 4,353 km were highways or main roads. The Central Highway runs from Pinar del Río in the west to Santiago, for a length of 1,144 km. In addition to this paved highway, there are a number of secondary and 'farm-to-market' roads. A small proportion of these secondary roads is paved but many can be used by motor vehicles only during the dry season.

SHIPPING

Cuba's principal ports are Havana (which handles 60% of all cargo), Santiago de Cuba, Cienfuegos, Nuevitas, Matanzas, Antilla, Guayabal and Mariel. Maritime transport has developed rapidly since 1959, and at 31 December 1998 Cuba had a merchant fleet of 105 ships (with a total displacement of 157,847 grt). In 2000 a US $100m. renovation and enlargement project for the port of Mariel was announced.

Coral Container Lines, SA: Oficios 170, 1°, Habana Vieja, Havana; tel. (7) 67-0854; fax (7) 67-0850; e-mail bfdez@coral.com.cu; f. 1994; liner services to Europe, Canada, Brazil and Mexico; 11 containers; Chair. and Man. Dir EVELIO GONZÁLEZ GONZÁLEZ.

Empresa Consignataria Mambisa: San José No 65, entre Prado y Zulueta, Habana Vieja, Havana; tel. (7) 62-2061; fax (7) 33-8111; e-mail denis@mambisas.transnet.cu; shipping agent, bunker suppliers; Man. Dir EDUARDO DENIS VALCÁRCEL; Commercial Operations Man. MERCEDES PÉREZ NEWHALL.

Empresa Cubana de Fletes (Cuflet): Calle Oficios No 170, entre Teniente Rey y Amargura, Apdo 6755, Havana; tel. (7) 61-2604; freight agents for Cuban cargo; Man. Dir CARLOS SÁNCHEZ PERDOMO.

Empresa de Navegación Caribe (Navecaribe): San Martín, 4°, Agramonte y Pasco de Martí, Habana Vieja, Havana; tel. (7) 62-5878; fax (7) 33-8564; f. 1966; operates Cuban coastal fleet; Dir RAMÓN DURÁN SUÁREZ.

Empresa de Navegación Mambisa: San Ignacio No 104, Apdo 543, Havana; tel. (7) 62-7031; fax (7) 61-0044; operates dry cargo, reefer and bulk carrier vessels; Gen. Man. GUMERSINDO GONZÁLEZ FELIÚ.

Naviera Frigorífica Marítima: Havana; tel. (7) 35743; fax (7) 33-5185.

Naviera Mar América: 5a Avda y 246, Barlovento, Playa; tel. (59)24-9053; fax (59) 24-8889; e-mail nubia@maramerica.fish navy.inf.eu.

Naviera Poseidon: Altos de la Aduana, San Pedro 1, Habana Vieja, Havana; tel. (7) 29-8073; fax (7) 24-8627; e-mail ccom@posei don.fishnavy.inf.cu.

Nexus Reefer: Avda de la Pesquera y Atarés, Puerto Pesquero de la Habana, Habana Vieja, Havana 1; tel. (7) 66-6561; fax (7) 33-8046; e-mail nexus@fishnavy.inf.cu; merchant reefer ships; Gen. Dir QUIRINO L. GUTIÉRREZ LÓPEZ.

CIVIL AVIATION

There are a total of 16 civilian airports, with 10 international airports, including Havana, Santiago de Cuba, Camagüey, Varadero and Holguín. The newest, Abel Santamaría International Airport, opened in Villa Clara in early 2001. Another international airport was being built in Cayo Coco, as part of a tourist 'offshore' centre.

Aerocaribbean: Calle 23, No 64 esq. a P. Vedado, Havana; tel. (7) 33-4543; fax (7) 33-5016; e-mail aerocarvpcr@iacc3.6ct.cma.net; f. 1982; international and domestic charter services; Chair. JULIÁN INFIESTA.

Aerogaviota: Avda 47, No 2814, Reparto Kolhy, Havana; tel. (7) 81-3068; fax (7) 33-2621; f. 1994; operated by Cuban air force.

Empresa Consolidada Cubana de Aviación (Cubana): Calle 23, Pt 64 Vedado, La Rampa, Havana 4; tel. (7) 78-4961; fax (7) 79-3333; internet www.cubana.cu; f. 1929; international services to North America, Central America, the Caribbean, South America and Europe; internal services from Havana to 14 other cities; Gen. Dir HERIBERTO PRIETO.

Instituto de Aeronáutica Civil de Cuba (IACC): Calle 23, No 64, La Rampa, Vedado, Havana; tel. (7) 33-4471; fax (7) 33-3082; f. 1985; Pres. ROGELIO ACEVEDO GONZÁLEZ.

Tourism

Tourism began to develop after 1977, with the easing of travel restrictions by the USA, and Cuba subsequently attracted European tourists. At the Fourth Congress of the PCC, held in 1991, emphasis was placed on the importance of expanding the tourism industry, and, in particular, on its promotion within Latin America. Receipts totalled an estimated US $1,338m. in 1997, when there were some 1,170,000 visitors. In 2000 there were an estimated 1,774,000 arrivals. The number of hotel rooms increased to 34,000 in 2000. In that year there were 189 hotels. A number of hotel tourism complexes were under construction in 2000/01.

Cubanacán: Calle 148, entre 11 y 13, Playa, Apdo 16046, Havana; tel. (7) 22-5512; fax (7) 22-8382; f. 1987; Pres. ABRAHAM MACIQUES MACIQUES.

Empresa de Turismo Internacional (Cubatur): Calle 23, No 156, entre N y O, Apdo 6560, Vedado, Havana; tel. (7) 35-4521; fax (7) 32-3157; f. 1968; Dir JOSÉ PADILLA.

Empresa de Turismo Nacional (Viajes Cuba): Calle 20, No 352, entre 21 y 23, Vedado, Havana; tel. (7) 30-0587; f. 1981; Dir ANA ELIS DE LA CRUZ GARCÍA.

Defence

At August 2000, according to Western estimates, Cuba's Revolutionary Armed Forces numbered 58,000 (including ready reserves serving 45 days per year to complete active and reserve units): Army 45,000, Navy 3,000 and Air Force 10,000. Army reserves were estimated at 39,000. Cuba's paramilitary forces included 20,000 State Security troops, 6,500 border guards, a civil defence force of 50,000 and a Youth Labour Army of some 65,000. A local militia organization (Milicias de Tropas Territoriales—MTT), comprising an estimated 1m. men and women, was formed in 1980. Despite Cuban hostility, the USA maintains a base at Guantánamo Bay, which comprised 590 naval and 490 marine personnel in 2000. In June 1993, in accordance with the unilateral decision of the then USSR in September 1991, the 3,000-strong military unit of the former USSR, which had been stationed in Cuba since 1962, was withdrawn. A number of Russian military personnel, an estimated 810 in 2000, remained to operate military-intelligence facilities. Following the political changes in Eastern Europe, previously high levels of military aid to Cuba were dramatically reduced, and the size of the Army was reduced by some 60,000 personnel. Conscription for military service is for a two-year period from 17 years of age, and conscripts also work on the land.

Defence Expenditure: Expenditure on defence and internal security for 1999 was estimated at US $750m.

Minister of the Revolutionary Armed Forces: Gen. RAÚL CASTRO RUZ.

Chief of Staff: Gen. ALVARO LÓPEZ MIERA.

Education

State education in Cuba is universal and free at all levels. Education is based on Marxist-Leninist principles and combines study with manual work. National schools at the pre-primary level are available for children of five years of age, and day nurseries are available for all children over 45 days old. Primary education is compulsory for children aged six to 11 years. Secondary education lasts from 12 to 17 years of age, comprising two cycles of three years each. In 1997 almost 100% of children in the appropriate age group (males 99.9%; females 99.9%) attended primary schools, while 69.9% of those in the relevant age group (males 67.2%; females 72.6%) were enrolled at secondary schools. In 1999/2000 there were an estimated 106,800 students enrolled in higher education. Workers attending university courses receive a state subsidy to provide for their dependants. Courses at intermediate and higher levels lay an emphasis on technology, agriculture and teacher training. In 1998, according to estimates by the World Bank, the illiteracy rate among persons aged 15 years and over was 3.6% (males 3.5%; females 3.7%). In 1999 budgetary expenditure on education was estimated at 1,865m. pesos (13.3% of total spending).

Bibliography

For works on the Caribbean generally, see Select Bibliography (Books).

Arboleya, J. *Havana–Miami: The US–Cuban Migration Conflict.* Melbourne, Ocean Press, 1996.

Balfour, S. *Castro: Profiles in Power.* London, Longman, 1995.

Blight, J. A., and Welch, D. A. (Eds). *Intelligence and the Cuban Missile Crisis.* London, Frank Cass, 1998.

Brenner, P., et al. *The Cuba Reader: The Making of a Revolutionary Society.* New York, NY, Grove Press, 1998.

Centeno, M. A., and Font, M. *Towards a New Cuba?* London, Lynne Reinner, 1997.

Cole, K. *Cuba: From Revolution to Development.* London, Pinter, 1998.

Cuba's Economic Reforms: Results and Future Prospects. London, Cuba Business, 1997.

'Cuba's Emerging Business Opportunities', in *Columbia Journal of World Business*, Spring. 1995.

Cuba: Evolucíon Económica durante 1996. United Nations Economic Commission for Latin America and the Caribbean, 1997.

Domínguez, J. I. *Cuba: Order and Revolution.* Cambridge, MA, and London, Harvard University Press, 1978.

(Ed.). *Cuba: Internal and International Affairs.* London, Sage Publications, 1982.

To Make the World Safe for Revolution: Cuba's Foreign Policy. London, Harvard University Press, 1989.

Erisman, H. M. *Cuba's International Relations: The Anatomy of a Nationalistic Foreign Policy*. Boulder, CO, Westview Press, 1987.

Evolución de la Economía Cubana en 1996. Havana, Centro de Estudios sobre la Economía Cubana, 1997.

Figueras, M. A. *Aspectos Estructurales de la Economía Cubana*. Havana, Editorial de Ciencias Sociales, 1994.

Franklin, J. *Cuba and the United States: A Chronological History*. Melbourne, Ocean Press, 1997.

Fuente, A. de la. *A Nation for All: Race, Inequality, and Politics in Twentieth-Century Cuba (Envisioning Cuba)*. Chapel Hill, NC, University of North Carolina Press, 2001.

Garciá Luis, J. (Ed.). *Cuban Revolution Reader: A Documentary History of 40 Years of Revolution*. Melbourne, Ocean Press, 2000.

Haines, L. *Reassessing Cuba: Emerging Opportunities and Operating Challenges*. New York, NY, Economist Intelligence Unit, 1997.

Horowitz, I. L. (Ed.). *Cuban Communism, 1959-1995*, 10th edn. New Brunswick, NJ, Transaction Books, 2001.

Jenkins, G., and Haines, L. *Cuba: Prospects for Reform, Trade and Investment*. New York, NY, Economist Intelligence Unit, 1995.

Kapcia, A. *Political Change in Cuba: Before and After the Exodus*. London, Institute of Latin American Studies, 1992.

Kaplowitz, D. R. (Ed.). *Cuba's Ties to a Changing World*. Boulder, CO, Lynne Rienner, 1993.

Mazarr, M. J. 'Prospects for Revolution in Post-Castro Cuba', in Journal of Interamerican Studies and World Affairs, Vol. 31, No. 4 (Winter). 1989

Meso-Lago, C. (Ed.). *Cuba after the Cold War*. Pittsburgh, PA, University of Pittsburgh Press, 1993.

Pérez, Jr, L. A. *Cuba: Between Reform and Revolution*, 2nd edn. Oxford, Oxford University Press, 1995.

Cuba and the United States: Ties of Singular Intimacy, 2nd edn. Athens, GA, University of Georgia Press, 1997.

Pérez-López, J. F. *Cuba at a Crossroads (Politics and Economics After the Fourth Party Congress)*. Gainesville, FL, University Press of Florida, 1994.

Pérez Sarduy, P., and Stubbs, J. (Eds.). *AfroCuba. An Anthology of Cuban Writing on Race, Politics and Culture*. Melbourne, Ocean Press, 1993.

Prince, R., and Taylor, S. *Turning with the Enemy*. London, Channel Four Television, 1998.

Rodríguez, J. C. *The Bay of Pigs*. Melbourne, Ocean Press, 1999.

Smith, W. S. *The Closest of Enemies: A Personal and Diplomatic History of US–Cuban Relations Since 1957*. New York, NY, W. W. Norton, 1987.

Szulc, T. *Fidel: A Critical Portrait*. New York, NY, William Morrow, 1986; London, Hutchinson, 1987.

Tangley, L. 'Sugar Cane: Cuba's 'Noble Crop' , in *Bioscience*, Vol. 36 (July/August). 1986.

Thomas, H. *Cuba or the Pursuit of Freedom,* revised edn. New York, NY, First Da Capo Press, 1998.

The Cuban Revolution, 2nd edn. London, Weidenfeld and Nicolson, 1986.

Tulchin, J. S., and Serbin, A. *Cuba and the Caribbean (Regional Issues and Trends in the Post-Cold War Era) Latin American Silhouettes*. Wilmington, DE, Scholarly Resources, 1997.

DOMINICA

Area: 751 sq km (290 sq miles).

Population (official estimate, mid-1998): 75,871.

Capital: Roseau; population 15,853 at 1991 census.

Language: English (official); a French patois is also used.

Religion: Christianity (mainly Roman Catholic).

Climate: Tropical; average temperature 27°C (80°F); average annual rainfall varies from 1,800 mm along the coast to 6,350 mm in the mountainous areas.

Time: GMT −4 hours.

Public Holidays: 2002: 1 January (New Year's Day), 2 January (Merchants' Holiday), 11–12 February (Masquerade, Carnival), 29 March (Good Friday), 1 April (Easter Monday), 6 May (for May or Labour Day), 20 May (Whit Monday), 5 August (Emancipation, August Monday), 3 November (Independence Day), 4 November (Community Service Day), 25–26 December (Christmas). **2003:** 1 January (New Year's Day), 2 January (Merchants' Holiday), 26–27 February (Masquerade, Carnival), 18 April (Good Friday), 21 April (Easter Monday), 5 May (for May or Labour Day), 9 June (Whit Monday), 4 August (Emancipation, August Monday), 3 November (Independence Day), 4 November (Community Service Day), 25–26 December (Christmas).

Currency: Eastern Caribbean dollar; US $1 = EC $2.70 (fixed rate since July 1976); EC $100 = £25.87 = US $37.04 = €41.73 (30 April 2001).

Weights and Measures: Imperial; metric system being introduced.

History

Dominica was first settled by Arawaks and then Caribs. The Caribs, British and French fiercely contested control of the island during the 17th and 18th centuries. The British eventually prevailed and Dominica formed part of the Leeward Islands federation until 1939 and then of the Windward Islands Federation until 1960, when it gained separate status and a new Constitution was introduced. The 1961 elections were won by the Labour Party of Dominica (LPD). The Chief Minister was redesignated Premier in 1967, when the island gained full internal autonomy. In 1974 Patrick John became the leader of the ruling LPD and, in November 1978, upon independence, the island's first Prime Minister. In 1980 the Dominica Freedom Party (DFP) won 17 of the 21 elective seats in parliament, and Eugenia (later Dame Eugenia) Charles became Prime Minister. There were two attempted coups against the Government in 1981, and three states of emergency were imposed during 1981–83. Former Prime Minister Patrick John was eventually imprisoned for his part in a plot to overthrow the Government. The DFP under Charles was returned to power in 1985 and 1990, but in the general election of June 1995 only gained five seats in the House of Assembly. The United Workers' Party (UWP) won 11 seats and formed an administration. Edison James was appointed Prime Minister. Brian Alleyne, elected to succeed Charles as leader of the DFP in 1993, himself resigned in 1996, but the by-election for his seat was won by the UWP candidate, thus increasing the Government's representation in the House of Assembly to 12 seats. In October 1998, following the end of President Sorhaindo's term in office, the House of Assembly elected Vernon Lorden Shaw, a former cabinet secretary in the previous administration of Eugenia Charles, to the presidency.

On 31 January 2000 a general election was held. The LPD won 10 of the 21 seats in the House of Assembly and received 42.9% of total votes cast. The UWP was narrowly defeated, receiving nine seats (with 43.4% of the votes) and the DFP won two seats. The LPD and the DFP formed a coalition Government and the leader of the LPD, Roosevelt (Rosie) Douglas, was appointed Prime Minister. Allegations of corruption were made against the previous Governments, when the treasury was found to be in financial difficulties. In March Douglas controversially announced that Dominica was to pursue a special status with the European Union, in order to improve trade links with Europe. Following its inclusion in an Organisation for Economic Co-operation and Development (OECD) 'blacklist' in early 2000, Dominica introduced anti-money 'laundering' legislation and amended existing laws governing the offshore financial sector. In December 2000 legislation was passed in the House of Assembly making the crime of money laundering punishable by up to seven years' imprisonment and a fine of EC $1m. In May 2001 the Government closed down an offshore institution, the British Trade and Commercial Bank. However, Dominica remained on the OECD list in July 2001.

On 1 October 2000 Douglas died of a heart attack. The Minister of Communications and Works, Pierre Charles, became Prime Minister, following a parliamentary vote later in the month. The challenges facing the new Prime Minister included the declining banana industry and the consequent need for economic diversification, and the diplomatic problems caused by Dominica's important role in the international whaling debate. In July 2000 Atherton Martin, the Minister for Agriculture, Planning and the Environment, resigned from his post after the Government voted against the establishment of a South Pacific whaling sanctuary at a meeting of the International Whaling Commission in Australia. The vote was reported to be contrary to a cabinet agreement to abstain. Martin claimed that Japan had threatened to withdraw funding for two fish processing plants in Dominica if the Government abstained in the vote, and accused the Japanese Government of 'international extortion'. In July 2001 the debate was set to intensify with the prospect of further Japanese aid.

Economy

The principal economic activity is agriculture, which accounted for an estimated 16.9% of gross domestic product (GDP) in 1999 and, in 1997, employed 23.7% of the labour force. The main crops are bananas, of which an estimated 30,000 metric tons were produced in 2000, with exports earning EC $46.3m. in 1998, coconuts and citrus fruits. A World Trade Organization ruling in September 1997, against Dominica's preferential access to European markets, was expected to adversely affect the banana industry. However, by June 2001 agreement had been reached between the USA and the European Union (EU), guaranteeing Dominica's banana quota for a further five years. In March 2000 the Dominican Banana Marketing Corporation (DBMC) announced new measures, including a reduction in prices, an increase in production and restructuring of the DBMC, to deal with the crisis. With bananas currently providing about 90% of the agricultural sector's output, efforts are also being made to exploit the island's timber reserves (more than 40% of the island's total land area is forest and woodland), and international aid agencies are encouraging the development of a balanced timber industry. In July 1997 construction of a fishing port and market in Roseau was completed. The GDP of the agricultural sector decreased at an average annual rate of 1.0% in 1990–99. In real terms, agricultural GDP declined by 1.5% in 1997, by 2.0% in 1998 and by 0.4% in 1999.

Industry is mainly small scale and dependent upon agriculture; soap is an important export. In 1996 60% of Dominica's energy requirements were satisfied by hydroelectric power; in December of that year the state electricity company, Dominica Electricity Services, was privatized. In September 2000 parliament approved measures to liberalize the telecommunications sector. Efforts to expand the country's economic base have been impeded by poor infrastructure and, in terms of tourism, a paucity of desirable beaches. However, by the late 1990s the tourist sector was expanding steadily, aided by an 'eco-tourism' development programme with EU funding. Moreover, the numbers of cruise-ship arrivals increased dramatically in the 1990s and the construction of a new international airport in the north-east of the island became a government priority. The 1999/2000 government budget allocated US $28m. to the new airport's construction, which would cost a total of $110m. However, in March 2000 the new legislature announced that the airport plans were to be abandoned. Tourism receipts in 1998 were EC $42m. In July 2000 the Government announced that value-added tax (VAT) would be introduced in 2001. However, in July 2001 the International Monetary Fund warned Dominica about its large fiscal deficit and called on the Government to further increase tax revenue and tighten expenditure controls.

In 1999, according to estimates by the World Bank, Dominica's gross national product (GNP), measured at average 1997–99 prices, was US $231m., equivalent to US $3,170 per head (or $4,825 per head on an international purchasing-power parity basis). Gross domestic product (GDP), in real terms, increased by an average of 2.2% per year in 1990–97. Real GDP growth was 2.0% in 1997, 3.5% in 1998 and an estimated 0.4% in 1999. In 1999 GDP stood at EC $601.3m. The slowdown in economic growth in this year was largely attributable to the weak performance of the major productive sectors, particularly those affected by 'Hurricane Lenny', and was further evidence of the need for diversification.

Statistical Survey

Sources (unless otherwise stated): Ministry of Finance, Roseau; OECS Economic Affairs Secretariat, *Annual Digest of Statistics*.

AREA AND POPULATION

Area: 751 sq km (290 sq miles).

Population: 69,548 at census of 7 April 1970; 73,795 at census of 7 April 1981; 71,183 (males 35,471, females 35,712) at census of 12 May 1991; 75,871 (official estimate) at mid-1998.

Density (mid-1998): 101.0 per sq km.

Population by Ethnic Group (*de jure* population, excl. those resident in institutions, 1981): Negro 67,272; Mixed race 4,433; Amerindian (Carib) 1,111; White 341; Total (incl. others) 73,795 (males 36,754, females 37,041). Source: UN, *Demographic Yearbook*.

Principal Town (population at 1991 census): Roseau (capital) 15,853.

Births, Marriages and Deaths (registrations, 1998): Live births 1,230 (birth rate 16.2 per 1,000); Marriages (1996) 230 (marriage rate 3.1 per 1,000); Deaths 595 (death rate 7.8 per 1,000). Source: UN *Demographic Yearbook* and *Vital Statistics Report*.

Expectation of Life (UN estimates, years at birth, 1990–95): 67.8 (males 64.1; females 71.4). Source: ECLAC Demography Unit.

Economically Active Population (rounded estimates, persons aged 15 years and over, 1997): Agriculture, hunting, forestry and fishing 6,000; Fishing 100; Manufacturing 2,250; Electricity, gas and water supply 280; Construction 2,150; Wholesale and retail trade 4,050; Hotels and restaurants 980; Transport, storage and communications 1,500; Financial intermediation 540; Real estate, renting and business activities 850; Public administration, defence and social security 1,530; Education 1,260; Health and social work 1,110; Other community, social and personal service activities 930; Private households with employed persons 1,080; Not classifiable by economic activity 1,090; Total employed 25,690; Unemployed 7,720; Total labour force 33,420 (males 18,120; females 15,300). Source: ILO.

AGRICULTURE, ETC.

Principal Crops (FAO estimates, '000 metric tons, 2000): Sweet potatoes 1.8; Cassava 0.9; Yams 7.8; Taro (Dasheen) 11.0; Other roots and tubers 5.5; Coconuts 1.0; Cabbages 0.6; Pumpkins 0.8; Cucumbers 1.6; Carrots 0.5; Other vegetables 2.8; Sugar cane 4.3; Oranges 8.4; Lemons and limes 1.0; Grapefruit 0.5; Mangoes 1.8; Bananas 30; Plantains 10.0. Source: FAO.

Livestock (FAO estimates, '000 head, year ending September 2000): Cattle 13; Pigs 5; Sheep 8; Goats 10. Source: FAO.

Livestock Products (FAO estimates, '000 metric tons, 2000): Beef and veal 1; Cows' milk 6. Source: FAO.

Fishing (metric tons, live weight, 1998): Capture 1,212 (Marine fishes 1,212); Aquaculture 5; Total catch 1,217. Source: FAO, *Yearbook of Fishery Statistics*.

MINING

Pumice ('000 metric tons, incl. volcanic ash): Estimated production 100 per year in 1988–99 (Source: US Geological Survey).

INDUSTRY

Production (1996, metric tons, unless otherwise indicated): Soap 14,815; Crude coconut oil 753 (estimate); Edible coconut oil 82 (estimate); Coconut meal 350 (estimate); Electricity 37 million kWh*.

* Source: UN, *Industrial Commodity Statistics Yearbook*.

FINANCE

Currency and Exchange Rates: 100 cents = 1 Eastern Caribbean dollar (EC $). *Sterling, US Dollar and Euro Equivalents* (30 April 2001): £1 sterling = EC $3.866; US $1 = EC $2.700; €1 = EC $2.397; EC $100 = £25.87 = US $37.04 = €41.73. *Exchange Rate:* Fixed at US $1 = EC $2.70 since July 1976.

Budget (estimates, EC $ million, 1999): *Revenue:* Tax revenue 168.4; Other current revenue 32.1; Capital revenue 3.1; Total 203.6, excl. grants received (11.6). *Expenditure:* Current expenditure 206.5 (Wages and salaries 116.5); Capital expenditure and net lending 82.7; Total 289.2. Source: Eastern Caribbean Central Bank, *Report and Statement of Accounts* (2000).

International Reserves (US $ million at 31 December 2000): Reserve position in IMF 0.01; Foreign exchange 29.36; Total 29.37. Source: IMF, *International Financial Statistics*.

Money Supply (EC $ million at 31 December 2000): Currency outside banks 35.45; Demand deposits at commercial banks 69.12; Total money (incl. others) 105.47. Source: IMF, *International Financial Statistics*.

Cost of Living (Retail Price Index, base: 1995 = 100): All items 105.2 in 1998; 106.4 in 1999; 107.3 in 2000. Source: IMF, *International Financial Statistics*.

National Accounts (EC $ million at current prices): Gross domestic product in purchasers' values 649.7 in 1997; 697.9 in 1998; 714.7 in 1999. Source: ECLAC, *Statistical Yearbook for Latin America and the Caribbean*.

Expenditure on the Gross Domestic Product (EC $ million at current prices, 1999): Government final consumption expenditure 152.1; Private final consumption expenditure 435.8; Gross fixed capital formation (incl. increase in stocks) 195.2; *Total domestic expenditure* 783.1; Exports of goods and services 371.3; *Less* Imports of goods and services 439.6; GDP in purchasers' values 714.7. Source: ECLAC, *Statistical Yearbook for Latin America and the Caribbean*.

Gross Domestic Product by Economic Activity (EC $ million at current prices, 1999): Agriculture, hunting, forestry and fishing 111.4; Mining and quarrying 4.9; Manufacturing 51.0; Electricity and water 33.4; Construction 46.0; Wholesale and retail trade 70.6; Restaurants and hotels 16.2; Transport 56.4; Communications 51.7; Finance and insurance 69.3; Real estate and housing 20.3; Government services 116.5; Other services 9.7; Sub-total 657.4; *Less* imputed bank service charge 56.1; GDP at factor cost 601.3. Source: Eastern Caribbean Central Bank, *Statistical Digest* (December 2000).

Balance of Payments (EC $ million, 1999): Exports of goods f.o.b. 147.44; Imports of goods f.o.b. –333.04; *Trade balance* –185.60; Exports of services 265.13; Imports of services –164.17; *Balance on goods and services* –84.64; Other income received 12.49; Other income paid –78.51; *Balance on goods, services and income* –150.66; Current transfers received 62.02; Current transfers paid –14.94; *Current balance* –103.58; Capital account (net) 34.07; Direct investment from abroad 48.48; Portfolio investment liabilities 102.39; Portfolio investment assets –26.22; Other investment liabilities 27.03; Other investment assets –55.30; Net errors and omissions –15.33; *Overall balance* –11.54. Source: Eastern Caribbean Central Bank, *Balance of Payments* (2000).

EXTERNAL TRADE

Principal Commodities (estimates, EC $ million, 1998): *Imports c.i.f.:* Food and live animals 71,305; Beverages and tobacco 14,186;

Crude materials (inedible) except fuels 9,937; Mineral fuels, lubricants, etc. 25,912; Animal and vegetable oils, fats and waxes 14,070; Chemicals and related products 53,734; Basic manufactures 63,709; Machinery and transport equipment 86,977; Miscellaneous manufactured articles 41,466; Total (incl. others) 381,299. *Exports f.o.b.*: Food and live animals 64,142; Crude materials (inedible) except fuels 3,075; Chemicals and related products 89,150; Miscellaneous manufactured articles 3,601; Total (incl. others) 164,972. Source: Organization of Eastern Caribbean States, *External Merchandise Trade Annual Report* (1998).

Principal Trading Partners (EC $ million, estimates, 1999): *Imports c.i.f.*: Barbados 14,558; Canada 7,865; France 9,880; Germany 5,085; Guadeloupe 4,545; Jamaica 5,589; Netherlands 5,772; Saint Lucia 6,903; Saint Vincent and the Grenadines 7,746; Trinidad and Tobago 52,999; United Kingdom 39,745; USA 145,922; Total (incl. others) 381,300. *Exports f.o.b.*: Antigua and Barbuda 11,152; Barbados 8,272; France 9,810; Grenada 1,443; Guadeloupe 8,671; Guyana 10,019; Jamaica 43,689; Saint Christopher and Nevis 3,367; Saint Lucia 6,238; Saint Vincent and the Grenadines 2,840; Trinidad and Tobago 9,580; United Kingdom 41,424; USA 5,679; Total (incl. others) 164,972.

TRANSPORT

Road Traffic (motor vehicles licensed in 1994): Private cars 6,491; Taxis 90; Buses 559; Motorcycles 94; Trucks 2,266; Jeeps 461; Tractors 24; Total 9,985.

Shipping: *Merchant Fleet* (registered at 31 December 2000): 7 vessels (total displacement 2,233 grt) (Source: Lloyd's Register of Shipping, *World Fleet Statistics*); *International freight traffic* ('000 metric tons, estimates, 1993): Goods loaded 103.2; Goods unloaded 181.2.

Civil Aviation (1997): Aircraft arrivals and departures 18,672; Freight loaded 363 metric tons; Freight unloaded 575 metric tons.

TOURISM

Tourist Arrivals: *Stop-overs:* 65,446 in 1997; 65,501 in 1998; 70,791 in 1999. *Cruise-ship passengers:* 230,581 in 1997; 240,905 in 1998; 202,003 in 1999. *Excursionists:* 3,310 in 1997; 1,447 in 1998; 3,924 in 1999. Source: Eastern Caribbean Central Bank, *Balance of Payments* (2000).

Tourism Receipts (EC $ million): 106.8 in 1997; 125.6 in 1998; 131.8 in 1999. Source: Eastern Caribbean Central Bank, *Balance of Payments* (2000).

COMMUNICATIONS MEDIA

Radio Receivers (1997): 45,000 in use.

Television Receivers (1997): 6,000 in use.

Telephones (1996): 19,000 main lines in use.

Telefax Stations (1996): 396 in use.

Non-daily Newspapers (1996): 1.

Source: mainly UNESCO, *Statistical Yearbook*.

EDUCATION

Institutions (1994/95): Pre-primary 72 (1992/93); Primary 64; Secondary 14; Tertiary 2.

Teachers: Pre-primary 131 (1992/93); Primary 628 (1994/95); Secondary 269 (1994/95); Tertiary 34 (1992/93).

Pupils (1997/98): Pre-primary 3,000 (1992/93); Primary 13,418; Secondary 5,772; Tertiary 461 (1995/96).

Sources: UNESCO, *Statistical Yearbook*; Caribbean Development Bank, *Selected Indicators of Development*; UN Economic Commission for Latin America and the Caribbean, *Statistical Yearbook*.

Directory

The Constitution

The Constitution came into effect at the independence of Dominica on 3 November 1978. Its main provisions are summarized below:

FUNDAMENTAL RIGHTS AND FREEDOMS

The Constitution guarantees the rights of life, liberty, security of the person, the protection of the law and respect for private property. The individual is entitled to freedom of conscience, of expression and assembly and has the right to an existence free from slavery, forced labour and torture. Protection against discrimination on the grounds of sex, race, place of origin, political opinion, colour or creed is assured.

THE PRESIDENT

The President is elected by the House of Assembly for a term of five years. A presidential candidate is nominated jointly by the Prime Minister and the Leader of the Opposition and on their concurrence is declared elected without any vote being taken; in the case of disagreement the choice will be made by secret ballot in the House of Assembly. Candidates must be citizens of Dominica aged at least 40 who have been resident in Dominica for five years prior to their nomination. A President may not hold office for more than two terms.

PARLIAMENT

Parliament consists of the President and the House of Assembly, composed of 21 elected Representatives and nine Senators. According to the wishes of Parliament, the latter may be appointed by the President—five on the advice of the Prime Minister and four on the advice of the Leader of the Opposition—or elected. The life of Parliament is five years.

Parliament has the power to amend the Constitution. Each constituency returns one Representative to the House who is directly elected in accordance with the Constitution. Every citizen over the age of 18 is eligible to vote.

THE EXECUTIVE

Executive authority is vested in the President. The President appoints as Prime Minister the elected member of the House who commands the support of a majority of its elected members, and other ministers on the advice of the Prime Minister. Not more than three ministers may be from among the appointed Senators. The President has the power to remove the Prime Minister from office if a resolution expressing 'no confidence' in the Government is adopted by the House and the Prime Minister does not resign within three days or advise the President to dissolve Parliament.

The Cabinet consists of the Prime Minister, other ministers and the Attorney-General in an ex officio capacity.

The Leader of the Opposition is appointed by the President as that elected member of the House who, in the President's judgement, is best able to command the support of a majority of the elected members who do not support the Government.

The Government

HEAD OF STATE

President: Vernon Lorden Shaw (assumed office 6 October 1998).

CABINET
(August 2001)

A coalition of the Labour Party of Dominica (LPD) and the Dominica Freedom Party (DFP).

Prime Minister and Minister of Foreign Affairs and Carib Affairs: Pierre Charles (LPD).

Minister of Housing, Communications and Aviation: Reginald Austrie (LPD).

Minister of Finance: Ambrose George (LPD).

Minister of Trade, Industry and Marketing: Osborne Riviere (LPD).

Minister of Community Development and Women's Affairs: Matthew Walter (LPD).

Minister of Agriculture and the Environment: Vince Henderson (LPD).

Minister of Sports and Youth Affairs: Roosevelt Skerrit (LPD).

Minister of Tourism: Charles Savarin (DFP).

Minister of Health and Social Security: Sen. Herbert Sabroache (DFP).

Attorney-General and Minister of Justice, Legal Affairs, Immigration and Labour: David Bruney (LPD).

Minister of State: Loreen Bannis-Roberts.

MINISTRIES

Office of the President: Morne Bruce, Roseau; tel. 4482054; fax 4498366.

Office of the Prime Minister: Government Headquarters, Kennedy Ave, Roseau; tel. 4482401; fax 4485200.

All other ministries are at Government Headquarters, Kennedy Ave, Roseau; tel. 4482401.

CARIB TERRITORY

This reserve of the remaining Amerindian population is located on the central east coast of the island. The Caribs enjoy a measure of local government and elect their chief.

Chief: GARNET JOSEPH.

Waitukubuli Karifuna Development Committee: Salybia, Carib Territory; tel. 4457336.

Legislature

HOUSE OF ASSEMBLY

Speaker: F. OSBORNE G. SYMES.

Clerk: ALEX F. PHILLIP.

Senators: 9.

Elected Members: 21.

General Election, 31 January 2000

Party	Votes cast	%	Seats
Labour Party of Dominica . .	15,362	42.9	10
Dominica United Workers' Party	15,555	43.4	9
Dominica Freedom Party . .	4,858	13.6	2
Independents	29	0.1	—
Total	35,804	100.0	21

Political Organizations

Dominica Freedom Party (DFP): Great George St, Roseau; tel. 4482104; Leader CHARLES SAVARIN.

Dominica United Workers' Party (UWP): 37 Cork St, Roseau; tel. 4485051; f. 1988; Leader EDISON JAMES; Chair. GARNET L. DIDIER.

Labour Party of Dominica (LPD): Cork St, Roseau; tel. 4488511; f. 1985 as a merger and reunification of left-wing groups, incl. the Dominica Labour Party (DLP; f. 1961); Leader PIERRE CHARLES.

Diplomatic Representation

EMBASSIES IN DOMINICA

China (Taiwan): Checkhall, Massacre, POB 56, Roseau; tel. 4491385; fax 4492085; e-mail rocemb@cwdom.dom; Chargé d'affaires: R. C. WU.

Venezuela: 37 Cork St, 3rd Floor, POB 770, Roseau; tel. 4483348; fax 4486198; Ambassador: HERNANI ESCOBAR.

Judicial System

Justice is administered by the Eastern Caribbean Supreme Court (based in Saint Lucia), consisting of the Court of Appeal and the High Court. One of the six puisne judges of the High Court is resident in Dominica and presides over the Court of Summary Jurisdiction. The District Magistrate Courts deal with summary offences and civil offences involving limited sums of money (specified by law).

Religion

Most of the population profess Christianity, but there are some Muslims, Bahá'ís and Jews. The largest denomination is the Roman Catholic Church (with some 80% of the inhabitants in 1991).

CHRISTIANITY

The Roman Catholic Church

Dominica comprises the single diocese of Roseau, suffragan to the archdiocese of Castries (Saint Lucia). At 31 December 1999 there were an estimated 59,707 adherents in the country, representing a large majority of the inhabitants. The Bishop participates in the Antilles Episcopal Conference (currently based in Port of Spain, Trinidad).

Bishop of Roseau: Rt Rev. EDWARD J. GILBERT; Bishop's House, Turkey Lane, POB 790, Roseau; tel. 4482837; fax 4483404; e-mail bishop@cwdom.dm.

The Anglican Communion

Anglicans in Dominica are adherents of the Church in the Province of the West Indies. The country forms part of the diocese of the North Eastern Caribbean and Aruba. The Bishop is resident in Antigua, and Archbishop of the Province is the Bishop of the Bahamas and the Turks and Caicos Islands.

Other Christian Churches

Christian Union Church of the West Indies: District 1, Rose St, Goodwill; tel. 4482725.

Other denominations include Methodist, Pentecostal, Baptist, Church of God, Presbyterian, the Assemblies of Brethren, Moravian and Seventh-day Adventist groups, and the Jehovah's Witnesses.

BAHÁ'Í FAITH

National Spiritual Assembly: 9 James Lane, POB 136, Roseau; tel. 4484269; fax 4483881; e-mail coolesp@cwdom.dm.

The Press

The Chronicle: Wallhouse, POB 1724, Roseau; tel. 4487887; fax 4480047; e-mail thechronicle@cwdom.dm; internet www.delphis.dm.chron.htm; f. 1996; Friday; progressive independent; Editor CHARLES HARDING; Gen. Man. J. ANTHONY WHITE; circ. 3,500.

The Independent Newspaper: POB 462, 9 Great Marlborough St, Roseau; tel. 4480221; fax 4484368; internet www.delphis.dm/indpub; weekly.

Official Gazette: Government Printery, Roseau; tel. 4482401, ext. 330; weekly; circ. 550.

The Sun: Sun Inc., POB 2255, Roseau; tel. 4484744; fax 4484764; e-mail acsun@cwdom.dm; f. 1998; Editor CHARLES JAMES.

The Tropical Star: POB 1998, Roseau; tel. 4484634; fax 4485984; e-mail tpl@cwdom.dm; weekly; circ. 3,000.

Broadcasting and Communications

TELECOMMUNICATIONS

Regulatory Authority

Eastern Caribbean Telecommunications Authority: Castries; f. 2000 to regulate telecommunications in Dominica, Grenada, Saint Christopher and Nevis, Saint Lucia and Saint Vincent and the Grenadines.

Major Service Providers

Cable & Wireless Dominica: Hanover St, POB 6, Roseau; tel. 448100; fax 4481111; internet www.tod.dm/index.htm; Gen. Man. CARL ROBERTS.

Telecommunications of Dominica (TOD): Mercury House, Hanover St, Roseau; tel. 4481024.

BROADCASTING

Radio

Dominica Broadcasting Corporation: Victoria St, POB 1, Roseau; tel. 4483283; fax 4482918; e-mail dbsradio@dbsradio.com; internet www.dbsradio.com; government station; daily broadcasts in English; 2 hrs daily in French patois; 10 kW transmitter on the medium wave band; FM service; programmes received throughout Caribbean excluding Jamaica and Guyana; Gen. Man. DENNIS JOSEPH; Programme Dir SHERMAINE GREEN-BROWN.

Kairi FM: Island Communications Corporation, Great George St, POB 931, Roseau; tel. 4487330; fax 4487332; e-mail kairfm@tod.dm; internet www.delphis.dm/kairi.htm; f. 1994.

Radio Enba Mango: Grand Bay; tel. 4463207.

Voice of Life Radio—ZGBC: Gospel Broadcasting Corpn, Loubiere, POB 205, Roseau; tel. 4487017; fax 4487094; e-mail volradio@tod.dm; linked to the US Christian Reformed Church; 112 hrs weekly AM, 24 hrs daily FM; Man. Dir GRANT HOEPPNER.

Television

There is no national television service, although there is a cable television network serving one-third of the island.

Marpin Telecom and Broadcasting: POB 2381, Roseau; tel. 4484107; fax 4482965; e-mail manager@marpin.dm; internet www.marpin.dm; commercial; cable service; Programme Man. RON ABRAHAM.

Finance

(cap. = capital; res = reserves; dep. = deposits; m. = million;
amounts in East Caribbean dollars)

The Eastern Caribbean Central Bank (see Part Three), based in Saint Christopher, is the central issuing and monetary authority for Dominica.

BANKS

Agricultural, Industrial and Development (AID) Bank: cnr Charles Avenue and Rawles Lane, Goodwill, POB 215, Roseau; tel. 4482853; fax 4484903; e-mail aidbank@cwdom.dm; f. 1971; responsible to Ministry of Finance; planned privatization suspended in 1997; cap. 9.5m. (1991); Chair. CRISPIN SORHAINDO; Man. PATRICIA CHARLES.

Bank of Nova Scotia—Scotiabank (Canada): 28 Hillsborough St, POB 520, Roseau; tel. 4485800; fax 4485805; Man. C. M. SMITH.

Banque Française Commerciale (France): Queen Mary St, Roseau; tel. 4484040; fax 4485335; e-mail bfc@cwd.dom.dm; Man. THIERRY FREY.

Barclays Bank PLC (United Kingdom): 2 Old St, POB 4, Roseau; tel. 4482571; fax 4483471; Man. LEROY L. DANGLAR; sub-br. in Portsmouth.

National Commercial Bank of Dominica: 64 Hillsborough St, POB 271, Roseau; tel. 4482571; fax 4483982; e-mail ncbdom@cwdom.dm; f. 1976; cap. 10.0m., res 10.0m., dep. 247.0m. (June 1999); 51% govt-owned; Chair. NICHOLAS WALDRON; Gen. Man. JULIUS CORBETT; 2 brs.

Royal Bank of Canada: Dame Mary Eugenia Charles Blvd, POB 19, Roseau; tel. 4482771; fax 4485398; Man. H. PINARD.

INSURANCE

Several British, regional and US companies have agents in Roseau. Local companies include the following:

First Domestic Insurance Co Ltd. 19–21 King George V St, POB 1931, Roseau; tel. 4488337; fax 4485778; e-mail: insurance@cwdom.dm.

Insurance Specialists and Consultants: 19–21 King George V St, POB 20, Roseau; tel. 4482022; fax 4485778.

J. B. Charles and Co Ltd: Old St, POB 121, Roseau; tel. 4482876.

Tonge Inc Ltd: 19–21 King George V St, POB 20, Roseau; tel. 4484027; fax 4485778.

Windward Islands Crop Insurance Co (Wincrop): Vanoulst House, Goodwill, POB 469, Roseau; tel. 4483955; fax 4484197; f. 1987; regional; coverage for weather destruction of, mainly, banana crops; Man. KERWIN FERREIRA; brs in Grenada, Saint Lucia and Saint Vincent.

Trade and Industry

DEVELOPMENT ORGANIZATIONS

National Development Corporation (NDC): Valley Rd, POB 293, Roseau; tel. 4482045; fax 4485840; e-mail ndc@cwdom.dm; internet www.dominica.dm; f. 1988 by merger of Industrial Development Corpn (f. 1974) and Tourist Board; promotes local and foreign investment to increase employment, production and exports; promotes and co-ordinates tourism development; Chair. ISAAC BAPTISTE; Gen. Man. SHERIDAN G. GREGOIRE.

Eastern Caribbean States Export Development and Agricultural Diversification Unit (EDADU): POB 769, Roseau; tel. 4486655; fax 4485554; e-mail oecsundp@cwdom.dm; internet www.oecs-edadu.org; f. 1990 as Eastern Caribbean States Export Development Agency; reformed as above in 1997; OECS regional development org.; Exec. Dir COLIN BULLY.

INDUSTRIAL AND TRADE ASSOCIATIONS

Dominica Association of Industry and Commerce (DAIC): POB 85, cnr Old St and Fields Lane, Roseau; tel. 4482874; fax 4486868; e-mail daic@marpin.dm; internet www.delphis.dm/daic.htm; f. 1972 by a merger of the Manufacturers' Association and the Chamber of Commerce; represents the business sector, liaises with the Government, and stimulates commerce and industry; 100 mems; Pres. MICHAEL ASTAPHAN; CEO JEANILIA R. V. DE SMET.

Dominica Banana Marketing Corporation (DBMC): Vanoulst House, POB 1620, Roseau; tel. 4482671; fax 4486445; internet www.delphis.dm/dbmc.htm; f. 1934 as Dominica Banana Growers' Association; restructured 1984; state-supported; Chair. Dr BERNARD YANKEY; Gen. Man. GREGORY SHILLINGFORD.

Dominica Export-Import Agency (Dexia): Bay Front, POB 173, Roseau; tel. 4483494; fax 4486308; e-mail dexia@cwdom.dm;

internet www.delphis.dm/dexia/trade.htm; f. 1986; replaced the Dominica Agricultural Marketing Board and the External Trade Bureau; exporter of Dominican agricultural products, trade facilitator and importer of bulk rice, sugar and other essential commodities; Gen. Man. GREGOIRE THOMAS (acting).

EMPLOYERS' ORGANIZATION

Dominica Employers' Federation: 14 Church St, POB 1783, Roseau; tel. 4482314; fax 4484474; e-mail def@cwdom.dm; Pres. LAMBERT LEWIS.

UTILITIES

Electricity

Dominica Electricity Services Ltd (DOMLEC): 18 Castle St, POB 1593, Roseau; tel. 4482681; fax 4485397; e-mail mandomlec@cwdom.dm; national electricity service; 72%-owned by the Commonwealth Development Corporation (United Kingdom); Gen. Man. MURRAY ROGERS.

Water

Dominica Water and Sewerage Co Ltd (DOWASCO): 3 High St, POB 185, Roseau; tel. 4484811; fax 4485813; Chair. DON CHRISTOPHER; Gen. Man. DAMIEN SHILLINGFORD.

TRADE UNIONS

Dominica Amalgamated Workers' Union (DAWU): 18 King George V St, POB 137, Roseau; tel. 4483048; fax 4485787; f. 1960; Gen. Sec. FEDELINE MOULON; 500 mems (1996).

Dominica Association of Teachers: 7 Boyd's Ave, Roseau; tel. 4488177; fax 4488177; e-mail DAT@cwdom.dm; Pres. CELIA NICHOLAS; 630 mems (1996).

Dominica Trade Union: 70–71 Independence St, Roseau; tel. 4498139; fax 4499060; f. 1945; Pres. HAROLD SEALEY; Gen. Sec. LEO J. BERNARD NICHOLAS; 400 mems (1995).

Media Workers' Association: Roseau; Pres. MATTHIAS PELTIER.

National Workers' Union: 69 Queen Mary St, Roseau; tel. 4484465; f. 1977; Pres. RAWLINS JERMOTT; Gen. Sec. PATRICK JOHN; 450 mems (1996).

Public Service Union: cnr Valley Rd and Windsor Lane, Roseau; tel. 4482102; fax 4488060; f. 1940 and registered as a trade union in 1960; representing all grades of civil servants, including firemen, prison officers, nurses, teachers and postal workers; Pres. SONIA D. WILLIAMS; Gen. Sec. THOMAS LETANG; 1,400 mems.

Waterfront and Allied Workers' Union: 43 Hillsborough St, Roseau; tel. 4482343; f. 1965; Pres. LOUIS BENOIT; Gen. Sec. NEVILLE LEE; 1,500 mems.

Transport

ROADS

In 1996 there were an estimated 780 km (485 miles) of roads, of which about 50.4% was paved; there were also numerous tracks. A road and bridge reconstruction project, costing an estimated EC $33m., was announced by the Government in 1997.

SHIPPING

A deep-water harbour at Woodbridge Bay serves Roseau, which is the principal port. Several foreign shipping lines call at Roseau, and there is a high-speed ferry service between Martinique and Guadeloupe which calls at Roseau eight times a week. Ships of the Geest Line call at Prince Rupert's Bay, Portsmouth, to collect bananas, and cruise-ship facilities were constructed there during 1990. There are other specialized berthing facilities on the west coast.

Dominica Ports Authority: POB 243, Roseau; tel. 4484431; fax 4486131; f. 1972; responsible to the Ministry of Communications and Works; pilotage and cargo handling.

CIVIL AVIATION

Melville Hall Airport, 64 km (40 miles) from Roseau, and Canefield Airport, 5 km (3 miles) from Roseau, are the two airports on the island. In 2001 proposals for the construction of an international airport were under review. Construction of the new airport was to be funded by the European Union. A feasibility study on the expansion and upgrading of Melville Hall Airport was completed in 1998. The construction of a new runway at the nearby village of Wesley was chosen in preference to an earlier plan to realign Melville Hall's existing runway. The EC $78m.-project was due to begin in late 1998. Canefield Airport was also to be improved. The regional airline, LIAT (based in Antigua and Barbuda, and in which Dominica is a shareholder), provides daily services and, with Air Caraibe, Air

Guadeloupe and Air BVI, connects Dominica with all the islands of the Eastern Caribbean, including the international airports of Puerto Rico, Antigua, Guadeloupe and Martinique.

Tourism

The Government has designated areas of the island as nature reserves, to preserve the beautiful, lush scenery and the rich, natural heritage that constitute Dominica's main tourist attractions. Birdlife is particularly prolific, and includes several rare and endangered species, such as the Imperial parrot. There are also two marine reserves. Tourism is not as developed as it is among Dominica's neighbours, but the country is being promoted as an 'eco-tourism' and cruise destination. There were an estimated 276,718 visitors in 1999 (of whom 202,003 were cruise-ship passengers), and in 1996 there were 764 hotel rooms. Receipts from tourism increased by 4.9% from EC $125.64m. in 1998 to EC $131.77m. in 1999.

National Development Corporation (NDC)—Division of Tourism: Valley Rd, POB 73, Roseau; tel. 4482045; fax 4485840; e-mail ndc@cwdom.dm; internet www.dominica.dm; f. 1988, when Tourist Board merged with Industrial Development Corpn; Dir of Tourism SOBERS ESPRIT.

Dominica Hotel and Tourism Association: POB 384, Roseau; tel. 4486565; fax 4480299; Pres. ATHERTON MARTIN.

Defence

The Dominican Defence Force was officially disbanded in 1981. There is a police force of about 300, which includes a coastguard service. The country participates in the US-sponsored Regional Security System.

Education

Education is free and is provided by both government and denominational schools. There are also a number of schools for the mentally and physically handicapped. Education is compulsory for 10 years between five and 15 years of age. Primary education begins at the age of five and lasts for seven years. Enrolment of children in the primary age-group was 70.7% in 1992. Secondary education, beginning at 12 years of age, lasts for five years. A teacher-training college and nursing school provide further education, and there is also a branch of the University of the West Indies on the island. In 1997 the Government announced plans to invest EC $17.9m. in a Basic Education Reform project. The rate of adult illiteracy was 6.0% in 1996.

THE DOMINICAN REPUBLIC

Area: 48,422 sq km (18,696 sq miles).

Population (official estimate at mid-2000): 8,518,483.

Capital: Santo Domingo, population 1,609,699 at census of 1993.

Language: Spanish (official).

Religion: Predominantly Christianity (more than 90% Roman Catholic).

Climate: Subtropical; average annual temperature is 27°C (80°F).

Time: GMT –4 hours.

Public Holidays

2002: 1 January (New Year's Day), 6 January (Epiphany), 21 January (Our Lady of Altagracia), 26 January (Duarte), 27 February (Independence), 29 March (Good Friday), 14 April (Pan-American Day), 1 May (Labour Day), 16 July (Foundation of Sociedad la Trinitaria), 16 August (Restoration Day), 24 September (Our Lady of Las Mercedes), 12 October (Columbus Day), 24 October (United Nations Day), 1 November (All Saints' Day), 6 November (Constitution Day), 25 December (Christmas Day).

2003: 1 January (New Year's Day), 6 January (Epiphany), 21 January (Our Lady of Altagracia), 26 January (Duarte), 27 February (Independence), 18 April (Good Friday), 14 April (Pan-American Day), 1 May (Labour Day), 16 July (Foundation of Sociedad la Trinitaria), 16 August (Restoration Day), 24 September (Our Lady of Las Mercedes), 12 October (Columbus Day), 24 October (United Nations Day), 1 November (All Saints' Day), 6 November (Constitution Day), 25 December (Christmas Day).

Currency: Dominican Republic peso; 1,000 pesos = £41.52 = US $59.45 = €66.98 (30 April 2001).

Weights and Measures: The metric system is in force, but US imperial measures are also used.

Basic Economic Indicators

	1998	1999	2000
Gross domestic product (million pesos at 1970 prices) .	5,723	6,227	6,633
GDP per head ('000 pesos at 1970 prices) .	n.a.	748.0	778.7
GDP (million pesos at current prices) .	241,910	278,939	322,866
GDP per head ('000 pesos at current prices) .	n.a.	33,506.4	37,904.8
Annual growth of real GDP (%) .	7.5	8.8	6.5
Annual growth of real GDP per head (%) .	n.a.	n.a.	4.1
Government budget (million pesos at current prices):			
Revenue.	38,564.8	43,483.6	51,271.3
Expenditure.	36,757.5	45,164.7	48,202.3
Consumer prices index (annual average; base: 1995 = 100) .	119.3	127.0	n.a.
Rate of inflation (annual average, %) .	4.5	6.5	n.a.
Foreign exchange reserves (US $ million at 31 December) .	501.6	689.1	625.1
Imports f.o.b. (US $ million) .	5,631	5,988	7,379
Exports f.o.b. (US $ million) .	880	805	966
Balance of payments (current account, US $ million) .	–338.4	–429.2	n.a.

Gross national product per head measured at purchasing power parity (PPP) (US dollars, converted by the PPP exchange rate, 1999): 4653.

Economically active population (FAO estimate, mid-1998): 3,553,000.

Unemployment (estimate, 1998): 14.3%.

Total external debt (1999): US $4,771m.

Life expectancy (UN estimates, years at birth, 1990–95): 69.3 (males 67.6, females 71.7).

Infant mortality rate (per 1,000 live births, 1997): 44.

Adult population with HIV/AIDS (15–49 years, 1999): 2.8%.

School enrolment ratio (6–17 years, 1997/98): 64%.

Adult literacy rate (15 years and over, 2000): 83.6% (males 83.6, females 83.6).

Energy consumption per head (kg of oil equivalent, 1998): 676.

Carbon dioxide emissions per head (metric tons, 1997): 1.7.

Passenger motor cars in use (estimate, per 1,000 of population, 1998): 45.

Television receivers in use (per 1,000 of population, 1997): 95.

History

JAMES FERGUSON

Based on an earlier article by ROD PRINCE

The island of Hispaniola (or Quisqueya, the Amerindian name), now divided between the Dominican Republic and Haiti, was inhabited by Taino Indians (Amerindians) when the first Europeans to visit the New World, a Spanish expedition led by Christopher Columbus, landed in 1492. Spanish settlement began in the following year. By the mid-16th century the Tainos were extinct as a separate people, having succumbed to the effects of smallpox, enslavement and repression after a 13-year insurrection against the Spanish. The importation of African slaves on a large scale began in the 1520s.

Spanish colonization of the island was less than energetic. During the 16th and 17th centuries French buccaneers established control over the western part, which was ceded to France as Saint-Domingue, by the Treaty of Ryswick in 1697. An English force, under Sir Francis Drake, sacked Santo Domingo in 1586 and by 1740 the area under Spanish control had a population of only 6,000, of whom only 2,000 were Spanish. Under a repopulation programme, the figure then increased to 100,000 in 40 years.

INDEPENDENCE

At the end of the 18th century Santo Domingo became involved in the conflicts arising from the French Revolution and the Saint-Domingue slave revolt, which led to Haitian independence in 1804. France gained nominal control of the whole island through the 1795 Treaty of Basle. However, it was the Haitians, under Toussaint L'Ouverture, who succeeded in occupying Santo Domingo from 1801 to 1803. After further changes in sovereignty, Haiti invaded again in 1822, remaining until the declaration of Dominican independence in 1844.

The Haitians led further invasions, in the years following independence, and the new Republic's precarious position caused President Pedro Santana to request the re-establishment of Spanish dominion in 1861. Independence was regained in 1865 after a 'War of Restoration'. There followed 50 years of political and economic instability; there were rapid changes of government, with the notable exception of the dictatorship of Ulises Heureaux (1882–99). The Republic's inability to pay foreign creditors was the occasion for the establishment, by the USA, of a customs receivership in 1905, with outright US occupation following between 1916 and 1924. A lasting result of the US occupation was the creation of a Dominican Army, the commanding general of which, Rafael Leonidas Trujillo Molina, was elected President in 1930.

THE TRUJILLO ERA

Trujillo swiftly established a dictatorship which lasted until his assassination in 1961. He ruled personally between 1930 and 1947, and indirectly through his brother, President Héctor Trujillo (1947–60), and Dr Joaquín Balaguer (August 1960–January 1962). Ruling by blackmail, bribery, torture and murder, Trujillo amassed a fortune. He became the country's largest landowner. The Trujillo family controlled two-thirds of the sugar industry, which underwent enormous expansion during his rule; their interests also covered many areas of manufacturing and commerce.

During the Trujillo era a substantial programme of industrialization and public works was executed, while the agreement to end the US customs receivership allowed Trujillo to assume the title of 'Restorer of Financial Independence'. High prices for Dominican produce during the Second World War enabled him to liquidate the country's outstanding debt in 1947 and to introduce a national currency, the peso. Relations with Haiti, however, deteriorated, owing to the massacre of several thousand Haitian migrant labourers in 1937.

After the dictator's assassination, the titular President, Joaquín Balaguer, engineered the exile of Trujillo's son, Ramfis, and other members of the family. The Trujillo properties were seized by the state. After some months of political tension, marked by coup attempts and street disturbances, elections were held in December 1962, which gave a clear victory to the left-of-centre Partido Revolucionario Dominicano (PRD—Dominican Revolutionary Party). The PRD leader, Juan Bosch Gaviño, became President in February 1963, remaining in office for only seven months before being overthrown in a military coup, led by Col (later Gen.) Elías Wessin y Wessin. Bosch, accused of being pro-Communist, was exiled and a three-man civilian junta, led by Donald Reid Cabral, assumed power.

On 24 April 1965 followers of the PRD, supported by a group of young colonels, launched an insurrection aimed at restoring constitutional government. Fierce fighting followed between the insurgents and the armed forces under Wessin y Wessin, and on 28 April the first of 23,000 US Marines landed on the island. The Organization of American States (OAS) was subsequently requested to form a peace force and to negotiate a settlement. The intervention of the USA and the OAS resulted in an end to the fighting and the peace force withdrew in September. A provisional Government took office, under Héctor García Godoy, pending presidential and congressional elections in June 1966.

THE BALAGUER PERIOD, 1966–78

The victor in the presidential contest was Balaguer, now of the Partido Reformista Social Cristiano (PRSC—Reformist Social Christian Party), who remained in office until 1978. His rule was marked by periodic outbreaks of right-wing terrorism, military coup attempts and left-wing guerrilla landings. President Balaguer encouraged closer economic links with the USA, symbolized by the powerful position obtained by Gulf and Western, the major private company in the country's sugar industry.

The PRD boycotted polls in 1970 and 1974, in protest at Balaguer's decision to seek further terms in office. Bosch resigned from the leadership of the PRD and formed his own party, the left-wing Partido de la Liberación Dominicana (PLD—Party of Dominican Liberation) in 1973. The presidential election of May 1978 was the first serious contest for 12 years. The PRD's Silvestre Antonio Guzmán Fernández was elected President, with Jacobo Majluta Azar as Vice-President. As Guzmán's victory became apparent, members of the police force attempted to stop the counting of votes. However, pressure from the US Government ensured that Guzmán was able to take office.

THE PRD IN POWER, 1978–1986

During his four years as President, Guzmán attempted to 'institutionalize' the armed forces, dismantling the powerful group of officers who had supported Trujillo and Balaguer. He also attempted to deal with the long-standing problem of corruption. However, in July 1982 after his successor, Salvador Jorge Blanco, also of the PRD, had been elected, Guzmán committed suicide, after learning that his daughter and son-in-law, who worked in the presidential secretariat, had been accused of corruption. Contrary to widespread fears, his suicide did not cause a military coup—a measure of his success in taming the Army—and Jorge Blanco took office, as scheduled, in August.

During Jorge Blanco's presidency, as in Guzmán's, the economy suffered severe difficulties and the PRD underwent prolonged factional disputes, with the left of the party accusing the Government of abandoning its election pledges. In April 1984 at least 60 people were killed in riots, following the announcement of price increases and other austerity measures. In May 1986, as the elections approached, the PRD split into factions.

BALAGUER AGAIN, 1986–1996

The beneficiary of the PRD's disarray was Balaguer, candidate of the PRSC, who won his fifth term as President on 16 May 1986 and appointed a Cabinet comprised largely of unaffiliated technocrats. President Balaguer's policy of fostering rapid economic growth through a substantial public-works programme, together with incentives for foreign investors in industry and tourism, encountered increasing difficulties after 1988. The rapid price increases announced in early 1988 caused nationwide strikes and riots, including a violent two-day general strike in June 1989. Nevertheless, Balaguer obtained a sixth term in office in the presidential election of 16 May 1990, defeating Bosch (PLD), José Francisco Peña Gómez (PRD) and Majluta, the candidate of the breakaway Partido Revolucionario Independiente (PRI—Independent Revolutionary Party), in highly controversial circumstances.

Widespread discontent at sharply rising consumer prices in 1990 led to an abrupt change of government economic policy, aimed at countering inflation and obtaining an agreement with the International Monetary Fund (IMF). By the end of 1991 the IMF had approved an 18-month stand-by programme and debt rescheduling had been negotiated with the 'Paris Club' of creditor nations. The new policy was successful in reducing inflation and in improving the real gross domestic product (GDP) growth rate. A further eight-month IMF programme was agreed in July 1993, but inflation increased once more while growth slowed. Although 87 years old and virtually blind, Balaguer sought a seventh term in office in the presidential election of 16 May 1994. His principal opponent was the PRD's Peña Gómez, with the 84-year old Bosch standing for the PLD. Once again, the election was marked by allegations of voting irregularities, and a delayed official result gave Balaguer a narrow and bitterly contested victory over Peña Gómez. The atmosphere of crisis was only relieved by the signing of an agreement on 10 August between Balaguer and Peña Gómez, providing for Balaguer's term to last only 18 months, with a fresh election to be held in November 1995; this agreement was subsequently amended by the Congreso Nacional (National Congress) to give Balaguer a two-year term and to prohibit future presidents from seeking consecutive terms in office.

THE PRESIDENCY OF LEONEL FERNÁNDEZ, 1996–2000

Following the volatile political atmosphere of 1995, the election of 16 May 1996 was the first for 30 years in which Balaguer did not stand, while Bosch was also absent, having resigned as PLD leader in June 1994. Another innovation was the adoption of a two-round voting system. In the first round, Peña Gómez won 45.9% of the ballot for the PRD, against 38.9% for the PLD's new candidate, Leonel Fernández Reyna, a 42-year old lawyer; the PRSC candidate, Vice-President Jacinto Peynado, won only 15.0% of the votes cast, after a campaign in which he had received only formal support from Balaguer.

In the second round of the election, on 30 June 1996, Fernández won 51.25% of the votes cast, having obtained the support of PRSC voters through an alliance with their party. Peña Gómez secured 48.75% of the ballot. The majority of 71,704 votes, although narrow, was the largest in any presidential election since 1982. However, the new Government was impeded by the lack of a congressional majority, since the PLD had won only one Senate seat in the 1994 election, and 13 of the 120 seats in the Chamber of Deputies. This meant that the PLD was dependent on the support of the PRSC (which held 50 seats in the lower house and 14 in the Senate) to implement planned reforms.

President Fernández had promised to wage war on corruption and modernize the administration, and during 1997 he oversaw a restructuring of both the police and the judiciary. On other issues, however, notably the deteriorating state of public services, the new President made less progress. The opposition of the Congreso Nacional, which rejected the 1997 budget, played a significant role in this. This resulted in widespread disturbances and industrial action throughout 1997, which led to the deaths

of several demonstrators during confrontations with security forces in July–September.

Elections to the Senate and to an enlarged Chamber of Deputies were held on 16 May 1998. The PRD (the leader of which, Peña Gómez, had died six days before) gained 83 of the 149 seats in the lower house and 24 in the Senate. President Fernández's PLD also increased its representation in the Congreso Nacional, to 49 deputies and four senators. The PRSC secured the remaining 17 seats in the lower house and two seats in the Senate. However, the PLD failed to gain a sufficient majority to secure passage of a possible constitutional amendment allowing President Fernández to seek re-election in 2000.

The new composition of the Congreso Nacional exacerbated inter-party hostilities. The PLD and PRSC again joined forces to combat the opposition PRD's dominance, and the PRD continued with a strategy of non-co-operation, guaranteeing severe difficulties for President Fernández in his attempt to execute the remainder of his legislative programme.

The PLD and PRSC targeted the Junta Central Electoral (JCE—Central Electoral Council), claiming that its composition, which had been forced through by the PRD-dominated Congreso Nacional in August 1998, was politically biased. In retaliation, PRD members of the legislature continued to delay government legislation, including the disbursement of loans and grants intended for reconstruction following the destruction caused by 'Hurricane Georges' in September 1998. Mediation from the Roman Catholic Church and other non-partisan bodies produced no immediate solution to the impasse, although in November 1998 both houses approved the 1999 budget, albeit with significant amendments to proposed increases in value added tax (VAT). During 1998 and the first six months of 1999 there were further strike actions in protest at social hardship and poor employment conditions for public-sector workers. Violent crime also rose significantly during this period. Frustrated by congressional opposition to public-sector restructuring and comprehensive reform of tariff and tax systems, President Fernández concentrated on foreign-policy objectives, signing free-trade agreements with the Central American Common Market (CACM) in April 1998 and with the Caribbean Community and Common Market (CARICOM) in August of that year. Progress in privatization plans was uneven, with tendering for the large state-owned companies being repeatedly postponed. However, in November 1998 a foreign consortium was awarded management contracts for four of the country's international airports and in May 1999 the long-delayed privatization of the ailing state power company, Corporación Dominicana de Electricidad, was begun, improving the outlook for business considerably.

THE PRD'S RETURN

Following a period of political tension in the early months of 1999, during which candidates within the PRD, the PLD and the PRSC contested their parties' nominations for the forthcoming presidential election, due to be held in May 2000, two candidates emerged as favourites. Rafael Hipólito Mejía Domínguez won the PRD presidential nomination, while the ruling PLD selected the former Secretary of State to the Presidency, Danilo Medina Sánchez, as its nominee. In July 1999 the PRSC controversially nominated Joaquín Balaguer as its presidential candidate, with the 92-year-old former President aiming for an eighth term in office.

The campaign was the most peaceful in the Republic's history, marred only by a small number of violent incidents. It was widely assumed that the election would go to a second round, even though Mejía would probably gain a clear lead in the first. In the event, he received 49.9% of the votes cast on 16 May 2000, while Medina won 24.9% and Balaguer 24.6%. In an unprecedented move, the JCE allowed Mejía to declare himself the winner, although he had failed to secure the constitutionally required 50%. The PLD-PRSC alliance, which had kept the PRD out of office in 1996, failed to materialize again in 2000, probably because most PRSC activists felt that they had received little from the PLD Government over the past four years.

President Mejía's political programme was radical, including tax reform, decentralization of power and the restructuring of the public sector. In the first months of his presidency, he also proved to be confrontational, clashing publicly with ministers as well as the media. The PRD crusade against the previous PLD administration's alleged corruption also proved controversial, creating open hostility between the two parties. In November former President Fernández led a protest, following the arrest of various former senior government officials, including Diandino Peña, Haivanjoe Ng Cortinas and Feliz Bautista, on charges of corruption. Fernández was later similarly accused and arrested; however, they were all subsequently released, owing to lack of evidence. With only 73 PRD supporters out of 149 deputies in the lower house (10 of the 83 elected in May 1998 had been expelled from the party), Mejía was dependent on the PRSC and Balaguer.

In late 2000 the Dominican Republic was to testify before the Inter-American Court of Human Rights (part of the OAS) regarding the mistreatment of Haitians. President Mejía stated that one of his Government's priorities was bilateral relations with Haiti. In early 2001, following an increase in tensions in Haiti, a plan to protect Dominican territory was implemented, while military forces deployed on the Dominican–Haitian border were reinforced to prevent both illegal immigration and drugs-trafficking.

Some significant reforms were introduced in the first year of the Mejía administration. A package of fiscal legislation increased VAT from 8% to 12%, introduced taxes on luxury goods and obliged larger companies to pay corporation taxes of 1.5% in stages throughout the year. The removal of the cumbersome 'fuel differential', the margin between the price paid by the Government and that paid by consumers, and its replacement by a fixed tax raised petrol prices, but there was no violent popular response. In recognition of the hardships caused to the poor by increased prices, the Government introduced a poverty mitigation programme of redistributive measures, including training, infrastructural programmes and health, education and housing reforms. Social security legislation was introduced, aimed at providing employees with improved pensions and other benefits. In February 2001 public hospital medical workers called a strike in opposition of the proposed welfare reforms. The Government also announced ambitious infrastructural schemes, including a railway from the Port of Haina via Santo Domingo to Santiago, and extensive new road building, to be part-funded by private interests.

However, if President Mejía enjoyed significant, if gradually decreasing, public popularity in 2001, he also attracted much criticism, especially from political opponents. It was alleged that far from cutting the public-sector wage bill, the new Government had created 70,000 new jobs for PRD supporters. Critics also claimed that the Government's recurrent and capital spending was outstripping revenue from taxation and that the fiscal deficit would reach crisis point. As congressional elections in May 2002 approached, President Mejía's task was to retain the loyalty of PRD supporters and those attracted by his promises of social reform, while reassuring business interests that steady growth and low inflation would be maintained.

Economy
JAMES FERGUSON

Based on an earlier article by ROD PRINCE

During the 1990s substantial investment in tourism and free-zone manufacturing occurred, bringing these sectors into prominence as leading contributors to gross domestic product (GDP) and as earners of foreign exchange. Agriculture, traditionally the major sector of the economy, remained fundamental, although its importance to the economy as a whole was in decline; in 2000, according to preliminary figures, the sector's share of GDP (including livestock, forestry and fishing) was 11.1%, compared with 17.0% for the manufacturing sector. Government investment in roads, power-stations and other infrastructural projects made a significant contribution to employment and to GDP. In September 1998 'Hurricane Georges' killed approximately 300 people and caused damage to agricultural production estimated at US $2,000m. The hurricane also adversely affected manufacturing and tourism.

The economy was marked in the late 1980s and early 1990s by large trade and budgetary deficits, a heavy burden of debt and increases in the rate of inflation. In 1991 the adoption of an economic programme, supported by the International Monetary Fund (IMF), to restore fiscal discipline, succeeded in reducing the average annual rate of inflation from 47.0% in 1991 to 4.3% in 1992. The programme brought the Government's accounts into surplus, while debt rescheduling and strong services earnings improved balance-of-payment and reserve positions. In the following three years, however, the inflation rate increased steadily, reaching 12.5% in 1995, but falling back to 5.4% in 1996, before increasing again to 8.3% in 1997. It was feared that inflation would increase sharply at the end of 1998, as a result of emergency imports necessitated by Hurricane Georges, but a rate of 4.5% was recorded over the year. The rate of inflation rose in 1999 to 6.5% and to an estimated 7.9% in 2000, largely as a consequence of higher oil prices. Government finances fluctuated in the late 1990s: in 1996 there was a budgetary deficit of 708m. pesos, which turned to a surplus of 813m. pesos in 1997, and of 2,110m. pesos in 1998. In 1999, however, a deficit of 1,287m. pesos was recorded. In the first nine months of 2000 the Government recorded a surplus of 3,127m. pesos, but this sum was immediately spent on debt servicing, which increased sharply after the expiry of a defer-ment granted by the 'Paris Club' of creditor nations in the wake of Hurricane Georges. The visible trade deficit increased steadily from US $1,070.5m. in 1991 to $2,904.4m. in 1999 and $3,752.7m. in 2000.

The late 1960s and early 1970s had been a period of economic recovery from the stagnation of Gen. Rafael Trujillo's dictator-ship and the upheaval that followed his assassination. Between 1968 and 1974 the average annual growth rate in real GDP was 10.6% (7.4% per head), supported by high sugar prices and significant international, particularly US, aid. In the late 1970s, owing to rising petroleum prices, the economy began to decline; the growth rate fluctuated considerably in the 1980s.

In 1988 a combination of rapid inflation and decreasing production in agriculture, manufacturing and mining reduced the economic growth rate to 1.7%. This recovered to 4.3% in 1989, before contracting dramatically, by 4.8%, in 1990, and only growing by 1.0% in 1991. Increasing inflation, the inadequate supply of electric power from the state electricity corporation, Corporación Dominicana de Electricidad (CDE), and the impact of the Government's austerity programme, introduced in August 1990, were all factors in the recession.

A strong economic recovery took place in 1992, with a real GDP growth rate of 8.0%, led by the construction, tourism, energy and manufacturing sectors. The impetus given to construction and tourism by the quincentenary celebrations of the discovery of the Americas by the European navigator, Christo-pher Columbus, was a major factor in the revival. However, the recovery slowed in 1993, with an economic growth rate of 2.9%. This was owing to the impact of high interest rates, which inhibited investment in some areas, notably domestic manufacturing and agriculture. There was also a severe decline in the mining sector. The growth rate increased to 4.3% in 1994 and to 4.8% in 1995.

Economic recovery gathered momentum in 1996, producing a real GDP growth rate of 7.3%, based on increased activity in tourism, construction, mining, agriculture and telecommunications, together with an improvement in electricity supply. The strong performance of the economy was maintained subsequently, with GDP growth of 8.2% recorded in 1997, although there was a marked deterioration in power supplies, as well as signs of diminishing business confidence, including increasing pressure on the peso–US dollar exchange rate. Tourism, construction and telecommunications were again among the leading sectors. In 1998, despite the impact of Hurricane Georges, real GDP increased by 7.5%, with construction experiencing sectoral growth of 19.6% over the year. This trend continued into 1999; GDP growth of 8.8% was led by post-hurricane construction and a burgeoning telecommunications sector. In 2000 growth of 6.5% was recorded.

The population at the census of September 1993 was 7,293,390, of whom 3,742,593 (51.3%) were female; the urban population accounted for 56% of the total population, while those aged 14 or under accounted for 36%. At mid-2000 the total population was officially estimated at 8,518,483, with a population density of 175.9 per sq km, one of the lowest in the Caribbean. The work-force in 1993 numbered 2,607,021 (56% of those aged 15 or more), of whom 532,509 (20.4%) were unemployed. By mid-1997 the total labour force had increased to an estimated 3,155,700. An estimated 16.0% of these were unemployed. Approximately 1.6m. people lived in Santo Domingo (2.2m. including the suburban areas) in 1993. The annual average population growth rate between 1990 and 1999 was 2.1%.

By the 1990s deforestation was thought to have reduced the wooded area to about 6,000 sq km, the main forests being in the two mountain ridges, the northern and the southern cordilleras, both running from west to east. However, in 2000 a report by the Secretariat of State for Agriculture estimated that 13,000 sq km of the country were wooded. There were about 20,000 sq km of pasture and 15,000 sq km of arable land; the main agricultural areas were the Cibao and Vega Real lands in the centre of the country, where cocoa, coffee, rice and other crops were cultivated, and the south-east plains, where sugar-cane plantations and pasturage were concentrated. Mineral extraction took place near Bonao, in the centre, and in the south-west.

Clandestine emigration, mainly to the USA via Puerto Rico, was estimated at up to 40,000 attempts annually. However, increased co-operation between Puerto Rican and Dominican coast guards was reported, in 1997–99, to have reduced the numbers. The number of Haitians resident in the Republic increased following the 1991 military coup in Haiti; more than 15,000 Haitians were deported in the first two months of 1997, following an increase in immigration prompted by an announcement from the state sugar corporation that it intended to recruit 16,000 Haitian cane cutters. About 10,000 Haitians were similarly recruited in January 1998, while 3,000 Haitians were expelled. The 1997 deportations aroused protests from the Haitian Government, and in late 1999 the two countries agreed on principles and procedures to govern deportations. The visit of President Leonel Fernández to Haiti in June 1998, the first by a Dominican head of state for 62 years, led to a marked improvement in relations. Relations continued to improve during the presidency of Rafael Hipólito Mejía Domínguez, and there were proposals for joint Dominican–Haitian development programmes in the border region, to be financed by the European Union (EU).

AGRICULTURE

Agriculture (including livestock, forestry and fishing) accounted for an estimated 11.1% of GDP in 2000. The sector's share of export earnings, which had been as high as 55% in 1984, decreased to less than one-half in the 1990s; in 1999 the four traditional export products (sugar, coffee, cocoa and tobacco) accounted for approximately 30% of exports, excluding free-zone exports. The decline in the agricultural sector was slowed by the development of new crops and by official measures to support agriculture, including the abolition of duty on imported inputs and a reduction of interest rates on loans to farmers. In the wake of Hurricane Georges, however, almost all agricultural production was badly affected, and the sector contributed only 29.4% of the value of exports in 1999. By 2001, however, there were signs of recovery, especially in crops such as citrus, coffee and cocoa.

The principal crop was sugar, although by the late 1990s it had been in decline for many years, mainly because of the inefficiency of the severely indebted state sugar company, Consejo Estatal de Azúcar (CEA). In the 1995/96 harvest the CEA recorded production of only 207,000 metric tons, compared with 345,000 tons produced by the privately owned Central Romana Corporación. In September 1998 the CEA estimated that about one-half of all sugar cane under cultivation had been destroyed by Hurricane Georges, and in January 1999 it was announced that the country would need to import some 50,000 tons of sugar for domestic consumption. In 1999 output from the CEA stood at only 50,935 tons, the lowest ever recorded figure, while private growers produced 325,331 tons that same year. Overall, sugar exports earned an estimated US $76.5m. in 1999, compared to $170m. in 1996. Tendering for parts of the CEA was underway by June 1999, and in September it was announced that nine sugar mills had been leased to a Mexican consortium and one to a Dominican–US–French concern. The new mill operators, it was agreed, would pay 2% of their gross annual income to the Government.

Several areas of agriculture, notably cattle raising, were adversely affected by drought during 1997 and then by hurricane damage in 1998. Coffee exports, which, according to UN trade figures, had reached US $170m. in value in 1995, declined to $67.9m. in 1997, when the volume exported was only 6,000 metric tons, the lowest for 30 years. In 1999 coffee exports totalled just $30.4m. Tobacco production increased in line with improved export marketing for cigars in the USA and the EU; export earnings, including those for cigars manufactured in free zones, reached some $100m. in 1996, but declined thereafter, standing at a provisional $54.6m. in 1999 (according to government figures). In 1999 bids from private companies were invited for the state-owned Compañía Anónima de Tabaco. Cocoa was another important export crop, earning an estimated $24.8m. in 1999, a decrease from the $85.6m. earned in the previous year. New or 'non-traditional' export crops, vegetables, cut flowers and ornamental plants, expanded considerably from the late 1980s, with exports reaching $186m. in 1995. These sectors were least affected by Hurricane Georges, as replanting took place quickly.

Food crops included rice, maize, beans, cassava, tomatoes, bananas, plantains, mangoes and other fruit. The annual harvest of paddy rice was 527,000 metric tons in 2000, an 8.3% decrease on the previous year's harvest. In 2000 the country's livestock included 1.9m. head of cattle and an estimated 42m. chickens; the pig population was an estimated 538,600. The fish catch in 1998 was 11,000 tons, having declined from 15,200 tons in 1997. Production figures for 1998 reflected the considerable damage caused by Hurricane Georges, with bananas, rice and citrus crops particularly affected; however, these had mostly recovered by 2001.

MINING

In 2000 the mining sector, dominated by ferro-nickel, contributed only an estimated 1.8% of GDP, compared with 4.5% in 1985. The sector had replaced agriculture as the main export earner between 1989 and 1990, and in 1989 ferro-nickel earnings had reached a record US $372m. Declining world prices subsequently pushed mining into second place, and in 1993 ferro-nickel mining was suspended for three months, leading to a decrease in export revenue to $128.2m. Recovery followed in 1994 and 1995, with earnings in the latter year reaching $242.2m., which represented 30.0% of exports by value in that year. Ferro-nickel exports earned $222.3m. in 1996. Another phase of low world prices began in 1998, and exports of ferro-nickel earned only $118.7m. that year. Earnings recovered to $144m. in 1999 and a short-lived surge in world prices encouraged increased production in 2000, following a temporary closure of the principal mine in 1999.

Similarly, 1993 saw the closure of the state-owned Sulfuros de Pueblo Viejo gold and silver mine, owing to exhaustion of deposits in the upper oxide zone. In this year export revenue was reduced to only US $4.1m. Following renovation work, the mine was reopened in mid-1994, with operations taking place in a lower zone. Earnings recovered to $48.7m. in 1996. In 1998 export values declined once again to $11.7m., before plummeting to $6.1m. in 1999. In 2001 the Government awarded a 25-year concession to operate the Sulfuros de PuebloViejo mine to Canadian-owned Placer Dome. There were also plans to develop other mines throughout the country. Ahead of agriculture in terms of export earnings in 1995, gold and ferro-nickel earnings remained in second place for the rest of the decade. The slump in world prices forced the ferro-nickel mine at Bonao to close in late 1998. Following an increase in prices in early 2000, the mine was reopened. The mine was operated by Falconbridge Dominicana, the majority of which was owned by Falconbridge of Toronto (Canada).

ENERGY

There is no domestic petroleum production. Petroleum imports in 1999 cost US $1,196m. (13% of total imports, excluding free-zone activity). Under the San José Agreement of 1980, Mexico and Venezuela were to provide 45,000 barrels per day (b/d) each, between them accounting for 90% of the Dominican Republic's petroleum imports. Under the Agreement, 20% of the cost of the petroleum was converted into a low-interest development loan. In October 2000 the signing of the Caracas energy accord gave the Dominican Republic the option to buy a further 20,000 b/d from Venezuela under San José Agreement terms. Owing to steeply rising world petroleum prices, the Government's budget was adversely affected by a shrinking differential between petroleum import prices, albeit subsidized under the San José Agreement, and the price paid by consumers. This so-called 'tax' raised 2,000m. pesos between January and May 1999, but this fell to 700m. pesos during the same period of 2000. Fearful of provoking a political backlash, the Fernández Government refused to raise fuel prices, although an increase was announced by the Mejía administration in late August 2000. However, the fuel differential was later abolished and replaced with a fixed tax on petroleum and other fuels.

The electricity-generating operations of the CDE were severely deficient throughout the 1990s. Production fell to about one-half of peak demand in 1990 and 1991, recovered in the next two years, but remained at around two-thirds of peak demand in 1996. The difficulties worsened in 1997 and 1998, with daily power cuts of between eight and 12 hours in Santo Domingo and other areas. The difficulties were caused by the frequent withdrawal from service of generating units, for repair and maintenance, together with low hydroelectric production, as a result of drought, and an inefficient distribution system, which resulted in one-half of the electricity produced being lost in transmission or through illegal connections. Private generating companies periodically reduced supplies to the CDE because of non-payment of debts. The CDE was estimated, in late 1997, to be operating at a loss of 300m. pesos per month; in mid-1996 it was estimated to have a total debt of 1,800m. pesos.

In May 1999 the first stage of the privatization of the CDE was completed, with the sale of 50% of the shares in the CDE's two generating and three distribution companies. New Caribbean Investment, a Chilean–US consortium, paid US $177.8m. for a 50% stake in the Itabo generating company, and a consortium of the Commonwealth Development Corporation (United Kingdom) and Enron (USA) paid $144.5m. for the same proportion of the Haina generating company. Unión Fenosa (Spain) paid a combined $211.9m. for 50% shares in the northern and southern distribution companies and AES Distribución Dominicana paid $109.3m. for its stake in the eastern company. The new operators pledged substantial investment to overcome persistent supply problems and the privatization was expected to bring benefits to all of the CDE's customers, and, therefore, to the economy of the Dominican Republic as a whole. In September the generating plant at Itabo was transferred to the Gener-Coastal group, completing the transfer of the CDE's generating and distribution role to the private sector.

In 2000 construction began on a 300 MW oil-fired power-station and a 300 MW gas-fired power-station, including a liquified natural gas terminal; both were to be completed by 2002. There were also plans to build a regasification plant and a 500 MW gas-fired power-station, costing US $550m. York Caribbean Windpower, a subsidiary of York Research (USA), was to construct a US $160m. wind park in Puerto Plata, to be completed by 2002. In July 2001 it was announced that a hydroelectric dam was to be built in Altagracia, to supply drinking water, irrigation and electricity to the province. It was also announced in mid-2001 that the Canadian-owned Dessau-Soprin International was to construct four mini-hydroelectric plants, together generating 16 MW.

In February 2001 the Senate passed legislation on the reform of the electricity sector; the bill had still to be approved by the Chamber of Deputies. In May a report presented to the Senate highlighted a series of irregularities in the electricity sector privatization. In June riots broke out in Santo Domingo over the continuing power cuts.

MANUFACTURING

Manufacturing, the Dominican Republic's largest economic sector, contributed 17.0% of GDP in 2000. Almost one-half of the contribution of the domestic manufacturing sector traditionally came from sugar refining, although this was seriously affected in 1998–2000 by uncertainties surrounding privatization and post-hurricane shortfalls in production; other important products included cement and other non-metallic minerals, textiles, clothing and footwear, leather goods, paper, glassware, food and drinks. The sector employed 12% of the labour force in 1999. From 1990 to 1999 it demonstrated average annual growth of 7.5%, compared with an annual growth rate of 1.4% in the 1980s. Growth in manufacturing of 6.4% was recorded in 1999, despite a significant contraction in sugar refining, and the sector grew by 9.0% in 2000. The most dynamic sector in 1998–99 was construction, especially cement production. Construction contributed 13.1% of GDP in 2000, with the emphasis on private-rather than public-sector investment.

The Dominican Republic had a substantial free-zone sub-sector, which numbered 490 companies at the beginning of 2001, housed in 46 zones and employing 194,000 people. Exports from the zones in 1999 amounted to US $3,200.4m., compared with $1,765m. in 1995. Estimated exports in 2000 stood at $3,509m., representing 81% of the Republic's manufacturing export earnings. Free-zone companies enjoy 'tax holidays' of up to 20 years, duty-free raw-material imports and other benefits. In the late 1990s about 60% of production was accounted for by garments and textiles, while footwear, leather goods and electronic components were also produced. In 1993 US and Canadian investors owned 47% of the free-zone companies, then numbering 424, while 22% were locally owned. Others were owned by South Korean (Republic of Korea) and Taiwanese (Republic of China) interests. In 1999 investors warned that growing competition from Mexico was jeopardizing Dominican exports into the US market, and the sector experienced a 1.5% decrease in exports in the first three quarters of that year. In 2000, however, 7.5% growth took place in the sector, with 10 new companies opening operations. The passage of USA–Africa–Caribbean trade legislation in May 2000, giving Dominican apparel exports to the USA tariff-free status, also aided the sector.

TRANSPORT INFRASTRUCTURE

Roads, totalling 12,600 km in 1998, were the main means of communication. The Mejía administration undertook an extensive road building programme from 2000, aiming primarily to reduce traffic congestion in Santo Domingo. In 1998 it was estimated that there were 45 vehicles per 1,000 people. In July 2001 the Government announced that a Colombian-led consortium, Consorcio Dominico–Colombiano Autopista del Nordeste, was to construct the 120 km Samana–Santo Domingo toll highway. The road, which was to be financed by the Central Bank of Colombia and the Government of the Dominican Republic, was to be completed in 2004. There were several private railway companies devoted to the transport of sugar cane, the largest of which was the Central Romana network. In April 2001 plans were announced to construct a 170 km railway line from the south coast port of Haina to Santiago, with the possibility of subsequent extension to Puerto Plata and Manzanillo; the plan was awaiting approval by the Congreso Nacional, while a Puerto Rican company had reportedly been awarded a 50-year concession to operate the railroad. The country had 14 ports, of which Santo Domingo was the largest, handling 80% of imports. In 1998 the country had a merchant fleet of 20 vessels with a total displacement of 8,989 grt. In that year the Government granted a concession to a joint-venture company for the construction of a new port and transhipment centre near the Las Americas international airport to the east of Santo Domingo, which was designed specifically for use by free-zone businesses. Work began in 2000 and construction was to be completed by 2003. There were two ports, Punta Caucedo and Haina, under construction in 2001. There are international airports at Santo Domingo, Puerto Plata, Barahona and La Romana, and several domestic airports. The privatization of the international airports took place in 1999, with investment from Canadian and Italian consortia.

TOURISM

Rapid growth of the tourism industry from the 1980s made it the Republic's leading foreign-exchange earner, with receipts increasing from US $173m. in 1980 to about $2,524m. in 1999. The total number of hotel rooms in 2001 was 52,000, while a further 7,000 rooms were under construction. In mid-1995 there were 24 hotels with more than 300 rooms each; 22 of these were managed by international chains, which owned or managed 20,896 rooms in hotels of more than 100 rooms. German, Hong Kong, Italian, Japanese, Spanish and US companies were involved. An estimated 141,000 people were employed in the tourism industry in 1999.

In 1999 stop-over visitors by air numbered 2,649,418. This was an increase of almost 50% on the 1995 figure of 1,775,872. Of these, approximately 501,676 were returning Dominicans. Further substantial hotel reconstruction projects occurred in 2000, financed by national and international hotel companies. Tourists from Europe increased throughout the 1990s, reaching about 50% of the total in 1999, with Canada accounting for 9.1% and the USA for 23.3%. However, arrivals failed to keep pace with the increase in hotel capacity, while tourist lengths of stay shortened on average, and annual occupancy rates fell, from 76.8% in 1995 to 69.7% in 1998 and 66.9% in 1999.

INVESTMENT AND FINANCE

For most years in the 1990s government accounts showed a small surplus, the largest being in 1992, when the surplus equalled 3.3% of GDP. In 1993 it was reduced to 0.2% of GDP and a deficit occurred in 1994, equivalent to 0.5% of GDP (a sharp, pre-election increase in expenditure was held responsible). The national monetary board intervened in late 1994 to reduce the financing of government deficits, and a surplus of 1.1% of GDP was achieved in 1995. However, this surplus fell to a marginal 0.3% of GDP (540.6m. pesos) in 1996. In 1997 an increased surplus of 2,038.0m. pesos was recorded, with improved tax collection and other revenue measures outweighing increased current expenditure, brought about by public-sector pay increases and large subsidies to state enterprises. In July 1998 the Government introduced emergency measures to restrain public expenditure; however, the damage to the economy caused by Hurricane Georges in September was a major reverse, forcing the Government to announce a 3,500m.-peso reconstruction programme. Nevertheless, the reconstruction was to be financed partly by foreign grants and the Government was still able to record a budget surplus of 2,109.8m. pesos in 1998 (equivalent to 0.9% of GDP). In 1999, however, there was a budgetary deficit of 1,286.6m. pesos, and despite an early surplus recorded in the first half of 2000, increased debt-servicing obligations led to a projected deficit for the year as a whole.

The average inflation rate fell sharply from 47.0% in 1991 to 4.3% in 1992, but gradually increased to 12.5% in 1995. Counter-inflationary measures by the Central Bank produced a reduction to 5.4% in 1996, but in 1997 there was an increase in the average annual inflation rate, to 8.3%. In 1998 prudence in central-government expenditure helped to limit inflation to 4.5% for the year, but in 1999 the rate increased again to 6.5% and was estimated at 7.9% in 2000. Interest rates were generally high throughout the 1990s; in late 1999 the average commercial bank lending rate was 25% and the 90-day deposit rate was 16.1%; both represented an increase on 1997 rates.

Private investment, external and domestic, was principally in the tourism industry, the free zones and the agricultural sector. In late 1997 a new foreign-investment law was enacted, providing for total repatriation of capital and profits, simplifying investment procedures and easing previous restrictions on the scope of foreign investment. By December 1998 foreign direct investment had reached a record US $1,100m., compared with $421m. in 1997. In 1999 approximately $1,400m. of foreign investment flowed into the economy, representing some 12% of GDP. At least $500m. was related to the privatization of the CDE. Regulations governing foreign-exchange transactions were relaxed in 1993 and 1994, and a reform of the financial system was proposed; however, this made slow progress in the Congreso Nacional. A securities exchange opened in 1992, as a first step towards a stock exchange.

FOREIGN TRADE AND BALANCE OF PAYMENTS

The Dominican Republic's trade was in deficit from 1976 onwards and from 1989 the deficit exceeded US $1,000m. Between 1991 and 1992 it increased by 50.6%, from $1,070.5m. to $1,611.8m. The trade deficit (including the activities of the processing or free zones) subsequently decreased, falling to $1,390.9m. in 1995. However, there was a major increase in both 1996 and 1997, and in 1998 it reached $2,616.8m., principally owing to a sharp rise in imports in the last quarter, as reconstruction of the damage caused by Hurricane Georges began. In 1999 the deficit was $2,904.4m., again worsened by post-hurricane imports and reduced exports. In 2000, despite rising exports, the deficit widened still further to $3,752.7m., principally owing to increases in the price of imported petroleum.

Exports (excluding the free zones) fell each year from 1989 to 1993, when they reached a low point of US $511m., but increased to $767m. in 1995, largely as a result of a recovery in ferro-nickel exports, which produced earnings of $183m. Exports increased again in 1996, to $817m. (including free-zone transactions, total exports increased by 7.2%, to $4,053m.). Exports increased in 1997 to $4,614m. (excluding the free zones, exports increased to $882m.), but decreased in the following year to $3,799.2m. ($780m. excluding free zones). Total exports increased slightly in 1999 to an estimated $3,838.6m. ($638m. excluding free zones). In 2000 total exports stood at an estimated $5,823.3m.

Imports (f.o.b.—again excluding the free zones) fluctuated around a rising trend, reaching US $2,175m. in 1992, a year which showed strong GDP growth, falling back to $2,118m. in 1993 as the growth rate slowed. Imports gradually increased to $3,205m. in 1996 (if the activities of the free zones are included, total imports increased by an annual average of 7.2% over the same period, to reach $5,727.2m. in 1996). In 1997 and 1998 the value of imports continued to increase, to $4,192m. and $4,897m., respectively. The total value of imports including the free zones grew to $7,597m. in 1998 and $8,214m. in 1999, with figures for 1998 and 1999 including many imports of basic foods and construction materials. In 1999 imports (excluding the free zones) reached $5,207m. Estimated imports for 2000 (including the zones) reached $9,576m., both as a result of strong growth and owing to high petroleum prices.

The trade deficits were partially offset by earnings from tourism and free-zone exports, together with remittances from Dominicans overseas (estimated at US $1,900m. in 2000). Nevertheless, the current account of the balance of payments was in deficit from 1966 to 1994, when the deficit was $283m., down from $533m. in 1993. By 1995 the deficit had decreased to $183m. In 1996 this figure increased to $213m., but in the following year the deficit decreased to $163m. In 1998 an increased deficit of $338m. was recorded (equivalent to 2.5% of GDP), while the deficit for 1999 stood at $429m. Preliminary figures for 2000 indicated an increase in the current account deficit to $1,183m.

The Dominican peso, historically at par with the US dollar, was devalued in 1985, 1988 and 1990, when it stood at 11.20 pesos to one US dollar. In 1991 a dual exchange rate was established, with an official rate of 12.67 pesos to the dollar; the IMF agreement of July 1991 unified the official and commercial systems at a market rate, which averaged about 12.70 pesos to the dollar until the end of 1993. Over the next four years the peso depreciated steadily, reaching an average rate for 1997 of 14.26 pesos to the dollar. In February 1998 the rate stood at 14.65 pesos, leading the Central Bank to introduce US $40m. into the foreign-exchange market in an unsuccessful stabilization attempt. By December 2000 the rate stood at 16.40 pesos, a marginal improvement on the 16.48 rate of March 1999.

The Dominican Republic's main sources of long-term development aid were the Inter-American Development Bank (IDB), the World Bank (International Bank for Reconstruction and Development—IBRD) and the EU—the country was admitted to the fourth Lomé Convention in 1989 (the Lomé Convention expired in February 2000 and was replaced by the Cotonou Agreement in June—see Part Three, Regional Organizations, European Union). In the first Lomé protocol (1990–95), under its national initiative programme, the Dominican Republic was allocated ECU 85m. This figure increased to ECU 106m. in the second protocol (1995–2000). Bilateral aid was also received from a variety of countries. In the aftermath of Hurricane Georges, the country received emergency reconstruction loans worth US $111m. from the World Bank, $60m. from Banco Español de Crédito and $105m. from the IDB, intended for the reconstruction of rural housing. The disbursement of the loans was delayed by the non-co-operation policy of the opposition-controlled Senate, but was eventually approved in May 1999. The country obtained further loans of $150m. and $100m. from the IDB in 2000–2001 for housing projects in Santo Domingo and to fund the 'social package' of poverty-alleviation measures which followed the price increases of 2000.

The external debt more than doubled during the 1980s and the Government suspended medium- and long-term debt servicing between 1986 and 1991. In 1991 it cleared its arrears to the IMF and World Bank and reached a rescheduling agreement on US $926m. of debt to the Paris Club. A renegotiation of $775m. in principal and $325m. in interest was signed with commercial-bank creditors in 1994. As a result, the total external debt, which had reached $4,860m. at the end of 1993, was reduced to $4,275m. at the end of 1994. However, short-term borrowing increased the total to an estimated $4,448m. in

1995 and $4,332m. in 1996, of which $3,529m. was long-term debt. Total external debt amounted to $4,451m. at the end of 1998and $4,771m. at the end of 1999. Total reserves, excluding gold, stood at $625.5m. at the end of 2000.

CONCLUSION

Continued expansion in tourism, construction and non-traditional agriculture was expected to produce further economic growth in the Dominican Republic in 2001 and 2002, albeit not at the rates achieved in 1999–2000. However, it was anticipated that the Mejía administration would have to combat increasing inflation and endure stronger restrictions on government finances and low commodity prices. Widespread demands for wage rises and expectations of increased spending in the wake of election pledges placed pressure on the Government to relax restraints on public expenditure, with potentially inflationary consequences. The Government was likely to continue with tariff and tax reforms, while major priorities included the deepening of regional trade integration and the search for parity with North American Free Trade Agreement (NAFTA) beneficiaries such as Mexico and positive involvement in the forthcoming Free Trade Area of the Americas (FTAA). Unemployment, poverty, poor housing, and health and education levels were among the social problems. In August 2000 President Mejía announced a programme of fiscal measures, including an increase in consumer taxes, a rise in tariffs on imported luxury goods, and a tax increase on cars, insurance, advertising, flights, security, commercial rents, gambling, cigarettes and beer (see above, in History). A World Bank report in 2001 classed 25% of the population as poor, living on US $1 per day (equal to 1976 levels). Social problems included endemic corruption, a thriving cocaine trade, widespread prostitution and a high rate of human immunodeficiency virus (HIV) infection.

Statistical Survey

Sources (unless otherwise stated): Oficina Nacional de Estadística, Edif. de Oficinas Gubernamentales, Avda México, esq. Leopoldo Navarro, Santo Domingo; tel. 682-7777; fax 685-4424; e-mail direccion@one.gov.do; internet www.one.gov.do; Banco Central de la República Dominicana, Calle Pedro Henríquez Ureña, esq. Leopoldo Navarro, Apdo 1347, Santo Domingo; tel. 221-9111; fax 686-7488; e-mail info@bancentral.gov.do; internet www.bancentral.gov.do.

Area and Population

AREA, POPULATION AND DENSITY

Area (sq km)	
Land	48,072
Inland water	350
Total	48,422*
Population (census results)†	
12 December 1981	5,647,977
24 September 1993	
Males	3,550,797
Females	3,742,593
Total	7,293,390
Population (official estimates at mid-year)‡	
1999	8,324,945
2000	8,518,483
Density (per sq km) at mid-2000	175.9

* 18,696 sq miles.
† Excluding adjustment for underenumeration.
‡ Not adjusted to take account of the results of the 1993 census.

PROVINCES (estimated population, 2000)

Distrito Nacional .	2,677,056		Maria Trinidad Sánchez	142,030
Santiago . . .	836,614		La Altagracia . .	. 128,627
San Cristóbal . .	519,906		Bahoruco . . .	. 124,592
La Vega . . .	390,314		Peravía . . .	. 113,273
Duarte . . .	318,151		San José de Ocoa .	. 110,000
Puerto Plata . .	302,799		Salcedo . . .	. 106,450
San Juan . . .	265,562		El Seybo . . .	. 105,447
San Pedro de Macorís	260,629		Monte Cristi . .	. 103,711
Azua	243,157		Hato Mayor . .	. 87,595
Espaillat . . .	228,173		Samaná . . .	. 82,135
La Romana . .	213,628		Dajabón . . .	. 78,045
Valverde . . .	198,979		Elias Piña . . .	. 66,267
Sánchez Ramírez .	194,282		Santiago Rodríguez.	. 65,853
Barahona . . .	179,945		Independencia . .	. 41,778
Monseñor Nouel .	174,923		Pedernales. . .	. 19,698
Monte Plata . .	174,126			

PRINCIPAL TOWNS (population at 1993 census)

Santo Domingo,			San Francisco de	
DN (capital) . .	1,609,699		Macorís . . .	. 108,485
Santiago de los			San Felipe de Puerto	
Caballeros . .	365,463		Plata . . .	. 89,423
La Romana . .	140,204		Beneménta de San	
San Pedro de			Cristóbal . .	. 88,605
Macorís . .	124,735		La Vega . . .	. 87,162

Births and deaths (1997): Registered live births 164,556 (birth rate 25.2 per 1,000); Registered deaths 26,301 (death rate 5.8 per 1,000).

Expectation of life (estimates, years at birth, 1998): 70.9 (males 69.2; females 73.3) (Source: UN Development Programme, *Human Development Report*).

ECONOMICALLY ACTIVE POPULATION

('000 persons aged 10 years and over, official estimates, 1997)

	Males	Females	Total
Agriculture, hunting and forestry } Fishing . . . . }	512.5	16.5	529.0
Mining and quarrying . . .	7.5	0.9	8.4
Manufacturing	332.7	150.7	483.3
Electricity, gas and water supply	13.7	6.6	20.3
Construction	150.4	3.1	153.6
Wholesale and retail trade .	356.1	176.1	532.3
Hotels and restaurants . .	59.5	55.8	115.3
Transport, storage and communications . . .	190.0	12.9	202.7
Financial intermediation . . . } Real estate, renting and business } activities . . . . . }	17.3	16.8	34.0
Public administration and defence	99.5	25.9	125.4
Education . . . . . . } Health and social work . . } Other community, social and } personal service activities . }	152.2	295.3	447.5
Total employed . . .	1,891.4	760.6	2,652.0
Unemployed	199.0	304.7	503.7
Total labour force	2,090.4	1,065.3	3,155.7

Source: ILO, *Yearbook of Labour Statistics.*

Mid-1998 (estimates in '000): Agriculture, etc. 644. Total labour force 3,553 (Source: FAO, *Production Yearbook*).

Agriculture

PRINCIPAL CROPS ('000 metric tons)

	1998	1999	2000
Rice (paddy)	474.6	574.4	527.0
Maize	34.2	29.1	23.9
Sorghum	21.7*	7.8	4.8
Potatoes	18.8	28.8	24.9
Sweet potatoes	44.2	22.0	36.8
Cassava (Manioc) . . .	126.5	126.5	125.0
Yams	13.0	11.0	13.6
Dry beans	24.3	25.8	22.1
Groundnuts (in shell) . .	6.3	4.8	2.3
Coconuts	160.2	184.4	172.7
Tomatoes	277.6	386.0	285.5
Sugar cane	5,028.1	4,446.9	4,784.8
Oranges	135.6	89.4	131.4
Lemons and limes . . .	8.5	8.5*	8.5*
Avocados	155.0*	89.4	81.7*
Mangoes	185.0	180.0*	180.0*
Pineapples	107.8	72.5	64.4
Bananas	359.0	432.0	422.2
Plantains	341.4	229.3	343.3
Coffee (green)	56.9	34.6	45.5
Cocoa beans	67.7	33.8	37.1
Tobacco (leaves)	43.3	16.5	17.2

* FAO estimate(s).

Source: FAO.

LIVESTOCK ('000 head, year ending September)

	1998	1999	2000
Horses*	330.0	330.0	330.0
Mules*	135.0	138.0	138.0
Asses*	144.5	145.0	145.0
Cattle	2,528.3	1,904.4	1,904.4
Pigs	960.0	539.6	538.6
Sheep	135.0	105.5	105.5
Goats	300.0*	163.5	170.0*

Chickens (million): 37.7 in 1998; 42.0 in 1999; 46.0 in 2000.

* FAO estimate(s).

Source: FAO.

LIVESTOCK PRODUCTS ('000 metric tons)

	1998	1999	2000
Beef and veal	80.0	82.7	68.9
Poultry meat	157.7	176.7	254.0
Cows' milk	358.4	411.1	397.8
Butter*	1.5	1.5	1.5
Cheese*	2.5	2.5	2.5
Hen eggs	48.9	53.6	60.9
Cattle hides (fresh) . . .	9.3	8.7	8.1

* FAO estimate(s).

Source: FAO.

Forestry

ROUNDWOOD REMOVALS ('000 cubic metres, excl. bark)

	1997	1998	1999
Sawlogs, veneer logs and logs for sleepers	4	4	4
Other industrial wood . . .	3	3	3
Fuel wood	556	556	556
Total	562	562	562

Source: FAO, *Yearbook of Forest Products.*

Fishing

('000 metric tons, live weight)

	1996	1997	1998
Capture	13.8	14.5	10.2
Mozambique tilapia . . .	—	0.3	0.4
Other tilapia	1.0	0.3	0.1
Groupers, seabasses . .	0.5	0.3	0.4
Southern red snapper . .	0.3	0.5	0.2
Yellowtail snapper . . .	0.8	0.5	0.2
Other snappers and jobfishes	0.1	0.2	0.9
Porgies	0.4	1.1	—
Wrasses, hogfishes, etc. .	0.5	1.5	0.1
Atlantic Spanish mackerel .	1.6	0.6	0.3
Northern bluefin tuna . .	0.1	0.6	0.2
Blackfish tuna . . .	0.5	0.3	0.1
Caribbean spiny lobster . .	0.4	1.1	0.9
Aquaculture	0.8	0.7	0.8
Total catch	14.6	15.2	11.0

Source: FAO, *Yearbook of Fishery Statistics.*

Mining

	1996	1997	1998
Ferro-nickel ('000 metric tons)* .	78	n.a.	n.a.
Gold (metric tons) . . .	3.3	3.5	3.5
Silver (million troy ounces) . .	0.5	0.4	0.2

* Source: US Bureau of Mines (Washington, DC).

Industry

SELECTED PRODUCTS
('000 metric tons, unless otherwise indicated)

	1995	1996	1997
Wheat flour	249	203	203
Refined sugar	98	112	114
Cement	1,450	1,642	1,835
Beer ('000 hectolitres)	2,082	2,199	2,593
Cigarettes (million)	4,070	4,068	3,972
Motor spirit (gasoline)	356	363	370
Electricity (million kWh)	6,506	6,847	7,335

Source: UN, *Industrial Commodity Statistics Yearbook.*

Finance

CURRENCY AND EXCHANGE RATES

Monetary Units
100 centavos = 1 Dominican Republic peso (RD $ or peso oro)

Sterling, Dollar and Euro Equivalents (30 April 2001)
£1 sterling = 24.08 pesos;
US $1 = 16.82 pesos;
€1 = 14.93 pesos;
1,000 Dominican Republic pesos = £41.52 = US $59.45 = €66.98.

Average Exchange Rate (RD $ per US $)
1998	15.267
1999	16.033
2000	16.415

BUDGET (RD $ million)

Revenue*	1995	1996	1997
Tax revenue	23,624.5	25,474.8	33,418.8
Taxes on income and profits	4,074.9	4,566.7	6,017.7
Taxes on goods and services	8,823.4	9,345.8	12,522.9
Taxes on international trade and transactions	9,521.9	10,183.2	13,126.6
Other current revenue	2,395.0	2,171.2	2,989.3
Property income	1,119.8	944.9	1,445.0
Fees and charges	1,082.5	1,032.9	1,189.6
Capital revenue	77.1	299.0	268.7
Total	26,096.6	27,945.0	36,676.8

Expenditure†	1995	1996	1997
General public services	1,654.9	1,739.6	4,193.3
Defence	940.3	1,149.0	1,682.1
Public order and safety	692.6	815.4	1,401.7
Education	3,150.0	3,610.3	5,114.7
Health	2,701.6	3,197.4	4,027.7
Social security and welfare	937.2	1,313.0	2,019.3
Housing and community amenities	3,619.8	3,783.3	4,730.0
Recreational, cultural and religious affairs and services	222.2	327.2	421.9
Economic affairs and services	8,629.7	10,482.3	10,821.4
Fuel and energy	1,216.2	1,343.0	2,354.8
Agriculture, forestry and fishing	1,956.2	2,555.9	3,266.9
Mining and mineral resources, manufacturing and construction	2,221.3	2,206.1	1,730.8
Transport and communications	3,043.2	3,871.0	2,627.9
Other purposes	1,511.6	1,054.1	1,113.3
Sub-total	24,059.9	27,471.6	35,525.4
Adjustment	924.2	1,181.5	338.9
Total	24,984.1	28,653.1	35,864.3
Current‡	14,090.4	16,446.2	24,907.8
Capital	10,510.9	11,613.6	9,203.2
Adjustment	382.8	593.3	1,753.3

* Excluding grants received (RD $ million): 152.5 in 1995; 213.7 in 1996; 125.6 in 1997.

† Excluding lending minus repayments (RD $ million): 18.5 in 1995; 23.8 in 1996; 93.3 in 1997.

‡ Including interest payments (RD $ million): 1,511.6 in 1995; 1,054.1 in 1996; 1,113.3 in 1997.

Source: IMF, *Government Finance Statistics Yearbook.*

INTERNATIONAL RESERVES (US $ million at 31 December)

	1998	1999	2000
Gold*	5.3	5.2	5.0
IMF special drawing rights	0.3	0.3	0.4
Foreign exchange	501.6	689.1	625.1
Total	507.2	694.6	630.5

* Valued at market-related prices.

Source: IMF, *International Financial Statistics.*

MONEY SUPPLY (RD $ million at 31 December)

	1998	1999	2000
Currency outside banks	12,568	16,889	15,076
Demand deposits at commercial banks	16,782	18,884	20,290
Total money (incl. others)	29,416	35,840	35,445

Source: IMF, *International Financial Statistics.*

COST OF LIVING
(Consumer Price Index; base: 1990 = 100)

	1995	1996	1997
Food	188.2	196.7	211.7
Clothing	181.3	186.0	189.3
Rent	222.0	237.4	255.5
All items (incl. others)	196.6	207.2	224.4

Source: ILO, *Yearbook of Labour Statistics.*

All items (base: 1995 = 100): 119.3 in 1998; 127.0 in 1999 (Source: IMF, *International Financial Statistics*).

NATIONAL ACCOUNTS
National Income and Product (RD $ million at current prices)

	1998	1999	2000
GDP in purchasers' values .	241,910	278,939	322,866
Net factor income from abroad .	−13,565	−15,616	−17,077
Gross national product (GNP) .	228,345	263,323	305,789
Less Consumption of fixed capital .	14,515	16,736	19,372
National income in market prices	213,830	246,587	286,417

Source: IMF, *International Financial Statistics*.

Expenditure on the Gross Domestic Product
(RD $ million at current prices)

	1998	1999	2000
Government final consumption expenditure	19,449	22,437	26,503
Private final consumption expenditure	187,525	207,271	250,634
Increase in stocks . . .	698	804	931
Gross fixed capital formation .	56,026	69,186	75,571
Total domestic expenditure .	263,698	299,698	353,639
Exports of goods and services .	113,752	127,887	146,941
Less Imports of goods and services	135,542	148,646	177,714
GDP in purchasers' values .	241,910	278,939	322,866
GDP at constant 1970 prices .	5,723	6,227	6,633

Source: IMF, *International Financial Statistics*.

Gross Domestic Product by Economic Activity
(RD $ million at constant 1970 prices)

	1998*	1999*	2000*
Agriculture, hunting, forestry and fishing	657.4	701.5	736.6
Mining and quarrying . .	111.5	109.8	119.9
Manufacturing	974.2	1,036.5	1,129.5
Electricity, gas and water† .	120.7	130.5	144.9
Construction	702.1	826.2	869.0
Wholesale and retail trade, restaurants and hotels . .	1,092.4	1,190.3	1,319.3
Transport, storage and communications . . .	666.6	735.8	835.3
Finance, insurance and real estate	500.2	516.4	530.8
Community, social, personal and business services‡ . . .	876.4	908.7	947.6
Total	5,701.4	6,155.5	6,632.7

* Preliminary figures.
† Refers to electricity and water only.
‡ Including gas.

BALANCE OF PAYMENTS (US $ million)

	1997	1998	1999
Exports of goods f.o.b. . . .	4,613.7	4,980.5	5,136.7
Imports of goods f.o.b. . . .	−6,608.7	−7,597.3	−8.041.1
Trade balance	−1,995.0	−2,616.8	−2,904.4
Exports of services . . .	2,446.6	2,501.5	2,850.3
Imports of services . . .	−1,171.3	−1,319.5	−1,248.0
Balance on goods and services .	−719.7	−1,434.8	−1,302.1
Other income received . . .	140.4	168.2	218.3
Other income paid . . .	−935.8	−1,058.3	−1,193.2
Balance on goods, services and income	−1,515.1	−2,324.9	−2,277.0
Current transfers received . .	1,373.1	2,016.9	1,997.1
Current transfers paid . . .	−21.0	−30.4	−149.3
Current balance	−163.0	−338.4	−429.2
Direct investment from abroad .	420.6	699.8	1,337.8
Portfolio investment assets . .	−5.6	−17.5	−433.0
Portfolio investment liabilities .	−1.9	−3.8	−3.8
Other investment assets . .	−220.1	−66.4	−53.4
Other investment liabilities . .	254.6	76.0	213.4
Net errors and omissions . .	−193.7	−338.6	−480.4
Overall balance	90.9	11.1	151.4

Source: IMF, *International Financial Statistics*.

External Trade

PRINCIPAL COMMODITIES

Imports f.o.b. (US $ '000)*	1984	1985	1986
Cars and other vehicles (incl. spares)	65,300	84,633	161,619
Chemical and pharmaceutical products	59,649	64,436	106,229
Cotton and manufactures . .	9,660	15,212	7,045
Foodstuffs	112,295	171,793	115,248
Petroleum and petroleum products	504,842	426,782	253,849
Iron and steel manufactures (excl. building materials) . . .	56,874	43,500	56,357
Machinery (incl. spares) . .	83,360	119,311	218,185
Total (incl. others) . . .	1,257,134	1,285,910	1,351,732

* Provisional figures.

Total imports f.o.b. (US $ million): 1,792.8 in 1990; 1,728.8 in 1991; 2,174.6 in 1992; 2,118.4 in 1993; 2,283.8 in 1994; 2,588.0 in 1995; 3,205.1 in 1996; 4,192.0 in 1997; 4,896.6 in 1998; 5,206.8 in 1999 (Source: IMF, *International Financial Statistics*). Note: Figures exclude imports into free-trade zones.

Exports f.o.b. (US $ million)*	1998	1999†
Vegetable products	140.3	104.2
Edible vegetables	21	21.3
Edible fruits and nuts, peel of citrus and melons	39.3	46.1
Coffee, tea, maté and spices	68.1	24.0
Prepared food; beverages, spirits and tobacco	331.9	220.5
Sugars and sugar confectionery	127.4	76.5
Cocoa and cocoa preparations	85.6	24.8
Preparations of vegetables, fruits and nuts, etc.	18.3	17.6
Beverages, spirits and vinegar	20.2	22.5
Tobacco and manufactured tobacco substitutes	66.3	54.6
Products of chemical or allied industries	33.9	31.9
Organic chemicals	14.8	14.5
Plastics and articles thereof	13.5	15.6
Textiles and textile articles	19.2	15.7
Pearls, stones, precious metals, imitation jewellery, coins	16.2	6.5
Base metals and articles of base metal.	145.9	161.2
Iron and steel	127.6	140.8
Re-exported products	13.5	19.3
Total (incl. others)	780.0	638.2

* Excluding exports from free-trade zones: (US $ million): 3,019.2 in 1998; 3,200.4 in 1999.
† Provisional figures.
Source: Centro Dominicano de Promoción de Exportaciones.

PRINCIPAL TRADING PARTNERS (US $ '000)

Imports c.i.f.	1997
Argentina	40,172.1
Japan	132,247.7
Mexico	88,409.6
Panama	89,141.3
Puerto Rico	68,673.6
USA	2,357,757.5
Venezuela	46,299.9
Total (incl. others)	3,689,269.1

Exports f.o.b.*	1996	1997†
Belgium–Luxembourg	40,860.6	102,032.5
Canada	19,163.5	21,673.5
Germany	8,531.7	6,152.2
Haiti	24,440.9	26,451.1
Honduras	5,490.0	9,973.7
Italy	12,970.7	16,840.2
Japan	16,489.4	24,693.6
Korea, Republic	46,948.2	43,603.9
Netherlands	87,166.2	18,492.9
Panama	13,227.6	7,380.5
Puerto Rico	60,682.3	121,412.1
Spain	12,584.0	10,422.6
USA	429,741.2	484,207.4
Total (incl. others)	835,712.9	958,229.3

* Excluding exports from free-trade zones.
† Provisional figures.

Transport

ROAD TRAFFIC (motor vehicles in use at 31 December, estimates)

	1997	1998
Passenger cars	305,477	353,177
Buses and coaches	27,380	32,619
Lorries and vans	147,523	167,728

SHIPPING

Merchant Fleet (registered at 31 December)

	1996	1997	1998
Number of vessels	27	25	20
Total displacement ('000 grt)	12.0	11.3	9.0

Source: Lloyd's Register of Shipping, *World Fleet Statistics*.

International Sea-borne Freight Traffic ('000 metric tons)

	1996	1997	1998
Goods loaded	112	152	139

Source: UN, *Monthly Bulletin of Statistics*.

CIVIL AVIATION (traffic on scheduled services)

	1995	1996	1997
Kilometres flown (million)	1	1	1
Passengers carried ('000)	67	30	34
Passengers-km (million)	28	14	16
Total ton-km (million)	3	1	1

Source: UN, *Statistical Yearbook*.

Tourism

ARRIVALS BY NATIONALITY

	1996	1997	1998
Canada	127,683	152,777	170,027
USA	412,016	402,039	437,803
Argentina	62,996	64,404	78,764
United Kingdom	121,778	216,790	188,184
Italy	104,218	118,551	110,332
Spain	91,367	106,398	110,782
Austria	40,262	36,753	30,017
Belgium	35,309	46,590	40,145
France	32,479	57,507	95,771
Germany	327,772	328,860	366,599
Total (incl. others)	1,948,464	2,184,688	2,334,493

Source: mainly World Tourism Organization, *Yearbook of Tourism Statistics*.

Receipts from Tourism (US $ million): 2,099.4 in 1997; 2,153.1 in 1998; 2,524.0 in 1999.

Arrivals ('000, 1999): Total 2,930 (by air 2,649; by sea 281).

Communications Media

	1995	1996	1997
Radio receivers ('000 in use) . .	1,380	1,410	1,440
Television receivers ('000 in use) .	728	750	770
Telephones ('000 main lines in use)	581	622	709
Telefax stations (number in use) .	n.a.	2,300	n.a.
Mobile cellular telephones (subscribers)	53,973	77,795	130,149

Daily newspapers: 12 in 1996 (estimated average circulation 416,000 copies).

Mobile cellular telephones (subscribers): 705,431 in 2000.

Telephones ('000 main lines in use): 894 in 2000.

Sources: mainly UNESCO, *Statistical Yearbook*; UN, *Statistical Yearbook*.

Education

(1996/97)

	Institu-tions	Teachers	Students		
			Males	Females	Total
Pre-primary*	n.a.	8,571	96,252	94,289	190,541
Primary . .	4,001†	39,860	691,675	668,369	1,360,044
Secondary:					
General . .	1,737	11,033	145,560*	184,384*	329,944*
Teacher-training† .	n.a.	86	549	743	1,292
Vocational† .	n.a.	1,211	9,147	12,356	21,503
Higher . . .	n.a.	9,041	75,223	101,772	176,995

* 1997/98 figure(s).   † 1994/95 figure(s).

Source: UNESCO, *Statistical Yearbook*.

Directory

The Constitution

The Constitution of the Dominican Republic was promulgated on 28 November 1966. Its main provisions are summarized below:

The Dominican Republic is a sovereign, free, independent state; no organizations set up by the State can bring about any act which might cause direct or indirect intervention in the internal or foreign affairs of the State or which might threaten the integrity of the State. The Dominican Republic recognizes and applies the norms of general and American international law and is in favour of and will support any initiative towards economic integration for the countries of America. The civil, republican, democratic, representative Government is divided into three independent powers: legislative, executive and judicial.

The territory of the Dominican Republic is as laid down in the Frontier Treaty of 1929 and its Protocol of Revision of 1936.

The life and property of the individual citizen are inviolable; there can be no sentence of death, torture nor any sentence which might cause physical harm to the individual. There is freedom of thought, of conscience, of religion, freedom to publish, freedom of unarmed association, provided that there is no subversion against public order, national security or decency. There is freedom of labour and trade unions; freedom to strike, except in the case of public services, according to the dispositions of the law.

The State will undertake agrarian reform, dedicating the land to useful interests and gradually eliminating the latifundios (large estates). The State will do all in its power to support all aspects of family life. Primary education is compulsory and all education is free. Social security services will be developed. Every Dominican has the duty to give what civil and military service the State may require. Every legally entitled citizen must exercise the right to vote, i.e. all persons over 18 years of age and all who are or have been married even if they are not yet 18.

GOVERNMENT

Legislative power is exercised by Congress which is made up of the Senate and Chamber of Deputies, elected by direct vote. Senators, one for each of the 30 Provinces and one for the Distrito Nacional, are elected for four years; they must be Dominicans in full exercise of their citizen's rights, and at least 25 years of age. Their duties are to elect judges, the President and other members of the Electoral and Accounts Councils, and to approve the nomination of diplomats. Deputies, one for every 50,000 inhabitants or fraction over 25,000 in each Province and the Distrito Nacional, are elected for four years and must fulfil the same conditions for election as Senators.

Decisions of Congress are taken by absolute majority of at least half the members of each house; urgent matters require a two-thirds' majority. Both houses normally meet on 27 February and 16 August each year for sessions of 90 days, which can be extended for a further 60 days.

Executive power is exercised by the President of the Republic, who is elected by direct vote for a four-year term. The President must be a Dominican citizen by birth or origin, over 30 years of age and in full exercise of citizen's rights. The President must not have engaged in any active military or police service for at least a year prior to election. The President takes office on 16 August following the election. The President of the Republic is Head of the Public Administration and Supreme Chief of the armed forces and police forces. The President's duties include nominating Secretaries and Assistant Secretaries of State and other public officials, promulgating and publishing laws and resolutions of Congress and seeing to their faithful execution, watching over the collection and just investment of national income, nominating, with the approval of the Senate, members of the Diplomatic Corps, receiving foreign Heads of State, presiding at national functions, decreeing a State of Siege or Emergency or any other measures necessary during a public crisis. The President may not leave the country for more than 15 days without authorization from Congress. In the absence of the President, the Vice-President will assume power, or failing him, the President of the Supreme Court of Justice.

LOCAL GOVERNMENT

Government in the Distrito Nacional and the Municipalities is in the hands of local councils, with members elected proportionally to the number of inhabitants, but numbering at least five. Each Province has a civil Governor, designated by the Executive.

JUDICIARY

Judicial power is exercised by the Supreme Court of Justice and the other Tribunals; no judicial official may hold another public office or employment, other than honorary or teaching. The Supreme Court is made up of at least nine judges, who must be Dominican citizens by birth or origin, at least 35 years old, in full exercise of their citizen's rights, graduates in law and have practised professionally for at least 12 years. There are also five Courts of Appeal, a Lands Tribunal and a Court of the First Instance in each judicial district; in each Municipality and in the Distrito Nacional there are also Justices of the Peace.

Elections are directed by the Central Electoral Board. The armed forces are essentially obedient and apolitical, created for the defence of national independence and the maintenance of public order and the Constitution and Laws.

The artistic and historical riches of the country, whoever owns them, are part of the cultural heritage of the country and are under the safe-keeping of the State. Mineral deposits belong to the State. There is freedom to form political parties, provided they conform to the principles laid down in the Constitution. Justice is administered without charge throughout the Republic.

This Constitution can be reformed if the proposal for reform is supported in Congress by one-third of the members of either house or by the Executive. A special session of Congress must be called and any resolutions must have a two-thirds' majority. There can be no reform of the method of government, which must always be civil, republican, democratic and representative.

Note: In August 1994 Congress resolved that the current President's term of office should be restricted to two years. Presidential elections were, therefore, scheduled for 1996. Other constitutional amendments included provisions for the prohibition of the re-election of the President to a consecutive term in office, the adoption of a two-round voting system for presidential elections, the reorganization of the judicial system and the replacement of the Central Electoral Board.

The Government

HEAD OF STATE

President: RAFAEL HIPÓLITO MEJÍA DOMÍNGUEZ (took office 16 August 2000).

Vice-President: Dra MILAGROS ORTIZ BOSCH.

CABINET
(August 2001)

Secretary of State to the Presidency: SERGIO GRULLÓN.

Secretary of State for External Relations: Dr HUGO TOLENTINO DIPP.

Secretary of State for the Interior and Police: Dr RAFAEL SUBERVÍ BONILLA.

Secretary of State for the Armed Forces: Maj.-Gen. JOSÉ MIGUEL SOTO JIMÉNEZ.

Secretary of State for Finance: FERNANDO ALVAREZ BOGAERT.

Secretary of State for Education: Dra MILAGROS ORTIZ BOSCH.

Secretary of State for Agriculture: ELIGIO JAQUEZ CRUZ.

Secretary of State for Public Works and Communications: MIGUEL VARGAS MALDONADO.

Secretary of State for Public Health and Social Welfare: Dr JOSÉ RODRÍGUEZ SOLDEVILLA.

Secretary of State for Industry and Commerce: HUGO GUILLIANI CURY.

Secretary of State for Labour: Dr MILTON RAY GUEVARA.

Secretary of State for Tourism: RAMÓN ALFREDO BORDAS.

Secretary of State for Sport, Physical Education and Recreation: CÉSAR CEDEÑO.

Secretary of State for Art and Culture: TONY RAFUL TEJADA.

Secretary of State for Women: Dra YADIRA HENRÍQUEZ.

Secretary of State for Youth: FRANCISCO ANTONIO PEÑA GUABA.

Secretary of State for the Environment and Natural Resources: FRANK MOYA PONS.

Secretaries of State without Portfolio: ANGEL MIOLAN, RAMÓN EMILIO JIMÉNEZ, ANTONIO TORRES, ELIAS WESSIN Y WESSIN.

SECRETARIATS OF STATE

Administrative Secretariat of the Presidency: Palacio Nacional, Avda México, esq. Dr Delgado, Santo Domingo, DN; tel. 686-4771; fax 688-2100; internet www.presidencia.gov.do.

Technical Secretariat of the Presidency: Avda México, esq. Dr Delgado, Santo Domingo, DN; tel. 221-5140; fax 221-8627.

Secretariat of State for Agriculture: Autopista Duarte, Km 6.5, Los Jardines del Norte, Santo Domingo, DN; tel. 547-3888; fax 227-1268; internet www.agricultura.gov.do.

Secretariat of State for the Armed Forces: Plaza de la Independencia, Avda 27 de Febrero, esq. Luperón, Santo Domingo, DN; tel. 530-5149; fax 531-1309.

Secretariat of State for Art and Culture: Avda Máximo Gómez 10, esq. Santiago, Santo Domingo, DN; tel. 688-9700; fax 689-8907.

Secretariat of State for Education: Avda Máximo Gómez 10, esq. Santiago, Santo Domingo, DN; tel. 688-9700; fax 689-8907.

Secretariat of State for External Relations: Avda Independencia 752, Santo Domingo, DN; tel. 535-6280; fax 533-5772; internet www.serex.gov.do.

Secretariat of State for the Environment and Natural Resources: Santo Domingo, DN.

Secretariat of State for Finance: Avda México 45, Santo Domingo, DN; tel. 687-5131; fax 688-6561.

Secretariat of State for Industry and Commerce: Edif. de Oficinas Gubernamentales, 7°, Avda Francia, esq. Leopoldo Navarro, Santo Domingo, DN; tel. 685-5171; fax 686-4741; e-mail ind.comerci o@codetel.net.do; internet www.seic.gov.do.

Secretariat of State for the Interior and Police: Edif. de Oficinas Gubernamentales, 3°, Avda Francia, esq. Leopoldo Navarro, Santo Domingo, DN; tel. 686-6251; fax 221-8234.

Secretariat of State for Labour: Centro de los Héroes, Calle Jiménez Moya 9, Santo Domingo, DN; tel. 535-4404; fax 535-4590; internet www.set.gov.do.

Secretariat of State for Public Health and Social Welfare: Avda Tiradentes, esq. San Cristóbal, Ensanche La Fe, Santo Domingo, DN; tel. 541-3121; fax 540-6445.

Secretariat of State for Public Works and Communications: Avda San Cristóbal, esq. Tiradentes, Ensanche La Fe, Santo Domingo, DN; tel. 565-2811; fax 562-3382.

Secretariat of State for Sport, Physical Education and Recreation: Avda Ortega y Gasset, Centro Olímpico, Santo Domingo, DN; tel. 540-4010; fax 563-6586.

Secretariat of State for Tourism: Bloque D, Edif. de Oficinas Gubernamentales, Avda México, esq. 30 de Marzo, Apdo 497, Santo Domingo, DN; tel. 221-4660; fax 682-3806; internet www.dominicana .com.do.

Secretariat of State for Women: Bloque D, Edif. de Oficinas Gubernamentales, Avda México, esq. 30 de Marzo, Santo Domingo, DN; tel. 685-3755; fax 686-0911.

Secretariat of State for Youth: Santo Domingo, DN.

President and Legislature

PRESIDENT

Election, 16 May 2000

Candidate	% of votes cast
RAFAEL HIPÓLITO MEJÍA DOMÍNGUEZ (PRD)	49.87
DANILO MEDINA SÁNCHEZ (PLD)	24.94
Dr JOAQUÍN BALAGUER RICARDO (PRSC).	24.60
Total (incl. others)	100.0

CONGRESO NACIONAL

The National Congress comprises a Senate and a Chamber of Deputies.

President of the Senate: RAFAEL ALBUQUERQUE RAMÍREZ (PRD).

President of the Chamber of Deputies: Dra RAFAELA ALBURQUERQUE DE GONZÁLEZ.

General Election, 16 May 1998

	Seats	
	Senate	Chamber of Deputies
Partido Revolucionario Dominicano (PRD)	24	83*
Partido de la Liberación Dominicana (PLD)	4	49
Partido Reformista Social Cristiano (PRSC)	2	17
Total	30	149

* 10 PRD deputies were subsequently expelled from the party.

Political Organizations

Alianza por la Democracia (APD): Santo Domingo, DN; f. 1992 by breakaway group of the PLD; split into two factions (led, respectively, by MAX PUIG and NÉLSIDA MARMOLEJOS) in 1993; Sec.-Gen. VICENTE BENGOA.

Fuerza Nacional Progresista (FNP): Santo Domingo, DN; rightwing; Leader MARIO VINICIO CASTILLO.

Fuerza de la Revolución: Avda Independencia 258, Apdo 2651, Santo Domingo, DN; e-mail fr@nodo50.ix.apc.org; internet www.no do50.org/fr; f. 2000 by merger of the Partido Communista Dominicano, Movimiento Liberador 12 de Enero, Fuerza de Resistencia y Liberación Popular, Fuerza Revolucionaria 21 de Julio and other revolutionary groups; Marxist-Leninist.

Movimiento de Conciliación Nacional (MCN): Calle Pina 207, Santo Domingo, DN; f. 1969; centre party; 659,277 mems; Pres. Dr JAIME M. FERNÁNDEZ; Sec. VÍCTOR MENA.

Movimiento de Integración Democrática (MIDA): Las Mercedes 607, Santo Domingo, DN; tel. 687-8895; centre-right; Leader Dr FRANCISCO AUGUSTO LORA.

Movimiento Popular Dominicano: Santo Domingo, DN; leftwing; Leader JULIO DE PEÑA VALDÉS.

Participación Ciudadana: Desiderio Arias 25, La Julia, Santo Domingo, DN; tel. 535-6200; fax 535-6631; e-mail p.ciudadana@code tel.net.do; internet www.pciudadana.com; f. 1993; Leaders JAVIER CABREJA POLANCO, MELBA BARNETT, JUAN BOLÍVAR DÍAZ.

Partido Demócrata Popular: Arz. Meriño 259, Santo Domingo, DN; tel. 685-2920; Leader LUIS HOMERO LÁJARA BURGOS.

Partido de la Liberación Dominicana (PLD): Avda Independencia 401, Santo Domingo, DN; tel. 685-3540; f. 1973 by breakaway group of PRD; left-wing; Leader LEONEL FERNÁNDEZ REYNA; Sec.-Gen. JOSÉ TOMÁS PÉREZ.

Partido Quisqueyano Demócrata (PQD): Bolivar 51, esq. Uruguay, Santo Domingo, DN; tel. 565-0244; internet www.geocities.com/CapitolHill/Senate/7090/; f. 1968; right-wing; 600,000 mems; Pres. Lic. PEDRO BERGÉS; Sec.-Gen. Dr ELÍAS WESSIN CHÁVEZ.

Partido Reformista Social Cristiano (PRSC): Avda San Cristóbal, Ensanche La Fe, Apdo 1332, Santo Domingo, DN; tel. 566-7089; f. 1964; centre-right party; Life Pres. Dr JOAQUÍN BALAGUER RICARDO.

Partido Revolucionario Dominicano (PRD): Espaillat 118, Santo Domingo, DN; tel. 687-2193; internet www.prd.partidos.com; f. 1939; democratic socialist; mem. of Socialist International; 400,000 mems; Pres. RAFAEL HIPÓLITO MEJÍA DOMÍNGUEZ; Sec.-Gen. HATUEY DECAMPS.

Partido Revolucionario Independiente (PRI): Santo Domingo; f. 1985 after split by the PRD's right-wing faction; Pres. JOSÉ RAFAEL MOLINA UREÑA; Sec.-Gen. STORMI REYNOSO.

Partido Revolucionario Social Cristiano: Santo Domingo, DN; f. 1961; left-wing; Pres. Dr CLAUDIO ISIDORO ACOSTA; Sec.-Gen. Dr ALFONSO LOCKWARD.

Partido de los Trabajadores Dominicanos: Avda Duarte 69 (Altos), Santo Domingo, DN; tel. 685-7705; f. 1979; workers' party; Sec.-Gen. JOSÉ GONZÁLEZ ESPINOZA.

Unidad Democrática (UD): Santo Domingo; Leader FERNANDO ALVAREZ BOGAERT.

Other parties include Unión Cívica Nacional (UCN), Partido Alianza Social Demócrata (ASD—Leader Dr JOSÉ RAFAEL ABINADER), Movimiento Nacional de Salvación (MNS—Leader LUIS JULIÁN PÉREZ), Partido Comunista del Trabajo de la República Dominicana (Sec.-Gen. RAFAEL CHALJUB MEJÍA), Partido de Veteranos Civiles (PVC), Partido Acción Constitucional (PAC), Partido Unión Patriótica (PUP—Leader ROBERTO SANTANA), Partido de Acción Nacional (right-wing) and Movimiento de Acción Social Cristiana (ASC).

Diplomatic Representation

EMBASSIES IN THE DOMINICAN REPUBLIC

Argentina: Avda Máximo Gómez 10, Apdo 1302, Santo Domingo, DN; tel. 682-2977; fax 221-2206; e-mail embarg@codetel.net.do; Ambassador: CARLOS PIÑEIRO IÑIGUEZ.

Brazil: Avda Winston Churchill 32, Edif. Franco-Acra y Asociados, 2°, Apdo 1655, Santo Domingo, DN; tel. 532-0868; Ambassador: P. G. VILAS-BÒAS CASTRO.

Chile: Avda Anacaona 11, Mirador del Sur, Santo Domingo, DN; tel. 532-7800; fax 530-8310; Ambassador: PATRICIO POZO RUIZ.

China (Taiwan): Edif. Palic, 1°, Avda Abraham Lincoln, esq. José Amado Soler, Apdo 4797, Santo Domingo, DN; tel. 562-5555; fax 563-4139; Ambassador: KUO KANG.

Colombia: Avda Abraham Lincoln 502, 2°, Santo Domingo, DN; tel. 567-6836; Ambassador: JOSÉ JOAQUÍN GORI CABRERA.

Costa Rica: Calle Malaquías Gil 11 Altos, Santo Domingo, DN; tel. 683-7209; fax 565-6467; e-mail emb.costarica@codetel.net.do; Ambassador: MARIO GARNIER BORELLA.

Ecuador: Calle Rafael Augusto Sánchez 17, Ensanche Naco, Apdo 808, Santo Domingo, DN; tel. 563-8363; fax 563-8153; e-mailmecuador@codetel.net.do; Ambassador: LUIS NARVÁEZ RIVADENEIRA.

El Salvador: Calle José A. Brea Peña 12, Ensanche Evaristo Morales, Santo Domingo, DN; tel. 565-4311; fax 541-7503; Ambassador: Dr BYRON F. LARIOS L.

France: Calle Las Damas 42, Zona Colonial, Santo Domingo, DN; tel. 689-2161; fax 221-8408; Ambassador: FRANÇOIS-XAVIER DENIAU.

Germany: Calle Rafael Augusto Sánchez 33, esq. Avda Lope de Vega, Ensanche Naco, Santo Domingo, DN; tel. 565-8811; fax 567-5014; Ambassador: IMMO VON KESSEL.

Guatemala: Z No 8, Ensanche Naco, Santo Domingo, DN; tel. 567-0110; fax 567-0115; Ambassador: Gen. ROBERTO MATA.

Haiti: 33 Juan Sánchez Ramírez, Santo Domingo, DN; tel. 686-5778; fax 686-6096; Chargé d'affaires: GUY G. LAMOTHE.

Holy See: Avda Máximo Gómez 27, Apdo 312, Santo Domingo, DN (Apostolic Nunciature); tel. 682-3773; fax 687-0287; Apostolic Nuncio: Most Rev. FRANÇOIS BACQUÉ, Titular Archbishop of Gradisca.

Honduras: Condominio Anacaona II, Edif. I, Apt 202, Avda Anacaona, Apdo 1486, Santo Domingo, DN; tel. 482-7992; fax 482-7505; Ambassador: ANDRÉS VÍCTOR ARTILES.

Israel: Pedro Henríquez Ureña 80, Santo Domingo, DN; tel. 541-8974; fax 562-3555; e-mail emb.israel@codetel.net.do; Ambassador: ELIAHU LÓPEZ.

Italy: Rodríguez Objío 4, Santo Domingo, DN; tel. 689-3684; fax 682-8296; e-mail ambital@codetel.net.do; Ambassador: STEFANO ALBERTO CANAVESIO.

Japan: Torre BHD, 8°, Avda Winston Churchill, esq. Luis F. Thomén, Santo Domingo, DN; tel. 567-3365; fax 566-8013; Ambassador: TSUNODA KATSUHIKO.

Korea, Republic: Avda Sarasota 98, Santo Domingo, DN; tel. 532-4314; fax 532-3807; Ambassador: JIM BAE.

Mexico: Rafael Hernández 11, Ensanche Naco, Santo Domingo, DN; tel. 565-2744; Ambassador: HUMBERTO LIRA MORA.

Nicaragua: Angel Cevero Cabral 32, Sánchez Juliete, Santo Domingo, DN; tel. 563-2311; fax 565-7961; Ambassador: ELSA ITALIA MEJÍA DE BERMUDEZ.

Panama: Hotel Embajador, Apdo 25338, Santo Domingo, DN; tel. 685-6950; Chargé d'affaires a.i.: Lic. ANTONIO PUELLO.

Peru: Cancillería, Avda Winston Churchill, Santo Domingo, DN; tel. 565-5851; Ambassador: RAÚL GUTIÉRREZ.

Russia: Santo Domingo, DN; Ambassador: VLADIMIR GONCHARENKO.

Spain: Independencia 1205, Santo Domingo, DN; tel. 535-1615; fax 535-1595; Ambassador: RICARDO DÍEZ HOCHLEITNER.

United Kingdom: Edif. Corominas Pepin, 7°, Avda 27 de Febrero 233, Santo Domingo; tel. 472-7111; fax 472-7574; e-mail brit.emb.sadom@codetel.net.do; Ambassador: DAVID WARD.

USA: César Nicolás Pensón, esq. Leopoldo Navarro, Santo Domingo, DN; tel. 541-2171; Ambassador: JANICE JACOBS (acting).

Uruguay: Avda México 169, Santo Domingo, DN; tel. 565-2669; Ambassador: JAIME WOLFSON KOT.

Venezuela: Cancillería, Avda Anaconda 7, Mirador Sur, Santo Domingo, DN; tel. 537-8578; fax 537-8780; Ambassador: Lic. MARÍA CLEMENCIA LÓPEZ-JIMÉNEZ.

Judicial System

The Judicial Power resides in the Supreme Court of Justice, the Courts of Appeal, the Tribunals of the First Instance, the municipal courts and the other judicial authorities provided by law. The Supreme Court is composed of at least nine judges (15 in December 1997) and the Attorney-General, and exercises disciplinary authority over all the members of the judiciary. The Attorney-General of the Republic is the Chief of Judicial Police and of the Public Ministry which he represents before the Supreme Court of Justice. The Consejo Nacional de la Magistratura (National Judiciary Council) appoints the members of the Supreme Court, which in turn appoints judges at all other levels of the judicial system.

Corte Suprema: Centro de los Héroes de Constanza, Santo Domingo, DN; tel. 533-3522; internet www.suprema.gov.do.

President: Dr JORGE SUBERO ISA.

Attorney-General: VIRGILIO BELLO ROSA.

Religion

The majority of the inhabitants belong to the Roman Catholic Church, but freedom of worship exists for all denominations. The Baptist, Evangelist and Seventh-day Adventist churches and the Jewish faith are also represented.

CHRISTIANITY

The Roman Catholic Church

The Dominican Republic comprises two archdioceses and nine dioceses. At 31 December 1999 adherents represented about 90.8% of the population.

Bishops' Conference: Conferencia del Episcopado Dominicano, Apdo 186, Santo Domingo, DN; tel. 685-3141; fax 689-9454; f. 1985; Pres. Cardinal NICOLÁS DE JESÚS LÓPEZ RODRÍGUEZ, Archbishop of Santo Domingo.

Archbishop of Santiago de los Caballeros: Most Rev. JUAN ANTONIO FLORES SANTANA, Arzobispado, Calle Duvergé 14, Apdo 679, Santiago de los Caballeros; tel. 582-2094; fax 581-3580; e-mail arzobisp.stgo@codetel.net.do.

Archbishop of Santo Domingo: Cardinal NICOLÁS DE JESÚS LÓPEZ RODRÍGUEZ, Arzobispado, Isabel la Católica 55, Apdo 186, Santo Domingo, DN; tel. 685-3141; fax 688-7270; e-mail arzobispado@codetel.net.do.

The Anglican Communion

Anglicans in the Dominican Republic are under the jurisdiction of the Episcopal Church in the USA. The country is classified as a missionary diocese, in Province IX.

Bishop of the Dominican Republic: Rt Rev. JULIO CÉSAR HOLGUÍN KHOURY, Calle Santiago 114, Apdo 764, Santo Domingo, DN; tel. 688-6016; fax 686-6364; e-mail h.khoury@codetel.net.do.

BAHÁ'Í FAITH

National Spiritual Assembly of the Bahá'ís of the Dominican Republic: Cambronal 152, esq. Beller, Santo Domingo, DN; f. 1961; tel. 687-1726; fax 687-7606; e-mail bahai.rd.aen@codetel.net.do; 402 localities.

The Press

Dirección General de Información, Publicidad y Prensa: Santo Domingo, DN; f. 1983; government supervisory body; Dir-Gen. LUIS GONZÁLEZ FABRA.

DAILIES
Santo Domingo, DN

El Caribe: Autopista Duarte, Km 7½, Apdo 416, Santo Domingo, DN; tel. 566-8161; fax 544-4003; f. 1948; morning; circ. 32,000; Editor ANTONIO EMILIO ORNÉS.

Diario Las Américas: Avda Tiradentes, Santo Domingo, DN; tel. 566-4577.

Hoy: Avda San Martín 236, Santo Domingo, DN; tel. 565-5581; fax 567-2424; f. 1981; morning; Dir MARIO ALVAREZ DUGAN; circ. 40,000.

Listín Diario: Paseo de los Periodistas 52, Ensanche Miraflores, Santo Domingo, DN; tel. 686-6688; fax 686-6595; e-mail listin.diario@codetel.net.do; internet www.codetel.net.do/listin-diario; f. 1889; morning; Dir RAFAEL MOLINA MORILLO; circ. 88,050.

El Nacional: San Martín 236, Apdo 1402, Santo Domingo, DN; tel. 565-5581; fax 565-4190; f. 1966; evening and Sunday; Dir MARIO ALVAREZ DUGAN; circ. 45,000.

La Noticia: Julio Verne 14, Santo Domingo, DN; tel. 535-0815; f. 1973; evening; Pres. JOSÉ A. BREA PEÑA; Dir BOLÍVAR BELLO.

El Nuevo Diario: Ensanche Gazcue, Santo Domingo, DN; tel. 687-6205; fax 688-0763; morning; Dir PERSIO MALDONADO.

El Siglo: Calle San Antonio 2, Zona Industrial de Herrera, Santo Domingo, DN; tel. 530-1000; fax 530-8412; e-mail editorial.golfo@codetel.net.do; morning; Dir FEDERICO HENRÍQUEZ GRATEREAUX.

El Sol: Santo Domingo, DN; morning; Pres. QUITERIO CEDEÑO; Dir-Gen. MIGUEL ANGEL CEDEÑO.

Ultima Hora: Paseo de los Periodistas 52, Ensanche Miraflores, Santo Domingo, DN; tel. 688-3361; fax 688-3019; e-mail ultimahora@codetel.net.do; internet www.codetel.net.do/ultimahora; f. 1970; evening; Dir RUDDY L. GONZÁLEZ C.; circ. 40,000.

Puerto Plata

El Porvenir: Calle Imbert 5, Apdo 614, Puerto Plata; f. 1872; Dir CARLOS ACEVEDO.

Santiago de los Caballeros, SD

La Información: Carretera Licey, Km 3, Santiago de los Caballeros, SD; tel. 581-1915; fax 581-7770; f. 1915; morning; Editor FERNANDO A. PÉREZ MEMÉN; circ. 15,000.

PERIODICALS AND REVIEWS

Agricultura: Santo Domingo, DN; organ of the State Secretariat of Agriculture; f. 1905; monthly; Dir MIGUEL RODRÍGUEZ, Jr.

Agroconocimiento: Apdo 345-2, Santo Domingo, DN; monthly; agricultural news and technical information; Dir DOMINGO MARTE; circ. 10,000.

¡Ahora!: San Martín 236, Apdo 1402, Santo Domingo, DN; tel. 565-5581; f. 1962; weekly; Dir MARIO ALVAREZ DUGAN.

La Campiña: San Martín 236, Apdo 1402, Santo Domingo, DN; f. 1967; Dir Ing. JUAN ULISES GARCÍA B.

Carta Dominicana: Avda Tiradentes 56, Santo Domingo, DN; tel. 566-0119; f. 1974; monthly; economics; Dir JUAN RAMÓN QUIÑONES M.

Deportes: San Martín 236, Apdo 1402, Santo Domingo, DN; f. 1967; sports; fortnightly; Dir L. R. CORDERO; circ. 5,000.

Eva: San Martín 236, Apdo 1402, Santo Domingo, DN; f. 1967; fortnightly; Dir MAGDA FLORENCIO.

Horizontes de América: Santo Domingo, DN; f. 1967; monthly; Dir ARMANDO LEMUS CASTILLO.

Letra Grande, Arte y Literatura: Leonardo da Vinci 13, Mirador del Sur, Avda 27 de Febrero, Santo Domingo, DN; tel. 531-2225; f. 1980; monthly; art and literature; Dir JUAN RAMÓN QUIÑONES M.

Renovación: Calle José Reyes, esq. El Conde, Santo Domingo, DN; fortnightly; Dir OLGA QUISQUEYA VIUDA MARTÍNEZ.

FOREIGN PRESS BUREAUX

Agencia EFE (Spain): Galerías Comerciales, 5°, Of. 507, Avda 27 de Febrero, Santo Domingo, DN; tel. 567-7617; Bureau Chief ANTONIO CASTILLO URBERUAGA.

Agenzia Nazionale Stampa Associata (ANSA) (Italy): Calle Leopoldo Navarro 79, 3°, Sala 17, Apdo 20324, Huanca, Santo Domingo, DN; tel. 685-8765; fax 685-8765; Bureau Chief HUMBER ANDRÉS SUAZO.

Inter Press Service (IPS) (Italy): Calle Cambronal, No. 4-1, Ciudad Nueva, Santo Domingo, DN; tel. 593-5153; Correspondent VIANCO MARTÍNEZ.

United Press International (UPI) (USA): Carrera A. Manoguaybo 16, Manoguaybo, DN; tel. 689-7171; Chief Correspondent SANTIAGO ESTRELLA VELOZ.

Publishers
Santo Domingo, DN

Arte y Cine, C por A: Isabel la Católica 42, Santo Domingo, DN.

Editora Alfa y Omega: José Contreras 69, Santo Domingo, DN; tel. 532-5577.

Editora de las Antillas: Calle Pedro Henríquez Ureña, Santo Domingo, DN; tel. 685-2197.

Editora Dominicana, SA: 23 Oeste, No 3 Lup., Santo Domingo, DN; tel. 688-0846.

Editora El Caribe, C por A: Autopista Duarte, Km 7½, Apdo 416, Santo Domingo, DN; tel. 566-8161; fax 544-4003; f. 1948; Man. Dir RAFAEL DUARTE.

Editora Hoy, C por A: San Martín, 236, Santo Domingo, DN; tel. 566-1147.

Editora Listín Diario, C por A: Paseo de los Periodistas 52, Ensanche Miraflores, Apdo 1455, Santo Domingo, DN; tel. 686-6688; fax 686-6595; f. 1889; Pres. Dr ROGELIO A. PELLERANO.

Editorama, SA: Calle Justiniano Bobea, esq. Eugenio Contreras, Apdo 2074, Santo Domingo, DN; tel. 596-6669; fax 594-1421.

Editorial Padilla: San F. de Macorís 14, Santo Domingo, DN; tel. 682-3101.

Editorial Santo Domingo: Santo Domingo, DN; tel. 532-9431.

Editorial Stella: 19 de Marzo, Santo Domingo, DN; tel. 682-2281.

Julio D. Postigo e Hijos: Santo Domingo, DN; f. 1949; fiction; Man. J. D. POSTIGO.

Publicaciones Ahora, C por A: Avda San Martín 236, Apdo 1402, Santo Domingo; tel. 565-5580; fax 565-4190; Pres. JULIO CASTAÑO.

Publicaciones América: Santo Domingo, DN; Dir PEDRO BISONÓ.

Santiago de los Caballeros, SD

Editora el País, SA: Carrera Sánchez, Km 6½, Santiago de los Caballeros, SD; tel. 532-9511.

Broadcasting and Communications

Dirección General de Telecomunicaciones: Isabel la Católica 73, Santo Domingo, DN; tel. 682-2244; fax 682-3493; government supervisory body; Dir-Gen. RUBÉN MONTAS; Dir-Gen. of Television NELSON ARTURO MARTE.

Instituto Dominicano de Telecomunicaciones (INDOTEL): Santo Domingo, DN; Pres. ORLANDO JORGE MERA.

TELECOMMUNICATIONS

Compañía Dominicana de Teléfonos (Codetel): Avda Lincoln 1101, Apdo 1377, Santo Domingo, DN; tel. 220-2000; fax 543-1301; e-mail e.burri@codetel.net.do; internet www.codetel.net.do; f. 1930; Pres. JORGE IVAN RAMÍREZ; Gen. Man. GUILLERMO AMORE.

Tricom Telecomunicaciones de Voz, Data y Video: Avda Lope de Vega 95, Santo Domingo, DN; tel. 542-7556; fax 567-4412; internet www.tricom.net; Pres. ARTURO PELLERANO; Chief of Int. Relations CÉSAR A. FRANCO.

BROADCASTING
Radio

There were some 130 commercial stations in 2000. The government-owned broadcasting network, Radio Televisión Dominicana, operates nine radio stations.

Asociación Dominicana de Radiodifusoras (ADORA): Calle Paul Harris 3, Centro de los Héroes, Santo Domingo; tel. 535-4057; Pres. IVELISE DE TORRES.

Television

Corporación Dominicana de Radio y Televisión, Canal 9: Calle Emilio A. Morel, esq. Luis E. Pérez, Ensanche La Fe, Apdo 30043, Santo Domingo, DN; tel. 566-5876; fax 544-3607; commercial station; Channel 9; Dir-Gen. MANUEL QUIROZ MIRANDA.

Radio Televisión Dominicana: Dr Tejada Florentino 8, Apdo 869, Santo Domingo, DN; tel. 689-2120; government station; three channels, two relay stations; Dir-Gen. NELSON ARTURO MARTE; Gen. Man. AGUSTÍN MERCADO.

Rahintel Televisión: Centro de los Héroes de Constanza, Avda Independencia, Apdo 1220, Santo Domingo, DN; tel. 532-2531; fax 535-4575; commercial station; two channels; Pres. LEONEL ALMONTE V.

Teleantillas, Canal 2: Autopista Duarte, Km 7½, Los Prados, Apdo 30404, Santo Domingo, DN; tel. 567-7751; fax 540-4912; Gen. Man. JOSÉ A. MORENO.

Telecentro, SA: Avda Pasteur 204, Santo Domingo, DN; tel. 687-9161; fax 542-7582; Channel 13 for Santo Domingo and east region; Pres. JASINTO PEYNADO.

Tele-Inde Canal 13: Avda Pasteur 101, Santo Domingo, DN; tel. 687-9161; commercial station; Dir JULIO HAZIM.

Telesistema, Canal 11: Avda 27 de Febrero 52, Sector Bergel, Santo Domingo, DN; tel. 563-6661; fax 472-1754; Pres. JOSÉ L. CORREPIO.

Finance

(cap. = capital; dep. = deposits; m = million; p.u. = paid up; res = reserves; amounts in pesos)

BANKING

Supervisory Body

Superintendencia de Bancos: Avda México, esq. Leopoldo Navarro, Apdo 1326, Santo Domingo, DN; tel. 685-8141; fax 685-0859; f. 1947; Superintendent Lic. ALBERTO ELÍS ATALA LAJAN.

Central Bank

Banco Central de la República Dominicana: Calle Pedro Henríquez Ureña, esq. Leopoldo Navarro, Apdo 1347, Santo Domingo, DN; tel. 689-7121; fax 687-7488; e-mail info@bancentral.gov.do; internet www.bancentral.gov.do; f. 1947; cap. 0.7m., res 92.3m., dep. 6,321.7m. (Dec. 1996); Gov. FRANCISCO MANUEL GUERRERO PRATS; Man. NIEVES MÁRMOL DE PERICHE.

Commercial Banks

Banco BHD, SA: Avda 27 de Febrero, esq. Winston Churchill, Apdo 266-2, Santo Domingo, DN; tel. 243-3232; fax 562-4396; e-mail bhd@codetel.net.do; internet www.codetel.net.do.bhd; f. 1972; total assets 11,902m. (1999); Pres. JOSÉ ANTONIO CARO; Gen. Man. LUIS MOLINA A.; 35 brs.

Banco Dominicano del Progreso, SA: Avda John F. Kennedy 3, Apdo 1329, Santo Domingo, DN; tel. 563-3233; fax 563-2455; f. 1974; total assets 9,947m. (1999); Chair. TOMÁS A. PASTORIZA; Exec. Vice-Pres. PEDRO E. CASTILLO L.; 17 brs.

Banco Fiduciario, SA: Avda 27 de Febrero 50, Santo Domingo, DN; tel. 473-9400; fax 472-1466; total assets 7,876m. (1999); f. 1983; Exec. Vice-Pres. GEORGE MANUEL HAZOURY PEÑA.

Banco Global, SA: Avda R. Batancourt 1, esq. Avda A. Lincoln, Santo Domingo, DN; tel. 532-3000; fax 535-7070; total assets 11,486m. (1999).

Banco Intercontinental, SA: Avda Abraham Lincoln Casias, esq. José Contreras, Santo Domingo, DN; tel. 535-5500; fax 532-2474; total assets 10,129m. (1999).

Banco Mercantil: Avda Pastoriza 303, Santo Domingo; tel. 567-4444; fax 549-6509; internet www.mercantil.com.do; total assets 9,579m. (1999); Pres. ANDRÉS AYBAR BÁEZ; Exec. Vice-Pres. JUAN R. OLLER; 11 brs.

Banco Metropolitano: Avda Lope de Vega, esq. Gustavo Mejía Ricart, Apdo 1872, Santo Domingo, DN; tel. 562-2442; fax 540-1566; f. 1974; total assets 12,055m. (1999); Pres. AGUSTÍN VERDEJA; Gen. Dir ADALBERTO PÉREZ PERDOMO; 7 brs.

Banco Nacional de Crédito, SA: Avda John F. Kennedy, esq. Tiradentes, Apdo 1408, Santo Domingo, DN; tel. 540-4441; fax 567-4854; e-mail info@bancredito.com; internet www.bancredito.com; f. 1981; total assets 10,365m. (1999); Pres. MÁXIMO PELLERANO; Vice-Pres. MARINA DE GARRIGÓ.

Banco Popular Dominicano: Avda John F. Kennedy 20, Torre Popular, Apdo 1441, Santo Domingo, DN; tel. 544-8000; fax 544-5899; internet www.bpd.com.do; f. 1963; total assets 9,905m. (1999); Pres. MANUEL ALEJANDRO GRULLÓN; 45 brs.

Banco de Reservas de la República Dominicana: Isabel la Católica 201, Apdo 1353, Santo Domingo, DN; tel. 687-5366; fax 685-0602; f. 1941; cap. 250.0m., res 681.8m., dep. 14,996.9m. (Dec. 1999); Chair. DANIEL TORIBIO M.; Gen. Administrator MANUEL ANTONIO LARA HERNÁNDEZ; 23 brs.

Development Banks

Banco Agrícola de la República Dominicana: Avda G. Washington 601, Apdo 1057, Santo Domingo, DN; tel. 533-1171; fax 535-8088; e-mail bagricola.refor@codetel.net.do; f. 1945; government agricultural development bank; Pres. Lic. RAFAEL ANGELES SUÁREZ; Gen. Administrator RADHAMÉS RODRÍGUEZ VALERIO.

Banco Hipotecario Bancomercio, SA: Avda Máximo Gómez, Santo Domingo, DN; tel. 541-6231.

Banco Hipotecario de la Construcción, SA (BANHICO): Avda Tiradentes (Altos Plaza Naco), Santo Domingo, DN; tel. 562-1281; f. 1977; Man. Dr JAIME ALVAREZ DUGAN.

Banco Hipotecario Popular, SA: Avda 27 de Febrero 261, Santo Domingo, DN; tel. 544-6700; f. 1978; Pres. MANUEL E. JIMÉNEZ F.

Banco Nacional de la Construcción: Avda Alma Mater, esq. Pedro Henríquez Ureña, Santo Domingo, DN; tel. 685-9776; f. 1977; Gen. Man. LUIS MANUEL PELLERANO.

Foreign Banks

Bank of Nova Scotia (Canada): Avda John F. Kennedy, esq. Lope de Vega, Apdo 1494, Santo Domingo, DN; tel. 544-1700; fax 567-5732; f. 1920; Vice-Pres. and Gen. Man. ARIEL D. PÉREZ; 13 brs.

Citibank NA (USA): Avda John F. Kennedy 1, Apdo 1492, Santo Domingo, DN; tel. 566-5611; fax 683-0906; f. 1962; Vice-Pres. and Gen. Man. HENRY COMBER; 7 brs.

STOCK EXCHANGE

Santo Domingo Securities Exchange Inc.: Edif. Disesa, Suite 302, Avda Abraham Lincoln, Santo Domingo; tel. 567-6694; fax 567-6697; Pres. FELIPE AUFFANT.

INSURANCE

Supervisory Body

Superintendencia de Seguros: Secretaría de Estado de Finanzas, Avda México, esq. Leopoldo Navarro, Santo Domingo, DN; tel. 688-1245; internet www.superseguro.gov.do; f. 1969; Superintendent Dr DOMINGO BATISTA.

Insurance Companies

American Life and General Insurance Co, C por A: Edif. ALICO, 5°, Avda Abraham Lincoln, Santo Domingo, DN; tel. 533-7131; fax 533-5969; general; Gen. Man. FRANK CABREJA.

La Americana, SA: Edif. La Cumbre, Avda Tiradentes, Apdo 25241, Santo Domingo, DN; tel. 567-1211; f. 1975; life; Pres. MARINO GINEBRA H.

Atlantica Insurance, SA: Avda 27 de Febrero 265A. 2°, Apdo 826, Santo Domingo, DN; tel. 565-5591; fax 565-4343; Pres. Lic. RHINA RAMÍREZ.

Bankers Security Life Insurance Society: Gustavo Mejia Ricart 61, Apdo 1123, Santo Domingo, DN; tel. 544-2626; fax 567-9389; Pres. VIRIATO FIALLO.

Bonanza Compañía de Seguros, SA: Edif. Santanita I, Of. 201, Avda San Martín 253, Santo Domingo, DN; tel. 565-5525; fax 565-5630; e-mail bonanza.seg@codetel.net.do; internet www.bonanza.dominicana.com.do; Pres. Lic. DARIO LAMA.

Britanica de Seguros, SA: Max Henríquez Ureña 35, Apdo 3637, Santo Domingo, DN; tel. 542-6863; fax 544-4542; e-mail wharper@codetel.net.do; Pres. JOHN HARPER SALETA.

Centro de Seguros La Popular, C por A: Gustavo Mejía Ricart 61, Apdo 1123, Santo Domingo, DN; tel. 566-1988; fax 567-9389; f. 1965; general except life; Pres. Lic. ROSA FIALLO.

La Colonial, SA: Edif. Haché, 2°, Avda John F. Kennedy, Santo Domingo, DN; tel. 565-9926; f. 1971; general; Pres. Dr MIGUEL FERIS IGLESIAS.

Compañía Nacional de Seguros, C por A: Avda Máximo Gómez 31, Apdo 916, Santo Domingo, DN; tel. 687-5390; fax 682-3269; e-mail infocns@bancredito.com; internet www.cns.com.do; f. 1964; general; Chair. Dr MÁXIMO A. PELLERANO.

Compañía de Seguros Palic, SA: Avda Abraham Lincoln, esq. José Amado Soler, Apdo 1132, Santo Domingo, DN; tel. 562-1271; fax 562-1825; e-mail cia.seg.palic2@codetel.net.do; Pres. Lic. EDUARDO TOLENTINO.

Confederación del Canada Dominicana: Salvador Sturla 17, Santo Domingo, DN; tel. 544-4144; fax 540-4740; Pres. Lic. MOISES A. FRANCO LLENAS.

Federal Insurance Company: Edif. La Cumbre, 4°, Avda Tiradentes, esq. Presidente González, Santo Domingo, DN; tel. 567-0181; fax 567-8909; Pres. DIEGO RAMÓN SOSA.

General de Seguros, SA: Avda Sarasota 55, Bella Vista, Santo Domingo, DN; tel. 535-8888; fax 532-4451; f. 1981; general; Pres. Dr FERNANDO A. BALLISTA DÍAZ.

La Intercontinental de Seguros, SA: Plaza Naco, 2°, Avda Tiradentes, Apdo 825, Santo Domingo, DN; tel. 562-1211; general; Pres. Lic. RAMÓN BÁEZ ROMANO.

Magna Compañía de Seguros, SA: Edif. Magna Motors, Avda Abraham Lincoln, esq. John F. Kennedy, Santo Domingo, DN; tel. 544-1400; fax 562-5723; f. 1974; general and life; Pres. E. ANTONIO LAMA S.; Man. MILAGROS DE LOS SANTOS.

La Mundial de Seguros, SA: Avda Máximo Gómez, No 31, Santo Domingo, DN; tel. 685-2121; fax 682-3269; general except life and financial; Pres. PEDRO D'ACUNHA.

La Peninsular de Seguros, SA: Edif. Corp. Cominas Pepín, 3°, Avda 27 de Febrero 233, Santo Domingo, DN; tel. 472-1166; fax 563-2349; general; Pres. Lic. ERNESTO ROMERO LANDRÓN.

Reaseguradora Hispaniola, SA: Avda 27 de Febrero 205, Of. 202, Santo Domingo, DN; tel. 683-6150; fax 540-5288; Pres. MANUEL DE JESÚS COLÓN.

Seguros La Antillana, SA: Avda Lope de Vega 36, esq. Andres Julio Aybar y Ensanche Piantini, Santo Domingo, DN; tel. 541-3366; fax 567-9398; f. 1947; general and life; Pres. Lic. OSCAR LAMA.

Seguros La Isleña, C por A: Edif. Centro Coordinador Empresarial, Avda Nuñez de Caceres, esq. Guarocuya, Santo Domingo, DN; tel. 567-7211; fax 565-1448; Pres. MARÍA DEL PILAR RODRÍGUEZ.

Seguros Pepín, SA: Edif. Corp. Cominas Pepín, Avda 27 de Febrero 233, Santo Domingo, DN; tel. 472-1006; general; Pres. Dr BIENVENIDO COROMINAS.

Seguros San Rafael, C por A: Leopoldo Navarro 61, esq. San Francisco de Macorís, Santo Domingo, DN; tel. 688-2231; general; Admin. VICTOR RODRÍGUEZ.

El Sol de Seguros, SA: Torre Hipotecaria, 2°, Avda Tiradentes 25, Santo Domingo, DN; tel. 542-6063; general; Pres. GUILLERMO ARMENTEROS.

Sudamericana de Seguros, SA: El Conde 105, frente al Parque Colón, Santo Domingo, DN; tel. 685-0141; fax 688-8074; Pres. VINCENZO MASTROLILLI.

Transglobal de Seguros, SA: Avda Lope de Vega 36, esq. Andres Julio Aybar y Ensanche Piantini, Apdo 1869, Santo Domingo, DN; tel. 541-3366; fax 567-9398; e-mail transglobal@codetel.net.do; Dirs JOSÉ MANUEL VARGAS, OSCAR LAMA.

Universal América, C por A: Santo Domingo, DN; tel. 544-7200; fax 544-7999; internet www.universal.com.do; f. 1964 as La Universal de Seguros; merged with Grupo Asegurador América in 2000; general; Pres. Ing. ERNESTO IZQUIERDO.

Insurance Association

Cámara Dominicana de Aseguradores y Reaseguradores, Inc: Edif. Torre BHD, 5°, Calle Luis F. Thomen, esq. Winston Churchill, Santo Domingo, DN; tel. 566-0019; fax 566-2600; e-mail cadoar@codetel.net.do; internet www.cadoar.org.do; f. 1972; Pres. Lic. NELSON HEDI HERNÁNDEZ.

Trade and Industry

GOVERNMENT AGENCIES

Comisión para la Reforma de la Empresa Pública: Santo Domingo, DN; commission charged with divestment and restructuring of state enterprises; Pres. JOSÉ DEL CARMEN MARCANO.

Consejo Estatal del Azúcar (CEA) (State Sugar Council): Centro de los Héroes, Apdo 1256/1258, Santo Domingo, DN; tel. 533-1161; fax 533-7393; f. 1966; management of operations contracted to private consortiums in 1999; Dir-Gen. VÍCTOR MANUEL BÁEZ.

Corporación Dominicana de Empresas Estatales (CORDE) (Dominican State Corporation): Avda General Antonio Duvergé, Apdo 1378, Santo Domingo, DN; tel. 533-5171; f. 1966 to administer, direct and develop state enterprises; Dir-Gen. FÉLIX CALVO.

Instituto de Estabilización de Precios (INESPRE): Avda Luperón, Santo Domingo, DN; tel. 530-0020; fax 530-0343; f. 1969; price commission; Dir PABLO MERCEDES.

Instituto Nacional de la Vivienda: Antiguo Edif. del Banco Central, Avda Pedro Henríquez Ureña, esq. Leopoldo Navarro, Apdo 1506, Santo Domingo, DN; tel. 685-4181; f. 1962; low-cost housing institute; Dir-Gen. Ing. JUAN ANTONIO VARGAS.

DEVELOPMENT ORGANIZATIONS

Consejo Nacional de Desarrollo Minería: Santo Domingo, DN; f. 2000; encourages the development of the mining sector; Exec. Dir MIGUEL PENA; Sec.-Gen. PEDRO VÁSQUEZ.

Departamento de Desarrollo y Financiamento de Proyectos—DEFINPRO: c/o Banco Central de la República Dominicana, Calle Pedro Henríquez Ureña, esq. Leopoldo Navarro, Apdo 1347, Santo Domingo, DN; tel. 221-9111; fax 687-7488; f. 1993; associated with AID, IDB, WB, KFW; encourages economic development in productive sectors of economy, excluding sugar; authorizes complementary financing to private sector for establishing and developing industrial and agricultural enterprises and free-zone industrial parks; Dir ANGEL NERY CASTILLO PIMENTEL.

Fundación Dominicana de Desarrollo (Dominican Development Foundation): Calle Mercedes No 4, Apdo 857, Santo Domingo, DN; f. 1962 to mobilize private resources for collaboration in financing small-scale development programmes; 384 mems; Dir Lic. ADA WISCOVITCH.

Instituto de Desarrollo y Crédito Cooperativo (IDECOOP): Centro de los Héroes, Apdo 1371, Santo Domingo, DN; tel. 533-8131; fax 535-5148; f. 1963 to encourage the development of co-operatives; Dir JAVIER PEÑA NUÑEZ.

CHAMBERS OF COMMERCE

Cámara de Comercio y Producción de Santo Domingo: Arz. Nouel 206, Zona Colonial, Apdo 815, Santo Domingo, DN; tel. 682-7206; fax 685-2228; e-mail cámara.sto.dgo.@codetel.net.do; f. 1910; 1,500 active mems; Pres. JOSÉ MANUEL ARMENTEROS; Exec. Dir MILAGROS J. PUELLO.

Cámara Americana de Comercio de la República Dominicana: Torre BHD, 4°, Avda Winston Churchill, Santo Domingo, DN; tel. 544-2222; fax 544-0502; e-mail amcham@codetel.net.do; internet www.amcham.org.do; Pres. ANDRÉS AYBAR BÁEZ.

There are official Chambers of Commerce in the larger towns.

INDUSTRIAL AND TRADE ASSOCIATIONS

Asociación Dominicana de Hacendados y Agricultores Inc: Avda Sarasota 20, Santo Domingo, DN; tel. 565-0542; farming and agricultural org.; Pres. Lic. CESARIO CONTRERAS.

Asociación de Industrias de la República Dominicana Inc: Avda Sarasota 20, Apdo 850, Santo Domingo, DN; tel. 535-9111; fax 533-7520; f. 1962; industrial org.; Pres. NASSIM ALEMANY.

Centro Dominicano de Promoción de Exportaciones (CEDOPEX): Plaza de la Bandera, Apdo 199-2, Santo Domingo, DN; tel. 530-5505; fax 530-8208; e-mail cedopex@codetel.net.do; internet www.cedopex.gov.do; organization for the promotion of exports; Dir ROLANDO GALVÁN.

Consejo Nacional de la Empresa Privada (CONEP): Santo Domingo, DN; Pres. Lic. MARINO GINEBRA.

Consejo Nacional de las Zonas Francas: Santo Domingo, DN; co-ordinating body for the free-trade zones; Exec. Dir JEANNETTE DOMÍNGUEZ ARISTY.

Consejo Promotor de Inversiones (Investment Promotion Council): Avda Abraham Lincoln, 2°, Santo Domingo; tel. 532-3281; fax 533-7029; Exec. Dir and CEO FREDERIC EMAM ZADÉ.

Corporación de Fomento Industrial (CFI): Avda 27 de Febrero, Plaza Independencia, Apdo 1452, Santo Domingo, DN; tel. 530-0010; fax 530-1303; f. 1962 to promote agro-industrial development; Dir-Gen. JOSÉ OVALLE.

Dirección General de Minería e Hidrocarburos: Edif. de Oficinas Gubernamentales, 10°, Avda México, esq. Leopoldo Navarro, Santo Domingo, DN; tel. 687-7557; fax 686-8327; f. 1947; government mining and hydrocarbon org.; Dir-Gen. PEDRO VÁSQUEZ.

Instituto Agrario Dominicano (IAD): Avda 27 de Febrero, Santo Domingo, DN; tel. 530-8272; Dir-Gen. TOMÁS HERNÁNDEZ ALBERTO.

Instituto Dominicano de Tecnología Industrial (INDOTEC): Avda Nuñez de Caceres, esq. Olof Palme, Santo Domingo, DN; tel. 566-8121; fax 227-8808; e-mail indotec@codetel.net.do; internet www.indotec.gov.do; Dir ANTONIO ALMONTE REYNOSO.

Instituto Nacional del Azúcar (INAZUCAR): Avda Jiménez Moya, Apdo 667, Santo Domingo, DN; tel. 532-5571; internet www.inazucar.gov.do; sugar institute; f. 1965; Dir-Gen. RAFAEL MONTILLA.

EMPLOYERS' ORGANIZATIONS

Confederación Patronal de la República Dominicana: Edif. Mella, Cambronal/G. Washington, Santo Domingo, DN; tel. 688-3017; Pres. Ing. HERIBERTO DE CASTRO.

Consejo Nacional de Hombres de Empresa Inc: Edif. Motorámbar, 7°, Avda Abraham Lincoln 1056, Santo Domingo, DN; tel. 562-1666; Pres. JOSÉ MANUEL PALIZA.

Federación Dominicana de Comerciantes: Carretera Sánchez Km 10, Santo Domingo, DN; tel. 533-2666; Pres. IVAN GARCÍA.

MAJOR COMPANIES

Cartonera Hernández, SA: Anibal Espinosa 366, Santo Domingo, DN; tel. 695-4008; fax 536-0725; f. 1946; manufacturers of cardboard and packaging materials; Pres. RICARDO HERNÁNDEZ ELMUDESI; 285 employees.

Cementos Nacionales, SA: Avda Charles Summer 51, Apdo 285, Santo Domingo, DN; tel. 567-8811; f. 1970; manufacturers of cement and cement products; Pres. JOSÉ OSVALDO OLLER CASTRO; Gen. Man. MIGUEL ANGEL TREVIÑO; 457 employees.

Central Romana Corporación: Apdo 891, La Romana, DN; tel. 523-3333; f. 1984; sugar-cane cultivation and processing; Pres. ALFONSO FANJUL; 21,200 employees.

Cervecería Nacional Dominicana, C por A: Avda Independencia Km 6½, Apdo 1086, Santo Domingo, DN; tel. 535-5555; fax 533-5815; f. 1929; manufacturers of beer and malt liquor; Pres. RAFAEL MENICUCCI; 2,500 employees.

Delta Comercial, C por A: Avda John F. Kennedy, Apdo 1376, Santo Domingo, DN; f. 1962; manufacturers and distributors of inner tubes and tyres; Pres. JACINTO B. REYNADO; 675 employees.

Falconbridge Dominicana, C por A: Avda Máximo Gómez 30, Santo Domingo, DN; tel. 682-9156; fax 687-4735; f. 1972; subsidiary of Falconbridge Ltd, Canada; nickel mining and smelting; Pres. RICHARD FAUCHER; Vice-Pres. and Gen. Man. JAMES H. CORRIGAN; 1,200 employees.

Ferretería Americana, C por A: San Martín 175, Apdo 1181, Santo Domingo, DN; tel. 567-6272; fax 567-7063; internet www .americana.com.do; f. 1944; distributors of hardware, houseware, animal food and construction materials; Pres. LUIS GARCÍA SAN MIGUEL; 400 employees.

Industria Textil del Caribe, C por A: Isabel Aguirre, Apdo 2347, Santo Domingo, DN; f. 1957; manufacturers of cotton fabrics; Pres. PEDRO Z. BENDEK; 876 employees.

Industrias Textiles Puig, SA: Anibal Espinosa 303, Apdo 954, Santo Domingo, DN; tel. 536-5800; fax 536-6579; f. 1958; producers of socks, hosiery, underwear and other clothing; Pres. JOSÉ MARÍA PUIG; Vice-Pres. DINO MARRANZINI PUIG; 343 employees.

Induveca: Santo Domingo, DN; f. 2000 by merger of Industrias Vegas and Mercasid; producer of meat products and edible oils.

Rosario Dominicano, SA: Avda Nuñez de Cáceres, Edif. Indotec, 1°, Santo Domingo, DN; tel. 567-5251; fax 565-5290; f. 1972; mine exploration and development; Pres. ANTONIO IMBERT BARRERAS; 1,000 employees.

Sociedad Industrial Dominicana, C por A: Avda Máximo Gómez 192, Apdo 726, Santo Domingo, DN; tel. 565-2151; fax 567-0422; f. 1937; producers of cooking oil, soap, detergents and margarine; Pres. JOSÉ ENRIQUE ARMENTERO; 1,100 employees.

UTILITIES
Electricity

Corporación Dominicana de Electricidad (CDE): Centro de los Héroes, Apdo 1428, Santo Domingo, DN; tel. 535-1100; fax 535-7472; f. 1955; state electricity company; partially privatized in 1999; Dir-Gen. MARCELO JORGE PÉREZ; Admin. CÉSAR DOMINGO SÁNCHEZ TORRES.

Superintendencia de Electricidad: Santo Domingo, DN; Superintendent JOSÉ D. OVALLE TEJADA.

Water

Instituto Nacional de Aguas Potables (INAPA): Santo Domingo, DN; Exec. Dir JUAN ROBERTO RODRÍGUEZ HERNÁNDEZ.

Instituto Nacional de Recursos Hidráulicos: Centro de los Héroes, Santo Domingo, DN; tel. 532-3271; f. 1965; Dir FRANK RODRÍGUEZ.

TRADE UNIONS

Central General de Trabajadores (CGT): Calle 26, esq. Duarte, Santo Domingo, DN; tel. 688-3932; f. 1972; 13 sections; Sec.-Gen. FRANCISCO ANTONIO SANTOS; 65,000 mems.

Central de Trabajadores Independientes (CTI): Calle Juan Erazo 133, Santo Domingo, DN; tel. 688-3932; f. 1978; left-wing; Sec.-Gen. RAFAEL SANTOS.

Central de Trabajadores Mayoritarias (CTM): Tunti Cáceres 222, Santo Domingo, DN; tel. 562-3392; Sec.-Gen. NÉLSIDA MARMOLEJOS.

Confederación Autónoma de Sindicatos Clasistas (CASC) (Autonomous Confederation of Trade Unions): J. Erazo 39, Santo Domingo, DN; tel. 687-8533; f. 1962; supports PRSC; Sec.-Gen. GABRIEL DEL RÍO.

Confederación Nacional de Trabajadores Dominicanos (CNTD) (National Confederation of Dominican Workers): Santo Domingo, DN; f. 1988 by merger; 11 provincial federations totalling 150 unions are affiliated; Sec.-Gen. JULIO DE PEÑA VÁLDEZ; 188,000 mems (est.).

Confederación de Trabajadores Unitaria (CTU) (United Workers' Confederation): Santo Domingo, DN; f. 1991.

Transport
RAILWAYS

In 2001 a proposal for the construction of a US $200m. passenger and freight railway between Santo Domingo and Santiago, with the possibility of extension to other areas, was under discussion.

Dirección General de Tránsito Terrestre: Avda San Cristóbal, Santo Domingo, DN; tel. 565-2811; f. 1966; operated by Secretary of State for Public Works and Communications; Dir-Gen. Ing. LUIS EMILIO PINA.

Ferrocarriles Unidos Dominicanos: Santo Domingo; government-owned; 142 km of track from La Vega to Sánchez and from Guayubín to Pepillo principally used for the transport of exports.

There are also a number of semi-autonomous and private railway companies for the transport of sugar cane, including:

Ferrocarril de Central Romana: La Romana; 375 km open; Pres. C. MORALES.

Ferrocarril Central Río Haina: Apdo 1258, Haina; 113 km open.

ROADS

In 1998 there were an estimated 12,600 km of roads, of which about 6,225 were paved. There is a direct route from Santo Domingo to Port-au-Prince in Haiti. In 2001 plans were proceeding for the construction of a toll road between Boca and San Pedro de Macorís at a cost of US $65m. A new bridge was to be constructed over the Ozama river in 2001.

Dirección General de Mantenimiento de Carreteras y Caminos Vecinales: Santo Domingo, DN; f. 1987; government supervisory body; Dir-Gen. JESÚS MARIA MARTÍNEZ.

SHIPPING

The Dominican Republic has 14 ports, of which Santo Domingo is by far the largest, handling about 80% of imports.

A number of foreign shipping companies operate services to the island.

Agencias Navieras B&R, SA: Avda Abraham Lincoln 504, Apdo 1221, Santo Domingo; tel. 544-2200; fax 562-3383; e-mail jperiche@navierasbr.com; internet www.navierasbr.com; f. 1919; shipping agents and export services; Man. JUAN PERICHE PIDAL.

Armadora Naval Dominicana, SA: Isabel la Católica 165, Apdo 2677, Santo Domingo, DN; tel. 689-6191; Man. Dir Capt. EINAR WETTRE.

Autoridad Portuaria Dominicana: Avda Máximo Gómez, Santo Domingo, DN; tel. 535-8462; Exec. Dir Prof. ANÍBAL GARCÍA DUVERGÉ.

Líneas Marítimas de Santo Domingo, SA: José Gabriel García 8, Apdo 1148, Santo Domingo, DN; tel. 689-9146; fax 685-4654; Pres.C. LLUBERES; Vice-Pres. JUAN T. TAVARES.

CIVIL AVIATION

There are international airports at Santo Domingo (Aeropuerto Internacional de las Américas José Francisco Peña Gómez), Puerto Plata and Barahona (Aeropuerto Internacional María Móntez). A further international airport, at Samaná, was under construction. In December 2000 a new 421m.-peso international airport opened in La Romana. The international airports were undergoing privatization in 1999–2000. Most main cities have domestic airports.

Dirección General de Aeronáutica Civil: Santo Domingo, DN; f. 1955; government supervisory body; Dir-Gen. Dr ANÍBAL AMPARO GARCÍA DÍAZ.

Aerochago: Aeropuerto Internacional de las Américas, Santo Domingo; tel. 549-0709; fax 549-0708; f. 1973; operates cargo and charter service in Central America and the Caribbean; Gen. Man. PEDRO RODRÍGUEZ.

Aerolíneas Argo: Santo Domingo, DN; f. 1971; cargo and mail services to the USA, Puerto Rico and the US Virgin Islands.

Aerolíneas Dominicanas (Dominair): Calle el Sol 62, Apdo 202, Santiago; tel. 581-8882; fax 582-5074; f. 1974; scheduled and charter passenger services; Pres. JOSÉ ARMANDO BERMÚDEZ; Gen. Man. MARÍA TERESA VELÁSQUEZ.

Aerolíneas Santo Domingo: Edif. J.P., Avda 27 de Febrero 272, esq. Calle Seminario, Santo Domingo; e-mail asd@codetel.net.do; internet www.airsantodomingo.com; f. 1996; operates scheduled and charter internal, regional and international flights; Pres. HENRY W. AZAR.

Aeromar Airlines: Aeropuerto Internacional de las Américas, Santo Domingo; tel. 549-0281; fax 542-0152; cargo services.

Compañía Dominicana de Aviación C por A: Avda Jiménez de Moya, esq. José Contreras, Apdo 1415, Santo Domingo, DN; tel. 532-8511; fax 535-1656; f. 1944; operates on international routes connecting Santo Domingo with the Netherlands Antilles, Aruba, the USA, Haiti and Venezuela; operations suspended 1995, privatization pending; Chair. Dr RODOLFO RINCÓN; CEO MARINA GINEBRA DE BONNELLY.

Tourism

Strenuous efforts were made in the 1980s and 1990s to improve the tourism infrastructure, with 200m. pesos spent on increasing the number of hotel rooms by 50%, road improvements and new developments. In 2001 the Government announced a tourist development in the south-western province of Pedernales, consisting of a preliminary 2,400 hotel rooms. The total number of visitors to the Dominican Republic in 1999 was 2,930,000, of whom 281,000 were cruise-ship passengers. In that year receipts from tourism totalled US $2,524m. There were 52,000 hotel rooms in the Dominican Republic in 2001, with a further 7,000 rooms under construction.

Secretaría de Estado de Turismo: Bloque D, Edif. de Oficinas Gubernamentales, Avda México, esq. 30 de Marzo, Apdo 497, Santo Domingo, DN; tel. 221-4660; fax 682-3806; Sec. of State for Tourism RAMÓN ALFREDO BORDAS.

Asociación Dominicana de Agencias de Viajes: Carrera Sánchez 201, Santo Domingo, DN; tel. 687-8984; Pres. RAMÓN PRIETO.

Consejo de Promoción Turística: Avda México 66, Santo Domingo, DN; tel. 687-4676; fax 687-4727; e-mail cpt@codetel.net.do.

Defence

In August 2000 the Dominican Republic's armed forces numbered 24,500: Army 15,000, Navy 4,000 (including naval infantry), Air Force 5,500. There were also paramilitary forces numbering 15,000. Military service is voluntary and lasts for four years.

Defence Expenditure: The budget allocation for 2000 was an estimated RD $2,400m. (US $105m.).

Secretary of State for the Armed Forces and General Chief of Staff: Maj.-Gen. JOSÉ MIGUEL JIMÉNEZ SOTO.

Army Chief of Staff: Maj.-Gen. MANUEL ERNESTO POLANCO SALVADOR.

Navy Chief of Staff: Vice-Adm. LUIS HUMEAU HIDALGO.

Air Force Chief of Staff: Maj.-Gen. RAFAEL GUILLERMO BUENO VÁSQUEZ.

Education

Education is, where possible, compulsory for children between the ages of six and 14 years. Primary education commences at the age of six and lasts for eight years. Secondary education, starting at 14 years of age, lasts for four years. In 1997 total enrolment at primary and secondary schools was equivalent to 84.9% of the school-age population (males 82.0%; females 87.9%). In that period total enrolment at primary level was equivalent to 91.3% of children in the relevant age-group (males 89.0%; females 93.6%), while secondary enrolment was equivalent to 78.5% of children in the relevant age-group (males 74.9%; females 82.1%). At the end of 1997 there were 6,424 primary schools and 1,021 secondary schools. There were eight universities. Budgetary expenditure on education in 1997 was RD $5,114.7m., representing 14.3% of total spending. In 1998, according to UNESCO estimates, the average rate of adult illiteracy was 17.2% (males 17.1%; females 17.2%).

Bibliography

For works on the Caribbean generally, see Select Bibliography (Books).

Atkins, G. P., and Wilson, L. C. *The Dominican Republic and the United States: From Imperialism to Transnationalism.* Athens, GA, University of Georgia Press, 1998.

Betances, E. *State and Society in the Dominican Republic.* Boulder, CO, Westview, 1995.

Black, J. K. *The Dominican Republic: Politics and Development in an Unsovereign State.* London, George Allen and Unwin, 1986.

Hartlyn, J. *The Struggle for Democratic Politics in the Dominican Republic.* Chapel Hill, NC, University of North Carolina Press, 1998.

Hillman, R. S., and D'Agostino, T. J. *Distant Neighbors: The Dominican Republic and Jamaica in Comparative Perspectives.* New York, NY, Praeger Publrs, 1992.

Itzigsohn, J. *Developing Poverty: The State, Labor Market Deregulation, and the Informal Economy in Costa Rica and the Dominican Republic.* University Park, PA, Pennsylvania State University Press, 2000.

Pope Atkins, G., and Wilson, L. C. *The Dominican Republic and the United States: From Imperialism to Transnationalism.* Athens, GA, University of Georgia Press, 1998.

Vedovato, C. *Politics, Foreign Trade and Economic Development: A Study of the Dominican Republic.* Beckenham, Croom Helm, 1986.

Wucker, M. *Why the Cocks Fight: Dominicans, Haitians and the Struggle for Hispaniola.* New York, NY, Hill and Wang Publishing, 2000.

The Politics of External Influence in the Dominican Republic. New York, NY, Praeger Publrs, 1988.

ECUADOR

Area: 272,045 sq km (105,037 sq miles).

Population (official estimate at mid-2000): 12,646,095.

Capital: Quito, population 1,444,363 (estimate at mid-1996).

Language: Spanish (official); Quechua and other indigenous Indian (Amerindian) languages are also widely used.

Religion: Predominantly Christianity (92.5% Roman Catholic).

Climate: Varies with altitude from tropical in the coastal lowlands to areas of permanent snow in the Andes.

Time: GMT –5 hours.

Public Holidays

2002: 1 January (New Year's Day), 6 January (Epiphany), 11–12 February (Carnival), 28 March (Maundy Thursday), 29 March (Good Friday), 30 March (Easter Saturday), 1 May (Labour Day), 24 May (Battle of Pichincha), 24 July (Birth of Simón Bolívar), 10 August (Independence of Quito), 9 October (Independence of Guayaquil), 12 October (Discovery of America), 1 November (All Saints' Day), 2 November (All Souls' Day), 3 November (Independence of Cuenca), 6 December (Foundation of Quito), 25 December (Christmas Day).

2003: 1 January (New Year's Day), 6 January (Epiphany), 3–4 March (Carnival), 17 April (Maundy Thursday), 18 April (Good Friday), 19 April (Easter Saturday), 1 May (Labour Day), 24 May (Battle of Pichincha), 24 July (Birth of Simón Bolívar), 10 August (Independence of Quito), 9 October (Independence of Guayaquil), 12 October (Discovery of America), 1 November (All Saints' Day), 2 November (All Souls' Day), 3 November (Independence of Cuenca), 6 December (Foundation of Quito), 25 December (Christmas Day).

Currency: US dollar (which replaced the sucre as the national currency from March 2000); US $100 = £69.84 = €112.66 (30 April 2001).

Weights and Measures: The metric system is in force.

Basic Economic Indicators

	1997	1998	1999
Gross domestic product (US $ million at 1975 prices)	9,120	n.a.	n.a.
GDP per head (US $ at 1975 prices)	749	n.a.	n.a.
GDP (US $ million at current prices)	19,723	n.a.	n.a.
GDP per head (US $ at current prices)	1,620	n.a.	n.a.
Annual growth of real GDP (%)	0.4	n.a.	n.a.
Annual growth of real GDP per head (%)	–1.6	n.a.	n.a.
Government budget (US $ million at 31 December):			
Revenue	3,280.3	2,780.3	3,056.6
Expenditure	3,211.6	2,804.1	2,966.6
Consumer price index (annual average; base: 1995 = 100)	221.1	336.7	660.2
Rate of inflation (annual average, %)	36.1	52.2	96.1
Foreign exchange reserves (US $ million at 31 December)	1.595.3	1,616.5	924.3
Imports c.i.f. (US $ million)	5.575.7	3.017.3	3,465.0
Exports f.o.b. (US $ million)	4,202.9	4,451.0	4,845.9
Balance of payments (current account, US $ million)	–2,169	955	n.a.

Gross national product per head measured at purchasing power parity (PPP) (US dollars, converted by the PPP exchange rate, 1999): 2,820

Economically active population (persons aged eight years and over, 1999): 3,769,581.

Unemployment (2000): 9.0%.

Total external debt (1999): US $14,506m.

Life expectancy (years at birth, 1999): 72 (males 69; females 74).

Infant mortality rate (per 1,000 live births, 1999): 31.

Adult population with HIV/AIDS (15–49 years, 1999): 0.29%.

School enrolment ratio (6–17 years, 1994): 80%.

Adult literacy rate (15 years and over, 2000): 91.9% (males 93.6; females 91.2%).

Energy consumption per head (kg of oil equivalent, 1998): 737.

Carbon dioxide emissions per head (metric tons, 1997): 1.8.

Passenger motor cars in use (per 1,000 of population, 1998): 40.7.

Television receivers in use (per 1,000 of population, 1997): 130.

Personal computers in use (per 1,000 of population, 1999): 20.1.

History

SANDY MARKWICK

Based on an earlier essay by DAVID CORKILL

Ecuador is one of the smaller South American republics, with a land area of 272,045 sq km (105,037 sq miles), slightly larger than the United Kingdom. In 2000 it had an estimated population of 12.6m. Despite its size, Ecuador has a varied geography and ecology derived from its position astride the Equator, from which the country takes its name. The contrasting geography has a profound impact upon political and economic life by creating barriers to national integration and encouraging the emergence of competing economic and social systems on the coastal lowlands or Costa, in the Andean highlands or Sierra and, in more recent times, in the eastern Oriente region.

After it became an independent republic, following the disintegration of Gran Colombia in 1830, Ecuador lost territory to its neighbours. Claiming an area totalling 706,000 sq km at the time of independence, Ecuador progressively lost disputed territory in border wars. These were fought against Colombia in the 1830s and in 1916, and Brazil in 1904. Following the 1941 war against Peru, Ecuador lost a Pacific coastal province and large tracts of land in the Oriente region. Although obliged to sign the Protocol of Rio de Janeiro under US pressure in 1942, which recognized most of Peru's seizures, Ecuador continued to claim sovereignty over the lost territories and demand sovereign access to the Amazon river until 1998, when an agreement with Peru appeared to represent a definitive solution to the dispute.

The issue had remained contentious prior to 1998, with opposing troops clashing briefly in January 1981 and again in August 1991, and more seriously in January 1995 along the undemarcated 78 km section of the border in the area known as the Cordillera del Cóndor. A cease-fire, to be overseen by the four guarantor countries of the Rio Protocol (Argentina, Brazil, Chile and the USA), was eventually agreed in Montevideo (Uruguay) in March and by mid-May the last remaining troops had been withdrawn from the border area. In that month Ecuador recognized the validity of the Rio Protocol for the first time and agreement on the delimitation of the demilitarized zone in the disputed area was reached in late July. Formal negotiations to find a definitive solution to the conflict began in January 1996. These negotiations led to the signing in Chile of a framework document, the Santiago Agreement, in October of that year.

Negotiations continued during 1997 and 1998, despite allegations on both sides relating to the continued use of land-mines and the covert procurement of armaments, and Peru's firm opposition to the Ecuadorean delegation's insistence that the issue of a sovereign outlet to the Amazon river be included. These talks culminated in the signing of a comprehensive accord on 26 October 1998 in Brasília (Brazil), in the presence of the two countries' Presidents and six other regional leaders. The accord recognized Peruvian claims regarding the delineation of the border, but granted Ecuador the right to establish two, non-sovereign, 150 ha commercial zones on the Amazon river in Peru and to use the river and its tributaries for trade and navigation. The two countries' Presidents hailed a new era of joint development and co-operation when they met in May 1999 to celebrate the placement of the final frontier marker in the Cordillera del Cóndor. However, public reaction was equivocal. While polls suggested that Ecuadoreans accepted, with some indignation, the abandonment of their sovereign claims, in Peru there was vociferous opposition to the accord, particularly in Iquitos, the capital of Peru's Amazon region.

Politically, Ecuador comprises 21 provinces, which are divided into over 900 urban and rural parishes, administered by political lieutenants. The country is divided, geographically, into three distinct regions, plus the Galápagos archipelago located about 1,000 km (600 miles) off shore to the west. The Sierra is dominated by two mountain ranges or cordilleras, with over 30 volcanoes, the highest peaks being Chimborazo (6,310 m), Cotopaxi (5,896 m—the highest active volcano in the world) and Cayambe (5,790 m). The capital, Quito, lies below the slopes of Pichincha, which erupted in 1982. It is the country's administrative centre and, particularly from the beginning of the petroleum era, underwent a significant expansion in its service and industrial sectors. The Sierra is no longer the most populous region, largely because of migration to the urban centres on the coast. The rural population density, exacerbated by inequitable land distribution, generated high levels of rural poverty, which caused the migration. Traditionally, agriculture served the domestic market and took the form of large, often inefficiently run, estates or haciendas which delayed the emergence of modern commercial agriculture. Small-scale subsistence farms run by Indian (Amerindian) peasants co-existed alongside the large estates. Efforts were made to modernize sierran agriculture, most notably through agrarian reform laws (passed in 1964, 1973 and 1994), although there was a noticeable failure to resolve the problem of the shortage of land. However, the agrarian structure belatedly underwent change, as some haciendas developed efficient commercial systems capable of responding to urban demand for dairy and beef products.

The Costa has the country's largest and fastest-growing population, in excess of 4m. by the 1990s. The growth is attributable to a combination of internal migration and a high natural increase, which saw the population of Guayaquil, the Pacific port on the Guayas river, grow from some 250,000 people in 1950 to almost 2m. people by mid-1997. Rapid expansion generated social problems, such as 'squatter' settlements or *suburbios* and a large urban population living on the margins of subsistence, from where Ecuador's populist politicians gained many votes. The region was involved in agro-exporting activities from colonial times and diversified into industry and banking in the late 19th century. Unlike the Sierra, there are few large estates and the agrarian structure is characterized by small- and medium-scale commercial farms.

Although a focus for development and colonization efforts, following the discovery of petroleum reserves in the late 1960s, the Oriente or lowland Amazon basin region remains sparsely populated, containing 4% of the national population, despite accounting for about 36% of Ecuador's total territory. Indigenous Indians, such as the Auca and Jivaro, still inhabit the Oriente. They have come under threat from imported diseases and the depletion of resources, particularly land, by newcomers *colonos* and multinational companies. From the late 1980s the increasingly organized Amerindian population grew in assertiveness. Groups representing highland and Amazonian Indians organized a campaign of disruption in 1990, led a march on Quito by several thousand Amerindians in 1992 and mobilized on several subsequent occasions. Their demands included the recognition of land and territorial rights, ownership rights over natural resources, greater political autonomy, stricter controls on petroleum companies' operations to prevent further environmental damage and the constitutional recognition of Indian rights. Some concessions were made, but the claim to subsoil ownership met with strong opposition, particularly from the military, which had vested interests in the petroleum industry.

The Galápagos archipelago was incorporated into Ecuador in 1830, and became a province in 1973, with its capital at Puerto Baquerizo Moreno. Only 0.1% of Ecuador's population live on the Galápagos Islands, although in 1991 the Government ended a ban on migration from the mainland and subsequent population growth was around 15% per year. The Islands are noted for their association with British naturalist Charles Darwin's theory of evolution and the giant tortoises found there (from which the islands take their name). In the 19th century the Galápagos served as a base for whalers and, during the Second World War, the US Air Force had a base on South Seymour island. The Galápagos were designated as Ecuador's first national park and they have also been declared a World Heritage site by the UN Educational, Scientific and Cultural Organization (UNESCO). The waters around the archipelago form part of the exclusive maritime zone claimed by Ecuador, Chile and Peru from 1952. The 200 nautical mile (370 km) maritime limit provoked incidents in 1971, during the 'tuna war', when US fishing boats were apprehended and fined.

INDEPENDENCE

Before the arrival of the Spanish, Ecuador was ruled by the Incas, who had incorporated the area into their empire some 50 years earlier. The Spanish conquest began in 1534 and Spain's 300-year rule commenced when Sebastián de Belalcázar captured Quito, after Francisco Pizarro's conquests of the Incas at Cajamarca and Cuzco, in Peru. Ecuador, administered from both Lima (Peru) and Santafé de Bogotá (Colombia), remained peripheral to the Spanish imperial system for many years.

Colonial rule ended when Simón Bolívar's forces, under the command of a Venezuelan general, José Antonio de Sucre, defeated the Spanish at the decisive battle of Pichincha (1822). Following a meeting between Bolívar and José de San Martín in Guayaquil, Ecuador was incorporated into the short-lived Federation of Gran Colombia. However, by 1830 it had become an independent republic. Ecuador endured economic stagnation and political instability for most of the 19th century and what development did occur was uncoordinated. The conservative Gabriel García Moreno (President in 1861–65 and 1869–75) attempted to install a form of theocratic state. However, he also promoted public works, including a railway linking the capital, Quito, with Guayaquil. It was not until the Liberals, under Gen. Eloy Alfaro, took power, following the 1895 revolution, that modernization began. Railways were constructed, foreign investment encouraged, the influence of the Roman Catholic Church reduced and capital punishment abolished.

POLITICAL AND ECONOMIC INSTABILITY

During the 20th century Ecuador earned its reputation as one of the most unstable countries in South America. Between 1830 and 1979 there were 18 changes of constitution. In the first 150 years after independence there were 88 heads of state. Only 17 elected Presidents completed their full term of office. This inability to establish a stable democratic system could be attributed, on the one hand, to the absence of a democratic political culture and weak political institutions and, on the other, to the country's dependent economy, vulnerable to external fluctuations in demand for primary products.

The collapse of the cocoa market in the 1920s and the economic recession, the Great Depression, of the 1930s generated 20 years of political instability. Between 1931 and 1948 Ecuador had 21 governments, none of which survived a full term. The period also produced the type of demagogic politician for which Ecuador became famous. José María Velasco Ibarra was elected President on five occasions, in 1934, 1944, 1952, 1960 and 1968, and was overthrown four times. Velasquismo failed to become an organized political movement and, despite the anti-oligarchic and anti-imperialist rhetoric, never posed a serious threat to the ruling élite. After the tumultuous years of the 1930s and 1940s, Ecuador had a 12-year period (1948–60) when relative economic prosperity and political stability almost became accepted practice. Three Presidents succeeded one another in office and developmental policies were pursued as Ecuador enjoyed the prosperity generated by banana exports. However, before the foundations of an industrial economy could be established, the prosperity ended. The 1960s produced two Velasco presidencies, intersected by a military junta (1963–66). The military rulers introduced an agrarian reform law and promoted industrial development, but were eventually forced out of office by protests and pressure from influential civilian groups.

MILITARY TAKE-OVER, ECONOMIC PROSPERITY, 1972–79

In February 1972 the military seized power again. This time, however, the context had changed dramatically. The country was about to enter a period of unprecedented prosperity, based on substantial petroleum reserves discovered in the Oriente jungle. The coup had been caused by a mixture of motives: fears that the anti-militarist, Asaad Bucaram, might win the forthcoming presidential elections; a conviction that the anticipated petroleum income could not be left to corrupt politicians; and the emergence of a 'nationalist' faction within the military institution. The military Government, led by Gen. Guillermo Rodríguez Lara, initiated a state-sponsored modernization strategy, funded by petroleum revenues. The military decreed a new agrarian reform law, increased public expenditure, sponsored industrialization and export diversification, and attempted to limit vulnerability to external pressures through membership of the Organization of the Petroleum Exporting Countries (OPEC) and the Andean Pact.

In 1976 Rodríguez was replaced by a three-man military junta whose leader, Vice-Adm. Alfredo Poveda Burbano, represented the constitutionalist wing in the Armed Forces which favoured a democratic restoration. The increasingly unpopular and divided military regime supervised the return to civilian rule, which began with a constitutional referendum in January 1978, followed by presidential and legislative elections in April 1979.

THE RETURN TO CIVILIAN GOVERNMENT, 1979

The decisive victor in the presidential election was Jaime Roldós Aguilera, who promised social and economic reforms. However, the new Government's prospects were severely constrained by an opposition majority in Congress and a division between Roldós and his party, the Consensus of Popular Forces (Concertación de Fuerzas Populares—CFP). Ecuadorean politics again degenerated into legislative paralysis and personality conflicts. President Roldós died in an aeroplane crash in May 1981, and was succeeded by Osvaldo Hurtado Larrea.

Hurtado inherited uneasy relations with Congress, a deteriorating economic situation and increasing trade-union militancy. He was unable to construct a lasting pro-government majority in the legislature, as his administration attempted to solve the first major economic crisis since the advent of the petroleum era. Austerity measures generated social unrest and widespread dissatisfaction with the Government. Hurtado concentrated on consolidating democratic procedures and ensuring a legitimate succession. Popular reaction against the severe adjustment policies required by the International Monetary Fund (IMF) marked the end of social-democratic reformism and permitted a right-wing populist, León Febres Cordero, to gain a narrow victory in the May 1984 presidential elections. Febres Cordero exploited the traditional patterns of Ecuadorean politics, shifting the focus away from political parties towards personalities, so that his aggressive style gave him a clear advantage over his opponent, Rodrigo Borja Cevallos.

THE FEBRES ERA, 1984–88

Febres Cordero, a former President of Guayaquil's Chamber of Industry and an outspoken champion of free enterprise, led Ecuador into an experiment in neo-liberal economic policies, 'Andean Thatcherism'. His economic strategy prioritized export promotion, incentives for foreign investors, reductions in public expenditure, a reduced role for the state in the economy and incentives for the private sector. Febres Cordero aligned Ecuador closely with the USA, especially with regard to the Central American crisis. He pursued a policy of prompt debt repayment in order to ensure good relations with international economic institutions. The social costs of the neo-liberal model were high, especially as such policies had only been applied previously in the authoritarian context of military government, in the Southern Cone countries during the 1970s. Febres Cordero's economic project involved increasingly authoritarian behaviour by the executive, the alleged abuse of civil liberties and human rights, constitutional violations and conflicts between the legislature and the President.

By 1986 President Febres Cordero had many problems. The petroleum price collapse destroyed hopes for sustained growth and revealed strains in Ecuador's relations with OPEC over production quota levels. Conflicts with Congress, over constitutional issues, economic policy and foreign affairs, occurred regularly, which helped to tarnish the image of the democratic process itself. In the June 1986 congressional elections Febres Cordero failed to win both a parliamentary majority and a plebiscite on constitutional reform. The Government lost support because of deflationary measures, made necessary by declining petroleum prices, and the controversy surrounding a rebellion by the dismissed Chief-of-Staff of the Armed Forces and Commander of the Air Force, Lt-Gen. Frank Vargas Pazzos, whose allegations of corruption had damaged the Government. In January 1987 Febres Cordero was kidnapped by rebel paratroopers demanding Vargas's release from detention; after 11 hours the President was released, in exchange for the granting of an amnesty to Vargas.

THE BORJA PRESIDENCY, 1988–92

In early 1988 Ecuador successfully conducted the third presidential and fourth congressional elections since the restoration of civilian government. It confirmed that democratic processes were established and were strong enough to survive Febres Cordero's authoritarian populism, a sharp economic recession and rumours that another military coup was imminent. A peaceful transfer of power from Febres Cordero to his successor, Borja Cevallos, of the Democratic Left (Izquierda Democrática—ID), testified to a new resilience underpinning Ecuadorean democracy. Borja defeated his opponent, Abdalá Bucaram Ortiz, in the second round of voting by taking 46% of the votes cast, against the 41% of his opponent. It was the first time since 1979 that the presidency had been won without securing a majority in Guayaquil. However, Borja was alone among recent presidents in enjoying majority support in Congress. Borja immediately distanced himself from the policies of his predecessor. In international relations he restored diplomatic relations with Nicaragua, realigned Ecuador with its Andean neighbours and joined the 'Group of Eight' club of Latin American debtors.

Borja proposed a *concertación*, or consensus, between government, business and labour, as a forum to attempt to resolve the growing economic crisis. In economic policy, there were two priority areas: to bring inflation under control and to renegotiate the foreign debt. In contrast to the radical market-orientated policies pursued by other Latin American regimes, President Borja introduced a programme of moderate social-democratic reforms known as *gradualismo*. Politically, the new President had to deal with the conflicting views of a small, but vociferous, labour movement and a hostile Guayaquil business community, which regarded Borja as a dangerous Quito-centred socialist. In attempting to solve these problems President Borja needed to balance policies to retain the support of the left without alienating the private sector. The Government pardoned the paratroopers responsible for Febres Cordero's abduction. The President also successfully concluded negotiations with Alfaro Lives, Damn It! (Alfaro Vive ¡Carajo!-AVC), one of Ecuador's small guerrilla movements, after it agreed to abandon the armed struggle and enter the legal political arena.

However, popular disillusionment with economic policy contributed to a major reverse for the Government in the mid-term congressional elections, held in June 1990, when the ID and its allies lost their majority in Congress. Effective government was severely impeded in the second half of the administration. Highly confrontational politics caused frequent impasses between the executive and the opposition-controlled Congress. The latter repeatedly resorted to its power to censure cabinet members. This resulted in the Government losing six senior ministers and the Chairman of the National Monetary Board being threatened with impeachment proceedings.

The failure to reduce inflation and the gradual decline in spending power caused increasing labour unrest, with strikes organized by the trade-union federation, Frente Unitario de Trabajadores (FUT). President Borja responded to such pressure with the rapid mobilization of troops, the closing of schools and the decreeing of public holidays to coincide with the national strikes. Relations with the labour movement deteriorated further after the November 1991 reforms to the 60-year-old labour code, which were intended to increase the competitiveness of Ecuador's exports in the Andean Pact free-trade zone.

VICTORY OF THE RIGHT, THE DURAN BALLÉN GOVERNMENT, 1992–96

The presidential and congressional elections of May 1992 resulted in defeat for the ID, the presidential candidate of which gained only 8.2% of the votes cast. Both second-round candidates were from the centre-right. On 5 July Sixto Durán Ballén, of the recently formed Unitary Republican Party (Partido Unitario Republicano—PUR), won the presidency, defeating Jaime Nebot Saadi, of the Social Christian Party (Partido Social Cristiano—PSC), with 58% of the votes cast. Durán had strong links with the business community, experience in government and was the only presidential contender with substantial support in both Quito and the Costa. He promised to abandon the *gradualismo* of the previous regime, in favour of accelerating free-market reforms and encouraging foreign investment, and his appointment of prominent business executives to the principal portfolios in his Cabinet reflected his commitment to these policies. The PUR, which gained 12 seats in Congress, formed an alliance with the Conservative Party (Partido Conservador—PC), which contributed a further five seats. As this still did not constitute a majority, support had to be sought from other centre-right parties, mainly from the PSC, the closest ideological ally and the party with the largest number of seats in Congress.

The new administration moved as quickly as its predecessor in instituting reform. In early September 1992 the Government announced a programme of austerity measures, aimed at restructuring the public sector, reducing the rate of inflation and normalizing relations with foreign creditors. In November the National Council of Modernization (Consejo Nacional de Modernización—CONAM), charged with reforming the State, was established. The country's long-delayed entry into the Andean Pact free-trade area was implemented, a new foreign investment code was announced and negotiations were initiated on the rescheduling of Ecuador's foreign debt, which led to an agreement on an IMF stand-by facility in 1994. The Government also resigned from OPEC, enabling it to produce and export petroleum without restrictions being imposed by the cartel.

Although support from the PSC secured passage of some of the Government's early legislative agenda, President Durán's attempts at reform were soon impeded not only by an increasingly uncooperative and hostile legislature, but also by a lack of consensus and allegations of corruption within his own Cabinet. At regular intervals ministers resigned, were asked to resign, or were threatened with impeachment proceedings by Congress: during the administration there were five finance ministers and four energy ministers. The Modernization Law, a crucial part of the controversial austerity programme was only enacted after eight months of legislative debate and a number of amendments, including the deletion of the petroleum, electricity and telecommunications sectors from the legislation's remit.

Following the trend of the two previous administrations, mid-term congressional elections in May 1994 resulted in a humiliating defeat for President Durán's PUR, which, in alliance with the PC, won only nine seats in the 77-seat Congress. The opposition parties effectively took charge of Congress, forming two power blocs in the process: the right-wing PSC supported by the populist Roldós Party of Ecuador (Partido Roldosista Ecuatoriano—PRE) and a centre-left alliance of ID, Popular Democracy (Democracia Popular—DP) and the Popular Democratic Movement (Movimiento Popular Democrático—MPD). In order to circumvent congressional obstructionism and to create a legal basis for some of the more controversial areas of the privatization programme, President Durán planned a referendum on constitutional reforms. However, the antagonism between the President, the legislature and the Supreme Electoral Tribunal (Tribunal Supremo Electoral—TSE) ensured that only the least controversial issues were included when the referendum was held on 28 August 1994 and that a further plebiscite was to be necessary. Although all but one of the proposed reforms were approved, the turn-out was low, reflecting widespread disillusionment among the electorate.

The eruption of cross-border conflict with Peru in January 1995 temporarily alleviated domestic political tensions. However, within days of the first cease-fire agreement in February, political dissent re-emerged over emergency measures that had been imposed by the Government in the previous month, particularly reductions in spending and the widespread tax increases. This situation was aggravated by allegations from the former President, Febres Cordero, that the Government had diverted some of these emergency 'war funds' to finance external debt payments.

In July 1995 a deep political crisis was provoked by Vice-President Alberto Dahik Garzozi's admission that the Government had paid deputies and judges and used patronage to ensure the passage of its legislative programme. Dahik refused to resign and used his revelations to draw attention to the widespread nature of corruption in the political system, simultaneously denouncing the PSC, Febres Cordero and two other opposition parties. The investigation that followed led to the dismissal of the President of the Supreme Court and two other justices, alleged by some to be an attempt to obstruct the case against Dahik, and the resignation of the Superintendent of Banks and several ministers. The finance minister, Mauricio Pinto, was impeached and criminal charges concerning the misuse of 'discretionary' funds proceeded against the Vice-President. He eventually resigned in October and sought political asylum in Costa Rica. However, threats of impeachment proceedings against the President over his alleged involvement in the affair came to nothing.

As a result of the crisis, there was an increasing mobilization of the population against the policies and practices of the Durán Government. The rejection of all 11 proposals in the second referendum on constitutional reform in November 1995, was widely seen as a rejection of a discredited administration. In the second half of 1995 alone there were militant protests in the Galápagos Islands in support of increased political and financial autonomy, violent demonstrations in the major cities to oppose government policies, including labour-code reforms and fuel-price increases, a number of bombings of public buildings by a guerrilla group, the Puka Inti Maoist Communist Party, prolonged industrial action in the public sector and three one-day national strikes. In January 1996 army units had to be deployed to prevent a worsening of the energy crisis, brought about by industrial action in the sector and a drought in late 1995, which paralysed vital hydroelectric capacity.

President Durán also had to accommodate the interests of the increasingly organized and vociferous indigenous movement, which acted to oppose agricultural development legislation that allowed for the commercialization of Amerindian lands for farming and resource extraction. In June 1994 the Amerindian 'umbrella' organization, the Council of the Indigenous Nationalities of Ecuador (Consejo de Nacionalidades Indígenas de Ecuador—CONAIE), in concert with the FUT, organized nation-wide demonstrations against the new law. Serious unrest and a general strike followed, during which a state of emergency was declared and the army mobilized, with several protesters killed in clashes with security forces. The following month the legislation was modified to extend the rights of the rural population. That such issues could no longer be ignored was shown in the 1996 election campaign and in the first round of voting, in May, in which the newly formed Pachakutik—New Country Movement (Movimiento Nuevo País—Pachakutik—MNPP), representing indigenous, environmental and social groups, gained eight seats in Congress and third place in the presidential vote with over one-fifth of the votes cast.

PRESIDENTS BUCARAM AND ALARCÓN, 1996–98

In the congressional elections of May 1996 the PSC won 27 of the 82 seats in the enlarged National Congress, while the PRE secured only 19 and the DP 12. The PRE-allied parties won a combined five seats, while the MNPP emerged as a significant new force with its eight seats. However, the populist Abdalá Bucaram Ortiz of the PRE was the unexpected victor of the 1996 presidential election, winning 54.5% of votes cast in the second round of voting on 7 July 1996.

Bucaram, a former olympic athlete, had held political office as mayor of Guayaquil in the 1980s and had contested three previous presidential elections. Known as 'El Loco' ('the madman') by friends and enemies alike, owing to a highly unconventional approach to politics, marked by a combination of extravagant showmanship and combative bravado, Bucaram's victory reflected widespread disillusionment with established party politics and a rejection of Nebot's electoral promise to

continue with the outgoing Government's economic policy. Bucaram's campaign had promised to establish 'a government for the poor', and included proposals to extend social-security benefits to indigenous families, to provide low-cost housing for 200,000 families, to increase the salaries of teachers and health workers and to introduce subsidies for rice, meat, milk and fuel. However, following his inauguration President Bucaram appointed three prominent Guayaquil businessmen to advise him and sought to allay fears among the business community of costly social reform. The PRE dominated the new administration, but there were also some representatives of the Independent Movement for an Authentic Republic (Movimiento Independiente para una República Auténtica—led by the Vice-President, Rosalia Arteaga) and other small parties, as well as independents. However, other cabinet appointments, which included the President's brother and brother-in-law and several close personal friends, provoked criticism.

Soon after his election Bucaram's support dwindled rapidly. Huge price rises for electricity, gas, public transport and telephone services, designed to reduce the US $1,200m. budget deficit, equal to 6% of gross domestic product (GDP), were widely opposed. A scandal at the Ministry of Finance in September 1996, which resulted in the arrest of seven senior officials on charges of embezzlement (estimated at more than $300m.), tainted the Government, and concern at the President's idiosyncratic style of leadership began to intensify in late 1996. President Bucaram offended nationalist sentiment following an unsuccessful diplomatic mission to Lima (Peru) designed to solve the border dispute and gave the impression that he had no understanding of the historical basis of the conflict. It was reported that Bucaram had failed to attend a number of important meetings, while his television appearances, which often involved the President dancing and performing rock music, became more frequent. By the end of 1996 President Bucaram's Government was widely regarded to be rife with corruption and nepotism. Moreover, a perceived inconsistency in his policies and the apparently arbitrary nature of his decisions, together with his use of undiplomatic language, combined to give the appearance of demagoguery. This contributed to the increasing prevalence of the opinion that the President was, in fact, mentally unfit to govern.

A 48-hour general strike in January 1997, prompted by increases of up to 600% in the price of various commodities and the climate of general dissatisfaction with President Bucaram's leadership, was followed by mass demonstrations in the capital, during which violent clashes took place between protesters and security personnel, leaving Bucaram barricaded inside the presidential palace. In the first week of February an estimated 2m. people marched in the streets demanding President Bucaram's resignation. On 6 February Congress voted by 44 votes to 34 to dismiss the President on the grounds of mental incapacity, a move which circumvented the normal impeachment requirements of a two-thirds' majority. A state of emergency was declared by the acting President, hitherto the speaker of Congress, Fabián Alarcón Rivera. Bucaram reportedly fled on 9 February and on the following day Vice-President Arteaga was declared interim President. The constitutional provisions regarding the succession were unclear, prompting a brief stand-off between Arteaga and Alarcón and fears of a military coup, despite a declaration of neutrality from the Armed Forces. However, by 11 February Arteaga had resigned and Congress formally elected Alarcón to the presidency, by 57 votes to two, with the agreement that a new presidential election would be held in August 1998.

President Alarcón acted quickly in an attempt to restore confidence in the administration. State employees dismissed by Bucaram were reinstated, the Armed Forces were given responsibility for eliminating corruption in the customs system, and in March Bucaram's extradition from Panama was sought, on charges of the misappropriation of US $90m. of public funds. However, the Supreme Court ruled that extradition would only be possible once a prison sentence had been issued and, so, in January 1998 Bucaram was sentenced *in absentia* to two years in prison, on different charges of slandering two political rivals. On 25 May 1997 a referendum comprising 14 questions revealed considerable support for the removal of Bucaram (75.7%), for the appointment of Alarcón (68.3%) and for the creation of a

National Assembly to consider constitutional reform (64.5%), although some 40.7% of the electorate did not participate.

Despite President Alarcón's apparent success in the referendum, his administration was soon beset by the problems that had discredited the political process in Ecuador and eroded public confidence in their elected representatives over the preceding decade. A congressional inquiry was to investigate allegations that drugs traffickers had contributed to political party funds and particularly to Alarcón's FRA. Confrontation between the legislature and the judiciary continued, with the dismissal of all 31 judges of the Supreme Court by Congress, which claimed that this was in accordance with the views on the depoliticization of the judiciary (hitherto nominated by the legislature) expressed in the referendum. The action was condemned as unconstitutional by the President of the Supreme Court. President Alarcón's problems were further exacerbated by charges of embezzlement filed against him in the Supreme Court by a former FRA colleague, Cecilia Calderón.

In August 1997 the announcement that the National Constituent Assembly would be convened the following August provoked a 48-hour strike, led by CONAIE, to protest against the slow pace of constitutional reform. In response to public pressure, the elections for the 70 representatives to the new body were brought forward to November 1997. In February 1998 the recently installed Assembly agreed a number of institutional reforms, including the enlargement of Congress from 82 to 121 seats, the extension of the presidential term (from the subsequent election) from four years to four years, five months and five days, and the abolition of mid-term elections.

PRESIDENT MAHUAD WITT, 1998–2000

In elections to the newly enlarged Congress, held on 31 May 1998, the DP emerged as the strongest party, securing 32 seats. The PSC won 27 seats, the PRE 24 and the ID 18. At the second round of voting in the presidential election, on 12 July, the DP's Jamil Mahuad Witt, mayor of Quito, narrowly defeated Alvaro Noboa Pontón of the PRE, with 51.2% of the votes. Mahuad was sworn in on 10 August and appointed a Cabinet consisting predominantly of independents.

Mahuad's popularity increased following a peace agreement with Peru in October 1998. The accord established a definitive border with Peru while granting Ecuador unlimited navigation rights on the Amazon river. It appeared likely that the agreement would mark a permanent solution to the border dispute and refocus significantly both countries' international relations towards commercial relations.

The President's popularity did not last long. The effects of a programme of stringent adjustment measures, introduced in September 1998, began to be felt and led to a general strike, organized by the FUT and CONAIE, in early October. The programme, including huge increases in public transport and utilities prices, was designed to stabilize the economy. Protests were prolonged and resulted in the deaths of several demonstrators in clashes with security forces. By early 1999 Ecuador's economic situation had become extremely grave. The fiscal deficit required immediate attention, the private banking system was close to collapse, the prospect of default on external debt obligations threatened to destroy investor confidence and the rapid decline in the value of the sucre was raising fears of 'hyperinflation'. At the same time, Congress continued to resist the politically unpopular austerity measures required by multilateral lenders for the release of funds and the country's militant labour unions and social organizations continued to mobilize substantial and organized resistance.

A 25% fall in the value of the sucre in the first week of March 1999, which prompted President Mahuad to decree a freeze on bank deposits, was followed by a two-day national strike, organized by trade unions to demand the reversal of austerity measures. In response to the industrial action, during which violent protests paralysed urban transport in Quito, Guayaquil and Cuenca and Amerindian groups blocked all roads into Colombia, the President declared a 60-day state of emergency, enabling the army to be deployed to maintain order. Aiming to satisfy the restructuring demands of the IMF, in order to facilitate the agreement of a US $400m. contingency loan, President Mahuad announced a package of economic stabilization measures. These included a 100% increase in fuel prices, to be

partially revoked if Congress approved proposed increases in value-added tax (VAT), and the partial suspension of bank-deposit withdrawals, intended to restore liquidity to the banking sector. However, following the announcement, four of the five members of the independent Central Bank board resigned, citing differences over policy towards the financial sector. Moreover, the fuel-price increase provoked an additional week of industrial action, this time by transport workers, and further violent clashes.

In May 1999 the release of US $500m. in rapid-disbursement loans from the World Bank, the Inter-American Development Bank (IDB) and the Andean Development Corporation had engendered some optimism, but the deadline of 31 May for the signing of a letter of intent on the IMF contingency loan was missed. That loan, which would have been likely to release up to $1,200m. in multilateral lending, and without which an external-debt default was probable, was dependent on additional fiscal reform, progress with privatization legislation and measures to guarantee the stability of the banking sector. Although a comprehensive package of tax reforms was passed, in June, Congress rejected a framework privatization bill, which would have enabled the Government to begin the divestment of public companies in the electricity and telecommunications sectors. Congress was influenced by protests against the privatization of state assets, organized the previous day by labour and grassroots organizations, and, signalling division within the ruling DP, three deputies of the ruling DP determined that proposed additional powers for the President to decide on the terms of the sales were unconstitutional and voted with the opposition. In July Congress again rejected proposed legislation, this time on banking reform. An effect of the veto was a postponement in the disbursement of the much-needed IMF loan. The failure to obtain IMF funding led to the announcement, in late August, that the Government intended to default on interest payments due to international creditors. Ecuador became the first country to default on its Brady bond commitments and, subsequently, to default on Eurobonds as the Government declared a moratorium on all foreign debt repayments.

On 5 July 1999 taxi drivers, public-transport workers and commercial drivers began industrial action to protest against additional austerity measures announced by the Government, including further fuel-price increases, and President Mahuad again declared a state of emergency. Unions and indigenous groups soon joined the striking transport workers in what CONAIE termed an 'uprising', which saw an armed clash between protesters and soldiers in the central Andean town of Lacatunga and the seizure of communications antennae in Ambato by a 2,000-strong contingent of Amerindian demonstrators. The target of the protests became the Government's economic policy generally and President Mahuad's resignation was demanded. Congress repealed the state of emergency on 14 July, only for the President to reimpose it a few hours later. On 16 July, the day after Amerindian groups began a symbolic 'occupation' of Quito and armoured vehicles were positioned to defend the presidential palace, the immediate crisis was averted when an agreement was signed to end the transport strike. The Government agreed to fix fuel prices until 31 December 2000, to allow taxi co-operatives and transport companies access to their bank deposits, to release those arrested during the strike and to lift the state of emergency.

In the final months of 1999 Mahuad's position deteriorated. A campaign financing scandal which linked him to a disgraced former head of the bankrupt Banco del Progreso was followed, in November, by accusations that Mahuad concluded a deal with the PRE, in order to win support for his 2000 budget, in which legal reforms would be introduced allowing former President Bucaram to return from exile in Panama under no threat of prosecution. Increasing inflation and a currency crisis towards the end of 1999 undermined living standards further. By the end of the year Mahuad's popularity had plumbed new depths with opinion polling organizations reporting single-figure approval ratings.

On 9 January 2000 Mahuad announced a decision to adopt the US dollar as the currency of Ecuador. Only days before, Mahuad had dismissed the idea and this, along with inadequate technical preparations, suggested that 'dollarization' was a desperate attempt to appeal to key business interests and to save his presidency. The President of the Central Bank, Pablo Better, resigned in protest: he claimed that the Bank could not support the proposed conversion rate of 25,000 sucres = US $1 and was angry that the independence of the Bank, established in the Constitution, had been so clearly violated.

A series of protests by Amerindian groups in January 2000 were given added significance by the support of sections of the military. This permitted thousands of protesters to occupy Congress on 21 January, following which the President of CONAIE, Antonio Vargas, and a group of army colonels decreed the end of Mahuad's presidency and the establishment of a new 'parliament of salvation'.

The episode revealed divisions within the military, as a group of politicized colonels were able to influence the position taken by the military high command. The Chief of Staff of the Armed Forces, Gen. Carlos Mendoza, had originally opposed any compromising of the constitutional order, but then agreed to join a short-lived ruling triumvirate with Vargas and a former Supreme Court president, Carlos Solorzano, before finally, on 22 January 2000, backing the transfer of power to former Vice-President Gustavo Noboa Bejeramo. However, both Mendoza and subsequently his successor as Chief of Staff of the Armed Forces, Gen. Telmo Sandoval, were replaced after revelations of their roles in the January coup.

PRESIDENT GUSTAVO NOBOA, 2000–

President Noboa embarked on a programme of reform at a rapid pace. One month following his accession to the presidency, Noboa secured congressional approval for the Ley de Transformación Económica (Economic Transformation Law), a significant economic reform programme which included dollarization, fiscal reform and an expanded policy of privatization. As a result of the Law and subsequent modifications governing interest rates, private debt restructuring and the timetable for adoption of Basel standards of capital adequacy for the banking sector, the IMF confirmed, in April 2000, a one-year stand-by agreement conditionally approving US $2,000m. in multilateral aid over the next two years.

Noboa also earned credibility for fighting corruption with his order, in late March 2000, to withdraw the EMELEC (Empresa de Electricidad del Ecuador) electric power concession for Guayaquil from Aspiazu Seminario, the disgraced former head of Banco del Progreso, and open it up for auction. The energetic start to Noboa's presidency restored some popularity to the office, though there remained a serious disillusionment with politicians, particularly as the Government attempted to implement free-market reform. CONAIE, which became more significant following its role in the removal of President Mahuad, continued to oppose dollarization and called for a referendum to dissolve Congress and the Supreme Court. CONAIE led demonstrations in order to protest against dollarization and a proposal to allow private participation in the social security system, as well as to demand amnesties for troops involved in the January coup.

In April 2000 the Government formally began the process of replacing the sucre with the US dollar as the unit of currency. Dollarization resulted in a stabilization of the exchange rate, a drop in interest rates and restored popular confidence, which was further enhanced by the release of 45% of small bank depositors' funds, frozen since March 1999. Some concessions to groups opposed to the Government's stabilization programme succeeded in diminishing popular discontent. The Government increased public-sector salaries while introducing a gradual programme of subsidy reductions. However, this did not prevent CONAIE from calling for mass demonstrations against the

Noboa Government in August to protest against proposed privatizations (see below) and dollarization. CONAIE entered into renewed negotiations with the Government in September after its actions of the previous month met with only moderate support.

Both the DP and the PSC performed well in municipal and provincial elections held in May 2000, even though the ID's Paco Moncayo won the mayoral election in Quito, suggesting significant popular acceptance of the structural reforms. In July the Government presented a second major reform package before Congress for approval, which included liberalization of rules governing private investment in health and social security, and of foreign investment in the oil, electricity and telecommunications sectors. A major threat to the Government's reform programme was the fragility of relations between the DP and the PSC. Relations came under increased strain in August when the independent Susana González was elected as President of Congress for the remaining two years of the current presidential term (until August 2002). González's defeat of the PSC's choice, Xavier Neira, was secured with the support of smaller left-wing parties. However, the vote was controversial and a Constitutional Tribunal was organized to determine the legality of the victory. The PSC claimed that, as the second largest party in Congress, its nominee should fill the position. In the same month Noboa's entire Cabinet offered to resign in what was interpreted as a gesture of support to the President in his difficulties with Congress. However, by the end of August the impasse between the Government and Congress was resolved when the Constitutional Tribunal ruled that a new election must be held and Congress subsequently elected Hugo Quevado of the PSC. (Quevado resigned in June 2001 following allegations of corruption and was replaced by José Cordero.) Institutional dysfunction again damaged popular perception of politics and threatened the democratic process.

Political tensions over the conditions imposed as part of the IMF stand-by agreement, particularly the increase in value-added tax (VAT), continued inside and outside government in 2000. The increase in oil revenues and the signing of contracts with foreign companies to invest in pipeline infrastructure made the political task of persuading Congress to accept fiscal and structural changes more difficult. In December the Minister of Finance and Public Credit, Luis Yturralde, resigned because he was opposed to the stringent conditions specified in the IMF agreement. He was replaced by Jorge Gallardo in January 2001. Under the terms of the IMF agreement, the Government pledged to reduce its deficit to 1.5% of GDP. Gallardo estimated that without the increase in VAT, the deficit would rise to 3.5%–4% of GDP. In February Ecuador made its first six-month interest payment on 30-year Global bonds, issued in September 2000 in the aftermath of Ecuador's default on its Brady bond payments.

Congressional opposition to plans to increase VAT continued to undermine the Government's ability to meet its commitments to the IMF to reduce the deficit. In April 2001 the 'Paris Club' of Western creditor nations suspended talks with the Government until the tax issue was resolved. The IMF followed suit shortly afterwards. In early May, the Government secured a 2% increase in VAT in an extraordinary congressional session. The victory for the Government resulted in the approval by the IMF of a US $48m. disbursement and an extension of the agreement to the end of 2001. However, there was still uncertainty amid a legal challenge from some legislators about the legitimacy of the tax increase. It was feared that a breakdown in the IMF agreement would also rule out the possibility of a further $500m. in finance from the World Bank and the IDB, set aside for bank restructuring, as well as a rescheduling of debt payments with the Paris Club.

Economy

SANDY MARKWICK

Based on an earlier essay by Prof. CLIFFORD T. SMITH

INTRODUCTION

Ecuador's population at mid-2000 was an estimated 12.6m., compared to 10.3m. at the 1990 census. During the 1960s and 1970s the population growth rate averaged over 3% annually. However, this slowed to an estimated 2.4% per year in the period 1990–98. The officially reported birth rate increased from 18.7 per 1,000 in 1990 to 35.7 per 1,000 in 1995, before falling to as low as 16.4 per 1,000 in 1998. At the same time, infant mortality declined and health standards, on the whole, improved. As a consequence, life expectancy increased steadily from 50 years in 1955–60, to an average of 68.5 years in 1990–95.

The annual growth rate of the economically active population was rising at a rate of 3.2% per year, marginally faster than population growth as a whole in the early 1990s, and in 1997 the total labour force was calculated at 3,373,810. The decrease in unemployment recorded in the early 1980s was not sustained and the unemployment rate was 9.0% during 2000. Underemployment was more extensive at an estimated 65.9%. The structure of employment underwent considerable change from the early 1970s. Agriculture was still the main source of employment, although its share was steadily declining as a result of internal migration, and labour shortages occurred in the rural sector. In 1999 26.5% of the work-force were employed in agriculture, including forestry and fishing, down from 62.6% in 1962.

Ecuador remained one of the poorer countries in South America, in terms of gross domestic product (GDP), despite the expansion in the petroleum sector enabling the country to enjoy a 7.5% annual average rate of increase in real GDP during the 1970s. However, it was problems in the petroleum sector and the international economic recession that meant a lower average rate of growth during the 1980s. In 1980–90 the annual average rate of increase in real GDP was 2.0%, contractions being registered in 1983 (world recession), 1987 (a petroleum price crisis and earthquake damage) and 1989 (government austerity measures). The performance of the economy during the 1990s was modest, with annual average real GDP growth of 2.2% in 1990–99. Agricultural exports led growth of 5.0% in 1991 and expansion of the extractive sector contributed to a 4.4% increase in real GDP in 1994, but otherwise GDP per head was largely stagnant. This trend continued in 1996–97, with real GDP growth averaging 3.2%. However, in 1998 real GDP growth fell by an estimated 0.4% as Ecuador felt the impact of the political crisis of 1997, along with a decline in world petroleum prices, Ecuador's principal source of foreign-exchange earnings. As social and political conflict worsened in 1998 and 1999 and the Government imposed severe austerity measures in an attempt to stabilize public finances, Ecuador plunged into economic crisis. Despite a slight recovery in the second half of the year, in 1999 real GDP contracted by 7.3%. The economy grew by an estimated 1.9% in 2000. The recovery was led by an increase in oil pipeline capacity leading to higher petroleum output.

Inflationary pressure only became a serious problem of economic management in the 1970s, when the prosperous petroleum market stimulated domestic demand and wage rises. During the 1980s inflation was increased by public-sector spending growth, currency devaluations and higher food prices. President León Febres Cordero succeeded in reducing annual inflation in 1984–86, to around 25%, but the acceleration in price rises resumed thereafter. By 1989 the average annual rate of inflation had risen to 76%, the highest level ever recorded in Ecuador. The average rate of inflation for 1990–99 was 37.4%, caused largely by weaknesses in the sucre and budget deficits. The Government of President Rodrigo Borja Cevallos was unable to maintain consistency in fiscal policy. The Government could not balance the demands of austerity, and the temptation to increase public spending was high. The last months leading to the 1992 presidential elections once again saw a relaxation of fiscal policies and lower-than-expected revenues. This resulted in an increase in both the public-sector deficit and in the monthly rate of inflation. The annual rate of inflation in 1992 increased to 54.6%. The Government of President Sixto Durán Ballén indicated its commitment to accelerating structural reform when it came to power in August 1992 by implementing an economic adjustment programme, intended to reduce inflation and the fiscal deficit, and to begin the reconstruction and privatization of the public sector. Policy was not helped by tensions between executive and legislative branches of government—thus, the President had to rely on increases in the price of fuel or in utility rates if Congress refused tax rises or impeded privatization. Nevertheless, inflation slowed in 1994, to 27.4%, the lowest annual rate since 1985.

In spite of extravagant campaign promises of increased subsidies and spending on basic services, which implied an abandonment of the fiscal caution that had reduced inflation from 60% to 23%, the short-lived Government of President Abdalá Bucaram Ortiz preferred continuity in macroeconomic policy after taking office in July 1996. However, the political crises of the Bucaram Government rendered it largely ineffective in dealing with the country's real economic difficulties, and even when Bucaram resigned, the Government of interim President Fabián Alarcón Rivera was soon subject to the same constraints. Popular opposition to economic reform dictated that policy was largely a case of crisis management, rather than the pursuit of essential, long-term economic objectives and, as a result, the rate of inflation increased to 30.6% in 1997. It had been hoped that the election of a new President in August 1998 would restore credibility to government planning, but the Government of Jamil Mahuad Witt immediately discovered that public opinion and the intransigence of the legislature made austerity measures virtually impossible to implement. The continuing depreciation of the sucre and falling revenue from petroleum exports resulted in a further increase in the rate of inflation, to 36.1%, in 1998.

Inflation rose to 52.2% in 1999, as a result of a large increase in the monetary base, fuelled by credit to rescue illiquid banks in the financial crisis that was affecting much of the region. Monetary growth saw the value of the sucre to the US dollar decline dramatically, further fuelling inflation. Fears of hyperinflation were a key reason for 'dollarization', the policy announced in January 1999 of replacing the sucre with the US dollar. In the month of the announcement of the policy prices rose by 14.3%, the highest monthly inflation rate on record, as producers and retailers passed on higher prices to customers. However, inflation subsequently stabilized as monetary expansion was reversed; nevertheless, the impact was still felt in 2000, when consumer prices rose by an annual average of 96.1%. President Gustavo Noboa Bejerano, who came to power following military-backed protests in January 2000, submitted structural reforms to Congress including reforms to support dollarization, fiscal reform and an accelerated programme of privatization. The successful implementation of the dollarization policy was expected to reduce inflation significantly by preventing the Central Bank from printing money to finance fiscal deficits. However, the reforms needed to implement dollarization faced obstacles in securing congressional approval because of political tensions between the parties. Meanwhile, inflation was expected to remain high even with the reforms, as they would take time to overcome the build up of inflationary pressures in the economy.

AGRICULTURE

Despite the importance of petroleum production to the Ecuadorean economy, agriculture (including fishing and forestry) in 1999 still accounted for about 50% of total exports. The agricultural sector employed an estimated 26.5% of the economically active population in 1999, more than any other sector. However, low levels of productivity and mechanization, and inadequate infrastructure, meant that agriculture, forestry and fishing contributed only 13.0% of GDP in both 1998 and 1999. The difficulty in securing financing for planting was behind the decline in agricultural output, particularly after adverse climatic conditions brought by the El Niño phenomenon (a periodic warming of the tropical Pacific Ocean), which was estimated to have cost the country some US $250m. in lost agricultural income in 1997–98. The sector declined by 1.3% in 1999 and despite a partial recovery in the first half of 2000, the annual performance was heading for stagnation.

Cocoa

About one-third of Ecuador's territory is put to agricultural use. The coast produced the main export crops: bananas, rice, coffee, cocoa, sugar and hemp. Cocoa, cultivated on coastal plantations, was first developed as an export crop in the 19th century and contributed up to three-quarters of Ecuador's exports, until disease and decreasing world demand affected production in the 1920s. The cocoa market revived during the 1980s, following the introduction of subsidies to encourage the processing of cocoa beans for export. Production reached a record level of 131,000 metric tons in 1985. The crop's vulnerability was demonstrated in 1987, when output decreased to 57,500 tons, as a result of climatic problems and demand fluctuations. By 1991 production had recovered to 100,400 tons. However, this improvement was not sustained. Cocoa exports were threatened by the December 1994 decision of the International Cocoa Organization (ICCO) to lower the aroma quality of Ecuadorean cocoa by 25%. In 1995 the sector embarked on a US $5.2m. European Union (EU)-financed project to improve quality and increase production. In 1996 there were approximately 350,000 ha of cocoa plantations under cultivation. Production in 1996 and 1997 increased to close to 100,000 tons, but 1998 production was affected dramatically by the flooding of coastal lowlands caused by El Niño, falling to less than 50,000 tons. Cocoa staged an equally dramatic recovery in 1999 to pre-El Niño levels of close to 100,000 tons, and continued to increase in 2000, to 136,000 tons. The value of cocoa exports declined by 28.4% in 2000 (from $106.3m. in 1999 to $76.2m.), again owing to a decline in the world price.

Bananas

Bananas succeeded cocoa as Ecuador's principal export crop in the 1940s, when the Central American plantations were affected by disease, hurricanes and labour problems. Banana exports were 2.9m. metric tons in 1970, but decreased during the next decade to a low point of 1.3m. tons in 1982. However, Ecuador regained its former position as the world's leading producer and exporter of bananas in 1985 and remained so in 2001. By 1988 exports had increased to 1.6m. tons, yielding US $298m. in revenue. In the early 1990s the banana industry continued to perform well, in spite of a threat from the EU (known as the European Community until November 1993) quota system, which came into effect on 1 July 1993 and granted trade preferences to banana imports from African, Caribbean and Pacific countries (for details, see the section on Bananas in Major Commodities of Latin America, in Part Three, and The Banana Trade Dispute in General Survey, Part One). Ecuadorean production expanded steadily from 3.5m. tons in 1991 to 5.4m. tons in 1995, setting new record levels each year as the acreage planted increased. Exports also performed well, reaching 2.6m. tons in 1993, the second highest level of sales ever, as Ecuador benefited from supply problems experienced by Central American and Caribbean producers and the Government made efforts to open new markets in Asia, Eastern Europe and the Middle East to counter the effect of the EU quota. However, fluctuations in world banana prices, particularly owing to the flooding of non-EU markets by Latin American producers, affected export revenues. Earnings from banana exports fell from $719.6m. in 1991 to $557.5m. in 1993, before recovering to $845.1m. in 1995 and increasing to a peak of $1,327m. in 1997. Export revenues from bananas then declined to $1,070m. in 1998 and $954.4m. in 1999. Banana exports declined by a further 14% in 2000, to $820.6m. This fall in export revenues was a result of lower international prices and came in spite a small increase in production volumes. In early 1999, following years of protests, initiated by Ecuador in 1995, the World Trade Organization (WTO) ruled that the EU's banana-import regime did not comply with international trade regulations. In April 2001 another step was taken to resolve the long-running dispute when the EU provided assurances to Ecuadorean producers over access to the EU market.

The main area of banana production was in the Guayas lowlands. However, new road construction and better irrigation extended the area under cultivation north and south of Guayaquil. Production expanded with the introduction of the disease-resistant and higher-yielding Cavendish variety of banana, which replaced the traditional Gros Michel variety. In contrast to the plantation-based production, typical of most banana cultivation elsewhere, the average size of banana holdings in Ecuador was only 50 ha, and one-half of the plantations were less than 10 ha in size. In the mid-1990s the rate of growth in the area harvested for bananas slowed. By 1995 the area harvested was 125,604 ha.

Coffee

Coffee actually overtook bananas as the most valuable export crop during the weather-ravaged year of 1983. Export earnings from coffee reached their highest point in 1986, at US $298.9m., only to decrease steadily thereafter, falling to $80m. in 1992. However, the long-awaited recovery in world coffee prices, aided by falling world supply and Ecuador's continued shift to higher-value varieties, raised coffee export value by 26%, to $101m., in 1993, despite an 8% fall in production. In January 1994 Ecuador adopted the plan to retain 20% of coffee production as agreed by the Association of Coffee Producing Countries, which had been formed in July 1993 by Latin American coffee producers. This retention plan was successful in increasing world coffee prices. Retention was reduced to 10% in April 1994 and then suspended in May. Coffee prices also improved when frosts damaged the Brazilian crop. Consequently, export earnings soared in 1994 to $414m. From 1994–99 export revenues from coffee declined steadily. Another retention plan was agreed in March 1995, after a further fall in prices. With coffee production down by one-fifth to 148,000 metric tons in that year, partly owing to a fall in the area under coffee cultivation and partly to poor yields, export revenues decreased to $243.9m. Coffee producers shifted to other crops with better prospects as the retention scheme failed to reinforce international prices and the industry's infrastructure was threatening to disintegrate. The majority of coffee plantations (63%) were more than 15 years old and 35% were between five and 15 years old. In 1996 both the area under cultivation and the yield increased, and production recovered to 191,000 tons. However, an abundant Brazilian harvest depressed prices and export earnings were just $159.1m. in that year. The adverse climatic conditions brought by El Niño in 1997 had a severe impact on the coffee crop. In 1998 Ecuador earned $105m. from coffee exports. Production of coffee remained depressed into 1999 in the aftermath of El Niño, with producers finding it difficult to finance replanting. Export earnings fell to $78m. and then declined by a further 42% to $45.3m. in 2000. There were belated signs of recovery in the sector in the latter half of 2000.

Other crops

Rice production increased steadily in the late 1980s and expanded rapidly after 1991, when Ecuador became self-sufficient. The area under cultivation, mainly located in the Guayas lowlands, totalled 396,000 ha by 1996. However, this figure decreased in 1997, to an unofficial 290,000 ha. Rice production was 781,000 metric tons in 1987 and had increased to 1,472,000 tons in 1997. An additional 106,000 ha was devoted to sugar-cane cultivation, and raw-sugar production totalled 319,000 metric tons in 1991, but decreased in 1992, leading to a decline in sugar exports. By the mid-1990s raw-sugar output had recovered, reaching 412,000 tons in 1996. After a decline in 1997 production increased thereafter, reaching 556,250 tons in 1999.

Cotton production was badly affected by drought in the late 1980s. Production recovered to 36,900 tons in 1990, but then declined year on year until it reached an estimated 6,000 metric tons in 1999. However, in 2000 output doubled to 12,000 tons. Falling international prices and rising production costs in the early 1990s had caused a 50% decrease in the area cultivated and, consequently, led to increased imports. When prices recovered in 1994, production did not expand immediately as the 1994 crop was sown at the end of 1993 and maize had been substituted for cotton. New agricultural products were being encouraged, including cut flowers, strawberries, mangoes, melons, asparagus, artichokes and cardamom. Exports of cut flowers grew particularly rapidly, with annual earnings rising from $526,000 in 1985 to $180m. in 1999.

In the Sierra the main crops were maize (in which Ecuador was self-sufficient, with a surplus for export), wheat and barley. However, Ecuador relied heavily on imports to meet the demand for wheat, usually satisfied by imports from the USA, and barley. The principal problem was the predominance of small-scale farming, largely for subsistence, on the economically unviable holdings of mainly Indian peasant communities. Structural problems notwithstanding, new crops were introduced to meet domestic demand, including soya and African palm, which substituted for imported vegetable oils. In 2000 soya production totalled 170,000 metric tons (more than double the previous year's crop).

FISHING

Fishing was one of the growth sectors of the Ecuadorean economy, although this was also affected by El Niño in 1997. The prospects of exploiting the rich and varied marine resources of Ecuador's offshore waters were responsible for the country's claims, made from the 1950s onwards, for an exclusive maritime zone within 200 nautical miles (370 km) of its coasts. By far the most dramatic expansion occurred in shrimp culture. The majority of the production came from farms in the Gulf of Guayaquil, which received substantial foreign investment. In 1986 Ecuador became the world's largest exporter of shrimps, selling mainly to the US market. However, low yields, decreasing world prices and increasing shipping costs severely affected exports in 1989. Although production recovered in 1990, with export volume rising to 57,500 metric tons, up 22% on the previous year, revenues increased by only 3.7%, to US $340m. As a result of the weak US dollar, successful efforts were made to diversify export markets, with sales to Europe, and especially to Spain, increasing. With the threat of a cholera outbreak in the shrimp sector remaining dormant in 1991, there was a considerable increase in export earnings, of 44%, to a record $491m. Although in 1992 shrimp farmers were badly affected by suspensions of power supplies as a result of drought and a manifestation of the El Niño phenomenon, export earnings reached $526m. Exports in 1993 were adversely affected, not only by rising costs and competition from Asia, but also by the Taura syndrome, a disease caused by fungicides used in the banana industry. Output was reduced by 16%, representing a $72m. loss in export revenue. However, measures to control or avoid the disease allowed exports to reach $539m. in 1994, up 14.5% on earnings in 1993 of $471m. Export revenue increased by 20.7% in 1995 to a new record of $673m. In 1996 there were positive signs that the sector was beginning to recover from power shortages in 1995, which affected the preservation of larvae, and the continuing problem of the Taura syndrome. Producers were pleased by the EU's decision to renew tariff preferences for Andean countries for three years, beginning in June 1996. Export revenues of $607m. in 1999, when shrimp production was damaged significantly by the Taura syndrome, represented a 30% decline from the $872m. earned in 1998. The sector continued to decline in 2000 with production down by an estimated 50%. Drastic measures to fight the virus included drying out farms. Shrimp export revenues were down 74% in the first quarter of 2000 compared to the same period in 1999. It is possible that shrimp production will never fully recover. Control of the disease requires significant investment and many producers have begun cultivating in other countries. Other exports included canned tuna, sardines, mackerel, anchovies and fishmeal. Non-canned fish earned $69m. in exports in 1999,

a decline from $83m. in 1998, while canned fish exports earned $263m. in 1999, up from $254m. in 1998.

MINING AND ENERGY

Conventional mining was little developed in Ecuador, contributing less than 1% of GDP, although the country's mineral resources include gold, silver, copper, sulphur, titanium, antimony, lead and zinc. Most metallic mining activity was centred on the Nambija gold deposits in the southern Oriente and on the deposits at Portovelo and Zaruma. In 1991 a new mining law was passed to give greater protection to domestic and foreign mining companies. It included the establishment of a new state company, Corporación de Desarrollo e Investigación Geológico-Minero-Metalúrgica (CODIGEM), which was to direct exploration and exploitation. Probably two-thirds of the gold and about one-half of the diamond production of Ecuador was usually lost to smugglers and did not feature in official production statistics. In 1995 production of gold and silver increased dramatically. However, efforts to expand mining production were hindered by corrupt business practices in the sector and government inertia in encouraging foreign investment. In October 1997 Rio Tinto, the world's largest mining group, announced that it would terminate its exploration programme in Ecuador because of delays in the issue of permits. Rio Tinto had acquired the Llano Largo gold prospect concession from BP Minerals in 1989 and subsequently invested considerable sums. The company had become frustrated as a result of anticipated delays in the issue of a permit for exploration on the El Alumbre prospect and thus decided to sell all or part of its concessions.

Energy consumption in Ecuador was dominated by petroleum and natural gas, although hydroelectricity production increased significantly in the late 1980s and early 1990s. Petroleum was produced along the Santa Elena peninsula, west of Guayaquil, from 1917, although the three oilfields still in operation in the area contributed less than 0.5% of total production in 1991. In 1967, after years of exploration, major petroleum reserves were discovered at Lago Agrio, in the Oriente region, by the US Texaco-Gulf consortium. In order to exploit the reserves, a trans-Andean pipeline was constructed, from Lago Agrio to a tanker terminal located off the port of Esmeraldas. Exports began in 1972, but production volumes varied quite considerably, according to economic and political circumstances. Ecuador joined the Organization of the Petroleum Exporting Countries (OPEC) in 1973 and adopted policies which discouraged investment and exploration. Consequently, proven reserves reached critically low levels and the state petroleum corporation, Corporación Estatal Petrolera Ecuatoriana (CEPE), became deeply in debt. Changes in the hydrocarbons law in 1983, to revive foreign interest, led to several petroleum companies signing contracts with CEPE in the mid-1980s and new discoveries were made in the south-east sector of the Oriente in 1987. OPEC-imposed production quotas were ignored as production was increased, in order to maximize revenues, at a time of decreasing petroleum prices and production disruptions.

In September 1989 a new, restructured state petroleum company, Petróleos del Ecuador (PETROECUADOR), was established, as a prelude to the centralization of control over the petroleum-production process. The following month, in accordance with agreements which stipulated that the State could assume control of joint ventures with one year's notice, the Government initiated the take-over of those parts of the industry controlled by foreign companies, including the trans-Andean pipeline. This was in keeping with the enlarged state role in the economy envisaged by President Borja, but was also seen as an attempt to deflect criticism from 100% increases in fuel prices. These increases were designed to assist exports by reducing domestic consumption and smuggling to neighbouring countries. However, declining export revenues in the early 1990s led to a reversal of the policy of foreign exclusion. In November 1992 the Durán administration relinquished Ecuador's full membership of OPEC, citing the organization's refusal to increase the country's output quota, and announced an ambitious production target of 576,000 barrels per day (b/d) by 1996, an increase of more than 55% over the 1992 figure. The introduction of a new foreign-investment code in January 1993 was aimed at liberalizing the petroleum sector and giving foreign companies greater access to the country's resources.

In the mid-1990s discoveries in the Amazon region almost tripled Ecuador's proven petroleum reserves and, subsequently, the Government signed contracts with numerous foreign companies for further drilling and exploration, including rights for areas in the eastern Amazon, which previously had been withheld as a result of indigenous and foreign environmental protest. However, although petroleum production increased from 341,774 b/d in 1993 to 386,725 b/d by 1995, this level of output still fell far short of government targets and further expansion of the industry was subject to innumerable constraints. Political uncertainties, principally caused by public antipathy to the reduction of state participation in the sector, led to long delays in the negotiation of contracts with foreign companies and potential investors were made wary by this inconsistency in policy and by the lack of infrastructure, which limited the potential for growth. Nevertheless, petroleum and its derivatives remained Ecuador's major exports: in 1996 some 84.4m. barrels of crude petroleum were exported, earning US $1,521m. in revenue. In 1997–99 petroleum production was adversely affected by continuing political instability and repeated industrial action by industry workers. Consequently, petroleum output, at 388,000 b/d in 1997 and 1998, had not increased since the discoveries of the eastern Amazon fields. In addition, world petroleum prices declined steadily over that time, which caused export revenues to fall substantially and deprived the sector of investment capital. Output increased during the 1990s, fuelled by both growing domestic consumption and exports. Ecuador exported 91m. barrels of crude petroleum in 1997 compared to 25m. barrels in 1992. Export earnings from petroleum and petroleum products declined, however, from $1,550m. in 1997 to $925m. in 1998. In 2000 86m. barrels of crude petroleum were exported, a 1.8% increase over 1999. Despite the stagnation in export volumes and nation-wide strikes in 1999, which reduced production, export revenues increased significantly, to $1,479.7m., in 1999 and by a further 65%, to $2,442.4m., in 2000. The increase in earnings stemmed from an increase in average price for the country's crude from $9.1 per barrel to $15.1 per barrel in 1999 and then up to $25.1 per barrel in 2000. In mid-1999 President Mahuad declared his Government's intention to encourage foreign investment and expand production to 800,000 b/d within six years. However, the success of this new initiative would be largely dependent on progress in improving industry infrastructure. Work to expand the capacity of the national Trans-Ecuadorean Oil Pipeline System (SOTE) from 350,000 b/d to 410,000 b/d was completed in July 2000. The expansion contributed to an increase in production by 8.2%, to 404,009 b/d, in 2000 compared with 373,405 b/d in 1999. Another proposed infrastructure project to boost Ecuador's petroleum sector was a second pipeline for heavy crudes (Oleoducto para Crudos Pesados—OCP). Following lengthy delays, the legislation was passed, allowing the participation of private investment, and technical studies were undertaken. In February 2001, the Government signed a contract with an international consortium (consisting of Agip of Italy, Alberta Energy of Canada, US companies Kerr-McGee and Occidental Petroleum, Techint of Argentina and the Spanish-Argentine company Repsol-YPF) to build the OCP. It was expected to take two years to complete the project. The design of the OCP was modified to expand its capacity to 450,000 b/d from its original capacity of 315,000 b/d.

There were large deposits of natural gas in the Gulf of Guayaquil, estimated at 6,100m. cu m of proven and 18,000m. cu m of probable reserves. Further deposits of gas were also associated with petroleum deposits in the Oriente. Plans existed for the exploitation of natural gas in the Gulf field, involving petrochemicals, plastics, fertilizers and synthetic protein. Imports were necessary to meet the national demand for gas. Ecuador had only limited refining capacity leading to government plans to restructure the sector and invite the participation of foreign companies to develop its reserves.

Energy use in Ecuador increased from 4,209,000 metric tons of oil equivalent in 1980 to 7,100,000 tons in 1998. Ecuador was a net exporter of energy, in 1998 exporting nearly twice the quantity of energy that was consumed domestically. Ecuador had much hydroelectric potential. In the late 1980s, operating through the state electrical company, Instituto Ecuatoriano de Electrificación (INECEL), the Government began to invest heavily in hydroelectric power, with the aim of producing 80% of its electricity from hydro sources. Up to 60% of Ecuador's electricity is now generated by the hydroelectric plant at Paute, east of Cuenca. Hydroelectric resources of the Guayas basin were being developed as part of a wider regional plan. A plant at Daule-Peripa, with a capacity of 200 MW, had started to produce electricity by 1998. Another plant, at Agoyn, had come into production in mid-1987. The decrease in the price of petroleum cast doubts over the advantages in creating new hydroelectric capacity and also caused financial difficulties for INECEL. The sector was repeatedly afflicted by supply problems, particularly concerning the Paute plant. Drought, heavy rains and mudslides resulted in the disruption of supply from the plant at various times in 1992–93, forcing the Government to introduce electricity rationing. Recurrent power failures in August and September 1994 were allegedly caused by a lack of maintenance at the plant, and in 1995 and 1997 drought again caused the plant to operate well below full capacity. In April 1999 the Government signed investment contracts, which, it was hoped, would alleviate power shortages in the future. Wärtsilä NSD (Finland) planned to construct a US $350m., 270-MW plant to generate electricity using residue from the state-owned Amazonas petroleum refinery, and Energy Development Corporation (USA) was to invest $170m. to extract natural gas from the Gulf of Guayaquil and pump it to a 240-MW generating plant on the mainland. The two plants were expected to supply the equivalent of some 28% of national demand in 2001.

MANUFACTURING

Industrialization began in the 1960s. However, the prosperous period for manufacturing came during the 1970s, when the adoption of import-substitution industrialization policies stimulated growth. Manufacturing production increased at an average annual rate of 9.5% in 1972–82, accounting for 19% of GDP in 1981. However, the subsequent economic recession ended sustained growth and, for the rest of the 1980s, output stagnated and even declined. Food processing, beverages, chemicals and metal products were particularly affected by President Febres Cordero's liberalization policies, and experienced a decline under his administration. In the 1990s the manufacturing sector recovered, largely owing to increasing consumer confidence and demand. The sector employed 11.2% of the total labour force at the time of the 1990 census. Manufacturing GDP increased by an annual average of 2.9% in 1991–98 and contributed 22.7% of GDP in 1999. The most important branches of manufacturing in 1997 were food, drink and tobacco products (accounting for 31.9% of the total), textiles, clothing and leather petroleum (20.7%), minerals and metals (13.1%) and paper and printing (8.0%). Growth, estimated at 2.6%, was restored to manufacturing in 2000.

Ecuador's industrial sector had a number of distinctive characteristics: it was highly concentrated geographically, with three-quarters of manufacturing enterprises situated in and around Quito and Guayaquil, despite many years of state encouragement for geographic diversification. Industrial development was heavily dependent on imports of capital goods, as well as raw or semi-finished goods. Nor did the industrial sector significantly contribute to export volumes. There was legislation offering tax incentives for new investment, with special emphasis on the encouragement of non-traditional industrial exports and efficient import substitution. In 1990 a *maquiladora* (assembly plant) programme was initiated as a result of Ecuador's inclusion in the Generalized System of Preferences. Since Ecuador's production costs were generally lower than those of its Andean trading partners, the Andean Pact offered great export opportunities. New markets stimulated growth in chemicals, minerals, paper and wood products and capital goods during the 1990s. Vehicle exports were the best performing category within the manufacturing sector in 2000. Export revenues from vehicles increased by 123%, to US $60.8m., in that year, compared with $27.2m. in 1999, as car manufacturers increased exports to neighbouring countries.

TRANSPORT

In 1997 the railway network covered 956 km (600 miles), but much of it required significant modernization and repair. Parts of the rail and road network, including the main Quito-Guayaquil and the Pan-American Highway, have been badly damaged by flooding associated with El Niño weather conditions, most recently in 1997–98. In March 1987 an earthquake caused damage to the roads and bridges linking Quito to Lago Agrio and the oilfields. Road traffic expanded steadily, from 76,000 motor vehicles in 1971 to 563,523 in 1998. Road building in the 1960s and 1970s opened up both the Oriente and the Costa for agriculture and settlement, but was given low priority thereafter. The road network was 43,197 km in length in 1999. In late 1998 several major projects were undertaken to repair roads damaged by the heavy rains and flooding brought about by El Niño.

The port of Guayaquil handled the vast majority of non-petroleum trade, but Puerto Bolívar, to the south, and Manta, Esmeraldas and San Lorenzo, to the north, were also important. Petroleum tankers could be handled at Balao and La Libertad, near Santa Elena. There were more than 200 airports, of which two, at Quito and Guayaquil, were international, and a number of domestic airlines, including Transportes Aéreos Militares Ecuatorianos (TAME), Sociedad Anónima Ecuatoriana de Transportes Aereos (SAETA) and Ecuatoriana.

TOURISM

Tourism has been a significant contributor to the national economy from the 1960s and became the country's fourth largest foreign exchange earner during the 1990s, behind petroleum, bananas and shrimps. In 1998, 32% of Ecuador's visitors came from Colombia, 6% from Peru, 10% from other Latin American countries, 22% from the USA and 21% from Europe. The number of tourists visiting Ecuador increased from 172,000 in 1975 to 510,627 in 1998. In 1998 tourism receipts were US $289m.

Until the early 1990s tourist promotion concentrated on attracting visitors to the Galápagos Islands, which, along with the Sangay National Park, in the Sierra region, have been awarded world natural heritage status by the UN Educational, Scientific and Cultural Organization (UNESCO). However, the development potential for 'Darwin's Islands', with their spectacular wildlife and ecology, was not infinite. Saturation point was being reached, with the number of visitors increasing from 12,000 in 1974 to an estimated 60,000 in 1993. Anxieties about environmental damage in the archipelago (generally accepted as primarily caused by the population needed to serve the tourist industry and by fishing in the area) were compounded by the potential environmental catastrophe of January 2001, when an oil tanker ran aground less than 1 km off the Islands and leaked almost 20,000 gallons of fuel oil into the sea. Favourable weather conditions limited the extent of the ecological damage, but the long-term effects of the spill were yet to be assessed.

FOREIGN INVESTMENT AND PLANNING

National planning was undertaken by the National Development Council (Consejo Nacional de Desarrollo—CONADE). However, co-ordination, with plans organized on a sectoral basis, was not always satisfactory and plans were undermined by political change and economic fluctuations. Regional planning was organized on an *ad hoc* basis, with projects designed to stimulate development, mainly by means of small-scale projects in agricultural extension, irrigation, colonization, artisan production and industrialization. Most provincial plans were poorly financed and largely unsuccessful. From 1970 a more ambitious programme of regional development was elaborated for the Guayas basin. This focused mainly on large-scale irrigation and hydroelectric power projects in the Babahoyo and Daule-Peripa valleys. A programme for the development of the dry southern provinces was also based on the concept of river-basin development and irrigation, in conjunction with Peru. Public investment, either directly through government ministries or through semi-autonomous organizations, became increasingly important with the benefit of petroleum revenues, particularly in the petroleum industry itself, but also in industrial development, electricity production, irrigation and transport. With the move toward free-market economics in the early 1990s, there was a greater emphasis on attracting private and foreign investment.

As Ecuador was a member of the Andean Group, foreign investment complied with the organization's legislation. The Febres Cordero administration relaxed certain regulations in order to attract foreign capital. Foreign participation up to 49% was allowed and the obligation upon foreign companies to become mixed or fully national was liberalized. Profit remittance limits were increased, from 20% to 30%, and the limit was waived for companies exporting 80% of their production and for those involved in the tourist industry. The Borja Government established two free-trade zones and revised the tariff system— both decisions conflicted with Andean Group membership. In June 1991 new direct foreign investment legislation was passed, including improved investment conditions for Andean Group members and opening up a number of sectors to foreign investors.

The Government of President Durán introduced a more accessible foreign-investment code in 1993 to replace the 1991 legislation. The new code opened up all sectors of the economy to foreign capital and sought to ensure that foreign investment would be treated in the same way as national capital. Prior government authorization for foreign investment was no longer required and profits could be freely repatriated and converted into foreign currencies. Foreign acquisition of domestic companies was facilitated by an assurance that all transfers of company shares would be automatically approved by the Government. All limits on profit remittances were removed, except for the mining sector, where a limit of 20% of capital stock remained. These measures, together with the Brady Plan agreed in May 1994 (see below), did much to reassure investors. Greater economic stability also increased investor confidence. However, high interest rates attracted short-term capital inflows rather than longer-term productive investment, and these were of an essentially unstable nature. A large amount of investment capital was transferred abroad when the conflict with Peru began in January 1995. This also reflected a drop in investor confidence in Latin America in general, owing to the dramatic devaluation of the Mexican peso in December 1994 (the 'tequila effect'), and the fact that successive governments in Ecuador had seemingly been powerless to prevent political instability caused by in-fighting and corruption scandals, and social unrest caused by economic adversity. The political and economic crises of 1997–2000 further damaged investor confidence. President Gustavo Noboa secured major reform in 2000 in the form of the Ley de Transformación Económica (Economic Transformation Law) to implement the dollarization policy, introduced by his predecessor, President Jamil Mahuad Witt, to support privatization plans. Dollarization, which replaced the sucre with the US dollar in March 2000, underlined the importance of stability and investor confidence as growth rates became directly linked to levels of foreign investment. The social and political climate remained a prime factor in attracting foreign investment.

DEBT

Ecuador began borrowing heavily from abroad during the 1970s, and accumulated substantial foreign debts. Beginning the decade at a modest US $242m., the debt increased steadily to reach $4,600m. by 1980. By 1979 the debt-service ratio (debt servicing compared with the total value of exports of goods and services) had risen to 38%. High interest rates and economic difficulties forced Ecuador to begin negotiations on debt rescheduling, and by 1984 agreement was reached on extending repayments over a 12-year period at favourable rates of interest. However, decreasing petroleum prices and the March 1987 earthquake (estimated to have cost $800m. in lost petroleum revenues) forced the Government to suspend repayments on the debt owed to commercial banks. The country's foreign debt continued to increase under President Febres Cordero, rising to $12,300m. by the end of 1988.

Ecuador resumed debt-service payments in June 1989 and by September a stand-by agreement had been reached with the IMF. However, in 1990 Ecuador was unable to comply with the IMF's fiscal targets and disbursements were suspended again. A further IMF facility, agreed in late 1991, was suspended when the Borja administration stopped all interest payments to commercial banks, because reserves had fallen to critical levels during the national elections. By 1993 total foreign debt had risen to US $14,110m., and Ecuador was again unable fully to meet principal and interest liabilities. In May 1994 agreement on the implementation of the Brady Plan (the initiative on debt relief originally proposed by the former US Treasury Secretary,

Nicholas Brady, in 1989) was finally reached with commercial-bank creditors and new deals with the IMF and the 'Paris Club' of creditor nations soon followed. However, plans to meet IMF targets of reducing inflation and balancing the public-sector budget were jeopardized in early 1995 by the costs of the conflict with Peru, estimated at over $500m., and a further rescheduling of Paris Club debt was necessary in that year. At the end of 1996 Ecuador's total external debt was $14,491m., of which $12,435m. was long-term public debt. Subsequently, the costs of repairing the damage caused by the El Niño weather phenomenon in 1997 and early 1998, along with rapidly declining revenues from petroleum exports and the depreciation of the sucre, precipitated a debt crisis. By the end of 1998 Ecuador's total foreign debt had reached $15,140m., but this stabilized in 1999 at $14,506m. In early 1999 negotiations with the IMF for a $400m. contingency facility, which was expected to release up to $1,200m. in multilateral loans, stalled repeatedly owing to political circumstances that prevented President Mahuad's Government from proceeding with privatization and fiscal reform. In May 1999 the pressure was eased by the release of $500m. in rapid-disbursement loans from the World Bank, the Inter-American Development Bank and the Andean Development Corporation. However, negotiations on the rescheduling of Paris Club debt could not begin until the IMF facility was activated and, in September 1999, the Ecuadorean Government became the first in the world to announce a default on Brady bond and Eurobond obligations. The new Government of President Noboa negotiated a stand-by agreement with the IMF in April 2000, following the passage of economic reforms through Congress in March. The IMF was to provide $2,000m. in aid over a two-year period. The IMF agreement was expected to help encourage wary creditors to take part in much-needed debt restructuring negotiations to reduce Ecuador's debt burden to manageable levels. However, there were doubts that the Government would fulfil its tax reform commitments to the IMF, including an increase in value-added tax (VAT) to 15%. Failure to secure tax reforms could undermine IMF support and any chance of a renegotiation of the Paris Club debt.

FOREIGN TRADE

After becoming a petroleum exporter, Ecuador's foreign-trade balance was generally in surplus. Petroleum accounted for almost 70% of export earnings until petroleum prices decreased. In 1986 petroleum's contribution to the total fell to 45%. It demonstrated the vulnerability of the Ecuadorean economy to international price fluctuations and world demand for its export income. The recovery of petroleum exports, import controls and low domestic demand resulted in a return to trade surplus, which, by 1990, was $852.6m., owing to higher world petroleum prices. The surplus declined in 1991, despite a strong rise in banana and shrimp exports, to $452.8m., owing to a decrease in petroleum revenues and a sharp rise in imports, following the Government's trade liberalization programme and higher domestic demand. Successive administrations attempted to diversify the export base through a series of export promotion and credit insurance measures. Commodities targeted for special encouragement were cut flowers, fresh vegetables and soft fruits. Between 1990 and 1994 earnings from non-traditional exports almost doubled and their share of the total rose from 6.8% to 17.8%. In the early part of the 1990s the share of exports going to Latin America, especially within the Andean Pact, and Asia rose, while that going to the USA fell. Ecuador remained dependent on the US market, however, with 37.0% of its total exports going there in 1999. In the mid-1990s Ecuador continued with efforts to increase economic integration with neighbouring countries. For example, agreements with Colombia and Brazil promised to increase transport infrastructure links. Greater regional integration would, ultimately, be in Ecuador's long-term trading interests. By 1996 Ecuador's trade surplus had increased to $1,220m., but this surplus fell back to $598m. in the following year, and in 1998 an exceptional deficit of $995m. was recorded, a result of the damage to agricultural exports caused by El Niño and the collapsing value of petroleum. A record trade surplus was restored in 1999 (amounting to $1,665m.), when imports slumped by 50% owing to the depreciation of the sucre, lack of financing and low aggregate demand. The trade surplus declined in 2000 to $1,457m. Despite a deficit in service, the current account balance registered a surplus of $1,223m. in 2000.

CONCLUSION

The modernization of Ecuador was greatly accelerated by its rich petroleum resources. Petroleum revenues made possible dramatic improvements to education, public health, irrigation, hydroelectric power, road building, urban construction and industrialization. However, unstable world petroleum prices and limited reserves suggested that the country had to prepare for a post-petroleum future. Commercial agriculture, especially in the coastal zone, was not neglected, but much of the Sierra still had a traditional structure of poverty-stricken peasant farming and backward *latifundia* (landed estates). Inequalities of wealth and income increased in the cities as well as in the countryside, even though average GDP per head generally rose. In the late 1990s and the early years of the 21st century political problems revealed that among the country's main impediments were legislative paralysis and government inconsistency.

Statistical Survey

Sources (unless otherwise stated): Banco Central del Ecuador, Quito; Ministerio de Industrias, Comercio, Integración y Pesquería, Quito; Instituto Nacional de Estadística y Censos, 10 de Agosto 229, Quito; tel. (2) 519-320; internet www.inec.gov.ec.

Area and Population

AREA, POPULATION AND DENSITY

Area (sq km)	272,045*
Population (census results)†	
28 November 1982	8,060,712
25 November 1990	
Males	4,796,412
Females	4,851,777
Total	9,648,189
Population (official estimates at mid-year)†	
1998	12,174,628
1999	12,411,232
2000	12,646,095
Density (per sq km) at mid-2000	46.5

* 105,037 sq miles.

† Figures exclude nomadic tribes of indigenous Indians. Census results also exclude any adjustment for underenumeration, estimated to have been 5.6% in 1982 and 6.3% in 1990.

PROVINCES (official estimates, mid-1999)*

	Population	Capital
Azuay	617,247	Cuenca
Bolívar.	180,035	Guaranda
Cañar	214,820	Azogues
Carchi	165,132	Tulcán
Cotopaxi	302,177	Latacunga
Chimborazo . . .	422,676	Riobamba
El Oro	548,121	Machala
Esmeraldas . . .	407,555	Esmeraldas
Guayas	3,346,804	Guayaquil
Imbabura . . .	325,475	Ibarra
Loja	425,490	Loja
Los Ríos	652,078	Babahoyo
Manabí	1,249,073	Portoviejo
Morona Santiago . .	139,531	Macas
Napo	155,375	Tena
Pastaza	60,527	Puyo
Pichincha	2,409,712	Quito
Sucumbíos	139,371	Nueva Loja
Tungurahua . . .	440,771	Ambato
Zamora Chinchipe . .	100,281	Zamora
Archipiélago de Colón		Puerto Baquerizo (Isla
(Galápagos) . . .	16,184	San Cristóbal)
Total	**12,318,435**	

* Figures exclude persons in unspecified areas, totalling 92,797.

PRINCIPAL TOWNS (estimated population at mid-1997)

Guayaquil . .	1,973,880		Manta. . .	156,981	
Quito (capital) .	1,444,363*		Eloy Alfaro . .	127,832*	
Cuenca . .	255,028		Quevedo . .	120,640	
Machala . .	197,350		Milagro . .	119,371	
Santo Domingo de			Esmeraldas .	117,722	
los Colorados .	183,219		Loja . .	117,365	
Portoviejo . .	167,956		Riobamba . .	114,322*	
Ambato . .	160,302		Ibarra . .	113,791*	

* Population at mid-1996.

Source: UN, *Demographic Yearbook*.

BIRTHS, MARRIAGES AND DEATHS*
(excluding nomadic Indian tribes)

	Registered live births		Registered marriages		Registered deaths	
	Number	Rate (per 1,000)	Number	Rate (per 1,000)	Number	Rate (per 1,000)
1994 . .	350,838	31.3	71,289	6.4	51,165	4.6
1995 . .	408,983	35.7	70,480	6.2	50,867	4.4
1996 . .	302,217	25.8	72,094	6.2	52,300	4.5
1997 . .	288,803	24.2	66,967	5.6	52,089	4.4
1998 . .	199,079	16.4	n.a.	n.a.	54,357	4.5

* Registrations incomplete.

Sources: Instituto Nacional de Estadística y Censos; UN, *Demographic Yearbook*.

Expectation of life (UN estimates, years at birth, 1990-95): 68.5 (males 66.4, females 71.4) (Source: UN, *World Population Prospects: The 1998 Revision*).

ECONOMICALLY ACTIVE POPULATION*
(ISIC Major Divisions, 1990 census)

	Males	Females	Total
Agriculture, hunting, forestry and fishing	904,701	131,011	1,035,712
Mining and quarrying . . .	18,849	2,021	20,870
Manufacturing	248,157	122,181	370,338
Electricity, gas and water. . .	10,741	1,919	12,660
Construction.	192,034	4,682	196,716
Trade, restaurants and hotels .	295,855	180,875	476,730
Transport, storage and communications . . .	123,807	7,277	131,084
Financing, insurance, real estate and business services . .	54,043	27,314	81,357
Community, social and personal services	483,821	354,308	838,129
Activities not adequately defined .	111,919	45,811	157,730
Total labour force	**2,443,927**	**877,399**	**3,321,326**

* Figures refer to persons aged 8 years and over, excluding those seeking work for the first time, totalling 38,441 (males 27,506; females 10,935).

1997: Total employed 3,062,185; Total unemployed 311,625; Total labour force 3,373,810.

Agriculture

PRINCIPAL CROPS ('000 metric tons)

	1998	1999	2000
Wheat	20	19	22
Rice (paddy)	1,043	1,290	1,520
Barley	36	34	38
Maize	382	568	747
Potatoes	534	563	788
Cassava (Manioc)	74	125	184
Dry beans	30	31	47
Soybeans (Soya beans)	10	77	170
Seed cotton	10	6	12
Coconuts	23	22	37
Palm kernels	45	28	33
Tomatoes	65	62	71
Pumpkins, squash and gourds*	40	41	41
Sugar cane	7,000*	7,864	6,200*
Apples	25	12	19
Oranges	122	122	157
Other citrus fruits	39	52	111
Pineapples	80	124	101
Mangoes	69	21	125
Avocados	24	21	24
Bananas	4,563	6,392	6,816
Plantains	466	658	476
Papayas	68	112	89
Coffee (green)	48	133	133
Cocoa beans	35	95	136

* FAO estimate(s).

Source: FAO.

LIVESTOCK ('000 head)

	1998	1999	2000
Cattle	5,076	5,106	5,110
Sheep	2,081	2,180	2,130
Pigs	2,708	2,786	2,870
Horses*	520	521	521
Goats	280	284	284
Asses*	268	269	269
Mules*	157	157	157
Poultry	100,233	130,200	130,200

* FAO estimates.

Source: FAO.

LIVESTOCK PRODUCTS ('000 metric tons)

	1998	1999	2000
Beef and veal	158	164	174
Mutton and lamb	6	8	6
Pig meat	100	110	108
Goat meat	1	1	2
Poultry meat	108	146	148
Cows' milk	1,983	1,994	1,996
Sheep's milk	6	6	6
Goats' milk	2	2	2
Butter	5	5	5*
Cheese	7	7	7
Hen eggs	60	55	57
Wool: greasy	2*	2*	2
Cattle hides (fresh)	32	33	35

* FAO estimate.

Source: FAO.

Forestry

ROUNDWOOD REMOVALS ('000 cubic metres, excluding bark)

	1997	1998	1999
Sawlogs, veneer logs and logs for sleepers	5,168	5,168	5,168
Pulpwood	682	682	682
Other industrial wood	70	70	70
Fuel wood	5,420	5,420	5,420
Total	11,340	11,340	11,340

Source: FAO, *Yearbook of Forest Products*.

SAWNWOOD PRODUCTION
('000 cubic metres, including railway sleepers)

	1997	1998	1999
Coniferous (softwood)	416	416	416
Broadleaved (hardwood)	1,663	1,663	1,663
Total	2,079	2,079	2,079

Source: FAO, *Yearbook of Forest Products*.

Fishing

('000 metric tons, live weight)

	1996	1997	1998
Capture	703.0	549.0	310.0
Chilean jack mackerel	56.8	30.3	25.9
South American pilchard	356.5	57.2	1.0
Red-eye round herring	34.3	1.1	8.9
Pacific thread herring	41.0	43.1	40.5
Pacific anchoveta	26.4	89.2	44.5
Skipjack tuna	37.5	67.4	67.5
Yellowfin tuna	19.3	19.6	31.1
Bigeye tuna	17.9	26.1	17.9
Chub mackerel	79.5	192.2	44.7
Aquaculture	108.7	135.3	146.6
Blue shrimp	10.0	13.3	14.4
Whiteleg shrimp	97.9	119.4	129.6
Total catch	811.7	684.3	456.6

Source: FAO, *Yearbook of Fishery Statistics*.

Mining

	1994	1995	1996
Crude petroleum ('000 metric tons)	17,391	20,100	19,243
Natural gas (petajoules)	15	15	26
Natural gasoline ('000 metric tons)	43	42*	42
Gold-bearing ores (kilograms)†	13,000	15,500	17,700

* Provisional or estimated figure.
† Estimated gold content (data from the US Bureau of Mines).

1997 (estimated figures): Natural gas (petajoules) 24; Gold-bearing ores (kilograms) 17,700.

Source: UN, *Industrial Commodity Statistics Yearbook*.

Industry

SELECTED PRODUCTS ('000 metric tons, unless otherwise indicated)

	1994	1995	1996
Jet fuels.	181	239	253
Kerosene	80	89	78
Motor spirit (gasoline)	1,302	1,567	1,937
Distillate fuel oils	1,533	1,562	1,812
Residual fuel oils	2,999	3,059	3,215
Liquefied petroleum gas	253	374	440
Crude steel	22	29	21
Cement	2,085	2,459	2,930
Electric energy (million kWh)	8,163	8,349	9,260

Source: partly UN, *Industrial Commodity Statistics Yearbook.*

Finance

CURRENCY AND EXCHANGE RATES

Monetary Units
United States currency is used: 100 cents = 1 US dollar ($).

Sterling and Euro Equivalents (30 April 2001)
£1 sterling = US $1.4318;
€1 = 88.76 US cents;
US $100 = £69.84 = €112.66.

Note: Ecuador's national currency was formerly the sucre. From 13 March 2000 the sucre was replaced by the US dollar, at an exchange rate of $1 = 25,000 sucres. Both currencies were officially in use for a transitional period of 180 days, but from 9 September sucres were withdrawn from circulation and the dollar became the sole legal tender. Some figures in this Survey are still in terms of sucres. The average exchange rate of sucres per dollar was: 5,446.6 in 1998; 11,786.8 in 1999; 24,988.4 in 2000.

BUDGET (million sucres)

Revenue	1992	1993	1994
Petroleum revenue	1,537,698	2,069,852	2,345,187
Tax revenue	68,627	31,197	42,965
Non-tax revenue	1,469,071	2,038,655	2,302,222
Price increases on petroleum by-products for internal consumption	470,993	851,920	1,172,573
For export	998,078	1,186,735	1,129,649
Non-petroleum revenue	1,570,059	2,162,669	3,138,030
Tax revenue	1,368,994	2,034,925	2,808,630
External trade	274,413	392,470	606,631
Exports	—	—	—
Imports	274,413	392,470	606,631
Domestic taxes	1,094,581	1,642,455	2,201,999
Income tax	253,415	331,231	503,864
Taxes on financial transactions.	66,246	43,013	110,576
Taxes on production and consumption	744,757	1,152,491	1,495,902
Other taxes	30,163	115,720	91,657
Non-tax revenue	201,065	127,744	329,400
Transfers	22,034	82,051	164,426
Total	3,129,791	4,314,572	5,647,643

Expenditure	1992	1993	1994
General services	736,416	1,144,175	1,679,092
Education and culture	605,075	746,993	1,066,535
Social welfare and labour.	43,092	99,421	134,697
Health and community development	200,421	202,593	319,470
Farming and livestock development	88,631	146,023	230,227
Natural and energy resources	14,121	31,323	47,144
Industry and trade	43,041	25,507	33,674
Transport and communications	126,629	327,585	446,366
Public debt interest	473,826	500,841	898,153
Other purposes	216,730	539,389	677,075
Total	2,547,982	3,763,850	5,532,433

Source: Banco Central del Ecuador.
1995 ('000 million sucres): Total revenue 8,030.4; Total expenditure 8,450.6.
1996 ('000 million sucres): Total revenue 10,633.9; Total expenditure 10,916.7.

1997 ('000 million sucres): Total revenue 13,515.3; Total expenditure 14,680.5.
1998 ('000 million sucres): Total revenue 17,866.6; Total expenditure 17,492.3.
1999 ('000 million sucres): Total revenue 31,884.4; Total expenditure 33,051.5.
Source (for 1995–99): IMF, *International Financial Statistics.*

INTERNATIONAL RESERVES (US $ million at 31 December)

	1998	1999	2000
Gold*	166.7	166.4	114.1
IMF special drawing rights	0.3	2.3	0.3
Reserve position in IMF	24.2	23.5	22.3
Foreign exchange	1,595.3	1,616.5	924.3
Total	1,786.5	1,808.7	1,061.0

* National valuation (US $403 per troy ounce at 31 December 1998; $402 per ounce at 31 December 1999; $275 per ounce at 31 December 2000).
Source: IMF, *International Financial Statistics.*

MONEY SUPPLY (US $ million at 31 December)

	1998	1999	2000
Currency outside banks	426.6	576.3	31.7
Demand deposits at deposit money banks.	729.0	614.9	996.7
Total money*	1,330.7	1,338.0	1,335.7

* Includes private-sector deposits at the Central Bank.
Source: IMF, *International Financial Statistics.*

COST OF LIVING
(Consumer Price Index; annual averages for middle- and low-income families in urban area; base: 1990 = 100)

	1996	1997	1998
Food (excl. beverages)	597.8	813.8	1,146.4
Fuel and light	313.2	502.8	961.8
Clothing (incl. footwear)	523.1	642.7	788.5
Rent	903.5	1,118.1	1,331.6
All items (incl. others)	648.8	847.4	1,153.1

1999: Food (excl. beverages) 1,574.1; All items 1,749.1.
Source: ILO, *Yearbook of Labour Statistics.*

NATIONAL ACCOUNTS

Expenditure on the Gross Domestic Product
('000 million sucres at current prices)

	1996	1997	1998
Government final consumption expenditure	7,146	9,147	12,524
Private final consumption expenditure	38,791	53,153	75,610
Increase in stocks	−300	902	3,938
Gross fixed capital formation	10,798	15,053	22,550
Statistical discrepancy	−1	—	—
Total domestic expenditure	56,436	78,255	114,622
Exports of goods and services	18,514	23,711	27,170
Less Imports of goods and services	14,223	22,926	34,371
GDP in purchasers' values	60,727	79,040	107,421
GDP at constant 1975 prices	219	227	228

Source: IMF, *International Financial Statistics.*

Gross Domestic Product by Economic Activity
('000 million sucres at current prices)

	1997	1998	1999
Agriculture, hunting, forestry and fishing	9,556.5	12,941.5	19,606.6
Petroleum and other mining	6,968.8	6,064.7	18,451.7
Manufacturing	16,878.4	23,501.0	34,290.8
Electricity, gas and water	215.4	302.5	441.3
Construction	3,667.5	5,289.7	7,295.8
Trade	15,655.5	21,691.4	29,632.2
Transport	7,359.8	10,259.9	15,109.3
Financial services	4,330.3	6,042.1	8,954.2
Government services	9,862.0	13,612.4	17,387.3
Sub-total	74,494.2	99,705.2	151,169.0
Adjustments	4,545.8	7,715.8	10,181.4
GDP in purchasers' values	79,040.0	107,421.0	161,350.3

BALANCE OF PAYMENTS (US $ million)

	1997	1998	1999
Exports of goods f.o.b.	5,264	4,203	4,451
Imports of goods f.o.b.	−4,666	−5,198	−2,786
Trade balance	598	−995	1,665
Exports of services	826	808	812
Imports of services	−1,459	−1,531	−1,304
Balance on goods and services	−35	−1,718	1,173
Other income received	102	82	49
Other income paid	−1,172	−1,309	−1,368
Balance on goods, services and income	−1,105	−2,945	−146
Current transfers received	438	840	1,151
Current transfers paid	−47	−64	−50
Current balance	−714	−2,169	955
Direct investment from abroad	625	814	690
Other investment liabilities	829	1,300	53
Net errors and omissions	−477	−352	−2,024
Overall balance	263	−407	−326

Source: IMF, *International Financial Statistics*.

External Trade

PRINCIPAL COMMODITIES (distribution by SITC, US $ million)

Imports c.i.f.	1996	1997	1998
Food and live animals	308.7	359.2	582.2
Cereals and cereal preparations	134.4	139.7	221.5
Wheat and meslin (unmilled)	86.0	88.3	88.4
Crude materials (inedible) except fuels	128.0	143.4	154.8
Mineral fuels, lubricants, etc.	165.6	385.2	335.4
Petroleum, petroleum products, etc.	53.1	299.0	247.4
Refined petroleum products	47.8	257.8	183.0
Kerosene and other medium oils	15.1	206.4	139.3
Gas (natural and manufactured)	112.3	86.1	87.6
Liquefied petroleum gases, etc.	111.6	86.1	87.5
Chemicals and related products	700.0	820.1	880.2
Organic chemicals	94.0	106.0	93.9
Medicinal and pharmaceutical products	173.3	206.9	235.8
Medicaments (incl. veterinary)	138.0	166.8	196.2
Artificial resins, plastic materials, etc.	120.6	144.7	141.2
Products of polymerization, etc.	93.8	113.2	108.1
Disinfectants, insecticides, fungicides, etc.	81.5	104.6	112.6
Basic manufactures	738.5	778.5	930.4
Paper, paperboard and manufactures	124.1	108.7	132.4
Paper and paperboard (not cut to size or shape)	100.6	82.0	103.5
Textile yarn, fabrics, etc.	65.4	86.4	110.1
Non-metallic mineral manufactures	82.4	83.0	107.8
Iron and steel	262.3	237.2	297.5
Ingots and other primary forms	84.8	65.4	79.2
Machinery and transport equipment	1,323.3	1,624.9	1,934.3
Power-generating machinery and equipment	133.5	167.1	179.3
Machinery specialized for particular industries	167.6	179.2	260.4
General industrial machinery, equipment and parts	231.0	282.3	318.0
Telecommunications and sound equipment	89.6	235.9	216.3
Other electrical machinery, apparatus, etc.	160.0	183.0	284.5
Road vehicles and parts*	440.6	454.1	494.2
Passenger motor cars (excl. buses)	218.1	222.4	186.2
Motor vehicles for goods transport and special purposes	121.0	147.1	170.7
Goods vehicles (lorries and trucks)	114.4	139.3	149.6
Miscellaneous manufactured articles	301.0	338.9	416.2
Total (incl. others)	3,733.0	4,510.7	5,502.8

* Data on parts exclude tyres, engines and electrical parts.

Exports f.o.b.	1996	1997	1998
Food and live animals . . .	2,415.1	2,953.0	2,586.1
Fish, crustaceans and molluscs .	871.0	1,155.1	1,190.7
Fresh, chilled or frozen fish . .	87.4	102.5	85.7
Fresh, chilled, frozen, salted or dried crustaceans and molluscs	631.4	874.5	853.9
Prepared or preserved fish, crustaceans and molluscs .	151.0	176.5	250.3
Prepared or preserved fish	150.3	175.0	243.7
Vegetables and fruit . .	1,054.4	1,420.0	1,169.5
Fresh or dried fruit and nuts (excl. oil nuts) . . .	985.1	1,331.8	1,080.4
Bananas and plantains .	973.0	1,327.0	1,070.2
Coffee, tea, cocoa and spices . .	324.3	246.8	152.4
Coffee and coffee substitutes .	159.1	114.1	104.4
Coffee (incl. husks and skins) and substitutes containing coffee	129.1	86.3	71.3
Unroasted coffee, husks and skins	129.0	86.3	71.2
Cocoa	157.5	126.3	42.9
Crude materials (inedible) except fuels	160.8	194.4	197.1
Cut flowers and foliage . . .	99.1	119.1	144.6
Mineral fuels, lubricants, etc. .	1,776.1	1,550.0	925.2
Petroleum, petroleum products, etc.	1,776.1	1,550.0	925.2
Crude petroleum oils, etc. . .	1,520.8	1,404.3	791.3
Refined petroleum products .	216.5	118.0	107.7
Gas oils (distillate fuels) .	185.6	117.4	106.7
Basic manufactures . . .	187.9	190.5	154.8
Machinery and transport equipment	87.5	106.0	97.1
Non-monetary gold (excl. ores and concentrates) . .	127.4	65.2	15.0
Total (incl. others) . . .	4,889.8	5,214.2	4,141.1

Source: UN, *International Trade Statistics Yearbook*.

PRINCIPAL TRADING PARTNERS (US $ million)

Imports c.i.f.	1996	1997	1998
Argentina	81.2	90.4	135.7
Aruba	4.4	80.9	33.2
Belgium-Luxembourg . .	64.5	46.4	62.4
Brazil	142.6	134.0	196.5
Canada	49.5	52.3	102.7
Chile	135.2	152.1	200.8
China, People's Republic . .	0.8	45.3	65.3
Colombia	378.5	478.9	591.5
France (incl. Monaco) . .	34.6	81.1	47.7
Germany	155.5	188.2	228.2
Italy	98.1	124.5	157.2
Japan	209.8	263.0	493.7
Korea, Republic	60.2	61.5	101.7
Mexico	197.7	149.9	155.7
Netherlands	49.8	49.2	57.7
Panama	97.1	112.3	179.9
Peru	40.4	59.7	98.3
Russian Federation . . .	19.6	35.6	67.2
Spain	170.1	161.1	112.2
Switzerland-Liechtenstein .	40.0	37.5	36.6
United Kingdom	45.7	54.3	63.9
USA	1,174.1	1,376.3	1,617.5
Venezuela	172.6	301.9	259.3
Total (incl. others) . . .	3,733.0	4,510.6	5,502.8

Exports f.o.b.	1996	1997	1998
Argentina	84.1	76.0	76.3
Belgium-Luxembourg . . .	108.2	98.9	88.8
Chile	220.5	237.9	137.7
China, People's Republic . . .	67.1	157.3	51.9
Colombia	300.5	352.1	274.3
El Salvador	53.5	76.1	39.3
France (incl. Monaco) . .	82.9	87.6	93.6
Germany	176.0	204.0	128.4
Italy	195.4	271.4	254.6
Japan	138.7	155.7	122.8
Korea, Republic	314.4	171.4	95.2
Mexico	57.7	41.8	46.4
Netherlands	77.4	86.7	80.7
Panama	211.7	175.0	128.0
Peru	53.3	222.8	201.4
Russia	82.5	141.2	112.5
Spain	133.2	127.5	136.2
United Kingdom	125.1	94.3	60.5
USA	1,851.5	1,992.0	1,609.4
Venezuela	72.4	49.8	57.7
Total (incl. others) . . .	4,889.8	5,214.1	4,141.0

Source: mainly UN, *International Trade Statistics Yearbook*.

1999 (US $ million): Total imports c.i.f. 3,017.3; Total exports f.o.b. 4,451.0. (Source: IMF, *International Financial Statistics*.)

Transport

RAILWAYS (traffic)

	1994	1995	1996
Passenger-kilometres (million) .	20	14	11
Net ton-kilometres (million) .	9	3	1

Source: UN, *Statistical Yearbook*.

ROAD TRAFFIC (motor vehicles in use at 31 December)

	1996	1997	1998
Passenger cars	464,902	483,897	495,060
Buses and coaches	8,688	8,504	9,910
Lorries and vans	43,942	41,327	55,249
Road tractors	2,959	2,930	3,304

Source: IRF, *World Road Statistics*.

SHIPPING
Merchant Fleet (registered at 31 December)

	1998	1999	2000
Number of vessels	167	174	171
Total displacement ('000 grt) . .	171.3	309.3	300.9

Source: Lloyd's Register of Shipping, *World Fleet Statistics*.

International Sea-borne Freight Traffic ('000 metric tons)

	1988*	1989*	1990
Goods loaded	8,402	10,020	11,783
Goods unloaded	2,518	2,573	1,958

* Source: UN, *Monthly Bulletin of Statistics*.

CIVIL AVIATION (traffic on scheduled services)

	1995	1996	1997
Kilometres flown (million) . .	15	15	23
Passengers carried ('000) . .	1,671	1,925	1,791
Passenger-km (million) . .	1,591	1,663	2,035
Total ton-km (million) . .	174	181	235

Source: UN, *Statistical Yearbook*.

Tourism

FOREIGN VISITOR ARRIVALS*

Country of residence	1996	1997	1998
Chile	13,417	15,740	14,349
Colombia	159,091	164,859	165,596
France	16,389	16,494	16,034
Germany	21,421	20,363	21,701
Peru	34,795	33,543	29,821
Spain	11,755	12,545	12,306
United Kingdom	12,152	12,321	12,051
USA	104,978	124,924	113,155
Venezuela	12,056	12,148	12,255
Total (incl. others) . . .	493,727	529,492	510,627

* Figures refer to total arrivals (including same-day visitors), except those of Ecuadorean nationals residing abroad.

Tourism receipts (US $ million): 252 in 1994; 255 in 1995; 281 in 1996.

Source: World Tourism Organization, *Yearbook of Tourism Statistics*.

Communications Media

	1995	1996	1997
Radio receivers ('000 in use) . .	3,800	4,000	4,150
Television receivers ('000 in use)	1,100	1,500	1,550
Mobile cellular telephones . .	49,776	59,852	160,061
Daily newspapers	24	29	n.a.
Telephones ('000 main lines in use)	748	857	899

Source: mainly UNESCO, *Statistical Yearbook*.

Telefax stations: 30,000 in use in 1996 (Source: UN, *Statistical Yearbook*).

Education

(1996/97)

	Teachers	Pupils/ Students
Pre-primary	9,980	156,772
Primary	74,601	1,888,172
Secondary:		
General	62,630*	765,073†
Teacher-training	258‡	802*
Vocational	13,949§	279,189*
Higher‖	12,856	206,541

* 1992/93 figure. † 1994/95 figure.
‡ 1980/81 figure. § 1985/86 figure.
‖ 1990/91 figures.

1997/98: Pre-primary teachers 10,992; Pre-primary pupils 167,582; Pre-primary schools 4,009.

In 1996/97 there were 17,367 primary schools.

Source: UNESCO, *Statistical Yearbook*.

Directory

The Constitution

The 1945 Constitution was suspended in June 1970. In January 1978 a referendum was held to choose between two draft Constitutions, prepared by various special constitutional committees. In a 90% poll, 43% voted for a proposed new Constitution and 32.1% voted for a revised version of the 1945 Constitution. The new Constitution came into force on 10 August 1979. In November 1997 a National Constituent Assembly was elected for the purpose of reviewing the Constitution, and a new Constitution, which retained many of the provisions of the 1979 Constitution, came into force on 10 August 1998. The main provisions of the Constitution are summarized below:

CHAMBER OF REPRESENTATIVES

The Constitution of 1998 states that legislative power is exercised by the Chamber of Representatives, which sits for a period of 60 days from 10 August. The Chamber is required to set up four full-time Legislative Commissions to consider draft laws when the House is in recess. Special sessions of the Chamber of Representatives may be called.

Representatives are elected for four years from lists of candidates drawn up by legally recognized parties. Twelve are elected nationally; two from each Province with over 100,000 inhabitants, one from each Province with fewer than 100,000; and one for every 200,000 citizens or fractions of over 150,000. Representatives are eligible for re-election.

In addition to its law-making duties, the Chamber ratifies treaties, elects members of the Supreme and Superior Courts, and (from panels presented by the President) the Comptroller-General, the Attorney-General and the Superintendent of Banks. It is also able to overrule the President's amendment of a bill that it has submitted for Presidential approval. It may reconsider a rejected bill after a year or request a referendum, and may revoke the President's declaration of a state of emergency. The budget is considered in the first instance by the appropriate Legislative Commission and disagreements are resolved in the Chamber.

PRESIDENT

The presidential term is four years (starting from 15 January of the year following his election), and there is no re-election. The President appoints the Cabinet, the Governors of Provinces, diplomatic representatives and certain administrative employees, and is responsible for the direction of international relations. In the event of foreign invasion or internal disturbance, the President may declare a state of emergency and must notify the Chamber, or the Tribunal for Constitutional Guarantees if the Chamber is not in session.

As in other post-war Latin-American Constitutions, particular emphasis is laid on the functions and duties of the State, which is given wide responsibilities with regard to the protection of labour; assisting in the expansion of production; protecting the Indian and peasant communities; and organizing the distribution and development of uncultivated lands, by expropriation where necessary.

Voting is compulsory for every Ecuadorean citizen who is literate and over 18 years of age. An optional vote has been extended to illiterates (under 15% of the population by 1981). The Constitution guarantees liberty of conscience in all its manifestations, and states that the law shall not make any discrimination for religious reasons.

The Government

HEAD OF STATE

President: Gustavo Noboa Bejerano (assumed office on 26 January 2000).

Vice-President: Pedro Pinto Rubianes.

CABINET
(August 2001)

Minister of National Defence: Adm. HUGO UNDA AGUIRRE.

Minister of the Interior: JUAN MANRIQUE MARTINEZ.

Minister of Foreign Affairs: Dr HEINZ MOELLER FREILE.

Minister of Finance and Public Credit: JORGE GALLARDO.

Minister of Foreign Trade, Industrialization and Fishing: RICHARD MOSS.

Minister of Labour and Social Action: MARTÍN INSUA-CHANG.

Minister of Energy and Mines: PABLO TERÁN RIBADENEIRA.

Minister of Agriculture: GALO PLAZA PALLARES.

Minister of Urban Development and Housing: NELSON MURGUEYTIO PEÑAHERRERA.

Minister of Education and Culture: ROBERTO HANSSE SALEM.

Minister of Public Health: FERNANDO BUSTAMENTE.

Minister of the Environment: LOURDES DUQUE DE JARAMILLA.

Minister of Tourism: ROCÍO VÁSQUEZ.

Minister of Public Works and Communications: JOSÉ MACHIAVELLO.

Minister of Social Welfare: RAÚL PATIÑO ARCOA.

The following are, *ex officio*, members of the Cabinet: the National Secretary of Administrative Development, the Co-ordinator of the Social Expenditure Fund (FISE), the State Comptroller-General, the State Procurator-General, the Chairman of the National Monetary Board, the General Manager of the State Bank, the General Manager of the Central Bank, the Secretary-General of the National Planning Council (CONADE), the President of the National Financial Corporation, the President of the National Modernization Council (CONAM), the Presidential Private Secretary, the Subsecretary-General of Public Administration and the Presidential Press Secretary.

MINISTRIES

Office of the President: Palacio Nacional, García Moreno 1043, Quito; tel. (2) 216-300.

Office of the Vice-President: Manuel Larrea y Arenas, Edif. Consejo Provincial de Pichincha, 21°, Quito; tel. (2) 504-953; fax (2) 503-379.

Ministry of Agriculture: Avda Eloy Alfaro y Amazonas, Quito; tel. (2) 504-433; fax (2) 564-531.

Ministry of Education and Culture: Mejía 322, Quito; tel. (2) 216-224; fax (2) 580-116.

Ministry of Energy and Mines: Juan León Mera y Orellana, 5°, Quito; tel. (2) 550-041; fax (2) 550-018; e-mail menergia2@andinanet.net.

Ministry of the Environment: Avda Eloy Alfaro y Amazonas, edificio M.A.G., Quito; tel. (2) 563-487; fax (2) 563-487; e-mail mma@ambiente.gov.ec.

Ministry of Finance and Public Credit: Avda 10 de Agosto 1661 y Jorge Washington, Quito; tel. (2) 544-500; fax (2) 530-703.

Ministry of Foreign Affairs: Avda 10 de Agosto y Carrión, Quito; tel. (2) 230-100; fax (2) 564-873; e-mail webmast@mmrree.gov.ec; internet www.mmrree.gov.ec.

Ministry of Foreign Trade, Industrialization and Fishing: Avda Eloy Alfaro y Amazonas, Quito; tel. (2) 527-988; fax (2) 503-549.

Ministry of the Interior: Espejo y Benalcázar, Quito; tel. (2) 580-970; fax (2) 442-771.

Ministry of Labour and Social Action: Clemente Ponce 255 y Piedrahita, Quito; tel. (2) 566-148; fax (2) 503-122; e-mail mintrab@accessinter.net.

Ministry of National Defence: Exposición 208, Quito; tel. (2) 216-150; fax (2) 569-386.

Ministry of Public Health: Juan Larrea 444, Quito; tel. (2) 529-163; fax 569-786; e-mail msp@accessinter.net; internet www.msp.gpv.ec.

Ministry of Public Works: Avda Juan León Mera y Orellana, Quito; tel. (2) 222-749; fax (2) 223-077.

Ministry of Urban Development and Housing: Avda 10 de Agosto 2270 y Corotero, Quito; tel. (2) 238-060; fax (2) 566-785.

Ministry of Tourism: Quito; **tel.** (2) 540-920; fax (2) 255-172.

Office for Public Administration: Palacio Nacional, García Morena 1043, Quito; tel. (2) 515-990.

President and Legislature
PRESIDENT*
Elections of 31 May and 12 July 1998

Candidate	% of votes cast in first ballot	% of votes cast in second ballot
JAMIL MAHUAD WITT (DP)	35.2	51.2
ALVARO NOBOA PONTÓN (PRE)	26.5	48.8
RODRIGO BORJA CEVALLOS (ID)	15.6	—
FREDDY EHLERS ZURITA (MNPP)	14.3	—
ROSHAUA ARTEAGA SERRANO (MIRA)	5.1	—
Total (incl. others).	100.0	100.0

* President Mahuad was deposed in a coup on 21 January 2000; the erstwhile Vice-President, Gustavo Noboa Bejerano, was sworn in as Ecuador's new President on 26 January.

CONGRESO NACIONAL
Cámara Nacional de Representantes

President: JOSÉ CORDERO.

Election, 31 May 1998

Political parties	Seats
Democracia Popular (DP)	32
Partido Social Cristiano (PSC)	27
Partido Roldosista Ecuatoriano (PRE)	24
Izquierda Democrática (ID)	18
Movimiento Nuevo País-Pachakutik (MNPP)	9
Frente Radical Alfarista (FRA)	5
Partido Conservador (PC)	3
Movimiento Popular Democrático (MPD)	2
Concentración de Fuerzas Populares (CFP)	1
Total	121

Political Organizations

Acción Popular Revolucionaria Ecuatoriana (APRE): centrist; Leader Lt-Gen. FRANK VARGAS PAZZOS.

Coalición Nacional Republicana (CNR): Quito; f. 1986; fmrly Coalición Institucionalista Demócrata (CID).

Concentración de Fuerzas Populares (CFP): Quito; f. 1946; Leader GALO VAYAS; Dir Dr AVERROES BUCARAM SAXIDA.

Democracia Popular (DP): Calle Luis Saá 153 y Hnos Pazmiño, Casilla 17-01-2300, Quito; tel. (2) 547-654; fax (2) 502-995; f. 1978 as Democracia Popular-Unión Demócrata Cristiana; Christian democrat; Leader Lic. ABSALÓN ROCHA.

Frente Radical Alfarista (FRA): Quito; f. 1972; liberal; Leader IVÁN CASTRO PATIÑO.

Izquierda Democrática (ID): Polonia 161, entre Vancouver y Eloy Alfaro, Quito; tel. (2) 564-436; fax (2) 569-295; f. 1977; absorbed Fuerzas Armadas Populares Eloy Alfaro—Alfaro Vive ¡Carajo! (AVC) (Eloy Alfaro Popular Armed Forces—Alfaro Lives, Damn It!) in 1991; Leader RODRIGO BORJA CEVALLOS; National Dir ANDRÉS VALLEJO.

Movimiento Independiente para una República Auténtica (MIRA): Quito; f. 1996; Leader Dra ROSALIA ARTEAGA SERRANO.

Movimiento Nuevo País-Pachakutik (MNPP): Quito; represents indigenous, environmental and social groups; Leader FREDDY EHLERS ZURITA.

Movimiento Popular Democrático (MPD): Maoist; Leader (vacant).

Partido Comunista Marxista-Leninista de Ecuador: Sec.-Gen. CAMILO ALMEYDA.

Partido Conservador (PC): Wilsón 578, Quito; tel.(2) 505-061; f. 1855; incorporated Partido Unidad Republicano in 1995; centre-right; Leader SEXTO DURÁN BALLÉN.

Partido Demócrata (PD): Quito; Leader Dr FRANCISCO HUERTA MONTALVO.

Partido Liberal Radical (PLR): Quito; f. 1895; held office from 1895 to 1944 as the Liberal Party, which subsequently divided into various factions; perpetuates the traditions of the Liberal Party; Leader CARLOS JULIO PLAZA A.

Partido Republicano (PR): Quito; Leader GUILLERMO SOTOMAYOR.

Partido Roldosista Ecuatoriano (PRE): Quito; f. 1982; populist; Dir ABDALÁ BUCARAM ORTIZ.

Partido Social Cristiano (PSC): Carrión 548 y Reina Victoria, Casilla 9454, Quito; tel. (2) 544-536; fax (2) 568-562; f. 1951; centre-right party; Pres. JAIME NEBOT SAADI; Leaders LEÓN FEBRES CORDERO RIVADENEIRA, Lic. CAMILO PONCE GANGOTENA, Dr HEINZ MOELLER FREILE, Lic. PASCUAL DEL CIOPPO ARAGUNDI.

Partido Socialista-Frente Amplia (PS-FA): Avda Gran Colombia y Yaguachi, Quito; tel. (2) 221-764; fax (2) 222-184; f. 1926; Pres. Dr MANUEL SALGADO TAMAYO.

Unión Alfarista-FRA: Quito; f. 1998; centrist; Leader CÉSAR VERDUGA VÉLEZ.

The following guerrilla groups are active:

Grupo de Combatientes Populares (GCP): claims to defend human rights and to fight poverty.

Montoneros Patria Libre (MPL): f. 1986; advocates an end to authoritarianism.

Partido Maoísta-Comunista 'Puka Inti': Sec.-Gen. RAMIRO CELI.

Diplomatic Representation

EMBASSIES IN ECUADOR

Argentina: Avda Amazonas 22-147 y Roca, 8°, Quito; tel. (2) 562-292; fax (2) 568-177; e-mail embarge2@andinanet.net; Ambassador: HERNÁN HIPÓLITO CORNEJO.

Belgium: Juan León Mera 23-103 y Wilson, Apdo. 17-21-532, Quito; tel. (2) 545-340; e-mail quito@diplobel.org; Ambassador: ROBERT VANREUSEL.

Bolivia: Avda Eloy Alfaro 2432 y Fernando Ayarza, Casilla 17-210003, Quito; tel: (2) 446-652; fax (2) 244-033; e-mail emboliviaquito@rree.gov.bo; Chargé d'affaires a.i.: CARLOS ANTONIO BARRIENTOS TERÁN.

Brazil: Avda Amazonas 1429 y Colón, Apdo 231, Quito; tel. (2) 563-846; fax (2) 509-468; e-mail ebrasil@uio.satnet.net; Ambassador: VERA PEDROSA MARTINS DE ALMEIDA.

Canada: Edif. Josueth Gonzales, Avda 6 de Diciembre 28-16 y Paul Rivet, 4°, Apdo 17-11-65-12, Quito; tel. (2) 506-162; e-mail quito@dfait-maeci.gc.ca; Ambassador: JOHN G. KNEALE.

Chile: Edif. Xerox, 4°, Juan Pablo Sanz y Amazonas, Quito; tel. (2) 249-403; e-mail embchile@waccom.nt.com; Ambassador: RODRIGO ASENJO ZEGERS.

China, People's Republic: Avda Atahualpa y Amazonas, Quito; tel. (2) 458-927; fax (2) 444-364; e-mail embchina@uio.telconet.net; Ambassador: LIU JUNXIU.

Colombia: Edif. Arista, Avda Colón 1133 y Amazonas, 7°, Apdo 17-07-9164, Quito; tel. (2) 228-926; Ambassador: ELISEO RESTREPO LONDOÑO.

Costa Rica: Rumipamba 692 y República, 2°, Apdo 17-03-301, Quito; tel. (2) 254-945; e-mail embajcr@uio.satnet; Ambassador: LUZ ARGENTINA CALDERÓN DE AGUILAR.

Cuba: Mercurio 365, entre La Razón y El Vengador, Quito; tel. (2) 456-936; fax (2) 430-594; Chargé d'affaires a.i.: FÉLIX RAÚL ROJAS CRUZ.

Dominican Republic: Edif. Albatros, Avda de los Shyris 1240 y Portugal, 2°, Apdo 17-01-387-A, Quito; Ambassador: RAFAEL JULIAN CEDANO.

Egypt: Edif. Araucaria, 9°, Baquedano 222 y Reina Victoria, Apdo 9355, Sucursal 7, Quito; tel. (2) 235-046; Ambassador: NAPOLEON THABET ABDUL-RAHIM.

El Salvador: Avda Republica de El Salvador 733 y Portugal, 201°, Quito; tel. (2) 433-670; Ambassador: RAFAEL A. ALFARO.

France: Plaza 107 y Avda Patria, Apdo 536, Quito; tel. (2) 560-789; fax (2) 566-424; e-mail francie@uio.satnet.net; Ambassador: SERGE PINOT.

Germany: Edif. Citiplaza, 14°, Avda Naciones Unidas y República de El Salvador, Casilla 17-17-536, Quito; tel. (2) 970-820; fax (2) 970-815; e-mail alemania@interactive.net.ec; Ambassador: WALTER NOCKER.

Guatemala: Edif. Gabriela III, Avda República de El Salvador 733 y Portugal, Apdo 17-03-294, Quito; tel. (2) 459-700; Ambassador: LUIS PEDRO QUEZADA.

Holy See: (Apostolic Nunciature), Avda Orellana 692, Apdo 17-07-8980, Quito; tel. (2) 505-200; fax (2) 564-810; e-mail nunapec@impsat.net.ec; Apostolic Nuncio: Most Rev. ALAIN PAUL LEBEAUPIN, Titular Archbishop of Vico Equense.

Honduras: Avda 12 de Octubre 1942 y Cordero, Apdo 17-03-4753, Quito; tel. (2) 223-985; Chargé d'affaires a.i.: HUMBERTO LÓPEZ VILLAMIL.

Israel: Edif. Plaza 2000, Avda 12 de Octubre y Fco. Salazar, Apdo 17-21-08, Quito; tel. (2) 237-474; e-mail isremuio@uio.telconet.net; Ambassador: YOSHEP HASEEN.

Italy: Calle La Isla 111 y Humberto Alborñoz, Casilla 17-03-72, Quito; tel. (2) 561-077; fax (2) 502-818; e-mail ambital@ambitalquito.org; Ambassador: PAOLO LEGNAIOLI.

Japan: Juan León Mera 130 y Avda Patria, 7°, Quito; tel. (2) 561-899; fax (2) 503-670; e-mail japembec@uio.satnet.net; Ambassador: MASANORI TODA.

Korea, Republic: Edif. Citiplaza, 8°, Avda Naciones Unidas y Avda de El Salvador, Quito; tel. (2) 970-625; fax (2) 970-630; e-mail ecemco@interactive.net.ec; Ambassador: PIL-JOO SUNG.

Mexico: Avda 6 de Diciembre 4843 y Naciones Unidas, Casilla 17-11-6371, Quito; tel. (2) 457-820; fax (2) 448-245; e-mail embmxec@uio.satnet.net; Ambassador: MANUEL MARTINEZ DEL SOBRAL.

Netherlands: Edif. WTC, 1°, Avda 12 de Octubre 1942 y Cordero, Quito; tel. (2) 229-230; fax (2) 567-917; e-mail holgui@ibm.net; internet www.embajadadeholanda.com/embassy.html; Ambassador: MAARTEN M. VAN DER GAAG.

Panama: Edif. Posada de las Artes, 3°, Diego de Almagro 1550 y Pradera, Apdo 17-07-9017, Quito; tel. (2) 565-234; fax (2) 566-449; e-mail pmaemecu@interactive.net.ec; Ambassador: ARMANDO TERÁN MORALES.

Paraguay: Avda Gaspar de Villarroel 2013 y Amazonas, Casilla 139A, Quito; tel. (2) 245-871; fax (2) 251-446; e-mail embapar@uiotelconet.net; Ambassador: Dr CARLOS VILLAGRA MARSAL.

Peru: Avda República de El Salvador 495 e Irlanda, Quito; tel. (2) 468-410; fax (2) 252-560; e-mail embpeecu@uio.satnet.net; Ambassador: OSCAR MAURTUA DE ROMAÑA.

Russia: Reina Victoria 462 y Roca, Quito; tel. (2) 561-361; e-mail embrusia@accessinter.net; Ambassador: GIORGII P. KOROLIOV.

Slovakia: Gen. Francisco Salazar 459 y Coruña, Quito.

Spain: La Pinta 455 y Amazonas, Casilla 9322, Quito; tel. (2) 237-132; e-mail embespec@uio.satnet.net; EDUARDO CERRO GODINHO.

Switzerland: Edif. Xerox, 2°, Juan Pablo Sanz 120 y Amazonas, Casilla 17-11-4815, Quito; tel. (2) 434-948; fax (2) 449-314; Ambassador: PETER VON GRAFFENRIED.

United Kingdom: Edif. Citiplaza, 14°, Avda Naciones Unidas y República de El Salvador, Casilla 17-01-314, Quito; tel. (2) 970-800; fax (2) 970-809; e-mail britembq@impsat.net.ec; internet www.britembquito.org.ec; Ambassador: IAN GERKEN.

USA: Avda 12 de Octubre y Patria 120, Quito; tel. (2) 562-890; fax (2) 502-052; internet www.usis.org.ec; Ambassador: GWEN C. CLARE.

Uruguay: Edif. Josueth González, 9°, Avda 6 de Diciembre 2816 y James Orton, Casilla 17-12-282, Quito; tel. (2) 563-762; fax (2) 563-763; e-mail emburugl@emburuguay.int.ec; Ambassador: DUNCAN B. CROCI DE MULA.

Venezuela: Avda Los Cabildos 115, Apdo 17-01-688, Quito; tel. (2) 268-636; fax (2) 502-630; e-mail embavenecua@interactive.net.ec; Ambassador: CARLOS RODOLFO SANTIAGO MARTÍNEZ.

Yugoslavia: Gen. Francisco Salazar 958 y 12 de Octubre, Quito; tel. (2) 526-218; Ambassador: SAMUILO PROTIĆ.

Judicial System

Attorney-General: RAMON JIMÉNEZ.

Supreme Court of Justice: Palacio de Justicia, Avda 6 de Diciembre y Piedrahita 332, Quito; tel. (2) 900-424; fax (2) 900-425; e-mail dni-cnj@access.net.ec; internet www.justiciaecuador.gov.ec; f. 1830; Pres. GALO PICO MANTILLA.

Higher or Divisional Courts: Ambato, Azogues, Babahoyo, Cuenca, Esmeraldas, Guaranda, Guayaquil, Ibarra, Latacunga, Loja, Machala, Portoviejo, Quito, Riobamba and Tulcán; 90 judges.

Provincial Courts: there are 40 Provincial Courts in 15 districts; other courts include 94 Criminal; 219 Civil; 29 dealing with labour disputes; 17 Rent Tribunals.

Special Courts: National Court for Juveniles.

Religion

There is no state religion but more than 90% of the population are Roman Catholics. There are representatives of various Protestant Churches and of the Jewish faith in Quito and Guayaquil.

CHRISTIANITY

The Roman Catholic Church

Ecuador comprises four archdioceses, 11 dioceses, seven Apostolic Vicariates and one Apostolic Prefecture. At 31 December 1999 there were an estimated 12,205,117 adherents in the country, equivalent to some 93.1% of the population.

Bishops' Conference: Conferencia Episcopal Ecuatoriana, Avda América 1805 y La Gasca, Apdo 17-01-1081, Quito; tel. (2) 524-568; fax (2) 501-429; e-mail confepec@uio.satnet.net; f. 1939 (statutes approved 1999); Pres. JOSÉ MARIO RUIZ NAVAS, Archbishop of Portoviejo.

Archbishop of Cuenca: VICENTE RODRIGO CISNEROS DURÁN, Arzobispado, Calle Bolívar 7-64, Apdo 01-01-0046, Cuenca; tel. (7) 831-651; fax (7) 844-436; e-mail dicuenca@confep.org.ec.

Archbishop of Guayaquil: JUAN IGNACIO LARREA HOLGUÍN, Arzobispado, Calle Clemente Ballén 501 y Chimborazo, Apdo 09-01-0254, Guayaquil; tel. (4) 322-778; fax (4) 329-695.

Archbishop of Portoviejo: JOSÉ MARIO RUIZ NAVAS, Arzobispado, Avda Universitaria, Apdo 24, Portoviejo; tel. (5) 630-404; fax (5) 634-428; e-mail arzobis@ecua.net.ec.

Archbishop of Quito: Cardinal ANTONIO JOSÉ GONZÁLEZ ZUMÁRRAGA, Arzobispado, Calle Chile 1140 y Venezuela, Apdo 17-01-00106, Quito; tel. (2) 284-429; fax (2) 580-973.

The Anglican Communion

Anglicans in Ecuador are under the jurisdiction of Province IX of the Episcopal Church in the USA. The country is divided into two dioceses, one of which, Central Ecuador, is a missionary diocese.

Bishop of Littoral Ecuador: Rt Rev. ALFREDO MORANTE, Calle Bogotá 1010, Barrio Centenario, Apdo 5250, Guayaquil.

Bishop of Central Ecuador: Rt Rev. JOSÉ NEPTALÍ LARREA MORENO, Apdo 17-11-6165, Quito; e-mail ecuacen@uio.satnet.net.

The Baptist Church

Baptist Convention of Ecuador: Casilla 3236, Guayaquil; tel. (4) 384-865; Pres. Rev. HAROLT SANTE MATA; Sec. JORGE MORENO CHAVARRÍA.

The Methodist Church

Methodist Church: Evangelical United Church, Rumipamba 915, Casilla 17-03-236, Quito; tel. (2) 456-714; fax (2) 529-933; 800 mems, 2,000 adherents.

BAHÁ'Í FAITH

National Spiritual Assembly of the Bahá'ís: Apdo 869A, Quito; tel. (2) 563-484; e-mail ecua9nsa@uio.satnet.net; mems resident in 1,121 localities.

The Press

PRINCIPAL DAILIES
Quito

El Comercio: Avda Pedro Vicente Maldonado 11515 y el Tablón, Casilla 17-01-57, Quito; tel. (2) 670-999; fax (2) 670-466; e-mail elcomercio@elcomercio.com; internet www.elcomercio.com; f. 1906; morning; independent; Proprs Compañía Anónima El Comercio; Pres. GUADALUPE MANTILLA DE ACQUAVIVA; circ. 160,000.

Hoy: Avda Occidental N71-345, Casilla 17-07-09069, Quito; tel. (2) 490-888; fax (2) 491-881; e-mail hoy@edimpres.com.ec; internet www.hoy.com.ec; f. 1982; morning; independent; Dir BENJAMÍN ORTIZ BRENNAN; Man. JAIME MANTILLA ANDERSON; circ. 72,000.

El Tiempo: Avda América y Villalengua, Apdo 3117, Quito; f. 1965; morning; independent; Proprs Editorial La Unión, CA; Pres. ANTONIO GRANDA CENTENO; Editor EDUARDO GRANDA GARCÉS; circ. 35,000.

Ultimas Noticias: Avda Pedro Vicente Maldonado 11515 y el Tablón, Casilla 17-01-57, Quito; tel. (2) 670-999; fax (2) 674-923; f. 1938; evening; independent; commercial; Proprs Compañía Anónima El Comercio; Dir DAVID MANTILLA CASHMORE; circ. 60,000.

Guayaquil

Expreso: Avda Carlos Julio Arosemena, Casilla 5890, Guayaquil; tel. (4) 201-100; fax (4) 200-291; f. 1973; morning; independent; Dir GALO MARTÍNEZ MERCHÁN; circ. 60,000.

El Extra: Avda Carlos Julio Arosemena, Casilla 5890, Guayaquil; tel. (4) 201-100; fax (4) 200-291; f. 1975; morning; Pres. ERROL CARTWRIGHT BETANCOURT; Gen. Man. GALO MARTÍNEZ MERCHÁN; circ. 200,000.

La Razón: Avda Constitución y las Americas, Casilla 5832, Guayaquil; tel. (4) 280-100; fax (4) 285-110; f. 1965; morning; independent; Propr ROBERTO ISAÍAS DASSUM; Dir JORGE E. PÉREZ PESANTES; circ. 35,000.

La Segunda: Calle Colón 526 y Boyacá, Casilla 6366, Guayaquil; tel. (4) 320-635; fax (4) 320-539; f. 1983; morning; Propr CARLOS MANSUR; Dir VICENTE ADUM ANTÓN; circ. 60,000.

El Telégrafo: Avda 10 de Agosto 601 y Boyacá, Casilla 415, Guayaquil; tel. (4) 326-500; fax (4) 323-265; e-mail cartas@telegrafo.com.ec; internet www.telegrafo.com.ec; f. 1884; morning; independent; commercial; Proprs El Telégrafo CA; Dir Dr ROBERTO HANZE SALEM; circ. 45,000 (weekdays), 55,000 (Sundays).

El Universo: Avda Domingo Comín y Alban, Casilla 09-01-531, Guayaquil; tel. (4) 490-000; fax (4) 491-034; e-mail editores@telconet.net; internet www.eluniverso.com; f. 1921; morning; independent; Pres. FRANCISCO PÉREZ FEBRES CORDERO; Dir CARLOS PÉREZ PERASSO; circ. 174,000 (weekdays), 290,000 (Sundays).

There are local daily newspapers of low circulation in other towns.

PERIODICALS
Quito

La Calle: Casilla 2010, Quito; f. 1956; weekly; politics; Dir CARLOS ENRIQUE CARRIÓN; circ. 20,000.

Cámara de Comercio de Quito: Avda Amazona y República, Casilla 202, Quito; tel. (2) 443-787; fax (2) 435-862; f. 1906; monthly; commerce; Pres. ANDRÉS PÉREZ ESPINOSA; Exec. Dir ARMANDO TOMASELLI; circ. 10,000.

Carta Económica del Ecuador: Toledo 1448 y Coruña, Apdo 3358, Quito; f. 1969; weekly; economic, financial and business information; Pres. Dr LINCOLN LARREA B.; circ. 8,000.

El Colegial: Calle Carlos Ibarra 206, Quito; tel. (2) 216-541; f. 1974; weekly; publ. of Student Press Association; Dir WILSON ALMEIDA MUÑOZ; circ. 20,000.

Ecuador Guía Turística: Mejía 438, Of. 43, Quito; f. 1969; fortnightly; tourist information in Spanish and English; Propr Prensa Informativa Turística; Dir JORGE VACA O.; circ. 30,000.

Integración: Solano 836, Quito; quarterly; economics of the Andean countries.

Letras del Ecuador: Casa de la Cultura Ecuatoriana, Avda 6 de Diciembre, Casilla 67, Quito; f. 1944; monthly; literature and art; non-political; Dir Dr TEODORO VANEGAS ANDRADE.

El Libertador: Olmedo 931 y García Moreno, Quito; f. 1926; monthly; Pres. Dr BENJAMÍN TERÁN VAREA.

Mensajero: Benalcázar 478, Apdo 17-01-4100, Quito; tel. (2) 219-555; f. 1884; monthly; religion, culture, economics and politics; Man. OSWALDO CARRERA LANDÁZURI; circ. 5,000.

Nueva: Apdo 3224, Quito; tel. (2) 542-244; f. 1971; monthly; leftwing; Dir MAGDALENA JARAMILLO DE ADOUM.

Quince Dias: Sociedad Periodistica Ecuatoriana, Los Pinos 315, Panamericana Norte km 51/2, Quito; tel. (2) 474-122; fax (2) 566-741; fortnightly; news and regional political analysis.

Solidaridad: Calle Oriente 725, Quito; tel. (2) 216-541; f. 1982; monthly; publ. of Confederation of Catholic Office Staff and Students of Ecuador; Dir WILSON ALMEIDA MUÑOZ; Man. JOHNY MERIZALDE; circ. 15,000.

Guayaquil

Análisis Semanal: Elizalde 119, 10°, Apdo 4925, Guayaquil; tel. (4) 326-590; fax (4) 326-842; e-mail wspurrie@gye.satnet.net; internet www.ecuadoranalysis.com; weekly; economic and political affairs; Editor WALTER SPURRIER BAQUERIZO.

Ecuador Ilustrado: Guayaquil; f. 1924; monthly; literary; illustrated.

El Financiero: Casilla 6666, Guayaquil; tel. (4) 304-050; weekly; business and economic news.

Revista Estadio: Aguirre 730 y Boyacá, Apdo 1239, Guayaquil; tel. (4) 327-200; fax (4) 320-499; e-mail estadio@vistazo.com; f. 1962; fortnightly; sport; Editor LUIS SÁNCHEZ; circ. 70,000.

Hogar: Aguirre 724 y Boyacá, Apdo 1239, Guayaquil; tel. (4) 327-200; f. 1964; monthly; Man. Editor ROSA AMELIA ALVARADO; circ. 35,000.

Vistazo: Aguirre 724 y Boyacá, Apdo 1239, Guayaquil; tel. (4) 327-200; fax (4) 320-499; e-mail vistazo@vistazo.com; f. 1957; fortnightly; general; Pres. XAVIER ALVARADO ROCA; circ. 85,000.

NEWS AGENCIES
Foreign Bureaux

Agencia EFE (Spain): Palacio Arzobispal, Chile 1178, Apdo 4043, Quito; tel. (2) 512-427; Bureau Chief EMILIO CRESPO.

Agenzia Nazionale Stampa Associata (ANSA) (Italy): Calle Venezuela 1013 y esq. Mejía, Of. 26, Quito; tel. (2) 580-794; fax (2) 580-782; Correspondent FERNANDO LARENAS.

Associated Press (AP) (USA): Edif. Sudamérica, 4°, Of. 44, Calle Venezuela 1018 y Mejía, Quito; tel. (2) 570-235; Correspondent CARLOS CISTERNAS.

Deutsche Presse-Agentur (dpa) (Germany): Edif. Atrium, Of. 5-7, González Suárez 894 y Gonnessiat, Quito; tel. (2) 568-986; Correspondent JORGE ORTIZ.

Informatsionnoye Telegrafnoye Agentstvo Rossii—Telegrafnoye Agentstvo Suverennykh Stran (ITAR—TASS) (Russia): Calle Roca 328 y 6 de Diciembre, 2°, Dep. 6, Quito; tel. (2) 511-631; Correspondent VLADIMIR GOSTEV.

Inter Press Service (IPS) (Italy): Urbanización Los Arrayanes Manzanas 20, Casa 15, Calle León Pontón y Pasaje E, Casilla 17-01-1284, Quito; tel. (2) 662-362; fax (2) 661-977; e-mail jfrias@uio.telconet.net; Correspondent KINTTO LUCAS.

Prensa Latina (Cuba): Edif. Sudamérica, 2°, Of. 24, Calle Venezuela 1018 y Mejía, Quito; tel. (2) 519-333; Bureau Chief ENRIQUE GARCÍA MEDINA.

Reuters (United Kingdom): Avda Amazonas 3655, 2°, Casilla 17-01-4112, Quito; tel. (2) 431-753; fax (2) 432-949; Correspondent JORGE AGUIRRE CHARVET.

United Press International (UPI) (USA): Quito; Correspondent RICARDO POLIT.

Xinhua (New China) News Agency (People's Republic of China): Edif. Portugal, Avda Portugal y Avda de la República del Salvador 730, 10°, Quito; Bureau Chief LIN MINZHONG.

Publishers

Artes Gráficas Ltda: Avda 12 de Octubre 1637, Apdo 533, Casilla 456A, Quito; Man. MANUEL DEL CASTILLO.

Centro de Educación Popular: Avda America 3584, Apdo 17-08-8604, Quito; tel. (2) 525-521; fax (2) 542-369; e-mail centro@cedep.ec; f. 1978; communications, economics; Dir DIEGO LANDÁZURI.

CEPLAES: Avda 6 de Diciembre 2912 y Alpallana, Apdo 17-11/6127, Quito; tel. (2) 548-547; fax (2) 566-207; f. 1978; agriculture, anthropology, education, health, social sciences, women's studies; Exec. Dir ALEXANDRA AYALA.

CIDAP: Hno Miguel 3-23, Casilla 01011943, Cuenca; tel. (7) 829-451; fax (7) 831-450; e-mail cidapl@cidap.org.ec; art, crafts, games, hobbies; Dir CLAUDIO MALO GONZALES.

CIESPAL (Centro Internacional de Estudios Superiores de Comunicación para America Latina): Avda Almagro y Andrade Marin, Apdo 17-01-548, Quito; tel. (2) 234-031; fax (2) 548-011; f. 1959; communications, technology; Dir Dr LUIS E. PROANO.

Corporación de Estudios y Publicaciónes: Acuna 168 y J. Agama, Casilla 17-21-0086, Quito; tel. (2) 221-711; fax (2) 226-256; e-mail cep@accessinter.net; f. 1963; law, public administration.

Corporación Editora Nacional: Apdo 17-12-886, Quito; tel. (2) 554-358; fax (2) 566-340; e-mail editoranacionecuador@excite.com; f. 1978; archaeology, economics, education, geography, political science, history, law, literature, philosophy, social sciences; Pres. ERNESTO ALBÁN.

Cromograf, SA: Coronel 2207, Casilla 4285, Guayaquil; tel. (4) 346-400; children's books, paperbacks, art productions.

Ediciones Abya-Yala: Avda 12 de Octubre 1430, Quito; tel. (2) 562-633; fax (2) 506-255; e-mail admin-info@abyayala.org; internet www.abyayala.org; f. 1975; anthropology, environmental studies, languages, theology; Dir Fr JUAN BOTTASSO.

Editorial de la Casa de la Cultura Ecuatoriana 'Benjamín Carrión': Avda 6 de Diciembre 679 y Patria, Apdo 67, Quito; tel. (2) 235-611; f. 1944; general fiction and non-fiction, general science; Pres. MÍLTON BARRAGÁN DUMET.

Editorial y Librería Selecciones: Avda 9 de Octubre 724 y Boyacá, Guayaquil; tel. (4) 305-807; history, geography and sociology.

Eguez-Pérez en Nombre Colectivo/Abrapalabra Editores: America 5378, Casilla 464A, Quito; tel. and fax (2) 544-178; f. 1990; drama, education, fiction, literature, science fiction, social sciences; Man. IVAN EGUEZ.

Libresa S A: Murgeon 364 y Ulloa, Quito; tel. (2) 230-925; fax (2) 502-992; e-mail libresa@interactive.net.ec; f. 1979; education, literature, philosophy; Pres. FAUSTO COBA ESTRELLA.

Libros Técnicos Litesa Cía Ltda: Avda América 542, Apdo 456A, Quito; tel. (2) 528-537; Man. MANUEL DEL CASTILLO.

Pontificia Universidad Católica del Ecuador, Centro de Publicaciones: Avda 12 de Octubre 1076 y Carrión, Apdo 17-01-2184, Quito; tel. (2) 529-250; fax (2) 567-117; e-mail puce@edu.ec; internet www.puce.edu.ec; f. 1946; literature, natural science, law, anthropology, sociology, politics, economics, theology, philosophy, history, archaeology, linguistics, languages and business; Rector Dr JOSÉ RIBADENEIRA ESPINOSA; Dir JESÚS AGUINAGA ZUMÁRRAGA.

Universidad Central del Ecuador: Departamento de Publicaciones, Servicio de Almacén Universitario, Ciudad Universitaria, Avda America y A. Perez Guerrero, POB 3291, Quito; tel. (2) 226-080; fax (2) 501-207.

Universidad de Guayaquil: Departamento de Publicaciones, Biblioteca General 'Luis de Tola y Avilés', Apdo 09-01-3834, Guayaquil; tel. (4) 516-296; f. 1930; general literature, history, philosophy, fiction; Man. Dir LEONOR VILLAO DE SANTANDER.

Broadcasting and Communications

TELECOMMUNICATIONS

Andinatel: Edif. Zeta, Avda Amazonas y Veitimilla, Quito; tel. (2) 561-004; fax (2) 562-240; e-mail wmaster@andinatel.com; internet www.andinatel.com; Exec. Pres. Ing. ALBERTO SANDOVAL.

Asociación Ecuatoriana de Radiodifusión (AER): Edif. Gran Pasaje, Avda 9 de Octubre 424, 9°, Oficina 915, Guayaquil; tel. and fax (4) 562-448; independent association; Pres. Abog. MARIO CANESSA ONETO.

Consejo Nacional de Telecomunicaciones (CONATEL): Avda Diego de Almagro 31-95 y Alpallana, Casilla 17-07-9777, Quito; tel. (2) 225-614; fax (2) 225-030; e-mail jpileggi@conatel.gov.ec; internet www.conatel.gov.ec; Pres. Dr JOSÉ PILEGGI VÉLIZ.

Pacifitel: Calle Panamá y Roca, Guayaquil; tel. (4) 308-724; Exec. Pres. Ing. WILSON CORREA.

Secretaría Nacional de Telecomunicaciones: Avda Diego de Almagro 31-95 y Alpallana, Casilla 17-07-9777, Quito; tel. (2) 502-197; fax (2) 901-010; Secretario Nacional de Telecomunicaciones Ing. CARLOS DEL POZO CAZAR.

Superintendencia de Telecomunicaciones: Edif. Olimpo, Avda 9 de Octubre 1645 y Berlín, Casilla 17-21-1797, Quito; tel. (2) 222-449; fax (2) 566-688; Superintendente de Telecomunicaciones Ing. HUGO RUIZ CORAL.

BROADCASTING
Regulatory Authority

Consejo Nacional de Radiodifusión y Televisión (CONARTEL): Calle La Pinta 225 y Rábida, Quito; tel. (2) 233-492; fax (2) 523-188; Pres. Ing. ALOO OTTATI PINO.

Radio

There are nearly 300 commercial stations, 10 cultural stations and 10 religious stations. The following are among the most important stations:

CRE (Cadena Radial Ecuatoriana): Edif. El Torreón, 9°, Avda Boyacá 642 y Padre Solano, Apdo 4144, Guayaquil; tel. (4) 564-290; fax (4) 560-386; e-mail aguerrero@cre.com.ec; Dir RAFAEL GUERRERO VALENZUELA.

Emisoras Gran Colombia: Calle Galápagos 112 y Guayaquil, Quito; tel. (2) 442-951; fax (2) 443-147; f. 1943; Pres. MARIO JOSÉ CANESSA ONETO.

Radio Católica Nacional: Avda América 1830 y Mercadillo, Casilla 17-03-540, Quito; tel. (2) 541-557; fax (2) 567-309; f. 1985; Pres. ANTONIO GONZÁLEZ.

Radio Centro: Avda República de El Salvador 836 y Portugal, Quito; tel. (2) 448-900; fax (2) 504-575; f. 1977; Pres. EDGAR YÁNEZ VILLALOBOS.

Radio Colón: Edif. Granda Centeno, Avda América OE4-22 y Villalengua, Casilla 17-08-8167, Quito; tel. (2) 247-467; fax (2) 241-994; f. 1934; Pres. JOSÉ ENRÍQUEZ ONTANEDA; Dir MARGARITA MOLINA GRANDA.

Radio Nacional del Ecuador: Mariano Echeverría 537 y Brasil, Casilla 17-01-82, Quito; tel. (2) 459-555; fax (2) 455-266; f. 1961; state-owned; Dir ANA MALDONADO ROBLES.

Radio Quito: Avda 10 de Agosto 2441 y Colón, Casilla 17-21-1971, Quito; tel. (2) 508-301; fax (2) 503-311; f. 1940; Pres. GUADALUPE MANTILLA MOSQUERA.

Radio Sonorama (HCAEL): Eloy Alfaro 5400 y Los Granados, Casilla 130B, Quito; tel. (2) 448-403; fax (2) 445-858; f. 1975; Pres. SANTIAGO PROAÑO.

Radio Sucre: JUAN Tanca Marengo, Casilla 117114, Guayaquil; tel. (4) 680-586; fax (4) 680-592; e-mail rsucre@gye.satnet.net; internet www.radiosucre.com.ec; f. 1983; Pres. VICENTE ARROBA DITTO.

Radio Zacaray: Avda Quito 1424 y Pasaje Aguavil, Santo Domingo de los Colorados; tel. (2) 750-140; fax (2) 449-207; f. 1959; Pres. HÓLGER VELASTEGUÍ DOMÍNGUEZ.

La Voz de los Andes (HCJB): Villalengua 884 y Avda 10 de Agosto, Casilla 17-17-691, Quito; tel. (2) 264-768; fax (2) 447-263; e-mail helpdesk@hcjb.org.ec; f. 1931; operated by World Radio Missionary Fellowship; programmes in 44 languages and dialects, including Spanish, English and Quechua; private, non-commercial, cultural, religious; Programme Dir GUILLERMO BOSSANO; Man. Dir GLEN VOLKHARDT.

Television

Corporación Ecuatoriana de Televisión—Ecuavisa Canal 2: Cerro El Carmen, Casilla 1239, Guayaquil; tel. (4) 300-150; fax (4) 303-677; f. 1967; Pres. XAVIER ALVARADO ROCA; Gen. Man. FRANCISCO AROSEMENA ROBLES.

Cadena Ecuatoriana de Televisión—TCTelevisión Canal 10: Avda de las Américas, frente al Aeropuerto, Casilla 09-01-673, Guayaquil; tel. (4) 397-664; fax (4) 287-544; e-mail tctvl@tctv.com.ec; f. 1969; commercial; Pres. ROBERTO ISAÍAS; Gen. Man. JORGE KRONFLE.

Televisora Nacional—Ecuavisa Canal 8: Bosmediano 447 y José Carbo, Bellavista, Quito; tel. (2) 446-472; fax (2) 445-488; commercial; f. 1970; Pres. PATRICIO JARAMILLO.

Televisión del Pacífico, SA—Gamavisión: Eloy Alfaro 5400 y Rio Coca, Quito; tel. (2) 262-222; fax (2) 440-259; e-mail gamavision @telconet.net; internet www.gamavision.com; Pres. MARCEL RIVAS SÁENZ.

Teleamazonas Cratel, CA: Granda Centeno y Brasil, Casilla 17-11-04844, Quito; tel. (2) 430-350; fax (2) 451-387; f. 1974; commercial; Pres. EDUARDO GRANDA GARCÉS.

Teleandina Canal 23: Avda de la Prensa 3920 y Fernández Salvador, Quito; tel. (2) 599-403; fax (2) 592-600; f. 1991; Pres. HUMBERTO ORTIZ FLORES; Dir PATRICIO AVILES.

Finance

(cap. = capital; p.u. = paid up; res = reserves;
dep. = deposits;m. = million; amounts in sucres)

Junta Monetaria Nacional (National Monetary Board): Quito; tel. (2) 514-833; fax (2) 570-258; f. 1927; Pres. FRANCISCO SWETT.

Supervisory Authority

Superintendencia de Bancos y Seguros: Avda 12 de Octubre 561 y Madrid, Quito; tel. (2) 541-326; fax (2) 506-812; e-mail alejo@e-mail.superban.gov.ec; internet www.superban.gov.ec; f. 1927; supervises national banking system, including state and private banks and other financial institutions; Superintendent JUAN FALCONI PUIG.

BANKING
Central Bank

Banco Central del Ecuador: Avda 10 de Agosto y Briceño, Plaza Bolívar, Casilla 339, Quito; tel. (2) 582-577; fax (2) 955-458; internet www.bce.fin.ec; f. 1927; cap. 1,482m., res 2,533m., dep. 666,608m. (Dec. 1987); Pres. JOSÉ LUIS YCAZA PAZMIÑO; Gen. Man. LEOPOLDO R. BÁEZ CARRERA; 19 brs.

Other State Banks

Banco del Pacífico: Francisco de P. Ycaza 200, Guayaquil; tel. (4) 566-010; fax (4) 564-636; internet www.bp.fin.ec; f. 1999 by merger of Banco del Pacífico and Banco Continental; Exec. Pres. MARCEL J. LANIADO.

Banco Ecuatoriano de la Vivienda: Avda 10 de Agosto 2270 y Cordero, Casilla 3244, Quito; tel. (2) 521-311; f. 1962; cap. 5,006m., res 952m., dep. 7,389m. (Dec. 1986); Pres. Abog. JUAN PABLO MONCAGATTA; Gen. Man. Dr PATRICIO CEVALLOS MORÁN.

Banco del Estado (BDE): Avda Atahualpa 628 y 10 de Agosto, Casilla 17-01-00373, Quito; tel. (2) 250-800; fax (2) 250-320; f. 1979; cap. 115,587.5m., res 8,481.5m. (Aug. 1991); Pres. Econ. CÉSAR ROBALINO; Gen. Man. Econ. MARTÍN COSTA MARCH.

Banco Nacional de Fomento: Ante 107 y 10 de Agosto, Casilla 685, Quito; tel. (2) 572-248; fax (2) 580-910; e-mail bnf1@bnfomento .fin.ec; f. 1928; cap. 3,000m., res 14,914m., dep. 117,067m. (Dec. 1987); Pres. Dr IGNACIO HIDALGO VILLAVICENCIO; Gen. Man. MARCELO PEÑA DURINI; 70 brs.

Corporación Financiera Nacional (CFN): Avda Juan León Mera 130 y Patria, Casilla 163, Quito; tel. (2) 564-900; fax (2) 562-519; e-mail pnoboa@cfn.fin.ec; f. 1964; cap. 2,000m., res 8,417m. (July 1987); Pres. MILTON SALGADO; Gen. Man. Ing. RAFAEL CUESTA ALVAREZ.

Commercial Banks
Quito

Banco Amazonas, SA: Avda Amazonas 4430 y Villalengua, Casilla 121, Quito; tel. (2) 260-400; fax (2) 255-123; e-mail basacomp@ porta.net; f. 1976; affiliated to Banque Paribas; cap. 21,400m., res 8,970m., dep. 145,740m. (Dec. 1994); Pres. RAFAEL FERRETTI BENÍTEZ; Vice-Pres. ROBERTO SEMINARIO.

Banco Caja de Crédito Agrícola Ganadero, SA: Avda 6 de Diciembre 225 y Piedrahita, Quito; tel. (2) 528-521; f. 1949; cap

132m., res 41m., dep. 592m. (Aug. 1984); Man. HUGO GRIJALVA GARZÓN; Pres. NICOLÁS GUILLÉN.

Banco Consolidado del Ecuador: Avda Patria 740 y 9 de Octubre, Casilla 9150, Suc. 7, Quito; tel. (2) 560-369; fax (2) 560-719; e-mail jcalarco@gnb.fin.ec; f. 1981; cap. 2,874m., res 4,338m., dep. 5,545m. (Oct. 1998); Chair. JAIME GILINSKI; Gen. Man. ANTONIO COY; 2 brs.

Banco General Rumiñahui: Avda Orellana y Amazonas, Casilla 2952, Quito; tel. (2) 505-446; fax (2) 505-366; Gen. Man. Gen. GUSTAVO HERRERA.

Banco Internacional, SA: Avda Patria E-421 y 9 de Octubre, Casilla 17-01-2114, Quito; tel. (2) 565-547; fax (2) 565-758; e-mail cromero@bancointernacional.com.ec; internet www .bancointernacional.com.ec; f. 1973; cap. US $8,600m. (Dec. 2000); Pres. DAMIÁN VALLEJO; Gen. Man. Econ. RAÚL GUERRERO ANDRADE; 58 brs.

Banco Pacífico Popular (BPP): Avda Amazonas 353 y Juan Pablo Sanz, Casilla 696, Quito; tel. (2) 444-700; fax (2) 444-794; f. 1998 by merger of Banco Popular del Ecuador, Banco del Pacífico and Banco COFIEC; cap. US $251m., dep. US $1,598m., total assets US $2,859m. (Nov. 1998); Chair. ARTURO QUIROS; Exec. Pres. NICOLÁS LANDÉS; Pres. FRANCISCO ROSALES.

Banco del Pichincha, CA: Avda Amazonas 4560 y Pereira, Casilla 261, Quito; tel. (2) 980-980; fax (2) 981-187; internet www.pichincha .com; f. 1906; cap. 153,000m., dep. 6,773,832m. (Dec. 1998); Exec. Pres. and Chair. Dr FIDEL EGAS GRIJALVA; Gen. Man. ANTONIO ACOSTA ESPINOSA; 127 brs.

Produbanco: Avda Amazonas 3775 y Japón, Casilla 17-03-38-A, Quito; tel. (2) 260-150; fax (2) 447-319; internet www .produbanco.com; f. 1978 as Banco de la Producción; name changed as above in 1996; cap. 112,000m., res 64,840m., dep. 906,613.2 (Dec. 1997); Exec. Pres. and Gen. Man. Econ. ABELARDO PACHANO BERTERO; Exec. Vice-Pres. FERNANDO VIVERO LOZA.

UniBanco: Avda 10 de Agosto 937 y Buenos Aires, Casilla 2244, Quito; tel. (2) 544-188; fax (2) 227-898; f. 1964 as Banco de Co-operativas del Ecuador, name changed as above in 1995; Pres. Dr JACINTO MONTERO ZAMORA; Vice-Pres. Dr HUGO ENRÍQUEZ; 4 brs.

Ambato

Banco de Tungurahua: Montalvo 630, Casilla 173, Ambato; tel. (2) 821-122; fax (2) 840-426; f. 1979; cap. 50m., res 2m., dep. 329m. (June 1984); Pres. GEORG SONNENHOLZNER; Gen. Man. Econ. CAMILO AMPUERO SÁNCHEZ.

Cuenca

Banco del Austro: Sucre y Borrero (esq.), Casilla 01-01-0167, Cuenca; tel. (7) 831-646; fax (7) 832-633; f. 1977; cap. 34,000m., dep. 141,000m. (July 1994); Pres. JUAN ELJURI ANTÓN; Gen. Man. PATRICIO ROBAYO IDROVO; 19 brs.

Guayaquil

Banco Bolivariano, CA: Junín 200 y Panamá, Casilla 09-01-10184, Guayaquil; tel. (4) 560-799; fax (4) 566-707; e-mail crivera @bolivariano.fin.ec; internet www.bolivariano.com; f. 1978; cap. 90,000m., res 23,470.9m., dep. 579,890.1m. (Dec. 1998); Chair. JOSÉ SALAZAR BARRAGÁN; Exec. Pres. MIGUEL BABRA LYON; 22 brs.

Banco Industrial y Comercial—Baninco: Pichincha 335 e Illingworth, Casilla 5817, Guayaquil; tel. (4) 323-488; f. 1965; cap. and res 2m., dep. 10m. (June 1988); Pres. Ing. CARLOS MANZUR PERES; Gen. Man. GABRIEL MARTÍNEZ INTRIAGO; 2 brs.

Banco Territorial, SA: Panamá 814 y V. M. Rendón, Casilla 09-01-227, Guayaquil; tel. (4) 566-695; fax (4) 566-695; f. 1886; cap. 3,800m., res 3,769m. (June 1993), dep. 516m. (Sept. 1991); Pres. ROBERTO GOLDBAUM; Gen. Man. Ing. GUSTAVO HEINERT.

Loja

Banco de Loja: esq. Bolívar y Rocafuerte, Casilla 11-01-300, Loja; tel. (4) 571-682; fax (4) 573-019; f. 1968; cap. 10,000m., res 4,207m., dep. 70,900m. (Dec. 1996); Pres. Lic. AUGUSTO EGUIGUREN EGUIGUREN; Man. Lic. FERNANDO BURBANO TORAL.

Machala

Banco de Machala, SA: Avda 9 de Mayo y Rocafuerte, Casilla 711, Machala; tel. (4) 930-100; fax (4) 922-744; f. 1972; Pres. Dr RODOLFO VINTIMILLA FLORES; Exec. Pres. and Gen. Man. ESTEBAN QUIROLA FIGUEROA; 2 brs.

Portoviejo

Banco Comercial de Manabí, SA: Avda 10 de Agosto 600 y 18 Octubre, Portoviejo; tel. (4) 653-888; fax (4) 635-527; f. 1980; cap. 117m., res 21m., dep. 720m. (June 1985); Pres. Dr RUBÉN DARÍO MORALES; Gen. Man. ARISTO ANDRADE DÍAZ.

Foreign Banks

ABN AMBO Bank NV (Netherlands): Avda Amazonas 4272, Casilla 17-17-1534, Quito; tel. (2) 266-666; fax (2) 443-151; internet www .abnamro.com.ec. f. 1960; cap. 23m.; Gen. Man. SJEF MARTINOT; 6 brs.

Citibank, NA (USA): Juan León Mera 130 y Patria, Casilla 17-01-1393, Quito; tel. (2) 563-300; fax (2) 566-895; f. 1959; cap. 7,000m., res 1,000m., dep. 62,000m. (Dec. 1996); Gen. Man. BENJAMÍN FRANCO; 3 brs.

ING Bank NV (Netherlands): Edificio Centro Financiero, Avda Amazonas 4545 y Pereira, Quito; tel. (2) 981-650; fax (2) 981-665.

Lloyds TSB (BLSA) Ltd (United Kingdom): Avda Amazonas 580, esq. Jerónimo Carrión, Casilla 17-03-556, Quito; tel. (2) 564-177; fax (2) 568-997; e-mail lloydsec@interactive.net.ec; f. 1988 (in succession to the Bank of London and South America, f. 1936); cap. US $1,500m., res US $8,300m., dep. US $80,000m. (Dec. 2000); Man. G. BELTRÁN M.

'Multibanco'

Banco de Guayaquil, SA: Plaza Ycaza 105 y Pichincha, Casilla 09-01-1300, Guayaquil; tel. (4) 517-100; fax (4) 514-406; e-mail servicios@bankguay.com; internet www.bankguay.com; f. 1923; absorbed the finance corpn, FINANSUR, in 1990 to become Ecuador's first 'multibanco', carrying out commercial and financial activities; cap. 145,000m., dep. 3,198,862m. (Dec. 1998); Exec. Pres. Dr GUILLERMO LASSO MENDOZA; Vice-Pres ANGELO CAPUTI, CARMEN SORIANO; 50 brs.

Finance Corporations

Financiera Guayaquil, SA: Carchi 702 y 9 de Octubre, 6°, Casilla 2167, Guayaquil; f. 1976; cap. 900m., res 142m. (June 1987); Gen. Man. Dr MIGUEL BABRA LYON.

FINANSA—Financiera Nacional, SA: Avda 6 de Diciembre 2417, entre Orellana y la Niña, Casilla 6420-CCI, Quito; tel. (2) 546-200; f. 1976; cap. 694m., res 103.6m. (June 1986); Gen. Man. RICHARD A. PEARSE; Dir LEONARDO STAGG.

Associations

Asociación de Bancos Privados del Ecuador: Edif. Delta, 7o, Avda República de El Salvador 890 y Suecia, Casilla 17-11-6708, Quito; tel. (2) 466-670; fax (2) 466-701; e-mail echiribo@asobancos .org.ec; f. 1965; 36 mems; Pres. ANTONIO ACOSTA ESPINOSA; Exec. Pres. ERNESTO CHIRIBOGA BLONDET (acting).

Asociación de Compañías Financieras del Ecuador—AFIN: Robles 653 y Amazonas, 13°, Of. 1310-1311, Casilla 17-07-9156, Quito; tel. (2) 550-623; fax (2) 567-912; Pres. Ing. FRANCISCO ORTEGA.

STOCK EXCHANGES

Bolsa de Valores de Guayaquil: 9 de Octubre 110 y Pichincha, Guayaquil; tel. (4) 564-30; fax (4) 561-871; internet www4.bvg.fin.ec /eng; CEO ENRIQUE AROSEMENA; Dir of Operations ERNESTO MURILLO.

Bolsa de Valores de Quito: Avda Amazonas 540 y J. Carrión, Quito; tel. (2) 526-805; fax (2) 526-048; e-mail pazosc@ccbvq.com; internet www.ccbvq.com; f. 1969; volume of operations US $1,700m. (1995); Pres GONZALO CHIRIBOGA CHÁVEZ; Exec. Pres. ARTURO QUIROZ RIUMALLÓ.

INSURANCE

Instituto Ecuatoriano de Seguridad Social: Avda 10 de Agosto y Bogotá, Apdo 2640, Quito; tel. (2) 547-400; fax (2) 504-572; f. 1928; various forms of state insurance provided; directs the Ecuadorean social insurance system; provides social benefits and medical service; Dir-Gen. Dr RAÚL ZAPATER HIDALGO.

National Companies

In 1992 there were some 35 insurance companies operating in Ecuador. The following is a list of the eight principal companies, selected by virtue of capital.

Amazonas Cía Anónima de Seguros: V. M. Rendón 401 y Córdova, Apdo 3285, Guayaquil; tel. (4) 566-300; fax (4) 563-192; e-mail contacto@segurosamazonas.com.ec; internet www .segurosamazonas.com.ec; f. 1966; Gen. Man. ANTONIO AROSEMENA.

Cía Reaseguradora del Ecuador, SA: Junín 105 y Malecón Simón Bolívar, Casilla 09-01-6776, Guayaquil; tel. (4) 566-326; fax (4) 564-454; e-mail oespinoz@ecuare.fin.ec; f. 1977; Man. Dir Ing. OMAR ESPINOSA ROMERO.

Cía de Seguros Condor, SA: Plaza Ycaza 302, Apdo 09-01-5007, Guayaquil; tel. (4) 565-888; fax (4) 560-144; f. 1966; Gen. Man. JAIME GUZMÁN ITURRALDE.

Cía de Seguros Ecuatoriano-Suiza, SA: Avda 9 de Octubre 2101 y Tulcán, Apdo 09-01-0937, Guayaquil; tel. (4) 372-222; fax (4) 500-209; f. 1954; Gen. Man. Econ. ENRIQUE SALAS CASTILLO.

La Nacional Cía de Seguros Generales, SA: Edif. World Trade Centre, Avda.fra de Arellana, 5°, Guayaquil; tel. (4) 630-170; fax (4) 630-175; f. 1940; Gen. Man. Dr MIGUEL BABRA LEÓN.

Panamericana del Ecuador, SA: Calle Portugal 305 y Eloy Alfaro, Quito; tel. (2) 469-460; fax (2) 469-650; f. 1973; Gen. Man. GERMAN DAVILA.

Seguros Rocafuerte, SA: Plaza Carbo 505 y 9 de Octubre, Apdo 6491, Guayaquil; f. 1967; Gen. Man. Ing. DANIEL CAÑIZARES AGUILAR.

La Unión Cía Nacional de Seguros: Km. 5½, Vía a la Costa, Apdo 09-01-1294, Guayaquil; tel. (4) 851-500; fax (4) 851-700;e-mail launion2@porta.net; f. 1943; Man. DAVID ALBERTO GOLDBAUM MORALES.

Trade and Industry

GOVERNMENT AGENCIES

Consejo Nacional de Modernización del Estado (CONAM): Edif. CFN, 9°, Avda Juan León Mera 130 y Patria, Quito; tel. (2) 509-432; fax (2) 228-450; e-mail cdelgado@uio.conam-pertal.gov.ec; f. 1994; Pres. Ing. RICARDO NOBOA; Exec. Dir Ing. ANTONIO PERÉ YCAZA.

Empresa de Comercio Exterior (ECE): Quito; f. 1980 to promote non-traditional exports; State owns 33% share in company; share capital 25m. sucres.

Fondo de Promoción de Exportaciones (FOPEX): Juan León Mera 130 y Patria, Casilla 163, Quito; tel. (2) 564-900; fax (2) 562-519; f. 1972; export promotion; Dir ELIANA SANTAMARÍA M.

Instituto Ecuatoriano de Reforma Agraria y Colonización (IERAC): f. 1973 to supervise the Agrarian Reform Law under the auspices and co-ordination of the Ministry of Agriculture; Dir LUIS LUNA GAYBOR.

Superintendencia de Compañías del Ecuador: Roca 660 y Amazonas, Casilla 17-21-0687, Quito; tel. (2) 541-606; fax (2) 566-685; e-mail estudi@q.supercias.gov.ec; f. 1964; responsible for the legal and accounting control of commercial enterprises; Supt Dr XAVIER MUÑOZ CHÁVEZ.

DEVELOPMENT ORGANIZATIONS

Centro Nacional de Promoción de la Pequeña Industria y Artesanía (CENAPIA): Quito; agency to develop small-scale industry and handicrafts; Dir Econ. EDGAR GUEVARA (acting).

Centro de Reconversión Económica del Azuay, Cañar y Morona Santiago (CREA): Avda México entre Unidad Nacional y las Américas, Casilla 01-01-1953, Cuenca; tel. (7) 817-500; fax (7) 817-134; f. 1959; development organization; Dir Dr JUAN TAMA.

Consejo Nacional de Desarrollo (CONADE): Juan Larrea y Arenas, Quito; formerly Junta Nacional de Planificación y Coordinación Económica; aims to formulate a general plan of economic and social development and supervise its execution; also to integrate local plans into the national; Chair. GALO ABRIL OJEDA; Sec. PABLO LUCIO PAREDES.

Fondo de Desarrollo del Sector Rural Marginal (FODERUMA): f. 1978 to allot funds to rural development programmes in poor areas.

Fondo Nacional de Desarrollo (FONADE): f. 1973; national development fund to finance projects as laid down in the five-year plan.

Instituto de Colonización de la Región Amazónica (INCREA): f. 1978 to encourage settlement in and economic development of the Amazon region; Dir Dr DIMAS GUZMÁN.

Instituto Ecuatoriano de Recursos Hidráulicos (INERHI): undertakes irrigation and hydroelectric projects; Man. Ing. EDUARDO GARCÍA GARCÍA.

Organización Comercial Ecuatoriana de Productos Artesanales (OCEPA): Carrión 1236 y Versalles, Casilla 17-01-2948, Quito; tel. (2) 541-992; fax (2) 565-961; f. 1964; to develop and promote handicrafts; Gen. Man. MARCELO RODRÍGUEZ.

Programa Nacional del Banano y Frutas Tropicales: Guayaquil; to promote the development of banana and tropical-fruit cultivation; Dir Ing. JORGE GIL CHANG.

Programa Regional de Desarrollo del Sur del Ecuador(PREDESUR): Pasaje María Eufrasia 100 y Mosquera Narváez, Quito; tel. (2) 544-415; f. 1972 to promote the development of the southern area of the country; Dir Ing. LUIS HERNÁN EGUIGUREN CARRIÓN.

CHAMBERS OF COMMERCE AND INDUSTRY

Federación Nacional de Cámaras de Comercio del Ecuador: Avda Olmedo 414 y Boyacá, Guayaquil; tel. (4) 323-130; fax (4) 323-478; Pres. Ing. LUIS TRUJILLO BUSTAMANTE; Exec. Vice-Pres. Dr ROBERTO ILLINGWORTH.

Cámara de Comercio de Cuenca: Avda Federico Malo 1-90, Casilla 4929, Cuenca; tel. (7) 827-531; fax (7) 833-891; f. 1919; 5,329 mems; Pres. ENRIQUE MORA VÁZQUEZ.

Cámara de Comercio de Quito: Edif. Las Cámaras, 6°, Avda República y Amazonas, Casilla 17-01-202, Quito; tel. (2) 443-787; fax (2) 435-862; e-mail ccq@uio.satnet.net; f. 1906; 8,000 mems; Chair. JAVIER ESPINOSA; Pres. DOMINGO CÓRDOVEZ PÉREZ.

Cámara de Comercio de Guayaquil: Avda Olmedo 414 y Boyacá, Guayaquil; tel. (4) 323-130; fax (4) 323-478; e-mail camcomg@ g.camcom.org.ec; f. 1889; 16,500 mems; Pres. Ing. LUIS TRUJILLO BUSTAMENTE; Exec. Sec. Dr ROBERTO ILLINGWORTH CABANILLA.

Federación Nacional de Cámaras de Industrias: Avda República y Amazonas, Casilla 2438, Quito; tel. (2) 452-994; fax (2) 448-118; f. 1974; Pres. Ing. PEDRO KOHN.

Cámara de Industrias de Cuenca: Edif. Las Cámaras, Avda Federico Malo 1-90, Casilla 01-01-326, Cuenca; tel. (7) 830-845; fax (7) 830-945; f. 1936; Pres. Ing. FRANK TOSI IÑIGUEZ.

Cámara de Industrias de Guayaquil: Avda 9 de Octubre 910 y Rumichaca, Casilla 09-01-4007, Guayaquil; tel. (4) 561-556; fax (4) 320-924; f. 1936; Pres. Ing. ERNESTO NOBOA BEJARANO.

INDUSTRIAL AND TRADE ASSOCIATIONS

Centro de Desarrollo Industrial del Ecuador (CENDES): Avda Orellana 1715 y 9 de Octubre, Casilla 2321, Quito; tel. (2) 527-100; f. 1962; carries out industrial feasibility studies, supplies technical and administrative assistance to industry, promotes new industries, supervises investment programmes; Gen. Man. CLAUDIO CREAMER GUILLÉN.

Corporación de Desarrollo e Investigación Geológico-Minero-Metalúrgica (CODIGEM): Avda 10 de Agosto 5844 y Pereira, Casilla 17-03-23, Quito; tel. (2) 254-673; fax (2) 254-674;e-mail prodemi2@prodeminca.org.ec; f. 1991 to direct mining exploration and exploitation; Exec. Pres. Ing. JORGE BARRAGÁN G.

Fondo Nacional de Preinversión (FONAPRE): Jorge Washington 624 y Amazonas, Casilla 17-01-3302, Quito; tel. (2) 563-261; f. 1973 to undertake feasibility projects before investment; Pres. LUIS PARODÍ VALVERDE; Gen. Man. Ing. EDUARDO MOLINA GRAZZIANI.

Petróleos del Ecuador (PETROECUADOR): Avda 6 de Diciembre, Casilla 5007-8, Quito; tel. (2) 229-043; state petroleum co; operations in at least seven oilfields were expected to be transferred to the private sector; Pres. RODOLFO BARNIOL.

EMPLOYERS' ORGANIZATIONS

Asociación de Cafecultores del Cantón Piñas: García Moreno y Abdón Calderón, Quito; coffee growers' association.

Asociación de Comerciantes e Industriales: Avda Boyacá 1416, Guayaquil; traders' and industrialists' association.

Asociación de Industriales Textiles del Ecuador (AITE): Edif. Las Cámaras, 8°, Avda República y Amazonas, Casilla 2893, Quito; f. 1938; textile manufacturers' association; 40 mems; Pres. Ing. RAMIRO LEÓN PAEZ; Exec. Pres. Dr ANTONIO JOSÉ COBO.

Asociación de Productores Bananeros del Ecuador (APROBANA): Malecón 2002, Guayaquil; banana growers' association; Pres. NICOLÁS CASTRO.

Asociación Nacional de Empresarios (ANDE): Edif. España, 6°, Of. 67, Avda Amazonas 1429 y Colón, Casilla 17-01-3489, Quito; tel. (2) 238-507; fax (2) 509-806; e-mail ande@vio.satnet.net; internet www.ande.net; national employers' association.

Asociación Nacional de Exportadores de Cacao y Café: Casilla 4774, Manta; cocoa and coffee exporters' association.

Asociación Nacional de Exportadores de Camarones: Pres. LUIS VILLACÍS.

Cámara de Agricultura: Casilla 17-21-322, Quito; tel. (2) 230-195; Pres. ALBERTO ENRÍQUEZ PORTILLA.

Consorcio Ecuatoriano de Exportadores de Cacao y Café: cocoa and coffee exporters' consortium.

Corporación Nacional de Exportadores de Cacao y Café: Guayaquil; cocoa and coffee exporters' corporation.

Federación Nacional de Cooperativas Cafetaleras: Quito; coffee co-operatives federation.

Unión Nacional de Periodistas: Joaquín Auxe Iñaquito, Quito; national press association.

There are several other coffee and cocoa organizations.

MAJOR COMPANIES

The following are some of the leading industrial and commercial companies currently operating in Ecuador.

Acero Comercial Ecuatoriano, SA: Avda 10 de Agosto 3653 y María de Jesús, Quito; tel. (2) 524-450; fax (2) 227-596; e-mail acero@telconet.net; f. 1957; production of construction materials; Gen. Man. JUAN PEDRO BLUHM; 260 employees.

Auto y Máquinas del Ecuador, SA (AYMESA): Avda Panamericana Sur, Km 91/2, Quito; tel. (2) 679-464; fax (2) 677-026; f. 1970;

subsidiary of General Motors Corpn, USA; manufacture of motor vehicles and spare parts; Pres. PETER HAZL; Dir-Gen. PATRICIO ACOSTA ESPINOZA; 440 employees.

Cementos Selva Alegre, SA: Edif. Banco La Previsora, Of. 402, Amazonas y Naciones Unidas, Quito; tel. (2) 459-140; fax (2) 440-944; e-mail compras@csa.com.ec; internet www.csa.com.ec; f. 1979; manufacture of cement; Gen. Man. JOSÉ ESPINOSA PÉREZ; 567 employees.

Compañía de Cervezas Nacionales, CA: Vía a Daule, Km 161/2, Casilla 09-01-519, Guayaquil; tel. (4) 893-088; fax (4) 893-263; e-mail cervece1@bismark.com.ec; f. 1921; brewing; Exec. Pres. JULIO MARIO SANTO DOMINGO; 440 employees.

Empresa Pesquera Nacional: Guayaquil; tel. (4) 524-913; state fishing enterprise.

Fábrica de Aceites La Favorita, SA: G. Francisco de Marcos 102 y E. Alvaro, Guayaquil; tel. (4) 402-840; fax (4) 414-507; e-mail eduardo.vallarino@unilever.com; f. 1941; production of vegetable oils; Dir XAVIER VALLARINO MARQUÉZ DE LA PLATA; Gen. Man. ERNESTO NOBOA BEJARANO; 480 employees.

Fábrica Automatica de Envases, SA: Casilla 9446, Guayaquil; tel. (4) 445-266; fax (4) 444-954; f. 1963; manufacture of metal cans and containers; Pres. JUAN JOSÉ VILASECA; 256 employees.

Hidalgo E Hidalgo, SA: Avda, 10 de Agosto y Algarrobos, Quito; tel. (2) 408-038; fax (2) 400-541; e-mail heh@hoy.net; f 1984; construction; Pres. JUAN FRANCISCO HIDALGO; GEN.MAN. JULIO HIDALGO GONZÁLEZ; 1,000 employees.

Hoechst Eteco, SA: Edif. Eteco, Avda 9 de Octubre 135 y Patria, Casilla 1408, Quito; tel. (2) 561-450; fax (2) 564-662; f. 1961; manufacture of pharmaceuticals, cosmetics, chemicals, fertilizers and pesticides; Gen. Man. NORBER OTIK; 600 employees.

Importadora El Rosado Cía Ltda: Calle 9 de Octubre 727 y Boyacá, Guayaquil; tel. (4) 322-555; fax (4) 328-196; e-mail luchoweb @elrosado.com; internet www.elrosado.com; f. 1954; retailing; Dir-Gen. JOHNNY CZARNINSKY; 4,000 employees.

Industria Ecuatoriana Productora de Alimentos (INEPACA): Calle Malecon, Casilla 13-05-4881, Manta; tel. (5) 626 144; fax (5) 624-870; e-mail alzambra@inepaca.com.ec; internet www.metatips .com/ecu/inepaca/; f 1949; fishing and processing of fish; Pres. EDGAR TEÁN; Gen. Man. CARLOS E. ZARATE; 987 employees.

Industria Textil San Vincente, SA: Avda 6 de Diciembre y Avda Los Granados, Quito; manufacture of textile products, cloth and carpets; Pres. WILLIAM ISAÍAS DASSUN; 300 employees.

Industrias Ales, CA: Avda Galo Plaza 8919, No 51–23, Quito; tel. (2) 402-600; fax (2) 408-344; manufacture of cooking oils, fats and soap; Gen. Man. PATRICIO ALVAREZ DROUET.

La Cemento Nacional Cía, CA: Vía a la Costa, Km 7, Casilla 09-01-04243, Guayaquil; tel. (4) 871-900; fax (4) 873-482; e-mail info@lcn.com.ec; internet www.lcn.com.ec; f. 1934; manufacture of cement; Gen. Man. PATRICK BREDTHAUER; 1,472 employees.

La International, SA: Maldonado 14-365, Casilla 17-01-372, Quito; tel. (2) 610-896; fax (2) 657-267; f 1992; manufacture of textiles; Gen. Man. DIEGO TERÁN; 1,470 employees.

La Universal, SA: Eloy Alfaro 1101 y Gómez Rendon, Guayaquil; tel. (4) 414-009; fax (4) 414-904; e-mail launiversal@launiversal .com.ec; f. 1889; manufacture of food products; Pres. DOMINGO NORERO; Gen. Man. FERNANDO GUZMÁN; 1.050 employees.

Lanafit, SA: Avda 6 de Diciembre, Sector El Inca, Quito; manufacture of clothing from synthetic fibres; Gen. Man. FUAD ALBERTO DASSUM ARMÉNDARIZ; 700 employees.

Petroproducción, SA: Avda 6 Diciembre 4226, Quito; tel. (2) 440-381; fax (2) 440-383; f. 1989; state petroleum and natural gas exploration enterprise; Gen. Man. LUIS ÁLBÁN; 1,300 employees.

Productura Cartonera, SA (PROCARSA): Vía a Durán-Tambo, Km 6½, Guayaquil; tel. (4) 800-200; fax (4) 801-092; e-mail tblanc@dia.com.ec; internet www.procarsa.com.ec; production of cardboard boxes; Pres. FRANCISCO AMADOR JOUVIN.

Siderúrgica Ecuatoriana, SA: Calle Sabanilla y Gen. Guerrero, Apdo 17-17-839, Sector Cotocollao, Quito; tel. (2) 532-100; fax (2) 591-796; f. 1940; operation of foundry and steel mill; Pres. JUAN ELJURI; Man. Ing. ALBERTO TAMARIZ; 120 employees.

Sociedad Agrícola e Industrial San Carlos, SA: Calle Gen. Elizalde 114, esq. Pichincha y Malecón, Guayaquil; tel. (4) 321-380; fax (4) 534-133; e-mail xmarcos@gu.pro.ec; f. 1897; processing and refining of sugar; Pres. MARIO GONZÁLEZ; Gen. Man. XAVIER MARCOS STAGG; 4,000 employees.

Supermercados La Favorita, CA (SUPERMAXI): Avigiras s/n y Avda Eloy Alfaro, Casilla 17-11-04910. Quito; tel. (2) 401-140; fax (2) 402-496; e-mail favorita@supermaxi.com; internet www .supermaxi.com; f. 1952; Pres. THOMAS WRIGHT; Gen. Man. TOMÁS DURÁN BALLÉN; 2,475 employees.

Tejidos Pintex, SA: Avda de la Prensa 3741 y Manuel Herrera, Quito; tel. (2) 448-334; fax (2) 448-335; e-mail pintex@access.net.ec;

internet www.textilespintex.com; f. 1959; manufacture of textiles; Pres. CRISTINA PINTO MANCHENO; Man. Ing. RAMIRO LEÓN PAEZ; 420 employees.

Texaco Petroleum Company: Avda 6 de Diciembre 2816 y James Orton, 10°, Quito; tel. (2) 563-761; fax (2) 501-660; internet www.texaco-andean.com.co/ecuador/index.html; f. 1963; exploration and exploitation of crude oil; Gen. Man. RAFAEL PEÑA; 765 employees.

Textil San Pedro, SA: Avda Napo y Pedro Pinto 709, Apdo 17-01-3002, Quito; tel. (2) 660-918; fax (2) 661-596; production of cotton textiles; Gen. Man. PEDRO J. PINTO CHIRIBOGA.

Textiles Nacionales, SA: Avda 6 de Diciembre 5919, Sector El Inca, Quito; tel. (2) 435-105; fax (2) 459-259; manufacture of textiles; Pres. JOSEPH S. HANDALL; 450 employees.

Váldez, SA: Edif. Torres del Rio, Junin 114 y Malecon, Guayaquil; tel. (4) 314-762; fax (4) 314-946; processing and refining of sugar; Gen. Man. EDMUNDO VÁLDEZ MURILLO; 3,100 employees.

UTILITIES
Regulatory Authorities

Ministry of Energy and Mines: see section on The Government (Ministries).

Comisión Ecuatoriana de Energía Atómica: Juan Larrea 534 y Riofrío, Casilla 17-01-2517, Quito; tel. (2) 545-861; fax (2) 563-336; e-mail comecenl@comecenat.gov.ec; atomic energy commission; Exec. Dir CELIANO ALMEIDA.

Consejo Nacional de Electricidad (CONELEC): Avda Amazonas 33-299 e Inglaterra, Quito; tel. (2) 268-746; fax (2) 268-737; e-mail conelec@conelec.gov.ec; internet www.conelec.gov.ec; f. 1999; supervises electricity industry following transfer of assets of the former Instituto Ecuatoriano de Electrificación (INECEL) to the Fondo de Solidaridad; pending privatization as six generating companies, one transmission company and 19 distribution companies in late 2000; Pres. DIEGO PÉREZ PALLARES.

Directorate of Alternative Energy (Ministry of Energy and Mines): Edif. Interandina, Ulpiano Paéz 24-06 y Mercadillo, POB 17-15-007C, Quito; tel. (2) 565-980; fax (2) 565-474; e-mail mbalseca@uio.satnet.net; f. 1995; research and development of new and renewable energy sources; Dir Ing. MILTON BALSECA G.

Directorate-General of Hydrocarbons: Avda 10 de Agosto 321, Quito; supervision of the enforcement of laws regarding the exploration and development of petroleum.

Electricity

Empresa de Electricidad del Ecuador (EMELEC): La Garzota, Sector 3, Manzana 47; tel. (4) 248-057; fax (4) 246-952; major producer and distributor of electricity, mostly using oil-fired or diesel generating capacity.

Empresa Eléctrica Quito, SA: Avda 10 de Agosto y Las Casas, Quito; tel (2) 543-833; fax (2) 503-817; internet www.eeq.com.ec; f. 1894; produces electricity for the region around Quito, mostly from hydroelectric plants; Gen. Man. HERNÁN ANDINO ROMERO.

Water

Instituto Ecuatoriano de Obras Sanitarias: Toledo 684 y Lérida, Troncal, Quito; tel. (2) 522-738.

TRADE UNIONS

Frente Unitario de Trabajadores (FUT): f. 1971; left-wing; 300,000 mems; Pres. EDGAR PONCE; comprises:

Confederación Ecuatoriana de Organizaciones Clasistas (CEDOC): Calle Río de Janeiro 407 y Juan Larrea, Casilla 3207, Quito; tel. (2) 548-086; f. 1938; affiliated to CMT and CLAT; humanist; Pres. RAMIRO ROSALES NARVÁEZ; Sec.-Gen. JORGE MUÑOZ; 150,000 mems (est.) organized in 20 provinces.

Confederación Ecuatoriana de Organizaciones Sindicales Libres (CEOSL): Casilla 17-01-1373, Quito; tel. (2) 522-511; fax (2) 500-836; e-mail ceosl@hoy.net.; f. 1962; affiliated to ICFTU and ORIT; Pres. JOSÉ CHÁVEZ CHÁVEZ; Sec.-Gen. WILSON BECERRA ROSERO.

Confederación de Trabajadores del Ecuador (CTE) (Confederation of Ecuadorean Workers): Nueve de Octubre 1248 y Marieta de Veintimilla, Casilla 4166, Quito; tel. (2) 520-456; fax (2) 520-445; f. 1944; admitted to WFTU and CPUSTAL; Pres. CARLOS HUMBERTO LUZARDO; 1,200 affiliated unions, 76 national federations.

Central Católica de Obreros: Avda 24 de Mayo 344, Quito; tel. (2) 213-704; f. 1906; craft and manual workers and intellectuals; Pres. CARLOS E. DÁVILA ZURITA.

A number of trade unions are not affiliated to the above groups. These include the Federación Nacional de Trabajadores Marítimos

y Portuarios del Ecuador (FNTMPE) (National Federation of Maritime and Port Workers of Ecuador) and both railway trade unions.

Transport

RAILWAYS

All railways are government-controlled. In 1997 the total length of track was 956 km.

Empresa Nacional de Ferrocarriles del Estado: Calle Bolívar 443, Casilla 159, Quito; tel. (2) 216-180; Gen. Man. M. ARIAS SALAZAR.

There are divisional state railway managements for the following lines: Guayaquil–Quito, Sibambe–Cuenca and Quito–San Lorenzo.

ROADS

There were 43,197 km of roads in 1999, of which 18.9% were paved. The Pan-American Highway runs north from Ambato to Quito and to the Colombian border at Tulcán and south to Cuenca and Loja. Major rebuilding projects were undertaken in late 1998 with finance from several development organizations to restore roads damaged by the effects of El Niño (a periodic warming of the tropical Pacific Ocean).

SHIPPING

The following are Ecuador's principal ports: Guayaquil, Esmeraldas, Manta and Puerto Bolívar.

Acotramar, CA: General Gómez 522 y Coronel Guayaquil, Casilla 4044, Guayaquil; tel. (4) 401-004; fax (4) 444-852.

Ecuanave, CA: Junin 415 y Córdova, 4°, Casilla 09-01-30H, Guayaquil; tel. (4) 293-808; fax (4) 289-257; e-mail ecuanav@ecua.net.ec.; Chair. Ing. P. ERNESTO ESCOBAR; Man. Dir A. GUILLERMO SERRANO.

Flota Bananera Ecuatoriana, SA: Edif. Gran Pasaje, 9°, Plaza Ycaza 437, Casilla 6883, Guayaquil; tel. (4) 309-333; f. 1967; owned by Govt and private stockholders; Pres. DIEGO SÁNCHEZ; Gen. Man. JORGE BARRIGA.

Flota Mercante Grancolombiana, SA: Calle 2 Aguirre 104 y Malecón Simón Bolívar, Guayaquil; tel. (4) 512-791; f. 1946 with Colombia and Venezuela; on Venezuela's withdrawal, in 1953, Ecuador's 10% interest was increased to 20%; operates services from Colombia and Ecuador to European ports, US Gulf ports and New York, Mexican Atlantic ports and East Canada; offices in Quito, Cuenca, Bahía, Manta and Esmeraldas; Man. Naval Capt. J. ALBERTO SÁNCHEZ.

Flota Petrolera Ecuatoriana—FLOPEC: Edif. FLOPEC, Avda Amazonas 1188 y Cordero, Casilla 535-A, Quito; tel. (2) 564-058; fax (2) 569-794; f. 1972; e-mail g.general@flopec.com.ec; internet www.flopec.com.ec; Gen. Man. Vice-Adm. JORGE DONOSO MORAN.

Logística Marítima, CA (LOGMAR): Avda Córdova 812 y V. M. Rendón, 1°, Casilla 9622, Guayaquil; tel. (4) 307-041; Pres. J. COELLOG; Man. IGNACIO RODRÍGUEZ BAQUERIZO.

Naviera del Pacífico, CA (NAPACA): El Oro 101 y La Ría, Casilla 09-01-529, Guayaquil; tel. (4) 342-055; Pres. LUIS ADOLFO NOBOA NARANJO.

Servicios Oceánicos Internacionales, SA: Avda Domingo Comin y Calle 11, Casilla 79, Guayaquil; Pres. CARLOS VALDANO RAFFO; Man. FERNANDO VALDANO TRUJILLO.

Transfuel, CA: Junin 415 y Cordova, 4°, Casilla 09-01-30H, Guayaquil; tel. (4) 304-142; Chair. Ing. ERNESTO ESCOBAR PALLARES; Man. Dir CARLOS MANRIQUE A.

Transportes Navieros Ecuatorianos—Transnave: Edif. Citibank, 4°–7°, Avda 9 de Octubre 416 y Chile, Casilla 4706, Guayaquil; tel. (4) 561-455; fax (4) 566-273; transports general cargo within the European South Pacific Magellan Conference, Japan West Coast South America Conference and Atlantic and Gulf West Coast South America Conference; Pres. Vice-Adm. YÉZID JARAMILLO SANTOS; Gen. Man. RUBÉN LANDÁZURI ZAMBRANO.

CIVIL AVIATION

There are two international airports: Mariscal Sucre, near Quito, and Simón Bolívar, near Guayaquil.

Ecuatoriana: Edif. Torres de Almagro, Avda Reina Victoria y Colón, Torres de Almagro, Casilla 17-07-8475, Quito; tel. (2) 563-003; fax (2) 563-920; e-mail eu@impsat.comec; f. 1974 as Empresa Ecuatoriana de Aviación; nationalized 1974; ceased operations in 1993, aircraft subsequently sold or repossessed, and routes to the USA assigned to SAETA; airline subsequently reactivated; scheduled domestic and international services to Latin America and the USA; Dir. RICARDO VIO GUERRERO.

SAETA Air Ecuador (Sociedad Anónima Ecuatoriana de Transportes Aereos): Avda. Carlos Julio Arosemena Km. 2½, Guayaquil; tel. (4) 201-152; fax (4) 201-153; e-mail ehbuzon@saeta .com.ec; internet www.saeta.com.ec; f. 1967; domestic and regional scheduled flights; charter cargo services; Chair. ROBERTO DUNN BARREIRO; Exec. Dir ROBERTO D. SUÁREZ.

Servicios Aereos Nacionales (SAN): Km. 21½, Avda Carlos Julio Arrosemena, Apdo 7138, Guayaquil; tel. (4) 202-832; fax (4) 201-152; f. 1964; scheduled passenger and cargo services linking Guayaquil with Quito and the Galápagos Islands and Quito with Cuenca; Dir of Operations Capt. LUGIEBRE JEPEZ.

Transportes Aéreos Militares Ecuatorianos (TAME): Avda Amazonas 1354 y Colón, 6°, Casilla 17-07-8736, Sucursal Almagro, Quito; tel. (2) 547-000; fax (2) 500-736; e-mail tame1@tame.com.ec; internet wwwpub4.ecua.net.ec/tame/; f. 1962; domestic scheduled and charter services for passengers and freight; Pres. WILLIAM BIRKETT.

The following airlines also offer national and regional services:

Aerotaxis Ecuatorianos, SA (ATESA); Cía Ecuatoriana de Transportes Aéreos (CEDTA); Ecuastol Servicios Aéreos, SA; Ecuavia Cía Ltda; Aeroturismo Cía Ltda (SAVAC).

Tourism

Tourism has become an increasingly important industry in Ecuador, with 510,627 foreign arrivals (including same-day visitors) in 1998. Of total visitors in that year, some 32% came from Colombia, 6% were from Peru, 10% from other Latin American countries, 22% from the USA and 21% from Europe. Receipts from the tourism industry amounted to US $281m. in 1996.

Asociación Ecuatoriana de Agencias de Viajes y Turismo—ASECUT: Edif. Banco del Pacífico, 5°, Avda Amazonas 720 y Veintimilla, Casilla 9421, Quito; tel. (2) 503-669; fax (2) 285-872; f. 1953; Pres. KATBE I. TOUMA ABUHAYAR.

Corporación Ecuatoriana de Turismo—CETUR: Avda Eloy Alfaro y Carlos Tobar, Quito; tel. (2) 507-555; fax (2) 507-564; f. 1964; govt-owned; Exec. Dir KATBE I. TOUMA ABUHAYAR.

Defence

At 1 August 2000 Ecuador's numbered 57,500: Army 50,000, Navy 4,500 (including 1,500 marines), Air Force 3,000. Paramilitary forces included 270 coastguards. Military service lasts for one year and is selective for men at the age of 20.
Defence Expenditure: an estimated US $400m. in 2000.
Chief of Staff of the Armed Forces: Vice-Adm. MIGUEL SAONA.

Education

Education in Ecuador is officially compulsory for six years, to be undertaken between six and 14 years of age. All public schools are free. Private schools feature prominently in the educational system. Primary education is available for children aged between six and 12 years. In 1994 the total enrolment at primary and secondary schools was equivalent to 80% of the school-age population. In 1996/97 a total of 1,888,172 children attended 17,367 primary schools. Secondary education, in general and specialized technical or humanities schools, is available for students aged 12 to 18. In 1993/94 there were 2,868 secondary schools, attended by a total of 785,522 pupils. University courses last for up to six years, and include programmes for teacher training. A number of adult schools and literacy centres were established with the aim of reducing the adult illiteracy rate, which averaged 26.1% in 1974, but only an estimated 9.9% in 1995. In many rural areas, Quechua and other indigenous Amerindian languages are used in education. Budgetary expenditure on education and culture by the central Government was estimated at 1,426,660m. sucres in 1995.

Bibliography

For works on South America generally, see Select Bibliography (Books).

Corkill, D., and Cubitt, D. *Ecuador: Fragile Democracy*. London, Latin America Bureau, 1988.

Cueva, A. *The Process of Political Domination in Ecuador* (trans. Danielle Salti). New Brunswick, NJ, Transaction Books, 1981.

Downes, R., and Marcella, G. *Security Cooperation in the Western Hemisphere: Resolving the Ecuador-Peru Conflict*. Boulder, CO, Lynne Rienner Publishers, 1999.

Hurtado, O. *Political Power in Ecuador 1972–1992*. Boulder, CO, Westview Press, 1985.

Kyle, D. *Transnational Peasants: Migrations, Networks and Ethnicity in Andean Ecuador*. Baltimore, MD, Johns Hopkins University Press, 2000.

Philip, G. *Oil and Politics in Latin America*. Cambridge, Cambridge University Press, 1982.

Pineo, R. *Social and Economic Reform in Ecuador: Life and Work in Guayaquil*. Gainesville, FL, University Press of Florida, 1996.

Redclift, M. R. *Agrarian Reform and Peasant Organizations on the Ecuadorian Coast*. London, Athlone Press, 1978.

Selverston-Scher, M. *Ethnopolitics in Ecuador: Indigenous Rights and the Strengthening of Democracy*. Boulder, CO, Lynne Rienner Publishers, 2001.

Wood, B. *Aggression and History: The Case of Ecuador and Peru*. New York, NY, Columbia University Press, Institute of Latin American Studies, 1978.

EL SALVADOR

Area: 21,041 sq km (8,124 sq miles).

Population (official estimate, mid-2000): 6,276,000.

Capital: San Salvador, population 415,346 at census of 1992.

Language: Spanish.

Religion: Mainly Christianity (some 86% Roman Catholic).

Climate: Tropical in the coastal lowlands, but temperate in the uplands; average annual rainfall is about 1,830 mm.

Time: GMT –6 hours.

Public Holidays

2002: 1 January (New Year's Day), 27–31 March (Easter), 1 May (Labour Day), 30 May (Corpus Christi), 4–6 August (El Salvador del Mundo Festival), 15 September (Independence Day), 12 October (Discovery of America), 2 November (All Souls' Day or Memorial Day), 5 November (Cry of Independence), 24–25 December (Christmas), 31 December (Bank Holiday).

2003: 1 January (New Year's Day), 16–20 April (Easter), 1 May (Labour Day), 19 June (Corpus Christi), 4–6 August (El Salvador del Mundo Festival), 15 September (Independence Day), 12 October (Discovery of America), 2 November (All Souls' Day or Memorial Day), 5 November (Cry of Independence), 24–25 December (Christmas), 31 December (Bank Holiday).

Currency: Salvadorean colón; 1,000 colones = £79.82 = US $114.29 = €128.76 (30 April 2001).

Weights and Measures: The metric system is officially in force, but some old Spanish measures are also used.

Basic Economic Indicators

	1998	1999	2000
Gross domestic product (million colones at 1990 prices)	54,028	55,883	56,985
GDP per head (colones at 1990 prices)	8,958.4	9,080.8	9,079.8
GDP (million colones at current prices)	104,907	109,086	115,647
GDP per head (colones at current prices)	17,394.6	17,726.0	18,426.9
Annual growth of real GDP (%)	3.5	3.4	2.0
Annual growth of real GDP per head (%)	1.7	1.4	–0.0
Government budget (million colones at current prices):			
Revenue	13,104.2	12,471.4	13,030.6
Expenditure	15,227.1	15,094.3	16,628.1
Consumer price index (base: 1995 = 100)	117.6	118.2	120.9
Rate of inflation (annual average, %)	2.5	0.5	2.3
Foreign exchange reserves (US $ million at 31 December)	1,577.9	1,969.5	1,889.8
Imports c.i.f. (US $ million)	3,112.4	3,129.8	3,795.7
Exports f.o.b. (US $ million)	1,262.8	1,164.1	1,341.5
Balance of payments (current account, US $ million)	–78.7	–241.9	n.a.

Gross national product per head measured at purchasing power parity (PPP) (US dollars, converted by the PPP exchange rate, 1999): 4,048.

Economically active population (persons aged 10 years and over, 1998): 2,403,200.

Unemployment (persons aged 10 years and over, 1999): 9%.

Total foreign debt (1999): US $3,705m.

Life expectancy (years at birth, 1998): 69.7 (males 66.7, females 72.7).

Infant mortality rate (per 1,000 live births, 1998): 32.

Adult population with HIV/AIDS (15–49 years, 1999): 0.60%.

School enrolment ratio (7–18 years, 1998): 78%.

Adult literacy rate (15 years and over, 2000): 79.7% (males 81.6; females 76.1).

Energy consumption per head (kg of oil equivalent, 1998): 640.

Carbon dioxide emissions (per head, metric tons, 1997): 1.7.

Passenger motor cars in use (per 1,000 of population, 1997): 61.3.

Television receivers in use (per 1,000 of population, 1997): 677.

Personal computers in use (per 1,000 population, 1999): 16.2.

History

ANDREW BOUNDS

Based on an earlier essay by Dr DAVID BROWNING

El Salvador's history has been dominated by the land question. The country is the smallest and most densely populated on mainland America and has very few natural resources. For thousands of years before the conquest by Spain between 1524–35 indigenous (Amerindian) races populated the country. Following the conquest, Spanish settlers established large plantations of cocoa and then indigo for export, and the native population was forced on to ever smaller areas of common land where they grew traditional subsistence crops such as rice, beans and yucca. This competition for a limited land base and the practice of planting export crops over as great an area as possible shaped El Salvador's society, politics and economy.

El Salvador achieved full political independence after the end of Spanish rule and the collapse of the United Provinces of Central America, which grouped it with Honduras, Guatemala, Nicaragua and Costa Rica from 1823–29. From the mid-19th century a small group of local landowners and merchants transformed the country into a specialized producer of agricultural exports. After the collapse of world demand for indigo in the 1860s coffee emerged as the mainstay of the national commercial economy, displacing traditional systems of local food production. In 1882 all common lands were abolished and three-quarters of all land passed into the private ownership of families comprising only about 2% of El Salvador's inhabitants. The majority of the population, displaced from their traditional lands, became permanent wage labourers on the new plantations or migratory seasonal workers.

In contrast to other countries in Central America, the agro-export economy of El Salvador was created by domestic, not foreign, capital and expertise. The economy was dominated by an interlocked élite of landowners and merchants (known as the 'Fourteen Families') who controlled the state, land, capital and markets. The formal democratic procedures of a constitutional republic were maintained, but governments were effectively appointed by the oligarchy to administer power in its own interests.

MILITARY DOMINATION OF GOVERNMENT, 1932–82

The events of 1931–32 challenged the basis of this power-structure. In 1931, against a background of national and international economic depression, relatively fair elections brought to office a reformist President, Arturo Araújo. The existence of widespread popular discontent and allegations that the Partido Comunista Salvadoreño (PCS—Salvadorean Communist Party), recently established under the leadership of Agustín Farabundo Martí, was promoting armed insurrection, provoked a conservative reaction. Araújo was deposed by a military coup in December 1931 and replaced by Gen. Maximiliano Hernández Martínez. A large-scale peasant uprising in January 1932 was violently suppressed; it was alleged that 30,000 people were killed. Farabundo Martí was arrested and executed. The land-owning élite, shaken by these perceived threats to its economic interest, abdicated its control of political power to the Army that had saved it.

For the next 50 years the relationship between the Armed Forces and the civilian oligarchy remained the central reality of the nation's power structure: the former guaranteed the privileges of the latter, while simultaneously promoting their own interests by establishing military rule as an institution. Shifts between 'conservative' and 'progressive' factions within the military led to a pattern of reform and repression. When abuses of presidential power threatened to provoke popular discontent, incumbent Presidents were removed by military coup: Gen. Hernández Martínez in 1944, Lt-Col José María Lemus in 1960 and Gen. Carlos Humberto Romero Mena in 1979. When reformist administrations were considered to be

too radical, they were removed by counter-coup—as in the overthrow of the military–civilian juntas of 1944 and 1960.

The economy continued to develop after 1945. A second period of export-led agricultural growth (based mainly on sugar, cotton and cattle) was accompanied by some industrialization. The latter was as a result of the creation of the Central American Common Market (CACM—see Regional Organizations, in Part Three) which increased market size. As in the past, this development was achieved primarily by Salvadorean capital and entrepreneurs, but the benefits accrued to a minority while the needs of the majority continued to be denied.

Between 1961 and 1979 the military leadership attempted to present its own party, the Partido de Conciliación Nacional (PCN—Party of National Conciliation), as the country's unifying force. Other parties were tolerated but repeated electoral manipulation ensured that PCN candidates—Lt-Col Julio Adalberto Rivera, Gen. Fidel Sánchez Hernández, Col Arturo Armando Molina Barraza and Gen. Romero—gained the presidency, and so retained power in the hands of the army. From 1960 the Partido Demócrata Cristiano (PDC—Christian Democratic Party), under the leadership of José Napoleón Duarte, consistently attracted the largest electoral support for any opposition party and grew in strength steadily.

In July 1969 a 13-day war with Honduras killed 2,000 people. The catalyst for the so-called 'soccer war' was a disputed decision in the third qualifying round of the soccer world cup. The roots of the conflict were territorial disputes and migration pressures. Some 300,000 Salvadoreans had emigrated to Honduras to farm. Honduras decided to expel them as it pressed a boundary claim. The frontier dispute was settled in September 1972 when Honduras was awarded two-thirds of the disputed land by international arbitration.

The return of the emigrants, now refugees, put more pressure on El Salvador's land. The number of landless peasants grew from 30,500 in 1961 (12% of the rural population) to 167,000 in 1975 (41% of the rural population). This combined with an economic depression, caused partly by the 1973 oil shock and its global consequences and partly by the loss of the Honduran market, to put heavy pressure on the regime. In the 1972 presidential election the opposition parties united behind Duarte but Col Molina unilaterally declared victory. Subsequent protests and an attempted coup were crushed and Duarte exiled. These events not only frustrated the hopes of fundamental reform by democratic means but also convinced many opponents of military rule that armed insurrection was inevitable.

In 1969 ORDEN, the first of a succession of extreme right-wing terrorist groups, was established to assassinate and intimidate those in support of reform and political change. In 1970 Cayetano Carpio, Secretary-General of the PCS, broke from the party to pursue a campaign of armed insurrection. His lead was followed by a number of distinct guerrilla groups on the extreme left, and in Cuba in 1980 they co-ordinated to form the Frente Farabundo Martí de Liberación Nacional (FMLN—Farabundo Martí National Liberation Front). The FMLN also established a political wing, the Frente Democrático Revolucionario (FDR—Democratic Revolutionary Front). Reforming politicians, previously strongly opposed to armed struggle, began to support the FMLN as the only available option for the pursuit of democratic change.

The Roman Catholic Church, which had been a supporter of the conservative regime, also became more identified with the opposition after the Medellín council of bishops in 1968 called for it to transform the lives of the poor and overcome injustice. The Church began to preach a message of social justice and organized bible study groups in each parish that became one of the few forms of social gathering permitted under the military regime. These groups moulded many resistance leaders.

Gen. Romero's victory in the presidential election of 1977 followed a campaign characterized by intimidation, fraud and violent suppression of subsequent public protests. Alarmed by the implications of the overthrow of the dictatorship of Gen. Anastasio Somoza Debayle in Nicaragua in July 1979, the military ousted President Romero in October. After a series of abortive civilian–military juntas, Duarte agreed to lead a provisional government, on the condition that fundamental reforms be introduced immediately and be guaranteed by the military and by the USA.

Duarte joined the junta in March 1980. In the same month the Government, assisted by the USA, expropriated one-quarter of all agricultural land, for conversion into peasant co-operatives, and nationalized the banks and major export institutions. This was the first stage of the most important change in the nation's economy since the abolition of common lands a century before. However, civil war was already imminent. Army and death-squad human-rights abuses were such that the population had little faith in the Government. At the end of March Oscar Romero y Galdames, Archbishop of San Salvador, whose Sunday homilies had regularly expressed support for the cause of the poor and oppressed, was assassinated in the act of celebrating Mass. At his funeral, without provocation, soldiers fired into the crowd of mourners, which numbered more than 250,000.

THE CIVIL WAR

The Effects of the War

In January 1980 the FMLN launched its 'Final Offensive', intended to achieve victory before the inauguration of President Ronald Reagan of the USA. It failed and the civil war continued at an increasing cost in human suffering and economic disruption. By 1992 more than 80,000 combatants and civilians had been killed, the vast majority by the Armed Forces; an estimated 550,000 (more than 10% of the population) had been displaced from their homes within the country, while in excess of 500,000 had fled the country as refugees. There was military stalemate. The Army, relying heavily on US support, was increased in size to 55,000 military and 15,000 paramilitary personnel. However, it was ill-led and relied on a strategy of sporadic infantry attacks, supported by aerial bombings across extensive 'free-fire' zones, thus alienating the civilian population. The FMLN relied on well-co-ordinated, dispersed ambush attacks, urban terrorism and economic sabotage, such as the destruction of power lines and crops and the mining of public highways, all of which increased the war's impact on civilians.

The economic cost of the conflict was so high that the collapse of the economy was only averted by direct US economic assistance. One-half of government budgets were committed to defence spending. Reduced export earnings and increased government deficits by 1987 resulted in servicing of the public-sector external debt exceeding 50% of annual export income. Unemployment and underemployment affected more than one-half of the adult population and per-head income decreased to levels of the 1960s. The crisis was exacerbated by two natural disasters: the 1986 earthquake that killed 1,500 people and the subsequent drought.

Meanwhile, political reform and US pressure required that the Armed Forces acquiesce in the transfer of power to civilian politicians by means of free elections under international supervision. In December 1980 the junta was reorganized and Duarte was appointed President of El Salvador. Elections for a constituent assembly in March 1982 divided power between the PDC and two major right-wing parties—the PCN and the Alianza Republicana Nacionalista (ARENA—Nationalist Republican Alliance), founded in 1981. In 1982 Alvaro Magaña Borja, a politically independent banker, was accepted by all parties as interim President. Under his guidance, in 1983 the major parties agreed to a new Constitution. This provided for a democratic political process and incorporated the essential principles of economic reform.

In May 1984 Duarte won the presidency in a direct electoral contest with the ARENA candidate, Maj. Roberto D'Aubuisson Arrieta. Elections in March 1985 gave the PDC an absolute majority in the Asamblea Nacional (Legislative Assembly). But Duarte failed to make progress towards a negotiated settlement of the war or social and economic reforms. In the 1988 election ARENA won control of the Asamblea Nacional and in 1989 its candidate, Alfredo Cristiani Burkard, was elected President.

Progress Towards Peace

Formal and informal contacts between the Government and the FDR-FMLN began as early as 1980. Each attempt at a negotiated peace, however, foundered on two key issues: the future role, control and structure of the military; and the integration of the FDR-FMLN into national political life. Despite his position as Commander-in-Chief of the Armed Forces, President Duarte did not control them and so could not guarantee the FDR-FMLN's conditions. His failure to do so was demonstrated by the terror tactics of the extreme right-wing 'death squads' which, aided by his senior officers, were responsible for the assassination of church leaders, trade unionists and political activists.

The FDR-FMLN also considered each of the six elections held between 1982 and 1989 as invalid. On each occasion the guerrillas disrupted balloting. From 1989 the FDR leaders accepted that there had been sufficient improvement in electoral conditions to allow them openly to participate in the election, as the Convergencia Democrática (CD—Democratic Convergence), but not until 1991 did one of its five constituent parties contest national elections.

The victory of ARENA in the elections of 1989 and 1991 caused widespread expectations that the conflict would escalate. Many of its senior members were openly committed to a military solution and there was a common belief that some party leaders, such as Roberto d'Aubuisson, were involved in the death squads. After President Cristiani's assumption of power in April 1989, the FMLN launched limited, but effective, offensives in May and June, accompanied by direct attacks against the ARENA leadership—notably the assassination of the Attorney-General in April and the Minister of the Presidency in July. The reaction of the right-wing extremists, orchestrated by groups within ARENA and the military, involved the assassination of trade-union leaders and suspected FMLN sympathizers. FMLN–ARENA negotiations in September broke down almost immediately and were followed by a nation-wide November offensive by the FMLN, which posed the most formidable challenge to the Government in 10 years of civil war. The FMLN gained temporary occupation of large areas of the capital. These successes provoked major reactions by right-wing extremists: the assassination of six Jesuit priests; the less-remarked killings of alleged FDR-FMLN sympathizers; and intimidation of church and human-rights groups and of left-wing politicians. In April 1990, however, representatives of the Government and the FDR-FMLN met in Geneva (Switzerland), under the chairmanship of the Secretary-General of the United Nations (UN). Following a series of difficult negotiations a comprehensive agreement was reached by 31 December 1991, leading to a cease-fire on 1 February 1992.

The ceasefire stemmed from domestic and international factors. The end of the cold war in 1989 ended US–Soviet confrontation in Central America and this allowed a regional solution by reviving the Esquipulas Accord, proposed by Costa Rica and endorsed by Central American Presidents in 1987. The Accord committed all five countries to adopt specific measures to achieve regional peace. These measures included: dialogue between governments and insurgent groups; commitments to democratic and pluralistic political systems; and cessation of support for insurgent groups from whatever source. The end of the cold war also allowed the UN to become actively involved in the task of conflict resolution in El Salvador: firstly, by sponsorship of negotiations; secondly, by the establishment of a resident UN Observer Mission in El Salvador (ONUSAL), to verify compliance with negotiated agreements. Finally, within El Salvador, the Government, and especially the military, came under intense US pressure to reach a settlement, while the FMLN, appreciating its increasing international and regional isolation, accepted the need for one.

This settlement was achieved in the UN-brokered agreement, announced in December 1991, and signed at Chapultepec Castle in Mexico City (Mexico) on 16 January 1992. The Chapultepec Accords provided a framework for the reconstruction of Salvadorean society. The peace agreement focused on the demilitarization and submission of the country to civilian control under the rule of law. On 1 February the formal cease-fire was implemented under the supervision of some 1,000 UN personnel and the National Commission for the Consolidation of Peace (COPAZ) was formally installed. COPAZ was composed of representatives from both government and guerrilla forces, as well as from all major political parties. Its aim was to supervise the enforcement of guarantees for the political integration of the FMLN.

As well as the immediate measures for the disengagement and demobilization of FMLN guerrillas, and the reform and reduction of the Salvadorean military, the Accords established a range of new civilian institutions and programmes. These included the participation of former FMLN members in a new Policía Nacional Civil (PNC—National Civilian Police), which replaced the paramilitary national police. A new National Council for the Defence of Human Rights was to be supported by an independent National Judiciary Council. A Land Transfer Programme for demobilized combatants and displaced civilians envisaged the transfer of some 10% of El Salvador's agricultural land to a total beneficiary population of about 47,500 people. A tripartite forum, representing the Government, workers and the private sector, was established in order to formulate social and economic policies.

Initial progress was made possible by a widespread desire for reconciliation and a willingness to seek concertación, or consensus. However, mutual allegations of failure to comply with the terms of the Accords persisted throughout 1992 and resulted in the negotiation of a revised timetable for disarmament. Nevertheless, the cease-fire was observed by both sides and, on 15 December (declared National Reconciliation Day), the conflict was formally concluded. On the same day the FMLN was officially registered and recognized as a legitimate political party.

POST-ACCORD POLITICS

Expectations over the Chapultepec Accords were only partially fulfilled. In November 1992 the Comisión de la Verdad (Truth Commission) released the names of 103 military personnel alleged to have participated in human-rights abuses in the civil war. The Government, however, was at first reluctant to remove from the Armed Forces those personnel identified by the Commission. The FMLN was prompted to delay the demobilization of its forces. The effective operation of the new civilian police was constrained by a lack of resources. A dramatic decline in political violence and human-rights violations was accompanied by increasing criminal violence. The independence and security of the judiciary, reformed on the recommendations of the Commission's report, had not yet been tested. In late 1993, following international pressure, the military personnel identified by the Commission were dismissed.

These issues posed the principal themes in the campaign leading to national elections on 20 March 1994, monitored by ONUSAL. In spite of problems in the organization of the elections, the people of El Salvador were provided with their first opportunity to express their political preferences in elections that were peaceful as well as free and fair. The three major contending parties were ARENA, the PDC and the FMLN, which in September 1993 had confirmed its political alliance with the CD, and later, in December, with the Movimiento Nacional Revolucionario (MNR—National Revolutionary Movement). Following a second-round 'run-off' contest on 24 April, Armando Calderón Sol, the ARENA candidate, was elected President, with 68.2% of the votes cast, compared with 31.6% for the FMLN candidate, Rubén Zamora Rivas. Calderón Sol was sworn in as President on 1 June.

Despite its success, serious divisions emerged within the FMLN in 1994. In December, two factions, the Resistencia Nacional (RN—National Resistance) and the Expresión Renovadora del Pueblo (ERP—Renewed Expression of the People), left the FMLN because of a difference in political interests. In March 1995 Joaquín Villalobos, the ERP Secretary-General, announced the formation of the Partido Demócrata (PD—Democrat Party), a centre-left grouping consisting of the ERP, the RN, the MNR and a dissident faction of the PDC. The PD co-operated with the ruling ARENA party. In June 1995 the support of five PD

deputies, as well as three independents, allowed the Government to gain legislative approval for an increase in value-added tax (VAT) to 13%, which had been opposed vehemently by others. However, a year later the PD withdrew from its pact with the Government, in protest at the latter's failure to soften its neo-liberal policies and boost expenditure on health and education.

Meanwhile, there was increasing dissatisfaction with the Government's failure to honour the terms of the Chapultepec Accords. Former soldiers alleged that they had not received financial compensation and other benefits promised in the 1992 agreement. In September 1994 retired soldiers occupied the parliament building and held a number of deputies hostage. The Government immediately pledged to enter into direct negotiations with the soldiers, and the siege ended peacefully. However, in January 1995 former soldiers again occupied the Asamblea Nacional and took a number of hostages. Once again the occupation ended swiftly and bloodlessly as the Government reiterated its promise to meet its obligations. However, the spectre of renewed armed conflict was still in the background.

A reduced ONUSAL contingent, known as MINUSAL, remained in El Salvador until 31 December 1996. In March 1997, contrary to expectation, the ruling ARENA party lost seats to the FMLN in municipal and legislative elections. ARENA gained only 28 seats in the 84-member Asamblea Nacional, compared with the FMLN's 27. The PCN won 11 of the remaining seats and the PDC seven. The FMLN also won control of 48 municipalities, experiencing a significant increase in support in the capital where the party won seven of the 16 contested seats, while ARENA won control of 161 municipalities. The candidate of an FMLN-led coalition, Héctor Silva, was elected as Mayor of San Salvador, on a programme of fiscal rectitude. However, the FMLN was deeply divided and unable to present a coherent alternative to ARENA nationally. In the presidential elections, held on 7 March 1999, Francisco Flores Pérez, the ARENA candidate, was elected President, with 52% of the votes cast. The FMLN candidate, Facundo Guardado, received 29% of the ballot. The election was characterized by the highest abstention rate in the country's history, with over 60% of the three million registered voters failing to turn out. Flores, a former professor of philosophy, was sworn in as President on 1 June.

Although in many respects the peace process in El Salvador had opened up the country's political arena to wider participation, and judicial and political reforms were planned, most of the population remained too overwhelmed by the daily struggle for economic survival to feel that politics had anything to do with them. Moreover, the levels of criminality in the country were of greater importance to the people than the electoral contest. The number of violent deaths in El Salvador was higher after the civil war then during it. President Flores announced that his main priority was to combat crime through the joint efforts of the PNC, the judicial system, the Government and the public. However, his first year in office was marred by a series of abductions for ransom, some apparently involving police officers, and numerous strikes and protests over his proposals for the privatization of the health service.

In one significant way the country had changed: it was rapidly becoming an urban society. The urban population surpassed the rural population in 1998 as people moved to find employment in the growing *maquila* (textile assembly plant) and service industries.

THE 2000 ELECTIONS

Voter dissatisfaction with the new Government as economic growth slowed resulted in an unexpected victory for the FMLN in legislative elections held on 12 March 2000, and it became the largest single party in the Asamblea Nacional, winning 31 of the 84 legislative seats. ARENA was the second-largest party, gaining 29 seats. However, the PCN came third, with 13 seats, giving the right wing a working majority in the legislature, although not guaranteeing it the 56 votes required for the approval of important legislation. Of the remaining seats, the PDC won six, while the Centro Democrático Unido (CDU—United Democratic Centre), an electoral alliance comprising the CD and the Partido Social Demócrata (PSD—Social Democratic Party) won three seats, and the Partido Acción Nacional (PAN—

National Action Party) won two. Once again there was a low voter turn-out, of about 33%. ARENA's poor electoral performance initiated an upheaval within the party, following the resignation of its President, Alfredo Cristiani, in May. The FMLN made further gains in concurrently-held municipal elections, winning control of 78 of the country's 262 municipalities, compared to ARENA's 127. Silva won a convincing re-election to the mayoralty of San Salvador, increasing the likelihood that he would stand as a candidate in the 2004 presidential election.

FMLN–ARENA TENSIONS

Relations between the FMLN and ARENA immediately became strained as the three right-wing parties combined to prevent the FMLN from claiming the presidency of the Asamblea Nacional, a post traditionally held by the largest party. To prevent a political impasse it was decided that the presidency was to be rotated annually among the three largest parties, the PCN, ARENA and the FMLN. In late 2000 President Flores responded to ARENA's electoral reverses by amending some of his more unpopular economic policies; he suspended the privatization of the two remaining state banks, announced new public spending in port infrastructure, and implemented a series of measures to protect the agricultural sector against cheap imports and to provide credit to the coffee sector. On 22 November President Flores unexpectedly announced that, from 1 January 2001, the US dollar would be introduced as an official currency alongside the colón, anchored to the colón at a fixed rate of exchange. The intention was to stabilize the economy, lower interest rates in order to stimulate the economy, and encourage domestic and foreign investment. The FMLN filed a case against the legislation with the Supreme Court of Justice; however, the so-called Law of Monetary Integration was approved by the Asamblea Nacional in December. Opinion polls held in 2001, following the introduction of the currency, showed that 80% of Salvadoreans were opposed to the use of the dollar alongside the colón, but that most had adapted to the use of the US currency.

Two severe earthquakes struck El Salvador on 13 January and 13 February 2001, measuring 7.6 and 6.6 on the Richter scale, respectively, and presenting the country with its most serious test since the civil war. More than 1,100 people were killed and damage was estimated at US $1,900m., representing 14% of gross domestic product (GDP) for that year. Around 1.5m. people (one-quarter of the population) were made homeless. The Government initially was overwhelmed; however, international and domestic criticism prompted President Flores to devolve much responsibility to the municipalities, declaring a state of emergency and establishing 87 medical and evacuee centres. Society grew closer through the national recovery effort and the efficient response of the police and army, which grew in popularity. Relations between ARENA and the FMLN worsened, however, and in the days immediately following the earthquake the parties continued a dispute over the budget, resulting in a delay in the distribution of aid. This dispute and the refusal by ARENA deputies to support a motion giving three days' worth of their salaries to earthquake reconstruction efforts increased people's disillusion with politicians. The housing, health and education services, and the communications sector were badly affected, while agriculture, industry and trade all suffered losses, particularly in the private sector. In March the Inter-American Development Bank pledged some $1,278.5m. in aid, for economic, social and environmental development projects. In that month the US immigration authorities granted a one-year protective status to Salvadorean illegal immigrants residing in the USA, releasing those held in custody.

In May 2001 the PCN supported the FMLN in granting US $1,000 each to 37,708 former village guards who had been recruited by the army during the civil war. However, this compensation was not covered in the peace accords and President Flores vetoed the bill, claiming that the country could not afford to pay compensation. The primary issue in 2001 remained the refugee problem, as it had been throughout Salvadorean history. The migrants' traditional options were emigration or revolt. Whether the Government could provide a third option would demonstrate how much the country had changed in nine years of peace.

Economy

Dr DAVID BROWNING

Revised for this edition by ANDREW BOUNDS

El Salvador is a small, densely populated country. With an area of only 21,041 sq km (8,124 sq miles) it had a population of 6.3m. in 2000. Population growth per year averaged 2.1% in 1991–2000. Infant mortality was 30 per 1,000 live births and life expectancy at birth was 69.7 years in 1998. Gross domestic product (GDP) per head in 2000 was 18,426.9 colones, placing El Salvador in the middle-range of the World Bank's (International Bank for Reconstruction and Development—IBRD) lower middle-income countries.

From 1992 the overriding priority for El Salvador was to reconstruct an economy devastated by a 12-year civil war. The war caused more than 80,000 deaths, over 1m. internal and external displaced people, a massive flight of capital and economic damage estimated at more than US $2,000m. Prior to the civil war El Salvador had achieved a period of sustained growth on the basis both of expansion and diversification of agro-exports and increases in manufacturing output. Between 1960 and 1970 the country's GDP expanded, in real terms, at an average annual rate of 5.6% and in the period 1970–78 the annual growth rate averaged 5%. Between 1978 and 1982, however, real GDP decreased by 22.3%. This decline, combined with the effects of a continuing population growth of 2.6% annually, reduced GDP per head by 1983 to levels comparable with those of the 1960s. From 1979 to 1982 investment, in real terms, decreased by 68% and consumption by 20%. Unemployment, combined with

underemployment, was estimated to affect more than 40% of the total work-force.

From 1983 there was a modest recovery, but the country continued to rely heavily on external financial assistance, mainly from the USA. Between 1980 and 1990 total external financial assistance to El Salvador was in excess of US $5,000m., with approximately 90% originating from the USA, making El Salvador the third-largest recipient of assistance from the USA at that time. In the same period real GDP growth averaged an annual 0.9%. One of the main purposes of US assistance was to offset economic sabotage by the Frente Farabundo Martí de Liberación Nacional (FMLN—Farabundo Martí National Liberation Front), which particularly affected the harvesting and export of the country's main export crop, coffee, and caused severe disruption of public transport and power transmission. Economic recovery was further impeded by the earthquake of October 1986, which caused material damage estimated at $900m. (mainly in San Salvador) and disrupted administration and public services.

The Government of President Alfredo Cristiani (1989–94) introduced major changes in economic policy that emphasized the role of the private sector and deregulation. Important sectors of the economy were returned to private ownership, including sugar refineries, distilleries, textile mills, hotels and fish processing plants, as well as most of the banks and financial institutions nationalized in 1980. There were reductions in public spending and controls on price increases by public utilities. At the same time there was removal of controls and subsidies on a range of products and, in some sectors, such as the local production of basic grains, output increased sharply. Other measures included the simplification of the tax system, a liberalization of import policy and the introduction of regulations against currency speculation. In 1990 agreement was reached with the International Monetary Fund (IMF) on stand-by loans of US $50m. The principal effects of these new policies were to stabilize a previously deteriorating situation, and to make the first moves towards recovery. Real growth in GDP improved to 5.3% in 1992.

The cessation of the war in the early 1990s provided real opportunities for the improvement of the economy. Real GDP growth rates increased to as much as 6.3% in 1995, but declined to 1.7% in the following year. In 1997 growth recovered somewhat to 4.2%, before decreasing to 3.5% in 1998, 3.4% in 1999 and 2.0% in 2000. Market reforms continued throughout the 1990s. In 1998 the state telecommunications company, Administración Nacional de Telecomunicaciones (ANTEL), was privatized, and in 1999 several electricity generating stations were sold off. Following serious public and trade-union protests in 1999 and 2000, and an electoral reverse in March 2000, President Francisco Flores Pérez, who assumed office in June 1999, retreated from further privatization in the health and banking sectors. However, in November 2000 he announced the radical and surprising step of 'dollarization', in an attempt to reactivate the economy. The legislation was approved in December and from 1 January 2001 the US dollar circulated freely with the colón at a fixed rate of 8.75. The Central Bank had maintained a fixed exchange rate of 8.79 since May 1995. The World Bank and the IMF supported the move. The aim was to integrate El Salvador into the global economy and to reduce real interest rates to US levels, in order to encourage investment to expand growth.

'Hurricane Mitch', which struck Central America in October 1998, resulted in the loss of an estimated 8% (about US $1,760m.) of El Salvador's GDP that year and accounted for some of the downturn, although its economic effects were felt mostly in 1999. In January and February 2001 two severe earthquakes hit the country, killing more than 1,100 people and leaving a further 1.5m. people homeless. Reconstruction costs were put at around $1,900m., or 14% of GDP. Donors in March promised $1,300m., mostly in loans, and the Government diverted $150m. from the 2001 budget. However, it would have to borrow heavily to finance reconstruction over the following five years. External debt was expected to rise from a comparatively low 23.1% of GDP in 2000 to 38.9% of GDP in 2005. This would put pressure on public finances. Moreover, 40,000 small businesses were damaged and 200,000 people left without temporary work in the fields, as crops and equipment were destroyed.

The earthquakes were likely to exacerbate poverty in the country. Although the poverty rate fell by 15 percentage points in the 1990s it remained at 51.1% in 2000, according to the World Bank, while rural poverty was 55%. By the end of 1999 unemployment had reached 9% and was increasing. At least 30% of the economically active population were under-employed. The average per head income in the rural sector was only US $460, according to a 1996 World Bank report, less than 50% of the national average. The same report found that over 20% of the higher income rural households received remittances from family members who had migrated, especially to the USA. Poor urban as well as rural households became increasingly dependent on this source of income, which helped to lessen the impact of macroeconomic adjustments. Remittances reached $1,370m. in 1999, and a record $1,750m. in 2000; they were expected to rise following the earthquakes.

AGRICULTURE

Agriculture (including hunting, forestry and fishing) remained an important economic activity in El Salvador, but the sector was contracting owing to mass migration to the cities of people attracted by an expanding financial and commercial sector and the rapidly expanding offshore *maquila* (textile assembly) industry. By 2000 some 59% of the population lived in urban

areas, an increase from 46% in 1997, and around 100,000 people were leaving the countryside every year. Agricultural growth fell significantly behind the rest of the economy in 1990–99, at an annual average of 0.9%. Its share of GDP fell from around 13% to around 10%. Following the impact of Hurricane Mitch, the sector contracted by 0.9% in 1998, but recovered strongly thereafter, growing by 6.6% in 1999, before contracting by 0.8% in 2000. The sector employed some 25.1% of the economically active population in 1998. In the same year agricultural exports accounted for only 22% of export revenues, owing to low coffee prices and the virtual disappearance of cotton production, along with the rise of the *maquila* sector. The area devoted to the cultivation of traditional products (beans, coffee, corn, cotton, rice, sorghum and sugar) fell by some 2% between 1980 and 1995; the area of land under coffee production fell by over 30% and that under cotton production by 83.2% over the same period; only land under sugar production increased, by 32%. Most basic food requirements of the national population were domestically produced. In 1995 70% of agricultural land was devoted to the cultivation of basic grains in which 68% of agricultural producers were engaged. Productivity increases in this sector were very low. According to a 1996 World Bank study on rural development, 63.7% of producers of basic grains cultivated areas of land of less than two hectares (ha). All available cultivable land was utilized, at varying rates of intensity, in a country with an increasing population density, which stood at 298.3 per sq km in mid-2000. Development of the agricultural sector was impeded by a scarcity of land for cultivation, its high level of degradation (31% in 1996, according to the World Bank), the high density of population and uneven rainfall, some 84% of which occurred during May–October.

The agricultural sector was a focus of major government reforms from 1980. In that year all plantations of more than 500 ha (20% of all agricultural land) were expropriated by the state-owned Instituto Salvadoreño de Transformación Agraria (Salvadorean Institute of Agrarian Transformation), for transfer to peasant-run co-operatives. In 1981 a programme of transfer of freehold title to tenant smallholders was introduced, and by 1985 had benefited over 35,000 peasants. In 1983 a statutory limit of 245 ha was placed upon the amount of land that could be owned by any Salvadorean national. The overall agrarian-reform programme was intended to benefit about one-half of the under-privileged rural population. These reforms were accompanied by nationalization of the domestic banks and crop-marketing institutions. Considerable disruption was caused by these major changes, although reductions in the scope of the reforms resulted in a revision of the number of people affected by the programme, and at most only 23% of the under-privileged population was expected to benefit from the over-centralized, bureaucratic and often corrupt agrarian-reform programme. In 1992, as part of the overall peace settlement, agreement was reached on the provision of land for the resettlement of combatants and refugees. It was estimated that some 10% of agricultural land was to be distributed to 45,000 heads of families, but by the end of 1994 only some 12,000 had received plots of 4–5 ha. In June 1996 a United Nations (UN) report criticized the failure of successive governments to implement the land-transfer programme. The programme was finally completed at the beginning of 1998, three years after the official deadline. However, there were many questions surrounding the economic sustainability of the land transfers, particularly if the land was planted with traditional peasant food crops. A move from such crops would require credits and technical assistance, but small farmers were not seen as a priority for the post-war governments of El Salvador.

Production of the major export crops was seriously affected by the internal conflict, a shortage of credit, increases in costs and declining profitability. Coffee production declined from the 1979 harvest of 4.1m. quintales (the old Spanish quintal, used in El Salvador, is equivalent to 46 kg), to 2.6m. quintales by 1988. A substantial proportion of the decline in coffee output during the 1980s was attributed to the campaign of sabotage by the guerrillas, which caused large areas under cultivation to be destroyed or abandoned. However, although coffee production increased in the early 1990s and in 1992 stood at 3.2m. quintales (approximately 147,000 metric tons) it declined in the wake of Hurricane Mitch to 117,200 tons in 1998, before increasing, according to the UN's Food and Agriculture Organization (FAO), to 160,800 tons in 1999. However, production declined again in 2000, to an estimated 138,300 tons. Export income from coffee was determined more by the fluctuations of world prices than by output. Income halved from US $517.5m. (38.2% of total export earnings) in 1997 to $247m. in 1999, according to Central Bank figures, before recovering to $298m. in 2000 (roughly 10% of total export earnings). In 1999 there were 22,000 producers of coffee in El Salvador, of which some 90% owned plots of less than 10 ha. In the same year the sector employed some 150,000 people. In May 2000 the Government announced a $115m. credit line for coffee producers, in an attempt to revive the sector and appease coffee producers. However, coffee exports fell by 60% in the first quarter of 2001.

Sugar cane, another important cash crop, also declined in output during the civil war. However, some recovery of the sector took place in the late 1990s. Total sugar cane production in 1998 was 5.5m. metric tons, compared to 4.6m. tons in 1997. However, output declined slightly in 1999 and 2000, to an estimated 5.1m. tons. Earlier in the decade low world prices and reductions in US import quotas adversely affected the prospects for sugar exports. The value of sugar exports was again reduced by falling prices to US $63.7m. in 1998 and to $46.0m. in 1999.Considerable attention was given to the development of possible new export crops, such as sesame seed, rubber, nuts, fruits and honey. The commercial fishing industry expanded considerably after the 1960s, reaching a record 21,542 metric tons by 1987. Although the total catch fell in the rest of that decade, it then gradually recovered to reach 14,533 tons in 1995. After declines in 1996 and 1997, in 1998 the total catch increased to 15,400 tons. In 1998 the total catch accounted for $39m. of export income. Non-traditional exports (including fodder, melons, pineapple and other products) increased their share of total exports considerably during the 1990s, particularly those to the Central American Common Market (CACM). These averaged some $300m. over the decade, roughly equivalent to the value of coffee production in 1998. Food production for the domestic market was dominated by the cultivation of maize, sorghum, beans and rice, primarily on agricultural smallholdings. Production levels declined after 1979, owing mainly to the security situation and the displacement of population. However, substantial increases were achieved after 1982, particularly on co-operatives in the reformed sector. Maize production increased by 3.8% in 1991–95, but fell from some 13.5m. quintales in 1996 to some 11.2m. quintales in 1997. Production then rose, reaching 651,900 tons (14.2m. quintales) in 1999, before falling slightly in 2000, according to the FAO, to 587,800 tons (about 12.8m. quintales). Along with maize, beans provide the staple food of most Salvadoreans. Owing to the effects of Hurricane Mitch, production decreased from 66,700 tons in 1997 to 46,100 tons in 1998. However, production increased again in 1999 and 2000, to 65,700 tons and 71,300 tons, respectively.

MINING AND POWER

Mining was of negligible importance in 2000 accounting for less than 0.1% of the total work-force and an estimated 0.3% of GDP. The main minerals produced were limestone, gypsum and salt.

From the construction of its first dam, on the River Lempa in 1950, El Salvador actively developed both its hydroelectric and its geothermal potential, to reduce dependence on imported petroleum as the primary source of power for commercial uses. Plans for the development of hydroelectricity centred on the San Lorenzo power-station, on the River Lempa, with a generating capacity of 180 MW. From 1979 the principal obstacles to realizing this potential were attacks by guerrilla forces on the stations and, more importantly, the repeated destruction of transmission lines. The sector was also adversely affected by the consequent lack of investment. The potential capacity of El Salvador's geothermal energy sources was estimated at 1,000 MW, but by 1985 only the Ahuachapan field had been developed. This had a capacity of 95 MW and became operational in 1980. The other principal geothermal fields to have been identified were in the eastern region of the country, which was one of the worst-affected zones during the civil war. In 1992 installed capacity was 740 MW: 50% hydroelectric, 37% thermal

and 13% geothermal. In 2000, a dry year, an estimated 30% of electricity production was contributed by hydroelectric installations, compared with 41.6% in 1998. In 2000 total electricity output was an estimated 3,504m. kWh.

The end of the war had a significant effect on the energy sector, the development of which was a high priority for the Government. In 1993 the Electric Power Emergency Project was launched. The Project was co-funded by the Inter-American Development Bank (IDB) and aimed to attract much-needed investment to the sector. Nevertheless, demand for electricity, which increased by 6% per year in the mid-1990s, still exceeded the increase in electrical energy generated. In January 1998 the Government sold 75% of the shares in four state-owned regional electricity-distribution companies. In early 1999 plans to construct an electricity inter-connection between El Salvador and Honduras were announced. The inter-connection was to form part of a regional power network covering the whole of Central America. Funding for the project, which was due to be completed by 2006, was provided partly by the IDB. In July 1999 the Government sold three petroleum-fuelled electricity generation plants to the US concern Duke Energy International for US $125m. The State still owned the nation's hydroelectric dams, but competition was allowed in thermal and geothermal production.

The end of the civil war also offered the opportunity to achieve a long-term transfer to hydroelectric and geothermal power and to reduce the country's heavy dependence on imports of crude petroleum for almost all its energy needs. In 2000 the imported fuel bill stood at US $210m., or 7% of the cost of merchandise exports. About 50% of El Salvador's petroleum imports were provided by Mexico and Venezuela at preferential rates, under the San José Agreement of 1980. In 1997 some 57% of energy consumption in El Salvador was derived from imported petroleum. In the same year commercial consumption of energy (oil equivalent) was 691 kg per head.

A very significant part of total non-commercial energy consumption was accounted for by the burning of wood and charcoal. El Salvador was almost entirely deforested and the incorporation of sustainable fuel-wood production into the rural economy received belated attention in the 1990s. In 1998 some 5.1m. cu m of timber were cut, mainly for fuel.

MANUFACTURING

The rapid growth of the manufacturing sector after 1960, within the context of the CACM, increased the sector's contribution to 15% of GDP by 1979. This expansion was subsequently halted and then reversed. The internal security situation caused a flight of capital (estimated at US $1,800m. in 1979–86) and the closure of industrial plants. In addition, shortages of foreign currency, the lack of supplier credits and short-term domestic credit, and reduced national and regional demand presented severe problems to the industrial sector. Between 1980 and 1984 the sector's contribution to GDP declined by one-third. In 1984 it was operating at only 52% of its capacity and output of the major components of industrial production—food, tobacco, beverages and textiles—declined by over 20% in that year alone.

From 1983 a series of measures was taken to revitalize the sector: promotion of exports within the regional market and, in the context of the US Government's Caribbean Basin Initiative (CBI), to the USA; development of credit lines for industrial companies, with particular emphasis on lending from foreign and multinational creditors; and consideration was given to combining compensation to previous owners of expropriated agricultural land with reinvestment of this compensation in industrial enterprises. Output slowly recovered and by 1987 manufacturing accounted for some 15% of GDP. In the post-war period, with a return of business confidence and private investment and with the development of regional markets in Central America, the development of the manufacturing sector had become an urgent priority. Exports of manufactures accounted for 60% of total exports in 1993, with three-quarters of these destined for Central American markets. Despite negative publicity in the USA over poor labour standards and the alleged repression of trade unions, the *maquila* sector, which mainly produced clothing items for the US market, became the highest value export sector by the late 1990s, generating the equivalent of 54.5% of total exports in 2000. In the same year restrictions on the sector were reduced when the Government granted it access to both domestic and regional markets. Previously, *maquila* manufacturers were only permitted to sell 15% of products in Central America. In May 2000 the *maquila* sector was boosted further when the USA agreed to broaden the terms of the CBI in order to provide North American Free Trade Agreement (NAFTA) parity to El Salvador and 23 other Latin American countries. The enhanced CBI provided duty-free access to the US market for a number of previously excluded categories of *maquila* garments. Exports grew by 21% in 2000 and the Government expected the number of jobs in *maquila* factories to rise from 70,000 in 2000 to 100,000 by 2004. The most important branches of manufacturing in 1996 were food products, chemical products, petroleum products, textiles, apparel (excluding footwear) and beverages. Manufacturing GDP grew by an annual average of 5.6% in 1990–99, by an estimated 3.7%, in real terms, in 1999, and by an estimated 4.5% in 2000. In 1999 the sector accounted for 22.6% of GDP, and employed 18.7% of the active labour force in 1998.

TRANSPORT AND TOURISM

There were some 9,977 km of roads in 1996, of which 306 km were part of the Pan-American Highway and 1,985 km were paved. In 1997 177,488 private cars and 33,087 commercial vehicles were registered. Improving the quality of existing roads through maintenance, rehabilitation and modernization was a major challenge for post-war El Salvador. A Vice-Ministry of Transport was established to direct and co-ordinate policy. The earthquakes of 2001 caused considerable damage to the road system, which, according to government estimates, would cost US $188m. to repair.

The Comisíon Ejecutiva Portuaria Autónoma (CEPA) is responsible for the administration of El Salvador's main ports, Acajutla and Cutuco, the El Salvador International Airport at Comalpa, Cuscatlán and the national railway system, which operated 602 km of track in the late 1990s, including the 429-km Salvadorean section of the International Railways of Central America. In 1998 the rail system carried 355,300 passengers and 239,800 metric tons of freight. CEPA improved its financial situation in the 1990s, but faced the problem of recovering traffic lost during the civil war, as well as competing with other Central American ports, particularly Puerto Quetzal in Guatemala. In 2000 the Government reversed its previous plans for privatization, agreeing a long-term loan with Japan to develop port facilities at Cutuco, on the Gulf of Fonseca. In 2001 the Government planned to offer as a concession a regular cargo ferry service from Cutuco across the Gulf of Fonseca to Potosi, Nicaragua.

Although, unlike other Central American countries, it has only a Pacific coastline, El Salvador, with its ruined temples and cities of the ancient Mayan civilization, volcanoes, mountain lakes and sandy beaches, has considerable tourism potential. Despite damage to the tourism industry during the civil war, the sector recovered strongly in the late 1990s. Tourist arrivals rose from 387,052 in 1997, to 541,863 in 1998 and 658,000 in 1999.

INVESTMENT AND FINANCE

In 2000 there was an estimated budget deficit of 3,473.4m. colones, equivalent to 3.0% of GDP. The country continued to depend on high levels of foreign aid and concessionary loans to finance much needed infrastructural development. The Government increased incentives for foreign investment as part of its programme for economic reactivation and stabilization; however, high crime levels and a violent death rate on a par with that experienced during the civil war deterred foreign investors.

In 1990–99 the average annual rate of inflation was 9.0%. In 1999 consumer prices decreased to 0.5%. In 2000 the extension of value-added tax (VAT) contributed to a 2.3% rise, but the introduction of the US dollar was expected to keep inflation close to US levels. Attainment of economic objectives during the 1990s was made more difficult by the cost of the implementation of the 1992 peace accords. In July 1995 the IMF approved a

stand-by agreement for some US $58m., to be made available to the Government for use in economic and financial programmes in 1995/96.

FOREIGN TRADE AND PAYMENTS

According to the Central Bank, imports in 2000 totalled US $4,948m. Intermediary goods accounted for $1,617m., consumer goods $1,218m., and capital goods $961m. The imports for the *maquila* industries accounted for $1,153m. The leading sources of imports in 1999 were the USA (51.7%), Guatemala (9.0%) and Mexico (5.8%). Exports in 2000 totalled $1,164m. Principal export destinations in 1999 were the USA (63.1%), Guatemala (10.9%), and Honduras (6.9%).

The trade surplus of former years gave way to a deficit from 1981, although declines in export revenues were accompanied by rigorous restrictions on 'non-essential' imports. After 1992 the deficit increased. In 2000 the trade deficit stood at US $1,718m., a significant increase on the previous year's $1,362m. The deterioration in the balance of trade during the war was offset by net inflows of capital, especially remittances from Salvadoreans working abroad, so that the country's reserves of foreign exchange, after reaching a low of $72m. at the end of 1981, increased to $414.8m. by the end of 1990. International reserves increased throughout the 1990s, from $489m. in 1991 to $1,942m. in 2000, enough to cover the monetary base and guarantee dollarization. Foreign direct investment increased considerably in the late 1990s as a result of the privatization of the telecommunications sector and the sale of shares in energy companies.

In May 2000 El Salvador signed a free-trade agreement with Mexico, Guatemala and Honduras, which came into effect in March 2001, with the aim of gradually opening up markets for industrial and agricultural products over a 12-year period. In May 2001 the Central American countries, including El Salvador, reached the basis of a deal with Mexico, the 'Plan Puebla–Panamá', to integrate the region through joint transport, industry and tourism projects.

Between 1990 and 1999 total external debt increased from US $2,148m. to $3,705m. Almost all of this debt was incurred on a medium- to long-term basis at low interest rates. In 2000 the cost of debt-servicing was estimated to be equivalent to 4.4% of the value of exports.

OUTLOOK

By 2001 El Salvador was financially stable and had recovered from the economic crisis of the 1980s. It was also the most liberal economy in Latin America. However, many challenges remained to be met, not least the effects of repeated natural disasters. While growth was impressive in the 1990s, GDP per head remained at pre-war levels and was not sufficient to reduce the high levels of poverty. The World Bank's 1996 report on El Salvador noted, in particular, the low human and physical resource accumulation, low levels of productivity and limited outward orientation and competitiveness. This would be accentuated by dollarization, which would make the country more expensive than its neighbours for manufacturing businesses. Similarly, in its 1998 report the IDB observed that while El Salvador demonstrated considerable success according to criteria of macroeconomic stabilization, success was less marked in terms of employment generation and development. Moreover, its balance of payments and the success of the dollarization process remained heavily dependent on continued high remittance flows from more than 1m. Salvadoreans working abroad, which totalled US $1,750m. in 2000. Added to the rapidly expanding *maquila* sector, this made the country heavily dependent on the US economy. High levels of poverty, agricultural stagnation, environmental damage and increasing crime and violence were all issues that the country needed to confront urgently. The Government faced a huge challenge in recovering from the earthquakes of early 2001, and its response would determine whether El Salvador could finally shake off the legacy of war and division and move the economy forward fast enough to reduce poverty.

Statistical Survey

Sources (unless otherwise stated): Banco Central de Reserva de El Salvador, Alameda Juan Pablo II y 17 Avda Norte, Apdo 01-106, San Salvador; tel. 271-0011; fax 271-4575; Dirección General de Estadística y Censos, Edif. Centro de Gobierno, Alameda Juan Pablo II y Calle Guadalupe, San Salvador; tel. 286-4260; fax 286-2505; internet www.minec.gob.sv/estadis.htm.

Area and Population

AREA, POPULATION AND DENSITY

Area (sq km)	
Land	20,721
Inland water	320
Total	21,041*
Population (census results)†	
28 June 1971	3,554,648
27 September 1992	
Males	2,485,613
Females	2,632,986
Total	5,118,599
Population (official estimates at mid-year)	
1998	6,031,000
1999	6,154,000
2000	6,276,000
Density (per sq km) at mid-2000	298.3

* 8,124 sq miles.
† Excluding adjustments for underenumeration.

PRINCIPAL TOWNS* (population at 1992 census)

San Salvador (capital)	415,346	San Miguel	127,696
Soyapango	261,122	Nueva San Salvador	116,575
Santa Ana	139,389	Ciudad Delgado	104,790
Mejicanos	131,972	Apopa	100,763

* Figures refer to *municipios*, which may each contain rural areas as well as an urban centre.

Source: UN, *Demographic Yearbook*.

BIRTHS, MARRIAGES AND DEATHS

	Registered live births		Registered marriages		Registered deaths	
	Number	Rate (per 1,000)	Number	Rate (per 1,000)	Number	Rate (per 1,000)
1991	151,210	28.3	22,658	4.2	27,066	5.1
1992	154,014	28.1	23,050	4.2	27,869	5.1
1993*	n.a.	29.9	n.a.	n.a.	n.a.	6.3
1994*	160,772	28.5	27,700	5.0	29,407	5.2
1995	159,336	27.7	25,245	4.5	29,130	6.1
1996	163,007	28.2	27,038	4.7	28,904	5.0
1997	164,143	27.8*	23,519	4.0	29,118	4.9*
1998	158,350	26.3	25,923	4.3	29,854†	5.0

* Rates based on UN population estimate.

† Preliminary figure.

Note: Registration is incomplete. According to UN estimates, the average annual rates in 1990–95 were: births 29.6 per 1,000; deaths 6.7 per 1,000.

Expectation of life (estimates, years at birth, 1998): 69.7 (males 66.7; females 72.7) (Source: UN Development Programme, *Human Development Report*).

ECONOMICALLY ACTIVE POPULATION

(ISIC Major Divisions, '000 persons aged 10 years and over)

	1996	1997	1998
Agriculture, hunting, forestry and fishing	578.5	547.1	558.0
Mining and quarrying	1.7	1.7	1.9
Manufacturing	370.6	334.1	415.6
Electricity, gas and water	8.1	15.2	8.7
Construction	131.9	138.7	121.2
Trade, restaurants and hotels	398.9	445.1	555.9
Transport, storage and communication	91.3	96.7	90.0
Financing, insurance, real estate and business services	27.1	30.3	82.6
Community, social and personal services	448.3	467.1	393.6
Total employed	2,056.4	2,076.0	2,227.5
Unemployed	171.0	180.0	175.7
Total labour force	2,227.4	2,256.0	2,403.2

Source: ILO, *Yearbook of Labour Statistics*.

Agriculture

PRINCIPAL CROPS ('000 metric tons)

	1998	1999	2000
Rice (paddy)	71.8	56.7	47.6
Maize	551.8	651.9	587.8
Sorghum	217.0	137.8	157.2
Dry beans	46.1	65.7	71.3
Sugar cane	5,650.9	5,145.4	5,145.0
Coffee (green)	117.2	160.8	138.3

Source: FAO.

LIVESTOCK ('000 head, year ending September)

	1998	1999	2000
Horses*	95.8	95.8	95.8
Mules*	23.8	23.8	23.8
Cattle	1,037.7	1,141.5	1,212.2
Pigs	312.0	248.5	300.0
Sheep*	5.2	5.2	5.2
Goats*	15.3	15.3	15.3

Poultry* (million): 8.5 in 1998; 8.8 in 1999; 8.1 in 2000.

* FAO estimate(s).

Source: FAO.

LIVESTOCK PRODUCTS ('000 metric tons)

	1998	1999	2000
Beef and veal	34.0	33.7	34.1
Pig meat	10.4	11.3	8.2
Poultry meat	47.9	46.2	47.6
Cows' milk	340.7	349.4	400.8
Butter and ghee	0.2	0.2	0.2*
Cheese	2.6	2.6	2.6*
Hen eggs*	50.8	52.3	53.0

* FAO estimate(s).

Source: FAO.

Forestry

ROUNDWOOD REMOVALS
('000 cubic metres, excl. bark)

	1997	1998	1999
Sawlogs, veneer logs and logs for sleepers	466	610	650
Other industrial wood	2006	—	—
Fuel wood	4,519	4,519	4,520
Total	5,185	5,129	5,170

Source: FAO, *Yearbook of Forest Products*.

SAWNWOOD PRODUCTION
(FAO estimates, '000 cubic metres, incl. railway sleepers)

	1997	1998	1999
Coniferous (softwood)	57	57	57
Broadleaved (hardwood)	14	14	14
Total	70	70	70

Source: FAO, *Yearbook of Forest Products*.

Fishing

('000 metric tons, live weight)

	1996	1997	1998
Capture	12.8	10.6	15.0
Nile tilapia	1.1	1.3	1.5
Jaguar guapote	0.6	0.4	0.4
Other freshwater fishes	1.1	1.1	1.2
Croakers and drums	0.3	0.3	0.3
Sharks, rays, skates, etc.	0.3	1.2	1.1
Whiteleg shrimp	0.5	n.a.	1.1
Penaeus shrimps	1.4	1.2	1.7
Pacific seabobs	4.8	2.1	6.1
Aquaculture	0.4	0.4	0.4
Total catch	13.2	11.0	15.4

Source: FAO, *Yearbook of Fishery Statistics*.

Industry

SELECTED PRODUCTS ('000 metric tons, unless otherwise indicated)

	1994	1995	1996
Raw sugar	323	302	310
Motor spirit (petrol)	185	178	202
Distillate fuel oils	264	218	107
Residual fuel oils	262	217	309
Cement	915	914	938
Electric energy (million kWh)	3,203	3,398	3,452

Source: UN, *Industrial Commodity Statistics Yearbook*.

Finance

CURRENCY AND EXCHANGE RATES
Monetary Units
100 centavos = 1 Salvadorean colón.

Sterling, Dollar and Euro Equivalents (30 April 2001)
£1 sterling = 12.528 colones;
US $1 = 8.750 colones;
€1 = 7.767 colones;
1,000 Salvadorean colones = £79.82 = $114.29 = €128.76.

Note: The foregoing information refers to the principal exchange rate, applicable to official receipts and payments, imports of petroleum and exports of coffee. In addition, there is a market exchange rate, applicable to other transactions. The principal rate was maintained at 8.755 colones per US dollar from May 1995 to December 2000. However, in January 2001, with the introduction of legislation making the US dollar legal tender, the rate was adjusted to $1 = 8.750 colones. Both currencies were to be accepted for a transitional period.

BUDGET (million colones)

Revenue*	1996	1997	1998
Current revenue†	10,321.7	11,195.1	11,296.6
Taxation	10,599.1	10,290.8	10,784.0
Taxes on income, profits and capital gains	3,054.0	2,911.7	2,999.1
Taxes on property	86.1	119.5	126.1
Domestic taxes on goods and services	6,014.1	5,909.2	6,355.6
Sales or turnover taxes	5,306.4	5,195.1	5,698.9
Excises	630.8	632.0	571.1
Taxes on international trade and transactions	1,424.6	1,307.5	1,268.8
Customs duties	1,411.3	1,305.2	1,268.1
Other current revenue	396.7	823.8	523.4
Entrepreneurial and property income	280.3	624.4	346.9
Administrative fees, non-industrial and incidental sales	89.3	92.6	90.4
Capital revenue	206.2	32.9	30.2
Capital transfers from non-governmental sources	194.8	—	—
Total	10,527.9	11,228.0	11,326.8

Expenditure‡	1995	1996	1997
General public services	1,779.3	1,674.0	1,639.0
Defence	848.9	843.2	853.2
Public order and safety	1,438.2	1,908.2	1,964.2
Education	1,655.8	2,006.4	2,361.9
Health	1,044.2	1,217.7	1,235.4
Social security and welfare	1,078.7	596.3	654.8
Housing and community amenities	148.5	670.5	219.5
Recreational, cultural and religious affairs and services	125.0	206.1	202.8
Economic services	1,541.7	1,831.9	2,053.8
Agriculture, forestry and fishing	192.1	355.3	263.1
Transport and communications	1,079.8	1,199.8	1,487.4
Other expenditure	1,188.5	1,346.1	1,431.1
Total expenditure	11,376.3	12,305.6	12,027.3
Current§	9,486.1	10,298.9	10,367.6
Capital‖	1,362.7	2,001.5	2,248.1

* Excluding grants received (million colones): 105.2 in 1996; 42.3 in 1997; 18.3 in 1998.

† Including adjustment (million colones): −674.1 in 1996; 80.5 in 1997; −10.8 in 1998.

‡ Excluding lending minus repayments (million colones): −747.2 in 1995; −1,209.6 in 1996; −176.3 in 1997.

§ Including interest payments (million colones): 1,188.5 in 1995; 1,346.1 in 1996; 1,431.1 in 1997.

‖ Excluding adjustment to cash basis and expenditure under previous budgets (million colones): 527.5 in 1995; 5.2 in 1996; −588.4 in 1997.

Source: IMF, *Government Finance Statistics Yearbook*.

1998 (million colones, provisional figures): Expenditure 15,261.3 (excl. lending minus repayments −103.9).

INTERNATIONAL RESERVES (US $ million at 31 December)

	1998	1999	2000
Gold*	19.8	19.8	19.8
IMF special drawing rights . .	35.2	34.3	32.6
Foreign exchange	1,577.9	1,969.5	1,889.8
Total	1,632.9	2,023.6	1,942.2

* Valued at US $42.22 per troy ounce.

Source: IMF, *International Financial Statistics.*

MONEY SUPPLY (million colones at 31 December)

	1998	1999	2000
Currency outside banks . . .	3,531	4,716	3,932
Demand deposits at deposit money banks	5,268	5,416	5,517
Total money (incl. others) . .	10,064	10,880	9,608

Source: IMF, *International Financial Statistics.*

COST OF LIVING
(Consumer Price Index; base: 1990 = 100)

	1997	1998	1999
Food	243.6	248.3	246.2
Rent	163.2	171.9	176.7
Fuel and light	155.2	176.1	176.2
Clothing.	153.9	153.0	151.4
All items (incl. others) . .	210.5	216.1	216.7

Source: ILO, *Yearbook of Labour Statistics.*

NATIONAL ACCOUNTS (million colones at current prices)
National Income and Product

	1991	1992	1993
Domestic factor incomes* .	39,747	46,232	55,844
Consumption of fixed capital . .	—	—	—
Gross domestic product at factor cost . .	42,594	49,841	60,522
Indirect taxes, *less* subsidies .	2,847	3,609	4,678
GDP in purchasers' values .	45,441	53,450	65,200
Net factor income from abroad .	—	—	—
Gross national product .	41,386	48,226	59,803
Less Consumption of fixed capital	—	—	—
National income in market prices	41,386	48,226	59,803

* Compensation of employees and the operating surplus of enterprises. The amount is obtained as a residual.

Source: UN, *National Accounts Statistics.*

Expenditure on the Gross Domestic Product

	1998	1999	2000
Government final consumption expenditure	10,178	10,981	11,760
Private final consumption expenditure	88,831	93,624	101,082
Increase in stocks . . .	990	123	−31
Gross fixed capital formation . .	17,365	17,619	19,636
Total domestic expenditure .	117,364	122,347	132,447
Exports of goods and services . .	26,407	27,432	32,077
Less Imports of goods and services	38,863	40,694	48,877
GDP in purchasers' values .	104,907	109,086	115,647
GDP at constant 1990 prices .	54,028	55,883	56,985

Source: IMF, *International Financial Statistics.*

Gross Domestic Product by Economic Activity

	1996	1997	1998*
Agriculture, hunting, forestry and fishing	11,746.4	12,744.3	12,388.0
Mining and quarrying . . .	406.5	438.4	411.8
Manufacturing	18,762.3	20,349.6	22,166.6
Construction	3,877.4	4,219.6	4,510.9
Electricity, gas and water . .	1,369.2	1,599.4	1,739.7
Transport, storage and communications . . .	6,822.5	7,756.7	8,446.1
Wholesale and retail trade . .	18,758.3	19,159.5	20,068.0
Finance, insurance, etc. . . .	3,026.1	3,601.2	3,894.2
Owner-occupied dwellings . .	6,938.1	7,785.6	8,378.1
Public administration . . .	5,982.3	6,533.7	7,026.1
Other	9,570.1	10,455.2	11,260.5
Sub-total	87,259.2	94,643.2	100,290.0
Import duties . . . . } Value-added tax . . . . }	6,717.7	7,128.0	7,677.9
Less Imputed bank service charge	2,928.7	3,843.0	4,155.7
Total	91,048.2	97,928.2	103,812.2

* Preliminary figures.

BALANCE OF PAYMENTS (US $ million)

	1997	1998	1999
Exports of goods f.o.b. . . .	2,429.2	2,459.7	2,500.4
Imports of goods f.o.b. . . .	−3,532.5	−3,762.7	−3,859.3
Trade balance	−1,103.3	−1,303.0	−1,358.9
Exports of services . . .	370.4	558.2	634.8
Imports of services . . .	−548.7	−678.8	−791.5
Balance on goods and services	−1,281.6	−1,423.6	−1,515.5
Other income received . . .	75.1	111.4	112.9
Other income paid . . .	−221.7	−266.8	−395.9
Balance on goods, services and income	−1,428.2	−1,579.0	−1,798.5
Current transfers received . .	1,363.6	1,507.6	1,565.6
Current transfers paid . . .	—	−7.3	−9.0
Current balance . . .	−64.6	−78.7	−241.9
Capital account (net). . . .	—	4.6	31.6
Direct investment abroad. . .	—	—	−2.9
Direct investment from abroad .	59.0	1,103.7	231.3
Portfolio investment assets . .	—	—	−2.1
Portfolio investment liabilities .	111.0	−221.5	75.4
Other investment assets . .	2.0	−8.0	−148.8
Other investment liabilities . .	457.6	136.2	461.5
Net errors and omissions . .	−202.4	−633.1	−199.9
Overall balance . . .	362.6	303.2	204.2

Source: IMF, *International Financial Statistics.*

External Trade

PRINCIPAL COMMODITIES (distribution by SITC, US $ million).

Imports c.i.f.	1996	1997	1998
Food and live animals . . .	358.6	403.0	405.5
Dairy products and birds' eggs .	52.0	61.4	60.8
Cereals and cereal preparations .	128.7	140.1	127.3
Crude materials (inedible) except fuels	95.2	100.3	117.9
Textile fibres and their wastes .	55.2	61.6	69.1
Mineral fuels, lubricants, etc. .	325.4	336.7	322.0
Petroleum, petroleum products, etc.	299.7	311.5	296.2
Crude petroleum	121.6	119.6	86.7
Refined petroleum products .	175.2	188.5	206.4
Residual fuel oils . . .	114.0	125.2	120.4
Animal and vegetable oils, fats and waxes	76.2	76.9	82.4
Chemicals and related products	455.4	503.4	472.4
Medicinal and pharmaceutical products	109.7	115.2	94.3
Medicaments	89.9	90.8	75.4
Perfumes and cleansing preparations, etc. . . .	70.6	80.3	76.2
Plastic materials, etc. . . .	85.2	95.3	106.4
Products of polymerization, etc.	71.8	80.2	87.1
Basic manufactures . .	435.4	499.5	572.4
Paper, paperboard and manufactures	90.3	94.1	112.5
Paper and paperboard . .	68.4	68.2	87.9
Textile yarn, fabrics, etc. . .	45.9	64.3	73.4
Iron and steel	99.0	111.6	134.8
Machinery and transport equipment	700.1	783.8	853.9
Power-generating machinery and equipment	58.1	44.0	65.2
Machinery specialized for particular industries . . .	87.2	136.0	127.1
General industrial machinery, equipment and parts . .	85.2	114.7	131.4
Office machines and automatic data-processing equipment . .	57.7	76.5	62.1
Telecommunications and sound equipment	68.5	67.2	84.2
Other electrical machinery, apparatus, etc. . . .	94.1	97.4	95.1
Road vehicles	237.2	234.6	260.8
Passenger motor cars (except buses)	79.0	78.5	91.9
Lorries and special purpose motor vehicles . . .	96.4	90.0	102.1
Lorries and trucks . . .	89.0	86.0	95.3
Miscellaneous manufactured articles	204.8	237.0	260.1
Total (incl. others)	2,670.1	2,961.5	3,108.1

Source: UN, *International Trade Statistics Yearbook.*

Exports f.o.b.	1996	1997	1998
Food and live animals . . .	509.1	715.5	557.1
Fish, crustaceans and molluscs .	43.7	34.2	38.6
Fresh, chilled, frozen, salted or dried crustaceans and molluscs	40.9	31.6	33.9
Cereals and cereal preparations	19.6	23.8	30.3
Cereal preparations, etc. .	17.6	21.9	25.6
Sugar, sugar preparations and honey	53.1	74.8	85.3
Sugar and honey . . .	45.7	68.0	77.7
Sugars, beet and cane (raw, solid)	31.6	52.9	63.7
Coffee, tea, cocoa, etc. . . .	341.9	519.8	328.1
Coffee and coffee substitutes .	340.0	517.5	324.6
Coffee (incl. husks and skins) and substitutes containing coffee	339.1	515.9	322.0
Mineral fuels, lubricants, etc. .	33.2	44.5	47.6
Petroleum, petroleum products, etc.	33.2	44.4	47.6
Refined petroleum products .	33.1	44.3	47.2
Chemicals and related products	141.2	166.5	178.0
Medicinal and pharmaceutical products	49.7	53.2	58.8
Medicaments	45.7	48.0	53.6
Perfumes and cleansing preparations, etc. . . .	48.4	63.7	68.7
Soap, etc.	33.8	42.9	46.1
Basic manufactures . .	188.6	232.6	252.7
Paper, paperboard and manufactures	57.0	64.4	64.6
Shaped or cut articles of paper and paperboard . . .	40.6	45.8	45.7
Textile yarn, fabrics, etc. . .	67.3	84.2	90.8
Iron and steel	21.6	26.9	34.8
Non-ferrous metals . . .	21.0	23.0	27.1
Aluminium	20.7	22.1	26.1
Machinery and transport equipment	35.3	50.2	50.0
Miscellaneous manufactured articles	77.3	98.5	130.9
Clothing and accessories . . .	27.5	39.4	54.9
Total (incl. others)	1,024.3	1,354.0	1,257.1

Source: UN, *International Trade Statistics Yearbook.*

PRINCIPAL TRADING PARTNERS
(US $ million)

Imports c.i.f.	1996	1997	1998
Brazil	29.4	23.6	26.0
China, People's Republic . . .	7.9	14.0	53.4
Colombia	19.0	42.2	32.8
Costa Rica	101.7	116.3	115.1
Ecuador	29.2	79.3	85.5
Germany	97.2	93.6	89.7
Guatemala	279.8	323.7	346.8
Honduras	70.3	85.1	87.8
Italy	31.2	31.2	31.6
Japan	114.1	91.2	145.1
Mexico	172.3	235.3	238.4
Netherlands	30.4	18.2	27.2
Netherlands Antilles	30.3	20.7	37.0
Nicaragua	54.1	51.1	49.4
Panama	175.9	65.5	106.1
Spain	24.2	39.5	49.0
USA	1,067.6	1,224.6	1,197.6
Venezuela	59.6	63.6	41.8
Total (incl. others)	2,670.1	2,961.5	3,108.0

Exports f.o.b.	1996	1997	1998
Belgium	60.6	60.9	24.7
Costa Rica	93.3	111.4	110.3
Dominican Republic . . .	8.1	11.4	13.4
France	4.7	16.8	13.2
Germany	159.0	237.5	139.9
Guatemala	210.7	264.1	282.5
Honduras	97.5	136.0	148.8
Japan	10.3	14.1	12.5
Mexico	12.6	17.8	17.3
Netherlands	31.3	29.1	21.9
Nicaragua	53.7	64.6	75.0
Panama	24.5	24.5	24.3
Russia	0.0	0.0	22.2
United Kingdom	9.9	29.9	19.4
USA	197.4	260.1	270.1
Total (incl. others) . . .	1,024.3	1,353.9	1,257.1

Source: UN, *International Trade Statistics Yearbook.*

Transport

RAILWAYS (traffic)

	1997	1998
Number of passengers ('000)	460.5	355.3
Passenger-kilometres (million) . . .	7.1	5.5
Freight ('000 metric tons)	161.1	239.8
Freight ton-kilometres (million) . . .	17.4	24.8

ROAD TRAFFIC (motor vehicles in use at 31 December)

	1995	1996	1997
Passenger cars	151,081	168,234	177,488
Buses and coaches . . .	29,293	32,238	33,087
Lorries and vans . . .	125,101	142,916	151,772
Motorcycles and mopeds . .	28,888	38,330	27,476

Source: IRF, *World Road Statistics.*

SHIPPING
Merchant Fleet (registered at 31 December)

	1996	1997	1998
Number of vessels . . .	12	12	12
Total displacement ('000 grt) . .	1.5	1.5	1.5

Source: Lloyd's Register of Shipping, *World Fleet Statistics.*

CIVIL AVIATION (traffic on scheduled services)

	1995	1996	1997
Kilometres flown (million) . .	21	22	20
Passengers carried ('000) . .	1,698	1,800	1,701
Passenger–km (million) . .	2,077	2,181	2,080
Total ton-km (million) . .	227	212	204

Source: UN, *Statistical Yearbook.*

Tourism

TOURIST ARRIVALS BY COUNTRY OF ORIGIN
(excluding Salvadorean nationals residing abroad)

	1996	1997	1998
Canada	8,855	9,052	9,282
Costa Rica	19,497	19,919	28,804
Guatemala	54,210	83,685	163,485
Honduras	20,644	36,515	84,299
Mexico	11,276	19,737	19,912
Nicaragua	14,104	24,546	60,735
Panama	9,050	6,883	10,498
Spain	8,242	8,779	7,631
USA	88,905	123,355	97,838
Total (incl. others)	282,835	387,052	541,863

Receipts from tourism (US $ million): 67 in 1997; 125 in 1998; 211 in 1999.

Arrivals ('000): 658 in 1999.

Sources: World Tourism Organization, *Yearbook of Tourism Statistics,* World Bank, *World Development Indicators.*

Communications Media

	1995	1996	1997
Radio receivers ('000 in use) . .	2,600	2,670	2,750
Television receivers ('000 in use) .	3,900	3,910	4,000
Telephones ('000 main lines in use)	285	325	n.a.
Mobile cellular telephones			
(subscribers)	13,475	23,270	40,163
Daily newspapers:			
Number	6	5	n.a.
Total circulation ('000) . .	280	278	n.a.
Non-daily newspapers:			
Number	6	6	n.a.
Total circulation ('000) . .	48	52	n.a.

Source: mainly UNESCO, *Statistical Yearbook.*

Education

(1997)

	Insti-tutions	Teachers	Students		
			Males	Females	Total
Pre-primary . . .	3,679*	6,009*	88,447	90,599	179,046
Primary . . .	5,025*	34,496*	610,528	580,524	1,191,052
Secondary . .	n.a.	9,255*	73,295	79,179	152,474
Tertiary:					
University level . .	32	5,610*	53,183*	54,292*	107,475*
Other higher . .	n.a.	309*	2,747*	2,044*	4,791*

* 1996 figure.

Source: UNESCO, *Statistical Yearbook.*

Directory

The Constitution

The Constitution of the Republic of El Salvador came into effect on 20 December 1983.

The Constitution provides for a republican, democratic and representative form of government, composed of three Powers—Legislative, Executive, and Judicial—which are to operate independently. Voting is a right and duty of all citizens over 18 years of age. Presidential and congressional elections may not be held simultaneously.

The Constitution binds the country, as part of the Central American Nation, to favour the total or partial reconstruction of the Republic of Central America. Integration in a unitary, federal or confederal form, provided that democratic and republican principles are respected and that basic rights of individuals are fully guaranteed, is subject to popular approval.

LEGISLATIVE ASSEMBLY

Legislative power is vested in a single chamber, the Asamblea Nacional, whose members are elected every three years and are eligible for re-election. The Asamblea's term of office begins on 1 May. The Asamblea's duties include the choosing of the President and Vice-President of the Republic from the two citizens who shall have gained the largest number of votes for each of these offices, if no candidate obtains an absolute majority in the election. It also selects the members of the Supreme and subsidiary courts; of the Elections Council; and the Accounts Court of the Republic. It determines taxes; ratifies treaties concluded by the Executive with other States and international organizations; sanctions the Budget; regulates the monetary system of the country; determines the conditions under which foreign currencies may circulate; and suspends and reimposes constitutional guarantees. The right to initiate legislation may be exercised by the Asamblea (as well as by the President, through the Council of Ministers, and by the Supreme Court). The Asamblea may override, with a two-thirds majority, the President's objections to a Bill which it has sent for presidential approval.

PRESIDENT

The President is elected for five years, the term beginning and expiring on 1 June. The principle of alternation in the presidential office is established in the Constitution, which states the action to be taken should this principle be violated. The Executive is responsible for the preparation of the Budget and its presentation to the Asamblea; the direction of foreign affairs; the organization of the armed and security forces; and the convening of extraordinary sessions of the Asamblea. In the event of the President's death, resignation, removal or other cause, the Vice-President takes office for the rest of the presidential term; and, in case of necessity, the Vice-President may be replaced by one of the two Designates elected by the Asamblea.

JUDICIARY

Judicial power is exercised by the Supreme Court and by other competent tribunals. The Magistrates of the Supreme Court are elected by the Legislature, their number to be determined by law. The Supreme Court alone is competent to decide whether laws, decrees and regulations are constitutional or not.

The Government

HEAD OF STATE

President: Francisco Flores Pérez (assumed office 1 June 1999).
Vice-President: Carlos Quintanilla Schmidt.

COUNCIL OF MINISTERS
(August 2001)

Chief of Staff and Minister of the Treasury: Dr Juan José Daboub.
Minister of Foreign Affairs: María Eugenia Brizuela de Avila.
Minister of the Interior: (vacant).
Minister of Public Security and Justice: Francisco Bertrand Galindo.
Minister of the Economy: Miguel Ernesto Lacayo Argüello.
Minister of Education: Ana Evelyn Jacir de Lovo.

Minister of National Defence: Maj. Gen. Juan Antonio Martínez Varela.
Minister of Labour and Social Security: Jorge Isidoro Nieto Menéndez.
Minister of Public Health and Social Welfare: José López Beltrán.
Minister of Agriculture and Livestock: Salvador Urrutia Loucel.
Minister of Public Works: José Angel Quiros.
Minister of the Environment and Natural Resources: Ana María Majano Guerrero.

MINISTRIES

Ministry for the Presidency: Avda Cuba, Calle Darió González 806, Barrio San Jacinto, San Salvador; tel. 221-8483; fax 771-0950; internet www.casapres.gob.sv.

Ministry of Agriculture and Livestock: Alameda Roosevelt, San Salvador; tel. 779-1579; fax 779-1941; internet www.mag.gob.sv.

Ministry of the Economy: Centro de Gobierno, Alameda Juan Pablo II y Calle Guadalupe, San Salvador; tel. 281-1122; fax 221-5446; internet www.minec.gob.sv.

Ministry of Education: Dirección de Publicaciones, 17 Avda Sur 430, San Salvador; tel. 222-0665; fax 271-1071; internet www.mined.gob.sv.

Ministry of the Environment and Natural Resources: Edif. Torre El Salvador, 3°, Alameda Roosevelt y 55 Avda Norte, San Salvador; tel. 260-8900; fax 260-3117; e-mail medioambiente@marn.gob.sv; internet www.marn.gob.sv.

Ministry of Foreign Affairs: 5500 Alameda Dr Manuel Enrique Araújo, Km 6, Carretera a Santa Tecla, San Salvador; tel. 243-3712; fax 243-3714; internet www.rree.gob.sv.

Ministry of the Interior: Centro de Gobierno, Alameda Juan Pablo II y Calle Guadalupe, San Salvador; tel. 222-5000; e-mail informacion@minter.gob.sv; internet www.minter.gob.sv.

Ministry of Labour and Social Security: Avda La Capilla 223, Col. San Benito, San Salvador; tel. 779-0388; fax 779-0877.

Ministry of National Defence: Alameda Dr Manuel Enrique Araújo, Km 5, Carretera a Santa Tecla, San Salvador; tel. 223-0233; fax 998-2005.

Ministry of Public Health and Social Welfare: Calle Arce 827, San Salvador; tel. 771-0008; internet www.mspas.gob.sv.

Ministry of Public Security and Justice: Centro de Gobierno, Edif. B-1, Alameda Juan Pablo II y Avda Norte 17, San Salvador; tel. 221-3688; fax 221-3956; e-mail mjministro@telemovil.com.

Ministry of Public Works: 1a Avda Sur 603, San Salvador; tel. 222-1505; fax 771-2881.

Ministry of the Treasury: Edif. Ministerio de Hacienda, Blvd Los Héroes 1231, San Salvador; tel. 225-5500; fax 225-7491; internet www.mh.gob.sv.

President and Legislature

PRESIDENT

Election, 7 March 1999

Candidates	% of votes cast
Francisco Flores Pérez (ARENA)	51.96
Facundo Guardado (FMLN/USC)	29.05
Rubén Ignacio Zamora (CD)	7.50
Rodolfo Parker (PDC)	5.68
Rafael Hernán Contreras (PCN)	3.82
Salvador Nelson García (LIDER)	1.63
Francisco Ayala de Paz (PUNTO)	0.36
Total	**100.00**

ASAMBLEA NACIONAL

President: CIRO CRUZ ZAPEDA.

General Election, 12 March 2000

Party	Seats
Frente Farabundo Martí para la Liberación Nacional (FMLN)	31
Alianza Republicana Nacionalista (ARENA) . . .	29
Partido de Conciliación Nacional (PCN) . . .	14
Partido Demócrata Cristiano (PDC)	5
Centro Democrático Unido (CDU)*	3
Partido Acción Nacional (PAN)	2
Total	**84**

* Electoral alliance comprising the Movimiento Nacional Revolucionario (MNR), the Movimiento Popular Social Cristiano (MPSC) and the Partido Social Demócrata (PSD).

Political Organizations

Alianza Republicana Nacionalista (ARENA): Prolongación Calle Arce 2423, entre 45 y 47 Avda Norte, San Salvador; tel. 260-4400; fax 260-5918; f. 1981; right-wing; Leader (vacant); Pres. Lic. WALTER ARAUJO.

Centro Democrática Unido (CDU): Blvd Tutunichapa y Calle Roberto Masferrer 1313, Urb. Médica, San Salvador; tel. 226-1928; fax 225-5883; f. 1987 as Convergencia Democrática (CD) electoral alliance of the Movimiento Nacional Revolucionario (MNR), the Movimiento Popular Social Cristiano (MPSC) and the Partido Social Demócrata (PSD); changed name as above in 2000; became political party in 2001; Leader VINICIO PEÑATE; Sec.-Gen. RUBEN ZAMORA.

Frente Farabundo Martí para la Liberación Nacional (FMLN): 27 Calle Poniente 1316 y 9a Avda Norte 229, San Salvador; tel. 226-5236; internet www.fmln.org.sv; f. 1980 as the FDR (Frente Democrático Revolucionario)-FMLN as a left-wing opposition front to the PDC-military coalition Government; the FDR was the political wing and the FMLN was the guerrilla front; military operations were co-ordinated by the Dirección Revolucionaria Unida (DRU); achieved legal recognition 1992; Co-ordinator FABIO CASTILLO; the front comprised c. 20 groups, of which the principal were:

Bloque Popular Revolucionario (BPR): guerrilla arm: Fuerzas Populares de Liberación (FPL; Leader 'Commander GERÓNIMO'); based in Chalatenango; First Sec. LEONEL GONZÁLEZ; Second Sec. DIMAS RODRÍGUEZ.

Frente de Acción Popular Unificado (FAPU): guerrilla arm: Fuerzas Armadas de la Resistencia Nacional (FARN); Leaders FERMÁN CIENFUEGOS, SAÚL VILLALTA.

Frente Pedro Pablo Castillo: f. 1985.

Ligas Populares del 28 de Febrero (LP-28): guerrilla arm: Ejército Revolucionario Popular (ERP); Leaders JOAQUÍN VILLALOBOS, ANA GUADALUPE MARTÍNEZ.

Movimiento Obrero Revolucionario Salvado Cayetano Carpio (MOR).

Unión Democrática Nacionalista (UDN): f. 1969; Communist; Sec.-Gen. MARIO AGUINADA CARRANZA.

Futuro, Fuerza y Fortaleza (FUERZA): Residencial Villa Olímpica Senda 'B' 28, Avda Olímpica, San Salvador; tel. 223-1216; fax 245-1600; Dir-Gen. EDGAR MAURICIO MEYER BELTRAND.

Liga Democrática Republicana (LIDER): San Salvador; republican.

Movimiento Auténtico Cristiano (MAC): San Salvador; f. 1988; Leader JULIO ADOLFO REY PRENDES.

Movimiento Estable Republicano Centrista (MERECEN): San Salvador; f. 1982; centre party; Sec.-Gen. JUAN RAMÓN ROSALES Y ROSALES.

Partido Acción Democrática (AD): San Salvador; f. 1981; centre-right; observer mem. of Liberal International; Leader RICARDO GONZÁLEZ CAMACHO.

Partido Acción Nacional (PAN): 3a Avda Norte 320, San Salvador; tel. 281-1955; Dir GUSTAVO ROGELIO SALINAS OLMEDO.

Partido Acción Renovadora (PAR): San Salvador; f. 1944; advocates a more just society; Leader ERNESTO OYARBIDE.

Partido Auténtico Institucional Salvadoreño (PAISA): San Salvador; f. 1982; formerly right-wing majority of the PCN; Sec.-Gen. Dr ROBERTO ESCOBAR GARCÍA.

Partido de Conciliación Nacional (PCN): 15 Avda Norte y 3a Calle Poniente 244, San Salvador; tel. 221-3752; fax 281-9272; f. 1961; right-wing; Leader FRANCISCO JOSÉ GUERRERO; Sec.-Gen. CIRO CRUZ ZEPEDA.

Partido Demócrata (PD): Blvd Héctor Silva 128, Urb. Médica, San Salvador; tel. 225-3166; f. 1995 by Movimiento Nacional Revolucionario and a dissident faction of the PDC, together with Expresión Renovadora del Pueblo (f. 1994, fmrly the ERP, see above) and Resistencia Nacional (f. 1994, fmrly the FARN, see above), following their withdrawal from the FMLN; centre-left; Leaders JORGE MELÉNDEZ, JUAN MEDRANO.

Partido Demócrata Cristiano (PDC): 3a Calle Poniente 924, San Salvador; tel. 222-8485; fax 998-1526; f. 1960; 150,000 mems; anti-imperialist, advocates self-determination and Latin American integration; Sec.-Gen. RENÉ NAPOLEÓN AGUILUZ.

Partido de Orientación Popular (POP): San Salvador; f. 1981; extreme right-wing.

Partido Liberal Democrático (PLD): Calle El Progreso y Col. El Rosal 11, San Salvador; tel. 224-2143; f. 1994; right-wing; Leader KIRIO WALDO SALGADO.

Partido Popular Laborista (PPL): Calle Poniente 23 y Col. Layco 1518, San Salvador; tel. 235-6260; f. 1997; Sec.-Gen. ERNESTO VILANOVA.

Partido Popular Salvadoreño (PPS): San Salvador; f. 1966; right-wing; represents business interests; Sec.-Gen. FRANCISCO QUIÑÓNEZ AVILA.

Partido Social Demócrata (PSD): Blvd Héctor Silva Romero 128, Urb. Clinicas Médicas, San Salvador; f. 1987; left-wing; contested 2000 elections as part of Centro Democrático Unido alliance; Sec.-Gen. JORGE MELÉNDEZ.

Partido Unificación Cristiana Democrática (UCD): 7a Calle Ote. 52, Col. Los Andes, San Marcos; tel. 213-0759; Sec.-Gen. JOSÉ ALEJANDRO DUARTE.

Partido Unionista Centroamericana (PUCA): San Salvador; advocates reunification of Central America; Pres. Dr GABRIEL PILOÑA ARAÚJO.

Pueblo Unido Nuevo Trato (PUNTO): San Salvador.

Unión Social Cristiana (USC): Calle Poniente 12 y Avda Sur 31, Col. Flor Blanca, San Salvador; tel. 222-0571; f. 1997 by merger of Movimiento de Unidad, Partido de Renovación Social Cristiano and Movimiento de Solidaridad Nacional; Leader ABRAHAM RODRÍGUEZ.

Other parties include Partido Centrista Salvadoreño (f. 1985; Leader TOMÁS CHAFOYA MARTÍNEZ); Partido de Empresarios, Campesinos y Obreros (ECO, Leader Dr LUIS ROLANDO LÓPEZ); Partido Independiente Democrático (PID, f. 1985; Leader EDUARDO GARCÍA TOBAR); Partido de la Revolución Salvadoreña (Sec.-Gen. JOAQUÍN VILLALOBOS); Patria Libre (f. 1985; right-wing; Leader HUGO BARRERA).

OTHER GROUPS

The following groups were active during the internal disturbances of the 1980s and early 1990s:

Partido de Liberación Nacional (PLN): political-military organization of the extreme right; the military wing was the Ejército Secreto Anti-comunista (ESA); Sec.-Gen. and C-in-C AQUILES BAIRES.

The following guerrilla groups were dissident factions of the Fuerzas Populares de Liberación (FPL):

Frente Clara Elizabeth Ramírez: f. 1983; Marxist-Leninist group.

Movimiento Laborista Cayetano Carpio: f. 1983.

There were also several right-wing guerrilla groups and 'death squads', including the Fuerza Nacionalista Roberto D'Aubuisson (FURODA), not officially linked to any of the right-wing parties.

Diplomatic Representation

EMBASSIES IN EL SALVADOR

Argentina: 79 Avda Norte 704, Col. Escalón, Apdo 384, San Salvador; tel. 263-3638; fax 263-3687; e-mail argensalv@saltel.net; Ambassador: JORGE TELESFORO PEREIRA.

Belize: Calle el Bosque Norte, Col. La Lima, San Salvador; tel. 248-1423; fax 248-1423; e-mail embassyofbelizeinelsalvar@yahoo.com; Ambassador: DARWIN GABOUREL.

Brazil: Blvd de Hipódromo 305, Col. San Benito, San Salvador; tel. 298-2751; fax 279-3934; e-mail brasembes@netcomsa.com; Ambassador: LUIS ENRIQUE PEREIRA DA FONSECA.

Canada: Centro Financiero Gigante, 63 Avda Sur y Alameda Roosevelt, San Salvador; tel. 279-4655; fax 279-0765; Ambassador: ALLAN CULHAM.

Chile: Pasaje Belle Vista 121, Entre 9a C.P. y 9a C.P. bis, Col. Escalón, San Salvador; tel. 263-4285; fax 263-4308; Ambassador: HECTOR HORACIO WOOD ARMAS.

China (Taiwan): Condominio Penthouse, 7°, Paseo General Escalón 5333, Col. Escalón, Apdo 956, San Salvador; tel. 263-1275; fax 263-1329; Ambassador: Gen. BING F. YEN.

Colombia: Calle El Mirador 5120, Col. Escalón, San Salvador; tel. 263-1936; fax 263-1942; Ambassador: GUILLERMO ORJUELA.

Costa Rica: 85 Avda Sur y Calle Cuscatlán 4415, Colonia Escalón, San Salvador; tel. 264-3863; fax 264-3866; e-mail embaricasal@ sicanet.org.sv; Ambassador: CARMEN MARÍA MADRIZ CONTRERAS.

Dominican Republic: Avda República Federal de Alemania 163, Col. Escalón, San Salvador; tel. 263-1816; fax 263-1816; Ambassador: JORGE ADALBERTO SANTIAGO PÉREZ.

Ecuador: 77 Avda Norte 208, Col. Escalón, San Salvador; tel. 263-5323; fax 263-5258; Ambassador: ENRIQUE GARCÉS FÉLIX.

Egypt: 9a Calle Poniente y 93 Avda Norte 12-97, Col. Escalón; tel. 263-2426; fax 263-2411; Chargé d'affaires a.i.: FAWZI MOHAMED ALSAID GOHAR.

France: 1 Calle Poniente 3718, Col. Escalón, Apdo 474, San Salvador; tel. 279-4016; fax 298-1536; e-mail ambafrance@es.com.sv; Ambassador: LYDIE GAZARIAN.

Germany: 7a Calle Poniente 3972 esq. 77a Avda Norte, Col. Escalón, Apdo 693, San Salvador; tel. 263-2088; fax 263-2091; Ambassador: SEPP WOELKER.

Guatemala: 15 Avda Norte 135, San Salvador; tel. 271-2225; fax 221-3019; Ambassador: OSCAR AUGUSTO ZELAYA CORONADO.

Holy See: 87a Avda Norte y 7a Calle Poniente, Col. Escalón, Apdo 01-95, San Salvador (Apostolic Nunciature); tel. 263-2931; fax 263-3010; e-mail nunapes@es.com.sv; Apostolic Nuncio: Most Rev. GIACINTO BERLOCO, Titular Archbishop of Fidene.

Honduras: 7a Calle Poniente 3697, Col. Escalón, San Salvador; tel. 264-7814; fax 223-2221; Ambassador: ROBERTO ARITA QUIÑONEZ.

Israel: Centro Financiero Gigante, Torre B, 11°, Alameda Roosevelt y Avda Sur 63, San Salvador; tel. 211-3434; fax 211-3443; Ambassador: ARYEH ZUR.

Italy: Calle la Reforma 158, Col. San Benito, Apdo 0199, San Salvador; tel. 223-4806; fax 298-3050; e-mail italemb@embitaliaes .org; internet www.embitaliaes.org; Ambassador: ROBERTO FALASCHI.

Japan: Calle Loma Linda 258, Col. San Benito, San Salvador; tel. 224-4740; fax 298-6685; Ambassador: SABURO YAZAWA.

Malta: Calle Juan José Cañas 251, entre 79 y 81 Avda Sur, Col. Escalón; tel. 216-0222; fax 216-0727; Ambassador: LOUIS CHIURATO.

Mexico: Calle Circunvalación y Pasaje 12, Col. San Benito, Apdo 432, San Salvador; tel. 243-3190; fax 243-0437; Ambassador: ANGONIO GUILLERMO VILLEGAS.

Nicaragua: 71a Avda Norte y 1a Calle Poniente 164, Col. Escalón, San Salvador; tel. 223-7729; fax 223-7201; Ambassador: JULIO ALEJANDRO ESPINAL.

Panama: Alameda Roosevelt 2838 y Avda Norte 55, Apdo 104, San Salvador; tel. 260-5452; fax 260-5453; Ambassador: RAFAEL ANTONIO MORENO.

Peru: 7a Calle Poniente 4111, Col. Escalón, San Salvador; tel. 263-3326; fax 263-3310; e-mail embperu@telesal.net; Ambassador: ANTONIO GRUTER VÁSQUEZ.

Spain: Calle La Reforma 167, Col. San Benito, San Salvador; tel. 298-1188; fax 298-0402; Ambassador: RICARDO PEIDRÓ CONDE.

United Kingdom: Edif. Inter-Inversiónes, Paseo General Escalón 4828, Apdo 1591, San Salvador; tel. 263-6527; fax 263-6516; e-mail britemb@sal.gbm.net; Ambassador: PATRICK MORGAN.

USA: Blvd Santa Elena Sur, Antiguo Cuscatlán, San Salvador; tel. 278-4444; fax 278-6011; internet www.usinfo.org.sv; Ambassador: ROSE M. LIKINS.

Uruguay: Edif. Gran Plaza, 4°, Blvd del Hipódromo, Col. San Benito, San Salvador; tel. 279-1627; fax 279-1626; Ambassador: Dr ENRIQUE DELGADO GENTA.

Venezuela: 7a Calle Poniente, entre 75 y 77 Avda Norte, Col. Escalón, San Salvador; tel. 263-3977; fax 263-3979; Ambassador: JUAN JOSÉ MONSANT.

Judicial System

Supreme Court of Justice: Centro de Gobierno José Simeón Cañas, San Salvador; tel. 771-3511; fax 771-3379; f. 1824; composed of 14 Magistrates, one of whom is its President. The Court is divided into four chambers: Constitutional Law, Civil Law, Penal Law and Litigation.

President: JOSÉ DOMINGO MÉNDEZ.

Chambers of 2nd Instance: 14 chambers composed of two Magistrates.

Courts of 1st Instance: 12 courts in all chief towns and districts.

Courts of Peace: 99 courts throughout the country.

Attorney-General: BELISARIO ARTIGA.

Secretary-General: ERNESTO VIDAL RIVERA GUZMÁN.

Attorney-General of the Poor: Dr VICENTE MACHADO SALGADO.

Religion

Roman Catholicism is the dominant religion, but other denominations are also permitted. In 1982 there were about 200,000 Protestants. Seventh-day Adventists, Jehovah's Witnesses, the Baptist Church and the Church of Jesus Christ of Latter-day Saints (Mormons) are represented.

CHRISTIANITY
The Roman Catholic Church

El Salvador comprises one archdiocese and seven dioceses. At 31 December 1999 Roman Catholics represented some 79.6% of the total population.

Bishops' Conference: Conferencia Episcopal de El Salvador, 15 Avda Norte 1420, Col. Layco, Apdo 1310, San Salvador; tel. 225-8997; fax 226-5330; f. 1974; Pres. Most Rev. FERNANDO SÁENZ LACALLE, Archbishop of San Salvador.

Archbishop of San Salvador: Most Rev. FERNANDO SÁENZ LACALLE, Arzobispado, Avda Dr Emilio Alvarez y Avda Dr Max Bloch, Col. Médica, Apdo 2253, San Salvador; tel. 226-6066; fax 226-4979; e-mail arzfsl@ejje.com.

The Anglican Communion

El Salvador comprises one of the five dioceses of the Iglesia Anglicana de la Región Central de América.

Bishop of El Salvador: Rt Rev. MARTÍN DE JESÚS BARAHONA PASCACIO, 47 Avda Sur, 723 Col. Flor Blanca, Apdo 01-274, San Salvador; tel. 223-2252; fax 223-7952; e-mail martinba@gbm.net.

The Baptist Church

Baptist Association of El Salvador: Avda Sierra Nevada 922, Col. Miramonte, Apdo 347, San Salvador; tel. 226-6287; f. 1933; Exec. Sec. Rev. CARLOS ISIDRO SÁNCHEZ.

Other Churches

Sínodo Luterano Salvadoreño (Salvadorean Lutheran Synod): Iglesia La Resurrección, Calle 5 de Noviembre 313, San Miguelito, San Salvador; tel. 225-1078; fax 225-4621; e-mail lutadco@netcomsa.com; Pres. Bishop MEDARDO E. GÓMEZ SOTO; 12,000 mems.

The Press

DAILY NEWSPAPERS
San Miguel

Diario de Oriente: Avda Gerardo Barrios 406, San Miguel.

San Salvador

Co Latino: 23a Avda Sur 225, Apdo 96, San Salvador; tel. 271-0671; fax 271-0971; e-mail colatino@es.com.sv; f. 1890; evening; Editor FRANCISCO ELÍAS VALENCIA; circ. 15,000.

El Diario de Hoy: 11 Calle Oriente 271, Apdo 495, San Salvador; tel. 271-0100; fax 271-2040; e-mail comedh@es.com.sv; internet www.elsalvador.com; f. 1936; morning; independent; Dir ENRIQUE ALTAMIRANO MADRIZ; circ. 115,000.

Diario Oficial: 4a Calle Poniente 829, San Salvador; tel. 221-9101; f. 1875; Dir LUD DREIKORN LÓPEZ; circ. 2,100.

El Mundo: 2a Avda Norte 211, Apdo 368, San Salvador; tel. 771-4400; fax 771-4342; internet www.sadecu.com/el-mundo; f. 1967; evening; Dir CRISTÓBAL IGLESIAS; circ. 58,032 (weekdays), 61,822 (Sundays).

La Noticia: Edif. España, Avda España 321, San Salvador; tel. 222-7906; fax 771-1650; f. 1986; evening; general information; independent; Dir CARLOS SAMAYOA MARTÍNEZ; circ. 30,000 (weekdays and Saturdays).

La Prensa Gráfica: 3a Calle Poniente 130, San Salvador; tel. 271-1010; fax 271-4242; e-mail lpg@gbm.net; internet www.laprensa .com.sv; f. 1915; general information; conservative, independent; Editor RODOLFO DUTRIZ; circ. 97,312 (weekdays), 115,564 (Sundays).

Santa Ana

Diario de Occidente: 1a Avda Sur 3, Santa Ana; tel. 441-2931; f. 1910; Editor ALEX E. MONTENEGRO; circ. 6,000.

PERIODICALS

Anaqueles: 8a Avda Norte y Calle Delgado, San Salvador; review of the National Library.

Cultura: Concultura, Ministerio de Educación, 17 Avda Sur 430, San Salvador; tel. 222-0665; fax 271-1071; quarterly; educational; Dir Dr RICARDO ROQUE BALDOVINOS.

El Salvador Filatélico: San Salvador; f. 1940; publ. quarterly by the Philatelic Society of El Salvador.

Orientación: 1a Calle Poniente 3412, San Salvador; tel. 998-6838; fax 224-5099; f. 1952; Catholic weekly; Dir P. FABIAN AMAYA TORRES; circ. 8,000.

Proceso: Universidad Centroamericana, Apdo 01-575, San Salvador; tel. 224-0011; fax 273-3556; f. 1980; weekly newsletter, published by the Documentation and Information Centre of the Universidad Centroamericana José Simeón Cañas; Dir LUIS ARMANDO GONZÁLEZ.

Revista del Ateneo de El Salvador: 13a Calle Poniente, Centro de Gobierno, San Salvador; tel. 222-9686; f. 1912; 3 a year; official organ of Salvadorean Athenaeum; Pres. Lic JOSÉ OSCAR RAMÍREZ PÉREZ; Sec.-Gen. Lic. RUBÉN REGALADO SERMEÑO.

Revista Judicial: Centro de Gobierno, San Salvador; tel. 222-4522; organ of the Supreme Court; Dir Dr MANUEL ARRIETA GALLEGOS.

PRESS ASSOCIATIONS

Asociación de Corresponsales Extranjeros en El Salvador: San Salvador; Dir CRISTINA HASBÚN.

Asociación de Periodistas de El Salvador (Press Association of El Salvador): Edif. Casa del Periodista, Paseo General Escalón 4130, San Salvador; tel. 223-8943; Pres. JORGE ARMANDO CONTRERAS.

FOREIGN NEWS AGENCIES

Agencia EFE (Spain): San Salvador; Bureau Chief CRISTINA HASBÚN DE MERINO.

Agenzia Nazionale Stampa Associata (ANSA) (Italy): Edif. 'Comercial 29', 29 Calle Poniente y 11 Avda Norte, San Salvador; tel. 226-8008; fax 774-5512; Bureau Chief RENÉ ALBERTO CONTRERAS.

Associated Press (AP) (USA): San Salvador; Correspondent ANA LEONOR CABRERA.

Deutsche Presse-Agentur (dpa) (Germany): San Salvador; Correspondent JORGE ARMANDO CONTRERAS.

Inter Press Service (IPS) (Italy): Apdo 05152, San Salvador; tel. 998-0760; Correspondent PABLO IACUB.

Reuters (United Kingdom): 5 Calle La Mascota, Carretera a Santa Tecla, San Salvador; tel. 223-4736; Bureau Chief ALBERTO BARRERA.

United Press International (UPI) (USA): Calle y Pasaje Palneral, Col. Toluca, Apdo 05-185, San Salvador; tel. 225-4033; Correspondent (vacant).

Publishers

CENITEC (Centro de Investigaciones Tecnológicas y Científicas): 85 Avda Norte 905 y 15C Pte, Col. Escalón, San Salvador; tel. 223-7928; f. 1985; politics, economics, social sciences; Dir IVO PRÍAMO ALVARENGA.

Clásicos Roxsil, SA de CV: 4a Avda Sur 2–3, Nueva San Salvador; tel. 229-6742; fax 228-1212; e-mail silviaa@navegante.com.sv; f. 1976; textbooks, literature; Dir ROSA VICTORIA SERRANO DE LÓPEZ.

Editorial Delgado: Universidad 'Dr José Matías Delgado', Km 8.5, Carretera a Santa Tecla, Ciudad Merliot; tel. 278-1011; f. 1984; Dir LUCÍA SÁNCHEZ.

Editorial Universitaria: Ciudad Universitaria de El Salvador, Apdo 1703, San Salvador; tel. 226-0017; f. 1963; Dir TÍRSO CANALES.

D'TEXE (Distribuidora de Textos Escolares): Edif. C, Col., Paseo y Condominio Miravalle, San Salvador; tel. 274-2031; f. 1985; educational; Dir JORGE A. LÓPEZ HIDALGO.

Dirección de Publicaciones e Impresos: Ministerio de Educación, 17a Avda Sur 430, San Salvador; tel. 222-0665; fax 271-1071; e-mail dpi@netcomsa.com; f. 1953; educational and general; Dir MIGUEL HUEZO MIXCO.

UCA Editores: Apdo 01-575, San Salvador; tel. 273-4400; fax 273-3556; f. 1975; social science, religion, economy, literature and textbooks; Dir RODOLFO CARDENAL.

PUBLISHERS' ASSOCIATIONS

Asociación Salvadoreña de Agencias de Publicidad: Centro Profesional Presidente Loc. 33a, Col. San Benito, San Salvador; tel. 243-3535; f. 1962; Dir ANA ALICIA DE GONZÁLEZ.

Cámara Salvadoreña del Libro: 4a Avda Sur 2–3, Apdo 2296, Nueva San Salvador; tel. 228-1832; fax 228-1212; f. 1974; Pres. ADELA CELARIÉ.

Broadcasting and Communications

TELECOMMUNICATIONS

Regulatory Authority

Superintendencia General de Electricidad y Telecomunicaciones (SIGET): Sexta Décima Calle Poniente y 37 Avda Sur 2001, Col. Flor Blanca; tel. 257-4438; internet www.siget.gob.sv /index.htm; f. 1996; Supt Lic. ERNESTO LIMA MENA.

Major Service Providers

Digicel: San Salvador; provider of mobile telecommunications; owned by Digicel (USA).

Telecom de El Salvador: 63 Avda Sur y Alameda Roosevelt, Centro Financiero Gigante, San Salvador; tel 271-7200; fax 221-4849; e-mail servicioalcliente@cte.com.sv; internet www.telecom .com.sv; terrestrial telecommunications network, fmrly part of Administración Nacional de Telecomunicaciones (Antel), which was divested in 1998; changed its name from CTE Antel Telecom in 1999; 51% owned by France Télécom; scheduled for completion of privatization in 2002; Pres. DOMINIQUE ST JEAN.

Telecom Personal: San Salvador; provider of mobile telecommunications; subsidiary of France Telecom.

Telefónica El Salvador: San Salvador; internet www.telefonica .com.sv; manages sale of telecommunications frequencies; fmrly Internacional de Telecomunicaciones (Intel), which was divested in 1998; controlling interest owned by Telefónica de España; allied with Amzak International in March 2000 to form Telefónica Multiservicios, offering cable-based television, telephone and internet access; Dir-Gen. LUIS ANTÓN.

Telefónica Movistar: San Salvador; provider of mobile telecommunications; subsidiary of Telefónica (Spain).

Telemóvil: San Salvador; provider of mobile telecommunications; subsidiary of Millicom International Cellular (Sweden).

Tricom, SA: San Salvador; provider of mobile telecommunications; owned by Tricom, SA (Dominican Republic).

RADIO

Asociación Salvadoreña de Radiodifusores (ASDER): Avda Izalco, Bloco 6 No 33, Residencial San Luis, San Salvador; tel. 222-0872; fax 274-6870; f. 1965; Pres. MANUEL A. FLORES B.

YSS Radio Nacional de El Salvador: Dirección General de Medios, Calle Monserrat, Plantel Ex-IVU, San Salvador; tel. 773-4170; non-commercial cultural station; Dir-Gen. ALFONSO PÉREZ GARCÍA.

There are 64 commercial radio stations. Radio Venceremos and Radio Farabundo Martí, operated by the former guerrilla group FMLN, were legalized in April 1992. Radio Mayavisión (operated by FMLN supporters), began broadcasting in November 1993.

TELEVISION

Canal 2, SA: Carretera a Nueva San Salvador, Apdo 720, San Salvador; tel. 223-6744; fax 998-6565; commercial; Pres. BORIS ESERSKI; Gen. Man. SALVADOR I. GADALA MARÍA.

Canal 4, SA: Carretera a Nueva San Salvador, Apdo 720, San Salvador; tel. 224-4555; commercial; Pres. BORIS ESERSKI; Man. RONALD CALVO.

Canal 6, SA: Km 6, Carretera Panamericana a Santa Tecla, San Salvador; tel. 243-3966; fax 243-3818; e-mail tv6@gbm.net; internet www.elnoticiero.com.sv; f. 1972; commercial; Exec. Dir JUAN CARLOS ESERSKI; Man. Dr PEDRO LEONEL MORENO MONGE.

Canal 8 and 10 (Televisión Cultural Educativa): Avda Robert Baden Powell, Apdo 104, Nueva San Salvador; tel. 228-0499; fax 228-0973; f. 1964; government station; Dir TOMÁS PANAMEÑO.

Canal 12: Urb. Santa Elena 12, Antiguo Cuscatlán, San Salvador; tel. 278-0622; fax 278-0722; f. 1984; Pres. RICARDO SALINAS PLIEGO.

Canal 15: 4a Avda Sur y 5a Calle Oriente 301, San Miguel; tel 661-3298; fax 661-3298; f. 1994; Gen. Man. JOAQUÍN APARICIO.

Canal 19 Sistemas de Video y Audio INDESI: Final Calle Los Abetos 1, Col. San Francisco, San Salvador; Gen. Man. MARIO CAÑAS.

Canal 21 (Megavisión): Final Calle Los Abetos 1, Col San Francisco, Apdo 2789, San Salvador; tel. 298-5311; fax 298-6492; f. 1993; Pres. OSCAR ANTONIO SAFIE; Dir HUGO ESCOBAR.

Canal 25 (Auvisa de El Salvador): Final Calle Libertad 100, Nueva San Salvador; commercial; Gen. Man. MANUEL BONILLA.

Canal 33 (Teleprensa): Istmania 262, Col Escalón, San Salvador; tel. 224-6040; fax 224-3193; f. 1957; Dir and Gen. Man. GUILLERMO DE LEÓN.

Finance

(cap. = capital; p.u. = paid up; res = reserves; dep. = deposits;
m. = million; brs = branches; amounts in colones unless
otherwise stated)

BANKING

The banking system was nationalized in March 1980. In June 1991
the Government initiated the transfer to private ownership of six
banks and seven savings and loans institutions, as part of a programme of economic reform, which was completed in 1994.

Supervisory Body

Superintendencia del Sistema Financiero: 7a Avda Norte 240,
Apdo 2942, San Salvador; tel. 281-2444; fax 281-1621; internet
www.ssf.gob.sv/princip.htm; Supt Lic. GUILLERMO ARGUMEDO.

Superintendencia de Valores: Antiguo Edif. BCR, 1a Calle Poniente y 7a Avda Norte, San Salvador; tel. 281-8900; fax 281-8912;
Supt Lic. JOSÉ ENRIQUE SORTO CAMPBELL.

Central Bank

Banco Central de Reserva de El Salvador: Alameda Juan Pablo
II y 17 Avda Norte, Apdo 01-106, San Salvador; tel. 281-8000; fax
281-8011; e-mail comunicaciones@bcr.gob.sv; internet
www.bcr.gob.sv; f. 1934; nationalized Dec. 1961; entered monetary
integration process 1 Jan. 2001; cap. 1,000m., res 2,000m., dep.
6,500m. (Sept. 2000); Pres. RAFAEL BARRAZA; First Vice-Pres. CARMEN
ELENA DE ALEMÁN.

Commercial and Mortgage Banks

Ahorromet Scotiabank: Edif. Torre Ahorromet, Avda Olímpica y
53 Avda Sur, San Salvador; tel. 245-1455; fax 224-2815; f. 1972;
Pres. Lic. JUAN FEDERICO SALAVERRÍA.

Banco Agrícola: Paseo General Escalón y 69 Avda Sur 3635,
Col. Escalón, San Salvador; tel. 267-5000; fax 267-5775; internet
www.bancoagricola.com; f. 1955; privately owned; cap. 324.0m., res
703.6m., dep. 11,947.9m. (Dec. 1998); merged with Banco Desarrollo
in July 2000; Pres. ARCHI BALDOCHI DUEÑAS; 150 brs world-wide.

Banco Capital: 1a Calle Poniente 3649, Col. Escalón, San Salvador;
tel. 298-5776; fax 298-0772; privately owned; Gen. Man. Lic.
ARTURO NÚÑEZ.

Banco de Comercio de El Salvador: Edif. Ex Americana, 25
Avda Norte y 21 Calle Poniente, San Salvador; tel. 226-4577; fax
226-9466; f. 1949; privately owned; total assets 9,074m. (1999); Pres.
JOSÉ GUSTAVO BELISMELIS VIDES; 23 brs.

Banco Credomatic: Edif. Credomatic, Avda Olímpica y 55 Avda
Sur, San Salvador; tel. 279-4344; fax 224-4138; Pres. RAÚL
ERNESTO CARDENAL.

Banco Cuscatlán: Edif. Pirámide Cuscatlán, Km 10, Carretera a
Santa Tecla, Apdo 626, San Salvador; tel. 212-3333; fax 228-5700;
e-mail cuscatlan@bancocuscatlan.com; internet www
.bancocuscatlan.com; f. 1972; privately owned; cap. 80m., res 68.9m.,
dep. 1,312.0m. (Dec. 2000); Pres. MAURICIO SAMAYOA RIVAS; Vice-Pres.
ROBERTO ORTIZ; 31 brs.

Banco Hipotecario de El Salvador: Pasaje Senda Florida Sur,
Col. Escalón, Apdo 999, San Salvador; tel. 298-2072; fax 298-0447;
f. 1935; state-owned mortgage and commercial bank; cap. 104.0m.,
dep. 1,852m. (Dec. 1998); Pres. Lic. GINO BETTAGLIO; 13 brs.

Banco Promérica: 71 Avda Sur y Paseo General Escalón 3669,
Col. Escalón, San Salvador; tel. 211-5501; fax 211-4257; privately
owned; Pres. Lic. EDUARDO ERNESTO VILANOVA.

Banco Salvadoreño, SA (BANCOSAL): Edif. Centro Financiero,
Avda Olímpica 3550, Apdo 06-73, San Salvador; tel. 298-4444; fax
298-0102; internet www.gbm.net/bancosal; f. 1885; privately-owned
commercial bank; cap. 12,000m., dep. 8,900m. (Aug. 2000); merged
with Banco de Construcción y Ahorro, SA (BANCASA) in July 2000;
Pres. Lic. FÉLIX SIMÁN JACIR; Vice-Pres. Ing. MOISÉS CASTRO MACEDA;
53 brs.

Banco UNO: Paseo General Escalón y 69 Avda Sur 3563, Col.
Escalón, San Salvador; tel. 245-0055; fax 245-0080; Pres. Ing.
ALBINO ROMÁN.

Citibank, NA: Edif. Century Plaza, Alameda Dr Manuel Enrique
Araujo, San Salvador; tel. 224-3011; fax 245-1842; Pres. STEVEN
J. PUIG.

Financiera Calpiá: 37 Avda Sur 2, Col. Flor Blanca, San Salvador;
tel. 260-6859; fax 260-6922; Pres. PEDRO DALMAU GORRITA.

First Commercial Bank: Centro Comercial Gigante, Torre Telefónica, 3°, 63 Avda Sur y Alameda Roosevelt, San Salvador; tel. 211-
2121; fax 211-3130; Vice-Pres. PETER MING-FUNG LAN.

UNIBANCO: Alameda Roosevelt, entre 47 y 49, Avda Sur 2511,
San Salvador; tel. 245-0651; fax 245-0655; privately owned; Pres.
Ing. JOSÉ ROBERTO NAVARRO.

Public Institutions

Banco de Fomento Agropecuario: Km 10.5, Carretera al Puerto
de la Libertad, Nueva San Salvador; tel. 228-5199; fax 229-2930;
e-mail rgprieto@gbm.net; f. 1973; state-owned; cap. 605.0m., dep.
872.0m. (Oct. 1997); Pres. JOSÉ GUILLERMO FUNES ARAUJO; Gen. Man.
JUAN A. MARTÍNEZ; 27 brs.

Banco Multisectoral de Inversiones: Alameda Manuel E. Araujo,
Century Plaza, San Salvador; tel. 267-0000; fax 267-0038; f. 1994;
Pres. Dr NICOLA ANGELUCCI.

Federación de Cajas de Crédito: 25 Avda Norte y 23 Calle
Poniente, San Salvador; tel. 225-5922; fax 226-7059; f. 1943; Pres.
Lic. MARCO TULIO RODRÍGUEZ MENA.

Fondo Social Para la Vivienda: Calle Rubén Darío y 17 Avda
Sur, San Salvador; tel. 271-2774; Pres. Lic. EDGAR RAMIRO MENDOZA.

Banking Association

Asociación Bancaria Salvadoreña—ABANSA: Pasaje Senda
Florida Norte 140, Col. Escalón, San Salvador; tel. 298-6938; fax
223-1079; Pres. Ing. MAURICIO SAMAYOA; Exec. Dir Dr CLAUDIO DE
ROSA FERREIRA.

STOCK EXCHANGE

**Mercado de Valores de El Salvador, SA de CV (Bolsa de
Valores):** Edif. La Centroamericana, 6°, Alameda Roosevelt 3107,
San Salvador; tel. 298-4244; fax 223-2898; internet www
.bolsavalores.com.sv; Pres. ROLANDO DUARTE SCHLAGETER.

INSURANCE

AIG Unión y Desarrollo, SA: Calle Loma Linda 265, Col. San
Benito, Apdo 92, San Salvador; tel. 298-5455; fax 298-5084; e-mail
jorge.guirola@uni-desa.com; f. 1998 following merger of Unión y
Desarrollo, SA and AIG; Pres. FRANCISCO R. DE SOLA.

American Life Insurance Co: Edif. Omnimotores, 2°, Km 4½,
Carretera a Santa Tecla, Apdo 169, San Salvador; tel. 223-4925;
f. 1963; Man. CARLOS F. PEREIRA.

Aseguradora Agrícola Comercial, SA: Alameda Roosevelt 3104,
Apdo 1855, San Salvador; tel. 260-3344; fax 260-5592; f. 1973; Pres.
LUIS ALFREDO ESCALANTE; Gen. Man. FEDERICO PERAZA F.

Aseguradora Popular, SA: Paseo General Escalón 5338, Col.
Escalón, San Salvador; tel. 998-0700; fax 224-6866; f. 1975; Exec.
Pres. Dr CARLOS ARMANDO LAHÚD.

Aseguradora Suiza Salvadoreña, SA: Calle la Reforma, Col.
San Benito, Apdo 1490, San Salvador; tel. 298-5222; fax 298-5060;
f. 1969; Pres. MAURICIO M. COHEN; Gen. Man. RODOLFO SCHILDKNECHT.

Internacional de Seguros, SA: Centro financiero Banco Salvadoreño, 5°, Avda Olímpica 3550, Col. Escalón, San Salvador; tel. 298-
0202; fax 224-6935; f. 1958; Pres. FÉLIX JOSÉ SIMÁN JACIR; Gen. Man.
ALEJANDRO CABRERA RIVAS.

La Centro Americana, SA, Cía Salvadoreña de Seguros: Alameda Roosevelt 3107, Apdo 527, San Salvador; tel. 223-6666; fax
223-2687; f. 1915; Pres. RUFINO GARAY.

Compañía Anglo Salvadoreña de Seguros, SA: Paseo General
Escalón 3848, San Salvador; tel. 224-2399; fax 224-4394; f. 1976;
Pres. JOSÉ ARTURO GÓMEZ; Vice-Pres. JULIO E. PAYES.

Compañía General de Seguros, SA: Calle Loma Linda 223, Col.
San Benito, Apdo 1004, San Salvador; tel. 779-2777; fax 998-2870;
f. 1955; Pres. JOSÉ GUSTAVO BELISMELIS VIDES; Gen. Man. Lic. HERIB-
ERTO PÉREZ AGUIRRE.

Seguros e Inversiones, SA (SISA): Alameda Dr Manuel Enrique
Araújo 3530, Apdo 1350, San Salvador; tel. 998-1199; fax 998-2882;
f. 1962; Pres. ALFREDO FÉLIX CRISTIANI BURKARD.

Seguros Universales, SA: Paseo Escalón y 81 Avda Norte 205,
Col. Escalón, San Salvador; tel. 779-3533; fax 779-1830; Pres. Dr
ENRIQUE GARCÍA PRIETO.

Trade and Industry

GOVERNMENT AGENCIES AND DEVELOPMENT ORGANIZATIONS

Consejo Nacional de Ciencia y Tecnología (CONACYT): Col.
Médica, Avda Dr Emilio Alvarez, Pasaje Dr Guillermo Rodríguez
Pacas 51, San Salvador; tel. 226-2800; fax 225-6255; internet
www.conacyt.gob.sv; f. 1992; formulation and guidance of national
policy on science and technology; Exec. Dir CARLOS FEDERICO
PAREDES CASTILLO.

Corporación de Exportadores de El Salvador (COEXPORT):
Condomínios del Mediterráneo, Edif. 'A', No 23, Col. Jardines de
Guadalupe, San Salvador; tel. 243-1328; fax 243-3159; e-mailinfo@
coexport.com; internet www.coexport.com; f. 1973 to promote Salvadorean exports; Exec. Dir Lic. SILVIA M. CUÉLLAR.

Corporación Salvadoreña de Inversiones (CORSAIN): 1a Calle Poniente, entre 43 y 45 Avda Norte, San Salvador; tel. 224-4242; fax 224-6877; Pres. Lic. MARIO EMILIO REDAELLI.

Fondo de Financiamiento y Garantía para la Pequeña Empresa (FIGAPE): 9a Avda Norte 225, Apdo 1990, San Salvador; tel. 771-1994; f. 1994; government body to assist small-sized industries; Pres. Lic. MARCO TULIO GUARDADO.

Fondo Social para la Vivienda (FSV): Calle Rubén Darío y 17 Avda Sur 455, San Salvador; tel. 271-1662; fax 271-2910; internet www.fsv.gob.sv; f. 1973; Pres. EDGAR RAMIRO MENDOZA JEREZ; Gen. Man. FRANCISCO ANTONIO GUEVARA.

Instituto Salvadoreño de Transformación Agraria (ISTA): Km 5½, Carretera a Santa Tecla, San Salvador; tel. 224-6000; fax 224-0259; f. 1976 to promote rural development; empowered to buy inefficiently cultivated land; Pres. JOSÉ ROBERTO MOLINA MORALES.

Instituto de Vivienda Urbana (IVU): San Salvador; f. 1950; government housing agency, transferred to private ownership in 1991; Pres. Lic. PEDRO ALBERTO HERNÁNDEZ P.

CHAMBER OF COMMERCE

Cámara de Comercio e Industria de El Salvador: 9a Avda Norte y 5a Calle Poniente, Apdo 1640, San Salvador; tel. 771-2055; fax 771-4461; internet www.camarasal.com; f. 1915; 1,800 mems; Pres. RICARDO SIMÁN; Exec. Dir Ing. FRANCISCO CASTRO FUNES; Gen. Man. ALBERO PADILLA; branch offices in San Miguel, Santa Ana and Sonsonate.

INDUSTRIAL AND TRADE ASSOCIATIONS

Asociación Cafetalera de El Salvador (ACES): 67 Avda Norte 116, Col. Escalón, San Salvador; tel. 223-3024; fax 223-7471; f. 1930; coffee growers' asscn; Pres. Ing. EDUARDO E. BARRIENTOS.

Asociación de Ganaderos de El Salvador: 1a Avda Norte 1332, San Salvador; tel. 225-7208; f. 1932; livestock breeders' asscn; Pres. Lic. CARLOS ARTURO MUYSHONDT.

Asociación Salvadoreña de Beneficiadores y Exportadores de Café (ABECAFE): 87a Avda Norte 720, Col. Escalón, Apdo A, San Salvador; tel. 223-3292; fax 223-3292; coffee producers' and exporters' asscn; Pres. VICTORIA DALTÓN DE DÍAZ.

Asociación Salvadoreña de Industriales: Calles Roma y Liverpool, Col. Roma, Apdo 48, San Salvador; tel. 279-2488; fax 279-2070; e-mail asi@asi.com.sv; internet www.asi.com.sv; f. 1958; 400 mems; manufacturers' asscn; Pres. LEONEL MEJÍA; Exec. Dir Lic. JORGE ARRIAZA.

Cooperativa Algodonera Salvadoreña, Ltda: San Salvador; f. 1940; 185 mems; cotton growers' asscn; Pres. ULISES FERNANDO GONZÁLEZ; Gen. Man. Lic. MANUEL RAFAEL ARCE.

Instituto Nacional del Azúcar: Paseo General Escalón y 87a Avda Norte, San Salvador; tel. 224-6044; fax 224-5132; national sugar institute, scheduled for privatization; Pres. Lic. JAIME ALVAREZ GOTÁN.

Instituto Nacional del Café (INCAFE): San Salvador; f. 1942; national coffee institute, scheduled for privatization; Pres. ROBERT SUÁREZ SUAY; Gen. Man. MIGUEL ANGEL AGUILAR.

UCAFES: San Salvador; union of coffee-growing co-operatives; Pres. FRANCISCO ALFARO CASTILLO.

EMPLOYERS' ORGANIZATIONS

There are several business associations, the most important of which is the **Asociación Nacional de Empresa Privada (ANEP—National Private Enterprise Association)**: 1a Calle Pte. y 71a Avda Norte 204, Col. Escalón, Apdo1204, San Salvador; tel. 224-1236; fax 223-8932; e-mail anep@telesal.net; internet www.anep .org.sv; national private enterprise association; Pres. RICARDO FÉLIX SIMÁN; Exec. Dir Lic. LUIS MARIO RODRÍGUEZ.

MAJOR COMPANIES

The following are some of the leading industrial and commercial companies currently operating in El Salvador:

Construction and Metals

Cemento de El Salvador, SA de CV: Avda El Espina y Blvd Sur, Urb. Madre Selva, Antigua Cuscatlán, La Libertad; tel. 243-7722; fax 243-7712; e-mail cessamer@cessa.com.sv; internet www.cessa .com.sv; f. 1949; manufacturers of Portland cement; Pres. CÉSAR CATANI; Gen. Man. RICARDO CHÁVEZ; 400 employees.

Conductores Eléctricos de Centro América, SA (CONELCA): Carretera Panamérica, Km 11, Ilopango, San Salvador; tel. 295-0866; fax 295-0859; subsidiary of Phelps Dodge Industries Inc., USA; manufacturers of steel; Gen. Man. CARLOS EDUARDO MELÉNDEZ; 250 employees.

Corporación Industrial de Centroaméricana, SA de CV (CORINCA): Carretera a Quezaltepeque, Km 25, San Salvador; tel. 310-2033; fax 310-2234; f. 1966; iron rods and wire, construction and building materials; Pres. SERGIO CATANI PAPINI; Gen. Man. CARLOS FRANCISCO ALVARADO; 350 employees.

Food and Beverages

La Constancia, SA: Final Paseo Independencia 526, Apdo 06-111, San Salvador; tel. 271-0733; fax 221-3225; e-mail equisol@es.com.sv; internet www.laconstancia.com.sv; f. 1906; produces and sells beer; Pres. ROBERTO H. MURRAY MEZA; Gen. Man. HERBERT BLANDON; 950 employees.

Diana, SA de CV, Productos Alimenticios: 12 Avda Sur, Jurisdicción de Soyapango, Apdo 177, San Salvador; tel. 227-1671; fax 227-1268; e-mail prodiana@sal.gbm.net; f. 1951; food processing; Pres. PABLO TESAK; Gen. Man. HUGO CÉSAR BARRERA; 1,450 employees.

Molinos de El Salvador, SA: Blvd del Ejército Nacional y 50a Avda Norte, Apdo 327, San Salvador; tel. 271-3166; fax 271-5378; e-mail molsal@gbm.net; f. 1959; production of wheat flour; Pres. ALFONSO ALVAREZ; Man. FERIT ZACARIAS MASSIS; 121 employees.

Sello de Oro, SA, Productos Alimenticios: Final Col. Luz, San Salvador; tel. 273-6114; fax 273-0018; f. 1967; food and food processing; Pres. CARMEN ELENA DEL SOL; Gen. Man. AGUSTÍN MARTÍNEZ; 1,285 employees.

Pharmaceuticals

Laboratorio Lopez, SA de CV: Blvd del Ejército Nacional, Km 5, Jurisdicción de Soyapango, San Salvador; tel. 277-8333; fax 227-2783; f. 1948; manufacturers of pharmaceutical products; Pres. GUSTAVO LÓPEZ RODRÍGUEZ.

Laboratorios Vijosa, SA de CV: Calle L-3, 10 Zona Industrial Merliot, Antiguo Cuscatlán; manufacturers of pharmaceutical products; Pres. Dr VÍCTOR JORGE SACA; 130 employees.

Textiles and Clothing

Almacenes Simán, SA de CV: 4a Calle Poniente 9a Avda Sur, San Salvador; tel. 271-3000; fax 222-9629; f. 1921; wholesale and retail sale of clothing; Pres. SALVADOR SIMÁN; 1,100 employees.

Cooperativa Algodonera Salvadoreña Ltda: 7a Avda Norte 418, San Salvador; tel. 222-0399; fax 222-7359; f. 1940; cotton manufacturer; Pres. ULISES FERNANDO GONZÁLEZ; Gen. Man. GUSTAVO PARRAGA SUAY; 290 employees.

Facalca Hiltex, SA de CV: Km 99½, Carretera a San Salvador, Ahuachapan; tel. 443-0033; fax 443-0461; f. 1964; thread mills; Pres. and Man. JORGE BAHAIT GHIA; 980 employees.

Industrias Sintéticas de Centroamérica, SA: Carretera Troncal del Norte, Km 12½, Apopa; tel. 216-0055; fax 216-0062; f. 1966; manufacturers of synthetic fibres; Pres. FÉLIX CASTILLO MAYORGA; 1,000 employees.

Industrias Unidas, SA (IUSA): Carretera Panamericana a Ote Km 11½, Ilopango, San Salvador; tel. 295-0555; fax 295-0846; f. 1955; manufacturers of thread; Pres. GERMÁN MARON GARCÍA; 1,600 employees.

Textiles San Andrés, SA de CV (Hilasal): Km 32, Carretera a Santa Ana, La Libertad; tel. 338-4099; fax 338-4064; e-mail exhilasa@es.com.sv; manufacturers of cotton goods and towelling; Pres. RICARDO SAGRERA; 1,000 employees.

Textufil, SA de CV: 12 Avda Sur, Jurisdicción de Soyapango, Apdo 1632, San Salvador; tel. 277-0066; fax 227-2308; e-mail exportadora@ejje.com; f. 1971; manufacturers of nylon and polyester textiles; Pres. JORGE ELIAS BAHAIA; Man. ELIAS JORGE BAHAIA SAMOUR.

Miscellaneous

Cigarrería Morazón, SA de CV: Blvd del Ejército Nacional, Km 7½, Jurisdicción de Soyapango, San Salvador; tel. 277-0444; fax 227-2534; f. 1926; cigarette manufacturer and tobacco exporter; Pres. and Gen. Man. RAFAEL MARQUEZ; 150 employees.

Compañia Quimica Industrial, SA de CV (COQUINSA): 14a Avda Norte 1621, Col. La Rabida, San Salvador; tel. 225-9527; fax 225-8430; f. 1979; manufacturers of adhesives, detergents, disinfectants, insecticides; Pres. MANUEL DE J. RODRÍGUEZ.

Distribuidora de Automóviles, SA de CV (DIDEA): Blvd Los Héroes, Edif. DIDEA, San Salvador; tel. 261-1133; fax 260-3516; e-mail dideauno@es.com.sv; internet www.didea.com; f. 1919; distributor of cars and car supplies; Pres. RICARDO POMA; Dir-Gen. CASILDO QUAN; 350 employees.

Empresas Adoc, SA: Blvd Ejército Nacional, Km 4½, Final Col. Montecarlo, Jurisdicción de Soyapango, San Salvador; tel. 277-2277; fax 277-0352; e-mail adocsa@es.com.sv; f. 1952; tannery, rubber, plastics, manufacturers of shoes and leather goods; retailers; Pres. ROBERTO PALOMO; Gen. Man. and Financial Dir RAFAEL ALVARADO CANO; 4,370 employees.

Muebles Metálicos Prado, SA de CV: 5 Calle El Boqueron, Urb. Santa Elena, Antiguo Cuscatlán, La Libertad; tel. 289-1711; fax 289-1717; f. 1952; manufacturers of metal furniture; Pres. Francisco José Prado M.; Gen. Man. Francisco José Prado R.; 500 employees.

Papelería Hispanoamérica, SA: 2a Avda Sur y Calle Oriente, San Salvador; tel. 222-5018; f. 1965; paper mill; Pres. Luis Emilio Simón Dada; 390 employees.

SIGMA, SA: 979 Calle La Mascota, Urb. Maquilishuat, San Salvador; tel. 263-5000; fax 263-9404; e-mail cgranillo@sigmaq.com; f. 1973; manufacturers of collapsible packaging; Chair. Henry Yarhi; Exec. Pres. Mario Andino; 957 employees.

SIMAN, SA de CV: Alameda Roosevelt 3114, San Salvador; tel. 245-2533; fax 298-3424; f. 1961; general contractors; Pres. Roberto Simán; Gen. Man. José Revilla; c. 900 employees.

Tabacalera de El Salvador, SA de CV: 69 Avda Norte 213, Colonia Escalon, San Salvador; tel. 298-5888; fax 224-3815; f. 1976; subsidiary of Philip Morris Inc, USA; manufacturers of cigarettes; Pres. Jorge Zableh Touche; 186 employees.

UTILITIES

Electricity

Comisión Ejecutiva Hidroeléctrica del Río Lempa (CEL): 9a Calle Poniente 950, San Salvador; tel. 271-0855; fax 228-1911; state energy agency dealing with electricity generation and transmission, and non-conventional energy sources; scheduled for privatization; Pres. Guillermo A. Sol Bang.

Superintendencia General de Electricidad y Telecomunicaciones (SIGET): Sexta Décima Calle Poniente y 37 Avda Sur 2001, Col. Flor Blanca, San Salvador; tel. 257-4438; internet www.siget.gob.sv/index.htm; f. 1996; Supt Lic. Ernesto Lima Mena.

Electricity Companies

In order to increase competition, the electricity-trading market was opened up in October 2000. Four companies (two domestic and two foreign) subsequently applied for licences to trade electricity in the wholesale market, from SIGET.

Cartotécnica: San Salvador; owned by Simán Group (El Salvador).

Comercializdora Eléctrica Centroamericana (CEC): San Salvador; licence approval pending.

CONEC: San Salvador; subsidiary of Energia Global (USA); provides electricity from sustainable sources, imported from Costa Rica.

Excelergy: San Salvador; joint US–Chilean owned.

Water

Administración Nacional de Acueductos y Alcantarillados (ANDA): Edif. ANDA, Final Avda Don Bosco, Col Libertad, San Salvador; tel. 225-3534; fax 225-3152; f. 1961; maintenance of water supply and sewerage systems; Pres. Carlos Augusto Perla.

TRADE UNIONS

Asociación de Sindicatos Independientes—ASIES (Association of Independent Trade Unions): San Salvador.

Central de Trabajadores Democráticos—CTD (Democratic Workers' Confederation): San Salvador; Pres. Salvador Carazo.

Central de Trabajadores Salvadoreños—CTS (Salvadorean Workers' Confederation): Calle Darío González 616, Barrio San Jacinto, San Salvador; f. 1966; Christian Democratic; 35,000 mems; Sec.-Gen. Miguel Angel Vásquez.

Confederación General de Sindicatos—CGS (General Confederation of Unions): 3a Calle Oriente 226, San Salvador; f. 1958; admitted to ICFTU/ORIT; 27,000 mems.

Confederación General del Trabajo—CGT (General Confederation of Workers): 2a Avda Norte 619, San Salvador; tel. 222-5980; f. 1983; 20 affiliated unions; Sec.-Gen. José Luis Grande Preza; 85,000 mems.

Coordinadora de Solidaridad de los Trabajadores—CST (Workers' Solidarity Co-ordination): San Salvador; f. 1985; conglomerate of independent left-wing trade unions.

Federación Campesina Cristiana de El Salvador-Unión de Trabajadores del Campo—FECCAS-UTC (Christian Peasant Federation of El Salvador—Union of Countryside Workers): Universidad Nacional, Apdo 4000, San Salvador; allied illegal Christian peasants' organizations.

Federación Nacional de Sindicatos de Trabajadores de El Salvador (FENASTRAS) (Salvadorean Workers' National Union Federation): San Salvador; f. 1975; left-wing; 35,000 mems in 16 affiliates.

Federación Revolucionaria de Sindicatos (Revolutionary Federation of Unions): San Salvador; Sec.-Gen. Salvador Chávez Escalante.

Federación Unitaria Sindical Salvadoreña—FUSS (United Salvadorean Union Federation): Centro de Gobierno, Apdo 2226, San Salvador; tel. and fax 225-3756; f. 1965; left-wing; Sec.-Gen. Juan Edito Genovez.

MUSYGES (United Union and Guild Movement): San Salvador; labour federation previously linked to FDR; 50,000 mems (est.).

Unión Comunal Salvadoreña—UCS (Salvadorean Communal Union): San Salvador; peasants' association; 100,000 mems; Gen. Sec. Guillermo Blanco.

Unidad Nacional de Trabajadores Salvadoreños—UNTS (National Unity of Salvadorean Workers): San Salvador; f. 1986; largest trade union conglomerate; Leader Marco Tulio Lima; affiliated unions include:

> **Unidad Popular Democrática—UPD** (Popular Democratic Unity): San Salvador; f. 1980; led by a committee of 10; 500,000 mems.

Unión Nacional Obrera-Campesina—UNOC (Worker-Peasant National Union): San Salvador; f. 1986; centre-left labour organization; 500,000 mems.

Some unions, such as those of the taxi drivers and bus owners, are affiliated to the Federación Nacional de Empresas Pequeñas Salvadoreñas—Fenapes, the association of small businesses.

Transport

Comisión Ejecutiva Portuaria Autónoma (CEPA): Edif. Torre Roble, Blvd de Los Héroes, Apdo 2667, San Salvador; tel. 224-1133; fax 224-0907; f. 1952; operates and administers the ports of Acajutla (on Pacific coast) and Cutuco (on Gulf of Fonseca) and the El Salvador International Airport, as well as Ferrocarriles Nacionales de El Salvador; Pres. Ruy César Miranda; Gen. Man. Lic. Arturo Germán Martínez.

RAILWAYS

In 1998 there were 547 km of railway track in the country. The main track links San Salvador with the ports of Acajutla and Cutuco and with San Jerónimo on the border with Guatemala. The 429 km Salvadorean section of the International Railways of Central America runs from Anguiatú on the El Salvador–Guatemala border to the Pacific ports of Acajutla and Cutuco and connects San Salvador with Guatemala City and the Guatemalan Atlantic ports of Puerto Barrios and Santo Tomás de Castilla. A project to connect the Salvadorean and Guatemalan railway systems between Santa Ana and Santa Lucia (in Guatemala) is under consideration.

Ferrocarriles Nacionales de El Salvador (FENADESAL): Avda Peralta 903, Apdo 2292, San Salvador; tel. 271-5632; fax 271-5650; 562 km open; in 1975 Ferrocarril de El Salvador and the Salvadorean section of International Railways of Central America (429 km open) were merged and are administered by the Railroad Division of CEPA (see above); Gen. Man. Tulio O. Vergara.

ROADS

The country's highway system is well integrated with its railway services. There were some 9,977 km of roads in 1996, including: the Pan-American Highway: 306 km; paved highways: 1,985 km. A coastal highway, with interconnecting roads, was under construction in the early 1990s. Following the earthquakes of early 2001, the Inter-American Development Bank (IDB) pledged some US $106.0m. to the transport sector for the restoration and reconstruction of roads and bridges.

SHIPPING

The port of Acajutla is administered by CEPA (see above). Services are also provided by foreign lines. The port of Cutuco has been inactive since 1996; however, in 2000 it was being considered for privatization.

CIVIL AVIATION

The El Salvador International Airport is located 40 km (25 miles) from San Salvador in Comalapa. An expansion of the airport was completed in 1998, with a second expansion phase of hotel and commercial space to be completed early in the 21st century. The former international airport at Ilopango is used for military and private civilian aircraft; there are an additional 88 private airports, four with permanent-surface runways.

AESA Aerolíneas de El Salvador, SA de CV: San Salvador; cargo and mail service between San Salvador and Miami; Pres. E. Cornejo López; Gen. Man. José Roberto Santana.

TACA International Airlines: Edif. Caribe, 2°, Col. Escalón, San Salvador; tel. 339-9155; fax 223-3757; f. 1939; passenger and cargo services to Central America and the USA; Pres. Federico Bloch; Gen. Man. Ben Baldanza.

Tourism

El Salvador was one of the centres of the ancient Mayan civilization, and the ruined temples and cities are of great interest. The volcanoes and lakes of the uplands provide magnificent scenery, while there are fine beaches along the Pacific coast. The civil war, from 1979 to 1992, severely affected the tourism industry. However, in the late 1990s the number of tourist arrivals increased from 282,835 in 1996 to 658,000 in 1999. Tourism receipts in 1999 were US $211m. Following the earthquakes of early 2001, the IDB pledged some US $3.6m. to the tourism and historical and cultural heritage sectors, for the reconstruction and renovation of recreational centres, the promotion of tourism, and the development of culture and heritage.

Buró de Convenciones y Visitantes de la Ciudad de San Salvador: Edif. Olimpic Plaza, 73 Avda Sur 28, 2°, San Salvador; tel. 224-0819; fax 223-4912; f. 1973; assists in organization of national and international events; Pres. (vacant); Exec. Dir Rosy Mejía de Marchesini.

Cámara Salvadoreña de Turismo: San Salvador; tel. 223-9992; Pres. Arnoldo Jiménez; co-ordinates:

> **Comité Nacional de Turismo (CONATUR):** San Salvador; comprises hotels, restaurants, tour operators, airlines and Instituto Salvadoreño de Turismo; Sec. Mercedes Meléndez.

> **Corporación de Turismo (CORSATUR):** 508 Blvd del Hipódromo, Col. San Benito, San Salvador; tel. 243-7835: fax 243-0427: internet www.elsalvadorturismo.gob.sv.

> **Feria Internacional de El Salvador (FIES):** Avda La Revolución 222, Col. San Benito, Apdo 493, San Salvador; tel. 243-0244; fax 243-3161; e-mail fies@es.com.sv; internet www.fies.gob.sv; Pres. José Carlos Liévano.

Instituto Salvadoreño de Turismo (ISTU) (National Tourism Institute): Calle Rubén Darío 619, San Salvador; tel. 222-0960; fax 222-1208; f. 1950; Pres. Carlos Hirlemann; Dir Eduardo López Rivera.

Defence

In August 2000 El Salvador's Armed Forces numbered 16,800: Army an estimated 15,000, Navy 700, Air Force 1,100. Paramilitary forces numbered some 12,000, and were to be increased to 16,000. Military service is by compulsory selective conscription of males between 18 and 30 years of age and lasts for one year.

Defence Budget: 980m. colones (US $112m.) in 2000.

Chief of Staff of the Armed Forces: Gen. Juan Martínez Varela.

Education

Education in El Salvador is provided free of charge in state schools (there are also numerous private schools), and is officially compulsory for children between seven and 16 years of age. Primary education begins at the age of seven years and lasts for nine years. Secondary education, from the age of 16, lasts for three years. In 1997 enrolment at primary schools was equivalent to 89.1% of children in the relevant age group (males 89.1%; females 89.1%). In that year enrolment at secondary schools was equivalent to just 36.4% of students in the relevant age group (males 36.1%; females 36.7%). In 1998, according to estimates by the UN Development Programme, the illiteracy rate among people aged 15 years and over was 22.2% (males 19.2%; females 25.0%). Budgetary expenditure on education by the central Government in 1997 was 2,361.9m. colones, equivalent to 19.6% of total expenditure.

Bibliography

For works on Central America generally, see Select Bibliography (Books).

Armstrong, R., and Schenk, J. *El Salvador: 'Face of Revolution'.* London, Pluto Press, 1982.

Bonner, R. *Weakness and Deceit: US Policy and El Salvador.* London, Hamish Hamilton, 1985.

Browning, D. 'Agrarian Reform in El Salvador', in *Journal of Latin American Studies,* Vol. 15, 2. Cambridge, 1983.

> *Conflicts in El Salvador.* London, Institute for the Study of Conflict, 1984.

Byrne, H. *El Salvador's Civil War: A Study of Revolution.* Boulder, CO, Lynne Rienner, 1996.

Chislett, W. *El Salvador: A New Opportunity.* London, Euromoney, 1998.

La Comisión de la Verdad para El Salvador. *De la Locura a la Esperanza: La Guerra de 12 Años en El Salvador.* San Salvador, United Nations, 1993.

Duarte, J. N. *My Story.* New York, NY, G. P. Putnam's Sons, 1986.

Dunkerley, J. *The Long War: Dictatorship and Revolution in El Salvador.* London, Junction Books, 1982.

Juhn, T. *Negotiating Peace in El Salvador: Civil–Military Relations and the Conspiracy to end the War.* London, Macmillan, 1998.

Krenn, M. L. *The Chains of Interdependence: US Policy toward Central America, 1945–1954.* Armonk, NY, M. E. Sharpe, 1996.

Lauria-Santiago, A. A. *An Agrarian Republic: Commercial Agriculture and the Politics of Peasant Communities in El Salvador, 1823–1914.* Pittsburgh, PA, University of Pittsburgh Press, 1999.

McClintock, C. *Revolutionary Movements in Latin America: El Salvador's FMLN and Peru's Shining Path.* Washington, DC, United States Institute of Peace, 1998.

McClintock, M. *The American Connection,* Vol. 1: *State Terror and Popular Resistance in El Salvador.* London, Zed Books, 1985.

Montgomery, T. S. *Revolution in El Salvador: Origins and Evolution.* Boulder, CO, Westview Press, 1982.

Murray, K. *El Salvador: Peace on Trial.* Oxford, Oxfam, 1997.

Pearce, J. *Promised Land: Peasant Rebellion in Chalatenango, El Salvador.* London, Latin America Bureau, 1986.

Pelupessy, W. *The Limits of Economic Reform in El Salvador.* Basingstoke, Macmillan, 1997.

Popkin, M. L. *Peace Without Justice: Obstacles to Building the Rule of Law in El Salvador.* University Park, PA, Pennsylvania University Press, 2000.

Towell, L. *El Salvador.* New York, NY, W. W. Norton, 1997.

Woodward, R. L. *El Salvador,* World Bibliographical Series. Oxford, Clio, 1988.

FALKLAND ISLANDS

Area: about 12,173 sq km (4,700 sq miles): East Falkland and adjacent islands 6,760 sq km (2,610 sq miles); West Falkland and adjacent islands 5,413 sq km (2,090 sq miles). There are about 200 islands in the group.

Population: 2,826 at July 2000 (estimate). (In addition there was a garrison of about 1,650 British troops.)

Capital: Stanley, East Falkland Island (population 1,636 in 1996).

Language: English.

Religion: Several Christian denominations (especially Anglican) and other sects are represented.

Climate: Generally cool; mean annual temperature 6°C (42°F); average annual rainfall 635 mm (25 in).

Time: GMT –4 hours.

Public Holidays: 2002: 1 January (New Year's Day), 29 March (Good Friday), 21 April (Queen's Birthday), 14 June (Liberation Day), 14 August (Falklands Day), 8 December (Anniversary of the Battle of the Falkland Islands in 1914), 25–26 December (Christmas). **2003:** 1 January (New Year's Day), 18 April (Good Friday), 21 April (Queen's Birthday), 14 June (Liberation Day), 14 August (Falklands Day), 8 December (Anniversary of the Battle of the Falkland Islands in 1914), 25–26 December (Christmas).

Currency: Falkland Islands pound (at par with sterling): FI £100 = £100.00 sterling = US $143.18 = €161.31 (30 April 2001).

Weights and Measures: Imperial and metric systems are used.

History

The islands are a United Kingdom Overseas Territory. From February 1998 the British Dependent Territories were referred to as the United Kingdom Overseas Territories, following the announcement of the interim findings of a British government review of the United Kingdom's relations with the Overseas Territories. The Governor of the islands, who is the representative of the British monarch, is advised by a six-member Executive Council; the separate post of Chief Executive (responsible to the Governor) was created in 1983. A new Constitution was introduced in 1985.

From the late 17th century the British, French and Spanish disputed sovereignty over the Falkland Islands (Islas Malvinas). Finally, in 1832 a British expedition expelled colonists from the recently independent Argentine Republic. The Falkland Islands became a British Crown Colony in 1833. Argentina continued to claim sovereignty over the islands.

In 1966 negotiations between Argentina and the United Kingdom were opened. Limited progress was made, but on 2 April 1982 Argentine forces invaded the islands, expelled the Governor and established a military governorship. A British naval task force was dispatched and the Argentine forces formally surrendered on 14 June; in the conflict about 750 Argentines, 255 British soldiers and three Falkland Islanders were killed. A Civil Commissioner (later restored to the title of Governor) resumed authority in the dependency and the British Government established a garrison of some 4,000 troops (later reduced).

The Argentine military Government refused to declare a formal cessation of hostilities until the United Kingdom agreed to negotiations on sovereignty, while the United Kingdom maintained that sovereignty was not negotiable and that the wishes of the Falkland Islanders were paramount (the Constitution of 1985 guaranteed the islanders' right to self-determination). It was only in October 1989 that the formal cessation of hostilities and the re-establishment of diplomatic relations at consular level were agreed. In February 1990 it was announced that full diplomatic relations were to be re-established and the naval protection zone around the islands was to be ended. Disputes over fishing areas and exclusion zones continued into the 1990s, but did not prevent some agreement between the United Kingdom and Argentina on the allocation of marine resources and the exploitation of hydrocarbons reserves.

In December 1996 the Argentine Government announced that it would consider joint sovereignty of the Falkland Islands with the United Kingdom. The proposal was rejected by both the British Government and the Falkland Islanders. In May 1999 delegations from the Falkland Islands and Argentina met in the United Kingdom for formal negotiations intended to improve relations between the two countries. The talks were chaired by Robin Cook, the British Secretary of State for Foreign and Commonwealth Affairs. Issues under discussion included co-operation in fishing and petroleum exploration, Argentine access to the islands and the resumption of air links with mainland South America. (In March Chile had ended its country's regular air services to the islands in protest at the British Government's continued detention of Gen. Pinochet; Uruguay subsequently agreed not to establish an air link with the islands unless flights were routed via the Argentine capital.) The sovereignty of the islands was not scheduled for discussion. In July an agreement was signed by Cook and his Argentine counterpart, Guido di Tella, which ended the ban on Argentine citizens visiting the islands and re-established direct flights there from Chile. Furthermore, Argentina and the islands were to co-operate in fishing conservation and in the prevention of poaching in the South Atlantic. Symbolic gestures included allowing the construction of a monument to the Argentine war dead at their cemetery on the islands, while in return the Argentine Government would cease to use the Spanish names given to Falklands locations during the 1982 occupation. The agreement did not affect claims to sovereignty. The arrival of the first flights carrying Argentine passengers in mid-October were greeted by protests.

In February 2000, in a meeting with the British Prime Minister, Tony Blair, the new Argentine President, Fernando de la Rua, reiterated his country's claim to sovereignty of the islands. The new Argentine Government indicated a less friendly attitude to the Falkland islanders, in contrast to the previous administration, when it announced in July that it would not engage in any dialogue with Falkland Island councillors that involved the British Government. In the same month the Anglo–Argentine dialogue on joint petroleum and gas exploration was suspended by mutual agreement for an indefinite period of time.

Economy

From 1982 the economy enjoyed a period of strong and sustained growth, notably after the introduction of the fisheries licensing scheme in 1987. The main economic activity of the islands was sheep-rearing and in the late 1990s annual exports of wool were valued at some £3.5m. From 1987, when a licensing system was introduced for foreign vessels fishing within a 150-nautical-mile conservation and management zone, the islands' annual income tripled. In 1993 it was proposed that this zone be extended to 200 miles. Revenue from licence sales totalled £25m. in 1991, but declined to £21.6m. in 1998/99, following the Argentine Government's commencement of the sale of fishing licences. The revenues, estimated at £22m. for the financial year 2000/2001, fund social provisions and economic development programmes, including subsidies to the wool industry, which is in long-term decline, owing to the oversupply of that commodity on the international market. Significant revenue was expected from the licences for petroleum and gas exploration, issued in October 1996 under an Argentine–British agreement of the previous year, although no commercial quantities of petroleum were found in the initial phase of drilling in 1998. The services sector expanded rapidly during the late 1990s, while the importance of the agricultural sector has decreased, not least because of its reliance on direct and indirect subsidies.

In 1998 the Falkland Islands recorded a trade deficit of £21,237,345. Wool, most of which is purchased by the United Kingdom, was the islands' only significant export. The annual rate of inflation averaged 4.5% in 1980–90; consumer prices increased by 3.6% in 1998. The Government's development plan for 2001–03 emphasized agricultural diversification and the promotion of tourism as its main economic aims. In early 2001 the Government brought 100 reindeer from the South Georgia Islands (with the aim of increasing the number to 10,000 over the next 20 years) in order to export venison to Scandinavia and Chile.

Statistical Survey

Source (unless otherwise stated): The Treasury of the Falkland Islands Government, Stanley; tel. 27143; fax 27144.

AREA AND POPULATION

Area: approx. 12,173 sq km (4,700 sq miles): East Falkland and adjacent islands 6,760 sq km (2,610 sq miles); West Falkland and adjacent islands 5,413 sq km (2,090 sq miles).

Population: 2,826 at July 2000 (estimate). *Principal town:* Stanley (capital), population 1,636 at 1996 census.

Density (2000): 0.23 per sq km.

Births and Deaths (1998): Live births 28; Deaths 9.

Economically Active Population (persons aged 15 years and over, 1996 census): 2,161 (males 1,239; females 922).

AGRICULTURE, ETC.

Livestock (FAO estimates, 2000): Sheep 707,596; Cattle 4,439; Horses 1,188. Source: FAO.

Livestock Products (metric tons, 2000): Mutton and lamb 828; Cow's milk 1,660 (FAO estimate); wool (greasy) 2,339 (FAO estimate). Source: FAO.

Fishing ('000 metric tons, live weight, 1998): Tadpole codling 1.5; Southern blue whiting 2.0; Patagonian grenadier 4.2; Patagonian toothfish 1.7; Patagonian squid 31.9; Total catch 44.7. Source: FAO, *Yearbook of Fishery Statistics*.

FINANCE

Currency and Exchange Rates: 100 pence (pennies) = 1 Falkland Islands pound (FI £). *Sterling, Dollar and Euro Equivalents* (30 April 2001): £1 sterling = FI £1.0000; US $1 = 69.84 pence; €1 = 61.99 pence; FI £100 = £100.00 sterling = $143.18 = €161.31. *Average Exchange Rate* (US $ per FI £): 1.6564 in 1998; 1.6182 in 1999; 1.5161 in 2000. Note: The Falkland Islands pound is at par with the pound sterling.

Budget (1998/99 estimates): Ordinary Revenue £37,432,780; Ordinary Expenditure £30,069,820.

Cost of Living (Retail Price Index for Stanley; base: 1990 = 100): 136.8 in 1996; 137.6 in 1997; 142.5 in 1998.

EXTERNAL TRADE

1998: *Imports:* £23,529,415, *Exports:* £2,292,070.

Wool is the principal export. Trade is mainly with the United Kingdom.

TRANSPORT

Shipping (1989): 1,833 ships (displacement 1,282,631 grt) entered and cleared. *Merchant Fleet* (at 31 December 1998): Vessels 27; Displacement 48,911 grt. Source: Stanley Register of Ships.

Road Traffic: 3,065 vehicles in use in 1995.

EDUCATION

1999 (Stanley): *Primary:* Teachers 13; Pupils 183, *Secondary:* Teachers 18; Pupils 157.

Directory

The Constitution

The present Constitution of the Falkland Islands came into force on 3 October 1985 (replacing that of 1977) and was amended in 1997. The Governor, who is the personal representative of the British monarch, is advised by the Executive Council, comprising six members: the Governor (presiding), three members elected by the Legislative Council, and two *ex-officio* members, the Chief Execu-

tive and the Financial Secretary of the Falkland Islands Government, who are non-voting. The Legislative Council is composed of eight elected members and the same two (non-voting) *ex-officio* members. One of the principal features of the Constitution is the reference in the preamble to the islanders' right to self-determination. The separate post of Chief Executive (responsible to the Governor) was created in 1983. The electoral principle was introduced, on the basis of universal adult suffrage, in 1949. The minimum voting age was lowered from 21 years to 18 years in 1977.

The Government

(August 2001)

Governor: DONALD A. LAMONT (took office May 1999).

Chief Executive of the Falkland Islands Government: Dr MICHAEL BLANCH.

Government Secretary: PETER T. KING.

Financial Secretary: DEREK F. HOWATT.

Attorney-General: DAVID G. LANG.

Military Commander: Air Cdre JOHN CLIFFE.

EXECUTIVE COUNCIL

The Council consists of six members (see Constitution, above).

LEGISLATIVE COUNCIL

Comprises the Governor, two *ex-officio* (non-voting) members and eight elected members.

GOVERNMENT OFFICES

Office of the Governor: Government House, Stanley; tel. 27433; fax 27434; e-mail gov.house@horizon.co.fk.

General Office: Secretariat, Stanley; tel. 27242; fax 27109; e-mail govsec.fig@horizon.co.fk: internet www.falklands.gov.fk.

London Office: Falkland Islands Government Office, Falkland House, 14 Broadway, London, SW1H 0BH, United Kingdom; tel. (020) 7222-2542; fax (020) 7222-2375; e-mail rep@figo.u-net.com.

Judicial System

The judicial system of the Falkland Islands is administered by the Supreme Court (presided over by the non-resident Chief Justice), the Magistrate's Court (presided over by the Senior Magistrate) and the Court of Summary Jurisdiction. The Court of Appeal for the Territory sits in England and appeals therefrom may be heard by the Judicial Committee of the Privy Council.

Chief Justice of the Supreme Court: JAMES WOOD.

Acting Judge of the Supreme Court and Senior Magistrate: KEITH WATSON.

Courts Administrator: LESLEY TITTERINGTON.

Registrar-General: JOHN ROWLAND.

FALKLAND ISLANDS COURT OF APPEAL

President: Sir LIONEL BRETT.

Registrar: MICHAEL J. ELKS.

Religion

CHRISTIANITY

The Anglican Communion, the Roman Catholic Church and the United Free Church predominate. Also represented are the Evangelist Church, Jehovah's Witnesses, the Lutheran Church, Seventh-day Adventists and the Bahá'í faith.

The Anglican Communion

The Archbishop of Canterbury, the Primate of All England, exercises episcopal jurisdiction over the Falkland Islands and South Georgia.

Rector: Rev. ALISTAIR MCHAFFIE, The Deanery, Christ Church Cathedral, Stanley; tel. 21100; fax 21842; e-mail deanery@horizon.co.fk.

The Roman Catholic Church

Prefect Apostolic of the Falkland Islands: Mgr ANTON AGREITER, St Mary's Presbytery, Ross Rd, Stanley; tel. 21204; fax 22242; e-mail stmarys@horizon.co.fk; f. 1764; 600 adherents (2000).

The Press

The Falkland Islands Gazette: Stanley; tel. 27242; fax 27109; e-mail govsec.fig@horizon.co.fk; internet www.falklands.gov.fk; govt publication.

Falkland Islands News Network: Stanley; tel. 21182; relays news daily via fax; Man. JUAN BROCK; publishes:

Teaberry Express: Stanley; tel. 21182; weekly.

Penguin News: Ross Rd, Stanley; tel. 22684: fax 22238; e-mail pnews@horizon.co.fk; f. 1979; weekly; publicly-supported newspaper; Man. Editor LISA RIDDELL; circ. 1,460.

Broadcasting and Communications

TELECOMMUNICATIONS

In 1989 Cable & Wireless PLC installed a £5.4m. digital telecommunications network covering the entire Falkland Islands. The Government contributed to the cost of the new system, which provides international services as well as a new domestic network. Further work to improve the domestic telephone system was completed in the late 1990s at a cost of £3,286,000. The VHF telephone system was changed to microwave, and the internet was introduced in 1997.

BROADCASTING

Radio

Falkland Islands Broadcasting Station (FIBS): Broadcasting Studios, Stanley; tel. 27277; fax 27279; e-mail fibs.fig@horizon.co.fk; 24-hour service, financed by local Govt in association with SSVC of London, United Kingdom; broadcasts in English; Broadcasting Officer TONY BURNETT (acting); Asst Producer CORINA GOSS.

British Forces Broadcasting Service (BFBS): BFBS Falkland Islands, Mount Pleasant, BFPO 655; tel. 32179; fax 32193; e-mail chris.pearson@bfbs.com; internet www.bfbs.com; 24-hour satellite service from the United Kingdom; Station Man. CHRIS PEARSON; Sr Engineer ADRIAN ALMOND.

Television

British Forces Broadcasting Service: BFBS Falkland Islands, Mount Pleasant, BFPO 655; tel. 32179; fax 32193; daily four-hour transmissions of taped broadcasts from BBC and ITV of London, United Kingdom; Sr Engineer: COLIN MCDONALD.

KTV: Stanley; tel. and fax 21049; satellite television broadcasting services; Man. MARIO ZUVIC BULIC.

Finance

BANK

Standard Chartered Bank PLC: Box 166, 597 Ross Rd, Stanley; tel. 21352; fax 21219; branch opened in 1983; Man. KEITH BILES.

INSURANCE

The British Commercial Union, Royal Insurance and Norman Tremellen companies maintain agencies in Stanley.

Consultancy Services Falklands Ltd: 44 John St, Stanley; tel. 22666; fax 22639; e-mail consultancy@horizon.co.uk; Man. ALISON BAKER.

Trade and Industry

DEVELOPMENT ORGANIZATION

Falkland Islands Development Corporation (FIDC): Stanley; tel. 27211; fax 27210; e-mail reception@fidc.org.fk; internet www.fidc.org.fk; f. 1983; provides loans and grants; encourages private-sector investment, inward investment and technology transfer; Gen. Man. HUGH NORMAND.

CHAMBER OF COMMERCE

Chamber of Commerce: West Hillside, Stanley; tel. 22264; fax 22265; e-mail commerce@horizon.co.uk; f. 1993; promotes private industry; operates DHL courier service; runs an employment agency; Pres. HAMISH WYLIE; 100 mems.

TRADING COMPANY

Falkland Islands Co Ltd (FIC): Crozier Place, Stanley; tel. 27600; fax 27603; e-mail fic@horizon.co.fk; f. 1851; part of Falkland Islands Holding PLC; the largest trading co; retailing, wholesaling, shipping, insurance and Land Rover sales and servicing; operates as agent for Lloyd's of London and general shipping concerns; travel services and hoteliers; wharf owners and operators; Dir and Gen. Man. TERENCE G. SPRUCE.

EMPLOYERS' ASSOCIATION

Sheep Owners' Association: Coast Ridge Farm, Fox Bay; tel. 42094; fax 42084; e-mail n.knight.coastridge@horizon.co.fk; asscn for sheep-station owners; Sec. N. KNIGHT.

TRADE UNION

Falkland Islands General Employees Union: Ross Rd, Stanley; tel. 21151; f. 1943; Sec. C. A. ROWLANDS; 100 mems.

CO-OPERATIVE SOCIETY

Stanley Co-operative Society: Stanley; f. 1952; open to all members of the public; Man. NORMA THOM.

Transport

RAILWAYS

There are no railways on the islands.

ROADS

There are 29 km (18 miles) of paved road in and around Stanley. There are 54 km (34 miles) of all-weather road linking Stanley and the Mount Pleasant airport (some of which has been surfaced with a bitumen substance), and a further 37 km of road as far as Goose Green. There are 300 km of arterial roads in the North Camp on East Falkland linking settlements, and a further 197 km of road on West Falkland. An ongoing roads network project to link remote farms is in progress. Where roads have still not been built, settlements are linked by tracks, which are passable by all-terrain motor vehicle or motor cycle except in the most severe weather conditions.

SHIPPING

There is a ship on charter to the Falkland Islands Co Ltd which makes the round trip to the United Kingdom four or five times a year, carrying cargo. A floating deep-water jetty was completed in 1984. The British Ministry of Defence charters ships, which sail for the Falkland Islands once every three weeks. There are irregular cargo services between the islands and southern Chile and Uruguay.

The Falkland Islands merchant fleet numbered 27 vessels, with a total displacement of 48,911 grt, at December 1998; 22 of the 27 vessels registered are deep-sea fishing vessels.

Stanley Port Authority: c/o Department of Fisheries, POB 598, Stanley; tel. 27260; fax 27265; e-mail fish.fig@horizon.co.fk; Harbour Master J. CLARK.

Private Companies

Byron Marine Ltd: 3° 'H' Jones Road, Stanley; tel. 22245; fax 22246; e-mail byron@horizon.co.fk.

Darwin Shipping Ltd: Stanley; tel. 27629; fax 27603; e-mail darwin@horizon.co.fk.

European South Atlantic Line (ESAL): Stanley; tel. 22622; fax 22623.

Sulivan Shipping Services Ltd: Stanley; tel. 22626; fax 22625; e-mail sulivan@horizon.co.fk.

CIVIL AVIATION

There are airports at Stanley and Mount Pleasant; the latter has a runway of 2,590m, and is capable of receiving wide-bodied jet aircraft. The British Royal Air Force operates three weekly flights from the United Kingdom. The Chilean carrier LanChile, operates weekly return flights from Punta Arenas.

Falkland Islands Government Air Service (FIGAS): Stanley Airport, Stanley; tel. 27219; fax 27309; f. 1948 to provide social, medical and postal services between the settlements and Stanley; aerial surveillance for Fishery Dept since 1990; Gen. Man. VERNON R. STEEN.

Tourism

Approximately 500 shore-based and 30,000 cruise-ship tourists visit the islands each year. Wildlife photography, bird-watching and hiking are popular tourist activities. The Falkland Islands Development Corpn plans to develop the sector, which currently generates some £3m. in turnover annually.

Falkland Islands Tourist Board: Shackleton House, West Hillside, Stanley; tel. 22215; fax 22619; e-mail manager@tourism.org.fk; internet www.tourism.org.fk; Man. JOHN A. T. FOWLER.

Defence

In August 2000 there were approximately 1,650 British troops stationed on the islands. The total cost of the conflict in 1982 and of building and maintaining a garrison for four years was estimated at £2,560m. The current annual cost of maintaining the garrison is approximately £68m. Further defence spending during 1985–88 was put at £1,700m. There is a Falkland Islands Defence Force, composed of islanders.

Education

Education is compulsory, and is provided free of charge, for children between the ages of five and 16 years. Facilities are available for further study beyond the statutory school-leaving age. In 1999 183 pupils were instructed by 13 teachers at the primary school in Stanley, while 157 pupils received instruction from 18 teachers at the secondary school in the capital; a further 46 pupils received education from 12 teachers in rural districts. Total expenditure on education and training was estimated at £3,337,000 for 1999/2000.

FRENCH GUIANA

Area: 83,534 sq km (32,253 sq miles).

Population (census result, March 1999): 157,213.

Capital: Cayenne; population 50,594 (1999 census).

Language: French (official); a creole patois is also spoken.

Religion: Predominantly Christian (Roman Catholic).

Climate: Hot and humid; average temperature at sea level 27°C (85°F); average annual rainfall 3,556 mm (140 in); the rainy seasons are April–July and December–January.

Time: GMT –3 hours.

Public Holidays

2002: 1 January (New Year's Day), 11–13 February (Lenten Carnival), 29 March–1 April (Easter), 1 May (Labour Day), 9 May (Ascension Day), 20 May (Whit Monday), 14 July (National Day), 11 November (Armistice Day), 25 December (Christmas Day).

2003: 1 January (New Year's Day), 3–5 March (Lenten Carnival), 18–21 April (Easter), 1 May (Labour Day), 29 May (Ascension Day), 9 June (Whit Monday), 14 July (National Day), 11 November (Armistice Day), 25 December (Christmas Day).

Currency: French franc; 1,000 francs = £94.51 = US $135.31 = €152.45 (30 April 2001).

Weights and Measures: The metric system is in force.

Basic Economic Indicators

	1996	1997	1998
Consumer price index (Cayenne; base: 1990 = 100)*	111.8	112.9	113.5
Rate of inflation (annual average, %)†	0.8	1.0	0.5
Imports c.i.f. (million French francs)	3,240.9	3,640.4	3,449.4
Exports f.o.b. (million French francs)	885.7	915.7	597.2

* 113.7 in 1999.
† 0.2% in 1999.

Gross domestic product (million US $ at current prices, 1996): 1,672.

GDP per head (US $ at current prices, 1996): 10,930.

Growth of real GDP (annual average, 1990–96): 4.3%.

Total labour force (1999): 62,634.

Unemployment (1998): 26.0%.

Public external debt (1988): US $45m.

Life expectancy (years at birth, 1997): 75.6 (males 72.4, females 78.7).

Infant mortality rate (per 1,000 live births, 1990): 16.8.

Adult literacy rate (15 years and over, 1992): Male 83%; Female 81%.

Passenger motor cars in use (per 1,000 of population, 1993): 209.

Television receivers in use (per 1,000 of population, 1997): 188.

History

PHILLIP WEARNE

Revised for this edition by the editorial staff.

The land that is now French Guiana (Guyane) was first sighted by Europeans at the end of the 15th century. The French began to settle the territory in 1604, but rumours of its potential gold and diamond wealth led to frequent changes of ownership. The Dutch, British and Portuguese all occupied the area, and there were frequent border disputes before the colony was definitively assigned to France by the Treaty of Paris in 1814. Subsequent border disputes were settled by arbitration in 1891, 1899 and 1915. In March 1946 the colony, hitherto known as Cayenne, became an Overseas Department, like Guadeloupe and Martinique, with the same laws and administration as a department of metropolitan France. The head of state is the President of France represented locally by a Commissioner of the Republic. The General Council with 19 seats and the Regional Council with 31 seats are the two local legislative houses. Both have Presidents, and the territory also sends two deputies to the National Assembly, one senator to the Senate in Paris and one representative to the European Parliament in Strasbourg.

The discovery of gold in the basin of the Approuague river brought a brief period of prosperity in the mid-19th century, but French Guiana's chief notoriety, until 1937, was as a penal colony. After arriving, prisoners were distributed to camps scattered throughout the territory. Devil's Island became the most infamous. Prisoners mingled freely with other settlers and the indigenous population during a period of exile after serving their sentences, but few could afford to return to France.

The practice of imprisoning convicts and political prisoners in French Guiana ceased in 1937. However, the territory's reputation as a political and economic 'backwater' persisted until the 1970s, when separatist pressure and racial tension exploded in demonstrations against French rule and the deteriorating economic situation. The French Government responded with a combination of strict security measures and the allocation of more economic aid—the traditional prescription for disturbances in the Caribbean overseas departments. Leading trade unionists and separatist politicians were arrested, while the Minister for Overseas Departments and Territories, introduced a wide-ranging plan for economic revitalization.

However, economic expansion failed to materialize and the rate of unemployment rose to more than 30%. This prompted further demands for greater autonomy by the leading Guianese Socialist Party (Parti Socialiste Guyanais—PSG), and for full independence by separatist groups, the most articulate legal spokesman for which was Alain Michel of the Guianese Popular National Party (Parti National Populaire Guyanais—PNPG). In 1980 there were several bomb attacks on government offices and buildings, for which the left-wing group, Let's Free Guiana (Fo nou Libéré la Guyane), claimed responsibility. In May 1983 several other small-scale bomb attacks were attributed to the Guadeloupe-based Caribbean Revolutionary Alliance (Alliance Révolutionnaire Caraïbe), which had frequently threatened to broaden its campaign to include France's other Caribbean possessions.

In elections to the Regional Council in 1983 the total separatist vote reached 9% of the total—the highest ever recorded in any of France's Caribbean departments. Moreover, the three separatist members of the Union of Guianese Workers (Union des Travailleurs Guyanais—UTG) held the balance of power. However, at the Regional Council elections of 1986, the separatists, now grouped together in the PNPG, had their proportion of the vote reduced by 60%, to only 3.3% of the total poll. From then and into the mid-1990s, opinion polls repeatedly indicated a majority in favour of greater autonomy, with an average of about 5% of the population favouring complete independence.

In the French presidential elections in April–May 1988, French Guiana followed the other Caribbean overseas departments in voting overwhelmingly for François Mitterrand, the Socialist candidate, who secured 60.4% of the poll. In June 1989, however, a split occurred in the PSG when Georges Othily, President of the Regional Council, was expelled from the party for unauthorized links with the opposition, along with five other senior party figures. Analysts believed that the revolt signified growing discontent with the PSG's increasingly partisan and corrupt 10-year domination of Guianese politics. The PSG split was at least partially responsible for the party's loss of support in the 1992 elections, when it lost two General Council seats and retained 10, though Elie Castor, leader of the PSG, remained President of the General Council and one of the territory's two representatives in the French National Assembly. In the Regional Council elections, the PSG won 16 seats, but Othily followers secured 10 seats.

Weakened by continued infighting, the decline of the PSG continued. In the 1993 National Assembly elections a political newcomer, Christiane Taubira-Delannon of the Walwari movement, a dissident Socialist who once favoured independence, defeated the PSG's candidate, Rodolfe Alexandre, for the Cayenne-Macouria seat. Léon Bertrand of the Rally for the Republic (Rassemblement pour la République—RPR), mayor of the territory's second-largest town, Saint-Laurent-du-Maroni, won a convincing 52.5% of the votes cast in the second constituency, Kourou–Saint-Laurent. PSG representation in the General Council fell to eight seats after the March 1994 elections. Castor left the party, but a PSG member, Stéphan Phinera-Horth, was elected President of the General Council. Taubira-Delannon was ousted by Antoine Karam, the PSG's Secretary-General, but in June she became the first woman from the Department to enter the European Parliament. She took her place as a representative of the Radical Energy (Energie Radicale) grouping, which led the poll with 36.3% of the votes, against the right-wing government list (21.5%) and the combined list of the left-wing Rally for Overseas and Minorities (Rassemblement d'Outre-Mer et des Minorités—17.2%).

French Guiana's traditionally Socialist loyalties changed in the 1995 presidential election. In the first round on 23 April Jacques Chirac of the RPR took the lead, winning 39.8% of the valid votes cast in the department, at the expense of Lionel Jospin (PS), who received 24.2%. In the second round on 7 May Chirac won 57.4% of the votes. In municipal elections in June Taubira-Delannon narrowly failed to be elected mayor of Cayenne and thus break 30 years of PSG control. In late May and early June 1997 Léon Bertrand, securing 63.3% of the votes cast, and Taubira-Delannon (64.8%), were both re-elected to the French National Assembly. Candidates from pro-independence parties notably gained increased support, winning slightly more than 10% of the votes cast in both constituencies.

The high rate of abstention in these elections and the re-emergence of separatist parties were symptoms of an increasing dissatisfaction with departmental politics and of rising tension between the department and metropolitan France. These developments precipitated, and were reinforced by, escalating social unrest. In November 1996 protests in Cayenne, in support of secondary-school pupils who were boycotting classes to demand improved study conditions, degenerated into rioting and looting. Violent clashes between protesters and anti-riot police sent from metropolitan France provoked a one-day general strike in Cayenne, organized by the UTG. These tensions worsened as pupils' representatives and local politicians criticized the actions of the police, and local officials alleged that separatist groups were working to exploit the crisis for their own ends. The situation was temporarily resolved when the French Government announced administrative reform and additional funding for the education system. However, in April 1997 the arrest of five pro-independence activists suspected of setting fire to the home of the public prosecutor during the disturbances of November 1996, and the subsequent detention of five others, including leading members of the UTG and the PNPG, led to further demonstrations and riots in Cayenne. In August 1997 the release of the five original detainees, who had been held on remand since April, signalled an end to the immediate crisis, although it seemed likely that unrest would resurface.

There were elections to the Regional and General Councils in March 1998. The PSG retained 11 of 16 seats in the 31-seat Regional Council, while a further 11 seats were won by other left-wing candidates, including six by the RPR and two by Walwari. The PSG's Antoine Karam defeated Georges Othily to be re-elected as the body's President. Othily was re-elected to the French Senate in September 1998. The PSG's representation in the 19-member General Council also declined, from eight seats to five, with an equal number won by other left-wing candidates. Independent candidates secured seven seats, a further indication of the Guianese electorate's disillusionment with traditional party politics in the Department, and André Lecante, an independent, left-wing councillor, was elected to the presidency of the General Council.

In January 1999 representatives from 10 separatist organizations from French Guiana, Guadeloupe and Martinique, including the PNPG and the Mouvement pour la Décolonisation et l'Emancipation Sociale (MDES), signed a joint declaration denouncing 'French colonialism'. They also stated their intention to campaign for the reinstatement of the three American Overseas Departments on the UN list of territories to be decolonized. The political and constitutional future of the Overseas Departments generated considerable debate and controversy throughout 1999, especially in French Guiana. In February members of the Regional and General Councils held a congress, which recommended the replacement of the two Councils with a single body, to which added powers and responsibilities in areas such as economic development, health and education would be transferred. In October however, the French Prime Minister, Lionel Jospin, ruled out the possibility of any such merger. In December Karam co-signed a declaration along with the Presidents of the Regional Councils of Guadeloupe and Martinique, stating their intention to propose to the French Government, legislative and constitutional amendments aimed at creating a new status of 'overseas region'. The amendments would also provide for greater financial autonomy. The declara-

tion and subsequent announcements by Karam and his counterparts were dismissed by Jean-Jack Queyranne, Secretary of State for Overseas Departments and Territories, in February 2000 as unconstitutional and exceeding the mandate of the politicians responsible. In March, during a visit to the Department by Queyranne, rioting broke out following his refusal to meet a delegation of separatist organizations. Later that month the Regional Council rejected, by 23 votes to seven, the reforms proposed by Queyranne in February, which included the creation of a Congress in French Guiana, as well as the extension of the Departments' powers in areas such as regional co-operation. Nevertheless, the proposals were provisionally accepted by the French National Assembly in May, and were subsequently adopted, by a narrow margin, by the French Senate, following a number of modifications. In November the National Assembly approved the changes and in December they were ratified by the Constitutional Council. At a referendum held in September, French Guiana voted in favour (80%) of reducing the presidential mandate from seven years to five.

In November 2000 riots took place in Cayenne. The demonstrations followed a march, organized by the UTG, demanding greater autonomy for French Guiana, as well as immediate negotiations with the new Secretary of State for Overseas Departments and Territories, Christian Paul. Protesters claimed they had been excluded from talks on French Guiana's status (Paul had invited leaders of various political parties in French Guiana to attend a meeting to be held in France in December, but the offer was rejected by MDES activists, who demanded the meeting be held in Cayenne). Nevertheless, discussions were held in mid-December in Paris at which Paul, various senior politicians from French Guiana and representatives from the PSG, the RPR, Walwari, and the Forces Démocratiques Guyanaises (FDG) were present. It was agreed that further talks were to be held between the Regional and General Councils of French Guiana before the end of 2001, eventually to be followed by a referendum in the Department; however, no constitutional changes were to be effected before the 2002 presidential and parliamentary elections. In early January 2001, following further consultations, it was agreed that a document detailing proposals for increased autonomy for French Guiana was to be drawn up by local officials and was to be presented to the French Government for approval.

At municipal elections held in March 2001, the PSG candidate for the mayorship of Cayenne, Jean-Claude Lafontaine, defeated the Walwari candidate, Christiane Taubira-Delannon. At concurrently-held elections to the presidency of the General Council the left-wing independent candidate, Joseph Ho-Ten-You, defeated André Lecante.

Economy

PHILLIP WEARNE

Revised for this edition by the editorial staff

French Guiana's main exports are shrimps, gold, rice, and aircraft. Mineral resources and hydroelectric potential remained unexploited and although the tourist sector expanded throughout the 1980s its growth is limited by the lack of infrastructure inland. Like Martinique and Guadeloupe the Department is highly dependent on France for its foreign trade and for aid transfers to reduce the balance-of-payments deficit. The impact of the aerospace sector on the economy from the 1970s was another unsettling factor.

In 2000 the department recorded a trade deficit of some 3,249.2m. French francs. The value of exports was 807.2m. francs, only one-fifth of the total value of imports, worth 4,056.4m. francs, although export earnings had more than doubled since 1991. The main market for exports was France, which received 62.0% of the total in 1997. France was also the single largest source of imports, accounting for 51.9% of their total value in that year. Other significant import sources were other

countries in the European Union (EU), notably Italy, the Netherlands and Germany, Trinidad and Tobago and the USA. Machinery and transport equipment, food and live animals, manufactured articles, chemicals, mineral fuels and lubricants, beverages and tobacco were among the Department's principal imports.

In 1992 there was a combined deficit on the budgets of French Guiana's state, regional, departmental and communal government authorities of 974m. francs. By 1988 the Department's foreign debt reached US $1,200m. The annual rate of inflation averaged 1.6% in 1990–98; consumer prices increased by an average of 1.0% in 1997, 0.5% in 1998 and 0.2% in 1999.

The agricultural sector, concentrated in forestry and fisheries, employed 11.4% of the work-force in 1990. In 1994 agricultural products accounted for about 22% of total export earnings, at 181m. francs, although the contribution from forestry declined in the 1990s. Shrimps remained the single most important agricultural export, accounting for 26.6% of total export revenue in 1998. After rapid expansion in the mid-1980s shrimp production fluctuated, reaching 4,000 metric tons in 1992, before falling to 3,672 tons by 1994 and then recovering to 4,209 tons in 1998.

The main crops grown for local consumption were cassava, vegetables, rice and sugar cane, the last for use in the making of rum. Livestock rearing was also largely for subsistence, although some beef farms were developed on coastal plains from the mid-1970s. In 1998 Guianese abattoirs produced some 2,091 metric tons of meat, mostly pork, poultry and beef. Rice, pineapples and citrus fruit continued to be cultivated for export. The value of the agricultural sector's contribution to gross domestic product (GDP) increased at an average rate of 1.6% per year in 1985–89; it was estimated at 9% in 1999.

Timber exports declined steadily from almost 15,000 cu m in 1985 to less than 2,500 cu m in 1993, although exports of sawlogs and finished products rose in 1994 to 4,483 cu m. Local sales also fell sharply, from 27,549 cu m in 1991 to just 7,425 cu m by 1994. In 1994 total wood extraction was 48,122 cu m, about one-half of the 1991 figure. There were several sawmills, but exploitation of timber resources was hampered by the lack of infrastructure in the forest. Local mills produced plywood and veneers, while rosewood, satinwood and mahogany were the major hardwood products. In 1999 roundwood removals totalled 120,000 cu m, while sawnwood production (including railway sleepers) amounted to 15,000 cu m.

Industry, including mining, manufacturing, construction and power, engaged 20.7% of the work-force in 1990. The mining sector was dominated by the extraction of gold, mostly in the Inini region, which involves small-scale alluvial operations and larger local and multinational mining concerns. Officially recorded gold exports contributed 37.0% of total export earnings in 1998. In that year 2.8 metric tons (90,020 troy oz) of gold were mined. Crushed rock for the construction industry was the only other mineral extracted in significant quantities, but exploratory drilling of known diamond deposits began in 1995. Bauxite, kaolin and columbo-tantalite were also present in commercial quantities, in particular on the Kaw plateau and near Saint-Laurent-du-Maroni. However, low market prices and the high cost of building the infrastructure necessary for the exploitation of such reserves hampered development.

There was little manufacturing activity in French Guiana, except for the processing of agricultural or seafood products, mainly shrimp-freezing and rum distillation. The value of the manufacturing sector's contribution to GDP declined at an average annual rate of 10.6% in 1980–85, and by 1.8% per year in 1985–89. However, a small quantity of sugar cane—2,953 metric tons in 1994—was processed to supply the sole rum distillery, which produced 1,376 hl of rum in that year. By 2000 production of rum had more than doubled to 3,072 hl. Activity in the construction industry was minimal, with planning permission granted for a total of 2,023 buildings in 1994. However, the Kourou space centre added activity to the sector and employed about 1,100 people in 1991. The centre's satellite-launching activities also increased exports in transport services and imports to serve construction demands. In 1990 such imports rose to 62% of French Guiana's economic resources. Such activities were considered likely to increase in the early 2000s, with the start of the *Ariane-5* commercial-launch programme in 1999.

Before the flooding of the Petit-Saut hydroelectric dam on the River Sinnamary in 1994 French Guiana depended heavily on imported fuels for the generation of energy. Together with existing plants, the 116-MW dam was expected to supply the Department's energy for 30 years. Imports of mineral fuels, however, still accounted for 5.3% of total imports in 1995.

French Guiana's economic development was hindered by its location, its poor infrastructure away from the coast and the lack of a skilled indigenous work-force, which left the potential for growth in agriculture, fishing, tourism, forestry and the energy sector largely unexploited. French Guiana's geographical characteristics, with large parts of the territory accessible only by river, made it difficult to regulate key sections of the economy, such as gold mining and forestry. There was considerable concern among environmentalists that this could have severe ecological consequences. Proposals for the creation of a national park, covering some 2.5m. ha of the south of French Guiana, with the aim of protecting an expanse of equatorial forest and due to be completed in 2000, were being hindered by the need to reconcile ecological concerns with economic priorities and the needs of the resident communities, notably the demands of gold prospectors. Pressure to reduce the high budget deficit increased the Department's dependence on metropolitan France, while the high demand for imported consumer goods among the relatively affluent civil-servant population tended to undermine any progress. The French Government announced its decision to increase expenditure in the education sector between 2000 and 2006, including €71m. on the construction of new school buildings.

Statistical Survey

Sources (unless otherwise stated): Institut national de la statistique et des études économiques (INSEE), Service Régional de Guyane, ave Pasteur, BP 6017, 97306 Cayenne Cédex; tel. 29-73-00; fax 29-73-01; internet www.insee.fr; Ministère des départements et territoires d'outre-mer, 27 rue Oudinot, 75358 Paris 07 SP; tel. 1-53-69-20-00; fax 1-43-06-60-30; internet www.outre-mer.gouv.fr.

AREA AND POPULATION

Area: 83,534 sq km (32,253 sq miles).

Population: 73,012 at census of 9 March 1982; 114,808 (males 59,799, females 55,009) at census of 15 March 1990; 157,213 at census of 8 March 1999.

Density (at 1999 census): 1.9 per sq km.

Principal Towns (population at 1999 census, provisional): Cayenne (capital) 50, 594; Saint-Laurent-du-Maroni 19,211; Kourou 19,107; Matoury 18,032; Remire-Montjoly 15,555; Maripasoula 12,010; Mana 5,445; Macouria 5,050 .

Births, Marriages and Deaths (1997): Registered live births 4,453 (birth rate 29.8 per 1,000); Registered marriages 671 (marriage rate 4.5 per 1,000); Registered deaths 562 (death rate 3.8 per 1,000).

Expectation of Life (years at birth, 1997): 75.6 (males 72.4; females 78.7).

Economically Active Population (persons aged 15 years and over, 1990 census): Agriculture, hunting, forestry and fishing 4,177; Industry and energy 3,130; Construction 4,440; Trade 3,152; Transport and telecommunications 1,857; Financial services 408; Other marketable services 7,352; Non-marketable services 12,068; Total civilians employed 36,584; Military personnel 417; Unemployed 11,722. Total labour force 48,723 (males 30,110, females 18,613).
1999: Total labour force 62,634 (males 35,186, females 27,448).

AGRICULTURE, ETC.

Principal Crops (FAO estimates, '000 metric tons, 2000): Sugar cane 5; Cassava 10; Other roots and tubers 4; Rice (paddy) 20. Source: FAO.

Livestock (FAO estimates, '000 head, year ending September 2000): Cattle 9; Pigs 11; Sheep 3; Goats 1. Source: FAO.

Livestock Products (metric tons, unless otherwise indicated, 2000): Beef and veal 400*; Pig meat 1,180*; Poultry meat 560; Cows' milk 250*; Hen eggs 450*.
* FAO estimate. Source: FAO.

Forestry ('000 cu m, 1999): *Roundwood removals* (excl. bark): Sawlogs, veneer logs and logs for sleepers 51; Other industrial wood 9; Fuel wood 60; Total 120. *Sawnwood production* (incl. railway sleepers): Total 15. Source: FAO, *Yearbook of Forest Products.*

Fishing (metric tons, live weight, 1998): Capture 7,709 (Marine fishes 3,500, Shrimps 4,209); Aquaculture 18; Total catch 7,727. Source: FAO, *Yearbook of Fishery Statistics.*

MINING

Production: Gold (metal content of ore, metric tons) 2.8 in 1998 (Source: Gold Fields Mineral Services Ltd, *Gold Survey 1999*); Sand and gravel ('000 metric tons) 3,000 in 1994 (Source: UN, *Industrial Commodity Statistics Yearbook*).

INDUSTRY

Production: Rum 3,072 hl in 2000; Electric energy 450 million kWh in 1996 (Source: partly UN, *Industrial Commodity Statistics Yearbook*).

FINANCE

Currency and Exchange Rates: 100 centimes = 1 French franc. *Sterling, Dollar and Euro Equivalents* (30 April 2001): £1 sterling = 10.5813 francs; US $1 = 7.3902 francs; €1 = 6.5596 francs; 1,000 French francs = £94.51 = $135.31 = €152.45. *Average Exchange Rate* (French francs per US dollar); 5.8995 in 1998; 6.1570 in 1999; 7.1198 in 2000.

Budget (million French francs, 1992): *French Government:* Revenue 706; Expenditure 1,505. *Regional Government:* Revenue 558; Expenditure 666. *Departmental Government:* Revenue 998; Expenditure 803. *Communes:* Revenue 998; Expenditure 982. **1997** (million French francs): *Regional Budget:* Expenditure 447.

Money Supply (million French francs at 31 December 1996): Currency outside banks 3,000; Demand deposits at banks 1,621; Total money 4,621.

Cost of Living (Consumer Price Index for Cayenne; base: 1990 = 100): 112.9 in 1997; 113.5 in 1998; 113.7 in 1999. Source: UN, *Monthly Bulletin of Statistics.*

Expenditure on the Gross Domestic Product (million French francs at current prices, 1995): Government final consumption expenditure 4,042; Private final consumption expenditure 5,898; Increase in stocks 121; Gross fixed capital formation 2,542; *Total domestic expenditure* 12,603; Exports of goods and services 7,746; *Less* Imports of goods and services 9,577; *GDP in purchasers' values* 10,772.

Gross Domestic Product by Economic Activity (million French francs at current prices, 1995): Agriculture, hunting, forestry and fishing 572; Mining, quarrying and manufacturing 988; Electricity, gas and water 139; Construction 858; Trade, restaurants and hotels 1,895; Transport, storage and communications 1,241; Finance, insurance, real estate and business services 815; Public administration 1,492; Other services 2,451; *Sub-total* 10,449; *Less* Imputed bank service charge 310; *GDP at basic prices* 10,139; Taxes, less subsidies, on products 633; *GDP in purchasers' values* 10,772.

EXTERNAL TRADE

Principal Commodities: *Imports c.i.f.* (US $ million, 1995): Food and live animals 104.3 (Meat and meat preparations 29.6, Dairy products and birds' eggs 15.6); Beverages and tobacco 39.0 (Beverages 34.3); Mineral fuels, lubricants, etc. 41.9 (Petroleum and petroleum products 40.5); Chemicals and related products 58.0 (Medicinal and pharmaceutical products 17.2); Basic manufactures 92.5; Machinery and transport equipment 330.0 (Power-generating machinery and equipment 27.0, General industrial machinery, equipment and parts 28.0, Office machines and automatic data-processing machines 22.2, Telecommunications and sound equipment 27.6, Road vehicles and parts 88.6, Other transport equipment 88.6); Miscellaneous manufactured articles 97.0 (Professional, scientific and controlling instruments, etc. 15.6); Total (incl. others) 783.3. Source: UN, *International Trade Statistics Yearbook. Exports f.o.b.:* (million French francs, 1998): Crustaceans 158.9; Rice 48.3; Parts for air and space vehicles 115.9; Gold 221.2; Total (incl. others) 597.22.

1998 (million French francs): *Imports:* 3,449.44.

2000 (million French francs): *Imports:* 4,056.4; *Exports* 807.2.

Principal Trading Partners (million French francs, 1997): *Imports c.i.f.:* Belgium-Luxembourg 42.2; France (metropolitan) 1,889.9; Germany 58.3; Italy 72.2; Japan 59.0; Netherlands 66.5; Trinidad and Tobago 218.9; USA 519.9; Total (incl. others) 3,640.4. *Exports f.o.b.:* Brazil 47.6; France (metropolitan) 567.3; Guadeloupe 49.6; Martinique 44.5; Spain 54.8; Switzerland 66.5; USA 21.4; Total (incl. others) 915.7.

TRANSPORT

Road Traffic ('000 motor vehicles in use, 1995): Passenger cars 26.5; Commercial vehicles 8.1. Source: UN, *Statistical Yearbook.*

International Sea-borne Shipping (traffic, 1998): Vessels entered 318; Goods loaded 75,000 metric tons; Goods unloaded 501,400 metric tons; Passengers carried 275,300.

Civil Aviation (1998): Freight carried 6,600 metric tons; Passengers carried 422,100.

TOURISM

Tourist Arrivals (1999): 68,211. Source: Comité du Tourisme de la Guyane.

COMMUNICATIONS MEDIA

Radio Receivers ('000 in use) 104 in 1997; **Television Receivers** ('000 in use) 30 in 1997; **Telephones** ('000 main lines in use) 47 in 1997; **Telefax Stations** (number in use) 185 in 1990; **Daily Newspaper** 1 in 1996 (average circulation 2,000 copies). Sources: UNESCO, *Statistical Yearbook*; UN, *Statistical Yearbook.*

EDUCATION

Pre-primary (1998/99): 42 institutions (1993/94); 10,431 students (9,584 state, 847 private).

Primary* (1998/99): 125 institutions (118 state, 7 private); 1,349 teachers; 18,802 students (17,339 state, 1,463 private).

Secondary (1998/99): 33 institutions (28 state, 5 public); 1,198 teachers; 19,132 students (17,572 state, 3,870 private).

Higher (1998/99): 666 students.

* Figures for institutions and teachers in primary education include pre-primary education.

Directory

The Government

(August 2001)

Prefect: HENRI MASSE, Préfecture, rue Fiedmont, BP 7008, 97307 Cayenne Cédex; tel. 39-45-00; fax 30-02-77.

President of the General Council: JOSEPH HO-TEN-YOU (Independent left), Hôtel du Département, place Léopold Heder, BP 5021, 97305 Cayenne Cédex; tel. 29-55-00; fax 29-55-25.

Deputies to the French National Assembly: CHRISTIANE TAUBIRA-DELANNON (Independent left), LÉON BERTRAND (RPR).

Representative to the French Senate: GEORGES OTHILY (FDG).

REGIONAL COUNCIL

Conseil Regional, 66 ave du Général de Gaulle, BP 7025, 97307 Cayenne Cédex; tel. 29-20-35; fax 31-95-22; e-mail caberg@nplus.gf.

President: ANTOINE KARAM (PSG).

Election, 15 March 1998

						Seats†
Parti Socialiste Guyanais (PSG)	.	.	.	.	.	11
Rassemblement pour la République (RPR)	.	.	.	.	.	6
Walwari	.	.	.	.	.	2
Others	.	.	.	.	.	12*
Total	.	.	.	.	.	**31**

* Three independents and nine left-wing candidates.

† In 2000 one PSG and one RPR candidate defected from their respective parties; thus the new distribution of seats changed to PSG 10, RPR five, Walwari two and Others 14.

Political Organizations

Action Démocratique Guyanaise (ADG): Cayenne; Leader ANDRÉ LECANTE.

Forces Démocratiques Guyanaises (FDG): Cayenne; f. 1989 by a split in the PSG; Leader GEORGES OTHILY.

Mouvement pour la Décolonisation et l'Emancipation Sociale (MDES): Cayenne; pro-independence party; Sec.-Gen. MAURICE PIN-DARD.

Parti National Populaire Guyanais (PNPG): Cayenne; f. 1985; pro-independence party; Leader JEAN-CLAUDE RINGUET.

Parti Socialiste: Cayenne; tel. 37-81-33; local branch of the national party; Leader PIERRE RIBARDIÈRE.

Parti Socialiste Guyanais (PSG): 1 Cité Césaire, Cayenne; f. 1956; Sec.-Gen. MARIE-CLAUDE VERDANT.

Rassemblement pour la République (RPR): Cayenne; tel. 31-66-60; f. 1946; local branch of the national party; Gaullist; Leader PAULIN BRUNE.

Union pour la Démocratie Française (UDF): Cayenne; tel. 31-17-10; f. 1979; local branch of the national party; centre-right; Leader R. CHOW-CHINE.

Union Socialiste Démocratique (USD): Cayenne; Leader THÉO-DORE ROUMILLAC.

Walwari: Cayenne; left-wing; Leader CHRISTIANE TAUBIRA-DELANNON.

Judicial System

Courts of Appeal: see Judicial System, Martinique.

Tribunal de Grande Instance: Palais de Justice, 9 ave du Général de Gaulle, 97300 Cayenne; Pres. J. FAHET; Procurator-Gen. ANNE KAYANAKIS.

Religion

CHRISTIANITY

The Roman Catholic Church

French Guiana comprises the single diocese of Cayenne, suffragan to the archdiocese of Fort-de-France, Martinique. At 31 December 1999 there were an estimated 150,000 adherents in French Guiana, representing some 75% of the total population. French Guiana participates in the Antilles Episcopal Conference, currently based in Port of Spain, Trinidad and Tobago.

Bishop of Cayenne: Rt Rev. LOUIS SANKALÉ, Evêché, 24 rue Madame Payé, BP 378, 97328 Cayenne Cédex; tel. 31-01-18; fax 30-20-33; e-mail louisankale@wanadoo.fr.

The Anglican Communion

Within the Church in the Province of the West Indies, French Guiana forms part of the diocese of Guyana. The Bishop is resident in Georgetown, Guyana.

Other Churches

Assembly of God: 1051 route de Raban, 97300 Cayenne; tel. 25-62-22; fax 35-23-05; Pres. JACQUES RHINO.

Church of Jesus Christ of Latter-day Saints (Mormons): chemin Constant Chlore, 97354 Rémire-Montjoly; tel. 30-55-92; Br. Pres. FRANÇOIS PRATIQUE, allée des Cigales, route de Montabo, 97300 Cayenne; tel. 31-21-86.

Quadrangular Gospel Church: 97300 Cayenne; tel. 37-84-81.

Seventh-day Adventist Church: Mission Adventiste de la Guyane, 39 rue Schoëlcher, BP 169, 97324 Cayenne Cédex; tel. 25-64-26; fax 37-93-02; e-mail mission.adventiste@wanadoo.fr.

The Jehovah's Witnesses are also represented.

The Press

France-Guyane: 88 bis ave du Général de Gaulle, 97300 Cayenne; tel. 29-85-86; fax 31-11-57; daily; Dir PHILIPPE HERSANT; circ. 5,500.

La Presse de Guyane: 26 rue du Lieutenant Brassé, BP 6012, 97300 Cayenne; tel. 29-59-90; fax 30-20-25; 4 a week; circ. 1,000.

Broadcasting and Communications

TELECOMMUNICATIONS

France Telecom: 76 ave Voltaire, 97300 Cayenne; tel. 39-91-14; fax 39-93-02; local branch of national telecommunications co.

BROADCASTING

Réseau France Outre-mer (RFO): 43 rue du Dr Devèze, BP 7013, 97305 Cayenne; tel. 29-99-00; fax 30-26-49; e-mail rfosaf@nplus.gf; internet www.rfo.fr; fmrly Société Nationale de Radio-Télévision Française d'Outre-mer, renamed as above 1998; Radio-Guyane Inter: broadcasts 18 hours daily; Téléguyane: 2 channels, 32 hours weekly; Pres. ANDRÉ-MICHEL BESSE; Regional Dir ANASTASIE BOURQUIN.

Radio

Six private FM radio stations are in operation.

Cayenne FM: 88 ave Général de Gaulle, BP 428, 97300 Cayenne; tel. 31-37-38; private radio station broadcasting 126 hours weekly.

Radio Nou Men: private station; broadcasts in Creole and Boni.

Radio Tout Moune: rue des Mandarines, 97300 Cayenne; tel. 31-80-74; fax 30-91-19; f. 1982; private station; broadcasts 24 hours a day; Pres. R. BATHILDE; Dir GUY SAINT-AIME.

Television

Antenne Créole: 31 ave Louis Pasteur, 97300 Cayenne; tel. 31-20-20; private television station.

Canal Plus Guyane: Cayenne; private 'coded' television station.

Finance

(cap. = capital; res = reserves; dep. = deposits; m. = million; brs = branches; amounts in French francs)

BANKING

Central Bank

Institut d'Emission des Départements d'Outre-mer (IEDOM): 8 rue Christophe Colomb, BP 6016, 97306 Cayenne Cédex; tel. 29-36-50; fax 30-02-76.

Commercial Banks

Banque Française Commerciale Antilles–Guyane (BFC Antilles–Guyane): 8 pl. des Palmistes, BP 111, 97345 Cayenne; tel. 29-11-11; fax 30-13-12 (see chapter on Guadeloupe).

BNP Paribas Guyane SA: 2 pl. Victor Schoëlcher, BP 35, 97300 Cayenne; tel. 39-63-00; fax 30-23-08; e-mail bnpg@mail.change-espace.fr; f. 1855; fmrly BNP Guyane; name changed July 2000; cap. 71.7m., res 100.0m., dep. 2,007m. (Dec. 1994); Man. Dir JEAN-CLAUDE HERIDE; 5 brs.

Caisse Centrale de Coopération Économique: route Baduel Heliconias, Cayenne; tel. 31-41-33; fax 30-63-32.

Crédit Populaire Guyanais: Caisse de Crédit Mutuel, 93 rue Lallouette, BP 818, 97338 Cayenne; tel. 30-15-32; fax 30-17-65.

Development Bank

Société financière pour le développement économique de la Guyane (SOFIDEG): PK 3, route de Baduel, BP 860, 97339 Cayenne Cédex; tel. 29-94-29; fax 30-60-44; f. 1982; Dir FRANÇOIS CHEVIL-LOTTE.

Trade and Industry

GOVERNMENT AGENCY

Direction Régionale de l'Industrie, de la Recherche et de l'Environnement (DRIRE): impasse Buzaré, BP 7001, 97307 Cayenne; tel. 29-75-00; fax 29-07-34; e-mail drire.antilles.guyane @wanadoo.fr; mining authority; responsible for assessing applications for and awarding exploration and exploitation rights; Regional Dir JEAN-CLAUDE BARA.

DEVELOPMENT ORGANIZATION

Agence Française de Développement (AFD): Cayenne; tel. 31-41-33; fmrly Caisse Française de Développement; Dir CLAUDE ALBINA.

CHAMBERS OF COMMERCE

Chambre d'Agriculture: 8 ave du Général de Gaulle, Cayenne; tel. 29-61-95; fax 31-00-01; Pres. Patrick Labranche.

Chambre de Commerce et d'Industrie: Hôtel Consulaire, pl. de l'Esplanade, BP 49, 97321 Cayenne Cédex; tel. 29-96-00; fax 29-96-34; internet www.guyane.cci.fr; Pres. JEAN-PAUL LEPELLETIER.

Chambre de Métiers de Guyane: Jardin Botanique, blvd de la République, BP 176, 97324 Cayenne Cédex; tel. 30-54-22; Pres. ALEX LASHLEY.

Jeune Chambre Economique de Cayenne: Cité A. Horth, route de Montabo, BP 683, Cayenne; tel. 31-62-99; fax 31-76-13; f. 1960; Pres. FRANCK VERSET.

EMPLOYERS' ORGANIZATIONS

Organisation des Producteurs Guyanais de Crevettes (OPG): Kourou; tel. 32-27-26; fax 32-19-18; shrimp producers' asscn and export business; Man. ROBERT COTONNEC.

Syndicat des Exploitants Forestiers et Scieurs de la Guyane (SEFSEG): Macouria; tel. 31-72-50; fax 30-08-27; f. 1987; asscn of

14 forestry developers (450 employees); timber processers; Man. M. POMIES.

Syndicat des Exportateurs de la Guyane: Z. I. de Dégrad-des-Cannes, 97354 Rémire-Montjoly; tel. 35-40-78; Pres. JEAN PATOZ.

Union Patronale de la Guyane (UPDG): c/o SOFIDEG, km 3 route de Baduel, BP 820, 97338 Cayenne Cédex; tel. 31-17-71; fax 30-32-13; e-mail updg@nplus.gf; Pres. ALAIN CHAUMET.

MAJOR COMPANIES

Air Liquide Spatial Guyane: Ensemble de Lancement Ariane, BP 826, 97388 Kourou; tel. 33-75-69; fax 33-75-77; manufacture of industrial gases; Man. J. P. POCHOLLE.

Ariane Espace, SA: Establissement de Kourou, Lancement No 2, BP 809, 97388 Kourou; tel. 33-68-79; fax 33-69-13; f. 1979; aerospace industry; Man. J. C. VINCENT.

Bamyrag: Lot Marengo, Z. I. Collery, 97300 Cayenne; tel. 36-26-00; fax 35-14-45; distribution of petroleum products.

CEGELEC: pl. Newton, 97321 Kourou; tel. 32-05-24; fax 32-31-39; electrical engineering; Man. J. FIGUERRE.

Ciments Guyanais: Z. I. Dégrad-des-Cannes, 97354 Rémire-Montjoly; tel. 35-54-97; fax 35-54-99; f. 1989; cement production; Man. P. VANDRESSE; 24 employees.

Compagnie Française de Pêche: Zone portuaire du Lavirot, BP 834, 97338 Cayenne; tel. 35-17-77; fax 35-10-42; fishing company; Gen. Man. P. FOILLARD.

Coopérative de Pécheurs de Guyane (CODEPEG): ave de la Liberté, Rive droite, BP 867, 97388 Cayenne; tel. 31-46-59; fax 30-30-46; e-mail codepeg@nplus.gf; f. 1983; fish-processing co-operative; Pres. RENÉ GUSTAVE; Dir-Gen. CHRISTIAN MADERE; 30 employees.

Dumez: Z. I. Pariacabo, BP 817, 97388 Kourou; tel. 32-00-10; fax 32-17-30; construction and civil engineering.

Maire, S. E. E.: Z. I. Dégrad-des-Cannes, 97354 Rémire, BP 612, 97334 Cayenne; tel. 31-28-26; fax 30-52-70; construction; Gen. Man. D. MAIRE.

Nofrayne: Parc d'Activités de Matounry, BP 1166, 97345 Cayenne; tel. 35-18-65; fax 35-18-60; construction and civil engineering.

Propadis: Z. I. Collery, 97300 Cayenne; tel. 35-17-17; fax 35-19-91; distribution of food products; Gen. Man. CHANG HING WING.

Regulus (CSG): BP 73, 97372 Cayenne; tel. 35-15-00; fax 32-49-42; space industry; Man. G. DELLA CORTE.

Tanon & CIE: route de Baduel, PK 1.5, BP 262, 97326 Cayenne; tel. 29-39-39; fax 31-37-20; e-mail guyaneautocenter@wanadoo.fr; f. 1892; distribution of motor vehicles and spare parts, agricultural products, petroleum products and air conditioners; Pres. RAYMOND ABCHEE; Gen. Man. ANDRÉ ABCHEE; 115 employees.

UTILITIES
Electricity

Électricité de France Guyane (EDF): blvd Jubelin, BP 6002, 97300 Cayenne; tel. 39-64-00; fax 30-10-81; state-owned; Gen. Man. GUY EHRMANN.

Water

SGDE: PK 3 route de Montabo, 97305 Cayenne; tel. 30-32-32; fax 30-59-60; Gen. Man. MARC THEPOT.

TRADE UNIONS

Centrale Démocratique des Travailleurs de la Guyane (CDTG): 99-100 Cité Césaire, BP 383, 97300 Cayenne; tel. 31-50-72; fax 31-81-05; Sec.-Gen. GÉRARD FAUBERT.

Force Ouvrière (FO): 107 rue Barthélemy, Cayenne; Sec.-Gen. M. XAVERO.

SE/FEN (Syndicat des enseignants): 52 rue F. Arago, Cayenne; Sec.-Gen. GEORGINA JUDICK-PIED.

Union des Travailleurs Guyanais (UTG): 7 ave Ronjon, Cayenne; tel. 31-26-42; Sec.-Gen. CHRISTIAN RAVIN.

Transport

RAILWAYS

There are no railways in French Guiana.

ROADS

In 1988 there were 1,137 km (707 miles) of roads in French Guiana, of which 371 km were main roads. Much of the network is concen-

trated along the coast, although proposals for a major new road into the interior of the Department were under consideration in late 1997.

SHIPPING

Dégrad-des-Cannes, on the estuary of the river Mahury, is the principal port, handling 80% of maritime traffic in 1989. There are other ports at Le Larivot, Saint-Laurent-du-Maroni and Kourou. Saint-Laurent is used primarily for the export of timber, and Larivot for fishing vessels. There are river ports on the Oyapock and on the Approuague. There is a ferry service across the Maroni river between Saint-Laurent and Albina, Suriname. The rivers provide the best means of access to the interior, although numerous rapids prevent navigation by large vessels.

Direction Départementale des Affaires Maritimes: 2 bis rue Mentel, BP 307, 97305 Cayenne Cédex; tel. 31-00-08; Dir PIERRE-YVES ANDRIEUX.

Société de Transport Maritime Guyanes: 13 ave Pt Gaston Monnerville, Cayenne.

Somarig: Z. I. de Dégrad-des-Cannes, Remire, BP 81, 97322 Cayenne Cédex; tel. 35-42-00; fax 35-53-44; joint venture between the Compagnie Générale Maritime and Delmas; Dir DANIEL DOURET.

CIVIL AVIATION

Rochambeau International Airport, situated 17.5 km (11 miles) from Cayenne, is equipped to handle the largest jet aircraft. Access to remote inland areas is frequently by helicopter.

Air Guyane: Aéroport de Rochambeau, 97300 Matoury; tel. 35-65-55; operates internal services.

Guyane Aéro Services: Aéroport de Rochambeau, 97307 Matoury; tel. 35-65-55; f. 1980; fmrly Guyane Air Transport; Pres. PIERRE PRÉVÔT; Dir PATRICK LENCLOE.

Tourism

The main attractions are the natural beauty of the tropical scenery and the Amerindian villages of the interior. In 2000 there were 28 hotels with 1,272 rooms; in 1999 68,211 tourist arrivals were recorded.

Comité du Tourisme de la Guyane: Pavillon du Tourisme, Jardin Botanique, 12 rue Lallouette, BP 801, 97338 Cayenne Cédex; tel. 29-65-00; fax 29-65-01; internet www.tourisme-guyane.gf.

Délégation Régionale au Tourisme, au Commerce et à l'Artisanat pour la Guyane: BP 7008, 97307 Cayenne; tel. 31-01-04; fax 31-84-91; e-mail drtguyan@nplus.gf; Delegate PATRICE MALLET.

Fédération des Offices de Tourisme et Syndicats d'Initiative de la Guyane (FOTSIG): 12 rue Lallouette, 97300 Cayenne; tel. 30-96-29; fax 31-23-43; e-mail fotsig@nplus.gf; internet www.guyane.net.

Defence

At 1 August 2000 France maintained a military force of about 3,250 in French Guiana. The headquarters is in Cayenne.

Education

Education is modelled on the French system, and is free and compulsory for children between six and 16 years of age. Between 1980 and 1993 the number of children attending primary school increased by more than 70%, and the number of children at secondary school by 87%. This expansion placed considerable pressure on the education system. In 1997 the French Government made available funds to improve secondary-school standards and increase the number of places in primary schools. In 1998/99 there were 125 primary and pre-primary schools, and 33 secondary schools. A major school-building programme was carried out in 1989–93. Higher education is provided by a branch of the Université Antilles-Guyane in Cayenne, which has faculties of law, administration and French language and literature. The university as a whole had 15,810 enrolled students in the 1995/96 academic year. There is also an Ecole Normale for teacher-training, an agricultural college and a technical college. Total expenditure on education amounted to 851m. francs in 1993. An Academy for French Guiana was established in January 1997.

GRENADA

Area: 344.5 sq km (133 sq miles), incl. a number of small islands.

Population (1991 census): 94,806; (official estimate, mid-1998): 100,100.

Capital: St George's; population 4,439 in 1991.

Language: English (official); a French patois is also spoken.

Religion: Christian (mainly Roman Catholic).

Climate: Subtropical; average temperature 28°C (82°F) on lowlands; average annual rainfall 1,500 mm on coast and 3,800 mm in mountains; most of the rainfall occurs June–December.

Time: GMT –4 hours.

Public Holidays: 2002: 1 January (New Year's Day), 7 February (Independence Day), 29 March (Good Friday), 1 April (Easter Monday), 1 May (Labour Day), 19 May (Whit Sunday), 20 May (Whit Monday), 30 May (Corpus Christi), 5–6 August (Emancipation), 25 October (Thanksgiving Day), 25–26 December (Christmas). **2003:** 1 January (New Year's Day), 7 February (Independence Day), 18 April (Good Friday), 21 April (Easter Monday), 1 May (Labour Day), 9 June (Whit Monday), 19 June (Corpus Christi), 4–5 August (Emancipation), 25 October (Thanksgiving Day), 25–26 December (Christmas).

Currency: Eastern Caribbean dollar; US $1 = EC $2.70 (fixed rate since July 1976); EC $100 = £25.87 = US $37.04 = €41.73 (30 April 2001).

Weights and Measures: Metric.

History

Although first colonized by the French, Grenada was a British colony from 1783 until 1958, when it joined the Federation of the West Indies. It gained full internal self-government and associated statehood in 1967. Grenada achieved independence in February 1974, with Eric (later Sir Eric) Gairy of the Grenada United Labour Party (GULP) as Prime Minister. Sir Eric was accused of being corrupt and autocratic; he was overthrown in March 1979 by the New Jewel Movement (NJM), led by Maurice Bishop, who became Prime Minister. The establishment of a People's Revolutionary Government led to a deterioration in relations with the USA and with the more conservative Caribbean countries. An internal struggle within the NJM culminated, in October 1983, with Bishop's removal from office and subsequent execution, in a coup led by Gen. Hudson Austin, the army commander. In the ensuing turmoil Grenada was invaded by US and Caribbean troops, the coup leaders were imprisoned and an interim, non-political administration appointed.

This interim Government, headed by Nicholas Braithwaite, supervised the December 1984 elections, which were won by the New National Party (NNP), led by Herbert Blaize, who became Prime Minister. By the time Blaize died in December 1989, he was leading a minority administration, owing to internal dissension and dissatisfaction with his leadership. Ben Jones became Prime Minister until the general election of 13 March 1990, in which no party achieved an absolute majority. Braithwaite, now leader of the National Democratic Congress (NDC—which won seven of the 15 seats), was appointed Prime Minister. He secured an overall majority in Parliament when two members defected from other parties to join his administration. At the beginning of 1995 Braithwaite resigned and was succeeded as NDC leader and Prime Minister by George Brizan, hitherto Minister of Agriculture, Trade and Industry. In the general election of 20 June 1995, however, the NNP secured eight of the 15 seats in the House of Representatives and the party's leader, Keith Mitchell, became Prime Minister. The NDC gained five seats (although one formed the Democratic Labour Party later in the year) and the GULP two. In 1996 Daniel (later Sir Daniel) Williams was appointed Governor-General, which provoked controversy owing to his past connections with the NNP.

In August 1997 Sir Eric Gairy, the leader of GULP, died and in April/May 1998 Herbert Preudhomme (a former Deputy Prime Minister) was elected as his successor. On 2 December 1998 Parliament was dissolved following the resignation from the Government and NNP of Raphael Fletcher, the Minister of Foreign Affairs, who was disenchanted with Mitchell and wished to join GULP. An early general election was held on 18 January 1999 in which the NNP obtained all 15 seats. Keith Mitchell retained his position as Prime Minister and appointed a new Cabinet. A cabinet reshuffle took place in November, when Mark Isaac was appointed Minister of Foreign Affairs and Anthony Boatswain Minister of Finance, Trade and Planning. In August 2000 Mitchell reshuffled the Cabinet, creating a Ministry of Implementation. In October Tilman Thomas was elected leader of the NDC.

In October 2000 the Trades Union Council (TUC) and opposition parties condemned proposed government changes to Grenada's labour laws. The proposals followed labour unrest in April and May when teachers staged a series of stoppages following a dispute over pay, and port workers voted in favour of strike action after negotiations over new contracts broke down. Furthermore, on 12 May the Technical and Allied Workers' Union organized a national rally to protest at the allegedly unfair dismissal of 26 employees of the Grenada Broadcasting Network.

In January 2001 the Minister of Foreign Affairs, Mark Isaac, was dismissed, reportedly following his decision to re-establish diplomatic relations with Libya without first gaining cabinet approval. He was succeeded by Elvin Nimrod. In March Raymond Anthony replaced Lawrence Joseph as Attorney-General and was also appointed Minister of Legal Affairs, a portfolio hitherto held by Nimrod. Joseph was appointed Minister of Labour and Local Government. At the same time, Nimrod was given the international trade portfolio. In the same month a new opposition party, the United Labour Congress (ULC) was formed, following the merger of GULP and the People's Progressive Action. Michael Baptiste was appointed the ULC's interim leader and Kenny Lalsingh its interim Chairman pending a formal launch later in the year.

Economy

From the mid-1980s attempts were made to diversify the economy. However, it remained largely dependent on agriculture, especially the production of nutmeg, bananas and cocoa. The economy's vulnerability to fluctuating world commodity prices was partly offset by the new nutmeg cartel agreement of 1991, between Grenada (the world's second-largest producer) and Indonesia (the largest producer). In 1997 a decline in production of nutmeg in Indonesia resulted in higher prices in the external market, stimulating an increase of 15% in Grenada's output. In this year, according to the IMF, sales of nutmeg and mace accounted for 33.8% of Grenada's export earnings. In the year to June 1999 Grenada earned US $9.2m. from nutmeg exports, compared with $5.5m. for the same period in 1998. Nevertheless, a fall in world prices was predicted for 2000. Nutmeg exports decreased by 46% in the second half of 2000, compared with the same period in 1999. The agricultural sector was also susceptible to adverse weather conditions or problems such as the banana disease, moko, and the pink mealy bug. The need for economic diversification was increased in the late 1990s by the potential loss of preferential access to European markets for banana producers of the African, Caribbean and Pacific (ACP) countries. Banana exports were suspended in early 1997, owing to poor quality. Although they resumed in late 1998, exports were still greatly reduced in 1999 although some recovery in the sector was anticipated in 2000. Agricultural gross domestic product (GDP) declined at an average annual rate of 1.1% in 1990–99. The sector's GDP contracted by 0.9% in 1997, and by a further 1.2% in 1998, owing to a reduction in output of cocoa and bananas. However, agricultural GDP grew by some 10.0% in 1999, largely owing to increased production of nutmeg, mace and bananas.

Development of the tourist industry was Grenada's main economic strategy in terms of diversification, and since 1984 the number of stop-over arrivals and cruise-ship visitors has more than doubled. In 1999, however, total visitor arrivals declined by 3.9%, to 376,535. The decrease was partly as a result of a 8.6% fall in cruise-ship arrivals. Despite this, stop-over arrivals increased by 8.2% in 1999. Of total stop-over visitors (excluding non-resident Grenadians) in 1999, 32.5% were from the USA, 20.1% from Caribbean countries and 24.5% from the United Kingdom. Tourism receipts totalled around EC$251.5m. in 1999. The growth in tourism, from which revenue more than doubled between 1990 and 1999 has, in turn, stimulated the construction sector, the GDP of which expanded by some 5.0% in 1999. However, growth in the sector was expected to slow in 2000/01, as major construction projects neared completion. Industry also contributes strongly to Grenada's economy (mining, manufacturing, construction and utilities) providing 20.8% of GDP in 1999, and engaging 23.9% of the employed labour force in 1998. Overall, industrial GDP increased by an average of 5.9% annually in 1990–99.

The Government also hoped to diversify the economy through expansion of the 'offshore' financial sector; in September 1999 the creation of a regulatory body for this sector was announced.

In July 1998 Grenada joined fellow members of the Organisation of Eastern Caribbean States (OECS) in applying for group membership of the Inter-American Development Bank. Since 1997 some 900 'offshore' financial companies (including 21 banks) have been registered in Grenada. In January 2000, moreover, the Government established the Grenada International Financial Services Authority (GIFSA) to regulate the international financial services sector. In the same year, following Grenada's inclusion on international money-laundering and tax havens blacklists and the collapse (and subsequent government takeover) of an 'offshore' bank, the Government introduced measures to strengthen the GIFSA. These included redoubling efforts to combat money-laundering and drugs-trafficking; the establishment of a bank supervision department to ensure that all financial institutions operated within the norms of the sector; and a review of all existing legislation governing the financial services sector to comply with the requirements of the Organisation for Economic Co-operation and Development by March 2001. As part of this effort, in this month the Government revoked the licences of 17 'offshore' banks.

Total GDP increased, in real terms, at an average annual rate of 3.6% in 1990–99. Real GDP increased by 4.2% in 1997, by 7.3% in 1998 and by an estimated 8.2% in 1999; growth was projected at 5.3% for 2000.

Statistical Survey

Source (unless otherwise stated): Central Statistical Office, Ministry of Finance, Lagoon Rd, St George's; tel. 440-2731; fax 440-4115.

AREA AND POPULATION

Area: 344.5 sq km (133.0 sq miles).

Population: 89,088 at census of 30 April 1981; 94,806 (males 46,637; females 48,169) at census of 12 May 1991 (excluding 537 persons in institutions and 33 persons in the foreign service); 100,100 (official estimate) at mid-1998.

Density (mid-1998): 290.6 per sq km.

Principal Town: St George's (capital), population 4,439 (1991 census).

Births and Deaths (1996): Registered live births 2,096 (birth rate 21.3 per 1,000); Registered deaths 782 (death rate 7.9 per 1,000).

Expectation of Life (years at birth, 2000): 71 (males 68; females 73). Source: *Population Reference Bureau*.

Employment (employees only, 1998): Agriculture, hunting, forestry and fishing 4,794; Mining and quarrying 58; Manufacturing 2,579; Electricity, gas and water 505; Construction 5,163; Wholesale and retail trade 6,324; Restaurants and hotels 1,974; Transport, storage and communications 2,043; Financing, insurance and real estate 1,312; Public administration, defence and social security 1,879; Community services 3,904; Other services 2,933; Activities not adequately defined 1,321; Total employed 34,789 (males 20,733; females 14,056).

AGRICULTURE, ETC.

Principal Crops (FAO estimates, '000 metric tons, 2000): Roots and tubers 4; Pulses 1; Coconuts 7; Vegetables 3; Sugar cane 7; Apples 1; Plums 1; Oranges 1; Grapefruit and pomelos 2; Other citrus fruits 1; Avocados 2; Mangoes 2; Bananas 4; Plantains 1; Other fruits 3; Cocoa beans 1. Source: FAO.

Official Estimates ('000 lb, 1999): Cocoa beans 2,073; Bananas 1,248; Nutmeg 5,876; Mace 459. Source: IMF, *Grenada: Statistical Annex* (August 2000).

Livestock (FAO estimates, '000 head, 2000): Cattle 4; Pigs 5; Sheep 13; Goats 7; Asses 1. Source: FAO.

Livestock Products (FAO estimates, '000 metric tons, 2000): Meat 1; Cows' milk 1; Hen eggs 1. Source: FAO.

Fishing (metric tons, live weight, 1998): Capture 1,718 (Groupers 52, Bigeye scads 53, Other scads 101, Common dolphinfish 153; Wahoos 59, Blackfin tuna 236, Yellowfish tuna 351, Atlantic sailfish 154, Atlantic blue marlin 61, Other marine fishes 165); Total catch 1,718. Source: FAO, *Yearbook of Fishery Statistics*.

INDUSTRY

Production (1994): Rum 3,000 hectolitres; Beer 24,000 hectolitres; Wheat flour 4,000 metric tons (1996); Cigarettes 15m.; Electricity 95 million kWh (1996). Source: mainly UN, *Industrial Commodity Statistics Yearbook*.

FINANCE

Currency and Exchange Rates: 100 cents = 1 Eastern Caribbean dollar (EC $). *Sterling, US Dollar and Euro Equivalents* (30 April 2001): £1 sterling = EC $3.866; US $1 = EC $2.700; €1 = EC $2.397; EC $100 = £25.87 = US $37.04 = €41.73. *Exchange Rate:* Fixed at US $1 = EC $2.70 since July 1976.

Budget (EC $ million 1999): *Revenue:* Tax revenue 232.0 (Taxes on income and profits 38.6, Taxes on property 7.1, Taxes on domestic goods and services 44.3, Taxes on international trade and transactions 142.0); Other current revenue 38.7; Capital revenue 3.6; Total 274.3, excluding grants received (17.8). *Expenditure:* Current expenditure 220.4 (Personal emoluments 119.4, Goods and services 30.2, Interest payments 23.0, Transfers and subsidies 47.8); Capital expenditure 104.2; Total 324.6. Source: Eastern Caribbean Central Bank, *Report and Statement of Accounts*.

2000 (projections, EC $ million): *Revenue:* Total 297.5 (Recurrent 297.5; Capital 0), excl. grants (30.1). *Expenditure:* Total 357.9 (Recurrent 242.9; Capital 115.0).

International Reserves (US $ million at 31 December 2000): IMF special drawing rights 0.00; Foreign exchange 57.66; Total 57.66. Source: IMF, *International Financial Statistics*.

Money Supply (EC $ million at 31 December 2000): Currency outside banks 71.14; Demand deposits at deposit money banks 134.20; Total money (incl. others) 205.44. Source: IMF, *International Financial Statistics*.

Cost of Living (Consumer Price Index; base: 1995 = 100): 103.3 in 1997; 104.7 in 1998; 105.0 in 1999. Source: IMF, *International Financial Statistics*.

Expenditure on the Gross Domestic Product (EC $ million at current prices, 1999): Government final consumption expenditure 147.5; Private final consumption expenditure 695.8; Gross fixed capital formation 391.3; Increase in stocks 14.0; *Total domestic expenditure* 1,248.6; Exports of goods and services, *less* Imports of goods and services –228.2; *GDP in purchasers' values* 1,020.4. Source: IMF, *International Financial Statistics*.

Gross Domestic Product by Economic Activity (EC $ million at current prices, 1999): Agriculture, hunting, forestry and fishing 67.2; Mining and quarrying 4.1; Manufacturing 60.5; Electricity and water 41.5; Construction 79.3; Wholesale and retail trade 93.7; Restaurants and hotels 74.5; Transport and communications 201.1; Finance and insurance 77.9; Real estate 29.1; Government services 139.0; Other community, social and personal services 22.6; *Subtotal* 890.4; *Less* Imputed bank service charge 56.7; *GDP at factor cost* 833.8. Source: Eastern Caribbean Central Bank, *Statistical Digest 2000*.

Balance of Payments (EC $ million, 1999): Exports of goods f.o.b. 152.96; Imports of goods f.o.b. –498.35; *Trade balance* –345.39; Exports of services 428.86; Imports of services –217.81; *Balance on goods and services* –134.34; Other income received 11.53; Other income paid –90.67; *Balance on goods, services and income* –213.48; Current transfers received 96.07; Current transfers paid –20.44; *Current balance* –137.85; Capital account (net) 74.22; Direct investment from abroad 125.17; Portfolio investment liabilities 2.03; Portfolio investment assets –0.96; Other investment liabilities 62.64; Other investment assets –85.09; Net errors and omissions –29.27; *Overall balance* –10.89. Source: Eastern Caribbean Central Bank, *Balance of Payments 2000*.

EXTERNAL TRADE

Principal Commodities (US $ million, preliminary, 1999): *Imports:* Food and live animals 45.2; Crude materials (inedible) except fuels 5.9; Mineral fuels, lubricants, etc. 16.6; Chemicals 15.6; Basic manufactures 44.8; Machinery and transport equipment 66.0; Miscellaneous manufactured articles 31.1; Total (incl. others) 230.4 (excl. unrecorded imports). *Exports:* Cocoa 1.4; Nutmeg 14.9; Mace 1.9; Fish 3.1; Paper products 1.7; Flour 3.3; Electronic components 14.2; Total (incl. others) 46.4 (excl. re-exports 3.3). Source: IMF, *Grenada: Statistical Annex* (August 2000).

Principal Trading Partners (EC $ million, 1998): *Imports c.i.f.:* Antigua and Barbuda 8.1; Barbados 14.1; Canada 17.3; Netherlands 7.2; Trinidad and Tobago 122.3; United Kingdom 52.0; USA 216.4; Total (incl. others) 550.1. *Exports f.o.b.:* Antigua and Barbuda 2.2; Barbados 6.0; Canada 1.5; Dominica 3.3; France 2.7; French West Indies 2.9; Germany 5.5; Jamaica 1.8; Netherlands 14.6; Republic of Ireland 6.4; Saint Lucia 8.6; Saint Vincent and the Grenadines 1.5; Trinidad and Tobago 3.4; United Kingdom 3.2; USA 41.1; Total (incl. others) 112.3. Source: OECS, *External Merchandise Trade Annual Report 1998*.

TRANSPORT

Road Traffic (1991): Motor vehicles registered 8,262.

Shipping: *Merchant Fleet* (registered at 31 December 2000): 6 vessels (total displacement 1,009 grt). Source: Lloyd's Register of Shipping, *World Fleet Statistics*. *International Sea-borne Freight Traffic* (estimates, '000 metric tons, 1995): Goods loaded 21.3; Goods unloaded 193.0. *Ship Arrivals* (1991): 1,254. *Fishing vessels* (registered, 1987): 635.

Civil Aviation (aircraft arrivals, 1995): 11,310.

TOURISM

Visitor Arrivals: 368,417 in 1997; 391,680 in 1998; 376,535 (125,291 stop-overs, 243,042 cruise-ship passengers, 8,202 excursionists) in 1999. Source: Eastern Caribbean Central Bank, *Balance of Payments 2000*.

Cruise-ship Calls: 328 in 1998.

Receipts from Tourism (EC $ million): 219.1 in 1997; 231.7 in 1998; 251.5 in 1999. Source: Eastern Caribbean Central Bank, *Balance of Payments 2000*.

COMMUNICATIONS MEDIA

Radio Receivers (1997): 57,000 in use*.

Television Receivers (1997): 33,000 in use*.

Telephones (1997): 27,000 main lines in use†.

Telefax Stations (1996): 270 in use†.

Mobile Cellular Telephones (1997): 976 subscribers†.

Non-Daily Newspapers (1996): 4; circulation 14,000*.

* Source: UNESCO, *Statistical Yearbook*.
† Source: UN, *Statistical Yearbook*.

EDUCATION

Pre-primary (1994): 74 schools; 158 teachers; 3,499 pupils.
Primary (1995): 57 schools; 849 teachers; 23,256 pupils.
Secondary (1995): 19 schools; 381 teachers; 7,260 pupils.
Higher (excluding figures for the Grenada Teachers' Training College, 1993): 66 teachers; 651 students.

Directory

The Constitution

The 1974 independence Constitution was suspended in March 1979, following the coup, and almost entirely restored between November 1983, after the overthrow of the Revolutionary Military Council, and the elections of December 1984. The main provisions of this Constitution are summarized below:

The Head of State is the British monarch, represented in Grenada by an appointed Governor-General. Legislative power is vested in the bicameral Parliament, comprising a Senate and a House of Representatives. The Senate consists of 13 Senators, seven of whom are appointed on the advice of the Prime Minister, three on the advice of the Leader of the Opposition and three on the advice of the Prime Minister after he has consulted interests which he considers Senators should be selected to represent. The Constitution does not specify the number of members of the House of Representatives, but the country consists of 15 single-member constituencies, for which representatives are elected for up to five years, on the basis of universal adult suffrage.

The Cabinet consists of a Prime Minister, who must be a member of the House of Representatives, and such other ministers as the Governor-General may appoint on the advice of the Prime Minister.

There is a Supreme Court and, in certain cases, a further appeal lies to Her Majesty in Council.

The Government

Head of State: HM Queen ELIZABETH II (succeeded to the throne 6 February 1952).

Governor-General: Sir DANIEL WILLIAMS (appointed 8 August 1996).

THE CABINET
(August 2001)

Prime Minister and Minister of National Security and Information: Dr KEITH CLAUDIUS MITCHELL.

Minister of Finance, Trade, Industry and Planning: ANTHONY BOATSWAIN.

Minister of Foreign Affairs and International Trade, and of Carriacou and Petit Martinique Affairs: Sen. ELVIN NIMROD.

Minister of Health and the Environment: CLARICE MODESTE-CURWEN.

Minister of Education: AUGUSTINE JOHN.

Minister of Youth, Sports and Community Development: ADRIAN MITCHELL.

Minister of Agriculture, Lands, Forestry and Fisheries: CLARIS CHARLES.

Minister of Tourism, Civil Aviation, Social Security, Gender and Family Affairs: BRENDA HOOD.

Minister of Housing, Social Services, Culture and Co-operatives: CUTHBERT BRIAN MCQUEEN.

Minister of Communications, Works and Public Utilities: Sen. GREGORY BOWEN.

Minister of Transport: OLIVER ARCHIBALD.

Minister of Implementation: JOSLYN WHITEMAN.

Minister of Labour and Local Government: Sen. LAWRENCE JOSEPH.

Attorney-General and Minister of Legal Affairs: Sen. RAYMOND ANTHONY.

MINISTRIES

Office of the Governor-General: Government House, St George's; tel. 440-2401; fax 440-6688.

Office of the Prime Minister: Ministerial Complex, 6th Floor, St George's; tel. 440-2255; fax 440-4116; e-mail gndpm@caribsurf.com.

Ministry of Agriculture, Lands, Forestry and Fisheries: Ministerial Complex, 2nd and 3rd Floors, St George's; tel. 440-2708; fax 440-4191; e-mail grenfish@caribsurf.com.

Ministry of Carriacou and Petit Martinique Affairs: Beauséjour, Carriacou; tel. 443-6026; fax 443-6040.

Ministry of Communications, Works and Public Utilities: Ministerial Complex, 4th Floor, St George's; tel. 440-2181; fax 440-4122; e-mail ministerworks@caribsurf.com.

Ministry of Education: Young St, St George's; tel. 440-2166; fax 440-6650; e-mail mail@mined.edu.gd.

Ministry of Finance, Trade, Industry and Planning: Financial Complex, Lagoon Rd, St George's; tel. 440-2731; fax 440-4115; e-mail plandev@caribsurf.com.

Ministry of Foreign Affairs and International Trade: Ministerial Complex, 4th Floor, Botanical Gardens, St. George's; tel. 440-2640; fax 440-4184; e-mail faffgnd@caribsurf.com.

Ministry of Health and the Environment: Ministerial Complex, 1st and 2nd Floors, Botanical Gardens, St. George's; tel. 440-2649; fax 440-4127; e-mail minhealthgrenada@caribsurf.com.

Ministry of Housing, Social Services, Culture and Co-operatives: Ministerial Complex, 1st and 2nd Floors, Botanical Gardens, St. George's; tel. 440-6917; fax 440-6924.

Ministry of Implementation: Ministerial Complex, 6th Floor, St George's; tel. 440-2255; fax 440-4116.

Ministry of Information: Ministerial Complex, 6th Floor, Botanical Gardens, St George's; tel. 440-2255; fax 440-4116.

Ministry of Labour and Local Government: St George's.

Ministry of Legal Affairs: Church St, St George's; tel. 440-2050; fax 440-6630; e-mail legalaffairs@caribsurf.com.

Ministry of National Security: Botanical Gardens, St George's; tel. 440-2255.

Ministry of Tourism, Civil Aviation, Social Security, Gender and Family Affairs: Ministerial Complex, 4th Floor, Botanical Gardens, St George's; tel. 440-0366, fax 440-0443; e-mail mot@caribsurf.com; internet www.spiceisle.com.users.mot.

Ministry of Transport: Young St, St. George's.

Ministry of Youth, Sports and Community Development: Ministerial Complex, 2nd Floor, Botanical Gardens, St George's; tel. 440-6917; fax 440-6924.

Legislature

PARLIAMENT

Houses of Parliament: Church St, St George's; tel. 440-2090; fax 440-4138.

Senate

President: Sen. Dr JOHN WATTS.

There are 13 appointed members.

House of Representatives

Speaker: Sir CURTIS STRACHAN.

General Election, 18 January 1999

	Votes	%	Seats
New National Party (NNP) .	25,897	62.2	15*
National Democratic Congress (NDC)	10,399	24.9	—
United Labour*† . . .	4,853	11.6	—
Others	455	1.1	—
Total	41,604	100.0	15

* In June 2000 the NNP's parliamentary representation was reduced to 14 seats after one of its deputies, Michael Baptiste, joined the opposition. As a consequence, United Labour gained one seat in the House of Representatives.

† Informal electoral alliance composed of the Grenada United Labour Party (GULP) and the Democratic Labour Party (DLP).

Political Organizations

Democratic Labour Party (DLP): St George's; f. 1995 by former members of the NDC; Leader Dr FRANCIS ALEXIS; Dep. Leader WAYNE FRANCIS.

Grenada Progressive Party: f. 1997; Leader PRESCOTT WILLIAMS.

Maurice Bishop Patriotic Movement (MBPM): St George's; f. 1984 by former members of the New Jewel Movement; socialist; Leader TERRENCE MARRYSHOW.

National Democratic Congress (NDC): St George's; f. 1987 by former members of the NNP and merger of Democratic Labour Congress and Grenada Democratic Labour Party; centrist; Leader TILLMAN THOMAS; Dep. Leader JOAN PURCELL.

The National Party (TNP): St George's; f. 1989 by Prime Minister Herbert Blaize and his supporters, following a split in the New National Party; Chair. GEORGE McGUIRE; Leader BEN JONES.

New National Party (NNP): St George's; f. 1984, following merger of Grenada Democratic Movement, Grenada National Party and National Democratic Party; Chair. LAWRENCE JOSEPH; Leader Dr KEITH MITCHELL; Dep. Leader GREGORY BOWEN.

United Labour Congress (ULC): St George's; f. 2001 following merger of Grenada United Labour Party (GULP, f. 1950) and People's Progressive Action Party; centrist; Chair. KENNY LALSINGH (acting); Leader MICHAEL BAPTISTE (acting).

United Republican Party (URP): St George's; f. 1993 by Grenadians residing in New York, USA; Leader ANTONIO LANGDON.

Diplomatic Representation

EMBASSIES AND HIGH COMMISSION IN GRENADA

China (Taiwan): Archibald Ave, POB 36, St George's; tel. 440-3054; e-mail rocemgnd@caribsurf.com; Ambassador: DAVID Y. L. LIN.

Cuba: St George's; Ambassador: HUMBERTO RIVERO.

United Kingdom: British High Commission, 14 Church St, St George's; tel. 440-3222; fax 440-4939; e-mail bhcgrenada@caribsurf.com (High Commissioner resident in Barbados).

USA: POB 54, St George's; tel. 444-1173; fax 444-4820; e-mail usembgd@caribsurf.com; internet www.spiceisle.com/homepages/usembgd/embinfo (Ambassador resident in Barbados).

Venezuela: Archibald Ave, POB 201, St George's; tel. 440-1721; fax 440-6657; Ambassador: TEOFILO LABRADOR.

Judicial System

Justice is administered by the West Indies Associated States Supreme Court, composed of a High Court of Justice and a Court of Appeal. The Itinerant Court of Appeal consists of three judges and sits three times a year; it hears appeals from the High Court and the Magistrates' Court. The Magistrates' Court administers summary jurisdiction.

In 1988 the OECS excluded the possibility of Grenada's readmittance to the East Caribbean court system until after the conclusion of appeals by the defendants in the Maurice Bishop murder trial (see Recent History). Following the conclusion of the case in 1991, Parliament voted to rejoin the system, thus also restoring the right of appeal to the Privy Council in the United Kingdom.

Attorney-General: ERROL THOMAS.

Puisne Judges: LYLE K. ST PAUL, BRIAN KEITH ALLEYNE.

Registrar of the Supreme Court: SANDRA BELFON.

President of the Court of Appeal: C. M. DENNIS BYRON.

Office of the Attorney-General: St George's; tel. 440-2050.

Religion

CHRISTIANITY

The Roman Catholic Church

Grenada comprises a single diocese, suffragan to the archdiocese of Castries (Saint Lucia). The Bishop participates in the Antilles Episcopal Conference (based in Port of Spain, Trinidad and Tobago). At 31 December 1999 there were an estimated 54,661 adherents in the diocese.

Bishop of St George's in Grenada: Rt Rev. SYDNEY ANICETUS CHARLES, Bishop's House, Morne Jaloux, POB 375, St George's; tel. 443-5299; fax 443-5758; e-mail bissac@caribsurf.com.

The Anglican Communion

Anglicans in Grenada are adherents of the Church in the Province of the West Indies, and represented 14% of the population at the time of the 1991 census. The country forms part of the diocese of the Windward Islands (the Bishop, the Rt Rev. SEHON GOODRIDGE, resides in Kingstown, Saint Vincent).

Other Christian Churches

The Presbyterian, Methodist, Plymouth Brethren, Baptist, Salvation Army, Jehovah's Witness, Pentecostal (7.2% of the population in 1991) and Seventh-day Adventist (8.5%) faiths are also represented.

The Press

NEWSPAPERS

Barnacle: Tyrell St, St George's; tel. 440-5151; monthly; Editor IAN GEORGE.

Business Eye: Young St, St George's; tel. 440-3425.

The Consumer: Melville St, POB 232, St George's; tel. 440-2305; weekly.

The Grenada Guardian: Upper Lucas St, St George's; tel. 444-3823; fax 444-2873; weekly.

The Grenada Informer: Market Hill, POB 622, St George's; tel. 440-5762; fax 440-4119; e-mail movanget@caribsurf.com; f. 1985; weekly; Editor CARLA BRIGGS; circ. 6,000.

Grenada Times: Market Hill, POB 622, St George's; tel. 440-5762; fax 440-4117; weekly; Editor JEROME McBARNETT.

Grenada Today: St John's St, POB 142, St George's; tel. 440-4401; internet www.belgrafix.com/gtoday98.htm; weekly; Editor GEORGE WORME.

The Grenadian Voice: 10 Melville St, POB 633, St George's; tel. 440-1498; fax 440-4117; e-mail gvoice@caribsurf.com; internet www.spiceisle.com/gvoice; weekly; Editor LESLIE PIERRE; circ. 3,000.

Government Gazette: St George's; weekly; official.

PRESS ASSOCIATION

Press Association of Grenada: St George's; f. 1986; Pres. LESLIE PIERRE.

Inter Press Service (IPS) (Italy) is also represented.

Publishers

Anansi Publications: Hillsborough St, St George's; tel. 440-0800; e-mail aclouden@caribsurf.com.

Grenada Publishers Ltd: Torchlight, Melville St, St George's; tel. 440-2305.

Broadcasting and Communications

TELECOMMUNICATIONS

Regulatory Authority

Eastern Caribbean Telecommunications Authority: Castries; f. 2000 to regulate telecommunications in Grenada, Dominica, Saint Christopher and Nevis, Saint Lucia and Saint Vincent and the Grenadines.

Major Service Providers

Cable and Wireless Grenada Ltd: POB 119, The Carenage, St. George's; tel. 440-1000; fax 440-4134; e-mail gndinfo@caribsurf.com; internet www.candw.gd; f. 1989; 30% govt-owned; Chair. NICK KOUMARIANOS; Man. DAVID WRIGHT.

Grenada Postal Corporation: Burns Point, St George's; tel. 440-2526; fax 440-4271; Chair. CUTHBERT JOHN; Man. LEO ROBERTS.

Grenada Telecommunications Ltd (Grentel): POB 119, St George's; tel. 444-2202; fax 444-4848; internet www.spiceisle.com; Gen. Man. NEVILLE CALLISTE.

BROADCASTING

Grenada Broadcasting Network: Observatory Rd, POB 535, St George's; tel. 440-2446; fax 440-4180; e-mail gbn@caribsurf.com; internet www2.spiceisle.com; f. 1972; 60% privately-owned, 40% govt-owned; Chair. KEN GORDON; Man. Dir HAMLET MARK.

Radio

Spice Capitol Radio FM 90: Springs, St George's; tel. 440-0162.

The Harbour Light of the Windwards: Carriacou; tel. and fax 443-7628; e-mail hbrlight@caribsurf.com; Station Man. RANDY CORNELIUS; Chief Engineer JOHN McPHERSON.

Television

Television programmes from Trinidad and from Barbados can be received on the island.

Grenada Broadcasting Corporation (Television): Morne Jaloux, POB 535, St. George's; tel. 444-5522; fax 444-5054; govt-owned; Man. Dir CECIL BENJAMIN; Programme Dir ANDRÉ JEROME.

Finance

(cap. = capital; res = reserves; dep. = deposits; amounts in Eastern Caribbean dollars)

The Eastern Caribbean Central Bank (see p. 875), based in Saint Christopher, is the central issuing and monetary authority for Grenada.

Eastern Caribbean Central Bank—Grenada Office: NIS Bldg, Melville St, St George's; tel. 440-3016; fax 440-6721.

BANKING

Grenada Bank of Commerce Ltd: Corner of Cross and Halifax Sts, POB 4, St George's; tel. 440-3521; fax 440-4153; e-mail gbcltd@caribsurf.com; f. 1983; 10% govt-owned; cap. 7.4m., res 8.8m., dep. 227.4m. (Dec. 1999); Chair. PETER JULY; Gen. Man. MORRIS MATHLIN.

Grenada Co-operative Bank Ltd: 8 Church St, POB 135, St George's; tel. 440-2111; fax 440-6600; e-mail co-opbank@ caribsurf.com; f. 1932; Man. Dir and Sec. G. V. STEELE; brs in St Andrew's and St Patrick's.

Grenada Development Bank: POB 734, Melville St, St George's; tel. 440-2382; fax 440-6610; e-mail gdbbank@caribsurf.com; f. 1976, following merger; Chair. ARNOLD CRUICKSHANK; Man. PATRICK La ROSE.

National Commercial Bank of Grenada Ltd: NCB House, POB 857, Grand Anse, St George's; tel. 444-2265; fax 444-5500; e-mail ncbgnd@caribsurf.com; internet www.ncbgrenada.com; f. 1979; 51% owned by Republic Bank Ltd, Port of Spain; cap. 15.0m., res 8.1m., dep. 333.1m. (Sept. 1999); Chair. RONALD HARFORD; Man. Dir MICHAEL B. ARCHIBALD; 9 brs.

Foreign Banks

Bank of Nova Scotia (Canada): Granby and Halifax Sts, POB 194, St George's; tel. 440-3274; fax 440-4173; Man. B. ROBINSON; 3 brs.

Barclays Bank PLC (United Kingdom): Church and Halifax Sts, POB 37, St George's; tel. 440-3232; fax 440-4103; Man. IVAN BROWNE; 3 sub-brs in Carriacou, Grenville and Grand Anse.

Caribbean Commercial Bank (Trinidad and Tobago): St George's; 1 br.

INSURANCE

Several foreign insurance companies operate in Grenada and the other islands of the group. Principal locally-owned companies include the following:

Grenada Insurance and Finance Co Ltd: Young St, POB 139, St George's; tel. 440-3004.

Grenada Motor and General Insurance Co Ltd: Scott St, St George's; tel. 440-3379.

Grenadian General Insurance Co Ltd: Corner of Young and Scott Sts, POB 47, St George's; tel. 440-2434; fax 440-6618.

Trade and Industry

CHAMBERS OF COMMERCE

Grenada Chamber of Industry and Commerce, Inc: DeCaul Bldg, Mt Gay, POB 129, St George's; tel. 440-2937; fax 440-6621; e-mail gcic@caribsurf.com; internet www.spiceisle.com/homepages /gcic; f. 1921, incorporated 1947; 180 mems; Pres. AZAM RAHAMAN; Exec. Dir CHRISTOPHER DeRIGGS.

Grenada Manufacturing Council: POB 129, St George's; tel. 440-2937; fax 440-6627; e-mail gcic@caribsurf.com; f. 1991 to replace Grenada Manufacturers' Asscn; Chair. CHRISTOPHER DeALLIE.

INDUSTRIAL AND TRADE ASSOCIATIONS

Grenada Cocoa Association: Scott St, St George's; tel. 440-2234; fax 440-1470; f. 1987, following merger; changed from co-operative to shareholding structure in late 1996; Chair. LAWRENCE GRENADE; Gen. Man. KEN-MARTIN WHITEMAN.

Grenada Co-operative Banana Society: Scott St, St George's; tel. 440-2486; fax 440-4199; f. 1955; a statutory body to control production and marketing of bananas; Exec. Chair. DANIEL LEWIS; Gen. Man. JOHN MARK (acting).

Grenada Co-operative Nutmeg Association: POB 160, St George's; tel. 440-2117; fax 440-6602; f. 1947; processes and markets all the nutmeg and mace grown on the island; to include the production of nutmeg oil; Chair. BYRON CAMPBELL; Man. (vacant).

Grenada Industrial Development Corporation: Frequente Industrial Park, Frequente, St David's; tel. 444-1035; fax 444-4828; e-mail gidc@caribsurf.com; internet www.spiceisle.com/users/gidc; f. 1985; Chair. RUPERT AGOSTINI; Man. TERENCE MOORE.

Marketing and National Importing Board: Young St, St George's; tel. 440-1791; fax 440-4152; e-mail mnib.com@ mailcaribsurf.com; f. 1974; govt-owned; imports basic food items, incl. sugar, rice and milk; Chair. ANTHONY BOATSWAIN; Man. FITZROY JAMES.

EMPLOYERS' ORGANIZATION

Grenada Employers' Federation: Mt Gay, POB 129, St George's; tel. 440-1832; 60 mems.

There are several marketing and trading co-operatives, mainly in the agricultural sector.

UTILITIES
Public Utilities Commission: St George's.

Electricity
Grenada Electricity Services Ltd (Grenlec): POB 381, Halifax St, St George's; tel. 440-2097; fax 440-4106; e-mail grenlec @caribsurf.com; internet elec.carilec.com.lc/grenlec; generation and distribution; 90% privately-owned, 10% govt-owned; Chair. G. ROBERT BLANCHARD; Gen. Man. NIGEL D. WARDLE.

Water
National Water and Sewerage Authority: The Carenage, St George's; tel. 440-2155; fax 440-4107; Chair. NELSON LOUISON; Man. LEROY NECKLES.

TRADE UNIONS
Grenada Trade Union Council (GTUC): Green St, POB 405, St George's; tel 440-3733; Pres. C. ERIC PIERRE; Gen. Sec. CLARIS CHARLES.

Commercial and Industrial Workers' Union: Bains Alley, St George's; tel. 440-3423; 492 mems; Pres. A. DE BOURG.

Grenada Union of Teachers (GUT): Marine Villa, St George's; f. 1913; Pres. CLARIS CHARLES; 1,300 mems.

Seamen and Waterfront Workers' Union: The Carenage, POB 154, St George's; tel. 440-2573; f. 1952; Pres. ALBERT JULIEN; Gen. Sec. ERIC PIERRE; 350 mems.

Technical and Allied Workers' Union (TAWU): Green St, POB 405, St George's; tel. 440-2231; fax 440-5878; f. 1958; Pres. Sen. CHESTER HUMPHREY.

Bank and General Workers' Union (BGWU): St George's; tel. 440-3563; Pres. DEREK ALLARD.

Grenada Manual, Maritime and Intellectual Workers' Union (GMMIWU): St George's; Pres. (vacant); Vice-Pres. RAYMOND ANTHONY.

Grenada Media Workers' Association: St George's; Pres. RAY ROBERTS.

Public Workers' Union (PWU): POB 420, St George's; tel. 440-2203; f. 1931; Pres. LAURET CLARKSON; Exec. Sec. ALVIN ST JOHN.

Transport

RAILWAYS
There are no railways in Grenada.

ROADS
In 1996 there were approximately 1,040 km (646 miles) of roads, more than half of which were suitable for motor traffic. Public transport is provided by small private operators, with a system covering the entire country. In 1996 a concessionary loan worth some US $29m. was secured from the Government of Japan for a project to improve the road between St George's and St Andrew's.

SHIPPING
The main port is St George's, with accommodation for two ocean-going vessels of up to 500 ft. A number of shipping lines call at St George's. Grenville, on Grenada, and Hillsborough, on Carriacou, are used mostly by small craft.

Grenada Ports Authority: POB 494, The Carenage, St George's; tel. 440-7678; fax 440-3418; e-mail grenport@caribsurf.com; internet www.grenadaports.com; Chair. WALTER ST JOHN; Man. AMBROSE PHILLIP.

CIVIL AVIATION
The Point Salines International Airport, 10 km (6 miles) from St George's, was opened in October 1984, and has scheduled flights to most East Caribbean destinations, including Venezuela, and to the United Kingdom and North America. Work on an EC $30m.-project to renovate and expand the airport began in early 2000. There is an airfield at Pearls, 30 km (18 miles) from St George's, and Lauriston Airport, on the island of Carriacou, offers regular scheduled services to Grenada, Saint Vincent and Palm Island (Grenadines of Saint Vincent).

Grenada is a shareholder in the regional airline, LIAT (see under Antigua and Barbuda). In 1987 Air Antilles (based in Saint Lucia) was designated as the national carrier.

Grenada Airports Authority: Point Salines Int. Airport, POB 385, St George's; f. 1985; tel. 444-4101; fax 444-4838; e-mail gaa @caribsurf.com; Chair. MICHAEL MCINTYRE; Gen. Man. DONALD MCPHAIL.

Tourism

Grenada has the attractions of both white sandy beaches and a scenic, mountainous interior with an extensive rain forest. There are also sites of historical interest, and the capital, St George's, is a noted beauty spot. In 1999 there were 376,535 visitor arrivals, of which 243,042 were cruise-ship passengers, and tourism earned some EC $252m. There were approximately 1,670 hotel rooms in 1996. In 1997 a joint venture between the Government of Grenada and the Caribbean Development Bank to upgrade and market some 50 unprofitable hotels was implemented. In addition, the Ministry of Tourism, in conjunction with the Board of Tourism and the Hotel Association, announced a 10-year development plan to increase hotel capacity from its present level to 2,500 rooms.

Grenada Board of Tourism: POB 293, Burns Point, St George's; tel. 440-2279; fax 440-6637; e-mail gbt@caribsurf.com; internet www.grenada.org; f. 1991; Chair. LYDEN RAMDHANNY; Dir WILLIAM JOSEPH.

Grenada Hotel Association Ltd: POB 440, St George's; tel. 444-1353; fax 444-4847; e-mail grenhota@caribsurf.com; internet www.grenadahotelsinfo.com; f. 1961; Pres. ESTHER NOEL; Dirs LEO GARBUTT, AUGUSTUS CRUICKSHANK.

Defence

A regional security unit was formed in late 1983, modelled on the British police force and trained by British officers. A paramilitary element, known as the Special Service Unit and trained by US advisers, acts as the defence contingent and participates in the Regional Security System, a defence pact with other East Caribbean states.

Commissioner of Police: FITZROY BEDEAU.

Education

Education is free and compulsory for children between the ages of five and 16 years. Primary education begins at five years of age and lasts for seven years. Secondary education, beginning at the age of 12, lasts for a further five years. In 1995 a total of 23,256 children received public primary education in 57 schools. There were 19 public secondary schools, with 7,260 pupils registered, in that year. Technical Centres have been established in St Patrick's, St David's and St John's, and the Grenada National College, the Mirabeau Agricultural School and the Teachers' Training College have been incorporated into the Technical and Vocational Institute in St George's. The Extra-Mural Department of the University of the West Indies has a branch in St George's. A School of Medicine has been established at St George's University (SGU), where a School of Arts and Sciences was also founded in 1997, while there is a School of Fishing at Victoria. The rate of adult literacy was estimated at around 96% in the late 1990s. In 1997 the World Bank agreed to finance a US $7.6m. loan for improvements to schools. Projected budgetary expenditure on education was EC $25m. in 1998 (equivalent to 11.5% of total recurrent expenditure).

GUADELOUPE

Area: 1,705 sq km (658.3 sq miles); the dependencies of Saint-Martin, Saint-Barthélemy, Marie-Galante, the Iles des Saintes (Les Saintes) and La Désirade comprise 269 sq km of this total.
Population (census result, March 1999): 422,496.
Capital: Basse-Terre; population 12,410 at the 1999 census.
Language: French (official); a creole patois is widely spoken.
Religion: Predominantly Christian (mainly Roman Catholic).
Climate: Tropical; average temperature 29°C (76°F); humid and wet season June–November.
Time: GMT −4 hours.
Public Holidays
2002: 1 January (New Year's Day), 11–13 February (Lenten Carnival), 29 March–1 April (Easter), 1 May (Labour Day), 8 May (Victory Day), 9 May (Ascension Day), 20 May (Whit Monday), 14 July (National Day), 21 July (Victor Schoëlcher Day), 15 August (Assumption), 1 November (All Saints' Day), 11 November (Armistice Day), 25 December (Christmas Day). **2003:** 1 January (New Year's Day), 3–5 March (Lenten Carnival), 18–21 April (Easter), 1 May (Labour Day), 8 May (Victory Day), 29 May (Ascension Day), 9 June (Whit Monday), 14 July (National Day), 21 July (Victor Schoëlcher Day), 15 August (Assumption), 1 November (All Saints' Day), 11 November (Armistice Day), 25 December (Christmas Day).

Currency: French franc; 1,000 francs = £94.51 = US $135.31 = €152.45 (30 April 2001).

Weights and Measures: The metric system is in force.

Basic Economic Indicators

	1995	1996	1997
Consumer price index (base: 1990 = 100)	112.4	114.0	115.3
Rate of inflation (annual average, %)	2.1	1.4	1.1
Imports c.i.f. (million French francs)*	9,590.5	9,981.7	10,236.6
Exports f.o.b. (million French francs)†	807.9	725.4	819.4

* 10,703.9 in 1998.
† 704.2 in 1998.

State budget (million francs at current prices, 1990): Revenue 2,494; Expenditure 4,776.

Gross domestic product (US $ million at current prices, 1996): 3,153.

GDP per head (US $ at current prices, 1996): 7,316.

Growth of real GDP (annual average, 1990–96): −4.1%.

Total labour force (1999): 191,367.

Unemployment (1998): 28.8%.

Public external debt (1988): US $41m.

Life expectancy (years at birth, 1994): 75.

Infant mortality rate (per 1,000 live births, 1990): 10.0.

Adult literacy rate (15 years and over, 1992): Male 89.7%; Female 90.5%.

Passenger motor cars in use (per 1,000 of population, 1993): 248.8.

Television receivers in use (per 1,000 of population, 1997): 270.

History

PHILLIP WEARNE

Revised for this edition by the editorial staff

Named after the Spanish Virgin of Guadeloupe by the European navigator Christopher Columbus in 1493, the island was occupied by the French, almost without interruption, from 1635. Guadeloupe and its dependencies—namely three offshore islands and Saint-Barthélemy and the northern part of Saint-Martin in the Leeward Islands—became a French Overseas Department in March 1946, but achieved some measure of autonomy in 1983 as a result of the decentralization reforms of President François Mitterrand's Socialist Government. The island was administered by a prefect, appointed by the French Ministry of the Interior. Local government was made up of a 42-seat General Council, elected for a six-year term to control the department's budget and domestic taxation, and a 41-seat Regional Council, consisting of local councillors and the two senators and four deputies Guadeloupe sends to the French parliament.

However, progress towards greater autonomy did not prevent an upsurge of nationalist sentiment during the 1980s, witnessed by the formation of several separatist groups, making Guadeloupe the most politicized of France's Caribbean possessions. These groups comprised two broad categories: those that claimed responsibility for a series of bomb attacks on government offices and economic targets such as hotels and restaurants; and those that campaigned by lawful means. Among the former, the most active were the Caribbean Revolutionary Alliance (Alliance Révolutionnaire Caraïbe—ARC) and, during 1983 and 1984, the Armed Liberation Group (Groupe Libération Armée). In 1984 the ARC merged with the Popular Movement for an Independent Guadeloupe (Mouvement Populaire pour une Guadeloupe Indépendante—MPGI), but continued its bombing campaign, using the MPGI as a legitimate 'cover' for its activities. In 1984 the leader of the ARC, Luc Reinette, was sentenced to 12 years in prison, for possession of arms and conspiracy to carry out more than 20 bomb attacks in 1983–85. He escaped in June 1985, but was recaptured in July 1987 and held in Paris, where he was due to go on trial with 13 other Guadeloupe separatists. In June 1989, however, after demonstrations demanding the release of political prisoners and after 'hunger strikes' by separatist activists, among them Reinette, the French National Assembly granted an amnesty to those imprisoned or accused in connection with politically motivated crimes committed before July 1988 in the Overseas Departments.

The amnesty, the failure of the independence groups at the polls and the Mitterrand administration's willingness to cede more autonomy to Guadeloupe's democratic left, in firm control of the island's General Council by 1988, formed the basis for a new political *modus vivendi* in Guadeloupe. The bombers, temporarily at least, changed tactics. Pressure from trade unionists, the support base of the socialist movement on the island, who attributed a further decline in the island's economy to the bombing campaign, seems to have played a crucial role.

As in other French possessions (such as New Caledonia, in the Pacific), nationalist pressure had a racial element. The original white planters represented only 5% of the population, yet they owned more than 80% of all land and property until 1945. The position of this group was consolidated, after 1946, by the arrival of French government officials and professionals. They not only altered the racial balance in favour of the whites, at a time when black national consciousness was growing, but also effectively blocked the advancement of the most able blacks and people of mixed descent by monopolizing the most desirable jobs. The problems of change in the racial balance of the island were compounded by the influx of up to 45,000 illegal immigrants from Dominica, Haiti and other neighbouring islands, attracted by the relatively high standard of living that Guadel-

oupeans enjoyed, and by work opportunities in the agricultural sector. Many native islanders preferred to emigrate or to seek work in the services sector rather than accept wages below the legal minimum on the land. However, salary levels remained high by Caribbean standards, being linked to those of metropolitan France. Emigration, meanwhile, continued at a rate of nearly 20,000 per year, with the result that perhaps 40% of all Guadeloupeans lived abroad by the early 1990s. Their remittances to relatives at home became a vital part of the island's economic structure.

The belief that the separatists had an influence out of all proportion to their numbers was borne out by the French presidential and parliamentary elections, which, along with local elections, took place in 1988. In all three gauges of public opinion, it was the moderate left—the Socialists—which made gains, although the independence movement claimed that the increased rate of abstention reflected growing support for their cause. For the presidency of the Republic, François Mitterrand gained 55% and 69.4% of the votes in Guadeloupe, in the first and second rounds of voting in April and May 1988, respectively. In the French National Assembly elections, held in June 1988, the Socialists made one gain, when Dominique Larifla, President of the General Council, defeated the sitting deputy of the conservative Rally of the Centre Union (Union du Rassemblement du Centre—URC), a local alliance between the main national parties of the right, the Rally for the Republic (Rassemblement pour la République—RPR) and the Union of Democrats for the Republic (Union des Démocrates pour la République). One Socialist and one Communist were re-elected, as was Lucette Michaux-Chevry of the URC. In the elections for the local General Council itself, the Socialist–Communist coalition increased its total by one seat, giving it 26 seats, against the 16 of the right-wing parties. Dominique Larifla was re-elected President of the General Council.

In March 1992 Dominique Larifla was returned as President of the General Council, but the Socialists suffered some reversal in the Regional Council elections, held simultaneously. The right-wing grouping, on this occasion known as Guadeloupe Objective (Objectif Guadeloupe), led by Michaux-Chevry, gained 15 of the 41 seats; two Socialist groups gained 16 between them, the Communists eight seats and the pro-independence Popular Union for the Liberation of Guadeloupe (Union Populaire pour la Libération de la Guadeloupe) two seats. A split on the Socialist side meant that Michaux-Chevry, with the support of six dissident left-wingers, was able to oust the Socialist Félix Proto from the Council presidency. The decline of the left-wing was consolidated when a repeat of the Regional Council election was required after a complaint was upheld that one party's candidates had been registered after the official deadline. Guadeloupe Objective took a further seven seats to push its tally up to 22, while the two left-wing parties retained only 10.

In the French National Assembly elections of March 1993 the local wing of the national Socialist Party (Parti Socialiste—PS) lost more ground when an independent right-wing candidate, Edouard Chammougon, defeated Larifla by just 273 votes. Chammougon, mayor of Baie-Mahault, was elected despite being implicated in several corruption scandals, which involved many leading figures in the Department during the early 1990s. However, further corruption charges and allegations of abuse and misappropriation of public funds led to Chammougon's membership of the National Assembly being revoked by the French Constitutional Council in November 1994, at which time Léo Andy of the 'dissident' PS was elected to his seat. In 1993 Lucette Michaux-Chevry retained her Assembly seat with 79.9% of the poll, while an anti-Larifla Socialist, Frédéric Jalton, and a dissident Communist, Ernest Moutoussamy, retained the other two seats. However, the Socialist–Communist coalition retained control of the General Council in March 1994 and Larifla was re-elected its President. In elections to the European Parliament in June left-wing parties won the largest share of the vote, a combined 37.2%.

In the 1995 national presidential election Jacques Chirac (RPR) took the lead in the first round, with 38.2% of the votes cast. Lionel Jospin (PS) came second, with 35.1%. However, owing to the support of all the left-wing parties, Jospin won 55.1% of the votes cast in the department in the second round on 7 May. In municipal elections held at the same time Michaux-Chevry defeated the Communist incumbent to become mayor of the capital, Basse-Terre. She and Larifla were elected to the French Senate in September and Philippe Chaulet of the RPR was subsequently elected to her seat in the National Assembly. Jean Barfleur became Guadeloupe's first pro-independence mayor when he won Port-Louis. The defeat of the Communist, Henri Bangou, was attributed to continuing divisions within the left.

At elections to the French National Assembly in late May and early June 1997, Moutoussamy, Andy and Chaulet all retained their seats, while Daniel Marsin, a candidate of the independent left, was elected in the Les Abymes–Pointe-à-Pitre constituency formerly held by the deceased Frédéric Jalton. An abstention rate of 52.5% was recorded. In March 1998 the RPR won 25 of the 41 seats in the Regional Council, although the PS increased its representation to 12 seats in the same elections. Michaux-Chevry was re-elected to the presidency of the Council. In concurrent elections to the General Council the Socialist–Communist coalition retained a 28-seat majority, although the RPR increased its representation to eight seats. Larifla was deposed from the Council's presidency and replaced by Marcellin Lubeth of the Progressive Democratic Party of Guadeloupe (Parti Progressiste Démocratique Guadeloupéen—PPDG), which had been formed in 1991, following a split in the Communist Party of Guadeloupe (Parti Communiste Guadeloupéen—PCG).

Guadeloupe experienced a wave of political and social unrest in 1999 surrounding the two-day visit of Prime Minister Jospin in October. In September riots broke out in Pointe-à-Pitre following the arrest and sentencing of Armand Toto, a leading member of the Union Générale des Travailleurs de la Guadeloupe (UGTG), who was accused of assaulting two policemen and threatening to kill another, while occupying the premises of a motor-vehicle company in support of a dismissed worker. Moreover, industrial action by banana producers, concerned at falling banana prices in the European market, also created widespread disruption. The workers demanded the disbursement of 100m. French francs, and additional assistance for the restructuring of their businesses, as compensation for a

significant decline in banana prices. Jospin later announced that his Government would introduce an emergency plan for the banana sector.

The issue of Guadeloupe's constitutional status also arose in 1999, following a series of meetings between the Presidents of the Regional Councils of Guadeloupe, Martinique and French Guiana. In December Michaux-Chevry co-signed a declaration, stating the intention of the three Presidents to propose, to the French Government, legislative and constitutional amendments aimed at creating a new status of 'overseas region' and providing for greater financial autonomy. The declaration and subsequent announcements by Michaux-Chevry and her counterparts were dismissed by Jean-Jack Queyranne, the French Secretary of State for Overseas Departments and Territories, in February 2000, as unconstitutional and exceeding the mandate of the politicians responsible. However, in May 2000 a number of proposals, including the extension of the Departments' powers in areas such as regional co-operation, were provisionally accepted by the French National Assembly; a modified version of the proposals was subsequently adopted, by a narrow margin, by the French Senate. In November the National Assembly approved the changes, and in December they were ratified by the Constitutional Council. At a referendum held in September, Guadeloupe voted overwhelmingly in favour (89%) of reducing the presidential mandate from seven years to five.

In municipal elections held in March 2001 Michaux-Chevry was re-elected mayor of Basse-Terre, despite corruption charges against her (in January Michaux-Chevry was acquitted of charges of forgery, however she was still under investigation for charges of embezzlement). Following her election, Michaux-Chevry relinquished the post to Pierre-Martin, in order to comply with regulations that no official may hold more than two elected posts simultaneously (she already held the positions of senator and President of the Regional Council). Henri Bangou of the PPDG was also re-elected to the mayoralty of Pointe-à-Pitre. In the concurrently-held election to the presidency of the General Council Jacques Gillot of Guadeloupe United, Socialism and Reality (Guadeloupe Unie, Socialisme et Réalité—GUSR) defeated Marcellin Lubeth of the PPDG.

In early June 2001 riots took place in Pointe-à-Pitre in which a number of people were injured, in protest at the arrest of the leader of the UGTG, Michel Madassamy; Madassamy had been charged in late May with vandalizing a number of shops that had remained open, in defiance of the UGTG's recommendations that businesses remain closed on 27 May (the anniversary of the abolition of slavery in Guadeloupe). The General Secretary of the UGTG subsequently called for a general strike to be held for the duration of Madassamy's incarceration. A period of severe drought, necessitating the rationing of water supplies, served to exacerbate the deteriorating social situation on the island.

Economy

PHILLIP WEARNE

Revised for this edition by the editorial staff

The structure of Guadeloupe's economy helps to explain why the separatist movement does not command greater support. The penalties that would normally be associated with huge trade deficits and low productivity do not apply in Guadeloupe as French aid and subsidies make up the difference, providing one of the highest standards of living in the Caribbean. In 1996 Guadeloupe's gross domestic product (GDP) per head was estimated at US $7,316, a figure that, it was calculated, would be dramatically reduced were France to withdraw its support of the economy. The average annual inflation rate, after falling from 14% in 1981 to just 1.3% in 1986, began to rise again in the late 1980s. Between 1990 and 1997 the annual rate of inflation averaged 2.1%. Consumer prices increased by an

average of 1.1% in 1997. In December 1998 some 28.8% of the work-force were unemployed.

Guadeloupe's trade deficit rose steadily in the 1980s and the 1990s. In 1980 the value of exports covered 14.5% of imports. By 1998 that figure had fallen to 6.6%. The deficit rose from 2,628m. francs in 1981 to 9,999.7m. francs by 1998. The main reason for this was Guadeloupe's increased consumption of high-value consumer products, such as electrical goods and cars. The principal imports in 1995 were machinery and transport equipment, food and livestock, manufactured goods and chemicals. In 1997 some 62.9% of imports came from metropolitan France. Imports of mineral fuels, the main source of the department's energy, increased from 2.1% of the total in 1993 to 5.8%

in 1995. The main exports in 1997 were bananas, sugar, rum, cereals and boats. In that year France took 60.7% of Guadeloupe's exports.

One possible solution to the island's deteriorating trade position was more regional integration. Closer co-operation with the Organisation of Eastern Caribbean States (OECS—a seven-state, Commonwealth-Caribbean group, using a common currency, the Eastern Caribbean dollar), was the most obvious option. At an OECS meeting in Antigua and Barbuda in 1989, it was agreed to establish a committee to examine the possibility of OECS countries using Guadeloupe and Martinique as entrepôts for exporting to Europe. Joint ventures were another possibility. However, the advent of the single market in Europe from 1993 neutralized some of the special advantages the French Overseas Departments and Territories had previously enjoyed, with all three French Caribbean possessions thenceforth being treated simply as less developed areas of Europe.

As in other states in the region, the economy is based on agriculture, tourism and some light industry, mostly the processing of food and beverages. Bananas and raw sugar were traditionally Guadeloupe's principal exports, although the volume of production fluctuated in the early and mid-1990s owing to variable climatic conditions. Production of bananas reached 148,296 metric tons in 1992, but in 1994 a combination of drought and the damage caused to plantations in September by 'Hurricane Debbie' devastated the crop. Banana exports, typically about 120,000 tons per year in the early 1990s, fell to 86,859 tons in 1994. Adverse climatic conditions again damaged the industry in September 1995, when 'Hurricanes Luis' and 'Marilyn' destroyed many plantations. In 1996 banana production recovered to an estimated 116,000 tons. In the late 1990s Guadeloupe's banana sector was adversely affected by declining prices on the European market, while a dispute between the USA and four major Latin American producers and the EU over the latter's banana import regime also threatened the sector (this dispute was resolved in April 2001). In 1997 production fell to an estimated 87,000 tons and exports provided 22.2% of total export earnings, down from 25.4% the previous year. However, by 2000 banana production had increased to some 141,000 tons.

The fall in international sugar prices of the mid-1980s made the production of sugar cane in Guadeloupe uneconomic. A five-year plan to provide subsidies and price guarantees to growers was largely unsuccessful in maintaining production levels, as equipment deteriorated and growers voluntarily reduced production. In 1995 Guadeloupe's worst sugar-cane harvest—except for 1990, the year after 'Hurricane Hugo'—saw production fall to less than 376,000 tons of cane and 33,000 tons of sugar, though exports of raw sugar still accounted for 11.5% of total export earnings in that year. However, in 1997 production of raw sugar recovered to 57,000 tons, when it accounted for 23.7% of total export earnings, before declining to 38,400 tons in 1998. In 2000 output of sugar cane reached 500,000 tons.

The most promising agricultural sector remained non-traditional crops. The production of pineapples increased by 26.5% in the four years to 1990, to reach 4,660 metric tons. Production of pineapples was estimated at 7,000 tons in 2000. Melon output more than doubled in the same period, with exports increasing more than fourfold, to 2,695 metric tons in 1992, though this figure fell to 1,277 tons in 1997. Production was estimated at some 4,000 tons in 1999. Output of aubergines, avocados, limes and cut flowers also increased from the 1980s, although many non-traditional sectors experienced problems in the 1990s. Yams, sweet potatoes and plantains were the main subsistence crops. The fishing sector, traditionally underdeveloped, responded to efforts to stimulate output. Fishing, mostly at an artisanal level, fulfilled about two-thirds of domestic requirements in the 1990s. The total catch rose to some 9,084 metric tons by 1998. Exports rose to 176.4 tons by 1992: the recovery

of shrimp exports—up to 12.8 metric tons in 1992—was a key factor.

The main industrial activity concerned the processing of the island's agricultural crops, particularly the refining of sugar and the distillation of rum, one of Guadeloupe's major manufactured exports. By 1998 rum production had fallen from its peak of 79,550 hl in 1989 to 62,679 hl, although exports still accounted for 4.9% of total export revenues in 1997. In December 1994 the European Commission proposed that quotas of light rum from the African, Caribbean and Pacific (ACP) states associated with the EU under the Lomé Conventions be abolished by February 1996, with a phased abolition of quotas of traditional rum by the end of the century. The proposals were understood to comply with requests from the French Government, which wanted to pre-empt potential competition with its rum suppliers in the overseas territories.

There was only limited activity in the textile, furniture, metal, cement, plastics and printing sub-sectors. Despite government efforts to expand the island's industrial base with the establishment of an industrial zone and free port at Jarry, and by the promotion of fiscal incentives, industry and construction continued to employ relatively few people. In 1998 some 16.5% of the economically active work-force of 126,300 were employed in industry (of which 10.2% worked in construction). Some 8,200, or 6.5%, of the employed work-force were engaged by the agricultural sector.

Tourism remained the major source of foreign exchange, although the number of visitors declined sharply as a result of the bomb attacks by the separatist movement in the mid-1980s. Nevertheless, in 1988 tourism replaced sugar production as the department's principal source of income and the sector continued to expand rapidly in the 1990s, with tourist arrivals increasing from 453,000 in 1993 to 693,000 in 1998. The Guadeloupean dependencies of Saint-Martin (an island shared with the Dutch territory of St Maarten, in the Netherlands Antilles) and Saint-Barthélemy were almost entirely dependent upon the tourist industry and were less affected by separatist troubles. The deregulation of air transport in November 1986, which ended Air France's monopoly on flights to Guadeloupe, was a major factor in attracting more visitors to the main island. However, the decision by AOM Compagnie Aérienne Française (now Air Liberté) to cease flights to St Maarten in March 2001 severely affected the tourism industry on the island. Moreover, concerns were expressed in Guadeloupe at the potentially adverse effects on the tourism industry that a renewed monopoly on flights by Air France might have. France remained the largest source of tourists. In 1998 83.3% of arrivals came from metropolitan France or dependent territories, a further 3.4% from the USA and 8.5% from European countries other than France. The number of hotels increased in line with the rise in tourism, growing by more than 50% in the four years to 1992, and numbering 168 in 1998. The number of rooms available in that year totalled 11,555, of which 8,371 were hotel rooms. In 1990 the service sector as a whole, but most notably restaurants and hotels, employed 96,200 people or 76.2% of the island's work-force.

As the economy was heavily dependent on France, so local commercial activity was heavily dependent on the spending power of French tourists and civil servants. More than one-half of the total salary payments made on the island went to civil servants or the French Government's contractors. Civil servants received a 40% bonus on their basic metropolitan earnings, which further increased their economic importance to the department, in terms of purchasing power. As a result, local investment interest remained concentrated on the import-export business or in the services sector (such as the discount stores which handled imported goods), rather than in productive investment. The 1996 alignment of the social-security systems of the Overseas Departments with that of metropolitan France was also of significant benefit to many Guadeloupeans.

Statistical Survey

Sources (unless otherwise stated): Institut national de la statistique et des études économiques (INSEE), ave Paul Lacavé, BP 96, 97102 Basse-Terre; tel. 99-0250; Service de Presse et d'Information, Ministère des départements et territoires d'outre-mer, 27 rue Oudinot, 75700 Paris 07 SP, France; tel. 1-53-69-20-00; fax 1-43-06-60-30; internet www.outre-mer.gouv.fr.

AREA AND POPULATION

Area: 1,705 sq km (658.3 sq miles), incl. dependencies (La Désirade, Les Saintes, Marie-Galante, Saint-Barthélemy, Saint-Martin).

Population: 327,002 (males 160,112, females 166,890) at census of 9 March 1982; 387,034 (males 189,187, females 197,847) at census of 15 March 1990; 422,496 at census of 8 March 1999.

Density (at 1999 census): 247.8 per sq km.

Principal Towns (population at 1999 census): Basse-Terre (capital) 12,410; Les Abymes 63,054; Saint-Martin 29,078; Le Gosier 25,360; Baie-Mahault 23,389; Pointe-à-Pitre 20,948;Le Moule 20,827; Petit Bourg 20,528; Sainte Anne 20,410.

Births, Marriages and Deaths (1997, provisional figures): Registered live births 7,554 (birth rate 17.4 per 1,000); Registered marriages 1,936 (marriage rate 4.7 per 1,000); Registered deaths 2,441 (death rate 5.6 per 1,000).

Expectation of Life (UN estimates, years at birth, 1990–95): 75.9 (males 72.4, females 80.1). Source: UN, *World Population Prospects: The 1998 Revision*.

Economically Active Population (persons aged 15 years and over, 1990 census): Agriculture, hunting, forestry and fishing 8,391; Industry and energy 9,630; Construction and public works 13,967; Trade 15,020; Transport and telecommunications 6,950; Financial services 2,802; Other marketable services 26,533; Non-marketable services 34,223; Total employed 117,516 (males 68,258, females 49,258); Unemployed 54,926 (males 25,691, females 29,235); Total labour force 172,442 (males 93,949, females 78,493).

1998: Agriculture 8,200; Industry 7,900; Construction 13,000; Services 96,200; Not available 1,000; Total employed 126,300; Unemployed 55,900; Total labour force 182,200.

1999: Total labour force 191,362 (males 97,329, females 94,033).

AGRICULTURE, ETC.

Principal Crops (FAO estimates, '000 metric tons, 2000): Sweet potatoes 3; Yams 9; Cassava 1; Other roots and tubers 3; Vegetables and melons 23; Watermelons 1; Pineapples 7; Bananas 141; Plantains 6; Sugar cane 500. Source: FAO.

Livestock (FAO estimates, '000 head, year ending September 2000): Cattle 80; Goats 63; Pigs 15; Sheep 4. Source: FAO.

Livestock Products (FAO estimates, '000 metric tons, 2000): Beef and veal 3; Pig meat 1; Poultry meat 1; Hen eggs 2. Source: FAO.

Forestry: Roundwood removals ('000 cu m, excl. bark, 1999): Total (fuel wood) 15. Source: FAO, *Yearbook of Forest Products*.

Fishing (metric tons, live weight, 1998): Capture 9,084 (Common dolphinfish 680, Blackfin tuna 470, Other mackerel-like fishes 1,450, Marine fishes 5,800, Stromboid conchs 550); Aquaculture 14; Total catch 9,098. Source: FAO, *Yearbook of Fishery Statistics*.

MINING

Production ('000 metric tons, 1995): Pozzolan 210.0. Source: UN, *Industrial Commodity Statistics Yearbook*.

INDUSTRY

Production: Raw sugar 38,400 metric tons in 1998; Rum 62,679 hl in 1998; Cement 283,000 metric tons in 1996; Electric energy (million kWh) 1,211 in 1997 (Source: UN, *Industrial Commodity Statistics Yearbook*).

FINANCE

Currency and Exchange Rates: French currency is used (see French Guiana).

Budget (million French francs): *State budget* (1990): Revenue 2,494; Expenditure 4,776. *Regional budget* (1997): Expenditure 1,700. *Departmental budget* (1989): Revenue 1,617; Expenditure 1,748.

Money Supply (million French francs at 31 December 1996): Currency outside banks 1,148; Demand deposits at banks 6,187; Total money 7,335.

Cost of Living (Consumer Price Index for urban areas; base: 1990 = 100): 112.4 in 1995; 114.0 in 1996; 115.3 in 1997. Source: ILO, *Yearbook of Labour Statistics*.

Expenditure on the Gross Domestic Product (million French francs at current prices, 1994): Government final consumption expenditure 5,721; Private final consumption expenditure 16,779; Increase in stocks 161; Gross fixed capital formation 5,218; *Total domestic expenditure* 27,879; Exports of goods and services 912; *Less* Imports of goods and services 9,040; *GDP in purchasers' values* 19,751.

Gross Domestic Product by Economic Activity (million French francs at current prices, 1992): Agriculture, hunting, forestry and fishing 1,206.9; Mining, quarrying and manufacturing 1,237.5; Electricity, gas and water 307.5; Construction 1,164.4; Trade, restaurants and hotels 2,907.9; Transport, storage and communications 1,415.4; Finance, insurance, real estate and business services 2,023.0; Government services 4,769.7; Other community, social and personal services 2,587.7; Other services 348.0; *Sub-total* 17,968.0; Import duties 699.4; Value-added tax 615.7; *Less* Imputed bank service charge 1,311.2; *GDP in purchasers' values* 17,972.0. Source: UN, *National Accounts Statistics*.

EXTERNAL TRADE

Principal Commodities: *Imports c.i.f.* (US $ million, 1995): Food and live animals 302.8 (Meat and meat preparations 74.7, Dairy products and birds eggs 51.9, Cereals and cereal preparations 55.6, Vegetables and fruit 51.4); Beverages and tobacco 88.1 (Beverages 78.8); Mineral fuels, lubricants, etc. 110.7 (Petroleum, petroleum products, etc. 52.5, Gas, natural and manufactured 58.0); Chemicals and related products 172.8 (Medicinal and pharmaceutical products 78.1); Basic manufactures 259.5 (Paper, paperboard and manufactures 39.3); Machinery and transport equipment 607.0 (Office machines and automatic data-processing equipment 40.7, Telecommunications and sound equipment 43.0, Road vehicles and parts 217.7, Other transport equipment 100.0); Miscellaneous manufactured articles 282.6 (Furniture and parts 47.2, Clothing and accessories, excl. footwear, 52.6, Printed matter 39.5); Total (incl. others) 1,901.3. Source: UN, *International Trade Statistics Yearbook*. *Exports f.o.b.* (million French francs, 1997): Bananas 179.7; Melons and fresh papayas 33.8; Sugar 193.9; Rum 40.2; Wheaten or rye flour 35.3; Yachts and sports boats 50.7; Total (incl. others) 819.4.

1998 (million French francs): *Imports:* 10,703.9; *Exports:* 704.2.

Principal Trading Partners (million French francs, 1997): *Imports c.i.f.:* Belgium-Luxembourg 161.8; Curaçao (Netherlands Antilles) 212.6; France (metropolitan) 6,435.7; Germany 445.5; Italy 395.0; Japan 247.6; Martinique 114.0; Spain 190.2; Trinidad and Tobago 189.3; United Kingdom 151.7; USA 315.4; Total (incl. others) 10,236.6. *Exports f.o.b.:* Belgium-Luxembourg 23.0; France (metropolitan) 497.2; French Guiana 20.6; Italy 21.7; Martinique 152.2; United Kingdom 18.7; USA 36.6; Total (incl. others) 819.4.

TRANSPORT

Road Traffic ('000 motor vehicles in use, 1995): Passenger cars 97.0; Commercial vehicles 28.9. Source: UN, *Statistical Yearbook*.

Shipping *Merchant Fleet* (vessels registered, '000 grt at 31 December 1992): Total displacement 6. Source: Lloyd's Register of Shipping. *International sea-borne traffic,* (1998): Vessels entered 3,319 (1996); Goods loaded 324,500 metric tons; Goods unloaded 2,518,200 metric tons; Passengers carried 1,308,800.

Civil Aviation (1998): Passengers carried 1,978,000; Freight carried 16,500 metric tons.

TOURISM

Tourist Arrivals ('000): 693 in 1998.

Receipts from Tourism (US $ million): 458 in 1995; 496 in 1996; 499 in 1997. Source: World Tourism Organization, *Yearbook of Tourism Statistics*.

COMMUNICATIONS MEDIA

Radio Receivers ('000 in use) 113 in 1997; **Television Receivers** ('000 in use) 118 in 1997; **Telephones** ('000 main lines in use) 171 in 1996; **Telefax Stations** (number in use) 3,400 in 1996; **Mobile Cellular Telephones** (subscribers) 814 in 1996; **Daily Newspaper** 1 (estimate) in 1996 (estimated average circulation 35,000 copies). Sources: UNESCO, *Statistical Yearbook*; UN, *Statistical Yearbook*.

EDUCATION

Pre-primary (1993/94): 121 institutions; 760 teachers; 22,678 students (1994/95).

Primary (1992/93): 219 institutions; 1,920 teachers; 38,332 students (1994/95).

Secondary (1994/95): 3,467 teachers (1992/93); 41,656 general students 9,243 vocational students.

Source: UNESCO, *Statistical Yearbook.*

Higher (1997): 5,800 students (Université Antilles-Guyane).

Directory

The Government

(August 2001)

Prefect: JEAN-FRANÇOIS CARENCO, Préfecture, Palais d'Orléans, rue Lardenoy, 97109 Basse-Terre Cédex; tel. 99-39-00; fax 81-58-32.

President of the General Council: JACQUES GILLOT (GUSR), Hôtel du Département, blvd Félix Eboué, 97109 Basse-Terre; tel. 99-77-77; fax 99-76-00; e-mail info@cg971.com; internet www.cg971.com.

President of the Economic and Social Committee: GUY FRÉDÉRIC.

Deputies to the French National Assembly: ERNEST MOUTOUSSAMY (PPDG), LÉO ANDY ('dissident' PS), PHILIPPE CHAULET (RPR), DANIEL MARSIN (Independent left).

Representatives to the French Senate: LUCETTE MICHAUX-CHEVRY (RPR), DOMINIQUE LARIFLA ('dissident' PS).

REGIONAL COUNCIL

ave Paul Lacavé, Petit-Paris, 97109 Basse-Terre; tel. 80-40-40; fax 81-34-19; internet www.cr-guadeloupe.fr.

President: LUCETTE MICHAUX-CHEVRY (RPR).

Election, 15 March 1998

					Seats
Rassemblement pour la République (RPR)	.	.	.		25
Parti Socialiste (PS)		.	.	.	12
Parti Communiste Guadeloupéen (PCG)	.	.			2
Others*	.	.	.	.	2
Total	.	.	.	.	**41**

* Other right-wing candidates.

Political Organizations

Fédération de la Guadeloupe du Rassemblement pour la République (RPR): Lotissement SIG, Sainte-Anne; Gaullist; Departmental Sec. ALDO BLAISE.

Fédération Guadeloupéenne du Parti Socialiste (PS): 801 Residence Collinette, Grand Camp, 97139 Les Abymes; tel. and fax 82-19-32; divided into two factions to contest the March 1992 and March 1993 elections; First Sec. GEORGES LOUISOR. A 'dissident' faction of the party is led by DOMINIQUE LARIFLA.

Fédération Guadeloupéenne de l'Union pour la Démocratie Française (UDF): Pointe-à-Pitre; centrist.

Guadeloupe Unie, Socialisme et Réalité (GUSR): Pointe-à-Pitre.

Konvwa pou Liberayson Nasyon Gwadloup (KLNG): Pointe-à-Pitre; pro-independence; Leader LUC REINETTE.

Parti Communiste Guadeloupéen (PCG): 119 rue Vatable, 97110 Pointe-à-Pitre; tel. 82-19-45; fax 83-69-90; f. 1944; Sec.-Gen. CHRISTIAN CÉLESTE.

Parti Progressiste Démocratique Guadeloupéen (PPDG): Pointe-à-Pitre; f. 1991; includes a breakaway group of PCG militants; Leaders HENRI BANGOU; DANIEL GENIES.

Union Populaire pour la Libération de la Guadeloupe (UPLG): Basse-Terre; f. 1978; favours increased autonomy for Guadeloupe; Sec.-Gen. ROLAND THESAUROS.

Judicial System

Cour d'Appel: Palais de Justice, 4 blvd Félix Eboué, 97100 Basse-Terre; tel. 80-63-36; fax 80-63-39; First Pres. B. BACOU; Procurator-Gen. M. ZIRNHELT; two Tribunaux de Grande Instance, four Tribunaux d'Instance.

Religion

The majority of the population belong to the Roman Catholic Church.

CHRISTIANITY

The Roman Catholic Church

Guadeloupe comprises the single diocese of Basse-Terre, suffragan to the archdiocese of Fort-de-France, Martinique. At 31 December 1999 there were an estimated 340,000 adherents, representing some 79.1% of the total population. The Bishop participates in the Antilles Episcopal Conference, currently based in Port of Spain, Trinidad and Tobago.

Bishop of Basse-Terre: Rt Rev. ERNEST MESMIN LUCIEN CABO, Evêché, pl. Saint-François, BP 369, 97106 Basse-Terre Cédex; tel. 81-36-69; fax 81-98-23.

Other Denominations

Apostles of Infinite Love: Plaines, 97116 Pointe-Noire; tel. 98-01-19.

Mission Baptiste: 101 Belcourt, 97122 Baie-Mahault; tel. and fax 26-15-71; e-mail al.gary@wanadoo.fr.

The Press

L'Etincelle: 119 rue Vatable, 97110 Pointe-à-Pitre; tel. 91-12-77; fax 83-69-90; f. 1944; weekly; organ of the PCG; Dir RAYMOND BARON; circ. 5,000.

France-Antilles: 1 rue Hincelin, BP 658, 97159 Pointe-à-Pitre; tel. 90-25-25; fax 91-78-31; daily; Dir FRANÇOIS MERCADER; circ. 25,000.

Guadeloupe 2000: Résidence Massabielle, 97110 Pointe-à-Pitre; tel. 82-36-42; fax 91-52-57; fortnightly; right-wing extremist; Dir EDOUARD BOULOGNE; circ. 3,500.

Jakata: Pointe-à-Pitre; f. 1977; fortnightly; Dir FRANTZ SUCCAB; circ. 6,000.

Match: 33 rue Peyrier, 97110 Pointe-à-Pitre; tel. and fax 82-01-87; fortnightly; Dir MARIE ANTONIA JABBOUR; circ. 6,000.

Newsmagazine Guadeloupéen: Résidence Vatable, Bâtiment B, BP 1286, 97178 Pointe-à-Pitre; tel. 91-16-94; fax 82-22-38; f. 1994; fmrly *Magwa*; fortnightly; independent; Editor DANNICK ZANDRONIS; circ. 4,000.

Le Progrès social: rue Toussaint L'Ouverture, 97100 Basse-Terre; tel. 81-10-41; weekly; Dir JEAN-CLAUDE RODES; circ. 5,000.

7 Mag: Immeuble SOCOGAR, 97122 Baie-Mahault; Dir JACQUES CANNEVAL.

TV Magazine Guadeloupe: 1 rue Paul Lacavé, BP 658, 97169 Pointe-à-Pitre; tel. 90-25-25; weekly.

NEWS AGENCIES

Agence Centrale Parisienne de Presse (ACP): Pointe-à-Pitre; tel. 82-14-76; fax 83-78-73; Rep. RENÉ CAZIMIR-JEANON.

Foreign Bureaux

Agencia EFE (Spain): Pointe-à-Pitre; Correspondent DANNICK ZANDRONIS.

United Press International (UPI) (USA): BP 658, 97159 Pointe-à-Pitre; Rep. STÉPHANE DELANNOY.

Broadcasting and Communications

BROADCASTING

Réseau France Outre-mer (RFO): BP 402, 97163 Pointe-à-Pitre Cédex; tel. 93-96-96; fax 93-96-82; internet www.rfo.fr; fmrly Société Nationale de Radio-Télévision Française d'Outre-mer, renamed as above 1998; 24 hours radio and 24 hours television broadcast daily; Pres. ANDRÉ-MICHEL BESSE; Regional Dir MICHEL MEYER.

Radio

More than 30 private FM radio stations are in operation.

Radio Actif: Jarry, 97122 Baie-Mahault; commercial; satellite link to Radio Monte-Carlo (Monaco and France).

Radio Caraïbes International (RCI): BP 1309, 97187 Point-à-Pitre Cédex; tel. 83-96-96; fax 83-96-97; two commercial stations broadcasting 24 hours daily; Dir JEAN-FRANÇOIS FERANDIER-SICARD.

Radio Saint-Martin: Port de Marigot, 97150 Saint-Martin; commercial station broadcasting 94 hours weekly; Man. H. COOKS.

Radio Voix Chrétiennes de Saint-Martin: BP 103, Marigot, 97150 Saint-Martin; tel. 87-13-59; religious; Man. Fr CORNELIUS CHARLES.

Television

Archipel 4: Résidence Les Palmiers, Gabarre 2, 97110 Pointe-à-Pitre; tel. 83-63-50; commercial station.

Canal Antilles: 2 Lotissement Les Jardins de Houelbourg, 97122 Baie-Mahault; tel. 26-81-79; private 'coded' station.

TCI Guadeloupe: Montauban, 97190 Grosier; commercial station.

Finance

(cap. = capital; res = reserves; dep. = deposits;
m. = million; brs = branches; amounts in French francs)

BANKING
Central Bank

Institut d'Emission des Départments d'Outre-mer: Pointe-à-Pitre.

Commercial Banks

Banque des Antilles Françaises: pl. de la Victoire, BP 696, 97110 Pointe-à-Pitre Cédex; tel. 81-25-34; fax 27-81-41; f. 1853; cap. 36.9m., res 44.2m., dep. 2,441.8m. (Dec. 1998); Chair. JACQUES GIRAULT; Gen. Man. JEAN TAUZIES.

Banque Française Commerciale Antilles-Guyane (BFC Antilles-Guyane): BP 13, 97151 Pointe-à-Pitre Cédex; tel. 21-56-70; fax 21-56-80; internet www.cosmobay.com/demo/bfcag; f. 1976 as branch of Banque Française Commerciale SA, separated 1984; total assets 3,609.1m (1998); Chair. YVES GUERIN; CEO and Gen. Man. FRANCIS LAMARQUE.

BNP Paribas, SA: pl. de la Rénovation, 97110 Pointe-à-Pitre; tel. 90-58-58; fax 90-04-07; Dir HENRI BETBEDER; 6 further brs in Guadeloupe.

Crédit Martiniquais: blvd Marquisat de Houelbourg, Zone Industrielle de Jarry, 97122 Baie-Mahault; tel. 25-45-00; fax 25-45-02; f. 1987; cap. 185.4m (1998)—see chapter on Martinique.

Société Générale de Banque aux Antilles (SGBA): 30 rue Frébault, BP 55, 97152 Pointe-à-Pitre; tel. 25-49-77; fax 25-49-78; e-mail sgba@wanadoo.fr; f. 1979; Chair. JEAN-LOUIS MATTEI; Gen. Man. BERNARD GILBERT; 8 brs in French West Indies.

INSURANCE

Mutuelle Antillaise d'Assurances, Société d'Assurances à forme mutuelle: 12 rue Gambetta, BP 409, 97110 Pointe-à-Pitre; tel. 83-23-32; fax 83-34-99; f. 1937; Dir-Gen. FÉLIX CHERDIEU D'ALEXIS; Man. A. ZOGG.

Foreign Companies

Some 30 of the principal European insurance companies are represented in Pointe-à-Pitre, and another six companies have offices in Basse-Terre.

Trade and Industry

DEVELOPMENT ORGANIZATIONS

Agence Française de Développement (AFD): Faubourg Frébault, BP 160, 97154 Pointe-à-Pitre; tel. 83-32-72; fmrly Caisse Française de Développement.

Agence pour la Promotion des Investissements en Guadeloupe (APRIGA): BP 514, 97165 Pointe-à-Pitre; tel. 83-48-97; fax 82-07-09; e-mail apriga@apriga.com; f. 1979 as Agence pour la Promotion de l'Industrie de la Guadeloupe; Pres. PATRICK DOQUIN; Dir CHARLY BLONDEAU.

Centre Technique Interprofessionnel de la Canne et du Sucre: Morne Epingle, Les Abymes, BP 397, 97162 Pointe-à-Pitre Cédex; tel. 82-94-70; fax 20-97-84; Pres. MICHEL MONTEIRO; Dir MICHEL MARCHAT.

CHAMBERS OF COMMERCE

Chambre de Commerce et d'Industrie de Pointe-à-Pitre: Hôtel Consulaire, rue Félix Eboué, 97159 Pointe-à-Pitre Cédex; tel. 93-76-00; fax 90-21-87; e-mail contacts@cci-pap.org; Pres. FÉLIX CLAIREVILLE; Dir-Gen. JACQUES GARRETA.

Chambre de Commerce et d'Industrie de Basse-Terre: 6 rue Victor Hugues, 97100 Basse-Terre; tel. 99-44-44; fax 81-21-17; internet www.basse-terre.cci.fr; f. 1832; 24 mems; Pres. JEAN-JACQUES FAYEL; Sec.-Gen. JEAN-CLAUDE BAPTISTIDE.

Chambre Départementale d'Agriculture de la Guadeloupe: 23 rue Lardenoy, 97100 Basse-Terre; tel. 81-34-61; Pres. MAURICE RAMASSAMY; Dir FRANCK LOMBION.

Chambre de Métiers de la Guadeloupe: route Choisy, BP 61, 97120 Saint-Claude; tel. 80-23-33; fax 80-08-93; Dir MAURICE SONGEONS.

EMPLOYERS' ORGANIZATIONS

Union Patronale de la Guadeloupe: Pointe-à-Pitre; Pres. MICHEL POMAREDE.

Syndicat des Producteurs-Exportateurs de Sucre et de Rhum de la Guadeloupe et Dépendances: Zone Industrielle de la Pointe Jarry, 97122 Baie-Mahault, BP 2015, 97191 Pointe-à-Pitre; tel. 26-62-12; fax 26-86-76; f. 1937; 4 mems; Pres. AMÉDÉE HUYGHUES-DESPOINTES.

MAJOR COMPANIES

Chantiers Audebert et Cie, SARL: Quaie Gatine, 97110 Pointe-à-Pitre; tel. 26-75-40; fax 26-75-43; f. 1904; construction equipment and materials; Man. ARNAULD AUDEBERT; 100 employees.

Compagnie Frigorifique de la Guadeloupe, SARL: Z. I. de la Pointe Jarry, 97122 Baie-Mahault; tel. 26-72-28; fax 26-80-91; f. 1973; manufacture of soft drinks; Man. Dir ALAIN HUYGUES DESPOINTES; 87 employees.

Compagnie Guadeloupéenne de Boissons Gazeuses, SARL: POB 400, Pointe-à-Pitre; manufacture of canned and bottled soft drinks; Pres. MARCEL ANDRÉ CLEMENT.

Damoiseau Frères: Bellevue, 97160 Le Moule; tel. 23-55-55; fax 23-48-50; f. 1942; import and production of alcoholic beverages; Man. Dir HENRI DOMOISEAU; 29 employees.

Guadeloupe International Paper Co: Pères Blancs Baillif, Basse-Terre; manufacture of paper products; Gen. Man. L. DENZENNE; 55 employees.

Liquoristerie Madras: Z. I. de la Pointe Jarry, 97122 Baie-Mahault; tel. 26-60-28; fax 26-76-69; f. 1983; production and bottling of cane syrup, rums and other beverages; Man. Dir HENRI BICCHARA-JABOUR; 20 employees.

Panigua, SA: Voie principale, Z. I. de la Pointe Jarry, 97122 Baie-Mahault; tel. 26-87-80; fax 26-89-67; f. 1988; production of frozen uncooked pastry dough; Mans MARIUS PHERON, BERCHEL DELTA; 30 employees.

SA Rio: Z. I. de la Pointe Jarry, 97122 Baie-Mahault; tel. 26-63-22; fax 26-86-60; f. 1992; production of meats and meat products; Man. MARIUS PHERON; 26 employees.

Société des Eaux Capes Dole: Dolé les bains, 97113 Gourbeyre; tel. 92-10-92; fax 92-26-19; f. 1968; bottling of mineral water; Man. PATRICK DOQUIN; 21 employees.

Société Tropicale d'Aménagement (STA): Z. I. de la Pointe Jarry, 97122 Baie-Mahault; tel. 26-68-02; fax 26-75-97; f. 1979; manufacture of household wooden products; Man. HENRI MOLINARD; 12 employees.

Somatco: Z. I. de la Pointe Jarry, 97122 Baie-Mahault; tel. 26-71-67; fax 26-86-24; f. 1980; industrial manufacture of construction materials; Man. CHRISTIAN BONNARDEL; 17 employees.

TRADE UNIONS

Centrale des Travailleurs Unis (CTU): Logement Test 14, BP 676, Bergevin, 97169 Pointe-à-Pitre; tel. 83-16-50; fax 91-78-02; affiliated to the Confédération Française Démocratique du Travail; Sec.-Gen. HENRI BERTHELOT.

Confédération Générale du Travail de la Guadeloupe (CGTG): 4 cité Artisanale de Bergevin, BP 779, 97173 Pointe-à-Pitre Cédex; tel. 82-34-61; fax 91-04-00; f. 1961; Sec.-Gen. CLAUDE MORVAN; 5,000 mems.

Union Départementale de la Confédération Française des Travailleurs Chrétiens: BP 245, 97159 Pointe-à-Pitre; tel. 82-04-01; f. 1937; Sec.-Gen. ALBERT SARKIS; 3,500 mems.

Union Départementale des Syndicats CGT-FO: 59 rue Lamartine, 97110 Pointe-à-Pitre; Gen. Sec. FERDINAND QUILLIN; 1,500 mems.

Union Générale des Travailleurs de la Guadeloupe: rue Paul Lacavé, 97110 Pointe-à-Pitre; tel. 83-10-07; confederation of pro-independence trade unions; Sec.-Gen. GABY CLAVIER; 4,000 mems.

Transport

RAILWAYS

There are no railways in Guadeloupe.

ROADS

In 1990 there were 2,069 km (1,286 miles) of roads in Guadeloupe, of which 323 km were Routes Nationales.

SHIPPING

The major port is at Pointe-à-Pitre, and a new port for the export of bananas has been built at Basse-Terre.

Compagnie Générale Maritime Antilles-Guyane: Z.I. de la Pointe Jarry, BP 92, 97100 Baie-Mahault; tel. 26-72-39; fax 26-74-62.

Direction Départementale des Affaires Maritimes de la Guadeloupe: 1 Quai Layrle, BP 473, 97164 Pointe-à-Pitre Cédex; tel. 82-03-13; fax 90-07-33; Dir RENÉ GOALLO.

Port Autonome de la Guadeloupe: Gare Maritime, BP 485, 97165 Pointe-à-Pitre Cédex; tel. 21-39-00; fax 21-39-69; e-mail webmaster @port-guadeloupe.com; internet www.port-guadeloupe.com; port authority; Gen. Man. PATRICK LAMBERT.

Société Guadeloupéenne de Consignation et Manutention (SGCM): 8 rue de la Chapelle, BP 2360, 97001 Jarry Cédex; tel. 38-05-55; fax 26-95-39; e-mail sgcma@outremer.com; f. 1994; shipping agents, stevedoring; Chair. LUC EMY; Gen. Man. MARTIN BUTRUILLE.

Société de Transport Maritimes Brudy Frères: 78 Centre St John Perse, 97110 Pointe-à-Pitre; tel. 82-52-25; fax 93-00-79.

CIVIL AVIATION

Raizet International Airport is situated 3 km (2 miles) from Pointe-à-Pitre and is equipped to handle jet-engined aircraft. There are smaller airports on the islands of Marie-Galante, La Désirade and Saint-Barthélémy.

Air Caraïbe: Aéroport du Raizet, Immeuble Le Caducet, 97139 Abymes; tel. 82-47-34; fax 82-47-48; f. 2000 following merger of Air St Martin, Air St Barts, Air Guadeloupe and Air Martinique; operates inter-island and regional services within the Eastern Caribbean and flights to Miami (USA).

Tourism

Guadeloupe is a popular tourist destination, especially for visitors from metropolitan France (who account for some 82% of tourists) and the USA. The main attractions are the beaches, the mountainous scenery and the unspoilt beauty of the island dependencies. In 1999 847,131 tourists visited Guadeloupe, and receipts from tourism totalled US $499m. in 1997. In 1998 there were 168 hotels, with 8,371 rooms.

Delégation Régionale au Tourisme: 5 rue Victor Hugues, 97100 Basse-Terre; tel. 81-15-60; fax 81-94-82; Dir HUGUES JONNIAUX.

Office du Tourisme: 5 square de la Banque, BP 1099, 97110 Pointe-à-Pitre Cédex; tel. 89-46-90; fax 83-89-22; Pres. PHILIPPE CHAULET.

Syndicat d'Initiative de la Guadeloupe: Pointe-à-Pitre; Pres. Dr EDOUARD CHARTOL.

Defence

At 1 August 2000 France maintained a military force of about 3,800 in the Antilles (headquartered in Martinique).

Education

Education is free and compulsory in state schools between the ages of six and 16 years. There were 38,332 pupils in primary education in 1994/95, while in secondary education there were 50,899 pupils (including 9,243 pupils in vocational education). Higher education is provided by a branch of the Université Antilles-Guyane at Pointe-à-Pitre, which has faculties of law, economics, sciences, medicine and Caribbean studies. There were also two teacher-training institutes, and colleges of agriculture, fisheries, hotel management, nursing, midwifery and child care. The Guadeloupe branch of the university had 5,800 enrolled students in 1997. An Academy for Guadeloupe was established in January 1997. Government expenditure on education totalled 2,842m. French francs in 1993.

GUATEMALA

Area: 108,889 sq km (42,042 sq miles).

Population (official estimate at mid-2000): 11,385,334.

Capital: Guatemala City, estimated population 1,015,303 at mid-2000.

Language: Spanish (official); indigenous Indian (Amerindian) languages are also widely spoken.

Religion: Predominantly Christianity (mostly Roman Catholic, but many Protestant Churches are represented).

Climate: Tropical in the coastal lowlands, but more temperate and drier in the central highlands; rainy season from May to October.

Time: GMT −6 hours (GMT −5 hours in summer).

Public Holidays

2002: 1 January (New Year's Day), 6 January (Epiphany), 29 March–1 April (Easter), 1 May (Labour Day), 30 June (Anniver-sary of the Revolution), 15 August (Assumption, Guatemala City only), 15 September (Independence Day), 12 October (Columbus Day), 20 October (Revolution Day), 1 November (All Saints' Day), 24–25 December (Christmas), 31 December (New Year's Eve).

2003: 1 January (New Year's Day), 6 January (Epiphany), 18–21 April (Easter), 1 May (Labour Day), 30 June (Anniversary of the Revolution), 15 August (Assumption, Guatemala City only), 15 September (Independence Day), 12 October (Columbus Day), 20 October (Revolution Day), 1 November (All Saints' Day), 24–25 December (Christmas), 31 December (New Year's Eve).

Currency: Quetzal; 1,000 quetzales = £89.62 = US $128.32 = €144.57 (30 April 2001).

Weights and Measures: The metric system is officially in force.

Basic Economic Indicators

	1998	1999	2000
Gross domestic product (million quetzales at 1958 prices)	4,716	4,887	5,048
GDP per head (quetzales at 1958 prices)	436.7	440.7	443.4
GDP (million quetzales at current prices)	124,022	135,214	147,890
GDP per head (quetzales at current prices)	11,484.4	12,194.2	12,989.5
Annual growth of real GDP (%)	5.0	3.6	3.3
Annual growth of real GDP per head (%)	2.3	0.9	0.6
Government budget (million quetzales at current prices):			
Revenue	12,714.0	14,735.7	15,953.3
Expenditure	15,517.1	18,728.1	18,916.1
Consumer price index (annual average; base: 1995 = 100)	129.3	136.1	144.2*
Rate of inflation (annual average, %)	7.0	4.9	6.0*
Foreign exchange reserves (US $ million at 31 December)	1,322.9	1,177.7	1,736.6
Imports c.i.f. (US $ million)	4,651.1	4,381.7	n.a.
Exports f.o.b. (US $ million)	2,581.6	2,397.5	n.a.
Balance of payments (current account, US $ million)	−1,039.1	−1,025.9	n.a.

* Estimate.

Gross national product per head measured at purchasing power parity (PPP) (GNP converted to US dollars by the PPP exchange rate, 1999): 3,517.

Economically active population (official estimate, 1998): 3,151,200.

Unemployment (official figure, number of persons, Guatemala City, 1995): 1,400.

Total foreign debt (1997): US $4,086m.

Life expectancy (years at birth, 1998): 64.7 (males 61.7, females 67.6).

Infant mortality rate (per 1,000 live births, 1997): 43.

Adult population with HIV/AIDS (15–49 years, 1999): 1.38%.

School enrolment ratio (7–18 years, 1998): 47%.

Adult literacy rate (15 years and over, 2000): 68.7% (males 76.2%; females 62.1%).

Energy consumption per head (kg of oil equivalent, 1998): 579.

Carbon dioxide emissions per head (metric tons, 1997): 0.8.

Passenger motor cars in use (per 1,000 of population, 1999): 52.0.

Television receivers in use (per 1,000 of population, 1997): 61.

Personal computers in use (per 1,000 of population, 1999): 9.9.

History

Prof. JENNY PEARCE

Revised for this edition by JO TUCKMAN

The Mayan civilization originated in the highlands of what is now Guatemala, and was at its zenith in AD 300–800. Maya culture was advanced in architecture, mathematics, astronomy and chronology, and had developed a hieroglyphic script. It is not known what caused the decline of this sophisticated civilization, but, by the time of the Spanish conquest of Guatemala (1523–25), led by Pedro de Alvarado, the Guatemalan Indians (Amerindians) were ruled by a Mexican people. There followed a period of stable colonial rule by governors who were answerable to the Viceroyalty of New Spain, based in Mexico City.

INDEPENDENCE

The revolution of 1820 in Spain was closely followed by independence for Central America. A declaration of independence was drafted in Guatemala City in 1821. However, Mexico invaded and held Guatemala until 1823, when a congress of Central American provinces met in Guatemala City and the United Provinces of Central America was formed. The congress drew up a Constitution based on that of the USA, under which the liberal Manuel José Arce became first President of the federation, based in Guatemala City. Other Central American states revolted against his policies, which included the abolition of slavery, and in 1829 Gen. Francisco Morazán from Honduras defeated the federal forces and captured Guatemala City. He established a dictatorship and, while he destroyed monasteries and seized land, he also implemented a progressive programme to expand trade and industry and to encourage settlement. Morazán declared himself President of the Central American federation in 1830.

There were several uprisings by ambitious military leaders and the following years were ones of constant war and unrest, resulting in the dissolution of the federation and the adoption, in 1838, of a resolution which allowed each province the government of its choosing. Rafael Carrera, a mestizo with a large Indian following, ruled in Guatemala from 1839 to 1865, except for a short period between 1848 and 1849. Carrera was a conservative who upheld the power of the ruling classes and restored the dominant position of the Roman Catholic Church.

Guatemala underwent a liberal revolution in the 1970s, headed by Justo Rufino Barrios, a charismatic military commander who regarded himself as a great reformer. Rufino Barrios secularized and modernized the education system, attacked the Church, professionalized the army, established an effective secret police, and oversaw a fundamental reorganization of the economy. Between 1870 and 1900 the volume of foreign trade increased 20-fold, largely owing to the rapid expansion of the coffee sector, encouraged by the new export-orientated infrastructure, and new legislation that forced much of the indigenous population off their land and onto the plantations.

Rufino Barrios, who was killed in 1885, was succeeded by a series of leaders, including Manuel Estrada Cabrera, who governed from 1898 to 1920, when he was ousted by a *coup d'état*. Jorge Ubico continued the dictatorial tradition from 1930. He was forced to resign by popular discontent in 1944, ushering in 10 years of social reform under a constitutional government.

DICTATORSHIP DEFEATS DEMOCRACY, 1944–85

Juan José Arévalo won the presidential election in 1944 and introduced what became known as 'spiritual socialism', which concentrated on education, health and labour reforms. He was followed in 1950 by Col Jacobo Arbenz Guzmán, who introduced agrarian reform, whereby large private estates were expropriated and the land was shared among the peasant population. Opposition was widespread among landowners, the largest of which was the United Fruit Company of Boston (USA), which had interests in large plantations. In 1954 Col Carlos Castillo Armas led a group of foreign-armed Guatemalan exiles in a coup and remained in power until his assassination in 1957. His take-over had the support of the USA, which had viewed the previous Government as a Communist threat to the region.

It was a further nine years before an election was held. However, even then, democracy was fragile and the presidencies of Julio César Méndez Montenegro (1966–70), Col (later Gen.) Carlos Araña Osorio (1970–74) and Gen. Kjell Laugerud García (1974–78) were dominated by the Armed Forces and by the excesses of extreme right-wing groups. The inauguration of Gen. Fernando Romeo Lucas García in 1978 heralded a new 'reign of terror', which was systematized during the brief but brutal rule of Gen. José Efraín Ríos Montt from March 1982 to August 1983. Together Lucas García and Ríos Montt eradicated the potential for success of the burgeoning guerrilla movement.

The Rise of Insurgency Prompts Unfettered Repression

The combination of a series of effectively military governments and the continuation of a highly unequal form of landownership led to the formation, from the 1960s, of left-wing guerrilla groups influenced by the success of the Cuban revolution in 1959. The guerrilla movements of the 1960s were quickly defeated, with the help of US counter-insurgency techniques developed in Viet Nam. However, there was a resurgence of groups in the 1970s. The guerrillas became active in both rural and urban areas; their principal targets were government officials and the Armed Forces. By the end of the decade, they came to attract support from the majority Amerindian population. Political polarization reached its height in the early 1980s, and in February 1982 the three leading guerrilla groups united to form the Unidad Revolucionaria Nacional Guatemalteca (URNG—Guatemalan National Revolutionary Unity), in the belief that they could take power.

However, as support for the insurgents grew, the army resorted to a strategy of repression, focused on indigenous communities in the rural highlands believed to be supporters, or potential supporters, of the guerrilla movement. The massacres were carried out with the help of community-based paramilitary groups called Patrullas de Autodefensa Civil (PACS—Civil Defence Patrols). Thousands of people were killed as a result of the military campaign and many thousands more fled to refugee camps in Mexico. In the wake of the devastation inflicted on indigenous highland communities, the Government introduced a pacification programme that combined civil defence with basic subsistence support, in an attempt to restore order and confidence in military rule.

As human-rights violations by the military regime escalated, relations with the USA deteriorated, prompting the US Congress to ban all aid to Guatemala in November 1983, although in reality aid continued, estimated at US $27.5m. in 1983 and $33.6m. in 1984. The US President, Ronald Reagan, sought increased aid for Guatemala, but congressional approval was not obtained. The need for increased US aid was believed to be one of the factors in the decision of the military leadership to renounce the leadership of the country. By 1990 US aid was an estimated $120.0m.

The Transition to Democracy and a Decade of Civilian Governments

President Ríos Montt was overthrown in August 1983 by Gen. Oscar Mejía Victores, who promised a return to democracy. Although the repression and violence continued during the Government of Mejía Victores, elections for a Constituent Assembly were held in 1984, and a new Constitution was drafted, along with legislation preparing the way for democratic elections in 1985. The presidential elections were won by Mario Vinicio Cerezo of the Partido de la Democracia Cristiana de Guatemala (PDCG—Christian Democratic Party) who took office on 14 January 1986.

However, President Cerezo (1986–90) soon proved himself unable to fulfil expectations of sweeping reform, preferring a cautious approach to both the behind-the-scenes power of the military and entrenched economic interests. Military officers responsible for human-rights violations remained in their posts. The military's powerful intelligence unit, known as the G-2 and once described as the 'bureaucracy of death', was renamed the D-2 and continued its activities as before. The Government retreated from commitments on state welfare, rather than risk a confrontation with the private sector. Meanwhile, various corruption scandals further eroded support.

Progress towards peace negotiations was slow; Guatemala was a signatory of the peace plan for Central America, which was signed in Guatemala City on 7 August 1987 by the Presidents of Costa Rica, El Salvador, Guatemala, Honduras and Nicaragua. Although the principal aim of the accord was to resolve the internal conflict in Nicaragua and El Salvador, the plan also applied to Guatemala's long-standing guerrilla war. A Commission of National Conciliation was formed, in compliance with the terms of the accord. However, during 1989 there was increased guerrilla activity by groups from both the left and right. President Cerezo refused to negotiate with the URNG while its members remained armed. Preliminary talks between the URNG and the Commission began in Oslo (Norway) in March 1990.

Despite the disappointing performance, the return of civilian government was accompanied by a significant relaxation of the political climate, with opposition movements able to organize more openly. However, by the end of the decade political violence was on the increase again, and Cerezo's Government ended its term thoroughly discredited. Nevertheless, the country was able to organize a civilian transfer of power via elections in 1989, which were won by Jorge Serrano Elías, of the Movimiento para Acción y Solidaridad (MAS—Movement for Action and Solidarity). The election was marked by a high abstention rate and many null votes. The victory of Serrano, a previously unknown evangelical Protestant, reflected both public disillusion with traditional parties and the vacuum left by the constitutional ban on Ríos Montt's presidential candidature owing to his involvement in the 1982 coup that first propelled him to power.

Like Cerezo before him, President Serrano demonstrated a reluctance to confront the power of the military or the human-rights issues. However, the pressure on him increased in both domestic and international circles. The international community became increasingly vocal in its condemnation of human-rights violations, following a report by the US Department of State and another by the European Parliament; and in 1992 the indigenous leader, Rigoberta Menchú, was awarded the Nobel Peace Prize.

On 25 May 1993, amid increasing popular protest, particularly in response to electricity and transport price rises, army pressure and accusations of corruption, President Serrano dissolved the Congreso Nacional (National Congress) and the Corte Suprema (Supreme Court) and announced that he would rule by decree, pending the drafting of a new constitution. President Serrano's constitutional coup provoked almost unanimous international condemnation, including the suspension of US and European aid programmes. Such pressure, together with overwhelming domestic opposition, led to the removal of Serrano from the presidency by the military on 1 June, sending him into exile. A reconvened Congreso Nacional elected human-rights ombudsman Ramiro de León Carpio to complete what remained of Serrano's term, which ended in January 1996.

De León began his presidency with huge public and international support, pledging to end human-rights violations, fight corruption and combat poverty; but ended his term with a reputation for weakness and lack of consistency. In late August 1993, in an effort to restore the confidence of the electorate in his Government, the President requested the voluntary resignation of the legislature and the Corte Suprema. Elections for a new parliament were held in August 1994, with only one-fifth of the electorate participating. Ríos Montt's Frente Republicano

Guatemalteco (FRG—Guatemalan Republican Front), won the greatest number of seats (32 out of a total of 80), followed by the modernizing right-wing Partido de Avanzada Nacional (PAN—National Advancement Party) and the PDCG.

President de León oversaw the signing in March 1994 of a human-rights accord with the URNG, which included a mandate for a United Nations mission, the Human Rights Verification Mission in Guatemala (MINUGUA), which was formally established in September to supervise the implementation of the accord. Nevertheless, little immediate improvement in the human-rights situation was noted. Another accord signed simultaneously was designed to revitalize the peace process; however, little progress was made.

TOWARDS PEACE

The 1995 legislative and presidential elections were won, respectively, by the PAN and its leader, Alvaro Enrique Arzú Irigoyen, who promoted a pro-peace, pro-private sector agenda developed from within the more modernizing business classes. The margin of victory was extremely narrow, just 30,000 votes, owing to a last minute surge in favour of the FRG's candidate, Alfonso Portillo. Portillo had joined the FRG after Ríos Montt was once again frustrated in his attempts to stand as a presidential candidate.

The principal issue for the first year of President Arzú's administration was the peace negotiations with the guerrilla movement, the URNG, and whether the army would support an agreement with them. One of the most notable features of the negotiations for peace in Guatemala was the role played by popular and indigenous organizations, which formed a 'Civil Society Assembly' through which they made proposals, although the Government refused them direct representation in the negotiations. The greatest achievement of the Assembly was the Indigenous Rights Accord, drawn up by the Co-ordination of Organizations of the Mayan People of Guatemala (COP-MAGUA), which was adopted in March 1995. The Accord recognized indigenous rights for the first time in the country's history, and acknowledged that Guatemala was a multi-cultural, multi-lingual and multi-ethnic country.

In March 1996 a temporary, open-ended cease-fire was announced by the guerrillas. This was followed, in May, by an agreement on social and agrarian reform. On 19 September the Government and the URNG came to an agreement, in Mexico, signalling a resolution to the 36-year-old civil war. The agreement provided for constitutional changes and legislation that would democratize the role of the military and intelligence services by making them subordinate to elected bodies. The Agreement for a Firm and Lasting Peace, which consisted of 11 peace accords, was signed by the Government and the URNG in Guatemala City on 29 December 1996.

POST-ACCORDS: DILEMMAS OF IMPLEMENTATION

The demobilization of the URNG successfully took place under UN observation in March–May 1997 and in 1998 the guerrilla movement was recognized as a political party. The widely criticized PACS were also formally demobilized, as were the Policía Ambulante Militar (Mobile Military Police), and a new civilian police force was created.

However, the momentum for change and reform soon began to dissipate and virtually faded away, to the extent that by mid-2001 many observers were openly referring to the Guatemalan peace process as a failure. Analysts blamed everything from lack of political will to an exaggeration of the ability of unprepared civil society organizations to retain the pressure within the country.

There was little progress on tackling impunity, human-rights violations carried out by the security forces continued, the military Estado Mayor Presidencial (EMP—Presidential General Staff) was not dismantled, and violent crime ensured that a climate of tension continued to pervade the country. The post-accord era was also accompanied by an increase in lynchings and attacks on judicial authorities. In 2001 MINUGUA estimated that some 200 people had been killed in extrajudicial executions since 1996. Meanwhile, little was done to improve government accountability, or meet promises of social improvements. In October 1998 the Congreso Nacional approved a series of constitutional reforms provided for in the

1996 peace accords. These changes concerned the rights of indigenous peoples, the role of the Armed Forces and the police, and the strengthening of the courts, and had to be ratified by a referendum, which was held on 16 May 1999. The sense of alienation of the majority of Guatemalans towards their government and political system was revealed when 81.5% of those registered to vote abstained from the ballot. Of those who did vote, over 50% rejected the proposals. Although supporters of the constitutional amendments declared that the failure to ratify them would delay efforts to consolidate peace in the country, many believed that the result of the referendum was not a rejection of the peace process, but of the political system. In December 1999 the UN stated that the Government of President Arzú had only complied with 36% of the agreements that were scheduled to be implemented before the end of that year. The Government of Alfonso Portillo, which took office in January 2000, pledged to revive the peace process; however, by June 2001 the European Union had threatened to reduce or even suspend aid owing to the lack of progress, while international finance organizations were becoming increasingly vocal about their concern over the Government's failure to fulfil the peace deal's pledge of increasing fiscal revenue.

THE PRESIDENCY OF ALFONSO PORTILLO, 2000–

Legislative and presidential elections were held on 7 November 1999. The far-right FRG won 63 of 113 congressional seats, while the PAN secured only 37. The Alianza Nueva Nación (ANN—New Nation Alliance), a left-wing grouping including the URNG, won nine congressional seats, while three minority parties gained the remaining four seats. In the first round of the presidential contest, Alfonso Portillo, once again the FRG's candidate, won 47.8% of the votes cast, compared with the PAN's presidential nominee, Oscar Berger Perdomo, the mayor of Guatemala City, who polled 30.6% of the ballot. Alvaro Colom Caballeros, the ANN candidate, received 12.3% of the ballot. However, as Portillo failed to gain the required 50% of the votes, a second round was held on 26 December, in which Portillo received 68.3% of the valid votes cast and won in all 22 departments. The PAN's resounding defeat reflected its declining popularity with voters, owing to its poor economic performance and a series of corruption scandals. Most Guatemalans hoped that an FRG Government would improve the economic situation, as well as implement legislation to combat the public-security crisis resulting from the widespread criminality.

The new Government, which took office on 14 January 2000, was notable for its inclusion of former PDCG, PAN and URNG political leaders, as well as several prominent human-rights activists. At the beginning of Portillo's term in office the promised demilitarization of the upper echelons of government began. A civilian, Edgar Gutiérrez, was appointed to the key planning and advisory post of the Secretariado de Análisis Estratégico (Secretariat for Strategic Analysis), and Ronald Ochaeta was made Guatemala's representative to the Organization of American States (OAS), in Washington, DC (USA). One of the President's first tasks was the retirement of 20 army generals. All this went some way to counter the criticisms of those concerned by the return to power of Ríos Montt, who became president of the Congreso Nacional. The replacement of the EMP with a civilian security force also got under way. However, by mid-year the President was accused of reneging on the implementation of this important peace accord, having retained the military members of the EMP.

On taking office, the Government of Alfonso Portillo specified that one of its priorities would be the narrowing of the fiscal deficit. In May 2000 it introduced a Fiscal Pact, a long-term public-spending strategy, as stipulated under the 1996 peace accords. Another priority announced by the Portillo administration was the introduction of a Governability Pact, defined by the Government as a mechanism to build consensus between the representative of the State and the country's political and social leaderships. The country's 330 mayors were encouraged to assume a leadership role in order to promote debate among civil society organizations. This debate would centre around six issues: citizen security, justice, demilitarization and human rights; decentralization, rural development and the environment; education, including changes to the national curriculum and a modification of the educational system to safeguard gender

and inter-ethnic relations; political reform and civil-society participation, including participation mechanisms and access to decision-making structures; integral human development; and the Fiscal Pact.

However, Portillo's Government was soon subject to political infighting. The resulting instability generated rumours of a coup in February 2001 severe enough to prompt a visit by the OAS Secretary-General, César Gaviria Trujillo, to demonstrate support for Portillo. The principal source of tension was the division between President Portillo and the FRG, controlled by Ríos Montt. This resulted in constant disputes both between the Government and the Congreso Nacional, and within the Cabinet. The result was virtual paralysis in policy-making and, in particular, the failure to raise fiscal revenues. The FRG majority in the Congreso Nacional rejected a proposed increase of value-added tax (VAT) in March 2001. A subsequent package of tax reform proposals was also met with vehement opposition, led by the powerful business groups that organized regular protests. However, in July the FRG approved the increase in VAT to 12%, while the opposition PAN boycotted the session in protest. The Government was also characterized by frequent cabinet reshuffles, prompted by internal tensions. In one notable case, the head of the Presidential Human-Rights Commission, Víctor Hugo Godoy, was dismissed by Vice-President Juan Francisco Reyes López while President Portillo was out of the country.

Corruption scandals also continued in 2001; in June the Minister of Communications, Transport and Public Works, Luis Rabbe, was dismissed following an investigation that identified irregularities in road contracts. Rabbe had also invited controversy regarding his marriage to the sister of the Mexican broadcasting magnate, Angel González, who controlled all three national television channels. The use of the monopoly to promote the Government had been condemned by an OAS special envoy for freedom of expression earlier in the year. The dismissal of Rabbe reduced the Government's coverage on the national news, but the media monopoly continued to generate concern.

Meanwhile, the public-security crisis continued unabated. Kidnappings and other violent crimes increased and human-rights organizations denounced attacks against their members, which appeared to be politically motivated. In the first half of 2001 these included the murder of US nun, Ann Ford, who had worked on human-rights projects in the region of El Quiché, and the attempted kidnap of an Amnesty International worker, Barbara Bocek. In mid-June 79 dangerous convicts escaped from a high security prison in one of a series of escapes. The President declared a 30-day state of emergency, suspending some constitutional rights, while the police and army searched the countryside looking for the escapees. The state of emergency was subsequently extended, owing to the limited success of the search.

In early 2001 institutional credibility was tested by the so-called 'Guategate' scandal, involving the amendment of alcohol tax legislation by FRG deputies, after its enactment by the Congreso Nacional. The revelation of the alteration, by the media, prompted legal proceedings against 23 members of the Congreso Nacional and Ríos Montt. In March the Court ruled that the accused members would lose their parliamentary immunity. Ríos Montt temporarily resigned as head of the Congreso Nacional. However, on 24 April the Court exonerated the members of all charges, ruling that there was no case to answer.

In 2001 the fragmentation and reformulation of alliances was leading to preparations for the next elections, which, although over two years away, were made more relevant by the political crisis and policy stagnation.

Another notable development in the post-peace era was the virtual disappearance of the URNG's political influence. The former guerrilla movement-turned-political party was gradually consumed by internal power struggles and the lack of democratization of its traditionally vertical command structures. The party was also notably silent on the topics at the top of the national political agenda. The failure of the URNG to recreate itself as a credible political force prompted many former sympathizers to seek new leadership.

HUMAN RIGHTS

The assassination of the auxiliary bishop of the metropolitan diocese of Guatemala City, Juan José Gerardi Conedera, on 26 April 1998 was viewed at the time as a chilling reminder of times past and a major step backwards in the peace process. Two days before his murder the Bishop Gerardi, who headed the Roman Catholic Church's Oficina de Derechos Humanos del Arzobispado (ODHA—Archbishopric's Human Rights Office), had presented a comprehensive report documenting atrocities committed during the civil war, for which army personnel were found to be responsible for some 80%.

The case finally went to trial in 2001, taking place under intense national and international scrutiny, and was heralded as an important step towards the rejuvenation of the Guatemalan justice system. On 8 June former intelligence chief Col (retd) Disrael Lima Estrada, his son, Capt. Byron Lima Oliva, and a former member of the presidential guard, José Obdulio Villanueva, were convicted of the murder of Bishop Gerardi, while a priest, Mario Orantes, was convicted of conspiring in his death. The generally pessimistic atmosphere within Guatemala prompted many observers to view the verdict as an exception to the rule, owing to the unusual pressure that surrounded the trial, rather than representative of the other human-rights cases remaining to be investigated. In early August the Chief Public Prosecutor, Leopoldo Zeissig, who was instrumental in bringing Bishop Gerardi's murderers to justice, was forced to flee the country after receiving death threats. He had taken over responsibility for the case in 2000 after his predecessor resigned and left Guatemala after similar threats.

In August 2000 the Government accepted responsibility for 44 out of 150 cases of human-rights violations being studied by the Inter-American Commission on Human Rights (IACHR), part of the OAS. It acknowledged that, either through its actions or failure to protect its citizens, it was responsible for the 44 cases that involved extrajudicial executions and forced disappearances. In January 2001 the Government paid compensation for the deaths of five street children who were attacked by privately-employed police officers in Guatemala City in 1990. In April 2000 the Government had also admitted responsibility for human-rights violations at the annual meeting of the UN High Commission for Human Rights, in Geneva (Switzerland). Bishop Mario Ríos Montt, brother of the former dictator and FRG leader, represented the ODHA at the meeting. In the same month the ODHA accused the Armed Forces of abducting and possibly trading in children during the civil war. In December the IACHR also ruled that the military was responsible for the torture and murder of guerrilla leader Efraín Bamaca Valásquez, following his capture in 1992. In the same month the ODHA filed a case against Ríos Montt for human-rights violations during his regime.

On 6 June 2001 11 Indian communities filed genocide charges against Ríos Montt and other senior officers in his command, for his role in a series of massacres by the army during his 1982–83 rule. It remained to be seen if the case would make any progress through even the initial phases of investigation. The complaint was similar to a case filed against Gen. Lucas García that has made little impact since it was filed in 2000.

On 2 December 1999 the Nobel Peace Prize winner Rigoberta Menchú filed a case before the Spanish courts accusing Ríos Montt and former military dictators Gen. Romeo Lucas García and Gen. Oscar Humberto Mejía Victores, as well as other military officers, of the crimes of genocide, state terrorism and torture. As in the cases pursued against former Chilean dictator, Gen. Augusto Pinochet, and various Argentine military officers, the charges involved Spanish citizens killed in Guatemala in the early 1980s. In December 2000 the courts rejected the case, ruling that there was no impediment to their trial within the Guatemalan justice system. Menchú was to launch an appeal against the ruling.

On 25 February 1999 a report published by the Comisión para el Esclarecimiento Histórico (CEH—Commission for Historical Clarification) reminded people of the extent of the atrocities committed during the war years. The establishment of the CEH had been agreed by the Government and the URNG in talks held in 1994, in Oslo (Norway). Its purpose was to investigate human-rights violations and acts of violence linked to the 33-year armed conflict, although it was not allowed to name those responsible for abuses. The CEH's final report was more critical of the State than had been expected. It found that 200,000 people had been killed or had 'disappeared' between 1962 and 1996, the vast majority of them Mayan Indians. It attributed responsibility for some 90% of these crimes to state military and paramilitary terrorism. The report called for a special commission to study the conduct of army and security-force officers active during the armed conflict.

RELATIONS WITH BELIZE

Until the return to civilian government in 1986, Guatemala steadfastly laid claim to Belize, which was granted independence by the United Kingdom in September 1981. As a result of this, Guatemala severed remaining diplomatic relations with the United Kingdom. The situation had improved somewhat by 1984, and it was agreed, in principle, to reopen consular relations, in an attempt to accelerate negotiations towards a settlement, and full diplomatic relations were resumed by December 1986. By that time the new 1985 Guatemalan Constitution had dropped the inclusion of Belize in its delineation of Guatemalan territory. The United Kingdom retained a garrison of 1,500 soldiers in Belize until May 1993.

A conference in Miami, Florida (USA) in November 1998, between Guatemala, Belize and the United Kingdom, led to the establishment of a permanent joint commission to formulate a draft treaty to resolve Guatemala's claims to Belize. Approval of the treaty was to be decided by referendum, to be held in both Guatemala and Belize.

Bilateral negotiations in early 2000 were overshadowed by renewed tensions, following an announcement by the Guatemalan Government that it was increasing its military presence near to the disputed territory. In May a panel of negotiators was installed at the headquarters of the OAS, in Washington, DC, to supervise the process of bilateral negotiations. There were further border incidents in late 2000, despite an agreement in November to stabilize relations and increase communications between the Armed Forces of both countries. In February 2001 the Pan-American Institute of Geography and History, in Mexico City (Mexico), issued a report that determined the location of the 'adjacency line' between Belize and Guatemala, which was subsequently accepted by both countries. Negotiations further focused on the issue of Guatemalans living in the disputed area, who, Belize believed, were being used by Guatemala to assert sovereignty over the territory; an agreement was later reached to relocate the families.

Economy

Prof. JENNY PEARCE

Revised for this edition by JO TUCKMAN

The Guatemalan economy remained dominated by agriculture, which typically contributed 23% of the gross domestic product (GDP) in 2000 and employed more than 40% of the economically active population. At the same time, however, compared to the rest of Central America, Guatemala had a relatively highly developed industrial sector, which in 2000 contributed about 20% of GDP and exported processed products to the USA and to the country's neighbours. Only a small proportion of the country's reserves of petroleum were exploited; copper, antimony, tungsten and nickel were also mined.

Economic growth declined in the late 1970s, after two decades of expansion, and the economy stagnated in the 1980s as war and violence escalated in Guatemala and the rest of Central America. In 1980–90 annual growth averaged 0.9%, while per-head GDP decreased by an annual average of 0.8% in real terms. The recession appeared to have passed its worst by the mid-1980s, although per-head GDP growth remained slow until the end of the decade. Average annual growth in 1990–99 was 4.2%, reaching its peak in 1998 with 5.0%, before falling to 3.6% in 1999 and 3.3% in 2000. Average per-head growth over the same period, however, was only about one-half overall GDP growth.

Growth was stimulated by an increase in non-traditional exports, which outperformed the principal traditional export, coffee, in 1990, and was also improved by a sudden increase in infrastructure development. The non-traditional export sector showed the most dynamism in cultivated seafood (seafood-farm products), wood furniture and vegetables. The total value of non-traditional exports increased throughout the 1990s. Nevertheless, Guatemala continued to show a large trade deficit, which increased from US $521m. in 1991 to $1,445.1m. in 1999 and $2,177m. in 2000. During the 1990s the country had failed to diversify its export products sufficiently, had been unable to nurture the skilled labour to use high technology and had not developed its manufacturing base. At the end of the decade the economy remained overly dependent on an external sector that was extremely vulnerable to world prices of the main export commodities (coffee, sugar, bananas, cotton and petroleum), which were depressed from the late 1980s and through the 1990s; coffee prices experienced record lows in 2000 and 2001.

Increasing levels of poverty remained a major constraint on economic development. It was estimated that Guatemala's poverty rate increased from 63.4% to 89.0% in 1980–90. Extreme poverty, defined as the percentage of people unable to meet basic nutritional requirements, more than doubled, from 31% in 1980, to 67% in 1990, with even higher figures among the country's majority indigenous population. There was growing concern by the early 1990s that the Guatemalan economy was increasingly supported by money from the drugs trade and from remittances from Guatemalans living abroad. Furthermore, there was insufficient private and public investment to strengthen the productive base of the economy or to improve the social indicators. There were slight improvements in indicators between 1995 and the end of the decade, with malnutrition in children under five years of age falling from 26.6% to 24.2%, adult male illiteracy decreasing from 27.2% to 24.4%, and the number of women unable to read and write fell from 42.6% to 39.5%.

A major problem for the economy was the low tax revenue, which, at around 7% of GDP, was the lowest in Latin America. Only 20% of government revenues came from income taxes. This resulted in high (41%) government expenditure on financing the country's internal debt and forced the Government to keep interest rates high, in real terms, impeding economic growth. The peace accords signed in December 1996 committed the Government to increase tax revenue to 12% of GDP, and the issue of tax reform was a principal point of conflict during the presidency of Alvaro Enrique Arzú Irigoyen (January 1996 to January 2000), and continued to be so during the subsequent administration of Alfonso Portillo Cabrera. Income tax revenue in 2000 was 10% of GDP, but that was insufficient for international lenders, who subsequently increased the pressure on the Portillo administration to raise fiscal revenue further. However, a series of proposed tax reforms were blocked by Portillo's own party, the Frente Republicano Guatemalteco (FRG—Guatemalan Republican Front) in the Congreso Nacional, and the proposals faced heavy opposition also from powerful national business associations, which capitalized on the popular scepticism of government accountability, fuelled by a series of corruption scandals.

AGRICULTURE

Agriculture, including hunting, forestry and fishing, was the main sector of the economy, contributing an estimated 23.0% of GDP in 2000. Coffee, sugar, bananas, oil and cardamom were the major agricultural exports, with coffee alone accounting for 21.4% of the total (in 1986 it had accounted for almost 50% of total exports). Coffee was followed in importance by sugar (7.1%), bananas (6.1%) and cardamom (2.9%—Guatemala was the world's largest producer, typically accounting for 90% of cardamom on international markets). Other exported agricultural products included meat, vegetables, cotton and, from the late 1980s, tea. Fluctuating world prices for many commodities had an adverse effect on agricultural exports throughout the 1990s.

Although the suspension of the International Coffee Organization quota system in 1989 was initially beneficial to Guatemala, it adversely affected coffee exports in the early 1990s. In 1992, as world prices reached their lowest levels since the 1970s, coffee exports totalled US $253m., compared to $502m. in 1986. There was some recovery in 1994 and 1995 to $346.0m. and $539.3m., respectively, and, despite a slight decrease to $472.6m. in 1996, exports increased again to $620.4m. in 1997. However, by 1998 prices and volumes had declined again. 'Hurricane Mitch', which struck Central America in October 1998 also contributed to a 6% decline in coffee exports in that year. Prices decreased significantly once again in 2000, prompting not only a fall in revenue, but also in volume of exports. Accumulated exports from October 2000 to June 2001 were 5.2% less than in the same period of the previous cycle. Small producers, representing around 100,000 families and contributing 30% of overall national production, were particularly badly affected.

The question of how best to sustain international coffee prices preoccupied all exporters following the collapse of the International Coffee Agreement. Guatemala opted not to support a Central American plan to withhold coffee exports in an attempt to stimulate growth in falling international prices. The National Coffee Association (Anacafé) adopted a 'hedged' loan programme, under which producers received financial support by selling coffee beans at or above a set minimum price, which would then cover the loan in the event of depressed market conditions. Low world prices had a devastating impact on the sector in 1996; the average level at which income justified cost was around 130 cents per lb for Guatemalan growers, but prices were around 115 cents for most of that year. In 1997 growers visited the Republic of Korea and Japan to increase exports of high-grade coffee to Asia; Japan already accounted for 8% of Guatemala's coffee exports. In 2001, with prices at an all-time low, Guatemala joined an agreement negotiated by Mexico, Colombia and the Central American nations in March, to withhold 5% of their lowest-quality beans from export and put them to other uses, for example, fertilizer or fuel for industry. The plan coincided with an international scheme to withhold 20% of the export goods that had failed to prevent the plunge in coffee prices. Meanwhile, some of the nation's growers explored the possibilities of internet auctions of quality beans.

From the early 1980s there was a substantial decline in the area planted with cotton, a trend accelerated by the guerrilla war and high production costs. Conversely, the area planted with sugar cane expanded by more than 10% in the late 1980s and early 1990s. In 1994 production of sugar cane was 11.9m. metric tons, primarily for the domestic mills, representing an increase of 1.4% on the previous year's output. Estimated production rose steadily in the 1990s, reaching 18.2m. tons in 1998. Production decreased slightly in 1999, to 16.4m. tons, but recovered to an estimated 17.2m. tons in 2000. Exports of sugar increased from US $220.4m. in 1996 to $336.8m. in 1998. The impact of 'Hurricane Mitch' in late 1998 adversely affected regional trade and resulted in a fall in coffee, sugar and petroleum prices in the following year. Sugar exports in 2000 were worth $191m., unaltered from the previous year, while exports for the 2000/2001 harvest were expected to show a modest 2.7% increase; while improved prices had allowed farmers to increase production, yields had fallen.

Banana export revenue stood at US $163.0m. in 2000, providing 6.1% of total exports by value, compared with $132.5m. in 1999. There was potential for profitable wood production, as more than one-third of the country was covered with forests, including valuable cedar and mahogany. Total roundwood removals in 1998 amounted to 13.0m. cu m, while sawnwood production was estimated at 355m. cu m.

MINING AND POWER

The mining sector was small, contributing an estimated 0.5% of GDP in 2000. The largest operation was a copper mine in Alta Verapaz Department, which began production in 1975, but had an unrealized potential of 150,000 metric tons per year. Lead and zinc output fell drastically and a nickel-mining project was suspended in 1980, after only three years of production, owing to low world prices and high production costs. Antimony and tungsten were mined and Guatemala had exploitable reserves of sulphur and marble. With the hope that guerrilla violence was over, in 1996 the Government began attempts to attract foreign investment to the mining sector. The energy and mines ministry drafted legislation to increase the profitability of mining operations for foreign investors (through reductions in government royalties for mining concessions and in the time taken to allocate permits for companies applying to move into exploitation after exploration). Australia's Broken Hill Proprietary (BHP) Co was granted a concession to explore for copper, lead, zinc and silver in Quiché and Alta Verapaz in 1996. Mining production decreased by 3.3% in 2000.

The main reserves of petroleum were found in the north of the country, across the border from Mexican production areas. Proven reserves totalled 22m. barrels, while potential reserves were believed to be 800m.–1,000m. barrels. Earnings from exports declined to US $14.6m. in 1989, providing only 1.4% of total export earnings in the latter year. Earnings, however, recovered to $20.0m. in 1992 and petroleum production increased during the 1990s, reaching some 25,000 barrels per day (b/d) in 1997, or $98.7m. (4.2% of total export value). However, in 1998 exports fell to $61.6m. (2.4%). The Bahamas-based Basic Petroleum International was the only petroleum company engaged in production in Guatemala in 1996. It commenced production from two new oil wells during that year and increased output from 12,000 b/d to 20,000 b/d. Work was also begun on plans to construct a pipeline connecting the company's oilfields and refinery with an existing pipeline to the Caribbean coast. Increased political stability following the final peace accord signed in December 1996 raised hopes that other foreign petroleum companies could be encouraged to conduct exploration in Guatemala. Triton Energy Ltd of Dallas, Texas (USA), announced its interest in drilling in north-west Guatemala. In March 1997 bidding was opened for petroleum exploration sites in two of 12 areas, with at least four foreign companies expressing interest. The optimistic plans for the petroleum sector were, however, confounded by the fall in oil prices in 1998 and the withdrawal of foreign investors. Triton Energy suspended exploration at the beginning of 1998. Guatemala was receiving $14.4 per barrel at that time; however, by the end of the year this figure had fallen to $6.8. Meanwhile, production had increased to an average of 22,000 b/d. High international prices resulted in a significant increase in oil export revenue in 1999 and 2000, when it reached $159m.

In the early 1990s petroleum supplied 35% of Guatemala's domestic energy consumption, fuel wood 59%, agricultural residues (mainly bagasse) 5% and the remaining 1% was supplied by hydroelectricity. From the 1980s priority had been given to the development of hydroelectricity, in an attempt to reduce petroleum imports. However, construction problems delayed the completion of power-stations at Chixoy (300 MW) and Aguacapa (90 MW), costing Guatemala US $75m. per year in extra petroleum imports. The station at Chixoy only began full operation in 1986 and contributed to a significant saving in petroleum imports. The planned Chulac project on the Cahabón river, with projected capacity of 446 MW, was cancelled, owing to lack of finance.

In 1992 the Inter-American Development Bank (IDB—based in New York, USA) approved a US $14.4m. loan to help manage and conserve renewable natural resources in the Chixoy river basin. A severe drought in the area in 1991 resulted in water and electricity rationing in Guatemala City. The Chixoy watershed is the country's main source of hydroelectric power. The programme planned to introduce soil and water conservation methods, improve farming and reduce the rate of deforestation in the region. It also intended to monitor the impact of erosion and sedimentation on the dam and the hydroelectric plant.

The privatization of the energy sector was a major objective of the Arzú Government: in July 1998 80% of the capital of the state-owned Empresa Eléctrica de Guatemala, SA was sold to foreign investors for US $520m. and in December the Instituto Nacional de Electrificación (INDE) was sold for $100m. However, the incoming Portillo Government did much to reverse the privatization policy of its predecessor (see below).

MANUFACTURING

Guatemala has the largest, and one of the most developed, of all national manufacturing sectors in Central America. It experienced rapid expansion in the 1960s and 1970s, under the stimulus of the Central America Common Market (CACM) and foreign investment. This growth had slowed by the late 1970s to around 5% per year. In the 1980s, manufacturing output was adversely affected by the contraction in demand from other Central American countries as a result of the civil wars in the region and a shortage of domestic credit. Some recovery was experienced between 1987 and 1998, by which time manufacturing contributed an estimated $81.8m., or 13.6% of GDP. It remained at this level in 1999 and 2000. Despite its relatively advanced industrial sector, however, insufficient investment raised a number of concerns about its future competitiveness. In the early 1990s it was noted, for instance, that some 60% of the country's technology was more than 20 years old, partly as a result of the purchase of obsolete equipment from other nations.

The industrial sector (including construction) employed 13.6% of the work-force by 1995 and contributed an estimated 19.5% of GDP in 2000. Small enterprises predominated producing consumer goods, such as food, beverages and tobacco; intermediate goods accounted for a further 35% and included the manufacture of building materials and textiles. The clothing assembly, or *maquila*, plants contributed to an increase in non-traditional exports from the late 1980s. Guatemala took second place, behind Costa Rica, as the region's leading apparel exporter. There were 280 apparel firms operating in Guatemala by the 1990s, 30 of which were of Korean origin; major US companies accounted for most of the rest. An estimated 80,000 workers were employed in the sector. The sector's dynamism depended considerably on special government incentives to investors and low wages for a non-unionized labour force. Attracting foreign investment remained a problem for Guatemala. In 1996 representatives of large Korean conglomerates (Daewoo, Hyundai and Samsung) focused on Argentina, Brazil, Chile and Peru during a trip to Latin America, but failed to consider Guatemala. There was still a belief that Guatemala lacked political and economic stability, the regulatory framework or the consumer market to attract investment. Nevertheless, the *maquila* sector continued to expand through the 1990s and into 2000, when, despite a lack of new investments, the sector grew by 22.4%.

Although manufacturing was traditionally orientated towards Central American markets, recession and the impact of conflict throughout the region resulted in reduced demand for Guatemalan goods (exports to Central America in 1986 were only an estimated 53% of their 1981 levels). The emphasis was transferred to expanding trade with the USA. However, this tendency was reversed during the late 1980s, when Central America entered a period of greater stability. In 1996 the Arzú Government began a tariff reduction programme aimed at placing the country's manufacturing sector on an equal level with those of Costa Rica and El Salvador, where imports of raw materials were subject to recently lowered tariffs. In 1998 CACM countries agreed a joint reduction of import duties from 19% to 17% for finished goods and 12% for intermediate goods. There were further reductions in January 1999 to 15% and 10%, respectively. In 2000, 37% of exports were destined for the USA, and 31% for Central America.

The construction sector was the most dynamic sector of the economy in the early 1990s, although there were suspicions that the sector was partly funded by money raised from the illegal drugs trade. However, by the mid-1990s there were fears that the expansion of the building trade had ended, with the capital area saturated with luxury construction. Given that almost 127,000 people were directly employed by the construction trade (4.1% of the total labour force) in 1995 and that a great many more were indirectly dependent on the industry, the contraction of the sector would have a serious effect on levels of employment. Nevertheless, there was renewed dynamism in construction in the late 1990s, as the sector expanded by an estimated 5.8% in 1998, by 11.0% in 1999 and by 17.0% in 2000.

TRANSPORT AND COMMUNICATIONS

In 1999 Guatemala had 14,021 km of roads, 22% of which were paved. Paved roads increased to 35% of total roads in 2000. The Guatemalan section of the Pan-American Highway was 518.7 km long and totally asphalted. Highways are concentrated in the producing areas of the Pacific and altiplano regions. In 1996 the IDB approved a US $150m. loan for modernization of the national system of road building and maintenance, and for the repair of roads in rural areas destroyed during the civil war. The main ports are Puerto Barrios and Santo Tomás de Castilla, on the Gulf of Mexico, and San José and Champerico, on the Pacific Ocean. There are several airports, the main international airport being La Aurora, near Guatemala City.

The Arzú Government placed much emphasis on the modernization of the country's infrastructure, which included the 1997 sale of the Ferrocarriles de Guatemala (FEGUA) rail network and the 1998 sale of a 50-year concession of the railroads to the Railroad Development Corporation (USA). The company's first task was to rehabilitate the Atlantic route from Guatemala City to Puerto Barrios with the aim of fully restoring the Atlantic–Pacific link. The Government also announced plans to appoint consultants to advise on the concession of airport operations to the private sector. Increasing amounts of Guatemala's imports and exports were transported by air. In October 1996 representative boards were replaced by private-sector managers at the country's ports and, as a result, export tonnage at Puerto Quetzal increased dramatically. There were plans to invest US $250m. in the country's port facilities, including a cruise-ship terminal, a container terminal and a coal-fired power-station.

In 1998 the sale, for US $700m., of 95% of the state telecommunication company, Empresa Guatemalteca de Telecomunicaciones (Guatel), was awarded to a group of mostly domestic investors and the Mexican operator Teléfonos de México (Telmex). However, in July 2000 the new President, Alfonso Portillo Cabrera, declared Guatel's sale to be damaging to national interests and referred it to the courts. Analysts pointed out that the revision of the privatization process could be time-consuming and suggested an outcome that would not be positive for either the telecommunications sector or the national economy. The Government announced that it would not limit its revision to the sale of Guatel, but would also examine other privatizations that took place during the Arzú administration, including that of the postal service, the railway network and the electricity company. These measures, which placed in doubt many of the decisions made by the previous Government, generated much uncertainty among the Guatemalan and international business sectors. While the telecommunications service in the country improved dramatically, with the number of telephones per 1,000 people increasing from 28.6 in 1995 to 55.0 in 1999, it nevertheless remained inadequate.

INVESTMENT AND FINANCE

Following the transfer of power to the civilian Government of President Vinicio Cerezo in 1986, a programme of austerity measures and financial reform was implemented. As a result, the economy began to show signs of revival after several years of decline. The foreign-debt total decreased and inflation fell to an annual average of 12.3%. At the end of 1986 international reserves amounted to US $362.1m. and, for the first time in four years, they were adequate to cover import needs.

However, these positive developments were adversely affected by the decrease in coffee prices in the late 1980s and the decline in international reserves. A single exchange rate was introduced to deal with the latter in February 1989, followed in November by the flotation of the Guatemalan currency unit, the quetzal. Inflationary pressures increased in the economy as the quetzal was devalued several times, and a series of austerity measures was introduced. Although the general value of the quetzal stabilized, the rate of inflation continued to increase. The level of generalized crisis in the economy was such that by the end of the Cerezo Government, per-head income was estimated to have decreased to its 1969 level. The Government of Jorge Serrano Elías (1990–93) succeeded in stabilizing the currency

and in increasing international reserves. In 1990–99 real annual GDP grew by an average of 4.2%. In 1998 the economy expanded by 5.0%, falling slightly in 1999 to 3.6%. and again in 2000 to 3.3%. The decrease in economic growth was mainly owing to falling prices for primary export products and was expected to continue into 2001 as a result of both low coffee prices and the resulting effects of the US economic downturn. The annual rate of inflation was over 60% in 1990, but in the course of the following decade this rate was brought under control. The average annual rate of inflation in 1990–99 was 12.1%, while consumer prices increased by an average of 4.9% in 1999 and by 6.0% in 2000.

Levels of investment were adversely affected by the political uncertainty of the 1980s, decreasing from the equivalent of 15% of GDP in 1978 to 10% in 1985. The Serrano Government encouraged renewed confidence and, by 1990, there were signs that flight capital was returning to the country, attracted by high interest rates. Serrano's successor, President Ramiro de León Carpio (1993–96), aimed, however, to stimulate private-sector investment as the engine of growth by lowering interest rates as well as maintaining a realistic and flexible exchange rate and introducing measures to modernize the financial system.

The signing of the final peace accord in December 1996 enabled Guatemala to attract international aid for reconstruction. Some US $1,900m. in grants and loans was finally agreed. The IDB promised $800m., the International Bank for Reconstruction and Development (IBRD—World Bank) $400m. and the European Union (EU) $250m. The Government committed itself to raising the shortfall ($700m. of the estimated $2,500m. needed to implement the peace accords) by raising tax revenues to 50% above the 1995 levels by 2000. Failure to meet the pledge to raise revenue prompted increasing pressure on the Government from international organizations; the EU gave an explicit warning in June 2001. In May 2001 the Executive Board of the International Monetary Fund (IMF) concluded that Guatemala's main problem was its failure to raise tax revenue to the 12% of GDP promised in the peace accords. The IMF recognized Portillo's efforts to maintain macroeconomic stability through strict monetary policy, and reductions in public-sector investment, which, together with the fall in economic activity, helped decrease the trade deficit. However, an acceleration in government expenditure on administrative costs in early 2001 was of concern, given the increasing fiscal deficit.

In December 2000 legislation was approved to allow the circulation of the US dollar and other convertible currencies, for use in a wide range of transactions, including bank transactions, the paying of salaries, and other business services, from 1 May 2001. However, many were opposed to the change, and in May a constitutional challenge to the legislation was made, arguing that it violated the constitutional requirement that the Central Bank remain in exclusive control of foreign exchange.

The Guatemalan financial sector remained fragile. Non-performing loans stood at 13% of the total at the end of 2000, and the whole sector was generally agreed to be inadequately regulated. The Central Bank had to intervene in the operations of three banks in early 2001, following a major banking scandal involving insufficiently guaranteed loans handed out to public officials and relatives of the banks' directors. In June 2001 the Financial Action Task Force on Money Laundering (FATF—based at the Organisation for Economic Co-operation and Development) added Guatemala to their 'blacklist' of countries targeted for international scrutiny regarding potential money laundering activities within the banking sector.

FOREIGN TRADE AND THE BALANCE OF PAYMENTS

Depressed international commodity prices caused Guatemala major problems in the export sector, as more than 70% of its export earnings were derived from sales of primary products, mainly coffee, sugar, cotton, bananas, cardamom and petroleum. The Cerezo Government attempted to alter the economy's dependence on exports of primary products, particularly coffee, by the implementation of an export-orientated strategy aimed at export diversification rather than import substitution, as had previously been the case. This policy achieved undoubted success with the development of non-traditional exports, which by 1988 had increased by 200% in two years.

The export sector was depressed in the early 1990s, but following efforts by the new administration of President de León, exports increased by 6.2% in 1993 and 13.7% in 1994. In 1997 growth in exports reached 16.3%, before slowing to 7.2% in 1998 and falling further to 6.7% in 2000. In the late 1990s import growth also accelerated to about 20% in real terms, resulting in a growing trade deficit, which stood at US $2,177m. in 2000, compared with $1,445.1m. in 1999. The deficit on the current account of the balance of payments rose from US $232.9m. in 1990 to $1,025.9m. in 1999, about 5% of GDP. Falling coffee and petroleum prices also had a negative impact. The USA was the principal market for Guatemalan exports, taking an estimated 37% in 2000. Other significant purchasers were El Salvador, Honduras, Costa Rica, Germany and Mexico. The USA was also the major import source, supplying 39% in 2000.

In 1993 and 1994 the administration of US President Bill Clinton threatened Guatemala with exclusion from a future free-trade agreement in Central America if it failed to reduce human-rights abuses and corruption. Guatemala considered inclusion in any regional trade agreement to be essential, as lucrative US markets were becoming available to the country's exporters. Guatemala's trading privileges under both the Generalized System of Preferences and the Caribbean Basin Initiative were kept under review by the USA from June 1993; the improvement of workers' rights and respect for international patents remained important areas of disagreement between the US and Guatemalan Governments. In 1997 Van Heusan became the first firm in Guatemala's assembly-plant sector to agree to negotiate with a trade union. The 1996 peace accords clearly constituted a move towards improving Guatemala's standing with the international community; however, the failure to implement them adversely affected the country's status.

The prospects for free trade with Mexico were considered a potential benefit to exports; imports from Mexico, however, totalled an estimated US $485.1m. in 1998 compared with exports to Mexico of only $105.3m. in the same year. In 1997 the 'northern triangle' countries of El Salvador, Guatemala and Honduras (the so-called CA-3 countries) held negotiations for a new trade agreement with Mexico. In April 2000 the three companies signed the free-trade agreement, which promised greater access to the Mexican market for Guatemala, with increased bilateral trade in the future. However, many Guatemalan economic analysts predicted that the major benefits would be reaped by Mexico with its far greater economy, to the detriment of Guatemalan industry and agriculture.

In May 2001 the Central American countries, including Guatemala, reached an agreement with Mexico, called the 'Plan Puebla–Panamá', to establish a series of joint transport, industry and tourism projects intended to integrate the region.

THE FISCAL PACT

In 1998, following the socio-economic component of the peace accords, President Arzú launched the proposal of a Fiscal Pact, envisaged as a multi-sectoral, long-term consensus between the principal political, economic and social bodies over the future tax regime and fiscal policies. To this end a Fiscal Pact Preparatory Committee (CPPF) was established which, in early 1999, organized a national debate on tax policy.

On 29 December 1999, the third anniversary of the peace accords, the CPPF presented its report. Arguing that increasing tax collection was the only means for Guatemala to meet peace accord goals and advance infrastructure development plans, the report contained 66 recommendations to be implemented by 2004. It proposed the narrowing of the fiscal deficit to 2% in 2000, attaining the 12% tax collection goal by 2000, formulating a tax policy based on taxpayers' capacity to contribute, and creating a stabilization fund to cover shortfalls in revenue stemming from business cycles. It also recommended that the Government establish mechanisms to audit the Superintendency for Tax Administration (SAT), create a body to curb tax evasion and strengthen the judiciary's capacity to process cases of tax evasion and fraud.

The incoming Government of President Portillo declared the signing of the Fiscal Pact to be a priority, including it as one of the six essential elements of the Governability Pact, announced in January 2000. On 25 May 2000 the Fiscal Pact was signed into being by the Pact's National Forum and the Government. The National Forum, incorporating the Civil Society Assembly, the Comité Coordinador de Asociaciones Agrícolas, Comerciales, Industriales y Financieras (CACIF—Co-ordinating Committee of Agricultural, Commercial, Industrial and Financial Associations) and other social, political, business and academic bodies, had been established as part of the socio-economic accord and had conducted its activities under the guidance of the Accompaniment Committee.

The Fiscal-Pact agreement comprised eight distinct areas: fiscal balance of payments; state revenue; tax administration; public spending; public debt; public property; supervision and control mechanisms; and fiscal decentralization. The agreement was criticized by various sectors, which claimed that participant groups in the process were given little or no time to discuss in depth any proposals. The governing Frente Republicano Guatemalteco (FRG) remained absent in most of the discussions surrounding the Pact. One of the main agreements of the Pact was to achieve a 12% tax collection goal by 2002 (the tax collection figure was 10% in 1999, an increase of 0.5% from 1998). Such a goal seemed unattainable without the Government increasing considerably the rate of value-added tax (VAT), which stood at 10% in 1999. However, efforts to increase VAT to 12% were blocked in the Congreso Nacional and were protested against by business-led groups. Further attempts to raise VAT in early 2001 were again met with protests, and there appeared little chance of approval, despite growing pressure from the international finance community; alternatives were suggested, including a 0.5% tax on credit cards and current account transactions and a tax on mobile telephone calls. However, at a congressional session held in July, and boycotted by the PAN in protest, the FRG approved the controversial legislation to increase VAT.

OUTLOOK

The economic priorities of the Government of President Portillo included: liberalizing the trade regime; reform of the financial services sector; overhauling Guatemala's public finances; simplifying the tax structure, enhancing tax compliance and broadening the tax base; improving the investment climate through procedural and regulatory simplification; and adopting a goal of concluding treaties to protect investment and intellectual property rights. The new administration pledged to address the country's fiscal deficit by improving tax collection and reducing public spending, while complying with the spending targets set forth in the peace accords.

A popular move on the part of President Portillo, and one which brought him into conflict with CACIF, was the announcement, on 26 January 2000, of a 200 quetzals (US $26) salary increase for all state and private-sector employees. This was later amended by the Congreso Nacional to 80 quetzals ($11) for urban workers and 120 quetzals ($16) for agricultural workers. On 8 March the legislature approved Portillo's proposal to reduce spending in that year's budget by 10% in an effort to lower the fiscal deficit to 1.3%.

After 18 months in power, most observers were satisfied with the Government's efforts to retain macroeconomic stability, but were increasingly concerned that these would not be enough if efforts to impose a new tax regime remained stalled and if the general climate of political crisis continued. Owing to the strict monetary policy and depressed consumer demand, inflation was not of particular concern. However, with economic growth in 2001 unlikely to reach 3%, and with a gradual relaxation of fiscal discipline, the climate of relative macroeconomic security was beginning to dissipate. The constant political tension centred on conflicts between President Portillo and his own party in the Congreso Nacional, headed by former dictator, Gen. José Efraín Ríos Montt, as well as a public-security crisis in early 2001 acted as a disincentive for future investment, and a potential motivation for international lenders. The uncertainty also directly affected certain economic sectors such as tourism, which suffered from the effects of rampant crime on the country's image abroad.

Statistical Survey

Sources (unless otherwise stated): Banco de Guatemala, 7a Avda 22-01, Zona 1, Apdo 365, Guatemala City; tel. 230-6222; fax 253-4035; internet www.banguat.gob.gt; Dirección General de Estadística, Edif. América 4°, 8a Calle 9-55, Zona 1, Guatemala City; tel. 232-6136; fax 232-4790; e-mail info-ine@ine.gob.gt; internet www.ine.gob.gt/indexbak.htm.

Area and Population

AREA, POPULATION AND DENSITY

Area (sq km)	
Land	108,429
Inland water	460
Total	108,889*
Population (census results)†	
26 March 1981	
Males	3,015,826
Females	3,038,401
Total	6,054,227
17 April 1994	8,322,051
Population (official estimates at mid-year)	
1998	10,799,132
1999	11,088,372
2000	11,385,334
Density (per sq km) at mid-2000	104.6

* 42,042 sq miles.

† Excluding adjustments for underenumeration, estimated to have been 13.7% in 1981.

DEPARTMENTS (estimated population at mid-2000)

Alta Verapaz	.	814,300	Petén . . .	333,389
Baja Verapaz	.	203,430	Quetzaltenango . .	678,251
Chimaltenango	.	427,602	Quiché . . .	588,831
Chiquimula	.	313,150	Retalhuleu . .	241,921
El Progreso	.	143,197	Sacatepéquez .	259,265
Escuintla	.	483,768	San Marcos . .	844,486
Guatemala	.	2,578,526	Santa Rosa . .	319,814
Huehuetenango	.	879,987	Solola . . .	307,791
Izabal	.	333,956	Suchitepéquez . .	403,609
Jalapa	.	270,055	Totonicapán . .	361,303
Jutiapa	.	385,909	Zacapa . . .	212,794

PRINCIPAL TOWNS (estimated population at mid-2000)

Guatemala City	.	1,015,303	San Juan	
Mixco	.	440,065	Sacatepéquez . .	137,136
Villa Nueva	.	363,574	Jalapa . . .	115,493
San Pedro Carcha		159,574	Escuintla . .	113,320
Coban	.	156,086	Totonicapán . .	103,173
Quetzaltenango	.	148,108		

BIRTHS, MARRIAGES AND DEATHS

	Registered live births		Registered marriages		Registered deaths	
	Number	Rate (per 1,000)	Number	Rate (per 1,000)	Number	Rate (per 1,000)
1991 . .	359,904	38.0	44,440	4.7	66,703	7.0
1992 . .	363,648	37.3	46,795	4.8	64,837	6.7
1993 . .	370,138	36.9	45,736	4.6	64,515	6.4
1994 . .	381,497	37.0	48,356	4.7	74,761	7.2
1995 . .	371,091	34.9	49,701	4.7	65,159	6.1
1996 . .	377,723	34.6	47,428	4.3	60,618	5.5
1997 . .	387,862	36.9	51,908	4.9	67,691	6.4
1998* . .	362,165	33.5	51,459	4.8	69,322	6.4

* Preliminary figures.

Expectation of life (estimates, years at birth, 1998): 64.4 (males 61.7; females 67.6) (Source: UN Development Programme, *Human Development Report*).

ECONOMICALLY ACTIVE POPULATION
(official estimates for 1995)

	Males	Females	Total
Agriculture, forestry, hunting and fishing	1,767,791	30,436	1,798,227
Mining and quarrying . . .	3,052	43	3,095
Manufacturing	329,033	91,895	420,928
Construction	126,234	664	126,898
Electricity, gas, water and sanitary services	9,023	262	9,285
Commerce	155,122	70,818	225,940
Transport, storage and communications . . .	75,563	1,814	77,377
Services	163,945	207,462	371,407
Activities not adequately described	48,408	13,493	61,901
Total	2,678,171	416,887	3,095,058

Agriculture

PRINCIPAL CROPS ('000 metric tons)

	1998	1999	2000
Sugar cane	18,189.4	16,350.0*	17,150.0*
Cotton (lint)	2.8†	0.7	0.7*
Maize	1,068.8	1,109.1	1,109.1*
Rice	30.7	38.7	38.7*
Dry beans	83.6	93.3	94.0*
Wheat	5.0†	3.0†	3.0*
Coffee†	235.0	293.5	295.2
Bananas	880.0*	732.5	732.5*
Plantains*	53.0	70.0	70.0

* FAO estimate(s). † Unofficial figure(s).

Source: FAO.

LIVESTOCK ('000 head, year ending September)

	1998	1999	2000
Horses*	119.0	119.0	120.0
Cattle	2,330.0†	2,300.0*	2,300.0*
Sheep*	551.2	551.3	551.0
Pigs	825.6	825.0*	825.0*
Goats*	109.2	109.3	110.0

Poultry* (million): 24.0 in 1998; 24.0 in 1999; 24.0 in 2000.

* FAO estimate(s). † Unofficial figure.

Source: FAO.

LIVESTOCK PRODUCTS ('000 metric tons)

	1998	1999	2000
Beef and veal	54.5	47.0†	45.0†
Pig meat	17.5	17.5*	17.5*
Poultry meat	120.2	129.0†	129.0*
Cheese*	11.1	11.1	11.1
Hen eggs*	109.0	109.0	109.0
Cattle hides*	7.6	7.6	8.0

* FAO estimate(s). † Unofficial figure.

Source: FAO.

Forestry

ROUNDWOOD REMOVALS ('000 cubic metres, excl. bark)

	1997	1998	1999
Sawlogs, veneer logs and logs for sleepers	159	159	504
Other industrial wood	42	42	2
Fuel wood	12,794	12,794	12,794
Total	12,995	12,995	13,300

Source: FAO, *Yearbook of Forest Products.*

SAWNWOOD PRODUCTION
('000 cubic metres, incl. railway sleepers)

	1997	1998	1999
Coniferous (softwood)	263	263	263
Broadleaved (hardwood)	92	92	92
Total	355	355	355

Source: FAO, *Yearbook of Forest Products.*

Fishing

('000 metric tons, live weight)

	1996	1997	1998
Capture	7.7	6.9	10.8
Penaeus shrimps	0.7	0.7	2.0
Pacific seabobs	2.2	0.4	1.3
Aquaculture	3.4	4.4	3.1
Nile tilapia	n.a.	n.a.	1.0
Other tilapias	1.5	1.8	0.5
Penaeus shrimps	1.4	2.0	1.4
Total catch	11.1	11.3	14.0

Source: FAO, *Yearbook of Fishery Statistics.*

Mining

SELECTED PRODUCTS ('000 metric tons, unless otherwise indicated)

	1995	1996	1997
Crude petroleum	467	729	975
Antimony ore (metric tons)	665	880	880
Limestone	1,407	1,280	1,500
Sand, silica and quartz	107	67	81
Gravel and crushed stone	1,063	1,233	1,000

Source: UN, *Industrial Commodity Statistics Yearbook.*

Industry

SELECTED PRODUCTS
('000 metric tons, unless otherwise indicated)

	1997	1998	1999
Cement	1,315	1,330	1,885
Sugar	613	580	899
Electricity (million kWh)	4,132	n.a.	n.a.
Cigarettes (million)	2,198	4,184	4,376

Finance

CURRENCY AND EXCHANGE RATES
Monetary Units
100 centavos = 1 quetzal.

Sterling, Dollar and Euro Equivalents (30 April 2001)
£1 sterling = 11.158 quetzales;
US $1 = 7.793 quetzales;
€1 = 6.917 quetzales;
1,000 quetzales = £89.62 = $128.32 = €144.57.

Average Exchange Rate (quetzales per US dollar)
1998   6.3947
1999   7.3856
2000   7.7632

Note: In December 2000 legislation was approved to allow the circulation of the US dollar and other convertible currencies, for use in a wide range of transactions, from 1 May 2001.

BUDGET (million quetzales)

Revenue*	1996	1997	1998
Current revenue	8,544.7	10,153.0	12,550.0
Taxation	8,144.0	9,382.5	11,623.3
Taxes on income, profits and capital gains	2,003.7	2,299.5	2,392.2
Individual	245.5	189.7	210.6
Corporate	1,182.1	1,091.5	1,364.6
Domestic taxes on goods and services	4,429.5	5,365.2	7,310.3
Sales or turnover taxes	3,437.3	4,208.9	5,299.1
Excises	863.7	1,004.1	1,674.7
Taxes on international trade and transactions	1,501.6	1,537.6	1,685.1
Customs duties	1,501.6	1,537.6	1,682.1
Other current revenue	400.7	770.5	926.7
Entrepreneurial and property income	185.2	66.0	402.0
Administrative fees, nonindustrial and incidental sales	26.3	495.2	289.7
Contributions to government employee pension and welfare funds within Government	187.5	204.6	213.2
Capital revenue			34.7
Total	8,445.1	9,627.7	11,856.2

Expenditure	1995	1996	1997†
General public services	2,033.7	2,384.9	n.a.
Internal security	289.2	n.a.	n.a.
Defence	842.9	1,074.3	n.a.
Education	1,352.0	1,433.0	1,670.5
Health	718.6	723.7	882.2
Social security and welfare	599.8	632.5	837.2
Housing and community services	505.1	669.4	1,084.5
Social funds	403.1	406.5	772.4
Economic services	1,105.1	1,113.7	n.a.
Agriculture	205.6	190.6	n.a.
Transportation and communications	797.1	849.0	n.a.
Total (incl. others)	8,096.9	8,936.6	10,916.9

* Excluding grants received (million quetzales): 53.7 in 1996; 55.3 in 1997; 92.93 in 1998.
† Estimates.
1998 (million quetzales): Expenditure 13,515.0 (incl. lending minus repayments 29.01).
Sources: IMF, *Guatemala: Recent Economic Developments*; IMF, *Government Finance Statistics Yearbook.*
1999 (million quetzales): Revenue 14,735.7 (incl. grants received 188.2); Expenditure (incl. lending minus repayments) 18,728.1.
2000 (million quetzales): Revenue 15,953.3 (incl. grants received 112.4); Expenditure (incl. lending minus repayments) 18,916.1.
Source: IMF, *International Financial Statistics.*

INTERNATIONAL RESERVES (US $ million at 31 December)

	1998	1999	2000
Gold*	9.1	9.1	9.1
IMF special drawing rights . .	12.2	11.5	9.8
Foreign exchange	1,322.9	1,177.7	1,736.6
Total	1,344.2	1,198.3	1,755.5

* Valued at US $42.22 per troy ounce.

Source: IMF, *International Financial Statistics.*

MONEY SUPPLY (million quetzales at 31 December)

	1998	1999	2000
Currency outside banks . . .	5,632.5	7,752.8	7,298.2
Demand deposits at deposit money banks	7,866.9	7,614.1	11,271.5
Total money (incl. others) . .	13,613.5	15,467.6	18,832.2

Source: IMF, *International Financial Statistics.*

COST OF LIVING
(Consumer Price Index; base: 1990 = 100)

	1997	1998	1999
Food	244.4	255.7	261.3
Clothing	189.6	200.1	207.0
Rent	232.5	255.0	278.0
All items (incl. others) . .	249.8	266.4	280.2

Source: ILO, *Yearbook of Labour Statistics.*

NATIONAL ACCOUNTS
Expenditure on the Gross Domestic Product
(million quetzales at current prices)

	1998	1999	2000
Government final consumption expenditure	7,041	8,440	9,581
Private final consumption expenditure	105,429	114,487	124,527
Increase in stocks	929	−625	200
Gross fixed capital formation .	20,645	24,215	25,340
Total domestic expenditure	134,044	146,517	159,648
Exports of goods and services .	22,537	25,705	29,625
Less Imports of goods and services	32,559	37,008	41,383
GDP in purchasers' values .	124,022	135,214	147,890

Source: IMF, *International Financial Statistics.*

Gross Domestic Product by Economic Activity
(million quetzales at constant 1958 prices)

	1998	1999*	2000†
Agriculture, hunting, forestry and fishing	1,105.3	1,127.8	1,159.1
Mining and quarrying . . .	29.4	28.9	27.3
Manufacturing	639.8	656.0	663.2
Electricity, gas and water . .	112.0	124.7	110.3
Construction	161.8	179.6	210.2
Trade, restaurants and hotels .	426.2	447.7	473.2
Transport, storage and communications . . .	1,162.8	1,198.4	1,239.9
Finance, insurance and real estate	244.9	257.6	266.6
Ownership of dwellings . . .	217.2	225.6	233.3
General government services . .	347.3	362.8	377.2
Other community, social and personal services	268.8	278.0	287.7
Total	4,715.5	4,887.1	5,048.0

* Preliminary figures. † Estimates.

BALANCE OF PAYMENTS (US $ million)

	1997	1998	1999
Exports of goods f.o.b. . .	2,602.9	2,846.9	2,780.6
Imports of goods f.o.b. . . .	−3,542.7	−4,255.7	−4,225.7
Trade balance . . .	−939.8	−1,408.8	−1,445.1
Exports of services . . .	588.8	639.9	699.5
Imports of services	−650.5	−791.8	−790.7
Balance on goods and services	−1,001.5	−1,560.7	−1,536.3
Other income received . .	72.4	91.4	76.2
Other income paid . . .	−311.1	−275.1	−280.7
Balance on goods, services and income	−1,240.2	−1,744.4	−1,740.8
Current transfers received .	628.8	742.9	754.4
Current transfers paid . . .	−22.1	−37.6	−39.5
Current balance . . .	−633.5	−1,039.1	−1,025.9
Capital account (net) . . .	85.0	71.0	68.4
Direct investment from abroad .	84.4	672.8	154.6
Portfolio investment assets .	−18.1	−11.6	−26.0
Portfolio investment liabilities .	249.7	65.8	136.5
Other investment assets . .	221.2	241.7	199.9
Other investment liabilities .	200.2	168.0	172.5
Net errors and omissions . .	40.7	66.8	195.0
Overall balance	229.6	235.4	−125.0

Source: IMF, *International Financial Statistics.*

External Trade

PRINCIPAL COMMODITIES (US $ million)

Imports c.i.f.	1996	1997	1998
Food and live animals	369.6	414.0	422.8
Cereals and cereal preparations	176.8	147.0	105.0
Wheat and meslin (unmilled)	84.8	54.8	12.0
Crude materials (inedible)			
except fuels	63.3	91.9	98.7
Mineral fuels, lubricants, etc.	466.7	412.6	385.7
Petroleum, petroleum products,			
etc.	423.4	366.3	343.7
Crude petroleum oils, etc.	128.1	126.4	90.9
Refined petroleum products	288.9	231.8	244.4
Gasoline and other light oils	123.7	33.4	79.0
Animal and vegetable oils, fats			
and waxes	49.7	58.2	84.2
Chemicals and related			
products	528.3	684.7	756.9
Medicinal and pharmaceutical			
products	107.4	124.6	161.8
Medicaments (incl. veterinary)	86.3	100.3	128.6
Essential oils, perfume materials			
and cleansing preparations	53.1	86.0	110.8
Manufactured fertilizers	67.2	94.8	68.1
Artificial resins, plastic materials,			
etc.	99.4	135.5	146.8
Products of polymerizations, etc.	82.7	117.1	127.5
Basic manufactures	500.8	672.3	898.6
Paper, paperboards and			
manufactures	117.2	161.5	204.1
Paper and paperboard (not cut			
to size or shape)	84.2	107.2	130.6
Iron and steel	116.9	154.6	253.0
Universals, plates and sheets	55.7	78.4	115.4
Machinery and transport			
equipment	921.3	1,187.4	1,600.1
Power-generating machinery and			
equipment	46.8	78.0	118.5
Machinery specialized for			
particular industries	113.0	159.0	219.8
Office machines and automatic			
data-processing equipment	71.2	90.9	112.9
Telecommunications and sound			
equipment	85.3	122.6	160.7
Road vehicles and parts	371.5	408.7	590.3
Passenger motor cars (excl.			
buses)	157.1	158.8	252.4
Lorries and special motor			
vehicles	126.1	143.4	187.5
Lorries and trucks	125.7	142.8	185.8
Miscellaneous manufactured			
articles	222.3	298.7	365.6
Total (incl. others)	3,146.3	3,852.0	4,650.9

Exports f.o.b.	1996	1997	1998
Food and live animals	1,139.2	1,323.2	1,463.8
Cereals and cereal preparations	53.2	77.4	67.8
Vegetables and fruit	251.8	248.5	317.3
Fresh or simply preserved			
vegetables	54.0	53.3	64.9
Fresh or dried fruit and nuts			
(excl. oil nuts)	185.5	182.1	237.5
Bananas and plantains	156.3	152.5	194.7
Sugar, sugar preparations and			
honey	228.9	278.1	336.8
Sugar and honey	222.0	272.1	332.3
Raw beet and cane sugars	202.1	255.4	316.7
Coffee, tea, cocoa and spices	514.8	629.9	625.6
Coffee and coffee substitutes	473.1	589.6	586.8
Coffee (incl. husks and skins)			
and substitutes containing			
coffee	473.0	589.6	586.7
Beverages and tobacco	38.2	52.0	59.2
Crude materials (inedible)			
except fuels	146.0	136.3	122.1
Crude rubber	48.7	38.7	27.5
Natural rubber and gums	48.6	38.7	27.5
Mineral fuels, lubricants, etc.	65.8	98.7	61.7
Petroleum, petroleum products,			
etc.	65.8	98.7	61.6
Crude petroleum oils, etc.	60.5	96.5	58.3
Chemicals and related			
products	236.7	263.4	292.7
Medicinal and pharmaceutical			
products	74.4	68.6	85.3
Medicaments (incl. veterinary)	70.3	64.7	81.8
Essential oils, perfume materials			
and cleansing preparations	69.4	84.2	100.5
Soap, cleansing and polishing			
preparations	36.0	41.9	55.0
Basic manufactures	232.9	261.9	321.8
Textile yarn, fabrics, etc.	50.3	45.5	73.3
Iron and steel	58.2	69.3	74.2
Machinery and transport			
equipment	37.4	52.6	62.3
Miscellaneous manufactured			
articles	118.9	133.3	175.0
Clothing and accessories (excl.			
footwear)	38.7	43.9	60.5
Total (incl. others)	2,030.8	2,344.1	2,581.7

PRINCIPAL TRADING PARTNERS (US $ million)

Imports c.i.f.	1996	1997	1998
Aruba	107.0	127.4	69.2
Brazil	42.8	38.9	62.0
Canada	56.2	72.1	56.1
Costa Rica	62.0	108.0	163.2
El Salvador	128.8	228.5	334.8
Germany	99.6	114.2	131.7
Honduras	44.0	65.6	96.1
Italy	38.5	52.2	45.1
Japan	99.3	130.0	209.2
Korea, Republic	27.8	26.3	46.8
Mexico	322.5	438.4	485.1
Netherlands	46.5	24.8	40.7
Panama	79.8	111.9	153.8
Spain	40.9	44.0	51.6
United Kingdom	31.5	43.1	51.5
USA	1,409.4	1,613.6	1,962.8
Venezuela	165.3	180.5	152.7
Total (incl. others)	3,146.2	3,851.9	4,650.8

Exports f.o.b.						1996	1997	1998
Belgium						27.3	36.2	30.7
Canada	.					37.7	51.2	53.9
Chile	.					13.5	26.8	11.8
Costa Rica	.					99.8	111.9	120.0
El Salvador	.					258.0	310.9	320.1
France	.					21.6	20.6	20.7
Germany						102.6	113.5	111.0
Honduras						140.2	177.3	215.9
Italy						21.2	27.0	29.7
Japan	.					42.1	53.3	57.4
Korea, Republic	.					2.8	5.1	52.8
Mexico	.					80.0	77.0	105.3
Netherlands	.					29.4	39.7	37.2
Nicaragua						79.9	83.2	92.6
Panama	.					46.3	42.6	67.7
Peru						29.5	13.2	48.5
Russian Federation	.					19.6	0.1	71.1
Sweden	.					21.5	22.3	19.4
United Kingdom	.					18.3	14.0	28.5
USA	.					746.7	841.2	841.8
Venezuela						12.5	34.6	26.7
Total (incl. others)		.	.	.		2,030.7	2,344.1	2,581.7

Source: UN, *International Trade Statistics Yearbook.*

Transport

RAILWAYS (traffic)

				1994	1995	1996
Passenger-km (million)	.	.	.	991	0	0
Freight ton-km (million)	.	.	.	25,295	14,242	836

Source: UN, *Statistical Yearbook.*

ROAD TRAFFIC (motor vehicles in use at 31 December)

				1997	1998	1999
Passenger cars	.	.	.	470,016	508,868	578,733
Buses and coaches	.	.	.	9,843	10,250	11,017
Lorries and vans	.	.	.	34,220	37,057	42,219
Motor cycles and mopeds	.	.	.	111,358	117,536	129,664

Source: IRF, *World Road Statistics.*

SHIPPING
Merchant Fleet (registered at 31 December)

				1996	1997	1998
Number of vessels	.	.	.	5	5	5
Total displacement ('000 grt)	.	.		0.8	0.8	0.8

Source: Lloyd's Register of Shipping, *World Fleet Statistics.*

International Sea-borne Freight Traffic ('000 metric tons)

				1992	1993	1994
Goods loaded	.	.	.	2,176	1,818	2,096
Goods unloaded	.	.	.	3,201	3,025	3,822

CIVIL AVIATION (traffic on scheduled services)

			1995	1996	1997
Kilometres flown (million)	.	.	6	6	5
Passengers carried ('000)	.	.	300	300	508
Passenger-km (million)	.	.	500	530	368
Total ton-km (million)	.	.	70	71	77

Source: UN, *Statistical Yearbook.*

Tourism

TOURIST ARRIVALS BY COUNTRY OF ORIGIN

					1997	1998	1999
Canada	.				16,603	19,721	19,149
Costa Rica	.				18,393	21,408	25,556
El Salvador	.				108,506	133,683	272,747
France	.				12,937	14,814	14,584
Germany	.				18,895	20,805	18,069
Honduras	.				30,520	37,433	59,545
Italy	.				17,752	18,003	17,225
Mexico	.				63,557	61,387	54,901
Nicaragua	.				13,821	15,621	30,497
Spain	.				15,525	14,928	18,289
USA	.				162,528	168,851	182,597
Total (incl. others)	.		.		576,362	636,276	822,695

Tourism receipts (US $ million): 325 in 1997; 394 in 1998; 570 in 1999.

Communications Media

			1995	1996	1997
Radio receivers ('000 in use)	.	.	750	800	835
Television receivers ('000 in use)	.		600	620	640
Daily newspapers: number	.	.	5	7	n.a.
Telephones ('000 main lines in use)	.		286	338	430
Telefax stations (number in use)	.		n.a.	10,000	n.a.
Mobile cellular telephones (subscribers)	.	.	29,999	43,421	64,194

Sources: UN, *Statistical Yearbook*, and UNESCO, *Statistical Yearbook.*

Education

(1999)

		Institutions	Teachers	Students
Pre-primary	.	9,607	11,813	308,240
Primary	. . . .	17,905	47,811	1,825,088
Secondary	. . . .	3,118	20,543	305,818
Tertiary	. . . .	1,462	13,105	146,291

Directory

The Constitution*

In December 1984 the Constituent Assembly drafted a new Constitution (based on that of 1965), which was approved in May 1985 and came into effect in January 1986. A series of amendments to the Constitution were approved by referendum in January 1994 and came into effect in April 1994. The Constitution's main provisions are summarized below:

Guatemala has a republican representative democratic system of government and power is exercised equally by the legislative, executive and judicial bodies. The official language is Spanish. Suffrage is universal and secret, obligatory for those who can read and write and optional for those who are illiterate. The free formation and growth of political parties whose aims are democratic is guaranteed. There is no discrimination on grounds of race, colour, sex, religion, birth, economic or social position or political opinions.

The State will give protection to capital and private enterprise in order to develop sources of labour and stimulate creative activity.

Monopolies are forbidden and the State will limit any enterprise which might prejudice the development of the community. The right to social security is recognized and it shall be on a national, unitary, obligatory basis.

Constitutional guarantees may be suspended in certain circumstances for up to 30 days (unlimited in the case of war).

CONGRESS

Legislative power rests with Congress, which is made up of 113 deputies, 91 of whom are elected according to departmental representation. The remaining 22 deputies are elected by national listing. Congress meets on 15 January each year and ordinary sessions last four months; extraordinary sessions can be called by the Permanent Commission or the Executive. All Congressional decisions must be taken by absolute majority of the members, except in special cases laid down by law. Deputies are elected for four years; they may be re-elected after a lapse of one session, but only once. Congress is responsible for all matters concerning the President and Vice-President and their execution of their offices; for all electoral matters; for all matters concerning the laws of the Republic; for approving the budget and decreeing taxes; for declaring war; for conferring honours, both civil and military; for fixing the coinage and the system of weights and measures; for approving, by two-thirds' majority, any international treaty or agreement affecting the law, sovereignty, financial status or security of the country.

PRESIDENT

The President is elected by universal suffrage, by absolute majority for a non-extendable period of four years. Re-election or prolongation of the presidential term of office are punishable by law. The President is responsible for national defence and security, fulfilling the Constitution, leading the armed forces, taking any necessary steps in time of national emergency, passing and executing laws, international policy, nominating and removing Ministers, officials and diplomats, co-ordinating the actions of Ministers of State. The Vice-President's duties include presiding over Congress and taking part in the discussions of the Council of Ministers.

ARMY

The Guatemalan Army is intended to maintain national independence, sovereignty and honour, territorial integrity and peace within the Republic. It is an indivisible, apolitical, non-deliberating body and is made up of land, sea and air forces.

LOCAL ADMINISTRATIVE DIVISIONS

For the purposes of administration the territory of the Republic is divided into 22 Departments and these into 330 Municipalities, but this division can be modified by Congress to suit interests and general development of the Nation without loss of municipal autonomy. Municipal authorities are elected every four years.

JUDICIARY

Justice is exercised exclusively by the Supreme Court of Justice and other tribunals. Administration of Justice is obligatory, free and independent of the other functions of State. The President of the Judiciary, judges and other officials are elected by Congress for five years. The Supreme Court of Justice is made up of 13 judges. The President of the Judiciary is also President of the Supreme Court.

The Supreme Court nominates all other judges. Under the Supreme Court come the Court of Appeal, the Administrative Disputes Tribunal, the Tribunal of Second Instance of Accounts, Jurisdiction Conflicts, First Instance and Military, the Extraordinary Tribunal of Protection. There is a Court of Constitutionality presided over by the President of the Supreme Court.

* Under the terms of an accord, signed with the URNG in September 1996, concerning civilian power and the role of the armed forces, the Government undertook to revise the Constitution to relieve the armed forces of responsibility for internal security. This role was assumed by a new National Civilian Police force from mid-1997.

The Government

HEAD OF STATE

President: ALFONSO ANTONIO PORTILLO CABRERA (took office 14 January 2000).
Vice-President: JUAN FRANCISCO REYES LÓPEZ.

CABINET
(August 2001)

Minister of Foreign Affairs: GABRIEL ORELLANA ROJAS.
Minister of the Interior: BYRON BARRIENTES.
Minister of National Defence: Brig.-Gen. EDUARDO ARÉVALO LACS.
Minister of Public Finance: EDUARDO WEYMANN FUENTES.
Minister of Economy: MARCO ANTONIO VENTURA.
Minister of Public Health and Social Welfare: MARIO BOLAÑOS.
Minister of Communications, Transport and Public Works: ALVARO ENRIQUE HEREDIA SILVA.
Minister of Agriculture, Livestock and Food: JORGE ROLANDO ESCOTO MARROQUÍN.
Minister of Education: MARIO ROLANDO TORRES.
Minister of Employment and Social Security: JUAN FRANCISCO ALFARO MIJANGOS.
Minister of Energy and Mines: RAÚL EDMUNDO ARCHILA SERRANO.
Minister of Culture and Sport: OTILIA LUX DE COTI.
Minister of the Environment: HAROLDO QUEJ CHEN.

MINISTRIES

Ministry of Agriculture, Livestock and Food: Edif. Monja Blanca, 7 Avda 12-90, Zona 13, Guatemala City; tel. 362-4764; fax 332-8302; e-mail magadest@intelnet.net.gt; internet www.maga .gob.gt.
Ministry of Communications, Transport and Public Works: Palacio Nacional, 6a Calle y 7a Avda, Zona 1, Guatemala City; tel. 22-1212; fax 28-1613.
Ministry of Culture and Sport: 24a Calle 3-81, Zona 1, Guatemala City; tel. 230-0718; fax 230-0758.
Ministry of Economy: 8a Avda 10-43, Zona 1, Guatemala City; tel. 238-3330; internet www.mineco.gob.gt.
Ministry of Education: Palacio Nacional, 6a Calle y 7a Avda, Zona 1, Guatemala City; tel. 22-0162; fax 253-7386; internet www.mineduc.gob.gt.
Ministry of Employment and Social Security: Edif. NASA, 14 Calle 5-49, Zona 1, Guatemala City; tel. 230-1361; fax 251-3559; internet www.mintrabajo.gob.gt.
Ministry of Energy and Mines: Diagonal 17, 29–78, Zona 11, Guatemala City; tel. 276-0679; fax 276-3175; e-mail informatica@ mem.gob.gt; internet www.mem.gob.gt.
Ministry of the Environment: Edif. Plaza Robi 3°, 5a Calle 4-31, Zona 1, 01001 Guatemala; tel. 230-1719; fax 230-1718.
Ministry of Foreign Affairs: 2a Avda 4-17, Zona 10, Guatemala City; tel. 332-1900; fax 332-0805; e-mail webmaster@minex.gob.gt; internet www.minex.gob.gt.
Ministry of the Interior: Palacio Nacional, 6a Calle y 7a Avda, Zona 1, Guatemala City; tel. 22-1212; fax 251-5368.
Ministry of National Defence: Palacio Nacional, 6a Calle y 7a Avda, Zona 1, Guatemala City; tel. 22-1212; fax 28-1613; internet www.mindef.mil.gt.

Ministry of Public Finance: Edif. de Fianzas, Centro Cívico, 8a Avda y Calle 21, Zona 1, Guatemala City; tel. 251-1380; fax 251-0987; internet www.minfin.gob.gt.

Ministry of Public Health and Social Welfare: Palacio Nacional, 6a Calle y 7a Avda, Zona 1, Guatemala City; tel. 22-1212; fax 22-2736.

President and Legislature

PRESIDENT

Election, 7 November 1999

	% of votes cast
Alfonso Antonio Portillo Cabrera (FRG)	47.8
Oscar Berger Perdomo (PAN)	30.3
Alvaro Colom Caballeros (ANN)	12.3
Acisclo Valladares Molina (PLP)	3.1
Juan Francisco Bianchi Castillo (ARDE) . . .	2.1
Ana Catalina Soberanis Reyes (FDNG) . . .	1.3
José Enrique Asturias Rudeke (LOV) . . .	1.1
Danilo Julián Roca Barillas (UCN) . . .	1.0
Total (incl. others)	**100.0**

Since none of the candidates achieved the required 50% of the votes necessary to win outright, a second round of voting was held on 26 December 1999. At this election Alfonso Antonio Portillo Cabrera (FRG) received 68.3% of the valid votes cast, while Oscar Berger Perdomo (PAN) won the remaining 31.7%.

CONGRESO NACIONAL

President: Gen. (retd) José Efraín Ríos Montt.

Vice-Presidents: César Leonel Soto Arango, Zury Mayté Ríos-Montt Sosa de López-Villatoro, Luis Alfonso Rosales Marroquín.

Election, 7 November 1999

	Seats
Frente Republicano Guatemalteco (FRG)	63
Partido de Avanzada Nacional (PAN)	37
Alianza Nueva Nación (ANN)	9
Partido Democracia Cristiana Guatemalteca (PDCG) .	2
Partido Liberal Progresista (PLP)	1
La Organización Verde (LOV)	1
Total	**113**

Political Organizations

Acción Reconciliadora Democrática (ARDE): 4a Avda 14-53, Zona 1, Guatemala City; tel. 232-0591; fax 251-4076; centre-right; Sec.-Gen. Herlindo Alvarez del Cid.

Alianza Democrática: 6 Avda 15-41, Zona 1, Guatemala City; tel. 591-4158; f. 1992; centre party; Leader Leopoldo Urrutia.

Alianza Nueva Nación (ANN): electoral alliance comprising:

> **Desarrollo Integral Auténtico (DIA):** 12a Calle 'A' 2-18, Zona 1, Guatemala City; tel. 232-8044; fax 232-8044; e-mail morlain@guate.net; left-wing party; Sec.-Gen. Jorge Luis Ortega Torres.

> **Unidad de Izquierda Democrática (UNID):** Guatemala City; left-wing party.

> **Unidad Revolucionaria Nacional Guatemalteca (URNG):** (see below).

Alianza Popular Cinco (AP5): 6a Avda 3-23, Zona 1, Guatemala City; tel. 231-6022; Sec.-Gen. Max Orlando Molina Narciso.

Central Auténtica Nacionalista (CAN): 15a Avda 4-31, Zona 1, Guatemala City; tel. 251-2992; f. 1980 from the CAO (Central Arañista Organizado); Leader Héctor Mayora Dawe; Sec.-Gen. Jorge Roberto Arana España.

Comité Guatemalteca de Unidad Patriota (CGUP): f. 1982; opposition coalition consisting of:

> **Frente Democrático Contra la Represión (FDCR):** Leader Rafael García.

> **Frente Popular 31 de Enero (FP-31):** f. 1980; left-wing amalgamation of student, peasant and trade union groups.

Frente de Avance Nacional (FAN): 3a Calle 'A' 1-66, Zona 10, Guatemala City; tel. 231-8036; right-wing group; Sec.-Gen. Federico Abundio Maldonado Gularte.

Frente Cívico Democrático (FCD): Guatemala City; Leader Jorge González del Valle.

Frente Demócrata Guatemalteco: Leader Clemente Marroquín Rojas.

Frente Democrático Nueva Guatemala (FDNG): left-wing faction of Partido Revolucionario; Pres. Jorge González del Valle; Sec.-Gen. Rafael Arriaga.

Frente Republicano Guatemalteco (FRG): 3a Calle 5-50, Zona 1, Guatemala City; tel. 238-0826; internet www.frg.com.gt; f. 1988; right-wing group; leader Gen. (retd) José Efraín Ríos Montt.

Frente de Unidad Nacional (FUN): 6a Avda 5-18, Zona 12, Guatemala City; tel. 271-4048; f. 1971; nationalist group; Leader Gabriel Girón Ortiz.

Fuerza Demócrata Popular: 11a Calle 4-13, Zona 1, Guatemala City; tel. 251-5496; f. 1983; democratic popular force; Sec. Lic. Francisco Reyes Ixcamey.

Fuerza Nueva: Leader Carlos Rafael Soto.

La Organización Verde (LOV): 5a Calle A 0-64, Zona 3, Guatemala City; tel. 230-3946; suspended in 2000; Sec.-Gen. Marcos Emilio Recinos Alvarez; electoral coalition comprising:

> **Unidad Social Demócrata**.

> **Unión Democrática (UD):** Of. E, 3°, Vista Hermosa II, 1a Calle 18-83, Zona 15, Guatemala City; tel. 369-7074; fax 369-3062; e-mail chea@infovia.com.gt; f. 1983; Sec.-Gen. Rodolfo Ernesto Paiz Andrade.

Movimiento de los Descamisados (MD): Avda J. R. Barrios L. 896 Sta Luisa, Zona 6, Guatemala City; Sec.-Gen. Enrique Morales Pérez.

Movimiento Humanista de Integración Demócrata: Guatemala City; f. 1983; Leader Victoriano Alvarez.

Movimiento de Liberación Nacional (MLN): 2a Avda 38-11, Zona 8, Guatemala City; tel. 22-6528; e-mail mln@wepa.com.gt; internet www.wepa.com.gt/mln; f. 1960; extreme right-wing; 95,000 mems; Leader Lic. Mario Sandóval Alarcón; Sec.-Gen. Ulysses Charles Dent Weissenberg.

Movimiento 20 de Octubre: Leader Marco Antonio Villamar Contreras.

Pantinamit: f. 1977; represents interests of Indian population; Leader Fernando Tezahuic Tohón.

Partido de Avanzada Nacional (PAN): 7a Avda 10-38, Zona 9, Guatemala City; tel. 334-1702; internet www.pan.org.gt; Leader Alvaro Enrique Arzú Irigoyen; Sec.-Gen. Leonel Eliseo López Rodas.

Partido de la Democracia Cristiana de Guatemala (PDCG): Avda Elena 20-66, Zona 3, Guatemala City; tel. 238-4988; f. 1955; 130,000 mems; suspended in 2000; Sec.-Gen. Marco Vinicio Cerezo Arevalo.

Partido Demócrata Guatemalteco (PDG): Guatemala City; Sec.-Gen. Jorge Antonio Reyna Castillo.

Partido Institucional Democrático (PID): Guatemala City; f. 1965; 60,000 mems; moderate conservative; Sec.-Gen. Oscar Humberto Rivas García; Dir Donaldo Alvarez Ruiz.

Partido Libertador Progresista (PLP): 5a Calle 5-44, Zona 1, Guatemala City; tel. 232-5548; e-mail plp@intelnet.net.gt; f. 1990; suspended in 2000; Sec.-Gen. Acisclo Valladares Molina.

Partido Petenero: Guatemala City; f. 1983; defends regional interests of El Petén.

Partido Progresista (PP): 1a Calle 6-77, Zona 2, Guatemala City; Sec.-Gen. José Ramón Fernández González.

Partido Reformador Guatemalteco (PREG): 3a Calle 9-59, Zona 1, Guatemala City; tel. 22-8759; Sec.-Gen. Miguel Angel Montepeque Contreras.

Partido Revolucionario de los Trabajadores Centro-americanos (PRTC): Guatemala City.

Partido Social Cristiano (PSC): P. Savoy, Of. 113, 8°, 8a Calle 9-41, Zona 1, Guatemala City; tel. 274-0577; f. 1983; Sec.-Gen. Alfonso Alonzo Barillas.

Partido Socialista Democrático (PSD): Guatemala City; f. 1978; Sec.-Gen. Sergio Alejandro Pérez Cruz.

Partido de Unificación Anticomunista (PUA): Guatemala City; right-wing party; Leader Leonel Sisniega Otero.

Unidad Nacional de Esperanza (UNE): Guatemala City; f. 2001 following a split within the PAN; Founder and Pres. Alvaro Colom Caballero.

Unidad Nacionalista (UN): 18 Calle 14-82, Zona 13, Guatemala City; tel. 362-7127; fax 362-7139; Sec.-Gen. Jorge Canale Nanne.

Unidad Nacionalista Organizada (UNO): Calzada Aguilar Batres 17-14, Zona 11, Guatemala City; Sec.-Gen. Mario Roberto Armando Ponciano Castillo.

Unión del Centro Nacional (UCN): 12a Calle 2-45, Zona 1, Guatemala City; tel. 253-6211; fax 253-4038; f. 1984; centre party; Sec.-Gen. EDMOND MULET.

Unión Reformista Social (URS): 5a Calle 'A' 0-64, Zona 3, Guatemala City; Sec.-Gen. MARCOS EMILIO RECINOS ALVAREZ.

In February 1982 the principal guerrilla groups unified to form the **Unidad Revolucionaria Nacional Guatemalteca (URNG) (Guatemalan National Revolutionary Unity):** Avda Simeón Cañas 8-01, Zona 2, Guatemala City; tel. 288-4440; fax 254-0572; e-mail prensaurng@guate.net; internet www.urng.com; has links with the PSD; Sec.-Gen. JORGE ISMALE SOTO. The political wing of the URNG was the **Representación Unitaria de la Oposición Guatemalteca (RUOG).** At the end of 1996 the URNG consisted of:

Ejército Guerrillero de los Pobres (EGP): f. 1972; draws main support from Indians of western highlands; works closely with the **Comité de Unidad Campesina (CUC)** (Committee of Peasant Unity) and radical Catholic groups; mems 4,000 armed, 12,000 unarmed.

Fuerzas Armadas Rebeldes (FAR): formed early 1960s; originally military commission of CGTG; associated with the CNT and CONUS trade unions; based in Guatemala City, Chimaltenango and El Petén; Commdr JORGE ISMAEL SOTO GARCÍA ('PABLO MONSANTO').

Organización del Pueblo en Armas (ORPA): f. 1979; military group active in San Marcos province; originally part of FAR; Commdr RODRIGO ASTURIAS ('GASPAR ILOM').

Partido Guatemalteco del Trabajo (PGT): communist party; divided into three armed factions: PGT-Camarilla (began actively participating in war in 1981); PGT-Núcleo de Conducción y Dirección; PGT-Comisión Nuclear; Gen. Sec. RICARDO ROSALES ('CARLOS GONZÁLEZ').

In December 1996 the Government and the URNG signed a definitive peace treaty, bringing the 36-year conflict to an end. The demobilization of the URNG guerrillas began in March 1997 and was completed by early May. In June the URNG registered as a political party in formation. In August the movement held elections to a provisional executive committee. The URNG applied for formal recognition as a political party in October 1998 and was formally registered in December. In May 1999 the URNG formed an alliance, the Alianza Nueva Nación, with the FDNG (which later withdrew from the alliance), the UNID and the DIA in order to contest legislative elections, scheduled to be held in November 1999.

Diplomatic Representation

EMBASSIES IN GUATEMALA

Argentina: 2a Avda 11-04, Zona 10, Apdo 112, Guatemala City; tel. 332-6419; fax 332-1654; e-mail embargen@pronet.net.gt; Ambassador: SUSANA SARA GRANÉ.

Austria: Edif. Plaza Marítima, 4°, 6a Avda 20-25, Zona 10, Guatemala City; tel. 368-1134; fax 333-6180; Ambassador: GABRIEL KRAMARICS.

Belgium: Avda de la Reforma 13-70, Zona 9, Apdo 3725, Guatemala City; tel. 225-6633; Ambassador: MICHEL DELFOSSE.

Belize: Edif. El Reformador, Suite 801, Avda de la Reforma 1-50, Zona 9, Guatemala City; tel. 334-5531; fax 334-5536; e-mail embelguate@guate.net; Ambassador: MOISES CAL.

Bolivia: 12a Avda 15-37, Zona 10, Guatemala City; Chargé d'affaires a.i.: Dr JOSÉ GABINA VILLANUEVA G.

Brazil: 18a Calle 2-22, Zona 14, Apdo 196-A, Guatemala City; tel. 337-0949; fax 337-3475; e-mail brasilgua@gua.gbm.net; Ambassador: SÉRGIO DAMASCENO VIEIRA.

Canada: Edif. Edyma Plaza, 8°, 13a Calle 8-44210, Guatemala City; tel. 333-6102; fax 333-6153; Ambassador: DANIEL LIVERMORE.

Chile: 14 Calle 15-21, Zona 13, Guatemala City; tel. 334-8273; fax 334-8276; e-mail echile.gu@intelnet.net.gt; Ambassador: JORGE MOLINA VALDIVIESO.

China (Taiwan): 4a Avda 'A' 13–25, Zona 9, Apdo 1646, Guatemala City; tel. 339-0711; fax 332-2668; e-mail embajada@micro.com.gt; Ambassador: ANDREW J. S. WU.

Colombia: Edif. Gemini 10, 12a Calle, 1a Avda, Zona 10, Guatemala City; tel. 335-3602; fax 335-3603; e-mail embajada.col@gold.guate.net; Ambassador: ANGELA ROBAYO BELLO.

Costa Rica: 3°, Of. 320, Avda de la Reforma 8-60, Zona 9, Guatemala City; tel. 331-9604; fax 332-1520; e-mail embarica@intelnet.net.gt; Ambassador: YOLANDA INGIANNA-MAINIERI.

Cuba: 13 Calle 5-72, Zona 10, Guatemala City; tel. 333-7679; fax 337-3282; Ambassador: PASTOR RODRÍGUEZ VALIENTE.

Dominican Republic: Vista Hermosa, 5°, 18 Avda 1-50, Zona 15, Guatemala City; tel. 369-3580; fax 365-7966; Ambassador: ROBERTO VICTORIA.

Ecuador: 4 Avda 12-04, Zona 14, Guatemala City; tel. 337-2994; fax 368-1831; e-mail embecuad@guate.net; Ambassador: EDUARDO CABEZAS MOLINA.

Egypt: Edif. Cobella 5°, 5 Avda 10-84, Zona 14, Apdo 502, Guatemala City; tel. 333-6296; fax 368-2808; Ambassador: MOHAMED ALI AFIFI.

El Salvador: 4a Avda 13-60, Zona 10, Guatemala City; tel. 366-6147; fax 366-2234; e-mail emsalva@pronet.net.gt; Ambassador: SALVADOR JOSÉ TRIGUEROS HIDALGO.

Finland: 2A Calle 18-37, Zona 15, Apdo 2, Guatemala City; tel. 365-9270; fax 365-8375; e-mail imesland@infovia.com.gt; Ambassador: RISTO VALTHEIM.

France: Edif. Marbella, 16a Calle 4-53, Zona 10, Guatemala City; tel. 337-3639; fax 337-3180; e-mail ambfrguate@pronet.net.gt; Ambassador: SERGE PINOT.

Germany: Edif. Plaza Marítima, 20 Calle 6-20, Zona 10, Guatemala City; tel. 333-6903; fax 337-0031; Ambassador: Dr JOACHIM NEUKIRCH.

Holy See: 10a Calle 4-47, Zona 9, Guatemala City (Apostolic Nunciature); tel. 332-4274; fax 334-1918; e-mail nuntius@gua.net; Apostolic Nuncio: Most Rev. RAMIRO MOLINER INGLÉS, Titular Archbishop of Sarda.

Honduras: 9a Avda 16-34, Zona 10, Guatemala City; tel. 368-0842; fax 337-3921; e-mail embhon@infovia.com.gt; Ambassador: YOLANDA PALAU DE FERNÁNDEZ.

Israel: 13a Avda 14-07, Zona 10, Guatemala City; tel. 333-4624; fax 333-6950; e-mail esrembgu@guaweb.net; Ambassador: SCHLOMO COHEN.

Italy: 5a Avda 8-59, Zona 14, Guatemala City; tel. 337-4557; fax 337-0795; e-mail embitaly@guatenet.net.gt; Ambassador: ALESSANDRO SERAFINI.

Japan: Edif. Torre Internacional, 10531, Avda La Reforma 16-85, Zona 10, Guatemala City; tel. 331-9666; fax 331-5462; Ambassador: HISATO MURAYAMA.

Korea, Republic: Edif. El Reformador, 7°, Avda La Reforma 1-50, Zona 9, Apdo 1649, Guatemala City; tel. 334-5480; fax 334-5481; Ambassador: TAE SHIK CHUNG.

Mexico: 15 Calle 3-20, Zona 10, Guatemala City; tel. 333-7254; fax 333-7615; Ambassador: SALVADOR ARRIOLA BARRENECHEA.

Nicaragua: 10a Avda 14-72, Zona 10, Guatemala City; tel. 368-0785; fax 337-4264; e-mail embanic-guat@intco.com.gt; Ambassador: FRANCISCO JAVIER RAMOS SÁNCHEZ.

Norway: Edif. Murano Center 15°, Of. 1501, 14 Calle 3-51, Zona 10, Apdo 1764, Guatemala City; tel. 366-5908; fax 366-5928; Ambassador: ARNE AASHEM.

Panama: Centro Empresarial Torre II, Of. 702, 5a Avda 15-45, Zona 10, Guatemala City; tel. 333-7176; fax 337-2446; Ambassador: ALONSO ROY.

Spain: 6a Calle 6-48, Zona 9, Guatemala City; tel. 334-3757; fax 332-2456; Ambassador: VÍCTOR LUIS FAGILDE GONZÁLEZ.

Sweden: 8a Avda 15-07, Zona 10, Guatemala City; tel. 333-6536; fax 333-7607; e-mail swedish-emb@gua.gbm.net; Ambassador: STAFFAN WRIGSTAD.

Switzerland: Torre Internacional, 14°, 16 Calle 0-55, Zona 10, 01010 Guatemala City; tel. 367-5520; fax 367-5811; e-mail swissemgua@c.net.gt; Ambassador: CHRISTIAN HAUSWIRTH.

United Kingdom: Edif. Torre Internacional, 11°, Avda La Reforma 16-00, Zona 10, Guatemala City; tel. 367-5425; fax 367-5430; e-mail embassy@terra.com.gt; Ambassador: ANDREW J. F. CAIE.

USA: Avda de la Reforma 7-01, Zona 10, Guatemala City; tel. 331-1541; fax 331-6660; Ambassador: DONALD J. PLANTY.

Uruguay: Edif. Plaza Marítima, 5°, Of. 5-3, 6a Avda 20-25, Zona 10, Guatemala City; tel. 337-0229; fax 333-7553; e-mail uruguate@guate.net; Ambassador: ALFREDO MENINI TERRA.

Judicial System

Corte Suprema: Centro Cívico, Guatemala City.

There are 13 members of the Supreme Court, appointed by the Congress.

President of the Supreme Court: JOSÉ ROLANDO QUESADA FERNÁNDEZ.

Civil Courts of Appeal: 10 courts, 5 in Guatemala City, 2 in Quezaltenango, 1 each in Jalapa, Zacapa and Antigua. The two Labour Courts of Appeal are in Guatemala City.

Judges of the First Instance: 7 civil and 10 penal in Guatemala City, 2 civil each in Quezaltenango, Escuintla, Jutiapa and San Marcos, 1 civil in each of the 18 remaining Departments of the Republic.

Religion

Almost all of the inhabitants profess Christianity, with a majority belonging to the Roman Catholic Church. In recent years the Protestant Churches have attracted a growing number of converts.

CHRISTIANITY
The Roman Catholic Church

For ecclesiastical purposes, Guatemala comprises two archdioceses, 10 dioceses and the Apostolic Vicariates of El Petén and Izabal. At 31 December 1999 adherents represented about 80.2% of the total population.

Bishops' Conference: Conferencia Episcopal de Guatemala, Secretariado General del Episcopado, Km 15, Calzada Roosevelt 4-54, Zona 7, Mixco, Apdo 1698, Guatemala City; tel. 593-1831; fax 593-1834; e-mail ceg@quetzal.net; internet www.iglesiacatolica.org.gt; f. 1973; Pres. VÍCTOR HUGO MARTÍNEZ CONTRERAS, Archbishop of Los Altos, Quetzaltenango-Totonicapán.

Archbishop of Guatemala City: PRÓSPERO PEÑADOS DEL BARRIO, Arzobispado, 7a Avda 6-21, Zona 1, Apdo 723, Guatemala City; tel. 232-1071; fax 238-0004.

Archbishop of Los Altos, Quetzaltenango—Totonicapán: VÍCTOR HUGO MARTÍNEZ CONTRERAS, Arzobispado, 11a Avda 6-27, Zona 1, Apdo 11, 09001 Quetzaltenango; tel. 761-2840; fax 761-6049.

The Anglican Communion

Guatemala comprises one of the five dioceses of the Iglesia Anglicana de la Región Central de América.

Bishop of Guatemala: Rt Rev. ARMANDO GUERRA SORIA, Avda Castellana 40–06, Zona 8, Apdo 58-A, Guatemala City; tel. 272-0852; fax 472-0764; e-mail diocesis@infovia.com.gt; diocese founded 1967.

Protestant Churches

The Baptist Church: Convention of Baptist Churches of Guatemala, 12a Calle 9–54, Zona 1, Apdo 322, Guatemala City; tel. 22-4227; f. 1946; Pres. Lic. JOSÉ MARROQUÍN R.

Church of Jesus Christ of Latter-day Saints: 12a Calle 3–37, Zona 9, Guatemala City; 17 bishoprics, 9 chapels; Regional Rep. GUILLERMO ENRIQUE RITTSCHER.

Congregación Luterana La Epifanía (Evangelical Lutheran Congregation La Epifanía): 2a Avda 15-31, Zona 10, Apdo 651, 01010 Guatemala City; tel. 368-0301; fax 366-4968; e-mail egeb@guate.net; Pres. Rev. ECKHARD GEBSER; 350 mems.

Lutheran Church: Consejo Nacional de Iglesias Luteranas, Apdo 1111, Guatemala City; tel. 22-3401; 3,077 mems; Pres. Rev. DAVID RODRÍGUEZ U.

Presbyterian Church: Iglesia Evangélica Presbiteriana Central, 6a Avda 'A' 4–68, Zona 1, Apdo 655, Guatemala City; tel. 232-0791; fax 232-2832; f. 1882; 36,000 mems; Pastor: Rev. JOSÉ RAMIRO BOLAÑOS RIVERA.

Union Church: 12 Calle 7–37, Plaza España, Zona 9, Apdo 150-A, Guatemala City; tel. 331-6904; fax 362-3961; e-mail unionchurch@guate.net; f. 1943; Pastor: W. KARL SMITH.

BAHÁ'Í FAITH

National Spiritual Assembly of the Bahá'ís: 3a Calle 4–54, Zona 1, Guatemala City; tel. 232-9673; fax 232-9673; e-mail aenguate@e-mailgua.com; mems resident in 464 localities; Sec. MARVIN E. ALVARADO E.

The Press

PRINCIPAL DAILIES

Al Día: Avda La Reforma 6–64, Zona 9, Guatemala City; tel. 339-0870; fax 339-1276; f. 1996; Pres. LIONEL TORIELLO NÁJERA; Dir GERARDO JIMÉNEZ ARDÓN.

Diario de Centroamérica: 18a Calle 6–72, Zona 1, Guatemala City; tel. 22-4418; f. 1880; morning; official; Dir LUIS MENDIZÁBAL; circ. 15,000.

La Hora: 9a Calle 'A' 1–56, Zona 1, Apdo 1593, Guatemala City; tel. 232-6864; fax 251-7084; e-mail lahora@tikal.net.gt; f. 1920; evening; independent; Dir OSCAR MARROQUÍN ROJAS; circ. 18,000.

Impacto: 9a Calle 'A' 1-56, Apdo 1593, Guatemala City; tel. 22-6864; fax 251-7084; daily.

La Nación: 1a Avda 11-12, Guatemala City.

El Periódico: 15a Avda 24–51, Zona 13, Guatemala City; tel. 362-0242; fax 332-9761; e-mail periodic@gold.guate.net; f. 1996; morning; independent; Pres. JOSÉ RUBÉN ZAMORA; Editors JUAN LUIS FONT, SYLVIA GEREDA; circ. 50,000.

Prensa Libre: 13a Calle 9–31, Zona 1, Apdo 2063, Guatemala City; tel. 230-5096; fax 251-8768; e-mail econtrer@infovia.com.gt; internet www.prensalibre.com; f. 1951; morning; independent; Gen. Man. EDGAR CONTRERAS MOLINA; Editor GONZALO MARROQUÍN GODOY; circ. 120,000.

Siglo Veintiuno: 7a Avda 11-63, Zona 9, Guatemala City; tel. 360-6704; fax 331-9145; e-mail buzon21@sigloxxi.com; internet www.sigloxxi.com; f. 1990; morning; Pres. LIONEL TORIELLO NÁJERA; circ. 65,000.

La Tarde: 14a Avda 4-33, Guatemala City.

PERIODICALS

AGA: 9a Calle 3–43, Zona 1, Guatemala City; monthly; agricultural.

Crónica Semanal: Edif. Torre Profesional II, Of. 312, 6a Avda 0-60, Guatemala City; tel. 235-2155; fax 235-2360; f. 1988; weekly; politics, economics, culture; Publr FRANCISCO PÉREZ.

Gerencia: La Asociación de Gerentes de Guatemala, Edif. Aseguradora General, 7°, 10a Calle 3-17, Guatemala City; tel. 231-1644; fax 231-1646; f. 1967; monthly; official organ of the Association of Guatemalan Managers; Editor MARGARITA SOLOGUREN.

El Industrial: 6a Ruta 9-21, Zona 4, Guatemala City; monthly; official organ of the Chamber of Industry.

Inforpress Centroamericana: Guatemala City; f. 1972; weekly; Spanish; regional political and economic news and analysis; Dir ARIEL DE LEÓN.

Panorama Internacional: 13a Calle 8-44, Zona 9, Apdo 611-A, Guatemala City; tel. 233-6367; fax 233-6203; weekly; politics, economics, culture.

PRESS ASSOCIATIONS

Asociación de Periodistas de Guatemala (APG): 14a Calle 3-29, Zona 1, Guatemala City; tel. 232-1813; fax 238-2781; e-mail apg@terra.com.gt; f. 1947; Pres. SALVADOR BONINI; Sec. MARIO DOMÍNGUEZ VALIENTE.

Cámara Guatemalteca de Periodismo (CGP): Guatemala City; Pres. EDUARDO DÍAZ REINA.

Círculo Nacional de Prensa (CNP): Guatemala City; Pres. ISRAEL TOBAR ALVARADO.

NEWS AGENCIES

Inforpress Centroamericana: 7a Avda 2-05, Zona 1, Guatemala City; tel. and fax 221-0301; e-mail inforpre@guate.net; internet www.worldcom.nl/CAR; f. 1972; independent news agency; publishes two weekly news bulletins, in English and Spanish.

Foreign Bureaux

ACAN-EFE (Central America): Edif. El Centro, 8°, Of. 8-21, 9a Calle y 7a Avda, Zona 1, Of. Guatemala City; tel. 251-9454; fax 251-9484: Man. ANA CAROLINA ALPÍREZ A.

Agenzia Nazionale Stampa Associata (ANSA) (Italy): Torre Norte, Edif. Geminis 10, Of. 805, 12a Calle 1-25, Zona 10, Guatemala City; tel. 235-3039; Chief ALFONSO ANZUETO LÓPEZ.

Deutsche Presse-Agentur (dpa) (Germany): 5a Calle 4-30, Zona 1, Apdo 2333, Guatemala City; tel. 251-7505; fax 251-7505; Correspondent JULIO CÉSAR ANZUETO.

Inter Press Service (IPS) (Italy): Edif. El Centro, 3°, Of. 13, 7a Avda 8-56, Zona 1, Guatemala City; tel. 253-8837; fax 251-4736; Correspondent GEORGE RODRÍGUEZ-OTEIZA.

United Press International (UPI) (USA): 6a Calle 4-17, Zona 1, Guatemala City; tel. and fax 251-4258; Correspondent AMAFREDO CASTELLANOS.

Publishers

Ediciones América: 12a Avda 14-55B, Zone 1, Guatemala City; tel. 251-4556; Man. Dir RAFAEL ESCOBAR ARGÜELLO.

Ediciones Gama: 5a Avda 14-46, Zone 1, Guatemala City; tel. 234-2331; Man. Dir SARA MONZÓN DE ECHEVERRÍA.

Ediciones Legales 'Commercio e Industria': 12a Avda 14-78, Zone 1, Guatemala City; tel. 253-5725; Man. Dir LUIS EMILIO BARRIOS.

Editorial del Ministerio de Educación: 15a Avda 3-22, Zona 1, Guatemala City.

Editorial Nueva Narrativa: Edif. El Patio, Of. 106, 7a Avda 7-07, Zona 4, Guatemala City; Man. Dir MAX ARAÚJO A.

Editorial Oscar de León Palacios: 6a Calle 'A' 10-12, Zona 11, Guatemala City; tel. 272-1636; educational texts; Man. Dir OSCAR DE LEÓN CASTILLO.

Editorial Palo de Hormigo: O Calle 16-40, Zone 15, Col. El Maestro, Guatemala City; tel. 369-2080; fax 369-8858; e-mail juanfercif@hotmail.com; f. 1990; Man. Dir JUAN FERNANDO CIFUENTES.

Editorial Universitaria: Edif. de la Editorial Universitaria, Universidad de San Carlos de Guatemala, Ciudad Universitaria, Zona 12, Guatemala City; tel. and fax 476-9628; literature, social sciences, health, pure and technical sciences, humanities, secondary and university educational textbooks; Editor RAÚL FIGUEROA SARTI.

F & G Editores: 30 Avda 'B' 4-50, Zona 7, Jardines de Tikal I, Guatemala City; fax 474-0214; e-mail fgeditor@guate.net; internet www.fygeditores.com; f. 1990 as Figueroa y Gallardo, changed name in 1993; law, literature and social sciences; Editor RAÚL FIGUEROA SARTI.

Piedra Santa: 5a Calle 7-55, Zona 1, Guatemala City; tel. 220-1524; fax 323-9053; f. 1947; children's literature, text books; Man. Dir IRENE PIEDRA SANTA.

Seminario de Integración Social Guatemalteco: 11a Calle 4-31, Zona 1, Guatemala City; tel. 22-9754; f. 1956; sociology, anthropology, social sciences, educational textbooks.

Broadcasting and Communications

TELECOMMUNICATIONS

Regulatory Authority

Superintendencia de Telecomunicaciones de Guatemala: Edif. Murano Center, 16°, 14a Calle 3-51, Zona 10, Guatemala City; tel. 366-5880; fax 366-5890; e-mail supertel@sit.gob.gt; internet www.sit.gob.gt; Superintendent JOSÉ ROMEO ORELLANA.

Major Service Providers

BellSouth: Guatemala City; provides mobile telecommunications services in Guatemala City.

Empresa Guatemalteca de Telecomunicaciones (Guatel): Guatemala City; internet www.guatel.com.gt; 95% share transferred to private ownership in 1998; Dir ALFREDO GUZMÁN.

BROADCASTING

Dirección General de Radiodifusión y Televisión Nacional: Edif. Tipografía Nacional, 3°, 18 de Septiembre 6-72, Zona 1, Guatemala City; tel. 253-2539; f. 1931; government supervisory body; Dir-Gen. ENRIQUE ALBERTO HERNÁNDEZ ESCOBAR.

Radio

There are five government and six educational stations, including:

La Voz de Guatemala: 18a Calle 6-72, Zona 1, Guatemala City; tel. 253-2539; government station; Dir ARTURO SOTO ECHEVERRÍA.

Radio Cultural TGN: 4a Avda 30-09, Zona 3, Apdo 601, Guatemala City; tel. 471-4378; fax 440-0260; e-mail ssywulka@guate.net; f. 1950; religious and cultural station; programmes in Spanish and English, Cakchiquel and Kekchí; Dir ESTEBAN SYWULKA; Man. ANTHONY WAYNE BERGER.

There are some 80 commercial stations, of which the most important are:

Emisoras Unidas de Guatemala: 4a Calle 6-84, Zona 13, Guatemala City; tel. 440-5133; fax 440-5159; e-mail rboileau@tikal.net.gt; f. 1964; Pres. JORGE EDGARDO ARCHILA MARROQUÍN; Vice-Pres. ROLANDO ARCHILA MARROQUÍN.

Radio Cinco Sesenta: 14a Calle 4-73, Zona 11, Guatemala City; Dir EDNA CASTILLO OBREGÓN.

Radio Continental: Guatemala City; Dir ROBERTO VIZCAÍNO R.

Radio Nuevo Mundo: 6a Avda 10-45, Zona 1, Apdo 281, Guatemala City; fax 232-2036; f. 1947; Man. ALFREDO GONZÁLEZ GAMARRA.

Radio Panamericana: 1a Avda 35-48, Zona 7, Guatemala City; Dir JAIME J. PANIAGUA.

La Voz de las Américas: 11a Calle 2-43, Zona 1, Guatemala City; Dir AUGUSTO LÓPEZ S.

Television

Canal 3—Radio-Televisión Guatemala, SA: 30a Avda 3-40, Zona 11, Guatemala City; tel. 292-2491; fax 294-7492; f. 1956; commercial station; Pres. Lic. MAX KESTLER FARNÉS; Vice-Pres. J. F. VILLANUEVA.

Canal 5—Televisión Cultural y Educativa, SA: 4a Calle 18-38, Zona 1, Guatemala City; tel. 238-1781; fax 232-7003; f. 1980; cultural and educational programmes; Dir ALFREDO HERRERA CABRERA.

Teleonce: 20a Calle 5-02, Zona 10, Guatemala City; tel. 368-2595; fax 337-0861; f. 1968; commercial; Gen. Dir JUAN CARLOS ORTIZ.

Televisiete, SA: Blvr Vista Hermosa 18-07, Zona 15, Apdo 1242, Guatemala City; tel. 369-0033; fax 369-1393; f. 1988; commercial station channel 7; Dir ABDÓN RODRÍGUEZ ZEA.

Trecevisión, SA: 3a Calle 10-70, Zona 10, Guatemala City; tel. 26-3266; commercial; Dir Ing. PEDRO MELGAR R.; Gen. Man. GILDA VALLADARES ORTIZ.

Finance

(cap. = capital; p.u. = paid up; res = reserves; dep. = deposits; m. = million; brs = branches; amounts in quetzales)

BANKING

Superintendencia de Bancos: 9a Avda 22-00, Zona 1, Apdo 2306, Guatemala City; tel. 232-0001; fax 232-5301; e-mail sibcos@guate.net; internet www.sib.gob.gt; f. 1946; Superintendent ROBERTO A. GUTIÉRREZ NÁJERA.

Central Bank

Banco de Guatemala: 7a Avda 22-01, Zona 1, Apdo 365, Guatemala City; tel. 230-6222; fax 253-4035; internet www.banguat.gob.gt; f. 1946; cap. and res 603.2m., dep. 12,040.6m. (Dec. 1997); Pres. LIZARDO ARTURO SOSA LÓPEZ; Man. EDWIN GIOVANNI VERBENA DE LEÓN; 8 brs.

State Commercial Bank

Crédito Hipotecario Nacional de Guatemala: 7a Avda 22-77, Zona 1, Apdo 242, Guatemala City; tel. 230-6542; fax 238-2041; e-mail mercchn@bancared.net.gt; internet www.bancared.com.gt; f. 1930; government-owned; Pres. FABIÁN PIRA ARRIVILLAGA; Gen. Man. SERGIO DURINI CÁRDENAS; 35 agencies.

Private Commercial Banks

Guatemala City

Banco Agrícola Mercantil, SA: 7a Avda 7-30, Zona 9, Guatemala City; tel. 362-3141; fax 251-0780; e-mail interbam@guate.net; internet www.bamguatemala.com; f. 1948; cap. 84.1m., res 2.5m., dep. 974.1m. (Dec. 1996); Gen. Man. ALFONSO VILLA DE VOTO; 2 brs, 8 agencies.

Banco del Agro, SA: 9a Calle 5-39, Zona 1, Apdo 1443, Guatemala City; tel. 251-4026; fax 232-4566; e-mail info@banagro.com.gt; internet www.banagro.com.gt; f. 1956; cap. 10.0m., res 19.4m., dep. 374.9m. (June 1991); Pres. JOSÉ MARÍA VALDÉS GARCÍA; Gen. Man. HÉCTOR ESTUARDO PIVARAL; 41 brs.

Banco del Café, SA: Avda de la Reforma 9-30, Zona 9, Apdo 831, Guatemala City; tel. 361-3645; fax 331-1418; e-mail mercadeo@bancafe.com.gt; internet www.bancafe.com.gt; f. 1978; total assets 6.63m. (1999); merged with Multibanco in 2000; Pres. EDUARDO MANUEL GONZÁLEZ RIVERA; Asst Gen. Man. INGO HABERLAND HAESLOOP.

Banco de Comercio: Edif. Centro Operativo, 6a Avda 8-00, Zona 9, Guatemala City; tel. 339-0504; fax 339-0555; internet www.bancared.gt; f. 1991; 33 brs.

Banco del Ejército, SA: 7a Avda 3-73, Zona 9, Apdo 1797, Guatemala City; tel. 362-7042; fax 362-7108; e-mail baneje@gua.net; internet www.banejer.com.gt; f. 1972; cap. 72.2m., res 22.2m., dep. 735.9m. (Dec. 1997); Pres. Col GUIDO FERNANDO ABDALA PEÑAGOS; 14 brs.

Banco de Exportación, SA: Avda de la Reforma 11-49, Zona 10, Guatemala City; tel. 231-9861; fax 232-2879; e-mail infbanex@banex.net.gt; internet www.banex.net.gt; f. 1985; cap. 71.8m., res 30.0m., dep. 731.3m. (Dec. 1993); Pres. Dr FRANCISCO MANSILLA CÓRDOVA; Man. Ing. RAFAEL VIEJO RODRÍGUEZ.

Banco Industrial, SA (BAINSA): Edif. Centro Financiero, Torre 1, 7a Avda 5-10, Zona 4, Apdo 744, Guatemala City; tel. 234-5111; fax 232-1712; f. 1964 to promote industrial development; total assets 7.91m. (1999); Pres. JUAN MIGUEL TORREBIARTE LANTZENDORFFER; Gen. Man. Lic. NORBERTO RODOLFO CASTELLANOS DÍAZ.

Banco Inmobilario, SA: 7a Avda 11-59, Zona 9, Apdo 1181, Guatemala City; tel. 332-1950; fax 332-2325; e-mail info@bancoinmob.com.gt; internet www.bcoinmob.com.gt; f. 1958; cap. 45.0m., res 6.2m., dep. 532.3m. (June 1992); Pres. EMILIO ANTONIO PERALTA PORTILLO; Man. MARCO ANTONIO OVANDO; 15 brs.

Banco Internacional, SA: Torre Internacional, Avda Reforma 15-85, Zona 10, Apdo 2588, Guatemala City; tel. 366-6666; fax 366-6743; e-mail binter60@gua.gbm.net; internet www.bcointer.com/gt; f. 1976; cap. 50.0m., res 15.4m., dep. 822.6m. (Dec. 1997); Pres. JUAN SKINNER-KLÉE; Gen. Man. JOSÉ MANUEL REQUEJO SÁNCHEZ; 28 brs.

Banco del Quetzal, SA: Edif. Plaza El Roble, 7a Ave 6-26, Zona 9, Apdo 1001-A, Guatemala City; tel. 231-8333; fax 232-6937; f. 1984; cap. 37.4m., dep. 342.7m. (July 1994); Pres. Lic. MARIO ROBERTO LEAL PIVARAL; Gen. Man. ALFONSO VILLA DEVOTO.

Banco Reformador, SA: 7a Avda 7-24, Zona 9, Guatemala City; tel. 362-0888; fax 362-0847; cap. 1,720; merged with Banco de la Construcción in 2000; 60 brs.

Banco SCI: Edif. SCI Centre, Avda La Reforma 9-76, Zona 9, Guatemala City; tel. 331-7515; fax 331-2262; e-mail atencion@ sci.net.gt; internet www.sci.com.gt; f. 1967.

Banco de los Trabajadores: 8a Avda 9-41, Zona 1, Apdo 1956, Guatemala City; tel. 22-4651; fax 251-8902; f. 1966; deals with loans for establishing and improving small industries as well as normal banking business; Pres. Lic. CÉSAR AMILCAR BÁRCENAS; Gen. Man. Lic. OSCAR H. ANDRADE ELIZONDO.

Banco Uno: Edif. Unicentro, 1°, Blvd Los Próceres, 18 Calle 5-56, Zona 10, Guatemala City; tel. 366-1818; e-mail bancouno@gua .pibnet.com; internet www.bancared.com.gt/Uno.

G & T Continental: 7a Avda 1-86, Zona 4, Guatemala City; tel. 331-2333; fax 332-9083; and Plaza Continental, 6a Avda 9-08, Zona 9, Guatemala City; tel. 339-2001; fax 339-2091; e-mail gfc@email .continet.com.gt; internet www.gyt.com.gt; f. 2000 following merger of Banco Continental and Banco Granai y Townson; total assets 11.4m. (2000); 130 brs.

Quezaltenango

Banco de Occidente, SA: 7a Ave 11-15, Zona 1, Quezaltenango; tel. (961) 53-1333; fax (961) 30-0970; e-mail occidente@occidente.com.gt; internet www.occidente.com.gt; f. 1881; total assets 12.45m. (1999); Pres. Dr LUIS BELTRANENA VALLADARES; Gen. Man. Ing. JOSÉ E. ASCOLI CÁCERES; 29 brs.

State Development Bank

Banco Nacional de Desarrollo Agrícola—BANDESA: 9a Calle 9-47, Zona 1, Apdo 350, Guatemala City; tel. 253-5222; fax 253-7927; f. 1971; agricultural development bank; Pres. Minister of Agriculture, Livestock and Food; Gen. Man. GUSTAVO ADOLFO LEAL CASTELLANOS.

Finance Corporations

Corporación Financiera Nacional (CORFINA): 11a Avda 3-14, Zona 1, Guatemala City; tel. 253-4550; fax 22-5805; f. 1973; provides assistance for the development of industry, mining and tourism; Pres. Lic. SERGIO A. GONZÁLEZ NAVAS; Gen. Man. Lic. MARIO ARMANDO MARTÍNEZ ZAMORA.

Financiera Guatemalteca, SA (FIGSA): 1a Avda 11-50, Zona 10, Apdo 2460, Guatemala City; tel. 232-1423; fax 231-0873; f. 1962; investment agency; Pres. CARLOS GONZÁLEZ BARRIOS; Gen. Man. Ing. ROBERTO FERNÁNDEZ BOTRÁN.

Financiera Industrial y Agropecuaria, SA (FIASA): Plaza Continental, 3°, 6a Avda 9-08, Zona 9, Guatemala City; tel. 239-1951; fax 239-2089; f. 1968; private development bank; medium- and long-term loans to private industrial enterprises in Central America; cap. 2.5m., res 27.1m. (Dec. 1994); Pres. JORGE CASTILLO LOVE; Gen. Man. Lic. ALEJANDRO MEJÍA AVILA.

Financiera Industrial, SA (FISA): Centro Financiero, Torre 2, 7a Avda 5-10, Zona 4, Apdo 744, Guatemala City; tel. 232-1750; fax 231-1773; f. 1981; cap. 3m., res 6.2m. (Aug. 1991); Pres. CARLOS ARÍAS MASSELLI; Gen. Man. Lic. ELDER F. CALDERÓN REYES.

Financiera de Inversión, SA: 11a Calle 7-44, Zona 9, Guatemala City; tel. 332-4020; fax 332-4320; f. 1981; investment agency; cap. 15.0m. (June 1997); Pres. Lic. MARIO AUGUSTO PORRAS GONZÁLEZ; Gen. Man. Lic. JOSÉ ROLANDO PORRAS GONZÁLEZ.

Foreign Bank

Lloyds TSB Group PLC (United Kingdom): Edif. Gran Vía, 6a Avda 9-51, Zona 9, Guatemala City; tel. 332-7580; fax 332-7641; f. 1959; cap. 18.7m., dep. 79.5m. (2000); Man. N. M. A. HUBBARD; 10 brs.

Banking Association

Asociación de Banqueros de Guatemala: Edif. Quinta Montúfar, 2°, 12a Calle 4-74, Zona 9, Guatemala City; tel. 231-8211; fax 231-9477; f. 1961; represents all state and private banks; Pres. Ing. RAFAEL VIEJO RODRÍGUEZ.

STOCK EXCHANGE

Guatemala Stock Exchange: 4a Calle 6-55, Zona 9, Guatemala City; tel. 234-2479; fax 231-4509; f. 1987; the exchange is commonly owned (one share per associate) and trades stocks from private companies, government bonds, letters of credit and other securities.

INSURANCE
National Companies

Aseguradora General, SA: 10a Calle 3-17, Zona 10, Guatemala City; tel. 332-5933; fax 334-2093; f. 1968; Pres. JUAN O. NIEMANN; Man. ENRIQUE NEUTZE A.

Aseguradora Guatemalteca, SA: Edif. Torre Azul, 10°, 4a Calle 7-53, Zona 9, Guatemala City; tel. 361-0206; fax 361-1093; e-mail

aseguate@guate.net; f. 1978; Pres. Gen. CARLOS E. PINEDA CARRANZA; Man. CÉSAR A. RUANO SANDOVAL.

Cía de Seguros Generales Granai & Townson, SA: 2a Ruta, 2-39, Zona 4, Guatemala City; tel. 334-1361; fax 332-2993; f. 1947; Pres. ERNESTO TOWNSON R.; Exec. Man. MARIO GRANAI FERNÁNDEZ.

Cía de Seguros Panamericana, SA: Avda de la Reforma 9-00, Zona 9, Guatemala City; tel. 232-5922; fax 231-5026; f. 1968; Pres. JOHN ROBERTS; Gen. Man. Lic. SALVADOR ORTEGA.

Cía de Seguros El Roble, SA: Torre 2, 7a Avda 5-10, Zona 4, Guatemala City; tel. 332-1702; fax 332-1629; f. 1973; Pres. FEDERICO KÖNG VIELMAN; Man. Ing. RICARDO ERALES CÓBAR.

Comercial Aseguradora Suizo-Americana, SA: 7a Avda 7-07, Zona 9, Apdo 132, Guatemala City; tel. 332-0666; fax 331-5495; f. 1946; Pres. WILLIAM BICKFORD B.; Gen. Man. MARIO AGUILAR.

Departamento de Seguros y Previsión del Crédito Hipotecario Nacional: 7a Avda 22-77, Zona 1, Centro Cívico, Guatemala City; tel. 250-0271; fax 253-8584; f. 1935; Pres. FABIÁN PIRA; Man. SERGIO DURINI.

Empresa Guatemalteca Cigna de Seguros, SA: Edif. Plaza Marítima 10, 6a Avda 20-25, Zona 10, Guatemala City; tel. 337-2285; fax 337-0121; f. 1951; Gen. Man. Lic. RICARDO ESTRADA DARDÓN.

La Seguridad de Centroamérica, SA: Avda de la Reforma 12-01, Zona 10, Guatemala City; tel. 231-7566; fax 231-7580; f. 1967; Pres. EDGARDO WAGNER D.; Vice-Pres. RICARDO CAU MARTÍNEZ.

Seguros Alianza, SA: Edif. Etisa, 6°, Plazuela España, Zona 9, Guatemala City; tel. 331-5475; fax 331-0023; f. 1968; Pres. LUIS FERNANDO SAMAYOA; Gen. Man. DAVID LEMUS PIVARAL.

Seguros de Occidente, SA: 7a Calle 'A' 7-14, Zona 9, Guatemala City; tel. 231-1222; fax 234-1413; f. 1979; Pres. Lic. PEDRO AGUIRRE; Gen. Man. CARLOS LAINFIESTA.

Seguros Universales, SA: 4a Calle 7-73, Zona 9, Apdo 1479, Guatemala City; tel. 334-0733; fax 332-3372; e-mail tato@ universales.net; f. 1962; Manager PEDRO NOLASCO SICILIA.

Insurance Association

Asociación Guatemalteca de Instituciones de Seguros (AGIS): Edif. Torre Profesional I, Of. 411, 4°, 6a Avda 0-60, Zona 4, Guatemala City; tel. 235-1657; fax 235-2021; f. 1953; 12 mems; Pres. ENRIQUE NUETZE A.; Man. Lic. FERNANDO RODRÍGUEZ TREJO.

Trade and Industry
DEVELOPMENT ORGANIZATIONS

Comisión Nacional Petrolera: Diagonal 17, 29-78, Zona 11, Guatemala City; tel. 276-0680; fax 276-3175; f. 1983; awards petroleum exploration licences.

Consejo Nacional de Planificación Económica: 9a Calle 10-44, Zona 1, Guatemala City; tel. 251-4549; fax 253-3127; e-mail mrayo@ns.concyt.gob.gt; f. 1954; prepares and supervises the implementation of the national economic development plan; Sec.-Gen. MARIANO RAYO MUÑOZ.

Corporación Financiera Nacional (CORFINA): see under Finance (Finance Corporations).

Empresa Nacional de Fomento y Desarrollo Económico de El Petén (FYDEP): 11a Avda 'B' 32-46, Zona 5, Guatemala City; tel. 231-6834; f. 1959; attached to the Presidency; economic development agency for the Department of El Petén; Dir FRANCISCO ANGEL CASTELLANOS GÓNGORA.

Instituto de Fomento de Hipotecas Aseguradas (FHA): Edif. Aristos Reforma, 2°, Avda Reforma 7-62, Zona 9, Guatemala City; tel. 362-9434; fax 362-9492; e-mail fha@guate.net; internet www.fha.centroamerica.com; f. 1961; insured mortgage institution for the promotion of house construction; Pres. Lic. HOMERO AUGUSTO GONZÁLEZ BARILLAS; Man. Lic. JOSÉ SALVADOR SAMAYOA AGUILAR.

Instituto Nacional de Administración Pública (INAP): 5a Avda 12-65, Zona 9, Apto 2753, Guatemala City; tel. 26-6339; f. 1964; provides technical experts to assist all branches of the Government in administrative reform programmes; provides in-service training for local and central government staff; has research programmes in administration, sociology, politics and economics; provides postgraduate education in public administration; Gen. Man. Dr ARIEL RIVERA IRÍAS.

Instituto Nacional de Transformación Agraria (INTA): 14a Calle 7-14, Zona 1, Guatemala City; tel. 28-0975; f. 1962 to carry out agrarian reform; current programme includes development of the 'Faja Transversal del Norte'; Pres. Ing. NERY ORLANDO SAMAYOA; Vice-Pres Ing. SERGIO FRANCISCO MORALES-JUÁREZ, ROBERTO EDMUNDO QUIÑÓNEZ LÓPEZ.

CHAMBERS OF COMMERCE AND INDUSTRY

Comité Coordinador de Asociaciones Agrícolas, Comerciales, Industriales y Financieras (CACIF): Edif. Cámara de Industria de Guatemala, 6a Ruta 9-21, Zona 4, Guatemala City; tel. 231-0651; co-ordinates work on problems and organization of free enterprise; mems: 6 chambers; Pres. JORGE BRIZ; Sec.-Gen. RAFAEL POLA.

Cámara de Comercio de Guatemala: 10a Calle 3-80, Zona 1, Guatemala City; tel. 28-2681; fax 251-4197; f. 1894; Gen. Man. EDGARDO RUIZ.

Cámara de Industria de Guatemala: 6a Ruta 9-21, 12°, Zona 4, Apdo 214, Guatemala City; tel. 334-0850; fax 334-1090; f. 1958; Pres. JUAN JOSÉ URRUELA KONG; Gen. Man. CARLOS PERALTA.

INDUSTRIAL AND TRADE ASSOCIATIONS

Asociación de Agricultores Productores de Aceites Esenciales: 6a Calle 1-36, Zona 10, Apdo 272, Guatemala City; tel. 234-7255; f. 1948; essential oils producers' asscn; 40 mems; Pres. FRANCISCO RALDA; Gen. Man. CARLOS FLORES PAGAZA.

Asociación de Azucareros de Guatemala (ASAZGUA): Edif. Tívoli Plaza, 6a Calle 6-38, Zona 9, Guatemala City; fax 231-8191; f. 1957; sugar producers' asscn; 19 mems; Gen. Man. Lic. ARMANDO BOESCHE.

Asociación de Exportadores de Café: 11a Calle 5-66, 3°, Zona 9, Guatemala City; coffee exporters' asscn; 37 mems; Pres. EDUARDO GONZÁLEZ RIVERA.

Asociación General de Agricultores: 9a Calle 3-43, Zona 1, Guatemala City; f. 1920; general farmers' asscn; 350 mems; Pres. DAVID ORDÓÑEZ; Man. PEDRO ARRIVILLAGA RADA.

Asociación Nacional de Avicultores (ANAVI): Edif. Galerías Reforma, Torre 2, 9°, Of. 904, Avda de la Reforma 8-60, Zona 9, Guatemala City; tel. 231-1381; fax 234-7576; f. 1964; national asscn of poultry farmers; 60 mems; Pres. Lic. FERNANDO ROJAS; Dir Dr MARIO A. MOTTA GONZÁLEZ.

Asociación Nacional de Fabricantes de Alcoholes y Licores (ANFAL): Km 16½, Carretera Roosevelt, Zona 10, Apdo 2065, Guatemala City; tel. 292-0430; f. 1947; distillers' asscn; Pres. FELIPE BOTRÁN MERINO; Man. Lic. JUAN GUILLERMO BORJA MOGOLLÓN.

Asociación Nacional del Café—Anacafé: Edif. Etisa, Plazuela España, Zona 9, Guatemala City; tel. 236-7180; fax 234-7023; f. 1960; national coffee asscn; Pres. WILLIAM STIXRUD.

Cámara del Agro: 15a Calle 'A' 7-65, Zona 9, Guatemala City; tel. 26-1473; f. 1973; Man. CÉSAR BUSTAMANTE ARAÚZ.

Consejo Nacional del Algodón: 11a Calle 6-49, Zona 9, Guatemala City; tel. 234-8390; fax 234-8393; f. 1964; consultative body for cultivation and classification of cotton; 119 mems; Pres. ROBERTO MARTÍNEZ R.; Man. ALFREDO GIL SPILLARI.

Gremial de Hueleros de Guatemala: Edif. Centroamericano, Of. 406, 7a Avda 7-78, Zona 4, Guatemala City; tel. 231-4917; f. 1970; rubber producers' guild; 125 mems; Pres. JOSÉ LUIS RALDA; Man. Lic. CÉSAR SOTO.

MAJOR COMPANIES

The following are some of the leading companies currently operating in Guatemala:

Construction

Cementos Progreso, SA: 15 Avda 18-01, Zona 6, Guatemala City; tel. 288-2702; fax 288-3987; f. 1899; cement manufacturers; sold to the Swiss Holderbank Financiere Glaris Ltd in 2000; Pres. FREDERICK C. E. MELVILLE NOVELLA; Gen. Man. PLINIO A. HERRERA CHACON; 1,550 employees.

Ingenieros Mayorga & Tejada: 4a Avda 8-40, Zona 9, Guatemala City; tel. 331-6749; fax 332-0959; f. 1966; heavy construction and civil engineering services; Man. Dir ENRIQUE TEJADA; 800 employees.

Food and Beverages

Alimentos Kern de Guatemala, SA: Km 7½, Carretera al Atlántico, Zona 18, Guatemala City; tel. 256-0537; fax 256-7978; f. 1959; manufacturers of canned fruit juices and fruit products; Pres. JESS JOAQUÍN PARDO VIADERO; Gen. Man. ALFONSO BOCALETTI ALVAREZ; 550 employees.

Cervecería Centroamericana, SA: 3a Avda Norte Final, Finca El Zapote, Zona 2, Guatemala City; tel. 227-0722; fax (2) 253-8061; internet www.cerveceria.com.gt; f. 1886; brewery; Pres. JORGE CASTILLO LOVE; 440 employees.

Compañía Industrial de Alimentos, SA (CINDAL): 6a Avda 4-64, Zona 4, Guatemala City; tel. 332-4152; fax 332-1322; f. 1969; subsidiary of Nestlé SA, Switzerland; producers of chocolate and dairy products; Gen. Man. LUIS CABARCOS GIL; 335 employees.

Embotelladora Central, SA: 26 Calle 6-01, Zona 11, Guatemala City; tel. 476-2228; fax 476-7326; f. 1985; bottling factory, producers of carbonated beverages; Pres. CARLOS H. PORRAS; 490 employees.

Embotelladora del Pacífico, SA: Km 166, Cutytenango-Suchitepeque, Guatemala City; tel. 472-0884; fax 472-0883; f. 1957; producers of soft drinks; Pres. OSCAR CASTRILLO VALENZUELA; 800 employees.

Frigoríficos de Guatemala, SA: Calzada Aguilar Batres 35-21, Zona 12, Guatemala City; tel. 476-5290; fax 476-8350; f. 1967; food processing, producers of fish and poultry products; Pres. DOMINGO MOREIRA MARTÍNEZ; Gen. Man. JUAN FRANCISCO GUTIÉRREZ ROY; 1,400 employees.

Ingenio Tulula, SA: 19 Calle 3-97, Zona 10, Guatemala City; tel. 334-7189; fax 332-0004; f. 1982; processing sugar cane; Pres. JOSÉ BOUSCAYOL; 1,600 employees.

Julia SA, Empresa Avicola: Las Tapias, Llavareda, Zona 18, Guatemala City; tel. 256-4741; fax 256-4742; f. 1975; poultry hatcheries; Pres. CARLOS ALFREDO PIÑEDA NAVAS; 670 employees.

Metals and Rubber

Gran Industria de Neumáticos Centroamericanos, SA (GINSA): 50 Calle 23-70, Zona 12, Guatemala City; tel. 477-5412; fax 477-5421; f. 1956; subsidiary of Goodyear Tyre and Rubber Co, USA; tyre manufacturers; Pres. ADOLFO BEHRENS MOTTA; 600 employees.

Hulera Centroamericana, SA: 24 Calle 24-75, Zona 12, Guatemala City; tel. 477-0531; fax 476-7375; e-mail hucasa@gua.gbm.net; f. 1958; manufacturers of rubber goods; Gen. Man. CARLOS TORREBIARTE; 250 employees.

Industria de Tubos y Perfiles, SA: 9a Avda 3-17, Zona 2 de Mixco, Mixco, Guatemala City 11; tel. 593-4433; fax 593-4437; f. 1961; subsidiary of United States Steel Corpn, USA; manufacturers of stainless steel tubes and electrical cables; Pres. JOSÉ LUIS GABRIEL ABULARACH; 200 employees.

Llantas Vifrio, SA: 42 Calle 20-64, Zona 12, Guatemala City; tel. 476-1212; fax 476-1960; f. 1967; repair and retreading of tyres; Pres. HUMBERTO SUÁREZ VALDEZ.

Pharmaceuticals

Colgate-Palmolive Central America, SA: Avda Ferrocarril 49-66, Zona 12, Guatemala City; tel. 477-5511; fax 477-5403; f. 1971; pharmaceuticals and consumer products; Pres. CARLOS VELÁSQUEZ; Gen. Man. LUIS GAMAMIEL GUTIÉRREZ; 465 employees.

Química Hoechst de Guatemala, SA: Km 15½, Carretera Roosevelt, Guatemala City; tel. 201-0011; fax 595-4016; f. 1965; manufacturers of pharmaceuticals, chemicals, cosmetics and agricultural and industrial products; Pres. POMPEYO CASTILLO; 400 employees.

Tobacco

Tabacalera Centroamericana, SA: Km 12½, Carretera a Villa Canales, Aldea Boca del Monte, Guatemala City; tel. 448-0651; fax 448-0154; f. 1945; subsidiary of Phillip Morris Int. Finance Corpn of the USA; manufacturers of cigarettes; Pres. JORGE SKINNER KLEE; 487 employees.

Tabacalera Nacional, SA: 15 Calle 17-17, Zona 1, Guatemala City; tel. 230-6474; fax 232-3191; f. 1928; subsidiary of BAT Industries PLC (United Kingdom); manufacturers of cigarettes; Gen. Man. FRANCIS CARLO; 345 employees.

Miscellaneous

Cervinia, SA: 5a Avda 9-62, Zona 1, Guatemala City; textile manufacturers; f. 1972; Pres. ANTONIO CABARRUS; 200 employees.

Duralux, SA: 7a Avda 6-26, Zona 9, Guatemala City; tel. 289-1764; fax 289-1765; f. 1959; subsidiary of ESB Inc, USA; manufacturers of batteries; Gen. Man. FRANKLIN ROBERTO MURGA GUNTER; 250 employees.

Fábrica de Jabones y Detergentes La Luz, SA: Km 18, Carretera Vieja a Antigua 16–81, Zona 1, Guatemala City; tel. 594-5115; fax 594-4750; e-mail laluz@infovia.com.gt; f. 1946; producers of soap and detergents; Pres. Ing. JUAN JOSÉ URRUELA VILLACORTA; 620 employees.

Industria Centroamericana de Vidrio, SA: Avda Petapa 48-01, Zona 12, Apdo 1759, Guatemala City; tel. 276-0406; producers of glass bottles and containers and tableware; Pres. EDGAR CASTILLO SINIBALDI; 670 employees.

Industria La Popular, SA: Vía 3 5-42, Zona 4, Guatemala City; tel. 331-3821; fax 332-4533; f. 1920; producers of soap and detergents; Pres. FEDERICO KONG VIELMAN; 555 employees.

Minas de Guatemala, SA: 4a Avda 8-53, Zona 9, Guatemala City; tel. 336-3976; f. 1969; metal ore mining; Gen. Man. RODOLFO MENDOZA TEJADA; 650 employees.

Zelaya Suárez Rafael: 36 Calle 14-80, Zona 12, Guatemala City; tel. 477-0273; f. 1981; manufacturers of polishes; Gen. Man. RAFAEL ZELAYA; 760 employees.

UTILITIES
Electricity

Empresa Eléctrica de Guatemala, SA: 6a Avda 8-14, Zona 1, Guatemala City; tel. 230-3050; fax 253-1746; f. 1972; state electricity producer; 80% share transferred to private ownership in 1998; Pres. RICARDO CASTILLO SINIBALDI.

Instituto Nacional de Electrificación (INDE): Edif. La Torre, 7a Avda 2-29, Zona 9, Guatemala City; tel. (2) 34-5711; fax (2) 34-5811; f. 1959; former state agency for the generation and distribution of hydroelectric power; principal electricity producer; privatized in 1998; Pres. GUILLERMO RODRÍGUEZ.

CO-OPERATIVES

Instituto Nacional de Cooperativas (INACOP): 4a Calle 4-37, Zona 9, 01001 Guatemala City; tel. 234-1097; fax 234-7536; technical and financial assistance in planning and devt of co-operatives; Man. CÉSAR AUGUSTO MASSELLA BARRERA.

TRADE UNIONS

Frente Nacional Sindical (FNS) (National Trade Union Front): Guatemala City; f. 1968 to achieve united action in labour matters; affiliated are two confederations and 11 federations, which represent 97% of the country's trade unions and whose General Secretaries form the governing council of the FNS. The affiliated organizations include:

Comité Nacional de Unidad Sindical Guatemalteca—CONUS: Leader MIGUEL ANGEL SOLÍS; Sec.-Gen. GERÓNIMO LÓPEZ DÍAZ.

Confederación General de Sindicatos (General Trade Union Confederation): 18a Calle 5-50, Zona 1, Apdo 959, Guatemala City.

Confederación Nacional de Trabajadores (National Workers' Confederation): Guatemala City; Sec.-Gen. MIGUEL ANGEL ALBIZÚREZ.

Consejo Sindical de Guatemala (Guatemalan Trade Union Council): 18a Calle 5-50, Zona 1, Apdo 959, Guatemala City; f. 1955; admitted to ICFTU and ORIT; Gen. Sec. JAIME V. MONGE DONIS; 30,000 mems in 105 affiliated unions.

Federación Autónoma Sindical Guatemalteca (Guatemalan Autonomous Trade Union Federation): Guatemala City; Gen. Sec. MIGUEL ANGEL SOLÍS.

Federación de Obreros Textiles (Textile Workers' Federation): Edif. Briz, Of. 503, 6a Avda 14-33, Zona 1, Guatemala City; f. 1957; Sec.-Gen. FACUNDO PINEDA.

Federación de Trabajadores de Guatemala (FTG) (Guatemalan Workers' Federation): 5a Calle 4-33, Zona 1, Guatemala City; tel. 22-6515; Promoter ADRIAN RAMÍREZ.

A number of unions exist without a national centre, including the Union of Chicle and Wood Workers, the Union of Coca-Cola Workers and the Union of Workers of the Enterprise of the United Fruit Company.

Central General de Trabajadores de Guatemala (CGTG): 3a Avda 12-22, Zona 1, Guatemala City; tel. 232-9234; fax 251-3212; f. 1987; Sec.-Gen. JOSÉ E. PINZÓN SALAZAR.

Central Nacional de Trabajadores (CNT): 9a Avda 4-29, Zona 1, Apdo 2472, Guatemala City; f. 1972; cover all sections of commerce, industry and agriculture including the public sector; clandestine since June 1980; Sec.-Gen. JULIO CELSO DE LEÓN; 23,735 mems.

Unidad de Acción Sindical y Popular (UASP): f. 1988; broad coalition of leading labour and peasant organizations; includes:

Comité de la Unidad Campesina (CUC) (Committee of Peasants' Unity).

Confederación de Unidad Sindical de Trabajadores de Guatemala (CUSG): 5a Calle 4-33, Zona 1, Guatemala City; tel. 22-6515; f. 1983; Sec.-Gen. FRANCISCO ALFARO MIJANGOS.

Federación Nacional de Sindicatos de Trabajadores del Estado de Guatemala (Fenasteg): Sec. ARMANDO SÁNCHEZ.

Sindicato de Trabajadores de la Educación Guatemaltecos (STEG).

Sindicato de Trabajadores de la Industria de la Electricidad (STINDE).

Sindicato de Trabajadores del Instituto Guatemalteco de Seguro Social (STIGSS).

Unidad Sindical de Trabajadores de Guatemala (UNSITRAGUA).

Transport

RAILWAYS

In 1998 there were 1,390 km of railway track in Guatemala, of which some 102 km were plantation lines.

Ferrocarriles de Guatemala—FEGUA: 9a Avda 18-03, Zona 1, Guatemala City; tel. 232-7720; fax 238-3039; e-mail feguarivera @hotmail.com; f. 1968; 50-year concession to rehabilitate and operate railway awarded in 1997 to the US Railroad Devt Corpn;

782 km from Puerto Barrios and Santo Tomás de Castilla on the Atlantic coast to Tecún Umán on the Mexican border, via Zacapa, Guatemala City and Santa María. Branch lines: Santa María–San José; Las Cruces–Champerico. From Zacapa another line branches southward to Anguiatú, on the border with El Salvador; owns the ports of Barrios (Atlantic) and San José (Pacific); first 65-km section, Guatemala City—El Chile, and a further 300-km section, extending to Barrios, reopened in 1999; Administrator RENÉ MINERA PÉREZ.

ROADS

In 1999 there were an estimated 14,021 km of roads, of which 3,081 km were paved. The Guatemalan section of the Pan-American highway is 518.7 km long and totally asphalted. In 1997 the privately-owned Palín–Escuintla toll road opened.

SHIPPING

Guatemala's major ports are Puerto Barrios and Santo Tomás de Castilla, on the Gulf of Mexico, San José and Champerico on the Pacific Ocean, and Puerto Quetzal, which was redeveloped in the late 1990s.

Armadora Marítima Guatemalteca, SA: 14a Calle 8-14, Zona 1, Apdo 1008, Guatemala City; tel. 230-4686; fax 253-7464; cargo services; Pres. and Gen. Man. L. R. CORONADO CONDE.

Empresa Portuaria 'Quetzal': Edif. Torre Azul, 1°, 4a Calle 7-53, Zona 9, Guatemala City; tel. 334-7101; fax 334-8172; e-mail pquetzal@terra.com.gt; internet www.puerto-quetzal.gob.gt; port and shipping co; Man. LEONEL MONTEJO.

Empresa Portuaria Nacional Santo Tomás de Castilla: Edif. Mini, 6a Avda 1-27, Zone 4, Guatemala City; tel. 232-3685; fax 232-6894; Man. ENRIQUE SALAZAR.

Flota Mercante Gran Centroamericana, SA: Edif. Canella, 5°, 1a Calle 7-21, Zona 9, Guatemala City; tel. 231-6666. 1959; services from Europe (in association with WITASS), Gulf of Mexico, US Atlantic and East Coast Central American ports; Pres. R. S. RAMÍREZ; Gen. Man. J. E. A. MORALES.

Líneas Marítimas de Guatemala, SA: Edif. Plaza Marítima, 8°, 6a Avda 20-25, Zona 10, Guatemala City; tel. 237-0166; cargo services; Pres. J. R. MATHEAU ESCOBAR; Gen. Man. F. HERRERÍAS.

Several foreign lines link Guatemala with Europe, the Far East and North America.

CIVIL AVIATION

There are two international airports, 'La Aurora' in Guatemala City and at Santa Elena Petén.

Aerolíneas de Guatemala—AVIATECA: Avda Hincapié 12-22, Aeropuerto 'La Aurora', Zona 13, Guatemala City; tel. 231-8261; fax 231-7412; internet www.flylatinamerica.com; f. 1945; internal services and external services to the USA, Mexico, and within Central America; transferred to private ownership in 1989; Pres. Ing. JULIO OBOLS GOMES; Gen. Man. ENRIQUE BELTRONERA.

Aeroquetzal: Avda Hincapié y 18a Calle, Lado Sur, Aeropuerto 'La Aurora', Zona 13, Guatemala City; tel. 231-8282; fax 232-1491; scheduled domestic passenger and cargo services, and external services to Mexico.

Aerovías: Avda Hincapié 4 y 18a Calle, Aeropuerta 'La Aurora', Zona 13, Guatemala City; tel. 232-5686; fax 234-7470; operates scheduled and charter cargo services; Pres. FERNANDO ALFONSO CASTILLO R.; Vice-Pres. NELSON C. PUENTE.

Aviones Comerciales de Guatemala (Avcom): Avda Hincapié, Aeropuerto 'La Aurora', Zona 13, Guatemala City; tel. 231-5821; fax 232-4946; domestic charter passenger services.

Tourism

As a result of violence in the country, the annual total of tourist arrivals declined from 504,000 in 1979, when tourist receipts were US $201m., to 192,000 in 1984 (receipts $56.6m.). After 1985, however, the number of arrivals recovered and were recorded as some 853,072 in 2000, when receipts were an estimated $751m.

Instituto Guatemalteco de Turismo (INGUAT) (Guatemala Tourist Commission): Centro Cívico, 7a Avda 1-17, Zona 4, Guatemala City; tel. 331-1333; fax 331-8893; e-mail inguat@guate.net; internet www.guatemala.travel.com.gt; f. 1967; policy and planning council: 11 mems representing the public and private sectors; Pres. ALEJANDRO BOTRÁN; Dir MARIANO BELTRANENA FALLA.

Asociación Guatemalteca de Agentes de Viajes (AGAV) (Guatemalan Association of Travel Agents): 6a Avda 8-41, Zona 9, Apdo 2735, Guatemala City; tel. 231-0320; Pres. MARÍA DEL CARMEN FERNÁNDEZ O.

Defence

At August 2000 Guatemala's active Armed Forces numbered an estimated 31,400: Army 29,200 (including an estimated 23,000 conscripts), Navy 1,500 (estimate, including 650 marines) and Air Force 700. There were paramilitary forces numbering 19,000. Military service is by conscription for up to 30 months.

Under the terms of a 1996 accord concluded between the Government and the opposition guerrilla forces, the Armed Forces were reduced in number by one-third during 1997. This included the disbanding of the Policía Ambulante Militar (Mobile Military Police), which was completed in late 1997. The accord also provided for the abolition of the Patrullas de Autodefensa Civil (PAC—Civil Self-Defence Patrols), an anti-guerrilla peasant militia, estimated to number some 202,000. The demobilization of the PAC was officially completed in December 1996.

Defence Expenditure: budgeted at 950m. quetzales (US $123m.) in 2000.

Chief of Staff of the Armed Forces: Gen. RUDY POZUELOS ALEGRÍA.

Education

Elementary education in Guatemala is free and, in urban areas, compulsory between seven and 14 years of age. Primary education begins at the age of seven and lasts for six years. Secondary education, beginning at 13 years of age, lasts for up to six years, comprising two cycles of three years each. In 1999 there were 9,607 pre-primary schools, 17,905 primary schools and 3,118 secondary schools. In 1997 73.8% of children aged seven to 13 years (males 77.4%; females 70.2%) attended primary schools. In the same year secondary enrolment was equivalent to 34.9% of those aged 13 to 19 (males 38.1%; females 31.7%). There are five universities. In 1998, according to estimates by the UN Development Programme, the average rate of illiteracy was 32.7% (males 25.1%; females 40.3%). According to preliminary figures, in 1997 budgetary expenditure on education was 1,670.5m. quetzales (15.3% of total spending).

Bibliography

For works on Central America generally, see Select Bibliography (Books).

Calvert, P. *Guatemala: A Nation in Turmoil*. Boulder, CO, Westview Press, 1985.

Guatemalan Insurgency and American Security. London, Institute for the Study of Conflict, 1984.

Chea, J. L. *La Cruz Fragmentada: La Iglesia y el Cambio Social en Guatemala*. Austin, TX, Central America Resource Center, 1988.

Dosal, P. J. *Doing Business with the Dictators: A Political History of United Fruits in Guatemala, 1899–1944*. Wilmington, DE, Scholarly Resources, 1993.

Gleijeses, P. 'The Agrarian Reform of Jacobo Arbenz [and American Reactions]', in *Journal of American Studies*, Vol. 21 (Oct.). 1989.

Grandin, G. *The Blood of Guatemala: A History of Race and Nation*. Durham, NC, Duke University Press, 2000.

Handy, J. 'Resurgent Democracy and the Guatemalan Military', in *Journal of Latin American Studies*, Vol. 18, 2 (Nov.). 1986.

Immerman, R. H. *CIA in Guatemala: The Foreign Policy of Intervention*. Austin, TX, University of Texas Press, 1982.

Manz, B. *Refugees of a Hidden War: The Aftermath of Counterinsurgency in Guatemala*. Albany, NY, State University of New York Press, 1988.

McCleary, R. M. *Dictating Democracy: Guatemala and the End of Violent Revolution*. Gainesville, FL, University Press of Florida, 1999.

McCreery, D. *Rural Guatemala 1760–1940*. Stanford, CA, Stanford University Press, 1994.

Menchú, R.. *Crossing Borders*, (translated and edited by A. Wright). Lewiston, NY, Mellen University Press, 1998.

Montejo, V. *Voices From Exile: Violence and Survival in Modern Maya History*. Norman, OK, University of Oklahoma Press, 1999.

Painter, J. *Guatemala: False Hope, False Freedom: The Rich, the Poor, and the Christian Democrats*. London, Latin America Bureau, 1987.

Shea, M. E. *Culture and Customs of Guatemala*. Westport, CT, Greenwood Publishing Group, 2000.

Sieder, R (Ed.). *Guatemala after the Peace Accords*. London, Institute of Latin American Studies, 1999.

Trudeau, R. H. *Guatemalan Politics: The Popular Struggle for Democracy*. Boulder, CO, Lynne Rienner, 1993.

Wearne, P. *The Maya of Guatemala*. London, Minority Rights Group, 1989.

GUYANA

Area: 214,969 sq km (83,000 sq miles).

Population (official estimate for mid-1999): 782,000.

Capital: Georgetown, estimated population 72,049 (metropolitan area 187,056) at mid-1976.

Language: English (official); Hindi, Urdu and Amerindian languages are also spoken.

Religion: The principal religions are Christianity, Hinduism and Islam.

Climate: Tropical, but moderated on the coast by sea breezes; average annual rainfall varies from 1,520 mm inland to 2,500 mm on the coast.

Time: GMT –3 hours.

Public Holidays

2002: 1 January (New Year's Day), 23 February (Mashramani, Republic Day), 23 February* (Id al-Adha, feast of the Sacrifice), 29 March (Good Friday), 1 April (Easter Monday), 1 May (Labour Day), 24 May* (Yum an-Nabi, birth of the Prophet), 5 May (Indian Heritage Day), 1 July (Caribbean Day), 1 July (Caricom Day), 5 August (Freedom Day), 25–26 December (Christmas), 6 December* (Id al-Fitr, end of Ramadan).

2003: 1 January (New Year's Day), 23 February (Mashramani, Republic Day), 12 February* (Id al-Adha, feast of the Sacrifice), 18 April (Good Friday), 21 April (Easter Monday), 1 May (Labour Day), 5 May (Indian Heritage Day), 14 May* (Yum an-Nabi, birth of the Prophet), 7 July (Caribbean Day), 1 July (Caricom Day), 4 August (Freedom Day), 26 November* (Id al-Fitr, end of Ramadan), 25–26 December (Christmas).

In addition, the Hindu festivals of Holi Phagwah (usually in March) and Divali (October or November) are celebrated. These festivals are dependent on sightings of the moon and their precise date is not known until two months before they take place.

* These holidays are dependent on the Islamic calendar and may vary by one or two days from the dates given.

Currency: Guyana dollar ($ G); 1,000 Guyana dollars = £3.766 = US $5.369 = €6.079 (30 March 2001).

Weights and Measures: The metric system is in force.

Basic Economic Indicators

	1997	1998	1999
Gross domestic product (million Guyana dollars at 1988 prices)	5,360	5,269	5,426
GDP (million Guyana dollars at current prices)	106,678	108,002	120,668
Annual growth of real GDP (%)	6.2	–1.7	3.0
Government budget (million Guyana dollars at current prices):			
Revenue	36,006	33,028	36,584
Expenditure	45,682	41,833	n.a.
Consumer price index (base: 1995 = 100)*	110.9	116.0	124.7
Rate of inflation (annual average, %) †	3.6	4.6	7.5
Foreign exchange reserves (US $ million at 31 December)	315.3	276.4	267.0
Imports c.i.f. (US $ million)	630	n.a.	n.a.
Exports f.o.b. (US $ million)	644	484	523
Balance of payments (current account, US $ million)	–91.1	–98.5	–75.2

* 132.4 in 2000.
† 6.1% in 2000.

Gross national product per head measured at purchasing power parity (PPP) (GNP converted to US dollars by the PPP exchange rate, 1999): 2,774.

Gross domestic product per head (US dollars at current prices, 1999): 760.

Total labour force (sample survey, June 1987): 270,074.

Unemployment (estimate, 1992): 11.7%.

Total foreign debt (1999): US $1,688m.

Life expectancy (years at birth, 2000): 64.1 (males 61.1; females 67.2).

Infant mortality rate (per 1,000 live births, UN estimate, 1990–95): 63.

Adult population with HIV/AIDS (15–49 years, 1999): 3.01%.

School enrolment ratio (6–16 years, 1996): 86%.

Adult literacy rate (15 years and over, 2000): 98.5% (males 99%; females 98.1%).

Energy consumption per head (kg of coal equivalent, 1998): 271.

Carbon dioxide emissions (per head, metric tons, 1996): 1.2.

Passenger motor cars in use (1993): 24,000.

Television receivers in use (per 1,000 of population, 1997): 55.

Personal computers in use (per 1,000 of population, 1999): 24.6.

History

JAMES McDONOUGH

The Dutch were the first European power to establish a presence in what is now Guyana. In 1616 they founded a settlement at Kyk-Over-Al, an island in the Essequibo river (the country's largest), where the remnants of a fort remain. A second colony was founded in 1627 at the mouth of the Berbice River located east of the Essequibo. Subsequently, a third colony, at the mouth of the Demerara River was also settled by the Dutch in 1741. These three coastal communities were later joined to form Dutch Guiana. The Dutch West India Company, which controlled the colony, introduced slavery in the 17th century for the cultivation of tobacco and, later, sugar. During the 18th and 19th centuries, the colonies were controlled variously by the British, Dutch and French. They came permanently under British jurisdiction in 1814 and became known as British Guiana. Following the abolition of slavery in 1834, the British introduced Portuguese and Chinese workers into the colony to ensure a continued supply of cheap labour.

In around 1680 the Dutch West India Company promulgated what is thought to have been the country's first Constitution. Under the document, the Commander of the Essequibo colony was given complete administrative authority over the land, but in the application of justice he was to be assisted by a Council consisting of the Sergeant of the Garrison and the captains of the ships that were then in port. Later, in 1732, the Berbice region also established a Constitution, which formed the basis of government for the colony for the next 200 years. The Berbice Constitution instituted a Governor, a Council of Government and two Councils of Justice. Members of the Council of Government were selected by the Governor from a list provided by the colonial planters. Together, the Governor and Council comprised the Council of Criminal Justice. A second group, more representative of planter interests, but chaired by the Governor, made up the Council of Civil Justice. The Constitution's recall provision allowed the planters to bring charges against the Governor and his administration, and petition his removal. This provision gave the colonial planter class a curb over the colony's executive authority. Persistent overspending by the colonial Government and a dramatic decrease in sugar prices after the First World War prompted the British, in 1928, to establish the Legislative Council, a majority of whose members were appointed by the British Colonial Office. Elected members of the Legislative Council were not to form a majority until after the extensions of the local voting franchise, which occurred in 1943 and again in 1945.

THE BIRTH OF ETHNIC POLITICS

The post-Second World War period was dominated by two personalities: Dr Cheddi Bharat Jagan, a US-trained dentist and the son of an 'East' Indian sugar plantation foreman; and Forbes Burnham, a London-trained barrister from a black lower middle-class Georgetown family. Together they worked to establish the People's Progressive Party (PPP) in 1950, the country's first mass-based political party. Jagan became the party's Leader and Burnham its Chairman. As a result of the elections of 1953, the first held under universal adult suffrage, the left-wing PPP received 51% of the popular vote and won 18 of the 24 seats in the colonial legislature. The PPP took power under a mandate for radical change and a pledge to end British colonial rule. Its pro-Marxist ideology not only brought it into direct conflict with British colonial authorities, but also aroused the concern of the USA, then undergoing a national anti-Communist purge. In October 1953, only six months after the election, the British colonial Governor, at the behest of the British Government, suspended the Constitution, claiming that the country was under threat of Communist subversion, and promptly removed Jagan and his colleagues from political office.

Personal rivalry, racial divisions and political differences between Jagan and Burnham prompted the latter to break away and form the People's National Congress (PNC) in 1957. Burnham took with him the allegiance of the country's Afro-Guyanese population, while Jagan retained the loyalty of the larger, 'East' Indian population. A revised Constitution was adopted in 1956, and another Constitution, providing for internal self-government, was introduced in 1961. Jagan and the PPP again won the elections held in 1957 and 1961. However, serious riots over budget proposals in 1962, a long general strike over labour legislation in 1963 and an explosion of racial violence during the sugar workers' strike of 1964, in which 176 workers died, led to a weakening of the PPP's electoral support. Jagan alleged that much of the social agitation was secretly organized and financed by the USA. Just prior to the 1964 elections, the United Kingdom imposed new electoral rules favouring Burnham's party. The PNC won enough seats to form a majority coalition and elect Burnham Prime Minister. Two years later, on 26 May 1966, the United Kingdom granted Guyana its independence.

BURNHAM'S RULE OF INDEPENDENT GUYANA

Once in power, Burnham adopted economic policies based on attracting foreign capital. To gain US favour, he severed the trade relations with Cuba, which had been strongly promoted under PPP rule. Elections in December 1968 enabled the PNC to gain a clear majority in the National Assembly. The voting was, however, tainted by opposition allegations of electoral fraud on a massive scale. In January 1969 a brief revolt by ranchers in the Rupununi region was suppressed by force. The incident emphasized Venezuela's claim to the Essequibo district, for the ranchers had received support from some Venezuelans. The revolt and threat of foreign intervention, enabled Burnham to broaden his support. However, as his original pro-capital, economic plans began to falter, Burnham became increasingly left wing and authoritarian. In February 1970 Guyana was proclaimed a Co-operative Republic, whereby the co-operative sector was to become the dominant element of the economy. Burnham, however, in spite of the rhetoric, never made any serious attempt to develop a co-operative-based economy, but instead moved to nationalize the local subsidiaries of multinational corporations. In 1974, in what is known as the Declaration of Sophia, Burnham committed his party to a stronger socialist line; two years later, he declared the PNC would create a Marxist–Leninist state.

In 1980 Guyana adopted a new Constitution, which provided for a strong executive presidency. In the December elections the PNC won 41 out of 53 seats in the National Assembly and elected Burnham to the newly created position of President. International observers, however, denounced the elections as fraudulent and Christian churches and human-rights groups began to mobilize against Burnham, who by this time had established a near totalitarian regime. In August 1985 Burnham died, and was succeeded as President by Hugh Desmond Hoyte, hitherto First Vice-President and Prime Minister.

THE HOYTE PRESIDENCY, 1985–92

Hoyte led the PNC to a decisive victory in the general election in December 1985, when his party won 42 of 53 elective seats in the National Assembly and received 79% of the total votes cast. As a result, President Hoyte not only strengthened his own position, but was able to initiate an economic programme reversing Burnham's socialist policies. President Hoyte found Guyana excluded from foreign monetary sources, because the country was in serious arrears on the repayment of its loans from the International Monetary Fund (IMF), the World Bank (International Bank for Reconstruction and Development— IBRD) and the Caribbean Development Bank. In 1987 President Hoyte adopted the Economic Recovery Programme (ERP), the result of negotiations with the IMF, which envisaged greater participation of private enterprise in the economy, incentives to attract foreign investment, reduction of government spending and a willingness to privatize public corporations. In 1991, after three years of decline, the country registered a 4.5% increase in gross national product (GNP).

With presidential elections scheduled for 1990, various Guyanese groups and leaders formed the Guyanese Action for Reform and Democracy (GUARD) to urge the Government to ensure that free and fair elections were held. In response, following mediation by the former US President, Jimmy Carter, the Government agreed to postpone the elections, in order to update the nation's electoral records. The Government and opposition parties also agreed to invite observers from the Carter Center of Atlanta, Georgia (USA), and from the Commonwealth to monitor the elections. In May 1991 a survey of the entire country was undertaken, to produce a new electoral register. Meanwhile, the National Assembly moved to sanction the political agreements between President Hoyte and the opposition parties through an amendment to the country's Constitution. The PPP, which had withdrawn from the National Assembly in September 1991, returned to participate in the debate and vote on the constitutional proposals. The party subsequently remained in the National Assembly, but limited its participation to purely electoral matters. The amendment guaranteed the electoral rights of all the parties, but also extended Parliament's term until the end of September 1992.

THE CHEDDI JAGAN PRESIDENCY, 1992–97

The 1992 elections, held on 5 October, were won by the PPP in coalition with CIVIC, a movement consisting principally of members of the business and professional community, thus ending the long authoritarian reign of the PNC. The Carter Center and the Commonwealth Secretariat declared that the elections were essentially free and fair, although marred by riots in Georgetown. Three demonstrators were killed by police, and another 200 arrested. After spending 28 years in political opposition, PPP leader Jagan was named President on 9 October 1992. He subsequently appointed the CIVIC leader, Samuel Hinds, as Prime Minister. The PPP/CIVIC coalition secured 28 of the national elective seats in the National Assembly (and 53.5% of the votes cast), compared to 23 seats for the PNC (42.3%). After conducting negotiations with independent legislators, the governing coalition eventually came to control 36 of the 65 seats in the National Assembly.

After his victory President Jagan attempted to rewrite the Constitution in concert with all the country's political parties. In 1995 the four political parties in the National Assembly—the PPP, the PNC, The United Force (TUF) and the Working People's Alliance (WPA)—agreed to a 1991 recommendation of the Carter Center, whereby the Chairman of the Elections Commission was to be selected from a list of nominees proposed by the opposition parties. The parties also agreed to expand the Commission to include three representatives of the ruling party and three from the opposition parties. Subsequently, PPP/CIVIC rejected the only candidate proposed by the opposition parties. This led to an electoral impasse and destroyed any possibility of electoral reform before the 1997 elections.

President Jagan expounded his economic agenda in the 1992–94 Policy Framework Paper, which expressed the new Government's strong commitment to the fundamental principles of the ERP. At the same time, the paper stressed the need for the development of the nation's human resources and efforts to reduce poverty. Guyana's GNP per head of US $530 in 1994 was one of the lowest in the Western hemisphere. Jagan also announced his commitment to ending racial discrimination in Guyana and to implementing programmes for the development of the country's Amerindian, or indigenous, community. To this effect, he established a Race Relations Board, but this effort faltered when he failed to consult with the PNC.

The 1992 election results had devastating consequences for the PNC. Immediately following the elections, public disagreement erupted between Hoyte and Hamilton Green, his former Prime Minister. Green was expelled from the party after a PNC disciplinary committee found him guilty of misconduct. He retaliated by founding a new political group called the Forum for Democracy (subsequently renamed Good and Green Guyana). The Forum contested seats in the municipal elections,

which were eventually held in August 1994, and Green was elected as mayor of Georgetown.

THE JANET JAGAN PRESIDENCY, 1997–99

In March 1997 Cheddi Jagan died at the age of 78, after suffering a heart attack. Some 100,000 Guyanese attended his funeral in tribute to the man who had dominated much of the country's political life for 50 years. Prime Minister Hinds was named President to complete Jagan's term. In September the PPP/CIVIC selected Janet Jagan, Cheddi Jagan's US-born wife and the Prime Minister, as its presidential candidate in the elections, scheduled to be held on 15 December. The other parties contesting the election were the PNC, led by former President Hoyte, the TUF, now led by Green, the Alliance for Guyana (AFG) and the Guyana Democratic Party (GDP). The elections were monitored by international observers from the Organization of American States (OAS), the Commonwealth and the International Foundation for Election Systems, a US-based non-governmental organization. The PPP/CIVIC won 55.26% of the votes cast, compared to 40.55% for the PNC, 1.48% for the TUF and 1.19% for the AFG. As a result, PPP/CIVIC secured 29 of the 53 elective seats in the National Assembly and the PNC won 22, with one each being obtained by the TUF and the AFG. The GDP obtained no national seats. With the results of the district elections, the PPP/CIVIC won a clear majority in the National Assembly and on 19 December, after counting some 90% of the votes, the Elections Commission declared Janet Jagan the President. Hoyte immediately challenged the Commission, claiming that the elections were fraudulent. Racial slurs were aimed at the new white President and the traditional racial divisions within the country again came to the fore. The PNC refused to take their seats in the National Assembly, and Hoyte called for massive demonstrations in Georgetown to protest against the election results, which quickly escalated into rioting and looting. With unrest increasing, the Government and the PNC agreed to take part in negotiations, under the auspices of the Caribbean Community and Common Market (CARICOM). In mid-January 1998 the two sides signed the Herdmanston Accord, whereby they agreed to allow CARICOM to conduct an independent audit of the election results, and to form a commission to draft revisions to the Constitution within 18 months. New elections were to be held within three years, cutting the normal presidential term by two years. At the same time, Hoyte agreed to curtail any further demonstrations. The elections were subsequently scheduled for 17 January 2001. In early June 1998 the CARICOM audit declared the election results fair, but public violence continued to escalate.

In July 1998, at its annual summit in Saint Lucia, CARICOM again mediated between the PPP and the PNC. The two parties signed the Saint Lucia Statement, in which they agreed to adopt measures intended to improve race relations in Guyana, to renew discussions on constitutional reform and to reinstate full legislative participation. Legislation designed to allow the PNC deputies to recover their seats in the legislature was formulated by both sides, and the PNC (except Hoyte, who continued to deny the legitimacy of Jagan's authority) rejoined the National Assembly on 14 July. In January 1999 a 20-member Constitutional Reform Commission was created, comprising members of the principal political parties and community groups. The Commission's task was to formulate recommendations for constitutional reform by mid-July 1999. In 2000 the two parties agreed to change the title of the parliamentary minority leader to Leader of the Opposition, decided on a process for appointing the head of the Election Commission, and agreed to a constitutional change limiting the power of the presidency. The PPP, using its parliamentary majority, approved a smaller regional representation in the parliament than that advocated by the PNC.

THE BHARRAT JAGDEO PRESIDENCY, 1999–

Despite Hoyte's promises to call for an end to the unrest, demonstrations and public violence continued in 1999. The level of discontent amongst supporters of the PNC was underlined at the end of April when public-service employees, demanding higher salaries, organized a strike lasting eight weeks. The Government accused the PNC of instigating the action, while the opposition criticized the Government for the harsh behaviour of the police in dealing with demonstrators. In August, following a mild heart attack, Janet Jagan resigned as President. Prime Minister Bharrat Jagdeo was immediately sworn into office to replace her. As President, Jagdeo committed his administration to public-service reform, the continued privatization of public enterprises, improved land surveys and major infrastructure projects such as the Berbice bridge, a deep-water port, and the Guyana–Brazil highway.

In June 2000 the Elections Commission reached an agreement on electoral reform, to be implemented for the forthcoming general election, scheduled for 17 January 2001. In July 2000 the National Assembly approved legislation making the electoral reform task force a permanent institution (to be known as the Guyana Elections Commission—GECOM). In August legislation allowing for the creation of the Ethnic Relations Commission was passed (although it was not officially established until December). In October the legislature unanimously approved a constitutional amendment establishing a mixed system of proportional representation combining regional constituencies and national candidate lists, and the abolition of the Supreme Congress of the People of Guyana and the National Congress of Local Democratic Organs. However, in November the elections were postponed until 19 March 2001 in order to implement the reforms. This resulted in a dispute regarding the status of the Government in the interim. In January 2001 a high court judge, Claudette Singh, declared the December 1997 elections to be null and void, ruling that the legislature had acted illegally in making the possession of a voter identification card a prerequisite for voting, and further alleging that there had been instances of electoral fraud. However, she subsequently ruled that the Government should remain in office until March, but that only legislation necessary for the election should be passed. In December 2000 the National Assembly approved a constitutional amendment removing the President's immunity from prosecution and limiting his power to appoint only four ministers from outside the Assembly.

The general and regional elections of 19 March 2001 were preceded by demonstrations over the late distribution of voter identification cards (despite an earlier announcement that voters would be allowed to use other forms of identification). The PPP/CIVIC gained 53.0% of the votes cast, a clear majority, as opposed to 41.6% for the PNC (which contested the elections as the PNC/Reform). Of the 65 parliamentary seats, the PPP/CIVIC won 34, the PNC/Reform garnered 27, the Guyana Action Party, in alliance with the WPA, gained two seats, while Rise, Organize and Rebuild Guyana Movement and the TUF each secured one seat. The PNC/Reform contested the election in the nation's High Court, alleging numerous irregularities. The case was accompanied by protests, arson attacks and street violence across Guyana. The US-based Carter Center, which had observed the election, found the elections to be generally free and fair. On 31 March the High Court rejected the PNC challenge, ordered an immediate declaration of the official results, and the PPP/CIVIC leader, Jagdeo, was sworn in as President for a five-year term. At his inauguration, Jagdeo pledged to convene a National Conference to discuss ways of taking Guyana forward on a bipartisan basis. He committed his administration to working with the PNC as equals, and to incorporating the programmes of Guyana's various political parties into a National Development Strategy. He also promised to accelerate the process of constitutional reform and to expand the role of the legislative arm of Government in a attempt to reassure PNC supporters. In a relatively successful attempt to reduce the intensity of the continuing violence, on 25 April Jagdeo and Hoyte announced confidence-building measures and the establishment of joint committees to examine and report on critical issues. In May the Government announced the depolitization of the social service, with a new head of the service being created, separate from the Office of the President.

INTERNATIONAL RELATIONS

In the early years of independence, Guyana developed close links with Cuba and allied Guyana with the non-aligned nations. President Burnham took a strong position against the pro-apartheid Government in South Africa. However, after Ronald Reagan won the 1980 US presidential elections, Guyana began to modify its pro-Cuban stance in order to appease the new US

President. International attention was focused on Guyana when, in November 1978, about 900 followers of the US-based People's Temple cult committed mass suicide, following the murder in Guyana of US Congressman Leo Ryan. Ryan had travelled to Guyana to inspect the Temple's commune at the behest of some of his constituents.

Guyana's relations with its neighbouring South American states—Venezuela to the west and Suriname to the east—were, to a large extent, defined by bitter, long-running border disputes. In 1962 Venezuela declared the decision of the Paris Arbitral Tribunal null and void. The Tribunal, made up of two British and two US jurists and headed by a Russian, had established the border between the two countries to the apparent satisfaction of both Venezuela and the United Kingdom, which then controlled Guyana. In repudiating the Paris decision, Venezuela laid claim to all territory west of the Essequibo River, some 130,000 sq km, or almost two-thirds of modern-day Guyana. In 1966, just prior to granting Guyana independence, the United Kingdom and Venezuela signed the Geneva Agreement, which committed the two sides to establishing a joint commission to recommend a solution to the boundary dispute. In 1970, following a border incident, Guyana and Venezuela signed the Protocol of Port of Spain, in which the two countries agreed to reduce tensions along the border, and to work for a peaceful and negotiated resolution of the boundary dispute. In 1982 tension between the two countries again increased, when Venezuela refused to renew the Port of Spain agreement. In November 1989 President Hoyte and his Venezuelan counterpart, Carlos Andrés Pérez, agreed to accept a proposal from the UN to appoint the Vice-Chancellor of the University of the West Indies, Alister McIntyre, as a mediator in the territorial dispute. Nevertheless, although negotiations were ongoing throughout 2000 and 2001, neither side had reached agreement on a common border. In fact, tensions increased following Guyana's agreement with the US-based Beal Aerospace Corporation to build the world's first private satellite-launching facility in the disputed territory. However, following objections by Venezuela and financial difficulties, the company abandoned the project. Nevertheless, in January 2001 Venezuela announced an oil exploration project in the same disputed zone. Later in the year the Venezuelan Government allegedly refused to grant Guyana entry to the Caracas energy accord for special oil concessions, as it had other Caribbean nations, owing to the border dispute. However, Guyana was later invited to join the accord.

The border dispute with Suriname was equally unresolved. In question was a triangular piece of land, called the New River area, that protrudes from Guyana into Suriname, and the offshore areas between the two countries. The boundary with Suriname was never formally settled between the United Kingdom and the Netherlands; the present boundary between Guyana and Suriname was based on a draft treaty that was agreed to by the British and Dutch Governments in 1939. Under this treaty the boundary was established on the left bank of the Corentyne and Cutari Rivers. In 1962 the Netherlands proposed an alternative boundary, which followed the Thalweg River, instead of the left bank of the Corentyne, and the westerly New River, instead of the Cutari. The proposal was rejected by the United Kingdom. Compounding the problems of the New River area were misunderstandings over the two nations' economic development zone, which extended 200 nautical miles offshore. In 1998 Guyana granted the Canadian-based CGX Energy Incorporated a concession to explore for petroleum and gas along the continental shelf. Part of this area, the Corentyne block, lay within territory claimed by Suriname. In May 2000 the Government of Suriname formally protested that Guyana had violated its sovereignty and territorial integrity by granting the CGX concession. A second diplomatic note from Suriname later in the same month stated that the petroleum-exploration activity 'constituted an illegal act', and invited Guyana to begin negotiations 'in order to clarify any misunderstanding on the maritime boundary'. Guyana claimed that the exploration activities were being conducted in its own territory, but was willing to enter negotiations. In June gunboats from the Suriname navy forced CGX to remove the drill rig from the disputed area. Guyana demanded drilling by the Canadian company be allowed to resume. Both countries agreed to establish immediately a Joint Technical Committee to work towards a settlement of the dispute. A meeting was held in Port of Spain (Trinidad and Tobago), but both sides remained at an impasse. At the insistence of CARICOM, negotiations opened in Kingston (Jamaica) on 14 July 2001, facilitated by the Jamaican Prime Minister, Percival J. Patterson. However, on 18 July the talks ended without any agreement between the two countries. The company was unable to continue its test drilling to confirm its discovery of two potentially large oil fields in the disputed area. In July, with an agreement between the two countries unlikely, CGX left the area.

Relations with Brazil improved from the late 1980s. In 1989 President Hoyte signed an agreement with Guyana's neighbour to the south to start a road project, which was to provide the first land link between the two countries. Twelve years later, that road project was still not completed. However, in 2000 Brazil did indicate a willingness to pay for the pavement of the road and for the construction of a deep-water port along Guyana's coast. The Governor of the Brazilian state of Roraima agreed to finance a bridge over the Takutu river. Guyana, along with Brazil and six other states, was a signatory of the Treaty for Amazonian Co-operation.

In 1967 Antigua, Barbados and Guyana were the original signatories to the document that established the Caribbean Free Trade Area, which, in 1973, became CARICOM, a grouping primarily of British Commonwealth Caribbean countries. CARICOM, in July 1991, signed a trade co-operation agreement with the USA. Similar agreements were signed between the

USA and some Latin American countries as the first step towards the USA's long-term objective of a free-trade zone in the Western hemisphere. Nevertheless, the region, including Guyana, remained concerned that a Free Trade Area of the Americas (FTAA), to be established by 2005, would divert investment and trade away from the Caribbean. As a consequence, President Cheddi Jagan urged the developed states of North America to establish a Regional Development Fund (later renamed a Regional Integration Fund) to assist the integration of the smaller economies into the proposed FTAA. At the third Summit of the Americas, which was held in Québec City (Canada) in April 2001, President Jagdeo reiterated the need for a fund to assist Caribbean nations in the transition to free trade.

A reduction in Guyana's external debt was a major concern for President Janet Jagan. Her efforts to achieve this were rewarded in May 1999, when the IMF and the World Bank announced that Guyana had met the requirements to receive US $440m. of debt-relief under a joint Heavily Indebted Poor Countries (HIPC) initiative. The debt-relief programme was also supported by the Inter-American Development Bank. As Minister of Finance under Jagan, Jagdeo had been the principal negotiator for debt relief, and, following his inauguration as President, he continued the Government's efforts to obtain further reductions in the nation's foreign debt. In 2001 he was also leading negotiations for Guyana's entrance into the World Trade Organization.

Economy

JAMES McDONOUGH

The Co-operative Republic of Guyana is one of the poorest countries in the Western hemisphere, with a per-head income of US $761 in 1999. It is classified by the World Bank (International Bank for Reconstruction and Development—IBRD) as a heavily indebted low-income country, one of 35 such countries in the world. In 1999 its gross domestic product (GDP) was US $679m., while its external debt stood at approximately US $1,688m., more than two times its GDP. Overall poverty declined from 43% in 1993 to 35% in 1999. However, while the decline was significant, the overall rate was still high when compared to other countries in the region. Also, poverty in the rural interior actually increased from 79% in 1993, to 92% in 1999. The country's economy is dominated by agriculture and mining and its major exports are sugar, rice, bauxite, gold and wood. Guyana is approximately 214,969 sq km., making it slightly smaller than the US state of Idaho. The country is divided into four natural regions. Most of the country's economic activity, except for mining and forestry, and about 90% of its population—which totalled an estimated 782,000 in 1999—are concentrated on the country's narrow coastal plain. The capital, Georgetown, and its environs contain about 25% of the population. A hilly sand and clay region lies south of the coastal plain in the eastern part of the country, where most of the bauxite deposits are located. A forested and highland region comprises 65% of Guyana and includes areas covered by dense tropical rain forest and the Parkarima Mountains. This region, which lies in the east and south along the border with Venezuela, is inhabited chiefly by Amerindians, native Guyanese, who are engaged in subsistence agriculture. The fourth region is the savannah, which is divided into two areas, the intermediate savannah found between the coastal plain and the hilly sand and clay area, and the interior, or Rupununi Savannah, located in the south-west to the Brazilian border. Cattle ranching and farming are two of the main activities of the Rupununi Savannah.

Since acquiring independence in 1966, Guyana's economic history can be divided into two distinct phases: the so-called socialist period, under the presidency of Forbes Burnham, and the market economy pursued by the Governments of Hugh Desmond Hoyte (1985–92), Dr Cheddi Jagan (1992–97), Janet Jagan (1997–99) and Bharrat Jagdeo (1999–). The policies of the

socialist period led to economic disaster and a swiftly expanding external debt, while under the latter economic regime, the country experienced steady, if unspectacular, growth.

In 1970, only four years after independence, the Burnham administration adopted a socialist orientation and proceeded, over the next 10 years, to nationalize 80% of the country's economy, including its two major export sectors—bauxite and sugar. By the end of the decade the Government had taken over 32 companies and established 12 new companies under the Guyana State Corporation, a state-owned holding company. However, after 1975, world prices for Guyana's main exports (sugar, bauxite and rice) began to fall. The Government slipped increasingly into debt, and inflation increased rapidly, reaching over 400% by 1983. Throughout the 1980s, real GDP declined by approximately 6% per year. By 1989, 67% of Guyana's population was living in poverty. When President Burnham died in office in 1985 the Government was deeply in debt and in arrears with its international creditors; its capacity to borrow new funds exhausted.

Hoyte, the country's new President, immediately entered into negotiations with the International Monetary Fund (IMF) in order to resolve the country's debt crisis and to revive the economy. In 1987 President Hoyte adopted the Economic Recovery Programme (ERP), which reversed the co-operative, socialist policies of the Burnham administration. Under the ERP the Guyanese Government committed itself to major economic reform (see Investment and Finance below) and promised to initiate a major programme of privatization of public assets, to reduce government employment and to raise taxes. By the end of 1999 14 state enterprises had been privatized, including: the Guyana Telephones and Telegraph Company; Demerara Timber Ltd, the state lumber company; the Guyana Airways Corporation (GAC—later known as Guyana Airways 2000, which suspended operations in mid-2001); and the Guyana Electricity Corporation (now called Guyana Power and Light Incorporated), Still pending privatization were the Linden Mining Enterprises Ltd (Linmine) and the Berbice Mining Enterprises Ltd (Bermine), the Government's two bauxite mining companies. State-owned companies that the Government did not intend to sell included the Guyana Oil Company (GUYOIL), the Guyana National Co-operative Bank and the Guyana Sugar Corporation

(Guysuco). In 1990 the Government introduced the Social Impact Amelioration Programme (SIMAP) to soften the impact of the largely IMF-imposed austerity measures on the Guyanese population.

Successive administrations continued to implement the Hoyte ERP. Guyana's economy began to show positive growth; real GDP increased by an annual average of 5.7% in 1989–99. In 1998, following an economic decline in the latter half of the previous year, GDP contracted by 1.7%. This decline resulted from the financial crisis in Asia, the unfavourable weather conditions brought on by the El Niño weather phenomenon and almost two years of public protest against Janet Jagan's presidency. The GDP recovered in 1999, registering a 3.0% growth rate, and in 2000 was estimated to have increased by 3.9%. Economic growth of 2.8% was forecast for 2001. The annual rate of inflation, which had been reduced from over 100% in the late 1980s, dropped to 3.6% in 1997 and 4.6% in 1998. However, by 1999 it had increased to 7.5%, although it decreased again in 2000, to 6.1%. President Jagdeo proposed to reform and modernize the country's civil service, provide for accurate surveying of land, expand the country's transportation and telecommunications infrastructure, and work more closely with the private sector.

AGRICULTURE

The total land area of Guyana in 1996 (according to the UN Food and Agriculture Organization—FAO) was 19.7m. ha, of which some 500,000 ha were suitable for agriculture but only 140,000 ha were under cultivation. The country had a further 1.2m. ha of land under permanent pasture and an estimated 16.5m. ha of forests and woodlands, most of which was inaccessible. Sugar-cane plantations and rice paddies occupied most of the narrow coastal plain. Farming along the coast was dependent on a system of dikes, because coastal land for almost 8 km. (5 miles) inland was below sea-level at high tide. Much of this low coastal land had been reclaimed and converted, through the construction of dikes, into fertile estates (polders) by the Dutch West India Company during the colonial period. Successive Governments committed considerable resources to repairing and maintaining the dike system to ensure the continued viability of the country's agricultural sector. In 1999 agriculture, including forestry and fishing, provided an estimated 41.7% of GDP, dropping below 50% for the first time. The sector employed an estimated 18.7% of the country's total labour force in 1998.

Sugar

Sugar was the single largest contributor to Guyana's gross national product (GNP) in 1999. The state-owned Guysuco owned 90% of the land used for the cultivation of sugar cane (approximately 52,000 ha) and all of the country's cane-crushing facilities. The rest of the sugar was grown on land owned by private farmers. From 1990 Guysuco's holdings were managed by the British company, Booker Tate, the successor to Booker McConnell Ltd, whose Guyana sugar holdings were nationalized in the 1970s. Owing to initiatives taken by Booker Tate, sugar production increased steadily during 1990–99. Production reached 321,438 metric tons in 1999, the highest production levels since 1978, before dropping to 306,000 tons in 2000. The fall in production was attributable to an unexpectedly low yield, added to the rising cost of oil and fertilizers.

The sugar industry in Guyana is probably one of the least mechanized in the world. At harvest time, cane is burned to remove foliage, then cut and bundled by hand and carried by the labourers to canals where it is put onto punts for transportation to the mills. Guysuco experimented with mechanical harvesting equipment, but found it unsuitable for Guyana's clay soil. Fertilizer is applied by hand. At peak season, cane labourers would number about 24,000, or more than one-fifth of the country's labour force. More than 90% of the sugar produced in Guyana is for the export market. Of its sugar exports, approximately three-quarters went to the European Union (EU), particularly to the United Kingdom, and to the USA under quotas at rates considerably above world prices. The annual export quota to the EU was 165,000 metric tons per year. The US quota stood at 14,859 tons per year. In 1999 Guyana exported 256,000 tons of sugar, worth US \$136.2m.) some 27% of the value of total domestic exports). However, the increased production in

sugar exports (a 19% increase on the previous year) was offset by a steep reduction in the average price, from US \$554.8 per ton in 1998 to US \$483.5 per ton in 1999. The price reduction led to a modest 4% increase in receipts. In 2000 sugar exports totalled \$118.8m. (23.5% of total domestic export value).

Rice

During the early 1990s Guyana was the third most important exporter of rice to the EU, after Thailand and the USA. In 1999 the country produced approximately 365,469 metric tons of milled rice, of which some 290,000 tons was exported, mainly to the EU, which gives preferential tariff treatment to Guyanese rice. In addition, Guyanese long-grain and extra-long-grain rice are popular in Europe, especially in the Netherlands, where they are sold at a premium. Nevertheless, rice producers were concerned about the future, as the country's EU tariff advantage was scheduled to be phased out by 2000, following the implementation of the General Agreement on Tariffs and Trade (GATT, known as the World Trade Organization—WTO from 1 January 1995) 'Uruguay Round' tariff reductions. By 1997 rice tariffs in the EU had already been cut by 35% and Guyana's preferential quota had been reduced. As a result, Guyana was turning to Latin America for new markets for its rice. In 1997 the country negotiated new rice contracts with Colombia, El Salvador, Haiti, Nicaragua and Trinidad and Tobago.

The cultivation of rice in Guyana was dominated by 'East' Indian (Asian-descended) small-scale farmers, whose ancestors came to Guyana as indentured workers to replace slave labour. There were approximately 24,000 rice farmers in Guyana. Rice was milled in about 75 to 80 privately-owned rice mills of varying sizes, including many small mills that processed rice for the domestic market. There were between 25 to 30 mills that milled at least some rice for export. Of these, only six had a daily capacity in excess of 10 metric tons. The annual output of rice between 1960 and 1980 had averaged 256,000 tons. In 1980–89 rice production had fallen to an average annual output of 156,000 tons, hitting a low of 93,400 tons in 1990. Rice production in Guyana increased during the 1990s. In 1991 total production reached 150,000 tons; and by 2000 the yield was an estimated 600,000 tons. The value of the country's rice exports was US \$13m. in 1990, rising to US \$95m. in 1996 before declining. In 1999 rice accounted for 7.7% of GNP, with a total value of US \$71.1m. (14.1% of the total domestic export value), some 25% less than the 1990 figure. In 2000 the value of rice exports decreased to \$51.8m., or about 10% of total domestic export value. Rice production was expected to decline, in the early 2000s, owing to lower commodity prices, rising production costs and the depreciation of the euro in the case of preferential markets.

Forestry

Tropical rain forest covers about 161,000 sq km, approximately three-quarters of Guyana's land area, and is composed of hundreds of hardwood species. At the beginning of the 1990s only about 40% of the forest areas were accessible and only 10% were being exploited; a total of 3.7m. ha was allocated for commercial use by 10 large companies and 250 medium-sized and small operators, which were supplying the domestic market and some member states of the Caribbean Community and Common Market (CARICOM). During the 1990s the development of the wood-processing industry was targeted as a high priority. The Government's strategy was to privatize the industry and seek outside investment. One of the first initiatives was the sale by the Hoyte administration of the state-owned logging company to Demerara Timber Ltd, a company controlled by the British Beaverbrook group, for US \$16.5m. In 1991 Guyana attracted its first major direct investment in forestry, when Barama Co—whose major investors are Sunkyoung Ltd of the Republic of Korea (South Korea) and Samling Co of Malaysia—agreed to invest US \$154m. in the timber and plywood project. Barama was given a concession to log 1.6m. ha of state-owned land, the largest tract of land ever leased by the Government to a private company. Barama represented the first large-scale investment by a 'Pacific Rim' country in a CARICOM country. The Jagan Government in 1997 signed a memorandum of understanding with Berjaya of Malaysia for the exploitation of 303,520 ha of forest land. Berjaya planned to invest US $150m. in the project. In the same year the Government also signed a memorandum of understanding with Solid Timber of Sarawak, Malaysia, for the exploitation of 307,567 ha of forest land. Solid Timber planned to invest US $250m. in the venture. In 2000 the Jagdeo administration signed an agreement with the Chinese-owned Jilin Company Guyana, Incorporated for a forest concession in the north-west district, approximately 167,125 ha in size. Jilin proposed to invest £1m. over the next three years to carry out a forest inventory and to develop a management plan. Upon acceptance of its plan, Jilin would invest up to US $20m. in saw-milling and other projects. The agreement represented the first large investment made by the People's Republic of China in Guyana. In 1996 Guyana exported 34,000 cu m of forestry products at a value of US $10m. In 1998, however, output of forestry products declined by 24% compared with the previous year, owing mainly to the East Asian economic crisis, which reduced demand from export markets. In 1999 forestry output recovered to reach 467,000 cu m, or 6% more than the previous year. Wood and timber export earnings also improved in 1999 and 2000, reaching US $37.3m. and US $41.0m., respectively.

Fishing

Fishing expanded in the late 1980s, with an increase in the production of shrimp for export. In 1994 US and Japanese companies operating in Guyana produced 6,000 metric tons of shrimps. Total export value of shrimps in 1994 was approximately US $15m. Guyana Fisheries Ltd, owner of the national fishing fleet and shore-based processing facilities, was privatized in 1990, when a Georgetown-based company, Vieira Investment Ltd, acquired a 70% share and a Japanese company the remainder. The fishing industry received fresh impetus in 1997 when the Caribbean Star Seafood Processing Plant opened a US $100m. plant at Rosignol, which aimed to process 5,000 lb of fish per day for US, Canadian and Caribbean markets. In 1998 the fishing sector registered growth of 11%. However, in 1999 the industry showed a growth of only 1%. In the late 1990s the Government sought technical assistance to determine the fish biomass in its waters, in order to develop a sustainable fishing industry and to attract additional capital.

MINING AND ENERGY

Mining, consisting mainly of bauxite, gold and diamonds, contributed an estimated 13.6% of GDP in 1999, making it the third most important sector after agriculture and services. In 1999, however, the mining sector contracted for the second consecutive year, owing to lower world prices for both gold and bauxite. Nevertheless, in 2000 the sector grew, registering a 12% increase over the previous year. In terms of exports mining was even more important, with bauxite and gold alone accounting for some 38.2% of the value of Guyana's exports in 2000. The country was dependent on outside investment to develop its mining industry. Foreign investment was first attracted to Guyana in the 1990s to exploit its high-grade bauxite deposits for the making of aluminium. Later in the 1990s considerable foreign investment was directed into the mining of gold, marked by the opening, in 1994, of the Omai Gold Mine operation on the Omai River by a Canadian-led partnership. Subsequently, local funds began to invest in the industry; in 2000 Mazaruni Granite Products, Ltd announced that it would invest US $34m. in the modernization of granite production. The bauxite sector failed to expand during the 1990s, as world demand remained constant.

Bauxite

Guyana's extensive bauxite deposits occur in an arcuate, or bow-like, belt along the southern margin of the country's coastal plain. The Demerara Bauxite Company Ltd (Demba), a subsidiary of the Aluminium Company of Canada (ALCAN), started mining these bauxite deposits in 1916. The main mining centre was at Linden, 120 km (74 miles) south of Georgetown. An industrial complex was established in association with the mining operations, for the purification and drying of the mineral, with one factory producing calcium carbonate and alumina. The industry underwent a period of rapid expansion in the 1920s when foreign companies invested heavily in three operations: the Linden operation, which produced high-quality and high-

value calcined bauxite, representing 31% (in 1994) of the total tonnage, but 63% of total industry sales; and the Berbice and Aroima operations, which produced lower-value metallurgic bauxite. At the end of the 1960s Demba was producing 75% of all bauxite ore mined in Guyana, including all of the carbonated bauxite, and had a work-force of 4,500. Reynolds (Guyana) Mines, a subsidiary of the US Reynolds Metal Company, began mining bauxite around Kawakwani in the Berbice region after the Second World War, and was producing 25% of the total bauxite mined by 1975. Demba and Reynolds (Guyana) Mines were nationalized, with compensation, in 1971 and 1974, respectively. In 1977 the state-owned firms were combined to form the Guyana Mining Enterprise Ltd (Guymine). The lack of a major electricity supply continued to prevent the production in Guyana of aluminium.

In the late 1970s Guyana lost its market dominance when the People's Republic of China entered the high-value refractory bauxite market and gained a significant share through a substantial reduction in prices. By the early 1980s, after failing to adjust to market conditions and modernize its operations, Guymine started to experience serious financial problems. Management responded by increasing indebtedness and drastically reducing investment and long-term maintenance. Guymine's share of the world market for calcined bauxite fell from 75% in 1975 to about 30% by 1989. Matters continued to deteriorate in 1990, particularly with the entry of Brazil into the calcined-bauxite trade. By the late 1990s, however, the market situation had somewhat improved. In 1996 Guyana produced 2.48m. metric tons of dried metal-grade bauxite. In 1999 this figure fell to 2.22m. tons. Although the 1999 production figure represented an increase of 4.1% over that of 1998, Guyana suffered sharp declines in the higher valued calcined and chemical grade bauxite. In 1996 the country exported 2.1m. tons of bauxite at a value of US $86m. However, the production of the more expensive calcined bauxite steadily decreased throughout the 1990s, from a peak of 316,000 tons in 1990 to 163,253 tons in 1997. The decline was mainly owing to competition from Brazil and the People's Republic of China, and to shrinking markets in Europe and the USA. In 2000 bauxite exports were valued at US $71.8m.

In 1989 the Government relinquished some control of the bauxite industry, when it entered into a joint venture with Reynolds International for the development and exploitation of new bauxite deposits in Aroima, along the west bank of the Berbice River some 120 km south-east of Linden. The agreement called for the creation of the Aroima Bauxite Company, which began operations in mid-1991 and, by the end of that year, had produced 800,000 metric tons of bauxite. In 1992 the debt-ridden and state-owned Guymine was dissolved and divided into the Linden Mining Enterprise, Ltd (Linmine), with operations at East Montgomery along the east bank of the Demerara River south of Linden, and the Berbice Mining Enterprise, Ltd (Bermine), with operations along the east bank of the Berbice River. The management of Linmine passed into the hands of Minproc Engineers, Ltd, of Australia as part of the restructuring arrangement with the World Bank. Guymine was separated into smaller companies to promote greater efficiency and make it easier to privatize. In 1992–94 employment at Linmine was reduced from 3,000 workers to 2,300. However, by mid-2001 the Government had yet to identify a suitable buyer for either of the two operations. In 2000 a seven-year programme was initiated to develop and regenerate one of the principal bauxite mining towns, Linden, through the promotion of non-bauxite enterprises.

Gold and Diamond

In the country's other important mining sector, gold, output rose during the 1990s. Total production of gold reached 454,485 troy oz in 1998, marking a dramatic increase for the gold industry, which had recorded a level of production of 6,800 troy oz in 1983. In terms of exports, gold constituted 6% of the value of all exports in 1990. This figure increased significantly to 28.6% in 1994, because of the Omai Gold Mine, Ltd, which opened operations along the Omai River (a tributary of the Essequibo River) in 1993. Cambior of Montreal (Canada) owned 65% of Omai, Golden Star Resources of Denver, CO (USA) owned 35% and the Guyanese Government owned 5%. The three parties agreed to a 5% royalty on all production. The accidental release of cyanide into the Omai and Essequibo Rivers in 1995 resulted in the closure of the operation for six months, causing a major reduction in production and a negative impact on the country's GNP in that year. The Omai mine recovered in 1999 and overall gold production for Guyana in that year was 414,905 troy oz. In 2000 gold exports were valued at US $120.3m., falling from US $137m. in 1997, but still accounting for almost 24% of the total domestic export value. The Omai mine continued to perform well in this year, producing 330,000 troy oz of gold, an 8% increase on 1999. The Government gave Omai Gold Mine, Ltd licences for operations in Quartz Hill and a further area of the Omai River, which, it was hoped, would extend the life of the mine beyond its projected termination date of 2008. Total production of gold was expected to increase by 4.6% in 2001.

Production of diamonds, Guyana's other principal mineral resource, also increased in the 1990s, after suffering a decline in the previous decade, reaching a peak of 50,000 carats in 1993. Preliminary figures placed production at 46,700 carats in 1996. Diamond exports in 1991 totalled 18,000 carats. A small increase in diamond production was expected in 2001.

Energy

Guyana was dependent on petroleum as its main energy source and imported most of its feed stock from Trinidad and Tobago and Venezuela. Electricity was supplied and distributed by the Guyana Electric Company (GEC) for domestic use, public lighting and small industries, while the sugar factories and bauxite companies generated their own electricity. The country suffered a severe shortage of electrical generating capacity, leading to frequent shortages and failures of the power supply. From the late 1980s Guyana was able to attract the interest of the international lending institutions to help modernize the industry. The Inter-American Development Bank (IDB—based in New York, USA) agreed to provide US $33m. to the GEC to improve the company's generation, transmission and distribution capacity. By 1997 GEC had doubled its 1992 capacity to reach 90 MW. It was hoped that the sale of 15% of GEC in mid-1999 would enable further modernization. Nevertheless, energy problems persisted when the Linden Power Co, a subsidiary of the US-based Texas Ohio Energy Co, experienced production difficulties, causing power cuts in the area around Linden in May 2000. Meanwhile, in 2000 the Canadian-based CGX Energy Incorporated announced a find of two potentially giant oilfields off the coast of Guyana. However, the company was not able to continue test drilling in the area owing to an international boundary dispute between Guyana and Suriname (see History). Despite the border dispute, in early 2001 Venezuela granted Guyana, along with a number of other Caribbean nations, entry to the Caracas energy accord for special oil concessions.

MANUFACTURING

The Guyana Manufacturing and Industrial Development Agency, created in 1984 to promote industrial development, was replaced, in 1994, by the less bureaucratic, quasi-governmental entity, Guyana Office for Investment (Go-Invest), a 'one-stop' agency designed to promote investment. The Government also began implementing supportive tax-reform measures and constructing industrial parks to attract private investment. Outside the state sector, there were a number of local industries and co-operatives producing consumer goods, especially food and clothing. Manufacturing (including power) accounted for 3.6% of GDP in 1999. Processing of bauxite, sugar, rice, shrimps and timber were the most important industries. Rum production was another traditional export industry. In 1990 Guyana exported 8m. litres of rum for a total value of US $5m. Rum exports increased to 20m. litres and US $10m. in 1994. In 1998, however, the manufacturing sector declined by some 11%, owing to a reduction in the production of corrugated cartons, processed foods, stoves and refrigerators. Nevertheless, the sector recovered in 1999 showing a 13.2% increase, through a combination of aggressive marketing techniques, greater processing capacity and increased use of technology.

TRANSPORT INFRASTRUCTURE

Internal communications presented a major obstacle to the economic development of Guyana. In 1996 there were some 7,970 km (4,589 miles) of roads. Most were gravel and earth roads, which could be used in good weather. The remainder were paved, with the main roads running from Georgetown (north-westward to Charity and south-eastward to New Amsterdam). Much of the road network was confined to the coastal region. In 1989 President Hoyte signed an agreement with Brazil for the construction of the Lethem–Kurupukari road, providing the first land route connecting Georgetown with the Brazilian frontier. Construction of the road, however, was slow, owing to a lack of financial resources, and by 2001 the Guyanese portion of the road had only been partly completed. However, in 2000 Brazil did indicate a willingness to pay for the pavement of the road and for the construction of a deep-water port along Guyana's coast. Also, the Governor of the Brazilian state of Roraima agreed to finance a bridge over the Takutu river. While Guyana acknowledged that its infrastructure shortcomings were unlikely to be redressed in the short term, owing to a lack of funding, the country was nevertheless committed to the long-term rehabilitation of its roads, bridges, ferries, sea defences (ongoing), drainage and irrigation systems, and water and electricity supplies.

Air transportation forms the main link within Guyana. By 1998 there were about 94 airstrips, most of which were located in the interior and catered for light aircraft. An airstrip at Ogle, close to the centre of Georgetown, was used primarily for travel between the capital and the interior. The national carrier, the Guyana Airways Corporation (GAC—known as Guyana Airways 2000 from June 1999, following the sale of a 51% stake in the company to a consortium of local businesses) suspended operations in June 2001. This terminated an agreement signed in 1996, consolidating the air links between Guyana and Suriname.

Guyana is served mainly by the port of Georgetown, which is located at the mouth of the Demerara river. Another important port is that at Linden on the Demerara, which serves as a transit point for bauxite products from the Demerara region. The port facilities at Georgetown were constructed initially to handle the colony's large sugar exports. New Amsterdam's port was improved for the transhipment of bauxite ore, taken to the coast by river from Linden and Everton. President Jagdeo also committed his administration to building a deep-water port, although a site had yet to be selected by late 2000. A ferry service between Guyana and Suriname, across the Corentyne River, began operating in 1998. The Government was also committed to building a bridge across the Berbice River to link the west side with the town of New Amsterdam, currently accessible only by river ferry. The Dutch company, Ballast Nedam, was selected by the Government to construct the bridge, which was scheduled to be completed by 2002. In early 2000 the Government signed a 99-year agreement with Beal Guyana Services, LLC, a subsidiary of the US-based Beal Aerospace Corporation, to build the world's first private satellite-launching facility in the north-western region of the country. However, in October the project was terminated, with the company citing US government help for competing sites, and the reluctance of the USA to approve the transfer of aerospace technology to Guyana. Additionally, there was continued controversy between Venezuela and Guyana regarding the ownership of the western Essequibo region, where the space port was to be located.

INVESTMENT AND FINANCE

Guyana's real GDP growth amounted to an average of only 0.4% per year between independence in 1966 and 1989, the lowest in the Commonwealth Caribbean. During that period the Government borrowed excessively, reaching a point when it was unable to meet its debt-service obligations. In 1985 the IMF formally declared Guyana ineligible for further assistance. The World Bank and the Caribbean Development Bank did the same. By the end of 1988 the public sector had accumulated arrears of US $1,031m. on its external debt of US $1,760m. In 1985, faced with such a deteriorating financial position, the Government began seriously to consider an IMF recovery plan, based on a complete repudiation of its 'socialist' policies. After long negotiations with the IMF, the Hoyte administration in 1987 announced the IMF-imposed Economic Recovery Plan (ERP), approved by the National Assembly in the following year. The ERP demanded reductions in government spending, curbs on government intervention in the economy, the establishment of a 'floating' (free) exchange rate for the Guyanese dollar, promotion of foreign investment and the privatization of state enterprises.

The IMF adopted a monitoring plan in 1989, with the approval of an international support group from the 'Paris Club' of Western creditor nations. In June 1990 a settlement was finally reached, enabling Guyana to repay US $141m. to the IMF, US $55m. to the World Bank and US $30m. to the Caribbean Development Bank. In July Guyana received new loans of US $81m. from the World Bank and US $44m. from the Caribbean Development Bank, together with new structural-adjustment arrangements from the IMF worth US $111m. In April 1992 the World Bank expressed continued confidence in the Guyanese economy by authorizing another US $14m. Guyana received further debt relief in May 1993, when the Paris Club and Trinidad and Tobago rescheduled Guyana's debt for 1993–95 under what became known as the 'Enhanced Toronto Terms'. Furthermore, in April 1996 these parties agreed to cancel 67% of the country's short-term bilateral debt. Guyana's success at the Paris Club owed much to the support of Trinidad and Tobago. In March 1997 the Government won further debt relief from Denmark and the United Kingdom. These countries agreed to reduce Guyana's debt by almost US $130m. and to reschedule payments on the remaining debt over a 23-year period. In 1992, when Cheddi Jagan took power, Guyana's external debt stood at US $2,000m., but by the end of 1999 it had fallen to US $1,688m. In May 1999 the IMF and the World Bank granted Guyana US $440m. in debt reduction under the Heavily Indebted Poor Countries (HIPC) initiative. The total assistance provided to Guyana reduced the country's external debt burden by some 24%. It was estimated that this reduction would, ultimately, translate into debt-service relief of some 3% of GDP per year in 1999–2003 and some 2% per year in 2004–09. In return, Guyana was required to reduce the size of the civil service, to introduce slower wage increases for civil servants, and to make the collection of taxes more efficient through the establishment of an independent tax-collection agency (the Guyana Revenue Authority was established in January 2000). However, following a decision by an arbitration tribunal, which mediated a civil service labour action, the new Jagdeo administration granted public employees a 26.6% increase in wages, effective from January 2000. The decision provoked a negative reaction from the IMF. Nevertheless, the HIPC initiative did not reduce Guyana's ratio of net present value of external debt to central government revenues below the target of 280%. As a result, Guyana became eligible for additional debt relief under the enhanced HIPC initiative in November 2000. Upon successful completion of a series of pre-arranged conditions, Guyana would qualify for additional debt relief totalling US $590m. The principal condition under the enhanced HIPC initiative was the development of the Poverty Reduction Strategy Paper (PRSP), a blueprint for promoting economic growth and attacking poverty. Another condition was the signing of the Social Impact Amelioration Program Third Stage (SIMAP III) loan agreement with the IDB in 2001.

FOREIGN TRADE AND THE BALANCE OF PAYMENTS

Guyana's exports grew significantly during the early 1990s, increasing from US $293m. in 1991 to US $525m. in 1998, US $505m. in 1999 and US $503m. in 2000. Imports during the same period also rose, from US $244m. in 1991 to a high of US $628m. in 1997. This figure fell slightly, to some US $601m. in 1998 and to US $550m. in 1999. In 1998 the principal destinations for the country's exports were Canada (US $141m.), the United Kingdom (US $108m.), Trinidad and Tobago (US $14m.) and the Netherlands (US $13m.). The principal origins of its imports were the USA (US $160m.), Trinidad and Tobago (US $121m.), the United Kingdom (US $43m.), Cuba (US $17m.) and the Netherlands (US $12m.). Its main imports were intermediate goods, including fuel and lubricants, capital goods and consumer goods. Exports of sugar and rice increased significantly after 1990, along with gold and timber. Guyana's balance of payments improved during the early 1990s. However, the economic crisis in East Asia, bad weather brought on by the El Niño phenomenon, and continued public violence contributed to an increase in the deficit on the balance of payments in 1997 and again in 1998, when it reached US $86m. Prudent public management and a good harvest narrowed the balance of payments to US $25m. in 1999, but this increased in the following year to US $80m. Net private investment increased from US $16m. in 1990 to US $41m. in 1992, and US $24m. in 1994. The country's international reserves also improved, in 1997 registering US $310m., equivalent in value to five months of imports, a level considered to be more than adequate by international lenders. Total international reserves stood at US $277.3m. at the end of 1999. In the future, however, the World Bank and IMF believed export growth would have to come from more diversified sources. The principal objective of the Jagan Government's economic policy was to open the country to more international investment. This policy was continued by the Jagdeo administration.

CONCLUSION

Following the 1997 decision by the Paris Club, the IMF and World Bank to offer Guyana significant debt reduction, the outlook for the Guyanese economy was promising. The country had experienced positive growth for most of the 1990s, while at the same time reducing inflation and controlling spending. The country had implemented most of the structural reforms demanded by the IMF and World Bank, thus regaining the trust of its international creditors. Nevertheless, in 2000, despite two generous debt-reduction packages from the World Bank and the IMF, Guyana's economic progress was still impeded by a large external debt, which would necessitate continued austerity measures and prevent the country from modernizing at a faster pace. At the same time, it faced falling prices for its export commodities, especially gold, bauxite and sugar, and rising prices for imported commodities, such as petroleum and manufactured goods. Although growth of 2.8% was forecast for 2001 the Government still faced serious economic challenges in reducing the debt burden and relieving the extreme poverty in the country.

Statistical Survey

Source (unless otherwise stated): Bank of Guyana, 1 Church St and Ave of the Republic, POB 1003, Georgetown; tel. 226-3261; fax 227-2965; e-mail communications@bankofguyana.org.gy; internet www.bankofguyana.org.gy.

AREA AND POPULATION

Area: 214,969 sq km (83,000 sq miles).

Population: 758,619 (males 375,481, females 382,778) at census of 12 May 1980; 701,704 (males 344,928, females 356,776) at census of 12 May 1991; 782,000 in 1999 (official estimate).

Density (1999): 3.6 per sq km.

Ethnic Groups (official estimates, 1999): 'East' Indians 51%, Africans 41%, Portuguese and Chinese 2%, Amerindians 6%, Others less than 1%.

Regions (estimated population, 1986): Barima–Waini 18,500; Pomeroon–Supenaam 42,000; Essequibo Islands–West Demerara 102,800; Demerara–Mahaica 310,800; Mahaica–Berbice 55,600; East Berbice–Corentyne 149,000; Cuyuni–Mazaruni 17,900; Potaro–Siparuni 5,700; Upper Takutu–Upper Essequibo 15,300; Upper Demerara–Berbice 38,600.

Births and Deaths (official estimates): Birth rate 24.9 per 1,000 in 1995–2000, 17.9 per 1,000 in 2000; Crude death rate 7.4 per 1,000 in 1995–2000, 8.4 per 1,000 in 2000.

Expectation of Life (official estimates, years at birth, 2000): 64.1 (males 61.1; females 67.2).

Economically Active Population (persons between 15 and 65 years of age, 1980 census): Agriculture, forestry and fishing 48,603; Mining and quarrying 9,389; Manufacturing 27,939; Electricity, gas and water 2,772; Construction 6,574; Trade, restaurants and hotels 14,690; Transport, storage and communications 9,160; Financing, insurance, real estate and business services 2,878; Community, social and personal services 57,416; Activities not adequately defined 15,260; Total employed 194,681 (males 153,645; females 41,036); Unemployed 44,650 (males 26,439, females 18,211); Total labour force 239,331 (males 180,084, females 59,247). *Mid-1998* (estimates): Agriculture, etc. 68,000; Total labour force 364,000 (Source: FAO, *Production Yearbook*).

AGRICULTURE, ETC.

Principal Crops (FAO estimates, '000 metric tons, 2000): Rice (paddy) 600; Maize 3; Roots and tubers 42; Coconuts 56; Sugar cane 3,000; Pulses 2; Vegetables 7; Oranges 3; Bananas 12; Plantains 14. Source: FAO.

Livestock (FAO estimates, '000 head, year ending September 2000): Cattle 220; Pigs 20; Sheep 130; Goats 79; Chickens 12,500. Source: FAO.

Livestock Products (FAO estimates, '000 metric tons, 2000): Beef and veal 3; Mutton and lamb 1; Pig meat 1; Poultry meat 12; Cows' milk 13; Hen eggs 7. Source: FAO.

Forestry ('000 cubic metres, 1999): Roundwood removals: Sawlogs, veneer logs and logs for sleepers 435, Pulpwood 2, Other industrial wood 19, Fuel wood 11; Total 467; Sawnwood production: Total 25. Source: FAO, *Yearbook of Forest Products*.

Fishing ('000 metric tons, live weight, 1998): Capture 57.0 (Marine fishes 38.3, Atlantic seabob 17.2); Aquaculture 0.2 (FAO estimate); Total catch 57.2. Source: FAO, *Yearbook of Fishery Statistics*.

MINING

Production (preliminary figures, 1999): Bauxite 2,215,281 metric tons; Gold 414,905 troy oz.

INDUSTRY

Selected Products (preliminary figures, 1996): Raw sugar 257,000 metric tons; Rum 237,000 hectolitres; Beer 112,000 hectolitres; Cigarettes 400.2m.; Electric energy 328m. kWh. Sources: UN, *Industrial Commodity Statistics Yearbook*; IMF, *Guyana: Statistical Appendix* (February 1998).

FINANCE

Currency and Exchange Rates: 100 cents = 1 Guyana dollar ($ G). *Sterling, US Dollar and Euro Equivalents* (30 March 2001): £1 sterling = $ G265.50; US $1 = $ G186.25; €1 = $ G164.50; $ G1,000 = £3.766 = US $5.369 = €6.079. *Average Exchange Rate* ($ G per US $): 150.5 in 1998; 178.0 in 1999; 182.4 in 2000.

Budget (estimates, $ G million, 1999): *Revenue:* Tax revenue 33,647 (Income tax 13,618, Property tax 607, Consumption tax 12,297, Taxes on international trade 4,590, Other tax 2,535); Other current revenue 2,388; Total 36,033, excl. grants received (5,320). *Expendi-*

ture: Current expenditure 32,922 (Personnel emoluments 11,821, Other goods and services 6,215, Interest 9,455, Transfers 5,430); Capital expenditure 11,222; Total (incl. lending minus repayments) 44,144. Source: IMF, *Guyana: Statistical Annex* (January 2001).

International Reserves (US $ million at 31 December 1999): IMF special drawing rights 1.27, Foreign exchange 276.01; Total 277.28. Source: IMF, *International Financial Statistics*.

Money Supply ($ G million at 31 December 1999): Currency outside banks 13,394, Demand deposits at commercial banks 9,949; Total money (including also private-sector deposits at the Bank of Guyana) 23,350. Source: IMF, *International Financial Statistics*.

Cost of Living (Urban Consumer Price Index; base: 1995 = 100): 116.0 in 1998; 124.7 in 1999; 132.4 in 2000. Source: IMF, *International Financial Statistics*.

Expenditure on the Gross Domestic Product (estimates, $ G million at current prices, 1998): Government final consumption expenditure 19,114; Private final consumption expenditure 70,843; Gross fixed capital formation 31,144; *Total domestic expenditure* 121,101; Exports of goods and services 103,920; *Less* Imports of goods and services, 116,557; *GDP in purchasers' values* 108,465. Source: IMF, *Guyana: Recent Economic Developments* (June 1999).

Gross Domestic Product by Economic Activity (estimates, $ G million at current factor cost, 1999): Agriculture (incl. forestry and fishing) 42,536; Mining and quarrying 13,923; Manufacturing (incl. power) 3,681; Construction 4,771; Distribution 4,268; Transport and communication 7,138; Rented dwellings 3,848; Financial services 3,387; Other services 1,570; Government 16,976; GDP at factor cost 102,098; Indirect taxes, *less* subsidies 18,570; GDP at market prices 120,668.

Balance of Payments (US $ million, 2000): Exports of goods f.o.b. 505.2; Imports of goods c.i.f. −585.4; *Trade balance* −80.2; Exports of services (net) −33.9; *Balance on goods and services* −114.1; Other income received (net) −48.2; *Balance on goods, services and income* −162.3; Current transfers received (net) 45.0; *Current balance* −117.3; Capital transfer 10.0; Government long-term capital (net) 64.5; Private long-term capital (net) 57.0; Short-term capital (net) 2.0; Net errors and omissions 7.8; *Overall balance* 24.0.

EXTERNAL TRADE

Principal Commodities (preliminary figures, US $ million, 1999): *Imports c.i.f.:* Capital goods 135.5; Consumer goods 174.9; Fuel and lubricants 88.5; Other intermediate goods 151.0; Total (incl. others) 550.2. *Exports f.o.b.:* Bauxite 77.2; Sugar 136.2; Rice 71.1; Gold 108.7; Shrimps 29.2; Timber 37.3; Total (incl. others, excl. re-exports) 504.8.

2000: Exports f.o.b.: Bauxite 71.8; Sugar 118.8; Rice 51.8; Gold 120.3; Shrimps 50.1; Timber 41.0; Total (incl. others, excl. re-exports) 502.7.

Principal Trading Partners (estimates, US $ million, 1998): *Imports:* Cuba 17; Netherlands 12; Trinidad and Tobago 121; United Kingdom 43; USA 160; Total (incl. others) 601. *Exports:* Canada 141; Netherlands 13; Trinidad and Tobago 14; United Kingdom 108; Total (incl. others) 525.

TRANSPORT

Road Traffic ('000 vehicles in use, 1993): Passenger cars 24.0; Commercial vehicles 9.0. Source: UN, *Statistical Yearbook*.

Shipping (international sea-borne freight traffic, estimates in '000 metric tons, 1990): Goods loaded 1,730; Goods unloaded 673. Source: UN, *Monthly Bulletin of Statistics*. *Merchant Fleet* (at 31 December 1998): Vessels 62; Displacement 16,260 grt. Source: Lloyd's Register of Shipping, *World Fleet Statistics*.

Civil Aviation (traffic on scheduled services, 1997): Kilometres flown (million) 3; passengers carried ('000) 126; passenger-km (million) 248; total ton-km (million) 26. Source: UN, *Statistical Yearbook*.

TOURISM

Visitor Arrivals ('000): 93 in 1997; 80 in 1998; 66 in 1999.

Tourist Receipts (US $ million): 39 in 1997; 60 in 1998; 52 in 1999. Source: World Bank, *World Development Indicators*.

COMMUNICATIONS MEDIA

Radio Receivers (1997): 420,000 in use*.

Television Receivers (1997): 46,000 in use*.

Telephones (1997): 55,000 main lines in use†.

Telefax Stations (1990): 195 in use†.

Mobile Cellular Telephones (1997): 1,400 subscribers†.

Daily Newspapers (1996): 2; estimated circulation 42,000*.

Non-daily Newspapers (1988): 6 (estimate); estimated circulation 84,000*.

Book Production (school textbooks, 1996): 1 title.

* Source: UNESCO, *Statistical Yearbook*.
† Source: UN, *Statistical Yearbook*.

EDUCATION

Pre-primary (1997/98): Institutions 305; Teachers 1,976; Students 33,366.

Primary (1997/98): Institutions 418; Teachers 3,710; Students 100,998.

General Secondary (1997/98): Institutions 416; Teachers 3,028; Students 61,253.

Special Education (1997/98): Institutions 6; Teachers 28; Students 585.

Technical and Vocational (1997/98): Institutions 6; Teachers 168; Students 3,307.

Teacher Training (1997/98): Institutions 1; Teachers 70; Students 1,235.

University (1997/98): Institutions 1; Teachers 383; Students 4,671.

Private Education (1997/98): Institutions 5; Teachers 138; Students 1,590.

Source: Ministry of Education.

Directory

The Constitution*

Guyana became a republic, within the Commonwealth, on 23 February 1970. A new Constitution was promulgated on 6 October 1980, and amended in 2000 and 2001. Its main provisions are summarized below:

The Constitution declares the Co-operative Republic of Guyana to be an indivisible, secular, democratic sovereign state in the course of transition from capitalism to socialism. The bases of the political, economic and social system are political and economic independence, involvement of citizens and socio-economic groups, such as co-operatives and trade unions, in the decision-making processes of the State and in management, social ownership of the means of production, national economic planning and co-operativism as the principle of socialist transformation. Personal property, inheritance, the right to work, with equal pay for men and women engaged in equal work, free medical attention, free education and social benefits for old age and disability are guaranteed. Additional rights include equality before the law, the right to strike and to demonstrate peacefully, the right of indigenous peoples to the protection and preservation of their culture, and a variety of gender and work-related rights. Individual political rights are subject to the principles of national sovereignty and democracy, and freedom of expression to the State's duty to ensure fairness and balance in the dissemination of information to the public. Relations with other countries are guided by respect for human rights, territorial integrity and non-intervention.

THE PRESIDENT

The President is the supreme executive authority, Head of State and Commander-in-Chief of the armed forces, elected for a term of office, usually of five years' duration, with no limit on re-election. The successful presidential candidate is the nominee of the party with the largest number of votes in the legislative elections. The President may prorogue or dissolve the National Assembly (in the case of dissolution, fresh elections must be held immediately) and has discretionary powers to postpone elections for up to one year at a time for up to five years. The President may be removed from office on medical grounds, or for violation of the Constitution (with a two-thirds' majority vote of the Assembly), or for gross misconduct (with a three-quarters' majority vote of the Assembly if allegations are upheld by a tribunal).

The President appoints a First Vice-President and Prime Minister who must be an elected member of the National Assembly, and a Cabinet of Ministers, which may include non-elected members and is collectively responsible to the legislature. The President also appoints a Leader of the Opposition, who is the elected member of the Assembly deemed by the President most able to command the support of the opposition.

THE LEGISLATURE

The legislative body is a unicameral National Assembly of 65 members; 53 members are elected by universal adult suffrage in a system of proportional representation, 10 members are elected by the 10 Regional Democratic Councils and two members are elected by the National Congress of Local Democratic Organs. The Assembly passes bills, which are then presented to the President, and may pass constitutional amendments.

LOCAL GOVERNMENT

Guyana is divided into 10 Regions, each having a Regional Democratic Council elected for a term of up to five years and four months, although it may be prematurely dissolved by the President. Local councillors elect from among themselves deputies to the National Congress of Democratic Organs. This Congress and the National Assembly together form the Supreme Congress of the People of Guyana, a deliberative body which may be summoned, dissolved or prorogued by the President and is automatically dissolved along with the National Assembly.

OTHER PROVISIONS

Impartial commissions exist for the judiciary, the public service and the police service. An Ombudsman is appointed, after consultation between the President and the Leader of the Opposition, to hold office for four years.

* In October 2000 several amendments to the Constitution were approved by the National Assembly. These included the introduction of a mixed system of proportional representation, combining regional constituencies and national candidate lists, and the abolition of the Supreme Congress of the People of Guyana and of the National Congress of Local Democratic Organs. In January 2001 the High Court ruled that the 1997 election of the legislature was null and void. However, it granted temporary validity to legislation passed after December 1997. In December 2000 the National Assembly approved a constitutional amendment removing a President's immunity from prosecution and limiting the presidential power to appoint ministers from outside the National Assembly to a maximum of four, and two parliamentary secretaries.

The Government

HEAD OF STATE

President: BHARRAT JAGDEO (sworn in 11 August 1999; re-elected 19 March 2001).

CABINET
(August 2001)

Prime Minister: SAMUEL A. HINDS.

Minister of Agriculture: NAVIN CHANDARPAL.

Minister of Amerindian Affairs: CAROLYN RODRIGUES.

Minister of Education: Dr HENRY JEFFREY.

Minister of Finance: SAISNARINE KOWLESSAR.

Minister of Fisheries, Crops and Livestock: SATYADEOW SAWH.

Minister of Foreign Affairs: RUDY INSANALLY.

Minister of Foreign Trade in the Ministry of Foreign Affairs: CLEMENT ROHEE.

Minister of Health: Dr LESLIE RAMSAMMY.

Minister of Home Affairs: RONALD GAJRAJ.

Minister of Housing and Water: SHAIK BAKSH.

Minister of Human Services, Social Security and Labour: Dr DALE BISNAUTH.

Minister of Information: BHARRAT JAGDEO.

Minister of Legal Affairs and Attorney-General: DOODNAUTH SINGH.

Minister of Local Government: HARRY PERSAUD NOKTA.

Minister of Parliamentary Affairs in the Office of the President: REEPU DAMAN PERSAUD.

Minister of Planning and Economic Development: (vacant).

Minister of Public Service Management: Dr JENNIFER WESTFORD.

Minister of Trade and Tourism: MANZOOR NADIR.

Minister of Transport, Communications and Hydraulics: CARL ANTHONY XAVIER.

Minister of Youth and Sports: GAIL TEIXEIRA.

Secretary to the Cabinet: Dr ROGER LUNCHEON.

MINISTRIES

Office of the President: New Garden St and South Rd, Georgetown; tel. 225-1330; fax 226-3395.

Office of the Prime Minister: Wights Lane, Georgetown; tel. 227-3101; fax 226-7563.

Office of Amerindian Affairs: see Ministry of Public Works and Communications.

Ministry of Agriculture: POB 1001, Regent and Vlissingen Rds, Georgetown; tel. 227-5527; fax 227-3638; e-mail guyagri @hotmail.com; internet www.sdnp.org.gy/minagri.

Ministry of Education: 26 Brickdam, Stabroek, POB 1014, Georgetown; tel. 226-3094; fax 225-8511; internet www.sdnp.org.gy/minedu.

Ministry of Finance: Main and Urquhart Sts, Georgetown; tel. 227-1114; fax 226-1284.

Ministry of Fisheries, Crops and Livestock: Regent and Vlissengen Rds, Georgetown; tel. 225-8310; fax 227-2928; e-mail minfcl@sdnp.org.gy; internet www.sdnp.org.gy/minagri.

Ministry of Foreign Affairs: Takuba Lodge, 254 South Rd and New Garden St, Georgetown; tel. 226-1606; fax 225-9192; e-mail minfor@sdnp.org.gy; internet www.minfor.gov.gy.

Ministry of Health: Brickdam, Stabroek, Georgetown; tel. 226-1560; fax 225-6958; internet www.sdnp.org.gy/moh.

Ministry of Home Affairs: 6 Brickdam, Stabroek, Georgetown; tel. 225-7270; fax 226-2740.

Ministry of Housing and Water: Georgetown.

Ministry of Human Services, Social Security and Labour: 1 Water and Cornhill Sts, Stabroek, Georgetown; tel. 225-7073; fax 227-1308; e-mail nrdocgd@sdnp.org.gy; internet www.sdnp.org.gy /mohss.

Ministry of Information: Area B, Homestretch Ave, Durban Park, Georgetown; tel. 227-1101; fax 226-4003; internet www.sdnp.org.gy/mininfo.

Ministry of Legal Affairs and Office of Attorney-General: 95 Carmichael St, Georgetown; tel. 225-3607; fax 225-0732.

Ministry of Local Government: De Winkle Bldgs, Fort St, Kingston, Georgetown; tel. 225-8621.

Ministry of Planning and Economic Development: Georgetown.

Ministry of Public Service Management: Wight's Lane, Kingston, Georgetown; tel. 227-2365; fax 225-6954.

Ministry of Trade and Tourism: 229 South Rd, Lacytown, Georgetown; tel. 226-2505; fax 225-4310; e-mail mtti@sdnp.org.gy; internet www.sdnp.org.gy/mtti.

Ministry of Transport, Communications and Hydraulics: Georgetown.

Ministry of Youth and Sports: 71 Main St, North Cummingsburg; tel. 226-0142; fax 226-5067.

President and Legislature

NATIONAL ASSEMBLY

Speaker: WINSLOW MARTIN ZEPHYR.

Deputy Speaker: CLARISSA RIEHL.

Election, 19 March 2001

Party	No. of seats		
	Regional	National	Total
People's Progressive Party/ CIVIC (PPP/CIVIC) . .	11	23	34
People's National Congress/ Reform (PNC/Reform) . .	13	14	27
Guyana Action Party/Working People's Alliance (GAP/WPA)	1	1	2
Rise, Organize and Rebuild Guyana Movement (ROAR) .	—	1	1
The United Force (TUF) . .	—	1	1
Total	**25**	**40**	**65**

Under Guyana's system of proportional representation, the nominated candidate of the party receiving the most number of votes was elected to the presidency. Thus, on 23 March 2001 the candidate of the PPP/CIVIC alliance, BHARRAT JAGDEO, was declared President-elect, defeating HUGH DESMOND HOYTE of the PNC/Reform alliance. JAGDEO was inaugurated as President on 31 March.

Political Organizations

CIVIC: New Garden St, Georgetown; social/political movement of businessmen and professionals; allied to PPP; Leader SAMUEL ARCHIBALD ANTHONY HINDS.

God Bless Guyana (GBG): Georgetown; Leader HARDAT SINGH.

Guyana Action Party (GAP): Georgetown; allied to WPA; Leader PAUL HARDY.

Guyana Democratic Party (GDP): Georgetown; f. 1996; Leaders ASGAR ALLY, NANDA K. GOPAUL.

Guyana Labour Party (GLP): Georgetown; f. 1992 by members of Guyanese Action for Reform and Democracy.

Guyana National Congress (GNC): Georgetown.

Guyana People's Party (GPP): Georgetown; f. 1996; Leader MAX MOHAMED.

Guyana Republican Party (GRP): Paprika East Bank, Essequibo; f. 1985; right-wing; Leader LESLIE PRINCE (resident in the USA).

Guyana's Alliance for Progress: 199 Charlotte Street, Georgetown; tel. 227-8845; e-mail guyanasalliance@yahoo.com; internet guyanese.webjump.com.

Horizon and Star (HAS): Georgetown.

Justice For All Party (JFAP): 73 Robb and Wellington Sts, Lacytown, Georgetown; tel. 226-5462; fax 227-3050; e-mail sharma@guyana.net.gy; internet www.jfa-gy.com; Leader CHANDRANARINE SHARMA.

National Democratic Front (NDF): Georgetown; Leader JOSEPH BACCHUS.

National Front Alliance: Georgetown.

National Independence Party: Georgetown; Leader SAPHIER HUSSIEN.

National Republican Party (NRP): Georgetown; f. 1990 after a split with URP; right-wing; Leader ROBERT GANGADEEN.

Patriotic Coalition for Democracy (PCD): Georgetown; f. 1986 by five opposition parties; the PCD campaigns for an end to alleged electoral malpractices; principal offices, including the chair of the collective leadership, rotate among the parties; now comprises the following three parties:

Democratic Labour Movement (DLM): 34 Robb and King Sts, 4th Floor, Lacytown, POB 10930, Georgetown; f. 1983; democratic-nationalist; Pres. PAUL NEHRU TENNASSEE.

People's Democratic Movement (PDM): Stabroek House, 10 Croal St, Georgetown; tel. 226-4707; fax 226-3002; f. 1973; centrist; Leader LLEWELLYN JOHN.

People's Progressive Party (PPP): Freedom House, 41 Robb St, Lacytown, Georgetown; tel. 227-2095; fax 227-2096; e-mail ppp@guyana.net.gy; internet www.pppcivic.org; f. 1950; Marxist-Leninist; allied to CIVIC; Leader JANET JAGAN; Gen. Sec. DONALD RAMOTAR.

People's National Congress/Reform (PNC/Reform): Congress Place, Sophia, POB 10330, Georgetown; tel. 225-7852; fax 225-6055; e-mail pnc@guyana-pnc.org; internet www.guyana-pnc.org; f. 1955 after a split with the PPP; Reform wing established in 2000; PNC Leader HUGH DESMOND HOYTE; PNC Chair ROBERT CORBIN; Reform Leader STANLEY MING; Reform Chair. JEROME KHAN.

People's Republic Party: POB 10162, Georgetown; e-mail info@ peoplesrepublicparty.com; internet www.mins.net/prp; Chair HARRY DAS.

People's Unity Party of Guyana (PUP): POB 10-1223, George-town; e-mail peter@ramsaroop.com; internet www
.peoplesunityparty.com; f. 1999; Leader PETER R. RAMSAROOP.

Rise, Organize and Rebuild Guyana Movement (ROAR): 186 Parafield, Leonora, West Coast Demerara, POB 101409, George-town; tel. 068-2452; e-mail guyroar@hotmail.com; internet www
.jaiag.com; f. 1999.

The United Force (TUF): 95 Robb and New Garden Sts, Bourda, Georgetown; tel. 226-2596; fax 225-2973; e-mail manzoornadir@-yahoo.com; internet tuf.homestead.com/index.htm; f. 1960; right-wing; advocates rapid industrialization through govt partnership and private capital; Leader MANZOOR NADIR.

United People's Party: 77 Winter Place, Brickdam, Georgetown; tel. 227-5217; fax 227-5166; e-mail unitedguyana@yahoo.com; internet upp.webjump.com.

United Republican Party (URP): Georgetown; f. 1985; right-wing; advocates federal govt; Leader Dr LESLIE RAMSAMMY.

United Workers' Party (UWP): Georgetown; f. 1991; Leader WIN-STON PAYNE.

Working People's Alliance (WPA): Walter Rodney House, Lot 80, Croal St, Stabroek, Georgetown; tel. 225-6624; internet www
.saxakali.com/wpa; originally popular pressure group, became polit-ical party 1979; independent Marxist; allied to GAP; Collective Leadership: EUSI KWAYANA, Dr CLIVE THOMAS, Dr RUPERT ROOPNARINE, WAZIR MOHAMED.

Diplomatic Representation

EMBASSIES AND HIGH COMMISSIONS IN GUYANA

Brazil: 308 Church St, Queenstown, POB 10489, Georgetown; tel. 225-7970; fax 226-9063; e-mail bragetown@solutions2000.net; Ambassador: CLAUDIO LYRA.

Canada: High and Young Sts, POB 10880, Georgetown; tel. 227-2081; fax 225-8380; e-mail grgtn@dfait-maecl.gc.ca; High Commis-sioner: JACQUES CRÊTE.

China, People's Republic: 108 Duke St, Kingston, Georgetown; tel. 227-1651; Ambassador: WANG FUYUAN.

Colombia: 306 Church and Peter Rose Sts, Queenstown, POB 10185, Georgetown; tel. 227-1410; fax 225-8198; e-mail embcolguy@ solutions2000.net; Ambassador: Dr LUIS GUILLERMO MARTÍNEZ FER-NÁNDEZ.

Cuba: 40 High St, Kingston, Georgetown; tel. 226-6732; Ambas-sador: RICARDO GARCIA DIAZ.

India: Bank of Baroda Bldg, 10 Ave of the Republic, POB 101148, Georgetown; tel. 226-3996; fax 225-7012; High Commissioner: Dr PRAKASH V. JOSHI.

Korea, Democratic People's Republic: 82 Premniranjan Place, Georgetown; tel. 226-0266; Ambassador: JON HYON CHAN.

Russia: 3 Public Rd, Kitty, Georgetown; tel. 226-9773; fax 227-2975; Ambassador: TAHIR BYASHIMOVICH DURDIYEV.

Suriname: 304 Church St, POB 10508, Georgetown; tel. 226-7844; Ambassador: HUMPHREY ABDUL RAFIK HASRAT.

United Kingdom: 44 Main St, POB 10849, Georgetown; tel. 226-5881; fax 225-3555; e-mail consular@georgetown.mail.fco.gov.uk; internet www.britain-un-guyana.org; High Commissioner: EDWARD C. GLOVER.

USA: Duke and Young Sts, Kingston, Georgetown; tel. 225-4900; fax 225-8497; Ambassador: RONALD GODARD.

Venezuela: 296 Thomas St, Georgetown; tel. 226-1543; Ambas-sador: JEAN-FRANÇOIS PULVENIS.

Judicial System

The Judicature of Guyana comprises the Supreme Court of Judica-ture, which consists of the Court of Appeal and the High Court (both of which are superior courts of record), and a number of Courts of Summary Jurisdiction.

The Court of Appeal, which came into operation in 1966, consists of the Chancellor as President, the Chief Justice, and such number of Justices of Appeal as may be prescribed by the National Assembly.

The High Court of the Supreme Court consists of the Chief Justice as President of the Court and Puisne Judges. Its jurisdiction is both original and appellate. It has criminal jurisdiction in matters brought before it on indictment. A person convicted by the Court has a right of appeal to the Guyana Court of Appeal. The High Court of the Supreme Court has unlimited jurisdiction in civil matters and exclusive jurisdiction in probate, divorce and admiralty and certain other matters. Under certain circumstances, appeal in civil matters lies either to the Full Court of the High Court of the Supreme Court, which is composed of not less than two judges, or to the Guyana Court of Appeal.

A magistrate has jurisdiction to determine claims where the amount involved does not exceed a certain sum of money, specified by law. Appeal lies to the Full Court.

Chancellor of Justice: CECIL KENNARD.

Chief Justice: DESIRÉE BERNARD.

High Court Justices: NANDRAM KISSOON, CARL SINGH, CLAUDETTE SINGH.

Attorney-General: DOODNAUTH SINGH.

Religion

CHRISTIANITY

Guyana Council of Churches: 26 Durban St, Lodge, Georgetown; tel. 225-3020; e-mail bishopedghill@hotmail.com; f. 1967 by merger of the Christian Social Council (f. 1937) and the Evangelical Council (f. 1960); 15 mem. churches, 1 assoc. mem.; Chair. Bishop JUAN A. EDGHILL; Sec. Rev. KEITH HALEY.

The Anglican Communion

Anglicans in Guyana are adherents of the Church in the Province of the West Indies, comprising eight dioceses. The Archbishop of the Province is the Bishop of the North Eastern Caribbean and Aruba, resident in St John's, Antigua. The diocese of Guyana also includes French Guiana and Suriname. In 1986 the estimated membership in the country was 125,000.

Bishop of Guyana: Rt Rev. RANDOLPH OSWALD GEORGE, Austin House, 49 High St, Georgetown 1; tel. 226-4183; fax 226-3353.

The Baptist Church

The Baptist Convention of Guyana: POB 10149, Georgetown; tel. 226-0428; Chair. Rev. ALFRED JULIEN.

The Lutheran Church

The Lutheran Church in Guyana: Lutheran Courts, POB 88, New Amsterdam; tel. (3) 3425; fax (3) 6479; e-mail lcg@guyana
.net.gy; f. 1947; 11,000 mems; Pres. Rev. ROY K. THAKURDYAL.

The Roman Catholic Church

Guyana comprises the single diocese of Georgetown, suffragan to the archdiocese of Port of Spain, Trinidad and Tobago. At 31 December 1999 adherents of the Roman Catholic Church comprised about 11% of the total population. The Bishop participates in the Antilles Episcopal Conference Secretariat, currently based in Port of Spain, Trinidad.

Bishop of Georgetown: G. BENEDICT SINGH, Bishop's House, 27 Brickdam, POB 10720, Stabroek, Georgetown; tel. 226-4469; fax 225-8519; e-mail rcbishop@solutions2000.net.

Other Christian Churches

Other denominations active in Guyana include the African Meth-odist Episcopal Church, the African Methodist Episcopal Zion Church, the Church of God, the Church of the Nazarene, the Ethi-opian Orthodox Church, the Guyana Baptist Mission, the Guyana Congregational Union, the Guyana Presbyterian Church, the Halle-lujah Church, the Methodist Church in the Caribbean and the Americas, the Moravian Church and the Presbytery of Guyana.

HINDUISM

Hindu Religious Centre: Maha Sabha, 162 Lamaha St, POB 10576, Georgetown; tel. 225-7443; f. 1934; Hindus account for about one-third of the population; Pres. RAMRAJ JAGNANDAN; Gen. Sec. CHRISHNA PERSAUD.

ISLAM

The Central Islamic Organization of Guyana (CIOG): M.Y.O. Bldg, Woolford Ave, Thomas Lands, POB 10245, Georgetown; tel. 225-8654; fax 225-7313; e-mail ciog@sdnp.org.gy; internet www
.ali.on.ca/ciog; Pres. Alhaji FAZEEL M. FEROUZ; Gen. Sec. MUJTABA NASIR.

Guyana United Sad'r Islamic Anjuman: 157 Alexander St, Kitty, POB 10715, Georgetown; tel. 226-9620; f. 1936; 120,000 mems; Pres. Haji A. H. RAHAMAN; Sec. YACOOB HUSSAIN.

The Press

DAILIES

Guyana Chronicle: 2A Lama Ave, Bel Air Park, POB 11, George-town; tel. 226-3243; fax 227-5208; e-mail khan@guyana.net.gy; internet www.guyanachronicle.com; f. 1881; govt-owned; also produces weekly *Sunday Chronicle* (tel. 226-3243); Editor-in-Chief SHARIEF KHAN; circ. 23,000 (weekdays), 43,000 (Sundays).

Stabroek News: 46–47 Robb St, Lacytown, Georgetown; tel. 225-7473; fax 225-4637; e-mail stabroeknews@stabroeknews.com; internet www.stabroeknews.com; f. 1986; also produces weekly *Sunday Stabroek*; liberal independent; Editor-in-Chief DAVID DE CAIRES; circ. 24,000 (weekdays), 40,000 (Sundays).

WEEKLIES AND PERIODICALS

The Catholic Standard: 293 Oronoque St, Queenstown, POB 10720, Georgetown; tel. 226-1540; f. 1905; weekly; Editor COLIN SMITH; circ. 10,000.

Diocesan Magazine: 144 Almond and Oronoque Sts, Queenstown, Georgetown; quarterly.

Guyana Business: 156 Waterloo St, POB 10110, Georgetown; tel. 225-6451; f. 1889; organ of the Georgetown Chamber of Commerce and Industry; quarterly; Editor C. D. KIRTON.

Guyana Review: 143 Oronoque St, POB 10386, Georgetown; tel. 226-3139; fax 227-3465; e-mail guyrev@networksgy.com; internet www.guyanareview.com; f. 1993; monthly.

Guynews: Georgetown; monthly.

Kaieteur News: 24 Saffon St, Charlestown; tel. 225-8452; fax 225-8473; f. 1994; independent weekly; Editor W. HENRY SKERRETT; circ. 30,000.

Mirror: Lot 8, Industrial Estate, Ruimveldt, Greater Georgetown; tel. 226-2471; fax 226-2472; internet www.mirrornews.org; owned by the New Guyana Co Ltd; Sundays and Wednesdays; Editor JANET JAGAN; circ. 25,000.

New Nation: Congress Place, Sophia, Georgetown; tel. 226-7891; f. 1955; organ of the People's National Congress; weekly; Editor FRANCIS WILLIAMS; circ. 26,000.

The Official Gazette of Guyana: Guyana National Printers Ltd, Lot 1, Public Road, La Penitence; weekly; circ. 450.

Thunder: Georgetown; f. 1950; organ of the People's Progressive Party; quarterly; Editor RALPH RAMKARRAN; circ. 5,000.

NEWS AGENCY

Guyana Information Services: Office of the President, New Garden St and South Rd, Georgetown; tel. 226-3389; fax 226-4003; f. 1993; Dir MILTON DREPAUL.

Foreign Bureaux

Inter Press Service (Italy): Georgetown; tel. 225-3213.

United Press International (UPI) (USA): Georgetown; tel. 226-5153.

Xinhua (New China) News Agency (People's Republic of China): 52 Brickdam, Stabroek, Georgetown; tel. 226-9965.

Associated Press (USA) and Informatsionnoye Telegrafnoye Agentstvo Rossii Telegrafnoye Agentstvo Suverennykh Stran (ITAR-TASS) (Russia) are also represented.

PRESS ASSOCIATION

Guyana Press Association: Georgetown; revived in 1990; Pres. ENRICO WOOLFORD.

Publishers

Guyana Free Press: POB 10386, Georgetown; tel. 226-3139; fax 227-3465; e-mail guyrev@networksgy.com; books and learned journals.

Guyana National Printers Ltd: 1 Public Rd, La Penitence, POB 10256, Greater Georgetown; tel. 225-3623; e-mail gnpl@guyana.net.gy; f. 1939; govt-owned printers and publishers; privatization pending; Chair. DESMOND N. MOHAMED.

Guyana Publications Inc.: 46/47 Robb St, Lacytown, Georgetown; tel. 225-7473; fax 225-4637.

Broadcasting and Communications

TELECOMMUNICATIONS

Caribbean Wireless Telecom (CWT): Georgetown; f. 1999; intends to launch a mobile cellular telephone service by 2001; CEO EARL SINGH.

Guyana Telephones and Telegraph Company (GT & T): 79 Brickdam, POB 10628, Georgetown; tel. 226-7840; fax 226-2457; internet www.gtt.co.gy; f. 1991; formerly state-owned Guyana Telecommunications Corpn; 80% ownership by Atlantic Tele-Network (USA); Gen. Man. SONITA JAGAN; Chair. CORNELIUS PRIOR.

BROADCASTING

Radio

Guyana Broadcasting Corporation (GBC): Broadcasting House, 44 High St, POB 10760, Georgetown; tel. 225-8734; fax 225-8756; f. 1979; operates channels GBC 1 (Coastal Service) and GBC 2 (National Service); Gen. Man. DAVID DE GROOT (acting).

Radio Roraima: Georgetown.

Voice of Guyana: Georgetown.

Television

In 2001 the Government implemented the regulation of all broadcast frequencies. All television broadcast operations were required to be fully licensed by 31 July 2001. Two private stations relay US satellite television programmes.

Guyana Television: 68 Hadfield St, Georgetown; tel. 226-9231; f. 1993; fmrly Guyana Television Corporation; govt-owned; limited service; Dir A. BREWSTER.

Finance

(dep. = deposits; m. = million; brs = branches; amounts in Guyana dollars)

BANKING

Central Bank

Bank of Guyana: 1 Church St and Ave of the Republic, POB 10280, Georgetown; tel. 226-3250; fax 227-2965; e-mail boglib@guyana.net.gy; internet www.bankofguyana.org.gy; f. 1965; cap. 1,000m., res 10,138m., dep. 86,717m. (Dec. 1998); central bank of issue; acts as regulatory authority for the banking sector; Gov. DOLLY S. SINGH; Dir LESLIE GLEN.

Commercial Banks

Demerara Bank Ltd: 230 Camp and South Sts, Georgetown; tel. 225-50610; fax 225-0601; e-mail banking@demerarabank.com; internet www.demerarabank.com; f. 1994; cap. 450m., res 52m., dep. 4,949m. (Sept. 1998); Chair. YESU PERSAUD; Man. AHMED M. KHAN.

Guyana Bank for Trade and Industry Ltd: 47–48 Water St, POB 10280, Georgetown; tel. 226-68431; fax 227-1612; e-mail banking@gbtibank.com; f. 1987 to absorb the operations of Barclays Bank; dep. $G 19,490m., res $G 1,789m., total assets $G 23,961m. (1998); CEO R. K. SHARMA; 6 brs.

Guyana National Co-operative Bank: 1 Lombard and Cornhill Sts, POB 10400, Georgetown; tel. 225-7810; fax 226-0231; f. 1970; merged with Guyana Co-operative Agricultural and Industrial Development Bank in 1995; scheduled for privatization in 2001; Gen. Man. ROSALIE A. ROBERTSON; 11 brs.

National Bank of Industry and Commerce (NBIC): 38–40 Water St, POB 10440, Georgetown; tel. 226-4091; fax 227-2921; 51% govt-owned; 17.5% owned by National Insurance Scheme; Man. Dir CONRAD PLUMMER; 5 brs.

Foreign Banks

Bank of Baroda (India): 10 Regent St and Ave of the Republic, POB 10768, Georgetown; tel. 226-4005; fax 225-1691; f. 1908; Chief Man. P. SAVID.

Bank of Nova Scotia (Canada): 104 Carmichael St, Georgetown; tel. 225-9222; fax 225-9309; e-mail bns.guyana@scotiabank.com; Man. FARRIED SULLIMAN; 5 brs.

Citizens' Bank Ltd (Jamaica): 201 Camp and Charlotte Sts, Lacytown, Georgetown; tel. 226-1705; fax 227-8251; internet citizens-carib.com/guyana.htm; f. 1994; Chair. DENNIS LALOR.

INSURANCE

Demerara Mutual Life Assurance Society Ltd: Demerara Life Bldg, 61–62 Robb St and Ave of the Republic, POB 10409, Georgetown; tel. 225-8991; fax 225-8288; f. 1891; Chair. RICHARD B. FIELDS; Gen. Man. EAWAN E. DEVONISH.

Diamond Fire and General Life: Georgetown; f. 2000; privately owned; cap. $G 100m.

Guyana Co-operative Insurance Service: 46 Main St, Georgetown; tel. 225-9153; f. 1976; 67% share offered for private ownership in 1996; Chair. G. A. LEE; Gen. Man. PAT BENDER.

Guyana and Trinidad Mutual Life Insurance Co Ltd: Lots 27–29, Robb and Hincks Sts, Georgetown; tel. 225-7910; fax 225-9397; e-mail gtmgroup@guyana.net.org; f. 1925; Chair. HAROLD B. DAVIS; Man. Dir R. E. CHEONG; affiliated company: Guyana and Trinidad Mutual Fire Insurance Co Ltd.

Hand-in-Hand Mutual Fire and Life Group: 1–4 Ave of the Republic, POB 10188, Georgetown; tel. 225-0462; fax 225-7519;

f. 1865; fire and life insurance; Chair. J. A. CHIN; Gen. Man. K. A. EVELYN.

Insurance Association

Insurance Association of Guyana: 54 Robb St, Bourda, POB 10741, Georgetown; tel. 226-3514; f. 1968.

STOCK EXCHANGE

In July 1989 the Government announced that it intended to establish a national securities exchange, with a view to becoming a member of the proposed regional stock exchange.

Trade and Industry

GOVERNMENT AGENCIES

Guyana Agency for the Environment: Georgetown; tel. 225-7523; fax 225-7524; f. 1988; formulates, implements and monitors policies on the environment; Dir Dr WALTER CHIN.

Guyana Marketing Corporation: 87 Robb and Alexander Sts, Georgetown; tel. 226-8255; fax 227-4114; e-mail newgmc@networksgy.com; Chair. CHANDRABALLI BISHESWAR; Gen. Man. ROX-ANNE GREENIDGE.

Guyana Public Communications Agency: Georgetown; tel. 227-2025; f. 1989; Exec. Chair. KESTER ALVES.

Trade and Investment Agency: Office of the President, New Garden St and South Rd, Georgetown; f. 2001; Chair. BHARRAT JAGDEO; CEO GEOFF DA SILVA.

DEVELOPMENT ORGANIZATIONS

Guyana Office for Investment (Go-Invest): 190 Camp and Church Sts, Georgetown; tel. 225-0658; fax 225-0655; e-mail goinvest@sdnp.org.gy; internet www.goinvest.gov.gy; f. 1994; provision of investment promotion service for foreign and local cos; under control of the Office of the President; Dir KHELLAWAN LALL.

State Planning Commission: 229 South St, Lacytown, Georgetown; tel. 226-8093; fax 227-2499; Chief Planning Officer CLYDE ROOPCHAND.

Institute of Private Enterprise Development (IPED): Georgetown; f. 1986 to help establish small businesses; total loans provided $G771m. and total jobs created 9,021 (1999); Chair. YESU PERSAUD.

CHAMBER OF COMMERCE

Georgetown Chamber of Commerce and Industry: 156 Waterloo St, Cummingsburg, POB 10110, Georgetown; tel. 225-5846; fax 226-3519; f. 1889; 122 mems; Pres. JOHN S. DE FREITAS; Chief Exec. G. C. FUNG-ON.

INDUSTRIAL AND TRADE ASSOCIATIONS

Bauxite Industry Development Company Ltd: 71 Main St, Georgetown; tel. 225-7780; fax 226-7413; f. 1976; Chair. J. I. F. BLACKMAN.

Guyana Rice Development Board: 117 Cowan St, Georgetown; tel. 225-8717; fax 225-6486; e-mail grdb@gol.net.gy; internet www.cra.cc/grdb; f. 1994 to assume operations of Guyana Rice Export Board and Guyana Rice Grading Centre; Chair. and CEO CHARLES KENNARD.

Livestock Development Co Ltd: 58 High St, Georgetown; tel. 226-1601.

EMPLOYERS' ORGANIZATIONS

Consultative Association of Guyanese Industry Ltd: 157 Waterloo St, POB 10730, Georgetown; tel. 226-4603; f. 1962; 193 mems, 3 mem. asscns, 159 assoc. mems; Chair. DAVID KING; Exec. Dir DAVID YANKANA.

Forest Products Association of Guyana: 157 Waterloo St, Georgetown; tel. 226-9848; f. 1944; 47 mems; Pres. L. J. P. WILLEMS; Exec. Officer WARREN PHOENIX.

Guyana Manufacturers' Association Ltd: 62 Main St, Cummingsburg, Georgetown; tel. 227-4295; fax 227-0670; f. 1967; 190 members; Pres. KIM KISSOON; Exec. Sec. TREVOR SHARPLES.

Guyana Rice Producers' Association: Lot 104, Regent St, Lacytown, Georgetown; tel. 226-4411; f. 1946; *c.* 35,000 families; Pres. BUDRAM MAHADEO.

MAJOR COMPANIES

The following are some of the major companies operating in Guyana:

Food and Beverages

Banks DIH Ltd: Thirst Park, Ruimveldt, Georgetown; tel. 226-2491; fax 226-6523; f. 1848; brewers and soft drinks and snacks manufacturers; sales of $ G6,706m. (1995/96); Chair. and Man. Dir CLIFFORD B. REIS; Vice-Chair. KATHLEEN D'AGUIAR; 1,100 employees.

Demerara Distillers Ltd: Diamond, East Bank, Demerara; tel. (65) 6000; fax (65) 3367; f. 1952; producer of alcoholic and non-alcoholic beverages; sales of $ G6,530m. (1998); Exec. Chair. YESU PERSAUD; 1,200 employees.

Edward Beharry & Co Ltd: 191 Charlotte St, Lacytown, Georgetown; tel. 227-0632; fax 225-6062; producer of confectionery, condiments and pasta.

Guyana Sugar Corpn Inc. (Guysuco): 22 Church St, POB 10547, Georgetown; tel. 225-6237; fax 225-7274; e-mail CEGSC@guyana.net.gy; f. 1976; from 1990 managed by Booker Tate (United Kingdom); sugar production; scheduled for privatization in 2001; Chair. VIC ODITT; Sec. A. L. LANCASTER.

Forestry and Timber

A. Mazharally and Sons Ltd: 22 Wight Lane, Kingston, Georgetown; tel. 226-0442; fax 226-4151; logs supplier.

Demerara Timber Ltd: 1 Water St and Battery Rd, Kingston, Georgetown; tel. 225-3835; fax 227-1663; fmrly state-owned logging co; privatized 1989; owned by Beaverbrook Group (United Kingdom).

OREU Timber and Trading Co Ltd: 3 Church St, South Cummingsburg, Georgetown; tel. 227-3103; production of timber.

Plywood Industries Ltd: 62 Main St, Georgetown; tel. 226-9262; fax 226-0351; production of plywood.

Toolsie Persaud Ltd: 1–4 Lombard St, Georgetown; tel. 226-4071; fax 226-2554; e-mail tpl@solutions2000.net; f. 1949; logging and quarrying co and manufacturer of construction materials; Pres. TOOLSIE PERSAUD; Man. Dir DAVID PERSAUD; 455 employees.

Willems Timber and Trading Co Ltd: 7 Water St, Werk-en-Rust, POB 10443, Georgetown; tel. 226-9252; fax 226-0983; production of timber and lumber.

Mining

Aroima Bauxite Company: Aroima; f. 1989 by joint-venture agreement between Govt and Reynolds International (USA); began mining of bauxite in 1991.

Berbice Mining Enterprise Ltd (Bermine): East Bank, Berbice; f. 1992, following separation of Guyana Mining Enterprise Ltd (Guymine) into Bermine and Linmine (Linden Mining Enterprise Ltd); scheduled for privatization; mining of bauxite.

Guyana Oil Company (GUYOIL): 166 Waterloo Street, Georgetown; tel. 225-3033; fax 225-2320; state-owned; petroleum exploration and production.

Linden Mining Enterprises Ltd (Linmine): POB 27, Linden; tel. (4) 3311; fax (4) 6103; f. 1992; scheduled for privatization in 2000; mining of bauxite; Chair. WILLIAM DRAPER; Pres. JULES DETATIBRA; 2,000 employees.

Omai Gold Mine Ltd: 176d Middle St, Cummingsburg, Georgetown; tel. 226-6463; fax 227-3810; f. 1990; owned by Canadian Cambior Ltd (65%), US Golden Star Resources (30%) and the Guyanese Govt (5%); Gen. Man. REJEAN GOURDE.

Miscellaneous

A. H. & L. Kissoon Ltd: 80 Camp and Robb Sts, Georgetown; tel. 226-0967; fax 227-5265; construction of wooden furniture and housing, rice cultivation, cattle rearing.

Beesons Industries Ltd: 101 Regent St, Georgetown; tel. 225-7630; fax 226-1939; clothing manufacturer.

Brass Aluminium and Cast Iron: Foundry Ltd, 11–14 West Ruimveldt, Gtr Georgetown; tel. 225-7531; fax 225-4341; producer of ferrous and non-ferrous metals.

Colgate-Palmolive (Guyana) Ltd: Ruimveldt, East Bank, Georgetown; tel. 226-2663; fax 225-6792; subsidiary of Colgate-Palmolive Co (USA); manufacturer of toothpaste and domestic cleaning products.

Demerara Tobacco Co Ltd: Eping Ave, Bel Air Park, POB 10262, Gtr Georgetown; tel. 226-5190; fax 226-9322; f. 1975; manufacturer of cigarettes; sales of $ G775m.; Chair. CHARLES R. QUINTIN; 200 employees.

Guyana Fisheries Ltd: Georgetown; tel. 225-8960; privatized April 1990; 70% owned by Vieira Investments Ltd; owners of 26 trawlers, landing and processing facilities; Man. Dir MICHAEL ELLIOT DAVIS.

Guyana Pharmaceutical Corpn Ltd: 1 Public Rd, La Penitence, East Bank, Georgetown, Demerara; tel. 226-3281; fax 225-7362; manufacturer of pharmaceuticals and cosmetics; Exec. Chair. Dr BUD MANGAL; Company Sec. D. SINGH.

Guyana Refrigerators Ltd: 15A Water and Holmes Sts, POB 10392, Georgetown; tel. 225-4934; fax 227-0302; manufacturer of refrigerators, freezers and ice buckets.

Guyana Stores Ltd (GSL): 19 Water St, Georgetown, Demerara-Mahaica; tel. 226-6171. 1976; offered for privatization in 1999; retailers (supermarket, department store, pharmacies), wholesalers of hardware, motor vehicle sales concessions; Chair. PAUL CHAN-A-SUE; 1,100 employees.

Lysons Industries Ltd: 1-2 Industrial Site, Ruimveldt, East Bank, Georgetown, Demerara; tel. 226-7276; fax 226-8813; manufacturer of clothing.

Sanata Textiles Ltd: Industrial Site, Ruimveldt, Georgetown; tel. 225-7342; fax 225-6707; fabrics manufacturer.

Torginol (Guyana) Ltd: Industrial Site, Ruimveldt, East Bank, Georgetown, Demerara; tel. 226-4041; fax 225-3568; manufacturer of paints.

UTILITIES
Electricity

Guyana Power and Light Inc: 40 Main St, POB 10390, Georgetown; tel. 225-4618; fax 227-1978; f. 1999; fmrly Guyana Electricity Corpn; 50% state-owned; 50% owned by the Commonwealth Devt Corpn and the Electricity Supply Bd International; Chair. ADAM HEDAYAT; CEO NOEL HATCH.

Water

Guyana Water Authority (GUYWA): Georgetown; CEO KARAN SINGH.

CO-OPERATIVE SOCIETIES

Chief Co-operatives Development Officer: Ministry of Human Services, Social Security and Labour, 1 Water and Cornhill Sts, Georgetown; tel. 225-8644; fax 225-3477; f. 1948; L. MILLER.

In October 1996 there were 1,324 registered co-operative societies, mainly savings clubs and agricultural credit societies, with a total membership of 95,950.

TRADE UNIONS

Trades Union Congress (TUC): Critchlow Labour College, Woolford Ave, Non-pareil Park, Georgetown; tel. 226-1493; fax 227-0254; f. 1940; national trade union body; 22 affiliated unions; merged with the Federation of Independent Trade Unions in Guyana in 1993; Pres. LAURIE LEWIS; Gen. Sec. JOSEPH H. POLLYDORE.

Amalgamated Transport and General Workers' Union: 46 Urquhart St, Georgetown; tel. 226-6243; Pres. RICHARD SAMUELS.

Clerical and Commercial Workers' Union (CCWU): Clerico House, 140 Quamina St, South Cummingsburg, POB 101045, Georgetown; tel. 227-0611; Gen. Sec. BIRCHMORE PHILADELPHIA.

Federative Union of Government Employees (FUGE): Georgetown.

General Workers' Union: 79 New North Rd, Georgetown; tel. 226-4879; f. 1954; terminated affiliation to People's National Congress in 1989; Pres. NORRIS WITTER; Gen. Sec. EDWIN JAMES; 3,000 mems.

Guyana Agricultural and General Workers' Union (GAWU): 104–106 Regent St, Lacytown, Georgetown; tel. 227-2091; fax 227-2093; e-mail gawu@networksgy.com; allied to the PPP; Pres. KOMAL CHAND; Gen. Sec. SEEPAUL NARINE; 20,000 mems.

Guyana Bauxite Supervisors' Union: Linden; Gen. Sec. LINCOLN LEWIS.

Guyana Labour Union: 198 Camp St, Georgetown; tel. 227-1196; Pres.-Gen. HUGH DESMOND HOYTE; 6,000 mems.

Guyana Mine Workers' Union: 56 Wismar St, Wismar; tel. (4) 2822; Pres. ASHTON ANGEL; Gen. Sec. CHRISTOPHER JAMES; 5,800 mems.

Guyana Postal and Telecommunication Workers' Union: 310 East St, POB 10352, Georgetown; tel. 226-5255; fax 225-1633; Pres. MAUREEN WALCOTT-FORTUNE; Gen. Sec. DIAN PRINCE-JOHNSON.

Guyana Public Service Union (GPSU): 160 Regent Rd and New Garden St, Georgetown; tel. 226-1770; Pres. PATRICK YARDE; Gen. Sec. RANDOLPH KIRTON; 11,600 mems.

Guyana Teachers' Union: Georgetown.

National Association of Agricultural, Commercial and Industrial Employees: 64 High St, Kingston, Georgetown; tel. 227-2301; f. 1946; Pres. B. KHUSIEL; *c.* 2,000 mems.

Printing Industry and Allied Workers' Union: Georgetown; Gen. Sec. LESLIE REECE.

University of Guyana Workers' Union: Turkeyen, Georgetown; supports Working People's Alliance; Pres. Dr CLIVE THOMAS; Chair. AL CREIGHTON.

Transport

RAILWAY

There are no public railways in Guyana.

Linmine Railway: Mackenzie, Linden; tel. (4) 2279; fax (4) 6795; bauxite transport; 15 km of line, Coomara to Linden; Superintendent O. BARNWELL.

ROADS

The coastal strip has a well-developed road system. In 1996 there were an estimated 7,970 km (4,859 miles) of paved and good-weather roads and trails.

SHIPPING

Guyana's principal ports are at Georgetown and New Amsterdam. The port at Linden serves for the transportation of bauxite products. A ferry service is operated between Guyana and Suriname. Communications with the interior are chiefly by river, although access is hindered by rapids and falls. There are 1,077 km (607 miles) of navigable rivers. The main rivers are the Mazaruni, the Potaro, the Essequibo, the Demerara and the Berbice. By 2002 a bridge was to be constructed across the Berbice River to link the west bank with the town of New Amsterdam, accessible only by ferry. In 2000 the Brazilian Government announced that it would finance the construction of both a deep-water port and another river bridge.

Transport and Harbours Department: Battery Rd, Kingston, Georgetown; tel. 225-9350; e-mail t&hd@solutions2000.net; Gen. Man. IVOR B. ENGLISH; Harbour Master STEPHEN THOMAS.

Shipping Association of Guyana Inc: 24 Water St, Georgetown; tel. 226-1505; fax 226-1881; e-mail ferna@guyana.net.gy; f. 1952; Pres. CHRISTOPHER FERNANDES; Sec. and Man. W. V. BRIDGEMOHAN; members:

Guyana National Industrial Company Inc.: 2–9 Lombard St, Charlestown, POB 10520, Georgetown; tel. 225-8428; fax 225-8526; metal foundry, ship building and repair, agents for a number of international transport cos; Man. Dir and CEO CLAUDE SAUL.

Guyana National Shipping Corporation Ltd: 5–9 Lombard St, La Penitence, POB 10988, Georgetown; tel. 226-1732; fax 225-3815; e-mail gnsc@guyana.net.gy; internet www.gnsc.com; govt-owned; Exec. Chair. DESMOND MOHAMED; Man. Dir M. F. BASCOM.

John Fernandes Ltd: 24 Water St, POB 10211, Georgetown; tel. 225-6294; fax 226-1881; e-mail chris@jf-ltd.com; ship agents, pier operators and stevedore contractors; Man. Dir C. J. FERNANDES.

CIVIL AVIATION

The main airport is Timehri International, 42 km (26 miles) from Georgetown. By 1998 there were some 94 airstrips.

Roraima Airways: 101 Cummings St, Bourda, Georgetown; tel. 225-9648; fax 225-9646; e-mail ral@roraimaairways.com; internet www.roraimaairways.com; f.1992; Owner GERALD GOUVEIA.

Tourism

Despite the beautiful scenery in the interior of the country, Guyana has limited tourist facilities, and began encouraging tourism only in the late 1980s. In the 1990s Guyana began to develop its considerable potential as an eco-tourism destination. However, tourist arrivals declined towards the end of the decade. The total number of visitors to Guyana in 1998 was 80,000. Tourism receipts totalled US $60m. in 1998.

Tourism and Hospitality Association of Guyana: 157 Waterloo Street, Georgetown; tel. 225-0807; fax 225-0817; e-mail thag@networksgy.com; internet www.exploreguyana.com; f. 1992; Exec. Dir INDIRA ANANDJIT.

Defence

The armed forces are united in a single service, the Combined Guyana Defence Force, which consisted of some 1,600 men (of whom 1,400 were in the army, 100 in the air force and about 100 in the navy) at 1 August 2000. The Guyana People's Militia, a paramilitary reserve force, totalled about 1,500. The President is Commander-in-Chief.

Defence Expenditure: $ G950m. in 2000.

Chief-of-Staff: Maj.-Gen. JOSEPH SINGH.

Education

Education is free and compulsory for children aged between six years and 14 years of age. Children receive primary education for a period of six years, followed by secondary education, beginning at 12 years of age. Secondary education in a general secondary school lasts for up to seven years, comprising an initial cycle of five years, followed by a cycle of two years. Alternatively, children may remain at primary school or a Community High School for an additional four-year period. In 1997 there were 365 nursery schools/classes and 420 primary schools/classes. Gross enrolment at primary schools in 1997 was equivalent to 92.8% of children in the relevant age group (males 92.6%; females 93.0%). Gross enrolment at secondary schools in that year was equivalent to 74.9% of children in the relevant age group (males 73.4%; females 76.4%).

Higher education is provided by five technical and vocational schools, one teacher-training college, and one school for home econo-mics and domestic crafts. Training in agriculture is provided by the Guyana School of Agriculture, at Mon Repos. The Burrowes School of Art offers education in fine art. The University of Guyana at Turkeyen has faculties of natural sciences, social sciences, arts, medicine, law, agriculture, technology and education. The University's Institute of Distance and Continuing Education offers training in a broad range of subjects ranging from home management to psychology and industrial relations. In 1996/97 3,701 students were enrolled in higher education.

In 2000, according to estimates by UNESCO, the average rate of adult illiteracy was only 1.5%, one of the lowest in the Western hemisphere. In 1998 the central Government allocated a total of $ G6,381m. to education.

Bibliography

Adamson, A. H. *Sugar without Slaves: The Political Economy of British Guiana, 1838–1904.* New Haven, CT, Yale University Press, 1972.

Bartilow, H. A. *The Debt Dilemma: IMF Negotiations in Jamaica, Grenada and Guyana.* Warwick, Warwick University Caribbean Studies, 1997.

Braveboy-Wagner, J. A. *The Venezuela–Guyana Border Dispute: Britain's Colonial Legacy in Latin America.* Boulder, CO, Westview Press, 1984.

Chambers, F. *Guyana (World Bibliographical Series, Vol. 96).* Oxford, Clio Press, 1989.

Colchester, M. *Guyana: Fragile Frontier.* Kingston, Ian Randle Publishers, 1997.

Cruickshank, J. G. *Scenes from the History of the Africans in Guyana.* Georgetown, Guyana Free Press, 1999.

David, W. L. *The Economic Development of Guyana, 1563–1964.* London, Oxford University Press, 1969.

Glasgow, R. A. *Guyana: Race and Politics among Africans and East Indians.* The Hague, Martinus Nijhoff, 1970.

Guyana: Fraudulent Revolution. London, Latin America Bureau, 1984.

Guyana: From Economic Recovery to Sustained Growth. Washington, DC, World Bank, 1993.

Granger, D. G. (Ed.). *Emancipation.* Georgetown, Guyana Free Press, 1999.

Guyana's Military Veterans: Promises, Problems and Prospects. Georgetown, Guyana Free Press, 1999.

Hope, K. R. *Development Policy in Guyana: Planning, Finance and Administration.* Boulder, CO, Westview Press, 1979.

Guyana: Politics and Development in an Emergent Socialist State. Oakville, Ontario, Mosaic Press, 1986.

Hoyte, D. H. *Guyana's Economic Recovery: Leadership, Will-power and Vision. Selected Speeches of Hugh Desmond Hoyte.* Georgetown, Guyana Free Press, 1997.

Jagan, C. B. *The West on Trial: The Fight for Guyana's Freedom*, revised edn. Berlin, Seven Seas, 1972.

Joseph, C. L. *Anglo-American Diplomacy and the Re-Opening of the Guyana–Venezuela Boundary Controversy, 1961–66.* Georgetown, Guyana Free Press, 1998.

Mandle, J. R. *The Plantation Economy: Population and Economic Change in Guyana, 1838–1960.* Philadelphia, PA, Temple University Press, 1973.

McGowan, W. F., et al (Eds). *Themes in African–Guyanese History.* Georgetown, Guyana Free Press, 1998.

Premdas, R. R. *Ethnic Conflict and Development: The Case of Guyana (Research in Ethnic Relations).* Brookfield, VT, Avebury, 1995.

Singh, C. *Guyana–Politics in a Plantation Society.* London, Praeger Publrs, 1988.

Smith, R. T. *British Guiana.* London, Oxford University Press, 1962.

Thompson, A. *Colonialism and Underdevelopment in Guyana, 1580–1803.* Bridgetown, Carib Research and Publications, 1987.

Whitehead, N. L. *Lords of the Tiger Spirit: A History of the Caribs in Colonial Venezuela and Guyana, 1498–1820.* Dordrecht, Foris Publications Holland, 1988.

HAITI

Area: 27,750 sq km (10,714 sq miles).

Population (official estimate at mid-2000): 7,180,294.

Capital: Port-au-Prince, estimated population 884,472 at mid-1996.

Language: French; the Creole patois spoken by the majority of the population has also been an official language since 1987.

Religion: Mainly Christianity (67% Roman Catholic); voodoo (vaudou) is the popular folk religion.

Climate: Tropical, but cooler in the mountains and on the coast; rainy season from May to November.

Time: GMT –5 hours.

Public Holidays

2002: 1 January (Independence Day), 2 January (Heroes of Independence/Ancestors' Day), 10–12 February (Carnival), 29 March (Good Friday), 14 April (Pan-American Day), 1 May (Labour Day), 18 May (Flag and University Day), 22 May (National Sovereignty), 15 August (Assumption), 24 October (United Nations Day), 1 November (All Saints' Day), 2 November (All Souls' Day), 18 November (Army Day and Commemoration of the Battle of Vertières), 5 December (Discovery Day), 25 December (Christmas Day).

2003: 1 January (Independence Day), 2 January (Heroes of Independence/Ancestors' Day), 2–4 March (Carnival), 14 April (Pan-American Day), 18 April (Good Friday), 1 May (Labour Day), 18 May (Flag and University Day), 22 May (National Sovereignty), 15 August (Assumption), 24 October (United Nations Day), 1 November (All Saints' Day), 2 November (All Souls' Day), 18 November (Army Day and Commemoration of the Battle of Vertières), 5 December (Discovery Day), 25 December (Christmas Day).

Currency: Gourde; 1,000 gourdes = £29.76 = US $42.62 = €48.01 (30 April 2001).

Weights and Measures: Officially the metric system is in force, but many US measures are also used.

Basic Economic Indicators

	1997	1998	1999
Gross domestic product (million gourdes at 1976 prices)	4,502	4,634	n.a.
GDP per head (gourdes at 1976 prices)	600.9	606.0	n.a.
GDP (million gourdes at current prices)*	51,578	59,055	68,550
GDP per head (gourdes at current prices)†	6,884	8,837	10,119
Annual growth of real GDP (%)	1.1	2.0	n.a.
Annual growth of real GDP per head (%)	–1.0	0.8	n.a.
Government budget (million gourdes at current prices):			
Revenue	4,781.8	5,330.0	6,211.2
Expenditure	5,796.9	6,751.2	7,905.9
Consumer price index (annual average; base: 1995 = 100)‡	145.4	160.8	174.8
Rate of inflation (annual average, %)§	20.6	10.6	8.7
Foreign exchange reserves (US $ million at 31 December)	77.0	n.a.	n.a.
Imports c.i.f. (US $ million) ‖	648	797	1,025
Exports f.o.b. (US $ million)¶	120	175	196
Balance of payments (current account, US $ million)	–47.7	–38.1	n.a.

* 79,464m. gourdes in 2000.
† 11,067 gourdes in 2000.
‡ 198.7 in 2000.
§ 13.7% in 2000.
‖ US $1,036m. in 2000.
¶ US $164m. in 2000.

Gross national product per head measured at purchasing power parity—PPP (US dollars, estimate, converted by the PPP exchange rate, 1999): 1,407.

Total labour force (FAO mid-year estimate, 1998): 3,418,000.

Unemployment (1997): 70%.

Total foreign debt (2000): US $1,340m.

Life expectancy (years at birth, 1998): 54.0 (males 51.5, females 56.4).

Infant mortality rate (per 1,000 live births, 1998): 91.

Adult population with HIV/AIDS (15–49 years, 1999): 5.17%.

School enrolment ratio (1990): 22% (6–12 years); equivalent to 21% (12–18 years).

Adult literacy rate (15 years and over, 2000): 48.6% (males 51.0%; females 46.5%).

Energy consumption per head (kg of oil equivalent, 1998): 271.

Carbon dioxide emissions per head (metric tons, 1997): 0.2.

Passenger motor cars in use (estimate, per 1,000 of population, 1996): 4.4.

Television receivers in use (per 1,000 of population, 1997): 4.8.

History

GREG CHAMBERLAIN

The western half of the island of Hispaniola was first colonized by the French in the late 17th century and its borders with the Spanish part of the island were agreed in the Treaty of Ryswick in 1697. Haiti became the world's first independent black republic on New Year's Day 1804 after a bloody 12-year rebellion by African-descended slaves led by Toussaint Louverture, which was one of the most dramatic by-products of the French Revolution. Haiti's first ruler, Jean-Jacques Dessalines, and his successor, Alexandre Pétion (1807–18), divided the estates of the departed French among the freed peasantry, laying the economic, social and psychological foundations of modern Haiti.

Despite this early establishment of national identity, the attainment of meaningful independence proved to be a struggle. Economic development was hampered for a century by repayment of a massive indemnity of 150m. francs demanded by France in exchange for recognition. However, there was no recognition from the USA until 1862. Greed and the legacy of violence and colour division between blacks and the ruling mulattos produced increasingly unstable and chaotic government. In the late 19th century Haiti's economic dependence led to growing involvement of US and European interests in the country's affairs. In 1915 the USA, fearing European (especially German) economic and political rivalry in its Caribbean sphere of influence, invaded Haiti, ostensibly to restore order. There followed a 19-year occupation of what one senior US official had once called 'a public nuisance at our doors'.

US military rule brought racial segregation and forced labour. These provoked sharp resistance and between 1918 and 1920 some 3,000 rebels and their leader, Charlemagne Péralte, were killed. The occupation entrenched the mulatto minority in power. This aroused strong nationalist and socialist sentiments among black intellectuals and liberal mulattos, which erupted into open discontent in 1946 when President Elie Lescot was overthrown. The country's first trade unions and left-wing parties were founded and the election of the liberal Dumarsais Estimé gave the emerging black bourgeoisie some political power. However, Estimé was overthrown in 1950 by the army commander, Gen. Paul Magloire, whose rule saw relative political peace, notable infrastructure development and social and economic advances.

'PAPA DOC' AND 'BABY DOC' DUVALIER

In 1957 Dr François ('Papa Doc') Duvalier, a black nationalist intellectual, was elected President. He resolved to end the mulattos' political power even if he could not break their dominance of the economy. He also sought to limit the influence of the Army, the Roman Catholic Church and the USA, which had traditionally been strong in Haitian society. More blacks entered the Government and a lumpen black militia, the National Security Volunteers (popularly known as the Tontons Macoutes, a Creole expression for 'bogeymen'), was created to counterbalance the Army, which was purged and tamed. Duvalier appointed the first Haitian head of the local Roman Catholic Church, until then controlled by French Breton clergy, many of whom Duvalier deported.

Partly in response to opposition, President Duvalier's rule soon degenerated into violence and killings, particularly of mulattos. By 1965 tens of thousands of Haitians had been murdered, tortured or had fled to North America, Africa and Europe. Duvalier expelled the US ambassador in 1963 and the USA suspended aid to Haiti. However, US governments continued to regard the Duvalier regime favourably for not aligning the country with neighbouring Cuba. Duvalier extended his tenure of office by declaring himself 'President-for-Life' in 1964. A dozen attempts at invasion or internal rebellion were crushed and when Duvalier died in April 1971, he bequeathed power to his 19-year-old son, Jean-Claude ('Baby Doc') Duvalier, also as President-for-Life. The young man's inexperience and initial lack of interest in his legacy was a problem, but rival factions kept him in office as a pliable arbiter of their quarrels. The USA resumed economic and military aid.

Repression eased, however, and dissidence appeared from 1977 onwards, partly encouraged by US President Jimmy Carter's human-rights policies. The press criticized government failures, symbolized by famine and the flight of thousands of 'boat people' to the USA, although the Duvaliers and their estimated US $500m. private fortune remained above criticism. The regime tolerated the foundation of two small political parties and a trade-union federation, held parliamentary elections (without opposition candidates) and freed political prisoners.

In November 1980 the Government arrested and deported all its main press critics and political opponents. Leadership of the opposition was assumed by progressive Roman Catholic priests and the Church's grass-roots organizations (Ti Legliz). The Church-run Radio Soleil became the country's most popular station, using the national language, Creole, rather than the official French favoured by the élite. The President's marriage in 1980 to a mulatto, Michèle Bennett, angered many Duvalierists, who saw it as a sign the old élite was re-establishing itself.

THE END OF THE DUVALIER ERA

The first anti-government demonstrations in 20 years broke out in 1984, when food warehouses were looted. After the USA threatened to reduce aid, the Government promised to lift restrictions on political activity. However, the killing of four schoolchildren by police in Gonaïves in November 1985 prompted a revolt and the regime lost control of the provinces. In January 1986 President Duvalier declared a state of siege and several hundred people were killed. The US Government, fearing radicalization of the revolt, had the Duvaliers flown into exile in France on 7 February.

A civilian–military junta, led by the army commander, Gen. Henri Namphy, assumed power with the approval of the USA and leading Duvalierists. Freedom of expression was restored and formal democracy promised. Hundreds of Macoutes were killed during several months of violent *déchoukaj* (uprooting) by Haitians of traces of the old regime. However, apart from some token trials, officials of the old dictatorship escaped punishment.

By mid-1987 officially-sanctioned violence had resumed. In July about 140 peasants were massacred near the town of Jean-Rabel. Under the new Constitution, leading Duvalierists were barred from contesting elections for 10 years. Haiti's first attempt at free elections, on 29 November, was thwarted when Duvalierist gangs attacked polling stations, killing more than a dozen voters. The election was cancelled in mid-vote and the country's main sources of aid (Canada, France and the USA) suspended donations in protest.

The Army organized new elections in January 1988 and, despite a widespread boycott, a university professor, Leslie Manigat, was declared to have won the presidency. He tried to eradicate the Army's extensive smuggling activities and in June dismissed Gen. Namphy as its commander. Manigat was deposed on 19 June and Namphy resumed control. In September Duvalierists massacred a dozen people during a church service conducted by a popular radical priest, Fr Jean-Bertrand Aristide. Disgusted young soldiers overthrew Namphy on 17 September and appointed Gen. Prosper Avril as President.

Avril promised to restore democracy. Rank-and-file troops overthrew their commanders, but their radical leaders were soon arrested. Meanwhile, conservative Church leaders engineered the expulsion of Fr Aristide from his order, the Salesians. Avril declared a state of siege in 1990 'to defend democracy'. However, the USA and a united opposition forced him to flee into exile on 10 March. A Supreme Court judge, Ertha Pascal-Trouillot, was appointed provisional President.

THE ARISTIDE EXPERIMENT

Haiti's first free presidential elections took place on 16 December 1990. Aristide won 67% of the votes cast, compared to only 14% for a US-backed conservative, Marc Bazin. In January 1991 the Duvaliers' former Minister of the Interior, Roger Lafontant, who had been barred from the election, took outgoing President Pascal-Trouillot hostage and tried to seize power. Street protests, accompanied by the death of nearly 100 people, many by 'necklacing' (killing with burning rubber tyres), prompted the Army to suppress the coup.

Fr Aristide assumed the presidency on 7 February 1991. His huge popular support was not matched by administrative experience and he distanced himself from the political groups that had supported him. His impatience with parliament and his failure to condemn 'necklacing' strongly also lost him support from the traditional ruling class. However, his Government reduced corruption and political violence, and won overwhelming favour with foreign aid donors. The adulation of the black majority and Aristide's advocacy of social justice greatly alarmed the old élite. Moreover, Aristide's attempts to reduce the defence budget and make the armed forces and police accountable to civilian authorities met opposition. On 30 September the police chief, Maj. Michel François, supported by the Army, led by Gen. Raoul Cédras, overthrew the President. Hundreds of his supporters were killed and Aristide was exiled. Foreign aid was again suspended and the Organization of American States (OAS) imposed economic sanctions in an attempt to force Aristide's reinstatement.

INTERNATIONAL ISOLATION

In February 1992 parliament agreed, at OAS prompting, to a phased restoration of Aristide's presidency, but the deal was rejected by the Army. In June Bazin, whom Aristide had defeated in the 1990 election, was appointed Prime Minister, in the hope that he could end Haiti's world-wide diplomatic isolation. Violations of the sanctions, notably by imports of petroleum, meanwhile strengthened the regime and the killing of Aristide supporters continued.

New sanctions resulted in an agreement at Governor's Island, New York (USA), in July 1993, under which the Army again agreed to Aristide's phased return to power. Aristide named a Prime Minister, Robert Malval, but the Army prevented him from governing and its agents murdered a leading Aristide supporter, Antoine Izméry, during a church service in September. In October the US President, Bill Clinton, ordered a ship bringing the first 200 US troops of a UN peace-keeping force not to dock for fear of attacks by pro-Army demonstrators. Two days later the Minister of Justice, Guy Malary, was assassinated. The UN authorized a blockade of Haiti by US warships.

Political killings, notably by an army-sponsored paramilitary group, the Front Revolutionnaire pour l'Avancement et le Progrès d'Haïti (FRAPH—Revolutionary Front for the Advancement and Progress of Haiti), increased. By mid-1994 about 4,000 supporters of Aristide were estimated to have been murdered. The main consideration in US policy, however, was the tens of thousands of Haitian boat people fleeing to the USA from poverty as well as political repression. In May 1992 the US President, George Bush, ordered all those intercepted at sea to be summarily returned to Haiti. In May 1994 his successor, Bill Clinton, agreed to resume offshore hearings for asylum applications. Most of the resulting daily flood of thousands of boat people were held at the US naval base at Guantánamo, in Cuba. President Clinton had declared full support for Aristide in April. Further UN sanctions were imposed in May, after the Army appointed the 81-year-old head of the Supreme Court, Émile Jonassaint, as President. In July the regime expelled UN observers, after which all air links with Haiti were suspended and the UN authorized an invasion to depose the military regime. In August the murder of a leading left-wing priest, Fr Jean-Marie Vincent, further inflamed international opinion. On 18 September a mission led by former US President Jimmy Carter negotiated the departure abroad of the regime's leaders. A total of 21,000 US troops began landing the next day, followed by several hundred from other countries. The Army and the police were dismantled and President Aristide returned to Haiti in triumph on 15 October.

THE RETURN TO CIVILIAN RULE

President Aristide soon criticized the USA for not systematically disarming the former soldiers, police and other agents of the dictatorship. Describing the Army as a 'cancer', he reduced its size from 7,500 to 1,500 and then pronounced it dissolved in April 1995. Violent crime, much of it by former soldiers, increased and retaliatory lynchings occurred. The USA, helped by Canada and France, concentrated on creating and training a new police force of 6,000 members. In March 1995 a 7,000-strong UN peace force took over from the US soldiers. It was commanded, however, by a US general and one-half of the troops were provided by the USA. In February 1996 most of the US troops withdrew from the UN force, which was reduced to some 2,000 members, mostly Canadians.

Aristide named as his Prime Minister a businessman, Smarck Michel, who pledged to modernize the Haitian economy. Foreign assistance was made conditional on privatization of state bodies and a reduction in the number of government employees. Opposition to this policy by Aristide prompted Michel to resign in October 1995. He was replaced by the foreign minister, Claudette Werleigh.

Despite growing discontent over government inaction and daily violence, legislative and municipal elections held on 25 June and 17 September 1995 produced a massive victory for the government coalition led by Aristide's Organisation Politique Lavalas (OPL—Lavalas Political Organization, renamed the Organisation du Peuple en Lutte in 1998). The coalition won 17 of the 18 contested seats in the 27-member Sénat (Senate) and 68 seats in the Chambre des Députés (Chamber of Deputies). The remaining 15 seats in the lower chamber were obtained by independents. The opposition boycotted the poll as 'fraudulent'. A presidential election on 17 December 1995 was overwhelmingly won by the OPL candidate, René Préval, who gained 87.9% of the votes in a low turn-out (28%). Préval, Prime Minister before the 1991 army coup, succeeded Aristide as President on 7 February 1996.

Préval named an agronomist, Rosny Smarth, as Prime Minister and pledged to enact a diluted version of the delayed austerity programme. The new President improved relations with the neighbouring Dominican Republic and moved against tax evasion. The killing of a right-wing politician in August 1996 aroused suspicions that government-sponsored 'death squads' were operating. A small number of US troops returned to Haiti in mid-1996, some of them helping Préval to purge his palace guard.

The ruling party split in November 1996, when Aristide founded Fanmi Lavalas (FL—Lavalas Family), accusing the Government of having lost contact with its grass-roots supporters. The split between the FL and the remaining OPL faction deepened in April 1997 when legislative by-elections were held. Accusations of fraud led to parliamentary and political deadlock.

Demonstrations and strikes, as well as increasing violence, led to Smarth's resignation as premier in June 1997. In November Hervé Denis, a former Minister of Information, was nominated as Prime Minister, but was rejected by the legislature in April 1998. Disbursement of hundreds of millions of dollars in foreign aid was delayed because of the crisis. In July Préval nominated the Minister of Education, Jacques Édouard Alexis, as premier. In December 1998 Alexis was finally declared eligible to assume the office of Prime Minister, subject to his nomination being approved by the legislature. However, in January 1999 Préval announced he would no longer recognize the legislature, and Alexis, who had been acting as head of Government for many months, formed a coalition Cabinet, including five small opposition parties, in March. Alexis' nomination was finally approved on 23 November 2000.

Political tension increased, with growing polarization between the FL and other political groups. The FL began a campaign to gain control of the police force, with the help of pressure from pro-Aristide street gangs, and citing incidents of police brutality, notably the execution in May 1999 of 11 people in a Port-au-Prince slum, on the orders of Jean Coles Rameau, the Chief of Police. Rameau was imprisoned for three years in September 2000; his was the first trial of any of the several hundred officers of the force who had been dismissed for murder, brutality and drugs-trafficking from 1995. Aristide forced the resignation in October 1999 of Robert Manuel, the Secretary of State for Public

Security, who at once fled abroad. The Deputy Chief of Police, Luc Eucher Joseph, was forced out of office in April 2000 and also left the country.

THE 2000 ELECTIONS

Legislative and municipal elections were held on 21 May 2000 after several postponements, during which the FL obtained changes in the electoral law in its favour and forced the departure of foreign election experts. The vote produced a clear majority for the FL and observers at first declared that the election had been conducted adequately. However, the OAS subsequently revealed that the first-round votes for the Sénat had been counted incorrectly, exaggerating the number of seats won by the FL and disregarding about 1.5m. votes (more than one-third of the total) for candidates of the fragmented opposition. Following pro-Aristide street protests, the President of the Conseil Electoral Provisoire (CEP—Provisional Electoral Council), Léon Manus, fled abroad, claiming that he had been threatened by Préval and Aristide when he refused to endorse the inaccurate count. According to official first round results, the FL won 16 of the 19 contested seats in the Sénat, and 26 of the 83 seats in the lower house. Despite criticism by the UN, the OAS and numerous foreign governments, a second round of voting went ahead on 9 July. Opposition protests and a boycott by the 15-party opposition coalition, Convergence Démocratique (CD—Democratic Convergence) resulted in low voter turn-out (an estimated 10%) and a high incidence of violence, with 10 separate bombs killing two people and wounding a further 17. According to official results, the FL won 72 of the 82 seats contested in the 83-seat Chambre des Députés, and 18 of the 19 seats contested in the 27-member Sénat, while also gaining control of some 80% of the town councils and most urban and rural local assemblies. The USA, the European Union and international organizations denounced the fraud, maintained their aid suspension and called for the result to be rectified. The Government rejected the protests, installed the new legislature and began preparations for the presidential election, which was scheduled to be held on 26 November, together with elections for eight seats in the Sénat and one in the Chambre des Députés. The CD, however, announced its intention to boycott the ballots.

The May 2000 election campaign had been conducted amid increasing violence, in which opposition offices were burned down, the country's leading radio journalist, Jean Dominique, was murdered, the President of the Chambre de Commerce et d'Industrie d'Haïti (Chamber of Commerce and Industry) fled abroad and Aristide supporters tried to impose their will by force in rural areas. In early August a group of 193 intellectuals and former Lavalas sympathizers warned of impending dictatorship. The political situation and the police force were also seriously undermined by the sums of money involved in large-scale trafficking of cocaine through Haiti to the USA with the help of hundreds of locally-based Colombian agents.

On 16 October 2000 an alleged attempt by members of the National Police Force to overthrow the Government of Préval was uncovered. The seven police officers accused of planning the coup fled to the Dominican Republic. Relations between the two countries were strained as a result of the Dominican Republic's refusal to extradite the officers, who were subsequently granted asylum in Ecuador. In response to the attempted coup, the Government replaced several senior police officers around the country. On 16 November 37 former senior army officers, including the former dictator, Gen. Cédras, were sentenced to life imprisonment with hard labour *in absentia* for their role in the murders of 15 people in the shanty town of Raboteau, in Gonaïves, in 1994.

At the presidential election of 26 November 2000, Aristide was elected with some 91.7% of the votes cast; the remaining six candidates all won less than 2.0%. The opposition boycotted the ballot, after the failure of OAS mediation attempts to resolve the impasse between the authorities and the opposition CD, while the USA and the UN refused to help finance or observe the election. The Government estimated the turn-out to be some 60.5%, although the opposition claimed a far lower participation. The only official observer, the Caribbean Community (CARICOM), estimated a 30% voter turn-out. In concurrently-held

elections, the FL also won the remaining eight seats in the Sénat, and the one remaining seat in the Chambre des Députés.

THE NEW GOVERNMENT

In December 2000 an eight-member Transition Committee was established to oversee the smooth transfer of power to Aristide, who was to take office on 7 February 2001. Also in December 2000, under pressure from the USA, Aristide pledged in a letter to the US President, Bill Clinton, to implement an eight-point package of political reforms. However, the CD continued to call for a complete re-run of all the elections held in that year. On 6 February 2001 the CD issued the 'Marlique Declaration' in which they announced the formation of an alternative, provisional Government, known as the 'Front Alternatif', headed by former justice minister, Gérard Gourgue, with the intention of holding fresh legislative and presidential elections within two years. The announcement provoked widespread violent demonstrations by Aristide supporters. Discussions between the President-elect and opposition leaders in early February ended without agreement.

Following his inauguration, Aristide appointed Jean-Marie Chérestal as Prime Minister and named a Cabinet that included his former election rival, Marc Bazin, and a number of former Duvalierists, including Stanley Théard, who had been indicted in 1986 but never tried for the alleged embezzlement of US $4.5m. in state funds. In April 2001, in an attempt to end the political impasse, Aristide appointed a new nine-member CEP to investigate the results of the disputed May 2000 elections. The CEP also included former Duvalierist members, while the CD was not represented.

On 14 March 2001 the new Minister of Foreign Affairs and Relations, Antonio Joseph, announced that in order to satisfy international and opposition criticism, and to restore the flow of suspended foreign aid, legislative elections would be held one year early, in November 2002. Following the announcement, violent protests broke out in Port-au-Prince, in which three people died and dozens were injured. At the same time, pro-government demonstrators attempted to burn down the CD's headquarters and called for Gourgue's arrest. Later in the same month, in a widely-condemned move, the Sénat passed a resolution calling for Gourgue's arrest. In early June further proposals put forward by Aristide were rejected by the CD. Continuing violence resulted in the arrest of a number of opposition party members on treason and terrorism charges. In July, after further OAS mediation, the Government announced that legislative and local elections would be held in 2002, although a timetable remained to be agreed; an accord was also reached on the composition of the new CEP. The CEP would additionally organize an election to the seven Sénat seats, vacated in the previous month, that had been controversially awarded in the May 2000 election.

In May 2001 the former dictator, Gen. Avril (1998–90), was arrested, accused of the torture of opponents during his rule. The investigation into the murder of Jean Dominique was obstructed by death threats and pressure from supporters of the principal suspect in the case, FL Senator and former police chief, Dany Toussaint. In June the judge assigned to the case resigned, complaining of constant threats and lack of security and support from the Government. However, he later resumed the inquiry. On 12 July the former dictator, Gen. Magloire, died.

Undemocratic government and political violence have long isolated Haiti from its more peaceful neighbours. More than 1m. Haitians live in the Dominican Republic, one-half of them illegally, and many cutting sugar cane in virtual slavery, while tens of thousands provide cheap labour in the Bahamas and French Guiana. The Dominican and Bahamian authorities deported thousands of Haitians every year; in January 2001 some 7,500 Haitians were forcibly repatriated from the Dominican Republic. However, from the mid-1990s contact with other countries in the region increased. Diplomatic relations with Cuba were resumed in 1996 after a 32-year gap and by mid-2000 there were about 800 Cuban doctors working as volunteers in Haiti. In July 1999 CARICOM agreed to admit Haiti as a member state, but the regional body expressed serious concern over the country's political crisis and full accession to membership was delayed.

Economy

GREG CHAMBERLAIN

Most of Haiti's 7.1m. inhabitants are among the poorest in the Americas, and the contrast in wealth between rulers and ruled is stark. In the late 18th century Haiti was France's richest colony. By the end of the 20th century the country had few material resources and was wracked by drought, hunger, severe deforestation (98.5%) and soil erosion (some 10,000 ha of land and 30m. trees were lost each year), aggravated by the international sanctions imposed during the 1991–94 military dictatorship and political paralysis since 1997. Foreign aid officials considered the country to be an ecological disaster with little chance of recovery.

These factors, together with high population density (258.7 per sq km in mid-2000), primitive methods of production and ever-shrinking size of plots of land, as inheritances were divided, ensured the steady decline of agriculture, the main economic sector. In the late 1990s 37% of Haitians lived in towns, compared with 12% 50 years earlier. Between 1970 and 2000 the population of Port-au-Prince, the capital, tripled in size, and by the late 1990s some two-thirds of that population lived in slums. Haiti was heavily dependent on foreign aid, including food relief, mainly from the USA. By 2000 more than one-10th of the population was being fed by international relief organizations. Haiti was the only Latin American country defined by the UN in 2000 as having a food emergency, while malnutrition was 62%, the third highest rate in the world, according to the Food and Agricultural Organization.

In the late 1990s unemployment and underemployment affected 85% of the labour force. Some 97% of Haitians, most of them in the countryside, were outside the formal economy. The average income per head was about US $400 and more than 80% of the population existed in extreme poverty (living on about $50 per year). The wealthiest 4% of Haitians accounted for nearly two-thirds of gross national product (GNP). Illiteracy was estimated at 52.2% in 1998 (unofficial estimates were far higher). Total school enrolment was 26.8% in 1997 and in 1998 only 7% of candidates passed the school-leaving examination. Life expectancy in 1998 was 54.0 years. One-eighth of all children died before reaching the age of five (the highest rate in the Americas) and one-third were severely malnourished. Less than one-half of the population had access to health-care and drinking water, which was eight times more expensive than in developed countries. Malaria, tuberculosis, acquired immunodeficiency syndrome (AIDS), measles, worms, meningitis and rabies were common. In 2001 the UN's Human Development Index placed Haiti 134th out of a total of 162 countries.

Industry, virtually all North American 'offshore' assembly operations, provided jobs in Port-au-Prince. There was little other foreign investment. Tourism virtually died out in the 1980s owing to political instability and publicity about poverty and the high incidence of AIDS. In 1997 the Government began a US $18m. project to develop tourism near Jacmel, in the south-east.

The Government raised the minimum wage in 1995 to 36 gourdes (US $2.12) per day, but enforcement was difficult because of high unemployment and weak trade unions. The increase was actually a fall of 17%, in real terms, from 1984, when the minimum wage was last raised.

From the early 1960s Haitians responded to their bleak prospects by emigrating, mostly to the USA and Canada. In 2000 the value of the remittances from this diaspora was estimated at some US $700m. per year. The outflow of skilled people, however, condemned those who remained in Haiti to even less promising economic conditions.

From 1980 onwards the economy steadily declined, mainly owing to political turmoil. It was also undermined by extensive smuggling. In 1991 installation of the country's first freely elected president, Fr Jean-Bertrand Aristide, revived business confidence. Corruption and inflation were reduced, more taxes collected and structural reform planned. However, President Aristide's overthrow, after seven months, ended all economic hopes. An international trade embargo, except for basic food and medical supplies, was imposed. Haiti's foreign assets were 'frozen', as the USA and Canada attempted to force Aristide's restoration. Many of the sanctions were made ineffective by smuggling, including clandestine supplies of petroleum from Europe and the Dominican Republic. Nearly 100,000 jobs were lost, however, and prices rose dramatically. Repression and the embargo increased poverty and starvation and exacerbated health conditions in the countryside, to which some 300,000 people fled from the capital, while many of the rich became even wealthier from their control of smuggling. Thousands of others fled the country as boat people. The economy contracted by nearly one-third between 1991 and 1994.

The restoration to power of Aristide in 1994 raised hopes of a substantial economic revival. These quickly faded as government incapacity and political impasse hampered foreign and domestic economic efforts and about US $500m. in foreign aid was suspended. Gross domestic product (GDP), however, increased by 1.2% in 2000. Meanwhile, huge profits from the smuggling of cocaine through Haiti from Colombia to the USA were playing an increasingly large role in the economy. About 8% of the cocaine that arrived in the USA in 2000 had passed through Haiti.

AGRICULTURE

Nearly two-thirds of Haiti's working population were engaged in agriculture in 1998, but the sector produced only 31.0% of the country's GDP in 1998/99, less than 10% of total exports and less than one-half of domestic food requirements. Only about one-third of Haiti's land area was considered arable, but, as a result of population pressure, one-half of total land was under cultivation in 2000, mostly in small plots. About one-quarter of the peasantry had no land and the poorest 60% owned only 1% of it. Tenure was difficult to prove and land seizures and disputes were, with rural taxes, a cause of political unrest. The disruptions caused by the 1991–94 embargo and military dictatorship reduced farm production by 40% and sent the peasantry into serious debt. The Government began an agrarian reform programme in 1996, redistributing state lands and financing irrigation and fertilizers in the Artibonite Valley and, from 1998, in the north-east and north-west of the country.

Owing to erosion, drought, primitive farming methods, poor maintenance and population density, soil fertility was low. Only one-half of the arable land was irrigated, most of it in the main valley, the Artibonite, and the Port-au-Prince and Les Cayes plains. Poverty and the country's mountainous terrain make mechanization impractical. The peasantry was badly affected by the killing of the entire pig population in 1981–82, under a US-sponsored programme to eradicate African swine fever and so protect the US livestock industry: pigs were often a family's only asset.

Coffee, the main cash crop, was sold through a system of intermediaries, speculators and large merchants, which involved high taxes, making production erratic, as farmers alternated between coffee and food crops, according to prices. A US Agency for International Development (USAID) project, begun in 1990, organized growers into co-operatives and increased production, as well as helping reforestation. Sugar cane was once the second cash crop, but falling quality and cheaper imports forced closure of all the country's major sugar factories, although one of them, at Darbonne, near Léogane, was reopened with Cuban help in January 2001. Coffee, cocoa and mangoes were exported, as were essential oils for use in the cosmetic and pharmaceutical industries.

The main food crops, apart from sugar, were maize, rice, bananas, avocados, sorghum, vegetables and some citrus fruits.

Shortfalls of rice, the national staple, in the 1980s, and increased foreign food aid, mainly of wheat, increased popular demand for bread and thus for imported flour, most of it from the USA. However, the official reopening of provincial ports in 1986 led to large-scale smuggling of cheap rice from the USA. By 1998 the agrarian reform programme had increased rice yields in the Artibonite Valley by 60%, but this was offset from 1999 by falling prices. The lowering of tariffs under the International Monetary Fund (IMF)-imposed reforms in 1994 increased imports of cheaper food products from the Dominican Republic, adversely affecting tens of thousands of small producers. In 2001 Cuban experts were advising the undeveloped fishing industry and the first national fishing congress was held in December 2000.

MINING AND POWER

Local timber and charcoal account for some two-thirds of the energy used in Haiti. The fuel embargo imposed on the 1991–94 dictatorship increased deforestation because remaining trees were felled for use as domestic fuel. Total roundwood removals in 1999 amounted to 6.5m. cu m, while sawnwood production was estimated at 14,000 cu m.

One-third of the country's public electricity came from the Péligre hydroelectric plant above the Artibonite Valley and the rest from several thermal plants in the Port-au-Prince area and the Saut-Mathurine dam near Les Cayes. However, the Péligre lake was slowly silting up from erosion, partly caused by the deforestation of hillsides to make charcoal, the principal household fuel. Only 10% of the total population (45% in the capital and 3% in rural areas) had electricity. Supply was severely limited even in the capital and many assembly industries, along with wealthier citizens, relied on private generators, which provided about one-third of the national total. More than one-half of the current produced by the state electricity company, Electricité d'Haïti, was stolen or illegally re-sold. Severe shortfalls in 2000–01 led the Government to contract Dominican and US–Haitian companies to add 70 MW to the national supply, increasing it by one-third.

The mining sector disappeared in 1983, when the US-owned Reynolds Company closed its bauxite mine at Miragoane, after 40 years of operation, because of low world prices. Copper and gold deposits in the north were occasionally mined.

MANUFACTURING

Owing to Haiti's extreme poverty, the domestic market for finished goods was small, and local factories produced only such staples as cooking oil, detergents, household utensils, shoes, beverages, cigarettes, cement and flour. There was also strong competition from smuggled goods.

From 1970 about 150 mostly US-controlled factories assembling light industrial products for re-export were established on the outskirts of the capital. They were attracted to Haiti by the lowest labour costs in the region and the virtual absence of trade unions. This created about 60,000 jobs (two-thirds of them held by women) for workers assembling mainly electronic components, clothing and toys. Such manufacturing was the most dynamic sector of the economy, but its contribution to government revenue was insignificant, as the companies, some of them joint ventures with Haitians, were exempt from taxation for up to 15 years and were free to repatriate profits. Manufacturing accounted for an estimated 7.4% of GDP in 1998/99.

Political turmoil after the fall of the Duvaliers and then President Aristide's overthrow in 1991 resulted in the closure of many factories, some of which moved operations to more stable neighbouring countries. The sector revived slowly after Aristide's return from exile in 1994 and by mid-2000 manufacturing employed some 35,000 people. Another branch of manufacturing was handicrafts, including paintings, furniture and carvings.

TRANSPORT AND INFRASTRUCTURE

The country's main roads, from the capital to Cap Haïtien in the north and to Les Cayes and Jacmel in the south, were paved in the 1970s and early 1980s. Of a total 4,160 km (2,585 miles) of roads, about one-quarter were paved. In 1996 the Government made road construction and repair a priority. Road transport

was in the hands of individuals or small operators, who ran trucks (lorries), vans and taxis. A single railway near the capital, used only to transport sugar, closed in the early 1950s.

Less than 2% of Haitians had telephones. Lines to the provinces were few and overall service was poor, despite the substantial profits made by the state-owned telephone company, Télécommunications d'Haïti (Téléco), from calls by the large number of Haitians living abroad. Sabotage and theft of lines was extensive. By the late 1990s Téléco was being overtaken by the establishment of many mobile-phone companies and by internet service providers. In 2000 the Aristide Government handed control of much of the Téléco service in the provinces to its own supporters.

A container terminal in Port-au-Prince handled most of the country's foreign trade. Provincial ports and the porous frontier with the Dominican Republic were the main centres of imported contraband. There were direct air links to North America, Europe and the rest of the Caribbean, but few regular services to provincial airfields, which were mostly grass strips.

INVESTMENT AND FINANCE

Most government expenditure was devoted to government operations and salaries for civil servants, who were often paid long in arrears, reducing their efficiency. There was little capital investment and public services were minimal. The USA was the principal foreign investor in Haiti, almost exclusively in the assembly sector.

Foreign aid generally accounted for two-thirds of the national budget, despite Haiti's notable inability to absorb it. Most of the aid came from the European Union (EU), the USA, Canada, France and Japan. These countries and the European Community (as the EU was known until 1993) suspended all but humanitarian assistance after the cancellation of the 1987 elections. Aid increased again as prospects for democracy improved and in 1991, under President Aristide, nearly US $500m. was promised, only to be suspended again after the military coup later that year. Following Aristide's return to power, the international community pledged more than $1,000m. to restore Haiti's shattered economy. Aid was made conditional on compliance with an IMF structural-adjustment programme involving the privatization of nine major state bodies, most of them overstaffed and in deficit, except for the highly profitable Téléco. The 46,000-strong government work-force, which included many non-existent employees, was to be reduced by 20% as part of a reform of government operations, including decentralization. President Aristide opposed the reforms, however, and negotiations with the IMF were suspended in October 1995.

President Préval revived the structural-adjustment programme and proposed a compromise involving recapitalization or partial privatization, allowing private management and the sharing of profits with provincial authorities. By 2001, however, only two of the nine state bodies—a flour mill and a cement company—had been sold and only about one-half of the total foreign aid had been disbursed (some was no longer available) owing to the Haitian legislature's inaction and failure to approve agreements. In May 1999 Prime Minister Jacques Édouard Alexis announced a US $311m. emergency economic revival plan, one-half of it to be funded by foreign loans and grants. In July the UN Economic and Social Council (ECOSOC) proposed a long-term international aid programme for Haiti. However, charges of fraud in the May 2000 legislative elections once again resulted in the suspension of most foreign assistance. The budgetary position worsened from mid-1999 with an increase in government spending, which increased further in 2000 with the cost of elections and fuel subsidies to offset the rising price of petroleum. In September 2000 the Government ended the fuel price subsidies, which had cost it more than $47m. (about one-quarter of total government revenues) since the start of the year. Pump prices rose by an average 44%, followed by sharp increases in prices for consumer goods.

The post-Duvalier regimes made some attempt at fiscal reform. Monopolies were ended and the tax system was simplified. However, state revenue halved under the 1991–94 military dictatorship. Fiscal order was restored to some extent, but parliamentary disputes prevented approval of a national budget between 1996 and 2000. While the 2000/01 budget was 22% lower than in 1996/97, the sum allocated to the presidency quadrupled. Tax collection became steadily more efficient from 1995, but 40% of potential revenue was still being lost in 1999 through corruption or evasion. In 2000 total tax revenue was only 8% of GDP, two-thirds of it derived from customs duties. In June 2001 the Government froze the accounts of a number of companies that owed taxes. The annual inflation rate fell from 39.3% in 1994 to 8.7% in 1999, but increased to 13.7% in 2000. Official increases in the money supply and the effects of the international trade embargo reduced the value of the gourde by about 80% between 1986 and 1994. Its value remained steady until mid-1999, when it decreased by 25% over several months. Two-thirds of Haiti's foreign debt was cancelled by the main creditor countries in 1994. In mid-2000 total foreign debt was estimated at US $1,340m., 84% of it owed to the World Bank (International Bank for Reconstruction and Development— IBRD) and the IMF. Two major Haitian banks, Sogebank and Unibank, began a 'microloan' programme in 1999–2000.

FOREIGN TRADE

Haiti's principal export in 1997/98 was light manufactures (86.1% of total exports) produced by 'offshore' assembly industries, followed by coffee (4.1%). The principal imports in that year were food and live animals (37.2% of all imports), manufactured goods (27.5%), machinery and transport equipment (15.5%), and fuel (10.0%). External trade figures were estimated to have remained at the same level in 1999. One major problem was the heavy burden caused by the import of luxury items by the wealthy and by their deposit of millions of US dollars outside the country. In 1999 the USA took 90% of Haiti's exports and

provided 60% of imports. Other major trading partners were France, Canada, Japan and the Dominican Republic. The Caribbean Basin Initiative, Haiti's membership of the EU's Lomé Convention (which expired in February 2000 and was replaced by the Cotonou Agreement in June—see Part Three, Regional Organizations, European Union) and its tentative admission in July 1999 to the Caribbean Community and Common Market (CARICOM), opened more export opportunities, although these were offset by the sharp reduction in Haiti's import tariffs after 1995. Trade figures were deceptive owing to large-scale smuggling, estimated in 2000 to account for two-thirds of Haiti's imports.

CONCLUSION

Division in the ruling Fanmi Lavalas (FL—Lavalas Family) and the development of a hard-line, internationally-encouraged opposition hindered efforts to establish democracy and political and economic stability from the restoration of President Aristide in 1994. President Aristide's efforts to move the country forward were offset by his resort to traditional undemocratic methods and to corruption, although the media remained prolific and essentially free; consequently, his return to power in the 2000 elections alienated both the international community and the divided domestic opposition. Prospects for a real transformation of Haitian society and economic improvement remained poor, despite President Aristide's dissolution of the Army in 1995, which had obstructed the country's development since independence. With few viable structures and institutions, and scant natural resources, Haiti's path to progress in 2001 still lay through carefully-co-ordinated international aid.

Statistical Survey

Sources (unless otherwise stated): Banque de la République d'Haïti, angle rue du Magasin d'État et rue des Miracles, BP 1570, Port-au-Prince; tel. 299-1000; fax 299-1145; e-mail webmaster@brh.net; internet www.brh.net; Ministère des Finances, Port-au-Prince.

Area and Population

AREA, POPULATION AND DENSITY

Area (sq km)	27,750*
Population (census results)†	
31 August 1971	4,329,991
30 August 1982	
Males	2,448,370
Females	2,605,422
Total	5,053,792
Population (official estimates at mid-year)‡	
1998	6,682,785
1999	6,774,081
2000	7,180,294
Density (per sq km) at mid-2000	258.7

* 10,714 sq miles.
† Excluding adjustment for underenumeration.
‡ Provisional figures.

DEPARTMENTS (population estimates, 2000)

Artibonite . .	1,013,779	North-West . .	420,971
Central . .	490,790	South . .	653,398
Grande-Anse .	641,399	South-East . .	457,013
North . . .	759,318	West . . .	2,494,862
North-East . .	248,764	**Total** . . .	7,180,294

PRINCIPAL TOWNS (estimated population at mid-1996)

Port-au-Prince (capital) .	884,472	Delmas . .	240,429
Carrefour	290,204	Cap-Haïtien . .	102,233

Source: UN, *Demographic Yearbook*.

BIRTHS AND DEATHS (World Bank estimates)

	1996	1997	1998
Crude birth rate (per 1,000) . .	32	32	31
Crude death rate (per 1,000) . .	12	13	13

Source: World Bank, *World Development Indicators*.

Expectation of life (estimates, years at birth, 1998): 54.0 (males 51.5; females 56.4) (Source: UN Development Programme, *Human Development Report*).

ECONOMICALLY ACTIVE POPULATION
(official estimates, persons aged 10 years and over, mid-1990)

	Males	Females	Total
Agriculture, hunting, forestry and fishing	1,077,191	458,253	1,535,444
Mining and quarrying . .	11,959	12,053	24,012
Manufacturing	83,180	68,207	151,387
Electricity, gas and water . .	1,643	934	2,577
Construction	23,584	4,417	28,001
Trade, restaurants and hotels .	81,632	271,338	352,970
Transport, storage and communications . . .	17,856	2,835	20,691
Financing, insurance, real estate and business services .	3,468	1,589	5,057
Community, social and personal services	81,897	73,450	155,347
Activities not adequately defined .	33,695	30,280	63,975
Total employed	1,416,105	923,356	2,339,461
Unemployed	191,333	148,346	339,679
Total labour force	1,607,438	1,071,702	2,679,140

Source: ILO, *Yearbook of Labour Statistics*.

Mid-1998 (estimates in '000): Agriculture, etc. 2,168; Total labour force 3,418 (Source: FAO, *Production Yearbook*).

Agriculture

PRINCIPAL CROPS ('000 metric tons)

	1998	1999*	2000
Rice (paddy)	101.3	100.0	130.0
Maize	206.1	250.0	202.5
Sweet potatoes	170.3	172.0	180.0
Dry beans	35.1	35.5	33.2
Sugar cane	1,000.1	1,000.0	800.0
Bananas	287.7	290.0	322.5
Coffee (green)	27.2	28.0	30.0
Cocoa beans	4.5	4.5	4.5

* FAO estimates.

Source: FAO.

LIVESTOCK ('000 head, year ending September)

	1998	1999	2000
Horses*	490.0	490.0	500.0
Mules*	80.0	80.0	82.0
Asses*	210.0	210.0	215.0
Cattle	1,300.0	1,300.0*	1,430.0
Pigs	800.0	800.0*	1,000.0
Sheep	138.0	138.0*	151.8
Goats	1,618.2†	1,619.0*	1,941.8

Poultry (million): 5.0 in 1998; 5.0* in 1999; 5.5 in 2000.

* FAO estimate(s).   † Unofficial figures.

Source: FAO.

LIVESTOCK PRODUCTS ('000 metric tons)

	1998	1999*	2000
Beef and veal	30.8	31.0*	40.3
Goat meat	5.4†	5.4*	6.5
Pig meat	26.9	26.9*	28.0
Horse meat	5.4	5.4	5.5
Poultry meat	7.6	7.6	7.6
Cows' milk	37.4*	37.5*	41.3
Goats' milk	20.0	20.0	24.0
Hen eggs	3.8*	3.8*	4.1
Cattle hides	4.8	4.8	5.8

* FAO estimate.   † Unofficial figure.

Source: FAO.

Forestry

ROUNDWOOD REMOVALS ('000 cubic metres, excl. bark)

	1997	1998	1999
Sawlogs, veneer logs and logs for sleepers*	224	224	224
Other industrial wood* . . .	15	15	15
Fuel wood	6,055	6,158	6,262
Total	6,294	6,397	6,501

* Annual output assumed to be unchanged since 1971.

Source: FAO, *Yearbook of Forest Products.*

SAWNWOOD PRODUCTION
(FAO estimates, '000 cubic metres, incl. railway sleepers)

	1997	1998	1999
Coniferous (softwood) . . .	8	8	8
Broadleaved (hardwood) . . .	6	6	6
Total	14	14	14

Source: FAO, *Yearbook of Forest Products.*

Fishing

(FAO estimates, metric tons, live weight)

	1996	1997	1998
Freshwater fishes	500	500	450
Marine fishes	4,000	4,000	4,000
Caribbean spiny lobster . . .	190	210	200
Inshore shrimps	150	150	160
Stromboid conchs	400	380	350
Total catch	5,245	5,311	5,219

Source: FAO, *Yearbook of Fishery Statistics.*

Industry

SELECTED PRODUCTS
(metric tons, unless otherwise indicated, year ending 30 September)

	1999/2000
Edible oils	38,839.6
Butter	2,972.2
Margarine	2,387.4
Cornflour	104,542.6
Soap	30,069.9
Detergent	4,506.1
Beer ('000 cases of 24 bottles)	784.5
Beverages ('000 cases of 24 bottles)	1,807.7
Rum ('000 750ml bottles)	2,009.5
Electric energy (million kWh)	697.6

Finance

CURRENCY AND EXCHANGE RATES

Monetary Units
100 centimes = 1 gourde.

Sterling, Dollar and Euro Equivalents (30 April 2001)
£1 sterling = 33.597 gourdes;
US $1 = 23.465 gourdes;
€1 = 20.828 gourdes;
1,000 gourdes = £29.76 = $42.62 = €48.01.

Average Exchange Rate (gourdes per US $)
1998   16.766
1999   16.938
2000   21.171

Note: The official rate of exchange was maintained at US $1 = 5 gourdes until September 1991, when the central bank ceased all operations at the official rate, thereby unifying the exchange system at the 'floating' free market rate.

BUDGET (million gourdes, year ending 30 September)

Revenue	1995/96	1996/97	1997/98
Current receipts	3,178	4,770	5,252
Internal receipts . . .	2,678	3,731	4,174
Income tax . . .	485	688	630
General sales tax . .	619	1,271	1,420
Excises	495	705	855
Other domestic receipts . .	235	1,056	1,225
Customs	499	1,039	1,078
Transfers from public enterprises .	238	57	119
Total	3,417	4,828	5,371

Expenditure	1995/96	1996/97	1997/98
Current expenditure	4,459	4,217	4,828
Wages and salaries . . .	2,083	2,689	2,815
Operations	895	1,242	1,434
Subsidies	622	272	243
Interest on public debt . . .	211	374	437
External debt . . .	143	206	215
Internal debt . . .	68	168	222
Other current expenditure . .	648	−360	−101
Capital expenditure	145	874	1,219
Total*	4,604	5,084	6,036

* Including net lending (million gourdes): 0.0 in 1995/96; −7.0 in 1996/97; −11 in 1997/98.

Source: IMF, *Haiti: Statistical Annex* (October 1999).

INTERNATIONAL RESERVES (US $ million at 31 December)*

	1995	1996	1997
IMF special drawing rights . .	0.5	0.1	0.1
Reserve position in IMF . . .	0.1	0.1	0.1
Foreign exchange	105.2	107.8	77.0
Total	105.8	107.9	77.2

* Excluding gold (valued at market-related prices, US $ million): 6.6 in 1989.

Source: IMF, *International Financial Statistics*.

MONEY SUPPLY (million gourdes at 31 December)*

	1998	1999	2000
Currency outside banks . . .	3,905.4	4,927.1	5,807.2
Demand deposits at commercial banks	2,544.2	3,241.3	3,251.2
Total money (incl. others) . .	6,650.9	8,422.8	9,220.2

* Beginning in September 1997, data are based on an improved sectorization of the accounts.

Source: IMF, *International Financial Statistics*.

COST OF LIVING

(Consumer Price Index, year ending 30 September; base: 1991 = 100)

	1991/92	1992/93	1993/94
Food	119.0	134.3	182.0
Clothing and footwear . . .	114.4	134.0	186.4
Furnishings	117.8	154.7	190.1
Housing, heating and light . .	108.3	138.9	204.9
Services	112.5	137.5	226.7
All items	115.6	137.3	186.9

All items (base: 1995 = 100): 160.8 in 1998; 174.8 in 1999; 198.7 in 2000 (Source: IMF, *International Financial Statistics*).

NATIONAL ACCOUNTS (million gourdes, year ending 30 September)
Expenditure on the Gross Domestic Product (at current prices)

	1997/98	1998/99	1999/2000
Final consumption expenditure .	60,543	70,069	81,227
Increase in stocks . . . }	7,596	8,924	10,069
Gross fixed capital formation . . }			
Total domestic expenditure .	68,139	78,993	91,296
Exports of goods and services . .	7,799	9,017	9,933
Less Imports of goods and services	16,883	19,460	21,765
GDP in purchasers' values . .	59,055	68,550	79,464
GDP at constant 1976 prices .	4,634	n.a.	n.a.

Source: IMF, *International Financial Statistics*.

Gross Domestic Product by Economic Activity
(at constant 1975/76 prices)

	1996/97*	1997/98†	1998/99†
Agriculture, hunting, forestry and fishing	1,373	1,403	1,418
Mining and quarrying . . .	9	9	10
Manufacturing	324	330	338
Electricity, gas and water . .	42	42	43
Construction	514	562	598
Trade, restaurants and hotels. .	607	623	635
Transport, storage and communication	97	98	105
Government services	820	829	826
Finance, insurance, real estate and business services . .	357	366	374
Other services	211	216	231
Sub-total	4,354	4,478	4,578
Import duties	161	174	184
GDP in purchasers' values	4,515	4,653	4,762

* Provisional figures.
† Estimates.

BALANCE OF PAYMENTS
(US $ million, year ending 30 September)

	1995/96	1996/97	1997/98
Exports of goods f.o.b. . . .	82.5	205.4	299.3
Imports of goods f.o.b. . . .	−498.6	−559.6	−640.7
Trade balance	−416.1	−354.2	−341.4
Exports of services . . .	109.1	173.7	180.0
Imports of services . . .	−283.3	−331.5	−380.6
Balance on goods and services	−590.3	−512.0	−542.0
Other income paid	−9.9	−13.6	−11.7
Balance on goods, services and income	−600.2	−525.6	−553.7
Current transfers received . .	462.5	477.9	515.6
Current balance	−137.7	−47.7	−38.1
Direct investment from abroad .	4.1	4.0	10.8
Other investment assets . .	−4.6	21.6	86.8
Other investment liabilities .	68.4	35.9	95.5
Net errors and omissions . .	19.4	16.0	−120.5
Overall balance	−50.4	29.8	34.5

Source: IMF, *International Financial Statistics*.

External Trade

PRINCIPAL COMMODITIES
(US $ million, year ending 30 September)

Imports c.i.f.	1995/96	1996/97	1997/98
Food and live animals . . .	343.0	318.4	301.5
Mineral fuels, lubricants, etc. . .	79.4	74.9	80.8
Machinery and transport equipment	125.0	111.5	125.8
Raw materials	7.9	17.2	22.5
Manufactured goods . . .	130.6	154.4	223.2
Total (incl. others) . . .	687.9	706.6	811.5

Exports f.o.b.	1995/96	1996/97	1997/98
Coffee	6.9	13.0	11.6
Essential oils	5.7	2.9	3.7
Light manufactures . . .	126.6	159.4	244.9
Total (incl. others) . . .	147.7	195.5	284.3

Source: IMF, *Haiti: Statistical Annex* (October 1999).

PRINCIPAL TRADING PARTNERS*
(US $ million, year ending 30 September)

Imports c.i.f.	1989/90	1990/91	1991/92
Belgium	3.4	3.7	2.9
Canada .	22.0	31.9	15.2
France .	24.5	32.4	17.2
Germany, Federal Republic	14.6	19.2	10.0
Japan	23.6	31.2	17.7
Netherlands .	11.2	13.9	8.7
United Kingdom .	5.6	6.7	4.2
USA	153.1	203.2	126.7
Total (incl. others)	332.2	400.5	277.2

Exports f.o.b.†	1989/90	1990/91	1991/92
Belgium	15.9	19.5	6.0
Canada .	4.5	4.7	2.3
France .	17.4	21.6	6.1
Germany, Federal Republic	5.4	6.6	2.4
Italy .	16.5	20.7	8.7
Japan	2.4	2.9	0.9
Netherlands .	3.4	4.3	1.4
United Kingdom .	2.3	2.3	0.7
USA	78.3	96.3	39.7
Total (incl. others)	163.7	198.7	74.7

* Provisional.
† Excluding re-exports.

Source: Administration Générale des Douanes.

Transport

ROAD TRAFFIC ('000 motor vehicles in use)

	1994	1995	1996
Passenger cars .	30.0	49.0	59.0
Commercial vehicles .	30.0	29.0	35.0

Source: UN, *Statistical Yearbook*.

SHIPPING
Merchant Fleet (registered at 31 December)

	1996	1997	1998
Number of vessels .	6	7	5
Total displacement ('000 grt) .	1.0	1.6	1.3

Source: Lloyd's Register of Shipping, *World Fleet Statistics*.

International Sea-borne Freight Traffic ('000 metric tons)

	1988	1989	1990
Goods loaded .	164	165	170
Goods unloaded .	684	659	704

Source: UN, *Monthly Bulletin of Statistics*.

CIVIL AVIATION

International flights, 1995: Passengers arriving 367,900; Passengers departing 368,330.

Tourism

TOURIST ARRIVALS BY COUNTRY OF ORIGIN

	1996	1997	1998
Canada .	14,783	15,825	15,489
Dominican Republic .	7,373	7,319	7,905
France .	7,471	7,179	6,984
USA .	96,253	94,783	93,978
Total (incl. others) .	150,147	148,735	146,837

Receipts from tourism (US $ million): 80 in 1997; 58 in 1998; 57 in 1999. **Arrivals** ('000): 147 in 1999.

Sources: World Tourism Organization, *Yearbook of Tourism Statistics* and World Bank, *World Development Indicators*.

Communications Media

	1995	1996	1997
Radio receivers ('000 in use) . .	380	400	415
Television receivers ('000 in use) .	35	36	38
Telephones ('000 main lines in use)*	60	60	60

Daily newspapers: 4 in 1996 (total circulation 20,000 copies).
Book production: 340 titles published in 1995.
* Estimates.

Sources: UNESCO, *Statistical Yearbook*; UN, *Statistical Yearbook*.

Education

(1994/95)

	Institutions	Teachers	Students
Pre-primary .	n.a.	n.a.	230,391*
Primary .	10,071	30,205	1,110,398
Secondary .	1,038	15,275	195,418
Tertiary .	n.a.	654*	6,288*

* 1990/91 figure.

Directory

The Constitution

The Constitution of the Republic of Haiti, which was approved by the electorate in a referendum held in March 1987, provided for a system of power-sharing between a President (who may not serve two consecutive five-year terms), a Prime Minister, a bicameral legislature and regional assemblies. The army and the police were no longer to be a combined force. The death penalty was abolished. Official status was given to the Creole language spoken by Haitians and to the folk religion, voodoo (vaudou). The Constitution was suspended after a military *coup d'état* in June 1988. It was restored when the military ruler, Brig.-Gen. Prosper Avril, fled in March 1990 and an interim President was appointed, pending a presiden-tial election in December 1990. Fr Jean-Bertrand Aristide was elected President, but was deposed in September 1991 by a military coup. In October a new President and Government were installed by the army. In June 1992 the presidency was declared to be vacant, but in May 1994 a pro-military faction of the Senate declared the head of the Supreme Court, Émile Jonassaint, provisional President. Following US mediation, US forces (officially an international peace-keeping force) arrived on the island on 19 September. Lt-Gen. Raoul Cédras, the Commander-in-Chief of the armed forces, resigned on 10 October, and Jonassaint resigned the following day. On 15 October President Aristide returned to Haiti, to begin the restoration of constitutional government. He declared the army dissolved in April 1995. The constitutional amendment formally abolishing it was due to be passed by the legislature elected in May and July 2000.

The Government

HEAD OF STATE

President: JEAN-BERTRAND ARISTIDE (assumed office on 7 February 2001).

CABINET
(August 2001)

Prime Minister: JEAN-MARIE CHÉRESTAL.

Minister of Agriculture and the Environment: SÉBASTIEN HILAIRE.

Minister of the Civil Service: WEBSTER PIERRE.

Minister of Culture and Communications: GUY PAUL.

Minister of Economy and Finance: GUSTAVE FAUBERT.

Minister of Foreign Affairs and Religion: JOSEPH ANTONIO.

Minister for Haitians Residing Abroad: LESLIE VOLTAIRE.

Minister of Health: HENRI-CLAUDE VOLTAIRE.

Minister of the Interior: HENRI-CLAUDE MÉNARD.

Minister of Justice: GARY LISSADE.

Minister of National Education, Youth and Sports: GEORGES MÉRISIER.

Minister of Planning and External Co-operation: MARC BAZIN.

Minister of Public Works: ERNST LARAQUE.

Minister of Social Affairs: EUDES SAINT-PREUX CRAAN.

Minister of Tourism: MARTINE DEVERSON.

Minister of Trade and Industry: STANLEY THÉARD.

Minister of Women's Affairs and Rights: GINETTE LUBIN.

Secretary of State for Labour: RONALD JOSEPH.

Secretary of State for Population: JEAN ANDRE.

Secretary of State for Public Security: GÉRARD DUBREUIL.

Secretary of State for Youth, Sports and Civic Service: EVANS LESCOUFLAIR.

Secretary of State for Finance: JOCELERME PRIVERT.

MINISTRIES

Office of the President: Palais National, Champ de Mars, Port-au-Prince; tel. 222-3024.

Office of the Prime Minister: Villa d'Accueil, Delmas 60, Musseau, Port-au-Prince; tel. 245-0007; fax 245-1624.

Ministry of Agriculture and the Environment: Rte Nationale 1, Damien, Port-au-Prince; tel. 222-3596.

Ministry of the Civil Service: Port-au-Prince.

Ministry of Culture and Communications: rue Roy 31, Port-au-Prince; tel. 222-7357.

Ministry of Economy and Finance: Palais des Ministères, Port-au-Prince; tel. 222-0724.

Ministry of Foreign Affairs and Religion: blvd Harry S Truman, Cité de l'Exposition, Port-au-Prince; tel. 222-8482; fax 223-1668.

Ministry for Haitians Residing Abroad: rue Duncombe 37, Port-au-Prince; tel. 245-1116; fax 245-3400.

Ministry of Health: Palais de Ministères, Port-au-Prince; tel. 222-1583; fax 222-4066.

Ministry of the Interior: Palais des Ministères, Port-au-Prince; tel. 222-6490; fax 223-5742.

Ministry of Justice: ave Charles Sumner 19, Port-au-Prince; tel. 245-1626.

Ministry of National Education, Youth and Sports: rue Audain, Port-au-Prince; tel. 222-1036; fax 223-7887.

Ministry of Planning and External Co-operation: Palais des Ministères, Port-au-Prince; tel. 222-4148; fax 223-4193.

Ministry of Public Works: Palais des Ministères, BP 2002, Port-au-Prince; tel. 222-2164; fax 223-4586.

Ministry of Social Affairs: rue de la Révolution 16, Port-au-Prince; tel. 222-1244.

Ministry of Tourism: Port-au-Prince.

Ministry of Trade and Industry: rue Légitime 26, Champ-de-Mars, Port-au-Prince; tel. 222-1628; fax 223-8402.

Ministry of Women's Affairs and Rights: Champ de Mars, Port-au-Prince; tel. 222-1479.

President and Legislature

PRESIDENT

Presidential Election, 26 November 2000

Candidates	% of votes
JEAN-BERTRAND ARISTIDE (FL)	91.7
JEAN-ARNOLD DUMAS	2.0
EVAN NICOLAS	1.6
SERGE SYLVAIN	1.3
CALIXTE DORISCA	1.3
JACQUES PHILIPPE DORCE	1.1
PAUL ARTHUR FLEURIVAL	1.0
Total (incl. others)	100.0

LEGISLATURE

Sénat
(Senate)

President: YVON NEPTUNE.

Elections, 21 May, 9 July and 26 November 2000

	Seats
La Fanmi Lavalas (FL)	26*
Pati Louvri Baryè (PLB)	1
Total	27

* In June 2001 seven FL senators resigned their seats.

Chambre des Députés
(Chamber of Deputies)

President: PIERRE PAUL COTIN.

Elections, 21 May, 9 July and 26 November 2000

	Seats
La Fanmi Lavalas (FL)	73
Mouvement Chrétien pour Batir une Nouvelle Haïti (MOCHRENA)	3
Espace de Concertation	2
Pati Louvri Baryè (PLB)	2
Koordinasyon Resistans Grandans (KOREGA-ESCANP)	1
Organisation du Peuple en Lutte (OPL)	1
Independent	1
Total	83

Political Organizations

Alliance pour l'Avancement d'Haïti (ALAH): BP 13350, Station de Delmas, Port-au-Prince; tel. 245-0446; fax 257-4804; Leader REYNOLD GEORGES.

L'Alternative pour le Changement (AC): Port-au-Prince; f. 2000; Leader GÉRARD BLOT.

Congrès National des Mouvements Démocratiques (KONAKOM): f. 1987; social democratic; Leader VICTOR BENOÎT.

Convergence Démocratique (CD): f. 2000; coalition of 15 anti-Lavalas parties; Leaders SERGE GILLES, EVANS PAUL, MICHA GAILLARD.

Espace de Concertation: f. 1999; centre-left coalition; Leader EVANS PAUL.

La Fanmi Lavalas: f. 1996; formed a coalition with the MOP, the OPL and the PLB; Leader JEAN-BERTRAND ARISTIDE.

Jeunesse Pouvoir Populaire (JPP): f. 1997; Leader RENÉ CIVIL.

Konfederasyon Inite Demokratik (KID): f. 1986; Leader EVANS PAUL.

Koordinasyon Resistans Grandans (KOREGA-ESCANP): regionally based; radical left; Leader Fr JOACHIM SAMEDI.

Mobilisation pour le Développement National (MDN): c/o CHISS, 33 rue Bonne Foi, BP 2497, Port-au-Prince; tel. 222-3829; e-mail info@mdnhaiti.org; internet www.mdnhaiti.org; f. 1986; Pres. HUBERT DE RONCERAY; Sec.-Gen. MAX CARRE.

Mouvement Chrétien pour Batir une Nouvelle Haïti (MOCHRENA): f. 1991; Leader LUC MÉSADIEU.

Mouvement Démocratique pour la Libération d'Haïti (MODELH): Leader François Latortue.

Mouvement pour l'Instauration de la Démocratie en Haïti (MIDH): 114 ave Jean Paul II, Port-au-Prince; tel. 245-8377; f. 1986; centre-right; Pres. Marc Bazin.

Mouvement pour l'Organisation du Pays (MOP): f. 1946; centre party; Leader Jean Molière.

Mouvement Patriotique pour le Sauvetage National (MPSN): f. 1998; right-wing coalition; Leader Hubert de Ronceray.

Mouvement pour la Reconstruction Nationale (MRN): f. 1991; Leader René Théodore.

Organisation du Peuple en Lutte (OPL): f. 1991 as Organisation Politique Lavalas; name changed as above 1998; Leaders Gérard Pierre-Charles, Sauveur Pierre-Étienne.

Parti Agricole et Industrie National (PAIN): Leader Louis Dejoie.

Parti des Démocrates Haïtiens (PADEMH): Leader Jean-Jacques Clark Parent.

Parti Démocratique et Chrétien d'Haïti (PDCH): f. 1979; Christian Democrat party; Leader Joachin Pierre.

Parti pour un Développement Alternatif (PADH): Leader Gérard Dalvius.

Parti National Progressiste Révolutionnaire (PANPRA): f. 1989; social-democratic; Leader Serge Gilles.

Parti Populaire National: f. 1999; Leader Ben Dupuy.

Parti Social Chrétien d'Haïti (PSCH): Leader Grégoire Eugène.

Pati Louvri Baryè (PLB): f. 1992; Leader Renaud Bernardin.

Rassemblement des Démocrates Chrétiens (RDC): Leader Eddy Volel.

Rassemblement des Démocrates Nationalistes et Progressistes (RDNP): f. 1979; centre party; Sec.-Gen. Leslie François Manigat.

Union Démocrates Patriotiques (UDP): Leader Rockefeller Guerre.

Diplomatic Representation

EMBASSIES IN HAITI

Argentina: 8 rue Mangones, Berthe, Pétionville, BP 1755, Port-au-Prince; tel. 257-5725; fax 257-8227; e-mail embarghaiti@hainet.net; Ambassador: Fernando Novillo Saravia.

Brazil: 37 rue Lamarre, Pétionville, BP 15845, Port-au-Prince; tel. 256-0900; fax 510-6111; Ambassador: Antônio Ferreira da Rocha.

Canada: 18 route de Delmas, BP 826, Port-au-Prince; tel. 223-2358; fax 223-8720; Ambassador: Gilles Bernier.

Chile: 384 route de Delmas, entre rues 42 et 44, Port-au-Prince; Ambassador: Lucho Larraín Cruz.

China (Taiwan): 16 rue Leon Nau, Pétionville, BP 655, Port-au-Prince; tel. 256-8063; fax 256-8067; e-mail ambrde@aen2.net; Ambassador: Michel Lu Ching-long.

Colombia: Complexe 384, No 7, route de Delmas, entre rues 42 et 44, Port-au-Prince; tel. 246-2599; fax 246-5595; Ambassador: Guillermo Triana Ayala.

Cuba: Port-au-Prince; Ambassador: Oscar Coet Blackstock.

Dominican Republic: rue Panaméricaine 121, BP 56, Pétionville, Port-au-Prince; tel. 257-0383; fax 257-9215; Ambassador: Alberto Emilio Despradel Cabral.

Ecuador: BP 2531, Port-au-Prince; tel. 222-4576; Chargé d'affaires: Adolfo Alvarez.

France: 51 place des Héros de l'Indépendance, BP 1312, Port-au-Prince; tel. 222-0951; fax 223-9858; Ambassador: Yves Gaudeul.

Germany: 2 impasse Claudinette, Bois Moquette, Pétionville, BP 1147, Port-au-Prince; tel. 257-7280; fax 257-4131; e-mail germanem @haitiworld.com; Ambassador: Julius Georg Luy.

Holy See: rue Louis Pouget, Morne Calvaire, BP 326, Port-au-Prince; tel. 257-6308; fax 257-3411; e-mail nonciature@ haitiworld.com; Apostolic Nuncio: Most Rev. Luigi Bonazzi, Titular Archbishop of Atella.

Japan: Villa Bella Vista 2, impasse Tulipe, Desprez, Port-au-Prince; tel. 245-3333; fax 245-8834; Ambassador: Hisanobu Hasama.

Mexico: Delmas 60, 2, BP 327, Port-au-Prince; tel. 257-8100; fax 256-6528; e-mail embmxhai@yahoo.com; Ambassador: Carlos Ferrer.

Spain: 54 rue Pacot, State Liles, BP 386, Port-au-Prince; tel. 245-4410; fax 245-3901; Ambassador: Rafael Matos González de Careaga.

USA: 5 blvd Harry S Truman, BP 1761, Port-au-Prince; tel. 223-5511; fax 223-5515; Ambassador: Brian Dean Curran.

Venezuela: blvd Harry S Truman, Cité de l'Exposition, BP 2158, Port-au-Prince; tel. 222-0973; Ambassador: Irma Antonini.

Judicial System

Law is based on the French Napoleonic Code, substantially modified during the presidency of François Duvalier.

Courts of Appeal and Civil Courts sit at Port-au-Prince and the three provincial capitals: Gonaïves, Cap Haïtien and Port de Paix. In principle each commune has a Magistrates' Court. Judges of the Supreme Court and Courts of Appeal are appointed by the President.

Supreme Court: Port-au-Prince; tel. 222-3212; Pres. Alexandre Bonifax.

Religion

Roman Catholicism and the folk religion voodoo (vaudou) are the official religions. There are various Protestant and other denominations.

CHRISTIANITY

The Roman Catholic Church

For ecclesiastical purposes, Haiti comprises two archdioceses and seven dioceses. At 31 December 1999 adherents represented some 66.9% of the population.

Bishops' Conference: Conférence Episcopale de Haïti, angle rues Piquant et Lamarre, BP 1572, Port-au-Prince; tel. 222-5194; fax 223-5318; e-mail cehd@haitiworld.com; f. 1977; Pres. Rt Rev. Hubert Constant, Bishop of Fort-Liberté.

Archbishop of Cap-Haïtien: Most Rev. François Gayot, Archevêché, rue 19–20 H, BP 22, Cap-Haïtien; tel. 262-1278; fax 262-0593.

Archbishop of Port-au-Prince: Most Rev. François-Wolff Ligondé, Archevêché, rue Dr Aubry, BP 538, Port-au-Prince; tel. 222-2043; e-mail archeveche.pap@globalsud.com.

The Anglican Communion

Anglicans in Haiti fall under the jurisdiction of a missionary diocese of Province II of the Episcopal Church in the USA.

Bishop of Haiti: Rt Rev. Jean Zache Duracin, Eglise Episcopale d'Haïti, BP 1309, Port-au-Prince; fax 257-3412; e-mail epihaiti@ globalsud.net.

Protestant Churches

Baptist Convention: BP 20, Cap-Haïtien; tel. 262-0567; f. 1964; Pres. Rev. Moïse Joël Dorsinville.

Lutheran Church: Petite Place Cuzeau, BP 13147, Delmas, Port-au-Prince; tel. 246-3179; f. 1975; Minister Ben Bichotte.

Other denominations active in Haiti include Methodists and the Church of God 'Eben-Ezer'.

The Press

DAILIES

Le Matin: 88 rue du Quai, BP 367, Port-au-Prince; tel. 222-2040; f. 1908; French; independent; circ. 5,000.

Le Nouvelliste: 198 rue du Centre, BP 1316, Port-au-Prince; tel. 223-2114; fax 223-2313; f. 1898; evening; French; independent; circ. 6,000.

PERIODICALS

Haïti en Marche: 8 ruelle Cheriez, Port-au-Prince; tel. 245-1910; fax 513-5688; internet www.haitienmarche.com; weekly; Editor Marcus Garcia.

Haïti Progrès: 11 rue Capois, Port-au-Prince; tel. 222-6513; internet www.haiti-progres.com; weekly; Dir Ben Dupuy.

Haïti Observateur: 98 ave John Brown, Port-au-Prince; tel. 228-0782; weekly; Editor Léo Joseph.

Le Messager du Nord-Ouest: Port de Paix; weekly.

Le Moniteur: BP 214 bis, Port-au-Prince; tel. 222-1744; 2 a week; French; the official gazette; circ. 2,000.

Optique: French Institute, BP 1316, Port-au-Prince; monthly; arts.

Le Septentrion: Cap-Haïtien; weekly; independent; Editor Nelson Bell; circ. 2,000.

NEWS AGENCIES

Agence Haïtienne de Presse (AHP): 6 rue Fernand, Port-au-Prince; tel. 245-7222; fax 245-5836; e-mail ahp@haitiworld.com; internet www.ahphaiti.org; Dir-Gen. Venel Remarais.

Foreign Bureaux

Agence France-Presse (AFP): 72 rue Pavée, BP 62, Port-au-Prince; tel. 222-3469; fax 222-3759; Bureau Chief DOMINIQUE LEVANTI.

Agencia EFE (Spain): Port-au-Prince; tel. 255-9517; Correspondent HEROLD JEAN-FRANÇOIS.

Associated Press (AP) (USA): BP 2443, Port-au-Prince; tel. 257-4240; Correspondent MIKE NORTON.

Inter Press Service (Italy): 16 rue Malval, Turgeau, BP 19046, Port-au-Prince; tel. 245-9393; fax 245-9292; e-mail ipshaiti@haitiweb.net; Correspondent IVES-MARIE CHANEL.

Prensa Latina (Cuba): Port-au-Prince; tel. 246-5149; internet www.prensa-latina.org; Correspondent JACQUELÍN TELEMAQUE.

Reuters (United Kingdom): Port-au-Prince; Correspondent TRENTON DANIEL.

Publishers

Editions des Antilles: route de l'Aéroport, Port-au-Prince.

Editions Caraïbes S.A.: 57, rue Pavée, BP 2013, Port-au-Prince; tel. 222-0032; Man. PIERRE J. ELIE.

Editions du Soleil: BP 2471, rue du Centre, Port-au-Prince; tel. 222-3147; education.

L'Imprimeur Deux: Le Nouvelliste, 198 rue du Centre, Port-au-Prince.

Maison Henri Deschamps—Les Entreprises Deschamps Frisch, SA: 25 rue Dr Martelly Seïde, BP 164, Port-au-Prince; tel. 223-2215; fax 223-4976; e-mail entreprisesdeschamps@globelsud.net; f. 1898; education and literature; Man. Dir JACQUES DESCHAMPS, Jr; CEO PETER J. FRISCH.

Natal: Imprimerie, rue Barbancourt, Port-au-Prince; Dir ROBERT MALVAL.

Théodore: Imprimerie, rue Dantes Destouches, Port-au-Prince.

Broadcasting and Communications

TELECOMMUNICATIONS

Conseil National des Télécommunications (CONATEL): 16 ave Marie Jeanne, Cité de l'Exposition, BP 2002, Port-au-Prince; tel. 222-0300; fax 222-0579; f. 1969; govt communications licensing authority; Dir-Gen. JEAN ARY CÉANT.

Télécommunications d'Haïti (Téléco): Blvd Jean-Jacques Dessalines, BP 814, Port-au-Prince; tel. 245–2200; fax 223-0002; Dir-Gen. (vacant).

BROADCASTING
Radio

Radio Antilles International: 175 rue du Centre, BP 2335, Port-au-Prince; tel. 223-0696; f. 1984; independent; Dir-Gen. JACQUES SAMPEUR.

Radio Cacique: 5 Bellevue, BP 1480, Port-au-Prince; tel. 245-2326; f. 1961; independent; Dir JEAN-CLAUDE CARRIÉ.

Radio Caraïbes: 19 rue Chavannes, Port-au-Prince; tel. 223-0644; f. 1973; independent.

Radio Galaxie: 17 rue Pavée, Port-au-Prince; independent; Dir YVES JEAN-BART.

Radio Haïti Inter: Delmas 66A, 522, en face de Delmas 91, BP 737, Port-au-Prince; tel. 257-3111; f. 1935; independent; Dir MICHÈLE MONTAS.

Radio Lakansyèl: 285 route de Delmas, Port-au-Prince; tel. 246-2020; independent; Dir ALEX SAINT-SURIN.

Radio Lumière: Côte-Plage 16, BP 1050, Port-au-Prince; f. 1959; tel. 234-0330; f. 1959; Protestant; independent.

Radio Magic Stéreo: 346 route de Delmas, Port-au-Prince; tel. 245-5404; independent; Dir FRITZ JOASSIN.

Radio Metropole: 8 Delmas 52, BP 62, Port-au-Prince; tel. 246-2626; fax 246-3130; f. 1970; independent; Dir-Gen. RICHARD WIDMAIER.

Radio Nationale d'Haïti: 174 rue du Magasin de l'Etat, BP 1143, Port-au-Prince; tel. 223-5712; fax 223-5911; govt-operated; Dir-Gen. MICHEL FAVARD.

Radio Plus: 85 rue Pavée, BP 1174, Port-au-Prince; tel. 222-1588; independent; Dir LIONEL BÉNJAMIN.

Radio Port-au-Prince: Stade Sylvio Cator, BP 863, Port-au-Prince; f. 1979; independent; Dir GEORGE L. HÉRARD.

Radio Signal FM: 127 rue Louverture, Petionville, BP 391, Port-au-Prince; tel. 298-4370; fax 298-4372; e-mail signalfm@netcourrier.com; f. 1991; independent; Dir-Gen. ANNE-MARIE ISSA.

Radio Soleil: BP 1362, Archevêché de Port-au-Prince; tel. 222-3062; fax 222-3516; f. 1978; Catholic; independent; educational; broadcasts in Creole and French; Dir Fr ARNOUX CHÉRY.

Radio Solidarité: Port-au-Prince; Dir VENEL REMARAIS.

Radio Superstar: 38 rue Safran, Delmas 68, Port-au-Prince; tel. 257-7219; independent; Dir ALBERT CHANCY.

Radio Tropic FM: 6 ave John Brown, Port-au-Prince; tel. 223-6565; independent; Dir GUY JEAN.

Radio Vision 2000: Port-au-Prince; internet www.radiovision2000.com; Dir LÉOPOLD BERLANGER.

Television

PVS Antenne 16: 137 rue Monseigneur Guilloux, Port-au-Prince; tel. and fax 222-1277; f. 1988; independent; Dir-Gen. RAYNALD DELERME.

Télé Haïti: blvd Harry S Truman, BP 1126, Port-au-Prince; tel. 222-3887; fax 222-9140; f. 1959; independent; pay-cable station with 33 channels; in French, Spanish and English; Dir MARIE CHRISTINE MOURRAL BLANC.

Télévision Nationale d'Haïti: Delmas 33, BP 13400, Port-au-Prince; tel. 246-2952; fax 246-0693; e-mail info@haiticulture.net; internet www.haiticulture.net/tnh/index.htm; f. 1979; govt-owned; cultural; 4 channels in Creole, French and Spanish; administered by four-mem. board; Dir RAYNALD LOUIS.

Trans-America: ruelle Roger, Gonaïves; f. 1990; tel 74-0113; independent; Dir-Gen. HÉBERT PELISSIER.

TVA: rue Liberté, Gonaïves; independent; cable station with three channels; Dir-Gen. GÉRARD LUC JEAN-BAPTISTE.

Finance

(cap. = capital; m. = million; res = reserves; dep. = deposits; amounts in gourdes; brs = branches)

BANKING
Central Bank

Banque de la République d'Haïti: angle rues du Magasin de l'Etat et des Miracles, BP 1570, Port-au-Prince; tel. 299-1000; fax 299-1145; e-mail brh_adm@brh.net; internet www.brh.net; f. 1911; bank of issue; cap. and res 6.5m., dep. 204m. (May 1994); Pres. FRITZ JEAN; Gen. Dir ROLAND PIERRE.

Commercial Banks

Banque Commerciale d'Haïti: Champ de Mars, Port-au-Prince; tel. 222-3931.

Banque Nationale de Crédit: angle rues du Quai et des Miracles, BP 1320, Port-au-Prince; tel. 299-4081; fax 222-3331; f. 1979; cap. 25m., dep. 729.9m. (Sept. 1989); Pres. EDOUARD RACINE; Gen. Man. SOCRATE L. DEVIME.

Banque Populaire Haïtienne: angle rues des Miracles et du Centre, Port-au-Prince; tel. 222-1800; fax 222-4389; f. 1955; state-owned; cap. and res 84m., dep. 210m. (July 1994); Dir-Gen. REGINALD MONDÉSIR.

Banque de Promotion Commerciale et Industrielle SA (PROMOBANK): ave John Brown et rue Lamarre, BP 2323, Port-au-Prince; tel. 299-8000; fax 223-0982; e-mail marketing@mail.promobank.net; f. 1974 as B.N.P. Haïti, name changed as above 1994; cap. 60.4m., res 16.4m., dep. 1,183.4m. (Dec. 1998); Pres. GILBERT BIGIO; Gen. Man. JEAN PERRE.

Banque de l'Union Haïtienne: angle rues du Quai et Bonne Foi, BP 275, Port-au-Prince; tel. 222-1300; fax 223-2852; f. 1973; cap. 30.1m., res 6.2m., dep. 1,296.7m. (Sept. 1997); Pres. OSWALD J. BRANDT II; 11 brs.

Capital Bank: 149-151 rue des Miracles, BP 2464, Port-au-Prince; tel. 222-2830; fax 222-2898; frmly Banque de Crédit Immobilier, SA; Pres. BERNARD ROY; Gen. Man. LILIANE C. DOMINIQUE.

Sogebank, SA (Société Générale Haïtienne de Banque, SA): rue des Miracles, BP 1315, Port-au-Prince; tel. 222-4800; fax 222-5366; f. 1986; cap. 79.5m.; Pres. JEAN CLAUDE NADAL; Dir-Gen. CHARLES CLERMONT; 7 brs.

Sogebel: route de l'Aéroport, BP 2409, Port-au-Prince; tel. 229-5353; fax 229-5352; f. 1988; cap. 15.1m., dep. 249.9m.; Gen. Man. CLAUDE PIERRE-LOUIS; 2 brs.

Unibank: 94 place Geffard, BP 46, Port-au-Prince; tel. 299-2300; fax 299-2332; e-mail info@unibank.net; f. 1993; cap. 100m., res 17.5m., dep. 3,366m. (Sept. 1999); Pres. F. CARL BRAUN; Dir-Gen. FRANCK HELMCKE; 20 brs.

Foreign Banks

Bank of Nova Scotia (Canada): 360 blvd J.J. Dessalines, BP 686, Port-au-Prince; tel. 222-4462; fax 222-9340; Dir-Gen. CLAUDE E. MARCEL; Man. B. A. THEARD; 3 brs.

Banque Nationale de Paris (France): ave John Brown et rue Lamarre, Port-au-Prince; tel. 222-2300; fax 222-6720; Dir-Gen. MARCEL GARCÍA; 2 brs.

Citibank, NA (USA): 242 route de Delmas, BP 1688, Port-au-Prince; tel. 246-2600; fax 246-0985; Vice-Pres. GLADYS M. COUPET.

Development Bank

Banque Nationale de Développement Agricole: Port-au-Prince; tel. 222-1969; Dir-Gen. YVES LEREBOURS.

INSURANCE
National Companies

L'Atout Assurance, SA: 77 rue Lamarre, Port-au-Prince; tel. 223-9378; Dir JEAN EVEILLARD.

Compagnie d'Assurances d'Haïti, SA (CAH): étage Dynamic Entreprise, route de l'Aéroport, BP 1489, Port-au-Prince; tel. 246-0700; fax 246-0236; f. 1978; Pres. PHILIPPE R. ARMAND.

Excelsior Assurance, SA: rue 6, no 24, Port-au-Prince; tel. 245-8881; fax 245-8598; Dir-Gen. EMMANUEL SANON.

Générale d'Assurance, SA: Champ de Mars, Port-au-Prince; tel. 222-5465; fax 222-6502; f. 1985; Dir-Gen. ROLAND ACRA.

Haïti Sécurité Assurance, SA: 16 rue des Miracles, BP 1754, Port-au-Prince; tel. 223-2118; Dir-Gen. WILLIAM PHIPPS.

International Assurance, SA (INASSA): angle rues des Miracles et Pétion, Port-au-Prince; tel. 222-1058; Dir-Gen. RAOUL MÉROVÉ-PIERRE.

Multi Assurances, SA: route de l'Aéroport, Port-au-Prince; tel. 246-0700; fax 246-0236; Dir-Gen. PHILIPPE ARMAND.

National Assurance, SA (NASSA): 153 rue des Miracles, BP 532, Port-au-Prince; tel. 223-1058; fax 223-1821; Dir-Gen. FRITZ DUPUY.

Office National d'Assurance Vieillesse (ONA): Champ de Mars, Port-au-Prince; tel. 222-1655; Dir-Gen. MARGARETH LAMUR.

Société de Commercialisation d'Assurance, SA (SOCOMAS): autoroute de Delmas, BP 636, Port-au-Prince; tel. 249-3090; Dir-Gen. JEAN DIDIER GARDÈRE.

Foreign Companies

Les Assurances Léger, SA (France): 40 rue Lamarre, BP 2120, Port-au-Prince; tel. 222-3451; fax 223-8634; Pres. GÉRARD N. LÉGER.

Cabinet d'Assurances Fritz de Catalogne (USA): angle rues du Peuple et des Miracles, BP 1644, Port-au-Prince; tel. 222-6695; fax 223-0827; Dir FRITZ DE CATALOGNE.

Capital Life Insurance Company Ltd (Bahamas): angle rues du Peuple et des Miracles, BP 1644, Port-au-Prince; tel. 222-6695; fax 223-0827; Agent FRITZ DE CATALOGNE.

Dupuy & Merové-Pierre (USA): angle rues des Miracles et Pétion 153, Port-au-Prince; tel. 223-1058; fax 223-1821; agents for Cigna International La Nationale d'Assurance SA; Dirs FRITZ DUPUY, RAOUL MÉROVÉ-PIERRE.

Groupement Français d'Assurances (France): Port-au-Prince; Agent ALBERT A. DUFORT.

National Western Life Insurance (USA): 13 rue Pie XII, Cité de l'Exposition, Port-au-Prince; tel. 223-0734; Agent VORBE BARRAU DUPUY.

Preservatrices Foncières Assurances (France): angle rues du Magasin de l'Etat et Eden, Place Geffrard 266, étage Stecher, Port-au-Prince; tel. 222-4210; Agent PHILIPPE GATION.

Union des Assurances de Paris (UAP) (France): Port-au-Prince; Agent YVES GARDÈRE.

Insurance Association

Association des Assureurs d'Haïti: c/o Les Assurances Léger, SA, 40 rue Lamarre, BP 2120, Port-au-Prince; tel. 223-2137; fax 223-8634; Dir GÉRARD N. LÉGER.

Trade and Industry
GOVERNMENT AGENCY

Centre de Promotion des Investissements et des Exportations Haïtiennes (PROMINEX): Port-au-Prince; Pres. CLAUDE LEVY.

DEVELOPMENT ORGANIZATIONS

Fonds de Développement Industriel (FDI): Immeuble PROMO-BANK, 4 étage, ave John Brown et rue Lamarre, BP 2597, Port-au-Prince; tel. 222-7852; fax 222-8301; f. 1981; Dir ROOSEVELT SAINT-DIC.

Société Financière Haïtienne de Développement, SA (SOFIHDES): 11 blvd Harry S Truman, BP 1399, Port-au-Prince; tel. 222-8904; fax 222-8997; f. 1983; industrial and agro-industrial project financing, accounting, data processing, management consultancy; cap. 7.5m. (1989); Dir-Gen. FAUBERT GUSTAVE; 1 br.

CHAMBERS OF COMMERCE

Chambre de Commerce et d'Industrie d'Haïti (CCIH): blvd Harry S Truman, Cité de l'Exposition, BP 982, Port-au-Prince; tel. 223-0786; fax 222-0281; e-mail ccih@compa.net; internet www.intervision2000.com/iv2-trop/index.html; f. 1895; Exec. Dir MICHAËLE BERROUET FIGNOLÉ.

Chambre de Commerce et d'Industrie Haïtiano-Américaine (HAMCHAM): First National City Bank, route de Delmas, BP 13486, Delmas, Port-au-Prince; tel. 246-2600; fax 246-0985; f. 1979; Pres. GLADYS COUPET.

Chambre de Commerce et d'Industrie des Professions du Nord: BP 244, Cap-Haïtien; tel. 262-2360; fax 262-2895.

Chambre Franco-Haïtienne de Commerce et d'Industrie (CFHCI): Le Plaza Holiday Inn, rue Capois, Champ de Mars, Port-au-Prince; tel. 223-8404; fax 223-8131; f. 1987; Pres. PATRICK VICTOR; Sec. AXAN ABELLARD.

INDUSTRIAL AND TRADE ORGANIZATIONS

Association des Industries d'Haïti (ADIH): 199 route de Delmas, entre Delmas 31 et 33, étage Galerie 128, BP 2568, Port-au-Prince; tel. 246-4509; fax 246-2211; f. 1980; Pres. RICHARD COLES; Exec. Dir MARLÈNE SAM.

Association Nationale des Distributeurs de Produits Pétroliers (ANADIPP): Centre Commercial Dubois, route de Delmas, Bureau 401, Port-au-Prince; tel. 246-1414; fax 245-0698; f. 1979; Pres. MAURICE LAFORTUNE.

Association Nationale des Importateurs et Distributeurs de Produits Pharmaceutiques (ANIDPP): c/o Maison Nadal, rue du Fort Per, Port-au-Prince; tel. 222-1418; fax 222-4767; Pres. BERNARD CRAAN.

Association des Producteurs Agricoles (APA): BP 1318, Port-au-Prince; tel. 246-1848; fax 246-0356; f. 1985; Pres. REYNOLD BONNEFIL.

Association des Producteurs Nationaux (APRONA): c/o Mosaïques Gardère, ave Hailé Sélassié, Port-au-Prince; tel. and fax 249-4433; Pres. FRANTZ GARDÈRE.

Association des Exportateurs de Café (ASDEC): c/o USMAN, ave Somoza/Delmas, BP B-65, Port-au-Prince; tel. 222-2627; fax 222-1394; Pres. FRITZ BRANDT.

MAJOR COMPANIES

Alpha Electronics: route de l'Aéroport, Port-au-Prince; tel. 246-2772; f. 1952; manufacture of transformers and electronics; Pres. ANDRÉ APAID; 976 employees.

Brasserie Nationale d'Haïti, SA: Airport Rd, Port-au-Prince; tel. 249-1873; fax 246-1302; f. 1975; brewery; Man. Dir MICHAEL MADSEN; 145 employees.

Ciment d'Haïti, SA: Fond Mobin, Port-au-Prince; tel. 222-7955; contolled since 1997 by a Colombian-Swiss consortium; cement manufacturers; Pres. GUY ORCELLI; 345 employees.

Filature Tissage et Confection d'Haïti, SA: Diquini, Port-au-Prince; tel. 234-0523; f. 1944; textile mill; Pres. CLIFFORD BRANDT; 378 employees.

Flambert Raymond: rue du Magasin de l'Etat 257, BP 896, Port-au-Prince; tel. 222-2138; fax 223-2138; manufacturers of building materials; Pres. RAYMOND FLAMBERT; 245 employees.

Haïti Metal, SA: BP 327, Port-au-Prince; tel. 240-412; fax 241-175; f. 1955; aluminium producers; Pres. RAYMOND L. ROY; 300 employees.

Industries Nationales Réunies, SA: Delmas 6 & 8, Port-au-Prince; tel. 222-0153; manufacturers of plastic products; Pres. ANDRÉ APAID; 455 employees.

Laboratoires 4C: BP 44, Port-au-Prince; tel. 222-6434; fax 246-5332; f. 1952; manufacturers of pharmaceuticals and paper products; Pres. and Gen. Man. MAURICE ACRE; 450 employees.

Modern Business Systems & Equipment, SA: rue des Miracles, Port-au-Prince; tel. 222-5374; f. 1975; industrial and commercial equipment; Man. Dir GERARD LELIO JOSEPH.

UTILITIES
Electricity

Electricité d'Haïti: rue Dante Destouches, Port-au-Prince; tel. 222-4600; state energy utility company; Dir ROSEMOND PRADEL.

Péligre Hydroelectric Plant: Artibonite Valley.

Saut-Mathurine Hydroelectric Plant: Les Cayes.

TRADE UNIONS

Centrale Autonome des Travailleurs Haïtiens (CATH): 93 rue des Casernes, Port-au-Prince; tel. 222-4506; f. 1980; Sec.-Gen. FIGNOLE SAINT-CYR.

Centrale des Travailleurs Haïtiens (CTH): f. 1989; Sec.-Gen. JEAN-CLAUDE LEBRUN.

Confédération Ouvriers Travailleurs Haïtiens (KOTA): 155 rue des Césars, Port-au-Prince.

Confédération Nationale des Educateurs Haïtiens (CNEH): rue Berne 21, Port-au-Prince; tel. 245-1552; fax 245-9536; f. 1986.

Fédération Haïtienne de Syndicats Chrétiens (FHSC): BP 416, Port-au-Prince; Pres. LÉONVIL LEBLANC.

Fédération des Ouvriers Syndiques (FOS): angle rues Dr Aubry et des Miracles 115, BP 371, Port-au-Prince; tel. 222-0035; f. 1984; Pres. JOSEPH J. SÉNAT.

Organisation Générale Indépendante des Travailleurs et Travailleuses d'Haïti (OGITH): 121, 2-3 étage, angle route Delmas et Delmas 11, Port-au-Prince; tel. 249-0575; f. 1988; Gen. Sec. JEAN-PHILIPPE GESNER.

Syndicat des Employés de l'EDH (SEEH): c/o EDH, rue Joseph Janvier, Port-au-Prince; tel. 222-3367.

Union Nationale des Ouvriers d'Haïti—UNOH: Delmas 11, 121 bis, Cité de l'Exposition, BP 3337, Port-au-Prince; f. 1951; Pres. MARCEL VINCENT; Sec.-Gen. FRITZNER ST VIL; 3,000 mems from 8 affiliated unions.

A number of unions are non-affiliated and without a national centre, including those organized on a company basis.

Transport

RAILWAYS

The railway service, for the transportation of sugar cane, closed during the early 1990s.

ROADS

In 1996, according to International Road Federation estimates, there were 4,160 km (2,585 miles) of roads, of which 24.3% was paved. All-weather roads from Port-au-Prince, to Cap-Haïtien, on the northern coast, and to Les Cayes, in the south, were completed by the 1980s, with finance from the World Bank. Another, connecting Port-au-Prince with the southern town of Jacmel, was built and financed by France.

SHIPPING

Many European and American shipping lines call at Haiti. The two principal ports are Port-au-Prince and Cap-Haïtien. There are also 12 minor ports.

Autorité Portuaire Nationale: blvd La Saline, BP 616, Port-au-Prince; tel. 222-1942; fax 223-2440; e-mail jjulio@mail.com; f. 1978; Dir-Gen. JULIO JULIEN.

CIVIL AVIATION

The international airport, situated 8 km (5 miles) outside Port-au-Prince, is the country's principal airport, and is served by many international airlines linking Haiti with the USA and other Caribbean islands. There is an airport at Cap-Haïtien, and smaller airfields at Jacmel, Jérémie, Les Cayes and Port-de-Paix.

Air Haïti: Aéroport International, Port-au-Prince; tel. 246-3311; f. 1969; began cargo charter operations 1970; scheduled cargo and mail services from Port-au-Prince to Cap-Haïtien, San Juan (Puerto Rico), Santo Domingo (Dominican Republic), Miami and New York (USA).

Caribintair: Aéroport International, Port-au-Prince; tel. 246-0778; scheduled domestic service and charter flights to Santo Domingo (Dominican Republic) and other Caribbean destinations.

Haiti Air Freight, SA: Aéroport International, BP 170, Port-au-Prince; tel. 246-2572; fax 246-0848; cargo carrier operating scheduled and charter services from Port-au-Prince and Cap-Haïtien to Miami (USA) and Puerto Rico.

Haïti Trans Air: Aéroport International, BP 2526, Port-au-Prince; tel. 246-0418; fax 238938; scheduled flights to Miami and New York (USA); Pres. CHARLES H. VOIGHT.

Tourism

Tourism was formerly Haiti's second largest source of foreign exchange. However, as a result of political instability, the number of cruise ships visiting Haiti declined considerably, causing a sharp decline in the number of tourist arrivals. With the restoration of democracy in late 1994, the development of the tourism industry was identified as a priority by the Government. In 1998 stop-over tourists totalled 146,837, while cruise-ship excursionists numbered 246,221. Receipts from tourism in that year totalled US $58m.

Secrétariat d'Etat au Tourisme: 8 rue Légitime, Champ de Mars, Port-au-Prince; tel. 223-5631; fax 223-5380; e-mail tourisme@ sethaiti.org; internet www.haititourisme.com; Secretary of State for Tourism MARYSE PÉNETTE KEDAR.

Association Haïtienne des Agences de Voyages: rue des Miracles 17, Port-au-Prince; tel. 222-8855; fax 222-2054.

Association Touristique d'Haïti: rue Lamarre, Choucoune Plaza, Pétionville, BP 2562, Port-au-Prince; tel. 257-4647; fax 257-4134; Pres. DOMINIQUE CARVONIS; Exec. Dir GILIANE CÉSAR JOUBERT.

Defence

Following the restoration of the democratically elected President Aristide in October 1994, the armed forces and police were disbanded and an Interim Public Security Force (IPSF) of 3,000 formed. All army equipment was destroyed by US troops in 1994 and a National Police Force of some 6,000 personnel began to be recruited and trained by US, Canadian, French and Swiss officers. In late 1999 plans were outlined for the expansion of the civilian police force to 9,000; however, in 2000 there were only some 5,300 personnel. In August 2000 the Navy numbered 30. The UN Civilian Police Mission in Haiti (MIPONUH), which succeeded the UN Transition Mission in Haiti (UNTMIH), comprised 300 civilian police officers, assisted by 72 international and 133 local support staff. MIPONUH's mission was to ensure a secure environment and to oversee the creation of the National Police Force. It was succeeded in March 2000 by the UN International Civilian Support Mission in Haiti (MICAH), an unarmed, non-uniformed group of about 150 democracy and development advisers.

Security Budget: an estimated US $49m. in 2000.

Education

Some 80% of education is provided by private or missionary schools and the rest by the State. Learning is based on the French model, and French is used as the language of instruction, although most Haitians speak only Creole. Primary education, which normally begins at six years of age and lasts for six years, is officially compulsory. Secondary education usually begins at 12 years of age and lasts for a further six years, comprising two cycles of three years each. In 1997 primary enrolment included only 19.4% of children in the relevant age-group (males 18.9%; females 19.9%). Enrolment at secondary schools in 1997 was equivalent to only 34.2% of children in the relevant age-group (males 35.2%; females 33.2%). Some basic adult education programmes, with instruction in Creole, were created in the late 1980s in an attempt to address the problem of adult illiteracy. In 1998, according to the UN Development Programme, the average rate of adult illiteracy was 52.2% (males 49.9%, females 54.4%). The rate was even higher in rural areas. Higher education is provided by 18 technical and vocational centres, 42 domestic-science schools, and by the Université d'Etat d'Haïti, which has faculties of law, medicine, dentistry, science, agronomy, pharmacy, economics, veterinary medicine and ethnology. Government expenditure on education in 1990 was 216m. gourdes, or 20% of total government expenditure.

Bibliography

For works on the Caribbean generally, see Select Bibliography (Books).

Aristide, J.-B. *In the Parish of the Poor.* New York, NY, Orbis Books, 1990.

Dash, J. M. *Literature and Ideology in Haiti 1915–61.* London, Macmillan, 1981.

Haiti and the United States. London, Macmillan, 1988.

Delince, K. *Les forces politiques en Haïti: manuel d'histoire contemporaine.* Paris, Editions Karthala, 1993.

Diederich, B., and Burt, A. *Papa Doc: Haiti and Its Dictator.* Princeton, NJ, Markus Wiener Publications, 1998.

Dupuy, A. *Haiti in the World Economy: Class, Race and Underdevelopment since 1700.* Boulder, CO, Westview Press, 1989.

Haiti in the New World Order: the Limits of the Democratic Revolution. Boulder, CO, Westview Press, 1997.

Ferguson, J. *Papa Doc, Baby Doc: Haiti and the Duvaliers.* Oxford, Basil Blackwell, 1988.

Greene, A. *The Catholic Church in Haiti: Political and Social Change.* East Lansing, MI, Michigan State University Press, 1993.

Heinl, R. D., and Gordon, N. *Written in Blood.* New York, University Press of America, 1995.

Hurbon, Laënnec. *Voodoo: Search for the Spirit.* New York, NY, Henry Abrams, 1993.

Kumar, C. *Building Peace in Haiti.* Boulder, CO, Lynn Reinner Publrs, 1998.

Laguerre, M. S. *The Military and Society in Haiti.* Basingstoke, Macmillan, 1993.

Nicholls, D. *From Dessalines to Duvalier: Race, Colour and National Dependence in Haiti.* London, Macmillan Caribbean, 1996.

Haiti in Caribbean Context: Ethnicity, Economy and Revolt. London, Macmillan, 1985.

Prince, R. *Haiti: Family Business.* London, Latin American Bureau, 1985.

Renda, M. *Taking Haiti: Military Occupation and the Culture of US Imperialism, 1915–1940.* Chapel Hill, NC, University of North Carolina Press, 2001.

Ridgeway, J. (Ed.). *The Haiti Files: Decoding the Crisis.* London, Latin American Bureau, 1994.

Rotberg, R. I. *Haiti Renewed: Political and Economic Prospects.* Washington, DC, Brookings Institute Press, 1997.

St Mery, M. L. E. *The Civilization that Perished: The Last Years of Colonial White Rule in Haiti.* Lanham, MD, University Press of America, 1986.

Schmidt, H. *The US Occupation of Haiti, 1915–34.* New Brunswick, NJ, Rutgers University Press, 1971.

Stotzky, I. P. *Silencing the Guns in Haiti: the Promise of Deliberative Democracy.* Chicago, IL, University of Chicago Press, 1997.

Trouillot, M.-R. *Haiti: State Against Nation.* New York, NY, Monthly Review Press, 1990.

Weinstein, B., and Segal, A. *Haiti: Political Failures, Cultural Successes.* New York, NY, Praeger Publrs, 1984.

Wilentz, A. *The Rainy Season: Haiti since Duvalier.* London, Jonathan Cape, 1989.

HONDURAS

Area: 112,492 sq km (43,433 sq miles).

Population (official estimate at mid-2000): 6,597,100.

Capital: Tegucigalpa, estimated population 1,037,600 at mid-2000.

Language: Spanish.

Religion: Mainly Christianity (mostly Roman Catholic).

Climate: Tropical in the coastal lowlands, but temperate in the mountainous regions.

Time: GMT –6 hours.

Public Holidays

2002: 1 January (New Year's Day), 28 March (Maundy Thursday), 29 March (Good Friday), 14 April (Day of the Americas), 1 May (Labour Day), 15 September (Independence Day), 3 October (Morazán Day), 12 October (Discovery Day), 21 October (Army Day), 25 December (Christmas Day).

2003: 1 January (New Year's Day), 14 April (Day of the Americas), 17 April (Maundy Thursday), 18 April (Good Friday), 1 May (Labour Day), 15 September (Independence Day), 3 October (Morazán Day), 12 October (Discovery Day), 21 October (Army Day), 25 December (Christmas Day).

Currency: Lempira; 1,000 lempiras = £45.55 = US $65.22 = €73.48 (30 April 2001).

Weights and Measures: The metric system is in force, but some old Spanish measures are also used.

Basic Economic Indicators

	1998	1999	2000
Gross domestic product (million lempiras at 1978 prices)	6,880	6,750	7,073
GDP per head (lempiras at 1978 prices)	1,113	1,057	1,072
GDP (million lempiras at current prices)	70,438	77,095	88,025
GDP per head (lempiras at current prices)	11,398	12,074	13,343
Annual growth of real GDP (%)	2.9	–1.9	4.8
Annual growth of real GDP per head (%)	2.2	–5.0	1.4
Government budget (million lempiras at current prices):			
Revenue	13,583.8	n.a.	n.a.
Expenditure	14,601.0	n.a.	n.a.
Consumer price index (base: 1995 = 100)	169.2	188.9	209.8
Rate of inflation (annual average, %)	13.7	11.7	11.1
Foreign exchange reserves (US $ million at 31 December)	818.0	1,244.8	1,301.7
Imports c.i.f. (US $ million)	2,500	2,728	2,885
Exports f.o.b. (US $ million)	1,577	1,249	1,322
Balance of payments (current account, US $ million)	–316.9	–536.8	n.a.

Gross national product per head measured at purchasing power parity (PPP) (GNP converted to US dollars by the PPP exchange rate, 1997): 2,140.

Economically active population (September 1999): 2,299,005.

Unemployment (persons aged 10 years and over, March 1999): 3.7%.

Total foreign debt (December 1999): US $5,356m.

Life expectancy (years at birth, 1998): 70.1 (males 67.7, females 72.5).

Infant mortality rate (per 1,000 live births, 1998): 33.

Adult population with HIV/AIDS (15–49 years, 1999): 1.92%.

School enrolment ratio (7–17 years, 1998): 58%.

Adult literacy rate (15 years and over, 2000): 72.2% (males 72.5%; females 72%).

Energy consumption per head (kg of oil equivalent, 1998): 542.

Carbon dioxide emissions per head (metric tons, 1997): 0.8.

Passenger cars in use (estimate, per 1,000 of population, 1999): 60.4.

Television receivers in use (per 1,000 of population, 1997): 95.

Personal computers in use (per 1,000 of population, 1997): 9.5.

History

HELEN SCHOOLEY

Honduras gained independence from Spain in 1821, in a federation with the other four Central American states. However, the federation split up in 1838, after a peasant revolt that started in Guatemala, and the countries became separate states. For the rest of the 19th century the political life of Honduras was dominated by the struggle between the Conservatives, who opposed renewal of the federation, and the Liberals, who supported it.

The Liberals held power briefly in 1852–55 and again in 1876–91, when they received the active support of the Liberal President Barrios of Guatemala. It was at his instigation that the Honduran Liberal, Marco Aurelio Soto, both became President in 1876 and was replaced in 1881, by Luis Bográn Baraona. This kind of intervention by the Central American states in each others' affairs persisted. Thus, in 1906 Honduras threatened war with Nicaragua, claiming that the Nicaraguan authorities were supporting Hondurans working from abroad against President Policarpo Bonilla. In the following year, with conflict taking place between February and December, Nicaraguan forces did help to replace the President with Miguel Dávila.

Honduran politics were also shaped by the development of the country's principal economic activity, the cultivation and export of bananas, which increased the economic and political influence of the USA in the country. In the late 19th and early 20th centuries vast tracts of land were granted to US companies, in particular the United Fruit Company (UFCO), on very advantageous terms, often in exchange for political support. In 1910 President Dávila, who tried to halt the drastic land concessions, was overthrown by a group of US adventurers. They replaced him with Manuel Bonilla, who was more inclined to the interests of the US companies.

DICTATORSHIP AND COUPS, 1932–80

In 1932 Gen. Tiburcio Carías Andino, who founded the Partido Nacional (PN— National Party) in the previous decade, was elected President and he held office for 16 years without further election. He was finally persuaded to resign in 1948, and was succeeded by Dr Juan Manuel Gálvez of the PN, the sole candidate in the election. After inconclusive elections held in 1954, Vice-President Julio Lozano Díaz dissolved the Congress, abrogated the Constitution and declared himself head of state. Lozano was overthrown in a bloodless coup two years later. After constituent elections in which the Partido Liberal (PL— Liberal Party) achieved a substantial majority, the PL leader, Dr José Ramón Villeda Morales, took office in 1957. The moderate social reforms he introduced aroused opposition from the traditional ruling class and he was overthrown in 1963 in a military coup led by Col (later Brig.-Gen.) Oswaldo López Arellano. A new Constitution was approved in June 1965 and Arellano was then appointed President.

The next elections, held in 1971, were won narrowly by the PN, and Dr Ramón Ernesto Cruz Uclés became President. This brief return to civilian rule followed a humiliating defeat for the Honduran military in the war that had broken out against El Salvador in 1969. Triggered by events after two football (soccer) World Cup qualifying matches, it became known as the 'Football War', although it had its roots in long-standing economic grievances between the two countries. Full-scale hostilities lasted only four days (during which the better-equipped and -prepared Salvadorean Army crossed into Honduras), but the final peace treaty was not signed until 1980. The treaty did not include a definitive demarcation of the Honduran-Salvadorean border, leaving a number of areas of land, known as bolsones territoriales (territorial pockets), along the frontier, and the island of Meanguera, in the Gulf of Fonseca, in dispute. In 1986 the dispute was referred to the International Court of Justice, at The Hague (Netherlands), which, in 1992, awarded about two-thirds of the disputed territories to Honduras. In

January 1998 both countries agreed to complete the final demarcation of the frontier within 12 months, and to guarantee nationality and property rights to those affected. The demarcation left an estimated 6,000 Salvadoreans and 2,000 Hondurans living outside their respective borders. By September 2000 232.5 km of the 374 km border had been demarcated and the Government announced that the demarcation would be completed within one year.

Gen. López Arellano returned to power in a coup in 1972, but in 1975 was overthrown by Col (later Gen.) Juan Melgar Castro. Only a few weeks before the 1975 coup López Arellano had been named in a bribery scandal with United Brands (as UFCO had become in 1970), to which the company later admitted. Col Melgar Castro's attempts to introduce a comprehensive land-reform programme provoked opposition from landed interests and he was removed from power in 1978, in a coup led by Gen. (later Lt-Gen.) Policarpo Paz García.

RETURN TO CIVILIAN GOVERNMENT

With much encouragement from the USA, constituent elections were held in 1980, resulting in a surprise victory for the Liberals. The PL leader, Roberto Suazo Córdova, was elected President in 1981 and a new Constitution promulgated in January 1982. However, in a series of amendments proposed by the Armed Forces and passed by Congress, the Army increased its political influence, by transferring the post of Commander-in-Chief from the President to the head of the Armed Forces (then Gen. Gustavo Adolfo Alvarez Martínez). Gen. Alvarez was widely regarded as the most powerful man in the country and, under his command, the Army was accused of carrying out a 'dirty war' against 'subversives' and of consequent human-rights abuses. In March 1984 Gen. Alvarez was removed from power by a group of junior officers, after growing disenchantment with his authoritarian policies (he was assassinated in January 1989).

A constitutional crisis in March 1985 over the law on the selection of presidential candidates resulted in the introduction, in September, of a law providing that the winner of the presidential election would be the leading candidate from the party receiving the largest number of votes. The presidential election in November was contested by four PL candidates and three PN candidates; the winner was José Simeón Azcona del Hoyo of the PL, although by far the highest number of votes was gained by Rafael Leonardo Callejas Romero of the PN. In the enlarged 134-member Asamblea Nacional (National Assembly) the PL won 67 seats, but only 46 of these were held by Azcona's supporters, and so he reached a working agreement with Callejas, whose supporters held 63 seats. Azcona was sworn into office in January 1986, the first occasion for 55 years in which one freely elected president had succeeded another.

Reforms Under Callejas and Reina

In a move to simplify the electoral process the two main parties for the first time pre-selected their presidential candidates for the general elections held in November 1989. Callejas won 51% of the votes cast, and assumed office in January 1990, although the PL held a majority in the Asamblea Nacional. President Callejas soon encountered opposition from the Armed Forces, which during the 1990s continued to demonstrate that their influence was stronger than political or judicial institutions. There were unsuccessful coup attempts in January 1991 and February 1993; the latter focused on military resentment of attempts to initiate judicial proceedings against them for human-rights abuses. A special commission to investigate human-rights crimes was formed in March 1993, which subsequently laid particular responsibility on special army units answerable to Gen. Alvarez and his successors for the 'disappearance' (illegal detention, torture and murder) of at least 184 people during the 1980s. The Callejas Government faced strong opposition to its economic structural-adjustment programme, not only from trade unions and peasant groups, but also from private business and the Roman Catholic Church. The Church was chiefly concerned with the matter of land distribution, and denounced the amassing of large estates by foreign companies, justified by the Government on the grounds of agricultural modernization. At the same time, a number of indigenous Amerindian groups became more vocal in their protests over their living and working conditions, and at the failure of the Government to fulfil land-rights agreements.

The increasingly unpopular PN was decisively defeated in the presidential and legislative elections of November 1993. The PL candidate, Carlos Roberto Reina Idiaquez, became President, and in the slightly contracted 128-seat Asamblea Nacional the PL won 71 seats and the PN 55. There had been little difference between the policies advocated by the two main parties, and about 35% of the electorate had abstained. During the electoral campaign the parties accused each other of involvement in human-rights abuses, and the regular practice of purchasing favourable press coverage was exposed.

Reina, a former President of the Inter-American Court of Human Rights (part of the Organization of American States—OAS), set out to reform the judicial system, to curb the power of the Army and to eradicate political corruption. In February 1995 a new civilian criminal investigation body, the Dirección de Investigación Criminal (Directorate of Criminal Investigations) replaced the Armed Forces' much-criticized secret counter-intelligence organization, the División Nacional de Investigaciones (DNI—National Division of Investigation). The post of Commander-in-Chief was transferred from the head of the Armed Forces to the defence minister and the Military High Council was abolished; these measures, announced in 1995, were finally ratified by constitutional amendment in September 1998. In October 1997 a new national police force was formed, outside direct military control; however, it faced considerable problems of under-funding and allegations of corruption and inadequacy.

The human-rights issue remained a major concern and in 1998 the independent Comité para la Defensa de Derechos Humanos en Honduras (CODEH—Committee for the Defence of Human Rights in Honduras), claimed that paramilitary 'death squad' activity had doubled since Reina became President. Despite initial attempts to press human-rights cases, the Army generally managed to evade the judicial process. The delay in processing human-rights cases also came from evident corruption within the judiciary, while some leading judicial figures received death threats. In January 1997 Honduras adopted the UN Convention against Torture, making torture a specific crime; however, this had no retroactive force.

THE FLORES PRESIDENCY

At the general election held on 30 November 1997 the PL retained the presidency, and its majority in the Asamblea Nacional, although with a reduced number of seats. The PL candidate, Carlos Roberto Flores Facussé, took office in January 1998, and 12 months later appointed Edgardo Dumas the country's first civilian defence minister. Dumas' attempts to curb military influence in politics included a call for an official audit into the activities of the military pension fund, which had wide-ranging interests throughout the economy and was accused of operating an extensive network of corruption. In October 2000 the former military intelligence chief, Roberto Núñez Montes, was charged with illegal enrichment while general manager of the state telecommunications company, Empresa Hondureña de Telecomunicaciones (Hondutel) in 1979–80; Hondutel was under the control of the Armed Forces from its formation in 1947 to 1993.

The appointment of Dumas provoked defiance in the military command, and in July 1999 Flores removed four senior officers and redeployed 33 more in order to reassert political supremacy over the Armed Forces. Tension between the civilian and military authorities increased with the announcement in August that a series of graves had been discovered at a former US-built military base at El Aguacate. The camp had been used for training right-wing Nicaraguan guerrillas (known as the 'Contras') and allegedly for the detention and torture of suspected left-wing activists. In September 2000 the authorities began exhuming the graves, which were estimated to contain

one-half of the 184 people who had disappeared. Early in November the Government made compensation payments totalling US $1.6m. to the families of 17 of the 184, thus complying with an order issued by the Inter-American Court of Human Rights in 1986. Later in that month Gen. (retd) Amilcar Zelaya, a member of the military junta in 1978–80, voluntarily entered custody to face charges connected with the illegal arrest, torture and attempted murder of five students in 1982. The charges were first made in 1995, from which time he had been in hiding, as had eight other soldiers and army officers similarly charged.

Another traditionally powerful sector of society consisted of major landowners and large business concerns; they, in turn, were opposed by the Amerindians, seeking to protect their land rights. A series of accords providing for the return of some 7,000 ha to these communities, along with many infrastructure projects on their land, was reached in 1994, but conflicted with vested interests. From 1996 regular protests were staged in Tegucigalpa to call for a full investigation into the murders of over 40 indigenous leaders who had come into conflict with cattle ranchers, logging interests, energy companies and tourism developers. In March 2000 four leaders of the Chortí people were shot and killed by the private security guards of a landowner in the western part of the country, and in September the Chortí staged a protest in Copan over the minimal implementation of the 1994 accords.

The country also faced a series of social problems. In 2001 a survey indicated that 66% of the population lived in poverty, with 48% classified as destitute, although this represented an overall improvement during the 1990s from the figure of 75% in poverty in 1991. Among children, some 43% had no access to school education, and many lived precariously on the margins of society; street children were at risk of summary brutality and execution, and many became involved with criminal gangs, particularly in drugs-trafficking. According to a report released in June 2000 by a local human-rights group, Casa Alianza, some 302 street children had been murdered since January 1998, allegedly by police and security forces, in a 'social cleansing' programme. Although the detention of juveniles in adult prisons had officially ended, it continued in practice, and the prisons were seriously overcrowded; some 90% of those in prison had not been convicted. In 2001, although figures were difficult to ascertain, Honduras faced a growing problem of child prostitution, integrated into the tourist market. The poorly-resourced police force proved unequal to combat the rising crime levels, and in November 2000 the Army was drafted in to carry out police work. Since 1994 the country had seen 200 kidnappings and over 30,000 murders. The number of people in the country suffering from acquired immunodeficiency syndrome (AIDS) rose from just over 2,500 in 1993 to over 14,000 in 1999, with over 70% of cases occurring in the 19–35 age-group. Poor living conditions contributed to other health problems, notably cholera, which struck the country several times in the 1990s.

Hurricane Mitch

These social problems were further exacerbated by 'Hurricane Mitch', which hit Central America in late October 1998, killing around 7,000 people, leaving nearly 2m. homeless, and destroying one-third of all roads and 169 bridges. The crisis was intensified by existing environmental problems: rivers dammed by large-scale rubbish dumping; erosion by rampant 'slash-and-burn' land clearance, which had contributed to major, uncontrollable fires earlier in the year; and a rising level of pesticides in the national waterways. Massive redundancies among banana workers prompted an increase in illegal immigration north to Mexico and the USA, and there was a rise in disease, malnourishment and the incidence of pests and fungi. Rebuilding efforts were further impeded by heavy rains in many parts of the country in September 2000 and the earthquake that hit El Salvador in January 2001.

The need for reconstruction finance accelerated the Flores Government's privatization programme, and international reaction to the hurricane damage led to a reassessment of the country's massive debt burden in 1999. Implementation of international aid focused attention on the country's inadequate existing housing and services provision, on the reluctance to organize major public works, and on the level of corruption. The thousands of people evacuated were assured that they would be rehoused within a year, but this promise was not met. In December protesters in the north-west of the country demanded the rebuilding of schools, hospitals, roads, electricity plants and water services, claiming that none of the international emergency aid had reached their area. In October the German-based organization, Transparency International, cited Honduras as the most corrupt country in Latin America.

General elections were scheduled to take place in November 2001, and in May the Asamblea Nacional approved a change in electoral legislation that would allow Honduran nationals living in the USA to vote in the election. By the beginning of May there were five candidates for the presidential contest. All contenders were expected to support a request due to be presented at the end of June to the International Monetary Fund and the World Bank (International Bank for Reconstruction and Development—IBRD) for debt reduction under the Heavily Indebted Poor Countries (HIPC) initiative.

RELATIONS WITH THE USA AND CENTRAL AMERICA

Honduras was drawn into the Central American conflicts of the 1980s when right-wing Nicaraguan Contras began using its territory as a base for military operations and sabotage missions against Sandinista-ruled Nicaragua. The Honduran Army gave the Contras at least tacit assistance, and Honduras acted as a channel for US aid to the Nicaraguan Contras, and to the Government of El Salvador. In consequence, US military aid was raised from US \$31.3m. in 1982 to about \$85m. in 1987, and the USA stationed 1,500 troops in Honduras.

The advent of peace in Central America, and the electoral defeat of the Sandinistas in April 1990, led to substantially improved relations between the Central American countries, with a rapid expansion of the Central American Common Market (CACM). Relations with the USA still featured allegations of US involvement in the 'dirty war' and regional security matters, with rumours that the USA would focus its military influence around the Palmerola air base in Honduras after the scheduled withdrawal of its forces from Panama in 1999. However, the issues between the two countries focused increasingly on economic matters. Early in 1997 the USA halted the deportation of illegal immigrants from El Salvador, Guatemala and Nicaragua, but over the next 18 months deported over 5,000 from Honduras, on the alleged grounds that those from the other countries had political reasons while those from Honduras did not. (The deportations were temporarily suspended after Hurricane Mitch and in mid-1999 there were an estimated

350,000 illegal Honduran immigrants in the USA.) In 1998 concerns were raised in Honduras over the use, by the US company, Standard Fruit, of the pesticide Nemagon, which was alleged to have detrimental health effects. Although Standard Fruit claimed it had ceased using Nemagon in the 1960s, a government investigation found evidence of its application as recently as 1981.

The legacy of the Central American civil wars in Honduras was a very powerful and, arguably, over-manned and over-equipped Armed Forces, which needed to redefine their role in the 1990s. The few and relatively small guerrilla groups formed in the country during the 1980s became largely inactive, and the loss of support from the US authorities left the military open to domestic criticism. Another long-term consequence of the regional conflict was the presence of an estimated 30,000 land-mines in the border area with Nicaragua, mostly planted by the Contras. A programme to clear the mines was begun in 1995, but by 1998 fewer than 2,000 had been moved, and Hurricane Mitch caused a large-scale displacement of many of these devices.

In November 1999 the Government provoked a new dispute with Nicaragua when it requested that the Asamblea Nacional ratify a treaty signed with Colombia in 1986, delineating maritime boundaries. The Nicaraguan Government protested that this move threatened its country's own maritime claims, and both countries posted troops on their joint border. The border area was demilitarized in February 2000 and, following OAS mediation, the two countries agreed to establish a maritime exclusion zone in the disputed area. In the following month representatives of the two countries met in Washington, DC (USA) to sign an accord on joint patrols in the Caribbean and the withdrawal of forces from the land border area. However, after a year of relative calm, in February 2001, bilateral relations deteriorated when the Nicaraguan Government accused Honduras of violating the agreement by holding military exercises and moving military supplies into the border region. The Honduran authorities refuted any aggressive intention, stating that the exercises were being carried out with US army units solely for infrastructure projects. The OAS again mediated meetings between the two countries in an attempt to ease the growing tension, and in June the foreign ministers of Honduras and Nicaragua met in Washington, DC to sign a confidence-building agreement. In mid-July an OAS verification mission arrived in Honduras to check the situation on both sides of the border.

Economy

PHILLIP WEARNE

With a national income per head of just US \$845 in 1999, Honduras remained one of the poorest and least-developed nations in Latin America. Despite some success in efforts to diversify the country's economic base in the 1990s, Honduras remained overly dependent on primary agricultural and fisheries exports such as coffee, bananas, meat, shrimp and lobster, as well as on large quantities of external finance. However, despite the country's narrow trading base and large subsistence-farming sector, increased agricultural production and high levels of government expenditure allowed for a steady 4%–5% growth in real gross domestic product (GDP) during the 1970s. This trend was seriously disrupted by the onset of world recession, from 1981. Government plans to diversify the economy and to expand non-traditional export capacity were thwarted by high interest rates, increases in petroleum prices and a precipitous decrease in the world price of the country's principal agricultural commodities. Increased political tension in the region, in particular the civil wars in the neighbouring El Salvador, Guatemala and Nicaragua, and the poor performance of both private and parastatal industries exacerbated deep-rooted economic problems.

GDP growth fell from 6.8% in 1979 to –1.7% in 1982, while the population growth rate continued to exceed 3% per year,

leading to a negative growth rate in GDP per head. Overall, average real GDP growth in 1980–90 was 2.3%. By 1990 the economy was stagnant, expanding by a mere 0.1%, compared with 4.3% in 1989. However, growth increased in 1991 and the country sustained steady rates of growth in the mid-1990s. Economic growth for 1998 was 2.9%, but the devastation caused by 'Hurricane Mitch' in October of that year completely reversed the economic growth trend thereafter. GDP increased, in real terms, at an average annual rate of 3.2% in 1989–99. GDP contracted by 1.9% in 1999, although a full recovery in terms of growth at least was achieved in 2000. Estimates put GDP growth in 2000 at 4.8%, although the Central Bank estimated a far higher figure. GDP growth was forecast at 3.5% in 2001.

Overall, population growth (averaging 3.3% in 1990–98 with the number of inhabitants estimated to be 6.6m. in mid-2000) offset much of the benefit of economic growth in the last decade of the 20th century and caused a steady rise in unemployment. Although the official unemployment rate was just 3.7% in 1999, it was estimated that more than 35% of the labour force were actually jobless, or underemployed. Some 60% of the agricultural work-force were believed to be underemployed, a result of the pressure on land, the increased mechanization of export agriculture and the seasonal nature of coffee, banana, sugar and fruit production. The maintenance of the fixed exchange rate, at two lempiras (the Honduran currency unit) per US dollar, and a reduction in the money supply kept the annual inflation rate below 5% between 1984 and 1988. However, massive devaluations of the lempira in 1990–91, combined with more gradual ones thereafter, took the annual inflation rate to a record 34% in 1991. Inflation was much lower in 1992 and 1993, but it increased dramatically in 1994 and in 1995, when the annual increase in consumer prices was 29.5%. It fell steadily thereafter, from 20.2% in 1997 and 13.7% in 1998, to 11.7% in 1999 and to 11.1% in 2000.

In the mid-1980s a fall in international petroleum prices and an increase in coffee revenues, combined with reductions in public-sector expenditure and increased inflows of US aid, renewed creditors' confidence in the economy. However, by 1989 the position had been reversed. As imports soared and coffee prices fell drastically, the World Bank (International Bank for Reconstruction and Development—IBRD) declared the country ineligible for further credits. This followed President José Simeón Azcona del Hoyo's (1986–90) unilateral suspension of all interest payments on the country's US $3,200m. foreign debt. The Government of President Rafael Leonardo Callejas Romero (1990–94) steadily recovered the situation, adhering to the economic prescriptions of the US Agency for International Development (USAID) more closely. An effective 100% devaluation of the lempira against the US dollar in March 1990 began the process.

By mid-1990 the credibility of the new Government had been rewarded by a stand-by agreement with the International Monetary Fund (IMF), a second structural-adjustment accord with the World Bank and a US $247m. bridging loan. In 1992 Honduras signed an Extended Structural Adjustment Facility (ESAF) loan agreement with the IMF, but deterioration in the fiscal accounts meant that the Government was soon missing targets and the incoming Government of President Carlos Roberto Reina Idiaquez (1994–98) was forced to repeat the initial measures of its predecessor. In February 1994 the tax base was widened, the lempira devalued and public expenditure further decreased, in an effort to reduce a fiscal deficit of $326m., equivalent to 10.6% of GDP.

By late 1995 the World Bank, the IMF and the Inter-American Development Bank (IDB) agreed that the Honduran economy was recovering. The rise in the rate of inflation was slowing and the fiscal deficit had been reduced to less than 4% of GDP. As a result, by early 1996 the IDB had made some US $160m. available for the modernization of the economy and the World Bank approved a further $60m. The IMF also disbursed a $15m. loan for balance-of-payments support and in May 1997 announced a partial agreement for the third year disbursement of funds under its ESAF agreement with Honduras.

Following Hurricane Mitch, in October 1998, a further ESAF agreement, worth US $215m., was agreed with the IMF in March 1999 to aid economic reconstruction. Honduras was further aided by a three-year deferral of bilateral debt-service payments to the 'Paris Club' of Western creditor countries and the establishment by the World Bank of a fund from which other debt-service payments could be made. However, this was not enough to prevent a substantial rise in the total debt burden. By the end of 2000 total external debt was $5,400m., a 0.8% rise on the $5,356m. figure in 1999. The country was formally approved for debt relief under the Heavily Indebted Poor Countries (HIPC) initiative in December 1999. Under this programme, the IMF and the World Bank announced in July 2000 that the country's debt service payments would be reduced by $900m. over 20 years.

AGRICULTURE

Agriculture remained the most important sector of the economy. In 1999 the sector (which includes hunting, forestry and fishing) employed 35.1% of the economically active population and accounted for 14.8% of GDP in 2000, compared with 19.1% in 1998. The sector remained underdeveloped—of a total land area of 11.2m. ha, only an estimated 1.7m. ha were utilized for arable farming, with a further 1.5m. ha under pasture. Despite the country's relatively low density of population, land shortages were a persistent problem. In 1999 some 650,000 peasant farmers in Honduras were estimated to be landless. As a result,

disturbances caused by the unofficial occupation of unused or underutilized agricultural land had become a marked feature of life in rural Honduras.

The rapid development of cash-crop farming, most notably coffee and bananas, as well as relatively stable world commodity prices, allowed for an average annual growth in agricultural production of 5.8% during the 1960s. Although the average annual rate of growth was reduced to 2.4% during the 1970s, significant gains were made in livestock farming and sugar production. Adverse weather conditions, falling commodity prices and the onset of world recession reduced the growth rate markedly during the 1980s. In the early 1990s the sector began to recover. However, Hurricane Mitch, which affected the agricultural sector more adversely than any other, ended the revival. Coffee and banana production were particularly badly affected. Losses in the sector were estimated at US $200m. in 1998, and a further $500m. in 1999, when the agriculture sector contracted by 8.9%. Some 70% of the banana crop was destroyed and coffee production fell.

In November 1983 the effective control of the banana industry by two US conglomerates, United Brands (formerly the United Fruit Company—UFCO) and Standard Fruit, was broken when agreements were reached for the sale of a large proportion of the national crop to local trading companies. This, combined with a government export-incentive scheme in the mid-1980s, an increase in demand following the collapse of the Communist bloc in Eastern Europe in the early 1990s, and the implementation of the free market within the European Community (EC, known as the European Union—EU from 1993) in 1992 acted as a potential stimulant to banana production. In 1990 the Anglo-Irish banana company, Fyffes, began financing new, independent banana co-operatives, in a further challenge to the monopoly of the two US companies.

Banana export earnings were US $358m. in 1990. In 1991, however, earnings decreased to $314m. and continued to fall. From 1995, however, banana export earnings began a substantive recovery, growing nearly 20% in that year to reach $214m. and rising a similar amount in 1996 to reach $280m. However, in 1997 earnings fell back to $212m. as export volumes decreased by more than 15%, before dropping to $220m. Figures for 1999 reflected the disastrous consequences of Hurricane Mitch, with the destruction of more than 70% of the total crop. Banana export earnings fell dramatically to $38m. In 2000 a recovery in the sector was under way: exports increased to $114m.

Exports were 35.5m. 40-lb boxes in 1991 and actually increased in 1992, in spite of the reduction in earnings, to 38.5m. 40-lb boxes. After 1992 a prolonged conflict over the EC/EU's banana import-quota system and major labour problems served as major disincentives to increasing production. In 1993 exports fell to 36.5m. 40-lb boxes and in 1994 bad weather, disease and import restrictions reduced this figure to just 27.4m. boxes. There was a real improvement in 1995, with volume increasing by more than 12%, to 31.7m. boxes, before exports reached 38.7m. boxes in the following year. In 1997 and 1998 this figure fell back to 33.1m. and 28.2m. boxes, respectively. The volume of exports in 1999 was 6.8m. boxes and the rehabilitation of the banana industry was slower than anticipated and was not expected to be complete before the 2001/02 season. In June 2000 Chiquita Brands announced a substantial reduction in its operations, following further weather damage and a depression in the market. Following the EU's failure to satisfy the World Trade Organization that its banana-import regime complied with international trade regulations, on 11 April 2001 the EU and the USA signed an accord ending the EU preferential market. From 1 July a transitional system, issuing licences according to historical trade patterns, was to be implemented, with the definitive tariff-only system entering into force on 1 January 2006.

In the mid-1980s the volume of coffee exports increased significantly under the combined stimuli of greatly improved international prices and the success of government efforts to eradicate diseases such as coffee rust. However, the improvement was more than offset by the consequences of the collapse of the International Coffee Agreement in July 1989. The disastrous fall in prices that followed did not begin to be reversed until mid-1994, when world shortages produced the highest coffee prices in a decade. Thus, while the volume of production increased by 21% in 1990, export earnings actually fell, to US \$180.9m. Three years later exports rose but earnings declined to \$124.6m. In 1994, as prices began to recover, exports of 2.24m. 46-kg bags earned \$200.1m.; the vagaries of the market being fully illustrated the following year in 1995, when a minimal rise in export volume produced an increase in earnings to \$349.3m. In 1996 earnings decreased dramatically, by more than 20% to US \$278.9m., despite a rise of more than 10% in export volumes. In 1997 the trend was reversed, with the volume of exports falling by nearly 20%, but earnings rising by nearly the same amount, to \$326.3m. The following year both volumes and value rose again with the export of 3.04m. bags earning the country an estimated \$429.8m. Although Hurricane Mitch had less impact on the coffee sector than the banana industry, the devastation combined with low prices cut earnings to just \$256.1m. in 1999, although they partially recovered in 2000 to \$340.6m. Export revenues were not expected to recover fully before 2002. In 2000 Central American coffee producers, along with Mexico, Colombia and Brazil, agreed to retain up to 10% of their stocks in order to allow the price to rise, although the arrangement proved difficult to enforce.

Poor prices and the consequent lower production caused the sugar, cotton and tobacco sectors to decrease dramatically in importance as export crops in the 1980s. By 1999 sugar exports were worth a mere US \$5.3m. and tobacco just \$10.5m. However, growth in some non-traditional agricultural sectors, particularly pineapples and melons, and substantial growth in the seafood industry during the 1990s helped to offset the deficit. Melon exports significantly increased in both volume and value in the late 1990s, reaching \$47.0m. in 1999 before decreasing to \$37.6m. in 2000. Pineapple exports were less dynamic, but earned \$19.2m. in 1999. Exports of shellfish, principally lobster and shrimp, more than tripled in little more than a decade. In 2000 shellfish exports earned the country \$177.3m. The shrimp farming industry, in particular, although badly hit by Hurricane Mitch, recovered rapidly.

In 1997 there were 7.6m. ha of forest and woodland in Honduras. In 1983 wood was the third-largest export. However, the timber industry, which was nationalized in 1974 and placed under the control of the Corporación Hondureña de Desarrollo Forestal (COHDEFOR—Honduran Corporation of Forestry Development), encountered a series of problems. Like other state corporations, COHDEFOR incurred huge financial losses and its principal sawmill, the Bonito timber project in Olancho province, was eventually sold to a US citizen for only 5m. lempiras, representing a loss of 18m. lempiras. This followed devastating fires at the beginning of the 1980s, as a consequence of which the value of timber exports declined from US \$44.7m. in 1982 to just \$19.0m. in 1995, a level at which exports stabilized in the mid-1990s. In 1999 wood exports earned Honduras \$12.6m. Almost all timber exports in the late 1990s were pine and softwoods. Efforts in the late 1980s to revive hardwood production were abandoned after fierce opposition. An estimated 2.5m. ha of Honduras were believed to be in need of reforestation, following the loss of more than 30% of the country's forests after 1970, at a rate of some 88,000 ha per year.

MINING AND POWER

Although no comprehensive geological survey had been undertaken, Honduras was reported to have substantial reserves of tin, iron ore, coal, pitchblende and antimony and exploitable reserves of gold. In recent years there was an increase in interest in the sector from foreign companies and even though the mining and quarrying sector contributed only 2.0% of GDP in 1999, the increased activity was reflected in some revival of exports. In 2001 Entremares Honduras, SA (a subsidiary of Glamis Golds Ltd of the USA), the Canadian company Geomaque and the national Coviasa were to begin mining operations in Honduras, joining the Canadian-owned American Pacific, which worked the El Mochito lead, zinc and copper mines.

Activity was confined to the extraction of lead, zinc and silver and small quantities of gold. Zinc exports increased dramatically from 61.5m. lbs in 1996 to 96.6m. lbs in 1997, which more than doubled export revenues, to US \$53.8m., although this fell in 1998 and 1999, when exports of 85.6m. lbs and 74.2m. lbs earned \$36.3m. and \$39.4m., respectively. In 2000 the value of zinc exports totalled \$47.5m. Production of lead underwent a similar

revival, with exports nearly doubling to 13.6m. lbs in 1997, earning \$4.6m., before falling in 1998 and 1999 to 10.4m. lbs and 8.6m. lbs, with earnings of \$3.2m. and \$2.6m., respectively. In silver production earnings experienced similar fluctuations. Earnings and production peaked in 1998 with Honduras exporting 1.53m. troy oz to earn \$7.8m. In 1999 exports fell to 1.08m. troy oz, earning \$5.4m.

The power industry in Honduras experienced a deep crisis in the 1990s as a result of water shortages and their impact on the country's crucial hydroelectricity sector. Underinvestment in new plants and mismanagement exacerbated the crisis in the sector. In 1994 electricity rationing was common as power output decreased by an estimated 50%. The problem began in the 1970s when two major hydroelectric systems, the El Cajón dam (capacity 292 MW) and the Río Lindo–Yojoa system (capacity 285 MW), were developed to increase the country's self-sufficiency in electricity generation and offset the adverse effects of petroleum price increases. Relatively limited savings in petroleum-import costs were, however, matched by an increase in demand, as well as the problems caused by drought and technical failures. Declining levels of water in both hydro-electric systems were blamed on deforestation, caused by logging and the clearing of woodland for agriculture in order to cope with the country's growing land crisis. In 1997–98 a drought caused by the El Niño weather phenomenon reduced El Cajón's generating capacity by 50%. The floods caused by Hurricane Mitch in 1998 then wreaked havoc with the power-distribution network, despite raising water levels and thus increasing power-generation capacity. In February 1999 a fire destroyed two of the turbines at the El Cajón hydroelectricity plant, causing a further six months of energy rationing.

From 1994 successive Governments attempted, with some success, to resolve the problems of the power sector. Electricity prices were increased several times and the state-owned Empresa Nacional de Energía Eléctrica (ENEE—National Electrical Energy Company) intensified efforts to collect more than 120m. lempiras in debts. In February 1996 a new 40 MW thermal electricity plant was inaugurated. However, plans for the development of other plants were postponed, and continued underinvestment in the transmission network meant that more than 20% of the power generated was lost. The damage caused by Hurricane Mitch proved a major obstacle to efforts to over-haul the distribution network to major cities. In April 1999 the Governments of Honduras and El Salvador agreed to construct a regional electricity grid by 2001, to be funded by US \$30m. from the IDB. In 1999 the country generated some 3,574 gWh, with state-owned hydroelectric plants generating more than two-thirds of the total, and state and privately-owned thermal plants generating the remainder. Distribution losses accounted for 21% of all power generated. National consumption was put at 2,819 gWh in 1999 and demand grew by up to 12% per year. In 2001 the US energy company, AES Global Power Co, began construction of the \$650m. 'El Faro' natural gas-fired electricity generating plant in Puerto Cortés. The plant was to be completed by early 2003 and would generate some 780 MW, to be distributed throughout Central America.

No commercially-viable petroleum deposits were found. Previous offshore exploration by the US companies, Texaco and Exxon, had proved disappointing. Another rush of speculative exploration ended in 1993 after three petroleum companies, Cambria Oil, Maraven and Hon-Tex, withdrew from concessions in different parts of the country. Texaco operated a small refinery at Puerto Cortés, producing 14,000 barrels per day, until the company withdrew, in 1993, on the grounds of expense.

MANUFACTURING

In the early 1980s the Honduran manufacturing sector was the smallest and least diversified in Central America. However, it was substantially expanded by the establishment of *maquila* (offshore assembly) plants producing goods for re-export. By 1999 some 230 *maquila* plants accounted for US \$545m. in export earnings, although the rate of growth had slowed in the 1990s. In the 1970s the manufacturing sector grew at an average rate of 5.8% per year, with development mainly in and around San Pedro Sula. However, more recently, the sector's contribution to GDP remained relatively stable as the decline in traditional manufacturing industries offset the growth in the offshore assembly plants. Manufacturing GDP increased at an average annual rate of 3.8% during 1989–99. The sector's contribution to overall GDP remained relatively stable, at 17.8% in 1992 and 19.8% in 2000.

Traditional manufacturing activity was based largely on agro-forestry products for both export and domestic consumption and included food processing, beverages, textiles, furniture making, cigarettes, sugar refining, seafood and meat processing and paper and pulp processing. Cement, textile fabric, beer, soft drinks, wheat flour and rum were some of the major products. Despite some initial damage to plants and markets as a result of Hurricane Mitch, much of the domestic manufacturing sector benefited substantially as a result of the reconstruction programme. Cement production increased by 18% in 1999 to 28.5m. bags, metal manufacturing by more than 20% and textile production by more than 27%.

In the 1990s it was the free-market and privatization policies of the Governments of Presidents Callejas and Reina that dominated prospects in the manufacturing sector. During 1991 several factories, including a cement and textile plant, were sold, following the liquidation of the Corporación Nacional de Inversiones (CONADI—National Investment Corporation), the government-established industrial development agency. Reductions in tariff protection in 1991 adversely affected industry, but, for exporters at least, the successive currency devaluations helped to increase competitiveness.

Another major stimulus was the creation of five free-trade zones from 1976 onwards. The success of these led to the creation of six private free-trade zones from 1987. All of the free-trade zones were concentrated near the coastal cities of San Pedro Sula and Puerto Cortés. Textile and assembly companies predominated in the sector, creating more than 20,000 jobs in 1990–92 alone. Most companies operated under the customs provisions of the USA's Caribbean Basin Initiative (CBI), which allowed for the duty-free importation of clothes assembled from US cloth. However, as elsewhere in the duty-free sector, diversification was proceeding apace. Electronics, furniture and metal-manufacturing assembly plants all increased in number in the 1990s; similarly, the country of origin of the investment diversified.

For the offshore manufacturing sector, 1999 was the most successful year in more than a decade. Output increased by more than 15%, with employment figures reaching more than 125,000 people. With Hurricane Mitch devastating traditional agricultural exports like bananas and coffee, export earnings of some US $545m. made the offshore manufacturing sector Honduras' most important foreign-exchange earner for the first time. The sector was further boosted in July 2000 by the extension of the North American Free Trade Agreement (NAFTA) import duty parity to Honduran-assembled goods. The extension of these provisions reduced the import tariff on Honduran-assembled goods into the US market by 15% and allowed the sector to diversify into textile operations such as dyeing and cutting. The move encouraged the Government to target $700m. in new investment into the sector over the subsequent five years, which, it hoped, would create up to 80,000 jobs. In November 2000 the Formosa Industrial Park, financed by the Republic of China (Taiwan), opened. However, the US economic slowdown in the early 2000s adversely affected the sector, with *maquila* plants closing in 2000 and a further 12 plants announcing their closure in the first half of 2001.

FOREIGN TRADE AND PAYMENTS

Throughout the 1980s Honduras recorded a persistently large current-account deficit. By 1994 this deficit had reached US $343.3m., and despite some improvement, to $272.2m. and $316.9m. in 1997 and 1998, respectively, the balance continued to deteriorate. In 1999, with exports affected by Hurricane Mitch, the deficit increased to $536.8m. and was estimated to have improved to only $443m. by 2000. The trade deficit has always fluctuated in line with the prices of major exports and the demand for imports; however, it increased dramatically after 1990, standing at $323.1m. in 1998 and dramatically increasing to $709.1m. in 1999 and to an estimated $749.7m. in 2000. Export earnings rose by more than 10% per year in the mid-1990s, but fell back substantially in 1998 and 1999 in the wake of Hurricane Mitch. In 1998 export earnings (including

the value added revenue from offshore assembly plants) were $2,017m., falling to $1,848.9m. in 1999, and increasing slightly to an estimated $2,048.6m. in 2000. The growth in imports continued more uniformly, increasing to an estimated $2,534.8m. in 1998, to an estimated $2,676.1m. in 1999 and to an estimated $2,884.7m. in 2000.

During 1984–87 the widening of the trade gap was accompanied by a substantial rise in capital inflows, particularly aid from the USA. This peaked in 1985, at US $296m., before falling by more than one-half to $121.3m. over the subsequent four years. Such inflows allowed the Government to successfully resist pressure from the IMF and the World Bank for a devaluation of the lempira. However, falls in export revenue, combined with a decline in aid inflows, caused an accumulation of repayment arrears in 1989, with both the World Bank and the IMF declaring the country ineligible for loans during the course of that year. In March 1990 the new Government of President Callejas announced an emergency economic programme, which included a devaluation of the lempira.

In June and July 1990 Honduras cleared its loan-repayment arrears with international lending bodies, thus becoming eligible once again to receive new loans and financial assistance. In July the IMF approved a new 12-month stand-by arrangement. However, targets were soon being missed again and the fiscal situation deteriorated markedly in the early 1990s. In early 1994 the new Reina Government made two successive devaluations of the currency, imposed a selective consumption tax and announced further privatizations, in order to secure a US $500m. loan agreement from the World Bank and the IMF. Multilateral and bilateral creditor support subsequently remained strong, despite the significant weakening of government finances in the wake of Hurricane Mitch. The most obvious demonstration of this was the country's achievement of HIPC status in mid-2000. The agreement promised debt-service relief of some $900m. in return for continued economic reform and adherence to an IMF- and World Bank-agreed Poverty Reduction and Growth Facility programme. One condition of the improved terms from creditors, investment liberalization, dramatically increased 10-fold direct foreign investment inflows during the 1990s. In 1999 direct foreign investment increased to $230m., equivalent to more than 4% of GDP.

External debt more than doubled in the 1980s, reaching US $3,700m. in 1990. By 1996 it was $4,500m. and by 2000 had reached $5,400m., nearly 80% of the estimated GDP in that year. However, rescheduling, renegotiation and relief steadily reduced the Honduran debt service ratio (debt service as a percentage of earnings from the export of goods and services) from as much as 35% in 1995 to 10% five years later. In December 1999 a little more than one-half of the country's debt was held by multilateral creditors, principally the World Bank and the IDB, 26% by bilateral creditors, and a further 23.5% by private creditors.

By 2001 it was increasingly clear that successive Honduran Governments had enjoyed some success in their efforts to diversify the economy and the country's sources of foreign exchange. Non-traditional agricultural and fishery exports soared, earnings from the *maquila* industry exceeded those from both coffee and bananas in 1999 for the first time, and invisibles, such as tourism and remittances from Hondurans living abroad (some $409m. in 2000), were making increasingly important contributions to the current account. Revenues from tourism grew particularly well, rising from US $31.8m. in 1992 to $165m. in 1999, when some 371,000 tourists visited the country. More than 80% of the arrivals were from North and Central America.

There was less success in the diversification of the direction of trade, with dependence on the USA, the country's principal market, remaining strong. In 1994 54.0% of the country's exports went to the USA, compared with just over 50% a decade earlier. By 2000 the figure was 39.9%. Germany, Belgium and Japan historically also took significant amounts of Honduran exports, but all three accounted for just 17.9% of the total in 2000. The major trade development was the growth of intra-regional trade; Costa Rica, Nicaragua, El Salvador and Guatemala took 19.5% of the country's total exports in 2000. Reliance on the USA for imports also remained strong. In 1994 47.4% of the country's total imports came from the USA and by 2000 the proportion, at 46.1%, had hardly altered. Other important suppliers were

Guatemala, El Salvador, Japan and Mexico, collectively accounting for 24.1% of the total.

Following four years of negotiations, in April 2000 the Central American countries of El Salvador, Guatemala and Honduras signed a free-trade agreement with Mexico, which promised greater access to the Mexican market and increased bilateral trade. In May 2001 the Central American countries, including Honduras, completed negotiations on an accord with Mexico, the 'Plan Puebla–Panamá', which intended to integrate the region through joint transport, industry and tourism projects.

CONCLUSION

On assuming office in January 1998 the Government of President Carlos Roberto Flores Facussé introduced an economic programme designed to reduce public expenditure, liberalize trade and investment, diversify the narrow economic base of the country, and cut the country's onerous debt burden. Corporate taxes and certain export taxes were reduced, value-added tax was increased to 5% to offset the loss of revenue and a privatization programme, which included the sale of international and local airports, the ENEE, and the state-owned telec-

ommunications concern, Empresa Hondureña de Telecomunicaciones (Hondutel), was announced. However, following numerous unsuccessful attempts to sell Hondutel, in 2001 the President announced that the divestment would be postponed indefinitely, until the next administration, which was due to take office following the November election.

Despite this set-back in the privatization programme and despite popular protests at job losses and the erosion of the protection enjoyed by domestic industry, the Government's economic programme enjoyed some success, with debt relief, diversification and closer integration into the world economy all yielding results. However, it remained a measure of the economy's fragility that throughout a period of acceptable, if modest, growth in the 1990s, essential economic indicators, such as the balance of payments and current account deficit, continued to deteriorate. The country's economic vulnerability was also emphasized by one natural disaster, Hurricane Mitch, in 1998, which wreaked extensive damage, costing the country an estimated US $5,000m. Although economic growth had recovered by 2000, many sectors—most notably agriculture and the country's major export crop, bananas—still had much ground to recover.

Statistical Survey

Source (unless otherwise stated): Department of Economic Studies, Banco Central de Honduras—BANTRAL, 6a y 7a Avda, 1a Calle, Apdo 3165, Tegucigalpa; tel. 237-2270; fax 238-0376.

Area and Population

AREA, POPULATION AND DENSITY

Area (sq km)	112,492*
Population (census results)†	
6 March 1974	2,656,948
29 May 1988	
Males	2,110,106
Females	2,138,455
Total	4,248,561
Population (official estimates at mid-year)	
1998	6,179,700
1999	6,385,000
2000	6,597,100
Density (per sq km) at mid-2000	58.6

* 43,433 sq miles.
† Excluding adjustments for underenumeration, estimated to have been 10% at the 1974 census.

PRINCIPAL TOWNS (estimated population, '000 at mid-2000)

Tegucigalpa	. .	1,037.6	Siguatepeque . . .	51.0
San Pedro Sula	.	471.0	Puerto Cortés . . .	35.6
El Progreso	.	109.4	Juticalpa . . .	33.3
La Ceiba	. .	107.2	Santa Rosa de	
Choluteca .	.	96.9	Copán . . .	27.8
Comayagua	.	73.2	Tela	26.3
Danlí	. . .	64.4	Olanchito . . .	22.9

BIRTHS AND DEATHS (World Bank estimates, annual averages)

	1997	1998	1999
Birth rate (per 1,000). . . .	32.6	31.9	31.1
Death rate (per 1,000) . .	5.7	5.5	5.3

Expectation of life (estimates, years at birth, 1998): 69.6; Males 67.7, Females 72.5 (Source: UN Development Programme, *Human Development Report*).

ECONOMICALLY ACTIVE POPULATION
('000 persons aged 10 years and over)

	1997	1998	1999
Agriculture, hunting, forestry and fishing	772.7	738.4	806.1
Mining and quarrying . .	3.1	4.5	3.8
Manufacturing	361.7	368.3	376.9
Electricity, gas and water . .	6.7	7.0	8.2
Construction	88.3	110.7	117.8
Trade, restaurants and hotels .	393.8	440.0	489.1
Transport, storage and communications . . .	46.8	54.6	56.0
Financing, insurance, real estate and business services . .	41.4	52.5	49.9
Community, social and personal services	374.1	359.1	391.1
Total employed	2,088.5	2,134.9	2,299.0
Unemployed	69.4	87.7	89.3
Total labour force . . .	2,157.9	2,222.6	2,388.3

Source: ILO, *Yearbook of Labour Statistics*.

Agriculture

PRINCIPAL CROPS ('000 metric tons)

	1998	1999	2000
Rice (paddy)	27.8	13.1	7.3
Maize	471.3	477.5	533.6
Sorghum	90.2	71.3	64.7
Dry beans	72.7	53.4	85.0
Sugar cane	3,778.5	3,755.8	3,896.4
Pineapples	72.6	70.1	71.0
Bananas	861.9	860.5	452.6
Plantains	217.6	250.0	250.0*
Coffee (green)	172.8	185.1	196.3
Tobacco	4.5	4.5	4.3

* FAO estimate.

Source: FAO.

LIVESTOCK ('000 head)

	1998	1999	2000
Cattle	2,200.0	2,060.8	1,950.0*
Pigs*	700.0	798.0	800.0
Horses*	177.0	178.0	179.0
Mules*	69.4	69.5	69.6

Poultry* (million): 16.5 in 1998; 18.0 in 1999; 18.0 in 2000.

* FAO estimate(s).

Source: FAO.

LIVESTOCK PRODUCTS ('000 metric tons)

	1998	1999	2000
Beef and veal	28.3	21.0*	21.0*
Pig meat	16.1	16.9	16.9†
Poultry meat	54.2	58.5	64.9
Cows' milk	604.9	674.2	729.0
Hen eggs†	40.9	41.4	41.4

* Unofficial figure.   † FAO estimate(s).

Source: FAO.

Forestry

ROUNDWOOD REMOVALS ('000 cubic metres, excluding bark)

	1997	1998	1999
Sawlogs, veneer logs and logs for sleepers	711	789	853
Other industrial wood . . .	8	6	3
Fuel wood	6,209	6,381	6,557
Total	6,928	7,176	7,413

Source: FAO, *Yearbook of Forest Products*.

SAWNWOOD PRODUCTION
('000 cubic metres, incl. railway sleepers)

	1997	1998	1999
Coniferous (softwood) . . .	357	352	404
Broadleaved (hardwood) . . .	22	17	17
Total	379	369	421

Source: FAO, *Yearbook of Forest Products*.

Fishing

('000 metric tons, live weight)

	1996	1997	1998
Capture*	14.9	17.3	14.9
Yellowfin tuna* . . .	1.9	1.9	1.9
Caribbean spiny lobster . .	0.5	1.0	0.3
Penaeus shrimps . . .	1.3	2.6	1.9
Stromboid conchs . . .	0.5	3.0	3.0
Cuttlefish, bobtail squids .	3.1	2.1	2.1
Octopuses, etc. . . .	1.0	0.5	0.5
Aquaculture*	10.1	9.3	8.1
Total catch*	25.0	26.6	23.0

Note: Figures exclude crocodiles, recorded by number rather than weight. The number of spectacled caimans caught was: 6,000 in 1996.

* FAO estimates.

Source: FAO, *Yearbook of Fishery Statistics*.

Mining

(metal content)

	1998	1999	2000
Lead ('000 metric tons) . . .	6	5	4
Zinc ('000 metric tons) . . .	41	41	36
Silver (metric tons) . . .	60	54	51

Industry

SELECTED PRODUCTS

	1996	1997	1998
Raw sugar ('000 quintales) . .	5,007	5,311	5,445
Cement ('000 bags of 42.5 kg) .	22,324	25,126	24,141
Cigarettes ('000 packets of 20) .	105,437	130,141	190,722
Beer ('000 12 oz bottles) . . .	237,612	293,899	279,382
Soft drinks ('000 12 oz bottles) .	1,147,189	1,319,886	1,218,911
Wheat flour ('000 quintales) . .	2,173	2,262	2,300
Fabric ('000 yards)	24,053	30,695	62,460
Other alcoholic drinks ('000 litres)	7,081	7,298	7,864
Vegetable oil and butter ('000 lb)	110,542	131,307	132,867

Finance

CURRENCY AND EXCHANGE RATES

Monetary Units
    100 centavos = 1 lempira.

Sterling, Dollar and Euro Equivalents (30 April 2001)
    £1 sterling = 21.953 lempiras;
    US $1 = 15.333 lempiras;
    €1 = 13.609 lempiras;
    1,000 lempiras = £45.55 = $65.22 = €73.48.

Average Exchange Rate (lempiras per US $)
    1998   13.3850
    1999   14.2132
    2000   14.8392

BUDGET (million lempiras)

Revenue	1997	1998	1999*
Current revenue	10,374.4	13,214.2	14,621.5
Taxes	8,652.1	11,973.0	13,538.1
Direct taxes	2,512.3	3,377.4	2,891.6
Income tax	2,293.3	3,110.2	2,646.7
Property tax . . .	219.0	267.2	244.9
Indirect taxes . . .	6,138.0	8,593.4	10,643.9
Exports	88.3	72.3	7.9
Imports	2,067.8	2,043.2	1,977.1
Non-tax revenue . . .	1,422.1	943.4	741.7
Transfers	300.2	297.8	341.7
Other revenue (incl. capital revenue)	3.4	3.2	0.0
Total	10,377.8	13,217.4	14,621.5

Expenditure	1997	1998	1999*
Current expenditure . . .	10,072.2	11,182.3	12,359.0
Consumption expenditure . .	5,421.8	6,692.5	8,177.5
Interest	2,697.8	2,314.3	1,700.4
Internal debt . . .	1,090.9	647.8	562.0
External debt . . .	1,606.9	1,666.5	1,138.4
Transfers	1,952.6	2,175.5	2,481.1
Capital expenditure . . .	2,912.8	3,569.2	5,601.1
Real investment . . .	1,661.2	1,811.9	2,294.1
Transfers	1,243.2	1,730.0	3,306.6
Net lending	740.9	540.0	237.6
Total	13,725.9	15,291.5	18,197.7

* Estimates.

CENTRAL BANK RESERVES (US $ million at 31 December)

	1998	1999	2000
Gold*	6.25	6.28	5.99
IMF special drawing rights	0.07	0.94	0.10
Foreign exchange	818.00	1,244.80	1,301.70
Reserve position in IMF	—	11.84	11.24
Total	824.32	1,263.86	1,319.03

* National valuation.

Source: IMF, *International Financial Statistics*.

MONEY SUPPLY (million lempiras at 31 December)

	1998	1999	2000
Currency outside banks	3,744	4,714	4,727
Demand deposits at commercial banks	4,841	5,666	6,180
Total money (incl. others)	9,349	11,050	11,954

Source: IMF, *International Financial Statistics*.

COST OF LIVING (Consumer Price Index; base: 1990 = 100)

	1997	1998	1999
Food	419.7	468.9	505.9
Fuel and power	382.0	374.0	340.0
Clothing and footwear	363.5	420.0	474.7
Rent	326.2	362.3	401.4
All items	378.4	430.2	480.4

Source: ILO, *Labour Statistics Yearbook*.

NATIONAL ACCOUNTS (million lempiras at current prices)
Expenditure on the Gross Domestic Product

	1998	1999	2000
Government final consumption expenditure	7,117	8,726	10,575
Private final consumption expenditure	47,183	53,058	61,101
Increase in stocks	1,910	3,258	4,511
Gross fixed capital formation	19,874	22,977	23,926
Total domestic expenditure	76,084	88,019	100,113
Exports of goods and services	32,447	32,233	37,122
Less Imports of goods and services	38,092	43,157	49,110
GDP in purchasers' values	70,438	77,095	88,025
GDP at constant 1978 prices	6,880	6,750	7,073

Source: IMF, *International Financial Statistics*.

Gross Domestic Product by Economic Activity

	1998*	1999†	2000†
Agriculture, hunting, forestry and fishing	11,493	10,500	11,235
Mining and quarrying	1,102	1,325	1,509
Manufacturing	11,186	12,916	14,996
Electricity, gas and water	3,093	3,208	3,555
Construction	3,043	3,863	4,326
Wholesale and retail trade	7,360	8,365	9,742
Transport, storage and communications	2,985	3,423	3,974
Finance, insurance and real estate	6,331	7,155	8,008
Owner-occupied dwellings	3,478	3,990	4,772
Public administration and defence	3,625	3,875	4,602
Other services	6,372	7,261	9,168
GDP at factor cost	60,068	65,881	75,887
Indirect taxes, *less* subsidies	10,370	11,214	12,138
GDP in purchasers' values	70,438	77,095	88,025

* Preliminary figures.   † Estimates.

BALANCE OF PAYMENTS (US $ million)

	1997	1998	1999
Exports of goods f.o.b.	1,856.5	2,016.5	1,848.9
Imports of goods f.o.b.	−2,150.4	−2,339.6	−2,558.0
Trade balance	−293.9	−323.1	−709.1
Exports of services	334.9	370.0	431.5
Imports of services	−360.9	−395.0	−497.6
Balance on goods and services	−319.9	−348.1	−775.2
Other income received	70.0	105.5	102.9
Other income paid	−281.8	−266.2	−228.5
Balance on goods, services and income	−531.7	−508.8	−900.8
Current transfers received	306.8	268.6	365.4
Current transfers paid	−47.3	−76.7	−1.4
Current balance	−272.2	−316.9	−536.8
Capital account (net)	14.6	47.6	75.2
Direct investment from abroad	121.5	84.0	230.0
Financial derivatives liabilities	—	−25.8	−16.8
Other investment assets	−53.4	−61.7	−135.0
Other investment liabilities	175.2	264.2	273.2
Net errors and omissions	196.5	6.7	52.5
Overall balance	182.2	−1.9	−57.7

Source: IMF, *International Financial Statistics*.

External Trade

PRINCIPAL COMMODITIES (US $ million, preliminary figures)

Imports c.i.f.	1998	1999	2000
Live animals and meat products	71.3	71.5	96.4
Vegetables and fruit	103.6	134.4	148.4
Crude materials (inedible) except fuels	260.3	260.1	269.4
Mineral fuels, lubricants, etc.	219.6	261.6	365.5
Chemicals and related products	336.5	351.7	399.5
Plastic and manufactures	144.7	147.4	169.6
Paper, paperboard and manufactures	125.3	120.9	145.9
Textile yarn, fabrics and manufactures	79.1	85.9	82.8
Metal and manufactures	204.9	245.2	206.4
Machinery and electrical appliances	514.9	519.3	476.7
Transport equipment	295.0	279.1	306.3
Total (incl. others)	2,534.8	2,676.1	2,884.7

Exports f.o.b.	1998	1999	2000
Bananas	219.6	38.1	113.6
Coffee	429.8	256.1	340.6
Zinc	36.3	50.2	47.5
Shellfish	188.7	189.3	177.3
Melons	43.8	47.0	37.6
Soaps and detergents	37.2	38.7	40.8
Total (incl. others)	1,532.8	1,164.4	1,322.2

PRINCIPAL TRADING PARTNERS (US $ million, preliminary figures)

Imports c.i.f.	1998	1999	2000
Brazil	23.5	30.9	26.8
Colombia	16.1	28.0	18.3
Costa Rica	87.9	97.8	96.8
El Salvador	156.4	180.4	189.4
Germany	33.5	46.4	38.2
Guatemala	232.5	224.7	235.9
Japan	117.1	107.2	133.4
Mexico	118.7	136.6	135.3
Netherlands	35.1	27.6	40.0
Nicaragua	24.9	38.0	32.0
Spain	26.7	30.6	30.4
USA	1,165.8	1,193.3	1,328.5
Venezuela	31.8	29.3	36.2
Total (incl. others)	2,534.8	2,676.1	2,884.7

Exports f.o.b.*	1998	1999	2000
Belgium	90.7	48.2	76.3
Costa Rica	24.6	27.3	28.1
El Salvador	83.3	83.3	121.3
France	15.6	12.1	13.1
Germany	124.4	42.9	104.7
Guatemala	88.7	72.9	71.1
Italy	30.9	24.8	26.0
Japan	66.7	55.6	56.1
Netherlands	14.9	16.1	12.5
Nicaragua	65.7	73.7	37.6
Spain	44.3	38.4	37.3
United Kingdom	32.9	12.6	27.7
USA	626.3	457.4	526.9
Total (incl. others)	1,532.8	1,164.4	1,322.2

Transport

ROAD TRAFFIC (motor vehicles in use)

	1997	1998	1999
Passenger cars	268,142	306,426	326,541
Buses and coaches	15,329	16,930	18,419
Lorries and vans	33,279	37,242	40,903
Motor cycles and bicycles	74,437	82,794	90,890

Source: IRF, *World Road Statistics*.

SHIPPING

Merchant Fleet (registered at 31 December)

	1996	1997	1998
Number of vessels	1,408	1,339	1,465
Total displacement ('000 grt)	1,197.8	1,053.0	1,083.2

Source: Lloyd's Register of Shipping, *World Fleet Statistics*.

International Sea-borne Freight Traffic ('000 metric tons)

	1988	1989	1990
Goods loaded	1,328	1,333	1,316
Goods unloaded	1,151	1,222	1,002

Source: UN, *Monthly Bulletin of Statistics*.

CIVIL AVIATION (traffic on scheduled services)

	1993	1994	1995
Kilometres flown (million)	4	5	5
Passengers carried ('000)	409	449	474
Passenger-km (million)	362	323	341
Total ton-km (million)	50	42	33

Source: UN, *Statistical Yearbook*.

Tourism

VISITOR ARRIVALS BY COUNTRY OF ORIGIN

	1996	1997	1998
Canada	7,711	9,300	8,025
Costa Rica	10,509	12,516	12,665
El Salvador	20,778	29,291	32,534
Germany	6,602	6,919	6,321
Guatemala	23,949	32,915	30,393
Mexico	7,698	9,285	10,185
Nicaragua	29,174	34,734	39,285
USA	107,389	118,357	127,303
Total (incl. others)	263,317	306,646	321,149

Receipts from tourism (US $ million): 120 in 1997; 164 in 1998; 165 in 1999.

Arrivals ('000): 371 in 1999.

Sources: World Tourism Organization, *Yearbook of Tourism Statistics*; World Bank, *World Development Indicators*.

Communications Media

	1995	1996	1997
Radio receivers ('000 in use)	2,310	2,380	2,450
Television receivers ('000 in use)	500	550	570
Telephones ('000 main lines in use)	161	190	234
Daily newspapers	6	6	6
Weekly newspapers	2	n.a.	3

Sources: partly UN, *Statistical Yearbook*, and UNESCO, *Statistical Yearbook*.

Education

(1998)

	Institutions	Teachers	Students
Pre-primary	2,401	3,184	89,537
Primary	8,743	32,519	1,077,333
Secondary	917	14,357	183,245
University level	10	5,088	76,573

Directory

The Constitution

Following the elections of April 1980, the 1965 Constitution was revised. The new Constitution was approved by the National Assembly in November 1982, and amended in 1995. The following are some of its main provisions:

Honduras is constituted as a democratic Republic. All Hondurans over 18 years of age are citizens.

THE SUFFRAGE AND POLITICAL PARTIES

The vote is direct and secret. Any political party that proclaims or practises doctrines contrary to the democratic spirit is forbidden. A National Electoral Council will be set up at the end of each presidential term. Its general function will be to supervise all elections and to register political parties. A proportional system of voting will be adopted for the election of Municipal Corporations.

INDIVIDUAL RIGHTS AND GUARANTEES

The right to life is declared inviolable; the death penalty is abolished. The Constitution recognizes the right of habeas corpus and arrests may be made only by judicial order. Remand for interrogation may not last more than six days, and no-one may be held incommunicado for more than 24 hours. The Constitution recognizes the rights of free expression of thought and opinion, the free circulation of information, of peaceful, unarmed association, of free movement within and out of the country, of political asylum and of religious and educational freedom. Civil marriage and divorce are recognized.

WORKERS' WELFARE

All have a right to work. Day work shall not exceed eight hours per day or 44 hours per week; night work shall not exceed six hours per night or 36 hours per week. Equal pay shall be given for equal work. The legality of trade unions and the right to strike are recognized.

EDUCATION

The State is responsible for education, which shall be free, lay, and, in the primary stage, compulsory. Private education is liable to inspection and regulation by the State.

LEGISLATIVE POWER

Deputies are obliged to vote, for or against, on any measure at the discussion of which they are present. The National Assembly has power to grant amnesties to political prisoners; approve or disapprove of the actions of the Executive; declare part or the whole of the Republic subject to a state of siege; declare war; approve or withhold approval of treaties; withhold approval of the accounts of public expenditure when these exceed the sums fixed in the budget; decree, interpret, repeal and amend laws, and pass legislation fixing the rate of exchange or stabilizing the national currency. The National Assembly may suspend certain guarantees in all or part of the Republic for 60 days in the case of grave danger from civil or foreign war, epidemics or any other calamity. Deputies are elected in the proportion of one deputy and one substitute for every 35,000 inhabitants, or fraction over 15,000. Congress may amend the basis in the light of increasing population.

EXECUTIVE POWER

Executive power is exercised by the President of the Republic, who is elected for four years by a simple majority of the people. No President may serve more than one term.

JUDICIAL POWER

The Judiciary consists of the Supreme Court, the Courts of Appeal and various lesser tribunals. The nine judges and seven substitute judges of the Supreme Court are elected by the National Assembly for a period of four years. The Supreme Court is empowered to declare laws unconstitutional.

THE ARMED FORCES

The Armed Forces are declared by the Constitution to be essentially professional and non-political. The President exercises direct authority over the military.

LOCAL ADMINISTRATION

The country is divided into 18 Departments for purposes of local administration, and these are subdivided into 290 autonomous Municipalities; the functions of local offices shall be only economic and administrative.

The Government

HEAD OF STATE

President: Carlos Roberto Flores Facussé (assumed office 27 January 1998).

Vice-President: Gladys Aida Caballero.

CABINET
(August 2001)

Minister of the Interior and Justice: Vera Sofia Rubí.

Minister in the Office of the President: Gustavo Adolfo Alfaro Zelaya.

Minister of Foreign Affairs: Roberto Flores Bermúdez.

Minister of Industry and Commerce: Oscar Kafati.

Minister of Finance: Gabriela Núñez López.

Minister of National Defence: Enrique Flores Valeriano.

Minister of Public Security: Gautama Fonseca Zuniga.

Minister of Labour and Social Welfare: Rosa América Miranda de Galo.

Minister of Health: Plutarco Castellanos.

Minister of Public Education: Ramón Cálix Figueroa.

Minister of Public Works, Transport and Housing: Sergio Canales Munguia.

Minister of Culture, Art and Sports: Hermán Allan Padgett.

Minister of Agriculture and Livestock: Guillermo Alvarado Downing.

Minister of Natural Resources and Environment: Silvia Xiomara Gómez de Caballero.

Minister of Tourism: Ana del Socorro Abarca de Perdomo.

Minister of International Co-operation: Glenda Gallardo.

MINISTRIES

Office of the President: Palacio José Cecilio del Valle, Blvd Juan Pablo II, Tegucigalpa; tel. 232-6282; fax 231-0097.

Ministry of Agriculture and Livestock: Tegucigalpa.

Ministry of Culture, Art and Sports: Avda La Paz, Apdo 3287, Tegucigalpa; tel. 236-9643; fax 236-9532; e-mail binah @sdnhon.org.hn; internet www.sdnhon.org.hn/miembros/cultura.

Ministry of Finance: 5a Avda, 3a Calle, Tegucigalpa; tel. 22-1278; fax 238-2309.

Ministry of Foreign Affairs: Centro Cívico Gubernamental, Antigua Casa Presidencial, Blvd Fuerzas Armadas, Tegucigalpa; tel. 234-1922; fax 234-1484; internet www.sre.hn.

Ministry of Health: 4a Avda, 3a Calle, Tegucigalpa; tel. 22-1386; fax 238-4141; internet www.paho-who.hn/ssalud.htm.

Ministry of Industry and Commerce: Edif. Salame, 5a Avda, 4a Calle, Tegucigalpa; tel. 238-2025; fax 237-2836.

Ministry of the Interior and Justice: Palacio de los Ministerios, 2°, Tegucigalpa; tel. 237-1130; fax 237-1121; e-mail dgaatm@sdnhon.org.hn; internet www.sdnhon.org.hn/~dgaatm.

Ministry of International Co-operation: Tegucigalpa.

Ministry of Labour and Social Welfare: 2a y 3a Avda, 7a Calle, Comayagüela, Tegucigalpa; tel. 22-8526; fax 22-3220.

Ministry of National Defence and Public Security: 5a Avda, 4a Calle, Tegucigalpa; tel. 22-8560; fax 238-0238.

Ministry of Natural Resources and Environment: 100 ms al sur del Estadio Nacional, Apdo 1389, Tegucigalpa; tel. 239-4296; fax 232-6250; e-mail oss@serna.gob.hn; internet www.serna.gob.hn.

Ministry of Public Education: 1a Avda, 2a y 3a Calle 201, Comayagüela, Tegucigalpa; tel. 22-8517; fax 237-4312.

Ministry of Public Works, Transport and Housing: Barrio La Bolsa, Comayagüela, Tegucigalpa; tel. 233-7690; fax 25-2227.

Ministry of Tourism: Edif. Salame, 5a Avda, 4a Calle, Tegucigalpa; tel. 238-2025; fax 237-2836.

President and Legislature

PRESIDENT

Election, 30 November 1997

Candidate			Votes cast	% of votes
CARLOS ROBERTO FLORES FACUSSÉ (PL)	.	.	1,039,567	52.70
ALBA NORA GÚNERA DE MELGAR (PN)	.	.	843,154	42.74
OLBAN F. VALLADARES (PINU)	.	.	41,463	2.10
ARTURO CORRALES ALVÁREZ (PDCH)	.	.	24,717	1.25
MATÍAS FUNES (PUD)	.	.	23,745	1.20
Total .	.	.	1,972,646	100.00

ASAMBLEA NACIONAL

President: RAFAEL PINEDA PONCE.

General Election, 30 November 1997

Party			Votes cast	% of votes	Seats
Partido Liberal (PL)	.	.	940,575	49.55	67
Partido Nacional (PN)	.	.	789,015	41.56	55
Partido Innovación y Unidad—Social Democracia (PINU)		.	78,495	4.13	3
Partido Demócrata Cristiano de Honduras (PDCH)		.	49,650	2.62	2
Partido de Unificación Democrática (PUD)	.	.	40,658	2.14	1
Total*	.	.	1,898,393	100.00	128

* There were, in addition, 108,635 blank votes and 55,431 spoiled votes.

Political Organizations

Asociación para el Progreso de Honduras (APROH): right-wing grouping of business interests and members of the armed forces; Vice-Pres. MIGUEL FACUSSÉ; Sec. OSWALDO RAMOS SOTO.

Francisco Morazán Frente Constitucional (FMFC): f. 1988; composed of labour, social, political and other organizations.

Frente Patriótico Hondureño (FPH): left-wing alliance comprising:

> **Partido de Acción Socialista de Honduras (PASOH):** Leaders MARIO VIRGILIO CARAS, ROGELIO MARTÍNEZ REINA.

> **Partido Comunista de Honduras—Marxista-Leninista (PCH—ML):** f. 1954; gained legal status 1981; linked with DNU; Leader RIGOBERTO PADILLA RUSH.

Partido Demócrata Cristiano de Honduras (PDCH): legally recognized in 1980; Pres. EFRAÍN DÍAZ ARRIVILLAGA; Leader Dr HERNÁN CORRALES PADILLA.

Partido Innovación y Unidad—Social Democracia (PINU): 29 Avda de Comayaguela 912, Apdo 105, Tegucigalpa; tel. 237-1357; fax 237-4245; f. 1970; legally recognized in 1978; Leader OLBAN F. VALLADARES.

Partido Liberal (PL): Col. Miramonte atrás del supermercado La Colonia, No 1, Tegucigalpa; tel. 232-0520; fax 232-0797; internet www.partido-liberal.hn; f. 1891; factions within the party include the Alianza Liberal del Pueblo, the Movimiento Florista (Leader CARLOS ROBERTO FLORES FACUSSÉ), and the Movimiento Liberal Democrático Revolucionario (Pres. JORGE ARTURO REINA); Pres. CARLOS ROBERTO FLORES FACUSSÉ; Sec.-Gen. ROBERTO MICHELETTI BAIN.

Partido Nacional (PN): Paseo el Obelisco, Comayaguela, Tegucigalpa; tel. 237-7310; fax 237-7365; f. 1902; traditional right-wing party; internal opposition tendencies include Movimiento Democratizador Nacionalista (MODENA), Movimiento de Unidad y Cambio (MUC), Movimiento Nacional de Reivindicación Callejista (MONARCA) and Tendencia Nacionalista de Trabajo; Pres. CARLOS URBIZO; Sec. MARIO AGUILAR GONZÁLEZ.

Partido de Unificación Democrática (PUD): f. 1993; left-wing coalition comprising Partido Revolucionario Hondureño, Partido Renovación Patriótica, Partido para la Transformación de Honduras and Partido Morazanista.

Pueblo Unido en Bloque por Honduras (PuebloH): Tegucigalpa; f. 1999; Leader RAMÓN CUSTODIO.

Unión Revolucionaria del Pueblo (URP): f. 1980 following split in Communist Party; peasant support.

The Dirección Nacional Unificada—Movimiento Revolucionario Hondureño (DNU—MRH) comprises the following guerrilla groups:

Fuerzas Populares Revolucionarias (FRP) Lorenzo Zelaya.
Frente Morazanista para la Liberación de Honduras (FMLH).
Froylan Turcios.
Movimiento Popular de Liberación Cinchonero (MPLC).
Movimiento de Unidad Revolucionaria (MUR).
Partido Revolucionario de los Trabajadores Centroamericanos de Honduras (PRTCH).

Other guerrilla forces include the **Alianza por Acción Anticomunista (AAA)** and the **Frente Popular de Liberación, Nueve de Mayo (FPL)**.

Diplomatic Representation

EMBASSIES IN HONDURAS

Argentina: Avda José María Medina 417, Col. Rubén Darío, Apdo 3208, Tegucigalpa; tel. 232-3376; fax 231-0376; e-mail emarho@hondudata.com; Ambassador: JUAN ANGEL PEÑA.

Brazil: Col. La Reforma, Calle La Salle 1309, Apdo 341, Tegucigalpa; tel. 236-5867; fax 236-5873; e-mail brastegu@hondudata.com; Chargé d'affaires a.i.: SERGIO ELIAS COURY.

Chile: Edif. Interamericana frente Los Castaños, Blvd Morazán, Apdo 222, Tegucigalpa; tel. 232-4095; fax 232-8853; e-mail echilehn@cablecolor.hn; Ambassador: GERMÁN CARRASCO.

China (Taiwan): Col. Palmira, Avda República de Panamá 2043, Tegucigalpa; tel. 239-5837; fax 232-7645; e-mail embchina@datum.hn; Ambassador: CHING-YEN CHANG.

Colombia: Edif. Palmira, 4°, Col. Palmira, Apdo 468, Tegucigalpa; tel. 232-9709; fax 232-8133; e-mail emcolhon@multivisionhn.net; Ambassador: GERMÁN RAMÍREZ BULLA.

Costa Rica: Residencial El Triángulo, 1a Calle 3451, Apdo 512, Tegucigalpa; tel. 232-1768; fax 232-1876; e-mail embacori@hondutel.hn; Chargé d'affaires a.i.: MÁXIMO SUÁREZ ULLOA.

Dominican Republic: Calle Principal frente al Banco Continental, Col. Miramontes, Tegucigalpa; tel. 239-0130; fax 239-1594; e-mail embadom@compunet.hn; Ambassador: ELADIO KNIPPING VICTORIA.

Ecuador: Col. Palmira, Avda Juan Lindo 122, Apdo 358, Tegucigalpa; tel. 236-5980; fax 236-6929; e-mail mecuahon@hondutel.hn; Chargé d'affaires a.i.: Dr MARCELO FABIAN HURTADO LOMAS.

El Salvador: Col. San Carlos, Calzada República del Uruguay 219, Apdo 1936, Tegucigalpa; tel. 239-0901; fax 239-9403; e-mail embasal@worksitsnet.net; Ambassador: SIGIFREDO OCHOA PÉREZ.

France: Col. Palmira, Avda Juan Lindo, Callejón Batres 337, Apdo 3441, Tegucigalpa; tel. 236-6800; fax 236-8051; e-mail ambafrance@cablecolor.hn; Ambassador: MICHEL AVIGNON.

Germany: Edif. Paysen, 3°, Blvd Morazán, Apdo 3145, Tegucigalpa; tel. 232-3161; fax 232-9518; e-mail embalema@netsys.hn; Ambassador: Dr THOMAS BRUNS.

Guatemala: Col. Las Minitas, Calle Arturo López Rodezno 2421, Tegucigalpa; tel. 232-5018; fax 232-8469; e-mail embaguahon3@cablecolor.hn; Ambassador: ERWIN FERNANDO GUZMÁN OVALLE.

Holy See: Palacio de la Nunciatura Apostólica, Col. Palmira, Avda Santa Sede 412, Apdo 324, Tegucigalpa; tel. 236-6613; fax 232-8280; e-mail nunciatureateg@hondudata.com; Apostolic Nuncio: Most Rev. GEORGE PANIKULAM, Titular Archbishop of Arpaia.

Italy: Col. Reforma, Avda Principal 2602, Apdo 317, Tegucigalpa; tel. 236-6810; fax 236-5659; e-mail ambtegus@cablecolor.hn; Ambassador: ESTEFANO MARÍA CACCIGUERRA.

Japan: Col. San Carlos, 3a y 4a Calles, contiguo estacionamiento Supermercado Sucasa, Apdo 125-C, Tegucigalpa; tel. 236-6828; fax 236-6100; Ambassador: MASAMI TAKEMOTO.

Mexico: Col. Palmira, Avda República de México 2402, Apdo 769, Tegucigalpa; tel. 232-4039; fax 232-4719; e-mail embamexhond@cablecolor.hn; Ambassador: BENITO ANDION SANCHO.

Nicaragua: Col. Tepeyac, Bloque M-1, Avda Choluteca 1130, Apdo 392, Tegucigalpa; tel. 232-7224; fax 231-1412; e-mail embanic@hondudata.com; Ambassador: Dr JOSÉ RENÉ GUTIÉRREZ HUETE.

Panama: Edif. Palmira, 2°, Col. Palmira, Apdo 397, Tegucigalpa; tel. 239-5508; fax 232-8147; e-mail ephon@hondudata.com; Ambassador: IRIS ONEYDA VEGA RAMOS.

Peru: Col. La Reforma, Calle Principal 2618, Tegucigalpa; tel. 221-0596; fax 236-6070; e-mail embaperu@netsys.hn; Chargé d'affaires a.i.: CARLOS ALBERTO YRIGOYEN FORNO.

Spain: Col. Matamoros, Calle Santander 801, Apdo 3223, Tegucigalpa; tel. 236-6875; fax 236-8682; e-mail embesphn@correo.mae.es; Ambassador: JAVIER NAGORE SAN MARTÍN.

United Kingdom: Edif. Financiero BANEXPO, 3°, Blvd San Juan Bosco, Col. Payaqui, Apdo 290, Tegucigalpa; tel. 232-0612; fax 232-5480; e-mail britembhon@si.hn; Ambassador: DAVID ALLAN OSBORNE.

USA: Avda La Paz, Apdo 3453, Tegucigalpa; tel. 232-3120; fax 232-0027; Ambassador: FRANK ALMAGUER.

Venezuela: Col. Rubén Darío, entre Avda Las Minitas y Avda Rubén Darío 2321, Apdo 775, Tegucigalpa; tel. 232-1879; fax 232-1016; e-mail emvenezue@hondutel.hn; Ambassador: MARÍA SALAZAR SANABRIA.

Judicial System

Justice is administered by the Supreme Court (which has nine judges), five Courts of Appeal, and departmental courts (which have their own local jurisdiction).

Tegucigalpa has two Courts of Appeal which have jurisdiction (1) in the department of Francisco Morazán, and (2) in the departments of Choluteca Valle, El Paraíso and Olancho.

The Appeal Court of San Pedro Sula has jurisdiction in the department of Cortés, that of Comayagua has jurisdiction in the departments of Comayagua, La Paz and Intibucá; and that of Santa Bárbara in the departments of Santa Bárbara, Lempira and Copán.

Supreme Court: Edif. Palacio de Justicia, contiguo Col. Miraflores, Centro Cívico Gubernamental, Tegucigalpa; tel. 233-9208; fax 233-6784.

President of the Supreme Court of Justice: OSCAR ARMANDO AVILA.

Attorney-General: EDMUNDO ORELLANA.

Religion

The majority of the population are Roman Catholics; the Constitution guarantees toleration to all forms of religious belief.

CHRISTIANITY
The Roman Catholic Church

Honduras comprises one archdiocese and six dioceses. At 31 December 1999 some 81.6% of the population were adherents.

Bishops' Conference: Conferencia Episcopal de Honduras, Los Laureles, Comayagüela, Apdo 3121, Tegucigalpa; tel. 229-1111; fax 229-1144; e-mail ceh@sdnhon.org.hn; f. 1929; Pres. Cardinal OSCAR ANDRÉS RODRÍGUEZ MARADIAGA, Archbishop of Tegucigalpa.

Archbishop of Tegucigalpa: Most Rev. HÉCTOR ENRIQUE SANTOS HERNÁNDEZ, Arzobispado, 3a y 2a Avda 1113, Apdo 106, Tegucigalpa; tel. 237-0353; fax 222-2337.

The Anglican Communion

Honduras comprises a single missionary diocese, in Province IX of the Episcopal Church in the USA.

Bishop of Honduras: Rt Rev. LEOPOLD FRADE, Apdo 586, San Pedro Sula; tel. 556-6155; fax 556-6467; e-mail episcopal@mayanet.hn.

The Baptist Church

Baptist Convention of Honduras: Apdo 2176, Tegucigalpa; tel. and fax 236-6717; Pres. TOMÁS MONTOYA.

Other Churches

Iglesia Cristiana Luterana de Honduras (Christian Lutheran Church of Honduras): Apdo 2861, Tegucigalpa; tel. and fax 237-4893; e-mail iclh@mayanet.hn; Pres. Rev. J. GUILLERMO FLORES V.; 1,000 mems.

BAHÁ'Í FAITH

National Spiritual Assembly: Sendero de los Naranjos 2801, Col. Castaños, Apdo 273, Tegucigalpa; tel. 232-6124; fax 231-1343; e-mail bahaihon@globenet.hn; mems resident in 667 localities.

The Press

DAILIES

El Faro Porteño: Puerto Cortés.

La Gaceta: Tegucigalpa; f. 1830; morning; official govt paper; Dir MARCIAL LAGOS; circ. 3,000.

El Heraldo: Avda los Próceres, Frente Instituto del Tórax, Barrio San Felipe, Apdo 1938, Tegucigalpa; tel. 236-6000; fax 21-0778; f. 1979; morning; independent; Dir JOSÉ FRANCISCO MORALES CÁLIX; circ. 45,000.

El Nuevo Día: 3a Avda, 11–12 Calles, San Pedro Sula; tel. 52-4298; fax 57-9457; e-mail elndia@hondutel.hn; f. 1994; morning; independent; Pres. ABRAHAM ANDONIE; Editor ARMANDO CERRATO; circ. 20,000.

El Periódico: Carretera al Batallón, Tegucigalpa; tel. 234-3086; fax 234-3090; f. 1993; morning; Pres. EMIN ABUFELE; Editor OSCAR ARMANDO MARTÍNEZ.

La Prensa: 3a Avda, 6a–7a Calles No 34, Apdo 143, San Pedro Sula; tel. 53-3101; fax 53-0778; e-mail laprensa@simon.intertel.hn; internet www.laprensahn.com; f. 1964; morning; independent; Pres. JORGE CANAHUATI LARACH; Editor NELSON EDGARDO FERNÁNDEZ; circ. 62,000.

El Tiempo: Altos del Centro Comercial Miramontes, Col. Miramontes, Tegucigalpa; tel. 231-0418; internet www.tiempo.hn; f. 1970; liberal; Dir MANUEL GAMERO; circ. 42,000.

El Tiempo: 1a Calle, 5a Avda 102, Santa Anita, Apdo 450, San Pedro Sula; tel. 53-3388; fax 53-4590; e-mail tiempo@simon.intertel.hn; internet www.tiempo.hn; f. 1960; morning; left-of-centre; Pres. JAIME ROSENTHAL OLIVA; Editor MANUEL GAMERO; circ. 35,000.

La Tribuna: Col. Santa Bárbara, Comayagüela, Apdo 1501, Tegucigalpa; tel. 233-1138; fax 233-1188; e-mail tribuna@david.intertel.hn; internet www.latribuna.hn; f. 1977; morning; independent; Dir ADÁN ELVIR FLORES; Pres. CARLOS ROBERTO FLORES FACUSSÉ; circ. 45,000.

PERIODICALS

Cambio Empresarial: Apdo 1111, Tegucigalpa; tel. 237-2853; fax 237-0480; monthly; economic, political, social; Editor JOAQUÍN MEDINA OVIEDO.

El Comercio: Cámara de Comercio e Industrias de Tegucigalpa, Blvd Centroamérica, Apdo 3444, Tegucigalpa; tel. 232-4200; fax 232-0759; f. 1970; monthly; commercial and industrial news; Dir-Gen. Lic. HÉCTOR MANUEL ORDÓÑEZ.

Cultura para Todos: San Pedro Sula; monthly.

Espectador: San Pedro Sula; weekly.

Extra: Tegucigalpa; tel. 237-2533; f. 1965; monthly; independent; current affairs; Editor VICENTE MACHADO VALLE.

Hablemos Claro: Edif. Abriendo Brecha, Blvd Suyapa, Tegucigalpa; tel. 232-8058; fax 239-7008; e-mail abrecha@hondutel.hn; f. 1990; weekly; Editor RODRIGO WONG ARÉVALO; circ. 15,000.

Hibueras: Apdo 955, Tegucigalpa; Dir RAÚL LANZA VALERIANO.

Presente: Tegucigalpa; monthly.

Revista Ideas: Tegucigalpa; 6 a year; women's interest.

Revista Prisma: Tegucigalpa; quarterly; cultural; Editor MARÍA LUISA CASTELLANOS.

Sucesos: Tegucigalpa; monthly.

Tribuna Sindical: Tegucigalpa; monthly.

PRESS ASSOCIATION

Asociación de Prensa Hondureña: 6a Calle (altos), Barrio Guanacaste, Apdo 893, Tegucigalpa; tel. 237-8345; f. 1930; Pres. MIGUEL OSMUNDO MEJA ERAZO.

FOREIGN NEWS AGENCIES

Agence France-Presse (AFP) (France): Tegucigalpa; Correspondent WINSTON CÁLIX.

Agencia EFE (Spain): Edif. Jiménez Castro, 5°, Of. 505, Tegucigalpa; tel. 22-0493; Bureau Chief ARMANDO ENRIQUE CERRATO CORTÉS.

Agenzia Nazionale Stampa Associata (ANSA) (Italy): Edif. La Plazuela, Barrio La Plazuela, Tegucigalpa; tel. 237-7701; Correspondent RAÚL MONCADA.

Deutsche Presse-Agentur (dpa) (Germany): Edif. Jiménez Castro, Of. 203, 4a Calle y 5a Avda, No 405, Apdo 3522, Tegucigalpa; tel. 237-8570; Correspondent WILFREDO GARCÍA CASTRO.

Inter Press Service (IPS) (Italy): Apdo 228, Tegucigalpa; tel. 232-5342; Correspondent JUAN RAMÓN DURÁN.

Reuters (United Kingdom): Edif. Palmira, frente Honduras Maya, 5°, Col. Palmira, Tegucigalpa; tel. 231-5329.

United Press International (UPI) (USA): c/o El Tiempo, Altos del Centro Comercial Miramontes, Col. Miramontes, Tegucigalpa; tel. 231-0418; Correspondent VILMA GLORIA ROSALES.

Publishers

Compañía Editora Nacional, SA: 5a Calle Oriente, No 410, Tegucigalpa.

Editora Cultural: 6a Avda Norte, 7a Calle, Comayagüela, Tegucigalpa.

Editorial Nuevo Continente: Tegucigalpa; tel. 22-5073; Dir LETICIA SILVA DE OYUELA.

Editorial Paulino Valladares, Carlota Vda de Valladares: 5a Avda, 5a y 6a Calle, Tegucigalpa.

Guaymuras: Apdo 1843, Tegucigalpa; tel. 237-5433; fax 237-4931; f. 1980; Dir ISOLDA ARITA MELZER; Admin. ROSENDO ANTÚNEZ.

Industria Editorial Lypsa: Apdo 167-C, Tegucigalpa; tel. 22-9775; Man. JOSÉ BENNATON.

Universidad Nacional Autónoma de Honduras: Blvd Suyapa, Tegucigalpa; tel. 231-4601; fax 231-4601; f. 1847.

Broadcasting and Communications

TELECOMMUNICATIONS

Comisión Nacional de Telecomunicaciones (Conatel): Apdo 15012, Tegucigalpa; tel. 221-3500; fax 221-0578; e-mail nhernandez @conatel.hn; Pres. NORMAN ROY HERNÁNDEZ D.; Exec. Sec. WALTER DAVID SANDOVAL.

Empresa Hondureña de Telecomunicaciones (Hondutel): Apdo 1794, Tegucigalpa; tel. 237-9802; fax 237-1111; scheduled for privatization in 2001; Gen. Man. ROBERTO MICHELLETTI BAIN.

BROADCASTING
Radio

Radio América: Col. Alameda, frente a la Droguería Mandofer, Apdo 259, Tegucigalpa; commercial station; tel. 232-7028; fax 231-4180; f. 1948; 13 relay stations; Pres. MANUEL ANDONIE FERNÁNDEZ; Gen. Man. BERNARDINO RIVERA.

Radio Nacional de Honduras: Zona El Olvido, Apdo 403, Tegucigalpa; tel. 238-5478; fax 237-9721; f. 1976; official station, operated by the Govt; Dir ROY ARTHURS LEYLOR.

Radio Tegucigalpa: Edif. Landa Blanca, Calle La Fuente, Tegucigalpa; tel. 238-3880; f. 1982; Dir NERY ARTEAGA; Gen. Man. ANTONIO CONDE MAZARIEGOS.

La Voz de Centroamérica: 9a Calle, 10a Avda 64, Apdo 120, San Pedro Sula; tel. 52-7660; fax 57-3257; f. 1955; commercial station; Gen. Man. NOEMI SIKAFFY.

La Voz de Honduras: Blvd Suyapa, Apdo 642, Tegucigalpa; commercial station; 23 relay stations; Gen. Man. NOEMI VALLADARES.

Television

Centroamericana de Televisión, Canal 7 y 4: Edif. Televicentro, Blvd Suyapa, Apdo 734, Tegucigalpa; tel. 239-2081; fax 232-0097; f. 1959; Pres. JOSÉ RAFAEL FERRARI; Gen. Man. RAFAEL ENRIQUE VILLEDA.

Compañía Televisora Hondureña, SA: Blvd Suyapa, Apdo 734, Tegucigalpa; tel. 232-7835; fax 232-0097; f. 1959; main station Channel 5; nine relay stations; Gen. Man. JOSÉ RAFAEL FERRARI.

Corporación Centroamericana de Comunicaciones, SA de CV: 9a Calle, 10A Avda 64, Barrio Guamilito, Apdo 120, San Pedro Sula; tel. 557-5033; fax 557-3257; e-mail info@vicatv.hn; internet www.vicatv.hn; f. 1986; Pres. BLANCA SIKAFFY.

Voz y Imagen de Centro América: 9a Calle, 10A Avda 64, Barrio Guamilito, Apdo 120, San Pedro Sula; tel. 52-7660; fax 57-3257; Channels 9, 2 and 13; Pres. BLANCA SIKAFFY.

Telesistema Hondureño, SA, Canal 3: Edif. Televicentro, Blvd Suyapa, Apdo 734, Tegucigalpa; tel. 232-7064; fax 232-5019; f. 1967; Pres. MANUEL VILLEDA TOLEDO; Gen. Man. RAFAEL ENRIQUE VILLEDA.

Telesistema Hondureño, Canal 7: Col. Tara, Apdo 208, San Pedro Sula; tel. 53-1229; fax 57-6343; f. 1967; Pres. MANUEL VILLEDA TOLEDO; Dir JOSÉ RAFAEL FERRARI.

Trecevisión: Apdo 393, Tegucigalpa; subscriber TV; one relay station in San Pedro Sula; Gen. Man. F. PON AGUILAR.

Finance

(cap. = capital; res = reserves; dep. = deposits; m. = million; brs = branches; amounts in lempiras unless otherwise stated)

BANKING
Central Bank

Banco Central de Honduras—BANTRAL: Avda Juan Ramón Molina, 7a Avda y 1a Calle, Apdo 3165, Tegucigalpa; tel. 237-2270; fax 237-1876; internet www.bch.hn; f. 1950; bank of issue; cap. 63.7m., res 373.5m., dep. 4,762.2m. (Dec. 1992); Pres. VICTORIA ASFURA DE DÍAZ; Vice-Pres. DANIEL ALFREDO FIGUEROA; 4 brs.

Commercial Banks

Banco Atlántida, SA (BANCATLAN): Blvd Centroamérica, Plaza Bancatlán, Apdo 3164, Tegucigalpa; tel. 232-1050; fax 232-6120; e-mail webmaster@bancatlan.hn; internet www.bancatlan.hn; f. 1913;

cap. 500.0m., res 170.3m., dep. 5,121.0m. (Dec. 2000); Exec. Pres. GUILLERMO BUESO; Exec. Vice-Pres SALVADOR GÓMEZ, ROLANDO FUNES, JUDITH B. DE SALAZAR; 17 brs.

Banco del Comercio, SA (BANCOMER): 6a Avda, Calle SO 1-2, Apdo 160, San Pedro Sula; tel. 54-3600; Pres. RODOLFO CÓRDOBA PINEDA; 4 brs.

Banco Continental, SA (BANCON): Edif. Continental, 3a Avda 7, entre 2a y 3a Calle, Apdo 390, San Pedro Sula; tel. 239-2288; fax 239-0388; f. 1974; cap. 100m., res 14.3m., dep. 304.5m. (Dec. 1994); Pres. JAIME ROSENTHAL OLIVA; 6 brs.

Banco de las Fuerzas Armadas, SA (BANFFAA): Centro Comercial Los Castaños, Blvd Morazán, Apdo 877, Tegucigalpa; tel. 232-0164; fax 232-4728; e-mail webmaster@banffaa.hn; internet www.banffaa.hn; f. 1979; cap. 10m., res 33.2m., dep. 428.1m. (Dec. 1992); Pres. ROBERTO LÁZARUS LOZANO; Gen. Man. CARLOS RIVERA XATRUCH; 15 brs.

Banco Futuro: Edif. La Plazuela, 3a y 4a Calle, 4a Avda 1205, Tegucigalpa; tel. 237-4000; fax 237-1835; internet www.futuro.hn.

Banco Grupo El Ahorro Hondureño (BGA): Avda Colón 714, Apdo 3185, Tegucigalpa; tel. 237-5161; fax 237-4638; e-mail bancahorro@bancahorro.hn; internet www.bancahorro.hn; f. 2000, following a merger of Banco del Ahorro Hondureño and Banco La Capitalizadora Hondureña; cap. 648m., dep. 366m.; 125 brs.

Banco de Honduras, SA: Blvd Suyapa, Col. Loma Linda Sur, Tegucigalpa; tel. 232-6122; fax 232-6167; f. 1889; total assets 15,106m. (1999); Gen. Man. PATRICIA FERRO; 3 brs.

Banco Mercantil, SA: Blvd Suyapa, frente a Emisoras Unidas, Apdo 116, Tegucigalpa; tel. 232-0006; fax 232-3137; internet www.bamernet.hn; Pres. JOSÉ LAMAS; Gen. Man. JACOBO ATALA.

Banco de Occidente, SA (BANCOCCI): 6a Avda, Calle 2-3, Apdo 3284; tel. 237-0310; fax 237-0486; e-mail boccipan@pty.com; f. 1951; cap. and res 69m., dep. 606m. (June 1994); Pres. and Gen. Man. JORGE BUESO ARIAS; Vice-Pres. EMILIO MEDINA R.; 6 brs.

Banco Sogerin, SA: 8a Avda, 1a Calle, Apdo 440, San Pedro Sula; tel. 550-3888; fax 550-2001; e-mail sogelba@hondutel.hn; f. 1969; cap. and res 150.8m., dep. 857.9m. (Dec. 2000); Pres. and Gen. Man. EDMOND BOGRÁN ACOSTA; 31 brs.

Banco de los Trabajadores, SA (BANCOTRAB): 3a Avda, 13a Calle, Paseo El Obelisco, Comayagüela, Apdo 3246, Tegucigalpa; tel. 237-8723; f. 1967; cap. and res US $6.6m., dep. $43.1m. (Dec. 1992); Pres. ROLANDO DEL CID VELÁSQUEZ; 13 brs.

Development Banks

Banco Centroamericano de Integración Económica: Edif. Sede BCIE, Blvd Suyapa, Apdo 772, Tegucigalpa; tel. 228-2182; fax 228-2183; internet www.bcie.org; f. 1960 to finance the economic development of the Central American Common Market and its mem. countries; mems Costa Rica, El Salvador, Guatemala, Honduras, Nicaragua; cap. and res US $1,005.7m. (June 1999); Exec. Pres. ALEJANDRO ARÉVALO.

Banco Financiera Centroamericana, SA (FICENSA): Edif. La Interamericana, Blvd Morazán, Apdo 1432, Tegucigalpa; tel. 238-1661; fax 238-1630; f. 1974; private org. providing finance for industry, commerce and transport; total assets 11,023m. (1999); Pres. OSWALDO LÓPEZ ARELLANO; Gen. Man. ROQUE RIVERA RIBAS.

Banco Hondureño del Café, SA (BANHCAFE): Calle República de Costa Rica, Blvd Juan Pablo II, Apdo 583, Tegucigalpa; tel. 232-8370; fax 232-8332; e-mail bcafeinf@hondutel.hn; f. 1981 to help finance coffee production; owned principally by private coffee producers; cap. 63.1m., res 110.3m., dep. 1,174.8m. (Dec. 2000); Pres. RAMÓN DAVID RIVERA; Gen. Man. RENÉ ARDÓN MATUTE; 50 brs.

Banco Municipal Autónomo (BANMA): 6a Avda, 6a Calle, Tegucigalpa; tel. 22-5963; fax 237-5187; f. 1963; Pres. JUSTO PASTOR CALDERÓN; 2 brs.

Banco Nacional de Desarrollo Agrícola (BANADESA): 4a Avda y 5a Avda, 13a y 14a Calles, Apdo 212, Tegucigalpa; tel. 237-2201; fax 237-5187; f. 1980; govt development bank (transfer to private ownership pending); loans to agricultural sector; cap. 34.5m., res 42.7m., dep. 126.9m. (March 1993); Pres. GUSTAVO A. ZELAYA CHÁVEZ; 34 brs.

Financiera Nacional de la Vivienda—FINAVI: Apdo 1194, Tegucigalpa; f. 1975; housing development bank; Exec. Pres. Lic. ELMAR LIZARDO.

Foreign Bank

Lloyds TSB Bank PLC (United Kingdom): Edif. Europa, Col. San Carlos, Calle República de México, Avda Ramón Ernesto Cruz, Apdo 3136, Tegucigalpa; tel. 236-6864; fax 236-6417; e-mail lloydstsb@honduras.hn; Man. G. JOHNS.

Banking Association

Asociación Hondureña de Instituciones Bancarias (AHIBA): Blvd Suyapa contiguo a CANNON, Apdo 1344, Tegucigalpa; tel.

235-6770; fax 239-0191; f. 1956; 22 mem. banks; Pres. JACOBO ATALA Z.; Exec. Sec. GUILLERMO MATAMOROS.

STOCK EXCHANGE

Bolsa Hondureña de Valores: Edif. Martínez Valenzuela, 1°, 2a Calle, 3a Avda, San Pedro Sula; tel. 553-4410; fax 553-4480; e-mail bhvsps@bhv.hn2.com; Gen. Man. MARCO TULIO LÓPEZ PEREIRA.

INSURANCE

American Home Assurance Co: Edif. Los Castaños, 4°, Blvd Morazán, Apdo 3220, Tegucigalpa; tel. 232-3938; fax 232-8169; f. 1958; Mans LEONARDO MOREIRA, EDGAR WAGNER.

Aseguradora Hondureña, SA: Edif. El Planetario, 4°, Col. Lomas de Guijarro Sur, Calle Madrid, Avda Paris, Apdo 312, Tegucigalpa; tel. 232-2729; fax 231-0982; e-mail gerencia@asegurahon.hn; f. 1954; Pres. JOSÉ MARÍA AGURCIA; Gen. Man. GERARDO CORRALES.

Compañía de Seguros El Ahorro Hondureño, SA: Edif. Trinidad, Avda Colón, Apdo 3643, Tegucigalpa; tel. 237-8219; fax 237-4780; e-mail elahorro@segurosel ahorro.hn; f. 1917; Pres. JORGE A. ALVARADO.

Interamericana de Seguros, SA: Col. Los Castaños, Apdo 593, Tegucigalpa; tel. 232-7614; fax 232-7762; f. 1957; Pres. CAMILO ATALA FARAJ; Gen. Man. LUIS ATALA FARAJ.

Pan American Life Insurance Co (PALIC): Edif. PALIC, Avda República de Chile 804, Tegucigalpa; tel. 220-5757; fax 232-3907; e-mail palic@david.intertel.hn; f. 1944; Gen. Man. ALBERTO AGURCIA.

Previsión y Seguros, SA: Edif. Maya, Col. Palmira, Apdo 770, Tegucigalpa; tel. 231-2127; fax 232-5215; f. 1982; Pres. Gen. HÉCTOR CASTRO CABUS; Gen. Man. P. M. ARTURO BOQUÍN OSEJO.

Seguros Atlántida: Edif. Sonisa, Costado Este Plaza Bancatlán, Tegucigalpa; tel. 232-4014; fax 232-3688; e-mail morellana@bancatlan.hn; f. 1986; Pres. GUILLERMO BUESO; Gen. Man. JUAN MIGUEL ORELLANA.

Seguros Continental, SA: 3A Avda 2 y 3, 7a Calle, Apdo 320, San Pedro Sula; tel. 52-0880; fax 52-2750; f. 1968; Pres. JAIME ROSENTHAL OLIVA; Gen. Man. MARIO R. SOLÍS.

Seguros Crefisa: Edif. Ficensa, 1°, Blvd Morazán, Apdo 3774, Tegucigalpa; tel. 238-1750; fax 238-1714; e-mail ggerencia@crefisa.hn; internet www.crefisa.hn; f. 1993; Pres. OSWALDO LÓPEZ ARELLANO; Gen. Man. MARIO BATRES PIÑEDA.

Insurance Association

Cámara Hondureña de Aseguradores (CAHDA): Edif. Los Jarros, Blvd Morazán, Local 313, Apdo 3290, Tegucigalpa; tel. 239-0342; fax 232-6020; e-mail cahda@gbm.hn; f. 1974; Man. JOSÉ LUIS MONCADA RODRÍGUEZ.

Trade and Industry

GOVERNMENT AGENCIES

Fondo Hondureño de Inversión Social (FHIS): Tegucigalpa; internet www.fhis.hn; social investment fund; Gen. Man. MANUEL ZELAYA ROSALES.

Fondo Social de la Vivienda (FOSOVI): Col. Florencia, Tegucigalpa; tel. 239-1605; social fund for housing, urbanization and devt; Gen. Man. MARIO MARTÍ.

Secretaria Técnica del Consejo Superior de Planificación Económica (CONSUPLANE): Edif. Bancatlán, 3°, Apdo 1327, Comayagüela, Tegucigalpa; tel. 22-8738; f. 1965; national planning office; Exec. Sec. FRANCISCO FIGUEROA ZÚÑIGA.

DEVELOPMENT ORGANIZATIONS

Consejo Hondureño de la Empresa Privada (COHEP): Edif. COHEP contiguo a Plaza Visión, Calle Yoro, Col. Tepeyac, Apdo 3240, Tegucigalpa; tel. 235-3336; fax 235-3344; e-mail presidencia@cohep.com; f. 1968; comprises 23 private enterprises; Pres. Dr JULIETTE HANDAL DE CASTILLO.

Corporación Financiera de Olancho: f. 1977 to co-ordinate and manage all financial aspects of the Olancho forests project; Pres. RAFAEL CALDERÓN LÓPEZ.

Corporación Hondureña de Desarrollo Forestal (COHDEFOR): Salida Carretera del Norte, Zona El Carrizal, Comayagüela, Apdo 1378, Tegucigalpa; tel. 22-8810; fax 22-2653; f. 1974; semi-autonomous org. exercising control and man. of the forestry industry; transfer of all sawmills to private ownership was proceeding in 1991; Gen. Man. PORFIRIO LOBO S.

Dirección General de Minas e Hidrocarburos (General Directorate of Mines and Hydrocarbons): Blvd Miraflores, Apdo 981, Tegucigalpa; tel. 232-7848; fax 232-7848; Dir-Gen. MIGUEL VILLEDA VILLELA.

Instituto Hondureño del Café (IHCAFE): Apdo 40-C, Tegucigalpa; tel. 237-3131; f. 1970; coffee devt programme; Gen. Man. FERNANDO D. MONTES M.

Instituto Hondureño de Mercadeo Agrícola (IHMA): Apdo 727, Tegucigalpa; tel. 235-3193; fax 235-5719; f. 1978; agricultural devt agency; Gen. Man. TULIO ROLANDO GIRÓN ROMERO.

Instituto Nacional Agrario (INA): Col. La Almeda, 4a Avda, entre 10a y 11a Calles, No 1009, Apdo 3391, Tegucigalpa; tel. 232-8400; fax 232-8398; agricultural devt programmes; Exec. Dir ANÍBAL DELGADO FIALLOS.

CHAMBERS OF COMMERCE

Cámara de Comercio e Industrias de Cortés: 17a Avda, 10a y 12a Calle, Apdo 14, San Pedro Sula; tel. 53-0761; f. 1931; 812 mems; Pres. ROBERTO REYES SILVA; Dir LUIS FERNANDO RIVERA.

Cámara de Comercio e Industrias de Tegucigalpa: Blvd Centroamérica, Apdo 3444, Tegucigalpa; tel. 232-4200; fax 232-0759; e-mail camara@ccit.hn; internet www.ccit.hn; Pres. ANTONIO TAVEL OTERO.

Federación de Cámaras de Comercio e Industrias de Honduras (FEDECAMARA): Edif. Castañito, 2°, Col. Castaño, Sur, 6a Avda, Calle Jamaica, Apdo 3393, Tegucigalpa; tel. 232-6083; fax 232-1870; e-mail fedecamara@sigmanet.hn; internet www.sieh.org; f. 1948; 1,200 mems; Pres. SERGIO EVENOR BONILLA; Exec. Dir DANILO ROMERO MARTÍNEZ.

INDUSTRIAL AND TRADE ASSOCIATIONS

Asociación de Bananeros Independientes (ANBI) (National Association of Independent Banana Producers): San Pedro Sula; tel. 22-7336; f. 1964; 62 mems; Pres. Ing. JORGE ALBERTO ALVARADO; Sec. CECILIO TRIMINIO TURCIOS.

Asociación Hondureña de Productores de Café (Coffee Producers' Association): 10a Avda, 6a Calle, Apdo 959, Tegucigalpa.

Asociación Nacional de Exportadores de Honduras (ANEXHON) (National Association of Exporters): Tegucigalpa; comprises 104 private enterprises; Pres. Dr RICHARD ZABLAH.

Asociación Nacional de Industriales (ANDI) (National Association of Manufacturers): Blvd Los Próceres 505, Apdo 20-C, Tegucigalpa; Pres. HÉCTOR BULNES; Exec. Sec. DORCAS DE GONZALES.

Asociación Nacional de Pequeños Industriales (ANPI) (National Association of Small Industries): Apdo 730, Tegucigalpa; Pres. JUAN RAFAEL CRUZ.

Federación Nacional de Agricultores y Ganaderos de Honduras (FENAGH) (Farmers and Livestock Breeders' Association): Tegucigalpa; tel. 231-1392; Pres. ROBERTO GALLARDO LARDIZÁBAL.

Federación Nacional de Cooperativas Cañeras (Fenacocal) (National Federation of Sugar Cane Co-operatives): Tegucigalpa.

MAJOR COMPANIES

The following are some of the major industrial companies currently operating in Honduras.

Azucarera Central, SA de CV: Edif. Banco Atlántida, Blvd Morazán, Tegucigalpa; tel. 232-3334; fax 232-2658; f. 1974; processing and refining of sugar cane; Pres. Lic. GILBERTO GOLDSTEIN; 975 employees.

Breakwater Resources: Apdo 342, San Pedro Sula; tel. 659-3051; fax 659-3059; Canadian mining co, owner/operator of El Mochito mine; Chair. GORDON BUB; Pres. COLIN BENNER; Gen. Man. ROBERT BYRD.

Cementos del Norte, SA de CV: Río Bijao, Choloma Cortés, Apdo 132; tel. 669-3640; fax 669-3639; cement producers; Dir and Pres. Lic. YANI ROSENTHAL; 470 employees.

Cervecería Hondureña, SA: Carretera a Puerto Cortés, Apdo 86, San Pedro Sula; tel. 553-3310; fax 552-2845; f. 1915; brewery and soft drink manufacturers; Pres. ROBERTO ZACARÍAS; 1,150 employees.

Compañía Azucarera Choluteca, SA de CV: Zona de los Mangos, Choluteca; tel. 882-0530; fax 882-0554; f. 1967; sugar-cane refining; Pres. SERGIO R. SALINAS S.; Gen. Man. BRAULIO CRUZ; 180 employees.

Compañía Azucarera Hondureña, SA: 3 Avda 36, Apdo 552, San Pedro Sula; tel. 553-3401; fax 552-7091; f. 1938; cultivation and refining of sugar cane; Dir-Gen. Lic. RODRIGO J. ARBIR; 560 employees.

Droguería Nacional, SA: 3a Avda, 2a Calle 10, San Pedro Sula; tel. 553-0004; fax 557-5244; f. 1936; manufacturers of pharmaceuticals, chemicals and cosmetic products; Pres. CONSTANTINO BARELTTA; 115 employees.

Hilos y Mechas, SA de CV: Carretera a Puerto Cortés, Apdo 118, San Pedro Sula; fax 552-2441; manufacturers of cotton fabrics, twine and thread; Gen. Man. ROBERT HANDAL; 856 employees.

Leche y Derivados, SA (LEYDE): Km 8 Carretera Ceiba–Tela, La Ceiba, Atlántida; tel. 443-2276; f. 1973; milk and dairy products; Pres. JOSÉ BONANO; 210 employees.

Motorola, Inc.: Tegucigalpa; tel. 237-9096; f. 1996; cellular telephone networks.

Planta de Productos Lácteos Sula, SA de CV: Carretera a Puerto Cortés, San Pedro Sula; dairy products; Pres. ROBERTO ZELAYA; 300 employees.

Químicas Dinant de Centroamérica, SA de CV: Edif. Conjunto Químicas Dinant, Barrio Morazán, Tegucigalpa; tel. 232-8070; fax 232-6127; f. 1962; producers of agricultural chemicals, soaps, cosmetics and coffee; Pres. MIGUEL FACUSSÉ BARJÚN; 170 employees.

Tabacalera Hondureña, SA: Carretera Chamelecon, Zona El Cacao, San Pedro Sula; tel. 556-6161; fax 556-6678; f. 1928; subsidiary of British-American Tobacco Ltd, United Kingdom; cigarette manufacturers; Pres. BARRY SELBY; 280 employees.

Tela Railroad Company: Edif. Banco del País, 5°, Blvd Suyapa, Apdo 155, Tegucigalpa; tel. 235-8084; fax 235-8083; Honduras' largest banana producers; a subsidiary of Chiquita Brands International.

Textiles Río Lindo, SA de CV: San José del Pedregal, Apdo 211, Tegucigalpa; tel. 233-1411; fax 233-5433; e-mail riolindo @ns.gbm.hn; f. 1951; manufacturers of textiles; CEO ADOLFO FACUSSÉ; Gen. Man. ROBERTO FACUSSÉ; 850 employees.

UTILITIES

Electricity

Empresa Nacional de Energía Eléctrica—ENEE (National Electrical Energy Co): 7a Calle, 1a Avda, Apdo 99, Tegucigalpa; tel. 238-5977; fax 237-9881; e-mail eneeger@enee.gn; internet www.enee.hn; f. 1957; state-owned electricity co; scheduled for privatization in 2001; Pres. XIOMARA GOMEZ.

TRADE UNIONS

Asociación Nacional de Empleados Públicos de Honduras (ANDEPH) (National Association of Public Employees of Honduras): Plaza Los Dolores, Tegucigalpa; tel. 237-4393; Pres. OSCAR MARTÍNEZ.

Confederación de Trabajadores de Honduras—CTH (Workers' Confederation of Honduras): Edif. FARAJ, 5°, Avda Lempira, Barrio La Fuente, Apdo 720, Tegucigalpa; tel. 238-7859; fax 237-4243; f. 1964; affiliated to CTCA, ORIT, CIOSL, FIAET and ICFTU; Pres. JOSÉ ANGEL MEZA; Sec.-Gen. FRANCISCO GUERRERO NÚÑEZ; 200,000 mems; comprises the following federations:

Federación Central de Sindicatos Libres de Honduras (FECESITLIH) (Honduran Federation of Free Trade Unions): 1a Avda, 1a Calle 102, Apdo 621, Comayagüela, Tegucigalpa; tel. 237-5601; Pres. JOSÉ ANGEL MEZA.

Federación Sindical de Trabajadores Nacionales de Honduras (FESITRANH) (Honduran Federation of Farmworkers): 10a Avda, 11a Calle, Barrio Los Andes, San Pedro Sula; tel. 57-2539; f. 1957; Pres. MARIO QUINTANILLA.

Sindicato Nacional de Motoristas de Equipo Pesado de Honduras (SINAMEQUIPH) (National Union of HGV Drivers): Tegucigalpa; tel. 237-4243; Pres. ERASMO FLORES.

Central General de Trabajadores de Honduras (CGTH) (General Confederation of Labour of Honduras): Calle Real de Comayagüela, Apdo 1236, Tegucigalpa; tel. 237-4398; attached to Partido Demócrata Cristiano; Sec.-Gen. FELICITO AVILA.

Federación Auténtica Sindical de Honduras (FASH): 1a Avda, 11a Calle 1102, Comayagüela, Tegucigalpa.

Federación de Trabajadores del Sur (FETRASUR) (Federation of Southern Workers): Choluteca.

Federación Unitaria de Trabajadores de Honduras (FUTH): 2a Avda entre 11a y 12a Calle, Casa 1127, frente a BANCAFE, Apdo 1663, Comayagüela, Tegucigalpa; tel. 237-6349; f. 1981; linked to left-wing electoral alliance Frente Patriótico Hondureño; Pres. HÉCTOR HERNÁNDEZ FUENTES; 45,000 mems.

Frente de Unidad Nacional Campesino de Honduras (FUNACAMH): f. 1980; group of farming co-operatives and six main peasant unions as follows:

Asociación Nacional de Campesinos Hondureños (ANACH) (National Association of Honduran Farmworkers): 3a Avda, entre 9a y 10a Calle, Barrio Barandillas, San Pedro Sula; tel. 53-1884; f. 1962; affiliated to ORIT; Pres. ANTONIO JULÍN MÉNDEZ; 80,000 mems.

Federación de Cooperativas Agropecuarias de la Reforma Agraria de Honduras (FECORAH): Barrio Guanacaste, Casa 1702, Tegucigalpa; tel. 237-5391; Pres. JOSÉ NAHUM CÁLIX.

Frente Nacional de Campesinos Independientes de Honduras.

Unión Nacional de Campesinos (UNC) (National Union of Farmworkers): 1a Avda, Comayagüela, Tegucigalpa; tel. 238-2435; linked to CLAT; Pres. MARCIAL REYES CABALLERO; *c.* 25,000 mems.

Unión Nacional de Campesinos Auténticos de Honduras (UNCAH).

Unión Nacional de Cooperativas Populares de Honduras (UNACOOPH).

Transport

RAILWAYS

The railway network is confined to the north of the country and most lines are used for fruit cargo.

Ferrocarril Nacional de Honduras (National Railway of Honduras): 1a Avda entre 1a y 2a Calle, Apdo 496, San Pedro Sula; tel. and fax 552-8001; f. 1870; govt-owned; 595 km of track; Gen. Man. M. A. QUINTANILLA.

Tela Railroad Co: La Lima; tel. 56-2037; Pres. RONALD F. WALKER; Gen. Man. FREDDY KOCH.

Vaccaro Railway: La Ceiba; tel. 43-0511; fax 43-0091; fmrly operated by Standard Fruit Co.

ROADS

In 1998 there were an estimated 14,602 km of roads in Honduras, of which 2,644 km were paved. Some routes have been constructed by the Instituto Hondureño del Café and COHDEFOR in order to facilitate access to coffee plantations and forestry development areas. In November 2000 the World Bank approved a US $66.5m. loan to repair roads and bridges damaged or destroyed by 'Hurricane Mitch' in 1998.

Dirección General de Caminos: Barrio La Bolsa, Comayagüela, Tegucigalpa; tel. 225-1703; fax 225-2469; f. 1915; Dir KATHYA M. PASTOR; highways board.

SHIPPING

The principal port is Puerto Cortés on the Caribbean coast, which is the largest and best-equipped port in Central America. Other ports include Tela, La Ceiba, Trujillo/Castilla, Roatán, Amapala and San Lorenzo; all are operated by the Empresa Nacional Portuaria. There are several minor shipping companies. A number of foreign shipping lines call at Honduran ports.

Empresa Nacional Portuaria (National Port Authority): Apdo 18, Puerto Cortés; tel. 55-0192; fax 55-0968; f. 1965; has jurisdiction over all ports in Honduras; a network of paved roads connects Puerto Cortés and San Lorenzo with the main cities of Honduras, and with the principal cities of Central America; Gen. Man. ROBERTO VALENZUELA SIMÓN.

CIVIL AVIATION

Local airlines in Honduras compensate for the deficiencies of road and rail transport, linking together small towns and inaccessible districts. There are four international airports: Golosón airport in La Ceiba, Ramón Villeda Morales airport in San Pedro Sula, Toncontín airport in Tegucigalpa, and Juan Manuel Gálvaz airport in Roatán. In 2001 it was announced that San Francisco Airport, USA, was to invest some US $150m. in the four airports over two years. In 2000 plans for a new airport inside the Copán Ruinas archaeological park, 400 km west of Tegucigalpa, were announced.

Honduras Airways: Tegucigalpa; f. 1994; operates domestic flights and scheduled services to the USA.

Isleña Airlines: Avda San Isidro, frente al Parque Central, Apdo 402, La Ceiba; tel. 43-2683; fax 43-2632; e-mail islena@caribe.hn; internet www.caribe.hn; domestic service and service to Guatemala, Nicaragua and the Cayman Islands; Pres. and CEO ARTURO ALVARADO WOOD.

Líneas Aéreas Nacionales, SA (LANSA): La Ceiba; f. 2001; scheduled international services and flights within Central America.

Tourism

Tourists are attracted by the Mayan ruins, the fishing and boating facilities in Trujillo Bay and Lake Yojoa, near San Pedro Sula, and the beaches on the northern coast. There is an increasing eco-tourism industry. In May 2001 the tomb of a Mayan king was discovered near the Copán Ruinas archaeological park; it was expected to become an important tourist attraction. Honduras received around 371,000 tourists in 1999, when tourism receipts totalled US $165m.

Instituto Hondureño de Turismo: Edif. Europa, 5°, Col. San Carlos, Apdo 3261, Tegucigalpa; tel. 222-2124; fax 222-6621; e-mail tourisminfo@iht.hn; internet www.letsgohonduras.hn; f. 1972; dept of the Secretaría de Cultura y Turismo; Dir-Gen. RICARDO MARTÍNEZ.

Defence

In August 2000 the Honduran Armed Forces numbered 8,300: Army 5,500, Navy 1,000 and Air Force some 1,800. Paramilitary Public Security and Defence Forces numbered 6,000. Military service was ended in 1995. From January 1999 the post of Commander-in-Chief was abolished and the military were brought under the authority of the President. The military budget was substantially reduced in the late 1990s. In August 2000 some 410 US troops were based in Honduras.

Defence Budget: 520m. lempiras (US $35m.) in 2000.

Chairman of the Joint Chiefs of Staff: Col DANIEL LÓPEZ CARBALLO.

Chief of Staff (Army): Col FIDEL VELÁZQUEZ.

Chief of Staff (Air Force): Col SANTOS VALLADARES.

Education

Primary education, beginning at seven years of age and lasting for six years, is officially compulsory and is provided free of charge. Secondary education is not compulsory and begins at the age of 13. It lasts for up to five years and comprises a first cycle of three years and a second of two years. On completion of the compulsory period of primary education, every student is required to teach at least two illiterate adults to read and write. In 1997 the enrolment at primary schools was 87.5% (males 86.4%; females 88.6%) of the relevant age-group, while enrolment at secondary schools in that year was equivalent to only 36.0% (males 34.1%; females 37.9%) of children in the appropriate age-group. There are eight universities, including the Autonomous National University in Tegucigalpa. In 1998, according to estimates by the UN Development Programme, adult illiteracy averaged 26.6% (males 26.6%; females 26.5%). Estimated spending on education in 1997 was US $157.7m. In December 2000 the Inter-American Development Bank approved a US $29.6m. loan to initiate an expansion and reform of the education system.

Bibliography

For works on Central America generally, see Select Bibliography (Books).

Euraque, D. A. *Reinterpreting the Banana Republic: Region and State in Honduras, 1870–1972.* Chapel Hill, NC, University of North Carolina Press, 1996.

Fasquelle, R. P. *Perfil de un nuevo discurso político.* San Pedro Sula, Centro Editorial, 1992.

Madden, F. (Ed.). *The End of Empire Dependencies Since 1948: The West Indies, British Honduras, Hong Kong, Fiji, Cyprus, Gibraltar, and the Falklands.* Westport, CT, Greenwood Publishing Group, 2000.

Meyer, H. K. (Ed.). *Historical Dictionary of Honduras.* Metuchen, NJ, Scarecrow Press, 1977.

Morris, J. A. *Honduras: Caudillo Politics and Military Rulers.* Boulder, CO, Westview Press, 1984.

Peckenham, N., and Street, A. (Eds). *Honduras: Portrait of a Captive Nation.* New York, NY, Praeger Publrs, 1985.

Simmons, D. C. Jr. *Confederate Settlements in British Honduras.* Jefferson, MC, McFarland & Co, 2001.

Thorpe, A. *Agrarian Modernisation in Honduras.* Lewiston, NY, Edwin Mellen Press, 2001.

JAMAICA

Area: 10,991 sq km (4,244 sq miles).

Population (official estimate at mid-2000): 2,597,600.

Capital: Kingston, population 538,144 in 1991.

Language: English (official); a creole patois is also spoken.

Religion: Predominantly Christianity, with the Anglican, Roman Catholic and Presbyterian Churches the principal denominations; there is also a growing community of Rastafarians.

Climate: Tropical at sea-level, but temperate in the mountains; average temperature is 27°C (80°F), and mean annual rainfall is 198 cm (78 ins).

Time: GMT −3 hours.

Public Holidays

2002: 1 January (New Year's Day), 13 February (Ash Wednesday), 29 March (Good Friday), 1 April (Easter Monday), 27 May (for National Labour Day), 4 August (Emancipation Day), 5 August (Independence Day), 21 October (National Heroes' Day), 25–26 December (Christmas).

2003: 1 January (New Year's Day), 5 March (Ash Wednesday), 18 April (Good Friday), 21 April (Easter Monday), 23 May (National Labour Day), 3 August (Emancipation Day), 4 August (Independence Day), 20 October (National Heroes' Day), 25–26 December (Christmas).

Currency: Jamaican dollar; 1,000 Jamaican dollars = £15.38 = US $21.93 = €24.83 (30 March 2001).

Weights and Measures: Both the imperial and metric systems are in use.

Basic Economic Indicators

	1998	1999	2000
Gross domestic product (J $ million at 1986 prices)	19,088	19,044	19,154
GDP per head (J $ at 1986 prices)	7,418.6	7,355.7	7,351.7
GDP (J $ million at current prices)	268,424	287,904	320,814
GDP per head (J $ at current prices)	104,323.4	111,202.8	123,134.3
Annual growth of real GDP (%)	−0.4	−0.2	0.6
Annual growth of real GDP per head (%)	−1.3	−0.8	−0.5
Government budget (J $ million at current prices)*:			
Revenue	74,096	n.a.	n.a.
Expenditure	93,267	n.a.	n.a.
Consumer price index (annual average; base: 1995 = 100)	150.6	159.5	172.6
Rate of inflation (annual average, %)	8.6	6.0	8.2
Foreign exchange reserves (US $ million at 31 December)	708.8	553.8	1,053.6
Imports c.i.f. (US $ million)	3,035	2,899	3,216
Exports f.o.b. (US $ million)	1,312	1,240	1,296
Balance of payments (current account, US $ million)	−302.4	−255.7	n.a.

* Year ending 31 March of the following year.

Gross national product per head measured at purchasing power parity (PPP) (US dollars, converted by the PPP exchange rate, 1999): 3,276.

Total labour force (estimate, 2000): 933,500.

Unemployment (1999): 15.8%.

Total foreign debt (1999): US $4,609m.

Life expectancy (years at birth, 1998): 75 (males 72, females 77).

Infant mortality rate (per 1,000 live births, 1998): 21.

Adult population with HIV/AIDS (15–49 years, 1999): 0.71%.

School enrolment ratio (6–18 years, 1996): 88%.

Adult literacy rate (15 years and over, 2000): 86.7% (males 82.5; females 90.7).

Energy consumption per head (kg of oil equivalent, 1998): 1,575.

Carbon dioxide emissions per head (metric tons, 1996): 7.4.

Passenger motor cars in use (estimate, per 1,000 of population, 1996): 39.6.

Television receivers in use (per 1,000 of population, 1997): 183.

Personal computers in use (per 1,000 of population, 1997): 43.0.

History

ROD PRINCE

Based on an earlier essay by Dr A. J. PAYNE and
revised for this edition by JAMES FERGUSON

The first Europeans to visit Jamaica were members of a Spanish expedition, led by the navigator Christopher Columbus, in 1494. Before then the island had been inhabited by the Amerindian Taino people, who are thought to have arrived there from AD 650 onwards. Jamaica was claimed for Spain, but came under English control in 1655, and remained a part of the British Empire for the next 300 years. Slaves were transported from Africa, and Jamaica became a slave plantation society, producing sugar for export. Its colonial history was marked by a series of conflicts between the authorities and slaves or runaway slave communities known as Maroons. Slavery was abolished in 1834, but the decades following emancipation witnessed outbreaks of conflict over economic and social issues, such as land rights, in a society dominated by white planters. The most significant of these events was the Morant Bay rebellion in 1865, which was suppressed at the cost of some 500 lives. The rebellion led to the abolition of the island's Assembly and the imposition of Crown Colony control from the United Kingdom. Thereafter Jamaica remained relatively untroubled until the economic conditions of the 1930s produced a number of popular disturbances.

THE DEVELOPMENT OF TWO-PARTY POLITICS

The unrest was contained and channelled into organized labour and political movements by two cousins of utterly different character. Alexander Bustamante was a self-educated money-lender, who relied for his political success on his charisma and empathy for the masses. In 1938 he founded a trade union, characteristically named after himself, and in 1943 established the Jamaica Labour Party (JLP), which, despite its name, became a right-wing, anti-Communist party. Norman Manley, by contrast, was an intellectual (educated at the University of Oxford, United Kingdom) and an eminent barrister when he founded the People's National Party (PNP) in 1938. The PNP became a party of the centre left and affiliated itself to Jamaica's other trade union, the National Workers' Union (NWU).

From this point onwards the path towards independence was both steady and peaceful, beginning in 1944 with the inauguration of a new Constitution, providing for universal adult suffrage. Progress was hindered only by the creation of the West Indies Federation, which comprised all the British dependencies in the region, between 1958 and 1962. However, this was brought to a sudden end in September 1961, when Bustamante campaigned for Jamaica's withdrawal from the Federation and won a referendum on the issue. Thus, on 6 August 1962 Jamaica became a separate, independent state, with Bustamante as its first Prime Minister, following the JLP's victory at elections held in April.

The JLP again won elections in 1967, establishing the post-emancipation tendency of the Jamaican electorate to nominate each Government for two terms. The JLP's foreign and economic policy was firmly pro-Western and pro-overseas investment. This remained unaltered when Bustamante effectively retired in 1964, owing to ill health, and was succeeded first by Donald Sangster and then, when Sangster unexpectedly died, by Hugh Shearer. Towards the end of its period in office the JLP Government's record became tarnished by allegations of corruption and by growing social tensions, generated by the inequalities in Jamaican society. The latter were the underlying cause of the Rodney riots in 1968, when several days of violence against people and property followed the expulsion of Walter Rodney, a university advocate of a 'Black Power' philosophy. A demand for social reform prepared the way for the electoral victory of the PNP in 1972, and the emergence of the party's new leader, Michael Manley (the son of Norman Manley), as Prime Minister.

THE FIRST MANLEY GOVERNMENT, 1972–80

Manley came to office with a mandate for change and in 1974 he declared his Government's commitment to 'democratic socialism'. This embraced policies of partial nationalization, increased welfare expenditure, agricultural reform and, in foreign affairs, 'Third Worldism' and close alliance with Cuba. Manley's radical stance caused concern in the USA, and there were allegations that the US Central Intelligence Agency (CIA) was attempting to destabilize Jamaican socialism. More pressing, however, were the economic problems caused by the 1973 rise in world petroleum prices and the ensuing global recession. The economy contracted, foreign exchange became unavailable and foreign investors withdrew, leading to massive unemployment and shortages of basic goods. Even so, the PNP won a clear victory at the 1976 general election. In his second term, however, difficulties intensified for Manley. Under the impact of the world recession, the Jamaican economy deteriorated further and opposition from the USA increased. Eventually, in 1978, the Government resorted to the assistance of the International Monetary Fund (IMF), from which point the country experienced a series of sharp deflationary policies. Under pressure from the left of his own party and from the small but articulate Communist Workers' Party of Jamaica, Manley dramatically rejected IMF policy in late 1979 and tried to find an alternative economic strategy. His Government survived precariously until, following intense party political violence, it was decisively defeated at a general election in October 1980, with its programme of reform utterly destroyed. The JLP received 57% of the votes cast and won 51 of the 60 seats in the House of Representatives. Almost 1,000 people died in politically motivated violence surrounding the elections.

THE JLP GOVERNMENT, 1980–89

The new JLP regime was led by Edward Seaga (who had been educated at the University of Harvard, USA), a former Minister of Finance with a reputation for economic expertise. His approach was to reverse the previous administration's policies: to realign Jamaica with the West (diplomatic relations with Cuba were severed in October 1981) and to establish the closest possible relations with the USA, in order to encourage the inflow of foreign investment, and to seek openly the assistance of the IMF. However, Prime Minister Seaga did not find it easy to revive the economy. He initiated a premature general election, at short notice, for December 1983, after his party's popularity had temporarily increased, owing to Jamaican involvement in the US-led invasion of Grenada. The PNP refused to participate, arguing that Seaga had reneged on a promise not to hold elections until a revised electoral register was ready. The JLP thus won all the seats in the House of Representatives.

Seaga's difficulties concerning economic policy continued in his second term. Austerity measures, including the withdrawal of food price subsidies, produced a deterioration in industrial relations and frequent protest demonstrations, culminating in a week-long general strike in June 1985. Unemployment that year was estimated at between 30% and 35%. Soon afterwards, Seaga commenced negotiations with the IMF over conditions attached to loans, and in May 1986 he reversed his economic policy, introducing an expansionary budget. Large arrears on the repayment of debts to the IMF led to the suspension of Jamaica's agreement in September 1986; the Government resisted IMF demands for a currency devaluation, but accepted other conditions, including a limit on public-sector pay increases, a reduced inflationary target and the progressive reduction of import duties. A new loan agreement was reached in January 1987.

After an overwhelming defeat for the JLP in local elections held in July 1986, in which the PNP won 57% of the votes cast, Seaga's popularity decreased dramatically, both with the electorate and his own party. After threatening to resign, he succeeded in obtaining a pledge of loyalty from the new Cabinet. With an election expected by the end of 1988, he used that year's budget to announce increased expenditure on health, education and social services, the areas most severely affected by austerity measures. In August 1988 Seaga and Manley signed a non-violence pact aimed at reducing political clashes during the election campaign.

THE RETURN OF THE PNP

The general election was not held until February 1989, owing to the upheaval caused by 'Hurricane Gilbert', which killed 45 people, destroyed some 100,000 homes and caused severe agricultural and other economic damage in September 1988. The results of the election returned the PNP to power, with 56% of the votes cast and 45 out of 60 seats in the House of Representatives. Manley was reappointed Prime Minister.

Manley had by now discarded much of the radicalism of the 1970s, and the new Government continued with IMF-inspired economic policies, obtaining new Fund programmes in July 1989 and January 1990, after agreeing to a devaluation of the Jamaican dollar. Despite international approval for the implementation of policies leading to economic growth, Manley's Government continued to experience problems with foreign-exchange policy and with a large foreign debt dating from the Seaga Government's borrowing in the 1980s. Under the aegis of the IMF, the Government introduced widespread financial deregulation between 1990 and 1992, including the 'floating' of the Jamaican dollar (that is, making it freely convertible), and in September 1991 all foreign-exchange controls were removed, in the most radical change yet. By early 1992, the Jamaican dollar was valued at some J $22 to US $1, compared with its fixed rate in January 1990 of J $7 to US $1. Under the impact of rapid price increases, the PNP lost popular support during 1991.

POLITICS IN THE 1990s

On 15 March 1992 Prime Minister Manley announced his retirement, on health grounds. The PNP swiftly held a party leadership election, which was won by Percival J. Patterson, the former Deputy Prime Minister. Continued stringency of financial policy ensured that the exchange rate stabilized during 1992, to reach an average rate for that year of J $22.96 to US $1. Moreover, the inflation rate declined considerably. An extended Fund facility was approved by the IMF in October 1992, providing US $153m. until December 1995, when IMF aid increased.

Capitalizing on a renewal of internal conflict in the JLP, Patterson opted for a general election to be held almost one year early in March 1993. The PNP received a record 60% of the votes cast, albeit on a low turn-out, and increased its parliamentary representation to 52 seats. Irregularities and violence marred the elections and the JLP announced that it would boycott any subsequent by-elections pending the introduction of electoral reforms. The controversy over electoral reform continued until July 1996, when a contract was signed with a US company to provide a computerized electoral register.

During 1995 differences within the JLP increased, culminating in the formation, in October, of a new party, the National Democratic Movement (NDM), which was headed by the former JLP Chairman and finance spokesman, Bruce Golding. Golding was joined by several prominent JLP figures, including one other member of parliament. A number of other JLP dissidents were expelled from the party at this time. The split led, in the first half of 1996, to a number of violent incidents between JLP and NDM supporters, notably in St Catherine, where Golding was one of the parish's nine members of parliament.

Throughout the PNP's second term, economic regulation remained its priority. High interest rates were adopted in 1994, in order to stabilize the exchange rate, increase foreign-exchange reserves and reduce inflation. By the end of 1997 these objectives had been achieved, with the exchange rate remaining at an average level of about J $36 to US $1, and the annual rate of inflation averaging 9.7% in 1997, compared with 26.4% in 1996 and 35.1% in 1994. However, the deflationary policy was maintained at the cost of marginal or negative gross-domestic-product performance, with 1996 showing a contraction of 1.8% and 1997 a further contraction of 2.1%; agriculture and manufacturing were severely affected, the former partly because of drought in 1997. The banking and insurance sector experienced prolonged upheaval from 1995, during which period the Government was obliged to spend some J $50,000m. to rescue and restructure a number of financial institutions that had become insolvent.

Despite the party's continued problems, the PNP was returned to power in the general election held on 18 December 1997, winning 56% of the votes cast, compared with the 39% of votes won by the JLP and the 5% of votes won by the NDM. It was the first election in Jamaican history to give power to a party for a third consecutive term. The PNP lost only two seats to the JLP, retaining 50 seats compared with the JLP's 10; the NDM won no seats. In spite of some concerns as to whether the new electoral register would be completed in time, the election was described by observers as free, fair and calm by the standards of previous polls. However, two people were killed on the day of the election, and a number of people were injured both on polling day itself and in the days prior to it. Patterson was duly sworn in as Prime Minister again.

The PNP continued its electoral success in local elections, held on 10 September 1998, gaining control of all 13 local councils and winning 157 seats, compared with the JLP's 90. Although the elections were peaceful, voter turn-out was less than 25%. The NDM demanded the introduction of further electoral reforms to prevent procedural abuses and thus did not contest the elections. Seaga resigned from the JLP leadership for three months in protest at the party's decision to contest the elections.

Despite the PNP's political dominance, violence broke out at the end of September 1998, when a well-known PNP activist was arrested in the capital, Kingston, on charges of attempted murder. Several days of rioting ensued, during which a soldier and two civilians were killed. There was more unrest in April 1999 following the announcement of details of that year's budget, which included an increase of some 30% in the price of fuel. Eight people were killed in violence between the police and demonstrators. The Government eventually agreed to rescind the proposed increases.

RECENT DEVELOPMENTS

On winning a third term in office at the end of 1997, Prime Minister Patterson announced plans to make Jamaica a republic within five years, replacing the British monarch as head of state with a ceremonial President. In April 2001 he also announced that the traditional swearing of allegiance by ministers to the Crown would be replaced, in 2002, by an oath of allegiance to Jamaica and its Constitution. A referendum on proposed constitutional reform was expected to be held in 2001, when the installation of a new electronic voting system was due to be completed. On 14 February 2001, following legislative approval in November 2000, Prime Minister Patterson and 10 other Caribbean leaders signed an agreement to establish a Caribbean Court of Justice, based in Trinidad and Tobago. The Court would replace the British Privy Council as the final court of appeal, and would allow the execution of convicted criminals. (The Privy Council had commuted the death sentences of six Jamaican prisoners in September 2000.) The JLP opposed the move, and demanded that a referendum be held on the issue.

Concern was expressed regarding Jamaica's high incidence of crime, epitomized by an increasing murder rate, which reached over 900 in 1997. In July 1999 the Government announced the stationing of army personnel in 15 areas of greater Kingston in an attempt to combat crime. Much of the country's crime was a result of drugs-trafficking and in 1998 there were more than 7,000 drugs-related arrests. In October 1999 the British Government announced that it would contribute £2.9m. in grant assistance towards a programme to reform and modernize the Jamaican Constabulary Force and in September 2000 the Prime Minister announced the formation of a specialized police unit to combat organized crime. In October an investigation was initiated in response to widespread allegations of corruption in the police force, which included involvement in drugs-trafficking and the illicit recording of ministerial telephone conversations. On 10 January 2001, following assurances that the police force would receive special training in the non-lethal apprehension of suspects, the British Government released a shipment of arms and ammunition, intended for the force, which had been held for over a year. However, on 14 March seven people were shot dead by the police in Kingston. Subsequently, various human-rights groups, including Amnesty International, criticized the procedures of the Jamaican police force, which was reported to have shot dead 151 suspects in 1999 and 140 in 2000. The rate of violent crime, however, remained high, with a 3% rise in reported murders in 2000 over the previous year's figure of 849. In early 2001 there were numerous outbreaks of politically-motivated violence in Denham Town and Hannah Town, and on 11 July the Jamaican Defence Force was called in to restore order, following politically-motivated disturbances of gang violence in west Kingston. Some 25 people (21 civilians, three police officers and one soldier) were killed in the five days of civil unrest. A Commission, headed by a judge of the Canadian Supreme Court, was subsequently established to enquire into the causes and consequences of the violence.

In early 2001 opinion polls revealed that the PNP had lost a substantial degree of popularity to the JLP, for the first time since the 1980s. Overall, 61% of those questioned were uncommitted to any party, suggesting a high level of disenchantment with the political process as a whole. The JLP's resurgent fortunes were confirmed in March 2001 in a by-election for the North-East St Ann parliamentary constituency, where the JLP overturned a PNP majority. In the same by-election, the disappointing results for the NDM led to the resignation of Bruce Golding, who was replaced as party leader by Hyacinth Bennett. The 2001/02 budget contained unpopular measures, incorporated by a Government struggling with large debt obligations and a continuing stagnation in the economy. With a general election constitutionally due by the end of 2002, by mid-2001 it remained unclear whether the PNP would seek an early election and an unprecedented fourth consecutive term in office or whether it would choose to postpone a decision on the election until public reaction to the undoubtedly unpopular measures contained in its 2001/02 budget had abated.

Economy

ROD PRINCE

Based on an earlier essay by Dr A. J. PAYNE and revised for this edition by JAMES FERGUSON

Jamaica has one of the larger and more diversified economies of the Commonwealth Caribbean. The days of a sugar monoculture and the resulting ascendancy of foreign plantation owners are long past. The prevailing pattern just before independence in 1962 was of an economy consisting mainly of traders importing finished goods in exchange for the export of primary products. These products, by that stage, extended beyond sugar, to include bananas, coffee, citrus fruits and, in particular, bauxite, production of which began in 1952. Even this pattern was subsequently substantially reformed. As in other parts of the region during the 1950s and 1960s, successive Governments pursued policies of industrialization, aimed at encouraging the establishment of both import-substitution and export-orientated manufacturing enterprises. In addition, tourism was assiduously promoted and became a major source of foreign exchange.

Important as they were, these changes did not, however, remove the basic external orientation of the economy. The result was that Jamaica prospered in times of international economic expansion and suffered in periods of recession. In the 1960s, stimulated primarily by inflows of foreign investment and expanding bauxite output, Jamaica's gross domestic product (GDP) grew, in real terms, by an average of nearly 6% per year. Between 1974 and 1980 the economy was affected by the rise in the price of petroleum and by other deflationary factors; there was a cumulative fall of 16% in real GDP. Generally there was economic growth during the 1980s, apart from in 1984 and 1985, and in 1988 owing to the impact of 'Hurricane Gilbert' (after a peak of growth in real GDP of 6.2% in the previous year). Overall, the average annual rate of growth in real GDP in 1980–90 was 1.6%, but, by the end of that period, the 1974 level of GDP had not been recovered. In the 1990s the impact of a strict economic adjustment programme and other factors, including low prices for bauxite and alumina exports and a high rate of inflation, held the real GDP growth rate to a 1990–99 average of 0.1%. The rate fell by 0.5% in 1995, 1.8% in 1996, in 1997 there was a decline of 2.1% and in 1998 a further contraction of 0.4% took place. In 1999 GDP contracted by 0.2%. In 2000 the economy expanded slightly, by 0.6%. This placed GDP at its 1990 level, but taking population growth into account, signified a steep fall in per head GDP in the 1990s and into 2000.

Population growth averaged 0.8% per year between 1982 and 1991, both of which were census years. The population stood at 2,314,479 at the 1991 census. During 1990–98 the population increased at an average annual rate of 1.0%. A mid-2000 estimate put the population at 2,597,600, with population growth that year of 0.6%. Jamaica was highly urbanized, with 56% of the population estimated to live in urban areas in 1999. In 1996 the population of Kingston and the surrounding urban parish of St Andrew was estimated at 691,600 (27.4% of the total population), and the adjoining parish of St Catherine, which included extensive suburban areas, had an estimated 402,500 inhabitants (15.9% of the total population). Spanish Town in St Catherine and Montego Bay on the north-west coast, were the two main towns outside Kingston. In 1999 net emigration from the country was estimated at 14,118, declining from 24,600 in 1990.

In the 1980s the rate of unemployment was often very high, even during periods of substantial growth. Until 1988, when the number of unemployed fell to 18.9% of the labour force, levels of between 20% and 30% were consistently recorded. By 2000 the unemployment rate was estimated at 16% of the workforce, or 190,000 people. The members of the labour force to suffer most from unemployment were women and those aged under 25 years. Despite high unemployment and declining per head GDP, a report by the International Monetary Fund (IMF) in 1999 suggested that poverty fell during the 1990s, with the percentage of Jamaicans defined as living in poverty decreasing from 44.6% in 1991 to 17% in 1999.

AGRICULTURE

Agriculture, including forestry and fishing, accounted for an estimated 6.5% of GDP in 2000, although the sector suffered severe problems as a result of prolonged drought in 1997–98 and again in 2000. In 2000 the sector provided work for an estimated 21.2% of the employed labour force. From the 1980s government policy put considerable emphasis on overcoming structural problems in agriculture and increasing production, both for export and domestic consumption. In February 2001 the Inter-American Development Bank (IDB, based in New York, USA) agreed a US $22m. loan to modernize the Ministry of Agriculture.

The sugar industry, historically the dominant sector of the Jamaican economy, was in serious decline by the 1980s, and in 1985 the state sugar corporation was contracted to the British company, Booker Tate, to manage. At the end of 1993 the Government sold four out of five state-owned sugar mills; three mills were sold to a multinational consortium, which included Booker Tate, and the other was sold to a wholly Jamaican group. In September 1998, however, the Government was obliged to repurchase the privatized mills for a nominal sum of J $1 in order to rescue the Sugar Company of Jamaica from bankruptcy and closure. It also pledged to invest US $100m. in the sugar industry's future development. In 2001 it was estimated that the Government had spent J $3,000m. annually since 1998 in subsidizing the sugar industry. In January 2001 a task force was established to review the industry and identify the necessary reforms; however, it was thought unlikely that the Government would seek widespread redundancies among the 40,000-strong work-force. After declining to 189,000 metric tons in 1987, sugar production averaged some 224,000 tons in the first years of the 1990s, but fell to 211,500 tons in 1995, a drought year. Production recovered in 1996 and 1997, but declined slightly in 1998 to 182,761 tons, owing to a number of adverse factors, in particular drought. Production recovered to 201,319 tons in 1999. Sugar export earnings in the year ending March 1997 were US $122m. This figure decreased to US $81m. in 1998, and recovered only slightly in 1999, to US $98m., with the European Union (EU) and the USA the principal customers under preferential quota arrangements. The sugar industry remained in crisis despite trade preferences, and in 2001 it was estimated that the cost of sugar production was 30% above the EU preferential price. These prices were, moreover, to be gradually phased out by the EU over the following decade.

Banana production and exports, which had suffered severely from Hurricane Gilbert in 1988 (when production was 28,057 metric tons) recovered in the 1990s, reaching an export volume of 88,917 tons in 1996, before declining slightly to 79,709 tons in 1997. In the first three months of 1999 banana production was 16,558 tons, a 3% increase on the same period in the previous year. Overall production stood at an estimated 130,000 tons in 1998 and remained at this level in 1999 and 2000. The value of banana exports in the year ending March 1998 was US $44m., but a fall in exports of 25% (to US $33m.) was registered in 1998/99 in the wake of drought and storms. A further fall was recorded in 1999/2000 with earnings of US $30m. from exports of 52,000 tons. In 1994 Jamaica Producers and the Anglo-Irish company, Fyffes, bought shareholdings of 55% and 40%, respectively, in two government-owned banana farms, with the aim of increasing production and exports. Uncertainty over the future of the industry, caused by the dispute between the EU and the World Trade Organization over compliance of the banana-import regime with international trade regulations, further reduced confidence in the industry, with the prospect of reduced preferences deterring some farmers from continued investment. On 11 April 2001 the EU and the USA signed an accord ending the EU preferential market. From 1 July a transitional system, issuing licences according to historical trade patterns, was to be implemented, with the definitive tariff-only system entering into force on 1 January 2006.

Coffee production, similarly reduced to some 15,000 bags (60 kg each) in 1988/89 because of Hurricane Gilbert, recovered to record exports of 2,985 metric tons in 1995/96. By the late 1990s the country was exporting some 20,000 bags of coffee per year. In the year ending March 1999 coffee exports totalled US $17m. Non-traditional agricultural production for export showed strong growth in the early 1990s, but was also adversely affected by the drought of 1997. In 1998 the citrus industry, threatened by *tristeza* disease, was allocated US $6.8m. in government assistance, to finance the replanting of 3,000 ha of orchards over a period of five years.

A programme of land reform and investment, announced in 1990 with the aim of increasing food production for the domestic market as well as for export, had some success. The production of food items reached 583,717 metric tons in 1993, compared with 473,000 tons in 1986. In 1997, however, drought caused a slight decline in food production to 550,928 tons. In 1998 food production decreased further, to be followed by a 1.4% increase in 1999, before drought reduced production once more in 2000.

In 1999 6% of Jamaica's land area, or 77,000 ha, was estimated to consist of undisturbed natural forest. Forest and woodland areas came under continuing pressure from urbanization.

MINING AND POWER

The bauxite and alumina industry was the dominant element in the mining sector, accounting for more than 90% of the total value of production in the late 1990s. In 2000 mining and quarrying contributed an estimated 4.3% of GDP and in 1998/99 bauxite and alumina exports were valued at US $670m., some 43.2% of total export earnings. In 1999 Jamaica was the fourth largest world producer of bauxite.

In the early 1980s, owing to depressed international conditions, the industry experienced great difficulties. Bauxite production fell from 12.0m. metric tons in 1980 to only 6.0m. tons in 1985. Production then underwent a gradual recovery, to reach 11.8m. tons in 1994. Industrial disputes and operational problems caused production to decline to 10.8m. tons in 1995, before recovering to 11.7m. tons in 1996, 12.0m. tons in 1997 and 12.7m. tons in 1998. Bauxite production was badly affected in 1999 and the first quarter of 2000, principally owing to a fire at the Kaiser Aluminium refinery in Texas (USA); production fell to 11.7m. tons in 1999. In early 2000 production had fallen by 47.3% compared with the same period in 1999, but the Government arranged a special sale of bauxite to a company in Ukraine. The re-opening of the Kaiser refinery in mid-2001 was expected to lead to a resumption of normal production. Alumina production likewise failed to expand in the 1980s, but increased to an annual average of some 3.0m. tons during the 1990s. Production increased to 3.4m. tons in 1996 and remained at this level in 1997 and 1998. Alumina production grew by 2% in 1999 to reach 3.6m. tons. Bauxite mining and alumina refining were carried out by three major companies: Alcan of Canada; Jamalco, a joint venture between Alcoa of the USA and the Jamaican Government; and Alumina Partners of Jamaica (Alpart), which was jointly owned by Kaiser (of the USA) and Norsk Hydro (of Norway).

Jamaica was a petroleum-importing country, consuming 20.6m. barrels of petroleum products in 1994, of which 8.1m. barrels were for the bauxite industry. In 2000 fuel imports, including petroleum, cost US $585m., representing 18.3% of all imports. Oil-fired electricity plants produced 94% of the power generated in 1999, which amounted to 3,100m. kWh. The remainder was hydroelectric power. Petroleum exploration in Jamaica did not produce any exploitable finds and official policy was directed towards energy conservation and the development of alternative energy sources. In 2001 the state-owned Petrojam oil refinery returned to full production, following closure owing to a fire in mid-2000. In March 2001 the Government sold 80% of the country's electricity company, Jamaica Public Service Co, to the US-based Mirant Corporation.

MANUFACTURING

Jamaica had a relatively well-developed light manufacturing sector. In 2000 manufacturing accounted for an estimated 13.4% of GDP and employed 72,500 people, or 7.8% of the employed labour force, compared to 12.9% in 1989. The Jamaica Labour Party (JLP) Government (1980–89) encouraged the development of manufacturing, particularly for export, within the context of its structural-adjustment programme. The deregulation policy involved the abolition of import restrictions and the allocation of more foreign exchange to the sector. Manufacturing free-trade zones were established in Kingston, Spanish Town and Montego Bay, and a promotional body (later reorganized as Jamaica Promotions Ltd—JAMPRO) was created to encourage export manufacturing. The same policies were pursued by the People's National Party (PNP) Government after 1989.

Traditional manufactured products included food, drinks and tobacco products, construction materials, metals, chemicals and fertilizers. However, after 1986 there was a major expansion of the textile and garments sector, principally in the free-trade zones. Investment in the free-trade zones was principally from the USA, the Republic of China (Taiwan) and Hong Kong. The textile and garment industry, which benefited from preferential entry arrangements with the USA, under the Caribbean Basin Initiative and the Section 807 textile and garment facility, employed about 32,000 people in 1994. However, the industry was subsequently affected severely by the high cost of borrowing and by competition from Mexican exports to the USA, after the creation of the North American Free Trade Agreement (NAFTA—which came into effect in 1994). Employment fell to

21,000 by mid-1996, in which year total export earnings from manufactures were US $488m. In 1997 the Government allocated J $360m. in assistance to garment manufacturers, but export earnings still fell to US $428m. In 1999, after a series of closures and redundancies in the export garment sector, earnings stood at US $162m. By early 2001 employment in this sector had fallen below 10,000, although there were hopes that US legislation, passed in May 2000, that granted Caribbean garment producers tariff parity with NAFTA producers, would reinvigorate the sector. Other manufactured products included electronic components, chemicals and processed foods.

TRANSPORT AND COMMUNICATIONS

By regional standards, Jamaica's transport infrastructure was relatively well-developed. There were two international airports, at Kingston and Montego Bay, which were serviced by several international airlines, including the national flag carrier, Air Jamaica Ltd. The main port was at Kingston, a major transhipment centre for the region. The 339-km railway network was principally used for the transport of bauxite; passenger services were suspended in 1992. In June 1999 it was announced that an Indian state-owned company was to help restore Jamaica's railways for the transport of both freight and passengers. The joint venture would cost US $27m. and aimed to connect Kingston, Spanish Town and Montego Bay. In 1998 there were an estimated 19,000 km (11,801 miles) of roads, of which 70.7% were main roads. A five-year programme to improve and maintain the condition of all arterial and secondary roads and 30% of minor roads began in 1999, but problems over private-sector financing of toll roads created delays. In 1999 there were some 223,000 registered motor vehicles, a significant increase compared to previous years, owing to the importation of used cars from Japan. From the mid-1980s the telecommunications system underwent considerable modernization and improvement. At the end of 1999 there were almost 700,000 telephone lines in use, compared to 251,000 in 1994. Parliament approved the liberalization of the telecommunications sector in September 1999, and the issuing of cellular licences began soon afterwards. Cellular telecommunications services were launched by two companies in 2001, Centennial Digital Jamaica Ltd and an Irish consortium, Mossel (Jamaica) Ltd, while the British company Cable & Wireless, traditionally the dominant supplier, remained in competition. Montego Bay had a 'teleport', a centre for data processing, mainly for North American companies.

TOURISM

The tourist industry expanded to become one of the major sectors of the economy, and the country's largest earner of foreign exchange. It was an important employer, accounting for a substantial proportion of those employed in the services sector; direct employment in the industry was estimated at 85,000 in 2000, with twice that number engaged in tourist-related industry.

The number of 'stop-over' tourist arrivals increased by an annual average of 11.3% in the 1980s, and totalled 840,777 in 1990. A slower rate of growth was maintained in the 1990s, except for a slight decline in 1994. Arrivals reached 1.2m. in 1999. Cruise-ship passenger arrivals showed a greater advance, with figures increasing from 133,400 in 1980 to 649,517 in 1992. After declining in 1993 and in 1994, total cruise-ship arrivals recovered in the rest of the decade, to reach 764,341 in 1999. In the first 10 months of 2000 stop-over arrivals increased by 5.9% over the preceding period, while cruise-ship arrivals grew by 20.4%. Total tourist expenditure in 1999 reached US $1,233m. The number of hotel rooms available for tourist use in 1995 was 29,376. The industry, however, had to counter problems ranging from the US economic recession to the harassment of visitors by 'hustlers' and petty drugs dealers. Episodes of political unrest or street violence, although normally confined to Kingston and not affecting tourist areas, at times caused a fall in the number of tourists. However, the Jamaica Tourist Board was energetic in its marketing campaigns, achieving particular success in increasing the number of visitors during the traditionally quieter summer season and in attracting more tourists from Europe. However, in 2001 tourist harassment led to the withdrawal of a number of cruise-ships. In 1999 visitors from the USA accounted for 69.7% of stop-over arrivals (including non-resident Jamaicans), while those from the United Kingdom accounted for 10% and those from Canada, 8%. In May 2001 the Minister of Tourism and Sport announced a $2,000m., 10-year programme to expand and improve the tourism sector.

INVESTMENT AND FINANCE

Between 1972 and 1980, under the leadership of Michael Manley, there were substantial increases in state spending on welfare, infrastructure and production. In 1980 the PNP Government rejected the terms of an IMF support programme, but the JLP Government reopened negotiations and secured a three-year agreement on assistance totalling US $650m. This was followed by a series of stand-by arrangements, starting in June 1984 and continuing under the PNP Government after 1989. On the expiry of the sixth stand-by agreement in June 1992, a three-year extended fund facility was negotiated, to provide US $153m. from October 1992 to December 1995.

JLP and PNP Governments alike followed adjustment programmes involving: reductions in government expenditure; currency devaluation; deregulation of foreign exchange and trade controls; and privatization of some state enterprises. However, following a period of popular unrest in 1985, the Government of Edward Seaga reverted, in its 1986/87 budget, to expansionary policies. After the PNP election victory in 1989, the Government of Michael Manley increased interest rates and imposed credit restrictions, in a return to stricter fiscal discipline. Nevertheless, in late 1989 the Jamaican dollar came under intense pressure, which led to a devaluation of the official rate of J $5.50 to the US dollar, in effect since 1985, to J $6.50. There was a further devaluation, to J $7.00, in January 1990, as part of the fifth IMF stand-by agreement. Targets under the agreement included a reduction of the public-sector budgetary deficit to the equivalent of 4.4% of GDP and a 12.5% limit on pay increases. Import duties, food prices and national insurance contributions were increased, and a general consumption tax (GCT—sales tax) of 10% was introduced from October 1991.

In September 1990 the Jamaican dollar was 'floated', that is, became freely convertible, as part of a series of measures deregulating the economy. Other measures included the removal of price controls and the setting of a new upper limit for the public-sector deficit of 3.3% of GDP. Commercial banks were allowed to trade in foreign exchange. After several modifications to the foreign-exchange purchase system, complete abolition of controls was announced on 21 September 1991, by which date the exchange rate, per US dollar, had reached some J $14. The rate continued to deteriorate, reaching J $29 in April 1992, before recovering to about J $22 in May, following an initiative by a number of private businesses to repatriate large sums of foreign exchange held overseas.

The 1992/93 budget increased indirect taxes, to offset a reduction in income tax, and a target of a fiscal surplus equivalent to 0.7% of GDP was announced. The 1993/94 budget included tax increases aimed at largely meeting the cost of public-sector pay rises. The 1994/95 budget imposed further indirect tax increases, and the 1995/96 budget increased GCT to 15%. In November 1994 a profit levy was imposed on banks and other financial institutions, to pay for wage rises to government employees. A fiscal surplus on recurrent expenditure was achieved in the 1995/96 financial year. The policy of high interest rates, which had been maintained from the early 1990s until being relaxed at the end of 1994, was renewed in late 1995, when a fall in the value of the Jamaican dollar required central bank intervention to stabilize the position. Steady depreciation of the exchange rate had been arrested between January 1994 and July 1995, during which time the rate held at J $33 to the US dollar, but the new fall took it to J $41 in November 1995. The rate remained at about J $40 until June 1996, when an increased supply of 'hard' (convertible) currency brought a revaluation to J $36, the first for several years. With slight fluctuations, the rate remained at about J $36 throughout the following year and into the first quarter of 1998, falling to J $37 by the end of the year. A further depreciation occurred in 1999 and by March 2001 the rate stood at J $45.608.

The deflationary policy was accompanied by instability in the financial sector, entailing government intervention in 1997 through the creation of a Financial Sector Adjustment Co

(FINSAC), which, by July 1998, had assumed a controlling stake in Jamaica's seven largest commercial banks. The high cost of FINSAC's operations and of compensation for depositors in failed companies, together with public-sector pay increases, contributed to a renewed fiscal deficit of J $16,026m. in 1996/97. A further large deficit of J $20,687 occurred in 1997/98, with an estimated deficit of J $19,171m. recorded in 1998/99. The 1999/2000 fiscal deficit was estimated to be much higher, at J $50,100m., despite cuts in capital expenditure. Interest payments alone increased from J $27,280m. in 1996/97 to J $34,889m. in 1998/99, rising steeply to J $41,900m. in 1999/2000. By late 2000 FINSAC was believed to have left the Government with debts of J $30,000m., and efforts were made to divest the company of several commercial banks and insurance companies to private buyers. However, the Government succeeded in a prime objective: the reduction of the inflation rate, which averaged 6.0% in 1999, compared to 26.4% in 1996. Inflation was 8.2% in 2000, an increase largely owing to rising oil prices. In the 2000 budget, published in April, the finance minister announced that the Government would be entering into a Staff Monitored Programme (SMP) with the IMF. While not involving disbursements from the IMF, nor politically sensitive conditionality, the SMP included policy advice and was believed to facilitate government access to IDB and World Bank (International Bank for Reconstruction and Development—IBRD) loans worth US $300m., as well as enabling the Government to raise foreign investment through a bond issue.

Jamaica's financial difficulties made external support vital. The World Bank, the IDB, the Barbados-based Caribbean Development Bank, the EU and other bodies provided substantial assistance. Jamaica's external debt, which had reached US $4,671m. by 1990, fell to US $4,111m. by the end of 1993, as the result of international debt-reduction initiatives. At the end of 1999 total external debt stood at US $4,069m. Of greater concern, however, was a mounting internal debt, caused mainly by the Government's FINSAC intervention.

FOREIGN TRADE AND BALANCE OF PAYMENTS

Jamaica's foreign trade balance was in deficit for at least 20 years, but between 1992 and 1996 the deficit was offset by revenue from tourism, remittances from overseas and capital inflows attracted by the country's high interest rates, resulting in an overall surplus on the balance of payments. Between 1992 and 1997 the trade deficit increased from US $721m. to US $1,132m., with exports of goods increasing by more than 50%, and imports of goods increasing by almost 83%. In 1999 the merchandise trade deficit stood at US $1,138m. Weaker export prices as well as the problems faced by agriculture and manufacturing, notably the garment sector, contributed to the poor export performance, while rising oil prices and a deprecia-

tion of the Jamaican dollar lay behind a drop in imports. Rising oil prices in 1999 and 2000 were reflected in a 10.4% increase in the value of imports in the first eight months of 2000, while the cost of oil imports in 1999 was US $408m., a 33% increase on the previous year.

The current account of the balance of payments showed a surplus of US $28.5m. in 1992 and US $6.9m. in 1994, but was otherwise in deficit. The deficit increased from US $111.6m. in 1996 to US $310.6m. in 1997, before falling to US $302.4m. in 1998. The deficit decreased further in 1999, to US $255.7m. Positive capital movements led to a steady increase in total foreign reserves (excluding gold) from US $324.1m. at the end of 1992 to US $880m. in 1996, when net international reserves stood at US $693m. The payments deficit of 1997, however, reduced foreign reserves to US $682m. in that year. In 1998 reserves recovered to US $710m., but fell to US $555m. by the end of 1999, increasing once more to US $1,053.7m. in 2000. Remittances from Jamaicans living overseas and other transfers amounted to US $648m. in 1999.

CONCLUSION

While Jamaica succeeded in maintaining positive growth rates from 1986 to 1995, it remained vulnerable to external factors. The Jamaican Government's achievement of a reduced inflation rate and a stable exchange rate in 1997 and 1998 came at the cost of stagnation in the productive sectors of the economy, with slight GDP expansion becoming negative growth from 1996–99 and fiscal deficits equal to almost 15% of GDP in certain years. The inevitable difficulties in financing this deficit and the even larger deficit expected in 2001/02 appeared likely to necessitate further currency devaluation and higher inflation in the longer term. The Government anticipated a marked inflow of foreign capital in the wake of the IMF agreement, generating a balance-of-payments surplus that would provide an opportunity to reduce interest rates and encourage GDP growth. Yet the Government also remained vulnerable to a large domestic debt, in part owing to the FINSAC intervention. Strengthening of export manufacturing and agriculture and the development of new enterprises in the services sector were needed to supplement reliance on the main foreign-exchange earners, bauxite/alumina and tourism. The country had also to contend with the increased international challenges presented by the creation of a Free Trade Area of the Americas by 2005, together with a revised framework for trade and co-operation with the EU, following the expiry of the Lomé Convention in February 2000 and its replacement by the Cotonou Agreement in June. Jamaica's immediate economic outlook depended largely on the projected slowdown in the US economy, which would entail a negative impact on alumina and bauxite demand and on tourist arrivals from the USA.

Statistical Survey

Sources (unless otherwise stated): Statistical Institute of Jamaica, 9 Swallowfield Rd, Kingston 5, Jamaica; tel. 926-2175; fax 926-4859; e-mail statinja@infochan.com; internet www.statinja.com; Jamaica Information Service, 58A Half Way Tree Rd, POB 2222, Kingston 10, Jamaica; tel. 926-3740; fax 926-6715; e-mail jis@jis.gov.jm; internet www.jis.gov.jm.

Area and Population

AREA, POPULATION AND DENSITY

Area (sq km)	10,991*
Population (census results)	
8 June 1982	2,205,507
7 April 1991	
Males	1,134,386
Females	1,180,093
Total	2,314,479
Population (official estimates at mid-year)	
1998	2,563,700
1999	2,581,700
2000	2,597,600
Density (per sq km) at mid-2000	236.3

* 4,243.6 sq miles.

PARISHES

	Area (sq miles)	Population (estimates, 1994)	Parish capitals (with population at 1991 census)
Kingston . .	8.406 ⎫	697,000	Kingston M.A. (587,800)
St Andrew . .	166.308 ⎭		
St Thomas . .	286.800	88,900	Morant Bay (9,600)
Portland . .	314.347	78,500	Port Antonio (13,200)
St Mary . .	235.745	113,700	Port Maria (7,700)
St Ann . .	468.213	154,500	St Ann's Bay (10,500)
Trelawny . .	337.651	74,100	Falmouth (8,000)
St James . .	229.728	166,000	Montego Bay (83,400)
Hanover . .	173.855	66,600	Lucea (5,400)
Westmoreland .	311.604	130,500	Savanna La Mar (16,600)
St Elizabeth .	468.085	146,600	Black River (3,600)
Manchester .	320.482	173,100	Mandeville (39,400)
Clarendon .	461.864	222,500	May Pen (46,800)
St Catherine .	460.396	370,600	Spanish Town (92,400)
Total . . .	**4,243.484**	**2,482,600**	—

BIRTHS, MARRIAGES AND DEATHS*

	Registered live births Number	Rate (per 1,000)	Registered marriages Number	Rate (per 1,000)	Registered deaths Number	Rate (per 1,000)
1990 . .	59,606	24.7	13,037	5.4	12,174	5.0
1991 . .	59,879	25.3	13,254	5.6	13,319	5.6
1992 . .	56,276	23.5	13,042	5.6	13,225	5.5
1993 . .	58,627	24.0	14,352	5.9	13,927	5.7
1994 . .	57,404	23.2	15,171	6.1	13,503	5.5
1995 . .	57,607	23.0	16,515	6.6	12,776	5.1
1996 . .	57,370	22.8	18,708	7.4	14,854	5.9
1997 . .	59,249	23.2	n.a.	n.a.	15,967	6.3

* Data are tabulated by year of registration rather than by year of occurrence.

Source: partly UN, *Demographic Yearbook*.

Expectation of life (estimates, years at birth, 1998): 75.0 (males 73.0; females 77.0) (Source: UN Development Programme, *Human Development Report*).

ECONOMICALLY ACTIVE POPULATION*
('000 persons aged 14 years and over)

	1998	1999	2000*
Agriculture, forestry and fishing .	203.8	200.0	197.6
Mining and quarrying . . .	5.6	5.5	4.7
Manufacturing	84.1	79.0	72.5
Electricity, gas and water . .	6.5	6.5	6.9
Construction	79.7	77.9	78.8
Trade, restaurants and hotels .	205.4	205.4	206.5
Transport, storage and communications	54.9	61.8	59.1
Financing, insurance, real estate and business services . . .	56.8	52.5	50.8
Community, social and personal services	255.5	259.6	249.3
Activities not adequately defined .	1.3	4.3	7.3
Total employed	**953.6**	**943.9**	**933.5**

* Preliminary figures.

Unemployed ('000 persons aged 10 years and over): 183.0 in 1996; 186.9 in 1997; 175.0 in 1998.

Source: IMF, *Jamaica: Statistical Appendix* (June 2001).

Agriculture

PRINCIPAL CROPS ('000 metric tons)

	1998	1999	2000
Sweet potatoes	27.1	25.0	25.0*
Cassava	15.0	17.4	17.4*
Yams	198.4	195.7	195.7*
Other roots and tubers* . . .	45.0	45.0	45.0
Coconuts*	115.0	115.0	115.0
Pumpkins, squash and gourds* .	42.0	42.0	42.0
Sugar cane*	2,284.0	2,400.0	2,600.0
Oranges*	72.0	72.0	72.0
Lemons and limes* . . .	24.0	24.0	24.0
Grapefruit and pomelo* . . .	42.0	42.0	42.0
Bananas*	130.0	130.0	130.0
Plantains*	33.5	33.5	33.5
Coffee (green)*	1.7	2.4	2.7
Cocoa beans	1.7	1.0	1.0*
Tobacco (leaves)	1.8†	1.8†	1.8*

* FAO estimate(s).   † Unofficial figure.

Source: FAO.

LIVESTOCK (FAO estimates, '000 head, year ending September)

	1998	1999	2000
Horses	4.0	4.0	4.0
Mules	10.0	10.0	10.0
Asses	23.0	23.0	23.0
Cattle	400.0	400.0	400.0
Pigs	180.0	180.0	180.0
Sheep	1.5	1.4	1.4
Goats	440.0	440.0	440.0

Poultry (FAO estimates, million): 9.5 in 1998; 11.0 in 1999; 11.0 in 2000.

Source: FAO.

LIVESTOCK PRODUCTS ('000 metric tons)

	1998	1999	2000
Beef and veal	14.3	14.7	14.6*
Goat meat*	1.7	1.7	1.7
Pig meat	6.8	6.9	6.9*
Poultry meat	63.2	72.9	73.0*
Cows' milk*	53.0	53.0	53.0
Hen eggs*	28.0	28.0	28.0

* FAO estimate(s).

Source: FAO.

Forestry

ROUNDWOOD REMOVALS ('000 cubic metres, excl. bark)

	1997	1998	1999
Sawlogs, veneer logs and logs for sleepers	42	42	42
Other industrial wood . . .	1	1	1
Fuel wood	300	300	300
Total	343	343	343

Source: FAO, *Yearbook of Forest Products*.

SAWNWOOD PRODUCTION ('000 cubic metres, incl. railway sleepers)

	1997	1998	1999
Total	12	12	12

Source: FAO, *Yearbook of Forest Products*.

Fishing

('000 metric tons, live weight)

	1996	1997	1998
Capture	12.8	8.4	6.7
Nile tilapia	0.7*	0.6	0.6
Marine fishes . . .	8.8*	5.6	4.2
Stromboid conchs . . .	2.9	1.8	1.7
Aquaculture*	3.1	3.1	3.4
Nile tilapia*	2.8	2.8	3.0
Total catch	15.9	11.5	10.1

* FAO estimate.

Source: FAO, *Yearbook of Fishery Statistics*.

Mining

('000 metric tons)

	1996	1997	1998
Bauxite*	11,757	11,987	12,675
Alumina	3,365	3,394	3,440
Crude gypsum	251	132	154

* Dried equivalent of crude ore.

Industry

SELECTED PRODUCTS

	1997	1998	1999
Edible oil ('000 litres) . . .	13,712	14,038	15,976
Flour (metric tons) . . .	147,961	135,859	130,885
Sugar (metric tons) . . .	232,798	182,761	201,319
Molasses (metric tons) . .	92,158	97,865	85,120
Rum ('000 litres)	22,362	22,171	19,709
Beer and stout ('000 litres) . .	67,434	66,933	65,573
Animal feed (metric tons) . .	186,955	191,765	232,351
Fertilizers (metric tons) . .	n.a.	27,918	43,897
Fuel oil ('000 litres) . . .	382,134	399,018	284,967
Asphalt ('000 litres) . . .	15,722	3,708	5,508
Gasoline (petrol) ('000 litres) .	143,061	146,224	86,683
Kerosene, turbo and jet fuel ('000 litres)	72,486	52,690	41,397
Auto diesel oil ('000 litres) . .	159,013	150,109	102,336
Cement ('000 metric tons) . .	588,118	588,001	503,053

Electric energy (million kWh): 6,038 in 1996.

Finance

CURRENCY AND EXCHANGE RATES

Monetary Units
 100 cents = 1 Jamaican dollar (J $).

Sterling, US Dollar and Euro Equivalents (30 March 2001)
 £1 sterling = J $65.014;
 US $1 = J $45.608;
 €1 = J $40.281;
 J $1,000 = £15.38 = US $21.93 = €24.83.

Average Exchange Rate (J $ per US $)
 1998   36.550
 1999   39.044
 2000   42.701

BUDGET (J $ million, year ending 31 March)*

Revenue†	1996/97	1997/98	1998/99‡
Tax revenue	55,191	59,224	66,971
Taxes on income and profits .	21,646	23,297	25,844
Taxes on production and consumption	17,139	18,415	20,974
Taxes on international trade .	16,006	17,513	20,154
Bauxite levy	2,798	2,872	2,787
Other current revenue . . .	3,310	3,097	3,085
Capital revenue	727	508	602
Total	62,026	65,701	73,444

Expenditure	1996/97	1997/98	1998/99‡
Current expenditure . . .	64,225	73,260	85,764
Wages and salaries . . .	24,043	29,066	31,913
Other goods and services . .			
Pensions	12,902	19,631	19,262
Other current transfers . .			
Interest payments . . .	27,280	24,564	34,889
Capital expenditure	13,498	13,128	7,503
Unallocated expenditure (net) .	329	—	—
Total	78,052	86,388	93,267

* Figures refer to budgetary transactions of the central Government, excluding the operations of the National Insurance Fund and other government units with individual budgets.

† Excluding grants received (J $ million): 1,060 in 1996/97; 725 in 1997/98; 652‡ in 1998/99.

‡ Preliminary.

Source: IMF, *Jamaica: Selected Issues* (February 2000).

INTERNATIONAL RESERVES (US $ million, at 31 December)

	1998	1999	2000
IMF special drawing rights	0.7	0.7	0.1
Foreign exchange	708.8	553.8	1,053.6
Total	709.5	554.5	1,053.7

Source: IMF, *International Financial Statistics*.

MONEY SUPPLY (J $ million at 31 December)

	1998	1999	2000
Currency outside banks	13,504	17,821	17,607
Demand deposits at commercial banks	23,160	27,221	30,289
Total money	36,664	45,042	47,897

Source: IMF, *International Financial Statistics*.

COST OF LIVING (Consumer Price Index; base: 1990 = 100)

	1996	1997	1998
Food (incl. beverages)	688.0	742.0	794.2
Fuel and household supplies	679.8	743.1	793.9
Clothing (incl. footwear)	690.2	804.0	846.4
Rent and household operation	316.5	427.2	512.0
All items (incl. others)	669.5	734.2	797.5

Source: ILO, *Labour Statistics Yearbook*.

NATIONAL ACCOUNTS (J $ million at current prices)
Expenditure on the Gross Domestic Product

	1998	1999	2000
Government final consumption expenditure	46,727	48,584	52,130
Private final consumption expenditure	176,968	194,354	217,945
Increase in stocks	296	204	608
Gross fixed capital formation	72,660	73,531	85,401
Total domestic expenditure	296,651	316,673	356,084
Exports of goods and services	114,038	120,898	141,351
Less Imports of goods and services	142,266	149,667	176,620
GDP in purchasers' values	268,424	287,904	320,814
GDP at constant 1986 prices	19,088	19,004	19,154

* Estimates.
Source: IMF, *International Financial Statistics*.

Gross Domestic Product by Economic Activity

	1998	1999	2000*
Agriculture, forestry and fishing	20,204	20,045	20,765
Mining and quarrying	11,242	12,013	13,827
Manufacturing	36,232	38,817	42,904
Electricity and water	8,105	10,246	12,877
Construction	26,236	27,667	30,925
Wholesale and retail trade	54,974	57,771	63,941
Hotels, restaurants and clubs	11,449	12,694	14,243
Transport, storage and communication	26,000	28,939	31,704
Finance, insurance, real estate and business services	32,674	38,376	42,756
Producers of government services	31,059	34,045	36,327
Household and private non-profit services	1,404	1,657	2,010
Other community, social and personal services	5,664	6,273	6,900
Sub-total	265,243	288,543	319,179
Value-added tax	19,344	19,743	22,132
Less Imputed bank service charge	16,163	20,383	20,498
GDP in purchasers' values	268,424	287,904	320,815

* Preliminary.
Source: IMF, *Jamaica: Statistical Appendix* (June 2001).

BALANCE OF PAYMENTS (US $ million)

	1997	1998	1999
Exports of goods f.o.b.	1,700.3	1,613.4	1,489.9
Imports of goods f.o.b.	−2,832.6	−2,743.9	−2,627.6
Trade balance	−1,132.3	−1,130.5	−1,137.7
Exports of services	1,714.6	1,786.1	1,865.8
Imports of services	−1,225.8	−1,284.9	−1,300.6
Balance on goods and services	−643.5	−629.3	−572.5
Other income received	147.3	156.3	165.8
Other income paid	−439.2	−464.4	−498.3
Balance on goods, services and income	−935.4	−937.4	−905.0
Current transfers received	705.7	732.1	756.3
Current transfers paid	−80.9	−97.1	−107.0
Current balance	−310.6	−302.4	−255.7
Capital account (net)	16.9	15.5	13.1
Direct investment abroad	−56.6	−82.0	−94.9
Direct investment from abroad	203.3	369.1	523.7
Portfolio investment (net)	5.7	7.0	4.9
Other investment assets	−113.2	−59.1	−122.7
Other investment liabilities	124.3	102.2	−138.4
Net errors and omissions	−40.2	−6.4	−66.4
Overall balance	−170.4	43.9	−136.4

Source: IMF, *International Financial Statistics*.

External Trade

PRINCIPAL COMMODITIES (US $ million)

Imports c.i.f.	1998	1999	2000
Consumer goods	929	965	978
Foods	274	274	263
Non-durable goods	368	405	418
Durable goods	287	286	298
Fuels	306	416	585
Raw materials	1,227	1,108	1,120
Capital goods	568	470	509
Construction materials	167	157	144
Transport equipment	127	87	107
Other machinery	273	227	257
Total	3,029	2,960	3,192

Source: IMF, *Jamaica: Statistical Appendix* (June 2001).

(US $ million, year ending 31 March)

Exports f.o.b.	1996/97	1997/98	1998/99*
Agricultural products	90	85	64
Bananas	44	44	33
Coffee	33	31	17
Minerals	667	729	670
Bauxite	79	72	83
Alumina	588	657	587
Manufactures	488	428	401
Sugar	122	81	98
Clothing	242	224	186
Other	444	461	416
Total	1,689	1,703	1,551

* Estimates.
Source: IMF, *Jamaica: Selected Issues* (February 2000).

PRINCIPAL TRADING PARTNERS (US $ million)

Imports c.i.f.	1998	1999	2000
Canada	95	97	98
Guyana	29	29	33
Japan	200	179	192
Trinidad and Tobago	230	289	320
United Kingdom	115	96	98
USA	1,523	1,437	1,431
Venezuela	46	53	125
Total (incl. others)	2,992	2,960	3,192

Exports f.o.b.	1998	1999	2000
Canada	151	136	133
Japan	17	22	30
Norway	88	80	119
Trinidad and Tobago	16	15	22
United Kingdom	159	154	149
USA	52	461	509
Total (incl. others)	1,316	1,246	1,300

Source: IMF, *Jamaica: Statistical Appendix* (June 2001).

Transport

RAILWAYS (traffic)

	1988	1989	1990
Passenger-km ('000)	36,146	37,995	n.a.
Freight ton-km ('000) . . .	115,076	28,609	1,931

Source: Jamaica Railway Corporation.

ROAD TRAFFIC ('000 motor vehicles in use)

	1995	1996	1997
Passenger cars	104.0	120.7	156.8
Commercial vehicles	49.1	52.8	56.1

Source: UN, *Statistical Yearbook*.

SHIPPING

Merchant Fleet (registered at 31 December)

	1996	1997	1998
Number of vessels	11	12	9
Total displacement ('000 grt) . .	9.3	9.6	3.6

Source: Lloyd's Register of Shipping, *World Fleet Statistics*.

International Sea-borne Freight Traffic (estimates, '000 metric tons)

	1989	1990	1991
Goods loaded	7,711	8,354	8,802
Goods unloaded	5,167	5,380	5,285

Source: Port Authority of Jamaica.

CIVIL AVIATION (traffic on scheduled services)

	1995	1996	1997
Kilometres flown (million) . .	12	17	22
Passengers carried ('000) . . .	1,060	1,322	1,400
Passenger-km (million) . . .	1,583	2,107	2,677
Total ton-km (million) . . .	166	216	264

Source: UN, *Statistical Yearbook*.

Tourism

VISITOR ARRIVALS BY COUNTRY OF ORIGIN

	1996	1997	1998
Canada	102,215	99,216	109,802
USA	773,846	804,361	829,330
United Kingdom	114,417	116,390	116,552
Italy	23,969	21,028	17,718
Germany	36,509	33,480	43,018
Total (incl. others) . . .	1,162,449	1,192,194	1,225,287

Receipts from tourism (US $ million): 1,131 in 1997; 1,197 in 1998; 1,233 in 1999.

Arrivals ('000): 1,248 in 1999.

Sources: World Tourism Organization, *Yearbook of Tourism Statistics*; World Bank, *World Development Indicators*.

Communications Media

	1995	1996	1997
Radio receivers ('000 in use) . .	1,080	1,200	1,215
Television receivers ('000 in use) .	400	450	460
Telephones (main lines in use, '000)*	292	353	n.a.
Mobile cellular telephones (subscribers)*	45,178	54,640	n.a.
Daily newspapers (number) . .	3	3	n.a.
Circulation (estimates, '000) .	160	158	n.a.

Telefax stations (number in use)*: 1,567 in 1992.

* Year beginning 1 April.

Sources: UNESCO, *Statistical Yearbook*, and UN, *Statistical Yearbook*.

Education

	Institutions	Teachers	Students
Pre-primary*	1,681	4,158†	133,687†
Primary‡	—	9,512†	293,863†
Secondary§	—	10,931	235,071
Tertiary‖	1	418	8,191

* Figures for 1990/91.
† Public sector only.
‡ Figures for 1996/97.
§ Figures for 1992/93.
‖ Figures for 1995/96.

Source: UNESCO, *Statistical Yearbook*.

Directory

The Constitution

The Constitution came into force at the independence of Jamaica on 6 August 1962. Amendments to the Constitution are enacted by Parliament, but certain entrenched provisions require ratification by a two-thirds' majority in both chambers of the legislature, and some (such as a change of the head of state) require the additional approval of a national referendum.

HEAD OF STATE

The Head of State is the British monarch, who is locally represented by a Governor-General, appointed by the British monarch, on the recommendation of the Jamaican Prime Minister in consultation with the Leader of the Opposition party.

THE LEGISLATURE

The Senate or Upper House consists of 21 Senators, of whom 13 will be appointed by the Governor-General on the advice of the Prime Minister and eight by the Governor-General on the advice of the Leader of the Opposition. (Legislation enacted in 1984 provided for eight independent Senators to be appointed, after consultations with the Prime Minister, in the eventuality of there being no Leader of the Opposition.)

The House of Representatives consists of 60 elected members called Members of Parliament.

A person is qualified for appointment to the Senate or for election to the House of Representatives if he or she is a citizen of Jamaica or other Commonwealth country, of the age of 21 or more and has been ordinarily resident in Jamaica for the immediately preceding 12 months.

THE PRIVY COUNCIL

The Privy Council consists of six members appointed by the Governor-General after consultation with the Prime Minister, of whom at least two are persons who hold or who have held public office. The functions of the Council are to advise the Governor-General on the exercise of the Royal Prerogative of Mercy and on appeals on disciplinary matters from the three Service Commissions.

THE EXECUTIVE

The Prime Minister is appointed from the House of Representatives by the Governor-General, and is the leader of the party that holds the majority of seats in the House of Representatives. The Leader of the party is voted in by the members of that party. The Leader of the Opposition is voted in by the members of the Opposition party.

The Cabinet consists of the Prime Minister and not fewer than 11 other ministers, not more than four of whom may sit in the Senate. The members of the Cabinet are appointed by the Governor-General on the advice of the Prime Minister.

THE JUDICATURE

The Judicature consists of a Supreme Court, a Court of Appeal and minor courts. Judicial matters, notably advice to the Governor-General on appointments, are considered by a Judicial Service Commission, the Chairman of which is the Chief Justice, members being the President of the Court of Appeal, the Chairman of the Public Service Commission and three others.

CITIZENSHIP

All persons born in Jamaica after independence automatically acquire Jamaican citizenship and there is also provision for the acquisition of citizenship by persons born outside Jamaica of Jamaican parents. Persons born in Jamaica (or persons born outside Jamaica of Jamaican parents) before independence who immediately prior to independence were citizens of the United Kingdom and colonies also automatically become citizens of Jamaica.

Appropriate provision is made which permits persons who do not automatically become citizens of Jamaica to be registered as such.

FUNDAMENTAL RIGHTS AND FREEDOMS

The Constitution includes provisions safeguarding the fundamental freedoms of the individual, irrespective of race, place of origin, political opinions, colour, creed or sex, subject only to respect for the rights and freedoms of others and for the public interest. The fundamental freedoms include the rights of life, liberty, security of the person and protection from arbitrary arrest or restriction of movement, the enjoyment of property and the protection of the law, freedom of conscience, of expression and of peaceful assembly and association, and respect for private and family life.

The Government

Head of State: HM Queen Elizabeth II (succeeded to the throne 6 February 1952).

Governor-General: Sir Howard Felix Hanlan Cooke (appointed 1 August 1991).

PRIVY COUNCIL OF JAMAICA

Dr Vernon Lindo, Ewart Forrest, G. Owen, W. H. Swaby, Dr Douglas Fletcher.

CABINET
(August 2000)

Prime Minister: Percival James Patterson.

Deputy Prime Minister and Minister of Land and the Environment: Seymour Mullings.

Minister of Finance and Planning: Dr Omar Davies.

Minister of Labour and Social Security: Donald Buchanan.

Minister of Tourism and Sport: Portia Simpson-Miller.

Minister of Local Government, Youth and Community Development: Arnold Bertram.

Minister of National Security and Justice: Keith (K. D.) Knight.

Minister of Agriculture: Roger Clarke.

Minister of Foreign Affairs: Dr Paul Robertson.

Minister of Foreign Trade: George Anthony Hylton.

Minister of Mining and Energy: Robert Pickersgill.

Minister of Health: John Junor.

Minister of Education, Youth and Culture: Burchell Whiteman.

Minister of Transport and Works: Dr Peter Phillips.

Minister of Water and Housing: Dr Karl Blythe.

Minister of Industry, Commerce and Technology: Phillip Paulwell.

Minister of Information: Maxine Henry-Wilson.

MINISTRIES

Office of the Governor-General: King's House, Hope Rd, Kingston 10; tel. 927-6424.

Office of the Prime Minister: Jamaica House, 1 Devon Rd, POB 272, Kingston 10; tel. 927-9941; fax 929-0005; e-mail pmo@opm.gov.jm.

Ministry of Agriculture: Hope Gardens, POB 480, Kingston 6; tel. 927-1731; fax 977-1879.

Ministry of Education, Youth and Culture: 2 National Heroes Circle, Kingston 4; tel. 922-1400; fax 922-9371; internet www.moec.gov.jm.

Ministry of Finance and Planning: 30 National Heroes Circle, Kingston 4; tel. 922-8600; fax 922-7097; e-mail info@mof.gov.jm; internet www.mof.gov.jm.

Ministry of Foreign Affairs and Foreign Trade: 21 Dominica Drive, POB 624, Kingston 5; tel. 926-4220; fax 929-6733; e-mail mfaftjam@cwjamaica.com; internet www.mfaft.gov.jm.

Ministry of Health: Oceana Hotel Complex, 2–4 King St, Kingston; tel. 967-1100; fax 967-7293; internet www.moh.gov.jm.

Ministry of Industry, Commerce and Technology: PCJ Bldg, 36 Trafalgar Rd, Kingston 10; tel. 929-8990; fax 960-1623; e-mail admin@mct.gov.jm; internet www.mct.gov.jm.

Ministry of Labour and Social Security: 1F North St, POB 10, Kingston; tel. 922-3904; fax 924-9560; e-mail manpower@minlab.gov.jm; internet www.minlab.gov.jm.

Ministry of Land and the Environment: 2 Hagley Park Rd, Kingston 10; tel. 926-1590; fax 926-2591; e-mail mehsys@hotmail.com.

Ministry of Local Government, Youth and Community Development: 85 Hagley Park Rd, Kingston 10; tel. 754-0994; fax 960-0725.

Ministry of Mining and Energy: PCJ Bldg, 36 Trafalgar Rd, Kingston 10; tel. 926-9170; fax 968-2082; e-mail hmme@cwjamaica.com.

Ministry of National Security and Justice: Mutual Life Bldg, North Tower, 2 Oxford Rd, Kingston 5; tel. 906-4909; fax 906-1713; e-mail information@mnsj.gov.jm; internet www.mnsj.gov.jm.

Ministry of Tourism and Sport: 64 Knutsford Blvd, Kingston 5; tel. 920-4956; fax 920-4944; e-mail opmt@cwjamaica.com.

Ministry of Transport and Works: 1C–1F Pawsey Place, Kingston 5; tel. 754-1900; fax 927-8763; e-mail ps@mtw.gov.jm; internet www.mtw.gov.jm.

Ministry of Water and Housing: 7th Floor, Island Life Bldg, 6 St Lucia Ave, Kingston 5; tel. 754-0971; fax 754-0975; e-mail prumow@cwjamaica.com.

Legislature

PARLIAMENT

Houses of Parliament: Gordon House, Duke St, Kingston; tel. 922-0200.

Senate

President: SYRINGA MARSHALL-BURNETT.
Vice-President: NOEL MONTEITH.
The Senate has 20 other members.

House of Representatives

Speaker: VIOLET NEILSON.
Deputy Speaker: O'NEIL T. WILLIAMS.

General Election, 18 December 1997*

	Votes cast	Seats
People's National Party (PNP) . . .	441,739	50
Jamaica Labour Party (JLP) . . .	312,471	10
National Democratic Movement (NDM) .	38,430	—
Total	792,640	60

* Following a by-election in the North-East St Ann constituency on 8 March 2001, and following a Court of Appeal ruling in July 2001 over a disputed result in the St Catherine constituency, the JLP increased its parliamentary representation to 12 seats, thus reducing the PNP's representation in the House of Representatives to 48.

Political Organizations

Jamaica Labour Party (JLP): 20 Belmont Rd, Kingston 5; tel. 929-1183; fax 968-0873; e-mail jlp@colis.com; internet www.thejlp.com; f. 1943; supports free enterprise in a mixed economy and close co-operation with the USA; Leader EDWARD SEAGA; Deputy Leader DWIGHT NELSON.

National Democratic Movement (NDM): NDM House, 3 Easton Ave, Kingston 5; e-mail mail@ndmjamaica.org; internet www.ndmjamaica.org; f. 1995; advocates a clear separation of powers between the central executive and elected representatives; supports private investment and a market economy; Pres. HYACINTH BENNETT; Chair. HUGH THOMPSON.

Natural Law Party: c/o 21st Century Integrated Medical Centre, Shop OF3, Overton Plaza, 49 Union St, Montego Bay; tel. 971-9107; fax 971-9109; e-mail nlp@cwjamaica.com; internet www.natural-law-party.org/jamaica/; f. 1996; Leader Dr. LEO CAMPBELL.

People's National Party (PNP): 89 Old Hope Rd, Kingston 5; tel. 978-1337; fax 927-4389; internet www.pnp.org.jm; f. 1938; socialist principles; affiliated with the National Workers' Union; Leader PERCIVAL J. PATTERSON; Gen. Sec. MAXINE HENRY-WILSON; First Vice-Pres. PETER PHILLIPS.

In 1999 a pressure group, **Citizens for a Civil Society (CCS)**, was formed by DARYL VAZ to lobby the Government on specific issues. Another pressure group, **Jamaicans for Justice**, headed by Dr CAROLYN GOMES, was formed in 2001.

Diplomatic Representation

EMBASSIES AND HIGH COMMISSIONS IN JAMAICA

Argentina: 6th Floor, Dyoll Bldg, 40 Knutsford Blvd, Kingston 5; tel. 926-5588; fax 926-0580; e-mail fejama@mrecic.gov.ar; Ambassador: ALFREDO ALCORTA.

Brazil: PCMB Bldg, 3rd Floor, 64 Knutsford Blvd, Kingston 5; tel. 929-8607; fax 929-1259; e-mail brasking@infochan.com; Ambassador: SÉRGIO ARRUDA.

Canada: 3 West Kings House Rd, POB 1500, Kingston 10; tel. 926-1500; e-mail kngtn@dfait-maeci.gc.ca; High Commissioner: JOHN ROBINSON.

Chile: Island Life Centre, 5th Floor, South 6th St, Lucia Ave, Kingston; tel. 968-0260; fax 968-0265; e-mail chilejam@cwjamaica.com; Ambassador: FERNANDO PARDO HUERTA.

China, People's Republic: 8 Seaview Ave, Kingston 10; tel. 927-0850; Ambassador: LI SHANGSHENG.

Colombia: Victoria Mutual Bldg, 3rd Floor, 53 Knutsford Blvd, Kingston 5; tel. 929-1702; fax 929-1701; Ambassador: RICARDO VARGAS TAYLOR.

Costa Rica: Belvedere House, Beverly Drive, Kingston 5; tel. 927-5988; fax 978-3946; e-mail cr_emb_jam@hotmail.com; Ambassador: RODRIGO CASTRO ECHEVERRIA.

Cuba: 9 Trafalgar Rd, Kingston 5; tel. 978-0931; fax 978-5372; Ambassador: DARÍO DE URRA.

France: 13 Hillcrest Ave, POB 93, Kingston 6; e-mail albert.salon@diplomatie.fr; Ambassador: ALBERT SALON.

Germany: 10 Waterloo Rd, POB 444, Kingston 10; tel. 926-6728; fax 929-8282; e-mail germanemb@cwjamaica.com; Ambassador: ADOLF EDERER.

Haiti: 2 Monroe Rd, Kingston 6; tel. 927-7595; Chargé d'affaires: ANDRÉ L. DORTONNE.

India: 4 Retreat Ave, POB 446, Kingston 6; tel. 927-0486; fax 978-2801; High Commissioner: V. B. SONI.

Italy: 10 Rovan Drive, Kingston 6; tel. 978-1273; fax 978-0675; Ambassador: STEFANO CANAVESIO.

Japan: Mutual Life Centre, North Tower, 6th Floor, 2 Oxford Rd, Kingston 10; tel. 929-3338; fax 968-1373; Ambassador: TAKASHI MATSUMOTO.

Korea, Democratic People's Republic: Kingston; tel. 927-7087; Ambassador: HAN PONG GU.

Mexico: PCJ Bldg, 36 Trafalgar Rd, Kingston 10; tel. 926-6891; fax 929-7995; e-mail mexico.j@cwjamaica.com; Ambassador: JOSE LUIS VALLARTA MARRON.

Netherlands: Victoria Mutual Bldg, 53 Knutsford Blvd, Kingston 5; tel. 926-2026; fax 926-1248; e-mail rnekst@cwjamaica.com; Ambassador: E. W. P. KLIPP.

Nigeria: 5 Waterloo Rd, Kingston 10; tel. 926-6400; fax 968-7371; e-mail nhckingston@mail-infochan.com; High Commissioner: FLORENTINA ADENIKE UKONGA.

Panama: 1 St Lucia Ave, Spanish Court, Office 26, Kingston 5; tel. 968-2928; fax 960-1618; Chargé d'affaires: JOSÉ DE JESÚS MARTÍNEZ.

Russia: 22 Norbrook Drive, Kingston 8; tel. 924-1048; Ambassador: IGOR YAKOVLEV.

Spain: 25 Dominica Drive, 10th Floor, Kingston 5; tel. 929-6710; Ambassador: FERNANDO DE LA SERNA INCIARTE.

Trinidad and Tobago: First Life Bldg, 3rd Floor, 60 Knutsford Blvd, Kingston 5; tel. 926-5730; fax 926-5801; e-mail t&thckgn@infochan.com; High Commissioner: DENNIS FRANCIS.

United Kingdom: 28 Trafalgar Rd, POB 575, Kingston 10; tel. 926-9050; fax 929-7869; e-mail bhckingston@cw.com; High Commissioner: ANTONY F. SMITH.

USA: Mutual Life Centre, 2 Oxford Rd, Kingston 5; tel. 929-4850; Ambassador: STANLEY L. McLELLAND.

Venezuela: Petroleum Corpn of Jamaica Bldg, 3rd Floor, 36 Trafalgar Rd, Kingston 10; tel. 926-5510; fax 926-7442; Chargé d'affaires a.i.: NÉSTOR CASTELLANOS.

Judicial System

The Judicial System is based on English common law and practice. Final appeal is to the Judicial Committee of the Privy Council in the United Kingdom, although in 2001 the Jamaican Government signed an agreement to establish a Caribbean Court of Justice to fulfil this function.

Justice is administered by the Privy Council, Court of Appeal, Supreme Court (which includes the Revenue Court and the Gun Court), Resident Magistrates' Court (which includes the Traffic Court), two Family Courts and the Courts of Petty Sessions.

Judicial Service Commission: Office of the Services Commissions, 63–67 Knutsford Blvd, Kingston 5; advises the Governor-General on judicial appointments, etc.; chaired by the Chief Justice.

Attorney-General: ARNOLD J. NICHOLSON.

SUPREME COURT
Public Building E, 134 Tower St, POB 491, Kingston; tel. 922-8300; fax 967-0669; e-mail webmaster@sc.gov.jm; internet www.sc.gov.jm.

Chief Justice: LENSLEY H. WOLFE.

Senior Puisne Judge: LLOYD B. ELLIS.

Master: CAROL BESWICK.

Registrar: CHRISTINE MCDONALD.

COURT OF APPEAL
POB 629, Kingston; tel. 922-8300.

President: R. CARL RATTRAY.

Registrar: G. P. LEVERS.

Religion

CHRISTIANITY

There are more than 100 Christian denominations active in Jamaica. According to the 1982 census, the largest religious bodies were the Church of God, Baptists, Anglicans and Seventh-day Adventists. Other denominations include the Methodist and Congregational Churches, the Ethiopian Orthodox Church, the Disciples of Christ, the Moravian Church, the Salvation Army and the Society of Friends (Quakers).

Jamaica Council of Churches: 14 South Ave, Kingston 10; tel. 926-0974; e-mail jchurch@yahoo.com; f. 1941; 10 member churches and three agencies; Pres. Rev. STANLEY CLARKE; Gen. Sec. NORMAN MILLS.

The Anglican Communion

Anglicans in Jamaica are adherents of the Church in the Province of the West Indies, comprising eight dioceses. The Archbishop of the Province is the Bishop of the North East Caribbean and Aruba. The Bishop of Jamaica, whose jurisdiction also includes Grand Cayman (in the Cayman Islands), is assisted by three suffragan Bishops (of Kingston, Mandeville and Montego Bay). The 1982 census recorded 154,548 Anglicans.

Bishop of Jamaica: Rt Rev. NEVILLE WORDSWORTH DE SOUZA, Church House, 2 Caledonia Ave, Kingston 5; tel. 926-6609; fax 968-0618.

The Roman Catholic Church

Jamaica comprises the archdiocese of Kingston in Jamaica (also including the Cayman Islands), and the dioceses of Montego Bay and Mandeville. At 31 December 1999 the estimated total of adherents in Jamaica and the Cayman Islands was 116,924, representing about 4.6% of the total population. The Archbishop and Bishops participate in the Antilles Episcopal Conference (currently based in Port of Spain, Trinidad and Tobago).

Archbishop of Kingston in Jamaica: Most Rev. EDGERTON ROLAND CLARKE, Archbishop's Residence, 21 Hopefield Ave, POB 43, Kingston 6; tel. 927-9915; fax 927-4487; e-mail rcabkgn@cwjamaica.com.

Other Christian Churches

Assembly of God: Evangel Temple, 3 Friendship Park Rd, Kingston 3; tel. 928-2728; Pastor WILSON.

Baptist Union: 6 Hope Rd, Kingston 10; tel. 926-1395; fax 968-7832; e-mail jbuaid@mail.infochan.com; internet www.jbu.org.jm; Pres. Rev. NEVILLE CALLAM; Gen. Sec. Rev. KARL JOHNSON .

Church of God in Jamaica: 35A Hope Rd, Kingston 10; tel. 927-8128; 400,379 adherents (1982 census).

First Church of Christ, Scientist: 17 National Heroes Circle, C.S.O., Kingston 4.

Methodist Church (Jamaica District): 143 Constant Spring Rd, POB 892, Kingston 8; tel. and fax 924-2560; f. 1789; 18,284 mems; Chair. Rev. BRUCE B. SWAPP; Synod Sec. Rev. GILBERT G. BOWEN.

Moravian Church in Jamaica: 3 Hector St, POB 8369, Kingston 5; tel. 928-1861; fax 928-8336; f. 1754; 30,000 mems; Pres. Rev. STANLEY G. CLARKE.

Seventh-day Adventist Church: 56 James St, Kingston; tel. 922-7440; f. 1901; 150,722 adherents (1982 census); Pastor Rev. E. H. THOMAS.

United Church in Jamaica and the Cayman Islands: 12 Carlton Cres., POB 359, Kingston 10; tel. 926-8734; fax 929-0826; f. 1965 by merger of the Congregational Union of Jamaica (f. 1877) and the Presbyterian Church of Jamaica and Grand Cayman to become United Church of Jamaica and Grand Cayman; merged with Disciples of Christ in Jamaica in 1992 when name changed as above; 20,000 mems; Gen. Sec. Rev. MAITLAND EVANS.

RASTAFARIANISM

Rastafarianism is an important influence in Jamaican culture. The cult is derived from Christianity and a belief in the divinity of Ras (Prince) Tafari Makonnen (later Emperor Haile Selassie) of Ethiopia. It advocates racial equality and non-violence, but causes controversy in its use of 'ganja' (marijuana) as a sacrament. The 1982 census recorded 14,249 Rastafarians (0.7% of the total population). Although the religion is largely unorganized, there are some denominations.

Royal Ethiopian Judah Coptic Church: Kingston; not officially incorporated, on account of its alleged use of marijuana; Leader ABUNA S. WHYTE.

BAHÁ'Í FAITH

National Spiritual Assembly: 208 Mountain View Ave, Kingston 6; tel. 927-7051; fax 978-2344; incorporated in 1970; 6,300 mems resident in 368 localities.

ISLAM

At the 1982 census there were 2,238 Muslims.

JUDAISM

The 1991 census recorded 250 Jews.

United Congregation of Israelites: 92 Duke St, Kingston; tel. 927-7948; fax 978-6240; f. 1655; c. 250 mems; Spiritual Leader and Sec. ERNEST H. DE SOUZA; Pres. WALLACE R. CAMPBELL.

The Press

DAILIES

Daily Gleaner: 7 North St, POB 40, Kingston; tel. 922-3400; fax 922-2058; e-mail ads@jamaica-gleaner.com; internet www.jamaica-gleaner.com; f. 1834; morning; independent; Chair. and Man.Dir OLIVER CLARKE; Editor-in-Chief GARFIELD GRANDISON; circ. 44,000.

Daily Star: 7 North St, POB 40, Kingston; tel. 922-3400; evening; Editor LEIGHTON LEVY; circ. 49,500.

Jamaica Herald: 29 Molynes Rd, Kingston 10; tel. 968-7721; fax 968-7722; Man. Editor FRANKLIN MCKNIGHT.

Jamaica Observer: 2 Fagan Ave, Kingston 8; tel. 931-5188; fax 931-5190; internet www.jamaicaobserver.com; f. 1993; Chair. GORDON 'BUTCH' STEWART; CEO Dr GEORGE T. PHILLIP.

PERIODICALS

Caribbean Challenge: 55 Church St, POB 186, Kingston; tel. 922-5636; f. 1957; monthly; Editor JOHN KEANE; circ. 18,000.

Caribbean Shipping: Creative Communications Inc, Kingston; tel. 968-7279; fax 926-2217; 2 a year.

Catholic Opinion: 21 Hopefield Ave, POB 43, Kingston 6; tel. 927-9915; fax 927-4487; e-mail rcabkgn@cwjamaica.com; 6 a year; religious; Editor Rev. MICHAEL LEWIS.

Children's Own: 7 North St, POB 40, Kingston; weekly during term time; circ. 120,188.

Government Gazette: POB 487, Kingston; f. 1868; Govt Printer RALPH BELL; circ. 1,350.

Inquirer: 7–11 West St, Kingston; tel. 922-3952; weekly; current affairs.

Jamaica Churchman: 2 Caledonia Ave, Kingston 5; tel. 926-6608; quarterly; Editor BARBARA GLOUDON; circ. 7,000.

Jamaica Journal: 4 Camp Rd, Kingston 4; tel. 929-4048; fax 926-8817; f. 1967; 3 a year; literary, historical and cultural review; publ. by Instit. of Jamaica Publs Ltd; Man. Dir PATRICIA ROBERTS; Editor LEETA HEARNE.

Jamaica Weekly Gleaner: 7 North St, POB 40, Kingston; tel. 922-3400; weekly; overseas; Chair. and Man. Dir OLIVER CLARKE; circ. 13,599.

The Siren: 1 River Bay Rd, PO Box 614, Montego Bay, St James; tel. 952-0997; f. 1990; weekly.

Sunday Gleaner: 7 North St, POB 40, Kingston; tel. 922-3400; weekly; Editor-in-Chief GARFIELD GRANDISON; circ. 488,000.

Sunday Herald: 86 Hagley Park Rd, Kingston 10; tel. 901-5022; fax 937-7313; f. 1997; weekly; Editor FRANKLYN MCKNIGHT; circ. 20,000.

Swing: 102 East St, Kingston; f. 1968; monthly; entertainment and culture; Editor ANDELL FORGIE; circ. 12,000.

The Vacationer: POB 614, Montego Bay; tel. 952-6006; f. 1987; monthly; Man. Editor EVELYN L. ROBINSON; circ. 8,000.

The Visitor Vacation Guide: 82 Barnett St, POB 1258, Montego Bay; tel. 952-5253; fax 952-6513; weekly; Editor LLOYD B. SMITH.

Weekend Star: 7 North St, POB 40, Kingston; tel. 922-3400; weekly; Editor LOLITA TRACEY-LONG; circ. 400,000.

The Western Mirror: 82 Barnett St, POB 1258, Montego Bay; tel. 952-5253; fax 952-6513; e-mail westernmirror@mail.infochan .com;f. 1980; 2 a week; Man. Dir and Editor LLOYD B. SMITH; circ. 16,000.

West Indian Medical Journal: Faculty of Medical Sciences, University of the West Indies, Kingston 7; tel. 927-1214; fax 927-1846; f. 1951; quarterly; Editor-in-Chief Dr. E. N. BARTON; circ. 2,000.

PRESS ASSOCIATION

Press Association of Jamaica (PAJ): 5 East Ave, Kingston; tel. 926-7584; f. 1943; 240 mems; Pres. DESMOND ALLEN; Sec. MONICA DIAS.

NEWS AGENCIES

Jampress Ltd: 3 Chelsea Ave, Kingston 10; tel. 926-8428; fax 929-6727; e-mail jamnews@infochan.com; f. 1984; govt news agency; Exec. Dir DESMOND ALLEN.

Foreign Bureaux

Inter Press Service (IPS) (Italy): Suite 1G, 2-6 Melmac Ave, Kingston 5; tel. 960-0604; fax 929-6889; Regional Editor CORINNE BARNES.

Associated Press (USA) and CANA (Caribbean News Agency) are also represented.

Publishers

Jamaica Publishing House Ltd: 97 Church St, Kingston; tel. 967-3866; fax 922-5412; e-mail jph@jol.com.jm; f. 1969; wholly-owned subsidiary of Jamaica Teachers' Asscn; educational, English language and literature, mathematics, history, geography, social sciences, music; Chair. WOODBURN MILLER; Man. ELAINE R. STENNETT.

Kingston Publishers Ltd: 7 Norman Road, Suite 10, LOJ Industrial Complex, Kingston CSO; tel. 928-8898; fax 928-5719; f. 1970; educational textbooks, general, travel, atlases, fiction, non-fiction, children's books; Chair. L. MICHAEL HENRY.

Western Publishers Ltd: 82 Barnett St, POB 1258, Montego Bay; tel. 952-5253; fax 952-6513; e-mail westernmirror@mail.infochan .com; f. 1980; Man. Dir and Editor-in-Chief LLOYD B. SMITH.

Government Publishing House

Jamaica Printing Services: 77 Duke St, Kingston; tel. 967-2250; Chair. EVADNE STERLING; Man. RALPH BELL.

Broadcasting and Communications

TELECOMMUNICATIONS

In September 1999 the Government announced a three-year transition period to a fully competitive telecommunications sector. The sector was to be regulated by the Office of Utilities Regulation (see Utilities).

Cable & Wireless Jamaica Ltd: 7 Cecilio Ave, Kingston 10; tel. 926-9450; fax 929-9530; f. 1989; in 1995 merged with Jamaica Telephone Co Ltd and Jamaica International Telecommunications Ltd, name changed as above 1995; 79% owned by Cable & Wireless; Pres. E. MILLER.

Cellular One Caribbean: Kingston; mobile cellular telephone operator; licence granted Dec. 1999.

Centennial Digital: Kingston; f. 2001; mobile cellular telephone operator; Chief Operations Officer JIM BENEDA.

Digicel: Kingston; mobile cellular telephone operator; owned by Irish consortium, Mossel (Jamaica) Ltd; f. 2001; Chair. DENIS O'BRIEN.

BROADCASTING

Television

CVM Television: 69 Constant Sprint Rd, Kingston 10; tel. 931-9400; fax 931-9417; e-mail manager@cvmtv.com.

Love Television: Kingston; f. 1997; religious programming; owned by religious Media Ltd.

Television Jamaica Limited (TVJ): 5–9 South Odeon Avenue, POB 100, Kingston 10; tel. 926-5620; fax 929-1029; e-mail tvjadmin@cwjamaica.com; internet www.radiojamaica.com; f. 1959 as Jamaica Broadcasting Corporation; privatized 1997, name changed as above; island-wide VHF transmission, 24 hrs a day; Gen. Man. MARCIA FORBES.

Radio

Educational Broadcasting Service: Multi-Media Centre, 37 Arnold Road, Kingston 4; tel. 922-9370; f. 1964; radio broadcasts during school term; Pres. OUIDA HYLTON-TOMLINSON.

Independent Radio: 6 Bradley Ave, Kingston 10; tel. 968-4880; fax 968-9165; commercial radio station; broadcasts 24 hrs a day on FM; Gen. Man. NEWTON JAMES.

IRIE FM: Coconut Grove, POB 282, Ocho Rios, St Ann; tel. 974-5051; fax 968-8332; f. 1991; commercial radio station; plays only raggae music.

Island Broadcasting Services Ltd: 41B Half Way Tree Rd, Kingston 5; tel. 929-1344; fax 929-1345; commercial; broadcasts 24 hrs a day on FM; Exec. Chair. NEVILLE JAMES.

KLAS-FM: 81 Knutsford Blvd, Kingston 5; f. 1991; commercial radio station.

Love 101: Kingston; f. 1997; commercial radio station, broadcasts religious programming on FM; owned by Religious Media Ltd.

Radio Jamaica Ltd (RJR): Broadcasting House, 32 Lyndhurst Rd, POB 23, Kingston 5; tel. 926-1100; fax 929-7467; e-mail rjr@ radiojamaica.com; internet www.radiojamaica.com; f. 1947; commercial, public service; three channels:

RJR Supreme '94: broadcasts on AM and FM, island-wide, 24 hrs a day; Exec. Producer NORMA BROWN-BELL.

FAME FM: broadcasts on FM, island-wide, 24 hrs a day; Exec. Producer FRANCOIS ST. JUSTE.

Radio 2: broadcasts on FM, island-wide, 24 hrs a day; Media Services Man. DONALD TOPPING.

Other stations broadcasting include Hot 102, Power 106 FM, Roots FM and TBC FM.

Finance

(cap. = capital; p.u. = paid up; res = reserves; dep. = deposits; m. = million; brs = branches; amounts in Jamaican dollars)

BANKING
Central Bank

Bank of Jamaica: Nethersole Place, POB 621, Kingston; tel. 922-0752; fax 922-0854; e-mail info@boj.org.jm; internet www.boj.org.jm; f. 1960; cap. 4.0m., res 159.9m., dep. 51,793.3m. (Dec. 1998); Gov. DERICK LATIBEAUDIÈRE.

Commercial Banks

Bank of Nova Scotia Jamaica Ltd (Canada): Scotiabank Centre Bldg, cnr Duke and Port Royal Sts, POB 709, Kingston; tel. 922-1000; fax 924-9294; f. 1967; cap. 1,463.6m., res 4,114.0m., dep. 47,628.4m. (Dec. 1998); Chair. BRUCE R. BIRMINGHAM; Man. Dir WILLIAM E. CLARKE; 36 brs.

CIBC Jamaica Ltd (Canada): CIBC Centre, 23–27 Knutsford Blvd, POB 762, Kingston 5; tel. 929-9310; fax 929-7751; 57% owned by Canadian Imperial Bank of Commerce; cap. 96.7m., res 516.2m., dep. 8,153.1m. (Oct. 1997); Man. Dir A. W. WEBB; 12 brs.

Citibank, NA (USA): 63–67 Knutsford Blvd, POB 286, Kingston 5; tel. 926-3270; fax 929-3745.

National Commercial Bank Jamaica Ltd: 'The Atrium', 32 Trafalgar Rd, POB 88, Kingston 10; tel. 929-9050; fax 929-8399; internet www.jncb.com; f. 1977; merged with Mutual Security Bank in 1996; cap. 433.0m., res 1,811.6m., dep. 67,471.9m. (Sept. 1998); Chair. GLORIA D. KNIGHT; Man. Dir REX JAMES; 33 brs.

Trafalgar Commercial Bank Ltd: 60 Knutsford Blvd, Kingston 5; tel. 968-5119.

Union Bank of Jamaica Ltd: 17 Dominica Dr., Kingston 5; tel. 960-1350; fax 960-2332; f. 2000 by merger of Citizens Bank Ltd, Eagle Commercial Bank Ltd, Island Victoria Bank Ltd, and Workers' Savings and Loan Bank; bought by the Royal Bank of Trinidad and Tobago in 2001; 6 brs.

Development Banks

Jamaica Mortgage Bank: 33 Tobago Ave, POB 950, Kingston 5; tel. 929-6350; fax 968-5428; f. 1971 by the Jamaican Govt and the US Agency for Int. Devt; govt-owned statutory org. since 1973; intended to function primarily as a secondary market facility for home mortgages and to mobilize long-term funds for housing devts in Jamaica; also insures home mortgage loans made by approved financial institutions, thus transferring risk of default on a loan to the Govt; Chair. PETER THOMAS; Man. Dir EVERTON HANSON.

National Development Bank of Jamaica Ltd: 11A–15 Oxford Rd, POB 8309, Kingston 5; tel. 929-6124; fax 929-6996; e-mail ndb@ndbjam.com; internet www.ndbjam.com; replaced Jamaica Development Bank, f. 1969; provides funds for medium- and long-term devt-orientated projects in the tourism, industrial, agro-industrial and mining sectors through financial intermediaries; Pres. NATAN RICHARDS; Chair. HUNTLEY MANHERTZ.

Agricultural Credit Bank of Jamaica: 11A–15 Oxford Rd, POB 466, Kingston 5; tel. 929-4010; fax 929-6055; f. 1981; provides loans to small farmers through co-operative banks; Man. Dir KINGSLEY THOMAS; Chair. ARTHUR BARRET.

Trafalgar Development Bank: The Towers, 3rd Floor, 25 Dominica Drive, Kingston 5; tel. 929-4760; e-mail tdbhrgen@cwjamaica.com.

Other Banks

National Export-Import Bank of Jamaica Ltd: 48 Duke St, POB 3, Kingston; tel. 922-9690; fax 922-9184; e-mail eximjam@cwjamaica.com; replaced Jamaica Export Credit Insurance Corpn; finances import and export of goods and services; Chair. Dr OWEN JEFFERSON.

National Investment Bank of Jamaica Ltd: 11 Oxford Rd, POB 889, Kingston 5; tel. 960-9691; fax 920-0379; e-mail nibj@infochan.com; Chair. DAVID COORE; Pres. Dr GAVIN CHEN.

Banking Association

Jamaica Bankers' Association: POB 1079, Kingston; tel. 929-9050; fax 929-8399; Pres. PETER MOSES.

Financial Sector Adjustment Company

FINSAC Ltd: 76 Knutsford Blvd, POB 54, Kingston 5; tel. 906-1809; fax 906-1822; e-mail info@finsac.com; internet www.finsac.com; f. 1997; state-owned; intervenes in the banking and insurance sectors to restore stability in the financial sector.

STOCK EXCHANGE

Jamaica Stock Exchange Ltd: 40 Harbour St, Kingston; tel. 967-3271; fax 922-6966; f. 1968; 50 listed cos (1995); Chair. RITA HUMPHRIES-LEWIN; Gen. Man. C. WAIN ITON.

INSURANCE

Office of the Superintendent of Insurance: 51 St Lucia Ave, POB 800, Kingston 5; tel. 926-1790; fax 968-4346; f. 1972; regulatory body; Superintendent ERROL MCLEAN (acting).

Jamaica Association of General Insurance Companies: 58 Half Way Tree Rd, POB 459, Kingston 10; tel. 929-8404; e-mail jagic@cwjamaica.com; Man. GLORIA M. GRANT; Chair. LESLIE CHUNG.

Principal Companies

British Caribbean Insurance Co Ltd: 36 Duke St, POB 170, Kingston; tel. 922-1260; fax 922-4475; internet www.bcicdirect.com; f. 1962; general insurance; Gen. Man. LESLIE W. CHUNG.

First Life Insurance Group: 60 Knutsford Blvd, Kingston 5; tel. 926-3700; fax 929-8523; e-mail info@firstlife.com.jm; internet www.firstlife.com.jm; division of the Pan-Jamaican Investment Trust Group; all branches.

Globe Insurance Co of the West Indies Ltd: 17 Dominica Drive, POB 401, Kingston 5; tel. 926-3720; fax 929-2727; Gen. Man. R. E. D. THWAITES.

Guardian Holdings: Kingston; pension and life policies.

Insurance Co of the West Indies Ltd (ICWI): 2 St Lucia Ave, POB 306, Kingston 5; tel. 926-9182; fax 929-6641; Chair. DENNIS LALOR; CEO KENNETH BLAKELEY.

Island Life Insurance Co: 6 St Lucia Ave, Kingston 5; tel. 968-6874; e-mail ceo@islandlife-ja-com.jm; 64% owned by Barbados Mutual Life Assurance Co; 26% owned by FINSAC; merged with Life of Jamaica Ltd in 2001.

Jamaica General Insurance Co Ltd: 9 Duke St, POB 408, Kingston; tel. 922-6420; fax 922-2073; Man. Dir A. C. LEVY.

Life of Jamaica Ltd: 28–48 Barbados Ave, Kingston 5; tel. 929-8920; fax 929-4730; f. 1970; life and health insurance, pensions; 76% owned by Barbados Mutual Life Assurance Co; merged with Island Life Insurance Co in 2001; Pres. R. D. WILLIAMS.

NEM Insurance Co (Jamaica) Ltd: NEM House, 9 King St, Kingston; tel. 922-1460; fax 922-4045; fmrly the National Employers' Mutual General Insurance Asscn; Gen. Man. NEVILLE HENRY.

Trade and Industry

GOVERNMENT AGENCIES

Jamaica Commodity Trading Co Ltd: Kingston; f. 1981 as successor to State Trading Corpn; oversees all importing on behalf of state; Chair. DAVID GAYNAIR; Man. Dir ANDREE NEMBHARD.

Jamaica Information Service (JIS): 58A Half Way Tree Rd, POB 2222, Kingston 10; tel. 926-3741; fax 920-7427; e-mail jis@jis.gov.jm; internet www.jis.gov.jm; f. 1963; information agency for govt policies

and programmes, ministries and public sector agencies; CEO CARMEN E. TIPLING.

DEVELOPMENT ORGANIZATIONS

Agricultural Development Corpn (ADC) Group of Companies: Mais House, Hope Rd, POB 552, Kingston; tel. 977-4412; fax 977-4411; f. 1989; manages and develops breeds of cattle, provides warehousing, cold storage, offices and information for exporters and distributors of non-traditional crops and ensures the proper utilization of agricultural lands under its control; Chair. Dr ASTON WOOD; Gen. Man. DUDLEY IRVING.

Coffee Industry Development Co: Marcus Garvey Drive, Kingston 15; tel. 923-5645; fax 923-7587; e-mail cofeboard-jam@cwjamaica.com; f. 1981; to implement coffee devt and rehabilitation programmes financed by international aid agencies; Sec. JOYCE CHANG.

Jamaica Promotions Corpn (JAMPRO): 35 Trafalgar Rd, Kingston 10; tel. 929-7190; fax 960-8082; e-mail jampro@investjamaica.com; f. 1988 by merger of Jamaica Industrial Development Corpn, Jamaica National Export Corpn and Jamaica Investment Promotion Ltd; trade and investment promotion agency; Pres. PATRICIA FRANCIS; Chair. JOSEPH A. MATALON.

National Development Agency Ltd: Kingston; tel. 922-5445.

Planning Institute of Jamaica: 8 Ocean Blvd, Kingston Mall; tel. 967-3690; fax 967-3688; e-mail doccen@mail.colis.com; f. 1955 as the Central Planning Unit; adopted current name in 1984; monitoring performance of the economy and the social sector; publishing of devt plans and social surveys; Dir-Gen. WESLEY HUGHES.

Urban Development Corpn: The Office Centre, 8th Floor, 12 Ocean Blvd, Kingston; tel. 922-8310; fax 922-9326; f. 1968; responsibility for urban renewal and devt within designated areas; Chair. Dr VINCENT LAWRENCE; Gen. Man. IVAN ANDERSON.

CHAMBERS OF COMMERCE

Associated Chambers of Commerce of Jamaica: 7–8 East Parade, POB 172, Kingston; tel. 922-0150; f. 1974; 12 associated Chambers of Commerce; Pres. RAY CAMPBELL.

Jamaica Chamber of Commerce: 7–8 East Parade, POB 172, Kingston; tel. 922-0150; fax 924-9056; f. 1779; 450 mems; Pres. HOWARD HAMILTON.

INDUSTRIAL AND TRADE ASSOCIATIONS

Cocoa Industry Board: Marcus Garvey Drive, POB 1039, Kingston 15; tel. 923-6411; fax 923-5837; e-mail cocoajam@cwjamaica.com; f. 1957; has statutory powers to regulate and develop the industry; owns and operates four central fermentaries; Chair. JOSEPH SUAH; Man. and Sec. NABURN NELSON.

Coconut Industry Board: 18 Waterloo Rd, Half Way Tree, Kingston 10; tel. 926-1770; fax 968-1360; f. 1945; 9 mems; Chair. R. A. JONES; Gen. Man. JAMES S. JOYLES.

Coffee Industry Board: Marcus Garvey Drive, POB 508, Kingston 15; tel. 923-5850; fax 923-7587; e-mail cibcommercial@cwjamaica.com; internet www.jamaicancoffee.gov.jm; f. 1950; 9 mems; has wide statutory powers to regulate and develop the industry; Chair. RICHARD DOWNER; CEO GONZALO HERNÁNDEZ.

Jamaica Bauxite Institute: Hope Gardens, POB 355, Kingston 6; tel. 927-2073; fax 927-1159; f. 1975; adviser to the Govt in the negotiation of agreements, consultancy services to clients in the bauxite/alumina and related industries, laboratory services for mineral and soil-related services, Pilot Plant services for materials and equipment testing, research and development; Chair. CARLTON DAVIS.

Jamaica Export Trading Co Ltd: 6 Waterloo Rd, POB 645, Kingston 10; tel. 929-4390; fax 926-1608; e-mail jetcoja@infochan.com; f. 1977; export trading in non-traditional products, incl. spices, fresh produce, furniture, garments, processed foods, minerals, etc.; Chair. JOSEPH A. MATALON; Man. Dir HERNAL HAMILTON.

Sugar Industry Authority: 5 Trevennion Park Rd, POB 127, Kingston 5; tel. 926-5930; fax 926-6149; e-mail sia@cwjamaica.com; f. 1970; statutory body under portfolio of Ministry of Agriculture; responsible for regulation and control of sugar industry and sugar marketing; conducts research through Sugar Industry Research Institute; Exec. Chair. ANDRÉE NEMBHARD.

Trade Board: 107 Constant Spring Rd, Kingston 10; tel. 969-0478; Admin. JEAN MORGAN.

EMPLOYERS' ORGANIZATIONS

All-Island Banana Growers' Association Ltd: Banana Industry Bldg, 10 South Ave, Kingston 4; tel. 922-5492; fax 922-5497; f. 1946; 1,500 mems (1997); Chair. BOBBY POTTINGER; Sec. I. CHANG.

All-Island Jamaica Cane Farmers' Association: 4 North Ave, Kingston 4; tel. 922-3010; fax 922-2077; f. 1941; registered cane farmers; 27,000 mems; Chair. KENNETH A. HAUGHTON; Man. DAVID BELINFANTI.

Banana Export Co (BECO): 1A Braemar Ave, Kingston 10; tel. 927-3402; fax 978-6096; f. 1985 to replace Banana Co of Jamaica; oversees the devt of the banana industry; Chair. Dr MARSHALL HALL.

Citrus Growers' Association Ltd: Kingston; f. 1944; 13,000 mems; Chair. IVAN H. TOMLINSON.

Jamaica Association of Sugar Technologists: c/o Sugar Industry Research Institute, Kendal Rd, Mandeville; tel. 962-2241; fax 962-1288; e-mail maureenwil@hotmail.com; f. 1936; 275 mems; Pres. GILBERT THORNE; Sec. Dr MAUREEN R. WILSON.

Jamaica Exporters' Association (JEA): 13 Dominica Drive, POB 9, Kingston 5; tel. 960-1675; fax 960-1465; e-mail sbed@cwjamaica.com; internet www.exportjamaica.org; Pres. KARL JAMES; Exec. Dir PAULINE GRAY.

Jamaica Livestock Association: Newport East, POB 36, Kingston; f. 1941; tel. 922-7130; fax 923-5046; 7,316 mems; Chair. Dr JOHN MASTERTON; Man. Dir and CEO HENRY J. RAINFORD.

Jamaica Manufacturers' Association Ltd: 85A Duke St, Kingston; tel. 922-8869; fax 922-0051; e-mail jma@toj.com; f. 1947; 400 mems; Pres. SAMEER YOUNIS.

Jamaica Producers' Group Ltd: 6A Oxford Rd, POB 237, Kingston 5; tel. 926-3503; fax 929-3636; e-mail cosecretary@jpjamaica.com; f. 1929; fmrly Jamaica Banana Producers' Assen; Chair. C. H. JOHNSTON; Man. Dir Dr MARSHALL HALL.

Private Sector Organization of Jamaica (PSOJ): 39 Hope Rd, POB 236, Kingston 10; tel. 927-6238; fax 927-5137; federative body of private business individuals, cos and assens; Pres. CLIFTON CAMERON; Exec. Dir CHARLES A. ROSS.

Small Businesses' Association of Jamaica (SBAJ): 2 Trafalgar Rd, Kingston 5; tel. 927-7071; fax 978-2738; Pres. ALBERT GRAY; Exec. Dir ESME L. BAILEY.

Sugar Manufacturing Corpn of Jamaica Ltd: 5 Trevennion Park Rd, Kingston 5; tel. 926-5930; fax 926-6149; established to represent the sugar manufacturers in Jamaica; deals with all aspects of the sugar industry and its by-products; provides liaison between the Govt, the Sugar Industry Authority and the All-Island Jamaica Cane Farmers' Assen; 9 mems; Chair. CHRISTOPHER BOVELL; Gen. Man. DERYCK T. BROWN.

MAJOR COMPANIES
Chemicals and Pharmaceuticals

Alkali Group of Cos: 259 Spanish Town Rd, POB 200, Kingston 11; tel. 923-6153; fax 923-4947; f. 1960; holding co concerned with the production of chemicals; Chair. R. DANVERS WILLIAMS; Man. Dir A. BARCLAY EWART; 800 employees.

Colgate Palmolive Co (Jamaica) Ltd: 216 Marcus Garvey Drive, POB 4, Kingston 11; tel. 923-5691; fax 923-4355; f. 1938; subsidiary of Colgate-Palmolive Co (USA); manufacturer of toiletries; Man. Dir TREVOR OTTEY; 160 employees.

Federated Pharmaceutical Co Ltd: 2 Torrington Ave, POB 432, Kingston; tel. 922-1060; fax 922-0183; f. 1958; manufacturer of pharmaceuticals and cosmetics; Chair. JAMES LINDSAY; Man. Dir BRUCE TERRIER; 210 employees.

Construction

Ashtrom Building Structures Ltd: Ensom City, POB 283, Kingston; tel. 984-2395; fax 984-2310; f. 1970; production and installation of pre-constructed commercial buildings; Chair. HOWARD HAMILTON.

B. & H. Structures Ltd: 3 Lady Huggins Ave, Kingston; tel. 988-1135; fax 969-5198; f. 1975; building and civil engineering; Man. STAFFORD HYDE; 455 employees.

Caribbean Cement Co Ltd: POB 448, Kingston; tel. 928-6232; fax 928-7381; internet www.caribcement.com; f. 1947; manufacturer of cement; sales of J $2,218m. (1995); Chair. PATRICK ROUSSEAU; Pres. and CEO COMPTON N. RODNEY; 285 employees.

Hardware and Lumber Ltd: 697 Spanish Town Rd, Kingston 11; tel. 923-8912; fax 923-8629; f. 1969; wholesale distribution of construction materials; sales of J $859m. (1996); Chair. RICHARD BYLES; Man. Dir A. ANTHONY HOLNESS; 197 employees.

Food and Beverages

Butterkist Ltd: 2 Valentine Dr., Kingston 19; tel. 931-0811; fax 925-9417; f. 1969; manufacturer of biscuits; Man. Dir WAYNE SUTHERLAND.

Dairy Industries (Jamaica) Ltd: 111 Washington Blvd, POB 336, Kingston 11; tel. 925-0010; fax 925-0013; f. 1964; subsidiary of Kraft Inc. (USA); manufacturer and distributor of dairy products; Chair. A. R. DIAZ; Gen. Man. REX GADSBY; 121 employees.

Desnoes and Geddes Ltd: 214 Spanish Town Rd, POB 190, Kingston 11; tel. 923-9291; fax 923-8599; f. 1918; brewery and soft-drinks bottlers; producers of Red Stripe lager; sales of J $4,615m.

(1995); Chair. PATRICK H. O. ROUSSEAU; Pres. JOHN IRVINE; 667 employees.

Eastern Banana Estates Ltd: 6A Oxford Rd, Kingston 5; tel. 926-3503; fax 926-3636; f. 1983; subsidiary of the Jamaica Producers' Group Ltd; producers and exporters of bananas; Chair. MARSHALL HALL; Gen. Man. EDWIN THOMPSON; 1,453 employees.

Grace Kennedy and Co PLC: 73 Harbour St, POB 86, Kingston; tel. 922-3440; fax 922-7567; f. 1922; holding co concerned with food processing and wholesale distribution, manufacturing, financial services, maritime activities, information technology; over 70 subsidiaries and related cos; sales of J $11,053m. (1995); Chair. and CEO DOUGLAS ORANE; 2,400 employees.

Jamaica Broilers Ltd: 15 Hope Rd, Kingston 10; tel. 926-2490; fax 929-3073; f. 1963; manufacturer of animal feed, producer of poultry, beef, tilapia and hatching eggs; sales of J $5,055,000m. (1998); Chair. ANDREW A. WILDISH; Pres. and CEO ROBERT E. LEVY; 1,300 employees.

Jamaica Flour Mills Ltd: 24 Trafalgar Rd, POB 28, Kingston; tel. 968-3824; fax 968-4504; f. 1966; milling of grain, including flour; sales of J $2,679.5m. (1995/96); Chair. HENRY A. FULLERTON; Man. Dirs HUGH C HART, V. CORRINE MCLARTY, DAVID H. BICKNELL, JOHN M. RULAND; 180 employees.

Jamaica Standard Products Co Ltd: POB 2, Williamsfield, Manchester; tel. 963-4211; fax 963-4309; e-mail sanco@colis.com.jm; internet www.caribplace.com; f. 1942; sales J $60m. (1995); production and export of coffee; Man. Dir JOHN O. MINOTT; 232 employees.

Long Pond Sugar Factory Ltd: Trelawny Estate, Clark's Town, Trelwany; fax 954-2436; f. 1978; production and processing of sugar cane; Chair. W. A. KENNEDY; 820 employees.

National Rums Jamaica Ltd: 25 Dominica Drive, Kingston; tel. 926-7548; fax 926-7499; f. 1979; manufacturer of distilled alcoholic drinks; Man. Dir R. EVON BROWN; 287 employees.

Nestlé (Jamaica) Ltd: 60 Knutsford Blvd, POB 281, Kingston; tel. 926-1300; fax 926-7388; f. 1986; subsidiary of Nestlé (Switzerland); manufacturer of milk products; Chair. ÉMILE GEORGE; Gen. Man. JOHN PRINGLE; 456 employees.

Walker's Wood Caribbean Foods ltd: Walkerswood PO, St Ann; tel. 917-2318; fax 917-2648; e-mail wcfoods@cwjamaica.com; internet www.caribplace.com/walkers.htm; manufacturer of food products; sales of J $50m. (1996); Chair. RHODERICK EDWARDS; Man. Dir WOODROW MITCHELL; 65 employees.

Wray and Nephew Group Ltd: 234 Spanish Town Rd, POB 39, Kingston 11; tel. 923-6141; fax 923-8619; f. 1960; sugar plantation and rum distillery; Chair. ÉMILE C. GEORGE; Man. Dir BRUCE TERRIER; 2,400 employees.

Mining and Power

Alumina Partners of Jamaica (Alpart): 13 Caledonia Ave, Kingston 5; tel. 962-3654; fax 962-9221; f. 1966; 65% owned by Kaiser Aluminium (USA), 35% owned by Norsk Hydro Aluminium (Norway); bauxite mining and processing, aluminium products; scheduled to merge with Jamalco (see below); Gen. Man. EUGENE MILLER; 1,400 employees.

Esso Standard Oil SA Ltd: 75–77 Marcus Garvey Drive, Kingston 15; tel. 923-6011; fax 923-0533; subsidiary of Esso (USA); manufacture of lubricants and petroleum products; Man. PATRICK PEART.

Jamalco: 13 Waterloo Rd, Kingston; tel. 926-3390; a joint venture between the Aluminium Co of America (Alcoa) and the Jamaican Govt.; bauxite mining and processing; scheduled to merge operations with Alpart; Chair. CARLTON DAVIS.

Kaiser (Jamaica) Bauxite Co: Discovery Bay, St Anns; tel. 973-2221; fax 973-2568; f. 1951; subsidiary of Kaiser Aluminium (USA); bauxite mining, processing and refining; Gen. Man. RAY GENDRON; 1,000 employees.

Petroleum Corpn of Jamaica (PCJ): 36 Trafalgar Rd, POB 579, Kingston 10; tel. 929-5380; fax 929-2409; e-mail ica@pcj.com; internet www.pcj.com; f. 1979; state-owned; owns and operates petroleum refinery; holds exploration rights to local petroleum and gas reserves; Chair. JOHN COOKE.

Petrojam Ltd: 96 Marcus Garvey Dr., POB 241, Kingston; tel. 923-8611; fax 923-5698; internet www.pcj.com/petrojam; f. 1964 by Esso, bought by Govt in 1982; wholly-owned subsidiary of PCJ; operates sole oil refinery in Jamaica.

Petroleum Co of Jamaica Ltd (PETCOM): 695 Spanish Town Rd, Kingston 11; tel. 934-6682; fax 934-6690; e-mail petcom@cwjamaica.com; internet www.pcj.com/petcom; f. 1985; markets gasoline, lubricants and petrochemicals and operates service stations.

West Indies Alumina Co (Windalco): Kirkvine PO, Manchester; tel. 962-3141; fax 962-0606; f. 1943 as Alcan Jamaica; sold in 2001 to Glencore (Switzerland); bauxite mining and processing, production of calcinated alumina; operates Kirkvine and Ewarton refineries; Man. Dir PATRICK MCINTOSH; 1,470 employees.

Textiles and Clothing

Broadway Import Export Co Ltd: 218 Marcus Garvey Drive, POB 449, Kingston 11; tel. 923-8705; fax 923-8684; f. 1968; manufacturer and distributor of household linen; Man. JOSEPHINE JONES; 341 employees.

Cotton Polyester Textiles Co Ltd: Rhoden's Pen, Old Harbour Rd, St Catherine; tel. 983-2401; fax 983-2405; f. 1978; yarn mills; Chair. WARREN G. WOODHAM; 650 employees.

Davon Corpn Ltd: 6 East Bell Rd, Kingston 11; tel. 923-8931; fax 923-8934; f. 1960; clothing manufacturer; Chair. DAVID CHIN; Pres. BILL CHING; 1,250 employees.

Miscellaneous

Berger Paints Jamaica Ltd: 256 Spanish Town Rd, POB 8, Kingston 11; tel. 923-9116; fax 923-5129; f. 1952; subsidiary of UB International Ltd (United Kingdom); manufacturer of paints; Chair. VIJAY MALLYA; 125 employees.

Caribbean Brake Products Ltd: 11 Bell Rd, POB 66, Kingston 11; tel. 923-7236; fax 923-6352; e-mail cbpsales@cwjamaica.com; f. 1959; production and distribution of automobile components; Chair. GORDON A. STEWART; Man. Dir PHILIP N. CRIMARCO; 170 employees.

Caribbean Casting and Engineering Ltd: 138 Spanish Town Rd, POB 163, Kingston 11; tel. 923-6558; fax 923-9538; f. 1970; producer of cast-iron products and machinery used for the manufacture of sugar; Man. Dir DENNIS FLETCHER; 123 employees.

Caribbean Steel Co Ltd: Brunswick Ave, Spanish Town, St Catherine; tel. 984-3021; fax 984-2842; f. 1962; manufacturer of steel products; sales of J $453m. (1995); Man. NEVILLE SCARLET; 23 employees.

CFL Ltd: Unit A, Freeport Industrial Complex, Montego Bay, St James; tel. 952-0565; f. 1982; informatics and data processing; Mans CHESTER SWANSON, YVONNE CAMPBELL; 450 employees.

Ciboney Hotels Ltd: 39–43 Barbados Ave, New Kingston, Kingston 5; tel. 929-6198; fax 929-2230; f. 1991; public co; hotel management; sales of J $782m. (1995); Chair. PATRICK HYLTON; CEO GEOFFREY MESSADO; 567 employees.

Cigarette Co of Jamaica Ltd: Twickenham Park, POB 100, Spanish Town; tel. 984-3051; fax 984-6571; f. 1924; subsidiary of Rothmans International Investments Ltd (Netherlands); manufacturer of tobacco products; Man. Dir MICHAEL BERNARD; 187 employees.

Goodyear (Jamaica) Ltd: 8 Oliver Rd, Kingston 8; tel. 924-6130; fax 924-6372; f. 1945; subsidiary of Goodyear Tire and Rubber Co (USA); manufacturer of automobile tyres; Man. Dir PETER GRAHAM; 223 employees.

Seprod Group of Companies: 4–8 Producers' Rd, POB 271/52, Kingston; tel. 922-1220; fax 922-6984; f. 1940; manufacturer and distributor of soap, detergents, edible oils and fats, animal feeds; processors of grain, cereals, glycerine, etc.; Chair. R. C. S. JACKSON; Man. Dir RAPHAEL BARRETT; 900 employees.

West Indies Pulp and Paper Ltd: 19 West Kings House Road, Kingston 10; tel. 926-7423; fax 929-6726; f. 1968; manufacturer of paper products; sales of J $679m. (1996); Chair. PAUL GEDDES; Man. Dir MICHAEL PICKERSGILL; 288 employees.

UTILITIES

Regulatory Authority

Office of Utilities Regulation (OUR): PCJ Resource Centre, 36 Trafalgar Rd, Kingston 10; tel. 960-6474; fax 968-8703; e-mail office@our.org.jm; internet www.our.org.jm; f. 1995; regulates provision of services in the following sectors: water, electricity, telecommunications, public passenger transportation, sewerage; Dir-Gen. WINSTON HAY.

Electricity

Jamaica Public Service Co (JPSCo): Dominion Life Bldg, 6 Knutsford Blvd, POB 54, Kingston 5; tel. 926-3190; fax 968-3337; responsible for the generation and supply of electricity to the island; 80% sold to Mirant Corpn (USA) in March 2001; Chair. GORDON SHIRLEY; Man. Dir DERRICK DYER.

Water

National Water Commission: 4A Marescaux Rd, Kingston 5; tel. 929-3540; internet www.nwcjamaica.com; statutory body; provides potable water and waste water services.

Water Resources Authority: Hope Gardens, POB 91, Kingston 7; tel. 927-0077; fax 977-0179; e-mail wra@colis.com; internet www.wra-ja.org; f. 1996; manages, protects and controls allocation and use of water supplies.

TRADE UNIONS

Bustamante Industrial Trade Union (BITU): 98 Duke St, Kingston; tel. 922-2443; fax 967-0120; f. 1938; Pres. HUGH SHEARER; Gen. Sec. GEORGE FYFFE; 60,000 mems.

National Workers' Union of Jamaica (NWU): 130–132 East St, Kingston 16; tel. 922-1150; e-mail nwyou@toj.com; f. 1952; affiliated to the International Confederation of Free Trade Unions, etc.; Pres. CLIVE DOBSON; Gen. Sec. LLOYD GOODLEIGH; 10,000 mems.

Trades Union Congress of Jamaica: 25 Sutton St, POB 19, Kingston; tel. 922-5313; fax 922-5468; affiliated to the Caribbean Congress of Labour and the International Confederation of Free Trade Unions; Pres. E. SMITH; Gen. Sec. HOPETON CRAVEN; 20,000 mems.

Principal Independent Unions

Dockers' and Marine Workers' Union: 48 East St, Kingston 16; tel. 922-6067; Pres. MILTON A. SCOTT.

Industrial Trade Union Action Council: 2 Wildman St, Kingston; Pres. RODERICK FRANCIS; Gen. Sec. KEITH COMRIE.

Jamaica Federation of Musicians' and Artistes' Unions: POB 1125, Montego Bay 1; tel. 952-3238; f. 1958; Pres. HEDLEY H. G. JONES; Sec. CARL AYTON; 2,000 mems.

Jamaica Local Government Officers' Union: c/o Public Service Commission, Knutsford Blvd, Kingston 5; Pres. E. LLOYD TAYLOR.

Jamaica Teachers' Association: 97 Church St, Kingston; tel. 922-1385; fax 922-3257; e-mail jta@toj.com; Pres. PATRICK SMITH.

Master Printers' Association of Jamaica: Kingston; f. 1943; 44 mems; Pres. HERMON SPOERRI; Sec. RALPH GORDON.

Union of Schools, Agricultural and Allied Workers (USAAW): 2 Wildman St, Kingston; tel. 967-2970; f. 1978; Pres. IAN HINES.

United Portworkers' and Seamen's Union: Kingston.

University and Allied Workers' Union (UAWU): Students' Union, University of West Indies, Mona; tel. 927-7968; affiliated to the WPJ; Gen. Sec. Dr TREVOR MUNROE.

There are also 35 associations registered as trade unions.

Transport

RAILWAYS

There are about 339 km (211 miles) of railway, all standard gauge, in Jamaica. Most of the system is operated by the Jamaica Railway Corpn, which is subsidized by the Government. The main lines are from Kingston to Montego Bay, and Spanish Town to Ewarton and Port Antonio. Passenger services were suspended in 1992; operations were scheduled to resume in 2000. There are four railways for the transport of bauxite.

Jamaica Railway Corpn (JRC): 142 Barry St, POB 489, Kingston; tel. 922-6620; fax 922-4539; f. 1845 as Jamaica Railway Co, the earliest British colonial railway; transferred to JRC in 1960; govt-owned, but autonomous, statutory corpn until 1990, when it was partly leased to Alcan Jamaica Co Ltd (subsequently West Indies Alumina Co) as the first stage of a privatization scheme; 207 km of railway; Chair. W. TAYLOR; Gen. Man. OWEN CROOKS.

Alcoa Railroads: Alcoa Minerals of Jamaica Inc, May Pen PO; tel. 986-2561; fax 986-2026; 43 km of standard-gauge railway; transport of bauxite; Superintendent RICHARD HECTOR; Man. FITZ CARTY (Railroad Operations and Maintenance).

Kaiser Jamaica Bauxite Co Railway: Discovery Bay PO, St Ann; tel. 973-2221; 25 km of standard-gauge railway; transport of bauxite; Gen. Man. GENE MILLER.

ROADS

Jamaica has a good network of tar-surfaced and metalled motoring roads. According to estimates by the International Road Federation, there were 19,000 km of roads in 1998, of which 70.7% were paved. A five-year programme to improve the condition of all arterial and secondary roads and 30% of minor roads was to begin in 1999. In September 1999 plans were announced for a 290 km-highway system linking major cities. In 2001 a consortium of two British companies, Kier International and Mabey & Johnson, was awarded a contract to supply the materials for and construct six road bridges in Kingston and Montego Bay, and a further 20 bridges in rural areas.

SHIPPING

The principal ports are Kingston, Montego Bay and Port Antonio. The port at Kingston has four container berths, and is a major transhipment terminal for the Caribbean area. Jamaica has interests in the multinational shipping line WISCO (West Indies Shipping Corpn—based in Trinidad and Tobago). Services are also provided by most major foreign lines serving the region.

Port Authority of Jamaica: 15–17 Duke St, Kingston; tel. 922-0290; fax 924-9437; e-mail pajmktg@infochan.com; internet www.seaportsofjamaica.com; f. 1966; Govt's principal maritime agency; responsible for monitoring and regulating the navigation of all vessels berthing at Jamaican ports, for regulating the tariffs on public wharves, and for the devt of industrial Free Zones in Jamaica; Pres. and Chair. NOEL HYLTON.

Kingston Free Zone Co Ltd: 27 Shannon Drive, POB 1025, Kingston 15; tel. 923-5274; fax 923-6023; f. 1976; subsidiary of Port Authority of Jamaica; management and promotion of an export-orientated industrial free trade zone for cos from various countries; Gen. Man. OWEN HIGGINS.

Montego Bay Export Free Zone: c/o Port Authority of Jamaica, 15–17 Duke St, Kingston; tel. 922-0290.

Shipping Association of Jamaica: 4 Fourth Ave, Newport West, POB 1050, Kingston 15; tel. 923-3491; fax 923-3421; e-mail shipping.assoc@cwjamaica.com; f. 1939; 63 mems; an employers' trade union which regulates the supply and management of stevedoring labour in Kingston; represents members in negotiations with govt and trade bodies; Pres. GRANTLEY STEPHENSON; Gen. Man. ALVIN C. HENRY.

Principal Shipping Companies

Jamaica Freight and Shipping Co Ltd (JFS): 80–82 Second St, Port Bustamante, POB 167, Kingston 13; tel. 923-9371; fax 923-4091; e-mail cshaw@toj.com; cargo services to and from the USA, Caribbean, Central and South America, the United Kingdom, Japan and Canada; Exec. Chair. CHARLES JOHNSTON; Man. Dir GRANTLEY STEPHENSON.

Petrojam Ltd: 96 Marcus Garvey Drive, POB 241, Kingston; tel. 923-8727; fax 923-5698; Man. Dir STEPHEN WEDDERBURN (acting).

Portcold Ltd: 122 Third St, Newport West, Kingston 13; tel. 923-7425; fax 923-5713; Chair. and Man. Dir ISHMAEL E. ROBERTSON.

CIVIL AVIATION

There are two international airports linking Jamaica with North America, Europe, and other Caribbean islands. The Norman Manley International Airport is situated 22.5 km (14 miles) outside Kingston. The Donald Sangster International Airport is 5 km (3 miles) from Montego Bay. A J $800m.-programme to expand and improve the latter was under consideration in 2001.

Air Jamaica Ltd: 72–76 Harbour St, Kingston; tel. 922-3460; fax 922-0107; internet www.airjamaica.com; f. 1968; privatized in 1994; services within the Caribbean and to Canada (in asscn with Air Canada), the USA and the United Kingdom; Chair. GORDON 'BUTCH' STEWART; CEO CHRISTOPHER ZACCA.

Air Jamaica Express: Tinson Pen Aerodrome, Kingston 11; tel. 923-6664; fax 937-3807; previously known as Trans-Jamaican Airlines; internal services between Kingston, Montego Bay, Negril, Ocho Rios and Port Antonio; Chair. GORDON 'BUTCH' STEWART; Man. Dir PAULO MOREIRA.

Airports Authority of Jamaica: Victoria Mutual Bldg, 53 Knutsford Blvd, POB 567, Kingston 5; tel. 926-1622; fax 929-8171; Chair. CEZLEY SAMPSON; Pres. LUCIEN RATTRAY.

Civil Aviation Authority: 4 Winchester Rd, Kingston 10; tel. 960-3948; fax 920-0194; e-mail jcivav@cwjamaica.com; internet www.jcaa.gov.jm.

Tourism

Tourists, mainly from the USA, visit Jamaica for its beaches, mountains, historic buildings and cultural heritage. In 2000 there were an estimated 2,018,347 visitors (of whom 812,572 were cruise-ship passengers). Tourist receipts were estimated to be US $1,300m. in that year. In 1995 there were some 29,376 hotel rooms. In 2000 a US $125m. luxury resort opened in Montego Bay.

Jamaica Tourist Board (JTB): ICWI Bldg, 2 St Lucia Ave, Kingston 5; tel. 929-9200; fax 929-9375; internet www.jamaicatravel.com; f. 1955; a statutory body set up by the Govt to develop all aspects of the tourist industry through marketing, promotional and advertising efforts; Chair. ADRIAN ROBINSON; Dir of Tourism FAY PICKERSGILL.

Jamaica Hotel and Tourist Association (JHTA): 2 Ardenne Rd, Kingston 10; tel. 926-2796; fax 929-1054; e-mail info@jhta.org; internet www.jobsnmore.com; f. 1961; trade asscn for hoteliers and other cos involved in Jamaican tourism; Pres. JAMES SAMUELS; Exec. Dir CAMILLE NEEDHAM.

Defence

In August 2000 the Jamaican Defence Force consisted of 2,830 men on active service. This included an army of 2,500, a coastguard of 190 and an air wing of 140 men. There were reserves of some 953.

Defence Expenditure: an estimated J $2,100m. in 2000.

Chief of Staff: Maj.-Gen. J. I. SIMMONDS.

Education

Primary education was compulsory in certain districts, and free education was ensured. The education system consisted of a primary cycle of six years, followed by two secondary cycles of three and four years, respectively. In 1997 enrolment at primary schools included 95.6% of children in the relevant age-group (males 95.5%; females 95.7%). In the same year enrolment at secondary schools was equivalent to 69.8% of children in the relevant age-group (males 67.5%; females 72.1%). In 1990 an estimated 1.6% of the adult population had received no schooling and in 2000 an estimated 13.3% of the adult population was illiterate. Higher education was provided by the College of Arts, Science and Technology, the College of Agriculture and the University of the West Indies, which had five faculties (arts and general studies, natural sciences, social sciences, medicine and a school of education) situated at its Mona campus, in Kingston. Government expenditure on education in 1997/98 was estimated at some J $16,400m., representing approximately 15% of total budgetary expenditure. Education was declared the first priority for special attention in the 1999/2000 budget proposals.

Bibliography

For works on the Caribbean generally, see Select Bibliography (Books).

Alleyne, M. *Roots of Jamaican Culture.* London, Pluto, 1989.

Bennett, K. M. 'External Debt, Capital Flight and Stabilization Policy: The Experience of Barbados, Guyana, Jamaica and Trinidad and Tobago', in *Social and Economic Studies*, Vol. 27 (Dec.). 1988.

Boyd, D. A. C. *Economic Management, Income Distribution and Poverty in Jamaica.* London, Praeger Publrs, 1988.

Brown, A. *Colour, Class and Politics in Jamaica.* New Brunswick, NJ, Transaction Books, 1979.

Edie, C. J. 'From Manley to Seaga: The Persistence of Clientist Policies in Jamaica', in *Social and Economic Studies*, Vol. 38 (June). 1989.

Garcia-Muniz, H. 'Defence Policy and Planning in the Commonwealth Caribbean: An Account of Jamaica on its 25th Independence Anniversary', in *Journal of Commonwealth and Comparative Politics*, Vol. 27 (March). 1989.

Hillman, R. S., and D'Agostino, T. J. *Distant Neighbors: The Dominican Republic and Jamaica in Comparative Perspectives.* New York, NY, Praeger Publrs, 1992.

Kaufman, M. *Jamaica Under Manley: Dilemmas of Socialism and Democracy.* London, Zed Books, 1985.

Kirton, C. *Jamaica: Debt and Poverty.* Oxford, Oxfam, 1992.

Kitchen, R. 'Administrative Reform in Jamaica: A Component of Structural Adjustment', in *Public Administration and Development*, Vol. 9 (Sept./Oct.). 1989.

Lacey, T. *Violence and Power in Jamaica, 1960–70.* Manchester, Manchester University Press, 1977.

Lalta, S., and Freckleton, M. (Eds). *Caribbean Economic Development: The First Generation.* Kingston, I. Randle, 1993.

Looney, R. *The Jamaican Economy in the 1980s: Economic Decline and Structural Adjustment.* Boulder, CO, Westview Press, 1986.

Lundy, P. *Debt and Adjustment: Social and Environmental Consequences in Jamaica*. Aldershot, Ashgate, 1999.

Manderson, P. et al. *The Story of the Jamaican People*. Kingston, Ian Randle Publrs, 1997.

Manley, M. *The Politics of Change: A Jamaican Testament*. Washington, DC, Howard University Press, Revised edn, 1990.

Jamaica: Struggle in the Periphery. London, Writers' and Readers' Publishing Co-operative Society, 1982.

Mason, P. *Jamaica in Focus*. London, Latin American Bureau, 2000.

Munroe, T. The Politics of Constitutional Decolonization: Jamaica, 1944–62. Kingston, 1972.

Renewing Democracy into the Millennium: The Jamaican Experience in Perspective. Kingston, University of the West Indies Press, 2000.

Nettleford, R. (Ed.). *Jamaica in Independence*. London, Heinemann, 1989.

Payne, A. J. *Politics in Jamaica*. Kingston, Ian Randle Publrs, Revised edn, 1994.

Persaud, R. B., and Cox, R. W. *Counter-Hegemony and Foreign Policy: The Dialectics of Marginalized and Global Forces in Jamaica*. Albany, NY, SUNY, 2001.

Shepherd, V. A. 'The Different Effects of the Abolition of Slavery in Jamaican Livestock Forms', in *Slavery and Abolition*, Vol. 10 (Sept.). 1989.

Starr, J. B. 'Slave Trading in Jamaica (Eye-Witness Account of December 1778)', in *Slavery and Abolition*, Vol. 10 (May). 1989.

Stephens, E. H. and J. D. *Democratic Socialism in Jamaica*. London, Macmillan, 1986.

Stone, C. *Class, Race and Political Behaviour in Urban Jamaica*. London, Praeger Publrs, 1986.

Weston, A., and Viswanathan, U. (Eds). *Jamaica after NAFTA: Trade Options and Sectoral Strategies*. Ottawa, North–South Institute, 1998.

MARTINIQUE

Area: 1,100 sq km (424.7 sq miles).

Population (census result, March 1999): 381,427.

Capital: Fort-de-France (population 94,049 at 1999 census).

Language: French (official); a creole patois is also spoken.

Religion: Predominantly Christianity (78% Roman Catholic).

Climate: Tropical, but tempered by easterly and north-easterly breezes; average temperature is 26°C (80°F).

Time: GMT –3 hours.

Public Holidays

2002: 1 January (New Year's Day), 11–13 February (Lenten Carnival), 29 March–1 April (Easter), 1 May (Labour Day), 8 May (Victory Day), 9 May (Ascension Day), 20 May (Whit Monday), 14 July (National Day), 15 August (Assumption), 1 November (All Saints' Day), 11 November (Armistice Day), 25 December (Christmas Day).

2003: 1 January (New Year's Day), 3–5 March (Lenten Carnival), 18–21 April (Easter), 1 May (Labour Day), 8 May (Victory Day), 29 May (Ascension Day), 9 June (Whit Monday), 14 July (National Day), 15 August (Assumption), 1 November (All Saints' Day), 11 November (Armistice Day), 25 December (Christmas Day).

Currency: French franc; 1,000 francs = £94.51 = US $135.31 = €152.45 (30 April 2001).

Weights and Measures: The metric system is in force.

Basic Economic Indicators

	1996	1997	1998
Consumer price index (annual average for Fort-de-France; base: 1990 = 100)* . . .	117.2	118.7	120.0
Rate of inflation (annual average, %)†	1.4	1.1	1.3
Imports c.i.f. (million French francs)	10,073	9,855	9,997
Exports f.o.b. (million French francs)	1,259	1,179	1,692

* 120.5 in 1999.
† 0.4% in 1999.

Gross domestic product (million US $ at current prices, 1996): 3,876.

GDP per head (US $ at current prices, 1996): 10,095.

Growth of real GDP (annual average, 1990–96): –4.7%.

Total labour force (1998): 164,592.

Unemployment (December 1999): 29.5%.

Public external debt (1987): US $30m.

Life expectancy (years at birth, 1997): 78.1 (males 74.9; females 81.3).

Infant mortality rate (per 1,000 live births, estimates, 1996): 9.0.

Passenger motor cars in use (per 1,000 of population, 1993): 287.

Television receivers in use (per 1,000 of population, 1997): 171.

History

PHILLIP WEARNE

Revised for this edition by the editorial staff

Martinique's name is either a corruption of the Amerindian (Carib) name of Madinina or a derivation of Saint Martin. The navigator Christopher Colombus sighted the island in 1493 or 1502—the date is disputed. It was first settled by the French in 1635, despite the hostility of the local Caribs, and was occupied with little interruption thereafter. Like Guadeloupe, Martinique was made an Overseas Department of France in 1946, its people becoming French citizens. The island's Governor was replaced with a Prefect and an elected General Council was constituted. Thereafter the French Government's policy of assimilation created a strongly French society, bound by linguistic, cultural and economic ties to metropolitan France. The island enjoyed a better infrastructure and a higher standard of living than its immediate Caribbean neighbours, but, in consequence, it also became heavily dependent on France. For many years economic power remained concentrated in the hands of the *békés* (descendants of white colonial settlers), who still owned most of the agricultural land and controlled the lucrative import-export market in the last decade of the 20th century. This led to little incentive for innovation or self-sufficiency and fostered resentment of lingering colonial attitudes.

The evolution of Martinique's political system was based on the French Government's response to the growth in nationalist sentiment during the latter half of the 20th century. In 1960 the mandate of the island's General Council was broadened, to permit discussion of political as well as administrative issues. In 1974 Martinique was granted regional status, as were Guadeloupe and French Guiana, and an indirectly elected Regional Council, with some control over the local economy, was established. In the early 1980s the Socialist Government of President François Mitterrand tried to curb the continued growth of nationalist pressure and the threat of civil disturbances by instituting a policy of greater decentralization. The two local Councils were given increased control over taxation, the local police and the economy.

In the first direct election to the Regional Council in February 1983 the Department's left-wing parties, which articulated nationalist sentiments while supporting the French Government's policy of decentralization, gained 21 of the 41 seats. That success weakened the threat posed by militant separatist challengers inside and outside the left-wing parties. The most vocal of the separatist parties, the Martinique Independence Movement (Mouvement Indépendantiste Martiniquais—MIM), won less than 3% of the votes cast.

One of the principal campaigners for greater autonomy, from the 1940s, was the veteran socialist writer and poet Aimé Césaire, leader of the Martinique Progressive Party (Parti Progressiste Martiniquais—PPM). Mayor of Fort-de-France, Césaire held a seat in the French National Assembly from 1945 until March 1993, when he was succeeded by Camille Darsières, the General Secretary of the PPM. With Louis-Joseph Dogué of the Socialist Federation of Martinique (Fédération Socialiste de la Martinique), the local wing of the national Socialist Party (Parti Socialiste—PS), standing down in the same election, the Gaullist Rally for the Republic (Rassemblement pour la République—RPR) was able to increase its representation to three of the four Martinique National Assembly seats, through the election of André Lesueur, mayor of Rivière-Salée, Pierre Petit and Anicet Turinay.

In September 1992 72.3% of voters in Martinique approved ratification of the Treaty on European Union (Maastricht Treaty). Two months later banana-growers in Guadeloupe and Martinique blocked access to ports and airports in protest at the threatened loss of special advantages under the Single European Act. Order was restored after four days, following assurances that subsidies would be maintained and banana exports protected.

The 1993 election results in Martinique reflected the increase in support for the right wing seen throughout France, reversing the trend of the late 1980s towards consolidation of the left-wing vote. In the 1988 presidential elections François Mitterrand attracted 70.9% of the valid poll on the island. Later in that year, in the General Council elections on the island, the left wing was able to secure control of the Council with a one-seat majority. The Council then had 23 left-wing members, 11 of them from the PPM, against 22 right-wingers, who had enjoyed a one-seat majority on the previous Council. Emile Maurice, from the conservative RPR, was elected President of the General Council, for his seventh term. However Maurice was ousted in the 1992 elections, to be replaced by the PPM candidate, Claude Lise. The left-wing predominance in local politics was further enhanced by the results of the Regional Council elections at the same time. Although the right-wing grouping was the largest single list, with 16 of the 41 seats, the parties of the left had a working majority.

Elections in March 1994 brought little change in the composition of the General Council. The PPM retained 10 seats, the RPR seven and the centrist Union pour la Démocratie Française three seats, with Claude Lise re-elected President of the General Council. However, in the June elections to the European Parliament, with an abstention rate of 82.2%, the conservative government list secured the greatest proportion of the votes cast (36.6%). A combined list of the parties of the left, the Rally for Overseas and Minorities (Rassemblement d'Outre-Mer et des Minorités), came second with 20.2% of the votes.

At the first round of voting in the 1995 national presidential election, which took place on 23 April, Martinique was the only French overseas possession in which the candidate of the PS, Lionel Jospin, received the greatest proportion of the valid votes cast (34.4%). Jospin, supported by all the parties of the left, took 58.9% of the votes cast at the second round on 7 May, which was contested against Jacques Chirac of the RPR. At municipal elections in June the PPM retained control of Martinique's principal towns. In September Lise was elected to the Senate, while the incumbent PPM representative, Rodolphe Désiré, was returned to office.

At elections to the French National Assembly in May and June 1997, Turinay and Pierre Petit of the RPR were re-elected, together with Camille Darsières of the PPM. Alfred Marie-Jeanne, the First Secretary and a founding member of the MIM, was elected in the Le François–Le Robert constituency (hitherto held by the RPR). In Regional Council elections in March 1998 the left retained a majority. The MIM increased its representation to 13 seats, while the PPM held seven seats, the RPR six and the Union pour la Démocratie Française—UDF five. Marie-Jeanne was elected to the presidency of the Regional Council. In concurrent elections to the General Council the parties of the left again performed well, increasing their representation from 26 to 29 seats, with right-wing candidates securing 14 seats and independents two. Claude Lise was re-elected President of the General Council.

Martinique was adversely affected by industrial action in 1998 and 1999, with strikes occurring among banana- and automobile-sector workers. The crisis in the banana industry was caused by falling prices in the European market; however, the two-month strike was ended in January 1999, when a pay agreement was reached. There was further conflict in the sector in October, however, when, prior to a two-day visit by French Prime Minister Lionel Jospin, banana producers occupied the headquarters of the French naval forces for several days, demanding the disbursement of exceptional aid to compensate for the adverse effect on their industry of a dramatic decline in prices on the European market. Marie-Jeanne, who was opposed to the limited nature of the Government's plans for institutional reform, refused to participate in the events organized for Jospin's visit. The Prime Minister announced an emergency plan for the banana sector and, while attending a conference on regional co-operation, agreed, in principle, to a proposal for greater autonomy for the local authorities in conducting relations with neighbouring countries and territories. The dispute at the Toyota motor company, where workers were demanding substantial pay increases and a reduction in working hours, lasted five months and involved secondary action and blockades by trade unionists, but was eventually settled in November 1999.

The issue of Martinique's constitutional status also arose in 1999, following a series of meetings between the Presidents of the Regional Councils of Martinique, Guadeloupe and French Guiana. In December Marie-Jeanne co-signed a declaration, stating the intention of the three Presidents to propose, to the French Government, legislative and constitutional amendments aimed at creating a new status of 'overseas region'. The declaration and subsequent announcements by Marie-Jeanne and his counterparts were dismissed by Jean-Jack Queyranne, Secretary of State for Overseas Affairs, in February 2000 as unconstitutional and exceeding the mandate of the politicians responsible. However, in May a number of proposals, including the extension of the Departments' powers in areas such as regional co-operation, were provisionally accepted by the French National Assembly; a modified version of the proposals was subsequently adopted, by a narrow margin, by the French Senate. In November the National Assembly approved the proposals and in December they were ratified by the Constitutional Council. At a referendum held in September, Martinique voted overwhelmingly in favour (91%) of reducing the presidential mandate from seven to five years.

At municipal elections held in March 2001 the PPM retained control of the majority of municipalities (including Fort-de-France, where Aimé Césaire, retiring as mayor after 56 years, was succeeded by a fellow PPM member, Serge Letchimy, who defeated Alfred Marie-Jeanne). In the concurrently-held election to the General Council, Claude Lise was re-elected as President.

Economy

PHILLIP WEARNE

Revised for this edition by the editorial staff

Like Guadeloupe, Martinique's economy is closely tied to that of France. Aid and subsidies, in various forms, are necessary to balance a huge deficit between visible exports and imports. In 1999 the trade deficit was 8,890.5m. French francs, with export earnings worth only 16.2% of the total value of imports. Some 45.1% of exports in 1997 went to France. The next largest market was Guadeloupe, with the European Union (EU) countries of Belgium, Luxembourg and the United Kingdom also significant purchasers. The main exports were bananas, refined petroleum products and rum. France was also the single largest source of imports, accounting for 62.1% of their total value in 1997. The bulk of the remainder came from other members of the EU, the USA and Venezuela. The principal imports in 1995 included machinery and transport equipment, food and live animals, manufactured goods, chemicals and mineral fuels. Agriculture was the primary economic activity, with sugar, bananas, fruit, vegetables and some flowers being the principal crops. There was some light industry, the largest export being rum. Tourism was a major source of convertible-currency revenue. Consumer prices increased by an average 0.4% in 1999.

As in French Guiana and Guadeloupe, the single European market, which took effect in 1993, neutralized some of the privileges that Martinique enjoyed as an overseas department. Thereafter the island was treated as a disadvantaged region of Europe.

AGRICULTURE

The sugar industry was Martinique's original source of prosperity. However, it was dealt a devastating blow by the volcanic eruption of Mont Pelée in 1902. Bananas then became the major export. Banana exports grew steadily in the late 1980s to reach 215,980 metric tons by 1990. In the early and mid-1990s the volume of exports fluctuated owing to variable climatic conditions. A significant decline in prices on the European market, and an ongoing dispute between the USA and four Latin American countries and the EU over the latter's banana import regime also threatened Martinique's banana-growing sector. Production recovered thereafter, increasing to 210,000 tons in 1996, according to estimates by the UN's Food and Agriculture Organization (FAO), and to 321,000 tons in 2000. In 1997 bananas contributed 36.9% of total export revenues.

Sugarcane remained the island's major agricultural crop, despite low world prices, under-investment and the diversification of some cane-growing land to the cultivation of other crops. By 1982 local production proved insufficient to supply domestic demand, causing a reversal of the policy of neglect and a dramatic increase in the cane harvest, to 217,000 metric tons by 1989. In the 1990s production declined, to 187,705 tons in 1991, and then recovered again, to reach 212,000 tons in 1996. In 2000 the cane harvest totalled an estimated 189,000 tons. Output of sugar fluctuated accordingly. Local consumption accounted for virtually all the harvest, with about one-third going on the production of rum, the island's major manufactured product. Output of rum historically varied according to the supply of sugar, but in the early 1990s fell precipitously. In 1990 it declined by almost 20%, to 84,828 hl (hectolitres). Production recovered to 78,000 hl in 1994, but had declined to 69,458 hl by 1998, and in 1997 rum sales accounted for 10.0% of export earnings.

In the 1980s agricultural diversification became official government policy and it contributed to efforts to increase export earnings and reduce the cost of food imports. Pineapples, avocados and aubergines became significant export crops, and flowers and citrus fruits, particularly limes, were also shipped abroad. The most dramatic growth was in the cultivation of melons and pineapples, output of the former doubling in 1990 to 2,390 metric tons, and production of the latter rising more than 20% to some 16,000 tons, compared to the previous year's totals. However, only melon exports were having a major economic impact by 1994, when 1,587 tons were shipped overseas; however, exports of melons decreased to some 1,091 tons in 1998. Some 265 tons of taro, 11 tons of pineapples, 21 tons of avocados and 882,000 cut flowers were exported in 1998.

With less land available for pasture than on Guadeloupe, a significant proportion of the island's meat and dairy products had to be imported, although the local administration claimed some success in boosting livestock production. In 2000, according to FAO estimates, some 3,000 metric tons of beef, 2,000 metric tons of pig meat and 2,000 metric tons of cows' milk were produced. This was produced from a livestock population put at 30,000 cattle, 42,000 sheep, 33,000 pigs and 22,000 goats in September of that year. The total fishing catch declined sharply in the late 1980s, to only 3,314 tons in 1989, but increased to 5,555 tons in 1998. The absence of a full marketing structure was cited as the main obstacle to further development of the sector.

INDUSTRY

Industry accounted for about 15.5% of gross domestic product (GDP) in 1992 and employed about 4.3% of the work-force in 1998, but the sector remained underdeveloped. Industry's total contribution to the economy was somewhat inflated by the petroleum refinery, which registered an output of 733,274 metric tons of liquid fuels in 1991, processing crude petroleum imported from Venezuela, Trinidad and Tobago and even Saudi Arabia. By 1997 exports of refined petroleum products accounted for 16.0% of the total value of exports. Energy was derived mainly from mineral fuels, imports of which accounted for 7.5% of the total value of imports in 1995. Martinique generated 1,078m. kWh of energy in 1995.

Other industrial activity was generally concentrated on food and drink processing, in particular fish and fruit canning, rum distillation, soft-drink manufacture and sugar refining. Some 45,586 hl of rum were exported in 1998 (compared with 53,324 hl in 1991); this decreased to 47,200 hl in 1999. The island did, however, boast a polyethelyne plant and a cement factory. The latter produced an estimated 233,600 metric tons of cement in 1998, virtually all of which was used locally. Martinique also boasted some small wood-furniture manufacturers, construction material producers and a paper-carton outlet.

TOURISM

Martinique's tourist attractions are its beaches and coastal scenery, its mountainous interior and the historic towns of Fort-de-France and St Pierre. In the early 1990s tourism remained one of the most important sources of foreign exchange, with a steady growth in numbers of arrivals. Most visitors were from Europe, although proportionally the number of visitors from the USA grew most. The hotel industry experienced rapid expan-sion, with the total number of rooms offered rising from 3,735 in 1991 to 4,880 by 1998. In that year some 80% of hotel clients were from metropolitan France, a further 3.1% from the USA, and 5.0% from European countries other than France. In 1999 the island welcomed 564,303 tourists. Tourist receipts in 1998 totalled an estimated 1,580.4m. French francs. The numbers of arrivals on cruise ships and same-day visitors remained fairly static in the 1990s and totalled an estimated 382,086 in 1999.

EMPLOYMENT

As in Guadeloupe, relatively high wages—tied to those of metro-politan France—coupled with the high levels of aid and imports from France served to restrict economic development. The des-cendants of the original colonial settlers, or *békés*, were rein-forced professionals, whose spending power, together with that of the foreign tourists, simply encouraged the development of the services sector and import businesses. On the other hand, the native black population was reinforced by illegal immigrants from Saint Lucia, Dominica and Haiti.

Thus, as the more labour-intensive agricultural sector con-tracted, emphasis on the services sector increased and unem-ployment rose, particularly as more young people entered the job market from the early 1970s. The lack of job prospects encouraged extensive emigration, to France and other Carib-bean islands. By 1993 the level of this exodus was estimated at about 18,000 per year of the island's estimated 372,000 population, most of the emigrants being under 25 years of age. Some 29.5% of the labour force was unemployed in December 1998.

Statistical Survey

Sources: Institut national de la statistique et des études économiques (INSEE), Service Régional de Martinique, Centre Delgrès, blvd de la Pointe des Sables, Les Hauts de Dillon, BP 641, 97262 Fort-de-France Cédex; tel. 60-73-60; Ministère des départements et territoires d'outre-mer, 27 rue Oudinot, 75700 Paris 07 SP; tel. 1-53-69-20-00; fax 1-43-06-60-30; internet www.outre-mer.gouv.fr.

AREA AND POPULATION

Area: 1,100 sq km (424.7 sq miles).

Population: 326,717 (males 158,415; females 168,302) at census of 9 March 1982; 359,579 (males 173,878; females 185,701) at census of 15 March 1990; 381,427 at census of 8 March 1999.

Density (at 1999 census): 346.8 per sq km.

Principal Towns (at 1999 census): Fort-de-France (capital) 94,049; Le Lamentin 35,460; Le Robert 21,240; Schoelcher 20,845; Sainte-Marie 20,098; Le François 18,559; Saint-Joseph 15,785; Ducos 15,240.

Births, Marriages and Deaths (1997, provisional figures): Regis-tered live births 5,735 (birth rate 15.2 per 1,000); Registered mar-riages 1,548 (marriage rate 4.1 per 1,000); Registered deaths 2,403 (death rate 6.4 per 1,000).

Expectation of Life (years at birth, 1997): 78.1 (males 74.9; fem-ales 81.3).

Economically Active Population (persons aged 15 years and over, 1998): Agriculture and fishing 7,650; Industry 7,103; Construc-tion and public works 10,405; Trade 16,196; Transport 4,383; Finan-cial services and real estate 3,354; Business services 8,376; Public services 14,179; Education 14,991; Health and social security 10,676; Administrative services 18,742; Total employed 116,055 (males 62,198; females 53,857); Unemployed 48,537 (males 22,628; females 25,909); Total labour force 164,592 (males 84,826; females 79,766). *1999:* Total employed 119,900; Unemployed 46,900; Total labour force 166,800.

AGRICULTURE, ETC.

Principal Crops (FAO estimates, '000 metric tons, 2000: Yams 5; Sweet potatoes 1; Other roots and tubers 12; Sugar cane 189; Bananas 321; Plantains 13; Pineapples 20; Oranges 1; Source: FAO.

Livestock (FAO estimates, '000 head, year ending September 2000): Cattle 30; Sheep 42; Pigs 33; Goats 22. Source: FAO.

Livestock Products (FAO estimates, '000 metric tons, 2000): Beef and veal 3; Pig meat 2; Poultry meat 1; Cows' milk 2; Hen eggs 2. Source: FAO.

Forestry: Roundwood removals ('000 cu m, excluding bark, 1999): Sawlogs, veneer logs and logs for sleepers 2; Fuel wood 10; Total 12. Source: FAO, *Yearbook of Forest Products.*

Fishing (metric tons, live weight, 1998, estimates): Capture 5,500 (Common dolphinfish 420, Atlantic bonito 1,030, Cero 420, Blackfin tuna 910, Marine fishes 2,397); Aquaculture 55; Total catch 5,555. Source: FAO, *Yearbook of Fishery Statistics.*

MINING

Production (1995, '000 metric tons): Pumice 130.0. Source: UN, *Industrial Commodity Statistics Yearbook.*

INDUSTRY

Production (1996, '000 metric tons, unless otherwise indicated): Pineapple juice 3.2 (1994); Canned or bottled pineapples 18.4 (1994); Raw sugar 7 (1997); Rum ('000 hl) 78 (1994); Motor spirit (petrol) 151 (estimate); Kerosene 132; Gas-diesel (distillate fuel) oils 158; Residual fuel oils 275; Liquefied petroleum gas 21; Cement 225 (estimate); Electric energy (million kWh) 1,078 (1997). Source: UN, *Industrial Commodity Statistics Yearbook.*

1996: Rum 64,985 hl.
1997: Rum 70,040 hl.
1998: Raw sugar 7,000 metric tons; Rum 69,458 hl; Cement 233,600 metric tons.

FINANCE

Currency and Exchange Rates: French currency is used (see French Guiana).

Budget (million French francs, 1998): *State budget:* Revenue 4,757, Expenditure 8,309; *Regional budget:* Revenue: 1,876, Expenditure 1,921; *Departmental budget:* Revenue 2,439, Expenditure 2,420.

Money Supply (million French francs at 31 December 1998): Cur-rency outside banks 924; Demand deposits at banks 6,330; Total money 7,254.

Cost of Living (Consumer Price Index; base: 1990 = 100): 118.5 in 1997; 120.0 in 1998; 120.5 in 1999. Source: UN, *Monthly Bulletin of Statistics.*

Expenditure on the Gross Domestic Product (million French francs at current prices, 1994): Government final consumption expenditure 6,962; Private final consumption expenditure 20,133; Increase in stocks 20; Gross fixed capital formation 5,102; *Total domestic expenditure* 32,217; Exports of goods and services 1,439; *Less* Imports of goods and services 9,150; *GDP in purchasers' values* 24,506.

Gross Domestic Product by Economic Activity (million French francs at current prices, 1992): Agriculture, hunting, forestry and fishing 1,106.3; Mining, quarrying and manufacturing 1,770.6; Electricity, gas and water 483.6; Construction 1,145.3; Trade, restaurants and hotels 4,022.1; Transport, storage and communications 1,427.6; Finance, insurance, real estate and business services 2,590.1; Government services 5,416.0; Other community, social and personal services 3,576.4; Other services 330.5; *Sub-total* 21,868.5; Import duties 791.0; Value-added tax 640.9; *Less* Imputed bank service charge 1,207.1; *GDP in purchasers' values* 22,093.4. Source UN, *National Accounts Statistics*.

EXTERNAL TRADE

Principal Commodities: *Imports c.i.f.* (US $ million, 1995): Food and live animals 319.6 (Meat and meat preparations 82.8, Dairy products and birds' eggs 53.6, Fish and fish preparations 38.6, Cereals and cereal preparations 45.6, Vegetables and fruit 49.1); Beverages and tobacco 52.0 (Beverages 45.0); Mineral fuels, lubricants, etc. 148.0 (Petroleum and petroleum products 146.2); Chemicals and related products 189.5 (Medicinal and pharmaceutical products 83.9); Basic manufactures 260.1 (Paper, paperboard and manufactures 45.1); Machinery and transport equipment 637.6 (Power-generating machinery and equipment 62.8, General industrial machinery, equipment and parts 83.2, Telecommunications and sound equipment 41.1, Road vehicles and parts 240.7, Ships and boats 50.3); Miscellaneous manufactured articles 288.5 (Furniture and parts 46.2, Clothing and accessories, excl. footwear 62.6); Total (incl. others) 1,969.8. Source: UN, *International Trade Statistics Yearbook*. *Exports f.o.b.* (million French francs, 1997): Bananas 462.2; Rum 126.7; Flavoured or sweetened water 78.8; Refined petroleum products 201.9; Yachts and sports boats 74.4; Total (incl. others) 1,263.3.

1997 (million French francs): *Imports:* 9,947.0; *Exports:* 1,239.0. *1998* (million French francs): *Imports:* 10,046.8; *Exports:* 1,701.4. *1999* (million French francs): *Imports:* 10,605.6; *Exports:* 1,715.1.

Source: Direction Générale des Douanes.

Principal Trading Partners (million French francs, 1997): *Imports c.i.f.:* France (metropolitan) 6,178.9; Germany 352.0; Italy 350.1; Japan 180.3; Trinidad and Tobago 159.6; United Kingdom 108.3; USA 263.6; Venezuela 607.8; Total (incl. others) 9,957.5. *Exports f.o.b.:* Belgium-Luxembourg 76.4; France (metropolitan) 569.7; French Guiana 54.8; Guadeloupe 357.2; United Kingdom 110.5; Total (incl. others) 1,263.3.

TRANSPORT

Road Traffic ('000 motor vehicles in use, 1995): Passenger cars 95.0; Commercial vehicles 21.5. Source: UN, *Statistical Yearbook*.

Shipping *Merchant Fleet* (vessels registered '000 grt at 31 December, 1992): 1. Source: Lloyd's Register of Shipping. *International Sea-borne Traffic* (1999, provisional): Goods loaded 809,000 metric tons; Goods unloaded 1,927,000 metric tons. Source: Direction Départementale de l'Équipement.

Civil Aviation (1998): Passengers carried 1,821,063; Freight carried 16,166 metric tons. Source: Chambre de Commerce et d'Industrie de la Martinique.

TOURISM

Tourist Arrivals (excl. same-day visitors and cruise-ship arrivals): 513,231 in 1997; 548,766 in 1998; 564,303 in 1999.

Tourist Arrivals by Country (excl. same-day visitors and cruise-ship arrivals, 1998): France 439,702, USA 16,820, Canada 3,978; Total (incl. others) 548,766.

Receipts from Tourism (US $ million): 384 in 1995; 382 in 1996; 400 in 1997. Source: World Tourism Organization, *Yearbook of Tourism Statistics*.
1998 (million French francs): 1,580.4.

COMMUNICATIONS MEDIA

Radio Receivers ('000 in use) 82 in 1997; **Television Receivers** ('000 in use) 66 in 1997; **Telephones** ('000 main lines in use) 170 in 1997; **Telefax Stations** (number in use) 5,200 in 1997; **Mobile Cellular Telephones** (subscribers) 15,000 in 1997; **Daily Newspaper** 1 (estimate) in 1996 (estimated average circulation 32,000 copies). Sources: UNESCO, *Statistical Yearbook*; UN, *Statistical Yearbook*.

EDUCATION

Pre-primary (1995/96): 86 institutions; 660 teachers; (1998/99) 19,766 students (18,841 state, 925 private).

Primary* (1999/2000): 273 institutions; 3,266 teachers (3,026 state, 240 private); 54,327 students.

Secondary (1999/2000): 76 institutions; 4,227 teachers (3,897 state, 330 private); 48,893 students.

Vocational (1998/99): 15 institutions (9 state, 6 private); 7,661 students (7,101 state, 560 private).

Higher (1999/2000): 11,199 students (Université Antilles-Guyane).
* Includes pre-primary.

Source: UNESCO, *Statistical Yearbook*, and Académie de la Martinique.

Directory

The Government
(August 2001)

Prefect: MICHEL CADOT, Préfecture, 82 rue Victor Sévère, BP 647, 97200 Fort-de-France Cédex; tel. 39-36-00; fax 71-40-29.

President of the General Council: CLAUDE LISE (PPM), Conseil Général de la Martinique, 20 ave des Caraïbes, BP 679, 97264 Fort-de-France Cédex; tel. 55-26-00; fax 73-59-32; internet www.cg972.fr.

Deputies to the French National Assembly: ANICET TURINAY (RPR), PIERRE PETIT (RPR), CAMILLE DARSIÈRES (PPM), ALFRED MARIE-JEANNE (MIM).

Representatives to the French Senate: CLAUDE LISE (PPM), RODOLPHE DÉSIRÉ (PPM).

REGIONAL COUNCIL
Hôtel de Région, rue Gaston Deferre, BP 601, 97200 Fort-de-France Cédex; tel. 59-63-00; fax 72-68-10; e-mail Crg72 .comext@wanadoo.fr; internet www.cr-martinique.fr.

President: ALFRED MARIE-JEANNE (MIM).

Election, 15 March 1998

	Seats
Mouvement Indépendantiste Martiniquais (MIM) . .	13
Parti Progressiste Martiniquais (PPM).	7
Rassemblement pour la République (RPR)	6
Union pour la Démocratie Française (UDF)* . . .	5
Parti Martiniquais Socialiste (PMS)	3
Others†	7
Total	**41**

* Re-established as the Forces Martiniquaises de Progrès in October 1998.

† Three of those elected were candidates of the right.

Political Organizations

Fédération Socialiste de la Martinique (FSM): Cité la Meynard, 97200 Fort-de-France; tel. 75-53-28; local branch of the **Parti Socialiste (PS)**; Sec.-Gen. JEAN CRUSOL.

Forces Martiniquaises de Progrès: f. 1998 to replace the local branch of the Union pour la Démocratie Française.

Groupe Révolution Socialiste (GRS): 97200 Fort-de-France; tel. 70-36-49; f. 1973; Trotskyist; Leader GILBERT PAGO.

Mouvement Indépendantiste Martiniquais (MIM): Fort-de-France; f. 1978; pro-independence party; First Sec. ALFRED MARIE-JEANNE.

Parti Communiste Martiniquais (PCM): Fort-de-France; f. 1920; affiliated to French Communist Party until 1957; Leader GEORGES ERICHOT.

Parti Martiniquais Socialiste (PMS): Fort-de-France; Pres. LOUIS JOSEPH DOGUÉ; Sec. ERNEST WAN AJOUHU.

Parti Progressiste Martiniquais (PPM): Fort-de-France; tel. 71-86-83; f. 1957; left-wing; Pres. AIMÉ CÉSAIRE; Sec.-Gen. CAMILLE DARSIÈRES.

Rassemblement pour la République (RPR): 97205 Fort-de-France; Gaullist.

Judicial System

Cour d'Appel de Fort-de-France: Fort-de-France; tel. 70-62-62; fax 63-52-13; e-mail ca-fort-de-france@justice.fr; highest court of appeal for Martinique and French Guiana; First Pres. CHRISTIAN AUDOUARD; Procurator-Gen. ROBERT FINIELZ.

There are two Tribunaux de Grande Instance, at Fort-de-France and Cayenne (French Guiana), and three Tribunaux d'Instance (two in Fort-de-France and one in Cayenne).

Religion

The majority of the population belong to the Roman Catholic Church.

CHRISTIANITY
The Roman Catholic Church

Martinique comprises the single archdiocese of Fort-de-France, with an estimated 297,515 adherents (some 78% of the total population) at 31 December 1999. The Archbishop participates in the Antilles Episcopal Conference, currently based in Port of Spain, Trinidad and Tobago.

Archbishop of Fort-de-France: Most Rev. MAURICE MARIE-SAINTE, Archevêché, 5–7 rue du Révérend Père Pinchon, BP 586, 97207 Fort-de-France Cédex; tel. 63-70-70; fax 63-75-21; e-mail diocesef@ais.mq.

Other Churches

Among the denominations active in Martinique are the Assembly of God, the Evangelical Church of the Nazarene and the Seventh-day Adventist Church.

The Press

Antilla: BP 46, Lamentin; tel. 75-48-68; fax 75-58-46; e-mail antilla.hebdo@wanadoo.fr; weekly; Dir ALFRED FORTUNE.

Aujourd'hui Dimanche: Presbytère de Bellevue, Fort-de-France; tel. 71-48-97; weekly; Dir Père GAUTHIER; circ. 12,000.

Carib Hebdo: 97200 Fort-de-France; f. 1989; Dir GISÈLE DE LA FARGUE.

Combat Ouvrier: Fort-de-France; weekly; Dir M. G. BEAUJOUR.

France-Antilles: pl. Stalingrad, 97200 Fort-de-France; tel. 59-08-83; fax 60-29-96; f. 1964; daily; Dir HENRI MERLE; circ. 30,000 (Martinique edition).

Justice: rue Andrè Aliker, 97200 Fort-de-France; tel. 71-86-83; weekly; organ of the PPM; Dir G. THIMOTÉE; circ. 8,000.

Le Naif: Fort-de-France; weekly; Dir R. LAOUCHEZ.

Le Progressiste: Fort-de-France; weekly; organ of the PPM; Dir PAUL GABOURG; circ. 13,000.

Révolution Socialiste: BP 1031, 97200 Fort-de-France; tel. 70-36-49; f. 1973; weekly; organ of the GRS; Dir PHILIPPE PIERRE CHARLES; circ. 2,500.

Télé Sept Jours: rond-point du Vietnam Héroïque, 97200 Fort-de-France; tel. 63-75-49; weekly.

Broadcasting and Communications

BROADCASTING

Réseau France Outre-mer (RFO): La Clairère, BP 662, 97263 Fort-de-France; tel. 59-52-00; fax 63-29-88; internet www.rfo.fr; fmrly Société Nationale de Radio-Télévision Française d'Outre-mer, renamed as above 1998; broadcasts 24 hours of radio programmes daily and 37 hours of television programmes weekly; Pres. ANDRÉ-MICHEL BESSE; Regional Dir MARIJOSÉ ALIE; Editor-in-Chief GÉRARD LE MOAL.

Radio

There are some 40 licensed private FM radio stations.

Radio Caraïbe International (RCI): 2 blvd de la Marne, 97200 Fort-de-France Cédex; tel. 63-98-70; fax 63-26-59; internet www.fwinet.com/rci.htm; commercial station broadcasting 24 hours daily; Dir YANN DUVAL.

Television

ATV Antilles Télévision: 28 rue Arawaks, 97200 Fort de France; tel. 75-44-44; fax 75-55-65; commercial station.

Canal Antilles: Centre Commerciale la Galléria, 97232 Le Lamentin; tel. 50-57-87; private commercial station.

TCI Martinique: Immeuble RCI/TCI, Zone Industrielle, 92232 Le Lamentin; tel. 51-06-06; fax 51-85-62; private commercial station.

Finance

(cap. = capital; res = reserves; dep. = deposits;
m. = million; brs = branches; amounts in French francs)

BANKING

Central Bank

Institut d'Emission des Départements d'Outre-mer: blvd du Général de Gaulle, BP 512, 97206 Fort-de-France Cédex; tel. 59-44-00; fax 59-44-04.

Major Commercial Banks

Banque des Antilles Françaises: 28–34 rue Lamartine, BP 582, 97207 Fort-de-France Cédéx; tel. 73-93-44; fax 63-58-94; f. 1853; cap. 32.6m., res 42.9m., dep. 2,243.6m. (Dec. 1996); Dir. ALBERT CLERMONT.

Banque Française Commerciale: BP 986, 97425 Fort-de-France; tel. 63-82-57; fax 70-51-15; Man. JACQUES FACHON.

BNP Paribas, SA: 72 ave des Caraïbes, 97200 Fort-de-France; tel. 59-46-00; fax 63-71-42; Dir JEAN PASCAL DUMANS; 12 further brs in Martinique.

BRED Banque Populaire: 5 Place Monseigneur Romero, 97200 Fort-de-France; tel. 63-77-63; internet www.bred.fr; Chair. STEVE GENTILI.

Crédit Agricole: rue Case Nègre—Place d'Armes, 97232 Le Lamentin Cédex 2; tel. 66-59-39; fax 66-59-67; internet www.credit-agricole.fr; Chair MARC BUÉ.

Crédit Martiniquais: 17 rue de la Liberté, Fort-de-France; tel. 59-93-00; fax 60-29-30; f. 1922; associated since 1987 with Chase Manhattan Bank (USA) and, since 1990, with Mutuelles du Mans Vie (France); cap. 185.4m. (1998); Administrator ALAIN DENNHARDT; 10 brs.

Société Générale de Banque aux Antilles: 19 rue de la Liberté, BP 408, 97200 Fort-de-France; tel. 71-69-83; f. 1979; cap. 15m.; Dir MICHEL SAMOUR.

INSURANCE

Cie Antillaise d'Assurances: 19 rue de la Liberté, 97205 Fort-de-France; tel. 73-04-50.

Caraïbe Assurances: 11 rue Victor Hugo, BP 210, 97202 Fort-de-France; tel. 63-92-29; fax 63-19-79.

Groupement Français d'Assurances Caraïbes (GFA Caraïbes): 46–48 rue Ernest Desproges, 97205 Fort-de-France; tel. 59-04-04; fax 73-19-72.

La Nationale (GAN): 30 blvd Général de Gaulle, BP 185, Fort-de-France; tel. 71-30-07; Reps MARCEL BOULLANGER, ROGER BOULLANGER.

Le Secours: 74 ave Duparquet, 97200 Fort-de-France; tel. 70-03-79; Dir Y. ANGANI.

Trade and Industry

DEVELOPMENT ORGANIZATIONS

Agence pour le Développement Economique de la Martinique: Fort-de-France; tel. 73-45-81; fax 72-41-38; f. 1979; promotion of industry.

Agence Française de Développement (AFD): 12 blvd du Général de Gaulle, BP 804, 97244 Fort-de-France Cédex; tel. 59-44-73; fax 59-44-88; fmrly Caisse Française de Développement; Dir JACQUES ALBUGUES; Regional Man. XAVIER BLANCHARD.

Bureau du Développement Economique: Préfecture, 97262 Fort-de-France; tel. 39-36-00; fax 71-40-29; research, documentation and technical and administrative advice on investment in industry and commerce; Chief VICTOR VÉLAIDOMESTRY.

Société de Crédit pour le Développement de la Martinique (SODEMA): 12 blvd du Général de Gaulle, BP 575, 97242 Fort-de-France Cédex; tel. 72-87-72; fax 72-87-70; e-mail sodema@compuserve.com; f. 1970; cap. 25m. frs; medium- and long-term finance; Dir-Gen. JACKIE BATHANY.

Société de Développement Régional Antilles-Guyane (SODERAG): 111–113 rue Ernest Desproges, BP 450, 97205 Fort-de-France Cédex; tel. 59-71-00; fax 63-38-88; Dir-Gen. FULVIO MAZZEO; Sec.-Gen. OLYMPE FRANCIL.

CHAMBERS OF COMMERCE

Chambre d'Agriculture: pl. d'Armes, BP 312, 97286 Le Lamentin; tel. 51-75-75; fax 51-93-42; Pres. GUY OVIDE-ETIENNE.

Chambre de Commerce et d'Industrie de la Martinique: 50–54 rue Ernest Desproges, BP 478, 97241 Fort-de-France; tel. 55-28-00; fax 60-66-68; e-mail ccim.doi@martinique.cci.fr; internet www.martinique.cci.fr; f. 1907; Pres. JEAN-CLAUDE LUBIN; Dir-Gen. FERNAND LERYCHARD.

Chambre des Métiers de la Martinique: 2 rue du Temple, Morne Tartenson, BP 1194, 97200 Fort-de-France; tel. 71-32-22; fax 70-47-30; f. 1970; Pres. CHRISTIAN CAYOL; 8,000 mems.

EMPLOYERS' ORGANIZATIONS

Groupement de Producteurs d'Ananas de la Martinique: Fort-de-France; f. 1967; Pres. C. DE GRYSE.

Ordre des Médecins de la Martinique: 80 rue de la République, 97200 Fort-de-France; tel. 63-27-01; Pres. Dr RENÉ LEGENDRI.

Ordre des Pharmaciens de la Martinique: BP 587, 97207 Fort-de-France Cédex; tel. 52-23-67; fax 52-20-92.

Société Coopérative d'Intérêt Collectif Agricole Bananière de la Martinique (SICABAM): Domaine de Montgéralde, La Dillon, 97200 Fort-de-France; f. 1961; Pres. ALEX ASSIER DE POMPIGNAN; Dir GÉRARD BALLY; 1,000 mems.

Syndicat des Distilleries Agricoles: Fort-de-France; tel. 71-25-46.

Syndicat des Producteurs de Rhum Agricole: La Dillon, 97200 Fort-de-France.

Union Départementale des Coopératives Agricoles de la Martinique: Fort-de-France; Pres. M. URSULET.

MAJOR COMPANIES

Biometal, SA: Usine de Robert, 97231 Le Robert; tel. 65-14-44; fax 65-10-01; f. 1979; manufacture of steel products; Pres. and Dir.-Gen. LIONEL DE LAGUARIGUE; 70 employees.

Biscuiterie Girard/Pomagel: Z. I. de la Lézarde, 97232 Le Lamentin; tel. 51-15-43; fax 51-15-11; bakery products; Man. C. MEDLOCK.

Crocquet, SA: BP 579, 97297 Fort-de-France; tel. and fax 63-54-54; f. 1988; sale of motor vehicles; Man. Dir PHILIPPE DESPOINTES; 143 employees.

Distillerie Dillon, SA: BP 212, Fort-de-France; tel. 75-20-20; fax 75-30-33; f. 1967; rum producer; Man. PATRICK HÉRY; 50 employees.

Esso Antilles Guyane, SA: pl. d'Armes, BP 272, 97285 Le Lamentin Cédex 2; tel. 66-90-60; fax 51-17-87; f. 1965; distribution of petroleum and petroleum products; Pres. JEAN FRANÇOIS DUSSOULIER; 35 employees.

Etablissements Bellonie Bourdillon: BP 10, Génipa Rivière Salée; tel. 56-82-82; fax 56-82-83; f. 1919; rum producer, markets other spirits and wines; Man. M. RANCEZ; 161 employees.

Etablissements Laurent de Laguarigue de Survilliers, SA: Centre Commercial de Dillon, Fort-de-France; producer of construction materials; Pres. JOSÉ DE LAGUARIGUE DE SURVILLIERS.

Etablissements Marsan, SA: 87 rue Lamartine, Fort-de-France; manufacturer of durable goods; Pres. RAPHAEL MARSAN, Jr.

Martinique International Paper Co, SA: Z. I., BP 184, Fort-de-France; pulp mills; subsidiary of International Paper Co, New York (USA).

Prochimie, SA: BP 233, 97284 Le Lamentin Cédex; tel. 50-32-82; fax 50-22-48; f. 1972; domestic and sanitary products and paper; Dir MARCEL PLISSONNEAU DUQUENE; 50 employees.

Royal, SA: Gros Morne; tel. 67-51-23; fax 67-67-56; f. 1934; food processing, fruit juices and preserves; Man. ANDRÉ TALMANN; 70 employees.

SAEM PSRM Le Galion: Usine Le Galion, Trinit,; tel. 58-20-65; fax 58-34-40; f. 1984; sugar refinery and distillery; Man. J. M. TOTO; 91 employees.

SCAR, SA: Z. A. L'Espérance, 97215 Rivière Salée; tel. 68-14-42; fax 68-21-03; f. 1976; medical and surgical products; Dir FRANCK LITTÉE; 9 employees.

Siapoc, SA: Usine de Bassignac, Trinité; tel. 58-21-18; fax 58-64-25; f. 1965; paints; Man. BRUNO MENCE; 65 employees.

SISAL, SA: Z. I. de Cocottes, 97224 Ducos; tel. 56-32-32; fax 56-33-19; f. 1983; furniture manufacturer; Dir ALAIN SYLVIUS; 35 employees.

SMPA: Z. I., place d'Armes, 97232 Le Lamentin; tel. 51-57-11; fax 51-70-43; f. 1987; industrial bakery products and frozen foods; Man. O. LENAIRE; 49 employees.

Socara, SARL: 2 ave des Arawaks, Fort-de-France; tel. 75-04-04; fax 75-04-76; f. 1948; fruit juices, wines, beer, spirits; Dir IVAN DE QUATREBARBES; 50 employees.

Société Nouvelle Antillaise de Construction et d'Equipment SARL (SNACE): Z. I. de la Lézarde, BP 432, 97232 Le Lamentin; tel. 51-17-64; fax 51-46-75; f. 1986 (formerly Casimir Petit et Cie); aluminium and wood products for the construction industry; Gen. Man. BÉRNARD DUVAL; 35 employees.

SOFECA, SA: Quartier Californie, 97232 Le Lamentin; tel. 50-30-00; fax 50-03-11; f. 1977; refrigeration, air-conditioning, solar heating, catering equipment; Man. CHARLES BLANCANEAUX; 27 employees.

TRADE UNIONS

Centrale Démocratique Martiniquaise des Travailleurs: BP 21, 97201 Fort-de-France; tel. 70-19-86; fax 71-32-25; Sec.-Gen. CATHERINE FELIX.

Confédération Générale des Travailleurs de la Martinique (1936): Maison des Syndicats, porte no 14, Jardin Desclieux, 97200 Fort-de-France; tel. 60-45-21; f. 1936; affiliated to World Federation of Trade Unions; Sec.-Gen. LUC BERNABÉ; *c.* 12,000 mems.

Syndicat des Enseignants de la Martinique: 31 rue Perrinon, 97200 Fort-de-France; tel. 70-24-52; fax 63-74-36; e-mail se-gen-972@cgit.com.

Union Départementale des Syndicats—FO: BP 1114, 97248 Fort-de-France Cédex; affiliated to International Confederation of Free Trade Unions; Sec.-Gen. ALBERT SABEL; *c.* 2,000 mems.

Transport

RAILWAYS

There are no railways in Martinique.

ROADS

There were 2,077 km of roads in 1998, of which 261 km were motorways and first-class roads.

SHIPPING

Direction des Concessions Services Portuaires: Quai de l'Hydro Base, BP 782, 97244 Fort-de-France Cédex; tel. 59-00-00; fax 71-35-73; port services management; Dir FRANTZ THODIARD; Operations Man. VICTOR ELISTACHE.

Direction Départementale des Affaires Maritimes: blvd Chevalier de Sainte-Marthe, BP 620, 97261 Fort-de-France Cédex; tel. 71-90-05; fax 63-67-30; Dir FRANÇOIS NIHOUL.

Alcoa Steamship Co, Alpine Line, Agdwa Line, Delta Line, Raymond Witcomb Co, Moore MacCormack, Eastern Steamship Co: c/o Etablissements Ren, Cottrell, Fort-de-France.

American President Lines: c/o Compagnie d'Agence Multiples Antillaise (CAMA), 44 rue Garnier Pages, 97205 Fort-de-France Cédex; tel. 71-31-00; fax 63-54-40.

CMA-CGM CGM Antilles-Guyane: 8 ave Maurice Bishop, BP 574, 97242 Fort-de-France Cédex; tel. 55-32-05; fax 60-47-84; e-mail fdf.jdurand@cma-cgm.com; internet www.cma-cgm.com; also represents other passenger and freight lines; Dir. JEAN-LUC DURAND.

Compagnie de Navigation Mixte: Immeuble Rocade, La Dillon, BP 1023, 97209 Fort-de-France; Rep. R. M. MICHAUX.

CIVIL AVIATION

Martinique's international airport is at Le Lamentin, 6 km from Fort-de-France. A new terminal was inaugurated in July 1995.

Air Caraïbe: see chapter on Guadeloupe (Civil Aviation).

Tourism

Martinique's tourist attractions are its beaches and coastal scenery, its mountainous interior, and the historic towns of Fort-de-France and Saint Pierre. In 1999 tourist arrivals totalled 564,303. Tourism receipts in 1998 totalled 1,580.4m. French francs. In 1999 there were 122 hotels, with some 6,051 rooms.

Agence Régionale pour le Développement du Tourisme en Martinique: Anse Gouraud, 97233 Schoelcher; tel. 61-61-77; fax 61-22-72.

Chambre Syndicale des Hôtels de Tourisme de la Martinique: Entrée Montgéralde, Route de Chateauboeuf, Fort-de-France; tel. 70-27-80.

Délégation Régionale au Tourisme: 41 rue Gabriel Périé 97200 Fort-de-France; tel. 63-18-61; Dir GILBERT LECURIEUK.

Fédération Martiniquaise des Offices de Tourisme et Syndicats d'Initiative (FMOTSI): Maison du Tourisme Vert, 9 blvd du Général de Gaulle, BP 491, 97207 Fort-de-France Cédex; tel. 63-18-54; fax 70-17-61; f. 1984; Pres. VICTOR GRANDIN.

Office Départemental du Tourisme de la Martinique: 2 rue Ernest Desproges, BP 520, 97206 Fort-de-France; tel. 63-79-60; fax 73-66-93.

Defence

At 1 August 2000 France maintained a military force of about 3,800 in the Antilles. The headquarters is in Fort-de-France.

Education

There is free and compulsory education in government schools for children aged between six and 16 years. In 1999/2000 there were 54,327 pupils in primary education and 48,893 in secondary education. Higher education in law, French language and literature, human sciences, economics, medicine and Creole studies is provided by a branch of the Université Antilles-Guyane. The University as a whole had 11,199 enrolled students in the 1999/2000 academic year. There are two teacher-training institutes and colleges of agriculture, fisheries, hotel management, nursing, midwifery and child care. Separate Academies for Martinique, French Guiana and Guadeloupe were established in January 1997, replacing the single Academy for the Antilles-Guyane, which was based in Fort-de-France.

Bibliography

For works on the Caribbean generally, see Select Bibliography (Books).

'Latin America and the West Indies', in *Historical Periodicals Directory*, Vol. 4. ABC-Clio, 1985.

Butel, R. 'Traditions and Changes in French Atlantic Trade (with West Indies) between 1780 and 1830', in *Renaissance and Modern Studies*, Vol. 30. 1986.

Laguerre, M. S. *Urban Poverty in the Caribbean (French Martinique as a Social Laboratory)*, New York, NY, Palgrave, 1990.

Miles, W. F. S. *Martinique and the French National Elections.* London, Praeger Publrs, 1985.

Elections and Ethnicity in French Martinique: A Paradox in Paradise. New York, NY, Praeger Publrs, 1986.

MEXICO

Area:1,953,162 sq km (754,120 sq miles).

Population (at census of February 2000, preliminary figure): 97,361,711.

Capital: Mexico City, DF (population at census of February 2000, preliminary figure 8,591,309).

Language: Spanish; some local Amerindian dialects are also spoken.

Religion: Predominantly Christianity (90% Roman Catholic).

Climate: Varies with altitude from tropical to arid desert; the central highlands are temperate.

Time: GMT –6 hours; but GMT –7 and GMT –8 hours in western states, and GMT –5 hours in Chetumal.

Public Holidays

2002: 1 January (New Year's Day), 5 February (Constitution Day), 21 March (Birth of Benito Juárez), 29 March–1 April (Easter), 1 May (Labour Day), 5 May (Anniversary of the Battle of Puebla)*, 16 September (Independence Day), 12 October (Discovery of America), 1 November (All Saints' Day)*, 2 November (All Souls' Day)*, 20 November (Anniversary of the Revolution), 12 December (Day of Our Lady of Guadalupe)*, 24–25 December (Christmas).

2003: 1 January (New Year's Day), 5 February (Constitution Day), 21 March (Birth of Benito Juárez)*, 18–21 April (Easter), 1 May (Labour Day), 5 May (Anniversary of the Battle of Puebla)*, 16 September (Independence Day), 12 October (Discovery of America), 1 November (All Saints' Day)*, 2 November (All Souls' Day)*, 20 November (Anniversary of the Revolution) 12 December (Day of Our Lady of Guadalupe)*, 24–25 December (Christmas).

* Widely-celebrated unofficial holidays.

Currency: Mexican nuevo (new) peso; 1,000 new pesos = £75.57 = US $107.91= €121.57 (30 April 2001).

Weights and Measures: The metric system is in force.

Basic Economic Indicators

	1998	1999	2000
Gross domestic product ('000 million new pesos at 1993 prices)	1,449.3	1,505.0	1,609.1
GDP per head (new pesos at 1993 prices)	n.a.	n.a.	16,527.4
Gross domestic product ('000 million new pesos at current prices)	3,848.2	4,588.5	5,432.4
GDP per head (new pesos at current prices)	n.a.	n.a.	55,795.7
Annual growth of real GDP (%)	4.9	3.8	6.9
Government budget (million new pesos at current prices):			
Revenue	488,959	620,135	791,040
Expenditure	556,079	689,921	848,484
Consumer price index (annual average; base: 1995 = 100)	187.9	219.1	239.9
Rate of inflation (annual average, %)	15.9	16.6	9.5
Foreign exchange reserves (US $ million at 31 December)	31,461	30,992	35,142
Imports f.o.b. (US $ million at 31 December)	130,948	148,648	n.a.
Exports f.o.b. (US $ million at 31 December)	117,460	136,391	n.a.
Balance of payments (current account, US $ million)	–15,724	–14,166	n.a.

Gross national product per head measured at purchasing power parity (PPP) (US dollars, converted by the PPP exchange rate, 1999): 7,719.

Total labour force (April–June 1999): 39,751,000.

Unemployment (estimate, 2000): 2.3%.

Total foreign debt (1999): US $166,600m.

Life expectancy (years at birth, 1990–95): 71.2 (males 68.5, females 74.5).

Infant mortality rate (per 1,000 live births, 1998): 28.

Adult population with HIV/AIDS (15–49 years, 1999): 0.29%.

School enrolment ratio (6–17 years, 1996): equivalent to 90%.

Adult literacy rate (15 years and over, 2000): 91% (males 93.1; females 89.1%).

Energy consumption per head (kg of oil equivalent, 1998): 1,552.

Carbon dioxide emissions per head (metric tons, 1997): 4.0.

Passenger motor cars in use (per 1,000 of population, 1999): 100.3.

Radio receivers in use (per 1,000 of population, 1997): 329.

Television receivers in use (per 1,000 of population, 1997): 272.

Personal computers in use (per 1,000 of population, 1999): 44.2.

History

Prof. GEORGE PHILIP

The pattern of Mexican history is quite different to that of the republics of South America. The enduring influences of the remarkably rich Middle American high culture, which existed prior to the arrival of the Spaniards in the 16th century, a bloody civil war in the second decade of the 20th century and Mexico's proximity to the USA have contributed to a distinct national identity. It is likely that the North American Free Trade Agreement (NAFTA) and other economic links will be the most important influence on change in Mexico into the 21st century.

THE SPANISH CONQUEST AND THE FORMATION OF MODERN MEXICO

Between 1519 and 1521 the empire of the Aztec monarch, Moctezuma II, was overthrown by a Spanish conquistador, Hernán Cortés. Following the conquest, enormous numbers of Indians died in epidemics, caused by their lack of immunity to the diseases introduced by the newcomers. However, Indian communities remained in existence in southern and central Mexico. Although there was much intermarriage with Mexicans of European origin, indigenous communities retained a definite identity. Some 10% of today's Mexican population is of indigenous origin and speaks Spanish only as a second language. The Spanish rulers of Mexico established an early form of export economy, based on low wages and an abundance of raw materials. Plundered bullion from the Aztec treasury was followed by a steady flow of new wealth, arising from the discovery of rich underground mineral resources, particularly of silver. Migrants moved to the mines, in the north and centre of the country, and new towns, such as Guanajuato, San Luis Potosí and Zacatecas, were founded. Mexico continued to be a leading supplier of minerals to the world's markets.

By the end of the 18th century Spanish sovereignty extended over large parts of what is now the USA, including Florida, the Louisiana territories (which, at that time, also included the vast Mississippi valley area), Texas, New Mexico, part of Colorado, Arizona, Utah and California. However, in 1800 Spain surrendered Louisiana to France, which sold it to the USA in 1803, and in 1819 Spain ceded Florida to the USA.

Miguel Hidalgo y Costilla, a parish priest, is celebrated as the founder of the nation for his early leadership of the Mexican Revolution in 1810–11. However, the war of independence was bloody and hard-fought, and its lack of early resolution contributed to the emergence of chronic political conflict in post-independence Mexico. The Empire of Mexico, under a former Spanish army commander, Agustín de Iturbide, lasted only until 1823 and in the following year a republican, federal Constitution was adopted. The dictatorial Gen. Antonio López de Santa Ana was President no less than five times between 1833 and 1855 and was usually the real power in the country even when not President. During this period Mexico lost much of its original territory. Texas rebelled against Santa Ana, when he abolished the federal system in 1835; it declared independence in the following year and was annexed by the USA in 1845. Following the Mexican–US War of 1846–47, Mexico ceded, by the Treaty of Guadalupe Hidalgo (1848), what are now New Mexico and parts of Arizona, California, Colorado and Utah to the USA, in exchange for US $15m. and cancellation of its debts. However, the one-half of Mexico's territorial area that was thus lost contained only 1% of the Mexican population.

The Reform movement of 1855, led by Benito Juárez (a Zapotec Indian from Oaxaca), was a reaction against government ineptitude and the privileges of the Roman Catholic Church. A civil war between Juárez's Liberals and the Church's defenders, the Conservatives, from 1858 to 1860, ended in victory for Juárez. However, the Government's revenues were exhausted and in 1861 Juárez suspended payments on Mexico's foreign debts. France, Spain and the United Kingdom, all major creditors, raised a joint force and disembarked troops at Veracruz in 1862. The French carried the fight inland and lost a disastrous battle at Puebla; they returned with reinforcements in the following year and succeeded in occupying Mexico City. The French-sponsored policy of imposing Habsburg rule on Mexico by installing Archduke Maximilian of Austria as Emperor did not survive for long after the French troops withdrew in 1867. Maximilian was captured and executed at Querétaro in June and Juárez returned to power.

A long period of political stability under Gen. Porfirio Díaz commenced in 1876. Díaz effectively ruled Mexico, for most of the time as President, for the next 35 years. Díaz initiated the first of three long periods of Mexican history with a form of rule that was economically effective, but politically corrupt and authoritarian. During the 'Porfiriato' Mexico became safe for outside capital and British and US investment was used to initiate Mexico's first real period of economic development. Many of the grand buildings of Mexico City date from the time of Díaz's rule. Although there clearly was some material progress, most Mexicans remained extremely poor, and racial prejudice reinforced capitalist economics in ensuring that the benefits of growth did not flow very far down the social scale. Meanwhile, some of those who did benefit from the resulting economic progress resented their political exclusion at the hands of an authoritarian regime.

A combination of political resentment (mainly in the north) and economic desperation (mainly in the south) triggered the Mexican Revolution at the end of 1910. However, early hopes that the Revolution would bring social progress evaporated as rival armies fought over Mexico and war imposed its horrendous social costs. Around one million Mexicans died prematurely as a result of the Revolution—either from violence, disease or hunger. Anarchy gave way to a semblance of order in 1916 and a new Constitution (based largely on that of 1857) was promulgated in 1917. It was under this Constitution (amended frequently thereafter) that Mexico was subsequently governed. The Constitution included provisions safeguarding the national interest in the land, subsoil and water, and specifically allowed the expropriation and redistribution of land. Article 123 established principles of labour relations, social welfare and of the duty of the state to provide universal education. The power of the Roman Catholic Church was further curtailed. However, the immediate post-Revolutionary years saw a return to some of the practices of the past—political authoritarianism, some economic recovery and large-scale economic corruption. One of the post-Revolutionary Presidents, Gen. Obregón, when asked how he kept peace within the army replied that he knew of no general who could withstand a barrage of 50,000 pesos. Evidently not everything had changed as a result of the Revolution.

It was not until the presidency of Lázaro Cárdenas (1934–40) that the radical promises of the new Constitution began to materialize. His Government accelerated the land redistribution programme, under which haciendas were divided into smallholdings (*ejidos*) for the peasants. The major part of the railway system and the petroleum industry were nationalized. Organized labour benefited from the establishment of the Confederation of Workers of Mexico (Confederación de Trabajadores de México—CTM). Agrarian interests were also organized into the National Confederation of Farmers (Confederación Nacional de Campesinos—CNC).

Cárdenas' policies of social reform were initially accepted but increasingly resented by the middle classes and propertied interests. By the end of the Cárdenas presidency political tensions were undoubtedly rising, and some feared the outbreak of renewed political violence. In order to avoid this, Cardenas chose a moderate politician, Avila Camacho, as his successor. This was a clear signal that the radical measures taken in the 1930s would be consolidated rather than developed further. In fact, the change of political direction after 1940 went much further than Cárdenas had envisaged. In 1941 Mexico entered the Second World War on the side of the Allies and thereafter became a strong ally of the USA.

ECONOMIC AND POLITICAL DEVELOPMENT, 1941–70

As a result of these changes, Mexico again turned its back on political radicalism, although there remained a strong rhetorical commitment to the Revolution. The Revolution did succeed in creating a sense of nationalism and ending the racial stratification which was such a feature of pre-1910 Mexico. However, in other ways, the pattern of government after 1940 somewhat resembled that of Porfirio Díaz. The economy was competently managed and achieved a considerable rate of economic growth. Mexican society changed and modernized as a result. However, politics remained corrupt and became increasingly authoritarian.

The consequences of a period of peace and relative prosperity included the rapid increase and mobility of Mexico's population and the transformation in the size and structure of its economy. In accordance with the Constitution, presidential elections were held every six years. However, all of those elected belonged to the same party, the Institutional Revolutionary Party (Partido Revolucionario Institutional—PRI) and all were nominated as candidates by the outgoing President. Elections served various functions, but political competition was not among them. If opposition candidates threatened to poll strongly, the results were simply 'rigged'. The PRI has its roots in the 1910–17 revolutionary period and was formally founded, as the National Revolutionary Party (Partido Revolucionario Nacional), in 1929, becoming the Party of the Mexican Revolution (Partido de la Revolución Mexicana) in 1938 and then the PRI in 1946. Until the mid-1980s the party's dominance of Mexican politics was so complete that the real struggle for power occurred within the party (rather than at the national or local election level), as in a one-party state. There were opposition candidates (notably those of the conservative National Action Party, Partido Acción Nacional—PAN), but PRI victories were always overwhelming.

Although the popular electoral rhetoric of the PRI appealed to an Indian heritage, rooted in the soil, and to the ideal of equality, the major material benefits which successive Governments brought were for the commercial and industrial sectors of the economy, the towns and the middle classes. This was partly because presidents pursued policies of industrialization, in the context of a mixed economy, and partly because rapid population growth in rural areas put the limited resources of the public sector under growing strain. Meanwhile, the agricultural sector increasingly divided between a traditional *ejido*-based south and a newly-colonized north, where medium-sized holdings were helped by irrigation schemes. These transformed life in the drier parts of the country and began a slow but cumulative northward shift in the balance of national economic power.

Mexico's population grew very rapidly from 1945. In 1955, when Mexico surpassed Spain as the most populous Spanish-speaking country in the world, there were about 32m. Mexicans; by 1970 there were about 51m. By 2000 the country's population was, according to preliminary census results, 97.4m., although the rate of population growth did slow markedly during the 1990s. Growth would have been significantly higher if it were not for considerable migration, both legal and illegal, to the USA. Moreover, whereas in 1950 only 10m. Mexicans were classed as urban, by 2000 the figure was about 75m., as a result of heavy migration from the country to the towns. Mexico City grew to become one of the largest cities in the world with a population of more than 20m. (including its metropolitan region).

A PERIOD OF UNRESOLVED POLITICAL CONFLICT, 1970–82

By the end of the 1960s the Mexican economy seemed to be progressing well. However, exactly as occurred at the end of the Porfirio Díaz period, the pattern of growth under authoritarian rule was meeting resistance from two groups. One was poorer Mexicans, especially those in rural areas, who objected to the growing inequality that characterized the process. Although not explicitly the object of discrimination, poorer country-dwellers in the south felt that the process of growth was increasingly marginalizing them from the rest of Mexican society. Opposition also came from the middle classes, particularly the student-age population at a time of international change, who felt that the political élite had become too remote, too authoritarian and unwilling to reform. Major student demonstrations in 1968 ended on 2 October, when a protest was fired upon by soldiers and hundreds were killed.

The Government did not liberalize politically after this, except perhaps marginally, but it did try to restore credibility among the rural population after 1970 by accelerating the redistribution of land and expanding the size of the public sector. In political terms, this response was a success. The PRI remained a well-organized party, with a basis of genuine support. Opposition forces, from the Marxist Left and the Catholic Right, seemed to have little appeal for the average Mexican. As a result, the authorities were able to maintain the old system with only minimal change. However, in economic terms, the 1970–82 period was a failure. The agrarian export economy, which had underpinned a long period of rising prosperity in the 1950s and 1960s, ran out of steam. Unorthodox economic management and a lack of rapport between government and business prevented the emergence of a lasting alternative model of development. The emergence of Mexico as a large-scale oil exporter seemed for a time to have solved this problem, but in the end only encouraged dependency on an export commodity prone to fluctuate in value. Inflation rose considerably after 1970. Moreover, even with the advantage of oil exports, the Government's policy of promoting the public sector as a leading economic sector led to a rapid build-up of foreign debt, which finally undermined the entire strategy.

ECONOMIC REFORM AND THE SHIFT TO POLITICAL PLURALISM SINCE 1982

Economic Reform

The Mexican financial crisis of 1982, and the subsequent austerity measures, created great pressures upon the economic and social fabric of the country. The Government of President de la Madrid inherited the problem of servicing the massive debts incurred by the policies of the López Portillo Government. President de la Madrid's economic austerity programme imposed severe financial constraints upon Mexico's middle and lower classes. Inflation remained high and the PRI began to lose favour with some of its traditional supporters. These strains intensified over time as the initial post-crisis austerity measures deepened into a thoroughgoing economic liberalization.

For the third time in a century, the Mexican authorities responded to a period of political turbulence by resorting to the formula of capable economic management allied to corruption and political authoritarianism. The economy was increasingly run by highly-trained economic technocrats, who relied upon trade-union leaders, PRI officials and local politicians to maintain the social order during a difficult period of economic change. However, the technocratic reforms carried out during the 1982–2000 period did not produce as much economic growth as was the case in earlier times. Indeed, whereas a marked reduction in extreme poverty was achieved in the 1940–70 period, the trend in 1982–2000 was the reverse: poverty actually increased. This was largely because, by 1982, Mexico had acquired a crippling foreign debt, which required major reductions in public spending, and, after 1985, the financial position of the public sector was adversely affected by the fall in world petroleum prices. However, the underlying economic strategy had also changed. In the past Mexico had followed a rather nationalist policy of relying on protectionism to achieve industrial growth. After 1982 Mexico gradually abandoned protectionism and sought deeper economic integration with the USA. Crucial landmarks were Mexico's entry into the General Agreement on Tariffs and Trade (GATT, renamed the World Trade Organization in 1995) in 1986 and into NAFTA in 1994.

Inevitably, a policy of economic integration must be judged over the long term. However, in the short term the policy of economic liberalization made some of Mexico's social problems more difficult to resolve because agriculture was kept short of funds and then had to be opened up increasingly to foreign competition. Mexico's poor farmers could not compete with imports from the USA and many of them abandoned their holdings and moved away, either to Mexico's growing cities or to the USA. Similar disaster overtook many small and poorly-capitalized Mexican manufacturing businesses. However, the big industrial companies flourished and there has been an enormous increase in manufacturing employment and exports. The north, and to some extent the centre, of Mexico have become considerably more prosperous and much more closely linked with the USA, while the south has, for the most part, remained poor and backward.

Progress towards Liberalism

While the authoritarian state was not truly challenged until the end of the 1990s, the electoral dimension of Mexican politics became increasingly significant after 1982. The first indication of change occurred in July 1983, when the PAN made significant gains at municipal elections. In mid-September 1985 a major earthquake struck Mexico City and five other states. The greatest loss of life and damage to property occurred in the capital, where official estimates claimed that 7,000 people died. In spite of substantial emergency aid from overseas, the Government was accused of failing to conduct a properly organized rescue operation. An additional source of public discontent was the disclosure that many of the buildings that had been destroyed had contravened construction regulations. The Government's inadequate response to the disaster contributed to the overwhelming defeat of the PRI in Mexico City in the 1988 elections.

By the mid-1980s the international political climate was changing. Democracy was coming to Latin America and the authoritarian Government in Mexico appeared increasingly anomalous. The Mexican authorities did not wish to abandon their system, but they did need to liberalize it in order to avoid problems with the USA. US support was required in order to resolve their economic problems, since the issue of foreign debt needed almost continuous renegotiation. As a result, there was for a time considerable conflict between the Mexican Government's economic and political strategies. This was particularly evident in 1986, when there was evidence of significant fraud in Chihuahua. Apparently acknowledging that the Government had gone too far in Chihuahua, President de la Madrid removed the head of the PRI in October 1986. He also allowed his Secretary of Government to introduce an electoral reform, which provided for proportional representation in state legislatures and for the state funding of all registered political parties. This gave the larger opposition parties the opportunity to assemble serious political machines, rather than simply being, as in the past, essentially vehicles for protest.

This change led to continuing moves towards a stronger party system. The left was strengthened in 1987 by the defection from the ruling party of Cuautéhmoc Cárdenas Solórzano and Porfirio Muñoz Ledo, who headed the so-called Democratic Current (Corriente Democrática—CD). Eventually, Cárdenas allied himself with the traditional left, which supported his presidential candidacy in 1988, when he gained a large number of votes and nearly won. Many Mexicans believed that the vote had been rigged to prevent a Cárdenas victory. In 1989 the majority of left-wing groups combined to form the Party of the Democratic Revolution (Partido de la Revolución Democrática—PRD). The left underwent a period of political decline after 1988, although it recovered again in the aftermath of the 1994 peso devaluation and the ensuing 'tequila crisis', which created great instability in financial markets throughout Latin America. An important step forward for the PRD came with its victory in elections for the Federal District in 1997. Meanwhile, the PAN quietly gained strength and won a number of significant regional and local elections after 1989.

Finally, the PRI itself became a far more disciplined and professional party than in the past. President Carlos Salinas de Gortari (1988–1994), in an effort to prepare the PRI for a more democratic era, ruthlessly purged the party of some of its more unpopular figures, while allowing younger leaders to emerge in several areas. The PRI after 1988 became less a collection of loyalists and time-servers and more of a serious political operation. The man chiefly responsible for this transformation, Luis Donaldo Colosio, received the PRI nomination for the presidency in the 1994 elections but was assassin-ated in March of that year. The assassination has never been fully explained.

Political Turbulence

On 1 January 1994 there was a different expression of opposition, when armed Indian groups numbering 1,000–3,000 took control of four municipalities of the southern state of Chiapas. The rebels identified themselves as the Zapatista National Liberation Army (Ejército Zapatista de Liberación Nacional—EZLN). They detailed a series of demands for economic and social change in the region, culminating in a declaration of war against the Government and a statement of intent to depose President Salinas. The insurgency coincided with the implementation of NAFTA, which the rebels claimed was the latest in a series of exclusionary government initiatives, adopted at the expense of indigenous groups. The Armed Forces did not respond until 3 January, and then engaged in a campaign of heavy bombardment until 10 January, when the Government declared a unilateral cease-fire and an amnesty, effective from 22 January, for those EZLN members prepared to surrender arms. On the same day Manuel Camacho Solís was appointed as head of a peace and reconciliation commission in Chiapas. Negotiations between Camacho and the rebels began on 22 February and were concluded on 2 March with the publication of a document detailing 34 demands of the EZLN, and the Government's response to them. Negotiations between guerrillas and the Government on cultural, linguistic and local-government rights for indigenous groups continued inconclusively until December 1997, when a massacre of 45 Indians took place in a village in Chenalhó, Chiapas. Some 58 residents of Chenalhó, allegedly members of pro-Government paramilitary groups, were subsequently arrested, including the mayor of the municipality. The Secretary of the Interior and the Governor of Chiapas were forced to resign in January 1998 over the killings. In the following month a new government peace negotiator, Emilio Rabasa, was appointed, and further conciliatory gestures were made towards the EZLN. Nevertheless, the military presence in Chiapas increased, purportedly to deter paramilitary activity in the region.

The year 1994 proved to be very troublesome in Mexican history. In spite of the Zapatista rising in January and the assassination of Donaldo Colosio in March, presidential elections went ahead, as scheduled, in August and were widely judged to be free and reasonably fair. On being declared the victor, with 48.8% of the votes cast, President-elect Ernesto Zedillo Ponce de León, from the PRI, promised to continue with democratic reforms. However, the political system received a further shock on 28 September, when José Ruiz Massieu, the former brother-in-law of the outgoing President, was shot and killed in the centre of Mexico City. This event, together with the earlier incidents, seriously frightened foreign investors. Moreover, a few days after his inauguration as President on 1 December, Zedillo had to confront a major economic and financial crisis, when what was intended to be a limited devaluation brought on speculative panic and national near-bankruptcy. Mexico was rescued by an emergency loan from the USA, the banking system entered a period of deep crisis and the PRI lost much of its popularity.

The economy did recover from the 1994 crisis, and the years 1996–2000 were quite positive from an economic viewpoint. Exports to the USA had at last grown to the point where they could act as a basis for broader-based economic recovery. The long US economic boom of the 1990s drew in goods and migrants from Mexico and encouraged US investment in Mexico itself. However, from a political viewpoint, the PRI system never fully recovered from the shocks which it received in 1994.

LAW AND ORDER

Mexico has long had a cultural tradition of weak law enforcement. As late as 1988 only seven people in the history of post-revolutionary Mexico had ever been charged with tax fraud. What made matters more difficult was the increasing use of Mexico by drugs traffickers to transport cocaine and other illegal substances from Colombia and other parts of South America to the USA. There were periodic attempts by the authorities to reduce this problem, but success was limited. Organized crime remained a major problem in Mexico and a significant contributor to political corruption, which was also of considerable concern.

In 1989 President Salinas ordered the arrest of one of the most powerful men in Mexico, the petroleum-workers' union leader, Joaquín Hernández de Galicia ('La Quina'), on a range of charges including corruption and murder. President Salinas subsequently also ordered the detention of a number of individuals accused of stock-market fraud. Another important arrest was that of Félix Gallardo, one of the largest cocaine dealers in Mexico. Gallardo's arrest was followed by the purging of a number of lesser figures associated with the drugs trade and the dismissal of one-third of the entire police force in the state of Sinaloa. However, despite this increasingly vigorous action from the authorities, the problem of drugs-related corruption did not diminish.

When Ernesto Zedillo was inaugurated as President in December 1994, he immediately had to cope with the aftermath of the assassination of José Francisco Ruiz Massieu. In November Ruiz Massieu's brother, Mario, had resigned from his post as Deputy Attorney-General, alleging that senior PRI officials had impeded his investigation into his brother's murder. However, Mario Ruiz Massieu was subsequently arrested in the USA on charges of corruption and drugs trafficking. In September he committed suicide in prison, while awaiting trial. An even more dramatic development occurred in February 1995, when Raúl Salinas de Gortari, brother of former President Carlos Salinas, was arrested on charges of complicity in the murder. In late 1995 Raúl Salinas was also alleged to have participated in the 'laundering' (processing into legitimate accounts) of funds earned in the trafficking of illicit drugs. The scandal took on macabre proportions in October 1996 when the discovery of a body, believed to be that of Manuel Muñoz Rocha, a federal deputy, in the grounds of Raúl Salinas' house, appeared to add further to the evidence against Salinas. Muñoz Rocha had disappeared in 1995, following accusations that he was also involved in the murder of the PRI Secretary-General. However, forensic evidence soon showed that the body found was not that of Muñoz Rocha, but rather a person who had died of natural causes. The deceased was, in fact, the relative of a fortune-teller who had 'predicted' that a body would be found in this location, and who was arrested when she claimed a reward. Eventually, however, in January 1999, Raúl Salinas was convicted of the murder of Ruiz Massieu and sentenced to a long period of imprisonment. Former President Salinas, while protesting that he knew nothing about these events, nevertheless found it prudent to live in Dublin, Ireland, for most of the Zedillo presidential period.

1997–2001: TOWARDS FULL DEMOCRACY?

A momentous development in Mexican history occurred on 2 July 2000 when Vicente Fox Quesada, the candidate of a PAN-led political alliance, the Alliance for Change (Alianza por el Cambio—AC), defeated the PRI candidate, Francisco Labastida Ochoa, in presidential elections. Fox won 43.47% of the valid votes cast, while Labastida secured 36.91%. This was the first time in Mexican history that a candidate of the ruling party had lost a national election, and marked the high point of a political transformation, which had reached its decisive point during the Zedillo presidency. Important earlier stages had included changes to the rules within the PRI itself, which, in effect, ended the system by which the President chose his successor. In November 1999 the PRI organized its own internal primary election, which Labastida won. Earlier, a far greater degree of contestation had been a notable feature of the July 1997 elections to Congress and for the governorship of the Federal District. Cuauhtémoc Cárdenas of the PRD was elected in Mexico City, while in the congressional elections the PRI lost its absolute majority in the Chamber of Deputies. Although the PRI remained the largest party in the Mexican Congress during 1997–2000, it had to face an opposition alliance which, at times, embarrassed the Government. In the 2000 congressional elections the AC became the largest force in the Chamber of Deputies, winning 223 seats (compared with the PRI's 209 seats), although it, too, fell well short of an overall majority. In the Senate, however, the PRI secured 60 of the 128 seats, while

the AC won 51 seats. As a result, Fox found himself in a minority in both houses of the legislature, and some of his more ambitious ideas had to be put on hold due to his lack of law-making power.

Fox's control of events was further undermined in March 2001 when the leader of the Zapatistas, subcommandante Marcos, led a peaceful demonstration over 3,000 km from Chiapas to Mexico City, where he addressed a rally attended by over 150,000 people in the central square, demanding constitutional recognition for the 10m. indigenous Mexicans, the withdrawal of Mexican troops from Chiapas and the release of all Zapatista prisoners. After an historic address of both chambers of Congress on 28 March, the rebels agreed to reopen formal dialogue with the Government on the constitutional reform. Marcos successfully negotiated the dismantling of the seven garrisons in Chiapas, and in April both houses of Congress approved legislation reforming six articles of the Constitution, recognizing and guaranteeing indigenous political, legal, social and economic rights. The new law, however, fell short of granting indigenous peoples the right to live by their own laws and was widely regarded as a diluted version of draft legislation rejected in 1996, leaving the questions of communal property and voting rights unresolved. As the proposed legislation involved a constitutional amendment, a majority of Mexico's 32 states needed to vote in favour of it before it could become law; 17 states had done so by July 2001, but almost all states with sizeable indigenous populations rejected the proposals and it was far from certain whether it would become law: even if the Constitution were to be amended, the debate on indigenous rights was unlikely to end.

The movement that led Fox to victory in some ways resembled other opposition movements of the past century, although it could be distinguished from them by the fact that it was both democratic and peaceful. However, Fox drew strength from two groups. There were many, mainly in the north, who approved of the PRI's economic policies, but disliked its record of corruption and its history of authoritarianism. There were others, mostly poorer Mexicans, who disliked the increasing social inequality that existed as a consequence of the economic strategy being pursued. In the past this kind of alliance soon collapsed when the new Government had to choose its strategy: it could hope to please one group, but not both. This time, however, prospects for the future were perhaps more optimistic, owing to Mexico's deep economic integration with the USA. It was possible that the new Mexican Government would be able to persuade the new administration of George W. Bush (2001–) in the USA to change its policies on some issues of great concern to Mexico. However, this would depend on the avoidance of serious economic recession in the USA. President Fox very much wanted the USA to adopt a more liberal policy on immigration from Mexico, which could, indeed, be the only practicable way of resolving the serious crisis in the Mexican countryside. President Fox has long wanted to guarantee rights for his countrymen in the USA and in 2001 support was steadily growing on the US side: In July President Bush spoke of an amnesty for all illegal Mexican immigrants in the USA (estimated at 2.7m. in 1996), and US trade unions, once opposed to amnesties on the grounds that illegal immigrants created a pool of cheap labour, indicated their support for such an idea. Presidents Fox and Bush were to meet in September 2001 to discuss the possibility of documentation for all Mexicans in the USA and closer co-operation to prevent illegal immigration, as well the longer-term goal of stimulating economic growth in Mexico in order to encourage more Mexicans to stay in Mexico.

It was clear in 2001 that Mexico was undergoing substantial political change. Economically, it was more than ever a part of North America. Export growth had been impressive, as had Mexico's ability to attract investment from the USA. The millions of migrants from Mexico in the USA, and remittances from Mexicans working abroad were possibly the most important single factor ameliorating poverty in Mexico. The Mexican political system had also become more like that of the USA, with more decentralization, more pluralism and an increasingly powerful Congress. It remained to be seen how well Mexico's rich history and powerful cultural traditions would adapt to this new reality.

Economy

SANDY MARKWICK

Occupying an area of 1.95m. sq km (754,120 sq miles), Mexico is the 14th largest country in the world. It shares a 3,100 km-long border with the USA in the north, and in the south is bounded by Guatemala and Belize. The Gulf of Mexico and the Caribbean Sea lie to the east, and the Pacific Ocean and the Gulf of California to the west. The climate and topography are extremely varied: the tropical southern region and coastal lowlands are hot and wet, while the highlands of the centre are temperate and much of the north and west is arid desert. Although conditions were not ideally suited to agriculture, Mexico was among the world's leading producers of a number of crops. However, by the 21st century the country had not yet effectively developed its forestry and fishing resources. Extensive mineral potential also remained largely unrealized, although this did not apply to petroleum reserves, extraction of which began at the start of the 20th century and accelerated in the 1970s, following important discoveries.

The population of Mexico was an estimated 98.8m. in February 2001. It was possible that the population would exceed 100m. before the end of 2001. A birth rate of approximately 1.5% per year is significantly lower than in recent decades, reflecting improving education and health care. The economy, which in the mid-1990s ranked about 11th in the world, in terms of gross domestic product (GDP), became increasingly industrialized in the second half of the 20th century. Successive Governments encouraged this trend with fiscal incentives and protection against imports. Supported by high government spending, considerable overseas investment and massive foreign borrowing, as well as by petroleum discoveries and increases in petroleum prices, the Mexican economy grew by over 6% per year, on average, between 1958 and 1982. However, rapid growth was accompanied by high fiscal deficits, a growing rate of inflation and increasing trade deficits. By 1982 Mexico's external debt totalled US $90,000m. Domestic investors, concerned about the Government's ability to manage the economy, withdrew massive amounts of capital from the country. With its foreign-exchange reserves all but exhausted, Mexico was forced to suspend debt-service payments. In late 1982 the incoming Government of President Miguel de la Madrid Hurtado was forced to implement austerity measures in order to secure the much-needed support of multilateral lending agencies and thus reschedule the debt. In 1983–88 consumer prices increased by almost 4,000%, while annual GDP growth averaged just 0.1%.

The Government of President Carlos Salinas de Gortari (1988–94) continued and advanced the structural-adjustment process. Deregulation introduced market forces, encouraged foreign investment and reduced the role of the state in numerous sectors of the economy, including finance, agriculture, transport and communications. The state's shares in many state-owned companies were sold to the private sector. In 1992 import licences were required for fewer than 2% of all imports, while the average tariff was some 11%, compared with 13% in 1986. Part of President Salinas' motives for trade liberalization were political: cheaper consumer imports restored the support of a significant proportion of the middle classes who had abandoned the ruling Institutional Revolutionary Party (Partido Revolucionario Institucional—PRI) in 1988. Trade liberalization was consolidated by the coming into effect, on 1 January 1994, of the North American Free Trade Agreement (NAFTA) between Mexico, the USA and Canada. Trade liberalization and an exchange-rate band system succeeded in reducing inflation from 113.9% in 1988 to around 7% in December 1994, when Salinas was succeeded as President by Ernesto Zedillo Ponce de León. The economy looked stronger, partly because of broadening the tax base and more efficient tax collection, but also because of wage and price restraints, which were the result of a pact with labour and business leaders. Another reason for the economic improvement was a reduction in domestic interest rates. The country's admittance into the Organisation for Economic Co-operation and Development (OECD) in June 1994 was intended to have a similar effect to that of admittance into NAFTA, by committing the Mexican economy to a free-market programme and ensuring that capital receipts remained substantial. Encouraged by the new regulatory environment, foreign direct investment increased to US $8,000m. by 1994. Private investment was mainly responsible for the modest annual average GDP growth in the early 1990s.

However, President Salinas' economic successes were based on an exchange-rate policy which, ultimately, proved unsustainable. The rate at which the peso was traded with the US dollar was allowed to 'float' (i.e., be made freely convertible) within a band, the floor of which was fixed at 3.0562 pesos to US $1, while the ceiling depreciated daily. President Salinas maintained this policy in spite of peso appreciation in real terms, rapidly increasing balance-of-payments problems and a current-account deficit which rose to US $29,662m. in 1994 (almost 8% of GDP). To cover the current-account shortfall, the Government maintained real interest rates in order to continue to attract capital inflows which were under threat because of fears of political instability in Mexico and because of higher interest rates in the USA. In 1994 dollar-linked bonds, Tesobonos, were introduced to strengthen inflows. The capital-account deficit was largely financed by volatile, speculative portfolio inflows. Domestic political instability resulted in a loss of confidence in the currency during 1994. There was a massive withdrawal of investment funds, from $28,400m. to less than $8,200m., and a rapid depletion of foreign-exchange reserves, from $24,886m. at the end of 1993 to $6,101m. one year later.

Overvaluation of the peso led to a devaluation crisis within just three weeks of President Zedillo assuming power in December 1994. With foreign reserves low, the Government opted for a limited devaluation by lifting the exchange-band ceiling to 4.10 pesos to US $1, but this failed to ease pressure on the peso. Two days later the Government allowed the peso to float freely. At the end of 1994 there were 5.33 pesos to $1 and this level continued to decrease in 1995. Investor nervousness was exacerbated by the Government's delay in producing a credible plan to control devaluation. The crisis led to fears that the Government would be unable to repay $29,000m. of short-term Tesobono debt due in early 1995 and that the banking system would collapse because of increases in external debt-servicing costs.

In late January 1995 the US Government's announcement of a rescue programme succeeded in preventing default on debt payments and in supporting the Mexican economy until it could develop firmer foundations. The US Government pledged US $20,000m., while the Bank for International Settlements (BIS) and the International Monetary Fund (IMF) agreed to extend a further $17,800m. Other financial institutions also agreed credit facilities. This rescue programme, the largest since the US Marshall Plan (European Reconstruction Program) to aid Europe following the Second World War, was agreed after the Zedillo administration committed itself to emergency stabilization measures, consisting of strict control of the money supply, reductions in public spending in order to create a public-sector surplus, increased taxes and wage constraints. The Government maintained its priority of reducing inflation by means of strict monetary policies.

The austerity measures succeeded in improving the balance of payments, but the Mexican economy entered a deep recession. The current-account deficit on the balance of payments decreased to US $1,576m., but the economy contracted by 6.2% in 1995. The annual rate of inflation, having averaged 18% per year in 1991–95, increased to 35.0% in 1995. The Government continued its strict monetary policies into 1996 to re-establish credibility and to regain the confidence of the financial markets and the IMF. Mexico began refinancing its public-sector external debt, which had increased by $15,636m. in 1995, to $95,167m. The successful issue of a floating-rate note supported by petroleum exports helped to raise $7,000m. towards repaying the US Treasury. As a result of the Government's repayments, Mexico was able to resume borrowing in international financial markets in June 1996.

The economy began to recover in 1996, registering a growth rate of 5.2% in that year and a robust 6.7% in 1997. The recovery was led by the manufacturing sector, which grew by 10.9% in 1996 and 9.8% in 1997. The construction, mining, communications and transport sectors also registered healthy growth during this two-year period. Export revenues increased by 21% in 1996 and by a further 15% in 1997. Following a trade deficit of US $18,464m. in 1994, Mexico recorded a trade surplus of $7,089m. in 1995 after the devaluation of the peso and domestic recession. Mexico maintained a trade surplus until mid-1997, after which Mexico registered a small surplus for the year of $623m. The account went into deficit for 1998 amounting to $7,915m., exacerbated by low petroleum prices. The trade deficit in 1999 was $5,581m., but increased marginally in 2000 to an estimated $6,000m., though both imports and exports expanded rapidly in that year. Appreciation of the peso encouraged an import boom, which continued thereafter, but this was offset by strong demand from the USA, maintaining exports. Net direct foreign investment reached a record $12,831m. in 1997. In 1999 $11,786m. entered Mexico in the form of direct foreign investment, and this figure was expected to increase further in 2000, to a record, $13,100m. Inflation fell from 35.0% in 1995 to 15.9% in 1998. After a consumer price increase of 16.6% in 1999, annual inflation in 2000 declined to 9.5%. This was the lowest rate since 1994 and below the central bank's target, though there were signs that the downwards trend had stabilized.

President Zedillo continued to adhere to prudent monetary and fiscal policies. Public spending was restricted to meet budget targets and foreign-exchange reserves restored, increasing from US $6,101m. at the end of 1994 to $35,142m in 2000. Although the current-account deficit doubled from 1997 to 1998, owing to a trade deficit of $7,915m. in the latter year, it was considered manageable at $15,724m. (equivalent to 3.8% of GDP). The current-account deficit declined slightly to $14,166m. in 1999, but increased in 2000 to an estimated $16,067m., fuelled particularly by interest payments on public debt. However, as the equivalent of 3.1% of GDP, the deficit was not a cause for alarm. High levels of foreign direct investment, increases in private consumption and strong demand in the US market stimulated output. Despite the volatility of the peso, as a result of the Asian financial crisis of 1997 and 1998, Mexico's floating exchange rate was considered a strength, ensuring quick corrections in response to external conditions.

GDP growth slowed to 4.9% in 1998 and to 3.8% in 1999, principally owing to turmoil in Asian markets and currency devaluations in Brazil and the Russian Federation, although Mexico benefited from sustained demand from the USA. Growth in 1999 was led by transport and communications, which increased by 8.8%, banking services (5.7%) and construction (4.5%). Only the mining sector experienced recession with output declining by 3.2%. Strong growth, estimated at 6.9%, was restored in 2000, led by commerce, restaurants and hotels, and again by the transport and communications sector. Fears of traditional fiscal indiscipline on the part of the incumbent Government in an election year proved unfounded, helped partly by the autonomy of the central bank. The new President, Vicente Fox Quesada, who assumed office in December 2000, was the first head of state to come from outside the traditional ruling Institutional Revolutionary Party (Partido Revolucionario Institutional—PRI). While this marked a watershed in modern Mexican history, the implications for immediate economic policy were few. President Fox, from the conservative National Action Party (Partido Acción Nacional—PAN), renewed the Government's broad commitment to macroeconomic orthodoxy and free market reform. The Fox administration's first budget proposal included a strict fiscal policy, while monetary policy remained rigorous under the continuing stewardship of the central bank governor, Guillermo Ortiz Martínez.

In spite of its recovery in the latter half of the 1990s, Mexico remained vulnerable to external conditions, particularly to changes in interest and growth rates in the USA, the source of most of the country's trade and investment. In addition, a decline in world petroleum prices in 1998 (dramatically reversed subsequently) threatened the country's fiscal and trade accounts. The structural reforms of the 1980s caused widespread social hardship, which persisted at the beginning of the 21st century. There was a marked deterioration in income distribution between 1984 and 1992, and in the late 1990s extreme poverty affected around 20% of the population, the problem being particularly acute in the rural south. At the depth of the recession in July 1995 more than 500,000 people became unemployed. Job creation accompanied economic recovery, but underemployment remained a significant issue. There were hopes that the stable transition to the first non-PRI Government represented a maturing democracy that would underpin economic stability.

EMPLOYMENT

Linked with the inequality of income distribution in Mexico was the problem of unemployment. As Mexico's population was predominantly a young one, the economy needed to grow by over 3% per year just to absorb the 0.8m.–1m. potential new arrivals on the labour market. The fact that the economy consistently did not achieve adequate growth rates for more than a decade was reflected in high unemployment rates and the existence of a thriving informal economy.

The official unemployment rate averaged 2.25% in 2000, compared with 2.5% in 1999, and 5.5% in 1996. However, official figures concealed the problem of underemployment. In November 2000 19.6% of the work-force worked fewer than 35 hours per week, although this represented a decline from an annual average of 23.2% in 1997. The most significant provider of new jobs in terms of the industrial sector was manufacturing, and in particular the *maquiladora* assembly plants (see Manufacturing below). The informal sector was very large, although difficult to quantify accurately.

AGRICULTURE, LIVESTOCK, FORESTRY AND FISHING

Mexico's complicated topography and wide variation of climates restricted the area which could be cultivated to about 13% of its total territory in 1992 (according to the UN's Food and Agriculture Organization). By contrast, more than 38% was pasture or brushland while almost 21% was forested. About 16% of the arable land was irrigated. In 1999 the agricultural sector (including livestock, forestry and fishing) employed 21% of the employed work-force, but accounted for no more than 4.6% of GDP in this year, compared with 20% in 1950. The decline in its share of GDP was largely a result of post-Second World War industrialization, but it also reflected low growth rates: in 1980–92 the sector achieved an average growth rate of only 0.6% per year, in real terms. This increased to an annual growth of 1.6% in 1990–99. There were several reasons for such poor performances, including decapitalization, inadequate transport facilities, low world prices, adverse weather conditions and, increasingly in the 1990s, unpaid debts. One fundamental problem was the *ejido* land-holding system, which arose from the agrarian reforms of the 1930s. This system allowed for individual plots to be cultivated on communally owned land. As the land was communally owned there was no provision for the individual plots to be sold or leased, although they could be passed on to descendants. The result was an increasingly uneconomical fragmentation of the 95m. ha of land in communal ownership (in 1988). In 1992 the Government amended the Constitution in order to allow *ejido* land to be rented or sold, or to be used as collateral security for raising finance.

Other impediments to agricultural growth were trade liberalization and the decrease in subsidies, which caused output of many crops to fall. In 1993 the Government sought to address this problem by ending price supports for basic grains and by introducing a new scheme that subsidized farmers according to the area of land they owned. Indebtedness was made worse by devaluation. Faced with demonstrations by farmers, the authorities also arranged for the restructuring of overdue bank loans, but debts and high interest rates continued to restrain growth. In 1995 President Zedillo introduced a programme of direct cash subsidies for the agricultural sector and followed this with measures designed to stimulate output, including debt rescheduling for producers and increases in financing and credit from state agencies.

After experiencing recession in 1995–96, the agricultural sector grew by 0.2% in 1997. The sector recovered to register 4.9% growth in 1998, 3.7% in 1999 and 3.4% in 2000. While devaluation resulted in a rare surplus being achieved in 1995, Mexico regularly recorded trade deficits in agricultural products. In 1999 the agricultural trade deficit was $359m., a decrease from $845m., in 1998. Crop production accounted for around 50% of agricultural output in 1999. Livestock products contributed some 30% and forestry products 21%. The contribution of fisheries to sectoral output was marginal.

Maize was the principal grain produced by Mexico: it typically accounted for about one-half of the volume and value of cereal-crop production. Annual maize production averaged around 18.0m. metric tons in the 1990s. Other staples included sorghum (6.4m. tons in 2000), wheat, down to 3.3m. tons in 2000, from 3.7m. in 1997), and dry beans (stable at 1.2m. tons in 2000). Barley, sugar, rice and soya beans were also grown. In the late 1990s coffee was the most valuable export crop; however, in late 1998 production in the main coffee-growing state of Chiapas was adversely affected by extensive flooding associated with the El Niño weather phenomenon (a warm ocean current which appears periodically in the Pacific) and total coffee output declined to an estimated 306,000 tons. Coffee exports earned US $761.8m. in that year. The contribution of agricultural produce to total export revenues declined steadily after 1995, when revenues of $4,016m. represented 5.0% of total export revenues. Agricultural exports were valued at $3,926m. in 1999, equivalent to 2.9% of total export revenues.

Fruit and vegetables increased their sales substantially in the first half of the 1990s, earning some US $2,251.3m. in 1995, compared with $935m. in 1988. The increase came about mainly owing to an expansion in exports to the USA. Mexico's fruit and vegetable production included citrus fruits, strawberries, mangoes, apples, pears, melons, pineapples and tomatoes. Owing to weak world prices, rising production costs and adverse climatic conditions, in 1992 cotton (lint) production collapsed to an estimated 33,000 metric tons, compared with 202,000 tons in 1991. By 1998 production had recovered to 247,000 tons, but fell back again thereafter, to an estimated 51,000 tons in 2000. The sugar industry also suffered from bad weather in the late 1980s and early 1990s, but the sector felt more keenly the effects of the privatization of the state-owned milling industry, which had previously encouraged production by offering subsidized credits to growers. However, after a process of adjustment, raw sugar production recovered, to around 4.2m. tons in 1993, from its lowest level of 3.3m. tons in 1990. In 2000 output was an estimated 5.0m. tons. Tobacco cultivation was yet another sector adversely affected by bad weather, with production decreasing to just 21,000 tons in 1992, from a 1986–90 annual average of 58,000 tons. Output continued to fluctuate in the 1990s, reaching 51,000 tons by 1999, before falling back to about 43,000 tons in 2000. In the livestock sub-sector, cattle-raising was the most important activity. Total meat production amounted to some 4.5m. metric tons in 2000. Production of cows' milk steadily increased from the late 1980s and reached some 9.5m. tons by 2000. Cattle stocks were unofficially recorded at 30.3m. head in 2000. From the 1980s there was a sharp increase in poultry stocks which was reflected by rising production of white meat (roughly 1.9m. tons in 2000, compared with 399,200 tons in 1980) and eggs (1.7m. in 2000, compared with 644,400 in 1980). Another product of the livestock sector was honey, an estimated 57,000 tons of which were produced in 2000, an increase on the previous year's output of 55,000 tons.

Only about 30% of Mexico's forest area was exploited in the early 1990s, neither the transport infrastructure nor the land-ownership system having encouraged investment in the sector. Forestry accounted for around 21% of the output of the agricultural sector in 2000. In 1999 roundwood removals were 24.1m. cu m, the vast majority of which was pine. Deforestation (which averaged at an annual rate of 1.4% in 1981–90) was a problem that the Government attempted to address in the 1990s. In 1999 forestry output grew by 4.9%. Poor planning and El Niño

meant that the sector was severely affected by widespread forest fires in 1998.

Although it has long Caribbean and Pacific coastlines and extensive inland waters, in the 1990s Mexico had yet to develop a modern fishing industry of any real importance. The annual catch increased gradually, to reach 1.53m. metric tons in 1997, but declined to 1.27m. tons in 1999. Among the leading varieties of fish caught were tuna (tunny), Californian pilchard (sardines), anchovy and shellfish. Exports of fish (including shellfish) earned US $672m. in 1999, compared with $676m. in 1998 and $784m. in 1997. There are around 103,000 vessels in Mexico's fishing fleet operating out of 62 fishing ports.

MINING AND POWER

Petroleum was by far the most important product of the extractive sector. Mexico was the world's fifth largest petroleum-producing country in 1999. The state oil company, Petróleos Mexicanos (PEMEX), provided 32.5% of federal government taxation revenues in 1999. However, in the 1980s and 1990s its contribution to the Mexican economy declined as world petroleum prices fell. Between 1986 and 1998 petroleum export revenues declined by an estimated 61%, from the equivalent of 5.7% of GDP to just 1.7%. In 1990 petroleum accounted for 35.6% of export earnings. By 1999 this figure had decreased to 7.3%. Nevertheless, petroleum production (and liquid gas equivalent) increased slightly during the 1990s, from 2.67m. barrels per day (b/d) in 1993 to 3.01m. b/d in 2000. Petroleum exports earned estimated revenues of US $16,371m. in 2000, a considerable increase on the $9,921m. earned in 1999. The increase stemmed from dramatic increases in the oil price in 2000. Having declined to their lowest level in two decades in December 1998, at $7.67 per barrel, prices for Mexican crude recovered to an average price of $15.62 per barrel during 1999 and reached $29.27 per barrel in March 2000. The Government raised its official budgeted assumed oil price from $16 per barrel to $20. PEMEX recorded pre-tax profits of $29,100m. in 2000; however, it recorded an actual loss after subtracting tax payments to the Government.

PEMEX enjoyed a monopoly on petroleum production, conferred by the Constitution. However, foreign petroleum companies did operate under service contracts with PEMEX, while US and Canadian concerns had the opportunity to enter into 'performance' contracts with the company. Plans to sell petrochemical assets proceeded slowly, owing to investor concern about low petroleum prices and domestic opposition to privatization in the industry. Around 56% of Mexico's petroleum came from off-shore sites in the Campeche Sound (Gulf of Mexico), 24% from the Chicontepec region and 15% from the states of Chiapas and Tabasco. Mexico's crude reserves stood at 58,200m. in 2000, up from 57,700m. in 1999, but down from 60,200m. barrels in 1998. Gas reserves were equivalent to 11,994,000m. barrels in 2000, down from 12,093,000m. barrels in 1999. Output of natural gas averaged 4,679m. cu ft per day in 2000 compared with annual averages of 4,791m. cu ft per day in 1998–99. Mexico hoped to continue to increase gas production in order to become a net exporter, although a decline in exploratory activity in the 1980s led to a diminution of reserves in the 1990s.

Apart from petroleum, Mexico produced an impressive amount of other minerals. It was the largest producer of silver in the world and was also a leading source of fluorite, celestite, and sodium sulphate, as well as bismuth, graphite, antimony, arsenic, barite, sulphur and copper. It also produced iron ore, lead, zinc and coal. However, despite the wealth of resources, the mining sector was not a major force in the economy, accounting for just 1.2% of GDP and 0.3% of exports in 2000. The sector expanded little in the 1980s, with annual growth averaging no more than 0.4%. Mining increased by 2.7% in 1998, but decreased by 3.2% in 1999, the only sector to suffer recession in that year. It recovered to register a 4.0% growth rate in 2000, though this was still below average for the economy as a whole. The sector was restrained by outdated technology, poor world prices and lack of finance. However, government regulations acted as a deterrent to private investment. The Salinas Government, therefore, focused on increasing private investment: it made available a large proportion of the country's mining reserves, relaxed curbs on foreign investment, lowered taxes and extended concession terms. Some US $4,370m. was allocated for the development of mining projects for the period 1996–2000. The country registered a deficit in its trade in metallic and non-metallic minerals. Mining products earned $453m. in export revenues in 1999.

Unlike mining, the utilities sector expanded relatively rapidly in the early 1990s, with growth averaging 3.5% per year in 1990–93. Utilities (electricity, gas and water) grew by 7.9% in 1999 before declining slightly to 6.2% in 2000. In 1999 the sector contributed 1.3% of GDP. Electricity production rose steadily, with increases in installed capacity, which totalled 34,800 MW in 1997, compared with 21,399 MW in 1986. In 1994 55.3% of electric power came from oil-fired plants, 15.3% from hydroelectric plants, 9.3% from coal-fired plants, 4.1% from geothermal plants and 3.4% from the Laguna Verde nuclear power-station. National distribution of electricity was uneven. In this sector too, with the challenge of expanding output to meet rising demand, from the late 1980s the Government gradually increased the opportunities for private enterprise, including foreign competition, both to collaborate with the state-owned power utility, Comisión Federal de Electricidad (CFE), in installing new plants, and to produce power on its own account. In 1998 the Commission for Energy Regulation (Comisión Reguladora de Energía) granted permits for the construction of two thermo-electric plants in Hermosillo and Tamaulipas. The permits were granted to foreign investors and brought to three the total number of such schemes, whereby private concerns financed, built and managed plants for a 27-year contract period. However, political opposition delayed the introduction of more comprehensive measures to increase private-sector involvement in the electricity industry. Opposition parties obstructed President Ernesto Zedillo's attempts to change the Constitution to allow the full participation of private investors in the sector. President Vicente Fox renewed efforts to liberalize the electricity sector from late 2000. His proposals were similar to those of his predecessor, including ending the CFE's monopoly and creating a free market for electricity surpluses. However, in an attempt to overcome political opposition, Fox departed from Zedillo's vision of a privatized CFE and pledged the company to public ownership.

MANUFACTURING

The manufacturing sector began to be developed after the Second World War, and for four decades it enjoyed a considerable degree of protection from outside competition. However, from the 1980s it was increasingly subjected to such competition, as trade barriers were dismantled. The results were mixed. Manufacturing exports grew quite strongly, but many sectors were unable to meet the challenge of competition on either the export or the domestic market. This was particularly the case with small and medium-sized enterprises, which accounted for the majority of manufacturing businesses and for more than 90% of official employment in the sector. The manufacturing sector contributed 20.8% of GDP in 2000 and generated 89.5% of total export earnings in that year. Manufacturing GDP increased by 7.1% in 2000 following growth of 4.1% in 1999. In 1991–96 the sector averaged annual growth of 2.9%, despite recession in 1993 and 1995.

The most important manufacturing branch, in terms of its contribution to sectoral GDP and employment, was metal products, machinery and equipment, which accounted for 31.5% of manufacturing output and 28.5% of sectoral employment in 2000. This branch of manufacturing grew by an annual average rate of 10.3% in 1995–2000 and out-performed other manufacturing areas in 2000, recording 13.9% growth. The metal-products sub-sector was led by the automotive industry, which expanded rapidly from the mid-1990s as transnational corporations established operations in Mexico, in order to take advantage of NAFTA and of growth in the Mexican market.

The food, drink and tobacco sub-sector produced 24.0% of manufacturing output in 2000, employing 24.7% of the manufacturing work-force. Key industries in this sub-sector, which drew on domestically produced raw materials, included grain-milling and bakeries, sugar processing, fruit and vegetable processing, cigarettes and beers and spirits. The chemicals industry (14.7% of sectoral GDP in 2000) was another major sub-sector, of which the petrochemicals division was a particularly dynamic component, but which also encompassed plastics, rubber and pharmaceuticals. One of the main traditional industrial activities was textiles and clothing, developed following the success of locally grown cotton and, later, of petroleum resources. In fact, in the 1990s synthetic fibre output far exceeded that of natural fibres. The industry had a considerable export market, but the domestically orientated segment had suffered considerably from import competition.

Mexico had a significant iron and steel industry, which used mainly national iron-ore resources to produce over 8m. metric tons of steel per year in the 1980s. The industry was privatized in 1989, after which production increased above overall rates of GDP, while the work-force was reduced by 40%. In 1996 the biggest producer, Altos Hornos de México (AHMSA), discovered a new iron deposit in the northern state of Coahuila which, according to company estimates, would enable it to increase annual steel production from 3.5m. tons to 4.5m. tons. In 1996 Mexico produced 13.2m. tons of steel. There was concern that Mexico's reserves of iron ore would last only a further 25 years at existing rates of steel production.

Mexico also developed silver-, copper-, lead-, zinc- and tin-processing facilities, while non-metallic mineral resources provided the basis for glass and cement industries. Mexico produced 29.8m. metric tons of cement in 1997, making it one of the world's largest manufacturers. The other main industrial activities were paper, printing and publishing, and wood and cork manufactures.

In 1965 the Government began to plan an 'in-bond' industry, allowing temporary imports of inputs (parts) which were then assembled for duty-free exports. Originally, the provisions only covered the northern border areas, but they were later extended to the whole country. This in-bond, or *maquiladora* (assembly plant), sector, which took advantage of Mexico's low wage rates, prospered from the early 1980s. In 1982 there were 588 in-bond plants in operation; by 2000 this figure had reached 3,667, employing some 1.33m. workers. The main activities with which the *maquiladora* industries were concerned were electrical and electronic machinery and equipment, transport equipment and textiles. The sector generated an appreciable amount of foreign exchange. In 1999 it earned a total of US $63,748m., which represented nearly 50% of overall manufacturing revenues ($122,185m. in 1999). However, since the *maquiladora* sector was orientated on the processing of imported inputs from the USA, its outlays were also high, which left net earnings in 1999 at $13,339m. Industrial recovery from 1996 was led by the *maquiladora* industry, fuelled by a cheap peso. The increase in exports, however, entailed an increase in imports. The value of the peso rose in 1997, thereby further increasing imports. The *maquiladora* industry was one of the principal destinations for overseas foreign investment in the 1990s.

CONSTRUCTION

The construction industry suffered from severe recession in 1995, contracting by 23.5%. However, the sector recovered to surpass all other industrial activities, with average growth of 9.6% in 1996–97. This followed higher than average growth in 1989–94. The sector was given impetus by such diverse factors as tourism developments, the expansion of the road network, port improvements and increased industrial building. Construction output grew by 5.0% in 2000, the same growth rate as in 1999 and an increase on the 4.2% growth recorded in 1998. The sector contributed 4.8% of GDP in 2000.

TRANSPORT AND COMMUNICATIONS

Road transport was the chief means of conveying passengers and freight in Mexico. By 2000 road building had increased the total network to some 442,553 km (276,596 miles), of which 33.4% was paved. In order to support the development of the export trade and to spread the benefits of economic growth more evenly, the Government pursued extensive road-building projects in the 1990s. It also attempted to encourage the private sector to participate in road building, by granting concessionaires the right to build, maintain and collect the fees from toll roads. An innovative scheme for raising finance by issuing bonds backed by toll receipts was introduced. In 1997 the Government announced plans to repurchase almost one-half of the road concessions issued, in order to prompt further road construction.

The railway system, covering 26,662 km in 2000, was operated by the state-owned company, Ferrocarriles Nacionales de México. Inadequate investment resulted in the deterioration of the service, with the volume of freight traffic decreasing by 13% between 1986 and 1992, to 49.8m. metric tons, before recovering to 80.4m. tons by 1999. Passenger numbers decreased by 40% between 1986 and 1992, and continued to decline dramatically from 14.7m. in 1992 to 0.25m. by 2000. However, numbers were considered likely to increase with new investment. The Government slowly opened the railway system to private-sector involvement as it prepared to link the Mexican system with that of the USA and Canada, under NAFTA. In 1997–98 the Government divided Ferrocarriles Nacionales de México into regional companies and transferred their management to the private sector under 50-year concessions.

Mexico had 108 maritime ports, but the majority of cargo shipments were handled by just nine of them. The need for port facilities to meet international standards induced the Government to offer their management to the private sector. In 1989–94 US $700m. was spent on port development, much of it from the private sector. In 1994–95 the management of the ports of Altamira, Acapulco, Guaymas, Tampico, Lázaro Cárdenas, Manzanillo and Veracruz was transferred to the private sector.

Mexico boasts one of the largest networks of airports in the world, with nearly every town or city of over 50,000 inhabitants having its own airport. In 2000 there were 55 international airports. There were more than 50 national air companies, of which Aerovías de México (Aeroméxico) and Compañía Mexicana de Aviación, SA de CV (Mexicana) were the two largest and together controlled around three-quarters of the domestic market. Formerly state-owned, the companies were bought out by a coalition of banks in the late 1980s under the auspices of a new government-owned holding company, Cintra. However, Cintra's monopolistic arrangement was reviewed by the Federal Competition Commission in 1999, and the debate in 2001 centred on whether to sell the company as a single entity or in parts, to foster competition. The Government also planned to allow the private sector to build and operate airports on 50-year, renewable contracts. In December 1998 a consortium including Danish, French and Spanish investors successfully bid in the first auction for management of airports, gaining control of nine southern airports, including Cancún. In August 1999 Mexican and Spanish investors won control of Pacific coast airports, including Guadalajara and Tijuana. In 2001 the Government had yet to decide on the location of a new international airport in Mexico City before offering it for tender.

The state-owned telephone company, Teléfonos de México, SA de CV (Telmex) was privatized in 1990. The number of telephone lines increased from 5.4m. in 1990 to an estimated 12.3m. in 2000. Further liberalization opened long-distance and cellular services to competition in 1996. In 2000 there were an estimated 12.1m. cellular telephone subscribers, expected to increase to over 30m. by 2005. In 1997 Telmex received a provisional licence to provide services in the USA, in conjunction with US telecommunications company, Sprint. The local market was opened to competition in 1998. However, Telmex restricted access to local markets for competitors following disputes over interconnection fees and debt payments. These financial disputes were resolved in January 2001, but the extra market access subsequently made available to competitors was insufficient to stop the USA challenging Mexico in the World Trade Organization (WTO).

TOURISM

Tourism was an important foreign-exchange earner, with receipts from tourism (excluding day-trippers) totalling an estimated US $4,400m. in 2000 (day-trippers added a further $1,700m.). This represented a decrease from the $5,425m. earned in 1999. An estimated 10.4m. foreign tourists visited Mexico in 1999, of whom around 90% came from the USA and Canada. Tourist numbers increased following the devaluation of the peso at the end of 1994, although the value of average expenditure fell, resulting in a decrease in revenue from $4,250m. in 1994 to $4,050m. in 1995. Mexico's attractions range from beach resorts such as Acapulco and Bahías de Huatulco on the Pacific coast and Cancún on the Caribbean coast, to a number of pre-Columbian sites including Teotihuacan and Chichén Itzá, as well as various colonial cities. From the late 1980s the Government made a concerted effort to encourage further 'open-skies' policy (a deregulated civil aviation market), while investment rules were liberalized for domestic and foreign investors alike. In 2000 tourism in Mexico supported employment for some 1.8m. people and captured an estimated 3%–4% of the global tourist market.

FINANCE

From the early 1980s there were dramatic changes in the financial sphere. In 1982 the Government nationalized the banking sector in an attempt to help overcome the debt crisis. A process of rationalization ensued, with the number of commercial banks being reduced from 58 to 18. Although in 1987 34% of their capital was returned to private ownership in the form of non-voting stock, these banks remained under government control until 1991, when reprivatization began. By July 1992 the process was complete. The banks were generally sold for a high price, reflecting the fact that they were very profitable. However, operating systems had become cumbersome and outmoded and the new owners had to invest in modernization.

An added incentive to increase the banking sector's competitiveness came in 1993, when the Government began to authorize the establishment of new domestic banks. Following the ratification of NAFTA in 1994, US and Canadian banks were allowed access to the Mexican financial sector, albeit with certain restrictions. In addition, investors from countries other than the USA and Canada could also gain entry to the Mexican market if they operated through a North American subsidiary. In 2000 there were 34 commercial banks in operation in Mexico.

The object of the financial-sector reforms was both to increase domestic savings and to reduce borrowing costs. Before the bank privatizations began, the rules on lending had been relaxed. This, combined with success in reducing the fiscal deficit, lowered interest rates from 95% in 1987 to 14% by the end of 1993. In April 1994 interest rates in particular, and the setting of monetary policy in general, became the preserve of an autonomous central bank, Banco de México (BANXICO). The Government believed that by giving BANXICO independence it was guaranteeing that price stability would be maintained. The Government intervened to support ailing commercial banks and to prevent a collapse in the banking sector owing to 'bad' debts, which multiplied following devaluation in late 1994. In early 1998 the Government submitted to Congress proposals to grant additional powers of autonomy to BANXICO. However, a further crisis in the financial sector was prompted following an investigation by the US authorities, which in May resulted in the arrest of several prominent bankers, accused of money laundering and cultivating links with drugs cartels.

The Government established the Banking Fund for the Protection of Savings (Fondo Bancario de Protección al Ahorro—Fobraproa) to assume bad banking debts in exchange for new capital injections from shareholders. By late 1999 Fobaproa had absorbed US $89,000m. of liabilities, of which only an estimated 20% of the value would be recovered. After much political wrangling in Congress, in 1999 a new agency was approved, the Bank Savings Protection Institute (Instituto de Protección al Ahorro Bancario—IPAB). IPAB continued to prop up bankrupt banks, notably the third-largest bank, Banca Serfin, which it sold to Spanish bank Banco Santander Central Hispano in May 2000. IPAB also introduced new insurance quotas for banks to cover deposits and auctioned the rights to manage and recover loans accumulated by Fobraproa.

FOREIGN TRADE AND BALANCE OF PAYMENTS

The economic adjustments made necessary by the debt crisis of the 1980s led to a distinct improvement in the foreign-trade balance. After an eight-year period of increasing deficits, surpluses were recorded each year between 1982 and 1989. However, from 1990 the balance of trade was in deficit once again. Trade liberalization measures and a foreign-exchange policy that tended to allow the peso to become over-valued were partly to blame. The recovery in domestic growth rates and weak commodity prices also had a negative impact. The trade deficit amounted to US $18,464m. in 1994, compared with a deficit of $881m. just four years earlier and a surplus of $405m. in 1989. Following devaluation of the peso in 1994, exports performed better than imports. In 1995 Mexico registered a trade surplus of $7,089m. This surplus declined slightly to $6,531m. in 1996, before falling more dramatically to $623m. in 1997 as the growth in non-petroleum exports stimulated demand for imports of intermediate goods. While the value of exports increased by 22% in 1996–98, the value of imports increased by 40% over the same period, resulting in the trade balance falling into deficit once again in 1998. In that year a deficit of $7,915m. was recorded, falling to $5,581m. in 1999, but increasing again to an estimated $6,001m. in 2000.

Petroleum was traditionally the most important export, but it was surpassed in the mid-1990s by manufactures. Crude petroleum and petroleum products accounted for 7.3% of the value of total exports in 1999, compared with a record 89.3% for manufactures (including *maquiladora* manufactures, which made up about 46.6% of total exports). However, the export performance of manufactures was inconsistent, with a deficit recorded in 1997, despite surpluses in the metal products, machinery and equipment, and textiles and clothing sub-sectors. This inconsistency suggested that the economy's competitiveness relied on cheap labour in the *maquiladora* sector. Agriculture (including livestock, forestry and fisheries) accounted for 2.9% of total exports in 1999, a decline from 5.0% in 1995. The contribution of mineral products to total exports remained stable at just 0.3% in 1999.

Imports consisted mainly of intermediate products required by the manufacturing sector. By 1999 these totalled US $109,358m., or 77% of total imports. Imports of capital goods, which rose during the 1990s to support the increase in investment activity, amounted to $20,527m. in 1999. In that year this accounted for 14.4% of total imports. In 1999 imports of consumer goods amounted to $12,174m., representing 8.5% of total imports.

The vast majority of Mexico's foreign trade was, unsurprisingly, with the USA, a pattern which was reinforced by NAFTA. In 2000 the USA was the destination for an estimated 89% of Mexico's exports and the origin of 74% of imports. In 1997 Mexico displaced Japan as the USA's second most important trading partner. Although NAFTA would also bring about a strengthening of trade flows with Canada, the Mexican Government endeavoured to prevent excessive dependence on its northern neighbours. To this end it entered into free-trade agreements with Bolivia, Chile, Colombia, Costa Rica and Venezuela. The Government also sought to foster closer trading relations with countries outside Latin America. Important overseas trading partners included Germany and Japan. In 1993 Mexico gained admission to the Asia-Pacific Economic Co-operation group.

As well as a trade deficit, Mexico had a perennial shortfall on its 'invisibles' account. The largest contributors to this deficit were interest payments on the foreign debt, which led to massive current-account deficits in the balance of payments. At the same time there was substantial new foreign borrowing by the public- and private-sector alike. The result was a rapid increase in the size of the foreign debt. During the 1980s the authorities embarked on various debt-rescheduling exercises with commercial-bank creditors. The most fruitful was an agreement reached in 1989, adopting the idea of debt relief proposed by Nicholas Brady, the US Treasury Secretary, under the so-called Brady Plan. Although the Brady Plan required new borrowing from the World Bank, the IMF and Japan to provide a certain amount of collateral, it did lead to a reduction in the stock of external debt. However, in the early 1990s the debt increased once more. Total public- and private-sector foreign debt amounted to $166,900m. in 2000. Meanwhile, the current-account deficit declined significantly to $1,576m. in 1995. However, a continuing deficit on the invisibles account offset a trade surplus to produce a current-account deficit of $2,330m. in 1996, which was covered by new debt and foreign investment. Between 1996–99, the current-account deficit increased, reaching $15,724m. in 1998, as imports increased faster than exports. The current-account deficit declined to $14,166m. in 1999, but increased to an estimated $16,900m. in 2000. Mexico continued to record deficits in the trade, services and income balances. The peso was appreciating as a result of inflows of foreign capital into the stock market and high petroleum prices raising prospects of a correction. However, the floating exchange rate and macroeconomic indicators suggested that any devaluation would be less drastic than previous devaluations.

CONCLUSION

Unquestionably, there was a dramatic transformation in the Mexican economy in the 1980s and 1990s. Particularly after 1989, when President Salinas came to power, the role of the state was steadily reduced and opportunities for private and foreign investment increased. However, it was too early to tell whether the 6.9% growth rate recorded in 2000 represented a sustained return to the higher growth rates that prevailed before the 1980s, or whether it was an exception, as the 6.8% growth registered in 1997 proved to be. Low growth in the 1990s saw the poorer sections of society, already adversely affected by the previous decade's austerity measures, steadily became poorer. Political instability in 1994 caused a deterioration in economic conditions. The new peso came under pressure, leading to the devaluation crisis of December and recession and economic crisis in 1995. However, the devaluation of the peso restored export growth and the imposition of strict austerity measures ensured that the economy was more solidly based. Assisted by substantial financial aid, the economy began to recover in 1996. In 1997–98 growth returned to the Mexican economy and inflation was brought under control, with few adverse effects from the Asian financial crisis and the decline in world petroleum prices as Mexico strengthened its economic links with its North American neighbours. While NAFTA and other free-trade agreements with Latin American and Pacific countries were expected to continue to provide an impetus to exports and to investment, it was the Government's hope that this investment would be increasingly directed to productive, rather than speculative, assets.

Clearly, the maintenance of political calm was crucial to Mexico's economic future. The defeat of the ruling PRI in the presidential elections of 2000 represented a profound watershed in Mexican history. Investor confidence in Mexican political stability was encouraged by an orderly transfer of power in December 2000. Among President Fox's economic objectives in his first year in office were GDP growth of 4.5%, a budget deficit of 0.5% of GDP and a reduction in the annual rate of inflation to 6.5%. He also declared his aim of reducing Mexican dependence on commerce with the USA by attracting increased investment from countries of the European Union. However, his lack of an absolute majority in Congress, as well as the expected downturn in the US economy in 2001, reduced the likelihood of these aims being easily realized.

Statistical Survey

Sources (unless otherwise stated): Dirección General de Estadística, Instituto Nacional de Estadística, Geografía e Informática (INEGI), Edif. Sede, Avda Prolongación Héroe de Nacozari 2301 Sur, 20270 Aguascalientes, Ags; tel. (14) 918-1948; fax (14) 918-0739; internet www.inegi.gob.mx; Banco de México, Avda 5 de Mayo 2, Apdo 98 bis, 06059 México, DF; tel. (5) 237-2000; fax (5) 237-2370; internet www.banxico.org.mx; Banco Nacional de Comercio Exterior, SNC, Avda Camino Santa Teresa 1679, Col. Jardines del Pedregal, Del. Alvaro Obregón, 01900 México, DF; tel. (5) 568-2122; fax (5) 652-6662; internet www.bancomext.com.

Area and Population

AREA, POPULATION AND DENSITY

Area (sq km)	1,953,162*
Population (census results)	
5 November 1995	91,158,290
14 February 2000 (preliminary results)	
Males	47,354,386
Females	50,007,325
Total	97,361,711
Density (per sq km) at February 2000 census . . .	49.8

* 754,120 sq miles.

ADMINISTRATIVE DIVISIONS
(at census of 14 February 2000)

States	Area (sq km)*	Estimated Population	Density (per sq km)	Capital
Aguascalientes (Ags) . .	5,197	944,285	181.7	Aguascalientes
Baja California (BC) . . .	71,576	2,487,367	34.8	Mexicali
Baja California Sur (BCS) . . .	71,428	424,041	5.9	La Paz
Campeche (Camp.)	56,798	690,689	12.2	Campeche
Chiapas (Chis) .	73,724	3,920,892	53.2	Tuxtla Gutiérrez
Chihuahua (Chih.)	245,945	3,052,907	12.4	Chihuahua
Coahuila (Coah.) .	149,511	2,298,070	15.4	Saltillo
Colima (Col.) . .	5,433	542,627	99.9	Colima
Distrito Federal (DF) . .	1,547	8,605,239	5,562.5	Mexico City
Durango (Dgo) .	121,776	1,448,661	11.9	Victoria de Durango
Guanajuato (Gto) .	30,768	4,663,032	151.6	Guanajuato
Guerrero (Gro) .	64,586	3,079,649	47.7	Chilpancingo de los Bravos
Hidalgo (Hgo) .	20,502	2,235,591	109.0	Pachuca de Soto
Jalisco (Jal.) . .	78,389	6,322,002	80.6	Guadalajara
México (Méx.) .	21,196	13,096,686	617.9	Toluca de Lerdo
Michoacán (Mich.).	58,200	3,985,667	68.4	Morelia
Morelos (Mor.) .	4,968	1,555,296	313.1	Cuernavaca
Nayarit (Nay.) .	26,908	920,185	34.2	Tepic
Nuevo León (NL) .	64,210	3,834,141	59.7	Monterrey
Oaxaca (Oax.) .	93,136	3,438,765	36.9	Oaxaca de Juárez
Puebla (Pue.) . .	33,995	5,076,686	149.3	Heroica Puebla de Zaragoza
Querétaro (Qro) .	11,978	1,404,306	117.2	Querétaro
Quintana Roo (Q.Roo) .	39,376	874,963	22.2	Ciudad Chetumal
San Luis Potosí (SLP) . .	63,038	2,299,360	36.5	San Luis Potosí
Sinaloa (Sin.) .	56,496	2,536,844	44.9	Culiacán Rosales
Sonora (Son.) .	180,833	2,216,969	12.3	Hermosillo
Tabasco (Tab.) .	24,578	1,891,829	77.0	Villahermosa
Tamaulipas (Tam.)	78,932	2,753,222	34.9	Ciudad Victoria
Tlaxcala (Tlax.) .	4,037	962,646	238.5	Tlaxcala de Xicohténcatl
Veracruz (Ver.) .	71,735	6,908,975	96.3	Jalapa Enríquez
Yucatán (Yuc.) .	43,257	1,658,210	38.3	Mérida
Zacatecas (Zac.) .	73,103	1,353,610	18.5	Zacatecas
Total . .	**1,947,156**	**97,483,412**	**50.1**	—

* Excluding islands.

PRINCIPAL TOWNS
(population at census of 14 February 2000, preliminary results)

Distrito Federal	8,591,309
Guadalajara	1,647,720
Escatepec de Morelos.	1,620,303
Heroica Puebla de Zaragoza (Puebla)	1,346,176
Nezahualcóyotl	1,224,924
Ciudad Juárez	1,217,818
Tijuana	1,212,232
León	1,133,576
Monterrey	1,108,499
Zapopan.	1,002,239
Nauculpan de Juárez.	857,511
Mexicali	764,902
Culiacán Rosales (Culiacán)	744,859
Acapulco de Juárez (Acapulco)	721,011
Tlalnepantla de Baz	720,755
Mérida	703,324
Chihuahua	670,208
San Luis Potosí	669,353
Guadalupe	668,780
Toluca de Lerdo (Toluca)	665,617
Aguascalientes	643,360
Querétaro	639,839
Morelia	619,958
Hermosillo	608,697
Saltillo	577,352
Torreón	529,023
Villahermosa	519,873
San Nicolás de los Garza	495,540
Victoria de Durango (Durango)	490,524
Chimalhuacán	490,245
Tlaquepaque.	475,472
Atizapán de Zarogoza	467,262
Veracruz Llave (Veracruz)	457,119
Cuautitlán Izxalli	452,976
Irapuato	440,039
Tuxtla Gutiérrez	433,544
Tultitlán	432,411
Reynosa	419,776
Benito Juárez	419,926
Matamoros	416,428

BIRTHS, MARRIAGES AND DEATHS*

	Registered live births		Registered marriages		Registered deaths	
	Number	Rate (per 1,000)	Number	Rate (per 1,000)	Number	Rate (per 1,000)
1990 .	2,735,312	31.7	642,201	7.5	422,803	4.9
1991 .	2,756,447	31.4	652,172	7.4	411,131	4.7
1992 .	2,797,397	31.2	667,598	7.5	409,814	4.6
1993 .	2,765,580	30.3	679,911	7.5	413,756	4.5
1994 .	2,904,389	31.2	671,640	7.2	419,074	4.5
1995 .	2,750,444	30.4	658,114	7.3	430,278	4.6
1996 .	2,707,718	28.0	670,523	6.9	436,321	4.5
1997 .	2,698,425	28.6	707,840	7.5	440,437	4.7

1998: Registered live births 2,668,429; Registered deaths 444,665.

1999: Registered live births 2,769,089; Registered marriages 743,856; Registered deaths 443,950.

* Data are tabulated by year of registration rather than by year of occurrence. Rates are calculated on the basis of unrevised population estimates. However, birth registration is incomplete. According to UN estimates, the average annual rates in 1985–90 were: births 29.3 per 1,000; deaths 5.7 per 1,000, and in 1990–1995: births 27.0 per 1,000; deaths 5.2 per 1,000.

Expectation of life (UN estimates, years at birth, 1990–95): 71.2 (males 68.5; females 74.5) (Source: UN, *World Population Prospects: The 1998 Revision*).

ECONOMICALLY ACTIVE POPULATION
(sample surveys, '000 persons aged 12 years and over, April– June)

	1997	1998	1999
Agriculture, hunting, forestry and fishing	9,020	7,817	8,209
Mining and quarrying	108	153	133
Manufacturing	6,265	6,984	7,345
Electricity, gas and water	188	183	193
Construction	1,759	2,126	2,158
Trade, restaurants and hotels	8,028	8,629	8,390
Transport, storage and communications	1,520	1,693	1,739
Financing, insurance, real estate and business services	1,513	1,472	1,459
Community, social and personal services	8,821	9,392	9,278
Activities not adequately defined	140	169	166
Total employed	37,360	38,618	39,069
Unemployed	985	890	682
Total labour force	38,345	39,507	39,751
Males	25,347	26,176	26,437
Females	12,998	13,331	13,314

Source: ILO, *Yearbook of Labour Statistics*.

Agriculture

PRINCIPAL CROPS ('000 metric tons)

	1998	1999	2000
Wheat	3,235	3,072	3,300†
Rice (paddy)	458	395	450
Barley	411	466	532
Maize	18,455	18,314	18,761
Oats	89	132	106
Sorghum	6,475	6,043	6,400†
Potatoes	1,281	1,468	1,593
Dry Beans	1,261	1,081	1,158
Chick-peas	98	211	210*
Soybeans (Soya beans)	150	133	114
Groundnuts (in shell)	131	135†	137
Coconuts*	1,303	1,100	1,313
Safflower seed	171	263	109
Cabbages	207	205*	205*
Lettuce	169	168*	168*
Tomatoes	2,252	2,431	2,400
Cauliflower	210*	210*	200*
Pumpkins, squash and gourds*	440	440	440
Cucumbers and gherkins	430	420	410
Green chillies and peppers	1,850	1,810	1,813
Green onions and shallots	885	1,247	1,200*
Onions (dry)	102*	100*	100*
Carrots	320	356	359
Green corn (maize)*	193	190	190
Bananas	1,526	1,737	1,802
Oranges	3,331	2,903	3,390
Tangerines, mandarins, clemintines and satsumas	296	250†	240*
Lemons and limes	1,186	1,215	1,297
Grapefruit	168	160†	160*
Apples	370	443	390†
Peaches and nectarines	116	115*	115*
Strawberries	119	141	166
Grapes	478	479	481
Watermelons	698	923	993
Melons*	500	500	500
Mangoes	1,474	1,449	1,529
Avocados	877	807	939
Pineapples	481	502	486
Papayas	576	459	636
Coffee (green)	306	311	354
Cocoa beans	44	37	43
Tobacco (leaves)	49	51	43
Cotton (lint)	247	148	51*

* FAO estimate(s).   † Unofficial figure(s).

Source: FAO.

LIVESTOCK ('000 head, year ending September)

	1998	1999	2000
Horses*	6,250	6,250	6,250
Mules*	3,270	3,270	3,270
Asses*	3,250	3,250	3,250
Cattle	30,500	30,293	30,293
Pigs	14,994	13,845	13,690
Sheep	5,990*	5,900*	5,900
Goats	9,381†	9,600*	9,600
Chickens*	431,000	450,000	476
Ducks*	8,000	8,000	8,000
Turkeys*	3,000	3,000	3,000

* FAO estimates.   † Unofficial figures.

Source: FAO.

LIVESTOCK PRODUCTS ('000 metric tons)

	1998	1999	2000
Beef and veal	1,380	1,401	1,415
Mutton and lamb . . .	30	31	32
Goat meat	38	37	39
Pig meat	961	992	1,035
Horse meat*	79	79*	79*
Poultry meat	1,633	1,767	1,896
Cows' milk	8,574	9,171	9,474
Goats' milk	128	131	134
Butter	55†	60†	60*
Cheese	130	138	148
Evaporated and condensed milk* .	137	137	137*
Hen eggs	1,461	1,635	1,666†
Cattle hides†	170	170	175
Honey	55	55	57

* FAO estimate(s).   † Unofficial figure(s).
Source: FAO.

Forestry

ROUNDWOOD REMOVALS ('000 cubic metres, excluding bark)

	1997	1998	1999
Sawlogs, veneer logs and logs for sleepers	5,921	6,520	6,520*
Pulpwood	1,217	1,210	1,210*
Other industrial wood . .	175	201	201*
Fuel wood	15,678	15,935	16,191
Total	22,991	23,866	24,122

* FAO estimate(s).
Source: FAO.

SAWNWOOD PRODUCTION ('000 cubic metres, incl. railway sleepers)

	1997	1998	1999*
Coniferous (softwood). . .	2,751	3,044	3,044
Broadleaved (hardwood) . .	210	216	216
Total	2,961	3,260	3,260

* FAO estimate(s).
Source: FAO.

Fishing

('000 metric tons, live weight)

	1996	1997	1998
Capture	1,464.1	1,489.0	1,181.4
Tilapias	74.4	74.8	69.7
California pilchard (sardine)	340.2	325.7	323.2
Yellowfin tuna . . .	127.8	140.3	117.8
Marine shrimps and prawns	65.6	71.1	66.6
Jumbo flying squid . .	108.0	120.9	26.6
Aquaculture	31.3	39.5	41.0
Total catch (incl. others) .	1,495.4	1,528.5	1,222.4

Note: Figures exclude aquatic plants ('000 metric tons, capture only): 34.6 in 1996; 42.1 in 1997; 12.5 in 1998. Also excluded are aquatic mammals and crocodiles (recorded by number rather than by weight), shells and corals. The number of Morelet's crocodiles caught was: 20 in 1996; 146 in 1997; 121 in 1998. The catch of marine shells (metric tons) was: 542 in 1996; 1,403 in 1997; 970 in 1998.

Source: FAO, *Yearbook of Fishery Statistics.*

Mining

(metric tons, unless otherwise indicated)

	1998	1999	2000
Antimony*	1,301	273	110
Arsenic*	2,573	2,419	2,468
Barytes	161,555	157,952	
Bismuth*	1,204	548	1,082
Cadmium*	1,739	1,311	1,311
Coal*	7,832,227	8,767,000	7,369,468
Coke*	2,202,558	2,227,531	2,241,345
Copper*	344,756	340,147	344,551
Crude petroleum ('000 barrels per day)	3,070	2,906	3,012
Dolomite	785,516	416,284	386,110
Feldspar	197,866	262,241	267,819
Fluorite	598,043	557,106	543,581
Gas (million cu ft per day) .	4,791	4,791	4,679
Gold (kg)*	25,983	23,476	26,557
Graphite	43,461	27,781	34,915
Iron*	6,334,257	6,885,217	6,794,778
Lead*	171,610	131,402	155,940
Manganese*	187,103	169,107	157,547
Molybdenum*	5,949	7,961	6,726
Phosphate rock	756,349	950,649	981,196
Silver*	2,868	2,456	2,790
Sulphur	912,825	855,483	851,427
Tungsten*	9,362	849	0
Zinc*	371,898	339,758	357,161

* Figures for metallic minerals refer to the metal content of ores.
Source (for crude petroleum and gas): PEMEX.

Industry

SELECTED PRODUCTS
('000 metric tons, unless otherwise indicated)

	1995	1996	1997
Wheat flour	2,696.2	2,596.5	2,591.8
Corn flour	2,318.6	2,580.5	2,214.4
Raw Sugar	4,205.1	4,606.9	4,565.1
Beer ('000 hectolitres) . .	44,204.8	48,111.5	48,444.2
Cigarettes (million units) . .	56,820.6	59,907.2	57,637.5
Lubricating oils . . .	365.5	388.8	407.1
Sulphuric acid . . .	371	511	n.a.
Tyres ('000 units)* . . .	9,292	10,772	11,665
Cement	25,294.8	28,174.3	29,765.1
Gas stoves—household ('000 units)	2,301.4	2,631.8	2,999.4
Refrigerators—household ('000 units)	1,256.1	1,447.5	1,933.2
Washing machines—household ('000 units)	882.4	1,091.2	1,435.7
Television receivers ('000 units) .	181.1	205.4	244.3
Cotton yarn (pure) . .	7.8	4.6	4.7
Electric energy (million kWh) .	135,593	145,628	154,340

* Tyres for road motor vehicles.

Finance

CURRENCY AND EXCHANGE RATES

Monetary Units

100 centavos = 1 Mexican nuevo peso.

Sterling, Dollar and Euro Equivalents (30 April 2001)
£1 sterling = 13.269 nuevos pesos;
US $1 = 9.267 nuevos pesos;
€1 = 8.225 nuevos pesos;
1,000 Mexican nuevos pesos = £75.37 = $107.91 = €121.57.

Average Exchange Rate (nuevos pesos per US $)
1998   9.1360
1999   9.5604
2000   9.4556

Note: Figures are given in terms of the nuevo (new) peso, introduced on 1 January 1993 and equivalent to 1,000 former pesos.

BUDGET (million new pesos)*

Revenue	1995	1996	1997
Taxation†	235,016	321,495	413,921
Taxes on income, profits and			
capital gains . . .	76,148	102,220	144,599
Social security contributions .	39,013	48,437	57,780
Value-added tax . . .	51,785	72,110	97,741
Excises	25,379	29,706	46,200
Import duties	11,145	14,855	18,103
Other current revenue . .	46,040	62,873	53,782
Property income . . .	42,465	56,638	45,341
Capital revenue	82	98	484
Total revenue	281,138	384,466	468,187

Expenditure‡	1995	1996	1997
General public services . .	16,151	19,845	36,071
Defence	11,477	14,202	18,321
Public order and safety . .	3,740	4,306	4,819
Education	70,524	95,010	114,169
Health	9,255	12,861	17,764
Social security and welfare .	58,513	74,789	93,216
Housing and community amenities	8,204	13,111	17,571
Recreational, cultural and			
religious affairs and services .	1,785	2,142	3,140
Economic affairs and services .	43,830	57,134	90,661
Fuel and energy . . .	7,163	6,713	6,798
Agriculture, forestry and fishing	9,833	16,353	24,141
Transport and communications .	11,254	16,494	37,034
Other purposes	78,428	109,940	150,323
Interest on public debt . .	53,008	72,287	70,709
Sub-total	301,907	403,340	546,055
Adjustment to cash basis . .	−9,428	−15,530	−29,825
Total expenditure . . .	292,479	387,810	516,230
Current	255,723	342,058	454,716
Capital	34,023	48,109	60,685
Adjustment	2,733	−2,357	829

* Figures refer to the consolidated accounts of the central Government, including government agencies and the national social security system. The budgets of state and local governments are excluded.
† Including adjustment (million new pesos): −49,115 in 1995; −70,841 in 1996; −94,528 in 1997.
‡ Excluding net lending (million new pesos): 3,325 in 1995; 2,906 in 1996; −11,697 in 1997.

Source: IMF, *Government Finance Statistics Yearbook*.
1998 (million new pesos): Total revenue (incl. grants) 488,959; total expenditure 556,079 (excl. net lending 11,529).
1999 (million new pesos): Total revenue (incl. grants) 620,135; total expenditure 689,921 (excl. net lending 1,503).
2000 (million new pesos): Total revenue (incl. grants) 791,040; total expenditure 848,484 (excl. net lending 11,811).
Source: IMF *International Financial Statistics*.

INTERNATIONAL RESERVES (US $ million at 31 December)*

	1998	1999	2000
IMF special drawing rights . .	337	790	366
Foreign exchange	31,461	30,992	35,142
Total	31,799	31,782	35,508

* Excluding gold reserves ($357 million at 30 September 1989).
Source: IMF, *International Financial Statistics*.

MONEY SUPPLY (million new pesos at 31 December)

	1998	1999	2000
Currency outside banks . . .	116,083	164,424	183,118
Demand deposits at deposit money			
banks	190,036	229,128	259,494
Total money (incl. others) . .	308,135	395,475	444,138

Source: IMF, *International Financial Statistics*.

COST OF LIVING (Consumer Price Index; base: 1995 = 100)

	1998	1999	2000
All items	187.9	219.1	239.9

Source: IMF, *International Financial Statistics*.

NATIONAL ACCOUNTS (million new pesos at current prices)
National Income and Product

	1993	1994	1995
Compensation of employees . .	436,483	501,897	571,354
Operating surplus . . .	597,279	667,538	889,692
Domestic factor incomes . .	1,033,762	1,169,435	1,461,046
Consumption of fixed capital . .	113,388	129,563	210,842
Gross domestic product at			
factor cost	1,147,150	1,298,998	1,671,888
Indirect taxes	119,862	131,036	178,982
Less Subsidies	10,816	9,875	13,094
GDP in purchasers' values .	1,256,196	1,420,159	1,837,775

Source: UN, *National Accounts Statistics*.

Expenditure on the Gross Domestic Product*

	1998	1999	2000
Government final consumption			
expenditure	399,960	500,800	596,520
Private final consumption			
expenditure	2,593,350	3,077,840	3,669,290
Increase in stocks . . .	133,280	108,690	130,210
Gross fixed capital formation . .	804,000	973,710	1,135,590
Total domestic expenditure .	3,930,590	3,687,330	5,531,610
Exports of goods and services .	1,180,390	1,414,340	1,705,710
Less Imports of goods and services	1,262,760	1,486,900	1,804,970
GDP in purchasers' values .	3,848,220	3,614,770	5,432,360
GDP at constant 1993 prices .	1,451,350	1,505,850	1,609,140

* Figures are rounded to the nearest 10 million new pesos.
Source: IMF, *International Financial Statistics*.

Gross Domestic Product by Economic Activity

	1997	1998	1999
Agriculture, forestry and fishing .	159,168	183,511	197,728
Mining and quarrying . . .	43,923	48,424	60,140
Manufacturing	615,478	749,293	884,527
Electricity, gas and water . .	34,340	44,298	55,515
Construction	128,022	165,013	207,277
Trade, restaurants and hotels .	613,546	701,090	837,562
Transport, storage and			
communications . . .	304,348	381,118	468,657
Finance, insurance, real estate			
and business services . .	384,189	481,762	546,964
Community, social and personal			
services	632,585	798,641	995,143
Sub-total	2,915,601	3,553,149	4,253,513
Less Imputed bank service charge	42,328	35,367	57,010
GDP at factor cost . . .	2,873,273	3,517,782	4,196,503
Indirect taxes, *less* subsidies . .	301,002	328,568	387,260
GDP in purchasers' values .	2,572,271	3,189,214	4,583,762

BALANCE OF PAYMENTS (US $ million)

	1997	1998	1999
Exports of goods f.o.b. . . .	110,431	117,459	136,392
Imports of goods f.o.b. . . .	−109,808	−125,374	141,973
Trade balance	623	−7,915	−5,581
Exports of services . . .	11,400	12,064	11,733
Imports of services . . .	−12,616	−13,067	−14,295
Balance on goods and services	−593	−8,918	−8,143
Other income received . .	4,430	4,911	4,890
Other income paid . . .	−16,538	−17,732	17,227
Balance on goods, services and income	−12,701	−21,739	−20,480
Current transfers received . .	5,272	6,042	6,341
Current transfers paid . . .	−25	−28	27
Current balance . . .	−7,454	−15,724	−14,166
Direct investment from abroad .	12,831	11,312	11,786
Portfolio investment assets .	−708	−768	−836
Portfolio investment liabilities .	5,038	−578	10,996
Other investment assets . .	7,425	1,201	−1,804
Other investment liabilities .	−5,333	7,373	−851
Net errors and omissions . .	2,198	378	−817
Overall balance . . .	13,997	3,193	4,278

Source: IMF, *International Financial Statistics.*

External Trade

PRINCIPAL COMMODITIES (distribution by SITC, US $ million)

Imports f.o.b.	1996	1997	1998
Food and live animals . . .	4,897.2	4,633.9	5,285.3
Cereals and cereal preparations .	2,281.8	1,438.4	1,793.4
Crude materials (inedible) except fuels	3,641.7	4,518.3	4,263.0
Mineral fuels, lubricants, etc. . .	1,808.9	2,995.4	2,747.3
Chemicals and related products	8,134.7	10,054.1	10,718.2
Organic chemicals . . .	2,139.5	2,687.1	2,589.8
Artificial resins, plastic materials, etc.	2,350.5	2,953.0	3,277.8
Basic manufactures . .	15,373.0	18,900.4	21,537.2
Paper, paperboard and manufactures	2,052.4	2,359.5	2,568.1
Textile yarn, fabrics, etc. . .	2,241.5	2,897.0	3,462.5
Iron and steel	2,519.8	3,106.2	3,509.6
Machinery and transport equipment	41,391.9	51,783.5	59,849.7
Power-generating machinery and equipment	3,461.7	4,002.2	4,311.0
Internal combustion piston engines	2,391.1	2,526.5	2,603.4
Machinery specialized for particular industries . .	2,891.9	4,055.7	4,687.4
General industrial machinery and equipment and parts . .	4,837.3	5,957.2	6,966.7
Office machines and automatic data-processing equipment . .	2,344.7	2,913.6	3,185.8
Telecommuncations and sound equipment	3,583.4	4,775.3	5,820.0
Other electrical machinery, apparatus, etc. . . .	16,141.3	19,356.1	22,406.0
Switchgear, resistors, printed circuits, switchboards, etc. .	3,743.7	4,476.4	5,310.5
Switchgear, switchboards, control panels and parts	2,468.2	3,039.7	3,535.6
Equipment for distributing electricity	2,550.8	3,038.2	3,098.9
Insulated electric wire, cable, etc.	2,087.6	2,455.3	2,523.0
Thermionic valves, tubes, etc. . .	5,577.1	6,505.1	7,891.7
Electronic microcircuits . .	2,896.0	3,275.5	3,946.6

Imports f.o.b. — *continued*	1996	1997	1998
Road vehicles and parts* . . .	6,990.9	9,274.5	9,993.0
Parts and accessories for cars, buses, lorries, etc.* . . .	5,578.9	6,638.4	6,623.9
Miscellaneous manufactured articles	11,139.1	14,293.7	15,772.6
Clothing and accessories (excl. footwear)	2,394.6	3,355.2	3,750.1
Professional, scientific and controlling instruments, etc.	1,884.5	2,222.3	2,518.6
Articles of plastic materials, etc.	3,469.8	4,349.5	4,582.4
Total (incl. others)	89,355.1	111,983.3	125,193.2

* Excluding tyres, engines and electrical parts.

Exports f.o.b.	1996	1997	1998
Food and live animals . . .	5,311.4	5,813.5	6,134.7
Vegetables and fruit . . .	2,601.8	2,651.2	3,214.1
Mineral fuels, lubricants, etc. .	11,442.0	11,036.4	6,979.6
Petroleum, petroleum products, etc.	11,219.3	10,970.4	6,926.6
Crude petroleum oils, etc. . .	10,705.4	10,332.7	6,398.9
Chemicals and related products	3,808.1	4,190.6	4,230.8
Basic manufactures	9,833.1	11,634.4	11,975.9
Iron and steel	2,337.4	2,667.8	2,347.3
Machinery and transport equipment	51,166.8	59,445.7	68,010.9
Power-generating machinery and equipment	4,215.8	4,416.2	5,043.2
Internal combustion piston engines and parts . .	2,820.1	2,808.9	3,038.4
General industrial machinery, equipment and parts . .	2,520.1	3,191.7	3,571.6
Office machines and automatic data-processing equipment .	4,241.5	6,044.1	7,535.6
Automatic data-processing machines and units . .	2,700.4	3,767.2	4,428.0
Parts and accessories for office machines, etc. . . .	1,154.3	1,897.7	2,696.7
Telecommunications and sound equipment	8,260.6	10,003.7	12,075.4
Television receivers . .	3,331.0	3,852.7	4,911.1
Colour television receivers	3,330.8	3,852.5	4,908.6
Other electrical machinery, apparatus, etc. . .	14,344.0	16,986.8	18,225.7
Switchgear, resistors, printed circuits, switchboards, etc.	2,451.5	2,727.8	3,050.7
Switchgear, switchboards, control panels and parts	2,017.6	2,294.5	2,632.8
Equipment for distributing electricity	4,472.8	4,959.1	5,223.2
Insulated electric wire, cable, etc.	4,454.7	4,936.2	5,200.1
Road vehicles and parts* . . .	16,495.0	17,704.0	19,510.0
Passenger motor cars (excl. buses)	9,673.0	9,700.1	10,974.2
Motor vehicles for goods transport, etc. . . .	3,426.9	3,995.3	3,595.8
Goods vehicles (lorries and trucks)	3,422.4	3,985.2	3,579.1
Parts and accessories for cars, buses, lorries, etc.* . . .	2,976.1	3,462.1	4,173.8
Miscellaneous manufactured articles	11,071.3	14,840.8	16,976.1
Clothing and accessories (excl. footwear)	3,754.1	5,637.1	6,603.7
Professional, scientific and controlling instruments, etc.	1,372.5	1,901.9	2,356.4
Total (incl. others)	95,661.2	110,047.0	117,325.4

* Excluding tyres, engines and electrical parts.

Source: UN, *International Trade Statistics Yearbook.*

PRINCIPAL TRADING PARTNERS (US $ million)*

Imports c.i.f.	1997	1998	1999†
Canada	1,968.0	2,292.1	2,948.9
China, People's Republic	1,247.4	1,616.5	1,921.1
France (incl. Monaco)	1,182.4	1,429.9	1,393.7
Germany	3,902.3	4,558.0	5,032.1
Italy	1,326.0	1,581.1	1,649.4
Japan	4,333.6	4,553.4	5,083.1
Korea, Republic	1,831.0	1,951.3	2,964.0
Spain	977.7	1,257.0	1,321.8
Taiwan	1,136.5	1,526.6	1,556.8
USA	82,001.2	93,225.1	105,356.5
Total (incl. others)	113,120.2	129,072.2	146,173.0

Exports f.o.b.	1997	1998	1999†
Canada	2,156.7	1,521.0	2,311.3
Japan	1,156.4	855.6	777.0
USA	94,379.0	103,113.2	120,609.6
Total (incl. others)	110,431.4	117,500.3	136,703.4

* Imports by country of origin; exports by country of destination.
† Preliminary data.

CIVIL AVIATION (traffic on scheduled services)

	1995	1996	1997
Kilometres flown (million)	231	245	300
Passengers carried ('000)	14,969	14,678	17,266
Passenger-km (million)	19,403	19,636	23,668
Total ton-km (million)	1,799	1,861	2,295

Source: UN, *Statistical Yearbook*.

Tourism*

	1997	1998	1999†
Tourist arrivals ('000)	9,794	10,192	10,407
Total expenditure (US $ million)	5,303	5,539	5,425

* Excluding border tourism.
† Estimates.
Source: Secretaría de Turismo de México.

Transport

RAILWAYS (traffic, '000)

	1994	1995	1996
Passengers carried	7,189	6,678	6,727
Passenger-kilometres	1,855,000	1,899,000	1,799,314
Freight ton-kilometres	37,314,411	35,661,557	41,723,101

1998 (million): Passenger-kilometres 1,089; (Freight ton-kilometres 31,747 (Source: UN, *Statistical Yearbook*).

ROAD TRAFFIC (estimates, vehicles in use at 31 December)

	1997	1998	1999
Passenger cars	8,997,503	9,378,587	9,842,006
Buses and coaches	107,193	108,690	109,929
Lorries and vans	4,191,401	4,403,953	4,639,860

Source: International Road Federation, *World Road Statistics*.

SHIPPING

Merchant Fleet (registered at 31 December)

	1998	1999	2000
Number of vessels	626	621	631
Total displacement ('000 grt)	1,085.2	917.9	883.2

Source: Lloyd's Register of Shipping, *World Fleet Statistics*.

Sea-borne Shipping
(domestic and international freight traffic, '000 metric tons)

	1993	1994	1995
Goods loaded	129,091	130,884	135,957
Goods unloaded	53,121	56,308	53,300

Communications Media

	1994	1995	1996
Radio receivers ('000 in use)	23,500	24,000	30,000
Television receivers ('000 in use)	15,000	20,000	25,000
Telephones ('000 lines in service)	8,355	8,801	8,826
Telefax stations ('000 in use)*	200	220	220
Mobile cellular telephones ('000 subscribers)	569.3	688.5	1,021.9
Daily newspapers			
Number	309	301	295
Average circulation ('000)	10,420	9,338	9,030
Non-daily newspapers			
Number	45	21	23
Average circulation ('000)	1,274	648	620

* Estimates.
1997: Radio receivers 31,000,000 in use; Television receivers 25,600,000 in use; Telephones 9,254,000 lines in service; Telefax stations 285,000 in use; Mobile cellular telephones 1,746,972 subscribers.
Sources: UNESCO, *Statistical Yearbook*; UN, *Statistical Yearbook*.

Education

(estimates, 2000/01)

	Institutions	Teachers	Students*
Pre-primary	72,650	155,777	3,456.1
Primary	99,176	545,717	14,808.3
Secondary	44,441	552,735	9,330.9
Higher	4,081	214,126	2,073.5

* Figures are in thousands.
Source: Secretariat of State for Public Education.

Directory

Note: The prefix 5 should be added to all telephone and fax numbers in the Distrito Federal when dialling locally. Long-distance and international calls to the Distrito remain unchanged.

The Constitution

The present Mexican Constitution was proclaimed on 5 February 1917, at the end of the revolution, which began in 1910, against the regime of Porfirio Díaz. Its provisions regarding religion, education and the ownership and exploitation of mineral wealth reflect the long revolutionary struggle against the concentration of power in the hands of the Roman Catholic Church and the large landowners, and the struggle which culminated, in the 1930s, in the expropriation of the properties of the foreign petroleum companies. It has been amended from time to time.

GOVERNMENT

The President and Congress

The President of the Republic, in agreement with the Cabinet and with the approval of the Congreso de la Unión (Congress) or of the Permanent Committee when the Congreso is not in session, may suspend constitutional guarantees in case of foreign invasion, serious disturbance, or any other emergency endangering the people.

The exercise of supreme executive authority is vested in the President, who is elected for six years and enters office on 1 December of the year of election. The presidential powers include the right to appoint and remove members of the Cabinet and the Attorney-General; to appoint, with the approval of the Senado (Senate), diplomatic officials, the higher officers of the army, and ministers of the supreme and higher courts of justice. The President is also empowered to dispose of the armed forces for the internal and external security of the federation.

The Congreso is composed of the Cámara Federal de Diputados (Federal Chamber of Deputies) elected every three years, and the Senado whose members hold office for six years. There is one deputy for every 250,000 people and for every fraction of over 125,000 people. The Senado is composed of two members for each state and two for the Distrito Federal. Regular sessions of the Congreso begin on 1 September and may not continue beyond 31 December of the same year. Extraordinary sessions may be convened by the Permanent Committee.

The powers of the Congreso include the right to: pass laws and regulations; impose taxes; specify the criteria on which the Executive may negotiate loans; declare war; raise, maintain and regulate the organization of the armed forces; establish and maintain schools of various types throughout the country; approve or reject the budget; sanction appointments submitted by the President of the Supreme Court and magistrates of the superior court of the Distrito Federal; approve or reject treaties and conventions made with foreign powers; and ratify diplomatic appointments.

The Permanent Committee, consisting of 29 members of the Congreso (15 of whom are deputies and 14 senators), officiates when the Congreso is in recess, and is responsible for the convening of extraordinary sessions of the Congreso.

The States

Governors are elected by popular vote in a general election every six years. The local legislature is formed by deputies, who are changed every three years. The judicature is specially appointed under the Constitution by the competent authority (it is never subject to the popular vote).

Each state is a separate unit, with the right to levy taxes and to legislate in certain matters. The states are not allowed to levy inter-state customs duties.

The Federal District

The Distrito Federal consists of Mexico City and several neighbouring small towns and villages. The first direct elections for the Governor of the Distrito Federal were held in July 1997; hitherto a Regent had been appointed by the President.

EDUCATION

According to the Constitution, the provision of educational facilities is the joint responsibility of the federation, the states and the municipalities. Education shall be democratic, and shall be directed to developing all the faculties of the individual students, while imbuing them with love of their country and a consciousness of international solidarity and justice. Religious bodies may not provide education, except training for the priesthood. Private educational institutions must conform to the requirements of the Constitution with regard to the nature of the teaching given. The education provided by the states shall be free of charge.

RELIGION

Religious bodies of whatever denomination shall not have the capacity to possess or administer real estate or capital invested therein. Churches are the property of the nation; the headquarters of bishops, seminaries, convents and other property used for the propagation of a religious creed shall pass into the hands of the state, to be dedicated to the public service of the federation or of the respective state. Institutions of charity, provided they are not connected with a religious body, may hold real property. The establishment of monastic orders is prohibited. Ministers of religion must be Mexican; they may not criticize the fundamental laws of the country in a public or private meeting; they may not vote or form associations for political purposes. Political meetings may not be held in places of worship.

A reform proposal, whereby constitutional restrictions on the Catholic Church were formally ended, received congressional approval in December 1991 and was promulgated as law in January 1992.

LAND AND MINERAL OWNERSHIP

Article 27 of the Constitution vests direct ownership of minerals and other products of the subsoil, including petroleum and water, in the nation, and reserves to the Federal Government alone the right to grant concessions in accordance with the laws to individuals and companies, on the condition that they establish regular work for the exploitation of the materials. At the same time, the right to acquire ownership of lands and waters belonging to the nation, or concessions for their exploitation, is limited to Mexican individuals and companies, although the State may concede similar rights to foreigners who agree not to invoke the protection of their governments to enforce such rights.

The same article declares null all alienations of lands, waters and forests belonging to towns or communities made by political chiefs or other local authorities in violation of the provisions of the law of 25 June 1856,* and all concessions or sales of communally-held lands, waters and forests made by the federal authorities after 1 December 1876. The population settlements which lack *ejidos* (state-owned smallholdings), or cannot obtain restitution of lands previously held, shall be granted lands in proportion to the needs of the population. The area of land granted to the individual may not be less than 10 hectares of irrigated or watered land, or the equivalent in other kinds of land.

The owners affected by decisions to divide and redistribute land (with the exception of the owners of farming or cattle-rearing properties) shall not have any right of redress, nor may they invoke the right of amparo† in protection of their interests. They may, however, apply to the Government for indemnification. Small properties, the areas of which are defined in the Constitution, will not be subject to expropriation. The Constitution leaves to the Congreso the duty of determining the maximum size of rural properties.

In March 1992 an agrarian reform amendment, whereby the programme of land-distribution established by the 1917 Constitution was abolished and the terms of the *ejido* system of tenant farmers were relaxed, was formally adopted.

Monopolies and measures to restrict competition in industry, commerce or public services are prohibited.

A section of the Constitution deals with work and social security.

On 30 December 1977 a Federal Law on Political Organizations and Electoral Procedure was promulgated. It includes the following provisions:

Legislative power is vested in the Congreso de la Unión which comprises the Cámara Federal de Diputados and the Senado. The Cámara shall comprise 300 deputies elected by majority vote within single-member electoral districts and up to 100 deputies (increased to 200 from July 1988) elected by a system of proportional representation from regional lists within multi-member constituencies. The Senado comprises two members for each state and two for the Distrito Federal, elected by majority vote.

Executive power is exercised by the President of the Republic of the United Mexican States, elected by majority vote.

Ordinary elections will be held every three years for the federal deputies and every six years for the senators and the President of the Republic on the first Sunday of July of the year in question. When a vacancy occurs among members of the Congreso elected by majority vote, the house in question shall call extraordinary elections, and when a vacancy occurs among members of the Cámara elected by proportional representation it shall be filled by the candidate of the same party who received the next highest number of votes at the last ordinary election.

Voting is the right and duty of every citizen, male or female, over the age of 18 years.

A political party shall be registered if it has at least 3,000 members in each one of at least half the states in Mexico or at least 300 members in each one of at least half of the single-member constituencies. In either case the total number of members must be no less than 65,000. A party can also obtain conditional registration if it has been active for at least four years. Registration is confirmed if the party obtains at least 1.5% of the popular vote. All political parties shall have free access to the media.

In September 1993 an amendment to the Law on Electoral Procedure provided for the expansion of the Senado to 128 seats, representing four members for each state and the Distrito Federal, three to be elected by majority vote and one by proportional representation.

* The Lerdo Law against ecclesiastical privilege, which became the basis of the Liberal Constitution of 1857.

† The Constitution provides for the procedure known as juicio de amparo, a wider form of habeas corpus, which the individual may invoke in protection of his constitutional rights.

The Government

HEAD OF STATE

President: VICENTE FOX QUESADA (took office 1 December 2000).

CABINET
(August 2001)

Secretary of the Interior: SANTIAGO CREEL MIRANDA.

Secretary of Foreign Affairs: JORGE CASTAÑEDA.

Secretary of National Defence: Gen. GERARDO VEGA.

Secretary of the Navy: Adm. MARCO ANTONIO PEYROT.

Secretary of Public Security and Judicial Services: ALEJANDRO GERTZ MANERO.

Secretary of Finance and Public Credit: FRANCISCO GIL DÍAZ.

Secretary of Social Development: JOSEFINA VÁZQUEZ MOTA.

Secretary of the Environment and Natural Resources: VÍCTOR LICHTINGER.

Secretary of Energy: ERNESTO MARTENS REBOLLEDO.

Secretary of Economy: LUIS ERNESTO DERBEZ BAUTISTA.

Secretary of Agriculture, Livestock, Rural Development, Fisheries and Food: JAVIER USABIAGA ARROYO.

Secretary of Communications and Transport: PEDRO CERISOLA Y WEBER.

Comptroller-General: FRANCISO JAVIER BARRIO TERRAZAS.

Secretary of Public Education: REYES TAMEZ GUERRA.

Secretary of Health: JULIO FRENK MORA.

Secretary of Labour and Social Welfare: CARLOS MARÍA ABASCAL CARRANZA.

Secretary of Agrarian Reform: MARÍA TERESA HERRERA TELLO.

Secretary of Tourism: LETICIA NAVARRO.

Attorney-General: Gen. RAFAEL MARCIAL MACEDO DE LA CONCHA.

SECRETARIATS OF STATE

Office of the President: Los Pinos, Puerta 1, Col. San Miguel Chapultepec, 11850 México, DF; tel. (5) 515-3717; fax (5) 510-8713; internet www.presidencia.gob.mx.

Secretariat of State for Agrarian Reform: Avda Dr Vertiz 800, 1°, Col. Narvarte, 03020 México, DF; tel. (5) 273-9180; fax (5) 273-2481; internet www.sra.gob.mx.

Secretariat of State for Agriculture, Livestock, Rural Development, Fisheries and Food: Insurgentes Sur 476, 13°, Col. Roma Sur, 06760 México, DF; tel. (5) 584-0096; fax (5) 584-0268; e-mail c.informacion@sagar.gob.mx; internet www.sagarpa.gob.mx.

Secretariat of State for the Economy: México, DF.

Secretariat of State for Energy: Insurgentes Sur 552, 3°, Col. Roma Sur, 06769 México, DF; tel. (5) 448-6033; fax (5) 448-6055; internet www.energia.gob.mx.

Secretariat of State for the Environment and Natural Resources: Anillo Periférico Sur 4209, 3°, Col. Jardines en la Montaña, 14210 México, DF; tel. (5) 628-0600; fax (5) 628-0644; internet www.semarnat.gob.mx.

Secretariat of State for Finance and Public Credit: Palacio Nacional, primer patio Mariano, 3°, Col. Centro, 06066 México, DF; tel. (5) 518-5420; fax (5) 542-2821; internet www.shcp.gob.mx.

Secretariat of State for Foreign Affairs: Avda Ricardo Flores Magón 2, 4°, Col. Nonoalco Tlatelolco, 09600 México, DF; tel. (5) 782-3982; fax (5) 782-4109; internet www.sre.gob.mx.

Secretariat of State for Health: Lieja 7, 1° Col. Juárez, 06600 México, DF; tel. (5) 553-0758; fax (5) 553-7917; internet www.ssa.gob.mx.

Secretariat of State for the Interior: Bucareli 99, 1°, Col. Juárez, 06069 México, DF; tel. (5) 592-1141; fax (5) 546-5350; internet www.gobernacion.gob.mx.

Secretariat of State for Labour and Social Welfare: Edif. A, 4°, Anillo Periférico Sur 4271, 4°, Col. Fuentes del Pedregal, 14149 México, DF; tel. (5) 645-3965; fax (5) 645-5594; internet www.stps.gob.mx.

Secretariat of State for National Defence: Manuel Avila Camacho, esq. Avda Industria Militar, 3°, Col. Lomas de Sotelo, 11600 México, DF; tel. (5) 395-5936; fax (5) 557-1370; internet www.sedena.gob.mx.

Secretariat of State for the Navy: Eje 2 Ote, Tramo Heroica, Escuela Naval Militar 861, Col. Los Cipreses, 04830 México, DF; tel. (5) 684-8188; fax (5) 679-6411; internet www.semar.gob.mx.

Secretariat of State for Public Education: República de Argentina 28, 2°, Col. Centro, 06029 México, DF; tel. (5) 510-2557; fax (5) 329-6873; internet www.sep.gob.mx.

Secretariat of State for Public Security and Judicial Services: México, DF.

Secretariat of State for Social Development: Edif. B, planta alta, Constituyentes 947, Col. Belén de las Flores, 01110 México, DF; tel. (5) 271-2650; fax (5) 271-8862; e-mail cc@sedesol.gob.mx; internet www.sedesol.gob.mx.

Secretariat of State for Tourism: Presidente Masarik 172, Col. Polanco, 11587 México, DF; tel. (5) 250-8555; fax (5) 255-3112; internet mexico-travel.com.

Secretariat of State for Communications and Transport: Avda Universidad y Xola, Cuerpo C, 1°, Col. Narvarte, 03028 México, DF; tel. (5) 519-1319; fax (5) 519-9748; internet www.sct.gob.mx.

Office of the Comptroller-General: Insurgentes Sur 1735, 10°, Col. Guadalupe Inn, 01020 México DF; tel. (5) 662-4762; fax (5) 662-4763; internet www.secodam.gob.mx.

Office of the Attorney-General: Paseo de la Reforma y Violeta 75, 2°, Col. Guerrero, 06300 México, DF; tel. (5) 626-9600; fax (5) 626-4447; internet www.pgr.gob.mx.

State Governors

(August 2001)

Aguascalientes: FELIPE GONZÁLEZ GONZALES (PAN).

Baja California: ALEJANDRO GONZÁLEZ ALCOCER (PAN).

Baja California Sur: LEONEL COTA MONTAÑO (PRD-PT-PVEM).

Campeche: Lic. JOSÉ ANTONIO GONZÁLEZ CURI (PRI).

Chiapas: PABLO SALAZAR MENDIGUCHÍA (Ind.).

Chihuahua: Lic. PATRICIO MARTÍNEZ GARCÍA (PRI).

Coahuila: ENRIQUE MARTÍNEZ Y MARTÍNEZ (PRI).

Colima: Lic. FERNANDO MORENO PEÑA (PRI).

Distrito Federal: ANDRÉS MANUEL LÓPEZ OBRADOR (PRD).

Durango: Lic. ANGEL SERGIO GUERRERO MIER (PRI).

Guanajuato: JUAN CARLOS ROMERO HICKS (PAN).

Guerrero: RENÉ JUÁREZ CISNEROS (PRI).

Hidalgo: MANUEL ANGEL NÚÑEZ SOTO (PRI).

Jalisco: Lic. FRANCISCO RAMIREZ ACUÑA (PAN).

México: Lic. ARTURO MONTIEL ROJAS (PRI).

Michoacán: Lic. VÍCTOR MANUEL TINOCO RUBÍ (PRI).

Morelos: Lic. SERGIO ESTRADA CAGIJAL (PAN).

Nayarit: ANTONIO ECHEVARRÍA (PAN-PRD-PT-PVEM).

Nuevo León: Lic. FERNANDO CANALES CLARIOND (PAN).

Oaxaca: JOSÉ MURAT CASAB (PRI).

Puebla: MELQUIADES MORALES FLORES (PRI).

Querétaro: Ing. IGNACIO LOYOLA VERA (PAN).

Quintana Roo: JOAQUÍN HENDRICKS DÍAZ (PRI).

San Luis Potosí: FERNANDO SILVA NIETO (PRI).

Sinaloa: JUAN S. MILLÁN LIZARRAGA (PRI).

Sonora: Lic. ARMANDO LÓPEZ NOGALES (PRI).

Tabasco: ENRIQUE PRIEGO OROPEZA (PRI)*.

Tamaulipas: TOMÁS YARRINGTON RUVALCABA (PRI).

Tlaxcala: ALFONSO SÁNCHEZ ANAYA (PRD-PT-PVEM).

Veracruz: MIGUEL ALEMÁN VELAZCO (PRI).

Yucatán: PATRICIO PATRÓN LAVIADA (PAN-PRD-PT-PVEM).

Zacatecas: Lic. RICARDO MONREAL AVILA (PRD).

* In October 2000 MANUEL ANDRADE DÍAZ of the PRI was elected Governor of Tabasco. However, following an investigation by the Federal Electoral Tribunal into alleged electoral irregularities, the contest was annulled and ENRIQUE PRIEGO OROPEZA was appointed interim Governor until further elections, scheduled to take place in November 2001, could be held.

President and Legislature

PRESIDENT

Election, 2 July 2000

Candidate	Number of votes	Percentage of votes
Vicente Fox Quesada (Alianza por el Cambio)	15,988,740	43.47
FRANCISCO LABASTIDA OCHOA (PRI)	13,576,385	36.91
CUAUHTÉMOC CÁRDENAS SOLÓRZANO (Alianza por México)	6,259,048	17.02
Others	957,455	2.60
Total	36,781,628	100.00

CONGRESO DE LA UNIÓN

Senado
(Senate)

President: ENRIQUE JACKSON RAMÍREZ.

Elections, 2 July 2000

Party	Seats
Partido Revolucionario Institucional (PRI)	60
Partido Acción Nacional (PAN)*	46
Partido de la Revolución Democrática (PRD)†	15
Partido Verde Ecologista de México (PVEM)*	5
Convergencia por la Democracia (CD)†	1
Partido del Trabajo (PT)†	1
Total	128

* Contested the elections jointly as the Alianza por el Cambio.
† Contested the elections as part of the Alianza por México.

Cámara Federal de Diputados
(Federal Chamber of Deputies)

President: RICARDO FRANCISCO GARCÍA CERVANTES.

Elections, 2 July 2000

Party	Seats
Partido Revolucionario Institucional (PRI)	209
Partido Acción Nacional (PAN)*	208
Partido de la Revolución Democrática (PRD)†	52
Partido Verde Ecologista de México (PVEM)*	15
Partido del Trabajo (PT)†	8
Convergencia por la Democracia (CD)†	3
Partido de la Sociedad Nacionalista (PSN)†	3
Partido Alianza Social (PAS)†	2
Total	500

* Contested the elections jointly as the Alianza por el Cambio.
† Contested the elections as part of the Alianza por México.

Political Organizations

To retain legal political registration, parties must secure at least 1.5% of total votes at two consecutive federal elections. Several of the parties listed below are no longer officially registered but continue to be politically active.

Convergencia por la Democracia: México, DF; internet www.convergencia.org.mx; f. 1995; Leader DANTE DELGADO.

Democracia Social: Bartolache 1062, Col. del Valle, 03100 México, DF; tel. (5) 555-9692; fax (5) 559-3037; e-mail correos@democraciasocial.org.mx; internet www.democraciasocial.org.mx; f. 1999; Pres. GILBERTO RINCÓN GALLARDO.

Partido Acción Nacional (PAN): Angel Urraza 812, Col. del Valle, 03100 México, DF; tel. (5) 559-6300; fax (5) 559-0159; e-mail correo@cen.org.mx; internet www.pan.org.mx; f. 1939; democratic party; 150,000 mems; Pres. LUIS FELIPE BRAVO MENA; Sec.-Gen. JORGE OCEJO MORENO.

Partido Alianza Social (PAS): internet www.pas.org.mx; Pres. GUILLERMO CALDERÓN DOMÍNGUEZ; Sec.-Gen. ADALBERTO ROSAS LÓPEZ.

Partido Auténtico de la Revolución Mexicana (PARM): México, DF; f. 1954 to sustain the ideology of the Mexican Political Constitution of 1917; 191,500 mems; Pres. CARLOS GUZMÁN PÉREZ.

Partido de Centro Democrático (PCD): Amores 923, Col. del Valle, Deleg. Benito Juárez, 03100 México, DF; tel. (5) 575-3101; fax (5) 575-8888; e-mail pcdcen@pcd2000.org.mx; internet www.pcd2000.org.mx; centrist party; f. 1997; Leader MANUEL CAMACHO SOLÍS.

Partido del Frente Cardenista de Reconstrucción Nacional (PFCRN): Avda México 199, Col. Hipódromo Condesa, 06170 México, DF; f. 1972; Marxist-Leninist; fmrly Partido Socialista de los Trabajadores; 132,000 mems; Pres. RAFAEL AGUILAR TALAMANTES; Sec.-Gen. GRACO RAMÍREZ ABREU.

Partido Popular Socialista (PPS): Avda Alvaro Obregón 185, Col. Roma, 06797 México, DF; tel. (5) 533-0816; fax (5) 525-7131; internet www.pps.org.mx; f. 1948; left-wing party; Sec.-Gen. MANUEL FERNÁNDEZ FLORES.

Partido de la Revolución Democrática (PRD): Monterrey 50, Col. Roma, 06700 México, DF; tel. (5) 525-6059; fax (5) 208-7833; internet www.prd.org.mx; f. 1989 by the Corriente Democrática (CD) and elements of the Partido Mexicano Socialista (PMS); centre-left; Pres. AMALIA GARCÍA MEDINA; Sec.-Gen. JESÚS ZAMBRANO GRIJALVA.

Partido Revolucionario Institucional (PRI): Insurgentes Norte 59, Edif. 2, subsótano, Col. Buenavista, 06359 México, DF; tel. (5) 591-1595; fax (5) 546-3552; internet www.pri.org.mx; f. 1929 as the Partido Nacional Revolucionario, but is regarded as the natural successor to the victorious parties of the revolutionary period; broadly based and centre govt party; Pres. DULCE MARÍA SAURI RIANCHO; Sec.-Gen. RODOLFO ECHEVERRÍA; opinion groups within the PRI include: the Corriente Crítica Progresista, the Corriente Crítica del Partido, the Corriente Constitucionalista Democratizadora, Corriente Nuevo PRI XIV Asamblea, Democracia 2000, México Nuevo and Galileo.

Partido Social Demócrata Mexicano (PSDM): Edisón 89, Col. Revolución, 06030 México, DF; tel. (5) 592-5688; fax (5) 535-0031; f. 1975 as Partido Demócrata Mexicano; adopted current name in 1998; Christian Democrat party; 450,000 mems; Pres. BALTASAR IGNACIO VALADEZ MONTOYA.

Partido de la Sociedad Nacionalista (PSN): Adolfo Prieto 428, Col. del Valle, 03100 México, DF; tel. (5) 523-0408; e-mail psn@psn.org.mx; internet www.psn.org.mx; Pres. GUSTAVO RIOJAS SANTANA.

Partido del Trabajo (PT): Avda Cuauhtémoc 47, Col. Roma, 06700 México, DF; tel. and fax (5) 525-8419; internet www.pt.org.mx; f. 1991; labour party; Leader ALBERTO ANAYA GUTIÉRREZ.

Partido Verde Ecologista de México (PVEM): San Luis Potosí 118, Col. Roma, 06700 México, DF; tel. and fax (5) 574-1516; e-mail pve@infosel.net.mx; internet www.pvem.org.mx; f. 1987; ecologist party; Leader JORGE GONZÁLEZ TORRES.

The following parties are not legally recognized:

Frente Zapatista de Liberación Nacional: f. 1996; political force embodying the ideology of the EZLN; Leader JAVIER ELORRIAGA.

Partido Social Demócrata (PSD): México, DF; lost its registration after the 1982 elections; Leader MANUEL MORENO SÁNCHEZ.

Illegal organizations active in Mexico include the following:

Ejército Popular Revolucionario (EPR): f. 1994; left-wing guerrilla group active in southern states.

Ejército Revolucionario Popular Insurgente (ERPI): f. 1996; left-wing guerrilla group active in Guerrero, Morelos and Oaxaca; Leader JACOBO SILVA NOGALES.

Ejército Zapatista de Liberación Nacional (EZLN): internet www.ezln.org; f. 1993; left-wing guerrilla group active in the Chiapas region.

Frente Democrático Oriental de México Emiliano Zapata (FDOMEZ): peasant org.

Partido Popular Revolucionario Democrático: f. 1996; political grouping representing the causes of 14 armed peasant orgs, including the EPR and the PROCUP.

Partido Revolucionario Obrerista y Clandestino de Unión Popular (PROCUP): peasant org.

Los Tecos: based at the University of Guadalajara; extreme right-wing group.

Diplomatic Representation

EMBASSIES IN MEXICO

Algeria: Sierra Madre 540, Col. Lomas de Chapultepec, 11000 México, DF; tel. (5) 520-6950; fax (5) 540-7579; e-mail embjargl @iwm.com.mx; Chargé d'affaires a.i. Mohammad Abdou Tebbal.

Angola: Schiller 503, Col. Polanco, 11560 México, DF; tel. (5) 545-5883; fax (5) 545-2733; e-mail info@palanca-negra.org; internet www.palanca-negra.org; Chargé d'affaires: Alfonso Evaristo Eduardo.

Argentina: Manuel Avila Camacho 1, 7°, Col. Lomas de Chapultepec, 11000 México, DF; tel. (5) 520-9430; fax (5) 540-5011; e-mail argentina@mail.internet.com.mx; Ambassador: Oscar Guillermo Galie.

Australia: Rubén Darío 55, Col. Polanco, 11580 México, DF; tel. (5) 531-5225; fax (5) 203-8431; e-mail austemb@inetcorp.net.mx; Ambassador: Robert J. B. Hamilton.

Austria: Sierra Tarahumara 420, Col. Lomas de Chapultepec, Del. Miguel Hidalgo, 11000 México, DF; tel. (5) 251-1606; fax (5)245-0198; e-mail obmexico@data.net.mx; internet www .embajadadeaustria.com.mx; Ambassador: Dr Rudolf Lennkh.

Belgium: Musset 41, Col. Polanco, 11550 México, DF; tel. (5) 280-0758; fax (5) 280-0208; e-mail ambelmex@mail.internet.com.mx; Ambassador: Gaston van Duyse-Adam.

Belize: Bernardo de Gálvez 215, Col. Lomas de Chapultepec, 11000 México, DF; tel. (5) 520-1274; fax (5) 520-6089; e-mail embelize@ prodigy.net.mx; Ambassador: Salvador Amín Figueroa.

Bolivia: Insurgentes Sur 263, 6°, esq. Alvaro Obregón, Col. Roma Sur, 06760 México, DF; tel. (5) 564-5415; fax (5) 564-5298; e-mail arukipa@data.net.mx; Ambassador: José Gabino Villanueva Gutiérrez.

Brazil: Lope de Armendariz 130, Col. Lomas Virreyes, 11000 México, DF; tel. (5) 202-7500; fax (5) 520-4929; e-mail embrasil@ ienlaces.com.mx; Ambassador: Luiz Filipe de Macedo Soares.

Bulgaria: Paseo de la Reforma 1990, Col. Lomas de Chapultepec, 11000 México, DF; tel. (5) 596-3283; fax (5) 596-1012; Chargé d'affaires: Ivan Christov.

Canada: Schiller 529, Col. Polanco, 11560 México, DF; tel. (5) 724-7900; fax (5) 724-7980; internet www.canada.org.mx; Ambassador: Keith H. Christie.

Chile: Andrés Bello 10, 18°, Col. Polanco, 11560 México, DF; tel. (5) 280-9681; fax (5) 280-9703; e-mail echilmex@prodigy.net.mx; Ambassador: Luis Maira Aguirre.

China, People's Republic: Avda Río Magdalena 172, Col. Tizapán, 01090 México, DF; tel. (5) 550-0823; fax (5) 616-0460; e-mail embchina @data.net.mx; Chargé d'affaires a.i.: Zeng Gang.

Colombia: Paseo de la Reforma 1620, Col. Lomas de Chapultepec, 11000 México, DF; tel. (5) 202-7299; fax (5) 520-9669; e-mail colmex @spin.com.mx; Ambassador: Rafael Carvajal Argaez.

Costa Rica: Río Po 113, Col. Cuauhtémoc, 06500 México, DF; tel. (5) 525-7764; fax (5) 511-9240; e-mail embcrica@ri.redint.com; Chargé d'affaires a.i.: Cecilia de Highland.

Cuba: Presidente Masarik 554, Col. Polanco, 11560 México, DF; tel. (5) 280-8039; fax (5) 280-0839; e-mail embacuba@netservice.com.mx; Ambassador: Mario Rodríguez Martínez.

Cyprus: Sierra Gorda 370, Col. Lomas de Chapultepec, 11000 México, DF; tel. (5) 202-7600; fax (5) 520-2693; e-mail chipre@data .net.mx; Ambassador: Antonis Toumazis.

Czech Republic: Cuvier 22, esq. Kepler, Col. Nueva Anzures, 11590 México, DF; tel. (5) 531-2777; fax (5) 531-1837; e-mail mexico @embassy.mzv.cz; Ambassador: Vera Zemanová.

Denmark: Tres Picos 43, Apdo 105-105, Col. Chapultepec Morales, 11580 México, DF; tel. (5) 255-3405; fax (5) 545-5797; e-mail embdinamarca@mexis.com; Ambassador: Peter Branner.

Dominican Republic: Galileo 101, Col. Polanco, 11560 México, DF; tel. (5) 280-4689; fax (5) 553-2492; Ambassador: Pablo A. Maríñez Alvarez.

Ecuador: Tennyson 217, Col. Polanco, 11560 México, DF; tel. (5) 545-3141; fax (5) 254-2442; e-mail mecuamex@mail.internet .com.mx; Ambassador: Gustavo Vega Delgado.

Egypt: Alejandro Dumas 131, Col. Polanco, 11560 México, DF; tel. (5) 281-0823; fax (5) 282-1294; e-mail embofegypt@mexis.com; Ambassador: Ahmed Khaled Hamdy.

El Salvador: Temistocles 88, Col. Polanco, 11560 México, DF; tel. (5) 281-5725; fax (5) 280-0657; e-mail embesmex@webtelmex.net.mx; Ambassador: Eduardo Cálix López.

Finland: Monte Pelvoux 111, 4°, Col. Lomas de Chapultepec, Del. Miguel Hidalgo, 11000 México, DF; tel. (5) 540-6036; fax (5) 540-0114; e-mail finmmex@prodigy.net.mx; internet www.finlandia .org.mx; Ambassador: Hannu Uusi-Videnoja.

France: Campos Elíseos 339, Col. Polanco, 11560 México, DF; tel. (5) 282-9700; fax (5) 282-9703; internet www.francia.org.mx; Ambassador: Philippe Faure.

Germany: Lord Byron 737, Col. Polanco, 11560 México, DF, Apdo 107-92, 06000 México, DF; tel. (5) 283-2200; fax (5) 281-2588; e-mail info@embajada-alemana.org.mx; internet www.embajada -alemana.org.mx; Ambassador: Wolf-Ruthart Born.

Greece: Paseo de las Palmas 2060, Col. Lomas Reforma, 11930 México, DF; tel. (5) 596-6333; fax (5) 251-3001; Ambassador: Stratos Doukas.

Guatemala: Esplanada 1025, Col. Lomas de Chapultepec, 11000 México, DF; tel. (5) 202-7951; fax (5) 202-1142; e-mail embaguate@ mexis.com; Ambassador: Romulo Caballeros Otero.

Haiti: Córdoba 23a, Col. Roma, 06700 México, DF; tel. (5) 511-4390; fax (5) 533-3896; e-mail embadh@mail.internet.com.mx; Chargé d'affaires: Guy Lamonthe.

Holy See: Calle Juan Pablo II 118, Col. Guadalupe Inn, Del. Alvaro Obregón, 01020 México, DF; tel. (5) 663-3999; fax (5) 663-5308; e-mail nuntiusmex@infosel.net.mx; Apostolic Nuncio: Most Rev. Giuseppe Bertello, Titular Archbishop of Urbisaglia.

Honduras: Alfonso Reyes 220, Col. Hipódromo Condesa, 06170 México, DF; tel. (5) 211-5747; fax (5) 211-5425; e-mail emhonmex@ mail.internet.com.mx; Chargé d'affaires a.i.: Rigoberto Paredes.

Hungary: Paseo de las Palmas 2005, Col. Lomas de Chapultepec, 11000 México, DF; tel. (5) 596-0523; fax (5) 596-2378; e-mail hung@ prodigy.net.mx; Ambassador: Gyula Németh.

India: Musset 325, Col. Polanco, 11560 México, DF; tel. (5) 531-1050; fax (5) 254-2349; e-mail embindia@data.net.mx; Ambassador: Ganesh Sankranarayana Iyer.

Indonesia: Julio Verne 27, Col. Polanco, 11560 México, DF; tel. (5) 280-6363; fax (5) 280-7062; e-mail kbrimex@data.net.mx; Ambassdor: Barnabas Suebu.

Iran: Paseo de la Reforma 2350, Col. Lomas Altas, 11950 México, DF; tel. (5) 596-5399; fax (5) 251-0731; e-mail iranembmex@ibm.net; Ambassador: Seyed Reza Tabatabai Shafii.

Iraq: Paseo de la Reforma 1875, Col. Lomas de Chapultepec, 11000 México, DF; tel. (5) 596-0980; fax (5) 596-0254; Chargé d'affaires: Falih A. Huzam.

Ireland: Manuel Avila Camacho 76, Col. Lomas de Chapultepec, 11000 México, DF; tel. (5) 520-5803; fax (5) 520-5892; e-mail embajada @irlanda.org.mx; Ambassador: Art Agnew.

Israel: Sierra Madre 215, Col. Lomas de Chapultepec, 11000 México, DF; tel. (5) 201-1500; fax (5) 201-1555; Ambassador: Joseph Amihud.

Italy: Paseo de las Palmas 1994, Col. Lomas de Chapultepec, 11000 México, DF; tel. (5) 596-3655; fax (5) 596-7710; e-mail embitaly@ data.net.mx; internet www.pentanet.com.mx/embitaly; Ambassador: Dr Bruno Cabras Melchiori.

Jamaica: Galileo 317, Col. Polanco, 11560 México, DF; e-mail embjamaicamex@infosel.net.mx; Chargé d'affaires a.i.: Valencio Lindsay.

Japan: Paseo de la Reforma 395, Col. Cuauhtémoc, Apdo 5-101, 06500 México, DF; tel. (5) 211-0028; fax (5) 207-7743; e-mail embjapmx@mail.internet.com.mx; Ambassador: Katsuyuki Tanaka.

Korea, Democratic People's Republic: Eugenio Sue 332, Col. Polanco, 11550 México, DF; tel. (5) 545-1871; fax (5) 203-0019; Chargé d'affaires: Choe Bok.

Korea, Republic: Lope de Armendariz 110, Col. Lomas Virreyes, 11000 México, DF; tel. (5) 202-9866; fax (5) 540-7446; Chargé d'affaires: Jungsoo Doo.

Lebanon: Julio Verne 8, Col. Polanco, 11560 México, DF; tel. (5) 280-5614; fax (5) 280-8870; e-mail embalib@prodigy.net.mx; Ambassador: Nouhad Mahmoud.

Malaysia: Calderón de la Barca 215, Col. Polanco, 11560 México, DF; tel. (5) 254-1118; fax (5) 254-1295; e-mail msmexico@mpsnet .com.mx; Ambassador: Tengku Idriss bin Tengku Ibrahim.

Morocco: Paseo de las Palmas 2020, Col. Lomas de Chapultepec, 11020 México, DF; tel. (5) 245-1786; fax (5) 245-1791; e-mail sifamx@onfosel.net.mx; Ambassador: Mohamed Ayachi.

Netherlands: Edif. Calakmul, Avda Vasco de Quiroga 3000, 7°, Col. Santa Fe, 01210 México, DF; tel. (5) 258-9921; fax (5) 258-8138; e-mail nlgovmex@nlgovmex.com; Ambassador: Robert Arthur Vornis.

New Zealand: J. L. Lagrange 103, 10°, Col. Polanco, 11510 México, DF; tel. (5) 281-5486; fax (5) 281-5212; e-mail kiwimexico@ compuserve.com.mx; Ambassador: Bronwen E. Chang.

Nicaragua: Payo de Rivera 120, Col. Lomas de Chapultepec, 11000 México, DF; tel. (5) 540-5625; fax (5) 520-6960; e-mail embanic@ prodigy.net.mx; Ambassador: Edgar Escobar Fornos.

Norway: Avda de los Virreyes 1460, Col. Lomas Virreyes, 11000 México, DF; tel. (5) 540-3486; fax (5) 202-3019; e-mail embajadano@ infosel.net.mx; Ambassador: BJORNAR S. UTHEIM.

Pakistan: Hegel 512, Col. Chapultepec Morales, 11570 México, DF; tel. (5) 203-3636; fax (5) 203-9907; Ambassador: AMIR MOHAMMAD KHAN.

Panama: Schiller 326, 8°, Col. Chapultepec Morales, 11570 México, DF; tel. (5) 531-5164; fax (5) 250-4674; e-mail embpanmx@avantel .net; Ambassador: DIONISO DE GRACIA GUILLÉN.

Paraguay: Homero 415, 1°, esq. Hegel, Col. Polanco, 11570 México, DF; tel. (5) 545-0405; fax (5) 531-9905; e-mail embapar@prodigy .net.mx; Ambassador: EFRAÍN ENRÍQUEZ GAMÓN.

Peru: Paseo de la Reforma 2601, Col. Lomas Reforma, 11000 México, DF; tel. (5) 570-2443; fax (5) 259-0530; e-mail embaperu@ data.net.mx; Ambassador: ARMANDO LECAROS DE COSSÍO.

Philippines: Avda de las Palmas 1950, Col. Lomas de Chapultepec, 11000 México, DF; tel. (5) 251-9759; fax (5) 251-9754; e-mail ambamexi@mail.internet.com.mx; Ambassador: ALICIA M. L. COSE-TENG.

Poland: Cracovia 40, Col. San Ángel, 01000 México, DF; tel. (5) 550-4700; fax (5) 616-0822; e-mail ambrpxml@mail.cpesa.com.mx; Ambassador: GABRIEL BESZŁEJ.

Portugal: Alejandro Dumas 311, Col. Polanco, 11550 México, DF; tel. (5) 545-6213; fax (5) 203-0790; e-mail embpomex@prodigy .net.mx; Ambassador: ANTÓNIO ANTAS DE CAMPOS.

Romania: Sofocles 311, Col. Polanco, 11560 México, DF; tel. (5) 280-0197; fax (5) 280-0343; e-mail ambromaniei@supernet.com.mx; Ambassador: GHEORGHE STANCOV.

Russia: José Vasconcelos 204, Col. Hipódromo Condesa, 06140 México, DF; tel. (5) 273-1305; fax (5) 273-1545; e-mail embrumex@ mail.internet.com.mx; Ambassador: KONSTANTIN MOZEL.

Saudi Arabia: Avda de las Palmas 2075, Col. Lomas de Chapultepec, 11000 México, DF; tel. (5) 251-0829; fax (5) 251-8587; e-mail saudiambmx@geoline.net; Ambassador: HASSAN TALAT NAZER.

Slovakia: Julio Verne 35, Col. Polanco, 11560 México, DF; tel. (5) 280-6669; fax (5) 280-6294; e-mail embslovakia@mexis.com; Chargé d'affaires: VILIAM ROSENBERG.

South Africa: Apdo 105–219, Col. Polanco, 11581 México, DF; tel. (5) 282-9260; fax (5) 282-9259; e-mail safrica@dfl.telmex.net.mx; Ambassador: PIETER A. SWANEPOEL.

Spain: Galileo 114, esq. Horacio, Col. Polanco, 11550 México, DF; tel. (5) 282-2271; fax (5) 282-1302; e-mail embaes@prodigy.net.mx; Ambassador: JOSÉ IGNACIO CARBAJAL GÁRATE.

Suriname: Calle Cicerón 609, Col. Los Morales, 11510 México, DF; tel. (5) 540-4371; Ambassador: HARVEY NAARENDORP.

Sweden: Paseo de las Palmas 1375, 11000 México, DF; tel. (5) 540-6393; fax (5) 540-3253; e-mail embsvecia@internet.com.mx; internet www.svecia.com.mx; Ambassador: JAN STAHL.

Switzerland: Avda de las Palmas 405, 11°, Torre Optima, Col. Lomas de Chapultepec, 11000 México, DF; tel. (5) 520-3003; fax (5) 520-8685; e-mail vertretung@mex.rep.admin.ch; Ambassador: MARCUS KAISER.

Thailand: Sierra Vertientes 1030, Col. Lomas de Chapultepec, 11000 México, DF; tel. (5) 596-1290; fax (5) 596-8236; Ambassador: ABINANT NA RANONG.

Turkey: Schiller 326, 5°, Col. Chapultepec Morales, 11570 México, DF; tel. (5) 203-8984; fax (5) 203-8622; e-mail turken@mail.internet .com.mx; Ambassador: ERGÜN PELIT.

United Kingdom: Río Lerma 71, Col. Cuauhtémoc, 06500 México, DF; tel. (5) 207-2089; fax (5) 207-7672; e-mail infogen@mail .embajadabritanica.com.mx; internet www.embajadabritanica.c-om.mx; Ambassador: ADRIAN CHARLES THORPE.

USA: Paseo de la Reforma 305, Col. Cuauhtémoc, 06500 México, DF; tel. (5) 209-9100; fax (5) 511-9980; internet www.usembassy -mexico.gov; Ambassador: JEFFREY DAVIDOW.

Uruguay: Hegel 149, 1°, Col. Chapultepec Morales, 11560 México, DF; tel. (5) 531-0880; fax (5) 531-4029; e-mail uruazte@ort.org.mx; Ambassador: SAMUEL LICHTENSZTEJN TEZLER.

Venezuela: Schiller 326, Col. Chapultepec Morales, 11570 México, DF; tel. (5) 203-4233; fax (5) 203-8614; e-mail embavenezmexico@ yahoo.com; Ambassador: LINO MARTÍNEZ SALAZAR.

Viet Nam: Sierra Ventana 255, Col. Lomas de Chapultepec, 11000 México, DF; tel. (5) 540-1632; fax (5) 540-1612; e-mail embviet @dsqun.spin.com.mx; Ambassador: NGUYEN VAN SANH.

Yugoslavia: Montañas Rocallosas Ote 515, Col. Lomas de Chapultepec, 11000 México, DF; tel. (5) 520-0524; fax (5) 520-9927; e-mail ambayumex@spin.com.mx; Chargé d'affaires a.i.: ZORAN STANOJEVIĆ.

Judicial System

The principle of the separation of the judiciary from the legislative and executive powers is embodied in the 1917 Constitution. The judicial system is divided into two areas: the federal, dealing with federal law, and the local, dealing only with state law within each state.

The federal judicial system has both ordinary and constitutional jurisdiction and judicial power is exercised by the Supreme Court of Justice, the Electoral Court, Collegiate and Unitary Circuit Courts and District Courts. The Supreme Court comprises two separate chambers: Civil and Criminal Affairs, and Administrative and Labour Affairs. The Federal Judicature Council is responsible for the administration, surveillance and discipline of the federal judiciary, except for the Supreme Court of Justice.

In March 2001 there were 146 Collegiate Circuit Courts (Tribunales Colegiados), 58 Unitary Circuit Courts (Tribunales Unitarios) and 219 District Courts (Juzgados de Distrito). Mexico is divided into 26 judicial circuits. The Circuit Courts may be collegiate, when dealing with the derecho de amparo (protection of constitutional rights of an individual), or unitary, when dealing with appeal cases. The Collegiate Circuit Courts comprise three magistrates with residence in the cities of México, Toluca, Guadalajara, Monterrey, Hermosillo, Puebla, Boca del Río, Xalapa, Torreón, San Luis Potosí, Villahermosa, Morelia, Mazatlán, Oaxaca, Mérida, Mexicali, Guanajuato, Chihuahua, Cuernavaca, Ciudad Victoria, Tuxtla Gutiérrez, Chilpancingo, Querétaro, Pachuca, Zacatecas, Aguascalientes, Tepic and Durango. The Unitary Circuit Courts comprise one magistrate with residence mostly in the same cities as given above.

SUPREME COURT OF JUSTICE

Pino Suárez 2, Col. Centro, Deleg. Cuauhtémoc, 06065 México, DF; tel. (5) 522-0096; fax (5) 522-0152; internet www.scjn.gob.mx.
Chief Justice: GENARO DAVID GÓNGORA PIMENTEL.

First Chamber—Civil and Criminal Affairs
President: JOSÉ DE JESÚS GUDIÑO PELAYO.

Second Chamber—Administrative and Labour Affairs
President: GUILLERMO I. ORTIZ MAYAGOITIA.

Religion

CHRISTIANITY
The Roman Catholic Church

The prevailing religion is Roman Catholicism, but the Church, disestablished in 1857, was for many years, under the Constitution of 1917, subject to state control. A constitutional amendment, promulgated in January 1992, officially removed all restrictions on the Church. For ecclesiastical purposes, Mexico comprises 14 archdioceses, 61 dioceses and six territorial prelatures. An estimated 90% of the population are adherents.

Bishops' Conference: Conferencia del Episcopado Mexicano (CEM), Prolongación Misterios 24, Col. Tepeyac, Insurgentes, 07020 México, DF; tel. (5) 781-8462; fax (5) 577-5489; e-mail segecem@mail .cem.org.mx; internet segecem.cem.org.mx; f. 1979; Pres. LUIS MORALES REYES, Archbishop of San Luis Potosí.

Archbishop of Acapulco: RAFAEL BELLO RUIZ, Arzobispado, Quebrada 16, Apdo 201, 39300 Acapulco, Gro; tel. and fax (748) 20763; e-mail buenpastor@acabtu.com.mx.

Archbishop of Antequera/Oaxaca: HÉCTOR GONZÁLEZ MARTÍNEZ, Independencia 700, Apdo 31, 68000 Oaxaca, Oax.; tel. (951) 64822; fax (951) 65580; e-mail antequera@oax1.telmex.net.mx;.

Archbishop of Chihuahua: JOSÉ FERNÁNDEZ ARTEAGA, Arzobispado, Avda Cuauhtémoc 1828, Apdo 7, 31020 Chihuahua, Chih.; tel. (14) 10-3202; fax (14) 10-5621; e-mail curiao1@chih1.telmex.net.mx.

Archbishop of Durango: JOSÉ TRINIDAD MEDEL PÉREZ, Arzobispado, 20 de Noviembre 306 Poniente, Apdo 116, 34000 Durango, Dgo; tel. (188) 114242; fax (188) 128881; e-mail arqdgo@logicnet.com.mx.

Archbishop of Guadalajara: Cardinal JUAN SANDOVAL IÑÍGUEZ, Arzobispado, Liceo 17, Apdo 1-331, 44100 Guadalajara, Jal.; tel. (3) 614-5504; fax (3) 658-2300; e-mail arzgdl@vianet.com.mx.

Archbishop of Hermosillo/Sonora: JOSÉ ULISES MACÍAS SALCEDO, Arzobispado, Dr Paliza 81, Apdo 1, 83260 Hermosillo, Son.; tel. (62) 13-2138; fax (62) 13-1327; e-mail obispohmo@infosel.net.mx.

Archbishop of Jalapa: SERGIO OBESO RIVERA, Arzobispado, Avda Manuel Avila Camacho 73, Apdo 359, 91000 Jalapa, Ver.; tel. (28) 12-0579; fax (28) 17-5578; e-mail diocjalapa@quetzal.net.

Archbishop of Mexico City: Cardinal NORBERTO RIVERA CARRERA, Curia del Arzobispado de México, Durango 90, 5°, Col. Roma, Apdo 24433, 06700 México, DF; tel. (5) 208-3200; fax (5) 208-5350; e-mail nrivera@mail.cem.org.mx.

Archbishop of Monterrey: Cardinal ADOLFO ANTONIO SUÁREZ RIVERA, Zuazua 1100 con Ocampo, Apdo 7, 64000 Monterrey, NL; tel. (8) 345-2466; fax (8) 345-3557; e-mail curia@sdm.net.mx.

Archbishop of Morelia: ALBERTO SUÁREZ INDA, Arzobispado, Apdo 17, 58000 Morelia, Mich.; tel. (43) 120523; fax (43) 123744; e-mail asuarezi@mich1.telmex.net.mx.

Archbishop of Puebla de los Angeles: ROSENDO HUESCA PACHECO, Avda 2 Sur 305, Apdo 235, 72000 Puebla, Pue.; tel. (22) 32-4591; fax (22) 46-2277; e-mail rhuesca@mail.cem.org.mx.

Archbishop of San Luis Potosí: LUIS MORALES REYES, Arzobispado, Francisco Madero 300, Apdo 1, 78000 San Luis Potosí, SLP; tel. (48) 12-4555; fax (48) 12-7979; e-mail lmorales@mail.cem.org.mx.

Archbishop of Tlalnepantla: RICARDO GUÍZAR DÍAZ, Arzobispado, Avda Juárez 42, Apdo 268, 54000 Tlalnepantla, Méx.; tel. (5) 565-3944; fax (5) 565-2751; e-mail rguizar@mail.cem.org.mx.

Archbishop of Yucatán: EMILIO CARLOS BERLIE BELAUNZARÁN, Arzobispado, Calle 58 501, 97000 Mérida, Yuc.; tel. (99) 28-5720; fax (99) 23-7983; e-mail acm@sureste.com.

The Anglican Communion

Mexico is divided into five dioceses, which form the Province of the Anglican Church in Mexico, established in 1995.

Bishop of Cuernavaca: MARTINIANO GARCÍA MONTIEL, Minerva 1, Las Delicias, 62330 Cuernavaca, Mor.; tel. and fax (73) 15-2870; e-mail diovca@giga.com.mx.

Bishop of Mexico City: SERGIO CARRANZA GÓMEZ, Avda San Jerónimo 117, Col. San Angel, 01000 México, DF; tel. and fax (5) 616-2205; e-mail diomex@avantel.net.

Bishop of Northern Mexico: GERMÁN MARTÍNEZ MÁRQUEZ, Simón Bolívar 2005 Nte, Col. Mitras Centro, 64460 Monterrey, NL; tel. and fax (83) 48-7362; e-mail dionte@infosel.com.mx.

Bishop of South-Eastern Mexico: BENITO JUÁREZ MARTÍNEZ, Avda Las Américas 73, Col. Aguacatl, 91130 Jalapa, Ver.; tel. and fax (28) 144387; e-mail dioste@prodigy.net.mx.

Bishop of Western Mexico: SAMUEL ESPINOZA VENEGAS, Apdo 2-366, 44280 Guadalajara, Jal.; tel. (3) 615-5070; fax (3) 616-4413: e-mail diocte@vianet.com.mx.

Other Protestant Churches

Federación Evangélica de México: Motolinia 8, Of. 107, Del. Cuauhtémoc, 1830, 06002, México, DF; tel. (5) 585-0594; f. 1926; Pres. Prof. MOISES MÉNDEZ; Exec. Sec. Rev. ISRAEL ORTIZ MURRIETA.

Iglesia Evangélica Luterana de México: Mina Pte 5808, Nuevo Larado, Tamps; Pres. ENCARNACIÓN ESTRADA; 3,000 mems.

Iglesia Metodista de México: Central Area: Miravalle 209, Col. Portales, 03570 México, DF; tel. (5) 539-3674; fax (5) 672-4278; f. 1930; 55,000 mems; 370 congregations; Bishop: GRACIELA ALVAREZ DELGADO; Northern Area: Fray Bartolomé de Olmedo 149, Quintas del Márquez, 76050 Querétaro, Qro; tel. (42) 13-3089; Bishop: OCTAVIANO ESPINOZA FIERRO; South-eastern Area: Pte 311, 4°, 72000 Puebla, Pue.; tel. (22) 42-1895; Bishop: FIDEL RAMÍREZ SÁNCHEZ; Central Area: Avda Morelos 524 Pte, Torreón, Coah.; tel. (17) 12-3471; fax (17) 16-2697; Bishop BALTASAR GONZÁLEZ CARRILLO; North-eastern Area: Cuernavaca 116, Col. San Benito, 83190 Hermosillo, Son.; tel. (62) 14-2780; Bishop: ANTONIO AGUIÑA MÁRQUEZ; Eastern Area: Galeana 430 Norte, 64000 Monterrey, NL; tel. (8) 342-5376; fax (8) 344-0055; Bishop RICARDO ESPARZA ZUNO.

National Baptist Convention of Mexico: Vizcaínas Ote 16, Altos, 06080 México, DF; tel. (5) 518-2691; fax (5) 521-0118; internet www.bautistas.org.mx/cnbm; f. 1903; Pres. ROLANDO GUTIÉRREZ CORTÉS.

BAHÁ'Í FAITH

National Spiritual Assembly of the Bahá'ís of Mexico: Emerson 421, Col. Chapultepec Morales, Del. Miguel Hidalgo, 11570 México, DF; tel. (5) 545-2155; fax (5) 255-5972; mems resident in 1,009 localities.

The Press

DAILY NEWSPAPERS
México, DF

La Afición: Ignacio Mariscal 23, Apdo 64 bis, Col. Tabacalera, 06030 México, DF; tel. (5) 546-4780; fax (5) 535-3025; f. 1930; sport, entertainment, news; Pres. Lic. JUAN FRANCISCO EALY ORTIZ; Gen. Man. ANTONIO GARCÍA SERRANO; circ. 85,000.

Cuestión: Laguna de Mayrán 410, Col. Anáhuac, 11320 México, DF; tel. (5) 260-0499; fax (5) 260-3645; e-mail cuestion@compuserve.com; internet www.cuestion.com.mx; f. 1980; midday; Dir-Gen. Lic. ALBERTO GONZÁLEZ PARRA; circ. 48,000.

El Día: Insurgentes Norte 1210, Col. Capultitlán, 07370 México, DF; tel. (5) 729-2155; fax (5) 537-6629; e-mail cduran@servidor

.unam.mx; f. 1962; morning; Dir-Gen. JOSÉ LUIS CAMACHO LÓPEZ; circ. 50,000.

Diario de México: Chimalpopoca 38, Col. Obrera, 06800 México, DF; tel. (5) 588-3831; fax (5) 578-7650; e-mail diamex@rtn.net.mx; f. 1948; morning; Dir-Gen. FEDERICO BRACAMONTES GÁLVEZ; Dir RAFAEL LIZARDI DURÁN; circ. 76,000.

Esto: Guillermo Prieto 7, 1°, 06470 México, DF; tel. (5) 535-2722; fax (5) 535-2687; e-mail info@oem.com.mx; internet www.esto.com.mx; f. 1941; morning; sport; Pres. Lic. MARIO VÁZQUEZ RAÑA; Dir CARLOS TRAPAGA BARRIENTOS; circ. 400,200, Mondays 450,000.

Excélsior: Reforma 18, Apdo 120 bis, Col. Centro, 06600 México, DF; tel. (5) 535-6552; fax (5) 546-0787; internet www.excelsior .com.mx; f. 1917; morning; independent; Dir REGINO DÍAZ REDONDO; Gen. Man. JUVENTINO OLIVERA LÓPEZ; circ. 200,000.

El Financiero: Lago Bolsena 176, Col. Anáhuac entre Lago Peypus y Lago Onega, 11320 México, DF; tel. (5) 227-7600; fax (5) 255-1881; internet www.elfinanciero.com.mx; f. 1981; financial; Dir Lic. ALEJANDRO RAMOS ESQUIVEL; circ. 135,000.

El Heraldo de México: Dr Lucio, esq. Dr Velasco, Col. Doctores, 06720 México, DF; tel. (5) 578-7022; fax (5) 578-9824; e-mail heraldo @iwm.com.mx; internet www.heraldo.com.mx; f. 1965; morning; Dir-Gen. GABRIEL ALARCÓN VELÁZQUEZ; circ. 209,600.

La Jornada: Francisco Petrarca 118, Col. Chapultepec Morales, 11570 México, DF; tel. (5) 262-4315; fax (5) 262-4350; internet www.jornada.unam.mx; f. 1984; morning; Dir-Gen. Lic. CARMEN LIRA SAADE; Gen. Man. Lic. JORGE MARTÍNEZ JIMÉNEZ; circ. 106,471, Sundays 100,924.

Novedades: Balderas 87, esq. Morelos, Col. Centro, 06040 México, DF; tel. (5) 518-5481; fax (5) 521-4505; internet www.unam.netgate .net/novedades; f. 1936; morning; independent; Pres. and Editor-in-Chief ROMULO O'FARRILL, Jr; Vice-Pres. JOSÉ ANTONIO O'FARRILL AVILA; circ. 42,990, Sundays 43,536.

Ovaciones: Lago Zirahuén 279, 20°, Col. Anáhuac, 11320 México, DF; tel. (5) 328-0700; fax (5) 328-0775; f. 1947; morning and evening editions; Pres. and Dir-Gen. Lic. ALBERTO VENTOSA AGUILERA; circ. 130,000; evening circ. 100,000.

La Prensa: Basilio Badillo 40, Col. Tabacalera, 06030 México, DF; tel. (5) 228-8947; fax (5) 228-8922; f. 1928; morning; Pres. and Dir-Gen. Lic. MARIO VÁZQUEZ RAÑA; circ. 208,147, Sundays 172,465.

Reforma: Avda México Coyoacán 40, Col. Sta Cruz Atoyac, 03310 México, DF; tel. (5) 628-7878; fax (5) 628-7511; internet www .reforma.com; f. 1993; morning; Pres. and Dir-Gen. ALEJANDRO JUNCO DE LA VEGA; circ. 115,000.

El Sol de México: Guillermo Prieto 7, 20°, Col. San Rafael, 06470 México, DF; tel. (5) 566-1511; fax (5) 535-5560; e-mail info@oem .com.mx; internet www.elsoldemexico.com.mx; f. 1965; morning and midday; Pres. and Dir-Gen. Lic. MARIO VÁZQUEZ RAÑA; Dir PILAR FERREIRA GARCÍA; circ. 76,000.

El Universal: Bucareli 8, Apdo 909, Col. Centro, 06040 México, DF; tel. (5) 709-1313; fax (5) 521-8080; e-mail rocklech@servidor .unam.mx; internet www.el-universal.com.mx; f. 1916; morning; independent; centre-left; Pres. and Dir-Gen. Lic. JUAN FRANCISCO EALY ORTIZ; circ. 170,356, Sundays 181,615.

Unomásuno: Retorno de Correggio 12, Col. Nochebuena, 03720 México, DF; tel. (5) 563-9911; fax (5) 598-8821; e-mail cduran@ servidor.unam.mx; f. 1977; morning; left-wing; Pres. MANUEL ALONSO MUÑOZ; Dir RAFAEL CARDONA S.; circ. 40,000.

PROVINCIAL DAILY NEWSPAPERS
Baja California

El Mexicano: Carretera al Aeropuerto s/n, Fracc. Alamar, Apdo 2333, 22540 Tijuana, BC; tel. (66) 21-3400; fax (66) 21-2944; f. 1959; morning; Dir and Gen. Man. ELIGIO VALENCIA ROQUE; circ. 80,000.

El Sol de Tijuana: Rufino Tamayo 4, Zona Río, 22320 Tijuana, BC; tel. (66) 34-3232; fax (66) 34-2234; internet www.oem.com.mx; f. 1989; morning; Pres. and Dir-Gen. Lic. MARIO VÁZQUEZ RAÑA; circ. 50,000.

La Voz de la Frontera: Avda Madero 1545, Col. Nueva, Apdo 946, 21100 Mexicali, BC; tel. (65) 53-4545; fax (65) 53-6912; e-mail lavoz@oem.com.mx; internet www.oem.com.mx; f. 1964; morning; independent; Pres. and Dir-Gen. MARIO VÁZQUEZ RAÑA; Gen. Man. Lic. MARIO VALDÉS HERNÁNDEZ; circ. 65,000.

Chihuahua

El Heraldo de Chihuahua: Avda Universidad 2507, Apdo 1515, 31240 Chihuahua, Chih.; tel. (14) 13-9339; fax (14) 13-5625; e-mail elheraldo@buzon.online.com.mx; f. 1927; morning; Pres. and Dir-Gen. Lic. MARIO VÁZQUEZ RAÑA; Dir. Lic. JAVIER CONTRERAS O.; circ. 27,520, Sundays 31,223.

Coahuila

La Opinión: Blvd Independencia 1492 Ote, Apdo 86, 27010 Torreón, Coah.; tel. (17) 13-8777; fax (17) 13-8164; internet www .editoriallaopinion.com.mx; f. 1917; morning; Pres. FRANCISCO A. GONZÁLEZ; circ. 40,000.

El Siglo de Torreón: Avda Matamoros 1056 Pte, Apdo 19, 27000 Torreón, Coah.; tel. (17) 12-8600; fax (17) 16-5909; internet www .elsiglodetorreon.com.mx; f. 1922; morning; Pres. OLGA DE JUAMBELZ Y HORCASITAS; circ. 38,611, Sundays 38,526.

Guanajuato

El Heraldo de León: Hermanos Aldama 222, Apdo 299, 37530 León, Gto; tel. (47) 13-3528; fax (47) 15-5411; internet www .heraldoadi.com.mx; f. 1957; morning; Dir-Gen. MAURICIO BERCÚN MELNIC; circ. 23,546.

El Nacional: Carretera Guanajuato–Juventino Rosas, km 9.5, Apdo 32, 36000 Guanajuato, Gto; tel. (47) 33-1286; fax (47) 33-1288; f. 1987; morning; Dir-Gen. ARNOLDO CUÉLLAR ORNELAS; circ. 60,000.

Jalisco

El Diario de Guadalajara: Calle 14 2550, Zona Industrial, 44940, Guadalajara, Jal.; tel. (3) 612-0043; fax (3) 612-0818; f. 1969; morning; Pres. and Dir-Gen. LUIS A. GONZÁLEZ BECERRA; circ. 78,000.

El Informador: Independencia 300, Apdo 3 bis, 44100 Guadalajara, Jal.; tel. (3) 614-6340; fax (3) 614-4653; internet www.informador .com.mx; f. 1917; morning; Editor JORGE ÁLVAREZ DEL CASTILLO; circ. 50,000.

El Occidental: Calzada Independencia Sur 324, Apdo 1-699, 44100 Guadalajara, Jal.; tel. (3) 613-0690; fax (3) 613-6796; f. 1942; morning; Dir Lic. RICARDO DEL VALLE DEL PERAL; circ. 49,400.

México

ABC: Avda Hidalgo Ote 1339, Centro Comercial, 50000 Toluca, Méx.; tel. (72) 179880; fax (72) 179646; e-mail miled1@mail .miled.com; internet www.miled.com; f. 1984; morning; Pres. and Editor MILED LIBIEN KAUI; circ. 65,000.

Diario de Toluca: Allende Sur 209, 50000 Toluca, Méx.; tel. (72) 142403; fax (72) 141523; f. 1980; morning; Editor ANUAR MACCISE DIB; circ. 22,200.

El Heraldo de Toluca: Salvador Díaz Mirón 700, Col. Sánchez Colín, 50150 Toluca, Méx.; tel. (72) 173453; fax (72) 122535; f. 1955; morning; Editor ALBERTO BARRAZA SÁNCHEZ A.; circ. 90,000.

El Mañana: Avda Hidalgo Ote 1339, Toluca, Méx.; tel. (72) 179880; fax (72) 178402; e-mail miled1@mail.miled.com; internet www .miled.com; f. 1986; morning; Pres. and Editor MILED LIBIEN KAUI; circ. 65,000.

Rumbo: Allende Sur 205, Toluca, Méx.; tel. (72) 142403; fax (72) 141523; f. 1968; morning; Editor ANUAR MACCISE DIB; circ. 10,800.

El Sol de Toluca: Santos Degollado 105, Apdo 54, 50050 Toluca, Méx.; tel. (72) 150340; fax (72) 147441; f. 1947; morning; Pres. and Dir-Gen. Lic. MARIO VÁZQUEZ RAÑA; circ. 42,000.

Michoacán

La Voz de Michoacán: Blvd del Periodismo 1270, Col. Arriaga Rivera, Apdo 121, 58190 Morelia, Mich.; tel. (43) 27-3712; fax (43) 27-3728; e-mail lavoz@mail.giga.com; f. 1948; morning; Dir-Gen. MIGUEL MEDINA ROBLES; circ. 50,000.

Morelos

El Diario de Morelos: Morelos Sur 817, Col. Las Palmas, 62000 Cuernavaca, Mor.; tel. (73) 14-2660; fax (73) 14-1253; internet www.diariodemorelos.com.mx; morning; Dir-Gen. FEDERICO BRACA-MONTES; circ. 47,000.

Nayarit

Meridiano de Nayarit: E. Zapata 73 Pte, Apdo 65, 63000 Tepic, Nay.; tel. (321) 20145; fax (321) 26630; f. 1942; morning; Dir Dr DAVID ALFARO; circ. 60,000.

El Observador: Allende 110 Ote, Despachos 203-204, 63000 Tepic, Nay.; tel. (321) 24309; fax (321) 24309; morning; Pres. and Dir-Gen. Lic. LUIS A. GONZÁLEZ BECERRA; circ. 55,000.

Nuevo León

ABC: Platón Sánchez Sur 411, 64000 Monterrey, NL; tel. (8) 344-4480; fax (8) 344-5990; e-mail abc2000@mexis.com; f. 1985; morning; Pres. GONZALO ESTRADA CRUZ; Dir-Gen. GONZALO ESTRADO TORRES; circ. 40,000, Sundays 45,000.

El Diario de Monterrey: Eugenio Garza Sada 2245 Sur, Col. Roma, Apdo 3128, 647000 Monterrey, NL; tel. (8) 359-2525; fax (8) 359-1414; internet www.diariodemonterrey.com; f. 1974; morning; Dir-Gen. Lic. FEDERICO ARREOLA; circ. 80,000.

El Norte: Washington 629 Ote, Apdo 186, 64000 Monterrey, NL; tel. (8) 345-3388; fax (8) 343-2476; internet www.elnorte.com.mx; f. 1938; morning; Man. Dir Lic. ALEJANDRO JUNCO DE LA VEGA; circ. 133,872, Sundays 154,951.

El Porvenir: Galeana Sur 344, Apdo 218, 64000 Monterrey, NL; tel. (8) 345-4080; fax (8) 345-7795; internet www.elporvenir.com.mx; f. 1919; morning; Dir-Gen. JOSÉ GERARDO CANTÚ ESCALANTE; circ. 75,000.

El Sol: Washington 629 Ote, Apdo 186, 64000 Monterrey, NL; tel. (8) 345-3388; fax (8) 343-2476; internet www.infosel.com.mx; f. 1922; evening (except Sundays); Man. Dir Lic. ALEJANDRO JUNCO DE LA VEGA; circ. 45,300.

Oaxaca

El Imparcial: Armenta y López 312, Apdo 322, 68000 Oaxaca, Oax.; tel. (951) 62812; fax (951) 60050; internet www.imparoax.com.mx; f. 1951; morning; Dir-Gen. Lic. BENJAMÍN FERNÁNDEZ PICHARDO; circ. 17,000, Sundays 20,000.

Puebla

El Sol de Puebla: Avda 3 Ote 201, Apdo 190, 72000 Puebla, Pue.; tel. (22) 42-4560; fax (22) 46-0869; internet www.oem.com.mx; f. 1944; morning; Pres. and Dir-Gen. Lic. MARIO VÁZQUEZ RAÑA; circ. 67,000.

San Luis Potosí

El Heraldo: Villerías 305, 78000 San Luis Potosí, SLP; tel. (48) 12-3312; fax (48) 12-2081; e-mail diario_heraldo@hotmail.com; internet www.elheraldodesanluis.com.mx; f. 1954; morning; Dir-Gen. ALE-JANDRO VILLASANA MENA; circ. 60,620.

Momento: Zenón Fernández y Leandro Valle, Col. Jardines del Estadio, 78280 San Luis Potosí, SLP; tel. (48) 14-4444; fax (48) 12-2020; f. 1975; morning; Dir-Gen. Lic. EMILIO MANUEL TRINIDAD ZALDÍVAR; circ. 60,000.

Pulso: Galeana 485, 78000 San Luis Potosí, SLP; tel. (48) 12-7575; fax (48) 12-3525; internet www.pulsoslp.com.mx; morning; Dir-Gen. MIGUEL VALLADARES GARCÍA; circ. 60,000.

El Sol de San Luis: Avda Universidad 565, Apdo 342, 78000 San Luis Potosí, SLP; tel. and fax (48) 12-4412; f. 1952; morning; Pres. and Dir-Gen. Lic. MARIO VÁZQUEZ RAÑA; Dir JOSÉ ANGEL MARTÍNEZ LIMÓN; circ. 60,000.

Sinaloa

El Debate de Culiacán: Madero 556 Pte, 80000 Culiacán, Sin.; tel. (67) 16-6353; fax (67) 15-7131; e-mail redaccion@debate.com.mx; internet www.debate.com.mx; f. 1972; morning; Dir ROSARIO I. ORO-PEZA; circ. 23,603, Sundays 23,838.

Noroeste Culiacán: Angel Flores 282 Ote, Apdo 90, 80000 Culi-acán, Sin.; tel. (67) 13-2100; fax (67) 12-8006; internet www.noroeste .com.mx; f. 1973; morning; Editor Lic. JOSÉ REFUGIO HARO HARO; circ. 25,000.

El Sol de Sinaloa: Blvd G. Leyva Lozano y Corona 320, Apdo 412, 80000 Culiacán, Sin.; tel. (67) 13-1621; f. 1956; morning; Pres. Lic. MARIO VÁZQUEZ RAÑA; Dir JORGE LUIS TÉLLEZ SALAZAR; circ. 30,000.

Sonora

El Imparcial: Sufragio Efectivo y Mina 71, Col. Centro, Apdo 66, 83000 Hermosillo, Son.; tel. (62) 59-4700; fax (62) 17-4483; e-mail impar@imparcial.com.mx; internet www.imparcial.com.mx; f. 1937; morning; Pres. and Dir-Gen. JOSÉ SANTIAGO HEALY LOERA; circ. 32,083, Sundays 32,444.

Tabasco

Tabasco Hoy: Avda de los Ríos 206, 86035 Villahermosa, Tab.; tel. (93) 16-3333; fax (93) 16-2135; internet www.tabascohoy.com.mx; f. 1987; morning; Dir-Gen. MIGUEL CANTÓN ZETINA; circ. 52,302.

Tamaulipas

El Bravo: Morelos y Primera 129, Apdo 483, 87300 Matamoros, Tamps; tel. (88) 160100; fax (88) 162007; e-mail elbravo@riogrande .net.mx; f. 1951; morning; Pres. and Dir-Gen. JOSÉ CARRETERO BALBOA; circ. 60,000.

El Diario de Nuevo Laredo: González 2409, Apdo 101, 88000 Nuevo Laredo, Tamps; tel. (87) 128444; fax (87) 128221; internet www.diario.net; f. 1948; morning; Editor RUPERTO VILLARREAL MONTE-MAYOR; circ. 68,130, Sundays 73,495.

Expresión: Calle 3a y Novedades 1, Col. Periodistas, 87300 Mata-moros, Tamps; tel. (88) 174330; fax (88) 173307; morning; circ. 50,000.

El Mañana de Reynosa: Prof. Lauro Aguirre con Matías Canales, Apdo 14, 88620 Ciudad Reynosa, Tamps; tel. (89) 251469; fax (89)

230198; internet www.elmananarey.com.mx; f. 1949; morning; Dir-Gen. HERIBERTO DEANDAR MARTÍNEZ; circ. 65,000.

El Mundo: Ejército Nacional 201, Col. Guadalupe, 89120 Tampico, Tamps; tel. (12) 134084; fax (12) 134136; f. 1918; morning; Dir-Gen. ANTONIO MANZUR MARÓN; circ. 54,000.

La Opinión de Matamoros: Blvd Lauro Villar 200, Apdo 486, 87400 Matamoros, Tamps; tel. (88) 123141; fax (88) 122132; e-mail opinion1@tamps1.telmex.net.mx; f. 1971; Pres. and Dir-Gen. JUAN B. GARCÍA GÓMEZ; circ. 50,000.

Prensa de Reynosa: Matamoros y González Ortega, 88500 Reynosa, Tamps; tel. (89) 23515; fax (89) 223823; f. 1963; morning; Dir-Gen. FÉLIX GARZA ELIZONDO; circ. 60,000.

El Sol de Tampico: Altamira 311 Pte, Apdo 434, 89000 Tampico, Tamps; tel. (12) 12-3566; fax (12) 12-6986; internet www.oem.com.mx; f. 1950; morning; Dir-Gen. Lic. RUBÉN DÍAZ DE LA GARZA; circ. 77,000.

Veracruz

Diario del Istmo: Avda Hidalgo 1115, 96400 Coatzacoalcos, Ver.; tel. (921) 48802; fax (921) 48514; e-mail info@istmo.com.mx; internet www.diariodelistmo.com; f. 1979; morning; Dir-Gen. JAÍR BENJAMÍN ROBLES BARAJAS; circ. 64,600.

El Dictamen: 16 de Septiembre y Arista, 91700 Veracruz, Ver.; tel. (29) 311745; fax (29) 315804; f. 1898; morning; Pres. CARLOS ANTONIO MALPICA MARTÍNEZ; circ. 38,000, Sundays 39,000.

Yucatán

Diario de Yucatán: Calle 60, No 521, 97000 Mérida, Yuc.; tel. (99) 23-8444; fax (99) 42-2204; internet www.yucatan.com.mx; f. 1925; morning; Dir-Gen. CARLOS R. MENÉNDEZ NAVARRETE; circ. 54,639, Sundays 65,399.

El Mundo al Día: Calle 62, No 514A, 97000 Mérida Yuc.; tel. (99) 23-9933; fax (99) 24-9629; e-mail nmerida@cancun.novenet.com.mx; f. 1964; morning; Pres. ROMULO O'FARRILL, Jr; Gen. Man. Lic. GERARDO GARCÍA GAMBOA; circ. 25,000.

Por Esto!: Calle 60, No 576 entre 73 y 71, 97000 Mérida, Yuc.; tel. (99) 24-7613; fax (99) 28-6514; internet www.poresto.net; f. 1991; morning; Dir-Gen. MARIO R. MENÉNDEZ RODRÍGUEZ; circ. 26,985, Sundays 28,727.

SELECTED WEEKLY NEWSPAPERS

Bolsa de Trabajo: San Francisco 657, 9A, Col. del Valle, 03100 México, DF; tel. (5) 536-8387; f. 1988; employment; Pres. and Dir-Gen. MÓNICA ELÍAS CALLES; circ. 30,000.

Segundamano: Insurgentes Sur 813-501, Col. Nápoles, 03810 México, DF; tel. (5) 729-3737; fax (5) 687-9635; f. 1986; Dir-Gen. LUIS MAGAÑA MAGA&NCIRC; A; circ. 105,000.

GENERAL-INTEREST PERIODICALS

Car and Driver: Alabama 113, Col. Nápoles, 03810 México, DF; tel. (5) 523-5201; fax (5) 536-6399; f. 1999; monthly; Pres. PEDRO VARGAS G., circ. 80,000.

Conozca Más: Vasco de Quiroga 2000, Col. Santa Fe, 01210 México, DF; tel. (5) 261-2600; fax (5) 261-2704; f. 1990; monthly; Dir EUGENIO MENDOZA; circ. 90,000.

Contenido: Buffon 46, 9°, Col. Anzures, 11590 México, DF; tel. (5) 531-3162; fax (5) 545-8300; f. 1963; monthly; popular appeal; Dir ARMANDO AYALA A.; circ. 124,190.

Cosmopolitan (México): Vasco de Quiroga 2000, Col. Santa Fe, 01210 México, DF; tel. (5) 261-2600; fax (5) 261-2704; f. 1973; monthly; women's magazine; Dir SARA MARÍA CASTANY; circ. 260,000.

Fama: Avda Eugenio Garza Sada 2245 Sur, Col. Roma, Apdo 3128, 64700 Monterrey, NL; tel. (8) 359-2525; fortnightly; show business; Pres. JESÚS D. GONZÁLEZ; Dir RAÚL MARTÍNEZ; circ. 350,000.

Impacto: Avda Ceylán 517, Col. Industrial Vallejo, Apdo 2986, 02300 México, DF; tel. (5) 587-3855; fax (5) 567-7781; f. 1949; weekly; politics; Man. and Dir-Gen. JUAN BUSTILLOS OROZCO; circ. 115,000.

Kena: Romero de Terreros 832, Col. del Valle, 03100 México, DF; tel. (5) 543-1032; fax (5) 669-3465; f. 1977; fortnightly; women's interest; Dir-Gen. Lic. LILIANA MORENO G.; circ. 76,925.

Marie Claire: Editorial Televisa, SA de CV, Vasco de Quiroga 2000, Col. Santa Fe, 01210 México, DF; tel. (5) 261-2600; fax (5) 261-2704; f. 1990; monthly; women's interest; Editor LOUISE MERELES; circ. 80,000.

Mecánica Popular: Vasco de Quiroga 2000, Edificio E, Col. Santa Fe, Avda Obregón, 01210 Mexico, DF; tel. (5) 262-2000; fax (5) 261-2730; e-mail mecanica.popular@siedi.spin.com.mx; f. 1947; monthly; crafts and home improvements; Dir ANDRÉS JORGE; circ. 70,000.

Men's Health: Vasco de Quiroga 2000, Col. Santa Fe, 01210 México, DF; tel. (5) 261-2600; fax (5) 261-2732; e-mail mens.health@editorial.televisa.com.mx; f. 1994; monthly; health; Editor JUAN ANTONIO SEMPERE; circ. 130,000.

Muy Interesante: Vasco de Quiroga 2000, Col. Santa Fe, 01210 México, DF; tel. (5) 261-2600; fax (5) 261-2704; f. 1984; monthly; scientific devt; Dir PILAR S. HOYOS; circ. 250,000.

Proceso: Fresas 7, Col. del Valle, 03100 México, DF; tel. (5) 629-2090; fax (5) 629-2092; f. 1976; weekly; news analysis; Pres. JULIO SCHERER GARCÍA; circ. 98,784.

Selecciones del Reader's Digest: Avda Lomas de Sotelo 1102, Col. Loma Hermosa, Apdo 552, Naucalpan, 11200 México, DF; tel. (5) 395-7444; fax (5) 395-3835; f. 1940; monthly; Dir AVDON CORIA; circ. 611,660.

Siempre!: Vallarta 20, Apdo 32-010, Col. Revolución, 06030 México, DF; tel. (5) 566-9355; fax (5) 546-5130; e-mail siempre@data.net.mx; f. 1953; weekly; left of centre; Dir Lic. BEATRIZ PAGÉS REBOLLAR DE NIETO; circ. 100,000.

Tele-Guía: Vasco de Quiroga 2000, Col. Santa Fe, 01210 México, DF; tel. (5) 261-2600; fax (5) 261-2704; f. 1952; weekly; television guide; Editor MARÍA EUGENIA HERNÁNDEZ; circ. 375,000.

Tiempo Libre: Holbein 75 bis, Col. Nochebuena, 03720 México, DF; tel. (5) 611-3874; fax (5) 611-2884; e-mail tpolibre@planet.com.mx; internet www.tiempolibre.com.mx; f. 1980; weekly; entertainment guide; Dir-Gen. ANGELES AGUILAR ZINSER; circ. 90,000.

Tú: Vasco de Quiroga 2000, Col. Santa Fe, 01210 México, DF; tel. (5) 261-2600; fax (5) 261-2704; f. 1980; monthly; Editor MARÍA ANTONIETA SALAMANCA; circ. 275,000.

TV y Novelas: Vasco de Quiroga 2000, Col. Santa Fe, 01210 México, DF; tel. (5) 261-2600; fax (5) 261-2704; f. 1982; weekly; television guide and short stories; Dir JESÚS GALLEGOS; circ. 460,000.

Ultima Moda: Morelos 16, 6°, Col. Centro, 06040 México, DF; tel. (5) 518-5481; fax (5) 512-8902; f. 1966; monthly; fashion; Pres. ROMULO O'FARRILL, Jr; Gen. Man. Lic. SAMUEL PODOLSKY RAPOPORT; circ. 110,548.

Vanidades: Vasco de Quiroga 2000, Col. Santa Fe, 01210 México, DF; tel. (5) 261-2600; fax (5) 261-2704; f. 1961; fortnightly; women's magazine; Dir SARA MARÍA BARCELÓ DE CASTANY; circ. 290,000.

Visión: Homero 411, 5°, Col. Polanco, 11570 México, DF; tel. (5) 531-4914; fax (5) 531-4915; e-mail 74174.3111@compuserve.com; offices in Santafé de Bogotá, Buenos Aires and Santiago de Chile; f. 1950; fortnightly; politics and economics; Gen. Man. ROBERTO BELLO; circ. 27,215.

SPECIALIST PERIODICALS

Boletín Industrial: Goldsmith 37-403, Col. Polanco, 11550 México, DF; tel. (5) 280-6463; fax (5) 280-3194; e-mail bolind@viernes.iwm.com.mx; internet www.bolind.com.mx; f. 1983; monthly; Dir-Gen. HUMBERTO VALADÉS DÍAZ; circ. 36,000.

Comercio: Río Tíber 87, 06500 México, DF; tel. (5) 514-0873; fax (5) 514-1008; f. 1960; monthly; business review; Dir RAÚL HORTA; circ. 40,000.

Gaceta Médica de México: Academia Nacional de Medicina, Unidad de Congresos del Centro Médico Nacional Siglo XXI, Bloque B, Avda Cuauhtémoc 330, Col. Doctores, 06725 México, DF; tel. (5) 578-2044; fax (5) 578-4271; e-mail gacetamx@starnet.net.mx; f. 1864; every 2 months; medicine; Editor Dr LUIS BENÍTEZ; circ. 20,000.

Manufactura: Sinaloa 149, 1°, Col. Roma, 06700 México, DF; tel. (5) 511-1537; fax (5) 208-1265; e-mail publicidad@expansion.com.mx; internet www.expansion.com.mx; f. 1994; monthly; industrial; Dir-Gen. ALEJANDRO SERNA BARRERA; circ. 29,751.

Negobancos (Negocios y Bancos): Bolívar 8-103, Apdo 1907, Col. Centro, 06000 México, DF; tel. (5) 510-1884; fax (5) 512-9411; e-mail nego_bancos@mexico.com; f. 1951; fortnightly; business, economics; Dir ALFREDO FARRUGIA REED; circ. 10,000.

Noticiario Industrial: Goldsmith 38-302, Col. Polanco, 11560 México, DF; tel. (5) 259-1448; fax (5) 540-0673; f. 1988; monthly; Dir NEAL W. BAKER; circ. 34,144.

ASSOCIATIONS

Asociación Nacional de Periodistas A.C.: Luis G. Obregón 17, Desp. 209, Col. Centro, 06020 México, DF; tel. (5) 702-1546.

Federación Latinoamericana de Periodistas (FELAP): Nuevo Leon 144, 1°, Col. Hipódromo Condesa, 06170 México, DF; tel. (5) 286-6055; fax (5) 286-6085.

NEWS AGENCIES

Agencia de Información Integral Periodística, SA (AIIP): Tabasco 263, Col. Roma, Apdo 7-1490, 06700 México, DF; tel. and fax (5) 688-7339; e-mail mherrera@spin.com.mx; internet spin.com.mx/"mherrera; f. 1990; Dir-Gen. MIGUEL HERRERA L.

Agencia Mexicana de Información (AMI): Avda Cuauhtémoc 16, Col. Doctores, 06720 México, DF; tel. (5) 761-9933; Dir-Gen. JOSÉ LUIS BECERRA LÓPEZ; Gen.-Man. EVA VÁZQUEZ LÓPEZ.

Notimex, SA de CV: Morena 110, 3°, Col. del Valle, 03100 México, DF; tel. (5) 420-1100; fax (5) 682-0005; e-mail comercial@notimex .com.mx; internet www.notimex.com.mx; f. 1968; services to press, radio and TV in Mexico and throughout the world; Dir JORGE MEDINA VIEDAS.

Foreign Bureaux

Agence France-Presse (AFP): Torre Latinoamericana, 9°, Lázaro Cárdenas y Madero, Apdo M10330, 06007 México, DF; tel. (5) 518-5494; fax (5) 510-4564; Bureau Chief ANDRÉ BIRUKOFF.

Agenzia Nazionale Stampa Associata (ANSA) (Italy): Emerson 150, 2°, Col. Chapultepec Morales, 11570 México, DF; tel. (5) 255-3696; fax (5) 255-3018; e-mail ansamexico@inserve.net.mx; Bureau Chief Dott. CARLO GIACOBBE.

Associated Press (AP) (USA): Edif. Bank of America, 8°, Of. 902-804, Paseo de la Reforma 116, Apdo 1181, México, DF; tel. (5) 566-3488; Bureau Chief ELOY O. AGUILAR.

Deutsche Presse-Agentur (dpa) (Germany): Avda Cuauhtémoc 16, Col. Doctores, 06720 México, DF; tel. (5) 578-4829; fax (5) 761-0762; Bureau Chief THOMAS VON MONILLARD.

EFE (Spain): Lafayette 69, Col. Anzures, 11590 México, DF; tel. (5) 545-8256; fax (5) 254-1412; e-mail manuel_r_mora@infosel .net.mx; Bureau Chief MANUEL RODRÍGUEZ MORA.

Informatsionnoye Telegrafnoye Agentstvo Rossii—Telegrafnoye Agentsvo Suverennykh Stran (ITAR—TASS) (Russia): México, DF; Correspondent IGOR GOLUBEV.

Inter Press Service (IPS) (Italy): Avda Cuauhtémoc 16-403, Col. Doctores, Del. Cuauhtémoc, 06720 México, DF; tel. (5) 578-0417; fax (5) 578-0099; Chief Correspondent JOSÉ L. ALCAZAR DE LA RIVA.

Jiji Tsushin-Sha (Japan): Sevilla 9, 2°, Col. Juárez, Del. Cuauhtémoc, 06600 México, DF; tel. (5) 528-9651; fax (5) 511-0062; Bureau Chief FUJIO IKEDA.

Kyodo Tsushin (Japan): Jardín 13, Col. Tlacopac, 01040 México, DF; tel. (5) 548-3295; Correspondent SEIICHI TODA.

Prensa Latina (Cuba): Edif. B, Dpto 504, Insurgentes Centro 125, Col. San Rafael, Del. Cuauhtémoc, 06470 México, DF; tel. (5) 546-6015; fax (5) 592-0570; e-mail plenmex@mail.internet.com.mx; Chief Correspondent Lic. AISSA GARCÍA GOREIA.

Reuters Ltd (United Kingdom): Monte Pelvoux 110, 3°, Lomas de Chapultepec, 11000 México, DF; tel. (5) 728-9500; fax (5) 540-3001; e-mail stott@reuters.com; Bureau Chief MICHAEL STOTT.

United Press International (UPI) (USA): Avda Cuauhtémoc 16, Col. Dóctores, Del. Cuauhtémoc, 06700 México, DF; tel. (5) 761-5365; Bureau Chief EDWIN VIDAL.

Xinhua (New China) News Agency (People's Republic of China): Francisco I. Madero 17, Col. Tlacopac, 01040 México, DF; tel. (5) 550-9860; Correspondents SHEN JIASONG, XUE HONG.

ASSOCIATION

Asociación de Corresponsales Extranjeros en México (ACEM): Avda Cuauhtemoc 16, 1°, Col. Doctores, Del. Cuauhtémoc, 06720 México, DF; tel. (5) 588-3241; fax (5) 588-6382.

Publishers

México, DF

Addison-Wesley Iberoamericana, SA de CV: Blvd de las Cataratas 3, 2°, Col. Jardines del Pedregal, 01900 México, DF; tel. (5) 568-3618; fax (5) 568-3202; f. 1986; educational textbooks; Man. Dir JONATAN ROSE.

Aguilar, Altea, Taurus, Alfaguara, SA de CV: Avda Universidad 767, Col. del Valle, 03100 México, DF; tel. (5) 688-8966; fax (5) 604-2304; e-mail sealtiel@santillana.com.mx; f. 1965; general literature; Dir SEALTIEL ALATRISTE.

Arbol Editorial, SA de CV: Avda Cuauhtémoc 1430, Col. Sta Cruz Atoyac, 03310 México, DF; tel. (5) 688-4828; fax (5) 605-7600; e-mail editorialpax@maxis.com; f. 1979; health, philosophy, theatre; Man. Dir GERARDO GALLY TEOMONFORD.

Editorial Avante, SA de CV: Luis G. Obregón 9, 1°, Apdo 45-796, Col. Centro, 06020 México, DF; tel. (5) 510-8804; fax (5) 521-5245; e-mail editorialavante@infosel.net.mx; f. 1950; educational, drama, linguistics; Man. Dir Lic. MARIO ALBERTO HINOJOSA SÁENZ.

Editorial Azteca, SA: Calle de la Luna 225–227, Col. Guerrero, 06300 México, DF; tel. (5) 526-1157; fax (5) 526-2557; f. 1956; religion, literature and technical; Man. Dir ALFONSO ALEMÓN JALOMO.

Librería y Ediciones Botas, SA de CV: Justo Sierra 52, Apdo 941, 06020 México, DF; tel. (5) 702-4083; fax (5) 702-5403; e-mail botas@mail.nextgeninter.net.mx; internet members.nbci.com/botas; f. 1910; history, law, philosophy, literature, fine arts, science, language, economics, medicine; Dir ANDRÉS BOTAS HERNÁNDEZ.

Cía Editorial Continental, SA de CV (CECSA): Renacimiento 180, Col. San Juan Tlihuaca, Azcapotzalco, 02400 México, DF; tel. (5) 561-8333; fax (5) 561-5231; e-mail info@patriacultural.com.mx; f. 1954; business, technology, general textbooks; Pres. CARLOS FRIGOLET LERMA.

Ediciones de Cultura Popular, SA: Odontología 76, Copilco Universidad, México, DF; f. 1969; history, politics, social sciences; Man. Dir URIEL JARQUÍN GALVEZ.

Ediciones CUPSA: Centro de Comunicación Cultural CUPSA, Apdo 97 bis, 06000 México, DF; tel. (5) 546-2100; f. 1958; Biblical studies, theology, church history, devotional materials, hymn-books; Dir ELISA TOSTADO.

Editorial Diana, SA de CV: Roberto Gayol 1219, Col. del Valle, Apdo 44986, 03100 México, DF; tel. (5) 575-0711; fax (5) 575-3211; e-mail editor@diana.com.mx; internet www.editorialdiana.com.mx; f. 1946; general trade and technical books; Pres. and CEO JOSÉ LUIS RAMÍREZ-COTA.

Ediciones Era, SA de CV: Calle del Trabajo 31, Col. La Fama, Tlalpan, 14269 México, DF; tel. (5) 528-1221; fax (5) 606-2904; e-mail edicionesera@laneta.apc.org; f. 1960; general and social science, art and literature; Gen. Man. NIEVES ESPRESATE XIRAU.

Editorial Everest Mexicana, SA: Calzada Ermita Iztapalapa 1631, Col. Barrio San Miguel del Iztapalapa, 09360 México, DF; tel. (5) 685-1966; fax (5) 685-3433; f. 1980; general textbooks; Gen. Man. JOSÉ LUIS HUIDOBRO LEÓN.

Espasa Calpe Mexicana, SA: Pitágoras 1139, Col. del Valle, 03100 México, DF; tel. (5) 575-5022; f. 1948; literature, music, economics, philosophy, encyclopaedia; Man. FRANCISCO CRUZ RUBIO.

Fernández Editores, SA de CV: Eje 1 Pte México-Coyoacán 321, Col. Xoco, 03330 México, DF; tel. (5) 605-6557; fax (5) 688-9173; f. 1943; children's literature, textbooks, educational toys, didactic material; Man. Dir LUIS GERARDO FERNÁNDEZ PÉREZ.

Editorial Fondo de Cultura Económica, SA de CV: Carretera Picacho-Ajusco 227, Col. Bosques del Pedregal, 14200 México, DF; tel. (5) 227-4672; fax (5) 227-4640; e-mail geditorial@fce.com.mx; f. 1934; economics, history, philosophy, children's books, science, politics, psychology, sociology, literature; Dir Lic. MIGUEL DE LA MADRID.

Editorial Grijalbo, SA de CV: Calzada San Bartolo-Naucalpan 282, Col. Argentina, Apdo 17-568, 11230 México, DF; tel. (5) 358-4355; fax (5) 576-3586; f. 1954; general fiction, history, sciences, philosophy, children's books; Man. Dir AGUSTÍN CENTENO RÍOS.

Nueva Editorial Interamericana, SA de CV: Cedro 512, Col. Atlampa, Apdo 4-140, 06450 México, DF; tel. (5) 541-6789; fax (5) 541-1603; f. 1944; medical publishing; Man. Dir RAFAEL SÁINZ.

Editorial Joaquín Mortiz, SA de CV: Insurgentes Sur 1162, 3°, Col. del Valle, 03100 México, DF; tel. (5) 575-8585; fax (5) 575-3483; f. 1962; general literature; Man. Dir Ing. HOMERO GAYOSO ANIMAS.

Editorial Jus, SA de CV: Plaza de Abasolo 14, Col. Guerrero, 06300 México, DF; tel. (5) 526-0616; fax (5) 529-0951; f. 1938; history of Mexico, law, philosophy, economy, religion; Man. TOMÁS G. REYNOSO.

Ediciones Larousse, SA de CV: Dinamarca 81, Col. Juárez, 06600 México, DF; tel. (5) 208-2005; fax (5) 208-6225; f. 1965; Man. Dir DOMINIQUE BERTÍN GARCÍA.

Editora Latino Americana, SA: Guatemala 10-220, México, DF; popular literature; Dir JORGE H. YÉPEZ.

Editorial Limusa, SA de CV: Balderas 95, 1°, Col. Centro, 06040 México, DF; tel. (5) 521-2105; fax (5) 512-2903; e-mail limusa@ noriega.com.mx; internet www.noriega.com.mx; f. 1962; science, general, textbooks; Pres. CARLOS NORIEGA MILERA.

Editorial Nuestro Tiempo, SA: Avda Universidad 771, Desp. 103-104, Col. del Valle, 03100 México, DF; tel. (5) 688-8768; fax (5) 688-6868; f. 1966; social sciences; Man. Dir ESPERANZA NACIF BARQUET.

Editorial Oasis, SA: Avda Oaxaca 28, 06700 México, DF; tel. (5) 528-8293; f. 1954; literature, pedagogy, poetry; Man. MARÍA TERESA ESTRADA DE FERNÁNDEZ DEL BUSTO.

Editorial Orión: Sierra Mojada 325, 11000 México, DF; tel. (5) 520-0224; f. 1942; archaeology, philosophy, psychology, literature, fiction; Man. Dir SILVA HERNÁNDEZ BALTAZAR.

Editorial Patria, SA de CV: Renacimiento 180, Col. San Juan Tlihuaca, Azcapotzalco, 02400 México, DF; tel. (5) 561-6042; fax (5) 561-5231; e-mail info@patriacultural.com.mx; f. 1933; fiction, general trade, children's books; Pres. CARLOS FRIGOLET LERMA.

Editorial Porrúa Hnos, SA: Argentina 15, 5°, 06020 México, DF; tel. (5) 702-4574; fax (5) 702-6529; e-mail servicios@porrua.com; internet www.porrua.com; f. 1944; general literature; Dir JOSÉ ANTONIO PÉREZ PORRÚA.

Editorial Posada, SA de CV: Eugenia 13, Desp. 501, Col. Nápoles, 03510 México, DF; tel. (5) 682-0660; f. 1968; general; Dir-Gen. CARLOS VIGIL ZUBIETA.

Editorial Quetzacoatl, SA: Medicina 37, Local 1 y 2, México, DF; tel. (5) 548-6180; Man. Dir ALBERTO RODRÍGUEZ VALDÉS.

Harmex, SA de CV: Lucio Blanco 435, Azcapotzalco, 02400 México, DF; tel. (5) 352-6538; fax (5) 352-8218; romantic fiction; Pres. GUSTAVO GONZÁLEZ LEWIS.

Medios Publicitarios Mexicanos, SA de CV: Avda México 99-103, Col. Hipódromo Condesa, 06170 México, DF; tel. (5) 574-2858; fax (5) 574-2668; e-mail editorial@mpm.com.mx; internet www.mpm.com.mx; f. 1958; advertising media rates and data; Man. FERNANDO VILLAMIL ÁVILA.

Reverté Ediciones, SA de CV: Río Pánuco 141A, 06500 México, DF; tel. (5) 533-5658; fax (5) 514-6799; e-mail 101545.2361@compuserve.com; f. 1955; science, technical, architecture; Man. RAMÓN REVERTÉ MASCÓ.

Salvat Mexicana de Ediciones, SA de CV: Presidente Masarik 101, 5°, 11570 México, DF; tel. (5) 250-6041; fax (5) 250-6861; medicine, encyclopaedic works; Dir GUILLERMO HERNÁNDEZ PÉREZ.

Siglo XXI Editores, SA de CV: Avda Cerro del Agua 248, Col. Romero de Terreros, Del. Coyoacán, 04310 México, DF; tel. (5) 658-7999; fax (5) 658-7599; f. 1966; art, economics, education, history, social sciences, literature, philology and linguistics, philosophy and political science; Dir-Gen. Lic. JAIME LABASTIDA OCHOA; Gen. Man. Ing. GUADALUPE ORTIZ ELGUEA.

Editorial Trillas, SA: Avda Río Churubusco 385 Pte, Col. Xoco, Apdo 10534, 03330 México, DF; tel. (5) 688-4233; fax (5) 601-1858; e-mail trillas@ovinet.com.mx; internet www.trillas.mx; f. 1954; science, technical, textbooks, children's books; Man. Dir FRANCISCO TRILLAS MERCADER.

Universidad Nacional Autónoma de México: Dirección General de Fomento Editorial, Avda del Iman 5, Ciudad Universitaria, 04510 México, DF; tel. (5) 622-6581; fax (5) 665-2778; f. 1935; publications in all fields; Dir-Gen. ARTURO VELÁZQUEZ JIMÉNEZ.

ASSOCIATIONS

Cámara Nacional de la Industria Editorial Mexicana: Holanda 13, Col. San Diego Churubusco, 04120 México, DF; tel. (5) 688-2011; fax (5) 604-3147; e-mail cepromex@caniem.com; internet www.caniem.com; f. 1964; Pres. ANTONIO RUANO FERNÁNDEZ; Gen. Man. CLAUDIA DOMÍNGUEZ MEJÍA.

Instituto Mexicano del Libro, AC: México, DF; tel. (5) 535-2061; Pres. KLAUS THIELE; Sec.-Gen. ISABEL RUIZ GONZÁLEZ.

Organización Editorial Mexicana, SA: Guillermo Prieto 7, 06470 México, DF; tel. (5) 566-1511; fax (5) 566-0694; e-mail info@oem.com.mx; internet www.oem.com.mx; Pres. Lic. MARIO VÁZQUEZ RAÑA.

Prensa Nacional Asociada, SA (PRENASA): Insurgentes Centro 114-411, 06030 México, DF; tel. (5) 546-7389.

Broadcasting and Communications

TELECOMMUNICATIONS
Regulatory Authorities

Comisión Federal de Telecomunicaciones (CFT): Bosque de Radiatas 44, 4°, Col. Bosques de las Lomas, 05120 México, DF; tel. (5) 261-4000; fax (5) 261-4125; e-mail buzon@cft.gob.mx; internet www.cft.gob.mx; Pres. JORGE NICOLÍN FISCHER.

Dirección General de Concesiones y Permisos de Telecomunicaciones: Unidad Contel Sga, Avda de las Telecomunicaciones s/n, Ixtapalapa, 09310 México, DF; tel. (5) 692-0077; Dir Ing. SERGIO CERVANTES.

Dirección General de Telecomunicaciones: Lázaro Cárdenas 567, 11°, Ala Norte, Col. Narvarte, 03020 México, DF; tel. (5) 519-9161; Dir-Gen. Ing. ENRIQUE LUENGAS H.

Principal Operators

Alestra: México, DF; internet www.alestra.com.mx; Dir.-Gen. ROLANDO ZUBIRÁN SHETLER.

Avantel: Liverpool 88, Col. Juárez, 06600 México, DF; internet www.avantel.net.mx; Dir-Gen. OSCAR RODRÍGUEZ MARTÍNEZ.

Iusacell, SA de CV: Avda Prolongación Paseo de la Reforma 1236, Col. Santa Fe, 05438 México, DF; internet www.iusacell.com.mx; operates mobile cellular telephone network; Pres. and Dir-Gen. FÚLVIO V. DEL VALLE.

Telecomunicaciones de México (TELECOM): Lázaro Cárdenas 567, 11°, Ala Norte, Col. Narvarte, 03020 México, DF; tel. (5) 629-1166; fax (5) 559-9812; Dir-Gen. Ing. CARLOS MIER Y TERÁN ORDIALES.

Teléfonos de México, SA de CV (Telmex): Parque Vía 198, Of. 701, Col. Cuauhtémoc, 06599 México, DF; tel. (5) 222-5462; fax (5) 545-5500; internet www.telmex.com.mx; Chair. CARLOS SLIM.

Televisa, SA: Dr Río de la Loza 182, 06720 México, DF; tel. (5) 588-1549; fax (5) 588-1479.

BROADCASTING
Regulatory Authorities

Cámara Nacional de la Industria de Radio y Televisión (CIRT): Horacio 1013, Col. Polanco, 11550 México, DF; tel. (5) 726-9909; fax (5) 545-6767; e-mail cirt@data.net.mx; internet www.cirt.com.mx; f. 1942; Pres. JOAQUÍN VARGAS GUAJARDO; Gen. Man. Lic. CÉSAR HERNÁNDEZ ESPEJO.

Dirección General de Radio, Televisión y Cine (RTC): Atletas 2, Col. Country Club, Del. Coyoacán, 04220 México, DF; tel. (5) 544-3768; Dir-Gen. Lic. MANUEL VILLA AGUILERA.

Dirección de Normas de Radiodifusión: Eugenia 197, 1°, Col. Narvarte, 03020 México, DF; tel. (5) 590-4372; e-mail amilpg@sct.gob.mx; internet www.sct.gob.mx; licence-issuing authority; Dir Dr ALFONSO AMILPAS.

Instituto Mexicano de Televisión: Anillo Periférico Sur 4121, Col. Fuentes del Pedregal, 14141 México, DF; tel. (5) 568-5684; Dir-Gen. Lic. JOSÉ ANTONIO ÁLVAREZ LIMA.

Radio

In 1993 there were 1,040 commercial radio stations in Mexico.
Among the most important commercial networks are:

ARTSA: Avda de Los Virreyes 1030, Col. Lomas de Chapultepec, 11000 México, DF; tel. (5) 202-3344; fax (5) 202-6940; Dir-Gen. Lic. GUSTAVO ECHEVARRÍA ARCE.

Cadena Crystal Cima, SA de CV: Montecito 59, Col. Nápoles, 03810 México, DF; tel. (5) 682-4370; Dir-Gen. Lic. FRANCISCO J. SÁNCHEZ CAMPUZANO.

Corporación Mexicana de Radiodifusión: Tetitla 23, esq. Calle Coapa, Col. Toriello Guerra, 14050 México, DF; tel. (5) 666-8405; fax (5) 666-5422; e-mail cmr@mail.internet.com.mx; internet www.cmr.com.mx; Pres. and Dir-Gen. ENRIQUE BERNAL SERVÍN.

Firme, SA: Gauss 10, Col. Nueva Anzures, 11590 México, DF; tel. (5) 250-7788; fax (5) 250-7788; Dir-Gen. LUIS IGNACIO SANTIBÁÑEZ.

Grupo Acir, SA: Monte Pirineos 770, Col. Lomas de Chapultepec, 11000 México, DF; tel. (5) 540-4291; fax (5) 540-4106; f. 1965; comprises 140 stations; Pres. FRANCISCO IBARRA LÓPEZ.

Grupo Radio Centro, SA de CV: Constituyentes 1154, Col. Lomas Atlas, Del. Miguel Hidalgo, 11950 México, DF; tel. (5) 728-4947; fax (5) 259-2915; f. 1965; comprises 100 radio stations; Pres. ADRIÁN AGUIRRE GÓMEZ; Dir-Gen. Ing. GILBERTO SOLÍS SILVA.

Instituto Mexicano de la Radio (IMER): Mayorazgo 83, 2°, Col. Xoco, 03330 México, DF; tel. (5) 628-1730; f. 1983; Dir-Gen. CARLOS LARA SUMANO.

MVS Radio Stereorey y FM Globo: Mariano Escobedo 532, Col. Anzures, 11590 México, DF; tel. (5) 203-4574; fax (5) 255-1425; e-mail vargas@data.net.mx; f. 1968; Pres. Lic. JOAQUÍN VARGAS G.; Vice-Pres. Lic. ADRIÁN VARGAS G.

Núcleo Radio Mil: Insurgentes Sur 1870, 01030 México, DF; tel. (5) 662-6060; f. 1960; comprises seven radio stations in Mexico City and three provincial radio stations; Pres. and Dir-Gen. Lic. E. GUILLERMO SALAS PEYRÓ.

Organización Radio Centro: Artículo 123, N° 90, Col. Centro, 06050 México, DF; tel. (5) 709-2220; fax (5) 512-8588; nine stations in Mexico City; Pres. MARÍA ESTHER GÓMEZ DE AGUIRRE.

Organización Radiofónica de México, SA: Tuxpan 39, 8°, Col. Roma Sur, 06760 México, DF; tel. (5) 264-2025; fax (5) 264-5720; Pres. JAIME FERNÁNDEZ ARMENDÁRIZ.

Radio Cadena Nacional, SA de CV (RCN): Avda Coyoacán 1899, Col. Acacias, 03240 México, DF; tel. (5) 534-2300; fax (5) 524-2753; e-mail rcn.mex@prodigy.net.mx; f. 1948; Pres. RAFAEL C. NAVARRO ARRONTE; Dir-Gen. SERGIO FAJARDO ORTIZ.

Radio Comerciales, SA de CV: Avda México y López Mateos, 44680 Guadalajara, Jal.; tel. (3) 615-0852; fax (3) 630-3487; 7 major commercial stations.

Radio Educación: Angel Urraza 622, Col. del Valle, 03100 México, DF; tel. (5) 559-6169; fax (5) 575-6566; f. 1924; Gen. Dir LUIS ERNESTO PI OROZCO.

Radio Fórmula, SA: Privada de Horacio 10, Col. Polanco, 11560 México, DF; tel. (5) 282-1016; Dir Lic. ROGERIO AZCÁRRAGA.

Radiodifusoras Asociadas, SA de CV (RASA): Durango 331, 2°, Col. Roma, 06700 México, DF; tel. (5) 553-6620; fax (5) 286-2774; f. 1956; Pres. JOSÉ LARIS ITURBIDE; Dir-Gen. JOSÉ LARIS RODRÍGUEZ.

Radiodifusores Asociados de Innovación y Organización, SA: Emerson 408, Col. Chapultepec Morales, 11570 México, DF; tel. (5) 203-5577; fax (5) 545-2078; Dir-Gen. Lic. CARLOS QUIÑONES ARMENDÁRIZ.

Radiorama, SA de CV: Reforma 56, 5°, 06600 México, DF; tel. (5) 566-1515; fax (5) 566-1454; Dir José Luis C. Reséndiz.

Representaciones Comerciales Integrales: Avda Chapultepec 431, Col. Juárez, 06600 México, DF; tel. (5) 533-6185; Dir-Gen. Alfonso Palma V.

Sistema Radio Juventud: Pablo Casals 567, Prados Providencia, 44670 Guadalajara, Jal.; tel. (3) 641-6677; fax (3) 641-3413; f. 1975; network of several stations including Estereo Soul 89.9 FM; Dirs Alberto Leal A., J. Jesús Orozco G., Gabriel Arregui V.

Sistema Radiofónico Nacional, SA: Baja California 163, Of. 602, 06760 México, DF; tel. (5) 574-0298; f. 1971; represents commercial radio networks; Dir-Gen. René C. de la Rosa.

Sociedad Mexicana de Radio, SA de CV (SOMER): Gutenberg 89, Col. Anzures, 11590 México, DF; tel. (5) 255-5297; fax (5) 545-0310; Dir-Gen. Edilberto Huesca Perrotin.

Television

In 1992 there were 752 television stations, including 115 cable television stations.

Among the most important are:

Asesoramiento y Servicios Técnicos Industriales, SA (ASTISA): México, DF; tel. (5) 585-3333; commercial; Dir Roberto Chávez Tinajero.

MVS (Multivisión): Blvd Puerto Aéreo 486, Col. Moctezuma, 15500 México, DF; tel. (5) 571-2835; subscriber-funded.

Once TV: Carpio 475, Col. Casco de Santo Tomás, 11340 México, DF; tel. (5) 356-1111; fax (5) 396-8001; e-mail canal11@vmredipn .ipn.mx; f. 1959; Dir-Gen. Alejandra Lajous Vargas.

Tele Cadena Mexicana, SA: Avda Chapultepec 18, 06724 México, DF; tel. (5) 535-1679; commercial, comprises about 80 stations; Dir Lic. Jorge Armando Piña Medina.

Televisa, SA de CV: Edif. Televicentro, Avda Chapultepec 28, Col. Doctores, 06724 México, DF; tel. (5) 709-3333; fax (5) 709-3021; e-mail webmaster@televisa.com.mx; internet www.televisa.com; f. 1973; commercial; began broadcasts to Europe via satellite in Dec. 1988 through its subsidiary, Galavisión; 406 affiliated stations; Chair. and CEO Emilio Azcárraga Jean; Vice-Pres. Alejandro Burillo Azcárraga.

Televisión Azteca, SA de CV: Anillo Periférico Sur 4121, Col. Fuentes del Pedregal, 14141 México, DF; tel. (5) 420-1313; fax (5) 645-4258; e-mail webtva@tvazteca.com; internet tvazteca.todito .com; f. 1992 to assume responsibility for former state-owned channels 7 and 13; Pres. Ricardo B. Salinas Pliego.

Televisión de la República Mexicana: Mina 24, Col. Guerrero, México, DF; tel. (5) 510-8590; cultural; Dir Eduardo Lizalde.

As a member of the Intelsat international consortium, Mexico has received communications via satellite since the 1960s. The launch of the Morelos I and Morelos II satellites, in 1985, provided Mexico with its own satellite communications system. The Morelos satellites were superseded by a new satellite network, Solidaridad, which was inaugurated in early 1994. In late 1997 Mexico's three satellites (grouped in a newly-formed company, SatMex) were transferred to private ownership.

Finance

(cap. = capital; dep. = deposits; m. = million; res = reserves; amounts in old pesos unless otherwise stated)

BANKING

The Mexican banking system is comprised of the Banco de México (the central bank of issue), multiple or commercial banking institutions and development banking institutions. Banking activity is regulated by the Federal Government.

Commercial banking institutions are constituted as *Sociedades Anónimas*, with wholly private social capital. Development banking institutions exist as *Sociedades Nacionales de Crédito*, participation in their capital is exclusive to the Federal Government, notwithstanding the possibility of accepting limited amounts of private capital. In 2000 there were 34 commercial banks operating in Mexico.

All private banks were nationalized in September 1982. By July 1992, however, the banking system had been completely returned to the private sector, with total revenue from the sale of 18 banks amounting to US $12,900m.

Total bank deposits, as at June 1994, were estimated at 625,000m. new pesos.

In October 1994 the Government approved the application for operating licences within Mexico of 18 foreign banks. Legislation removing all restrictions on foreign ownership of banks received congressional approval in 1999.

Supervisory Authority

Comisión Nacional Bancaria y de Valores (National Banking and Securities Commission): Insurgentes Sur 1971, Torre Norte, 10°, México, DF; tel. and fax (5) 724-6000; e-mail info@cnbv.gob.mx; internet www.cnbv.gob.mx; f. 1924; govt commission controlling all credit institutions in Mexico; Pres. Jonathan Davis Arzac.

Central Bank

Banco de México (BANXICO): Avda 5 de Mayo 2, Apdo 98 bis, 06059 México, DF; tel. (5) 237-2000; fax (5) 237-2370; e-mail comsoc@banxico.org.mx; internet www.banxico.org.mx; f. 1925; currency issuing authority; became autonomous on 1 April 1994; res US $7,854m. (March 1995); Gov. Guillermo Ortiz Martínez; 9 brs.

Commercial Banks

Banca Promex, SA: Manuel Acuña 2937, Col. Providencia, 44670 Guadalajara, Jal.; tel. (3) 669-5821; fax (3) 669-5889; f. 1940; multiple bank; cap. 250,000m., res 237,000m., dep. 2,519,000m. (Dec. 1992); Pres. Eduardo A. Carrillo Díaz; 388 brs.

Banca Serfín, SA: Paseo de la Reforma 500, Mod. 409, 4°, Col. Lomas de Santa Fe, 01219 México, DF; tel. (5) 257-8000; fax (5) 257-8387; internet www.serfin.com.mx; f. 1864; merged with Banco Continental Ganadero in 1985; transferred to private ownership in Jan. 1992; acquired by Banco Santander Central Hispano (Spain) in May 2000; cap. 16,958.6m. new pesos, res −8,052.9m. new pesos, dep. 152,053.4m. new pesos (Dec. 1998); CEO Adolfo Lago Espinosa; 542 brs.

Banco del Bajío, SA: Avda Paseo del Moral 506, Col. Jardines del Moral, 37160 León, Gto; tel. (47) 10-4600; fax (47) 10-4693; e-mail info@bajionet.com.mx; internet www.bajionet.com.mx; f. 1994; cap. 395.6m. new pesos, res −48.7m. new pesos, dep. 2,837.2m. new pesos (Dec. 1998); Gen. Man. Carlos de la Cerda Serrano.

Banco BCH, SA: Paseo de la Reforma 364, 2°, Col. Juárez, 06694 México, DF; tel. (5) 533-0434; fax (5) 533-4701; f. 1941; merged with Banco Sofimex in 1985; transferred to private ownership in 1991; cap. 605,000m., res 419,000m., dep. 6,685m. (Dec. 1992); Chair. Francisco Suárez Dávila; 130 brs.

Banco Mercantil del Norte, SA: Zaragoza Sur 920, 64000 Monterrey, NL; tel. (8) 319-5200; fax (8) 319-5221; internet www.gfnorte .com.mx; f. 1899; merged with Banco Regional del Norte in 1985; cap. 2,111.8m. new pesos, res −37.1m. new pesos, dep. 29,993.9m. new pesos (Dec. 1997); Chair. Roberto González Barrera; 166 brs.

Banco Nacional de México, SA (Banamex): Avda Isabel la Católica 44, 1°, 06089 México, DF; tel. (5) 225-3191; fax (5) 720-7297; internet www.banamex.com; f. 1884; transferred to private ownership in 1991; cap. 41,790.8m. new pesos, res −17,382.8m. new pesos, dep. 243,630.6m. new pesos (Dec. 1998); Dir-Gen. Roberto Hernández Ramírez; 1,260 brs.

Banco Obrero, SA: Paseo de la Reforma 136, 17°, Col. Juárez, 06600 México, DF; tel. (5) 627-0600; fax (5) 535-1756; f. 1977; cap. 125,000m., res 6,000m., dep. 2,181,000m. (Dec. 1992); 24 brs.

Banco de Oriente, SA (Banorie): Avda 2 Ote 10, Apdo 30, 72000 Puebla, Pue.; tel. (22) 46-2801; fax (22) 42-0401; f. 1944; transferred to private ownership in 1991; cap. 49.9m. new pesos, res 119.9m. new pesos, dep. 2,266.5m. new pesos (Sept. 1993); Chair. Ricardo Margaín Berlanga; 48 brs.

Bancrecer, SA: Paseo de la Reforma 116, Col. Juárez, 06600 México, DF; tel. (5) 328-5000; fax (5) 703-0605.

Banpaís, SNC: Paseo de la Reforma 359, Col. Cuauhtémoc, 06500 México, DF; tel. (5) 208-2044; fax (5) 533-1223; f. 1892 as Banco de Nuevo León, present name 1978; merged with Banco Latino in 1985; transferred to private ownership in 1991; cap. 636,000m., res 28,000m., dep. 8,390,000m. (Dec. 1992); Chair. Lic. Carlos Sales Gutiérrez; 160 brs.

Grupo Financiero Bital, SA: Paseo de la Reforma 156, 06600 México; DF; tel. (5) 721-2222; fax (5) 721-2983; internet www.bital .com.mx; f. 1941 as Banco Internacional, SA; merged with Hipotecaria Internacional in 1977 and changed name to Banco Internacional, SNC in 1982; adopted current name in 1998; cap. 440.0m. new pesos, res 2,027.7m. new pesos, dep. 43,215.6m. new pesos (Dec. 1996); Pres. Antonio del Valle Ruiz; 1,533 brs.

Scotiabank Inverlat, SA: Plaza Inverlat, Miguel Avila Camacho 1, Col. Chapultepec Polanco, 11560 México, DF; tel. (5) 229-2929; fax (5) 229-2337; internet www.inverlat.com.mx; f. 1977 as Multibanco Comermex, SA; changed name to Banco Inverlat, SA 1995; 55% holding acquired by Scotiabank Group (Canada) and name changed as above 2000; Pres. Peter Cardinal.

Development Banks

Banco Nacional de Comercio Exterior, SNC (BANCOMEXT): Avda Camino Santa Teresa 1679, 12°, Col. Jardines del Pedregal, Del. Alvaro Obregón, 01900 México, DF; tel. (5) 652-8422; fax (5)

652-9408; f. 1937; cap. 13,308.5m. new pesos, res −5,212.3m. new pesos, dep. 28,772.6m. new pesos (Dec. 1998); Dir-Gen. ENRIQUE VILATELA RIBA.

Banco Nacional de Crédito Rural, SNC (BANRURAL): Agrarismo 227, Col. Escandón, 11800 México, DF; tel. (5) 273-1465; fax (5) 584-2664; f. 1975; provides financing for agriculture and normal banking services; cap. 1,791,569m., res −155,439m., dep. 623,402m. (Sep. 1992); Dir-Gen. Ing. JAIME DE LA MORA GÓMEZ; 187 brs.

Banco Nacional del Ejército, Fuerza Aérea y Armada, SNC (BANJERCITO): Avda Industria Militar 1055, 2°, Col. Lomas de Sotelo, 11200 México, DF; tel. (5) 557-5728; fax (5) 395-0909; f. 1947; cap. 11,035m., res 1,780.7m., dep. 139,184.5m. (Sept. 1990); Dir-Gen. Gral. RAFAEL PAZ DEL CAMPO; 17 brs.

Banco Nacional de Obras y Servicios Públicos, SNC (BANOBRAS): Tecoyotitla 100, 4°, esq. Francia, Col. Florida, 01030 México, DF; tel. (5) 723-6000; fax (5) 723-6177; f. 1933; cap. 255.6m. new pesos, res 5,297.4m. new pesos, dep. 65,049.3m. new pesos (Dec. 1996); Chair. GUILLERMO ORTIZ MARTÍNEZ.

BBVA-Bancomer, SA: Centro Bancomer, Avda Universidad 1200, Apdo 9 bis, 03339 México, DF; tel. (5) 534-0034; fax (5) 621-3230; internet www.bancomer.com.mx; f. 2000 by merger of Bancomer (f. 1864) and Mexican operations of Banco Bilbao Vizcaya Argentaria (Spain); cap. 10,375m. new pesos, res 7,086m. new pesos, dep. 199,247m. new pesos (Dec. 1997); CEO VITALINO M. NAFRÍA AZNAR; Pres. Ing. RICARDO GUAJARDO TOUCHÉ; 1,357 brs.

Financiera Nacional Azucarera, SNC (FINA, SNC): Insurgentes Sur 716, Col. del Valle, Apdo 10764, 03100 México, DF; tel. (5) 325-6000; fax (5) 325-7383; f. 1953; cap. 159,662m., res 52,724m., dep. 2,252,660m. (Sept. 1992); Dir-Gen. Lic. OSCAR ESPINOSA VILLARREAL.

Nacional Financiera, SNC: Insurgentes Sur 1971, Torre IV, 13°, Col. Guadalupe Inn, 01020 México, DF; tel. (5) 325-6700; fax (5) 661-8418; internet www.nafin.com.mx: f. 1934; Dir-Gen. CARLOS SALES GUTIÉRREZ; 37 brs.

Foreign Banks

Citibank NA (USA): Paseo de la Reforma 390, 18°, 06695 México, DF; tel. (5) 211-3030; fax (5) 525-1457; cap. 102,000m., res 6,000m., dep. 1,005,000m. (Dec. 1992); Dir-Gen. GABRIEL JARAMILLO; 235 brs.

Dresdner Bank Mexico, SA: Bosque de Alisos 47B, 4°, Col. Bosques de las Lomas, 05120 México, DF; tel. (5) 258-3000; fax (5) 258-3100; e-mail aespinos@ny.dresdner.com; f. 1995; Man. Dir LUIS NIÑO DE RIVERA.

BANKERS' ASSOCIATION

Asociación Mexicana de Bancos: Torre Latinoamericana, 9°, Madero y Lázaro Cárdenas, Apdo 89 bis, 06007 México, DF; tel. (5) 521-4080; fax (5) 521-5229; f. 1928; Pres. ANTONIO DEL VALLE RUIZ; Dir-Gen. RAFAEL OLIVERA ESCALONA; 52 mems.

STOCK EXCHANGE

Comisión Nacional de Valores (National Securities Commission): Barranca del Muerto 275, Col. San José Insurgentes, 03900 México, DF; tel. (5) 651-0129; f. 1946; a federal commission to regulate the stock exchange system; Pres. Lic. PATRICIO AYALA; Vice-Pres. GUILLERMO NÚÑEZ HERRERA.

In 1976 the three stock exchanges of Mexico City, Guadalajara and Monterrey were amalgamated into a single organization:

Bolsa Mexicana de Valores, SA de CV: Paseo de la Reforma 255, Col. Cuauhtémoc, 06500 México, DF; tel. (5) 726-6600; fax (5) 591-0642; e-mail cinforma@bmv.com.mx; f. 1894; Pres. Lic. MANUEL ROBELDA GONZALES DE CASTILLA; Dir-Gen. Ing. GERARDO FLORES DEUCHLER.

INSURANCE
México, DF

Aseguradora Banpaís, SA: Insurgentes Sur 1443, 7°, México, DF; f. 1958; Pres. Lic. ADRIÁN SADA GONZÁLEZ; Dir-Gen. RODRIGO M. SADA GÓMEZ.

Aseguradora Cuauhtémoc, SA: Manuel Avila Camacho 164, 11570 México, DF; tel. (5) 250-9800; fax (5) 540-3204; f. 1944; general; Exec. Pres. JUAN B. RIVEROLL; Dir-Gen. JAVIER COMPEÁN AMEZCUA.

Aseguradora Hidalgo, SA: Presidente Masarik 111, Col. Polanco, Del. Miguel Hidalgo, 11570 México, DF; f. 1931; life; Dir-Gen. JOSÉ GÓMEZ GORDOA; Man. Dir HUMBERTO ROQUE VILLANUEVA.

Aseguradora Mexicana (Asemex): México, DF; general, except life; transferred to private ownership in 1990.

La Continental Seguros, SA: Francisco I. Madero, 1, 10°, 06007 México, DF; tel. (5) 518-1670; fax (5) 510-3259; f. 1936; general; Pres.

Ing. TEODORO AMERLINCK Y ZIRIÓN; Vice-Pres. Ing. RODRIGO AMERLINCK Y ASSERETO.

La Nacional, Cía de Seguros, SA: México, DF; f. 1901; life, etc.; Pres. CLEMENTE CABELLO; Chair. Lic. ALBERTO BAILLERES.

Pan American de México, Cía de Seguros, SA: México, DF; f. 1940; Pres. Lic. JESS N. DALTON; Dir-Gen. GILBERTO ESCOBEDA PAZ.

Previsión Obrera, Sociedad Mutualista de Seguros sobre la Vida: Avda Ricardo Flores Magón 206, México, DF; f. 1934; life; Man. ANTONIO CASTELLANOS TOVAR.

Seguros América Banamex, SA: Avda Revolución 1508, Col. Guadalupe Inn, 01020 México, DF; f. 1933; Pres. AGUSTÍN F. LEGORRETA; Dir-Gen. JUAN OROZCO GÓMEZ PORTUGAL.

Seguros Atlántida Multiba, SA: Independencia 37, 2°, Apdo 152, 06050 México, DF; tel. (5) 510-8810; fax (5) 512-4091; f. 1941; general, except life; Pres. BORIS SIGAL BOULAYEVSKY; Dir-Gen. ALFONSO DE ORDUÑA Y PÉREZ.

Seguros Azteca, SA: Insurgentes 102, México, DF; f. 1933; general including life; Pres. JUAN CAMPO RODRÍGUEZ.

Seguros Cigna, SA: Arquimedes 199, 10°, Col. Polanco, 11560 México, DF; f. 1990; Pres. REMIGIO GÓMEZ SOTRES; Dir-Gen. ROBERTO HIDALGO.

Seguros La Comercial, SA: Insurgentes Sur 3900, Del. Tlalpan, 14000 México, DF; f. 1936; life, etc.; Pres. ELOY S. VALLINA; Dir-Gen. HÉCTOR GONZÁLEZ VALENZUELA.

Seguros Constitución, SA: Avda Revolución 2042, Col. La Otra Banda, 01090 México, DF; tel. (5) 550-7910; f. 1937; life, accident; Pres. ISIDORO RODRÍGUEZ RUIZ; Dir-Gen. ALFONSO DE ORDUÑA Y PÉREZ.

Seguros el Fénix, SA: México, DF; f. 1937; Pres. VICTORIANO OLAZÁBAL E.; Dir-Gen. JAIME MATUTE LABRADOR.

Seguros Internacional, SA: Abraham González 67, México, DF; f. 1945; general; Pres. Lic. GUSTAVO ROMERO KOLBECK.

Seguros de México, SA: Insurgentes Sur 3496, Col. Peña Pobre, 14060 México, DF; tel. (5) 679-3855; f. 1957; life, etc.; Dir-Gen. Lic. ANTONIO MIJARES RICCI.

Seguros Protección Mutua, SA: Constituyentes 357, 11830 México DF; tel. (5) 277-7100; f. 1933; general; Dir-Gen. GUSTAVO GONZÁLEZ NOGUÉS.

Seguros La Provincial, SA: México, DF; f. 1936; general; Pres. CLEMENTE CABELLO; Chair. ALBERTO BAILLERES.

Seguros La República, SA: Paseo de la Reforma 383, México, DF; f. 1966; general; 43% owned by Commercial Union (UK); Pres. LUCIANO ARECHEDERRA QUINTANA; Gen. Man. JUAN ANTONIO DE ARRIETA MENDIZÁBAL.

Guadalajara, Jal.

Nueva Galicia, Compañía de Seguros Generales, SA: Guadalajara, Jal.; f. 1946; fire; Pres. SALVADOR VEYTIA Y VEYTIA.

Seguros La Comercial, SA, División Centro: Avda Lerdo de Tejada 2007, 3°, Guadalajara, Jal.; tel. (36) 16-4460; f. 1940; fire; Pres. ELOY S. VALLINA; Dir-Gen. HÉCTOR GONZÁLEZ VALENZUELA.

Monterrey, NL

Seguros Monterrey Aetna, SA: Avda Diagonal Sta Engracia 221 Ote, Col. Lomas de San Francisco, 64710 Monterrey, NL; tel. (8) 319-1111; fax (8) 363-0428; f. 1940; casualty, life, etc.; Dir-Gen. FEDERICO REYES GARCÍA.

Seguros La Comercial del Norte, SA: Zaragoza Sur 1000, 1°, Condominio 'Acero Monterrey', Apdo 944, Monterrey, NL; f. 1939; general; Pres. MANUEL L. BARRAGÁN; Dir-Gen. SALIM FARAH SESSIN.

Seguros Monterrey del Círculo Mercantil, SA, Sociedad General de Seguros: Padre Mier Pte 276, Monterrey, NL; f. 1941; life; Gen. Man. CARMEN G. MASSO DE NAVARRO.

Insurance Association

Asociación Mexicana de Instituciones de Seguros, AC: Ejército Nacional 904, 6°, México, DF; f. 1946; all insurance cos operating in Mexico are members; Pres. KURT VOGT SARTORIUS.

Trade and Industry

GOVERNMENT AGENCIES

Comisión Nacional de Precios: Avda Juárez 101, 17°, México 1, DF; tel. (5) 510-0436; f. 1977; national prices commission; Dir-Gen. JESÚS SÁNCHEZ JIMÉNEZ.

Comisión Nacional de los Salarios Mínimos: Avda Cuauhtémoc 14, 2°, Col. Doctores, 06720 México 7, DF; tel. (5) 578-9021; fax (5) 578-5775; f. 1962 in accordance with Section VI of Article 123 of the Constitution; national commission on minimum salaries; Pres. Lic. BASILIO GONZÁLEZ-NUÑEZ; Tech. Dir ALIDA BERNAL COSIO.

Consejo Nacional de Comercio Exterior, AC (CONACEX): Avda Parque Fundidora 501, Of. 95ᴇ, Edif. CINTERMEX, Col. Obrera, 64010 Monterrey, NL; tel. (8) 369-0284; fax (8) 369-0293; e-mail conacex@technet.net.mx; internet www.technet.net.mx /conacex; f. 1962 to promote national exports; Chair. Ing. JAVIER PRIETO DE LA FUENTE; Pres. Lic. JUAN MANUEL QUIROGA LAM.

Consejo Nacional de Recursos Minerales: Avda Niños Héroes 139, 06720 México, DF; tel. (5) 568-6112; f. 1957; govt agency for the devt of mineral resources; Dir Ing. FERNANDO CASTILLO NIETO.

Dirección General de Política e Inversiones Industriales: México, DF; govt body established to direct industrial policy; took over the functions of the Comisión Coordinadora para el Desarrollo de la Industria de Maquinaria y Equipo, Comisión Nacional Coordinadora para el Desarrollo Industrial; Dir-Gen. Lic. VLADIMIRO BRAILOVSKY F.

Instituto Nacional del Consumidor: Insurgentes Sur 1228, 10°, Col. del Valle Tlacoquemecatl, 03210 México, DF; tel. (5) 559-2478; fax (5) 559-0123; f. 1976; national institute for consumer protection; Dir-Gen. MARGARITA ORTEGA VILLA.

Instituto Nacional de Investigaciones Nucleares (ININ): Apdo 111, 52000 Lerma, Méx.; tel. (5) 521-9402; internet www.inin.mx; f. 1979 to plan research and devt of nuclear science and technology, as well as the peaceful uses of nuclear energy, for the social, scientific and technological devt of the country; administers the Secondary Standard Dosimetry Laboratory, the Centro de Información y Documentación Nuclear (CIDN), which serves Mexico's entire scientific community; the 1 MW research reactor which came into operation, in 1967, supplies part of Mexico's requirements for radioactive isotopes; also operates a 12 MV Tandem van de Graaff. Mexico has two nuclear reactors, each with a generating capacity of 654 MW; the first, at Laguna Verde, became operational in 1989 and is administered by the Comisión Federal de Electricidad (CFE); Dir-Gen. Dr JULIÁN SÁNCHEZ GUTIÉRREZ.

Instituto Nacional de Pesca (National Fishery Institute): Alvaro Obregón 269, 10°, Col. Roma, 06709 México, DF; tel. (5) 211-0063; f. 1962; Dir ALICIA BARCENA IBARRA.

Laboratorios Nacionales de Fomento Industrial: México, DF; tel. (5) 589-0199; fax (5) 589-7162; f. 1948; conducts scientific research for industrial devt; Dir Dr MANUEL RUIZ DE CHÁVEZ.

Procuraduría Federal del Consumidor: Dr Carmona y Valle 11, Col. Doctores, 06720 México, DF; tel. (5) 761-3021; f. 1975; consumer protection; Dir IGNACIO PICHARDO PAGAZA.

Uranio Mexicano (URAMEX): Insurgentes Sur 1079, 3°, México, DF; tel. (5) 563-7100; supervises the use of uranium; Dir-Gen. ALBERTO ESCOGET ARTIGAS.

DEVELOPMENT ORGANIZATIONS

Comisión Coordinadora de la Industria Siderúrgica: México, DF; f. 1972; co-ordinating commission for the devt of the iron and steel industries; Dir-Gen. Lic. ALFREDO ADE TOMASINI.

Comisión Nacional de las Zonas Aridas: México, DF; tel. (5) 525-9360; internet www.conaza.gob.mx; f. 1970; commission to co-ordinate the devt and use of arid areas; Dir Ing. MANUEL AGUSTÍN REED SEGOVIA.

Fideicomisos Instituídos en Relación con la Agricultura (FIRA): México, DF; tel. (5) 550-7011; internet www.fira.gob.mx; Dir Ing. ANTONIO BACA DÍAZ; a group of devt funds to aid agricultural financing, under the Banco de México, comprising:

Fondo de Garantía y Fomento para la Agricultura, Ganadería y Avicultura (FOGAGA): f. 1954.

Fondo Especial para Financiamientos Agropecuarios (FEFA): f. 1965.

Fondo Especial de Asistencia Técnica y Garantía para Créditos Agropecuarios (FEGA): f. 1972.

Instituto Mexicano del Petróleo (IMP): Avda Eje Central Lázaro Cárdenas 152, Apdo 14-805, 07730 México, DF; tel. (5) 567-6600; fax (5) 567-6047; internet www.imp.mx; f. 1965 to foster devt of the petroleum, chemical and petrochemical industries; Dir GUSTAVO CHAPELA CASTAÑARES.

CHAMBERS OF COMMERCE

Confederación de Cámaras Nacionales de Comercio, Servicios y Turismo (CONCANACO) (Confederation of National Chambers of Commerce): Balderas 144, 3°, Col. Centro, 06079 México, DF; tel. (5) 709-1559; fax (5) 709-1152; f. 1917; Pres. JOSÉ YAMIL HALLAL ZEPEDA; Dir-Gen. Ing. ALEJANDRO AGUILERA GÓMEZ; comprises 283 regional Chambers.

Cámara Nacional de Comercio de la Ciudad de México (CANACO) (National Chamber of Commerce of Mexico City): Paseo de la Reforma 42, 3°, Col. Centro, Apdo 32005, 06048 México, DF; tel. (5) 592-2677; fax (5) 592-2279; f. 1874; 50,000 mems; Pres. VICENTE MAYO GARCÍA; Dir-Gen. Ing. MARCOS PÉREZ ARENAS.

Cámara Nacional de la Industria y de la Transformación (CANACINTRA): Calle Vallarta 21, 3°, México, DF; tel. (5) 566-9333; represents majority of smaller manufacturing businesses; Pres. VÍCTOR MANUEL TERRONES LÓPEZ.

Chambers of Commerce exist in the chief town of each State as well as in the larger centres of commercial activity.

CHAMBERS OF INDUSTRY

The 64 Industrial Chambers and 32 Associations, many of which are located in the Federal District, are representative of the major industries of the country.

Central Confederation

Confederación de Cámaras Industriales de los Estados Unidos Mexicanos—CONCAMIN (Confed. of Industrial Chambers): Manuel María Contreras 133, 8°, Col. Cuauhtémoc, 06500 México, DF; tel. (5) 566-7822; fax (5) 535-6871; e-mail cetin@ solar.sar.net; internet www.concamin.org.mx; f. 1918; represents and promotes the activities of the entire industrial sector; Pres. ALEJANDRO MARTÍNEZ GALLARDO; Dir-Gen. RENÉ ESPINOSA Y TORRES ESTRADA.

INDUSTRIAL AND TRADE ASSOCIATIONS

Asociación Nacional de Importadores y Exportadores de la República Mexicana (ANIERM) (National Association of Importers and Exporters): Monterrey 130, Col. Roma-Cuauhtémoc, 06700 México, DF; tel. (5) 564-8618; fax (5) 584-5317; f. 1944; Pres. RODRIGO GUERRA B.; Vice-Pres. Lic. HUMBERTO SIMONEEN ARDILA.

Azúcar, SA de CV: Insurgentes Sur 1079, Col. Nochebuena, 03910 México, DF; tel. (5) 563-7100; f. 1983 to develop the sugar industry; Dir Ing. EDUARDO A. MACGREGOR BELTRÁN.

Comisión de Fomento Minero: Puente de Tecamachalco 26, Lomas de Chapultepec, 11000 México, DF; tel. (5) 540-2906; f. 1934; to promote the devt of the mining sector; Dir Lic. LUIS DE PABLO SERNA.

Comisión Nacional del Cacao (Conadeca): México, DF; tel. (5) 286-9495; f. 1973 to promote the cultivation, industrialization and the marketing of cocoa; Dir-Gen. Lic. JULIO DERBEZ DEL PINO.

Comisión Nacional de Fruticultura (Conafrut): Querétaro, Qro; tel. (463) 570-2499; f. 1961 to develop the production, industrialization and marketing of fruits; Dir Lic. FRANCISCO MERINO RÁBAGO.

Comisión Nacional de Inversiones Extranjeras: Blvd Avila Camacho 1, 11°, 11000 México, DF; tel. (5) 540-1426; fax (5) 286-1551; f. 1973; commission to co-ordinate foreign investment; Exec. Sec. Dr CARLOS CAMACHO GAOS.

Comisión Nacional de Seguridad Nuclear y Salvaguardias (CNSNS): Dr Barragán 779, Col. Narvarte, 03020 México, DF; tel. (5) 590-4181; fax (5) 590-6103; e-mail dg1@servidor.unam.mx; f. 1979; nuclear regulatory agency; Dir-Gen. JOSÉ LUIS DELGADO GUARDADO.

Comisión Petroquímica Mexicana: México, DF; to promote the devt of the petrochemical industry; Tech. Sec. Ing. JUAN ANTONIO BARGÉS MESTRES.

Compañía Nacional de Subsistencias Populares (CONASUPO): Avda Insurgentes Sur 489, 4°, Col. Hipódromo Condesa, 06100 México, DF; tel. (5) 272-0472; fax (5) 272-0607; f. 1965 to protect the income of small farmers, improve the marketing of basic farm commodities and supervise the operation of rural co-operative stores; Dir Lic. JAVIER BONILLA GARCÍA.

Consejo Empresarial Mexicano para Asuntos Internacionales (CEMAI): Homero 517, 7°, Col. Polanco, 11570 México, DF; tel. (5) 250-7033; fax (5) 531-1590.

Fondo de Operación y Financiamiento Bancario a la Vivienda: Ejército Nacional 180, 7°, 8° y 11°, Col. Anzures, 11590 México, DF; tel. (5) 255-4199; fax (5) 203-7304; f. 1963 to promote the construction of low-cost housing through savings and credit schemes; devt fund under the Banco de México; Dir-Gen. Lic. MANUEL ZEPEDA PAYERAS.

Instituto del Fondo Nacional de la Vivienda para los Trabajadores (INFONAVIT): Barranca del Muerto 280, 4°, Col. Guadalupe Inn., Del. Alvaro Obregón, 01029 México, DF; tel. (5) 660-2423; f. 1972 to finance the construction of low-cost housing for the working classes; Dir JOSÉ JUAN DE OLLOQUI Y LABASTIDA.

Instituto Mexicano del Café (Inmecafé): Carretera Jalapa-Veracruz km 4, Campo Experimental Garnica, Jalapa, Ver.; Lago Merú 32, Col. Granada, México, DF; tel. (5) 250-5543; f. 1958; sponsors cultivation to increase domestic and foreign sales of coffee; Dir-Gen. JESÚS SALAZAR TOLEDANO.

Instituto Nacional de Investigaciones Forestales y Agropecuarias—INIFAP (National Forestry and Agricultural Research Institute): Apdo 6-882, 06600 México, DF; tel. (5) 687-7451; f. 1985; conducts research into plant genetics, management of species and conservation; Exec. Dir Dr MANUEL R. VILLA ISSA.

Tabacos Mexicanos, SA de CV (TABAMEX): México, DF; tel. (5) 395-5477; fax (5) 395-6836; f. 1972 to foster the cultivation, industrialization and marketing of tobacco; Dir-Gen. Gustavo Carvajal Moreno.

EMPLOYERS' ORGANIZATIONS

Confederación Patronal de la República Mexicana (COPARMEX) (Employers' Federation): Insurgentes Sur 950, 2°, Col. del Valle, 03100 México, DF; tel. (5) 687-6493; fax (5) 687-2821; e-mail coparmex@albec.com.mx; internet www.coparmex.org.mx; f. 1929; national syndicate of free affiliated business people organized to promote economic devt; Chair. Alberto Fernández-Garza; Dir-Gen. Lorenzo Peláez-Dorantes; 36,000 mems.

Consejo Coordinador Empresarial (CCE): Paseo de la Reforma 255, 11°, Col. Cuauhtémoc, 06500 México, DF; tel. (5) 592-3910; fax (5) 592-3857; f. 1974; co-ordinating body of private sector; Pres. Luis Germán Cárcoba; Dir Francisco Calderón.

Consejo Mexicano de Hombres de Negocios (CMHN): México, DF; represents leading businesspeople; affiliated to CCE; Pres. Eugenio Clariond Reyes.

STATE HYDROCARBONS COMPANY

Petróleos Mexicanos (PEMEX): Avda Marina Nacional 329, 44°, Col. Huasteca, 11300 México, DF; tel. (5) 254-2044; fax (5) 531-6354; internet www.pemex.com; f. 1938; govt agency for the exploitation of Mexico's petroleum and natural gas resources; Dir-Gen. Raúl Muñoz Leos; 106,900 employees.

MAJOR COMPANIES
Mining and Metals

Altos Hornos de México, SA: Prolongación Juárez s/n, Col. La Loma, Monclova, Coah.; tel. (86) 49-3000; fax (86) 33-8452; internet www.gan.com.mx; f. 1942; former state-owned iron and steel foundry and rolling mill; privatized in the early 1990s; Pres. Xavier Autrey Maza; 11,069 employees.

Empresas Frisco, SA de CV: Jaime Balmes 11, 5°, Col. Los Morales Polanco, 11510 México, DF; tel. (5) 626-7799; fax (5) 557-1591; f. 1973; mining co; Man. Dir Jesús Gutiérrez Bastida; 1,600 employees.

Fundidora Monterrey, SA: Adolfo Prieto s/n, Col. Obrero, 64011 Monterrey, NL; fax (8) 355-3655; f. 1900; iron foundry; Pres. Francisco Labastida Ochoa; 9,000 employees.

Grupo Industrial Saltillo, SA de CV: Chiapas 375, Col. República, 25280 Saltillo, Coah.; tel. (84) 111-000; fax (84) 158-096; internet www.gis.com.mx; f. 1966; steel producers; Chair. Isidro López del Bosque; 9,900 employees.

Grupo de México, SA: Avda Baja California 200, Col. Roma Sur, 06760 México, DF; tel. (5) 564-7066; fax (5) 574-7677; internet www.gmexico.com; holding co with interests in extraction and processing of metallic ores; Chair. and CEO German Larrea Mota Velasco; 22,000 employees.

Grupo Simec, SA de CV: Calzado Lázaro Cárdenas 601, Col. La Nogalera, 44460 Guadalajara, Jal.; tel. (3) 669-5735; fax (3) 669-5726; e-mail mktcsg@sidek.com.mx; internet www.simec.com.mx; steel producers; Man. Dir Luis García Limón; 1,906 employees.

Industrias Peñoles, SA de CV: Río de la Plata 48, 15°, Col. Cuauhtémoc, 06500 México, DF; tel. (5) 231-3131; fax (5) 231-3636; f. 1969; mining co; Chair. Alberto Baillères; 7,924 employees.

Nacional de Cobre, SA de CV (Nacobre): Poniente 134, No 719, Col. Industria Vallejo, 02300 México, DF; tel. (5) 567-1144; fax (5) 587-7711; f. 1951; copper producers; Gen. Man. Alejandro Ochoa Abarca; 715 employees.

Tubacero, SA de CV: Avda Guerrero 3729 Norte, Col. del Norte, 64500 Monterrey, NL; tel. (8) 351-8100; fax (8) 351-3550; f. 1943; manufacturers of piping; Dir-Gen. León Gutiérrez Vela; 299 employees.

Tubos de Acero de México, SA: Campos Eliseos 400, 11560 México, DF; fax (5) 592-6059; manufacturers of seamless steel tubes and bars; Pres. Ernesto Fernández Hurtado; 2,200 employees.

Motor Vehicles

BMW de México, SA: Plaza Arquímedes 130, 10°, Col. Polanco, 11560 México, DF; tel. (5) 282-8700; fax (5) 282-8731; subsidiary of Bayerische Moteorn Werke AG of Germany; motor-vehicles and motor-parts manufacturers; Man. Dir Franz Baumgartner; 266 employees.

Chrysler de México, SA: Lago Alberto 320, Col. Anahuac, 11320 México, DF; tel. (5) 729-1000; fax (5) 729-1461; internet www.chrysler.com.mx; f. 1938; subsidiary of the Chrysler Corpn, USA; automobile assembly; Man. Dir Miles Brijant III; 11,000 employees.

Ford Motor Company, SA de CV: Paseo de la Reforma 333, Col. Cuauhtémoc, 06500 México, DF; tel. (5) 326-0000; fax (5) 525-3840; subsidiary of Ford Motor Co, USA; manufacturers of motor-vehicle, truck and tractor parts; Chair. Kathleen Legocki; 7,765 employees.

General Motors de México, SA de CV: Lago Victoria 74, 8°, Col. Granada, 11520 México, DF; tel. (5) 625-3000; fax (5) 625-3335; internet www.gm.com.mx; f. 1935; subsidiary of General Motors Corpn of the USA; automobile assembly; Pres. and Dir-Gen. Troy Clarke; 10,445 employees.

Mercedes-Benz México, SA de CV: División Automovil, Edif. Corporativo, Km 23.7, Carretera Santiago Tianguistengo, Santiago Tianguistenco, 52600 México, DF; tel. (7) 279-2400; fax (7) 279-2493; f. 1968; subsidiary of Mercedes-Benz AG of Germany; Man. Dir José Diere; 900 employees.

Nissan Mexicana, SA de CV: Avda Insurgentes Sur 1958, Col. Florida, 01030 México, DF; tel. (5) 661-6120; fax (5) 628-2690; f. 1961; subsidiary of Nissan Motors Co Ltd, Japan; automobile assembly plant; Chair. Jirosha Yuriocha; 2,987 employees.

Transmisiones y Equipos Mecánicos, SA de CV: Avda 5 de Febrero 2115, Zona Industrial, 76120 Querétaro, Qro; tel. (42) 170-717; fax (42) 170-345; f. 1964; makers of motor-vehicle components; Pres. Bernardo Quintana Isaac; 1,800 employees.

Volkswagen de Mexico, SA de CV: Km 116, Autopista México–Puebla, Apdo 875, 72008 Puebla, Pue.; tel. (22) 308-111; fax (22) 308-468; internet www.vw.com.mx; f. 1964; subsidiary of Volkswagen AG of Germany; manufacture of motor vehicles; Chair. Bernd Leissner; 16,000 employees.

Food and Drink, etc.

Coca-Cola Femsa, SA de CV: Rio Amazonas 43, 8°, Col. Cuauhtémoc, 06500 México, DF; tel. (5) 209-0909; fax (5) 705-5508; internet www.cocacola-femsa.com.mx; f. 1991; subsidiary of Coca-Cola Export Co, USA; soft-drink manufacturer; CEO Alfredo Martínez Urdal; 12,000 employees.

Femsa Cerveza, SA de CV: Alfonso Reyes 2202 Norte, 64442 Monterrey, NL; tel. (8) 328-5000; fax (8) 328-5253; e-mail invrel@mail.femsa.com; internet www.femsa.com; f. 1991; beer producers; CEO Alfredo Martínez Urdal; 14,600 employees.

Gruma, SA: Calzada del Valle 407 Oeste, Col. del Valle, 66220 Garza García, NL; tel. (8) 399-3300; fax (8) 399-3359; e-mail acruz@gruma.com; internet www.gruma.com; tortilla and corn-flour products manufacturers and distributors; Pres. Roberto González Barrera; 13,652 employees.

Grupo Industrial Bimbo, SA de CV: Elienne Sabet 10000, Col. Santa Fe, 01210 México, DF; tel. (5) 229-6600; fax (5) 229-6697; f. 1966; confectionery and canned food manufacturers; Chair. Lorenzo Servitje Sendra; 44,090 employees.

Grupo Industrial Maseca, SA de CV: Edif. Delta, 1°, Avda La Clinica 2520, Col. Sertoma, 64710 Monterrey, NL; tel. (8) 333-6022; fax (8) 333-7435; f. 1949; production and sale of corn flour; Pres. Roberto González Barrera; 3,541 employees.

Grupo Modelo, SA: Campo Eliseos 400, 18°, Col. Lomas de Chapultepec, 01100 México, DF; tel. (5) 281-0114; fax (5) 280-6718; e-mail invrelations@gmodelo.com.mx; internet www.gmodelo.com.mx; beer producers; Pres. Antonio Fernández Rodríguez; 44,040 employees.

Molinos Azteca, SA de CV: Ruiz Cortines Oriente, 67119 Guadalupe, NL; tel. (8) 377-6100; fax (8) 399-3994; f. 1950; flour mill; Gen. Man. Gerardo Gómez; 250 employees.

Sistema Argos, SA de CV: Simona Barba 6615, Fracción Villahermosa, 32510 Ciudad Juárez, Chih.; tel. (16) 291-228; fax (16) 291-294; e-mail info-argos@argos.com.mx; www.argos.com.mx; f. 1981; soft drinks; Dir-Gen. Miguel Fernández I.; 4,300 employees.

Electrical Goods

Grupo Condumex, SA de CV: Paseo del Río 186, 01070 México, DF; tel. (5) 326-5100; fax (5) 328-5898; f. 1952; electrical equipment; Pres. Julio Gutiérrez Trujillo; 12,000 employees.

Teleindustria Ericsson, SA de CV: Dr Gustavo Baz 2160, Col. La Loma, Tlalnepantia, 54060 Méxica, DF; tel. (5) 726-2000; fax (5) 726-2333; f. 1963; subsidiary of Telefonaktiebolaget L. M. Ericsson of Sweden; makers of telecommunications equipment; Man. Dir Gerhard Skladal; 3,565 employees.

Cement and Construction

Apasco, SA de CV: Campos Eliseos 345, 18°, Col. Polanco Chapultepec, 11560 México, DF; tel. (5) 724-0000; fax (5) 724-0288; internet www.apsco.com.mx; f. 1963; manufacture and distribution of construction materials; Pres. Pierre Froidevaux; 2,600 employees.

Cemex, SA de CV: Constitución 44 Pte, 64000 Monterrey, NL; tel. (8) 328-3000; fax (8) 328-3188; internet www.cemex.com; f. 1906; manufacturers and distributors of cement, concrete and building materials; Pres. and Dir.-Gen. LORENZO H. ZAMBRANO; 17,000 employees.

Corporación GEO, SA de CV: Margaritas 433, Col. Chimalistac, 01050 México, DF; tel. (5) 480-0523; fax (5) 554-6064; construction and real estate; Chair. LUIS ORVAÑANOS L.; 12,329 employees.

Empresas ICA Sociedad Controladora, SA: Edif. D, 4°, Minería 145, 11800 México, DF; tel. (5) 272-9991; fax (5) 271-1607; internet www.ica.com.mx; f. 1947; holding co with interests in the construction industry; Pres. BERNARDO QUINTANA ISAAC; 25,267 employees.

Grupo Empresarial Maya, SA de CV: Avda Constitución 444 Pte, 64900 Monterrey, NL; tel. (8) 345-3000; fax (8) 345-2025; f. 1987; cement manufacturers; Pres. MARCELO ZAMBRANO; 1,990 employees.

Tolmex, SA de CV: Avda Constitución 444 Pte, 64900 Monterrey, NL; tel. (8) 328-3000; fax (8) 328-3886; f. 1989; cement and ready-made concrete manufacturers; Dir-Gen. LORENZO ZAMBRANO; 4,400 employees.

Retail

Cifra, SA de CV: Blvd Manuel Avila Camacho, Delegación Miguel Hidalgo, 11220 México, DF; tel. (5) 283-0100; fax (5) 327-9211; f. 1958; retail co; Dir. Henry Davis; 47,129 employees.

Controladora Comercial Mexicana, SA de CV: Avda Revolución 780, Módulo 2, Col. San Juan, 03730 México, DF; tel. (5) 371-7312; fax (5) 371-7302; internet www.comerci.com.mx; f. 1944; retail traders; Pres. CARLOS GONZÁLEZ NOVA; 24,000 employees.

El Puerto de Liverpool, SA: Avda Mariano Escobedo 425, Col. Chapultepec Morales, 11570 México, DF; tel. (5) 328-6400; fax (5) 254-5688; internet www.liverpool.com.mx; f. 1944; retail traders; Pres. ENRIQUE BREMOND; 13,200 employees.

Far-Ben, SA de CV: J. Cantú Leal 1528, Col. Cerro de la Silla, 64810 Monterrey, NL; tel. (8) 359-6215; fax (8) 359-5150; e-mail adriano@benavides.com.mx; internet www.benavides.com.mx; f. 1917; retail chemists (pharmacies); Chair. JAIME M. BENAVIDES-POMPA; 8,200 employees.

Grupo Gigante, SA de CV: Ejército Nacional 769-A, Delegación M. Hidalgo, 11560 México, DF; tel. (5) 724-8000; fax (5) 724-8308; internet www.gigante.com.mx; f. 1962; retail traders; Pres. ANGEL LOSADA GÓMEZ; 20,200 employees.

Organización Soriana, SA de CV: Alejandro de Rodas 3102-A, Col. Las Cumbres, 8 Sector, 64610 Monterrey, NL; tel. (8) 329-9000; fax (8) 329-9128; e-mail pmejia@soriana.com.mx; internet www.soriana.com.mx; f. 1982; holding co with interests in the grocery trade; Pres. FRANCISCO J. MARTÍN BRINGAS; 27,300 employees.

Sears Roebuck de México, SA de CV: San Luis Potosí 214, Col. Romas, 06700 México, DF; tel. (5) 247-7500; fax (5) 584-6848; f. 1947; subsidiary of Sears Roebuck and Co of the USA; department stores; Pres. THURMON A. WILLIAMS STEWART; 10,000 employees.

Miscellaneous

Alfa, SA de CV: Gómez Morín 1111, 66254 Garza García, NL; tel. (8) 152-1111; fax (8) 152-2552; internet www.alfa.com.mx; holding co with interests in steel, petrochemicals, food products and telecommunications; Chair. and CEO DIONISIO GARZA MEDINA; 35,615 employees.

Berol, SA de CV: Apdo Postal 829, Tlalnepantia, Estado de México, DF; tel. (5) 729-3400; fax (5) 729-3433; f. 1970; stationery manufacturers; Pres. CARLOS MORENO RIVAS; 600 employees.

Compañía Industrial de San Cristobal, SA de CV: Manuel María Contreras 133, 3°, Col. San Rafael, 06470 México, DF; tel. (5) 326-2200; fax (5) 326-2262; f. 1951; paper products; Dir-Gen. LUIS REBOLLAR CORONA; 2,700 employees.

CYDSA, SA y Subsidarias: Ricardo Margáin Zozaya 325, Col. Valle del Campestre, 66250 Garza García, NL; tel. (8) 335-9090; fax (8) 335-3330; internet www.cydsa.com; f. 1945; manufacturers of rayon fibre and packaging materials; Chair. TOMÁS GONZÁLEZ SADA; 10,838 employees.

John Deere, SA de CV: Blvd Díaz Ordáz 500, Garza García, NL; tel. (8) 336-1212; fax (8) 336-0851; f. 1955; subsidiary of Deere and Co of the USA; farming machinery and equipment makers; Pres. AGUSTÍN SANTAMARINA VÁZQUEZ; 1,215 employees.

Desc, SA de CV: Paseo de los Tamarindos 400B, Bosque de las Lomas, 05120 México, DF; tel. (5) 261-8000; fax (5) 261-8096; e-mail desc@mail.desc.com.mx; internet www.desc.com.mx; f. 1973; holding co with interests in agribusiness, construction and manufacturing of consumer products; Chair. and CEO FERNANDO SENDEROS MESTRE; 22,152 employees.

Empaques Ponderosa, Sa de CV: Paseo de Las Palmas 405-103, Col. Lomas de Chapultepec, 11000 México, DF; tel. (5) 201-1000; fax (5) 201-1003; e-mail amurrieta@empaq.com.mx; f. 1989; cardboard manufacturers; Chair. ALFONSO ROMO GARZA; 858 employees.

Empresas La Moderna, SA de CV: Avda Francisco I. Madero Pte 2750, Apdo 384, 64000 Monterrey, NL; tel. (8) 356-9229; fax (8) 356-

7929; f. 1971; holding co with interests in agrobiotechnology and manufacturing of cigarettes and packaging; Chair. and CEO ALFONSO ROMO GARZA; 11,259 employees.

Grupo Carso, SA de CV: Insurgentes 3500, POB 03, Col. Pena Pobre, 14060 Mexico, DF; tel. (5) 202-8838; fax (5) 238 0601; f. 1980; tobacco producers; Pres. CARLOS SLIM HELÚ; 30,840 employees.

Grupo Casa Autrey, SA de CV: Netzahualcoyotl 79, Col. Centro, 06080 México, DF; tel. (5) 227-4500; fax (5) 227-4523; internet www.autrey.com; pharmaceutical co; Man. Dir SERGIO AUTREY MAZA; 5,700 employees.

Grupo Celanese, SA: Tecoyotitla 412, Col. Chimalistac, 01050 México, DF; tel. (5) 480-9100; fax (5) 480-9324; e-mail aorduna3@celanese.com.mx; internet www.celanese.com.mx; f. 1944; holding co with interests in chemicals and packaging manufacturing; CEO FRANCISCO PUENTE; 2,464 employees.

Grupo Situr, SA de CV: Circ. Agustín Yañez 2343, 3°, Col. Moderna, 44100 Guadalajara, Jal.; tel. (3) 678-5985; fax (3) 678-5920; e-mail sidek@sidek.com.mx; internet www.sidek.com.mx; f. 1989; hotel owners; Chair. LUIS REBOLLAR CORONA; 4,717 employees.

Internacional de Cerámica, SA de CV: Avda Pacheco y Vías FFCC CH-P, 31080 Chihuahua, Chih.; tel. (14) 291-111; fax (14) 291-166; f. 1978; makers of floor tiles; Chair. OSCAR ALMEIDA CHABRE; 2,900 employees.

Kimberly-Clark de México, SA de CV: José Luis Lagrange 103, 3°, Col. Los Morales, 11510 Mexico, DF; tel. (5) 282-7300; fax (2) 282-7272; f. 1955; subsidiary of Kimberly Clark Corpn of the USA; paper manufacturers; Dir-Gen. CLAUDIO XAVIER GONZÁLEZ LAPORTE; 6,273 employees.

Vitro, SA: Avda Roble 660, Col. Valle del Campestre, 66265 Garza García, NL; tel. (8) 329-1210; fax (8) 335-7210; internet www.vto.com; f. 1936; manufacturers of glass, glass bottles and containers; Pres. ADRIÁN SADA GONZÁLEZ; 33,300 employees.

UTILITIES
Regulatory Authorities

Comisión Nacional de Energía: Francisco Márquez 160, Col. Hipódromo Condesa, México, DF; f. 1973; commission to control energy policy and planning; Chair. FERNANDO HIRIART VALDERRAMA.

Secretariat of State for Energy: see section on The Government (Secretariats of State).

Electricity

Comisión Federal de Electricidad (CFE): Río Ródano 14, 7°, Col. Cuauhtémoc, 06598 México, DF; tel. (5) 207-3704; fax (5) 553-6424; internet www.cfe.gob.mx; state-owned power utility; Dir-Gen. ALFREDO ELÍAS AYUB.

Luz y Fuerza del Centro: Melchor Ocampo 171, 7°, Col. Tlaxpana, 11379 México, DF; tel. (5) 629-7100; fax (5) 518-0083; internet www.lfc.gob.mx; operates electricity network in the centre of the country; Dir-Gen. ALFONSO CASO AGUILAR.

Gas

Gas Natural México (GNM): Monterrey, NL; natural gas distributor; subsidiary of Spanish co Gas Natural.

Petróleos Mexicanos (PEMEX) (see State Hydrocarbons Company, above): distributes natural gas.

TRADE UNIONS

Congreso del Trabajo (CT): Avda Ricardo Flores Magón 44, Col. Guerrero, 06300 México 37, DF; tel. (5) 583-3817; f. 1966; trade union congress comprising trade union federations, confederations, etc.; Pres. Lic. HÉCTOR VALDÉS ROMO.

Confederación Regional Obrera Mexicana—CROM (Regional Confederation of Mexican Workers): República de Cuba 60, México, DF; f. 1918; Sec.-Gen. IGNACIO CUAUHTÉMOC PALETA; 120,000 mems, 900 affiliated syndicates.

Confederación Revolucionaria de Obreros y Campesinos—CROC (Revolutionary Confederation of Workers and Farmers): Hamburgo 250, Col. Juárez, 06600 México, DF; f. 1952; Sec.-Gen. ALBERTO JUÁREZ BLANCAS; 120,000 mems in 22 state federations and 8 national unions.

Confederación Revolucionaria de Trabajadores—CRT (Revolutionary Confederation of Workers): Dr Jiménez 218, Col. Doctores, México, DF; f. 1954; Sec.-Gen. MARIO SUÁREZ GARCÍA; 10,000 mems; 10 federations and 192 syndicates.

Confederación de Trabajadores de México—CTM (Confederation of Mexican Workers): Vallarta 8, México, DF; f. 1936; admitted to ICFTU; Sec.-Gen. LEONARDO RODRÍGUEZ ALCAINE; 5.5m. mems.

Federación Obrera de Organizaciones Femeniles—FOOF (Workers' Federation of Women's Organizations): Vallarta 8,

México, DF; f. 1950; a women workers' union within CTM; Sec.-Gen. HILDA ANDERSON NEVÁREZ; 400,000 mems.

Federación Nacional de Sindicatos Independientes (National Federation of Independent Trade Unions): Isaac Garza 311 Ote, 64000 Monterrey, NL; tel. (8) 375-6677; internet www.fnsi.org.mx; f. 1936; Sec.-Gen. JACINTO PADILLA VALDEZ; 230,000 mems.

Federación de Sindicatos de Trabajadores al Servicio del Estado—FSTSE (Federation of Unions of Govt Workers): Gómez Farías 40, Col. San Rafael, 06470 México, DF; f. 1938; Sec.-Gen. Lic. HÉCTOR VALDÉS ROMO; 2.5m. mems; 89 unions.

Frente Unida Sindical por la Defensa de los Trabajadores y la Constitución (United Union Front in Defence of the Workers and the Constitution): f. 1990 by more than 120 trade orgs to support the implementation of workers' constitutional rights.

Unión General de Obreros y Campesinos de México—UGOCM (General Union of Workers and Farmers of Mexico): José María Marroquí 8, 2°, 06050 México, DF; tel. (5) 518-3015; f. 1949; admitted to WFTU/CSTAL; Sec.-Gen. JUAN RODRÍGUEZ GONZÁLEZ; 7,500 mems, over 2,500 syndicates.

Unión Nacional de Trabajadores—UNT (National Union of Workers): México, DF; internet www.unt.org.mx; f. 1998; Leader FRANCISCO HERNÁNDEZ JUÁREZ.

A number of major unions are non-affiliated; they include:

Frente Auténtico de los Trabajadores (FAT).

Pacto de Unidad Sindical Solidaridad (PAUSS): comprises 10 independent trade unions.

Sindicato Nacional de Trabajadores Mineros, Metalúrgicos y Similares de la República Mexicana (Industrial Union of Mine, Metallurgical and Related Workers of the Republic of Mexico): Avda Dr Vertiz 668, Col. Narvarte, 03020 México, DF; tel. (5) 519-5690; f. 1933; Sec.-Gen. NAPOLEON GÓMEZ SADA; 86,000 mems.

Sindicato Nacional de Trabajadores de la Educación (SNTE): Venezuela 44, Col. Centro, México, DF; tel. (5) 702-0005; fax (5) 702-6303; teachers' union; Sec.-Gen. TOMÁS VÁZQUEZ VIGIL; 1.2m. mems.

Coordinadora Nacional de Trabajadores de la Educación (CNTE): dissident faction; Leader TEODORO PALOMINO.

Sindicato de Trabajadores Petroleros de la República Mexicana—STPRM (Union of Petroleum Workers of the Republic of Mexico): Zaragoza 15, Col. Guerrero, 06300 México, DF; tel. (5) 546-0912; close links with PEMEX; Sec.-Gen. CARLOS ROMERO DESCHAMPS; 110,000 mems; includes:

Movimiento Nacional Petrolero: reformist faction; Leader HEBRAÍCAZ VÁSQUEZ.

Sindicato de Trabajadores Ferrocarrileros de la República Mexicana—STFRM (Union of Railroad Workers of the Republic of Mexico): Avda Ricardo Flores Magón 206, Col. Guerrero, México 3, DF; tel. (5) 597-1011; f. 1933; Sec.-Gen. VÍCTOR F. FLORES MORALES; 100,000 mems.

Sindicato Unico de Trabajadores Electricistas de la República Mexicana—SUTERM (Sole Union of Electricity Workers of the Republic of Mexico): Río Guadalquivir 106, Col. Cuauhtémoc, 06500 México, DF; tel. (5) 207-0578; Sec.-Gen. LEONARDO RODRÍGUEZ ALCAINE.

Sindicato Unico de Trabajadores de la Industria Nuclear (SUTIN): Viaducto Río Becerra 139, Col. Nápoles, 03810 México, DF; tel. (5) 523-8048; fax (5) 687-6353; e-mail sutin@nuclear.inin.mx; internet www.prodigyweb.net.mx/sutin; Sec.-Gen. RICARDO FLORES BELLO.

Unión Obrera Independiente (UOI): non-aligned.

The major agricultural unions are:

Central Campesina Independiente: Dr E. González Martínez 101, México, DF; Leader ALFONSO GARZÓN SANTIBÁÑEZ.

Confederación Nacional Campesina—CNC: Mariano Azuela 121, Col. Santa María de la Ribera, México, DF; Sec.-Gen. Lic. BEATRIZ PAREDES RANGEL.

Confederación Nacional Ganadera: Calzada Mariano Escobedo 714, Col. Anzures, México, DF; tel. (5) 203-3506; Pres. Ing. CÉSAR GONZÁLEZ QUIROGA; 300,000 mems.

Consejo Agrarista Mexicano: México, DF; Sec.-Gen. HUMBERTO SERRANO.

Unión Nacional de Trabajadores Agriculturas (UNTA).

Transport

Road transport accounts for about 98% of all public passenger traffic and for about 80% of freight traffic (approximately 12.3m. passengers and 35,001m. ton-km of freight in 1993). Mexico's terrain is difficult for overland travel. As a result, there has been an expansion of air transport and there were 83 international and national airports, plus 2,418 landing fields and feeder airports, in

1992. International flights are provided by a large number of national and foreign airlines. In 1990 Mexico's Airports and Auxiliary Services agency (ASA) announced that, as part of a long-term policy of decentralization, landing rights for wide-bodied civil airliners could be transferred from the capital's Benito Juárez airport to a vastly expanded facility at Toluca, some 65 km from the capital, by 1991. Mexico has 140 seaports, 29 river docks and a further 29 lake shelters. More than 85% of Mexico's foreign trade is conducted through maritime transport. During 1984–88 the Government developed the main industrial ports of Tampico, Coatzacoalcos, Lázaro Cárdenas, Altamira, Laguna de Ostión and Salina Cruz in an attempt to redirect growth and to facilitate exports. The port at Dos Bocas, on the Gulf of Mexico, is intended to be the largest in Latin America when it is opened. A 300-km railway link across the isthmus of Tehuantepec connects the Caribbean port of Coatzacoalcos with the Pacific port of Salina Cruz.

In 1992, as part of an ambitious divestment programme, the Government announced that concessions would be offered for sale to the private sector, in 1993, to operate nine ports and 61 of the country's airports. The national ports authority was to be disbanded, responsibility for each port being transferred to Administraciones Portuarias Integrales (APIs). In early 1998 plans were announced for public share offerings in 35 airports.

Secretaría de Transportes y Comunicaciones: see section on The Government (Secretariats of State).

Aeropuertos y Servicios Auxiliares (ASA): Dir ALFREDO ELIAS.

Caminos y Puentes Federales de Ingresos (CPFI): Dir GUSTAVO PETRICIOLI.

STATE RAILWAYS

In 2000 there were 26,662 km of main line track. In 1999 the railway system carried 80.4m. metric tons of freight and an estimated 0.7m. passengers.

Ferrocarriles Nacionales de México (National Railways of Mexico): Centro Administrativo, Avda Jesús García Corona 140, 13°, Ala 'A', Col. Buenavista, 06358 México, DF; tel. (5) 547-6857; fax (5) 541-6054; f. 1873; govt-owned since 1937; restructuring and privatization of national railways commenced in 1996 (see below); responsibility for signalling to be held by the Ferrocarril Terminal Valle de México; construction work on new railway links in the state of Guanajuato (at an estimated cost of US $830m.) was scheduled to begin in the late 1990s; Gen. Dir LUIS DE PABLOS.

Ferrocarril del Noreste: Avda Manuel L. Barragán 4850, 64420 Monterrey, NL; tel. (83) 51-1204; concession awarded to TFM Kansas City Southern in 1996; links Mexico City with the ports of Lázaro Cárdenas, Veracruz and Tampico, and the US border at Laredo; transports more than 40% of Mexico's rail freight; Pres. M. MOHAR.

Ferrocarril Pacifico-Norte: Avda Enrique Díaz de Leon 336, Col. Moderna, 44100 Guadalajara, Jal.; tel. (3) 825-6664; 50-year concession awarded to Grupo Ferroviario Mexicano, SA, commencing in 1998.

Ferrocarril del Sureste: Montesino 1 altos, Col. Centro, 91700 Veracruz, Ver.; tel. (29) 32-6144; 50-year concession awarded to Triturados Basálticos y Derivados, SA in 1998.

Servicio de Transportes Eléctricos del Distrito Federal (STE): Avda Municipio Libre 402, Col. San Andrés Tetepilco, México, DF; tel. (5) 539-6500; fax (5) 672-4758; suburban tram route with 17 stops upgraded to light rail standard to act as a feeder to the metro; also operates bus and trolleybus networks; Dir-Gen. J. ORTEGA CUEVAS.

Sistema de Transporte Colectivo (Metro): Delicias 67, 06070 México, DF; tel. (5) 709-1133; fax (5) 512-3601; internet www.metro.df.gob.mx; f. 1967; the first stage of a combined underground and surface railway system in Mexico City was opened in 1969; 10 lines, covering 158 km, were operating, in 1998, and five new lines, bringing the total distance to 315 km, are to be completed by 2010; the system is wholly state-owned and the fares are partially subsidized; Dir-Gen. Dr JAVIER GONZÁLEZ GARZA.

ROADS

In 2000 there were an estimated 442,553 km of roads, of which 33.4% were paved. The construction of some 4,000 km of new four-lane toll highways, through the granting of govt concessions to the private sector, was undertaken during 1989–93. In mid-1997 the Govt announced that it would repurchase almost one-half of the road concessions granted in an attempt to stimulate road construction.

Long-distance buses form one of the principal methods of transport in Mexico, and there are some 600 lines operating services throughout the country.

Dirección General de Autotransporte Federal: Calzada de las Bombas 411, 11°, Col. San Bartolo Coapa, 04800 México, DF; tel. (5) 684-0757; co-ordinates long distance bus services.

SHIPPING

At the end of 1998 Mexico's registered merchant fleet numbered 626 vessels, with a total displacement of 1,085,153 grt. The Government operates the facilities of seaports. In 1989–94 US $700m. was spent on port development, much of it from the private sector. In 1994–95 management of several ports were transferred to the private sector.

Coordinadora General de Puertos y Marina Mercante: Avda Municipio Libre 377, 12°, Ala 'B', Col. Santa Cruz Atoyac, Del. Cuauhtémoc, 03310 México, DF; tel. (5) 688-5047; fax (5) 688-7520; Dir PEDRO PABLO ZEPEDA.

Port of Acapulco: Puertos Mexicanos, Malecón Fiscal s/n, Acapulco, Gro.; tel. (748) 22067; fax (748) 31648; Harbour Master Capt. RENÉ F. NOVALES BETANZOS.

Port of Coatzacoalcos: Administración Portuaria Integral de Coatzacoalcos, SA de CV, Interior Recinto Portuario, Coatzacoalcos, 96400 Ver.; tel. (921) 46744; fax (921) 46758; e-mail apicoa@moomsa .com.mx; Dir Lic. CARLOS G. MIRANDA SÁNCHEZ.

Port of Manzanillo: Administración Portuaria Integral de Manzanillo, SA de CV, Avda Tte Azueta 9, Fracc. Playa Azul, 28250 Manzanillo, Col.; tel. (333) 21254; fax (333) 21005; e-mail apiman@ bay.net.mx; Port Supt CARLOS CABANILLAS TIRADO.

Port of Tampico: Administración Portuaria Integral de Tampico, SA de CV, Edif. API de Tampico, 1°, Recinto Portuario, 89000 Tampico, Tamps; tel. (12) 12-4660; fax (12) 12-5744; e-mail apitam@ puertodetampico.com.mx; Gen. Dir ENRIQUE GARCÍA PICAZO.

Port of Veracruz: Administración Porturia Integral de Veracruz, SA de CV, Marina Mercante 210, 7°, 91700 Veracruz, Ver.; tel. (29) 32-1319; fax (29) 32-3040; e-mail portverc@infosel.net.mx; privatized in 1994; Port Dir JUAN JOSÉ SÁNCHEZ ESQUEDA.

Petróleos Mexicanos (PEMEX): Edif. 1917, 2°, Avda Marina Nacional 329, 44°, Col. Anáhuac, 11300 México, DF; tel. (5) 531-6053; Dir-Gen. J. R. MOCTEZUMA.

Transportación Marítima Mexicana, SA de CV: Avda de la Cúspide 4755, Col. Parques del Pedregal, Del. Tlalpan, 14010 México, DF; tel. (5) 652-4111; fax (5) 665-3566; internet www.tmm.com.mx; f. 1955; cargo services to Europe, the Mediterranean, Scandinavia, the USA, South and Central America, the Caribbean and the Far East; Pres. JUAN CARLOS MERODIO; Dir-Gen. JAVIER SEGOVIA.

CIVIL AVIATION

Aerocalifornia: Aquiles Serdán 1955, 23000 La Paz, BCS; tel. (112) 26655; fax (112) 53993; e-mail aeroll@aerocalifornia.uabcs.mx; f. 1960; regional carrier with scheduled passenger and cargo services in Mexico and the USA; Chair. PAUL A. ARECHIGA.

Aerocancún: Edif. Oasis 29, Avda Kukulcan, esq. Cenzontle, Zona Hotelera, 77500 Cancún, Q. Roo; tel. (988) 32475; fax (988) 32558; charter services to the USA, South America, the Caribbean and Europe; Dir-Gen. JAVIER MARANON.

Aerocaribe: Aeropuerto Internacional, Zona Hangares, 97291 Mérida, Yuc.; tel. (99) 46-1307; fax (99) 46-1330; e-mail qamsc@ mail.interaccess.mx.com; internet www.aerocaribe.com; f. 1975; operates a network of domestic passenger flights from Cancún and Mérida; subsidiary of Mexicana; Pres. JAIME VALENZUELA TAMARIZ.

Aerocozumel: Aeropuerto Internacional, Apdo 322, Cozumel, 77600 Q. Roo; tel. (987) 23456; fax (987) 20877; f. 1978; charter airline; subsidiary of Mexicana; Dir JAIME VALENZUELA TAMARIZ.

Aeromar, Transportes Aeromar: Aeropuerto Internacional, Zona E, Hangar 7, 15620 México, DF; tel. (5) 756-0282; fax (5) 756-0174; e-mail dirplan@netmex.com; f. 1987; scheduled domestic passenger and cargo services; Dir-Gen. JUAN I. STETA.

Aerovías de México (Aeroméxico): Paseo de la Reforma 445, 3°, Torre B, Col. Cuauhtémoc, 06500 México, DF; tel. (5) 133-4000; fax (5) 133-4619; internet www.aeromexico.com; f. 1934 as Aeronaves de México, nationalized 1959; fmrly Aeroméxico until 1988, when, following bankruptcy, the Govt sold a 75% stake to private investors and a 25% stake to the Asociación Sindical de Pilotos de México; services between most principal cities of Mexico and the USA, Brazil, Peru, France and Spain; CEO ARTURO BARAHONA; Pres. and Chair. ALFONSO PASQUEL.

Mexicana (Compañía Mexicana de Aviación, SA de CV): Xola 535, 30°, Col. del Valle, Apdo 12813, 03100 México, DF; tel. (5) 448-3000; telex 01771247; fax (5) 687-8786; e-mail dirgenmx@mexicana .com.mx; internet www.mexicana.com; f. 1921; operated as private co, until July 1982, when the Govt took a 58% stake; in 1989 it was returned to private ownership; international services between Mexico City and the USA, Central America and the Caribbean; domestic services; Pres. and CEO FERNANDO P. FLORES.

Tourism

Tourism remains one of Mexico's principal sources of foreign exchange. Mexico received an estimated 10.4m. foreign visitors in 1999, and receipts from tourists in that year were estimated at US $5,425m. More than 90% of visitors come from the USA and Canada. The country is famous for volcanoes, coastal scenery and the great Sierra Nevada (Sierra Madre) mountain range. The relics of the Mayan and Aztec civilizations and of Spanish Colonial Mexico are of historic and artistic interest. Zihuatanejo, on the Pacific coast, and Cancún, on the Caribbean, were developed as tourist resorts by the Government. In 1998 there were about 392,402 hotel rooms in Mexico. The government tourism agency, FONATUR, encourages the renovation and expansion of old hotels and provides attractive incentives for the industry. FONATUR is also the main developer of major resorts in Mexico.

Secretaría de Turismo (Secretariat of State for Tourism): Presidente Masarik 172, 11587 México, DF; tel. (5) 250-8555; fax (5) 255-3112; internet mexico-travel.com.

Fondo Nacional de Fomento al Turismo (FONATUR): Insurgentes Sur 800, 17°, Col. del Valle, 03100 México, DF; tel. (5) 687-2697; f. 1956 to finance and promote the devt of tourism; Dir-Gen. Dr KEMIL A. RIZK.

Defence

In August 2000 Mexico's regular Armed Forces numbered 192,770: Army 144,000, Navy 37,000 (including naval air force and marines) and Air Force 11,770. There were also 300,000 reserves. There is a rural defence militia numbering 14,000. Military service, on a part-time basis, is by a lottery and lasts for one year.

Defence Budget: 28,400m. new pesos (US $43,000m.) in 2000.

Chief of Staff of the Armed Forces: Maj. JUAN HARIBERTO SALINAS ALTES.

Education

State education in Mexico is free and compulsory at primary and secondary level. Primary education lasts for six years between the ages of six and 11. Secondary education lasts for up to 6 years. Children aged four years and over may attend nursery school. As a proportion of children between six and 17 years of age, the total enrolment at primary and secondary schools was equivalent to 90% (males 90%; females 89%) in 1996. In that year an estimated 101% of children in the relevant age-group were enrolled in primary education (males 101%; females 102%), while the equivalent of 64% of children in the relevant age-group were enrolled in secondary schools (males 64%; females 64%). In 1998/99 there were 66,801 nursery schools, 97,627 primary schools and 39,225 secondary schools, including 13,555 commercial and technical colleges. In addition, in 2000/01 there were an estimated 4,081 institutes of higher education. There were 56 universities in 1999. In 1989–91 more than 37,000 new educational facilities were built, and there was a scholarship scheme to encourage continued school attendance by indigenous and rural children. In 1997 there were 16,592 nursery and primary schools for the indigenous population. However, in spite of the existence of more than 80 indigenous languages in Mexico, there were few bilingual secondary schools. Special emphasis was placed on a campaign to promote literacy. Much was done in the field of adult education and the illiteracy rate declined from 34.6% in 1960, to 10.5% (males 8.2%; females 12.8%) in 1995, according to UNESCO estimates. Federal expenditure on education in the 2000 budget was an estimated 220,171m. new pesos.

Bibliography

Alder Hellman, J. *Mexican Lives*. New Press, New York, NY, 1994.

Aspe Armella, P. *Economic Transformation the Mexican Way*. London, MIT Press, 1993.

Bartra, R. *Agrarian Structure and Political Power in Mexico*. Baltimore, MD, Johns Hopkins University Press, 1993.

Brading, D. (Ed.). *Caudillo and Peasant in the Mexican Revolution*. Cambridge, Cambridge University Press, 1980.

Brown, J. C. *Oil and Revolution in Mexico*. Berkeley, CA, University of California Press, 1993.

Camp, R. A. *Politics in Mexico*, 2nd Edn. Oxford, Oxford University Press, 1996.

Cockcroft, J. D. *Mexico: Class Formation, Capital Accumulation and the State*. New York, NY, Monthly Review Press, 1983.

Fatemi, K. (Ed.). *US–Mexican Economic Relations: Prospects and Problems*. New York, NY, Praeger Publrs, 1988.

Franco, J. *Plotting Women: Gender and Representation in Mexico*. London, Verso, 1989.

Fuentes, C. *A New Time for Mexico*. Bloomsbury, London, 1997.

Garber, P. M. (Ed.). *The Mexico–US Free Trade Agreement*. London, MIT Press, 1993.

Gentleman, J. (Ed.). *Mexican Politics in Transition*. Boulder, CO, Westview Press, 1986.

Guzmán, O., et al. *Energy Efficiency and Conservation in Mexico: Perspectives on Efficiency and Conservation Policies*. Boulder, CO, Westview Press, 1986.

Krauze, E. *Mexico: Biography of Power. A History of Modern Mexico, 1810–1996*. London, HarperCollins, 1997.

La Botz, D. *The Crisis of Mexican Labor*. New York, NY, Praeger Publrs, 1988.

Levy, D., and Szekeky, G. *Mexico: Paradoxes of Stability and Change*. Boulder, CO, Westview Press, 1983.

Meyer, M. C., and Sherman, W. L. *The Course of Mexican History*, 2nd Edn. Oxford, Oxford University Press, 1983.

Miller, R. R. *Mexico: A History*. Norman, OK, University of Oklahoma Press, 1985.

Newman, G., and Szterenfeld, A. *Business International's Guide to Doing Business in Mexico*. London, McGraw-Hill, 1993.

O'Malley, I. V. *The Myth of the Revolution: Hero Cults and the Institutionalization of the Mexican State, 1920–1940*. London, Greenwood, 1986.

Orme, Jr, W. A. *Continental Shift, Free Trade and the New North America*. Washington, DC, The Washington Post, 1993.

Raat, D. W., and Beezeley, W. H. (Eds). *Twentieth Century Mexico*. Lincoln, NE, University of Nebraska Press, 1986.

Ramirez, M. D. *Development Banking in Mexico: The Case of the Nacional Financiera, SA*. New York, NY, Praeger Publrs, 1986.

Riding, A. *Mexico: Inside the Volcano*. London, I. B. Tauris, 1987.

Poulson, B. W. 'The Mexican Debt Crisis: A Case Study in Public Sector Failure', in *Journal of Social, Political and Economic Studies*, Vol. 13 (Winter). 1988.

Story, D. *Mexico's Ruling Party: Stability and Authority*. New York, NY, Praeger Publrs, 1986.

Thomas, H. *The Conquest of Mexico*. London, Hutchinson, 1993.

Twomey, M. J. *Multinational Corporations and the North America Free Trade Agreement*. London, Praeger Publrs, 1993.

Velasco S., J.-A. *Impacts of Mexican Oil Policy on Economic and Political Developments*. Lexington, MA, Lexington Books, 1983.

Ward, P. *Welfare Politics in Mexico: Papering over the Cracks*. London, Allen and Unwin, 1986.

Weintraub, S. *A Marriage of Convenience*. Oxford, Oxford University Press, 1990.

MONTSERRAT

Area: 102 sq km (39.5 sq miles).

Population (official estimate in February 2000): 5,000.

Capital: Plymouth (population 1,478 in 1980).

Language: English.

Religion: Several Christian denominations are represented.

Climate: Generally warm; average annual rainfall about 1,475 mm (58.0 ins).

Time: GMT −4 hours.

Public Holidays: 2002: 1 January (New Year's Day), 18 March (for St Patrick's Day), 29 March (Good Friday), 1 April (Easter Monday), 6 May (Labour Day), 20 May (Whit Monday), 5 August (August Monday), 23 November (Liberation Day), 25–26 December (Christmas), 31 December (Festival Day). **2003:** 1 January (New Year's Day), 17 March (St Patrick's Day), 18 April (Good Friday), 21 April (Easter Monday), 5 May (Labour Day), 9 June (Whit Monday), 4 August (August Monday), 23 November (Liberation Day), 25–26 December (Christmas), 31 December (Festival Day).

Currency: Eastern Caribbean dollar; US $1 = EC $2.70 (fixed rate since July 1976); EC $100 = £25.87 = US $37.04 = €41.73 (30 April 2001).

Weights and Measures: Imperial; metric system being introduced.

History

Montserrat is a United Kingdom Overseas Territory, and the Governor, who is the representative of the British monarch, presides over the Executive Council. From February 1998 the British Dependent Territories were referred to as the United Kingdom Overseas Territories, following the announcement of the interim findings of a British government review of the United Kingdom's relations with the Overseas Territories.

British settlers first arrived in Montserrat in 1632. Between 1871 and 1956 the island was part of the Leeward Islands Federation. In 1960 a Constitution was introduced, and an Administrator appointed (later redesignated Governor). In 1978 the People's Liberation Movement (PLM) won all seven elective seats in the Legislative Council and the party leader, John Osborne, became Chief Minister. The PLM won five seats in the 1983 general election and four in 1987. In 1989 the island was devastated by 'Hurricane Hugo' and an investigation into Montserrat's offshore-finance sector culminated in the closure of many offshore banks. The British authorities then proposed amendments to the Constitution, granting extra powers to the Governor to control financial services, which provisions became effective in February 1990. Resignations over allegations of corruption caused the Osborne Government to lose its majority and to hold elections in October 1991. The newly formed National Progressive Party (NPP) won the election, with four seats, and its leader, Reuben Meade, became Chief Minister. At the general election of 11 November 1996, however, the NPP retained only one seat, while the Progressive People's Alliance of John Osborne and the Movement of National Reconstruction (MNR) of Austin Bramble (Chief Minister 1970–78) each won two seats. The MNR agreed to support an administration with an independent member of the legislature, Bertrand Osborne, as Chief Minister.

In 1995 all affairs on Montserrat came to be dominated by the threat of eruption of the Soufrière Hills volcano, Chance's Peak. Volcanic activity left two-thirds of Montserrat uninhabitable and destroyed Plymouth. Islanders were evacuated to 'safe areas' in the north of the territory. Intensified geological activity in June 1997 provoked criticism of both the British Government and of the local administration. On 21 August Osborne resigned as Chief Minister after protests over his handling of the crisis. On the same day the British Government announced details of its voluntary evacuation scheme for those wishing to leave the island. However, the scheme was criticized as inadequate by both islanders and by Osborne's successor, David Brandt, who accused the United Kingdom of showing insufficient commitment to the redevelopment of Montserrat. By mid-February 1998 the island's population had declined to an estimated 2,850.

In May 1998 the British Government announced that all citizens of Montserrat, except those already resident in other countries, would be entitled to settle in the United Kingdom. In early July the Soufrière Hills volcano erupted again, postponing plans to re-open parts of Plymouth to residents. There was further criticism of the British Government in January 1999 when an inquest into the 19 deaths during the eruptions found that, in nine cases, the Government was in part to blame. The jury criticized the Government's failure to provide farming land in the 'safe area', which had led to some farmers choosing to risk their lives rather than abandon their farms. In the same month the implementation of a £75m. three-year redevelopment programme in the north of the island was announced. In February it was suggested that the number of areas of the island suitable for redevelopment might be further limited by the threat to health from long-term exposure to the volcanic ash which contained silica, the cause of the lung disease, silicosis.

In July 1999 the commanding officer of the Royal Montserrat Defence Force, Maj. Michael Duberry, resigned, following the cancellation of a parade to commemorate the Queen's Birthday, owing to protests from the force's soldiers over living conditions. Later in the year Brunel Meade of the PPA was appointed Minister of Agriculture, Lands, Housing and the Environment, following the dismissal of Austin Bramble. In mid-2000 Montserrat was included in an Organisation of Economic Co-operation and Development (OECD) investigation into harmful tax regimes. The Chief Minister acknowledged the island's duty to enforce legislation and encourage administrative transparency; however, he also declared that the administration would not act on the report without receiving adequate proof of the allegations. In December Brandt declared his wish for responsibility for managing and monitoring Montserrat's financial services sector to be transferred to the Eastern Caribbean Central Bank (ECCB), and for policy matters to fall under the Ministry of Finance portfolio.

In August 2000 Montserrat signed up to a British mortgage assistance programme, which would provide housing subsidies and loans to residents who had been made homeless as a result of volcanic activity. Many residents were still paying mortgages on homes in an off-limits zone of the island as well as paying rent for new accommodation. At a conference in October in Anguilla, the Chief Minister called for the right for each of the United Kingdom's Overseas Territories to have a representative in the British Parliament to represent each territory's particular concerns. There was, however, no immediate reaction from the British Government. In November 2000 it was announced that Tony Abbott would be retiring as Governor in May 2001. He was succeeded by Anthony Longrigg.

In February 2001 Chief Minister Brandt's coalition Government collapsed following the resignations of Adelina Tuitt, the Minister of Education, Health and Community Services, and Rupert Weekes, the Deputy Chief Minister and Minister of Communications, Works and Sports. The two accused Brandt of making decisions, in particular about a proposed new airport, without consulting other ministers. Their resignations forced Brandt to dissolve the Executive Council and announce that an early general election would be held on 2 April, under the new system of the nine-member single constituency. In mid-March Brandt announced that he would not be seeking re-election, citing as one of his reasons a recurring sports injury to the knee. The main contestants in the election were former Chief Minister Reuben Meade's NPP, and former Chief Minister John Osborne's newly-formed New People's Liberation Movement (NPLM). There was anger following the announcement that Montserratians who had left the island following the volcanic eruptions would not be entitled to vote. At the elections the NPLM won seven of the nine seats and 52% of the votes cast. The NPP won the remaining two seats. Turn-out was put at 77.6% of the 2,955 islanders registered to vote. Osborne was sworn in as Chief Minister on 5 April and an Executive Council was subsequently formed. One of Osborne's first statements as Chief Minister called on the United Kingdom to increase its grants to the island.

Economy

As only about 50% of potential agricultural land was under cultivation, the Government had made agricultural development a priority. However, the eruption of the Soufrière Hills volcano in June 1997, and subsequent volcanic activity, caused a 81.3% decline in agricultural production, and a return to subsistence farming. The sector contracted by a further 2.0% in 1998, but increased by 16.5% in 1999. The agricultural sector's contribution to GDP was 1.3% in 1999. Light industry was also encouraged prior to the eruptions. However, many industrial sites were destroyed in 1997, causing a decline in output of 45.2% in that year and of 85.0% in 1998. The assembly of electrical components, which accounted for 69% of export earnings in 1993, ceased in 1998, following further volcanic activity. However, in 1999 the industrial sector improved by 10.6%.

Service industries dominated Montserrat's economy in the early 1990s. Tourism contributed about 25% of gross domestic product (GDP) annually in the early 1990s, and the island was also an important communications, technology and media centre for the region. However, the activity of the Soufrière Hills volcano in the mid-1990s devastated this sector as well (tourism in particular). The tourism sector, which earned an estimated EC $8.3m. in 1999, remains important to the island, and it is hoped to establish Montserrat as a centre for environmental tourism. Output from the hotel and restaurant sector decreased by an annual average of 19.2% between 1993–99, but declined dramatically in 1996 and 1997 (by 78.2% and 42.9%, respectively), although increases of 45.0% and 66.7% were recorded in 1998 and 1999, respectively. It is also hoped to re-establish Montserrat as a data-processing centre, and as a centre for financial services, which previously provided an important source of government revenue.

The volcanic eruption destroyed much of the country's infrastructure, including the main port and airport. In August 2000 the British Government announced a five-year reconstruction programme for the development of the 'safe areas' in the north of the island. However, by mid-February 1998 the population of Montserrat had declined to just 2,850 (the population was an estimated 11,581 in 1994) owing to the lack of employment prospects and to poor living conditions. Of the remaining workforce, some 25% were employed by the Government or statutory bodies. The population was reported to have increased to some 5,000 by early 2000, and it was hoped that a reduction in volcanic activity would encourage Monserratians resident abroad to return home, thereby stimulating the economy. The remaining population came to be concentrated in the less fertile and less developed north of the island. The territory was dependent on emergency aid and food aid, mainly from the United Kingdom. The already large trade deficit (which totalled EC $48.42m. in 1997) was largely offset by this aid and by remittances from workers abroad and the incomes of foreign residents (mainly aid workers from the mid-1990s).

In July 1999 the Montserrat Volcano Observatory warned that volcanic activity showed no signs of decline and reported further explosions of ash and minor eruptions of lava. In September the Government announced proposals to establish a new capital at Little Bay, in the north-west of the island. In early 2000 it was hoped that a reduction in volcanic activity would encourage Monserratians to return; measures implemented to assist those displaced by the crisis included a work-permit scheme to ensure employment and a subsidized mortgage scheme. However, in March 2000 the dome of lava, which had been covering the Soufrière Hills volcano, collapsed, producing lava flows and mudslides in the west of the island, and covering much of the 'safe area' with ash. In late 2000 the British Government's Department for International Development awarded funds of EC $7.5m., and the European Union (EU) allocated EC $19m. to finance re-development projects. Montserrat's economic prospects depend entirely on the activity of the volcano, and although reconstruction work is in progress, other areas of the economy are likely to remain at extremely low levels of output for some years. In December 2000 one of Montserrat's main hotels, which was forced to close in 1997, reopened. The economy was expected to contract by 6.3% in 2000.

Statistical Survey

Sources (unless otherwise stated): Government Information Service, Media Centre, Chief Minister's Office, Old Towne; tel. 491-2702; fax 491-2711; Eastern Caribbean Central Bank, POB 89, Basseterre, Saint Christopher; OECS Economic Affairs Secretariat, *Statistical Digest.*

AREA AND POPULATION

Area: 102 sq km (39.5 sq miles).

Population: 10,639 (males 5,290; females 5,349) at census of 12 May 1991; 11,851 (official estimate) in 1994, 5,000 (official estimate) in February 2000.

Density (Feb. 2000): 49.0 per sq km.

Births and Deaths (1986): 200 live births (birth rate 16.8 per 1,000); 123 deaths (death rate 10.3 per 1,000).

Employment (1992): Agriculture, forestry and fishing 298; Mining and manufacturing 254; Electricity, gas and water 68; Wholesale and retail trade 1,666; Restaurants and hotels 234; Transport and communication 417; Finance, insurance and business services 242; Public defence 390; Other community, social and personal services 952; Total 4,521. Source: *The Commonwealth Yearbook.*
1998: The labour force is estimated at 1,500.

AGRICULTURE, ETC.

Principal Crops (estimate, metric tons, 2000): Fruit excl. melons 710. Source: FAO.

Livestock ('000 head, estimates, 2000): Cattle 10; Sheep 5; Goats 7; Pigs 1. Source: FAO.

Livestock Products (estimates, '000 metric tons, 2000): Beef and veal 1; Cows' milk 1. Source: FAO.

Fishing (metric tons, live weight, 1998): Marine fishes 50; Total catch 50. Source: FAO, *Yearbook of Fishery Statistics.*

INDUSTRY

Electric Energy (production, million kWh): 16 in 1993; 16 in 1994; 17 in 1995. Source: UN, *Industrial Commodity Statistics Yearbook.*

FINANCE

Currency and Exchange Rates: 100 cents = 1 East Caribbean dollar (EC $). *Sterling, US Dollar and Euro Equivalents* (30 April 2001): £1 sterling = EC $3.866; US $1 = EC $2.700; €1 = EC $2.397; EC $100 = £25.87 = US $37.04 = €41.73. *Exchange Rate:* Fixed at US $1 = EC $2.70 since July 1976.

Budget (EC $ million, 1999): *Revenue:* Revenue from taxation 24.3 (Taxes on income and profits 7.6, Taxes on international trade and transactions 12.8); Non-tax revenue 2.5; Grants 46.7; Total 73.5. *Expenditure:* Current expenditure 57.9 (Personal emoluments 19.9, Goods and services 31.3, Transfers and subsidies 5.9, Interest payments 0.8); Capital expenditure 13.8; Total 71.7. Source: Eastern Caribbean Central Bank, *Report and Statement of Accounts.*

Cost of Living (consumer price index; base: Sept. 1982 = 100): 155.7 in 1994; 162.6 in 1995; 172.7 in 1996.

Gross Domestic Product (EC $ million at current factor cost): 95.8 in 1997; 92.5 in 1998; 93.5 (provisional) in 1999. Source: Eastern Caribbean Central Bank, *Report and Statement of Accounts.*

Gross Domestic Product by Economic Activity (EC $ million at current factor cost, 1999): Agriculture, forestry and fishing 1.22; Mining and quarrying 0.07; Manufacturing 0.62; Electricity, gas and water 5.83; Construction 19.97; Wholesale and retail trade 7.29; Restaurants and hotels 1.35; Transport 9.01; Communications 5.81; Banks and insurance 7.86; Real estate and housing 9.40; Government services 23.55; Other services 5.39; Sub-total 97.37; *Less* Imputed service charge 3.86; GDP at factor cost 93.51. Source: Eastern Caribbean Central Bank, *National Accounts.*

Balance of Payments (EC $ million, 1999): Exports of goods f.o.b. 3.41; Imports of goods f.o.b. –64.91; *Trade balance* –61.50; Exports of services 53.81; Imports of services –57.98; *Balance on goods and services* –65.67; Other income received 3.21; Other income paid –10.77; *Balance on goods, services and income* –73.23; Current transfers received 65.67; Current transfers paid –7.26; *Current balance* –14.82; Capital account (net) 4.25; Direct investment (net)

22.18; Other investment (net) −38.11; Net errors and omissions −2.53; *Overall balance* −29.03. Source: Eastern Caribbean Central Bank, *Balance of Payments*.

EXTERNAL TRADE

Principal Commodities (EC $ '000): *Imports c.i.f. (1998):* Food and live animals 6,960; Beverages and tobacco 3,171; Crude materials (inedible) except fuels 4,404; Mineral fuels, lubricants, etc. 4,714; Chemicals 3,779; Basic manufactures 13,691; Machinery and transport equipment 13,372; Miscellaneous manufactured articles 14,137; Total (incl. others) 64,335. *Exports f.o.b. (1997):* Food and live animals 8,221; Basic manufactures 8,362; Machinery and transport equipment 6,719; Miscellaneous manufactured articles 1,749; Total (incl. others) 29,939.

Principal Trading Partners (EC $ '000): *Imports c.i.f. (1998):* Canada 775; Jamaica 772; Saint Vincent and the Grenadines 1,279; Trinidad and Tobago 8,150; United Kingdom 8,977; USA 30,505; Total (incl. others) 64,335. *Exports f.o.b. (1996):* Antigua and Barbuda 1,294; Belgium 5,442; Ireland 3,683; Martinique 2,104; Spain 7,519; United Kingdom 27,000; USA 62,789; Total (incl. others) 111,597.

Source: OECS, *External Merchandise Trade Annual Report*.

TOURISM

Visitor Arrivals: 7,467 in 1998; 9,900 in 1999; 14,356 (excursionists 4,019; stay-over visitors 10,337) in 2000. Sources: World Tourism Organization, *Yearbook of Tourism Statistics* and Ministry of Finance, Economic Development and Trade, *Budget Statement 2001*.

Tourist receipts (EC $ million): 11.88 in 1997; 11.49 in 1998; 8.25 in 1999. Source: Eastern Caribbean Central Bank, *Balance of Payments*.

TRANSPORT

Road Traffic (vehicles in use, 1990): Passenger cars 1,823; Goods vehicles 54; Public service vehicles 4; Motor cycles 21; Miscellaneous 806.

Shipping *International freight traffic* ('000 metric tons, 1990): Goods loaded 6; Goods unloaded 49. Source: UN, *Monthly Bulletin of Statistics*.

Civil Aviation (1985): Aircraft arrivals 4,422; passengers 25,380; air cargo 132.4 metric tons.

COMMUNICATIONS MEDIA

Radio Receivers (1997): 7,000 in use.

Television Receivers (1997): 3,000 in use.

Telephones (1995): 5,000 main lines in use.

Mobile Cellular Telephones (estimate, 1994): 70 subscribers.

Non-Daily Newspapers (1996): 2 (estimated circulation 3,000).

Sources: UNESCO, *Statistical Yearbook*; UN, *Statistical Yearbook*.

EDUCATION

Pre-primary (1993/94): 12 schools; 31 teachers; 407 pupils.

Primary (1993/94): 11 schools; 85 teachers; 1,525 pupils.

Secondary (1993/94): 2 schools (1989); 80 teachers; 905 pupils.

Source: UNESCO, *Statistical Yearbook*.

Directory

The eruption in June 1997 of the Soufrière Hills volcano, and subsequent volcanic activity, rendered some two-thirds of Montserrat uninhabitable and destroyed the capital, Plymouth. Islanders were evacuated to a 'safe zone' in the north of the island.

The Constitution

The present Constitution came into force on 19 December 1989 and made few amendments to the constitutional order established in 1960. The Constitution now guarantees the fundamental rights and freedoms of the individual and grants the Territory the right of self-determination. Montserrat is governed by a Governor and has its own Executive and Legislative Councils. The Governor retains responsibility for defence, external affairs (including international financial affairs) and internal security. The Executive Council consists of the Governor as President, the Chief Minister and three other Ministers, the Attorney-General and the Financial Secretary. The Legislative Council consists of the Speaker (chosen from outside the Council), nine elected, two official and two nominated members.

The Government

Governor: ANTHONY LONGRIGG (appointed May 2001).

EXECUTIVE COUNCIL
(August 2001)

President: The Governor.

Official Members:

    Attorney-General: BRIAN COTTLE.

    Financial Secretary: JOHN SKERRIT.

Chief Minister and Minister of Finance, Economic Development, Trade, Tourism and Media: JOHN A. OSBORNE.

Minister of Agriculture and the Environment: MARGARET DYER-HOWE.

Minister of Communications and Works, Land, Housing and Disaster Mitigation: LOWELL LEWIS.

Minister of Education, Health, Community Services, Sports and Culture: IDABELLE MEADE.

Clerk to the Executive Council: CLAUDETTE WEEKES.

MINISTRIES

Office of the Governor: McChesney's Estate, Olveston; tel. 491-2688; fax 491-4553; e-mail govoff@candw.ag.

Office of the Chief Minister: Government Headquarters, POB 292; tel. 491-3463; fax 491-6780.

Ministry of Agriculture and the Environment: tel. 491-2546; fax 491-7275.

Ministry of Communications and Works, Land, Housing and Disaster Mitigation: tel. 491-2521; fax 491-4534.

Ministry of Education, Health, Community Services, Sports and Culture: Government Headquarters, POB 24; tel. 491-2880; fax 491-3131.

Ministry of Finance, Economic Development, Trade, Tourism and Media: POB 292; tel. 491-2066; fax 491-4632.

LEGISLATIVE COUNCIL

Speaker: Dr HOWARD A. FERGUS (acting).

Election, 2 April 2001

Party	Seats
New People's Liberation Movement (NPLM) .	7
National Progressive Party (NPP)	2

There are also two *ex-officio* members (the Attorney-General and the Financial Secretary), and two nominated members.

Political Organizations

Movement for National Reconstruction (MNR): f. 1996; Leader AUSTIN BRAMBLE.

National Progressive Party (NPP): POB 280; tel. 491-2444; f. 1991; Leader REUBEN T. MEADE.

New People's Liberation Movement (NPLM): f. 2001, as successor party to People's Progressive Alliance; Leader JOHN A. OSBORNE.

Judicial System

Justice is administered by the Eastern Caribbean Supreme Court (based in Saint Lucia), the Court of Summary Jurisdiction and the Magistrate's Court.

Puisne Judge (Montserrat Circuit): NEVILLE L. SMITH.

Magistrate: ANNA B. RYAN.

Registrar: EULALIE GREENAWAY.

Religion

CHRISTIANITY

The Montserrat Christian Council: St Peter's, POB 227; tel. 491-4864; fax 491-2813; e-mail 113057.1074@compuserve.com.

The Anglican Communion

Anglicans are adherents of the Church in the Province of the West Indies, comprising eight dioceses. Montserrat forms part of the diocese of the North Eastern Caribbean and Aruba. The Bishop is resident in The Valley, Anguilla.

The Roman Catholic Church

Montserrat forms part of the diocese of St John's-Basseterre, suffragan to the archdiocese of Castries (Saint Lucia). The Bishop is resident in St John's, Antigua.

Other Christian Churches

There are Baptist, Methodist, Pentecostal and Seventh-day Adventist churches and other places of worship on the island.

The Press

The Montserrat Reporter: POB 306, Olveston; tel. 491-4715; fax 491-2052; internet www.montserratreporter.com; weekly on Fridays; circ. 2,000.

The Montserrat Times: POB 28; tel. 491-2501; fax 491-6069; weekly on Fridays; circ. 1,000.

Montserrat Today: government information publication.

Broadcasting and Communications

TELECOMMUNICATIONS

Cable and Wireless: Sweeney's; tel. 491-1000; fax 491-3599.

BROADCASTING

Prior to the volcanic eruption of June 1997 there were three radio stations operating in Montserrat. Television services can also be obtained from Saint Christopher and Nevis, Puerto Rico, and from Antigua (ABS).

Radio

Radio Montserrat—ZJB: POB 51, Sweeney's; tel. 491-2885; fax 491-9250; e-mail radmon@candw.ag; f. 1952, first broadcast 1957; govt station; Station Man. ROSE WILLOCK; CEO LOWELL MASON.

Radio Antilles: POB 35/930; tel. 491-2755; fax 491-2724; f. 1963; in 1989 the Govt of Montserrat, on behalf of the OECS, acquired the station; has one of the most powerful transmitters in the region; commercial; regional; broadcasts in English and French; Chair. Dr H. FELLHAUER; Man. Dir KRISTIAN KNAACK; Gen. Man. KEITH GREAVES.

Gem Radio Network: Barzey's, POB 488; tel. 491-5728; fax 491-5729; f. 1984; commercial; Station Man. KEVIN LEWIS; Man. Dir KENNETH LEE.

Television

Antilles Television Ltd: POB 342; tel. 491-2226; fax 491-4511; 2 channels for region; Gen. Man. KARNEY OSBORNE; Technical Dir Z. A. JOSEPH.

Cable Television of Montserrat Ltd: POB 447, Olveston; tel. 491-2507; fax 491-3081; Man. SYLVIA WHITE.

Montserrat Television Foundation: POB 447; tel. 491-7767; fax 491-3081.

Finance

The Eastern Caribbean Central Bank (see Part Three), based in Saint Christopher, is the central issuing and monetary authority for Montserrat.

Financial Services Centre: POB 292; tel. 491-3057; fax 491-3757; e-mail minfin@candw.ag.

BANKING

Bank of Montserrat Ltd: POB 10, Parliament St, Plymouth; tel. 491-3843; fax 491-3163; e-mail bom@candw.ag; CEO GREGORY DE GANNES.

Barclays Bank PLC: POB 131; tel. 491-2501; fax 491-3801; Man. NORRIS VIDAL.

Government Savings Bank: 2,026 depositors (March 1998).

Royal Bank of Canada: tel. 491-2426; fax 491-3991; Man. J. R. GILBERT.

INSURANCE

Insurance Services (Montserrat) Ltd: POB 185, Sweeney's; tel. 491-2103; fax 491-6013.

United Insurance Co Ltd: Jacquie Ryan Enterprises Ltd, Woodlands; tel. 491-2055; fax 491-3257.

Trade and Industry

CHAMBER OF COMMERCE

Montserrat Chamber of Commerce and Industry: POB 384, Olveston; tel. 491-3640; fax 491-6602; refounded 1971; 22 company mems, 8 individual mems; Pres. BRUCE FARARA.

UTILITIES

Gas

Grant Enterprises and Trading: Brades, POB 350; tel. 491-9654; fax 491-4854; e-mail granten@candw.ag; domestic gas supplies.

TRADE UNIONS

Montserrat Allied Workers' Union (MAWU): Banks; tel. 491-2919; f. 1973; private-sector employees; Gen. Sec. HYLROY BRAMBLE; 1,000 mems.

Montserrat Seamen's and Waterfront Workers' Union: tel. 491-6335; fax 491-6335; f. 1980; Sec.-Gen. CHEDMOND BROWNE; 100 mems.

Montserrat Union of Teachers: POB 460; tel. 491-7034; fax 491-5779; e-mail hcb@candw.ag; f. 1978; Pres. GREGORY JULIUS (acting); Gen. Sec. HYACINTH BRAMBLE-BROWNE; 46 mems.

Transport

The eruption in June 1997 of the Soufrière Hills volcano, and subsequent volcanic activity, destroyed much of the infrastructure in the southern two-thirds of the island, including the country's principal port and airport facilities, as well as the road network.

ROADS

Prior to the volcanic eruption of June 1997 Montserrat had an extensive and well-constructed road network. There were 203 km (126 miles) of good surfaced main roads, 24 km (15 miles) of secondary unsurfaced roads and 42 km (26 miles) of rough tracks.

SHIPPING

The principal port at Plymouth was destroyed by the volcanic activity of June 1997. An emergency jetty was constructed at Little Bay in the north of the island. Regular trans-shipment steamship services are provided by Harrison Line and Nedlloyd Line. The Bermuth Line and the West Indies Shipping Service link Montserrat with Miami, USA and with neighbouring territories. A twice-daily ferry service is in operation between Montserrat and Antigua.

Port Authority of Montserrat: Little Bay; tel. 491-2791; fax 491-8063.

Montserrat Shipping Services: POB 46, Carr's Bay; tel. 491-3614; fax 491-3617.

CIVIL AVIATION

The main airport, Blackburne at Trants, 13 km (8 miles) from Plymouth, was destroyed by the volcanic activity of June 1997. The airport is to be rebuilt, and it was hoped to complete the renovation work in 2001. A helicopter port at Gerald's in the north of the island was completed in 2000. Montserrat is linked to Antigua by a helicopter service, which operates three times a day. Montserrat is a shareholder in the regional airline, LIAT (based in Antigua and Barbuda).

Montserrat Airways Ltd: tel. 491-6494; fax 491-6205; charter services.

Montserrat Aviation Services Ltd: Nixon's, POB 257; tel. 491-2533; fax 491-7186; f. 1981; ceased operating its own flights in 1988; handling agent.

Tourism

Since the 1997 volcanic activity, Montserrat has been marketed as an eco-tourism destination. Known as the 'Emerald Isle of the Caribbean', Montserrat is noted for its Irish connections, and for its range of flora and fauna. In 2000 there were 10,337 tourist arrivals. In 1997 some 44% of tourist arrivals were from Caribbean countries, 24% from the USA, 19% from the United Kingdom and 5% from Canada. A large proportion of visitors are estimated to be Montserrat nationals residing overseas. In 1999 earnings from the sector amounted to some EC $8.3m.

Montserrat Tourist Board: POB 7; tel. 491-2230; fax 491-7430; e-mail mrattouristboard@candw.ag; f. 1961; Chair. E. CHARLES EDGECOMBE; Dir of Tourism ERNESTINE CASSELL.

Education

Education, beginning at five years of age, is compulsory up to the age of 14. In 1993 there were 11 primary schools, including 10 government schools. Secondary education begins at 12 years of age, and comprises a first cycle of five years and a second, two-year cycle. In 1989 there was one government secondary school and one private secondary school. In addition, in 1993 there were 12 nursery schools, sponsored by a government-financed organization, and a Technical College, which provided vocational and technical training for school-leavers. There was also an extra-mural department of the University of the West Indies in Plymouth. Current expenditure on education totalled EC $7m. in 1993, equivalent to 18.8% of total current expenditure.

NETHERLANDS ANTILLES

Area: 800 sq km (309 sq miles).

Population (official estimate, 1999): 214,800.

Capital: Willemstad, estimated population 144,097 at 1992 census.

Language: Dutch, Papiamento and English (official languages); English is the principal language of the 'Windward Islands'; Spanish is also widely spoken; Papiamento is the dominant language of Aruba and the 'Leeward Islands'.

Religion: Predominantly Christianity (mainly Protestantism on St Eustatius and St Maarten).

Climate: Tropical; average annual temperature 27°C (81°F); average annual rainfall (Bonaire and Curaçao) 510 mm; (St Maarten, St Eustatius and Saba) 1,100 mm.

Time: GMT –4 hours.

Public Holidays

2002: 1 January (New Year's Day), 11 February (Curaçao and Bonaire only: Lenten Carnival), 29 March–1 April (Easter), 30 April (Queen's Day), 1 May (Labour Day), 9 May (Ascension Day), 20 May (St Maarten, Saba and St Eustatius only: Whit Monday), 2 July (Curaçao Day), 6 September (Bonaire Day), 11 November (St Maarten Day), 18 November (for St Eustatius Day), 6 December (Saba Day), 25–26 December (Christmas).

2003: 1 January (New Year's Day), 3 March (Curaçao and Bonaire only: Lenten Carnival), 18–21 April (Easter), 30 April (Queen's Day), 1 May (Labour Day), 29 May (Ascension Day), 9 June (St Maarten, Saba and St Eustatius only: Whit Monday), 2 July (Curaçao Day), 8 September (for Bonaire Day), 11 November (St Maarten Day), 17 November (for St Eustatius Day), 8 December (for Saba Day), 25–26 December (Christmas).

Currency: Gulden (guilder) or florin; 100 guilders = £39.02 = US $55.87 = €62.94 (30 April 2001).

Weights and Measures: The metric system is in force.

Basic Economic Indicators

	1998	1999	2000
Government budget (NA Fl. million at current prices):			
Revenue.	555.7	498.3	n.a.
Expenditure.	592.4	547.4	n.a.
Consumer price index (base: 1995 = 100)	108.2	108.6	114.9
Rate of inflation (annual average, %)	1.1	0.4	5.8
Foreign exchange reserves (US $ million at 31 December)	248	265	261
Balance of payments (current account, million NA Fl.)	–100.0	–363.0	n.a.

Gross domestic product: NA Fl. 4,537.1m. at current prices in 1997; average real growth rate in 1999: –2.9%.

Total labour force (estimate, 1998): 98,444.

Unemployment (2000): 14.9%.

Total foreign debt (estimate, 1996): US $1,354m.

Life expectancy: (World Bank estimate, years at birth, 1999) 76.

Infant mortality rate (excl. St Eustatius—per 1,000 live births, 1998): 13.5.

Adult literacy rate (estimate, 2000): 96.6%.

Energy consumption per head (kg of coal equivalent, 1998): 8,153.

Carbon dioxide emissions per head (metric tons, 1997): 6,430.

Passenger motor cars in use (per 1,000 of population, 1996): 357.

Television receivers in use (per 1,000 of population, 1997): 328.

History

RENÉ VAN DONGEN

The Netherlands Antilles, sometimes also referred to as the 'Antilles of the Five', consist of two groups of islands. Bonaire and Curaçao are situated approximately 70 km off the coast of Venezuela and are known as the 'Leeward (*Benedenwindse*) Islands'. Sint (St) Maarten, St Eustatius and Saba (also referred to as the 'S' Islands) are located nearly 900 km north-east from Aruba and Curaçao and make up the 'Windward (*Bovenwindse*) Islands' part of the Netherlands Antilles. Because of the vast distance between these two groups of islands, there are great differences in physical geographical conditions. Bonaire and Curaçao are rather flat limestone islands, with a semi-arid climate (with an average annual rainfall of 510 mm) and a vegetation type suited to these rather dry conditions. St Maarten, St Eustatius and Saba are volcanic in origin with a rainfall pattern and vegetation type suited to more humid tropical conditions (average annual rainfall approximately 1,100 mm). St Maarten, St Eustatius and Saba are located in the middle of the Atlantic hurricane zone, whereas Curaçao and Bonaire are located near the southern border of this zone.

EARLY OCCUPATION

The first inhabitants of the island of Curaçao were small groups of Amerindians (most likely from the Caquetíos tribe), who had crossed over from Venezuela. Some of their artefacts found on Curaçao can be dated back to 2500 BC. Another group of Amerindians (most likely Arawaks) had settled on Aruba, Bonaire and Curaçao around AD 900. These Amerindians clashed several times with groups of Caribs who were roaming around the Caribbean Sea. A few Amerindian artefacts were found on the 'S' Islands (near Norman Estate on St Maarten), which greatly resembled Amerindian artefacts found in Venezuela. By the time the first European settlers set foot on the 'S' Islands, the Amerindians had disappeared.

The first written source of information about the Netherlands Antilles was from the Italian sailor, Amerigo Vespucci. He travelled through the Caribbean in 1499 together with Alonso de Ojeda and the cartographer, Juan de la Cosa, and reported an encounter with Amerindians on the islands of Bonaire and Curaçao. Between 1499 and 1526 these Amerindians were captured as slaves by the Spaniards and put to work on other islands. The Spaniards considered Bonaire and Curaçao to be *islas inútiles*, or 'useless islands', and used them mainly to graze sheep, goats and horses. They also started to grow fruit trees and tobacco on the islands. They took no interest in St Maarten, Saba and St Eustatius, perhaps also because the influence of the French and English was much stronger in the northern part of the Caribbean.

UNDER THE RULE OF THE WEST INDIAN COMPANY

Dutch sailors belonging to the West-Indische Compagnie (WIC—West Indian Company) began visiting the islands of Bonaire and St Maarten from around 1624, with the sole purpose of collecting salt in the natural salt pans there. St Maarten, St Eustatius and Saba were captured by the Dutch in 1630, 1635 and 1640, respectively. Curaçao was captured by the Dutch in 1634, without experiencing any resistance from the Spanish. Bonaire came under Dutch rule for the first time in 1636.

Like so many territories in the Caribbean, the ownership and administration of the islands was far from stable. The British and the Dutch governed Curaçao and Bonaire for alternating periods between the early 17th and the early 19th century. The Government of St Maarten, St Eustatius and Saba changed hands several times between the Dutch, French and British (and, in the case of St Maarten, the Spanish, between 1633 and 1648). St Eustatius changed flag 22 times before the Dutch claimed uncontested sovereignty in 1816. The most famous Governor of one of the five Antillean islands was Peter Stuyvesant, who was Director-General of New Holland and Curaçao

from 1647 until 1664, before he moved on to the newly established Dutch colony of New Amsterdam, which later changed name and ownership and became New York (USA). The most influential Governor who brought prosperity to Curaçao was Jan Doncker (1673–79). Under his leadership trade and agriculture (important to feed the growing number of slaves) flourished.

From the beginning the interest of the Dutch in the Caribbean was confined to (legal and illegal) trade. Anything that would fetch a price or could find a buyer either in Europe, in other parts of the Caribbean, on the South American mainland and, during the American War of Independence (1775–83), on the North American continent, was traded. The range of goods transported varied from salt (an essential preservative) and lumber (Bonaire and Curaçao), to sugar, tobacco and cotton (St Maarten, St Eustatius and Saba) and slaves.

Slave trade to the Caribbean commenced in 1501, by Spanish and Portuguese slavers. The Dutch West Indian Company began the transportation of slaves from West Africa to Brazil in 1637. Curaçao became the centre of the Dutch slave trade in 1648 after the Spanish traders lost ground to the Portuguese in Brazil. In 1675 Curaçao achieved the status of 'free-trade zone', whereby traders from all nations could come to buy or sell. Between 1685 and 1713 the majority of the slaves transported from West Africa into the Caribbean passed through Curaçao. In the 18th century, St Eustatius took over this role from Curaçao, supplying slaves to plantations in Suriname and the counties of Essequibo, Demerara and Berbice (located in what is now known as Guyana). In the 17th century the Dutch traders transported 100,000 slaves from Africa to the Americas. Together with the 400,000 slaves they expatriated in the 18th century this represents 5% of the total Atlantic slave trade which took place from the 16th century until its abolition in the 19th century.

Although the islands of Aruba, Bonaire and Curaçao were not really suited for the cultivation of any crops, planters came to these islands in the 17th century. The majority of these white planters originated from the Protestant south-west of the Netherlands (Zeeland) and were referred to as 'high Protestants'. Also, Jews from Portugal and Portuguese Jews from former Dutch colonies in Brazil arrived in Curaçao to buy land and establish plantations. Together with these successful white settlers came Europeans who had left or had been forced to leave Europe for a variety of other reasons. These settlers made up the group of so-called 'low Protestants', or 'poor whites'. Small groups of refugees from Colombia and Venezuela also took up residence on the islands.

The Protestant traders from Zeeland were also the first Europeans to colonize the 'S' Islands. Because British and French influence was more pronounced in this part of the Caribbean, a mixture of white Europeans (mainly English, Irish and Scottish and, on St Maarten, some French and English-Americans) occupied these islands in the 17th and 18th centuries. These settlers also brought knowledge about the cultivation of sugar cane, a crop that was introduced in 1650.

During the American War of Independence the island of St Eustatius became well known for supplying the rebels from the American colonies (later to become the USA) with goods, which enabled them to continue the war against the British. This continued supply to the rebels through St Eustatius, as well as the island's official recognition of the flag of the rebel American colonies in 1776, forced the British to declare war on the Dutch Republic. The conflict that followed was the beginning of the end of the success of Dutch trading in the Caribbean in general, and the shipment and transhipment of goods and slaves through St Eustatius, in particular.

19TH CENTURY: SEARCHING FOR A NEW DIRECTION

The rule of the Dutch West India Company came to an end in 1828 and the Dutch Crown assumed responsibility for the islands. By that time the commercial value of the Dutch West Indies had lessened considerably, particularly compared with the attractions of the Dutch East Indies (now Indonesia). The Dutch territories were the last to abolish slavery in 1863, after the slave trade had ceased to exist in the Dutch colonies in 1818. The main reasons at that time to abolish slavery were the static or declining profits in the sugar industry. The growers of cane sugar could not compete with large producers such as Cuba and the discovery of beet sugar in 1747 also meant that Europe was no longer dependent on imports of cane sugar from the Caribbean.

As a result, the old plantocracy system slowly began to decline in the second half of the 19th century. After the abolition of slavery, many former slaves stayed on as wage-labourers on the plantations or in the salt pans. Others obtained or rented small pieces of land and became small farmers. One of the very few new economic opportunities which were created during this period was the mining of newly discovered deposits of phosphate on Little Curaçao. Trade with Venezuela became very difficult at the end of the 19th century, when the Venezuelan President, Antonio Guzmán Blanco, implemented regulations in order to protect Venezuela's economy.

In the early part of the 19th century the Dutch Crown possessed three colonies in the West Indies: the colony of Suriname, the colony of Curaçao (including Little Curaçao, Aruba and Bonaire) and the islands of St Maarten, St Eustatius and Saba, which were grouped together as one colony. In order to stimulate unity between these three colonies, a form of Government was attempted, with a Governor-General, seated in Paramaribo (Suriname), overlooking all three colonies. In practice, however, it proved impossible to govern the colonies in unison. Therefore, in 1845 the islands now forming the Netherlands Antilles, together with Aruba, were placed under one Governor (based in Curaçao) for the first time. The Governor was appointed by the King and, later, by the Dutch Government, which remained the major source of funding and thus retained a considerable amount of influence.

CHANGE IN FORTUNE

A sharp change in fortune for Curaçao came with the discovery of significant petroleum deposits in and around Lake Maracaibo, in Venezuela, at the turn of the 20th century. Because oil tankers could not pass over a large sandbar at the entrance to the shallow lake and since Venezuela was regarded by the Royal Dutch-Shell Company as politically unstable, a petroleum refinery was built on Curaçao in 1915. The refining industry was very successful and attracted labour from the other islands of the Netherlands Antilles and many other countries.

The people of the Netherlands Antilles had to wait until 1936 before they were given some form of self-governance and it was not until 1948 that the first real parliament (called the Staten) for the Netherlands Antilles was elected and appointed. The movement for (more) independence from the Netherlands started long before the Second World War, but gained real momentum with the foundation of the Democratic Party (Democratische Partij—DP) in 1944, which campaigned actively for independence from the Netherlands. Similar parties were established in Aruba. Following the first Round Table Conference in The Hague (Netherlands) in 1948 and the second Conference in 1954, the Statute of the Kingdom of the Netherlands was produced. This important document provided a legal framework for greater autonomy of the Netherlands Antilles and Suriname, except for matters pertaining to foreign affairs, defence, security and migration. It also created the opportunity for the Netherlands Antilles to introduce their own currency, the Netherlands Antillean guilder or florin and their own system of taxation and social security. Efraín Jonckheer became the first Prime Minister of the Netherlands Antilles in 1954, a position he held until 1968. The Statute regulations with Suriname became redundant in 1975 when Suriname gained independence.

Although the petroleum industry brought wealth and prosperity to the Netherlands Antilles in general and to Curaçao and Bonaire in particular, not everybody profited in equal terms.

This became very apparent in May 1969 when the high level of unemployment caused by the contraction of the refining industry provoked serious riots in Willemstad, necessitating the dispatch of Dutch marines to restore order. The riots revealed the existence of racial tensions but also led to a new sense of awareness, especially for the Afro-Antillean part of the population. It also resulted in a decrease in influence of the 'old white élite' (white Protestants, Portuguese Jews and Catholic leaders) and an increase in the influence of the labour movement. In the Netherlands the riots and its effects confirmed the views of many Dutch politicians that the Netherlands Antilles should be given independence as soon as possible.

TRYING OUT NEW FORMS OF CO-OPERATION

The independence movement in the Netherlands Dependencies gained momentum in Aruba when the People's Electoral Movement (Movimentu Electoral di Pueblo—MEP) gained large support under the charismatic leadership of Gilberto (Betico) Croes in the 1970s. The MEP was determined to leave the Antillean Federation and, by doing so, free itself from control by Willemstad. Croes argued that Aruba was unfairly treated by Curaçao and Aruba's budgetary contributions were excessive. The MEP's cause was endorsed by a referendum in Aruba in 1977, in which 82% of voters supported separation from the Netherlands Antilles. In 1983 it was agreed that Aruba would leave the federation in 1986 and obtain a *status aparte*, on the condition that Aruba would gain full independence by 1996. This clause was abandoned in 1993 and Aruba's *status aparte* remained more or less permanent.

Although some politicians favoured the idea of a *status aparte* for Curaçao in the early 1990s, a referendum in Curaçao in November 1993 revealed that 75% of the island's inhabitants wished to remain part of the Netherlands Antilles. On Bonaire, Saba and St Eustatius a large majority of the people voted, in October 1994, in favour of the idea to remain part of the Federation (88%, 91% and 86%, respectively). In the simultaneously held referendum on St Maarten, however, only 60% of those voting were in favour of maintaining the *status quo*. Moreover, in a subsequent referendum, held on 23 June 2000, only 4% of the people of St Maarten favoured maintaining the *status quo*. Some 69% favoured obtaining *status aparte* within the Kingdom of the Netherlands, 14% favoured complete independence and 12% preferred a restructuring of the Antilles of the Five. Although the Dutch Government was reluctant to grant *status aparte* to St Maarten, the results did indicate a need for change. Alternative scenarios for the future governance of the Antilles of the Five were expected to be proposed by the Government of the Netherlands Antilles for discussion with the Government of the Netherlands in the second half of 2001.

There was a strong tradition of migration between the islands of the Antilles. For instance, when Royal Dutch-Shell opened its petroleum refineries on Bonaire and Curaçao, many skilled and unskilled workers from St Eustatius, Saba and St Maarten went there to take up jobs. The first wave of migration from the Netherlands Antilles to the Netherlands occurred in the 1960s and 1970s, following large-scale redundancies in the petroleum industry as a result of automation and scale reductions. After the closure of the main refineries on Curaçao in 1985 the number of emigrants to the Netherlands more than doubled. The number of people from the Antilles of the Five and Aruba living in the Netherlands in 1997 was about 90,000, compared with 11,000 in 1972. Of particular concern for the Dutch Government in the 1990s was the increased influx of low-educated, young Antilleans (sometimes under-age and unaccompanied) into the Netherlands. In order to facilitate the smooth integration of this group into Dutch society, the process of acculturation was begun in the Antilles, with language and other courses that would help people to settle and find work in the Netherlands.

In 1999 alone, more than 8,000 people left the Netherlands Antilles. Similar emigration figures were expected for 2000 and 2001. According to one survey carried out in 2000, one out of five adults in the Netherlands Antilles (approximately 20,000 people) was thinking about leaving the islands. However, more Dutch people were expected to migrate to the Netherlands Antilles, following an agreement signed in July 2000 between the Governments of the Netherlands and the Netherlands

Antilles, making it easier for Dutch people to work and live in the Netherlands Antilles.

The island of St Maarten experienced great economic development in the 1970s under the leadership of Claude Wathey, the leader of the Democratic Party of St Maarten (DP—StM), who led the campaign for the island's secession. However, by the 1990s there was growing evidence to support allegations of gross economic mismanagement, drugs trafficking and corruption by Wathey and other senior DP—StM figures. In 1991 popular protests against Wathey forced him to resign and in 1994 he was convicted of charges of perjury and forgery and sentenced to 18 months' imprisonment. In 1992 the Dutch Government imposed 'higher supervision', which limited the island Government's power to make decisions on expenditure. That regime remained in place until October 1995, when it was rescinded in order to facilitate reconstruction efforts following the destruction caused in the previous month by Hurricanes Luis and Marilyn. In 1998 Hurricane José caused more damage on St Maarten and in November 1999 Hurricane Lenny caused considerable damage just before the start of the main tourist season.

In 1994 the newly appointed Prime Minister of the Netherlands Antilles, Miguel A. Pourier, negotiated a structural-adjustment programme with the International Monetary Fund (IMF). A stringent set of economic measures was introduced, designed to reduce the budget deficit, which led to public discontent, culminating in November 1995, when some 15,000 public- and private-sector workers held a strike in Curaçao, to protest against the increases in public-utility rates and petroleum prices. At elections in January 1998 Pourier's party, the Restructured Antilles Party (Partido Antía Restrukturá—PAR) lost four of its eight seats in the 22-seat legislature and won only 18.9% of the total votes cast (compared with 38.9% in 1994). The National People's Party (Partido Nashonal di Pueblo—PNP) retained its three seats, while the newly-formed Popular Workers' Crusade Party (Partido Laboral Krusado Popular—PLKP) also gained three seats. A new coalition Government (without the PAR) finally took office on 1 June 1998, under the leadership of Susanne F. C. Camelia-Römer of the PNP. A committee advising the Government produced a National Recovery Plan (*Plan Nasional*), in which very stringent measures were proposed in order to revitalize the Antillean economy. The *Plan Nasional* aimed to reduce Government spending drastically by streamlining the civil service, changing the tax system and merging and/or nationalizing government institutions and departments.

However, the *Plan Nasional* failed to show immediate visible results and in October 1999 the Government of Camelia-Römer was forced to resign. The new coalition Government, which took office in November 1999, again under the leadership of Miguel Pourier, consisted of nine coalition parties. Camelia-Römer was appointed Minister for the National Recovery Plan and Economic Affairs. An important agreement between the Government of the Netherlands Antilles and the IMF was signed in September 2000 and assessed in March 2001. This was intended to prepare the way for the design and implementation of a multi-year adjustment programme.

In a policy paper entitled 'A Future in Co-operation 1999–2002', the Dutch Government stated that the central aim of the co-operation effort between the Netherlands, the Netherlands Antilles and Aruba was to promote the self-reliance of the Kingdom partners. It emphasized the need of the Antilles of the Five to improve the quality of its administration ('good governance') and education systems, the need for the Netherlands Antilles to finance its own capital investments and to improve the efficiency of the deployment of aid money. The Dutch Government also intended that part of the aid given be used for law enforcement, in the form of providing assistance to the judiciary and the Public Prosecution Service, the Coast Guard and the prison system.

Economy

RENÉ VAN DONGEN

The mainstays of the economy of the Netherlands Antilles are the tourism industry, offshore finance activities and the petroleum-refining and transport industry. Tourism and the offshore financial sectors were the main cause of economic expansion from the 1960s. No reliable long-term economic data were available for the Netherlands Antilles, but from 1996 the growth in gross domestic product (GDP) was negative. The economic contraction was caused by a combination of factors: the damage inflicted by Hurricanes Luis and Marilyn in September 1995; the subsequent implementation of stricter monetary policy by the Government of Miguel A. Pourier; large debt accumulation; and uncertainty over a tax treaty with the USA, which depressed activity in the offshore sector. Total external debt in 1999 was an estimated NA Fl. 527.3m. (12.6% of GDP), owed mostly to the Netherlands. Financial aid from the Netherlands was likely to remain important to the islands' economies into the 21st century. More than $125m. of aid was made available by the Dutch Government in 1998 and, in the same year the European Union (EU) granted €26.6m. to the Netherlands Antilles in order to improve infrastructure. In addition, in September 2000, the Netherlands Antilles Government and a team from the International Monetary Fund (IMF) agreed upon a comprehensive medium-term economic adjustment and reform programme. As a result, the Netherlands released NA Fl. 110m. in liquidity support. The first assessment by the IMF and subsequent further measures were announced in March 2001.

In 1997 the annual rate of inflation in the Netherlands Antilles was 3.3%. This figure decreased to 1.1% in 1998, the lowest since 1992, as a result of lower inflation rates in the islands' main trading partners (Venezuela, the USA and the Netherlands) and decreasing world petroleum prices. There was a further decrease in the annual rate of inflation in 1999, to 0.4%. However, inflation rose sharply in 2000 to 5.8%, mainly owing to increases in turnover tax rates, petroleum prices and in the inflation rates of the main trading partners. Unemployment on the islands remained high, at around 14.9% of the workforce in 2000, despite massive migration to the Netherlands. On the island of Curaçao, the rate of unemployment among young people reached 35% in 1998. Most employment opportunities existed in the trade sector, where at least middle, and sometimes higher, levels of education were required. The internal market was very limited and relied heavily on imports. In 1997 the principal source of imports was Venezuela, followed by the USA, Mexico, the Netherlands and Italy. Over 60% of Curaçao's exports went to the USA in 1997, with smaller quantities being exported to Honduras, Belgium, Luxembourg, Italy and the Netherlands.

The secession of Aruba from the six-island Antillean federation in 1986 was followed by economic disruption in the region, in the form of 'capital flight' (the withdrawal of funds and investments), mostly by local citizens. The 'Antilles of the Five' had to provide Aruba with nearly one-third of the assets and 27% of the gold and foreign reserves of the former federation of six islands.

Following its election in 1994, the Pourier administration negotiated a structural-adjustment programme with the IMF, which was intended to reduce the fiscal deficit over a period of four years, from 1996. Measures included the privatization of loss-making Government services, a reduction in the number of civil servants (over 60% of the work-force was employed by the Government), a 'freeze' on salaries and a reduction in holiday allowance in 1996–98, and a reform of civil-service pensions. Furthermore, petrol and motor-fuel duties and utility prices were to be increased, and a 6% sales tax was to be introduced. Public- and private-sector workers reacted to the announced austerity measures by organizing a series of strikes in November

1995. The fiscal deficit, which had increased from US $16.3m. in 1994 to $32m. in 1995, fell sharply in 1997 as a result of the adjustment programme. By 1999, however, it had risen to $53.1m., mainly because of reduced tax, income inefficiencies in the system of tax collection and the overall economic recession.

Although the Government of Susanne F. C. Camelia-Römer (which took office in June 1998) was instrumental in the design of a National Recovery Plan (*Plan Nasional*), the Government coalition parties were unable to reach consensus on the necessary measures for a structural reduction of expenditure. This caused the collapse of the governing coalition in October 1999. A new Government, appointed in the following month and once again led by Pourier, enthusiastically began the implementation of the *Plan Nasional*, under the watchful eyes of the IMF, the Inter-American Development Bank (IDB) and the Dutch Government. In its first month in office the new coalition administration dismissed 850 civil servants and replaced the sales tax with a turnover tax, which was raised from 2% to 5% in October 1999. In order to address the economic crisis, an important piece of legislation was approved by the Staten in July 2000 for a period of one year (until August 2001). This special legislation would enable the Government of the Netherlands Antilles to accelerate considerably the processing of tax and finance laws.

The agreement signed in September 2000 between the IMF and the Government of the Netherlands Antilles sought to simplify the tax system, restructure the pension schemes and create a more flexible labour market. Furthermore, agreement was reached on a maximum limit for the fiscal deficit for 2001, the dismissal of a further 394 civil servants and the implementation of more stringent controls of the contracting of consultants. In addition, legislation was introduced preventing the cabinet from taking political decisions when the financial consequences or budgetary implications were not clear. Measures to encourage foreign investment were also announced (including the elimination of market protection and the simplification of import procedures and bureaucracy for new investors). The IMF's first assessment of the efficacy of these measures in March 2001 showed that the Government of the Netherlands Antilles needed to implement even more stringent measures to keep the 2001/02 budget deficit within the agreed limits.

TOURISM

Although the most important growth in the tourism industry took place on Aruba, the sector was a major contributor to the economy of the Netherlands Antilles. The tourist sector was the largest employer (28.1% in 1992) after the public sector. From 1995 foreign-exchange earnings from tourism increased by about 15% annually, with a total of NA Fl.1,284.1m. in 1998. The total number of stay-over tourists in the Netherlands Antilles (including Saba and St Eustatius) decreased from 738,082 in 1998 to 690,917 in 2000. The largest decreases took place in Saba (33%) and Bonaire (17%), while St Eustatius actually experienced an increase in the number of stay-over tourists (5%) over the same period. St Maarten still attracted the largest number of stay-over tourists: 432,292 in 2000. The total number of cruise passengers decreased significantly for St Maarten in 1999 as a result of the damage done by Hurricane Lenny. However, numbers had almost returned to 1998 levels by the end of 2000. The total number of cruise passengers visiting the Netherlands Antilles (excluding Saba and St Eustatius) in 2000 was the highest ever for the Antilles of the Five: 1,221,168. In particular, Bonaire is becoming increasingly popular as a cruise-ship destination: 43,477 cruise passengers visited in 2000, compared to 11,832 in 1998. Some 50% of the tourists staying over on St Maarten in 2000 were from the USA and Canada, 10.6% from other parts of the Caribbean and 3.1% from the Netherlands. Most of the tourists (29.3%) staying over on Curaçao in 2000 came from the Netherlands, with 17.5% from the USA and Canada and 15.5% from Venezuela. The number of visitors from Europe (especially the Netherlands) decreased in 2001 owing to the depreciation of the euro against the US dollar. However, more tourists arrived in Curaçao from North and South American countries.

The main attractions of Curaçao were the (largely man-made) beaches and the modern and numerous shopping facilities. Although Curaçao and Bonaire experienced a steady decline in stay-over tourists between 1996 and 2000, cruise tourism grew by 80% between 1995 and 2000. Curacao continued to invest in its tourism industry, with several large hotel complexes and a golf course under construction in 2001. At the entrance to the Curaçao harbour, a 'mega-pier' was being built, aimed at accommodating large cruise ships. The project was being funded with assistance from the EU, the Dutch Government and local resources. With additional major new tourism investments planned (Brionplein Hotel, Kura Hulanda, Cornelisbaai, Jan Thiel Baai) in the early 2000s, the prospects for the sector on Curaçao were bright.

St Maarten, with its fine beaches and exceptional duty-free port (and a large airport) had a highly developed tourist industry, accounting for approximately 65% of total tourism activities in the Netherlands Antilles in 1999. The destruction caused to St Maarten by Hurricanes Luis and Marilyn in 1995 and by Hurricane George in September 1998 resulted in a decline in the sector in the late 1990s. In 1999 the tourism sector of the Windward Islands again suffered from the impact of two hurricanes (José and Lenny), incurring a decline in numbers of stay-over and cruise tourists in 1999 and closing down some hotels for most of 2000. On the neighbouring islands of Saba and St Eustatius the tourism industry was small but very important for the local economy. Overall, the tourism sector in St Eustatius, Saba and St Maarten produced more favourable results in the 1990s than that of Curaçao and Bonaire. Prospects for the tourism industry on St Maarten for 2001 and beyond were expected to improve, with most of the room capacity restored.

FINANCIAL SERVICES AND FOREIGN TRADE

From the early 1970s banking and financial services in the Netherlands Antilles changed from an almost completely locally owned industry to a sophisticated global network. By the late 1990s many foreign banks were well-established on the islands and were specializing in 'offshore' banking facilities. In 1988 a major international trade centre opened, capitalizing upon years of accumulated financial expertise. The financial intermediation sector employed 6.9% of the working population in 1998 and contributed 11.3% of GDP in 1997. In 1994 and 1995 financial services were the second-largest net foreign-exchange earner, outstripping tourism. The 'tax-haven' facilities established on Curaçao in the 1960s offered an attractive incentive for foreign companies to channel their money through the island. Interest on overseas investments was tax-free for all US companies registered in Curaçao. Furthermore, a tax treaty signed in 1963 between the USA and the Netherlands Antilles made it possible for US companies to spend money banked in Curaçao in other countries without having to pay tax in the recipient country. These favourable tax treaties were abrogated in the late 1980s, leading to an immediate decline of Curaçao as a tax haven.

From the late 1980s the finance industry concentrated on the promotion of trade brokerage, counter-trade finance, trusts and private companies, over 40,000 of which were registered in 1995. Most transactions in the offshore finance sector were legal, but money 'laundering', involving drug cartels, became a serious problem by the mid-1990s. Legislation was introduced in 1995 aimed at combating financial crime. In 1998 the Bank of the Netherlands Antilles conducted a number of checks at several international credit institutions to ensure that sufficient efforts were being undertaken to deter and detect use of their facilities for money-laundering purposes. The Bank received assistance in this matter from the Financial Action Task Force on Money Laundering (FATF, based at the Secretariat of the Organisation for Economic Co-operation and Development, OECD) and the Caribbean Financial Action Task Force (CFATF, also based at the OECD).

In 1998–2000 the international financial and business services sector continued to perform poorly. This weak performance was reflected by a decline in both income received for services rendered and profit taxes transferred to the Government. However, following the introduction, in November 1998, of legislation to promote proper functioning of the stock-exchange markets, the introduction of a new tax regime (New Fiscal Regime—NFR) and the conclusion of a new tax arrangement for the Kingdom of the Netherlands, laid the groundwork for improvements in this sector.

Although new jurisdiction for the adequate supervision of financial institutions was introduced and much effort and capital was invested to comply with international standards of effective banking supervision, in May 2000 the Financial Stability Forum (FSF) categorized the Netherlands Antilles in group III (the lowest group) in May 2000. The FSF report focused mainly on licensing and admission processes for financial institutions, local supervisory infrastructure and instruments used to combat and prevent money laundering. In June 2000, the OECD urged the Netherlands Antilles to improve further the accountability and transparency of the financial services it was providing and in January 2001 the Netherlands Antilles, under pressure from the FATF, agreed to conform to the OECD's rules on combating harmful tax practices.

The free-trade zones at Schottegat Harbour and at Curaçao's Hato International Airport recorded a marked increase in re-exports and the number of visits in 1998. Goods destined for a market outside the Netherlands Antilles could be traded in these free-trade zones, without having to pay import duty. The increase in merchandise exports for 1998 was related almost entirely to the increased re-exporting activities of some of the main free-zone companies on Curaçao and was the main factor responsible for an improved deficit on the current account of the balance of payments in the same year. After five consecutive years of expansion, free-zone activities deteriorated significantly in 1999, mainly owing to set-backs in re-exports, increased competition from other free zones in the region and the economic downturn in some of the main export markets. However, the steep decrease in the number of free-zone visits slowed in the third quarter of 2000, when they declined by 1.1%, compared to 15.3% for the same period in 1999. Furthermore, legislation on e-commerce and on the establishment of economic zones (so-called E-zones) was adopted by the Staten in 2000 in order to promote business development.

PETROLEUM INDUSTRY

The refining industry began on Curaçao in 1915, with the construction of the plant by the Royal Dutch-Shell Company. Most of the crude petroleum for the refineries came from the nearby Venezuelan field and the refined products were mainly shipped to the USA. At its peak, in the 1950s, the industry produced 400,000 barrels per day (b/d), accounting for about one-third of employment and 40% of the Antillean gross national product (GNP). During the 1970s the industry diversified into petroleum transhipment and petroleum storage. Huge terminals were built on Curaçao to handle supertankers carrying African and Middle Eastern crude petroleum and petroleum products. The terminal at Bullen Bay on Curaçao remained one of the world's largest into the 1990s. Since US ports on the eastern seaboard could not handle heavy tankers, the deep-water facilities of the two islands were ideal. Smaller terminals were also built on Bonaire and St Eustatius, and by 1980 the revenue from transhiping almost equalled that of refining. However, the refining industry suffered a reverse when, in the early 1980s, the US federal authorities permitted the construction of large offshore terminals on the US Gulf of Mexico and eastern coasts.

The situation deteriorated further in the 1980s, as the new US terminals often fed into US refineries. As the price of petroleum fell and with reductions in supplies by Venezuela, as a result of production quotas by the Organization of the Petroleum Exporting Countries (OPEC), the Netherlands Antilles' refining industry became unprofitable. In September 1985, the Government purchased the plant for a nominal one guilder (plus US $47m. for stocks and machinery), after which it was leased to the Venezuelan state petroleum company, Petróleos de Venezuela, SA (PDVSA) for 10 years. Of the 1,900 jobs at the plant, 1,700 were saved when the refinery reopened as the Refinería Isla (Curazao), SA, with PDVSA responsible for operating and maintenance costs. In November 1987 PDVSA agreed to spend $25m. to adapt the refinery to process heavy crude petroleum. In 1991 capacity increased to 470,000 b/d, from the original 320,000 b/d, mostly destined for markets in Latin American and the Caribbean. In 1989 PDVSA also leased the huge 7.7m.-barrel storage facility on Bonaire.

However, there was considerable concern that PDVSA would not renew the refinery's lease. The plant, located in an urban area, was a major contributor to pollution on the island and required significant investment in order to meet more stringent

environmental standards. Moreover, the market demanded cleaner fuels by the 1990s, and the Venezuelan Government, lacking capital, was already committed to upgrading two refineries in Venezuela. Nevertheless, in 1995 PDVSA extended the lease for a further 20 years, ensuring that Curaçao would not be entirely dependent upon Dutch financial support. PDVSA planned to invest at the plant through a build-operate-own scheme. In 1995 petroleum accounted for 54.6% of imports and 84.3% of exports. Although there was no increase on the previous year in the total amount of foreign exchange generated by the refining industry in 1998 (NA Fl.206.6m.), the petroleum industry managed to produce at lower operational costs. Upgrading programmes begun in the late 1990s were intended to secure the refinery's long-term viability. The third quarter results for 2000 for the petroleum sector were favourable. Petroleum refining grew by 5.9% in contrast to a fall of 11.7% in the same period in 1999.

TRANSPORT

The performance of the national carrier of the Netherlands Antilles, Antilliaanse Luchtvaart Maatschappij (ALM—Antillean Airlines), deteriorated from 1999 and the privatization of the airline, which the Antillean Government agreed on in 1999, seemed inevitable by July 2001. Regional and international transit arrivals at Curaçao's airport increased in the late 1990s, particularly following the establishment of a free-trade zone there in 1998.

The port of Curaçao was one of the largest natural ports in the world and played an important role in Caribbean petroleum transhipment. After a slight increase in harbour activities in Curaçao and St. Eustatius in 1998, performance for all harbours in the Netherlands Antilles deteriorated in 1999. For the third quarter of 2000, Curaçao's ship-repair industry grew, following a decline in the corresponding quarter of 1999. Furthermore, the number of ships piloted into the harbour rose in the third quarter of 2000, in particular owing to an increase in the number of tankers, cruise ships and other types of vessels using the port.

MANUFACTURING AND AGRICULTURE

The Netherlands Antilles has a very small, highly-protected manufacturing sector. Its main sub-sectors were food processing, the production of Curaçao liqueur and the manufacture of paper, plastics and textiles. There was also a dry dock at Curaçao. In 1997 manufacturing contributed 5.7% of GDP and employed 8.8% of the economically active population on Curaçao in 1998. The mining sector only employed 0.2% of the working population on Curaçao in 1998. The poor quality of the soils, combined with water shortages (especially on Curaçao and Bonaire) restricted agricultural development. The major crops and products used to be aloes, charcoal, goat meat, goatskins, sorghum and divi-divi nuts (nuts from the Casealpinia coriaria tree used in the tanning industry). Aloe (Aloe barbadensis) was used in the pharmaceutical industry and Bonaire was a major exporter until 1973, when production ended.

By the late 1990s cultivation of groundnuts, beans, fresh vegetables and tropical fruit was very limited. The Government of the Netherlands Antilles imposed restrictions on the imports of certain products (notably cucumbers, hot peppers and aubergines) in an attempt to stimulate domestic production. Irrigation with water from wells and pipe water took place on a very limited scale. Fresh water on Bonaire and Curaçao was an expensive commodity (it was manufactured in large desalination plants), making cultivation using large-scale irrigation unlikely. Agriculture, forestry and fishing employed 0.9% of the Curaçao working population in 1998.

OUTLOOK

The Netherlands Antilles experienced great difficulties in adapting to altered economic fortunes at the end of the 20th century, despite great efforts to generate new business and to diversify its activities. Curaçao suffered from high salary levels, a vestige of the petroleum-refining industry, and only moderate productivity levels. For example, in 1993 labour charges in the large but financially troubled Curaçao dry-dock company were US $20 per hour, compared to an average $12 in Western Europe. However, in the early part of 2001 prospects for Curaçao appeared more positive. Estimates from the island's Chamber of Commerce and Industry suggested that, for the first time since 1997, large-scale investment in the tourist industry, petroleum refineries and the energy sector were returning. In addition, the Caribbean Rim Investment Initiative (a three-year OECD programme , launched in April 2001) aimed to maximize foreign investment in the Caribbean and Latin America.

The economic situation on the island of Bonaire was at least as serious as on Curaçao. St Maarten demonstrated great economic resilience after being hit by several hurricanes in the 1990s. That island's economic success, as well as the results of the referendum which took place on the 23 June 2000, again raised the issue of St Maarten's proposed *status aparte* within the Antilles of the Five. Developments on St Eustatius and Saba remained stable, with tourism the most important economic activity.

The structural-adjustment programme, designed and implemented with the help of the IMF and the Dutch Government in 1996, did attempt to improve public finances, restore government credibility, attain a sustainable level of external reserves and reduce the number of civil servants. Although the Government employed a large number of people, the shortage of skilled personnel in the islands' bureaucracies limited economic planning. However, by 1999 the programme had failed to revive economic activity, which declined for a fourth consecutive year. A committee advising the Camelia-Römer Government wrote a National Recovery Plan (*Plan Nasional*), outlining strategies

to control state spending and implement practices of 'good governance'. A further elaboration of corrective measures was imperative if the persistent downturn in economic activities was to be halted and a deepening of the recession avoided. The IDB advised measures, including a reduction in state bureaucracy, the removal of market-protection safeguards and a relaxation of labour-market restrictions, complemented with a strengthening of telecommunication infrastructure and education standards, with the aim of attracting investment.

The Pourier Government, which took office in November 1999, showed that it was able to take unpopular and bold steps to ensure implementation of the National Recovery Plan. For the Plan to be implemented in full, more steps still had to be taken to improve the collection of taxes, restructure pension schemes, privatize companies, reform the labour market, phase out the market-protection regime, and make government services more cost effective. An IMF assessment of the implementation of the economic adjustment and reform programme in early 2001 showed that the Netherlands Antilles had made a strong start, but that there was still a great deal left to be done.

The conclusion of the negotiations with the IMF on a multi-year adjustment programme and the full and timely implementation of the proposed measures, would certainly help to restore confidence in the Antillean economy. Before private businesses, donor agencies and the Dutch Government would be disposed to invest money or grant additional financial support, however, important conditions would have to be met.

Statistical Survey

Sources (unless otherwise stated): Centraal Bureau voor de Statistiek, Fort Amsterdam, Willemstad, Curaçao; tel. (9) 61-1329; internet www.gov.an/cbs; Bank van de Nederlandse Antillen, Breedestraat 1, Willemstad, Curaçao; tel. (9) 434-5500; fax (9) 461-5004; e-mail info@centralbank.an; internet centralbank.an.

AREA AND POPULATION

Area (sq km): Curaçao 444; Bonaire 288; St Maarten (Dutch sector) 34; St Eustatius 21; Saba 13; Total 800 (309 sq miles).

Population: 171,620 (males 82,808; females 88,812) at census of 1 February 1981 (excluding adjustment for underenumeration, estimated at 2.0%); 189,474 (males 90,707; females 98,767) at census of 27 January 1992 (excluding adjustment for underenumeration, estimated at 3.2%); 207,175 (males 99,662; females 107,513) at 31 December 1996 (official estimate). *By island* (estimate, 31 December 1996): Curaçao 152,700; Bonaire 14,169; St Maarten (Dutch sector) 36,231; St Eustatius 2,609; Saba 1,466.

Density (per sq km, 31 December 1996): Curaçao 344; Bonaire 49; St Maarten (Dutch sector) 1,066; St Eustatius 124; Saba 113; Total 259.

Principal Town (1992): Willemstad (capital), population 2,345. Source: UN, *Demographic Yearbook*.

Births, Marriages and Deaths (1996): Registered live births 3,756; Registered marriages 1,418; Registered deaths 1,323.

Expectation of Life (World Bank estimates, years at birth, 1999): 76. Source: World Bank, *World Development Indicators*.

Economically Active Population (Curaçao only, persons aged 15 years and over, 1998): Agriculture, forestry and fishing 534; Mining and quarrying 95; Manufacturing 4,789; Electricity, gas and water 906; Construction 4,280; Wholesale and retail trade, repairs 10,362; Hotels and restaurants 3,673; Transport, storage and communications 4,092; Financial intermediation 3,716; Real estate, renting and business activities 3,958; Public administration, defence and social security 5,683; Education 2,791; Health and social work 4,207; Other community, social and personal services 3,046; Private households with employed persons 1,971; Total employed 54,181 (males 29,526, females 24,655); Unemployed 10,827 (males 4,841, females 5,986); Total labour force 65,008 (males 34,367, females 30,641).
Total employed (Curaçao, Bonaire, St Maarten, St Eustatius, Saba) 82,980. Source: ILO.

AGRICULTURE, ETC.

Livestock (FAO estimates, '000 head, 2000: Asses 3; Cattle 1; Pigs 2; Goats 13; Sheep 7. Source: FAO.

Livestock Products ('000 metric tons, 2000): Meat 1; Hen eggs 1 (FAO estimate). Source: FAO.

Fishing (FAO estimates, metric tons, live weight, 1998): Capture 1,020 (Wahoo 200, Skipjack tuna 40, Blackfin tuna 50, Yellowfin tuna 150, Atlantic blue marlin 50, Other marine fishes 520); Aquaculture 5; Total catch 1,025. Source: FAO, *Yearbook of Fishery Statistics*.

MINING

Production ('000 metric tons, 1996, estimate): Salt (unrefined) 366. Source: UN, *Industrial Commodity Statistics Yearbook*.

INDUSTRY

Production ('000 metric tons, unless otherwise indicated, 1996, estimates): Kerosene 38; Jet fuel 820; Residual fuel oils 5,013; Lubricating oils 377; Petroleum bitumen (asphalt) 464; Liquefied petroleum gas 63; Motor spirit (petrol) 1,790; Aviation gasoline 10; Distillate fuel oils (gas oil) 2,218; Sulphur (recovered) 120 (1993); Electric energy (million kWh) 1,482. Source: UN, *Industrial Commodity Statistics Yearbook*.

FINANCE

Currency and Exchange Rates: 100 cents = 1 Netherlands Antilles gulden (guilder) or florin (NA Fl.). *Sterling, Dollar and Euro Equivalents* (30 April 2001): £1 sterling = NA Fl. 2.563; US $1 = NA Fl. 1.790; €1 = NA Fl. 1.589; NA Fl. 100 = £39.02 = $55.87 = €62.94. *Exchange Rate:* In December 1971 the central bank's midpoint rate was fixed at US $1 = NA Fl. 1.80. In 1989 this was adjusted to $1 = NA Fl. 1.79. The US dollar also circulates on St Maarten.

Central Government Budget (NA Fl. million, 2000): *Revenue:* Tax revenue 519.0 (Taxes on property 17.0, Taxes on goods and services 363.5, Sales tax 231.8, Licences 16.6, Taxes on international trade and transactions 128.1, Other taxes 10.4); Non-tax and capital revenue 92.3; Total 611.3 (excl. grants received 10.0). *Expenditure:* Wages and salaries 262.8; Other goods and services 96.1; Interest payments 77.2; Subsidies to public companies 10.8; Current transfers 241.5; Capital expenditure (incl. transfers and net lending) 55.3; Total 743.7.

Note: Total General Government budget (incl. island governments, NA Fl. million, 2000): *Revenue:* 1,223.3; *Expenditure:* 1,367.2.

Source: IMF, *Netherlands Antilles: Recent Developments, Selected Issues and Statistical Appendix* (May 2001).

International Reserves (US $ million at 31 December 2000): Gold (national valuation) 78; Foreign exchange 261; Total 339. Source: IMF, *International Financial Statistics*.

Money Supply (NA Fl. million at 31 December 2000): Currency outside banks 188.9; Demand deposits at commercial banks 806.8; Total (incl. others) 1,000. Source: IMF, *International Financial Statistics*.

Cost of Living (Consumer Price Index; base: 1995 = 100): All items 108.2 in 1998; 108.6 in 1999; 114.9 in 2000. Source: IMF, *International Financial Statistics*.

Gross Domestic Product (million NA Fl. at current prices, 1997): Agriculture, fishing, mining, etc. 28.7; Manufacturing 271.0; Electricity, gas and water 194.4; Construction 330.6; Wholesale and retail trade 926.4; Hotels and restaurants 163.2; Transport, storage and communications 500.1; Financial intermediation 538.7; Real estate, renting and business activities 634.4; Healthcare and social services 199.5; Other community, social and personal services 196.8; Services to households 26.9; Government services 748.1; *Sub-total* 4,758.8; *Less* Imputed bank service charge 221.7; *Gross domestic product* 4,537.1. Source: IMF, *Netherlands Antilles: Recent Developments, Selected Issues and Statistical Appendix* (May 2001).

Balance of Payments (cash basis, NA Fl. million, 1999): Exports of goods f.o.b. 752.7; Imports of goods f.o.b. −2,458.5; *Trade balance* −1,705.8; Exports of services 2,618.5; Imports of services −1,283.8; *Balance on goods and services* −371.1; Other income received 180.9; Other income paid −168.4; *Balance on goods, services and income* −363.0; Current transfers received 324.0; Current transfers paid −328.4; *Current balance* −363.0; Direct investment abroad 6.0; Direct investment from abroad 11.0; Portfolio investment inflow 487.1; Portfolio investment outflow −505.4; Other capital inflow 590.4; Other capital outflow −461.2; Net errors and omissions 19.3; *Overall balance* 22.1. Source: Bank van de Nederlandse Antillen *Quarterly Bulletin*.

EXTERNAL TRADE

Principal Commodities (US $ million, 1995): *Imports c.i.f.:* Petroleum, petroleum products, etc. 1,000.9 (Crude petroleum 889.6); Machinery and transport equipment 232.6; Total (incl. others) 1,832.5. *Exports f.o.b.:* Petroleum, petroleum products etc. 1,143.3 (Refined petroleum products 1,086.8); Total (incl. others) 1,355.8.

Principal Trading Partners (US $ million, 1995): *Imports c.i.f.:* Netherlands 195.3; USA 363.8; Venezuela 1,006.2; Total (incl. others) 1,832.5. *Exports f.o.b.:* Bahamas 41.0; Belgium-Luxembourg 44.7; Canada 33.3; Colombia 71.3; Costa Rica 63.3; Dominican Republic 73.4; Guadeloupe 47.7; Guatemala 55.5; Guyana 48.2;

Honduras 87.9; Jamaica 29.6; Netherlands 98.0; Panama 28.3; USA 188.5; Venezuela 42.6; Total (incl. others) 1,355.7. Source: UN, *International Trade Statistics Yearbook*.

TRANSPORT

Road Traffic (motor vehicles registered, 1996): Passenger cars 75,105, Lorries 17,031, Buses 722, Taxis 430, Other cars 2,842, Motor cycles 1,541, Total 97,671.

Shipping: *International Freight Traffic* (Curaçao, '000 metric tons, excl. petroleum, 1997): Goods loaded 215.2; Goods unloaded 516.7. *Merchant Fleet* (registered at 31 December 1998): Number of vessels 144; Total displacement 970,587 grt. (Source: Lloyd's Register of Shipping, *World Fleet Statistics*).

TOURISM

Tourist Arrivals: (Bonaire, Curaçao and St Maarten only): *Stopovers* ('000s): 718.8 in 1998; 704.6 in 1999; 674.8 in 2000. *Cruiseship passengers:* 1,124,266 in 1998; 850,825 in 1999; 1,221,168 in 2000.

Source: IMF, *Netherlands Antilles: Recent Developments, Selected Issues and Statistical Appendix* (May 2001).

COMMUNICATIONS MEDIA

Radio Receivers (1997): 217,000 in use.

Television Receivers (1997): 69,000 in use.

Telephones (1996): 80,000 main lines in use.

Mobile Cellular Telephones (1996): 13,977 subscribers.

Daily Newspapers (1996): 6 titles (estimated circulation 70,000 copies per issue).

Sources: UNESCO, *Statistical Yearbook*, UN, *Statistical Yearbook*.

EDUCATION

Pre-primary (1996): 77 schools; 7,720 pupils; 342 teachers.

Primary (1996): 85 schools; 24,286 pupils; 1,139 teachers.

Junior High (1996): 16 schools; 5,282 pupils; 261 teachers.

Senior High (1996): 5 schools; 3,141 pupils; 200 teachers.

Technical and Vocational (1996): 37 institutions; 8,875 pupils; 623 teachers.

Special Education (1996): 18 schools; 1,616 pupils; 204 teachers.

Teacher Training (1996): 1 institution; 217 students; 26 teachers.

University of the Netherlands Antilles (1996): 671 students; 92 teachers.

Directory

The Constitution

The form of government for the Netherlands Antilles is embodied in the Charter of the Kingdom of the Netherlands, which came into force on 20 December 1954. The Netherlands, the Netherlands Antilles and, since 1986, Aruba each enjoy full autonomy in domestic and internal affairs and are united on a basis of equality for the protection of their common interests and the granting of mutual assistance.

The monarch of the Netherlands is represented in the Netherlands Antilles by the Governor, who is appointed by the Dutch Crown for a term of six years. The central Government of the Netherlands Antilles appoints a Minister Plenipotentiary to represent the Antilles in the Government of the Kingdom. Whenever the Netherlands Council of Ministers is dealing with matters coming under the heading of joint affairs of the realm (in practice mainly foreign affairs and defence), the Council assumes the status of Council of Ministers of the Kingdom. In that event, the Minister Plenipotentiary appointed by the Government of the Netherlands Antilles takes part, with full voting powers, in the deliberations.

A legislative proposal regarding affairs of the realm and applying to the Netherlands Antilles as well as to the 'metropolitan' Netherlands is sent, simultaneously with its submission, to the Staten Generaal (the Netherlands parliament) and to the Staten (parliament) of the Netherlands Antilles. The latter body can report in writing to the Staten Generaal on the draft Kingdom Statute and designate one or more special delegates to attend the debates and furnish information in the meetings of the Chambers of the Staten Generaal. Before the final vote on a draft the Minister Plenipotentiary has the right to express an opinion on it. If he disapproves of the draft, and if in the Second Chamber a three-fifths' majority of the votes cast is not obtained, the discussions on the draft are

suspended and further deliberations take place in the Council of Ministers of the Kingdom. When special delegates attend the meetings of the Chambers this right devolves upon the delegates of the parliamentary body designated for this purpose.

The Governor has executive power in external affairs, which he exercises in co-operation with the Council of Ministers. He is assisted by an advisory council, which consists of at least five members appointed by him.

Executive power in internal affairs is vested in the nominated Council of Ministers, responsible to the Staten. The Netherlands Antilles Staten consists of 22 members, who are elected by universal adult suffrage for four years (subject to dissolution). Each island forms an electoral district. Curaçao elects 14 members, Bonaire three members, St Maarten three members and Saba and St Eustatius one member each. In the islands where more than one member is elected, the election is by proportional representation. Inhabitants have the right to vote if they have Dutch nationality and have reached 18 years of age. Voting is not compulsory. Each island territory also elects its Island Council (Curaçao 21 members, Bonaire 9, St Maarten 7, St Eustatius and Saba 5), and its internal affairs are managed by an executive council, consisting of the Gezaghebber (Lieutenant-Governor), and a number of commissioners. The central Government of the Netherlands Antilles has the right to annul any local island decision which is in conflict with the public interest or the Constitution. Control of the police, communications, monetary affairs, health and education remain under the jurisdiction of the central Government.

On 1 January 1986 Aruba acquired separate status (*status aparte*) within the Kingdom of the Netherlands. However, in economic and monetary affairs there is a co-operative union between Aruba and the Antilles of the Five, known as the 'Union of the Netherlands Antilles and Aruba'.

The Government

HEAD OF STATE

HM Queen BEATRIX of the Netherlands.
Governor: JAIME M. SALEH.

COUNCIL OF MINISTERS

The Government comprised a nine-party coalition of the Partido Antía Restrukturá (PAR), Partido Nashonal di Pueblo (PNP), the Frente Obrero i Liberashon 30 di mei (FOL), the Movimentu Antiyos Nobo (MAN), the Democratic Party—St Maarten (DP—StM), the Democratische Partij—Bonaire (DP—B), the Unión Patriótico Bonairiano (UPB), the Saint Eustatius Alliance (SEA), and the Windward Islands People's Movement (WIPM).

(August 2001)

Prime Minister, Minister of General Affairs and Development Co-operation: MIGUEL A. POURIER (PAR).

Minister of the Interior, Labour and Social Affairs: LUCILLE ANDREA GEORGE-WOUT (PAR).

Minister of Finance: W. RUSSELL VOGES (DP—StM).

Minister of Justice: Dr RUTSEL S. J. MARTHA (PNP).

Minister of Education, Culture, Youth and Sports: Dr STANLEY M. LAMP (MAN).

Minister of Traffic and Transport: MAURICE H. P. P. ADRIAENS (FOL).

Minister of Public Health and Hygiene: LAURENSO (TOON) A. ABRAHAM (DP—B).

Minister for the National Recovery Plan and Economic Affairs: SUSANNE (SUZI) F. C. CAMELIA-RÖMER (PNP).

Minister Plenipotentiary and Member of the Council of Ministers of the Realm of the Netherlands Antilles: CAREL DE HASETH (PAR).

GEZAGHEBBERS
(Lieutenant-Governors)

Bonaire: RICHARD N. HART, Wilhelminaplein 1, Kralendijk, Bonaire; tel. (7) 175330; fax (7) 175100; e-mail gezag@bonairelive.com.

Curaçao: STANLEY BETRIAN, Centraal Bestuurskantoor, Concordiastraat 24, Willemstad, Curaçao; tel. (9) 461-2900.

Saba: ANTOINE J.M. SOLAGNIER, The Bottom, Saba; tel. (416) 3215.

St Eustatius: IRWIN E. TEMMER, Oranjestad, St Eustatius; tel. (3) 2213.

St Maarten: DENNIS RICHARDSON, Central Administration, Secretariat, Philipsburg, St Maarten; tel. (5) 22233.

MINISTRIES

Office of the Governor: Fort Amsterdam 2, Willemstad, Curaçao; tel. (9) 461-2000; fax (9) 461-1412.

Ministry of Education, Culture, Youth and Sports: Boerhavestraat 16, Otrobanda, Willemstad, Curaçao; tel. (9) 462-4777; fax (9) 462-4471.

Ministry of Finance: Pietermaai 4–4A, Willemstad, Curaçao; tel. (9) 432-8000; fax (9) 461-3339.

Ministry of General Affairs and Development Co-operation: Plasa Horacio Hoyer 9, Willemstad, Curaçao; tel. (9) 461-1866; fax (9) 461-1268.

Ministry of the Interior, Labour and Social Affairs: Schouwburgweg 24, Gaito, Willemstad, Curaçao; tel. (9) 461-6211; fax (9) 461-5553.

Ministry of Justice: Willhelminaplein, Willemstad, Curaçao; tel. (9) 463-0299; fax (9) 465-8083.

Ministry for the National Recovery Plan and Economic Affairs: Scharlooweg 106, Willemstad, Curaçao; tel. (9) 465-6236; fax (9) 465-6316; e-mail info.DEZ@ibm.net.

Ministry of Public Health and Hygiene: Heelsumstraat, Willemstad, Curaçao; tel. (9) 461-4555; fax (9) 461-2388.

Ministry of Traffic and Transport: Fort Amsterdam 17, Willemstad, Curaçao; tel. (9) 461-3988.

Office of the Minister Plenipotentiary of the Netherlands Antilles: Antillenhuis, Badhuisweg 173–175, 2597 JP The Hague, the Netherlands; tel. (70) 306-6111; fax (70) 306-6110.

Legislature
STATEN

Speaker: ERROL COVA.

General Election, 30 January 1998

Party	% of votes	Seats
Partido Antía Restrukturá . . .	18.9	4
Partido Nashonal di Pueblo . . .	14.9	3
Partido Laboral Krusado Popular . .	13.9	3
Frente Obrero i Liberashon 30 di mei .	10.4	2
Movimentu Antiyas Nobo . . .	8.4	2
Democratic Party—St Maarten . .	5.3	2
Democratische Partij—Bonaire . .	2.8	2
St Maarten Patriotic Alliance . .	3.7	1
Unión Patriótico Bonairiano . . .	2.5	1
Saint Eustatius Alliance . . .	0.5	1
Windward Islands People's Movement . .	0.4	1
Others	18.3	—
Total	**100.0**	**22**

Political Organizations

Democratic Party—St Maarten (DP—StM): Tamarind Tree Drive 4, Union Rd, Cole Bay, St Maarten; tel. (5) 31166; fax (5) 24296; Leader SARAH WESCOTT-WILLIAMS.

Democratic Party—Statia (DP—StE): Oranjestad, St Eustatius; Leader KENNETH VAN PUTTEN.

Democratische Partij—Bonaire (DP—B) (Democratic Party—Bonaire): Kaya America 13A, POB 294, Kralendijk, Bonaire; tel. (7) 5923; fax (7) 7341; f. 1954; also known as Partido Democratico Boneriano; Leader JOPIE ABRAHAM.

Democratische Partij—Curaçao (DP—C) (Democratic Party—Curaçao): Neptunusweg 28, Willemstad, Curaçao; tel. (9) 75432; f. 1944; Leader RAYMOND BENTOERA.

Frente Obrero i Liberashon 30 di mei (FOL) (Workers' Liberation Front of 30 May): Mayaguanaweg 16, Willemstad, Curaçao; tel. (9) 461-8105; f. 1969; Leaders ANTHONY GODETT, RIGNALD LAK, EDITHA WRIGHT.

Movimentu Antiyas Nobo (MAN) (Movement for a New Antilles): Landhuis Morgenster, Willemstad, Curaçao; tel. (9) 468-4781; f. 1971; socialist; Leader DOMINICO (DON) F. MARTINA.

Nos Patria (Our Fatherland): Willemstad, Curaçao; Leader CHIN BEHILIA.

Partido Antía Restrukturá (PAR) (Restructured Antilles Party): Fokkerweg 28, Willemstad, Curaçao; tel. (9) 465-2566; fax (9) 465-2622; e-mail par@partidopar.com; internet www.partidopar.com; f. 1993; social-Christian ideology; Pres. MIGUEL A. POURIER; Sec. PEDRO J. ATACHO.

Partido Kousa Akshan Sosial (KAS): Santa Rasaweg Naast 156, Willemstad, Curaçao; tel. (9) 747-2660; Leader BERNARD S. A. DEMEI.

Partido Laboral Krusado Popular (PLKP): Schouwburgweg 44, Willemstad, Curaçao; tel. (9) 737-0644; fax (9) 737-0831; internet www.cur.net/krusado; f. 1997; Leader ERROL A. COVA.

Partido Nashonal di Pueblo (PNP) (National People's Party): Winston Churchillweg 133, Willemstad, Curaçao; tel. (9) 869-6777; fax (9) 869-6688; f. 1948; also known as Nationale Volkspartij; Social Christian Party; Pres. MARIA LIBERIA-PETERS; Leader SUSANNE F. C. CAMELIA-RÖMER.

Partido Obrero di Bonaire (Bonaire Workers' Party): Kralendijk, Bonaire.

Partido Union den Reino Ulandés (PURU): Binnenweg 11, Willemstad, Curaçao; Leader FREDDY I. ANTERSUN.

People's Democratic Party (PDP): Philipsburg, St Maarten; tel. (5) 22696; Leader MILLICENT DE WEEVER.

Saba Democratic Labour Movement (SDLM): Saba; tel. (4) 63311; fax (4) 63434; Leader STEVE HASSELL.

Saint Eustatius Alliance (SEA): Oranjestad, St Eustatius; Leader INGRID WHITFIELD.

Serious Alternative People's Party (SAPP): St Maarten; Leader JULIAN ROLLOCKS.

St Maarten Patriotic Alliance (SPA): Frontstraat 69, Philipsburg, St Maarten; tel. (5) 31064; fax (5) 31065; Leader VANCE JAMES, Jr.

Social Independiente (SI): Willemstad, Curaçao; f. 1986 by fmr PNP mems in Curaçao; formed electoral alliance with FOL for 1990 election; Leader GEORGE HUECK.

Unión Patriótico Bonairiano (UPB) (Patriotic Union of Bonaire): Kaya Sabana 22, Kralendijk, Bonaire; tel. (7) 8906; fax (7) 5552; 2,134 mems; Leader Ramonsito T. Booi; Sec.-Gen. C. V. Winklaar.

Windward Islands People's Movement (WIPM): Windwardside, POB 525, Saba; tel. (4) 2244; Chair. and Leader Will Johnston; Sec.-Gen. Dave Levenstone.

Judicial System

Legal authority is exercised by the Court of First Instance (which sits in all the islands) and in appeal by the Joint High Court of Justice of the Netherlands Antilles and Aruba. The members of the Joint High Court of Justice sit singly as judges in the Courts of First Instance. The Chief Justice of the Joint High Court of Justice, its members (a maximum of 30) and the Attorneys-General of the Netherlands Antilles and of Aruba are appointed for life by the Dutch monarch, after consultation with the Governments of the Netherlands Antilles and Aruba.

Joint High Court of Justice: Wilhelminaplein 4, Willemstad, Curaçao; tel. (9) 463-4111; fax (9) 461-8341.

Chief Justice of the Joint High Court: Dr L. A. J. de Lannoy.

Attorney-General of the Netherlands Antilles: Dr F. M. D. L. S. Goedgedrag.

Secretary-Executive of the Joint High Court: Dr N. V. Ribeiro.

Religion

CHRISTIANITY

Most of the population were Christian, the predominant denomination being Roman Catholicism. According to the 1992 census, Roman Catholics formed the largest single group on four of the five islands: 82% of the population of Bonaire, 81% on Curaçao, 65% on Saba and 41% on St Maarten. On St Eustatius the Methodists formed the largest single denomination (31%). Of the other denominations, the main ones were the Anglicans and the Dutch Reformed Church. There were also small communities of Jews, Muslims and Bahá'ís.

Curaçaose Raad van Kerken (Curaçao Council of Churches): Barenblaan 11, Willemstad, Curaçao; tel. (9) 737-3070; fax (9) 7362183; f. 1958; six member churches; Chair. Ida Visser; Exec. Sec. Paul van der Waal.

The Roman Catholic Church

The Netherlands Antilles and Aruba together form the diocese of Willemstad, suffragan to the archdiocese of Port of Spain (Trinidad and Tobago). At 31 December 1999 the diocese numbered an estimated 235,526 adherents (some 79% of the total population). The Bishop participates in the Antilles Episcopal Conference, currently based in Trinidad and Tobago.

Bishop of Willemstad: Rt Rev. Willem Michel Ellis, Bisdom, Breedestraat 31, Otrobanda, Willemstad, Curaçao; tel. (9) 462-5857; fax (9) 462-7437; e-mail bisdomwstad@curinfo.an.

The Anglican Communion

Saba, St Eustatius and St Maarten form part of the diocese of the North Eastern Caribbean and Aruba, within the Church in the Province of the West Indies. The Bishop is resident in The Valley, Anguilla.

Other Churches

Iglesia Protestant Uni (United Protestant Church): Fortkerk, Fort Amsterdam, Willemstad, Curaçao; tel. (9) 461-1139; fax (9) 465-7481; f. 1825 by union of Dutch Reformed and Evangelical Lutheran Churches; Pres. D. J. Lopes; 3 congregations; 11,280 adherents.

Methodist Church: Oranjestad, St Eustatius.

Other denominations active in the islands include the Moravian, Apostolic Faith, Wesleyan Holiness and Norwegian Seamen's Churches, the Baptists, Calvinists, Jehovah's Witnesses, Evangelists, Seventh-day Adventists, the Church of Christ and the New Testament Church of God.

JUDAISM

Reconstructionist Shephardi Congregation Mikvé Israel-Emanuel: Hanchi di Snoa 29, POB 322, Willemstad, Curaçao; tel. (9) 461-1067; fax (9) 465-4141; e-mail board@snoa.com; internet www.snoa.com; f. 1732 on present site; about 350 mems.

Orthodox Ashkenazi Congregation Shaarei Tsedek: Leliweg 1a, Willemstad, Curaçao; tel. (9) 737-5738; 100 mems.

The Press

Algemeen Dagblad: Daphneweg 44, POB 725, Willemstad, Curaçao; tel. (9) 747-2200; fax (9) 747-2257; e-mail adcarib@cura.net; internet www.ad-caribbean.com; daily; Dutch: Editor Noud Köper.

Amigoe: Scherpenheuvel z/n, POB 577, Willemstad, Curaçao; tel. (9) 467-2000; fax (9) 467-4524; e-mail amigoe@amigoe.com; internet www.amigoe.com; f. 1884; Christian; daily; evening; Dutch; Dir Ingrid de Maayer-Hollander; Chief Editor Norbert Hendrikse; circ. 12,000.

Bala: Noord Zapateer nst 13, Willemstad, Curaçao; tel. (9) 467-1646; fax (9) 467-1041; daily; Papiamento.

Beurs- en Nieuwsberichten: A. M. Chumaceiro Blvd 5, POB 741, Willemstad, Curaçao; tel. (9) 465-4544; fax (9) 465-3411; f. 1935; daily; evening; Dutch; Editor L. Schenk; circ. 8,000.

Bonaire Holiday: POB 569, Curaçao; tel. (9) 767-1403; fax (9) 767-2003; f. 1971; tourist guide; English; 3 a year; circ. 95,000.

The Business Journal: Indjuweg 30A, Willemstad, Curaçao; tel. (9) 461-1367; fax (9) 461-1955; monthly; English.

The Chronicle: Pointe Blanche, Philipsburg, St Maarten; tel. (5) 23919; daily; English.

Colors: Liberty Publications, Curaçao; tel. and fax (9) 869-6066; e-mail colors@curacao-online.net; internet www.curacao-online.net/colors; f. 1998; general interest magazine; 4 a year; Publr Tirzah Z. B. Libert.

De Curaçaosche Courant: Frederikstraat 123, POB 15, Willemstad, Curaçao; tel. (9) 461-2766; fax (9) 462-6535; f. 1812; weekly; Dutch; Editor J. Koridon.

Curaçao Holiday: POB 569, Curaçao; tel. (9) 767-1403; fax (9) 767-2003; f. 1960; tourist guide; English; 3 a year; circ. 300,000.

Daily Herald: Front St 17, POB 828, Philipsburg, St Maarten; tel. (5) 25253; fax (5) 25913; e-mail editorial@thedailyherald.com; internet www.thedailyherald.com; daily; English.

Extra: W. I. Compagniestraat 41, Willemstad, Curaçao; tel. (9) 462-4595; fax (9) 462-7575; daily; morning; Papiamento; Man. R. Yrausquin; Editor Mike Oehlers; circ. 20,000.

Know-How: Schottegatweg Oost 56, POB 473, Willemstad, Curaçao; tel. (9) 736-7079; fax (9) 736-7080; monthly; English.

Newsletter of Curaçao Trade and Industry Association: Kaya Junior Salas 1, POB 49, Willemstad, Curaçao; tel. (9) 461-1210; fax (9) 461-5422; f. 1972; monthly; English and Dutch; economic and industrial paper.

Nobo: Scherpenheuvel w/n, POB 323, Willemstad, Curaçao; tel. (9) 467-3500; fax (9) 467-2783; daily; evening; Papiamento; Editor Carlos Daantje; circ. 15,000.

Nos Isla: Refineria Isla (Curazao) SA, Emmastad, Curaçao; 2 a month; Papiamento; circ. 1,200.

Noticiero: Willemstad, Curaçao; tel. (9) 461-7744; fax (9) 461-7811; daily; Papiamento; Editor Rigoberto Galan Melendrez.

La Prensa: W. I. Compagniestraat 41, Willemstad, Curaçao; tel. (9) 462-3850; fax (9) 462-5983; e-mail webmaster@laprensacur.com; internet www.laprensacur.com; f. 1929; daily; evening; Papiamento; Man. R. Yrausquin; Editor Sigfried Rigaud; circ. 10,750.

Saba Herald: The Level, Saba; tel. (4) 2244; f. 1968; monthly; news, local history; Editor Will Johnson; circ. 500.

St Maarten Guardian: Vlaun Bldg, Pondfill, POB 1046, Philipsburg, St Maarten; tel. (5) 26022; fax (5) 26043; e-mail guardian@sintmaarten.net; f. 1989; daily; English; Man. Dir Richard F. Gibson; Man. Editor Joseph Dominique; circ. 4,000.

St Maarten Holiday: POB 569, Curaçao; tel. (9) 767-1403; fax (9) 767-2003; f. 1968; tourist guide; English; 3 a year; circ. 175,000.

Teen Times: St Maarten; e-mail info@teentimes.com; internet www.teentimes.com; for teenagers by teenagers; sponsored by The Daily Herald; English; Editor-in-Chief Michael Granger.

Ultimo Noticia: Frederikstraat 123, Willemstad, Curaçao; tel. (9) 462-3444; fax (9) 462-6535; daily; morning; Papiamento; Editor A. A. Jonckheer.

La Unión: Rotaprint NV, Willemstad, Curaçao; weekly; Papiamento.

NEWS AGENCIES

Algemeen Nederlands Persbureau (ANP) (The Netherlands): Panoramaweg 5, POB 439, Willemstad, Curaçao; tel. (9) 461-2233; fax (9) 461-7431; Representative Ronnie Rens.

Associated Press (AP) (USA): Roodeweg 64, Willemstad, Curaçao; tel. (9) 462-6586; Representative Orlando Cuales.

Publishers

Curaçao Drukkerij en Uitgevers Maatschappij: Willemstad, Curaçao.

Ediciones Populares: W. I. Compagniestraat 41, Willemstad, Curaçao; f. 1929; Dir RONALD YRAUSQUIN.

Drukkerij Scherpenheuvel, NV: Scherpenheuvel, POB 60, Willemstad, Curaçao; tel. (9) 467-1134.

Drukkerij de Stad NV: W. I. Compagniestraat 41, Willemstad, Curaçao; tel. (9) 462-3878; fax (9) 462-2175; e-mail destad@ibm.net; f. 1929; Dir KENRICK YRAUSQUIN.

Holiday Publications: POB 569, Curaçao; tel. (9) 767-1403; fax (9) 767-2003.

Offsetdrukkerij Intergrafia, NV: Essoweg 54, Willemstad,Curaçao; tel. (9) 464-3180.

Broadcasting and Communications

TELECOMMUNICATIONS

Antelecom N.V.: Schouwburgweg 22, POB 103, Willemstad,Curaçao; tel. (9) 463-1111; fax (9) 463-1321.

Servicio de Telekomunikashon (SETEL): F. D. Rooseveltweg 337, POB 3177, Willemstad, Curaçao; tel. (9) 833-1222; fax (9) 868-2596; e-mail setel@curinfo.an; internet www.curinfo.an; f. 1979; telecommunications equipment and network provider; state-owned, but expected to be privatized; Pres. ANGEL R. KOOK; Man. Dir JULIO CONSTANSIA; 400 employees.

Smitcoms N.V.: Dr A. C. Wathey Cruise & Cargo Facility, St Maarten; tel. (54) 29140; fax (54) 29141; e-mail matthews@sintmaarten.net; internet smitcomsltd.com; f. 2000; international telephone network provider; Man. Dir CURTIS K. HAYNES.

St Maarten Telephone Co (TelEm): C. A. Cannegieter St 17, Philipsburg, St Maarten; tel. (54) 22278; fax (54) 30101; e-mail lpeters@telem.an; f. 1975; local landline and value-added services, also operates TelCell digital cellular service; 15,000 subscribers; Man. Dir CURTIS K. HAYNES.

BROADCASTING

Radio

Easy 97.9 FM: Arikokweg 19A, Willemstad, Curaçao; tel. (9) 462-3162; fax (9) 462-8712; e-mail radio@easyfm.com; internet www.easyfm.com; Dir KEVIN CARTHY.

Radio Caribe: Ledaweg 35, Brievengat, Willemstad, Curaçao; tel. (9) 736-9555; fax (9) 736-9569; f. 1955; commercial station; programmes in Dutch, English, Spanish and Papiamento; Dir-Gen. C. R. HEILLEGGER.

Radio Curom (Curaçaose Radio-Omroep Vereniging): Roodeweg 64, POB 2169, Willemstad, Curaçao; tel. (9) 462-6586; fax (9) 462-5796; f. 1933; broadcasts in Papiamento; Dir ORLANDO CUALES.

Radiodifusión Boneriana NV: Kaya Gobernador Debrot 2, Kralendijk, Bonaire; tel. (7) 8273; fax (7) 8220; e-mail vozdibon@bonairenet.com; Owner FELICIANO DA SILVA PILOTO.

Voz di Bonaire—PJB2 (Voice of Bonaire): broadcasts in Papiamento, Spanish and Dutch.

Ritme FM—PJB4: broadcasts in Dutch.

Radio Exito: Wolkstraat 15, Willemstad, Curaçao; tel. (9) 462-5577; fax (9) 462-5580.

Radio Hoyer NV: Plasa Horacio Hoyer 21, Willemstad, Curaçao; tel. (9) 461-1678; fax (9) 461-6528; e-mail hoyer@cura.net; internet www.radiohoyer.com; f. 1954; commercial; two stations: Radio Hoyer I (mainly Papiamento, also Spanish) and II (mainly Dutch, also English) in Curaçao; Man. Dir HELEN HOYER.

Radio Korsou FM: Bataljonweg 7, POB 3250, Willemstad, Curaçao; tel. (9) 737-3012; fax (9) 737-2888; e-mail master@korsou.com; internet www.korsou.com; 24 hrs a day; programmes in Papiamento and Dutch; Gen. Man. ALAN H. EVERTSZ.

Laser 101 (101.1 FM): tel. (9) 737-7139; fax (9) 737-5215; e-mail master@laser101.com; 24 hours a day; music; English and Papiamento; Gen. Man. ALAN H. EVERTSZ.

Radio Paradise: ITC Building, Piscadera Bay, POB 6103, Curaçao; tel. (9) 463-6103; fax (9) 463-6404; Man. Dir J. A. VISSER.

Radio Statia—PJE3: St Eustatius Broadcasting NV, St Eustatius; tel. (3) 82262; 121@fb2 hrs daily.

Radio Tropical: Willemstad, Curaçao; tel. (9) 652467; fax (9) 652470; Dir DWIGHT RUDOLPHINA.

Semiya Broadcasting: Klipstraat 2, POB 4709, Willemstad,Curaçao; tel. (9) 462-8488; fax (9) 464-8390; Dir FERRIS THODE.

Trans World Radio (TWR): Kaya Gouverneur N. Debrotweg 64, Kralendijk, Bonaire; tel. (717) 8800; fax (717) 8808; e-mail 800am@twr.org; internet www.twr.org; religious, educational and cultural station; programmes to South, Central and North America, Caribbean in six languages; Pres. THOMAS J. LOWELL, Jr; Station Dir H. EUGENE WILLIAMS.

Voice of St Maarten—PJD2 Radio: Plaza 21, Backstreet, POB 366, Philipsburg, St Maarten; tel. (5) 22580; fax (5) 24905; also operates **PJD3** on FM (24 hrs); commercial; programmes in English; Gen. Man. DON R. HUGHES.

Voice of Saba—PJF1: The Bottom, POB 1, Saba; studio in St Maarten; tel. (5) 63213; also operates The Voice of Saba FM; Man. MAX W. NICHOLSON.

There is a relay station for Radio Nederland on Bonaire.

Television

Leeward Broadcasting Corporation—Television: Philipsburg, St Maarten; tel. (5) 23491; transmissions for approx. 10 hours daily.

Antilliaanse Televisie Mij NV (Antilles Television Co): Berg Arraret, POB 415, Willemstad, Curaçao; tel. (9) 461-1288; fax (9) 461-4138; f. 1960; operates Tele-Curaçao (formerly operated Tele-Aruba); commercial; govt-owned; also operates cable service, offering programmes from US satellite television and two Venezuelan channels; Dir JOSÉ M. CLJNTJE; Gen. Man. NORMAN K. RICHARDS.

Five television channels can be received on Curaçao, in total. Relay stations provide Bonaire with programmes from Curaçao, St Maarten with programmes from Puerto Rico, and Saba and St Eustatius with programmes from St Maarten and neighbouring islands. Curaçao has a publicly-owned cable television service, TDS.

Finance

(cap. = capital; res = reserves; dep. = deposits; m. = million; brs = branches; amounts in Netherlands Antilles guilders unless otherwise stated)

BANKING

Central Bank

Bank van de Nederlandse Antillen (Bank of the Netherlands Antilles): Breedestraat 1, Willemstad, Curaçao; tel. (9) 434-5500; fax (9) 461-5004; e-mail info@centralbank.an; internet centralbank.an; f. 1828 as Curaçaosche Bank; name changed as above 1962; cap. 30m., res 112m., dep. 439m. (Dec. 2000); Chair. M. NICOLINA; Pres. EMSLEY TROMP; brs on St Maarten and Bonaire.

Commercial Banks

ABN AMRO Bank NV: Kaya Flamboyan 1, POB 3144, Willemstad, Curaçao; tel. (9) 763-8000; fax (9) 737-0620; f. 1964; Gen. Man. H. V. IGNACIO; 6 brs.

Antilles Banking Corpn (Curaçao) NV: Wilhelminaplein 14–16, POB 763, Willemstad, Curaçao; tel. (9) 461-2822; fax (9) 461-2820; f. 1989 as McLaughlin Bank NV; name changed as above in 1997; Pres. SHAFFIE WIHBY; 3 brs.

Antilles Banking Corpn (St Maarten) NV: Cannegieterstreet, POB 465, Philipsburg, St Maarten; tel. (5) 25908; fax (5) 25964; f. 1988; Man. Dirs F. BOWMAN, C. A. GREIGG-DUNCAN.

Banco di Caribe: Schottegatweg Oost 205, POB 3786, Willemstad, Curaçao; tel. (9) 432-3000; fax (9) 461-5220; e-mail info@bancodicaribe.com; internet www.bancodicaribe.com; f. 1973; cap. 2.0m., res 30.0m., dep. 482.5m. (Dec. 1998); Gen. Man. Dir E. DE KORT, Man. R. HENRIQUEZ; 5 brs.

Banco Mercantil CA, SACA (Curaçao): Abraham de Veerstraat 1, POB 565, Willemstad, Curaçao; tel. (9) 461-8241; fax (9) 461-1824; f. 1988; Gen. Man. FRANK GIRIGORI.

Banco de Venezuela NV: POB 131, c/o Amicorp NV, Caracasbaaiweg 199, Willemstad, Curaçao; tel. (9) 434-3500; fax (9) 434-3533; f. 1993; Man. Dirs H. P. F. VON AESCH, R. YANES V., E. BORBERG.

Bank of Nova Scotia NV (Canada): Backstreet 54, POB 303, Philipsburg, St Maarten; tel. (5) 23317; fax (5) 22562; f. 1969; Man. ROBERT G. JUDD.

Barclays Bank plc (UK): 29 Front St, POB 941, Philipsburg, St Maarten; tel. (5) 23511; fax (5) 24531; f. 1959; Man. EDWARD ARMOGAN; offices in Saba and St Eustatius.

Chase Manhattan Bank NA (USA): Chase Financial Center, Vlaun Building, Cannegieter Road (Pondfill) and Mullet Bay Hotel, POB 921, Philipsburg, St Maarten; tel. (5) 23726; fax (5) 23692; f. 1971; Gen. Man. K. BUTLER.

CITCO Banking Corporation NV: Kaya Flamboyan 9, POB 707, Willemstad, Curaçao; tel. (9) 732-2322; fax (9) 732-2330; e-mail cbc@citco.com; f. 1980 as Curaçao Banking Corporation NV; Man. Dir R. F. IRAUSQUIN.

Giro Curaçao NV: Scharlooweg 35, Willemstad, Curaçao; tel. (9) 433-9999; fax (9) 461-7861; Gen. Dir L. C. BERGMAN; Financial Dir H. L. MARTHA.

ING Bank NV (Internationale Nederlanden Bank NV): Kaya W. F. G. (Jombi) Mensing 14, POB 3895, Willemstad, Curaçao; tel.

(9) 732-7000; fax (9) 732-7502; f. 1989 as Nederlandse Midden-standsbank NV: name changed as above 1992; Gen. Man. MARK SCHNEIDERS.

Maduro & Curiel's Bank NV: Plaza Jojo Correa 2–4, POB 305, Willemstad, Curaçao; tel. (9) 466-1100; fax (9) 466-1122; e-mail info@mcb-bank.com; internet www.mcb-bank.com; f. 1916 as NV Maduro's Bank, 1931 merged with Curiel's Bank; affiliated with Bank of Nova Scotia NV, Toronto; cap. 50.0m., res 87.7m., dep. 2,300.6m. (Dec. 1999); Man. Dirs W. H. L. FABRO, R. GOMES CASSERES; Pres. and CEO LIONEL CAPRILES; 17 brs.

MeesPierson (Curaçao) NV: Berg Arrarat 1, POB 3889, Willemstad, Curaçao; tel. (9) 463-9300; fax (9) 461-3769; internet www.meespierson.com; f. 1952 as Pierson, Heldring and Pierson (Curação) NV; name changed as above 1993; international banking/trust company; Gen. Man. J. F. C. BLANKVOORT.

Orco Bank NV: Dr Henry Fergusonweg 10, POB 4928, Willemstad, Curaçao; tel. (9) 737-2000; fax (9) 737-6741; e-mail info@orcobank.com; f. 1986; cap. 30.7m., res 27.5m., dep. 523.9m. (Dec. 1999); Chair. E. L. GARCIA; Man. Dir I. D. SIMON.

Rabobank Curaçao NV: Zeelandia Office Park, Kaya W.F.G. (Jombi), Mensing 14, POB 3876, Willemstad, Curaçao; tel. (9) 465-2011; fax (9) 465-2066; f. 1978; cap. 100.0m., res –21.4m., dep. 4,876.1m. (Dec. 1998); Chair. H. W. E. RIEDLIN; Gen. Man. WILLEM WAGNER.

SFT Bank NV: Schottegatweg Oost 44, POB 707, Willemstad, Curaçao; tel. (9) 732-2900; fax (9) 732-2902.

Windward Islands Bank Ltd: Clem Labega Square 7, POB 220, Philipsburg, St Maarten; affiliated to Maduro and Curiel's Bank NV; tel. (5) 22313; fax (5) 24761; f. 1960; cap. and res 3.6m., dep. 53.6m. (Dec. 1984); Man. Dirs V. P. HENRÍQUEZ, W. G. H. STRIJBOSCH.

'Offshore' Banks
(without permission to operate locally)

ABN AMRO Bank Asset Management (Curaçao) NV: Kaya Flamboyan 1, POB 3144, Willemstad, Curaçao; tel. (9) 736-6755; fax (9) 736-9246; f. 1976; Man. D. M. VROEGINDEWEY.

Abu Dhabi International Bank Inc: Kaya W. F. G. (Jombi) Mensing 36, POB 3141, Willemstad, Curaçao; tel. (9) 461-1299; fax (9) 461-5392; internet www.adibwash.com; f. 1979; cap. US $20m., res $30m., dep. $302m. (Dec. 1998); Pres. QAMBAR AL MULLA.

Banco Caracas NV: Kaya W.F.G. (Jombi) Mensing 36, POB 3141, Willemstad, Curaçao; tel. (9) 461-1299; fax (9) 461-5392; f. 1984; Pres. GEORGE L. REEVES.

Banco Consolidado NV: Handelskrade 12, POB 3141, Willemstad, Curaçao; tel. (9) 461-3423; f. 1978.

Banco Continental Overseas NV: Kaya Urdal 3, Willemstad, Curaçao; tel. (9) 736-7299; fax (9) 737-5046; f. 1981; Man. Dir HENDRIK SCHUTTE.

Banco Latino NV: De Ruyterkade 61, POB 785, Willemstad,Curaçao; tel. (9) 461-2987; fax (9) 461-6163; f. 1978; cap. US $25.0m., res $12.3m., dep. $450.8m. (Nov. 1992); Chair. Dr GUSTAVO GÓMEZ LÓPEZ; Pres. FOLCO FALCHI.

Banco Provincial Overseas NV: Santa Rosaweg 51–55, POB 5312, Willemstad, Curaçao; tel. (9) 737-6011; fax (9) 737-6346; Man. E. SUARES.

Banque Artesia Curaçao NV: Castorweg 22-24, POB 155, Willemstad, Curaçao; tel. (9) 461-8061; fax (9) 461-5151; f. 1976 as Banque Paribas Curaçao NV; name changed as above 1998.

Caribbean American Bank NV: POB 6087, TM1 10, WTC Bldg, Piscadera Bay, Willemstad, Curaçao; tel. (9) 463-6380; fax (9) 463-6556; Man. Dir Dr MARCO TULIO HENRÍQUEZ.

Crédit Lyonnais Bank Nederland NV: Office Park Zeelandia, Kaya W.F.G. (Jombi) Mensing 18, POB 599, Willemstad, Curaçao; tel. (9) 461-1122; fax (9) 465-6265; Gen. Man. J. A. BROUWER.

F. Van Lanschot Bankiers (Curaçao) NV: Schottegatweg Oost 32, POB 4799, Willemstad, Curaçao; tel. (9) 737-1011; fax (9) 737-1086; f. 1962; Man. A. VAN GEEST.

First Curaçao International Bank NV: Office Park Zeelandia, Kaya W.F.G. (Jombi) Mensing 18, POB 299, Willemstad, Curaçao; tel. (9) 737-2100; fax (9) 737-2018; f. 1973; cap. and res US $55m., dep. $244m. (1988); Pres. and CEO J. CH. DEUSS; Man. M. NEUMAN-ROUIRA.

Toronto Dominion (Curaçao) NV: c/o SCRIBA NV, Polarisweg 31–33, POB 703, Willemstad, Curaçao; tel. (9) 461-3199; fax (9) 461-1099; f. 1981; Man. E. L. GOULDING.

Union Bancaire Privée–TDB: J. B. Gorsiraweg 14, POB 3889, Willemstad, Curaçao; tel. (9) 463-9300; fax (9) 461-4129.

Other 'offshore' banks in the Netherlands Antilles include American Express Overseas Credit Corporation NV, Banco Aliado NV, Banco del Orinoco NV, Banco Mercantil Venezolano NV, Banco Principal NV, Banco Provincial International NV, Banunion NV, CFM Bank NV, Citco Banking Corporation NV, Compagnie Bancaire des Antilles NV, Deutche Bank Finance NV, Ebna Bank NV, Exprinter International Bank NV, Integra Bank NV, Lavoro Bank Overseas NV, Lombard-Atlantic Bank NV, Middenbank (Curaçao) NV, Netherlands Caribbean Bank NV, Noro Bank NV, Premier Bank International NV.

Development Banks

Ontwikkelingsbank van de Nederlandse Antillen NV: Salinja 206, POB 267, Willemstad, Curaçao; tel. (9) 461-5551; fax (9) 461-2802; f. 1981.

Stichting Korporashon pa Desaroyo di Korsou (KORPDEKO): Breedestraat 29c, POB 656, Willemstad, Curaçao; tel. (9) 461-6699; fax (9) 461-3013.

Other Banks

Postspaarbank van de Nederlandse Antillen: Waaigatplein 7, Willemstad, Curaçao; tel. (9) 461-1126; fax (9) 461-7561; f. 1905; post office savings' bank; Chair. H. J. J. VICTORIA; cap. 21m.; 20 brs.

Spaar- en Beleenbank van Curaçao NV: MCB Salinja Bldg, Schottegatweg Oost 130, Willemstad, Curaçao; tel. (9) 466-1585; fax (9) 466-1590.

There are also several mortgage banks and credit unions.

Banking Associations

Association of International Bankers in the Netherlands Antilles: Berg Arrarat 1, POB 3889, Curaçao; tel. (9) 461-5367; fax (9) 461-5369; e-mail mellis@attglobal.net; internet www.ibna.an; Pres. HANS BLANKVOORT.

Bonaire Bankers' Association: POB 288, Kralendijk, Bonaire.

Curaçao Bankers' Association (CBA): Plasa Jojo Correa 2–4, Willemstad, Curaçao; tel. (9) 466-1119; fax (9) 466-1122; Pres. L. CAPRILES.

Federashon di Kooperativanan di Spar i Kredito Antiyano (Fekoskan): Curaçaostraat 50, Willemstad, Curaçao; tel. (9) 462-3676; fax (9) 462-4995; e-mail fekoskan@attglobal.net.

International Bankers' Association in the Netherlands Antilles: Scharlooweg 55, Willemstad, Curaçao.

The Windward Islands Bankers' Association: Clem Labega Square, Philipsburg, St Maarten; tel. (5) 22313; fax (5) 24761.

INSURANCE

Amersfoortse Antillen NV: Kaya W.F.G. Mensing 19, Willemstad, Curaçao; tel. (9) 461-6399; fax 461-6709.

Aseguro di Kooperativa Antiyano (ASKA) NV: Scharlooweg 15, Willemstad, Curaçao; tel. (9) 461-7765; fax (9) 461-5991; accident and health, motor vehicle, property.

Assurantiekantoor van der Lubbe: Buncamper Rd 33, Philipsburg, St Maarten; tel. (5) 22737; fax (5) 23979; all branches except life.

Ennia Caribe Schaden NV: J.B.Gorsiraweg 6, Willemstad, Curaçao; tel. (9) 434-3800; fax (9) 434-3873; general; life insurance as Ennia Caribe Leven NV.

ING Fatum: Cas Coraweg 2, Willemstad, Curaçao; tel. (9) 777-7777; fax (9) 461-2023; property insurance.

MCB Group Insurance NV: MCB Bldg Scharloo, Scharloo, Willemstad, Curaçao; tel. (9) 466-1370; fax (9) 466-1327.

Netherlands Antilles and Aruba Assurance Company (NA&A) NV: Pietermaai 135, Willemstad, Curaçao; tel. (9) 465-7146; fax (9) 461-6269; accident and health, motor vehicle, property.

Seguros Antilliano NV: S.b.N.Doormanweg/Reigerweg 5, Willemstad, Curaçao; tel. (9) 736-6877; fax 736-5794; general.

A number of foreign companies also have offices in Curaçao, mainly British, Canadian, Dutch and US firms.

Insurance Association

Insurance Association of the Netherlands Antilles (NAVV): c/o Ing Fatum, POB 3002, Cas Coraweg 2, Willemstad, Curaçao; tel. (9) 777-7777; fax (9) 736-9658; Pres. R. C. MARTINA-JOE.

Trade and Industry

DEVELOPMENT ORGANIZATIONS

Curaçao Industrial and International Trade Development Company NV–CURINDE: Emancipatie Blvd 7, Landhuis Koninsplein, Curaçao; tel. (9) 737-6000; fax (9) 737-1336; e-mail curinde@attglobal.net; internet curinde.com; f. 1980; state-owned; manages the harbor free zone, the airport free zone and the industrial zone; Man. Dir E. R. SMEULDERS.

Foreign Investment Agency Curaçao—FIAC: Scharlooweg 174, Curaçao; tel. (9) 465-7044; fax (9) 461-5788; e-mail fiac@curinfo.an.

World Trade Center Curaçao: POB 6005, Piscadera Bay, Curaçao; tel. (9) 463-6100; fax (9) 462-4408; e-mail wtccur@attglobal.net; Man. Dir HUGO DE FRANÇA.

CHAMBERS OF COMMERCE

Bonaire Chamber of Commerce and Industry: Princess Mariestraat, POB 52, Kralendijk, Bonaire; tel. (7) 5595; fax (7) 8995.

Curaçao Chamber of Commerce and Industry: Kaya Junior Salas 1, POB 10, Willemstad, Curaçao; tel. (9) 461-1451; fax (9) 461-5652; e-mail businessinfo@curacao-chamber.an; internet www.curacao-chamber.an; f. 1884; Pres. HERMAN BEHR; Exec. Dir P. R. J. COMENENCIA.

St Maarten Chamber of Commerce and Industry: C. A. Cannegieterstraat 11, POB 454, Philipsburg, St Maarten; tel. (542) 3590; fax (542) 3512; e-mail coci@sintmaarten.net; f. 1979; Exec. Dir J. M. ARRINDELL VAN WINDT.

INDUSTRIAL AND TRADE ASSOCIATIONS

Association of Industrialists of the Netherlands Antilles (ASINA): Kaya Junior Salas 1, Willemstad, Curaçao; tel. (9) 461-2353; fax (9) 465-8040; Pres. R. M. LUCIA.

Bonaire Trade and Industry Asscn (Vereniging Bedrijfsleven Bonaire): POB 371, Kralendijk, Bonaire.

Curaçao Exporters' Asscn: World Trade Center Curaçao, POB 6049, Piscadera Bay, Curaçao; tel. (9) 463-6151; fax (9) 463-6451; e-mail cea@curacao-inc.an; f. 1903; Business Dir MURIEL M. LARMONIE.

Curaçao Trade and Industry Asscn (Vereniging Bedrijfsleven Curaçao—VBC): Kaya Junior Salas 1, POB 49, Willemstad, Curaçao; tel. (9) 461-1210; fax (9) 461-5652; Pres. DEANNA CHEMALY; Exec. Dir R. P. J. LIEUW.

Offshore Association of the Netherlands Antilles (VOB): c/o Holland Intertrust (Antilles) NV, De Ruyterkade 58A, Willemstad, Curaçao; tel. (9) 461-3277; fax (9) 461-1061; Pres. G. E. ELIAS.

MAJOR COMPANIES

The following are some of the leading industrial and commercial companies currently operating in the Netherlands Antilles:

Alesie Curaçao NV: Brionwerf/Emancipatie Blvd z/n, POB 3293, Willemstad, Curaçao; tel. (9) 61-6869; fax (9) 61-6868; f. 1984; rice mill, produces semi-milled rice, white rice, bran and broken rice; Man. R. BOTTSE; 85 employees.

Antilliaanse Brouwerij NV: Rijkseenheid Blvd w/n, POB 465, Willemstad, Curaçao; tel. (9) 461-2944; fax (9) 461-2035; f. 1958; manufacture and distribution of beer and soft drinks; Man. Dir JOHANNES BRUNING; 121 employees.

Antillean Paper and Plastic Co NV: Industrial Park Brievengat, POB 3505, Curaçao; tel. (9) 37-6422; fax (9) 37-2424; f. 1976; plastics, paper; subsidiaries produce plastic containers and soaps; Mans HUBERT VAN GRIEKEN, E. J. HALABI, J. B. M. KOOL; 56 employees.

Antillean Soap Co NV: Industrial Park Brievengat, Willemstad, Curaçao; tel. (9) 37-7177; fax (9) 37-7191; f. 1976; manufactures powder and liquid soap, disinfectants, abrasives, industrial cleaners; Man. Dir EDWARD J. HALABI; 87 employees.

Antilliaanse Emballago Fabrick NV: Westwerf, POB 3247, Curaçao; f. 1961; manufactures packaging materials such as cans, foils and plastic bags, solvents, margarine and milk powder; Man. E. A. BRUSSEN; 25 employees.

Antilliaanse Verffabrick NV: Asteroidenweg z/n, POB 3944, Curaçao; tel. (9) 37-9866; fax (9) 37-2048; f. 1956; manufactures paint products; Man. E. VAN ARKEL; 47 employees.

Azko Nobel Salt Company: Bonaire; salt mining.

Betonbouw NV: Baai Macolaweg 8, POB 3884, Willemstad. Curaçao; tel. (9) 61-1295; fax (9) 61-2354; f. 1975; construction; Man. Dir CO KLEYN; 376 employees.

BOPEC—Bonaire Petroleum Corporation NV: Kralendijk, POB 117, Bonaire; tel. (7) 8177; fax (7) 8266; oil terminal with storage capacity of 10.1m. barrels; bought by PDVSA (Venezuela) in 1989; Gen. Man. ELIELER COLMENARES.

Cargill Salt Bonaire NV: Bonaire; salt production and export; operates Solar Salt Works.

Caribbean Bottling Co Ltd/Pop Beverages, Inc.: Kaminda André J. E. Kusters 6, POB 302, Willemstad, Curaçao; tel. (9) 461-2488; fax (9) 465-1377; e-mail pop@cura.net; internet www.cura.net/pop; produces carbonated drinks; Man. A. MADURO; 110 employees.

Caribbean Metal Products Inc.: Industrial Park Brievengat, POB 4054, Curaçao; tel. (9) 37-0633; fax (9) 37-0106; f. 1989; manufactures masonry nails, galvanized common nails and umbrella nails; Man. R. LUCIA; 17 employees.

Carnefco Group: Kaya Buena Vista w/n, POB 3121, Willemstad, Curaçao; tel. (9) 869-2121; fax (9) 869-2486; f. 1973; ship maintenance, grit-blasting, wet-blasting, high-pressure water blasting, internal coatings, etc.; Man. Dir W. VOS; 60 employees.

Continental Milling Co (Netherlands Antille) NV: Brionwerf/Emancipatie Blvd w/n, POB 290, Willemstad, Curaçao; tel. (9) 61-6627; fax (9) 61-6116; f. 1971; millers for bakeries, producers of animal feeds; Man. JON D. STUEWE; 70 employees.

Curaçao Beverage Bottling Co NV: Rijkseenheid Blvd 6, POB 95, Willemstad, Curaçao; tel. (9) 63-3311; fax (9) 61-1310; f. 1938; bottlers and manufacturers of soft drinks, many under licence; Man. Dir VICTOR PINEDO; 112 employees.

Curaçao Mining Co Inc.: Nieuwpoort z/n, POB 3078, Curaçao; tel. (9) 767-3400; fax (9) 767-6721; f. 1875; produces phosphate, limestone pebbles in five sizes, sand; Man. D. J. JANSE; 130 employees.

Curaçao Oil NV (CUROIL): A.M. Chumaceiro Blvd 15, POB 3927, Curaçao; tel. (9) 432-0000; fax (9) 461-3335; e-mail curoil@curoil.com; internet www.curoil.com; f. 1985; fuel and petroleum lubricants marketing company; supplies automotive, marine, aviation and industrial fuels and lubricants; Man. Dir M. J. NICOLINA; 80 employees.

Curaçao Wire Products: Industrial Park Zeelandia, POB 3712, Curaçao; tel. (9) 61-3780; fax (9) 61-8732; f. 1977; produces wire mesh, chain link fencing, etc.; Man. R. LUCIA; 32 employees.

Kooijman NV: Kaya W. F. G. (Jombi) Mensing 44, POB 3062, Willemstad, Curaçao; tel. (9) 461-3433; fax (9) 461-5806; e-mail kooyman@kooyman.an; f. 1939; building supplies, hardware, steel/aluminium goods, glass, timber goods, etc.; Man. Dir BASTIAAN KOOIJMAN; 200 employees.

Lovers Industrial Corporation NV: Industrial Park Brievengat, Curaçao; tel. (9) 37-0499; fax (9) 37-1747; f. 1984; produces fruit juices, ice cream, frozen yoghurt; Man. O. VAN DER DIJS; 169 employees.

Otto Senior NV: Scharlooweg 25–27, Willemstad, Curaçao; tel. (9) 61-1701; fax (9) 61-5978; e-mail dserphos@cura.net; f. 1938; 'Ritz' trade name; dairy products, fruit juices, processed foods, catering supplies; Mans I. F. SERPHOS, D. I. SERPHOS, R. H. SERPHOS; 112 employees.

Plastico NV: Industrial Park Brievengat, POB 3561, Curaçao; tel. (9) 737-9568; fax (9) 737-5843; f. 1985; manufactures polythene pipes for water-distribution and irrigation purposes; Man. L. LIEUW-SJONG; 20 employees.

Refinería Isla (Curazao) SA: Margrietlaan, Emmastad, POB 3843, Curaçao; tel. (9) 466-2273; fax (9) 466-2488; e-mail jhdsisl@ccopl.pdv.com; f. 1985; refinery established in 1915 by Royal Dutch-Shell Co, but from 1985 operated by PDVSA (Venezuela); petroleum products; Man. J. HERNÁNDEZ; 1,300 employees.

Refineria di Korsou NV: Ara Hilltop Office Complex, POB 3627, Curaçao; tel. (9) 61-1050; fax (9) 61-1250; f. 1985; owner co of the former Shell Curaçao Refinery and the former Curaçao Oil Terminal; Man. H. PARISIUS; 16 employees.

Softex Products NV: Industrial Park Brievengat, POB 3795, Curaçao; tel. (9) 37-7811; fax (9) 37-7903; f. 1976; produces paper towels, napkins, etc.; Man. P. LIEUW; 35 employees.

Vasos Antillanos NV: Industrial Park Brievengat, Curaçao; tel. (9) 37-7488; fax (9) 37-2424; f. 1986; produces plastic cold-drink cups; Man. H. VAN GRIEKEN; 20 employees.

VERF—Antilliaanse Verffabriek NV: Asteroidenweg w/n, POB 3944, Willemstad, Curaçao; tel. (9) 37-9866; fax (9) 37-2048; f. 1961; paints; Gen. Man. E. VAN ARKEL; 60 employees.

WIMCO—West India Mercantile Co Ltd: POB 74, Willemstad, Curaçao; tel. (9) 461-1833; fax (9) 461-1627; f. 1928; wholesale and retail of household electrodomestic goods; Man. Dir VICTOR HENRÍQUEZ; 132 employees.

UTILITIES
Electricity and Water

GEBE NV: Pond Fill, W. J. A. Nisbeth Rd, St Maarten; tel. (5) 22213.

Kompania di Awa i Elektrisidat di Korsou NV (KAE): POB 2097, Curaçao; tel. (9) 433-2200; fax (9) 462-6685; e-mail kaenv@cura.net; internet www.kaenv.com.

Water & Energiebedrijf Bonaire (WEB) NV: Carlos Nicolaas 3, Kralendijk; tel. (7) 8244.

TRADE UNIONS

Algemene Bond van Overheidspersoneel—ABVO (General Union of Civil Servants): POB 3604, Willemstad, Curaçao; tel. (9) 76097; f. 1936; Pres. F. S. BRITTO; Sec. S. J. HEERENVEEN; 5,000 mems.

Algemene Federatie van Bonaireaanse Werknemers (AFBW): Kralendijk, Bonaire.

Central General di Trahado di Corsow—CGTC (General Head-quarters for Workers of Curaçao): POB 2078, Willemstad, Curaçao; tel. (9) 462-3995; fax (9) 462-7700; f. 1949; Sec.-Gen. OSCAR I. SEMEREL.

Curaçaosche Federatie van Werknemers (Curaçao Federation of Workers): Schouwburgweg 44, Willemstad, Curaçao; tel. (9) 76300; f. 1964; Pres. WILFRED SPENCER; Sec.-Gen. RONCHI ISENIA; 204 affiliated unions; about 2,000 mems.

Federashon Bonaireana di Trabou (FEDEBON): Kaya Krabè 6, Nikiboko, POB 324, Bonaire; tel. and fax (7) 8845; Pres. GEROLD BERNABELA.

Petroleum Workers' Federation of Curaçao: Willemstad, Cura-çao; affiliated to Int. Petroleum and Chemical Workers' Fed.; tel. (9) 737-0255; fax (9) 737-5250; f. 1955; Pres. R. G. GIJSBERTHA; about 1,500 mems.

Sentral di Sindikatonan di Korsou—SSK (Confederation of Curaçao Trade Unions): Schouwburgweg 44, POB 3036, Willemstad; tel. (9) 737-0794; 6,000 mems.

Sindikato di Trahado den Edukashon na Korsou—SITEK (Curaçao Schoolteachers' Trade Union): Landhuis Stenen Koraal, Willemstad, Curaçao; tel. (9) 4682902; fax (9) 4690552; 1,234 mems.

Windward Islands' Federation of Labour (WIFOL): Pond Fill, Long Wall Rd, POB 1097, St Maarten; tel. (54) 22797; fax (54) 26631; e-mail wifol@sintmaarten.net; Pres. THEOPHILUS THOMPSON.

Transport

RAILWAYS

There are no railways.

ROADS

All the islands have a good system of all-weather roads. There were 590 km of roads in 1992, of which 300 km were paved.

SHIPPING

Curaçao is an important centre for the refining and transhipment of Venezuelan and Middle Eastern petroleum. Willemstad is served by the Schottegat harbour, set in a wide bay with a long channel and deep water. Facilities for handling containerized traffic at Willemstad were inaugurated in 1984. A Mega Cruise Facility, with capacity for the largest cruise ships, is under construction on the Otrobanda side of St Anna Bay. Curaçao is also served by ports at Bullen Bay and Caracas Bay. St Maarten is one of the Caribbean's leading ports for visits by cruise ships and in January 2001 new pier facilities were opened which could accommodate up to four cruise ships and add more cargo space. Each of the other islands has a good harbour, except for Saba which has one inlet, equipped with a large pier. Many foreign shipping lines call at ports in the Netherlands Antilles.

Curaçao Ports Authority: Werf de Wilde, POB 3266, Willemstad, Curaçao; tel. (9) 461-4422; fax (9) 461-3907; e-mail cpamanag@cura.net; internet curports.com; Man. Dir RICHARD LOPEZ-RAMIREZ.

Harbour Corporation of St Maarten: Emmaplein, Philipsburg, St Maarten; tel. (5) 22472; port authority.

Curaçao Shipping Association: Kaya Flamboyan 11, Willemstad, Curaçao; tel. (9) 737-0600; fax (9) 737-3875; Pres. K. PONSEN.

Principal Shipping Companies

Caribbean Cargo Services NV: Jan Thiel w/n, POB 442, Willemstad, Curaçao; tel. (9) 467-2588.

Curaçao Dry-dock Company Inc.: POB 3012, Curaçao; tel. (9) 733-0000; fax (9) 737-9950; e-mail cdmna@ibm.net; internet www.curacao-drydock.com.

Curaçao Ports Authority (CPA) NV: Werf de Wilde z/n, POB 689, Curaçao; tel. (9) 434-5999; fax (9) 461-3907; e-mail cpamanag@cura.net; internet www.curports.com; Man. Dir RICHARD LOPEZ-RAMIREZ.

Curaçao Ports Services Inc. NV—CPS: Curaçao Container Terminal, POB 170, Curaçao; tel. (9) 461-5079; fax (9) 461-6536; e-mail cps@ibm.net; Man. Dir KAREL JAN O. ASTER.

Dammers & van der Heide, Shipping and Trading (Antilles) Inc.: Kaya Flamboyan 11, POB 3018, Willemstad, Curaçao; tel. (9) 737-0600; fax (9) 737-3875; e-mail general@dammers-curacao.com; Man. Dir J. J. PONSEN.

Gomez Transport NV: Zeelandia, Willemstad, Curaçao; tel. (9) 461-5260; fax (9) 461-3358; e-mail gomez-shipping@ibm.net; Man. FERNANDO DA COSTA GOMEZ.

Hal Antillen NV: De Ruyterkade 63, POB 812, Curaçao.

Intermodal Container Services NV: Fokkerweg 30, Willemstad, POB 3747, Curaçao; tel. (9) 461-3330; fax (9) 461-3432; Mans A. R. BEAUJON, N. N. HARMS.

Kroonvlag Curaçao NV: Maduro Plaza, POB 231, Curaçao; tel. (9) 737-6900; fax (9) 737-1266; e-mail hekro@cura.net.

Lagendijk Maritime Services: POB 3481, Curaçao; tel. (9) 465-5766; fax (9) 465-5998; e-mail ims@ibm.net.

S. E. L. Maduro & Sons (Curaçao) Inc: Maduro Plaza, POB 3304, Willemstad, Curaçao; tel. (9) 733-1501; fax (9) 733-1506; e-mail hmeijer@madurosons.com; Man. Dir H. MEIJER; Vice Pres. R. CORSEN.

St Maarten Port Services: POB 270, Philipsburg, St Maarten; tel. (5) 22304.

Anthony Veder & Co NV: Zeelandia, POB 3677, Curaçao; tel. (9) 461-4700; fax (9) 461-2576; e-mail anveder@ibm.net; Man. Dir JOOP VAN VLIET.

CIVIL AVIATION

There are international airports at Curaçao (Dr A. Plesman, or Hato, 12 km (7.5 miles) from Willemstad), Bonaire (Flamingo Field) and St Maarten (Princess Juliana, 16 km (10 miles) from Philipsburg); and airfields for inter-island flights at St Eustatius and Saba. In 1998 a free trade zone was inaugurated at the international airport on Curaçao.

AIR ALM: Hato International Airport, Curaçao; tel. (9) 733-8888; fax (9) 733-8300; internet www.airalm.com; f. 1964 to assume responsibilities of the Caribbean division of KLM (the Netherlands); majority govt-owned since 1969; internal services between Bonaire, Curaçao and St Maarten; external services to destinations in North and South America and within the Caribbean; Pres. and CEO Ir MARIO R. EVERTSZ.

Windward Islands Airways International (WIA—Winair) NV: Princess Juliana Airport, POB 2088, Philipsburg, St Maarten; tel. (5) 452568; fax (5) 454229; e-mail info@fly-winair.com; internet www.fly-winair.com; f. 1961; govt-owned since 1974; scheduled and charter flights throughout north-eastern Caribbean; Man. Dir JOHN STRUGNELL.

Tourism

Tourism is a major industry on all the islands. The principal attractions for tourists are the white, sandy beaches, marine wildlife and diving facilities. There are marine parks in the waters around Curaçao, Bonaire and Saba. The numerous historic sites are of interest to visitors. The largest number of tourists visit St Maarten, Curaçao and Bonaire. In 1998 these three islands received 718,774 stop-over visitors (of whom 63.8% were on St Maarten) and 1,124,266 cruise-ship passengers (of whom 78.4% were on St Maarten). Saba had an estimated 10,674 stop-over visitors in 1998 and 14,153 cruise-ship passengers in 1994; St Eustatius received an estimated 8,634 stop-over visitors in 1998 and 3,351 cruise-ship passengers in 1988. Receipts from tourism totalled some NA Fl. 1,000m. in 1993. The destruction caused on St Maarten by Hurricanes Luis and Marilyn in September 1995 caused a drastic decrease in tourism arrivals to the Netherlands Antilles in 1995, compared to the previous year, while there was a concomitant fall in tourism earnings of 12.1%. By December 1995, however, 85% of hotels on St Maarten had reportedly reopened in time for the important winter season, and tourist arrivals recovered to pre-hurricane levels by the end of 1998.

Bonaire Tourism Corporation: Kaya Simon Bolivar 12, Kralendijk, Bonaire; tel. (7) 8322; fax (7) 8408; e-mail tcbinfo@bonairelive.com; Dir RONNIE PIETERS.

Curaçao Tourism Development Bureau (CTDB): Pietermaai 19, POB 3266, Willemstad, Curaçao; tel. (9) 461-6000; fax (9) 461-2305; e-mail ctdbcur@attglobal.net; internet www.curacao-tourism.com; f. 1989; Dir PIETER SAMPSON.

Saba Tourist Office: Windwardside, POB 527, Saba; tel. (4) 162231; fax (4) 162350; e-mail iluvsaba@unspoiledqueen.com; internet www.turq.com/saba; Dir GLENN C. HOLM.

St Eustatius Tourism Development Foundation: Fort Oranje Straat z/n, Oranjestad, St Eustatius; tel. (3) 182701; fax (3) 182433; e-mail euxtour@goldenrock.net; internet www.turov.com/statia; Dir ALIDA FRANCIS.

St Maarten Tourist Bureau: Vineyard Office Park, W. G. Buncamper Rd 33, Philipsburg, St Maarten; tel. (5) 22337; fax (5) 22734; Dir CORNELIUS DE WEEVER.

HOTEL ASSOCIATIONS

Bonaire Hotel and Tourism Association: Kralendijk, Bonaire; Man. Dir HUGO GERHARTS.

Curaçao Hotel and Tourism Association (CHATA): Kaya Junior Salas 1, Piscadera Bay, POB 6115, Curaçao; tel. (9) 465-1005; fax (9) 465-1052; e-mail andre@chata.org; internet www.chata.org; Pres. JAN VAN BEURDEN.

St Maarten Hospitality and Trade Association: W. J. A. Nisbeth Rd 33a, POB 486, Philipsburg, St Maarten; tel. (542) 0108; fax (542) 0107; e-mail info@shta.com; internet www.shta.com.

Defence

Defence is the responsibility of the Netherlands, and military service is compulsory. The Governor is the Commander-in-Chief of the armed forces in the islands, and a Dutch naval contingent is based in Curaçao.

Commander of the Navy: Brig.-Gen. WILLEM A. J. PRINS.

Education

From 1992 education was compulsory for all children between the ages of six and 16 years. The education system is the same as that in the Netherlands. Primary education begins at six years of age and lasts for six years. Secondary education lasts for a further five years. Dutch is used as the principal language of instruction in schools on the 'Leeward Islands', while English is used in schools on the 'Windward Islands'. Instruction in Papiamento (using a different standardization of spelling to that adopted in Aruba) was introduced in primary schools. In 1996 there were 77 pre-primary, 85 primary, 16 junior high and five senior high schools; altogether there were 40,429 pupils in the primary and secondary sectors. In addition, there were technical, vocational, teacher-training and special-needs institutions. The University of the Netherlands Antilles, based in Curaçao, had 671 students in 1996. In 1995 total government expenditure on education in the Antilles of the Five was NA Fl. 178.9m. (19.3%).

Bibliography

For works on the Caribbean generally, see Select Bibliography (Books).

Hartog, J. *History of St Eustatius*. Aruba, De Wit, 1976.

Ferguson, J. *Eastern Caribbean*. Latin American Bureau, New York, NY, 1997.

Keinders, A. *Politieke Geschiedenis van de Nederlandse Antillen en Aruba, 1950–93*. Zutphen, Walburg Press, 1993.

Klomp, A. *Politics on Bonaire*. Assen (Netherlands), Van Gorcum, 1986.

Koulen, I. *Netherlands Antilles and Aruba: A Research Guide*. London, ICP Publishing Ltd, 1987.

Schoenhais, K. *Netherlands Antilles and Aruba*, World Bibliographical Series. Oxford, Clio Press, 1993.

NICARAGUA

Area: 120,254 sq km (46,430 sq miles).

Population (official estimate, 2000): 5,071,700.

Capital: Managua, estimated population 819,700 in 1995.

Language: Spanish; some English also spoken.

Religion: Mainly Christianity (Roman Catholicism predominates).

Climate: Tropical; average annual temperature is 25.5°C, rainy season between May and October.

Time: GMT –6 hours.

Public Holidays

2002: 1 January (New Year's Day), 28 March (Maundy Thursday), 29 March (Good Friday), 1 May (Labour Day), 19 July (Liberation Day), 1 and 10 August (Managua local holiday), 16 September (for Battle of San Jacinto), 17 September (for Independence Day), 4 November (for Day of the Dead), 8 December (Immaculate Conception), 25 December (Christmas).

2003: 1 January (New Year's Day), 17 April (Maundy Thursday), 18 April (Good Friday), 1 May (Labour Day), 21 July (for Liberation Day), 1 and 11 August (Managua local holiday), 15 September (for Battle of San Jacinto), 16 September (for Independence Day), 3 November (for Day of the Dead), 8 December (Immaculate Conception), 25 December (Christmas).

Currency: Gold córdoba; 1,000 gold córdobas = £52.47 = US $75.13 = €84.65 (30 April 2001).

Weights and Measures: The metric system is officially in force, although some old Spanish and local units are also in general use.

Basic Economic Indicators

	1998	1999	2000
Gross domestic product (million córdobas at 1980 prices)	22,367.7	24,014.7	25,046.0
GDP per head ('000 córdobas at 1980 prices)	4,653.2	4,863.2	4,936.1
GDP (million gold córdobas at current prices)	19,127	22,500	26,782
GDP per head ('000 gold córdobas at current prices)	3,979.0	4,556.5	5,278.3
Annual growth of real GDP (%)	4.1	7.4	4.3
Annual growth of real GDP per head (%)	1.3	4.5	1.5
Government budget (million gold córdobas at current prices):			
Revenue	6,580.6	n.a.	n.a.
Expenditure (incl. net lending)	7,037.2	n.a.	n.a.
Consumer price index (annual average; base: 1995 = 100)	138	153	n.a.
Rate of inflation (annual average, %)	13.0	11.2	n.a.
Foreign exchange reserves (US $ million at 31 December)	350.2	509.4	488.4
Imports c.i.f. (US $ million)	1,491.6	1,861.9	n.a.
Exports f.o.b. (US $ million)	573.2	545.3	n.a.
Balance of payments (current account, US $ million)	–498.2	–652.2	n.a.

Gross national product per head measured at purchasing power parity (PPP) (US dollars, converted by the PPP exchange rate, 1999 estimate): 2,154.

Economically active population (estimate, 2000): 1,637,300.

Unemployment (official estimate, persons aged 10 years and over, 2000): 9.8%.

Total foreign debt (estimate, 1999): US $6,458m.

Life expectancy (years at birth, 1996): 68.5 (males 66.1, females 70.9).

Infant mortality rate (per 1,000 live births, 1997): 43.

School enrolment ratio (7–17 years, 1998): 82%.

Adult literacy rate (15 years and over, 1999): 68.6% (males 66.9; females 71.2).

Adult population with HIV/AIDS (15–49 years, 1999): 0.2%.

Commercial energy consumption per head (kg of oil equivalent, 1998): 553.

Carbon dioxide emissions per head (metric tons, 1997): 0.7.

Passenger cars in use (estimate, per 1,000 of population, 1999): 10.4.

Television receivers in use (per 1,000 of population, 1997): 68.

Personal computers in use (per 1,000 of population, 1999): 8.1.

History

LUCIANO BARACCO

Revised for this edition by DENNIS RODGERS

Nicaragua, Central America's largest republic, gained independence from Spain in 1821, briefly becoming part of the Mexican Empire (1821–23) and then part of the short-lived United Provinces of Central America (1823–38). The country can be divided into three zones: the Pacific Slope, which contains the centre of government and commerce; the Central Highlands, which historically were the centre of rebellion; and the Atlantic Coast, populated by a number of indigenous Indian (Amerindian) groups. The country's boundaries underwent a number of alterations after independence: Guanacaste was ceded to Costa Rica in 1858; in the 20th century the islands of San Andreas and Providencia were ceded to Colombia, and a large piece of territory in north-eastern Nicaragua was granted to Honduras by the World Court in the 1960s.

NICARAGUA, 1838–1936

The first decades of independence became known as the 'Age of Anarchy', owing to successive civil wars between the Liberals of León and the Conservatives of Granada. With these two cities acting like autonomous states, the emergence of a national state apparatus was severely impeded. In 1854 Leonese Liberals recruited a group of North American mercenaries, led by William Walker, to fight their Granadan rivals. After defeating the Granadan Conservatives, Walker turned on his Liberal patrons, declared himself President, reintroduced slavery and established English as the official language. However, his ambitions of regional domination united the rest of Central America against him. The expulsion of Walker, in a struggle referred to as the National War (1855–57), acted as a catalyst to unite Nicaragua's feuding élite behind its first coherent nation-building project. An Oligarchic Pact brought stability by ensuring the rotation of Liberals and Conservatives in the presidency. This period also saw the arrival in Nicaragua of the first signs of modernity, with the building of railways, port facilities and telegraph networks, and the introduction of coffee as a valuable export crop.

This period of peace was ended by the Liberal Revolution (1893–1909), led by José Santos Zelaya. The pace of modernization quickened under Zelaya's regime, as he introduced a Constitution separating the Church from the State, developed state services, modernized the Army, gained control of the Atlantic Coast from the United Kingdom, and encouraged foreign capital investment. However, the courting of European and Japanese capital for the construction of an inter-oceanic canal in southern Nicaragua provoked a US-supported rebellion by Nicaragua's Conservatives, which forced Zelaya into exile in 1909. The Bryan–Chamorro Treaty of 1916 granted the USA exclusive rights in perpetuity to construct a canal, safeguarding the Panamanian canal from a rival Nicaraguan project.

In 1912 a Liberal rebellion led the USA to send military forces to support the Conservative regime; these remained in Nicaragua until 1925. In 1926 the US military returned, following a new rebellion, led by the Liberal general, José María Moncada. An agreement was reached with Moncada in 1927, however, which included US-supervised elections, the continued presence of US troops, and the training of a non-partisan National Guard. One of Moncada's lieutenants, Augusto César Sandino, rejected these measures, and with a 300-strong 'Defending Army of National Sovereignty' fought a guerrilla war against the regime until 1933. New peace accords were signed in this year guaranteeing the withdrawal of US troops and new elections. The peace was short-lived, however, as the Commander of the National Guard, Anastasio Somoza García, ordered Sandino's murder in 1934 and seized power two years later, becoming President in 1937.

THE SOMOZA DYNASTY

The Somoza family ruled Nicaragua until 1979. They proved to be skilful manipulators of successive US administrations, and utilized a mix of coercion and strategies of accommodation with the traditional oligarchy to sustain their dictatorship. Following Anastasio Somoza García's assassination in 1956 by the poet Rigoberto López Pérez, he was succeeded as President by his son, Luís Somoza Debayle, while his youngest son, Anastasio Somoza Debayle, became Commander-in-Chief of the National Guard. After the death of Luís Somoza Debayle in 1967, Anastasio Somoza Debayle assumed the presidency.

Exploiting their control of the National Guard and good relations with the USA, the Somozas constructed a business empire that monopolized the most modern sectors of the economy. It was estimated that by 1979 the Somozas owned around 40% of Nicaragua's economy. With US assistance the dynasty assembled the most efficient state apparatus Nicaragua had ever possessed. However, the main function of this apparatus was to service Somoza business interests (known as 'Somocismo'), rather than to achieve national development.

The regime began to fragment in the 1970s as the dictatorship's increasing authoritarianism agitated the Nicaraguan people as well as President Somoza's international supporters. His corrupt misuse of humanitarian aid, following an earthquake that destroyed Managua in 1972, combined with the assassination of the Conservative opposition leader, Pedro Joaquín Chamorro, in 1978, united internal opposition (see below). Moreover, President Somoza's actions led to international criticism, especially from the administration of US President Jimmy Carter (1977–81). Facing international isolation, a growing popular insurrection and a disintegrating National Guard, Anastasio Somoza Debayle resigned the presidency in July 1979. He fled to Paraguay, where he was assassinated in September 1980.

THE SANDINISTA NATIONAL LIBERATION FRONT

The overthrow of the Somoza dictatorship represented one of the most broadly based and popular insurrections in Latin America's history. In 1961, inspired by the Cuban revolution, a group of students from the University of León, together with surviving members of Sandino's Defending Army, formed the Frente Sandinista de Liberación Nacional (FSLN—Sandinista National Liberation Front). Despite the fact that many of its founders were Marxists, the FSLN rapidly broadened its ideological base, and its politics represented a mix of nationalism, radical Christianity and a brand of socialism that owed more to cultural practices peculiar to Latin America than to the USSR. The FSLN became the hegemonic group within an extremely broad revolutionary alliance, which also included the non-Somocista business élite, sections of the Roman Catholic Church, left-wing activists and intellectuals, and which mobilized large numbers of the urban poor and the rural peasantry.

The Somoza regime remained firmly in control of the country until the mid-1970s, inflicting serious losses on the FSLN in the late 1960s and early 1970s. By 1974 most of the FSLN's founders were dead or imprisoned, many of its underground networks had been destroyed, and the organization was internally divided. However, the dictator's increasingly brutal and arbitrary repression brought unqualified condemnation from almost every sector of Nicaraguan society, and the murder of Chamorro in 1978 provoked a full-scale insurrection. In late 1978 the Sandinista-led opposition instigated a series of uprisings in the major cities. The National Guard began to disintegrate and, sensing the imminent fall of Somoza, President Carter attempted to negotiate his replacement with members of the non-Sandinista opposition. However, owing to the growing popularity of the FSLN, and the refusal of President Somoza to accept this proposal, the plan failed and by July Nicaragua was ruled by a Government of National Reconstruction.

SANDINISTA GOVERNMENT, 1979–80

The guiding principles of the new regime were the pursuit of political pluralism, a mixed economy, popular participation, and a non-aligned foreign policy. The state was to function according to the 'logic of the majority', with a priority given to the interests of the poor. The five-member governing Junta consisted of two members of the anti-Somoza bourgeoisie and three Sandinistas, among them the General Secretary of the FSLN, Daniel Ortega Saavedra, who became *de facto* President of Nicaragua. The 1974 Constitution was abrogated, the bicameral Congreso Nacional (National Congress) was dissolved and the National Guard was replaced with the Sandinista People's Army. In May 1980 a 47-seat Council of State was convened (increased to 51 seats in May 1981) to act as a legislative body. The new assembly consisted of representatives of various mass organizations active within Nicaraguan civil society. Although the Sandinistas enjoyed an institutionalized parliamentary majority, the non-Sandinista business sectors and constitutional opposition parties were also represented. The new Constitution guaranteed a range of civil liberties common to liberal democracies, abolished the death penalty and established an independent judiciary.

Elections to the presidency and to a new 96-seat Asamblea Nacional (National Assembly) were held on 4 November 1984. The FSLN presidential candidate, Ortega, received 67% of the votes cast, and the FSLN won 61 seats in the Asamblea Nacional. Most national and international observers endorsed the legitimacy of the elections (with the significant exception of the USA) and they were undoubtedly indicative of the high level of popular support enjoyed by the Sandinistas in the mid-1980s, particularly among the beneficiaries of agricultural, health and educational reforms.

Under the Sandinista Government, Nicaragua was characterized by a series of popular consultations and Asamblea Nacional debates, which led to the promulgation of a new Constitution on 9 January 1987. Prominent amongst its provisions was the granting of autonomy to the indigenous population of the Atlantic coast, following the initial centralizing policies that had prompted armed resistance by various indigenous groups, including the Miskito 'Yatama' group. Initially, the regime promoted governance on a local community level; however, the management demands of the conflict against the Contras (see below) led to increasingly authoritarian tendencies from the mid-1980s.

Economically, the Sandinista regime pursued a number of redistributive policies, which included subsidies on basic goods and nationalization; however, the public sector never accounted for more than 40% of the economy during the Sandinista period, and the private sector was encouraged. An agrarian reform programme was also undertaken, with the aim of redistributing some state lands to landless peasants, both in the form of co-operative farms and individual land holdings, and many unauthorized urban inhabitants of unoccupied land or premises were legalized and received materials with which to construct houses.

By 1988 the effects of the US trade embargo, imposed in 1985, and the conflict with the Contras had made the original Sandinista economic model unsustainable. The annual rate of inflation reached 7,778%, 50% of the national budget was being spent on the war, and the foreign debt stood at almost US $6,700m., in a country with an average gross national product of $2,500m. An economic adjustment plan was instituted, which reduced public-sector employment and state subsidies, and devalued the currency. The initiation of peace negotiations also resulted in significant reductions in military expenditure. Despite these measures, however, the economy failed to improve by the 1990 elections.

OPPOSITION AND THE WAR

The Movimiento Democrático Nicaragüense (MDN—Nicaraguan Democratic Movement) and the Fuerzas Democráticas Nicaragüenses (FDN—Nicaraguan Democratic Forces), based in Honduras, formed the major counter-revolutionary forces ('Contras') against the Sandinista regime. From 1981 the Contras, which initially consisted of about 2,000 former National Guards, successfully recruited significant numbers of peasants disaffected by the Sandinistas' agrarian reform programme. By 1985 the Contras had recruited up to 10,000 members. A smaller force, the Alianza Revolucionaria Democrática (ARDE—Democratic Revolutionary Alliance), led by a disillusioned Sandinista commander, Edén Pastora Gómez, was based in Costa Rica. With the support of the Honduran army and financial aid from the USA, the Contras were able to organize numerous incursions into Nicaragua from the early 1980s.

The USA was implacably opposed to the Sandinista regime and claimed that the Contras' actions were in the international interest, given the Nicaraguan Government's left-wing policies and its links with the Soviet bloc. From 1982 the US Government allocated funds to the Contras and to the US Central Intelligence Agency (CIA) for the purpose of destabilizing the Sandinista regime. In 1986 increasing US congressional opposition to such funding and growing international censure, provoked elements of the administration of US President Ronald Reagan (1981–89) to become involved in the illegal transfer to the Contras, of the proceeds of clandestine sales of military equipment to Iran. The eventual exposure of these actions, known as the Iran–Contra scandal, contributed to the strengthening of the congressional ban on aid to the Contras.

Despite their destructive impact on the Sandinista economic project, the failure of the Contras to achieve a decisive military victory, combined with the end of US aid, prompted them to enter into peace negotiations. The first in a series of agreements, known as the Esquipulas Peace Accords, was signed in 1987. These accords laid the foundations for a general disarmament process, with international observation by the Organization of American States (OAS). Subsequent accords (Esquipulas II and III) led to further disarmament and provided the framework for the 1990 elections.

THE 1990 ELECTIONS

The presidential, legislative and municipal elections of February 1990 were a landmark in Nicaraguan history. Recognized to have been free and fair by international observers, the Sandinistas abided by the results. Such peaceful transitions of power were rare in Nicaraguan history. The ballot produced an unexpected victory for the Unión Nacional Opositora (UNO—National Opposition Union), a hastily prepared coalition of 14 anti-Sandinista parties. The UNO's presidential candidate, Violeta Barrios de Chamorro, widow of the assassinated Pedro Joaquín Chamorro, won 55% of the votes cast, compared to President Ortega's 41%. The opposition alliance also gained 51 seats in the 92-seat Asamblea Nacional and 101 of a total of 132 municipal councils. The Sandinistas obtained 39 congressional seats. The belief that a Sandinista victory would mean the continuation of war and economic hardship, the unpopularity of military conscription and increasing authoritarianism of the Sandinista leadership were the principal causes of the Government's electoral defeat.

The new head of state, Violeta Chamorro, a former member of the Government of National Reconstruction, was seen as a figure of national reconciliation. On assuming the presidency she avoided confrontation with the FSLN by reappointing Sandinista Gen. Humberto Ortega as Commander-in-Chief of the Armed Forces, and by agreeing to uphold the 1987 Constitution. President Chamorro's actions led to tensions with more extremist factions within the UNO coalition, led by the Vice-President, Virgilio Godoy Reyes, and the newly elected Mayor of Managua, Arnoldo Alemán Lacayo. This infighting within the governing coalition led to the collapse of the UNO as a coherent political force in early 1993. Following the failure of the UNO, a new consensus was reached between a number of former UNO deputies, the FSLN, the Partido Conservador de Nicaragua (PCN—Conservative Party of Nicaragua), and the President. Right-wing UNO deputies re-formed as the Alianza Política Opositora (Political Opposition Alliance) in February 1993 and boycotted the Asamblea Nacional, demanding the dismissal of Gen. Ortega and of the Minister to the Presidency, Antonio Lacayo Oyanguren.

THE UNO GOVERNMENT

Although the victory of the UNO coalition generated fears of a loss of civil liberty, owing to the extremism of some of its component parties, government policy quickly dispelled such misapprehensions. The architect of government policy was Antonio Lacayo, the son-in-law of President Chamorro and *de facto* prime minister. Lacayo represented Nicaragua's modernizing bourgeoisie and sought to pragmatically implement a range of market-orientated economic reforms, while recognizing the continued influence of the FSLN. However, a number of factors prevented the successful implementation of Lacayo's 'centrist solution'. President Chamorro's conciliatory stance towards the Sandinistas led to the suspension of US aid on the advice of the Chairman of the US Senate's Foreign Relations Committee, Jesse Helms. Moreover, vital loans from the International Monetary Fund (IMF) were contingent on the implementation of economic-liberalization measures and public-expenditure reductions, which provoked industrial action by opposition-led trade unions and popular organizations. By mid-1991 Lacayo's strategic policy of market-led modernization had been replaced by short-term crisis management. Further economic reforms were enacted only after lengthy negotiations with the Sandinistas.

THE FSLN IN OPPOSITION

Despite their electoral defeat the Sandinistas remained the largest single party in the Asamblea Nacional and the most experienced, organized political party in Nicaragua. They continued to exert informal influence over the police and the army, both of which were led by prominent Sandinistas. The FSLN also exercised considerable influence among the trade unions and civil associations. However, the party's popularity among the wider population suffered considerably from what became known as 'la piñata', a process whereby large amounts of state and government property was transferred to the leadership of the FSLN, during the two-month transition period between the FSLN and UNO Governments.

In 1994 internal divisions within the FSLN over its co-operation with the Chamorro Government led to the formation of two factions. The Izquierda Democrática Sandinista (Sandinista Democratic Left), led by Daniel Ortega, supported a more orthodox revolutionary outlook and carried the support of mass organizations, the trade unions and the urban and rural poor. This faction was opposed by the more socio-democratic, 'renewalist' faction, led by a former Vice-President and leader of the FSLN in the Asamblea Nacional, Sergio Ramírez Mercado. The Ortega faction emerged successful from the ensuing political struggle, and in January 1995, Ramírez left the FSLN to form the Movimiento de Renovación Sandinista (MRS—Sandinista Renewal Movement). The majority of the Sandinista deputies in the Asamblea Nacional moved to the MRS, leaving the FSLN with just eight deputies. However, the overwhelming majority of the grassroots membership remained loyal to the FSLN.

OPPOSITION TO THE CHAMORRO GOVERNMENT

As well as constitutional opposition, the Chamorro presidency was challenged by an increasing number of armed opposition groups. Following the 1990 elections, the OAS supervised a progressive demobilization of Contra forces, and the Nicaraguan Army was reduced from 90,000 to 15,000 troops. The resettlement into civilian life of both former Contras and former Sandinista soldiers proved problematic, however, and promises guaranteed in the Esquipulas Accords to provide land, social services and credit to facilitate this process were not fulfilled.

As a result, the Government faced its first major military crisis in July 1993, following the occupation of the town of Estelí by a pro-Sandinista armed group. The security forces recaptured the town by force, resulting in 22 deaths. In August a rearmed group of former Contras, Frente Norte 3-80 (FN—Northern Front 3-80), kidnapped a number of deputies who had gone to the northern town of Quilalí to negotiate its disarmament. The FN demanded the resignations of Gen. Humberto Ortega and Antonio Lacayo. In response, former Sandinista soldiers kidnapped a group of right-wing deputies in Managua, including Vice-President Godoy. A peaceful resolution was negotiated by the OAS and a general amnesty was granted. In late 1993 Gen.

Ortega was replaced as Commander-in-Chief of the Armed Forces by Gen. Joaquín Cuadra Lacayo, also a Sandinista.

A further source of tension for the UNO Government centred on the status of land that peasant families had received through the Sandinista agrarian reform programme. Most of this land had been owned by the Somozas or their allies who fled the country during the revolution. Following the UNO election victory, demands for the return of such lands to their original owners began to increase. In 1994–95 violence also erupted sporadically among the student population, in protest at the Government's failure to spend 6% of the national budget on higher education, as stated in the Constitution.

CONSTITUTIONAL REFORM

In November 1994 a series of constitutional amendments were proposed by a coalition of opposition deputies. The proposals aimed: to reduce presidential powers; to give the Asamblea Nacional the authority to veto international agreements and to set the national budget; to establish a second round of voting in presidential elections if no candidate gained more than 45% of votes cast in the first round; and to prevent the President serving two consecutive terms. A further proposed amendment prohibited close relatives of a serving President from presenting their candidacy in a presidential election, a move widely considered to be specifically intended to prevent Lacayo from standing in the 1996 elections.

Although President Chamorro refused to give the proposed amendments her assent, they were enacted by the Asamblea Nacional in February 1995. This the President declared to be unconstitutional. The legal disputes lasted until June, when a political accord, which moderated many of the reforms, was signed by the Government and legislature. Lacayo's case against the consanguinity clause in the amended Constitution was rejected by the Court of Appeal. In February 1996 the Supreme Court ruled that the issue should be resolved by the Consejo Supremo Electoral (CSE—Supreme Electoral Council), which decided that Lacayo was not eligible to contest the forthcoming presidential election of October.

THE 1996 ELECTIONS

Presidential and legislative elections were held on 20 October 1996. Owing to the discovery of various procedural irregularities, including significant quantities of missing votes, the provisional results of the presidential contest, which indicated a victory for Arnoldo Alemán Lacayo, the candidate of the Alianza Liberal (AL—Liberal Alliance) coalition, were alleged to be fraudulent by the FSLN and several other parties. However, although the election process was undoubtedly characterized by administrative incompetence and logistical difficulties, there was no indication of a systematic attempt to manipulate the poll, and international observers declared the ballot to have been generally free and fair. Although many of the provisional results were subsequently revised, the CSE, announcing the definitive results on 22 November, declared that these anomalies had not affected the overall result. Alemán was declared the winner, with 51.0% of the valid votes cast, compared with 37.8% for the FSLN candidate and former President, Daniel Ortega. The remaining 21 presidential candidates shared the remainder of the votes. In the legislative elections, the AL gained 42 of the 90 elective seats in the Asamblea Nacional and control of 92 municipalities. The FSLN obtained 35 legislative seats and 51 municipalities and the Camino Cristiano Nicaragüense (CCN—Nicaraguan Christian Way) won three seats in the legislature. The FSLN, the CCN and the PCN were each allocated a further seat, on the basis of votes received by their respective presidential candidates, while the remaining 10 elective seats were shared by eight other parties. Alemán was inaugurated as President on 10 January 1997.

THE ALEMÁN ADMINISTRATION

In contrast to the conciliatory figure of President Chamorro, President Alemán had an openly anti-Sandinista agenda. Indeed, Alemán's association with the Somoza family, as well as the inclusion of Somoza's former Partido Liberal Nacionalista (PLN—Nationalist Liberal Party) within the AL prompted some to label him a Somocista. He immediately adopted a more abrasive style of Government; the eviction of families occupying land confiscated by the Sandinistas, under the new Government's policy of returning the land to its previous owners, prompted the FSLN to organize national protests in April 1997. Meanwhile, unemployment continued to increase, despite President Alemán's campaign promise to create 100,000 jobs per year, and the establishment of a multi-party commission to seek solutions to social hardship caused by austerity measures produced few tangible benefits. In June 1997 the Government convened a 'national dialogue', involving representatives of more than 50 political parties and civic organizations, to examine poverty, unemployment and property-rights issues. However, it was boycotted by the FSLN and anti-government demonstrations continued, including, from late June 1997, violent clashes between security forces and students protesting against the Government's failure to fulfil a constitutional requirement to allocate a minimum 6% of the national budget for university education.

During 1998 continuing economic and social problems were accompanied by an increase in allegations of corruption against the Alemán administration. The work of the Comptroller-General, Agustín Jarquín Anaya, was systematically obstructed by President Alemán who was, together with members of his family, the subject of a number of investigations by Jarquín's office. In February 1999 allegations against the President gained credence with the publication of a report by the Comptroller-General's office, which revealed that Alemán's personal wealth had increased by some 900% during his terms of office as Mayor of Managua and as President. However, the campaign of obstruction against Jarquín was aided by senior figures from the FSLN, who were also under investigation concerning their acquisition of former state assets. This culminated in Jarquín's imprisonment in November 1999 on charges of illegal use of state funds to employ an investigative journalist to examine President Alemán's finances. Although the FSLN remained silent on the matter, a groundswell of protest among other opposition parties and the international community led to his release after less than three weeks in custody.

HURRICANE MITCH

The weakness of Nicaragua's public institutions was amply illustrated following the impact of 'Hurricane Mitch' in October 1998. The hurricane devastated the north-western parts of the country, killing almost 3,000 people and causing massive infrastructural damage. Initially, President Alemán refused to declare a state of emergency and questioned the severity of the disaster. When the full consequences of the disaster became known, international donors adopted a strategy to deliver humanitarian aid directly to non-governmental organizations (NGOs), owing to concerns over the possible misappropriation of funds by the Government. In response, the President threatened to impose a tax of up to 40% on all aid entering the country, a threat universally condemned and subsequently withdrawn. The aftermath of the hurricane also exposed an increasing distance between the FSLN and the social organizations from which it traditionally drew its core support. Ortega, along with President Alemán, was criticized by the NGOs for using the disaster for political purposes; the apparent lack of input by the FSLN leadership in the mass mobilization of volunteers illustrated the extent of the FSLN's transformation from a mass social movement to a parliamentary party.

The confused response to this disaster and the subsequent inefficiency of the Government's reconstruction plans brought criticism from various quarters. The Stockholm Consultative Group, established by international donors, the Nicaraguan Government and NGOs to co-ordinate reconstruction efforts, was highly critical of the Alemán administration's repeated inability to present detailed proposals on how aid would be spent. Growing accusations of corruption and incompetence in the allocation of post-hurricane reconstruction funds, as well as the attacks on the Comptroller-General's office led members of this group, specifically the Scandinavian countries, to suspend a number of aid programmes. Nicaragua's inclusion in the World Bank (International Bank for Reconstruction and Development—IBRD) and IMF 'Heavily Indebted Poor Countries' (HIPC) initiative, which proposed to reduce the country's debt-servicing payments by one-half and to cut the principal of its

debt by 80%, in exchange for adherence to a specific programme of economic and political reform, was, nevertheless, eventually approved on 18 December 2000, more in order to avoid discrediting the initiative as a whole rather than owing to any improvement in government performance. In July 2001 the IMF permitted the release of loans and donations that had been held since November 2000.

THE PLC–FSLN PACT

During 1998 the FSLN maintained strong vocal opposition to President Alemán's Government, but the party's apparent lack of long-term strategy, combined with failure in the March 1998 Atlantic Coast Autonomous Assemblies election, led to renewed divisions within the FSLN command. Although Ortega was re-elected Secretary-General of the party at the FSLN's congress in May 1998, opposition to his leadership intensified when he subsequently entered into negotiations with President Alemán on political co-operation with the PLC. These negotiations, concluded in October 1999, centred on changes to the Constitution and to the electoral system. It was agreed that the PLC and FSLN would appoint their own members to important institutions such as the CSE and the Supreme Court, and that elaborate procedures for the granting of legal status to political parties would be established in order to make it more difficult for smaller parties to function, thereby institutionalizing a two-party system consisting of the PLC and the FSLN. The proposed principal changes to the electoral laws included the following provisions: each party must obtain 75,000 signatures in order to gain legal recognition (in the case of an alliance, 75,000 signatures must be collected for each party included in the alliance); each party must gain 4% of the popular vote in order to retain legal status after an election; and all parties must have a presence in all 150 municipalities. Moreover, the threshold for a first-round victory in the presidential elections was reduced from 45% to 35%, albeit on the condition that the victor have a 5% lead over the second placed candidate; and all former Presidents were granted a life seat in the Asamblea Nacional (and with it, comprehensive parliamentary immunity). Other reforms transformed the Comptroller-General's office into a collegiate body of five Comptrollers, chosen by the PLC and FSLN, thus effectively marginalizing the existing Comptroller-General, Agustín Jarquín, who, as a result, resigned in June 2000.

OPPOSITION TO THE PLC–FSLN PACT

The PLC–FSLN pact was initiated in the context of a growing crisis within both the Sandinista party and the PLC. In March 2000 Daniel Ortega's stepdaughter, Zoilamérica Narváez Murillo, accused him of having abused her as a child during the 1980s and early 1990s. Ortega claimed that the accusations were politically motivated and that Narváez was manipulated by his political rivals within the FSLN. However, his decision to avoid trial by invoking his parliamentary immunity deepened the divisions in the FSLN command, with a number of leading figures being removed from prominent positions owing to their criticism of Ortega's refusal to answer the charges. Also in early 2000 President Alemán was implicated in the 'narcojet scandal', a complex affair involving a stolen plane, drugs trafficking, and the falsification of government documents. He similarly refused to respond to the accusations. As a result, the opportunist PLC–FSLN pact deepened divisions within both parties, the PLC losing the support of several of its deputies in the Asamblea Nacional, and the FSLN expelling some of its senior figures, while others resigned.

The European Union (EU), Scandinavian governments and the USA all expressed concern regarding the impact of the PLC–FSLN pact on the transparency of government administration, and in June 2000 the countries constituting the Stockholm Consultative Group informed the Alemán Government that although they would fulfil their existing aid commitments, no additional aid would be forthcoming. In particular, the Group pointed out that the failure of the new Comptroller-General's office to investigate clearly documented cases of corruption involving government officials played a significant part in its decision to suspend further aid.

In February 2000, a number of small parties entered into negotiations to open up what they referred to as a 'Third Way', through the creation of an electoral alliance, the Movimiento

Democrático Nicaragüense (MDN—Nicaraguan Democratic Movement). The initiative attracted a number of public figures from all parties, but rapidly collapsed, owing to the need for the parties to formally merge in order to avoid the requirements of a political alliance outlined in the PLC–FSLN pact. The ideological differences between the parties made a formal merger an impossibility. In June 2000, the recently retired general, Joaquín Cuadra, who had been seen as a potential MDN presidential candidate, announced the formation of a new, broad-based 'anti-pact' party, the Movimiento Unidad Nacional (MUN—National Unity Movement) and soon afterwards the former Minister of National Defence, José Antonio Alvarado, left the PLC to form the Partido Liberal Democrático (PLD—Democratic Liberal Party). However, the CSE subsequently denied legal status to all political parties except for the FSLN, the PLC, the PCN, the CCN, and two small Atlantic Coast indigenous parties, and declared that the municipal elections of 5 November 2000 would be contested only by these parties.

ELECTION FEVER

The decision to deny legal status to the new parties caused widespread outrage and was seen as blatant political manipulation on the part of the FSLN and the PLC. Partly as a result, the municipal elections of 5 November 2000 were marked by a high rate of abstention. The result of the election was widely portrayed as a 'technical draw'. The FSLN did qualitatively better than the PLC, winning in 11 of the 17 departmental capitals, including Managua. However, the PLC gained 41.5% of the vote, compared to the 40.4% gained by the FSLN, and won control of 97 of the municipalities; the FSLN won 49 and the PCN won five. The political parties prepared, meanwhile, for the general and presidential elections that were due to be held on 4 November 2001.

In January 2001 the FSLN held primary elections to select its candidates for the November 2001 presidential elections. Former President Daniel Ortega won with 70% of the vote. Meanwhile, the PLC selected Vice-President Enrique Bolaños Geyer (who subsequently resigned his position in order to run in the election) and liberal coffee magnate, José Rizo Castellón, as its presidential and vice-presidential candidates. Both parties sought to broaden their base of appeal in 2001. Following the inconclusive results of the November 2000 municipal elections, in February 2001 the PLC suggested a possible electoral alliance with the PCN. After a month of negotiations, however, this project collapsed, leading to an acrimonious internal debate within the PCN and the resignation of its President, Pedro Solórzano, who consequently joined the PLC. The FSLN formalized an alliance with the Unión Social Cristiana (USC—Social Christian Union), led by the former Comptroller-General Jarquín, who in April 2001 was declared the alliance's vice-presidential candidate, with Ortega as presidential nominee, in the presidential election.

Although in mid-2001 rumours circulated in Nicaragua of a compromise 'anti-pact' candidacy by former President Violeta Chamorro, the November 2001 elections seemed likely to be contested by the FSLN, the PLC and the PCN. Opinion polls in early 2001 suggested that the FSLN would win, although it was believed that the institutional paralysis would remain unchanged. The FSLN was no longer considered a programmatic revolutionary party, but rather the political expression of an economic interest group whose interests lay more in a maintenance of the status quo. This impression was reinforced by the perception that President Alemán was preparing to take up his guaranteed Asamblea Nacional seat, in order to make a bid for re-election in 2006. In many ways, however, this was simply a return to the 'caudillismo' (government by one man) style of politics that was characteristic of Nicaraguan, and indeed Latin American, history.

Economy

PHILLIP WEARNE

The mid- to late 1990s marked a period of gradual economic recovery for Nicaragua, despite a pause in a number of positive economic trends, a result of the devastation caused by 'Hurricane Mitch' in October 1998. Following more than a decade of gross domestic product (GDP) decline, real GDP increased by 4.3% in 1995, 4.7% in 1996 and 5.2% in 1997. This trend continued when in 1998 GDP grew by 4.1%, then 7.4% and 4.3% in 1999 and 2000, respectively. In the same period, the annual rate of inflation was brought under control, standing at 11.6% in 1996, before rising to 13.0% in 1998 and falling again to 11.2% in 1999 and 11.5% in 2000. Exports nearly doubled in the three years to 1997, rising from US $351.7m. in 1994 to $576.8m. in 1997, but declined to $573.2m. in 1998 and $545.3m. in 1999, largely as a result of the disruption caused by Hurricane Mitch, before recovering to $630.7m. in 2000.

Nicaragua's recovery in the latter half of the 1990s followed one of the most prolonged and profound economic crises ever witnessed in the world. By the early 1990s Nicaragua had been in a state of economic crisis bordering on collapse for more than 15 years. This was the result of a prolonged civil war, the imposition of economic sanctions against the country and government mismanagement. All these factors served to accentuate a traditional dependence on imports and external financing. Moreover, economic performance remained excessively reliant on the level of Nicaragua's earnings of convertible currency from the country's narrow range of agricultural commodity exports, the most important of which were bananas, coffee, cotton, meat and sugar. By 1994 gross national product (GNP) per head in Nicaragua was just US $330, making the country the second poorest in the Western hemisphere, after Haiti. By 2000 Nicaraguan GDP per head, just $445, remained pitifully low, at little more than one-half that of the next poorest Central American country, Honduras.

After the revolution of 1979, which overthrew the dictator Anastasio Somoza Debayle, the size of the state sector increased dramatically and significant social reforms were undertaken. However, the Sandinista Government also actively encouraged the expansion of the private sector, which continued to account for more than 50% of economic activity throughout its time in office. The principal economic success of the Sandinista Government occurred in rural areas in the early 1980s. Here agrarian reforms, including expropriation and redistribution of land, stimulated a significant improvement in the standard of living of the peasantry. However, the subsequent US-funded 'Contra' war against the Sandinista Government and the economic boycott of the nation by multilateral lending agencies caused great damage to the Nicaraguan economy, damage from which it had still to recover at the beginning of the 21st century.

Nicaragua's GDP decreased, in real terms, by an annual average of 6.1% in 1985–94. Despite the onset of world recession and the downward pressure on agricultural export prices, the initial restructuring and rehabilitation of the economy following the revolution increased growth in the early 1980s. However, a reduction in external financing, a decrease in agricultural output and growing trade and budget deficits placed immense pressure on available resources. As a result, real GDP gradually declined from 1984, until 1988, when the economy went into deep recession, with GDP contracting by 18.6% in just two years. It was not until 1992 that positive growth, of 0.3%, was recorded. The cumulative impact of the economic contraction of the late 1980s and early 1990s was devastating. By 1994 economic output was more than 60% below that of 1977. In the same year real GDP per head was estimated to be less than one-third of its level 15 years earlier.

In 2000 the population of Nicaragua was estimated at 5.1m., of which about two-thirds resided in urban areas in 1999, principally Managua, Matagalpa, Chinandega, Leon and Masaya, which together accounted for some 2m. people. The important factors in the large increase in urban population levels were the economic recession and, during the 1980s, the Contra war in the countryside. These tendencies, as well as 'hyperinflation' of up to 36,000% per year in 1988, offset the early economic and social success of the 1979 revolution. One such achievement was the Sandinista's literacy campaign. Begun in 1980, it raised the proportion of literate Nicaraguans to 88%. However, by 1999 much of the improvement had been reversed, with the United Nations (UN) estimating that the literacy rate had fallen to just 68.6%.

AGRICULTURE

The agricultural sector was, along with the rest of the economy, deeply depressed in the 1980s and early 1990s. Thereafter it recovered only modestly, impeded by a scarcity of inputs, credit and continuing political instability in many rural areas. Nevertheless, the sector (including hunting, forestry and fishing) remained the mainstay of the economy, employing an estimated 40.0% of the economically active population and accounting for 32.3% of GDP in 2000, when the sector posted an 8.4% increase in output. Production in all sectors of agriculture in 1998 and 1999 reflected the widespread damage and disruption caused by Hurricane Mitch in October 1998; however, production figures appeared to have recovered by 2000.

Production of all Nicaragua's major staple crops increased in the mid-1990s, but the performance of the sector was more variable thereafter. In 1999 production was not good, with output of rice, beans and maize all falling and only the sorghum yield increasing. The output of export crops was similarly variable in the late 1990s. In 2000 the coffee harvest decreased from 91,800 metric tons to an estimated 81,800 tons, but banana production increased from 75,100 tons in 1999 to an estimated 91,600 tons in 2000. The sugar cane harvest also increased from 3.7m. tons in 1999 to an estimated 4.0m. tons in 2000.

After the 1979 revolution, the state expropriated more than 1m. ha of land, of which about 70% was converted into state farms, with the remainder transferred to peasant co-operatives. Large areas of underutilized and idle land were expropriated during the second stage of the Government's land-reform programme in mid-1981. By the end of 1985 some 1.8m. ha, of which about two-thirds were in the Atlantic Coast area, had been redistributed. As a result, the share of farm land in the possession of major landowners was reduced from 36% to 11%, while smallholders increased their proportion 10-fold, to 20%. From 1986 the emphasis was on production from co-operatives, or individual smallholders, with the Government continuing to exercise considerable control through its monopoly purchases of export crops.

The Government of President Violeta Barrios de Chamorro (1990–97) adopted a pragmatic approach, privatizing a number of large state farms but declining to reverse the Sandinista land reforms that had granted land to co-operatives and smallholders. However, the demands of resettling former Contras, who were given land from former state farms, took priority. The administration of President Arnoldo Alemán Lacayo, which took power in January 1997, endorsed this flexibility, reaching an agreement with the Sandinista opposition, which sanctioned the land and property distribution, to legitimize beneficiaries of the Sandinista reforms. At the same time, the new Government established an arbitration mechanism to adjudicate the claims of many larger property owners who insisted that they had been victims of asset seizures by senior Sandinistas. Meanwhile, the cycle of claims and counter-claims continued to be a major disincentive to significant private investment in agriculture.

Agricultural production in Nicaragua remained subject to all the normal variables in Central America: weather, labour shortages, fluctuating world commodity prices and crop disease. However, the sector had the additional burden of almost continuous war, or its effects, from the late 1970s, in the country's most important agricultural zones. During the early 1970s, agricultural production increased, on average, by 7.8% per year, with rapid growth in the production of beef, bananas, sugar, cotton and coffee. Such production was export-orientated and did little to improve the country's growing food deficit. Fluctuating world commodity prices, labour shortages at harvest time and

adverse weather conditions reduced the annual growth rate to around 2.5% per year during the late 1970s. In 1978–79 agricultural production fell dramatically, as the civil war intensified. With the aid of large state subsidies, production was restored to pre-revolutionary levels in 1981. However, agricultural output subsequently deteriorated, with floods and drought contributing to a fall of 8% in 1982 alone.

Food imports continued to increase, while production of the principal cash crop, coffee, declined steadily after 1984. Coffee production reached a nadir in 1990, but recovered fairly steadily thereafter, with the harvest virtually doubling in 1994–96, to reach 1.3m. quintals. In 1997, however, coffee output declined to 1.2m. quintals before rising to 1.4m. quintals in 1998 and falling back slightly to 1.4m. quintals in 1999. Coffee export earnings followed a similar pattern, affected not only by lower volumes of exports but by the dramatic price decrease after 1989, and the sudden price increase in 1994–95. In 1993 export earnings were just US $34.5m. This figure increased to $73m. in the following year and increased once again, to reach $131.3m. in 1995, $128.0m. in 1996 and $123.6m. in 1997. However, good harvests yielded by an expansion programme begun several years earlier produced earnings of $167.1m. in 1998. Exports fell to $135.3m. in 1999, before recovering to $169.5m. in 2000. Owing to the adverse affect on the sector of problematic harvests and variable world prices, in early 2001 the Government announced an aid plan for the sector of special loans to export producers.

The cotton industry fared rather worse and by 1998 had virtually ceased to exist. Export earnings declined from US $44.4m. in 1991, when the country produced 30,000 metric tons of cotton lint, to just $400,000 in 1993 (an estimated 1,000 tons). Some recovery occurred thereafter, with an increase in world prices stimulating planting. Export earnings rose to $10.1m. by 1996. However, another cycle of low prices had a predictable effect on the area planted and export earnings. In 1998 the latter were just $300,000, less than one-10th the level of the previous year. Sugar, bananas and sesame seeds were among other significant agricultural exports. Sugar export earnings decreased from $38.6m. in 1990 to $15.8m. in 1994, despite remarkably stable annual production averaging 2.4m. tons. However, earnings increased steadily to reach $53.2m. in 1997 before falling back to $39.7m. in 1998 and some $30.4m. in 1999. Export revenue from bananas followed a similar pattern, reaching a low of $5.5m. in 1993 before recovering to $22.3m. in 1996 and $21.9m. in 1998. Preliminary results put export revenues at $13.6m. in 1999 and just $10.6m. in 2000. Sesame seed production decreased significantly in the late 1990s with export revenues falling similarly. Exports were worth just $3.9m. in 1999, less than one-third of their $14.7m. value in 1996.

In 2000 the livestock industry, like other sectors, had yet to recover fully from the shortage of foreign exchange for foreign machinery and other essential products, during the Contra war in the 1980s. Compounding this, the sector was excluded from government credit schemes in the early 1990s, and it seemed unlikely to recover its former position in terms of export importance. Some sub-sectors did show improvement, however. Thus, beef and veal output was estimated at 51,000 metric tons in 1994, producing a rise in export earnings, to US $67.6m. in that year. However, the improvement was not maintained, with meat exports earning just $38.8m. in 1998 and $41.8m. in 1999.

Nicaragua possessed substantial supplies of timber, including considerable reserves of hardwoods such as mahogany, cedar, rosewood, caoba and oak. In the 1990s roundwood production averaged about 4.0m. cu m annually, rising slightly in 1999 to 4.3m. cu m. Concern about overexploitation in the mid-1990s led the National Assembly to ban further logging concessions in 1996. The development of the fishing industry was a major priority in the late 20th century. Three fish-processing plants were rehabilitated and commercial fishing of crab, crayfish, shrimp, lobster and tuna was encouraged. By 1998 the total shrimp catch had doubled in just five years to 15.8m. lbs, although it fell to 13.0m. lbs in 1999. The fish catch remained fairly stable during the late 1990s, fluctuating between 12.6m. lbs and 15.2m. lbs, while lobster production reached a new peak of 3.9m. lbs in 1999. Earnings from lobster and shrimp exports also remained stable, rising slightly to $84.1m. in 1999.

MINING AND POWER

The mining sector was completely nationalized in 1979. However, after the end of the Sandinista regime, successive Governments ceded the rights of exploitation of all natural resources to private companies under long-term lease agreements. The policy met with some success: an estimated US $70m. of private investment was directed into the sector in the 1990s. The contribution of the mining sector to overall GDP reflected the investment, rising from 0.6% in 1994 to 1.0% in 1999, although this fell in 2000 to 0.7% of GDP. Increases in gold production were in line with sectoral performance, a 51% expansion resulting in output of 123,300 troy oz in 1998. The sector recorded a further rise in 1999, with output of 143,000 troy oz, but a fall in 2000 to 118,100 troy oz. After two years of rapidly declining output, silver production increased by almost 50% in 1997, rising to 34,600 troy oz, before increasing to 62,600 troy oz in 1998. However, output fell to 57,200 troy oz in 1999 and to 51,100 troy oz in 2000. This level of output remained well below the 84,500 troy oz mined in 1994, although official sources predicted that exports could triple in the early 21st century, as some of the six closed gold and silver mines returned to production.

Dependence on imported energy sources, particularly petroleum, proved a major problem for successive Nicaraguan Governments. During much of its time in office, the Sandinista Government relied on cheap or bartered petroleum from Mexico or the former USSR. However, Mexico suspended supplies when even 'soft-term' payments became overdue and in 1987 the USSR announced large reductions in supplies, causing severe energy problems. In the late 1990s, as the country's credit rating was somewhat restored, much of Nicaragua's petroleum needs were met by Venezuela and Mexico under the concessionary terms of the 1980 San José Agreement. Despite ambitious diversification efforts, in particular the inauguration of the Momotombo geothermal plant in 1984 and the Asturias hydroelectric scheme five years later, oil and fuel imports remained crucial throughout the 1980s and 1990s, costing the country as much as US $273.4m. in 2000, compared with the $181.5m. required in 1998. In 1999 hydroelectricity provided 27.8% of Nicaragua's total production of 1,410.8 gWh, with geothermal plants contributing just over 3% of this total. In 1999 both total electricity generation (down by 22%) and the contribution of geothermal plants declined seriously on 1998.

Net electrical generating capacity was estimated to be 503 MW in 1999, an increase of almost 30% on the previous year, largely a result of a number of new private power-plants coming on stream. The new capacity was expected to alleviate the frequent power shortages so common in the 1990s when supply covered just one-half of consumer demand. Foreign companies had been required to restrict output to 30 MW per year until 1999, but in that year the US company, Amfels, was given permission to increase capacity at its Puerto Sandino plant to 57 MW. At the same time, Ormat Industries of Israel signed a 15-year operating contract for the Momotombo geothermal plant with the state power company, Empresa Nicaragüense de Electricidad (ENEL). The Israeli firm pledged to invest an initial US $15m., with up to $30m. to follow, and announced plans to increase the plant's capacity from 13 MW to 70 MW. In 1999 ENEL was divided into three generating companies (one hydroelectric and two thermal plants) and two distribution companies, in preparation for privatization, for which tenders were solicited in May 2000. Meanwhile, ENEL continued to increase spending on the rehabilitation and repair of existing plant and transmission lines and a regional electricity grid, the core of which already existed in the import and export of power to Honduras and Panama. The dilapidated state of the power-distribution system in Nicaragua was responsible for the loss of up to 25% of all power generated during the 1990s. The distribution companies were sold to the Spanish company, Unión Fenosa, in November 2000; however, the Government failed to sell the generating companies, the privatization of which was still pending in 2001.

MANUFACTURING AND INDUSTRY

Manufacturing activity in Nicaragua centred on the processing and packing of local agricultural produce, although some heavy industries, such as chemical and cement production, also existed. In 2000 manufacturing accounted for an estimated 14.4% of GDP, an increase of 2.0% on the previous year. The rapid expansion of import-substitution industries during the 1960s was short-lived and the average annual rate of manufacturing growth decreased from 11.4% in 1960–70 to 2.5% in 1970–82. However, as political strife, hyperinflation and shortages of raw materials, imported machinery and skilled personnel took full effect, manufacturing contracted by an average of 4.9% per year between 1983 and 1989. The sector's overall contribution to GDP decreased accordingly. The contraction persisted into the early 1990s and, although it subsequently recovered, recording growth greater than 10% in five successive years from 1994, by 2000 the sector had still to reach the levels attained 20 years earlier.

The civil war seriously disrupted manufacturing activity and production was estimated to have decreased by 26.4%, in real terms, during 1979. Growth after the revolution was sporadic and uneven. While the shifting of the economy on to a permanent war footing stimulated the production of consumer goods for the armed forces and of construction materials for the repair of roads and buildings, other import-dependent industries suffered from the reduction in consumer spending and from Nicaragua's chronic shortage of foreign exchange. By 1985 the private sector had contracted by about 20% and was operating at little more than 50% of capacity. After a brief respite in 1986–87, manufacturing was again badly affected by the 1988–89 recession. Industrial production was estimated to have contracted by some 20% in 1989 alone.

The end of the civil war, a sharp fall in import tariffs and renewed access to the US market provided new opportunities in manufacturing, with many Nicaraguan exiles returning to take advantage of them. However, the continued contraction in the domestic market acted as a restraint, particularly in production sectors such as beverages, processed foods and cigarettes. Fluctuations were common, with a 6.4% growth in manufacturing in 1991 being followed by a 5.0% contraction in 1992. Thenceforth, output of manufactured food and beverage products increased modestly but steadily, while tobacco and textile production contracted dramatically. Overall, the sector grew by some 3.7% in 1999 and 2.1% in 2000, with the building materials sub-sector expanding nearly 40% in the wake of the rebuilding efforts following Hurricane Mitch. The varied performance reflected a major restructuring of the Nicaraguan manufacturing sector, following economic liberalization efforts. An importation tariff reform brought cheap imports and, unable to compete, many traditional manufacturing businesses closed, diversified or formed joint ventures with foreign firms or returning exiles attracted into the country by a more favourable foreign investment environment.

Rapid expansion was seen, however, in the *maquila*, or offshore assembly, sector. The Las Mercedes free-trade zone, the country's first, doubled its total exports to US $80m. in 1995, although subsequent growth was more modest, averaging 3% per year in 1996–99. Although its principal product was clothing assembled from US-imported textiles, the plants also produced footwear, aluminium frames and jewellery, with companies from Hong Kong and the Republic of China (Taiwan) augmenting those from the USA. The Chamorro Government privatized some of the state agro-business projects completed by the Sandinistas, including the $500m.-Tititapa/Malacatoya sugar mill, the Chiltepe dairy project and a fruit and vegetable processing and canning factory in the Sebaco valley. However, the sale of these enterprises had little impact on the manufacturing sector. The plants that were transferred experienced the same problems in the private sector as they had under public ownership. In 2001 the Court of Appeal ruled against a *maquila* company, Chentex (based in the Republic of China, Taiwan), for illegally dismissing nine employees who had organized a strike in May 2000. However, this landmark ruling was not welcomed by the Nicaraguan business sector, as it was seen as a potential threat to further foreign investment in the *maquila* sector.

Until 1988 the construction sector continued to grow, accounting for 3% of total GDP in that year. Much of the investment during the 1980s was strategic, including roads, airfields and a deep-water port at El Bluff, on the Atlantic coast, which was built with Bulgarian assistance. By 1990, however, the industry appeared to be contracting rapidly, decreasing by

11% in 1989, and an estimated 9% in the following year. The Chamorro Government's reconstruction programme reversed the decline in the early 1990s and the sector expanded by 10% in 1992. The fluctuations continued in the mid-1990s and in 1998 the sector accounted for 4.4% of GDP.

However, the assistance given the sector by reconstruction efforts in the wake of Hurricane Mitch, combined with several large-scale projects in the tourism and transport sectors, dramatically expanded construction in 1999 and 2000, when it accounted for 6.0% and 6.3% of overall GDP, respectively. In 2000 the construction industry employed 5.4% of the economically active population. The production of basic materials also greatly expanded; cement production increased by 24.2% in 1999, to 11.8m. quintals, while concrete production nearly doubled in the three years to 1999 and asphalt output increased by 42% in 1999, reaching 67,600 barrels. With work continuing to replace and rebuild the 200,000 homes destroyed or damaged in the hurricane and several more large private investment construction projects, the construction industry seemed assured of further substantive growth.

PUBLIC FINANCE AND PAYMENTS

The Government of President Chamorro had some success in controlling one of the highest current-account budget deficits ever recorded. Access to external funds from the USA and multilateral lending agencies, a dramatic decrease in inflation, severe reductions in public spending, as well as privatization of state enterprises, improved tax collection and the retirement or renegotiation of some of the country's massive foreign debt combined to help reduce the budget deficit from the average 25% of GDP it had reached in the 1980s. By 1994 the budget deficit (before grants) was equivalent to 9.7% of GDP and it fell sharply to 5.6% and 4.5% of GDP (before grants) in 1997 and 1998, respectively, before increasing to 11.7% of GDP in 1999. Much of this was financed by foreign grants and concessionary loans, which in turn contributed substantially to a capital expenditure programme that, with the International Monetary Fund's (IMF) permission, almost doubled to 20.9% of GDP in 1999 in the wake of reconstruction and emergency spending required as a result of Hurricane Mitch.

Many of the policies of the Chamorro Government were in fact implemented by the previous administration. Although the Sandinista Government had attempted to offset the increase in state spending on defence in the 1980s by increasing taxation on profits, workers' remittances and non-essential imports, the Government was forced to implement a programme of austerity measures in 1988–89, in an attempt to solve the growing budget crisis. The two programmes included large devaluations, the creation of new currencies, wide-ranging price increases and, in the latter case, budget reductions that involved a large number of job losses in the public sector. There were also job losses under the Chamorro Government, as attempts were made to reduce the deficit as part of its stabilization programme of March 1991. The programme's only lasting achievement, however, was to reduce the rate of inflation. The official rate of unemployment fell almost steadily from 1994 and was estimated to be 9.8% in 2000. Underemployment, as defined by the Ministry of Employment, remained static; it was 12.1% in 1998.

On assuming the presidency in 1997, Arnoldo Alemán Lacayo continued to limit public spending. In addition, tax collection improved markedly in the late 1990s, with revenue rising by 28% in 1998 and a further 14.9% in 1999, largely owing to a substantial rise in import tax and general sales tax revenue as reconstruction efforts stimulated demand. Capital spending in 1999 was double that of the previous year, but was nominally at least covered by the international donations and grants made available in the wake of Hurricane Mitch. The Sandinistas had always had recourse to the Central Bank to print money to fund such spending. Rapid growth in the money supply, which increased by 189% in 1985 and grew still further, to expand by 644% in 1987 and 11,762% in 1988, was the inevitable consequence. This, in turn, led to an increasing parallel or informal economy, the 'black market', which traded in both US dollars and consumer goods. The country's money-supply problems during the 1980s were worsened by the fact that perhaps two-thirds of the money in use circulated outside the formal economy. The increase in the money supply, combined

with acute shortages of goods, caused high rates of inflation. The consumer price index rose by 25% in 1982, and the rate of increase continued, until it reached the highest rate ever recorded in the world, 36,000%, in 1988. However, by 1990 it had decreased to a mere 7,485%, responding well thereafter to the monetary control exerted by the Government. In the late 1990s the money supply grew relatively modestly, with the highest growth of 33% in 1996, and the lowest of 17% in 1998. Partly as a result, inflation moderated between 9.2% in 1997 and 11.2% in 1999. In 2000 inflation was 11.5%.

The growing deficits in the budget and on the current account of the balance of payments forced the Sandinista Government to increase its foreign borrowing during the 1980s. As a result, the external debt of US $1,600m., which was inherited from the Somoza dictatorship in 1979, increased to more than $9,300m. by 1989. The main problem was the Sandinistas' refusal to enter into an agreement with the IMF and the country's consequent exclusion from access to Western loans. With access to multilateral loans from the IDB restricted by US opposition, Nicaragua became dependent on bilateral credits from Western states and countries that were members of the Council for Mutual Economic Assistance (CMEA). Following initial rescheduling, a moratorium on public-sector debt-service payments had, by September 1982, become inevitable. In June 1983 Nicaragua failed to repay $45m. and requested the renegotiation of $180m. in interest payments due in 1984. Unable to pay either interest or principal on its debt, Nicaragua entered a state of 'passive default'. However, in 1988–89 the Sandinista Government implemented many of the measures traditionally demanded by the IMF as part of its own austerity programme.

These measures facilitated the implementation of the new policies of the Chamorro Government. In 1992, with the USA agreeing to waive payment of US $259.5m. in bilateral debt and the 'Paris Club' of Western creditor nations reducing an $830m. debt to $207m., the new Government was able to pay arrears to the World Bank (International Bank for Reconstruction and Development—IBRD) and the IDB. This, in turn, opened a series of loan opportunities. The IMF ended its 12-year boycott of Nicaragua by approving a $55.7m. stand-by loan and the IDB approved a $132.5m. loan to support adjustment programmes in the trade and financial sectors. Restructuring of debt payments with various major bilateral creditors such as Mexico, the Russian Federation (as the principal successor state of the USSR) and several European countries followed in 1992. However, by 1993 Nicaragua was again defaulting on repayment. Continued contraction of the economy and widening of the trade deficit was followed by a severe decline in foreign aid inflows in 1992–93. Of the $612m. of foreign aid received in 1993, 80% was assigned to servicing the country's ever-growing foreign-debt arrears. It was in this context that the Chamorro Government reached agreement with the IMF on a $120m. enhanced structural-adjustment loan in early 1994 and redoubled its efforts to secure debt renegotiation and cancellation. In 1994 Nicaragua's external debt totalled $11,019m. In 1995 the Government secured the purchase of more than 80% of its commercial debt at eight cents in the dollar, effectively paying US $112m. to cancel $1,400m. in debt. This followed the restructuring of debts of $633m. in March 1995 by the Paris Club, some $560m. of which was owed to Germany. In 1998 the Club agreed to a further two-year postponement of $201m. in debt-service payments. In April 1996 Nicaragua finally reached agreement with Russia over its $3,500m. debt to the former USSR, with 95% of the outstanding amount being forgiven. Later that year Mexico followed suit, agreeing to waive 91% of the $1,100m. that it was owed by Nicaragua. Agreement was also reached with the IMF in 1998 on a second enhanced structural-adjustment loan. In November 1998 a number of countries pardoned or softened terms on bilateral debt they were owed, in the wake of Hurricane Mitch. Cuba, Austria and France, in particular, waived a total of US $157m. in bilateral debt. France then waived a further $90m. in outstanding debt in February 2000.

In September 1999 Nicaragua was declared eligible for inclusion in the IMF–World Bank Heavily Indebted Poor Countries (HIPC) debt-relief initiative, which made the cancellation of 80%–90% of the country's foreign debt possible. However, the timing remained uncertain. Fulfilment of economic targets were expected to lead to inclusion and further debt reduction, already initiated by the Banco Centroamericano de Integración Económica (BCIE), which waived some US $101m. in debt under the HIPC initiative in September 1997. However, the war, sanctions and natural disasters meant that the scale of Nicaragua's debt problem remained unique: the country remained one of the most highly-indebted in the world, with an external debt as a proportion of GNP of over 300% in 1999, and arrears on debt service an economic fact of life for more than two decades. Despite all the debt forgiveness and renegotiation, in 2000 the country's foreign debt was still one of the highest in the world, at an estimated $6,427m.

FOREIGN TRADE

Nicaragua's export trade was dominated by agricultural commodities, mainly coffee, cotton, sugar, beef, bananas and, increasingly, seafood. Import trade was dominated by petroleum, other raw materials, non-durable consumer goods and machinery. However, the civil war halted foreign trading activity and reserves of convertible currency were exhausted by 1980. The enormous cost of the war, increased purchases of petroleum and reduced income from exports (chiefly owing to low prices for coffee, sugar and cotton) resulted in a trade deficit of US $482.6m. in 1988. Exports, which earned $508m. in 1981, declined to $236m. by 1988. They increased slowly, to $340m. in 1990, but decreased steadily again, to $222m. by 1992. Thenceforth, there was substantial improvement, with revenue from exports rising steadily to $660.2m. in 1996 and $666.7m. in 1997. However, the damage caused to export crops by Hurricane Mitch resulted in a fall in revenues in 1998, to $573m.; there was another decrease to an estimated $545m. in 1999, but export revenues recovered to $630.7m. in 2000.

Imports of goods, which were worth US $94.2m. (f.o.b.) in 1981, reached $807m. by 1988 and did not decline as markedly as expected in the late 1980s, despite the dramatic deterioration in economic activity. By 1993 imports stood at $659.4m. This figure continued to increase throughout the rest of the decade, reaching $1,469.8m. in 1997 and $1,383.1m. in 1998. In 1999, fuelled by the reconstruction and repair needs resulting from Hurricane Mitch, Nicaragua's imports increased to $1,683.2m., before falling slightly to $1,629.1m. in 2000. The only substantial new source of income that helped defray the trade deficit was tourism revenue. In 1999 income reached $113m., an increase of 25.6% on the previous year, while arrivals increased by 15.4% to reach 468,000.

Fighting in the border regions disrupted Nicaragua's trade with neighbouring Central American countries during the 1980s. Non-traditional exports to the Central American Common Market (CACM) suffered most, decreasing by more than 75% in 1982–85. The irregular availability of foreign exchange was the principal problem, but the continued economic recession throughout the region was also a contributory factor. Trade with Argentina and Brazil increased, owing to the extension of trade credits for Nicaragua's prime agricultural exports. With the exception of bananas, Nicaragua's trade with the USA fell dramatically, from 31% in 1980, when US imports to

Nicaragua were valued at US $242m., to less than 1% in 1987 (valued at $160m.).

However, with the US trade embargo lifted in 1990, trade with Nicaragua's most natural trading partner rapidly began to improve. Initially, it seemed clear that the resumption of relations with the USA was more likely to increase imports than exports. However, by 1993 exports to the USA represented 48.1% of Nicaragua's total exports, while the value of goods from the USA rose to 26.6% of total imports. By 1999, however, with total imports increasing more quickly than exports, these figures moved into balance, with trade with the USA accounting for 37.6% of exports and 33.9% of imports. Trade with Nicaragua's neighbours recovered substantially; in 1999 Central American states accounted for 27.1% of Nicaragua's exports and 35.5% of the country's imports. El Salvador became Nicaragua's second-largest export market, taking 12.5% of its goods in 1999. In May 2001 the Central American countries, including Nicaragua, reached an accord with Mexico, known as the 'Plan Puebla–Panamá', under which the region would be integrated through joint transport, industry and tourism projects.

CONCLUSION

From the mid-1980s repeated promises that the Nicaraguan economy would improve went unfulfilled. However, by mid-2001 there was a general consensus that, despite the huge set-backs caused by Hurricane Mitch, most economic indicators were encouraging. The economy was expected to maintain its momentum in 2001–02 and retain the 4.3% growth achieved in 2000. While the increase in the level of imports was expected to slow down, the value of exports was also expected to rise, resulting in some amelioration of the large trade deficit. Meanwhile, the rate of inflation, which was virtually static in 2000 at 11.5% was not expected to alter significantly, owing to the elimination of the shortages caused by Hurricane Mitch. There were, however, real dangers to the generally positive economic trend. The most obvious was a deterioration in foreign trade, which Nicaragua had suffered in recent years, owing to diverse prices of basic commodities like coffee and oil. Another potential threat stemmed from the relative economic success of recent years: that the positive economic trend might tempt the Government to increase public spending and to deviate from the fiscal path laid down by the IMF, especially in the election year of 2001.

Even without the additional complication of an election in which the Sandinistas could return to power, Nicaragua's political climate remained polarized. The scale of devastation that the country suffered in the 1970s and 1980s, not to mention that caused by Hurricane Mitch, left huge political, economic and developmental challenges. Real wages continued to fall, rising just 4.4% in 1999 in the face of inflation of 11.2% and national income per head, at just US $445 in 2000, was the second lowest in Latin America. The scale of the problem was reflected in the fact that a massive 72.6% of households remained impoverished or severely impoverished (as measured by UN criteria, focusing on unmet basic needs). Poverty and polarization were perhaps, then, the principal threats to continued economic progress in Nicaragua.

Statistical Survey

Sources (unless otherwise stated): Banco Central de Nicaragua, Carretera Sur, Km 7, Apdos 2252/3, Zona 5, Managua; tel. (2) 65-0500; fax (2) 65-2272; e-mail bcn@cabcn.gob.ni; internet www.bcn.gob.ni; Instituto Nacional de Estadísticas y Censos (INEC), Las Brisas, Frente Hospital Fonseca, Managua; tel. (2) 66-2031.

Area and Population

AREA, POPULATION AND DENSITY

Area (sq km)	
Land	109,004
Inland water	11,250
Total	120,254*
Population (census results)	
20 April 1971	1,877,952
25 April 1995	
Males	2,147,105
Females	2,209,994
Total	4,357,099
Population (official estimates at mid-year)	
1998	4,803,100
1999	4,935,600
2000	5,071,700
Density (per sq km) at mid-2000	42.2

* 46,430 sq miles.

DEPARTMENTS (estimated population at mid-1995)

Boaco	124,500	Managua . . .	1,056,700
Carazo . . .	141,800	Masaya	236,100
Chinandega . .	349,000	Matagalpa . . .	364,800
Chontales . . .	137,500	Nueva Segovia . .	151,300
Estelí	168,900	Río San Juan . .	70,900
Granada . . .	153,200	Rivas	141,800
Jinotega . . .	214,100	Zelaya Norte . .	175,400
León	330,200	Zelaya Sur . . .	223,500
Madríz . . .	99,800	**Total** . . .	4,139,500

PRINCIPAL TOWN

Managua (capital), estimated population 819,700 at mid-1995.

BIRTHS AND DEATHS (World Bank estimates)

		1996	1997	1998
Birth rate (per 1,000)	. . .	33	32	31
Death rate (per 1,000)	. .	6	5	5

Expectation of life (World Bank estimates, years at birth): 68 in 1996; 68 in 1997; 68 in 1998.

Source: World Bank, *World Development Indicators*.

ECONOMICALLY ACTIVE POPULATION ('000 persons)

	1998	1999	2000*
Agriculture, forestry and fishing .	609.2	655.3	711.8
Mining and quarrying . . .	9.7	11.7	9.4
Manufacturing	122.0	125.3	127.8
Electricity, gas and water . .	5.8	5.8	5.9
Construction	63.2	88.1	97.3
Trade, restaurants and hotels .	245.5	259.2	268.3
Transport and communications .	46.8	49.7	51.2
Financial services . . .	17.4	20.1	21.8
Government services . . .	71.2	67.5	65.0
Other services	251.0	261.5	278.8
Total employed . . .	**1,441.8**	**1,544.2**	**1,637.3**
Unemployed	219.5	184.7	178.0
Total labour force . . .	**1,661.3**	**1,728.9**	**1,815.3**

* Preliminary figures.

Agriculture

PRINCIPAL CROPS ('000 metric tons)

	1998	1999	2000
Rice (paddy)	265.9	193.0	285.3
Maize	300.5	290.8	363.6
Sorghum	51.4	75.4	102.3
Cassava (Manioc)* . . .	51.0	51.5	52.0
Dry beans	149.1	134.5	113.6
Tomatoes	2.2	2.4	6.2
Oranges*	71.0	71.0	71.0
Pineapples*	46.0	46.0	47.0
Bananas	87.9	75.1	91.6
Plantains*	38.0	39.0	40.0
Sugar cane	3,459.2	3,687.1	4,000.0
Coffee (green) . . .	65.4	91.8	81.8
Cotton (lint)	1.7	2.0*	2.0*

* FAO estimate(s).
Source: FAO.

LIVESTOCK ('000 head, year ending September)

	1998	1999	2000
Cattle*	1,668.0	1,693.0	1,660.0
Pigs†	400.0	400.0	400.0
Goats†	6.4	6.4	6.5
Horses†	245.0	245.0	245.0
Asses†	8.5	8.5	8.5
Mules†	45.6	45.7	45.7

* Unofficial figure. † FAO estimates.
Poultry† (million): 9.3 in 1998; 10.6 in 1999; 10.0 in 2000.
Source: FAO.

LIVESTOCK PRODUCTS ('000 metric tons)

	1998	1999	2000
Beef and veal	45.8	47.9	48.8
Pig meat	5.6	5.7	6.0
Poultry meat	32.0	36.8	38.5
Cows' milk	218.1	224.0	230.6
Butter	0.9	0.9	0.9
Cheese	7.9	11.3	11.3*
Hen eggs	30.3	30.3*	30.3*
Cattle hides*	7.1	7.1	7.1

* FAO estimate(s).
Source: FAO.

Forestry

ROUNDWOOD REMOVALS
('000 cubic metres, excluding bark)

	1997	1998	1999
Sawlogs, veneer logs and logs for sleepers	228	228	228
Fuel wood	3,864	3,970	4,078
Total	**4,092**	**4,198**	**4,306**

Source: FAO, *Yearbook of Forest Products*.

SAWNWOOD PRODUCTION
('000 cubic metres, incl. railway sleepers)

	1997	1998	1999
Coniferous	104	104	104
Broadleaved	44	44	44
Total	**148**	**148**	**148**

Source: FAO, *Yearbook of Forest Products*.

Fishing

(metric tons, live weight)

	1996	1997	1998
Capture .	15,442	16,176	19,892
Freshwater fishes .	1,142	1,293	1,256
Marine fishes .	5,859	6,886	9,530
Spiny lobsters .	4,458	4,164	3,795
Shrimps .	3,983	3,833	4,904
Aquaculture .	2,573	3,773	4,789
Whiteleg shrimp .	2,568	3,570	4,545
Total catch .	18,015	19,949	24,681

Source: FAO, *Yearbook of Fishery Statistics*.

Mining

	1998	1999*	2000*
Gold ('000 troy ounces) .	123.3	143.0	118.1
Silver ('000 troy ounces) .	62.6	57.2	51.1
Sand ('000 cubic metres) .	695.8	737.3	535.6
Limestone ('000 cubic metres) .	295.5	250.8	261.3
Gypsum ('000 metric tons) .	22.7	26.9	28.2

* Provisional figures.

Industry

SELECTED PRODUCTS

('000 metric tons, unless otherwise indicated)

	1995	1996	1997
Raw sugar .	297	349	351
Motor spirit .	102	102	97
Kerosene .	13	17	16
Jet fuel .	18	19	18
Distillate fuel oils .	217	174	220
Residual fuel oils .	184	250	355
Bitumen (asphalt) .	14*	14*	14
Electric energy (million kWh)† .	1,796	1,919	1,907
Soap (metric tons) .	14,318	21,796	9,488
Rum ('000 litres) .	12,014	12,381	11,374
Cigarettes (million) .	1,521	1,510	1,580

* Provisional figure(s).

Sources: UN, *Industrial Commodity Statistics Yearbook*; Central Bank.

Finance

CURRENCY AND EXCHANGE RATES

Monetary Units
100 centavos = 1 córdoba oro (gold córdoba).

Sterling, Dollar and Euro Equivalents (30 April 2001)
£1 sterling = 19.06 gold córdobas;
US $1 = 13.31 gold córdobas;
€1 = 11.81 gold córdobas;
1,000 gold córdobas = £52.47 = $75.13 = €84.65.

Average Exchange Rate (gold córdobas per US dollar)
1998	10.58
1999	11.81
2000	12.69

Note: In February 1988 a new córdoba, equivalent to 1,000 of the former units, was introduced, and a uniform exchange rate of US $1 = 10 new córdobas was established. Subsequently, the exchange rate was frequently adjusted. A new currency, the córdoba oro (gold córdoba), was introduced as a unit of account in May 1990 and began to be circulated in August. The value of the gold córdoba was initially fixed at par with the US dollar, but in March 1991 the exchange rate was revised to $1 = 25,000,000 new córdobas (or 5 gold córdobas). On 30 April 1991 the gold córdoba became the sole legal tender.

BUDGET (million gold córdobas)

Revenue*	1996	1997	1998
Taxation .	3,637.0	4,624.3	5,638.9
Direct taxes .	513.7	679.5	814.1
Taxes on income and profits	511.3	675.3	810.3
Taxes on goods and services	2,157.8	2,653.7	3,085.4
General sales tax .	519.4	703.3	931.4
Excise and selective consumption tax .	1,375.1	1,756.3	2,137.3
Petroleum products .	667.6	858.8	1,099.4
Stamp taxes .	263.2	194.1	16.7
Taxes on international trade and transactions .	778.9	1,058.8	1,514.0
Earmarked revenue.	186.6	232.3	225.5
Other current revenue .	138.6	241.8	247.3
Transfers .	21.2	0.6	—
Capital revenue .	42.1	24.6	19.4
Total .	3,838.9	4,891.3	5,905.6

Expenditure†	1996	1997	1998
Current expenditure .	3,758.5	4,411.0	4,729.8
Personnel emoluments .	1,085.9	1,176.8	1,367.2
Goods and services .	1,194.2	986.3	1,052.7
Interest payments .	584.4	1,071.9	1,003.9
Current transfers .	894.0	1,176.0	1,306.0
Capital expenditure .	1,774.2	1,919.1	2,224.2
Fixed capital formation .	1,059.3	955.4	1,267.2
Capital transfers .	715.0	963.7	957.0
Total .	5,532.7	6,330.1	6,954.0

* Excluding grants received (million gold córdobas): 1,019.5 in 1996; 821.7 in 1997; 675.0 in 1998.
† Excluding net lending (million gold córdobas): 2.5 in 1996; 5.6 in 1997; 83.2 in 1998.

Source: IMF, *Nicaragua: Recent Economic Developments and Statistical Annex* (October 1999).

CENTRAL BANK RESERVES (US $ million at 31 December)*

	1998	1999	2000
IMF special drawing rights .	0.21	0.21	0.06
Foreign exchange .	350.20	509.50	488.40
Total .	350.41	509.71	488.46

* Excluding gold reserves (US $ million at 31 December): 4.10 in 1993.

Source: IMF, *International Financial Statistics*.

MONEY SUPPLY (million gold córdobas at 31 December)

	1997	1998	1999
Currency outside banks .	1,096	1,340	1,735
Demand deposits at commercial banks .	959	1,196	1,406
Total money (incl. others) .	2,064	2,551	3,151

Source: IMF, *International Financial Statistics*.

COST OF LIVING

(Consumer Price Index for Managua. Base: 1994 = 100)

	1997	1998	1999
Food, beverages and tobacco .	136.0	155.5	163.9
Clothing .	101.9	110.9	123.9
Housing .	172.4	198.9	253.3
All items (incl. others) .	135.2	152.9	170.0

Source: ILO, *Yearbook of Labour Statistics*.

NATIONAL ACCOUNTS

Expenditure on the Gross Domestic Product
(million gold córdobas at current prices)

	1997	1998	1999
Government final consumption expenditure	3,176	3,657	4,928
Private final consumption expenditure	17,484	20,862	25,131
Increase in stocks	49	142	79
Gross fixed capital formation	5,788	7,301	11,386
Total domestic expenditure	26,497	31,962	41,524
Exports of goods and services	7,434	8,057	9,004
Less Imports of goods and services	14,805	17,519	23,746
GDP in purchasers' values	19,127	22,500	26,782
GDP at constant 1980 prices*	4.3	4.6	4.8

* In gold córdobas.

Source: IMF, *International Financial Statistics.*

Gross Domestic Product by Economic Activity
(million gold córdobas at current prices)

	1998	1999	2000*
Agriculture, hunting, forestry and fishing	7,087.7	8,248.0	9,817.6
Mining and quarrying	215.1	256.1	220.5
Manufacturing	3,405.3	3,878.4	4,389.5
Electricity, gas and water	265.9	297.6	338.7
Construction	952.0	1,559.5	1,920.5
Wholesale and retail trade	5,149.3	6,001.6	6,867.2
Transport and communications	767.3	893.6	1,023.4
Finance, insurance, real estate and business services	1,166.6	1,347.2	1,560.8
Public administration and defence	1,645.0	2,226.2	2,615.2
Other services	1,227.2	1,417.9	1,641.9
Total	21,881.4	26,126.1	30,395.0

* Preliminary figures.

BALANCE OF PAYMENTS (US $ million)

	1997	1998	1999
Exports of goods f.o.b.	630.9	579.4	550.0
Imports of goods f.o.b.	−1,329.3	−1,383.1	−1,683.2
Trade balance	−698.4	−803.7	−1,133.2
Exports of services	216.6	251.1	288.7
Imports of services	−237.1	−271.9	−327.7
Balance on goods and services	−718.9	−824.5	−1,172.2
Other income received	14.7	19.5	27.0
Other income paid	−279.4	−211.2	−227.0
Balance on goods, services and income	−983.6	−1,016.2	−1,372.2
Current transfers received	427.4	518.0	720.0
Current balance	−556.2	−498.2	−652.2
Direct investment from abroad	173.1	183.7	300.0
Other investment assets	−70.8	55.2	22.2
Other investment liabilities	−163.3	−155.3	69.7
Net errors and omissions	322.6	13.8	−192.8
Overall balance	−294.6	−400.8	−453.1

Source: IMF, *International Financial Statistics.*

External Trade

PRINCIPAL COMMODITIES (distribution by SITC, US $ million)

Imports c.i.f.	1996	1997	1998
Food and live animals	152.4	158.7	204.1
Cereals and cereal preparations	84.9	74.0	86.1
Wheat (incl. spelt) and meslin, unmilled	26.4	14.6	22.2
Rice	32.5	34.4	26.9
Rice, semi-milled, milled	28.7	30.9	12.1
Mineral fuels, lubricants and related materials	97.4	178.9	181.5
Petroleum, petroleum products and related materials	92.4	172.2	175.1
Crude petroleum	43.0	117.3	121.2
Petroleum products, refined	48.6	53.8	—
Gas oils	27.7	—	—
Animal and vegetable oils, fats and waxes	39.3	42.2	48.1
Fixed vegetable oils and fats	24.7	30.7	33.5
Fixed vegetable oils, 'soft,' crude, refined or purified	13.6	17.6	16.4
Chemicals and related products	197.3	275.6	230.2
Dyeing, tanning and colouring materials	10.7	35.1	8.9
Medicinal and pharmaceutical products	75.0	75.3	80.0
Medicaments (incl. veterinary)	64.3	63.9	69.1
Essential oils and perfume materials; toilet, polishing and cleansing preparations	25.7	34.8	40.8
Fertilizers, manufactured	17.7	30.6	23.1
Plastic materials	31.1	54.4	23.7
Basic manufactures	179.2	234.9	238.5
Paper, paperboard and manufactures	31.9	37.7	41.3
Iron and steel	49.3	50.7	52.9
Machinery and transport equipment	287.2	395.9	467.6
Power-generating machinery and equipment	16.0	30.5	54.2
Machinery specialized for particular industries	35.5	49.2	48.5
Telecommunications and sound equipment	26.2	42.2	22.8
Telecommunications equipment	18.4	33.8	12.3
Road vehicles and parts	91.5	132.0	183.2
Passenger motor cars (excl. buses)	39.9	58.3	78.0
Lorries, trucks and special purpose vehicles	35.0	49.0	69.6
Lorries and trucks	31.1	47.1	68.8
Miscellaneous manufactured articles	101.3	152.2	124.6
Total (incl. others)	1,076.2	1,469.8	1,532.2

Exports f.o.b.	1996	1997	1998
Food and live animals . .	343.9	380.6	403.7
Meat and meat preparations . .	42.1	42.5	39.0
Meat, fresh, chilled or frozen .	41.9	42.2	38.8
Bovine meat, fresh, chilled or frozen	40.8	40.8	37.7
Dairy products and birds' eggs .	11.0	13.9	18.0
Cheese and curd	8.1	12.4	15.0
Fish, crustaceans and molluscs .	78.4	81.9	85.0
Fish, fresh, chilled or frozen .	10.8	10.7	12.1
Shell fish, fresh or frozen .	64.0	63.8	72.6
Vegetables and fruit	33.2	36.8	33.8
Vegetables, fresh, chilled, frozen or simply preserved .	7.5	16.4	7.3
Fruit and nuts, fresh or dried .	25.5	20.4	26.5
Bananas (incl. plantains), fresh or dried . . .	22.3	16.0	21.9
Sugar, sugar preparations and honey	37.1	56.8	44.1
Sugar and honey	37.0	56.7	43.9
Sugars, beet and cane, raw, solid	33.5	53.2	39.7
Coffee, tea, cocoa, spices and manufactures	129.8	126.1	167.3
Coffee and coffee substitutes .	128.0	123.6	167.1
Green and roasted coffee, and substitutes	126.3	123.6	164.7
Beverages and tobacco . .	17.1	45.1	25.0
Tobacco and tobacco manufactures	14.6	42.6	23.8
Tobacco, manufactured . . .	10.7	31.6	15.4
Cigars and cheroots; cigarillos	10.5	31.1	14.8
Crude materials (inedible) except fuels	65.6	56.7	42.8
Oil seeds and oleaginous fruit .	29.8	28.1	26.4
Seeds for 'soft' fixed oil . .	28.2	25.2	24.7
Groundnuts, green . . .	13.4	14.8	19.1
Sesame seeds	14.7	10.3	5.5
Cork and wood	18.0	19.5	12.5
Wood, shaped, and sleepers .	17.9	19.5	12.5
Basic manufactures . . .	12.6	13.8	12.5
Machinery and transport equipment	63.1	50.3	8.9
Office machines and automatic data-processing equipment . .	41.0	23.8	0.3
Office and automatic data-processing parts and accessories	41.0	23.8	0.1
Office machine parts . . .	41.0	23.7	0.1
Miscellaneous manufactured articles	138.5	90.8	11.1
Precision instruments . . .	0.1	16.6	0.1
Medical instruments . . .	0.1	16.5	0.1
Office supplies	52.0	27.9	0.1
Gold, silverware, jewellery .	36.8	22.5	—
Precious jewellery, gold and silverware	36.8	16.0	—
Musical instruments and parts .	43.2	16.5	0.1
Prepared media for sound or similar recording . . .	43.2	16.5	—
Total (incl. others) . . .	660.2	666.7	552.9

Source: UN, *International Trade Statistics Yearbook*.

1999 (US $ million, preliminary figures, excl. franc zone): *Imports c.i.f.:* Non-durable consumer goods 439.2; Durable consumer goods 102.4; Petroleum 108.5; Fuels and lubricants (incl. electrical energy) 72.0; Intermediate goods for agriculture 78.7; Intermediate goods for industry 353.0; Intermediate goods for construction 111.3; Capital goods for agriculture 39.6; Capital goods for industry 352.5; Capital goods for transport 202.2; Total (incl. others) 1,861.7,. *Exports f.o.b.:* Coffee 135; Sugar 30; Meat 42; Shrimps 45; Lobster 40; Bananas 14; Gold 30; Groundnuts 19; Miscellaneous manufactured goods 110; Total (incl. others) 545.

PRINCIPAL TRADING PARTNERS (US $ million)*

Imports c.i.f.	1997	1998	1999
Argentina	31.8	4.5	5.2
Canada	19.8	16.7	20.8
Chile	14.8	1.6	4.6
Colombia	16.0	33.2	11.3
Costa Rica	131.9	164.4	211.0
El Salvador	60.8	75.2	101.5
Germany	23.4	24.4	28.0
Guatemala	97.7	115.8	135.7
Honduras	57.8	71.6	80.9
Japan	57.8	86.6	98.9
Mexico	73.2	69.4	76.9
Netherlands	2.2	26.8	5.6
Panama	103.0	101.3	131.6
Spain	63.8	21.8	17.0
USA	541.4	464.0	631.1
Venezuela	48.4	98.1	128.7
Total (incl. others) . . .	1,454.0	1,491.7	1,861.7

Exports f.o.b.	1997†	1998†	1999†
Belgium	17.6	20.1	19.9
Canada	3.2	8.4	7.0
Costa Rica	24.1	26.0	27.5
Dominican Republic . . .	8.8	3.7	4.0
El Salvador	58.4	57.5	68.2
France	8.9	13.0	11.4
Germany	61.7	69.5	53.5
Guatemala	14.3	16.6	15.0
Honduras	28.3	22.9	37.0
Mexico	13.1	11.6	14.9
Netherlands	4.8	11.0	5.2
Spain	19.7	23.9	13.4
United Kingdom	0.6	8.5	6.2
USA	237.1	214.3	205.2
Total (incl. others) . . .	576.7	573.2	545.2

* Imports by country of provenance; exports by country of final destination.

† Preliminary figures.

Transport

RAILWAYS (traffic)

	1983	1984	1985*
Passenger-km (million) . .	45	60	66
Freight ton-km (million) . .	2	5	4

Passenger-km (million): 3 in 1990; 3 in 1991; 6 in 1992.
Source: UN, *Statistical Yearbook*.

ROAD TRAFFIC (motor vehicles in use at 31 December)

	1997	1998	1999
Cars	47,992	52,220	12,671
Buses and coaches . . .	3,853	4,450	4,385
Goods vehicles	61,793	68,952	34,488
Motorcycles and mopeds . .	17,408	19,303	7,842

Source: IRF, *World Road Statistics*.

SHIPPING

Merchant fleet (registered at 31 December)

	1996	1997	1998
Number of vessels . . .	27	27	28
Total displacement ('000 grt) .	4.2	4.2	4.3

Source: Lloyd's Register of Shipping, *World Fleet Statistics*.

International Sea-Borne Freight Traffic ('000 metric tons)

	1997	1998	1999
Imports	1,272.7	1,964.7	1,180.7
Exports	329.3	204.5	183.6

CIVIL AVIATION (traffic on scheduled services)

	1995	1996	1997
Kilometres flown (million) . .	1	1	1
Passengers carried ('000) . .	48	51	51
Passenger-km (million) . .	79	85	85
Total ton-km (million) . .	16	17	17

Source: UN, *Statistical Yearbook*.

Tourism

TOURIST ARRIVALS BY COUNTRY OF ORIGIN

	1996	1997	1998
Canada	6,822	8,255	7,565
Costa Rica	48,414	56,058	64,792
El Salvador	35,814	44,450	49,829
Guatemala	20,971	24,157	27,676
Honduras	82,635	105,465	119,710
Panama	6,104	7,138	9,026
Spain	7,056	7,535	8,024
USA	50,121	58,943	66,460
Total (incl. others)	266,880	322,241	405,702

Receipts from tourism (US $ million): 74 in 1997; 90 in 1998; 113 in 1999.
Arrivals ('000): 468 in 1999.

Sources: World Tourism Organization, *Yearbook of Tourism Statistics*; World Bank, *World Development Indicators*.

Communications Media

	1995	1996	1997
Radio receivers ('000 in use) . .	1,155	1,200	1,240
Television receivers ('000 in use) .	300	310	320
Telephones ('000 main lines in use)	97	111	128
Mobile cellular telephones (subscribers)	4,400	5,100	7,911
Daily newspapers			
Number	4	4	n.a.
Average circulation ('000 copies)	130	135	n.a.

Sources: UNESCO, *Statistical Yearbook*; UN, *Statistical Yearbook*.

Education

(2000, unless otherwise indicated)

	Institu-tions	Teach-ers	Students		
			Males	Females	Total
Pre-primary . . .	3,968*	3,672†	83,342	83,373	166,715
Primary . . .	7,224*	21,020†	423,928	414,509	838,437
Secondary					
General . . .	n.a.	5,970†	147,394	167,960	315,354
Tertiary‡					
University level .	n.a.	3,630	22,441	6,317	48,758
Other higher . .	n.a.	210	4,360	3,440	7,800

* 1998 figures.   † 1996 figures.   ‡ 1997 figures.

Sources: UNESCO, *Statistical Yearbook*; Ministry of Education.

Directory

The Constitution*

Shortly after taking office on 20 July 1979, the Government of National Reconstruction abrogated the 1974 Constitution. On 22 August 1979 the revolutionary junta issued a 'Statute on Rights and Guarantees for the Citizens of Nicaragua', providing for the basic freedoms of the individual, religious freedom and freedom of the press and abolishing the death penalty. The intention of the Statute was formally to re-establish rights which had been violated under the deposed Somoza regime. A fundamental Statute took effect from 20 July 1980 and remained in force until the Council of State drafted a political constitution and proposed an electoral law. A new Constitution was approved by the National Constituent Assembly on 19 November 1986 and promulgated on 9 January 1987. Amendments to the Constitution were approved by the Asamblea Nacional (National Assembly) in July 1995 and January 2000. The following are some of the main points of the Constitution:

Nicaragua is an independent, free, sovereign and indivisible state. All Nicaraguans who have reached 16 years of age are full citizens.

POLITICAL RIGHTS

There shall be absolute equality between men and women. It is the obligation of the State to remove obstacles that impede effective participation of Nicaraguans in the political, economic and social life of the country. Citizens have the right to vote and to be elected at elections and to offer themselves for public office. Citizens may organize or affiliate with political parties, with the objective of participating in, exercising or vying for power. The supremacy of civilian authority is enshrined in the Constitution.

SOCIAL RIGHTS

The Nicaraguan people have the right to work, to education and to culture. They have the right to decent, comfortable and safe housing, and to seek accurate information. This right comprises the freedom

to seek, receive and disseminate information and ideas, both spoken and written, in graphic or any other form. The mass media are at the service of national interests. No Nicaraguan citizen may disobey the law or prevent others from exercising their rights and fulfilling their duties by invoking religious beliefs or inclinations.

LABOUR RIGHTS

All have a right to work, and to participate in the management of their enterprises. Equal pay shall be given for equal work. The State shall strive for full and productive employment under conditions that guarantee the fundamental rights of the individual. There shall be an eight-hour working day, weekly rest, vacations, remuneration for national holidays and a bonus payment equivalent to one month's salary, in conformity with the law.

EDUCATION

Education is an obligatory function of the State. Planning, direction and organization of the secular education system is the responsibility of the State. All Nicaraguans have free and equal access to education. Private education centres may function at all levels.

LEGISLATIVE POWER

The Asamblea Nacional exercises Legislative Power through representative popular mandate. The Asamblea Nacional is composed of 90 representatives elected by direct secret vote by means of a system of proportional representation, of which 70 are elected at regional level and 20 at national level. The number of representatives may be increased in accordance with the general census of the population, in conformity with the law. Representatives shall be elected for a period of five years. The functions of the Asamblea Nacional are to draft and approve laws and decrees; to decree amnesties and pardons; to consider, discuss and approve the General Budget of the Republic; to elect judges to the Supreme Court of Justice and the Supreme Electoral Council; to fill permanent vacancies for the Presidency or Vice-Presidency; and to determine the political and administrative division of the country. The Presidency of the Republic may partially or totally veto a legislative proposal within a period of 15 days following its approval by the Assembly.

EXECUTIVE POWER

The Executive Power is exercised by the President of the Republic (assisted by the Vice-President), who is the Head of State, Head of Government and Commander-in-Chief of the Defence and Security Forces of the Nation. The election of the President (and Vice-President) is by equal, direct and free universal suffrage in secret ballot. Should a single candidate in a presidential election fail to secure the necessary 35% of the vote to win outright in the first round, a second ballot shall be held. Close relatives of a serving President are prohibited from contesting a presidential election. The President shall serve for a period of five years and may not serve for two consecutive terms. All outgoing Presidents are granted a seat in the Asamblea Nacional.

JUDICIAL POWER

The Judiciary consists of the Supreme Court of Justice, Courts of Appeal and other courts of the Republic. The Supreme Court is composed of at least seven judges, elected by the Asamblea Nacional, who shall serve for a term of six years. The functions of the Supreme Court are to organize and direct the administration of justice. There are 12 Supreme Court justices, appointed for a period of seven years.

LOCAL ADMINISTRATION

The country is divided into regions, departments and municipalities for administrative purposes. The municipal governments shall be elected by universal suffrage in secret ballot and will serve a six-year term. The communities of the Atlantic Coast have the right to live and develop in accordance with a social organization which corresponds to their historical and cultural traditions. The State shall implement, by legal means, autonomous governments in the regions inhabited by the communities of the Atlantic Coast, in order that the communities may exercise their rights.

*In January 2000 a constitutional amendment established a constitutional assembly to effect further reform of the Constitution, following amendments in 1995 and 2000.

The Government

HEAD OF STATE

President: Arnoldo Alemán Lacayo (took office 10 January 1997).
Vice-President: Leopoldo Navarro Bermúdez.

CABINET
(August 2001)

Minister of Foreign Affairs: Francisco Aguirre Sacasa.
Minister of Government: José Marenco.
Minister of National Defence: José Adán Guerra.
Minister of Finance: Estebán Duque Estrada.
Minister of Development, Industry and Trade: Noel Sacasa Cruz.
Minister of Labour: Manuel Martínez.
Minister of the Environment and Natural Resources: Roberto Stadhagen V.
Minister of Transport and Infrastructure: Edgard Bohorquez Ocampo.
Minister of Agriculture and Forestry: José Augusto Navarro.
Minister of Health: Mariangeles Arguello.
Minister of Education, Culture and Sports: Fernando Robleto.
Minister of Social Action: Jamilet Bonilla.
Minister of Tourism: Lorenzo Guerrero.
Secretary to the Presidency: David Castillo.
There are, in addition, four Secretaries of State.

MINISTRIES

Ministry of Agriculture and Forestry: Km 8½, Carretera a Masaya, Managua; tel. (2) 76-0235; internet www.mag.gob.ni.
Ministry of Development, Industry and Trade: Edif. Central, Km 6, Carretera a Masaya, Apdo 8, Managua; tel. (2) 78-8702; fax (2) 70-095; internet www.mific.gob.ni.
Ministry of Education, Culture and Sports: Complejo Cívico Camilo Ortega Saavedra, Managua; tel. (2) 65-1577; internet www.med.gob.ni.
Ministry of the Environment and Natural Resources: Km 12½, Carretera Norte, Apdo 5123, Managua; tel. (2) 63-1271; fax (2) 63-1274.

Ministry of Finance: Frente a la Asamblea Nacional, Apdo 2170, Managua; tel. (2) 22-6530; fax (2) 22-6430; e-mail gobid@ibw.com.ni; internet www.hacienda.gob.ni.
Ministry of Foreign Affairs: Detrás de restaurante Los Ranchos, Managua; tel. (2) 66-1159; e-mail gabriela.hernandez@cancilleria.gob.ni; internet www.cancilleria.gob.ni.
Ministry of Government: Apdo 68, Managua; tel. (2) 28-5005.
Ministry of Health: Complejo Cívico Camilo Ortega Saavedra, Managua; tel. (2) 89-7164.
Ministry of Labour: Estadio Nacional, 400 m al Norte, Apdo 487, Managua; tel. (2) 28-2028; fax (2) 28-2103.
Ministry of National Defence: Casa de la Presidencia, Managua; tel. (2) 66-3580; fax (2) 28-7911.
Ministry of Social Action: Managua.
Ministry of Tourism: Managua; internet www.intur.gob.ni.
Ministry of Transport and Infrastructure: Frente al Estadio Nacional, Apdo 26, Managua; tel. (2) 28-2061; fax (2) 28-2060; e-mail webmaster@mti.gob.ni; internet www.mti.gob.ni.

President and Legislature

PRESIDENT

Election, 20 October 1996

Candidate	Votes	% of total
Arnoldo Alemán Lacayo (Alianza Liberal)	904,908	51.03
Daniel Ortega Saavedra (Frente Sandinista de Liberación Nacional)	669,443	37.75
Guillermo Antonio Osorno Molina (Camino Cristiano Nicaragüense)	72,621	4.10
Noel José Vidaurre (Partido Conservador de Nicaragua)	40,096	2.26
Others*	86,333	4.87
Total valid votes	1,773,401	100.00

* There were 19 other candidates.

ASAMBLEA NACIONAL
(National Assembly)

Asamblea Nacional: Avda Bolívar, Contiguo a la Presidencia de la República; e-mail webmaster@correo.asamblea.gob.ni; internet www.asamblea.gob.ni.
President: Oscar Moncada Reyes.
First Vice-President: Dr Damicis Sirias.
Second Vice-President: Edwin Castro.
Third Vice-President: Angeles Castellón.

Election, 20 October 1996

Party	Seats
Alianza Liberal (AL)	42
Frente Sandinista de Liberación Nacional (FSLN)	35
Camino Cristiano Nicaragüense (CCN)	3
Partido Conservador de Nicaragua (PCN)	2
Proyecto Nacional (PRONAL)	2
Partido Liberal Independiente (PLI)	1
Acción Nacional Conservadora (ANC)	1
Partido Resistencia Nicaragüense (PRN)	1
Movimiento Renovador Sandinista (MRS)	1
Alianza Unidad (AU)	1
Unión Nacional Opositora 96 (UNO 96)	1
Total	90*

* In addition to the 90 elected members, supplementary seats in the Asamblea Nacional are awarded to unsuccessful candidates at the presidential election who were not nominated for the legislature but who received, in the presidential poll, a number of votes at least equal to the average required for one of the 70 legislative seats decided at a regional level. On this basis, the FSLN, the CCN and the PCN each obtained one additional seat in the Asamblea Nacional, bringing the total to 93.

Political Organizations

Acción Nacional Conservadora (ANC): Costado Oeste SNTV, Managua; tel. (2) 66-8755; Pres. Dr Frank Duarte Tapia.
Alianza Liberal (AL): f. 1996 as electoral alliance; comprises the following parties:
Conservadores por la Democracia.

Convergencia Liberal: f. 1996 by former mems of Partido Liberal Independiente.

Partido Liberal Constitucionalista (PLC): Semáforos Country Club 100 m al Este, Apdo 4569, Managua; tel. (2) 78-8705; fax (2) 78-1800; e-mail plc@ibw.com.ni; internet www.nfdd.org; f. 1967; Pres. Dr LEOPOLDO NAVARRO BERMÚDEZ; Exec. Dir EDMOND H. PALLAIS.

Partido Liberal Independiente de Unidad Nacional (PLIUN): Munich, 2½ c. Arriba, Managua; tel. (2) 61672; f. 1988; splinter group of PLI; Pres. EDUARDO CORONADO PÉREZ; Sec.-Gen. CARLOS ALONSO.

Partido Neo-Liberal (Pali): Cine Dorado, 2 c. al Sur, 50 m Arriba, Managua; tel. (2) 66-5166; f. 1986; Pres. Dr RICARDO VEGA GARCÍA.

Partido Unionista Centroamericano (PUCA): Cine Cabrera, 1a c. al Este, 20 m al Norte, Managua; tel. (2) 27472; f. 1904; Pres. BLANCA ROJAS ECHAVERRY.

Alianza Unidad (AU): f. 1996; an alliance of parties with social democrat tendencies.

Frente Sandinista de Liberación Nacional (FSLN) (Sandinista National Liberation Front): Costado Oeste Parque El Carmen, Managua; tel. (2) 66-0845; fax (2) 66-1560; internet www.fsln.org.ni; f. 1960; led by a 15-member directorate; embraces Izquierda Democrática Sandinista 'orthodox revolutionary' faction, led by DANIEL ORTEGA SAAVEDRA; 120,000 mems; Gen. Sec. DANIEL ORTEGA SAAVEDRA.

Movimiento de Acción Democrática (MAD): Managua; f. 1993; Leader EDÉN PASTORA GÓMEZ.

Movimiento Democrático Nicaragüense (MDN): f. 2000 as electoral alliance; comprises the following parties:

Camino Cristiano Nicaragüense (CCN): Managua; Pres. GUILLERMO ANTONIO OSORNO MOLINA.

Movimiento Democrático Nicaragüense (MDN): Casa L-39, Ciudad Jardín Bnd, 50 m al Sur, Managua; tel. (2) 43898; f. 1978; Leader ROBERTO URROZ CASTILLO.

Movimiento Renovador Sandinista (MRS): Tienda Katty 1 c. Abajo, Apdo 24, Managua; tel. (2) 78-0279; fax (2) 78-0268; f. 1995; former faction of Frente Sandinista de Liberación Nacional; Pres. Dr SERGIO RAMÍREZ MERCADO.

Partido Conservador de Nicaragua (PCN): Colegio Centroamérica 500 m al Sur, Managua; tel. (2) 67-0484; f. 1992 as result of merger between Partido Conservador Demócrata (PCD) and Partido Socialconservadurismo; Pres. Dr FERNANDO AGÜERO ROCHA.

Partido de Unidad Social Cristiano (PUSC).

Proyecto Nacional (PRONAL): Managua; formed an alliance with MDN, MRS and PUSC in February 2000; Leader BENJAMÍN LANZAS.

Movimiento Patria: Managua; alliance of centre parties, formed in 1998; comprising:

Alianza Popular Conservadora (APC): Iglesia El Carmen 50 m Arriba, Managua; tel. (2) 28-1247; f. 1856 as Partido Conservador de Nicaragua, name changed as above 1989; Pres. EDUARDO PALADINO CABRERA; Sec.-Gen. MYRIAM ARGÜELLO MORALES.

Movimiento Nueva Alternativa (MNA).

Partido Liberal Independiente (PLI): Ciudad Jardín, H-4, Calle Principal, Managua; tel. (2) 44-3556; fax (2) 48-0012; f. 1944; Leader VIRGILIO GODOY REYES.

Partido Resistencia Nicaragüense (PRN): Optica Nicaragüense, 100 m al Lago, Managua; f. 1991; tel. (2) 66-8098; Pres. ENRIQUE QUIÑONES.

Partido Nacional Conservador (PNC): Frente Costado Sur Galería Internacional, Managua; tel. (2) 66-9979; f. 1979; Leader Dr SILVIANO MATAMOROS LACAYO; Pres. ADOLFO CALERO PORTOCARRERO.

Partido Popular Nicaragüense (PPN): Managua; centrist; Leader ALVARO RAMÍREZ.

Partido de los Pueblos Costeños (PPC): Bluefields; f. 1997; multi-ethnic; Pres. HUGO SUJO.

Partido Social Cristiano Nicaragüense (PSCN): Ciudad Jardín, Pizza María, 1 c. al Lago, Managua; tel. (2) 22026; f. 1957; 42,000 mems; Pres. GERMÁN ALFARO OCAMPO.

Partido Social Demócrata (PSD): Frente al Teatro Aguerri, Managua; tel. (2) 28-1277; f. 1979; Pres. ADOLFO JARQUÍN ORTEL; Sec.-Gen. Dr JOSÉ PALLAIS ARANA.

Partido Socialista Nicaragüense (PSN): Hospital Militar, 100 m al Norte, 100 m al Oeste, 100 m al Sur, Managua; tel. (2) 66-2321; fax (2) 66-2936; f. 1944; social democratic party; Sec.-Gen. Dr GUSTAVO TABLADA ZELAYA.

Unión Demócrata Cristiana (UDC): De Iglesia Santa Ana, 2 c. Abajo, Barrio Santa Ana, Apdo 3089, Managua; tel. (2) 66-2576; f. 1976 as Partido Popular Social Cristiano; name officially changed

as above December 1993; Pres. Dr LUIS HUMBERTO GUZMÁN; Political Sec. Dr PEDRO ARCEDA PICADO.

Unión Nacional Opositora 96 (UNO 96): f. 1996; frmly Partido Nacional Demócrata; no relation to former governing UNO; Pres. ALFREDO CÉSAR AGUIRRE.

Diplomatic Representation

EMBASSIES IN NICARAGUA

Argentina: Reparto Las Colinas, Km 8, Carretera a Masaya, de la TEXACO 1 c. Arriba, Apdo 703, Managua; tel. (2) 76-0156; fax (2) 76-0116; e-mail embargsc@tmx.com.ni; Ambassador: HORACIO ALBERTO AMOROSO.

Brazil: Km 7¾, Carretera Sur, Quinta los Pinos, Apdo 264, Managua; tel. (2) 50035; Chargé d'affaires: PATRICIA MARIA DE OLIVEIRA LIMA SERAPIÃO.

Bulgaria: Reparto Las Colinas, Calle Los Mangos 195, Managua; Ambassador: KIRIL ZLATKOV NIKOLOV.

Cambodia: Managua; Ambassador: LONG VISALO.

Chile: Km 13.8, Carretera Sur, 200 m a Mano Izquierda, Apdo 1704, Managua; Chargé d'affaires a.i.: EDUARDO VEGA BEZANILLA.

China (Taiwan): Planes de Altamira, 19-20, frente de la Cancha de Tenis, Apdo 4653 Managua 5; tel. (2) 70-6054; fax (2) 67-4025; Ambassador: ANTONIO T. S. TSAI.

Colombia: Reparto Los Robles, Apdo 1062, Managua; tel. (2) 70247; Ambassador: NEIVA MAYOR GUILLERMO PLAZAS ALCID.

Costa Rica: De la Estatua de Montoya 2 c. al Lago y 1 c. Arriba (Callejón Zelaya), Managua; tel. (2) 66-2404; fax (2) 68-1479; e-mail embcr@ibw.com.ni; Ambassador: JAVIER SOLIS HERRARA.

Cuba: Carretera a Masaya, 3a Entrada a las Colinas, Managua; tel. (2) 71182; fax (2) 76-0166; Ambassador: JULIÁN LÓPEZ DÍAZ.

Czech Republic: Managua; Ambassador: GUSTAV STOPKA.

Denmark: De la Plaza España 1 c. Abajo, 2 c. al Lago, ½ c. Abajo, Apdo 4942, Managua; tel. (2) 68-0250; fax (2) 66-8095; e-mail danembassy@denmark.org.ni; internet www.denmark.org.ni; Ambassador: ANDERS SERUP RASMUSSEN.

Dominican Republic: Reparto Las Colinas, Prado Ecuestre 100, con Curva de los Gallos, Apdo 614, Managua; Ambassador: MIGUEL ANGEL DECAMPS.

Ecuador: De los Pipitos 1½ c. Abajo, Apdo C-33, Managua; tel. (2) 68-1098; fax (2) 66-8081; Ambassador: FRANCISCO PROAÑO ARANDI.

El Salvador: Reparto Las Colinas, Avda Las Colinas y Pasaje Los Cerros, Apdo 149, Managua; tel. (2) 76-0712; fax (2) 76-0711; Ambassador: JOSÉ ROBERTO FRANCISCO IMENDIA.

Finland: Del Hospital Militar 1 c. al norte, 1½ c almoeste, Reparto Bolonia, Managua; tel. (2) 66-7947; fax (2) 66-3416; Chargé d'affaires: SIRPQA MAENPAA.

France: Km 13½, Carretera del Sur, Apdo 1227, Managua; tel. (2) 22-6210; fax (2) 28-1056; e-mail ambafrance@tmx.com.ni; Ambassador: MICHEL VANDEPOORTER.

Germany: De Plaza España, 1 c. al Lago, Contiguo a Optica Nicaragüense, Apdo 29, Managua; tel. (2) 66-3917; fax (2) 66-7667; e-mail diploger@tmx.com.ni; Ambassador: HANS PETERSMANN.

Guatemala: Km 11½, Carretera a Masaya, Apdo E-1, Managua; tel. (2) 79609; fax (2) 79610; Ambassador BERNA ROLANDO MÉNDEZ MORA.

Holy See: Km 10.8, Carretera Sur, Apdo 506, Managua (Apostolic Nunciature); tel. (2) 65-0552; fax (2) 65-7416; e-mail nuntius@tmx.com.ni; Apostolic Nuncio: Most Rev. LUIGI TRAVAGLINO, Titular Archbishop of Lettere.

Honduras: Km 7½, Carretera Sur, Reparto Barcelona, Apdo 321, Managua; Ambassador: HERMINIO PINEDA.

Iran: Calle Vista Alegre 93, Las Colinas, Managua; Ambassador: MUHAMMAD JAMSHIDI-GOHARI.

Italy: Rotonda El Güegüense, 1 c. al norte, Apdo 2092, ½ c. Abajo, Managua 4; tel. (2) 66-2961; fax (2) 66-3987; e-mail italdipl@tmx.com.ni; Ambassador: Dr MAURIZIO FRATINI.

Japan: Del Portón del Hospital Militar, 1 c. al Lago y 1½ c. Abajo, Mano Izquierda, Bolonia, Apdo 1789, Managua; tel. (2) 62-3092; fax (2) 62-7393; Ambassador: YOSHIZO KONISHI.

Korea, Democratic People's Republic: Managua; Ambassador: KIM SUNG RYONG.

Libya: Mansión Teodolinda, 6 c. al Sur, ½ c. Abajo, Managua; Secretary of the People's Bureau: IBRAHIM MOHAMED FARHAT.

Mexico: Frente Oficinas Telcor de Altamira, Km 4½ Carretera a Masaya, Apdo 834, Managua; tel. (2) 78-1859; fax (2) 78-2886; Ambassador: EDGARDO FLORES RIVAS.

Mongolia: Managua; Ambassador: G. DASHDAAVA.

Netherlands: Col. los Robles III etapa, de Plaza el Sol 1 c. al sur 1½ c. al oeste, Apdo 3688, Managua; tel. (2) 70-4505; fax (2) 70-0399; e-mail mng-az@minbuza.nl; Ambassador: HENRICUS GAJENTAAN.

Panama: Reparto San Juan, Calle El Carmen 619, Managua; tel. (2) 66-2224; fax (2) 66-8633; Ambassador: JOSEFA MARÍN DIEZ.

Peru: Frente a Procuraduría General de Justicia, Bolonia, Apdo 211, Managua; tel. (2) 22376; fax (2) 22381; Ambassador: MANUEL BOZA HECK.

Russia: Reparto Las Colinas, Calle Vista Alegre 214, Entre Avda Central y Paseo del Club, Managua; tel. (2) 76-0374; fax (2) 76-0179; e-mail rossia@tmx.com.ni; Ambassador: ANATOLI P. KUZNETSOV.

Spain: Avda Central 13, Las Colinas, Apdo 284, Managua; tel. (2) 76-0966; fax (2) 76-0937; e-mail espana@tmx.com.ni; Ambassador: IGNACIO JESÚS MATELLANES MARTINEZ.

Sweden: Rotonda El Güegüense, 1 c. Abajo, 2 c. al Lago y ½ c. Abajo, Lado Derecho, Apdo 2307, Managua; tel. (2) 66-2762; fax (2) 66-6778; Ambassador: KLAS MARKENSTEN.

United Kingdom: Plaza Churchill, Reparto Los Robles, Apdo A-169, Managua; tel. (2) 78-0014; fax (2) 78-4085; e-mail britemb @ibw.com.ni; Ambassador: HARRY WILES.

USA: Km 4½, Carretera Sur, Apdo 327, Managua; tel. (2) 66-6010; Ambassador: OLIVER GARZA .

Uruguay: Managua; **tel**. (2) 25542; Ambassador: ALFREDO LAFONE.

Venezuela: Edif. Málaga, 2°, Plaza España, Módulo A-13, Apdo 406, Managua; Ambassador: LUIS RAFAEL ZAPATA LUIGI.

Viet Nam: Zona Residencial Planetarium, Paseo Saturno, Casa CS 10, esq. Vía Láctea, Managua; Ambassador: LE DUC CANG.

Yugoslavia: Apdo 3463, Managua; tel. (2) 72847; Ambassador: DUŠAN TRIFUNOVIĆ.

Judicial System

The Supreme Court: Km 7½, Carretera Norte, Managua; tel. (2) 43562; fax (2) 33-0581; internet www.csj.gob.ni; deals with both civil and criminal cases, acts as a Court of Cassation, appoints Judges of First Instance, and generally supervises the legal administration of the country.

President: Dr FRANCISCO PLATA LÓPEZ.

Vice-President: Dr YADIRA CENTENO GONZÁLEZ.

Attorney-General: JULIO CENTENO GÓMEZ.

Religion

All religions are tolerated. Almost all of Nicaragua's inhabitants profess Christianity, and the great majority belong to the Roman Catholic Church. The Moravian Church predominates on the Caribbean coast.

CHRISTIANITY
The Roman Catholic Church

Nicaragua comprises one archdiocese, six dioceses and the Apostolic Vicariate of Bluefields. At 31 December 1999 there were an estimated 4,603,801 adherents.

Bishops' Conference: Conferencia Episcopal de Nicaragua, Ferretería Lang 1 c. al Norte, l c. al Este, Zona 3, Las Piedrecitas, Apdo 2407, Managua; tel. (2) 66-6292; fax (2) 66-8069; e-mail cen@tmx.com.ni; f. 1975 (statute approved 1987); Pres. Cardinal MIGUEL OBANDO Y BRAVO, Archbishop of Managua.

Archbishop of Managua: Cardinal MIGUEL OBANDO Y BRAVO, Arzobispado, Apdo 3058, Managua; tel. (2) 77-1754; fax (2) 76-0130.

The Anglican Communion

Nicaragua comprises one of the five dioceses of the Iglesia Anglicana de la Región Central de América.

Bishop of Nicaragua: Rt Rev. STURDIE W. DOWNS, Apdo 1207, Managua; tel. (2) 25174; fax (2) 22-6701.

Protestant Churches

Baptist Convention of Nicaragua: Apdo 2593, Managua; tel. (2) 25785; fax (2) 24131; f. 1917; 35,000 mems (1988); Pres. Rev. ELÍAS SÁNCHEZ; Gen. Sec. TOMÁS H. TÉLLEZ.

The Nicaraguan Lutheran Church of Faith and Hope: Apdo 151, Managua; tel. (2) 66-1329; fax (2) 66-4609; e-mail luterana@ nicarao.org.ni; f. 1994; 4,000 mems (2000); Pres. Rev. VICTORIA CORTEZ RODRÍGUEZ.

The Press

NEWSPAPERS AND PERIODICALS

Acción: Managua; **of**ficial publication of the Partido Social Demócrata.

Alternativa Liberal: Managua; f. 1984; official publication of the Partido Liberal Independiente.

Avance: Ciudad Jardín 0-30, Apdo 4231, Managua; tel. (2) 43750; f. 1972; weekly publication of the Partido Comunista de Nicaragua; circ. 10,000.

Barricada: Camino del Oriente, Apdo 576, Managua; tel. (2) 67-4885; fax (2) 67-3941; e-mail barricada@ibw.com.ni; internet www.barricada.com.ni; f. 1979; morning, daily; also publ. in English; temporary closure announced Jan. 1998; Dir TOMÁS BORGE; Editor JUAN RAMÓN HUERTA; circ. 95,000.

El Centroamericano: 4a Calle Norte, Apdo 52, León; f. 1917; evening; independent; Dir R. ABAUNZA SALINAS; circ. 3,500.

La Crónica: Managua; f. 1988; weekly; independent; Dir LUIS HUMBERTO GUZMÁN.

Diario El Pueblo: Apdo 2346, Managua; tel. (2) 23480; f. 1979; daily; owned by a co-operative; Dir CARLOS CUADRA; circ. 7,000.

La Gaceta, Diario Oficial: Avda Central Sur 604, Managua; f. 1912; morning; official.

La Información: León; weekly.

La Nación Nicaragüense: Camino de Oriente, Managua; weekly.

Novedades: Pista P. Joaquín Chamorro, Km 4, Carretera Norte, Apdo 576, Managua; daily; evening.

Nuevo Diario: Pista P. Joaquín Chamorro, Km 4, Carretera Norte, Apdo 4591, Managua; tel. (2) 49-1190; fax (2) 49-0700; e-mail ndiario @ibw.com.ni; internet www.elnuevodiario.com.ni; f. 1980; morning; daily; independent; Editor XAVIER CHAMORRO CARDENAL; circ. 45,000.

El Observador: Apdo 1482, Managua; weekly.

Paso a Paso: Managua; weekly; Dir JOAQUÍN MEJÍA.

Poder Sandinista: Managua; f. 1980; weekly.

El Popular: Managua; monthly; official publication of the Partido Socialista Nicaragüense.

La Prensa: Km 4½, Carretera Norte, Apdo 192, Managua; tel. (2) 49-8405; fax (2) 49-6926; e-mail info@laprensa.com.ni; internet www.laprensa.com.ni; f. 1926; morning; daily; independent; Pres. JAIME CHAMORRO CARDENAL; Editor PABLO ANTONIO CUADRA; circ. 30,000.

Prensa Proletaria: Managua; fortnightly; official publication of the Movimiento de Acción Popular Marxista-Leninista.

El Reportero: Managua; resumed publication Jan. 1988; Editor ARILO MEJÍA.

Revista del Pensamiento Centroamericano: Apdo 2108, Managua; quarterly; centre-left; Editor XAVIER ZAVALA CUADRA.

La Semana Cómica: Centro Comercial Bello Horizonte, Módulos 7 y 9, Apdo SV-3, Managua; tel. (2) 44909; f. 1980; weekly; Dir RÓGER SÁNCHEZ; circ. 45,000.

El Socialista: Managua; fortnightly; official publication of the Partido Revolucionario de los Trabajadores.

La Tribuna: Detrás del Banco Mercantil, Plaza España, Apdo 1469, Managua; tel. (2) 66-7583; fax (2) 66-9089; e-mail tribuna@latribuna .com.ni; internet www.latribuna.com.ni; f. 1993; morning; daily; Dir HAROLDO J. MONTEALEGRE; Gen. Man. MARIO GONZÁLEZ.

Association

Unión de Periodistas de Nicaragua (UPN): Apdo 4006, Managua; Leader LILLY SOTO VÁSQUEZ.

NEWS AGENCIES

Agencia Nicaragüense de Noticias (ANN): Managua; Dir-Gen. ROBERTO GARCÍA.

Foreign Bureaux

Agencia EFE (Spain): Ciudad Jardín S-22, Apdo 1951, Managua; tel. (2) 24928; Bureau Chief FILADELFO MARTÍNEZ FLORES.

Agenzia Nazionale Stampa Associata (ANSA) (Italy): c/o La Prensa, Km 4½, Carretera Norte, Apdo 192, Managua; tel. (2) 40139; Correspondent MARCIO VARGAS.

Deutsche Presse-Agentur (dpa) (Germany): Apdo 2095, Managua; tel. (2) 78-1862; fax (2) 78-1863; Correspondent JOSÉ ESTEBAN QUEZADA.

Informatsionnoye Telegrafnoye Agentstvo Rossii—Telegrafnoye Agentstvo Suverennykh Stran (ITAR—TASS) (Russia): Col. Los Robles, Casa 17, Managua; Correspondent ALEKSANDR TRUSHIN.

Inter Press Service (IPS) (Italy): Residencia El Dorado, Casa 337, Clínica San Rafael, 2½ c. al Lago, Managua; tel. (2) 42933; Correspondent FELIPE JAIME.

Prensa Latina (Cuba): De los Semáforos del Portón de Telcor de Villa Fontana, 25 m al Este, 2 c. al Lago, Casa 280, Managua; tel. (2) 72697; Correspondent MARIO MAINADE MARTÍNEZ.

Reuters (United Kingdom): Apdo A-150, Managua; tel. (2) 27070; Correspondent M. CAMPBELL.

United Press International (UPI) (USA): Reparto Serrano 1166, Managua; tel. (2) 24192; Bureau Chief DOUGLAS TWEEDALE.

Xinhua (New China) News Agency (People's Republic of China): De Policlínica Nicaragüense, 80 m al Sur, Apdo 5899, Managua; tel. (2) 62155; Bureau Chief LIU RIUCHANG.

Publishers

Academia Nicaragüense de la Lengua: Calle Central, Reparto Las Colinas, Apdo 2711, Managua; f. 1928; languages; Dir PABLO ANTONIO CUADRA; Sec. JULIO YCAZA TIGERINO.

Editora de Publicaciones, SA (EDIPSA): Detrás Edif. Corporación Industrial del Pueblo, Pista de la Resistencia Sur, Managua.

Editorial Alemana, SA: Centro Comercial, Módulo B 30, Km 18½, Carretera a Masaya, Apdo E-10, Managua.

Editorial América, SA: Ciudad Jardín K-24, Frente al Juzgado, Managua.

Editorial Artes Gráficas: Managua.

Editorial El Socorro: Cine Aguerri, 1 c. Abajo, 2½ c. al Lago, No 618, Managua.

Editorial Flórez: Centro Taller Las Palmas, 75 m al Norte, Managua; Dir JOSÉ MARÍA FLÓREZ MORALES.

Editorial Impresora Comercial: Julio C. Orozco L., 9 C.S.E. Entre 27a y 28a Avda, Apdo 10-11, Managua; tel. (2) 42258; art.

Editorial José Martí: De donde fue Bunge, 2 c. al Lago, Managua.

Editorial Lacayo: 2a Avda Sureste 507, Managua; religion.

Editorial Nueva Nicaragua: Paseo Salvador Allende, Km 3½, Carretera Sur, Apdo 073, Managua; fax (2) 66-6520; f. 1981; Pres. Dr SERGIO RAMÍREZ MERCADO; Dir-Gen. ROBERTO DÍAZ CASTILLO.

Editorial Rodríguez: Iglesia Santa Faz, 1½ c. Abajo, B. Costa Rica, Apdo 4702, Managua.

Editorial San José: Calle Central Este 607, Managua.

Editorial Unión: Avda Central Norte, Managua; travel.

Editorial Universitaria Centroamérica: Col. Centroamérica, K-752, Managua.

Editorial Vilma Morales M.: Academia Militar David Tejada, 2 c. Abajo y ½ c. al Lago, Bello Horizonte K-1-19.

Librería y Editorial, Universidad Nacional de Nicaragua: León; tel. (311) 2612; education, history, sciences, law, literature, politics.

Broadcasting and Communications

TELECOMMUNICATIONS

Dirección de Telecomunicaciones (Telcor): Apdo 2264, Managua; tel. (2) 70041; government supervisory body; Dir MARIO MONTENEGRO.

Empresa Nicaragüense de Telecomunicaciones (Enitel): Managua; privatization pending in 2001; Exec. Pres. GABRIEL LEVY.

Grupo Salinas: Managua; mobile cellular telephone operator; Mexican owned.

Telefonía Celular de Nicaragua (Nicacel): Managua; mobile cellular telephone operator; owned by BellSouth (USA).

BROADCASTING

Radio

Radio Cadena de Oro: Altamira 73, Managua; tel. (2) 78-1633; fax (2) 78-1220; f. 1990; Dir ALLAN DAVID TEFEL ALBA.

Radio Católica: Altamira D'Este 621, 3°, Apdo 2183, Managua; tel. (2) 78-0836; fax (2) 78-2544; e-mail catolica@ibw.com.ni; f. 1961; controlled by Conferencia Episcopal de Nicaragua; Dir Fr JOSÉ BISMARCK CARBALLO; Gen. Man. ALBERTO CARBALLO MADRIGAL.

Radio Corporación: Ciudad Jardín Q-20, Apdo 2442, Managua; tel. (2) 49-1619; fax (2) 44-3824; internet www.rc540.com.ni; Dir JOSÉ CASTILLOS OSEJO; Man. FABIO GADEA MANTILLA.

Radio Minuto: Ciudad Jardín Q-20, Apdo 2442, Managua; tel. (2) 40869; Dir CARLOS GADEA MANTILLA.

Radio Mundial: 36 Avda Oeste, Reparto Loma Verde, Apdo 3170, Managua; tel. (2) 66-6767; fax (2) 66-4630; commercial; Pres. MANUEL ARANA VALLE; Dir-Gen. ALMA ROSA ARANA HARTIG.

Radio Nicaragua: Villa Fontana, Contiguo a Telcor, Apdo 4665, Managua; tel. (2) 67-3630; fax (2) 67-1448; f. 1979; government station; Dir LORENZO CARDENAL VARGAS.

Radio Noticias: Col. Robles 92, 4°, Apdo A-150, Managua; tel. (2) 49-5914; fax (2) 49-6393; e-mail fuentes@ibw.com.ni; Dir AGUSTÍN FUENTES SEQUEIRA.

Radio Ondas de Luz: Costado Sur del Hospital Bautista, Apdo 607, Managua; tel. and fax (2) 49-7058; f. 1959; religious and cultural station; Pres. GUILLERMO OSORNO MOLINA; Dir EDUARDO GUTIÉRREZ NARVÁEZ.

Radio Sandino: Paseo Tiscapa Este, Contiguo al Restaurante Mirador, Apdo 4776, Managua; tel. (2) 28-1330; fax (2) 62-4052; f. 1977; station controlled by the Frente Sandinista de Liberación Nacional; Pres. BAYARDO ARCE CASTAÑO; Dir CONRADO PINEDA AGUILAR.

Radio Tiempo: Reparto Pancasan 217, 7°, Apdo 2735, Managua; tel. (2) 78-2540; f. 1976; Pres. ERNESTO CRUZ; Gen. Man. MARIANO VALLE PETERS.

Radio Universidad: Del transfer de la UNAN 800 m al Sur, Apdo 2883, Managua; tel. (2) 78-4743; fax (2) 77-5057; f. 1984; Dir LUIS LÓPEZ RUIZ.

Radio Ya: Pista de la Resistencia, Frente a la Universidad Centroamericana, Managua; tel. (2) 78-5600; fax (2) 78-6000; f. 1990; Dir CARLOS JOSÉ GUADAMUZ P.

There are some 50 other radio stations.

Television

Nicavisión, Canal 12: Apdo 2766, Managua; tel. (2) 66-0691; fax (2) 66-1424; e-mail info@tv12-nic.com; internet www.tv12-nic.com; f. 1993; Dir MARIANO VALLE PETERS.

Nueva Imagen, Canal 4: Montoya, 1 c. Sur, 1 c. Arriba, Managua; tel. (2) 66-3420; fax (2) 66-3467; Pres. DIONISIO MARENCO; Gen. Man. ORLANDO CASTILLLO.

Sistema Nacional de Televisión (SNTV): Km 3½, Carretera Sur, Contiguo a Shell, Las Palmas, Apdo 1505, Managua; tel. (2) 66-1520; fax (2) 66-2712; Dir MARIO AMADOR RIVAS.

Televisora Nicaragüense, S.A., Telenica 8: De la Mansión Teodolinda, 1 c. al Sur, ½ c. Abajo, Bolonia, Apdo 3611, Managua; tel. (2) 66-5021; fax (2) 66-5024; e-mail cbriceno@nicanet.com.ni; f. 1989; Pres. CARLOS A. BRICEÑO LOVO.

Televisión Internacional, Canal 23: Planes de Altamira 7, del Sorbet-Inn 30 m Abajo, Apdo 444, Managua; tel. (2) 67-0171; fax (2) 67-0179; e-mail canal23@ibw.com.ni; f. 1993; Pres. CÉSAR RIGUERO.

Televicentro de Nicaragua, S.A., Canal 2: Casa del Obrero, 6½ c. al Sur, Apdo 688, Managua; tel. (2) 68-2222; fax (2) 66-3688; e-mail canal2@canal2.com.ni; internet www.canal2.com.ni; f. 1965; Pres. OCTAVIO SACASA.

Unitel, S.A., Canal 13: Calle Principal de Altamira, Managua; tel. (2) 66-5530; fax (2) 66-4862; Pres. ARNOLDO RÍOS.

Finance

(cap. = capital; res = reserves; dep. = deposits; m. = million; amounts in gold córdobas unless otherwise stated)

BANKING

All Nicaraguan banks were nationalized in July 1979. Foreign banks operating in the country are no longer permitted to secure local deposits. All foreign exchange transactions must be made through the Banco Central or its agencies. Under a decree issued in May 1985, the establishment of private exchange houses was permitted. In 1990 legislation allowing for the establishment of private banks was enacted.

Supervisory Authority

Superintendencia de Bancos y de Otras Instituciones Financieras: Edif. SBOIF, Km 7, Carretera Sur, Apdo 788, Managua; tel. (2) 65-1555; fax (2) 65-0965; e-mail superinten@interlink.com.ni; internet www.superintendencia.gob.ni; f. 1991; Superintendent NOEL J. SACASA CRUZ.

Central Bank

Banco Central de Nicaragua: Carretera Sur, Km 7, Apdos 2252/3, Zona 5, Managua; tel. (2) 65-0500; fax (2) 65-0561; e-mail bcn@bcn.gob.ni; internet www.bcn.gob.ni; f. 1961; bank of issue and Government fiscal agent; cap. and res 272.6m., dep. 5,590.9m. (Dec. 1998); Pres. Dr NOEL RAMÍREZ SÁNCHEZ; Dir SILVIO CONRADO.

Private Banks

Banco de América Central (BAC): Pista Sub-Urbana, Frente a Lotería Popular, Managua; tel. (2) 77-3624; fax (2) 77-3696; f. 1991; total assets 10,516m. (1999); Man. CARLOS MATUS.

Banco Caley Dagnall; Km 3 Carretera Sur 1, Managua; tel. (2) 68-0068; fax (2) 68-0069; e-mail bancaley@ibw.com.ni; total assets 8,350m. (1999).

Banco de Crédito Centroamericano (BANCENTRO): Edif. BANCENTRO, Km 4½, Carretera a Masaya, Managua; tel. (2) 78-0353; fax (2) 78-8030; internet www.bancentro.com; total assets 5,249m. (1999); Gen. Man. JULIO CÁRDENAS.

Banco Europeo de Centro América: Del Hospital Dávila Bolaños 20 m Abajo, Apdo 188, Managua; tel. (2) 66-5401; fax (2) 66-5405.

Banco de la Exportación (BANEXPO): Plaza España, Rotonda el Güegüense 20 m al Oeste, Managua; tel. (2) 78-7171; fax (2) 77-3154; e-mail info@banexpo.com.ni; total assets 6,134m. (1999); Man. GILBERTO WONG.

Banco de Finanzas: Frente Hotel Intercontinental, Apdo 6020, Managua; tel. (2) 28-3045; fax (2) 28-3056; total assets 5,608m. (1999); merged with Banco del Café in Nov. 2000; Pres. WILLIAM GRAHAM.

Banco Mercantil, SA (BAMER): Plaza Banco Mercantil, Rotonda El Güegüense 1 c. al Sur, Managua; tel. (2) 66-8558; fax (2) 67-2041; e-mail bamer@tmx.com.ni; f. 1991; total assets 6,372m. (1999); Pres. HAROLDO J. MONTEALEGRE; 6 brs.

Banco Nicaragüense de Industria y Comercio (BANIC): Centro BANIC, Carretera a Masaya, Km 5½, Apdo 549, Managua; tel. (2) 67-2107; fax (2) 67-2308; e-mail rolacayo@ibw.com.ni; f. 1953; cap. and res 78.5m., dep. 1,421.9m. (Dec. 1997); Pres. RONALD LACAYO; Gen. Man. ARMANDO NÚÑEZ BRUX; 21 brs.

Banco de Préstamos (BANPRES): Esq. Opuesta, Hotel Intercontinental, Managua; tel. (2) 28-3045; fax (2) 28-3056; Man. NERVO BERMEO C.

Banco de la Producción, SA (BANPRO): Edif. Plaza Libertad, Frente a Plaza El Sol, Managua; tel. (2) 78-7532; fax (2) 77-3996; e-mail ejg@banpro.com.ni; f. 1991; total assets 6,083m.; merged with Banco Intercontinental in Nov. 2000; Man. ARTURO ARANA.

INTERBANK: Frente a Lotería Nacional, Managua; tel. (2) 78-5959; fax (2) 78-3536; f. 1991; cap. 34.7m., res 38.8m., dep. 1,636.7m. (Dec. 1998); Pres. ENRIQUE DESHON DUQUE-ESTRADA; Gen. Man. JOSÉ FÉLIX PADILLA.

Foreign Bank

Citibank NA (USA): Del Sandy's ½ c. Arriba, Km 3½, Carretera a Masaya, 75 m Arriba, Apdo 3102, Managua; tel. (2) 72124; f. 1967; cap. 10.5m., dep. 33.1m. (Oct. 1980); Man. ENRIQUE ALANIZ D.; 1 br.

STOCK EXCHANGE

Bolsa de Valores de Nicaragua: Edif. Oscar Pérez Cassar, Centro BANIC, Km 5½, Carretera a Masaya, Managua; tel. (2) 78-3830; fax (2) 78-3836; e-mail info@bolsanic.com; f. 1993; Pres. Dr RAÚL LACAYO; Gen. Man. CAROLINA SOLÓRZANO DE BARRIOS.

INSURANCE
State Company

Instituto Nicaragüense de Seguros y Reaseguros (INISER): Centro Comercial Camino de Oriente, Km 6, Carretera a Masaya, Apdo 1147, Managua; tel. (2) 72-2772; fax (2) 67-2121; internet www.iniser.gob.ni; f. 1979 to assume the activities of all the pre-revolution national private insurance companies; Exec. Pres. LUIS GONZÁLEZ RAMÍREZ.

Foreign Companies

American Life Insurance Company: Metrocentro Módulo 7, Apdo 601, Managua; tel. (2) 73356; Admin. Man. DOLORES LEZAMA.

British American Insurance Co.: Altamira D'Este 360, Apdo A-56, Managua; Gen. Man. CECIL E. GILL.

Citizens Standard Life Insurance Co.: Iglesia El Carmen, 2 c. al Lago, ½ c. Abajo, No 1410, Apdo 3199, Managua; Man. YAGALÍ RIVAS ALEGRÍA.

Pan American Life Insurance Co.: Edif. Kodak, Plaza de Compras, Col. Centroamérica, Managua; Man. ALEJANDRO LEIVA CABEZAS.

Trade and Industry

GOVERNMENT AGENCIES

Dirección General de Promoción de Exportaciones: Km 6, Carretera a Masaya, Apdo 8, Managua; tel. (2) 67-0150; fax (2) 67-0095; promotion of non-traditional exports, responsible to Ministry of Economy and Development; Dir-Gen. Lic. ALEJANDRO CARRIÓN M.

Empresa Nicaragüense de Alimentos Básicos (ENABAS): Salida a Carretera Norte, Apdo 1041, Managua; tel. (2) 23082; fax

(2) 26185; f. 1979; controls trading in basic foodstuffs; Dir Lic. IGNACIO VÉLEZ LACAYO.

Empresa Nicaragüense del Azúcar (ENAZUCAR): Ministerio de Defensa Nacional, El Chipote, Complejo Germán Pomares, Managua; tel. (2) 27261; f. 1979; controls sugar trading; Dir NOEL CHAMORRO CUADRA.

Empresa Nicaragüense del Banano (BANANIC): Edif. Málaga, Plaza España, Apdo 3433, Managua; tel. (2) 678311; fax (2) 73633; f. 1979; controls banana trading; Dir EDUARDO HOLMANN.

Empresa Nicaragüense del Café (ENCAFE): Plaza de Compras, Contiguo al Banco de Londres (Lloyds Bank), Col. Centroamérica, Apdo 2482, Managua; tel. (2) 70337; fax (2) 67-2604; f. 1979; controls coffee trading; Dir Dr ARMANDO JARQUÍN SEQUIERA.

Empresa Nicaragüense de la Carne (ENCAR): Frente al Edif. Pérez Cassar, Apdo C-11, Managua; tel. (2) 70519; fax (2) 70621; f. 1979; controls trading and export of meat and meat products; Exec. Dir ORLANDO N. BONILLA.

Empresa Nicaragüense de Insumos Agropecuarios (ENIA): Distribuidora Vicky, 2 c. Oeste, Apdo C-11, Managua; tel. (2) 71724; f. 1979; agricultural investment goods board; Dir EDUARDO FONSECA FÁBREGAS.

Empresa Nicaragüense de Productos del Mar (ENMAR): Frente al Cine Aguerri, Apdo 356, Managua; tel. (2) 23572; f. 1979; controls trading in all seafood products; Dir FRANKLIN MENDIETA MEDINA.

Instituto Nicaragüense de Apoyo a la Pequeña y Mediana Empresa (INPYME): De la Shell Plaza el Sol, 1 c. al Sur, 300 m Abajo, Apdo 449, Managua; tel. (2) 77-0598; fax (2) 70-1406; internet www.inpyme.gob.ni; supports small and medium-sized enterprises; Exec. Dir Dr RICARDO ALVARADO N.

Instituto Nicaragüense de Minas (INMINE): Pista de la Resistencia, Antiguo Centro Comercial El Punto, Contiguo a Migración y Extranjera, Apdo 195, Managua; tel. (2) 65-2073; fax (2) 51043; f. 1979; mines and hydrocarbons; Dir IVAN ORTEGA.

Instituto Nicaragüense de Reforma Agraria (INRA): Km 8, Entrada a Sierrita Santo Domingo, Managua; tel. (2) 73210; agrarian reform; Dir VIRGILIO GURDIÁN CASTELLÓN.

Instituto Nicaragüense de Seguridad Social (INSS): Frente Cementerio San Pedro, Edif. INSS, Apdo 1649, Managua; tel. (2) 22-7454; fax (2) 22-7445; f. 1955; social security and welfare; Exec. Pres. OSCAR MARTÍN AGUADO ARGÜELLO.

Instituto Nicaragüense de Tecnología Agropecuaria (INTA): Managua; internet www.inta.gob.ni; f. 1993; Dir HENRY PEDROZA PACHECO.

MEDEPESCA: Km 6½, Carretera Sur, Managua; tel. (2) 67-3490; state fishing agency; Dir Ing. EMILIO OLIVARES.

DEVELOPMENT ORGANIZATIONS

Asociación Nicaragüense de Productores y Exportadores de Productos No Tradicionales (APPEN): Del Hotel Intercontinental, 2 c. al Sur y 2 c. Abajo, Bolonia, Managua; tel. (2) 66-5038; fax (2) 66-5039; Pres. SAMUEL MANSELL.

Cámara de Industrias de Nicaragua: Rotonda el Güegüense, 300 m al Sur, Apdo 1436, Managua; tel. (2) 66-8847; Pres. ENRIQUE SALVO H.

Cámara Nacional de la Mediana y Pequeña Industria (CONAPI): Plaza 19 de Julio, Frente a la UCA, Apdo 153, Managua; tel. (2) 78-4892; fax (2) 67-0192; Pres. ANTONIO CHÁVEZ JIMÉNEZ.

Cámara Nicaragüense de la Construcción (CNC): 2° Callejón, Col. Mántica 239, Apdo 3016, Managua; tel. (2) 62-2071; f. 1961; construction industry; Pres. Ing. PABLO VIGIL.; Exec. Sec. Lic. FELIPE LAU G.

Instituto Nicaragüense de Fomento Municipal: Managua; Pres. Ing. SANTIAGO RIVAS LECLAIR.

CHAMBERS OF COMMERCE

Cámara de Comercio de Nicaragua: Rotonda El Gueguense 300 m al Sur, 20 m al Oeste; tel. (505) 268-3505; fax (505) 268-3600; e-mail comercio@ibw.com.ni; f. 1892; 530 mems; Pres. MARCO A. MAYORGA L.; Gen. Man. MARIO ALEGRÍA.

Cámara de Comercio Americana de Nicaragua: Semáforos ENEL Central, 500 m al Sur, Apdo 2720, Managua; tel. (2) 67-3099; fax (2) 67-3098; e-mail amcham@ns.tmx.com.ni; f. 1974; Pres. HUMBERTO CORRALES M.

Cámara Oficial Española de Comercio de Nicaragua: Restaurante la Marseilleisa, ½ c. Arriba, Los Robles, Apdo 4103, Managua; tel. (2) 78-9047; fax (2) 78-9088; e-mail camacoes@tmx.com.ni; Pres. RAMÓN HERNÁNDEZ ULLÁN; Sec.-Gen. AUXILIADORA MIRANDA DE GUERRERO.

EMPLOYERS' ORGANIZATIONS

Asociación de Productores de Café Nicaragüenses: coffee producers; Pres. Dr NICOLÁS BOLAÑOS.

Consejo Superior de la Empresa Privada (COSEP): De Telcor Zacarías Guerra, 1 c. Abajo, Apdo 5430, Managua; tel. (2) 62-2030; fax (2) 62-2041; private businesses; consists of Cámara de Industrias de Nicaragua (CADIN), Unión de Productores Agropecuarios de Nicaragua (UPANIC), Cámara de Comercio, Cámara de la Construcción, Confederación Nacional de Profesionales (CONAPRO), Instituto Nicaragüense de Desarrollo (INDE); mem. of Coordinadora Democrática Nicaragüense; Pres. GILBERTO CUADRA S.; Sec. ORESTES ROMERO ROJAS.

Instituto Nicaragüense de Desarrollo (INDE): Ofs de Montoya, 1 c. al Norte, ½ c. al Oeste, Apdo 2598, Managua; tel. (2) 24047; f. 1963; organization of private businessmen; 650 mems; Pres. Ing. GILBERTO CUADRA; Exec. Sec. CARLOS ANTONIO NOGUERA P.

Unión de Productores Agropecuarios de Nicaragua (UPANIC): Los Robles, Galería 3 Mundos, 1 c. Abajo, ½ c. al Sur, Casa 300, Apdo 2351, Managua; tel. (2) 78-2586; fax (2) 78-3382; private agriculturalists' association; Pres. GERARDO SALINAS CASTRILLO; Exec. Sec. ROSENDO DÍAZ.

MAJOR COMPANIES

Azucarera Lacayo Montealegre Hermanos, SA: Mansión Teodolinda, 1 c. Abajo, Managua; tel. (2) 66-5110; fax (2) 66-8858; f. 1944; sugar and molasses production; Pres. RAÚL LACAYO SOLÓRZANO; Gen. Man. FRANCISCO BALTODANO.

Café Soluble, SA: Km 8½, Carretera Norte, Apdo 429, Managua; tel. (2) 63-1100; fax (2) 63-1195; e-mail info@cafesoluble.com; internet www.cafesoluble.com; f. 1958; instant-coffee manufacturers; Gen. Man. GERARDO BALTODANO; 200 employees.

Comercializadora del Banano Nicaragüense, SA (COMBANISA): De la Vichy, 75 m al Sur, Altamira del Este, Managua; tel. (2) 67-8311; fax (2) 67-3633; f. 1979; wholesale fruit trading; Gen. Man. BLANCO OLIVIA LÓPEZ; 4,000 employees.

Compañía Cervecera de Nicaragua, SA: Km 6½, Carretera Norte, Frente a ENABAS, Managua; tel. (2) 48-5080; fax (2) 48-5120; internet www.victoria.com.ni; brewery; f. 1926; Gen. Man. JAIME ROSALES P; 751 employees.

Compañía Licorera de Nicaragua, SA: Camino Oriente, Casilla 1494, Managua; tel. (2) 78-3270; fax (2) 77-3649; e-mail cia.licorera @nic.gbm.net; internet www.cln.com.ni; f. 1890; producers of rum; Gen. Man. LUIS A. CHAMORRO.

Corporación Nicaragüense del Banano: Altamira del Este, Managua; tel. (2) 67-8312; fax (2) 77-3633; f. 1988; fruit growers and sellers; Gen. Man. BLANCO OLIVIA LÓPEZ; 6,000 employees.

Embotelladora Nacional, SA (ENSA): Km 7½, Carretera Norte, Apdo 471, Managua; tel. (2) 33-1260; fax (2) 63-1320; f. 1944; bottlers of carbonated beverages; Pres. SILVIO PELLAS CHAMORRO; Gen. Man. MILTON CALDERA CARDENAL; 700 employees.

Empresa Bananera de Occidente: Frente al Centro de Salud, Chinandega, Corinto; f. 1981; fruit growers and sellers; Gen. Man. ROBERTO HURTADO; 3,350 employees.

Esso Standard Oil Ltd, SA: Base de la Cuesta de los Mártires, Apdo 343, Managua; tel. (2) 66-1101; fax (2) 66-6104; subsidiary of Exxon Corpn of USA; petroleum products; Gen. Man. AGUSTÍN FUENTES P.

Industria Nacional de Clavos y Alambres de Púas, SA (INCA): Apdo 14, Masaya, Masaya; tel. (2) 62-2605; f. 1961; producers of nails, wire and meshwork; Man. Dir RAMÓN ORLANDO GARCÍA PÉREZ; 560 employees.

Manufacturera Centroamericana (MACEN): Km 141/2, Carretera a los Brasiles, Managua; tel. (2) 69-9213; fax (2) 69-9217; e-mail macen@interlink.com.ni; internet www.interlink.com.ni; f. 1957; producers of sacking, string, linings and hammocks; Mans ALBERTO MACGREGOR, ADOLFO MACGREGOR, DONALD SPENCER; 200 employees.

Metales y Estructuras, SA (METASA): Km 28, Carretera Norte, Tipitapa, Managua; tel. (2) 21-1124; f. 1958; production of metals; Dir HERSÁN GARCÍA; 498 employees.

Molinos de Nicaragua, SA (MONISA): Parque Sandino 2, 1–2 c. al Lago, Apdo 45, Granada; tel. and fax (55) 22-291; e-mail monisa @tmx.com.ni; internet www.echamorro.com; f. 1964; flour producers; Gen. Man. CARLOS GERMAN SEQUEIRA.

Nabisco de Nicaragua, SA: Km 5, Carretera Norte, Apdo 1689, Managua; tel. (2) 49-2740; fax (2) 48-0704; e-mail nabisco @tmx.com.ni; internet www.nabisco.com.ni; f. 1949; subsidiary of Nabisco of the USA; makers of biscuits and puddings; Gen. Man. ARÓN GUERRERO.

NICALIT: Km 3½, Carretera Sur, Apdo 2964, Managua; tel. (2) 66-1551; fax (2) 66-2534; f. 1967; makers of asbestos products; Pres. FERNANDO MONTES OROZCO; Gen. Man. CAMILO LÓPEZ; 300 employees.

Nicaragua Sugar Estate Ltd: Ingenio San Antonio, Chichigalpa, Chinandega; tel. (2) 78-3270; fax (2) 67-2874; e-mail c.pellas@ nic.gbm.net; internet www.nicaraguasugar.com; f. 1890; sugar refi-

nery; Pres. CARLOS PELLAS; Gen. Man. XAVIER ARGUELLO; 3,500 employees.

Plásticos de Nicaragua, SA (PLASTINIC): Km 1½, Carretera Norte, Apdo 2286, Managua; tel. (2) 49-5695; fax (2) 49-5698; f. 1968; plastic-bag manufacturers; Gen. Man. RENÉ LACAYO; 245 employees.

Tabacalera Nicaragüense, SA (TANIC): Km 7½, Carretera Norte, Apdo 1049, Managua; tel. (2) 63-1900; fax (2) 63-1642; f. 1934; cigarette manufacturers; Gen. Man. MIGUEL TRIVELLI; 1,100 employees.

UTILITIES

Electricity

Unidad de Reestructuración de la Empresa Nicaragüense de Electricidad (URE): Altamira d'Este 141, de la Vicky 1 c. Abajo, 1 c. al Sur, Managua; tel (2) 70-9989; fax (2) 78-2284; e-mail ure@ ibw.com.ni; internet www.ure.gob.ni; f. 1999 to oversee the privatization of the state-owned distribution and generation companies of ENEL; Exec. Dir SALVADOR QUINTANILLA.

Empresa Nicaragüense de Electricidad (ENEL): Ofs Centrales, Pista Juan Pablo II y Avda Bolívar, Managua; tel. (2) 67-4159; fax (2) 67-2686; e-mail relapub@ibw.com.ni; internet www.enitel.gob.ni; responsible for planning, organization, management, administration, research and development of energy resources; split into two distribution companies and three generation companies in 1999:

DISNORTE, SA: electricity distribution company; distributes some 802 gWh; sold to Union Fenosa (Spain) in 2000.

DISSUR, SA: electricity distribution company; distributes some 658 gWh; sold to Union Fenosa (Spain) in 2000.

GECSA: electricity generation company; 79 MW capacity thermal plant; scheduled for privatization in 2001.

GEOSA: electricity generation company; 112 MW capacity thermal plant; scheduled for privatization in 2001.

HIDROGESA: electricity generation company; 94 MW capacity hydro-electric plant; scheduled for privatization in 2001.

Instituto Nicaragüense de Energía (INE): Edif. Petronic, 4° piso, Managua; tel. (2) 28-1142; fax (2) 28-2049; internet www.ine .gob.ni; Dirs OCTAVIO SALINAS, GONZALO PÉREZ, ARTURO ROA.

Water

Instituto Nicaragüense de Acueductos y Alcantarillados (INAA): De la Mansión Teodolinda, 3 c. al Sur, Bolonia, Apdo 1084, Managua; tel. (2) 66-7916; fax (2) 66-7917; e-mail pres .ejinaa@tmx.com.ni; internet www.inaa.gob.ni; f. 1979; water and sewerage; Exec. Pres. JORGE ENRIQUE HAŸN VOGL.

CO-OPERATIVES

Cooperativa de Algodoneros de Managua, RL: Km 3½, Carretera Norte, Apdo 483, Managua; tel. (2) 4515; cotton-growers; Pres. Ing. GUILLERMO LACAYO; Sec. Ing. CARLOS ORTEGA M.

Cooperativa de Mercadeo de los Artesanos del Calzado: Managua; tel. (2) 4196; shoemakers and leatherworkers; Dir FÉLIX LECHADO CASTRILLO.

Empresa Cooperativa de Productores Agropecuarios: Managua; represents 13,000 members from 48 affiliated co-operatives; Chair. DANIEL NÚÑEZ.

TRADE UNIONS

Asociación de Trabajadores del Campo—ATC (Association of Rural Workers): Apdo A-244, Managua; tel. (2) 23221; f. 1977; Gen. Sec. EDGARDO GARCÍA; 52,000 mems.

Central de Trabajadores Nicaragüenses—CTN (Nicaraguan Workers' Congress): Iglesia Santa Ana, 1½ c. al Oeste, Managua; tel. (2) 25981; f. 1962; mem. of Coordinadora Democrática Nicaragüense; Leader CARLOS HUENDES; Sec.-Gen. ANTONIO JARQUÍN.

Confederación General de Trabajo (Independiente)—CGT(I) (Independent General Confederation of Labour): Calle 11 de Julio, Managua; f. 1953; Sec.-Gen. CARLOS SALGADO MEMBRENO; 4,843 mems (est.) from six federations with 40 local unions, and six non-federated local unions.

Confederación de Unificación Sindical—CUS (Confederation of United Trade Unions): Apdo 4845, Managua; tel. (2) 42039; f. 1972; affiliated to the Inter-American Regional Organization of Workers, etc.; mem. of Coordinadora Democrática Nicaragüense; Leader ALVIN GUTHRIE RIVEZ; Sec. SANTOS TIJERINO.

Congreso Permanente de los Trabajadores—CPT (Permanent Workers' Congress): 'umbrella' group for four trade unions, incl. the CTG(I) and CTN.

Consejo de Acción y Unidad Sindical—CAUS (Council for Trade Union Action and Unity): Pauterizadora 'La Perfecta', 3 c. Abajo, Residencial Bello Horizonte, Managua; tel. (2) 44-2587; fax (2) 22-

2623; f. 1973; trade-union wing of Partido Comunista de Nicaragua; Sec.-Gen. Pío Santos Murillo González.

Federación de Trabajadores de la Salud—FETSALUD (Federation of Health Workers): Optica Nicaragüense, 2 c. Arriba ½ c. al Sur, Apdo 1402, Managua; tel. and fax (2) 66-3065; Dir Gustavo Porras Cortez.

Federación de Trabajadores Nicaragüenses—FTN: workers' federation; Leader Zacarías Hernández.

Federación de Transportadores Unidos Nicaragüense—FTUN (United Transport Workers' Federation of Nicaragua): De donde fue el Vocacional, esq. Este, 30 m al Sur, Apdo 945, Managua; f. 1952; Pres. Manuel Saballos; 2,880 mems (est.) from 21 affiliated associations.

Frente Nacional de Trabajadores—FNT (National Workers' Front): Calle Colón, Iglesia del Carmen, 1 c. Abajo, 20 m al Sur, Managua; tel. (2) 26484; f. 1979; affiliated to Frente Sandinista de Liberación Nacional; Leader Roberto González; Gen. Sec. Lucio Jiménez.

Frente Obrero—FO (Workers' Front): f. 1974; radical Marxist-Leninist trade union.

Frente de Trabajadores Socialcristiano—FRETRA SC (Social-Christian Workers' Front): f. 1980; trade-union wing of the Partido Social Cristiano Nicaragüense.

Solidaridad de Trabajadores Cristianos—STC: Christian workers; Leader Donald Castillo.

Unión Nacional de Agricultores y Ganaderos—UNAG (National Union of Agricultural and Livestock Workers): De donde fue el Cine Dorado, 1 c. Este, ½ c. Norte, frente al Restaurante Rincón Marino, Apdo 4526, Managua; tel. (2) 28-1403; fax (2) 28-1404; e-mail unag@unag.org.ni; internet www.unag.org.ni; f. 1981; Pres. Daniel Núñez Rodríguez.

Unión Nacional de Caficultores de Nicaragua—UNCAFENIC (National Union of Coffee Growers of Nicaragua): Reparto San Juan, Casa 300, Apdo 3447, Managua; tel. (2) 78-2586; fax (2) 78-2587; Pres. Gerardo Salinas C.

Unión Nacional Campesina—UNC (National Union of Rural Workers): f. 1983; affiliated to the Unión Demócrata Cristiana.

Unión de Productores Agropecuarios de Nicaragua (Union of Agricultural Producers of Nicaragua): Reparto San Juan, Casa 300, Apdo 2351, Managua; tel. (2) 78-3382; fax (2) 78-2587; Pres. Gerardo Salinas C.

Transport

Plans for the construction of a 377 km 'dry canal' or rail link between the Atlantic and Pacific oceans, at an estimated cost of US $1,400m., were being pursued in 2001. The plans included the construction of two deep-water ports, at Punta Mono (Atlantic) and Gigante (Pacific).

RAILWAYS

Ferrocarril de Nicaragua: Plantel Central Casimiro Sotelo, Del Parque San Sebastián, 5 c. al Lago, Apdo 5, Managua; tel. (2) 22-2160; fax (2) 22-2542; f. 1881; government-owned; main line from León via Managua to Granada on Lake Nicaragua (132 km), southern branch line between Masaya and Diriamba (44 km), northern branch line between León and Río Grande (86 km) and Puerto Sandino branch line between Ceiba Mocha and Puerto Sandino (25 km); total length 287 km; reported to have ceased operations in 1994; Gen. Man. N. Estrada.

Ferrocarril del Pacífico de Nicaragua: Plantel Central Casimiro Sotelo, Del Parque San Sebastián, 5 c. al Lago, Apdo 5, Managua; tel. (2) 22-2530; fax (2) 22-2542; Pacific railway co.

ROADS

In 1999 there were an estimated 25,000 km of roads of which 4,000 km were paved. Of the total only some 9,000–10,000 km were accessible throughout the entire year. Some 8,000 km of roads were damaged by 'Hurricane Mitch', which struck in late 1998. The Pan-American Highway runs for 384 km in Nicaragua and links Managua with the Honduran and Costa Rican frontiers and the Atlantic and Pacific Highways connecting Managua with the coastal regions.

SHIPPING

Corinto, Puerto Sandino and San Juan del Sur, on the Pacific, and Puerto Cabezas, El Bluff and El Rama on the Caribbean, are the principal ports. Corinto deals with about 60% of trade. In 2001 the US-based company Delasa was given a 25-year concession to develop and modernize Puerto Cabezas port. It was to invest some US $200m.

Comisión Ejecutiva Portuaria Autónoma: Edif. Torre Roble, Blvd Los Héroes. San Salvador; tel. (2) 60-3320; fax (2) 60-3321; internet www.cepasal.com.

Administración Portuaria de Corinto: De Telcor, 1 c. al Oeste, Corinto; tel. (342) 211; f. 1956; port authority at Corinto.

CIVIL AVIATION

The principal airport is the Augusto Sandino International Airport, in Managua. There are some 185 additional airports in Nicaragua.

Aerolíneas Nicaragüenses (AERONICA): Contiguo Aeropuerto Internacional Augusto C. Sandino, Apdo 6018, Managua; tel. (2) 63-1929; fax (2) 63-1822; f. 1981; domestic services and international services to El Salvador, Costa Rica, Panama, Mexico and USA; Gen. Man. Julio Rocha.

Nicaragüenses de Aviación (NICA): Apdo 6018, Managua; tel. (2) 63-1929; fax (2) 63-1822; internet www.flylatinamerica.com; f. 1992; domestic services and international services to Panama, Costa Rica, Honduras, El Salvador, Guatemala and USA; Pres. Enrique Dreyfus; Gen. Man. Mario Medrano.

Tourism

In 1988 a campaign to attract more tourists to Nicaragua was launched, including a tourist development at Montelimar, which was supported by a US $10m. loan from Spanish investors. In 1998 tourist arrivals totalled 405,702 and receipts from tourism totalled around $90m.

Instituto Nicaragüense de Turismo (INTUR): Avda Bolívar Sur, Apdo 122, Managua; tel. (2) 22-5436; fax (2) 28-1187; internet www.intur.gob.ni; f. 1967; Min. Lorenzo Guerrero.

Asociación Nicaragüense de Agencias de Viajes (ANAVIT): Apdo 1045, Managua; Pres. Antonio Espino.

Cámara Nacional de Turismo: Contiguo al Ministerio de Turismo, Apdo 2105, Managua; tel. (2) 66-5071; fax (2) 66-5071; e-mail canatur@munditel.com.ni; f. 1976; Pres. Mario Medrano M.

Defence

In August 2000 Nicaragua's professional Armed Forces numbered an estimated 16,000: Army 14,000, Navy 800 (estimated) and Air Force 1,200. Conscription was introduced in September 1983, but was abolished in April 1990. There is a voluntary military service which lasts 18–36 months.

Defence Budget: 329m. gold córdobas (US $26m.) in 2000.

Commander-in-Chief: Maj.-Gen. Javier Carrión.

Education

From 1979 primary and secondary education in Nicaragua were provided free of charge. Primary education, which is officially compulsory, begins at seven years of age and lasts for six years. Secondary education, beginning at the age of 13, lasts for up to five years, comprising a first cycle of three years and a second of two years. In 1997 the total enrolment at primary school was equivalent to 64.6% of children in the appropriate age-group (males 62.7%; females 66.4%), while the total enrolment in secondary school was 57.0% (males 52.0%; females 62.0%). There are many commercial schools and four universities. In 1998 56,558 students attended universities and other higher education institutes. According to UNESCO, the rate of adult illiteracy averaged 37.2% (males 37.2%; females 37.2%) in 1999. In 1997 expenditure on education accounted for 8.8% of total government expenditure.

Bibliography

For works on Central America generally, see Select Bibliography (Books).

Arnove, R. F. *Education and Revolution in Nicaragua*. New York, NY, Praeger Publrs, 1986.

Booth, J. A. *End and the Beginning: Nicaraguan Revolution*. Boulder, CO, Westview Press, 1981.

Cardenal, E. *Nicaraguan New Time*. London, Journeyman Press, 1988.

Close, D. *Nicaragua: The Chamorro Years*. Boulder, CO, Lynne Rienner, 1998.

Edmisten, P. *Nicaragua Divided: La Prensa and the Chamorro Legacy*. Gainesville, FL, University Press of Florida, 1990.

Field, L. W. *The Grimace of MacHo Raton: Artisans, Identity and Nation in Late Twentieth-Century Western Nicaragua*. Durham, NC, Duke University Press, 1999.

Freeland, J. 'Nationalist Revolution and Ethnic Right: The Miskitu Indians of Nicaragua's Atlantic Coast', in *Third World Quarterly*, Vol. 11 (October), 1989.

Heyck, D. L. D. *Life Stories of the Nicaraguan Revolution*. London, Routledge, 1990.

Jones, J. *Brigadista: Harvest and War in Nicaragua*. London, Praeger Publrs, 1986.

MacAulay, N. *The Sandino Affair*. Micanopy, FL, Wacahoota Press, 1998.

Morley, M. H. *Washington, Somoza and the Sandinistas: State and Regime in US Policy towards Nicaragua, 1969–1981*. Cambridge, Cambridge University Press, 1994.

O'Shaughnessy, L. N., and Serra, L. H. *The Church and Revolution in Nicaragua*. Athens, OH, Ohio University Press, 1986.

Raou, M. 'The Origins and Evolution of the Nicaraguan Insurgencies 1979–85', in *Orbis* (Winter). 1986.

Ruchwarger, G. *People in Power: Forging a Grassroots Democracy in Nicaragua*. South Hadley, MA, Bergin and Garvey, 1986.

Smith, H. *Nicaragua: Self-Determination and Survival*. London, Pluto Press, 1992.

Vanderlaan, M. B. *Revolution and Foreign Policy in Nicaragua*. Boulder, CO, Westview Press, 1986.

Walker, T. W. (Ed.). *Nicaragua: The First Five Years*. London, Praeger Publrs, 1985.

Nicaragua Without Illusions: Regime Transition and Structural Adjustment in the 1990s. Wilmington, DE, Scholarly Resources, 1997.

PANAMA

Area: 75,517 sq km (29,157 sq miles).

Population (census of 14 May 2000): 2,839,177.

Capital: Panamá, population 708,438 at census of 14 May 2000.

Language: Spanish (official).

Religion: Mainly Christianity (Roman Catholicism predominates).

Climate: Tropical; but tempered by sea breezes; rainy season from April until December.

Time: GMT –5 hours.

Public Holidays

2002: 1 January (New Year's Day), 9 January (National Martyrs' Day), 11–12 February (Carnival), 13 February (Ash Wednesday), 28 March (Maundy Thursday), 29 March (Good Friday), 1 May (Labour Day), 15 August (Foundation of Panamá; Panamá only)*, 2 November (Day of the Dead), 3 November (Independence from Colombia), 4 November (Flag Day)*, 5 November (Independence Day; Colón only), 10 November (First Call for Independence), 28 November (Independence from Spain), 8 December (Immaculate Conception, Mothers' Day), 25 December (Christmas).

2003: 1 January (New Year's Day), 9 January (National Martyrs' Day), 3–4 March (Carnival), 5 March (Ash Wednesday), 17 April (Maundy Thursday), 18 April (Good Friday), 1 May (Labour Day), 15 August (Foundation of Panamá; Panamá only)*, 2 November (Day of the Dead), 3 November (Independence from Colombia), 4 November (Flag Day)*, 5 November (Independence Day; Colón only), 10 November (First Call for Independence), 28 November (Independence from Spain), 8 December (Immaculate Conception, Mothers' Day), 25 December (Christmas).

* Official holiday: banks and government offices closed.

Currency: Balboa; 100 balboas = £69.84 = US $100.00 = €112.66 (30 April 2001).

Weights and Measures: Both the metric and imperial systems are in use.

Basic Economic Indicators

	1998	1999	2000
Gross domestic product (million balboas at 1982 prices)	6,947.2	7,152.2	7,341.8
GDP per head (balboas at 1982 prices)	2,513.8	2,545.9	n.a.
GDP (million balboas at current prices)	9,344.7	9,556.6	n.a
GDP per head (balboas at current prices)	3,381.3	3,401.8	n.a
Annual growth of real GDP (%)	4.4	3.0	2.7
Annual growth of real GDP per head (%)	2.7	1.3	n.a.
Government budget estimates (million balboas at current prices):			
Revenue	2,331.2	n.a.	n.a.
Expenditure	2,606.8	n.a.	n.a.
Consumer price index (base: 1995 = 100)	103.2	104.5	106.0
Rate of inflation (annual average, %)	0.6	1.3	1.4
Foreign exchange reserves (US $ million at 31 December)	937.7	805.5	706.8
Imports c.i.f. (US $ million)	3,398	3,516	3,379
Exports f.o.b. (US $ million)	784	822	860
Balance of payments (current account, US $ million)	–1,175.9	–1,376.0	–926.8

Gross national product per head measured at purchasing power parity (PPP) (US dollars, converted by the PPP exchange rate, 1999): 5,016.

Economically active population (2000): 1,119,100.

Unemployment (persons aged 12 years and over, 1999): 11.8%.

Total foreign debt (estimate, 1999): US $7,100m.

Life expectancy (years at birth, 1998): 73.8 (males 71.9, females 76.5).

Infant mortality rate (per 1,000 live births, 1998): 18.

Adult population with HIV/AIDS (15–49 years, 1999): 1.54%.

School enrolment ratio (6–17 years, 1998): 73%.

Adult literacy rate (15 years and over, 2000): 91.9% (males 92.6, females 91.3).

Energy consumption per head (kg of oil equivalent, 1998): 862.

Carbon dioxide emissions per head (metric tons, 1997): 2.9.

Passenger motor cars in use (per 1,000 of population, 1996): 102.0.

Television receivers in use (per 1,000 of population, 1997): 187.

Personal computers in use (per 1,000 of population, 1999): 32.0.

History

HELEN SCHOOLEY

Geographically, Panama is part of Central America, but, as a result of Spanish colonial divisions and the construction of the Panama Canal through its territory, its history was very different from that of its northern neighbours. The question of the Canal dominated the country's history and, as a result, Panama gained political independence, first from Spain and then from Colombia, only to experience 150 years of US involvement in its national life. The USA was concerned less with the country's internal politics than with the protection of US interests in the operation of the Canal, and with US security policy throughout Latin America. The cession of the Canal to Panama on 1 January 2000 marked a decline in US interest in both the political life and, coincidentally, in the national economy of Panama. The Spanish arrived in Panama in 1502, and made it the centre of viceregal government over an area stretching as far south as Peru from 1533 to 1751, when the seat of government was moved to Santafé de Bogotá (Colombia). In 1821, along with the rest of Central America, Panama declared independence from Spain, but instead of joining the Central American Federation (1823–38) it opted for incorporation into the Federation of Gran (Greater) Colombia, which also included Venezuela and Ecuador, both of which seceded in 1830, while Panama, despite a number of revolts, continued under Colombian rule for a further 70 years.

CONSTRUCTION OF THE CANAL

The idea of constructing a transisthmian route was originated by the Spanish, who hoped to build a trading passage for Peruvian silver. The idea gained renewed prominence in the 1840s as a result of the California gold-rush, and led to the construction of the Panama railway in 1850–55 by a US company. The USA directly intervened in the country's internal politics on five occasions between 1860 and 1902, to protect the railway under the terms of a US–Colombian treaty of 1846. The original contract to build a canal was held by the French Panama Canal Co, but the work begun in 1879 proved so much more complex and costly, in terms of human lives, than anticipated that it was suspended in 1888. The Canal was finished by US interests and finally opened in 1914.

INDEPENDENCE

In 1903 Panama achieved independence from Colombia, largely at the instigation of the USA. Earlier in that year the US Government negotiated a treaty with Colombia, gaining the canal concession for the sum of US $10m., together with a 100-year lease on a 1,432 sq km strip of Panamanian territory (known as the Canal Zone), extending for eight km on either side of the Panama Canal route. The Colombian Congress raised objections to the treaty, causing a revolt in Panama, which then received US assistance in declaring independence in November. The USA concluded a similar treaty with the new Panamanian Government, according Panama sovereignty and the USA 'sovereign rights', creating an ambiguity that was to cause considerable disagreement between the two countries in the following years. The USA retained the right to military intervention to protect the Canal and, within the Zone, it had its own military bases, police force, laws, currency and postal service; it also maintained a direct political role in Panama's internal political life until 1918. After more than two decades of relatively stable political life in Panama, constitutional government was disrupted in the 1940s. In 1941 President Arnulfo Arias Madrid was overthrown in a bloodless coup and replaced by Adolfo de la Guardia, who refused to resign at the expiry of his term of office and was, in turn, replaced in 1945 by Enrique Jiménez. In the 1948 presidential election Domingo Díaz Arosemena was declared the winner, over Arias Madrid, but there were many allegations of fraud on both sides. After Díaz's death in 1949, Arias Madrid was installed in a bloodless coup, led by Col José

Antonio Remón, formerly the Chief of Police. President Arias Madrid pursued a series of right-wing policies, but after a vain attempt to suspend the right of habeas corpus, he was impeached in 1950 and banned from public life. Remón was elected President in 1952 and enacted a programme of moderate reforms until his assassination in January 1955. During this period the USA established the School of the Americas (SOA), a military base in Panama which acquired a formidable reputation for its training of anti-insurgency forces from several Latin American countries; the SOA was moved to the USA in 1984.

THE TORRIJOS ERA, 1968–81

After 12 years of uninterrupted elected government, political turbulence erupted again in 1968. Arias Madrid won the presidential election, but after 11 days in office he was deposed in a military coup led by the National Guard under the command of Col (later Brig.-Gen.) Omar Torrijos Herrera. (The National Guard, which wielded considerable political influence in the country, functioned as the national defence force, since the formation of an army had been proscribed in the 1904 Constitution.) Freedoms of the press, and of speech and assembly were suspended for one year, and party political activity was banned from February 1969 until October 1978. The National Guard retained power, first with military, and subsequently with civilian, appointees. Torrijos took the executive title of Chief of Government in 1972, and legislative power was vested in a 505-member Asamblea Nacional de Representantes de Corregimientos (National Assembly of Community Representatives, elected in August on a non-party basis). Under Torrijos, Panama enjoyed a greater degree of internal stability; his Government adopted more broadly left-wing sympathies in foreign policy and undertook considerable agrarian reform, while its most important achievement was the negotiation of a new Canal Treaty with the USA.

The Revision of the Canal Treaty

Despite revisions of the Canal Treaty in 1936 and 1955, which included an increase in the annual rent paid by the USA, the 1903 Treaty continued to be a focus for anti-US sentiment within the country. After repeated pressure from Panama and a number of other Latin American countries, negotiations on a new treaty began in 1973. Two draft treaties were signed in September 1977, in which the USA agreed to cede the Canal to the Government of Panama at noon on 31 December 1999. Prior to that, there would be a phased withdrawal of US troops, with Panama eventually taking control of all US military bases in the Canal Zone. The Zone itself would be abolished forthwith (although 40% of the land would remain under US control until the transition) and the former Canal Zone would be renamed the Canal Area. The Panama Canal Co would be replaced by a nine-member Panama Canal Commission, a non-profit US government agency with a board of Panamanian and US directors approved by the US Senate, on which the USA was to retain majority representation until 1989. In addition, Panama and the USA were to be jointly responsible for guaranteeing the Canal's permanent neutrality. The treaties were approved by a national referendum in Panama in October 1977, but opposition within the US Congress delayed their ratification in the USA until October 1979. In 1978 Gen. Torrijos announced plans to return Panama to elected government. He resigned as Chief of Government in October (retaining the post of National Guard Commander), when a newly-elected Asamblea Nacional endorsed his nominee, Dr Arístides Royo Sánchez, as President for a six-year term. However, Gen. Torrijos maintained his hold on power when, at elections in August to the 19-seat Consejo Nacional de Legislación (National Legislative Council) (an upper house that also contained 38 members nominated by the Asamblea Nacional), the Partido Revolucionario Democrático (PRD—

Revolutionary Democratic Party, led by Torrijos) obtained 10 seats. The elections were boycotted by Arias Madrid's Partido Panameñista Auténtico (PPA—Authentic Panamanian Party). In July 1981 Gen. Torrijos was killed in an aeroplane crash, which was assumed to be accidental, although there were allegations of US Central Intelligence Agency (CIA) involvement.

THE RISE AND FALL OF NORIEGA

After the death of Gen. Torrijos, relations between the presidency and the National Guard deteriorated, especially after the appointment as Commander, in March 1982, of Gen. Rubén Darío Paredes, a much keener advocate of pro-US foreign policy than President Royo. In July Gen. Paredes forced Royo from office, and the First Vice-President, Ricardo de la Espriella, became President. In the following year Paredes withdrew from the National Guard in order to contest the 1984 presidential election and was replaced by Gen. Manuel Noriega Morena. Dr Jorge Illueca, who took over as President in February 1984, was also highly critical of the USA and its alleged violations of the new Canal Treaties.

Constitutional amendments introduced in 1983 provided for the direct election of the President and Consejo Legislativo Nacional, replaced the 505-member Asamblea Nacional de Representantes de Corregimientos with a 67-seat Asamblea Legislativa (Legislative Assembly), reduced the presidential term of office to five years and prevented members of the National Defence Forces (as the National Guard was renamed) from standing as political candidates. In the May 1984 elections the PRD, in coalition with five other parties, won a majority in the Asamblea Legislativa and its candidate, Nicolás Ardito Barletta, was elected President. President Ardito resigned in September 1985, however, amid rumours that the National Defence Forces had assisted his election; it was then alleged that Gen. Noriega had removed him in order to disrupt an investigation into the murder, in the same month, of a leading politician, Hugo Spadáfora, in which the armed forces' command was implicated. Ardito Barletta was succeeded by the First Vice-President, Eric Delvalle, who promised 'a return to Torrijista principles', but faced strong opposition to his economic policies. His main problems, however, were the growing power of Gen. Noriega, and Panamanian claims that the USA was trying to renege on its commitment to withdraw from the Canal area and also failing to hand over Panama's rightful share of profits.

Despite mounting criticism of Gen. Noriega within Panama, US pressure for an investigation into allegations against him merely increased anti-US sentiment. In February 1988 President Delvalle attempted to dismiss Noriega, following his indictment in the USA on drugs-trafficking charges. Instead, Noriega deposed Delvalle and replaced him with Manuel Solís Palma. Delvalle went into hiding, but continued to be recognized as head of state by the opposition and the US administration. The May 1989 elections were contested entirely on the issue of Noriega's continuance in power, between two hastily formed coalitions: the government Coalición de Liberación Nacional (COLINA—National Liberation Coalition) and the Alianza Democrática de Oposición Civilista (ADOC—Civic Opposition Democratic Alliance). There were reports of substantial fraud on the part of COLINA and, when the ADOC presidential candidate, Guillermo Endara Gallimany, claimed victory, the counting was suspended and the whole election annulled. As ADOC refused to accept the annulment, COLINA formed a provisional Government.

US Military Intervention

In December 1989 Gen. Noriega was declared Head of Government. He announced that Panama was at war with the USA, and on 20 December US forces intervened to overthrow him and Endara was installed as President. US economic sanctions (in force since 1987) were ended and full diplomatic relations restored. Although Noriega himself had few allies abroad, the US action was condemned by most Latin American countries, and by the United Nations (UN) General Assembly, as a violation of Panamanian sovereignty. The official death toll resulting from the intervention was 527, excluding 27 US troops; the economic cost to Panama was estimated to be at least US $2,000m.

Noriega eventually gave himself up in return for an assurance that he would receive a fair trial and would not face the death penalty. He was then flown to the USA, found guilty on charges relating to drugs-trafficking and money laundering, and in July 1992 was sentenced to 40 years' imprisonment. In October 1994 he was sentenced *in absentia* by a Panamanian court to 20 years' imprisonment for the murder of a senior military officer in 1989. However, in March 1999 Noriega's US sentence was reduced to 30 years, after an appeal by his lawyers that he had given years of service to the USA as an 'asset' of the CIA.

RESTORATION OF THE DEMOCRATIC PROCESS

In order to regain the confidence of the international community, a new Asamblea Legislativa was formed in February 1990, based on the results of the May 1989 elections; ADOC was awarded 51 seats and COLINA six, while fresh elections were held for the remaining seats. The National Defence Forces were dissolved and a new Public Force created, consisting of the National Police, the National Air Force and the National Maritime Service. President Endara's Government, however, lacked domestic confidence, and was criticized for its inadequate social policy. The Roman Catholic Church urged the introduction of measures to reduce both political corruption and poverty; according to the Church, some 54.4% of the population lived on, or below, the poverty line. There was also a sharp increase in the rate of violent crime, with between 250 and 300 violent deaths every year, the majority of them linked to the drugs trade. Furthermore, in 1993 various ethnic groups (which formed about 8% of the population) increased their demands for land rights and accused the Government of failing to honour a commitment, made in February 1992, to prevent settlers encroaching on indigenous Amerindian lands.

The PRD returned to power after the May 1994 elections, although it failed to secure an outright majority in either the presidential or legislative polls. The party's presidential candidate, Ernesto Pérez Balladares, won 33.2% of the votes cast, ahead of Mireya Moscoso de Gruber (widow of former President Arias Madrid) of the Partido Arnulfista (PA—Arnulfist Party, the leading member of the ADOC coalition) with 29.1%. In the enlarged 72-seat legislature the PRD reached an agreement with minority parties to command just 36 seats. President Pérez's social and economic policies were highly controversial. A legislative proposal introduced in November 1995 (the third such proposal in five years), sought to extend an amnesty to nearly 1,000 former officials of the Noriega regime (some already convicted of murder, torture and embezzlement), but the bill was abandoned in June 1996. Meanwhile, the unions opposed the Government's attempts to liberalize the labour market and to implement a privatization programme, and the President's apparent endorsement of a system of political favours damaged public confidence in the administration. A draft constitutional amendment allowing a president to stand for re-election was passed by the legislature in late 1997, but was rejected by a ratio of nearly two to one in a referendum held in August 1998; the result was widely considered to reflect public opposition to the neo-liberal policies of the Pérez administration.

In the mid-1990s protests by indigenous groups increased, forcing greater concessions from the Government. The Kuna Indians and the Guaymí (also known as the Ngöbe-Buglé) were granted a degree of autonomy in June 1996 and March 1997, respectively. The agreement allowed them self-rule but not, as the Guaymí had demanded, any powers over either mineral rights or exploitation. Another social issue to arouse widespread concern in 1997 was that of prison overcrowding, a chronic situation which provoked a series of prison riots. National prisons held nearly five times their optimum number of inmates, and some 80% of detainees were still awaiting trial.

THE 1999 ELECTIONS

The presidential election of 2 May 1999 was a contest between representatives of traditional forces in national politics, with Moscoso de Gruber standing for the PA-led Unión por Panamá (UPP—Union for Panama) alliance against PRD nominee Martín Torrijos, son of Gen. Torrijos, the candidate of its Nueva Nación (NN—New Nation) grouping. The candidates did not differ substantially on policy, both undertaking to continue with free-market reforms, while seeking to ameliorate their economic consequences, and Moscoso's unexpected victory was perceived as an endorsement of her more populist style and greater emphasis on social justice. Although Moscoso emerged as the clear leader in the presidential ballot, the UPP won only 24 of the 71 contested legislative seats, with the result that the NN secured the largest representation (41 seats) in the Asamblea Legislativa. Moscoso took office on 1 September 1999, becoming Panama's first female President. On the same day a new Government was formed, known as a 'Government of national unity' and comprising members of the Partido Solidaridad (Solidarity Party), the Partido Liberal Nacional (PLN—National Liberal Party), the Partido Demócrata Cristiano (PDC—Christian Democratic Party) and the Partido Renovación Civilista (PRC—Civil Renewal Party). Moscoso reached an agreement with six minority parties in order to achieve a working parliamentary majority, albeit of just one seat. In September 2000, however, the PRD and the PDC formed an alliance, thus removing the governing coalition's small majority.

Following the discovery of human remains in a former military barracks in Tocumen, on 27 December 2000, President Moscoso announced the establishment of a Truth Commission to investigate human-rights abuses under former military leaders. Human rights groups estimated the number of 'disappearances' under the military dictatorships during 1968–89 to be some 150. Little effort had been made to investigate these cases, and there were allegations that the US authorities wished to avoid further scrutiny of their association with Noriega. The seven-member Commission was to be headed by Alberto Santiago Almanza Henríquez and, following a six-month investigation, was to present a report of recommended action to the Attorney-General. In September 2000 the human-rights issue returned to prominence, when the Peruvian former intelligence chief, Vladimiro Montesinos, arrived in Panama and requested political asylum to avoid charges of corruption. Many Panamanians resented their country's growing reputation as a refuge for allegedly corrupt or ruthless foreign politicians, and despite pressure from the USA and the Organization of American States to grant Montesinos' request, in October President Moscoso took the decision to return him to Peru.

Stronger opposition to the Government was founded on the state of the national economy. In September President Moscoso travelled to the town of Changuinola (in western Panama) after residents' peaceful demands for improved health, education, water and other public services degenerated into violent protests; and in May 2001 a strike in the capital over government-approved bus fare increases triggered similar unrest.

TRANSFER OF THE CANAL TO PANAMANIAN SOVEREIGNTY

The final US base in the Canal Area was closed at the end of November 1999, and the Canal was formally transferred to Panamanian sovereignty on 31 December. The Canal also became a fully commercial operation; under US control it had been run on a non-profit basis. The official ceremony was held on 14 December, and the US delegation was headed by former President Jimmy Carter. The absence of US President Bill Clinton, or any other senior officials, was interpreted in Panama as a diplomatic snub, and a concession to US right-wing interests still opposed to the hand-over. In the late 1990s several objections had been raised in the USA to the assumption of full Panamanian control, focusing on the issues of drugs-trafficking, the activities of Colombian paramilitary groups (see below), and the fear of an escalation of Chinese influence in Panama. This latter concern related to a contract awarded in 1996 to the Hong Kong-based company, Hutchinson Whampoa, to operate the ports at either end of the Canal.

A new 11-member Autoridad del Canal de Panamá (ACP—Panama Canal Authority) was created in 1994, and succeeded the Panama Canal Commission in December 1999. In early 2000 a five-year canal-modernization project was announced, including the development of technology to raise capacity, a general improvement of facilities, the construction of a second bridge over the Canal, and the widening of the narrowest section of the Canal, at Culebra Cut.

INTERNATIONAL RELATIONS

During the 1990s political wrangling over the possibility and benefits of a continued US military presence from 2000 was ongoing in both Panama and the USA, and relations between the two countries were further complicated by developments in Panama's relationship with Colombia. One legacy of the Central American civil wars of the 1980s was a vast surplus of arms and ammunition in the region, and Panama became a point of passage for arms-trafficking to Colombia and drugs-trafficking to the USA. The presence of left-wing Colombian guerrillas just inside the Panamanian border, in the province of Darién, had been tacitly accepted since 1993, although under President Pérez Panama appeared to offer more assistance to Colombia's right-wing paramilitary groups. In September 1999 there was a sharp increase in activity by these groups, which some Panamanians alleged were part of an orchestrated scheme to strengthen the case for a continued US military presence. In 2000 the Colombian Government launched the anti-drugs project, 'Plan Colombia', which was expected to have serious implications for Darién province, increasing the number of Colombian refugees crossing into Panama (some 8,000 refugees were thought already to have crossed the border since 1996). Border incursions continued in 2000; in November Colombian paramilitary forces attacked the town of Nazaret, in Darién province, leaving one person dead and nine injured. Following renewed death threats from Colombian groups, local schools were closed to protect the pupils. However, in November the Colombian President, Andrés Pastrana Arango, proposed a development plan for the province, partially in an attempt to prevent further border incidents.

Although plans were announced to turn a number of former US bases in Panama into tourist developments, some of these were affected by the presence of US chemical and biological weapons and munitions left behind. US forces had tested chemical and biological weapons in Panama during 1930–68, including napalm and 'Agent Orange' (the defoliant used by the USA during the Viet Nam War). In February 2000 the USA maintained that there were insufficient technological resources available to them at that time to ensure the safe removal of the weapons. The Panamanian Government declared its intention to pursue the matter through the machinery of the Chemical Weapons Convention, to which both countries were signatories.

On 17 November 2000 four people were arrested in Panama City following allegations of a plot to assassinate the Cuban head of state, Fidel Castro Ruz, who was attending the 10th Ibero-American Summit. Among those detained was Luis Posada Carriles, an alleged member of the Cuban-American National Foundation. Both Cuba and Venezuela sought the extradition of the detainees; however, in March 2001 the Panamanian Government rejected these requests, announcing that the legal process would take place in Panama.

Both the staging of the 10th Ibero-American Summit in Panama in November 2000, and the establishment in Panama in 2001 of the temporary headquarters for negotiations regarding the establishment of the Free-Trade Area of the Americas, were seen as an indication of the country's growing independence from the USA. Although the USA remained the Canal's principal customer, Panama sought to strengthen trading links with the rest of Latin America and with Europe, while moderating its relations with Asia. Like other Central American countries Panama accorded diplomatic recognition to the Republic of China (Taiwan), receiving considerable investment in return; however, the country also extended links to the People's Republic of China, which was the third greatest user of the Canal and accounted for one-third of exports to Panama's duty-free re-export zone.

Economy

PHILLIP WEARNE

Panama's geographic location enabled it to develop as one of the most important shipping crossroads and entrepôts in the world. The country's most famous asset was the 82 km-long Panama Canal, which traversed the Darién isthmus, thus linking the Pacific Ocean with the Caribbean Sea and enabling shipping to avoid the lengthy Cape Horn route around the South American landmass. The Canal itself, however, diminished in importance with the advent of supertankers and freighters, as the largest of the modern oil and bulk-cargo tankers could not use it. In June 1986 a commission was established to study the possibilities of enlarging the Canal, or even constructing a new one, but by early 1994 it had been decided that there would be no major improvements before 2010. Nevertheless, Panama's continued role as a 'land-bridge' was assured with the opening, in October 1982, of a transisthmian pipeline to carry petroleum deemed economically impractical for transit in the usual way.

For a relatively small country, Panama possessed abundant natural resources, including high-quality fishing grounds, mineral deposits, forests and, above all, a topography and climate that were ideal for the development of hydroelectric power. Substantial reserves of gold, copper and coal were under exploited and, apart from some manufacturing in the Colón Free Zone (CFZ—the second largest free-trade zone in the world, after Hong Kong), the primary and secondary sectors of the productive economy were also grossly underdeveloped. Panama was thus traditionally a service-based economy, reliant on revenues from the Canal and contributions from 'offshore' banking activities. From 1997 services accounted for more than 75% of gross domestic product (GDP) each year; some of the largest individual sub-sectors were transport, storage and communications (which contributed an estimated 15.8% of GDP in 1999), and the financial sector (which accounted for some 25.3% of GDP in the same year). Agriculture (including hunting, forestry and fishing), manufacturing and construction together accounted for only 19.3% of GDP in 1999.

Panama's currency was, effectively, the US dollar, although a nominal local currency, the balboa, existed at par with the dollar. The country's banknote supply was thus determined exclusively by trading relations and capital flows. Balance-of-payment surpluses automatically increased the money supply, while deficits caused it to dwindle. The country's central bank, the Banco Nacional de Panamá, could only influence the credit-creation constituent of the money supply (although it could issue local coinage) and the Government was unable to use currency devaluation or revaluation as an instrument of economic management.

The Government's economic policies were largely dictated by the International Monetary Fund (IMF), the World Bank (International Bank of Reconstruction and Development—IBRD) and the Inter-American Development Bank (IDB), all of which were involved in structural-readjustment programmes from 1985. One of the principal aims of these programmes was to correct Panama's lack of international competitiveness by removing distortions and inefficiencies in the tax regime and labour market. Import substitution in industry and agriculture was considered an important means of closing the gap between an over-regulated domestic economy and an underregulated international services sector. To this end Panama joined the World Trade Organization in September 1997 and began to dismantle its protective import tariff regime. At the same time, there was some effort (from the mid-1980s) to diversify the Panamanian services-orientated economic model. Revenues from the Panama Canal were by no means guaranteed and the credibility of the offshore banking sector was damaged by its perceived association with drugs-traffickers. Furthermore, the CFZ's exclusive advantages were being increasingly challenged by the creation of free-trade ports and zones all over Latin America. It seemed clear, therefore, that the Panamanian econ-

omic base had to adapt to avoid a steady decline. From the mid-1980s the contribution of the services sector to the Panamanian economy remained fairly steady; however, there was considerable diversification within the sector itself, with tourism a particularly robust growth area.

Policies originating in the 1980s were designed to curb the budget deficit by reducing subsidies, rationalizing employment in the public sector and stimulating export growth, particularly in agriculture, by eliminating bureaucracy and offering better incentives. The initial implementation of such policies, however, produced a high level of political instability in Panama. This led to the resignation of President Ardito Barletta in September 1985 and the ousting of his successor, Eric Arturo Delvalle, by the then Commander of the Panamanian Defence Forces, Gen. Manuel Antonio Noriega, in February 1988. There could be little doubt that the economic situation, worsened immeasurably by the US economic boycott of 1988–89, also played a crucial role in the downfall of Noriega himself, who was ousted by, and surrendered to, US troops during a brief but devastating invasion of the country in December 1989.

Panama withstood the general global recession of the early 1980s fairly well until 1983–84. In 1983 GDP grew by only 0.4% then contracted by the same amount in 1984, before a recovery in the services sector and manufacturing output from the CFZ stimulated growth of 4.7% in 1985. Expansion decreased to just 2.3% in 1987, before US economic sanctions provoked a precipitous 15.6% decline in the following year. There was a contraction of 0.4% in 1989, before the lifting of US sanctions and a more realistic economic policy in 1990 and 1991 stimulated economic growth of 4.6% and 9.6%, respectively. The recovery was maintained, although it slowed progressively, and after growing by 8.5% in 1992 the economy expanded by just 5.6% in 1993, before growth halved to 2.9% in 1994 and fell to just 1.8% in 1995. There was, however, a subsequent revival, with GDP expanding by 2.8% and 4.5% in 1996 and 1997, respectively. Steady progress was maintained in 1998 when GDP increased by 4.4%, before falling to 3.0% in 1999 and 2.7% in 2000. The rate of increase in consumer prices remained low in the late 1990s. In 1997 the annual rise in inflation was 1.3%, decreasing to just 0.7% in 1998, and rising to 1.3% in 1999 and 1.4% in 2000.

Panama had one of the highest foreign debts per head of population in the world (partly because it needed to borrow the money that it could not print). At the end of 2000 total external debt was an estimated US $7,600m., more than 80% of which was public debt. Total internal debt in the same year was an estimated $2,200m., of which almost one-half was owed to the central bank. High real interest rates significantly increased the debt-service ratio (annual amortization and interest, expressed as a proportion of foreign-exchange earnings on goods and non-factor services) on Panama's external debt during the 1980s, and in 1988 the country suspended all debt-service payments. By the end of 1990 arrears to the IMF, the World Bank and the IDB had reached $610m. Despite a series of financial reforms in 1991–92, the situation continued to deteriorate. Total arrears were estimated at $3,000m. in early 1994, before the Government intensified its efforts to reach an agreement with commercial and multilateral creditors.

In May 1995 a Brady Plan debt-restructuring agreement was announced (the initiative on debt relief originally proposed by the then US Treasury Secretary, Nicholas Brady, in 1989), which covered a total of US $3,230m. in principal and interest arrears. The agreement, whereby Panama exchanged debt for new bonds with virtually all its commercial creditors, reduced the country's debt by more than $400m. and opened the way for fresh credit. In 1997 the country further reduced its debt by renegotiating more than $300m. in petroleum-supply debts incurred with Mexico and Venezuela under the San José Agreement of 1980. This restructuring gave Panama access to concessionary finance from the IMF, the World Bank and the IDB and allowed the country access to international capital markets. Panama took advantage of this in March 1999, when it sold $500m.-worth of 30-year global bonds, using 40% of the receipts to buy back more foreign debt, and in February 2001, when it sold $750m.-worth of 10-year global bonds.

AGRICULTURE, FORESTRY AND FISHING

Agriculture and fishing were vitally important to the success of the economic diversification effort in Panama. This fact was recognized in the country's 1986 development plan, which set out to reverse a steady economic decline originating in the early 1970s. In 2000 an estimated 19.4% of the working population were employed in agriculture, forestry and fishing, but the sector contributed just 6.7% to GDP in 1999. About 23% of Panama's 7.6m. ha of land were cultivated, while another 21% were permanent pasture land and 44% were forest and wood-land, (more than one-half of which was declared protected park, woodland and forest in the past 25 years).

Bananas, sugar cane and coffee were the principal export crops. In 1999 Panama's exports of bananas, the leading export commodity, earned US $182.2m., an increase of 31% on the previous year, and accounted for 21.1% of total exports. However, in 2000 the value of exports fell by 18.6% to the more typical level of $148.3m. The figures represented yet another decline in the relative importance of banana exports since 1992, when they earned $212.5m., accounting for 44.2% of total revenue; the decline was largely attributed to falling international prices, industrial action in the sector and the adverse effects of the El Niño weather phenomenon (the warm current that periodically appears in the Pacific Ocean, altering normal weather patterns). In the late 1990s two subsidiaries of a US company, Chiquita Brands, was responsible for about 80% of Panama's banana production and exports, with private Panamanian producers accounting for the remainder. In 2000 the sector employed some 15,000 people directly, with a further 60,000 people dependent on the industry.

Traditionally, sugar was the second-highest agricultural export earner. However, revenues declined dramatically from the late 1980s as a result of depressed world prices and dramatic annual reductions in the USA's sugar import quota. Revenue decreased from US $41.3m. in 1983 to $10.2m. in 1989, although it recovered thereafter, reaching $28.7m. in 1997 following significant increases in Panama's share of the US sugar import quota, which increased by more than 25% in 1996, to 51,000 metric tons. In 1998 export revenue decreased slightly to $25.5m., before declining dramatically in 1999 to $14.4m., when it accounted for just 1.7% of export revenue. In 2000 the industry recovered slightly, with the value of exports reaching $20.0m. Coffee production remained stable at about 11,000 tons throughout the 1990s, but earnings fluctuated owing to international price movements. In 1995 earnings more than doubled to $33.4m., before declining to $18.8m. in 1996, rising slightly to $23.9m. in 1998, and declining again to $18.5m. in 1999 and $16.0m. in 2000. In May 2001 the Specialty Coffee Association of America successfully introduced the auction of gourmet Panamanian beans on the Internet.

The Government recognized the urgent need to increase agricultural production in its agreements with the IMF and the World Bank. A five-year agricultural development plan announced in 1985 envisaged investment of US $482m. by 1989 to counteract the effects of under-investment resulting from price controls on rice, meat, potatoes and dairy products. Diversification of both crops and markets was given a high priority, and new crops such as African palm (oil palm), cocoa, coconuts, various winter vegetables and tropical fruits were promoted. With political stability apparently returning, there were some signs that the renewed commitment to agriculture was taking effect, with agricultural GDP increasing by an annual average of 2.1% in 1989–99. In 1998 the sector expanded by 6.3%, despite industrial action in the banana industry early in the year; however, the sector contracted by 0.4% in 1999.The livestock sector underwent particularly rapid expansion, averaging 4.0% annual growth in the late 1980s and early 1990s. However, the sector subsequently suffered from credit problems and export restrictions, and in 1994 export earnings from livestock products fell dramatically to just US $5m., from $16m. in the previous

year. The sector recovered slowly, thereafter. Panama's fishing industry was stimulated by the completion of a new port and fishing terminal at Vacamonte in 1979. In 1999 Panama claimed to be the world's third-largest exporter of shrimps, with exports of shellfish more than doubling in the five years to 1998, when shrimp revenues reached $136.7m. However, in 1999 the value of shrimp and shellfish exports fell dramatically, to just $76.6m., owing to a severe outbreak of white spot virus among shrimp stocks. Fish exports, also declined in 1999, following a decrease in the tuna and anchovy catch.

MINING AND ENERGY

Despite valuable mineral deposits that included gold, silver, copper and coal, mineral extraction was traditionally limited to clay, limestone and salt for local consumption. In 2000 mining contributed only an estimated 0.2% of GDP, employing the same proportion of the employed labour force. With a return to political and economic stability in the mid-1990s, and studies indicating potential export earnings from gold, silver and copper of some US $500m. per year, Panama's mining potential began to attract the interest of foreign investors. However, in 2001 the sector remained undeveloped, with potential investors discouraged by low world metal prices and the high cost of initial exploratory and extractive activity. Panama had about 1,300m. metric tons of proven and probable reserves of copper ore, reserves that included the world's 12th largest copper deposit, at Cerro Colorado, in the western Chiriquí province. In 1997 the owners of Cerro Colorado, Panacobre (a subsidiary of the Canadian-owned Tiomin Resources), began a $150m. first-phase investment at the site. However, work was suspended indefinitely in December of that year, owing to a decline in the international price of copper.

Gold mining in Panama tended to be small-scale, but gold mining concessions were more attractive to foreign investors owing to the lower capital costs. Nevertheless, by mid-1999 Panama had only one gold mine in production, the Santa Rosa mine in Veraguas province. Following an initial investment of US $25m. in 1995, the Santa Rosa mine yielded some 57,000 troy oz in 1997, producing $20m. in export revenue. In 1998 output fell with exports earning a mere $14m. It was anticipated that the Cerro Quema gold mining concession, acquired by the Canadian-owned Campbell Resources in 1996, would eventually yield a similar output for an initial outlay of $33m.

Panama had enormous hydroelectric potential and aimed eventually to eliminate petroleum-powered electricity generation. The opening in April 1984 of the La Fortuna (now Edwin Fabrega) hydroelectricity plant brought this aim closer. The plant cost US $500m. and was the third major hydroelectricity plant to come into operation in the country. However, the value of the plant, in terms of savings on petroleum imports, was reduced by the decrease in international petroleum prices in the late 1980s and by fluctuating rainfall levels, which led to a crisis in the hydroelectricity sector. Plans for another 120 MW plant in Esti, in western Panama, were abandoned in 1994. By 1999 hydroelectricity accounted for 551 MW of the country's 959 MW generating capacity, with demand growing at an average of 6% per year.

During periods of low hydroelectric output Panama was dependent on power generated from imported petroleum products. The cost of petroleum imports, which had been as high as US $350m. in 1982–83, had fallen to less than $125m. by 1994, owing to increased hydroelectric capacity and lower world petroleum prices. However, the poor performance of the hydroelectricity sector and a rise in the price of crude petroleum resulted in the cost of petroleum imports increasing to $262m. in 1997. Although the cost of petroleum imports fell to $184m. in 1998, they increased by 64% in 1999 to $302m. The cost of importing petroleum was expected, however, to be offset by the construction of a new 190 MW thermoelectric plant near the city of La Chorrera. The $92m. private plant, owned by US electricity firms and built by a Finnish company, was expected to come on stream by 2002.

MANUFACTURING AND CONSTRUCTION

Manufacturing accounted for 7.6% of GDP in 1999 and employed 9.3% of the country's employed labour force in 2000. The sector was based on agricultural processing and light manufacturing, particularly food and beverages, clothing, household goods and construction materials. Growth in the sector fluctuated considerably in the 1980s and early 1990s, successively depressed by a stagnant internal market, political instability and foreign competition, and then buoyed by the removal or neutralization of such impediments. In 1989–99 manufacturing GDP increased by an annual average of 4.5%, but contracted by 5.8% in 1999. Industrial activity was concentrated in the corridor of land running between Panama City and Colón (roughly following the line of the Canal), known as the Colón Free Zone (CFZ). This was by far the most important manufacturing area in Panama, covering 400 ha and accommodating some 1,890 companies. These enterprises employed an estimated 15,000 people in 1998 and accounted for between 13% and 14% of GDP, compared to the 9% contributed by revenues from the Canal.

Although it expanded in the mid-1980s, the CFZ was seriously affected by the regional economic crisis of the latter half of the decade. However, it survived the national political and economic crises of 1988–89 better than some other sectors. Following the consolidation of the Government of President Arturo Endara Gallimany (1989–94), ambitious expansion plans costing more than US $65m. were initiated. There was a corresponding increase in confidence and private-sector investment, with total trade—the sum of imported and re-exported goods—increasing from $5,100m. in 1990 to $11,197m. in 1998. Nevertheless, in the late 1990s competition from other free-trade zones and the increasing removal of trade barriers within the region, combined with the severe financial crises that crippled Latin America and Asia, threatened the long-term competitiveness of the CFZ, which responded by emphasizing its geographical location and seeking to reposition itself in the free-trade zone market as a transhipment hub. In 2000 earnings from re-exports were $4,777m., with imports at $4,430m. In June 2001 a concession was tendered to design, construct and operate a private airport in the CFZ.

The construction sector underwent a substantial expansion in the late 1990s. The most recent boost was the conversion or restoration of a large number of buildings in the Canal Area (known as the Canal Zone until 1979), transferred to Panamanian control when US troops and personnel withdrew from the Canal on 31 December 1999. Investment in construction increased by 50% in 1999 and the pattern seemed set to continue, with several major projects including hotels, container ports, two transisthmian railway container shipment points, retail outlets, a service centre for air cargo, and a new bridge over the Canal in progress or under consideration. However, the fortunes of the sector had been predictably erratic during the previous 20 years. Activity expanded by 28.2% in 1982, largely owing to the inauguration of the transisthmian pipeline, and the sector contributed 8.6% to GDP. As the benefits derived from major construction projects began to decline, the construction sector contracted in the late 1980s and activity all but ceased. In 1990, however, as the economy began to improve, rebuilding work following the US invasion stimulated rapid expansion, with the development of valuable condominiums and a building programme of low and medium-cost housing. In 1999 the sector contributed almost 5% of GDP, and more than 8% of the employed population were engaged in construction activity in 2000.

TRANSPORT AND TOURISM

Economic sanctions against the Noriega regime severely damaged Panama's ship registration industry, but it had more than recovered by the mid-1990s. Panama's open registry fleet grew by 4.5%–5.0% per year in the 1980s and by 1990 the number of vessels registered, including tankers, was 12,149. However, although the country's shipping registry remained the largest in the world, by 1999 this figure had fallen to less than 9,000 owing to fierce competition from other countries. Earnings from ship-registration fees also declined, to an estimated $51m., in 1999. Nevertheless, these figures represented a complete recovery from the disastrous US sanctions of the late 1980s, when Panamanian ships were banned from US ports. Thousands of ships transferred to other registers before the Endara Government waived re-registration fees for a year in 1990, in an effort to recover market share. Further measures enacted in 1995 included offering volume discounts of up to 50% in fees to

shipowners whose registry was over 100,000 grt in total. Most shipping remained foreign-owned, reflecting the preferential tax treatment available to shipping companies in Panama. Cristóbal and Balboa, ports in the Canal area, could accommodate ocean-going freighters and passenger ships, following their redevelopment in 1996. Such investment made Panama one of the busiest container transhipment locations in the world. The country handled some 1.3m. 20 ft equivalent container units (TEUs) in 1999. The Manzanillo International Terminal, Evergreen and Panamá ports were the three largest container ports in Latin America. Late 2000 saw the successful inauguration of Panama's first cruise-ship terminals, at both ends of the Canal.

In 1997 the road network totalled 11,301 km, of which about 32% was paved; and there were an estimated 310,000 vehicles in use in 1999. The Pan-American Highway ran for 545 km in Panama, from the Costa Rican border through Panama City, to Chepo. In 2001 the Highway was being extended towards Colombia, which would expand the potential for overland transport development in Panama. Three railways served the banana plantations and other agricultural areas in the western parts of Bocas del Toro and Chiriquí, which bordered Costa Rica. On ratification of the 1977 Canal Treaties, Panama also acquired control of the Panama Railroad, which connected Panama City and Colón. The 83-km railroad re-opened on 1 July 2001, operating daily passenger and cargo container services. It was operated by Ferrocarril de Panamá, a subsidiary of Kansas City Southern Railway (USA). The Tocumen International Airport (formerly Omar Torrijos) was officially opened in August 1978. In 1997 Panama recorded 1.7m. journeys by air; some 76,300 metric tons of air freight were moved in the same year.

Two long, varied coastlines with good beaches and 700 tropical islands offered vast tourist potential. The southern (Pacific) coast of Panama offered some of the best deep-sea fishing in the world. Other tourist attractions included the mountains and volcanic scenery, the ruins of the original Panama City and the Panama Canal. Although tourism declined steadily throughout the 1980s, a strong recovery was established in the early 1990s, with arrivals increasing steadily, from 221,677 in 1990 to 507,895 in 2000. In 1999 tourist revenues reached $379m. The construction of six hotels and 120 tourist villas in the former US military base at Fort Amador, at the entrance to the Canal, was expected to increase the country's hotel capacity by one-third; the $450m., four-stage scheme was begun in 1997. In addition, in 1999 the Government approved another major scheme, a $68.5m. resort development at Rio Hato by Decameron Hotels of Colombia. In 2000 hotel and recreation projects worth more than $600m. were underway in Panama. In 2001 the Government was to promote tourism heavily and seek to improve facilities and employment in the sector.

THE CANAL AREA

The Canal Area (known as the Canal Zone until 1979) was a strip of land, 16 km wide, between the Pacific and Caribbean coasts, running north-west to south-east. The Canal itself was 82 km long, and raised or lowered ships through 26 m by means of six pairs of locks. An average passage took about eight hours. The Canal could accommodate ships with a maximum draught of 12.0 m and beams of 32.3 m. Improvements to the Canal increased the transit capacity to 42 vessels per day in the mid-1990s. Canal operations—tolls, transit-related services and sales of surplus water and electricity—accounted for about 7% of Panama's GDP in 1999 (some US $752m.).

Almost 70% of all traffic through the Canal either originated from, or was destined for, the USA (moving between Asia and the east coast of the USA). Japan was the second most regular user of the Canal, followed by Canada, Chile and the People's Republic of China. In 1986 Japan, the USA and Panama established a commission to consider the future of the Canal. However, the commission's report, published in early 1994, concluded that no major development work would be necessary before 2010. It estimated that traffic was likely to increase by no more than 0.8%–1.0% per year in the early 2000s, making the construction of a third set of high-rise locks unnecessary until at least 2010. Such a project was likely to cost about US $5,000m. In 1996 a report by the US Army Corps of Engineers, commissioned in preparation for the transfer of full control of the Canal to Panama on 31 December 1999, listed more than 1,000 maintenance repairs and equipment upgrades that required immediate attention. As a result, the Panama Canal Commission (replaced by the Autoridad del Canal de Panamá, ACP—Panama Canal Authority, in December 1999) initiated a $1,000m. modernization programme (expected to take up to six years to complete and to increase capacity by one-fifth), which was to be financed entirely from the Canal's revenue, and which significantly increased employment in the area.

Under the Canal Treaties of 1977, which came into force in October 1979, the neutrality of the Canal Area was guaranteed, so as to ensure the continuous and clear transit of traffic. Panama was to administer the Canal from December 1999, although the USA reserved the right to protect the Canal by military force if necessary, and assumed a majority on the nine-member PCC in 1990. The vessels that used the Canal were predominantly bulk cargo carriers carrying grain, petroleum and related products. In 1999 canal transit fees earned Panama US $568.9m., derived from some 14,337 commercial transits of 196.0m. long tons. All three sets of figures were virtually unchanged from the previous year when total fees reached $556.9m. This represented an increase of nearly $100m. over 1995 ($460m.), owing to the dramatic increase in transit charges, while the number of transits and cargo figures remained virtually static from 1995. The Canal's first year under Panamanian control was widely acknowledged to have been both financially and organizationally successful.

The transisthmian pipeline was completed in October 1982. With a length of 130 km and diameter of 0.9 m, it had a maximum capacity of 830,000 barrels per day (b/d). The pipeline ran from the Pacific petroleum terminal of Puerto Armuelles to Chiriquí Grande on the Caribbean coast. Each terminal had a storage capacity of 2.5m. barrels. The pipeline derived its major business from pumping Alaskan crude petroleum into a relay of tankers bound for the east coast of the USA. The operation of the pipeline was one of the principal factors in the decline in Canal traffic in the 1980s. From 1987 the pipeline faced considerable competition from the US Celerosa Oil Co's 'All-American Pipeline' (capacity 300,000 b/d), which extended across the USA for a distance of 1,971 km, from Santa Barbara, in California, to McCarney, in Texas. Such competition, as well as changes in the international petroleum market, caused severe fluctuations in the flow of petroleum through the pipeline in the 1980s. In the early 1990s the volume of petroleum transported declined steadily and in 1992 was just 70m. barrels, barely one-half the total in 1988. By 1994 the volume had decreased again to just 29.3m. barrels.

EXTERNAL TRADE AND FINANCE

Panama regularly incurred a large deficit on its merchandise trade account as a result of its heavy dependence on imported fuel and 'invisibles' (banking, ship registration, canal fees and re-exports). This was, however, partially offset by a surplus on transactions in services. The trade deficit grew inexorably from 1988, and reached US $1,415.0m. in 1999, before decreasing slightly, to $1,290.9m., in 2000. In 1994 imports (c.i.f.) totalled $2,404m. and increased to $3,379m. in 2000. Exports (f.o.b.— including those from the CFZ) grew from $6,045m. in 1994 to some $6,655m. in 1997 before falling to $5,300m. in 1999, and rising again to some $5,749m. in 2000. Exports, excluding those from the CFZ, were a mere $540m. in 1994 increasing to an estimated $707m. in 1999. In 1999 the principal merchandise exports were bananas, shrimps, fish, clothing and raw sugar. The principal imports were capital goods, in particular electrical and electronic equipment, transport equipment, mineral products and chemicals and chemical products. The current account registered increasing deficits in the late 1990s. In 2000 the deficit on the current account of the balance of payments was $926.8m., compared with $1,376.0m. in 1999.

Panama tended to be heavily dependent on capital inflows, such as IMF assistance. This was partly because its unusually liberal economic system made it particularly vulnerable to lower world-trading activity during periods of recession. Furthermore, because of its use of the US dollar, Panama was unable to resort to currency devaluation in order to correct trading imbalances. In 1997 the World Bank estimated the country's total external debt at US $6,338m. This figure increased to $7,334m. at the end of 1999 and $7,600m. at the end of 2000. Between 1981 and

1986 the debt-service ratio (debt servicing compared with the total value of exports of goods and services) fluctuated between 43% and 55%, but declined steadily thereafter following renegotiation and rescheduling. In 1998 the debt-service ratio was 7.6%, less than one-half of the 16.3% in the previous year, reflecting the Brady Plan debt-restructuring of 1996. In the late 1990s, however, it increased again, and in 2000 it was an estimated 10.9%.

Panama traditionally encouraged foreign investment, a policy that was intensified after 1990, as part of efforts to improve the economy and counterbalance the legacy of sanctions and the US invasion. Many restrictions were ended in the late 1980s and early 1990s as part of the Government's privatization programme. A new foreign-investment protection law in 1991 added to the relative attractiveness of Panama (which had introduced measures to encourage industry in 1986). Panama exercised no exchange controls, and transfers of funds were never prevented. There were no restrictions on the transfer of profits, dividends, interest, royalties or fees, nor on the repatriation of capital nor the repayment of principal. A 10% withholding tax was levied on dividends from operations in Panama (excluding the CFZ), but Panama did not levy tax on income earned in offshore financial dealings. In 1997–98 foreign capital inflows increased to an annual average of more than US $1,200m. Although this figure was somewhat distorted by the purchase of a 49% stake in the state telecommunications monopoly, Instituto Nacional de Telecomunicaciones (INTEL), by Cable & Wireless (United Kingdom) for $652m., the incidence of such major investments was increasing. For example, the sale of toll-road concessions to two Mexican companies in 1998 secured future inward investment in excess of $600m., while the sale of electricity assets in the same year yielded $603m. Other important sales and joint-venture investments, including many tourism and infrastructure developments linked to redevelopment of military and Canal sites following the withdrawal of US personnel, were expected to help maintain a healthy level of capital investment. However, the completion of a number of major investment projects in 2000 caused a decline in direct foreign investment from $517m. to $393m.

From the late 1960s onwards Panama developed its potential as an international finance centre, based on the full transferability of its currency, the country's favourable tax laws and the absence of state controls. The offshore business, foreign exchange, money and reinsurance markets expanded in the early 1980s and in 2000 the sector accounted for an estimated 11% of GDP. However, in the last two decades of the 20th century the offshore banking sector experienced difficulties caused by political and economic instability and radical changes in business. Both domestic and international confidence in the stability of Panama's banking sector was undermined by the political unrest of 1987. The sector was particularly affected by rumours of 'capital flight', amounting to between US $1,000m. and $4,000m. Such reports were denied by the banking authorities, but the situation was exacerbated by the absence of both exchange controls and government regulation of disinvestments by private and corporate investors. By March 1988 capital outflows were so great that the country's regulatory body, the Comisión Bancaria Nacional (National Banking Commission, superseded by the Superintendencia de Bancos in 1998), suspended most banking operations for more than a year. Some estimates of deposit outflow in 1986–89 were as high as $16,000m. Some confidence returned with the inauguration of the Endara Government, but the signing of the Mutual Legal Assistance Treaty with the USA in April 1991, which affected secrecy laws, was another obstacle to the redevelopment of the sector. By December 1999 the total assets of the finance sector had reached US $37,048m. (representing an increase of more than 80% over the figure for 1993), but this amount was still well below the levels of the mid-1980s, when total assets amounted to $49,000m. In 2000 the number of banks registered was 84, significantly fewer than the 129 registered in 1983, and the importance and performance of Panama's offshore banking sector seemed unlikely to recover to mid-1980s levels. As general financial liberalization eroded Panama's competitiveness, in the 1990s, competitors in Latin American and the Caribbean were establishing themselves. The relaxation of financial restrictions globally meant that many banks in the USA and Europe began to deal directly with clients in Latin America, denying Panama's banks one of their principal roles. In 1998 an Organisation of Economic Co-operation and Development (OECD) investigation into tax 'havens' and business secrecy prompted a further investigation by the Financial Action Task Force on Money Laundering (FATF, established by the G7 group of major industrialized nations), and a 'blacklist' of those jurisdictions (including Panama) considered harmful tax regimes was drawn up. In early 2000 the OECD postponed publication of the list. Meanwhile, Panama protested its inclusion and subsequently modified its legislation to introduce greater legal and administrative transparency in the financial sector. In the FATF follow-up report published in June 2001, Panama was removed from the list, having satisfactorily implemented the necessary legislation.

From 1983 Panama's fiscal policies required IMF approval. However, such approval was difficult to secure, because the Panamanian Government had difficulty in achieving IMF targets for the budget deficit. Successful rescheduling negotiations and new loans from the IMF were achieved in the mid-1980s. However, these were gained not only because of budgetary austerity, but also because of the Government's commitment to certain reforms opposed by the trade unions and by the private sector. Satisfaction with the Government's efforts at economic restructuring was signalled by the resumption of lending to the country by the World Bank in December 1986. However, in June 1987 the Government began to withhold payments to bilateral creditors and by March 1988 the country's IMF agreement had lapsed, with no new accord negotiated to replace it. By the end of that year accumulated interest and principal arrears on public-sector debt were estimated at US $1,400m.

Although in mid-1989 the IMF declared Panama ineligible to receive further credits, owing to payment arrears, by early 1991 the Endara Government had rescheduled US $520m. in bilateral debts with the 'Paris Club' of Western creditor nations. In 1990–91 the Government used some of the $1,000m. in aid promised by the USA, Japan and the European Community (EC—known as the European Union from November 1993) to pay part of the $610m. in arrears to the IMF, the World Bank and the IDB, making the country eligible for further credits during 1992–93. In February 1992 the IMF disbursed $50.4m. in support of the Government's economic programme. The trend was consolidated in April 1995 when Panama signed a debt-rescheduling agreement based on the Brady Plan. The accord covered $2,000m. in principal arrears and $1,500m. in interest

arrears, offering creditors a variety of options with the IMF, the World Bank and the IDB, which were all actively supporting the agreement.

Thereafter, Panama repurchased or exchanged US $1,220m. of this Brady-bond debt for its own 30-year government bonds. In December 1997 the IMF approved a credit of $162m., under the Extended Fund Facility, in support of the Government's economic programme for 1998–2000. In March 2000 Panama began negotiations with other Central American countries on a free-trade accord. Negotiations continued in 2001. In May 2001, following further extensive discussions, the Central American countries, including Panama, reached an agreement with Mexico to establish the 'Plan Puebla–Panamá'. The World Bank-funded Plan was intended to integrate the region through development, and extended from the Mexican state of Puebla, to Panama. The Plan promoted joint projects in environmental protection, tourism, trade, energy, transport and infrastructure.

CONCLUSION

Real economic growth slowed dramatically in Panama in the first half of the 1990s and in 1995 was only one-fifth of that recorded in 1991 (9.6%). Although the country's economic performance improved subsequently, with growth of 4.5% and 4.4% and 3.0% in 1997, 1998 and 1999, respectively, by the late 1990s Panama had not recovered fully from the effects of the US sanctions and invasion of the late 1980s. In 2000 GDP growth had slowed to 2.7%, little more than one-half of that in 1997, and the Government forecast GDP of 3.0% in 2001. With unprecedented pressure on its traditional economic base of 'invisibles', it was clear that major economic diversification was essential if Panama was to recover the relative prosperity it had enjoyed in the past. The social price of the economic adjustment already achieved was high, with poverty and unemployment increasing rapidly and Panamanians finding themselves less protected from the trends affecting the whole continent in the 21st century than they had been hitherto. The Government of President Mireya Moscoso de Gruber took office in September 1999 with a populist mandate and a commitment to social justice. Midway through her term, it remained to be seen whether the new administration could contain inflation and maintain the strict budgetary control necessary to retain the goodwill of international lenders and investors, while completing the adjustments necessary for longer term economic revival and meeting its commitments to tackling poverty and inequality.

Statistical Survey

Sources (unless otherwise stated): Dirección de Estadística y Censo, Contraloría General de la República, Avda Balboa y Federico Boyd, Apdo 5213, Panamá 5; tel. 210-4777; internet www.contraloria.gob.pa; Banco Nacional de Panamá, Casa Matriz, Vía España, Apdo 5220, Panamá; tel. 263-5151.

Note: The former Canal Zone was incorporated into Panama on 1 October 1979.

Area and Population

AREA, POPULATION AND DENSITY

Area (sq km)	75,517*
Population (census results)	
13 May 1990	2,329,329
14 May 2000	
Males	1,432,566
Females	1,406,611
Total	2,839,177
Population (official estimates at mid-year)	
1997	2,718,686
1998	2,763,612
1999	2,809,280
Density (per sq km) at May 2000	37.6

* 29,157 sq miles.

ADMINISTRATIVE DIVISIONS (population at census of May 2000)

Province	Population	Capital (and population)*
Bocas del Toro . . .	89,269	Bocas del Toro (9,916)
Chiriquí	368,790	David (124,280)
Coclé	202,461	Penonomé (72,448)
Colón	204,208	Colón (42,133)
Comarca Emberá . . .	8,246	–
Comarca Kuna Yala . .	32,446	–
Comarca Ngöbe Buglé . .	110,080	–
Darién	40,284	Chepigana (27,461)
Herrera	102,465	Chitré (42,467)
Los Santos	83,495	Las Tablas (24,298)
Panamá	1,388,357	Panamá (708,438)
Veraguas	209,076	Santiago (74,679)
Total	**2,839,177**	

* Population of district in which capital is located.

Note: Population figures include the former Canal Zone.

BIRTHS, MARRIAGES AND DEATHS

	Registered live births		Registered marriages*		Registered deaths	
	Number	Rate (per 1,000)	Number	Rate (per 1,000)	Number	Rate (per 1,000)
1991 . .	60,080	24.6	11,714	5.1	9,683	4.0
1992 . .	59,905	24.1	12,547	5.4	10,143	4.1
1993 . .	59,191	23.3	13,744	5.8	10,669	4.2
1994 . .	59,947	23.2	13,523	5.2	10,983	4.3
1995 . .	61,939	23.5	8,841	3.4	11,032	5.1
1996 . .	61,401	23.7	10,206	3.8	11,161	4.2
1997 . .	51,164	18.8	10,357	3.8	9,720†	3.6†
1998† . .	61,756	22.3	n.a.	n.a.	14,036	5.1

* Excludes tribal Indian population.
† Estimates.
Source: mainly UN, *Demographic Yearbook*.

Expectation of life (years at birth, 1998): 73.8 (males 71.9; females 76.5)
(Source: UN Development Programme, *Human Development Report*).

EMPLOYMENT ('000 persons aged 15 years and over, August of each year)

	1997	1998	1999
Agriculture, hunting and forestry	159.9	157.0	157.2
Fishing	9.7	9.3	10.4
Mining and quarrying . .	2.0	0.8	0.9
Manufacturing	96.2	92.2	94.0
Electricity, gas and water supply .	9.1	9.1	7.0
Construction	59.6	67.2	73.0
Wholesale and retail trade; repair of motor vehicles, motorcycles and personal and household goods	168.1	177.8	182.7
Hotels and restaurants . .	34.2	33.8	39.5
Transport, storage and communications . . .	62.1	63.3	73.0
Financial intermediation . .	22.8	24.1	23.9
Real estate, renting and business activities	28.6	34.1	39.4
Public administration and defence; compulsory social service	69.2	67.9	68.1
Education	48.1	52.1	50.2
Health and social work . .	28.8	31.4	30.8
Other community, social and personal service activities . .	52.8	61.0	57.5
Private households with employed persons	52.2	52.9	51.2
Extra-territorial organizations and bodies.	5.8	2.5	2.4
Total employed . . .	909.1	936.5	961.4
Unemployed	140.3	147.1	128.4
Total labour force . . .	1,049.4	1,083.6	1,089.4

Source: ILO, *Yearbook of Labour Statistics*.

2000 ('000 persons aged 10 years and over): Agriculture, hunting and forestry 204.2; Fishing 12.8; Mining and quarrying 2.0; Manufacturing 104.3; Electricity, gas and water 9.1; Construction 90.3; Wholesale and retail trade 201.5; Hotels and restaurants 49.1; Transport, storage and communications 78.2; Financial intermediation 26.5; Real estate and business activities 45.8; Public administration and defence and compulsory social service 70.1; Education 56.8; Health and social work 36.8; Other community and social activities 48.6; Self-employed 65.6; Extra-territorial activities 1.5; Activities not adequately defined 15.8; *Total employed* 1,119.1.

Agriculture

PRINCIPAL CROPS ('000 metric tons)

	1998	1999	2000
Dry beans	3.4	4.0	4.0
Coffee (green)	10.8	11.4	9.4
Maize	88.6	80.3	80.3
Rice (paddy)	232.4	224.3	319.1
Sugar cane	1,954.8	1,773.9	2,000.0*
Bananas	650.0†	750.0†	807.4
Tobacco (leaves)	2.2*	1.8*	1.8

* Unofficial figure.   † FAO estimate.
Source: FAO.

LIVESTOCK ('000 head, year ending September)

	1998	1999	2000
Horses*	165.0	166.0	166.0
Mules*	4.0	4.0	4.0
Cattle	1,382.2	1,359.8	1,359.8
Pigs	251.8	278.3	279.5
Goats	5.2*	5.3*	5.2

Poultry (million): 12.5 in 1998; 11.8 in 1999; 11.8* in 2000.
* FAO estimate(s).
Source: FAO.

LIVESTOCK PRODUCTS ('000 metric tons)

	1998	1999	2000
Beef and veal . . .	63.5	60.3	57.4
Pig meat	18.7	20.5*	20.5*
Poultry meat	58.5*	58.5*	58.5
Cows' milk	157.0	150.0*	174.2
Cheese	8.8	9.5*	9.4
Hen eggs	19.0*	17.0*	14.4

* FAO estimate.
Source: FAO.

Forestry

ROUNDWOOD REMOVALS ('000 cubic metres, excluding bark)

	1997	1998	1999
Sawlogs, veneer logs and logs for sleepers	37	5	35
Other industrial wood . . .	60	–	–
Fuel wood	985	1,001	1,017
Total	1,082	1,006	1,052

Source: FAO, *Yearbook of Forest Products*.

SAWNWOOD PRODUCTION
('000 cubic metres, incl. railway sleepers)

	1997	1998	1999
Total	17	8	24

Source: FAO, *Yearbook of Forest Products*.

Fishing

('000 metric tons, live weight)

	1996	1997	1998
Capture	140.3	166.6	208.8
Pacific thread herring . .	32.5	26.3	49.5
Pacific anchoveta . .	60.3	77.7	107.7
Skipjack tuna . . .	7.3	8.6	5.7
Yellowfin tuna . . .	10.0	11.7	7.7
Natantian decapods . .	4.1	5.3	0.9
Aquaculture	5.1	7.2	10.2
Whiteleg shrimp . . .	4.4	6.4	9.1
Total catch	145.4	173.8	219.0

Source: FAO, *Yearbook of Fishery Statistics*.

Industry

SELECTED PRODUCTS
('000 metric tons, unless otherwise indicated)

	1994	1995	1996
Salt	22.0	22.0	22.0
Alcoholic beverages (million litres)	139.6	137.8	134.3
Sugar	141.8	121.2	136.7
Condensed, evaporated, or powdered milk . . .	25.4	25.6	26.0
Tomato derivatives . . .	13.8	14.4	13.8
Fishmeal (metric tons) . .	27.8	30.8	23.1
Fish oil (metric tons) . . .	13.9	9.0	3.2
Cigarettes (million) . . .	1,197.7	1,136.4	1,253.2
Electricity (million kWh) . .	3,360.7	3,519.3	3,824.6

Finance

CURRENCY AND EXCHANGE RATES

Monetary Units
100 centésimos = 1 balboa (B).

Sterling, Dollar and Euro Equivalents (30 April 2001)
£1 sterling = 1.4318 balboas;
US $1 = 1.0000 balboas;
€1 = 88.76 centésimos;
100 balboas = £69.84 = $100.00 = €112.66.

Exchange Rate
The balboa's value is fixed at par with that of the US dollar.

BUDGET ESTIMATES ('000 balboas)

Revenue	1997	1998	1999
Direct taxes	510,293	454,944	568,080
Indirect taxes	573,304	649,194	643,119
Income from assets . . .	36,963	37,339	38,205
Income from state enterprises .	71,679	64,369	135,921
Other sources of income . .	253,607	267,561	302,487
Total current revenue . . .	1,575,146	1,663,286	1,908,959
National resources . . .	27,432	68,111	32,286
Loans	1,006,453	840,871	605,197
Other capital revenue . . .	63,504	72,317	6,800
Total revenue	2,691,260	2,726,274	2,570,240

Expenditure	1997	1998	1999
National Assembly . . .	27,652	36,885	36,966
Inspectorate of Taxes . . .	25,958	27,560	28,676
President's Office . . .	28,668	30,703	34,975
Home Affairs and Justice . .	162,137	156,624	160,789
Foreign Affairs	29,539	27,915	27,490
Treasury	33,496	48,435	24,482
Education	364,145	405,331	405,046
Public Works	25,027	23,487	24,236
Agriculture and Livestock . .	31,534	33,944	32,837
Ministry of Youth, Women, Family and Childhood	—	9,796	10,046
Health	252,534	440,240	299,493
Commerce and Industry . .	61,015	18,734	13,360
Labour and Social Security . .	10,168	6,550	6,325
Ministry of Housing . . .	10,522	13,420	12,462
Ministry of Planning and Economic Policy	15,346	16,268	15,677
Law Courts	27,677	30,042	30,956
Public Services	28,978	30,507	31,967
Electoral Tribunal . . .	11,406	29,578	29,367
Debt Service	1,139,684	903,830	935,492
Capital Expenditure . . .	232,414	249,395	248,907
Total expenditure	2,557,350	2,586,584	2,454,679

INTERNATIONAL RESERVES (US $ million at 31 December)*

	1998	1999	2000
IMF special drawing rights .	0.1	1.6	0.3
Reserve position in IMF . .	16.7	16.3	15.5
Foreign exchange . . .	937.7	805.0	706.8
Total	954.5	822.9	722.6

* Excludes gold, valued at US $476,000 in 1991–93.

Source: IMF, *International Financial Statistics*.

Note: US treasury notes and coins form the bulk of the currency in circulation in Panama.

COST OF LIVING
(Consumer Price Index, Panamá (Panama City); base: 1990 = 100)

	1997	1998	1999
Food (incl. beverages) . .	110.0	110.4	110.6
Fuel and light	102.2	101.7	103.1
Clothing (incl. footwear) . .	104.0	105.4	105.7
Rent	112.5	115.7	121.1
All items (incl. others) . .	108.6	109.3	110.7

Source: ILO, *Yearbook of Labour Statistics*.

All items (base: 1995 = 100) 104.5 in 1999; 106.0 in 2000 (Source: IMF, *International Financial Statistics*).

NATIONAL ACCOUNTS

National Income and Product (million balboas at current prices)

	1997	1998	1999
Compensation of employees . .	4,318.3	4,724.2	4,832.9
Operating surplus . . .	3,002.7	3,103.9	3,120.4
Domestic factor incomes . .	7,321.0	7,828.1	7,953.3
Consumption of fixed capital . .	601.1	667.8	717.0
Gross domestic product (GDP) at factor cost . . .	7,922.1	8,495.9	8,670.3
Indirect taxes	805.5	891.2	935.2
Less Subsidies	70.1	42.4	48.9
GDP in purchasers' values . .	8,657.5	9,344.7	9,556.6
Factor income received from abroad *Less* Factor income paid abroad .	−451.4	−608.8	−790.0
Gross national product . .	8,206.1	8,735.9	8,766.6
Less Consumption of fixed capital .	601.1	667.8	717.0
National income in market prices .	7,605.0	8,068.1	8,049.6
Other current transfers from abroad (net)	150.6	159.0	164.2
National disposable income .	7,755.6	8,227.1	8,213.8

Source: UN Economic Commission for Latin America and the Caribbean, *Statistical Yearbook*.

Expenditure on the Gross Domestic Product (million balboas)

	1997	1998	1999
Government final consumption expenditure	1,402.6	1,507.6	1,487.0
Private final consumption expenditure	4,699.1	5,283.4	5,449.2
Increase in stocks	396.1	372.3	278.0
Gross fixed capital formation . .	2,295.0	2,624.9	2,831.2
Total domestic expenditure . .	8,792.8	9,788.2	10,045.4
Exports of goods and services . .	8,494.6	8,396.4	7,306.9
Less Imports of goods and services	8,629.9	8,839.9	7,795.7
GDP in purchasers' values . .	8,657.5	9,344.7	9,556.6
GDP at constant 1982 prices . .	6,657.5	6,947.2	7,152.2

2000 (million balboas): GDP at constant 1982 prices 7,341.8.

Source: IMF, *International Financial Statistics*.

Gross Domestic Product by Economic Activity
(million balboas at current prices)

	1997	1998	1999
Agriculture, hunting, forestry and fishing	603.5	659.1	649.1
Mining and quarrying	22.3	37.2	49.6
Manufacturing	755.6	753.7	731.6
Electricity, gas and water	317.2	320.4	354.3
Construction	376.3	427.9	480.5
Wholesale and retail trade, restaurants and hotels	1,811.7	1,826.1	1,725.8
Transport, storage and communications	1,206.5	1,389.7	1,524.9
Finance, insurance, real estate and business services	2,063.5	2,332.6	2,434.7
Government, community, social and personal services	1,536.0	1,644.4	1,683.0
Sub-total	8,693.0	9,391.0	9,633.5
Import duties and other taxes	308.0	307.8	306.8
Less Imputed bank service charge	343.1	354.1	383.7
GDP in purchasers' values	8,657.5	9,344.7	9,556.6

Source: UN Economic Commission for Latin America and the Caribbean, *Statistical Yearbook*.

BALANCE OF PAYMENTS (US $ million)*

	1998	1999	2000
Exports of goods f.o.b.	6,349.7	5,299.5	5,748.8
Imports of goods f.o.b.	−7,711.2	−6,714.5	−7,039.7
Trade balance	−1,361.5	−1,415.0	−1,290.9
Exports of services	1,728.1	1,714.5	1,765.8
Imports of services	−1,146.3	−1,099.1	−1,047.1
Balance on goods and services	−779.7	−799.6	−572.2
Other income received	1,725.2	1,546.7	1,622.8
Other income paid	−2,280.4	−2,287.3	−2,143.6
Balance on goods, services and income	−1,334.9	−1,540.2	−1,093.0
Current transfers received	195.2	202.7	206.4
Current transfers paid	−36.2	−38.5	−40.2
Current balance	−1,175.9	−1,376.0	−926.8
Capital account (net)	50.9	3.0	1.7
Direct investment from abroad	1,218.7	516.9	393.3
Portfolio investment assets	437.7	−542.1	−103.8
Portfolio investment liabilities	−65.5	−99.2	−86.8
Other investment assets	678.9	2,068.4	128.3
Other investment liabilities	−1,363.6	−574.8	−392.1
Net errors and omissions	−244.4	−144.0	659.5
Overall balance	−463.2	−147.8	−326.7

* Including the transactions of enterprises operating in the Colón Free Zone.

Source: IMF, *International Financial Statistics*.

External Trade

PRINCIPAL COMMODITIES ('000 balboas)

Imports c.i.f.	1996	1997	1998*
Vegetable products	104,135	90,448	121,936
Food products, beverages and tobacco	155,315	171,838	211,703
Mineral products	455,636	440,978	349,300
Chemicals and chemical products	318,330	324,638	327,051
Plastics and synthetic resins	130,202	149,742	161,573
Paper and paper products	129,487	126,911	134,181
Textiles and textile manufactures	153,293	168,556	188,398
Basic metals and metal manufactures	174,567	205,382	210,073
Electrical and electronic equipment	498,163	580,378	779,238
Transport equipment	354,184	402,686	514,808
Optical, photographic and measuring instruments, clocks and watches	61,383	63,015	68,532
Total (incl. others)	2,781,071	2,992,404	3,398,342

Exports f.o.b.	1996	1997	1998*
Raw sugar	22,598	28,669	25,549
Bananas	184,031	179,841	138,748
Coffee	18,794	22,425	23,931
Shrimps	74,555	96,493	136,730
Fish (fresh, dried and frozen)	26,069	41,063	61,924
Clothing	20,182	24,801	25,635
Petroleum products	28,033	25,461	24,827
Pharmaceuticals	13,192	13,525	16,082
Total (incl. others)	566,409	647,919	705,458

* Preliminary figures.

1999 (million balboas): *Exports f.o.b.*: Raw sugar 14.4; Bananas 182.2; Coffee 18.5; Shrimps 68.9; Fish (fresh, dried and frozen) 63.9; Clothing 21.9; Petroleum products 152.3; Total (incl. others) 864.6.

Total imports (million balboas): 3,398.3 in 1998; 3,515.8 in 1999; 3,378.7 in 2000 (Source: IMF, *International Financial Statistics*).

Total exports (million balboas): 784.1 in 1998; 822.1 in 1999; 859.5 in 2000 (Source: IMF, *International Financial Statistics*).

PRINCIPAL TRADING PARTNERS (US $ '000)

Imports c.i.f.	1997	1998	1999*
Colombia	78,100	65,044	91,097
Costa Rica	88,102	101,861	114,423
Ecuador	166,821	108,754	185,236
Finland	1,546	1,741	52,813
France	45,797	32,063	24,344
Germany	39,314	45,110	47,542
Guatemala	47,758	55,590	63,414
Hong Kong	25,826	33,971	27,971
Japan	210,734	304,256	254,119
Korea, Republic	62,421	89,162	123,760
Mexico	146,983	163,932	172,293
Spain	40,059	44,634	53,961
Taiwan	30,707	32,191	27,934
Trinidad and Tobago	19,939	8,375	43,619
United Kingdom	25,526	39,830	34,651
USA	1,103,192	1,349,990	1,241,865
Venezuela	119,857	106,900	100,403
Total (incl. others)	2,965,797	3,365,510	3,515,766

Exports f.o.b.	1997	1998	1999*
Belgium-Luxembourg . . .	34,948	30,347	31,258
Colombia	11,298	9,857	10,431
Costa Rica	40,996	46,408	37,380
Dominican Republic . . .	3,873	5,570	13,445
Ecuador	5,842	8,222	3,423
El Salvador	11,658	11,340	9,098
Germany	20,091	24,284	75,932
Guatemala	12,536	18,014	14,897
Honduras	27,184	22,233	23,008
Hong Kong	3,135	4,090	8,131
Italy	4,464	19,291	28,980
Japan	5,265	4,355	7,168
Mexico	4,247	7,062	19,185
Nicaragua	8,153	13,021	19,630
Portugal	3,721	15,619	695
Puerto Rico	18,932	15,795	17,194
Spain	24,699	38,231	4,109
Sweden	54,413	50,902	8,022
Taiwan	648	2,741	7,921
USA	303,966	281,922	298,735
Total (incl. others) . . .	658,052	705,458	707,131

* Preliminary figures.

Transport

RAILWAYS (traffic)

	1995	1996	1997
Passenger-km (million)* . .	39,240	11,740	5,684
Freight ton-km (million)† . .	34,119	27,971	24,115

* Panama Railway and National Railway of Chiriquí.
† Panama Railway only.

Source: UN, *Statistical Yearbook*.

ROAD TRAFFIC (motor vehicles registered)

	1996	1997*	1998*
Cars	203,760	214,899	228,722
Buses	15,492	16,181	16,072
Lorries	59,145	62,057	67,948
Others	7,243	7,532	n.a.

* Estimates.
Source: IRF, *World Road Statistics*.

SHIPPING
Merchant Fleet (registered at 31 December)

	1996	1997	1998
Number of vessels . . .	6,105	6,188	6,143
Total displacement ('000 grt) . .	82,130.7	91,127.9	98,222.4

Source: Lloyd's Register of Shipping, *World Fleet Statistics*.

International Sea-borne Freight Traffic ('000 metric tons)

	1995*	1996	1997*
Goods loaded	1,645.0	362.2	2,916.5
Goods unloaded	2,167.8	3,255.4	4,440.3

* Preliminary figures.

Panama Canal Traffic

	1998	1999	2000
Transits	14,243	14,337	13,653
Cargo (million long tons) . . .	192.2	196.0	193.7

Source: Panama Canal Authority.

CIVIL AVIATION (traffic on scheduled services)

	1995	1996	1997
Kilometres flown (million) . .	14	14	18
Passengers carried ('000) . .	661	689	772
Passengers-km (million) . .	862	872	1,094
Total ton-km (million) . . .	111	114	152

Source: UN, *Statistical Yearbook*.

Tourism

VISITOR ARRIVALS BY COUNTRY OF ORIGIN

	1996	1997	1998
Canada	9,491	8,898	6,779
Colombia	62,517	75,769	66,419
Costa Rica	41,839	47,311	54,840
Dominican Republic . . .	8,028	8,786	8,131
Ecuador	11,968	16,896	20,631
El Salvador	7,826	7,976	8,028
Guatemala	8,335	9,827	10,279
Jamaica	10,769	11,889	10,189
Mexico	12,577	14,813	16,122
Nicaragua	10,670	10,561	10,982
USA	99,014	100,385	100,909
Venezuela	8,355	12,368	15,018
Total (incl. others) . . .	376,672	418,846	422,228

Receipts from tourism (US $ million): 343 in 1996; 374 in 1997; 379 in 1998.

Sources: World Tourism Organization, *Yearbook of Tourism Statistics*; World Bank, *World Development Indicators*.

Arrivals: 476,274 in 1999; 507,895 in 2000.

Communications Media

	1995	1996	1997
Radio receivers ('000 in use) .	600	800	815
Television receivers ('000 in use) .	460	500	510
Daily newspapers (number) . .	7	7	7
Telephones ('000 main lines in use)	304	325	366
Mobile cellular telephones (subscribers)	n.a.	7,000	17,000

Sources: UNESCO, *Statistical Yearbook*; UN, *Statistical Yearbook*.

Education
(1997)

	Institutions	Teachers	Pupils
Pre-primary	1,084	2,063	45,340
Primary	2,866	15,058	377,898
Secondary	417	12,327	223,155
University	5	5,454	84,452
Special*	24	483	6,205
Supplementary*	27	206	4,819

* 1996 figures.
Sources: Ministry of Education; UNESCO, *Statistical Yearbook*.

Directory

The Constitution

Under the terms of the amendments to the Constitution, implemented by the adoption of Reform Acts No 1 and No 2 in October 1978, and by the approval by referendum of the Constitutional Act in April 1983, the 67 (later 71) members of the unicameral Asamblea Legislativa (Legislative Assembly) are elected by popular vote every five years. Executive power is exercised by the President of the Republic, who is also elected by popular vote for a term of five years. Two Vice-Presidents are elected by popular vote to assist the President. The President appoints the Cabinet. The armed forces are barred from participating in elections.

The Government

HEAD OF STATE

President: MIREYA ELISA MOSCOSO DE GRUBER (took office 1 September 1999).
First Vice-President: ARTURO ULISES VALLARINO.
Second Vice-President: DOMINADOR KAISER BALDOMERO BAZÁN.

THE CABINET
(August 2001)

Minister of the Interior and Justice: Dr WINSTON SPADAFORA.
Minister of Foreign Affairs: JOSÉ MIGUEL ALEMÁN.
Minister of Public Works: VICTOR NELSON JULIAO GELONCH.
Minister of Finance and the Treasury: NORBERTO DELGADO DURÁN.
Minister of Agricultural Development: PEDRO ADÁN GORDON SARASQUETA.
Minister of Commerce and Industry: JOAQUÍN JÁCOME DÍEZ.
Minister of Public Health: FERNANDO GRACIA GARCÍA.
Minister of Labour and Social Welfare: JOAQUÍN JOSÉ VALLARINO III.
Minister of Education: Dr DORIS ROSAS DE MATA.
Minister of Housing: MIGUEL ANGEL CÁRDENAS.
Minister of the Presidency: IVONNE YOUNG VALDÉS.
Minister of Youth, Women, Family and Childhood: ALBA ESTER TEJADA DE ROLLA.
Minister of Canal Affairs: RICARDO MARTINELLI BERROCAL.

MINISTRIES

Office of the President: Palacio Presidencial, Valija 50, Panamá 1; tel. 227-4062; fax 227-0076.
Ministry of Agricultural Development: Edif. 576, Altos de Curundú, Apdo 5390, Panamá 5; tel. 232-5037; fax 232-5778; internet www.mida.gob.pa.
Ministry of Canal Affairs: Panamá.
Ministry of Commerce and Industry: El Paical 2° y 3°, Plaza Edison, Apdo 9658, Panamá 4; tel. 360-0600; fax 360-0700; e-mail uti@mici.gob.pa; internet www.mici.gob.pa.
Ministry of Education: Edif. Poli y Los Rios, Avda Justo Arosemena, Calles 26 y 27, Apdo 2440, Panamá 3; tel. 262-2645; fax 262-9087; e-mail me@sinfo.net; internet www.educacion.gob.pa.
Ministry of Finance and the Treasury: Central Postal Balboa, Ancón, Apdo 5245, Panamá 5; tel. 225-3431; fax 227-2357; e-mail mhyt@mhyt.gob.pa; internet www.mhyt.gob.pa.
Ministry of Foreign Affairs: Panamá 4; tel. 227-0013; fax 227-4725; e-mail infoweb@mire.gob.pa; internet www.mire.gob.pa.
Ministry of Housing: Apdo 5228, Panamá 5; tel. 262-6470; fax 262-9250.
Ministry of the Interior and Justice: Apdo 1628, Panamá 1; tel. 222-8973; fax 262-7877; internet www.gobiernoyjusticia.gob.pa.
Ministry of Labour and Social Welfare: Apdo 2441, Panamá 3; tel. 269-4250; fax 263-8125; e-mail mitrabs2@sinfo.net; internet www.mitrabs.gob.pa.
Ministry of the Presidency: Valija 50, Apdo 2189, Panamá 1; tel. 222-0520; fax 237-4119.
Ministry of Public Health: Apdo 2048, Panamá 1; tel. 225-6080; fax 227-5276; e-mail daimimsa@ihpanama.com.

Ministry of Public Works: Apdo 1632, Panamá 1; tel. 232-5505; fax 232-5776; internet www.mop.gob.pa.
Ministry of Youth, Women, Family and Childhood: Panamá; internet www.dinamu.gob.pa.

President and Legislature

PRESIDENT

Election, 2 May 1999

Candidate	Votes	% of votes
MIREYA MOSCOSO DE GRUBER (Unión por Panamá)	572,717	44.8
MARTÍN TORRIJOS ESPINO (Nueva Nación) .	483,501	37.8
ALBERTO VALLARINO (Acción Opositora) .	222,250	17.4
Total	1,278,486	100.0

ASAMBLEA LEGISLATIVA
(Legislative Assembly)

President: LAURENTINO CORTIZO (PS).

General Election, 2 May 1999

Affiliation/Party	% of votes	Seats
Nueva Nación		
Partido Revolucionario Democrático (PRD)	47.9	34
Partido Solidaridad	5.6	4
Partido Liberal Nacional (PLN) . .	4.2	3
Unión por Panamá		
Partido Arnulfista (PA) . . .	25.3	18
Movimiento Liberal Republicano Nacionalista (MOLIRENA) . .	4.2	3
Cambio Democrático	2.8	2
Movimiento de Renovación Nacional (Morena)	1.4	1
Acción Opositora		
Partido Demócrata Cristiano (PDC) .	7.0	5
Partido Renovación Civilista (PRC) .	1.4	1
Total (incl. others)	100.0	71

Political Organizations

Cambio Democrático (CD): Panamá; formally registered 1998.
Movimiento Laborista Agrario (MOLA): Panamá; tel. 263-7055; fax 264-5981; formally registered 1993; Pres. CARLOS ELETA A.
Movimiento Liberal Republicano Nacionalista (MOLIRENA): Calle Venezuela, entre Vía España y Calle 50, Panamá; tel. 213-5928; fax 265-6004; internet www.sinfo.net/molirena; formally registered 1982; conservative; Pres. RAMÓN MORALES.
Movimiento de Renovación Nacional (Morena): Panamá; tel. 236-4930; formally registered 1993; Pres. PEDRO VALLARINO COX; Sec.-Gen. DEMETRIO DECEREGA.
Partido Arnulfista (PA): Avda Perú y Calle 38E, No 37-41, (al lado de Casa la Esperanza), Panamá; tel. 227-1267; f. 1990; formed by Arnulfista faction of the Partido Panameñista Auténtico; Pres. MIREYA MOSCOSO DE GRUBER; Sec.-Gen. VÍCTOR JULIAO.
Partido Demócrata Cristiano (PDC): Avda Perú (frente al Parque Porras), Apdo 6322, Panamá 5; tel. 227-3204; fax 227-3944; f. 1960; Pres. RUBÉN AROSEMENA.
Partido Liberal Auténtico (PLA): Vía España y Calle 46 (frente a la Clínica Dental Arrocha), Panamá; tel. 227-1041; fax 227-4119; formally registered 1988; Pres. ARNULFO ESCALONA RIOS; Sec.-Gen. JULIO C. HARRIS.
Partido Liberal Nacional (PLN): El Dorado, Apdo 7363, Panamá 6; tel. 229-7523; fax 229-7524; e-mail pln@sinfo.net; internet www.sinfo.net/liberal-nacional; f. 1979; mem. of Liberal International, and founding mem. of Federación Liberal de Centroamérica y el Caribe (FELICA); 40,645 mems; Pres. RAÚL ARANGO GASTEAZORO; Sec.-Exec. Lic. OSCAR UCROS.

Partido Liberal Republicano (Libre): Panamá; tel. 261-4659; formally registered 1993; Pres. GONZALO TAPIA COLLANTE; Sec.-Gen. CARLOS ORILLAC.

Partido Revolucionario Democrático (PRD): Avda 7a Central (frente al Edif. Novey), Apdo 2650, Panamá 9; tel. 225-1050; f. 1979; supports policies of late Gen. Omar Torrijos Herrera; combination of Marxists, Christian Democrats and some business interests; Pres. GERARDO GONZÁLEZ VERNAZA; Sec.-Gen. MARTÍN TORRIJOS ESPINO.

Partido Solidaridad: Edif. Plaza Balboa, Panamá; tel. 263-4097; internet www.sinfo.net/solidaridad; formally registered 1993; Pres. SAMUEL LEWIS GALINDO; Sec.-Gen. ENRIQUE LAU CORTÉS.

The following political alliances were formed to contest presidential and legislative elections conducted on 2 May 1999:

Acción Opositora (AO): comprising the PDC, the Partido Renovación Civilista (PRC), the Partido Liberal (PL) and the Partido Nacionalista Popular (PNP); Presidential Candidate ALBERTO VALLARINO (PDC).

Nueva Nación (NN): comprising the PRD, Partido Solidaridad, the PLN and the Movimiento Papa Egoró (MPE); Presidential Candidate MARTÍN TORRIJOS (PRD).

Unión por Panamá (UPP): comprising the PA, MOLIRENA, Morena and CD; Presidential Candidate MIREYA MOSCOSO DE GRUBER (PA).

Diplomatic Representation

EMBASSIES IN PANAMA

Argentina: Edif. del Banco de Iberoamérica, 7°, Avda 50 y Calle 53, Apdo 1271, Panamá 1; tel. 264-6561; fax 269-5331; Ambassador: ERNESTO MARIO PFIRTER.

Belize: Villa de las Fuentes 1, F-32, Avda 22 norte, Apdo 205, Panamá; tel. 236-3762; fax 236-4132; Chargé d'affaires a.i.: NAIM MUSA.

Bolivia: Calle Eric Arturo del Valle, Bella Vista 1, Panamá; tel. 269-0274; fax 264-3868; e-mail embolivia-panama@rree.gov.bo; Ambassador: CARLOS BEJAR MOLINA.

Brazil: Edif. El Dorado, 1°, Calle Elvira Méndez y Avda Ricardo Arango, Urb. Campo Alegre, Apdo 4287, Panamá 5; tel. 263-5322; fax 269-6316; e-mail brasemb@sifo; Ambassador: PEDRO PAULO PINTO ASSUMPÇAO.

Canada: Edif. World Trade Center, Galería Comercial, 1°, Urb. Marbella, Apdo 0832-2446, Panamá; tel. 264-7115; fax 263-8083; Ambassador: DANIEL DALEY.

Chile: Edif. Banco de Boston, 11°, Calle Elvira Méndez y Vía España, Apdo 7341; Panamá 5; tel. 223-9748; fax 263-5530; e-mail echilepa@cw.panama.net; Ambassador: LEOPOLDO DURÁN.

China (Taiwan): Edif. Torre Hong Kong Bank, 10°, Avda Samuel Lewis, Apdo 4285, Panamá 5; tel. 223-3424; fax 263-5534; e-mail embchina@hotmail.com; Ambassador: DAVID C. Y. HU.

Colombia: Edif. World Trade Center, Of. 1802, Calle 53, Urb. Marbella, Panamá; tel. 264-9644; fax 223-1134; e-mail emcolpan@sinfo.net; Ambassador: RAMÓN JESÚS MARTÍNEZ DE LEÓN.

Costa Rica: Edif. Plaza Omega, 3°, Calle Samuel Lewis, Apdo 8963, Panamá; tel. 264-2980; fax 264-4057; e-mail embarica@pan.gbm.net; Ambassador: ALVARO DE LA CRUZ MARTÍNEZ.

Cuba: Avda Cuba y Ecuador 33, Apdo 6-2291, El Dorado, Panamá; tel. 227-5277; fax 225-6681; e-mail embacuba@cableonda.net; Chargé d'affaires: CARLOS RAFAEL ZAMORA RODRÍGUEZ.

Dominican Republic: Casa 40A, Calle 75, Apdo 6250, Panamá 5; tel. 270-3884; fax 270-3886; e-mail embajdom@sinfo.net; Ambassador: RODOLFO LEYBA POLANCO.

Ecuador: Edif. Banco Central Hispano, 5°, Of. 13, Avda Samuel Lewis, Panamá; e-mail eecuador@cabledonda.net; tel. 264-2654; fax 223-0159; Ambassador: SUSANA ALVEAR CRUZ DE ACOSTA.

Egypt: Calle 55, No 15, El Cangrejo, Panamá; tel. 263-5020; Ambassador: MOUSTAFA MOHAMED AHMED EL HATEER.

El Salvador: Edif. Metropolis, 4°, Avda Espinosa Batista, Panamá; tel. 223-3020; fax 264-1433; e-mail patriasa@sinfo.net; Ambassador: AIDA ELENA MINERO REYES.

France: Plaza de Francia 1, Las Bovedas, San Felipe, Apdo 869, Panamá 1; tel. 228-8290; fax 228-7852; Ambassador: PATRICK BOURSIN.

Germany: Edif. World Trade Center, 20°, Calle 53E, Marbella, Apdo 0832-0536, Panamá 5; tel. 263-7733; fax 223-6664; e-mail germpanama@cwp.net; Ambassador: GEORG HEINRICH VON NEUBRONNER.

Guatemala: Edif. Versalles, Avda Federico Boyd y Calle 48 de Bella Vista, Apdo 2352, Panamá 9A; tel. 269-3475; fax 223-1922; Ambassador: GUISELA GODÍNEZ SAZO.

Haiti: Edif. Dora Luz, 2°, Calle 1, El Cangrejo, Apdo 442, Panamá 9; tel. 269-3443; fax 223-1767; Chargé d'affaires: GEORGES H. BARBEROUSSE.

Holy See: Punta Paitilla, Avda Balboa y Vía Italia, Apdo 4251, Panamá 5 (Apostolic Nunciature); tel. 269-2102; fax 264-2116; e-mail nuncio@sinfo.net; Apostolic Nuncio: Most Rev. GUIDO OTTONELLO GIACOMO Titular Archbishop of Sasaben.

Honduras: Edif. Tapia, 2°, Of. 202, Calle 31 y Justo Arosemena, Apdo 8704, Panamá 5; tel. 225-8200; fax 225-8200; Ambassador: HILARIO RENE VALLEJO HERNÁNDEZ.

India: Avda Federico Boy y Calle 51, Alado de Torre Universal, Panamá; tel. 264-3043; fax 264-2855; e-mail indempn@panama.c-com.net; Ambassador: TARA SINGH.

Israel: Edif. Grobman, 5°, Calle Manuel María Icaza 12, Apdo 6357, Panamá 5; tel. 264-8022; fax 264-2706; e-mail panama@israel.org; Ambassador: EMANUEL SERI.

Italy: Torre Banco Exterior, 25°, Avda Balboa, Apdo 2369, Panamá 9A; tel. 225-8950; fax 227-4906; e-mail panitamb@cwp.net.pa; Ambassador: MASSIMO SPINETTI.

Jamaica: Edif. del Seguro Simón, planta baja, Avda de Los Mártires, Apdo A1, Panamá 9A; tel. 225-4441; e-mail geosimp@sinfo.net; Chargé d'affaires: GEORGE P. SIMPSON.

Japan: Calle 50, Frente al Credicor Bank, Panamá 1; tel. 263-6155; fax 263-6019; e-mail taiship2@sinfo.net; internet www.embjapon.net; Chargé d'affaires: MASATO MATSUI.

Korea, Republic: Edif. Plaza, planta baja, Calle Ricardo Arias y Calle 51E, Campo Alegre, Apdo 8096, Panamá 7; tel. 264-8203; fax 264-8825; e-mail korm@cwp.net.pa; Ambassador: KEUN SEOP OHM.

Libya: Avda Balboa y Calle 32 (frente al Edif. Atalaya), Apdo 6-894 El Dorado, Panamá; tel. 227-3365; Chargé d'affaires: ABDULMAJID MILUD SHAHIN.

Mexico: Plaza Credicorp Bank, 27°, Calle 50, Apdo 8373, Panamá 7; tel. 210-1523; fax 210-1526; e-mail embamex@pan.gbm.net; Ambassador: ALFREDO PÉREZ BRAVO.

Nicaragua: Quarry Heights, 16, Ancon, Apdo 772, Zona 1, Panamá; tel. 211-2113; fax 211-2116; e-mail embapana@sinfo.net; Ambassador: ALVARO SEVILLA SIERO.

Peru: Edif. World Trade Center, 12°, Panamá; tel. 223-1112; fax 269-6809; e-mail embaperu@pananet.com; Ambassador: JOSÉ ANTONIO BELLINA ACEVEDO.

Russia: Torre IBC, 10°, Avda Manuel Espinosa Batista, Apdo 6-4697, El Dorado, Panamá; tel. 264-1408; fax 264-1588; e-mail emruspan@sinfo.net; Ambassador: NIKOLAY MIKHAYLOVICH VLADIMIR.

Saudi Arabia: Calle Manuel M. Icaza y Avda Samuel Lewis; tel. 263-2599; fax 264-2116; Ambassador: SOULIMAN TAYEB AHMED SALEM.

Spain: Calle 53 y Avda Perú (frente a la Plaza Porras), Apdo 1857, Panamá 1; tel. 227-5122; fax 227-6284; e-mail embespa@cwp.net.pa; Ambassador: CARLOS DE LOJENDIO Y PARDO MANUEL DE VILLENA.

United Kingdom: Torre Swiss Bank, 4°, Urb. Marbella, Calle 53,Apdo 889, Panamá 1; tel. 269-0866; fax 223-0730; e-mail britemb@cwp.net.pa; Ambassador: ROBERT HAROLD GLYN DAVIES.

USA: Avda Balboa y Calle 38, Apdo 6959, Panamá 5; tel. 207-7000; fax 227-1964; e-mail usembisc@cwp.net.pa; Chargé d'affaires: FREDERICK A. BECKER.

Uruguay: Edif. Vallarino, 5°, Of. 4, Calle 32 y Avda Justo Arosemena, Apdo 8898, Panamá 5; tel. 225-0049; fax 225-9087; e-mail urupanan@sinfo.net; Ambassador: TABARÉ BOCALANDRO.

Venezuela: Torre Banco Unión, 5°, Avda Samuel Lewis, Apdo 661, Panamá 1; tel. 269-1014; fax 269-1916; e-mail embvenp@panama.ce.net; Chargé d'Affaires: EMMA TOLEDO PADILLA.

Judicial System

The judiciary in Panama comprises the following courts and judges: Corte Suprema de Justicia (Supreme Court of Justice), with nine judges appointed for a 10-year term; 10 Tribunales Superiores de Distrito Judicial (High Courts) with 36 magistrates; 54 Jueces de Circuito (Circuit Judges) and 89 Jueces Municipales (Municipal Judges).

Panama is divided into four judicial districts and has seven High Courts of Appeal. The first judicial district covers the provinces of Panamá, Colón, Darién and the region of Kuna Yala and contains two High Courts of Appeal, one dealing with criminal cases, the other dealing with civil cases. The second judicial district covers the provinces of Coclé and Veraguas and contains the third High Court of Appeal, located in Penonomé. The third judicial district covers the provinces of Chiriquí and Bocas del Toro and contains the fourth High Court of Appeal, located in David. The fourth judicial district covers the provinces of Herrera and Los Santos and contains the fifth High Court of Appeal, located in Las Tablas. Each of these courts deals with civil and criminal cases in their respective provinces. There are two additional special High Courts of Appeal. The first hears maritime, labour, family and infancy cases; the second deals with antitrust cases and consumer affairs.

Corte Suprema de Justicia: Edif. 236, Ancón, Calle Culebra, Apdo 1770, Panamá 1; tel. 262-9833; e-mail orgjudrp@sinfo.net; internet www.sinfo.net/orgjup.

President of the Supreme Court of Justice: MIRTZA ANGELICA FRANCESCHI DE AGUILERA.

Attorney-General: JOSÉ ANTONIO SOSSA.

Religion

The Constitution recognizes freedom of worship and the Roman Catholic Church as the religion of the majority of the population.

CHRISTIANITY

The Roman Catholic Church

For ecclesiastical purposes, Panama comprises one archdiocese, five dioceses, the territorial prelature of Bocas del Toro and the Apostolic Vicariate of Darién. There were an estimated 2,441,678 adherents at 31 December 1999.

Bishops' Conference: Conferencia Episcopal de Panamá, Secretariado General, Apdo 870933, Panamá 7, tel. 223-0075; fax 223-0042; f. 1958 (statutes approved 1986); Pres. Rt Rev. JOSÉ LUIS LACUNZA MAESTROJUÁN, Bishop of David.

Archbishop of Panamá: Most Rev. JOSÉ DIMAS CEDEÑO DELGADO, Arzobispado Metropolitano, Calle 1a Sur Carrasquilla, Apdo 6386, Panamá 5; tel. 261-0002; fax 261-0820.

The Baptist Church

The Baptist Convention of Panama (Convención Bautista de Panamá): Apdo 6212, Panamá 5; tel. 264-5585; fax 264-4945; f. 1959; Pres. Rev. DIMAS JIMÉNEZ; Exec. Sec. Rev. EDUARDO HENNINGHAM.

The Anglican Communion

Panama comprises one of the five dioceses of the Iglesia Anglicana de la Región Central de América.

Bishop of Panama: Rt Rev. CLARENCE W. HAYES-DEWAR, Box R, Balboa; fax 262-2097; e-mail furriola@sinfo.net.

BAHÁ'Í FAITH

National Spiritual Assembly of the Bahá'ís: Apdo 815-0143, Panamá 15; tel. 231-1191; fax 231-6909; e-mail panbahai@sinfo.net; mems resident in 550 localities; National Sec. ÉMELINA RODRÍGUEZ.

The Press

DAILIES

Crítica Libre: Vía Ricardo J. Alfaro, al lado de la USMA, Apdo B-4, Panamá 9A; tel. 230-1666; fax 230-0132; e-mail esotop@epasa.com; internet www.epasa.com; f. 1925; morning; independent; Pres. ROSARIO ARIAS DE GALINDO; Editor ANTONIO AMAT; circ. 40,000.

La Estrella de Panamá: Calle Alejandro A. Duque G. esq. Avda Frangipani y Vía S. Bolívar, Panamá; tel. 227-0555; fax 227-1026; f. 1853; morning; independent; Pres. ALEJANDRO A. DUQUE; Editor JAMES APARICIO; circ. 20,000.

El Matutino: Vía Fernández de Córdoba, Apdo B-4, Panamá 9A; tel. 261-2300; morning; pro-Govt; circ. 7,000.

El Panamá América: Vía Ricardo J. Alfaro, al lado de la USMA, Apdo B-4, Panamá 9A; tel. 230-1666; fax 230-1035; e-mail director@epasa.com; internet www.epasa.com; f. 1958; morning; independent; Pres. ROSARIO ARIAS DE GALINDO; Editor OCTAVIO AMAT; circ. 25,000.

La Prensa: Avda 11 de Octubre y Calle C. Hato Pintado, Apdo 6-4586, El Dorado, Panamá; tel. 221-7515; fax 221-7328; e-mail editor@prensa.com; internet www.prensa.com; f. 1980; morning; independent; closed by Govt 1988–90; Pres. JUAN A. ARIAS; Editor WINSTON ROBLES C.; circ. 38,000.

La República: Vía Fernández de Córdoba, Apdo B-4, Panamá 9A; tel. 261-0813; evening; circ. 5,000.

El Siglo: Calle 58, Urb. Obarrio, No 12, Apdo W, Panamá 4; tel. 269-3311; fax 269-6954; e-mail siglonet@pananet.com; f. 1985; morning; independent; Editor JAIME PADILLA BÉLIZ; circ. 42,000.

El Universal: Avda Justo Arosemena entre Calles 29 y 30, Panamá; tel. 225-7010; fax 225-6994; e-mail eluniver@sinfo.net; f. 1995; Pres. TOMÁS GERARDO DUQUE ZERR; Editor MILTON HENRÍQUEZ; circ. 16,000.

PERIODICALS

Análisis: Edif. Señorial, Calle 50, Apdo 8038, Panamá 7; tel. 226-0073; fax 226-3758; monthly; economics and politics; Dir MARIO A. ROGNONI.

El Camaleón: Calle 58E, No 12, Apdo W, Panamá 4; tel. 269-3311; fax 269-6954; weekly; satire; Editor JAIME PADILLA BÉLIZ; circ. 80,000.

Diálogo Social: Apdo 9A-192, Panamá; tel. 229-1542; fax 261-0215; f. 1967; published by the Centro de Capacitación Social; monthly; religion, economics and current affairs; Pres. CELIA SANJUR; circ. 3,000.

Estadística Panameña: Apdo 5213, Panamá 5; tel. 210-4800; fax 210-4801; e-mail cgrdec@contraloría.gob.pa; internet www.contraloria.gob.pa; f. 1941; published by the Contraloría General de la República; statistical survey in series according to subjects; Controller-General ALVIN WEEDEN GAMBOA; Dir of Statistics and Census LUIS ENRIQUE QUESADA.

FOB Colón Free Zone: Apdo 6-3287, El Dorado, Panamá; tel. 225-6638; fax 225-0466; e-mail focusint@sinfo.net; internet www.colonfreezone.com; annual; bilingual trade directory; circ. 35,000.

Focus on Panama: Apdo 6-3287, Panamá; tel. 225-6638; fax 225-0466; e-mail focusint@sinfo.net; internet www.focuspublicationsint.com; f. 1970; 2 a year; visitor's guide; separate English and Spanish editions; Dir KENNETH JONES; circ. 70,000.

Informativo Industrial: Apdo 6-4798, El Dorado, Panamá 1; tel. 230-0482; fax 230-0805; monthly; organ of the Sindicato de Industriales de Panamá; Pres. ALBERTO PONS Z.

Maga: Panamá 4; monthly; literature, art and sociology; Dir ENRIQUE JARAMILLO LEVY.

Sucesos: Calle 58E, No 12, Apdo W, Panamá 4; tel. 269-3311; fax 269-6854; three a week; Editor JAIME PADILLA BÉLIZ; circ. 50,000.

Unidad: Calle 1a, Apdo 2705, Perejil, Panamá 3; fax 227-3525; f. 1977; fortnightly; publ. of Partido del Pueblo de Panamá; Dir CARLOS F. CHANGMARÍN.

PRESS ASSOCIATION

Sindicato de Periodistas de Panamá: Avda Ecuador y Calle 33, Apdo 2096, Panamá 1; tel. 225-0234; fax 225-0857; f. 1949; Sec.-Gen. EUCLIDES FUENTES ARROYO.

FOREIGN NEWS BUREAUX

Agence-France Presse (AFP): Panamá; tel. 261-2300; Correspondent ROBERTO R. RODRÍGUEZ.

Agencia EFE (Spain): Edif. Comosa, 22°, Avda Samuel Lewis y Calle Manuel María Icaza, Apdo 479, Panamá 9; tel. 223-9020; fax 264-8442; Bureau Chief HUGO FABIÁN ORTIZ DURÁN.

Agenzia Nazionale Stampa Associata (ANSA) (Italy): Edif. Banco de Boston, 17°, Vía España 601, Panamá; tel. 260-6166; Dir LUIS LAMBOGLIA.

Central News Agency (Taiwan): Apdo 6-693, El Dorado, Panamá; tel. 223-8837; Correspondent HUANG KWANG CHUN.

Deutsche Press-Agentur (dpa) (Germany): Panamá; tel. 233-0396; fax 233-5393.

Informatsionnoye Telegrafnoye Agentstvo Rossii—Telegrafnoye Agentstvo Suverennykh Stran (ITAR—TASS) (Russia): Panamá; tel. 269-1993; Bureau Chief ELIDAR ABDULAYEV.

Inter Press Service (IPS) (Italy): Panamá; tel. 225-1673; fax 264-7033; Correspondent SILVIO HERNÁNDEZ.

Prensa Latina (Cuba): Edif. Doña Luz, Apto 3, Avda Quinta Norte 35, Apdo 6-2799, Panamá; tel. 264-3647; Correspondent RAIMUNDO LÓPEZ MEDINA.

Rossiyskoye Informatsionnoye Agentstvo—Novosti (RIA-Novosti) (Russia): Apdo 1190, Panamá 1; tel. 227-4596; Dir RAMIRO OCHOA LÓPEZ.

United Press International (UPI) (USA): Altos de Miraflores 4-H, Apdo 393, Panamá 9A; tel. 229-3443; fax 229-3279; Dir TOMÁS A. CUPAS.

Xinhua (New China) News Agency (People's Republic of China): Vía Cincuentenario 48, Viña del Mar, Panamá 1; tel. 226-4501; Dir HU TAIRAN.

Publishers

Editora 'La Estrella de Panamá': Avda 9a Sur 7-38, Apdo 159, Panamá 1; tel. 222-0900; f. 1853.

Editora Renovación, SA: Vía Fernández de Córdoba, Apdo B-4, Panamá 9A; tel. 261-2300; newspapers; govt-owned; Exec. Man. ESCOLÁSTICO CALVO.

Editora Sibauste, SA: Edif. Panchita 3°, 101 Perejil, Apdo 3375, Panamá 3; tel. 269-0983; Dir ENRIQUE SIBAUSTE BARRÍA.

Editorial Litográfica, SA (Edilito): Panamá 10; tel. 224-3087; Pres. EDUARDO AVILES C.

Editorial Universitaria: Vía José de Fábrega, Panamá; tel. 264-2087; f. 1969; history, geography, law, sciences, literature; Dir CARLOS MANUEL GASTEAZORO.

Focus Publications: Apdo 6-3287, El Dorado, Panamá; tel. 225-6638; fax 225-0466; e-mail focusint@sinfo.net; internet www.focuspublicationsint.com; f. 1970; guides, trade directories and yearbooks.

Fondo Educativo Interamericano: Edif. Eastern, 6°, Avda Federico Boyd 10 y Calle 51, Apdo 6-3099, El Dorado, Panamá; tel. 269-1511; educational and reference; Dir ALICIA CHAVARRÍA.

Industrial Gráfica, SA: Vía España entre Calles 95 y 96 (al lado de Orange Crush), Apdo 810014, Panamá 10; tel. 224-3994; Pres. EDUARDO AVILES C.

Publicaciones Panameñas, SA: Edif. YASA, 2°, Of. 1, Urb. Obarrio, Calle 59, Apdo 9-103, Panamá 9; tel. 263-5190; Dir EMPERATRIZ S. DE CÁRDENAS.

Publicar Centroamericana, SA: Edif. Banco de Boston, 7°, Vía España 200 y Calle Elvira Méndez, Apdo 4919, Panamá 5; tel. 223-9655; fax 269-1964.

Government Publishing House

Editorial Mariano Arosemena: Instituto Nacional de Cultura, Apdo 662, Panamá 1; tel. 222-3233; f. 1974; literature, anthropology, social sciences, archaeology; Dir ESTHER URIETA DE REAL.

Broadcasting and Communications

TELECOMMUNICATIONS

Dirección Nacional de Medios de Comunicación Social: Avda 7a Central y Calle 3a, Apdo 1628, Panamá 1; tel. 262-3197; fax 262-9495; Dir EDWIN CABRERA.

Instituto Nacional de Telecomunicaciones (INTEL): Gerencia Executiva Internacional, Apdo 659, Panamá 9A; tel. 269-0656; fax 264-5743; f. 1973; 49% share acquired by Cable & Wireless (United Kingdom) in 1997; Gen. Man. JUAN RAMÓN PORRAS; 3,600 employees.

BROADCASTING

Radio

In March 1990 the Government approved the creation of the National State Radio Broadcasting Directorate, which was to be a department of the Ministry of the Presidency.

Asociación Panameña de Radiodifusión: Apdo 7387, Estafeta de Paitilla, Panamá; tel. 263-5252; fax 226-4396; Pres. FERNANDO ELETA CASSANOVA.

In 1995 there were 88 AM (Medium Wave) and 118 FM stations in Pamana. Most stations are commercial.

Television

Fundación para la Educación en la Televisión—FETV (Canal 5): Edif. Proconsa, 8°, Calle 51 y Calle Manuel María Icaza, Apdo 6-7295, El Dorado, Panamá; tel. 264-6555; fax 223-5966; e-mail fetvadm@sinfo.net; f. 1992; Dir MANUEL BLANQUER; Gen. Man. MARÍA EUGENIA FONSECA M.

Medcom: Calle 50, No. 6, Apdo 116, Panamá 8; tel. 210-6700; fax 210-6797; e-mail murrutia@medcom.com.pa; f. 1998 by merger of RPC Televisión (Canal 4) and Telemetro (Canal 13); commercial; also owns Cable Onda 90; Pres. FERNANDO ELETA; CEO NICOLÁS GONZÁLEZ-REVILLA.

Panavisión del Istmo, SA: Torre Plaza Regency, Vía España, Apdo 6-2605, El Dorado, Panamá 8; tel. 269-6816; f. 1983; Dir ALFONSO DE LA ESPRIELLA.

Sistema de Televisión Educativa (Canal 11): Universidad de Panamá, Estafeta Universitaria, Calle José de Fábrega, Panamá; tel. 269-3755; fax 223-2921; f. 1978; educational and cultural; Pres. GERARDO MALLONEY; Dir-Gen. I. VELÁSQUEZ DE CORTES.

Southern Command Network—SCN (Canal 8): Edif. 209, Fuerte Clayton, Apdo 919, Panamá; tel. 287-4209; f. 1943; broadcasting in English for US military personnel; Dir Maj. BENJAMIN C. FRAZIER.

Tele-Carrier Inc.: Panamá; f. 2000; commercial; Pres. JOSÉ GUANTI.

Televisora Nacional—TVN (Canal 2): Vía Bolívar, Apdo 6-3092, El Dorado, Panamá; tel. 236-2222; fax 236-2987; f. 1962; Dir JAIME ALBERTO ARIAS.

In 1995 there were 32 television channels broadcasting in Panama.

Finance

(cap. = capital; res = reserves; dep. = deposits; m. = million; amounts in balboas, unless otherwise stated)

BANKING

In February 1998 new banking legislation was approved, providing for greater supervision of banking activity in the country, including the creation of a Superintendency of Banks. In January 2001 a total of 85 banks operated in Panama, including two official banks, 48 with general licence, 18 with international licence, and two representative offices.

Superintendencia de Bancos (Banking Superintendency): Torre HSBC, 18°, Apdo 2397, Panamá 1; tel. 206-7800; fax 264-9422; internet www.superbancos.gob.pa; f. 1970 as Comisión Bancaria Nacional (National Banking Commission) to license and control banking activities within and from Panamanian territory; Comisión Bancaria Nacional superseded by Superintendencia de Bancos June 1998 with enhanced powers to supervise banking activity; Superintendent CARLOS VALLARINO.

National Bank

Banco Nacional de Panamá: Torre BNP, Vía España, Apdo 5220, Panamá 5; tel. 263-5151; fax 269-0091; e-mail bnpvalores@cwp.net.pa; internet www.banconal.com.pa; f. 1904; govt-owned; cap. 500.0m., res 6.8m., dep. 2,708m. (Dec. 1998); Pres. ROOSEVELT THAYER G.; Man. BOLIVAR PARIENTE; 51 brs.

Development Banks

Banco de Desarrollo Agropecuario—BDA: Avda de los Mártires, Apdo 5282, Panamá 5; tel. 262-0140; fax 262-1713; f. 1973; govt-sponsored agricultural and livestock credit org.; Pres. Minister of Agricultural Development; Gen. Man. ABELARDO AMO ZAKAY.

Banco Hipotecario Nacional: Edif. Peña Prieta, Avda Balboa y Calle 40 Bella Vista, Apdo 222, Panamá 1; tel. 227-0055; fax 225-6956; e-mail bhn@sinfo.net; f. 1973; govt-sponsored; finances national housing projects and regulates national savings system; Pres. Minister of Housing; Gen. Man. WALDO ARROCHA.

Savings Banks

Banco General, SA: Calle Aquilino de la Guardia, Apdo 4592, Panamá 5; tel. 227-3200; fax 265-0210; e-mail info@banco-general.com; internet www.bgeneral.com; f. 1955; total assets 2,300m. (2000); purchased Banco Comercial de Panamá (BANCOMER) in 1999; Chair. and CEO FEDERICO HUMBERT, Jr; Exec. Vice-Pres. and Gen. Man. RAÚL ALEMÁN Z.; 14 brs.

Banco Panameño de la Vivienda: Avda Chile y Calle 41, Apdo 8639, Panamá 5; tel. 227-4020; fax 227-5433; f. 1981; cap. and res 3.2m., dep. 30.7m., total assets 45.1m. (Dec. 1987); Gen. Man. MARIO L. FÁBREGA AROSEMENA; 3 brs.

Banco Provincial, SA: Avda Rodolfo Chiari, Apdo 122, Aguadulce; tel. 997-5010; fax 997-6433; f. 1987; cap. US $2.5m., dep. $18.6m. (Dec. 1994); Gen. Man. J. PEDRO M. BARRAGÁN.

Caja de Ahorros: Vía España y Calle Thais de Pons, Apdo 1740, Panamá 1; tel. 205-1000; fax 269-3674; f. 1934; govt-owned; cap. and res 10.1m., dep. 310.7m., total assets 359.6m. (1987); Chair. RAMÓN MORALES; Gen. Man. WILBERT BAZÁN KODAT; 37 brs.

Domestic Private Banks

Banco Continental de Panamá, SA: Calle 50 y Avda Aquilino de la Guardia, Apdo 135, Panamá 9A; tel. 215-7000; fax 215-7134; e-mail bcp@bcocontinental.com; internet www.bcocontinental.com; f. 1972; cap. 57.0m., res 12.6m., dep. 471.4m., total assets 728.3m. (Dec. 1998); Pres. ROBERTO MOTTA; Gen. Man. OSVALDO MOUYNÉS; 7 brs.

Banco Disa, SA: Calle 51E, Campo Alegre, Apdo 7201, Panamá 5; tel. 263-5933; fax 264-1084; internet www.bdisa.com; f. 1986; Gen. Man. FÉLIX RIERA.

Banco Internacional de Panamá (BIPAN): Complejo Plaza Marbella, Avda Aquilino de la Guardia y Calles 47 y 48, Apdo 11181, Panamá 6; tel. 263-9000; fax 263-9514; e-mail bipan@bipan.com; internet www.bipan.com; f. 1973; cap. US $39.4m., dep. $370.4m., total assets $472.5m. (Dec. 2000); Gen. Man. RENÉ A. DÍAZ; 10 brs.

Banco Mercantil del Istmo, SA: Apdo 484, Panamá 9A; tel. 263-6262; fax 263-7553; e-mail mguerra@banistmo.com; internet www.banistmo.com; f. 1967 as Banco de Santander y Panamá; name changed as above in 1992; cap. 13.5m., res 4.5m., dep. 155.1m., total assets 184.6m. (Dec. 1995); Pres. SAMUEL LEWIS GALINDO; Gen. Man. MANUEL JOSÉ BARREDO MARTÍNEZ.

Banco Panamericano, SA (PANABANK): Edif. Panabank, Casa Matriz, Calle 50, Apdo 1828, Panamá 1; tel. 263-9266; fax 269-1537; e-mail panabank@sinfo.net; internet www.panabank.com; f. 1983; cap. and res 3.2m., dep. 42.5m., total assets 46.0m. (June 1991); Exec. Vice-Pres. GUIDO J. MARTINELLI, Jr.

Banco de Santa Cruz de la Sierra (Panamá), SA: Torre Banco Unión, 11°, Calle Samuel Lewis, Apdo 6-4416, El Dorado, Panamá; tel. 263-8477; fax 263-8404; f. 1980; cap. 3.0m., res 1.1m., dep. 74.5m. (Dec. 1994); Chair. JUAN MANUEL PARADA PERDRIEL; Gen. Man. JULIO ANTELO SALMÓN.

Banco Transatlántico, SA: Calles Ricardo Arias y Manuel María Icaza, Apdo 7655, Panamá 5; tel. 269-2318; fax 269-4948; f. 1979; cap. and res 3.5m., dep. 31.9m., total assets 34.6m. (Dec. 1987); Gen. Man. RAÚL DE MENA; 2brs.

Global Bank Corporation: Torre Global Bank, Calle 50, Apdo 55-1843, Paitilla, Panamá; tel. 206-2000; fax 263-3518; e-mail global@pan.gbm.net; internet www.globalbank.com.pa; f. 1994; total assets 5,433m.; Gen. Man. JORGE VALLARINO S.

Multi Credit Bank Inc.: Edif. Prosperidad, planta baja, Vía España 127, Apdo 8210, Panamá 7; tel. 269-0188; fax 264-4014; internet www.grupomulticredit.com; f. 1990; cap. and res 29.7m., dep. 172.7m. (Dec. 1997); Gen. Man. MOISÉS D. COHEN M.

Primer Banco del Istmo, SA: Panamá; f. 2000 following a merger of Primer Grupo Nacional and Banco del Istmo; total assets 3,700m. (2000).

Republic National Bank Inc.: Calle 51 entre Avda Federico Boyd y Calle 47 (Colombia), Apdo 8962, Panamá 5; tel. 264-7777; fax 264-3722; f. 1969; cap. 4.0m., res 0.8m., dep. 30.0m. (Dec. 1987); Pres. ESTEFANO ISAIAS DASSUM; Gen. Man. LUIS E. GUIZADO.

Towerbank International Inc.: Edif. Tower Plaza, Calle 50 y Beatriz M de Cabal, Apdo 6-6039; Panamá; tel. 269-6900; fax 269-6800; e-mail towerbank@towerbank.com; internet www.towerbank.com; f. 1971; cap. and res US $20.2m., dep. $97.8m., total assets $242.2m. (Dec. 1997); Pres. SAM KARDONSKI; Gen. Man. GYSBERTUS ANTONIUS DE WOLF; 1 br.

Foreign Banks
Principal Foreign Banks with General Licence

ABN AMRO Bank, NV (Netherlands): Calle Manuel María Icaza 4, Apdo 10147, Panamá 4; tel. 263-6200; fax 269-0526; e-mail stef.merckx@abnamro.com; internet www.abnamro.com; Gen. Man. STEF MERCKX.

BAC International Bank (Panamá), Inc. (USA): Avda de la Guardia, planta baja, Apdo 6-3654, Panamá; tel. 213-0822; fax 269-3879; e-mail rcucalon@bacbank.com; internet www.bacbank.com; Vice-Pres. RICARDO E. CUCALON U.

BANCAFE (Panamá), SA (Colombia): Avda Manuel María Icaza y Calle 52E, No 18, Apdo 384, Panamá 9A; tel. 264-6066; fax 263-6115; e-mail bancafe@bancafe-panama.com; internet www.bancafe-pa.com; f. 1966 as Banco Cafetero; name changed as above 1995; cap. 27.6m., dep. 299.5m. (Dec. 1994); Gen. Man. ALVARO NARANJO SALAZAR; 2 brs.

Banco Aliado, SA: Apdo 55-2109, Paitilla, Panamá; tel. 263-9777; fax 263-9677; e-mail bkaliado@panama.phoenix.net; internet bancoaliado.com; f. 1992; Gen. Man. ALEXIS A. ARJONA.

Banco Atlántico, SA: Apdo 6553, Panamá 5; tel. 263-5366; fax 269-1616; e-mail yisaza@iberban.com; internet www.batlantico.com.pa; f. 1975; Gen. Man. JAVIER GALLARDO VILAJUANA.

Banco Bilbao Vizcaya (Panama) SA (Spain): Apdo 8673, Panamá 5; tel. 227-1122; fax 227-3663; e-mail fperezp@bbvapanama.com; internet www.bbvapanama.com; f. 1982; cap. 10.0m., res 34.1m., dep. 355.4m. (Dec. 1997); Gen. Man. FÉLIX PÉREZ PARRA.

Banco de Bogotá, SA (Colombia): Centro Comercial Plaza Paitilla, Avda Balboa y Vía Italia, Apdo 8653, Panamá 5; tel. 264-6000; fax 263-8037; e-mail banbogo@sinfo.net; internet www.bancobogota-panama.com; f. 1967; cap. 17.7m., res 351.3m., total assets 394.8m. (Dec. 1999); merged with Banco del Comercio, SA (Colombia) in 1994; Gen. Man. FABIO RIAÑO.

Banco do Brasil, SA: Edif. Interseco, planta baja, Calle Elvira Méndez 10, Apdo 87-1123, Panamá 7; tel. 263-6566; fax 269-9867; e-mail bdbrasil@bbpanama.com; internet www.bancodobrasil.com.br; f. 1973; cap. and res 52.3m., dep. 1,248.1m., total assets 1,320.2m. (Dec. 1993); Gen. Man. LUIZ EDUARDO JACOBINA; 1 br.

Banco Internacional de Costa Rica, SA Apdo 600, Panamá 1; tel. 263-6822; fax 263-6393; e-mail bicsapty@pananet.com; internet www.bicsa.com; f. 1976; total assets 15,382m. (1999); Gen. Man. JOSÉ FRANCISCO ULATE.

Banco de Latinoamerica, SA (BANCOLAT): Apdo 4401, Panamá 5; tel. 210-7100; fax 263-7368; e-mail bancolat@bancolat.com; internet www.bancolat.com; f. 1982; total assets 11,060m. (1999); Gen. Man. RAFAEL ARIAS CHIARI.

Banco Latinoamericano de Exportaciones (BLADEX) (Multinational): Casa Matriz, Calles 50 y Aquilino de la Guardia, Apdo 6-1497, El Dorado, Panamá; tel. 210-8500; fax 269-6333; e-mail infobla@blx.com; internet www.blx.com; f. 1979; groups together 254 Latin American commercial and central banks, 22 international banks and some 3,000 New York Stock Exchange shareholders; cap. US $606.5m., dep. $1,706.0m., total assets $5,587.7m. (Dec. 1998); Exec. Pres. JOSÉ CASTAÑEDA VELEZ.

Banco Santander Central Hispano, SA: Apdo 1630, Panamá 1; tel. 206-6500; fax 206-6587; e-mail santander@info.net; formed by merger of Banco Santander (Panama) and Banco Central Hispano; Gen. Man. JUAN R. DE DIANOUS HENRÍQUEZ.

Banco Unión, SACA (Venezuela): Torre Hongkong Bank, 1°, Avda Samuel Lewis, Apdo 'A', Panamá 5; tel. 264-9133; fax 263-9985; e-mail bcounion@orbi.net; internet www.bancunion.com; f. 1974; cap. and res 15.6m., dep. 177.1m. (Dec. 1993); Gen. Man. MARÍA M. DE MÉNDEZ; 1 br.

Banco Uno, SA Apdo 3844, Panamá 7; tel. 206-5333; fax 223-5338; e-mail banexpo@sinfo.net; internet www.bepma.com; f. 1995; Gen. Man. JUAN ANTONIO NIÑO.

Bancolombia (Panama), SA: Apdo 8593, Panamá 5; tel. 263-6955; fax 269-1138; e-mail mdebetan.bicpma@mail.bic.com.co; internet www.bancolombia.com; f. 1973; Gen. Man. SANTIAGO EDUARDO VILLA CARDONA.

Bank of China: Apdo 87-1056, Panamá 7; tel. 263-5522; fax 223-9960; f. 1994; Gen. Man. QI REN HE.

Bank Leumi Le-Israel, BM (Israel): Edif. Grobman, planta baja, Calle Manuel María Icaza, Apdo 6-4518, El Dorado, Panamá; tel. 263-9377; fax 269-2674; Gen. Man. YAACOV OSMO.

Bank of Boston (USA): Edif. Banco de Boston, Vía España 122, Apdo 5368, Panamá 5; tel. 265-6077; fax 265-7400; e-maillnavarro@bkb.com; internet www.bkbpanama.com; f. 1973; fmrly The First National Bank of Boston; cap. and res 3.7m., dep. 80.6m., total assets 79.2m. (Dec. 1987); Gen. Man. LUIS A. NAVARRO LINARES; 2 brs.

Bank of Nova Scotia (Canada): Edif. P.H. Scotia Plaza, Avda Federico Boyd y Calle 51, Apdo 7327, Panamá 5; tel. 263-6255; fax 263-8636; e-mail scotiabk@sinfo.net; Gen. Man. TERENCE S. McCOY.

Bank of Tokyo-Mitsubishi Ltd (Japan): Vía España y Calle Aquilino de la Guardia, Apdo 1313, Panamá 1; tel. 263-6777; fax 263-5269; f. 1973; cap. and res 8.3m., dep. 1,574.0m., total assets 1,615.8m. (Mar. 1998); Gen. Man. SHIGEYUKI ONISHI.

Banque Sudameris, SA (Multinational): Avda Balboa y Calle 41, Apdo 1847, Panamá 9A; tel. 227-2777; fax 227-5828; e-mail banque.sudameris@sudameris.com.pa; internet www.sudameris.com.pa; Gen. Man. JULIO A. CORTÉS; 2 brs.

BNP Paribas (Panama), SA: Apdo 1774, Panamá 1; tel. 263-6600; fax 263-6970; e-mail bnpfil@sinfo.net; f. 1948; Gen. Man. CHRISTIAN GIRAUDON.

Citibank NA (USA): Vía España 124, Apdo 555, Panamá 9A; tel. 210-5900; fax 210-5901; internet www.citibank.com.pa; f. 1904; cap. and res 8.0m., dep. 236.0m., total assets 259.8m. (Dec. 1988); Gen. Man. FRANCISCO CONTO; 10 brs.

Credicorp Bank, SA Apdo 833-0125, Panamá; tel. 210-1111; fax 210-0069; e-mail sistemas@plazapan.com; internet www.credicorpbank.com; f. 1993; Gen. Man. CARLOS GUEVARA.

Dai Ichi Kangyo Bank, SA (Japan): Edif. Plaza Internacional, Vía España, Apdo 2637, Panamá 9A; tel. 269-6111; fax 269-6815; f. 1979; cap. and res 2.0m., dep. 216.1m., total assets 218.4m. (Sept. 1991); Gen. Man. GAKUO FUKUTOMI.

Dresdner Bank (Germany): Torre Banco Germánico, Calles 50 y 55E, Apdo 5400, Panamá 5; tel. 206-8100; fax 206-8109; e-mail panama@dbla.com; internet www.dbla.com; f. 1971; affiliated to Dresdner Bank AG; cap. 5.0m., dep. 1,131.4m., total assets 1,186.1m. (Dec. 1992); Gen. Man. KLAUS MÜLLER.

GNB Bank (Panama), SA: Apdo 4213, Panamá 5; tel. 215-7550; fax 215-7560; e-mail cveraste@sinfo.net; f. 1964; Gen. Man. CAMILO VERASTEGUI CARVAJAL.

HSBC Bank plc (United Kingdom): Apdo 9A-76, Panamá 9A; tel. 263-5855; fax 263-6009; e-mail hsbcpnm@sinfo.net; internet www.hsbcpnm.com; dep. 477m. (1999); in 2000 it acquired the 11 branch operations of the Chase Manhattan Bank, with assets of US $752m.; Gen. Man. JOSEPH L. SALTERIO; 3 brs.

International Commerical Bank of China (Taiwan): Calles 50 y 56E, Apdo 4453, Panamá 5; tel. 263-8565; fax 263-8392; Gen. Man. SHOW-LOONG HWANG.

Korea Exchange Bank (Republic of Korea): Torre Global Bank, Calle 50, Apdo 8358, Panamá 7; tel. 269-9966; fax 264-4224; Gen. Man. KWANG-SUCK KOH.

Lloyds TSB Bank Plc (United Kingdom): Calles Aquilino de la Guardia y 48, Apdo 8522, Panamá 5; tel. 263-6277; fax 264-7931; e-mail lloydspa@sinfo.net; Gen. Man. STEPHEN R. ROBINSON; 3 brs.

Metrobank, SA: Apdo B, Panamá 5; tel. 223-1666; fax 223-2020; f. 1991; Gen. Man. ALBERTO JOSÉ PAREDES.

Principal Foreign Banks with International Licence

Atlantic Security Bank: Apdo 6-8934, El Dorado, Panamá; tel. 215-7311; fax 215-7323; internet www.credicorpnet.com; f. 1984; Gen. Man. JORG PONCE S.

Austrobank Overseas (Panama), SA: Apdo 6-3197, El Dorado, Panamá; tel. 223-5105; fax 264-6918; f. 1995; Gen. Man. NODIER I. ARAÚZ PERIGAULT.

Banco Agricola Comercial de El Salvador, SA: Apdo 6-2637, ElDorado, Panamá; tel. 263-5863; fax 263-5626; e-mail bacsalv@pan.gbm.net; internet www2.gbm.net/bancoagricola; f. 1995; Gen. Man. José Alfonso Espinoza.

Banco Alemán Platina, SA: Edif. BAP, Avdas Federico Boyd y 4A, A Sur, Apdo 6-3197, Panamá 5; tel. 223-8005; fax 269-0910; e-mail baplatina@balppa.com; f. 1965; as Banco Alemán-Panameño, current name adopted in 1993; cap. US $12.0m., res $10.3m., dep. $214.7m. (Aug. 1997); Gen. Man. Ralf Fischer.

Banco de Crédito (Panama), SA: Apdo 0832-1700, Panamá; tel. 214-9613; fax 214-9715; internet www.bancredito.com; f. 1998; Gen. Man. Carlos Humberto Rojas Martínez.

Banco de la Nación Argentina: Avda Federico Boyd y Calle 51, Apdo 6-3298, El Dorado, Panamá; tel. 269-4666; fax 269-6719; e-mail bna@panama.phoenix.net; internet www.bna.com.ar; f. 1977; cap. and res 183.1m., dep. 1,015.2m. (Dec. 1984); total assets 3,314.7m. (Dec. 1985); Gen. Man. Luis Alejandro Ubalde.

Banco de Occidente (Panama), SA Apdo 6-7430, El Dorado, Panamá; tel. 263-8144; fax 269-3261; e-mail boccipan@pty.com; f. 1982; Gen. Man. Oscar Luna G.

Banco del Pacífico (Panama), SA: Apdo 6-3100, El Dorado, Panamá; tel. 263-5833; fax 269-2640; e-mail bpacificopanama@pacifico.fin.ec; f. 1980; Gen. Man. José Chung.

Banco de la Provincia de Buenos Aires (Argentina): Torre Banco Continental, 26°, Calle 50, Apdo 6-4592, El Dorado, Panamá; tel. 215-7703; fax 215-7718; e-mail bpbapma@pananet.com; internet www.bapro.com; f. 1982; total assets 15,000m. (Dec. 2000); Gen. Man. Juan Carlos Sturlesi.

Bancredito (Panama), SA: Apdo 6-6010, El Dorado, Panamá; tel. 223-2977; fax 264-6781; e-mail bancred@sinfo.net; f. 1987; Vice-Pres. Raisa Gil De Fondeur.

Banesco Internacional (Panama), SA: Apdo 8384, Panamá 7; tel. 269-3301; fax 269-3302; e-mail banesco@info.net; f. 1993; Gen. Man. Rafael Amar G.

BNP Paribas: Apdo 201, Panamá; tel. 264-8555; fax 263-6970; e-mail bnpsuc@sinfo.net; f. 1972; Gen. Man. Christian Giruadon.

Commerce Overseas Bank, SA: Apdo 6A-2414, El Dorado, Panamá; tel. 269-9565; fax 269-9563; e-mail kbarrios@bancomer.fi.cr; f. 1994; Gen. Man. Humberto Arcia W.

Filanbanco Trust Banking, Corp.: Apdo 87-3940, Panamá 7; tel. 269-4080; fax 269-9141; f. 1994; Gen. Man. Olga Arosemena de Guizado.

Interbank Overseas Ltd: Apdo 87-0553, Panamá 7; tel. 265-7300; fax 223-3333; e-mail rinigo@pan.gbm.net; f. 1997; Gen. Man. Raúl Iñigo Tizón.

Popular Bank and Trust Ltd: Apdo 5404, Panamá 5; tel. 269-4166; fax 269-1309; e-mail gversari@mail.pananet.com; f. 1983; Gen. Man. Gianni Versari.

Societé Générale: Apdo 6-3689, El Dorado, Panamá; tel. 264-9611; fax 264-0295; e-mail panama.branch@pa.socgen.com; f. 1981; Gen. Man. Celestin Cuq.

UBS (Panama), SA: Apdo 61, Panamá 9A; tel. 206-7100; fax 206-7100; internet www.ubs.com/panama; f. 1971; Gen. Man. Fritz Christen.

Banking Association

Asociación Bancaria de Panamá (ABP): Torre Hong Kong Bank, 15°, Avda Samuel Lewis, Apdo 4554, Panamá 5; tel. 263-7044; fax 223-5800; e-mail abp@orbi.net; internet www.asociacionbancaria.com; f. 1962; 79 mems; Pres. Luis A. Navarro L.; Exec. Vice-President Mario de Diego, Jr.

STOCK EXCHANGE

Bolsa de Valores de Panamá: Edif. Vallarino, planta baja, Calles Elvira Méndez y 52, Apdo 87-0878, Panamá; tel. 269-1966; fax 269-2457; e-mail bvp@pty.com; f. 1960; Gen. Man. Roberto Branes P.

INSURANCE

Aseguradora Mundial, SA: Edif. Aseguradora Mundial, Avda Balboa y Calle 41, Apdo 8911, Panamá 5; tel. 227-4444; fax 225-8176; general; f. 1937; Man. Orlando Sánchez Avilés.

ASSA Cía de Seguros, SA: Edif. ASSA, Avda Nicanor de Obarrio (Calle 50), Apdo 5371, Panamá 5; tel. 269-0443; fax 263-9623; f. 1973; Pres. Lorenzo Romagosa; Gen. Man. Carlos A. Rabat Mallol.

Cía Internacional de Seguros, SA: Avda Cuba y Calles 35 y 36, Apdo 1036, Panamá 1; tel. 227-4000; f. 1910; Pres. Richard A. Ford; Gen. Man. Manuel A. Eskildsen.

Cía Nacional de Seguros, SA: Calles 47 y Aquilino de la Guardia, Plaza Marbella, Apdo 5303, Panamá 5; tel. 263-8222; fax 269-6568; f. 1957; Pres. Gabriel J. de la Guardia; Gen. Man. Raúl Novey.

Cía de Seguros Chagres, SA: Edif. Chagres, Avda 4a Sur No 62, Apdo 6-1599, El Dorado, Panamá; tel. 263-7433; fax 263-9106; Man. Raúl Novey.

La Seguridad de Panamá, Cía de Seguros SA: Edif. American International, Calle 50 esq. Aquilino de la Guardia, Apdo 5306, Panamá 5; tel. 263-6700; Man. Courtney Stempel.

LARSA Latin American Reinsurance Co Inc.: Apdo 810, Panamá 1; tel. 263-5866; fax 263-5713; Pres. Laurencio Jaén O.

Trade and Industry

Colón Free Zone (CFZ): Avda Roosevelt, Apdo 1118, Colón; tel. 445-1033; fax 445-2165; f. 1948 to manufacture, import, handle and re-export all types of merchandise; some 1,780 companies were established by mid-1999. Well-known international banks operate in the CFZ, where there are also customs, postal and telegraph services. In 1998 the value of imports was an estimated US $5,319m. Re-exports amounted to an estimated $5,969m. The main exporters to the CFZ are Japan, the USA, Hong Kong, Taiwan, the Republic of Korea, Colombia, France, Italy and the United Kingdom. The main importers from the CFZ are Brazil, Venezuela, Mexico, Ecuador, the Netherlands Dependencies, Bolivia, the USA, Chile, Argentina and Colombia. In view of the rapid expansion in turnover of the CFZ in recent years, the total area of 138.2 ha was to be extended to 485.3 ha. Gen. Man. Ricardo Alemán.

GOVERNMENT AGENCIES

Consejo Nacional de Inversiones (CNI): Edif. Banco Nacional de Panamá, Apdo 2350, Panamá; tel. 264-7211; f. 1982; national investment council; promotes private local and foreign investments; Exec. Dir Lic. Julio E. Sosa.

Corporación Financiera Nacional—COFINA: Apdo 6-2191, Estafeta El Dorado, Panamá; f. 1976 to develop state and private undertakings in productive sectors; Dir-Gen. Winston Welch.

Instituto Panameño de Comercio Exterior (IPCE): Edif. Banco Exterior, Torre Chica, 3° y 4°, Apdo 55-2359, Paitilla, Panamá; tel. 225-7244; fax 225-2193; f. 1984; foreign trade and investment promotion organization; Dir Kenia Jaén Rivera.

CHAMBER OF COMMERCE

Cámara de Comercio, Industrias y Agricultura de Panamá: Avda Cuba y Ecuador 33A, Apdo 74, Panamá 1; tel. 227-1233; fax 227-4186; f. 1915; Pres. Juan José Vallarino A.; Exec. Dir Ing. José Ramón Varela; 1,300 mems.

INDUSTRIAL AND TRADE ASSOCIATIONS

Cámara Oficial Española de Comercio: Calle 33E, Apdo 1857, Panamá 1; tel. 225-1487; Pres. Edelmiro García Villa Verde; Sec.-Gen. Atiliano Alfonso Martínez.

Cámara Panameña de la Construcción: Calle Aquilino de la Guardia No 19, Apdo 6793, Panamá 5; tel. 265-2500; fax 265-2571; e-mail ryburilo@pty.com; represents interests of construction sector; Pres. Ing. José A. Sosa.

Codemín: Panamá; tel. 263-7475; state mining organization; Dir Jaime Roquebert.

Corporación Azucarera La Victoria: Calle II Juegos Centroamericanos, Apdo 1228, Panamá 1; tel. 233-3833; state sugar corpn; scheduled for transfer to private ownership; Dir Prof. Alejandro Vernaza.

Corporación para el Desarrollo Integral del Bayano: Avda Balboa, al lado de la estación del tren, Estafeta El Dorado, Panamá 2; tel. 232-6160; f. 1978; state agriculture, forestry and cattle-breeding corpn; Dir Ing. José María Chaverri.

Dirección General de Industrias: Edif. de la Lotería, 19°, Apdo 9658, Panamá 4; tel. 227-4403; govt body which undertakes feasibility studies, analyses and promotion; Dir-Gen. Lucía de Ferguson; National Dir of Business Development Ulpiano Prado.

Sindicato de Industriales de Panamá: Vía Ricardo J. Alfaro, Entrada Urb. Sara Sotillo, Apdo 6-4798, Estafeta El Dorado, Panamá; tel. 230-0169; fax 230-0805; e-mail sip@sinfo.net; f. 1945; represents and promotes activities of industrial sector; Pres. Antonio Miro E.

EMPLOYERS' ORGANIZATIONS

Asociación Panameña de Ejecutivos de Empresas (APEDE): Edif. APEDE, Calle 42, Bella Vista y Avda Balboa, Apdo 1331, Panamá 1; tel. 227-3511; fax 227-1872; e-mail apede@sinfo.net; Pres. Irving H. Bennett N.

Consejo Nacional de la Empresa Privada (CONEP): Calle 41, Bella Vista, Apdo 1276, Panamá 1; tel. 225-5306; fax 225-2663; Pres. Darío Selles.

Consejo Nacional para el Desarrollo de la Pequeña Empresa: Ministry of Commerce and Industry, Apdo 9658, Panamá 4; tel.

227-3559; fax 225-1201; f. 1983; advisory and consultative board to the Ministry of Commerce and Industry.

MAJOR COMPANIES
Beverages and Tobacco

Cervecería Nacional, SA: Carrera Transísmica y Vía Ricardo J. Alfaro, Panamá 1; tel. 236-1400; fax 236-1527; internet www .cerveceria-nacional.com; f. 1909; brewing; Pres. ROBERTO R. ALÉMAN; 400 employees.

Compañía Embotelladora Coca Cola de Panamá, SA: Parque Industrial San Cristóbal, Calle Santa Rosa, Panamá 9A; tel. 260-7000; fax 260-3504; f. 1913; bottlers of soft drinks; Pres. JOAQUÍN J. VALLARINO; 500 employees.

Tabacalera Nacional, SA: La Rinconada, Vía Tocumén, Apdo 5976, Panamá 1; tel. 220-7077; fax 220-3877; f. 1955; manufacture of cigarettes; Pres. CARLOS ELETA ALMARÁN; 200 employees.

Varela Hermanos, SA: Calle 85, Urb. Industrial Los Angeles entre Coagro y Fósforos El Gallo, Panamá; tel. 217-3111; fax 217-3627; f. 1950; distillation and bottling of liquors; Pres. JUAN ANTONIO VARELA C.; 300 employees.

Food Products

Compañía Azucarera La Estrella, SA: La Locería y Nata, Calle Arturo del Valle, Apdo 8404, Panamá 7; tel. 236-2577; fax 236-1308; f. 1949; sugar mill and refinery; Chair. ERIC A. DELVALLE; 2,390 employees.

Compañía Panameña de Alimentos, SA: Avda 5a, 5-05, Panamá 9A; manufacturers and processors of food products; canning factory; Pres. ROBERTO R. ALÉMAN; 700 employees.

Industrias Lácteas, SA: Vía Simón Bolívar, Apdo 4362, Panamá 5; tel. 229-1122; fax 261-6883; f. 1956; dairy products; Pres. RICARDO CHIARI; 780 employees.

Nestlé Panamá, SA and Kraft Foods, SA: Calle 69O 74D, Urb. La Loma, Panamá 9A; tel. 229-1333; fax 229-1982; f. 1937; subsidiary of Nestlé Co SA (Switzerland); manufacture and wholesale of food products; Gen. Man. LUIS CARBARCOS GIL; 760 employees (Nestlé Panamá, SA).

Productos Alimenticios Pascual, SA: Avda José Agustín Arango, Apdo 8422, Panamá 7; tel. 217-2133; fax 233-2825; e-mail pashnos@ sinfo.net; f. 1946; food and food processing; Pres. VICENTE ESTEVEZ PASCUAL; Gen. Man. JUAN ALBERTO PASCUAL; 448 employees.

Paper and Paper Products

Compañía Atlas, SA: Edif. 40, Calle 16½, Apdo 6-1092, El Dorado, Panamá; tel. 445-2787; fax 441-4610; holding co with interests in the wholesale manufacture, import and distribution of stationery; Gen. Man. ROBERTO C. HENRÍQUEZ; 110 employees.

L. Rodríguez y Cía, SA: Calle 36E y Final Avda México, POB 1170, Zona 1, Panamá; Urb. Industrial Tocumen, Calle Las Mañanitas, Panamá; printers and manufacturers of cardboard boxes; Pres. LEOPOLDO F. RODRÍGUEZ; 46 employees.

Textile Manufactures

Dayan Hermanos, SA: Vía Fernández de Córdoba, Panamá 5; tel. 229-3730; fax 261-7776; f. 1956; manufacture and distribution of clothing; Pres. RAYMOND DAYAN; 500 employees.

Fábrica de Colchones Simons, SA: Urb. Industrial, Calle El Gorrión, Panamá 5; manufacturers of mattresses, bed linen; Pres. IDELFONSO RIANDE PEÑA; 103 employees.

Tejidos y Confecciones, SA: Edif. Durex Carrasquilla, Calle 2a, Panamá; Apdo X, Panamá 9A; tel. 263-8888; fax 264-5022; e-mail teyco@teyco.com; internet www.teyco.com; f. 1963; manufacturers of men's and children's clothing; Pres. MAYER ATTIE CHAYO; Dir RAMY ATTIE; 500 employees.

Miscellaneous

Cemento Panamá: Edif. Cemento Panamá, Avda Manuel Batista, Apdo 1755, Panamá 1; tel. 229-2555; fax 229-3151; f. 1943; manufacturers of portland cement; Pres. ROY ICAZA; Gen. Man. JOSÉ A. MOSCOSO; 280 employees.

Constructora Frantoni, SA: Edif. Cipeles, Vía Ricardo J. Alfaro, Panamá; construction contractors; Pres. TOMÁS GUERRA CEDENO; 88 employees.

Durex, SA: Edif. Durex Carrasquilla, Calle 2a, Panamá; tel. 263-8888; fax 264-5022; rubber and plastics manufacturers.

Lindo y Maduro, SA: Apdo 5300, Panamá 5; tel. 227-0100; fax 227-2935; e-mail prllm@sinfo.net; manufacturers and distributors of non-durable goods and perfumery; Pres. RALPH J. LINDO; 60 employees.

Melo y Cía, SA: Vía España, Río Abajo 2313, Panamá; tel. 221-0033; fax 224-8972; vendors of veterinary, agricultural and agrochemical products, building materials and household goods; Pres. ARTURO DONALDO MELO S.; Gen. Man. FEDERICO MELO K.; 400 employees.

Petroterminal de Panamá, SA: Edif. Scotia Plaza, 1°, Calle 51 y Federico Boyd, Panamá; tel. 263-7777; fax 263-9949; f. 1977; petroleum and gas field services and petroleum storage facilities; Dir Gen. LUIS ROQUEFORT; 80 employees.

Syntex Corporation: Edif. Bank of America, 9°, Calle 50, Panamá; tel. 263-5255; fax 441-4568; f. 1944; wholesale import and distribution of pharmaceuticals; Man. PAUL FREIMAN; 32 employees.

Tractomovil, SA: Vía Ricardo J. Alfaro, Panamá; manufacturers of farm machinery and equipment; Pres. SIMÓN BOLÍVAR ALEMÁN; 75 employees.

UTILITIES
Electricity

Instituto de Recursos Hidráulicos y Electrificación (IRHE): Edif. Poli, Avda Justo Arosemena y 26E, Apdo 5285, Panamá 5; tel. 262-6272; state organization responsible for the national public electricity supply; partial divestment of generation and distribution operations completed Dec. 1998; transmission operations remain under complete state control; Dir-Gen. Dr FERNANDO ARAMBURÚ PORRAS.

Water

Instituto de Acueductos y Alcantarillados Nacionales— IDAAN (National Waterworks and Sewage Systems Institute): Panamá; Dir-Gen. ELIDA DÍ.

TRADE UNIONS

In 1981 the Labour Code which had been promulgated in 1977 was amended, establishing the right to strike and increasing compensation for dismissal. Collective bargaining is permitted and employers must pay workers' salaries during the whole period of a legal strike.

Central Istmeña de Trabajadores—CIT (Isthmian Labour Confederation): Vía España 16, Of. 1, Apdo 6308, Panamá 5; tel. 264-0509; f. 1971; Sec.-Gen. JULIO CÉSAR PINZÓN.

Confederación de Trabajadores de la República de Panamá— CTRP (Confederation of Workers of the Republic of Panama): Calle 31 entre Avdas México y Justo Arosemena 3-50, Apdo 8929, Panamá 5; tel. 225-0293; fax 225-0259; f. 1956; admitted to ICFTU/ORIT; Sec.-Gen. ANIANO PINZÓN REAL; 62,000 mems from 13 affiliated groups.

Consejo Nacional de Trabajadores Organizados—CONATO (National Council of Organized Labour): Ancón 777, 2°, Panamá; tel. 228-0224; e-mail conato@sinfo.net; 150,000 mems.

Federación Nacional de Asociaciones de Empleados Públicos—FENASEP (National Federation of Associations of Public Employees): Panamá; Pres. HÉCTOR ALEMÁN.

A number of unions exist without affiliation to a national centre.

Transport
RAILWAYS

In 1998 there were an estimated 485 km of track in Panama. In 2000 a US $75m. project to modernize the line between the ports at either end of the Panama Canal began. It was to be completed by 2001. In July 2001 the 83-km trans-isthmian railway, originally founded in 1855, reopened.

Chiriquí Land Co: Apdo 87-1733, Estafeta El Dorado, Panamá; tel. 770-7243; fax 770-8064; operates two lines: the Northern Line (Almirante–Guabito in Bocas del Toro Province) and the Southern Line (Puerto Armuelles–David in Chiriquí Province); purchased by the Govt in 1978; Gen. Man. FRED JOHNSON.

Ferrocarril Nacional de Chiriquí: Apdo 12B, David City, Chiriquí; tel. 775-4241; fax 775-4105; 126 km linking Puerto Armuelles and David; Gen. Man. M. ALVARENGA.

Ferrocarril de Panamá: Apdo 2023, Estafeta de Balboa, Panamá; tel. 232-6000; fax 232-5343; govt-owned; 83 km linking Panama City and Colón, running parallel to Panama Canal; operation on concession by Kansas City Southern (USA); modernization programme completed in 2001; operates daily passenger and cargo service; Dir-Gen. VÍCTOR MANUEL DANELO.

ROADS

In 1998 there were an estimated 11,400 km of roads, of which some 3,910 km were paved. The two most important highways are the Pan-American Highway and the Boyd-Roosevelt or Trans-Isthmian, linking Panama City and Colón. The Pan-American Highway to Mexico City runs for 545 km in Panama was being extended towards Colombia. There is a highway to San José, Costa Rica.

SHIPPING

The Panama Canal opened in 1914. In 1984 more than 4% of all the world's seaborne trade passed through the waterway. It is 82 km long, and ships take an average of eight hours to complete a transit. In 2000 some 13,653 transits were recorded. The Canal can accommodate ships with a maximum draught of 12 m and beams of up to approximately 32.3 m (106 ft) and lengths of up to about 290 m (950 ft), roughly equivalent to ships with a maximum capacity of 65,000–70,000 dwt. In early 2000 a five-year modernization project was begun. The project included: a general improvement of facilities; the implementation of a satellite traffic-management system; the construction of a bridge; and the widening of the narrowest section of the Canal, the Culebra Cut (to be completed by October 2001). Plans were also announced to construct a 203 ha international cargo-handing platform at the Atlantic end of the Canal, including terminals, a railway and an international airport. Terminal ports are Balboa, on the Pacific Ocean, and Cristóbal, on the Caribbean Sea.

Autoridad del Canal de Panamá (ACP): Balboa Heights, Panamá; tel. 272-3202; fax 272-2122; e-mail info@pancanal.com; internet www.pancanal.com; in October 1979 the Panama Canal Commission, a US Govt agency, was established to perform the mission, previously accomplished by the Panama Canal Co, of managing, operating and maintaining the Panama Canal. The Autoridad del Canal de Panamá (ACP) was founded in 1997 and succeeded the Panama Canal Commission on 31 December 1999, when the waterway was ceded to the Govt of Panama. The ACP is the autonomous agency of the Govt of Panama; there is a Board of 11 mems; Chair Ricardo Martinelli; Administrator Alberto Alemán Zubieta; Deputy Administrator Ricaurte Vásquez.

Autoridad Marítima de Panamá: Edif. 5534, Antigua escuela de Diablo, Ancón, Apdo 8062, Panama 7; tel. 232-5528; fax 232-5527; e-mail autoport@sinfo.net; f. 1998 to unite and optimize the function of all state institutions with involvement in maritime sector; Admin. Jerry Salazar.

Autoridad de la Región Interoceánica (ARI): Panamá; tel. 228-5668; fax 228-7488; e-mail ari@sinfo.net; f. 1993; govt body created to administer the land and property of the former Canal Zone following their transfer from US to Panamanian control, after 1999; legislation approved in early 1995 transferred control of the ARI to the President of the Republic; Pres. Alfredo Arias.

Panama City Port Authority and Foreign Trade Zone 65: Apdo 15095, Panamá; FL 32406, USA; Dir Rudy Etheredge.

There are deep-water ports at Balboa and Cristóbal (including general cargo ships, containers, shipyards, industrial facilities); Coco Solo (general cargo and containers); Bahía Las Minas (general bulk and containers); Vacamonte (main port for fishing industry); Puerto Armuelles and Almirante (bananas); Aguadulce and Pedregal (export of crude sugar and molasses, transport of fertilizers and chemical products); and Charco Azul and Chiriquí Grande (crude oil).

The Panamanian merchant fleet was the second largest (after Japan) in the world in December 1998, numbering 6,143 vessels with an aggregate displacement of 98.2m. gross registered tons. It was estimated to be the largest fleet in 2000. In November 2000 construction was completed on the largest container terminal in Latin America, in Balboa.

CIVIL AVIATION

Tocumen (formerly Omar Torrijos) International Airport situated 19 km (12 miles) outside Panamá (Panama City), is the country's principal airport and is served by many international airlines. The France Airport in Colón and the Rio Hato Airport in Coclé province have both been declared international airports. There are also 11 smaller airports in the country.

Aerolíneas Pacífico Atlántico, SA (Aeroperlas): Apdo 6-3596, El Dorado, Panamá; tel. 315-7500; fax 315-0331; e-mail apfly@aeroperlas.com; internet www.aeroperlas.com; operates scheduled regional and domestic flights; in 2000 initiated international flights; fmrly state-owned, transferred to private ownership in 1987; Pres. George F. Novey; Gen. Man. Eduardo Stagg.

Compañía Panameña de Aviación, SA (COPA): Avda Justo Arosemena 230 y Calle 39, Apdo 1572, Panamá 1; tel. 227-2522; fax 227-1952; e-mail proquebert@mail.copa.com.pa; internet www.copaair.com; f. 1947; scheduled passenger and cargo services from Panamá (Panama City) to Central America, South America, the Caribbean and the USA; Chair. Alberto Motta; Exec. Pres. Pedro O. Heilbron.

Dirección de Aeronaútica Civil: Apdo 7615, Panamá 7; tel. 226-1622; directorate for civil aviation; Dir-Gen. Jaime Ignacio.

Panama Air International, SA: Avda Justo Arosemena y Calle 34, Panamá 5; tel. 227-2371; fax 227-2281; f. 1967; fmrly state-owned (as Air Panama International), transferred to private ownership in Dec. 1991; services from Panamá (Panama City) to destinations throughout the Americas; Pres. Joaquín J. Vallarino.

Trans Canal Airways: Suite 4, B-18 Calle A, Apdo 7528, Panamá 5; tel. 223-7676; fax 263-6743; f. 1991; domestic flights and scheduled passenger and cargo services to Miami (USA); Chair. Franz R. Manfredi; Man. Dir Carlos DePuy.

Tourism

Panama's attractions include Panamá (Panama City), the ruins of Portobelo and 800 sandy tropical islands, including the resort of Contadora, one of the Pearl Islands in the Gulf of Panama, and the San Blas Islands, lying off the Atlantic coast. The number of foreign visitors to Panama declined from 370,369 in 1982 to 200,436 in 1989, partly as a result of internal and regional instability. By 1998 the number of visitors had increased to 422,228. Income from tourism was some US $379m. in 1998. In 2000 there were some 5,700 hotel rooms in Panama. In 2000 hotel and recreation projects to the value of $600m. were under way in Panama; these included plans for a cruise-ship terminal at either end of the Canal.

Instituto Panameño de Turismo (IPAT): Centro de Convenciones ATLAPA, Vía Israel, Apdo 4421, Panamá 5; tel. 226-7000; fax 226-3483; f. 1960; Dir-Gen. César Tribaldos.

Asociación Panameña de Agencias de Viajes y Turismo (APAVIT): Apdo 55-1000 Paitilla, Panamá 3; tel. 269-9584; fax 264-0309; Pres. Michelle de Guizado.

Defence

In 1990, following the overthrow of Gen. Manuel Antonio Noriega Morena, the National Defence Forces were disbanded and a new Public Force (numbering an estimated 11,800 men at 1 August 2000), comprising the National Police (11,000 men), the National Air Service (an estimated 400 men) and the National Maritime Service (an estimated 400 men), was created. The new force was representative of the size of the population and affiliated to no political party.

Security Expenditure: In 2000 the security budget was an estimated US $135m.

Commander-in-Chief of Public Forces: Col Eduardo Herrera Hassán.

Air Force Commander: Maj. Augusto Villalaz.

Education

The education system in Panama is divided into elementary, secondary and university schooling, each of six years' duration. Education is free up to university level and is officially compulsory between six and 15 years of age. Primary education begins at the age of six and secondary education, which comprises two three-year cycles, at the age of 12. In 1997 the enrolment at primary schools was 89.9% of children in the relevant age group (males 89.6%; females 90.2%), while secondary enrolment was 71.3% of children in the relevant age group (males 70.9%; females 71.7%). There are three universities, with regional centres in the provinces. Adult illiteracy in 1998 was an estimated 8.6% (males 7.9%; females 9.2%). Of total budgetary expenditure by the central Government in 1999, 405.0m. balboas (16.5%) was allocated to education.

Bibliography

For works on Central America generally, see Select Bibliography (Books).

Dinges, J. *Our Man in Panama: How General Noriega Fooled the United States and Made Millions in Drugs and Arms.* New York, NY, Random House, 1990.

Dudley Gold, S. *The Panama Canal Transfer: Controversy at the Crossroads.* Austin, TX, Raintree/Steck Vaughn, 1999.

Farnsworth, D. N., and McKenney, J. W. *US–Panama Relations, 1903–1978: A Study in Linkage Politics.* Boulder, CO, Westview Press, 1983.

Guevara Mann, C. *Panamanian Militarism: A Historical Interpretation.* Athens, OH, Ohio University Press, 1996.

Habeeb, W. M., and Artman, I. W. *The Panama Canal Negotiations*, FBI Case Studies, No. 1. Washington, DC, Foreign Policy Institute (Johns Hopkins University), 1986.

Harding II, R. C. *Military Foundations of Panamanian Politics.* Piscataway, NJ, Transaction Publishers, 2001.

Johns, C. J., and Ward Johnson, P. *State Crime, the Media and the Invasion of Panama.* London, Praeger Publrs, 1994.

Kempe, F. *Divorcing the Dictator: America's Bungled Affair with Noriega.* New York, NY, G. P. Putnam's Sons, 1990.

Major, J. *Prize Possession: The United States and the Panama Canal, 1903–1979.* Cambridge, Cambridge University Press, 1993.

McCullough, D. *Path Between the Seas: Creation of the Panama Canal, 1870–1914.* New York, NY, Simon and Schuster, 1999.

Pearcy, T. L. *We Answer Only to God: Politics and the Military in Panama, 1903–1947.* Albuquerque, NM, University of New Mexico Press, 1998.

Perez, O. J. (Ed.). *Post-Invasion Panama.* Lexington, MA, Lexington Books, 2000.

Venero, A. P. *Before the Five Frontiers: Panama from 1821–1903.* New York, NY, AMS Press, 1980.

Wali, A. *Kilowatts and Crisis: A Study of Development and Social Change in Panama.* Boulder, CO, Westview Press, 1986.

Weeks, J. *Panama: Made in the USA.* London, Latin American Bureau, 1990.

PARAGUAY

Area: 406,752 sq km (157,048 sq miles).

Population (official estimate at mid-2000): 5,496,450.

Capital: Asunción, estimated population, 1997: 550,060.

Language: Spanish (official); but the majority of the population speak Guaraní, a local Indian language.

Religion: Mainly Christianity (85% Roman Catholic).

Climate: Subtropical; but hot between January and March; rainy season between October and April.

Time: GMT –4 hours.

Public Holidays

2002: 1 January (New Year's Day), 3 February (San Blás, Patron Saint of Paraguay), 1 March (Heroes' Day), 28 March (Maundy Thursday), 29 March (Good Friday), 1 May (Labour Day), 9 May (Ascension Day), 14–15 May (Independence Day celebrations), 22 June (Corpus Christi), 12 June (Peace of Chaco), 15 August (Foundation of Asunción), 25 August (Constitution Day), 29 September (Battle of Boquerón), 12 October (Day of the Race, anniversary of the discovery of America), 1 November (All Saints' Day), 8 December (Immaculate Conception), 25 December (Christmas Day).

2003: 1 January (New Year's Day), 3 February (San Blás, Patron Saint of Paraguay), 1 March (Heroes' Day), 17 April (Maundy Thursday), 18 April (Good Friday), 1 May (Labour Day), 14–15 May (Independence Day celebrations), 29 May (Ascension Day), 12 June (Peace of Chaco), 19 June (Corpus Christi), 15 August (Foundation of Asunción), 25 August (Constitution Day), 29 September (Battle of Boquerón), 12 October (Day of the Race, anniversary of the discovery of America), 1 November (All Saints' Day), 8 December (Immaculate Conception), 25 December (Christmas Day).

Currency: Guaraní; 10,000 guaraníes = £1.838 = US $2.632 = €2.965 (30 April 2001).

Weights and Measures: The metric system is in force.

Basic Economic Indicators

	1998	1999	2000
Gross domestic product ('000 million guaraníes at 1982 prices)	1,125.0	1,130.4	1,125.8
GDP per head ('000 guaraníes at 1982 prices)	215.6	211.1	204.8
GDP ('000 million guaraníes at current prices)	23,436.9	24,144.3	26,114.0
GDP per head ('000 guaraníes at current prices)	4,409.7	4,507.9	4,751.1
Annual growth of real GDP (%)	–0.4	0.4	–0.4
Annual growth of real GDP per head (%)	–2.9	–2.1	–3.0
Government budget ('000 million guaraníes at current prices):			
Revenue	3,795.0	4,093.8	4,287.3
Expenditure	4,022.2	4,959.0	5,467.2
Consumer price index (base: 1995 = 100)	131.0	139.9	152.4
Rate of inflation (annual average, %)	11.5	6.8	8.9
Foreign exchange reserves (US $ million at 31 December)	732.9	845.9	630.4
Imports c.i.f. (US $ million)	2,470.8	1,725.1	n.a.
Exports f.o.b. (US $ million)	1,014.0	740.9	n.a.
Balance of payments (current account, US $ million)	–56.2	–63.6	n.a.

Gross national product per head measured at purchasing power parity (PPP) (US dollars, converted by the PPP exchange rate, 1999): 4,380.

Economically active population (1999): 2,195,931.

Unemployment (December 2000): 16%.

Total foreign debt (1999): US $2,897m.

Life expectancy (years at birth, estimates, 1995-2000): 69.6 (females 72.0, males 67.5).

Infant mortality rate (per 1,000 live births, 1999): 36.

Adult population with HIV/AIDS (15–49 years, 1999): 0.11%.

School enrolment ratio (6–17 years, 1996): 80%.

Adult literacy rate (15 years and over, 2000): 93.3% (males 94.4; females 92.2).

Energy consumption per head (kg of oil equivalent, 1998): 819

Carbon dioxide emissions per head (metric tons, 1997): 0.8.

Passenger motor cars in use (estimate, per 1,000 of population, 1996): 14.3.

Television receivers in use (per 1,000 of population, 1997): 101.

Personal computers in use (per 1,000 of population, 1999): 11.2.

History

Prof. PETER CALVERT

Paraguay was already well populated when the Spanish first arrived in 1524. In 1537 the Spanish founded Asunción. The city enjoyed a brief period of importance until the foundation of Buenos Aires, in what is now Argentina, in 1580, when the seat of regional government was moved to the new port city. In the absence of important resources that were of interest to the Spanish, Paraguay remained economically undeveloped throughout the colonial period, and was politically and economically dependent on Buenos Aires. The indigenous Indians (Amerindians) established good relations with the Spanish and many intermarried; however, they retained their own language, Guaraní.

Jesuit missionaries soon arrived in the country. Indians converted to Christianity were resettled in missions, each farming the surrounding land. They built churches and created a unique, theocratic society. In 1767 the Jesuits were expelled and, for the first time, the Indians were directly exposed to Spanish rule. In 1810 Buenos Aires declared self-government and on 14 May 1811 Paraguay became the first Spanish territory in the Americas to achieve independence.

The newly independent country was governed by Dr José Gaspar Rodríguez de Francia. De Francia, known as 'El Supremo', closed Paraguay's borders to the outside world, thus ensuring Paraguayan sovereignty (despite Argentine plans for annexation), proclaimed Guaraní the sole language and ruled alone until his death in 1840. His successor, Carlos Antonio López (President, 1842–62), reopened Paraguay's borders. No less a dictator than his predecessor, López encouraged trade, built Paraguay's first railway and abolished slavery. López's son, Francisco Solano López, succeeded him as President-for-life, and during his rule Paraguay was defeated in the War of the Triple Alliance (1865–70) by the combined forces of Argentina, Brazil and Uruguay. The War, which became known in Paraguay as the 'National Epic' (*Epopeya Nacional*), resulted in the loss of 90% of the country's male population and left the economy devastated. Marshal López himself perished and was buried on the battlefield of Cerro Cora.

International rivalry for control of a defeated Paraguay began with the emergence of national political parties; Anglo-Argentine capital supported the Liberal Party (Partido Liberal), while Brazilian interests supported the National Republican Association—Colorado Party (Asociación Nacional Republicana—Partido Colorado). The conservative Colorados remained in power between 1870 and 1904. The 1883 Law of Sale of Public Land enclosed land which had previously been accessible to all and turned it into vast private estates. Peasants were either forced to leave or to work for a pittance. In 1904 a revolution brought the Liberals to power, but achieved little else. The period from 1870 to 1940 was marked by a tumultuous series of coups and countercoups, as rival groups within each party vied for political control of the riches to be gained from widespread foreign ownership of the national territory.

Of the 45 Presidents who governed between 1870 and 1979, all achieved power by force or by fraud and most were ousted by violence or the threat of it. Factionalism, inability to compromise and the relative weakness of the parties in government made the Army the central institution in Paraguayan politics. Paraguay's historic need to defend its borders justified the role of the armed forces and led to one of the highest ratios in the world of military and police to population.

THE CHACO WAR AND ITS AFTERMATH

Paraguay gradually extended its control west of the River Paraguay, into the arid Chaco region. In response, Bolivia, which also claimed possession of the region, sent troops into the disputed territory. In the ensuing Chaco War (1932–35), Paraguay defeated Bolivia, and under the terms of a 1938 peace treaty, brokered by Argentina, was awarded three-quarters of the disputed territory.

Dissatisfaction with the Liberal war effort, however, led to the overthrow, by a military coup, of the Government of Eusebio Ayala in February 1936. The coup, led by Col Rafael Franco and supported by war veterans, brought to power the reformist Government of the February Revolution Party (Partido Revolucionario Febrerista—PRF). Although the Government did manage to seize and redistribute some land, its tenure was short-lived and the Febreristas, as Franco's followers soon became known, were overthrown in 1937 by army officers loyal to the Liberals.

Following a two-year interim presidency, Marshal José Félix Estigarribia (the Liberal leader in the Chaco War) became President. Estigarribia was a reformist nationalist, popular with both the military and peasants. Nevertheless, his restoration of political freedoms was met with generalized unrest, including strikes, attacks by the press and conspiracies by some military cliques, amongst which the Febrerista movement survived. Estigarribia therefore declared himself a temporary dictator, repressed opposition and announced a developmentalist land programme that included land expropriation. A new corporatist Constitution, which came into force in August 1940, strengthened executive powers and permitted the President to serve a second term. Estigarribia did not benefit from these constitutional changes, however, as both he and his wife were killed in an aeroplane crash only three weeks after the Constitution was approved.

Estigarribia's former Minister of War, Gen. Higinio Morínigo, assumed power following Estigarribia's death. Initially, Morínigo was regarded as a reasonably benevolent autocrat who faced the unenviable task of balancing opposing political forces to retain control of the nation. However, he soon assumed absolute powers, banning all political parties, repressing the activities of the trade-union movement and dissolving the legislature. Eminent Liberals were forced into exile and Febrerista uprisings were suppressed.

The Allied victory in the Second World War, however, gave rise to a military movement in 1946, which was directed against the Axis sympathizers behind Morínigo. Exiles were allowed to return and some conservative Colorados as well as young, developmentalist Febrerista officers were invited to join a Colorado–PRF coalition Government, under Morínigo's nominal control. From 1946 there was an increase in public unrest. Threatened by a growth in popular political activity and the emergence of a strong left-wing movement, Morínigo excluded the PRF from the Government and openly sided with the Colorados. An attempted coup late in 1946 was followed by the disintegration of the coalition Government in early 1947. Declaring a state of siege, Morínigo formed a new military cabinet; on the rebel side, Liberals and Communists joined Febrerista forces, led by Col Rafael Franco, in a civil war which broke out in March 1947 and which divided the armed forces, with some four-fifths of officers defecting to the rebel side. The Colorados triumphed over the combined rebel forces, partly owing to support from the Argentine Government of Gen. Juan Domingo Perón Sosa.

The defeat of the rebels gave the Colorados control of the Army and thus of the country. A number of coups followed, the first of which, in 1948, removed Morínigo from power. Presidential elections were held in the same year, but the only candidate was the Colorado, Juan Natalicio González. President González was supported by an all-Colorado legislature; Paraguay had become a one-party state. Although Morínigo went into exile, factional infighting continued. There were uprisings by Colorado officers against the González Government. Eventually González, too, fled abroad. Another Colorado faction, led by Dr Federico Chávez, assumed power.

In October 1951 President Chávez appointed Gen. Alfredo Stroessner Mattiauda, a veteran of the Chaco War, as Commander-in-Chief of the Armed Forces. Paraguay's economy began to deteriorate, however, and as inflation rose, so did political opposition. On 4 May 1954 Stroessner deposed Chávez in a military coup and in the July presidential elections Stroessner, a Colorado candidate, was elected unopposed to complete Chávez's term of office.

THE RULE OF GEN. STROESSNER

Gen. Stroessner immediately established a dictatorship, assuming extensive powers. Restrictions were placed on all political activities and the Febrerista and Liberal opposition groups were ruthlessly suppressed. In 1956 Stroessner forced his principal rival within the Colorado Party, Epifanio Méndez Fleitas, into exile. A state of siege was imposed. For over 30 years, until 1987, this state of siege was renewed every 60 days to comply with constitutional requirements. The unaccustomed sense of order which existed during Stroessner's dictatorship was advantageous to both domestic and foreign companies and his commitment to the International Monetary Fund (IMF) austerity measures contributed to the stabilization of the guaraní by 1957. In 1958 Stroessner, as the sole candidate of the only permitted party, was re-elected President and continued to be re-elected in this way every five years until 1988. Opposition continued, but it originated mostly from outside Paraguay; attacks from Argentina by exiles were repelled in 1959 and 1960.

Stroessner's command of the armed forces and of the economy contributed to the strength of his position. Increasing confidence in the economy in the 1960s led to the encouragement of some limited political activity. Stroessner encouraged the pretence of democracy by allowing a dissident wing of the Liberal Party, the Renovation (Renovación) wing, to participate in controlled legislative elections, in which it received one-third of the seats in the legislature. This did not in any way diminish the President's personal dominance of Paraguayan politics, since he controlled the ruling Colorado Party which held the remaining two-thirds of the parliament. In 1959 some 400 Colorado politicians who opposed Stroessner had been imprisoned or had fled into exile, where they formed the Colorado Popular Movement (Movimiento Popular Colorado—MOPOCO), under the leadership of Méndez Fleitas. The President then reorganized the purged Colorado Party in order to facilitate the entrenchment of an authoritarian style of government. By 1967 the Colorado Party constituted only members loyal to Stroessner. In that year the President changed the Constitution of 1940 to permit his legal re-election to a fourth term of office.

In the late 1960s the overtly autocratic nature of Stroessner's regime encouraged criticism from the Roman Catholic Church in Paraguay, which, in turn, resulted in popular unrest. However, the upturn in the economy experienced in the 1970s contained much of the opposition. The majority of opposition parties boycotted the presidential and legislative elections of February 1983, enabling Stroessner to obtain more than 90% of the votes cast in the presidential poll, and in August he formally took office for a seventh five-year term. In the mid-1980s the question of who would succeed Stroessner became increasingly important; his son was considered a likely candidate. In April 1987 the President announced that the state of siege was to be ended, since extraordinary security powers were no longer necessary to maintain peace. His decision to seek re-election in the February 1988 presidential elections, for an eighth consecutive term, precipitated the final crisis of Stroessner's regime. Although it was announced that he had received 88.6% of the votes cast, opposition leaders complained of electoral malpractice, and denounced his re-election as fraudulent. On 3 February 1989 Stroessner was overthrown in a coup, led by his son-in-law, Gen. Andrés Rodríguez, the second-in-command of the armed forces.

DEMOCRATIZATION

On 1 May 1989 Gen. Rodríguez was elected President, as the official candidate of the Colorado Party with 74.2% of the votes cast. The Colorado Party, having won 72.8% of the votes in the congressional elections, automatically took two-thirds of the seats in both the Chamber of Deputies (Cámara de Diputados) and the Senate (Senado—48 and 24 seats, respectively). How-

ever, the process of democratization continued. In Paraguay's first ever municipal elections, which took place on 26 May 1991, the Colorados gained only 43% of the votes cast in 154 of the 206 municipalities, compared with 29% gained by the opposition Authentic Radical Liberal Party (Partido Liberal Radical Auténtico—PLRA). The Government's neo-liberal austerity programme accelerated the formation of both new trade-union and peasant movements, which carried out a series of illegal land occupations. On 20 June 1992 a new Constitution was promulgated before the National Constituent Assembly, despite the absence of Rodríguez. The presidential boycott was the result of a dispute between Rodríguez and the Constituent Assembly concerning a 'transitory clause', introduced by the latter, that extended an eventual ban on the re-election of the President to include the current term of office.

Luis María Argaña Ferraro, leader of the conservative Movement of Colorado Reconciliation (Movimiento de Reconciliación Colorado—MRC) faction, was nominated in December 1992 as the Colorado Party candidate for the presidential elections due in August 1993. His nomination, however, was reversed following pressure from President Rodríguez and from the Commander of the First Corps, Gen. Lino César Oviedo Silva, who had political ambitions of his own. Argaña took refuge in Brazil, urging his supporters not to vote for his rival. On 9 May 1993, however, the new official candidate, Juan Carlos Wasmosy, a former business associate of President Rodríguez but a political novice, won the presidential election with 40% of the votes cast. International observers agreed that the elections were generally fair, despite the partisanship of Gen. Oviedo, and Wasmosy thus became the first civilian President of Paraguay for 39 years.

THE GOVERNMENT OF PRESIDENT WASMOSY

Wasmosy was inaugurated as President on 15 August 1993. There was widespread concern over the composition of Wasmosy's first Council of Ministers, many of whom had served in the administrations of Rodríguez and Stroessner. Despite the new President's apparent desire to restrict the influence of the military, the appointment on 18 August of Gen. Oviedo as Commander of the Army provoked further criticism. As a result, the PLRA refused to co-operate with the Colorados and there were violent demonstrations outside the Congress building. In September 1994 President Wasmosy carried out a reshuffle of the command of the armed forces, strengthening the position of Gen. Oviedo, but tensions remained high between the two men and, on 22 April 1996, the President finally requested that Oviedo resign. Oviedo had begun to campaign for the leadership of the Colorado Party and hoped to succeed Wasmosy as President in 1998. He refused to step down and, with the support of some 5,000 troops, in turn demanded the resignation of the President who sought asylum in the US Embassy. Strengthened by popular demonstrations in support of his position, and by the backing of other regional powers, on 24 April the President agreed to a compromise by which Oviedo would retire from active service in exchange for the offer of the post of defence minister.

Congress, however, refused to ratify Oviedo's appointment, which was withdrawn. The new Commander of the Army, Gen. Oscar Díaz Delmas, did not intervene and three days later Argaña was again elected President of the Colorado Party. A purge of senior military commanders followed. On 13 June 1996 Gen. Oviedo was arrested and detained on a charge of sedition, of which he was subsequently cleared by the Courts of Appeal on 7 August and freed. In September he narrowly defeated Argaña in the election to become the Colorado Party's presidential candidate. Following Oviedo's victory in the primary election the President attempted to exclude him from the presidential contest. In October an arrest order was issued against Oviedo on charges of making inflammatory public statements. Nevertheless, the general eluded capture until mid-December, when he surrendered.

In March 1998 the Special Military Tribunal convened by President Wasmosy found Gen. Oviedo guilty of rebellion and sentenced him to 10 years' imprisonment and dishonourable discharge. On 1 September a specially constituted Military Tribunal attempted to reverse the verdict, but its decision was ruled invalid by the Supreme Court, which had already confirmed the original decision on 17 April. On 18 April the Supreme Electoral Tribunal annulled Oviedo's presidential candidacy. The nomination of the Colorado Party was assumed by Raúl Cubas Grau, a wealthy engineer. Argaña was to be the new candidate for the vice-presidency. Despite public protests the elections were held as planned on 10 May 1998. Cubas Grau obtained 55.4% of the votes cast, ahead of the candidate of the Democratic Alliance (Alianza Democrática), Domingo Laíno, who received 43.9% of the votes.

DEMOCRATIZATION FALTERS

Cubas Grau assumed office on 15 August 1998 and a new Council of Ministers, including two pro-Oviedo generals, was sworn in on the same day. On 18 August the President issued a decree commuting Gen. Oviedo's prison sentence to time already served. The new Congress immediately voted to condemn the decree and to initiate proceedings to impeach the President for unconstitutional behaviour. On 2 December the Supreme Court ruled the decree unconstitutional. Three days later the Argaña faction-controlled central apparatus of the Colorados expelled Oviedo from the party. While the Congress was unable to muster the two-thirds' majority support necessary to impeach President Cubas Grau, the country remained in effective political deadlock, heightened by the fact that the economy had been in recession since 1997.

On 23 March 1999, however, the political impasse ended dramatically when Vice-President Argaña was assassinated in the capital, Asunción, by three men in military uniform (one of whom was later arrested, while a second died in a shoot-out with police). The 66 year-old Vice-President and his supporters had just succeeded in regaining control of the Colorado Party headquarters, from which they had been expelled on 14 March by supporters of Gen. Oviedo and President Cubas Grau, who were immediately accused by supporters of Argaña of being at least the 'moral instigators' of the assassination. Large crowds took to the streets to demand the President's resignation and the situation was further inflamed when six protesters, demonstrating outside the Congress building on 25 March, were killed, apparently by an official at the finance ministry, who was filmed firing at the crowds from a building near the Congress.

On 28 March, however, hours before Congress was due to vote on his impeachment, President Cubas Grau resigned and fled to Brazil, where he was granted political asylum. At the same time, Gen. Oviedo was granted asylum in Argentina. The President of the Congress, the pro-Argaña Colorado Party senator, Luis González Macchi, became head of state for the remainder of Cubas Grau's presidential term (scheduled to end in 2003). Hoping to overcome the disagreements existing within the Colorado Party and between the Government and opposition in the legislature, on 30 March he announced the composition of a multi-party Government of National Unity. On 12 July Gen. Oviedo was officially expelled from the Colorado Party. His arrest was ordered three days later but the Argentine authorities twice refused to extradite him and on 9 December he left Argentina to avoid being extradited by the new Government of Fernando de la Rúa.

Oviedo's supporters in the Army continued to present problems for President González Macchi's Government. Firstly, tensions between Argaña's son, Nelson Argaña, the Minister of National Defence, and Gen. Eligio Torres Heyn, the head of the Armed Forces, over the reorganization of the military high command, led to the latter's resignation. In May 1999 the new President forcibly retired more than 100 army officers, including

several high-ranking supporters of Oviedo. Nevertheless, in November the Government denied rumours that an attempted military coup had taken place even though 14 military officers were arrested. On 18 May 2000 rebellious soldiers thought to be sympathetic to Oviedo seized the First Cavalry Division barracks and other strategic points. The coup was swiftly suppressed by the Government, which declared a 30-day nationwide state of emergency, assuming extraordinary powers that resulted in the arrest of more than 70 people, mostly members of the security forces. However, on 11 June Oviedo himself was arrested in Foz do Iguaçu (Brazil) by the Brazilian authorities and was held in Brasília pending a Supreme Court ruling on extradition to Paraguay.

In April 1999 the Supreme Court ruled that elections for a new Vice-President would be held on 21 November 1999, but these were subsequently postponed. The PLRA withdrew from the government coalition in February 2000 when it became clear that, contrary to the national unity agreement, the Colorado Party would contest them. In April the Colorados nominated Félix Argaña, another son of the late Vice-President, to be their party's candidate. However, at the elections, which were finally held on 13 August, the 53-year Colorado monopoly on power was ended when Argaña was narrowly defeated (by less than 1% of the votes cast) by the PLRA candidate, Julio César Franco. The election of Franco, whose candidacy was endorsed by Oviedo, resulted in the resignation in September of the defence minister and the public works minister, José Alberto Planás. Planás was replaced by Walter Bower, hitherto interior minister. His portfolio was assumed by Julio César Fanego. The Minister of Finance, Federico Zayas, was replaced by Francisco Oviedo Brítez.

In February 2001 the Minister of Education and Culture, Nicanor Duarte Frutos, resigned in order to campaign for the presidency of the Partido Colorado, which he secured, with almost 50% of the vote, in elections in early May. At the same time, the Government was further undermined by tensions between the President and the Vice-President; Franco, as the most senior elected government official, demanded the resignation of President González Macchi in the name of democratic legitimacy. In March the Government's problems intensified when the three Encuentro Nacional (EN) representatives in the Council of Ministers threatened to resign in response to allegations that the President's car was a stolen vehicle, illegally smuggled into the country. In an attempt to restore confidence, González Macchi swiftly carried out a cabinet reshuffle in which José Antonio Moreno Rufinelli was appointed to the post of Minister of Foreign Affairs, replacing Juan Esteban Aguirre. On the same day, some 10,000 farmers marched through Asunción to protest against the Government's economic policy and to demand greater action on rural issues. Furthermore, at the end of March, several thousand rural workers who had been camping outside the parliament building in protest at depressed cotton prices, returned home after securing government concessions. Another corruption scandal emerged in early May which forced the President of the Central Bank of Paraguay, Washington Ashwell, to resign over his alleged involvement in the fraudulent transfer of US $16m. to a US bank account. Later that month, in response to allegations that the President had been a beneficiary of the misappropriated funds, opposition parties launched a bid to impeach him. It remained unclear whether an increasingly divided Colorado Party would unite behind González Macchi in order to save his presidency.

Economy

Prof. PETER CALVERT

Paraguay has a land area of 406,752 sq km (157,048 sq miles) and is one of the smaller republics of South America, considerably smaller than neighbouring Brazil and Argentina. Together with Bolivia, it is one of the sub-continent's two land-locked countries, with Brazil to the north and east, Argentina to the south and Bolivia to the west. It had an estimated population

of 5.5m. in mid-2000 and a population density of 13.5 persons per sq km. The country is divided into two distinct geographical regions by the River Paraguay, which joins the River Paraná at an altitude of 46 m above sea level. The majority of the population live within 160 km of the capital, Asunción, to the east of the river. This region consists of grassy plains and low hills and has a temperate climate. It is divided into two zones by a ridge of hills, to the east of which lies the Paraná plateau, which ranges from 600 m to 2,300 m in height. West of the ridge lie gently rolling hills. To the west of the River Paraguay is the Chaco region; an arid, marshy plain extending to the foothills of the Andes and to the country's border with Bolivia. The Chaco accounts for 61% of Paraguay's land area but is inhabited by less than 2% of the population.

In the 1980s Paraguay had one of the highest population growth rates in Latin America. The rate later decreased but remained high, at 2.6% in 2000. In 1999 the estimated birth rate was 31.9 births per 1,000 and the death rate was 5.2 deaths per 1,000. In the same year the infant mortality rate per 1,000 live births was 36.4. However, estimates of life expectancy at birth for 1995–2000 were 72.4 years (females 74.5, males 70.5), reflecting a generally healthy climate, though water pollution presented a health risk for many urban residents and only some 39% of the population had access to safe drinking water. In 1996 there was one doctor for every 2,174 inhabitants.

Owing to the fertility of eastern Paraguay, economic activity was widespread but unevenly distributed. Historically, the main concentration of activity was around Asunción, with a secondary, more recent economic zone based in the industrial park, Parque Industrial Oriente, 23 km from Ciudad del Este (formerly Puerto Presidente Stroessner). The Chaco region accounted for less than 3% of economic activity. In the late 1990s the percentage of the population below the national poverty line was 22%; however, according to a survey published by the Government's own statistical service, this figure included some 70% of Paraguayans in rural areas, thus demonstrating that although poverty was widespread, it was not necessarily as acute as in other countries. Spending on social welfare in the Stroessner era (1954–89) was very low, resulting in a poorly funded education system, inadequate health care and limited sanitation. The literacy rate, however, was relatively impressive by 2000, at 93.3%. In 1999 gross national product (GNP) per head was US $1,560 ($4,380 by purchasing power parity), placing Paraguay among the World Bank's rankings of lower middle-income countries.

AGRICULTURE

Agriculture (including hunting and fishing, but excluding forestry) was fundamental to the Paraguayan economy, accounting for an estimated 22.0% of gross domestic product (GDP) in 1999 and virtually all export earnings. During 1990–99 the agricultural sector grew by an annual average of 2.8%. In 1999 the sector(including forestry) employed an estimated 30.4% of the employed labour force. Some 9m. ha of land was classified as arable, of which only some 30% was cultivated. There was no attempt at agrarian reform and the ownership of land, therefore, remained one of the most unequal in Latin America. The 1991 agricultural census showed that 351 landowners controlled some 40% of the country's arable land. There was a large subsistence sector, including more than 200,000 families. A further 200,000 rural families were landless.

Paraguay is largely self-sufficient in basic foodstuffs. Maize, cassava (manioc) and wheat are the main food crops. In 2000, the largest area, 1,254,000 ha, was planted with oil crops, of which 579,560 metric tons were harvested. In the same year 561,000 ha of cereal crops were planted, yielding a total of 1,266,000 tons, of which wheat accounted for 250,000 tons and maize 900,000 tons. Some 240,000 ha was cultivated with cassava, of which 3.5m. tons were produced.

The main products grown for export were cotton, sugar cane and soya beans. Production of cotton and soya beans increased dramatically with the colonization of the eastern border region in the 1970s, and the area planted continued to expand at the beginning of the 21st century. Production of soya beans reached a new record of 3.3m. metric tons in 1999 but declined to 2.8m. tons in 2000. Production of cotton lint also declined in 2000, to 67,500 tons, from 220,000 tons in the previous year. In 2000 170,000 ha were dedicated to fibre crops and 67,500 tons harvested. Sugar cane covered 59,000 ha and 2.9m. tons were grown. Among tree crops, two were of particular note in 2000: 42,000 tons of tung nuts were grown on 10,000 ha and 4,800 tons of green coffee were produced on 6,000 ha of land.

The gently undulating plains of eastern Paraguay are good ranching country. Beef, pork, eggs and milk are produced for domestic consumption. Stocks recorded by the UN's Food and Agriculture Organization (FAO) in 2000 included 9.91m. head of cattle, 412,500 sheep, 137,500 goats and 2.70m. pigs, as well as 25m. chickens. Some 400,000 horses were also listed. Like land ownership, possession of livestock in Paraguay was unevenly distributed, with nearly two-thirds (58%) of cattle owned by 1% of the producers. Cattle-ranching used to be the most important sector of the Paraguayan economy, but the establishment of the European Union's (EU) Common Agricultural Policy (CAP) and the signing of the Lomé Agreement (which was succeeded by the Cotonou Convention in 2000) led to the closure of all meat-packing plants by 1981. In the late 20th century the success of cattle-ranching was subject to the changing fortunes of the Argentina and Brazilian markets. Only 21,614 metric tons were exported in 1999, with a value of US $35.4m., approximately one-half the previous year's return. The fishing catch in 1998 totalled some 26,000 tons, almost all of which was for domestic consumption.

Paraguay's once abundant forest resources were severely depleted in recent years by competitive logging for export. The damage was most extreme in eastern Paraguay, where less than one-quarter was still forested by the late 1990s. Transport costs acted as a deterrent in the Chaco region, where some 10.5m. ha of primary forest cover remained. Official figures almost certainly understated the amount of damage done and the quantities involved; they showed that, in 1999, the country produced 8.1m. cu m of roundwood and 4.2m. cu m of fuelwood, including charcoal, for domestic consumption. In the same year, sawnwood production was 550,000 cu m, nearly all of which (414,000 cu m) was exported. However, given the continued illegal logging trade and the absence of a systematic reafforestation programme, World Bank (International Bank for Reconstruction and Development—IBRD) sources predicted that the primary forest cover of eastern Paraguay would completely disappear by 2005. The sector accounted for about 3.2% of GDP in 1999.

MINING AND ENERGY

Paraguay had few proven mineral resources. From 1964 limestone was mined for the manufacture of portland cement by the state-owned Industria Nacional de Cemento at Vallemí, in the Department of Concepción. Deposits of bauxite, copper, iron ore and manganese were known to exist. Deposits of uranium have been found in both the east and west of the country.

Total electricity consumption in 1999 was 4,327m. kWh, an average of 808 kWh per inhabitant. Paraguay, bordered by two of the great rivers of South America (the Paraguay and Paraná), had abundant potential hydroelectric generating capacity, which was developed to create substantial revenue. Installed capacity in 1995 was 6,500 MW. Of the 40,050m. kWh generated in that year 92%, or 36,960m. kWh, was exported to Brazil. The most important source of power was the Paraguayan–Brazilian Itaipú project on the River Paraná. An agreement to build the plant was signed in 1973, providing for a generating capacity of 12,600 MW. The first stage was inaugurated in November 1982 and the final turbine came into operation in May 1991. Under the terms of the agreement Paraguay and Brazil were each to receive one-half of the energy generated; any that they could not consume was then to be offered to the other country at a preferential rate. Paraguay, however, did not benefit from the arrangement as much as was expected, as persistent financial crises meant that the Brazilian Government was often late in settling its account. In 1995 Paraguay finally succeeded in revising the agreement to allow the sale of part of its share in the Itaipú project to Argentina.

A similar agreement for a hydroelectric project with an installed capacity of 2,760 MW (later upgraded to 3,100 MW) was signed by Paraguay and Argentina in 1983. Owing to civil disturbances and an economic crisis in Argentina, the Yacyretá project was delayed and exceeded its budget, but the final turbine was installed in October 1997 and came 'on stream' in February 1998. However, later that year cracks in the dam walls were discovered, which led to three turbines being taken out of production. In 2001 generating capacity was seriously impaired by drought.

Following the Chaco War (1932–35) there were repeated hopes that petroleum deposits might be found in that part of the Chaco plain adjoining the southern Bolivian oilfields. These hopes were reactivated by the discovery of petroleum deposits in the northern Argentine province of Formosa in 1984. However, exploratory wells in the Chaco proved to be dry, and in July 1996 the US company Phillips Petroleum abandoned its search. Paraguay consumed some 14,000 barrels per day of petroleum products, all of which were imported.

MANUFACTURING

During 1990–99 the manufacturing sector grew by an average of only 0.5% per year. Manufacturing accounted for 13.6% of GDP in 1999. The sector was dominated by the processing of agricultural inputs, including sugar and wood products. There were also many small companies engaged in import substitution for the domestic market, particularly in the cement, textiles and beverages sub-sectors. From 1995 the country's membership of Mercosur (Mercado Común del Sur—Southern Common Market) brought significant export advantages, but also increased competition from Argentine and Brazilian imports. At the end of 2000 the official rate of unemployment was 16%.

There were two steel mills. The formerly state-owned Aceros del Paraguay (ACEPAR) was privatized in 1997; a second, built by a Brazilian company, Ioscape, to process ore from Corumbá (Brazil), began operations in 1994. There was some production of metal goods and machinery. In the 1990s there was substantial investment in the production of cotton yarn and paper.

COMMERCE

The main feature of the economic upturn of the 1970s was the joint development with Brazil of the Itaipú hydroelectric project on the River Paraná, which involved a good deal of construction work and attracted many Brazilian settlers. The opening of road links with Brazil stimulated trade, both legal and illegal. Although inflation was high, the second half of the 1970s generated annual GDP growth rates of more than 10%. This growth ended abruptly, however, when the Brazilian economy entered a period of crisis in 1982. GDP growth fell to 1.6% per year and although work continued at Itaipú, the huge revenues anticipated from the sale of Paraguay's share of its power to Brazil's developing south did not materialize.

In the late 1980s Paraguay, taking advantage of its geographical position, was able to re-establish itself as an entrepôt for intra-regional trade. A busy commercial sector was well-established, engaged in the import of consumer goods from the USA, Japan and other Asian countries, for re-export to neighbouring countries. The services sector accounted for 48.9% of GDP in 1999 and grew by an annual average of 1.9% during 1990–99.

Paraguay's informal economy was believed to be as extensive as its formal one. Vastly improved road links with Brazil had contributed to Paraguay becoming a major centre for contraband activities. Much of the informal economy consisted of profit from the smuggling of valuable electronic goods, spirits and tobacco into Argentina and Brazil. Paraguay was also an illicit producer of marijuana (cannabis) for the international market, and in recent years played an increasingly significant role in the transhipment of cocaine from Colombia to the USA and Europe. One of the consequences of this 'black' economy was a persistent increase in the rate of inflation. In 1998 consumer prices rose by 11.5% and in January of that year the exchange rate to the US dollar was 2,528.8 guaraníes, compared with 2,191.0 guaraníes in 1997 and 1,744.4 guaraníes in 1993. The annual rate of inflation was 8.9% in 2000.

TRANSPORT AND COMMUNICATIONS

Historically, waterways provided the main mode of transport for foreign trade in Paraguay, although in the 1980s road transport became more important and by 1999 the leading point of exit for exports of cereals and vegetables was Ciudad del Este (869,373 metric tons). The country had 3,100 km of waterways, with ports at the capital, Asunción, San Antonio, Encarnación and Villeta. In 2000 the merchant fleet consisted of 44 vessels with a total displacement of 44,962 grt, including two oil tankers. The country had free-port facilities at Nueva Palmira in Uru-

guay, although in the 1990s services on the Paraguay–Paraná network became both irregular and expensive. From 1994 Paraguay was linked with the Brazilian port of Santos on the Atlantic Ocean by the Hidrovía project, a network of canals and waterways sponsored by Mercosur.

Paraguay's principal road network was a triangle linking Asunción, Encarnación and Ciudad del Este. The Trans-Chaco Highway linked Asunción to the Bolivian border and there were links with Argentina and Brazil via the international bridge over the River Paraná at Ciudad del Este. However, of the estimated 60,901 km of roads, only 3,067 km were paved in 1998. Excessive reliance on road-hauled container traffic continued to cause congestion on the bridge at Ciudad del Este, despite the opening, in October 1995, of a new container port at Hernandarias on the banks of Lake Itaipú.

The state-owned railway, Ferrocarril Presidente Carlos Antonio López, owned a 370-km (274 miles) line linking Asunción with Encarnación, on the Argentine border. In 1998 a regular steam service operated only as far as Ypacaraí, 35 km from Asunción. A number of other lines, mostly privately owned, made up the remainder of the nominally-operated 971 km of track.

There were 10 airports with paved runways, three of which had runways of more than 3,047 m. The main international airport, Aeropuerto Internacional Silvio Pettirossi, was situated 15 km from Asunción. The state-owned international airline, Líneas Aéreas Paraguayas (LAPSA), was privatized in October 1994; in 1997 its name changed to Transportes Aéreos del Mercosur (TAM Paraguay) and 80% of ownership was transferred to Transportes Aéreos of Brazil. A private airline, Aerolíneas Paraguayas (ARPA), also operated daily flights between Paraguay's major cities.

The state-owned telephone service, Administración Nacional de Telecomunicaciones (ANTELCO), had a long history of overstaffing and low productivity. In November 1995 (when the number of people waiting for telephone lines was twice as many as the number of existing subscribers) ANTELCO signed an agreement with the German company, Siemens, to modernize the telephone system. By 1999, however, the network was still inadequate, although two cellular telephone companies were by then in operation. In 1997 515,000 households had televisions, compared with 390,000 in 1993, and in 1995 there were 45,000 subscribers to the cable-television network, although given Paraguay's central role in the regional smuggling of electrical goods, this figure seemed rather low.

BANKING AND FINANCIAL SERVICES

There was a rapid expansion in the provision of banks and finance companies in the country after 1990, and in 1997 there were 33 banks and 54 finance companies registered. The expansion was generally believed to be directly related to the reorientation of the drugs trade from Colombia's Andean highlands to Paraguay and the subsequent increase in illegal funds flowing through the country. In late 1995 the Central Bank announced a temporary 'freeze' on the opening of new banks and finance companies, on the grounds that the local market was saturated.

In 1995 a major banking crisis occurred which had a significant recessionary impact on the economy. In April a US $3.8m. fraud was uncovered in the Central Bank of Paraguay. The scandal involved a well-established practice under which obligatory commercial-bank deposits lodged with the Central Bank as part of legal reserve requirements were lent for short periods on the flourishing parallel, or 'black', market, through non-registered finance houses. Here they earned rates of return of over 30% for the high-ranking bank officials involved. Following the disclosure of the arrangement Banco Comercial Paraguayo (BANCOPAR) and Banco General were required to return missing funds to the Central Bank at short notice. The banking superintendency intervened to rescue both banks, but the crisis continued and by the end of 1995 four banks, 10 finance houses, two mortgage companies and two private pension schemes were experiencing difficulties. Both the Central Bank and the International Monetary Fund (IMF) argued strongly against further subsidies for these institutions and eventually the Government agreed to their closure, while strengthening the regulatory regime in the banking sector.

Fears that the 1995 banking crisis had not been overcome were confirmed in June 1997 when both Ahorros Paraguayos, a mortgage company, and its parent company, Banco Unión, collapsed as a result of the earlier crisis. Banco Unión, the second largest bank in the country, had a large number of repossessed properties valued at over US $50m., all with low liquidity, which it was unable to sell. Its past-due portfolio increased from 6% of all loans at the end of 1996, to 9% by June 1997. Owing to a loss of confidence in the country's economy, foreign investment in Paraguay fell by some 56% in 1997. Gross domestic investment fell by 4.7% in 1998 and by 5.7% in 1999.

GOVERNMENT FINANCE AND INVESTMENT

According to official government statistics GDP grew by some 2.6% in real terms in 1997, compared with a growth rate of 1.3% in 1996. However, there was a slight decrease in GDP per head in 1997, of 0.1%. In 1998 the economy contracted slightly, by 0.4%. In 1999 GDP expanded again, but only by 0.5%, and GDP contracted by 0.4% in 2000. In 1998, 1999 and 2000 there were contractions in GDP per head (of 2.9%, 2.1% and 3.0%, respectively). The total public-sector budget was US $3,750m. in 1997. This represented about one-third of GDP; 60% of the budget went to state-owned corporations and companies indirectly controlled by the state, and the balance to central government.

Unlike many lower middle-income countries, Paraguay was not heavily indebted. At the end of 1999 total outstanding and disbursed external debt stood at US $2,897m., compared with $2,305m. one year earlier. The cost of debt-servicing in 1999 was $282m., up from $165m. in 1998. According to the World Bank, total debt as a percentage of GDP was 36.9% in 1999, up from 22.2% in the previous year, and the cost of debt-servicing was equivalent to 8.5% of the total value of exports of goods and services. Reserves fell significantly from the third quarter of 1997 as the Central Bank was obliged to sell foreign exchange to arrest speculative attacks on the local currency, caused by growing political uncertainty. By the end of 1998 foreign exchange reserves totalled $732.9m. This figure increased to $845.9m. at the end of 1999 but declined to $630.4m. in 2000. There was a continuing decline in net government reserves in both 1998 and 1999, and in early 2001 the economy was still stagnant.

FOREIGN TRADE AND BALANCE OF PAYMENTS

In 1997 Paraguay's most important trading partner was Brazil, which accounted for around one-third of all imports and two-fifths of all exports. However, there were substantial differences both between exports and imports and from one year to the next. In 1999 the total value of registered exports (f.o.b.) was US $740.8m. The main exports were cotton ($69.1m.), soya beans ($312.9m.), timber, vegetable oils, meat products, coffee and tung oil. The main destinations were Argentina (27.0% of legal exports), Brazil (25.4%), the Netherlands (7.6%), Chile (4.6%) and the USA (4.6%).

Paraguay imported foodstuffs, raw materials, fuels and lubricants, and tobacco, much of which was illegally re-exported. The total value of registered imports (f.o.b.) in 1999 was US $1,725.1m. Capital goods accounted for $614.4m. in value, indicative of a small, but growing, economy, while the value of consumer goods was $691.2m. Machinery and motors accounted for $418.6m., fuel and energy for $194.8m. and beverages and tobacco for $220.2m. In the same year the main sources of imports were Brazil (28.0%), Argentina (20.7%) and the USA (20.0%).

Exports of goods and services accounted for US $3,267.4m. in 1999. Imports of goods and services were somewhat higher, at $3,533.2m. As a result, the country had a negative resource balance of $265.8m. and a deficit of $63.6m. on the current account of the balance of payments, compared with a deficit of $56.2m. in 1998. This checked a worrying trend, established in 1992, of gently rising export levels being overtaken by a steep and continuing increase in the value of imports, a pattern which led to a widening deficit on the balance of trade in the mid-1990s (which reached $586.5m. in 1996). In 1998 the trade deficit decreased to $289.2m., but in 1999 it increased to $334.4m. while imports of goods and services fell by 7.0% in 1998 and by 26.7% in 1999. It was uncertain, however, what the impact of Paraguay's informal trading activity would be on this pattern.

CONCLUSION

Paraguay's geographical position placed its economy at a competitive disadvantage while also offering opportunities which the informal sector was quick to seize. Its main economic problems remained the extent of its informal sector, the crisis in the banking system and the resulting loss of confidence among investors, the vagaries of climate and the low value of the country's principal agricultural exports. From the late 1980s successive Governments attempted to resolve at least some of these problems and Paraguay was likely to benefit substantially from its incorporation into Mercosur. Political instability, however, left Governments with little option but to delay or postpone the reform measures recommended by the IMF and, therefore, to retain the problems created by an under-funded and inefficient public sector.

Statistical Survey

Sources (unless otherwise stated): Dirección General de Estadística y Censos, Humaitá 473, Asunción; tel. (21) 47900; internet www.dgeec.gov.py/index.htm; Banco Central del Paraguay, Avda Pablo VI y Avda Sargento Marecos, Casilla 861, Asunción; tel. (21) 60-8019; fax (21) 60-8150; internet www.bcp.gov.py; Secretaría Técnica de Planificación, Presidencia de la República, Iturbe y Eligio Ayala, Asunción.

Area and Population

AREA, POPULATION AND DENSITY

Area (sq km)	406,752*
Population (census results)†	
11 July 1982	3,029,830
26 August 1992	
Males	2,085,905
Females	2,066,683
Total	4,152,588
Population (official estimates at mid-year)‡	
1998	5,219,000
1999	5,356,000
2000	5,496,450
Density (per sq km) at mid-2000	13.5

* 157,048 sq miles.
† Excluding adjustments for underenumeration.
‡ Not revised to take account of the 1992 census results.

DEPARTMENTS (1 July 1997)

	Area (sq km)	Population (estim- ated)	Density (per sq km)	Capital
Alto Paraguay (incl. Chaco). . . .	82,349	13,831	0.2	Fuerte Olimoo
Alto Paraná . . .	14,895	595,276	40.0	Ciudad del Este
Amambay . . .	12,933	127,011	9.8	Pedro Juan Caballero
Asunción. . . .	117	454,881	3,887.9	—
Boquerón (incl. Nueva Asunción) . .	91,669	35,238	0.4	Doctor Pedro P. Peña
Caaguazú . . .	11,474	442,161	38.5	Coronel Oviedo
Caazapá . . .	9,496	141,559	14.9	Caazapá
Canindeyú . . .	14,667	133,075	9.1	Salto del Guairá
Central . . .	2,465	1,174,212	476.4	Asunción
Concepción . . .	18,051	185,496	10.3	Concepción
Cordillera . . .	4,948	215,663	43.6	Caacupé
Guairá . . .	3,846	173,668	45.2	Villarrica
Itapúa . . .	16,525	454,757	27.5	Encarnación
Misiones. . . .	9,556	98,607	10.3	San Juan Bautista
Ñeembucú . . .	12,147	86,965	7.2	Pilar
Paraguarí . . .	8,705	247,675	28.5	Paraguarí
Presidente Hayes. .	72,907	77,145	1.1	Pozo Colorado
San Pedro . . .	20,002	332,926	16.6	San Pedro
Total . . .	**406,752**	**5,085,325**	**12.5**	**—**

PRINCIPAL TOWNS (population at 1992 census)

Asunción (capital) .	500,938	Luque.	84,877
Ciudad del Este* .	133,881	Capiatá . . .	83,773
San Lorenzo . .	133,395	Encarnación . .	56,261
Lambaré . . .	99,572	Pedro Juan Caballero .	53,566
Fernando de la Mora .	95,072		

* Formerly Puerto Presidente Stroessner.

BIRTHS, MARRIAGES AND DEATHS

	Estimated live births		Registered marriages*		Estimated deaths	
	Number	Rate (per 1,000)	Number	Rate (per 1,000)	Number	Rate (per 1,000)
1983 . .	121,500	35.3	13,394	3.9	23,800	6.7
1984 . .	124,500	35.2	16,354	4.6	24,400	6.7
1985 . .	127,500	35.2	18,370	5.0	25,000	6.7
1986 . .	130,500	35.1	16,050	4.2	25,600	6.6
1987 . .	133,500	35.0	17,741	4.5	26,200	6.6
1988 . .	136,500	34.9	15,659	3.9	26,800	6.5
1989 . .	143,400	34.5	12,627	3.0	27,400	6.5
1990 . .	142,500	34.1	7,708	1.8	28,000	6.5

* Source: *Anuario Estadístico del Paraguay*.

Expectation of life (UN estimates, years at birth, 1995–2000): 69.6 (males 67.5; females 72.0) (Source: UN, *World Population Prospects: The 1998 Revision*).

ECONOMICALLY ACTIVE POPULATION
(Household survey, August–November 1999)

Agriculture, hunting, forestry and fishing	667,961
Mining and quarrying	3,738
Manufacturing	269,327
Electricity, gas and water	10,599
Construction	114,490
Trade, restaurants and hotels	466,473
Transport, storage and communications	94,524
Financing, insurance, real estate and business services . .	77,797
Community, social and personal services	490,861
Activities not adequately described	161
Total employed	**2,195,931**

Agriculture

PRINCIPAL CROPS ('000 metric tons)

	1998	1999	2000
Wheat	231	231	250*
Rice (paddy). . . .	92	92	93*
Maize	874	817	900*
Sorghum	21	23	23*
Sweet potatoes . . .	77	79	80*
Cassava (Manioc) . .	3,300	3,500	3,500*
Soybeans (Soya beans) .	2,856	3,304	2,750†
Groundnuts	30	28	35*
Seed cotton	222	202	205*
Tomatoes	65	60*	60*
Avocados*	15	n.a.	12
Watermelons* . . .	108	110	110
Sugar cane	2,800	2,872	2,850*
Oranges	208	231	209*
Tangerines	27	30	30*
Grapefruit and pomelo .	60	60	60*
Mangoes*	29	30	30
Pineapples	39	41	41*
Grapes*	24	24	24
Bananas	71	70	70*

* FAO estimate(s).   † Unofficial figure.

Source: FAO.

LIVESTOCK ('000 head, year ending September)

	1998	1999	2000
Cattle*	9,863	9,863	9,910
Horses†	400	400	400
Pigs†	2,300	2,500	2,700
Sheep	395	395*	413*
Goats*	131	132	138
Chickens†	15,000	15,000	25,000
Ducks†	710	710	710
Geese†	75	75	75

* Unofficial figure.   † FAO estimates.

Source: FAO.

LIVESTOCK PRODUCTS ('000 metric tons)

	1998	1999	2000
Beef and veal	231*	246*	239
Pig meat	119	120	148
Poultry meat	38	38	58
Cows' milk	445†	445†	330
Hen eggs	46†	46†	68
Cattle hides	36	38	39

* Unofficial figure.   † FAO estimates.

Source: FAO.

Forestry

ROUNDWOOD REMOVALS
('000 cubic metres, excluding bark)

	1993	1994	1995
Sawlogs, veneer logs and logs for sleepers	3,322	3,413	3,413
Other industrial wood . .	452	464	464
Fuel wood	5,608	4,220	4,220
Total	9,382	8,097	8,097

1996–99: Annual production as in 1995.

Source: FAO, *Yearbook of Forest Products*.

SAWNWOOD PRODUCTION
('000 cubic metres, including railway sleepers)

	1995	1996	1997
Total (all broadleaved) . . .	400	500	550

1998–99: Annual production as in 1997.

Source: FAO, *Yearbook of Forest Products*.

Fishing

('000 metric tons, live weight)

	1996	1997	1998
Capture	21.7	27.7	26.0*
Characins* . . .	8.4	10.7	10.0
Freshwater siluroids* . .	9.1	11.6	11.0
Other freshwater fishes* . .	4.2	5.4	5.0
Aquaculture	0.4*	0.4*	0.1
Total catch	22.0	28.0	26.1

Note: Figures exclude crocodiles, recorded by number rather than by weight. The number of spectacled caimans caught was: 725 in 1996; 503 in 1997; 4,345 in 1998.

* FAO estimate(s).

Source: FAO, *Yearbook of Fishery Statistics*.

Industry

SELECTED PRODUCTS
(metric tons, unless otherwise indicated)

	1990	1991	1992
Soya bean oil (refined) . . .	15,517	22,886	82,357
Alcohol (100%)	21,220	36,913	27,953
Fuel alcohol	2,604	3,575	4,561
Sugar (refined)	103,705	135,845	133,417
Portland cement	343,661	340,737	475,758
Beer	107,583	113,933	114,144
Electricity (million kWh) . .	27,228	29,400	27,136
Cotton thread	442	570	576
Cotton fabrics ('000 metres) . .	14,648	18,967	19,170

1993: Soya bean oil (refined) 50,000 metric tons; Sugar (refined) 109,000 metric tons; Portland cement 480,000 metric tons; Electricity 31,454 million kWh; Cotton fabrics 20,100,000 metres.
1994: Sugar (refined) 96,000 metric tons*; Portland cement 529,000 metric tons; Electricity 36,420 million kWh.
1995 (provisional figures): Sugar (refined) 90,000 metric tons*; Portland cement 625,000 metric tons; Electricity 42,236 million kWh.
1996: Sugar (refined) 111,000 metric tons*; Electricity 48,200 million kWh.
1997: Electricity 50,619 million kWh.

* Data from the FAO.

Source (for 1993–97): UN, *Industrial Commodity Statistics Yearbook*.

Finance

CURRENCY AND EXCHANGE RATES

Monetary Units
100 céntimos = 1 guaraní (G).

Sterling, Dollar and Euro Equivalents (30 April 2001)
£1 sterling = 5,439.8 guaraníes;
US $1 = 3,799.3 guaraníes;
€1 = 3,372.3 guaraníes;
10,000 guaraníes = £1.838 = \$2.632 = €2.965.

Average Exchange Rate (guaraníes per US dollar)
1998   2,726.5
1999   3,119.1
2000   3,486.4

BUDGET ('000 million guaraníes)

Revenue	1998	1999	2000
Taxation	2,729.1	2,685.7	2,975.4
Taxes on net income and profits .	474.4	552.2	513.6
Government payroll taxes .	244.6	288.0	300.4
Taxes on goods and services .	1,483.5	1,446.7	1,664.3
Selective excises on goods .	302.7	308.2	454.5
Value-added tax . . .	1,063.7	1,048.4	1,112.2
Stamp taxes . . .	76.1	68.8	68.9
Taxes on international trade and transactions . . .	526.6	398.8	497.2
Import duties . . .	526.6	398.8	497.2
Other current revenue . .	1,028.7	1,364.7	1,261.5
Capital revenue . . .	37.4	43.4	50.4
Total	3,795.2	4,093.8	4,287.3

Expenditure	1998	1999	2000
Current expenditure . . .	3,199.7	3,549.5	4,163.8
Wages and salaries . . .	1,818.0	2,021.4	2,338.6
Goods and services . . .	332.2	250.4	307.8
Interest payments . . .	170.4	193.2	310.7
Subsidies and other transfers .	774.9	1,009.5	1,170.3
Capital expenditure . . .	822.5	1,409.5	1,303.4
Capital formation . . .	728.0	978.9	1,188.9
Transfers	94.3	430.4	113.8
Total	4,022.2	4,959.0	5,467.2

Source: IMF, *Paraguay: Recent Economic Developments* (June 2001).

INTERNATIONAL RESERVES
(US $ million at 31 December)

	1998	1999	2000
Gold*	10.03	10.15	9.60
IMF special drawing rights .	111.44	102.68	102.26
Reserve position in IMF .	20.45	29.48	27.98
Foreign exchange . . .	732.85	845.90	630.40
Total	874.77	988.21	770.24

* National valuation of gold reserves (35,000 troy ounces in each year), based on market-related prices.

Source: IMF, *International Financial Statistics*.

MONEY SUPPLY ('000 million guaraníes at 31 December)

	1998	1999	2000
Currency outside banks . .	1,264.08	1,398.68	1,327.19
Demand deposits at commercial banks	682.36	733.47	1,254.79
Total money (incl. others) . .	2,020.46	2,206.86	2,664.98

Source: IMF, *International Financial Statistics*.

COST OF LIVING
(Consumer Price Index for Asunción; base: 1990 = 100)

	1996	1997	1998
Food (incl. beverages) . .	237.0	247.4	275.1
Housing (incl. fuel and light) . .	272.6	297.7	327.7
Clothing (incl. footwear) . .	206.7	212.9	221.9
All items (incl. others) . .	253.9	271.7	303.1

Source: ILO, *Yearbook of Labour Statistics*.

All items (base: previous year = 100): 106.8 in 1999; 109.0 in 2000 (Source: IMF, *International Financial Statistics*).

NATIONAL ACCOUNTS ('000 million guaraníes at current prices)
National Income and Product

	1997	1998	1999
Compensation of employees . .	6,610.5	7,360.3	7,764.3
Operating surplus* . . .	10,912.5	12,331.2	12,736.9
Domestic factor incomes . .	17,523.0	19,691.5	20,501.2
Consumption of fixed capital .	1,639.2	1,835.0	1,889.6
Gross domestic product (GDP) at factor cost	19,162.2	21,526.5	22,390.8
Indirect taxes, *less* subsidies . .	1,772.2	1,910.4	1,753.6
GDP in purchasers' values .	20,934.4	23,437.0	24,144.3
Factor income received from abroad, *less* factor income paid abroad .	221.7	304.5	132.2
Gross national product .	21,156.1	23,741.5	24,276.5
Less Consumption of fixed capital	1,639.2	1,835.0	1,889.6
National income in market prices	19,516.9	21,906.5	22,386.9

* Obtained as a residual.

Expenditure on the Gross Domestic Product

	1997	1998	1999
Government final consumption expenditure	1,693.0	1,928.3	2,135.4
Private final consumption expenditure	17,704.2	20,101.4	19,762.5
Increase in stocks . . .	181.0	205.6	221.7
Gross fixed capital formation .	4,749.1	5,168.2	5,342.1
Total domestic expenditure .	24,327.3	27,403.5	27,461.7
Exports of goods and services .	5,696.2	6,613.7	5,548.6
Less Imports of goods and services	9,089.3	10,580.0	8,866.1
GDP in purchasers' values	20,934.3	23,436.9	24,144.3
GDP at constant 1982 prices .	1,129.7	1,125.0	1,130.7

2000 ('000 million guaraníes): GDP in purchasers' values 26,114.0; GDP at constant 1982 prices 1,125.8.

Source: IMF, *International Financial Statistics*.

Gross Domestic Product by Economic Activity

	1997	1998	1999
Agriculture, hunting and fishing .	4,505.2	4,991.3	5,300.6
Forestry	640.8	725.0	767.1
Mining	71.8	79.5	89.0
Manufacturing	3,193.1	3,631.5	3,272.1
Construction	1,308.2	1,433.1	1,502.9
Electricity, gas and water . .	985.7	1,148.9	1,394.9
Trade, finance and insurance . .	5,787.4	6,309.9	5,887.1
Transport, storage and communications . . .	808.1	913.9	1,063.4
Government services . . .	1,065.4	1,181.8	1,360.3
Real estate and housing . .	466.2	515.8	561.5
Other services	2,102.6	2,506.2	2,945.3
GDP in purchasers' values	20,934.4	23,437.0	24,144.3

Source: IMF, *Paraguay: Recent Economic Developments* (June 2001).

BALANCE OF PAYMENTS (US $ million)

	1997	1998	1999
Exports of goods f.o.b. . .	3,880.0	3,652.3	2,707.1
Imports of goods f.o.b. . .	−4,192.4	−3,941.5	−3,041.5
Trade balance	312.4	−289.2	−334.4
Exports of services . . .	655.0	625.5	560.3
Imports of services . . .	−654.6	−575.9	−491.7
Balance on goods and services .	−312.0	−239.6	−265.8
Other income received . .	278.1	266.3	210.2
Other income paid . . .	−245.1	−260.2	−179.1
Balance on goods, services and income	−279.0	−233.5	−234.7
Current transfers received . .	182.2	178.3	172.6
Current transfers paid . . .	−1.3	−1.0	−1.5
Current balance . . .	−98.1	−56.2	−63.6
Capital account (net) . . .	7.5	5.4	19.6
Direct investment abroad . .	−5.7	−5.6	−5.6
Direct investment from abroad .	235.8	341.9	71.6
Portfolio investment assets . .	−4.3	9.0	−20.9
Other investment assets . .	72.9	5.0	−86.9
Investment liabilities . . .	122.7	−27.4	131.7
Net errors and omissions . .	−546.7	−245.4	−348.9
Overall balance . . .	−215.9	16.7	−303.0

Source: IMF, *International Financial Statistics*.

External Trade

PRINCIPAL COMMODITIES (distribution by SITC, US $ million)

Imports c.i.f.	1995	1996	1997
Food and live animals . . .	217.5	199.6	182.2
Beverages and tobacco . .	355.9	429.8	476.7
Beverages	158.0	136.4	132.4
Alcoholic beverages . .	146.8	125.8	120.9
Distilled alcoholic beverages .	94.7	71.4	65.0
Whisky	87.2	64.4	55.2
Tobacco and manufactures . .	197.9	293.5	344.3
Tobacco, manufactured . . .	190.6	283.0	330.1
Cigarettes	190.1	276.4	328.0
Mineral fuels, lubricants and related materials . .	206.5	252.6	332.6
Petroleum, petroleum products and related materials . .	192.5	236.9	313.1
Petroleum products, refined .	157.8	208.6	278.8
Gasoline, other light oils .	108.6	153.2	233.6
Chemicals and related products	278.6	322.8	358.7
Pesticides, disinfectants, etc. . .	47.0	65.5	71.6
Basic manufactures . . .	372.1	346.6	436.6
Rubber manufactures . .	64.0	61.5	73.3
Paper, paperboard and manufactures . . .	71.4	68.5	75.0
Machinery and transport equipment	1,323.6	1,124.3	1,226.9
Machinery specialized for particular industries . .	100.5	113.2	133.3
General industrial machinery, equipment and parts . .	99.0	114.3	161.6
Office machines and automatic data-processing equipment .	152.1	131.9	84.6
Automatic data-processing machines and units . .	119.4	98.3	59.9
Telecommunications and sound equipment. . .	428.8	239.9	159.4
Television receivers . .	118.5	35.8	19.8
Colour television receivers .	96.9	21.3	18.8
Radio-broadcast receivers .	143.9	77.4	46.3
Road vehicles and parts . .	336.3	307.1	454.5
Passenger motor cars (excl. buses)	135.3	139.5	199.3
Goods vehicles and specialized purpose motor vehicles .	99.4	86.9	116.3
Goods vehicles . . .	92.8	84.4	110.5
Miscellaneous manufactured articles	354.2	318.3	357.4
Baby carriages, toys, games and sporting goods	97.2	81.4	88.5
Total (incl. others) . . .	3,135.9	3,107.4	3,403.4

Exports f.o.b.	1995	1996	1997
Food and live animals . . .	152.2	189.0	246.9
Live animals for food . . .	12.2	10.7	23.8
Cattle and buffaloes . .	12.1	10.7	23.8
Meat and preparations . . .	54.9	46.9	49.2
Meat, fresh, chilled or frozen .	51.1	45.9	47.7
Bovine meat, fresh, chilled or frozen	48.1	44.3	45.8
Bovine meat, boneless . .	34.1	28.4	34.6
Cereals and preparations . .	26.9	26.6	51.6
Wheat and meslin (unmilled) .	5.0	7.2	26.4
Feeding stuff for animals . .	43.4	91.2	107.2
Oil-cake and other residues . .	40.9	87.8	103.5
Oil-cake and residues of soya beans	38.0	81.0	100.9
Crude materials (inedible) except fuels	514.5	583.7	647.9
Oil seeds and oleaginous fruit. .	177.8	325.7	496.7
Seeds for 'soft' fixed vegetable oils	177.6	325.3	496.2
Soya beans	176.0	324.2	493.6
Cork and wood	57.7	62.2	68.2
Wood, simply worked, and railway sleepers . . .	57.1	61.2	67.6
Wood, shaped, non-coniferous	56.8	60.9	66.2
Wood, sawn, non-coniferous	29.3	32.8	36.1
Wood, planed, non-coniferous	27.5	28.1	30.2
Textile fibres and waste . . .	274.0	190.7	75.1
Cotton	271.1	189.8	74.0
Cotton (excl. linters) . .	268.1	188.2	72.9
Animal and vegetable oils, fats and waxes	64.4	74.4	62.0
Fixed vegetable oils and fats . .	64.0	73.6	61.3
Fixed vegetable oils, 'soft' . .	59.5	67.8	52.8
Soya bean oil	57.8	58.2	48.0
Chemicals and related products	23.6	22.3	29.8
Basic manufactures . . .	134.7	130.4	117.1
Leather and manufactures, dressed furskins	55.7	40.8	41.6
Leather	54.8	38.2	39.3
Cork and wood manufactures . .	31.3	31.2	31.1
Veneers, plywood, etc. . . .	25.9	28.0	26.4
Plywood of wood sheets . .	15.3	20.1	22.6
Textile yarn, fabrics, etc. . . .	28.2	30.9	26.8
Total (incl. others)	919.4	1,043.0	1,141.1

Source: UN, *International Trade Statistics Yearbook.*

1998 (US $ million): *Imports f.o.b.*: Foodstuffs, beverages and tobacco 584.5; Other consumer goods 618.7 (Automobiles 139.7); Intermediate goods 512.0 (Chemicals 133.7, Fuels and lubricants 188.7); Capital goods 755.5 (Transportation equipment 200.0, Machinery and motors 500.1); Total 2,470.8. *Exports f.o.b.*: Livestock products 110.9 (Processed meat 72.1, Hides 38.8); Agricultural products 578.2 (Cotton fibres 92.1, Soya bean seeds 443.0); Manufactured products 316.0 (Lumber 69.7, Soya bean oil 81.5); Total (incl. others) 1,014.1.

1999 (US $ million): *Imports f.o.b.*: Foodstuffs, beverages and tobacco 298.4; Other consumer goods 392.8 (Automobiles 79.0); Intermediate goods 419.4 (Chemicals 102.3, Fuels and lubricants 194.8); Capital goods 614.4 (Transportation equipment 160.0, Machinery and motors 418.6); Total 1,725.1. *Exports f.o.b.*: Livestock products 75.3 (Processed meat 38.3, Hides 37.0); Agricultural products 404.4 (Cotton fibres 69.1; Soya bean seeds 312.9); Manufactured products 248.8 (Lumber 58.8, Soya bean oil 59.8); Total (incl. others) 740.8. Source: IMF, *Paraguay: Recent Economic Developments* (June 2001).

PRINCIPAL TRADING PARTNERS
(countries of first and last consignments, US $ million)

Imports c.i.f.		1995	1996	1997
Argentina		518.6	587.4	676.2
Brazil		681.3	982.0	1,008.5
Chile		85.2	71.7	67.3
France (incl. Monaco) . . .		37.8	28.3	38.7
Germany		83.3	103.4	112.0
Hong Kong		169.7	71.6	58.9
Italy		66.2	33.5	149.9
Japan		272.5	204.4	266.9
Korea, Republic		207.2	109.5	71.3
Singapore		36.3	11.1	10.3
United Kingdom		96.1	86.8	69.5
USA		392.4	348.3	361.5
Uruguay		36.9	63.2	67.4
Total (incl. others) . . .		3,135.9	3,107.4	3,403.4

Exports f.o.b.		1995	1996	1997
Argentina		83.3	95.4	103.4
Bermuda		11.5	1.7	43.2
Brazil		410.8	520.7	457.6
Cayman Islands		1.6	4.4	19.7
Chile		31.1	24.8	34.3
France (incl. Monaco) . . .		19.7	11.6	9.9
Germany		10.5	7.4	3.5
Italy		29.1	20.1	17.9
Japan		0.7	0.7	11.0
Netherlands		89.7	172.7	276.6
USA		43.9	37.5	58.1
Uruguay		33.9	43.5	23.8
Venezuela		21.6	14.7	11.1
Total (incl. others) . . .		919.3	1,043.0	1,141.0

Source: UN, *International Trade Statistics Yearbook*.

Transport

RAILWAYS (traffic)

	1988	1989	1990
Passengers carried . . .	178,159	196,019	125,685
Freight (metric tons) . . .	200,213	164,980	289,099

1991: Passenger-km 1m.; Net ton-km 3m.
1992: Passenger-km 1m.; Net ton-km 3m.
1993: Passenger-km 1m.; Net ton-km 3m.

(Source: UN, *Statistical Yearbook*).

ROAD TRAFFIC (vehicles in use)

	1988	1989	1990
Cars	60,246	108,001	117,067
Buses	2,734	3,151	3,375
Lorries	1,863	n.a.	n.a.
Vans	22,327	41,264	45,660
Jeeps	978	2,268	2,278
Motorcycles	16,025	n.a.	n.a.

1991: 190,900 passenger cars; 30,700 commercial vehicles.
1992: 221,100 passenger cars; 34,900 commercial vehicles.
1993: 250,700 passenger cars; 37,700 commercial vehicles.

Source (for 1991–93): UN, *Statistical Yearbook*.

SHIPPING
Merchant Fleet (registered at 31 December)

	1998	1999	2000
Number of vessels	47	40	44
Total displacement ('000 grt) . .	44.9	39.4	45.0

Source: Lloyd's Register of Shipping, *World Fleet Statistics*.

CIVIL AVIATION (traffic on scheduled services)

		1995	1996	1997
Kilometres flown (million) . .		4	7	4
Passengers carried ('000) . . .		105	260	196
Passenger-km (million) . . .		283	474	215
Total ton-km (million) . . .		32	42	19

Source: UN, *Statistical Yearbook*.

Tourism

ARRIVALS BY NATIONALITY

		1996	1997	1998
Argentina		144,550	125,194	111,006
Brazil		87,313	83,989	77,304
Chile		53,528	43,417	45,997
Germany		10,255	15,051	7,093
Spain		8,250	7,545	5,806
USA		18,576	17,620	15,066
Uruguay		15,024	18,331	11,022
Total (incl. others) . . .		425,561	395,058	349,592

Tourism receipts (US $ million): 869 in 1996; 753 in 1997.

Source: World Tourism Organization, *Yearbook of Tourism Statistics*.

Communications Media

	1995	1996	1997
Radio receivers ('000 in use) . .	870	900	925
Television receivers ('000 in use)	450	500	515
Telephones ('000 main lines in use)	167	176	218
Mobile cellular telephones (subscribers)	15,807	32,860	84,240

Telefax stations (number in use): 1,691 in 1992.
Daily newspapers: 5* in 1996 (average circulation 213,000* copies).
Non-daily newspapers: 2 in 1988 (average circulation 16,000* copies).
Book production: 152 titles (incl. 23 pamphlets) in 1993.
* Estimates.

Sources: UNESCO, *Statistical Yearbook*; UN, *Statistical Yearbook*.

Education

(1998, unless otherwise indicated)

	Insti-tutions	Teachers	Students Males	Females	Total
Pre-primary . .	3,530	3,203*	56,214	55,905	112,119
Primary . .	6,143	59,423	479,927	453,362	933,289
Secondary					
General . .	1,846	17,668†	164,692	168,011	332,703
Vocational . .	n.a.	n.a.	12,842	11,390	24,232
Tertiary‡					
University level .	n.a.	n.a.	n.a.	n.a.	36,626
Other higher .	n.a.	n.a.	3,383	9,974	13,357

* 1996 figure.
† 1994 figure.
‡ Excluding private universities.

Source: partly UNESCO, *Statistical Yearbook*.

Directory

The Constitution

A new Constitution for the Republic of Paraguay came into force on 22 June 1992, replacing the Constitution of 25 August 1967.

FUNDAMENTAL RIGHTS, DUTIES AND FREEDOMS

Paraguay is an independent republic whose form of government is representative democracy. The powers accorded to the legislature, executive and judiciary are exercised in a system of independence, equilibrium, co-ordination and reciprocal control. Sovereignty resides in the people, who exercise it through universal, free, direct, equal and secret vote. All citizens over 18 years of age and resident in the national territory are entitled to vote.

All citizens are equal before the law and have freedom of conscience, travel, residence, expression, and the right to privacy. The freedom of the press is guaranteed. The freedom of religion and ideology is guaranteed. Relations between the State and the Catholic Church are based on independence, co-operation and autonomy. All citizens have the right to assemble and demonstrate peacefully. All public- and private-sector workers, with the exception of the Armed Forces and the police, have the right to form a trade union and to strike. All citizens have the right to associate freely in political parties or movements.

The rights of the indigenous peoples to preserve and develop their ethnic identity in their respective habitat are guaranteed.

LEGISLATURE

The legislature (Congreso Nacional—National Congress) comprises the Senado (Senate) and the Cámara de Diputados (Chamber of Deputies). The Senado is composed of 45 members, the Cámara of 80 members, elected directly by the people. Legislation concerning national defence and international agreements may be initiated in the Senado. Departmental and municipal legislation may be initiated in the Cámara. Both chambers of the Congreso are elected for a period of five years.

GOVERNMENT

Executive power is exercised by the President of the Republic. The President and the Vice-President are elected jointly and directly by the people, by a simple majority of votes, for a period of five years. They may not be elected for a second term. The President and the Vice-President govern with the assistance of an appointed Council of Ministers. The President participates in the formulation of legislation and enacts it. The President is empowered to veto legislation sanctioned by the Congreso, to nominate or remove ministers, to direct the foreign relations of the Republic, and to convene extraordinary sessions of the Congreso. The President is Commander-in-Chief of the Armed Forces.

JUDICIARY

Judicial power is exercised by the Supreme Court of Justice and by the tribunals. The Supreme Court is composed of nine members who are appointed on the proposal of the Consejo de la Magistratura, and has the power to declare legislation unconstitutional.

The Government

HEAD OF STATE

President: Luis González Macchi (took office 28 March 1999).

Vice-President: Dr Julio César ('Yoyito') Franco (took office 2 September 2000).

Note: Raúl Cubas Grau and Luis María Argaña took office as President and Vice-President, respectively, on 15 August 1998, following their victory at elections on 10 May. However, the President of the Congreso Nacional, Luis González Macchi, assumed the presidency following the assassination of Argaña on 23 March and the resignation of Cubas Grau on 28 March.

COUNCIL OF MINISTERS
(August 2001)

A Government comprising members of various factions of the Partido Colorado and Encuentro Nacional (EN).

Minister of the Interior: Julio César Fanego.

Minister of Foreign Affairs: José Antonio Moreno Rufinelli.

Minister of Finance: Francisco Oviedo Brítez.

Minister of Industry and Commerce: Eúclides Acevedo.

Minister of Public Works and Communications: Alcides Luciano Gimenez.

Minister of National Defence: Adm. Miguel Angel Candia Fleitas.

Minister of Public Health and Social Welfare: Martín Antonio Chiola.

Minister of Justice and Labour: Silvio Ferreira Fernández.

Minister of Agriculture and Livestock: Pedro Lino Morel.

Minister of Education and Culture: Dario Zárate Arellano.

MINISTRIES

Ministry of Agriculture and Livestock: Presidente Franco 472, Asunción; tel. (21) 44-9614; fax (21) 49-7965.

Ministry of Education and Culture: Chile, Humaitá y Piribebuy, Asunción; tel. (21) 44-3078; fax (21) 44-3919; internet www2.paraguaygobierno.gov.py/mec.

Ministry of Finance: Chile 128 esq. Palmas, Asunción; tel. (21) 44-0010; fax (21) 44-8283; e-mail info@hacienda.gov.py; internet www.hacienda.gov.py.

Ministry of Foreign Affairs: Juan E. O'Leary y Presidente Franco, Asunción; tel. (21) 49-4593; fax (21) 49-3910; internet www.mre.gov.py.

Ministry of Industry and Commerce: Avda España 323, Asunción; tel. (21) 20-4638; fax (21) 21-3529; internet www.mic.gov.py.

Ministry of the Interior: Estrella y Montevideo, Asunción; tel. (21) 49-3661; fax (21) 44-8446.

Ministry of Justice and Labour: G. R. de Francia y Estados Unidos, Asunción; tel. (21) 49-3515; fax (21) 20-8469; e-mail mjt@conexion.com.py.

Ministry of National Defence: Avda Mariscal López y Vice-Presidente Sánchez, Asunción; tel. (21) 20-4771; fax (21) 21-1583.

Ministry of Public Health and Social Welfare: Avda Pettirossi y Brasil, Asunción; tel. (21) 20-7328; fax (21) 20-6700; internet www.mspbs.gov.py.

Ministry of Public Works and Communications: Oliva y Alberdi, Asunción; tel. (21) 44-4411; fax (21) 44-4421; internet www.mopc.gov.py.

President and Legislature

PRESIDENT

Election, 10 May 1998

Candidate	% of votes
Raúl Cubas Grau (Partido Colorado)	55.4
Dr Domingo Laino (Alianza Democrática)	43.9

CONGRESO NACIONAL
(National Congress)

President: Candido Vera Bejarano.

General Election, 10 May 1998

Party	Seats	
	Cámara de Diputados	Senado
Partido Colorado	45	24
Partido Liberal Radical Auténtico* . . .	27	13
Encuentro Nacional*	8	7
Partido Blanco	—	1
Total	**80**	**45**

* Contested the election jointly as the Alianza Democrática (AD).

Political Organizations

Alianza Democrática (AD): Asunción; electoral alliance f. 1997 to contest general election of May 1998; comprises:

Encuentro Nacional (EN): Asunción; coalition comprising factions of PRF, PDC, APT and a dissident faction of the Partido Colorado formed to contest presidential and legislative elections of May 1993; Leader EÚCLIDES ACEVEDO.

Partido Liberal Radical Auténtico (PLRA): Asunción; f. 1978; centre party; Pres. MIGUEL ABDÓN SAGUIER.

Asociación Nacional Republicana—Partido Colorado (National Republican Party): Asunción; f. 19th century, ruling party since 1940; principal factions include: Movimiento de Reconciliación Colorada; Coloradismo Unido, led by Dr ANGEL ROBERTO SEIFART; Coloradismo Democrático, led by BLÁS RIQUELME; Acción Democrática Republicana, led by CARLOS FACETTI MASULLI; Unión Nacional de Colorados Eticos, led by Gen. (retd) LINO CÉSAR OVIEDO SILVA (expelled from party by Movimiento de Reconciliación Colorada faction in Dec. 1998, went into exile in Argentina in March 1999, arrested in Brazil in June 2000); Frente Republicano de Unidad Nacional, led by WÁLTER BOWER MONTALTO: 947,430 mems (1991); Pres. NICANOR DUARTE FRUTOS.

Asunción Para Todos (APT): Asunción; f. 1991 to contest municipal elections; also campaigned nationally; Leader Dr CARLOS FILIZZOLA.

Partido Comunista Paraguayo (PCP): Asunción; f. 1928; banned 1928–46, 1947–89; Sec.-Gen. ANANÍAS MAIDANA.

Partido de los Trabajadores (PT): Asunción; f. 1989; Socialist.

Partido Demócrata Cristiano (PDC): Colón 871, Casilla 1318, Asunción; f. 1960; 20,500 mems; Pres. Prof. Dr JERÓNIMO IRALA BURGOS; Vice-Pres Dr JOSÉ M. BONÍN, JUAN C. DESCALZO BUONGERMINI; Gen. Sec. Dr LUIS M. ANDRADA NOGUÉS.

Partido Revolucionario Febrerista (PRF): Casa del Pueblo, Manduvira 552, Asunción; tel. (21) 494041; e-mail partyce@mixmail.com; f. 1951; social democratic party; affiliated to the Socialist International; President CARLOS MARÍA LJUBETIC.

Diplomatic Representation

EMBASSIES IN PARAGUAY

Argentina: Avda España esq. Avda Perú, Asunción; tel. (21) 21-2320; fax (21) 21-1029; e-mail embarpy@pla.net.py; internet www.pla.net.py/embarpy; Ambassador: JOSÉ MARÍA BERRO.

Bolivia: America 200 y Mariscal Lopez, Asunción; tel. (21) 22-7213; fax (21) 21-0440; e-mail embolivia-asuncion@rree.gov.bo; Ambassador: EMILIO ANTELO PEREIRA.

Brazil: Col Irrazábal esq. Eligio Ayala, Asunción; tel. (21) 21-4534; fax (21) 21-2693; Ambassador: LUIZ CASTRO NEVES.

Chile: Guido Spano 1687, Calle Juan B. Motta, Asunción; tel. (21) 66-0344; Ambassador: EMILIO RUIZ TAGLE.

China (Taiwan): Avda Mariscal López 1043, Casilla 503, Asunción; tel. (21) 21-3362; fax (21) 21-3681; e-mail giopy@telesurf.com.py; internet www.roc-taiwan.org.py; Ambassador: Gen. AGUSTIN TING-TSU LIU.

Colombia: Avda Mariscal López 2240, Asunción; tel. (21) 62162; Ambassador: GUILLERMO TRIANA AYALA.

Costa Rica: San José 447, Casilla 1936, Asunción; tel. and fax (21) 21-3535; Ambassador: FERNANDO JOSÉ GUARDIA.

Ecuador: Edif. Inter-Express, 9°, Of. 901, Herrera 195 esq. Yegros, Asunción; tel. (21) 46150; Ambassador: ROBERTO PONCE ALVARADO.

El Salvador: Edif. Líder W, 11°, Estrella 692 y Juan E. O'Leary, Apdo 115, Asunción; tel. (21) 95503; Ambassador: JOSÉ MAURICIO ANGULO.

France: Avda España 893, Calle Pucheu, Casilla 97, Asunción; tel. (21) 21-2449; fax (21) 21-1690; e-mail chancellerie@ambafran.gov.py; Ambassador: JEAN-PIERRE DANIEL LAFOSSE.

Germany: Avda Venezuela 241, Casilla 471, Asunción; tel. (21) 21-4009; fax (21) 21-2863; Ambassador: JOSEF RUSNAK.

Holy See: Calle Ciudad del Vaticano 350, casi con 25 de Mayo, Casilla 83, Asunción (Apostolic Nunciature); tel. (21) 21-5139; fax (21) 21-2590; e-mail nunapos@conexion.com; Apostolic Nuncio: Most Rev. ANTONIO LUCIBELLO, Titular Archbishop of Thurio.

Israel: Edif. San Rafael, 8°, Yegros 437, Asunción; tel. (21) 49-5097; fax (21) 49-6355; e-mail israel@quanta.com.py; Ambassador: MERON REUBEN.

Italy: Calle Luis Morales 680, esq. Luis de León, Apdo 521, Asunción; tel. (21) 20-7429; (21) 21-2630; e-mail ambasu@uninet.com.py; Ambassador: GIULIO CESARE PICCIRILLI.

Japan: Avda Mariscal López 2364, Casilla 1957, Asunción; tel. (21) 60-4616; fax (21) 60-6901; Ambassador: SHOSUKE ITO.

Korea, Republic: Avda Rep. Argentina 678, Asunción; tel. (21) 60-5606; fax (21) 60-1376; Ambassador: CHOU UCK KIM.

Mexico: Edif. Parapití, 5°, Estrella y Juan E. O'Leary, Asunción; tel. (21) 44-4421; fax (21) 44-1877; Ambassador: SERGIO ROMERO CUEVAS.

Panama: Edif. Betón I, 11B°, Calle Eduardo Víctor Haedo 179, Asunción; tel. (21) 44-5545; fax (21) 44-6192; Ambassador: REYMUNDO HURTADO.

Peru: Agustín Barrios 852, Barrio Manorá, Asunción; tel. (21) 60-7431; fax (21) 60-7327; Ambassador: NORAH NALVARTE CHÁVEZ.

Spain: Yegros 437, Asunción; tel. (21) 90686; Ambassador: IGNACIO GARCÍA-VALDECASAS.

Switzerland: Edif. Parapití, 4°, Juan E. O'Leary 409 y Estrella, Asunción; tel. (21) 48022; e-mail swiemasu@pla.net.py; Ambassador: URS STEMMLER.

United Kingdom: Avda. Boggiani 5848, C/R 16 Boquerón, Asunción; tel. (21) 61-2611; fax (21) 60-5007; e-mail brembasu@rieder.net.py; Ambassador: ANDREW N. GEORGE.

USA: Avda Mariscal López 1776, Casilla 402, Asunción; tel. (21) 21-3715; fax (21) 21-3728; internet www.usembparaguay.gov.py; Ambassador: DAVID N. GREENLEE.

Uruguay: 25 de Mayo 1894 esq. General Aquino, Asunción; tel. (21) 25391; fax (21) 23970; Ambassador: RODOLFO OLAVARRIA.

Venezuela: Edif. Delime II, 1°, Juan E. O'Leary esq. Eduardo Víctor Haedo, Apdo 94, Asunción; tel. (21) 44242; Ambassador: NELSON PINEDA.

Yugoslavia: Mariscal Estigarribia 1023, Asunción; tel (21) 44-4243; fax (21) 49-0515; Ambassador: GOJKO CELEBIĆ.

Judicial System

The Corte Suprema de Justicia (Supreme Court of Justice) is composed of judges (usually nine) appointed on the recommendation of the Consejo de la Magistratura (Council of the Magistracy).

Corte Suprema de Justicia: Palacio de Justicia, Asunción; CARLOS FERNÁNDEZ GADEA (President), ENRIQUE SOSA, FELIPE SANTIAGO PAREDES, RAÚL SAPENA BRUGADA, WILDO RIENZI, BONIFACIO RÍOS, JERÓNIMO IRALA BURGOS, LUIS LEZCANO CLAUDE, ELIXENO AYALA.

Consejo de la Magistratura: Palacio de Justicia, Asunción; FEDERICO CALLIZO NICORA (President), CÉSAR MANUEL DIESEL (Vice-President), CARLOS FERNÁNDEZ GADEA, EVELIO FERNÁNDEZ AREVALOS, MARCELO DUARTE, FLORENTÍN LÓPEZ C., SIXTO VOLPE RÍOS, RAÚL SILVA ALONSO.

Attorney-General: OSCAR LATORRE.

Under the Supreme Court are the Courts of Appeal, the Tribunal of Jurors and Judges of First Instance, the Judges of Arbitration, the Magistrates (Jueces de Instrucción), and the Justices of the Peace.

Religion

The Roman Catholic Church is the established religion, although all sects are tolerated.

CHRISTIANITY
The Roman Catholic Church

For ecclesiastical purposes, Paraguay comprises one archdiocese, 11 dioceses and two Apostolic Vicariates. At 31 December 1999 there were an estimated 4,923,015 adherents in the country, representing about 87% of the total population.

Bishops' Conference: Conferencia Episcopal Paraguaya, Calle Alberdi 782, Casilla 1436, Asunción; tel. (21) 49-0920; fax (21) 49-5115; e-mail cep@infonet.com.py; f. 1977 (statutes approved 2000); Pres. Rt Rev. JORGE ADOLFO CARLOS LIVIERES BANKS, Bishop of Encarnación.

Archbishop of Asunción: Most Rev. FELIPE SANTIAGO BENÍTEZ AVALOS, Arzobispado, Avda Mariscal López 130 esq. Independencia Nacional, Casilla 654, Asunción; tel. (21) 44-4150; fax (21) 44-7510.

The Anglican Communion

Paraguay constitutes a single diocese of the Iglesia Anglicana del Cono Sur de América (Anglican Church of the Southern Cone of America). The Presiding Bishop of the Church is the Bishop of Northern Argentina.

Bishop of Paraguay: Rt Rev. JOHN ELLISON, Iglesia Anglicana, Casilla 1124, Asunción; tel. (21) 20-0933; fax (21) 21-4328; e-mail jellison@pla.net.py.

The Baptist Church

Baptist Evangelical Convention of Paraguay: Casilla 1194, Asunción; tel. (21) 27110; Exec. Sec. Lic. RAFAEL ALTAMIRANO.

BAHÁ'Í FAITH

National Spiritual Assembly of the Bahá'ís of Paraguay: Eligio Ayala 1456, Apdo 742, Asunción; tel. (21) 22-0250; fax (21) 22-5747; e-mail bahai@uninet.com.py; Sec. MIRNA LLAMOSAS DE RIQUELME.

The Press

DAILIES

ABC Color: Yegros 745, Asunción; tel. (21) 49-1160; fax (21) 49-3059; e-mail azeta@abc.una.py; internet www.ubc.com.py; f. 1967; independent; Propr ALDO ZUCCOLILLO; circ. 75,000.

El Día: Avda Mariscal López 2948, Asunción; tel. (21) 60-3401; fax (21) 66-0385; e-mail eldia@infonet.com.py; Dir HUGO OSCAR ARANDA; circ. 12,000.

La Nación: Avda Zavala Cue y Cerro Col, Fernando de la Mora, Asunción; tel. (21) 51-2520; fax (21) 44-4827; e-mail lanacion@infonet.com.py; internet www.lanacion.com.py; f. 1995; Dir-Gen. OSVALDO DOMÍNGUEZ DIBB; circ. 10,000.

Noticias: Avda Artigas y Avda Brasilia, Casilla 3017, Asunción; tel. (21) 29-2721; fax (21) 29-2841; e-mail director@diarionoticias.com.py; internet www.diarionoticias.com.py; f. 1984; independent; Dir NÉSTOR LÓPEZ MOREIRA; circ. 55,000.

Patria: Tacuari 443, Asunción; tel. (21) 92011; f. 1946; Colorado Party; Dir JUAN RAMÓN CHÁVEZ; circ. 8,000.

Popular: Avda Mariscal López 2948, Asunción; tel. (21) 60-3401; fax (21) 60-3400; Dir HUGO OSCAR ARANDA; circ. 125,000.

Ultima Hora: Benjamín Constant 658, Asunción; tel. (21) 49-6261; fax (21) 44-7071; e-mail ultimahora@uhora.com.py; internet www.ultimahora.com; f. 1973; independent; Dir DEMETRIO ROJAS; circ. 45,000.

PERIODICALS

Acción: Casilla 1072, Asunción; tel. (21) 37-0753; e-mail oliva@uninet.com.py; internet www.uninet.com.py/accion; monthly; Dir MARIANO GARCÍA.

La Opinión: Boggiani esq. Luis Alberto de Herrera, Asuncíon; tel. (21) 50-7501; fax (21) 50-2297; weekly; Dir FRANCISCO LAWS; Editor BERNARDO NERI.

Tiempo 14: Mariscal Estigarribia 4187, Asunción; tel. (21) 60-4308; fax (21) 60-9394; weekly; Dir HUMBERTO RUBÍN; Editor ALBERTOPERALTA.

NEWS AGENCIES

Agencia Paraguaya de Noticias (APN): Asunción; e-mail apn@supernet.com.py; internet www.supernet.com.py/usuarios/apn.

Foreign Bureaux

Agence France-Presse (AFP): Edif. Segesa, Of. 602, Oliva y Alberdi, Asunción; tel. (21) 44-3725; fax (21) 44-4312; Correspondent HUGO RUIZ OLAZAR.

Agencia EFE (Spain): Yegros 437, Asunción; tel. (21) 49-2730; fax (21) 49-1268; Bureau Chief LUCIO GÓMEZ-OLMEDO.

Agenzia Nazionale Stampa Associata (ANSA) (Italy): Edif. Interexpress, 4°, Of. 403, Luis Alberto de Herrera 195, Asunción; tel. (21) 44-9286; fax (21) 44-2986; Agent VÍCTOR E. CARUGATI.

Associated Press (AP) (USA): Calle Caballero 742, Casilla 264, Asunción; tel. (21) 60-6334.

Deutsche Presse-Agentur (dpa) (Germany): Edif. Segesa, Of. 705, Oliva 309, Asunción; tel. (21) 45-0329; fax (21) 44-8116; Correspondent EDUARDO ARCE.

Inter Press Service (IPS) (Italy): Edif. Segesa, 3°, Of. 5, Oliva 393 y Alberdi, Asunción; tel. and fax (21) 44-6350; Legal Rep. CLARA ROSA GAGLIARDONE.

United Press International (UPI) (USA): Azara 1098, Asunción; tel. (21) 21-2710; Correspondent JOSÉ GALEANO.

TELAM (Argentina) is also represented in Paraguay.

Publishers

La Colmena, SA: Asunción; tel. (21) 20-0428; Dir DAUMAS LADOUCE.

Ediciones Diálogo: Calle Brasil 1391, Asunción; tel. (21) 20-0428; f. 1957; fine arts, literature, poetry, criticism; Man. MIGUEL ANGEL FERNÁNDEZ.

Ediciones Nizza: Eligio Ayala 1073, Casilla 2596, Asunción; tel. (21) 47160; medicine; Pres. Dr JOSÉ FERREIRA MARTÍNEZ.

Editorial Comuneros: Cerro Corá 289, Casilla 930, Asunción; tel. (21) 44-6176; fax (21) 44-4667; e-mail rolon@conexion.com.py; f. 1963; social history, poetry, literature, law; Man. OSCAR R. ROLÓN.

Intercontinental Editora: Caballero 270, Asunción; tel. (21) 49-6991; fax (21) 44-9738; political science, law, literature, poetry; Dir ALEJANDRO GATTI.

R. P. Ediciones: Eduardo Víctor Haedo 427, Ascunción; tel. (21) 49-8040; Man. RAFAEL PERONI.

ASSOCIATION

Cámara Paraguaya del Libro: Nuestra Señora de la Asunción 697 esq. Eduardo Víctor Haedo, Asunción; tel. (21) 44-4104; fax (21) 44-7053; Pres. PABLO LEÓN BURIAN; Sec. EMA DE VIEDMA.

Broadcasting and Communications

TELECOMMUNICATIONS

Administración Nacional De Telecomunicaciones (ANTELCO): Edif. Morotí, 1°–2°, esq. Gen. Bruguéz y Teodoro S. Mongelos, Casilla 2042, Asunción; tel. (21) 20-3800; fax (21) 20-3888; scheduled for privatization in 2001; Pres. JUAN WILFRED GÓMEZ ARGAÑA.

Comisión Nacional de Telecomunicaciones (CONATEL): Edif. San Rafael, 2° Yegros 437 y 25 de Mayo, Asunción; tel. (21) 44-0020; fax (21) 49-8982; Pres. VICTOR ALCIDES BOGADO.

BROADCASTING

Radio

FM 99: Edif. Líder III, Antequera 652, 9°, Asunción; tel. (21) 44-3324; fax (21) 44-4367; f. 1980; Gen. Man. EFRÉN MELLO.

Radio Apyzandú: Mcal López y Capitán del Puerto San Ignacio, Misiones; tel. (82) 374; fax (82) 384; f. 1982; Gen. Man. AUGUSTO DOS SANTOS.

Radio Asunción: Avda Artigas y Capitán Lombardo 174, Asunción; tel. (21) 29-0618; Dir MIGUEL G. FERNÁNDEZ.

Radio Cáritas: Kubitschek y Azara, Casilla 1313, Asunción; tel. (21) 21-3570; fax (21) 20-4161; f. 1936; station of the Franciscan order; medium-wave; Pres. Most Rev. FELIPE SANTIAGO BENÍTEZ AVALOS (Archbishop of Asunción); Dir CRISTÓBAL LÓPEZ.

Radio Cardenal Stéreo: Río Paraguay 1334 y Guariníes Lambaré, Casilla 2532, Asunción; tel. (21) 31-1240; fax (21) 31-0556; f. 1991; Pres. NÉSTOR LÓPEZ MOREIRA.

Radio Chaco Boreal: Avda Mariscal López 2948, Asunción; tel. (21) 66-2616; f. 1968; Gen. Man. CARMEN BIGORDA.

Radio Concepción: Coronel Panchito López 241, entre Schreiber y Profesor Guillermo A. Cabral, Casilla 78, Concepción; tel. (31) 42318; fax (31) 42254; f. 1963; medium-wave; Dir SERGIO E. DACAK; Gen. Man. JULIÁN MARTÍ IBÁÑEZ.

Radio Encarnación: General Artigas 798 y Caballero, Encarnación; tel. (71) 3345; fax (71) 4099; commercial but owned by ANTELCO; medium- and short-wave; Dir PEDRO GÓMEZ FALCÓN.

Radio Guairá: Presidente Franco 788 y Alejo García, Villarica; tel. (541) 2385; fax (541) 2130; f. 1950; medium-, long- and short-wave; Dir LÍDICE RODRÍGUEZ DE TRAVERSI.

Radio Guaraní: Avda José F. Bogado y Batallón 40, Asunción; tel. (21) 24313; medium- and short-wave; Dir ESTEBAN CÁCERES ALMADA.

Radio Horizonte: Carlos A. López C/B Caballero Caaguazú, Caaguazú; tel. (522) 2359; fax (522) 2070; f. 1990; Dir ROQUE A. GÓMEZ LÓPEZ.

Radio Itapirú S.R.L.: Avda San Blás, esq. Coronel Julián Sánchez, ciudad del Este, Alto Paraná; tel. (61) 57-2206; fax (61) 57-2210; f. 1969; Pres. FABIÁN ARANDA ENCINA.

Radio La Voz de Amambay: 14 de Mayo y Cerro León, Pedro Juan Caballero, Amambay; tel. (36) 2537; fax (36) 4004; f. 1959; Gen. Man. DIANA ROLÓN DOS SANTOS.

Radio Nacional del Paraguay: Niamad Blas Garay 241 y Iturbe, Asunción; tel. (21) 39-0374; medium- and short-wave and FM; Dir GILBERTO ORTIZ.

Radio Ñandutí: Choferes del Chaco 1194, esq. Mariscal Estigarribia, Casilla 1179, Asunción; tel. (21) 60-4308; fax (21) 60-6074; internet www.infonet.com.py/holding/nanduam/; f. 1962; Dirs HUMBERTO RUBÍN, GLORIA RUBÍN.

Radio Nuevo Mundo: Coronel Romero y Flórida, San Lorenzo, Asunción; tel. (21) 58-6258; fax (21) 58-2424; f. 1972; Dir JULIO CÉSAR PEREIRA BOBADILLA.

Radio Paraguay: Avda General Santos 2525 y 18 de Julio, Asunción; tel. (21) 34591; medium-wave and FM; Dir ROQUE A. FLEITAS T.

Radio Parque: Ruta Internacional Dr Francia, Km 10, Ciudad del Este, Alto Paraná; tel. (61) 57-0262; fax (61) 57-1237; f. 1964; Gen. Man. ELVA BARRETO DE BEJARANO.

Radio Primero de Marzo: Avda General Perón y Felicidad, Casilla 1456, Asunción; tel. (21) 31-0564; fax (21) 33-2750; Dir-Gen. ANGEL GUERREROS A.

Radio Santa Mónica FM: Avda Boggiani y Herrera, 3°, Asunción; tel. (21) 51-3935; fax (21) 51-3936; f. 1973; Gen. Man. OSCAR RAMÍREZ.

Radio Venus: República Argentina y Souza, Asunción; tel. (21) 61-0151; e-mail venus@infonet.com.py; internet www.venus.com.py; f. 1987; Gen. Man. RICHARD ROJAS.

Television

Teledifusora Paraguaya—Canal 13: Chile 993, Asunción; tel. (21) 33-2823; fax (21) 33-1695; f. 1980; Gen. Man. NESTOR LÓPEZ MOREIGA.

Televisión Cerro Corá—Canal 9: Avda Carlos A. López 572, Asunción; tel. (21) 42-4222; fax (21) 44-2345; f. 1965; commercial; Dir MIRTHA RODRÍGUEZ DE SABA.

Televisora del Este: San Pedro, Calle Pilar, Area 5, Ciudad del Este; commercial; tel. (61) 8859; Dir Lic. JALIL SAFUAN; Gen. Man. A. VILLALBA V.

Televisión Itapúa—Canal 7: Avda Gen. Irrazábal y 25 de Mayo, Barrio Ipvu, Encarnación; tel. (71) 20-4450; commercial; Dir Lic. JALIL SAFUAN; Station Man. JORGE MATEO GRANADA.

Finance

(cap. = capital; res = reserves; dep. = deposits;m. = million; amounts in guaraníes, unless otherwise indicated)

BANKING

Superintendencia de Bancos: Edif. Banco Central del Paraguay, Avda Federacíon Rusa y Avda Sargento Marecos, Barrio Santo Domingo, Asunción; tel. (21) 60-8011; fax (21) 60-8149; e-mailsup ban@bcp.gov.py; internet www.bcp.gov.py/supban/principal.htm; Superintendent ANGEL GABRIEL GÓNZALEZ.

Central Bank

Banco Central del Paraguay: Avda Federación Rusa y Sargento Marecos, Casilla 861, Barrio Santo Domingo, Asunción; tel. (21) 60-8011; fax (21) 60-8149; e-mail bcp@uninet.com.py; internet www.bcp.com.py; f. 1952; cap. and res 19,300m. (June 1985); Pres. RAÚL JOSÉ VERA BOGADO; Gen. Man. EDGAR CACERES VERA.

Development Banks

Banco de Desarrollo del Paraguay, SA: Eduardo Víctor Haedo 195, Casilla 1531, Asunción; tel. (21) 44-8222; fax (21) 44-4885; f. 1970; cap. 3,000m., res 10,310.3m., dep. 142,435.9m. (Dec. 1995); Pres. EVELIO GONZÁLEZ PÉREZ; Gen. Man. JOSÉ GASPAR GÓMEZ .

Banco Nacional de Fomento: Independencia Nacional y Cerro Corá, Casilla 134, Asunción; tel. (21) 44-3762; fax (21) 44-4502; f. 1961 to take over the deposit and private banking activities of the Banco del Paraguay; cap. 59,168m., res 49,120m., dep. 807,587m. (Dec. 1997); Pres. JUAN JOSÉ GALEANO; 52 brs.

Banco Paraguayo Oriental de Inversión y de Fomento ECASA: Azara 197 y Yegros, Casilla 1496, Asunción; tel. (21) 44-4212; fax (21) 44-6820; f. 1988; cap. 22,992m., res 1,321.9m., dep. 189,832.7m. (Dec. 1995); Pres. CHAN WAI FU; Gen. Man. NELSON MÉNDEZ MORINIGO; 6 brs.

Banco Union SA de Inversión y Fomento (BUSAIF): Calles España y Brasil, Apdo 2973, Asunción; tel. (21) 21-1471; fax (21) 21-2587; Gen. Man. Dr RAÚL CASSIGNOL.

Crédito Agrícola de Habilitación: Caríos 362 y Willam Richardson, Asunción; tel. (21) 56-9010; fax (21) 55-4956; e-mail cah@quanta.com.py; f. 1943; Pres. Ing. Agr. WALBERTO FERREIRA.

Fondo Ganadero: Avda Artigas 1921, Asunción; tel. (21) 29-4361; fax (21) 44-6922; Pres. GUILLERMO SERRATTI G.

Commercial Banks

Banco Continental, SA: Estrella 621, Casilla 2260, Asunción; tel. (21) 44-2002; fax (21) 44-2001; f. 1980; total assets $53.7m. (Dec. 1998); Pres. CARLOS A. GOBERMAN; Gen. Man. JULIO C. CRISTALDO.

Banco Corporación SA: Eduardo Víctor Haedo 103 esq. Independencia Nacional, Casilla 317, Asunción; tel. (21) 44-9388; fax (21) 49-3772; f. 1987; dep. 112,452.7m., total assets 103,712.3m. (Dec. 1995); Pres. MIGUEL A. LARREINEGABE LESME; Gen. Man. Dr NELSON MENDOZA.

Banco Finamérica SA: Chile y Oliva, Casilla 1321, Asunción; tel. (21) 49-1021; fax (21) 44-5199; f. 1988; Pres. Dr GUILLERMO HEISECKE VELÁZQUEZ; Gen. Man. ENRIQUE FERNÁNDEZ ROMAY.

Banco Nacional de Trabajadores (BNT): 15 de Agosto 629, Casilla 1822, Asunción; tel. (21) 49-2214; fax (21) 44-8327; f. 1973 to make credit available to workers and to encourage savings; cap. 22,670m., dep. 89,337m. (Feb. 1994); Pres. Dr DOMINGO TORRES.

Interbanco, SA: Oliva y Chile 349, Casilla 392, Asunción; tel. (21) 49-4992; fax (21) 44-8587; e-mail interban@infonet.com.py; internet www.interbanco.com.py; f. 1978; cap. 19,000.0m., res 3,655.4m., dep. 233,734.9m. (Dec. 1997); Pres. FERNANDO SOTELINO; Gen. Man. CARLOS EDUARDO CASTRO; 5 brs.

Foreign Banks

ABN AMRO Bank NV (Netherlands): Alberdi y Estrella, Casilla 1180, Asunción; tel. (21) 49-0001; fax (21) 49-1734; internet www.abnamronet.com; f. 1965; Gen. Man. PETER BALTUSSEN.

Argentaria Banco Exterior, SA (Spain): Yegros 437 y 25 de Mayo, Casilla 824, Asunción; tel. (21) 49-2072; fax (21) 44-8103; e-mail bexpy@mmail.com.py; f. 1961 as Banco Exterior de España, S.A; name changed to above in 1999; cap. 1,126m., res 1,931m., dep. 30,455m. (Dec. 1987); Pres. JOSÉ IGNACIO LEYUN; Gen. Man. LUIS YAGÜE JIMENO; 5 brs.

Banco Alemán Paraguayo SA (Germany): Estrella 505 y 14 de Mayo, Casilla 1426, Asunción; tel. (21) 49-0166; fax (21) 44-7645; e-mail fpeterlik@bancoaleman.com.py; internet www.bancoaleman.com.py; f. 1989; cap. US$8.5m.; res $8.5m.; dep $216.7m. (Dec. 2000); Pres. JUAN PEIRANO; Gen. Man. FERNANDO SORRENTINO.

Banco de Asunción, SA: Palma esq. 14 de Mayo, Asunción; tel. (21) 49-3191; fax (21) 49-3190; f. 1964; major shareholder Banco Central Hispano (Spain); cap. 10,000.0m., res 62,588.1m., dep. 434,799.0m. (Dec. 1999); Pres. LIZARDO PELÁEZ ACERO; Gen. Man. RODRIGO CORREA GONZÁLEZ; 2 brs.

Banco do Brasil, SA: Oliva y Nuestra Señora de la Asunción, Casilla 667, Asunción; tel. (21) 44-1863; fax (21) 44-8761; f. 1941; Gen. Man. ANISIO LEITE JUNIOR.

Banco Central Hispano (Spain): Palma esq. 14 de Mayo, Asunción; tel. (21) 49-3191; fax (21) 49-3190.

Banco do Estado de São Paulo SA (BANESPA) (Brazil): Independencia Nacional esq. Fulgencio R. Moreno, Casilla 2211, Asunción; tel. (21) 49-4981; fax (21) 49-4985; e-mail banesspa@infonet.com.py; Gen. Man. AROLDO SALOMÃO.

Banco de la Nación Argentina: Chile y Palma, Asunción; tel. (21) 44-8566; fax (21) 44-4365; f. 1942; Man. EDUARDO V. FERNÁNDEZ; 3 brs.

Banco del Paraná, SA: Chile esq Eduardo V. Haedo 2298, Asunción; tel. (21) 44-6691; fax (21) 44-8909; e-mail int@mmail.com.py; internet www.bancodelparana.com.py; f. 1980; cap. US $9.9m., res US $2.2m., dep. US $70.0m. (Dec. 1999); Pres. ANTONIO CARLOS GENOVEZE; Dir ANISIO RESENDE DE SOUZA; 5 brs.

Banco Sudameris Paraguay, SA: Independencia Nacional y Cerro Corá, Casilla 1433, Asunción; tel. (21) 49-4542; fax (21) 44-8670; e-mail sudameri@conexion.com.py; f. 1961; savings and commercial bank; subsidiary of Banque Sudameris; cap. 33,038m., res 15,768m., dep. 481,246m. (Dec. 1998); Pres. Dr JOSÉ ANTONIO MORENO RUFFINELLI; Man. GIUSEPPE DI FRANCESCO; 6 brs.

Citibank NA (USA): Chile y Estrella 345, Asunción; tel. (21) 49-4951; fax (21) 44-4820; f. 1958; dep. 55,942.2m.; total assets 1,316,258.1m. (Dec. 1997); Vice-Pres. and Gen. Man. FELIPE CAVALCANTI.

Lloyds Bank PLC (United Kingdom): Palma esq. Juan E. O'Leary, Apdo 696, Asunción; tel. (21) 49-1090; fax (21) 44-3569; f. 1920; Man. STUART DUNCAN.

Banking Associations

Asociación de Bancos del Paraguay: Jorge Berges 229 esq. EEUU, Asunción; tel. (21) 21-4951; fax (21) 20-5050; e-mail abp.par @pla.net.py; mems: Paraguayan banks and foreign banks with brs in Asunción; Pres. CELIO TUNHOLI.

Cámara de Bancos Paraguayos: 25 de Mayo esq. 22 de Setiembre, Asunción; tel. (21) 22-2373; Pres. MIGUEL ANGEL LARREINEGABE.

STOCK EXCHANGE

Bolsa de Valores y Productos de Asunción SA: Estrella 540, Asunción; tel. (21) 44-2445; fax (21) 44-2446; e-mail bupasa@pla.net.py; f. 1977; Pres. GALO EGUEZ.

INSURANCE

La Agrícola SA de Seguros Generales: Mariscal Estigarribia 1173, Casilla 1349, Asunción; tel. (21) 21-3746; fax (21) 21-3685; f. 1982; general; Pres. Dr VICENTE OSVALDO BERGUES; Gen. Man. CARLOS ALBERTO LEVI SOSA.

Aseguradora Paraguaya, SA: Israel 309 esq. Rio de Janeiro, Casilla 277, Asunción; tel. (21) 21-5086; fax (21) 22-2217; e-mail asepasa@asepasa.com.py; f. 1976; life and risk; Pres. GERARDO TORCIDA CONEJERO.

Atalaya SA de Seguros Generales: Independencia Nacional 565, 1°, esq. Azara y Cerro Corá, Asunción; tel. (21) 49-2811; fax (21) 49-6966; e-mail ataseg@quanta.com.py; f. 1964; general; Pres. KARIN M. DOLL.

Central SA de Seguros: Edif. Betón I, 1° y 2°, Eduardo Víctor Haedo 179, Independencia Nacional, Casilla 1802, Asunción; tel. (21) 49-4654; fax (21) 49-4655; e-mail censeg@conexion.com.py; f. 1977; general; Pres. MIGUEL JACOBO VILLASANTI; Dir Dr FÉLIX AVEIRO.

Cigna Worldwide Insurance Company: Humaitá 937 y Montevideo, Casilla 730, Asunción; tel. (21) 44-5595; fax (21) 49-5209; f. 1989; general; Gen. Man. Dra TERESA Ma G. B. DE ROMERO PEREIRA.

El Comercio Paraguayo SA Cía de Seguros Generales: Alberdi 453 y Oliva, Asunción; tel. (21) 49-2324; fax (21) 49-3562; e-mail elcomericopy@mmail.com.py; f. 1947; life and risk; Dir Dr BRAULIO OSCAR ELIZECHE.

La Consolidada SA de Seguros y Reaseguros: Chile 719 y Eduardo Víctor Haedo, Casilla 1182, Asunción; tel. (21) 44-5788; fax (21) 44-5795; e-mail conso@higuray.com.py; f. 1961; life and risk; Pres. Dr JUAN DE JESÚS BIBOLINI; Gen. Man. Lic. JORGE PATRICIO FERREIRA FERREIRA.

La Continental Paraguaya SA de Seguros y Reaseguros: Chile 680 y Eduardo Víctor Haedo, 3°, Asunción; tel. (21) 44-6210; fax (21) 44-6210; f. 1986; life and risk; Pres. GUILLERMO HEISECKE VELÁZQUEZ; Man. JORGE A. LLORET.

La Independencia de Seguros y Reaseguros, SA: Edif. Parapatí, 1°, Juan E. O'Leary 409 esq. Estrella, Casilla 980, Asunción; tel. (21) 44-7021; fax (21) 44-8996; e-mail la_independencia@par.net.py; f. 1965; general; Pres. REGINO MOSCARDA; Gen. Man. JUAN FRANCISCO FRANCO LÓPEZ.

Intercontinental SA de Seguros y Reaseguros: Iturbe 1047, Teniente Fariña, Altos, Asunción; tel. (21) 49-2348; fax (21) 49-1227; e-mail intercontinentalseguros@usa.net.py; f. 1978; Pres. Dr JUAN MODICA.

Mundo SA de Seguros: Estrella 917 y Montevideo, Asunción; tel. (21) 49-2787; fax (21) 44-5486; f. 1970; risk; Pres. JUAN MARTÍN VILLALBA DE LOS RÍOS; Gen.-Man. BLÁS MARCIAL CABRAL BARRIOS.

Nanawa SA de Seguros y Reaseguros: Edif. Nanawa, Oliva 756, Casilla 2003, Asunción; tel. (21) 49-4961; fax (21) 44-9673; f. 1975; Pres. ROBERTO SALOMÓN; Gen. Man. JOSÉ LUIS CUEVAS.

Ñane Reta SA de Seguros y Reaseguros: Teniente Fariña 768 y Tacuari, Asunción; Casilla 1658, Asunción; tel. (21) 44-9745; fax (21) 44-7042; f. 1980; Pres. WERNER BÄERTSCHI; Gen. Man. CARLOS MOLINA LATERRA.

La Paraguaya SA de Seguros: Estrella 675, 7°, Asunción; tel. (21) 49-1367; fax (21) 44-8235; e-mail lps@rieder.net.py; f. 1905; life and risk; CEO JUAN BOSCH.

Patria SA de Seguros y Reaseguros: Edif. San Rafael, 9°, Yegros 437 esq. 25 de Mayo, Casilla 2735, Asunción; tel. (21) 44-5389; fax (21) 44-8230; e-mail patria@infonet.com.py; f. 1968; general; Pres. ROLF DIETER KEMPER; Exec. Dir Dr MARCOS PERERA R.

La Previsora SA de Seguros Generales: Estrella 1003, 5°, Asunción; tel. (21) 49-2442; fax (21) 49-4791; e-mail laprevisiora@laprevisiora.com.py; f. 1964; general; Pres. RUBÉN ODILIO DOMECQ M.; Man. JORGE EDUARDO DOMECQ F.

Real Paraguaya de Seguros, SA: Edif. Banco Real, 1°, Estrella esq. Alberdi, Casilla 1442, Asunción; tel. (21) 49-3171; fax (21) 49-8129; e-mail realscc@pla.net.py; f. 1974; general; Chair. CELIO TUNHOLI; Man. Dir JOSÉ CARLOS UTWARI.

Rumbos SA de Seguros: Estrella 851, Ayolas, Casilla 1017, Asunción; tel. (21) 44-9488; fax (21) 44-9492; e-mail rumbos@conexion.com.py; f. 1960; general; Pres. Dr ANTONIO SOLJANCIC; Man. Dir ROBERTO GÓMEZ VERLANGIERI.

La Rural del Paraguay SA Paraguaya de Seguros: Avda Mariscal López 1082 esq. Mayor Bullo, Casilla 21, Asunción; tel. (21) 49-1917; fax (21) 44-1592; e-mail larural@mmail.com.py; f. 1920; general; Pres. YUSAKU MATSUMIYA; Gen. Man. EDUARDO BARRIOS PERINI.

Seguros Chaco SA de Seguros y Reaseguros: Mariscal Estigarribia 982, Casilla 3248, Asunción; tel. (21) 44-7118; fax (21) 44-9551; e-mail segucha@conexion.com.py; f. 1977; general; Pres. EMILIO VELILLA LACONICH; Exec. Dir ALBERTO R. ZARZA TABOADA.

Seguros Generales, SA (SEGESA): Edif. SEGESA, 1°, Oliva 393 esq. Alberdi, Casilla 802, Asunción; tel. (21) 49-1362; fax (21) 49-1360; e-mail segesa@conexion.com.py; f. 1956; life and risk; Gen. Man. CÉSAR AVALOS.

Universo de Seguros y Reaseguros, SA: Edif. de la Encarnación, 9°, 14 de Mayo esq. General Díaz, Casilla 788, Asunción; tel. (21) 44-8530; fax (21) 44-7278; f. 1979; Pres. DANIEL CEREZUELA SÁNCHEZ.

Yacyretá SA de Seguros y Reaseguros: Padre Juan Pucheu 556, Avda España, Casilla 2487, Asunción; tel. (21) 20-8407; fax (21) 21-3108; f. 1980; Pres. Dr ERNESTO ROTELA PRIETO; Gen. Man. BENITO GIMÉNEZ CABALLERO.

Insurance Association

Asociación Paraguaya de Cías de Seguros: 15 de Agosto esq. Lugano, Casilla 1435, Asunción; tel. (21) 44-6474; fax (21) 44-4343; e-mail apcs@uninet.com.py; f. 1963; Pres. EMILIO VELILIA LACONICH; Sec. Lic. JUAN FRANCISCO FRANCO LÓPEZ.

Trade and Industry

GOVERNMENT AGENCIES

Consejo Nacional para las Exportaciones: Asunción; f. 1986; founded to eradicate irregular trading practices; Dir Minister of Industry and Commerce.

Consejo de Privatización: Edif. Ybaga, 10°, Presidente Franco 173, Asunción; fax (21) 44-9157; responsible for the privatization of state-owned enterprises; Exec. Dir RUBÉN MORALES PAOLI.

Instituto Nacional de Tecnología y Normalización (INTN) (National Institute of Technology and Standardization): Avda General Artigas 3973 y General Roa, Casilla 967, Asunción; tel. (21) 29-3748; fax (21) 29-0873; national standards institute; Dir. Gen. JOSÉ MARTINO.

Instituto de Previsión Social: Constitución y Luis Alberto de Herrera, Casilla 437, Asunción; tel. (21) 22-5719; fax (21) 22-3654; f. 1943; responsible for employees' welfare and health insurance scheme; Pres. Lic. BONIFACIO IRALA AMARILLA.

DEVELOPMENT ORGANIZATIONS

Secretaría Técnica de Planificación de la Presidencia de la República: Edif. AYFRA, 3°, Presidente Franco y Ayolas, Asunción; tel. (21) 44-8074; fax (21) 49-6510; govt body responsible for overall economic and social planning; Exec. Sec. Dr GUILLERMO SOSA; Sec.-Gen. Dr MARÍA VICTORIA DIESEL DE COSCIA.

Consejo Nacional de Coordinación Económica: Presidencia de la República, Paraguayo Independiente y Juan E. O'Leary, Asunción; responsible for overall economic policy; Sec. FULVIO MONGES OCAMPOS.

Consejo Nacional de Desarrollo Industrial (National Council for Industrial Development): Asunción; national planning institution.

Instituto de Bienestar Rural (IBR): Tacuary 276, Asunción; tel. (21) 44-0578; fax (21) 44-6534; responsible for rural welfare and colonization; Pres. ANTONIO IBAÑEZ.

Instituto Nacional del Indígena (INDI): Don Bosco 745, Asunción; tel. (21) 49-7137; fax (21) 447-154; f. 1981; responsible for welfare of Indian population; Pres. ELENA PANE PÉREZ.

ProParaguay: Edif. Ayfra, 12°, Pdte Franco y Ayolas, Asunción; tel. (21) 49-3625; fax (21) 49-3862; e-mail ppy@proparaguay.gov.py; internet www.proparaguay.gov.py; f. 1991; responsible for promoting investment in Paraguay and the export of national products; Exec. Dir Ing. FRANCISCO GUTIÉRREZ CAMPOS.

CHAMBER OF COMMERCE

Cámara y Bolsa de Comercio: Estrella 540, Asunción; tel. (21) 49-3321; fax (21) 44-0817; f. 1898; Pres. NICOLÁS GONZÁLEZ ODDONE; Gen. Man. Dr RICARDO FRANCO L.

EMPLOYERS' ORGANIZATIONS

Federación de la Producción, Industria y Comercio (FEPRINCO): Palma 751 y 15 de Agosto, Asunción; tel. (21) 46638; organization of private sector business executives; Pres. GUILLERMO STANLEY.

Unión Industrial Paraguaya (UIP): Cerro Corá 1038, Casilla 782, Asunción; tel. (21) 21-2556; fax 21-3360; f. 1936; organization of business entrepreneurs; Pres. NÉSTOR MÉNDEZ NÚÑEZ.

MAJOR COMPANIES

Automotive Importadora y Exportadora, SA: Estigarribia 1126 y Pitantuta F. de la Mora, Asunción; tel. (21) 51-0480; fax (21) 51-0949; e-mail automoti@infonet.com.py; f. 1954; wholesale and retail distribution of vehicle spare parts, tyres and lubricants; Chair. AGUSTÍN BELLON; Man. Dir ALEJANDRO BELLON; 160 employees.

Azucarera Paraguaya, SA: Avda General Artigas 552, Asunción; tel. (21) 21-3778; fax (21) 21-3150; e-mail azpa@azpa.com.py; internet www.azucareraparaguaya.com; f. 1905; refining and wholesale distribution of cane sugar; Pres. JUAN BOSCH; Dir-Gen. RAÚL HOECKLE; 1,000 employees.

Cervecería Paraguaya, SA: Palma 1139 con Hernanadarias, Asunción; tel. (21) 44-4424; fax (21) 49-3298; f. 1910; brewing and bottling beer; Man. DEMETRIO AYALA; 430 employees.

Compañía Algodonera Paraguaya, SA (CAPSA): Aviadora del Chaco 1846, Asunción; tel. (21) 44-4156; fax (21) 608-750; f. 1951; manufacture of edible vegetable oils, wholesale of tobacco and cotton; CEO THOMAS DOETWYLER; 800 employees.

Consorcio de Ingeniería Electromecanica, SA: Casilla 2078, Asunción; tel. (21) 64-2850; fax (21) 64-4130; e-mail ventas@cie.com.py; internet www.cie.com.py; f. 1978; manufacture of sheet metal work; Pres. HUGO ARANDA NÚÑEZ; 800 employees.

Empresa Distribuidora Especializada, SA (EDESA): Avda Eusebio Ayala 1690 esq. Prof Conradi, Asunción; tel. (21) 50-1652; fax (21) 50-8549; e-mail edesa@pla.net.py; f. 1981; wholesale distribution of durable goods; Pres. RAÚL ALBERTO DÍZ DE ESPADA; 450 employees.

Fenix, SA: Avda Boggiani 5086, Asunción; tel. (21) 66-0517; fax (21) 66-3375; f. 1968; import and manufacture of clothing and general merchandise; Pres. Dr ROLANDO NIELLA; 1,800 employees.

Grandes Tiendas La Riojana, SA: Avda Mariscal Estigarribia 165/171, Asunción; tel. (21) 49-2211; fax (21) 49-2212; e-mail riojana@rieder.net.py; retailing; CEO Lázaro Morga Lacalle; 480 employees.

Industria Nacional de Cemento: Humaitá 357, Asunción; cement manufacturers; Pres. Ramón Centurión Núñez; 776 employees.

Industrializadora Guaraní, SA: Madame Lynch y Sucre, Asunción; tel. (21) 67-1561; fax (21) 50-1761; f. 1967; manufacture of canned and bottled soft drinks; Man. Nery Lovera Pérez Ramírez; 1,170 employees.

La Vencedora, SA: Manduvira y Alberdi, Asunción; tel. (21) 49-2225; fax (21) 44-8036; internet www.lavencedora.com.py; f. 1895; cigarette manufacturers; Pres. Eduardo Nicolás Bo; 200 employees.

Las Palmas: Avda República Argentina 2154, Asunción; tel. (21) 55-3438; fax (21) 55-3403; f. 1943; production of cotton and manufacture of cotton linens; Pres. and Gen. Man. Dr Alejandro González; 965 employees.

Paraguay Refrescos, SA: 3°, Ruta Ñemby Barcequillo Km 3, San Lorenzo; tel. (21) 50-4121; fax (21) 50-3608; f. 1964; manufacture of soft drinks; Pres. Carlos Miguens Bemberg; 700 employees.

Petróleos Paraguayos, SA (PETROPAR): Edif. Oga Rapé, Chile 753, 9°, Asunción; tel. (21) 44-8503; fax (21) 46-9232; f. 1986; petroleum refining; Pres. Julio Gutiérrez ; 400 employees.

Scavone Hermanos, SA: Santa Ana 431, Asunción; tel. (21) 60-8171; fax (21) 66-2976; e-mail scavonehnos@online.uninet.com.py; f. 1905; manufacture and retail distribution of pharmaceuticals; Pres. Amadeo Scavone; 530 employees.

Shell Paraguay Ltda: Calle Presidente Franco e Ayolas, 15°, Asunción; tel. (21) 49-1111; fax (21) 44-9253; f. 1953; wholesale distribution of petroleum products; Dir-Gen. Adrian Hearle; 119 employees.

Tecno Electric, SA: Tte Molinas con Itapua, Asunción; tel. (21) 29-4114; fax (21) 29-2863; e-mail tesa@highway.com.py; f. 1968; manufacture of electrical equipment; Pres. Guido Boettner Balansa; 200 employees.

Vargas Peña Apezteguia y Compañía, SAIC: Quesada 5240 y Cruz del Chaco, Asunción; tel. (21) 60-2841; fax (21) 60-0262; e-mail abgvm@rieder.net.py; f. 1977; production of cotton and edible oils; Pres. José María Hernan Vargas Peña Apezteguia; 600 employees.

UTILITIES
Electricity

Administración Nacional de Electricidad (ANDE): Avda España 1268, Asunción; tel. (21) 21-1001; fax (21) 21-2371; e-mail ande@ande.gov.py; internet www.ande.gov.py; f. 1949; national electricity board, scheduled for privatization in 2001; Pres. Mario César Orue Delgado.

Water

Corporación de Obras Sanitarias (CORPOSANA): José Berges 516, entre Brasil y San José, Asunción; tel. (21) 21-0319; fax 21-5061; internet www.corposana.com; responsible for public water supply, sewage disposal and drainage, scheduled for privatization in 2001; Pres. Carlos Antonio López Rodríguez.

TRADE UNIONS

Central Nacional de Trabajadores (CNT): Piribebuy 1078, Asunción; tel. (21) 44-4084; fax (21) 49-2154; e-mail cnt@uninet.com.py; Sec.-Gen. Eduardo Ojeda.

Central de Sindicatos de Trabajadores del Estado Paraguayo (Cesitep): Asunción.

Central Unica de Trabajadores (CUT): San Carlos 836, Asunción; tel. (21) 44-3936; fax (21) 44-4195; f. 1989; Pres. Alan Flores; Sec.-Gen. Jorge Alvarenga.

Confederación Paraguaya de Trabajadores—CPT (Confederation of Paraguayan Workers): Yegros 1309-33 y Simón Bolívar, Asunción; tel. (21) 44-3184; f. 1951; Pres. Gerónimo López; Sec.-Gen. Julio Etcheverry Espinola; 43,500 mems from 189 affiliated groups.

Federación Nacional Campesina de Paraguay (FNC): Asunción; national peasants' federation; Sec.-Gen. Aberto Areco.

Transport

RAILWAYS

Ferrocarril Presidente Carlos Antonio López: México 145, Casilla 453, Asunción; tel. (21) 44-3273; fax (21) 44-7848; f. 1854, state-owned since 1961; 370 km of track, of which 8 km, from Encarnación to Argentine border, in service in 1997; scheduled for privatization in 2001; Pres. Jorge Jara Servían.

ROADS

In 1999 there were an estimated 29,500 km of roads, of which 3,067 km were paved. The Pan-American Highway runs for over 700 km in Paraguay and the Trans-Chaco Highway extends from Asunción to Bolivia.

SHIPPING

Administración Nacional de Navegación y Puertos—ANNP (National Shipping and Ports Administration): Cólon y El Paraguayo Independiente, Asunción; tel. (21) 49-5086; fax (21) 49-7485; e-mail annp@mail.pla.net.py; internet www.annp.gov.py; f. 1965; responsible for ports services and maintaining navigable channels in rivers and for improving navigation on the Rivers Paraguay and Paraná; Pres. Milciades Rabery Ocampos.

Inland Waterways

Flota Mercante Paraguaya SA (FLOMEPASA): Estrella 672-686, Casilla 454, Asunción; tel. (21) 44-7409; fax (21) 44-6010; boats and barges up to 1,000 tons displacement on Paraguay and Paraná rivers; cold storage ships for use Asunción–Buenos Aires-Montevideo; Pres. Capt. Aníbal Gino Pertile R.; Commercial Dir Dr Emigdio Duarte Sostoa.

Ocean Shipping

Compañía Paraguaya de Navegación de Ultramar, SA: Presidente Franco 625, 2°, Casilla 77, Asunción; tel. (21) 49-2137; fax (21) 44-5013; f. 1963 to operate between Asunción, USA and European ports; 10 vessel; Exec. Pres. Juan Bosch B.

Navemar S.R.L.: B. Constant 536, 2°, Casilla 273, Asunción; tel. (21) 49-3122; 5 vessels.

Transporte Fluvial Paraguayo S.A.C.I.: Edif. de la Encarnación, 13°, 14 de Mayo 563, Asunción; tel. (21) 49-3411; fax (21) 49-8218; e-mail tfpsaci@tm.com.py; Admin. Man. Daniella Charbonnier; 1 vessel.

CIVIL AVIATION

The major international airport, Aeropuerto Internacional Silvio Pettirossi is situated 15 km from Asunción. A second airport, Aeropuerto Internacional Guaraní, 30 km from Ciudad del Este, was inaugurated in January 1996.

National Airlines

Aerolíneas Paraguayas (ARPA): Terminal ARPA, Aeropuerto Internacional Silvio Pettirossi, Asunción; tel. (21) 21-5072; fax (21) 21-5111; f. 1994; domestic service; wholly-owned by Transportes Aéreos Regionais (Brazil); Pres. Miguel Candia; Dir-Gen. Aníbal Gómez de la Fuente.

Transportes Aéreos del Mercosur (TAM Mercosur): Aeropuerto Internacional Silvio Pettirossi, Hangar TAM/ARPA, Luque, Asunción; tel. (21) 49-1039; fax (21) 64-5146; e-mail tammercosur@uninet.com.py; f. 1963 as Líneas Aéreas Paraguayas (LAP), name changed as above 1997; services to destinations within South America; 80% owned by Transportes Aéreos Regionais (Brazil); Pres. Miguel Candia.

Tourism

Tourism is undeveloped, but, with recent improvements in the infrastructure, efforts were being made to promote the sector. Tourist arrivals in Paraguay in 1998 totalled 349,592. In 1997 tourist receipts were US $753m.

Dirección General de Turismo: Ministerio de Obras Públicas y Comunicaciones, Palma 468, Asunción; tel. (21) 44-1530; fax (21) 49-1230; f. 1940; Pres. and Dir of Tourism Hugo O. Cataldo.

Defence

At 1 August 2000 Paraguay's Armed Forces numbered 20,200, including an army of 14,900 and an air force of 1,700. The navy, which operates on the rivers, had 3,600 members, including 900 marines. There were 14,800 men in the paramilitary police force. Military service, which is compulsory, lasts for 12 months in the army and two years in the navy.

Defence Budget: 290,000m. guaraníes in 2000.

Commander-in-Chief of the Armed Forces: President of the Republic.

Chairman of the Joint Chiefs of Staff: Gen. Expedito Garrigoza.

Education

Education in Paraguay is, where possible, compulsory for six years, to be undertaken between six and 12 years of age, but there are insufficient schools, particularly in the remote parts of the country. Primary education commences at the age of six and lasts for six years. Secondary education, beginning at 12 years of age, lasts for a further six years, comprising two cycles of three years each. In 1996 91% of children in the relevant age-group attended primary schools, while secondary enrolment in the same year was 38%. There were 5,928 primary schools in 1996 and 801 secondary schools in 1990. There is one state and one Roman Catholic university in Asunción. In 1995, according to estimates by UNESCO, the rate of adult illiteracy averaged 7.9%. Education accounted for some 18.6% of total government expenditure in 1996.

Bibliography

For works on South America generally, see Select Bibliography (Books).

Box, P. H. *The Origins of the Paraguayan War*. New York, NY, Russell and Russell, 1967.

Burton, R. *Letters from the Battlefields of Paraguay*. London, Tinsley Brothers, 1870.

Clarke, E., and Horrock, N. *Contrabandista: The Busting of a Heroin Empire*. London, Paul Elek, 1975.

Lambert, P., and Nickson, A. *The Transition to Democracy in Paraguay*. Basingstoke, Palgrave, 1997.

Lewis, P. H. *Paraguay under Stroessner*. Chapel Hill, NC, University of North Carolina Press, 1980.

Socialism, Liberalism and Dictatorship in Paraguay. New York, NY, Praeger Publrs, 1982.

Nickson, R. A. *Paraguay*. Oxford, Clio, 1999.

Paraguay: Power Game. London, Latin American Bureau, 1980.

Turner, B. *Politics and Peasant-State Relations in Paraguay*. Lanham, MD, University Press of America, 1993.

White, R. A. *Paraguay's Autonomous Revolution, 1810–1840*. Albuquerque, NM, University of New Mexico, 1978.

Williams, J. H. *Rise and Fall of the Paraguayan Republic, 1800–70*. Austin, TX, University of Texas Press, 1980.

PERU

Area: 1,285,216 sq km (496,225 sq miles).

Population (official estimate at mid-2000): 25,662,000.

Capital: Lima (population of metropolitan area, Gran Lima, 7,060,600 at 1 July 1998).

Language: Spanish and Quechua (official).

Religion: Mainly Christianity (predominantly Roman Catholicism).

Climate: Varies with altitude from tropical in the coastal plain to cool in the Andes; rainy season from October to April.

Time: GMT –5 hours.

Public Holidays

2002: 1 January (New Year's Day), 28 March (Maundy Thursday), 29 March (Good Friday), 1 May (Labour Day), 24 June (Day of the Peasant, half-day only), 29 June (SS Peter and Paul), 28–29 July (Independence), 30 August (St Rose of Lima), 1 November (All Saints' Day), 8 December (Immaculate Conception), 25 December (Christmas Day).

2003: 1 January (New Year's Day), 17 April (Maundy Thursday), 18 April (Good Friday), 1 May (Labour Day), 24 June (Day of the Peasant, half-day only), 29 June (SS Peter and Paul), 28–29 July (Independence), 30 August (St Rose of Lima), 1 November (All Saints' Day), 8 December (Immaculate Conception), 25 December (Christmas Day).

Currency: Nuevo sol (new sol); 100 nuevos soles = £19.47 = US $27.88 = €31.41 (30 April 2001).

Weights and Measures: The metric system is in force.

Basic Economic Indicators

	1998	1999	2000
Gross domestic product (million new soles at 1994 prices)	118,595	118,210	122,473
GDP per head (new soles at 1994 prices)	4,781.9	4,684.9	4,772.5
GDP (million new soles at current prices)	167,026	175,856	188,209
GDP per head (new soles at current prices)	6,734.7	6,989.6	7,334.2
Annual growth of real GDP (%)	1.3	–0.3	3.6
Annual growth of real GDP per head (%)	–0.5	–0.2	1.9
Government budget estimates (million new soles at current prices):			
Revenue	29,637	n.a.	n.a.
Expenditure	30,130	n.a.	n.a.
Consumer price index (base: 1995 = 100)	129.9	134.4	139.4
Rate of inflation (annual average, %)	7.3	3.5	3.7
Foreign exchange reserves (US $ million at 31 December)	9,563.4	8,730.1	8,372.5
Imports c.i.f. (US $ million)	9,866.9	8,074.8	8,796.8
Exports f.o.b. (US $ million)	5,756.7	6,112.6	7,001.6
Balance of payments (current account, US $ million)	–3,638	–1,822	–1,648

Gross national product per head measured at purchasing power parity (PPP) (US dollars, converted by the PPP exchange rate, 1999): 4,480.

Economically active population (1999): 10,076,800.

Unemployment (1999): 8.0%.

Total foreign debt (estimate, 2000): US $32,200m.

Life expectancy (years at birth, 1998): 69 (males 66, females 71).

Infant mortality rate (per 1,000 live births, 1999): 42.

Adult population with HIV/AIDS (15–49 years, 1999): 0.35%.

School enrolment ratio (6–16 years, 1997): 100%.

Adult literacy rate (15 years and over, 2000): 89.9% (males 94.7; females 85.4).

Energy consumption per head (kg of oil equivalent, 1998): 581.

Carbon dioxide emissions per head (metric tons, 1997): 1.2.

Passenger motor cars in use (per 1,000 of population, 1999): 270.

Television receivers in use (per 1,000 of population, 1997): 126.

Personal computers in use (per 1,000 of population, 1997): 12.9.

History

SANDY MARKWICK

In 1532, when Francisco Pizarro began the conquest of modern-day Peru on behalf of the Spanish, the Inca empire was engaged in civil war. After the death of the Inca ruler, Huayna Capac, a dispute over the succession was fought out between the northern forces, led by Atahualpa, and those under the command of his half-brother, Huásca, who controlled the southern part of the empire from Cuzco. The territory of the Inca empire, Tahuantin-suyo, had grown too large to control, stretching, at its peak, 5,000 km, from modern-day Colombia to central Chile. Under Pachacuti, who became ruler in 1432, imperial expansion had accelerated as neighbouring societies and cultures were subjugated by the military might and despotism of the Incas. Centred on the fertile Cuzco region, Inca control was based on a strong pyramidal system of government. A sophisticated network of stone roads, bridges and tunnels, and intensive systems of irrigation and agriculture, based on a communal productive unit known as the ayllu, supported a high-density population (estimates vary between 12m. and 32m.). Maize and potatoes were the principal crops. The metals worked were gold, silver and bronze. Agricultural tribute and labour was demanded through local chieftains, or kurakas, in return for military and divine protection from the emperors, who were deified as sun-gods.

Pizarro's forces captured Atahualpa and killed some 7,000 of his troops after luring them into a trap in Cajamarca. The conquistadors, fearing the arrival of an Inca army to rescue Atahualpa, demanded riches from him before carrying out his public execution. The Cuzco region fell to Pizarro's forces in 1533, and in 1544 the Viceroyalty of Peru was formally established, with its capital in Lima. Sporadic resistance continued until the Incas were finally defeated in 1572, when Tupac Amarú I, the last Inca emperor, was captured at the fall of Vilcabamba, taken to Cuzco and beheaded. The Spanish colonial administration, having completed its military conquest (despite intermittent uprisings), embarked on a repressive programme of Christianization. Indigenous Indian (Amerindian) religious traditions survived, however, either assimilated into the new Roman Catholic order or concealed from the Church hierarchy. During the colonial period, the Andean tradition of communalism was weakened, as mining for export became the dominant economic activity, and the new criollo (Creole) élite of Spanish origin established large agricultural estates (haciendas) on the most fertile lands, to supply produce for mining and coastal towns. The defeat of the Incas by the Spanish greatly influenced the character of modern Peru, where sharp divisions follow ethnic lines and long-established resentments occasionally escalate into violence.

INDEPENDENCE

At the end of the 18th century an independence movement grew among the criollos, who resented their inferior status as well as the restrictive trade regulations and high taxes imposed by Spanish government. Peru declared independence from Spain on 28 July 1821, helped by the republican forces of the Argentine general, José de San Martín. The republicans, assisted by Great Britain, defeated Spain at the decisive Battle of Ayacucho in 1824. Political instability characterized the first half-century of independence. In the aftermath of the war, political office was held by regional military leaders (caudillos) who, having fought against a common enemy—the Spanish—now fought each other in the contest for central power. After independence Peru was highly regionalized, with economic power vested in the hacienda and political control exercised by hacienda owners in alliance with local caudillos. The weakness of the central state prevented governments from consolidating national political control and forced them to work in co-operation with regional leaders to rule at local level. Government in Lima represented a series of shifting alliances between caudillos and regional groupings

of the criollo élite of merchants and landowners. Successive Presidents failed to create a consensus to permit the emergence of relatively stable government, and rival groups competed for power and the resources of the state. Between 1826 and 1865 some 34 Presidents, including 27 military officers, held office. One such contender for power was a Bolivian President, Gen. Andrés Santa Cruz, who, allied with southern Peruvian landowners, proclaimed the Peruvian–Bolivian Confederation in 1836, with its capital in Lima. Chile, viewing the Confederation as a threat to its interests in the Pacific, declared war. The Confederation was finally defeated and, subsequently, dissolved by Chilean forces in 1839. The most successful leader during the immediate post-independence era, who achieved relative political stability, was Marshal Ramón Castilla, President in 1845–51 and 1855–60.

THE GUANO YEARS

The emergence of the guano trade ended a period of economic stagnation. International demand for the fertilizing properties of guano (the accumulated nitrate-rich deposits of bird colonies on the offshore islands) escalated with the development of capital-intensive commercial agriculture in Europe. The Peruvian Government established a state monopoly over the exploitation of guano. However, despite average economic growth rates of over 5% between 1840 and 1878, resulting largely from the trade, the success of the guano industry was not fully exploited. Revenue from guano was spent on the expansion of the bureaucracy, the military and the servicing of the Government's foreign debt, which had accumulated to finance imports. The colonial character of production on large estates and the self-sufficient nature of peasant economies remained intact. This perpetuated deep ethnic and class divisions and prevented the emergence of a strong internal market which would have provided Peru's productive sectors with the domestic stimulus for growth. Internal demand among élite consumers, which developed after the dramatic expansion of guano exports, could not be satisfied by the domestic productive sector and resulted in increased imports. The railways brought Peruvian products closer to the international market, but did not fundamentally alter the development model. The most lucrative years of the guano trade came to an end in the 1870s, as the result of competition from cheaper nitrates and synthetic fertilizers. Peru was under threat of bankruptcy, with a huge external debt of US $35m. and no access to foreign loans. The crisis culminated in another military defeat of Peru and Bolivia by Chile, in the War of the Pacific (1879–83), which resulted from a dispute over nitrate resources in the Atacama desert. Chile occupied much of Peru, including Lima, in 1881. Under the terms of the peace settlement, Chile annexed the province of Tarapac as well as the Bolivian department of Antofagasta.

THE RISE OF A COASTAL OLIGARCHY

Post-war reconstruction led to the expansion of coastal haciendas and the rise of an oligarchy of merchants, financiers and landowners, better adapted to a new capitalist age, whose interests centred on the production and export of primary products. The coastal oligarchy (comprising some 50 extended families), allied to foreign capital and semi-feudal landowners of the sierra, exercised widespread influence and control over government until 1968, when a modernizing military regime seized power. The reconstruction of archaic productive capacity after the War of the Pacific was facilitated by the demands for raw materials and outlets for surplus investment from Europe and North America, in a period of world capitalist expansion. Raw material prices grew at an average of 7% per year between 1890 and 1929. Peru's reconstruction after the War of the Pacific also received substantial support from the so-called Grace Contract, which was finally approved in 1889. The Contract, negotiated by a British businessman, Michael Grace, provided for the cancellation of Peru's national debt in return for the Government ceding control over its railway network to the largely British-owned Peruvian Corporation. The export-led development of Peru in this period was more broad-based than that undertaken when guano dominated. Sugar and cotton were the principal exports, but wool, rubber, silver, copper and petroleum each accounted for more than 15% of total export earnings at various times between 1890 and 1929.

Peru's first modern political party, the Civil Party (Partido Civil), was created in 1871 to represent the interests of the new oligarchy. The civilistas were opposed to military government and rejected the unproductive use of resources from guano. In 1872 Manuel Pardo was elected as the first civilista President. The Partido Civil, guided by liberal, *laissez-faire* doctrines, and the rival Democratic Party (Partido Democrático), which was more pro-Church and conservative, led Peru through a period of export-orientated development and rapid economic and social change during the next half-century. Formal parliamentary democracy was, in practice, extremely limited, applying to no more than some 3% of the total population. During this period, however, the military was professionalized and, at least between 1895 and 1919, was brought under civilian control. The government was reorganized to conform better to the demands of a modern export economy. Democratic government was interrupted by the dictatorship of Augusto Bernardino Leguia, which lasted from 1919 until 1930. From this period, marked by economic prosperity and relative political stability, the structure of contemporary Peru emerged. The advance of capitalism saw peasants migrate to the cities, while traditional haciendas and small-scale mining operations were transformed into more modern agro-industrial or mining complexes. During this export-led expansion, which was allied to foreign capital, the USA replaced the Great Britain as Peru's main trading partner and source of direct investment. By the 1920s over one-third of Peruvian exports went to the USA and almost one-half of its imports came from the USA. Direct foreign investment was increasingly attracted to areas of production in export sectors, particularly mining. US firms accounted for the majority of foreign ownership.

THE RISE OF APRA

The export-led model of the Peruvian economy was seriously affected by the collapse of world commodity prices in 1929. From this time there was a growing realization that export dependency was fundamental to the country's underdevelopment. The debate over methods of resolving the problem of development was led by the reformist, Víctor Raúl Haya de la Torre, and the revolutionary, José Carlos Mariátegui. De la Torre founded the left-wing and populist American Popular Revolutionary Alliance (Alianza Popular Revolucionaria Americana—APRA, also known as the Partido Aprista Peruano—PAP). Mariátegui founded the Peruvian Communist Party (Partido Comunista Peruano—PCP) in 1928. The emergence of APRA reflected the increasing radicalism among the Peruvian masses as world economic crisis in 1929 led to depression. APRA was a left-wing, populist and anti-imperialist organization claiming to represent peasants, workers and the progressive middle classes whose interests were not being served by the governing élite. When Leguia's regime was deposed by a military coup led by Col Luis Sánchez Cerro, a popular military caudillo, the oligarchical élite, conscious of the threat from APRA, gave its support to the military. The take-over inaugurated a period of political instability in national politics between the 1930s and the 1960s, as an emerging national industrial bourgeoisie and Peru's popular sectors challenged the old alliance of the Peruvian agrarian oligarchy and foreign capital which had dominated the Peruvian state. The increasing strength of the industrial bourgeoisie, which sought to generate an internal market, resulted in a gradual shift in the balance of political power away from the traditional élites. This was reflected in the increase in popularity of APRA, which became an important political force and often had the largest representation in Congress (Congreso). An alliance of old oligarch and military forces prevented APRA from forming a government by means of electoral fraud, repression (APRA was declared illegal in 1931–45

and 1948–56) and finally, in July 1962, a pre-emptive *coup d'état* (which annulled the elections of the previous month).

MILITARY GOVERNMENT 1968–80

In October 1968 a left-wing military regime led by the Army Chief of Staff, Gen. Juan Velasco, supplanted President Fernando Belaúnde Terry of the reformist Popular Action (Acción Popular—AP). Belaúnde had been elected President in June 1963, as the joint candidate of AP and of the Christian Democratic Party (Partido Demócrata Cristiano—PDC). Until 1968 government in Peru had continued broadly to reflect the priorities of the old export-orientated élites. However, a developmentalist ideology, which emerged from within the Peruvian Armed Forces, coincided more closely with the priorities of industrial interests. Velasco and other ranking officers in the Army held the old élites responsible for Peru's underdevelopment and assumed the role of modernizers. The new regime aimed to expand the internal market and to abolish traditional and inadequate systems of production. The military Government introduced land reform and nationalized banks, telecommunications, the railways, electricity production, fisheries and heavy industry. Large haciendas were partitioned and converted into agricultural co-operatives. This policy of nationalization was presented as a nationalist, socialist and anti-imperialist struggle, partly in order to inspire popular support for the reforms.

In international relations Peru improved its links with the USSR and became less involved with the USA. The Velasco regime nationalized companies that had been crucial to the export-orientated economy controlled by the traditional élites. Foreign mining and energy companies seen as part of the old power bloc—notably the Cerro de Pasco Corporation, the US-owned Marcona Mining Company and the International Petroleum Company—were nationalized.

As opposition to the Velasco regime increased, attention became focused on the Government's restrictions on education, its controls on currency and imports, and the failure of its agrarian reform. Agricultural co-operatives proved to be poorly conceived, corrupt and badly managed, resulting in rebellions in rural areas. Velasco was replaced, in August 1975, by Gen. Francisco Morales Bermúdez, in an internal military coup. The new Government abandoned the former regime's anti-imperialist image and pledged a return to civilian democracy. A new Constitution was drafted by a Constituent Assembly, which was elected in June 1978. The draft Constitution, which, for the first time, granted universal adult suffrage, was adopted by the Assembly in July of the following year. In May 1980 military rule came to an end and Belaúnde was elected President for a second term, winning 45.4% of the votes cast. The Constitution came into effect in July.

SENDERO LUMINOSO AND THE GUERRILLA WAR

On the eve of presidential elections in May 1980 the Maoist insurgent group, Shining Path (Sendero Luminoso), initiated a strategy of 'people's war', with the burning of ballot boxes in the rural community of Chuschi, in Ayacucho department. Subsequently, Sendero Luminoso extended its influence to most other departments. By the mid-1990s the movement's destructive campaign and the Army's counter-insurgency were estimated to have caused some 30,000 deaths. The origins of Sendero Luminoso lay in the worsening of relations between the USSR and the People's Republic of China in the 1960s. Sendero Luminoso left the pro-Soviet PCP in 1970 under the leadership of its founder and ideological force, Abimael Guzmán Reynoso (known as 'Chairman Gonzalo'). It penetrated universities and teacher-training colleges and expanded its influence through Huamanga University in Ayacucho, the underdeveloped and neglected region chosen for the group's inception as a peasant movement. Through the infiltration of peasant communities, Sendero Luminoso won endorsement from sectors of the peasantry, drawing on Amerindian traditions and centuries-old resentment against Lima and against foreign conquerors, to enlist support. From these rural origins it infiltrated the student movement, labour unions and shanty-town organizations in order to develop further support bases.

The rapid increase in support for Sendero Luminoso was assisted by the incomplete and largely unsuccessful land reform under Velasco, and by a fragmentation among the parties of the left over the issue of reform. Sendero Luminoso emphasized revolutionary violence as the fundamental mechanism for obtaining political change. Its use of extreme brutality brought a response in kind from the Army. The movement regarded as a legitimate target any body or person that collaborated with the Peruvian state, participated in state-organized activities or was involved in interests allied to it. Sendero Luminoso's strategy was to mobilize first the peasantry, through political work and intimidation, then the urban proletariat and the *petit bourgeoisie*. At its First Congress in 1988, Sendero Luminoso decided to change its focus from the countryside to the cities. This move represented a modification of orthodox Maoism, which elevated Guzmán's status to that of the 'fourth sword of Marxism' (after Karl Marx, Lenin and Mao Zedong) and his interpretation of Marxism-Leninism-Maoism to that of *pensamiento Gonzalo* (Gonzalo Thought). Sendero Luminoso grew to represent a genuine threat to the country's internal security, particularly since it increased the risk of a military take-over.

GARCÍA LEADS APRA TO GOVERNMENT

The Belaúnde Government became increasingly unpopular, owing, in particular, to the measures it imposed to deal with Peru's considerable economic problems and its ineffectiveness in combating Sendero Luminoso. Following the presidential election in April 1985, at which he received 45.7% of the votes cast, APRA candidate Alan García took office on 28 July. The Army accepted García's election victory and demonstrated that it was prepared to adhere to the Constitution. President García introduced radical economic policies, including a limit on debt repayments, designed to control inflation. However, the economy continued to deteriorate and guerrilla violence from Sendero Luminoso and a second insurgent group, the Tupac Amarú Revolutionary Movement (Movimiento Revolucionario Tupac Amarú—MRTA), continued to increase. Support for the United Left (Izquierda Unida—IU, a coalition of seven left-wing parties formed in 1980) increased and trade unions organized a series of general strikes in 1987 and 1988. Right-wing opposition to the Government also increased as a result of the decision, announced in July 1987, to nationalize the financial sector. A 'freedom movement', Liberty (Libertad), expressing opposition to the nationalization plans, was formed under the leadership of the novelist, Mario Vargas Llosa.

INFLUENCE OF THE MILITARY RESTORED UNDER FUJIMORI

Alberto Fujimori, an independent candidate, was the unexpected victor in the presidential election of June 1990, and he was inaugurated in July of that year. An agricultural economist of Japanese descent, he had never previously held political office. Fujimori's main rival in the elections was Vargas Llosa, representing the centre-right Democratic Front alliance (Frente Democrático—FREDEMO, established in early 1988 by the AP, Libertad and the Popular Christian Party—Partido Popular Cristiano). Fujimori's victory, following a second round of voting in which he gained 57% of the votes cast, reflected a widespread disillusionment with traditional party politics. Fujimori lacked the benefit of a party machine when he entered politics, and therefore established the Change 90 (Cambio 90—C90) party to contest the elections. The party consisted largely of members of Protestant movements and centrists dissatisfied with the inefficiency and corruption of APRA and other traditional parties. Although C90 lacked a coherent ideology or programme, Fujimori won the election because he represented a more populist alternative to Vargas Llosa, who was identified with a Lima-based élite. During the election campaign Fujimori had advocated 'hard work, honesty and technology' and promised an economic-reform programme which was markedly less harsh than the one proposed by Vargas Llosa. However, shortly after taking office, Fujimori broke his campaign pledges and introduced an uncompromisingly orthodox economic reform programme, which became known as the 'Fujishock'. He reduced state subsidies, freed the exchange rate, and, in December, began negotiations with international lending agencies. In addition, President Fujimori liberalized the economy to encourage foreign investment and embarked on an ambitious privatization programme involving all the state's productive ventures.

The lack of a coherent organizational support base meant that the Army's loyalty was crucial. As soon as Fujimori came to power he attempted to win the support of the Army in order to reduce the risk of a military coup and to secure a powerful political ally in the event of widespread unrest. He gave the Army increased powers and autonomy in the counter-insurgency campaign and appointed Army generals to his cabinet (Council of Ministers). On 5 April 1992 President Fujimori launched an *autogolpe*, an incumbent's coup, when he suspended the 1979 Constitution, dissolved parliament, suspended the authority of the judiciary and assumed wide powers of decree, with the endorsement of the Armed Forces. He justified his actions by claiming that the traditional political élite was blocking the reforms necessary to combat the economic crisis and ultra-leftist insurgencies. When President Fujimori suspended the legislature he appealed for, and received, mass popular approval, in direct defiance of the political class. He claimed that popular support for his presidency and the demands of guerrilla war and economic crisis overrode any concern about the constitutionality of his actions. The political class in Peru denounced this as demagoguery. The mainstream opposition maintained that he had forfeited his position and, in accordance with the 1979 Constitution, declared First Vice-President Máximo San Román Cáceres to be the new President. Similarly, the USA and other foreign powers urged the early restoration of democratic government. However, the Organization of American States (OAS) failed to give its unreserved support to the opposition, and did not impose the requested sanctions on the Fujimori Government.

Following the suspension of international financial aid to Peru, which threatened Fujimori's radical economic-reform programme, the President was forced to hold elections to the Democratic Constituent Congress (Congreso Constituyente Democrático—CCD), a constituent assembly, in November 1992. The pro-Fujimori alliance of C90 and the New Majority (Nueva Mayoría—NM) received some 40% of the votes cast, and won 44 seats in the 80-seat chamber. APRA and AP boycotted the CCD elections, as did Libertad and small leftist parties. Of the significant political parties, only the Partido Popular Cristiano participated, winning eight seats. The assembly was inaugurated in December. In early January 1993 the CCD exonerated Fujimori for his coup and confirmed him as head of state.

The final draft of the proposed new Constitution was approved by the CCD in early September 1993. It was endorsed by the electorate, with 52.2% of the votes cast, in a national referendum held in October. The new Constitution consolidated President Fujimori's position by at least partially restoring his democratic legitimacy and by permitting him to be re-elected for a successive five-year term. All presidential decrees issued during the interim period were declared ratified until revised or revoked by the CCD. Foreign aid to Peru, which had been withdrawn in protest against the coup, was largely restored. The CCD acted as the legislature until the end of President Fujimori's existing term of office.

In 1993 the Armed Forces were deeply divided over Fujimori's actions. Discontent stemmed in part from the President's interference in military promotions, postings and retirements under the influence of his controversial security adviser, Vladimiro Montesinos. Meanwhile, loyal military officers claimed to have uncovered military plots to depose the President in November 1992 and January 1993.

A dispute over human rights, which developed in mid-1993 and continued into 1994, was evidence of the extent to which President Fujimori was beholden to the Armed Forces. From the time of his election the President was under pressure from the USA to improve Peru's poor human-rights record, but in doing so he risked undermining military support. On 21–22 April 1993 the Army deployed tanks and armed personnel at strategic locations throughout Lima, as a demonstration of support for Gen. Nicolás de Bari Hermoza Ríos, the Army chief and also head of the Armed Forces' joint command. Parliamentary deputies had demanded that Gen. Hermoza testify in investigations into the disappearance of 10 suspected supporters of Sendero Luminoso from La Cantuta University in Lima in July 1992. New legislation promulgated in February 1994 allowed the La Cantuta case to be heard in a closed military court instead of a civilian court, thus averting a requirement for Montesinos and Hermoza to give testimony, despite receiving insufficient approval in the Supreme Court.

President Fujimori consistently protected the Armed Forces from accusations of human-rights abuses. The extent to which the military influenced government policy was further revealed by an amnesty law in June 1995. Unexpectedly, the legislation was hastily passed by Congress, without a committee stage to allow the opportunity for debate. The law extended amnesty to the military for human rights offences committed during the previous 15 years of counter-insurgency, and included members of the military 'death squad' convicted of the La Cantuta killings. Meanwhile, the President's power *vis-à-vis* the military was consolidated by a change in the law, granting him the power to appoint all generals and admirals. Under previous governments, the Armed Forces had always appointed its own high command.

Border War with Ecuador

The Armed Forces' support for President Fujimori was tested by a short, undeclared border war with Ecuador in January–February 1995, in which more than 100 soldiers were killed. A cease-fire was brokered in Montevideo (Uruguay) in March by the guarantors of the 1942 Rio Protocol (Argentina, Brazil, Chile and the USA), which ended an earlier war with Ecuador in 1941. This short stretch of unmarked border in the Condor mountain range remained a source of tension between Peru and Ecuador, with occasional accusations from both sides of incursions and skirmishes, until in October 1998 in Brasília (Brazil), Peru and Ecuador signed a peace deal to end the long-standing dispute. The accord recognized Peruvian claims regarding the delineation of the border, but granted Ecuador navigation rights in Peruvian Amazonia. In addition, Peru ceded one sq km of territory around the former Ecuadorean outpost of Tiwintza, the burial site of many Ecuadorean soldiers killed during the fighting of 1995. While opponents of the accord in Peru protested vociferously that the ceding of territory to Ecuador was incompatible with national dignity and security, its broad acceptance in both countries raised hopes that the peace would endure. The physical demarcation of the frontier, which was begun in mid-January 1999, was completed by May of that year.

CAPTURE OF GUZMÁN

The capture, on 12 September 1992, of Abimael Guzmán and other members of Sendero Luminoso's Central Committee (the organization's highest decision-making body) and, subsequently, many others from among its senior leaders, inflicted serious damage on the movement from which it seemed unlikely to recover. Arrested along with Guzmán, in a raid on a house in Lima, were two of the three members of Sendero Luminoso's Permanent Committee. The arrests came at a crucial time, when Sendero Luminoso had been escalating its terrorist campaign in Lima and planning further offensives as part of its 'sixth military plan'. A large car bomb in Miraflores in July had killed 21 and injured 250 in the worst single terrorist incident in 12 years of guerrilla war. The bombing was designed to cause indiscriminate civilian casualties and to intimidate the wealthy and the middle class of Lima, which had largely escaped the worst effects of terrorism. After Guzmán's arrest the overall scale of guerrilla violence decreased by approximately 50% in the latter half of 1992, and violence continued to decline before stabilizing at a significantly reduced rate. Sendero Luminoso experienced a devastating decline in the geographical extent of its influence, which became confined to shanty towns in Lima and coca-growing areas in the Huallaga Valley and central sierra, and other isolated areas.

In September 1993 Guzmán offered to commence peace negotiations with the Government, in what appeared to be an extraordinary capitulation for the dogmatic, lifelong radical, who scorned most other revolutionaries as 'paper tigers'. It was likely, however, that he had a tactical objective in offering peace. His action might have been designed to encourage the Sendero Luminoso leadership at large to retreat to a defensive position from which it could begin to rebuild the organization. Following Guzmán's offer of peace negotiations, the number of guerrillas surrendering in order to take advantage of the lenient sentences offered as part of the Government's Repentance Law increased significantly. Guzmán's advances to the Government gave rise to

divisions within Sendero Luminoso. Although he succeeded in persuading imprisoned followers to support his demand for peace, an extremist faction, which controlled much of the organization outside prison, opposed him, and remained committed to the popular war. This faction, under the leadership of Oscar Ramírez Durand, continued to wage guerrilla insurgency in the mid- and late 1990s, although attacks were smaller and less frequent than in previous years. Sendero Luminoso was no longer considered to represent a serious threat to the stability of the Government or to the state long before the capture of Durand by the security forces in July 1999.

FUJIMORI'S SECOND TERM

President Fujimori was re-elected in April 1995 for a second five-year term of office, with 64.4% of the votes cast. His main challenger, former UN Secretary-General Javier Pérez de Cuéllar, supported by an independent movement, Union for Peru (Unión Por el Perú—UPP), received 21% of the ballot and conceded the clear popular mandate that the vote gave to Fujimori. Minor irregularities were reported, but did not undermine the legitimacy of the result. The restoration of economic growth and success against the insurgencies in Fujimori's first term of office ensured the President's popularity. Meanwhile, the traditional parties had lost their support base and the opposition was divided.

Fujimori intended to pursue the liberal, free-market reforms introduced since his accession to the presidency in 1990, although he pledged to use funds from privatization to alleviate poverty. A cabinet reshuffle in April 1996 reconfirmed the Government's commitment to these reforms. However, divisions within the administration over economic policy widened as a result of the contraction of Peru's economy and a growth in inflation, after three years of rapid economic growth.

The threat of left-wing insurgency re-emerged dramatically in December 1996, with the seizure of the Japanese ambassador's residence in Lima and some 600 hostages by 14 MRTA guerrillas. The guerrillas, led by Nestor Cerpa Cartolini, released most of the hostages within days, but continued to hold the remaining 72 hostages, among them high-level government officials, foreign diplomats and businessmen, until the residence was stormed by Peruvian commandos in April 1997, resulting in the deaths of all 14 guerrillas and one hostage. Cerpa had demanded the release of MRTA prisoners, including the group's leader, Víctor Polay Campos, a ransom payment and safe passage; the raid appeared to mark an end to MRTA insurgent activity. Allegations that security forces had summarily executed the guerrillas during the rescue operation would later be added to the list of charges of human-rights abuses levelled against Fujimori's administration. President Fujimori's style of government continued to be personal and autocratic, with few restraints or moderations to his rule. His NM/C90 supporters enjoyed an absolute majority in the new 120-seat Congress, which made the passage of legislation and even constitutional reform straightforward. In addition, opposition political parties were in disarray, the judiciary was discredited, the trade unions largely defeated, regional and municipal authorities powerless and the Council of Ministers generally weak and subservient. The judiciary and prosecution services were widely accused of becoming tools of the executive. Civilian democracy was weakened, moreover, by the lack of vibrant political parties and civic organizations through which popular demands could be articulated. The President's approach was to appeal directly to the public, rather than seek agreement and compromise with rival political groups. He travelled widely throughout Peru, addressing problems at local level. This populist approach was illustrated, in particular, by President Fujimori's personal involvement in helping poor communities to defend themselves against flooding caused by El Niño (an aberrant current which periodically causes the warming of the Pacific coast of South America, disrupting usual weather patterns) in 1997–98.

Disaffection with President Fujimori's authoritarian tendencies became evident from mid-1997, following a series of controversies, including allegations of the clandestine recording by the security services of the telephone conversations of opposition politicians. A vote by Congress in August 1996, allowing Fujimori to stand for re-election in 2000 for a third presidential term was also challenged, but was ultimately successful, despite a clearly-stated limit in the Constitution, which allowed a President to serve only two consecutive terms of office. However, the pro-government NM/C90 alliance claimed that Fujimori's first term of office should be discounted, because it had commenced under the 1979 Constitution. In mid-1997 a Constitutional Tribunal ruled that the law allowing President Fujimori to stand in 2000 was illegal. Opponents of re-election among members of the Constitutional Tribunal were dismissed following the ruling, provoking outrage among opposition groups. In February 1998 the Supreme Court overturned the ruling of the Constitutional Tribunal. In July a 7,000-strong opposition delegation presented a petition with 1.4m. signatures to the National Electoral Board (Jurado Nacional Electoral—JNE), in support of a proposal to decide Fujimori's eligibility by a national referendum. However, the JNE, which opposition politicians alleged was now subject to the executive's sprawling influence, rejected the petition and a motion to hold a referendum on the issue was defeated in Congress in September.

During 1998 President Fujimori repeatedly altered the composition of his administration in an attempt to consolidate his position and restore public confidence in his leadership. In June 1998 the President's decision to appoint as Prime Minister a former opposition senator, Javier Valle Riestra, who had been highly critical of the Fujimori Government's autocratic style, was widely perceived as an attempt to demonstrate an increased commitment to political tolerance. However, the reverse was indicated by Valle Riestra's resignation two months later, forced by his overt opposition to President Fujimori's plan to stand for re-election and sundry other conflicts with the President's allies in the Government and the Armed Forces. In August the President moved to reinforce his control of the levers of state power and strengthen his democratic credentials with the unexpected dismissal of Gen. Hermoza, who had come to be seen as one of a ruling triumvirate, along with President Fujimori and his security chief, Montesinos.

In spite of President Fujimori's political manoeuvring, the Government's popularity continued to wane and a major reshuffle of the Council of Ministers, in January 1999, which saw politically inexperienced technocrats appointed to a number of ministerial positions, could not reverse the trend. In fact, in April allegations of organized corruption within the Peruvian customs authority brought by the Minister of Labour and Social Promotion, Jorge Mufarech, a former industrialist, were challenged by other prominent members of the Government, causing a rift which precipitated the resignation of the entire Council of Ministers. With the administration increasingly perceived as authoritarian in attitude and constrained by neo-liberal dogma in its handling of a deteriorating economy, the early signs were not encouraging for President Fujimori's anticipated attempt to secure a third successive term of office in the presidential election scheduled for April 2000.

FUJIMORI WINS DISCREDITED ELECTIONS FOR THIRD TERM

The first round of elections was held on 9 April 2000. Official results gave Fujimori just less than the 50% of votes required for an outright victory. Fujimori's main rival was an economist, Alejandro Toledo, of Perú Posible—PP (Possible Peru), who received just over 40% of the votes cast. Toledo's campaign focused on what he referred to as Fujimori's record of authoritarianism and abuse of power, rather than on any significant economic or political differences. All other candidates, including the Mayor of Lima, Alberto Andrade, of Somos Perú—SP (We Are Peru) and the former head of the Social Security Institute, Luis Casteñeda Lossio, of Solidaridad Nacional—SN (National Solidarity), registered less than 4% of the votes cast. Toledo came from relative obscurity, having himself received less than 4% of votes cast as a candidate in the 1995 presidential election, to eclipse the challenges of Andrade and Casteñeda, who failed to muster nation-wide support. Toledo's mestizo (mixed race) ethnicity and impoverished background attracted support from many poor Peruvians. The April vote was marred by allegations, made by the opposition candidates, of large-scale irregularities in the vote count. These allegations received widespread support from international observers and representatives of foreign governments, including, in particular, the US Government. Complaints made by opposition candidates included government manipulation of the media to deny the opposition equal access, the use of state resources (including the military and the intelligence services) to promote Fujimori's campaign, and the alleged falsification of more than 1m. signatures by members of Perú 2000 (a new movement formed to support the incumbent's re-election campaign) to facilitate registration of Fujimori's candidacy. Suspicions of electoral fraud provoked street protests by opposition supporters. Elections to Congress, also held on 9 April, resulted in 52 seats for Fujimori's Perú 2000 alliance, short of the 61 needed for an absolute majority. Toledo's PP was the second largest group, with 29 seats.

A second presidential ballot, between Fujimori and Toledo, was scheduled for 28 May, despite efforts by Toledo and the Organization of American States (OAS) to postpone the vote for 10 days to ensure that the conditions for fair elections were in place. Toledo withdrew from the election and called on his supporters to spoil their ballot papers in protest at electoral fraud. The JNE refused the postponement request and, as a result, the OAS issued a statement that the elections could not be considered free and fair. The OAS and other international observers from the US-based Carter Center and the European Union withdrew their missions. Fujimori won an uncontested election (although the JNE ruled that Toledo remained a candidate and refused to remove his name from the ballot papers) with 51.2% of votes; Toledo received 17.7%. Excluding spoilt (29.9%) and blank (1.2%) papers, the incumbent was thus returned to office with 74.3% of the valid votes cast. An estimated 18% of the electorate did not participate. The result was denounced as invalid by the political opposition. For its part, the OAS decided against the imposition of economic sanctions, instead dispatching a mission to Peru to explore options for strengthening democracy. Fujimori's inauguration on 28 July was accompanied by violent protests in Lima.

However, Fujimori's term of office was prematurely curtailed by the disclosure, in September 2000, of apparent video evidence of Montesinos bribing an opposition member of Congress. In response, on 16 September Fujimori declared that new elections would be organized, in which he would not participate. He also announced that the national intelligence service, which Montesinos headed, would be disbanded. Montesinos' close links with the military high command led to fears of a military coup, but these concerns subsided after the military publicly supported Fujimori's decision. Demonstrations, led by Toledo, demanded the immediate resignation of Fujimori and the arrest of Montesinos, who fled to Panama. At the same time, 10 Perú 2000 members of Congress defected, thus depriving Fujimori of his majority in the legislature. On 5 October Congress approved OAS-mediated proposals preparing the way for power to be transferred from Fujimori to his successor (as well as the dissolution of Congress to make way for a newly-elected legislature) in mid-2001. The political crisis deepened in late October 2000, when Montesinos returned from Panama, after failing to secure political asylum there. At the same time, the first Vice-President, Francisco Tudela, resigned in protest at government attempts to tie new elections to a military amnesty, and middle-ranking officers in southern Peru staged an isolated rebellion demanding the resignation of Fujimori. Under pressure, the Government launched an investigation into Montesinos' activities, considering allegations including torture and murder, as well as corruption, gun running and money laundering. By this time Montesinos had gone into hiding. Fujimori's attempts to consolidate political support focused on distancing himself from Montesinos, and included the staging of highly public operation to arrest the former intelligence chief and to dismiss his allies in the military high command. Meanwhile, Montesinos' whereabouts remained unknown, and these actions failed to assuage Fujimori's critics, and the defection of a number of Fujimori's supporters led to a shift in power in Congress, which appointed Valentin Paniagua, a moderate opposition legislator, as President of the legislature. Paniagua immediately reinstated judges dismissed for challenging the constitutionality of Fujimori's third consecutive term of office.

A NEW ERA

Fujimori resigned from the presidency during a visit to Japan in November 2000, prompting speculation that he would seek political asylum in the home of his ancestors. The Japanese authorities confirmed that Fujimori was entitled to Japanese citizenship and could stay indefinitely. Congress, meanwhile, rejected his resignation, and instead voted to dismiss him, declaring him 'morally unfit' to hold office. Congress appointed Paniagua as interim President of Peru, and he immediately named former UN Secretary-General and presidential candidate Javier Pérez de Cuellar as Prime Minister. The new President, lacking a democratic mandate to pursue a legislative agenda, pledged to act only as an 'administrator' overseeing new elections in April 2001. Paniagua continued the process of purging the military of Montesinos' influence in order to ensure the impartiality of the military in the transition towards a newly elected government. The end of the Fujimori era was widely embraced as an opportunity to restore the rule of law and the integrity of democratic institutions.

The election, scheduled for 8 April 2001, offered Alejandro Toledo a second chance to win the presidency, following the disputed vote the previous year. The election also presented the opportunity for an unlikely political comeback to former President Alan García, who returned from exile to contest the poll. The other leading candidate was the conservative, Lourdes

Flores Nano, of the Unidad Nacional—UN (National Unity) alliance. Toledo won 36.5% of the first round vote, García 25.8% and Flores 24.3%, thereby eliminating Flores from a second round of elections which was held on 3 June. Toledo emerged victorious, polling 53.1%, ahead of Garcia's 46.9%. The PP gained 45 seats in the concurrently-held legislative elections but, together with allied parties, failed to secure a majority in the 120-seat Congress, leaving the prospect of coalition government. The inauguration of President Alejandro Toledo took place on 28 July, and two days earlier the composition of a new, broad-based 15-member cabinet headed by a lawyer, Roberto Danino, was announced.

In June 2001 Venezuelan military intelligence officers, assisted by the US Federal Bureau of Investigation and the Peruvian police force, arrested Montesinos in Caracas (Venezuela). The President of Venezuela, Hugo Chávez Frías, denied allegations that his security forces had obstructed the arrest and had only co-operated following widespread diplomatic intervention. In late June, the interim Government of Pérez de Cuellar had increased diplomatic pressure on Japan to allow the extradition of Fujimori by recalling its ambassador to Japan.

Economy

SANDY MARKWICK

Peru is the fourth-largest country in Latin America in terms of geographical area (1.3m. sq km, or just under 500,000 sq miles) and, with a population estimated at 25.7m. in mid-2000, the fifth most populous. Peru's economy was ranked seventh in Latin America in terms of gross domestic product (GDP), estimated at US $54,000m. in 2000, and eighth in terms of GDP per head (estimated at $2,100 in 2000).

Peru divides into three distinct geographic regions. A coastal strip extends the 2,800-km length of Peru west of the Andean sierra and is characterized by extremely low rainfall. Despite the arid conditions agriculture thrives, owing to irrigation from some 50 rivers, which drain from the Andes. Low average annual rainfall (of just 41 mm) and relatively low average temperatures for a latitude of 12 degrees south of the Equator are caused by high atmospheric pressure in the south-east Pacific and the cold Humboldt ocean current. A warm surface current from the western Pacific, El Niño, periodically replaces cold water and brings heavy rains, causing considerable damage to crops, most recently in 1997–98. The Andean sierra extends from the Bolivian border in the south to the border with Ecuador in the north and runs roughly parallel to the coast, as close as 100 km at some points. The high plains of the south and central Peruvian Andes at 4,200 m–4,400 m support llama and alpaca, but are too high for crop farming or sheep rearing. Most agricultural and population centres in the Andes are located in deep river valleys. The climate varies considerably depending on altitude and aspect. At 3,000 m above sea level the mean annual temperature is approximately 14°C (57°F), but there is a wide daily temperature range. Frosts can damage agriculture. Rainfall is variable. Extremes of drought and flooding are common. Moving east from the Andean sierra, the landscape changes rapidly from semi-arid vegetation to lush jungle. Higher rates of rainfall support dense tree growth and present favourable conditions for agriculture. Further east and at lower altitudes is the Amazonian tropical rain forest with meandering river floodplains.

In the 1990s the population grew by an average of 1.7% per year and this rate of growth was expected to remain steady over the next few years. Peru has a young population, one-third of which is under 15 years. The birth rate fell from 46 per 1,000 in 1960 to an estimated 24.2 per 1,000 in 1999, by which time life expectancy had risen to 69 years (from 47 years in 1960). However, health and nutritional standards were poor, as reflected by a high (although diminishing) infant mortality rate of 42 per 1,000 live births in 1999. In the mid-1980s some 37.5% of children under six years were estimated to suffer from chronic malnutrition. In 1991 several thousands died in a cholera epid-

emic, the first to afflict Latin America since the beginning of the 20th century.

The geographical distribution of the population shifted dramatically in favour of the coastal region after 1940, when 64% of the population lived in the sierra and 30% on the coast. By 1981 the proportion of Peruvians living in the sierra had fallen to 35%, while the coastal population had risen to 55% of the total, as migrants sought improved standards of living, better employment prospects and access to infrastructure in the cities concentrated along the coastal strip. The population of eastern Amazonia increased to 6% of the total over the same period as new agricultural land was developed, encouraged by government road-building projects. The proportion of Peruvians living in cities was estimated to have risen from 46% in 1960 to 70% in the mid-1990s. Economic activity was highly concentrated in the capital city, Lima. The population of metropolitan Lima (Gran Lima), including its neighbouring port of Callao, was recorded as 6.34m. at the 1993 census, compared to 4.7m. in 1980 and less than 1m. in 1940. Lima was almost 10 times the size of Peru's second-largest city, Arequipa (with an estimated 619,000 inhabitants), at the 1993 census. Peru's coastal strip is highly urbanized, containing the seven largest cities in the country. Cuzco and Huancayo (256,000 and 258,000 inhabitants, respectively) are the most important cities in the sierra. Iquitos (275,000), a river port on the Amazon, is the only large town in the eastern jungle region. Peru's indigenous Amerindian population lives predominantly in the sierra regions, where native languages, particularly Quechua, are widely spoken.

From the 1950s a strategy of government industrialization replaced the prevailing *laissez-faire* economy characterized by little direct government participation and few regulations. Thereafter, governments attempted to nurture domestic manufacturing by preventing an influx of cheap foreign goods through the imposition of high import tariffs. Industry grew at a faster pace than other sectors of the economy. Broadly, Peru experienced positive growth in GDP until the late 1970s. Real GDP increased by an annual average of 5.3% in the 1960s and 4.5% in the 1970s, but a decrease in the value of exports, an increase in imports and an expensive nationalization programme prompted a recession in 1977–78. Between 1980 and 1985 GDP fell, in real terms, at an annual average rate of 0.5%, signalling the worst economic performance since the 1930s. In 1984 GDP per head fell below the 1972 level. Average annual inflation doubled from 51% per year between 1975 and 1980 to 102% between 1980 and 1985. President Alan García (1985–90) stimulated demand-led growth by increasing real wages and extending import controls to encourage import substitution. The economy grew by an average of 6.4% between 1986 and 1987. However, by 1988 a balance-of-payments deficit, an overvalued exchange rate, fiscal difficulties and rising inflation led the Government to adopt a more orthodox free-market approach to economic management until President García, concerned about the outcome of the April 1990 elections, allowed wages to rise, causing an increase in inflation.

On taking office in 1990, García's successor, President Alberto Fujimori, implemented a rigid stabilization policy aimed at combating inflation by reducing the fiscal deficit. Subsidies were eliminated, causing the rate of inflation in the short term to increase to a record monthly figure of 397% in August 1990, by dramatically raising the prices of public services. However, the measures resulted in a reduced annual inflation rate of 11.1% by 1995. In 1996 the rate increased slightly, to 11.5%, but thereafter decreased each year to 3.5% in 1999. President Fujimori's austerity measures prompted a modest increase in output in 1991, but recession followed in 1992, as the economy contracted by 2.3%. High growth (6.4%) was restored in 1993, followed by growth of 13.1% in 1994 and 7.4% in 1995. Stringent economic stabilization policies, implemented in response to a widening current-account deficit on the balance of payments, led to reduced demand and a slower growth rate (2.5%) in 1996. Growth rates recovered to 6.9% in 1997, owing in particular to the construction sector, which grew by 21.3%, and the water and electricity sectors, which grew by 20.9%. However, the scale of unemployment led observers to question the rates of growth recorded by official statistics. Some 7.7% of the work-force was unemployed in 1998, while a further 40% was estimated to be underemployed. More than 60% of the urban work-force was estimated to be employed in the informal sector, contributing as much as 40% to the national economy. GDP growth slowed to just 1.3% in 1998, and the economy contracted by 0.3% in 1999, only to recover in 2000, when it registered an official rate of 3.6%. This renewed growth reflected a return to more typical performance in the primary sector, following the effects of El Niño in 1997–98 and financial crises in Asia, Brazil and the Russian Federation, which led to high interest rates and weakened demand in international markets.

AGRICULTURE

Irrigation and a temperate climate along Peru's arid coastline supported traditional crops of rice, sugar and cotton from the 1860s, but by the 1990s they increasingly supported a modern and varied agro-industrial sector of non-traditional agricultural produce such as asparagus, cocoa and fruit. There are extensive pasture lands in the Andean sierra although some crops, notably maize, barley and potatoes, are cultivated in deeper valley basins while tea, coffee and coca are grown on lower eastern-facing slopes. The tropical forests east of the Andes have enormous agricultural potential, but a lack of transport and infrastructure meant that they remained largely unexploited. Of the 1.3m. ha under cultivation in Peru, 53% was in the Andean sierra, 30% in the coastal region and 17% in the eastern rain forests. There is little room for expansion in the sierra region.

Land reform introduced under the regime of Gen. Juan Velasco between 1968 and 1975 turned huge privately-owned coastal haciendas into co-operatives alongside single family smallholdings (minifundios). The reforms, however, were largely unsuccessful. Increasing inefficiency and growing demand converted Peru into a net importer of cotton, sugar and rice, which it had traditionally exported in large quantities. Attempts by subsequent Presidents to reactivate agriculture were limited, owing to a lack of resources to provide credit to farmers and the overvaluation of the currency. President Fujimori introduced free-market reforms into the agricultural sector by declaring land to be a freely tradable commodity, exchanged under market conditions. Strict landholding limits were relaxed and subsidized credit, tax rebates and export credits were removed. Foreign investors in agriculture faced the same rules as Peruvian nationals. President Fujimori's policy was designed to promote higher agricultural output more efficiently, by favouring medium-sized commercial farms producing for export at the expense of traditional smallholdings.

The contribution of agriculture to GDP declined after the 1950s, when it accounted for more than 20% of GDP. By 1970 agriculture had fallen below 15% and from 1980 into the 1990s

it represented between 11% and 14% of GDP. In 2000 the sector (excluding fishing) accounted for an estimated 8.9%% of GDP. However, the absolute value of agriculture's contribution to the economy grew, in real terms, by 10% in the 1980s. The area under cultivation increased by about one-third between 1970 and 1988. In the 1980s agriculture grew at an average rate of 2.2% per year compared to the previous decade, when the sector declined by an average 0.6% per year. Agriculture in Peru, particularly production on non-irrigated land, was vulnerable to unpredictable weather conditions. The El Niño offshore current, in 1982–83, 1992 and 1997–98, caused widespread rainfall and flooding in some parts of Peru, and drought in others, resulting in reduced output. Agricultural output recovered from the effects of El Niño in 1993 because of strong domestic demand, growing by 13.9% in 1994, 7.6% in 1995 and 5.8% in 1996. In spite of the severe impact of El Niño in 1997 and 1998, the agricultural sector still managed to record growth of 4.9% and 3.6% in those years and in 1999 output increased by 12.0%, with substantial year-on-year increases in the production of cotton, rice, coffee and potatoes. More modest growth of 6.% was recorded in 2000, led particularly by the production of maize and cotton.

In the early 1990s modern productive commercial agro-industry in Peru was located in the coastal region, where irrigation projects enhanced the agricultural potential of the coast. The cultivation of high-price export crops could be maintained all year: mangoes, bananas, passion fruit and lemons and limes on the northern coast; asparagus, broccoli, green beans, snow-peas (mange-touts) and grapes in the central coastal area; and beans, garlic, onions and oregano in the south. Sugar estates, concentrated in the northern coastal area, were able to produce all year round with careful control of irrigation. Cotton required less water and could be grown where supplies were seasonal. The importance of cotton and sugar as export crops diminished, although they continued to rank second and third in terms of legal export earnings. The volume of agricultural exports in 1992 was just 15% of that in 1982. Peru became a net importer of sugar because of rising domestic consumption, inefficient methods of production, weak prices and a reduction in the US sugar quota. A dramatic fall in the export earnings of traditional crops saw non-traditional crops overtake sugar, cotton and rice for the first time in 1992. However, exports of traditional crops again earned more in 1994–95 and in 1997, when non-traditional produce earned US $340m., compared to $472m. earned by traditional crops. The best performer in the new range of crops was asparagus, with significant quantities of mangoes, mandarin oranges, grapes, apples and bananas also exported.

Agricultural production in the sierra was based on predominantly subsistence-orientated smallholdings and large estates for livestock. The major crops were maize, potatoes, barley and wheat. Low productivity, scarce capital and limited land resources perpetuated rural poverty. In the eastern rain forests, new road construction was followed by internal migration and agricultural colonization. In this area there was a variety of crops produced for the domestic market, including cassava, rice, bananas, oranges, tea, cacao (cocoa plant), beef, rubber and oil palm. Coffee, Peru's most valuable legal agricultural export commodity, was produced in this region. The land area devoted to coffee increased from 76,000 ha in 1960, producing an output of 32,000 metric tons, to 180,000 ha in 1996, producing 107,000 tons. Most coffee production was exported, earning US $223m. in 1996 from exports of 100,000 tons. Earnings reached $397m. in 1997 from 98,000 tons. Subsequently, lower international prices meant that despite a rise in total coffee production to 155,300 tons in 2000, export earnings of $223m. in that year only matched those of 1996.

Coca is grown on lower, eastern-facing slopes where the sierra descends to meet the eastern rain forests. Coca is a traditional crop used for centuries in its leaf form as a stimulant by Amerindians of the sierra. The role of coca as the raw material for cocaine resulted in a dramatic increase in cultivation after the 1960s, as world demand for cocaine expanded. In 1970 an estimated 5,000 ha of land was under coca cultivation. This figure increased, by some estimates, to as much as 300,000 ha by the mid-1990s, although it was estimated by the US State Department that total coca production occupied some 115,000 ha of land (with potential production of an estimated 460m. metric tons). About one-half of the coca-producing land was located in the Upper Huallaga Valley in San Martín department. However, in the early 1990s coca production increasingly spread south to the departments of Ucayali, Huánuco, Pasco, Junín, Ayacucho and the La Convención valley in Cuzco to escape the attentions of the authorities. By this time some 300,000 peasant farmers were growing coca either exclusively or to supplement other crops such as coffee, tea and cacao. Peru was one of the world's principal suppliers of coca for the production of cocaine. Official export figures do not record earnings from coca, an illegal trade, though earnings were estimated to be as high as US $600m.–$800m. per year in the mid-1990s. Crop-substitution programmes and dwindling prices led to a reduction in coca production after 1995, with the US State Department estimating the area under cultivation at 51,000 ha in 1998.

FISHING

An abundance of fish in the cold Humboldt current, and investment since the 1960s in industrial processing plants, made Peru one of the world's largest exporters of fish products. The anchoveta (Peruvian anchovy) was used to produce fishmeal for animal feed and fertilizers and was the most important species fuelling the fishmeal industry. Other species, principally sardines and pilchards, were caught after the mid-1980s for human consumption. Peru's main fishing ports are Chimbote, Tambo de Mora, Pisco, Callao, Supe and Ilo.

In the 1960s and early 1970s fish and fishmeal were significant foreign-exchange earners. An average of some 10m. metric tons of anchovy were caught each year during this period, producing some 2m. tons of fishmeal. The appearance of the warm-water El Niño current in 1973 reduced the nutrient supply that supported the anchovy and caused the catch to decline to 1.5m. tons in 1973. The return of El Niño in 1982 forced the industry to focus on sardines and pilchards, and these catches remained high despite a return of the Humboldt current. The anchovy catch returned to high levels in the mid-1980s and the total quantity of fish caught remained stable from the mid-1980s to the early 1990s at between 5m. and 7m. tons per year. The El Niño current again seriously damaged fisheries in 1997–98. The total catch was 7.9m. tons in 1997, 17.3% below 1996 levels. Despite the small catch, export earnings increased by 21.5% in 1997 because of high world market prices and increased canning capacity. Fishmeal was the most important legal export in 1997, surpassing copper, when earnings amounted to US $1,031.5m. from exports of 1.9m. tons of fishmeal, which accounted for 15.3% of export revenues. In 1998 the continuing effects of El Niño caused a devastating% decline in output and export earnings, with fishmeal and fish oil the worst affected subsectors. In 1998 fishmeal exports declined to a volume of 662,000 tons, earning just $397m. in revenues. Fisheries' production and exports recovered strongly in 1999 and production increased by around 5% in 2000, fuelled by a significantly improved anchovy catch. In 2000 fishing accounted for 0.6% of total GDP, compared with 0.9% in 1997 and 1.1% in 1996. Fish products earned $1,173m. in export revenues in 2000 (some 16.8% of the total).

In 1995 the Government imposed restrictions on fishing in order to replenish stocks, owing to fears of over-exploitation. Despite smaller catches in 1995–96, earnings were stable because of higher international prices. There was also potential for growth in mackerel fishing. At that time huge stocks of mackerel remained unexploited owing to shortcomings in the national fishing fleet. It seemed that investment in larger, refrigerated deep-sea trawlers might increase opportunities for mackerel fishing. Shrimp, trout, turbot and frozen fish provided other opportunities for diversification in the industry. Foreign investment was increasing in fisheries and Peru granted concessions to foreign fishing operations to exploit Peruvian waters for species not consumed locally. Japanese and Korean boats fished for giant squid. Fishing contracts were awarded on the basis of open and competitive international tender. Furthermore, in 1995 the Government sold fishmeal plants belonging to the state fishing concern, PescaPerú. The fisheries were estimated to be carrying debts totalling US $1,500m. as a result of high levels of investment during the 1990s, the El Niño-affected catch of 1998 and a general tightening of credit terms and conditions. The Government was in the process of developing a plan to finance a reduction in the fishing fleet in order to reduce the pressure on anchovy and sardine stocks.

MINING AND ENERGY

Mining is an important contributor to export earnings, owing to Peru's varied and considerable mineral wealth. In 2000 the mining sector (excluding petroleum) accounted for 45.5% of Peru's total export revenue, earning some US $3,192.8m. Gold, copper and zinc ranked respectively first, third and fifth most significant export earners in 2000. In 1998 gold overtook copper as Peru's most important mineral export. In 2000 Peru earned $1,144m. from gold exports and $931m. from copper. In 1999 and 2000 the mining sector contributed 5.5% of GDP. Despite the importance of mining, there was potential for even greater production. Peru was among the world's leading mining countries, yet less than one-fifth of its reserves were under exploitation.

The US-owned mining companies, Southern Peru Copper Corporation (SPCC), Cerro de Pasco Corporation and Marcona Mining Company, played the major role in the expansion of the mining industry, helped by the 1950 Mining Code, which fostered a favourable investment climate. However, by the 1970s the mining industry had begun to stagnate. Productivity declined dramatically and many smaller firms abandoned operations. The state mining company, MineroPerú (Empresa Minera del Perú), was created in 1970 to participate directly in areas of production where foreign investment was not forthcoming. Those foreign mining companies that failed to invest and were considered to form part of the old power bloc were nationalized. In 1974 Peru took over the Cerro de Pasco complex under its new name, Centromín. The Marcona Mining Co was nationalized in 1975 and its name changed to HierroPerú. At the same time, the Government negotiated terms with SPCC for one of the world's largest investments in the copper industry.

In 1991 President Fujimori declared the mining sector, heavily undercapitalized, to be in a state of crisis. Successive Governments had overburdened the industry as a source of tax revenue. With heavy taxes on gross sales rather than profits and high fuel taxes, most local companies became seriously indebted. Currency overvaluation damaged the export sector as a whole. Hyperinflation, restrictions on profit remittances and an oversized state bureaucracy under President García saw the mining sector deteriorate further. Mining's share of GDP fell from 3.2% in 1986 to 2.1% in 1991, and in 1992 it was still only 2.2%. By mid-1991 exploration had ceased altogether; some 90% of small mines had closed and many medium-sized mines were temporarily or permanently closed. The sector as a whole, supported by the Government, sought salvation through foreign investment, and many large companies subsequently entered into discussions to explore joint-venture possibilities. Until the early 1990s foreign investment in the mining sector was relatively limited. Best estimates indicate that total foreign investment in Peru over the 15 years to 1992 amounted to only US $700m. The most important foreign company in the mining sector was SPCC, which consistently produced around two-thirds of Peru's copper. It was one of the world's 10 largest copper-production companies and owned and operated two huge open-pit mines in southern Peru, at Cuajone and Toquepala. In December 1991 SPCC signed an agreement with the Peruvian state resolving a long-standing conflict over the contract for SPCC's Cuajone operation. As part of the agreement SPCC committed itself to a minimum investment of $300m. over five years. The agreement improved conditions for investment in mining, and production of metals rose considerably in 1993, reflecting new investment through privatizations and through the granting of concessions to private companies, despite generally poor world prices for minerals. In May 1997 SPCC began a two-stage expansion project to increase production at the Cuajone mine. Total investment was projected to reach some $1,000m.

In 1992 a new Mining Law liberalized restrictions on foreign investment in mining and curbed the state's traditionally interventionist role. The law was designed to give Peru an advantage over other countries competing for investment and was intended as a forerunner to privatization, which was aided by the sale, in November 1992, of HierroPerú to the Shougang Corporation of the People's Republic of China. Some key assets of the other state mining concerns–MineroPerú and Centromín—were subsequently privatized. These, along with Shougang Hierro-Perú and SPCC, accounted for two-thirds of total output and two-fifths of exports in the mid-1990s. The remainder comprised some 40 medium-sized concerns and 500 small mining firms.

Copper production (404,700 metric tons in 2000) was led by SPCC, but other important sources of copper were: La Oroya complex in Junín department (a subsidiary of Centromín, undergoing transfer to private ownership by the Mexican Industrías Peñoles Mining Co in the late 1990s); Cerro Verde; and the Tintaya mine south of Cuzco. Peru was one of the world's largest suppliers of zinc; in 2000 730,100 metric tons was produced, mostly for export. Centromín dominated zinc production in the early 1990s, accounting for 35% of the total, which was extracted largely from its Cerro de Pasco mine in Pasco department. Revenues for zinc sales declined from $539.3m. in 1997 to $462m. in 1999, but rose again to $496m. in 2000. Centromín was also the main producer of lead. In 2000 Peru produced total lead output of 256,200 tons and earned US $103.7m. from exports. In May 1999 Peruvian-owned zinc producer, Volcán Compañia Minera, bid successfully for the huge Cerro de Pasco zinc and lead mine, which had been renamed Paragsha. The Volcán–Paragsha operation became the largest zinc producer in Latin America. A copper and zinc mine, Antamina, operated by three Canadian mining firms, Rio Algom Ltd, Noranda Inc. and Teck Corporation, since its privatization in 1998, was expected to compete with Volcán–Paragsha, in terms of zinc output, by 2002. The sole producer of iron ore was Shougang HierroPerú. Iron-ore production in 2000 amounted to 2,611m. metric tons, representing a significant decline from the 1994 peak of 4,700m. tons. Iron ore exports amounted to $36.6m. in 2000, representing a 7.7% increase over 1999, despite a 12% decline in output.

In the late 1990s Peru was the most important gold-producing country in Latin America and gold was the most significant mineral export. The growth in the gold sector was the result of new investment. In August 1993 a consortium made up of Newmont Mining of the USA, BRGM of France and the local Buenaventura group invested US $37m. in the Yanacocha gold-mine in the northern department of Cajamarca. Other foreign companies investing in Peruvian gold deposits were Canadian companies, Cambior, LAC Minerals and Placer Dome, and in early 1998 the Sociedad Nacional de Minera y Petróleo announced that a further $206m. was to be invested in the gold-production sector. In November 1998 the Pierina gold mine, owned by Canadian firm Barrick Gold, came into production. In 1999 it produced 837,407 troy oz (26.0 metric tons). Silver production increased by 8.7% in 2000, to 2,460.0 kg from 2,263.5 kg in 1999. Silver production contrasted with other major minerals as the sector was dominated by small and medium-sized mines. Peru earned $103.7m. in silver exports in 2000. Export earnings varied between $60m. and $98m. during 1987–95.

After high growth in the late 1970s, petroleum production declined from its highest point of 204,000 barrels per day (b/d) in 1980 to 115,593 b/d in 1998 and fell further to an estimated 99,489 b/d in 2000. The latest decline stemmed from the depletion of light crude reserves in the northern jungle, which had the further effect of making production of some heavy crudes no longer economical. Proven reserves fell to 650m. barrels in 1997, from 900m. in 1996, as new operations failed to compensate for the depletion of existing fields. Peru was a net petroleum importer from 1992, when it was forced to import increasing amounts of light crude petroleum because of rising domestic demand, declining production and a lower quality of extracted crude.

A damaging dispute between the García Government and three foreign companies discouraged new investments in the petroleum and natural-gas sector. The Government, claiming breach of contract, expropriated the US-owned Belco petroleum company in 1987. Another long-running contractual dispute occurred in the late 1980s over pricing with the US corporation, Occidental. Furthermore, the British–Dutch company, Royal Dutch-Shell, withdrew from negotiations over the Camisea natural-gas field (Cuzco-Ucayali) in 1987, after the Government failed to deliver sufficient guarantees to the company for a long-term commitment.

However, encouraged by President Fujimori's new liberal hydrocarbons law, the petroleum sector, like mining, began to recover. The Fujimori Government came to an agreement with Belco's insurers over compensation and Occidental embarked on a US $60m. investment programme for drilling a series of new wells after settling its dispute with the Government. Ninety per cent of output stemmed from the operations of four companies: Occidental Petroleum; Petrotech of New York, USA; Pluspetrol (a predominantly Argentine concern); and Perez Companc (also Argentine). New investment in the petroleum sector was slow initially, but the pace increased in the mid-1990s; 20 exploration and drilling contracts were signed in 1996. In March 1993 Occidental signed a further $34m. contract with the Peruvian Government for exploration in the Amazon basin. Two smaller US petroleum companies, Great Western Resources (GWR) of Houston, Texas, and Petrotech, signed contracts in 1993 for petroleum concessions. Mobil of the USA also signed an exploration concession contract in Madre de Díos department.

Petroleum was drilled in three principal areas. Most crude was extracted from fields in the eastern jungle (64.2% in 1990). Northern coastal fields (19.2%) and the continental shelf comprised the other two key zones. Decline in petroleum production was most marked in the eastern jungle region. In the late 1990s petroleum production continued to be dominated by the state company, PetroPerú (Empresa de Petróleos de Perú), and Occidental, although new investments were diversifying the operators. The Fujimori Government initiated the gradual privatization of PetroPerú in 1996. The first parts to be sold were the La Pampilla petroleum refinery, which was purchased by a consortium comprising Repsol of Spain, Yacimientos Petrolíferos Fiscales (YPF) of Argentina and Mobil. At the same time, Pluspetrol won an option on a block for petroleum extraction. A new pipeline between Andoas in Ecuador and Station No. 5 in Peru, to be financed by the Canadian Petroleum Institute, was planned following the 1998 peace agreement with Ecuador.

An agreement between the Government and a consortium of Shell International Gas and Mobil Power Inc., for the development of the huge Camisea natural-gas field in the southern jungles of Cuzco, was signed in May 1996. Camisea was estimated to contain sufficient reserves for 100 years' production at average consumption rates, and additional reserves of 700m. barrels of condensates. It was planned that a 300-MW thermal power plant was later to be constructed by EnerPerú (a joint venture between Shell, Mobil and InterGen, an affiliate of the US company, Bechtel). An estimated investment of US $2,000m. was required to develop Camisea, representing one of the largest single investments in the history of Peru. However, in July 1998 the Shell–Mobil consortium announced its withdrawal from the project because of disagreements with the Government over distribution and export sales. In February 2000 the contract for first-phase exploration of natural gas and hydrocarbon deposits was won by a consortium of Pluspetrol, Hunt Oil of the US and SK Corporation of South Korea. The consortium has the right to develop the field for 40 years. The consortium plans to invest $1,600m. during this phase. The state-owned electricity company guaranteed a domestic market for the fuel. The contract for the transport and distribution phase of the Camisea project was won by the same consortium in October.

Peru has a huge potential to secure hydroelectric power because of its abundance of steep running rivers. Electricity generation rose steadily in the latter half of the 1990s from production of 17,440m. kWh in 1995 to 19,507m. kWh in 1999. However, installed hydroelectric capacity represented only a fraction of the potential, estimated at 60,000m. kWh. Hydroelectric plants at Santa Eulalia, Marcapomachocha and the Mantaro valley produced Lima's electricity supplies. Hydroelectric power accounted for over 80% of the total electricity generated, rendering the electricity supply vulnerable to climatic conditions. A lack of rainfall in 1991 resulted in severe rationing and an estimated loss of US $150m. per month in production. The electricity network in Peru suffered from a lack of investment. Between 1985 and 1991 the electricity supply expanded by an average of just 3.3% per year. In 1994 only 25% of homes were supplied with electricity. At that time, annual consumption per head was 610 kWh, one of the lowest levels in Latin America. In 1998 an estimated 30% of the population were still without power, despite new investment. The Government was encouraging the private sector to generate and supply electricity to fulfil demand and embarked on the privatization of electricity assets in 1995, beginning with Cahua, a 40-MW hydroelectric plant, and Edegel, the 700-MW generating unit of former state company, Electrolima. In late 1997 an amendment to the electricity law was passed by Congress which allowed the Government to veto any private investment considered monopolistic or to pose a risk to national interests. In 1998 the Government changed its plan to privatize Mantaro, deciding instead to offer a concession to operate the plant.

MANUFACTURING AND CONSTRUCTION

In the early 1970s manufacturing output grew at an annual rate of 10%, although at a long-term cost to efficiency, as industry was protected by high tariff barriers. In the late 1970s growth slowed. When protectionism was reduced under President Fernando Belaúnde Terry from 1980, manufacturing output declined dramatically. The Government returned to its policy of protectionist growth in 1984. High growth rates, averaging 16.0% per year in 1986–87, were followed by a sharp fall in 1988, owing to a lack of foreign exchange with which to buy imports for the manufacturing process. The sector declined by an annual average of 16.1% in 1988–89. Between 1965 and 1980 the industry grew by an annual average of 3.8%, in real terms, but contracted by an average of 0.5% per year between 1980 and 1990. Average growth in 1990–95 was 3.6%. Manufacturing contributed 15.0% to GDP in 1999, having contributed an average of 21.6% between 1994 and 1999.

Prior to the military regime, manufacturing largely comprised the processing of agricultural and mineral products. A policy of import-substitution industrialization, introduced under the Velasco regime, encouraged the development of domestic industry by raising the cost of imports. The military's developmentalist outlook saw the beginnings of heavy industry, including petroleum refining, chemicals, non-ferrous metals and electrical industries. Velasco made SiderPerú a state monopoly and the most important element of his industrialization policy. An overvalued exchange rate reduced Peru's competitiveness in export markets, while a decline in the real value of domestic wages reduced local demand and damaged manufacturing.

In the early 1990s the principal manufacturing sectors in Peru were food, metalworking, steel, textiles, chemicals, cement, automobile assembly, fish processing and petroleum refining. The food industry, accounting for about one-fifth of manufacturing output in the late 1980s, was heavily dependent on agricultural performance. The main products were processed fish, coffee, cocoa and sugar. In 1986–87 iron and steel output reached a peak, and production subsequently declined, owing to a lack of spare parts, a damaging pricing policy and the consequent effect of a decline in other manufacturing and construction activities. The textile industry, accounting for about 10% of industrial output, was the most significant non-traditional exporter, earning an average of US $347m. per year in 1989–92. However, the sector suffered in the early 1990s, along with other export products.

Under President Fujimori's leadership manufacturing was exposed to greater foreign competition and underwent a process of restructuring. However, there was a wide divergence in performance between industries. The output of textiles and other export-orientated sectors was lower in 1993 than in 1990. The foodstuffs industry for the domestic market grew by 11% in 1993. Manufacturing in general performed well, with high growth rates in 1993 (4.8%) and 1994 (15.7%). In 1990–94 output of consumer and intermediate goods increased while, in the same period, capital-goods production declined as domestic producers were unable to meet increased demand. Overall, manufacturing registered a moderate rate of growth in 1995–96, averaging 3.6%, but subsequently recovered to grow by 6.7% in 1997, fuelled by increased consumer-goods output. The sector declined by 3.0% in 1998, largely owing to the severe impact of El Niño on fishmeal production. Excluding figures for fishmeal, however, the sector grew by 0.2% in 1998, reflecting low rates of domestic demand. Manufacturing GDP grew by 0.3% in 1999, and by 6.9% in 2000. The primary resource sub-sector grew by 8.9% in 2000 fuelled by a strong performance in fisheries and sugar processing. Non-primary resource industries increased

their output by 5.8% in the same year, with paper, textiles, metal machinery and equipment leading the way.

President Belaúnde initiated an ambitious programme of housing and public works (including road-building, hydroelectric and irrigation schemes), which expanded the construction industry. Construction experienced similarly high growth rates in the first years of President García's administration, also owing to investment in public works, most notably an ambitious electric-train project for Lima, subsequently postponed because of lack of funds. Recession affected the construction industry from 1988, with increases in the price of building materials and in interest rates. After leading GDP growth in 1992–95, the construction sector went into recession, but recovered strongly in 1997 with growth of 18.9%. Sectoral growth slowed dramatically to 2.3% in 1998, with an overall decline in demand. The sector subsequently contracted as a result of lows levels of both public and private investment. There was a 3.8% decline in construction GDP in 2000.

TRANSPORT AND COMMUNICATIONS

In 1994 Peru had some 2,399 km of railway track, run by the state national railway enterprise, Empresa Nacional de Ferrocarriles del Perú (Enafer-Perú), following nationalization in 1972. The railways were largely used for transporting minerals. The Central Railway (Ferrocarril del Centro del Perú) connected Lima to Huancayo (Junín) with a branch to the mining operations at Cerro de Pasco. The railway rose to a high point of 4,775 m above sea-level. The Southern Railway (Ferrocarril del Sur del Perú ENAFER, SA) ran from Matarani, through Arequipa, to Juliaca, with branches running to Puno and Cuzco. The Cuzco line ran through the Urubamba valley, bypassing Machu Picchu, to Quillabamba. Passenger use declined in the 1990s, both in terms of total numbers and in distances travelled. The use of railways for cargo was largely stagnant, with 6,300m. metric tons transported in 1998 compared with 6,100m. in 1994. In the late 1990s the Government began offering concessions to run ENAFER routes to private operators.

The road system was greatly improved after 1960. However, until the early 1990s the network lacked adequate investment to ensure basic maintenance or expansion. Only about 10% of the road network was asphalted. However, from 1993, as a result of new investment from the Inter-American Development Bank (IDB, based in New York, USA) and the Government, road repairs were begun. The major road links were: the coastal Pan-American Highway, which linked Peru to Ecuador and Chile; the Central Highway from Lima to Pucallpa, which ran alongside the Ucayali river via Oroya, Huanuco and Tingo María; the northern Trans-Andean Highway from Olmos to Yurimaguas on the Huallaga river; and the Carretera Marginal de la Selva, which was built to provide access to new settlements in the east. The Fujimori Government declared road-building central to its aims of integration, development and pacification. It was hoped that repairs to the Central Highway between Huanuco, Tingo María and Pucallpa would reduce transport costs and encourage coca-growers to cultivate alternative crops. In 1998 the road network was an estimated 77,999 km, of which 12.9% was paved. In 2001 the Government announced an auction for a 25-year concession to manage the Ancon–Pativilca section of Highway 5.

In 1999 there were 21 ports in Peru, of which Lima's neighbouring port of Callao was by far the most important. The deregulation of ports under President Fujimori reduced costs and increased competitiveness with ports in neighbouring Ecuador and Chile. River transport was important in the Amazon region. The port of Iquitos was accessible to ocean-going shipping from the Atlantic Ocean. River traffic extended from there as far as Pucallpa and Yurimaguas, where new ports were constructed in the 1980s. In 1999 the Government offered for tender the management of the ports of Ilo, Paita, Pisco, Salaverry and Chimbote, but the process was slow and there was a lack of interest from potential bidders.

Air services were well developed and particularly important in eastern Peru, where the road and railway networks were less extensive than those in other areas. Peru has five international airports and over 300 domestic airports and airfields in operation, used, officially, by over 50 air operators. The major Peruvian airline, AeroPerú, became heavily indebted and was forced to cease operations in March 1999. Aero Continente subsequently became Peru's principal domestic carrier.

Telefónica of Spain bought a controlling interest in Peru's two former state telecommunications companies, Empresa Nacional de Telecomunicaciones del Perú (ENTEL PERU) and Compañía Peruana de Teléfonos (CPT), in early 1994. The Government's objective was to modernize the service and to expand the provision of telephone lines, which, at 2.5 lines per 100 inhabitants in 1994, was the worst in Latin America. Improved communications were considered to be a fundamental requirement for developing poor provincial communities. Telefónica was obliged to increase Peru's existing 637,000 lines nearly three-fold within 10 years and to guarantee that each town of 500 inhabitants or more had telephone provision. In 1999 there were more than 2m. fixed lines. In 1996 the telecommunications market regulator also obliged Telefónica to provide a cellular-communications infrastructure in the provinces. In the late 1990s the sector was being opened to greater competition. Bell South of the USA acquired an interest in cellular operator Tele 2000 and a third cellular operation was licensed to TIM Peru, a subsidiary of Telecom Italia Mobile, in 2000. The new investment was expected to increase rapidly cellular telephony penetration in Peru which, at 4%, was relatively low for the region. In 2001 AT&T started a fixed line service specifically for the business market.

GOVERNMENT FINANCE AND INVESTMENT

Investment declined in the 1980s, particularly under President García, when there was virtually no foreign investment, owing to restrictions on profit remittances, and little external funding. The ratio of domestic investment to GDP decreased during the 1980s as corporate profits declined, private assets were sent overseas and government savings became negative. During the 1980s domestic savings were the main source of investment, with loans to the Government making up most of the remainder. The level of central government investment declined from 18% of total expenditure to 3% and annual direct private-sector investments declined from US $125m. in 1981 to $34m. in 1990. Under President Fujimori foreign investment increased dramatically. A new liberal foreign-investment regime lifted restrictions on remittances and provided foreign investors with the same opportunities as national investors. In addition, the Government began an ambitious privatization programme, which aimed to sell virtually all of the state's productive ventures. The sale of the state iron company, HierroPerú, to the Chinese Shougang Corporation for $312m., in November 1992, was the first major privatization. Subsequent large-scale privatizations included a 49% share of the national air carrier, Aero-Perú, sold to the Mexican Cintra Group in 1993 for $54m.; the Cerro Verde copper mine, sold to Cyprus Minerals for $37m. in November 1993; and the Entel and CPT telephone companies, sold to Telefónica of Spain for $2,000m. in 1994. Telefónica's investment brought total direct foreign investment (excluding investment on the stock exchange) between 1993 and 1998 to $3,600m. The investment made telecommunications the leading sector in securing foreign investment (followed by mining, industry, finance and commerce) and made Spain the greatest source of foreign investment. Other principal sources were the USA, the United Kingdom and Chile. At least 18 smaller state companies, including pharmaceutical companies, were sold in 1997. Railways, insurance, electricity and airports were expected to be the next sectors to undergo at least partial privatization. The Government intended to use a proportion of the revenue received for anti-poverty programmes and job-creation schemes, although a large part was to be used for debt servicing. The sale of state-owned assets generated $7,180m. in 1991–97 and foreign direct investment totalled $1,830m. in 1998. The international financial crisis reduced the availability of international credit, and foreign direct investment in 1999 was just $779.2m., despite an increase in privatization receipts from $60m. to $219m. Foreign direct investment remained low throughout 2000, amounting to just $360m. during the year, as investors remained cautious in the aftermath of the international crisis and in the context of political instability in Peru. The Government earned $229m. from privatization receipts in the same year. The annual trading value of stock exchange activity incre-

ased from $70m. in 1991 to $4,033m. in 1997, but then declined to $2,289m. in 1999. Total market capitalization rose to $17,586m. in 1997, declined to $11,645m. in 1998 and rose to $13,332m. in 1999. Foreign exchange reserves, which were negative in 1988, stood at $9,563m. in 1998, but declined to $8,730m. in 1999 and then to $8,373m. in 2000, the lowest level for four years.

The García administration's policy of extending subsidies while reducing taxes required the Government to finance a wide public-sector deficit and gave rise to hyperinflation at a level of 667.0% in 1988, 3,398.7% in 1989 and 7,481.7% in 1990. Central government revenues fell from 14.1% of GDP in 1985 to 6.5% in 1989. In 1989 government expenditure was equivalent to 12.8% of GDP. President Fujimori's policy of maintaining fiscal equilibrium as part of a wider monetarist policy of reducing public-sector wages, delaying payments and decreasing investments, lowered the public-sector deficit. In addition, President Fujimori introduced reforms to increase revenues and simplify tax collection. The tax-collection agency, Sunat, reported nearly US $4,000m. of revenue in 1993, a 53.2% increase over the previous year. Tax revenues increased by 23.8% in the first four months of 1994 compared with the same period in 1993. When Fujimori assumed office, tax collection amounted to 4.4% of GDP. By 1997 this had increased to 14%. However, this figure declined to 12% in 2000, partly as a result of low levels of confidence in the integrity of the tax authority, Sunat.

Consistently high inflation resulted in the introduction of two new currencies between 1985 and 1991. Firstly, the inti replaced the sol in 1985 at a rate of one inti per 1,000 soles. In 1991 the new sol replaced the inti at a rate of one new sol per 1m. intis. Between 1978 and 1985 the sol had been gradually devalued by means of a 'crawling-peg' mechanism of mini-devaluations (i.e., the exchange rate changed in response to market pressure, but only by limited amounts over set periods). Multiple exchange rates, designed to favour priority imports and manufacturing exports over traditional exports, were introduced in the mid-1980s. These were simplified to a two-rate system under President García, with a series of crawling-peg mini-devaluations for the official rate and a floating rate for all other transactions. President Fujimori further simplified the exchange-rate mechanism by adopting a free-floating, single-rate system. The new sol appreciated in real terms against the dollar from 1993 as capital inflows maintained a balance of payments surplus. The exchange rate was affected by the inflow of dollars from the illegal drugs trade. High real interest rates tended to maintain the overvaluation of the new sol. The strength of the sol helped control inflation, but weakened exports. A lack of confidence in the new sol, along with fears that the problem of inflation had not yet been fully solved, encouraged the 'dollarization' of the economy, made possible by President Fujimori's deregulation of the financial system. In 1993 more than 80% of bank deposits were made in US dollars. Financial reform implemented by the Fujimori Government gave foreign commercial banks equal status with local private banks.

FOREIGN DEBT

Heavy public spending in the mid-1970s resulted in a rapid accumulation of foreign debt. Foreign debt increased further in the 1980s, because of the need to meet large debt-service payments and finance large public-sector deficits. In 1982 Peru secured a three-year extended fund facility from the International Monetary Fund (IMF). However, the country's failure to meet its commitments resulted in the suspension of the agreement one year later. In 1984 a 15-month stand-by loan agreement with the IMF collapsed after three months. Furthermore, Peru failed to meet bilateral commitments to member countries of the 'Paris Club' of creditor nations, following a rescheduling of debts worth US $1,046m. in 1984. In 1985 President García announced that a maximum of 10% of export earnings would be reserved for debt servicing and that no agreement with the IMF would be sought. Payment arrears affected multilateral as well as commercial-bank debt. The IMF declared Peru ineligible for further lending in August 1986, closely followed by the IDB and the World Bank. Foreign creditor banks ruled Peru ineligible for rescheduling negotiations. On taking office, President Fujimori immediately sought to re-establish good relations with the international financial community. In September 1990 he agreed to resume debt repayments and introduced a programme of economic restructuring. A support group, including the USA and Japan, provided a $2,000m. 'bridging' loan to enable Peru to clear part of its arrears. In 1991 Peru rescheduled payment of $6,660m. in principal debts, interest and arrears owed to the Paris Club. The IMF agreed to support the Government's economic reforms, thereby enabling credits from the World Bank and the IDB. Agreements with the Paris Club in July 1996 rescheduled $7,000m. in bilateral debts contracted before 1983. The agreement was to reduce the annual servicing bill by one-half, to $450m. over 20 years. In October 1995 Peru announced a debt-restructuring scheme for debts amounting to $10,560m. ($4,400m. principal and $6,160m. interest and arrears) with commercial-bank creditors. The scheme, implemented in March 1997, normalized relations between Peru and the international financial community and reopened private- and public-sector access to international capital markets. At the end of 2000 Peru's total external debt was estimated at $32,200m.

FOREIGN TRADE AND BALANCE OF PAYMENTS

The slow increase in the value of exports since the 1970s reflected Peru's vulnerability to international prices of raw materials. Exports declined and stagnated in the 1980s, from their highest figure of US $3,916m. in 1980 to $2,691m. in 1988. The value of exports increased slightly after 1988, owing to changes in government trading policy and more favourable metal prices. An overvalued new sol, recession and weak commodity prices had resulted in retarded export growth during the 1990s, but buoyancy returned in 1994 because of larger volumes and higher commodity prices. However, the value of exports declined to $5,757m. in 1998, owing to the effects of El Niño, low commodity prices and diminished overseas demand. Exports increased to $6,112m. in 1999 owing to the recovery in fishing and strength in mining exports. Export earnings increased further, to $6,999m., in 2000 owing to increased output in the fisheries sector and higher international prices for fishmeal and oil. Non-traditional exports, particularly textiles and metals, also contributed to the overall increase.

Imports stood at US $3,000m. in 1982. By 1985 the value of imports had fallen to $1,529m., owing to the debt crisis. Imports only recovered their nominal 1982 value in 1991. During the 1980s and 1990s imports were subject to inconsistent government policies. Protectionism prevented an increase in imports in 1984–85. This was followed by a dramatic increase in economic activity, resulting from the overvaluation of the inti (the currency in use between May 1985 and July 1991, before the new sol was introduced), which led to sharp increases in imports in 1986–87. However, severe recession caused a contraction of imports in 1988–89. In 1990 a strategy by President García to provoke a demand-led recovery (in an election year) resulted in a 26% increase in the value of imports. Imports increased further in 1991–92 as President Fujimori's Government reduced tariffs and other trade barriers. In 1997 the two tariff rates were cut from 15% to 12% and from 25% to 20%. Most non-tariff barriers were eliminated. Imports were further encouraged by the strength of the new sol. The value of imports was $8,554m. in 1997, declining to $8,220m. in 1998 and $6,729m. in 1999 because of reduced domestic demand. The value of imports grew to $7,334m. in 2000, mainly as a result of higher international oil prices.

Peru's balance of payments remained favourable while high tariffs discouraged imports. However, the lowering of protective barriers, begun in 1991, resulted in consumer-driven imports and successive years of trade deficit. The strength of the new sol against the US dollar further encouraged imports and damaged exports by reducing their competitiveness. Export growth of 7.4% in 1995, compared to 26.4% growth for imports, caused the trade deficit to more than double, to a record US $2,168m. Fuelled by the trade balance, the current-account deficit also grew in 1990–95 to a record $4,314m. The implementation of a stricter fiscal and monetary policy slowed imports and reduced the trade deficit, but the substantial fall in exports in 1998 caused the trade deficit to widen once again, to $2,463m. In 1999 the trade deficit fell to $617m. because of the sharp decline in imports, which contributed towards a reduced current-account deficit. The current-account deficit increased from 5.2% of GDP in 1997 to 6.4% in 1998, or $3,638m. In 1999 the current-account deficit stood at $1,822m., or 3.5% of GDP. The trend continued in 2000 as the trade deficit fell by 45.7% to $335m. helping the current account deficit to fall by 9.5% to $1,648m., equivalent to 3.1% of GDP.

In 1970 primary products (excluding fuel) accounted for 98% of all exports. Of this amount, some two-thirds was comprised of minerals, with copper alone accounting for 23%. Agriculture accounted for one-fifth of exports, led by sugar, cotton and coffee. Fishmeal accounted for 13% of exports. Manufacturing amounted to only 1.30% and fuels 0.67%. The composition of exports thereafter shifted away from traditional commodities to non-traditional exports, principally finished and agro-industrial products. The decline in traditional exports largely reflected developments in agriculture, which was affected by land reform under the military Government of 1968–75 and by a fall in world prices. Copper and zinc maintained their share of total exports, as did fishmeal, despite intervening fluctuations. The performance of these commodities reflected long-term increases in world prices. Even within the primary-products sector, new exports made gains on the traditional commodities of rice, sugar and cotton. In 1992 non-traditional agricultural produce, such as asparagus, cocoa and fruit, overtook historically more important crops. However, traditional exports recovered in 1994, when they represented 70% of the total. In 2000 traditional exports contributed 68.6% of total export revenues. In 2000 raw materials and intermediate goods accounted for 50.2% of total import costs, representing the largest share. This was followed by capital goods, which accounted for 28.4%. The relative importance of consumer-product imports increased, owing to the Government's trade liberalization policies. Consumer imports were valued at US $1,451.6m. in 2000, equivalent to 19.7% of the total value of imports, compared to $289m. in 1988, which was equivalent to 11% of the total cost of imports.

In the mid-1990s the USA continued to be Peru's main trading partner, although its importance had declined over several decades. In 1970 the USA was the source of just under one-third of all imports and the destination for just over one-third of exports. The USA accounted for 29.8% of imports and 26.8% of exports in 2000. The next most important export markets were the United Kingdom (8.5% of exports in 2000), Switzerland (8.0%) and the People's Republic of China (6.8%). From 1970 Peru diversified trading partners, creating a greater role for other Latin American countries as sources of imports, reflecting the growing trade among Andean Pact members. In 2000 Chile, Colombia and Venezuela were respectively the third, fourth and fifth most important sources of imports. The USA was the most important source, ahead of Spain.

TOURISM

The number of tourists visiting Peru grew steadily from an estimated 134,000 in 1970 to 373,000 in 1980. After a decline in 1980–83, numbers reached almost 360,000 by 1988, when the industry accounted for earnings of US $448m. A decline after 1988 resulted from a combination of guerrilla violence and an outbreak of cholera. The number of visitors to Peru in 1992 was 217,000, the lowest since 1972. However, a dramatic improvement in Peru's image after 1992 improved the fortunes of the industry. As the threat from cholera and Sendero Luminoso guerrillas diminished, the numbers of tourist arrivals and business visitors increased by 25.8%, to 273,000, in 1993, and by 1999 arrivals had risen to 943,900. In 1997 receipts from tourism totalled an estimated $805m. Even the Easter Festival in Ayacucho, previously home to numerous supporters of Sendero Luminoso, began to attract tourists in significant numbers. Tourists were attracted by Peru's Inca heritage, Amerindian cultural traditions and varied topography. The Amazonian rain forest and the Andean sierra are rich in flora and fauna. The most popular places to visit were the former Inca capital, Cuzco(which retained original Inca structures alongside Spanish colonial architecture), the spectacular Inca-period city of Machu Picchu and the mysterious earth designs at Nazca. The gold-filled tombs of the ancient Moche culture of Sipan, excavated and exhibited in museums world-wide, greatly enhanced the tourist industry.

In the late 1990s the Peruvian Government continued to promote the expansion of the tourist sector. Greater competition between airlines had been introduced and the Government was investing increased sums to improve infrastructure for tourism, including airports and railways. Furthermore, the Government encouraged foreign investment in hotels and hotel construction. At that time, however, underdeveloped infrastructure and services remained an obstacle to the expansion of the sector. Investment in hotels increased throughout the 1990s, but infrastructure remained insufficient to meet the Government's proposed expansion.

CONCLUSION

There was a significant economic revival during the 1990s. Inflation was reduced from 7,481.7% in 1990 to 3.7% in 2000, and real GDP growth was restored. Following recession in 1992, GDP grew by an annual average of 6.7% in 1993–98. In 2000 GDP grew by 3.6%. The challenge for the Government was to distribute the benefits of restored economic growth, in order to reduce poverty and avoid social unrest. This task was made more difficult by the pace of population growth. Job creation remained an acute problem, with almost 50% of the work-force either unemployed or underemployed. Despite an increase in exports, the trade account remained in deficit as imports increased because of economic growth and trade liberalization. Fiscal conditions remained reasonable and government initiatives to help companies restructure short-term loans helped to avert a banking crisis. It was hoped that a further political crisis, which had led to economic uncertainty, had been averted by the resignation and self-imposed exile in Japan of President Fujimori in 2000, and the subsequent election of Alejandro Toledo to the presidency in June 2001.

Statistical Survey

Sources (unless otherwise stated): Banco Central de Reserva del Perú, Jirón Miró Quesada 441, Lima 1; tel. (1) 4276250; Instituto Nacional de Estadística e Informática, Avda General Garzón 658; tel. (1) 4334223; fax (1) 4333159; internet www.inei.gob.pe.

Area and Population

AREA, POPULATION AND DENSITY
(excluding Indian jungle population)

Area (sq km)	
Land	1,280,000
Inland water	5,216
Total	1,285,216*
Population (census results)†	
12 July 1981	17,005,210
11 July 1993	
Males	10,956,375
Females	11,091,981
Total	22,048,356
Population (official estimates at mid-year)	
1998	24,800,768
1999	25,232,000
2000	25,662,000
Density (per sq km) at mid-2000	20.0

* 496,225 sq miles.

† Excluding adjustment for underenumeration, estimated at 4.1% in 1981 and 2.35% in 1993.

DEPARTMENTS (1 July 1998)

	Area (sq km)	Population (estimated)	Density (per sq km)	Capital
Amazonas	39,249	391,078	10.0	Chachapoyas
Ancash	35,826	1,045,921	29.2	Huaráz
Apurimac	20,896	418,775	20.0	Abancay
Arequipa	63,345	1,035,773	16.4	Arequipa
Ayacucho	43,814	525,601	12.0	Ayacucho
Cajamarca	33,247	1,377,297	41.4	Cajamarca
Callao*	147	736,243	5,008.5	Callao
Cusco	71,892	1,131,061	15.7	Cusco
Huancavelica	22,131	423,041	19.1	Huancavelica
Huánuco	36,938	747,263	20.2	Huánuco
Ica	21,328	628,684	29.5	Ica
Junín	44,410	1,161,581	26.2	Huancayo
La Libertad	25,570	1,415,512	54.4	Trujillo
Lambayeque	14,231	1,050,280	73.8	Chiclayo
Lima	34,802	7,194,816	206.7	Lima
Loreto	368,852	839,748	2.3	Iquitos
Madre de Dios	85,183	79,172	0.9	Puerto Maldonado
Moquegua	15,734	142,475	9.1	Moquegua
Pasco	25,320	245,651	9.7	Cerro de Pasco

— continued	Area (sq km)	Population (estimated)	Density (per sq km)	Capital
Piura	35,892	1,506,716	42.0	Piura
Puno	71,999	1,171,838	16.3	Puno
San Martín	51,253	692,408	13.5	Moyabamba
Tacna	16,076	261,336	16.3	Tacna
Tumbes	4,669	183,609	40.0	Tumbes
Ucayali	102,411	394,889	3.9	Pucallpa
Total	1,285,216	24,800,768	19.3	

* Province.

PRINCIPAL TOWNS
(estimated population of towns and urban environs at 1 July 1998)

Lima (capital)	7,060,600*	Piura	308,155
Arequipa	710,103	Huancayo	305,039
Trujillo	603,657	Chimbote	298,800
Callao	515,200†	Cusco	278,590
Chiclayo	469,200	Pucallpa	220,866
Iquitos	334,013	Tacna	215,683

* Metropolitan area (Gran Lima) only.

† Estimated population of town, excluding urban environs, at mid-1985.

BIRTHS AND DEATHS*
(excluding Indian jungle population)

	Registered live births		Registered deaths	
	Number	Rate (per 1,000)	Number	Rate (per 1,000)
1992 . . .	658,884	29.3	172,899	7.7
1993 . . .	661,061	29.1	172,188	7.6
1994 . . .	663,239	28.7	171,476	7.4
1995 . . .	617,300	26.2	156,000	6.6
1996. . .	615,300	25.7	156,800	6.5
1997† . . .	613,500	25.2	157,500	6.5
1998† . . .	611,600	24.7	158,500	6.4
1999 . . .	609,800	24.2	159,900	6.3

* Data are tabulated by year of registration rather than by year of occurrence. Registration is incomplete but the figures include an upward adjustment for under-registration.
† Provisional.

Expectation of life (excluding Indian jungle population, years at birth, 1990–95): males 62.74; females 66.55.

Source: partly UN, *Demographic Yearbook* and *Population and Vital Statistics Report*.

ECONOMICALLY ACTIVE POPULATION
('000 persons)

	1990	1991	1992
Agriculture, hunting, forestry and fishing	2,575	2,604	2,658
Mining and quarrying . .	181	190	198
Manufacturing	792	816	840
Electricity, gas and water . .	23	24	25
Construction	280	288	300
Business services . . .	1,176	1,235	1,297
Transport	332	345	355
Financial services . . .	181	187	192
Other services . . .	2,036	2,118	2,199
Total labour force . . .	**7,576**	**7,807**	**8,064**

1999 ('000 persons aged 15 years and over): Total labour force 10,076.8.

Agriculture

PRINCIPAL CROPS ('000 metric tons)

	1998	1999	2000
Wheat	146.3	169.9	165.0*
Rice (paddy)	1,548.8	1,955.0	1,664.7
Barley	165.8	169.8	175.0*
Maize	932.9	1,058.7	1,271.1
Potatoes	2,589.3	3,066.2	3,186.9*
Sweet potatoes . . .	221.6	244.2	230.0*
Cassava	884.4	868.1	985.5
Dry beans	73.8	81.0†	112.5
Seed cotton	95.3	134.9	175.0
Tomatoes	117.9	165.5	196.9
Onions (dry)	315.7	366.1	366.5
Sugar cane†	6,300.0	6,900.0	7,750.0
Apples	126.8	150.0	171.0
Oranges	233.8	257.4	318.4
Mandarins	89.5	116.8	118.0
Lemons and limes . . .	220.8	236.9	310.0
Avocados	68.2	79.1	75.0*
Mangoes	137.6	191.5	180.0*
Plantains	1,321.9	1,385.0	1,414.9
Coffee (green)	119.9	144.9	155.3

* Unofficial figure.   † FAO estimate(s).

Source: partly FAO.

LIVESTOCK ('000 head, year ending September)

	1998	1999	2000*
Horses*	665.0	675.0	690.0
Mules*	224.0	235.0	250.0
Asses*	520.0	535.0	550.0
Cattle	4,656.8	4,903.0	4,903.0
Pigs	2,531.5	2,788.0	2,788.0
Sheep	13,558.0	14,400.0	14,400.0
Goats	2,019.4	2,068.3	2,068.3
Poultry	80,120.0	81,304.0	81,304.0

* FAO estimates.
Source: FAO.

LIVESTOCK PRODUCTS ('000 metric tons)

	1998	1999	2000
Beef and veal . . .	123.9	133.5	136.3
Mutton and lamb . . .	22.6	29.8	30.8
Pig meat	90.7	92.9	95.0
Poultry meat . . .	490.3	553.6	580.0
Cows' milk	998.1	1,013.3	1,048.1
Poultry eggs . . .	154.5	161.3	162.6
Wool (greasy) . . .	12.9	12.0	12.6

Source: FAO.

Forestry

ROUNDWOOD REMOVALS
('000 cubic metres, excluding bark)

	1997	1998	1999
Sawlogs, veneer logs and logs for sleepers	916	1,617	1,617
Other industrial wood . .	203	212	212
Fuel wood	7,291	7,328	7,328
Total	**8,410**	**9,157**	**9,157**

Source: FAO, *Yearbook of Forest Products*.

SAWNWOOD PRODUCTION
('000 cubic metres, including railway sleepers)

	1997	1998	1999
Total (all broadleaved) . .	482	590	282

Source: FAO, *Yearbook of Forest Products*.

Fishing

('000 metric tons, live weight)

	1996	1997	1998
Capture	9,515.0	7,869.9	4,338.4
Chilean jack mackerel . .	438.7	649.8	386.9
South American pilchard .	1,056.4	625.1	908.3
Anchoveta (Peruvian anchovy) .	7,463.1	5,927.6	1,206.3
Other anchovies . .	59.6	24.7	706.2
Chub mackerel . . .	49.2	206.2	401.9
Aquaculture	6.9	7.4	7.7
Total catch	**9,521.9**	**7,877.3**	**4,346.1**

Note: Figures exclude aquatic plants ('000 metric tons): 0.5 (capture 0.3, aquaculture 0.2) in 1996; 0.3 (capture 0.2, aquaculture 0.1) in 1997; 1.8 (capture 1.7, aquaculture 0.1) in 1998. Also excluded are aquatic mammals, recorded by number rather than by weight. The number of toothed whales caught was: 15 in 1996; 8 in 1997; 56 in 1998.

Source: FAO, *Yearbook of Fishery Statistics*.

Mining*

('000 metric tons, unless otherwise indicated)

	1998	1999	2000
Crude petroleum ('000 barrels) .	42,191.4	38,663.4	36,828.9
Copper	356.2	393.5	404.7
Lead	242.7	254.8	256.2
Zinc	693.9	718.5	730.1
Iron ore	3,296.6	2,636.2	2,611.4
Silver (kg)	2,067.0	2,263.5	2,460.0

Gold (metric tons): 64.9 in 1996; 77.9 in 1997; 94.2 in 1998.

* Figures for metallic minerals refer to metal content only.

Sources: Peruvian Ministry of Energy and Mines; Central Reserve Bank of Peru.

Industry

SELECTED PRODUCTS

('000 metric tons, unless otherwise indicated)

	1995	1996	1997
Canned fish	57.4	59.4	n.a.
Prepared animal feeds . .	1,049	n.a.	n.a.
Wheat flour	793	820	805
Raw sugar	643	603	674
Beer ('000 hectolitres) .	7,815	7,493	7,428
Cigarettes (million) . . .	2,968	3,279	2,808
Rubber tyres ('000)* . .	814	799	n.a.
Motor spirit (petrol) . .	1,000	1,188	1,175
Kerosene	1,077	1,102	644
Distillate fuel oils . .	1,704	1,769	1,869
Residual fuel oils . . .	2,599	2,656	2,561
Cement	3,647	3,679	n.a.
Crude steel† . . .	515	510	510
Copper (refined)‡ . . .	282.0	342.0	n.a.
Lead (refined)‡ . . .	89.6	94.3	86.0
Zinc (refined)† . . .	159.0	173.1	166.1
Electric energy (million kWh) .	17,440§	20,038	17,951

* Tyres for road motor vehicles.
† Data from the US Bureau of Mines.
‡ Data from *World Metal Statistics, London.*
§ Provisional or estimated figure.

Source: UN, *Industrial Commodity Statistics Yearbook.*

Finance

CURRENCY AND EXCHANGE RATES

Monetary Units

100 céntimos = 1 nuevo sol (new sol).

Sterling, Dollar and Euro Equivalents (30 April 2001)

£1 sterling = 5.136 new soles;
US $1 = 3.587 new soles;
€1 = 3.184 new soles;
100 new soles = £19.47 = $27.88 = €31.41.

Average Exchange Rate (new soles per US $)

1998   2.930
1999   3.383
2000   3.490

Note: On 1 February 1985 Peru replaced its former currency, the sol, by the inti, valued at 1,000 soles. A new currency, the nuevo sol (equivalent to 1m. intis), was introduced in July 1991.

GENERAL BUDGET (million new soles)

Revenue	1998	1999	2000
Taxation	22,995	21,873	22,514
Taxes on income, profits, etc. .	5,861	5,072	5,126
Taxes on payroll and work force.	984	1,000	1,036
Domestic taxes on goods and			
services	14,467	14,475	15,351
Value-added tax . . .	11,040	11,029	11,976
Excises	3,427	3,446	3,375
Taxes on international trade and			
transactions	2,891	2,848	2,871
Import duties . . .	2,891	2,848	2,871
Other taxes	586	579	825
Adjustment to tax revenue . .	−1,794	−2,101	−2,695
Other current revenue . .	3,179	3,461	4,785
Resources of ministries and			
other non-tax revenues .	2,810	3,193	4,620
Interest on privatization funds	369	268	165
Capital revenue	612	624	679
Total (incl. grants) . . .	26,785	25,957	27,978

Expenditure	1998	1999	2000
Current expenditure . . .	22,875	25,471	27,815
Labour services . . .	10,416	11,778	12,403
Wages and salaries . .	6,979	7,774	8,187
Pensions	2,894	3,281	3,420
Social security contributions	543	724	796
Goods and non-labour services	5,418	5,598	6,378
Transfers	3,922	4,421	4,890
Private sector . . .	930	1,095	1,130
Non-financial public sector	2,992	3,326	3,760
Interest payments . . .	3,119	3,674	4,144
Capital expenditure . . .	5,623	5,900	5,085
Gross capital formation. .	4,964	5,652	4,590
Total	28,498	31,371	32,900

Source: IMF, *Peru: Selected Issues* (March 2001).

INTERNATIONAL RESERVES

(US $ million at 31 December)

	1998	1999	2000
Gold*	268.8	270.9	254.1
IMF special drawing rights . .	2.1	0.4	1.5
Foreign exchange . . .	9,563.4	8,730.1	8,372.5
Total	9,834.3	9,001.4	8,628.1

* National valuation.

Source: IMF, *International Financial Statistics.*

MONEY SUPPLY (million new soles at 31 December)

	1998	1999	2000
Currency outside banks . . .	3,950	4,609	4,537
Demand deposits at commercial			
and development banks .	10,174	11,018	9,556
Total money (incl. others) . .	19,165	22,273	21,518

Source: IMF, *International Financial Statistics.*

COST OF LIVING

(Consumer Price Index, Lima metropolitan area; base: 1990 = 100)

	1997	1998	1999
Food (incl. beverages) . .	1,776.0	1,923.4	1,918.1
Housing (incl. fuel and light) .	5,495.0	5,665.5	6,303.9
Clothing (incl. footwear) . .	1,592.5	1,681.0	1,686.1
All items (incl. others) . .	2,187.3	2,346.0	2,427.4

Source: ILO, *Yearbook of Labour Statistics.*

All items (base: 1995 = 100): 134.4 in 1999; 139.4 in 2000 (Source: IMF, *International Financial Statistics*).

NATIONAL ACCOUNTS

National Income and Product
('000 new soles at current prices)

	1989	1990	1991
Compensation of employees . .	31,356	1,719,943	5,533,638
Operating surplus . . .	70,543	4,407,995	25,106,377
Domestic factor incomes . .	101,899	6,127,938	30,640,015
Consumption of fixed capital .	7,818	431,058	2,180,329
Gross domestic product (GDP) **at factor cost** . . .	109,717	6,558,996	32,820,344
Indirect taxes	6,495	517,980	2,359,192
Less Subsidies	1,097	35,976	27,829
GDP in purchasers' values .	115,115	7,041,000	35,151,707
Factor income received from abroad	881	35,086 ⎫	−751,738
Less Factor income paid abroad .	2,498	212,567 ⎭	
Gross national product . .	113,498	6,863,519	34,399,969
Less Consumption of fixed capital .	7,818	431,058	2,180,328
National income in market **prices**	105,680	6,432,461	32,219,641
Other current transfers from abroad	835	47,317 ⎫	174,731
Less Other current transfers paid abroad	55	834 ⎭	
National disposable income .	106,460	6,478,944	32,394,372

Source: UN, *National Accounts Statistics.*

Expenditure on the Gross Domestic Product
(million new soles at current prices)

	1998	1999	2000
Government final consumption expenditure	17,546	19,156	20,980
Private final consumption expenditure	117,953	122,102	131,891
Increase in stocks . . .	678	643	1,559
Gross fixed capital formation . .	39,787	37,985	37,234
Total domestic expenditure .	175,964	179,886	191,664
Exports of goods and services .	22,076	25,900	29,918
Less Imports of goods and services	31,014	29,931	33,373
GDP in purchasers' values .	167,026	175,856	188,209
GDP at constant 1994 prices .	118,595	118,210	122,473

Source: IMF, *International Financial Statistics.*

Gross Domestic Product by Economic Activity
(million new soles at constant 1994 prices)

	1998	1999	2000*
Agriculture	9,175	10,274	10,895
Fishing	499	643	699
Mining	5,815	6,501	6,724
Manufacturing	17,112	17,170	18,352
Construction	7,295	6,509	6,261
Commerce	16,982	16,702	17,535
Government services . . .	7,128	7,385	7,713
Other services	52,589	53,026	54,323
Total	118,595	118,210	122,502

* Provisional.

Source: IMF, *Peru: Selected Issues* (March 2001).

BALANCE OF PAYMENTS (US $ million)

	1998	1999	2000
Exports of goods f.o.b. . . .	5,757	6,112	6,999
Imports of goods f.o.b. . . .	−8,220	−6,729	−7,334
Trade balance	−2,463	−617	−335
Exports of services . . .	1,745	1,524	1,550
Imports of services . . .	−2,344	−2,124	−2,243
Balance on goods and services .	−3,062	−1,217	−1,028
Other income received . .	778	656	754
Other income paid	−2,267	−2,204	−2,351
Balance on goods, services and **income**	−4,551	−2,765	−2,625
Current transfers received . .	924	970	985
Current transfers paid . . .	−11	−27	−8
Current balance	−3,638	−1,822	−1,648
Capital account (net) . . .	−87	−94	−113
Direct investment abroad . .	−24	—	—
Direct investment from abroad .	1,905	1,969	558
Portfolio investment assets . .	−149	−240	−518
Portfolio investment liabilities .	−199	−132	95
Other investment assets . .	65	130	177
Other investment liabilities . .	103	−1,006	756
Net errors and omissions . .	662	337	563
Overall balance	−1,362	−858	−130

Source: IMF, *International Financial Statistics.*

External Trade

PRINCIPAL COMMODITIES (distribution by SITC, US $ million)

Imports c.i.f.	1996	1997	1998
Food and live animals . .	1,195.8	1,044.9	1,111.7
Cereals and cereal preparations .	681.5	555.8	535.5
Wheat and meslin (unmilled) .	264.2	217.2	197.4
Sugar, sugar preparations and honey	143.8	109.7	179.0
Crude materials (inedible) **except fuels**	139.8	159.4	208.8
Mineral fuels, lubricants, etc. .	806.9	888.2	651.3
Petroleum, petroleum products, etc.	733.4	816.5	590.0
Crude petroleum oils, etc. . .	426.7	507.5	403.4
Refined petroleum products .	296.6	299.1	176.7
Gas oils (distillate fuels) .	233.7	217.4	128.2
Animal and vegetable oils, fats **and waxes**	73.3	114.8	166.4
Chemicals and related **products**	963.1	1,085.5	1,047.5
Medicinal and pharmaceutical products	151.7	179.6	194.6
Artificial resins, plastic materials, etc.	246.9	279.9	247.0
Products of polymerization, etc. .	191.4	216.1	182.2
Basic manufactures . . .	1,156.9	1,248.5	1,256.2
Paper, paperboard and manufactures	244.4	229.5	227.6
Paper and paperboard (not cut to size or shape) . . .	181.1	169.3	169.6

Imports c.i.f. — *continued*	1996	1997	1998
Iron and steel	280.3	308.7	338.1
Machinery and transport equipment	2,955.8	3,274.3	3,071.8
Power-generating machinery and equipment	232.5	283.0	176.8
Machinery specialized for particular industries . .	444.4	532.0	541.6
Civil engineering and contractors' plant and equipment	145.9	197.4	206.3
General industrial machinery, equipment and parts . .	471.0	515.0	500.2
Office machines and automatic data-processing equipment . .	259.7	299.9	290.4
Automatic data-processing machines and units . .	182.0	216.4	212.0
Telecommunications and sound equipment	490.3	525.2	412.9
Parts and accessories for telecommunications and sound equipment . . .	356.5	406.7	300.3
Television and radio transmitters, etc. . .	85.8	198.6	137.7
Other electrical machinery, apparatus, etc. . .	347.2	344.9	318.8
Road vehicles and parts (excl. tyres, engines and electrical parts)	652.4	698.5	767.7
Passenger motor cars (excl. buses)	291.2	328.6	333.8
Motor vehicles for goods transport, etc. . . .	190.5	218.5	250.3
Goods vehicles (lorries and trucks) . . .	173.0	194.1	237.0
Miscellaneous manufactured articles	618.6	699.0	667.5
Total (incl. others)	7,947.2	8,558.4	8,220.3

Exports f.o.b.	1996	1997	1998
Food and live animals . .	1,573.2	2,029.4	1,201.8
Fish and fish preparations . .	209.2	276.7	224.2
Fresh and frozen shellfish .	76.3	124.6	125.7
Vegetables and fruit . .	207.5	215.7	199.6
Coffee, tea, cocoa and spices .	247.5	421.1	313.2
Coffee and coffee substitutes .	223.5	397.3	288.8
Coffee (green), husks and skins . . .	222.6	396.9	287.5
Feeding stuff for animals (excl. unmilled cereals) . .	856.2	1,058.7	413.3
Flours and meals of meat, fish, etc. (unfit for human consumption) . . .	836.1	1,031.5	396.8
Flours and meals of fish, crustaceans or molluscs .	836.1	1,031.5	396.8
Crude materials (inedible) except fuels . . .	973.8	1,095.8	846.1
Metalliferous ores and metal scrap	823.2	909.7	717.9
Ores and concentrates of base metals . . .	711.0	806.3	605.0
Copper ores and concentrates, etc.	137.4	153.1	82.6
Lead ores and concentrates .	183.3	159.2	142.0
Zinc ores and concentrates	273.3	397.4	315.3
Mineral fuels, lubricants, etc. .	384.8	401.9	252.2
Petroleum, petroleum products, etc.	384.8	401.9	252.2
Crude petroleum oils, etc. .	236.6	239.6	126.2
Refined petroleum products .	146.9	159.9	125.2
Chemicals and related products	153.5	180.8	173.6
Basic manufactures . .	1,605.5	1,770.7	1,536.6
Textile yarn, fabrics, etc. . .	159.3	196.1	164.4
Non-ferrous metals . .	1,376.1	1,477.5	1,255.7
Silver, platinum, etc. . .	125.3	121.7	197.3
Unwrought silver . .	124.8	111.0	159.6

Exports f.o.b. — *continued*	1996	1997	1998
Copper and copper alloys . .	959.7	1,001.3	751.6
Unwrought copper and alloys .	911.3	938.6	699.4
Unrefined copper (excl. cement copper) . . .	175.4	122.8	74.4
Refined copper (excl. master alloys) . . .	735.9	815.9	625.0
Zinc and zinc alloys . .	193.1	219.3	195.0
Unwrought zinc and alloys .	162.5	179.2	162.8
Miscellaneous manufactured articles	416.7	492.2	593.4
Clothing and accessories (excl. footwear)	256.8	325.8	336.4
Knitted or crocheted undergarments (incl. foundation garments of non-knitted fabrics) . . .	143.1	193.2	214.6
Jewellery, goldsmiths' and silversmiths' wares, etc. .	126.6	129.5	144.4
Non-monetary gold (excl. gold ores and concentrates) . .	609.2	644.9	954.5
Total (incl. others)	5,835.0	6,759.4	5,671.9

Source: UN, *International Trade Statistics Yearbook*.

1999 (US $ million): *Imports f.o.b.*: Consumer goods 1,438.8 (Non-durable 932.3, Durable 506.1); Raw materials and intermediate goods 3,015.4 (Fuels 640.6, Raw materials for agriculture 185.1, Raw materials for industry 2,189.7); Capital goods 2,139.5 (Construction materials 198.8, Capital goods for industry 1,396.6, Transportation equipment 478.5); Other goods 135.6; Total 6,728.9. *Exports f.o.b.*: Traditional products 4,142.8 (Minerals 3,008.0, Petroleum and derivatives 251.3, Agricultural products 281.9, Fishing 601.5); Non-traditional products 1,874.2 (Agriculture and livestock 405.4, Textiles 574.9, Fishing products 190.2, Chemicals 194.4, Steel and metallurgical products 197.9, Other 184.9); Other 96.7; Total 6,112.7.

2000 (US $ million): *Imports f.o.b.*: Consumer goods 1,451.6 (Non-durable 876.2, Durable 575.4); Raw materials and intermediate goods 3,702.9 (Fuels 1,078.2, Raw materials for agriculture 213.4, Raw materials for industry 2,411.4); Capital goods 2,091.3 (Construction materials 212.8, Capital goods for industry 1,407.6, Transportation equipment 441.1); Other goods 125.8; Total 7,371.6. *Exports f.o.b.*: Traditional products 4,815.3 (Minerals 3,192.8, Petroleum and derivatives 405.8, Agricultural products 240.3, Fishing 976.4); Non-traditional products 2,042.1 (Agriculture and livestock 425.3, Textiles 670.0, Fishing products 196.6, Chemicals 206.3, Steel and metallurgical products 212.9, Other 197.1); Other 158.8; Total 7,016.2. (Source: IMF, *Peru: Selected Issues*, March 2001).

PRINCIPAL TRADING PARTNERS (US $ million)

Imports c.i.f.	1996	1997	1998
Argentina	278.8	360.7	372.3
Bolivia	124.3	151.3	128.8
Brazil	363.5	375.3	381.5
Canada	210.1	289.9	217.5
Chile	284.6	311.3	285.6
China, People's Republic . .	190.0	216.5	213.3
Colombia	677.2	613.3	440.8
Ecuador	44.5	240.3	206.4
France (incl. Monaco) . .	142.1	156.6	188.0
Germany	305.8	302.8	319.1
Italy	185.4	213.4	187.1
Japan	439.7	479.4	536.4
Korea, Republic . . .	241.2	253.9	309.0
Mexico	272.4	350.1	298.9
Spain	338.4	257.2	220.0
Sweden	79.6	79.5	100.1
Switzerland-Liechtenstein .	52.6	75.2	83.5
United Kingdom . . .	109.7	119.8	99.9
USA	2,089.3	2,271.3	2,233.3
Venezuela	591.0	566.8	406.1
Total (incl. others) . . .	7,947.2	8,558.3	8,220.3

Exports f.o.b.			1996	1997	1998
Belgium-Luxembourg	.	. .	154.2	183.3	138.7
Bolivia .	.	. . .	101.2	111.3	115.5
Brazil .	.	. . .	239.3	256.1	180.3
Canada .	.	. . .	157.8	119.7	126.0
Chile .	.	. . .	123.2	132.3	138.5
China, People's Republic .		. .	419.4	490.6	233.2
Colombia	.	. . .	120.3	154.6	143.4
Ecuador .		. . .	70.3	111.2	106.4
France (incl. Monaco)		. .	80.1	91.3	88.2
Germany	.	. . .	300.7	386.9	230.2
Italy .	.	. . .	198.7	229.4	189.8
Japan .	.	. . .	388.0	473.6	216.4
Korea, Republic .		. .	145.1	91.5	42.0
Malaysia	.	. . .	73.8	59.8	20.0
Mexico .	.	. . .	95.6	114.2	137.3
Netherlands .		. . .	208.4	219.3	135.7
Spain .	.	. . .	139.9	157.8	150.7
Switzerland-Liechtenstein		. .	291.2	412.6	484.0
United Kingdom .		. .	424.2	299.6	272.2
USA .	.	. . .	1,159.6	1,597.6	1,835.2
Venezuela	.	. . .	125.7	138.6	108.0
Total (incl. others)	.	. .	5,835.0	6,759.4	5,671.8

Source: UN, *International Trade Statistics Yearbook*.

Tourism

ARRIVALS BY NATIONALITY

			1996	1997	1998
Argentina	.	. . .	28,705	32,595	36,039
Bolivia .	.	. .	24,671	27,082	25,553
Brazil .	.	. . .	19,557	21,936	23,894
Canada .		. . .	14,393	16,601	18,232
Chile .	.	. . .	88,698	117,052	136,763
Colombia	.	. . .	17,595	20,266	19,339
Ecuador .		. . .	15,998	17,526	15,860
France .	.	. .	23,841	23,144	29,976
Germany	.	. . .	27,768	28,084	28,865
Italy .	.	. . .	20,046	18,995	21,528
Japan .	.	. . .	21,012	14,560	13,970
Mexico .	.	. . .	10,985	13,174	15,641
Spain .	.	. . .	25,362	25,210	28,732
United Kingdom .		. .	19,720	22,888	29,603
USA .	.	. . .	125,603	141,577	162,039
Venezuela	.	. . .	11,472	12,568	12,995
Total (incl. others)	.	. .	584,388	649,287	723,668

Tourism receipts (US $ million): 632 in 1996; 805 in 1997.

Source: World Tourism Organization, *Yearbook of Tourism Statistics*.

Transport

RAILWAYS (traffic)

			1995	1996	1997
Passenger-km (million)	.	.	231	222	206
Freight ton-km (million) .		.	864	856	829

Source: UN, *Statistical Yearbook*.

ROAD TRAFFIC (motor vehicles in use)

			1997	1998	1999
Passenger cars	.	. .	595,825	645,934	684.533
Buses and coaches	.	. .	43,506	43,366	44,192
Lorries and vans	.	. .	325,121	343,195	359,460

Source: IRF, *World Road Statistics*.

SHIPPING
Merchant Fleet (registered at 31 December)

			1998	1999	2000
Number of vessels	.	. .	719	724	721
Total displacement ('000 grt) .		.	269.7	284.9	256.5

Source: Lloyd's Register of Shipping, *World Fleet Statistics*.

International Sea-borne Freight Traffic ('000 metric tons)

			1988	1989	1990
Goods loaded	.	. .	8,851	9,402	10,197
Goods unloaded .	.	. .	5,020	5,059	5,077

Source: UN, *Monthly Bulletin of Statistics*.

CIVIL AVIATION (traffic on scheduled services)

			1995	1996	1997
Kilometres flown (million)	.	.	34	33	40
Passengers carried ('000) .		.	2,508	2,328	2,725
Passenger-km (million)	.	.	2,884	2,634	2,964
Total ton-km (million)	.	.	286	251	276

Source: UN, *Statistical Yearbook*.

Communications Media

	1995	1996	1997
Radio receivers ('000 in use) . .	6,100	6,500	6,650
Television receivers ('000 in use) .	2,500	3,000	3,060
Telephones ('000 main lines in use)	1,109	1,435	1,646
Telefax stations (number in use) .	15,000	n.a.	n.a.
Mobile cellular telephones (subscribers)	73,543	200,972	435,691
Book production: titles . .	1,294	612	n.a.
Daily newspapers: number .	48	74	n.a.

Non-daily newspapers (estimates, 1988): 12 titles (average circulation 374,000 copies).
Other periodicals (1988): 45 titles (average circulation 90,000 copies).

Sources: UNESCO, *Statistical Yearbook*; UN, *Statistical Yearbook*.

Education

(1997)

			Institutions	Teachers	Pupils
Nursery .	.	. . .	14,000*	30,736	688,425
Primary .	.	. . .	33,017	153,951	4,163,180
Secondary†	.	. . .	n.a.	106,614	1,969,501
Higher:					
Universities, etc.	.	. .	n.a.	25,795	352,909
Other third-level	.	. .	n.a.	19,648	304,677

* Figure for 1995.
† Including adult education.

Source: UNESCO, *Statistical Yearbook*.

Directory

The Constitution

In 1993 the Congreso Constituyente Democrático (CCD) began drafting a new constitution to replace the 1979 Constitution. The CCD approved the final document in September 1993, and the Constitution was endorsed by a popular national referendum that was conducted on 31 October. The Constitution was promulgated on 29 December 1993.

EXECUTIVE POWER

Executive power is vested in the President, who is elected for a five-year term of office by universal adult suffrage; this mandate is renewable once.* The successful presidential candidate must obtain at least 50% of the votes cast, and a second round of voting is held if necessary. Two Vice-Presidents are elected in simultaneous rounds of voting. The President is competent to initiate and submit draft bills, to review laws drafted by the legislature (Congreso) and, if delegated by the Congreso, to enact laws. The President is empowered to appoint ambassadors and senior military officials without congressional ratification, and retains the right to dissolve parliament if two or more ministers have been censured or have received a vote of 'no confidence' from the Congreso. In certain circumstances the President may, in accordance with the Council of Ministers, declare a state of emergency for a period of 60 days, during which individual constitutional rights are suspended and the armed forces may assume control of civil order. The President appoints the Council of Ministers.

LEGISLATIVE POWER

Legislative power is vested in a single-chamber Congreso (removing the distinction in the 1979 Constitution of an upper and lower house) consisting of 120 members. The members of the Congreso are elected for a five-year term by universal adult suffrage from national party lists.† The Congreso is responsible for approving the budget, for endorsing loans and international treaties and for drafting and approving bills. It may conduct investigations into matters of public concern, and question and censure the Council of Ministers and its individual members. Members of the Congreso elect a Standing Committee, to consist of not more than 25% of the total number of members (representation being proportional to the different political groupings in the legislature), which is empowered to make certain official appointments, approve credit loans and transfers relating to the budget during a parliamentary recess, and conduct other business as delegated by parliament.

ELECTORAL SYSTEM

All citizens aged 18 years and above, including illiterate persons, are eligible to vote. Voting in elections is compulsory for all citizens aged 18–70, and is optional thereafter.

JUDICIAL POWER

Judicial power is vested in the Supreme Court of Justice and other tribunals. The Constitution provides for the establishment of a National Council of the Judiciary, consisting of nine independently elected members, which is empowered to appoint judges to the Supreme Court. An independent Constitutional Court, comprising seven members elected by the Congreso for a five-year term, may interpret the Constitution and declare legislation and acts of government to be unconstitutional.

The death penalty may be applied by the Judiciary in cases of terrorism or of treason (the latter in times of war).

Under the Constitution, a People's Counsel is elected by the Congreso with a five-year mandate which authorizes the Counsel to defend the constitutional and fundamental rights of the individual. The Counsel may draft laws and present evidence to the legislature.

According to the Constitution, the State promotes economic and social development, particularly in the areas of employment, health, education, security, public services and infrastructure. The State recognizes a plurality of economic ownership and activity, supports free competition, and promotes the growth of small businesses. Private initiative is permitted within the framework of a social market economy. The State also guarantees the free exchange of foreign currency.

* In October 2000 the Congreso passed a motion to prohibit Presidents from serving two consecutive five-year terms.

† In December 2000 the Congreso voted to change the system for election of members to one based on geographic constituencies.

The Government

HEAD OF STATE

President: ALEJANDRO TOLEDO (took office 28 July 2001).

First Vice-President and Minister of Industry, Tourism, Integration and International Trade: RAÚL DÍEZ CANESCO TERRY.

Second Vice-President and Minister of Defence: DAVID WAISMAN RJAVINSTHI.

COUNCIL OF MINISTERS
(August 2001)

President of the Council of Ministers: ROBERTO ENRIQUE DAÑINO ZAPATA.

Minister of Foreign Affairs: DIEGO GARCÍA SAYÁN.

Minister of the Interior: FERNANDO ROSPIGLIOSI.

Minister of Justice: FERNANDO OLIVERA VEGA.

Minister of Economy and Finance: PEDRO PABLO KUCZYNSKI.

Minister of Labour and Social Promotion: FERNANDO VILLARÁN.

Minister of Transport, Communications, Housing and Construction: LUIS CHANG REYES.

Minister of Health: LUIS SOLARI.

Minister of Agriculture: ALVARO QUIJANDRÍA.

Minister of Energy and Mines: JAIME QUIJANDRÍA.

Minister of the Presidency: CARLOS BRUCE.

Minister of Fisheries: JAVIER REÁTEGUI.

Minister of Education: NICOLÁS LYNCH GAMERO.

Minister for the Advancement of Women and Human Development: DORIS SÁNCHEZ.

MINISTRIES

Prime Minister's Office: Ucayali 363, Lima; tel. (1) 4273860; fax (1) 4323266.

Ministry for the Advancement of Women and Human Development: Avda Emancipación 235, esq. Jirón Camaná 616, Lima 1; tel. (1) 4289800; fax (1) 4261665; e-mail postmaster@lima .promudeh.gob.pe; internet www.promudeh.gob.pe.

Ministry of Agriculture: Avda Salaverry s/n, Jesús María, Lima 11; tel. (1) 4333034; fax (1) 4329098; e-mail postmast@oia.minag .gob.pe; internet www.minag.gob.pe.

Ministry of Defence: Avda Arequipa 291, Lima 14; tel and fax (1) 4335150.

Ministry of Economy and Finance: Jirón Junín 339, 4°, Lima; tel. (1) 4273930; fax (1) 4282509; e-mail postmaster@mef.gob.pe; internet www.mef.gob.pe.

Ministry of Education: Avda Van Develde 160, (Cuadra 33 Javier Prado Este), San Borja, Lima 41; tel. (1) 4361240; fax (1) 4330230; e-mail postmaster@minedu.gob.pe; internet www.minedu.gob.pe.

Ministry of Energy and Mines: Avda Las Artes s/n, San Borja, Apdo 2600, Lima 41; tel. (1) 4750206; fax (1) 4750689; internet www.mem.gob.pe.

Ministry of Fisheries: Calle 1 Oeste 60, Urb. Corpac, San Isidro, Lima 27; tel. (1) 2243336; fax (1) 2243233; e-mail percy@mail .tambo.com.pe; internet www.minpes.gob.pe.

Ministry of Foreign Affairs: Palacio de Torre Tagle, Jirón Ucayali 363, Lima 1; tel. (1) 4273860; fax (1) 4263266; internet www.rree .gob.pe.

Ministry of Health: Avda Salaverry Cuadra 8, Jesús María, Lima 11; tel. (1) 4310410; fax (1) 4315338; e-mail MLOPEZ@minsa.gob.pe; internet www.minsa.gob.pe.

Ministry of Industry, Tourism, Integration and International Trade Negotiations: Calle 1 Oeste, Urb. Corpac, San Isidro, Lima 27; tel. (1) 2243347; fax (1) 2243264; internet www.mitinci.gob.pe.

Ministry of the Interior: Plaza 30 de Agosto 150, San Isidro, Lima 27; tel. (1) 4752995; fax (1) 4415128.

Ministry of Justice: Scipion Llona 350, Miraflores, Lima 18; tel. (1) 4404310; fax (1) 4417320; internet www.minjus.gob.pe.

Ministry of Labour and of Social Promotion: Avda Salaverry Cuadra 8, Jesús María, Lima 11; tel. (1) 4332512; fax (1) 4338126; internet www.mtps.gob.pe.

Ministry of the Presidency: Avda Paseo de la República 4297, Lima 1; tel. (1) 4465886; fax (1) 4470379.

Ministry of Transport, Communications, Housing and Construction: Avda 28 de Julio 800, Lima 1; tel. (1) 4331212; fax (1) 4339378; internet www.mtc.gob.pe.

President and Legislature

PRESIDENT

Elections, 8 April 2001 and 3 June 2001

Candidate	First round % of votes	Second round % of votes
ALEJANDRO TOLEDO (PP)	36.51	53.08
ALAN GARCÍA (APRA)	25.78	46.92
LOURDES FLORES (UN) . . .	24.30	—
FERNANDO OLIVERA VEGA (FIM) . .	9.85	—
CARLOS BOLOÑA (Solución Popular) . .	1.69	—
CIRO A. GÁLVEZ (Renacimiento Andino) .	0.81	—
MARCO A. ARRUNATEGUI (Proyecto País) .	0.75	—
RICARDO NORIEGA (Todos por la Victoria)	0.31	—
Total	100.00	100.00

CONGRESO

President: CARLOS FERRERO COSTA.

General Election, 8 April 2001

Political Parties	Seats
Perú Posible (PP)	45
Alianza Popular Revolucionaria Americana (APRA) .	27
Unidad Nacional (UN)	17
Frente Independiente Moralizador (FIM). . .	12
Unión por el Perú	6
Somos Perú	4
Acción Popular (AP)	3
Cambio 90-Nueva Mayoría (C90-NM) . . .	3
Renacimiento Andino	1
Solución Popular	1
Todos por la Victoria	1
Total	120

Political Organizations

Acción Popular (AP): Paseo Colón 218, Lima 1; tel. (1) 4234177; e-mail accionpopular2000@yahoo.com; internet www.geocities.com/accionpopular_2000; f. 1956; 1.2m. mems; pro-USA; liberal; Leader FERNANDO BELAÚNDE TERRY; Sec.-Gen. JAVIER DÍAZ ORIHUELA.

Alianza Popular Revolucionaria Americana (APRA): Avda Alfonso Ugarte 1012, Lima 5; tel. (1) 4328022; f. in Mexico 1924, in Peru 1930 as Partido Aprista Peruano (PAP); legalized 1945; democratic left-wing party; Sec.-Gen. AGUSTÍN MANTILLA CAMPOS; 700,000 mems.

Cambio 90 (C90): Lima; group of independents formed to contest the 1990 elections, entered into coalition with Nueva Mayoría (see below) in 1992 to contest elections to the CCD, local elections in 1993, the presidential and congressional elections in 1995 and 2000 and the 2001 congressional elections; Leader PABLO CORREA.

Confluencia Socialista: Lima; f. 1991; left-wing alliance comprising:

   Acción Política Socialista (APS).

   Movimiento de Acción Socialista (MAS).

   Movimiento No Partidarizado (MNP).

   Partido Mariateguista Revolucionario (PMR).

Coordinación Democrática (CODE): Lima; f. 1992 by dissident APRA members; Leader JOSÉ BARBA CABALLERO.

Frente Independiente Moralizador (FIM): Lima; right-wing; e-mail fim@fr.fm; internet www.fim.fr.fm; Leader FERNANDO OLIVERA VEGA.

Fuerza Democrática: Lima; f. 1998 to contest municipal elections.

Izquierda Nacionalista: Lima; f. 1984; left-wing party; Leader PEDRO REYNALDO CÁCERES VELÁSQUEZ.

Izquierda Socialista: Lima; coalition of left-wing groups which broke away from Izquierda Unida before the elections of April 1990; Leader Dr ALFONSO BARRANTES LINGÁN.

   Unidad Democrática Popular (UDP): Plaza 2 de Mayo 46, Lima 1; tel. (1) 4230309; f. 1978; extreme left-wing; Leader Dr ALFONSO BARRANTES LINGÁN.

Izquierda Unida (IU) (Unified Left): Avda Grau 184, Lima 23; tel. (1) 4278340; f. 1980; Leader GUSTAVO MOHOME; left-wing alliance comprising:

   Frente Nacional de Trabajadores y Campesinos (FNTC/FRENATRACA): Avda Colonial 105, Lima 1; tel. (1) 4272868; f. 1968; left-wing party; Pres. Dr RÓGER CÁCERES VELÁSQUEZ; Sec.-Gen. Dr EDMUNDO HUANQUI MEDINA.

   Partido Comunista Peruano (PCP): Jirón Lampa 774, Lima 1; f. 1928; Pres. JORGE DEL PRADO.

   Unión de Izquierda Revolucionaria (UNIR) (Union of the Revolutionary Left): Jirón Puno 258, Apdo 1165, Lima 1; tel. (1) 4274072; f. 1979; Chair. Senator ROLANDO BREÑA PANTOJA; Gen. Sec. JORGE HURTADO POZO.

Libertad en Democracia Real (Lider): Lima; f. 1998; represents interests of Peru's estimated 2m. evangelical Protestants.

Movimiento de Bases Hayistas (MBH): Pasaje Velarde 180, Lima; f. 1982; faction of APRA, which supports fundamental policies of APRA's founder, Dr Víctor Raúl Haya de la Torre; Leader Dr ANDRÉS TOWNSEND EZCURRA.

Nueva Mayoría: Lima; f. 1992; group of independents, including former cabinet ministers, formed coalition with Cambio 90 in 1992 in order to contest elections to the CCD, and local elections in 1993; Leader JAIME YOSHIYAMA TANAKA.

Partido Aprista Peruano (PAP): see entry for APRA.

Partido Demócrata Cristiano (PDC): Avda España 321, Lima 1; tel. (1) 4238042; f. 1956; 95,000 mems; Chair. CARLOS BLANCAS BUSTAMANTE.

Partido Liberal (PL): Lima; f. 1987; right-wing; formerly Libertad movement; Sec.-Gen. MIGUEL CRUCHAGA.

Partido Obrero Revolucionario Marxista-Partido Socialista de los Trabajadores (PORM-PST): Jirón Apurimac 465, Lima 1; tel. (1) 4280443; PORM f. 1971; PST f. 1974; unified 1982; Trotskyist; Leaders Senator RICARDO NAPURÍ, ENRIQUE FERNÁNDEZ CHACÓN.

Partido Popular Cristiano (PPC): Avda Alfonso Ugarte 1484, Lima; tel. (1) 4238723; fax (1) 4236582; e-mail efa@hamtech.com.pe; f. 1966; splinter group of Partido Demócrata Cristiano; 200,000 mems; Pres. Dr ANTERO FLORES-ARAOZ; Vice-Pres ALEXANDER KOURI, RAÚL CASTRO STAGNARO, EMMA VARGAS DE BENAVIDES.

Partido Revolucionario de los Trabajadores (PRT): Plaza 2 de Mayo 38, Apdo 2449, Lima 100; f. 1978; Trotskyist; Leader HUGO BLANCO; 5,000 mems.

Partido Socialista del Perú (PSP): Jirón Azángaro 105, Lima 1; f. 1930; left-wing; Leader Dr MARÍA CABREDO DE CASTILLO.

Perú Posible (PP): Bajada Balta 131, Miraflores, Lima; tel. (1) 2419307; fax (21) 2419473; e-mail prensa@peruposible.org.pe; internet www.peruposible.org; f. 1995 to support Toledo's candidacy for the 1995 presidential election in alliance with CODE, contested the 2000 and 2001 presidential and congressional elections unaligned; Leader ALEJANDRO TOLEDO.

Proyecto País: Avda General Garzón 820, Lima; tel. (1) 423-3996; internet www.proyectopais.org.pe; f. 1998; Leader MARCO A. ARRUNATEGUI.

Renovación: c/o Edif. Complejo 510, Avda Abancay 251, Lima; tel. (1) 4264260; fax (1) 4263023; f. 1992; Leader RAFAEL REY REY.

Solidaridad Nacional (SN): Los Jilgueros 209, La Molina, Lima; tel. (1) 3494828; e-mail psnpt@hotmail.com; internet www.psn.org.pe; f. 1999; centre-left; Leader LUIS CASTAÑEDA LOSSIO.

Solución Popular: Avda Santa Cruz 398, San Isidro, Lima; tel. (1) 2220884; fax (1) 2223079; internet www.solucionpopular.com; Leader CARLOS BOLOÑA.

Somos Perú (SP): Lima; f. 1999; Leader ALBERTO ANDRADE.

Unidad Nacional (UN): Lima; f. 2000; centrist alliance; Leader LOURDES FLORES.

Unión Nacional Odriísta (UNO): right-wing; Leader FERNANDO NORIEGA.

Unión por el Perú (UPP): c/o Edif. Reyser 3°, Jirón Junin 330, Lima; independent movement; f. 1995 to contest presidential and legislative elections.

Vamos Vecino: Lima; f. 1998; Leader ABSALON VÁSQUEZ.

Other parties include the Marxist Acción Socialista Revolucionaria (ASR), Partido Comunista del Perú—Bandera Roja, Movimiento de Izquierda Revolucionaria (MIR), Vanguardia Revolucionaria, the right-wing Movimiento Democrático Peruano (MDP), Frente Obrero, Campesino Estudiantil y Popular (FOCEP), Partido Comunista

Revolucionario (PCR), Partido Integración Nacional (PADIN), Partido Socialista Revolucionario (PSR), Partido Unificado Mariateguista (PUM), Frente de Liberación Nacional (FLN), Movimiento de Izquierda Revolucionaria (MIR-Perú—Patria Roja, Movimiento de Solidaridad y Democracia, Movimiento Libertad, Partido Unificado, Movimiento Democrático de Izquierda (MDI), Movimiento Obras Cívicas (MOC), Movimiento Independiente Agrario, Frente Popular Agrícola del Perú (Frepap), Renacimiento Andino and Todos por la Victoria.

Guerrilla groups

Sendero Luminoso (Shining Path): f. 1970; began armed struggle 1980; splinter group of PCP; based in Ayacucho; advocates the policies of the late Mao Zedong and his radical followers, including the 'Gang of Four' in the People's Republic of China; founder Dr ABIMAEL GUZMÁN REYNOSO (alias Commdr GONZALO—arrested September 1992); Current leaders MARGIE CLAVO PERALTA (arrested March 1995), PEDRO DOMINGO QUINTEROS AYLLÓN (alias Comrade LUIS—arrested April 1998).

Sendero Rojo (Red Path): dissident faction of Sendero Luminoso opposed to leadership of Abimael Guzmán; Leader FILOMENO CERRÓN CARDOSO (alias Comrade ARTEMIO).

Movimiento Revolucionario Tupac Amarú (MRTA): f. 1984; began negotiations with the Government to end its armed struggle in September 1990; Leader VÍCTOR POLAY CAMPOS (alias Comandante ROLANDO—arrested Feb. 1989; escaped in 1990; rearrested 1992).

Diplomatic Representation

EMBASSIES IN PERU

Argentina: Avda 28 de Julio 828, Lima; tel. (1) 4339966; fax (1) 4330769; Ambassador: ANSELMO MARINI.

Austria: Avda Central 643, 5°, San Isidro, Lima 27; tel. (1) 4420503; fax (1) 4428851; e-mail austria@terra.com.pe; Ambassador: WOLFGANG DONAT.

Belgium: Avda Angamos 392, Lima 18; tel. (1) 2417566; fax (1) 4474478; Ambassador: WILLY TILEMANS.

Bolivia: Los Castaños 235, San Isidro, Lima 27; tel. (1) 4423836; fax (1) 4402298; e-mail jemis@emboli.firstcom.com.pe; Ambassador: FRANZ ONDARZA LINARES.

Brazil: Avda Pardo 850, Miraflores, Lima; tel. (1) 4216763; fax (1) 4452421; e-mail braslim@telematic.edu.pe; Ambassador: CARLOS LUIZ PERES.

Bulgaria: Jirón Paul Harris 289, San Isidro, Lima; tel. and fax (1) 4221145; Ambassador: DIMITAR STANOEV.

Canada: Calle Libertad 130, Miraflores, Lima 18; tel. (1) 4444015; fax (1) 4444347; e-mail lima-gr@dfait-maeci.gc.ca; Ambassador: GRAEME C. CLARK.

Chile: Avda Javier Prado Oeste 790, San Isidro, Lima; tel. (1) 2212080; fax (1) 2211258; e-mail emchile@terra.com.pe; internet www.civila.com/chile/chileper; Ambassador: FRANCISCO PÉREZ WALKER.

China, People's Republic: Jirón José Granda 150, San Isidro, Lima 27; tel. (1) 4429458; fax (1) 4429467; Ambassador: REN JINGYU.

Colombia: Avda J. Basadre 1580, San Isidro, Lima 27; tel. (1) 4410954; fax (1) 4419806; e-mail emperu@telematic.edu.pe; Ambassador: LUIS GUILLERMO GRILLO.

Costa Rica: Avda Emilio Cavanecia 175, Miraflores, Lima; tel. and fax (1) 4409982; Ambassador: TOMÁS SOLEY SOLER.

Cuba: Coronel Portillo 110, San Isidro, Lima; tel. (1) 2642053; fax (1) 2644525; e-mail embacuba@chavin.rcp.net.pe; Ambassador: BENIGNO PÉREZ FERNÁNDEZ.

Czech Republic: Baltazar La Torre 398, San Isidro, Lima 27; tel. (1) 2643381; fax (1) 2641708; e-mail lima@embassy.mzv.pe; Ambassador: JAN KOPECKÝ.

Dominican Republic: Avda 28 de Julio 779, 2°, Lima 1; tel. (1) 4225218; fax (1) 4332856; Ambassador: JOSÉ RAMÓN DÍAZ VALDEPARES.

Ecuador: Las Palmeras 356 y Javier Prado Oeste, San Isidro, Lima; tel. (1) 4409991; fax (1) 4411144; e-mail embjecua@amauta .rcp.net.pe; Ambassador: HORACIO SEVILLA.

Egypt: Avda Jorge Basadre 1470, San Isidro, Lima 27; tel. (1) 4402642; fax (1) 4402547; Ambassador: SAMEER ABDEL SALAM.

El Salvador: Calle Rubens 205, San Borja Norte, Lima; tel. (1) 4758673; fax (1) 4759050; Ambassador: ROBERTO ARTURO CASTRILLO HIDALGO.

Finland: Avda Víctor Andrés Belaúnde 147, Edif. Real Tres, 502°, San Isidro, Lima; tel. (1) 2224466; fax. (1) 2224463; e-mailembajada @finlandiaperu.org.pe; internet www.finlandiaperu.org.pe; Ambassador: MIKKO PYHÁLÁ.

France: Avda Arequipa 3415, Lima; tel. (1) 2158400; fax (1) 2158410; e-mail france.embajada@computextos.com.pe; internet www.ambafrance-pe.org/index.html/; Ambassador: ANTOINE BLANCA.

Germany: Avda Arequipa 4210, Miraflores, Lima 18; tel. (1) 4224919; fax (1) 4226475; Ambassador: Dr HERIBERT WÖCKEL.

Greece: Avda Arequipa 2450, Edif. El Dorado, Of. 1605, Lima; tel. (1) 4218569; fax (1) 4218569; Ambassador: ALKIVIADIS KAROKIS.

Guatemala: Inca Ripac 309, Lima 27; tel. (1) 4602078; fax (1) 4635885; e-mail popolvuh@amauta.rcp.net.pe; Ambassador: CARLOS ARMANDO MOREIRA LÓPEZ.

Haiti: Avda Orrantia 910, San Isidro, Lima; tel. (1) 4223362; Ambassador: ANTOINE BERNARD.

Holy See: Avda Salaverry 6a cuadra, Apdo 397, Lima 100 (Apostolic Nunciature); tel. (1) 4319436; fax (1) 4315704; e-mail nuntius@ amauta.rop.net.pe; Apostolic Nuncio: Most Rev. FORTUNATO BALDELLI, Titular Archbishop of Bevagna.

Honduras: Avda Larco 1013, Miraflores, Lima 18; tel. (1) 4442345; fax (1) 4466577; Ambassador: JOSÉ EDUARDO MARTELL MEJIA.

Hungary: Avda Jorge Basadre 1580, San Isidro, Lima; tel. (1) 4410954; fax (1) 4419806; Ambassador: JÁNOS TÓTH.

India: Avda Salaverry 3006, San Isidro, Lima 27; tel. (1) 4602289; fax (1) 4610374; internet www.indembassy.org.pe; Ambassador: BUTSHIKAN SINGH.

Israel: Edif. El Pacifico, 6°, Plaza Washington, Natalio Sánchez 125, Santa Beatriz, Lima; tel. (1) 4334431; fax (1) 4338925; e-mail emisrael@electrodata.com.pe; Ambassador: YUVAL METSER.

Italy: Avda Gregorio Escobedo 298, Apdo 0490, Lima 11; tel. (1) 4632727; fax (1) 4635317; e-mail italemb@chavin.rcp.net.pe; internet www.italembperu.org.pe; Ambassador: GIUSEPPE M. BORGA.

Japan: Avda San Felipe 312, Apdo 3708, Jesús María, Lima; tel. (1) 4630000; fax (1) 4630302; Ambassador: YOSHIZO KONISHI.

Korea, Democratic People's Republic: Los Nogales 227, San Isidro, Lima; tel. (1) 4411120; fax (1) 4409877; Ambassador: RI IN CHUN.

Korea, Republic: Avda Principal 190, 7°, Lima 13; tel. (1) 4760815; fax (1) 4760950; e-mail korembj@telematic.com.pe; Ambassador: HEE-JOO PARK.

Malaysia: Avda Benavides 415, Miraflores, Lima; tel. (1) 4447272; fax (1) 4441137; Ambassador: MOKHTAR SELAT.

Mexico: Avda Jorge Basadre 710, San Isidro, Lima; tel. (1) 2211173; fax (1) 4404740; e-mail embmexper@embamex.com; Ambassador: MANUEL JOSÉ IGNACIO PIÑA.

Morocco: Avda Javier Prado Oeste 2108, San Isidro, Lima; tel. (1) 4402655; fax (1) 4417762; e-mail sifamlim@chavin.rcp.net.pe; Ambassador: TAIEB CHAOUDRI.

Netherlands: Avda Principal 190, 4°, Urb. Santa Catalina, La Victoria, Lima; tel. (1) 4761069; fax (1) 4756536; e-mail nlgovlim@ terra.com.pe; internet www.terra.com.pe/nl; Ambassador: S. E. RAMONDT.

Nicaragua: Pasaje Los Piños 156, Miraflores, Lima 18; tel. (1) 4461555; fax (1) 4459274; Ambassador: MAURICIO CUADRA SCHULZ.

Panama: Coronel Portillo 521, San Isidro, Lima; tel. (1) 4404874; fax (1) 4406592.

Paraguay: Avda del Rosario 415, San Isidro, Lima; tel. (1) 4418154; fax (1) 4224990; Ambassador: Dr JULIO PEÑA.

Philippines: José del Llano Zapata, Miraflores, Lima 18; tel. (1) 4416318; fax (1) 4420432; Ambassador: ROMEO A. ARGUELLES.

Poland: Avda Salaverry 1978, Jesús María, Lima; tel. (1) 4713920; fax (1) 4713925; Ambassador: WOJCIECH TOMASZEWSKI.

Portugal: Avda Central 643, 4°, Lima 27; tel. (1) 4409905; fax (1) 4429655; Ambassador: Dr ALEXANDRE DE ALMEIDA FERNANDES.

Romania: Avda Jorge Basadre 690, San Isidro, Lima; tel. (1) 4224587; fax (1) 4210609; e-mail amb-rom@computextos.com.pe; Ambassador: ION CIUCU.

Russia: Avda Salaverry 3424, San Isidro, Lima 27; tel. (1) 2640038; fax (1) 2640130; e-mail embrusa@bellnet.com.pe; Ambassador: VIKTOR A. TKACHENKO.

Slovakia: Avda Angamos 1626, San Isidro, Lima 27; tel. (1) 4418272; fax (1) 4222249; Chargé d'affaires: Dr PAVOL SÍPKA.

Spain: Jorge Basadre 498, San Isidro, Lima 27; tel. (1) 2125155; fax (1) 4410084; Ambassador: GONZALO DE BENITO.

Sweden: Centro Camino Real, Torre El Pilar, 9°, Avda Camino Real, San Isidro, Lima 27; tel. (1) 4213400; fax (1) 4429547; Ambassador: ULF LEWIN.

Switzerland: Avda Salaverry 3240, San Isidro, Lima 27; tel. (1) 2640305; fax (1) 2641319; e-mail vertretung@lim.rep.admin.ch; Ambassador: ERIC MARTIN.

United Kingdom: Edif. El Pacífico, 12°, Plaza Washington, Natalio Sánchez 125, Lima; tel. (1) 4334738; fax (1) 4334735; e-mail britemb@terra.com.pe; Ambassador: ROGER HART.

USA: Avda La Encalada 17, Surco, Lima 33; tel. (1) 4343000; fax (1) 4343037; internet ekeko.rcp.net.pe/usa; internet usembassy.state .gov/lima; Ambassador: JOHN R. HAMILTON.

Uruguay: Avda Larco 1013, Dptos 201-202, Miraflores, Lima 18; tel. (1) 4462047; fax (1) 4475065; e-mail emb-uruguay@viaexpresa .com.pe; Ambassador: TABARE BOCALANDRO.

Venezuela: Avda Arequipa 298, Lima; tel. (1) 4334511; fax (1) 4331191; e-mail embavenez@amauta.rcp.net.pe; Ambassador: RODRIGO ARCAYA SMITH.

Yugoslavia: Carlos Porras Osores 360, San Isidro, Lima 27; Apdo 0392, Lima 18; tel. (1) 4212423; fax (1) 4212427; Chargé d'affaires a.i.: ZORAN RAICEVIĆ.

Judicial System

The Supreme Court consists of a President and 17 members. There are also Higher Courts and Courts of First Instance in provincial capitals. A comprehensive restructuring of the judiciary was being implemented during the late 1990s.

SUPREME COURT

Corte Suprema: Palacio de Justicia, 2°, Avda Paseo de la República, Lima 1; tel. (1) 4284457.

President: MARIO URRELO ALVAREZ.

Attorney-General: NELLY CALIDERÓN NAVARRO.

Religion

CHRISTIANITY
The Roman Catholic Church

For ecclesiastical purposes, Peru comprises seven archdioceses, 18 dioceses, 11 territorial prelatures and eight Apostolic Vicariates. At 31 December 1999 89% of the country's population (an estimated 26.6m.) were adherents of the Roman Catholic Church.

Bishops' Conference: Conferencia Episcopal Peruana, Jr. Estados Unidos 838, Apdo 310, Lima 100; tel. (1) 4631010; fax (1) 4636125; e-mail sgc@iglesiacatolica.org.pe; internet ekeko.rcp.net.pe/IAL/cep; f. 1981 (statutes approved 1987, revised 1992 and 2000); Pres. Mgr LUIS BAMBARÉN GASTELUMENDI, Bishop of Chimbote.

Archbishop of Arequipa: LUIS SÁNCHEZ-MORENO LIRA, Arzobispado, Moral San Francisco 118, Apdo 149, Arequipa; tel. (54) 234094; fax (54) 242721; e-mail coam_aqp@mail.interplace.

Archbishop of Ayacucho or Huamanga: Mgr FEDERICO RICHTER FERNÁNDEZ-PRADA, Arzobispado, Jirón 28 de Julio 148, Apdo 30, Ayacucho; tel. and fax (64) 812367; e-mail arzaya@mail.udep.edu.pe.

Archbishop of Cuzco: ALCIDES MENDOZA CASTRO, Arzobispado, Herrajes, Apdo 148, Cuzco; tel. (84) 225211; fax (84) 222781; e-mail arzobisp@telser.com.pe.

Archbishop of Huancayo: JOSÉ PAULINO RÍOS REYNOSO, Arzobispado, Jirón Puno 430, Apdo 245, Huancayo; tel. (64) 234952; fax (64) 239189; e-mail arzohyo@lima.business.com.pe.

Archbishop of Lima: Cardinal JUAN LUIS CIPRIANI THORNE, Arzobispado, Plaza de Armas, Apdo 1512, Lima 100; tel. (1) 4275980; fax (1) 4271967; e-mail arzolimas@amauta.terra.pe.

Archbishop of Piura: OSCAR ROLANDO CANTUARIAS PASTOR, Arzobispado, Libertad 1105, Apdo 197, Piura; tel. and fax (74) 327561; e-mail ocordova@upiura.edu.pe.

Archbishop of Trujillo: MIGUEL CABREJOS VIDARTE, Arzobispado, Jirón Mariscal de Orbegoso 451, Apdo 42, Trujillo; tel. (44) 231474; fax (44) 231473; e-mail arzobispado_tr@starclar.edu.pe.

The Anglican Communion

The Iglesia Anglicana del Cono Sur de América (Anglican Church of the Southern Cone of America), formally inaugurated in April 1983, comprises seven dioceses, including Peru. The Presiding Bishop of the Church is the Bishop of Northern Argentina.

Bishop of Peru: Rt. Rev. HAROLD WILLIAM GODFREY, Apdo 18-1032, Miraflores, Lima 18; tel. (1) 4229160; fax (1) 4408540; e-mail wgodfrey@amauta.rcp.net.pe.

The Methodist Church

There are an estimated 4,200 adherents of the Iglesia Metodista del Perú.

President: Rev. JORGE FIGUEROA, Baylones 186, Lima 5; Apdo 1386, Lima 100; tel. (1) 4245970; fax (1) 4318995; e-mail iglesiamp@computextos.com.pe.

Other Protestant Churches

Among the most popular are the Asamblea de Dios, the Iglesia Evangélica del Perú, the Iglesia del Nazareno, the Alianza Cristiana y Misionera, and the Iglesia de Dios del Perú.

BAHÁ'Í FAITH

National Spiritual Assembly of the Bahá'ís of Peru: Horacio Urteaga 827, Jesús María, Apdo 11-0209, Lima 11; tel. (1) 4316077; fax (1) 4333005; mems resident in 1,888 localities.

The Press

DAILIES
Lima

El Bocón: Jirón Jorge Salazar Araoz 171, Urb. Santa Catalina, Apdo 152, Lima 1; tel. (1) 4756355; fax (1) 4758780; f. 1994; Editorial Dir JORGE ESTÉVES ALFARO; circ. 90,000.

El Comercio: Empresa Editora 'El Comercio', SA, Jirón Antonio Miró Quesada 300, Lima; tel. (1) 4264676; fax (1) 4260810; e-mail www@comercio.com.pe; internet www.rcp.net.pe/elcomercio/; f. 1839; morning; Editorial Dir AURELIO MIRÓ QUESADA; Gen. Man. CÉSAR PARDO-FIGUEROA; circ. 150,000 weekdays, 220,000 Sundays.

Expreso: Jirón Libertad 117, Miraflores, Lima; tel. (1) 4447088; fax (1) 4447117; e-mail direccion@expreso.com.pe; f. 1961; morning; conservative; Editor-in-Chief MANUEL D'ORNELLAS; circ. 100,000.

Extra: Jirón Libertad 117, Miraflores, Lima; tel. (1) 4447088; fax (1) 4447117; e-mail extra@expreso.com.pe; f. 1964; evening edition of *Expreso*; Dir CARLOS SÁNCHEZ; circ. 80,000.

Gestión: Avda Salaverry 156, Miraflores, Lima 18; tel. (1) 4776919; fax (1) 4476569; e-mail gestion@gestion.com.pe; internet www .gestion.com.pe; f. 1990; News Editor JULIO LIRA; Gen. Man. OSCAR ROMERO CARO; circ. 131,200.

Ojo: Jirón Jorge Salazar Araoz 171, Urb. Santa Catalina, Apdo 152, Lima; tel. (1) 4709696; fax (1) 4761605; f. 1968; morning; Editorial Dir AGUSTÍN FIGUEROA BENZA; circ. 100,000.

El Peruano (Diario Oficial): Avda Alfonso Ugarte, cuadra 7, Lima 7; tel. (1) 4283460; fax (1) 4249507; f. 1825; morning; official State Gazette; Editorial Dir ENRIQUE SÁNCHEZ HERNANI; circ. 27,000.

La República: Jirón Camaná 320, Lima 1; tel. (1) 4276455; fax (1) 4265678; e-mail otxoa@larepublica.com.pe; internet www .larepublica.com.pe; f. 1982; left-wing; Dir GUSTAVO MOHME SEMINARIO; circ. 50,000.

Arequipa

Arequipa al Día: Avda Jorge Chávez 201, IV, Centenario, Arequipa; tel. (54) 215515; fax (54) 217810; f. 1991; Editorial Dir CARLOS MENESES CORNEJO.

Correo de Arequipa: Calle Bolívar 204, Arequipa; tel. (54) 235150; e-mail correoperu@mail.interplace.com.pe; Editorial Dir MARTHA VALENCIA; circ. 70,000.

El Pueblo: Sucre 213, Apdo 35, Arequipa; tel. (54) 211500; fax (54) 213361; f. 1905; morning; independent; Editorial Dir EDUARDO LAIME VALDIVIA; circ. 70,000.

Chiclayo

La Industria: Tacna 610, Chiclayo; tel. (74) 238592; fax (74) 235493; f. 1952; Dir JOSÉ RAMIREZ RUIZ; circ. 20,000.

Cuzco

El Comercio: Apdo 70, Cuzco; f. 1896; evening; independent; Dir ABEL RAMOS PEREA; circ. 60,000.

Huacho

El Imparcial: Avda Grau 203, Huacho; f. 1891; tel. (34) 239-2187; fax (34) 232-1352; e-mail el.imparcial@USA.net; evening; Dir ADAN MANRIQUE ROMERO; circ. 5,000.

Huancayo

Correo de Huancayo: Jirón Cuzco 337, Huancayo; tel. (64) 235792; fax (64) 233811; evening; Editorial Dir RODOLFO OROSCO.

La Opinión Popular: Huancas 251, Huancayo; tel. (64) 231149; f. 1922; Dir MIGUEL BERNABÉ SUÁREZ OSORIO.

Ica

La Opinión: Avda Los Maestros 801, Apdo 186, Ica; tel. (34) 235571; f. 1922; evening; independent; Dir GONZALO TUEROS RAMÍREZ.

La Voz de Ica: Castrovirreyna 193, Ica; f. 1918; tel. (34) 232112; Dir ATILIO NIERI BOGGIANO; circ. 4,500.

Pacasmayo

Ultimas Noticias: 2 de Mayo 33, Pacasmayo; tel. and fax (44) 522060; e-mail ballena@misti.lared.net.pe; f. 1973; evening; independent; Dir LUIS ALBERTO BALLENA SÁNCHEZ; circ. 3,000.

Piura

Correo: Zona Industrial Mzna 246, Lote 6, Piura; tel. (74) 321681; fax (74) 324881; Editorial Dir ROLANDO RODRICH ARANGO; circ. 12,000.

El Tiempo: Ayacucho 751, Piura; tel. (74) 325141; fax (74) 327478; e-mail eltiempo@mail.cosapidata.com.pe; f. 1916; morning; independent; Dir LUZ MARÍA HELGUERO; circ. 18,000.

Tacna

Correo: Jirón Hipólito Unanue 636, Tacna; tel. (54) 711671; fax (54) 713955; Editorial Dir RUBÉN COLLAZOS ROMERO; circ. 8,000.

Trujillo

La Industria: Gamarra 443, Trujillo; tel. (44) 234720; fax (44) 427761; e-mail industri@united.net.pe; internet www.unitru.edu.pe/-eelitsa/; f. 1895; morning; independent; Gen. Man. ISABEL CERRO DE BURGA; circ. 8,000.

PERIODICALS AND REVIEWS
Lima

Alerta Agrario: Avda Salaverry 818, Lima 11; tel. (1) 4336610; fax (1) 4331744; f. 1987 by Centro Peruano de Estudios Sociales; monthly review of rural problems; Dir BERTHA CONSIGLIERI; circ. 100,000.

Amautá: Jirón Lampa 1115, Of. 605, Lima; fortnightly; Dir FLORENTINO GÓMEZ VALERIO; circ. 10,000.

The Andean Report: Pasaje Los Pinos 156, Of. B6, Miraflores, Apdo 531, Lima; tel. (1) 4472552; fax (1) 4467888; e-mail perutimes @amauta.rcp.net.pe; internet www.perutimes.com; f. 1975; weekly newsletter; economics, trade and commerce; English; Publisher ELEANOR GRIFFIS DE ZÚÑIGA; circ. 1,000.

Caretas: Jirón Huallaya 122, Portal de Botoneros, Plaza de Armas, Lima 1; Apdo 737, Lima 100; tel. (1) 4289490; fax (1) 4262524; weekly; current affairs; Editor ENRIQUE ZILERI GIBSON; circ. 90,000.

Debate: Apdo 671, Lima 100; tel. (1) 4467070; fax (1) 4455946; f. 1980; every 2 months; Editor AUGUSTO ALVAREZ-RODRICH.

Debate Agrario: Avda Salaverry 818, Lima 11; tel. (1) 4336610; fax (1) 4331744; e-mail cepes@cepes.org.pe; f. 1987 by Centro Peruano de Estudios Sociales; every 4 months; rural issues; Dir FERNANDO EGUREN L.

Gente: Eduardo de Habich 170, Miraflores, Lima 18; tel. (1) 4465046; fax (1) 4461173; e-mail correo@genteperu-com; internet www.genteperu.com; f. 1958; weekly; circ. 25,000.

Hora del Hombre: Apdo 2378, Lima 1; tel. (1) 4220208; f. 1943; monthly; cultural and political journal; illustrated; Dir JORGE FALCÓN.

Industria Peruana: Los Laureles 365, San Isidro, Apdo 632, Lima 27; f. 1896; monthly publication of the Sociedad de Industrias; Editor ROLANDO CELI BURNEO.

Lima Times: Pasaje Los Pinos 156, Of. B 6, Miraflores, Apdo 531, Lima 100; tel. (1) 4469120; fax (1) 4467888; e-mail perutimes@ amauta.rcp.net.pe; internet www.perutimes.com; f. 1975; monthly; travel, cultural events, general news on Peru; English; Editor ELEANOR GRIFFIS DE ZÚÑIGA; circ. 10,000.

Mercado Internacional: El Rosario 115, Miraflores, Lima; tel. (1) 4445395; business.

Monos y Monadas: San Martín 135, Lima; tel. (1) 4773483; f. 1981; fortnightly; satirical; Editor NICOLÁS YEROVI; circ. 17,000.

Oiga: Pedro Venturo 353, Urb. Aurora, Miraflores, Lima; tel. (1) 4475851; weekly; right-wing; Dir FRANCISCO IGARTUA; circ. 60,000.

Onda: Jorge Vanderghen 299, Miraflores, Lima; tel. (1) 4227008; f. 1959; monthly cultural review; Dir JOSÉ ALEJANDRO VALENCIA-ARENAS; circ. 5,000.

Orbita: Parque Rochdale 129, Lima; tel. (1) 4610676; weekly; f. 1970; Dir LUZ CHÁVEZ MENDOZA; circ. 10,000.

Perú Económico: Apdo 671, Lima 100; tel. (1) 4467070; fax (1) 4455946; f. 1978; monthly; Editor AUGUSTO ALVAREZ-RODRICH.

Quehacer: León de la Fuente 110, Lima 17; tel. (1) 2641316; fax (1) 2640128; e-mail postmaster@desco.org.pe; f. 1979; 6 a year; supported by Desco research and development agency; circ. 5,000.

Runa: Apdo 3724, Lima; f. 1977; monthly; review of the Instituto Nacional de Cultura; Dir MARIO RAZZETO; circ. 10,000.

Semana Económica: Apdo 671, Lima 100; tel. (1) 4455237; fax (1) 4455946; f. 1985; weekly; Editor AUGUSTO ALVAREZ-RODRICH.

Unidad: Jirón Lampa 271, Of. 703, Lima; tel. (1) 4270355; weekly; Communist; Dir GUSTAVO ESTEVES OSTOLAZA; circ. 20,000.

Vecino: Avda Petit Thouars 1944, Of. 15, Lima 14; tel. (1) 4706787; f. 1981; fortnightly; supported by Yunta research and urban publishing institute; Dirs PATRICIA CÓRDOVA, MARIO ZOLEZZI; circ. 5,000.

NEWS AGENCIES
Government News Agency

Agencia de Noticias Andina: Jirón de la Unión 264, Lima; tel. (1) 4273602.

Foreign Bureaux

Agence France-Presse (AFP): F. Masías 544, San Isidro, Lima; tel. (1) 4214012; fax (1) 4424390; e-mail yllorca@amautarcp.net.pe; Bureau Chief YVES-CLAUDE LLORCA.

Agencia EFE (Spain): Manuel González Olaechea 207, San Isidro, Lima; tel. (1) 4412094; fax (1) 4412422; Bureau Chief FRANCISCO RUBIO FIGUEROA.

Agenzia Nazionale Stampa Associata (ANSA) (Italy): Avda Gen. Córdoba 2594, Lince, Lima 14; tel. (1) 4225130; fax (1) 4229087; Correspondent ALBERTO KU-KING MATURANA.

Associated Press (AP) (USA): Jirón Cailloma 377, Apdo 119, Lima; tel. (1) 4277775; Bureau Chief MONTE HAYES.

Deutsche Presse-agentur (dpa) (Germany): Schell 343, Of. 707, Miraflores, Apdo 1362, Lima 18; tel. (1) 4441437; fax (1) 4443775; Bureau Chief GONZALO RUIZ TOVAR.

Informatsionnoye Telegrafnoye Agentstvo Rossii—Telegrafnoye Agentstvo Suverennykh Stran (ITAR—TASS) (Russia): Aurelio Miró Quezada 576, San Isidro, Apdo 1402, Lima; Chief VITALII GLOBA.

Inter Press Service (IPS) (Italy): Daniel Olaechea y Olaechea 285, Lima 11; tel. and fax (1) 4631021; Correspondent ABRAHAM LAMA.

Prensa Latina (Cuba): Edif. Astoria, Of. 303, Avda Tacna 482, Apdo 5567, Lima; tel. (1) 4233908; Correspondent LUIS MANUEL ARCE ISAAC.

Reuters (United Kingdom): Avda Paseo de la República 3505, 4°, San Isidro, Lima 27; tel. (1) 2212111; fax (1) 4418992; Man. EDUARDO HILGERT.

United Press International (UPI) Inc. (USA): Avda La Paz 374A, 2°, Miraflores, Lima 18; tel. (1) 4445100; fax (1) 4445095; Bureau Man. JANE HOLLIGAN.

Xinhua (New China) News Agency (People's Republic of China): Parque Javier Prado 181, San Isidro, Lima; tel. (1) 4403463; Bureau Chief WANG SHUBO.

PRESS ASSOCIATIONS

Asociación Nacional de Periodistas del Perú: Jirón Huancavélica 320, Apdo 2079, Lima 1; tel. (1) 4270687; fax (1) 4278493; e-mail anpofip@attmail.com; f. 1928; 7,400 mems; Pres. and Sec.-Gen. ROBERTO MEJÍA ALARCÓN.

Federación de Periodistas del Perú (FPP): Avda Abancay 173, Lima; tel. (1) 4284373; f. 1950; Pres. ALBERTO DELGADO ORÉ; Sec.-Gen. JORGE PAREDES CABADA.

Publishers

Asociación Editorial Bruño: Avda Arica 751, Breña, Lima 5; tel. (1) 4244134; fax (1) 4251248; f. 1950; educational; Man. FEDERICO DÍAZ PINEDO.

Biblioteca Nacional del Perú: Avda Abancay 4a c., Apdo 2335, Lima 1; tel. (1) 44287690; fax (1) 44277331; f. 1821; general nonfiction, directories; Dir MARTHA FERNÁNDEZ DE LÓPEZ.

Colección Artes y Tesoros del Perú: Calle Centenario 156, Urb. Las Laderas de Melgarejo, La Molina, Lima 12; tel. (1) 3493128; fax (1) 3490579; e-mail acarulla@bcp.com.pe; f. 1971; Dir ALVARO CARULLA.

Editorial Amarú: Jirón Canta 651, Lima 13; f. 1981; Dir CARLOS MATTA.

Ediciones Ave: Yauli 1440, Chacra Ríos Norte, Lima; Man. AUGUSTO VILLANUEVA P.

Editorial Colegio Militar Leoncio Prado: Avda Costanera 1541, La Perla, Callao; f. 1946; textbooks and official publications; Man. OSCAR MORALES QUINA.

Editorial D.E.S.A.: General Varela 1577, Breña, Lima; f. 1955; textbooks and official publications; Man. ENRIQUE MIRANDA.

Editorial Desarrollo, SA: Ica 242, 1°, Apdo 3824, Lima; tel. and fax (1) 4286628; f. 1965; business administration, accounting, auditing, industrial engineering, English textbooks, dictionaries, and technical reference; Dir LUIS SOSA NÚÑEZ.

Editorial Horizonte: Avda Nicolás de Piérola 995, Lima 1; tel. (1) 4279364; fax (1) 4274341; e-mail damonte@terra.com.pe; f. 1968; social sciences, literature, politics; Man. HUMBERTO DAMONTE.

Editorial Labrusa, SA: Los Frutales Avda 670-Ate, Lima; tel. (1) 4358443; fax (1) 4372925; f. 1988; literature, educational, cultural; Gen. Man. ADRIÁN REUILLA CALVO; Man. FEDERICO DÍAZ TINEO.

Ediciones Médicas Peruanas, SA: Avda Angamos Oeste 371, Of. 405, Miraflores, Apdo 6150, Lima 18; f. 1965; medical; Man. ALBERTO LOZANO REYES.

Editorial Milla Batres, SA: Lima; **f.** 1963; history, literature, art, archaeology, linguistics and encyclopaedias on Peru; Dir-Gen. CARLOS MILLA BATRES.

Editorial Navarrete SRL-Industria del Offset: Manuel Tellería 1842, Apdo 4173, Lima; tel. (1) 4319040; fax (1) 4230991; Man. LUIS NAVARRETE LECHUGA.

Editorial Salesiana: Avda Brasil 218, Apdo 0071, Lima 5; tel. (1) 4235225; f. 1918; religious and general textbooks; Man. Dir Dr FRANCESCO VACARELLO.

Editorial Universo, SA: Avda Nicolás Arriola 2285, Urb. Apolo, La Victoria, Apdo 241, Lima; f. 1967; literature, technical, educational; Pres. CLEMENTE AQUINO; Gen. Man. Ing. JOSÉ A. AQUINO BENAVIDES.

Fundación del Banco Continental para el Fomento de la Educación y la Cultura (EDUBANCO): Avda República de Panamá 3055, San Isidro, Apdo 4687, Lima 27; tel. (1) 2111000; fax (1) 2112479; f. 1973; Pres. PEDRO BRESCIA CAFFERATA; Man. FERNANDO PORTOCARRERO.

Industrial Gráfica, SA: Jirón Chavín 45, Breña, Lima 5; fax (1) 4324413; f. 1981; Pres. JAIME CAMPODONICO V.

INIDE: Van de Velde 160, Urb. San Borja, Lima; f. 1981; owned by National Research and Development Institute; educational books; Editor-in-Chief ANA AYALA.

Librerías ABC, SA: Avda Paseo de la República 3440, Local B-32, Lima 27; tel. (1) 4422900; fax (1) 4422901; f. 1956; history, Peruvian art and archaeology; Man. Dir HERBERT H. MOLL.

Librería San Pablo: Jirón Callao 198, Lima 1; tel. (1) 4269493; fax (1) 4269496; e-mail paulinaslperu@hys.com.pe; f. 1981; religious and scholastic texts; Man. Sister MARÍA GRACIA CAPALBO.

Librería Studium, SA: Plaza Francia 1164, Lima; tel. (1) 4326278; fax (1) 4325354; f. 1936; textbooks and general culture; Man. Dir EDUARDO RIZO PATRÓN RECAVARREN.

Pablo Villanueva Ediciones: Yauli 1440, Chacra Ríos Norte, Lima; f. 1938; literature, history, law etc.; Man. AUGUSTO VILLA-NUEVA PACHECO.

Pontificia Universidad Católica: Fondo Editorial, Avda Universitaria, 18c., San Miguel, Lima; tel. 4602870; fax (1) 4600872; Dir DANTE ANTONIOLI DELUCCHI.

Sociedad Bíblica Peruana, AC: Avda Petit Thouars 991, Apdo 14-0295, Lima 100; tel. (1) 4335815; fax (1) 4336389; internet www.members.tripod.com/sbpac; f. 1821; Christian literature and bibles; Gen. Sec. PEDRO ARANA-QUIROZ.

Universidad Nacional Mayor de San Marcos: Oficina General de Editorial, Avda República de Chile 295, 5°, Of. 508, Lima; tel. (1) 4319689; f. 1850; textbooks, education; Man. Dir JORGE CAMPOS REY DE CASTRO.

Association

Cámara Peruana del Libro: Avda Cuba 427, Apdo 10253, Lima 11; tel. (1) 2650737; fax (1) 2650735; e-mail cp-libro@amauta.rcp.net.pe; f. 1946; 120 mems; Pres. CARLOS A. BENVIDES AGUIJE; Exec. Dir LOYDA MORÁN BUSTAMANTE.

Broadcasting and Communications

TELECOMMUNICATIONS

Regulatory Authorities

Dirección de Administración de Frecuencias: Ministerio de Transportes, Comunicaciones, Vivienda y Construcción, Avda 28 de Julio 800, Lima 1; tel. (1) 4331990; e-mail dgcdir@mtc.gob.pe; manages and allocates radio frequencies; Dir JOSÉ VILLA GAMBOA.

Dirección General de Telecomunicaciones: Ministerio de Transportes, Comunicaciones, Vivienda y Construcción, Avda 28 de Julio 800, Lima 1; tel. (1) 4330752; fax (1) 4331450; e-mail dgtdir@mtc.gob.pe; Dir-Gen. MIGUEL OSAKI SUEMITSU.

Instituto Nacional de Investigación y Capacitación de Telecomunicaciones (INICTEL): Avda San Luis 17, esq. Bailetti, San Borja, Lima 41; tel. (1) 3360993; fax (1) 3369281; e-mailpostmaster@inictel.gob.pe; Pres. MANUEL ADRIANZEN.

Organismo Supervisor de Inversión Privada en Telecomunicaciones (OSIPTEL): Calle de la Prosz 136, San Borja, Lima 41; tel. (1) 2251313; fax (1) 4760563; e-mail jkunigami@ospitel.gob.pe; internet www.ospitel.gob.pe; body established by the Peruvian Telecommunications Act to oversee competition and tariffs, to monitor the quality of services and to settle disputes in the sector; Pres. JORGE KUNIGAMI K.

Major Service Provider

Telefónica del Perú, SA: Avda Arequipa 1155, Santa Beatriz, Lima 1; tel. (1) 2101013; fax (1) 4705950; e-mail mgarcia@tp.com.pe; Exec. Pres. MANUEL GARCÍA G.

BROADCASTING

In 1996 there were 1,277 radio stations, 59 television transmitters and 476 television relay stations in Peru.

Regulatory Authorities

Asociación de Radio y Televisión del Perú (AR&TV): Avda Roma 140, San Isidro, Lima 27; tel. (1) 4703734; Pres. HUMBERTO MALDONADO BALBÍN; Dir DANIEL LINARES BAZÁN.

Coordinadora Nacional de Radio: Santa Sabina 441, Urb. Santa Emma, Apdo 2179, Lima 100; tel. (1) 5640760; fax (1) 5640059; e-mail postmaster@cnr.org.pe; internet www.cnr.org.pe; f. 1978; Pres. RODOLFO AQUINO RUIZ.

Instituto Nacional de Comunicación Social: Jirón de la Unión 264, Lima; Dir HERNÁN VALDIZÁN.

Unión de Radioemisoras de Provincias del Perú (UNRAP): Mariano Carranza 754, Santa Beatriz, Lima 1.

Radio

Radio Agricultura del Perú, SA—La Peruanísima: Avda Alfonso Ugarte 1428, Of. 202, Casilla 625, Lima 5; tel. (1) 4244302; fax (1) 4246677; e-mail radioagriculturadelperu@yahoo.com; f. 1963; Pres. BARTOLOMÉ DEXTRE FREYLE; Dir LUZ ISABEL DEXTRE NÚÑEZ.

Radio América: Montero Rosas 1099, Santa Beatriz, Lima 1; tel. (1) 2653841; fax (1) 2653844; e-mail kcrous@americatv.com.pe; f. 1943; Dir-Gen. KAREN CROUSILLAT.

Radio Cadena Nacional: Los Angeles 129, Miraflores, Lima; tel. (1) 4220905; fax (1) 4221067; Pres. MIGUEL DÍEZ CANSECO; Gen. Man. CÉSAR LECCA ARRIETA.

Cadena Peruana de Noticias: Paseo de la República 3662, San Isidro, Lima; tel. (1) 2218339; fax (1) 2218337; Pres. JOSÉ PASTOR AMPUERO; Gen. Man. WILLY CONTRERAS LÓPEZ.

Radio Cutivalú, La Voz del Desierto: Jirón Ignacio de Loyola 300, Urb. Miraflores, Castilla, Piura; tel. (74) 342802; fax (74) 342965; e-mail postmaster@cipcaperu-pe; f. 1986; Pres. MARÍA ISABEL REMY SIMATOVIC; Dir RODOLFO AQUINO RUIZ.

Emisoras 'Cruz del Perú': Victorino Laynes 1402, Urb. Elio, Lima 1; tel. (1) 4521028; Pres. FERNANDO CRUZ MENDOZA; Gen. Man. MARCO CRUZ MENDOZA M.

Emisoras Nacionales: León Velarde 1140, Lince, Lima 1; tel. (1) 4714948; fax (1) 4728182; Gen. Man. CÉSAR COLOMA R.

Radio Inca del Perú: Jirón Bernardo Alcedo 375, Lince, Lima 14; tel. (1) 4723882; fax (1) 4708384; f. 1951; Gen. Man. AUGUSTO SHOZEN IREI SHIMABUKURO.

Radio Nacional del Perú: Avda Petit Thouars 447, Santa Beatriz, Lima; tel. (1) 4331712; fax (1) 4338952; Pres. LUIS ALBERTO MARAVÍ SÁENZ; Gen. Man. CARLOS PIZANO PANIAGUA.

Radio Panamericana: Paseo Parodi 340, San Isidro, Lima 27; tel. (1) 4226768; fax (1) 4221182; e-mail mad@tci.net.pe; f. 1953; RAQUEL DELGADO DE ALCÁNTARA.

Radio Programas del Perú: Alejandro Tirado 217, 7°, Santa Beatriz, Lima; tel. (1) 4338720; Pres. MANUEL DELGADO PARKER; Gen. Man. ROLANDO ESTREMADOYRO.

Radio Santa Rosa: Jirón Camaná 170, Apdo 206, Lima; tel. (1) 4277488; fax (1) 4269219; e-mail santarosa@viaexpresa.com.pe; f. 1958; Dir P. JUAN SOKOLICH ALVARADO.

Sonograbaciones Maldonado: Mariano Carranza 754, Santa Beatriz, Lima; tel. (1) 4715163; fax (1) 4727491; Pres. HUMBERTO MALDONADO B.; Gen. Man. LUIS HUMBERTO MALDONADO.

Television

América Televisión, Canal 4: Jirón Montero Rosas 1099, Santa Beatriz, Lima; tel. (1) 4717512; Gen. Man. JOSÉ CROUSILLAT.

ATV, Canal 9: Avda Arequipa 3570, San Isidro, Lima; tel. (1) 4426666; fax (1) 4217263; e-mail andinatelevision@atv.com.pe; f. 1983; Man. MARÍA ELENA VERA ABAD.

Frecuencia Latina, Canal 2: Avda San Felipe 968, Jesús María, Lima; tel. (1) 4707272; fax (1) 4714187; Pres. BARUCH IVCHER.

Global Televisión, Canal 13: Gen. Orbegoso 140, Breña, Lima; tel. (1) 3303040; fax (1) 4238202; f. 1989; Pres. GENARO DELGADO PARKER; Gen. Man. RAFAEL LEGUÍA.

Nor Peruana de Radiodifusión, SA: Avda Arequipa 3520, San Isidro, Lima 27; tel. (1) 403365; fax (1) 419844; f. 1991; Dir FRANCO PALERMO IBARGUENGOITIA; Gen. Man. FELIPE BERNINZÓN VALLARINO.

Panamericana Televisión SA, Canal 5: Alejandro Tirado 217, Santa Beatriz, Lima; tel. (1) 4708555; fax (1) 4334787; Pres. MANUEL DELGADO PARKER.

Cía Peruana de Radiodifusión, Canal 4 TV: Mariano Carranza y Montero Rosas 1099, Santa Beatriz, Lima; tel. (1) 4728985; fax (1) 4710099; f. 1958; Dir JOSÉ FRANCISCO CROUSILLAT CARREÑO.

RBC Televisión, Canal 11: Avda Manco Cápac 333, La Victoria, Lima; tel. (1) 4310169; fax (1) 4331237; Pres. FERNANDO GONZÁLEZ DEL CAMPO; Gen. Man. JUAN SÁENZ MARÓN.

Radio Televisión Peruana, Canal 7: Avda José Galvez 1040, Santa Beatriz, Lima 1; tel. (1) 4718000; fax (1) 4726799; f. 1957; Pres. LUIS ALBERTO MARAVÍ SÁENZ; Gen. Man. CARLOS ALBERTO PIZZANO P.

Cía de Radiodifusión Arequipa SA, Canal 9: Centro Comercial Cayma, R2, Arequipa; tel. (54) 252525; fax (54) 254959; e-mail crasa@ibm.net; f. 1986; Dir ENRIQUE MENDOZA NÚÑEZ; Gen. Man. ENRIQUE MENDOZA DEL SOLAR.

Uranio, Canal 15: Avda Arequipa 3570, 6°, San Isidro, Lima; e-mail agamarra@atv.com.pe; Gen. Man. ADELA GAMARRA VASQUEZ.

Finance

In April 1991 a new banking law was introduced, which relaxed state control of the financial sector and reopened the sector to foreign banks (which had been excluded from the sector by a nationalization law promulgated in 1987).

BANKING

(cap. = capital; res = reserves; dep. = deposits; m. = million; amounts in new soles, unless otherwise stated)

Superintendencia de Banca y Seguros: Jirón Huancavelica 240, Lima 1; tel. (1) 4288210; fax (1) 4287259; e-mail mostos@sbs.gob.pe; internet www.sbs.gob.pe; f. 1931; Superintendent MANUEL VÁSQUEZ PERALES; Sec.-Gen. TOMÁS MORÁN ORTEGA.

Central Bank

Banco Central de Reserva del Perú: Jirón Antonio Miró Quesada 441, Lima 1; tel. (1) 4276250; fax (1) 4275880; internet www.bcrp.gob.pe; f. 1922; refounded 1931; cap. 50.0m.; res 300.9m., dep. 31,803.1m. (Dec. 1998); Pres. RICHARD WEBB; Gen. Man. JAVIER DE LA ROCHA MARIE; 7 brs.

Other Government Banks

Banco Central Hipotecario del Perú: Carabaya 421, Apdo 1005, Lima; tel. (1) 4273845; fax (1) 4319729; f. 1929; Pres. AUSEJO RONCAGLIOLO CARLOS; 63 brs.

Banco de la Nación: Avda Nicolás de Piérola 1065, Lima 1; Apdo 1835, Lima 100; tel. (1) 4261133; fax (1) 4268099; e-mail gergeneral@bn.com.pe; f. 1966; cap. 500.4m., res 188.0m., dep. 3,144.1m. (Dec. 1999); conducts all commercial banking operations of official government agencies; Pres. ALFREDO JALILIE AWAPARA; Gen. Man. JOSÉ LUIS MIGUEL DE PRIEGO PALOMINO; 385 brs.

Corporación Financiera de Desarrollo (COFIDE): Augusto Tamayo 160, San Isidro, Lima 27; tel. (1) 4422500; fax (1) 4423374; e-mail postmaster@cofide.com.pe; f. 1971; Pres. AURELIO LORET DE MOLA BÖHME; Gen. Man. MARCO CASTILLO TORRES; 11 brs.

Development Banks

Banco Industrial del Perú: Jirón Lampa 535–545, Apdo 1230, Lima 1; tel. (1) 4288080; fax (1) 4282213; f. 1936; cap. 54,862, res 6.0m., dep. 12.7m., total assets 503.6m. (Dec. 1990); Pres. REYNALDO SUSANO LUCERO; Gen. Man. MARIO VIZCARRA VILLAVICENCIO; 34 brs.

Banco de la Vivienda del Perú: Jirón Camaná 616, Apdo 5425, Lima 100; tel. (1) 4276655; f. 1962; cap. and res 10,926.7, dep. 2,989.9 (July 1988); Pres. RAMÓN ARROSPIDE MEJÍA; Man. VÍCTOR CASTRO MUÑOZ; 5 brs.

Commercial Banks

Banco de Comercio: Avda Paseo de la República 3705, San Isidro, Lima; tel. (1) 4229800; fax (1) 4405458; e-mail postmaster@bancomercio.com.pe; internet www.bancomercio.com.pe; f. 1967; formerly Banco Peruano de Comercio y Construcción; cap. 41.0m., res. 5.9m., dep. 411.4m. (Dec. 1998); Chair. PERCY TABORY; Gen. Man. HÉCTOR QUEZADA M. ILLA; 24 brs.

Banco Continental: Avda República de Panamá 3050–3065, San Isidro, Lima 27; tel. (1) 2111000; fax (1) 2111788; e-mail telematica@grupobbv.com.pe; internet www.continental.grupobbv.com.pe; f. 1951; cap. 652.3m., res 127.2m., dep. 7,872.2m. (Dec. 1998); Pres. PEDRO BESCIA CAFFERATA; Dir-Gen. JOSÉ ANTONIO COLOMER GUIU; 190 brs.

Banco de Crédito del Perú: Calle Centenario 156, Urb. Las Laderas de Melgarejo, Apdo 12–067, Lima 12; tel. (1) 3490606; fax (1) 4266543; internet www.bcp.com.pe; f. 1889; cap. 983.7m., res

545.6m., dep. 17,579.1m., total assets 21,307.7m. (Dec. 1999); Pres. DIONISIO ROMERO SEMINARIO; Gen. Man. RAIMUNDO MORALES DASSO; 215 brs.

Banco Exterior de los Andes y de España (EXTEBANDES): Avda Enrique Canaval y Moreyra 454, Lima 27; tel. (1) 4422121; f. 1982; cap. and res US $53.0m., dep. $371.9m. (Dec. 1987); Pres. ROSARIO ORELLANA YÉPEZ; Regional Gen. Man. HENRY BARCLAY REY DE CASTRO; 3 brs.

Banco Latino (BCOLATIN): Avda Paseo de la República 3505–3515, Lima 27; tel. (1) 4221290; fax (1) 4426200; e-mail clientelatino@bcolatino.com.pe; internet www.bcolatino.com.pe; f. 1982; cap. 229.9m., res 7.0m., dep. 815.5m. (Nov. 1999); Pres. RICHARD WEBB DUARTE; Gen. Man. HENRY BARCLAY REY DE CASTRO; 10 brs.

Banco del Libertador: Avda Paseo de la República 3245, San Isidro, Lima 27; tel. (1) 4421661; fax (1) 4428280; f. 1979 as Financiera Nacional; Pres. and Chair. ALBERTO BEDOYA SÁENZ; Gen. Man. JOSÉ MACCHIAVELLO RODRÍGUEZ.

Banco Santander Central Hispano Perú: Avda Riviera Navarrete 698, San Isidro, Lima; tel. (1) 2158000; fax (1) 2222980; f. 1995 as Banco Santander Perú following acquisition by Banco Santander of Banco Mercantil del Perú and Banco Interandino; name changed to above in 2000 following merger with Bancosur; cap. and res 453.5m., dep. 2,695.3m. (Dec. 2000); CEO LEOPOLDO QUINTANO; 25 brs.

Banco Solventa: Avda Aviación 2401, San Borja, Lima; tel. (1) 4758899; fax (1) 4756644.

Banco Sudamericano: Avda Camino Real 815, San Isidro, Lima 27; tel. (1) 2211111; fax (1) 4423892; e-mail servicios@bansud.com.pe; internet www.bansud.com.pe; f. 1981; cap. 101.2m., res 28.4m., dep. 1,431.1m. (Dec. 1998); Pres. ROBERTO CALDA CAVANNA; Gen. Man. RICARDO WENZEL FERRADAS; 9 brs.

Banco del Trabajo: Avda Paseo de la República 3587, San Isidro, Lima; tel. (1) 4219000; fax (1) 2214096; e-mail bravo@bantra.com.pe; Chair. CARLOS CARRILLO QUIÑONES; Gen. Man. JORGE SABAG SABAG; 46 brs.

Banco Wiese Sudameris: Jirón Cuzco 245, Apdo 1235, Lima 100; tel. (1) 4286000; fax (1) 4263977; internet www.wiese.com.pe; f. 1943; cap. 251.9m., dep. 6,647.2m., total assets 10,656.7m. (Dec. 1998); taken over by Govt in Oct. 1987; returned to private ownership in Oct. 1988 as Banco Wiese Ltdo; merged with Banco de Lima-Sudameris in Sept. 1999; Pres. and Chair. AUGUSTO FELIPE WIESE DE OSMA; Dir and Gen. Man. EUGENIO BERTINI VINCI.

INTERBANK (Banco Internacional del Perú): Jirón de la Unión 600, Lima 1; Apdo 148, Lima 100; tel. (1) 4272000; fax (1) 4262630; e-mail krubin@intercorp.com.pe; internet www.interbank.com.pe; f. 1897; commercial bank; cap. 299.8m., res. 91.4m., dep. 4,687.8m. (Dec. 1999); Pres. CARLOS RODRÍGUEZ PASTOR; Gen. Man. ISMAEL BENAVIDES FERREYROS; 139 brs.

NBK Bank: Av. República de Panamá 3655, Lima 27; tel. (1) 2153000; fax (1) 2210292, internet www.nbkbank.com; f. 1960; cap. 215m., dep. 750.5m., total assets 1,963.9m. (Dec. 1999); Chair. FRANCISCO GONZÁLEZ GARCÍA; Gen. Man. ANDY ALTENA.

Provincial Banks

Banco Regional del Norte: Esq. Libertad e Ica 723, Apdo 131, Piura; tel. (74) 325992; fax (74) 332742; f. 1960; cap. and res US $9.6m., dep. $67.6m. (Dec. 1992); Pres. JUAN ARTURO ATKINS MORALES; CEO FRANCISCO GONZÁLEZ GARCÍA; 10 brs.

Savings Bank

Caja de Ahorros de Lima: Jirón Augusto N. Wiese 638, Apdo 297, Lima 100; tel. (1) 4276663; f. 1868; cap. and res 114.5m., dep. 942.0m. (Dec. 1986); Pres. RICARDO LA PUENTE ROBLES; Gen. Man. Ing. DAVID ELLENBOGEN SCHAUER; 5 brs.

Foreign Banks

Banco do Brasil, SA: Avda Camino Real 348, San Isidro, Lima; tel. (1) 2212280; fax (1) 4424208.

Banco Arabe Latinoamericano (ARLABANK): Calle Juan de Arona 830, San Isidro, Apdo 10070, Lima 100; tel. (1) 4413150; fax (1) 4414277; f. 1977; Chair. CÉSAR RODRÍGUEZ BATILE; Gen. Man. FERNANDO ACCAME FEIJOO.

Citibank NA (USA): Torre Real, 5°, Avda Camino Real 456, Lima 27; tel. (1) 4214000; fax (1) 4409044; internet www.citibank.com/peru/homepage/index-e-htm; f. 1920; cap. US $47,520m., res $1,936m., dep. $139,627m. (Nov. 1997); Vice-Pres. GUSTAVO MARÍN; 1 br.

Banking Association

Asociación de Bancos del Perú: Calle 41, No 975, Urb. Corpac, San Isidro, Lima 27; tel. (1) 2241718; fax (1) 2241707; f. 1929;

refounded 1967; Pres. José Nicolini Lorenzoni; Gen. Man. Juan Klingenberger Lomellini.

STOCK EXCHANGE

Bolsa de Valores de Lima: Pasaje Acuña 106, Lima 100; tel. (1) 4260714; fax (1) 4267650; e-mail tfreire@bvl.com.pe; f. 1860; Exec. Pres. Carlos Seminario Pizzorni; CEO Miguel Rivera Aguirre.

INSURANCE

Lima

Cía de Seguros La Fénix Peruana: Avda Cte Espinar 689, Miraflores, Lima 18; Apdo 1356, Lima 100; tel. (1) 2412430; fax (1) 4455840; e-mail fenix@lafenix.com.pe; internet www.lafenix.com; f. 1927; Pres. Raúl Barrios Orbegoso; Gen. Man. Rafael Padial.

Cía de Seguros La Nacional: Esq. Avda La Fontana con La Molina, Apdo 275, Lima 1; tel. (1) 4369100; fax (1) 4369258; f. 1904; Pres. Ing. Roberto Calda Cavanna; Gen. Man. Renzo Calda Giurato.

Generali Perú, Cía de Segurosy Reaseguros: Jirón Antonio Miró Quesada 191, Apdo 1751, Lima 100; tel. (1) 3111000; fax (1) 3111004; e-mail boac@generali-peru-com.pe; f. 1942; Pres. Piero Sacchi Checcuci; Gen. Man. Bruno Orlandini Alvarez Calderón.

El Pacífico-Peruano Suiza, Cía de Seguros y Reaseguros: Avda Arequipa 660, Apdo 595, Lima 100; tel. (1) 4333626; fax (1) 4333388; f. 1993 by merger; Pres. Calixto Romero Seminario; Gen. Man. Arturo Rodrigo Santistevan.

Panamericana Cía de Seguros y Reaseguros: Jirón Augusto Tamayo 180, San Isidro, Lima; tel. (1) 4715070; fax (1) 4703769; f. 1958; Pres. Juan Banchero Rossi; Gen. Man. Rodolfo Gordillo Tordoya.

Popular y Porvenir, Cía de Seguros: Jirón Augusto Tamayo 125, San Isidro, Lima; tel. (1) 4219557; fax (1) 4218843; f. 1904; Pres. Augusto Miyagusuku Miagui; Gen. Man. Victor Rendón Valencia.

La Positiva Cía de Seguros y Reaseguros SA: Esq., Javier Prado Este y Francisco Masías, Apdo 1456, Lima 27; tel. (1) 4426250; fax (1) 4401124; f. 1937; Pres. Ing. Juan Manuel Peña Roca; Gen. Man. Jaime Pérez Rodríguez.

La Real, Cía de Seguros Generales, SA: Avda San Luis 2000, San Borja, Lima; tel. (1) 4758650; fax (1) 4769941; e-mail segureal @cbd.com.pe; f. 1980; Pres. César Vilchez Vivanco Cahuas Bonino; Gen. Man. José Antonio León Roca.

Reaseguradora Peruana, SA: Chinchón 890, San Isidro, Apdo 3672, Lima 100; tel. (1) 4425065; fax (1) 4417959; f. 1965; state-controlled; Pres. Rafael Villegas Cerro; Gen. Man. Ernesto Becerra Mejía.

Rimac Internacional, Cía de Seguros: Las Begonias 475, 3°, San Isidro, Lima 27; Apdo 245, Lima 100; tel. (1) 4222780; fax (1) 4210570; internet www.rimac.com; f. 1896; Pres. Ing. Pedro Brescia Cafferata; Gen. Man. Alex Fort Brescia.

SECREX, Cía de Seguro de Crédito y Garantías: Avda Angamos Oeste 1234, Miraflores, Apdo 0511, Lima 18; tel. (1) 4424033; fax (1) 4423890; e-mail ciaseg@secrex.com.pe; f. 1980; Pres. Dr Raúl Ferrero Costa; Gen. Man. Juan A. Giannoni.

El Sol, Nacional Cía de Seguros y Reaseguros: Avda 28 de Julio 873, Miraflores, Apdo 323, Lima 100; tel. (1) 4444515; fax (1) 4468456; f. 1950; Pres. Ing. Roberto Calda Cavanna; Gen. Man. Renzo Calda Giurato.

Sul América Cía de Seguros, SA—Sul América Seguros: Jirón Sinchi Roca 2728, Apdo 5569, Lince, Lima 14; tel. (1) 4210515; fax (1) 4418730; e-mail postmaster@sulamerica.com.pe; internet www.sulamerica.com; f. 1954; Pres. Oswaldo Mario Pego de Amorim Azevedo; Gen. Man. Luis Salcedo Marsano.

La Vitalicia, Cía de Seguros: Avda Ricardo Rivera Navarrete 791, San Isidro, Apdo 5597, Lima 27; tel. (1) 4422424; fax (1) 4422766; f. 1950; Pres. Benjamín Perelman Zelter; Gen. Man. Raúl Carvallo Rey.

Wiese Aetna, Cia de Seguros: Calle Tudela y Varela 102, San Isidro, Lima; tel. (1) 2222222; fax (1) 4427550; e-mail seguros@wieseaetna.com; internet www.wieseaetna.com; f. 1980 as Cía de Seguros Condor; changed name to above in 1996; Pres. Gonzalo de la Puente y Lavalle; Gen. Man. José Antonio Cacho-Sousa de Cárdenas.

Insurance Association

Asociación Peruana de Empresas de Seguros (APESEG): Arias Araguez 146, Miraflores, Apdo 1684, Lima 100; tel. (1) 4442294; fax (1) 4468538; f. 1904; Pres. Guillermo Carrillo Flecha; Gen. Man. Manuel Portugal Mariátegui.

Trade and Industry

GOVERNMENT AGENCIES

Consejo Nacional de Conciliación Agraria (CNCA): Lima; f. 1988; acts as mediator between the Government and producers in agricultural sector; Pres. Minister of Agriculture.

Instituto de Comercio Exterior—ICE: Avda Grau 501, Lima 1; tel. (1) 4479877; f. 1986; responsible for supervision and promotion of foreign trade; Pres. (vacant).

Enci (Empresa Nacional de Comercialización de Insumos): Galerías San Felipe 111, Cuadra 7, Avda Gregorio Escobedo, Apdo 1834, Lima 11; tel. (1) 4632122; fax (1) 4626242; f. 1974; controls the import, export and national distribution of agricultural and basic food products; Gen. Man. Juan Masao Okuma Isa.

DEVELOPMENT ORGANIZATIONS

Asociación de Dirigentes de Ventas y Mercadotecnia del Perú (ADV—PERU): Avda Belén 158, Apdo 1280, Lima 27; tel. (1) 4419988; fax (1) 4410303; f. 1958; Pres. Franco Carabelli Pace; Gen. Man. Stefan Arie Singer; 1,500 mems.

Asociación de Exportadores (ADEX): Javier Prado Este 2875, Lima 41; Apdo 1806, Lima 1; tel. (1) 3462530; fax (1) 3461879; e-mail postmaster@adexperu.org.pe; internet www.adexperu.org.pe; f. 1973. Pres. Carlos Bruce Montes de Oca; Gen. Man. Jaime Rodríguez Favarato; 600 mems.

Comisión de Promoción de la Inversión Privada (COPRI): Avda Las Artes Sur 260, San Borja, Lima; fax (1) 4750078; internet www.copri.org; Dir Minister of Labour and Social Promotion.

Consejo Nacional de Desarrollo—CONADE: Avda Agusto Tamayo 160, Lima 27; national development council; Chair. José Palomino.

Sociedad Nacional de Industrias (SNI) (National Industrial Association): Los Laureles 365, San Isidro, Apdo 632, Lima 27; tel. (1) 4218830; fax (1) 4422573; f. 1896; comprises permanent commissions covering various aspects of industry including labour, integration, fairs and exhibitions, industrial promotion; its Small Industry Committee groups over 2,000 small enterprises; Pres. Ing. Emilio Navarro Castañeda; Gen. Man. Pablo Carriquiry Blondet; 90 dirs (reps of firms); 2,500 mems; 60 sectorial committees.

Centro de Desarrollo Industrial (CDI): c/o SNI; tel. (1) 4419101; fax (1) 4407702; supports industrial development and programmes to develop industrial companies; Exec. Dir Luis Tenorio Puentes.

CHAMBER OF COMMERCE

Cámara de Comercio de Lima (Lima Chamber of Commerce): Avda Gregorio Escobedo 398, Lima 11; tel. (1) 4633434; fax (1) 4632820; internet www.camaralima.org.pe; f. 1888; Pres. Samuel Gleiser Katz; Gen. Man. Dr Jorge Chian Chong; 3,500 mems.

There are also Chambers of Commerce in Arequipa, Cuzco, Callao and many other cities.

INDUSTRIAL AND TRADE ASSOCIATIONS

Epsep (Empresa Peruana de Servicios Pesqueros): Las Tunas, Salamanca, Lima; tel. (1) 4362770; fax (1) 4362112; edible fish; Pres. Antonio Hudtwalcker Texeira; Gen. Man. Antonio Romano Thantawatae.

Minpeco, SA (Empresa Comercializadora de Productos Mineros): Jirón Scipión Llona 350, Miraflores, Apdo 0274, Lima 18; tel. (1) 4473561; fax (1) 4402840; f. 1974 as the state mining marketing agency to be responsible for the sale of traditional and non-traditional mining products; in 1981 Minpeco lost its monopoly; Chair. Lic. Fermín Bustamente Moscoso; Gen. Man. Mario Mesia.

EMPLOYERS' ORGANIZATIONS

Asociación Automotriz del Perú: Dos de Mayo 299, Apdo 1248, Lima 27; tel. (1) 4404119; fax (1) 4428865; e-mail aap@terra.com.pe; f. 1926; association of importers of motor cars and accessories; 360 mems; Pres. Carlos Bambarén García-Maldonado; Gen. Man. César Martín Barreda.

Asociación de Ganaderos del Perú (Association of Stock Farmers of Peru): Pumacahua 877, 3°, Jesús María, Lima; f. 1915; Gen. Man. Ing. Miguel J. Fort.

Comité de Minería de la Cámara de Comercio e Industria de Arequipa: Apdo 508, Arequipa; mining association; Pres. F. Ch. Willfort.

Confederación Nacional de Instituciones Empresariales Privadas (CONFIEP): Avda Victor Andrés Belaunde 147, Lima; e-mail postmaster@confiep.com.pe; internet www.cosapi.com.pe/instituciones/Confiep/index.htm; f. 1984; association of private companies; Pres. Roque Benavides.

Instituto Peruano del Café: Lima; f. 1965; representatives of Government and industrial coffee growers.

Sociedad Nacional de Minería y Petróleo: Francisco Graña 671, Lima 17; tel. (1) 4601560; fax (1) 4601616; e-mail infsnmp@mail.cosapidata.com.pe; internet www.snmpe.org.pe/; f. 1940; Pres. Hans Flury; Vice-Pres. Kurt Schultze-Rhonhof; Gen. Man. Carlos Diez

CANSECO; association of companies involved in mining, petroleum and energy; 205 mems.

Sociedad Nacional de Pesquería (SNP): Lima; f. 1952; private sector fishing interests; Pres. JOSÉ SARMIENTO MADUEÑO.

MAJOR COMPANIES

The following is a selection of the principal industrial companies operating in Peru.

Metals, Mining and Petroleum

Aceros Arequipa, SA (Acersa): Avda Jacinto Ibañez 111, Parque Industrial, Arequipa; tel. (54) 232430; fax (54) 219796; internet www.acerosarequipa.com.pe; f. 1964; iron and steel manufacturer; sales of 261m. new soles (1995); Exec. Pres. RICARDO CILLONIZ OBERTI; 792 employees.

Centromín-Perú, SA (Empresa Minera del Centro del Perú): Edif. Solgas, Avda Javier Prado Este 2175, San Borja, Apdo 2142, Lima 41; tel. (1) 4367014; fax (1) 4767715; internet www.centromin.com.pe; f. 1902; fmr state-owned mining corpn, transferred to private ownership in 1997; Pres. JUAN ASSERETO; Gen. Man. JUAN CARLOS BARCELLOS MILLA ; 11,527 employees.

Compañía de Minas Buenaventura, SA: Avda Carlos Villarán 790, La Victoria, Lima 13; tel. (1) 4717278; fax (1) 4717349; internet www.buenaventura.com; f. 1953; mining of silver ores; Pres. ALBERTO BENAVIDES DE LA QUINTINA; Man. Dir JORGE BENAVIDES DE LA QUINTANA; 1,400 employees.

Compañía Minera Antamina, SA: La Floresta 497, 4°, Urb. Chacarilla del Estanque, San Borja, Lima 41; tel. (1) 2173000; fax (1) 3726317; operates a copper and zinc mine; 401 employees.

Compañía Minera Atacocha, SA: Avda Javier Prado Oeste 980, San Isidro, Lima; tel. (1) 4402595; fax (1) 4409937; f. 1936; mining of lead and zinc; Chair. FRANCISCO J. GALLO ATARD; Gen. Man. MANUEL GALUP; 1,270 employees.

Compañía Minera Huaron, SA: Avda República de Panamá 3055, San Isidro, Lima; tel. (1) 2212727; fax (1) 2212747; f. 1912; lead, copper and zinc mining; Pres. EDUARDO HOCHSCHILD B.; Gen. Man. GERMAN ARCE SIPÁN; 1,000 employees.

Compañía Minera del Madrigal, SA: Morelli 181, 3°, Lima 41; f. 1967; tel. (1) 4414700; fax (1) 4751349; copper mining; Man. MIGUEL ACLEN; 760 employees.

Compañía Minera Milpo, SA: San Martín 864, 4°, Lima 1; tel. (1) 4442020; fax (1) 4443044; f. 1946; lead, silver and zinc mining; sales of 132.8m. new soles (1996); Man. Dir MANUEL MONTORI ALFARO; 475 employees.

Compañía Rex, SA: Avda Alfreo Mendiola 1879, San Martín de Porres, Lima 31; tel. (1) 5342143; fax (1) 5342295; f. 1958; clay mining; Gen. Man. FRANCISCO ARANETA LAVINZ; 445 employees.

Corporación Minera Nor Perú, SA: Canaral y Moreyra 654, San Isidro, Lima; tel. (1) 4752186; fax (1) 4756940; copper, gold, silver, lead and zinc mining; Chair. JAVIER NUÑEZ CARVALLO; Gen. Man. MARIO DEL RIO A.; 1,070 employees.

Empresa Minera Especial Tintaya, SA: Avda San Martin, Cuzco; tel. (54) 244436; fax (54) 246592; mining; 1,456 employees.

Empresa Siderúrgica del Perú: Avda Tacna 543, Lima; fax (1) 4330807; f. 1971; processing of steel; Gen. Man. CESAR GARAY GHILARDI; 4,195 employees.

Fábrica de Aluminio y Metales del Perú, SA (Fam Perú): Carretera Central Km 8, Ate Vitarte, Lima 3; tel. (1) 3513399; fax (1) 4942541; f. 1957; processing of aluminium; sales of 441.4m. new soles (1995); Pres. MANUEL A. GONZÁLEZ; Gen. Man. PERCY M. GONZÁLEZ CASTRO; 300 employees.

Minas de Arcata, SA: Avda República de Panamá 3055, 15°, San Isidro, Lima; tel. (1) 2212727; fax (1) 2212747; f. 1961; silver mining; Pres. ERNESTRO BAERTI MONTORI; Gen. Man. CARLOS ORTÍZ UGARTE; 460 employees.

MineroPerú (Empresa Minera del Perú): Bernardo Monteagudo 222, Apdo 4332, Lima 17; tel. (1) 4620740; fax (1) 4611895; f. 1970; transferred to private ownership in 1993; mining co; Man. RAÚL OTERO BOSSANO; 1,400 employees.

Occidental Petroleum Corpn of Peru: Los Forestales 910, Lima 1; tel. (1) 3480600; fax (1) 3480500; f. 1970; principal shareholder Occidental Petroleum Corpn of the USA; petroleum and natural-gas exploration and extraction; Man. RICARDO SILVA CHUECA; 970 employees.

PetroPerú (Empresa de Petróleos de Perú, SA): Avda Passeo de la República 3361, San Isidro, Apdo 3126/1081, Lima 27; tel. (1) 4425000; fax (1) 4425416; f. 1969; state-owned petroleum co; transfer to private ownership commenced in 1996; Pres. JORGE KAWAMURO; Gen. Man. Ing. DONALD SALAZOR; 1,500 employees.

Shougang HierroPerú, SA: Avda República de Chile 262, Jesús María, Lima 1; tel. (1) 3304600; fax (1) 3305136; f. 1992; owned by Shougang Corpn (People's Republic of China); mining, processing and shipment of iron ore; sales of 281m. new soles (1999); Chair. JIN YONG HUN; Gen. Man. WANG BAO JUN; 1,988 employees.

Southern Peru Copper Corporation (SPCC): Avda Luna Pizarro 208, Vallecito, Arequipa; tel. (54) 214646; fax (54) 246215; f. 1995; copper mining; owned by the US cos Asarco (54.1%), Marmon Corpn and Phelps Dodge; sales of 1,833m. new soles (1999); Chair. RICHARD J. OSBORNE; Pres. and CEO CHARLES G. PREBLE; 5,000 employees.

Volcán Compañía Minera, SA: Gregorio Escobedo 710, Of. 301, Lima 11; tel. (1) 2617718; fax (1) 2613113; f. 1943; lead, zinc and silver mining; bought Paragsha zinc and lead mine in 1999; Chair. ROBERTO LETTS COLMENARES; Gen. Man. EDUARDO LLOSA B.; 545 employees.

Food and Drink

Arturo Field y La Estrella Ltda, SA: Avda Venezuela 2470, Lima 1; tel. (1) 4317510; fax (1) 4247184; f. 1864; production of confectionery; Pres. NICANOR ARTEAGA DOMINGUEZ; 560 employees.

Cervecería San Juan, SA: Carretera Federico Basadre Km 13, Provincia Cnel Portillo, Ucayali; tel. (64) 571131; fax (64) 573798; f. 1971; brewery; Pres. ELIAS BENTÍN PERAL; Gen. Man. ERIC COMBE C.

Compañía Cervecera del Sur del Perú, SA (Cervesur): Variante de Uchumayo 1801, Castilla 43, Arequipa; tel. (54) 470000; fax (54) 449602; e-mail cervesur@ibm.net; f. 1898; brewery; sales of 267m. new soles (1997); Pres. Dr JOSÉ GARCÍA CALDERÓN; 866 employees.

Compañía Embotelladora del Pacífico, SA: Avda Venezuela 2221-2223, Lima 1; tel. (1) 4313010; fax (1) 4325280; f. 1951; bottlers of soft drinks; Pres. and Dir-Gen. JOSÉ CONSTANTINO HEREDÍA GARCÍA; 600 employees.

Compañía Nacional de Cerveza, SA: Avda Oscar R. Benavides 3866, Bellavista, Callao 2, Apdo 256; tel. (1) 4511700; fax (1) 4521700; f. 1863; brewery; Chair. VICTOR MONTORI; Gen. Man. JOSÉ DE BERNARDIS; 900 employees.

Compañía Oleaginosa del Perú, SA: Calle Chinchón 980, San Isidro, Lima; tel. (1) 4422552; fax (1) 4425686; e-mail psacchi@alicorp.com.pe; f. 1946; manufacturers of edible oils, lard and soaps; Gen. Man. LESLIE PIERCE; 3,000 employees.

Del Mar, SA: Aristides Aljovin 690, Lima 18; tel. (1) 4457829; fax (1) 4471350; e-mail delmart@amauta.rcp.net.pe; f. 1979; canning and processing of fish; Gen. Man. JUAN LUIS KRUGER CARRION; 900 employees.

D'Onofrio, SA: Avda Venezuela 2580, Lima 1; tel. (1) 4313510; fax (1) 4315852; e-mail joscoa@donofrio.com.pe; internet www.donofrio.com.pe; f. 1933; manufacturers of desserts, confectionery and biscuits; sales of 173.2m. new soles (1995); Pres. VITO RODRIGUEZ RODRIGUEZ; Gen. Man. ALBERTO HAITO MOARRI; 1,254 employees.

Empresa de la Sal, SA: Avda Nestor Gambetta, Km 8.5 Carretera Ventanilla, Callao; tel. (1) 5770685; fax (1) 5770669; f. 1969; salt production; Chair. MARCOS FISHMAN C.; Gen. Man. JOSÉ C. DE LOS RÍOS O.; 500 employees.

Flota Pesquera Peruana, SA: Avda Argentina 4090, Callao; tel. (1) 4299808; fax (1) 4640170; f. 1986; fishing co; Gen. Man. JORGE LAINES DE LA CRUZ; 564 employees.

Rubber and Cement

Cementos Lima, SA: Avda Atocongo 2440, Villa María del Triunfo, Lima; tel. (1) 9541900; fax (1) 9541297; e-mail postmaster@cementolima.com.pe; internet www.cementoslima.com.pe; f. 1967; cement producers; Pres. JAIME RIZO-PATRÓN; Gen. Man. CARLOS UGAS D.; 500 employees.

Cementos Norte Pacasmayo, SA: Pasaje El Carmen 180, Santiago de Surco, Lima 33; tel (1) 3172000; fax (1) 4375009; f. 1974; cement producers; Pres. Alberto Beeck Ulloa; Man. Dir LINO ABRAM CABALLERINO; 495 employees.

Lima Caucho, SA: Carretera Central No. 349, Km 1, Santa Anita, Lima 3; tel. (1) 3623845; fax (1) 3623810; internet www.limacaucho.com.pe; f. 1955; manufacturers of tyres and industrial rubber products; Pres. HUGO ESPINOSA ROJAS; Gen. Man. ELLIS WAYNE BROWN; 300 employees.

Textiles and Clothing

Compañía Industrial Nuevo Mondo, SA: Jr José Calendón 750, Lima; tel. (1) 3367964; fax (1) 3368193; e-mail nmtex@lp.edu.pe; internet www.lp.edu.pe/nmtex; f. 1949; manufacturers of textiles; sales of 163.7m. new soles (1999); 700 employees.

Consorcio Textil del Pacífico, SA: Avda Argentina 2400, Lima 1; tel. (1) 3368429; fax (1) 3368431; f. 1993; textiles and clothing manufacturer; sales of 77.9m. new soles (1999); Pres. MICHAEL MICHELL STAFFORD; 1,350 employees.

Fábrica de Calzado Peruano, SA: Carretera Central Km 4.400, Lima 3; tel. (1) 4350343; fax (1) 4351048; f. 1939; shoe manufacturers; Man. Dir FRANÇOIS MELS; 1,800 employees.

Fábrica Nacional Textil el Amazona: Avda Argentina 1440, Lima 1; tel. (1) 3367776; fax (1) 3367947; f. 1943; yarn mills; Man. GIANNO FAVIO GERBOLINI ISOLA; 1,000 employees.

Fábrica de Tejidos La Unión Ltda, SA: Avda Nicolás Ayllón 2681, Lima 10; tel. (1) 3624055; fax (1) 3624056; e-mail launion@computextos.com.pe; manufacturers of thread, cloth and clothing; sales of 18.3m. new soles (1997); Pres. and Dir Gen. ESAC MOORE MAC TERVET; 1,617 employees.

Michell y Compañía, SA: Avda Juan de la Torre 101, San Lázaro, Arequipa; tel. (54) 214170; fax (54) 219877; e-mail michell@michell.com.pe; internet www.michell.com.pe; f. 1957; yarn mills; Exec. Pres. MICHAEL MICHELL STAFFORD; Gen. Man. GONZALO BEDOYA STAFFORD; 419 employees.

Universal Textil, SA: Avda Venezuela 2505, Apdo 554, Lima 1; tel. (1) 3375260; fax (1) 3375270; e-mail postmaster@utsanet.com.pe; f. 1952; manufacturers of synthetic fabrics for outerwear; sales of 79.6m. new soles (1999); Chair. DIONISIO ROMERO SEMINARIO; Man. Dir GEORGE R. SCHOFIELD; 733 employees.

Miscellaneous

Bayer Peru, SA: Avda Paseo de la República 3074, San Isidro, Lima; tel. (1) 4213381; fax (1) 4213384; f. 1969; chemicals, plastics and pharmaceuticals manufacturer; sales of 117.2m. new soles (1999); Chair. MATHIAS MALLMANN; Gen. Man. KLAUS D. MARTENS; 755 employees.

Indeco, SA: Avda Universitaria 683, Lima 1; tel. (1) 4642570; fax (1) 4522326; e-mail postmaster@indeco.com.pe; internet www.indeco.com.pe; f. 1952; manufacturers of electrical cables; sales of 98.9m. new soles (1998); Pres. ERNESTO MONTORI; Gen. Man. JUAN ENRIQUE RIVERA; 247 employees.

Industrias Eletroquímicas, SA (Ieqsa): Avda Elmer Faucett 1920, Callao, Lima; tel. (1) 5720113; fax (1) 5720118; e-mail export@ieqsa.com.pe; internet www.ieqsa.com.pe; f. 1963; manufacturers of batteries; Pres. and Dir Gen. CARLOS GLIKSMAN L.; 600 employees.

Industrias Militares del Perú, SA: Avda Oscar Benavides 3006, Lima 1; tel. (1) 4528503; fax (1) 4527714; f. 1978; manufacturers of ammunition; Pres. MANUEL ALVAREZ PERALTA; 2,170 employees.

Industrias Pacocha, SA: Francisco Graña 155, Urb. Santa Catalina, La Victoria, Lima; tel. (1) 4708000; fax (1) 4752590; f. 1971; manufacturers of detergents, soaps, fats and vegetable oils; Man. Dir EDUARDO MONTERO ARAMBURÚ; Gen. Man. MOISES DANNON LEVY; 675 employees.

Ingenieros Constratistas Cosapi, SA : Nicolás Arriola 500, Lima 13; tel. (1) 2113500; fax (1) 2248665; e-mail wgpiazza@cosapi.com.pe; internet www.cosapi.com.pe; f. 1967; engineering; sales of 211.9m. new soles (1995); Pres. WALTER PIAZZA TANGUIS; 4,350 employees.

Nissan Motors del Perú, SA: Avda Tomás Valle 601, Lima 31; fax (1) 4325818; subsidiary of Nissan Motors of Japan; automobile assembly plant; Man. YOKI TASHANUKI; 435 employees.

Sociedad Paramonga Ltd, SA: Avda Nestor Gambetta 8585, Callao; tel. (1) 5770700; fax (1) 5770273; e-mail quimpac@panasa.com.pe; f. 1898; pulp mills; Man. CARLOS ORAMS BASADRE; 3,000 employees.

Tabacalera Nacional, SA: Avenida La Molina 140, Ate, Lima 3; tel. (1) 4360388; fax (1) 4370066; f. 1964; cigarette manufacturers; sales of 115.4m. new soles (1999); Pres. MANUEL ISABEL ROCA; Man. Dir JULIO CAIPO GUERRERO; 205 employees.

UTILITIES

Regulatory Authority

Comisión de Tarifas Eléctricas (CTE): Avda Canadá 1470, San Borja, Lima 41; tel. (1) 2240487; fax (1) 2240491.

Electricity

Electrolima, SA: Jirón Zorritos 1301, Lima 5; tel. (1) 4324153; fax (1) 4323042; f. 1906; produces and supplies electricity for Lima and the surrounding districts; Pres. LUIS CARLOS RODRÍGUEZ MARTÍNEZ.

ElectroPerú: Avda Pedro Miotta, Ant. Carretera Panamericana Sur, km 14.5, Lima 29; tel. (1) 4661849; fax (1) 4661899; state-owned; Pres. JESÚS BEOUTIS LEDESMA; Gen. Man. LUIS NICHO DÍAZ.

Empresa Regional de Servicio Público de Electricidad Norte Electronorte, SA: Vicente de la Vega 318, Chiclayo; tel. (74) 231580; fax (74) 243260; Gen. Man. HERACLIO PRADA MARTÍNEZ.

Sociedad Eléctrica del Sur-Oeste, SA: Consuelo 310, Arequipa; tel. (54) 6460; fax (54) 219020; f. 1905; Man. ADOLFO VÉLEZ DE CÓRDOVA.

TRADE UNIONS

The right to strike was restored in the Constitution of July 1979. In 1982 the Government recognized the right of public employees to form trade unions.

Central Unica de Trabajadores Peruanos (CUTP): Lima; f. 1992; comprises:

> **Central de Trabajadores de la Revolución Peruana (CTRP):** Lima.

Confederación General de Trabajadores del Perú (CGTP): Ayacucho 173, Lima; tel. (1) 4282253; f. 1968; Pres. VALENTÍN PACHO QUISPE; Sec.-Gen. TEÓDULO HERNÁNDEZ VALLE.

Confederación Nacional de Trabajadores (CNT): Avda Iquitos 1198, Lima; tel. (1) 4711385; affiliated to the PPC; 12,000 mems (est.); Sec.-Gen. ANTONIO GALLARDO EGOAVIL.

Confederación de Trabajadores Peruanos (CTP): Lima; affiliated to APRA; Gen. Sec. JULIO CRUZADO EZCURRA.

Confederación Intersectorial de Trabajadores Estatales (CITE) (Union of Public Sector Workers): Jirón Callao 326, Apdo 2178, Lima; tel. (1) 4245525; f. 1978; Leader CÉSAR PASSALACQUA PEREYRA; Sec.-Gen. RAÚL CABALLERO VARGAS; 600,000 mems.

Federación de Empleados Bancarios (FEB) (Union of Bank Employees): Leader ANTONIO ZÚÑIGA; Sec.-Gen. AUGUSTO GARCÍA DUQUE.

Federación Nacional de Trabajadores Mineros, Metalúrgicos y Siderúrgicos—FNTMMS (Federation of Peruvian Mine-workers): Lima; Pres. VÍCTOR TAIPE; Vice-Pres. LEONARDO RAMÍREZ; 70,000 mems.

Movimiento de Trabajadores y Obreros de Clase (MTOC): Lima.

Sindicato Unico de Trabajadores de Educación del Perú—SUTEP (Union of Peruvian Teachers): Lima; fax (1) 4762792; Sec.-Gen. JOSÉ RAMOS.

Independent unions, representing an estimated 37% of trade unionists, include: Comité para la Coordinación Clasista y la Unificación Sindical, Confederación de Campesinos Peruanos (CCP—Sec.-Gen. ANDRÉS LUNA VARGAS), Confederación Nacional Agraria (Pres. FELIPE HUMÁN YAYAHUANCA).

Confederación Nacional de Comunidades Industriales (CONACI): Lima; co-ordinates worker participation in industrial management and profit-sharing.

The following agricultural organizations exist:

Consejo Unitario Nacional Agrario (CUNA): f. 1983; represents 36 farmers' and peasants' organizations, including:

Confederación Campesina del Perú (CCP): radical left-wing; Pres. ANDRÉS LUNA VARGAS; Sec. HUGO BLANCO (arrested Feb. 1989).

Organización Nacional Agraria (ONA): organization of dairy farmers and cattle-breeders.

Transport

RAILWAYS

In 1998 there were some 1,903 km of track. A programme to develop a national railway network (Sistema Nacional Ferroviario) was begun in the early 1980s, aimed at increasing the length of track to about 5,000 km initially. The Government also plans to electrify the railway system and extend the Central and Southern Railways.

Ministerio de Transportes, Comunicaciones, Vivienda y Construcción: see section on The Government (Ministries).

Consorcio de Ferrocarriles del Peru: following the privatization of the state railway company Enafer, the above consortium won a 30-year concession in July 1999 to operate the following lines:

> **Empresa Minera del Centro del Perú SA—División Ferrocarriles (Centromín-Perú SA)** (fmrly Cerro de Pasco Railway): Edif. Solgas, Avda Javier Prado Este 2175, San Borja, Apdo 2412, Lima 41; tel. (1) 4761010; fax (1) 4769757; 212.2 km; acquired by Enafer-Perú in 1997; Pres. HERNÁN BARRETO; Gen. Man. GUILLERMO GUANILO.

> **Ferrocarril del Centro del Perú** (Central Railway of Peru): Ancash 201, Apdo 1379, Lima; tel. (1) 4276620; fax (1) 4281075; 591 km open; Man. DAVID SAN ROMÁN B.

> **Ferrocarril del Sur del Perú ENAFER, SA** (Southern Railway): Avda Tacna y Arica 200, Apdo 194, Arequipa; tel. (54) 215350; fax (54) 231603; 915 km open; also operates steamship service on Lake Titicaca; Man. C. NORIEGA.

> **Tacna–Arica Ferrocarril** (Tacna–Arica Railway): Avda Aldarracín 484, Tacna; 62 km open.

Ferrocarril Pimentel (Pimentel Railway): Pimentel, Chiclayo, Apdo 310; 56 km open; owned by Empresa Nacional de Puertos; cargo services only; Pres. R. MONTENEGRO; Man. LUIS DE LA PIEDRA ALVIZURI.

Private Railways

Ferrocarril Ilo–Toquepala–Cuajone: Apdo 2640, Lima; 219 km open, incl. five tunnels totalling 27 km; owned by the Southern Peru

Copper Corporation for transporting copper supplies and concentrates only; Pres. OSCAR GONZÁLEZ ROCHA; Gen. Man. WILLIAM TORRES.

Ferrocarril Supe–Barranca–Alpas: Barranca; 40 km open; Dirs CARLOS GARCÍA GASTAÑETA, LUIS G. MIRANDA.

ROADS

In 1999 there were an estimated 72,900 km of roads in Peru, of which approximately 13% were paved. The most important highways are: the Pan-American Highway (3,008 km), which runs southward from the Ecuadorean border along the coast to Lima; Camino del Inca Highway (3,193 km) from Piura to Puno; Marginal de la Selva (1,688 km) from Cajamarca to Madre de Dios; and the Trans-Andean Highway (834 km), which runs from Lima to Pucallpa on the River Ucayali via Oroya, Cerro de Pasco and Tingo María.

SHIPPING

Most trade is through the port of Callao but there are 13 deep-water ports, mainly in northern Peru (including Salaverry, Pacasmayo and Paita) and in the south (including the iron ore port of San Juan). There are river ports at Iquitos, Pucallpa and Yurimaguas, aimed at improving communications between Lima and Iquitos, and a further port is under construction at Puerto Maldonado.

Empresa Nacional de Puertos, SA (Enapu): Edif. Administrativo, 3°, Terminal Marítimo del Callao, Apdo 260, Callao; tel. (1) 4299210; fax (1) 4656415; e-mail enapu@inconet.net.pe; f. 1970; government agency administering all coastal and river ports; Pres. CARLOS GUSTAVO SALCEDO WILLIAMS; Gen. Man. MANUEL LORES LEMQUE.

Asociación Marítima del Perú: Avda Javier Prado Este 897, Of. 33, San Isidro, Apdo 3520, Lima 27; tel. and fax (1) 4221904; f. 1957; association of 20 international and Peruvian shipping companies; Pres. LUIS FELIPE VILLENA GUTIÉRREZ.

Consorcio Naviero Peruano, SA: Avda Central 643, San Isidro, Apdo 929, Lima 1; tel. (1) 4116500; fax (1) 4116599; e-mail cnp@cnpsa.com; f. 1959.

Naviera Humboldt, SA: Edif. Pacífico–Washington, 9°, Natalio Sánchez 125, Apdo 3639, Lima 1; tel. (1) 4334005; fax (1) 4337151; e-mail postmast@sorcomar.com.pe; internet www.humbolt.com.pe; f. 1970; cargo services; Pres. AUGUSTO BEDOYA CAMERE; Man. Dir LUIS FREIRE R.

Agencia Naviera Maynas, SA: Avda San Borja Norte 761, San Borja, Lima 41; tel. (1) 4752033; fax (1) 4759680; e-mail lima@navieramaynas.com.pe; f. 1996; Pres. R. USSEGLIO D.; Gen. Man. ROBERTO MELGAR B.

Naviera Universal, SA: Calle 41 No 894, Urb. Corpac, San Isidro, Apdo 10307, Lima 100; tel. (1) 4757020; fax (1) 4755233; Chair. HERBERT C. BUERGER.

Petrolera Transoceánica, SA (PETRANSO): Víctor Maúrtua 135, Lima 27; tel. (1) 4422007; fax (1) 4403922; internet www.petranso.com.pe; Gen. Man. JUAN VILLARÁN.

A number of foreign lines call at Peruvian ports.

CIVIL AVIATION

Of Peru's 294 airports, the major international airport is Jorge Chávez Airport near Lima. Other important international airports are Coronel Francisco Secada Vignetta Airport, near Iquitos, Velasco Astete Airport, near Cuzco, and Rodríguez Ballón Airport, near Arequipa.

Domestic Airlines

Aero Condor: Juan de Arona 781, San Isidro, Lima; tel. (1) 4411354; fax (1) 4429487; e-mail acondor@ibm.net; domestic services; Pres. CARLOS PALACÍN FERNÁNDEZ.

Aero Continente: Avda José Pardo 651, Lima 18; tel. (1) 2424260; fax (1) 4467638; internet www.aerocontinente.com.pe; f. 1992; domestic services; Pres. LUPE L. Z. GONZALES.

AeroPerú: Avda José Pardo 601, Miraflores, Lima 18; tel. (1) 4478900; fax (1) 4443974; f. 1973 as the national airline, partially 'privatized', in 1981; 49% share sold to Cintra Group (Mexico) in 1993; operates internal services and international routes to Central and South America and the USA; operations suspended owing to insolvency in March 1999; Pres. ROBERTO ABUSADA; Gen. Man. ALEJANDRO GÓMEZ MONROY.

Aeronaves del Perú, SA: Jirón José Cálvez 711, Lima 18; tel. (1) 4476488; fax (1) 4479558; f. 1965; scheduled cargo services and charter flights between Lima and Miami (USA); Pres. ALFREDO ZANATTI.

Americana de Aviación (Americana), SA: Avda Larco 345, 3°, Lima 18; tel. (1) 2412929; fax (1) 4442761; f. 1991; regional and domestic scheduled passenger and cargo services to eight cities; Chair. LEANDRO CHIOK CHANG; Gen. Man. CARLOS MORALES.

Aviandina: Jr. Bolognesi 125, Of. 604, Miraflores, Lima; tel. (1) 2428823; fax (1) 2413049; internet www.aviandina.com; scheduled domestic passenger service; Pres. ZADI DESME.

Compañia de Aviación Faucett: Aeropuerto Jorge Chávez, Apdo 1429, Lima; tel. (1) 5750961; fax (1) 5750970; f. 1928; scheduled internal passenger services, cargo and passenger services to Miami (USA) via Panama City and Iquitos and passenger and cargo charters; Pres. ROBERTO LEIGH.

Tourism

Tourism is centred on Lima, with its Spanish colonial architecture, and Cuzco, with its pre-Inca and Inca civilization, notably the 'lost city' of Machu Picchu. Lake Titicaca, lying at an altitude of 3,850 m. above sea-level, and the Amazon jungle region to the north-east also form popular resorts. In the mid-1990s there was evidence of a marked recovery in the tourist sector, which had been adversely affected by health and security concerns. In 1997 Peru received 649,287 visitors, generating receipts of US $805m. In 1998 the number of visitors had increased to 723,668.

Fondo de Promoción Turística (FOPTUR): Calle Uno, 14°, Urb. Corpac, San Isidro, Lima; tel. (1) 2243146; fax (1) 2243276; f. 1979; Pres. JUAN LIRA; Gen. Man. JUAN MANUEL ECHEVERRÍA.

Defence

At 1 August 2000 Peru's Armed Forces numbered 115,000 (including an estimated 64,000 conscripts): Army 75,000 (including 52,000 conscripts), Navy 25,000 (including some 800 Naval Aviation personnel, 3,000 marines and 10,000 conscripts), Air Force 15,000 (including 2,000 conscripts). Paramilitary forces numbered 77,000. There were 188,000 army reserves. Military service was selective and lasted for two years.

Defence Budget: An estimated 2,900m. new soles in 2000.

President of the Joint Command of the Armed Forces and Commander of the Army: Gen. VICTOR BUSTAMENTE REATEGUI.

Commander of the Air Force: Lt-Gen. JORGE DEL CARPIO.

Commander of the Navy: Vice-Adm. ALFREDO PALACIOS.

Education

Education in Peru is based on a series of reforms introduced after the 1968 revolution. The educational system is divided into three levels: the first level is for children up to six years of age in either nurseries or kindergartens. Basic education is provided at the second level. It is free and, where possible, compulsory between six and 15 years of age. Primary education lasts for six years. Secondary education, beginning at the age of 12, is divided into two stages, of two and three years respectively. Total enrolment at primary schools, in 1995, was equivalent to 91% of children in the relevant age group, while an estimated 53% of children in the relevant age-group attended secondary schools. Higher education includes the pre-university and university levels. In 1998 there were 28 public and 42 private universities. There is also provision for adult literacy programmes and bilingual education.

In 1972 adult illiteracy averaged 27.5% (males 16.7%; females 38.2%), but in rural areas the rate was 50.9%. By 1995 the national rate of adult illiteracy had declined to some 9%. In the 1999 budget the Government allocated some 1,600m. new soles to the education sector.

Bibliography

For works on South America generally, see Select Bibliography (Books).

Alberts, T. *Agrarian Reform and Rural Poverty: A Case Study of Peru*. Boulder, CO, Westview Press, 1983.

Booth, D., and Sorj, B. (Eds). *Military Reformism and Social Classes: the Peruvian Experience 1968–80*. London, Macmillan, 1983.

Brass, T. 'Trotskyism, Hugo Blanc and the Ideology of a Peruvian Peasant Movement', in *Journal of Peasant Studies*, Vol. 16, No. 2 (Jan.). 1989.

Cane, M. A. 'El Niño', in *Annual Review of Earth and Planetary Science*, Vol. 4. 1986.

'Caught between Two Fires', Peru briefing. London, Amnesty International, 1989.

Crabtree, J., and Thomas, J. (Eds). *Fujimori's Peru*. London, Institute of Latin American Studies, 1998.

Daeschner, J. *The War of the End of Democracy: Mario Vargas Llosa vs Alberto Fujimori*. Lima, Peru Reporting, 1993.

Dore, E. W. *The Peruvian Mining Industry: Growth, Stagnation and Crisis*. Boulder, CO, Westview Press, 1986.

Durand, F. *Business and Politics in Peru: The State and the National Bourgeoisie*. Oxford, Westview Press, 1994.

Feige, W. 'Irrigation Projects in the Andes and Highlands of Peru', in *Applied Geography and Development*, Vol. 34, (Oct). 1989.

Fisher, J. *Peru (World bibliographical series, Vol. 109)*. Oxford, Clio Press, 1989.

Fitzgerald, E. V. K. *The Political Economy of Peru, 1956–78*. Cambridge, Cambridge University Press, 1979.

Flores Galindo, A. *Buscando un Inca: Identidad y Utopia en los Andes*. Lima, Edition Instituto de Apoyo Agrario, 1987.

Gertler, P., and Glewwe, P. *The Willingness to Pay for Education in Developing Countries: Evidence from Rural Peru*. Washington, DC, The World Bank, 1989.

Glewwe, P., and Tray, D. de. *The Poor in Latin America during Adjustment: A Case Study of Peru*. Washington, DC, The World Bank, 1989.

Gorman, S. M. (Ed.). *Post-Revolutionary Peru: The Politics of Transformation*. Boulder, CO, Westview Press, 1982.

Hemming, J. *Conquest of the Incas*, Revised Edn. London, Penguin, 1983.

Kimura, R. *Alberto Fujimori of Peru: The President Who Dared to Dream*. Woodstock, NY, Beekman Publishers, 1998.

Klaren, P. *Peru: Society and Nationhood in the Andes*. Oxford, Oxford University Press, 1999.

Labrousse, A., and Hertoghe, A. *Le sentier lumineux du pérou*. Paris, La Découverte, 1989.

Long, N., and Roberts, B. *Miners, Peasants and Entrepreneurs: Regional Development in the Central Highlands of Peru*. Cambridge, Cambridge University Press, 1984.

Morales, E. 'Coca and Cocaine Economy and Social Change in the Andes of Peru', in *Economic Development and Cultural Change*, Vol. 35, No. 1 (Oct.). 1986.

Parodi, J., and Conaghan, C. *To Be A Worker: Identity and Politics in Peru*. Chapel Hill, NC, University of North Carolina Press, 2000.

Radcliffe, S. A. *'Así es una mujer del pueblo': low-income women's organizations under APRA, 1985–1987*. Cambridge, Cambridge University, Centre of Latin American Studies, 1988.

Reid, M. *Peru: Paths to Poverty*. London, Latin America Bureau, 1985.

Roberts, K. *Deepening Democracy?: The Modern Left and Social Movements in Chile and Peru*. Stanford, CA, University of California Press, 1999.

Scheetz, T. *Peru and the International Monetary Fund*. Pittsburgh, PA, University of Pittsburgh Press, 1986.

Schmidt, G. D. 'Political Variables and Governmental Decentralization in Peru, 1949–1988', in *Journal of Interamerican Studies and World Affairs*, Vol. 31 (Spring/Summer). 1989.

Slater, D. *Territory and State Power in Latin America: the Peruvian Case*. Basingstoke, Macmillan, 1989.

Smith, G. *Livelihood and Resistance: Peasants and the Politics of the Land in Peru*. Berkeley, CA, University of California Press, 1989.

Stelender, M., *et al*. 'A Switching Regression Model of Public-Private Sector Wage Differentials in Peru, 1985–86', in *Journal of Human Resources*, Vol. 24 (Summer). 1989.

Stern, S. *Shining and Other Paths: War and Society in Peru, 1980–95*. Durham, NC, Duke University Press, 1998.

Strong, S. *Shining Path, the World's Deadliest Revolutionary Force*. London, Fontana, 1993.

Taylor, L. *Maoism in the Andes: Sendero Luminoso and the Contemporary Guerrilla Movement in Peru*. Liverpool, Centre for Latin American Studies.

Tickell, J., and O. *Cuzco, Peru*. London, Tauris Parke Books, 1989.

Uriarte, J. M. *Transnational Banks and the Dynamics of the Peruvian Foreign Debt and Inflation*. New York, NY, Praeger Publrs, 1985.

PUERTO RICO

Area: 8,959 sq km (3,459 sq miles).

Population (2000): 3,808,610.

Capital: San Juan (population 421,958 in 2000).

Language: Spanish and English are both official languages.

Religion: Predominantly Christianity (about 81% of the population is Roman Catholic).

Climate: Maritime-tropical; average temperature 24°C (75°F), generally ranging between 17°C and 36°C (63°F to 97°F).

Time: GMT −3 hours.

Public Holidays

2002: 1 January (New Year's Day), 6 January (Epiphany), 14 January (for Birthday of Eugenio María de Hostos), 21 January (Martin Luther King, Jr Day), 18 February (Presidents' Day), 22 March (Emancipation of the Slaves), 29 March (Good Friday), 15 April (for Birthday of José de Diego), 27 May (Memorial Day), 24 June (Feast of St John the Baptist), 4 July (US Independence Day), 15 July (for Birthday of Luis Muñoz Rivera), 22 July (for Birthday of José Celso Barbosa), 25 July (Constitution Day), 2 September (Labor Day), 14 October (Columbus Day), 11 November (Veterans' Day), 19 November (Discovery of Puerto Rico Day), 28 November (Thanksgiving Day), 25 December (Christmas Day).

2003: 1 January (New Year's Day), 6 January (Epiphany), 14 January (for Birthday of Eugenio María de Hostos), 21 January (Martin Luther King, Jr Day), 18 February (Presidents' Day), 22 March (Emancipation of the Slaves), 25 April (Good Friday), 15 April (for Birthday of José de Diego), 27 May (Memorial Day), 24 June (Feast of St John the Baptist), 4 July (US Independence Day), 15 July (for Birthday of Luis Muñoz Rivera), 22 July (for Birthday of José Celso Barbosa), 25 July (Constitution Day), 2 September (Labor Day), 14 October (Columbus Day), 11 November (Veterans' Day), 19 November (Discovery of Puerto Rico Day), 28 November (Thanksgiving Day), 25 December (Christmas Day).

Currency: US dollar ($); $100 = £69.84 = €112.66 (30 April 2001).

Weights and Measures: The US system is officially in force.

Basic Economic Indicators

	1996	1997	1998
Gross domestic product (US $ million at 1954 prices)*	8,291.8	8,677.8	9,239.7†
GDP per head (US $ at 1954 prices)*‡	2,221.2	2,280.6	2,410.6†
GDP (US $ million at current prices)*	45,511.4	48,096.2	53,825.4†
Annual growth of real GDP (%)*	2.8	4.7	6.5†
Annual growth of real GDP per head (%)*‡	2.4	2.7	5.7†
Consumer price index (annual average; base: 1990 = 100)§	124.5	131.3	138.2
Rate of inflation (annual average, %)‖	6.5	6.8	6.9
Imports f.o.b. (US $ million)*	21,873.9	24,204.3	27,308.7¶
Exports f.o.b. (US $ million)*	25,675.5	26,874.5	33,416.4¶
Balance of payments (current account, US $ million)*	−5,394.3	−6,456.2	−5,505.9¶

* Twelve months ending 30 June of year stated.
† Preliminary figure.
‡ The figures for GDP per head are based on official estimates of mid-year population: 3.733m. in 1996; 3.805m. in 1997; 3.833m. in 1998.
§ 146.1 in 1999.
‖ 5.7% in 1999.
¶ Provisional figure.

Economically active population (1999): 1,302,000.

Unemployment (2000): 10%.

Life expectancy (years at birth, 1990–95): 73.6 (males 69.4, females 78.5).

Infant mortality rate (per 1,000 live births, 1996): 10.5.

Adult literacy rate (15 years and over, 1995): 92.8%.

Energy consumption per head (kg of coal equivalent, 1992): 2,018.

Carbon dioxide emissions per head (metric tons, 1997): 4.5.

Passenger motor cars in use (estimate, per 1,000 of population, 1996): 280.1.

Television receivers in use (per 1,000 of population, 1997): 270.

History

JAMES McDONOUGH

INTRODUCTION

Puerto Rico was discovered by a Spanish expedition, led by the navigator Christopher Columbus, in 1493, and subsequently conquered and settled by the Spanish. The island served as an important Spanish military outpost, which by the 19th century had also developed a significant coffee and sugar industry. In 1897 the island gained a considerable degree of self-government, when Spain granted its colony a Carta Autonómica (Autonomy Charter). However, Puerto Rico's new-found autonomy ended a year later when, as a result of the Spanish–American War, the Caribbean possession was ceded to the USA by the Treaty of Paris. In 1900 the USA replaced the military Government, which had ruled since 1898, with a civil Government, under US authority. Under the new arrangement, Puerto Rico became subject to most laws of the US Congress, and the Governor and members of the Island's Executive Council, which functioned as an upper house of the legislative branch, were appointed by the US President. The lower house was elected by popular vote. In 1917 Congress extended US citizenship to the island's inhabitants over the objections of the lower house, and provided for the popular election of the members of an upper house or Senate. The island's Governor, however, still remained a presidential appointee. Further internal self-government was achieved under President Harry S Truman in 1947, when Congress approved a law giving the people of Puerto Rico the right to elect their own Governor. One year later Luis Muñoz Marín, recognized as the 'father of modern Puerto Rico', was chosen as the island's first elected Governor. In 1950, in yet another move towards greater internal autonomy, Congress approved Law 600, allowing Puerto Rico to draft its own constitution, although this was subject to congressional review. This process culminated in 1952, when, in a special referendum, the people of Puerto Rico approved the island's first Constitution under US rule. Puerto Rico was given the status of a 'Commonwealth' (Estado Libre Asociado) in its relation to the USA, and became self-governing. Although Puerto Rico enjoyed wide powers of organization over its internal affairs, the USA retained full sovereignty over the island and most federal laws continued to apply to Puerto Rico. The Commonwealth status, although more liberal than earlier forms of US rule, afforded less powers of self-government than Puerto Rico enjoyed under Spain's Carta Autonómica.

DOMESTIC POLITICS

Since 1898 the Puerto Rican political spectrum has been divided on the question of the island's political relationship with the USA. The island's two dominant parties both favour continued strong links with the USA. The Popular Democratic Party (Partido Popular Democrático—PPD) supports the existing Commonwealth status with 'enhancements', such as greater autonomy, while the New Progressive Party (Partido Nuevo Progresista—PNP) favours Puerto Rico's inclusion as a state of the USA. The island's third and smallest party, the Puerto Rican Independence Party (Partido Independentista Puertorriqueño—PIP) endorses national sovereignty for Puerto Rico.

Historically, various clandestine, pro-independence forces have operated in Puerto Rico outside the electoral process. During the 1940s and 1950s the most influential of these groups was the Nationalist Party (Partido Nacionalista), led by the charismatic Pedro Albizu Campos. The Partido Nacionalista was responsible for an uprising in Puerto Rico in 1950, involving an armed attack on La Fortaleza, the seat of government, and a later attempt on the life of President Truman. It also carried out an armed assault on members of the US Congress in 1954. In the 1970s another pro-independence group, the Puerto Rican Socialist Party (Partido Socialista Puertorriqueño—PSP) was instrumental in bringing the question of Puerto Rico's colonial status before the UN's Decolonization Committee and the Con-

ference of Non-Aligned Nations. With the active participation of Cuba, the Decolonization Committee approved a resolution recognizing Puerto Rico's inalienable right to self-determination and independence. However, the USA was able to prevent the UN General Assembly returning Puerto Rico to the list of political dependencies, from which it was removed in 1953, following the approval of the Commonwealth Constitution. In the early 1980s the most important non-electoral pro-independence group was the Puerto Rican Popular Army (Ejército Popular Boricua), generally known as Los Macheteros. This clandestine group claimed responsibility for armed attacks in the USA and Puerto Rico against military targets. However, in 1985 the group fragmented, following a series of raids by the US Federal Bureau of Investigation (FBI), in both Puerto Rico and the USA. Seventeen members of Los Macheteros, including its leadership, were arrested and imprisoned. However, the group's most important leader, Filiberto Ojeda, remained a fugitive.

The PPD, under the leadership of Muñoz Marín, dominated Puerto Rican electoral politics from 1940 to 1968. Muñoz Marín voluntarily retired from the leadership of the party in 1964, after serving four terms as Governor. He nominated his successor, then Secretary of State, Roberto Sánchez Vilella, who was elected Governor in 1964. A division in the PPD allowed the gubernatorial candidate of the newly formed PNP, Luis A. Ferré, to win the governorship in 1968. In the gubernatorial election held in 1972 the PPD returned to power under the leadership of Senate President Rafael Hernández Colón. He was defeated in 1976 by the PNP Mayor of San Juan, Carlos Romero Barceló, who had taken over the party's leadership following Ferré's defeat in 1972. Romero Barceló won again in 1980 by a mere 3,500 votes, in the narrowest election win in Puerto Rican history. The PPD, however, won a majority in both the House of Representatives and the Senate, thus preventing Romero Barceló from holding a status referendum to determine whether people favoured US statehood for Puerto Rico.

During 1981 dissatisfaction with Romero Barceló's leadership developed, following the murder of two independence activists, allegedly by Puerto Rican police. This brought into question the role of Governor Romero Barceló in the affair. Romero Barceló faced additional problems from his own party, when the Mayor of San Juan, Hernán Padilla Ramírez, left the PNP over the issue of internal party democracy and formed a new political grouping, the Puerto Rican Renewal Party (Partido de Renovación Puertorriqueño—PRP). Padilla entered the 1984 gubernatorial election as the PRP candidate and received some 70,000 votes (about 4% of the total votes cast). The division in the PNP was great enough to ensure the election of former Governor Hernández Colón, the PPD candidate. Hernández Colón dedicated his second term in office to the resolution of economic problems. In 1986 he successfully persuaded the US Congress to retain a special tax benefit for US corporations operating in Puerto Rico, although this was rescinded in 1996 (see Economy below).

The Mayor of San Juan, Baltasar Corrada del Río, assumed control of the PNP following Romero Barceló's electoral defeat in 1984. He was the party's candidate in the 1988 election, but was defeated by Hernández Colón by some 50,000 votes. For the first time in 20 years the PNP lost its traditional bastion of power, the island's capital city of San Juan, by a mere 300 votes, to the PPD candidate, Héctor Luis Acevedo. At his third gubernatorial inauguration, in January 1989, Hernández Colón announced that he would seek congressional approval for a status plebiscite, to be held in mid-1991. Subsequently, the leaders of the island's three political parties formally petitioned the US Congress to approve legislation to authorize and implement a status referendum for Puerto Rico. In late 1989, after the US House of Representatives had approved a non-binding status plebiscite bill for Puerto Rico, the US Senate's Energy and Natural Resources Committee, which had jurisdiction over territorial matters, defeated a binding status referendum bill in a dramatic tied vote, thus ending the de-colonialization initiative. In Puerto Rico the defeat of the plebiscite measure was attributed to the reluctance of the US Congress to approve a referendum that could lead to statehood for Puerto Rico.

Following the defeat of the status legislation in the US Congress, Hernández Colón's administration, which held a majority in both legislative chambers, introduced legislation establishing a charter of 'democratic rights'. This included guarantees of US citizenship regardless of future changes in the island's constitutional status, and the declaration of Spanish as the only official language of Puerto Rico. The new legislation abrogated a 1902 law that had established both Spanish and English as the island's official languages. The PPD also approved legislation, opposed by the PNP, to hold a plebiscite to amend the island's constitution by adding six 'principles of self-determination'. The electorate rejected the proposed amendment by a vote of 53.6% against to 45.4% in favour. The referendum represented a major defeat for Governor Hernández Colón, and a victory for the new PNP leader, Dr Pedro J. Rosselló, a 48 year-old physician and former prominent tennis player. On 8 January 1992, one year before his gubernatorial term expired, Hernández Colón resigned as leader of the PPD, a position which he had occupied almost continuously since 1969. He was succeeded by Victoria Muñoz Mendoza, the daughter of the former Governor, Luis Muñoz Marín.

In the 1992 election campaign the pro-statehood PNP candidate, Rosselló, pledged to reduce crime, privatize the island's public-health system and lower taxes for the middle classes and for small businesses. He also promised to hold a Puerto Rican-sponsored plebiscite between the three traditional status options: statehood, enhanced Commonwealth and independence. His PPD rival, Victoria Muñoz, pledged to reform government bureaucracy and to encourage economic development. In the gubernatorial election, held on 3 November, Rosselló secured 49.9% of the votes cast, defeating Muñoz, who won 45.9% of the ballot. Former Governor Romero Barceló was also elected as the Island's Resident Commissioner in the US Congress. At the same time, the PNP won control of both the Senate and the House of Representatives, as well as 58 of the island's 78 municipalities. The PPD had suffered a major political reverse.

THE STATUS ISSUE

Upon taking office on 2 January 1993, the first bill passed by the PNP-dominated legislature restored English as an official language of the island. Rosselló moved to fulfil his election promise to reduce crime by mobilizing the National Guard in several residential areas of San Juan with high crime rates. He also moved to privatize the island's public-health system by subsidizing private health insurance for the poor and selling or renting out the Government's health-care facilities. Legislation presented by Rosselló to enable a status plebiscite to be held was overwhelmingly endorsed in the island legislature. The ensuing referendum, which was held on 14 November, resulted in a 48.6% vote for the retention of Commonwealth status, with 46.3% of voters supporting statehood and 4% advocating independence. Some 73% of all registered voters participated in the plebiscite. The results were disappointing for the governing PNP, which had hoped to win a mandate to urge the US Congress to grant the island statehood. Those in favour of continued Commonwealth status, which included the PPD, were equally disappointed that their formula had not received a clear majority and shocked to see their 60% majority in the 1967 plebiscite decline so substantially. For the 1996 election the PPD nominated the Mayor of San Juan, Héctor Acevedo, to oppose Rosselló, who was standing for a second term. On 5 November Rosselló was re-elected by an even greater margin than in 1992, with 51% of the votes cast compared to 44% for Acevedo. The PNP retained control of both houses of the island legislature and won 54 of the 78 island municipalities. Romero Barceló was also re-elected to the post of Resident Commissioner, soundly defeating his PPD opponent, Celeste Benítez.

In November 1994 the Republicans won control of both the US House of Representatives and the Senate. In the following year the Republican Don Young, newly appointed Chairman of

the House Resources Committee with jurisdiction over Puerto Rico, introduced a bill which required Puerto Rico to hold periodic plebiscites until the issue of the island's status was resolved. The legislation was withdrawn in late 1996 at the insistence of Romero Barceló, after it had been amended to make English the sole official language of a future US state of Puerto Rico. It was revived in 1997, but was opposed by the PPD, owing to the bill's categorization of the Commonwealth as a territory of the USA. The PPD argued that when the Commonwealth was established in 1952, Puerto Rico ceased to be a colonial dependency of the USA, an interpretation which has been continually challenged by both the PNP and the PIP. On 4 March 1998, however, the bill was passed in the US House of Representatives by one vote. The law authorized a plebiscite to be held in 1998 to allow Puerto Rico to choose between Commonwealth status, independence and statehood. In the event of the electorate voting for the Commonwealth formula, a plebiscite was to be held every 10 years until the island chose either independence or statehood. However, the bill was never voted on in the Senate, the leadership of which opposed the measure. Subsequently, Governor Rosselló held a Puerto Rican-sponsored plebiscite on 13 December 1998. The plebiscite allowed a choice between the existing Commonwealth status, which was defined as territorial, independence, statehood, a free association with the USA (whereby the USA would yield sovereignty over Puerto Rico), or 'none of the above'. The PPD campaigned for the last of the five options, 'none of the above', which won the plebiscite with 50.2% of the vote, compared with 46.5% in favour of statehood, 2.5% in favour of independence, and less than 1% supporting free association or the existing Commonwealth status.

In June 2000 US President Bill Clinton (1993–2001) met with representatives of the island's three major political parties to discuss a formula for resolving the status issue. However, the Republican congressional leadership boycotted the meeting and the Majority Leader of the Senate, Trent Lott, stated that the US legislature was not interested in dealing with Puerto Rico's status during the current Congress.

VIEQUES

In April 1999 a US navy bomb accidentally fell on an observation tower on the small island of Vieques, which lies off the eastern coast of Puerto Rico. Since the end of the Second World War the US Navy has been using most of Vieques, which has 10,000 civilian inhabitants, as a live firing range. The killing of a civilian prompted angry public protests in Puerto Rico, which ultimately led to the illegal occupation of the firing range by Puerto Ricans and a general outcry for the Navy to leave Vieques. In January 2000 Rosselló reached an agreement with the President Clinton to allow the Navy to continue bombing practice with inert or dummy ordnance until a referendum could be held on Vieques to allow the population to choose between the Navy staying and renewing live bombing practice, or leaving the island altogether by May 2003. The US Government was also to provide immediate development aid to Vieques of US $40m., which would increase to $90m. if residents agreed to the resumption of live ammunition testing. In return, Rosselló promised to help the federal authorities remove the protesters, who had been occupying the firing range since the incident. In May 2000, in anticipation of the recommencement of (dummy) ammunition testing, protests were held on Vieques. US Federal Government agents were deployed on the island to remove forcibly the protesters. Further protests were held throughout 2000.

On 7 November 2000 Sila María Calderón of the PPD was elected to the governorship, securing 48.5% of the votes cast, while the PNP candidate, Carlos I. Pesquera Morales, won 45.7%. Aníbal Acevedo Vilá of the PPD was elected to the post of Resident Commissioner, defeating the incumbent, Romero Barceló. The PPD also gained control of the Senate, the House of Representatives and 46 of the 78 municipalities. While mayor of San Juan, Calderón had questioned Rosselló's Vieques agreement with President Clinton and, following her election as governor, she adopted a firm stance with the US Navy on the issue of Vieques. She immediately renounced the agreement reached between her predecessor and President Clinton, and called for the immediate withdrawal of the US Navy from the island, claiming that bombing over the years has caused serious health problems for the residents. Military exercises were resumed on the island in May 2001. Following legal challenges and protests, operations were suspended, but resumed again on 18 June, prompting further protests. In early July the new US President, George W. Bush, announced that the US Navy would leave the island by May 2003, as planned. However, a non-binding referendum on the issue, organized by the Calderón Government, took place on 29 July, in which 68% of islanders voted for an immediate cessation of bombing. The US Navy's activities received endorsement from only 2% of voters. The binding referendum, agreed by Rosselló and Clinton in 2000, was still scheduled to take place in November 2001.

Economy

JAMES McDONOUGH

Puerto Rico has been a US territory since 1898, and its economy is closely bound to that of the USA. It is a mountainous island measuring 117 km (110 miles) long by 56 km (35 miles) wide, with a relatively flat and narrow coastal belt. It is the smallest of the three Caribbean islands making up the Greater Antilles. In 2000 Puerto Rico's population stood at 3.8m. inhabitants, with a population density of around 425.1 per sq km, making the island one of the most densely populated areas in the world. Until the 1950s Puerto Rico's economy was traditionally based on agriculture; in the 19th and early 20th centuries its principal cash crops were coffee, sugar and tobacco. However, in the 1940s the Government decided to seek economic growth through industrialization. The governing Popular Democratic Party (Partido Popular Democrático—PPD) decided to seek external capital, mainly from the USA, to spur economic growth. US capital was encouraged to invest in manufacturing facilities on the island through a unique combination of local and federal tax exemption and low wages. The results were immediate and astonishing, and became known throughout the world as 'Operation Bootstrap'. Real gross national product (GNP) increased by 68% in the 1950s, and by 90% in the 1960s. The average annual growth in GNP was approximately 6% during these two decades. Living standards rose accordingly, with personal income per head rising from US $342 per year in 1950, to $1,511 per year in 1971 and to $7,454 per year in 1997. By 1970 manufacturing constituted 40% of the island's gross domestic product (GDP) and remained around this level for the next three decades. Meanwhile, earnings from agriculture fell to less than 1% of GDP by 1999. In 1970 unemployment declined to 10% of the labour force, astonishing progress given the island's traditional agricultural economy with its massive seasonal unemployment and widespread underemployment.

The extraordinary growth produced by Operation Bootstrap ended following the petroleum crisis of 1973. The dramatic increases in petroleum prices imposed by the Organization of Petroleum Exporting Countries (OPEC) severely impeded Puerto Rico's capacity to sustain high economic growth as it is dependent on imported oil and gas to meet its energy needs. At the same time, wage increases and reduced US tariffs on foreign products hampered Puerto Rico's ability to attract US capital. Governor Rafael Hernández Colón (1972–76) attempted to combat the economic slowdown through aggressive government intervention in the economy. Under his leadership, the Government purchased the Puerto Rico Telephone Company, the two major shipping lines serving Puerto Rico and US ports, and most of the island's sugar mills. Nevertheless, these efforts did not slow the economic decline and the island's growth rate dropped to 1.8% between 1974 and 1984. For the first time since Operation Bootstrap began, the island experienced a decline in real GNP in 1975, 1982 and 1983. Economic disaster was avoided only by a massive increase in federal funds, which offset the drop in growth in the productive sectors. Federal aid to Puerto Rico increased from US $558m in 1970 to $4,500 by 1985. (In 2000 federal transfers to Puerto Rico were estimated at $7,165m.)

Governor Hernández Colón won his second term in office in the 1984 gubernatorial election on the strength of his pledge to make job creation his main priority. His new term of office coincided with the recovery of the USA from the 1981 recession.

Recuperation of the US economy was accompanied by a decrease in world petroleum prices. Nevertheless, he was faced with a serious challenge from the US administration of President Ronald Reagan (1981–89), which sought to eliminate the special tax incentives for US investment in Puerto Rico. Many in the administration and in the US Congress argued that the tax incentives were too expensive a mechanism for job creation. To thwart the offensive against the tax breaks, Hernández Colón embarked on an ambitious 'twin-plant' programme to promote industrial development in the Caribbean. His idea was to use the capital generated by the operations of US companies in Puerto Rico to invest in secondary Caribbean plants that would feed the companies' Puerto Rico operations. His programme won the approval of the Reagan administration and efforts to eliminate the federal tax incentives for Puerto Rico were postponed. At the same time, the Governor moved to restore most of the local tax benefits that had been curtailed by the previous pro-statehood administration. The success of Hernández Colón's policies was reflected in an annual average growth rate in real GDP of 3.8% in 1984–88. However, economic growth slowed considerably during Hernández Colón's second and third terms in office, mainly because of the advent of a world recession. Puerto Rico's real GDP grew by 2.0% per year between 1989 and 1992. Slower growth led to an increase in unemployment, which reached 16.6% in 1992, and remained consistently high throughout the early 1990s.

In 1993 the incoming administration of Governor Pedro J. Rosselló structured a new economic development programme in which the private sector was to be the primary vehicle for economic development. Rosselló moved to change the role of government from being a provider of most basic services, to that of a facilitator for private-sector initiatives. In 1994 the Governor introduced his 'new economic model', advocating reduced government regulation of businesses, the privatization of public enterprises, greater promotion of tourism, and the encouragement of local investment and local industry. In 1993–99 Puerto Rico's GDP grew, in real terms, by an average of 3.3% per year, as the island mirrored the general success of the US economy over the same period. During this period total employment increased by 169,000 jobs, and unemployment decreased from 16.8% in 1993 to 12.5% in 1999. In 1999 the annual rate of increase in consumer prices was 5.7%.

In keeping with its privatization policy, the Rosselló administration sold the government-owned shipping company, a major state-owned hotel property, the public sugar corporation and majority control of the state-owned Puerto Rico Telephone Company. However, in 1996, in a major reversal for the island, the US Congress approved legislation ending the possessions tax credit, the powerful federal tax incentive used to attract manufacturing investment from US corporations to Puerto Rico. Since the elimination of the tax incentive, Puerto Rico has lost at least 36,600 manufacturing jobs. In early 2001 total manufacturing employment stood at 135,600 (down from an historic high of 172,000 jobs in 1995). Faced with this massive loss of factory jobs, a slowing economy and an increase in unemployment from 10% in 2000 to 11.4% in 2001, Puerto Rico's new Governor, Sila María Calderón, who took office in 2001, committed her administration to securing new tax incentives from the US Congress. Meanwhile, she has retained former US Secretary of State, Henry Kissinger, and former US Federal Reserve Board Chairman, Paul Volker, to draw up a 10-year economic development plan for the island.

MANUFACTURING

The growth of manufacturing in Puerto Rico was almost entirely the result of special tax benefits from both the US and Puerto Rican Governments. Under US law (Section 936 of the US Tax Code), the income of a subsidiary of a US corporation operating a manufacturing facility in Puerto Rico is eligible to receive a federal tax credit, which practically exempts the corporation from the payment of US income taxes on its Puerto Rican earnings. The Puerto Rico Government in 1948 matched the federal possessions tax credit with its own equally generous tax incentive programme. The combined incentives created a powerful lure to attract US corporate investment to Puerto Rico. In the early years of Operation Bootstrap, the island attracted the labour-intensive textiles and apparel industries. However, over the years, and as the federal incentive grew more generous, Puerto Rico manufacturing became more capital intensive and diversified, marked by substantial investment in sectors such as pharmaceuticals, scientific instruments, computers, microprocessors, medical products and electrical goods.

In 2000 manufacturing still employed 12.5% of the island's working population, but accounted for an estimated 43.4%% of GDP, some US $27,441m. in gross income. However, since 1996 Puerto Rico's industrialization programme stagnated, owing to the elimination of the federal possessions tax credit. Nevertheless, the full impact of the credit's elimination will not be felt until the end of the 10-year 'grace' period granted to companies operating in Puerto Rico at the time of the tax credit's demise. Growth in the manufacturing sector in the late 1990s resulted mainly from the expansion of those US companies that could still take advantage of the tax incentive. To offset the negative impact of the elimination of Section 936, the Rosselló administration won legislative approval in 1998 for a revision in the island's tax incentive law. The new law reduced the effective Puerto Rico tax burden on manufacturing companies from 14.5% to 7%, in effect eliminating the 10% 'tollgate tax' the island had imposed on the repatriation of earnings from Puerto Rico to the USA. For labour-intensive firms the reduction of the Puerto Rican tax burden was even greater, reaching 4%, and, in some special cases, as low as 2%. The law also provided for generous tax incentives for research and development and training. In 1999 the Rosselló administration was able to persuade Congress to extend federal credits for research and development to Puerto Rico. The Rosselló administration also embarked on a campaign to convince the US Congress to extend the federal wage credit granted to US companies already operating in Puerto Rico beyond 2005, when it was to expire, and to open the wage credit incentive to start-up companies. Governor Calderón abandoned Rosselló administration's efforts to extend the wage credit, and instead is attempting to win new incentives for Puerto Rico under the Controlled Foreign Corporation (CFC) provisions of the federal tax code. Following the elimination of the federal tax incentives in 1996, some 57 large manufacturing firms operating in Puerto Rico, many in the pharmaceutical sector, took advantage of Puerto Rico's status as a foreign tax jurisdiction to re-incorporate as CFCs. Under federal tax law, the earnings of CFCs are not subject to federal taxation as long as they remain 'off-shore'. The larger companies use their Puerto Rican earnings to strengthen their non-US subsidiaries in other countries. In mid-2001 Calderón was seeking US congressional approval to allow these Puerto Rican CFCs to repatriate their earnings to their US corporate shareholders at a preferential 10% tax rate.

COMMERCE

Wholesale and retail trade played a significant role in Puerto Rico's economy. In 2000 the sector contributed 13.3% of total GDP. With 239,000 workers in 2000, commerce represented the third largest source of employment on the island, after services and government. In 2000 this sector generated US $8,437m. in total revenues. Shopping centres dominated the retail trade; total space available increased from 9.2m. sq ft in 1980 to 15.9m. sq ft in 1995. During the same period shopping-centre sales volume per sq ft increased by 4.8%. The island's first 'megastore' was built in the mid-1990s, consisting of several businesses which had previously operated individually, but were now gathered under one roof. This phenomenon spread and could be seen in the incorporation of pharmacies and banking service centres into department stores, as well as in fast-food establishments.

FINANCE

Finance, insurance and real estate contributed an estimated 14.1% to the island's GDP in 2000. However, the sector faced an uncertain future because of the elimination of the possessions tax credit (see above). US corporations with a total of about US $13,000m. deposited in Puerto Rican financial institutions were expected to repatriate their funds, since the federal tax credit on the interest income was eliminated. The banks would have to replace these funds with more costly alternatives, which could cause an increase in interest rates and competition. There were 20 commercial banks and trust companies operating in Puerto Rico in the mid-1990s, of which three were major US money-centre banks. Canadian and Spanish banks also operated on the island, along with some 14 local banks and trust companies. Assets of these banks totalled $29,878m. in 1995. In 2000 the finance, insurance and real-estate sector generated an estimated US $.8,920m. and employed a total of 42,000 workers.

SERVICES

The services sector (including public utilities) contributed an estimated 53.1% of GDP in 1999. Puerto Rico experienced significant growth in services, in terms of both income and employment, throughout the 1980s and 1990s. Between 1970 and 1980 the average annual GDP growth of the sector was 3.2%. However, in 1980–92 annual growth increased to 4.7%. In 2000 services generated some US $6,678m, and employed an estimated 307,000 workers, an increase of more than 100,000 from 1980.

TOURISM

Tourism forms an increasingly important, but still small, part of Puerto Rico's economy. In 2000 the tourism industry constituted approximately 6% of the island's GDP. Approximately 14,000 people, or 1.2% of the island's work-force, is employed by the tourism industry. During the early years of Operation Bootstrap the Government utilized a combination of direct government and private investment to create the necessary infrastructure for tourism. It invested directly in the construction of hotels, but contracted with US corporations for the hotel management. In 1959 the industry was favourably affected by the Cuban Revolution, which led to the US economic embargo and the diversion of much of Cuba's US tourism to other Caribbean destinations. The island's traditional emphasis has been on relatively expensive casinos and hotels located along the beaches. However, in the late 1970s the Government developed a unique system of country inns to move tourism out of San Juan, and improved the transportation facilities, including the expansion of the airport and new tourism piers in San Juan's harbour. In 2000 some 1,741m. visitors stayed in the island's hotels, which registered a healthy 68.7% occupancy rate. In 1992, the year before Governor Rosselló took power, visitor expenditure totalled US $1,452m. By 2000. his last year in office, this figure had risen to $2,388m. In 2000 the island received approximately 1,69m. cruise-ship visitors, making San Juan the second largest cruise-ship port in the world in terms of total number of visitors. Nevertheless, over the last 10 years Puerto Rico has lost market share to other Caribbean destinations. In 1989 Puerto Rico was the leading Caribbean destination with a 19.6% market share of visitors to the region, followed by the Mexican-Caribbean coast (17%). By 1998, however, the Mexican-Caribbean coast had risen to first place with 22.9% of visitors, followed by Puerto Rico with 16.8%.

The development of tourism was a priority for the Rosselló administration, who extended additional tax credits to the sector to encourage hotel construction. At the same time Rosselló created a new subsidiary of the Government Development Bank to encourage and promote investment in new hotels. As a result, the number of hotel rooms increased every year—except in 1998, when Hurricane Georges resulted in the closure of several major hotels—under his administration, reaching 11,915 by mid-2000. The Rosselló administration was particularly successful in decentralizing tourism outside San Juan. New projects were built or planned east of San Juan, extending along the coast to

Fajardo, and new tourism enclaves were appearing along the west coast between San Juan and Aguadilla. In 1999 the Rosselló administration announced plans to create an ambitious tourism and trade centre, to be known as the Golden Triangle, on the Isla Grande peninsular in San Juan. Plans involved the construction of a 159,000 sq ft convention centre and 800-room hotel, a world trade centre, as well as condominiums, residences and an entertainment centre. The total cost of the project is expected to exceed US $600m. The Calderón administration continued with the project, signing a $200m. agreement with LCOR, Inc., for the construction of two hotels, the trade centre and a retail and entertainment area.

Puerto Rico's Luis Muñoz Marín International Airport, in San Juan, was served by 45 US and international airlines. In 1996 the airport served approximately 4.6m. passengers and moved 142,000m. kg of freight. The airport offered daily direct air services between San Juan and more than seven US cities, and regular scheduled services to other Caribbean islands and major Latin American and European cities. However, the airport suffered a reverse in late 1997, when American Airlines, the island's biggest passenger carrier, transferred its Caribbean hub.

THE PUBLIC SECTOR

The government sector was the second largest area of employment. In 2000 the sector employed approximately 249,000 people, or 21% of the total labour force. The sector accounted for US $5,477m., or 8.6%, of Puerto Rico's GDP in 2000. One major reason for Puerto Rico's ability to maintain such high public-sector employment was the economic aid it received from the USA. Federal disbursements to Puerto Rico increased from $2,900m. in 1979 to $7,156m. in 2000. Governor Rosselló modernized the government bureaucracy by creating 'super agencies', which grouped previously independent agencies under an overarching structure. Such was the case in the creation of the Department of Economic Development and Commerce, which included the Economic Development Administration, the Department of Commerce and the Department of Tourism. Besides selling off publicly-owned industries, Rosselló also opened the government-owned and -operated electricity system, the Electrical Energy Authority of Puerto Rico (Autoridad de Energía Eléctrica de Puerto Rico), to private co-generators. In early 1998 the Enron Corporation of Houston, Texas (USA), began construction on a US $600m., 507 MW, liquefied natural gas (LNG) co-generation plant, a desalination plant and an LNG storage facility. Located on the southern coast of the island, the facility became operational in 2001. The water from the desalination plant is used to cool the turbines and the excess sold as fresh water to the Government's Water and Sewer Authority. In November 1999 construction also began on an $850m., coal-burning, co-generation plant, to be built by the USA's AES Corporation, and expected to open by mid-2001. Both plants have a contract with the Electrical Energy Authority of Puerto Rico to sell their output to the government network. Construction of the plants was encouraged by the Government, in an attempt to diversify the island's electrical generation, which hitherto had been completely dependent on imported petroleum as its fuel source.

In terms of public works, in 1996 construction began of a 'super-aqueduct' to bring water from the western part of the island to the San Juan metropolitan area, where traditional water supplies were insufficient to handle the city's growing population. In the same year the Government also began the construction of a US $1,200m., 16.6-km (10.3-mile), mass transit system for the San Juan area, which was scheduled to become

operational in 2002. The project was made possible by a $300m. commitment by the US Government. In early 2000 plans were also announced for the construction of a deep-water megaport in Guayanilla on the south coast. The new administration embraced the project and broadened the reach of the port to include the neighbouring ports of Ponce and Peñuelas. Governor Calderón planned to spend US 1,000m. to build the 'Port of the Américas', which will provide deepwater docking and on-shore warehouse space and factory sites for assembly and re-export of semi-finished goods.

PUBLIC FINANCE

Puerto Rico is constitutionally required to operate within a balanced budget. The island's Constitution provided for a limitation on the amount of general debt that could be issued, equal to 15% of the average annual revenues raised over the previous two years. Historically, Puerto Rico kept within its constitutional bounds. Nevertheless, under the Rosselló administration, public-sector debt increased from $13,822m. in 1992 to $23,821m. in 2000. Most of this was spent on the construction of roads and other infrastructure projects.

TRADE

Puerto Rico lies within the customs barrier of the USA. Consequently, exports and imports are dominated by the USA. In 2000 Puerto Rico exported goods valued at US $38,305m. and imported goods worth $27,042m. Puerto Rico's export trade consisted mainly of manufactured goods. From 1982 until the present the island has operated with an annual trade surplus. In 2000 its favourable balance of trade equalled $11,263m. The percentage of exports to the USA remained relatively constant from the 1950s to the end of the 1990s, at around 90% of the total. However, goods shipped from the USA decreased from 92% of total imports in 1950 to 60.7% in 1997/98.

After the USA, Puerto Rico's biggest external markets in 1997 were the Dominican Republic (US $712m.), Japan ($234m.), Germany ($148m.), Belgium ($139m.), the Netherlands ($138m.), Canada ($123m.), Switzerland ($116m.), the US Virgin Islands ($91m.) and Mexico ($89m.). With respect to imports, following the USA in 1997 were Japan ($1,182m.), the Dominican Republic ($882m.), Venezuela ($699m.), the United Kingdom ($588m.), Ireland ($508m.), the US Virgin Islands ($444m.), Italy ($247m.), South Korea (Republic of Korea— $221m.) and Mexico ($217m.). With the start of the 'twin-plant' programme in 1986, Puerto Rico also moved to increase trade with its Caribbean and Central American neighbours. In 1988 Puerto Rico's exports to 13 Caribbean and Central American countries totalled $657m. and its imports $620.5m. By 1997 Puerto Rican exports to the this region totalled $1,017m. The Rosselló administration also attempted to increase trade with Latin America, including Mexico. However, the participation of the Caribbean and Latin America in Puerto Rico's overall exports was relatively small, representing on average 5% of total exports of merchandise. Puerto Rico also invested $747m. in the Caribbean area between 1985 and 1995, with Jamaica and the Dominican Republic receiving the largest share of the funds. However, the elimination of the possessions tax credit adversely affected the loan programme. After the elimination of the possessions tax credit, the source of capital for the loan programme diminished as US companies repatriated Puerto Rican profits, instead of investing the money in the Caribbean. In addition, at the end of the 1990s Puerto Rico was yet to benefit substantially from the implementation of NAFTA. Despite encouraging government predictions, in 2000 Puerto Rico still maintained an unfavourable balance of trade with Mexico.

Statistical Survey

Source (unless otherwise stated): Puerto Rico Planning Board, POB 41119, San Juan, 00940-1119; tel. (787) 723-6200; internet www.jp.gov.pr.

Area and Population

AREA, POPULATION AND DENSITY

Area (sq km)	8,959*
Population (census results)	
1 April 1980	3,196,520
1 April 1990	
Males	1,705,642
Females	1,816,395
Total	3,522,037
1 April 2000	3,808,610
Population (official estimates at mid-year)	
1997	3,827,038
1998	3,860,091
1999	3,889,507
Density (per sq km) at 1 April 2000	425.1

* 3,459 sq miles.

PRINCIPAL TOWNS (Census 1 April 2000).

San Juan (capital)	421,958	Carolina		168,164
Bayamón	203,499	Ponce		155,038

Source: Bureau of the Census, US Department of Commerce.

BIRTHS, MARRIAGES AND DEATHS

	Registered live births		Registered marriages		Registered deaths	
	Number	Rate (per 1,000)	Number	Rate (per 1,000)	Number	Rate (per 1,000)
1993	65,242	18.0	33,262	9.2	28,494	7.9
1994	64,325	17.5	33,200	9.0	28,444	7.7
1995*	64,000	17.1	n.a.	n.a.	30,000	8.1
1996	63,259	16.9	32,572	8.7	29,871	8.0
1997*	64,000	16.9	n.a.	n.a.	29,000	7.7
1998*	64,000	16.6	n.a.	n.a.	30,000	7.8

* Provisional.

ECONOMICALLY ACTIVE POPULATION
('000 persons aged 16 years and over)

	1997	1998	1999
Agriculture, hunting, forestry and fishing	32	28	25
Manufacturing	163	160	157
Electricity, gas and water	15	14	13
Construction	66	74	84
Trade and restaurants	233	231	231
Transport, storage and communications	43	46	44
Financing, insurance, real estate and business services	38	41	42
Community, social and personal services (incl. hotels)	541	543	552
Total employed (incl. others)	1,132	1,138	1,149
Unemployed	176	175	153
Total labour force	1,308	1,313	1,302

* Source: ILO, *Yearbook of Labour Statistics*.

Agriculture

PRINCIPAL CROPS ('000 metric tons)

	1995	1996	1997
Sugar cane	504.2	404.6	307.4
Tomatoes	10.3	8.7	9.9
Pumpkins, squash and gourds	17.5	16.3	16.3*
Bananas	48.3	48.0	38.2
Plantains	65.3	76.1	76.1*
Oranges	17.4	16.7	16.1
Mangoes	9.1	15.3	17.4
Pineapples	24.1	18.9	19.2
Coffee (green)	12.7	12.2	11.6

* FAO estimate(s).

1998–2000 (FAO estimates): data as for 1997.

LIVESTOCK ('000 head, year ending September)

	1995	1996	1997
Cattle	367.7	370.6	388.3
Goats	17.9	8.4	13.0*
Pigs	204.6	182.2	174.7
Chickens (million)	12.3	12.4	11.6
Horses	23.5*	23.5*	23.5*

* FAO estimate(s).

1998–2000 (FAO estimates): data as for 1997.

Fishing

(metric tons, live weight)

	1996	1997	1998
Fishes	1,938	2,301	1,752
Crustaceans	189	171	184
Molluscs	184	162	182
Total catch	2,311	2,634	2,118

Source: FAO, *Yearbook of Fishery Statistics*.

Industry

SELECTED PRODUCTS (year ending 30 June)

	1995/96	1996/97	1997/98*
Distilled spirits ('000 proof gallons)	25,343	36,292	33,471
Beer ('000 wine gallons)	7,923	6,973	5,784

* Preliminary.

Cement ('000 metric tons): 1,398 in 1995; 1,508 in 1996 (Source: UN, *Industrial Commodity Statistics Yearbook*).
Electricity (million kWh): 20,140.8 in 1998/99; 21,459.8 in 1999/2000.

Finance

CURRENCY AND EXCHANGE RATES
Monetary Units
United States currency: 100 cents = 1 US dollar (US $).

Sterling and Euro Equivalents (30 April 2001)
£1 sterling = US $1.4318;
€1 = 88.76 US cents;
$100 = £69.84 = €112.66.

BUDGET (US $ million, year ending 30 June)

Revenue	1995/96	1996/97	1997/98*
Taxation	4,880	5,203	5,515
Income taxes	3,384	3,633	3,996
Property taxes	78	38	74
Excise taxes	1,357	1,455	1,362
Licences	60	73	82
Intergovernmental transfers	2,579	2,824	2,786
Other receipts	393	433	483
Total	7,852	8,460	8,784

Expenditure	1989/90
General government	318
Public safety	542
Health	219
Public housing and welfare	1,606
Education	1,270
Economic development	678
Aid to municipalities	246
Lottery prizes	316
Capital outlays	504
Debt service	564
Total	6,263

*Provisional.
Source: Department of the Treasury, Commonwealth of Puerto Rico.

COST OF LIVING (Consumer Price Index; base: 1990 = 100)

	1997	1998	1999
Food (incl. beverages)	168.6	187.8	206.4
Fuel and light	103.6	100.4	101.9
Rent	114.7	121.9	124.1
Clothing (incl. footwear)	87.9	86.8	85.5
All items (incl. others)	131.3	138.2	146.1

Source: ILO, *Yearbook of Labour Statistics.*

NATIONAL ACCOUNTS
(US $ million at current prices, year ending 30 June)
Expenditure on the Gross Domestic Product

	1995/96	1996/97	1997/98*
Government final consumption expenditure	6,493.4	6,925.4	7,176.1
Private final consumption expenditure	27,819.5	29,876.6	31,351.0
Increase in stocks	324.4	417.7	31.2
Gross fixed capital formation	7,589.9	8,510.6	9,236.8
Total domestic expenditure	42,227.2	45,730.3	47,795.1
Exports of goods and services . *Less* Imports of goods and services	3,284.2	2,365.9	6,030.3
GDP in purchasers' values	45,511.4	48,096.2	53,825.4
GDP at constant 1954 prices	8,291.8	8,677.8	9,239.7

* Preliminary.

Gross Domestic Product by Economic Activity

	1997	1998	1999*
Agriculture	466	457	324
Manufacturing	19,302	22,961	26,439
Construction and mining†	1,257	1,327	1,515
Transportation and public utilities‡	3,751	3,983	4,353
Trade	6,724	7,353	7,876
Finance, insurance and real estate	6,917	7,372	8,207
Services	5,314	5,693	6,014
Government§	5,220	5,251	5,523
Sub-total	48,951	50,424	60,251
Statistical discrepancy	−765	−532	−304
Total	48,186	49,892	59,947

* Preliminary.
† Mining includes only quarries.
‡ Includes radio and television broadcasting.
§ Includes public enterprises not classified elsewhere.

BALANCE OF PAYMENTS (US $ million, year ending 30 June)

	1995/96	1996/97	1997/98*
Merchandise exports f.o.b.	25,675.5	26,874.5	33,416.4
Merchandise imports f.o.b.	−21,873.9	−24,204.3	−27,308.7
Trade balance	3,801.6	2,670.2	6,107.7
Investment income received	1,185.2	932.9	1,082.3
Investment income paid	−17,107.2	−17,682.3	−20,864.5
Services and other income (net)	224.1	444.5	696.3
Unrequited transfers (net)	6,720.9	7,420.9	7,731.6
Net interest of Commonwealth and municipal governments	−218.9	−242.5	−259.3
Current balance	−5,394.3	−6,456.2	−5,505.9

* Provisional.

External Trade

PRINCIPAL COMMODITIES (US $ million, year ending 30 June)*

Imports	1995/96	1996/97	1997/98
Mining products	506.8	329.1	133.3
Manufacturing products	18,103.7	20,532.2	21,165.6
Food	2,149.9	2,192.7	2,226.5
Clothing and textiles	840.3	813.8	915.9
Paper, printing and publishing	541.4	508.9	531.5
Chemical products	4,151.7	5,416.3	5,842.0
Drugs and pharmaceutical preparations	1,910.8	3,206.1	3,644.2
Petroleum refining and related products	1,159.4	1,572.3	1,579.2
Rubber and plastic products	509.7	516.9	508.6
Primary metal products	404.5	474.7	490.0
Machinery, except electrical	1,382.4	1,370.4	1,489.6
Electronic computers	456.3	317.4	375.6
Electrical machinery	2,447.2	2,423.8	2,578.8
Transport equipment	1,764.5	2,241.2	2,097.2
Professional and scientific instruments	856.7	901.8	876.2
Total (incl. others)	19,060.9	21,387.4	21,797.5

Exports			1995/96	1996/97	1997/98
Manufacturing products	.	.	22,852.0	23,837.3	30,108.7
Food	.	.	3,319.6	3,386.4	3,645.3
Clothing and textiles	.	.	832.1	805.4	805.1
Chemical products	.	.	9,923.9	10,627.8	15,748.9
Drugs and pharmaceutical preparations	.	.	7,514.1	8,328.5	13,203.6
Machinery, except electrical	.		3,254.7	3,490.0	3,997.8
Electronic computers	.	.	2,999.6	3,062.5	3,290.2
Electrical machines	.	.	2,202.3	2,204.4	2,380.6
Professional and scientific instruments	.	.	1,629.6	1,625.5	1,682.8
Total (incl. others)	.	.	22,944.4	23,946.8	30,272.9

* Figures refer to recorded transactions only. Adjusted totals (in US $ million) are: Imports f.o.b. 21,873.9 in 1995/96, 24,204.3 in 1996/97, 27,308.7 (provisional) in 1997/98; Exports f.o.b. 25,675.5 in 1995/96, 26,874.5 in 1996/97; 33,416.4 (provisional) in 1997/98.

PRINCIPAL TRADING PARTNERS (US $ million)*

	1994/95		1995/96	
	Imports	Exports	Imports	Exports
Belgium . . .	53.2	165.2	122.9	205.9
Canada . . .	187.5	74.2	197.8	75.5
Dominican Repub. . .	664.2	693.7	768.1	677.4
France . . .	130.3	86.1	194.1	103.6
Germany . . .	207.0	280.8	175.7	233.8
Ireland . . .	180.8	27.4	278.8	19.6
Italy . . .	203.8	58.3	279.0	56.7
Japan . . .	1,278.5	91.1	1,222.8	184.5
Korea, Repub. . .	216.8	43.8	236.7	61.1
Mexico . . .	202.2	90.7	181.3	106.0
Netherlands . .	93.1	157.2	100.2	119.1
United Kingdom .	708.3	178.0	560.8	159.0
USA	12,158.1	21,106.9	11,909.3	20,148.6
US Virgin Islands .	307.0	164.8	366.8	137.3
Venezuela . . .	424.0	43.1	509.5	35.8
Total (incl. others) .	18,816.6	23,811.3	19,060.9	22,944.4

* Recorded trade only.
1996/97 (US $ million): *Imports:* USA 13,317.8; Total (incl. others) 21,387.4. *Exports:* USA 21,187.3; Total (incl. others) 23,946.8.
1997/98 (US $ million): *Imports:* USA 13,225.9; Total (incl. others) 21,797.5. *Exports:* USA 27,397.4; Total (incl. others) 30,272.9.

Transport

ROAD TRAFFIC (vehicles in use)

		1987/88	1988/89	1989/90
Cars				
Private	. . . . .	1,322,069	1,289,873	1,305,074
For hire	. . . .	14,814	11,033	10,513
Trucks				
Private	. . . .	15,790	13,273	12,577
For hire	. . . .	4,131	3,933	3,283
Light trucks .	. . .	176,583	174,277	189,705
Other vehicles	. . .	75,155	74,930	60,929
Total	. . . . .	1,608,542	1,567,319	1,582,081

1996 (estimates): Passenger cars 878,000; Lorries and vans 190,000.

SHIPPING (year ending 30 June)

		1985/86	1986/87	1987/88
Passengers arriving .	. .	29,559	59,089	33,737
Passengers departing	. .	33,683	63,987	35,627
Cruise visitors .	. . .	448,973	584,429	723,724

1988/89: Cruise visitors: 777,405.
1989/90: Cruise visitors: 866,090.
1990/91: Cruise visitors: 891,348.
Source: Puerto Rico Ports Authority.

CIVIL AVIATION (year ending 30 June)

		1988/89	1989/90	1990/91
Passengers arriving .	. . .	4,064,762	4,282,324	4,245,137
Passengers departing	. . .	4,072,828	4,297,521	4,262,154
Freight (tons)*	. . . .	173,126	208,586	222,172

* Handled by the Luis Muñoz Marín International Airport.
Source: Puerto Rico Ports Authority.

Tourism

(year ending 30 June)

		1995/96	1996/97	1997/98*
Total visitors ('000)†	. . .	4,110.2	4,349.7	4,670.8
From USA‡	. . .	2,211.3	2,443.9	2,544.4
From US Virgin Islands‡	. .	26.2	30.5	25.2
From other countries‡ .	. .	827.5	767.3	826.5
Expenditure ($ million)	. .	1,898.3	2,046.3	2,232.9

* Figures are preliminary.
† Including cruise-ship visitors and transient military personnel ('000): 1,045.1 in 1995/96; 1,107.9 in 1996/97; 1,274.7 (preliminary) in 1997/98.
‡ Excluding cruise-ship visitors.
1999/2000: Number of visitors 4,221.3; Expenditure (US $ million) 2,138.5.

Communications Media

	1994	1995	1996
Radio receivers ('000 in use) . .	2,600	2,636	2,670
Television receivers ('000 in use) .	973	1,000	1,010
Telephones ('000 main lines in use)*	1,130	1,196	1,254
Telefax stations ('000 in use) . .	n.a.	n.a.	543
Mobile cellular telephones ('000 subscribers)	109	171	169
Daily newspapers:			
Number	3	3	3
Average circulation ('000 copies)	475	475	475

Non-daily newspapers (estimates, 1988): 4 titles (average circulation 106,000 copies).
1997 ('000 in use): Radio receivers 2,700; Television receivers 1,021.
* Data refer to switched access lines.
Sources: UNESCO, *Statistical Yearbook*; UN, *Statistical Yearbook*.

Education

	1993/94	1994/95	1995/96
Total number of students . .	933,183	934,406	947,249
Public day schools . . .	631,460	621,370	627,620
Private schools (accredited)* .	140,034	145,864	148,004
University of Puerto Rico† . .	53,935	54,353	62,341
Private colleges and universities	107,754	112,819	109,284
Number of teachers‡	39,816	40,003	39,328

* Includes public and private accredited schools not administered by the Department of Education.
† Includes all university-level students.
‡ School teachers only.

Directory

The Constitution

RELATIONSHIP WITH THE USA

On 3 July 1950 the Congress of the United States of America adopted Public Law No. 600, which was to allow 'the people of Puerto Rico to organize a government pursuant to a constitution of their own adoption'. This Law was submitted to the voters of Puerto Rico in a referendum and was accepted in the summer of 1951. A new Constitution was drafted in which Puerto Rico was styled as a commonwealth, or estado libre asociado, 'a state which is free of superior authority in the management of its own local affairs', though it remained in association with the USA. This Constitution, with its amendments and resolutions, was ratified by the people of Puerto Rico on 3 March 1952, and by the Congress of the USA on 3 July 1952; and the Commonwealth of Puerto Rico was established on 25 July 1952.

Under the terms of the political and economic union between the USA and Puerto Rico, US citizens in Puerto Rico enjoy the same privileges and immunities as if Puerto Rico were a member state of the Union. Puerto Rican citizens are citizens of the USA and may freely enter and leave that country.

The Congress of the USA has no control of, and may not intervene in, the internal affairs of Puerto Rico.

Puerto Rico is exempted from the tax laws of the USA, although most other federal legislation does apply to the island. Puerto Rico is represented in the US House of Representatives by a non-voting delegate, the Resident Commissioner, who is directly elected for a four-year term. The island has no representation in the US Senate.

There are no customs duties between the USA and Puerto Rico. Foreign products entering Puerto Rico—with the single exception of coffee, which is subject to customs duty in Puerto Rico, but not in the USA—pay the same customs duties as would be paid on their entry into the USA.

The US social security system is extended to Puerto Rico, except for unemployment insurance provisions. Laws providing for economic co-operation between the Federal Government and the States of the Union for the construction of roads, schools, public health services and similar purposes are extended to Puerto Rico. Such joint programmes are administered by the Commonwealth Government.

Amendments to the Constitution are not subject to approval by the US Congress, provided that they are consistent with the US Federal Constitution, the Federal Relations Act defining federal relations with Puerto Rico, and Public Law No. 600. Subject to these limitations, the Constitution may be amended by a two-thirds vote of the Puerto Rican Legislature and by the subsequent majority approval of the electorate.

BILL OF RIGHTS

No discrimination shall be made on account of race, colour, sex, birth, social origin or condition, or political or religious ideas. Suffrage shall be direct, equal and universal for all over the age of 18. Public property and funds shall not be used to support schools other than State schools. The death penalty shall not exist. The rights of the individual, of the family and of property are guaranteed. The Constitution establishes trial by jury in all cases of felony, as well as the right of habeas corpus. Every person is to receive free elementary and secondary education. Social protection is to be afforded to the old, the disabled, the sick and the unemployed.

THE LEGISLATURE

The Legislative Assembly consists of two chambers, whose members are elected by direct vote for a four-year term. The Senate is composed of 27 members, the House of Representatives of 51 members. Senators must be over 30 years of age, and Representatives over 25 years of age. The Constitution guarantees the minority parties additional representation in the Legislature, which may fluctuate from one quarter to one third of the seats in each House.

The Senate elects a President and the House of Representatives a Speaker from their respective members. The sessions of each house are public. A majority of the total number of members of each house constitutes a quorum. Either house can initiate legislation, although bills for raising revenue must originate in the House of Representatives. Once passed by both Houses, a bill is submitted to the Governor, who can either sign it into law or return it, with his reasons for refusal, within 10 days. If it is returned, the Houses may pass it again by a two-thirds majority, in which case the Governor must accept it.

The House of Representatives, or the Senate, can impeach one of its members for treason, bribery, other felonies and 'misdemeanours involving moral turpitude'. A two-thirds majority is necessary before an indictment may be brought. The cases are tried by the Senate. If a Representative or Senator is declared guilty, he is deprived of his office and becomes punishable by law.

THE EXECUTIVE

The Governor, who must be at least 35 years of age, is elected by direct suffrage and serves for four years. Responsible for the execution of laws, the Governor is Commander-in-Chief of the militia and has the power to proclaim martial law. At the beginning of every regular session of the Assembly, in January, the Governor presents a report on the state of the treasury, and on proposed expenditure. The Governor chooses the Secretaries of Departments, subject to the approval of the Legislative Assembly. These are led by the Secretary of State, who replaces the Governor at need.

LOCAL GOVERNMENT

The island is divided into 78 municipal districts for the purposes of local administration. The municipalities comprise both urban areas and the surrounding neighbourhood. They are governed by a mayor and a municipal assembly, both elected for a four-year term.

The Government

HEAD OF STATE

Governor: Sila María Calderón (took office 2 January 2001).

EXECUTIVE
(August 2001)

Governor: Sila María Calderón.

Secretary of State: Fernando Mercado Ramos.

Secretary of Justice: Anabele Rodríguez.

Secretary of the Treasury: Juan A. Flores Galarza.

Secretary of Education: César Rey Hernández.

Secretary of Labor and Human Resources: Victor Rivera Hernández.

Secretary of Transportation and Public Works: José M. Izquierdo Encarnación.

Secretary of Health: Johnny Rullán.

Secretary of Agriculture: Fernando Toledo.

Secretary of Housing: Ileana Echegoyen.

Secretary of Natural and Environmental Resources: Carlos M. Padín.

Secretary of Consumer Affairs: Fernando Torres Ramírez.

Secretary of Recreation and Sports: Jorge L. Rosario.

Secretary of Economic Development and Commerce: Ramón Cantero Frau.

Secretary of Prisons and Rehabilitation: Victor M. Rivera González.

Secretary of the Family: Yolanda Zayas.

Resident Commissioner in Washington: Aníbal Acevedo Vilá.

GOVERNMENT OFFICES

Office of the Governor: La Fortaleza, PR 00901; tel. (787) 721-7000; fax (787) 721-7483; e-mail webmaster@govpr.org; internet www.fortaleza.gobierno.pr.

Department of Agriculture: POB 10163, San Juan, PR 00908-1163; tel. (787) 721-2120; fax (787) 723-9747.

Department of Consumer Affairs: POB 41059, San Juan, PR 00940-1059; tel. (787) 722-7555; fax (787) 726-6576.

Department of Economic Development and Commerce: POB 4435, San Juan, PR 00902-4435; tel. (787) 721-2400; fax (787) 725-4417.

Department of Education: POB 190759, San Juan, PR 00919; tel. (787) 758-4949; fax (787) 250-0275.

Department of the Family: POB 11398, Santurce, San Juan, PR 00910; tel. (787) 722-7400.

Department of Health: POB 70184, San Juan, PR 00936; tel. (787) 766-1616.

Department of Housing: POB 21365, San Juan, PR 00928-1365; tel. (787) 274-2004; fax (787) 758-9263.

Department of Justice: POB 192, San Juan, PR 00902; tel. (787) 721-2900; fax (787) 724-4770.

Department of Labor and Human Resources: 505 Muñoz Rivera Ave, San Juan, PR 00918; tel. (787) 754-5353; fax (787) 753-9550.

Department of Natural and Environmental Resources: POB 9066600, San Juan, PR 00906-6600; tel. (787) 724-8774; fax (787) 723-4255.

Department of Recreation and Sports: POB 3207, San Juan, PR 00904; tel. (787) 721-2800.

Department of State: POB 3271, San Juan, PR 00902-3271; tel. (787) 722-2121; fax (787) 725-7303.

Department of Transportation and Public Works: POB 41269, San Juan, PR 00940; tel. (787) 722-2929; fax (787) 728-8963.

Department of the Treasury: POB 4515, San Juan, PR 009012; tel. (787) 721-2020; fax (787) 723-6213.

Gubernatorial Election, 7 November 2000

Candidate	Votes	%
Sila María Calderón (PPD)	978,860	48.65
Carlos I. Pesquera (PNP)	919,194	45.68
Rubén Berríos Martínez (PIP) . . .	104,705	5.20
Others†	9,376	0.47
Total	2,012,135	100.00

† Including 4,103 blank votes and 4,564 invalid votes.

Legislature

LEGISLATIVE ASSEMBLY
Senate
(28 members)

President of the Senate: Antonio J. Fas Alzamora.

Election, 7 November 2000

Party	Seats
PPD	19
PNP	8
PIP	1

House of Representatives
(51 members)

Speaker of the House: Carlos Vizcarrondo Irrizarry.

Election, 7 November 2000

Party	Seats
PPD	27
PNP	23
PIP	1

Political Organizations

Partido Comunista Puertorriqueño (PCP) (Puerto Rican Communist Party): f. 1934; seeks full independence and severance of ties with the USA.

Partido Independentista Puertorriqueño (PIP) (Puerto Rican Independence Party): 963 F. D. Roosevelt Ave, Hato Rey, San Juan PR 00918; internet www.independencia.net.; f. 1946; advocates full independence for Puerto Rico as a socialist-democratic republic; c. 60,000 mems; Leader Rubén Berríos Martínez.

Partido Nuevo Progresista (PNP) (New Progressive Party): POB 1992, Fernández Zuncos Station, San Juan 00910-1992; tel. (787) 289-2000; internet www.pnp.org; f. 1967; advocates eventual admission of Puerto Rico as a federated state of the USA; Pres. Leo Díaz Urbina; Sec.-Gen. Hugo Pérez; c. 225,000 mems.

Partido Popular Democrático (PPD) (Popular Democratic Party): 403 Ponce de León Ave, POB 5788, Puerta de Tierra, San Juan, PR 00906; f. 1938; supports continuation and improvement of the present Commonwealth status of Puerto Rico; Pres. and Leader Sila María Calderón; c. 660,000 mems.

Partido Socialista Puertorriqueño (PSP) (Puerto Rican Socialist Party): f. 1971; seeks the establishment of an independent socialist republic; Pres. and Leader Carlos Gallisá; c. 6,000 mems.

Pro Patria National Union: seeks independence for Puerto Rico; encourages assertion of distinct Puerto Rican citizenship as recognized by US Supreme Court in Nov. 1997; Leader Fufi Santori.

Puerto Rican Republican Party: POB 366108, San Juan, PR 00936-6108; tel. (787) 793-4040; Chair. Luis A. Ferré.

Puerto Rico Democratic Party: POB 5788, San Juan, PR 00906; tel. (787) 722-4952; Pres. William Miranda Marín.

The Fuerzas Armadas de Liberación Nacional Puertorriqueña (FALN) (Puerto Rican National Liberation Armed Forces) and the Ejército Popular Boricua (Macheteros; f. 1978; Leader Filiberto Ojeda Ríos), which seek to attain independence through non-electoral means, are not incorporated or registered as political parties.

Judicial System

The Judiciary is vested in the Supreme Court and other courts as may be established by law. The Supreme Court comprises a Chief Justice and six Associate Justices, appointed by the Governor with the consent of the Senate. The lower Judiciary consists of Superior and District Courts and Municipal Justices equally appointed.

There is also a US Federal District Court, whose judges are appointed by the President of the USA. Judges of the US Territorial District Court are appointed by the Governor.

SUPREME COURT OF PUERTO RICO
(POB 2392, Puerta de Tierra, San Juan, PR 00902-2392; tel. (787) 724-3551; fax (787) 725-4910)

Chief Justice: José A. Andréu García.

Justices: Federico Hernández Denton, Myriam Naveira de Rodón, Antonio S. Negrón García, Francisco Rebollo López, Jaime B. Fuster Berlingeri, Baltasar Corrada del Río.

US TERRITORIAL DISTRICT COURT FOR PUERTO RICO
(Federico Degetau Federal Bldg, Carlos Chardón Ave, Hato Rey, PR 00918; tel. (787) 772-3011; internet www.prd.uscourts.gov).

Judges: Héctor M. Laffitte (Chief Judge), Juan M. Pérez-Giménez, José A. Fusté, Salvador E. Casellas, Daniel R. Domínguez, Carmen C. Cerezo; Jay A. García-Gregory.

Religion

About 74% of the population belonged to the Roman Catholic Church at the end of 1999. The Protestant churches active in Puerto Rico include the Episcopalian, Baptist, Presbyterian, Methodist, Seventh-day Adventist, Lutheran, Mennonite, Salvation Army and Christian Science. There is a small Jewish community.

CHRISTIANITY
The Roman Catholic Church

Puerto Rico comprises one archdiocese and four dioceses. At 31 December 1999 there were an estimated 2,705,197 adherents.

Bishops' Conference of Puerto Rico: POB 40682, San Juan, PR 00940-0682; tel. (787) 728-1650; fax (787) 728-1654; f. 1966; Pres. Rt Rev. Roberto Octavio González Nieves, Archbishop of San Juan de Puerto Rico.

Archbishop of San Juan de Puerto Rico: Roberto Octavio González Nieves, Arzobispado, Calle San Jorge 201, Santurce, San Juan, POB 902-1967; tel. (787) 725,4975; fax (787) 723-4040.

Other Christian Churches

Episcopal Church of Puerto Rico: POB 902, St Just, PR 00978; tel. (787) 761-9800; fax (787) 761-0320; e-mail iep@centennialpr.net; internet www.iepanglicom.org.; diocese of the Episcopal Church in the USA, part of the Anglican Communion; Bishop Rt Rev. David Andrés Alvarez.

Evangelical Council of Puerto Rico: Calle El Roble 54, Apdo 21343, Río Piedras, San Juan, PR 00928; tel. (787) 765-6030; fax (787) 765-5977; f. 1954; 6 mem. churches; Pres. Rev. Harry del Valle; Exec. Sec. Rev. Moisés Rosa-Ramos.

BAHÁ'Í FAITH

Spiritual Assembly: POB 11603, San Juan, PR 00910-2703; tel. (787) 763-0982; fax (787) 753-4449; e-mail bahaispr@caribe.net.

JUDAISM

Jewish Community Center: 903 Ponce de León Ave, San Juan, PR 00907; tel. (787) 724-4157; fax (787) 722-4157; e-mail jccpr@coqui.net; f. 1953; conservative congregation with 250 families; Rabbi Alfredo Winter.

There is also a reform congregation with 60 families.

The Press

Puerto Rico has high readership figures for its few newspapers and magazines, as well as for mainland US periodicals. Several newspapers have large additional readerships among the immigrant communities in New York.

DAILIES
(M = morning; S = Sunday)

El Nuevo Día: 404 Ponce de León Ave, POB S-297, San Juan, PR 00902; tel. (787) 793-7070; fax (787) 793-8850; internet www.endi.zonai.com; f. 1970; Publr and Editor ANTONIO LUIS FERRÉ; circ. 220,000 (M), 223,000 (S).

The San Juan Star: POB 364187, San Juan, PR 00936-4187; tel. (787) 793-7152; fax (787) 783-5788; internet www.thesanjuanstar.com; f. 1959; English; Publr ADOLFO COMAS BACARDI; Editor SCOTT WARE; circ. 35,000 (M), 37,000 (S).

El Vocero de Puerto Rico: 206 Ponce de León Ave, POB 3831, San Juan, PR 00902-3831; tel. (787) 721-2300; fax (787) 725-8422; internet www.vocero.com; f. 1974; Publr and Editor GASPAR ROCA; circ 259,000 (M).

PERIODICALS

Buena Salud: 1700 Fernández Juncos Ave, San Juan, PR 00909; tel. (787) 728-7325; f. 1990; monthly; Editor IVONNE LONGUEIRA; circ. 59,000.

Caribbean Business: 1700 Fernández Juncos Ave, San Juan, PR 00909; tel. (787) 728-3000; fax (787) 728-7325; f. 1973; weekly; business and finance; Man. Editor MANUEL A. CASIANO, Jr; circ. 47,000.

Educación: c/o Dept of Education, POB 190759, Hato Rey Station, San Juan, PR 00919; f. 1960; 2 a year; Spanish; Editor JOSÉ GALARZA RODRÍGUEZ; circ. 28,000.

Imagen: 1700 Fernández Juncos Ave, Stop 25, San Juan, PR 00909-2999; tel. (787) 728-4545; fax (787) 728-7325; f. 1986; monthly; women's interest; Editor LIZZY FONFRÍAS; circ. 70,000.

Qué Pasa: POB 4435, Old San Juan Station, San Juan, PR 00905; tel. (787) 721-2400; fax (787) 721-3878; f. 1948; quarterly; English; publ. by Puerto Rico Tourism Co; official tourist guide; Editor KATHRYN ROBINSON; circ. 180,000.

Revista Colegio de Abogados de Puerto Rico: POB 9021900, San Juan, PR 00902-1900; tel. (787) 721-3358; fax (787) 725-0330; e-mail abogados@prtc.net; f. 1914; quarterly; Spanish; law; Editor Lic. ALBERTO MEDINA; circ. 10,000.

Revista del Instituto de Cultura Puertorriqueña: POB 9024184, San Juan, PR 00902-4184; tel. (787) 721-0901; e-mail revista@icp.prstar.net; internet icp.prstar.net; f. 1958; biannual; Spanish; arts, literature, history, theatre, Puerto Rican culture; Editor GLORIA TAPIA; circ. 3,000.

La Torre: POB 23322, UPR Station, San Juan, PR 00931-3322; tel. (787) 250-0000; fax (787) 753-9116; f. 1953; publ. by University of Puerto Rico; quarterly; literary criticism, linguistics, humanities; Editor J. MARTÍNEZ; circ. 1,000.

Vea: POB 190240, San Juan, PR 00919-0240; tel. (787) 721-0095; fax (787) 725-1940; f. 1969; weekly; Spanish; TV and Cable-TV programmes; Editor ENRIQUE PIZZI; circ. 88,000.

El Visitante: POB 41305, San Juan, PR 00940-1305; tel. (787) 728-3710; fax (787) 728-3656; e-mail jortizv@coqui.net; internet www.elvisitante.com; f. 1975; weekly; publ. by the Puerto Rican Conf. of Roman Catholic Bishops; Dir JOSÉ R. ORTIZ VALLADARES; Editor Rev. EFRAÍN ZABALA; circ. 64,000.

FOREIGN NEWS BUREAUX

Agencia EFE (Spain): Cobian's Plaza, Suite 214, Santurce, PR 00910; tel. (787) 723-6023; fax (787) 725-8651; Dir ELÍAS GARCÍA.

Associated Press (USA): Metro Office Park 8, 1 St 108, Guaynabo, PR 00968.

United Press International (UPI) (USA): POB 9655, Santurce, San Juan, PR 00908; tel. (787) 725-4460; Bureau Chief VIRGILIO ESPETIA.

Publishers

Ediciones Huracán Inc.: González 1002, Río Piedras, San Juan, PR 00925; tel. (787) 763-7407; fax (787) 763-7407; f. 1975; textbooks, literature, social studies, history; Dir CARMEN RIVERA-IZCOA.

Editorial Académica, Inc.: 67 Santa Anastacia St, El Vigía, Río Piedras, PR 00926; tel. (787) 760-3879; f. 1988; regional history, politics, government, educational materials, fiction; Dir FIDELIO CALDERÓN.

Editorial Coquí: POB 21992, UPR Station, San Juan, PR 00931.

Editorial Cordillera, Inc.: POB 192363, San Juan, PR 00919-2363; tel. (787) 767-6188; fax (787) 767-8646; e-mail info@editorialcordillera.com; internet www.editorialcordillera.com; f. 1962; Pres. and Treas. CARLOS E. SERRANO.

Editorial Cultural Inc.: POB 21056, Río Piedras, San Juan, PR 00928; tel. (787) 765-9767; f. 1949; general literature; Dir FRANCISCO M. VÁZQUEZ.

Editorial Edil, Inc.: POB 23088, UPR Station, Río Piedras, PR 00931; tel. (787) 753-9381; fax (787) 250-1407; e-mail editedil@coqui.net; internet www.editorialedil.com; f. 1967; university texts, literature, technical and official publs; Man. Dir CONSUELO ANDINO ORTIZ.

Librería y Tienda de Artesanias Instituto de Cultura Puertorriqueña: POB 9024184, San Juan, PR 00902-4184; tel. (787) 724-4295; fax (787) 723-0168; f. 1955; literature, history, poetry, music, textbooks, arts and crafts; Man. Dir MAIRA PIAZZA.

University of Puerto Rico Press (EDUPR): POB 23322, UPR Station, Río Piedras, San Juan, PR 00931-3322; tel. (787) 250-0550; fax (787) 753-9116; f. 1932; general literature, children's literature, Caribbean studies, law, philosophy, science, educational; Dir CARLOS D'ALZINA.

Broadcasting and Communications

TELECOMMUNICATIONS

Puerto Rico Telephone Co (PRTC): GPO Box 360998, San Juan, PR 00936-0998; tel. (787) 782-8282; fax (787) 758-0575; provides all telecommunications services in Puerto Rico; majority control transferred from govt to private-sector GTE Corpn in March 1999.

RADIO AND TELEVISION

There were 120 radio stations and 15 television stations operating in early 2001. The only non-commercial stations are the radio station and the two television stations operated by the Puerto Rico Department of Education. The US Armed Forces also operate a radio station and three television channels. All television services are in colour.

Asociación de Radiodifusores de Puerto Rico (Puerto Rican Radio Broadcasters' Asscn): Caparra Terrace, Delta 1305, San Juan, PR 00920; tel. (787) 783-8810; fax (787) 781-7647; e-mail prbroadcasters@centennialpr.net; f. 1947; 90 mems; Pres. EFRAÍN ARCHILLA DIEZ; Exec. Dir JOSÉ A. RIBAS DOMINICCI.

Finance

(cap. = capital; res = reserves; dep. = deposits; brs = branches; amounts in US dollars)

BANKING
Government Bank

Government Development Bank for Puerto Rico: POB 42001, Minillas Station, San Juan, PR 00940-2001; tel. (787) 728-9200; fax (787) 268-5496; e-mail gdbcomm@prstar.net; internet www.gdb-pur.com; f. 1942; an independent govt agency; acts as fiscal (borrowing) agent to the Commonwealth Govt and its public corpns and provides long- and medium-term loans to private businesses; cap. 1,325.0m., res 219.6m., dep. 4,857.1m. (June 1999); Pres. JUAN AGOSTO ALICEA.

Commercial Banks

Banco Bilbao Vizcaya Puerto Rico: Mendez Vigo St, Mayagüez, PR, 00936; cap. and res 307.5m. dep. 2,594.1m.

Banco Popular: Banco Popular Centre, 209 Muñoz Rivera Ave, San Juan, PR 00936; tel. (787) 765-9800; fax (787) 754-7803; internet www.bancopopular.com; f. 1893; cap. and res 1,345m., dep. 10,696m. (Dec. 2000); Chair., Pres. and CEO RICHARD L. CARRIÓN; 160 brs.

Banco Santander Puerto Rico: 207 Ponce de León Ave, Hato Rey, PR 00918; tel. (787) 759-7070; fax (787) 763-1366; f. 1976; cap. 171.5m., res 232.1m., dep. 4,966.9m. (Dec. 2000); Chair., Pres. and CEO BENITO CANTALAPIEDRA; 76 brs.

Banco de la Vivienda: POB 345, Hato Rey, San Juan, PR 00919; tel. (787) 765-2537; f. 1961; housing bank and finance agency; helps low-income families to purchase houses; cap. and res 44m. (June 1989); Pres. CARMEN S. MELERO; 7 brs.

Royal Bank of Canada: Royal Bank Centre, 225 Ponce de León Ave, POB 190819, San Juan, PR 00919-0819; tel. (787) 250-3900; fax (787) 230-3971; f. 1927; cap. and res 34m., dep. 471.5m. (Oct. 1991); Regional Rep. R. W. BRYDON; 17 brs.

Scotiabank de Puerto Rico: Plaza Scotiabank, 273 Ponce de León Ave, Hato Rey, PR 00918; tel. (787) 758-8989; fax (787) 766-7879; f. 1979; cap. 23.2m., res 128.0m., dep. 915.8m. (Dec. 2000); Chair. D. F. BABENSEE; Pres. I. A. MÉNDEZ; 13 brs.

Savings Banks

FirstBank Puerto Rico: First Federal Bldg, 1519 Ponce de León Ave, POB 9146, Santurce, PR 00908-0146; tel. (787) 729-8200; fax (787) 729-8139; internet www.lbankpr.com; f. 1948; cap. and res 368.3m., dep. 3,363.0m. (Dec. 2000); Pres. ANGEL ALVAREZ-PÉREZ; 40 brs.

Oriental Federal Savings Bank: 2 Hoya y Hernández, POB 1952, Humacao, PR 00792; tel. (787) 852-0378; fax (787) 850-8280; Chair., Pres. and CEO JOSÉ ENRIQUE FERNÁNDEZ.

Ponce Federal Bank, FSB: Villa esq. Concordia, POB 1024, Ponce, PR 00733; tel. (787) 844-8100; fax (787) 848-5380; f. 1958; total assets 1,197.4m. (Sept. 1991); Pres. and CEO HANS H. HERTELL; 19 brs.

R & G Federal Savings Bank: POB 2510, Guaynabo, PR 00970; tel. (787) 766-6677; fax (787) 766-8175; Chair., Pres. and CEO VÍCTOR J. GALÁN.

US Banks in Puerto Rico

Chase Manhattan Bank NA: 254 Muñoz Rivera Ave, San Juan, PR 00936; tel. (787) 753-3400; Man. Dir and Gen. Man. ROBERT C. DÁVILA; 1 br.

Citibank NA: 252 Ponce de León Ave, San Juan, PR 00926; tel. (787) 753-5555; fax (787) 766-3880; Gen. Man. HORACIO IGUST; 7 brs.

SAVINGS AND LOAN ASSOCIATIONS

Caguas Central Federal Savings of Puerto Rico: POB 7199, Caguas, PR 00626; tel. (787) 783-3370; f. 1959; assets 800m.; Pres. LORENZO MUÑOZ FRANCO.

United Federal Savings and Loan Association of Puerto Rico: POB 2647, San Juan, PR 00936; f. 1957; cap. and res 151.4m., assets 164.1m.; Pres. GUILLERMO S. MARQUÉS; 8 brs.

Westernbank Puerto Rico: 19 West McKinley St, Mayagüez, PR 00680; tel. (787) 834-8000; fax (787) 831-5958; cap. and res 250.6m., dep. 2,610.4m. (Dec. 2000); Chair. and CEO Lic. FRANK C. STIPES; 31 brs.

Banking Organization

Puerto Rico Bankers' Association: 820 Banco Popular, San Juan, PR 00918; tel. (787) 753-8630; fax (787) 754-6077; Pres. JUAN A. NET; Exec. Vice-Pres. ARTURO L. CARRIÓN.

INSURANCE

Atlantic Southern Insurance Co: POB 362889, San Juan, PR 00936-2889; tel. (787) 767-9750; fax (787) 764-4707; f. 1945; Chair. DIANE BEAN SCHWARTZ; Pres. RAMÓN L. GALANES.

Caribbean American Life Assurance Co: Scotiabank Plaza, Suite 350, POB 195167, Hato Rey, PR 00919; tel. (787) 250-6470; fax (787) 250-7680; Pres. HARRY LEWIS.

Caribbean Bankers Life Insurance Co: POB 7145, Ponce, PR 00732-7145.

Cooperativa de Seguros Multiples de Puerto Rico: POB 3846, San Juan, PR 00936; general insurance; Pres. EDWIN QUIÑONES SUÁREZ.

La Cruz Azul de Puerto Rico: Road 1, Río Piedras, POB 366068, San Juan, PR 00936-6068; tel. (787) 272-9898; fax (787) 751-5545; health; Exec. Dir JOSÉ JULIÁN ALVAREZ.

General Accident Life Assurance Co of Puerto Rico: POB 363786, San Juan, PR 00936-3786; tel. (787) 758-4888; fax (787) 766-1985; Pres. HERMES VARGAS.

Pan American Life Insurance Co: POB 364865, San Juan, PR 00936-4865; tel. (787) 724-5354; fax (787) 722-0253; e-mail palicpr@prtc.net; Man. MAITE MUÑOZGUREN.

Puerto Rican–American Insurance Co: POB 70333, San Juan, PR 00936-8333; tel. (787) 250-6500; fax (787) 250-5380; f. 1920; total assets 119.9m. (1993); Chair. and CEO RAFAEL A. ROCA; Pres. RODOLFO E. CRISCUOLO.

Security National Life Insurance Co: POB 193309, Hato Rey, PR 00919; tel. (787) 753-6161; fax (787) 758-7409; Pres. CARLOS FERNÁNDEZ.

There are numerous agents, representing Puerto Rican, US and foreign companies.

Trade and Industry

DEVELOPMENT ORGANIZATION

Puerto Rico Industrial Development Co (PRIDCO): POB 362350, San Juan, PR 00936-2350; 355 Roosevelt Ave, Hato Rey, San Juan, PR 00918; tel. (787) 758-4747; fax (787) 764-1415; internet www.pridco.com; public agency responsible for the govt-sponsored industrial development programme; Exec. Dir RAMÓN CANTERO FRAU.

CHAMBERS OF COMMERCE

Chamber of Commerce of Puerto Rico: 100 Calle Tetuán, POB 9024033, San Juan, PR 00902-4033; tel. (787) 721-6060; fax (787) 723-1891; f. 1913; 1,800 mems; Pres. LUIS TORRES LLOMPART; Exec. Vice-Pres. EDGARDO BIGAS.

Chamber of Commerce of Bayamón: POB 2007, Bayamón, PR 00619; tel. (787) 786-4320; 350 mems; Pres. IVÁN A. MARRERO; Exec. Sec. ANGELICA B. DE REMÍREZ.

Chamber of Commerce of Ponce and the South of Puerto Rico: POB 7455, Ponce, PR 00732-7455; tel. (787) 844-4000; fax (787) 844-4705; f. 1885; 500 mems; Pres. CÁNDIDO R. RIVERA TOLLINCHE.

Chamber of Commerce of Río Piedras: 1057 Ponce de León Ave, San Juan, PR 00923; f. 1960; 300 mems; Pres. NEFTALÍ GONZÁLEZ PÉREZ.

Chamber of Commerce of the West of Puerto Rico Inc.: POB 9, Mayagüez, PR 00681; tel. (787) 832-3749; fax (787) 832-4287; e-mail ccopr@coqui.net; f. 1962; 220 mems; Pres. RAFAEL MOLINA.

Official Chamber of Commerce of Spain: POB 894, San Juan, PR 00902; tel. (787) 725-5178; fax (787) 724-0527; f. 1966; promotes Spanish goods; provides information for Spanish exporters and Puerto Rican importers; 300 mems; Pres. MANUEL GARCÍA; Gen. Sec. ANTONIO TRUJILO.

INDUSTRIAL AND TRADE ASSOCIATIONS

Home Builders' Association of Puerto Rico: 1605 Ponce de León Ave, Condominium San Martín, Santurce, San Juan, PR 00909; tel. (787) 723-0279; 150 mems; Pres. FRANKLIN D. LÓPEZ; Exec. Dir WANDA I. NAVAJAS.

Puerto Rico Farm Bureau: Cond. San Martín, 16054 Ponce de León Ave, Suite 403, San Juan, PR 00909-1895; tel. (787) 721-5970; fax (787) 724-6932; f. 1925; over 1,500 mems; Pres. ANTONIO ALVAREZ.

Puerto Rico Manufacturers' Association (PRMA): POB 195477, San Juan, PR 00919-5477; tel. (787) 759-9445; fax (787) 756-7670; e-mail prma@i-lan.com.

Puerto Rico United Retailers Center: POB 190127, San Juan, PR 00919-0127; tel. (787) 759-8405; fax (787) 763-9494; e-mail etorres@centraunido.org; internet www.centraunido.org.; f. 1891; 20,000 mems; Pres. EMILIO TORRES; Exec. Dir RUTH GRACIA.

MAJOR COMPANIES

The following is a selection of some of the principal industrial and commercial companies operating in Puerto Rico.

Construction

Aireko Construction Corpn: Calle 2, Lote 119, El Tuque Ponce 00731; tel. (787) 844-4001; fax (787) 793-3555; e-mail aireko@aireko.com; internet www.aireko.com; f. 1963; construction of commercial, industrial and institutional buildings; sales of US $42m. (1996); Pres. JOSÉ ROSSI; 520 employees.

Hormigonera Mayaguezana Inc.: 637 Calle Post, POB 1343, Mayaguez 00681; tel. (787) 834-6666; fax (787) 834-8380; f. 1953; manufacturers of concrete; sales of US $31m. (1993); Pres. JOSÉ BECHARA; 266 employees.

Massó Enterprises: Calle Rafael Cordero, POB 446, Caguas; tel. (787) 746-1251; fax (787) 743-0707; f. 1963; wholesale of construction materials; sales of US $200m. (1996); Pres. GILDO MASSÓ APONTE; 2,000 employees.

Puerto Rican Cement Co Inc.: POB 364487, San Juan, PR 00936-4487; tel. (787) 783-3000; fax (787) 781-8850; internet www.prcement.com; f. 1938; cement hydraulics; sales of US $148.3m. (1998); Chair. ANTONIO LUIS FERRÉ; Pres. and CEO MIGUEL NAZARIO; 1,069 employees.

Electronics and Computers

Digital Equipment Corporation de Puerto Rico: Rd 362, Km 0.5, POB 11038, Fernández Juncos Station, Santurce 00910; tel. (787) 892-1946; electronic computing equipment; Man. Dir EUTEMIO TOUCET; 1,900 employees.

EMEC Computer and Communication Systems: 1F 30 Lomas Verdes Ave, Royal Palm, Bayamón, PR 00956; tel. (787) 740-4745; fax (787) 740-3425; Pres. RAFAEL HERNÁNDEZ.

ETS/Technical House Inc.: 1723 Piñero Ave, Summit Hills, Rio Piedras, PR 00920; tel. (787) 781-1313; fax (787) 781-2020; e-mail ets@coqui.net; distributors of electronic components and equipment; Pres. JORGE DONATO.

Hewlett-Packard Puerto Rico Co: Carretera 110, Km 5.1, Barrio Aguacate, POB 4048, Aguadilla 00605; tel. (787) 890-6000; fax (787) 890-6262; f. 1980; subsidiary of Hewlett-Packard Co, USA; manufacturers of computer hardware; Man. LUCY CRESPO; 1,700 employees.

Intel Puerto Rico Inc.: Carretera 183, Km 21.2, POB 125, Las Piedras 00771; tel. (787) 733-8080; fax (787) 733-8020; f. 1982; subsidiary of Intel Corpn of the USA; manufacturers of computer parts; Chair. GORDON MOORE; Man. PABLO RODRÍGUEZ; 1,065 employees.

Microsoft Puerto Rico Inc.: Humacao Industrial Park, Road 3, Km 77.8, Humacao 00792; tel. (787) 850-1600; fax (787) 852-7076; f. 1990; subsidiary of Microsoft Corpn of the USA; manufacturers of computer software; Pres. RODOLFO ACEVEDO; 100 employees.

Sensormatic Electronics Corpn Puerto Rico: Carretera 110, Km 5.8, POB 627, San Antonio, Aguadilla 00690; tel. (787) 890-9091; fax (787) 819-2093; f. 1989; subsidiary of Sensormatic Electronic Corpn of the USA; manufacturers of electronic goods, including surveillance equipment; Chair. RONALD ASSAF; Man. JORGE A. SANTOS; 1,500 employees.

Suttle Caribe Inc.: Carretera 3, Km 82.3, Humacao 00791; tel. (787) 852-0643; fax (787) 850-7930; f. 1978; manufacturers of telecommunications equipment; Pres. ALBERTO DOMÍNGUEZ; Man. ADALBERTO SIERRA; 254 employees.

Food and Beverages

Bacardi Corpn: Carretera 165, Km 2.6, Cataño 00962; tel. (787) 788-1500; fax (787) 788-0340; internet www.bacardi.com; f. 1992; distillers and distributors of rum; Pres. ANGEL TORRES; 1,200 employees.

BMJ Foods Puerto Rico Inc.: 1046 Calle Federico Costas, San Juan 00918; tel. (787) 759-9210; fax (787) 763-2000; f. 1989; manages fast-food restaurants; Pres. SAMUEL JOSÉ; 1,100 employees.

Cervecería India Inc.: Blvd Alfonso Valdez 100, Mayaguez 00680; tel. (787) 834-1000; fax (787) 265-7740; f. 1937; brewery and soft drinks manufacturer; sales of US $107m. (1993); Chair. GRACE G. VALDÉS; Exec. Vice-Pres. ISRAEL HILERIO; 400 employees.

Destilería Serralles Inc.: Main Rd 1, Mercedita, San Juan 00715; tel. (787) 840-1000; fax (787) 840-1155; f. 1955; manufacturers of distilled alcoholic beverages; sales of US $80m. (1993); Pres. FELIX SERRALLES; 355 employees.

Fernández & Hermanos Inc., B: Urbanización Industrial Lucetti 305, Carretera 5, Bayamón; tel. (787) 792-7272; fax (787) 288-7291; f. 1888; wholesale of alcoholic beverages and food products; sales of US $270m. (1993); Pres. JOSÉ ANGEL MÉNDEZ; 265 employees.

Goya de Puerto Rico Inc.: Urbanización Industrial Lucetti, Carretera 167, Bayamón 00961; tel. (787) 740-9000; fax (787) 740-5040; f. 1949; manufacturers of canned fruit and vegetables; sales of US $120m. (1993); Pres. FRANCISCO UNANUE; 465 employees.

Star Kist Caribe Inc.: Carretera 341, Barrio Malecon, POB 3690, Marina Santa, Mayaguez 00681; tel. (787) 834-2424; fax (787) 833-5427; f. 1960; subsidiary of H. J. Heinz Co, USA; canned and cured seafood; Pres. ALFREDO CRISTY; Man. MAURICE CALLAGHAN; 4,000 employees.

Pharmaceuticals and Medical Supplies

Abbott Chemicals Inc.: Carretera 2, Km 58, Cruce Davila, POB 278, Barceloneta 00617; tel. (787) 846-3500; fax (787) 846-5132; f. 1968; subsidiary of Abbott Laboratories, USA; manufacturers of pharmaceuticals; Man. JOSÉ LUIS RODRÍGUEZ; 2,400 employees.

Eli Lilly Industries Inc.: Carretera 3, Km 12.6, POB 1198, Pueblo Sta 00986; tel. (787) 257-5555; fax (787) 251-5929; f. 1985; subsidiary of Eli Lilly & Co of the USA; producers of pharmaceuticals; Chair. VAUGHAN BRYSON; Man. MIKE KENDALL; 1,000 employees.

Ethicon Johnson & Johnson Profesional: Carretera 183, Km 8.3, POB 982, San Lorenzo 00754; tel. (787) 783-7070; fax (787) 749-0200; f. 1988; subsidiary of Johnson & Johnson, USA; manufacturers of medical supplies; Man. ARMANDO SOSA; 1,500 employees.

McGaw of Puerto Rico Inc.: Carretera 2, Km 215.7, Parque Industrial El Rayo, POB 729, Sabana Grande 00637; tel. (787) 833-0100; fax (787) 783-3207; f. 1974; subsidiary of Ivax Corpn of the USA; producers of medical supplies; sales of US $88.8m. (1995); Pres. JAMES SWEENEY; Man. ADRIAN RANDS; 925 employees.

Merck Sharpe & Dohme Química de Puerto Rico: Carretera 2, Km 56.7, POB 601, Barceloneta 00617; tel. (787) 846-4110; fax (787) 846-8905; f. 1984; subsidiary of Merck & Co Inc. of the USA; pharmaceuticals manufacturers; Man. EDWIN RODRÍGUEZ; 1,643 employees.

Mova Pharmaceutical Corpn: Carretera 1, Km 34.8, Calle A, Urbanización Villa Blanca, Caguas 00726; tel. (787) 746-8500; fax (787) 743-7669; f. 1968; manufacture and distribution of pharma-

ceuticals; sales of US $50m. (1996); Pres. JOAQUÍN B. VISO; 750 employees.

Upjohn Manufacturing Co Inc.: Carretera 2, Km 60.0, POB 11307, Barceloneta 00617; tel. (787) 782-3578; fax (787) 846-2510; f. 1971; pharmaceutical preparations; Pres. MANUEL HORMAZA;Man. J. MARTIN; 655 employees.

Miscellaneous

Almacenes Pitusa Inc.: Julio N. Matos Industrial Park, Carolina 00985; tel. (787) 757-2800; fax (787) 757-9000; f. 1975; department stores; sales of US $120.2m. (1993); Pres. ISRAEL KOPEL; 3,000 employees.

Avon Mirabella Inc.: POB 3918, Aguadilla 00605; tel. (787) 891-3066; fax (787) 891-3125; f. 1975; manufacturers of jewellery; Chair. and CEO JAMES E. PRESTON; Vice-Pres. and Gen. Man. JOSÉ QUIÑONES; 1,100 employees.

Charlie Auto Sales Inc.: Carretera 168, Km 0.3, Hato Tejas, Bayamón; tel. (787) 798-4660; fax (787) 785-2730; f. 1975; automobile traders; sales of US $93.7m. (1993); Pres. CHARLIE LA COSTA;67 employees.

Colgate-Palmolive (Puerto Rico) Inc.: Puente de Jobos, POB 540, Guayama 00784; tel. (787) 723-5625; fax (787) 864-5053; f. 1988; subsidiary of Colgate-Palmolive Co, USA; manufacturers of toiletries and cleaning products; Man. VÍCTOR SUÁREZ; 90 employees.

Empresas Cordero Badillo Inc.: Avda Ponce de Léon 56, Barrio Amelia, Guaynabo 00962; tel. (787) 749-1400; fax (787) 749-1500; f. 1975; supermarkets; sales of US $300m. (1993); Chair. ATILANO CORDERO BADILLO; 1,400 employees.

Hilton International of Puerto Rico (Caribe Hilton International Hotel): Los Rosales, San Juan 00901; tel. and fax (787) 721-0303; internet www.caribehilton.com; f. 1981; hotel management; Man. RAÚL BUSTAMANTE; 875 employees.

Industrias Vassallo Inc.: POB 473, Coto Laurel, PR 00780; tel. (787) 848-1515; fax (787) 259-1302; internet www.vassalloindustries .com; f. 1969; manufacturers of plastics; sales US $40m. (1996); Pres. and Gen. Man. SALVADOR VASSALLO; 300 employees.

Olympic Mills Corpn: Carretera 20, Km 3.8, POB 1669, Guaynabo 00970; tel. (787) 720-1000; fax (787) 720-5166; internet www .olympicmills.com; f. 1949; manufacturers of clothing; sales of US $31.2m. (1995); Chair. FRANCISCO CARVAJAL; Pres. DENNIS D. BRADFORD; 1,200 employees.

Phillips Puerto Rico Corpn Inc.: Carretera 710, Km 1, Guayama, PR 00784; tel. (787) 864-1515; fax (787) 864-2302; f. 1967; subsidiary of Phillips Petroleum Co, USA; petroleum refining; Pres. JOHN R. HENNON; 284 employees.

UTILITIES
Electricity

Autoridad de Energía Eléctrica de Puerto Rico: POB 364267, San Juan, PR 00936-4267: tel. (787) 289-4666; fax (787) 289-4665; internet www.prepa.com; govt-owned electricity corpn, opened to private co-generators in the mid-1990s; installed capacity of 4,389 MW; Chair. MIGUEL A. CORDERO LÓPEZ.

TRADE UNIONS

American Federation of Labor–Congress of Industrial Organizations (AFL–CIO): San Juan; c. 60,000 mems; Regional Dir AGUSTÍN BENÍTEZ.

Central Puertorriqueña de Trabajadores (CPT): POB 364084, San Juan, PR 00936-4084; tel. (787) 781-6649; fax (787) 277-9290; f. 1982; Pres. FEDERICO TORRES MONTALVO.

Confederación General de Trabajadores de Puerto Rico: 620 San Antonio St, San Juan, PR 00907; f. 1939; Pres. FRANCISCO COLÓN GORDIANY; 35,000 mems.

Federación del Trabajo de Puerto Rico (AFL-CIO): POB S-1648, San Juan, PR 00903; tel. (787) 722-4012; f. 1952; Pres. HIPÓLITO MARCANO; Sec.-Treas. CLIFFORD W. DEPIN; 200,000 mems.

Puerto Rico Industrial Workers' Union, Inc.: POB 22014, UPR Station, San Juan, PR 00931; Pres. DAVID MUÑOZ HERNÁNDEZ.

Sindicato Empleados de Equipo Pesado, Construcción y Ramas Anexas de Puerto Rico, Inc. (Construction and Allied Trades Union): Calle Hicaco 95–Urb. Milaville, Río Piedras, San Juan, PR 00926; f. 1954; Pres. JESÚS M. AGOSTO; 950 mems.

Sindicato de Obreros Unidos del Sur de Puerto Rico (United Workers' Union of South Puerto Rico): POB 106, Salinas, PR 00751; f. 1961; Pres. JOSÉ CARABALLO; 52,000 mems.

Unión General de Trabajadores de Puerto Rico: Apdo 29247, Estación de Infantería, Río Piedras, San Juan, PR 00929; tel. (787) 751-5350; fax (787) 751-7604; f. 1965; Pres. JUAN G. ELIZA-COLÓN; Sec.-Treas. OSVALDO ROMERO-PIZARRO.

Unión de Trabajadores de la Industría Eléctrica y Riego de Puerto Rico: POB 13068, Santurce, San Juan, PR 00908; tel. (787) 721-1700; Pres. HERMINIO MARTÍNEZ RODRÍGUEZ; Sec.-Treas. RAFAEL ORTEGA; 6,000 mems.

Transport

There are no passenger railways in Puerto Rico, although in 1996 construction began of a 16.6-km (10.3-mile) urban rail system in greater San Juan. The system, which would cost US \$1,200m., was expected to become operational in 2001.

Ponce and Guayama Railway: Aguirre, PR 00608; tel. (787) 853-3810; owned by the Corporación Azucarera de Puerto Rico; transports sugar cane over 96 km of track route; Exec. Dir A. MARTÍNEZ; Gen. Supt J. RODRÍGUEZ.

ROADS

The road network totalled 14,400 km (8,950 miles) in 1996. A modern highway system links all cities and towns along the coast and cross-country. A highways authority oversees the design and construction of roads, highways and bridges. In 2001 improvements to Routes 53 and 66 were underway.

SHIPPING

There are nine major ports in the island, the principal ones being San Juan, Ponce and Mayagüez. Other ports include Guayama, Guayanilla, Guánica, Yabucoa, Aguirre, Aguadilla, Fajardo, Arecibo, Humacao and Arroyo. San Juan, one of the finest and longest all-weather natural harbours in the Caribbean, is the main port of entry for foodstuffs and raw materials and for shipping finished industrial products. In 1992 it handled 14.3m. tons of cargo. Passenger traffic is limited to tourist cruise vessels, which brought an estimated 1.0m. visitors to Puerto Rico in 1997.

Puerto Rico Ports Authority: POB 362829, San Juan, PR 00936-2829; tel. (787) 729-8805; fax (787) 722-7867; manages and administers all ports and airports; Exec. Dir Dr HERMAN SULSONA.

CIVIL AVIATION

The principal airports are at San Juan (Carolina), Ponce, Mayagüez and Aguadilla.

Tourism

An estimated 4,221,300 tourists visited Puerto Rico in 1999/2000, when revenue from this source was estimated at US \$2,139m. About three-quarters of tourist visitors (excluding cruise-ship passengers) were from the mainland USA. In mid-2001 several major tourist developments were under construction.

Commonwealth of Puerto Rico Tourism Co: POB 9023960, San Juan, PR 00902-3960; tel. (787) 721-2400; fax (787) 725-4417; internet www.prtourism.com; Exec. Dir JOSÉ A. CORUJO.

Defence

The USA is responsible for the defence of Puerto Rico. The US Navy maintains a large base at Roosevelt Roads in eastern Puerto Rico, which includes large sections of the nearby island of Vieques. Puerto Rico has a paramilitary National Guard of some 11,000 men, which is funded mainly by the US Department of Defense.

Education

The public education system is centrally administered by the Department of Education. Education is compulsory for children between six and 16 years of age. The 12-year curriculum, beginning at five years of age, is subdivided into six grades of elementary school, three years at junior high school and three years at senior high school. Vocational schools at the high school level and kindergartens also form part of the public education system. Instruction is conducted in Spanish, but English is a required subject at all levels. In 1985 there were 1,782 public day schools, 818 private elementary and secondary schools and 69 public and private institutions of higher education. The State University system consists of three principal campuses and six regional colleges. In the academic year 1995/96 there were 627,620 pupils attending public day schools and 148,004 pupils were enrolled at accredited private schools. In 1989/90 more than 20% of the Commonwealth budget was allocated to education. In 1995, according to estimates by UNESCO, the average rate of adult illiteracy was 7.2% (males 7.3%; females 7.2%).

Bibliography

For works on the Caribbean generally, see Select Bibliography (Books).

Acosta-Belen, E. *The Puerto Rican Woman: Perspectives on Culture, History and Society.* New York, NY, Praeger Publrs, 1986.

Baver, S. L. *The Political Economy of Colonialism, the State and Industrialization in Puerto Rico.* London, Praeger Publrs, 1993.

Caban, P. A. 'Industrial Transformation and Labour Relations in Puerto Rico from the Operation Bootstrap to the 1970s', in *Journal of Latin American Studies*, Vol. 21, 3 (Oct.). 1989.

Constructing a Colonial People: Puerto Rico and the United States, 1898–1932. Boulder, CO, Westview Press, 1999.

Carr, R. *Puerto Rico: A Colonial Experiment.* New York, NY, Vintage Books, 1984.

Cruz Monclova, L. *Historia de Puerto Rico.* San Juan, Editorial Universitaria, 1963.

Dietz, J. L. *Economic History of Puerto Rico: Institutional Change and Capitalist Development.* Princeton, NJ, Princeton University Press, 1987.

Duffy Burnett, C., and Marshall, B. (Eds). *Foreign in a Domestic Sense : Puerto Rico, American Expansion, and the Constitution.* American Encounters/Global Interactions, Durham, MC, Duke University Press, 2001.

Fernández, R. *The Disenchanted Island: Puerto Rico and the United States in the Twentieth Century.* London, Praeger Publrs, 1993.

Fernández, R., Méndez Méndez, S., and Cueto, G. *Puerto Rico Past and Present: An Encyclopedia.* Westport, CT, Greenwood Press, 1998.

Fernández Méndez, E. *Historia cultural de Puerto Rico.* San Juan, Ediciones Cemí, 1970.

Fowlie-Flores, F. (Ed). *Index to Puerto Rican Collective Biography.* London, Greenwood, 1987.

González, J. L. *El país de cuatro pisos.* Río Piedras, Ediciones Piedras, 1980.

Lewis, G. K. *Puerto Rico: Freedom and Power in the Caribbean.* New York, NY, Monthly Review Press, 1963.

Maldonado-Denis, M. *Puerto Rico: A Socio-Historic Interpretation.* New York, NY, Vintage Press, 1972.

Monge, J. T. *Puerto Rico: The Trials of the Oldest Colony in the World.* New Haven, Yale, CT, Universal Press, 1999

Morales, V. J. *Puerto Rican Poverty and Migration.* New York, NY, Praeger Publrs, 1986.

Morales-Carrión, A. *Puerto Rico: A Political and Cultural History.* New York, NY, N. W. Norton & Co, 1983.

Pantojas, G. E. 'Puerto Rican Population Revisited: The PPD During the 1940s', in *Journal of Latin American Studies*, Vol. 21, 3 (Oct.). 1989.

Perloff, H. S. *Puerto Rico's Economic Future: A Study in Planned Development.* Chicago, IL, University of Chicago Press, 1950.

Rivera, A. I. 'A Hesitant Unveiling of America's Colonial Problems in Puerto Rico', in *Journal of Latin American Studies*, Vol. 18, 2 (Nov.). 1986.

Rodríguez, C. E., and Sánchez K. V. (Eds). *Historical Perspectives on Puerto Rican Survival in the United States.* Princeton, NJ, Markus Weiner, 1996.

Santiago, E. *America's Dream.* London, Virago, 1997.

Schmidt-Nowara, C. *Empire and Antislavery; Spain, Cuba and Puerto Rico, 1833–1874.* Pittsburgh, PA, University of Pittsburgh Press, 1999.

Wells, H. *The Modernization of Puerto Rico: A Political Study of Changing Values and Institutions.* Cambridge, MA, Harvard University Press, 1969.

SAINT CHRISTOPHER* AND NEVIS

Area: 261.6 sq km (102.2 sq miles): Saint Christopher 168.4 sq km, Nevis 93.2 sq km.

Population (World Bank estimate, 1999): 40,880.

Capital: Basseterre (estimated population 12,220 in 1994), on Saint Christopher.

Language: English.

Religion: Predominantly Christianity; the main denomination is the (Anglican) Church in the Province of the West Indies.

Climate: Tropical, tempered by sea winds; temperature varies between 17°C and 33°C (62°F–92°F); average annual rainfall 1,400 mm (55 in) on Saint Christopher and 1,220 mm (48 in) on Nevis.

Time: GMT –4 hours.

Public Holidays: 2002: 1 January (New Year's Day), 2 January (Carnival), 29 March (Good Friday), 1 April (Easter Monday), 6 May (Labour Day), 20 May (Whit Monday), 8 June (Queen's Official Birthday), 5 August (August Monday), 6 August (Culturama, Nevis only), 19 September (Independence Day), 14 November (Prince of Wales' Birthday), 25–26 December (Christmas), 31 December (Carnival). **2003:** 1 January (New Year's Day), 2 January (Carnival), 18 April (Good Friday), 21 April (Easter Monday), 5 May (Labour Day), 9 June (Whit Monday), 14 June (Queen's Official Birthday), 4 August (August Monday), 5 August (Culturama, Nevis only), 19 September (Independence Day), 14 November (Prince of Wales' Birthday), 25–26 December (Christmas), 31 December (Carnival).

Currency: Eastern Caribbean dollar; US $1 = EC $2.70 (fixed rate since July 1976); EC $100 = £25.87 = US $37.04 = €41.73 (30 April 2001).

Weights and Measures: Imperial.

History

From 1816 Saint Christopher, Nevis, Anguilla and the British Virgin Islands were administered as a single colony, prior to the formation of the Leeward Islands Federation in 1871. Saint Christopher–Nevis–Anguilla belonged to the West Indies Federation in 1958–62 and gained associated statehood in 1967. However, Anguilla rejected rule from Saint Christopher in 1967 and reverted to the state of a *de facto* British dependency in 1971 (see Anguilla chapter). Full independence for the two remaining islands was originally scheduled for 1980, but was delayed in order to grant a greater degree of autonomy to Nevis. The Federation of Saint Christopher and Nevis finally became independent on 19 September 1983.

The Government was led for nearly 30 years by the Labour Party, which was replaced in the 1980 elections by a coalition of the People's Action Movement (PAM) and the Nevis Reformation Party (NRP), under the leadership of Dr Kennedy A. Simmonds of the PAM. The PAM/NRP coalition retained power after the 1984 and 1989 general elections, and as a minority administration after the 1993 election. This unstable political situation, as well as escalating concern about rising levels of drugs-related crime, prompted an early general election, on 3 July 1995. The Labour Party returned to power under Denzil Douglas, having won seven of the 11 elected seats. The National Assembly also contained three or four nominated Senators. Under the federal system, there was a separate Nevis Island Assembly, dominated by the Concerned Citizens' Movement under Vance Amory, who was the Premier of the Nevis Island Administration. Deteriorating relations between Amory and the central Government prompted the initiation of secessionary legislative proposals in the Nevis Island Assembly in July 1996. A referendum on the issue of secession was held on 10 August 1998, with 61.7%, less than the two-thirds' majority required by the Constitution, voting for secession. The leaders of the two islands immediately announced that they would work to improve relations. In

December the Government appointed a seven-member Constitutional Task Force to draft a new constitution. In March 1999 the Task Force met with political leaders from both islands, and a process of public consultation was initiated throughout the islands. On 21 September 1998 'Hurricane Georges' struck Saint Christopher and Nevis, causing great destruction to the islands' infrastructure. Preliminary estimates indicated that the overall damage amounted to US $400m. The country attracted international criticism in July 1998, upon the reintroduction of capital punishment.

At the general election of 6 March 2000, the Labour Party won all eight seats available on St Christopher (with 64.5% of the votes cast), gaining the seat previously held by the PAM, which won 35.5% of the votes. There was no change in the position on Nevis, where the CCM retained its two seats to the NRP's one. The PAM subsequently accused the Government of widespread electoral fraud, and announced that the party would not contest any future elections until the electoral register had been revised and voter identification cards issued. In June 2000 the USA announced plans to seek the extradition of Kenrick Simmonds, son of the then PAM leader, Kennedy Simmonds, on cocaine-trafficking charges. In February 2001 a 10pm government curfew for all children under 15 was introduced in an effort to reduce youth crime and the spread of HIV infection. In June 2001, with crime becoming an increasing problem on the island and affecting the tourist industry, the Government sought to persuade the US Navy to relocate one of its bases to St Christopher. Douglas hoped the islands would derive 'economic, social and financial' benefits from the US presence.

Economy

The islands' principal economic activity is the sugar industry (nationalized in 1975), with sugar and sugar products accounting for an estimated 21% of total export earnings in 1999. 'Hurricane Georges', which struck Saint Christopher and Nevis in September 1998, resulted in the loss of an estimated 25% of the 1999 sugar crop. In 1998 the sugar cane harvest totalled 240,077 metric tons. However, by 2000 production had fallen to 188,373 metric tons. In December 2000 the Saint Christopher and Nevis Chamber of Commerce recommended the closure of the islands' state-owned sugar industry, which continued to run up significant losses. The Government attempted to diversify the agricultural sector to reduce the economy's vulnerability to fluctuations in the world price of sugar. As well as encouraging greater production of traditional crops, such as sweet potatoes, yams and bananas, the cultivation of groundnuts, rice and coffee was developed in the 1980s. Sea-island cotton and coconuts replaced the traditional sugar crop on the smallholdings of Nevis. Fishing became an increasingly important commercial activity. Nevertheless, the agricultural sector (including forestry and fishing) provided only 3.4% of gross domestic product (GDP) in 1999, although it employed some 14.7% of the work-force in 1994

The Government encouraged the development of manufacturing activity, which provided some 15% of GDP by the beginning of the 1990s, though this figure declined to 9.6% by 1999. The decrease in the manufacturing sector was, in part, owing to a decline in activity in the sugar-processing sector. In 1999, however, manufacturing GDP increased by an estimated 8.0%. Industry as a whole (including mining, manufacturing, construction and public utilities) provided an estimated 23.4% of GDP in 1999. Excluding sugar manufacturing, the sector employed 21.0% of the working population in 1994. Activity is mainly connected with the construction industry (the GDP of which expanded by 7.0% in 1998 and by an estimated 6.8% in 1999). Remittances sent home by workers abroad provided another important source of income.

Tourism was an increasingly major contributor to the economy throughout the 1990s, and in 1998 tourism accounted for an estimated 8.7% of GDP and in 1994 some 12.8% of the employed

---

* While this island is officially called Saint Christopher as part of the state, the name is usually abbreviated to St Kitts.

population were engaged in tourism-related activities. In 1999 the number of yacht and cruise-ship visitors increased by 58.5%, to 162,800, while the number of stop-over tourists increased by 5.5%, to 93,190. Visitor numbers declined, however, in 1999, while tourist revenues, which had increased by 6.2% in 1998, declined by 11.7% in 1999 to EC $182.1m. However, as the hurricane-damaged tourist infrastructure of the island is rebuilt, the tourist sector is expected to recover. In May 2000 the Financial Stability Forum (FSF) categorized Saint Christopher and Nevis's banking supervision in the lowest group. In June the Organisation for Economic Co-operation and Development (OECD) included Saint Christopher and Nevis on a list of tax havens and in the same month it was also included on a list of 'non-co-operative' governments in the fight against 'money-laundering' by the Financial Action Task Force (FATF, based

at the OECD Secretariat). By July 2001, Saint Christopher and Nevis remained on the FATF report. Following an assessment of the islands' economic performance by the International Monetary Fund in December 2000, which emphasized the need to reduce the public sector deficit, Prime Minister Douglas raised consumption tax by 5%, although he exempted a number of basic wage goods. He also announced investment incentives for companies, cutting corporation tax to 35% from 2002. According to a Caribbean Development Bank report of June 2001, Saint Christopher and Nevis' economy grew by 7.5% in 2000, mainly as a result of the increase in the construction sector in the aftermath of hurricane damage. In July 2001 Prime Minister Douglas announced that trade liberalization, oil price rises and retraining the work-force in the declining sugar industry were his Government's economic priorities.

Statistical Survey

Source (unless otherwise stated): St Kitts and Nevis Information Service, Ministry of Tourism, Information, Telecommunications, Commerce and Consumer Affairs, Church St, POB 186, Basseterre; tel. 465-2521; e-mail skninfo@caribsurf.com.

AREA AND POPULATION

Area (sq km): 269.4 (St Christopher 176.1, Nevis 93.3).

Population: 40,618 (males 19,933; females 20,685) at census of 12 May 1991; 42,460 (official estimate) at mid-1999.

Density (mid-1999): 157.6 per sq km.

Principal Town (estimated population, 1994): Basseterre (capital) 12,220.

Births and Deaths (1999): Registered live births 864 (estimated birth rate 20.3 per 1,000); Registered deaths 418 (estimated death rate 9.8 per 1,000).

Expectation of life (years at birth, 1999) males 68.02; females 71.88.

Employment (labour force survey, 1994): Sugar cane production/manufacturing 1,525; Non-sugar agriculture 914; Mining and quarrying 29; Manufacturing (excl. sugar) 1,290; Electricity, gas and water 416; Construction 1,745; Trade (except tourism) 1,249; Tourism 2,118; Transport and communications 534; Business and general services 3,708; Government services 2,738; Other statutory bodies 342; *Total* 16,608 (Saint Christopher 12,516, Nevis 4,092). Source: IMF, *St Kitts and Nevis: Recent Economic Developments* (August 1997).

AGRICULTURE, ETC.

Principal Crops ('000 metric tons, 2000): Roots and tubers 1; Coconuts 1; Vegetables and melons 1; Sugar cane 188; Fruits and berries 1 (FAO estimate). Source: FAO.

Livestock ('000 head, estimates, 2000): Cattle 3.6; Sheep 5.5; Goats 5.6.

Fishing (metric tons, live weight, 1998): Capture 281 (Groupers 11, Surgeonfishes 9, Needlefishes, etc. 60, Flyingfishes 38, Bigeye scad 20, Common dolphinfish 34, Tuna-like fishes 10, Caribbean spiny lobster 21, Stromboid conchs 22); Aquaculture 4 (FAO estimate); Total catch 285. Figures exclude aquatic plants and mammals. Source: FAO, *Yearbook of Fishery Statistics*.
1999: Total catch 264 metric tons.

INDUSTRY

Raw Sugar (2000): 18,051 metric tons.

Electric Energy (1999): 96.7 million kWh.

FINANCE

Currency and Exchange Rates: 100 cents = 1 Eastern Caribbean dollar (EC $). *Sterling, US Dollar and Euro Equivalents* (30 April 2001): £1 sterling = EC $3.866; US $1 = EC $2.700; €1 = EC $2.396; EC $100 = £25.87 = US $37.04 = €41.73. *Exchange Rate:* Fixed at US $1 = EC $2.70 since July 1976.

Budget (preliminary, EC $ million, 1999): *Revenue:* Revenue from taxation 183.5 (of which, Taxes on international trade and transactions 93.0); Other current revenue 67.0; Capital revenue 1.1; Foreign grants 1.2; Total 252.9. *Expenditure:* Personal emoluments 91.6; Wages 30.3; Goods and services 84.8; Public debt charges 32.0; Transfers 23.6; Capital expenditure and net lending 36.5; Total

298.8. Source: IMF, *St Kitts and Nevis: Recent Economic Developments* (November 2000).

International Reserves (US $ million at 31 December 2000): Reserve position in IMF 0.11; Foreign exchange 45.09; Total 45.20. Source: IMF, *International Financial Statistics*.

Money Supply (EC $ million at 31 December 2000): Currency outside banks 40.59; Demand deposits at deposit money banks 79.30; Total money (incl. others) 120.98. Source: IMF, *International Financial Statistics*.

Cost of Living (Consumer price index; base: 1995 = 100): 111.2 in 1997; 115.0 in 1998; 119.5 in 1999.

Gross Domestic Product (EC $ million at current prices): 625.07 in 1997; 652.04 in 1998; 693.34 in 1999.

Expenditure on the Gross Domestic Product (EC $ million, 1999): Government final consumption expenditure 174.6; Private final consumption expenditure 525.5; Gross capital formation 303.4; *Total domestic expenditure* 1,003.5; Exports of goods and services 375.3; *Less* Imports of goods and services 566.9; *GDP in purchasers' values* 811.8. Source: IMF, *International Financial Statistics*.

Gross Domestic Product by Economic Activity (EC $ million at current factor cost, preliminary, 1999): Agriculture, hunting, forestry and fishing 24.9; Mining and quarrying 2.3; Manufacturing 70.5; Electricity and water 12.9; Construction 89.4; Wholesale and retail trade 107.2; Restaurants and hotels 55.6; Transport 51.2; Communications 45.2; Finance and insurance 93.6; Real estate and housing 19.2; Government services 129.5; Other community, social and personal services 29.5; Sub-total 731.1; *Less* Imputed bank service charge 48.6; Total 682.5.

Balance of Payments (EC $ million, 2000): Exports of goods f.o.b. 143.4; Imports of goods f.o.b. −438.7; *Trade balance* −295.3; Exports of services 278.6; Imports of services −193.1; *Balance on goods and services* −209.7; Other income received (net) −82.4; *Balance on goods, services and income* −292.1; Current transfers received (net) 81.3; *Current balance* −210.7; Capital account (net) 15.6; Direct investment from abroad (net) 342.2; Portfolio investment (net) 0.0; Other investment (net) 8.7; Net errors and omissions −144.3; *Overall balance* 11.4.

EXTERNAL TRADE

Principal Commodities (EC $ million, estimates, 1999): *Imports c.i.f.:* Food and live animals 60.2; Beverages and tobacco 12.1; Crude materials (inedible) except fuels 8.7; Mineral fuels, lubricants, etc. 23.7; Chemicals 29.5; Basic manufactures 80.6; Machinery and transport equipment 106.7; Miscellaneous manufactured articles 66.4; Total (incl. others) 391.7. *Exports f.o.b.:* Food and live animals 62.1; Machinery and transport equipment 47.7; Miscellaneous manufactured articles 5.0; Total (incl. others) 129.2. Source: IMF, *St Kitts and Nevis: Recent Economic Developments* (November 2000).

Principal Trading Partners (EC $ million, 2000): *Imports:* Canada 37.9; Japan 17.7; Puerto Rico 22.5; Trinidad and Tobago 52.8; United Kingdom 30.4; USA 255.3; Total (incl. others) 477.5. *Exports* (excl. re-exports): Dominica 1.3; United Kingdom 16.1; USA 49.6; Total (incl. others) 73.9.

TRANSPORT

Road Traffic (registered motor vehicles): 7,398 in 1997; 11,352 in 1998; 12,432 in 1999.

Shipping: *Arrivals* (1999): 1,911. *International Freight Traffic* ('000 metric tons, 1999): Goods loaded 27.2; Goods unloaded 202.2.

Civil Aviation (aircraft arrivals): 26,400 in 1997; 24,800 in 1998; 23,500 in 1999.

TOURISM

Tourist Arrivals: ('000): 194.3 (88.3 stop-over visitors, 102.7 yacht and cruise-ship passengers, 3.3 excursionists) in 1997; 258.9 (93.2 stop-over visitors, 162.8 yacht and cruise-ship passengers, 2.9 excursionists) in 1998: 230.8 (84.0 stop-over visitors, 143.8 yacht and cruise-ship passengers, 3.0 excursionists) in 1999.

Tourist Receipts (EC $ million): 194.2 in 1997; 206.2 in 1998; 182.1 in 1999.

COMMUNICATIONS MEDIA

Non-Daily Newspapers (1999): Titles 4; Circulation 34,000 (1996).
Radio Receivers ('000 in use, 1997): 28.
Television Receivers ('000 in use, 1997): 10.
Telephones ('000 main lines in use, 1999): 18.3.
Mobile Cellular Telephones (subscribers, 1996): 300.
Telefax Stations (1996): 450.
Sources: mainly UNESCO, *Statistical Yearbook*; UN, *Statistical Yearbook*.

EDUCATION

Pre-primary (1999/2000): 77 schools; 184 teachers; 2,649 pupils.
Primary (1998/99): 23 schools; 293 teachers; 5,497 pupils.
Secondary (1998/99): 7 schools; 345 teachers; 4,258 pupils.
Tertiary (1999/2000): 1 institution; 64 teachers (1992/93); 518 students.

Directory

The Constitution

The Constitution of the Federation of Saint Christopher and Nevis took effect from 19 September 1983, when the territory achieved independence. Its main provisions are summarized below:

FUNDAMENTAL RIGHTS AND FREEDOMS

Regardless of race, place of origin, political opinion, colour, creed or sex, but subject to respect for the rights and freedoms of others and for the public interest, every person in Saint Christopher and Nevis is entitled to the rights of life, liberty, security of person, equality before the law and the protection of the law. Freedom of conscience, of expression, of assembly and association is guaranteed, and the inviolability of personal privacy, family life and property is maintained. Protection is afforded from slavery, forced labour, torture and inhuman treatment.

THE GOVERNOR-GENERAL

The Governor-General is appointed by the British monarch, whom the Governor-General represents locally. The Governor-General must be a citizen of Saint Christopher and Nevis, and must appoint a Deputy Governor-General, in accordance with the wishes of the Premier of Nevis, to represent the Governor-General on that island.

PARLIAMENT

Parliament consists of the British monarch, represented by the Governor-General, and the National Assembly, which includes a Speaker, three (or, if a nominated member is Attorney-General, four) nominated members (Senators) and 11 elected members (Representatives). Senators are appointed by the Governor-General; one on the advice of the Leader of the Opposition, and the other two in accordance with the wishes of the Prime Minister. The Representatives are elected by universal suffrage, one from each of the 11 single-member constituencies.

Every citizen over the age of 18 years is eligible to vote. Parliament may alter any of the provisions of the Constitution.

THE EXECUTIVE

Executive authority is vested in the British monarch, as Head of State, and is exercised on the monarch's behalf by the Governor-General, either directly or through subordinate officers. The Governor-General appoints as Prime Minister that Representative who, in the Governor-General's opinion, appears to be best able to command the support of the majority of the Representatives. Other ministerial appointments are made by the Governor-General, in consultation with the Prime Minister, from among the members of the National Assembly. The Governor-General may remove the Prime Minister from office if a resolution of 'no confidence' in the Government is passed by the National Assembly and if the Prime Minister does not resign within three days or advise the Governor-General to dissolve Parliament.

The Cabinet consists of the Prime Minister and other Ministers. When the office of Attorney-General is a public office, the Attorney-General shall, by virtue of holding that office, be a member of the Cabinet in addition to the other Ministers. The Governor-General appoints as Leader of the Opposition in the National Assembly that Representative who, in the Governor-General's opinion, appears to be best able to command the support of the majority of the Representatives who do not support the Government.

CITIZENSHIP

All persons born in Saint Christopher and Nevis before independence who, immediately before independence, were citizens of the United Kingdom and Colonies automatically become citizens of Saint Christopher and Nevis. All persons born in Saint Christopher and Nevis after independence automatically acquire citizenship, as do those born outside Saint Christopher and Nevis after independence to a parent possessing citizenship. There are provisions for the acquisition of citizenship by those to whom it is not automatically granted.

THE ISLAND OF NEVIS

There is a Legislature for the island of Nevis which consists of the British monarch, represented by the Governor-General, and the Nevis Island Assembly. The Assembly consists of three nominated members (one appointed by the Governor-General in accordance with the advice of the Leader of the Opposition in the Assembly, and two appointed by the Governor-General in accordance with the advice of the Premier) and such number of elected members as corresponds directly with the number of electoral districts on the island.

There is a Nevis Island Administration, consisting of a premier and two other members who are appointed by the Governor-General. The Governor-General appoints the Premier as the person who, in the Governor-General's opinion, is best able to command the support of the majority of the elected members of the Assembly. The other members of the Administration are appointed by the Governor-General, acting in accordance with the wishes of the Premier. The Administration has exclusive responsibility for administration within the island of Nevis, in accordance with the provisions of any relevant laws.

The Nevis Island Legislature may provide that the island of Nevis is to cease to belong to the Federation of Saint Christopher and Nevis, in which case this Constitution would cease to have effect in the island of Nevis. Provisions for the possible secession of the island contain the following requirements: that the island must give full and detailed proposals for the future Constitution of the island of Nevis, which must be laid before the Assembly for a period of at least six months prior to the proposed date of secession; that a two-thirds majority has been gained in a referendum which is to be held after the Assembly has passed the motion.

The Government

Head of State: HM Queen ELIZABETH II.

Governor-General: Sir CUTHBERT MONTROVILLE SEBASTIAN (took office 1 January 1996).

CABINET
(August 2001)

Prime Minister and Minister of Finance, Development, Planning and National Security: Dr DENZIL DOUGLAS.

Deputy Prime Minister and Minister of CARICOM Affairs, International Trade, Labour, Social Security, Telecommunications and Technology: SAM CONDOR.

Minister of Tourism, Commerce and Consumer Affairs: G. A. DWYER ASTAPHAN.

Minister of Health and the Environment: Dr EARL ASIM MARTIN.

Minister of Agriculture, Fisheries, Co-operatives, Lands and Housing: CEDRIC ROY LIBURD.

Minister of Information, Youth, Sports and Culture: JACINTH LORNA HENRY-MARTIN.

Minister of Public Works, Utilities, Transport and Posts: HALVA HENDRICKSON.

Minister of Social Development, Community and Gender Affairs: RUPERT EMANUEL HERBERT.

Minister of Education and Foreign Affairs: TIMOTHY HARRIS.

Attorney-General and Minister of Justice and Legal Affairs: DELANO BART.

MINISTRIES

Office of the Governor-General: Government House, Basseterre; tel. 465-2315.

Government Headquarters: Church St, POB 186, Basseterre; tel. 465-2521; fax 465-1001; e-mail sknis@stkittsnevis.net; internet www.stkittsnevis.net.

Ministry of Agriculture, Fisheries, Co-operatives, Lands and Housing: Church St, POB 186, Basseterre; tel. 465-2521; fax 465-0604.

Ministry of Communications, Works and Public Utilities: Church St, POB 186, Basseterre; tel. 465-2521; fax 465-9069.

Ministry of Education, Labour and Social Security: Church St, POB 186, Basseterre; tel. 465-2521; fax 465-2635; e-mail minelsc@caribsurf.com.

Ministry of Finance, Development, Planning and National Security: Church St, POB 186, Basseterre; tel. 465-2521; fax 465-1532; e-mail skbmof@caribsurf.com; internet www.fsd.gov.kn.

Ministry of Foreign and CARICOM Affairs, International Trade, Community and Social Development: Church St, POB 186, Basseterre; tel. 465-2521; fax 465-1778; e-mail foreigna@caribsurf.com.

Ministry of Health and the Environment: Church St, POB 186, Basseterre; tel. 465-2521; fax 465-1316.

Ministry of Tourism, Information, Telecommunications, Commerce and Consumer Affairs: Pelican Mall, Basseterre; tel. 465-4040; fax 465-8794; e-mail skninfo@caribsurf.com.

Ministry of Youth, Sports and Culture: Church St, POB 186, Basseterre; tel. 465-2521; fax 465-7075.

NEVIS ISLAND ADMINISTRATION

Premier: VANCE AMORY.

There are also two appointed members.

Administrative Centre: Administration Bldg, Main St, Charlestown, Nevis; tel. 469-5221; fax 469-1207; e-mail nevisinfo@nevisweb.kn; internet www.nevisweb.kn.

Legislature

NATIONAL ASSEMBLY

Speaker: IVAN BUCHANAN.

Elected members: 11. Nominated members: 3. Ex-officio members: 1.

Election, 6 March 2000

Party	Votes	Seats
Labour Party	11,762	8
Concerned Citizens' Movement	1,901	2
Nevis Reformation Party	1,710	1
People's Action Movement	6,468	—
Total	21,841	11

NEVIS ISLAND ASSEMBLY

Elected members: 5. Nominated members: 3.

Elections to the Nevis Island Assembly took place in February 1997. The Concerned Citizens' Movement took three seats, and the Nevis Reformation Party retained two seats.

Political Organizations

Concerned Citizens' Movement (CCM): Charlestown, Nevis; alliance of four parties; Leader VANCE AMORY.

Labour Party (Workers' League): Masses House, Church St, POB 239, Basseterre; tel. 465-2229; internet www.sknlabourparty.org; f. 1932; socialist party; Chair. HERBERT WYCLIFFE-MORTON; Leader Dr DENZIL DOUGLAS.

Nevis Reformation Party (NRP): Government Rd, POB 480, Charlestown, Nevis; tel. 469-0630; f. 1970; Leader JOSEPH PARRY; Sec. LEVI MORTON.

People's Action Movement (PAM): Basseterre; e-mail exec@pamskb.com; internet www.pamskb.com; f. 1965; Leader LINDSAY GRANT.

United People's Party (UPP): Basseterre; f. 1993; Leader MICHAEL POWELL.

Diplomatic Representation

EMBASSIES IN SAINT CHRISTOPHER AND NEVIS

China (Taiwan): Taylor's Range, POB 119, Basseterre; tel. 465-2421; fax 465-7921; e-mail rocemb@caribsurf.com; Ambassador: KATHARINE CHANG.

Venezuela: Delisle St, POB 435, Basseterre; tel. 465-2073; fax 465-5452; Charge d'affairés a.i.: SHELANGEL CARREÑO.

Diplomatic relations with other countries are maintained at consular level, or with ambassadors and high commissioners resident in other countries of the region, or directly with the other country.

Judicial System

Justice is administered by the Eastern Caribbean Supreme Court, based in Saint Lucia and consisting of a Court of Appeal and a High Court. One of the nine puisne judges of the High Court is responsible for Saint Christopher and Nevis and presides over the Court of Summary Jurisdiction. The Magistrates' Courts deal with summary offences and civil offences involving sums of not more than EC $5,000. In 1998 the death penalty was employed in Saint Christopher and Nevis for the first time since 1985.

Puisne Judge: NEVILLE SMITH.

Magistrates' Office: Losack Rd, Basseterre; tel. 465-2926.

Religion

CHRISTIANITY

St Kitts Christian Council: Victoria Rd, POB 48, Basseterre; tel. 465-2504; Chair. Rev. CHARLES SEATON.

St Kitts Evangelical Association: Princess St, POB 773, Basseterre.

The Anglican Communion

Anglicans in Saint Christopher and Nevis are adherents of the Church in the Province of the West Indies. The islands form part of the diocese of the North Eastern Caribbean and Aruba. The Bishop is resident in The Valley, Anguilla.

The Roman Catholic Church

The diocese of Saint John's-Basseterre, suffragan to the archdiocese of Castries (Saint Lucia), includes Anguilla, Antigua and Barbuda, the British Virgin Islands, Montserrat and Saint Christopher and Nevis. At 31 December 1999 the diocese contained an estimated 14,402 adherents. The Bishop participates in the Antilles Episcopal Conference (currently based in Port of Spain, Trinidad and Tobago).

Bishop of Saint John's-Basseterre: Rt Rev. DONALD JAMES REECE (resident in St John's, Antigua).

Other Churches

There are also communities of Methodists, Moravians, Seventh-day Adventists, Baptists, Pilgrim Holiness, the Church of God, Apostolic Faith and Plymouth Brethren.

The Press

The Democrat: Cayon St, POB 30, Basseterre; tel. 465-2091; fax 465-0857; f. 1948; weekly on Saturdays; organ of PAM; Dir Capt. J. L. WIGLEY; Editor FITZROY P. JONES; circ. 3,000.

The Labour Spokesman: Masses House, Church St, POB 239, Basseterre; tel. 465-2229; fax 466-9866; e-mail sknunion@caribsurf.com; f. 1957; Wednesdays and Saturdays; organ of St Kitts-Nevis Trades and Labour Union; Editor DAWUD BYRON; Man. WALFORD GUMBS; circ. 6,000.

The St Kitts and Nevis Observer: Basseterre; weekly.

FOREIGN NEWS AGENCIES

Associated Press (USA), Inter Press Service (IPS) (Italy) and United Press International (UPI) (USA) are represented in Basseterre.

Publishers

Caribbean Publishing Co (St Kitts-Nevis) Ltd: Dr William Herbert Complex, Frigate Bay Rd, POB 745, Basseterre; tel. 465-5178; fax 466-0307; e-mail lsk-sales@caribsurf.com.

MacPennies Publishing Co: 10A Cayon St East, POB 318, Basseterre; tel. 465-2274; fax 465-8668.

Broadcasting and Communications

TELECOMMUNICATIONS

Regulatory Authority

Eastern Caribbean Telecommunications Authority: based on Castries, Saint Lucia; f. 2000 to regulate telecommunications in Saint Christopher and Nevis, Dominica, Grenada, Saint Lucia and Saint Vincent and the Grenadines.

Major Service Provider

Cable & Wireless St Kitts and Nevis: Cayon St, POB 86, Basseterre; tel. 465-1000; fax 465-1106; internet www.candw.kn; f. 1985; fmrly St Kitts and Nevis Telecommunications Co Ltd (SKANTEL); 65% owned by Cable & Wireless plc; 17% state-owned; Chair. (vacant).

BROADCASTING

Radio

Radio Paradise: Charlestown, POB 423, Nevis; tel. 469-1994; owned by US co (POB A, Santa Ana, CA 92711); religious; Dir R. A. Mayer.

Trinity Broadcasting Ltd: Bath Plain Rd, Charlestown, Nevis; tel. 469-5425; fax 469-1723.

Voice of Nevis (VON) Radio 895 AM: Bath Plain, Bath Village, POB 195, Charlestown, Nevis; tel. 469-1616; fax 469-5329; e-mail vonradio@caribsurf.com; internet www.skbee.com/vonlive.html.

ZIZ Radio and Television: Springfield, POB 331, Basseterre; tel. 465-2621; fax 465-5624; f. 1961, television from 1972; commercial; govt-owned; Dir of Broadcasting Clement Liburd, Jr.

Television

ZIZ Radio and Television: (see Radio); Gen. Man Claudette Manchester.

Finance

BANKING

Central Bank

Eastern Caribbean Central Bank (ECCB): Headquarters Bldg, Bird Rock, POB 89, Basseterre; tel. 465-2537-9; fax 465-5615; e-mail eccberu@caribsurf.com; internet www.eccb-centralbank.org; f. 1965 as East Caribbean Currency Authority; expanded responsibilities and changed name 1983; responsible for issue of currency in Anguilla, Antigua and Barbuda, Dominica, Grenada, Montserrat, Saint Christopher and Nevis, Saint Lucia and Saint Vincent and the Grenadines; res EC $109.0m., dep. EC $35.1m., total assets EC $1,188.9m. (March 2000); Gov. and Chair. K. Dwight Venner.

Local Banks

Bank of Nevis Ltd: Main St, POB 450, Charlestown, Nevis; tel. 469-5564; fax 469-5798; e-mail bon@caribsurf.com.

Caribbean Banking Corporation (SKN) Ltd: Chapel St, POB 60, Charlestown; tel. 469-5277; fax 469-5795.

National Bank Ltd: Central St, POB 343, Basseterre; tel. 465-2204; fax 466-1050; 2 brs.

Nevis Co-operative Banking Co Ltd: Chapel St, POB 60, Charlestown, Nevis; tel. 469-5277; fax 469-1493; f. 1955; Man. Dir I. Walwyn.

Foreign Banks

Bank of Nova Scotia: Fort St, POB 433, Basseterre; tel. 465-4141; fax 465-8600; Man. W. A. Christie.

Barclays Bank PLC (UK): The Circus, POB 42, Basseterre; tel. 465-2449; fax 465-1041; Man. Philip Li; 2 brs.

Royal Bank of Canada: cnr Bay and Fort St, POB 91, Basseterre; tel. 465-2259; fax 465-1040.

Development Bank

Development Bank of St Kitts and Nevis: Church St, POB 249, Basseterre; tel. 465-2288; fax 465-4016; e-mail dbskskn@caribsurf.com; f. 1981; cap. EC $8.0m., res EC $1.8m., dep. EC$2.5m.; Gen. Man. Auckland Hector.

INSURANCE

National Caribbean Insurance Co Ltd: Central St, POB 374, Basseterre; tel. 465-2694; fax 465-3659.

St Kitts-Nevis Insurance Co Ltd: Central St, POB 142, Basseterre; tel. 465-2845; fax 465-5410.

Several foreign companies also have offices in Saint Christopher and Nevis.

Trade and Industry

GOVERNMENT AGENCIES

Central Marketing Corpn (CEMACO): Pond's Pastire, Basseterre; tel. 465-2326; fax 465-2326; Man. Maxwell Griffin.

The Department of Planning and Development: The Cotton House, Market St, Charlestown, Nevis; tel. 469-5521; fax 469-1273; e-mail planevis@caribsurf.com.

Frigate Bay Development Corporation: Frigate Bay, POB 315, Basseterre; tel. 465-8339; fax 465-4463; promotes tourist and residential developments.

Investment Promotion Agency: Investment Promotion Division, Ministry of Trade and Industry, Church St, POB 186, Basseterre; tel. 465-4106; fax 465-1778; f. 1987.

St Kitts Sugar Manufacturing Corpn: St Kitts Sugar Factory, POB 96, Basseterre; tel. 466-8503; merged with National Agricultural Corpn in 1986; Gen. Man. J. E. S. Alfred.

Social Security Board: Bay Rd, POB 79, Basseterre; tel. 465-6000; fax 465-5051; e-mail ssbcomrm@caribsurf.com; f. 1977; Dir Sephlin Lawrence.

CHAMBER OF COMMERCE

St Kitts-Nevis Chamber of Industry and Commerce: South Independence Sq. St, POB 332, Basseterre; tel. 465-2980; fax 465-4490; e-mail sknchamber@caribsurf.com; incorporated 1949; 120 mems; Pres. Michael Morton; Exec. Dir Wendy Phipps.

EMPLOYERS' ORGANIZATIONS

Building Contractors' Association: Anthony Evelyn Business Complex, Paul Southwell Industrial Park, POB 1046, Basseterre; tel. 465-6897; fax 465-5623; e-mail SKNBCA@caribsurf.com; Pres. Anthony E. Evelyn.

Nevis Cotton Growers' Association Ltd: Charlestown, Nevis; Pres. Ivor Stevens.

Small Business Association: Anthony Evelyn Business Complex, Paul Southwell Industrial Park, POB 367, Basseterre; tel. 465-8630; fax 465-6661; e-mail SB-Association@caribsurf.com; Pres. Eustace Warner.

TRADE UNIONS

St Kitts-Nevis Trades and Labour Union: Masses House, Church St, POB 239, Basseterre; tel. 465-2229; fax 466-9866; f. 1940; affiliated to Caribbean Maritime and Aviation Council, Caribbean Congress of Labour, International Federation of Plantation, Agricultural and Allied Workers and International Confederation of Free Trade Unions; associated with Labour Party; Pres. Lee L. Moore; Gen. Sec. Stanley R. Franks; about 3,000 mems.

United Workers' Union (UWU): Market St, Basseterre; tel. 465-4130; associated with People's Action Movement.

Transport

RAILWAYS

There are 58 km (36 miles) of narrow-gauge light railway on Saint Christopher, serving the sugar plantations.

St Kitts Sugar Railway: St Kitts Sugar Manufacturing Corpn, POB 96, Basseterre; tel. 465-8099; fax 465-1059; Gen. Man. J. E. S. Alfred.

ROADS

There are 320 km (199 miles) of road in Saint Christopher and Nevis, of which approximately 136 km (84 miles) are paved.

SHIPPING

The Government maintains a commercial motor boat service between the islands, and numerous regional and international shipping lines call at the islands. A deep-water port, Port Zante, was opened at Basseterre in 1981. Work is ongoing on port development projects to improve facilities for cargo ships and cruise ships in Basseterre and to repair the ports of Charlestown and Long Point on Nevis, which were damaged in 1999 by Hurricane Lenny.

St Kitts Air and Sea Ports Authority: Administration Bldg, Deep Water Port, Bird Rock, Basseterre; tel. 465-8121; fax 465-8124; f. 1993 combining St Kitts Port Authority and Airports Authority; Gen. Man. SIDNEY OSBORNE; Airport Man. EDWARD HUGHES; Sea Port Man. CARL BRAZIER-CLARKE.

Shipping Companies

Delisle Walwyn and Co Ltd: Liverpool Row, POB 44, Basseterre; tel. 465-2631; fax 465-1125; e-mail delwal@caribsurf.com; internet www.delisleco.com.

Sea Atlantic Cargo Shipping Corp.: Main St, POB 556, Charlestown, Nevis.

Tony's Ltd: Main St, POB 564, Charlestown, Nevis; tel. 469-5953; fax 469-5413.

CIVIL AVIATION

Robert Llewellyn Bradshaw (formerly Golden Rock) International Airport, 4 km (2½ miles) from Basseterre, is equipped to handle jet aircraft and is served by scheduled links with most Caribbean destinations, the United Kingdom, the USA and Canada. Saint Christopher and Nevis is a shareholder in the regional airline, LIAT (see chapter on Antigua and Barbuda). Newcastle Airfield, 11 km (7 miles) from Charlestown, Nevis, has regular scheduled services to St Kitts and other islands in the region. A new airport, Castle Airport, was opened on Nevis in 1998.

St Kitts Air and Sea Ports Authority: (see Shipping).

Private Airlines

Air St Kitts-Nevis: New Castle Airport, New Castle, Nevis; tel. 469-9241; fax 469-9018.

Nevis Express Ltd: Newcastle Airport, Newcastle, Nevis; tel. 469-9756; fax 469-9751; e-mail reservations@nevisexpress.com; internet www.nevisexpress.com; passenger and cargo charter services to all Caribbean destinations; St Kitts-Nevis shuttle service.

Tourism

The introduction of regular air services to Miami and New York has opened up the islands as a tourist destination. Visitors are attracted by the excellent beaches on Saint Christopher and the spectacular mountain scenery of Nevis, the historical Brimstone Hill Fortress National Park on Saint Christopher and the islands' associations with Lord Nelson and Alexander Hamilton. In 1999 there were 230,800 visitors, of whom 143,800 were yacht and cruise-ship passengers. Receipts from tourism were estimated at EC $182.1m. in 1999. There were 1,508 rooms in hotels and guest houses in Saint Christopher and Nevis in 1999. This number was expected to increase by a further 1,500 rooms by the end of 2001.

Nevis Tourism Bureau: Main St, Charlestown; tel. 469-1042; fax 469-1066; e-mail nevtour@caribsurf.com; internet www .nevisweb.kn.

St Kitts-Nevis Department of Tourism: Pelican Mall, Bay Rd, POB 132, Basseterre; tel. 465-4040; fax 465-8794; Permanent Sec. HILARY WATTLEY.

St Kitts-Nevis Hotel and Tourism Association: Liverpool Row, POB 438, Basseterre; tel. 465-5304; fax 465-7746; e-mail stkitnevhta @caribsurf.com; f. 1972; Pres. LARKLAND RICHARD; Exec. Dir VAL HENRY.

Defence

The small army was disbanded by the Government in 1981, and its duties were absorbed by the Volunteer Defence Force and a special tactical unit of the police. In July 1997 the National Assembly approved legislation to re-establish a full-time defence force. Coastguard operations were to be brought under military command; the defence force was also to include cadet and reserve forces. St Christopher and Nevis participates in the US-sponsored Regional Security System, comprising police, coastguards and army units, which was established by independent East Caribbean states in 1982. Budgetary expenditure on national security in 1998 was approximately EC $23.8m.

Education

Education is compulsory for 12 years between five and 17 years of age. Primary education begins at the age of five, and lasts for seven years. Secondary education, from the age of 12, generally comprises a first cycle of four years, followed by a second cycle of two years. In 1993 enrolment at all levels of education was estimated to be equivalent to 78% of the school-age population. There are 30 state, eight private and five denominational schools. There is also a technical college. Budgetary expenditure on education by the central Government in 1998 was projected to be EC $25m. (6.7% of total government expenditure). In 1998 the average rate of adult illiteracy was estimated to be 2.0%. In September 2000 a privately financed offshore medical college, the Medical University of the Americas, opened in Nevis with 40 students registered.

SAINT LUCIA

Area: 616.3 sq km (238 sq miles).

Population (official estimate, mid-1999): 153,703.

Capital: Castries (estimate of population 61,823 in 1999).

Language: English (official); a large proportion of the population speaks only a French-based patois.

Religion: Predominantly Christianity (mainly Roman Catholicism).

Climate: Average temperature 26°C (79°F); dry season January–May, rainy season May–August; average annual rainfall varies from 1,500 mm (60 ins) in low-lying areas to 3,500 mm (138 ins) in the mountains.

Time: GMT –4 hours.

Public Holidays: 2003: 1–2 January (New Year), 22 February (Independence Day), 3–4 March (Carnival), 18 April (Good Friday), 21 April (Easter Monday), 1 May (Labour Day), 9 June (Whit Monday), 14 June (Queen's Official Birthday), 19 June (Corpus Christi), 1 August (Emancipation Day), 3 October (Thanksgiving Day), 1 November (All Saints Day), 2 November (All Souls Day), 22 November (Feast of St Cecilia), 13 December (St Lucia Day), 25–26 December (Christmas). **2002:** 1–2 January (New Year), 11–12 February (Carnival), 22 February (Independence Day), 29 March (Good Friday), 1 April (Easter Monday), 1 May (Labour Day), 20 May (Whit Monday), 30 May (Corpus Christi), 8 June (Queen's Official Birthday), 2 August (Emancipation Day), 4 October (Thanksgiving Day), 1 November (All Saints Day), 2 November (All Souls Day), 22 November (Feast of St Cecilia), 13 December (St Lucia Day), 25–26 December (Christmas).

Currency: Eastern Caribbean dollar: US $1 = EC $2.70 (fixed rate since July 1976); EC $100 = £25.87 = US $37.04 = €41.73 (30 April 2001).

Weights and Measures: Imperial.

History

After two centuries of Anglo-French dispute, Saint Lucia was finally ceded to Britain in 1814. The island belonged to the Windward Islands Federation until 1959, and to the West Indies Federation from 1958 to 1962. Saint Lucia became one of the West Indies Associated States in March 1967, with full autonomy in internal affairs, and gained independence on 22 February 1979, with John Compton of the conservative United Workers' Party (UWP) as Prime Minister. The Saint Lucia Labour Party (SLP) won the general election of July 1979, but was defeated in May 1982, after allegations of corruption had forced the Government to resign. The UWP was returned to power, with Compton again becoming Prime Minister, and subsequently retained power for 15 years, winning general elections in 1987 and 1992. Compton remained Prime Minister until his resignation at the end of March 1996, when he was succeeded by Dr Vaughan Lewis. However, the SLP won a decisive victory in the May 1997 general election, securing 16 of the 17 seats in the House of Assembly. Kenny Anthony was inaugurated as Prime Minister. In August the Governor-General, Sir George Mallet, resigned. His appointment, in June 1996, had been opposed by the SLP, on the grounds that the post's tradition of neutrality would be compromised—Mallet had previously been Deputy Prime Minister. In mid-September 1998 Saint Lucia's first female Governor-General, Dr Perlette Louisy, was appointed. In the same month an inquiry into allegations of corruption under the UWP began. In September 1999 the inquiry cleared former Prime Ministers Compton and Lewis of corruption.

In March 2000 the Prime Minister announced a cabinet reshuffle, appointing Menissa Rambally as Minister of Tourism and Civil Aviation. In the same month the Constituency Boundaries Commission recommended that two new constituencies be created, increasing the total to 19, in time for the next general election in 2002. In early October the leader of the opposition UWP, Vaughan Lewis, resigned his post. He was subsequently replaced by Dr Morella Joseph. In early October 2000 Vaughan Lewis unexpectedly announced his resignation as leader of the UWP stating as his reason his commitments to his overseas employment at the University of the West Indies. Morella Joseph, one of the two deputy leaders of the UWP, was elected unopposed to the leadership at the annual party convention later in the month. Eldridge Stephens, a former junior minister, was elected to succeed Romanus Lansiquot as party chairman. Joseph called on the party to examine its policies and structure and improve its public relations strategy. In January 2001, following a increase of tourist cancellations, Kenny Anthony announced a series of measures aimed at reducing the rising crime rate in Saint Lucia. These measures included the establishment of a National Anti-Crime Commission, the creation of a 10-member police 'rapid response unit', a review of the penal code and reforms to the police service. In March 2001 the Foreign Minister, George Odlum, left the Government to join the new opposition 'Alliance', headed by former Prime Minister Sir John Compton and the UWP leader Morella Joseph. Prime Minister Anthony stated that he had dismissed Odlum from his post, although Odlum himself claimed that he had resigned from the Government. Odlum was replaced by Julian Hunte, a former ambassador to the UN in New York.

Economy

The island's principal economic activity was agriculture, which employed some 17.2% of the working population in 1998. Bananas were the principal cash crop and, in 1999, accounted for 62.5% of the value of merchandise exports. The productivity of the sector was affected by disputes over the administration of the industry during the mid-1990s, but bananas remained the leading export. In 1999 banana production declined by 11%. In July 1999 the Government founded a Banana Industry Trust, which was to oversee the improvement of farming practices in the banana sector and to manage the financial resources available to the industry, including EC $21m. in funds provided by the European Union. However, in September 2000 the Government announced that subsidies would no longer be available to the banana industry. In July 2001, following the resolution of the dispute in the industry between the USA and the European Union, it was announced that the banana sector was to be restructured in an attempt to increase competitiveness. Other important crops include coconuts, mangoes, citrus fruit, cocoa and spices. Commercial fishing is also being developed. During 1993–99 agricultural gross domestic product (GDP) decreased by an estimated annual average of 7.3%. A decline, in real terms, of 17.9% was recorded in the sector's GDP in 1997 (largely as a result of a decline in the banana sector). Although in 1998 growth of 2.6% was recorded, in 1999 GDP was estimated to have again declined, by 11.6%. In 1999 agriculture as a whole (including forestry and fishing) accounted for 6.8% of GDP and employed some 20.8% of the working population in 2000.

Manufacturing output increased in the late 1980s, but was more erratic in the 1990s, although it was encouraged by the establishment of 'free zones'. In 1999 the sector accounted for 5.3% of GDP and employed 9.3% of the working population in 2000. Overall, industry (including mining, manufacturing, public utilities and construction) accounted for 17.9% of GDP in 1999 and employed some 37.6% of the working population.

The services sector, of which tourism is increasingly the most important industry, contributed an estimated 75.3% of GDP in 1999. During 1993–99 the GDP of the services sector increased by an estimated annual average of 3.5%. Investment in the island's infrastructure was seen as essential for attracting foreign investment and further expanding the tourist industry. Tourism became an important sector of the economy, with receipts of EC $736.0m. in 1999, equivalent to 72.8% of the value of total exports of goods and services. By the late 1990s the industry had become the principal source of foreign exchange.

At the beginning of the 21st century the Government intended to establish Saint Lucia as a centre for international financial services and the necessary legislation was approved in late 1999. In February 2001 the Government approved the registration of Saint Lucia's first 'offshore' bank, Bank Crozier International Ltd. However, in September 2000 Philip Pierre, the Financial Services Minister, announced that the International Monetary Fund was to assess the country's financial services jurisdiction, following the inclusion of Saint Lucia on a list of 'tax havens' compiled by the Organisation for Economic Co-operation and Development (OECD) in June. Pierre accused the OECD of attempting to 'cripple the financial services sector in the Caribbean'.

Saint Lucia's GDP increased, in real terms, by an estimated average of 3.1% annually during 1991–98. Despite the decline in banana production, the economy continued to expand at the same rate in 1999, primarily owing to growth in the tourism and construction sectors. In April 2000 the Government was able to present a virtually balanced budget for 2000/01, which was intended to stimulate further growth. Unemployment was reported to have fallen from a peak of 21% of the work-force in 1998 to 15% at the end of 2000.

Statistical Survey

Source (unless otherwise indicated): St Lucian Government Statistics Department, Block A, Government Bldgs, Castries Waterfront, Castries; tel. 452-6653; fax 451-8254; e-mail statsdept@candw.lc; internet www.stats.gov.lc.

AREA AND POPULATION

Area: 616.3 sq km (238 sq miles).

Population: 120,300 at census of 12 May 1980; 135,685 (males 65,988; females 69,697) at census of 12 May 1991; 153,703 (official estimate) at mid-1999. *By District* (official estimates, 1999): Castries 61,823; Anse La Raye 6,203; Canaries 1,923; Soufrière 8,953; Choiseul 7,255; Laborie 8,727; Vieux-Fort 14,624; Micoud 17,423; Dennery 12,778; Gros Islet 13,994; Total 153,703.

Density (mid-1999): 249.4 per sq km.

Principal Towns (estimated population, 1999): Castries (capital) 61,823; Vieux-Fort 13,791 (1993); Soufrière 8,064 (1993).

Births, Marriages and Deaths (1999): Registered live births 2,906 (birth rate 18.9 per 1,000); Registered marriages 661 (marriage rate 4.2 per 1,000); Registered deaths 963 (death rate 6.3 per 1,000).

Expectation of life (years at birth, 1999) males 69.5; females 73.2.

Economically Active Population (persons aged 15 years and over, labour survey for January–June 2000: Agriculture, hunting and forestry 13,040; Fishing 790; Manufacturing 5,790; Electricity, gas and water 840; Construction 5,530; Wholesale and retail trade; repair of motor vehicles, motorcycles and personal and household goods 11,600; Hotels and restaurants 7,030; Transport, storage and communications 3,650; Financial intermediation 1,100; Real estate, renting and business activities 1,160; Public administration and defence; compulsory social security 6,880; Education 890; Health and social work 750; Other community, social and personal service activities 1,880; Private households with employed persons 1,520; Activities not adequately defined 120; Total employed 62,570 (males 34,440, females 28,130); Unemployed 11,440; Total labour force 74,010.

AGRICULTURE, ETC

Principal Crops (FAO estimates, '000 metric tons, 2000): Cassava 1; Yams 5; Other roots and tubers 5; Coconuts 12; Vegetables 1; Oranges 1; Grapefruit 1; Mangoes 28; Bananas 92; Plantains 1. Source: FAO.

Livestock (FAO estimates, '000 head, year ending September 2000): Horses 1; Mules 1; Asses 1; Cattle 12; Pigs 15; Sheep 13; Goats 10. Source: FAO.

Livestock Products (FAO estimates, '000 metric tons, 2000): Pig meat 1; Poultry meat 1; Cows' milk 1; Hen eggs 1. Source: FAO.

Fishing (metric tons, live weight, 1998): Capture 1,314 (Flyingfishes 112, Common dolphinfish 264, Wahoo 245, Skipjack tuna 144, Blackfin tuna 53, Yellowfin tuna 147); Aquaculture 2; Total catch 1,316. Figures exclude aquatic plants and mammals. Source: FAO, *Yearbook of Fishery Statistics*.

INDUSTRY

Production (estimates, 1998): Electric energy 235.9 million kWh; Copra 1,484 metric tons; Coconut oil (unrefined) 292,000 litres; Coconut oil (refined) 194,000 litres; Coconut meal 558,000 kg; Rum 328,600 gallons (1997). Source: mainly IMF, *St Lucia: Statistical Annex* (May 1999).

FINANCE

Currency and Exchange Rates: 100 cents = 1 Eastern Caribbean dollar (EC $). *Sterling, US Dollar and Euro Equivalents* (30 April 2001): £1 sterling = EC $3.866; US $1 = EC $2.700; €1 = EC $2.396; EC $100 = £25.87 = US $37.04 = €41.73. *Exchange Rate:* Fixed at US $1 = EC $2.70 since July 1976.

Budget (EC $ million, preliminary figures, year ending 31 March 1999): *Revenue:* Tax revenue 419.7 (Taxes on income and profits 127.0, Taxes on domestic goods and services 59.5, Taxes on international trade and transactions 232.5); Other current revenue 77.9; Capital revenue 2.5; Grants 62.1; Total 562.2. *Expenditure:* Current expenditure 358.9 (Personal emoluments 200.1, Goods and services 68.4, Interest payments 24.9, Transfers 65.6); Capital expenditure and net lending 155.7; Total 514.6. Source: Eastern Caribbean Central Bank, *Report and Statement of Accounts*.

International Reserves (US $ million at 31 December 2000): IMF special drawing rights 1.87; Foreign exchange 76.96; Total 78.83. Source: IMF, *International Financial Statistics*.

Money Supply (EC $ million at 31 December 2000): Currency outside banks 84.60; Demand deposits at deposit money banks 229.15; Total money (incl. others) 314.99. Source: IMF, *International Financial Statistics*.

Cost of Living (Consumer Price Index; base: 1995 = 100): 102.0 in 1997; 104.2 in 1998; 109.7 in 1999. Source: IMF, *International Financial Statistics*.

Gross Domestic Product (EC $ million at current prices): 1,672.6 in 1998; 1,820.2 in 1999; 1,893.2 in 2000. Source: IMF, *International Financial Statistics*.

Expenditure on the Gross Domestic Product (EC $ million at current prices, 1998, estimates): Government final consumption expenditure 250; Private final consumption expenditure 1,132; Gross capital formation 318; *Total domestic expenditure* 1,700; Exports of goods and services 1,069; *Less* Imports of goods and services 1,123; *GDP at market prices* 1,646. Source: IMF, *St Lucia: Statistical Annex* (May 1999).

Gross Domestic Product by Economic Activity (EC $ million at current factor cost, 1999): Agriculture, hunting, forestry and fishing 110.28; Mining and quarrying 6.02; Manufacturing 84.88; Electricity and water 66.47; Construction 130.98; Wholesale and retail trade 210.76; Restaurants and hotels 201.32; Transport 176.85; Communications 104.79; Banking and insurance 139.18; Real estate and housing 89.71; Government services 220.63; Other services 73.04; Sub-total 1,614.91; *Less* Imputed bank service charge 118.33; Total 1,496.58. Source: Eastern Caribbean Central Bank, *National Accounts*.

Balance of Payments (EC $ million, 1999): Exports of goods f.o.b. 164.5; Imports of goods f.o.b. –842.42; *Trade balance* –667.92; Exports of services 847.12; Imports of services –359.49; *Balance on goods and services* –190.29; Other income received 6.43; Other income paid 120.98; *Balance on goods, services and income* –304.84; Current transfers received 85.43; Current transfers paid –26.00; *Current balance* –245.41; Capital account (net) 70.35; Direct investment from abroad (net) 253.96; Portfolio investment (net) –7.84; Other investments (net) –61.56; Net errors and omissions 0.88; *Overall balance* –10.38. Source: Eastern Caribbean Central Bank, *Balance of Payments*.

EXTERNAL TRADE

Principal Commodities (EC $ million, 1999): *Imports c.i.f.:* Food and live animals 191.3; Beverages and tobacco 32.6; Crude materials (inedible) except fuels 28.6; Mineral fuels, lubricants, etc. 65.1; Chemicals and related products 87.3; Basic manufactures 194.7; Machinery and transport equipment 221.2; Miscellaneous manufactured articles 134.1; Total (incl. others) 957.3. *Exports f.o.b.:* Bananas 87.7; Beer 17.7; Paper and paperboard 6.2; Electrical machinery 5.6; Clothing and accessories 9.1; Total (incl. others) 140.3 (excl. re-exports 10.0).

Principal Trading Partners (EC $ million, 1999): *Imports c.i.f.:* Barbados 29.2; Canada 31.7; China, People's Republic 15.5; France 13.3; Japan 53.5; Netherlands 11.1; Saint Vincent and the Grenadines 11.6; Trinidad and Tobago 135.0; United Kingdom 100.4; USA 379.4; US Virgin Islands 22.1; Total (incl. others) 957.3. *Exports f.o.b.:* Antigua and Barbuda 4.5; Barbados 10.0; Dominica 3.6; Grenada 3.3; Trinidad and Tobago 5.4; United Kingdom 89.0; USA 17.0; Total (incl. others) 140.3.

TRANSPORT

Road Traffic (registered motor vehicles, 1999): Goods vehicles 8,840; Taxis and hired vehicles 1,805; Motorcycles 769; Private vehicles 17,763; Passenger vans 3,150; Total (incl. others) 32,650.

Shipping: *Arrivals* (1999): 2,328 vessels. *International Freight Traffic* ('000 metric tons, 1999): Goods loaded 117; Goods unloaded 666.

Civil Aviation (aircraft movements): 41,702 in 1996; 41,160 in 1997; 42,040 in 1998.

TOURISM

Tourist Arrivals: 572,738 (248,406 stop-over visitors, 319,256 cruise-ship passengers, 4,963 excursionists) in 1997; 638,550 (252,237 stop-over visitors, 381,020 cruise-ship passengers, 5,293 excursionists) in 1998; 664,984 (260,583 stop-over visitors, 394,148 cruise-ship passengers, 10,253 excursionists) in 1999.

Tourist Receipts (EC $ million): 683.91 in 1997; 749.64 in 1998; 736.02 in 1999. Source: Eastern Caribbean Central Bank, *Balance of Payments*.

COMMUNICATIONS MEDIA

Non-daily Newspapers (1996): 5 (circulation 34,000 copies).
Radio Receivers (1997): 111,000 in use.
Television Receivers (1997): 32,000 in use.
Telephones (1999): 44,465 main lines in use.
Mobile Cellular Telephones (year beginning 1 April 1996): 1,400.
Sources: UN, *Statistical Yearbook*; UNESCO, *Statistical Yearbook*.

EDUCATION

(state institutions only, 1999/2000)
Pre-primary: 105 schools; 325 teachers; 4,288 pupils.
Primary: 82 schools; 1,081 teachers; 28,975 pupils.
General Secondary: 18 schools; 645 teachers; 12,817 pupils.
Special Education: 4 schools; 36 teachers; 162 students.
Adult Education: 21 centres; 94 facilitators; 662 learners.
Tertiary (including part-time): 133 teachers; 1,458 students.

Directory

The Constitution

The Constitution came into force at the independence of Saint Lucia on 22 February 1979. Its main provisions are summarized below:

FUNDAMENTAL RIGHTS AND FREEDOMS

Regardless of race, place of origin, political opinion, colour, creed or sex but subject to respect for the rights and freedoms of others and for the public interest, every person in Saint Lucia is entitled to the rights of life, liberty, security of the person, equality before the law and the protection of the law. Freedom of conscience, of expression, of assembly and association is guaranteed and the inviolability of personal privacy, family life and property is maintained. Protection is afforded from slavery, forced labour, torture and inhuman treatment.

THE GOVERNOR-GENERAL

The British monarch, as Head of State, is represented in Saint Lucia by the Governor-General.

PARLIAMENT

Parliament consists of the British monarch, represented by the Governor-General, the 11-member Senate and the House of Assembly, composed of 17 elected Representatives. Senators are appointed by the Governor-General: six on the advice of the Prime Minister, three on the advice of the Leader of the Opposition and two acting on his own deliberate judgement. The life of Parliament is five years.

Each constituency returns one Representative to the House who is directly elected in accordance with the Constitution.

At a time when the office of Attorney-General is a public office, the Attorney-General is an *ex-officio* member of the House.

Every citizen over the age of 21 is eligible to vote.

Parliament may alter any of the provisions of the Constitution.

THE EXECUTIVE

Executive authority is vested in the British monarch and exercisable by the Governor-General. The Governor-General appoints as Prime Minister that member of the House who, in the Governor-General's view, is best able to command the support of the majority of the members of the House, and other Ministers on the advice of the Prime Minister. The Governor-General may remove the Prime Minister from office if the House approves a resolution expressing no confidence in the Government, and if the Prime Minister does not resign within three days or advise the Governor-General to dissolve Parliament.

The Cabinet consists of the Prime Minister and other Ministers, and the Attorney-General as an *ex-officio* member at a time when the office of Attorney-General is a public office.

The Leader of the Opposition is appointed by the Governor-General as that member of the House who, in the Governor-General's view, is best able to command the support of a majority of members of the house who do not support the Government.

CITIZENSHIP

All persons born in Saint Lucia before independence who immediately prior to independence were citizens of the United Kingdom and Colonies automatically become citizens of Saint Lucia. All persons born in Saint Lucia after independence automatically acquire Saint Lucian citizenship, as do those born outside Saint Lucia after independence to a parent possessing Saint Lucian citizenship. Provision is made for the acquisition of citizenship by those to whom it is not automatically granted.

The Government

Head of State: HM Queen ELIZABETH II.

Governor-General: Dame PEARLETTE LOUISY (took office 17 September 1997).

CABINET
(August 2001)

Prime Minister, Minister of Finance, Economic Affairs and Information: Dr KENNY ANTHONY.

Deputy Prime Minister and Minister of Education, Human Resource Development, Youth and Sports: MARIO MICHEL.

Minister of Commerce, International Financial Services and Consumer Affairs: PHILLIP J. PIERRE.

Minister of Agriculture, Forestry and Fisheries: CASSIUS B. ELIAS.

Minister of Health, Human Services, Family Affairs and Women: SARAH L. FLOOD.

Minister of Development, Planning, the Environment and Housing: WALTER F. FRANÇOIS.

Minister of Communications, Works, Transport and Public Utilities: CALIXTE GEORGE.

Minister of Community Development, Culture, Local Government and Co-operatives: DAMIAN E. GREAVES.

Minister of Legal Affairs, Home Affairs and Labour: VELON L. JOHN.

Minister of Foreign Affairs and International Trade: JULIAN HUNTE.

Minister of Tourism and Civil Aviation: MENISSA RAMBALLY.

Attorney-General, Minister for the Public Service: PETRUS COMPTON.

MINISTRIES

Office of the Prime Minister: New Government Bldgs, Castries; tel. 452-3980; fax 453-7352; internet www.stlucia.gov.lc.

Ministry of Agriculture, Forestry and Fisheries: 5th floor, NIS Bldg, Waterfront, Castries; tel. 452-2526; fax 453-6314; e-mail admin@slumaffe.org; internet www.slumaffe.org.

Ministry of Commerce, International Financial Services and Consumer Affairs: 4th Floor, Block B, NIS Bldg, John Compton Highway, Castries; tel. 452-2611; fax 453-7347; e-mail mitandt@candw.lc; internet www.geocities.com/WallStreet/Floor/7020.

Ministry of Communications, Works, Transport and Public Utilities: Williams Bldg, Bridge St, Castries; tel. 452-2429; fax 453-2769.

Ministry of Community Development, Culture, Local Government and Co-operatives: 4th Floor, New Government Bldgs, John Compton Highway, Castries; tel. 453-1487; fax 453-7921.

Ministry of Development, Planning, the Environment and Housing: POB 709, Waterfront, Castries; tel. 451-6957; fax 452-2506.

Ministry of Education, Human Resource Development, Youth and Sports: New NIS Bldg, The Waterfront, Castries; tel. 452-2476; fax 453-2299; e-mail mineduc@candw.lc.

Ministry of Finance, Economic Affairs and Information: Old Government Bldgs, Laborie St, Castries; tel. 452-5315; fax 453-1648.

Ministry of Foreign Affairs and International Trade: New Government Bldgs, John Compton Highway, Castries; tel. 452-1178.

Ministry of Health, Human Services, Family Affairs and Women: Chaussee Rd, Castries; tel. 452-2827.

Ministry of Legal Affairs, Home Affairs and Labour: Old Government Bldgs, Laborie St, Castries.

Ministry of Tourism and Civil Aviation: Government Bldg, John Compton Highway, Castries; tel. 451-6849; fax 451-6986.

Legislature

PARLIAMENT
Senate

The Senate has nine nominated members and two independent members.

President: NEVILLE CENAC.

House of Assembly

Speaker: WILFRED ST CLAIR DANIEL.

Clerk: DORIS BAILEY.

Election, 23 May 1997

Party	Votes	% of votes	Seats
Saint Lucia Labour Party . .	44,063	61.30	16
United Workers' Party . . .	26,325	36.62	1
Independents	1,494	2.08	—
Total	71,882	100.00	17

Political Organizations

National Alliance (NA): Castries; f. 2001; opposition electoral alliance; Pres. Sir JOHN COMPTON; Vice-Pres. Dr MORELLA JOSEPH; Political Leader GEORGE ODLUM.

Reform Party: Castries; f. 1999; campaigns against the political establishment; Spokesman MARTINUS FRANÇOIS.

Saint Lucia Labour Party (SLP): 2nd Floor, Tom Walcott Bldg, Jeremie St. POB 427, Castries; tel. 451-8446; fax 451-9389; e-mail slp@candw.lc; internet www.geocities.com/~slp; f. 1946; socialist party; Leader Dr KENNY ANTHONY.

United Workers' Party (UWP): 1 Riverside Rd, Castries; tel. 452-3438; e-mail uwp@iname.com; internet www.geocities.com/CapitolHill/8393; f. 1964; right-wing party; Chair. ELDRIDGE STEPHENS; Leader Dr MORELLA JOSEPH.

Diplomatic Representation

EMBASSIES AND HIGH COMMISSION IN SAINT LUCIA

China, People's Republic: Cap Estate, Gros Islet, POB GM 999, Castries; tel. 452-0903; fax 452-9495; Ambassador: LIANG JAINMING.

France: French Embassy to the OECS, Vigie, Castries; tel. 452-2462; fax 452-7899; e-mail frenchembassy@candw.lc; Ambassador: HENRI VIDAL.

United Kingdom: NIS Bldg, Waterfront, POB 227, Castries; tel. 452-2484; fax 453-1543; e-mail britishhc@candw.lc; (High Commissioner resident in Barbados); Resident Acting High Commissioner: PETER HUGHES.

Venezuela: Vigie, BOP 494, Castries; tel. 452-4033; fax 453-6747; Chargé d'affaires a.i.: RAFAEL BARRETO.

Judicial System

SUPREME COURT

Eastern Caribbean Supreme Court: Waterfront, Government Bldgs, POB 1093, Castries; tel. 452-2574; fax 452-5475; e-mail appeal@candw.lc. The West Indies Associated States Supreme Court was established in 1967 and was known as the Supreme Court of Grenada and the West Indies Associated States from 1974 until 1979, when it became the Eastern Caribbean Supreme Court. Its jurisdiction extends to Anguilla, Antigua and Barbuda, the British Virgin Islands, Dominica, Grenada (which rejoined in 1991), Montserrat, Saint Christopher and Nevis, Saint Lucia and Saint Vincent and the Grenadines. It is composed of the High Court of Justice and the Court of Appeal. The High Court is composed of the Chief Justice and 13 High Court Judges. The Court of Appeal is presided over by the Chief Justice and includes three other Justices of Appeal. Jurisdiction of the High Court includes fundamental rights and freedoms, membership of the parliaments, and matters concerning the interpretation of constitutions. Appeals from the Court of Appeal lie to the Judicial Committee of the Privy Council, based in the United Kingdom.

Chief Justice: C.M. DENNIS BYRON (acting).

Attorney-General: PETROS COMPTON.

Religion

CHRISTIANITY
The Roman Catholic Church

Saint Lucia forms a single archdiocese. The Archbishop participates in the Antilles Episcopal Conference (currently based in Port of Spain, Trinidad and Tobago). At 31 December 1999 there were an estimated 115,000 adherents, equivalent to some 78% of the population.

Archbishop of Castries: KELVIN EDWARD FELIX, Archbishop's Office, POB 267, Castries; tel. 452-2416; fax 452-3697; e-mail archbishop@candw.lc.

The Anglican Communion

Anglicans in Saint Lucia are adherents of the Church in the Province of the West Indies, comprising eight dioceses. The Archbishop of the West Indies is the Bishop of Nassau and the Bahamas. Saint Lucia forms part of the diocese of the Windward Islands (the Bishop is resident in Kingstown, Saint Vincent).

Other Christian Churches

Seventh-day Adventist Church: St Louis St, POB 117, Castries; tel. 452-4408; e-mail adventist@candw.lc; Pastor THEODORE JARIA.

Trinity Evangelical Lutheran Church: Gablewoods, POB GM 858, Castries; tel. 450-1484; fax 450-3382; e-mail jaegerj@candw.lc; Pastor J. JAEGER.

Baptist, Christian Science, Methodist, Pentecostal and other churches are also represented in Saint Lucia.

The Press

The Catholic Chronicle: POB 778, Castries; f. 1957; monthly; Editor Rev. PATRICK A. B. ANTHONY; circ. 3,000.

The Crusader: 19 St Louis St, Castries; tel. 452-2203; fax 452-1986; f. 1934; weekly; Editor GEORGE ODLUM; circ. 4,000.

The Mirror: Bisee Industrial Estate, Castries; tel. 451-6181; fax 451-6197; e-mail webmaster@stluciamirror.com; internet www.stluciamirror.com; f. 1994; weekly on Fridays; Man. Editor GUY ELLIS.

One Caribbean: POB 852, Castries; e-mail dabread@candw.lc; internet www.onecaribbean.com; Editor D. SINCLAIR DABREO.

The Star: Rodney Bay Industrial Estate, Gros Islet, POB 1146, Castries; tel. 450-7827; fax 450-8694; e-mail starpub@candw.lc; internet www.stluciastar.com; weekly; Propr RICK WAYNE.

The Vanguard: Hospital Rd, Castries; fortnightly; Editor ANDREW SEALY; circ. 2,000.

Visions Magazine: POB 947, Castries; tel. 453-0427; fax 452-1522; e-mail visions@candw.lc; internet www.sluonestop.com/visions; official tourist guide; published by St Lucia Hotel and Tourism Association.

The Voice of St Lucia: Odessa Bldg, Darling Rd, POB 104, Castries; tel. 452-2590; fax 453-1453; f. 1885; 2 a week; circ. 8,000.

The Weekend Voice: Odessa Bldg, Darling Rd, POB 104, Castries; tel. 452-2590; fax 453-1453; weekly on Saturdays; circ. 8,000.

NEWS AGENCY

Caribbean News Agency: Bisee Rd, Castries; tel. 453-7162.

FOREIGN NEWS AGENCIES

Inter Press Service (IPS) (Italy): Hospital Rd, Castries; tel. 452-2770.

United Press International (UPI) (USA): Castries; tel. 452-3556.

Publishers

Caribbean Publishing Co Ltd: American Drywall Bldg, Vide Boutielle Highway, POB 104, Castries; tel. 452-3188; fax 452-3181; e-mail publish@candw.lc; f. 1978; publishes telephone directories and magazines.

Crusader Publishing Co Ltd: 19 St Louis St, Castries; tel. 452-2203; fax 452-1986.

Island Visions: Sans Soucis, POB 947, Castries; tel. 453-0427; fax 452-1522; e-mail visions@candw.lc; internet www.sluonestop.com/visions.

Mirror Publishing Co Ltd: POB 1782, Bisee Industrial Estate, Castries; tel. 451-6181; fax 451-6503; e-mail webmaster@stluciamirror.com; internet www.stluciamirror.com; Man. Editor GUY ELLIS.

Star Publishing Co: Massade Industrial Park, Gros Islet, POB 1146, Castries; tel. 450-7827; fax 450-8694; e-mail starpub@candw.lc.

Voice Publishing Co Ltd: Odessa Bldg, Darling Rd, POB 104, Castries; tel. 452-2590; fax 453-1453.

Broadcasting and Communications

TELECOMMUNICATIONS
Regulatory Authority

Eastern Caribbean Telecommunications Authority: Castries; f. 2000 to regulate telecommunications in Saint Lucia, Dominica, Grenada, Saint Christopher and Nevis and Saint Vincent and the Grenadines.

Major Service Providers

Cable & Wireless (St Lucia) Ltd: Bridge St, POB 111, Castries; tel. 453-9000; fax 453-9700; e-mail talk2us@candw.lc; internet www.candw.lc; also operates a mobile cellular telephone service. (In February 2001 Cable & Wireless announced it was to cease operations in Saint Lucia when its current licence expired and relocate its regional call centres to Barbados and Anguilla.)

St Lucia Boatphone Ltd: POB 2136, Gros Islet; tel. 452-0361; fax 452-0394; e-mail boatphone@candw.lc.

BROADCASTING
Radio

Gem Radio Network: POB 1146, Castries; tel. 459-0609.

Radio Caribbean International: 11 Mongiraud St, POB 121, Castries; tel. 452-2636; fax 452-2637; e-mail rci@candw.lc; internet www.candw.lc/homepage/rci.htm; operates Radio Caraïbes; English and Creole services; broadcasts 24 hrs; Pres. H. COQUERELLE; Station Man. WINSTON FOSTER.

Radyo Koulibwi: POB 20, Morne Du Don, Castries; tel. 451-7814; fax 453-1983; f. 1990.

Saint Lucia Broadcasting Corporation: Morne Fortune, POB 660, Castries; tel. 452-2337; fax 453-1568; govt-owned; Man. KEITH WEEKES.

> **Radio 100-Helen FM:** Morne Fortune, POB 621, Castries; tel. 451-7260; fax 453-1737.

Radio Saint Lucia (RSL): Morne Fortune, POB 660, Castries; tel. 452-7415; fax 453-1568; English and Creole services; Chair. VAUGHN LOUIS FERNAND; Man. KEITH WEEKES.

Trinity Broadcasting Network: Plateau Castries; tel. 450-5979.

Television

Cablevision: George Gordon Bldg, Bridge St, POB 111, Castries; tel. 452-3301; fax 453-2544.

Catholic TV Broadcasting Service: Micoud St, Castries; tel. 452-7050.

Daher Broadcasting Service Ltd: Vigie, POB 1623, Castries; tel. 453-2705; fax 452-3544; Man. Dir LINDA DAHER.

Helen Television System (HTS): National Television Service of St Lucia, POB 621, The Morne, Castries; tel. 452-2693; fax 454-1737; e-mail hts@candw.lc; internet www.htsstlucia.com; f. 1967; commercial station; Man. Dir LINFORD FEVRIERE; Prog. Dir VALERIE ALBERT.

Finance

(cap. = capital; m. = million; br. = branch)

BANKING

The Eastern Caribbean Central Bank (see Part Three), based in Saint Christopher, is the central issuing and monetary authority for Saint Lucia. Total deposits at commercial banks were EC $922.3m. at the end of 1992, of which amount EC $69.3m. was deposited by non-residents.

Local Banks

Caribbean Banking Corporation Ltd: Gobblewoods Mall, POB 1531, Castries; tel. 451-7469; fax 451-1668; f. 1985; owned by Royal Bank of Trinidad and Tobago Ltd; Chair. PETER JULY; 4 brs.

National Commercial Bank of Saint Lucia: Financial Centre, Bridge St, POB 1860, Castries; tel. 452-2103; fax 453-1604; e-mail ncbslu@candw.lc; internet ncbstlucia.com; f. 1981; cap. US $0.4m.; 52% state-owned; Chair. VICTOR EUDOXIE; Man. Dir MARIUS ST ROSE; 5 brs.

Saint Lucia Co-operative Bank Ltd: 21 Bridge St, POB 168, Castries; tel. 452-2880; fax 453-1630; e-mail coopbank@candw.lc; incorporated 1937; commercial bank; auth. cap. EC $5,000,000; Pres. FERREL CHARLES; 3 brs.

Development Bank

Saint Lucia Development Bank: Financial Centre, 1 Bridge St, POB 368, Castries; tel. 457-7532; fax 457-7299; f. 1981; merged with former Agricultural and Industrial Development Bank; provides credit for agriculture, industry, tourism, housing and workforce training; Man. Dir DANIEL GIRARD.

Foreign Banks

Bank of Nova Scotia Ltd (Canada): 6 William Peter Blvd, POB 301, Castries; tel. 456-2100; fax 456-2130; e-mail bns@candw.lc; Man. S. COZIER; 3 brs.

Barclays Bank PLC (United Kingdom): Bridge St, POB 335, Castries; tel. 452-3306; fax 452-6860; e-mail Barclays@candw.lc; Man. T. T. KING; 6 brs.

Canadian Imperial Bank of Commerce (CIBC): Clarke St, POB 244, Vieux Fort; tel. 454-6262; fax 454-5309; Man. F. D. ROCK; 2 brs.

Royal Bank of Canada: Laborie St and William Peter Blvd, POB 280, Castries; tel. 452-2245; fax 452-7855; Man. JOHN MILLER.

'Offshore' Bank

Bank Crozier International Ltd: Crozier Bldg, Brazil St, Castries; e-mail p.johansson@bankcrozier.com; internet www.bankcrozier.com; CEO PETER JOHANSSON.

INSURANCE

There were 25 insurance companies operating in Saint Lucia in 1990. Local companies include the following:

Caribbean General Insurance Ltd: Laborie St, POB 290; Castries; tel. 452-2410; fax 452-3649.

Eastern Caribbean Insurance Ltd: Laborie St, POB 290, Castries; tel. 452-2410; fax 452-3649; e-mail gci.ltd@candw.lc.

Saint Lucia Insurances Ltd: 48 Micoud St, POB 1084, Castries; tel. 452-3240; fax 452-2240.

Saint Lucia Motor and General Insurance Co Ltd: 38 Micoud St, POB 767, Castries; tel. 452-3323; fax 452-6072.

Trade and Industry

DEVELOPMENT ORGANIZATION

National Development Corporation (NDC): Block B, First Floor, Govt. Bldgs, The Waterfront, POB 495, Castries; tel 452-3614; fax 452-1841; e-mail devcorp@candw.lc; internet www.stluciandc.com; f. 1971 to promote the economic development of Saint Lucia; owns and manages four industrial estates; br. in New York, USA; Chair. MATTHEW BEAUBRUN; Gen. Man. JACQUELINE EMMANUEL-ALBERTINIE.

CHAMBER OF COMMERCE

Saint Lucia Chamber of Commerce, Industry and Agriculture: Vide Bouteille, POB 482, Castries; tel. 452-3165; fax 453-6907; e-mail chamber@candw.lc; internet www.sluchamber.com.lc; f. 1884; 150 mems; Pres. LINFORD FEVRIER.

INDUSTRIAL AND TRADE ASSOCIATIONS

Saint Lucia Banana Corporation (SLBC): Castries; f. 1998 following privatization of Saint Lucia Banana Growers' Asscn (f. 1967); Sec. FREEMONT LAWRENCE.

Saint Lucia Industrial and Small Business Association: 2nd Floor, Ivy Crick Memorial Bldg, POB 312, Castries; tel. 453-1392; Pres. LEO CLARKE; Exec. Dir Dr URBAN SERAPHINE.

EMPLOYERS' ASSOCIATIONS

Saint Lucia Agriculturists' Association Ltd: Mongiraud St, POB 153, Castries; tel. 452-2494; Chair. and Man. Dir C. ALCINDOR; Sec. R. RAVENEAU.

Saint Lucia Coconut Growers' Association Ltd: Manoel St, POB 259, Castries; tel. 452-2360; fax 453-1499; Chair. JOHANNES LEONCE; Man. N. E. EDMUNDS.

Saint Lucia Employers' Federation: Morgan's Bldg, Maurice Mason Ave, POB 160, Castries; tel. 452-2190; fax 452-7335.

Saint Lucia Fish Marketing Corpn: Castries; tel. 452-1341; fax 451-7073.

Saint Lucia Marketing Board: Conway, POB 441, Castries; tel. 452-3214; fax 453-1424; Chair. DAVID DEMAQUE; Man. MICHAEL WILLIAMS.

Windward Islands Banana Development and Exporting Co (Wibdeco): POB 115, Castries; tel. 452-2651; f. 1994 in succession to the Windward Islands Banana Growers' Association (WINBAN); regional organization dealing with banana development and marketing; jointly owned by the Windward governments and island banana associations; Chair. ARNHIM EUSTACE.

UTILITIES

Electricity

Caribbean Electric Utility Services Corpn (CARILEC): 16–19 Orange Park Centre, POB 2056, Bois D'Orange, Gros Islet; tel. 452-0140; fax 452-0142; e-mail admin@carilec.org; internet www.carilec.org.

St Lucia Electricity Services Ltd (LUCELEC): Lucelec Bldg, John Compton Highway, POB 230, Castries; tel. 452-2324; fax 452-1127.

Water

Water and Sewerage Co Inc.: L'Anse Rd, POB 1481, Castries; tel. 452-5344; fax 452-6844: e-mail wasco@candw.lc; f. 1999.

TRADE UNIONS

Farmers' and Farm Workers' Union: St Louis St, Castries; Pres. Senator FRANCES MICHEL; Sec. CATHERINE BURT; 3,500 mems.

National Workers' Union: POB 713, Castries; tel. 452-3664; represents daily-paid workers; affiliated to World Federation of Trade Unions; Pres. TYRONE MAYNARD; Gen. Sec. GEORGE GODDARD; 3,000 mems (1996).

Saint Lucia Civil Service Association: POB 244, Castries; tel. 452-3903; fax 453-6061; e-mail csa@candw.lc; f. 1951; Pres. TERENCE LEONARD; Gen. Sec. LAWRENCE POYOTTE; 1,950 mems.

Saint Lucia Media Workers' Association: Castries; provides training for media workers in partnership with the Government.

Saint Lucia Nurses' Association: POB 819, Castries; tel. 452-1403; fax 453-0960; f. 1947; Pres. LILIA HARRACKSINGH; Gen. Sec. ESTHER FELIX.

Saint Lucia Seamen, Waterfront and General Workers' Trade Union: 24 Chaussee Rd, POB 166, Castries; tel. 452-1669; fax 452-5452; f. 1945; affiliated to International Confederation of Free Trade Unions (ICFTU), International Transport Federation (ITF) and Caribbean Congress of Labour; Pres. MICHAEL HIPPOLYTE; Sec. CRESCENTIA PHILLIPS; 1,000 mems.

Saint Lucia Teachers' Union: POB 821, Castries; tel. 452-4469; fax 453-6668; e-mail sltu@candw.lc; internet www.sltu.org; f. 1934; Pres. URBAN DOLOR; Gen.-Sec. KENTRY D. J. PIERRE.

Saint Lucia Workers' Union: Reclamation Grounds, Conway, Castries; tel. 452-2620; f. 1939; affiliated to ICFTU; Pres. GEORGE LOUIS; Sec. TITUS FRANCIS; 1,000 mems.

Vieux Fort General and Dock Workers' Union: New Dock Rd, POB 224, Vieux Fort; tel. 454-6193; fax 454-5128; f. 1954; Pres. JOSEPH GRIFFITH; 846 mems (1996).

Transport

RAILWAYS

There are no railways in Saint Lucia.

ROADS

In 2000 there was an estimated total road network of 910 km, of which 150 km were main road and 127 km were secondary roads. In that year only 5.2% of roads were paved. The main highway passes through every town and village on the island. A construction project of a coastal highway, to link Castries with Cul de Sac Bay, was completed in February 2000. Internal transport is handled by private concerns and controlled by Government. A major five-year road maintenance programme was due to commence in 2000 to rehabilitate the estimated 60% of roads which were on the point of collapse. The programme was to be partially funded by the Caribbean Development Bank.

SHIPPING

The ports at Castries and Vieux Fort have been fully mechanized. Castries has six berths with a total length of 2,470 ft (753 metres). The two dolphin berths at the Pointe Seraphine cruise-ship terminal have been upgraded to a solid berth of 1000 ft (305 metres) and one of 850 ft (259 metres). A project to upgrade the port at Vieux Fort to a full deep-water container port was completed in mid-1993. The port of Soufrière has a deep-water anchorage, but no alongside berth for ocean-going vessels. There is a petroleum transhipment terminal at Cul de Sac Bay. In 1999 394,148 cruise-ship passengers called at Saint Lucia. Regular services are provided by a number of shipping lines, including ferry services to neighbouring islands.

Saint Lucia Air and Sea Ports Authority: Manoel St, POB 651, Castries; tel. 452-2893; fax 452-2062; e-mail slaspa@candw.lc; Gen. Man. VINCENT HIPPOLYTE.

St Lucia Marine Terminals Ltd: POB 355, Vieux Fort; tel. 454-8738; fax 454-8745; e-mail slumarterm@candw.lc; f. 1995; private port management co.

CIVIL AVIATION

There are two airports in use: Hewanorra International (formerly Beane Field near Vieux Fort), 64 km (40 miles) from Castries, which is equipped to handle large jet aircraft; and George F. L. Charles Airport, which is at Vigie, in Castries, and which is capable of handling medium-range jets. Saint Lucia is served by scheduled flights to the USA, Canada, Europe and most destinations in the Caribbean. The country is a shareholder in the regional airline LIAT (see chapter on Antigua and Barbuda).

Saint Lucia Air and Sea Ports Authority: (see above).

Air Antilles: Laborie St, POB 1065, Castries; f. 1985; designated as national carrier of Grenada in 1987; flights to destinations in the Caribbean, the United Kingdom and North America; charter co.

Caribbean Air Transport: POB 253, Castries; f. 1975 as Saint Lucia Airways; local shuttle service, charter flights.

Eagle Air Services Ltd: Vigie Airport, POB 838, Castries; tel. 452-1900; fax 452-9683; e-mail eagleairslu@candw.lc; internet www.eagleairslu.com; charter flights; Man. Dir Capt. EWART F. HINKSON.

Helenair Corpn Ltd: POB 253, Castries; tel. 452-1958; fax 451-7360; e-mail helenair@candw.lc; internet www.stluciatravel.com.lc/helenair.htm; f. 1987; charter and scheduled flights to major Caribbean destinations; Man. ARTHUR NEPTUNE.

Tourism

Saint Lucia possesses spectacular mountain scenery, a tropical climate and sandy beaches. Historical sites, rich birdlife and the sulphur baths at Soufrière are other attractions. Tourist arrivals totalled 664,984 in 1999. Tourist receipts in 1999 were EC $736.02m. The USA is the principal market (32% of total stop-over visitors in 1998), followed by the United Kingdom and Canada. There were an estimated 3,760 hotel rooms in 1997, although expansion of hotel capacity remains a government priority, and it was hoped that 5,000 rooms would be available in 2000.

Saint Lucia Tourist Board: Top floor, Sureline Bldg, Vide Bouti-elle, POB 221, Castries; tel. 452-5968; fax 453-1121; e-mail slutour@candw.lc; internet www.stlucia.org; 2 brs overseas; Chair. DESMOND SKEETE; Dir HILARY MODESTE.

Saint Lucia Hotel and Tourism Association: POB 545, Castries; tel. 452-5978; fax 452-7967; e-mail slhta@candw.lc; internet www.stluciatravel.com.lc; f. 1962; Pres. NOEL CADASSE; Exec. Vice Pres. HILARY MODESTE.

Defence

The Royal Saint Lucia Police Force, which numbers about 300 men, includes a Special Service Unit for purposes of defence. Saint Lucia participates in the US-sponsored Regional Security System, comprising police, coastguards and army units, which was established by independent East Caribbean states in 1982. There are also two patrol vessels for coastguard duties.

Education

Education is compulsory for 10 years between five and 15 years of age. Primary education begins at the age of five and lasts for seven years. Secondary education, beginning at 12 years of age, lasts for five years, comprising a first cycle of three years and a second cycle of two years. Free education is provided in more than 90 government-assisted schools. Facilities for industrial, technical and teacher-training are available at the Sir Arthur Lewis Community College at Morne Fortune, which also houses an extra-mural branch of the University of the West Indies. The rate of adult illiteracy is estimated at 19% for males and 18% for females. EC $22m. was allocated to education in the 1999/2000 budget.

SAINT VINCENT AND THE GRENADINES

Area: 389.3 sq km (150.3 sq miles); Saint Vincent covers 344 sq km, and the country also includes some of the Grenadines, an island chain stretching between Saint Vincent and Grenada.

Population (IMF estimate, 1999): 110,000.

Capital: Kingstown (population 16,132 in 1996).

Language: English.

Religion: Predominantly Christianity; the main denominations are the Anglican, Methodist and Roman Catholic Churches.

Climate: Tropical; temperature ranges between 18°C and 32°C (64°–90°F); annual rainfall on Saint Vincent varies between 1,500 mm in the south and 3,750 mm in the mountainous interior.

Time: GMT –4 hours.

Public Holidays: 2002: 1 January (New Year's Day), 22 January (Saint Vincent and the Grenadines Day), 29 March (Good Friday), 1 April (Easter Monday), 6 May (Labour Day), 20 May (Whit Monday), 1 July (Caricom Day), 2 July (Carnival Tuesday), 5 August (Emancipation Day), 27 October (National Day), 25–26 December (Christmas). **2003:** 1 January (New Year's Day), 22 January (Saint Vincent and the Grenadines Day), 18 April (Good Friday), 21 April (Easter Monday), 5 May (Labour Day), 9 June (Whit Monday), 1 July (Carnival Tuesday), 7 July (Caricom Day), 4 August (Emancipation Day), 27 October (National Day), 25–26 December (Christmas).

Currency: Eastern Caribbean dollar; US \$1 = EC \$2.70 (fixed rate since July 1976); EC \$100 = £25.88 = US \$37.04 = €41.73 (30 April 2001).

Weights and Measures: Imperial.

History

The islands became a British possession in the 18th century, belonged to the Windward Islands Federation until 1959 and the West Indies Federation between 1958 and 1962. Under the name of St Vincent, the territory became an Associated State, with full internal autonomy in October 1969 with Milton Cato, leader of the Saint Vincent Labour Party (SVLP) and formerly Chief Minister, as the first Premier. At elections in April 1972, James Mitchell, standing as an independent, held the balance of power between the SVLP and the People's Political Party (PPP). The PPP formed a Government with Mitchell as Premier. In 1974 Mitchell's Government collapsed, and in the subsequent December elections the SVLP was returned to power with 10 seats, and Cato became Premier of a coalition Government with the PPP. The islands attained full independence on 27 October 1979, when Cato became Prime Minister. After winning elections in December 1979, the SVLP gradually lost popularity, owing to its economic and taxation policies, and to reported scandals surrounding the Cato administration. In the elections of July 1984 the centrist New Democratic Party (NDP), founded by former Premier Mitchell, won nine of the 13 elective seats in the House of Assembly, and Mitchell became Prime Minister. The success of the NDP's economic policies contributed to an overwhelming victory in the general election of May 1989, in which it won all 15 seats in the newly enlarged House of Assembly. At a general election in February 1994 the NDP secured 12 seats, ensuring its third consecutive term of office. The three remaining seats were won by an alliance between the SVLP and the Movement for National Unity, which formally merged as the United Labour Party (ULP) in September, led by Vincent Beache. He led criticism of the Government over the crisis in the banana industry and, in 1995, during the scandal that caused the resignation of Parnell R. Campbell, the Deputy Prime Minister, following allegations of financial impropriety. Nevertheless, Mitchell retained power after the general election of 15 June 1998, the NDP winning eight seats and the ULP seven. On 9 July, at the opening of the first session of the House of Assembly, several hundred protesters demonstrated against the new Government. In December Ralph Gonsalves, the deputy leader of the ULP, was elected party leader following the resignation of Vincent Beache. In early December US marines and troops provided by the Regional Security System destroyed marijuana crops during a two-week operation, despite opposition from growers.

In April 2000 the introduction of legislation increasing the salaries and benefits of members of the House of Assembly provoked protests throughout the islands. An agreement was reached in May, whereby further legislative elections were to be held before March 2001. On 20 August finance minister Arnhim Eustace took over the presidency of the NDP from Mitchell, and, in October, Mitchell stood down as Prime Minister in favour of Eustace. In January 2001 the US air carrier American Eagle suspended its service between Puerto Rico and Saint Vincent, following a safety audit of E. T. Joshua airport by the US Federal Aviation Authority. Over half of all stop-over tourists arrived on American Eagle flights. The Government had plans to expand the airport to take larger aircraft.

Parliament was dissolved on 5 March 2001 for elections to be held on 28 March. Prime Minister Eustace and ULP leader Gonsalvez called for a peaceful campaign after a ULP supporter was shot and wounded by a supporter of the NDP. The ULP accused the NDP in mid-March of trying to create a situation in which a national emergency could be declared, troops from the Regional Security System bought in, and the elections postponed. However, at the election the ULP secured an overwhelming victory, winning 12 of the 15 parliamentary seats and 57% of the votes cast, with the NDP, which had been in power since 1984, securing the remaining three and 40.9% of the votes cast. Eustace only narrowly avoided losing his own seat. The newly formed PPM failed to win any seats. Voter turn-out was 68.7%. Gonsalves stated that the new Government's priorities would be job creation, education and health. In June Gonsalves announced his intention to establish a constitutional review commission. Among the issues to be addressed by the commission were local government organization and finance, civil service reform and the electoral system.

Economy

Agriculture (including forestry and fishing) contributed a projected 9.8% of GDP in 2000. The sector employed 25.1% of the working population at the census of 1991, and agricultural products account for the largest share of export revenue, although Vincentian crops were badly affected by mealybug infestation, which led to the suspension of some exports from 1996 to March 1999. The country's main crop was bananas, which contributed a projected 40.1% of the value of merchandise exports in 2000. Furthermore, despite some decline in production the islands remained the world's leading producer of arrowroot. Real agricultural GDP (which is heavily reliant on weather conditions and banana production) fluctuated throughout the last decade, but was projected to increase by 4.8% in 2000. There was also a small manufacturing sector, which expanded throughout most of the 1990s, although decreases were recorded in 1997–99. However, the sector was expected to continue to account for 6.3% of GDP in 2000. The main activities included a garment industry, the assembling of electrical components and the processing of agricultural products. One of the main limits on industry was the need to import most energy (89% in 1992). However, the industrial sector accounted for 25.5% of GDP in 2000.

Investment in infrastructure assisted agricultural development and was seen as essential for the encouragement of tourism. The latter sector contributed 2.3% of GDP in 1997. Tourist activity remained concentrated in the Grenadines and catered mainly for the luxury market. Visitors aboard yachts remain the most important sector, although the numbers of stop-over and cruise-ship visitors have steadily increased in recent years, by an estimated 13.6% in 1998 and by 33.0% in 1999. In addition, there is a small 'offshore' financial sector. The services sector as a whole contributed a projected 66.7% of GDP in 2000 and engaged 53.8% of the employed population at the time of the 1991 census.

According to data published by the International Monetary Fund (IMF), real GDP increased by an estimated average of 4.1% during 1996–2000. However growth slowed slightly in 2000, decreasing to 3.0% compared with 4.0% in 1999. This largely reflected continuing decline in the banana industry. In July 2001 the Government announced that the banana industry was to be restructured in a bid to increase competitiveness in the period leading up to the end of the tariff/quota system in 2006. The prospects for long-term economic growth remain dependent on the health of the agricultural sector and further growth in tourism. In May 2000 the Financial Stability Forum (FSF) categorized Saint Vincent and the Grenadines' banking supervision in the lowest group. In June the Organisation for Economic Co-operation and Development (OECD) included Saint Vincent and the Grenadines in a report on countries with harmful tax policies and in the same month it was also included on a list of 'non-co-operative' governments in the fight against money 'laundering' by the Financial Action Task Force (FATF, based a the OECD Secretariat). In July the Offshore Finance Authority revoked the licences of six offshore banks in an immediate response to an advisory by the US Department of the Treasury. The Government also announced that it would take further steps to improve its regulatory and advisory mechanisms. However, by July 2001 Saint Vincent and the Grenadines remained on the FATF's list.

Statistical Survey

Sources (unless otherwise stated): Statistical Office, Ministry of Finance and Planning, Government Bldgs, Kingstown; tel. 456-1111.

AREA, POPULATION AND DENSITY

Area: 389.3 sq km (150.3 sq miles). The island of Saint Vincent covers 344 sq km (133 sq miles).

Population: 97,845 at census of 12 May 1980; 106,499 (males 53,165; females 53,334) at census of 12 May 1991; 110,000 (IMF estimate) at mid-1999.

Density (mid-1999): 282.6 per sq km.

Principal Town: Kingstown (capital), population 16,132 (1996).

Births and Deaths (preliminary, registrations, 1998): Live births 2,002 (birth rate 18.0 per 1,000); Deaths 813 (death rate 7.3 per 1,000). Source: UN, *Population and Vital Statistics Report.*

Economically Active Population (persons aged 15 years and over, 1991 census): Agriculture, hunting, forestry and fishing 8,377; Mining and quarrying 98; Manufacturing 2,822; Electricity, gas and water 586; Construction 3,535; Trade, restaurants and hotels 6,544; Transport, storage and communications 2,279; Financing, insurance, real estate and business services 1,418; Community, social and personal services 7,696; Total employed 33,355 (males 21,656; females 11,699); Unemployed 8,327 (males 5,078, females 3,249); Total labour force 41,682 (males 26,734, females 14,948). Source: ILO, *Yearbook of Labour Statistics.*

AGRICULTURE, ETC.

Principal Crops (metric tons, 1994): Nutmeg and mace 104; Arrowroot starch 115; Ginger 489; Taro (Dasheen, Eddo) 2,591; Tannias 270.

2000 (FAO estimates, '000 metric tons): Maize 2; Sweet potatoes 2; Yams 1; Other roots and tubers 9; Coconuts 24; Vegetables 4; Sugar cane 20; Apples 1; Oranges 1; Lemons and limes 1; Mangoes 1; Bananas 43; Plantains 1. Source: FAO.

Livestock (FAO estimates, '000 head, year ending September 2000): Asses 1; Cattle 6; Pigs 10; Sheep 13; Goats 6. Source: FAO.

Livestock Products (FAO estimates; '000 metric tons, 2000): Pig meat 1; Cows' milk 1; Hen eggs 1. Source: FAO.

Fishing (metric tons, live weight, 1998): Total catch 1,329 (European pilchard 46, Wahoo 72, Skipjack tuna 63, Yellowfin tuna 54.) Source: FAO, *Yearbook of Fishery Statistics.*

INDUSTRY

Selected Products ('000 metric tons, 1998, unless otherwise indicated): Copra 1 (FAO estimate); Raw sugar 2 (FAO estimate); Rum 163,000 proof gallons; Electric energy 89.5 million kWh (IMF estimate, 1999). Source: partly FAO: *Production Yearbook.*

FINANCE

Currency and Exchange Rates: 100 cents = 1 Eastern Caribbean dollar (EC $). *Sterling, US Dollar and Euro Equivalents* (30 April 2001): £1 sterling = EC $3.866; US $1 = EC $2.700; €1 = EC $2.397; EC $100 = £25.88 = US $37.04 = €41.73. *Exchange rate:* Fixed at US $1 = EC $2.70 since July 1976.

Budget (EC $ million, estimates, 1999): *Revenue:* Revenue from taxation 222 (Taxes on international trade and transactions 105); Other current revenue 30; Capital revenue 2; Foreign grants 11; Total 264. *Expenditure:* Personal emoluments 118; Other goods and services 44; Interest payments 20; Transfers and subsidies 33; Capital expenditure and net lending 62; Total 277. Source: IMF, *St Vincent and the Grenadines: Recent Economic Developments* (December 2000).

International Reserves (US $ million at 31 December 2000): IMF special drawing rights 0.08; Reserve position in IMF 0.65; Foreign exchange 54.45; Total 55.18. Source: IMF, *International Financial Statistics.*

Money Supply (EC $ million at 31 December 2000): Currency outside banks 52.11; Demand deposits at deposit money banks 183.10; Total money (incl. others) 235.34. Source: IMF, *International Financial Statistics.*

Cost of Living (Consumer Price Index; base: 1995 = 100): 107.1 in 1998; 108.2 in 1999; 108.4 in 2000. Source: IMF, *International Financial Statistics.*

Gross Domestic Product (EC $ million at current prices): 793.1 in 1997; 856.6 in 1998; 887.2 in 1999. Source: IMF, *St Vincent and the Grenadines: Recent Economic Developments* (December 2000).

Expenditure on the Gross Domestic Product (estimates, EC $ million at current prices, 1999): Government final consumption expenditure 163.3; Private final consumption expenditure 637.3; Gross fixed capital formation 253.7; *Total domestic expenditure* 1,054.4; Exports of goods and services 484.2; *Less* Imports of goods and services 651.4; *Gross domestic product in purchasers' values* 887.2. Source: IMF, *St Vincent and the Grenadines: Recent Economic Developments* (December 2000).

Gross Domestic Product by Economic Activity (estimates, EC $ million at current prices, 1999): Agriculture, hunting, forestry and fishing 77.7; Mining and quarrying 2.2; Manufacturing 48.8; Electricity and water 44.1; Construction 97.2; Wholesale and retail trade 127.7; Hotels and restaurants 17.0; Transport 102.9; Communications 53.0; Banks and insurance 56.0; Real estate and housing 18.0; Government services 132.4; Other community, social and personal services 13.9; *Sub-total* 701.2; *Less* Imputed bank service charge 44.8; *GDP at factor cost* 746.0; Indirect taxes, *less* subsidies 141.3; *GDP in purchasers' values* 887.2. Source: IMF, *St Vincent and the Grenadines: Recent Economic Developments* (December 2000).

Balance of Payments (estimates, US $ million, 1999): Exports of goods f.o.b. 49.6; Imports of goods f.o.b. –177.1; *Trade balance* –127.4; Exports of services 129.7; Imports of services –64.2; *Balance on goods and services* –62.0; Other income received 3.0; Other income paid –22.9; *Balance on goods, services and income* –81.9; Current transfers (net) 15.6; *Current balance* –66.2; Capital account (net) 7.8; Financial account 42.0; Net errors and omissions 20.3; *Overall balance* 3.9. Source: IMF, *St Vincent and the Grenadines: Recent Economic Developments* (December 2000).

EXTERNAL TRADE

Principal Commodities (US $ million, estimates, 1999): *Imports:* Food and live animals 41.3; Beverages and tobacco 4.0; Crude materials (inedible) except fuels 6.1; Mineral fuels, lubricants, etc. 11.1; Chemicals and related products 20.1; Basic manufactures 68.8; Machinery and transport equipment 48.8; Total (incl. others) 200.8. *Exports:* Bananas 20.4; Eddoes and dasheens 1.9; Flour 6.7; Rice 5.0; Total domestic exports (incl. others) 44.8; Re-exports 4.6; Total 49.4. Source: IMF, *St Vincent and the Grenadines: Recent Economic Developments* (December 2000).

Principal Trading Partners (US $ million, estimates, 1999): *Imports:* Barbados 7.6; Canada 5.0; Guyana 2.9; Japan 9.2; Netherlands 2.1; Trinidad and Tobago 31.8; United Kingdom 24.3; USA 75.8; Total (incl. others) 200.8. *Exports:* Antigua and Barbuda 3.3; Barbados 4.3; Dominica 1.7; Guyana 0.5; Jamaica 1.5; Saint Lucia 4.3; Trinidad and Tobago 5.1; United Kingdom 19.9; USA 1.6; Total (incl. others) 49.4. Source: IMF, *St Vincent and the Grenadines: Recent Economic Developments* (December 2000).

TRANSPORT

Road Traffic (motor vehicles in use, 1996): Passenger cars 5,023; Commercial vehicles 6,109.

Shipping: *Arrivals* (1996): Vessels 996. *International Freight Traffic* ('000 metric tons, 1996): Goods loaded 72; Goods unloaded 128. *Merchant Fleet* (vessels registered at 31 December 2000): Number 1,366; Total displacement 7,026,538 grt (Source: Lloyd's Register of Shipping).

Civil Aviation (visitor arrivals): 88,110 in 1998; 85,761 in 1999; 97,117 in 2000. Source: IMF, *St Vincent and the Grenadines: Recent Economic Developments* (December 2000).

TOURISM

Visitor Arrivals: 226,900 (62,195 stop-over arrivals, 33,372 excursionists, 67,639 cruise-ship passengers, 76,918 visitors aboard yachts) in 1997; 202,100 (67,227 stop-over arrivals, 20,882 excursionists, 34,903 cruise-ship passengers, 81,946 visitors aboard yachts) in 1998; 223,125 (68,293 stop-over arivals, 17,468 excursionists, 47,743 cruise-ship passengers, 89,621 visitors aboard yachts) in 1999. Source: IMF, *St Vincent and the Grenadines: Recent Economic Developments* (December 2000).

Hotel Rooms: 554 in 1996.

Tourist Receipts: (EC $ million): 186.68 in 1997; 197.69 in 1998; 212.93 in 1999. Source: IMF, *St Vincent and the Grenadines: Recent Economic Developments* (December 2000).

COMMUNICATIONS MEDIA

Daily newspapers (1996): 1; average circ. 1,000.

Non-daily newspapers (1996): 6; average circ. 34,000.

Radio Receivers (1997): 77,000 in use.

Television Receivers (1997): 18,000 in use.

Telephones (1998): 20,500 main lines in use.

Telefax Stations (year beginning 1 April 1996): 1,500 in use.

Mobile Cellular Telephones (year beginning 1 April 1993): 83 subscribers.

Sources: mainly UNESCO, *Statistical Yearbook*, and UN, *Statistical Yearbook*.

EDUCATION

Pre-primary (1993/94): 97 schools; 175 teachers; 2,500 pupils.

Primary (1996): 60 schools; 1,169 teachers; 22,149 pupils.

Secondary (1996): 21 schools; 394 teachers; 7,639 pupils.

Teacher-Training (1996): 1 institution; 10 teachers; 162 students.

Technical College (1996): 1 institution; 22 teachers; 213 students.

Source: partly UNESCO, *Statistical Yearbook*.

Directory

The Constitution

The Constitution came into force at the independence of Saint Vincent and the Grenadines on 27 October 1979. The following is a summary of its main provisions:

FUNDAMENTAL RIGHTS AND FREEDOMS

Regardless of race, place of origin, political opinion, colour, creed or sex, but subject to respect for the rights and freedoms of others and for the public interest, every person in Saint Vincent and the Grenadines is entitled to the rights of life, liberty, security of the person and the protection of the law. Freedom of conscience, of expression, of assembly and association is guaranteed and the inviolability of a person's home and other property is maintained. Protection is afforded from slavery, forced labour, torture and inhuman treatment.

THE GOVERNOR-GENERAL

The British Monarch is represented in Saint Vincent and the Grenadines by the Governor-General.

PARLIAMENT

Parliament consists of the British monarch, represented by the Governor-General, and the House of Assembly, comprising 15 elected Representatives (increased from 13 under the provisions of an amendment approved in 1986) and six Senators. Senators are appointed by the Governor-General—four on the advice of the Prime Minister and two on the advice of the Leader of the Opposition. The life of Parliament is five years. Each constituency returns one Representative to the House who is directly elected in accordance with the Constitution. The Attorney-General is an *ex-officio* member of the House. Every citizen over the age of 18 is eligible to vote. Parliament may alter any of the provisions of the Constitution.

THE EXECUTIVE

Executive authority is vested in the British monarch and is exercisable by the Governor-General. The Governor-General appoints as Prime Minister that member of the House who, in the Governor-General's view, is the best able to command the support of the majority of the members of the House, and selects other Ministers on the advice of the Prime Minister. The Governor-General may remove the Prime Minister from office if a resolution of no confidence in the Government is passed by the House and the Prime Minister does not either resign within three days or advise the Governor-General to dissolve Parliament.

The Cabinet consists of the Prime Minister and other Ministers and the Attorney-General as an *ex-officio* member. The Leader of the Opposition is appointed by the Governor-General as that member of the House who, in the Governor-General's view, is best able to command the support of a majority of members of the House who do not support the Government.

CITIZENSHIP

All persons born in Saint Vincent and the Grenadines before independence who, immediately prior to independence, were citizens of the United Kingdom and Colonies automatically become citizens of Saint Vincent and the Grenadines. All persons born outside the country after independence to a parent possessing citizenship of Saint Vincent and the Grenadines automatically acquire citizenship, as do those born in the country after independence. Citizenship can be acquired by those to whom it would not automatically be granted.

The Government

Head of State: HM Queen ELIZABETH II.

Governor-General: Sir CHARLES ANTROBUS (took office in 1996).

CABINET
(August 2001)

Prime Minister and Minister of Finance, Planning, Economic Development, Labour and Information: Dr RALPH GONSALVES.

Deputy Prime Minister and Minister of Foreign Affairs, Commerce and Trade: LOUIS STRAKER.

Minister of National Security, the Public Service, Seaports and Airports and Air Development: VINCENT BEACHE.

Minister of Education, Youth Affairs and Sports: MIKE BROWN.

Minister of Social Development, the Family, Gender Affairs and Ecclesiastical Affairs: GIRLYN MIGUEL.

Minister of Agriculture, Land and Fisheries: SELMON WALTERS.

Minister of Tourism and Culture: RENÉ BAPTISTE.

Minister of Health and the Environment: Dr DOUGLAS SLATER.

Minister of Telecommunications, Science, Technology and Industry: Dr JERROL THOMPSON.

Minister of Transport, Works and Housing: JULIAN FRANCIS.

Attorney-General: JUDITH JONES-MORGAN.

MINISTRIES

Office of the Governor-General: Government Bldgs, Kingstown; tel. 456-1401.

Office of the Prime Minister: Administrative Centre, Kingstown; tel. 456-1703; fax 457-2152.

Office of the Attorney-General: Government Bldgs, Kingstown; tel. 457-2807.

Ministry of Agriculture, Land and Fisheries: Government Bldgs, Kingstown; tel. 457-1380; fax 457-1688.

Ministry of Commerce and Trade: Government Bldgs, Kingstown; tel. 456-1223; fax 457-2880; e-mail mtrade@caribsurf.com.

Ministry of Education, Youth Affairs and Sports: Government Bldgs, Kingstown; tel. 457-1104; e-mail mined@caribsurf.com.

Ministry of Finance, Planning, Economic Development, Labour and Information: Government Bldgs, Kingstown; tel. 456-1111.

Ministry of Foreign Affairs: Administrative Centre, Kingstown; tel. 456-2060; fax 456-2610; e-mail svgforeign@caribsurf.com.

Ministry of Health and the Environment: Government Bldgs, Kingstown; tel. 457-2586; fax 457-2684.

Ministry of National Security, the Public Service, Seaports and Airports and Air Development: Government Bldgs, Kingstown.

Ministry of Social Development, the Family, Gender Affairs and Ecclesiastical Affairs: Government Bldgs, Kingstown; tel. 426-2949.

Ministry of Telecommunications, Science, Technology and Industry: Government Bldgs, Kingstown; tel. 457-2039.

Ministry of Tourism and Culture: Government Bldgs, Kingstown.

Ministry of Transport, Works and Housing: Government Bldgs, Kingstown.

Legislature

HOUSE OF ASSEMBLY

Senators: 6.

Elected Members: 15.

Election, 28 April 2001

Party	% of votes	Seats
Unity Labour Party (ULP)	57.0	12
New Democratic Party (NDP)	40.9	3
People's Progressive Movement (PPM) . . .	2.1	—
Total	100.0	15

Political Organizations

Canouan Progressive Movement: Kingstown; Leader TERRY BYNOE.

New Democratic Party (NDP): Murray Rd, POB 1300, Kingstown; tel. 457-2647; f. 1975; democratic party supporting political unity in the Caribbean, social development and free enterprise; Pres. ARNHIM EUSTACE; Sec.-Gen. STUART NANTON; 7,000 mems.

People's Progressive Movement (PPM): Kingstown; f. 2000 following split from ULP; Leader KEN BOYEA.

People's Working Party: Kingstown; Leader BURTON WILLIAMS.

Unity Labour Party (ULP): Beachmont, Kingstown; tel. 457-2761; fax 456-2811; e-mail ulpweb@aol.com; internet www.ulp.org; f. 1994 by merger of Movement for National Unity (MNU) and the Saint Vincent Labour Party (SVLP); moderate, social-democratic party; Leader Dr RALPH E. GONSALVES.

In 2000 the **Organization in Defence of Democracy (ODD),** an umbrella group of trade unions and non-governmental organizations, was formed to protest against government policy.

Diplomatic Representation

EMBASSIES AND HIGH COMMISSION IN SAINT VINCENT AND THE GRENADINES

China (Taiwan): Murray Road, POB 878, Kingstown; tel. 456-2431; fax 456-2913; Chargé d'affaires a.i.: TOM CHOU.

United Kingdom: Granby St, POB 132, Kingstown; tel. 457-1701; fax 456-2750; (High Commissioner resident in Barbados); Resident Acting High Commissioner: BRIAN ROBERTSON.

Venezuela: Baynes Bros Bldg, Granby St, POB 852, Kingstown; tel. 456-1374; fax 457-1934; e-mail lvccsvg@caribsurf.com; Chargé d'affaires a.i.: RICHARD ESPINOZA.

Judicial System

Justice is administered by the Eastern Caribbean Supreme Court, based in Saint Lucia and consisting of a Court of Appeal and a High Court. Two puisne judges are resident in Saint Vincent. There are five Magistrates, including the Registrar of the Supreme Court, who acts as an additional Magistrate.

Puisne Judges: ODEL ADAMS, IAN DONALDSON MITCHELL.

Office of the Registrar of the Supreme Court: Registry Dept, Court House, Kingstown; tel. 457-1220; fax 457-1888; Registrar JUDITH S. JONES-MORGAN.

Chief Magistrate: BRIDGET NURSE.

Magistrates: ERROL MOUNSEY, SIMONE CHURUMAN, REGINALD JAMES.

Director of Public Prosecutions: HAYMANT BALROOP.

Religion

CHRISTIANITY

Saint Vincent Christian Council: Melville St, POB 445, Kingstown; tel. 456-1408; f. 1969; four mem. churches; Chair. Mgr RENISON HOWELL.

The Anglican Communion

Anglicans in Saint Vincent and the Grenadines are adherents of the Church in the Province of the West Indies, comprising eight dioceses. The Archbishop of the West Indies is the Bishop of Nassau and the Bahamas, and is resident in Nassau. The diocese of the Windward Islands includes Grenada, Saint Lucia and Saint Vincent and the Grenadines.

Bishop of the Windward Islands: Rt Rev. SEHON GOODRIDGE, Bishop's Court, POB 502, Kingstown; tel. 456-1895; fax 456-2591; e-mail diocesewi@vincysurf.com.

The Roman Catholic Church

Saint Vincent and the Grenadines comprises a single diocese (formed when the diocese of Bridgetown-Kingstown was divided in October 1989), which is suffragan to the archdiocese of Castries (Saint Lucia). The Bishop participates in the Antilles Episcopal Conference, currently based in Port of Spain, Trinidad and Tobago. At 31 December 1999 there were an estimated 10,000 adherents in the diocese, comprising about 9% of the population.

Bishop of Kingstown: Rt Rev. ROBERT RIVAS, Bishop's Office, POB 862, Edinboro, Kingstown; tel. 457-2363; fax 457-1903; e-mail rcdok @caribsurf.com.

Other Christian Churches

The Methodists, Seventh-day Adventists, Baptists and other denominations also have places of worship.

BAHÁ'Í FAITH

National Spiritual Assembly: POB 1043, Kingstown; tel. 456-4717.

The Press

DAILY

The Herald: Blue Caribbean Bldg, Kingstown; tel. 456-1242; fax 456-1046; e-mail herald@caribsurf.com; internet www .heraldsvg.com; daily; internationally distributed.

SELECTED WEEKLIES

The Independent Weekly: 85 Sharpe St, Kingstown; tel. 457-2866; Man. Editor CONLEY ROSE.

Justice: POB 519, Kingstown; weekly; organ of the United People's Movement; Editor RENWICK ROSE.

The New Times: POB 1300, Kingstown; f. 1984; Thursdays; organ of the New Democratic Party.

The News: McCoy St, POB 1078, Kingstown; tel. 456-2942; fax 456-2941; e-mail thenews@caribsurf.com; weekly.

Searchlight: Cnr Bay & Egmont St, POB 152, Kingstown; tel. 456-1558; fax 457-2250; e-mail search@caribsurf.com; weekly on Fridays.

The Star: POB 854, Kingstown.

The Vincentian: Paul's Ave, POB 592, Kingstown; tel. 457-7430; f. 1919; weekly; owned by the Vincentian Publishing Co; Man. Dir EGERTON M. RICHARDS; Editor-in-Chief TERRANCE PARRIS; circ. 6,000.

The Westindian Crusader: Kingstown; tel. 456-9315; fax 456-9315; e-mail crusader@caribsurf.com; weekly.

SELECTED PERIODICALS

Caribbean Compass: POB 175, Bequia; tel. 457-3409; fax 457-3410; e-mail compass@caribsurf.com; internet www .caribbeancompass.com; marine news; monthly; free distribution in Caribbean from Puerto Rico to Panama; circ. 12,000.

Government Bulletin: Government Information Service, Kingstown; tel. 456-3410; circ. 300.

Government Gazette: POB 12, Kingstown; tel. 457-1840; f. 1868; Government Printer HAROLD LLEWELLYN; circ. 492.

Unity: Middle & Melville St, POB 854, Kingstown; tel. 456-1049; fortnightly; organ of the United Labour Party.

Publishers

CJW Communications: Frenches Gate, Kingstown; tel. 456-2942; fax 456-2941.

Great Works Depot: Commission A Bldg, Granby St, POB 1849, Kingstown; tel. 456-2057; fax 457-2055; e-mail gwd@caribsurf.com.

The Vincentian Publishing Co Ltd: St George's Place; POB 592, Kingstown; tel. 456-1123; Man. Dir EGERTON M. RICHARDS.

Broadcasting and Communications

TELECOMMUNICATIONS

Regulatory Authority

Eastern Caribbean Telecommunications Authority: based in Castries, Saint Lucia; f. 2000 to regulate telecommunications in Saint Vincent and the Grenadines, Dominica, Grenada, Saint Christopher and Nevis and Saint Lucia.

Major Service Providers

Cable & Wireless (WI) Ltd: Halifax St, Kingstown; tel. 457-1901; fax 457-2777; Man. IAN KYLE.

Cable & Wireless Caribbean Cellular: Halifax St, Kingstown; tel. 457-4600; fax 457-4940; cellular telephone service.

BROADCASTING

National Broadcasting Corporation of Saint Vincent and the Grenadines: Dorsetshire Hill, POB 617, Kingstown; tel. 456-1078; fax 456-1015; e-mail svgbc@caribsurf.com; internet www .nbcsvg.com; govt-owned; Chair. ST CLAIR LEACOCK; controls:

Radio 705: Richmond Hill, POB 705, Kingstown; tel. 457-1111; fax 456-2749; commercial; broadcasts BBC World Service (United Kingdom) and local programmes.

Television

National Broadcasting Corporation of Saint Vincent and the Grenadines: (see Radio).

SVG Television: Dorsetshire Hill, POB 617, Kingstown; tel. 456-1078; fax 456-1015; e-mail svgbc@caribsurf.com; broadcasts US and local programmes; Chief Engineer R. P. MACLEISH.

Television services from Barbados can be received in parts of the islands.

Finance

(cap. = capital; res = reserves; dep. = deposits; m. = million; br. = branch)

BANKING

The Eastern Caribbean Central Bank (see Part III), based in Saint Christopher, is the central issuing and monetary authority for Saint Vincent and the Grenadines.

Principal Banks

Caribbean Banking Corporation Ltd: 81 South River Rd, POB 118, Kingstown; tel. 456-1501; fax 456-2141; f. 1985; cap. EC $7.9m., res $1.0m., dep. $89.4m. (July 1992); Gen. Man. FRANCIS V. BOWMAN; Chair. PETER JULY; 2 brs.

First Saint Vincent Bank Ltd: Lot 112, Granby St, POB 154, Kingstown; tel. 456-1873; fax 456-2675; f. 1988; fmrly Saint Vincent Agricultural Credit and Loan Bank; Man. Dir O. R. SYLVESTER.

National Commercial Bank (SVG) Ltd: Bedford St, POB 880, Kingstown; tel. 457-1844; fax 456-2612; e-mail natbank@ caribsurf.com; f. 1977; govt-owned; cap. EC $26.6m., dep. $352.7m. (June 1999); Chair. RICHARD JOACHIM; Man. DIGBY AMBRIS; 8 brs.

New Bank Ltd: 16 South River Rd and Bay St, POB 1628, Kingstown; tel. 457-1411; fax 457-1357; e-mail nbl.adnw@caribsurf.com; internet www.nbltd.com.

Owens Bank Ltd: Blue Caribbean Bldg, Bay St, POB 1045, Kingstown; tel. 457-1230; fax 457-2610; f. 1926.

Saint Vincent Co-operative Bank: Cnr Long Lane (Upper) and South River Rd, POB 886, Kingstown; tel. 456-1894; fax 457-2183.

Foreign Banks

Bank of Nova Scotia Ltd (Canada): 76 Halifax St, POB 237, Kingstown; tel. 457-1601; fax 457-2623; Man. S. K. SUBRAMANIAM.

Barclays Bank PLC (United Kingdom): Halifax St, POB 604, Kingstown; tel. 456-1706; fax 457-2985; Man. KARL HAYWOOD; 5 brs.

Canadian Imperial Bank of Commerce: Halifax St, POB 212, Kingstown; tel. 457-1587; fax 457-2873; Man. W. G. LYONS.

INSURANCE

A number of foreign insurance companies have offices in Kingstown. Local companies include the following:

Abbott's Insurance Co: cnr Sharpe and Bay St, POB 124, Kingstown; tel. 456-1511; fax 456-2462.

BMC Agencies Ltd: Sharpe St, POB 1436, Kingstown; tel. 457-2041; fax 457-2103.

Durrant Insurance Services: South River Rd, Kingstown; tel. 457-2426.

Haydock Insurances Ltd: Granby St, POB 1179, Kingstown; tel. 457-2903; fax 456-2952.

Metrocint General Insurance Co Ltd: St Georges Place, POB 692, Kingstown; tel. 456-1821.

Saint Hill Insurance Co Ltd: Bay St, POB 1741, Kingstown; tel. 457-1227; fax 456-2374.

Saint Vincent Insurances Ltd: Lot 69, Grenville St, POB 210, Kingstown; tel. 456-1733; fax 456-2225; e-mail vinsure@ caribsurf.com.

'OFFSHORE' FINANCIAL SECTOR

Legislation permitting the development of an 'offshore' financial sector was introduced in 1976 and revised in 1996 and 1998. International banks are required to have a place of business on the islands and to designate a licensed registered agent. International business companies registered in Saint Vincent and the Grenadines are exempt from taxation for 25 years. Legislation also guarantees total confidentiality.

Saint Vincent and the Grenadines Offshore Finance Authority: Administrative Center, POB 356, Kingstown; tel. 456-2577; fax 457-2568.

Saint Vincent Trust Service: Trust House, 112 Bonadie St, POB 613, Kingstown; tel. 457-1027; fax 457-1961; e-mail trusthouse@ saint-vincent-trust.com; internet www.saint-vincent-trust.com; br. in Liechtenstein; Pres. BRYAN JEEVES.

Trade and Industry

DEVELOPMENT ORGANIZATION

Saint Vincent Development Corporation (Devco): Grenville St, POB 841, Kingstown; tel. 457-1358; fax 457-2838; f. 1970; finances industry, agriculture, fisheries, tourism; Chair. SAMUEL GOODLUCK; Man. CLAUDE M. LEACH.

CHAMBER OF COMMERCE

Saint Vincent and the Grenadines Chamber of Industry and Commerce (Inc): Hillsboro St, POB 134, Kingstown; tel. 457-1464; fax 456-2944; e-mail svgcic@caribsurf.com; internet www .svgcic.com; f. 1925; Pres. JEFFREY PROVIDENCE; Exec. Dir LEROY ROSE.

INDUSTRIAL AND TRADE ASSOCIATION

Saint Vincent Marketing Corporation: Upper Bay St, Kingstown; tel. 457-1603; fax 456-2673.

EMPLOYERS' ORGANIZATIONS

Saint Vincent Arrowroot Industry Association: Upper Bay St, Kingstown; tel. 457-1511; f. 1930; producers, manufacturers and sellers; 186 mems; Chair. GEORGE O. WALKER.

Saint Vincent Banana Growers' Association: Sharpe St, POB 10, Kingstown; tel. 457-1605; fax 456-2585; f. 1955; over 7,000 mems; Chair. LESLINE BEST; Gen. Man. HENRY KEIZER.

Saint Vincent Employers' Federation: Halifax St, POB 348, Kingstown; tel. 456-1269; Dir ST CLAIR LEACOCK.

UTILITIES

Saint Vincent Electricity Services Ltd (VINLEC): Paul's Ave, POB 856, Kingstown; tel. 456-1701; fax 456-2436.

Water

Central Water and Sewerage Authority: New Montrose, POB 363, Kingstown; tel. 456-2946; fax 456-2552; e-mail cwsa@ caribsurf.com.

CO-OPERATIVES

There are 26 Agricultural Credit Societies, which receive loans from the Government, and five Registered Co-operative Societies.

TRADE UNIONS

Commercial, Technical and Allied Workers' Union (CTAWU): Lower Middle St, POB 245, Kingstown; tel. 456-1525; fax 457-1676; f. 1962; affiliated to CCL, ICFTU and other international workers' organizations; Pres. ALICE MANDEVILLE; Gen. Sec. LLOYD SMALL; 2,500 mems.

National Labour Congress: POB 1290, Kingstown; tel. 457-1950; five affiliated unions; Chair. FITZ JONES.

National Workers' Movement: Grenville St, POB 1290, Kingstown; tel. 457-1950; fax 456-2858; e-mail natwok@caribsurf.com; Gen. Sec. NOEL C. JACKSON.

Public Services Union of Saint Vincent and the Grenadines: McKies Hill, POB 875, Kingstown; tel. 457-1950; fax 456-2858; f. 1943; Pres. CONRAD SAYERS; Exec. Sec. ROBERT I. SAMUEL; 738 mems.

Saint Vincent Union of Teachers: POB 304, Kingstown; tel. 457-1062; f. 1952; members of Caribbean Union of Teachers affiliated to FISE; Pres. TYRONE BURKE; 1,250 mems.

Transport

RAILWAYS

There are no railways in the islands.

ROADS

In 1996 there was an estimated total road network of 1,040 km (646 miles), of which 319 km (198 miles) was paved.

SHIPPING

The deep-water harbour at Kingstown can accommodate two ocean-going vessels and about five motor vessels. There are regular motor-vessel services between the Grenadines and Saint Vincent. A weekly service to the United Kingdom was operated by Geest Industries, formerly the major banana purchaser. Numerous shipping lines also call at Kingstown harbour. Some exports are flown to Barbados to link up with international shipping lines. A new marina and shipyard complex at Ottley Hall, Kingstown, was completed during 1995. A new container port at Campden Park, near Kingstown, was opened in May 1995. A new dedicated Cruise Terminal was scheduled to open in June 1999, which would permit two cruise ships to berth at the same time.

Saint Vincent and the Grenadines Port Authority: POB 1237, Kingstown; tel. 456-1830; fax 456-2732; e-mail svgport@ caribsurf.com.

CIVIL AVIATION

There is a civilian airport, E. T. Joshua Airport, at Arnos Vale, situated about 3 km (2 miles) south-east of Kingstown. Projects to upgrade the airports on the islands of Bequia and Union were completed in 1992. The islands of Mustique and Canouan have landing strips for light aircraft only, although a project to upgrade Canouan Airport began in May 1997. In late 1999 the Government began the process of raising finance for the extension of E. T. Joshua Airport in order to permit the use of long-haul jet aircraft. It was hoped to complete the project by 2003.

American Eagle: POB 1232, E.T. Joshua Airport, Arnos Vale; tel. 456-5555; fax 456-5616.

Mustique Airways: POB 1232, E. T. Joshua Airport, Arnos Vale; tel. 456-4380; fax 456-4586; e-mail info@mustique.com; internet mustique.com; f. 1979; charter flights; Chair. JONATHAN PALMER.

Saint Vincent and the Grenadines Air (1990) Ltd (SVG Air): POB 39, E.T. Joshua Airport, Arnos Vale; tel. 457-5124; fax 457-5077; e-mail info@svgair.com; internet www.svgair.com; f. 1990; charter and scheduled flights; CEO J. E. BARNARD.

Tourism

The island chain of the Grenadines is the country's main tourist asset. There are superior yachting facilities, but the lack of major air links with countries outside the region has resulted in a relatively slow development for tourism. In 1999 Saint Vincent and the Grenadines received 223,125 tourists (including 47,743 cruise-ship passengers and 89,621 visitors aboard yachts). Tourist receipts totalled EC $212.9m. in 1999.

Department of Tourism: Bay St, POB 834, Kingstown; tel. 457-1502; fax 456-2610; e-mail tourism@caribsurf.com; internet www.svgtourism.com; Dir VERA-ANN BRERETON.

Saint Vincent and the Grenadines Hotel and Tourism Association: E. T. Joshua Airport; tel. 458-4379; fax 456-4456; e-mail office@svghotels.com; internet www.svghotel.com; Exec. Dir DAWN SMITH.

Defence

Saint Vincent and the Grenadines participates in the US-sponsored Regional Security System, comprising police, coastguards and army units, which was established by independent East Caribbean states in 1982. Since 1984, however, the paramilitary Special Service Unit has had strictly limited deployment. Government current expenditure on public order and safety was estimated at EC $20.8m. in 1998.

Education

Free primary education, beginning at five years of age and lasting for seven years, is available to all children in government schools, although it is not compulsory and attendance is low. There are 60 government, and five private, primary schools. Secondary education, beginning at 12 years of age, comprises a first cycle of five years and a second, two-year cycle. However, government facilities at this level are limited, and much secondary education is provided in schools administered by religious organizations, with government assistance. There are also a number of junior secondary schools. There is a teacher-training college and a technical college. In 1994/95 76% and 24% of children in the relevant age-groups were attending primary and secondary schools, respectively. In 1994 the average rate of adult illiteracy was estimated at 18%. Current expenditure on education by the central Government was an estimated EC $43.5m. (17.6% of total current expenditure) in 1997 and a projected EC $46.4m. in 1998.

SOUTH GEORGIA AND THE SOUTH SANDWICH ISLANDS

South Georgia, an island of 3,592 sq km (1,387 sq miles), lies in the South Atlantic Ocean, about 1,300 km (800 miles) east-south-east of the Falkland Islands. The South Sandwich Islands, which have an area of 311 sq km (120 sq miles), lie about 750 km (470 miles) south-east of South Georgia.

The United Kingdom annexed South Georgia and the South Sandwich Islands in 1775. With a segment of the Antarctic mainland and other nearby islands (now the British Antarctic Territory), they were constituted as the Falkland Islands Dependencies in 1908. Argentina made formal claim to South Georgia in 1927, and to the South Sandwich Islands in 1948. In 1955 the United Kingdom unilaterally submitted the dispute over sovereignty to the International Court of Justice (based in the Netherlands), which decided not to hear the application in view of Argentina's refusal to submit to the Court's jurisdiction. South Georgia was the site of a British Antarctic Survey base (staffed by 22 scientists and support personnel) until it was invaded in April 1982 by Argentine forces, who occupied the island until its recapture by British forces three weeks later. The South Sandwich Islands were uninhabited until the occupation of Southern Thule in December 1976 by about 50 Argentines, reported to be scientists. Argentine personnel remained until removed by British forces in June 1982.

In mid-1989 it was reported that the British Government was considering the imposition of a conservation zone extending to 200 nautical miles (370 km) around South Georgia, similar to that which surrounds the Falkland Islands, in an attempt to prevent the threatened extinction of certain types of marine life.

Under the provisions of the South Georgia and South Sandwich Islands Order of 1985, the islands ceased to be governed as dependencies of the Falkland Islands on 3 October 1985. The Governor of the Falkland Islands is, *ex officio*, Commissioner for the territory.

In May 1993, in response to the Argentine Government's decision to commence the sale of fishing licences for the region's waters, the British Government announced an extension, from 12 to 200 nautical miles, of its territorial jurisdiction in the waters surrounding the islands, in order to conserve crucial fishing stocks.

In September 1998 the British Government announced that it would withdraw its military detachment from South Georgia in 2000, while it would increase its scientific presence on the island with the installation of a permanent team from the British Antarctic Survey to investigate the fisheries around the island for possible exploitation. The small military detachment finally withdrew in March 2001. The British garrison stationed in the Falkland Islands would remain responsible for the security of South Georgia and the South Sandwich Islands.

Commissioner: DONALD A. LAMONT (Stanley, Falkland Islands).
Assistant Commissioner and Director of Fisheries: ROSS T. JARVIS (Stanley, Falkland Islands).

SURINAME

Area: 163,265 sq km (63,037 sq miles).

Population (official estimate, mid-1999): 430,000.

Capital: Paramaribo, population 67,718 at census of 1 July 1980.

Language: Dutch (official); Hindustani, Javanese, Chinese, English, French, Spanish and the local language, Sranang Tongo, are also widely spoken.

Religion: The principal religions are Christianity, Hinduism and Islam.

Climate: Tropical, but tempered on the coast by trade winds; average annual temperature is about 27°C (80°F), and average annual rainfall is 2,340 mm.

Time: GMT –3½ hours.

Public Holidays

2002: 1 January (New Year's Day), March* (Phagwa), 29 March–1 April (Easter), 1 May (Labour Day), 1 July (National Union Day), 25 November (Independence Day), 6 December* (Id al-Fitr, end of Ramadan), 25–26 December (Christmas).

2003: 1 January (New Year's Day), March* (Phagwa), 18–21 April (Easter), 1 May (Labour Day), 1 July (National Union Day), 25 November (Independence Day), 26 November* (Id al-Fitr, end of Ramadan), 25–26 December (Christmas).

* Exact date dependent upon sightings of the moon.

Currency: Suriname gulden (guilder) or florin; 10,000 Suriname guilders = £3.206 = US $4.590 = €5.172 (30 April 2001).

Weights and Measures: The metric system is in force.

Basic Economic Indicators

	1996	1997	1998
Gross domestic product (million Suriname guilders at 1980 prices) .	1,407.3	1,554.1	1,582.4
GDP (million Suriname guilders at current prices) .	299,609	362,110	328,080
Annual growth of real GDP (%) .	13.1	10.1	3.1*
Government budget ('000 million Suriname guilders at current prices):			
Revenue .	122.8	113.1	137.2†
Expenditure .	116.3	130.4	188.0
Consumer price index (annual average for Paramaribo; base: 1995 = 100)‡ .	99.3	106.4	126.6
Rate of inflation (annual average, %)§ .	–0.7	7.1	19.0
Foreign exchange reserves (US $ million at 31 December) .	96.3	109.1	106.1
Imports c.i.f. (US $ million) .	501	658	552
Exports f.o.b. (US $ million) .	433	701	436
Balance of payments (current account, US $ million) .	9.5	24.7	–154.9

* Preliminary figure.
† Estimate.
‡ 251.8 in 1999.
§ 98.9% in 1999; 64.3% in 2000.

Gross national product (purchasing power parity of GNP per head, USA = 100, 1995): 8.3.

Economically active population (1998): 88,244.

Unemployment (1998): 10.6%.

Total foreign debt (1999): US $248m.

Life expectancy (years at birth, 1998): 70.

Infant mortality rate (per 1,000 live births, World Bank estimate, 1998): 28.

Adult population with HIV/AIDS (15–49 years, 1999): 1.26%.

School enrolment ratio (6–17 years, 1988): 87%.

Adult literacy rate (15 years and over, 2000): 94.2% (males 4.1%; females 7.4%).

Energy consumption per head (kg of coal equivalent, 1984): 1,773.

Carbon dioxide emissions per head (metric tons, 1997): 5.2.

Passenger motor cars in use (estimate, per 1,000 of population, 1996): 143.7.

Television receivers in use (per 1,000 of population, 1997): 153.

History

JAMES McDONOUGH

In the 15th century the only inhabitants of Suriname were Carib, Arawak and Awarao Indians (Amerindians). Another tribe, the Surinas, who inhabited the country at an earlier time, is considered the source of the name Suriname. In 1499 Alonso de Ojeada, a Spanish lieutenant serving the Italian navigator Amerigo Vespucci, landed on the north-eastern coast of South America, which was called Guiana by the Amerindians. The Spanish claimed possession of the coast, but no actual settlement was attempted. During the next century the Dutch began establishing trading posts along the Commewijn and Corantijn rivers (now in Suriname), and later along the Essequibo and Berbice (now in Guyana). The French were attempting to establish settlements along the Cayenne River (now in French Guiana). During this period, lumbering and tobacco farming were the chief commercial activities. It was the English, however, who founded the first successful colony in Suriname, as the result of an expedition financed by Lord Francis Willoughby, the colonial Governor of the flourishing but overcrowded English sugar island of Barbados. The group of English planters and their slaves established a large settlement on the Suriname River, near what is now Paramaribo. The British Crown ceded its Suriname colony to the Netherlands in the Treaty of Breda (1667), in exchange for the colony of Nieuw Amsterdam (now New York, USA). The colony remained under Dutch rule for the next 300 years, except for two brief periods of British control in 1799–1802 and 1804–14, during the Napoleonic wars.

The territory became known as Dutch Guiana, and was flanked to the west by British Guiana (now Guyana) and to the east by French Guiana. The colony was administered by a Governor, with the assistance of the Political Council, the members of which were appointed by the Governor, following nomination by the colonial planter-class. In 1828 the administration of all Dutch West Indies colonies was centralized under a Governor-General, stationed in Suriname, who reported directly to the Colonial Office in the Netherlands. During this period the colony flourished on the basis of large, Dutch-owned sugar plantations, worked by African slave labour. Between 1650 and 1820 some 300,000 West African slaves were brought into Suriname. Nevertheless, the plantations suffered a continual labour drain owing to escaping slaves, who would seek refuge from the authorities in the vast and underdeveloped interior of the country. By 1728 these runaway slaves, known as 'Boschnegers' (Bush Negroes) or maroons, had established a number of settlements based on African tribal customs and were warring with the white plantation owners and the colonial authorities. Expeditions were sent into the jungle to subdue them, but without success. Finally, in 1761 the Dutch signed a treaty with the Boschnegers, guaranteeing their liberty and supplying them with yearly shipments of arms. In return, the Boschnegers promised to return all future runaway slaves and never to appear in Paramaribo in armed groups of more than six persons. From that time, the Boschnegers led an isolated, independent life in the Suriname interior.

The abolition of slavery in neighbouring British Guiana in 1834 and in French Guiana in 1848 produced a period of unrest among Suriname's slaves. These events led King William III of the Netherlands finally to abolish slavery in 1863. To solve the problem of labour shortage created by the abolition of slavery, the Dutch turned to overseas contract or indentured labour. Between 1873 and 1917 some 37,000 indentured labourers were brought to Suriname from India. A similar influx of contract labourers, numbering about 33,000, were brought from the Dutch East Indies (now Indonesia) between 1893 and 1939. Furthermore, the Dutch encouraged the immigration of Chinese, Portuguese and, later, Lebanese workers. Suriname's ethnic and racial make-up reflected the plantation colony's historic need for cheap labour. The census in 1980 recorded that 33.49% of Suriname's population were of Indian descent (known locally as Hindustani, 34.70% were Creole (urban dwellers of African descent), 16.33% were Indonesian-descended 'Javanese', 9.55% Boschneger, 3.10% Amerindian and 1.55% Chinese. The country also had European and other minorities, amounting to about 1.28% of the population. Suriname comprised seven different ethnic groups, speaking more than 15 languages. It was the most fragmented country in the Latin American and Caribbean region and among the 20 most fragmented countries in the world. This ethnic fragmentation also existed in the political arena, where the majority of political parties were organized along ethnic lines.

INDEPENDENCE AND POLITICAL DEVELOPMENT

In 1866 the Koloniale Staten (Colonial Assembly, also known as the Staten van Surnimae), was established. A representative body with limited local power, its members were elected from a small group of colonial planters, who were extended the franchise on the basis of a poll tax. While ultimate power continued to reside in The Hague, the Koloniale Staten remained the principal administrative body in Suriname until the colony gained independence. In the 20th century the exploitation of Suriname's large bauxite reserves and the cultivation of rice replaced sugar as the principal foreign-exchange earner, although the Dutch Government found it necessary to subsidize an ever-increasing share of the colony's budget. In 1950 the Dutch Government granted Suriname internal self-government. Then in 1954, Suriname became an overseas territory of the Dutch 'Tripartite Kingdom', composed of the Netherlands, the Netherlands Antilles (now the Netherlands Antilles and Aruba) and Suriname. Full and complete independence was granted to Suriname by the Dutch on 25 November 1975.

Local political parties began forming during the Second World War, at the time of the promise of local autonomy. Further political participation was stimulated by the introduction of universal suffrage for the general election of 1949. The Nationale Partij Suriname (NPS—Suriname National Party), representing the country's Creole population, won the majority of the seats in the Koloniale Staten, under the leadership of Johan Pengel. During the 1950s the Verenigde Hindostaanse Partij (VHP—United Hindustani Party), representing the Hindustani population, gained prominence under the leadership of Jaggernath Lachmon. The NPS and VHP formed an alliance during the 1960s, which gave Suriname a long period of stability under the principle of ethnic *verbroedering* (fraternization). In the 1973 general election the NPS formed the Nationale Partij Kombinatie (NPK—Combined National Party) alliance with three other parties and won 22 of 39 seats in the Koloniale Staten. Henck Arron, who had replaced Pengel as party leader upon the latter's death in 1970, was named Prime Minister and was in power when the country gained independence in 1975.

Dutch aid, worth 3,500m. guilders, gave considerable support to the economy of the new republic. However, the international economic recession of the mid-1970s, brought on by the petroleum crisis, and the fall of the world price of bauxite, caused growing concern that Suriname would be unable to promote economic development, despite the country's large natural resources and relatively small population. Moreover, more than 40,000 persons, mostly the well-educated and well-trained, emigrated to the Netherlands on the eve of independence, in order to qualify for Dutch citizenship. A series of strikes underlined the growing dissatisfaction of the people, while corruption scandals involving cabinet ministers undermined the Government. Nevertheless, in the general election of 1977, the NPK again won 22 seats, with the remaining 17 seats going to a left-wing opposition front, led by Lachmon and the VHP.

MILITARY TAKE-OVER, 1980–87

On 25 February 1980 the Armed Forces took control of government in a *coup d'état*. The coup followed the civilian Government's refusal to recognize demands of members of the military to form a trade union. The take-over was led by a junior army officer, Sgt-Maj. (later Lt-Col) Désiré (Desi) Bouterse, who seized power in alliance with the left-wing Partij Nationalistiche Republiek (PNR—Nationalist Republican Party). Dr Henk Chin-A-Sen, a PNR leader, was chosen as Prime Minister, presiding over a PNR-assembled Government and the eight-member Nationale Militaire Raad (NMR—National Military Council) named by Bouterse. In August 1980, following a disagreement over policy, Bouterse strengthened his control over the Government by dissolving the legislature and declaring a state of emergency. In March 1981 Sgt-Maj. Wilfred Hawker led an unsuccessful Hindustani-inspired, right-wing coup against Bouterse. In December Bouterse launched the Revolutionaire Volksfront (Revolutionary People's Front) and in February 1982 Chin-A-Sen, who earlier had been named President, was dismissed along with his civilian Government. In March, a second coup attempt by Sgt-Maj. Hawker failed, resulting in his execution.

As a result of the coup attempt, Bouterse declared a state of siege and imposed martial law. However, to prevent the Netherlands from suspending aid under the terms of the independence treaty, the military regime appointed a 12-member Council of Ministers with a civilian majority, and Henry Neyhorst, a moderate economist, became Prime Minister. The failure to solve Suriname's economic difficulties lost Bouterse the support of the left-wing groups and the trade unions, and soon the country was plagued by strikes, demonstrations, and calls for an end to military rule. Bouterse promised to hold elections for a constituent assembly to draft a new constitution. On 8 December 1982, members of the Armed Forces burned down Paramaribo offices of the Bouterse opposition. In the ensuing disturbances some 15 leading politicians, trade unionists, lawyers, journalists and academics were killed, in what became known as the 'December Murders'.

In response to the December Murders, the Dutch Government suspended its large aid programme to the country. The USA and the European Community (EC—known as the European Union from November 1993) immediately followed suit and the Council of Ministers resigned. Bouterse, however, retained the loyalty of the 3,000-man military by dismissing two-thirds of the officer corps. In February 1983 he formed a new civilian–military Council of Ministers, with Dr Errol Alibux (a former Minister of Social Affairs) as Prime Minister. The new Government was composed of two left-wing parties, the Progressieve Arbeiders en Landbouwers Unie (PALU—Progressive Workers' and Farm Labourers' Union) and the Revolutionaire Volkspartij (Revolutionary Peoples' Party).

In foreign affairs, the Bouterse Government followed a non-alignment policy, establishing close relations with Cuba and Libya, to balance the historically close links with the USA and the Netherlands. These moves alarmed both the French and the US authorities. The French saw potential danger to its Kourou space centre, the launching site for the European Ariane rocket, which was located close to the Surinamese border in French Guiana. The USA, determined to stop the spread of 'Communist' governments in the Western hemisphere, was very wary of Suriname's growing ties with Cuba and the large presence of Cuban advisers in the country. George Schultz, former US Secretary of State under President Ronald Reagan (1981–89), revealed in a 1993 memoir that the US administration had been ready to intervene militarily as a result of the 1982 December Murders; however, US plans for the military overthrow of the Bouterse regime were abandoned after the Netherlands refused to participate.

CIVILIAN RESTORATION

In August 1984 the state of emergency imposed in 1982 was lifted, as the military Government began to move the country towards civilian rule. In December plans were announced for the formation of a supreme deliberating council, the Topberaad, consisting of representatives of the trade unions, the business sector and Standvaste, a new movement Bouterse had established in November 1983 as a political power base. The Top-

beraad met in January 1985, with the main task of drafting a new constitution. In March 1987 a draft document consisting of some 186 articles was completed. The Constitution was approved by referendum in September of that year, and a general election was held in November, for the first time in eight years.

In July 1987 Standvaste was reconstituted as the Nationale Democratische Partij (NDP—National Democratic Party), under the leadership of Jules Wijdenbosch. Wijdenbosch was Prime Minister in the last Bouterse-appointed Cabinet of Ministers prior to the November election. In August the three major opposition parties, the Creole NPS, the Hindustani VHP and the Kaum-Tani Persuatan Indonesia (KTPI—Javanese Indonesian Farmers' Union), formed an electoral alliance, the Front voor Demokratie en Ontwikkeling (FDO—Front for Democracy and Development). With the restoration of electoral politics, Suriname's ethnic parties, which had dominated the political scene prior to the 1980 military coup, returned to prominence. At the 25 November election, the FDO won a decisive victory, taking 40 seats in the new 51-seat National Assembly. The PALU and the Progressieve Bosneger Partij (PBP—Progressive Boschneger Party) each won four seats and the NDP won only three. The National Assembly took over political control in January 1988 and unanimously elected Ramsewak Shankar of the VHP to the presidency. Henck Arron of the NPS was elected Vice-President and Prime Minister, heading a 14-member Cabinet of Ministers.

THE BOSCHNEGER REVOLT

The return to constitutional rule did not end Suriname's internal conflicts. From 1986 the military was fighting against a Boschneger insurgency in the interior of the country, which threatened the successful move to constitutional government. The insurgency was led by Ronnie Brunswijk, a Boschneger who was once a member of the presidential bodyguard. He claimed that plans to develop the interior of the country violated the autonomy of the Boschneger society, which had been guaranteed by the 1761 treaty and subsequent agreements signed between the Boschneger and the colonial Dutch. In 1987 Brunswijk's Surinamese Liberation Army (SLA—popularly known as the Jungle Commando) attacked economic targets, causing severe disruption, including the closure of the main bauxite smelting and refining plants.

Bouterse retaliated against the insurgency with raids into the interior; the rebels claimed that the Army massacred Boschnegers in several interior villages. The Army also moved to arm about 1,000 Amerindians, leading to armed clashes between the Boschneger and the Tucayana Amerindians. As a result of the fighting, some 10,000 Boschnegers took refuge in French Guiana and the French reinforced the border with Suriname with paratroopers and legionnaires, refusing to let the Suriname military pursue the insurgents across the border.

In June 1988 negotiations began between the Government and representatives of the SLA. Bouterse's willingness to negotiate was attributed by many to the announcement that there would be an amnesty for personnel from both sides involved in the conflict, which the SLA claimed would prevent investigation of alleged abuses of human rights by the Army. Nevertheless, in July 1989 the SLA and the Suriname Government signed a peace accord at Kourou (French Guiana). The provisions of the so-called Kourou Accord included a general amnesty for those involved in the conflict, the ending of the state of emergency established in December 1986, the incorporation of members of the SLA into the national police and measures to provide for the safe return of the Surinamese refugees in French Guiana. However, the Accord failed when Bouterse vetoed the clause demanding the integration of Brunswijk's fighting force into the national police, and the Amerindians refused to abide by its terms. In addition, the Boschneger refugees refused to move back to Suriname, fearing reprisals by either the Army or the Amerindians once they left the protection of French territory.

The Kourou Accord included proposals for a Consultative Council for the Development of the Interior. Much of the interior's infrastructure had been destroyed and development suspended during the insurgency, but it was not until late 1995 that the Council was appointed. The Government failed, however, to consult the Boschneger and Amerindian representatives about the granting of gold and timber concessions on their land. The Boschneger and Amerindians complained that small-scale mining operations, mainly by illegal Brazilian gold miners, were disrupting tribal and community life. They were concerned in particular about the damaging effects on the food chain by the gold miners' widespread use of mercury.

THE MILITARY INTERREGNUM

In 1990 the US State Department noted, in its annual report to the US Congress on human rights, that the Surinamese military had 're-established itself as the dominant political force in the country'. Only a few of the 120 new laws required to implement the Constitution had been passed by the Assembly, and the Constitutional Court, which was to interpret the Constitution and rule on human-rights issues, had not been established. Moreover, the Government had not taken steps to deprive the military of such powers as the investigation and detention of civilians, the issue of visas and the supervision of customs and immigration at airports and harbours. Of concern to the USA was the growing military involvement in the international trafficking of illicit drugs. By the end of 1991 Western intelligence sources reported that Suriname had become a major centre of the illegal drugs trade, serving as a transhipment point for increasing quantities of cocaine intended for Europe and the USA. The country also served as a transhipment point for the sale of illegal arms to the Colombian drugs cartels. Sources in the USA and in Suriname alleged that Bouterse and the Army were behind the illegal trade in drugs and arms.

In early 1990 President Shankar's Government renewed contacts with the SLA, following the failure of the Kourou Accord. With a presidential guarantee of safety, Ronnie Brunswijk travelled to Paramaribo to negotiate. However, Bouterse violated the guarantee and arrested Brunswijk. Although Brunswijk was later released on the insistence of President Shankar, the action of the military showed the weakness of the civilian Government and eventually led to its downfall. On 24 December the military overthrew the Shankar Government and installed leaders of the NDP in the executive. Jules Wijdenbosch held the posts of Vice-President, Prime Minister and Minister of Finance until the elections of May 1991. In August 1992 the new administration signed an accord with the SLA, finally ending the insurgency. The former rebels recognized the Government's authority over the entire country, while the Government promised to honour the rights of the Boschnegers, including their right to engage in gold prospecting and forestry, and to join the Army.

THE VENETIAAN GOVERNMENT

A general election was held on 25 May 1991, monitored by a delegation from the Organization of American States (OAS). The Nieuw Front coalition (NF—New Front, formerly the FDO), consisting of the dominant NPS, the VHP, the KTPI and the Surinaamse Partij van de Arbeid (SPA—Suriname Labour Party), won 30 of the 51 seats in parliament. Bouterse's NDP won 12 seats and the Democratisch Alternatief 1991 (DA '91—Democratic Alternative 1991) the remaining nine seats. The NPS leader, Runaldo Ronald Venetiaan, was elected President and Jules Adjodhia, Prime Minister. Venetiaan took office on 6 September.

In March 1992 the Government requested that the National Assembly remove references in the Constitution that allowed the Army to act in a way that contravened the proper democratic functioning of the State. The action to curb the military was taken as a measure designed to improve relations with the Netherlands, Suriname's main international benefactor. With the restoration of democracy in 1987, the Dutch Government had renewed aid to Suriname, but under more restrictive conditions than those imposed at the time of independence. The Dutch agreed to disburse funds for only specific projects, a policy which limited the amount of overall aid. In early 1990 some US $700m., which had accumulated over the period of outright military control, had yet to be disbursed by the Netherlands. At a meeting with Dutch officials in November 1991 on Bonaire (Netherlands Antilles), President Venetiaan asked for the release of all or part of these funds. In 1992 the Netherlands agreed to renew economic assistance, but required the Government to implement the International Monetary Fund's (IMF) structural-adjustment

programme, a stringent monetary policy that included reduced public spending, increased taxes and the removal of food and fuel subsidies. The structural-adjustment programme, implemented in 1994, proved highly successful and by 1995 the depreciation of the Suriname guilder had been halted and Central Bank reserves had reached a healthy $100m. In 1994 the average annual rate of inflation was 368.5%, but by 1996 Suriname was experiencing deflation, with the average change in consumer prices for the year at 0.7%. However, the economic reforms caused widespread hardship and the Government became increasingly unpopular.

THE WIJDENBOSCH GOVERNMENT

The results of the elections to the National Assembly, held on 23 May 1996 represented a reverse for the ruling NF. It won 24 seats, six less than in 1991, while Bouterse's NDP won 16 seats, four more than in the previous legislature. The DA '91 and the Pendawa Lima won four seats each and the Alliantie electoral coalition gained three seats. The election was also important because Amerindians were elected to the Assembly for the first time. In an attempt to secure broader support, the NDP chose Jules Wijdenbosch, instead of Bouterse, as its candidate to contest the presidency. In the National Assembly's first vote for President, Venetiaan gained more support than Wijdenbosch, but not the two-thirds' majority necessary to win the election outright. Responsibility for electing the President then passed to the United People's Assembly, a body comprising national, regional and local representatives. With only a simple majority required, Wijdenbosch won 438 votes, compared with 407 votes for Venetiaan. He was inaugurated as President on 14 September. The NF alliance disintegrated, with the VHP and the KTPI joining an NDP-led coalition, on condition that Bouterse should not hold office in the new administration. The new coalition Government was appointed on 20 September, comprising representatives of four different political groupings.

The Wijdenbosch Government soon became characterized by internal political crisis and increasing pressure from diverse opposition groups. In August 1997, the dismissal of the finance minister, Motilal Mungra, following his outspoken criticism of the President's extravagant use of public funds, including the purchase of a presidential yacht, prompted Mungra's Beweging voor Vernieuwing en Democratie (BVD—Movement for Renewal and Democracy) and two other small parties to announce their withdrawal from the governing coalition. Following negotiations with the three parties concerned and other smaller opposition parties, President Wijdenbosch was able to secure sufficient support to maintain his Government's parliamentary majority. However, the Government's instability was apparent and the withdrawal of support for the administration by four members of the National Assembly precipitated a further reorganization of the coalition in February 1998. President Wijdenbosch also drew accusations of political corruption when he revealed, under considerable pressure from local and international human-rights groups, that a five-member committee, appointed to investigate past human-rights abuses, in particular the 1982 December Murders, was being led by a former Bouterse lawyer.

In July 1998 the President attracted further criticism, following his controversial appointment of a new President of the Court of Justice and Prosecutor-General, without consultation with, and disregarding the objections of, the sitting justices. The members of the Court refused to recognize the appointments; however, despite the objections, President Wijdenbosch named additional justices in December, and in May 1999 the appointed President of the Court of Justice swore in himself and then the new justices. Meanwhile, the Government's mismanagement of the economy was causing increasing public unrest. A strike by petroleum workers in May 1998 was followed by widespread industrial action in June, in support of the Trade and Manufacturers' Association's demands for the resignation of the Government in favour of a non-political administration.

THE RE-ELECTION OF VENETIAAN

In early 1999 the economic situation became extremely grave, with spiralling inflation caused by an ever-widening budget deficit and a decline in the international price of bauxite, by far Suriname's most important source of foreign-exchange earnings. The Dutch Government continued to withhold the US $300m.

in aid that had accumulated after it suspended payments in 1998, stating that the beneficial use of the funds by the Surinamese Government could not be assured. Under pressure from the Netherlands, in April 1999 President Wijdenbosch dismissed Bouterse, a precursor to his dismissal of his entire Cabinet of Ministers in the following month in an attempt to avoid demands for his own resignation. However, on 31 May some 30,000 protesters gathered in Paramaribo to demand President Wijdenbosch's removal, while a general strike paralysed the country. On 1 June the National Assembly passed a vote of 'no confidence' in the Government by 27 votes to 14 (with 10 abstentions). The vote, however, fell short of the two-thirds' majority (34 votes) needed to remove the President from office. President Wijdenbosch refused to resign, but did agree to hold new elections on 25 May 2000, one year earlier than was constitutionally required.

In the elections the NF, led by Venetiaan, secured 33 of the 51 seats in the National Assembly. The Millenium Combinatie (MC—Millennium Alliance, an alliance that included the NDP) won 10 seats, and the Democratisch Nationaal Platform 2000 (DNP—National Democratic Platform 2000), which had been formed by President Wijdenbosch in an apparent attempt to distance himself from Bouterse, took three seats. Nevertheless, Bouterse, as an NDP candidate, won a seat in the National Assembly, even as a Dutch appeals court upheld an earlier drugs-trafficking conviction (see below). As the NF narrowly failed to win the two-thirds' majority to appoint a new President directly, it immediately began coalition negotiations with smaller parties. Following the conclusion of these negotiations, on 4 August 2000 Venetiaan was elected to the presidency for the second time, winning 37 of the 51 votes cast in the National Assembly. A new Cabinet of Ministers was sworn in on 12 August. The conflict between the Government and the Judiciary precipitated by President Wijdenbosch's controversial and unilateral judicial appointments was resolved, when the disputed judges resigned. President Venetiaan also took steps to establish the independent constitutional court required by the 1987 Constitution. In late 2000 the Venetiaan Government was selecting the judges to sit in the Court.

In its electoral campaign, the NF had pledged to revitalize the faltering economy; soon after taking office, the new administration instituted a series of economic reforms aimed at reversing the failed economic policies of the Wijdenbosch administration. However, while the Venetiaan administration made progress in stabilizing the economy in 2000 and 2001, tensions within the coalition and the impatience of the populace impeded its efforts.

INTERNATIONAL RELATIONS

Relations with the Government of the Netherlands deteriorated rapidly under President Wijdenbosch, principally owing to his administration's continued links with Bouterse. In 1997 the President appointed Bouterse an adviser to the Government of Suriname, a cabinet-level position, despite an ongoing investigation by the Dutch Government into drugs-trafficking allegations against the former dictator. In March 1999 the Dutch authorities began legal proceedings against Bouterse, and on 16 July a Dutch court convicted Bouterse *in absentia* of leading a Surinamese cartel that had attempted to smuggle about two metric tons of cocaine seized at Dutch and Belgian ports and airports in 1989–97. Bouterse received a sentence of 16 years' imprisonment (later reduced to 11 years) and US $2.2m. fine. The Dutch Government secured a warrant from the International Criminal Police Commission (Interpol) for Bouterse's arrest on drugs-trafficking charges with hopes of detaining him in a third country, since the Surinamese Constitution barred extradition of its nationals. The Attorney-General of the Netherlands filed further charges (this time for torture resulting in death) against Bouterse in January 2000. The new suit concerned the December Murders in 1982 and arose because of a complaint filed by relatives of the victims.

Following the election of Venetiaan, there were calls for the new Government to investigate the December Murders, before the 18-year statute of limitations expired in December 2000. In October the country's highest court, the Court of Justice, began hearings on the December Murders, in response to a request by relatives of the victims. The Court heard testimony from the victims' relatives, human-rights activists and the prosecutor's office, which had not yet made any investigation into the case. Following an order from the Court of Justice, an examining judge called for a full investigation into the 1982 Murders, including the involvement of 36 individuals. Consequently, relations between Suriname and the Netherlands improved, and in October the Dutch Government agreed to resume aid to Suriname, suspended since 1998. On 8 February 2001 President Venetiaan announced his intention to seek the amendment of an article in the Constitution that banned the extradition of Surinamese citizens to other countries for trial.

The Wijdenbosch Government made efforts to combat illegal drugs-trafficking, in order to appease both its European and its US allies. In June 1997 the President installed a commission to monitor the drugs trade. In June 1998 the Government signed the Anti-Drugs Strategy for the Western Hemisphere that had been prepared by the OAS. In January 1999 new legislation was passed, providing for heavier sentences for drugs-trafficking. Finally, the Government prepared a 'Drugs Masterplan 1997–2002', which, among other things, proposed that money laundering be made a criminal offence. Notwithstanding these and other measures, the Government was unable effectively to stem the tide of drugs-trafficking; according to official estimates, roughly 26,000 kgs of cocaine, with a street value of slightly over US $1,000m., were shipped to Europe each year.

The Wijdenbosch administration also came into conflict with Guyana over the two countries' common border. The present boundary between Guyana and Suriname was based on a draft treaty agreed, but never ratified, between the United Kingdom and the Netherlands in 1939. Under the draft treaty the boundary between the two countries was established on the left bank of the Corantijn and Cutari rivers. In 1962 the Netherlands questioned Guyana's sovereignty over an area of land that protrudes from Guyana into Suriname. The Dutch proposed a modification of the treaty, favouring a boundary that followed the Thalweg, instead of the left bank of the Corantijn, and the westerly New River, instead of the Cutari. The British Government, however, refused to reopen the issue. In June 1998 a new border dispute erupted between Suriname and Guyana. Guyana had granted the Canadian-based CGX Energy Incorporated a concession to explore for petroleum and gas along the continental shelf off Guyana. Part of the area, designated the Corantijn block, lay within waters claimed by Suriname. In May 2000 the Surinamese Government made a formal protest against the CGX concession, claiming it violated Suriname's sovereignty and territorial integrity. A second diplomatic note from Suriname claimed that the petroleum exploration activity 'constituted an illegal act', and invited Guyana to begin negotiations 'to clarify any misunderstanding on the maritime boundary'. The Guyanese Government maintained that the exploration activities were being conducted in Guyanan territory, but was prepared to attend talks. In early June gunboats of the Suriname Navy forced CGX to remove the drill rig from the disputed waters. At a meeting held on 6 June in Port of Spain, Trinidad and Tobago, representatives from the two countries agreed that a Joint Technical Committee be established to resolve the dispute, but both sides remained at an impasse. Further talks, held later in the month in Jamaica, also ended in deadlock, and with an agreement between the two countries unlikely, CGX Energy Incorporated abandoned the area. It was agreed that talks would resume once the new Government took office. In September 2000 Guyana reported an alleged intrusion into its territory by Surinamese soldiers. In June 2001 the Minister of Foreign Affairs, Marie E. Levens, invited her Guyanan counterpart to visit Suriname. Following a subsequent declaration by the Presidents of both countries of their commitment to peace and co-operation, President Bharrat Jagdeo of Guyana accepted an invitation to visit Suriname in the near future in order to resolve the dispute.

Economy

JAMES McDONOUGH

Suriname occupies 163,265 sq km (63,037 sq miles) on the north-east coast of South America, lying between Guyana to the west and French Guiana to the east. Suriname's economy is based on bauxite and agriculture. Bauxite, or rather its derivative, alumina, from which aluminium is made, generally accounted for some 70% of the total value of Suriname's exports and about 15% of gross domestic product (GDP). As a result, Suriname's economy was susceptible to 'boom and bust' cycles caused by variations in the international price of alumina. The tax receipts that Suriname received from the export of alumina and aluminium (hardly any unrefined bauxite was exported from Suriname) provided the revenue to support the large civil service, which employed close to 50% of the working population of about 100,000 in 2000. The interruption of Dutch aid in 1982–86 and in the late 1990s, and the six-year civil war in the 1980s, inhibited economic and social development. Exacerbating the country's economic problems were the poor fiscal policies adopted by the Wijdenbosch administration in 1996–2000. These policies included borrowing from the Centrale Bank van Suriname (Central Bank of Suriname) to cover the budget deficit. Inflation soared during those years, reaching 98.9% in 1999. Further adding to Suriname's economic difficulties was a decline in the world price of alumina. The average price of alumina decreased from US $190 per metric ton in 1995–97 to $160 per ton in 1999. As a result, Suriname's GDP declined by 5.0% in 1999 and by 5.6% in 2000. In 1999 Suriname's GDP per head was approximately $848, the fourth-lowest of the Inter-American Development Bank's (IDB) member countries. Its per head income in 1999 was estimated at $2,500, and it was officially estimated that up to one-half of the population was living in poverty.

AGRICULTURE

In the 18th century Suriname's economy was based on the sugar industry, but by the 19th century coffee, cocoa and cotton were the country's main commodities. With the decline of large-scale plantation agriculture in the 20th century the former contract labourers from India and Indonesia were induced to remain in Suriname by the offer of free land. The Government distributed small plots of land for the growing of rice along the country's rich coastal plain. In the 1990s rice was the country's principal agricultural export, followed by bananas. The coastal polders (land that had been drained) remained the country's focus of agricultural activity and settlement. At least 70% of Suriname's population, estimated to total some 430,000 in mid-1999, lived on the estuarine lands of the Suriname River, within 25 km of the capital, Paramaribo, while a further 15% lived along the coastal plain.

The majority of Suriname's 58,000 ha of cultivated land, which represented only 0.4% of the country's total land area, was on the coastal plain. One-half of the cultivated area was in the polders close to Paramaribo, between the Commewijne and Saramacca estuaries. The country's agricultural potential was far from being realized, partly because of the inaccessibility of the interior savannahs, but also because of the unequal pattern of land tenure. In the 1980s, of the total number of land holdings, 46% were less than 2 ha in area and a further 27% were between 2 ha and 4 ha. At the other end of the scale, one-half of the agricultural land was occupied by 139 large holdings averaging 370 ha. Nevertheless, during 1980–85 agricultural production increased by an average of 6.1% per year. From 1986–90, as a result of the disruption caused by guerrilla activity, production declined by 6.4% per year. There was a brief recovery at the start of the 1990s, but the agricultural sector registered a decline of 1.0% in 1996, 5.6% in 1998 and 2.2% in 1999, owing to a fall in paddy-rice prices, which led to a sharp reduction in the cultivated acreage. In 1999 agriculture (including hunting, forestry and fishing) contributed 11% of GDP and in 1998 employed an estimated 5.6% of the working population, which represented a notable diminution in the importance of the sector during the 1990s.

At the beginning of the 1990s rice remained the crop of greatest commercial value in Suriname. About 50% of all cultivated land was devoted to rice, chiefly in the western polders of the Nickerie district. Much of the rice was produced by Hindustanis and Javanese on plots of less than 1 ha, located on the older polders. On the new polders, land holdings were typically of 80 ha or more and cultivation was mechanized and well managed. The fully-mechanized rice farm at Wageningen was one of the largest in the world.

The annual output of paddy rice increased from 174,845 metric tons in 1975, to 301,975 tons in 1984. Output declined after 1985, however, owing to a lack of government resources to rebuild and expand the country's decaying canal system. Rice production declined in the 1990s, falling to 175,000 tons in 2000, according to UN Food and Agriculture Organization (FAO) estimates. In addition, the port of Nickerie was in need of dredging and major capital improvements; in the early 1990s rice was being off-loaded onto barges because transoceanic ships could not dock at the port's piers. In 1998 export earnings from rice totalled US $19.6m., equivalent to 4.7% of total export earnings.

Bananas and plantains (in Suriname usage, an eating banana is referred to as a *bacove*, while *banaan* is a cooking variety), which together comprised the next most important export crop, were grown on plantations in the Paramaribo region. In 1998 Suriname exported bananas and plantains with a total value of US $6.7m., 1.6% of export earnings. In 2000 the production of bananas reached 55,000 metric tons and that of plantains, 11,000 tons. The cultivation of oil palm expanded rapidly from 1975, when only 625 tons of palm oil were produced from 1,645 ha planted with palms. By 1985 oil-palm plantations covered 6,184 ha and annual output of palm oil had increased to 7,958 tons. Palm oil was mostly used for domestic consumption, but exports, valued at over $300,000 per year, commenced in 1979. However, production of palm oil was greatly reduced after 1986, as plantations were located mostly in rebel-held territory, falling to a mere 60 tons by 1989. As security problems eased, production recovered, reaching 6,890 tons by 1994 and increasing slowly thereafter. Sugar was a very important crop during the colonial period, but by the mid-1990s it was produced only for local consumption.

Livestock received little attention and the output of livestock products was insufficient for local needs. The few cattle that were reared by small-scale farmers were not of high quality and were used more as draught animals than for the production of either beef or milk. In 2000 there were 106,000 head of cattle. Some efforts were made by the Government to breed stock of better quality and there were experiments to cross the Holstein breed of cattle with the Santa Gertrudi. On the initiative of the Suriname Aluminium Company (Suralco), a scientifically-operated dairy farm was established at Moengo. The ideal location for cattle would be the interior savannah, but the lack of access roads has, so far, prevented such development. In 2000 the country produced 2,300 metric tons of beef and veal.

Fishing played a small, though significant, role in the economy. There was a modern fishing industry, located in Paramaribo. This industry was dominated by Japanese and Korean companies, which exported most of their catch to the USA and Canada. Shrimps were the most important, single, fish export, although the industry suffered a decline in the early 1990s. In 1991 the USA banned shrimp imports from Suriname because the country refused to take the necessary measures to protect the sea turtle, an endangered species, from the fishing practices of the Suriname fishermen. Nevertheless, the sector remained an important source of export revenue, with shrimps contri-

SURINAME

buting an estimated US $29.4m. in 1998, or 7% of total export earnings.

More than 80% of Suriname is covered by forest, making it one of the most densely forested countries in the world. The first administration of President Runaldo Ronald Venetiaan (1991–96) moved to exploit this resource in the early 1990s. In January 1994 the Government granted Mitra Usaha Sejati Abadi, a private Indonesian logging company, a timber concession for 125,000 ha in western Suriname, the maximum amount permitted without the approval of the National Assembly. The Government then formulated plans to grant concessions to three Asian companies that would permit over 3m. ha (over 7.4m. acres) to be logged. These plans provoked protests from local interest groups, international environmental organizations and many in the country's legislature. The indigenous Amerindian peoples and the 'Boschnegers' (Bush Negroes) protested against the proposed concessions, maintaining that they infringed upon the economic zones promised under the 1992 peace accord that the Government had signed with various insurgent groups. Environmentalists urged the Government to consider alternative strategies, such as the exploitation of 'eco-tourism'. As a result of the opposition, President Jules Wijdenbosch (1996–2000) announced in January 1997 that Suriname would not proceed with the huge logging concessions. In 1998 lumber contributed only US $6.5m. to export revenue, equivalent to 1.3% of total exports by value.

MINING

Mining, dominated by the extraction of bauxite, was the single most important economic activity in Suriname. Bauxite, from which aluminium is made, was mined from deposits found along the northern edge of the central plateau, close to the Cottica river (the Moengo deposit) and the Suriname river (the Paranam and Onverwacht deposits). In Suriname the mining of bauxite and its refining into alumina and aluminium was controlled by two multinational companies, one US and the other Dutch. Mining began in 1915, by Suralco, a wholly owned subsidiary of the Aluminum Company of America (Alcoa), the world's largest producer of aluminium. In 1939 Billiton Maatschappij Suriname (BMS), a subsidiary of the Royal Dutch Shell-owned Billiton Company, initiated bauxite mining operations in Suriname's Para District, some 35 km south of Paramaribo. In 1983 BMS bought 46% of Suralco's Paranam refinery on the bank of the Suriname River, 100 km from its mouth, and Suralco purchased 24% of BMS's bauxite mining operations. In 1997 BMS opened the Lelydorp III deposit in the Paranam area. The Paranam refinery included installations for the extraction of alumina (1.7m. metric tons per year) from bauxite ore, as well as a smelter for the production of aluminium using alumina. However, in 1999 Suralco closed the smelter, which had a capacity of 30,000 tons per year. The closure was influenced by the high relative cost of the smelter and low rainfall affecting power generation. The company used hydroelectric power generated by the Brokopondo–Afobaka dam on the Suriname river to run the manufacturing operations. The dam was built by Suralco in the 1960s at a cost of US $150m., creating a 1,560-sq km lake, one of the largest artificial lakes in the world. BMS estimated that it would have enough bauxite for the Paranam refinery until 2006. In 2001 it was looking for more sites in and outside Suriname to continue to supply the Paranam facility beyond the depletion of its current bauxite reserves.

The bauxite industry was heavily taxed and in 1990 accounted for over 40% of the Government's revenue. Suriname's traditional markets for bauxite derivatives were the USA, Canada and Norway. Suriname's annual bauxite output increased steadily in the 1990s, reaching 3.9m. metric tons in 1998, before falling to 3.7m. tons in 1999. Suriname's alumina production remained fairly constant during the 1990s, with an average annual production of about 1.5m. tons. Aluminium production in 1997 reached 29,000 tons. In 2000 alumina constituted 72% of the value of Suriname's exports, generating income of US $483.6m.

Other mineral resources included iron ore, nickel, platinum, tin, copper, manganese, diamonds and gold. Gold and diamonds were extracted in small quantities from the river beds by private prospectors. In June 1994 the Government signed an agreement with Golden Star Resources Incorporated (USA) and Cambior

(Canada), envisaging the large-scale exploitation of gold in the central-eastern part of the country. The Gross Rosebud gold mine began operations in mid-2001 and company sources anticipated that it would produce an annual output of between 160,000 and 200,000 troy oz (4,980 kg–6,220 kg). The total reserves of the mine area were estimated at 42.5 metric tons.

Petroleum was discovered in the Saramacca district in 1981, by the Gulf Oil Corporation of the USA. As a result, a Suriname State Oil Company (Staatsolie) was formed to exploit the reserves. Suriname exported small quantities of crude petroleum and imported refined petroleum products, as the country lacked refining capacity. In 1988 Staatsolie reported that 99 of the 112 wells were in operation, with production of 3,888 barrels per day (b/d). Output in the early 2000s was 12,000 b/d, and regional geology suggested additional potential. Staatsolie was actively seeking international joint-venture partners, but with little success. In June 2001 a consortium of foreign oil companies halted exploration in waters off Suriname after deciding it was too high-risk an operation.

MANUFACTURING

The industrial sector was dominated by the production of alumina and aluminium. However, the country manufactured some foodstuffs (flour, margarine, cattle fodder), tobacco products, beverages, construction materials, clothing and furniture, using chiefly local raw materials, but imported machinery. Manufacturing, aside from alumina, grew only marginally in the 1990s owing to shortages caused by lack of foreign exchange, and increased competition from the Caribbean Community and Common Market (CARICOM) countries. In February 1995 Suriname was granted full membership of CARICOM, the first member from outside the English-speaking countries of the region. Suriname accepted CARICOM economic obligations on 1 January 1996 and on 1 January 1997 CARICOM's maximum common external tariff was reduced to 25%. Manufacturing employed 8.0% of the working population and contributed 10.1% of GDP in 1998.

TRANSPORT AND COMMUNICATIONS INFRASTRUCTURE

Suriname's first 10-Year Development Plan, covering the period 1955–65, placed emphasis on improving the infrastructure. Projects included the modernization of Paramaribo's port and Zanderij airport. In addition, a coastal road was constructed from Albina to Nieuw Nickerie, and another from Paramaribo, 110 km along the Suriname river, to the Brokopondo dam. This latter road formed the first part of a projected highway to Brazil. There were two railway lines, one a narrow-gauge line between Onverwacht and Brownsweg, the other a 70-km track between the bauxite deposits in the west, and Apoera on the Corantijn river, opened in 1980. However, owing to the abandonment of plans to mine bauxite in the Backhuis mountains, the latter railway remained inoperative. Despite the major improvements made in 1955–65, the infrastructure remained only minimally developed in Suriname. In 1996 there were an estimated 4,530 km of roads, mainly in the north of the country. In the late 1980s a ferry link between Suriname and Guyana, across the Corantijn, was opened. Relative to Suriname's population and level of economic development, there was a large number of telephones, with 64,000 in use in 1997.

FOREIGN TRADE AND BALANCE OF PAYMENTS

Exports were dominated by alumina and aluminium, which accounted for four-fifths of Suriname's total export earnings. The remaining exports included rice, crude petroleum, bananas, shrimps and timber products. Imports consisted largely of food and beverages, mineral fuels and basic manufactures, as well as vehicles, machinery and other industrial equipment. Imports declined steeply in the 1980s and early 1990s, owing to official regulation and a shortage of foreign exchange, and the balance of trade was generally in Suriname's favour as a result. Imports began to recover in 1996, and remained strong until 1999, although exports decreased in the same period. From 1996 to 1999, the value of imports increased from US $426.3m. to an estimated $694m. During this same period, the total value of exports increased from $434.3m to an estimated $518m. As a result, the country's trade deficit increased from $22m in 1996 to $176m. in 1999. The current-account deficit was largely financed by official external borrowing and by a decline in Suriname's international reserves. Total public external debt grew from $175.6m. in 1998 to $248m by the end of 1999. In the same period, the country's international reserves declined by $17m. On assuming office in August 2000, the new Venetiaan administration discovered that the bulk of Suriname's gold reserves had been converted into dollars. A mere 2% (146 kg) of the country's gold reserves remained.

In 1998 the principal destinations for Suriname's exports were to Norway (an estimated 12.5% of the total), the USA (an estimated 16.7%) and the Netherlands (an estimated 14.6%). Norway was the leading recipient of Suriname's exports because most of Alcoa's production of alumina was shipped to that country for refining into aluminium. In the same year imports came chiefly from the USA (an estimated 31.2%), the Netherlands (an estimated 17.3%) and Trinidad and Tobago (an estimated 16.1%).

INVESTMENT AND FINANCE

Prior to independence the country's two 10-Year Development Plans, beginning in 1955, served to stimulate economic growth. During this period the Brokopondo dam was built to supply hydroelectric power for the bauxite industry, the irrigation of polders was perfected and the country's infrastructure improved. Scientific techniques were introduced in agriculture, and social programmes, particularly in education, were funded. In the 1980s Suriname's economy began to decline. Official capital imports came to a virtual halt in 1982, when the Netherlands suspended its development co-operation because of the political murders by the military regime, which had taken power in 1980. A reduction in foreign capital investment and in exports, owing to the weakness of the world market for alumina and aluminium products, was reflected in a 20% fall in government revenues. Nevertheless, the military Government increased expenditure excessively, doubling the level of spending during the 1980s. The number of public employees increased by one-fifth, with the result that by 1994 nearly one-half of the active labour force consisted of civil servants. By contrast, spending on development projects collapsed. Over 50% of total government spending in the early 1990s was estimated to go on wages, with another 30% used to buy materials. The Government was able to devote a mere 2% to development projects.

Suriname's budget deficit increased from the equivalent of barely 5% of GNP in 1980 to over 25% in 1992. The Government financed its expenditures first with international reserves and then by printing money, which by 1994 had precipitated a 'hyperinflationary' crisis, with the annual rate of inflation at 368.5%. Subsequently, the implementation of a stringent austerity programme and an increase in revenues caused by a rise in the world price of bauxite derivatives brought about dramatic improvement in the country's economic situation. By 1996 the depreciation of the Surinamese guilder had been halted, international reserves had reached almost US $100m. and the country was experiencing deflation. In that year there was a budget surplus equivalent to 2% of GDP. However, in the late 1990s a decline in revenues from exports of alumina and aluminium, along with increased government spending and a relaxation of fiscal controls by the Wijdenbosch administration, combined to recreate the conditions of an economic crisis. In 1998 the budget deficit increased to an estimated Sf 50,700m., equivalent to 11.1% of GDP, financed mainly through domestic borrowing. In 1999 a reduction in government expenditure reduced the deficit to 8.8% of GDP. Nevertheless, inflation, which had been brought under control in 1996, increased to 19.0% in 1998, 98.9% in 1999 and 64.3% in 2000. The guilder depreciated rapidly, despite a 43% devaluation on 1 January 1999. The differential between the official and parallel exchange rate, which had all but been eliminated with the devaluation,

reached an average of 82% in 1999–2000. In an attempt to halt the economic decline, the second Venetiaan administration, which assumed power in August 2000, devalued the official exchange rate by 89%. The new Government also ended government borrowing from the Central Bank, eliminated subsidies on petroleum products, substantially increased electricity and water rates, rationalized the list of price controls on 12 basic food items, and increased the tax on cigarettes, alcohol and soft drinks. President Venetiaan also dismissed the President of the Central Bank for financing the previous administration's budget deficits.

FINANCIAL AID

Suriname's fractured political spectrum and its weak financial situation combined to deny the country access to significant financial aid through the major international lending institutions. Suriname had no loans from the International Monetary Fund (IMF) or the World Bank (International Bank for Reconstruction and Development—IBRD). It had a series of small loans with the IDB, mainly to upgrade its financial and tax operations. Most of its other loans came from bilateral arrangements with individual countries, including Brazil, Japan and the Netherlands. The Framework Treaty of 1975, by which Suriname gained its independence from the Netherlands, provided for substantial amounts of economic aid to assist the development of the new republic. According to the Treaty, the Dutch were to provide US $1,700m. in the form of outright grants to implement a general development programme, and 500m. guilders as import guarantees for a period of 10–15 years. An additional 300m. guilders were to be available for matching grants to be financed from savings in Suriname. However, the Dutch suspended the treaty aid in 1982, as a result of the 'December Murders' (see History).

Upon the approval of a new Constitution in 1987, the Dutch agreed to resume their aid, but on a limited basis. Prior to 1989 some US $100m. had been disbursed, but about $700m., which had accumulated during the six years of military rule, remained undisbursed. The Netherlands insisted that aid would be provided only on a project-by-project basis until the Suriname Government implemented the IMF's structural-adjustment programme, considered necessary to correct the hyperinflationary crisis of the early 1990s and provide long-term stability for the economy. In 1998 the aid payments were suspended once again, owing to disagreements relating to the attempts of the Dutch Government to arrest Lt-Col Désiré (Desi) Bouterse, Suriname's former military ruler, and to Bouterse's continued presence in government. In 2000, with the advent of a new administration, the Dutch Government revised the structure of their aid to Suriname in support of sectoral priorities rather than individual projects. The Venetiaan administration was not in favour of that approach, and the two Governments began negotiations on the issue.

OUTLOOK

Suriname's economic prospects, based on prevailing trends, were bleak. The economy was expected to grow by 2% in 2001 on the strength of an expansion in the mining sector and some recovery in manufacturing and agriculture. However, much depended on the world price of alumina, the ability of the country to revive its agricultural sector and the overall health of the world economy. The IMF wished the Venetiaan Government to institute a public-sector reform programme to institutionalize its short-term reforms. According to the IMF, Suriname also needed to rationalize the civil service, encourage privatization and institute a public-sector investment programme. Essential to the country's progress was the need to promote agricultural development and exports. President Venetiaan's reforms gained the approval of the international lending agencies, but met with resistance at home. Much would depend on his ability to build a national consensus for basic financial reform.

Statistical Survey

Sources (unless otherwise stated): Algemeen Bureau voor de Statistiek, Kromme Elleboogstraat 10, POB 244, Paramaribo; tel. 473927; fax 425004; e-mail statistics@cq-link.sr; Ministry of Trade and Industry: Nieuwe Haven, POB 557, Paramaribo; tel. 475080; fax 477602.

AREA, POPULATION AND DENSITY

Area: 163,265 sq km (63,037 sq miles).

Population: 355,240 (males 175,814; females 179,426) at census of 1 July 1980; 430,000 at mid-1999 (official estimate).

Density (mid-1999): 2.6 per sq km.

Ethnic Groups (1980 census, percentage): Creole 34.70; Hindustani 33.49; Javanese 16.33; Bush Negro 9.55; Amerindian 3.10; Chinese 1.55; European 0.44; Others 0.84.

Administrative Districts (population at 1980 census, according to new boundaries of 1985): Paramaribo 169,980; Nickerie 32,725; Coronie 2,780; Saramacca 10,820; Wanica 60,790; Commewijne 20,084; Marowijne 16,142; Brokopondo 6,628; Para 12,040; Sipaliwini 23,251.

Births and Deaths (1999): Registered live births 10,144 (birth rate 23.6 per 1,000); Registered deaths 2,992 (death rate 7.0 per 1,000).

Expectation of Life (estimates, years at birth, 1998): 70.3 (males 67.7; females 72.9). Source: UN Development Programme, *Human Development Report*.

Economically Active Population (labour force sample survey, '000 persons aged between 15 and 66 years, 1998): Agriculture, hunting, forestry and fishing 4,926; Mining and quarrying 3,442; Manufacturing 7,095; Electricity, gas and water 1,640; Construction 9,898; Trade, restaurants and hotels 16,473; Public administration and defence 3,762; Financing, insurance, real estate and business services 5,791; Commercial, social and personal services 31,956; Activities not adequately defined 3,261; *Total employed* 88,244 (males 59,773; females 28,471); Unemployed 10,475 (males 4,627; females 5,848); *Total labour force* 98,719 (males 64,400; females 34,319).

AGRICULTURE, ETC.

Principal Crops ('000 metric tons, 2000): Rice (paddy) 175; Citrus fruit 14; Bananas 55; Plantains 11; Coconuts 9; Roots and tubers 5; Vegetables 15 (FAO estimate). Source: FAO.

Livestock ('000 head, 2000): Cattle 106; Goats 12; Sheep 12; Pigs 32; Poultry 2,000 (FAO estimate). Source: FAO.

Livestock Products ('000 metric tons, 2000): Cows' milk 13; Hen eggs 5; Beef and veal 2; Pig meat 2. Source: FAO.

Forestry ('000 cu metres, 1999): Roundwood removals: Sawlogs, veneer logs and logs for sleepers 90; Other industrial wood 2; Fuel wood 1; *Total* 93. Sawnwood production: Total (incl. railway sleepers) 30. Source: FAO, *Yearbook of Forest Products*.

Fishing (FAO estimates, '000 metric tons, 1998): Capture 13.0 (Marine fishes 12.5); Total catch 13.0. Source: FAO, *Yearbook of Fishery Statistics*.

MINING

Production ('000 metric tons, 1999): Bauxite 3,715.

INDUSTRY

Production ('000 hectolitres, 1996): Soft drinks 230; Beer 72. ('000 metric tons, 1996): Alumina 1,643; Aluminium 28.8; Raw sugar 2 (FAO figure); Cement 50 (1995 estimate). Other products: Palm oil ('000 litres, 1994 estimate) 1,051; Cigarettes 483 million (1996); Shoes (pairs, 1995 estimate) 98,990; Plywood ('000 cubic metres) 7 (1996); Particle board (cubic metres) 106 (1991); Electricity (million kWh) 1,614 (1995). Source: partly UN, *Industrial Commodity Statistics Yearbook*.

FINANCE

Currency and Exchange Rates: 100 cents = 1 Suriname gulden (guilder) or florin (Sf). *Sterling, Dollar and Euro Equivalents* (30 April 2001): £1 sterling = 3,119.2 guilders; US $1 = 2,178.5 guilders; €1 = 1,933.6 guilders; 10,000 Suriname guilders = £3.206 = $4.590 = €5.172. *Average Exchange Rate* (Suriname guilders per US $): 401.26 in 1996; 401.00 in 1997; 401.00 in 1998. *Note:* Between 1971 and 1993 the official market rate was US $1 = 1.785 guilders. A new free market rate was introduced in June 1993, and a unified, market-determined rate took effect in July 1994. A mid-point rate of US $1 = 401.0 guilders was in effect between September 1996 and January 1999.

Budget (Sf '000 million, 1998, estimates): *Revenue:* Direct taxation 49.6; Indirect taxation 55.4; Other revenue (incl. bauxite levy) 15;

Grants 17.2; Total 137.2. *Expenditure:* Compensation of employees 73.6; Subsidies 21.9; Goods and services 61.6; Interest payments 2.5; Capital 18.4; Net lending 10; Total 188.0. Source: IMF, *Suriname: Selected Issues* (August 1999).

International Reserves (US $ million at 31 December 1999): Gold (national valuation) 73.81; IMF special drawing rights 2.75; Reserve position in IMF 8.41; Foreign exchange n.a. Source: IMF, *International Financial Statistics*.

Money Supply (Sf million at 31 December 1999): Currency outside banks 81,853; Demand deposits at deposit money banks 51,367; Total money (incl. others) 138,523. Source: IMF, *International Financial Statistics*.

Cost of Living (Consumer Price Index; base: 1995 = 100): 106.4 in 1997; 126.6 in 1998; 251.8 in 1999. Source: IMF, *International Financial Statistics*.

Expenditure on the Gross Domestic Product (Sf million at current prices, excl. informal sector, 1998): Government final consumption expenditure 144,384.0; Private final consumption expenditure 151,400.0; Gross capital formation 41,248.1; *Total domestic expenditure* 337,032.1; Exports of goods and services 67,308.1; *Less* Imports of goods and services 80,418.5; *GDP at factor cost* 323,921.7.

Gross Domestic Product by Economic Activity (Sf million at current prices, 1998): Agriculture, forestry and fishing 26,079.3; Mining and quarrying 14,833.7; Manufacturing 33,559.5; Electricity, gas and water 16,549.0; Construction 22,181.6; Trade, restaurants and hotels 560.1; Transport, storage and communications 31,360.4; Finance, insurance, real estate and business services 52,504.2; Government services 81,501.0; Community, social, personal and other services 1,823.9; Sub-total 333,452.8; *Less* Imputed bank service charge 9,531.0; GDP at factor cost 323,921.8; Indirect taxes, less subsidies 42,846.2; GDP in purchasers' values 366,768.0. Note: Figures exclude the GDP of the informal sector (Sf million): 89,199.0 (incl. Gold 48,106.0). Source: IMF, *Suriname: Selected Issues* (August 1999).

Balance of Payments (US $ million, 1998): Exports of goods f.o.b. 349.7; Imports of goods f.o.b. −376.9; *Trade balance* −27.2; Exports of services 72.0; Imports of services −196.9; *Balance on goods and services* −152.1; Other income received 6.5; Other income paid −7.0; *Balance on goods, services and income* −152.6; Current transfers received 1.3; Current transfers paid −3.6; *Current balance* −154.9; Capital account (net) 6.6; Direct investment from abroad 9.1; Other investment assets 18.6; Other investment liabilities 2.8; Net errors and omissions 125.9; *Overall balance* 8.1. Source: IMF, *International Financial Statistics*.

EXTERNAL TRADE

Principal Commodities (US $ million): *Imports* (1997): Food and live animals 62.3; Beverages and tobacco 18.2; Crude materials (inedible) except fuels 4.4; Mineral fuels, lubricants, etc. 87.7; Animal and vegetable oils, fats and waxes 6.0; Chemicals and related products 47.4; Basic manufactures 89.0; Machinery and transport equipment 228.0; Miscellaneous manufactured articles 55.6; Total (incl. others) 604.7. *Exports* (incl. re-exports, 1998, estimates): Alumina 296.6; Aluminium 39.4; Rice 19.6; Shrimps 29.4; Bananas and plantains 6.7; Crude petroleum 15.6; Total (incl. others) 417.4. Source: partly IMF, *Suriname: Selected Issues* (August 1999).

Principal Trading Partners (US $ million, 1998, preliminary figures): *Imports:* Brazil 10.0; Germany 4.2; Hong Kong 3.7; Japan 34.2; Netherlands 123.9; Trinidad and Tobago 51.1; United Kingdom 8.4; USA 112.6; Total (incl. others) 461.4. *Exports:* France 29.6; Japan 19.7; Netherlands 96.7; Norway 97.6; United Kingdom 9.1; USA 88.0; Total (incl. others) 406.1. Source: IMF, *Suriname: Selected Issues* (August 1999).

TRANSPORT

Road Traffic (registered motor vehicles, 1999 estimates): Passenger cars 59,890; Buses and coaches 2,333; Lorries and vans 19,909; Motor cycles and mopeds 31,428.

Shipping: *International Freight Traffic* (estimates, '000 metric tons, 1999): Goods loaded 2,391; Goods unloaded 1,344. *Merchant Fleet* (registered at 31 December 1999): Number of vessels 17; Total displacement 6,154 grt. Source: Lloyd's Register of Shipping, *World Fleet Statistics*.

Civil Aviation (traffic on scheduled services, 1997): Kilometres flown (million) 7; Passengers carried ('000) 279; Passenger-km (million) 1,068; Total ton-km (million) 127. Source: UN, *Statistical Yearbook*.

TOURISM

Tourist Arrivals ('000): 90 in 1997; 54 in 1998; 54 in 1999.
Tourism Receipts (US $ million): 17 in 1997; 45 in 1998; 44 in 1999. Source: World Bank, *World Development Indicators*.

COMMUNICATIONS MEDIA

Radio Receivers (1997): 300,000 in use. Source: UNESCO, *Statistical Yearbook*.
Television Receivers (1997): 63,000 in use. Source: UNESCO, *Statistical Yearbook*.
Telephones (1997): 64,000 in use.

Telefax Stations (1996): 800 in use. Source: UN, *Statistical Yearbook*.
Mobile Cellular Telephones (1997): 4,090 subscribers. Source: UN, *Statistical Yearbook*.
Daily Newspapers (2000): 2.
Non-daily Newspapers (2000): 10.

EDUCATION

Pre-primary (1997/98): 539 teachers; 15,767 pupils.
Primary (1997/98, incl. special education): 280 schools; 2,565 teachers; 67,414 pupils.
General Secondary (1997/98, incl. teacher-training): 123 schools; 2,056 teachers (1994/95); 34,003 pupils.
University (1999/2000): 1 institution; 2,581 students.
Other Higher (1999/2000): 3 institutions; 1,456 students.

Directory

The Constitution

The 1987 Constitution was approved by the National Assembly on 31 March and by 93% of voters in a national referendum in September.

THE LEGISLATURE

Legislative power is exercised jointly by the National Assembly and the Government. The National Assembly comprises 51 members, elected for a five-year term by universal adult suffrage. The Assembly elects a President and a Vice-President and has the right of amendment in any proposal of law by the Government. The approval of a majority of at least two-thirds of the number of members of the National Assembly is required for the amendment of the Constitution, the election of the President or the Vice-President, the decision to organize a plebiscite and a People's Congress and for the amendment of electoral law. If it is unable to obtain a two-thirds' majority following two rounds of voting, the Assembly may convene a People's Congress and supplement its numbers with members of local councils. The approval by a simple majority is sufficient in the People's Congress.

THE EXECUTIVE

Executive authority is vested in the President, who is elected for a term of five years as Head of State, Head of Government, Head of the Armed Forces, Chairman of the Council of State, the Cabinet of Ministers and the Security Council.

The Government comprises the President, the Vice-President and the Cabinet of Ministers. The Cabinet of Ministers is appointed by the President from among the members of the National Assembly. The Vice-President is the Prime Minister and leader of the Cabinet, and is responsible to the President.

In the event of war, a state of siege, or exceptional circumstances to be determined by law, a Security Council assumes all government functions.

THE COUNCIL OF STATE

The Council of State comprises the President (its Chairman) and 14 additional members, composed of two representatives of the combined trade unions, one representative of the associations of employers, one representative of the National Army and 10 representatives of the political parties in the National Assembly. Its duties are to advise the President and the legislature and to supervise the correct execution by the Government of the decisions of the National Assembly. The Council may present proposals of law or of general administrative measures to the Government. The Council has the authority to suspend any legislation approved by the National Assembly which, in the opinion of the Council, is in violation of the Constitution. In this event, the President must decide within one month whether or not to ratify the Council's decision.

The Government

President: RUNALDO RONALD VENETIAAN (assumed office 12 August 2000).
Council of State: Chair. President of the Republic; 14 mems (10 to represent the political parties in the National Assembly, one for the Armed Forces, two for the trade unions and one for employers).

CABINET OF MINISTERS
(August 2001)

Vice-President: JULES RATTANKOEMAR AJODHIA (VHP).
Minister of Finance: HUMPHREY HILDENBERG (NPS).
Minister of Foreign Affairs: MARIE E. LEVENS (NPS).
Minster of Defence: RONALD ASSEN (NPS).
Minister of the Interior: URMILA JOELLA-SEWNUNDUN (VHP).
Minister of Justice and the Police: SIEGFRIED F. GLIDS (SPA).
Minister of Planning and Development Co-operation: KEREMCHAND RAGHOEBARSINGH (VHP).
Minister of Agriculture, Livestock and Fisheries: GEETAPERSAD GANGARAM PANDAY (VHP).
Minister of Transport, Communications and Tourism: GUNO H. G. CASTELEN (SPA).
Minister of Public Works: DEWANAND BALESAR (VHP).
Minister of Social Affairs and Housing: SLAMET PAUL SOMOHARDJO (PL).
Minister of Trade and Industry: JACK TJONG TJIN JOE (PL).
Minister of Regional Development: ROMEO W. VAN RUSSEL (NPS).
Minister of Education and Community Development: WALTER T. SANDRIMAN (PL).
Minister of Health: MOHAMED RAKIEB KHUDABUX (VHP).
Minister of Labour, Technological Development and the Environment: CLIFFORD MARICA (SPA).
Minister of Natural Resources and Energy: FRANCO R. DEMON (NPS).

MINISTRIES

Ministry of Agriculture, Livestock and Fisheries: Letitia Vriesdelaan, Paramaribo; tel. 477698; fax 470301.
Ministry of Defence: Kwattaweg 29, Paramaribo; tel. 474244; fax 420055.
Ministry of Education and Community Development: Dr Samuel Kafilludistraat 117–123, Paramaribo; tel. 498383; fax 495083.
Ministry of Finance: Tamarindelaan 3, Paramaribo; tel. 472610; fax 476314.
Ministry of Foreign Affairs: Gravenstraat, POB 25, Paramaribo; tel. 471209; fax 410411.
Ministry of Health: Gravenstraat 64 boven, POB 201, Paramaribo; tel. 474841; fax 410702.
Ministry of the Interior: Wilhelminastraat 3, Paramaribo; tel. 476461; fax 421170.
Ministry of Justice and the Police: Gravenstraat 1, Paramaribo; tel. 473033; fax 412109.
Ministry of Labour, Technological Development and the Environment: Wagenwegstraat 22, POB 911, Paramaribo; tel. 475241; fax 410465; e-mail arbeid@sr.net.
Ministry of Natural Resources and Energy: Dr J. C. de Mirandastraat 11–15, Paramaribo; tel. 473428; fax 472911.
Ministry of Planning and Development Co-operation: Dr S. Redmondstraat 118, Paramaribo; tel. 473628; fax 421056.
Ministry of Public Works: Verlengde Coppenamestraat 167, Paramaribo; tel. 462500; fax 464901.

Ministry of Regional Development: Van Rooseveltkade 2, Paramaribo; tel. 471574; fax 424517.

Ministry of Social Affairs and Housing: Waterkant 30–32, Paramaribo; tel. 472610; fax 476314.

Ministry of Trade and Industry: Nieuwe Haven, POB 9354, Paramaribo; tel. 404776; fax 402602; internet www.sr.net/users /dirhi.

Ministry of Transport, Communications and Tourism: Prins Hendrikstraat 26–28, Paramaribo; tel. 411951; fax 420425.

President and Legislature

PRESIDENT

Election, 4 August 2000

On 4 August 2000 the National Assembly (see below) held an election to the presidency. RUNALDO RONALD VENETIAAN, of the New Front coalition, won 37 of the 51 votes cast. His main opponent, RACHID DOEKHIE, the candidate of the National Democratic Party, attracted 10 votes. Having secured the two-thirds' majority necessary to avoid a further round of voting in the Vereinigde Volksvergadering (United People's Assembly—convened to elect the head of state when the National Assembly failed to do so), VENETIAAN was thus elected President. He assumed office on 12 August.

NATIONAL ASSEMBLY

Chairman: JAGGERNATH LACHMON.

General Election, 25 May 2000

Party	Seats
Nieuwe Front (NF)*	33
Millenium Combinatie (MC)†	10
Democratisch Nationaal Platform 2000 (DNP 2000)‡	3
Democratisch Alternatief 1991 (DA '91)§	2
Politieke Vleugel van de FAL (PVF)	2
Progressieve Arbeiders en Landbouwers Unie (PALU)	1
Total	**51**

* An alliance of the Nationale Partij Suriname (NPS), the Pertajah Luhur (PL), the Surinaamse Partij van de Arbeid (SPA), and the Vooruitstrevende Hervormingspartij (VHP).
† An alliance of the Nationale Democratische Partij (NDP), Kerukanan Tulodo Pranatan Ingigil (KTPI) and Democratisch Alternatief.
‡ The list of DNP 2000 included candidates of the Democratische Partij (DP) and of Democraten Van de 21 (D21).
§ The list of DA '91 included candidates from the Broederschap en Eenheid in de Politiek (BEP).

Political Organizations

Algemene Bevrijdings- en Ontwikkeling Partij (ABOP) (General Liberation and Development Party): Jaguarstraat 15, Paramaribo; f. 1986.

Alternatief Forum (AF) (Alternative Forum): Gladiolenstraat 26–28, Paramaribo; tel. 432342; Chair. WINSTON JESSURUN.

Amazone Partij Suriname (APS) (Suriname Amazon Party): Wilhelminastraat 91, Paramaribo; tel. 452081.

Basispartij voor Vernieuwing en Democratie (BVD) (Base Party for Renewal and Democracy): Tunalaan 7, Paramaribo; Chair. TJAN GOBARDHAN.

Broederschap en Eenheid in Politiek (BEP): Paramaribo; f. 1986; contested the 2000 election in alliance with DA '91; Chair. CAPRINO ALLENDY.

Democratisch Alternatief 1991 (DA '91) (Democratic Alternative 1991): POB 91, Paramaribo; tel. 470276; fax 493121; internet www.da91.sr; f. 1991; contested the 2000 election in alliance with the BEP; social-democratic; Chair. S. RAMKHELAWAN.

Democratisch Nationaal Platform 2000 (DNP) (National Democratic Platform 2000): Gemenlandsweg 83, Paramaribo; f. 2000; alliance including:

Democratische Partij (DP) (Democratic Party): Paramaribo; f. 1992; Leader FRANK PLAYFAIR.

Democraten Van de 21 (D21) (Democrats of the 21st Century): Goudstraat 22, Paramaribo; f. 1986.

Hernieuwde Progressieve Partij (HPP) (Renewed Progressive Party): Tourtonnelaan 51, Paramaribo; tel. 426965; e-mail hpp@cq-link.sr; internet www.cq-link.net/hpp; f. 1986; Chair. HARRY KISOENSINGH.

Millenium Combinatie (MC) (Millennium Alliance): f. 2000; alliance including:

Democratisch Alternatief (Democratic Alternative): Jadnanansinghlaan 5, Paramaribo.

Kerukanan Tulodo Pranatan Ingigil (KTPI) (Party for National Unity and Solidarity): Bonistraat 64, Geyersvlijt, Paramaribo; tel. 456116; f. 1947 as the Kaum-Tani Persuatan Indonesia; largely Indonesian; Leader WILLY SOEMITA.

Nationale Democratische Partij (NDP) (National Democratic Party): Benjaminstraat 17, Paramaribo; tel. 499183; fax 432174; e-mail ndpsur@sr.net; internet www.sr.net/users/ndp.sur; f. 1987 by Standvaste (the 25 February Movement); army-supported; Chair. Lt-Col DÉSIRÉ (DESI) BOUTERSE.

Nationale Hervormingspartij (NHP) (National Reform Party): Waterkant 54, Paramaribo; tel. 471624.

Nationale Partij Voor Leiderschap en Ontwikkeling (NPLO) (National Party for Leaderhip and Development): Tropicaweg 1, Paramaribo; tel. 551252; f. 1986.

Naya Kadam (New Choice): Naarstraat 5, Paramaribo; tel. 482014; fax 481012.

Nieuw Front (NF) (New Front): Paramaribo; f. 1987 as Front voor Demokratie en Ontwikkeling (FDO—Front for Democracy and Development), an alliance comprising:

Nationale Partij Suriname (NPS) (Suriname National Party): Wanicastraat 77, Paramaribo; tel. 477302; fax 475796; e-mail nps@sr.net; internet www.nps.sr; f. 1946; predominantly Creole; Sec. OTMAR ROEL RODGERS.

Pertajah Luhur (PL) (Full Confidence Party): Hoek Gemenlandsweg-Daniel Coutinhostraat, Paramaribo; tel. 401087; fax 420394.

Surinaamse Partij van de Arbeid (SPA) (Suriname Labour Party): Rust en vredestraat 64, Paramaribo; tel. 425912; fax 420394; f. 1987; affiliated with C-47 trade union; social democratic party; joined FDO in early 1991; Leader (vacant).

Vooruitstrevende Hervormings Partij (VHP) (Progressive Reform Party): Coppenamestraat 130, Paramaribo; tel. 425912; fax 420394; f. 1949; leading left-wing party; predominantly Indian; Leader JAGGERNATH LACHMON.

Partij voor Demokratie en Ontwikkeling in Eenheid (DOE) (Party for Democracy through Unity and Development): Kamperfoeliestraat 23, Paramaribo; internet www.angelfire.com/nv /DOE; f. 1999.

Pendawa Lima: Bonistraat 115, Geyersvlijt, Paramaribo; tel. 551802; f. 1975; predominantly Indonesian; Chair. SALAM SOMOHARDJO.

Politieke Vleugel van de Fal (PVF): Keizerstraat 150, Paramaribo; Chair. JIWAN SITAL.

Progressieve Arbeiders en Landbouwers Unie (PALU) (Progressive Workers' and Farm Labourers' Union): Dr S. Kafiluddistraat 27, Paramaribo; tel. 400115; socialist party; Chair. Ir IWAN KROLIS.

Progressieve Bosneger Partij (PBP): f. 1968; resumed political activities 1987; represents members of the Bush Negro (Boschneger) ethnic group; associated with the Pendawa Lima (see above).

Progressieve Surinaamse Volkspartij (PSV) (Suriname Progressive People's Party): Keizerstraat 122, Paramaribo; tel. 472979; f. 1946; resumed political activities 1987; Christian democratic party; Chair. W. WONG LOI SING.

Insurgent groups are as follows:

Angula: f. 1990; composed mainly of Saramaccaner Bush Negro clan; Leader CARLOS MAASSI.

Mandela Bush Negro Liberation Movement (BBM): Upper Saramacca region; f. 1989 by mems of the Mataurièr Bush Negro clan; Leader 'BIKO' (LEENDERT ADAMS).

Suriname Liberation Front: Leader CORNELIS MAISI.

Surinamese Liberation Army (SLA—Jungle Commando): Langetabbetje (Suriname), via St Laurent du Maroni, French Guiana; f. 1986; Bush Negro guerrilla group; Leader RONNIE BRUNSWIJK.

Tucayana Amazonica: Bigi Poika; f. 1989 by Amerindian insurgents objecting to Kourou Accord between Govt and Bush Negroes of the SLA; Leader THOMAS SABAJO ('Commander THOMAS'); Chair. of Tucayana Advisory Group (Commission of Eight) ALEX JUBITANA.

Union for Liberation and Democracy (UBD): Moengo; f. 1989 by radical elements of SLA; Bush Negro; Leader KOFI AJONGPONG.

Diplomatic Representation

EMBASSIES IN SURINAME

Brazil: Maratakkastraat 2, POB 925, Paramaribo; tel. 400200; fax 400205; e-mail brasemb@sr.net; Ambassador: RICARDO LUIZ VEANA DE CARVALHO.

China, People's Republic: Anton Dragtenweg 154, POB 3042 Paramaribo; tel. 451570; fax 452540; Ambassador: HU SHOUQIN.

France: Gravenstraat 5–7 boven, POB 2648, Paramaribo; tel. 476455; fax 471208; internet www.amfrance@sr.net; Ambassador: OLIVIER MAITLAND PELEN.

Guyana: Gravenstraat 82, POB 785, Paramaribo; tel. 475209; fax 472679; Ambassador: KARSHANJEE ARJUN.

India: Rode Kruislaan 10, POB 1329, Paramaribo; tel. 498344; fax 491106; Ambassador: UDAI SINGH.

Indonesia: Van Brussellaan 3, POB 157, Paramaribo; tel. 431230; fax 498234; Ambassador: SUBAGIYO WIRYOHADISUBROTO.

Japan: Gravenstraat 23–25, POB 2921, Paramaribo; tel. 474860; fax 412208; Ambassador: HATSUHIKO SHIGIMITSU.

Libya (People's Bureau): Dario Saveedralaan 4, Paramaribo; tel. 490717; fax 464923; Chargé d'affaires: A. TAHER AFTEES.

Netherlands: Van Roseveltkade 5; tel. 477211; fax 477792; Ambassador: RUDOLF TREFFERS.

Russia: Anton Dragtenweg 7, POB 8127, Paramaribo; tel. 472387; fax 472387; Chargé d'affaires a.i.: V. SHCHERBAKOV.

USA: Dr Sophie Redmondstraat 129, POB 1821, Paramaribo; tel. 472900; fax 420800; e-mail embuscen@sr.net; Ambassador: DANIEL JOHNSON.

Venezuela: Gravenstraat 23–25, POB 3001, Paramaribo; tel. 475401; fax 475602; Ambassador: FRANCISCO DE JESÚS SIMANCAS.

Judicial System

The administration of justice is entrusted to a Court of Justice, the six members of which are nominated for life, and three Cantonal Courts.

President of the Court of Justice: ALFRED VELDEMA.

Attorney-General: C. G. DE RANDAMIE.

Religion

Many religions are represented in Suriname. Christianity, Hinduism and Islam predominate.

CHRISTIANITY

Committee of Christian Churches: Paramaribo; Chair. Rev. JOHN KENT (Praeses of the Moravian Church).

The Roman Catholic Church

For ecclesiastical purposes, Suriname comprises the single diocese of Paramaribo, suffragan to the archdiocese of Port of Spain (Trinidad and Tobago). The Bishop participates in the Antilles Episcopal Conference (currently based in Port of Spain, Trinidad and Tobago). At 31 December 1999 there were an estimated 101,660 adherents in the diocese, representing about 23% of the population.

Bishop of Paramaribo: Rt Rev. ALOYSIUS FERDINANDUS ZICHEM, Bisschopshuis, Gravenstraat 12, POB 1230, Paramaribo; tel. 473306; fax 471602; e-mail azichem@sr.net.

The Anglican Communion

Within the Church in the Province of the West Indies, Suriname forms part of the diocese of Guyana. The Episcopal Church is also represented.

Anglican Church: St Bridget's, Hoogestraat 44, Paramaribo.

Protestant Churches

Evangelisch-Lutherse Kerk in Suriname: Waterkant 102, POB 585, Paramaribo; tel. 425503; fax 481856; e-mail elks@sr.net; Pres. RAYMON LESLIE WIMPEL; 4,000 mems.

Moravian Church in Suriname: Maagdenstraat 50, POB 1811, Paramaribo; tel. 473073; fax 475797; e-mail ebgs@sr.net; f. 1735; Praeses HESDIE ZAMUEL; Gen. Sec. LILIAN TRUIDEMAN; 57,400 mems (1985).

Also represented are the Christian Reformed Church, the Dutch Reformed Church, the Evangelical Methodist Church, Pentecostal Missions, the Seventh-day Adventists and the Wesleyan Methodist Congregation.

HINDUISM

Sanatan Dharm: Koningstraat 31–33, POB 760, Paramaribo; tel. 404190; f. 1930; Pres. Dr R. M. NANNAN PANDAY; Sec. A. GAJADHARSING; over 150,000 mems.

ISLAM

Surinaamse Moeslim Associatie: Kankantriestraat 55–57, Paramaribo; Chair. A. ABDOELBASHIRE.

Surinaamse Islamitische Organisatie (SIO): Watermolenstraat 10, POB 278, Paramaribo; tel. 475220; f. 1978; Pres. Dr I. JAMALUDIN; Sec. K. M. HOESSEIN; 6 brs.

Stichting Islamitische Gemeenten Suriname: Verlengde Mahonielaan 39, Paramaribo; Chair. Dr T. SOWIRONO.

Federatie Islamitische Gemeenten in Suriname: Paramaribo; Chair. K. KAAIMAN.

JUDAISM

The Dutch Jewish Congregation and the Dutch Portuguese-Jewish Congregation are represented in Suriname.

Jewish Community: The Synagogue Neve Shalom, Keizerstraat, POB 1834, Paramaribo; tel. 400236; fax 402380; e-mail rene-fernandes@cq-link.sr; f. 1854; Pres. RENÉ FERNANDES.

OTHER RELIGIONS

Arya Dewaker: Dr S. Kafilludistraat 1, Paramaribo; tel. 400706; members preach the Vedic Dharma; disciples of Maha Rishi Swami Dayanand Sarswati, the founder of the Arya Samaj in India; f. 1929; Chair. Dr R. BANSRADJ; Sec. D. CHEDAMMI.

The Bahá'í faith is also represented.

The Press

DAILIES

De Ware Tijd: Malebatrumstraat 7–9, POB 1200, Paramaribo; tel. 472823; fax 411169; internet www.dwt.net; f. 1957; morning; Dutch; independent/liberal; Editors NITA RAMCHARAN, DENNIS SAMSON.

De West: Dr J. C. de Mirandastraat 2–6, POB 176, Paramaribo; tel. 473338; fax 470322; f. 1909; midday; Dutch; liberal; Editors G. D. C. FINDLAY, L. KETTIE; circ. 15,000–18,000.

PERIODICALS

Advertentieblad van de Republiek Suriname: Gravenstraat 120, POB 56, Paramaribo; tel. 473501; fax 454782; f. 1871; 2 a week; Dutch; government and official information bulletin; Editor E. D. FINDLAY; circ. 1,000.

CLO Bulletin: Gemenelandsweg 95, Paramaribo; f. 1973; irregular; Dutch; labour information published by civil servants' union.

Hervormd Suriname: POB 2542, Paramaribo; tel. 472344; f. 1895; monthly; religious.

Kerkbode: Burenstraat 17–19, POB 219, Paramaribo; tel. 473079; fax 475635; e-mail stadje@sr.net; f. 1906; weekly; religious; circ. 2,000.

Omhoog: Gravenstraat 21, POB 1802, Paramaribo; tel. 472521; fax 473904; weekly; Dutch; Catholic bulletin; Editor S. MULDER.

NEWS AGENCIES

Surinaams Nieuws Agentschap (SNA) (Suriname News Agency): Paramaribo; two daily bulletins in Dutch, one in English; Dir E. G. J. DE MEES.

Foreign Bureau

Inter Press Service (IPS) (Italy): Malebatrumstraat 1–5, POB 5065, Paramaribo; tel. 471818; Correspondent ERIC KARWOFODI.

Publishers

Anton de Kom Universiteit van Suriname: Universiteitscomplex, Leysweg 1, POB 9212, Paramaribo; tel. 465558; fax 462291.

Educatieve Uitgeverij Sorava NV: Latourweg 10, POB 8382, Paramaribo; tel. and fax 480808.

Publishing Services Suriname: Van Idsingastraat 133, Paramaribo; tel. 472746; e-mail pssmoniz@sr.net; fmrly I. Krishnadath.

Ministerie van Onderwijs en Volksontwikkeling (Ministry of Education and Community Development): Dr Samuel Kafilludistraat 117-123, Paramaribo; tel. 498850; fax 495083.

Pkin Fowru Productions: Jupiterstraat 30, Paramaribo; tel. 455792.

Stichting Al Qalam: Lawtonlaan 6, Paramaribo.

Stichting Volksboekwinkel: Keizerstraat 197, POB 3040, Paramaribo; tel. 472469.

Stichting Volkslectuur: Dr S. Redmondstraat 231, Paramaribo; tel. 497935.

Stichting Wetenschappelijke Informatie: Prins Hendrikstraat 38, Paramaribo; tel. 475232; fax 422195; e-mail swin@sr.net; f. 1977.

VACO, NV: Domineestraat 26, POB 1841, Paramaribo; tel. 472545; fax 410563; f. 1952; Dir EDUARD HOGENBOOM.

PUBLISHERS' ASSOCIATION

Publishers' Association Suriname: Domineestraat 32, POB 1841, Paramaribo; tel. 472545; fax 410563.

Broadcasting and Communications

TELECOMMUNICATIONS

Telecommunication Corporation Suriname (Telesur): Heiligenweg 1, POB 1839, Paramaribo; tel. 473944; fax 404800; supervisory body; Dir Ir LEONARD C. JOHANNS.

BROADCASTING

Radio

Ampi's Broadcasting Corporation (ABC): Maystraat 57, Paramaribo; tel. 465092; f. 1975; re-opened in 1993; commercial; Dutch and some local languages; Dir J. KAMPERVEEN.

Kara's Broadcasting Co (KBC): Verlengde Keizerstraat 5–7, POB 3025, Paramaribo; tel. 475032; fax 474946; f. 1985; commercial; Dutch and some local languages; Dir ORLANDO KARAMAT ALI.

Radio Apintie: Verlengde Gemenelandsweg 37, POB 595, Paramaribo; tel. 400500; fax 400684; e-mail apintie@sr.net; f. 1958; commercial; Dutch and some local languages; Gen. Man. CH. VERVUURT.

Radio Boskopou: Roseveltkade 1, Paramaribo; tel. 410300; govt-owned; Sranang Tongo and Dutch; Head Mr VAN VARSEVELD.

Radio Garuda: Goudstraat 14-16, Paramaribo; tel. 422422; Dir T. RADJI.

Radio Nickerie (RANI): Waterloostraat 3, Nieuw Nickerie; tel. 231462; commercial; Hindi and Dutch; Dir. DJOTIES LALTA.

Radio Paramaribo: Verlengde Coppenamestraat 34, POB 975, Paramaribo; tel. 499995; fax 493121; f. 1957; commercial; Dutch and some local languages; Dir R. PIERKHAN.

Radio Radhika: Indira Gandhiweg 165, Paramaribo; tel. 482910; re-opened in 1989; Dutch, Hindi; Dir ROSHNI RADHAKISUN.

Radio Sangeet Mala: Indira Gandhiweg 40, Paramaribo; tel. 423902; Dutch, Hindi; Dir RADJEN SOEKHRADJ.

Stichting Radio Omroep Suriname (SRS): Jacques van Eerstraat 20, POB 271, Paramaribo; tel. 498115; fax 498116; f. 1965; commercial; govt-owned; Dutch and some local languages; Dir L. DARTHUIZEN.

Other stations include: Radika Radio, Radio 10, Radio Bersama, Radio Koyeba, Radio Pertjaya, Radio Sjalom, Radio Sun, and SRS.

Television

Algemene Televisie Verzorging (ATV): Adrianusstraat 55, POB 2995, Paramaribo; tel. 404611; fax 402660; e-mail cooman@sr.net; f. 1985; govt-owned; commercial; Dutch, English, Portuguese, Spanish and some local languages; Man. GUNO COOMAN.

Surinaamse Televisie Stichting (STVS): Cultuurtuinlaan 34, POB 535, Paramaribo; tel. 473100; fax 477216; f. 1965; govt-owned; commercial; local languages, Dutch and English; Dir FRITS J. PENGEL.

Finance

(cap. = capital; res = reserves; dep. = deposits; m. = million; amounts in Suriname guilders unless otherwise stated)

BANKING

Central Bank

Centrale Bank van Suriname: 18–20 Waterkant, POB 1801, Paramaribo; tel. 473741; fax 476444; f. 1957; e-mail cbvsprv@sr.net; cap. and res 34.5m. (Dec. 1987); Pres. ANDRE TELTING.

Commercial Banks

ABN AMRO Bank NV: Kerkplein 1, POB 1836, Paramaribo; tel. 471555; fax 411325; f. 1970; Man. J. M. J. HUISMAN; 8 brs.

Finansbank NV: Dr Sophie Redmondstraat 59–61, Paramaribo; tel. 476111; fax 410471.

Handels-Krediet- en Industriebank (Hakrinbank NV): Dr Sophie Redmondstraat 11–13, POB 1813, Paramaribo; tel. 477722;

fax 472066; e-mail hakrindp@sr.net; f. 1936; cap. 50.4m., res 3,391.3m., dep. 24,112.6m. (Dec. 1999); Pres. S. GIRJASING; Man. Dir F. W. M. THIJM; 7 brs.

Landbouwbank NV: Postraat 28–30, POB 929, Paramaribo; tel. 475945; fax 411965; e-mail lbbank@sr.net; f. 1972; agricultural bank; cap. 5m., res 4.6m., dep. 76.0m. (Dec. 1987); Chair. R. KAIMAN; Pres. J. G. BUNDEL.

De Surinaamsche Bank NV: Gravenstraat 26–30, POB 1806, Paramaribo; tel. 471100; fax 411750; internet www.dsbbank.sr; f. 1865; cap. 48.3m., res 2,239.9m., dep. 69,580.5m. (Dec. 1998); Chair. A. R. FRIJMERSUM; Pres. Drs E. J. MÜLLER; 6 brs.

Surinaamse Postspaarbank: Knuffelsgracht 10–14, POB 1879, Paramaribo; tel. 472256; fax 472952; f. 1904; savings and commercial bank; cap. and res 50.3m., dep. 269.7m. (Dec. 1992); Man. RUDI R. LO FO WONG (acting); 2 brs.

Surinaamse Volkscredietbank: Waterkant 104, POB 1804, Paramaribo; tel. 472616; fax 473257; e-mail btlsvcb@sr.net; f. 1949; cap. and res 170.3m. (Dec. 1997); Man. Dir THAKOERDIEN RAMLAKHAN; 3 brs.

Development Bank

Nationale Ontwikkelingsbank van Suriname NV: Coppenamestraat 160–162, POB 677, Paramaribo; tel. 465000; fax 497192; f. 1963; govt-supported development bank; cap. and res 34m. (Dec. 1992); Man. Dir J. TSAI MEU CHONG.

INSURANCE

American Life Insurance Company (ALICO): Paramaribo; Gen. Man. ABDOEL HAFIZKHAN.

Assuria NV: Grote Combeweg 37, POB 1501, Paramaribo; tel. 477955; fax 472390; f. 1961; life and indemnity insurance; Man. Dir Dr S. SMIT.

Assuria Schadeverzekering NV: Gravenstraat 5–7, POB 1030, Paramaribo; tel. 473400; fax 476669; e-mail assuria@sr.net; Dir. M. R. CABENDA.

British American Insurance Company: Klipstenenstraat 29, POB 370, Paramaribo; tel. 476523; Man. H. W. SOESMAN.

CLICO Life Insurance Company (SA) Ltd: Klipstenenstraat 29, POB 3026, Paramaribo; tel. 472525; fax 477219; Gen. Man. C. ABDOELHAFIEZKHAN.

The Manufacturers' Life Insurance Company: c/o Assuria NV, Grote Combeweg 37, Paramaribo; tel. 473400; fax 472390; Man. S. SMIT.

Nationale Nederlanden Levensverzekering Maatschappij NV: Noorderkerkstraat 5–7, POB 1845, Paramaribo; tel. 471541; f. 1955; subsidiary: Fatum Schadeverzekering NV; Man. Dir N. W. LALBIHARIE.

Parsasco N.V.: Gravenstraat 117 boven, Paramaribo; tel. 421212; e-mail parsasco@sr.net; internet www.parsasco.com; Dir L. KHEDOE.

Self Reliance: Herenstraat 22, Paramaribo; tel. 472582; life insurance; Dir N. J. VEIRA.

Suram NV (Suriname American International Insurance Company): Lim A Postraat 7, Paramaribo; tel. 473908; Man. P. J. KAPPEL.

Trade and Industry

DEVELOPMENT ORGANIZATIONS

Centre for Industrial Development and Export Promotion: Rust en Vredestraat 79–81, POB 1275, Paramaribo; tel. 474830; fax 476311; f. 1981; Man. R. A. LETER.

Stichting Planbureau Suriname (National Planning Bureau of Suriname): Dr Sophie Redmondstraat 118, POB 172, Paramaribo; tel. 476241; fax 475001; responsible for financial administration of development programmes and projects; long- and short-term planning; Gen. Sec. A. J. S. HOK A HIN.

CHAMBER OF COMMERCE

Kamer van Koophandel en Fabrieken (Chamber of Commerce and Industry): Dr J. C. de Mirandastraat 10, POB 149, Paramaribo; tel. 473526; fax 474779; e-mail chamber@sr.net; internet www.srnet/chamber; f. 1910; Pres. R. L. A. AMEERALI; Sec. R. RAMDAT; 16,109 mems.

Surinaams–Nederlandse Kamer voor Handel en Industrie (Suriname–Netherlands Chamber of Commerce and Industry): Coppenamestraat 158, Paramaribo; tel. 463201; fax 463241.

INDUSTRIAL AND TRADE ASSOCIATION

Associatie van Surinaamse Fabrikanten (ASFA) (Suriname Manufacturers' Asscn): Domineestraat 33 boven, POB 3046, Paramaribo; tel. 476585; fax 421160; Sec. E. VEGA; 317 mems.

EMPLOYERS' ASSOCIATION

Vereniging Surinaams Bedrijfsleven (VSB) (Suriname Trade and Industry Association): Prins Hendrikstraat 18, POB 111, Paramaribo; tel. 475286; fax 472287; f. 1950; Chair. M. A. MEYER; 290 mems.

MAJOR COMPANIES

The following are some of the major enterprises operating in Suriname:

NV Billiton Maatschappij Suriname: Nickeriestraat 8, POB 1053, Paramaribo; tel. 423277; subsidiary of Royal Dutch-Shell (Netherlands); bauxite mining and refining; Supervisor and Dir PAUL MICHAEL EVERARD; 1,000 employees.

British American Tobacco Company Ltd Suriname: Kan Kawastraat 7, POB 1913, Paramaribo; tel. 481444; fax 483170; subsidiary of BAT Industries (United Kingdom); cigarette manufacturers.

Bruynzeel Suriname Houtmaatschappij NV: Slangenhoutstraat, POB 1831, Paramaribo; tel. 478811; fax 411304; timber merchants; producers of sawnwood, plywood and precut and prefabricated houses.

CHM Suriname NV: Dr Sophie Redmondstraat 2–14, POB 1819, Paramaribo; tel. 471166; fax 471534; subsidiary of Handelen Industrie Mij Ceteco NV (Netherlands); electrical appliances, televisions and radios; importer of Toyota automobiles; 136 employees.

NV Consolidated Industries Corporation: Industrieweg-zuid BR 34, POB 365, Paramaribo; tel. 482050; fax 481431; manufacturers of detergents and disinfectants, packaging materials and cosmetics and toiletries; Pres. PIETER SONNEVELD; 135 employees.

Fernandes Concern Beheer NV: Klipstenenstraat 2–10, Paramaribo; holding co; subsidiary cos: Fernandes Bottling Co NV, Ephraimszegan, Paramaribo (fax 471154); Fernandes & Sons Bakery, Kernkampweg (fax 492177); Handelmaatschappij Fernandes & Sons NV, Klipstenenstraat 2–10, Paramaribo (fax 471154); Gen. Man. RENE FERNANDES; 800 employees.

H. J. de Vries Beheersmaatschappij NV: Waterkant 90–94, Paramaribo; tel. 471222; fax 475718; durable goods; Gen. Man. W. A. TIRION; 384 employees.

C. Kersten en Co NV: Steenbakkerijstraat 27, POB 1808, Paramaribo; tel. 471133; fax 478524; durable goods; Man. Dir F. R. FRIDSMERSUM; 1,265 employees.

Kirplani's Kleding Industrie NV: Domineestraat 52–56, POB 1917, Paramaribo; tel. 471400; textile and clothing producers; Gen. Man. GHAMATMAL T. KIRPALANI; 636 employees.

Nameco NV Nationale Metaal-& Construktie Maatschappij NV: POB 1560, Paramaribo; tel. 482014; construction and civil engineering projects.

Reli NV: Steenbakkerijstraat 56, Paramaribo; durable goods; Man. Dir RUDI CHIN A. LIEN; 800 employees.

Shell Suriname Verkoopmaatschappij NV: Sir Winston Churchill weg Livorno, Paramaribo; tel. 482927; fax 482569; f. 1975; producers of fuel oil and lubricants; Man. Dir YOUNG CAN PETEN; 190 employees.

Staatsolie Maatschappij Suriname NV: Industrieterrein 21, POB 4069, Flora, Paramaribo; tel. 499649; fax 491105; f. 1981; state petroleum exploration and exploitation co; Pres. HUGO GEORG COLERIDGE; 300 employees.

Suriname Aluminium Company (Suralco): van 't Hogerhuystraat, POB 1810, Paramaribo; tel. 477660; subsidiary of Alcoa (USA); bauxite mining and refining, alumina production; Gen. Man. GEORGE STEPHENS.

Suriname-Amerikaanse Industrie NV (SAIL): Cornelis Jongbawstraat 48, POB 3045, Paramaribo; tel. 474014; fax 473521; e-mail sail@sr.net; f. 1955; subsidiary of Castle & Cooke Inc (USA); processors and exporters of marine and farm-raised shrimps and fish; Pres. E. K. MANNES; 280 employees.

NV Suriname Food and Flavor Industries: Rossignollaan 3, POB 863, Paramaribo; tel. 462090; fax 464889; f. 1982; food processors; sauces, flavourings and spices; Gen. Man. HANSRAJ SINGH.

Varossieau Suriname NV: van 't Hogerhuystraat 63, POB 995, Paramaribo; tel. 478308; manufacturers of industrial paints and enamels; Pres. HUERA MILANO CLEVIUS BERGEN.

TRADE UNIONS

Council of the Surinamese Federation of Trade Unions (RVS): f. 1987; comprises:

Algemeen Verbond van Vakverenigingen in Suriname 'De Moederbond' (AVVS) (General Confederation of Trade Unions): Verlengde Coppenamestraat 134, POB 230, Paramaribo; right-wing; Chair. A. W. KOORNAAR; 15,000 mems.

Centrale 47 (C-47): Wanicastraat 230, Paramaribo; includes bauxite workers; Chair. (vacant); 7,654 mems.

Centrale Landsdienaren Organisatie (CLO) (Central Organization for Civil Service Employees): Gemenelandsweg 93, Paramaribo; Pres. HENDRIK SYLVESTER; 13,000 mems.

Progressieve Werknemers Organisatie (PWO) (Progressive Workers' Organization): Limesgracht 80, Paramaribo; f. 1948; covers the commercial, hotel and banking sectors; Chair. RAMON W. CRUDEN; Sec. M. E. MENT; 4,000 mems.

Transport

RAILWAYS

There are no public railways operating in Suriname.

Paramaribo Government Railway: Paramaribo; single-track narrow-gauge railway from Onverwacht, via Zanderij, to Brownsweg (87 km—54 miles); operational between Onverwacht and Republiek (13 km—8 miles); Dir S. R. C. VITERLOO.

Suriname Bauxite Railway: POB 1893, Paramaribo; fax 475148; 70 km (44 miles), standard gauge, from the Backhuis Mountains to Apoera on the Corantijn River; owing to the abandonment of plans to mine bauxite in the Backhuis mountains, the railway transports timber and crushed stone; Pres. EMRO R. HOLDER.

ROADS

In 1996 Suriname had an estimated 4,530 km (2,815 miles) of roads, of which 1,178 km (732 miles) were main roads. The principal east–west road, 390 km (242 miles) in length, links Albina, on the eastern border, with Nieuw Nickerie, in the west. An east–west road, further to the south, was completed in 1978.

SHIPPING

Suriname is served by many shipping companies and has about 1,500 km (930 miles) of navigable rivers and canals. A number of shipping companies conduct regular international services (principally for freight) to and from Paramaribo including EWL, Fyffesgroup, the Alcoa Steamship Co, Marli Marine Lines, Bic Line, Nedlloyd Line, Maersk Lines and Tecmarine Lines (in addition to those listed below). There are also two ferry services linking Suriname with Guyana, across the Corentijn River, and with French Guiana, across the Marowijne River.

Dienst voor de Scheepvaart (Suriname Maritime Authority): Cornelis Jongbawstraat 2, POB 888, Paramaribo; tel. 476769; fax 472940; e-mail dvsmas@sr.net; government authority supervising and controlling shipping in Surinamese waters; Dir of Maritime Affairs E. FITZ-JIM.

Scheepvaart Maatschappij Suriname NV (SMS) (Suriname Shipping Line Ltd): Waterkant 44, POB 1824, Paramaribo; tel. 472447; fax 474814; f. 1936; regular cargo and passenger services in the interior; Chair. F. VAN DER JAGT; Man. Dir. M. E. LIEUW A. PAW.

NV VSH Scheepvaartmij United Suriname Shipping Company: Van het Hogerhuysstraat 9–11, POB 1860, Paramaribo; tel. 402558; fax 403515; e-mail united@sr.net; shipping agents and freight carriers; Man. PATRICK HEALY.

Staatsolie Maatschappij Suriname NV: Industrieterrein 21, Flora, POB 4069, Paramaribo; tel. 480333; fax 480811; Chair. H. G. COLERIDGE; Man. Dir Dr S. E. JHARAP.

Suriname Coast Traders NV: Flocislaan 4, Industrieterrein Flora, POB 9216, Paramaribo; tel. 463020; fax 463040; f. 1981.

CIVIL AVIATION

The main airport is Johan Adolf Pengel International Airport (formerly Zanderij International Airport), 45 km from Paramaribo. Domestic flights operate from Zorg-en-Hoop Airport, located in a suburb of Paramaribo. There are 35 airstrips throughout the country.

Surinaamse Luchtvaart Maatschappij NV (SLM) (Suriname Airways): Coppenamestraat 136, POB 2029, Paramaribo; tel. 433273; fax 491213; e-mail c.cairo@slm.firm.sr; internet www.slm.firm.sr; f. 1962; services to Amsterdam (the Netherlands) and to destinations in North America, South America and the Caribbean; Pres. HENK JESSURUN (acting); Vice-Pres. JAN HOLLUM.

Gonini Air Service Ltd: Doekhiweg 1, Zorg-en-Hoop Airport, POB 1614, Paramaribo; tel. 499098; fax 498363; f. 1976; privately-owned; licensed for scheduled and unscheduled national and international services (charters, lease, etc.); Man. Dir GERARD BRUNINGS.

Gum Air NV: Rijweg naar Kwatta 254, Paramaribo; tel. 497670; privately-owned; unscheduled domestic flights; Man. Mr GUMMELS.

Tourism

Efforts were made to promote the previously undeveloped tourism sector in the 1990s. Attractions include the varied cultural activities, a number of historical sites and an unspoiled interior with many varieties of plants, birds and animals. There are 13 nature reserves and one nature park. There were 54,000 foreign tourist arrivals at the international airport in 1999, when tourism receipts totalled US $44m.

Suriname Tourism Foundation: Dr J. F. Nassylaan 2, Paramaribo; tel. 410357; e-mail stsur@sr.net; f. 1996; Exec. Dir Dr H. EDWARD ESSED.

Defence

The National Army numbered an estimated 2,040 men and women in August 2000. There is an army of 1,600, a navy of 240 and an air force of some 200.

Defence Budget: US $11m. in 2000.

Commander-in-Chief: Lt-Col ARTHY GORRÉ.

Education

Education is compulsory for children between the ages of seven and 12. Primary education lasts for six years, and is followed by a further seven years of secondary education, comprising a junior secondary cycle of four years followed by a senior cycle of three years. All education in government and denominational schools is provided free of charge. In 1997 the total enrolment in primary, secondary and tertiary education was equivalent to 76.0% of the population in the relevant age group, while total enrolment in primary education was equivalent to 99.9% of children in the relevant age group (males 99.9%; females 99.9%). In the 1990s, owing to political events in the country, some schools in Suriname were closed, particularly in the interior of the country. As a result, enrolment rates declined. In 1999 there were 448 primary and pre-primary schools, 106 junior secondary schools and 18 senior secondary schools. The traditional educational system, inherited from the Dutch, was amended after the 1980 revolution to place greater emphasis on serving the needs of Suriname's population. This included a literacy campaign and programmes of adult education. In 2000, according to a UNESCO estimate, the rate of adult illiteracy was only 5.8% (males 4.1%; females 7.4%). Higher education was provided by four technical and vocational schools and by the University of Suriname at Paramaribo, which had faculties of law, social and technological sciences, economics and medicine. Expenditure on education by all levels of government in 1996 was an estimated Sf 3,840m. (3.2% of GNP).

Bibliography

For works on the region generally, see Select Bibliography (Books).

Brana-Shute, G. 'Back to the Barricades? Five Years 'Revo' in Suriname', in *Journal of Interamerican Studies*, Vol. 28, 1 (Spring). 1986.

Derveld, F. E. R. *Politics and Surinam Migration*. Gröningen, Instituut voor Economisch Onderzoek, 1980.

Dew, E. *The Difficult Flowering of Surinam: Ethnicity and Politics in a Plural Society*. The Hague, Martinus Nijhoff, 1978.

Goslinga, C. Ch. *A Short History of the Netherlands Antilles and Surinam*. The Hague, Martinus Nijhoff, 1979.

Hira, S. 'Class Formation and Class Struggle in Suriname: The Background and Development of the coup d'état', in Ambursley, F., and Cohen, R. (Eds). *Crisis in the Caribbean*. London, Heinemann, 1983.

Lier, R. A. J. van. *Frontier Society: A Social Analysis of The History of Surinam*, 2nd edn. The Hague, Martinus Nijhoff, 1971.

Meel, P. *Tussen autonomie en onafhankelijkheid: Nederlands-Surinaamse betrekkingen 1954-1961*. Leiden, KITLV Uitgeverij, 1999.

Oostindie, G. (Ed.). *Het verleden onder ogen: herdenking van de slavernij*. Amsterdam, Arena.

Schultz, G. *Turmoil and Triumph: Diplomacy, Power and the Victory of the American Ideal*. New York, NY, Touchstone, 1996.

Sizer, N., and Rice, R. *Backs to the Wall in Suriname: Forest Policy in a Country in Crisis*. Washington, DC, World Resources Institute, 1995.

Suriname: Policies to Meet the Social Debt. Santiago (Chile), PREALC, 1992.

TRINIDAD AND TOBAGO

Area: 5,128 sq km (1,980 sq miles); of which Tobago is 300 sq km (116 sq miles).

Population (official estimate at September 2000): 1,294,000.

Capital: Port of Spain, estimated population 51,076 at mid-1991.

Language: English (official); French, Spanish, Hindi and Chinese are also spoken.

Religion: 40% Christian (29% Roman Catholic), 24% Hindu, 6% Muslim.

Climate: Tropical; average annual temperature is 29°C (84°F); annual average rainfall is 1,630 mm.

Time: GMT −4 hours.

Public Holidays

2002: 1 January (New Year's Day), 11–12 February (Carnival), 30 March (Spiritual Baptist Shouters' Liberation Day), 29 March–1 April (Easter), 30 May (Indian Arrival Day), 30 May (Corpus Christi), 19 June (Labour Day), 1 August (Emancipation Day), 2 September (for Independence Day), 6 December* (Id al-Fitr, end of Ramadan), 25–26 December (Christmas).

2003: 1 January (New Year's Day), 3–4 March (Carnival), 31 March (for Spiritual Baptist Shouters' Liberation Day), 18–21 April (Easter), 30 May (Indian Arrival Day), 19 June (Corpus Christi), 19 June (Labour Day), 1 August (Emancipation Day), 1 September (for Independence Day), 26 November* (Id al-Fitr, end of Ramadan), 25–26 December (Christmas).

In addition, the Hindu festival of Divali is celebrated, in October or November. This festival is dependent on sightings of the moon and its precise date is not known until two months before it takes place.

* Dependent on the Islamic lunar calendar and may vary by one or two days from the dates given.

Currency: Trinidad and Tobago dollar; TT $1,000 = £111.58 = US $159.75 = €179.98 (30 April 2001).

Weights and Measures: The imperial system is in force, but the metric system is being introduced.

Basic Economic Indicators

	1996	1997	1998
Gross domestic product (million Trinidad and Tobago dollars at 1985 prices)	17,950	18,507	19,327
GDP per head (Trinidad and Tobago dollars at 1985 prices)*	14,246.0	14,458.6	15,099.2
Annual growth of real GDP (%)	3.8	3.1	4.4
Annual growth of real GDP per head (%)	3.8	1.5	4.4
Government budget (million Trinidad and Tobago dollars at current prices):			
Revenue	9,446.5	9,259.6	10,482.6†
Expenditure	8,623.7	8,906.1	9,062.5†
Consumer price index (annual average; base: 1995 = 100)‡	103.4	107.2	113.2
Rate of inflation (annual average, %)§	3.4	3.6	5.6
Foreign exchange reserves (US $ million at 31 December)	543.8	706.2	783.0
Imports f.o.b. (million Trinidad and Tobago dollars)	12,866.8	18,705.9	18,886.8
Exports f.o.b. (million Trinidad and Tobago dollars)	15,014.4	15,887.6	14,220.5
Balance of payments (current account, US $ million)	105.1	−613.6	−643.5

* Figures for GDP per head are based on official estimates of mid-year population: 1.26m. in 1996; 1.28m. in 1997; 1.28m. in 1998.
† Provisional figures.
‡ 117.1 in 1999 and 121.2 in 2000.
§ 3.4% in 1999 and 3.6% in 2000.

Gross national product per head measured at purchasing power parity (PPP) (GNP converted to US dollars by the PPP exchange rate, 1999): 7,262.

Economically Active Population (1998): 479,300.

Unemployment (December 2000): 12.1%.

Total foreign debt (2000): US $1,680m.

Infant mortality rate (per 1,000 live births, 1998): 16.

Life expectancy (years at birth, 1998): 74.1 (males 71.7; females 76.4).

Adult population with HIV/AIDS (15–49 years, 1999): 1.1%.

School enrolment ratio (5–16 years, 1998): 66%.

Adult literacy rate (15 years and over, 2000): 98.2% (males 99.0; females 97.5).

Commercial energy consumption per head (kg of oil equivalent, 1998): 6,964.

Carbon dioxide emissions per head (metric tons, 1997): 17.4.

Passenger motor cars in use (estimate, per 1,000 of population, 1996): 107.9.

Television receivers in use (per 1,000 of population, 1997): 333.

Personal computers in use (per 1,000 of population, 1999): 54.2.

History

MARK WILSON

Based on an earlier article by ROD PRINCE

The two islands that constitute the modern state of Trinidad and Tobago were both first settled by Carib and other Amerindian populations from the South American mainland. Contact with Europe and North America dates from the third voyage of the Spanish navigator Christopher Columbus, in 1498. Small Spanish settlements were established from 1592, which formed an insignificant part of the Viceroyalty of New Granada, based in Bogotá (Santafé de Bogotá, Colombia).

Larger scale settlement began from 1776, when Spain began to encourage settlers from Grenada and other former French possessions that had passed to British rule. Later, settlers came from Martinique and Guadeloupe, where slavery had been temporarily abolished as a result of the French Revolution. A Spanish cedula of 1783 established a system of land grants for French planters, with additional allocations for those who brought slaves. Coffee, cocoa and sugar plantations were established, and there was considerable growth in trade. Until the late 19th century French creole remained the main spoken vernacular. At the end of the 20th century Roman Catholicism remained the main Christian denomination.

Trinidad was captured by the United Kingdom in 1797 and was formally ceded to that country by Spain in 1802. Tobago was colonized by the Dutch in 1628, but then claimed by a succession of European navies until the British took possession in 1762, following 100 years of French occupation; France ceded the island to the United Kingdom in the following year. However, it was not until 1814 that the British gained the island in perpetuity. Throughout the 19th century in Trinidad there remained a latent conflict between the British administration and a mainly French planter and commercial class. For this reason, Trinidad, unlike most West Indian colonies, had no elected Assembly.

The abolition of slavery in 1834 was followed by four years in which slaves were forced to remain on the plantations under an 'apprenticeship' system. From 1838, however, many former slaves moved to Port of Spain or established peasant farms on unoccupied land; as did a large number of immigrants from other West Indian colonies. With a labour shortage developing on the plantations, from 1845 the Government encouraged the immigration of indentured labourers, mainly Indian, but also Chinese and Madeiran. On the expiry of a 10-year period, of which the first five were contracted to a single employer, the workers received either their passage home or title to a small plot of land. This form of immigration continued until 1917 and the majority of the rural population in modern Trinidad was descended from Indian indentured labourers. Tobago's sugar industry performed badly after emancipation, and was close to collapse by the 1880s. For this reason, the smaller colony was attached to Trinidad from 1889.

Agitation for increased political rights began in Trinidad from the 1880s, earlier than in most other West Indian colonies. From 1896, the Trinidad Workingmen's Association played an important role in political life. Against this background, in 1899 the colonial authorities unwisely abolished the elected Borough Council in Port of Spain. In 1914 the Council was re-established and, from 1925, there were elected members on the Legislative Council, although the electoral roll was limited by property qualifications.

THE MOVE TO INDEPENDENCE

Disturbances resulting from the depressed economic situation of the 1930s provided suitable conditions for the foundation of the labour movements. These, in turn, evolved into political movements, particularly after the introduction of universal adult suffrage in 1946. The People's National Movement (PNM), founded in 1956 by Dr Eric Williams, won 39% of the votes cast in legislative elections held in 1956, and gained control of the Legislative Council (securing 13 of the 24 elected seats), under the provision of the new constitutional arrangements that provided for self-government. Dr Williams became Trinidad and Tobago's Chief Minister.

Along with most other British Caribbean colonies, Trinidad and Tobago joined the Federation of the West Indies in 1958. However, when Jamaica left the grouping in 1961 in order to seek independence individually, Trinidad and Tobago also withdrew, reluctant to take financial responsibility for the other, and, at that time, poorer, islands, in the north of the region, and the Federation collapsed. Internal self-government for Trinidad and Tobago in 1961 was followed by independence on 31 August 1962.

THE PNM AND PARTY POLITICS

Elective politics in Trinidad and Tobago mostly ran along racial lines, although there was some attempt by all parties to win at least token support from other groups. The PNM was mainly urban and Afro-Trinidadian, with some backing from Muslim and Christian Indians. Its early opponent, the Democratic Labour Party (DLP), led by Rudranath Capildeo, was based in the Hindu section of the Indian-origin community. Although Indo- and Afro-Trinidadians were roughly equal numerically, support from minority and mixed-race voters, together with the pattern of constituency boundaries, was enough to give the PNM a secure parliamentary majority over the DLP and its ethnically-based successor parties until 1986. Dr Williams remained Prime Minister until his death in 1981.

The PNM's strongest challenge in this period came from the 'Black Power' movement, which came to prominence on the islands in 1970. Influenced to some extent by African-American radicalism, support for the movement stemmed mainly from a well-established perception that, eight years after independence, there was significant discrimination against Afro-Trinidadians in private-sector employment, and that insufficient respect was given to black people and their culture. A series of demonstrations in 1970 was accompanied by some violence, and a state of emergency was declared. Unrest extended to junior army officers, who unsuccessfully attempted to overthrow the Government. The leaders of the Black Power movement were imprisoned without trial, and marches were banned. Nevertheless, many of their aims were achieved in the 1970s, when there were broader economic opportunities and more attention to cultural development.

Political difficulties persisted for some time, however, and there was an opposition boycott of the 1971 elections. In September 1973 Dr Williams announced his resignation, but was persuaded to rescind it. A new Constitution came into effect on 1 August 1976, making Trinidad and Tobago a republic within the Commonwealth. In elections to the House of Representatives in the following month, the PNM won 24 of the 36 seats, while an alliance of petroleum and sugar workers within the newly-formed United Labour Front (ULF), a mainly Indian party with trade-union support led by Basdeo Panday, secured 10 seats. The two Tobago seats were won by the Democratic Action Congress (DAC), led by A. N. R. Robinson, a former PNM cabinet minister. The former Governor-General, Ellis Clarke, was sworn in as the islands' first President in December.

At this time, the PNM was presiding over a buoyant economy, following steep rises in the world price of petroleum in 1973 and 1974 that transformed Trinidad and Tobago's relatively small reserves of petroleum into a major financial and political asset. Petroleum prices remained high until 1981, by which time the PNM's dominance of national politics was such that, at his death in March of that year, Williams was without serious rivals.

THE RISE OF THE NATIONAL ALLIANCE FOR RECONSTRUCTION

Williams was succeeded as Prime Minister by George Chambers, one of the three deputy leaders of the PNM. Chambers was seen as moderate and generally fair, but failed to command enthusiastic support. He presided over another election victory for the PNM in November 1981, winning 26 seats in the parliament. The DAC and the ULF, as well as an intellectual pressure group, the Tapia House Movement, formed the National Alliance and took the two Tobago seats and eight, mainly Indian, rural seats, gaining 20.7% of the votes cast. The middle class, conservative, Organization for National Reconstruction (ONR), led by another former PNM minister, Karl Hudson-Phillips, won 22.3% of the ballot but took no seats, because its mainly middle-class support was evenly spread across a large number of constituencies.

In August 1983 the four opposition parties formed an alliance to contest local elections and won 66 of the 120 local council seats. A united opposition party, the National Alliance for Reconstruction (NAR), was formed a year later. The NAR aimed to offer a credible alternative to the Government, at a time when stagnant and then decreasing petroleum prices were severely reducing government revenues and highlighting the defects of the policies pursued during the increase in prices of the previous decade. In the November 1984 elections to the Tobago House of Assembly, which had been formed in 1980, the DAC (part of the NAR) reduced the PNM's share of the 12 elective seats from four to one. Prime Minister Chambers was increasingly losing political respect, and his position was not strengthened by his failure to support the US-led military intervention in Grenada in October 1983. A 33% devaluation of the currency in December 1985 was deeply unpopular, and was seen as further eroding purchasing power in what was still an import-dependent economy.

Accusations of government economic mismanagement and corruption increased in the months preceding the December 1986 general election, intensified by the Government's failure to publish an official report on drugs-trafficking. The NAR, led by Robinson, won an overwhelming victory, gaining 33 of the 36 seats in the House of Representatives, and 67% of the votes. The PNM's parliamentary representation was reduced to just three seats, owing to residual support in urban strongholds in eastern Port of Spain and in San Fernando. The party retained 33% of the popular vote, nevertheless, which formed the basis for a later recovery under the former energy minister, Patrick Manning, who was appointed PNM leader in January 1987. Robinson was appointed premier.

THE GOVERNMENT OF A. N. R. ROBINSON

The NAR Government was an unwieldy coalition of the ULF, the ONR, the DAC and the Tapia House Movement, a grouping of university radicals. Divisions emerged almost immediately over the allocation of cabinet portfolios and positions on state boards, and extended to policy matters, as the Government was forced to implement unpopular measures in response to a deepening economic crisis. There were also accusations that Indo-Trinidadians, who formed a majority of NAR voters, were being excluded from positions of real power.

The small Tapia House Movement left the NAR in June 1987, while John Humphrey, a former ULF member, was removed from his post as Minister of Public Works and Settlement in November. The external affairs minister and former ULF leader, Basdeo Panday, was dismissed in February 1988, along with one cabinet colleague and a junior minister. All three accused the NAR leadership of racism and were expelled from the party in October. In April 1989 Panday announced the formation of a new party, the United National Congress (UNC), which became the official opposition in September 1990, by virtue of holding six seats to the PNM's three. The UNC at this time was widely perceived to be a rural, Indo-Trinidadian party with strong links to the sugar workers' trade union.

The Government's unpopularity increased as it was forced to take further austerity measures. A compensatory financing agreement with the International Monetary Fund (IMF) was

followed by stand-by agreements in 1989 and 1990. There was a further 15% currency devaluation in August 1988, which increased retail-price levels. Government expenditure was cut, and the budget of January 1989 imposed a 10% reduction on public-sector pay. This last measure aroused the hostility of the trade unions, which successfully challenged its legality.

In July 1990 a group of insurgents from the Jamaat al Muslimeen, a sect of mainly Afro-Trinidadian Muslim converts led by Yasin Abu Bakr, a former policeman, stormed the parliament building during a session of the House of Representatives, taking 46 hostages including the Prime Minister and most of the Cabinet. At the same time, they blew up the police headquarters building and took over what was then the sole television station, using it to broadcast their demands that the Prime Minister should resign, and his deputy lead an interim Government into elections within 90 days. Widespread looting and fires began almost immediately in the capital and some suburban centres. The siege lasted for five days, during which time 23 people were killed and 500 wounded, most of them looters shot by the police. The Prime Minister was shot in the leg by the rebels after refusing to sign a letter of resignation. However, the acting President was induced to sign an amnesty for the rebels, which was delivered to them in the parliament building.

Following the surrender of the Jamaat al Muslimeen, the Government announced that the amnesty agreement had been made under duress and was therefore invalid. Abu Bakr and 113 others were charged with murder and treason. The Judicial Committee of the Privy Council (the country's final court of appeal, and based in London, United Kingdom) ruled, in November 1992, that the validity of the presidential amnesty should be determined before the case came to trial. In July 1992 the High Court ruled that the pardon was valid, and ordered the release of the accused. In October 1993 the Government lost an appeal against the ruling, but a year later the Privy Council ruled that the Jamaat al Muslimeen had invalidated the pardon by failing to surrender as soon as it was agreed, instead continuing the siege in an attempt to win further concessions. However, it was also ruled that it would be an abuse of process for the accused to be rearrested and tried. In January 2000 the Jamaat al Muslimeen was ordered to pay TT $20m. for damage incurred during the insurrection. In May 2001, however, the High Court awarded TT $625,000 in compensation to the group for damage done to its headquarters, in addition to an earlier payment of TT $1.5m.

THE RETURN OF THE PNM

One member of parliament was killed in the siege, and the NAR lost a by-election to elect his successor. This highlighted the Government's loss of support, but there was some surprise at the scale of the NAR's rout in the general election that followed in December 1991, when the party gained only 24.4% of the valid votes cast and secured only the two seats on Robinson's home island, Tobago. The PNM won 21 legislative seats and 45.1% of the popular vote, mainly in urban areas with an Afro-Trinidadian majority, while the UNC took 29.1% of the ballot and 13, mainly rural, seats in central and southern Trinidad.

The new PNM Government, led by Patrick Manning, contained few members of previous PNM administrations. Economic policies reversed many aspects of the party's previous policies, focusing on financial and trade liberalization, divestment of state enterprises and foreign investment, particularly in heavy industries based on 'offshore' natural-gas resources.

In April 1993 the Trinidad and Tobago dollar was made convertible, in a strictly-managed float against the US dollar. In contrast with Jamaica and Guyana, the currency remained stable, in spite of occasional shortages on the foreign-exchange markets. The fiscal current account was in surplus from 1993 and the economy moved back into steady growth from 1994. A protracted dispute with the trade unions over repayment of the TT $3,000m. in salary arrears incurred through the NAR's attempt in 1991 to reduce public-sector salaries was settled in 1995 for teachers, and in the following year for other public servants, who were able to claim either no-interest bonds, additional leave, or other non-cash benefits.

In spite of its relative economic success, however, the PNM lost an important by-election in a marginal seat in May 1994.

This was followed by a serious dispute with the Speaker of the House of Representatives, Occah Seapaul, who was the subject of damaging financial allegations, and who responded to attempts to replace her by suspending a government minister from parliament for six months. A state of emergency was briefly declared on 3 August 1995, in order to allow the Government to remove her from office. This, in turn, led to the defection from the Government, on the following day, of her brother, Ralph Maraj, the Minister of Public Utilities (and former Minister of Foreign Affairs). With only a narrow majority now remaining—the UNC had previously won an additional seat in a by-election—the Prime Minister responded by announcing that a general election was to be held on 6 November 1995, one year earlier than was necessary.

THE ELECTION OF THE UNC

In the elections, although the PNM increased its share of the votes to 48.8%, its support was concentrated heavily in its urban strongholds. The UNC received enthusiastic backing from some important members of the business community, and raised its share of the ballot to 45.8%. The UNC secured control of three marginal constituencies, which left each party with 17 of the 34 Trinidad seats. The NAR's remaining support in Trinidad had collapsed, but with the support of the two Tobago members, the UNC was able to form a Government and Basdeo Panday became Prime Minister. In spite of the electoral defeat, Manning resisted continuing demands from within the PNM for his resignation as party leader, winning a further five-year term in the post in 1996. However, he lost the support of important sections of the PNM, which weakened his ability to organize an effective opposition to Panday's Government.

The new administration continued most of the economic policies of its predecessor. The new finance minister, Brian Kuei Tung, and the foreign minister, Ralph Maraj, had both been members of the previous Cabinet. In February 1997 the Government's parliamentary position was strengthened by the defection of two PNM members, who subsequently sat as independents and were appointed junior ministers. The Government presided over a period of strong economic growth, averaging 5.6% in 1995–2000. However, there were persistent and widespread reports of corruption and mismanagement. On 14 February an electoral college of both houses of parliament elected Robinson as President. He immediately relinquished his parliamentary and cabinet seats, as well as the leadership of the NAR. The PNM was opposed to a head of state who had, until his nomination, played an active role in party politics, and for the first time a presidential election was contested. However, the PNM candidate, a serving high-court judge, received 18 votes to Robinson's 46. The NAR retained President Robinson's former seat at a by-election in May. However, in April the representative of the other Tobago seat, Pamela Nicholson, resigned from the Government and from the NAR to sit as an independent. She was later followed by three members of Tobago's House of Assembly, still controlled by the NAR, who also left that party to sit as independents. As a result of these changes, from mid-1997 the Government could command the support of 20 members of the House of Representatives. However, while the UNC was expected to perform well in local government elections, held on 12 July 1999, instead the PNM made significant gains at the cost of the ruling party, winning 66 of the 124 districts being contested.

A serious dispute between the Government and the Chief Justice, Michael de la Bastide, began in September 1999 when he claimed that the independence of the judiciary was threatened by an attempt by the Attorney-General, Ramesh Lawrence Maharaj, to tighten administrative and financial controls. The Chief Justice was supported by 28 of the country's 29 judges, but not by the President of the Bar Association, Karl Hudson-Phillips. The Government responded in December by announcing that a former British Lord Chancellor, Lord Mackay of Clashfern, would lead a three-member Commission of Inquiry into the administration of justice on the islands. President Robinson, clearly unhappy with this decision, did not appoint the Commission until February 2000, signalling an unprecedented breach between the largely ceremonial Head of State and the Cabinet. This was all the more surprising owing to the fact that President Robinson had himself been a senior member

of Panday's Cabinet in 1995–97 and had been nominated as President by Panday's Government. The Commission announced its findings and recommendations in October 2000, clearing the Attorney-General of seeking to undermine the independence of the judiciary, but apparently failing to settle the fundamental disagreement between de la Bastide and Maharaj.

The conflict between Prime Minister Panday and President Robinson intensified in 2000 and 2001; both the President and the Chief Justice were alleged by Panday to be 'enemies' of his administration, along with Ken Gordon, Chairman of the Caribbean Communications Network media group, who, as a consequence, won damages of TT $600,000 in a libel suit against Panday in October 2000.

In January 2000 the Prime Minister decided to revoke the appointment of two Tobagonians as government senators, on the basis that they had voted against his administration; the President, himself a Tobagonian, delayed before acting on this decision, believing that their dismissal would be a breach of the understanding reached in 1995 between the UNC and the NAR. Following the mediation of the Archbishop of Port of Spain, the Most Rev. Anthony Pantin, Robinson agreed to revoke the senators' appointments, replacing them with two Tobagonians nominated by Panday.

In early January 2000 Hansraj Sumairsingh, a member of the UNC and leader of one of Trinidad's nine regional corporations, was found murdered. It was subsequently reported that Sumairsingh had written to the Prime Minister several times regarding threats made to him by the Minister of Local Government, Dhanraj Singh, following Sumairsingh's revelation of alleged corruption in the unemployment relief programme administered by Singh's ministry. Although Panday said that he could not remember having received such letters, a copy of one was later produced by a PNM member. A full investigation was initiated and in October Singh was dismissed from his government post. Singh left unexpectedly for the USA for medical treatment for stress and high blood pressure. However, he returned to Trinidad in January 2001, and was charged with corruption in the unemployment relief programme and, on 19 February, with the murder of Sumairsingh. Singh was subsequently moved to a mental institution, suffering from depression.

THE RE-ELECTION OF THE UNC

The general election of 11 December 2000 was won by the UNC with 51.5% of the votes cast, compared to 46.2% for the PNM. The UNC gained two marginal seats on Trinidad, bringing its total in the 36-seat House of Representatives to 19, while the PNM won 16 seats and the NAR gained one. On 20 December, following a delay owing to a recount of votes, Panday was inaugurated as Prime Minister for the second time.

The December 2000 general election was marred by allegations of fraud. Opposition charges that the electoral list had been manipulated were highlighted by police investigations of prominent government supporters and arrests were made following attempted manipulation of the electoral register. The opposition also challenged the election of two of the UNC's winning candidates, Winston Peters and William Chaitan, as they had failed to declare their dual nationality (US and Canadian, respectively). However, this challenge remained delayed in mid-2001, leaving some legal doubt about the election result. In January 2001 Panday announced his Cabinet and his nominations to the Senate. However, President Robinson refused to approve the senate nominations of seven UNC members, declaring them to be unconstitutional, as they had been defeated as candidates in the congressional election. His refusal was widely felt to be outside the President's discretionary powers under the Constitution and, despite threats of widespread demonstrations by the Jamaat al Muslimeen, should the seven nominations be approved, on 14 February the President acceded to the Prime Minister's wishes, although he urged the Prime Minister not to appoint any of the seven senators to the Cabinet.

Panday appointed a private-sector banker, Gerald Yetming, to the Ministry of Finance, Planning and Development portfolio. This appointment was interpreted as a further increase in the influence of businessmen and technocrats within the Government, and a move away from the party's traditional rural, Indo-Trinidadian and trade union origins. However, despite its election victory and the continuing growth of the economy, the UNC Government continued to be dogged by allegations of corruption in early 2001, including alleged fraud within the North West Regional Health Authority and irregularities at the state-owned Petroleum Company of Trinidad and Tobago Ltd (Petrotrin).

At elections to the Tobago House of Assembly, held on 29 January 2001, the PNM took control of the Assembly for the first time, with 46.7% of the vote and eight of the 12 seats. The NAR retained 38.4% of the vote and four seats, while the UNC, contesting the election for the first time, won minimal support, as did the People's Empowerment Party, formed by former NAR dissidents.

Rumours of a planned coup attempt circulated in early 2001, and in April the acting Commissioner of Police revealed that evidence of a plot had been discovered. Evidence of arms-trafficking and a further plot to overthrow the Government were discovered in June.

In March 2001, owing to health problems, Panday reduced his workload, relinquishing parts of his portfolio. Despite his ill health, however, his leadership was not challenged at the internal party election held in June. Attorney-General Maharaj, representing the party's traditional rural, Indo-Trinidadian base, was elected deputy leader with 41.6% of the votes cast. Carlos John, widely believed to be favoured by Panday as a possible successor, was third-placed in the leadership ballot, with 25.7% of the vote, behind the education minister, Kamla Persad-Bissessar.

In May 2001, following the suspension of opposition member Keith Rowley, for 'objectionable' behaviour and disrespect towards the Speaker, opposition members withdrew from the House of Representatives in protest. An agreement was subsequently reached by Panday and Manning, whereby Rowley would be reinstated; according to the agreement Manning would abandon a motion of censure against the Prime Minister, while Panday would take no further action against the Opposition Chief Whip, Ken Valley, for previous objectionable behaviour.

INTERNATIONAL RELATIONS

In April 2000 Trinidad and Tobago received widespread international condemnation, following a government announcement that the country was to withdraw from the first optional protocol to the International Covenant on Civil and Political Rights, owing to its continued support of capital punishment. The Government stated that the withdrawal was intended to prevent condemned murderers from addressing lengthy appeals. At the end of April a meeting was held between Hochoy Charles, the Chief Secretary of the Tobago House of Assembly, and the Prime Minister, to discuss the deterioration in the relationship between the two islands. It was decided that a 'task force' would be created to consider the constitutional and legal position of Tobago and to resolve the problems of governance.

Talks were held in July 2000 to demarcate the maritime boundary between Trinidad and Barbados, but no conclusive result had been achieved by mid-2001. In July 2001 a joint commission was established to negotiate the maritime boundary between Trinidad and Tobago and Grenada.

On 14 February 2001, at a Caribbean Community and Common Market (CARICOM) summit in Barbados, the leaders of 11 Caribbean states signed an agreement to establish the Caribbean Court of Justice. The Court would replace the British Privy Council as the final court of appeal, and was to be based in Trinidad. The Court would be established upon ratification by three states, at the annual summit in July; the Government of Trinidad and Tobago had already stated that it would ratify the agreement. However, the Court was unlikely to be fully established before 2003.

Economy

MARK WILSON

At the beginning of the 21st century the economy of Trinidad and Tobago contrasted sharply with those of its Caribbean neighbours. Although no longer dependent on the extraction and refining of petroleum, it remained underpinned by the energy sector, with the extraction of natural gas and crude oil providing the basis for processing and manufacturing industries. Tourism, 'offshore' finance and agriculture, by contrast, were less well developed.

A phase of rapid economic development began when petroleum prices rose from US $1.3 in 1970 to US $33.5 in 1982. This led to rapid growth in gross domestic product (GDP) in this period, at an average annual rate of 5.5%. Expansion of GDP, in turn, had strong positive effects on foreign-exchange earnings and on government revenue, which grew from TT $888m. in 1974 to TT $4,253m. in 1981. The Government attempted to spread the benefits of the increase in petroleum prices through spending on infrastructure, investment in state-owned, heavy industries and other capital projects. Imports were restricted in an effort to encourage local manufacturing, while protection extended also to services such as insurance. Real wages grew by an average of 5.2% per year from 1974 to 1984.

Domestic petroleum production, although insignificant by world standards, nevertheless reached 230,000 barrels per day (b/d) in 1978, owing to increases in world-wide prices of the commodity. However, from 1981 world oil prices stabilized and, from 1983, fell sharply, while new facilities for crude petroleum imports to the USA had already prompted the removal of that country's strategically motivated tax incentives for petroleum products refined in the Caribbean. By 1988–90 production had decreased to a level of 150,000 b/d, with a further decline to 125,000 b/d in 1993. While fluctuating slightly, production remained at around this level throughout the 1990s and averaged 119,100 b/d in 2000. However, there were also some important discoveries, including, in January 1998, the largest newly identified reservoir for 25 years; there were also substantial amounts of condensate associated with recent gas finds. In early 2001 proven oil reserves were 716m. barrels, with possible reserves of between 1,150m. and 2,600m. barrels.

GDP declined at an average annual rate of 6.1% in 1982–87, necessitating a painful period of readjustment. There were strict controls on domestic consumption, imports, foreign exchange, and public expenditure. The National Alliance for Reconstruction (NAR) formed a Government from 1986, which adopted a structural-adjustment programme and negotiated two successive stand-by agreements with the International Monetary Fund (IMF). The unemployment rate rose to 22.3% in 1987. Real wages declined as inflation accelerated under the impact of currency devaluations in 1985 and 1987. However, even at its weakest, Trinidad and Tobago's economy avoided the precipitous, uncontrolled decline experienced at times by the economies of Guyana, Jamaica, and neighbouring Venezuela.

The IMF programme was followed in 1990 by debt-rescheduling agreements with lending agencies and a US $850m. loan agreement with the Inter-American Development Bank (IDB). These measures, along with enhanced use of natural-gas resources, contributed to an economic recovery in 1990, when there was growth of 1.5%. Following further growth of 2.7% in 1991, GDP fell by 1.6% and 1.5% in 1992 and 1993, respectively. However, steady and continuous economic expansion resumed and growth averaged 3.3% in 1994–98, rising to 5.1% in 1999, before falling to 4.0% in 2000. Import restrictions were gradually liberalized from the early 1990s, while foreign-exchange controls were abolished in April 1993 as the Trinidad and Tobago dollar moved from a fixed rate against the US currency to a strictly-managed float. The currency moved sharply from a rate of TT $4.25 to TT $5.74, but remained stable thereafter, with the rate at TT $6.29 from early 1997 to mid-2000 and appreciating slightly to TT $6.24 by June 2001. There was increased activity from the early 1990s in other manufacturing sectors, as well as the construction and financial sectors. Unemployment fell to 12.1% in 2000.

In late 1998 and early 1999 there was some concern over international petroleum prices, which had a negative effect on exploration and production activity and on government revenues, and led to redundancies in the sector. Prices for heavy chemicals, particularly methanol, were also low, and the revenues of the National Gas Company of Trinidad and Tobago Ltd, whose contracts were tied to end-use prices, were also adversely affected. Steel prices were also low, which affected investment plans and brought the threat of plant closures. In mid-1999 to 2001, however, a strong recovery in oil prices had a positive effect on government revenues. Chemicals and steel prices also recovered slightly, although they remained below peak levels. Methanol, a key product, decreased from US $268 per metric ton in 1995 to a low point of US $94 per ton in mid-1999, before recovering to US $220 per ton in mid-2001.

The population was estimated at 1.296m. in mid-2001, with a population density (per sq km) of 253. Approximately one-half of the population lived in an urbanized 'east–west corridor', stretching from Diego Martin in the west, through Port of Spain to Arima in the east. One-sixth of the population lived in other urban areas, principally the San Fernando conurbation in southern Trinidad and Chaguanas in the centre of the country. The average annual population growth rate was 0.6% in 1991–2001. At the 1990 census 40.3% of the population was of South Asian origin, 39.6% was of African descent, with 18.5% of mixed origin and 1.6% of European, Chinese or Arab descent.

AGRICULTURE

The strength of the energy-based economy led to the relative neglect of agriculture, particularly in the 1970s and early 1980s, while agricultural wage rates could not compete with other areas of employment. As a result, in 2000 the sector contributed only 1.7% of GDP (down from 6.9% in 1972), but employed 8.8% of the labour force.

The principal commercial crop was sugar, which generated 3.4% of total employment in 2000 (including seasonal employees and cane farmers). The main producer was a state-owned company, Caroni (1975) Ltd, which operated two sugar factories. However, smaller, independent farmers grew 56% of the island's cane in 1999. Exports, which went mainly to Europe at the preferential price agreed under the European Union's (EU) Lomé Convention (which expired in February 2000 and was replaced by the Cotonou Agreement in June—see Part Three, Regional Organizations, European Union) accounted for 60,976 metric tons in 2000, with a value of TT $227.5m.; some sugar for the local market was imported in most years. Raw sugar production reached 227,400 tons in 1965, declining to 48,300 tons in 1982, at the end of the period of increase in petroleum prices. Renewed interest in agriculture resulted in a recovery in production of 169,100 tons in 1994. However, in 1995–99 the industry was affected by poor weather, a failed pest-control programme, and technical problems at the sugar factories. As a result, output fell to 101,000 tons in 1998. Output recovered to 112,100 tons in 1999 and 162,500 tons in 2000. Furthermore, subsidies to the sector rose from US $7.5m. in 1995 to an estimated US $25m. three years later. Efforts to improve the company's position through diversification proved unsuccessful, and land sales for industrial development were seen as an important source of cash, as was a proposal to divest the company's valuable rum business. In mid-2001 the Government was investigating the future of the industry, with closure among the wide range of options under consideration.

Premium-quality cocoa was a traditional export, but production fell from 7,542 metric tons in 1972 to 1,160 tons in 1999, recovering slightly to an estimated 1,200 tons in 2000. Low-grade robusta coffee was grown: production was 4,586 tons in 1968, but had fallen to 553 tons in 2000, none of which was exported. There were some floriculture exports, mainly of orchids and anthuriums to North America. A wide variety of vegetables and fruits, particularly citrus, were grown for the local market, as well as some rice. Local producers supplied virtually the entire domestic market with eggs and broiler chicken, as well as just under one-half of milk supplies.

Teak was the main forestry product, and was used extensively in the yacht-repair industry. Most lumber requirements, however, were imported. In 1999 roundwood removals totalled 44,000 cu m. The fishing sector also was small-scale, employing approximately 3,140 people in 2000. Exports, mainly of large shrimp, were worth US $15.5m. in 1999. Trinidad was also used as a base by Asian vessels for deep-sea fishing in the Caribbean and mid-Atlantic.

PETROLEUM AND GAS

Energy-based industries were of central importance to the Trinidad and Tobago economy throughout the 20th century. Commercial petroleum production started in 1908, although the first oil well was sunk as early as 1857. Refining of local and imported petroleum was well established by the 1930s, and the sector accounted for 29.2% of GDP by 1955. The energy sector's contribution to GDP increased to 42.8% in 1980, at the height of the increase in petroleum prices. In 2000 the petroleum and asphalt sector (including mining and refining) accounted for an estimated 26.0% of GDP, but employed only 3.2% of the economically-active population. In the same year fuels and chemicals accounted for 83.7% of total exports. Offshore petroleum production began in 1955. By the 1980s most petroleum and gas was produced on the east coast continental shelf.

In 2001 16 international companies were involved in petroleum and gas exploration and production in Trinidad and Tobago's offshore areas. The state-owned Petroleum Company of Trinidad and Tobago Ltd (Petrotrin) and the National Gas Company of Trinidad and Tobago Ltd, as well as small, local, privately-owned producers, operated both onshore and offshore. Most (42%) crude-petroleum output came from BP Energy Company of Trinidad and Tobago and from Trinidad and Tobago Marine Petroleum Company Ltd (Trinmar), which contributed about 28% of production. Following the closure of two smaller plants, in the late 1990s there was just one refinery, at Pointe-à-Pierre, owned by Petrotrin, which had been fully upgraded in the mid-1990s, and which refined imported, as well as local, crude petroleum. Most of BP's local crude was refined overseas, although, from 1999, some was processed by Petrotrin.

Natural-gas use increased at an average annual rate of 8.7% in 1977–97, and by an annual average rate of 18% in 1997–2001. The discovery in the late 1990s of several significant deposits of natural gas led to the development of a major liquefied natural gas (LNG) plant. The Atlantic LNG Company of Trinidad and Tobago, came 'on-stream' in April 1999, purchasing 450m. cu ft per day of natural gas directly from BP. The plant was owned by a consortium of BP, British Gas Trinidad and Tobago Ltd (BG), Repsol of Spain, Tractebel of the USA and the National Gas Company, which had a 10% shareholding. The capital cost of the project was US $950m. In March 2000 an agreement was reached for an expansion project, scheduled for completion by mid-2003. The proposed expansion was expected to increase gas consumption to approximately 1,400m. cu ft per day, with 37.5% of gas used by the LNG plant supplied by British Gas and its partners, using a new pipeline that would allow Trinidad's north coast gas fields to be exploited for the first time. Upon completion of the expansion, Atlantic LNG was expected to be the fifth largest LNG plant in the world. The expansion would create 2,000–3,000 jobs during the construction phase, with total employment falling to approximately 250 upon completion.

In September 2000 BP announced the discovery of a natural gas deposit of 3,000,000m. cu ft, and in May 2001 a further deposit of 1,000,000m. cu ft was discovered. Proven natural-gas reserves in early 2001 were 23,450,000m. cu ft, with a reserves-to-production ratio of 47 years, rising to 71 years if discounted possible and probable reserves were included. However, this ratio was expected to fall to 21 years by 2003, with the expansion of petrochemical and LNG operations. This prompted some concern that reserves were being exploited too rapidly, although other industry sources projected probable eventual finds totalling 100,000,000m. cu ft, which would justify rapid expansion of gas-using industries.

Most of the natural gas produced in Trinidad and Tobago was purchased by the National Gas Company, which operated a 620-km pipeline system, supplying the needs of all end-users except the LNG plant. The company's gas purchases were 931m. cu ft per day in 2000, of which 49% was supplied by BP,

25% by a BG joint venture with Texaco, 16% by Enron Gas and Oil Trinidad Ltd, and 10% by the National Gas Company's own offshore compression operations. In 1999 some 64% of the company's gas was used in the manufacture of ammonia and methanol, 20% in electric power generation, 6% in the iron and steel industry, 9% in other heavy manufacturing, including oil refining and the extraction of propane and butane from the gas stream, and 1% in light manufacturing, commerce and transport. There were no plans to establish a piped gas supply system for domestic household use.

MANUFACTURING

Trinidad and Tobago became the world's largest methanol exporter in 2000. The first methanol plant was established in 1984, under state ownership, and was sold in 1997 to a consortium of a local financial company, CL Financial, and two German companies, Ferrostaal AG and Helm AG. In 2000 these companies owned three other methanol plants. The islands' fifth and largest methanol plant, owned by Titan Methanol, was completed in December 1999. Total production increased from 963,000 metric tons in 1995 to 2.4m. tons in 2000, with a projected figure of more than 2.9m. tons in 2001. Two further methanol plants, each with a capacity of 1.7m. tons, were under development in mid-2001. Other gas-linked projects under consideration in 2001 included: a gas-to-liquids plant; an ethylene complex, which was seen as a step towards the development of a value-added plastics industry; the development of an aluminium smelter; and other metals and heavy-chemicals ventures.

Trinidad was also the world's principal exporter of ammonia, with the Russian Federation a close rival. There were eight ammonia plants operating in 2001, the oldest dating from 1959, with a ninth under construction. The plants were owned by Norsk Hydro of Norway (three plants), the Canadian PCS (Potash Corporation of Saskatchewan) Nitrogen Ltd (four plants), and the Farmland and Mississippi Chemical Corporation of the USA (one plant).

The state-owned Iron and Steel Company of Trinidad and Tobago, established in 1981, made large losses until the commencement of lease arrangement with the local subsidiary of an Indian company, Ispat, in 1989. Caribbean Ispat Ltd subsequently acquired the plant in 1994; by 1999 it comprised three directly reduced iron units with a total capacity of 2.2m. metric tons, as well as mills for billets and wire rods. Cliffs and Associates, a US-German joint venture, was operating a US $150m., 500,000 ton iron-briquette facility, using new fluidized-bed technology.

Low-cost natural gas assisted the development of other manufacturing industries. Trinidad Cement Ltd (TCL) used locally quarried limestone in gas-fired kilns; in 2000 cement production totalled 742,700 metric tons, of which 290,000 tons was exported to regional markets. The company also owned cement plants in Barbados and Jamaica. Carib Glassworks was another manufacturing concern to benefit from cheap energy, producing bottles for national and export markets, while low-cost electricity from gas-powered generating stations allowed local soft-drink manufacturers to operate competitively for export to the wider Caribbean. There was also a wide range of consumer goods, foods and other industries.

There were efforts to broaden the range of import substitution in the 1970s and 1980s by protecting local automobile-assembly plants and similar industries. However, this practice resulted in the production of high-cost and frequently outdated goods, and was ended in the 1990s, as a result of trade liberalization. In contrast to Jamaica and some other Caribbean islands, there were very few labour-intensive export industries in Trinidad and Tobago. The clothing industry and the informatics sector were both underdeveloped. In 2000 the manufacturing sector (excluding sugar and petroleum) contributed a provisional 7.7% of GDP and employed 10.9% of the total labour force.

TRANSPORT AND COMMUNICATIONS

In 1999 there were 7,900 km (4,910 miles) of roads in Trinidad and Tobago. Major routes were covered by four-lane highways, which, however, suffered from heavy congestion. The road system had to accommodate a huge increase in use after the growth of the petroleum sector in the 1970s. The main international ports were at Port of Spain (container, cargo and cruise ships), Point Lisas (mainly specialized bulk cargo piers, but also container cargo) and, in Tobago, Scarborough (general cargo, ferry service and cruise ships). There were also specialized port facilities at Point Fortin (LNG), Pointe-à-Pierre (crude petroleum and refinery products), Claxton Bay (cement) and Tembladora (transhipment of Guyanese bauxite).

Trinidad's airport at Piarco offered direct connections to North America, Europe, most other Caribbean islands, Guyana, Suriname and Venezuela. A far reaching but controversial US $250m. improvement project was completed in May 2001; however, plans to develop Trinidad as a regional air transport hub were delayed when the US Federal Aviation Authority downgraded Trinidad and Tobago to Category II status on air safety grounds, preventing local carriers from expanding services to the USA. In 1996 some 1.4m. passengers used the airport. There was a frequent service to Crown Point airport in Tobago, which was also served by direct connections to the United Kingdom, Puerto Rico, and some neighbouring Caribbean islands. The state-owned airline BWIA International Airways Ltd was privatized in 1996, with the Government retaining a 33.5% share.

Trinidad and Tobago was linked to the Americas I and II fibre-optic systems and also benefited from international satellite telecommunications links. The telecommunications sector was still a monopoly in 2001, controlled by Telecommunication Services of Trinidad and Tobago (TSTT) Ltd, 51% of which was owned by the Government and 49% by a British company, Cable & Wireless. Charges were high and new connections were not available in many suburban and rural areas. There were independent internet providers, however. In June 2000 the Government was accused of lacking transparency in the liberalization process of the telecommunications sector. There was controversy in the bidding process for cellular licences, following the removal of the Caribbean Communications Network from the bidding shortlist, and the successful bid of Open Telecom Ltd, owned by the family of government minister Lindsay Gillette. It was also believed that the licences should not be awarded until appropriate legislation for the telecommunications sector was in place; however, a new Telecommunications Act was passed in May 2001 and there were hopes that new cellular licences might be issued by the end of the year.

TOURISM

For many years the full tourist potential of Trinidad and Tobago was not promoted. From 1983, however, successive Governments placed greater emphasis on the sector, providing new facilities, including a cruise-ship terminal in Port of Spain, and conducting more effective promotional campaigns. Nevertheless, in 2001 the industry remained significantly less developed than that of other Caribbean islands; of the 358,800 stop-over arrivals in 1999, 17.1% were business travellers, while 55.5% were visiting friends and relatives and only 21.6% were vacation tourists staying in hotels and guest houses. Net earnings from tourism were a negative balance of payments item until 1996, but were equivalent to 4.7% of merchandise imports in 1999. Hotels and guest houses accounted for 1.4% of GDP in 2000 and tourist receipts totalled US $201m. in 1999. In 1999 there were 63,251 cruise-ship passenger arrivals.

Tobago was the main centre for leisure tourism, with 51% of the 4,236 hotel rooms in 1999. In 1995–99 the number of hotel rooms increased by 22% in Trinidad and 44% in Tobago. On Trinidad the main hotels catered principally for business visitors, although the annual pre-Lenten carnival was a major attraction. There was an important yacht- and powerboat-service industry based at marinas on the north-west peninsula of the island. For insurance purposes, Trinidad was outside the hurricane belt. This factor, as well as a combination of competitive wage rates and engineering skills, produced an attractive environment for repair services, which generated an estimated US $24m. per year. Yacht arrivals increased from 637 in 1990 to 3,249 in 2000.

PUBLIC FINANCE

From a very strong fiscal position in the 1970s government finances deteriorated sharply from 1983. Successive austerity and emergency budgets reduced expenditure and increased taxation, while the Government made use of IMF compensatory financing and stand-by credit. The 1989 budget announced a 10% reduction in public-sector pay, which was later ruled illegal by the courts. Value-added tax was introduced at the rate of 15% on 1 January 1990. This was followed, in April 1990, by a further stand-by agreement with the IMF, providing US $111m. over 11 months. In the same month the IDB agreed to lend US $850m. over four years for housing, infrastructure development, and for major energy investments, including a full upgrade of the Pointe-à-Pierre petroleum refinery. The IDB's conditions emphasized relaxation of import and foreign-exchange controls, reduced tariffs, currency liberalization, and privatization of state-owned industries.

The overall fiscal account was in deficit from 1982 to 1992. There were smaller deficits in 1993 and 1994, although the recurrent finances registered a surplus. A small, overall surplus was achieved in 1995–97. Partly as a result of a fall in energy and chemical prices, the overall account moved into a deficit equivalent to 3.1% of GDP in 1999, with the current account also in deficit. In 2000 the fiscal account returned to surplus, equivalent to 1.8% of GDP, with a recovery in energy-based revenues more than compensating for an increase in both current and capital expenditure. However, there were concerns over the medium-term fiscal implications of increased spending on salaries and on infrastructural projects, and of debts incurred by state-owned enterprises. An interim Revenue Stabilization Fund was established in 2000 with TT $415m. of energy sector revenue, equivalent to 1% of GDP.

The inflation rate, which had increased from 3.8% in 1991 to 10.8% in 1993 as a result of the depreciation of the local currency, subsequently decreased to 3.6% in 1997. After increasing to 5.6% in 1998, the rate fell to 3.4% in 1999 and 3.6% in 2000. The average rate for 2001 was forecast at 4.0%.

FINANCIAL SERVICES

Trinidad and Tobago had a strong domestic banking sector. Of the five main commercial banks, the two largest, Republic Bank Ltd and Royal Bank of Trinidad and Tobago Ltd, were in local private-sector ownership; Scotiabank Trinidad and Tobago Ltd was the local subsidiary of the Canadian Bank of Nova Scotia; First Citizens Bank Ltd was state-owned; and Citibank (Trinidad and Tobago) Ltd specialized in services for international corporate clients. In the late 1990s there was increased activity in the commercial banking and finance sector.

Trinidad and Tobago was a regional centre for some financial services. Republic Bank held 20% of shares in CIBC West Indies, which owned commercial banks in other countries in the Caribbean region and, in July 2001, announced a planned merger with the regional operations of Barclays Bank (United Kingdom). It also had a majority shareholding in commercial banks in Grenada and Guyana. Royal Bank had subsidiaries in several English- and Dutch-speaking Caribbean countries and provided, as did Citibank and Republic Bank, public-and private-sector merchant-banking services throughout the region. In 2000 financial institutions based in Trinidad and Tobago raised almost US $200m. in finance for regional governments and the private sector. In mid-1999 the Trinidad and Tobago Stock Exchange listed 26 local and four Barbadian or Jamaican companies. In 2001 there were plans for closer links to other regional exchanges and for an electronic trading and depository system.

A small number of private-sector companies played a dominant role in the local economy. The largest local conglomerate, ANSA McAL, had life- and general-insurance subsidiaries, as well as interests in brewing and glass-making, importing, distribution and media sectors. There were a number of locally-owned insurance companies, of which the largest were active in other regional markets and had important local investments in real estate and equities. CL Financial, an unlisted company that grew out of the Colonial Life Insurance Company, had a dominant 34% shareholding in the Republic Bank and interests in property, supermarkets, media, rum, foods, and in four of the islands' methanol plants (and in a further methanol plant and an ammonia plant, both in development in 2001). It also had subsidiaries in several other Caribbean countries. Guardian Holdings, also insurance-based, had important real-estate interests in Trinidad and Tobago and, in 1999, bought three insurance companies in Jamaica. Neal & Massy Holdings Ltd

scaled down its activities in the mid-1990s, but retained important regional interests, and in 1998 agreed a 20% reciprocal shareholding with the dominant Barbados conglomerate, Barbados Shipping and Trading Company Ltd.

FOREIGN TRADE, DEBT AND BALANCE OF PAYMENTS

In 1982 Trinidad and Tobago's foreign trade and payments accounts moved into deficit, owing to the reversal experienced in the Government's finances. In this year the balance of visible trade was transformed from surplus to deficit for the first time since 1973. There was another deficit in 1983, but, from 1984, the trade balance returned to surplus, albeit a fluctuating one. While imports declined steadily from 1984 to 1990, reflecting the severity of the recession, exports, although declining between 1984 and 1986, increased in the rest of the decade. In 1990 there was a trade surplus of US $1,012.5m. However, the subsequent decrease in exports and increase in imports reduced the trade surplus by 1996. In 1997 and 1998 visible trade deficits of US $528.6m. and US $740.8m., respectively, resulted from imports of capital goods for investment in heavy manufacturing. This deficit was covered on the balance of payments capital account by large foreign direct investment inflows. In 1999, with the completion of several projects, exports increased and imports of capital goods decreased sharply, resulting in a trade surplus of US $63.6m., increasing to an estimated US $663m. in 2000, as a result of higher export prices and with some new plants in operation for the first full year. In 2000 the current account balance of payments surplus was an estimated US $519.6m., equivalent to 7.3% of GDP.

With the manufacturing sector strong and the tourist sector weak, Trinidad and Tobago's balance of payments contrasted in its structure with that of most other Caribbean islands. There was a positive balance in merchandise trade from 1987, with the exception of 1997–98, when there were exceptional imports of capital goods for energy-related investment projects. In 2000 the principal merchandise exports were: fuels (66.0%, of which crude petroleum made up 13.4%, natural gas liquids 12.5%, refined petroleum products 40.1%); chemicals (17.7%, of which methanol 6.4%, ammonia 8.7%, urea 1.5%); iron and steel (4.1%); other manufactured goods, including cement (6.5%); sugar (0.9%); other foods (2.7%); and beverages, mainly rum (1.9%). The services account was in deficit until 1991; in 1999 the estimated positive balance of US $286m. on non-factor services was sufficient to cover 8.0% of merchandise imports. The main positive items were travel, transport, and communications, followed by insurance services. Long-term investment income was a strong outflow item, equivalent, in 2000, to 9.1% of merchandise imports. In 2001 capital goods made up 27.7% of merchandise imports, followed by raw materials and intermediate goods (21.9%), fuels, mainly crude petroleum for local refining (15.6%), non-food consumer goods (8.7%), and foods (5.4%).

External debt increased through the 1980s, reaching US $2,510m. in 1990. As a result of debt relief and amortization, this figure was reduced to US $1,467m. representing 54% of GDP, at the end of 1998. However, borrowing for capital projects in 1998–2000 increased public debt to 60% of GDP or US $1,680m. at the end of 2000. Debt servicing peaked in 1993, equivalent to 49.2% of current government revenue and 30.6% of exports of goods and services in that year. By 2000 these ratios had declined to 18.3% and 6.9%, respectively.

Net official foreign reserves reached US $3,347.5m. at the end of 1981, before falling to US $127.1m. at the end of 1988. Thereafter, strong exports and foreign direct investment inflows increased net official reserves to US $1,508.0m. by the end of March 2001.

CONCLUSION

Trinidad and Tobago's natural gas resources provided the basis for strong economic growth from 1994, with falling unemployment, a stable exchange rate, and a stable rate of inflation, high investment inflows, and increasing foreign exchange reserves. High energy prices in 1999–2001 greatly improved the fiscal position, allowing an increase in both current and capital spending; however, there were concerns over the increasing public-sector debt, while inefficient state enterprises, including some, such as telecommunications, which were partially divested, remained a burden on the economy. The planned restructuring of some nationalized companies would, it was hoped, go some way towards alleviating the problem, but it was clear that an acceleration in the rate of privatization and the introduction of competition for public- and private-sector mono-

polies, were necessary. However, the strong resource base would continue to attract additional foreign investment. A strong manufacturing, banking and insurance sector meant that Trinidad and Tobago was advantageously placed to benefit from the creation of a Caribbean single market.

Statistical Survey

Source (unless otherwise stated): Central Statistical Office, 35-41 Queen St, POB 98, Port of Spain; tel. 623-7069.

Area and Population

AREA, POPULATION AND DENSITY

Area (sq km)	5,128*
Population (census results)	
12 May 1980	1,079,791
2 May 1990	
Males	606,388
Females	607,345
Total	1,213,733
Population (official estimates at September)	
1998	1,277,000
1999	1,286,000
2000	1,294,000
Density (per sq km) at September 2000	252.3

* 1,980 sq miles. Of the total area, Trinidad is 4,828 sq km (1,864 sq miles) and Tobago 300 sq km (116 sq miles).

POPULATION BY ETHNIC GROUP

(1990 census*)

	Males	Females	Total	%
African	223,561	221,883	445,444	39.59
Chinese	2,317	1,997	4,314	0.38
'East' Indian . . .	226,967	226,102	453,069	40.27
Lebanese . . .	493	441	934	0.08
Mixed	100,842	106,716	207,558	18.45
White	3,483	3,771	7,254	0.64
Other	886	838	1,724	0.15
Unknown . . .	2,385	2,446	4,831	0.43
Total	560,934	564,194	1,125,128	100.00

* Excludes some institutional population and members of unenumerated households, totalling 44,444.

Principal towns (population at mid-1991): Port of Spain (capital) 51,076; San Fernando 30,115; Arima (borough) 29,483.
1996: Port of Spain 43,396.

BIRTHS AND DEATHS (official estimates, annual averages)

	1996	1997	1998
Birth rate (per 1,000) . . .	14.2	14.3	13.9
Death rate (per 1,000) . . .	7.4	7.1	7.2

Expectation of life (estimates, years at birth, 1998): 74.0 (males 71.7; females 76.4) (Source: UN Development Programme, *Human Development Report*).

EMPLOYMENT

('000 persons aged 15 years and over)

	1996	1997	1998
Agriculture, forestry, hunting and fishing	42.6	43.7	39.0
Mining and quarrying . . .	17.2	17.6	18.5
Manufacturing	44.7	46.8	51.5
Electricity, gas and water . .	7.5	6.1	6.3
Construction	44.0	50.8	58.8
Wholesale and retail trade, restaurants and hotels . .	81.6	81.0	83.3
Transport, storage and communication . . .	30.7	31.8	35.5
Finance, insurance, real estate and business services .	36.4	38.8	39.0
Community, social and personal services	139.5	143.1	147.1
Activities not adequately defined	0.1	0.3	0.3
Total employed . . .	444.2	459.8	479.3
Unemployed	86.1	81.2	79.4
Total labour force . . .	530.3	541.0	558.7

Source: ILO, *Yearbook of Labour Statistics*.

Agriculture

PRINCIPAL CROPS ('000 metric tons)

	1998	1999	2000
Maize*	5.0	5.0	5.0
Roots and tubers* . . .	11.6	11.6	11.6
Pulses*	3.7	3.7	3.7
Tomatoes	1.5	2.7	2.7*
Sugar cane	1,056.9	1,255.9	1,500.0*
Cocoa	1.3	1.2	1.2*
Coffee (green) . . .	0.4	0.3	0.5†
Coconuts*	23.0	23.0	23.0
Pumpkins, squash and gourds	7.7	7.7*	7.7*
Cucumbers and gherkins . .	3.9	2.6	2.6*
Watermelons . . .	2.7	2.8*	2.8*
Oranges*	15.0	19.5	19.5
Grapefruit and pomelos . .	7.9	7.9	7.9
Pineapples* . . .	3.4	3.4	3.4
Bananas*	6.0	6.0	6.0
Plantains*	3.9	3.9	3.9
Rice (paddy)	7.0	7.0*	7.0*

* FAO estimate(s). † Unofficial figure.

Source: FAO.

LIVESTOCK (FAO estimates, '000 head, year ending September)

	1998	1999	2000
Horses	1.0	1.0	1.0
Mules	1.7	1.7	1.7
Asses	2.0	2.0	2.0
Cattle	34.0	35.0	35.0
Buffaloes	5.4	5.4	5.4
Pigs	40.0	41.0	41.0
Sheep	12.0	12.0	12.0
Goats	59.0	59.0	59.0

Poultry (million): 10.0 in 1998; 10.0 in 1999; 10.0 in 2000.

Source: FAO.

LIVESTOCK PRODUCTS ('000 metric tons)

	1998	1999	2000*
Beef and veal	0.9	1.0	1.0
Pig meat	1.9	1.9	1.9
Poultry meat	26.2	26.2*	26.2
Cows' milk	10.0	10.2	10.2
Hen eggs*	9.0	9.0	9.0

* FAO estimate(s).

Source: FAO.

Forestry

ROUNDWOOD REMOVALS ('000 cubic metres, excl. bark)

	1997	1998	1999
Sawlogs, veneer logs and logs for sleepers	71	35	34
Other industrial wood	2	—	—
Fuel wood	10	10	10
Total	83	45	44

Source: FAO, *Yearbook of Forest Products*.

SAWNWOOD PRODUCTION

('000 cubic metres, incl. railway sleepers)

	1997	1998	1999
Coniferous (softwood)	10	10	10
Broadleaved (hardwood)	28	17	17
Total	38	27	27

Source: FAO, *Yearbook of Forest Products*.

Fishing

('000 metric tons, live weight)

	1996	1997	1998*
Demersal percomorphs	2.7	2.6	2.5
Jacks and crevalles	0.5	0.6	0.5
King mackerel	1.0	0.9	0.8
Serra Spanish mackerel	1.6	1.7	1.6
Other seerfishes	1.4	1.4	1.4
Albacore	0.7	0.7	0.7
Sharks, rays, skates, etc.	0.6	0.6	0.5
Penaeus shrimps	0.3	0.8	0.7
Total catch	14.4	15.0	14.5

* FAO estimate(s).

Source: FAO, *Yearbook of Fishery Statistics*.

Mining

('000 metric tons, unless otherwise indicated)

	1994	1995	1996
Crude petroleum	6,769	6,746	6,673
Natural gasoline	36	35*	35
Natural gas (petajoules)	300	303	353

* Provisional figure.

Source: UN, *Industrial Commodity Statistics Yearbook*.

1997: ('000 cu metres): Crude petroleum 7,181.2; Natural gasoline 1,722.3.
1998: ('000 cu metres): Crude petroleum 7,136.9; Natural gasoline 2,563.7.

Source: UN Economic Commission for Latin America and the Caribbean, *Statistical Yearbook*.

Industry

SELECTED PRODUCTS

('000 metric tons, unless otherwise indicated)

	1996	1997	1998*
Raw sugar	134	137	101
Rum ('000 proof gallons)	4,499	4,726	5,425
Beer and stout ('000 hectolitres)	296	369	391
Cigarettes (metric tons)	812	1,043	1,282
Nitrogenous fertilizers	2,674	2,691	3,247
Jet fuels and kerosene ('000 barrels)	4,069	3,287	5,501
Motor spirit—petrol ('000 barrels)	5,708	7,547	10,653
Gas-diesel (distillate fuel) oil ('000 barrels)	7,793	8,338	11,103
Residual fuel oils ('000 barrels)	17,000	14,271	19,864
Lubricating oils ('000 barrels)	523	129	379
Cement	617	652	690
Wire rods	575	668	650
Gas cookers (number)	10,211	11,658	n.a.
Television receivers (number)	2,887	1,012	n.a.
Electric energy (million kWh)	4,488	4,841	5,194

* Provisional figures.

Finance

CURRENCY AND EXCHANGE RATES

Monetary Units

100 cents = 1 Trinidad and Tobago dollar (TT $).

Sterling, US Dollar and Euro Equivalents (30 April 2001)

£1 sterling = TT $8.962;
US $1 = TT $6.260;
€1 = TT $5.556;
TT $1,000 = £111.58 = US $159.75 = €179.98.

Average Exchange Rate (TT $ per US $)

1998   6.2983
1999   6.2989
2000   6.2998

BUDGET (TT $ million)

Revenue	1996	1997	1998*
Oil sector	3,009.3	2,144.1	2,324.6
Corporation tax	1,901.6	955.1	163.4
Royalties	678.9	526.9	588.4
Other	428.8	662.1	1,572.7
Non-oil sector	6,437.2	7,076.8	7,486.0
Taxes on income	3,045.9	3,152.4	3,060.0
Taxes on property	58.9	56.8	62.7
Taxes on goods and services	1,983.6	2,266.2	2,280.8
Taxes on international trade	496.2	570.0	584.8
Other taxes	68.1	104.6	95.3
Non-tax revenue	1,548.5	1,672.1	2,351.8
Capital revenue	5.7	38.7	672.0
Total	9,446.5	9,259.6	10,482.6

Expenditure	1996	1997	1998*
Current expenditure	7,594.9	7,155.2	7,982.7
Wages and salaries . . .	2,847.4	2,688.6	2,979.8
Goods and services . . .	907.6	886.7	1,011.9
Interest	1,580.6	1,690.0	1,697.6
Transfers and subsidies . .	2,259.3	1,889.9	2,293.4
Capital expenditure	1,028.8	1,750.9	1,079.8
Total	8,623.7	8,906.1	9,062.5

* Provisional figures.

INTERNATIONAL RESERVES (US $ million at 31 December)

	1997	1998	1999
Gold*	1.3	—	—
IMF special drawing rights . .	0.1	0.1	—
Foreign exchange . . .	706.2	783.0	945.4
Total	707.6	783.1	945.4

* National valuation of gold reserves.

Source: IMF, *International Financial Statistics.*

MONEY SUPPLY (TT $ million at 31 December)

	1998	1999	2000
Currency outside banks . . .	1,046.8	1,292.4	1,270.6
Demand deposits at commercial banks	2,819.7	3,182.0	3,718.7
Total money (incl. others) . .	4,724.8	5,306.8	5,653.8

Source: IMF, *International Financial Statistics.*

COST OF LIVING
(Consumer Price Index; base: 1990 = 100)

	1997	1998	1999
Food (incl. beverages and tobacco)	228.1	262.4	285.2
Fuel and light .	110.8	110.8	n.a.
Clothing (incl. footwear) . .	95.3	94.7	92.2
Rent	107.4	110.2	111.7
All items (incl. others) . . .	150.2	158.7	164.1

Source: ILO, *Yearbook of Labour Statistics.*

NATIONAL ACCOUNTS (TT $ million at current prices)
Expenditure on the Gross Domestic Product

	1996	1997	1998
Government final consumption expenditure	5,473	5,579	6,281
Private final consumption expenditure	19,536	22,302	23,862
Increase in stocks . . .	129	225	232
Gross fixed capital formation . .	5,717	9,582	9,839
Total domestic expenditure .	30,855	37,688	40,214
Exports of goods and services . .	17,778	19,306	18,453
Less Imports of goods and services .	14,184	20,441	20,470
GDP in purchasers' values .	34,448	36,552	38,197
GDP at constant 1985 prices .	17,950	18,570	19,327

Source: IMF, *International Financial Statistics.*

Gross Domestic Product by Economic Activity

	1997	1998	1999
Agriculture, hunting, forestry and fishing	618.8	567.5	629.8
Mining and quarrying . . .	4,811.1	3,769.8	4,367.7
Manufacturing	5,699.1	5,584.7	6,320.1
Electricity, gas and water . .	587.0	820.1	848.7
Construction	3,674.3	4,156.6	4,701.9
Wholesale and retail trade, restaurants and hotels . .	7,192.8	8,026.0	8,764.3
Transport, storage and communications . . .	3,294.0	3,391.3	3,758.6
Finance, insurance, real estate and business services . .	5,193.9	5,622.2	5,706.1
Community, social and personal services	5,190.9	5,583.6	6,032.2
Sub-total	36,261.9	37,521.8	41,129.4
Less Imputed bank service charges	1,373.7	1,645.5	1,844.4
Value-added tax	1,624.0	2,160.4	1,749.0
GDP in purchaser's values .	36,512.2	38,036.7	41,034.0

Source: UN Economic Commission for Latin America and the Caribbean, *Statistical Yearbook.*

BALANCE OF PAYMENTS (US $ million)

	1996	1997	1998
Exports of goods f.o.b. . .	2,354.1	2,448.0	2,258.0
Imports of goods f.o.b. . . .	−1,971.6	−2,976.6	−2,998.9
Trade balance	382.4	−528.6	−740.8
Exports of services . . .	461.2	546.5	671.7
Imports of services . . .	−217.5	−254.1	−255.4
Balance on goods and services	626.2	−236.2	−324.5
Other income received . . .	39.1	63.8	64.0
Other income paid . . .	−553.1	−445.0	−405.3
Balance on goods, services and income	112.2	−617.4	−665.8
Current transfers received . .	34.2	37.0	58.4
Current transfers paid . . .	−41.3	−33.2	−36.2
Current balance	105.1	−613.6	−643.5
Direct investment from abroad .	355.4	999.3	729.8
Portfolio investment assets . .	—	—	−0.4
Other investment assets . .	3.0	32.6	1.0
Other investment liabilities . .	−315.4	−334.7	−258.8
Net errors and omissions . .	90.0	110.0	252.2
Overall balance	238.1	193.6	80.2

Source: IMF, *International Financial Statistics.*

External Trade

PRINCIPAL COMMODITIES (US $ million)

Imports c.i.f.	1996	1997	1998*
Consumer goods	410	428	500
Foodstuffs	173	165	190
Raw materials and intermediate goods .	990	1,147	1,198
Fuels	305	320	300
Construction materials . . .	92	113	123
Capital goods	552	1,372	1,206
Transport equipment . .	89	112	151
Oil-refining and mining machinery	28	62	88
Total†	2,090	3,036	3,012

Exports f.o.b.		1996	1997	1998*
Fuels		1,261	1,171	1,002
Crude petroleum . .	.	429	443	247
National gas liquids	.	52	62	63
Refined petroleum products	.	780	666	692
Chemicals	.	568	609	495
Anhydrous ammonia	. .	293	277	248
Urea	.	111	84	50
Methanol . . .	.	120	202	148
Manufactures . .	.	279	340	352
Steel products . .	.	178	187	206
Food and live animals	. .	121	151	145
Sugar . . .	.	25	43	32
Beverages and tobacco	. .	69	74	88
Total (incl. others)‡ .	. .	2,506	2,542	2,335

* Preliminary figures.
† Including imports for processing: 139 in 1996; 89 in 1997; 108 in 1998.
‡ Including re-exports: 110 in 1996; 116 in 1997; 166 in 1998.

PRINCIPAL TRADING PARTNERS (US $ million)

Imports c.i.f.		1996	1997	1998*
Barbados		17	16	24
Canada		78	80	105
France		20	18	56
Germany		108	136	89
Guyana		12	13	11
Jamaica		19	17	18
Japan		88	107	145
Latin America . .		512	497	572
United Kingdom . . .		129	148	148
USA		817	1,564	1,340
Total (incl. others) . . .		2,090	3,036	3,012

Exports f.o.b.		1996	1997	1998*
Barbados		87	94	127
Canada		56	23	26
Guyana		88	109	84
Jamaica		216	210	237
Latin America . . .		207	261	251
USA		1,101	999	825
Total (incl. others) . . .		2,506	2,542	2,335

* Preliminary figures.
Source: IMF, *Trinidad and Tobago: Selected Issues and Statistical Appendix* (July 1999).

Transport

ROAD TRAFFIC (motor vehicles in use)

	1994	1995	1996
Passenger cars	122,000	122,000	122,000
Lorries and vans	24,000	24,000	24,000

Source: IRF, *World Road Statistics*.
Total number of registered vehicles: 215,895 in 1995; 226,380 in 1996; 237,299 in 1997.

SHIPPING
Merchant Fleet (registered at 31 December)

	1996	1997	1998
Number of vessels . . .	51	50	50
Total displacement ('000 grt) . .	18.5	18.7	18.6

Source: Lloyd's Register of Shipping, *World Fleet Statistics*.

International Sea-borne Freight Traffic
(estimates, '000 metric tons)

	1988	1989	1990
Goods loaded	7,736	7,992	9,622
Goods unloaded	4,076	4,091	10,961

Source: UN, *Monthly Bulletin of Statistics*.
1998: Port of Spain handled 3.3m. metric tons of cargo.

CIVIL AVIATION (traffic on scheduled services)

	1995	1996	1997
Kilometres flown (million) . .	33	20	18
Passengers carried ('000) . .	1,280	897	807
Passenger-km (million) . .	4,300	2,658	2,392
Total ton-km (million) . . .	425	265	239

Source: UN, *Statistical Yearbook*.

Tourism

FOREIGN TOURIST ARRIVALS*

Country of Origin	1996	1997	1998
Barbados	16,839	19,051	23,524
Canada	36,382	38,945	40,167
Germany	11,172	14,114	11,474
Grenada	10,200	12,159	12,639
Guyana	15,992	17,789	19,581
St Vincent and Grenadines . .	6,415	11,041	11,370
United Kingdom	27,960	38,403	47,764
USA	90,973	112,344	116,549
Venezuela	6,887	8,157	10,445
Total (incl. others) . . .	265,900	324,293	347,705

* Arrivals by air only.
Receipts from tourism (US $ million): 74 in 1996; 108 in 1997; 201 in 1998.
Source: World Tourism Organization, *Yearbook of Tourism Statistics*.

Communications Media

	1995	1996	1997
Radio receivers ('000 in use) . .	650	670	680
Television receivers ('000 in use) .	415	419	425
Telephones ('000 main lines in use)	209	220	243
Telefax stations (number in use)	2,023	2,100	2,400
Mobile cellular telephones			
(subscribers)	5,615	14,000	17,411
Daily newspapers			
Number	4*	4*	4
Average circulation ('000 copies)	150*	156	n.a.
Non-daily newspapers			
Number	n.a.	5	5
Average circulation ('000 copies)	n.a.	150*	n.a.

* Estimate.

Source: UN, *Statistical Yearbook*; UNESCO, *Statistical Yearbook*.

Education

(1996/97, unless otherwise indicated)

	Insti-tutions	Teachers	Students		
			Males	Females	Total
Pre-primary*† . .	50	126	727	691	1,418
Primary*	476	7,311	92,015	89,015	181,030
Secondary					
General	} 101‡ {	5,070	51,096	53,253	104,349
Vocational† . .		n.a.	575	113	688
University and					
equivalent . . .	3§	421§	2,727	3,280	6,007

* Government-maintained and government-aided schools only.
† 1992/93.
‡ 1993/94.
§ 1995/96.

Source: mainly UNESCO, *Statistical Yearbook*.

Directory

The Constitution

Trinidad and Tobago became a republic, within the Commonwealth, under a new Constitution on 1 August 1976. The Constitution provides for a President and a bicameral Parliament comprising a Senate and a House of Representatives. The President is elected by an Electoral College of members of both the Senate and the House of Representatives. The Senate consists of 31 members appointed by the President: 16 on the advice of the Prime Minister, six on the advice of the Leader of the Opposition and nine at the President's own discretion from among outstanding persons from economic, social or community organizations. The House of Representatives consists of 36 members who are elected by universal adult suffrage. The duration of a Parliament is five years. The Cabinet, presided over by the Prime Minister, is responsible for the general direction and control of the Government. It is collectively responsible to Parliament.

The Government

HEAD OF STATE

President: ARTHUR NAPOLEON RAYMOND ROBINSON (took office 19 March 1997).

THE CABINET
(August 2001)

Prime Minister and Minister of National Security: BASDEO PANDAY.

Attorney-General and Minister of Legal Affairs: RAMESH LAWRENCE MAHARAJ.

Minister of Communications and Information Technology: RALPH MARAJ.

Minister of Community Empowerment, Sport and Consumer Affairs: MANOHAR RAMSARAN.

Minister of Education: KAMLA PERSAD-BISSESSAR.

Minister of Energy and Energy Industries: LINDSAY GILLETTE.

Minister of the Environment: Dr ADESH NANAN.

Minister of Finance: GERALD YETMING.

Minister of Food Production and Marine Resources: TREVOR SUDAMA.

Minister of Foreign Affairs and Enterprise Development: MERVYN ASSAM.

Minister of Health: Dr HAMZA RAFEEQ.

Minister of Housing and Settlements: SADIQ BAKSH.

Minister of Human Development, Youth and Culture: GANGA SINGH.

Minister of Infrastructure Development and Local Government: CARLOS JOHN.

Minister of Integrated Planning and Development: JOHN HUMPHREY.

Minister of Labour, Manpower Development and Industrial Relations: HARRY PARTAP.

Minister of Tourism and Tobago Affairs and of Transport: JERLEAN JOHN.

MINISTRIES

Office of the President: President's House, Circular Rd, St Ann's, Port of Spain; tel. 624-1261; fax 625-7950; e-mail presoftt@carib-link.net.

Office of the Prime Minister: Whitehall, Maraval Rd, Port of Spain; tel. 622-1625; fax 622-0055; e-mail opm@trinidad.net; internet www.opm.gov.tt.

Office of the Attorney-General and Ministry of Legal Affairs: Cabildo Chambers, 23–27 St Vincent St, Port of Spain; tel. 623-7010; fax 625-0470.

Ministry of Communications and Information Technology: Kent House, Long Circular Rd, Maraval; tel. 628-1323; fax 622-4783.

Ministry of Community Empowerment, Sport and Consumer Affairs: Autorama Bldg, El Socorro Rd, San Juan; tel. 675-6728; fax 674-4021.

Ministry of Education: 18 Alexandra St, St Clair, Port of Spain; tel. 622-2181; fax 622-7818.

Ministry of Energy and Energy Industries: Level 9, Riverside Plaza, cnr Besson and Piccadilly Sts, Port of Spain; tel. 623-6708; fax 623-2726; e-mail admin@energy.gov.tt.

Ministry of the Environment: Level 16, Eric Williams Financial Bldg, Eric Williams Plaza, Independence Sq., Port of Spain; tel. 627-8389; fax 625-1585.

Ministry of Finance: Eric Williams Finance Bldg, Independence Sq., Port of Spain; tel. 627-9700; fax 627-6108.

Ministry of Food Production and Marine Resources: St Clair Circle, St Clair, Port of Spain; tel. 622-1221; fax 622-8202; e-mail apdmalmr@trinidad.net.

Ministry of Foreign Affairs and Enterprise Development: Knowsley Bldg, 1 Queen's Park West, Port of Spain; tel. 623-4116; fax 627-0571.

Ministry of Health: IDC Bldg, 10–12 Independence Sq., Port of Spain; tel. 627-0012; fax 623-9528.

Ministry of Housing and Settlements: 44–46 South Quay, Port of Spain; tel. 624-5058; fax 625-2793.

Ministry of Human Development, Youth and Culture: Sacred Heart Bldg, 16–18 Sackville St, Port of Spain; tel. 624-2000; fax 625-7003.

Ministry of Infrastructure Development and Local Government: Kent House, Long Circular Rd, Maraval; tel. 628-1325; fax 622-7410; e-mail molg1@carib-link.net; internet www.molg.bizland.com.

Ministry of Integrated Planning and Development: Level 14, Eric Williams Finance Bldg, Independence Sq., Port of Spain; tel. 627-9700; fax 623-8123.

Ministry of Labour, Manpower Development and Industrial Relations: Level 11, Riverside Plaza, Cnr Besson and Piccadilly Sts, Port of Spain; tel. 623-4451; fax 624-4091.

Ministry of Tobago Affairs: 10 St Vincent St, Port of Spain; tel. 624-1403; fax 625-0437; internet www.tobagoaffairs.gov.tt.

Ministry of Tourism: 45A-C St Vincent St, Port of Spain; tel. 627-0002; fax 625-6404.

Ministry of Transport: Cnr Richmond and London Sts, Port of Spain; tel. 625-1225; fax 627-9886.

Legislature

PARLIAMENT

Senate

President: GANACE RAMDIAL.

House of Representatives

Speaker: RUPERT GRIFFITH.

Election, 11 December 2000

Party	Seats
United National Congress	19
People's National Movement	16
National Alliance for Reconstruction	1
Total	36

TOBAGO HOUSE OF ASSEMBLY

The House is elected for a four-year term of office and consists of 12 elected members and three members selected by the majority party.

Chief Secretary: ORVILLE LONDON.

Election, 29 January 2001

Party	Seats
People's National Movement	8
National Alliance for Reconstruction	4
Total	12

Political Organizations

Lavantille Out-Reach for Vertical Enrichment: L. P. 50, Juman Drive, Morvant; tel. 625-7840; f. 2000; Leader: LENNOX SMITH; Gen. Sec. VAUGHN CATON.

The Mercy Society: L. P. 216, Mount Zion, Luango Village, Maracas; tel. 628 1753.

National Alliance for Reconstruction (NAR): 37 Victoria Square, Port of Spain; tel. 627-6163; f. 1983 as a coalition of moderate opposition parties; reorganized as a single party in 1986; Leader ANTHONY SMART; Chair. ABDOOL WAHAB.

New National Democratic Organization (NNDO): L. P. 2 Freedom St, Enterprise, Chaguanas; f. 2000; Leader ENOCH JOHN; Sec. JANET CHARLES.

People's Empowerment Party (PEP): Miggins Chamber, Young St, Scarborough; tel. 639-3175; f. by independent mems of the Tobago House of Assembly; Leader DEBORAH MOORE-MIGGINS.

People's National Movement (PNM): 1 Tranquillity St, Port of Spain; tel. 625-1533; e-mail pnm@carib-link.net; internet www.pnm.org.tt; f. 1956; moderate nationalist party; Leader PATRICK MANNING; Chair. Dr LINDA BABOOLAL; Gen. Sec. MARTIN JOSEPH.

United National Congress (UNC): Rienzi Complex, 78-81 Southern Main Rd, Couva; tel. 636-8145; e-mail unc@tstt.net.tt; internet www.unc.org.tt; f. 1989; social-democratic; Leader BASDEO PANDAY; Deputy Leader RAMESH LAWRENCE MAHARAJ; Chair. WADE MARK; Gen. Sec. FAZAL KARIM.

Diplomatic Representation

EMBASSIES AND HIGH COMMISSIONS IN TRINIDAD AND TOBAGO

Argentina: TATIL Bldg, 4th Floor, 11 Maraval Rd, POB 162; Port of Spain; tel. 628-7557; fax 628-7544; e-mail embargen-pos@carib-link.net; Ambassador: JULIO ALBERTO MILLER.

Brazil: 18 Sweet Briar Rd, St Clair, POB 382, Port of Spain; tel. 622-5779; fax 622-4323; e-mail brastt@wow.net; Ambassador: JOSÉ MARCUS VINÍCIUS DE SOUSA.

Canada: Maple House, 3-3A Sweet Briar Rd, St Clair, POB 1246, Port of Spain; tel. 622-6232; fax 628-1830; e-mail chcpspan@opus.co.tt; High Commissioner: SIMON WADE.

China, People's Republic: 39 Alexandra St, St Clair, Port of Spain; tel. 622-6976; fax 622-7613; e-mail tian@wow.net; Ambassador: ZHANG SONGXIAN.

Colombia: The Mutual Centre, Ground Floor, 16 Queen's Park West, Port of Spain; tel. 622-5904; fax 622-5938; e-mail emtrinidad@trinidad.net; Ambassador: Dr JUAN ANTONIO LIEVANO RANGEL.

Cuba: Furness Bldg, 2nd Floor, 90 Independence Sq., Port of Spain; tel. 627-1306; fax 627-3515; Chargé d'affaires: FRANCISCO A. MARCHANTE.

Dominican Republic: Suite 8, 1 Dere St, Queen's Park West, Port of Spain; tel. 624-7930; fax 623-7779; Ambassador: Jorge Luis Pérez Alvarado.

France: TATIL Bldg, 6th Floor, 11 Maraval Rd, Port of Spain; tel. 622-7447; fax 628-2632; e-mail francett@wow.net; Ambassador: ALAIN GIRMA.

Germany: 7–9 Marli St, Newtown, POB 828, Port of Spain; tel. 628-1630; fax 628-5278; internet www.germanemb-portofspain.de; Ambassador: ULRICH NITZSCHKE.

Holy See: 11 Mary St, St Clair, POB 854, Port of Spain; tel. 622-5009; fax 628-5457; e-mail apnun@trinidad.net; Apostolic Pro-Nuncio: Most Rev. EMIL PAUL TSCHERRIG, Titular Archbishop of Tiddi.

India: 6 Victoria Ave, POB 530, Port of Spain; tel. 627-7480; fax 627-6985; e-mail hcipos@tstt.net.tt; High Commissioner: Prof. PARIMAL KUMAR DAS.

Jamaica: 2 Newbold St, St Clair, Port of Spain; tel. 622-4995; fax 628-9043; e-mail jhctnt@tstt.net.tt; High Commissioner: LORNE MCDONNOUGH.

Japan: 5 Hayes St, St Clair, Port of Spain; tel. 628-5991; fax 622-0858; e-mail jpemb@wow.net; Ambassador: YOSHIO YAMAGISHI.

Korea, Republic: Ground Floor, Albion Court, 61 Dundonald St, Port of Spain; tel. 627-6791; fax 627-6363; e-mail koemtt@trinidad.net; Ambassador: JON HYON CHAN.

Mexico: 4th Floor, Algico Bldg, 91–93 St Vincent St, Port of Spain; tel. 627-6988; fax 627-1028; e-mail embamex@carib-link.net; Ambassador: ISABEL TÉLLEZ DE ORTEGA.

Netherlands: Life of Barbados Bldg, 3rd Floor, 69–71 Edward St, POB 870, Port of Spain; tel. 625-1210; fax 625-1704; e-mail nlgovpor@wow.net; internet community.wow.net/nlgovpor; Chargé d'affaires: ARJEN J. VAN DEN BERG.

Nigeria: 3 Maxwell-Phillip St, St Clair, Port of Spain; tel. 622-4002; fax 622-7162; High Commissioner: NNE FURO KURUBO.

Panama: Suite 6, 1A Dere St, Port of Spain; tel. 623-3435; fax 623-3440; e-mail embapatt@wow.net; Ambassador: VASCO DEL MAR HUERTA.

Suriname: TATIL Bldg, 5th Floor, Maraval Rd, Port of Spain; tel. 628-0704; fax 628-0086; e-mail ambsurpde@opus.co.tt; Chargé d'affaires: EDWARD R. HALFHUID.

United Kingdom: 19 St Clair Circle, St Clair, POB 778, Port of Spain; tel. 622-2748; fax 622-4555; e-mail ppabhc@opus.co.tt; High Commissioner: PETER HARBORNE.

USA: 15 Queen's Park West, POB 752, Port of Spain; tel. 622-6371; fax 625-5462; e-mail usispos@trinidad.net; Chargé d'affaires: DAVID C. STEWART.

Venezuela: 16 Victoria Ave, POB 1300, Port of Spain; tel. 627-9821; fax 624-2508; e-mail embaveneztt@carib-link.net; Ambassador: HÉCTOR AZÓCAR.

Judicial System

The Chief Justice, who has overall responsibility for the administration of justice in Trinidad and Tobago, is appointed by the President after consultation with the Prime Minister and the Leader of the Opposition. The President appoints and promotes judges on the advice of the Judicial and Legal Service Commission. The Judicial and Legal Service Commission, which comprises the Chief Justice as chairman, the chairman of the Public Service Commission, two former judges and a senior member of the bar, appoints all judicial and legal officers. The Judiciary comprises the higher judiciary (the Supreme Court) and the lower judiciary (the Magistracy).

Chief Justice: MICHAEL DE LA BASTIDE.

Supreme Court of Judicature: Knox St, Port of Spain; tel. 623-2417; fax 627-5477; e-mail ttlaw@wow.net; internet www.ttlaw-courts.org. The Supreme Court consists of the High Court of Justice and the Court of Appeal. The Supreme Court is housed in four locations: Port of Spain, San Fernando, Chaguaramas and Tobago. There are 20 Supreme Court Puisne Judges who sit in criminal, civil, and matrimonial divisions. Registrar: EVELYN PETERSEN.

Court of Appeal: The Court of Appeal hears appeals against decisions of the Magistracy and the High Court. Further appeals are directed to the Judicial Committee of the Privy Council of the United Kingdom, sometimes as of right and sometimes with leave of the Court. The Court of Appeal consists of the Chief Justice, who is President, and six other Justices of Appeal.

The Magistracy and High Court of Justice: The Magistracy and the High Court exercise original jurisdiction in civil and criminal matters. The High Court hears indictable criminal matters, family matters where the parties are married, and civil matters involving sums over the petty civil court limit. High Court judges are referred to as either Judges of the High Court or Puisne Judges. The Masters of the High Court, of which there are three, have the jurisdiction of judges in civil chamber courts. The Magistracy (in its petty civil division) deals with civil matters involving sums less than TT \$15,000. It exercises summary jurisdiction in criminal matters and hears preliminary inquiries in indictable matters. The Magistracy, which is divided into 13 districts, consists of a Chief Magistrate, a Deputy Chief Magistrate 13 Senior Magistrates and 29 Magistrates.

Chief Magistrate: SHERMAN McNICHOLLS, Magistrate's Court, St Vincent St, Port of Spain; tel. 625-2781.

Director of Public Prosecutions: MARK MOHAMMED.

Attorney-General: RAMESH LAWRENCE MAHARAJ.

Religion

In 1990 it was estimated that 29.4% of the population were members of the Roman Catholic Church, 23.8% Hindus, 10.9% Anglicans, 5.8% Muslims and 3.4% Presbyterians.

CHRISTIANITY

Christian Council of Trinidad and Tobago: Hayes Court, 21 Maraval Rd, Port of Spain; tel. 637-9329; f. 1967; church unity organization formed by the Roman Catholic, Anglican, Presbyterian, Methodist, African Methodist, Spiritual Baptist and Moravian Churches, the Church of Scotland and the Salvation Army, with the Ethiopian Orthodox Church and the Baptist Union as observers; Pres. Rev. SHELDON DEWSBURY, Supt of Methodist Church, North Trinidad circuit; Sec. GRACE STEELE.

The Anglican Communion

Anglicans are adherents of the Church in the Province of the West Indies, comprising eight dioceses. The Archbishop of the West Indies is the Bishop of Nassau and the Bahamas.

Bishop of Trinidad and Tobago: The Rt Rev. RAWLE E. DOUGLIN, Hayes Court, 21 Maraval Rd, Port of Spain; tel. 622-7387; fax 628-1319; e-mail red@trinidad.net.

Protestant Churches

Presbyterian Church in Trinidad and Tobago: POB 92, Paradise Hill, San Fernando; tel. and fax 652-4829; e-mail pctt@tstt.net.tt; f. 1868; Moderator Rt Rev. ALLISON KEN NOBBEE; 45,000 mems.

Baptist Union of Trinidad and Tobago: 104 High St, Princes Town; tel. 655-2291; f. 1816; Pres. Rev. ALBERT EARL-ELLIS; Gen. Sec. Rev. ANSLEM WARRICK.

The Roman Catholic Church

For ecclesiastical purposes, Trinidad and Tobago comprises the single archdiocese of Port of Spain. At 31 December 1999 there were some 395,000 adherents in the country, representing about 31.6% of the total population.

Antilles Episcopal Conference: 9A Gray St, Port of Spain; tel. 622-2932; fax 622-8255; e-mail aec@carib-link.net; internet www.opus.co.tt/aec; f. 1975; 20 mems from the Caribbean and Central American regions; Pres. Most Rev. EDGERTON ROLAND CLARKE, Archbishop of Kingston (Jamaica).

Archbishop of Port of Spain: EDWARD J. GILBERT, 27 Maraval Rd, Port of Spain; tel. 622-1103; fax 622-1165; e-mail abishop@carib-link.net.

HINDUISM

Hindu immigrants from India first arrived in Trinidad and Tobago in 1845. The vast majority of migrants, who were generally from Uttar Pradesh, were Vishnavite Hindus, who belonged to sects such as the Ramanandi, the Kabir and the Sieunaraini. The majority of Hindus, estimated in 1990 at 23.8% of the total population, currently subscribe to the doctrine of Sanathan Dharma, which evolved from Ramanandi teaching.

Arya Pratinidhi Sabha of Trinidad Inc. (Arya Samaj): Seereeram Memorial Vedic School, Old Southern Main Rd, Montrose Village, Chaguanas; tel. 663-1721; e-mail sadananramnarine@hotmail.com; Pres. SADANAN RAMNARINE.

Pandits' Parishad (Council of Pandits): Maha Sabha Headquarters, Eastern Main Rd, St Augustine; tel. 645-3240; works towards the co-ordination of temple activities and the standardization of ritual procedure; affiliated to the Maha Sabha; 200 mems.

Sanathan Dharma Maha Sabha of Trinidad and Tobago Inc.: Maha Sabha Headquarters, Eastern Main Rd, St Augustine; tel. 645-3240; e-mail mahasabha@ttemail.com; internet www.websitetech.com/mahasabha; f. 1952; Hindu pressure group and public organization; organizes the provision of Hindu education; Pres. Dr D. OMAH MAHARAJH; Sec. Gen. SATNARAYAN MAHARAJ.

The Press

DAILIES

Newsday: 19–21 Chacon St, Port of Spain; tel. 623-4949; fax 625-8362; f. 1993; CEO and Editor-in-Chief THERESE MILLS.

Trinidad Guardian: 22 St Vincent St, POB 122, Port of Spain; tel. 623-8870; e-mail letters@guardian.co.tt; internet www.guardian.co.tt; f. 1917; morning; independent; Editor-in-Chief LENNOX GRANT; circ. 52,617.

Trinidad and Tobago Express: 35 Independence Sq., Port of Spain; tel. 623-1711; fax 627-1451; e-mail express@trinidadexpress.com; internet www.trinidadexpress.com; f. 1967; morning; CEO KEN GORDON; Editor KEITH SMITH; circ. 55,000.

PERIODICALS

Blast: 5–6 Hingoo Lane, El Socorro, San Juan; tel. 674-4414; weekly; Editor ZAID MOHAMMED; circ. 22,000.

The Boca: Crews Inn Marina and Boatyard, Village Sq., Chaguaramas; tel. 634-2055; fax 634-2056; e-mail boaters@trinidad.net; internet www.boatersenterprise.com/boca; monthly; magazine of the sailing and boating community.

The Bomb: Southern Main Rd, Curepe; tel. 645-2744; weekly.

Caribbean Beat: 6 Prospect Ave, Maraval, Port of Spain; tel. 622-3821; fax 628-0639; e-mail mep@wow.net; internet www.caribbeanbeat.com; 6 a year; distributed by BWIA International Airways Ltd; Editor JEREMY TAYLOR.

Catholic News: 31 Independence Sq., Port of Spain; tel. 623-6093; fax 623-9468; e-mail cathnews@trinidad.net; internet www.trinidad.net/catholicnews; f. 1892; weekly; Editor Fr MICHEL DE VERTEUIL; circ. 15,600.

Naturalist: Port of Spain; tel. 622-3428; f. 1975; 9 a year; natural heritage and conservation in the Caribbean; Publr/Editor-in-Chief STEPHEN MOHAMMED; circ. 25,000.

Quarterly Economic Bulletin: 35–41 Queen St, POB 98, Port of Spain; tel. 623-7069; fax 625-3802; f. 1950; issued by the Central Statistical Office.

Showtime: Cnr 9th St and 9th Ave, Barataria; tel. 674-1692; fax 674-3228; circ. 30,000.

Sunday Express: 35 Independence Sq., Port of Spain; tel. 623-1711; fax 627-1451; e-mail express@trinidadexpress.com; internet www.trinidadexpress.com; f. 1967; Editor OMATIE LYDER; circ. 60,000.

Sunday Guardian: POB 122, Port of Spain; tel. 623-8870; fax 625-7211; e-mail letters@ttol.co.tt; f. 1917; independent; morning; Editor-in-Chief LENNOX GRANT; circ. 43,502.

Sunday Punch: Cnr 9th St and 9th Ave, Barataria; tel. 674-1692; weekly; fax 674-3228; Editor ANTHONY ALEXIS; circ. 40,000.

Tobago News: Milford Rd, Scarborough; tel. 639-5565; f. 1985; weekly; Editor COMPTON DELPH.

Trinidad and Tobago Exporter: 6 Prospect Ave, Maraval, Port of Spain; tel. 622-3821; fax 628-0639; e-mail mep@wow.net; internet www.readcaribbean.com; f. 1996; quarterly; promotes exports from Trinidad and Tobago and the Caribbean; Man. Dir JEREMY TAYLOR.

Trinidad and Tobago Gazette: 2–4 Victoria Ave, Port of Spain; tel. 625-4139; weekly; official government paper; circ. 3,300.

Trinidad and Tobago Mirror: Cnr 9th St and 9th Ave, Barataria; tel. 674-1692; fax 674-3228; two a week; Editors KEN ALI, KEITH SHEPHERD; circ. 35,000.

Tropical Agriculture: Faculty of Agriculture and Natural Sciences, University of the West Indies, St Augustine; tel. and fax 645-3640; e-mail trop-agric@hotmail.com; f. 1924; journal of the School of Agriculture (fmrly Imperial College of Tropical Agriculture); quarterly; Editor-in-Chief Prof. FRANK A. GUMBS.

Weekend Heat: Southern Main Rd, Curepe; tel. 645-2744; weekly; Editor STAN MORA.

NEWS AGENCY

Caribbean News Agency (CANA) (Barbados): 92 Queen St, Port of Spain; tel. 627-2262; Correspondent LYNDA HUTCHINSON.

Publishers

Caribbean Book Distributors (1996) Ltd: 10 Boundary Rd, San Juan, POB 462, Port of Spain; tel. 674-4720; fax 674-0497; publish and distribute school textbooks and general books; Man. GERRY BABOOLAL.

Caribbean Children's Press: 1 A. Lazare St, St James; tel. 628-4248.

Caribbean Educational Publishers: 49 High St, San Fernando; tel. 657-1012; fax 657-5620.

Charran Educational Publishers: 53 Eastern Main Rd, Port of Spain; tel. 663-1884.

Lexicon Trinidad Ltd: 53 Boundary Rd, San Juan; tel. 675-3395.

Media and Editorial Projects Ltd: 6 Prospect Ave, Maraval, Port of Spain; tel. 622-3821; fax 628-0639; e-mail mep@wow.net; internet www.readcaribbean.com; f. 1991; magazine and book publishing; Man. Dir JEREMY TAYLOR.

Trinidad Publishing Co Ltd: 22–24 St Vincent St, Port of Spain; tel. 623-8870; fax 625-7211; e-mail guardian@ttol.co.tt; internet www.guardian.co.tt; f. 1917; Gen. Man. and CEO GRENFELL KISSOON.

University of the West Indies: St Augustine; tel. 663-1334; fax 663-9684; e-mail campreg@centre.uwi.tt; f. 1960; academic books and periodicals; Principal Pro-Vice Chancellor COMPTON BOURNE.

Broadcasting and Communications

TELECOMMUNICATIONS

Telecommunication Services of Trinidad and Tobago (TSTT) Ltd: 1 Edward St, POB 3, Port of Spain; tel. 625-4431; fax 627-0856; e-mail tsttceo@tstt.net.tt; internet www.tstt.co.tt; 51% state-owned, 49% by Cable & Wireless (United Kingdom); 51% privatization pending; CEO SAMUEL A. MARTIN.

TSTT Cellnet: 114 Frederick St, Port of Spain; fax 625-5807; internet www.tstt.co.tt/cellservices.html; f. 1991; mobile cellular telephone operator.

Caribbean Communications Network (CCN): 10 Nook Ave, Port of Spain; tel. 624-5735; Chair. KEN GORDON.

Open Telecom Ltd: 88 Edward St, Port of Spain; tel. 627-6559.

BROADCASTING

Radio

Central Radio 90.5: 1 Morequito Ave, Port of Spain; tel. 662-4309.

Hott 93 FM: Cumulus Broadcasting Inc., 3A Queens Park West, Port of Spain; tel. 623-4688; fax 624-3234; e-mail studio@gemradio.com.

Love 94 88–90 and Power 102 FM: 88–90 Abercromby St, Port of Spain; tel. 627-6937.

MW & C Radio 97: Long Circular Rd, St James; tel. 622-9797.

National Broadcasting Networks Ltd (FM 100, Yes 98.9 FM, Swar Milan 91.1, Radio 610): Television House, 11A Maraval Rd, POB 665, Port of Spain; tel. 622-4141; fax 622-0344; e-mail ttt@trinidad.net; internet www.icn.co.tt; f. 1957; AM and FM transmitters at Chaguanas, Cumberland Hill, Hospedales and French Fort, Tobago; govt-owned; CEO INGRID ISAAC; Programme Man. BRENDA DE SILVA; est. regular audience 105,000.

Trinidad Broadcasting Radio Network (Radio Trinidad, Rhythm Radio, Caribbean Tempo and **Sangeet 106.1 FM):** 22 St Vincent St, Port of Spain; tel. 623-9202; fax 622-2380; internet www.ttol.co.tt/caribbeantempo; f. 1947; commercial; three programmes; Man. Dir GRENFELL KISSOON.

Trinidad and Tobago Radio Network: 35 Independence Sq., Port of Spain; tel. 624-7078.

Television

CCN TV6: 35 Independence Sq., Port of Spain; tel. 627-8806; fax 627-2721; f. 1991; owned by Caribbean Communications Network (CCN); CEO KEN GORDON; Gen. Man. BERNARD PANTIN.

Trinidad & Tobago Television Co Ltd: Television House, 11A Maraval Rd, POB 665, Port of Spain; tel. 622-4141; fax 622-0344; f. 1962; state-owned commercial station; Gen. Man. GRENFELL KISSOON.

Finance

(cap. = capital; dep. = deposits; res = reserves; m. = million; brs = branches; amounts in TT $)

BANKING

Central Bank

Central Bank of Trinidad and Tobago: Eric Williams Plaza, Independence Sq., POB 1250, Port of Spain; tel. 625-4835; fax 627-4696; e-mail info@central-bank.org.tt; internet www.central-bank.org.tt; f. 1964; cap. 67.3m., res 57.1m., dep. 4,987m. (Sept. 1999); Gov. WINSTON DOOKERAN.

Commercial Banks

Citibank (Trinidad and Tobago) Ltd: 12 Queen's Park East, POB 1249, Port of Spain; tel. 625-1046; fax 624-8131; internet www.citicorp.com; f. 1983; fmrly The United Bank of Trinidad and Tobago Ltd; name changed as above 1989; owned by Citicorp Merchant Bank Ltd; cap. 30.0m., res 14.7m., dep. 455.5m. (Dec. 1996); Chair. IAN E. DASENT; Man. Dir STEVE BIDESHI; 2 brs.

First Citizens Bank Ltd: 62 Independence Sq., Port of Spain; tel. 625-2893; fax 623-3393; e-mail treasfcb@trinidad.net; internet www.firstcitizenstt.com; f. 1993 as merger of National Commercial Bank of Trinidad and Tobago Ltd, Trinidad Co-operative Bank Ltd and Workers' Bank of Trinidad and Tobago; state-owned; cap. 340.0m., res 35.3m., dep. 2,009.7m. (Sept. 1997); CEO LARRY HOWAI; 22 brs.

Republic Bank Ltd: 9–17 Park St, POB 1153, Port of Spain; tel. 625-3611; fax 624-1323; e-mail email@republictt.com; internet www.republictt.com; f. 1837 as Colonial Bank; 1972 Barclays Bank; 1981 name changed as above; 1997 merged with Bank of Commerce Trinidad and Tobago Ltd; cap. 76.9m., res 220.2m., dep. 1,374.5m. (Sept. 2000); Chair. FRANK A. BARSOTTI; Man. Dir RONALD HARFORD; 47 brs.

Royal Bank of Trinidad and Tobago Ltd: Royal Court, 19–21 Park St, POB 287, Port of Spain; tel. 623-1322; fax 625-3764; e-mail royalinfo@rbtt.co.tt; internet www.rbtt.com; f. 1972 to take over local branches of Royal Bank of Canada; cap. 404.0m., res 467.8m., dep. 9,462.8m. (March 1998); Chair. HERMAN P. URICH; Man. Dir PETER J. JULY; 21 brs.

Scotiabank Trinidad and Tobago Ltd: Cnr of Park and Richmond Sts, POB 621, Port of Spain; tel. 625-3566; fax 627-5278; e-mail scotiamain@carib.link.net; internet www.scotiabanktt.com; cap. 117.6m., res 109.7m., dep. 3,950m. (Oct. 1999); Chair. B. R. BIRMINGHAM; Man. Dir R. P. YOUNG; 23 brs.

Development Banks

Agricultural Development Bank of Trinidad and Tobago: 87 Henry St, POB 154, Port of Spain; tel. 623-6261; fax 624-3087; f. 1968; provides long-, medium- and short-term loans to farmers and the agri-business sector; Chair. NITYANAND MAHARAJ; CEO KRISHNA GOORIESINGH.

Development Finance Ltd (DFL): 10 Cipriani Blvd, POB 187, Port of Spain; tel. 623-4665; fax 624-3563; e-mail dfinbank@dflpos.com; internet www.dflpos.com; provides short- and long-term finance, and equity financing for projects in manufacturing, agro-processing, tourism, industrial and commercial enterprises; total assets US $84.2m. (Dec. 1998); Man. Dir GERARD M. PEMBERTON.

Credit Union

Co-operative Credit Union League of Trinidad and Tobago Ltd: 32-34 Maraval Rd, St Clair; tel. 622-3100; fax 622-4800; e-mail culeague@tstt.net.tt.

INSURANCE

American Life and General Insurance Co (Trinidad and Tobago) Ltd: ALGICO Plaza, 91–93 St Vincent St, POB 943, Port of Spain; tel. 625-4425; fax 623-6218; e-mail algico@wow.net.

Bankers Insurance Co of Trinidad and Tobago Ltd: 177 Tragarete Rd, Port of Spain; tel. 622-4613; fax 628-6808.

Barbados Mutual Life Assurance Society: The Mutual Centre, 16 Queen's Park West, POB 356, Port of Spain; tel. 628-1636; Gen. Man. HUGH MAZELY.

Capital Insurance Ltd: 38–42 Cipero St, San Fernando; tel. 657-8077; fax 652-7306; f. 1958; motor and fire insurance; total assets TT $65m.; 10 brs and 9 agencies.

Caribbean Home Insurance Co Ltd: 63 Park St, Port of Spain; tel. 625-4461; fax 625-5985; e-mail insure@caribbeanhome.com; f. 1973; cap. 100m.; general and group life; Chair. DAVID N. COLLENS; Man. Dir FRANKLIN DE MOBRIGA.

Colonial Life Insurance Co (Trinidad) Ltd: Colonial Life Bldg, 29 St Vincent St, POB 443, Port of Spain; tel. 623-1421; fax 627-3821; e-mail info@clico.com; internet www.clico.com; f. 1936; Chair. LAWRENCE A. DUPREY; Man. Dir A. CLAUDE MUSAIB-ALI.

CUNA Caribbean Insurance Services Ltd: 2 Rust St, St Clair, Port of Spain; tel. 628-2862; fax 628-0841; e-mail cunaweb@trinidad.net; internet www.cunacaribbean.com; f. 1991; marine aviation and transport; motor vehicle, personal accident, property; Gen. Man. ERIC PHILLIP; 3 brs.

Furness Anchorage General Insurance Ltd: 11–13 Milling Ave, Sea Lots, POB 283, Port of Spain; tel. 623-0868; fax 625-1243; e-mail furness@wow.net; internet www.furnessgroup.com; f. 1979; general; Man. Dir ROBERT I. FERREIRA.

Great Northern Insurance Co Ltd: 29A Edward St, Port of Spain; tel. 625-1116.

GTM Fire Insurance Co Ltd: 95–97 Queen St, Port of Spain; tel. 623-1525.

Guardian Life of the Caribbean: 80 Independence Sq., Port of Spain; tel. 625-5433.

Gulf Insurance Ltd: 1 Gray St, St Clair, Port of Spain; tel. 622-5878; fax 628-0272; e-mail gulf@wow.net; f. 1974; general.

Maritime Financial Group: Maritime Centre, Tenth Ave, Barataria; tel. 674-0130; f. 1978; property and casualty; CEO RICHARD ESPINET.

Motor and General Insurance Co Ltd: 1–3 Havelock St, St Clair, Port of Spain; tel. 622-2637; fax 622-5345.

NEMWIL: NEMWIL House, 12 Abercromby St, Port of Spain; tel. 623-4741; fax 623-4320; e-mail info@nemwil.com; internet www.nemwil.com; f. 1960; general insurer; Chair. KRISHNA NARINE-SINGH; CEO and Man. Dir GERRARD LEE-INNIS; 3 brs.

New India Assurance Co (T & T) Ltd: 22 St Vincent St, Port of Spain; tel. 623-1326; fax 625-0670; e-mail newindia@wow.net.

Presidential Insurance Co Ltd: 54 Richmond St, Port of Spain; tel. 625-4788.

Royal Caribbean Insurance Ltd: 109 St Vincent St, Port of Spain; tel. 625-9980; fax 623-7895; e-mail rci@trinidad.net; f. 1977.

Trinidad and Tobago Export Credit Insurance Co Ltd: 14-17 Victoria Park Suites, 5th Floor, Victoria Sq., Port of Spain; tel. and fax 624-0028; CEO ROGER MIKE.

Trinidad and Tobago Insurance Ltd (TATIL): 11 Maraval Rd, POB 1004, Port of Spain; tel. 622-5351; fax 628-0035; Chair. JOHN JARDIM; Man. Dir GERRY BROOKS.

INSURANCE ORGANIZATIONS

Association of Trinidad and Tobago Insurance Companies: 22 Cotton Hill, Port of Spain; tel. 622-8994.

National Insurance Board: Cipriani Place, 2A Cipriani Blvd, POB 1195, Port of Spain; tel. 625-2171; fax 624-0276; f. 1971; statutory corporation; Chair. EDWARD BAYLEY; Exec. Dir TREVOR J. ROMANO.

STOCK EXCHANGE

Trinidad and Tobago Stock Exchange Ltd: 1st Floor, 1 Ajax St, Port of Spain; tel. 625-5107; fax 623-0089; e-mail ttstockx@tstt.net.tt; internet www.stockex.co.tt; f. 1981; 28 companies listed (April 1999); electronic depository system came into operation in 1999; Chair. RONALD HUGGINS; Gen. Man. HUGH EDWARDS.

Trade and Industry

GOVERNMENT AGENCIES

Caribbean Food Corporation (CFC): 30 Queen's Park West, POB 264B, Port of Spain; tel. 622-5211; fax 622-4430; e-mail cfc@trinidad.net; f. 1976; promotion of agricultural development; Man.Dir E. C. CLYDE PARRIS.

Caroni (1975) Ltd: Brechin Castle, Couva; tel. 636-2311; fax 636-1259; sugar-cane plantations and mills; producers of rum and other sugar by-products; Chair. Dr JOE RAMKISSOON; Gen. Man. J. R. WOTHERSPOON.

Cocoa and Coffee Industry Board: 27 Frederick St, POB 1, Port of Spain; tel. 625-0289; fax 627-4172; e-mail ccib@carib-link.net; f. 1962; marketing of coffee and cocoa beans, regulation of cocoa and coffee industry; Man. KENT VILLAFANA.

Export-Import Bank of Trinidad and Tobago Ltd (EXIM-BANK): 5th Floor, Victoria Park Suites, 14–17 Victoria Sq., Port of Spain; tel. 625-3946; fax 624-0028; e-mail eximbank@wow.net; CEO ROGER MIKE; Gen. Man. JOSEPHINE IBLE.

Trinidad and Tobago Forest Products Ltd (TANTEAK): Connector Rd, Carlsen Field, Chaguanas; tel. 665-0078; fax 665-6645; f. 1975; harvesting, processing and marketing of state plantation-grown teak and pine; privatization pending; Chair. RUSKIN PUNCH; Man. Dir CLARENCE BACCHUS.

DEVELOPMENT ORGANIZATIONS

National Energy Corporation of Trinidad and Tobago Ltd: PLIPDECO House, Orinoco Drive, POB 191, Point Lisas, Couva; tel. 636-4662; fax 679-2384; e-mail infocent@carib-link.net; f. 1979; Chair. KENNETH BIRCHWOOD.

National Housing Authority: 44–46 South Quay, POB 555, Port of Spain; tel. 627-1703; fax 625-3963; f. 1962; Chair. BRIAN GEORGE; Exec. Dir Dr KEITH BAILEY.

Point Lisas Industrial Port Development Corporation Ltd (PLIPDECO): PLIPDECO House, Orinoco Drive, POB 191, Point Lisas, Couva; tel. 636-2201; fax 636-4008; e-mail plipdeco@plipdeco.com; internet www.plipdeco.com; f. 1966, privatized in the late 1990s; deep-water port handling general cargo, liquid and dry bulk, to serve adjacent industrial estate, which now includes iron and steel complex, methanol, ammonia, urea and related downstream industries; Chair. NIRMAL RAMPERSAD; CEO NEIL ROLINGSON.

Tourism and Industrial Development Company of Trinidad and Tobago (TIDCO): 10–14 Philipps St, POB 222, Port of Spain; tel. 623-6022; fax 624-8124; e-mail invest-info@tidco.co.tt; internet www.tidco.co.tt; Pres. (vacant).

CHAMBERS OF COMMERCE

South Trinidad Chamber of Industry and Commerce: Suite 311, Cross Crossing Shopping Centre, Lady Hailes Ave, San Fernando; tel. 652-5613; e-mail secretariat@southchamber.com; internet www.southchamber.com; f. 1956; Pres. BRIAN SAMLALSINGH.

Trinidad and Tobago Chamber of Industry and Commerce (Inc): Chamber Bldg, Columbus Circle, Westmoorings, POB 499, Port of Spain; tel. 627-6966; fax 637-7425; f. 1891; Pres. MICHAEL ARNEAUD; CEO DAVID MARTIN; Gen. Man. CARMENA BAIRD; 299 mems.

INDUSTRIAL AND TRADE ASSOCIATIONS

Agricultural Society of Trinidad and Tobago: 2A Alexandra St, Port of Spain; tel. 628-2486.

Coconut Growers' Association (CGA) Ltd: Eastern Main Rd, Laventille, POB 229, Port of Spain; tel. 623-5207; fax 623-2359; e-mail cgaltd@tstt.net.tt; f. 1936; 354 mems; Chair. PHILLIP AGOSTINI.

Co-operative Citrus Growers' Association of Trinidad and Tobago Ltd: Eastern Main Rd, POB 174, Laventille, Port of Spain; tel. 623-2255; fax 623-2487; e-mail ccga@wow.net; f. 1932; 437 mems; Pres. AINSLEY NICHOLS; Sec. N. WEEKES.

Pan Trinbago: 75 Edward St, Port of Spain; tel. 623-4486; fax 625-6715; e-mail pantrngo@wow.net; f. 1971; official body for Trinidad and Tobago steelbands; Pres. PATRICK LOUIS ARNOLD; Sec. VERNON MORANCIE.

Shipping Association of Trinidad and Tobago: Wrightson Rd, Port of Spain; tel. 623-8570; f. 1938; Pres. NOEL JENVEY; Exec. Sec. S. JULUMSINGH.

Sugar Association of the Caribbean: Brechin Castle, Couva; tel. 636-2449; fax 636-2847; f. 1942; promotes and protects sugar industry in the Caribbean; 6 mem. associations; Chair. KARL JAMES; Sec. A. MOHAMMED.

Trinidad and Tobago Contractors' Association: 8 Stanmore Ave, Port of Spain; tel. 625-0196; fax 625-0247; internet www.ttca.com; f. 1968; represents contractors and manufacturers and suppliers to the sector.

Trinidad and Tobago Manufacturers' Association: 8 Stanmore Ave, St Clair, POB 971, Port of Spain; tel. 623-1029; fax 623-1031; e-mail ttmagm@opus.co.tt; internet www.ttma.com; f. 1956; 260 mems; Pres. AMJAD ALI.

EMPLOYERS' ORGANIZATION

Employers' Consultative Association of Trinidad and Tobago (ECA): 43 Dundonald St, POB 911, Port of Spain; tel. 625-4723; fax 625-4891; e-mail eca@wow.net; internet www.wow.net/community/eca; f. 1959; CEO GERARD PINARD; 156 mems.

STATE HYDROCARBONS COMPANIES

National Gas Co of Trinidad and Tobago Ltd: Goodrich Bay Rd, Point Lisas, POB 1127, Port of Spain; tel. 636-4662; fax 679-2384; e-mail infocent@carib-link.net; f. 1975; purchases, sells, compresses, transmits and distributes natural gas to consumers; Pres. FRANK LOOK KIN.

Petroleum Company of Trinidad and Tobago Ltd (Petrotrin): Petrotrin Administration Bldg, cnr Queen's Park West and Cipriani Blvd, Port of Spain; tel. 625-5240; fax 624-4661; e-mail petroprd@petrotrin.com; internet www.petrotrin.com; f. 1993 following merger between Trinidad and Tobago Oil Company Ltd (Trintoc) and Trinidad and Tobago Petroleum Company Ltd (Trintopec); petroleum and gas exploration and production; operates refineries and a manufacturing complex, producing a variety of petroleum and petrochemical products; Chair. RODERICK PARRIAG; Pres. RODNEY JAGAI; Vice-Pres ALEEM HOSEIN, WAYNE BERTRAND, SOLOMON SINANAN.

Trinidad and Tobago Marine Petroleum Company Ltd (Trinmar): Administration Bldg, Port Fortin; tel. 648-2127; fax 648-2519; internet www.trinmar.com; f. 1962; owned by Petrotrin; marine petroleum and natural gas co; Gen. Man. ALEEM HOSEIN; 455 employees.

MAJOR COMPANIES

The following is a selection of major industrial and commercial companies operating in Trinidad and Tobago:

Food and Beverages

Angostura Holding Ltd: Industrial Centre, Eastern Main Rd, Lavantille; POB 62, Port of Spain; tel. 623-1841; fax 623-1847; f. 1921; manufacturers of rum, Angostura aromatic bitters and other alcoholic beverages; sales of TT $240.9m. (1995); Chair. THOMAS A. GATCLIFFE; Man. Dir and CEO KEITH MCLACHLAN; 35 employees.

Bermudez Biscuit Co Ltd: 6 Maloney St, POB 885, Port of Spain; tel. 638-3336; fax 638-5911; e-mail bermudez@opus.co.tt; f. 1950; producers of biscuits and other food products; Man. Dirs ROBERT BERMUDEZ, BERNARDO BERMUDEZ; 367 employees.

Kiss Baking Co Ltd: 12–14 Gaston St, POB 776, Lange Park, Chaguanas; tel. 671-5477; fax 672-3840; e-mail kissbaking @cariblink.net; f. 1975; bakery; Chair. ROBERT BERMUDEZ; Man. Dir WAYNE YIP-CHOY; 2,890 employees.

National Flour Mills Ltd: 27–29 Wrightson Rd, POB 1154, Port of Spain; tel. 625-2416; fax 625-4389; e-mail flourmil@catstt.net.tt; f. 1972; milling of flour and grains; manufacturers of rice, edible oils and animal feed; sales of TT $738.3m. (1996); Chair WINSTON CONNELL; 275 employees.

Metals

Bhagwansingh's Hardware and Steel Industries Ltd: Beetham Highway, Sea Lots, Port of Spain; tel. 625-2981; fax 623-0804; f. 1974; manufacturers of aluminium products; wholesale of steel and electrical products; sales of TT $153.0m. (1996); Chair. HELEN BHAGWANSINGH; Man. Dir HUBERT BHAGWANSINGH; 310 employees.

Caribbean Ispat Ltd: Point Lisas Industrial Estate, POB 476, Couva; tel. 636-2213; fax 636-5696; f. 1988; Indian-owned; formerly Iron and Steel Co of Trinidad and Tobago Ltd; divested in 1994; production of iron and steel wire and rods; Chair. MOHAMMED LAL MITTAL; Man. Dir RAM SHANKER MISRA; 985 employees.

Cliffs and Associates: POB 96, Caribbean Dr, California; tel. 636-5826; fax 679-5047; US-German joint venture; iron and steel producers.

Petroleum, Natural Gas and Asphalt
(see also State Hydrocarbons Companies above)

Atlantic LNG Co of Trinidad and Tobago: 6A Queen's Park West, Port of Spain; tel. 625-5707; fax 625-5641; internet www.alng.com; f. 1995; owned by BP Amoco Energy Co (34%), BG (British Gas Trinidad and Tobago Ltd—26%), Repsol of Spain (20%), the US-owned Cabot Trinidad LNG (10%) and the National Gas Co of Trinidad and Tobago (10%); production of liquefied natural gas; Chair. JOHN ANDREWS; Pres. GERALD PEEREBOOM; 140 employees.

BP Energy Company of Trinidad and Tobago: 5–5A Queen's Park West Plaza, Port of Spain; tel. 623-2862; fax 628-5058; internet www.bp.com; f. 1960; exploration and extraction of natural gas and petroleum; Pres. ROBERT RILEY.

BG (British Gas Trinidad and Tobago Ltd): BG House, 6 Stanmore Ave, Port of Spain; tel. 627-8106; fax 627-8102; e-mail jacques .robinson@cabgep.co.uk; extraction of natural gas; Pres. and Gen. Man. PETER DRANFIELD; 110 employees.

Enron Gas and Oil Trinidad Ltd: Mutual Centre, 16 Queen's Park West, Port of Spain; tel. 622-8653; fax 628-4215; exploration and extraction of petroleum and natural gas; Man. Dir LINDELL LOOGER.

Lake Asphalt of Trinidad and Tobago (1978) Ltd: Brighton, La Brea; tel. 648-7555; fax 648-7433; e-mail lakeasphalt@trinidad.net; internet www.trinidadlakeasphalt.com; state-owned; manufacturers of asphalt; Chair WINSTON MOOTOO.

Mora Oil Ventures: L. P. 13/1, Bobb Street-on-Sea, La Romain; tel. 657-5058; fax 657-6991; e-mail kpamora@trinidad.net; oil production; Chair. GEORGE STEPHEN WATTLEY; CEO KRISHNA PERSAD.

Petrochemicals

Conoco Trinidad B.V.: POB 225, Port of Spain; tel. 624-9205; fax 623-6025; natural gas liquid processing; Man. Dir Paul Warwick.

Farmland Mississippi Chemical Corporation: North Caspian Drive, PO Bag 38, Point Lisas, Couva; tel. 679-4045; fax 679-2452; e-mail fmcl@carib-link.net; opened ammonia plant in 1999; Pres. LARRY HOLLEY.

Methanol Holdings Trinidad and Tobago Ltd: Atlantic Ave, POB 457, Point Lisas Industrial Estate, Couva; tel. 636-2803; fax 636-4501; e-mail rmotilal@tstt.net.tt; methanol production; CEO RAMPERSAND MOTILAL.

PCS (Potash Corpn of Saskatchewan) Nitrogen Ltd: Goodrich Bay Rd, Point Lisas, Couva; tel. 636-2205; fax 636-2052; f. 1977; formerly state-owned Fertilizers of Trinidad and Tobago (Fertrin) Ltd, bought by Arcadian Partners (USA) in 1993; Arcadian Partners bought by PCS in 1997; manufacturers of fertilizers; Chair. T. BOOP-SINGH; Man. Dir IAN WELCH; 355 employees.

Titan Methanol: Maracaibo Drive, Point Lisas, Couva; tel. 679-5052; fax 679-5065; e-mail titanmc@carib-link.net; owns Trinidad and Tobago's largest methanol plant; Pres. MALCOLM JONES.

Trinidad and Tobago Methanol Co Ltd (TTMC): POB 457, Couva Caroni, Port of Spain; tel. 623-2101; fax 623-1847; f. 1984; formerly state-owned; privatized in stages from 1994; fully divested in 1997; owned by the German companies Ferrostaal (62.5%) and Helm (26.25%), and CL Financial (11.25%); planned merger with the Caribbean Methanol Co, Fertrin and TTUC announced in 1997; manufacturers and distributors of methanol; sales of TT $532.3m. (1995); Chair. ANTHONY CHAN TACK; Gen. Man. ASHRAM BEHARRY; 195 employees.

Trinidad and Tobago Urea Company Ltd (TTUC): Port of Spain; formerly state-owned, bought by Arcadian Partners (USA) in 1993.

Miscellaneous

A. S. Bryden and Sons (Trinidad) Ltd: POB 607, Port of Spain; tel. 623-2312; fax 627-5655; e-mail asbryden@trinidad.net; internet www.caribinfo.com; f. 1928; importers and distributors of alcoholic beverages, food products, household goods and pharmaceuticals; sales of TT $121.0m. (1996/97); Chair. HAROLD L. BRYDEN; Man. Dir KEITH MAINGOT; 92 employees.

Agostini's Ltd: 4 Nelson St, POB 191, Port of Spain; tel. 623-2236; fax 624-6751; e-mail agostini@catstt.net.tt; f. 1925; importers and wholesale distributors of construction materials, foodstuffs and pharmaceuticals; sales of TT $208m. (1997/98); Chair. RAYMOND BERNARD; Man. Dir GEOFFREY AGOSTINI; 450 employees.

Automotive Components Ltd: O'Meara Rd, POB 1298, Arima; tel. 642-3268; fax 646-1956; internet www.neal-and-massy.com /autocomp; f. 1966; manufacturers of automobile components; owned by Neal & Massy Holdings Ltd (see below); sales of TT $80m. (1996); Chair. BERNARD DULAL-WHITEWAY; Man. Dir GORDON RAUSEO; 250 employees.

Berger Paints Trinidad Ltd: 11 Concessions Rd, Sea Lots, POB 546, Port of Spain; tel. 623-2231; fax 623-1682; e-mail berger@tstt.net.tt; internet www.trinidad.net/berger; f. 1760; manufacturers of paint, wood stains, wood preservatives, auto refinishes; Man. Dir KISHORE S. ADVANI; 100 employees.

Carib Glassworks Ltd: Eastern Main Rd, POB 1287, Champs Fleurs, St George's; tel. 662-2231; fax 663-1779; f. 1955; glass manufacturers; Chair. STEPHEN WEBSTER; 455 employees.

Conglomerates ANSA McAL: Queen and Henry St, Port of Spain; tel. 625-2201; activities include glass making, construction, finance, media; owns Caribbean Devt Co brewery; Group Chair. ANTHONY SABGA; CEO A. NORMAN SABGA.

Fujitsu-ICL Caribbean (Trinidad) Ltd: 46 Park St, POB 195, Port of Spain; tel. 623-2826; fax 623-4314; subsidiary of Fujitsu Ltd of Japan; manufacturers of computers and telecommunications equipment; Gen. Man. IAN GALT.

Johnson and Johnson (Trinidad) Ltd: New Trincity Industrial Estate, Trincity, St George's; tel. 640-3772; fax 640-3777; f. 1965; subsidiary of Johnson and Johnson of the USA; manufacturers of pharmaceuticals; Chair. SURT SELQUIST; Man. CLIVE ANNANDSINGH; 135 employees.

Lever Brothers (West Indies) Ltd: Eastern Main Rd, POB 295, Champ Fleurs, Port of Spain; tel. 663-1787; fax 662-1780; f. 1964; subsidiary of Unilever PLC of the United Kingdom; manufacturers of soaps, detergents, cosmetic products and foods; Chair. and Man. Dir GARY N. VOSS; 600 employees.

Neal & Massy Holdings Ltd: 63 Park St, POB 1298, Port of Spain; tel. 625-3426; fax 627-9061; f. 1923; industrial, trading and financial group involved in metals, engineering and automobile assembly; sales of US $507.2m. (1995); Chair. WILFRED SIDNEY ROX; Man. Dir JESÚS PAZOS; 6,500 employees.

Trinidad Cement Ltd (TCL): Southern Main Rd, Claxton Bay; tel. 659-2381; fax 659-2540; internet www.tclgroup.com; f. 1954; manufacture and sale of Portland, sulphate-resisting and oil-well cement and paper sacks and bags; sales of TT $364.2m. (1996); Chair. ANDY J. BHAJAN; Man. Dir and CEO SHARMA LALLA; 400 employees.

Trinidad and Tobago National Petroleum Marketing Co Ltd: National Drive, POB 666, Sealots, Port of Spain; tel. 627-2975; fax 627-4028; e-mail npmc@trinidad.net; marketing of petroleum products; state-owned; Chair. CAROLYN SEEPERSAD-BACHAN.

Trintomar Ltd: 1 East St, Pointe-à-Pierre; tel. 658-4322; fax 658-0911; state-owned; develops offshore petroleum sector.

L. J. Williams Ltd: 122 St Vincent St, Port of Spain; tel. 623-2865; fax 625-6782; e-mail ljw@caopus.co.tt; f. 1925; manufacturers of glues and sealants; distribution of groceries and beverages; sales of TT $135.0m. (1996); Chair. J. G. FURNESS-SMITH; Man. Dir RONALD JAY WILLIAMS; 500 employees.

West Indian Tobacco Co Ltd (WITCO): Eastern Main Rd, POB 177, Champ Fleurs, Port of Spain; tel. 662-2271; fax 663-5451; f. 1904; subsidiary of British-American Tobacco Co Ltd of the United Kingdom; cigarette manufacturers; sales of TT $219.6m. (1995); Chair. HECTOR CASCO; 165 employees.

UTILITIES
Regulatory Authority

Public Utilities Commission: 90 Independence Sq., Port of Spain; tel. 627-0821.

Electricity

Inncogen Ltd: 10 Marine Villas, Columbus Blvd, West Moorings by the Sea; tel. 632-7339; fax 632-7341; Chair. ROBERT PALEDINE.

Power Generation Co of Trinidad and Tobago (PowerGen): 6A Queen's Park West, Port of Spain; tel. 624-0383; fax 625-3759; Gen. Man. LARRY PORTER.

Trinidad and Tobago Electricity Commission (TTEC): 63 Frederick St, POB 121, Port of Spain; tel. 623-2611; fax 623-3759; e-mail ttecisd@trinidad.net; state-owned electricity transmission and distribution company; 51% owned by Power Generation Company of Trinidad and Tobago, 49% owned by Southern Electric Int./Amoco; Chair. DEVANAND RAMLAL; Gen. Man. DENIS SINGH (acting).

Gas

National Gas Co of Trinidad and Tobago Ltd: (see State Hydrocarbons Companies above).

Water

Water and Sewerage Authority (WASA): Farm Rd, St Joseph; tel. 662-9272; fax 652-1253.

TRADE UNIONS

National Trade Union Centre (NATUC): c/o NUGFW Complex, 145–147 Henry St, Port of Spain; tel. 623-4591; fax 625-7756; f. June 1991 as umbrella organization unifying entire trade-union movement, including former Trinidad and Tobago Labour Congress and Council of Progressive Trade Unions; Pres. ERROL K. MCLEOD; Gen. Sec. SELWYN JOHN.

Principal Affiliates

All-Trinidad Sugar and General Workers' Trade Union (ATSGWTU): Rienzi Complex, Exchange Village, Southern Main Rd, Couva; tel. 636-2354; fax 636-3372; e-mail atsgwtu@opus.co.tt; f. 1937; Pres. BOYSIE MOORE JONES; Gen. Sec. RUDRANATH INDARSINGH; 8,500 mems.

Amalgamated Workers' Union: 16 New St, Port of Spain; tel. 627-8993; f. 1953; Pres.-Gen. CYRIL LOPEZ; Sec. FLAVIUS NURSE; c. 7,000 mems.

Aviation, Communication and Allied Workers' Union: 315 McConie St, Dinsley Village, Tacarigua; tel. 669-1762; f. 1982; Pres. PAUL HARRISON; Gen. Sec. MARTIN ELIGON.

Bank and General Workers' Union: 27 Borde St, Woodbrook, Port of Spain; tel. 627-3931; fax 627-0278; e-mail bgwu@cariblink.net; f. 1974; Pres. VINCENT CABRERA; Gen. Sec. CHRISTOPHER JACKSON-SMITH.

Communication Workers' Union: 146 Henry St, Port of Spain; tel. 623-5588; f. 1953; Pres. LAWRENCE BROWN; Gen. Sec. LYLE TOWNSEND; c. 2,100 mems.

National Union of Government and Federated Workers: 145–147 Henry St, Port of Spain; tel. 623-4591; fax 625-7756; f. 1937; Pres. SELWYN JOHN; Gen. Sec. CECIL MCNEIL; c. 20,000 mems.

Oilfield Workers' Trade Union: Paramount Bldg, 99A Circular Rd, San Fernando; tel. 652-2701; fax 652-7170; e-mail owtu@carib-link.net; f. 1937; Pres. ERROL MCLEOD; Gen. Sec. DOODNATH MAHARAJ; 10,000 mems.

Public Services Association: 89–91 Abercromby St, POB 353, Port of Spain; tel. 623-7987; fax 627-2980; f. 1938; Pres. JENNIFER BAPTISTE; c. 15,000 mems.

Seamen and Waterfront Workers' Trade Union: 1D Wrightson Rd, Port of Spain; tel. 625-1182; f. 1937; Pres.-Gen. FRANCIS MUNGROO; Sec.-Gen. ROSS ALEXANDER; c. 3,000 mems.

Transport and Industrial Workers' Union of Trinidad and Tobago: 114 Eastern Main St, Laventille, Port of Spain; tel. 623-4943; fax 623-2361; f. 1962; Pres. ALBERT ABERDEEN; Gen Sec. DESMOND O. BISHOP; c. 5,000 mems.

Trinidad and Tobago Postmen's Union: c/o General Post Office, Wrightson Rd, POB 692, Port of Spain; Pres. KENNETH SOOKOO; Gen. Sec. EVERALD SAMUEL.

Trinidad and Tobago Unified Teachers' Association: Cnr Fowler and Southern Main Rd, Curepe; tel. 645-2134; fax 662-1813; Pres. ANTHONY GARCIA; Gen. Sec. FRANK RAMNANAN.

Union of Commercial and Industrial Workers: 130–132 Henry St, Port of Spain; tel. 623-8381; f. 1951; Asst Sec. M. WILSON; c. 1,500 mems.

Transport

RAILWAYS
The railway service was discontinued in 1968.

ROADS
In 1999 there were 7,900 km (4,910 miles) of roads in Trinidad and Tobago.

Public Transport Service Corporation: Railway Bldgs, South Quay, POB 391, Port of Spain; tel. 623-2341; fax 625-6502; f. 1965 to operate national bus services; Chair. (vacant); Gen. Man. EDISON ISAAC; operates a fleet of buses.

SHIPPING
The chief ports are Port of Spain, Pointe-à-Pierre and Point Lisas in Trinidad and Scarborough in Tobago. Port of Spain handles 85% of all container traffic, and all international cruise arrivals. In 1998 Port of Spain handled 3.3m. metric tons of cargo. Port of Spain and Scarborough each have a deep-water wharf. Port of Spain possesses a dedicated container terminal, with two large overhead cranes. Plans were in place in 2001 for an expansion of operations, through the purchase of an additional crane, the computerization of operations, and the deepening of the harbour (from 9.75m to 12m).

Caribbean Drydock Ltd: Port Chaguaramas, Western Main Rd, Chaguaramas; tel. 634-4127; fax 625-1215; e-mail caridoc@trinidad.org; internet www.caridoc.org; ship repair, marine transport, barge and boat construction.

Point Lisas Industrial Port Development Corporation Ltd (PLIPDECO): see Development Organizations.

Port Authority of Trinidad and Tobago: Dock Rd, POB 549, Port of Spain; tel. 623-2901; fax 627-2666; e-mail patt@wow.net; internet www.patnt.com; f. 1962; Chair. ISAAC T. MCLEOD; Gen. Man. COLIN LUCAS.

Shipping Association of Trinidad and Tobago: 1st level, Cruise Ship Complex, Wrightson Rd, Port of Spain; tel. 623-3352; fax 623-8570; Pres. RAWLE BADDALOO; Exec. Sec. S. JULUMSINGH.

CIVIL AVIATION
Piarco International Airport is situated 25.7 km (16 miles) southeast of Port of Spain and is used by numerous airlines. The airport was expanded and a new terminal was constructed in 2001. Piarco remains the principal air transportation facility in Trinidad and Tobago. However, following extensive aerodrome development at Crown Point Airport (located 13 km from Scarborough) in 1992 the airport was opened to jet aircraft. It is now officially named Crown Point International Airport. A further re-development of the airport was to begin in 2001–02. There is a domestic service between Trinidad and Tobago.

Airports Authority of Trinidad and Tobago (AATT): Airport Administration Centre, Piarco International Airport; tel. 669-8047; fax 669-2319; e-mail airport@tstt.net.tt; internet www.airporttnt.com; administers Piarco and Crown Point International Airports; Chair. TYRONE GOPEE.

BWIA International Airways Ltd (Trinidad and Tobago): Administration Bldg, Golden Grove Rd, Piarco International Airport, POB 604, Port of Spain; tel. 669-3000; fax 669-1865; e-mail mail@bwee.com; internet www.bwee.com; f. 1980 as merger of BWIA International (f. 1940) and Trinidad and Tobago Air Services (f. 1974); 51% owned by consortium headed by Acker Group (USA), 33.5% state-owned; operates scheduled passenger and cargo services linking destinations in the Caribbean region, South America, North

America and Europe; began service between Trinidad and Tobago, the Tobago Express, in March 2001; Chair. LAWRENCE DUPREY; Pres. and CEO CONRAD ALEONG.

Tourism

The climate and coastline attract visitors to Trinidad and Tobago. The latter island is generally believed to be the more beautiful and is less developed. The annual pre-Lenten carnival is a major attraction. In 1999 there were an estimated 360,000 foreign visitors, excluding cruise-ship passengers, and tourist receipts were estimated at US $180m. In 2000 there were an estimated 82,859 cruise-ship passenger arrivals. In 1999 there were 4,236 hotel rooms in Trinidad and Tobago. The sector experienced growth in 1999 and 2000. The Government announced plans to increase first-class hotel room accommodation by 8,000 in 2001, marketing the islands as a sophisticated cultural destination. There were additional tourism developments in Chaguaramas and Toco Bay.

Tourism and Industrial Development Company of Trinidad and Tobago (TIDCO): see Development Organizations.

Trinidad and Tobago Hotel and Tourism Association (TTHTA): Unit 'B', 36 Scott Bushe St, POB 243, Port of Spain; tel. 627-4515; fax 627-4516; e-mail hotelassoc@wow.net; internet www.tnthotels.com; Pres. SHAZAM ALI; Exec. Dir GREER ASSAM.

> **Tobago Chapter:** Goddard's Bldg, Auchenskeoch, Carnbee; tel. and fax 639-9543; e-mail tthtatob@tstt.net.tt; Vice-Pres. RENE SEEPERSADSINGH.

Defence

At 1 August 2000 the Trinidad and Tobago Defence Force consisted of 2,700 active members: an Army of an estimated 2,000 men and a coastguard of 700. Included in the coastguard was an air wing of 50.

Defence Budget: TT $390m. (US $62m.) in 2000.

Chief of Defence Staff: Brig.-Gen. JOHN CHRYSOSTOM EDMUND SANDY.

Education

Primary and secondary education is free. Many schools are run jointly by the State and religious bodies. Attendance at school is officially compulsory for children between five and 12 years of age. Primary education begins at the age of five and lasts for seven years. In 1997 99.9% of children in this age group (males 99.9%; females 99.9%) were enrolled at primary schools. Secondary education, beginning at 12 years of age, lasts for up to five years, comprising a first cycle of three years and a second of two years. In 1999 the ratio for secondary enrolment was 69% of those in the relevant age-group. Entrance to secondary schools is determined by the Common Entrance Examination. Many schools are administered jointly by the State and religious bodies. In mid-1999 the Inter-American Development Bank approved a US $105m. loan for a programme to construct 20 new secondary schools and improve the facilities of the 100 existing secondary schools in Trinidad and Tobago. In 2000 the Government announced an education reform programme to improve access to and levels of education. A school-to-work apprenticeship programme was also to be established.

The Trinidad campus of the University of the West Indies (UWI), at St Augustine, includes an engineering faculty. The UWI Institute of Business offers postgraduate courses and develops programmes for local companies. Other institutions of higher education are the Eric Williams Medical Sciences Complex, the Polytechnic Institute and the Eastern Caribbean Farm Institute. The country has one teacher-training college and three government technical institutes and vocational centres, including the Trinidad and Tobago Hotel School. In the late 1990s the Government established the Trinidad and Tobago Institute of Technology, and the College of Science, Technology and Applied Arts of Trinidad and Tobago. Distance learning was also being expanded. Government expenditure on education in 2000 was TT $2,111.0m.

Bibliography

For works on the Caribbean generally, see Select Bibliography (Books).

Anthony, M. *Profile Trinidad: A Historical Survey from the Discovery to 1900.* London, Macmillan, 1986.

Birbalsingh, F. (Ed). *Indo-Caribbean Resistance.* Toronto, TSAR, 1993.

Boodhoe, K. I. (Ed.). *Eric Williams: The Man and the Leader.* Lanham, MD, University Press of America, 1986.

Brereton, B. *A History of Modern Trinidad, 1783–1962.* London, Heinemann Educational Books, 1981.

Klass, M. *Singing With Sai Baba: Politics of Revitalization in Trinidad.* Prospect Heights, IL, Waveland Press, 1996.

Macdonald, S. B. *Trinidad and Tobago: Democracy and Development.* New York, NY, Praeger Publrs, 1986.

Oxaal, I. *Black Intellectuals Come to Power: The Rise of Creole Nationalism in Trinidad and Tobago.* Cambridge, MA, Schenkman Publishing, 1968.

Regis, L. *The Political Calypso: True Opposition in Trinidad and Tobago.* Gainesville, FL, University Press of Florida, 1999.

Ryan, S. *Race and Nationalism in Trinidad and Tobago: A Study of Decolonisation in a Multi-racial Society.* Toronto, University of Toronto Press, 1974.

Stuempfle, S. *The Steelband Movement: The Forging of a National Art in Trinidad and Tobago.* Philadelphia, PA, University of Pennsylvania Press, 1996.

Winer, L. *Trinidad and Tobago.* Amsterdam, Benjamins, 1993.

TURKS AND CAICOS ISLANDS

Area: 430 sq km (166 sq miles); consists of more than 30 islands.

Population (official estimate, mid-2000): 17,502. By island (1980): Grand Turk 3,098, South Caicos 1,380, Middle Caicos 396, North Caicos 1,278, Salt Cay 284, Providenciales 977 (Total 7,435).

Capital: Cockburn Town (Grand Turk), population (estimate, 1987) 2,500.

Language: English; a creole tongue is also spoken.

Religion: Several Christian denominations are represented.

Climate: Warm; average temperature 27°C (82°F); average annual rainfall varies from 530 mm (21 in) in the eastern islands to 1,000 mm (40 in) in the western islands.

Time: GMT –5 hours.

Public Holidays: 2002: 1 January (New Year's Day), 11 March (Commonwealth Day), 29 March (Good Friday), 1 April (Easter Monday), 27 May (National Heroes' Day), 6 June (J. A. G. S. McCartney Memorial Day), 8 June (Queen's Official Birthday), 5 August (Emancipation Day), 30 September (National Youth Day), 14 October (for Columbus Day), 10 December (International Human Rights Day), 25–26 December (Christmas). **2003:** 1 January (New Year's Day), 10 March (Commonwealth Day), 18 April (Good Friday), 21 April (Easter Monday), 26 May (National Heroes' Day), 6 June (J. A. G. S. McCartney Memorial Day), 14 June (Queen's Official Birthday), 4 August (Emancipation Day), 30 September (National Youth Day), 17 October (for Columbus Day), 10 December (International Human Rights Day), 25–26 December (Christmas).

Currency: US dollar; US $100 = £69.84 = €112.66 (30 April 2001).

Weights and Measures: Imperial.

History

The Turks and Caicos Islands constitute a United Kingdom Overseas Territory and the British monarch is represented locally by a Governor who presides over the Executive Council. From February 1998 the British Dependent Territories were referred to as the United Kingdom Overseas Territories, following the announcement of the interim findings of a British government review of the United Kingdom's relations with the Overseas Territories.

The islands, which had been a Jamaican dependency from 1874 until 1959, became a separate colony in 1962, following Jamaican independence. They were accorded their own resident Governor in 1972. At the 1976 elections the pro-independence People's Democratic Movement (PDM) won a majority of seats in the Legislative Council, and the party leader, J. A. G. S. McCartney, became Chief Minister. In 1980 the PDM reached an agreement with the United Kingdom that, if it won the next election, the islands would be granted independence. However, the election was won by the opposition Progressive National Party (PNP), which is committed to continued dependent status. In the 1984 election the PNP, led by Norman Saunders, maintained its lead.

In March 1985 Saunders was arrested in Miami (Florida, USA) on charges involving illicit drugs and accepting a bribe. He resigned as Chief Minister and was replaced by Nathaniel Francis. In July 1986 an official report on the destruction of a government building by fire in December 1985 forced the resignation of Francis and two other ministers and discredited the Government amidst allegations of unconstitutional behaviour and ministerial malpractice. The Governor proceeded to dissolve the Government and an Order-in-Council authorized him to replace the Executive Council with an interim Advisory Council. In March 1987 the British Government announced that it had accepted a constitutional commission's central recommendations and a general election was held in March 1988, after which there was a return to ministerial government.

The PDM won 11 of the 13 seats on the Legislative Council in the 1988 elections and Oswald Skippings, the leader of the PDM, was appointed Chief Minister. In the April 1991 general election the PNP secured eight seats and Skippings was replaced as Chief Minister by Washington Misick, the PNP leader. In January 1995 the PDM, now led by Derek Taylor, gained eight seats, while the PNP won four and the remaining seat went to Saunders, who had stood as an independent.

From mid-1995 relations between the Governor, Martin Bourke, and the Legislative Council deteriorated to such an extent that in February 1996 all government and opposition deputies signed a petition requesting the British Foreign and Commonwealth Office to replace the Governor. He did not, however, leave office until the end of his three-year term in September 1996, when he was replaced by John Kelly. At legislative elections, held on 4 March 1999, the PDM won 52.2% of the votes cast. Norman Saunders, who had secured nomination as a PDM candidate, retained the seat that he had held as an independent, increasing the PDM's representation in the Legislative Council to nine seats. The PNP won the other four seats, with 40.9% of the ballot. In the same month the British Government published draft legislation on its future relationship with its Overseas Dependencies, which had been referred to as United Kingdom Overseas Territories since February 1998. The Government announced that in future citizens of Overseas Territories would have the right to reside in the United Kingdom, provided they meet international standards in the areas of human rights and the regulation of the financial services sector. In mid-March 1999 Taylor appointed a new Executive Council. In January 2000 Mervyn Jones replaced John Kelly as Governor. In June 2000 pressure increased on the Government to introduce fiscal reform when the Organisation for Economic Co-operation and Development (OECD) included the islands on a list of territories operating harmful tax regimes; the OECD urged greater legal and administrative transparency to prevent companies using the countries' tax systems in an attempt to launder money or avoid income tax.

Economy

Salt produced by solar evaporation was the principal export until 1964; however, by the early 1990s the activity had virtually ceased. In the late 1990s the underwater extraction of aragonite was being investigated. Agriculture is not practised on any significant scale in the Turks Islands or on South Caicos (the most populous island of the Territory). The other islands of the Caicos group grow some beans, maize and a few fruits and vegetables. There is some livestock-rearing, but the islands' principal natural resource is fisheries, which account for almost all commodity exports, the principal species caught being the spiny lobster (an estimated 230 metric tons in 1998) and the conch (an estimated 788 metric tons in that year). Conches are now being developed commercially (on the largest conch farm in the world), and there is potential for larger-scale fishing. Exports of lobster and conch earned US $3.4m. in 1995, which constituted an increase of more than 14% compared with the previous year's earnings. However, agricultural possibilities were limited and most foodstuffs were imported. Industrial activity consists mainly of construction (especially for the tourist industry) and fish-processing.

The principal economic sector is the service industry. This is dominated by the expanding tourist sector, which is concentrated on the island of Providenciales. The market is for wealthier visitors, most of whom come from the USA. Tourist arrivals increased from 110,855 in 1998 to 120,898 in 1999. As a result of the growth in tourism throughout the late 1990s many new hotels and resorts have been developed. Concern has, however, been expressed that the islands are in danger of becoming overdeveloped and thereby of damaging their reputation as an unspoilt tourist location. An 'offshore' financial sector was encouraged in the 1980s, and new regulatory legislation was ratified in 1989. In early 2000 there were some 8,000 overseas companies registered in the islands. Earnings from some 2,858 new registrations totalled US $2.3m. in 1995. However, in June 2000 the Turks and the Caicos was included in the list of harmful tax regimes compiled by the OECD. Jurisdictions included in the list were required to make legislative changes, introducing greater legal and administrative transparency.

In 1999 GDP growth of 8.7% was recorded. Overall the economy, and also the population, were estimated to have doubled in size during the 1990s, making the islands one of the region's most dynamic economies. The remarkable economic growth experienced by the islands was chiefly owing to the increasing significance of the tourism and international financial services sectors, both of which benefited from the perceived stability of United Kingdom Overseas Territory status. However, a source of disquiet is the exclusion of many inhabitants from the benefits of economic growth; it is estimated that the economic situation of the majority of 'belongers' has improved only marginally during the 1990s, as newly-created jobs were often taken by low-wage migrant workers or by highly-skilled expatriate workers. It has also been noted that the Territory's growth is highly dependent on exterior factors, and the OECD's proposals to force comprehensive reforms of offshore financial services centres are therefore of particular concern.

Statistical Survey

Source: Chief Secretary's Office, Grand Turk; tel. 946-2300; fax 946-2886.

AREA AND POPULATION

Area: 430 sq km (166 sq miles).

Population: 7,435 (males 3,602; females 3,833) at census of 12 May 1980; 12,350 (males 6,289; females 6,061) at census of 31 May 1990; 16,863 (official estimate) at mid-1999. *By island* (1980): Grand Turk 3,098; South Caicos 1,380; Middle Caicos 396; North Caicos 1,278; Salt Cay 284; Providenciales 977. (1990): Grand Turk 3,761; Providenciales 5,586.

Density: 39.2 per sq km (at mid-1999).

Principal Towns: Cockburn Town (capital, on Grand Turk), population 2,500 (estimate, 1987); Cockburn Harbour (South Caicos), population 1,000.

Births and Deaths (registrations, 1990): Live births 240; Deaths 37; (rates per 1,000, 1998) Births 27.14; Deaths 4.98.

Expectation of Life (years at birth, 1998): Males 70.21; Females 74.20.

Economically Active Population (1990 census): 4,848 (males 2,306; females 2,542).

AGRICULTURE, ETC.

Fishing (metric tons, live weight, 1998): Capture 1,318 (Marine fishes 300, Caribbean spiny lobster 230, Stromboid conchs 788); Aquaculture 4; Total catch 1,322. Figures exclude aquatic plants and mammals. Source: FAO, *Yearbook of Fishery Statistics*.

INDUSTRY

Electric Energy (estimated production, million kWh): 5 in 1993; 5 in 1994; 5 in 1995. Source: UN, *Industrial Commodity Statistics Yearbook*.

FINANCE

Currency and Exchange Rate: United States currency is used: 100 cents = 1 US dollar ($). *Sterling and Euro Equivalents* (30 April 2001): £1 sterling = US $1.4318; €1 = 88.76 US cents; $100 = £69.84 = €112.66.

Budget (provisional, $ million, 2000/01): Total revenue 67.05; Total expenditure 67.11.

EXTERNAL TRADE

1993 ($ million): *Imports:* 46.6. *Exports:* 4.6.

TRANSPORT

Road Traffic (1984): 1,563 registered motor vehicles.

Shipping *International freight traffic* (estimates in '000 metric tons, 1990): Goods loaded 135; Goods unloaded 149. *Merchant Fleet* (vessels registered at 31 December 2000): 5; Total displacement 975

grt. Sources: UN, *Monthly Bulletin of Statistics*; Lloyd's Register of Shipping, *World Fleet Statistics*.

TOURISM

Tourist Arrivals: 93,011 in 1997; 110,855 in 1998; 120,898 in 1999. Source: World Tourism Organization, *Yearbook of Tourism Statistics*.

COMMUNICATIONS MEDIA

Radio Receivers (1997): 8,000 in use.

Telephones (1994): 3,000 main lines in use.

Telefax Stations (1992): 200 in use.

Non-daily Newspapers (1996): 1; (estimated circulation 5,000). Sources: UNESCO, *Statistical Yearbook*; UN, *Statistical Yearbook*.

EDUCATION

Pre-primary: (1996/97): 21 schools; 797 pupils.

Primary (1996/97): 21 schools; 86 teachers (1993/94); 1,573 pupils.

General Secondary (1996/97): 5 schools (1990); 101 teachers (1993/94); 1,028 pupils.

Vocational Education: (1993/94) 30 teachers; 89 pupils.

Source: UNESCO, *Statistical Yearbook*.

Directory
The Constitution

The Order in Council of July 1986 enabled the Governor to suspend the ministerial form of government, for which the Constitution of 1976 made provision. Ministerial government was restored in March 1988, following amendments to the Constitution, recommended by a constitutional commission.

The revised Constitution of 1988 provides for an Executive Council and a Legislative Council. Executive authority is vested in the British monarch and is exercised by the Governor (the monarch's appointed representative), who also holds responsibility for external affairs, internal security, defence, the appointment of any person to any public office and the suspension and termination of appointment of any public officer.

The Executive Council comprises: three *ex-officio* members (the Financial Secretary, the Chief Secretary and the Attorney-General); a Chief Minister (appointed by the Governor) who is, in the judgement of the Governor, the leader of that political party represented in the Legislative Council which commands the support of a majority of the elected members of the Council; and four other ministers, appointed by the Governor, on the advice of the Chief Minister. The Executive Council is presided over by the Governor.

The Legislative Council consists of the Speaker, the three *ex-officio* members of the Executive Council, 13 members elected by residents aged 18 and over, and three nominated members (appointed by the Governor, one on the advice of the Chief Minister, one on the advice of the Leader of the Opposition and one at the Governor's discretion).

For the purposes of elections to the Legislative Council, the islands are divided into five electoral districts. In 1988 and 1991 a multiple voting system was used, whereby three districts elected three members each, while the remaining five districts each elected two members. However, in the 1995 election a single-member constituency system was used.

The Government

Governor: MERVYN JONES (sworn in 27 January 2000).

EXECUTIVE COUNCIL
(August 2001)

President: The Governor.

Ex-Officio Members:

Financial Secretary: AUSTIN ROBINSON.

Attorney-General: DAVID J. JEREMIAH.

Chief Secretary: CYNTHIA ASTWOOD.

Chief Minister and Minister of Finance, Development and Commerce: DEREK TAYLOR.

Deputy Chief Minister and Minister of Home Affairs, Labour and Immigration: HILLY EWING.

Minister of Transport, Communications, Tourism, Information and CARICOM Affairs: OSWALD O. SKIPPINGS.

Minister of Education, Health, Youth, Sports, Social Welfare and National Insurance: CLARENCE SELVER.

Minister of Natural Resources, Planning, Heritage, Agriculture and Fisheries and Environment and Coastal Resources: LARRY COALBROOKE.

Minister of Public Works and Utilities: NOEL SKIPPINGS.

GOVERNMENT OFFICES

Office of the Governor: Government House, Waterloo, Grand Turk; tel. 946-2308; fax 946-2903; e-mail governoroffice@tciway.tc.

Office of the Chief Minister: Government Compound, Grand Turk; tel. 946-2801; fax 946-2777; e-mail unfptc@tciway.tc.

Chief Secretary's Office: Government Secretariat, Grand Turk; tel. 946-2702; fax 946-2886.

Office of the Permanent Secretary: Finance Department, Chief Minister's Office, Government Buildings, Front St, Grand Turk; tel. 946-1115; fax 946-2777.

LEGISLATIVE COUNCIL

Speaker: WINSTON R. OUTTEN.

Election, 4 March 1999

Party	% of vote	Seats
People's Democratic Movement . . .	52.2	9
Progressive National Party . . .	40.9	4
Independents	6.9	—
Total	100.0	13

There are three *ex-officio* members (the Chief Secretary, the Financial Secretary and the Attorney-General), three appointed members, and a Speaker chosen from outside the Council.

Political Organizations

People's Democratic Movement (PDM): POB 38, Grand Turk; favours internal self-government and eventual independence; Leader DEREK TAYLOR.

Progressive National Party (PNP): Grand Turk; supports full internal self-government; Chair. N. B. SAUNDERS; Leader C. WASHINGTON MISICK.

United Democratic Party (UDP): Grand Turk; f. 1993; Leader WENDAL SWANN.

Judicial System

Justice is administered by the Supreme Court of the islands, presided over by the Chief Justice. Following the suspension of the Constitution in 1986, an inquiry recommended that the Chief Justice should reside in the Territory. There is a Chief Magistrate resident on Grand Turk, who also acts as Judge of the Supreme Court. There are also three Deputy Magistrates.

The Court of Appeal held its first sitting in February 1995. Previously the islands had shared a court of appeal in Nassau, Bahamas. In certain cases, appeals are made to the Judicial Committee of the Privy Council (based in the United Kingdom).

Judicial Dept: Grand Turk; tel. 946-2114; fax 946-2720.

Chief Justice: DAVID HALLCHURCH.

Magistrate: DEREK REDMAN.

Attorney-General's Chambers: Grand Turk; tel. 946-2096; fax 946-2588; e-mail attorney-general@tciway.tc.

Religion

CHRISTIANITY

The Anglican Communion

Within the Church in the Province of the West Indies, the territory forms part of the diocese of Nassau and the Bahamas. The Bishop is resident in Nassau. According to census results, there were 1,465 adherents in 1990.

Anglican Church: St Mary's Church, Front St, Grand Turk; tel. 946-2289.

The Roman Catholic Church

The Bishop of Nassau, Bahamas (suffragan to the archdiocese of Kingston in Jamaica), has jurisdiction in the Turks and Caicos Islands, as Superior of the Mission to the Territory (founded in June 1984).

Roman Catholic Mission: Leeward Highway, POB 340, Providenciales; e-mail rcmission@tciway.tc; churches on Grand Turk and on Providenciales; 132 adherents in 1990 (according to census results); Superior: Archbishop of Newark.

Protestant Churches

The Baptist, Jehovah's Witness, Methodist, Church of God and Seventh-day Adventist faiths are represented on the islands.

Baptist Union of the Turks and Caicos Islands: South Caicos; tel. 946-3220; 3,153 adherents in 1990 (according to census results).

Jehovah's Witnesses: Kingdom Hall, Intersection of Turtle Cove and Bridge Rd, POB 400, Providenciales; tel. 941-5583.

Methodist Church: The Ridge, Grand Turk; tel. 946-2115; 1,238 adherents in 1990 (according to census results).

New Testament Church of God: Orea Alley, Grand Turk; tel. 946-2175.

The Press

Free Press: Caribbean Place, POB 179, Providenciales; tel. 946-5615; fax 941-3402; e-mail frepress@tciway.tc; internet www.turksandcaicos.tc/FreePress; f. 1991; weekly; Man. Editor YASMIN BLUES; Editor FAITH HAMER; circ. 2,000.

Times of the Islands Magazine: Caribbean Place, POB 234, Providenciales; tel. 946-4788; fax 941-3402; e-mail timespub@tciway.tc; internet www.timespub.tc; f. 1988; quarterly; circ. 7,000.

Turks and Caicos Times: Southern Shores Bldg, Providenciales; tel. 946-4257; e-mail times@tciway.tc.

Turks and Caicos Weekly News: POB 52, Cheshire House, Providenciales; tel. 946-4664; fax 946-4661; e-mail tcnews@tcway.tc.

Where, When, How: POB 192, Providenciales; tel. 946-4815; fax 941-3497; e-mail wwh@provo.net; internet www.wherewhenhow.com; monthly; travel magazine.

Broadcasting and Communications

TELECOMMUNICATIONS

Cable and Wireless (Turks and Caicos) Ltd: Grand Turk; tel. 946-2222; fax 946-2497; e-mail cwtci@tciway.tc; internet www.cw.tc; f. 1973.

Radio

Caribbean Christian Radio: POB 200, Grand Turk; tel. 946-1095; fax 946-1095; operates under licence from West Indies Broadcasting; Gen. Man. REO STUBBS; Station Man. BUDDY TUCKER; CEO JERRY KIEFER.

Radio Providenciales: Leeward Highway, POB 32, Providenciales; tel. 946-4496; fax 946-4108; commercial.

Radio Turks and Caicos (RTC): POB 69, Grand Turk; tel. 946-1705; fax 946-1120; govt-owned; commercial; broadcasts 105 hrs weekly; Man. LYNETTE SMITH.

Radio Visión Cristiana Internacional: North End, South Caicos; tel. 946-6601; fax 946-6600; commercial; Man. WENDELL SEYMOUR.

Victory in Christ (VIC) Radio: Butterfield Sq., POB 32, Providenciales; tel. 946-4496; religious.

WIV FM Radio: POB 108, Providenciales.

WPRT Radio: Leeward Highway, POB 262, Providenciales; tel. 946-4267; commercial; Station Man. PETER STUBBS.

Television

Television programmes are available from a cabled network, and broadcasts from the Bahamas can be received in the islands.

Turks and Caicos Television: Pond St, POB 80, Grand Turk; tel. 946-1530; fax 946-2896.

WIV Cable TV: Tower Raza, Leeward Highway, POB 679, Providenciales; tel. 946-4273; fax 946-4790.

Finance

Financial Services Commission (FSC): POB 173, Post Office Bldg, Front St, Grand Turk; tel. 946-2791; fax 946-2821; e-mail fsc@tciway.tc; regulates local and 'offshore' financial services sector; Supt PAUL DE WEERD.

BANKING

Barclays Bank (International) PLC (United Kingdom): Cockburn Town, POB 61, Grand Turk; tel. 946-2831; fax 946-2695; e-mail barclays@tciway.tc; Man. PAUL WILLIAMS; 3 brs.

Bordier International Bank and Trust Ltd: Caribbean Place, Leeward Highway, POB 5, Providenciales; tel. 946-4535; fax 946-4540; e-mail bibt@tciway.tc; Man. ELISE HARTSHORN.

First National Bank Ltd: The Arch Plaza, Leeward Highway, POB 58, Providenciales; tel. 946-4060; fax 946-4061; e-mail fnb@tciway.tc.

Scotiabank (Canada): Harbour House, Front St, Cockburn Town, POB 132, Grand Turk; tel. 946-2506; fax 946-2667; Man. C. COAL-BROOKE; br. on Providenciales.

Turks and Caicos Banking Co Ltd: Duke St North, POB 123, Grand Turk; tel. 946-2368; fax 946-2365; f. 1980; cap. $2.7m., dep. $9.7m.; Man. Dir ANTON FAESSLER.

INSURANCE

Turks and Caicos Islands National Insurance Board: Church Folly, POB 250, Grand Turk; tel. 946-1045; fax 946-1362; e-mail nib@tciway.tc; 3 brs.

Several foreign (mainly US and British) companies have offices in the Turks and Caicos islands. Some 1,491 insurance companies were registered at the end of 1993.

Financial Association

United Belongers in Financial Services: Grand Turk; f. 2000.

Trade and Industry

GOVERNMENT AGENCY

Financial Services Commission (FSC): (see Finance, above).

General Trading Company (Turks and Caicos) Ltd: PMBI, Cockburn Town, Grand Turk; tel. 946-2464; fax 946-2799; shipping agents, importers, air freight handlers; wholesale distributor of petroleum products, wines and spirits.

Turks Islands Importers Ltd (TIMCO): Front St, POB 72, Grand Turk; tel. 946-2480; fax 946-2481; f. 1952; agents for Lloyds of London, importers and distributors of food, beer, liquor, building materials, hardware and appliances; Dir H. E. MAGNUS.

DEVELOPMENT ORGANIZATION

Turks and Caicos Islands Investment Agency (TC Invest): Hibiscus Sq., Pond St, POB 105, Grand Turk; tel. 946-2058; fax 946-1464; e-mail TCInvest@caribsurf.com; internet www.tcinvest.tc; f. 1974 as Development Board of the Turks and Caicos Islands; statutory body; development finance for private sector; promotion and management of internal investment; Chair. LILLIAN MISICK; Pres. and CEO COLIN R. HEARTWELL.

CHAMBER OF COMMERCE

Chamber of Commerce: POB 148, Grand Turk; tel. 946-2324; fax 946-2714; Pres. GLENN CLARKE; also on Providenciales; tel. 946-4650; fax 946-4565.

UTILITIES

Electricity and Gas

Atlantic Equipment and Power (Turks and Caicos) Ltd: New Airport Rd, Airport Area, South Caicos; tel. 946-3201; fax 946-3202.

North Caicos Power Co: Bottle Creek, North Caicos; tel. 946-7234.

PPC Ltd: Town Centre Mall, POB 132, Providenciales; tel. 946-4313; fax 946-4532.

Turks and Caicos Utilities Ltd: Pond St, POB 80, Grand Turk; tel. 946-2402; fax 946-2896.

Water

Provo Water Co: Grace Bay Rd, POB 124, Providenciales; tel. 946-5202; fax 946-5204.

Turks and Caicos Water Co: Provo Golf Clubhouse, Grace Bay Rd, POB 124, Providenciales; tel. 946-5126; fax 946-5127.

TRADE UNION

Turks and Caicos Workers' Labour Trade Union: Grand Turk; all professions; f. 2000; Leader CALVIN HANDFIELD.

Transport

ROADS

There are 121 km (75 miles) of road in the islands, of which 24 km (15 miles), on Grand Turk, South Caicos and Providenciales, are tarmac.

SHIPPING

There are regular freight services from Miami, Florida. The main sea ports are Grand Turk, Providenciales, Salt Cay and Cockburn

Harbour on South Caicos. Harbour facilities on South Caicos and Providenciales are being improved, and there are plans for a new port on North Caicos. Plans are also under way for a deep-water port on East Caicos for cruise liners and a transhipment port on South Caicos.

Cargo Express Shipping Service Ltd: Butterfield Sq., POB 645, Providenciales; tel. 941-3865; fax 941-5062; Man. GRANTLEY HINDS.

Ocean Research and Recovery Ltd: The Mariner, POB 64, Providenciales; tel. 946-4109; fax 946-4939.

Seacair Ltd: Churchill Bldg, POB 170, Grand Turk; tel. 946-2591; fax 946-2226.

Seacorp Shipping Ltd: Grand Turk; tel. 946-2226; fax 946-2226.

Southeast and Caribbean Shipping Co Ltd: Churchill Bldg, Front St, POB 1, Grand Turk; tel. 946-2355.

Tropical Shipping: Butterfield Sq., Providenciales; tel. 941-3865; fax 941-5062; e-mail vgonzalez@tropical.com; internet www.tropical.com; Man. VINCE GONZALEZ.

Turks and Caicos National Shipping and Development Co Ltd: Front St, POB 103, Grand Turk; tel. 946-2194.

CIVIL AVIATION

There are international airfields on Grand Turk, South Caicos, North Caicos and Providenciales, the last being the most important; there are also landing strips on Middle Caicos, Pine Cay, Parrot Cay and Salt Cay.

Department of Civil Aviation: Off Waterloo Rd, Grand Turk; tel. 946-2801; fax 946-1185; e-mail gtws@tciway.tc.

Caicos Caribbean Airlines: South Caicos; tel. 946-3283; fax 946-3377; freight to Miami (USA).

Cairsea Services Ltd: Old Airport Rd, POB 138, Providenciales; tel. 946-4205; fax 946-4504; internet www.cairsea.com.

Flamingo Air Services Ltd: Grand Turk Int. Airport, POB 162, Grand Turk; tel. 946-2109; fax 946-2188.

Inter-Island Airways: POB 191, Providenciales; tel. 946-4181.

Sky King: POB 398, Providenciales; tel. 941-5170.

Turks Air Ltd: Providenciales; tel. 946-4504; fax 946-4504; (Head Office: 7294 NW 41st, Miami, Florida, 33166, USA; tel. 593-8847; fax 871-1622); twice-weekly cargo service to and from Miami; Grand Turk Local Agent CRIS NEWTON.

Turks and Caicos Airways Ltd: Providenciales International Airport, POB 114, Providenciales; tel. 946-4255; fax 946-4438; f. 1976 as Air Turks and Caicos, privatized 1983; scheduled daily inter-island service to each of the Caicos Islands, charter flights; Dir-Gen. C. MOSER.

Tourism

The islands' main tourist attractions are the numerous unspoilt beaches, and the opportunities for diving. Salt Cay has been designated a World Heritage site by UNESCO. Hotel accommodation is available on Grand Turk, Salt Cay, South Caicos, Pine Cay and Providenciales. In 1999 there were 120,898 tourist arrivals (an increase of some 9%, compared with the previous year). In 1997 69.3% of tourists were from the USA. In 1995 there were 1,561 hotel rooms (some 80% of which were on Providenciales). Revenue from the sector in 1997 totalled US $118m.

Turks and Caicos Islands Tourist Board: Front St, POB 128, Grand Turk; tel. 946-2321; fax 946-2733; e-mail tcitourism@tciway.tc; internet www.turksandcaicostourism.com; f. 1970; Dir JOHN SKIPPINGS.

Turks and Caicos Hotel Association: Third Turtle Inn, Providenciales; tel. 946-4230.

Education

Primary education, beginning at seven years of age and lasting seven years, is compulsory, and is provided free of charge in government schools. Secondary education, from the age of 14, lasts for five years, and is also free. In 1997 there were 14 primary schools, and in 1990 one private secondary school and four government secondary schools. In 1997 the Caribbean Development Bank approved a loan of just under US $4m. to fund the establishment of a permanent campus for the Turks and Caicos Community College. Expenditure on education in 1985 was US $1.4m., or 11.2% of total government spending.

UNITED STATES VIRGIN ISLANDS

Area: 347.1 sq km (134 sq miles): St Croix 215 sq km (83 sq miles), St Thomas 80.3 sq km (31 sq miles), St John 51.8 sq km (20 sq miles); there are about 50 smaller islands, mostly uninhabited.

Population (estimate, 2000): 121,000.

Capital: Charlotte Amalie (population 12,331 in 1990), on St Thomas.

Language: English (official); Spanish and Creole are also used.

Religion: Predominantly Christian (mainly Protestant).

Climate: Tropical, tempered by trade winds; average temperature 26°C (79°F); low rainfall.

Time: GMT –4 hours.

Public Holidays: 2002: 1 January (New Year's Day), 6 January (Three Kings' Day), 21 January (Martin Luther King, Jr Day), 18 February (Presidents' Day), 1 April (for Transfer Day), 28 March–1 April (Easter), 27 May (Memorial Day), 20 June (Organic Act Day), 3 July (Danish West Indies Emancipation Day), 4 July (US Independence Day), 23 July (Hurricane Supplication Day), 2 September (Labor Day), 11 November (Veterans' Day), 28 November (US Thanksgiving Day), 25–26 December (Christmas). **2003:** 1 January (New Year's Day), 6 January (Three Kings' Day), 20 January (Martin Luther King, Jr Day), 17 February (Presidents' Day), 31 March (Transfer Day), 17–21 April (Easter), 26 May (Memorial Day), 20 June (Organic Act Day), 3 July (Danish West Indies Emancipation Day), 4 July (US Independence Day), 23 July (Hurricane Supplication Day), 1 September (Labor Day), 11 November (Veterans' Day), 27 November (US Thanksgiving Day), 25–26 December (Christmas).

Currency: US dollar; US $100 = £69.84 = €112.66 (30 April 2001).

Weights and Measures: US imperial.

History

The Virgin Islands constitute a US external territory. Executive power is vested in the popularly-elected Governor and there is a Legislature of 15 Senators; the islands send a non-voting delegate to the US House of Representatives.

Originally inhabited by Carib and Arawak Indians (Amerindians), the islands came under Danish control. In 1917 they were sold by Denmark to the USA for US $25m. The islands were granted a measure of self-government in 1954, but subsequent attempts to give them greater autonomy were all rejected by popular referendum. The Democratic Party held a majority in the Legislature for many years, although a member of the Independent Citizens' Movement (which split from the Democratic Party), Cyril E. King, was elected Governor in 1974. On King's death in 1978, Juan Luis became Governor, being elected in his own right in 1982. The governorship returned to the Democratic Party with the election of Alexander Farrelly in 1986; he was re-elected in 1990. A further referendum on the islands' status, postponed following the disruption caused by 'Hurricane Hugo', eventually took place in October 1993; however, the result was invalidated by the low turn-out: only 27.4% of voters took part (50% participation was required for the referendum to be valid). In 1994 an Independent, Dr Roy Schneider, was elected to succeed Farrelly as Governor. The governorship was regained by a Democrat, Charles Turnbull, in the 1998 elections was re-elected to the post in 2000. Following the presentation of legislation to create a constitutional convention to the US Virgin Islands Senate, in May 2000 a committee of the US House of Representatives was considering a range of measures to enlarge the scope of local self-government in the Territory.

In January 2001 the acting Commissioner of Health, Lucien Moolennar, was charged with the theft of more than US $102,000 from the Government over a five-year period. He immediately resigned his post.

Economy

The islands are heavily dependent on links to the US mainland; more than 90% of trade is conducted with Puerto Rico and the USA. St Croix has one of the world's largest petroleum refineries (with a capacity of 550,000 barrels per day), although it was operating at reduced levels of throughput from 1981. An alumina processing plant on St Croix, closed in 1994, was acquired by the US company, Alcoa, in 1995 and re-opened briefly before closing again in 2001. Rum is an important product, earning money from refunded US excise duty at the rate of about US $40m. per year, but considered likely to suffer from increasing competition from Mexico as the NAFTA internal market becomes established. Some fruit and food crops (notably sorghum) are also grown. However, the major source of income and employment is tourism, with the emphasis on the visiting cruise-ship business and the sale of duty-free products to visitors from the US mainland. The sector is estimated to account for more than 60% of GDP, although storm damage can cause visitor numbers to fluctuate, as in 1995 when 'Hurricane Marilyn' saw tourist arrivals decrease by 9.7% on the previous year. In 1989 'Hurricane Hugo' was estimated to have caused US $1,000m.-worth of property damage, although subsequent rebuilding revitalized employment in the construction industry. Serious damage was caused again in the late 1990s. The budget deficit, which peaked at US $300m. in 1999, was reduced to nearer $200m. in 2001 following the introduction of a Five-Year Strategic and Financial Operating Plan to reduce government expenditure and enhance the effectiveness of procedures for revenue collection.

Statistical Survey

Sources (unless otherwise stated): Office of Public Relations, Office of the Governor, Charlotte Amalie, VI 00802; tel. (340) 774-0294; fax (340) 774-4988; Bureau of Economic Research, Department of Economic Development and Agriculture, POB 6400, Charlotte Amalie, VI 00804; tel. (340) 774-8784.

AREA AND POPULATION

Area: 347.1 sq km (134 sq miles): St Croix 215 sq km (83 sq miles); St Thomas 80.3 sq km (31 sq miles); St John 51.8 sq km (20 sq miles).

Population: 101,809 (males 49,210; females 52,599) at census of 1 April 1990; 121,000 in 2000 (estimate). *Distribution by island* (1990 census): St Croix 50,139, St Thomas 48,166, St John 3,504.

Capital: Charlotte Amalie (population 12,331 at 1990 census).

Births and Deaths (1998): Registered live births 1,800; Registered deaths 622. Source: US Census Bureau.

Economically Active Population (persons aged 16 years and over, 1990 census): Agriculture, hunting, forestry and fishing 576; Mining and quarrying 30; Manufacturing 2,916; Electricity, gas and water 731; Construction 5,712; Trade, restaurants and hotels 10,343; Transport, storage and communications 3,715; Financing, insurance, real estate and business services 3,631; Community, social and personal services 12,883; Activities not adequately defined 6,906; Total labour force 47,443 (males 24,762; females 22,681). Source: ILO, *Yearbook of Labour Statistics*.

1995 (excl. armed forces): Total employed 45,070; Unemployed 2,740; Total labour force 47,810.

AGRICULTURE, ETC

Livestock (estimates, 2000): Cattle 8,000; Sheep 3,200; Pigs 2,600; Goats 4,000; Chickens 35,000. Source: FAO.

Fishing (FAO estimates, metric tons, live weight): Total catch 900 in 1996; 930 in 1997; 910 in 1998. Source: FAO, *Yearbook of Fishery Statistics*.

INDUSTRY

Production ('000 metric tons, unless otherwise indicated, 1996): Jet fuels 1,585; Motor spirit (petrol) 2,310; Kerosene 62; Gas-diesel (distillate fuel) oil 2,885; Residual fuel oils 3,812; Liquefied petroleum gas 142; Electric energy 1,075 million kWh (net production). Source: UN, *Industrial Commodity Statistics Yearbook*.

FINANCE

Currency and Exchange Rates: 100 cents = 1 United States dollar (US $). *Sterling and Euro Equivalents* (30 April 2001): £1 sterling = US $1.4318; €1 = 88.76 US cents; $100 = £69.84 = €112.66.

Budget (projection US $ million, year ending 30 September 2001): Total revenue 522.4 Total expenditure 503.9.

EXTERNAL TRADE

Total (US $ million): *Imports*: 2,625.6 in 1993; 3,108.4 in 1994; 3,200.3 in 1995. *Exports*: 2,191.4 in 1993; 2,847.7 in 1994; 3,026.3 in 1995. The main import is crude petroleum ($1,802.1m. in 1993), while the principal exports are refined petroleum products.

Trade with the USA (US $ million): *Imports*: 976.5 in 1993; 1,021.4 in 1994; 1,045.0 in 1995. *Exports*: 2,014.7 in 1993; 2,666.9 in 1994; 2,805.8 in 1995.

TRANSPORT

Road Traffic (registered motor vehicles, 1993): 63,332.

Shipping (2000): Cruise-ship arrivals 1,014; Passenger arrivals 1,768,402.

Civil Aviation (2000): Visitor arrivals 629,760.

TOURISM

Tourist Arrivals (tourists staying in hotels): 229,237 in 1996; 386,740 in 1997; 480,064 in 1998.

Tourism Receipts (US $ million): 921 in 1998.

COMMUNICATIONS MEDIA

Radio Receivers (1997): 107,000 in use.

Television Receivers (1997): 68,000 in use.

Telephones (1997): 62,000 main lines in use.

Mobile Cellular Telephones (1992): 2,000 subscribers.

Daily Newspapers (1996): 3 titles (combined average circulation 42,000 copies).

Non-daily Newspapers (estimates, 1988): 2 titles (combined average circulation 4,000 copies).

Sources: UNESCO, *Statistical Yearbook;* UN, *Statistical Yearbook.*

EDUCATION

Pre-primary (1992/93): 62 schools; 121 teachers; 2,606 students.

Elementary (1992/93): 62 schools; 790 teachers (public schools only); 14,544 students.

Secondary: 541 teachers (public schools only, 1990); 12,502 students (1992/93).

Higher education (1992/93): 266 teachers; 2,924 students.

In 1990 there were also 44 private schools, with 7,016 students. In 2000 the University of the Virgin Islands had an enrolment of 2,610 students. In 1995 there were 28,749 students enrolled in primary and secondary schools.

Source: mainly UNESCO, *Statistical Yearbook.*

Directory
The Constitution

The Government of the US Virgin Islands is organized under the provisions of the Organic Act of the Virgin Islands, passed by the Congress of the United States in 1936 and revised in 1954. Subsequent amendments provided for the popular election of the Governor and Lieutenant-Governor of the Virgin Islands in 1970, and, since 1973, for representation in the US House of Representatives by a popularly-elected Delegate. The Delegate has voting powers only in committees of the House. Executive power is vested in the Governor, who is elected for a term of four years by universal adult suffrage and who appoints, with the advice and consent of the Legislature, the heads of the executive departments. The Governor may also appoint administrative assistants as his representatives on St John and St Croix. Legislative power is vested in the Legislature of the Virgin Islands, a unicameral body comprising 15 Senators, elected for a two-year term by popular vote. Legislation is subject to the approval of the Governor, whose veto can be overridden by a two-thirds vote of the Legislature. All residents of the islands, who are citizens of the United States and at least 18 years of age, have the right to vote in local elections but not in national elections. In 1976 the Virgin Islands were granted the right to draft their own constitution, subject to the approval of the US President and Congress. A Constitution permitting a degree of autonomy was drawn up in 1978 and gained the necessary approval, but was then rejected by the people of the Virgin Islands in a referendum in March 1979. A fourth draft, providing for greater autonomy than the 1978 draft, was rejected in a referendum in November 1981.

The Government
EXECUTIVE
(August 2001)

Governor: CHARLES WESLEY TURNBULL.

Lieutenant-Governor: GERARD AMWUR 'LUZ' JAMES, II.

Commissioner of Agriculture: HENRY SCHUSTER, Jr.

Commissioner of Education: RUBY SIMMONDS.

Commissioner of Finance: BERNICE TURNBULL.

Commissioner of Health: MAVIS MATTHEW (acting).

Commissioner of Housing, Parks and Recreation: IRA M. HOBSON.

Commissioner of Human Services: SEDONIE HALBERT.

Commissioner of Labor: CECIL R. BENJAMIN (acting).

Commissioner of Licensing and Consumer Affairs: ANDREW RUTNIK.

Commissioner of Planning and Natural Resources: DEAN C. PLASKETT.

Commissioner of Police: FRANZ CHRISTIAN Sr.

Commissioner of Property and Procurement: MARC BIGGS.

Commissioner of Public Works: WAYNE D. CALLWOOD (acting).

Commissioner of Tourism: PAMELA C. RICHARDS (acting).

Attorney-General: IVER A. STRIDIRON.

US Virgin Islands Delegate to the US Congress: DONNA M. CHRISTIAN CHRISTENSEN.

GOVERNMENT OFFICES

Office of the Governor: Government House, 21–22 Kongens Gade, Charlotte Amalie, VI 00802; tel. (340) 774-0001; fax (340) 774-1361.

Office of the Lieutenant-Governor: Government Hill, 18 Kongens Gade, Charlotte Amalie, VI 00802; tel. (340) 774-2991; fax (340) 774-6953.

Department of Agriculture: Estate Lower Love, Kingshill, St Croix, VI 00850; tel. (340) 774-0997; fax (340) 774-5182; e-mail agriculture@usvi,org.

Department of Economic Development: 81 AB Kronprindsens Gade, POB 6400, Charlotte Amalie, VI 00801; tel. (340) 774-8784; fax (340) 774-4390.

Department of Education: 44–46 Kongens Gade, Charlotte Amalie, VI 00802; tel. (340) 774-0100; fax (340) 779-7153; e-mail education@usvi.org.

Department of Finance: GERS Bldg, 2nd Floor, 76 Kronprindsens Gade, Charlotte Amalie, VI 00802; tel. (340) 774-4750; fax (340) 776-4028.

Department of Health: 48 Sugar Estate, Charlotte Amalie, VI 00802; tel. (340) 774-0117; fax (340) 777-4001.

Department of Housing, Parks and Recreation: Property & Procurement Bldg No. 1, Sub Base, 2nd Floor, Rm 206, Charlotte Amalie, VI 00802; tel. (340) 774-0255; fax (340) 774-4600.

Department of Human Services: Knud Hansen Complex Bldg A 1303, Hospital Ground, Charlotte Amalie, VI 00802; tel. (340) 774-0930; fax (340) 774-3466; e-mail humanservices@usvi.org.

Department of Justice: GERS Bldg, 2nd Floor, 48B–50C Kronprindsens Gade, Charlotte Amalie, VI 00802; tel. (340) 774-5666; fax (340) 774-9710; e-mail justice@usvi.org.

Department of Labor: 21–31 Hospital St, Christiansted, St Croix, VI 00802; tel. (340) 774-3700; fax (340) 776-0529; e-mail labor@usvi.org.

Department of Licensing and Consumer Affairs: Property & Procurement Bldg No. 1, Sub Base, RM 205, Charlotte Amalie, VI 00802; tel. (340) 774-3130; fax (340) 776-0675.

Department of Planning and Natural Resources: 396-1 Anna's Retreat–Foster Bldg, Charlotte Amalie, VI 00802; tel. (340) 774-3320; fax (340) 775-5706.

Department of Police: 8172 Sub Base, St Thomas, VI 00802; tel. (340) 774-2211; fax (340) 778-2211; e-mail police@usvi.org.

Department of Property and Procurement: Property & Procurement Bldg No. 1, Sub Base, 3rd Floor, Charlotte Amalie, VI 00802; tel. (340) 774-0828; fax (340) 774-9704; e-mail pnp@usvi.org.

Department of Public Works: No. 8 Sub Base, Charlotte Amalie, VI 00802; tel. (340) 773-1290; fax (340) 774-5869; e-mail publicworks@usvi.org.

Department of Tourism: 78-123 Estate Contant, POB 6400, Charlotte Amalie, VI 00802; tel. (340) 774-8784; fax (340) 774-4390; e-mail tourism@usvi.org; internet www.usvi.org.

Legislature

LEGISLATIVE ASSEMBLY

Senate

(15 members)

President of the Senate: ALMANDO LIBURD.

Election, 7 November 2000

Party	Seats
Democrats	6
Independent Citizens Movement	2
Independent	7

Political Organizations

Democratic Party of the Virgin Islands: POB 3739, Charlotte Amalie, VI 00801; tel. (340) 774-3130; affiliated to the Democratic Party in the USA; Chair. MARYLYN A. STAPLETON.

Independent Citizens Movement: Charlotte Amalie, VI 00801; Chair. VIRDIN C. BROWN.

Republican Party of the Virgin Islands: Charlotte Amalie, VI 00801; tel. (340) 776-7660; affiliated to the Republican Party in the USA; Chair. SHERON E. HODGE; Exec. Dir KRIM BALLENTINE.

Judicial System

US Federal District Court of the Virgin Islands: Federal Bldg and US Courthouse, 5500 Veteran's Drive, Charlotte Amalie, VI 00802; tel. (340) 774-0640; jurisdiction in civil, criminal and federal actions; the judges are appointed by the President of the United States with the advice and consent of the Senate.

US Territorial District Court of the Virgin Islands: Alexander A. Farrelly Justice Center, POB 70, Charlotte Amalie, VI 00802; tel. (340) 774-6680; jurisdiction in violations of police and executive regulations, in criminal cases and civil actions involving not more than $200,000, in domestic and juvenile matters concurrently with the US Federal District Court; judges are appointed by the Governor.

Judges: RAYMOND L. FINCH (Chief Judge), THOMAS K. MOORE.

Religion

The population is mainly Christian. The main churches with followings in the islands are the Roman Catholic (with an estimated 30,000 adherents in 1999), Episcopalian, Lutheran, Methodist, Moravian and Seventh-day Adventist. There is also a small Jewish community.

CHRISTIANITY

The Roman Catholic Church

The US Virgin Islands comprise a single diocese, suffragan to the archdiocese of Washington, DC, USA. At 31 December 1999 there were an estimated 30,000 adherents in the territory

Bishop of St Thomas: Most Rev. GEORGE V. MURRY, Bishop's Residence, 68 Kronprindsens Gade, POB 301825, Charlotte Amalie, VI 00803; tel. (340) 774-3166; fax (340) 774-5816; e-mail chancery@islands.vi.

The Anglican Communion

Episcopal Church of the Virgin Islands: Bishop: Rt Rev. THEODORE A. DANIELS, POB 10437, St Thomas. VI 00801; fax (340) 777-8485; e-mail tad@aol.com.

The Press

Pride Magazine: 22A Norre Gade, POB 7908, Charlotte Amalie, VI 00801; tel. (340) 776-4106; f. 1983; monthly; Editor JUDITH WILLIAMS; circ. 4,000.

St Croix Avis: La Grande Princesse, Christiansted, St Croix, VI 00820; tel. (340) 773-2300; f. 1944; morning; independent; Editor RENA BROADHURST-KNIGHT; circ. 10,000.

Tradewinds: POB 1500, Cruz Bay, St John, VI 00831; tel. (340) 776-6496; internet www.tradewinds.vi; f. 1972; fortnightly; Editor THOMAS C. OAT; circ. 2,000.

Virgin Islands Business Journal: 69 Kronprindsens Gade, POB 1208, Charlotte Amalie, VI 00804; tel. (340) 776-2874; fax (340) 774-3636; f. 1986; weekly; independent; Man. Editor LUCY NEILAN GUNTHER; circ. 10,000.

Virgin Islands Daily News: 49 and 52A Estate Thomas, POB 7760, Charlotte Amalie, VI 00801; tel. (340) 774-8772; fax (340) 776-0740; f. 1930; morning; CEO RON DILLMAN; Publr and Editor ARIEL MELCHIOR, Jr; circ. 17,000.

Broadcasting and Communications

TELECOMMUNICATIONS

Virgin Islands Telephone Corporation (Vitelco): POB 1141, Charlotte Amalie, VI 00801; tel. (340) 774-5555; owned by Atlantic Tele-Network; provides telephone services throughout the islands.

RADIO

WAVI—FM: POB 25016, Gallows Bay Station, St Croix, VI 00824; tel. (340) 773-3693; commercial; Gen. Man. DOUG HARRIS.

WGOD: Crown Mountain, POB 5012, Charlotte Amalie, VI 00803; tel. (340) 774-4498; fax (340) 776-0877; commercial; Gen. Man. PETER RICHARDSON.

WJKC—FM: 5020 Anchor Way, POB 25680, Christiansted, St Croix, VI 00824-1680; tel. (340) 773-0995; e-mail jkc95@aol.com; internet www.wjkcisle95.com; commercial; Gen. Man. JONATHAN COHEN.

WSTA: Sub Base 121, POB 1340, St Thomas, VI 00804; tel. (340) 774-1340; fax (340) 776-1316; e-mail addie@wsta.com; internet www.wsta.com; commercial; Gen. Man. ATHNIEL C. OTTLEY.

WVWI (Knight Communications): 13 Crown Bay Fill, POB 305678, Charlotte Amalie, VI 00803-5678; tel. (340) 776-1000; fax (340) 776-5357; e-mail knightvi@viaccess.net; f. 1962; commercial; Pres. and Gen. Man. RANDOLPH H. KNIGHT.

TELEVISION

Caribbean Communications Corporation: One Beltjen Place, Charlotte Amalie, VI 00802-6735; tel. (340) 776-2150; fax (340) 774-5029; f. 1966; cable service, 72 channels; Gen. Man. ANDREA L. MARTIN.

St Croix, VI Cable TV: Heron Commercial Park, POB 5968, Sunny Isle, St Croix, VI 00823; f. 1981; 32 channels; Gen. Man. JACK WHITE.

WSVI—TV: Sunny Isle, POB 8ABC, Christiansted, St Croix, VI 00823; tel. (340) 778-5008; fax (340) 778-5011; f. 1965; one channel and one translator; Gen. Man. BARAKAT SALEH.

WTJX—TV (Public Television Service): Barbel Plaza, POB 7879, Charlotte Amalie, VI 00801; tel. (340) 774-6255; fax (340) 774-7092; e-mail wtjx@usvi.net; one channel; Gen. Man. CALVIN BASTIAN.

Finance

BANKING

Banco Popular de Puerto Rico: Church St, Christiansted, St Croix, VI 00820; tel. (340) 773-0077; 6 brs.

Bank of Nova Scotia (Canada): 214C Altona and Welgunst, POB 420, Charlotte Amalie, VI 00804; tel. (340) 774-0037; fax (340) 776-5997; Man. R. HAINES; 9 brs.

Barclays Bank PLC (UK): POB 6880, Charlotte Amalie, VI 00804; tel. (340) 776-5080; fax (340) 776-5922; Man. JOHN INGRAM.

Chase Manhattan Bank, NA (USA): Waterfront, Charlotte Amalie, VI 00801; tel. (340) 776-2222; Gen. Man. WARREN BEER; brs in St Croix and St John.

Citibank, NA (USA): Veterans Drive, Charlotte Amalie, VI 00801; tel. (340) 774-4800; Vice-Pres. ALBERT MALAVE.

First Federal Savings Bank: Veterans Drive, Charlotte Amalie, VI; tel. (340) 774-2022; fax (340) 776-1313; Man. ALFRED LESLIE; br. in St Croix.

First Virgin Islands Federal Savings Bank: GERS Bldg, 50 Kronprindsens Gade, Charlotte Amalie, VI 00803-5468; tel. (340) 776-9494; fax (340) 776-3447; Sr Vice-Pres. JAMES E. CRITES.

Virgin Islands Community Bank: 12–13 King St, Christiansted, St Croix, VI 00820; tel. (340) 773-0440; fax (340) 773-4028; Pres. and CEO MICHAEL J. DOW.

INSURANCE

A number of mainland US companies have agencies in the Virgin Islands.

Trade and Industry

GOVERNMENT AGENCY

US Virgin Islands Industrial Development Commission: Government Development Bank, Bldg, 1050 Norre Gade, POB 305038, St Thomas; VI 00803, tel. (340) 774-8104; e-mail idc@usvi.org; govt agency; offices in St Thomas and St Croix.

CHAMBERS OF COMMERCE

St Croix Chamber of Commerce: POB 4369, Kings Hill, St Croix, VI 00851; tel. and fax (340) 773-1435; f. 1925; 450 mems; Exec. Dir RACHEL HAINES.

St Thomas–St John Chamber of Commerce: 6–7 Dronning Gade, POB 324, Charlotte Amalie, VI 00804; tel. (340) 776-0010; fax (340) 776-8630; Pres. JOHN DE JONGH, Jr; Exec. Dir JOSEPH S. AUBAIN.

UTILITIES

Electricity

Virgin Islands Energy Office: Old Custom House, 200 Strand St, Frederiksted, St Croix, VI 00840; tel. (340) 722-2616; fax (340) 722-2133; Dir ALICIA BARNES-JAMES.

Water

Virgin Islands Water and Power Authority: POB 1450, Charlotte Amalie, VI 00804; tel. (340) 774-3552; fax (340) 774-3422; f. 1964; public corpn; manufactures and distributes electric power and desalinated sea water; Exec. Dir RAYMOND GEORGE.

Transport

ROADS

The islands' road network totals approximately 855.5 km (531.6 miles).

SHIPPING

The US Virgin Islands are a popular port of call for cruise ships. The bulk of cargo traffic is handled at a container port on St Croix. A ferry service provides frequent daily connections between St Thomas and St John and between St Thomas and Tortola (British Virgin Islands).

Virgin Islands Port Authority: POB 301707, Charlotte Amalie, VI 00803; tel. (340) 774-1629; fax (340) 774-0025; also at POB 1134, Christiansted, St Croix, VI 00821; tel. (340) 778-1012; fax (340) 778-1033; f. 1968; semi-autonomous govt agency; maintains, operates and develops marine and airport facilities; Exec. Dir GORDON A. FINCH.

CIVIL AVIATION

There are airports on St Thomas and St Croix, and an airfield on St John. Seaplane services link the three islands. The runways at Cyril E. King Airport, St Thomas, and Alexander Hamilton Airport, St Croix, can accommodate intercontinental flights.

Tourism

The islands have a well developed tourist infrastructure, offering excellent facilities for fishing, yachting and other aquatic sports. A National Park covers about two-thirds of St John. There were 5,148 hotel rooms in 1995, when 1,733,300 tourists (including 1,171,300 cruise-ship passengers) visited the islands. Tourist expenditure in 1998 totalled US $921m.

Hotel Association of St Croix: POB 3869, Christiansted, St Croix, VI 00820; tel. (340) 773-7117.

Hotel Association of St Thomas–St John: POB 2300, Charlotte Amalie, VI 00803; tel. (340) 774-6835.

Education

Education is compulsory up to the age of 16 years. It generally comprises eight years at primary school and four years at secondary school. In 1990 there were 28,691 elementary and secondary students at public and private schools, and 1,762 public school teachers. The University of the Virgin Islands, with campuses on St Thomas and St Croix, had 2,610 students in 2000.

URUGUAY

Area: 176,215 sq km (68,037 sq miles).

Population (official estimate at mid-1999): 3,313,000.

Capital: Montevideo (population 1,251,647 at census of 23 October 1985).

Language: Spanish.

Religion: Predominantly Christianity (Roman Catholicism is the largest denomination).

Climate: Temperate; average winter temperature of 15°C (59°F), average summer temperature of 21°–28°C (70°–82°F); average annual rainfall of 1,200 mm.

Time: GMT –3 hours.

Public Holidays

2002: 1 January (New Year's Day), 6 January (Epiphany), 29 March (Good Friday), 22 April (for Landing of the 33 Patriots), 1 May (Labour Day), 20 May (for Battle of Las Piedras), 17 June (for Birth of Gen. Artigas), 18 July (Constitution Day), 25 August (National Independence Day), 14 October (for Discovery of America), 4 November (for All Souls' Day), 9 December (for Blessing of the Waters), 25 December (Christmas).

2003: 1 January (New Year's Day), 6 January (Epiphany), 18 April (Good Friday), 21 April (for Landing of the 33 Patriots), 1 May (Labour Day), 19 May (for Battle of Las Piedras), 23 June (for Birth of Gen. Artigas), 18 July (Constitution Day), 25 August (National Independence Day), 13 October (for Discovery of America), 3 November (for All Souls' Day), 8 December (Blessing of the Waters), 25 December (Christmas).

Note: Many businesses close during Carnival week (11 February–15 February 2002 and 3 March–7 March 2003) and Holy Week (including Good Friday, 25–29 March 2002 and 14–18 April 2003).

Currency: Peso uruguayo; 1,000 pesos uruguayos = £53.97 = US $77.28 = €87.07 (30 April 2001).

Weights and Measures: The metric system is in force.

Basic Economic Indicators

	1998	1999	2000
Gross domestic product (million pesos* at 1983 prices)	299	291	287
GDP per head (pesos* at 1983 prices)	91.0	88.1	86.3
GDP (million pesos* at current prices)	234,267	237,143	242,636
GDP per head (pesos* at 1983 prices)	71.3	71.8	73.1
Annual growth of real GDP (%)	4.5	–2.7	–1.4
Annual growth of real GDP per head (%)	3.9	–3.2	–2.0
Government budget (million pesos* at current prices):			
Revenue	70,664	n.a.	n.a.
Expenditure	72,673	n.a.	n.a.
Consumer price index (annual average; base: December 1995 = 100)	170.4	180.0	188.6
Rate of inflation (annual average, %)	10.8	5.7	4.8
Foreign exchange reserves (US $ million at 31 December)	2,051	2,031	2,400
Imports c.i.f. (US $ million)	3,811	3,357	3,466
Exports f.o.b. (US $ million)	2,771	2,237	2,295
Balance of payments (current account, US $ million)	–475.5	–605.0	n.a.

* Figures are in terms of the peso uruguayo, introduced on 1 March 1993 and equivalent to 1,000 former new pesos.

Gross national product per head measured at purchasing power parity (PPP) (US dollars, converted by the PPP exchange rate, 1999): 8,750.

Economically active population (estimate, mid-1998): 1,472,000.

Unemployment (persons over 14 years, urban only, November 1999): 11.3%.

Total foreign debt (1999): US $7,447m.

Infant mortality rate (per 1,000 live births, 1999): 13.

Life expectancy (years at birth, 1999): 75.8 (males 72; females 79).

Adult population with HIV/AIDS (15–49 years, 1999): 0.33%.

School enrolment ratio (6–17 years, 1996): 97%.

Adult literacy rate (15 years and over, 2000): 97.8% (male 97.4; female 98.2).

Energy consumption per head (kg of oil equivalent, 1998): 910.

Carbon dioxide emissions (per head, metric tons, 1998): 1.8.

Passenger cars in use (estimate, per 1,000 of population, 1996): 169.3.

Television receivers in use (per 1,000 of population, 1997): 239.

Personal computers in use (per 1,000 of population, 1999): 99.6.

History

HELEN SCHOOLEY

During the early 20th century Uruguay acquired a reputation as one of the most stable, prosperous and democratic countries in Latin America. That image, albeit tarnished by a period of military rule between 1973 and 1985, was at variance with the country's early history. From the 16th century to the early 19th century the territory changed hands between the Spanish and Portuguese several times. In 1776 the territory of Uruguay became part of the newly created Spanish Viceroyalty of Río de la Plata. Uruguay's attainment of independence, proclaimed in 1825 and recognized in 1828, was promoted by the British Government to provide a buffer state between Brazil and Argentina. However, both countries continued to influence domestic affairs through their support of rival rulers (caudillos). The first 50 years of nationhood was a period of anarchy, as the rival bands of Blancos ('Whites') and Colorados ('Reds'), the respective forerunners of the modern conservative and liberal political groupings, struggled for land and power.

The transition from anarchy to stability began in the 1870s, with the creation of the apparatus of a modern state. As world demand for wool and hides increased, Uruguayan landowners began to seek protection from the losses that persistently warring factions inflicted on livestock. Trading interests, strong in Montevideo because of the port's natural advantages in the River Plate region, also sought peace. The replacement of weak civilian government by a military regime (1876–86) and the introduction of modern armaments, railways and telegraph services secured the dominance of central authority in Montevideo over regional caudillos. British capital was loaned to the Government and invested directly in public utilities, and foreign trade expanded. Ironically, the modernization of the rural export economy involved the displacement of much of the labour force. The men who had been so displaced were to form the armies of the Blanco rebels and the Colorado Government, which fought Uruguay's most recent civil war, in 1904.

THE RULE AND INFLUENCE OF JOSÉ BATLLE

The Colorados' victory confirmed the authority of José Batlle y Ordóñez, who was twice President (1903–07 and 1911–15) and the dominant figure in Uruguayan politics until his death in 1929. His policies were nationalist and reformist and, under his rule, Uruguay became South America's first welfare state. The country's social structure was transformed by immigrants from the Mediterranean countries of Europe, and its economic prosperity was founded on export growth. Within the country, Batlle tried to limit the power of British capital by the encouragement of domestic investment in manufacturing and by cultivating closer relations with the USA as a counter-weight.

Batlle's radicalism, drawing support from the middle and working classes, antagonized foreign and domestic capital and alarmed his own Partido Colorado (PC—Colorado Party). His proposals for constitutional reform, which, in modified form, were embodied in the 1919 Constitution, led to the emergence of the batllistas and other factions in the party. The Constitution, which divided the executive branch of government between a President and eight other members of a National Council of Government, remained in force until its overthrow by a *coup d'état*, led by Gabriel Terra, in 1933. Terra claimed that he was acting against the inadequacies of the Council, but it was more probable that the coup was a reflection of the anxiety of landowners to maintain access to the British market for their beef exports.

Terra was influenced by, and attempted to follow, the policies being pursued by Benito Mussolini, the Fascist leader of Italy. During the 1930s Uruguayan economic expansionism had some success. For most of the Second World War, Uruguay was formally neutral, although its political sympathies (in addition to commercial advantage) lay with the Allies, led by the USA and the United Kingdom. In 1942 further political and constitutional

change saw the restoration to power of the batllistas, who represented the interests of the urban economy, rather than those of rural exporters. As had also been the case in the First World War, Uruguay found easy markets for its exports, and commercial relations with the USA became very close. Following the War, the United Kingdom again became an important export market, but the special relationship between the two countries declined with the sale of the mainly British-built railways to the Uruguayan Government in 1948.

THE DEVELOPMENT OF TWO-PARTY DOMINANCE

The manufacturing sector of the economy expanded rapidly in the decade following the War. However, Uruguay's export earnings did not keep pace with industrial growth and in 1956 the country entered a period of economic stagnation, which lasted until the early 1970s. The political parties proved to be adept at staying in power by the distribution of rewards to political clienteles, but showed little ability to devise new policies. In 1959, however, the Partido Nacional (PN—National Party, or Blancos) defeated the Colorados and took power for the first time in the 20th century. Despite the adoption of an austerity programme sponsored by the International Monetary Fund (IMF), the new Government failed to halt the country's economic decline. Political and social frustration intensified in the 1960s. The political left, small in electoral terms but strong in the trade-union movement, became more militant.

In November 1966 a new Constitution was approved by a referendum. It reintroduced the presidential system of government, following 15 years of a collegiate executive (whereby the presidency was rotated, on an annual basis, among the nine members of the National Council of Government). A simultaneous presidential election was won by Gen. Oscar Daniel Gestido of the PC, who took office in March 1967, but his term only lasted until his death in December. His successor, Jorge Pacheco Areco, used emergency powers to confront students and organized labour and to reduce the influence of professional politicians. With political life radicalized, the Tupamaro urban guerrilla movement increased its operations and was not defeated until the Armed Forces took control of internal security in 1972.

MILITARY DICTATORSHIP, 1973–85

The official winner of the November 1971 presidential election was a Colorado, Juan María Bordaberry Arocena; the Colorado candidates had gained the greatest number of votes, even though Wilson Ferreira Aldunate of the PN was the most popular individual candidate. President Bordaberry took office in March 1972, but was little more than a figure-head President. In February 1973 he accepted the Armed Forces' demand for military participation in political affairs. In June both chambers of the elected Congress were dissolved and in December the President appointed a new legislature, the Council of State, composed of 25 (later 35) nominated members. All left-wing groups were banned and political activity suspended. With an estimated 6,000 political prisoners detained by 1976, the military-supported regime came to be regarded as one of the most repressive in South America. In June 1976 President Bordaberry was deposed by the Army because of his refusal to consider any return to constitutional rule. The newly formed Council of the Nation, comprising the Council of State and the 21-member Joint Council of the Armed Forces, chose Dr Aparicio Méndez Manfredini (a former Minister of Health) as the new President, and he took office in September. Under military rule, economic growth resumed, but real wages declined sharply and about 10% of the population emigrated, for economic or political reasons. Close political and commercial links developed with neighbouring Brazil and Argentina, but the previously good relations with the USA were strained during US President

Jimmy Carter's administration (1977–81), as a result of his criticism of the Uruguayan regime's flagrant violations of human rights.

In 1977 the military leadership embarked on a plan to restore democratic rule to the country, submitting a draft constitution to a referendum in November 1980, and allowing political meetings to take place for the first time since 1973. Large sections of the traditional Colorado and Blanco parties campaigned against the military's proposals, on the grounds that they institutionalized the Army's role in security matters. When the proposed document was rejected, by 57.8% of those voting, the military leadership was forced to consult with leaders of the recognized parties on the constitutional future of the country.

THE RETURN TO CIVILIAN RULE

The Armed Forces appointed Lt-Gen. Gregorio Álvarez Armellino to the presidency in September 1981. Restrictions on political activity were eased, and in June 1982 the PC, the PN (Blanco) and the smaller Unión Cívica (Civic Union) were allowed to operate, although left-wing parties remained banned, and censorship was increased. Constitutional negotiations foundered in 1983 over the attempts by the military leaders to preserve their authority in future governments, and in August the Government suspended all political activity for up to two years. Distinctions between the two main parties, the liberal PC and the more conservative PN, gradually eroded, and pro- and anti-military tendencies developed within each of them. Two national days of protest were organized by the opposition in November 1983, and the Plenario Intersindical de Trabajadores—Convención Nacional de Trabajadores (PIT—CNT, Intersyndical Plenary of Workers—National Convention of Workers), the country's main trade-union federation, organized the first industrial action in the country for 10 years in September. The PIT was banned in January 1984, following a 24-hour strike protesting against a 28% increase in prices and, more generally, against the continued political repression.

Negotiations between the Government and the PC, the still-proscribed Frente Amplio (Broad Front, a left-wing coalition) and the Unión Cívica resumed in July 1984. However, the PN refused to participate while its leader, Wilson Ferreira Aldunate, was detained (he had been arrested in June, on returning from an 11-year exile). In August the Government withdrew its suspension of political activity and began to release some political prisoners (who at that time numbered between 600 and 900), but Ferreira and Gen. Líber Seregni Mosquera, the leader of the Frente Amplio, were banned from political activity. In November the presidential election was won by Dr Julio María Sanguinetti Cairolo of the PC's Unidad y Reforma (Unity and Reform) faction. In the legislative elections, however, the PC did not gain an absolute majority in either the Federal Chamber of Deputies or the Senate. In preparation for the full restoration of civilian rule, most remaining political prisoners, including Ferreira Aldunate, were released in November, and the Tupamaro leader, Raúl Sendic, was freed in March 1985. In December the Tupamaros formally agreed to become a political party, the Movimiento de Liberación Nacional (MLN—National Liberation Movement), and voted to join the Frente Amplio.

THE AMNESTY LAW

President Sanguinetti was inaugurated on 1 March 1985, and formed a Council of Ministers including two members of the PN and one of the Unión Cívica. The Partido Comunista (Communist Party) and other previously outlawed organizations were legalized, and remaining restrictions on press freedom were lifted. Trade unions were quick to demand more rapid liberalization, and the new Government was criticized within Congress for its economic policies. In January 1986 the PN, the Unión Cívica and the Frente Amplio obstructed legislative approval of the annual budget proposals, forcing the President to reach a consensus with opposition leaders, in order to implement a three-year economic recovery programme.

The most controversial issue for the Sanguinetti administration was the introduction in August 1986 of a draft amnesty law, which protected all members of the security forces from prosecution for alleged violations of human rights during the period of military rule. (A more limited amnesty had already been agreed between the military regime and civilian political leaders in 1984.) After considerable debate a revised version of the original proposals was passed by both houses in December, despite violent outbursts in the streets of Montevideo and within the Chamber of Deputies itself. The 'Punto Final' (Full Stop) legislation, as the final law was known, ended current military trials and made President Sanguinetti responsible for any further investigations into the whereabouts of the 'disappeared'. Under military rule over 170 Uruguayan citizens had apparently been seized by the military, and subsequently murdered; 33 had disappeared within Uruguay, 132 in Argentina and the remainder in Paraguay and Chile. Public opposition to the legislation continued to increase and by March 1988 a sufficient number of signatures (a minimum of 25% of the electorate) had been gathered to force a referendum, which was held in April 1989. For the first time in a national referendum voting was declared compulsory, and the law was confirmed by a vote of 57% in favour.

ECONOMIC LIBERALIZATION

The resolution of the amnesty question once again made economic policy the Government's chief concern. The trade unions criticized the Government for adhering to the dictates of the international monetary agencies, at the expense of the domestic work-force, and organized general strikes in November 1987 and June 1988. The Government's economic performance cost the Colorados the elections, held on 26 November 1989 (the first free elections since 1972), even though there was little material difference between the economic manifestos of the two leading presidential candidates. Luis Alberto Lacalle Herrera of the Blancos gained 37% of the votes cast, compared with 30% for Jorge Batlle Ibáñez of the Colorados and 21% for Líber Seregni of the Frente Amplio.

The PN could form only a minority Government, with 39 out of 99 seats in the Chamber of Deputies and 13 of the 31 seats in the Senate. Although Lacalle reached a power-sharing agreement with the PC, taking office in March 1990, the PC publicly expressed its opposition to parts of the Government's economic policy, as did a number of PN deputies. The most contentious economic issue was the proposed privatization programme (see Economy below), which gained little support within the main parties and was suspended in 1992. President Lacalle remained committed to privatization, however, and despite opposition, the process of eroding the country's large state sector was set in motion, albeit at a far gentler pace than in many neighbouring countries.

The Government provoked further outcry in 1992 when it attempted to impose a programme of wage restraint on public-sector workers, but exempted the police and the Armed Forces. In March 1993 two PN factions withdrew their congressional support, Vice-President Gonzalo Aguirre Ramírez left the Government, and the PIT–CNT led a 24-hour general strike. The crisis was averted by the introduction of a fiscal-reform programme, but in May the Government was defeated in a congressional vote on finance policy, leaving President Lacalle to rely on his own faction of the PN and a right-wing PC faction for support in Congress. The divisions within the PN were further exacerbated by the attempts of other Blanco politicians to distance themselves from the Lacalle administration before the 1994 election campaign began. A measure of President Lacalle's isolation was the series of corruption charges brought against former members of his Government, and even against his wife (who was accused of illegally profiting from the sale of shares in a privatized bank), following the end of his term of office in 1995.

Lacking reliable political support, President Lacalle's Government became more sympathetic to the Armed Forces. The Government prepared legislation extending military powers and displayed reluctance in pursuing investigations into violent incidents implicating members of the Armed Forces. One such incident was the disappearance in June 1993 of a former Chilean secret agent, Eugenio Berríos Sagredo, wanted in Chile in connection with the murder of Orlando Letelier in 1976, and apparently abducted by Uruguayan, Argentine and Chilean security forces. President Lacalle allowed the Uruguayan officers charged in the affair to be tried by a military, rather than a civilian, court, and ordered a confidential investigation into the affair, rather than the public inquiry demanded by the opposition.

ELECTORAL REFORM

The presidential and legislative elections of 27 November 1994 marked an end to traditional two-party politics. The vote was almost evenly split between the PC (32.5%), the PN (31.4%) and a third political force, the Encuentro Progresista (Progressive Congress, 30.8%), a predominantly left-wing alliance of the parties of the Frente Amplio, dissidents of the PN (Blancos), and other minority parties. In the Chamber of Representatives the PC won 32 seats, and the PN and Encuentro Progresista 31 seats each. Sanguinetti, the leading Colorado presidential candidate, was again elected President, and was obliged to form a coalition administration. The new Government, which took office in March 1995, contained seven Colorado ministers, four Blancos and a minister each from the Unión Cívica and the Partido por el Gobierno del Pueblo—Lista 99 (Party for the People's Government). The Encuentro Progresista party was left as the main opposition force. However, the principal member of this alliance, the Frente Amplio, reportedly gave an undertaking to co-operate with the new administration in return for government consideration of its views when determining social policy.

The new Government's first initiative was to introduce a proposal for electoral reform. Under the existing system, each party could present multiple presidential candidates, with the leading candidate in each party assuming the total number of votes for candidates in that party. This system had long been criticized for promoting factionalism within political parties and for yielding an unclear result. Under the proposed reform each party would present a single candidate and, in the event of no candidate securing an absolute majority, a second round of voting would take place. Negotiations on reform had begun in the late 1980s, but the two traditional parties had hitherto been reluctant to change the system until prompted by the narrowness of the Colorados' victory in the 1994 election. Agreement between the Government and the legislative opposition on electoral reform was reached in July 1995, although it faced growing opposition within the Frente Amplio, which claimed that the change was a deliberate attempt to deny any left-wing group the chance to win the presidency. The amendment was passed in Congress in October 1996, and was narrowly approved (by 50.5%) in a plebiscite held in December. The amendment came into effect in January 1997.

The other programme, begun in March 1995, was a restructuring of the social-security system, President Sanguinetti's fifth attempt at such a reform (see also Economy below). The fiscal burden of the pension system was growing to such an extent that on this occasion the proposed reform received support from the two larger parties. The draft legislation was introduced in June and, in spite of union opposition and resistance from the Frente Amplio, was approved in August. Confident that the reform would be generally unpopular, the Frente Amplio had requested that it be submitted to a referendum, but in March 1996 the Electoral Court rejected this demand. In the event, the new system proved to have a far greater appeal than expected, and within a year of its introduction nearly one-third of the work-force had subscribed.

In May 1996 the 'governability pact' between the Colorados and the Blancos was given a more formal basis following a meeting between the leaders of the two parties to discuss social and economic policy. The attempt to establish a common political agenda between the two parties was the first such occurrence in 160 years and underlined the shift away from the traditional two-party rivalry. Ironically, this move was accompanied by the emergence of divisions within the Frente Amplio. In September 1997 the Front's leader, Tabaré Vázquez, threatened to resign after party in-fighting over the issue of privatization. Although his grouping generally opposed privatization, the Frente Amplio-controlled authorities in Montevideo had begun to offer contracts to private tender, to the annoyance of the more left-wing member organizations.

In April 1997 Frente Amplio senator, Felipe Michelini, whose father was among the disappeared, called for an investigation into allegations that 32 of the victims of the dictatorship had been interred in the grounds of military property and covertly

removed from the burial sites in 1985–86. A judicial ruling in the same month promised to facilitate such an inquiry and in May 20,000 people attended a rally in Montevideo to demand that the Government and the Armed Forces acquiesce. However, in June a court of appeal overturned the ruling on the grounds that it contravened the Punto Final amnesty law. Under pressure, particularly from the Nuevo Espacio (New Space) party, in October the Government conceded that it had not kept its undertaking in the 1986 amnesty to ascertain where the disappeared had been buried. The Armed Forces made it clear that they would obstruct any attempts by the civilian judiciary to conduct investigations involving military property or personnel. Although President Sanguinetti decided in December 1997 to compensate 41 former army officers dismissed from service during the military dictatorship owing to their political beliefs, and reduced the size of all three branches of the Armed Forces, no investigations into human-rights abuses during military rule were launched during his administration.

The human-rights issue continued to be prominent in 1998. In May the country's principal religious and human-rights groups published a National Reconciliation Declaration, which made explicit their opposition to the amnesty law. In July a former intelligence chief, Rear-Adm. (retd) Eladio Moll, caused a diplomatic crisis when he alleged that US military officers had instructed the Uruguayan security forces on the detention and torture of Tupamaro suspects, and that Uruguayan officers had resisted US demands that the suspects be killed after interrogation. In October the detention of the former Chilean military dictator, Gen. (retd) Augusto Pinochet Ugarte, in the United Kingdom had repercussions throughout the region. The Spanish judiciary, which was attempting to extradite Pinochet to face charges relating to alleged crimes committed under his regime, ordered an investigation into the involvement of other Southern Cone countries in the 1970s anti-terrorist programme, code-named 'Operation Condor'.

Following the re-establishment of democratic rule, there were frequent strikes on a number of political, social and economic issues. Most of these were organized by the PIT–CNT, which was weakened in November 1996 by the defection of several major trade unions, particularly those representing public-sector workers, who constituted a considerable section of the work-force. In 1997 there was a marked increase in violent protests in rural areas, which had previously been peaceful, similar to trends in Argentina and Chile. In common with a number of other Latin American nations, Uruguay's prison system suffered from chronic overcrowding. In 1997 it was estimated that up to 90% of the country's prison inmates had not received finalized sentences, and many had not even come to trial. Meanwhile, the integrity of the police had been undermined by reports of numerous instances in which serving and retired police officers had colluded with criminal groups.

THE 1999 ELECTIONS

In accordance with the Sanguinetti Government's electoral reforms, a primary election was held on 25 April 1999 to select candidates for the presidential contest due in October. The PC gained 38% of the total, and its nomination was won by Jorge Batlle Ibáñez. His closest Colorado rival, Luis Hierro López, subsequently became his vice-presidential candidate. The Encuentro Progresista—Frente Amplio (EP—FA) secured 30% of the total votes in the primary election and its leader, Tabaré Vázquez, was selected as the coalition's candidate. For the PN, the campaign for the primary election was seriously divisive, which contributed to its third place overall, with 29% of the total ballot. During the campaign the PC candidate, former President Luis Alberto Lacalle, had been accused of corruption, and in the months preceding the elections it became clear that the presidential contest would be, in effect, a contest between Batlle and Vázquez. During the election campaign the Colorados and Blancos attempted to portray Vázquez (an eminent oncologist) as a Marxist, and claimed that he would destroy the country's economy. His main manifesto promises were government-led job creation, and the rather less popular introduction of a universal income-tax system. Although the EP—FA's main area of support was in Montevideo, Vázquez also campaigned in the countryside in a bid to gain the support of farmers demanding government assistance.

Presidential and legislative elections were held on 31 October 1999. The EP—FA emerged as the leading party, winning a simple majority in both the Chamber of Deputies (40 of the 99 seats) and in the Senate (12 of the 30 seats). The PC secured 33 and 10 seats, and the PN secured only 22 seats in the lower house and seven senate seats (however, the party performed well in local and regional elections in May 2000, securing control of 13 of the 19 departments). In the presidential ballot Vázquez gained 38.5% of the vote, compared with 31.3% for Batlle and 21.3% for Lacalle. Under the system operating until 1995 Vázquez would have been elected President; however, under the new electoral law, a second round of voting was required, which was held on 28 November. In the event, most of the Blanco support was transferred to the Colorado candidate, and Batlle won with 51.6% of the votes cast.

THE BATLLE IBÁÑEZ PRESIDENCY, 2000–

Batlle's inauguration speech of 1 March 2000 included undertakings to reduce public spending, address the farming crisis, investigate the fate of the disappeared, and institutionalize the Southern Common Market (Mercado Común del Sur—Mercosur). His new Government comprised eight PC and five PN members. In April he dismissed Gen. Manuel Fernández, who had sought to justify the military repression of the 1970s and had spoken of a renewed struggle against left-wing extremists. In August a six-member Commission for Peace was formed to investigate the disappearance of 170 people during the military dictatorship. In May 2001 the bodies of two Uruguayan exiles were found in Argentine soil; it was reported that some 140 of the 'disappeared' had been killed in Argentina by members of that country's Armed Forces, acting in co-operation with the Uruguayan military authorities. In a speech to mark his first anniversary in office Batlle renewed his commitment to clarifying the fate of the disappeared. Meanwhile, in January 2001 Gen. Juan Geymonat was dismissed as Commander-in-Chief of the Armed Forces; it was widely believed that the dismissal would pave the way for a military modernization programme advocated by Batlle.

During 2000 the Batlle administration encountered opposition from trade unions, not least because of the deterioration in social and economic conditions. In June 2000 the PIT—CNT organized a general strike to demand action on unemployment and additional finance for education and health care, as well as to protest at emergency legislation, passed that month, that would allow the partial privatization of some public services. Although a more widespread strike was held in December, the EP—FA failed to force a referendum on the controversial legislation, owing to lack of public support. The PIT—CNT led a further general strike in July 2001.

Economy

HELEN SCHOOLEY

Based on an earlier article by Dr M. H. J. Finch

From the late 19th century Uruguay developed as an agricultural export economy by selling wool, beef and hides, mainly to European countries. Owing to favourable natural conditions and a low density of population, export values per head were high. Government policy also encouraged domestic manufacturing, and protection was intensified in the 1930s and after the Second World War, in the late 1940s. However, the rate of growth of exports was low and the small size of the domestic market meant that the strategy of industrialization by import substitution was exhausted by the mid-1950s. A period of economic stagnation, with falling average income per head, followed and continued into the early 1970s. The economic policies of the military regime after 1973, based on reduction in the public sector and incentives to non-traditional exports, helped to stimulate growth in the gross domestic product (GDP) averaging 4.5% per year between 1974 and 1980. However, attempts to control inflation and the general effects of the world recession halted economic expansion, and GDP registered negative growth between 1982 and 1984. Overall, GDP expanded by an average of 0.3% per year in 1980–90.

The chief factor in the performance of the economy was export growth and the balance of trade. GDP growth resumed in the 1990s, with notable rises of 7.9% in 1992 and 6.3% in 1994, although negative rates were recorded in 1995, when GDP contracted by 1.8% owing primarily to a sharp downturn in construction and services, and again in 1999, when the devaluation of the Brazilian currency resulted in a 2.7% fall in GDP. The consequent recession in Argentina and continued low world prices for agricultural exports caused a further decline in 2000 (1.4%), but the International Monetary Fund (IMF) forecast a growth rate of 2% for 2001. Although the economy was always strongly linked to the economies of neighbouring countries, the establishment in 1995 of the Southern Common Market (Mercado Común del Sur—Mercosur, or, in Portuguese, Mercado Comum do Sul—Mercosul) had accentuated the influence of markets in Brazil and Argentina. Uruguay maintained one of the highest levels of GDP per head in Latin America, at US $6,350 in 1998. Consumption rose by 62% over the 10 years to 1997, and Uruguay was the only country in Latin America where the gap between the wealthiest and the poorest did not increase during the 1990s. The level of trade-union membership was substantial for the region, and the rate of unemployment was relatively high, increasing from 11.3% in November 1999 to 15% by early 2001.

A relatively small country, with an area of 176,215 sq km (68,037 sq miles), Uruguay had an estimated population of around 3.3m. in 2001. The average population growth of 0.8% was the lowest in Latin America, whereas the proportion of urban population in 1999 was 91% of the total, the highest in the region, with 45% of the population living in Montevideo. Although over 80% of the national territory was cultivable, thin soils limited the area potentially capable of bearing an annual crop to about 20% of total productive land. Moreover, a report released in mid-1995 indicated that the country was facing an erosion problem, losing more than 50m. metric tons of topsoil per year. Horticulture and vineyards were concentrated in the area adjacent to Montevideo, with dairy farming in the south-western departments of San José and Colonia, and cereals in the west. Citrus fruit was grown in the department of Salto and rice in the east, near Laguna Merim. By far the greatest area was devoted to sheep- and cattle-raising.

AGRICULTURE

Agriculture traditionally formed the basis of the Uruguayan economy, and accounted (directly or indirectly) for almost all commodity export earnings. An estimated 12.8% of the working population were employed in the sector in mid-1999, compared with 20% in 1965. Following a severe drought in 1988–89, the sector performed strongly in the early and mid-1990s, including an 8% increase in agricultural GDP in 1996, largely owing to substantial investment in infrastructure and production. In 1999 agriculture and fishing accounted for 5.4% of national GDP.

Uruguay's two main export products were meat (especially beef) and wool. Meat was also an important item of the local diet, with an annual average consumption per head of about 70 kg in 1990. Meat exports raised US $478.2m. in 1999, and the main markets for Uruguayan beef were Brazil, Chile, the European Union (EU) and Israel. In 1999 exports of live animals, animal products, skins and hides contributed 39.4% of export revenue. The dairy sector was comparatively very small, although it grew rapidly in the 1980s and produced exportable surpluses. Milk yields more than doubled between 1981 and 1997, and wool production rose by over 50% from the early 1970s to the mid-1990s. Between 1988 and 1994 Uruguay's share of wool production in the Southern Cone region increased from 32% to 41%, although the region's total output declined by 30% in the same period.

The arable sector, which was confined to a relatively small area and had low yields, was also adversely affected by the drought of 1988–89. Traditionally, the main crop was wheat, and yields had risen sharply in the late 1980s, falling in the early 1990s, but recovering by the end of the decade. Other main crops, such as maize and oil seeds, declined in importance, but rice production expanded during the 1980s and 1990s, owing principally to demand from Brazil. Output of paddy rice trebled between 1990 and 2000, although 1998 crop yields were hit by flooding in the west of the country caused by El Niño (the warm current that periodically appears along the Pacific coast of South America). Fruit crop levels increased in 1992, and subsequently remained stable, as a result of favourable weather conditions and the beginning of production on newly cultivated land. There were also efforts to increase timber production, with a view to the export market, although in the late 1990s output remained relatively static, despite government investment in the industry's infrastructure.

Although small scale, the fishing industry grew rapidly in the late 1970s and early 1980s. In 1982 an estimated 119,201 metric tons were caught, compared with 26,000 tons in 1975, and about 90% of the total catch was exported. Production peaked at 143,700 tons in 1991, but by the mid-1990s was more or less stagnant, at about 125,000 tons per year. The total catch increased to 136,900 tons in 1997, and to 140,600 in the following year, although there was a sharp decline, to 97,631 tons, in 1999. Concern over dwindling fishery reserves in the late 1990s prompted attempts at diversification, including a plan to begin farming caviar in the Baygorria reservoir, 200 km north of Montevideo, using sturgeon eggs imported from Russia.

By the end of the 1990s weak world markets for Uruguay's traditional meat and dairy products had precipitated a crisis in the farming sector. Indebted farmers demanded government action to improve their situation, prompting the resignation, in August 1999, of the agriculture minister. In an attempt to alleviate the financial plight of agricultural producers, whose amalgamated debt was estimated at about US $1,200m., the Government reduced certain taxes and introduced refinancing arrangements, but the farmers renewed their protests in November. Problems in the livestock sector were compounded by an outbreak of foot-and-mouth disease in October 2000. Two weeks after the outbreak was first announced meat exports were temporarily halted and 6,500 employees in the meat and dairy industry lost their jobs. Although exports resumed following the slaughter of some 20,000 animals, they were suspended once again in April 2001, when a second outbreak of the disease spread rapidly across the country. The Government was forced to adopt a mass vaccination programme, thereby reducing the value of future meat exports. Some analysts estimated that revenue from meat exports might decline by $600m. over the following four years. In July the EU lifted the ban on Uruguayan beef imports.

MINING AND POWER

The absence of any commercially viable deposits of petroleum, natural gas or coal made Uruguay heavily dependent on the import of foreign crude petroleum, which accounted for about two-thirds of the country's energy requirements. Prospecting for oil began in the 1940s, and resumed in the 1970s in the wake of the oil crisis, when attention was focused on offshore possibilities. Deep-water deposits were judged to be economically unviable, and the same conclusion was drawn in the early 1990s. In 1999, however, in the wake of a further round of oil price increases, a new initiative was announced within Mercosur to investigate the deposits.

In an attempt to reduce the dependence on imported petroleum, successive Governments promoted the use of hydroelectricity; by 1996 petroleum supplied 58% of national energy requirements and electricity (mostly hydroelectricity) 19%. Exploitation of hydroelectric resources had begun in the 1930s, but substantial development came in the 1970s as a result of

major investments in the 1,800 MW Salto Grande project with Argentina, and the 300 MW Palmar installation with Brazil. The output from these two plants and two others on the Río Negro made Uruguay a net exporter of electric energy by the 1980s. The opening of another new hydroelectric plant in 1991 increased not only domestic power resources, but by quadrupling electricity sales to Argentina, made hydroelectric power an important factor in the country's balance of payments from 1992. Uruguay also developed its gas resources for export. In November 2000 construction began on a US $135m. gas pipeline from Buenos Aires (Argentina) to Montevideo, as part of a greater scheme to link the gas network of the Mercosur countries. The next likely market for Uruguayan gas exports was Brazil.

Apart from quarrying for marble and other construction materials, there was little mining activity. A survey suggested that Uruguay might possess reserves of gold, manganese, copper, lead and zinc, but the only mineral extracted was iron ore. Work was begun at two sites: at Zapucay, in the north, deposits were estimated at 400m. metric tons of ore, with an iron content of over 40%; and at Valentines, in the south-east, proven deposits totalled 30m. tons of 40% ore, with a further 15m. tons estimated. Feasibility studies were undertaken in the early 1990s for the installation of a US $140m. iron and steel complex at Valentines. According to the central bank, the GDP of the mining sector increased by an annual average of 11.2% in 1990–99.

MANUFACTURING

From the 1970s manufacturing was the largest sector of the Uruguayan economy, accounting for 16.0% of GDP in 1999. In the early 1990s the country's widening trade deficit prompted a programme of investment and re-organization in the sector. Industrial activity was concentrated in Montevideo and accounted for about one-quarter of the capital's total employed population. Measured by the value of output, the most important branch of manufacturing was food products (mainly processed meat for export, accounting for one-third of the total), along with textiles and clothing, chemicals, petroleum and coal products, beverages, leather and fur products, and printing and publishing. Between 1965 and 1997 the proportion of the workforce employed in industry declined from 29% to 16%, reflecting both greater productivity (with a consequent loss of jobs) and a major rise in the service sector. By 2000 the number of people working in industry was only one-half the level of 1988, and in the textile sector the number fell to below one-third. Between 1973 and 1980 industrial output increased by 36%. The sector was adversely affected by the recession of the early 1980s, but grew rapidly in the later part of the decade, chiefly as a result of an increase in car manufacturing and, to a lesser degree, in textiles and parts for the petroleum industry. During the 1990s the sector fluctuated, with expansion in the food processing and textile sectors in 1992, an increase in car production in 1994–95, and a marked upturn in the chemical sector in 1997. In total industrial output there were rises of 4% in 1994 and 1996, and of 6% in 1997, but declines of 9% in 1993, 2.8% in 1995 and 8.4% in 1999.

TRANSPORT, INFRASTRUCTURE AND COMMUNICATIONS

Montevideo was the focal point of all Uruguay's transport systems, and the city's port was the principal gateway for foreign trade, but during the 1980s the transport systems suffered from neglect. Major improvements began in the 1990s, stimulated by the growth of tourism and the investment in non-traditional exports, and by the end of the decade there was a rolling programme of road, rail and port extension. The sector was a growth area even though the country's freight shipment costs were currently the highest in Mercosur.

The railway system was relatively extensive, with 3,002 route-km radiating from Montevideo, and links to the Argentine and Brazilian networks. By 1987 passenger traffic had fallen to one-third of the 1978 level, and passenger services were halted completely in 1988. However, passenger services linking Montevideo with Florida and Canelones were resumed in mid-1993. Apart from livestock, principal freight items were stone, cement, rice, and fuel, and in 1996 a project was launched for a freight railway scheme to connect the forestry industry in the north east of the country with the coast. Like the railways, Uruguay's roads linked interior centres with the capital, rather than with each other. In 1996 a scheme was announced for the improvement and maintenance programme of rural roads, as part of a plan to modernize the dairy industry. In August 1999 Congress gave final approval for the construction of a 41-km toll bridge over the Río de la Plata (River Plate), between Colonia del Sacramento in Uruguay and Punta Lara in Argentina.

The transport, storage and communications sector contributed 8.4% of GDP in 1999, and during the 1990s recorded an average annual growth rate of 8%, owing chiefly to the telecommunications sector. There was substantial investment in modern technology in the early 1990s. The communications sector was in the vanguard of government free-market reforms. Although opposition to privatization halted the proposed sale of the state telecommunications concern, Administración Nacional de Telecomunicaciones (ANTEL, see below), cellular-telephone services, road maintenance, port and airport administration and the new passenger railway services were opened to private-sector participation in the mid-1990s.

PRIVATIZATION

The process of privatization in Uruguayan was much slower than in other South American countries, partly because the state sector had been more efficient than its counterparts and partly because the political opposition to the policy was more effective. Government attempts to introduce a major privatization programme in the early 1990s met with resistance from the Frente Amplio and the trade unions, which were initially successful in reversing plans by demanding a referendum on individual sales. In 1992 the Government was forced to suspend the sale of shares in the state telecommunications company, ANTEL, and to adopt a more gradual approach to privatization, encouraging competition and the use of private capital in state concerns. The state monopolies on insurance and the financing and construction of new homes were ended in 1993 and 1996, respectively, and the national airline, Primeras Líneas Uruguayas de Navegación Aérea (PLUNA) was privatized in 1995.

The restructuring of the social-security system undertaken by the Government of Julio María Sanguinetti (1995–2000) proved less controversial. President Sanguinetti had made four previous attempts at such a reform, and his arguments were reinforced by the pressing need to alleviate the fiscal pressure exerted by pensions. In 1995 only 65% of the social-security budget was raised by contributions from those currently employed, while the number of people of pensionable age was over one-half of the economically active population. The new legislation, approved in August 1996, increased the period of contribution, raised the retirement age and established a mixed capitalization and distribution system. The reforms aimed to eliminate the system's structural deficit within 10 years. The first pension-fund administration company (fondo de ahorro previsional—Afap) was inaugurated in April 1996 and by 2000 some 85% of the work-force had joined the new private pension scheme.

In 1996 the state oil concern, Administración Nacional de Combustibles Alcohol y Portland (ANCAP), lost its monopoly over the manufacture of alcohol and cement, and private companies were invited to tender for contracts to run the port and airport. In 1997 the Government introduced legislation to deregulate the electricity industry, ending the state monopoly on the generation of electricity and introducing legislation allowing the use of private capital in electricity distribution. Despite a campaign on the part of the Frente Amplio and the trade unions, the energy reform law received a positive vote in a referendum held in June 1998.

When President Jorge Batlle Ibáñez came to office in March 2000 he continued a cautious liberalization policy, opting for the introduction of competition rather than the dismantling of state concerns, although this policy was still opposed by the Frente Amplio and the trade unions. Further efforts were made to deregulate the telecommunications sector and the Government made it possible for ANCAP to use private-sector partners to develop its refining capacity, and also announced its intention to end ANCAP's monopoly on oil imports. Deregulation of the banking sector was expected to be delayed by the volume of indebtedness among the farming community.

INVESTMENT AND FINANCE

In the 1970s Uruguay experienced a high level of public-sector investment, largely in hydroelectricity and bridge-construction programmes, but during the 1980s and 1990s an increasing amount of investment came from the private sector. A law passed in 1987 allowed for the establishment of free-trade zones, both publicly and privately owned, for various manufacturing and service industries. In the mid-1990s the opening up of the public sector to private capitalization and joint venture schemes encouraged significant levels of foreign direct investment for the first time. A new investment law, approved in 1998, promised further opportunities for private finance, with incentives including tax and tariff exemptions and reduction of employers' social security contributions. Its main consequence was to boost foreign investment, although indications were that investment funds were growing in response to the decline in interest rates and inflation and the pegging of the exchange rate. Like internal investment, domestic savings and stock-exchange trading were relatively low for the region. In 1999 the financial sector accounted for 9.8% of GDP.

In conformity with the terms of agreements reached with the International Monetary Fund (IMF) in 1985, 1990, 1992 and 1996, successive Governments reduced the fiscal deficit, which reached 1.4% of GDP in 1998. The first major factor in this fall was the reduction of the number of public-sector employees from 240,000 in 1990 to 150,000 in 1997 through a series of retirement packages. The second factor was the 1996 reform of the social-security system, which was projected to achieve annual savings of US $80m., and to reduce the social-security deficit within the budget to 1% of GDP. The Sanguinetti Government increased value-added tax (VAT) and personal income tax, introduced performance-related pay for civil servants and raised tax receipts by 5.7% in 1996. The Government introduced further reductions in public spending in January 1999 to offset the adverse effects of the Brazilian devaluation, prompting the IMF to approve a further stand-by credit, worth $95m. This was supplemented in May 2000 by the approval by the IMF of another stand-by credit, valued at $197m., to support the economic programme for 2000–01 of the incoming Batlle Government.

Another priority of the Lacalle Government was reducing inflation, which had risen from an annual average of 72.1% in 1985 to 112.5% in 1990. The rate was brought down to 44.7% in 1994, mainly through the use of exchange controls and public-sector wage restraints. With effect from 1 March 1993, the peso uruguayo was introduced, replacing the peso nuevo, which had been in circulation since July 1975; the peso uruguayo was equivalent to 1,000 pesos nuevos. The currency entered a floating exchange-rate system, supervised by the Government at a monthly devaluation rate of approximately 1%. The annual rate of inflation decreased to 28.3% in 1996, to 19.8% in 1997 and to 10.8% in 1998 (the lowest level since 1956). A level of 5.7% was recorded in 1999, and of 4.8% in 2000, assisted by the recession in Brazil and Argentina.

DEBT

Uruguay's total foreign debt rose from US $2,156m. in 1981 to $4,279m. by the end of 1987; nearly 90% of it was publicly held. In July 1986 an accord was signed with a consortium of creditor banks, in conjunction with the World Bank and the IMF, effectively reducing debt-service payments from 60% to 40% of export revenue. The agreement was superseded in 1987 by an accord with international creditor banks, with easier repayment terms. A further round of rescheduling concluded in 1991, also reduced interest payments. As a result of these measures, and of stricter control of public-sector spending, the overall debt figure fell in the late 1980s and totalled $3,707m. in 1990. Following an increase in the early 1990s, foreign debt stood at $5,320m. in 1995, although this represented a decline from the equivalent of 54% of GDP in 1990 to some 30% of GDP in 1995. A rise in international reserves actually reduced the net external debt to $5,000m. in 1996, and although the total debt increased to $6,713m. in 1997, the country's debt profile had improved sufficiently for it to be accorded an investment-grade rating on the international financial markets. In 1999 total external debt stood at $7,447m., a slight decrease on the previous year.

FOREIGN TRADE, TOURISM AND THE BALANCE OF PAYMENTS

Uruguay's traditional exports were meat, wool and other unprocessed animal products, which, until the mid-1970s, provided about 80% of the country's total export earnings. By the 1990s that proportion had fallen to 20%–25%, although these primary commodities were still basic to overall export performance. Non-traditional exports included textiles, leather goods, fish and rice, and by the 1990s hydroelectric power and tourism had also become major contributors. Despite this growth, however, the trade balance, which had recorded surpluses in 1991 and 1990, registered a deficit in the rest of the 1990s, chiefly because of rising imports of capital goods. In 1999 the imbalance increased to US $868m., largely as a result of the Brazilian devaluation; reduced demand in Brazil helped to cut exports by 24%, while imports declined by only 14%. The figures for 2000 were expected to reflect the adverse effect of the rise in oil prices, which would raise the country's petroleum import bill by 66%.

In the 1990s the main export markets for Uruguayan meat were Brazil, the EU and Middle Eastern countries, and during the 1990s trade with the USA grew by 50%. Bilateral trade agreements were concluded with Argentina and Brazil in the 1970s, and by 1992 these two countries accounted for almost 43% of Uruguay's imports and about one-third of the country's exports. This trend continued with the establishment of Mercosur (see below), and in 1999 Mercosur accounted for 50% of Uruguay's exports and the EU for 20%.

After more than one decade in deficit, the current account of the balance of payments was in surplus every year from 1986 to 1991, with the exception of 1987. The surplus reached US $169.9m. in 1990 and fell to $42.5m. in the following year. The deteriorating trade balance caused by an increase in imports resulted in a deficit on the current account of $8.8m. in 1992. The current account stayed in deficit thereafter, rising from $475.5m. in 1998 to $605.0m. in 1999.

MERCOSUR

Argentina, Brazil, Paraguay and Uruguay signed the Treaty of Asunción in March 1991, forming a regional common market, Mercosur, with its headquarters in Montevideo, which came into effect on 1 January 1995. In preparation for the implementation of Mercosur, Uruguay continued to liberalize its trade, reducing its three-tier tariffs in March 1992 and again in January 1993. The country generally recorded a trade deficit within Mercosur, and closer ties increased Uruguay's vulnerability to economic events in the other member countries, notably the Argentine economic crisis in 1995, austerity measures in Brazil in 1996 and the Brazilian devaluation in January 1999. Membership of the common market did, however, bring economic advantages through the presence of the Mercosur secretariat in Uruguay, reduced tariffs and interest in investment from a number of multinational companies. By the end of the 1990s most duties between the member countries had been eliminated and a common external tariff (CET) had been established for trade outside Mercosur. In April 2000 Uruguay joined Paraguay in protesting against a bilateral agreement between Brazil and Argentina to raise the CET on automobiles from 20% to 35%. By the time of the Mercosur Heads of State Summit in December 2000 there were evident strains within the organization. The previous month Chile, an associate member since 1996, had announced its intention to seek bilateral trade talks with the USA, and there were indications that economic recession would lead Argentina to take a similar path. Brazil, on the other hand, favoured strengthening Mercosur as a trading bloc to boost its regional position against the USA, and in particular sought the establishment of the Free Trade Area of the Americas (FTAA).

TOURISM

By the mid-1990s tourism and financial services had become the major contributors to the country's balance of payments, with tourist revenues outstripping receipts from exports of wool and meat. Uruguay's principal attractions for tourists were the fashionable resort of Punta del Este and the chain of beaches between it and Montevideo. The sector expanded considerably in the 1980s, with the number of summer-season visitors rising from just over 316,000 in 1980/81, to nearly 690,000 in 1990/91. In 1999 Uruguay received 2.3m. visitors, and receipts from the sector amounted to US $653m. Although the 1990s saw an increase in visitors from other neighbouring countries, and also the USA and Europe, at the end of the decade Argentine tourists still accounted for 75% of the total. Traditionally Punta del Este had catered for the wealthy end of the market, but by the end of the 1990s tourist patterns were changing, with shorter stays and partially successful moves by hotel-owners to attract middle-range visitors from Brazil, Chile and Paraguay. The recession in both Argentina and Brazil severely affected tourist receipts in both the 1999/2000 and 2000/2001 seasons.

ENVIRONMENT

In the mid-1980s Uruguay lodged protests with Brazil over the acid-rain damage caused in the border area by the chemicals discharged from a Brazilian power plant. By the mid-1990s certain recreational areas in Montevideo were severely damaged by industrial pollution in the Miguelete River. There was also concern over the possible consequences of a proposed five-nation (the Mercosur countries and Bolivia) scheme to dredge a waterway to allow large shipping into the interior up the River Plate Estuary as far as the Bolivian border. In December 2000 a Brazilian judge suspended licences for dredging and construction projects along the waterway out of concern for wildlife in the Pantanal, a 140,000 sq km area in western Brazil. A petroleum spill which occurred 20 km off the coast of the tourist resort of Punta del Este in February 1998 polluted not only the beach, but also affected local seal and sea-lion colonies. Moreover, the oil leak halted the harvesting of mussels, which accounted for a major part of the country's shellfish catch. Like other Latin American countries, Uruguay suffered from abnormal weather conditions caused by El Niño in 1997–98, and the consequences were expected to be far-reaching. In Uruguay's case the principal problem was severe flooding in the west of the country, and a notable casualty was the rice crop.

CONCLUSION

Following severe recession in 1981–85, the Uruguayan economy showed a marked improvement in the second half of the 1980s, despite the attendant steep rise in the rate of inflation. In the early 1990s the Government's policies were assisted by substantial economic growth in 1992 and 1994, although in 1993 the reduction of trade tariffs contributed to a continuous increase in imports. The launch of the privatization programme in 1991, albeit in the face of initial hostility, marked a move away from the relatively high level of protectionism within the economy. The coalition Government that came to power in 1995 was able to reach a greater consensus on its economic policies, and, notably, to introduce the social-security reforms which had eluded previous Governments.

On taking office in March 2000, President Batlle promised to reduce the rate of VAT, make further cuts in public spending, continue the privatization programme, extend unemployment benefit and maintain a phased decrease in the social-security contributions made by employers. He inherited an economy with the advantages of the lowest rate of inflation for over 50 years, a substantially reduced budget deficit, and the future benefits of the pension reform for budget resources. However, the reduced inflation rate was also a measure of the economic difficulties facing the country, especially the increase in the price of oil, the effects of economic difficulties in Brazil, with their consequent effects in Argentina, and the weak world market for Uruguay's main exports. The economy registered negative rates of growth in both 1999 and 2000, the already high rate of unemployment rose, and prospects for 2001 were curbed by the outbreak of foot-and-mouth disease in October 2000 and in April 2001. Meanwhile, in late 2000 the Government embarked on a major campaign to combat contraband and corruption among customs officials, as the vast quantity of merchandise brought into the country illegally was adversely affecting the local economy. In his first anniversary speech, Batlle renewed his pledge to reduce the public sector, and advocated a greater emphasis on service exports, and the active encouragement of high technology development.

Statistical Survey

Sources (unless otherwise stated): CENCI-Uruguay, Misiones 1361, Casilla 1510, Montevideo; tel. (2) 9152930; fax (2) 9154578; e-mail cenci@adinet.com.uy; Banco Central del Uruguay, Avda Juan P. Fabini, esq. Florida 777, Casilla 1467, 11100 Montevideo; tel. (2) 9017112; fax (2) 9021634; Cámara Nacional de Comercio y Servicios del Uruguay, Edif. Bolsa de Comercio, Rincón 454, 2°, Casilla 1000, 11000 Montevideo; tel. (2) 9161277; fax (2) 9161243; e-mail canadeco@adinet.com.uy; internet www.davanet.com.uy/canadeco.

Area and Population

AREA, POPULATION AND DENSITY*

Area (sq km)	
Total	176,215†
Population (census results)	
23 October 1985	2,955,241
22 May 1996	
Males	1,532,288
Females	1,631,475
Total	3,163,763
Population (official estimates at mid-year, preliminary figures)	
1999	3,302,843
2000	3,322,141
2001	3,341,521
Density (per sq km) at mid-2001	19.0

* Census results exclude, and estimates include, adjustment for underenumeration, estimated at 2.6% at 1985 census.
† 68,037 sq miles.

DEPARTMENTS (population at 22 May 1996 census)

	Area (sq km)	Population	Density (per sq km)	Capital
Artigas . . .	11,928	75,059	6.3	Artigas
Canelones . .	4,536	443,053	97.7	Canelones
Cerro Largo .	13,648	82,510	6.0	Melo
Colonia . .	6,106	120,541	19.7	Colonia del Sacramento
Durazno . .	11,643	55,716	4.8	Durazno
Flores . .	5,144	25,030	4.9	Trinidad
Florida . .	10,417	66,503	6.4	Florida
Lavalleja . .	10,016	61,085	6.1	Minas
Maldonado . .	4,793	127,502	26.6	Maldonado
Montevideo . .	530	1,344,839	2,537.4	Montevideo
Paysandú . .	13,922	111,509	8.0	Paysandú
Río Negro . .	9,282	51,713	5.6	Fray Bentos
Rivera . .	9,370	98,472	10.5	Rivera
Rocha . .	10,551	70,292	6.7	Rocha
Salto . .	14,163	117,597	8.3	Salto
San José . .	4,992	96,664	19.4	San José de Mayo
Soriano . .	9,008	81,557	9.1	Mercedes
Tacuarembó .	15,438	84,919	5.5	Tacuarembó
Treinta y Tres .	9,529	49,502	5.2	Treinta y Tres
Total . . .	**175,016**	**3,163,763**	**18.1**	

PRINCIPAL TOWNS (population at 22 May 1996 census)

Montevideo		Rivera . . .	63,370
(capital) . .	1,378,707	Mercedes . . .	50,800
Salto . . .	93,420	Maldonado . .	50,420
Paysandú . .	84,160	Melo . . .	47,160
Las Piedras . .	66,100	Tacuarembó . .	42,580

BIRTHS, MARRIAGES AND DEATHS

	Registered live births*		Registered marriages		Registered deaths	
	Number	Rate (per 1,000)	Number	Rate (per 1,000)	Number	Rate (per 1,000)
1991 . .	54,754	17.6	20,502	6.6	29,774	9.6
1992 . .	54,190	17.3	19,376	6.2	30,008	9.6
1993 . .	55,958	17.8	n.a.	n.a.	31,616	10.0
1994 . .	55,990	17.7	n.a.	n.a.	30,209	9.5
1995 . .	55,664	17.5	n.a.	n.a.	31,715	10.0
1996 . .	56,928	17.8	n.a.	n.a.	30,888	9.6
1997 . .	58,032	18.0	n.a.	n.a.	30,917	9.5
1998 . .	54,760	16.6	n.a.	n.a.	32,082	9.8

* Data are tabulated by year of registration rather than by year of occurrence.

1999: Live births 54,055 (birth rate 16.3 per 1,000).

Source: UN, mainly *Demographic Yearbook*.

Expectation of life (UN estimates, years at birth, 1990–95): 72.8 (males 69.2; females 76.9) (Source: UN, *World Population Prospects: The 1998 Revision*).

ECONOMICALLY ACTIVE POPULATION (ISIC Major Divisions, persons aged 12 years and over, 1985 census*)

	Males	Females	Total
Agriculture, hunting, forestry and fishing	155,801	14,382	170,183
Mining and quarrying . . .	1,711	60	1,771
Manufacturing	142,134	72,811	214,945
Electricity, gas and water. . .	14,632	2,745	17,377
Construction.	63,509	876	64,385
Trade, restaurants and hotels. .	92,734	46,508	139,242
Transport, storage and communications . . .	51,425	7,864	59,289
Financing, insurance, real estate and business services . . .	28,324	14,364	42,688
Community, social and personal services†	169,749	199,511	369,260
Activities not adequately defined .	55,510	24,369	79,879
Total	**785,944**	**390,864**	**1,176,808**

* Figures exclude 17,789 persons (10,415 males; 7,374 females) seeking their first job but include about 60,000 other unemployed.
† Including armed forces, totalling 28,500 (27,600 males; 900 females).

Mid-1999 (estimates in '000): Agriculture, etc. 190; Total labour force 1,487 (Source: FAO, *Production Yearbook*).

Agriculture

PRINCIPAL CROPS ('000 metric tons)

	1998	1999	2000
Wheat	559	377	310
Maize	203	243	65
Barley	196	110	200
Oats	45	45*	45*
Sorghum	91	106	20
Rice (paddy)	950	1,302	1,175
Potatoes	145	159	110
Sugar cane	167	160	160*
Sunflower seed	79	161	33
Linseed	2†	3*	3*

* FAO estimate.　　† Unofficial figure.

Source: FAO.

LIVESTOCK ('000 head)

	1998	1999	2000
Cattle	10,297	10,504	10,800*
Sheep	16,495	14,409	13,032
Pigs†	330	360	380
Horses†	500	500	500
Chickens†	12,000	13,000	13,000

* Unofficial figure.　　† FAO estimate.

Source: FAO.

LIVESTOCK PRODUCTS ('000 metric tons)

	1998	1999	2000
Beef and veal	450	458	453
Mutton and lamb*	55	51	51
Pigmeat	26	27	26
Poultry meat	53	58	53
Cows' milk	1,468	1,479	1,422
Poultry eggs	33	37	37
Wool: greasy	76	60	55
Cattle hides	60	58	60
Sheepskins	19	16	15

* Unofficial figures.

Source: FAO.

Forestry

ROUNDWOOD REMOVALS ('000 cu m)

	1996	1997	1998
Sawlogs, veneer logs and logs for sleepers	909	1,130	1,374
Pulpwood	217	217	380
Other industrial wood	49	60	74
Fuel wood	2,866	3,563	4,335
Total	4,041	4,970	6,163

1999: Annual removals as in 1998 (FAO estimates).

Source: FAO, *Yearbook of Forest Products.*

SAWNWOOD PRODUCTION
('000 cu m, incl. railway sleepers)

	1990	1991	1992
Coniferous (softwood)	77	67	84
Broadleaved (hardwood)	152	138	185
Total	229	205	269

1993–99: Annual production as in 1992 (FAO estimates).

Source: FAO, *Yearbook of Forest Products.*

Fishing

('000 metric tons, live weight)

	1996	1997	1998
Argentine hake	57.9	48.4	49.1
Striped weakfish	12.7	15.2	15.3
Whitemouth croaker	25.7	23.7	22.3
Castaneta	2.9	4.1	9.7
Blackbelly rosefish	2.2	3.4	4.4
Argentine shortfin squid	5.7	20.9	13.2
Total catch	123.3	136.9	140.6

Source: FAO, *Yearbook of Fishery Statistics.*

Total catch (metric tons): 97,631 in 1999.

Industry

SELECTED PRODUCTS
('000 metric tons, unless otherwise indicated)

	1995	1996	1997
Raw sugar*	17	15	20
Wine	85	95	103
Cigarettes (million)	3,561	6,044	n.a.
Jet fuels	25	41	37
Motor spirit (petrol)	257	235	265
Kerosene	30	36	21
Distillate fuel oils	413	608	431
Residual fuel oils	496†	587	487
Cement	593	656	n.a.
Electric energy (million kWh)	6,306†	6,668	7,147

* FAO estimate.
† Provisional.

1998 (FAO estimates, '000 metric tons): Raw sugar 12; Wine 105.
1999 (FAO estimates, '000 metric tons): Raw sugar 10; Wine 105.

Source: mainly UN, *Industrial Commodity Statistics Yearbook.*

Finance

CURRENCY AND EXCHANGE RATES

Monetary Units
　100 centésimos = 1 peso uruguayo.

Sterling, Dollar and Euro Equivalents (30 April 2001)
　£1 sterling = 18.527 pesos;
　US $1 = 12.940 pesos;
　€1 = 11.486 pesos;
　1,000 pesos uruguayos = £53.97 = $77.28 = €87.07.

Average Exchange Rate (pesos per US $)
　1998　10.4719
　1999　11.3393
　2000　12.0996

Note: On 1 March 1993 a new currency, the peso uruguayo (equivalent to 1,000 former new pesos), was introduced.

BUDGET (million pesos uruguayos)*

Revenue	1996	1997	1998
Taxation†	42,276	55,313	65,359
Taxes on income, profits, etc. .	5,991	7,154	8,891
Individual taxes . . .	2,660	3,114	3,444
Corporate taxes . . .	3,173	3,839	5,203
Social security contributions .	13,899	17,335	20,212
Taxes on payroll and work-force.	430	352	405
Taxes on property	2,200	3,328	3,520
Domestic taxes on goods and services .	14,890	24,101	27,828
Value-added tax . . .	9,597	17,103	20,164
Excises	4,852	6,567	7,289
Taxes on international trade .	1,583	2,159	2,604
Import duties . . .	1,456	1,977	2,394
Export duties	12	21	14
Other taxes	2,158	3,379	4,214
Other current revenue . . .	3,014	4,428	5,030
Property income	1,224	2,104	1,930
Administrative fees, charges, etc.	572	1,075	938
Capital revenue	245	424	275
Total	**45,535**	**60,165**	**70,664**

Expenditure	1997	1998	1999
General public services‡ . .	5,995	7,745	8,485
Defence	2,638	2,847	3,115
Education	4,314	5,061	5,902
Health	3,513	4,209	4,459
Social security and welfare . .	38,681	44,628	45,115
Housing and community amenities	852	1,073	1,258
Other community and social services	279	241	523
Economic services	3,712	4,277	4,305
Other purposes	3,763	4,246	5,178
Sub-total	**65,661**	**76,698**	**78,340**
Less Government contribution as employer	1,384	1,654	2,261
Total	**64,277**	**78,352**	**76,079**
Current§	59,233	68,975	n.a.
Capital	3,130	3,698	n.a.

* Figures represent the consolidated accounts of the central Government, comprising the General Budget, the Directorate General of Social Security and three other social security funds.
† Including adjustments to a cash basis (million pesos uruguayos): 1,125 in 1996; –2,495 in 1997; –2,315 in 1998.
‡ Including public order and safety.
§ Including interest payments (million pesos uruguayos): 3,005 in 1997; 3,426 in 1998; 4,708 in 1999.

Source: IMF, mainly *Government Finance Statistics Yearbook*.

INTERNATIONAL RESERVES (US $ million at 31 December)

	1998	1999	2000
Gold	517	518	315
IMF special drawing rights . .	1	1	—
Reserve position in the IMF . .	22	49	46
Foreign exchange	2,051	2,031	2,400
Total	**2,590**	**2,599**	**2,761**

Source: IMF, *International Financial Statistics*.

MONEY SUPPLY (million pesos uruguayos at 31 December)

	1998	1999	2000
Currency outside banks . . .	7,084.0	7,639.0	7,324.0
Demand deposits at commercial banks	7,314.2	7,216.6	7,241.0
Total money (incl. others) . .	**14,420.3**	**14,873.9**	**14,583.1**

Source: IMF, *International Financial Statistics*.

COST OF LIVING (Consumer Price Index for Montevideo; base: 1990 = 100)

	1997	1998	1999
Food	1,307.5	1,444.4	1,497.5
All items (incl. others) . . .	**1,660.7**	**1,839.4**	**1,943.5**

Source: UN, *Monthly Bulletin of Statistics*.

2000 (base: 1999 = 100): All items 104.8 (Source: IMF, *International Financial Statistics*].

NATIONAL ACCOUNTS

Composition of the Gross National Product
(million pesos uruguayos at current prices)

	1989	1990	1991
Compensation of employees . .	1,943.0	3,880.9	8,397.4
Operating surplus . . . . }	2,163.5	4,126.5	7,139.4
Consumption of fixed capital . . }			
Gross domestic product (GDP) at factor cost .	**4,106.5**	**8,007.4**	**15,536.8**
Indirect taxes, *less* subsidies . .	732.9	1,690.7	3,598.7
GDP in purchasers' values .	**4,839.4**	**9,698.1**	**19,135.5**
Net factor income from abroad .	–211.6	–377.1	–470.2
Gross national product .	**4,627.8**	**932.1**	**18,665.3**

Source: UN, *National Accounts Statistics*.

Expenditure on the Gross Domestic Product
(million pesos uruguayos at current prices)

	1997	1998	1999
Government final consumption expenditure	25,411	29,546	33,027
Private final consumption expenditure	148,676	170,874	173,285
Increase in stocks	1,585	1,555	1,561
Gross fixed capital formation . .	29,244	35,137	34,809
Total domestic expenditure .	**204,916**	**237,112**	**242,682**
Exports of goods and services .	42,109	46,511	42,965
Less Imports of goods and services	42,088	48,230	46,827
GDP in purchasers' values .	**204,938**	**235,393**	**238,820**
GDP at constant 1983 prices .	**286**	**299**	**289**

Source: IMF, *International Financial Statistics*.

Gross Domestic Product by Economic Activity
(million pesos uruguayos at current prices)

	1997	1998	1999
Agriculture	15,118	16,376	13,288
Fishing	319	448	299
Mining and quarrying . . .	449	578	621
Manufacturing	39,006	44,319	39,852
Electricity, gas and water. .	10,854	13,375	14,916
Construction.	7,772	9,307	9,465
Commerce	30,238	33,009	33,741
Transport, storage and communications	16,067	18,904	20,967
Finance, insurance and real estate	16,902	21,007	24,430
Other services	73,645	85,596	92,467
Sub-total	**209,920**	**242,339**	**249,425**
Adjustments.	–4,982	–6,946	–10,605
GDP in purchasers' values .	**204,938**	**235,393**	**238,820**

BALANCE OF PAYMENTS (US $ million)

	1997	1998	1999
Exports of goods f.o.b.	2,793.1	2,829.3	2,304.5
Imports of goods f.o.b.	−3,497.5	−3,601.4	−3,172.9
Trade balance	**−704.4**	**−772.1**	**−868.4**
Exports of services	1,424.1	1,319.1	1,281.5
Imports of services	−888.6	−883.6	−896.6
Balance on goods and services	**−168.9**	**−336.6**	**−483.5**
Other income received	547.3	608.0	647.6
Other income paid	−740.0	−805.9	−839.1
Balance on goods, services and income	**−361.6**	**−534.5**	**−675.0**
Current transfers received	83.0	75.0	78.4
Current transfers paid	−8.8	−16.0	−8.4
Current balance	**−287.4**	**−475.5**	**−605.0**
Direct investment from abroad	126.4	164.1	228.8
Portfolio investment liabilities	209.6	—	—
Other investment assets	−626.6	−428.0	110.8
Other investment liabilities	912.5	550.2	−92.0
Net errors and omissions	78.8	134.0	222.6
Overall balance	**400.1**	**−64.3**	**−134.8**

Source: IMF, *International Financial Statistics.*

External Trade

PRINCIPAL COMMODITIES (US $ '000)

Imports c.i.f.	1997	1998	1999
Vegetable products	119,045	118,507	97,086
Foodstuffs, beverages and tobacco	239,242	256,523	239,528
Mineral products	368,615	242,355	390,387
Chemical products	491,846	512,390	489,681
Synthetic plastic, resins and rubber	254,172	257,900	234,869
Raw materials for paper production and paper products	128,499	144,840	136,664
Textiles and textile products	215,283	207,023	155,389
Base metals and products	194,465	226,769	161,743
Machinery and appliances	841,913	852,797	745,254
Transport equipment	471,621	553,394	304,256
Optical and photographic apparatus	84,211	89,150	75,066
Total (incl. others)	**3,726,757**	**3,810,501**	**3,356,770**

Exports f.o.b.	1997	1998	1999
Live animals and animal products	729,156	823,147	663,229
Vegetable products	478,378	439,875	353,608
Foodstuffs, beverages and tobacco	113,099	149,238	120,801
Chemical products	112,490	120,743	97,095
Synthetic plastics, resins and rubber	91,076	97,005	88,924
Hides, skins, leather products, etc.	278,359	249,123	218,347
Raw materials for paper production and paper products	60,684	68,457	62,776
Textiles and textile products	479,689	356,521	264,599
Machinery and appliances	70,838	58,007	39,065
Transport equipment	82,727	178,706	130,236
Total (incl. others)	**2,725,741**	**2,768,737**	**2,236,798**

PRINCIPAL TRADING PARTNERS (US $ '000)

Imports c.i.f.	1997	1998	1999
Argentina	790,697	839,336	795,491
Brazil	801,944	793,379	651,638
Chile	62,873	59,136	54,828
China. People's Republic	63,872	78,717	89,020
Ecuador	14,458	39,786	9,985
France	119,862	177,525	140,400
Germany	117,669	125,098	97,852
Hong Kong	44,169	44,718	31,422
Italy	170,584	176,473	123,760
Japan	97,125	92,662	69,445
Korea, Republic	78,398	81,680	54,954
Mexico	52,372	43,427	38,682
Spain	116,560	140,655	113,340
Sweden	38,083	25,660	20,755
Taiwan	42,503	44,056	27,496
United Kingdom	65,717	58,950	45,602
USA	432,189	459,750	375,428
Venezuela	88,488	38,113	124,315
Total (incl. others)	**3,716,020**	**3,808,151**	**3,356,770**

Exports f.o.b.	1997	1998	1999
Argentina	354,303	513,192	368,614
Brazil	940,155	935,246	557,119
Canada	28,843	24,351	44,985
Chile	56,739	73,382	46,499
China, People's Republic	123,200	76,466	61,860
France	24,559	20,721	18,397
Germany	120,391	112,123	110,955
Hong Kong	60,486	46,348	35,057
Israel	66,392	75,943	69,215
Italy	91,069	78,740	72,109
Japan	28,742	21,874	23,544
Mexico	32,438	25,812	43,417
Netherlands	58,189	53,750	49,468
Paraguay	60,665	83,860	81,139
Peru	31,944	32,962	17,524
Spain	58,680	55,226	69,545
United Kingdom	116,549	94,034	80,452
USA	160,812	158,424	140,767
Venezuela	15,141	27,716	27,994
Total (incl. others)	**2,729,521**	**2,768,737**	**2,236,798**

Transport

RAILWAYS (traffic)

	1993	1994	1995
Passenger-km (million)	221	467	n.a.
Freight ton-km (million)	178	188	184

Freight ton-km (million): 182 in 1996; 204 in 1997.

Source: UN, *Statistical Yearbook.*

ROAD TRAFFIC (motor vehicles in use at 31 December)

	1995	1996	1997
Passenger cars	464,547	485,109	516,889
Buses and coaches	4,409	4,752	4,984
Lorries and vans	41,417	43,656	45,280
Road tractors	12,511	14,628	15,514
Motorcycles and mopeds	300,850	328,406	359,824

Source: International Road Federation: *World Road Statistics.*

SHIPPING

Merchant Fleet (registered at 31 December)

	1998	1999	2000
Number of vessels	91	90	88
Total displacement ('000 grt) . .	106.9	61.8	67.5

Source: Lloyd's Register of Shipping, *World Fleet Statistics*.

International Sea-borne Freight Traffic ('000 metric tons)*

	1988	1989	1990
Goods loaded	670	680	710
Goods unloaded	1,415	1,395	1,450

* Port of Montevideo only.

Source: UN, *Monthly Bulletin of Statistics*.

CIVIL AVIATION (traffic on scheduled services)

	1995	1996	1997
Kilometres flown (million) . .	5	5	6
Passengers carried ('000) . .	477	504	544
Passenger-km (million) . .	636	640	627
Total ton-km (million) . .	62	62	57

Source: UN, *Statistical Yearbook*.

Communications Media

	1995	1996	1997
Radio receivers ('000 in use) . .	1,940	1,955	1,970
Television receivers ('000 in use) .	750	775	782
Telephones ('000 main lines in use)	622	669	761
Telefax stations ('000 in use) . .	11,000	n.a.	n.a.
Mobile cellular telephones (subscribers)	39,904	79,701	149,740
Daily newspapers Number	36	36	n.a.
Average circulation ('000 copies)*	950	950	n.a.

* Estimates.

Book production: 934 titles in 1996.

Sources: UNESCO, *Statistical Yearbook*; UN, *Statistical Yearbook*.

Tourism

ARRIVALS BY NATIONALITY ('000)*

	1997	1998	1999
Argentina	1,602.8	1,513.6	1,532.7
Brazil	200.3	212.2	153.7
Total (incl. others) . . .	2,462.5	2,324.0	2,273.2

* Figures refer to arrivals at frontiers of visitors from abroad.

Sources: World Tourism Organization, *Yearbook of Tourism Statistics*, and Ministerio de Turismo.

Tourism receipts (million US $): 759 in 1997; 695 in 1998; 653 in 1999 (Source: World Bank, *World Bank Atlas*).

Education

(1999)

	Institutions	Teachers	Students
Pre-primary	1,267	3,207	99,999
Primary	2,415	17,023	349,647
Secondary			
General	392	23,605*	229,390
Vocational	106	n.a.	54,241
Tertiary†			
University and equivalent institutions	6	7,364*	77,454

* Public education only.

Directory

The Constitution

The Constitution of Uruguay was ratified by plebiscite, on 27 November 1966, when the country voted to return to the presidential form of government after 15 years of 'collegiate' government. The main points of the Constitution, as amended in January 1997, are as follows:

General Provisions

Uruguay shall have a democratic republican form of government, sovereignty being exercised directly by the Electoral Body in cases of election, by initiative or by referendum, and indirectly by representative powers established by the Constitution, according to the rules set out therein.

There shall be freedom of religion; there is no state religion; property shall be inviolable; there shall be freedom of thought. Anyone may enter Uruguay. There are two forms of citizenship: natural, being persons born in Uruguay or of Uruguayan parents, and legal, being people established in Uruguay with at least three years' residence in the case of those with family, and five years' for those without family. Every citizen has the right and obligation to vote.

Legislature

Legislative power is vested in the Congreso (Congress or General Assembly), comprising two houses, which may act separately or together according to the dispositions of the Constitution. It elects in joint session the members of the Supreme Court of Justice, of the Electoral Court, Tribunals, Administrative Litigation and the Accounts Tribunal.

Elections for both houses, the President and the Vice-President shall take place every five years on the last Sunday in October; sessions of the Assembly begin on 1 March each year and last until 15 December (15 September in election years, in which case the new Congress takes office on 15 February). Extraordinary sessions can be convened only in case of extreme urgency.

Chamber of Representatives

The Chamber of Representatives has 99 members elected by direct suffrage according to the system of proportional representation, with at least two representatives for each Department. The number of representatives can be altered by law by a two-thirds' majority in both houses. Their term of office is five years and they must be over 25 years of age and be natural citizens or legal citizens with five years' exercise of their citizenship. Representatives have the right to bring accusations against any member of the Government or judiciary for violation of the Constitution or any other serious offence.

Senate

The Senate comprises 31 members, including the Vice-President, who sits as President of the Senate, and 30 members elected directly by proportional representation on the same lists as the representatives, for a term of five years. They must be natural citizens or legal citizens with seven years' exercise of their rights, and be over 30 years of age. The Senate is responsible for hearing cases brought by the representatives and can deprive a guilty person of a post by a two-thirds' majority.

The Executive

Executive power is exercised by the President and the Council of Ministers. There is a Vice-President, who is also President of the Congress and of the Senate. The President and Vice-President are directly elected by absolute majority, and remain in office for five years. They must be over 35 years of age and be natural citizens.

The Council of Ministers comprises the office holders in the ministries or their deputies, and is responsible for all acts of government and administration. It is presided over by the President of the Republic, who has a vote.

The Judiciary

Judicial power is exercised by the five-member Supreme Court of Justice and by Tribunals and local courts; members of the Supreme Court must be over 40 years of age and be natural citizens, or legal citizens with 10 years' exercise and 25 years' residence, and must be lawyers of 10 years' standing, eight of them in public or fiscal ministry or judicature. Members serve for 10 years and can be re-elected after a break of five years. The Court nominates all other judges and judicial officials.

The Government

HEAD OF STATE

President: Jorge Luis Batlle Ibáñez (took office 1 March 2000).
Vice-President: Luis Hierro López.

COUNCIL OF MINISTERS
(August 2001)

The Council of Ministers is composed of members of the Partido Colorado (PC) and the Partido Nacional (PN).

Minister of the Interior: Guillermo Stirling (PC).
Minister of Foreign Affairs: Dr Didier Opertti (PC).
Minister of National Defence: Luis Brezzo (PC).
Minister of Economy and Finance: Alberto Bensión (PC).
Director of Planning and Budget Office: Ariel Davrieux (PC).
Minister of Industry, Energy and Mining: Sergio Abreu (PN).
Minister of Livestock, Agriculture and Fishing: Gonzalo González (PN).
Minister of Transport and Public Works: Lucio Cáceres Behrens (PC).
Minister of Labour and Social Security: Alvaro Alonso Tellechea (PN).
Minister of Tourism: Alfonso Varela (PC).
Minister of Education and Culture: Antonio Mercader (PN).
Minister of Public Health: Luis Fraschini (PC).
Minister of Housing, Territorial Regulation and the Environment: Carlos Cat (PN).

MINISTRIES

Office of the President: Casa de Gobierno, Edif. Libertad, Avda Luis Alberto de Herrera 3350, Montevideo; tel. (2) 4872110; fax (2) 4809397.
Ministry of Economy and Finance: Colonia 1089, 3°, Montevideo; tel. (2) 9021017; fax (2) 9021277.
Ministry of Education and Culture: Reconquista 535, Montevideo; tel. (2) 9150103; fax (2) 9162632; e-mail webmaster@mec.gub.uy; internet chana.mec.gub.uy.
Ministry of Foreign Affairs: Avda 18 de Julio 1205, Montevideo; tel. (2) 9021007; fax (2) 9021327; e-mail webmaster@mrree.gub.uy; internet www.mrree.gub.uy.
Ministry of Housing, Territorial Regulation and the Environment: Zabala 1427, 11000 Montevideo; tel. (2) 9150211; fax (2) 9162914; e-mail computos@mvotma.gub.uy; internet www.mvotma.gub.uy.
Ministry of Industry, Energy and Mining: Rincón 723, 11000 Montevideo; tel. (2) 9000231; fax (2) 9021245.
Ministry of the Interior: Mercedes 993, Montevideo; tel. (2) 9089024; fax (2) 9020716; internet www.minterior.gub.uy.

Ministry of Labour and Social Security: Juncal 1511, 4°, 11000 Montevideo; tel. (2) 9162681; fax (2) 9162708; e-mail webmtss@mtss.gub.uy; internet www.mtss.gub.uy.
Ministry of Livestock, Agriculture and Fishing: Avda Constituyente 1476, 11900 Montevideo; tel. (2) 4004155; fax (2) 4099623; e-mail informatica@mgap.gub.uy; internet www.mgap.gub.uy.
Ministry of National Defence: Edif. General Artigas, Avda 8 de Octubre 2628, Montevideo; tel. (2) 4809707; fax (2) 4809397.
Ministry of Public Health: Avda 18 de Julio 1892, Montevideo; tel. (2) 4000101; fax (2) 4088676; e-mail msp@msp.gub.uy; internet www.msp.gub.uy.
Ministry of Tourism: Avda Libertador 1409, 11100 Montevideo; tel. (2) 9089105; fax (2) 9021624; e-mail cecom@turismo.gub.uy; internet www.turismo.gub.uy.
Ministry of Transport and Public Works: Rincón 575, 4° y 5°, 11000 Montevideo; tel. (2) 9150509; fax (2) 9162883; e-mail info@dnt.gub.uy; internet www.dnt.gub.uy.
Office of Planning and Budget: Fondo de las Americas, Convención 1366, Montevideo; tel. (2) 9000461; fax (2) 2099730; e-mail diropp@presidencia.gub.uy.

President and Legislature
PRESIDENT

Election, 31 October and 28 November 1999

Candidate	First ballot % of vote	Second ballot % of vote
Jorge Luis Batlle Ibáñez (Partido Colorado)	31.32	51.59
Tabaré Vázquez (Encuentro Progresista—Frente Amplio)	38.51	44.07
Luis Alberto Lacalle (Partido Nacional)	21.29	—
Rafael Michelini (Nuevo Espacio)	4.36	—
Luis Pieri (Unión Cívica)	0.23	—
Invalid votes	4.29	4.34
Total	100.00	100.00

CONGRESO
Senate

Election, 31 October 1999

Party	Seats
Encuentro Progresista—Frente Amplio	12
Partido Colorado	10
Partido Nacional	7
Nuevo Espacio	1
Total*	30

* An additional seat is reserved for the Vice-President, who sits as President of the Senate.

Chamber of Representatives

Election, 31 October 1999

Party	Seats
Encuentro Progresista—Frente Amplio	40
Partido Colorado	33
Partido Nacional	22
Nuevo Espacio	4
Total	99

Political Organizations

Alianza Libertadora Nacionalista: Montevideo; extreme right-wing; Leader Osvaldo Martínez Jaume.
Encuentro Progresista—Frente Amplio (EP—FA): Colonia 1367, 2°, Montevideo; tel. (2) 9022176; f. 1971; left-wing grouping; Pres. Tabaré Vázquez; members include:

Frente Izquierda de Liberación (FIDEL): Montevideo; f. 1962; socialist; Leader Adolfo Aguirre González.

Grupo Pregón: Montevideo; left-wing liberal party; Leaders SERGIO PREVITALI, ENRIQUE MORAS.

Movimiento de Acción Nacionalista (MAN): Montevideo; left-wing nationalist org.; Leader JOSÉ DURÁN MATOS.

Movimiento Blanco Popular y Progresista (MBPP): Montevideo; moderate left-wing; Leader A. FRANCISCO RODRÍGUEZ CAMUSSO.

Movimiento de Liberación Nacional (MLN)—Tupamaros: Montevideo; f. 1962; radical socialist; during 1962–73 the MLN, operating under its popular name of the **Tupamaros**, conducted a campaign of urban guerrilla warfare until it was defeated by the Armed Forces in late 1973; following the return to civilian rule, in 1985, the MLN announced its decision to abandon its armed struggle; legally recognized in May 1989; Sec.-Gen. JOSÉ MUJICA.

Movimiento 26 de Marzo: Durazno 1118, Montevideo; tel. (2) 9011584; f. 1971; socialist; Pres. EDUARDO RUBIO; Sec.-Gen. FERNANDO VÁZQUEZ.

Partido Comunista: Río Negro 1525, Montevideo; tel. (2) 9017171; fax (2) 9011050; f. 1920; Sec.-Gen. MARINA ARISMENDI; 42,000 mems (est.).

Partido de Democracia Avanzada: Montevideo; Communist.

Partido Socialista del Uruguay: Casa del Pueblo, Soriano 1218, Montevideo; tel. (2) 9013344; fax (2) 9082548; f. 1910; Pres. (vacant); Sec.-Gen. DR. MANUEL LAGUARDA.

Nuevo Espacio: Eduardo Acevedo 1615, Montevideo; tel. (2) 4026989; fax (2) 4026991; e-mail larosa@adinet.com.uy; internet www.nuevoespacio.org.uy; f. 1989 by parties withdrawing from the Frente Amplio; moderate left-wing; Leader RAFAEL MICHELINI; Pres. HÉCTOR PÉREZ PIERA; Sec. EDGARDO CARVALHO; members include:

Partido Demócrata Cristiano (PDC): Aquiles Lanza 1318 bis, Montevideo; tel. and fax (2) 9030704; e-mail pdc@chasque.apc.org; internet www.chasque.apc.org/pdc; fmrly Unión Cívica del Uruguay; f. 1962; Pres. Dr HÉCTOR LESCANO; Sec.-Gen. FRANCISCO OTTONELLI.

Partido por el Gobierno del Pueblo (Lista 99): Ejido 1480, Montevideo; tel. (2) 9082534; f. 1962; left-wing; Leader RAFAEL MICHELINI.

Unión Cívica: Río Branco 1486, Montevideo; tel. (2) 9005535; f. 1912; recognized Christian Democrat faction which split from the Partido Demócrata Cristiano in 1980.

Partido Azul (PA): Paul Harris 1722, Montevideo; tel. and fax (2) 6016327; f. 1993; Leader Dr ROBERTO CANESSA; Gen. Sec. Ing. ARMANDO VAL.

Partido Colorado: Andrés Martínez Trueba 1271, Montevideo; tel. (2) 4090180; f. 1836; Sec.-Gen. JORGE BATLLE IBÁÑEZ; Leader JOSÉ LUIS BATLLE; factions include:

Batllismo Radical: Leader JORGE BATLLE IBÁÑEZ.

Cruzada 94: Leader PABLO MILLOR.

Foro Batllista: Colonia 1243, Montevideo; tel. (2) 9030154; Leader Dr JULIO MARÍA SANGUINETTI CAIROLO.

Unión Colorada y Batllista (Pachequista): Buenos Aires 594, Montevideo; tel. (2) 9164648; right-wing.

Partido Justiciero: Montevideo; extreme right-wing; Leader BOLÍVAR ESPÍNDOLA.

Partido Nacional (Blanco): Juan Carlos Gómez 1384, Montevideo; tel. (2) 9163831; fax (2) 9163758; f. 1836; Leader ALBERTO VOLONTÉ; Sec.-Gen. ALBERTO ZUMARÁN; tendencies within the party include:

Consejo Nacional Herrerista: Leaders LUIS ALBERTO LACALLE, IGNACIO DE POSADAS.

Divisa Blanca: conservative; Leader EDUARDO PONS ETCHEVERRY.

Manos a la Obra: Plaza Cagancha 1145, Montevideo; tel. (2) 9028149; Leader ALBERTO VOLONTÉ.

Movimiento Nacional de Rocha—Corriente Popular Nacionalista: Avda Uruguay 1324, Montevideo; tel. (2) 9027502; Leaders CARLOS JULIO PEREYRA, JUAN PIVEL DEVOTO.

Partido Nacional—Barrán.

Renovación y Victoria: Leader Dr GONZALO AGUIRRE RAMÍREZ.

Sector por la Patria: Leader ALBERTO ZUMARÁN.

Partido del Sol: Peatonal Yi 1385, Montevideo; tel. (2) 9001616; fax (2) 9006739; e-mail sol@adinet.com.uy; ecologist, federal, pacifist; Leader HOMERO MIERES.

Partido de los Trabajadores: Convención 1196, Montevideo; tel. (2) 9082624; f. 1980; extreme left-wing; Leader JUAN VITAL ANDRADE.

Diplomatic Representation

EMBASSIES IN URUGUAY

Argentina: Cuareim 1470, 11800 Montevideo; tel. (2) 9028166; fax (2) 9028172; Ambassador: Dra ALICIA MARTÍNEZ RÍOS.

Belgium: Leyenda Patria 2880, 4°, Montevideo; tel. (2) 7101571; Ambassador: ROGER TYBERGHEIN.

Bolivia: Dr Prudencio de Pena 2469, Montevideo; tel. (2) 7083573; fax (2) 7080066; e-mail emburu@adinet.com.uy; Ambassador: FERNANDO ROJAS ALAIZA.

Brazil: Blvr Artigas 1328, Montevideo; tel. (2) 7072119; fax (2) 7072086; Ambassador: RENATO PRADO GUIMARÃES.

Bulgaria: Rambla Mahatma Gandhi 647, 5°, Casilla 502, Montevideo; tel. (2) 7111627; Ambassador: LIUBOMIR ILIEV IVANOV.

Chile: Andes 1365, 1°, Montevideo; tel. (2) 9082223; fax (2) 9021649; Ambassador: AUGUSTO BERMÚDEZ ARANCIBIA.

China, People's Republic: Miraflores 1508, Casilla 18966, Montevideo; tel. (2) 6016126; fax (2) 6018508; e-mail embchina@adinet.com.uy; Ambassador: WANG ZHEN.

Colombia: Juncal 1305, 18°, Montevideo; tel. (2) 9154434; fax (2) 9161594; Ambassador: MANUEL JOSÉ CÁRDENAS.

Costa Rica: José Martí 3295, Apt 102, Casilla 12242, Montevideo; tel. (2) 7083645; fax (2) 7089714; Ambassador: JUAN W. VALENZUELA C.

Cuba: Francisco Vidal 677, Montevideo; tel. (2) 7124668; fax (2) 4082140; Ambassador: (vacant).

Czech Republic: Luis B. Cavia 2996, Casilla 12262, Montevideo; tel. (2) 7087808; Ambassador: PAVEL ZRUST.

Dominican Republic: T. de Tezanos 1186, Montevideo; tel. (2) 6287766; fax (2) 7114265; Ambassador: Dr JESÚS MARÍA HERNÁNDEZ SÁNCHEZ.

Ecuador: Guayaquí 3428, Montevideo; tel. (2) 7076463; fax (2) 9021409; Ambassador: EDUARDO CABEZAS MOLINA.

Egypt: Avda Brasil 2663, Montevideo; tel. (2) 7081553; fax (2) 7080977; Ambassador: AMINA HUSSEIN FARID.

France: Avda Uruguay 853, Casilla 290, 11100 Montevideo; tel. (2) 9020077; fax (2) 9023711; e-mail ambfra@adinet.com.uy; internet hlm.le-village.com/ambassadedefrance; Ambassador: THIERRY REYNARD.

Germany: La Cumparsita 1435, Casilla 20014, 11200 Montevideo; tel. (2) 9025222; fax (2) 9023422; e-mail deubot@montevideo.com.uy; internet www.emb-alemania.com; Ambassador: Dr HORST HEUBAUM.

Guatemala: General French 1695, Montevideo; tel. (2) 6287880; fax (2) 6287568; Ambassador: GUILLERMO ESTRADA STRECKER.

Holy See: Blvr Artigas 1270, Casilla 1503, Montevideo (Apostolic Nunciature); tel. (2) 7072016; fax (2) 7072209; Apostolic Nuncio: Most Rev. JANUSZ BOLONEK, Titular Archbishop of Madaurus.

Hungary: Dr Prudencio de Pena 2469, Montevideo; tel. (2) 7086173; Ambassador: Dr BÉLA SZABÓ.

Israel: Blvr Artigas 1585, Montevideo; tel. (2) 4004164; Ambassador: AVRAHAM TOLEDO.

Italy: José B. Lamas 2857, Casilla 268, Montevideo; tel. (2) 7084916; fax (2) 7085994; e-mail amburuit@netgate.com.uy; internet www.ambitalia.com.uy; Ambassador: ALBERTO BONIVER.

Japan: Blvr Artigas 953, Montevideo; tel. (2) 4087645; fax (2) 4087980; Ambassador: KATSUHIKO TSUNODA.

Lebanon: Avda Gral Rivera 2278, Montevideo; tel. and fax (2) 4086365; Chargé d'affaires: MILIA JABBOUR.

Mexico: Andes 1365, 7°, Montevideo; tel. (2) 9020791; fax (2) 9021232; e-mail embmexur@netgate.com.uy; internet www.rau.edu.uy/embamex; Ambassador: ROGELIO GRANGUILLHOME MORFIN.

Netherlands: Leyenda Patria 2880/202, Casilla 1519, 11300 Montevideo; tel. (2) 7112956; fax (2) 7113301; e-mail nlgovmtv@multi.com.uy; Ambassador: J. W. C. ZANDVLIET.

Nicaragua: Rambla República del Perú 1139, Montevideo; Chargé d'affaires a.i.: MARIO DUARTE ZAMORA.

Panama: Rambla Mahatma Gandhi 509, Casilla 404, Montevideo; Ambassador: ALEXIS CABRERA QUINTERO.

Paraguay: Blvr Artigas 1256, Montevideo; tel. (2) 7072138; fax (2) 7083682; Ambassador: Dr HORACIO NOGUÉS ZUBIZARRETA.

Peru: Soriano 1124, Casilla 126, Montevideo; tel. (2) 9021194; fax (2) 9021194; Ambassador: GUILLERMO DEL SOLAR ROJAS.

Poland: Jorge Canning 2389, Casilla 1538, 11600 Montevideo; tel. (2) 4801313; fax (2) 4873389; e-mail ambmonte@netgate.com.uy; Ambassador: JAROSLAVW GUGALA.

Portugal: Avda Dr Francisco Soca 1128, Casilla 701, 11300 Montevideo; tel. (2) 7084061; fax (2) 7096456; Ambassador: Dr JOSÉ DUARTE SEQUEIRA E SERPA.

Romania: Echevarriarza 3452, Montevideo; tel. (2) 6220876; fax (2) 6220135; Chargé d'affaires: ANTON DONCIU.

Russia: Blvr España 2741, Montevideo; tel. (2) 7081884; fax (2) 7086597; e-mail embaru@montevideo.com.uy; internet www.rusiaoficial.org.uy; Ambassador: YAN A. BURLIAY.

South Africa: Echevarriarza 3335, Casilla 498, Montevideo; tel. (2) 6230161; fax (2) 6230066; e-mail safem@netgate.com.uy; Chargé d'affaires a.i.: KRISHNALAL CHOONILAL KAPITAN.

Spain: Avda Brasil 2786, Montevideo; tel. (2) 7086010; Ambassador: Joaquín María de Arístegui.

Switzerland: Ing. Federico Abadie 2936/40, 11300 Montevideo; tel. (2) 7104315; fax (2) 7115031; Ambassador: Urs Stemmler.

United Kingdom: Marco Bruto 1073, Casilla 16024, 11300 Montevideo; tel. (2) 6223650; fax (2) 6227815; e-mail bemonte@internet .com.uy; internet www.britishembassy.org.uy; Ambassador: Andrew R. Murray.

USA: Lauro Muller 1776, 11200 Montevideo; tel. (2) 2036061; fax (2) 4088611; internet www.embeeuu.gub.uy; Chargé d'affaires a.i.: Marianne M. Myles.

Venezuela: Araucana 1265, Montevideo; tel. (2) 6007986; fax (2) 6018608; e-mail embaven@adinet.com.uy; Ambassador: Juan Enrique Moreno Gómez.

Judicial System

The Supreme Court of Justice comprises five members appointed at the suggestion of the executive, for a period of five years. It has original jurisdiction in constitutional, international and admiralty cases, and hears appeals from the appellate courts, of which there are seven, each with three judges.

Cases involving the functioning of the state administration are heard in the ordinary Administrative Courts and in the Supreme Administrative Court, which consists of five members appointed in the same way as members of the Supreme Court of Justice.

In Montevideo there are 19 civil courts, 10 criminal and correctional courts, 19 courts presided over by justices of the peace, three juvenile courts, three labour courts and courts for government and other cases. Each departmental capital, and some other cities, has a departmental court; each of the 224 judicial divisions has a justice of the peace.

The administration of justice became free of charge in 1980, with the placing of attorneys-at-law in all courts to assist those unable to pay for the services of a lawyer.

Supreme Court of Justice: Gutiérrez Ruiz 1310, 11100 Montevideo; tel. (2) 9001041; fax (2) 9023549.

President of the Supreme Court of Justice: Dr Luis Tonello.

Supreme Administrative Court: Mercedes 961, Montevideo; tel. (2) 9008047; fax (2) 9080539.

Religion

Under the Constitution, the Church and the State were declared separate and toleration for all forms of worship was proclaimed. Roman Catholicism predominates.

CHRISTIANITY

Federación de Iglesias Evangélicas del Uruguay: Estero Bellaco 2676, 11600 Montevideo; tel. (2) 4873375; fax (2) 4872181; f. 1956; eight mem. churches; Pres. Luis Rosso; Sec. Alfredo Servetti.

The Roman Catholic Church

Uruguay comprises one archdiocese and nine dioceses. At 31 December 1999 there were an estimated 2,325,148 adherents in the country, representing about 73% of the total population.

Bishops' Conference: Conferencia Episcopal Uruguaya, Avda Uruguay 1319, 11100 Montevideo; tel. (2) 9002642; fax (2) 9011802; e-mail ceusecre@adinet.com.uy; internet www.iglesiauruguaya.com; f. 1972; Pres. Rt Rev. Carlos María Collazzi Irazábal, Bishop of Mercedes.

Archbishop of Montevideo: Most Rev. Nicolás Cotugno Fanizzi, Arzobispado, Treinta y Tres 1368, Casilla 356, 11000 Montevideo; tel. (2) 9158127; fax (2) 9158926; e-mail arzmvdeo@sicoar.com.uy; internet www.iglesia-mvdo.org.

The Anglican Communion

Uruguay is the newest diocese in the Province of the Southern Cone of America, having been established in 1988. The presiding Bishop of the Iglesia Anglicana del Cono Sur de América, is the Bishop of Northern Argentina.

Bishop of Uruguay: Rt Rev. Miguel Tamayo Zaldivar, Centro Diocesano, Reconquista 522, Casilla 6108, 11000 Montevideo; tel. (2) 9159627; fax (2) 9162519; e-mail mtamayo@netgate.com.uy.

Other Churches

Baptist Evangelical Convention of Uruguay: Mercedes 1487, Montevideo; tel. and fax (2) 2167012; e-mail suspasos@adinet .com.uy; f. 1948; Pres: Dr Juan Carlos Otormín.

Iglesia Adventista (Adventist Church): Castro 167, Montevideo; f. 1901; 4,000 mems; Principal officers Dr Guillermo Durán, Dr Alexis Piro.

Iglesia Evangélica Metodista en el Uruguay (Evangelical Methodist Church in Uruguay): Estero Bellaco 2678, 11600 Montevideo; tel. (2) 4800984; fax (2) 4872181; e-mail iemu@adinet .com.uy; f. 1878; 1,193 mems (1997); Pres. Beatriz Ferrari.

Iglesia Evangélica Valdense (Waldensian Evangelical Church): Avda 8 de Octubre 3039, 11600 Montevideo; tel. and fax (2) 4879406; e-mail ievm@internet.com.uy; f. 1952; 15,000 mems; Pastor Alvaro Michelin Salomón.

Iglesia Pentecostal Unida Internacional en Uruguay (United Pentecostal Church International in Uruguay): Helvecia 4032, Piedras Blancas, 12200 Montevideo; tel. (2) 5133618; e-mail lrodrigu@montevideo.com.uy; internet members.tripod.com /"lrodrigu; Pastor Luis Rodriguez.

Primera Iglesia Bautista (First Baptist Church): Avda Daniel Fernández Crespo 1741, Casilla 5051, 11200 Montevideo; tel. (2) 4098744; fax (2) 4002694; f. 1911; 350 mems; Pastor Lemuel J.Larrosa.

Other denominations active in Uruguay include the Iglesia Evangélica del Río de la Plata and the Iglesia Evangélica Menonita (Evangelical Mennonite Church).

BAHÁ'Í FAITH

National Spiritual Assembly of the Bahá'ís: Blvr Artigas 2440, 11600 Montevideo; tel. (2) 4875890; fax (2) 4802165; e-mail bahai@ multi.com.uy; f. 1938; mems resident in 140 localities.

The Press

DAILIES

Montevideo

El Diario: Rincón 712, 11000 Montevideo; tel. (2) 9030465; fax (2) 9030637; e-mail joterom@adinet.com.uy; f. 1923; evening; independent; Editor Jorge Otero; circ. 80,000.

El Diario Español: Cerrito 551–555, Casilla 899, 11000 Montevideo; tel. (2) 9159481; fax (2) 9159545; f. 1905; morning (except Monday); newspaper of the Spanish community; Editor Carlos Reinante; circ. 20,000.

Diario Oficial: Florida 1178, Montevideo; f. 1905; morning; publishes laws, official decrees, parliamentary debates, judicial decisions and legal transactions; Dir Sra Zain Nassif de Zarumbe.

Gaceta Comercial: Juncal 1391, 11000 Montevideo; tel. (2) 9165618; fax (2) 9165619; f. 1916; morning (Mon.–Fri.); Dir Milton Sans; Editor Pablo Sans; circ. 4,500.

La Mañana: Paysandú 926, Montevideo; tel. (2) 9029055; fax (2) 9021326; f. 1917; supports the Partido Colorado; Editor Dr Salvador Alabán Demare; circ. 40,000.

Mundocolor: Cuareim 1287, 11800 Montevideo; f. 1976; evening (except Sunday); Dir Daniel Herrera Lussich; circ. 4,500.

El Observador: Cuareim 2052, 11800 Montevideo; tel. (2) 9247000; fax (2) 9248698; e-mail elobservador@observador.com.uy; internet www.observador.com.uy; f. 1991; morning; Editor Ricardo Peirano; circ. 26,000.

Observador Económico: Soriano 791, Montevideo; tel. (2) 9030690; fax (2) 9030691.

El País: Plaza Cagancha 1162, 11100 Montevideo; tel. (2) 9011929; fax (2) 9020632; e-mail epais@adinet.com.uy; internet www .diarioelpais.com; f. 1918; morning; supports the Partido Nacional; Editor Martín Aguirre; circ. 106,000.

La República: Avda Gral Garibaldi 2579, 11600 Montevideo; tel. (2) 4873565; fax (2) 4872419; internet www.multi.com.uy/republica; f. 1988; morning; Editor Federico Fasano Mertens.

Ultimas Noticias: Paysandú 1179, Montevideo; tel. (2) 9020452; fax (2) 9024669; f. 1981; evening (except Saturday); owned by Impresora Polo Ltd; Publr Dr Alphonse Emanuiloff-Max; circ. 25,000.

Florida

El Heraldo: Independencia 824, 94000 Florida; tel (35) 22229; fax (35) 24546; e-mail heraldo@adinet.com.uy; f. 1919; evening (except Sunday); independent; Dir Alvaro Riva Rey; circ. 1,800.

Minas

La Unión: Florencio Sánchez 569, Minas; tel. (442) 2065; fax (442) 4011; e-mail union@chasque.apc.org; f. 1877; evening (except Sunday); Dir Laura Puchet Martínez; Editor Alejandro Maya Sosa; circ. 2,600.

Maldonado

Correo de Punta del Este: Michelini 815 bis, 20000 Maldonado; tel. and fax (42) 35633; e-mail gallardo@adinet.com.uy; f. 1993; morning; Editor María P. Rodríguez Zanoni; circ. 2,500.

Paysandú

El Telégrafo: 18 de Julio 1027, 60000 Paysandú; tel. (722) 2314; fax (722) 7999; e-mail correo@eltelegrafo.com; internet www .eltelegrafo.com; f. 1910; morning; independent; Dir Fernando M. Baccaro; circ. 10,000.

Salto

Tribuna Salteña: Joaquín Suárez 71, Salto; f. 1906; morning; Dir Modesto Llantada Fabini; circ. 3,000.

PERIODICALS

Montevideo

Aquí: Zabala 1322, Of. 102, 11000 Montevideo; weekly; supports the Encuentro Progresista—Frente Amplio; Dir Francisco José O'Honelli.

Brecha: Avda Uruguay 844, 11100 Montevideo; tel. (2) 9025042; fax (2) 9020388; e-mail brecha@brecha.com.uy; internet www .brecha.com.uy; f. 1985; weekly; politics, current affairs; circ. 14,500; Dir Guillermo González; Editor-in-Chief Daniel Gatti.

Búsqueda: Avda Uruguay 1146, 11100 Montevideo; tel. (2) 9021300; fax (2) 9022036; e-mail busqueda@adinet.com.uy; f. 1972; weekly; independent; politics and economics; Dir Danilo Arbilla Frachia; circ. 25,000.

Charoná: Gutiérrez Ruiz 1276, Of. 201, Montevideo; f. 1968; tel. (2) 9086665; f. 1968; fortnightly; children's; Dir Sergio Boffano; circ. 25,000.

Colorín Colorado: Dalmiro Costa 4482, Montevideo; f. 1980; monthly; children's; Dir Sara Minster de Murninkas; circ. 3,000.

Crónicas Económicas: Avda Libertador Brig.-Gen. Lavalleja 1532, Montevideo; tel. (2) 9004790; f. 1981; weekly; independent; economics; Dirs Julio Ariel Franco, Walter Hugo Pagés, Jorge Estellano.

La Democracia: Colonia 1308, Montevideo; f. 1981; weekly; organ of the Partido Nacional; Editor Alberto Zumarán; circ. 17,000.

La Gaceta Militar Naval: Montevideo; monthly.

Indice Industrial-Anuario de la Industria Uruguaya: Sarandí 456, Montevideo; tel. (2) 9151963; f. 1957; annually; Dir W. M. Trias; circ. 6,000.

La Justicia Uruguaya: 25 de Mayo 555, 11000 Montevideo; tel. (2) 9157587; fax (2) 9159721; e-mail justicia@isoft.com.uy; internet www.lajusticiauruguaya.com.uy; f. 1940; bimonthly; jurisprudence; Dirs Eduardo Albanell, Adolfo Albanell, Susana Arias; circ. 3,000.

La Juventud: Durazno 1118, Montevideo; tel. (2) 9011584; weekly; supports the Movimiento 26 de Marzo.

Marketing Directo: Mario Cassinoni 1157, 11200 Montevideo; tel. (2) 4012174; fax 4087221; e-mail consumo@adinet.com.uy; f. 1988; monthly; Dir Edgardo Martínez Zimarioff; circ. 9,500.

Mate Amargo: Tristán Narvaja 1578 bis, Montevideo; f. 1986; organ of the Movimiento de Liberación Nacional; circ. 22,500.

Opción: J. Barrios Amorín 1531, Casilla 102, Montevideo; f. 1981; weekly; Dir Francisco José Ottonelli; circ. 15,000.

Patatín y Patatán: Montevideo; f. 1977; weekly; children's; Dir Juan José Ravaioli; circ. 3,000.

La Propaganda Rural: Arenal Grande 1341, Montevideo; tel. (2) 4001752; fax (2) 4001753; f. 1902; monthly; cattle, agriculture and industry; Dirs Oscar Martín, Alberto R. Conde; circ. 5,000.

Revista Naval: Soriano 1117, Montevideo; tel. (2) 9087884; f. 1988; 3 a year; military; Editor Gustavo Vanzini; circ. 1,000.

PRESS ASSOCIATIONS

Asociación de Diarios del Uruguay: Río Negro 1308, 6°, Montevideo; f. 1922; Pres. Batlle T. Barbato.

Asociación de la Prensa Uruguaya: Avda Uruguay 1255, Montevideo; tel. and fax (2) 9013695; f. 1944; Pres. Gustavo Aguirre.

PRESS AGENCIES

Foreign Bureaux

Agence France-Presse (AFP): Plaza Independencia 831, Montevideo; tel. (2) 9005095; Chief Jupiter Puyo.

Agencia EFE (Spain): Wilson Ferreira Aldunate 1294, Of. 501, 11200 Montevideo; tel. (2) 9020322; fax (2) 9026726; e-mail efeuru @adinet.com.uy; Correspondent Ana Rosa Mengotti Meaurio.

Agenzia Nazionale Stampa Associata (ANSA) (Italy): Florida 1408, Montevideo; tel. (2) 9011032; fax (2) 9081950; Bureau Chief Juan Atella.

Associated Press (AP) (USA): Avda 18 de Julio 1076, Montevideo; tel. (2) 9018291; Correspondent Daniel Gianelli.

Deutsche Presse-Agentur (dpa) (Germany): Avda 18 de Julio 994, 4°, Montevideo; tel. (2) 9028052; fax (2) 9022662; e-mail dpaurc@montevideo.com.uy; Correspondent María Isabel Rivero de los Campos.

Inter Press Service (IPS) (Italy): Juan Carlos Gómez 1445, Of. 102, 1°, 11000 Montevideo; tel. (2) 9164397; fax (2) 9163598; e-mail ips@tips.org.uy; internet www.ips.org; f. 1964; Dir Mario Lubetkin.

Reuters (United Kingdom): Plaza Independencia 831, Of. 907-908, Montevideo; tel. (2) 9020336; fax (2) 9027912; Correspondent Anahi Rama.

Prensa Latina (Cuba): Montevideo; tel. (2) 7092955; Correspondent Osvaldo Burgos.

United Press International (UPI) (USA): Avda 18 de Julio 1224, 2°, Montevideo; Chief Carlos Díaz.

Publishers

Editorial Arca SRL: Andes 1118, Montevideo; tel. (2) 9024468; fax (2) 9030188; f. 1963; general literature, social science and history; Man. Dir Claudio Rama.

Ediciones de la Banda Oriental: Gaboto 1582, 11200 Montevideo; tel. (2) 4098138; general literature; Man. Dir Heber Raviolo.

Barreiro y Ramos, SA: 25 de Mayo 604, Casilla 15, 11000 Montevideo; tel. (2) 9150150; fax (2) 9162358; f. 1871; general; Man. Dir Gastón Barreiro Zorrilla.

CENCI—Uruguay (Centro de Estadísticas Nacionales y Comercio Internacional): Misiones 1361, Casilla 1510, Montevideo; tel. (2) 9152930; fax (2) 9154578; e-mail cenci@adinet.com.uy; f. 1956; economics, statistics; Dirs Cristina Z. de Vertesi, Kenneth Brunner.

Editorial y Librería Jurídica Amalio M. Fernández SRL: 25 de Mayo 589, 11000 Montevideo; tel. and fax (2) 9151782; f. 1951; law and sociology; Man. Dir Carlos W. Deamestoy.

Fundación de Cultura Universitaria: 25 de Mayo 568, Casilla 1155, 11000 Montevideo; tel. (2) 9161152; fax (2) 9152549; e-mail fcuventa@multi.com.uy; internet www.fcu.com.uy; f. 1968; law and social sciences; Man. Dir Nelson Rojas.

Hemisferio Sur: Buenos Aires 335, Casilla 1755, 11000 Montevideo; tel. (2) 9164515; fax (2) 9164520; e-mail librperi@adinet .com.uy; f. 1951; agronomy and veterinary science.

Editorial Idea: Misiones 1424, 5°, Montevideo; law; Dir Dr Guillermo Vezcovi.

Editorial Kapelusz: Avda Uruguay 1331, Montevideo; educational.

Editorial Medina SRL: Gaboto 1521, Montevideo; tel. (2) 4085800; f. 1933; general; Pres. Marcos Medina Vidal.

A. Monteverde & Cía, SA: 25 de Mayo 577, Casilla 371, 11000 Montevideo; tel. (2) 9159019; fax (2) 9157543; f. 1879; educational; Man. Dir Liliana Mussini.

Mosca Hnos SA: Avda 18 de Julio 1578, 11300 Montevideo; tel. (2) 4093141; fax (2) 4088059; e-mail mosca@attmail.com.uy; f. 1888; general; Pres. Lic. Zsolt Agardy.

Editorial Nuestra Tierra: Cerrito 566, Casilla 1603, 11000 Montevideo; tel. and fax (2) 9157528; f. 1968; general; Man. Dir Daniel Aljanati.

Librería Selecta Editorial: Guayabo 1865, 11200 Montevideo; tel. (2) 4086989; fax (2) 4086831; f. 1950; academic books; Dir Fernando Masa.

PUBLISHERS' ASSOCIATION

Cámara Uruguaya del Libro: Juan D. Jackson 1118, 11200 Montevideo; tel. (2) 4015732; fax (2) 4011860; e-mail camurlib @adinet.com.uy; f. 1944; Pres. Vicente Porcelli; Man. Ana Cristina Rodríguez.

Broadcasting and Communications

TELECOMMUNICATIONS

Administración Nacional de Telecomunicaciones (ANTEL): Avda Daniel Fernández Crespo 1534, 9°, 11200 Montevideo; tel. (2) 4000407; fax (2) 4012703; e-mail kely@adinet.com.uy; internet www.antel.com.uy; f. 1974; state-owned; Pres. Fernando Braco; Gen. Man. José Luis Saldías.

ANCEL: Pablo Galarza 3537, Montevideo; internet www.ancel .com.uy; f. 1994; state-owned mobile telephone co; scheduled for partial (40%) privatization in 2001.

Dirección Nacional de Comunicaciones (DNC): Blvr Artigas 1520, POB 927, 11600 Montevideo; tel. (2) 7073662; fax (2) 7073591; e-mail dnc@dnc.gub.uy; internet www.dnc.gub.ny.

BROADCASTING

Regulatory Authorities

Asociación Nacional de Broadcasters Uruguayos (ANDEBU): Yi 1264, 11100 Montevideo; tel. (2) 9000053; f. 1933; 101 mems; Pres. Raúl Fontaina; Sec.-Gen. Dr Rafael Inchausti.

Dirección Nacional de Comunicaciones: Blvr Artigas 1520, Casilla 927, 11600 Montevideo; tel. (2) 7073662; fax (2) 7073591; e-mail dnc@dnc.gub.uy; internet www.dnc.gub.uy; f. 1984; Dir Dr Fernando Omar Pérez Tabo.

Radio

El Espectador: Río Branco 1481, 11100 Montevideo; tel. (2) 9023531; fax (2) 9083044; e-mail am810@espectador.com.uy; internet www.espectador.com; f. 1923; commercial; Pres. María A. Mastrángelo; Dir-Gen. Javier Massa.

Radio Carve: Mercedes 973, 11100 Montevideo; tel. (2) 9020911; fax (2) 9022839; e-mail carve@mailer.distrinet.com.uy; internet www.urunet.com.uy/carve; f. 1928; commercial; Dir Pablo Fontaina Minelli.

Radio Montecarlo: Avda 18 de Julio 1224, 1°, 11100 Montevideo; tel. (2) 9014433; fax (2) 9017762; e-mail cx20@netgate.comintur.com.uy; internet netgate.comintur.com.uy/x20; f. 1928; commercial; Dir Daniel Romay.

Radio Sarandí: Enriqueta Compte y Riqué 1250, 11800 Montevideo; tel. (2) 2082612; fax (2) 2036906; e-mail sarandi@netgate.com.uy; internet isa.isa.com.uy/sarandi; f. 1931; commercial; Pres. Ramiro Rodríguez Vallamil Riviere.

Radio Universal: Avda 18 de Julio 1220, 3°, 11100 Montevideo; tel. (2) 9032222; fax (2) 9026050; f. 1929; commercial; Pres. Oscar Imperio.

Radiodifusión Nacional SODRE: Sarandí 430, 11000 Montevideo; tel. (2) 957865; fax (2) 9161933; f. 1929; state-owned; Pres. Adela R. Sosa Díaz.

In 1998 there were some 23 medium- and short-wave radio stations and 14 FM stations in the Montevideo area. In addition, there were approximately 70 medium- and short-wave radio stations and more than 90 FM stations outside the capital.

Television

Canal 4 Montecarlo: Paraguay 2253, 11800 Montevideo; tel. (2) 9244591; fax (2) 9242001; f. 1961; Dir Hugo Romay Salvo.

SAETA TV—Canal 10: Dr Lorenzo Carnelli 1234, 11200 Montevideo; tel. (2) 4002120; fax (2) 4009771; internet multi.com.uy/canal10/index.htm; f. 1956; Pres. Jorge de Feo.

SODRE—Servicio Oficial de Difusión Radiotelevisión y Espectáculos: Blvr Artigas 2552, 11600 Montevideo; tel. (2) 4806448; fax (2) 4808515; f. 1963; Dir Víctor Ganón; Gen. Man. Julio Frade.

Teledoce Televisora Color—Canal 12: Enriqueta Compte y Riqué 1276, 11800 Montevideo; tel. (2) 2035856; fax (2) 20037623; internet web2mil/intercanal.com/teledoce@hs; f. 1962; Dir Alejandra Morgan; Gen. Man. Horacio Scheck.

In 1999 there were 21 television stations outside the capital.

Finance

BANKING

(cap. = capital; res = reserves; dep. = deposits; m. = million; amounts in pesos, unless otherwise indicated)

State Banks

Banco Central del Uruguay: Avda Juan P. Fabini 777, Casilla 1467, 11100 Montevideo; tel. (2) 9082090; fax (2) 9021782; e-mail secgral@bcu.gub.uy; internet www.bcu.gub.uy; f. 1967; note-issuing bank, also controls private banking; Pres. César Rodríguez Batlle; Gen. Man. Gualberto De León.

Banco Hipotecario del Uruguay (BHU): Avda Daniel Fernández Crespo 1508, Montevideo; tel. (2) 4090000; fax (2) 4005675; e-mail info@bhu.net; internet www.bhu.com.uy; f. 1892; state mortgage bank; in 1977 assumed responsibility for housing projects in Uruguay; Pres. Ariel Lausarot; Gen. Man. Enrique Ruíz Corbo.

Banco de la República Oriental del Uruguay (BROU): Cerrito 351, 11000 Montevideo; tel. (2) 9150157; fax (2) 9163708; internet www.brounet.com.uy; f. 1896; a state institution; cap. and res 8,149.0m., dep. 45,263.1m. (Dec. 1999); Pres. Juan I. García Peluffo; 107 brs.

Principal Commercial Banks

Banco Comercial, SA: Cerrito 400, Casilla 34, 11000 Montevideo; tel. (2) 9160541; fax (2) 9153569; e-mail dne@bancocomercial.com.uy; internet www.bancocomercial.com.uy; f. 1857; privatized in Oct. 1990; acquired ING Bank (Uruguay), SA in Oct. 2000; cap. US \$155.5m., res \$21.0m., dep. \$1,457.9m. (Dec. 2000); Pres. Dr Armando M. Braun Estrugamon; Vice-Pres. and CEO Carlos Rohm Conte; 65 brs.

Banco de Crédito SA: Avda 18 de Julio 1451, 11200 Montevideo; tel. (2) 4004141; fax (2) 4019353; e-mail departamento.internacional@bdc.com.uy; internet www.bancodecredito.com.uy; f. 1908; cap. 47.6m., res 216.4m., dep. 4,606.4m. (Dec. 1997); intervened by Banco Central del Uruguay in June 1998; acquired Banco Pan de Azúcar in Dec. 1998; Pres. José Felix Iglesias; 42 brs.

Banco Exterior de América SA—Uruguay: Rincón 493, Casilla 914, 11000 Montevideo; tel. (2) 9160042; fax (2) 9161089; f. 1982; cap. 587.3m., res 14.2m., dep. 1,761.7m. (Dec. 1998); Pres. José Ignacio Leyún González; Gen. Man. Pedro Guida Castro; 21 brs.

Banco Francés (Uruguay) SA: 25 de Mayo 401, 11000 Montevideo; tel. (2) 9156368; fax (2) 9160838; e-mail bfrances@adinet.com.uy; f. 1968; formerly Unión de Bancos del Uruguay, and later Banesto Banco Uruguay, SA; adopted current name in 1995; cap. 70m., res 451.6m. dep. 4,769.4m. (Dec. 1997); Pres. Rodolvo Corvi; Gen. Man. Néstor Gessaga; 9 brs.

Banco La Caja Obrera: 25 de Mayo 500, Casilla 1201, 11000 Montevideo; tel. (2) 9154114; fax (2) 9163657; e-mail intlblco@adinet.com.uy; internet www.bancocajaobrera.com.uy; f. 1905; taken over by BROU in 1987; cap. 18.0m., res 79.5m., dep. 3,835.3m. (Dec. 1998); Pres. and Gen. Man. Eduardo Rocca Couture; Vice-Chair. Jorge Fodere; 30 brs.

Banco de Montevideo: Misiones 1399, Casilla 612, 11000 Montevideo; tel. (2) 1881; fax (2) 9160952; e-mail bmvd@davanet.com.uy; internet www.bancomontevideo.com.uy; f. 1941; cap. 67.9m., res 351.5m., dep. 6,832.5m. (Dec. 1999); Pres. Mario San Cristóbal; Gen. Man. Alejandro Suzacq; 8 brs.

Banco Santander Uruguay, SA: Cerrito 449, 11000 Montevideo; tel. (2) 9170970; fax (2) 9163685; e-mail bsantander@icorp.com.uy; internet www.icorp.com.uy/santander/default.htm; 100% owned by Banco Santander (Spain); cap. 1.4m.; res. 472.0m.; dep. 7,682.7m. (Dec. 1999); Vice-Pres. Miguel Estrugo Santaeugenia; Dir Jorge Jourdán Peyronel; 28 brs.

Banco Surinvest SA: Rincón 530, 11000 Montevideo; tel. (2) 9160177; fax (2) 9160241; e-mail lblanco@surinvest.com.uy; f. 1981 as Surinvest Casa Bancaria, name changed as above 1991; cap. 35.2m., res 86.5m., dep. 2,170.6m. (Dec. 1998); Chair. and CEO Juan Martín Etchegoyhen; Gen. Man. José Luis Rubio.

Foreign Banks

ABN AMRO Bank NV (Netherlands): Avda 18 de Julio 999, Casilla 888, 11100 Montevideo; tel. (2) 9009799; fax (2) 9009798; internet www.abnamro.com.uy; Gen. Man. Eric Simon.

American Express Bank, SA (USA): Edif. Presidente, Rincón 473, 8°, 11000 Montevideo; tel. (2) 9160103; fax (2) 9162245; e-mail aeburuguay@amex.com.uy; Pres. Sergio J. Masvidal; Gen. Man. Mara Mattozo 1 br.

Banco de la Nación Argentina: Juan C. Gómez 1372, 11000 Montevideo; tel. (2) 9158760; fax (2) 9160078; Gen. Man. Jorge Humberto Rossi; 2 brs.

Banco Sudameris (France): Rincón 500, 11000 Montevideo; tel. (2) 9150095; fax (2) 9162509; Pres. Dr Sagunto Pérez Fontana; Gen. Man. Paul Pinelli; 6 brs.

BankBoston NA (USA): Zabala 1463, 11000 Montevideo; tel. (2) 9160127; fax (2) 9162209; took over Banco Internacional in 1978; cap. US \$10.8m., dep. \$179.9m. (May 1990); Gen. Man. Horacio Vilaró; 11 brs.

Citibank NA (USA): Cerrito 455, Casilla 690, 11000 Montevideo; tel. (2) 9001981; fax (2) 9163665; Dir-Gen. Gustavo Cardoni; 3 brs.

Discount Bank (Latin America), SA (USA): Rincón 390, 11000 Montevideo; tel. (2) 9164848; fax (2) 9160890; e-mail mensajes@discbank.com.uy; internet www.discbank.com.uy; f. 1958; cap. 46.0m., res 152.1m., dep. 3,081.7m. (Dec. 1999); Pres. and Chair. Arie Sheer; Gen. Man. Bitoush Menahem; 4 brs.

Exprinter Uruguay, SA (Luxembourg): Sarandí 700, Casilla 69, 11000 Montevideo; tel. (2) 9162011; fax (2) 9162087; f. 1958 as Exprinter Casa Bancaria; adopted current name in 1997; cap. 12,635m., res 44,510m., dep. 714,753m. (Dec. 1994); Chair. Jorge Supeveille; Gen. Man. Marcelo S. Studer.

HSBC Banco Roberts (Uruguay) SAIFE (Argentina): Rincón 477, Of. 201, 11000 Montevideo; tel. (2) 9164802; fax (2) 9164805; e-mail roberts@adinet.com.uy; f. 1995; cap. US \$18.0m., res \$16.6m., dep. \$311.9m. (June 1998); Pres. and Chair. Antonio M. Losada; Gen. Man. Leonel Juan Puppo.

Leumi (Latin America) SA: 25 de Mayo 549, 11000 Montevideo; tel. (2) 9160223; fax (2) 9170673; e-mail leumont@montevideo.com.uy; f. 1980; cap. 775m., res 6,902m., dep. 74,942m. (Dec. 1991); Chair. Dr Zalman Segal; Gen. Man. Mordechai Kessous; 1 br.

Lloyds Bank (BLSA) Ltd (United Kingdom): Zabala 1500, Casilla 204, 11000 Montevideo; tel. (2) 9160976; fax (2) 9161262; f. 1862; fmrly Bank of London and South America; Man. CHRISTOPHER GOLBY.

Bankers' Association

Asociación de Bancos del Uruguay (Bank Association of Uruguay): Rincón 468, 2°, 11000 Montevideo; tel. (2) 9162342; fax (2) 9162329; e-mail uy340424@adinet.com.uy; internet www.abu .org.uy; f. 1945; 15 mem. banks; Pres. Dr CARLOS GARCÍA AROCENA.

STOCK EXCHANGE

Bolsa de Valores de Montevideo: Edif. Bolsa de Comercio, Misiones 1400, 11000 Montevideo; tel. (2) 9165051; fax (2) 9161900; e-mail bvm@netgate.com.uy; internet www.bvm.com.uy; f. 1867; 75 mems; Pres. IGNACIO ROSPIDE.

INSURANCE

In late 1993 legislation was introduced providing for an end to the state monopoly of most types of insurance. With effect from mid-1994 the Banco de Seguros del Estado lost its monopoly on all insurance except life, sea transport and fire risks, which have been traditionally open to private underwriters.

Banco de Seguros del Estado: Avda Libertador Brig.-General Lavalleja 1465, 11000 Montevideo; tel. (2) 9089303; fax (2) 9021063; e-mail proyectointernet@bse.com.uy; internet www.bse.com.uy; f. 1912; state insurance org.; all risks; Pres. ALBERTO IGLESIAS; Vice-Pres. ENRIQUE ROIG.

Real Uruguaya de Seguros SA: Julio Herrera y Obes 1365, 2°, Montevideo; tel. (2) 9025858; fax (2) 9024515; e-mail realseg@ realseguros.com.uy; f. 1900; life and property; Pres. PAUL ELBERSE; Gen. Man. EIJI AJIMURA.

Trade and Industry

GOVERNMENT AGENCY

Oficina de Planeamiento y Presupuesto de la Presidencia de la República: Fondo de las Americas, Convención 1366, Montevideo; tel. (2) 9000461; fax (2) 2099730; f. 1976; responsible for the implementation of devt plans; co-ordinates the policies of the various ministries; advises on the preparation of the budget of public enterprises; Dir ARIEL DAVRIEUX.

DEVELOPMENT ORGANIZATION

Corporación Nacional para el Desarrollo: Rincón 528, 7°, Casilla 977, 11000 Montevideo; tel. (2) 9155764; fax (2) 9159662; e-mail cnd01@adinet.com.uy; f. 1985; national devt corpn; mixed-capital org.; obtains 60% of funding from state; Pres. MILKA BARBATO; Vice-Pres. JULIO GEMELLI; Dirs SERVANDO ARRILLAGA, ANGEL ALEGRE.

CHAMBERS OF COMMERCE

Cámara de Industrias del Uruguay (Chamber of Industries): Avda Libertador Brig.-General Lavalleja 1672, 11100 Montevideo; tel. (2) 9023402; fax (2) 9022567; e-mail ciu@ciu.com.uy; internet www.ciu.com.uy; f. 1898; Pres. GUALBERTO ROCCO.

Cámara Nacional de Comercio y Servicios del Uruguay (National Chamber of Commerce): Edif. Bolsa de Comercio, Rincón 454, 2°, Casilla 1000, 11000 Montevideo; tel. (2) 9161277; fax (2) 9161243; e-mail canadeco@adinet.com.uy; internet www.davanet .com.uy/canadeco; f. 1867; 1,500 mems; Pres. Dr JORGE PEIRANO BASSO; Sec. and Man. Dr CLAUDIO PIACENZA.

Cámara Mercantil de Productos del País (Chamber of Commerce for Local Products): Avda General Rondeau 1908, 11800 Montevideo; tel. (2) 9240644; fax (2) 9240673; e-mail cmpp@davanet .com.uy; internet www.davanet.com.uy/cmpp; f. 1891; 180 mems; Pres. CHRISTIAN BOLZ; Dir-Gen. GONZALO GONZÁLEZ PIEDRAS.

TRADE ASSOCIATION

Instituto Nacional de Pesca (INAPE): Avda Constituyente 1497, 11200 Montevideo; tel. (2) 4004689; fax (2) 4013216; national fisheries institute; Dir-Gen. Dr ENRIQUE BERTULLO.

EMPLOYERS' ORGANIZATIONS

Asociación de Importadores y Mayoristas de Almacén (Importers' and Wholesalers' Asscn): Edif. Bolsa de Comercio, Of. 317/319, Rincón 454, 11000 Montevideo; tel. (2) 9156103; fax (2) 9160796; f. 1926; 52 mems; Pres. FERNANDO MELISSARI.

Asociación Rural del Uruguay: Avda Uruguay 864, 11100 Montevideo; tel. (2) 9020484; fax (2) 9020489; e-mail aru@netgate.com.uy; internet www.aru.org.uy; f. 1871; 1,800 mems; Pres. ROBERTO SYMONDS.

Comisión Patronal del Uruguay de Asuntos Relacionados con la OIT (Commission of Uruguayan Employers for Affairs of the ILO): Edif. Bolsa de Comercio, Rincón 454, 2°, Casilla 1000, 11000 Montevideo; tel. (2) 9161277; fax (2) 9161243; e-mail canadeco@adinet.com.uy; internet www.davanet.com.uy/canadeco; f. 1954; mem. of Cámara Nacional de Comercio y Servicios del Uruguay; Sec. and Man. Dr CLAUDIO PIACENZA.

Federación Rural del Uruguay: Avda 18 de Julio 965, 1°, Montevideo; tel. (2) 9005583; fax (2) 9004791; e-mail fedrural@adinet .com.uy; f. 1915; 2,000 mems; Pres. CARLOS SECCO GUTIÉRREZ.

Unión de Exportadores del Uruguay (Uruguayan Exporters' Asscn): Edif. Bolsa de Comercio, Of. 401, 4°, Rincón 454, 11000 Montevideo; tel. (2) 9170105; fax (2) 9161117; e-mail ueu@adinet .com.uy; Pres. DANIEL SOLODUCHO; Exec. Sec. TERESA AISHEMBERG.

MAJOR COMPANIES

Azucarera del Litoral, SA: 25 de Mayo 444, 1°, 11000 Montevideo; tel. (2) 9160868; fax (2) 9161192; f. 1943; processors of raw cane sugar; Gen. Man. RAÚL CONCELO; 495 employees.

Cinoca, SA: Avda Libertador Brig. Juan A. Lavalleja 1641, Of. 403, Montevideo; tel. (2) 9083635; fax (2) 9083610; f. 1932; producers of oxygen and steel piping; Pres. ANTONIO JOSÉ TERRA; 380 employees.

Compañía Industrial de Tabacos Monte Paz, SA: San Ramón 716, Montevideo; tel. (2) 2008821; fax (2) 2037890; e-mail montepaz@zfm.uy; internet www.montepaz.com; f. 1930; tobacco and cigarette manufacturers; Pres. JORGE LUIS MAILHOS; 425 employees.

Compañía Sudamericana de Empresas Eléctricas, Mecanicas y Obras Públicas (SACEEM): Treinta y Tres 1468, 11800 Montevideo; tel. (2) 9160208; fax (2) 9163939; e-mail saceem@uyweb .com.uy; f. 1951; construction of industrial buildings and warehouses; Chair. GERMÁN VILLAR; 850 employees.

Compañía Uruguaya de Transportes Colectivos, SA (CUTCSA): Sarandí 528, Montevideo; tel. (2) 9087821; fax (2) 9162807; e-mail cutcsa@adinet.com.uy; f. 1937; passenger transport services; Pres. CARLOS LAGO FACAL; 5,000 employees.

Cooperativa Nacional de Productores de Leche, SA (CONAPROLE): Magallanes 1871, Montevideo; tel. (2) 9247171; fax (2) 9246672; internet www.conaprole.com.uy; f. 1935; manufacturers and wholesalers of milk and dairy products; Pres. JORGE PANIZZA TORRENS; 2,750 employees.

Cybaran, SA: Lima 1200, Montevideo; tel. (2) 9240688; fax (2) 9140721; f. 1962; processors and wholesalers of meat; Pres. MARCO ANDRÉS DUTRA; 700 employees.

Dymac, SA: Thompson 3077, Montevideo; tel. (2) 4870812; fax (2) 4872786; f. 1962; clothing manufacturers; Pres. DANIEL DYMENSTEIN; 520 employees.

Fábrica Nacional de Papel, SA (FANAPEL): Avda General Rondeau 1799, Casilla 509, 11800 Montevideo; tel. (2) 9240917; fax (2) 9240919; internet www.fanapel.com; f. 1913; pulp and paper mill; Pres. RICARDO ZERBINO CAVAJANI; 680 employees.

Fábrica Uruguaya de Neumáticos, SA (FUNSA): Corrales 3076, Casilla 15175, Montevideo; tel. (2) 5083141; fax (2) 5070611; e-mail funsa@ciu.com.uy; f. 1935; manufacturers of rubber tyres, shoes and insulated electrical cables; Gen. Man. ANTONIO J. MUJICA; 600 employees.

Fábricas Nacionales de Cerveza, SA (FNC): Entre Ríos 1060, Montevideo; tel. (2) 2001683; fax (2) 2034525; f. 1932; brewery; Pres. JUAN D. GANG; 400 employees.

Frigorífico Modelo, SA: Tomás Gomensoro 2906, Montevideo; tel. (2) 4873017; fax (2) 4873114; e-mail frimosa@adinet.com.uy; f. 1930; food processing and production; Pres. LUIS FERNANDO ECHEVERRÍA; 400 employees.

FRIPUR, SA: Avda General Rondeau 2260, Montevideo; tel. (2) 9243112; fax (2) 9243149; internet www.fripur.com.uy; f. 1976; food processing; Pres. MAXIMO FERNÁNDEZ ALONSO; 1,185 employees.

Industria Lanera del Uruguay, SA (ILDUSA): José de Béjar 2600, Montevideo; tel. (2) 5083161; fax (2) 5071068; f. 1932; manufacturers of woollen textiles; Pres. ALBERTO PUIG TERRA; 980 employees.

Industrias Philips del Uruguay, SA: Avda Uruguay 1287, 11100 Montevideo; tel. (2) 9019000; fax (2) 9020601; f. 1957; subsidiary of NV Philips (Netherlands); manufacturers of lighting and other electrical goods; Pres. GUIDO MICHELIN SALOMON; 300 employees.

Metzen y Sena, SA: Cerro Largo 877, Montevideo; tel. (2) 9021536; fax (2) 9016366; f. 1937; manufacturers of ceramic tiles; Pres. CARLOS METZEN; 1,460 employees.

Montevideo Refrescos, SA: Camino Carrasco 6173, Montevideo; tel. (2) 5008401; fax (2) 5007321; f. 1946; producers of carbonated beverages; Pres. Ing. GREGORIO AZNARES; 560 employees.

Paysandú Industrias del Cuero, SA (PAYCUEROS): Cerro Largo 777, Montevideo; tel. (2) 9020139; fax (2) 9021321; tannery, manufacturing handbags and other leather products; Pres. CONRADO OLASO MARÍN; 1,160 employees.

Sociedad Anónima Arroceros Nacionales (SAMAN): Rambla Baltasar Brum 2772, Montevideo; tel. (2) 2081421; fax (2) 2037087; f. 1951; rice mills; Pres. RICARDO FERRÉS BLANCO; 538 employees.

UTILITIES
Electricity

Administración Nacional de Usinas y Transmisiones Eléctricas (UTE): Paraguay 2431, Montevideo; tel. (2) 2097685; fax (2) 2080708; e-mail ute@ute.com.uy; internet www.ute.com.uy; f. 1912; autonomous state body; sole purveyor of electricity; Pres. RICARDO SCAGLIA.

Gas

Gaseba Uruguay (Gaz de France): 25 de Mayo 702, 11000 Montevideo; tel. (2) 9017454; gas producers and service providers.

Water

Obras Sanitarias del Estado (OSE): Carlos Roxlo 1275, 11200 Montevideo; tel. (2) 4001151; fax (2) 4088069; f. 1962; processing and distribution of drinking water, sinking wells, supplying industrial zones of the country; Pres. JUAN JUSTO AMARO.

TRADE UNIONS

All trade-union activity was under strict control during 1973–85. In June 1973 the central organization (Confederación Nacional de Trabajadores), which claimed some 400,000 members, was declared illegal. In December 1979 a new labour law was submitted to the Council of State allowing three levels of association and optional union membership. A further law, introduced in October 1981, allows for the holding of secret ballots to elect union officials, and the establishment of company unions in firms with 15 or more employees. On taking office in March 1985, President Julio María Sanguinetti ordered the restoration of the legal status of the principal workers' and university students' federations.

Plenario Intersindical de Trabajadores—Convención Nacional de Trabajadores (PIT—CNT): Avda 18 de Julio 2190, Montevideo; tel. (2) 4096680; fax (2) 4004160; f. 1966; org. comprising 83 trade unions, 17 labour federations; 320,000 mems; Pres. JOSÉ D'ELÍA; Exec.-Sec. VÍCTOR SEMPRONI.

Transport

Dirección Nacional de Transporte: Rincón 575, 5°, 11000 Montevideo; tel. (2) 9162940; fax (2) 9163122; e-mail info@dnt.gub.uy; internet www.dnt.gub.uy; co-ordinates national and international transport services.

RAILWAYS

Administración de los Ferrocarriles del Estado (AFE): La Paz 1095, Casilla 419, Montevideo; tel. (2) 9240805; fax (2) 9240847; e-mail affegg@adinet.com.uy; f. 1952; state org.; 3,002 km of track connecting all parts of the country; there are connections with the Argentine and Brazilian networks; passenger services ceased in 1988; passenger services linking Montevideo with Florida and Canelones were resumed in mid-1993; Pres. JORGE GARCÍA CARRERE; Gen. Man. MARÍA ANASTASIA.

ROADS

In 1997 Uruguay had 8,683 km of motorways (forming the most dense motorway network in South America), connecting Montevideo with the main towns of the interior and the Argentine and Brazilian frontiers. There was also a network of approximately 40,000 km of paved roads under departmental control. Construction work on a 41-km bridge across the River Plate (linking Colonia del Sacramento in Uruguay with Punta Lara in Argentina) was scheduled to begin in 1999; however, no progress had been made by mid-2001.

INLAND WATERWAYS

There are about 1,250 km of navigable waterways, which provide an important means of transport.

Nobleza Naviera, SA: Avda General Rondeau 2257, Montevideo; tel. (2) 9243042; fax (2) 9243218; e-mail nobleza@netgate.com.uy; operates cargo services on the River Plate, and the Uruguay and Paraná rivers; Chair. AMÉRICO DEAMBROSI; Man. Dir DORIS FERRARI.

SHIPPING

Administración Nacional de Combustibles, Alcohol y Portland (ANCAP): Paysandú y Avda Libertador Brig.-General Lavalleja, Casilla 1090, Montevideo; tel. (2) 9024192; fax (2) 9021136; e-

mail webmaster@ancap.com.uy; internet www.ancap.com.uy; f. 1931; deals with transport, refining and sale of petroleum products, and the manufacture of alcohol, spirit and cement; tanker services, also river transport; Pres. JORGE SANGUINETTI; Gen. Man. BENITO PIÑEIRO.

Administración Nacional de Puertos (ANP): Rambla 25 de Agosto de 1825 160, Montevideo; tel. (2) 91664747; fax (2) 9161704; e-mail presidencia@anp.com.uy; internet www.anp.gub.uy; f. 1916; national ports admin.; Pres. JOSÉ AGUSTÍN AGUERRE.

Prefectura Nacional Naval: Edif. Comando General de la Armada, 5°, Rambla 25 de Agosto de 1825 s/n, esq. Maciel, Montevideo; tel. (2) 9160741; fax (2) 9163969; f. 1829; maritime supervisory body, responsible for rescue services, protection of sea against pollution, etc.; Commdr Rear-Adm. RICARDO MURIALDO.

Navegación Atlántida, SA: Río Branco 1373, Montevideo; tel. (2) 9084449; f. 1967; ferry services for passengers and vehicles between Argentina and Uruguay; Pres. H. C. PIETRANERA.

Transportadora Marítima de Combustibles SA (TRAMACO, SA): Treinta y Tres 1383, 1°, 11000 Montevideo; tel. (2) 9165754; fax (2) 9165755; Pres. J. FERNÁNDEZ BAUBETA.

CIVIL AVIATION

Civil aviation is controlled by the following: Dirección General de Aviación Civil; Dirección General de Infraestructura Aeronáutica.

The main airport is at Carrasco, 21 km from Montevideo, and there are also airports at Paysandú, Rivera, Salto, Melo, Artigas, Punta del Este and Durazno.

Aero Uruguaya SA: Florida 1280, Casilla 206, Montevideo; tel. (2) 9020212; fax (2) 2002298; cargo charter services to the USA, Europe, Africa and other destinations in South America; Chair. Col ATILIO BONELLI.

Primeras Líneas Uruguayas de Navegación Aérea (PLUNA): Puntas de Santiago 1604, Casilla 1360, 11500 Montevideo; tel. (2) 6042244; fax (2) 6042247; e-mail pumkt@adinet.com.uy; internet www.pluna.com.uy; f. 1936, nationalized 1951; transferred to private ownership in 1995, with the controlling stake (51%) acquired by consortium led by Varig, SA (Brazil); operates international services to Argentina, Brazil, Chile, El Salvador, Paraguay, Spain and the USA; Pres. MILTON RODRÍGUEZ.

Tourism

The sandy beaches and woodlands on the coast and the grasslands of the interior, with their variety of fauna and flora, provide the main tourist attractions. About 80% of tourists come from Argentina, and 10% from Brazil. Uruguay received 2.3m. visitors in 1999. Revenue from the sector amounted to US $653m. in that year.

Asociación Uruguaya de Agencias de Viajes (AUDAVI): Río Branco 1407, Of. 205, Montevideo; tel. (2) 9012326; fax (2) 9021972; e-mail audavi@k-bell.com.uy; f. 1951; 100 mems; Pres. FEDERICO GAMBARDELLA; Man. MÓNICA W. DE RAIJ.

Cámara Uruguaya de Turismo: Martín C. Martínez 1865, Montevideo; tel. (2) 4016404; fax (2) 4016013.

Uruguayan Hotel Association: Gutiérrez Ruiz 1213, Montevideo; tel. (2) 4080139; fax (2) 9082317; e-mail ahru@montevideo.com.uy.

Defence

In August 2000 Uruguay's Armed Forces consisted of 23,700 volunteers between the ages of 18 and 45 who contract for one or two years of service. There was an Army of 15,200, a Navy of 5,500 (including a coastguard service of 1,600) and an Air Force of 3,000. There were also paramilitary forces numbering 920.

Defence Budget: an estimated 2,700m. pesos uruguayos (US $227m.) in 2000.

Commander-in-Chief of the Armed Forces: Lt.-Gen. JUAN GEYMONAT.

Commander-in-Chief of the Navy: Vice-Adm. CARLOS GIANI.

Commander-in-Chief of the Air Force: Lt.-Gen. MIGUEL A. SUÑOL.

Education

All education in Uruguay, including university tuition, is provided free of charge. Education is officially compulsory for six years between six and 14 years of age. Primary education begins at the age of six and lasts for six years. Secondary education, beginning at 12 years of age, lasts for a further six years, comprising two cycles of three years each. In 1996 the total enrolment at both primary and secondary schools was equivalent to 97% of the school-age population. Primary enrolment in that year included an estimated 93% of children in the relevant age-group (males 92%; females 93%), while secondary enrolment was equivalent to 85% of the population in the appropriate age-group (males 77%; females 92%).

The programmes of instruction are the same in both public and private schools and private schools are subject to certain state controls. There are two universities. Expenditure on education by the central Government in 1999 was 5,902m. pesos uruguayos (7.8% of total government spending).

Bibliography

For works on South America generally, see Select Bibliography (Books).

Achard, D. *La Transición en Uruguay*. Montevideo, Ingenio de Servicios de Comunicación y Marketing, 1992.

Barahona de Brito, A. *Human Rights and Democratization in Latin America: Uruguay and Chile*. Oxford, Oxford University Press, 1997.

Barrán, J. P., and Nahum, B. *Batlle, Los Estancieros, y el Imperio Británico*, in five vols. Montevideo, Ediciones de la Banda Oriental, 1979–84.

Bronstein, A. S. 'The Evolution of Labour Relations in Uruguay: Achievements and Challenge', in *International Labour Review*, Vol. 128. 1989.

La Crisis Uruguaya y el Problema Nacional. Montevideo, Ediciones de la Banda Oriental, 1984.

Faraone, R. *De la Prosperidad a la Ruina. Introducción a la Historia Económica del Uruguay*. Montevideo, Ediciones Arca, 1987.

Finch, M. H. J. *A Political Economy of Uruguay since 1870*. London, Macmillan, and New York, NY, St Martin's Press, 1981.

'Back to Utopia?', in *Third World Quarterly*. 1986.

Gillespie, C. G. 'Negotiating Democracy (Politicians and Generals in Uruguay)', in *Cambridge Latin American Studies No 72*. Cambridge, Cambridge University Press, 1992.

González, L. E. *Political Structures and Democracy in Uruguay*. Notre Dame, The University of Notre Dame Press, 1991.

Minsburg, N. *El Mercosur, un Problema Complejo*. Buenos Aires, Centro Editor de America Latina, 1993.

Pendle, G. *Uruguay*. Westport, CT, Greenwood Press, 1986.

Portes, A., et al. 'The Urban Informal Sector in Uruguay: Internal Structure, Characteristics and Effects', in *World Development*, Vol. 14, 6 (June). 1986.

Siete Enfoques Sobre la Concertación. Montevideo, Ediciones de la Banda Oriental, 1984.

Roniger, L., and Sznajder, M. *The Legacy of Human-Rights Violations in the Southern Cone: Argentina, Chile and Uruguay*. Oxford, Oxford University Press, 1999.

Smyla, J. O. 'Placing Uruguayan Corrections in Context, 1979–1984: A Note on the Visiting Criminologist's Role (Uruguay's Criminal Justice)', in *Journal of Criminal Justice*, Vol. 17, 6.

Uruguay: The Private Sector. Washington, DC, World Bank, 1994.

Uruguay, Trade Reform and Economic Efficiency. Washington, DC, World Bank, 1993.

Villareal, N. *La Izquierda en Uruguay, Impactos y Reformulaciones (1989–1992)*. Montevideo, Observatorio del Sur, 1992.

VENEZUELA

Area: 912,050 sq km (352,144 sq miles).

Population (official estimate at mid-2000): 24,169,744.

Capital: Caracas, estimated population 3,435,795 (metropolitan area) at 30 June 1990.

Language: Spanish.

Religion: Mainly Christianity (Roman Catholicism predominates).

Climate: Varies with altitude from tropical to temperate; coastal areas more humid; annual average temperature in Caracas is 21°C (69°F).

Time: GMT −4 hours.

Public Holidays

2002: 1 January (New Year's Day), 11–12 February (Carnival), 10 March (La Guaira only), 29 March–1 April (Easter), 19 April (Declaration of Independence),1 May (Labour Day), 24 June (Battle of Carabobo), 5 July (Independence Day), 24 July (Birth of Simón Bolívar and Battle of Lago de Maracaibo), 12 October (Discovery of America), 24 October (Maracaibo only), 19 November (Maracaibo only), 24–25 December (Christmas), 31 December (New Year's Eve).

2003: 1 January (New Year's Day), 3–4 March (Carnival), 10 March (La Guaira only), 18–21 April (Easter), 19 April (Declaration of Independence), 1 May (Labour Day), 24 June (Battle of Carabobo), 5 July (Independence Day), 24 July (Birth of Simón Bolívar and Battle of Lago de Maracaibo), 12 October (Discovery of America), 24 October (Maracaibo only), 19 November (Maracaibo only), 24–25 December (Christmas), 31 December (New Year's Eve).

Banks and insurance companies will also close on: 6 January (Epiphany), 19 March (St Joseph), 9 May 2002 and 29 May 2003 (for Ascension), 29 June (SS Peter and Paul), 15 August (Assumption), 1 November (All Saints' Day), 8 December (Immaculate Conception).

Currency: Bolívar; 1,000 bolívares = £9.813 = US $14.050 = €15.829 (30 April 2001).

Weights and Measures: The metric system is in force.

Basic Economic Indicators

	1998	1999	2000
Gross domestic product ('000 million bolívares at 1984 prices)	602.6	565.9	584.1
GDP per head ('000 bolívares at 1984 prices)	25,925.5	23,871.2	24,165.1
GDP ('000 million bolívares at current prices)	52,482.5	62,577.0	81,924.2
GDP per head ('000 bolívares at current prices)	2,258,088.8	2,639,711.5	3,389,499.4
Annual growth of real GDP (%)	0.2	−6.1	3.2
Annual growth of real GDP per head (%)	−1.8	−7.9	1.2
Government budget ('000 million bolívares at current prices):			
Revenue	9,017.5	n.a.	n.a.
Expenditure	10,281.0	n.a.	n.a.
Consumer price index (annual average; base: 1995 = 100)	407.2	503.2	584.7
Rate of inflation (annual average, %)	35.8	23.6	16.2
Foreign exchange reserves (US $ million at 31 December)	11,612	11,708	12,633
Imports c.i.f. (US $ million)	15,818	14,064	n.a.
Exports f.o.b. (US $ million)	17,193	20,190	31,802
Balance of payments (current account, US $ million)	−3,253	−3,689	−13,365

Gross national product per head measured at purchasing power parity (PPP) (US dollars, converted by the PPP exchange rate, 1999): 5,420.

Total labour force (estimate, 2000): 10.3m.

Unemployment (estimate, 2000): 13.2%.

Total foreign debt (1998): US $37,003m.

Infant mortality rate (per 1,000 live births, 1996): 22.

Life expectancy (years at birth, 1999): 73 (males 70; females 76).

Adult population with HIV/AIDS (15–29 years, 1999): 0.49%.

School enrolment ratio (6–16 years, 1996): 83%.

Adult literacy rate (15 years and over, 2000): 93.0% (males 93.3; females 92.7).

Energy consumption per head (kg of oil equivalent, 1998): 2,433.

Carbon dioxide emissions per head (metric tons, 1997): 8.4.

Passenger motor cars in use (estimate, per 1,000 of population, 1996): 69.3.

Television receivers in use (per 1,000 of population, 1997): 180.

Personal computers in use (per 1,000 of population, 1999): 42.2.

History

Dr JULIA BUXTON

The coast of Venezuela was first sighted by Europeans in 1498, during the navigator Christopher Columbus's third Spanish expedition to the New World. In 1499 a Spanish conquistador, Alonso de Ojeda, reached Lake Maracaibo. The Amerindian villages constructed on poles over the lake reminded him of a little Venice—hence the name Venezuela. Initially, the region was an economic disappointment. It lacked both good mining potential and settled and exploitable agricultural tribes; the indigenous Amerindian population, largely Carib and Arawak, was scattered, unlike those of Mexico, Peru or neighbouring Nueva Granada (modern Colombia). The mythical land of El Dorado was thought to lie somewhere in the Orinoco delta, and such rumours aroused some interest in the territory.

INDEPENDENCE

Until the foundation of Nueva Granada as a Viceroyalty in 1739, Venezuela was administered from Lima, Peru. In 1777 Venezuela became a Spanish Captaincy-General, with an enhanced degree of administrative autonomy from Bogotá, the capital of Nueva Granada. In 1724 a company of Basque merchants, the Caracas Company, obtained a monopoly of the territory's foreign trade, anticipating the growth of commercial prosperity in the territory as the Company developed new markets in Europe and the Caribbean for local produce, including cocoa and coffee. The export market fostered a small élite of European planters, the so-called 'Marqueses de Chocolate', and it was a member of this class, Simón Bolívar, who emerged as the leader of the movement for independence in all northern Spanish America. Venezuela gained independence from Spain in 1819 and joined with Colombia, Ecuador and Panama to form the 'Gran Colombia' federation. Bolívar perceived regional unification as an essential counter to the emerging power of the United States, a vision that later influenced the more contemporary foreign policy of President Hugo Chávez Frías (1999–). Bolívar's objective was, however, undermined by political infighting, and in 1830 the federation was dissolved and Venezuela became a separate republic.

The next one hundred years of Venezuelan history were characterized by authoritarian rule, encompassing the regimes of José Antonio Páez (1830–46 and 1861–63), Antonio Guzmán Blanco (1870–88) and Juan Vicente Gómez (1908–35). It was during the Gómez period that the democratic opposition emerged from the middle-class student movement. Two prominent figures in student politics, Romulo Betancourt and Dr Rafael Caldera Rodríguez formed what were to become the country's leading political parties: the social democrat Democratic Action (Acción Democrática—AD) party and the christian democrat Committee of Independent Electoral Political Organization (Comité de Organización Política Electoral Independiente—COPEI). Both parties found it difficult to organize in the repressive political climate of the Gómez regime and developed hierarchical and centralized internal structures controlled by the party elite, or *cogollo*, to counter infiltration. Collaboration between AD and progressive elements of the military led to a coup in 1945 that brought democratic elections and propelled AD to power for three years. A military coup in 1948 curtailed the regime, which was weakened by intense partisan conflict. The corruption and oppression of General Marcos Pérez Jiménez, who governed Venezuela for the following 10 years, led the previously antagonistic political parties to form the Pact of Punto Fijo in 1957. The Pact committed AD and COPEI to share positions in the state administration, to respect the outcome of democratic elections and to control their respective constituencies. Following a military rebellion and general strike in January 1958, Pérez Jiménez fled the country, and in the elections that ensued, Romulo Betancourt was elected President. It was the capacity for negotiation and policy consensus, the so-called 'coincidencia', between AD and COPEI that ensured

democratic stability after 1958. The Presidency of Rafael Caldera in 1969–74 was characterized by strong elements of continuity with the previous AD Governments.

THE DEVELOPMENT OF PETROLEUM RESOURCES

Venezuela had been the world's third-largest producer of coffee in the 19th century, after Brazil and Java (the latter now part of Indonesia). By the mid-1930s the importance of petroleum to the Venezuelan economy had overtaken that of coffee, following the discovery and exploitation of those mineral resources at the beginning of the 20th century. Venezuela's importance as a petroleum exporter was enhanced by the nationalization of Mexico's oil industry in 1938 and by the outbreak of the Second World War in Europe in 1939. As a result, Venezuela became increasingly skilled in international negotiation, and was considered responsible for much of the preliminary planning that culminated in the creation of the Organization of the Petroleum Exporting Countries (OPEC—see Part Three, Regional Organizations), of which Venezuela was one of five founder member nations. OPEC was formally constituted at a conference in Venezuela in January 1961. Venezuela's petroleum industry was nationalized in 1976 in a gradual process that was co-ordinated with the petroleum companies operating in the country. Despite nationalist opposition, the deteriorating economic situation led the second Caldera Government (1994–99) to initiate a selective opening to foreign and domestic private capital of the state petroleum company, Petróleos de Venezuela, SA (PDVSA) in 1995. The incorporation of private capital into the petroleum sector was reviewed by the incoming Government of President Hugo Chávez Frías (1999–), which was highly critical of the 'state within a state' which PDVSA was accused of representing. The new administration significantly reduced PDVSA's autonomy, as well as its budget, and introduced legislation to help end Venezuela's dependence on the petroleum sector, through diversification. Strengthening relations with oil-exporting countries became a central aspect of the Government's energy and foreign policy, and the Minister of Energy and Mines, Ali Rodríguez Araque, who assumed the presidency of OPEC in 2000, was successful in introducing a petroleum price band system within the organization. Following industrial unrest in the petroleum sector in October 2000, President Chávez appointed General Guacaipuro Lameda to the presidency of PDVSA, a move that prompted concerns that the industry was being militarized.

The predominance of petroleum in the Venezuelan economy had inevitable political consequences. The Venezuelan Government traditionally received much higher revenues than neighbouring countries, without burdening its citizens with heavy taxes. One consequence was the enormous patronage that Government could dispense. This was directed through a network of party-affiliated organizations, including trade unions and business organizations. Whilst the distribution of petroleum revenue initially facilitated the consolidation of the democratic system and helped to increase support for the centrist political parties, a negative side-effect was the creation of an association between access to patronage, redistributive policies and governmental legitimacy. This made it particularly difficult for successive Governments to reduce public expenditure when petroleum prices were low. However, Venezuela's wealth was intelligently used in restructuring civil–military relations and in promoting many advances in welfare and education. Public liberties were secure and Venezuela enjoyed one of the best records in the Americas for respecting human rights.

THE ADMINISTRATION OF CARLOS ANDRÉS PÉREZ RODRÍGUEZ

Following the national elections of 1973, at which the AD candidate, Carlos Andrés Pérez, won the presidency, Venezuela experienced a dramatic change in economic fortunes. The Arab-Israeli war prompted an acute increase in world oil prices, and this coincided with the nationalization of the Venezuelan petroleum industry; central government revenues increased by an estimated 170%. The petroleum earnings were channelled into state subsidies and social investment, with particular advances in health, housing and education. Unfortunately, the extraordinary levels of revenue also exacerbated corruption, and led the national administration to became excessively bureaucratized and inefficient. In addition, the Government began to borrow from international creditors in order to sustain investment projects when the price of petroleum began to fall, towards the end of Pérez's term in office. Despite the steady deterioration in the oil price and increasingly negative international borrowing conditions, the successive COPEI and AD Governments of Luís Herrera Campins (1978–83) and Jaíme Lusinchi (1983–88) were reluctant to reduce fiscal spending. This was related to concerns that economic adjustment would undermine support for the parties and the legitimacy of the political system.

Throughout the 1980s, previously high levels of electoral participation declined, and opinion poll surveys indicated mounting popular disaffection with AD and COPEI. The parties were seen as corrupt, unrepresentative and ineffective in their handling of the economy. Despite the increasingly negative evaluation of their performance, they remained the dominant political forces. This was determined by a number of factors. As a result of the 1958 Pact, the two parties shared control of appointments in the judiciary, the military, the state bureaucracy and the electoral administration, creating powerful vested interests in their political pre-eminence. In addition, their central role in the dispersion of the petroleum revenues created a network of corrupt and clientelistic interests, particularly among the country's leading economic groups. The dominance of AD and COPEI was further reinforced by the electoral system, which was highly restrictive. The operations of the political and electoral system consequently limited the opportunities for the electorate to turn to new, competing organizations such as the Movement to Socialism (Movimiento al Socialismo—MAS) party and the Radical Cause (La Causa Radical—Causa R).

In 1988 Carlos Andrés Pérez was re-elected to the presidency. This owed much to a campaign that drew strongly on nostalgia for the prosperity enjoyed during his previous term of office. Hopes that his second term would herald a renewed era of national prosperity were frustrated within one month of his inauguration in 1989. In February an orthodox programme of liberal economic reform was introduced, reflecting a trend throughout Latin America, as the continent attempted to emerge from the debt crisis of the 1980s. The strict austerity policy, in particular increased fuel and transport prices, combined with disappointed popular expectations, provoking the most serious civil disturbances in Venezuela's recent history in February 1989. At least 300 people were killed in conflicts with security forces in the capital, Caracas. The riots were not led by any political movement, nor were they anticipated by the centrist parties, indicating that the political control exercised by AD and COPEI over the Venezuelan people had weakened. President Pérez found it difficult to secure the support of his own party, AD, and the trade-union movement for his International Monetary Fund (IMF)-inspired adjustment policies. AD was opposed to economic policies such as privatization, which would restrict its ability to dispense patronage. Traditionally, labour unrest was not a serious problem in Venezuela and organized labour was an important sector of support for democracy. Some 22% of the work-force was unionized, mostly in the pro-AD Venezuelan Workers' Confederation (Confederación de Trabajadores de Venezuela—CTV), or the pro-COPEI Confederation of Autonomous Workers (Confederación de Sindicatos Autónomos de Venezuela—CODESA). Members of the CTV and CODESA enjoyed a greater range of benefits than other workers because of extensive government patronage. However, in May 1989 the CTV organized the first general strike for 31 years, in order to demand pro-labour reforms. The CTV's hostility to the Government's economic programme was motivated by the fear that a reduction in patronage would undermine the Confederation's control of the labour force. This weakening of CTV authority was already evident in the strategically important region of

Guyana, where Causa R pioneered new forms of autonomous union representation in protest at corruption and limited representation within the CTV.

In an attempt to stabilize the political system the Pérez Government introduced a series of major reforms, including measures to promote decentralization of power and changes to the electoral system. These initiatives were approved in Congress, despite the opposition of President Pérez's AD, which viewed them as a threat to its political dominance. Such concerns were justified by the subsequent success of Causa R and the MAS in the first state governorship elections, which were organized in 1989. Nevertheless, despite allowing political hostility to the dominant parties to be expressed through institutional channels, the reforms failed to improve support for the political system.

Failed Military Coup

The stability of Venezuela's democracy was shaken by an attempted *coup d'état* in February 1992. The rebels belonged to a nationalist faction of junior officers known as the Bolivarian Revolutionary Movement 200 (Movimiento Bolivariano Revolucionario 200—MBR-200), which was led by Lt-Col Hugo Chávez Frías and Lt-Col Francisco Arias Cárdenas, and had been in existence since the early 1980s. The MBR-200 was opposed to government economic reforms and to alleged corruption within the political system and the higher echelons of the military, where promotion was dependent on political support in Congress. They were encouraged to organize the coup attempt by increased social unrest, and were supported by sections of Causa R. Although the coup failed, its size and the level of conspiracy were significant. Furthermore, there was a degree of sympathy within the mainstream military for the rebels and, despite his subsequent imprisonment, Chávez was transformed into a popular hero.

President Pérez came under considerable pressure to resign following the coup attempt. His opponents in Congress, including former President Rafael Caldera, condemned him for endangering democracy, and the leadership of Pérez's own AD party called for his term of office to be reduced. In November a second coup attempt led by forces loosely connected to the MBR-200 further weakened the President's credibility, and in May 1993 he was suspended from office by Congress, following allegations of corruption. In May 1996 Pérez was found guilty of misuse of public funds and sentenced to two years and four months under house arrest (two years of this sentence having been already served).

THE ADMINISTRATION OF RAFAEL CALDERA RODRÍGUEZ

Following the suspension of Pérez, in June 1993 Congress elected Ramón José Velásquez, an independent senator, as interim President until fresh elections could be held in December. Rafael Caldera Rodríguez, who contested the election as an independent candidate following his expulsion from COPEI in June, won the presidency with the support of a 17-party anti-liberal alliance, National Convergence (Convergencia Nacional—CN). The octogenarian Caldera emphasized his reputation as one of the founding fathers of Venezuelan democracy during the election, which he won with 30% of the votes cast. The AD and COPEI presidential candidates garnered 23.6% and 22.7% of the votes respectively, marking the first time since 1958 that neither of the two parties controlled the executive. They remained, however, the dominant force in the bicameral legislature, and together took 119 of the total 248 seats. In contrast, CN captured only 10 seats in the 49-seat Senate and 50 of the 199 seats in the Chamber of Deputies. Causa R also became a powerful political force; its presidential candidate, Andrés Velásquez, officially gained 22% of the votes cast. The party's performance, which built on extensive gains made at local elections in 1989 and 1992, was another indication that the traditional dominance of AD and COPEI was coming to an end.

Caldera was elected, like Pérez before him, on a platform of opposition to the IMF and neo-liberal policies. As a committed advocate of 'social justice', on assuming office in February 1994 Caldera promised to abolish value-added tax (sales tax) and to halt the aggressive privatization programme introduced by his predecessor. One of Caldera's immediate priorities was to placate the military, particularly the junior officers: on taking office he replaced the entire military high command and released the coup plotters of 1992. Lt-Col Chávez was pardoned for his role in the February coup, but was not allowed to re-enter the Army. (Chávez subsequently focused on political mobilization, and encouraged mass abstention in elections as a means to overthrow the political system.)

Caldera inherited a severe crisis in the banking sector. In January 1994, one month before the new President took office, Banco Latino, the country's second largest commercial bank, collapsed exposing the poor regulation and solvency problems inherent in the domestic banking system. The Government intervened in Banco Latino and seven other financial institutions, together accounting for 38% of Venezuela's financial market. In March an emergency finance law guaranteed the security of savers' deposits. However, confidence in the banking system was severely damaged. In June a further eight financial institutions were rescued by government intervention. The financial system was subsequently placed under the control of the Bank Deposits Guarantee Fund (FOGADE), which was created by presidential decree. This measure prompted accusations that the Government had all but nationalized the sector. Despite declaring an end to the crisis in August 1994, in January 1995 the Government intervened in a further three commercial banks.

As well as instability in the banking sector, in 1994 the Government encountered violent social unrest. As a result of the economic crisis and the general climate of mounting lawlessness, in June the Government announced that it was to assume extraordinary powers. These included the suspension of six articles of the Constitution, which concerned guarantees of freedom of movement, freedom from arbitrary arrest and the right to own property and to participate in legal economic activity. Price controls and a fixed exchange rate were also introduced, in an attempt to stabilize the rapidly depreciating currency and to augment foreign-exchange reserves. In July the legislature voted to restore five of the six guarantees of the Constitution suspended in the previous month but, in spite of protests, the Government immediately reintroduced the measures. Later in the month the legislative opposition, with the exception of Causa R, which withdrew from the Congress in protest, endorsed the emergency financial measures as a prelude to the restoration of full constitutional rights to the whole country, with the exception of areas along the border with Colombia, where criminal activity was reported to be rife.

Caldera's administration, like that of his predecessor, was forced to renege on electoral promises and introduce an IMF-negotiated US $1,400m. stand-by agreement in July 1996. The series of economic and structural reforms, the so-called Agenda Venezuela, provoked considerable popular discontent and there were numerous large anti-Government demonstrations in 1996 and 1997. Meanwhile, the Government found it difficult to ensure congressional support for important economic proposals. Outraged by the imposition of the Agenda, the MAS entered a 'tripartite alliance' with COPEI and Causa R which forced President Caldera to rely on AD for support in the legislature. This dependence became acute after March 1997, following the defection of five CN deputies, reducing the alliance's representation in the lower house to just 19.

Unlike the experience of 1989, the adoption of the IMF-sponsored reforms did not lead to violence. This was largely owing to a rise in the oil price, which provided the Government with the fiscal resources to maintain public spending and defer structural adjustment. The Government also attempted to balance the conflicting demands of the IMF and the public sector through the creation of tripartite commissions, which linked business, government and the highly unrepresentative official trade-union confederation, the CTV. This allowed agreements on the minimum wage and on labour and social-security reform. However, Causa R and the unofficial trade-union movement condemned the measures. The modification of the labour legislation ended the system of retroactive severance payments, a crucial form of welfare provision, whilst the planned social-security reforms and minimum wage increases did not include workers in the informal labour sector, which by 1995, constituted one-half of the country's total work-force.

The relative political and economic stability of 1997 was reversed in 1998, when a deterioration in the price of petroleum forced the Government into spending cuts of US $6,000m. in the weeks preceding national and regional elections scheduled for 6 December. As an indication of the profound popular hostility to the established political parties, all the leading presidential candidates contested the election as independents, with the leading contender, Hugo Chávez Frías, promising a radical reform of the political system. In an attempt to prevent a decisive Chávez victory, in May COPEI and AD used their congressional majority to pass a revision of the electoral schedule. This separated the legislative and gubernatorial elections, which were brought forward to 8 November, from the presidential election in December.

The two leading contenders in the presidential contest were Chávez and Henrique Salas Römer. Salas, who campaigned on a platform of neo-liberal reform was a former Governor of Carabobo state and was supported by the Venezuela Project party (Proyecto Venezuela—PRVZL). Chávez, the former coup leader, was backed by his Fifth Republic Movement (Movimiento V República—MVR), which he created in 1995 as the electoral arm of the MBR-200. His presidential bid was supported by a dissident faction of Causa R, the Homeland For All party (Patria Para Todos—PPT), the MAS and the PCV, which together formed the Patriotic Pole (Polo Patriótico—PP) alliance. Chávez enjoyed enormous popular support, owing partly to his nationalist, populist rhetoric, which capitalized on hostility to the Government's economic policy, but also as a result of his pledge to abolish Congress and hold elections for a Constituent Assembly, if approved in a referendum.

In the November 1998 elections AD gained 21.7% of the votes cast, secured the most congressional seats (55 of the 189 seats in the Chamber of Deputies, 19 of the 48 seats in the Senate) and won eight of the 23 state governorships. The MVR also performed strongly, gaining 21.3% of the votes cast, 49 lower-house seats and 12 seats in the Senate. The MAS and the PPT won a total of 21 seats in the Chamber of Deputies and six seats in the Senate, increasing to 70 the number of pro-Chávez deputies. In contrast, Salas Römer's PRVZL gained 24 seats in the Chamber of Deputies and just one senate seat. In a final, desperate effort to avert a presidential victory for Chávez, and thus forestall the loss of their long-standing political predominance, AD and COPEI withdrew their support for their own candidates (Luis Alfaro Ucero, the party Secretary-General of the AD and Irene Sáez, respectively) and united in support of Salas Römer. However, Chávez had engaged the popular imagination, and was elected President with 56.2% of the votes cast, ahead of Salas Römer, who received the support of 40% of voters.

THE ADMINISTRATIONS OF HUGO CHÁVEZ FRÍAS

On assuming office in February 1999 President Chávez immediately decreed that a national referendum on the convening of a Constituent Assembly to draft a new constitution be held. His preference for an 'organic' assembly, which would replace the existing state institutions, in contrast to a 'derivative' assembly, which would work alongside existing institutions, generated a major constitutional debate in the country. Opponents of the Government, including AD, COPEI and the PRVZL, attempted to prevent the referendum by appealing to the Supreme Court. This body, however, accepted the legality of Chávez's referendum decree, although the electorate was not asked to vote on the remit of the Constituent Assembly's powers. In the plebiscite, held on 25 April 1999, 81.5% of voters endorsed the convening of a Constituent Assembly and 80.0% supported Chávez's proposals for electoral procedures. The success of the referendum was marred by an abstention rate of 60%.

In elections to the 131-member Constituent Assembly held on 27 July 1999, supporters of Chávez won 121 of the seats. The Constituent Assembly was formally convened on 3 August 1999 and, in a symbolic act intended to demonstrate the sovereignty of the Assembly, Chávez tendered his resignation. The Assembly immediately reappointed him to the presidency. In response to the convening of the Assembly, Congress declared itself in recess, thereby avoiding an impasse between the executive and the legislature. The Constituent Assembly created 20 commissions to draft separate sections of a new constitution and completed its work in November. The new Constitution introduced a number of radical changes to the institutional framework of the Venezuelan state. These included the introduction of a renewable six-year term for the President (replacing the traditional non-renewable five-year term), the replacement of the bicameral legislative arrangements with a 165-seat unicameral chamber (the National Assembly), and the abolition of the Supreme Court, which was to be superseded by the Supreme Justice Tribunal (Tribunal Suprema de Justicia—TSJ). In addition, two new powers were created, the Moral Republican Council (Consejo Moral Republicano), whose principal duty was to uphold the Constitution, and the National Electoral Council (Consejo Nacional Electoral—CNE, awarded constitutional status). For the first time, the post of Vice-President was created, and serving military officers were given the right to vote, with military promotions removed from the hands of the legislature and given to the President. In a move that attracted criticism from senior figures in the Armed Forces, the army, navy and air force were merged into a single unified command,. The Constitution also changed the official name of the country to the Bolivarian Republic of Venezuela.

The new Constitution was approved by 71% of voters in a referendum held on 15 December 1999. The voting process was disrupted by the worst natural disaster experienced by Venezuela, with an estimated 20,000 people killed and 250,000 made homeless by mudslides that followed torrential rainstorms along a 60 km stretch of the north-east coast. Following the promulgation of the new Constitution, the Constituent Assembly was replaced by a 21-person 'mini-congress' (congresillo), pending fresh elections, scheduled for May 2000, to re-legitimize all elective authorities. The leader of the Constituent Assembly, Luís Miquilena (a close confidant of President Chávez), was appointed to head the unelected congresillo. He was criticized for a number of appointments he made to strategic positions, with the opposition alleging that those selected were closely linked to the Government. Such criticism increased following the appointments of a number of military officers to senior cabinet and administrative positions, and led to the withdrawal of the PPT from the PP, in protest.

The economic situation inherited by President Chávez was bleak, with petroleum prices falling to a nine-year low at the beginning of 1999. Despite populist speeches, Chávez demonstrated an immediate commitment to fiscal prudence. The President's popularity limited efforts by the opposition-controlled trade-union confederations to mobilize support against the Government's economic measures. A social policy initiative, the Social Emergency and Internal Defence and Development Plan, popularly known as the 'Proyecto Bolívar 2000', launched in February, intended to rehabilitate public property and land, and led to the deployment of the Armed Forces in local communities to build schools and hospitals. The project initially prompted concerns that President Chávez was seeking to politicize the Armed Forces and to expand their role in civilian affairs, and provoked a series of rural and urban land occupations.

Throughout 1999 opposition towards President Chávez was uncoordinated, discredited and inchoate. Initially, it seemed that he would encounter no legitimate opposition in the presidential election, scheduled for May 2000. However, in early 2000 a challenger emerged from an unexpected quarter. On the eighth anniversary of the February military coup attempt, Francisco Arias Cárdenas, a former close colleague of President Chávez, and five other prominent figures within MBR-200 issued the Declaration of Maracay. This condemned corruption within the Government and called on Chávez to dismiss Miquilena and a number of other civilian ministers, in addition to criticising Chávez for betraying the democratic ideals of MBR-200. Arias subsequently announced his intention to contest the Presidency.

The 2000 Elections

The elections scheduled for May 2000 were popularly known as the 'mega-elections', since they were the largest and most complex in the country's history , with more than 6,000 posts to be decided. Arias's candidacy was supported by an unruly coalition that included Causa R and a left-wing guerrilla movement, Bandera Roja (Red Flag). On 25 May, three days before the elections were to be held, the TSJ ruled in favour of an injunction

against the elections introduced by a number of civil society organizations, on the grounds that the CNE was not technically competent to administer the process. The decision was seen to reflect a measure of autonomy within the judiciary and was an embarrassment for President Chávez. Following the postponement of the election, the CNE executive was replaced by new authorities, selected by a 'table of dialogue' comprising members of the opposition, civil society groups and the MVR. The CNE decided to separate the election of the President, legislative assembly, state governors and mayors from those for regional and municipal legislatures.

The presidential elections proceeded on 30 July 2000, following a bitter campaign that was dominated by rumours of an imminent military coup that gained credence following the dissemination of video footage in June that appeared to show a serving national guardsman calling on President Chávez to resign or risk a popular uprising. Chávez received 59.7% of the votes cast, compared with the 37.5% secured by Arias. Claudio Fermín, the candidate of the National Encounter (Encuentro Nacional—EN) party, came third with less than 3% of the ballot. The severe economic contraction experienced in 1999 failed to diminish support for President Chávez among the most marginalized sectors of Venezuelan society, which endorsed his anti-corruption drive and vitriolic verbal attacks on the traditional parties. In elections to the new, 165-seat National Assembly the MVR-led PP alliance won the three-fifths' majority required to make appointments to the position of Fiscal- and Comptroller-General and to the judiciary. AD emerged as the largest opposition party, winning 32 seats, while COPEI was eliminated as a significant political force, securing just five assembly seats. The PP won control of 13 regional executives in the state governorship elections, which were beset by allegations of electoral fraud proceeding from AD. In early August the congresillo was dissolved and the National Assembly convened for the first time. The primary task of the legislature was to modify existing legislation to accord with the new Constitution. In November the National Assembly granted 'enabling powers' to the executive for one year, allowing President Chávez to legislate by decree in a range of areas, without the need for congressional approval.

The start of President Chávez's second term was characterized by heightened political conflict between the Government and an increasingly coherent opposition. This incorporated the Roman Catholic Church, the private sector, sections of the media, the CTV union confederation and civil society organizations. Sectoral mobilization against the Government substituted for organization by the weak and discredited opposition parties. Whilst popular support for President Chávez remained high amongst the numerically dominant marginalized sectors, there was growing frustration at the limited progress made in policy areas allegedly prioritized by the Government, including job creation and reductions in crime and corruption. This owed much to the administration's proclivity for centralized authority and President Chávez's reluctance to decentralize responsibility outside of his core group of select government colleagues. Despite 'fast-track' legislative powers, by June 2001, the Council of Ministers had approved only 12 economic and administrative bills, of which amount only 8 had been enacted as law; more than 40 pieces of legislation were awaiting further considerations. The executive also demonstrated a tendency to circumvent its own constitutional obligations and impose controversial policy reform without consultation. This served to weaken private-sector confidence and generated allegations of authoritarianism.

In October 2000 President Chávez decreed a referendum to approve measures to reform the trade-union movement through the introduction of direct internal elections and the creation of a single, unified confederation. The proposed referendum was criticized by the International Labour Organization and the CTV as a violation of the constitutional provision of freedom from state interference for private organizations. The planned changes were interpreted as an attempt to replace the AD-affiliated CTV with a new trade-union movement loyal to President Chávez called the Bolivarian Workers Front (Frente Bolivariana de Trabajadores—FBT). Opposition to the proposed referendum led to a resurrection in the political fortunes of the discredited CTV, which stepped up demands for improved working conditions, triggering a wave of stoppages by trade unions affiliated to the confederation. This included a damaging four-day strike by petroleum workers in October, which culminated in President Chávez dimissing the President of PDVSA, Héctor Civaldini, for his handling of the dispute. The referendum, which went ahead in December, registered the endorsement of 63% of voters: however, with an abstention rate of 78%, the legitimacy of the Government's reforms were considered somewhat questionable. Elections for a unified confederation were delayed until September 2001 (beyond the 180 days stipulated in the decree), because of the low level of support for the FBT, which struggled to recruit its target of 1m. members. In the vacuum created by the delay, industrial unrest increased as over 2,740 separate trade unions mobilized worker interests in the hope of reaping electoral dividends.

The numerous demonstrations organized by the CTV were supported by other interest groups, including teachers, the church and parents, who protested against a decree amending the Education Act also introduced in December 2000. Decree 1011 ended state payment for religious instruction in schools and created the position of school inspectors, appointed by the education ministry, empowered to assess educational provision in both public and private institutions. The measure was intended to tackle the high 'drop out' and absenteeism rates, but it was interpreted by opponents as an indication of the Government's authoritarian inclinations. These fears were fuelled by changes to educational texts, the recruitment of Cuban teachers and the introduction of marching and drill practice in schools. A further area of contention was the Government's Land Reform Bill, which President Chávez claimed would allow for the expropriation of idle land in the national interest. As with Decree 1011, debate on the underlying rationale of the reform, which, in this instance, was to reduce the highest concentration of landownership in Latin America, was undermined by the conflict between an opposition alleging authoritarianism and the Government, which attacked the resistance of the 'old oligarchy'.

In May 2001 President Chávez generated intense constitutional debate when he announced that he was considering emergency powers to tackle corruption and crime. The proposal was criticized by MAS party members, partners with MVR in the PP, prompting President Chávez to exclude them from the alliance. Chávez did not pursue the proposals and turned his attention to reforming his organizational base. Concerned by mounting allegations of corruption within the military and his MVR party, Chávez announced his intention to relaunch MBR-200 and to create neighbourhood groups of ideologically committed activists called Bolivarian Circles in June 2001. Although Chávez emphasised that MVR would continue to exist as an electoral organization, the creation of the Bolivarian Circles was interpreted as recognition that MVR was incapable of consolidating grassroots support for the President.

INTERNATIONAL RELATIONS

In 1998 Venezuela cemented a bilateral agreement with Chile to promote a free-trade pact. As a member of the Andean Community of Nations (known as the Andean Pact until 1996), Venezuela took a leading role in negotiations between fellow pact members (Bolivia, Colombia, Ecuador and Peru) and with the countries of the Southern Common Market (Mercado Común del Sur—Mercosur—Argentina, Brazil, Paraguay and Uruguay as full members and Bolivia and Chile as associate members) to form a single free-trade area. In April 1998 a trade-liberalization agreement, committing the two regional trading blocs to the creation of a free-trade area by 1 January 2000, was signed. Integration, however, was delayed, prompting the Venezuelan Government to pursue unilateral entry into Mercosur, a move supported by the Brazilian Government. In June 1999 President Chávez proposed the creation of a political confederation grouping Latin American and Caribbean countries by 2010. Following the American Heads of State Summit in Ottawa (Canada) in May 2001, at which agreement was reached on creating a Free Trade Area of the Americas (FTAA) by 2005, the Andean Community of Nations endorsed moves to strengthen regional integration at a meeting in Venezuela in June 2001. This included co-ordination on anti-drugs, social and educational policies and the creation of a common passport by 2005.

The intensification of regional ties was viewed as a means of increasing the voice of Andean countries in the FTAA discussions. President Chávez's Government was also committed to improving relations with Cuba and supported that country's integration into regional trade associations.

In March 1999 PDVSA began negotiating a subsidized petroleum supply contract with Cuba, with the preferential terms negotiated subsequently extended to other Caribbean nations under the Caracas Energy Accord of 2000. Relations with other OPEC member countries worsened in 1998, when Saudi Arabia accused Venezuela of exceeding OPEC production quotas by more than 30%, forcing petroleum prices to fall to a nine-year low. However, when President Chávez took office in February 1999, good relations with OPEC were prioritized and Venezuela played a leading role in the negotiation of successive rounds of petroleum-production cuts, in 1999 and 2000, which applied to OPEC and non-OPEC nations. This enhanced Venezuela's standing within the organization and the country's energy minister, Alí Rodríguez was elected to the OPEC presidency in March 2000. In August 2000 President Chávez undertook a controversial tour of the Middle East, during which he visited Iraq and Libya to extend personally invitations to Presidents Saddam Hussein and Muammar al-Qaddafi to attend the OPEC heads of state summit, held in Caracas in the following month. President Chávez became the first elected head of state to meet the Iraqi leader since sanctions were imposed on that country following the war in the region of the Persian (Arabian) Gulf in 1991. The USA condemned the meeting.

In contrast to the cordial links between Venezuela and Brazil, relations with the other neighbouring countries of Guyana and Colombia were strained by territorial and border disputes. Venezuela had historical claims to all territory west of the Essequibo river in Guyana. In November 1989 a UN mediator was appointed to resolve this territorial dispute. Limited progress was made and in October 1999 Venezuela renewed its claims to the disputed land. Relations deteriorated in July 2000 when Venezuela strongly protested against the decision by the Government of Guyana to lease land to a US company in the disputed Essequibo delta for the purpose of developing a satellite-launch facility. In addition, Venezuela had a claim to some islands in the Dutch Caribbean. A territorial dispute with Colombia concerning maritime boundaries in the Gulf of Venezuela came to prominence in September 1987 when Venezuela closed its border with Colombia. Diplomatic relations between the two countries were strained by continued border confrontations between Colombian guerrillas and right-wing paramilitaries and units of the Venezuelan Armed Forces. In 1996 bilateral discussions on the demarcation and control of the Venezuelan–Colombian border began. This was followed by an emergency summit of defence ministers and military commanders from the two countries in April 1997, at which it was agreed to strengthen military co-operation. Agreement was subsequently reached on intelligence sharing. In late 1998 government representatives attended the peace talks held between the Colombian Government of President Andrés Pastrana Arango and the left-wing guerrilla group, the Revolutionary Armed Forces of Colombia (Fuerzas Armadas Revolucionarias de Colombia—FARC). The Venezuelan Government committed itself to facilitating dialogue with the guerrillas. This led to a souring of diplomatic relations between Venezuela and Colombia, with President Pastrana accusing Venezuela of interfering in Colombian affairs. Relations between the two countries were further strained when Venezuela violated trade agreements with Colombia and refused to end a blockade of cross-border haulage, introduced in March 1999. In May 2000 Presidents Chávez and Pastrana signed the Declaration of Santa Marta, which committed the two countries to co-operate to resolve border disputes and to strengthen bilateral trade and political relations.

Relations with the USA deteriorated following the accession of Chávez to the presidency. The new Government's decision to deny the US Air Force permission to enter Venezuelan airspace to undertake anti-drugs and aerial surveillance exercises was condemned by the US administration. Relations were further exacerbated in mid-1999, following the Venezuelan foreign minister's criticism of the USA's anti-drugs strategy. Venezuela maintained a position of open hostility to the US-proposed 'Plan

Colombia', intended to combat the Colombian drugs trade. The Venezuelan Government feared an escalation of the Colombian civil conflict as a result and, therefore, a greater influx of refugees into Venezuela, and strengthened its border in preparation. In May 2001 Venezuela revised its opposition to Plan Colombia in exchange for financial assistance for border areas.

Venezuela and the USA also came into conflict over the embargoes imposed on Iraq and Cuba. As part of its strategy of diluting the country's commercial dependence on the USA, the Venezuelan Government signed a number of bilateral trade and cultural agreements with the People's Republic of China, India, Iran and Russia in mid-2001.

Economy

Dr JULIA BUXTON

Venezuela has the sixth largest proven oil reserves in the world and petroleum has been the mainstay of the economy since the discovery of deposits at the end of the 19th century. There have been a number of failed attempts to diversify the economic base. These included a programme of state-led industrialization focusing on heavy industrial development in the mid-1970s, and policies to encourage non-oil export growth, led by the private sector, in the early 1990s. The Government of Hugo Chávez Frías sought to diversify into 'downstream' and agricultural activities. However, by 2000 petroleum accounted for 84.2% of export revenue and 28.0% of the gross domestic product (GDP). Such heavy dependence on petroleum rendered Venezuela vulnerable to changes in the international economy. The domestic economy was subject to 'boom and bust' cycles, with high petroleum prices leading to expansionary spending policies, only to result in severe fiscal problems when the petroleum price fell. The channelling of petroleum revenue through central government spending resulted in high rates of economic growth in the 1960s and 1970s. Real GDP grew by an annual average of 3.7% between 1965 and 1980. However, because of a high rate of population increase over the same period (2.5%), per-caput growth was not as strong. During 1980–2000 GDP growth averaged 0.9% per year, suggesting a decline in real income levels.

The 10-fold increase in world petroleum prices in the early 1970s, which coincided with nationalization of the oil industry in Venezuela, led to a reversal in the trend of steady economic growth. The temporary abundance of petroleum revenue in 1973–74 and 1979, led to heavy external borrowing to finance state-led expansion. This, in turn, increased debt and exacerbated import dependence. However, difficulties only increased as petroleum prices declined; revenues were reduced and deflationary policies were necessary to control public-sector deficits. Such difficulties prevailed in the 1980s. Successive governments found it politically difficult to reduce spending, because of popular expectations of petroleum-induced wealth. As a result, austerity policies were repeatedly deferred, and foreign debt accumulated when the petroleum price temporarily increased.

In 1986–88 GDP expanded briefly, but in 1989 real GDP fell by 7.8%, this decline coinciding with the imposition of an International Monetary Fund (IMF) austerity programme. This three-year programme led to a new debt-repayment arrangement with commercial-bank creditors in June 1990. In the same year the country benefited from the increase in world petroleum prices following the Iraqi invasion of Kuwait in August. Real GDP growth in 1992 was 7.3% but, thereafter, GDP declined every year until 1995, when a modest improvement in the economy was reflected in GDP growth of 4.0%. In 1996 there was a contraction of 0.2% in real GDP, corresponding with the adoption of a one-year stand-by agreement with the IMF in July. Nevertheless, the petroleum sector experienced an expansion of 8.8% following its opening to private investors, leading to real GDP growth of 6.4% in 1997. Following the decline of world petroleum prices and a weak performance by the non-petroleum sector, growth contracted by 0.2% in 1998. Despite a sharp rise in oil prices in 1999, GDP contracted by a further 6.1% in that year as a result of a 7.4% decline in the oil sector owing to production cuts, an 8% decline in the non-oil export sector and recession in the domestic economy. This negative performance was reversed in 2000, with growth in the non-oil sector, led by telecommunications, combining with a 3.4% expansion of the oil sector to produce GDP growth of 3.2%.

Venezuela traditionally had one of the highest average annual population growth rates in Latin America, at 2.6% per year, and, as a result, from 1958–98, the population increased five-fold, to 23.2m. A high birth rate, comparatively low death rate and significant immigration to Venezuela were the main factors behind this trend. By 2000, the growth rate had slowed to 1.6%. A decline in the birth rate from 24 births per 1,000 inhabitants in 1998 to 21 births per 1,000 in 2000, a rise in infant mortality from 21 per 1,000 live births in 1999 to 26 in 2000, and an increase in the death rate from 4.5 deaths per 1,000 people in 1999 to 4.9 in 2000 were the principal factors behind the fall. In 2000 61.5% of the population was under the age of 30, and the total labour force was some 10.3m. Indeed the labour force, with an average rate of increase of 3.8% per year, was expanding at a faster rate than the population. However, unemployment remained a problem during the 1990s as a result of limited economic growth, reduced domestic demand and an increase in labour supply. In 2000 the estimated rate of unemployment was 13.2%. Informal sector employment is one of the highest in Latin America, at an estimated 53.2% of the population. The structure of employment and the distribution of the population in the late 1990s were markedly different from the 1960s. Whilst 35% of the total employed labour force was employed in agriculture (including hunting, forestry and fishing) in 1960, by 2000 this figure had fallen to 11%. In 2000 87% of the total population was located in urban areas, underlining a consistent trend of migration from rural to urban locations. In the same year 67% of the employed labour force was employed in the services sector, while 23% worked in industry. Despite repeated agreements between the IMF and the Government to reduce the number of public-sector workers, in 2000 this figure remained high, at 17% of the total work-force. The prevalence of public-sector employment was related to the resistance of the trade-union movement to rationalization and the reluctance of the Government to increase unemployment figures. The major industry in economic terms, petroleum production and processing, employed only 40,000 workers in 2000, less than 1% of the working population.

According to the Inter-American Development Bank (IDB), during 1981–98 there was an accumulated fall in real wages of 68%. Economic decline and informal sector growth has contributed to the trend of rising poverty in Venezuela, which has been exacerbated by the weakness of the social security system. The monthly salaries of formal sector workers are 62% higher than those in the informal sector. An estimated 86% of the population live in conditions of general poverty, an increase of 50% since 1990. Extreme poverty affects 20.7% of the population; women are the most likely to live in conditions of poverty, and the salaries of female workers in the informal sector are 70% less than those earned by men. Rural poverty is also a major problem, with 82% of residents in rural areas living in impoverished conditions.

Public-sector industrial action pressured the Government into large sectoral wage increases, including a 150% wage increase for doctors and oil workers in January 1998. In March 1997 a tripartite commission comprising government, business and trade-union representatives signed an agreement to reform the system of social security and the 1936 labour law. Under the modifications to social security, legislation was introduced to replace public provision with a combined public and private system, but this was not extended to cover informal sector workers. The tripartite commission also increased the minimum wage by 44%, and this was increased by a further 33% in February 1998. In May 1999 the Government further increased the monthly minimum wage by 20%, to US \$200. In October 2000 a significant increase in salaries was agreed for employees in the petroleum sector, after a four-day strike by more than three-quarters of Venezuela's oil workers. Tensions continued to mount between the trade unions and the Government. Meanwhile, a new social security bill, to incorporate provisions for informal sector workers, was under consideration in 2001, the changes to the social security system formulated by the Caldera administration having been blocked by the Chávez Government.

AGRICULTURE

The agriculture sector was characterized by inefficiency, limited investment in modern farm technology and, with 70% of agricultural land in the hands of 3% of proprietors, the second highest concentration of land ownership in Latin America and the Caribbean. The agriculture sector, including hunting, forestry and fishing, accounted for 5.0% of Venezuela's GDP in 2000, and engaged 10.6% of the employed labour force in the same year. According to estimates by the UN's Food and Agriculture Organization (FAO), in 2000 only 24% of Venezuela's land area was utilized for agriculture, of which amount more than 80% was devoted to pasture. Some 50% of all agricultural revenue was derived from cattle ranching, with grains, fruit, vegetables, dairy products and poultry farming accounting for 40%, and forestry and fishing for the remaining 10%.

The country was not self-sufficient in most areas of agricultural production, and in 1999 67% of food consumed was imported. From the mid-1980s, however, Venezuela was virtually self-sufficient in cereals. Maize production stood at 900,000 metric tons in 2000, and rice production rose from 716,000 metric tons in 1998 to 737,000 tons in 2000. Sugar production increased during the 1990s as a result of the Government's efforts to achieve self-sufficiency, and in 2000 production totalled 7.0m. metric tons. Livestock and dairy farming showed promising growth in the 1980s, with self-sufficiency being achieved in pork and poultry meat. The number of pigs rose from 4.4m. in 1996 to 4.9m. in 2000. Annual milk production in the same year was 1.3m. metric tons, when there were an estimated 15.8m. cattle.

The powerful agro-industrial lobby benefited from a series of currency devaluations in the 1980s, and exports of livestock and cash crops (mainly coffee and cocoa) increased. During the Peréz administration government policy on agriculture concentrated on greater liberalization and competitiveness, and many subsidies were gradually withdrawn. In 1994 and 1997 the Government reintroduced the policy of fixing prices above international levels on a number of agricultural products. This, in conjunction with an overvalued bolívar, had a detrimental impact on agricultural production. In 1997 the Government ended its policy of offering subsidized credit to farmers, further increasing imports of agricultural goods. In 1998 development of the agricultural sector was prioritized; five areas—fishing, forestry, maize, palm oil and sugar—received special funding and, in May 1999, constitutionally mandated protectionist tariffs on imports of these products were introduced. The measures boosted production of coffee (by 5.1%) and maize (by 35.7%) in 2000, but aroused concern and controversy at the World Trade Organization and the Andean Community of Nations (Comunidad Andina de Naciones—CAN). Meanwhile, although the Government distributed US \$15m. to those seeking to establish farms in semi-urban areas, with additional land being made available for purchase from the National Agrarian Institute, land ownership remained a contentious issue and over 300 cases of squatting were reported between 1998 and 2000. In 2001 the Government drafted a controversial land reform bill, recommending the expropriation of 'idle land' in the 'social interest', in line with ownership provisions of the 1999 Constitution.

MINING AND POWER

Metallic Minerals

Venezuela possessed vast metallic mineral wealth. In 2000 estimated reserves of iron ore and bauxite totalled 19.5m. metric tons and 5.2m. metric tons, respectively. There were also deposits of zinc, copper, lead, phosphorus, nickel, diamond, silver

and uranium. In 1997 and 1998, in an attempt to improve production output in the sector, the Government introduced a series of measures to encourage foreign investment, which exempted foreign companies from paying 16.5% in value-added tax (VAT) during the first five years of pre-production activities. In 2000 a reform of the 1941 mining law enhanced legal security and streamlined the concession-granting process. Revenues from mining activities increased from US \$3.1m. in 1999 to \$4.6m. in 2000. The Government pursued a number of public-private partnerships to increase aluminium and iron ore production. These included a \$208m. agreement with the French firm Pechiney to expand production capacity at the state-owned bauxite plant, Bauxilum, from 1.7m. to 2.1m. metric tons per year, and a \$400m. project with the Korean firm Phang Steel to increase iron ore production, which totalled 20.1m. metric tons in 2000.

Venezuela has estimated gold reserves of 10,000 metric tons. Exploitation has suffered from prohibitive mining legislation, contested ownership claims and environmental impact disputes. The sector has also been negatively affected by the activities of an estimated 50,000 illegal miners. These problems led to a contraction in exploration spending and a consequent decline in production, which fell from 22.3m. grams in 1997 to 5.4m. grams in 1999. Production is expected to increase following the award of a number of new concessions in the sector; these include a US \$13m. investment in the Sosa Méndez gold mine by the Chinese Yankuang and Shandong mining groups, while 510 small-scale miners were awarded exploration and extraction permits in 2001 as part of the Government's strategy of formalizing illegal production.

Venezuela is the third largest coal producer in Latin America and has estimated reserves of 10,200m. metric tons. Since 1985 the Petróleos de Venezuela, SA (PDVSA) subsidiary Carbozulia has been responsible for the mining industry, but poor transport links in the east of the country, where 80% of reserves are located, and low investment ratios, have limited the development of the sector. In 1999 the Government announced plans to increase coal production, in collaboration with private-sector partners, to 21m. tons by 2008. Coal production increased from 5.5m. tons in 1999 to 7.7m. tons in 2000.

Electricity

Venezuela's electricity consumption levels were among the highest in Latin America (more than 90% of households have electricity). Some 75% of electric generating power was derived from hydroelectric projects, including the Guri Dam in Guyana and dams on the Caroní River. Three further hydroelectric projects, expected to add an estimated 8 gW of hydropower, were under consideration in 2001. Development of the electricity industry was state-led; however, declining central-government revenues made it difficult to maintain investment in the sector, which, in turn, led to problems within the transmission and distribution infrastructure. In 1998 the Government introduced the National Electrical Service Law, which formed the regulatory basis for the privatization of the sector. In October the sale of electricity assets began with the privatization of Sistema Eléctrico de Nueva Esparta (Seneca), at a cost of US \$63m. This was followed in 1999 by the privatization of a 70% stake in several regional electricity distributors. In June 2000 the electricity distributor for the capital, Electricidad de Caracas (EDC), was taken over by US energy group AES Corporation. In 2001 the energy ministry estimated that the sector required investment of \$5,300m. over the next three years.

Petroleum and Natural Gas

With 77,000m. barrels of proven oil reserves, and recoverable reserves of an estimated 100,000m. barrels of heavy crude, Venezuela has the largest oil reserves in the western hemisphere. The petroleum industry was traditionally the mainstay of the economy, providing 80% of government revenue. The oil industry was nationalized in 1975 and the state oil company, Petróleos de Venezuela, SA (PDVSA), and its subsidiaries were exclusively responsible for extracting and refining Venezuelan petroleum. PDVSA paid 73% of profits to the Government as taxes, royalties and special dividend payments; this tax contribution rose from US \$6,200m. in 1999 to \$13,000m. in 2000. Successive Venezuelan Governments brought different ideological perspectives to the question of how the country should best exploit its oil wealth, and this resulted in volatile production levels and relations with the Organization of the Petroleum Exporting Countries (OPEC).

Production of crude petroleum, which derived mostly from the Maracaibo, Apure-Barinas and Eastern Venezuela basins, steadily declined from a peak annual average of 3.7m. barrels per day (b/d) in 1970, to 1.55m. b/d in 1985. In 1986, OPEC increased production quotas and Venezuelan crude output rose in line with the revised targets, reaching 1.57m. b/d in 1988. Venezuela's quota increased to just below 2m. b/d in 1990 following the Iraqi invasion of Kuwait, which resulted in a suspension of supplies from those two countries. The subsequent increase in petroleum prices led to Venezuela exceeding its agreed quota, with actual production increasing to 2.26m. b/d in September 1990. Under President Caldera, a strategy of maximising output was pursued, and Venezuela continued to exceed its OPEC quota. Production in 1997 totalled 3.2m. b/d, in keeping with PDVSA's plans to double total output to 7m. b/d by 2007. The steep decline in petroleum prices in 1998 forced Venezuela to embrace OPEC-negotiated production cuts in an attempt to rescue prices. Under President Chávez, Venezuelan oil policy was revised, with emphasis transferred to reducing production in order to maintain stable and high prices in agreement with other OPEC members. In 1998 and 1999 OPEC and non-OPEC countries agreed to three successive rounds of reductions in petroleum production. Venezuela complied with the agreement to reduce petroleum production by a total of 650,000 b/d. The production cuts were effective in bolstering prices to their highest level since 1991. In March 2000 OPEC adopted a Venezuelan proposal to regulate output in order to maintain a price band of US $22–$28 per barrel, and member countries agreed to a total production increase of 1.7m. b/d. This was followed by a further 710,000 b/d increase in June. Venezuela's share of the increase in production amounted to 81,000 b/d, increasing its overall quota to 2.93m. b/d. However, it was estimated that under-investment in the industry was resulting in the loss of 300,000 b/d–500,000 b/d in production capacity. In 2000 Venezuelan petroleum production averaged 3.1m. b/d, of which 83.3% was exported. The largest market for petroleum exports was the USA, which absorbed 57.7% of Venezuelan petroleum exports in 2000. Exports to the Caribbean and Central America were also significant, partly owing to the 2000 Caracas Energy Accord, which committed PDVSA to supply subsidized petroleum to Caribbean nations, including Cuba. In July 2001 OPEC agreed to reduce total production by 1m. b/d, effective from September. Venezuela's overall quota decreased to 2.7m. b/d as a result.

In 1985 export earnings from petroleum and its derivatives totalled US $12,900m. An increase in Venezuela's production output, together with rising petroleum prices, generated a substantial increase in petroleum export revenue, which by 1996 reached $23,400m., whilst the average export price of Venezuelan crude petroleum had increased to $18.4 per barrel. In 1997 and 1998 this fell to $16.3 and $10.6 per barrel, respectively, as a result of seasonal factors, the Asian economic crisis and oversupply. Consensus on production cuts between OPEC and non-OPEC countries increased the price of Venezuelan crude petroleum to an average of $16.1 per barrel in 1999, producing export earnings of $16,419m. for the year. Compliance with production quotas and an increase in global petroleum demand led to a steep increase in the price of Venezuelan petroleum in 2000, which rose to $26.28 per barrel, increasing export earnings by 69.3%, to $28,356m.

In 1991 a policy of opening ('apertura') the petroleum sector to private participation began, and in 1992 it was announced that foreign companies would be allowed to hold a majority stake in future joint ventures. However, the apertura policy still required PDVSA to maintain a shareholding in any private-sector venture and, subsequently, the 1999 Constitution prohibited the privatization of the company. PDVSA suffered from persistent liquidity problems, although it continued to be profitable; the steep rise in oil prices in the late 1990s increased PDVSA earnings to US $2,600m. in 1999, from $766m. in 1998. The new Chávez Government introduced a series of measures intended to restrict the operating autonomy of PDVSA, which was condemned as 'a state within a state' by the President.

The Ministry of Energy and Mines proposed the implementation of a series of policies intended to reduce Venezuelan dependence on petroleum revenue through diversification into petrochemicals, coal and gas production. In order to reverse the ratio of crude petroleum and petroleum-derivative exports from 60:40 to 40:60, expenditure on exploration and production in PDVSA's 10-year business plan was reduced, with funds redirected to the gas and petrochemicals sectors.

Natural bitumen reserves were estimated at 42,000m. metric tons in 2000. Under its diversification plans, the Government of President Chávez sought to increase the production of Orimulsion (an alternative boiler fuel derived from a mixture of bitumen and water) to 20m. tons by 2006. Orimulsion exports rose sharply in 2000, to 6.2m tons, following the signing of a series of supply contracts with Canada, the People's Republic of China, Denmark, Germany, Italy, Japan, the Republic of Korea (South Korea) and Lithuania. Production in 2001 was at full installed capacity and two new joint ventures with the Chinese National Petroleum Corporation and Enel (Italy) were being pursued for the construction of new plants.

Venezuela had proven natural gas reserves of 143,000,000m. cu ft and estimated total deposits of 458,000,000m. cu ft, the seventh largest in the world. Some 90% of gas production was extracted from oil wells, with production capacity averaging 6,100m. cu ft per day in 2000. From 1971 the exploitation and production of natural gas was undertaken by Corpoven, a subsidiary of PDVSA (known as PDV Servicios from January 1998). The price of natural gas was fixed at artificially low levels, making it an attractive energy source. Output and domestic sales increased significantly from the mid-1980s. However, the petroleum industry remained the largest consumer, absorbing 60% of domestically produced gas for re-injection into oilfields for flaring. In 1997 the Government offered financial incentives to taxi drivers and bus operators to fund the cost of conversion to natural gas for vehicles, as part of its promotion of the commodity as an alternative vehicle fuel.

Construction of the Nurgas pipeline, designed to carry 22m. cu m of gas per day between extraction terminals in the Paria Peninsula and industrial towns in the central and western parts of the country, was completed in 1990. In 1990 PDVSA announced an investment plan of US $2,400m. for the development of gas production, and a $3,000m. public-private initiative, the Cristóbal Colón project, was inaugurated to develop gas reserves in the Gulf of Paria. Following a change of policy in 1994, foreign investors assumed a majority share in the project, which was scheduled to begin in the late 1990s, with the aim of producing 4.4m. metric tons of gas for export. The natural-gas industry was opened to private investment in June 1998. In July a concession was awarded to a private-sector conglomerate to build and operate two natural gas liquids-extraction facilities, the Accro III and IV plants, at a cost of $450m. In January 1999 a second presidential decree opened the processing, transportation, distribution and marketing of methane and ethane to private investment. As part of its strategy of diversification from the petroleum economy, the Government introduced a revision of the hydrocarbons legislation in August 1999, intended to regulate production and exploration activities, industrialization, transportation and the distribution of natural gas. A new industry regulator, Enagas, was also created. Under the new legislation, to be effective from 2001, the corporate tax rate was reduced from 67.5% to 40%, and royalty payments increased from 16.7% to 20%. PDVSA made firm commitments to invest $20,000m. in the gas industry in the following 10 years. In December 2000 an auction of 11 exploration and production licences in the Orinoco belt was suspended pending the publication of an official pricing policy framework by the Government. The framework was released in March 2001, and 23 foreign and 8 domestic companies successfully fulfilled pre-qualification criteria, allowing them to bid for the licences.

FINANCE

Venezuela's finance sector underwent major restructuring following a banking crisis in 1994, which forced the Government to intervene in one-third of the country's financial institutions (see History). Following the introduction of legislation in 1996 to improve supervision of the sector and create universal banks, many of the largest banks were privatized. This led to increased foreign presence in the sector, which appeared to stabilize following a series of mergers and acquisitions that continued into 2001, resulting in an estimated 40,000 job losses. There are 37 private banks operating in the country. The four largest together accounted for 60% of system deposits in 2000, prompting an inquiry by the Competition Superintendency in January 2001. Although it was concluded that the banks were not operating as a cartel, relations between the Government and the industry remained strained, particularly after the Government threatened to impose interest rate controls in May 2001.

Foreign participation in the insurance sector increased noticeably following the introduction of the Insurance and Reinsurance Company Law of 1994, which removed restrictions on foreign shareholdings. As with the banking system, this led to an increase in mergers, and to acquisitions by foreign companies. The development of the equity market was fostered by the structural-reform programme introduced by President Pérez in 1989, which led to an increase in trading activity. In 1992 an automated trading system was introduced and changes in legislation allowed the shares of privatized companies to be traded on the Caracas Stock Exchange (Bolsa de Valores de Caracas—BVC). Political and economic uncertainty reduced activity on the severely undercapitalized stock market thereafter and the equity market dwindled, with the BVC recording one of the worst performances in the world in 1998, with a dollar loss of 51%. Two of the country's three stock markets closed in 2000, and 40 of the 63 seats on the BVC remained inactive.

TELECOMMUNICATIONS

Telecommunications was one of the fastest growing sectors outside of the petroleum industry. Dissatisfaction with the fixed-line service provided by the state telecommunications company, Compañía Anónima Nacional Teléfonos de Venezuela (CANTV), which was privatized in 1991, led to a surge in mobile cellular telephone usage after the awarding of mobile telephone concessions in 1991 and 1992. Two service providers, the US- and Venezuelan-owned Telcel, and the CANTV-owned company, Movilnet, dominated the cellular market of an estimated 3.8m. subscribers (although the Venezuelan-Italian Digitel registered growth of 200% in 2000, increasing its market share to 6%). In November 2000 CANTV lost its monopoly of fixed line telephony services in accordance with the 1991 privatization contract, providing the Government with the opportunity to restructure the sector. In June 2000 a new Telecommunications Law was introduced to replace legislation dating from 1940. Following an auction in 2001 of regional bands to be operated using Wireless Local Loop (WLL), the Government raised US $20.1m., with further investment totalling $400m. anticipated in the sector. The expansion of the telecommunications sector led to one of the highest rates of growth in Internet usage in South America, with an estimated 1.6m. subscribers in 2000. Some 500,000 of the 4.1m. televisions in Venezuela were connected to a cable network in 2000, representing a rapid expansion of the cable industry, which was dominated by SuperCable, Inter-Cable, Cabletel and DIRECTV.

MANUFACTURING

The manufacturing sector contributed 19.8% of GDP in 2000 and engaged 13.3% of the employed labour force in the same year. Most of the major capital-intensive industries were state-owned and were located in the Ciudad Guayana development region, in the east of the country. The private sector was dominated by small- and medium-scale industries and was mainly involved in import substitution. Private concerns concentrated on the production of consumer goods for the domestic market. There was also a growing capital-goods sector. Structural reform in 1989 and free-trade agreements within the CAN generated strong manufacturing growth at the beginning of the 1990s. However, this declined in 1996 as the imposition of stabilization and adjustment measures reduced demand for manufactured goods. Economic recovery in 1997 led to manufacturing growth of 4.4%, a performance which was subsequently reversed as the country entered recession in 1998 and 1999, leading to a sectoral contraction of 5.6% and 9.2% respectively. There was a pronounced decline in the automotive industry in

1999, where sales of domestically manufactured and imported vehicles declined by 46.6% compared with 1998. Manufacturing GDP increased by 3.6% in 2000.

CONSTRUCTION

Growth in Venezuela's construction industry traditionally followed trends in the petroleum economy, with periods of inflated oil prices leading to increased levels of public spending. The industry expanded in the 1970s as a result of public works projects, only to suffer a marked decline in the 1980s as the petroleum price fell and the economy contracted.

Despite major government building projects and official encouragement of low-cost housing, the industry remained relatively depressed in the second half of the 1980s, especially in the private sector. Overall conditions improved in the early 1990s, but the recession of 1994–95 and the high cost of borrowing limited growth of the sector. However, the liberalization of the petroleum sector resulted in an increase in growth in the sector from mid-1997, particularly in the east of the country. Construction led growth in the non-petroleum private sector in 1997, expanding by 12.6%. In 1998 the construction sector again faced serious problems following the sharp rise in interest rates, a policy intended to prevent capital flight before the 1998 legislative and presidential elections. In September interest rates reached 77%, provoking a steep contraction in borrowing. Such rises, coupled with reductions in public spending and the investment budget, provoked a crisis in the sector. In 1999 the sector contracted by 16.5%, and unemployment among construction workers was estimated at 30%. The sector was expected to benefit from the large-scale reconstruction required following the devastating mudslides of December 1999 that left an estimated 125,000 homeless in the north. However, delays in securing funding for public works projects, in addition to political infighting between the central and state governments, contributed to a further GDP contraction of 4.9% in the sector in 2000.

TRANSPORT

The abundance of petroleum in Venezuela and the low cost of domestic fuel led to high levels of automobile usage at the expense of a fully integrated transport system. This was reflected in the extensive network of highways, which totalled 96,155 km in 2000, and the large number of passenger cars in use (2.1m. in the same year). Even though responsibility for highway maintenance was devolved to state governments in 1989, anticipated improvements in the road infrastructure failed to materialize, and the south of the country remained largely inaccessible by land. The railway network was small, at 584 km, half of which was privately owned. Under plans announced in December 2000, a railroad linking industrial towns in the east to the northern Caribbean coast was to be constructed in collaboration with a Brazilian consortium. In 1982 a subway system opened in Caracas, which was efficiently managed subsequently, with new lines added in the 1990s. Responsibility for airports (of which there are 366—including 11 of international standard) was also decentralized, in 1989. There was substantive growth in the airline industry following the elimination of state airline monopolies and the deregulation of fares in 1989. Venezuela now has 14 private domestic airlines which operate within a fiercely competitive sector. The country has 13 major ports and harbours, with La Guaira, Puerto Cabello, and Maracaibo handling 80% of bulk trade. The Orinoco river was navigable for about 1,120 km, and in 2000 a US $10m. study began to investigate suitable areas for development in order to increase barge transport.

TOURISM

Despite a vast array of potential tourist attractions, including the world's highest waterfall (Angel Falls, with an overall drop of 979 m), a 2,718 km Caribbean coastline and an Andean mountain range running from the south-west to the north-east of the country, the Venezuelan tourism industry remained underdeveloped. Facilities for tourists were limited, and the strong currency increased the cost of travel to Venezuela. In the late 1990s the sector accounted for an estimated 6% of GDP, with the USA the principal market. As a result of the number of Venezuelans travelling abroad, the country experienced an annual deficit of about US $1,000m. on its international travel account. Political instability, civil unrest and problems of personal security have adversely affected the tourism industry over the last 10 years, despite aggressive marketing by the Office of Tourism Corporation (Corporación de Turismo de Venezuela—Corpoturismo) and the designation of the sector as a priority area by the Government. Tourist numbers fell by 18.5% in 2000, to 478,300 visitors, a decline exacerbated by the mudslides of December 1999.

PUBLIC FINANCE

Throughout the latter half of the 1970s increased income from the petroleum sector allowed for high levels of public spending. Budget deficit financing formed a major part of the Government's expansionary policies and provided an important stimulus to economic growth. However, in line with the Government's deflationary policies, the budget was kept in surplus between 1979 and 1981, although reduced petroleum revenues and a growing public-sector debt resulted in a deficit in 1982. There were budget surpluses in 1983 and 1984, but falling government revenues, increasing outflows of capital and an expanding public debt were growing problems in the mid-1980s, and in 1988 the fiscal deficit rose to the equivalent of 8.0% of GDP.

Following the adoption of an IMF-sponsored austerity programme in 1989, the deficit was reduced to 1.1% of GDP. This was transformed into a modest surplus of 0.2% and 0.7% of GDP in 1990 and 1991 respectively, owing to the proceeds from privatization and general economic recovery. An increase in public spending and a decline in petroleum exports generated a deficit equivalent to 5.8% of GDP in 1992, which was reduced to 2.9% of GDP in 1993. A slump in petroleum prices in 1994 and the imposition of a fixed exchange rate regime contributed to a fiscal deficit of 6% of GDP in 1995. The adoption of a further IMF adjustment programme in 1996, combined with an increase in world petroleum prices, improved revenue in 1996 and, despite large pay increases in 1997, a budget surplus was maintained. This was made possible by congressional approval of two credits to fund unbudgeted expenditure. A collapse in petroleum prices in 1998 reduced revenue from that sector by 43.5% of the total in 1997. The Government was forced into a drastic revision of its budget and attempts were made to boost ordinary fiscal revenues, including the introduction of higher excise duties and improved methods of taxation collection. This failed to overcome the shortfall created by the decline in petroleum income and a budget deficit of 4.2% was recorded in that year. Petroleum production cuts and economic recession offset an increase in the petroleum price in 1999, leading to a deficit of 3.1%. In 2000 a dramatic recovery in the petroleum price led to a 106.5% increase in petroleum revenue. The fiscal accounts, however, registered a deficit of 1.8% of GDP, owing to a 46% increase in public spending as the Government attempted to accelerate economic recovery.

The non-petroleum tax base in Venezuela accounted for less than 10% of GDP and was a source of fiscal weakness. Tax evasion remained a major problem. Evasion of VAT, levied at 14.5%, was estimated by the National Tax Superintendency (Seniat) to be 40% in 2000; income tax evasion was estimated at 60% and evasion of customs duties at 60% in the same year. The Government of Hugo Chávez declared improvements in tax collection to be a central element of its fiscal policy. In 2000 tax revenues increased by 35%; however, 85% of this stemmed from the petroleum sector. In March 2001 a reform of the Fiscal Organic Code was introduced. This imposed custodial sentences on tax evaders and improved auditing techniques. Seniat also announced plans to collect VAT from informal street sellers, and in 2001 automated procedures were introduced in the customs service to increase efficiency.

COST OF LIVING

Foreign currency earnings, derived from petroleum exports, made it possible for Venezuela to avoid the bouts of hyperinflation afflicting other countries in the region in the 1980s. However, inadequate macroeconomic management generated an overvalued currency, which precipitated recurrent devaluations and consequently created inflationary cycles. Restrictive monetary policies and rigid price controls, introduced in 1980 in order to deflate the economy, at first succeeded in repressing

inflationary pressures. However, after the devaluation of the currency and the imposition of foreign-exchange controls in February 1983, the money supply resumed its growth. By 1988 the annual rate of inflation stood at 29.5%. The adjustment programme and liberalization of the exchange rate in 1989 led to a surge in inflation, which reached 84% at the end of the year. The upward trend was reversed in 1990 and 1991, but increases in public-sector tariffs, including petroleum prices, in 1992, resulted in an inflation rate of 31.4% for that year and 38.1% in 1993. The devaluation of the bolívar in early 1994, coupled with wage rises, prompted inflation to increase dramatically, to 60.8%. In 1995 the average annual rate inflation decreased only slightly, to 59.9%, but in the following year this rate increased dramatically, to 99.9%, fuelled by revenue from privatization, higher than anticipated petroleum income and price rises in public-sector utilities.

In 1996 the Central Bank adopted a new anti-inflationary strategy. A 'crawling peg' banded exchange rate was introduced. In conjunction with depressed domestic demand, this succeeded in gradually reducing the rate of inflation. A series of public-sector wage rises in 1997 prevented the Government from meeting that year's 20% inflation target agreed with the IMF, with annual inflation standing at 50%. The Government resisted pressure to devalue the bolívar in 1998, despite the fact that devaluation was traditionally a method of restoring balance in the fiscal accounts. Nevertheless, inflation fell to 35.8%. Progress on meeting the 1999 inflation target of 20%–24% was facilitated by depressed domestic demand, and the Government's decision to keep the increase in the minimum wage below inflation resulted in consumer prices increasing by 23.6%. The downward trend in inflation was maintained in 2000, when an average annual rate of 16.2% was recorded.

FOREIGN DEBT

Declining petroleum revenues, an overvalued bolívar and the accumulation of debt maturities made it increasingly difficult for Venezuela to service its US $38,000m. foreign debt during the 1980s. In December 1990 the country restructured $21,000m. of its external debt under the Brady debt relief programme. Despite maintaining a stable reserve position in 1992 and 1993, reserves decreased dramatically in early 1994, following the collapse of the Banco Latino. Foreign-exchange reserves fell from $8,531m. at the end of 1993, to $7,393m. one year later. By the mid-1990s, Venezuela had fallen behind on repayment of its Paris Club obligations. In April 1996 President Caldera introduced a structural adjustment programme, which secured a $1,400m. stand-by agreement from the IMF. This enabled the Government to issue new foreign debt to cover its arrears. In 1997 the finance minister, Luis Matos Azócar, negotiated a controversial $4,400m. Brady bond 'buyback' and a $325m. Eurobond issue in exchange for $4,000m. in new global bonds. However, Matos Azócar was forced to resign when it was revealed that the deal had released $1,300m. in Brady bond collateral but at the cost of a net increase in the value of the public debt. In November 1998 Congress approved a proposal to create a macroeconomic stabilization fund (Fondo de Inversión para la Estabilidad Macroeconómica—FIEM). This set aside 'windfall' oil revenues proceeding from periods when the average oil price exceeded the budgeted level. The surplus was divided between two separate accounts; the debt-redemption fund, used to pay outstanding external liabilities, and a macroeconomic stabilization fund to cover government revenue shortfalls in periods of depressed oil prices. The new Government of Hugo Chávez pledged to reschedule the debt burden. However, little progress was made in this area in 1999, and prospects for a prompt resolution of the situation were slim, given Venezuela's heavy foreign debt repayment schedule, with payments of $4,300m. and $3,900m. falling due in 2000 and 2001, respectively. In March 2000 Venezuela issued a five-year $475m. Euro bond followed by two successive seven-year Euro issues of €300m. and €200m. in February and March 2001. In May 2000 the Prosecutor-General launched an investigation during which it was suggested that the rules determining when the Government could draw on the funds from the FIEM were unclear. The Government subsequently acknowledged that it had used funds from the FIEM to finance the fiscal deficit in 1999.

BALANCE OF PAYMENTS AND TRADE

Venezuela's external trade was dominated by petroleum, which provided 84% of export earnings in 2000. Petroleum traditionally ensured that the country maintained a large trade and current account surplus. The performance of the non-oil sector was persistently weak owing to the small and uncompetitive profile of the private sector and the overvaluation of the bolívar. This, in turn, increased reliance on petroleum revenues and generated a high level of import dependence.

The Venezuelan import bill expanded at an average rate of 22% annually during the 1970s, against a background of rising petroleum revenues and increased public and private spending. Until 1982 increases in petroleum export earnings offset the rise in imports. However, recurrent falls in world petroleum prices and a rising external debt narrowed the balance of trade dramatically in that year. The Government introduced a series of corrective measures in February 1983. Combined with a contraction in petroleum revenues and a corresponding decrease in economic activity, this slowed the rate of import growth and allowed the current account of the balance of payments to return to a surplus in the mid-1980s. In 1986 low world petroleum prices led to a trade surplus of just over US $1,000m. and a current-account deficit of $1,471m. Imports initially remained steady in the mid-1980s, before beginning to rise, resulting in balance-of-payments deficits in 1987 and 1988.

Import growth contracted with the implementation of an adjustment programme and devaluation during 1989. Stronger international petroleum prices resulted in trade and current-account surpluses in 1989 and 1990. Conversely, reduced petroleum export prices in 1991 and a sharp increase in imports, reduced both surpluses in that year. In 1994 the Government introduced exchange controls, which led to a fall in imports. As a result, the trade surplus increased, to US $7,606m., and the current account moved out of deficit, registering a surplus of $2,451m. A recovery in petroleum prices and a 15% increase in non-traditional exports in 1996–97 led to an improvement in export earnings. The trade surplus expanded to $13,770m. in 1996 while the current-account surplus grew to $8,914m. Expectations of a currency devaluation in 1998 precipitated a sharp increase in imports, while oil export revenue was halved from $12,000m. in 1997 to $6,000m. This led to a contraction in the trade surplus to $10,025m., while the current account recorded a surplus of $3,467m. in 1997. Imports reached a record high of $15,105m. in 1998, whilst a 33% decline in petroleum prices and a 2.1% fall in non-traditional exports led to a sharp deterioration in the trade surplus to $2,471m., and the current account registered a deficit of $3,253m. In 1999 a 37.3% increase in the price of petroleum boosted oil export earnings, which rose to $16,419m. Combined with a deep recession, which reduced import demand by 20.7%, this moved the current account back into a surplus totalling $3,689m. Non-traditional exports registered a strong performance in 2000, increasing by 29.1% following a recovery in demand in the Andean market. Imports grew by 21.7% as a result of improved domestic demand. This was offset by a 72% increase in petroleum export revenues as petroleum prices rose sharply and export volumes increased. The trade balance consequently registered a surplus of $17,965m. whilst the current account registered $13,365m., the largest surplus since 1980.

The USA was Venezuela's main trading partner, providing 35.8% of imports in 2000, and taking 46.8% of Venezuela's exports in 1999. Much of this trade took place under the provisions of a 'most-favoured nation' treaty signed in 1972. Petroleum production reductions in 1999 led Venezuela to lose its market share in the USA and, by 2000, Venezuela had fallen from second to fourth largest supplier, behind Canada, Saudi Arabia and Mexico. In 1999 Venezuela's exports to the USA totalled an estimated US $9,748m. Trade with Colombia increased from the late 1980s and was augmented by the signing of a free-trade agreement in 1991. In 1998 the balance of trade tipped in favour of Colombia and in 1999 exports to Colombia totalled $798m. whilst imports from Colombia rose from $739m. in 1999 to $1,088m. in 2000. Trading relations with Brazil increased significantly, rising by 130% between 1994 and 1998. Exports to Cuba also saw a marked increase, rising from $91m. in 1994 to $429m. in 1999.

Venezuela was a member of the Andean Pact (known as the Andean Community of Nations, Comunidad Andina de Naciones—CAN from 1996), which, under revised rules, operated a four-tier Common External Tariff agreement from February 1995. Venezuela was also, with Mexico and Colombia, a member of the 'Group of Three', which implemented a free-trade agreement in early 1994. Venezuela participated in the Latin American Economic System, which promoted intra-regional economic and social co-operation. In April 1998 CAN and the Southern Common Market (Mercado Común del Sur—Mercosur, or, in Portuguese, Mercado Comum do Sul—Mercosul) signed an accord to establish a free-trade area by 1 January 2000. The agreement, which would lead to the creation of the largest market in Latin America, was subsequently delayed by technical problems, leading Venezuela to pursue unilateral entry in 2000.

CONCLUSION

In 1999 the new Government of Hugo Chávez inherited a dire economic legacy and an acutely polarized society. The country's stock of flight capital stood at US $50,000m., larger than the foreign debt. Growing poverty, informality and unemployment were the main trends after a decade of political and economic turmoil. Two central objectives; reducing dependence on petroleum export revenue and improving distribution to the most deprived sectors of society, shaped government economic policy. Strategies to overcome the profound inequalities that characterized Venezuelan society were negatively received by the wealthiest sectors. Initiatives in areas such as tax collection and land reform were perceived as politically motivated attacks on historically privileged groups, leading to a spiral of conflict between the Government and opposition. This further reduced private-sector confidence in the country and accelerated capital flight. Although the economy appeared fundamentally sound by mid-2001, concerns persisted that Venezuela was still overly dependent on its petroleum export revenue. The generation of a fiscal deficit in 2000, a year of high petroleum prices, in addition to extensive domestic debt issues and the withdrawal of funds from the Macroeconomic Stabilization Fund, exacerbated these concerns.

Statistical Survey

Sources (unless otherwise stated): Oficina Central de Estadística e Informática (formerly Dirección General de Estadística y Censos Nacionales), Edif. Fundación La Salle, Avda Boyacá, Caracas 1050; tel. (212) 782-1133; fax (212) 782-2243; e-mail ocei@platino.gov.ve; internet www.ocei.gov.ve; Banco Central de Venezuela, Avda Urdaneta esq. de las Carmelitas, Caracas 1010; tel. (212) 801-5111; fax (212) 861-0048; e-mail mbatista@bcv.org.ve; internet www.bcv.org.ve.

Area and Population

AREA, POPULATION AND DENSITY

Area (sq km)	
Land	882,050
Inland waters	30,000
Total	912,050*
Population (census results)†	
20 October 1981	14,516,735
20 October 1990	
Males	9,019,757
Females	9,085,508
Total	18,105,265
Population (official estimates at mid-year)†	
1998	23,242,000
1999	23,706,000
2000	24,169,744
Density (per sq km) at mid-2000	26.5

* 352,144 sq miles.
† Excluding Indian jungle inhabitants, estimated at 140,562 in 1982. Census results also exclude an adjustment for underenumeration, estimated at 6.7% in 1990.

ADMINISTRATIVE DIVISIONS
(population at 1990 census)

State	Population	Capital	Population of capital
Federal District . .	2,103,661	Caracas	1,824,892
Amazonas . . .	55,717	Puerto Ayacucho . .	35,865
Anzoátegui . . .	859,758	Barcelona . . .	109,061
Apure . . .	285,412	San Fernando . .	72,733
Aragua . . .	1,120,132	Maracay . . .	354,428
Barinas . . .	424,491	Barinas . . .	152,853
Bolívar . . .	900,310	Ciudad Bolívar . .	225,846
Carabobo . . .	1,453,232	Valencia . . .	903,076
Cojedes . . .	182,066	San Carlos . .	50,339
Delta Amacuro . .	84,564	Tucupita . . .	40,946
Falcón . . .	599,185	Coro . . .	124,616
Guárico . . .	488,623	San Juan de los Morros	67,645
Lara . . .	1,193,161	Barquisimeto . .	602,622
Mérida . . .	570,215	Mérida . . .	167,992
Miranda . . .	1,871,093	Los Teques . .	143,519
Monagas . . .	470,157	Maturín . . .	207,382
Nueva Esparta . .	263,748	La Asunción . .	16,585
Portuguesa . .	576,435	Guanare . . .	83,380
Sucre . . .	679,595	Cumaná . . .	212,492
Táchira . . .	807,712	San Cristóbal . .	220,697
Trujillo . . .	493,912	Trujillo . . .	32,683
Yaracuy . . .	384,536	San Felipe . .	65,793
Zulia . . .	2,235,305	Maracaibo . .	1,207,513
Federal Dependencies	2,245	—	
Total . . .	18,105,265		

PRINCIPAL TOWNS
(city proper, estimated population at 1 July 2000)

Caracas (capital)	.	1,975,787	Mérida . . .	230,101
Maracaibo .	.	1,764,038	Barinas . . .	228,598
Valencia . .	.	1,338,833	Turmero . . .	226,084
Barquisimeto .	.	875,790	Cabimas . . .	214,000
Ciudad Guayana	.	704,168	Baruta . . .	213,373
Petare . .	.	520,982	Puerto la Cruz . .	205,635
Maracay . .	.	459,007	Los Teques . .	183,142
Ciudad Bolívar .	.	312,691	Guarenas . . .	170,204
Barcelona . .	.	311,475	Puerto Cabello . .	169,959
San Cristóbal .	.	307,184	Acarigua . . .	166,720
Maturín . .	.	283,318	Coro . . .	158,763
Cumaná . .	.	269,428		

BIRTHS, MARRIAGES AND DEATHS*

	Registered live births		Registered marriages		Registered deaths	
	Number	Rate (per 1,000)	Number	Rate (per 1,000)	Number	Rate (per 1,000)
1989 . .	529,015	28.0	111,970	5.9	84,761	4.5
1990 . .	577,976	29.9	106,303	5.5	89,830	4.6
1991 . .	602,024	30.4	107,136	5.4	88,634	4.5
1992 . .	559,950	27.4	108,965	5.3	90,566	4.5
1993 . .	524,387	25.1	100,042	4.8	92,273	4.4
1994 . .	547,819	25.6	97,674	4.6	98,911	4.6
1995 . .	520,584	24.1	83,735	3.9	n.a.	n.a.
1996 . .	595,816†	26.2†	73,064†	3.2†	93,839	4.2

1997†: Live births 575,832; Rate (per 1,000) 25.3.
* Excluding Indian jungle population.
† Provisional.

Expectation of life (UN estimates, years at birth, 1990–95): 71.4 (males 69.0; females 74.7) (Source: UN, *World Population Prospects: The 1998 Revision*).

ECONOMICALLY ACTIVE POPULATION (household surveys, '000 persons aged 15 years and over, July–December)*

	1998	1999	2000†
Agriculture, hunting, forestry and fishing	881	890	950
Mining and quarrying . . .	83	57	53
Manufacturing	1,226	1,202	1,191
Electricity, gas and water . .	58	59	58
Construction	772	665	741
Transport, storage and communications	574	604	608
Financing, insurance, real estate, business services and trade . .	2,687	2,742	2,752
Community, social and personal services	2,516	2,514	2,598
Activities not adequately defined .	19	7	10
Total employed	8,816	8,742	8,961
Unemployed	1,091	1,483	1,366
Total labour force	9,907	10,225	10,327

* Figures exclude members of the Armed Forces.
† Provisional.

Agriculture

PRINCIPAL CROPS ('000 metric tons)

	1998	1999	2000
Maize	983	1,024	900*
Rice (paddy)	716	740	737*
Sorghum	449	402	320*
Potatoes	272	352	352†
Sesame seed	27	28	28†
Seed cotton	29	20	20†
Cotton (lint)	11*	7†	6*
Coffee (green)	67	67	55
Cocoa beans	17	19	19
Tobacco	14	11	11†
Cassava (Manioc)	488	448	448†
Oranges	398	332	332†
Tomatoes	174	188	188†
Coconuts	133	105	105
Avocados	48	46	46†
Bananas	948	1,000	1,000*
Plantains	578	551	551†
Sugar cane	7,701	7,989	6,950*

* Unofficial figure.   † FAO estimate.

Source: FAO.

LIVESTOCK ('000 head, year ending September)

	1998	1999	2000
Horses*	500	500	500
Asses*	440	440	440
Cattle	15,661	15,992	15,800*
Pigs*	4,800	4,900	4,900
Sheep	747	781	781*
Goats*	3,900	3,600	3,600
Chickens*	100,000	105,000	110,000

* FAO estimate(s).

Source: FAO.

LIVESTOCK PRODUCTS ('000 metric tons)

	1998	1999	2000
Beef and veal	406	384	360*
Pig meat	113	114	114*
Poultry meat	491	516	516*
Cows' milk	1,440	1,311	1,311*
Cheese	100	87	89*
Hen eggs	158	168	168*
Cattle hides (fresh)	47	44	41

* FAO estimate.

Source: FAO.

Forestry

ROUNDWOOD REMOVALS ('000 cubic metres, excl. bark)

	1997	1998	1999
Sawlogs, veneer logs and logs for sleepers	1,313	1,067	1,620
Pulpwood	46	140	181
Other industrial wood	27	—	—
Fuel wood	876	894	912
Total	2,262	2,101	2,713

Source: FAO, *Yearbook of Forest Products*.

SAWNWOOD PRODUCTION
('000 cubic metres, incl. railway sleepers)

	1997	1998	1999
Coniferous (softwood)	10	—	—
Broadleaved (hardwood)	240	174	261
Total	250	174	261

Source: FAO, *Yearbook of Forest Products*.

Fishing

('000 metric tons, live weight)

	1996	1997	1998
Capture	484.5	463.2	506.1
Prochilods	18.7	11.0	15.7
Sea catfishes	17.0	9.0	10.1
Round sardinella	153.8	140.6	186.1
Yellowfin tuna	71.2	72.5	79.2
Ark clams	31.2	39.1	28.0
Aquaculture	7.3	8.6	10.7
Total catch	491.8	471.8	516.8

Source: FAO, *Yearbook of Fishery Statistics*.

Mining

PRODUCTION ('000 metric tons, unless otherwise indicated)

	1995	1996	1997
Iron ore (gross weight)*	22,617	21,974	20,566
Hard coal	4,168	3,823	4,626
Crude petroleum	143,584	144,862	146,300†
Natural gas (petajoules)	1,626	1,749	1,939
Gold (kg)	14,212	16,544	17,896
Diamonds ('000 metric carats)	268,187	225,283	356,398
Bauxite	5,020	4,834	4,926

* The estimated iron content is 64%.
† Provisional figure.

Sources: IMF, *Venezuela: Recent Economic Developments* (October 1998), and UN, *Industrial Commodity Statistics Yearbook*.

Industry

PETROLEUM PRODUCTS ('000 metric tons)

	1994	1995	1996
Motor spirit (petrol)	16,829	18,810	16,933
Kerosene	390*	395*	398
Jet fuel	3,700*	3,400*	3,920
Distillate fuel oils	10,675	12,218	12,497
Residual fuel oils	14,400	14,433	14,670

* Provisional figure.
Source: UN, *Industrial Commodity Statistics Yearbook*.

SELECTED OTHER PRODUCTS
('000 metric tons, unless otherwise indicated)

	1995	1996	1997
Raw sugar*	484	594	614
Rubber tyres ('000)† . .	5,361	5,162	5,717
Nitrogenous fertilizers‡ . .	456	473	n.a.
Cement†	7,672	7,568	7,867
Crude steel§	3,568	3,941	4,019
Aluminium‖	627	635	641
Electric energy (million kWh) .	74,886¶	74,968	n.a.

1998 ('000 metric tons): Raw sugar 590*; Rubber tyres ('000) 5,383†; Cement 7,869†.
1999 ('000 metric tons): Raw sugar 660*.

* FAO figure(s).
† Data from UN Economic Commission for Latin America and the Caribbean.
‡ Output in terms of nitrogen.
§ Provisional figures.
‖ Data from US Bureau of Mines (Washington, DC).
¶ Data from *World Metal Statistics* (London).

Finance

CURRENCY AND EXCHANGE RATES

Monetary Units
100 céntimos = 1 bolívar.

Sterling, Dollar and Euro Equivalents (30 April 2001)
£1 sterling = 1,019.08 bolívares;
US $1 = 711.75 bolívares;
€1 = 631.75 bolívares;
10,000 bolívares = £9.813 = $14.050 = €15.829.

Average Exchange Rate (bolívares per US dollar)
1998   547.556
1999   605.717
2000   679.960

Note: Between July 1994 and December 1995 a fixed rate of US $1 = 170 bolívares was maintained.

BUDGET (million bolívares)*

Revenue	1996	1997	1998
Tax revenue†	4,070,195	7,487,817	6,637,579
Taxes on income, profits and capital gains . .	2,203,347	3,971,733	2,047,703
Social security contributions .	94,493	160,012	372,441
Domestic taxes on goods and services	1,602,322	3,092,291	3,571,799
Sales tax	1,327,467	2,379,518	2,789,624
Excises	110,591	163,197	215,919
Import duties . . .	397,952	694,966	1,025,967
Other current revenue . .	1,697,600	2,753,145	2,379,896
Property income . . .	1,647,225	2,597,259	2,244,837
Total	5,767,795	10,240,962	9,017,475

Expenditure‡	1996	1997	1998
Current expenditure . . .	4,285,149	7,421,993	8,302,434
Expenditure on goods and services	1,015,092	2,114,514	2,498,142
Wages and salaries . .	814,168	1,763,574	1,915,793
Interest payments . . .	1,100,204	1,033,830	1,229,658
Subsidies and other current transfers . . .	2,169,853	4,273,649	4,574,634
Capital expenditure . . .	679,018	1,472,312	1,978,609
Capital transfers . . .	507,473	1,111,533	1,405,094
Total	4,964,167	8,894,305	10,281,043

* Figures represent the consolidated accounts of the central Government, comprising the operations of the General Budget, government agencies and social security funds.
† Including adjustments (million bolívares): –232,979 in 1996; –436,925 in 1997; –393,346 in 1998.
‡ Excluding lending minus repayments (million bolívares): 347,131 in 1996; 391,182 in 1997; 179,192 in 1998.
Source: IMF, *Government Finance Statistics Yearbook*.

CENTRAL BANK RESERVES (US $ million at 31 December)

	1998	1999	2000
Gold*	2,929	2,887	2,794
IMF special drawing rights . .	104	127	36
Reserve position in IMF . . .	204	442	419
Foreign exchange . . .	11,612	11,708	12,633
Total	14,849	15,164	15,882

* Valued at $300 per troy ounce.
Source: IMF, *International Financial Statistics*.

MONEY SUPPLY (million bolívares at 31 December)*

	1998	1999	2000
Currency outside banks . . .	1,235,050	1,816,790	1,997,610
Demand deposits at commercial banks	3,715,030	4,260,830	5,813,370
Total (incl. others) . . .	5,181,040	6,496,660	9,500,230

* Figures rounded to the nearest 10m. bolívares.
Source: IMF, *International Financial Statistics*.

COST OF LIVING
(Consumer Price Index; Base: 1990 = 100)

	1995	1996	1997
Food	585.3	1,095.8	1,585.4
Fuel and light	555.8	896.8	2,722.9
Clothing.	471.5	895.9	1,313.6
Rent	597.0	1,212.8	2,229.6
All items (incl. others) . . .	609.4	1,223.8	1,818.8

1998: Food 2,181.5; Clothing 1,590.7; All items 2,447.8.
1999: Food 2,516.4; Clothing 1,864.4; All items 2,986.4.
Source: ILO, *Yearbook of Labour Statistics*.

NATIONAL ACCOUNTS

National Income and Product (million bolívares at current prices)

	1992	1993	1994
Compensation of employees . .	1,432,489	1,863,825	2,715,315
Operating surplus . . .	2,213,625	2,909,020	4,654,086
Domestic factor incomes . .	3,646,114	4,772,845	7,369,401
Consumption of fixed capital .	309,272	422,389	634,070
Gross domestic product (GDP) at factor cost.	3,955,386	5,195,234	8,003,471
Indirect taxes	188,384	271,176	664,081
Less Subsidies	12,287	12,507	16,252
GDP in purchasers' values .	4,131,483	5,453,903	8,651,300
Factor income received from abroad	103,420	138,056	247,363
Less Factor income paid abroad .	227,195	300,494	524,613
Gross national product .	4,007,708	5,291,465	8,374,050
Less Consumption of fixed capital	309,272	422,389	634,070
National income in market prices . . .	3,389,164	4,869,076	7,739,980
Other current transfers from abroad	35,440	41,625	64,824
Less Other current transfers paid abroad	59,660	71,402	87,929
National disposable income .	3,364,944	4,839,299	7,716,875

Source: UN, *National Accounts Statistics*.

Expenditure on the Gross Domestic Product
('000 million bolívares at current prices)

	1998	1999	2000
Government final consumption expenditure	3,957.6	4,700.3	5,766.9
Private final consumption expenditure	37,685.0	43,236.9	51,667.8
Increase in stocks	1,485.0	1,477.2	2,464.2
Gross fixed capital formation . .	9,991.3	9,850.6	11,902.9
Total domestic expenditure .	53,118.9	59,265.0	71,801.8
Exports of goods and services .	10,441.8	13,546.0	24,072.0
Less Imports of goods and services	11,078.2	10,233.9	13,949.6
GDP in purchasers' values .	52,482.5	62,577.0	81,924.2
GDP at constant 1984 prices .	602.6	565.9	584.1

Source: IMF, *International Financial Statistics*.

Gross Domestic Product by Economic Activity
(million bolívares at constant 1984 prices)

	1998	1999	2000‡
Agriculture, hunting, forestry and fishing	28,356	27,748	28,359
Mining and quarrying* . . .	141,531	128,066	134,937
Manufacturing†	119,097	111,495	113,168
Electricity and water . . .	10,593	10,711	10,933
Construction	36,462	30,428	28,935
Trade, restaurants and hotels . .	65,687	59,396	61,690
Transport, storage and communication . . .	32,896	33,436	36,545
Finance, insurance, real estate and business services . .	54,496	52,967	53,719
Government services . . .	43,948	44,454	45,848
Other services	58,454	57,331	58,172
Sub-total	591,520	556,032	572,306
Import duties	15,535	13,917	16,009
Less Imputed bank service charge	4,497	4,061	4,241
Total	602,558	565,888	584,074

* Includes crude petroleum and natural gas production.
† Includes petroleum refining.
‡ Preliminary figures.

BALANCE OF PAYMENTS (US $ million)

	1998	1999	2000
Exports of goods f.o.b. . . .	17,576	20,819	34,038
Imports of goods f.o.b. . . .	−15,105	−13,213	−16,073
Trade balance . . .	2,471	7,606	17,965
Exports of services . . .	1,461	1,303	1,201
Imports of services . . .	−5,146	−3,772	−4,510
Balance on goods and services	−1,214	5,137	14,656
Other income received . .	2,286	2,120	2,893
Other income paid . . .	−4,217	−3,638	−4,045
Balance on goods, services and income	−3,145	3,619	13,504
Current transfers received .	275	331	317
Current transfers paid . .	−383	−261	−456
Current balance . . .	−3,253	3,689	13,365
Direct investment abroad . .	−233	−518	−321
Direct investment from abroad .	4,495	3,187	4,110
Portfolio investment assets .	1,070	280	−265
Portfolio investment liabilities .	219	1,179	−1,138
Other investment assets . .	−3,413	−6,470	−5,011
Other investment liabilities .	−374	686	−1,045
Net errors and omissions . .	−1,442	−992	−3,719
Overall balance . . .	−2,931	1,041	5,976

Source: IMF, *International Financial Statistics*.

External Trade

PRINCIPAL COMMODITIES (US $ million)

Imports f.o.b.	1995	1996	1997
Food and live animals . . .	1,165.0	1,123.0	1,087.8
Cereals and cereal preparations .	428.2	529.5	454.3
Wheat and meslin, unmilled .	193.8	201.1	181.1
Maize unmilled . . .	144.6	222.0	176.0
Crude materials (inedible) except fuels . . .	671.0	440.5	460.3
Pulp and waste paper . . .	254.7	113.0	107.8
Mineral fuels	125.1	131.7	440.3
Petroleum and products . .	105.7	114.8	415.8
Chemicals and related products	1,735.0	1,320.4	1,655.6
Organic chemicals . . .	507.0	357.5	466.3
Artificial resins and plastic materials	276.9	200.8	218.6
Basic manufactures . . .	1,808.7	1,523.9	2,108.9
Paper, paperboard and manufactures	245.6	166.0	216.5
Textile yarn, fabrics, etc . .	276.2	205.3	257.0
Iron and steel	463.3	492.4	662.1
Iron and steel tubes, pipes and fittings	206.2	276.4	379.4
Non-ferrous metals . . .	270.5	165.6	206.0
Other metal manufactures . .	263.3	232.6	357.4
Machinery and transport equipment	3,983.2	3,380.4	5,982.3
Power-generating machinery and equipment	297.7	233.3	309.1
Machinery specialized for particular industries . .	356.7	339.5	752.3
General industrial machinery, equipment and parts . .	914.2	917.1	1,202.3
Non-electrical parts and accessories of machinery . .	268.3	278.0	374.6
Office machines and automatic data-processing equipment . .	341.3	292.4	399.8
Automatic data-processing equipment	218.9	205.0	276.6
Telecommunications and sound recording and reproducing equipment	305.4	270.3	529.4
Telecommunications equipment parts and accessories . .	196.0	193.9	417.5
Other electrical machinery, apparatus, etc. . .	514.0	427.9	720.4
Road vehicles	1,061.7	803.2	1,818.0
Passenger motor vehicles (except buses) . . .	637.3	444.2	1,038.3
Lorries and special purpose motor vehicles . .	249.7	208.6	369.1
Lorries and trucks . . .	231.4	190.2	331.1
Miscellaneous manufactured articles	988.7	758.8	1,130.4
Clothing and accessories . . .	275.3	147.9	209.8
Total (incl. others) . . .	10,791.3	8,902.3	13,158.9

Total imports (US $ million): 14,250 in 1998; 12,670 in 1999 (Source: IMF, *International Financial Statistics*).

Exports f.o.b.	1995	1996	1997
Food and live animals . . .	347.7	365.7	388.6
Mineral fuels, lubricants and related materials . .	14,559.3	18,634.0	18,064.9
Petroleum, petroleum products and related materials . . .	14,441.8	18,543.3	17,957.6
Crude petroleum . . .	8,576.3	12,615.5	12,176.8
Petroleum products, refined .	5,863.0	5,924.2	5,773.7
Chemicals and related products	788.9	810.4	841.7
Basic manufactures . . .	2,135.3	2,133.4	2,345.9
Iron and steel	621.8	729.3	827.2
Non-ferrous metals	929.3	784.2	781.7
Aluminium	913.7	765.6	766.7
Aluminium and aluminium alloys, unwrought . . .	728.4	586.9	553.3
Machinery and transport equipment . . .	537.0	491.3	528.8
Road vehicles	440.3	381.2	388.2
Total (incl. others)	18,914.2	22,900.7	22,729.4

Source: UN, *International Trade Statistics Yearbook*.

1998 (preliminary figures, US $ million): *Exports f.o.b.:* Petroleum 12,230; Iron ore 198; Coffee 27; Cocoa 15; Aluminium 705; Steel 780; Chemical products 860; Total (incl. others) 17,534. Source: IMF, *Venezuela: Statistical Appendix* (September 1999).

1999 (US $ million): *Exports f.o.b.:* Petroleum 16,419; Iron ore 124; Coffee 49; Cocoa 9; Aluminium 672; Chemical products 550; Total (incl. others) 20,819.

2000 (US $ mllion): *Exports:* Petroleum 26,772; Total (incl. others) 31,802 (Source: IMF, *International Financial Statistics*).

PRINCIPAL TRADING PARTNERS (US $ million)

Imports f.o.b.	1998	1999	2000*
Brazil	618	457	725
Canada	275	290	n.a.
Chile	174	198	n.a.
Colombia	797	739	1,088
France	n.a.	n.a.	247
Germany	687	604	503
Italy	n.a.	n.a.	620
Japan	633	388	463
Mexico	609	486	n.a.
Netherlands	231	186	n.a.
Netherlands Antilles . . .	116	163	n.a.
Spain	322	406	373
United Kingdom	286	209	301
USA	6,291	5,351	5,756
Total (incl. others) . . .	15,105	13,213	16,073

Exports f.o.b.	1998	1999*
Brazil	700	901
Canada	366	559
Chile	189	193
Colombia	1,427	798
Germany	227	204
Japan	209	236
Mexico	226	185
Netherlands	173	200
Netherlands Antilles	1,152	959
Puerto Rico	509	590
United Kingdom	355	168
USA	7,999	9,748
Total (incl. others)	17,576	20,819

* Provisional.

Transport

RAILWAYS (traffic)

	1994	1995	1996
Passenger-kilometres (million) .	31.4	12.5	0.1
Freight ton-kilometres (million) .	46.8	53.3	45.5

Freight ton-kilometres (million): 54.5 in 1997; 79.5 in 1998.

Source: UN Economic Commission for Latin America and the Caribbean.

ROAD TRAFFIC ('000 motor vehicles in use at 31 December)

	1991	1992	1993
Passenger cars	1,540	1,566	1,579
Buses and coaches	18	20	20
Goods vehicles	431	436	440
Motor cycles, scooters and mopeds	295	298	301

1994–96 (estimates, '000 motor vehicles in use): 1,520 passenger cars; 434 commercial vehicles (Source: IRF, *World Road Statistics*).

SHIPPING
Merchant Fleet (registered at 31 December)

	1998	1999	2000
Number of vessels	246	250	262
Total displacement ('000 grt) . .	665.3	657.4	666.6

Source: Lloyd's Register of Shipping, *World Fleet Statistics*.

International Sea-borne Freight Traffic (estimates, '000 metric tons)

	1988	1989	1990
Goods loaded	82,082	88,920	101,435
Goods unloaded	17,566	18,160	17,932

Source: UN, *Monthly Bulletin of Statistics*.

CIVIL AVIATION (traffic on scheduled services)

	1995	1996	1997
Kilometres flown (million) . .	68	80	63
Passengers carried ('000) . .	4,445	4,487	4,020
Passenger-km (million) . .	6,120	5,800	4,444
Total ton-km (million) . .	724	639	483

Source: UN, *Statistical Yearbook*.

Tourism

ARRIVALS BY NATIONALITY

	1996	1997	1998
Argentina	42,544	59,565	41,534
Brazil	31,090	31,932	28,125
Canada	64,893	74,629	33,034
Chile	6,471	6,290	16,346
Colombia	27,422	29,259	26,245
France	24,856	25,565	27,841
Germany	72,255	77,073	67,063
Italy	36,232	35,767	43,540
Mexico	7,733	8,030	18,774
Netherlands	66,310	70,996	46,931
Spain	40,004	37,288	15,345
Trinidad and Tobago	46,037	47,655	8,984
United Kingdom	30,733	30,008	35,570
USA	153,844	152,696	158,265
Total (incl. others)	758,503	813,862	685,429

Tourism receipts (US $ million): 811 in 1995; 945 in 1996; 1,086 in 1997.
Source: World Tourism Organization, *Yearbook of Tourism Statistics*.

Communications Media

	1995	1996	1997
Radio receivers ('000 in use)*	10,000	10,500	10,750
Television receivers ('000 in use)*	3,700	4,000	4,100
Telephones ('000 main lines in use)	2,463	2,667	2,703
Telefax stations (number in use)	35,000	50,000	70,000
Mobile cellular telephones (subscribers)	403,800	581,700	1,071,900
Daily newspapers			
Number	89	86	n.a.
Average circulation ('000 copies)*	4,500	4,600	n.a.
Book production (titles)†	4,225	3,468	n.a.

* Estimates. † First editions only.

Sources: UNESCO, *Statistical Yearbook*; UN, *Statistical Yearbook*.

Education

(1996/97)

	Institutions	Teachers	Students		
			Males	Females	Total
Pre-primary	7,917*	46,291†	374,334	364,511	738,845
Primary	15,984‡	202,195	2,145,506	2,116,715	4,262,221
Secondary	1,517*	33,692§	160,090	217,894	377,984
Higher	99*	43,833‖	n.a.	n.a.	550,783‖

* 1990/91 figure.
† Figures refer to teaching posts.
‡ 1992/93 figure.
§ 1993/94 figure.
‖ 1991/92 figure.

Source: mainly UNESCO, *Statistical Yearbook*.

Directory

The Constitution

The Bolivarian Constitution of Venezuela was promulgated on 30 December 1999.

The Bolivarian Republic of Venezuela is divided into 23 States, one Federal District and 72 Federal Dependencies. The States are autonomous but must comply with the laws and Constitution of the Republic.

LEGISLATURE

Legislative power is exercised by the unicameral Asamblea Nacional (National Assembly). This replaced the bicameral Congreso Nacional (National Congress) following the introduction of the 1999 Constitution.

Deputies are elected by direct universal and secret suffrage, the number representing each State being determined by population size on a proportional basis. A deputy must be of Venezuelan nationality and be over 21 years of age. Indigenous minorities have the right to select three representatives. Ordinary sessions of the Asamblea Nacional begin on the fifth day of January of each year and continue until the fifteenth day of the following August; thereafter, sessions are renewed from the fifteenth day of September to the fifteenth day of December, both dates inclusive. The Asamblea is empowered to initiate legislation. The Asamblea also elects a Comptroller-General to preside over the Audit Office (Contraloría de la Nación), which investigates Treasury income and expenditure, and the finances of the autonomous institutes.

GOVERNMENT

Executive power is vested in a President of the Republic elected by universal suffrage every six years, who may serve one additional term. The President is empowered to discharge the Constitution and the laws, to nominate or remove Ministers, to take supreme command of the Armed Forces, to direct foreign relations of the State, to declare a state of emergency and withdraw the civil guarantees laid down in the Constitution, to convene extraordinary sessions of the Asamblea Nacional and to administer national finance.

JUDICIARY

Judicial power is exercised by the Supreme Tribunal of Justice (Tribunal Suprema Justicia) and by the other tribunals. The Supreme Tribunal forms the highest court of the Republic and the Magistrates of the Supreme Tribunal are appointed by the Asamblea Nacional following recommendations from the Committee for Judicial Postulations, which consults with civil society groups. Magistrates serve a maximum of twelve years.

The 1999 Constitution created two new elements of power. The Moral Republican Council (Consejo Moral Republicano) is comprised of the Comptroller-General, the Attorney-General and the Peoples' Defender (or ombudsman). Its principle duty is to uphold the Constitution. The National Electoral Council (Consejo Nacional Electoral) administers and supervises elections.

The Government

HEAD OF STATE

President of the Republic: Lt-Col (retd) HUGO CHÁVEZ FRÍAS (took office 2 February 1999; re-elected 30 July 2000).

Vice-President: ADINA BASTIDAS.

COUNCIL OF MINISTERS
(August 2001)

Minister of Foreign Affairs: LUIS ALFONSO DÁVILA.

Minister of the Interior and of Justice: LUIS MIQUILENA.

Minister of National Defence: JOSÉ VICENTE RANGEL.

Minister of Finance: NELSON MERENTES.

Minister of Energy and Mines: ALVARO SILVA CALDERON.

Minister of Health and Social Development: MARÍA LOURDES URBANEJA.

Minister of Education, Culture and Sport: HÉCTOR NAVARRO DÍAZ.

Minister of Labour: BLANCA NIEVE PORTOCARRERO.

Minister of Production and Commerce: LUISA ROMERO BERMÚDEZ.

Minister of Infrastructure: Gen. ISMAEL ELIÉZER HURTADO SUCRE.

Minister of the Environment and Natural Resources: ANA ELISA OSORIO GRANADOS.

Minister of Planning and Development: JORGE GIORDANI.

Minister of Science and Technology: CARLOS GENATIOS SEQUERA.

Minister for the Secretariat of the Presidency: DIOSDADO CABELLO.

Minister of State for the Central Information Office of the Presidency: FREDDY BALZÁN.

Minister of State and President of the Venezuelan Investment Fund: ANTONIO GINER.

MINISTRIES

Central Information Office of the Presidency: Torre Oeste, 18°, Parque Central, Caracas 1010; tel. (212) 572-7110; fax (212) 572-2675.

Ministry of Education, Culture and Sport: Edif. Ministerio de Educación, Esquina de Salas, Caracas 1010; tel. (212) 564-0025; fax (212) 562-0175; internet www.me.gov.ve.

Ministry of Energy and Mines: Torre Oeste, 16°, Avda Lecuna, Parque Central, Caracas 1010; tel. (212) 507-6080; fax (212) 571-3953.

Ministry of the Environment and Natural Resources: Torre Sur, 18°, Centro Simón Bolívar, Caracas 1010; tel. (212) 481-7008; fax (212) 408-1464.

Ministry of Finance: Edif. Norte, 3°, Centro Simón Bolívar, Caracas 1010; tel. (212) 41-9406; fax (212) 481-5953.

Ministry of Foreign Affairs: Edif. MRE, Avda Urdaneta, Esq. Carmelitas, Caracas 1010; tel. (212) 862-1085; fax (212) 83-3633; internet www.mre.gov.ve.

Ministry of Health and Social Development: Torre Sur, 8°, Centro Simón Bolívar, Caracas 1010; tel. (212) 481-8250; fax (212) 483-4016.

Ministry of Infrastructure: Torre Este, 50°, Parque Central, Caracas 1010; tel. (212) 509-1076; fax (212) 509-1004.

Ministry of the Interior and Justice: Avda Urdaneta, Esq. Carmelitas, Caracas 1010; tel. (212) 862-9728; fax (212) 861-1967; internet www.minjusticia.gov.ve.

Ministry of Labour: Torre Sur, 5°, Centro Simón Bolívar, Caracas 1010; tel. (212) 481-1368; fax (212) 483-8914.

Ministry of National Defence: Fuerte Tiuna, Conejo Blanco, El Valle, Caracas 1090; tel. (212) 607-1604; fax (212) 662-8829.

Ministry of Planning and Development: Torre Oeste, 26°, Avda Lecuna, Parque Central, Caracas 1010; tel. (212) 507-7901; fax (212) 573-6419.

Ministry of Production and Commerce: Avda Lecuna, Torre Este, 16°, Parque Central, Caracas; tel. (212) 509-0241; fax (212) 509-0118.

Ministry of Science and Technology: Edif. Maploca 1, 4°, Final Av. Principal de los Cortijos de Lourdes, Caracas; tel. (212) 239-6475; fax (212) 239-8766.

Government Agencies

Office of the National Council for Culture: Torre Norte, 16°, Centro Simón Bolívar, Caracas 1010; tel. (212) 483-1195; fax (212) 481-8946.

Office of the Presidential Commission for State Reform: Torre Oeste, 38°, Parque Central, Caracas; tel. (212) 507-8923; fax (212) 572-3178.

Office of the Tourism Corporation (Corporación de Turismo de Venezuela—Corpoturismo): Torre Oeste, 35°–37°, Avda Lecuna, Parque Central, Caracas 1010; tel. (212) 576-5696; fax (212) 574-2679; e-mail corpoturismo@platino.gov.ve.

Office of the Venezuelan Corporation of Guayana: Edif. General, 2°, Avda La Estancia, Chuao, Caracas 1060; tel. (212) 91-3444.

Office of the Venezuelan Investment Fund: Torre Financiera del Banco Central de Venezuela, 20°, Avda Urdaneta esq. de las Carmelitas, Caracas 1010; tel. (212) 83-5390; fax (212) 83-4689.

President

Presidential Election, 30 July 2000

Candidates					% of valid votes
Lt-Col (retd) HUGO CHÁVEZ FRÍAS (MVR)	.	.	.	.	59.7
FRANCISCO ARIAS CÁRDENAS (Causa R)	.	.	.	.	37.5
CLAUDIO FERMÍN (EN)	.	.	.	.	2.7
Others	.	.	.	.	0.1
Total	.	.	.	.	100.00

Legislature

ASAMBLEA NACIONAL
(National Assembly)

President: WILLIAM LARA.

First Vice-President: LEOPOLDO PUCHI.

Second Vice-President: GERARDO SAER.

Election, 30 July 2000

Party						Seats
Movimiento V República (MVR)	.	.	.	.	.	93
Acción Democrática (AD)	.	.	.	.	.	32
Proyecto Venezuela (PRVZL)	.	.	.	.	.	8
Movimiento al Socialismo (MAS)	.	.	.	.	.	6
Partido Social-Cristiano (COPEI)	.	.	.	.	.	5
Primero Justicia (PJ)	.	.	.	.	.	5
Causa Radical (Causa R)	.	.	.	.	.	3
Indigenous groups	.	.	.	.	.	3
Others	.	.	.	.	.	10
Total	.	.	.	.	.	165

Political Organizations

Acción Democrática (AD): Casa Nacional Acción Democrática, Calle Los Cedros, La Florida, Caracas 1050; internet www.ad.org.ve; f. 1936 as Partido Democrático Nacional; adopted present name and obtained legal recognition in 1941; member of Socialist International; 1,450,000 mems; Pres. HENRY RAMOS ALLUP; Leader HUMBERTO CELLI; Sec.-Gen. TIMOTEO ZAMBRANO.

Apertura y Participación Nacional: Caracas; f. 1997; Leader CARLOS ANDRÉS PÉREZ RODRÍGUEZ.

Causa Radical (Causa R): Caracas; tel. (212) 541-2412; Leader ANDRÉS VELÁSQUEZ.

Convergencia Nacional (CN): Edif. Tajamar, Mezzanina, Parque Central, Avda Lecuna, El Conde, Caracas 1010; tel. (212) 576-9879; fax (212) 576-8214; f. 1993; Leader Dr RAFAEL CALDERA RODRÍGUEZ; Gen. Co-ordinator JUAN JOSÉ CALDERA.

Derecha Emergente de Venezuela (DEV): Caracas; f. 1989; right-wing legislative coalition, comprising Nueva Generación Democrática, Fórmula Uno and Organización Renovadora Auténtica; Leaders VLADIMIR GESSEN, RHONA OTTOLINA, GODOFREDO MARÍN.

Encuentro Nacional (EN): Caracas.

Integración, Renovación y Nueva Esperanza (IRENE): Calle los Cahguaramos con Avda Mohedano, Urb. La Castelana, Caracas; tel. (212) 267-4512; f. 1998 to represent the political agenda of 1998 presidential candidate IRENE SÁEZ.

Movimiento Electoral del Pueblo (MEP): Caracas; f. 1967 by left-wing AD dissidents; 100,000 mems; Pres. Dr LUIS BELTRÁN PRIETO FIGUEROA; Sec-Gen. Dr JESÚS ÁNGEL PAZ GALARRAGA.

Movimiento de Integración Nacional (MIN): Edif. José María Vargas, 1°, esq. Pajarito, Caracas; tel. (212) 563-7504; fax (212) 563-7553; f. 1977; Sec.-Gen. GONZALO PÉREZ HERNÁNDEZ.

Movimiento de Izquierda Revolucionaria (MIR): c/o Fracción Parlamentaria MIR, Edif. Tribunales, esq. Pajaritos, Caracas; f. 1960 by splinter group from AD; left-wing; Sec.-Gen. MOISÉS MOLEIRO.

Movimiento Primero Justicia: Caracas; f. 2000.

Movimiento V República (MVR): Calle Lima, cruce con Avda Libertador, Los Caobos, Caracas; tel. (212) 782-3808; fax (212) 782-9720; f. 1998 to support the presidential candidacy of Lt-Col (retd) HUGO CHÁVEZ FRÍAS.

Movimiento al Socialismo (MAS): Quinta Alemar, Avda Valencia, Las Palmas, Caracas; tel. (212) 782-4022; fax (212) 782-9720; f. 1971 by PCV dissidents; democratic-socialist party; 220,000 mems; Pres. FELIPE MÚJICA; Sec.-Gen. LEOPOLDO PUCHI.

Nueva Alternativa (NA): Edif. José María Vargas, esq. Pajaritos, Apdo 20193, San Martín, Caracas; tel. (212) 563-7675; f. 1982; Leaders EDUARDO MACHADO, CLEMENTE CASTRO, ANTONIO GARCÍA PONCE, PEDRO TROCONIS; Sec.-Gen. GUILLERMO GARCÍA PONCE; alliance of democratic left comprising:

Constancia Gremial.

MIR: dissident faction of party listed above.

Movimiento Patria Socialista (MPS): Caracas; f. 1983; splinter group formed by MAS dissidents, and members of the extreme left-wing Vanguardia Unitaria, Causa R and the Grupo de Acción Revolucionaria.

Movimiento Revolucionario Popular (MRP).

Vanguardia Unitaria: Apdo 20193, San Martín, Caracas; f. 1974 by PCV dissidents; Pres. EDUARDO MACHADO; Sec.-Gen. GUILLERMO GARCÍA PONCE.

Opinión Nacional (OPINA): Pájaro a Curamichate 92, 2°, Caracas 101; f. 1961; 22,000 mems; Pres. Dr PEDRO LUIS BLANCO PEÑALVER; Sec.-Gen. Prof. AMADO CORNEILLES.

Partido Comunista de Venezuela (PCV): Edif. Cantaclaro, esq. San Pedro, San Juan, Apdo 20428, Caracas; tel. (212) 484-0061; fax (212) 481-9737; f. 1931; Sec.-Gen. OSCAR FIGUERA.

Partido Devolucionario de Venezuela: Caracas; f. 1998.

Partido Social-Cristiano (Comité de Organización Política Electoral Independiente) (COPEI): esq. San Miguel, Avda Panteón cruce con Fuerzas Armadas, San José, Caracas 1010; tel. (212) 51-6022; fax (212) 52-1876; f. 1946; Christian Democratic; more than 1,500,000 mems; Pres. Dr LUIS HERRERA CAMPÍNS; Sec.-Gen. Dr DONALD RAMÍREZ.

Partido Unión: Caracas; f. 2001; Leader Francisco Arias Cárdenas.

Patria Para Todos (PPT): Caracas; tel. (212) 577-4545; e-mail ppt@cantv.net; internet www.patriaparatodos.org/index.htm; breakaway faction of Causa Radical; Leaders ARISTÓBULO ISTÚRIZ, PABLO MEDINA.

Polo Patriótico: f. 1998; grouping of small, mainly left-wing and nationalist political parties, including the MVR, in support of presidential election campaign of Lt-Col (retd) HUGO CHÁVEZ FRÍAS.

Proyecto Venezuela (PRVZL): f. 1998 to support the presidential candidacy of HENRIQUE SALAS RÖMER.

Tradición, Familia y Propiedad (TFP)*: Caracas; f. 1960; right-wing ultramontane Roman Catholic group (also active in Brazil and Argentina); 200 mems.

Unión Republicana Democrática (URD): Caracas; f. 1946; moderate left; Leader ISMENIA VILLALBA.

Other parties include: Fuerza Espiritual Venezolana Orientadora (Leader RÓMULO ABREU FUERTE); Liga Socialista (f. 1974; Pres. CARMELO LABORIT; Tercer Camino* (Third Way—Marxist; Leader DOUGLAS BRAVO); Bandera Roja* (Red Flag—f. 1968; Marxist-Leninist); Poder Independiente (right-wing; Leader LEOPOLDO DÍAZ BRUZUAL); Rescate Nacional (right-wing; Leader Gen. (retd) LUIS ENRIQUE RANGEL BOURGOIN); Fuerzas Bolivarianos de Liberación*; Los Justicieros de Venezuela*; Movimiento Bolivariano Revolucionario 200 (MBR-200).

* Illegal organizations.

Diplomatic Representation

EMBASSIES IN VENEZUELA

Algeria: Transversal con Avda San Juan Bosco Quinta Tatau, Altamira, Caracas 1060; tel. (212) 263-9771; fax (212) 263-8482; e-mail ambalgcar@ccs.fast-link.net; Ambassador: MOHAMMED GHALIB NEDJARI.

Argentina: Edif. FEDECAMARAS, 3°, Avda El Empalme, El Bosque, Apdo 569, Caracas; tel. (212) 731-3311; fax (212) 731-2659; Ambassador: JUAN CARLOS VIGLIONE.

Australia: Quinta Yolanda, Avda Luis Roche entre 6 y 7 transversales, Caracas 1060-A; tel. (212) 263-4033; fax (212) 261-3448; e-mail ausembcrcs@cantv.net; Ambassador: JOHN WOODS.

Austria: Edif. Torre Las Mercedes, 4°, Of. 408, Avda La Estancia, Chuao, Apdo 61381, Caracas 1060-A; tel. (212) 991-3863; fax (212) 959-9804; e-mail e.austria@cantv.net; internet www.internet.ve /austria; Ambassador: Dr JOHANNES SKRIWAN.

Barbados: Edif. Los Frailes, 5°, Of. 501, Calle La Guairita, Chuao, Caracas; tel. (212) 992-0545; fax (212) 991-0333; e-mail caracas@ foreign.gov.bb; Ambassador: SONJA P. J. WELCH.

Belgium: Quinta la Azulita, Avda 11, entre 6 y 7 transversales, Apdo del Este 61550, Altamira, Caracas 1060; tel. (212) 263-3334; fax (212) 261-0309; e-mail ambelven@sa.omnes.net; Ambassador: Baron ANDRE DE VIRON.

Bolivia: Avda Luis Roche con 6 transversal, Altamira, Caracas; tel. (212) 261-4563; fax (212) 261-3386; e-mail embabolivia@cantv.net; Ambassador: JAIME PONCE CABALLERO.

Brazil: Avda Mohedano con Calle Los Chaguaramos, Centro Gerencial Mohedano, 6°, La Castellana, Caracas; tel. (212) 261-5505; fax (212) 261-9601; e-mail brasembcaracas@cantv.net; internet www.brasil-ve.org; Ambassador: RUY NUNES PINTO NOQUEIRA.

Canada: Avda de Altamira 6 entre 3 y 5 transversal, Altamira, Caracas 1062; tel. (212) 264-0833; fax (212) 261-8741; e-mail embajada.canada@crcas01.X400.gc.ca; Ambassador: ALLAN STEWART.

Chile: Edif. Torre La Noria, 10°, Calle Paseo Enrique Eraso, Las Mercedes, Caracas; tel. (212) 991-1967; fax (212) 991-1621; e-mail echileve@cantv.net; Ambassador: OTTO ALEJANDRO BOYE SOTO.

China, People's Republic: Prados del Este, Apdo 80665, Caracas 1080-A; tel. (212) 977-4949; fax (212) 978-0876; e-mail embcnven@ att.com.ven; Ambassador: LIU BOMING.

Colombia: Torre Credival, 11°, 2a Calle de Campo Alegre con Avda Francisco de Miranda, Apdo 60887, Caracas; tel. (212) 261-6592; fax (212) 261-1358; e-mail Colombia@telcel.net.ve; Ambassador: GERMAN BULA.

Costa Rica: Avda San Juan Bosco, entre 1 y 2 transversal, Edif. For You P.H., Altamira, Apdo 62239, Caracas; tel. (212) 267-1104; fax (212) 262-0038; e-mail embcostar@cantv.net; Ambassador: RICARDO LIZANO CALZADA.

Cuba: Calle Roraima E Río de Janeiro y Choroni, Chuao, Caracas 1060; tel. (212) 991-2911; Ambassador: GERMÁN SÁNCHEZ OTERO.

Czech Republic: Avda Luis Roche 41, 5 transversal, Altamira, Caracas; tel. (212) 33-9866.

Denmark: Torre Centuria, 7°, Avda Venezuela con Calle Mohedano, El Rosal, Caracas 1060-A; tel. (212) 951-4618; fax (212) 951-5278; e-mail danmark@cantv.net; internet www.dinamarca.com; Ambassador: SØREN VOSS.

Dominican Republic: Edif. Humboldt, 6°, Of. 26, Avda Francisco de Miranda, Altamira, Caracas; tel. (212) 284-2443; fax (212) 283-3965; e-mail embaredo@telcel.net.ve; Ambassador: ANTONIO OCAÑA RODRÍGUEZ.

Ecuador: Centro Andrés Bello, Torre Oeste, 13°, Avda Andrés Bello, Maripérez, Apdo 62124, Caracas 1060; tel. (212) 781-3180; fax (212) 782-7978; e-mail embajado@viptel.com; Ambassador: MARCELO FERNÁNDEZ DE CÓRDOBA PONCE.

Egypt: Quinta Maribel, Calle Guaicaipuro, Las Mercedes, Caracas; tel. (212) 992-6259; fax (212) 993-1555; e-mail egyptianembassy@ cantv.net; Ambassador: KAMEL KHALIL.

El Salvador: Quinta Cuzcatlán, Calle Amazonas, final Avda Principal de Prados del Este, Caracas; tel. (212) 959-0817; fax (212) 959-3920; Ambassador: MARGARITA ESCOBAR.

Finland: Edif. Atrium, 1°, Calle Sorocaima, entre Avdas Venezuela y Tamanaco, El Rosal, Apdo 61118-A, Caracas 1060; tel. (212) 952-4111; fax (212) 952-7536; e-mail finland@viptel.com; internet www.finlandia-caracas.com; Ambassador: IIVO SALMI.

France: Calle Madrid con Avda Trinidad-las-Mercedes, Apdo 60385, Caracas 1060; tel. (212) 993-6666; fax (212) 993-3483; e-mail consulat@telul.net.ve; internet www.ambafrance.org.ve; Ambassador: LAURENT AUBLIN.

Germany: Edif. Panavén, 2°, Avda San Juan Bosco, esq. 3 transversal, Altamira, Apdo 2078, Caracas; tel. (212) 261-0181; fax (212) 261-0641; Ambassador: EDMUND DUCKWITZ.

Greece: Quinta La Cañada, 1a Avda El Casquillo, esq. con Calle Unión, Alta Florida, Caracas; tel. (212) 730-3833; fax (212) 731-0429; Ambassador: LAZAROS NANOS.

Grenada: Edif. Los Frailes, 3°, Of. 34, Calle La Guairita, Chuao, Caracas; tel. (212) 991-0933; fax (212) 991-8907; e-mail egrenada @cantv.net; Chargé d'affaires: MARGARET HARRIS.

Guatemala: Edif. Los Frailes, 6°, Calle La Guairita, Chuao, Apdo 80238, Caracas 1080-A; tel. (212) 952-1166; fax (212) 952-1992; e-mail guateven@ven.net; Ambassador: LARS PIRA PÉREZ.

Guyana: Quinta 'Roraima', Avda El Paseo, Prados del Este, Apdo 51054, Caracas; tel. (212) 978-2781; fax (212) 976-3765; Ambassador: BAYNEY RAM KARRAN.

Haiti: Quinta Flor 59, Avda Las Rosas, La Florida, Apdo 60213, Caracas; tel. (212) 730-7220; fax (212) 730-4605; Chargé d'affaires: MARIO BRIERRE.

Holy See: Avda La Salle, Los Caobos, Apdo 29, Caracas 1010-A (Apostolic Nunciature); tel. (212) 781-8939; fax (212) 793-2403; e-mail nunapos@cantv.net; Apostolic Nuncio: Most Rev. ANDRÉ DUPUY, Titular Archbishop of Selsea.

Honduras: Edif. Excelsior, Avda San Juan Bosco, 5°, Altamira, Apdo 68259, Caracas; tel. (212) 284-5593; fax (212) 266-1935; e-mail embhondv@truevision.net; Ambassador: Dr CARLOS ALEJANDRO SOSA COELLO.

India: Apdo 61585, Chacao, Caracas 1060-A, Caracas; tel. (212) 285-7887; fax (212) 286-5131; e-mail embindia@eldish.net; Ambassador: N. N. DESAI.

Indonesia: Quinta La Trinidad, Avda El Paseo, Prados del Este, Apdo 80807, Caracas 1080; tel. (212) 976-2725; fax (212) 976-0550; Ambassador: GHAFFAR FADYL.

Iran: Quinta Ommat, Calle Kemal Ataturk, Valle Arriba, Caracas; tel. (212) 992-3575; fax (212) 992-9989; e-mail kesmavrz@sa.omnes.net; Ambassador: MOHAMMAD KESHAVARZZADEH.

Iraq: Quinta Babilonia, Avda Nicolas Cópernico con Calle Los Malabares, Valle Arriba, Caracas; tel. (212) 991-1627; fax (212) 992-0268; Ambassador: GHAZI KARIM KHALIFA.

Israel: Centro Empresarial Miranda, 4°, Avda Principal de los Ruices cruce con Francisco de Miranda, Apdo 70081, Los Ruices, Caracas; tel. (212) 239-4511; fax (212) 239-4320; e-mail embajo01@cantv.net; Ambassador: ARIE TENNE.

Italy: Edif. Atrium, Calle Sorocaima, entre Avdas Tamanaco y Venezuela, El Rosal, Apdo 3995, Caracas; tel. (212) 952-7311; fax (212) 952-7120; e-mail ambcara@italamb.org.ve; internet www.italamb.org.ve; Ambassador: ADRIANO BENEDETTI.

Jamaica: Edif. Los Frailes, 5°, Calle La Guairita, Urb. Chuao, Caracas 1062; tel. (212) 991-6955; fax (212) 991-5798; e-mail embjaven@cantv.net; Ambassador: PAUL A. ROBOTHAM.

Japan: Quinta Sakura, Avda San Juan Bosco, entre 8a y 9a Transversales, Altamira, Apdo 68790, Caracas 1062; tel. (212) 261-8333; fax (212) 261-6780; Ambassador: MASAAKI KUNIYASU.

Korea, Democratic People's Republic: Caracas; Ambassador: KIM KIL HWANG.

Korea, Republic: Edif. Atrium, 3°, Avda Sorocaima con Avda Venezuela, El Rosal, Apdo 80671, Caracas; tel. (212) 954-1270; fax (212) 954-0619; e-mail venadmi@viptel.com; Ambassador: DONG-CHUL CHANG.

Kuwait: Quinta El-Kuwait, Avda Las Magnolias con Calle Los Olivos, Los Chorros, Caracas; tel. (212) 235-1257; fax (212) 239-3127; Ambassador: YOUSUF AL-ONAIZI.

Lebanon: Quinta el Cedro del Lebanon, Avda Primera, Colinas Bello Monte, Calle Motatán, Caracas 1050; tel. (212) 751-5943; fax (212) 753-0726; e-mail embajada@libano.org.ve; Ambassador: MUSTAPHA HRAIBEH.

Libya: 3a Avda entre 9a y 10a transversales, Quinta Los Leones, Altamira, Apdo 68946, Caracas 1060; tel. (212) 261-1290; fax (212) 261-7271; Ambassador: AHMED TAHER TABIB.

Lithuania: Centro Plaza, Torre A, Avda Francisco de Miranda, 9°, Apdo 62818, Caracas; tel. (212) 286-2649; fax (212) 286-1268; e-mail lrambven@sa.omnes.net; Ambassador: VYTAUTAS A. DAMBRAVA.

Mexico: Edif. Forum, Calle Guaicaipuro con Principal de las Mercedes, 5°, El Rosal, Apdo 61371, Caracas; tel. (212) 952-5777; fax (212) 952-3003; e-mail prensa@eldish.net; internet www.embamexven@eldish.net; Ambassador: JESÚS PUENTE LEYVA.

Morocco: Torre Multinvest, Plaza Isabel La Católica, Avda Eugenio Mendoza, 2°, La Castellana, Caracas; tel. (212) 266-7543; fax (212) 266-4681; Ambassador: MOHAMED MAOULAININE.

Netherlands: Edif. San Juan Bosco, 9°, San Juan Bosco con 2 transversal de Altamira, Caracas; tel. (212) 263-3622; fax (212) 263-0462; e-mail nlgovcar@internet.ve; Ambassador: N. P. VAN ZUTPHEN.

Nicaragua: Quinta Teocal, Calle Codazzi, Prados del Este, Caracas; tel. (212) 977-2459; fax (212) 979-9167; e-mail embnicve@mail.lat.net; Ambassador: ALVARO SANSON-ROMAN.

Nigeria: Quinta Leticia, Calle Chivacoa cruce con Calle Taría, San Román, Caracas; tel. (212) 263-4816; fax (212) 263-4635; Ambassador: ADEYOMBO OLUBONMI OYESOLA.

Norway: Centro Lido, Torre A-92A, Avda Francisco de Miranda, El Rosal, Apdo 60532, Caracas 1060-A; tel. (212) 953-0671; fax (212) 953-6877; e-mail emb.caracas@mfa.no; Ambassador: DAG MORK-ULNES.

Panama: Edif. Los Frailes, 6°, Calle La Guairita, Chuao, Apdo 1989, Caracas; tel. (212) 992-9093; fax (212) 992-8107; Chargé d'affaires: JACINTA RIVERA URRIOLA.

Paraguay: Quinta Lily, 8a Avda de Altamira norte entre 7 y 8 transversales, Apdo 80668, Caracas; tel. (212) 781-8213; fax (212) 793-3017; e-mail embaparven@cantv.net; Ambassador: LICINIO RODOLFO GILL DUARTE.

Peru: Avda San Juan Bosco, 5°, Altamira, Caracas; tel. (212) 264-1483; fax (212) 265-7592; e-mail embaperu123@cantv.net; Ambassador: JULIO BALBUENA LÓPEZ-ALFARO.

Philippines: Quinta Taray, Avda Tropical, La Floresta, Caracas; tel. (212) 284-2006; Ambassador: PABLO A. ARAQUE.

Poland: Quinta Ambar, Final Avda Nicolás Copérnico, Sector Los Naranjos, Las Mercedes, Apdo 62293, Caracas; tel. (212) 991-1461; fax (212) 992-2164; e-mail ambcarac@ven.net; Ambassador: JACEK PERLIN.

Portugal: Edif. FEDECAMARAS, 1°, Avda El Empalme, El Bosque, Caracas 1062; tel. (212) 731-0539; fax (212) 731-0543; e-mail embport@etheron.net; Ambassador: FERNANDO DE CASTRO BRANDÃO.

Romania: Calle El Pedregal (Alto), La Castellana, Caracas; tel. (212) 261-2769; fax (212) 263-7594; e-mail ambarove@infoline.wtfe.com; Ambassador: GEORGHE STOICA.

Russia: Quinta Soyuz, Calle Las Lomas, Las Mercedes, Caracas; tel. (212) 993-4395; fax (212) 993-6526; e-mail emruscar@cantv.net; Ambassador: VALERY MOROZOV.

Saudi Arabia: Calle Andrés Pietri, Los Chorros, Caracas 1071; tel. (212) 239-0290; fax (212) 239-6494; e-mail arabsaudi@eldish.net; Ambassador: MARWAN BIN BASHIR AL-ROUMI.

South Africa: Centro Profesional Eurobuilding, Calle La Guiarita, 4°, Chuao, Caracas 1064; tel. (212) 991-6822; fax (212) 911-5555; e-mail rsaven@eldish.net; Ambassador: THANDI LUTHULI-GCABASHE.

Spain: Avda Mohedano entre la y 2a transversal, La Castellana, Caracas; tel. (212) 263-2855; fax (212) 261-0892; Ambassador: MIGUEL ANGEL FERNÁNDEZ MAZARAMBROZ Y BERNABEU.

Suriname: 4a Avda entre 7a y 8a transversal, Quinta 41, Altamira, Caracas; Apdo 61140, Chacao, Caracas; tel. (212) 261-2724; fax (212) 263-9006; e-mail emsurl@contv.net; Chargé d'affaires: LAURENCE E. NEEDE.

Sweden: Torre Europa, 8°, Of. A, Avda Francisco de Miranda, Chacaíto, Caracas; tel. (212) 952-2111; fax (212) 952-2057; e-mail embsueciave@cantv.net; Ambassador: MAGNUS NORDBÄCK.

Switzerland: Torre Ing-Bank, Avda Eugenio Mendoza y San Felipe, 15°, Apdo 62555, Caracas 1060-A; tel. (212) 267-9585; fax (212) 267-7745; e-mail vertretung@car.rep.admin.ch; Ambassador: Dr ERNST ITEN.

Syria: Quinta Damasco, Avda Casiquare, Colinas de Bello Monte, Caracas; tel. (212) 752-6687; fax (212) 751-6146; Chargé d'affaires: NADER NADER.

Trinidad and Tobago: Quinta Serrana, 4a Avda entre 7 y 8 transversales, Altamira, Caracas; tel. (212) 261-4772; fax (212) 261-9801; e-mail embtt@caracas.c-com.net; Ambassador: PHILIP SEALY.

Turkey: Calle Kemal Atatürk, Quinta Turquesa 6, Valle Arriba, Apdo 62078; Caracas 1060-A; tel. (212) 991-0075; fax (212) 992-0442; e-mail turkishemb@cantv.net; Ambassador: TANJU ÜLGEN.

United Kingdom: Torre Las Mercedes, 3°, Avda La Estancia, Chuao, Apdo 1246, Caracas 1061; tel. (212) 993-4111; fax (212) 993-9989; e-mail britishembassy@internet.ve; internet www.britain.org.ve; Ambassador: Dr EDGAR JOHN HUGHES.

USA: Calle Suapure con Calle F, Colinas de Valle Arriba, Caracas; tel. (212) 975-6411; fax (212) 975-9429; e-mail embajada@usia.gov; internet http://usembassy.state.gov/venezuela; Ambassador: DONNA HRINAK.

Uruguay: Torre Delta, 8°, Of. A y B, Avda Francisco de Miranda, Altamira Sur, Apdo 60366, Caracas 1060-A; tel. (212) 261-5352; fax (212) 266-9233; Ambassador: JUAN SAENZ DE ZUMARÁN.

Yugoslavia: Quinta No 13, 4°, Avda de Campo Alegre, Caracas; tel. (212) 266-7995; fax (212) 266-9957; e-mail yuembven@att.com.ve; Ambassador: SLAVKO SUKOVIĆ.

Judicial System

The judicature is headed by the Supreme Tribunal of Justice, which replaced the Supreme Court of Justice after the promulgation of the December 1999 Constitution. The judges are divided into penal and civil and mercantile judges; there are military, juvenile, labour, administrative litigation, finance and agrarian tribunals. In each state there is a superior court and several secondary courts which act on civil and criminal cases. A number of reforms to the judicial system were introduced under the Organic Criminal Trial Code of March 1998. The Code replaced the inquisitorial system, based on the Napoleonic code, with an adversarial system in July 1999. In addition, citizen participation as lay judges and trial by jury was introduced, with training financed by the World Bank.

SUPREME TRIBUNAL OF JUSTICE

The Supreme Tribunal comprises 20 judges appointed by the Asamblea Nacional for 12 years. It is divided into three courts, each with five judges: political-administrative; civil, constitutional and social cassation; penal cassation. When these three act together the court is in full session. It has the power to abrogate any laws, regulations or other acts of the executive or legislative branches conflicting with the Constitution. It hears accusations against members of the Government and high public officials, cases involving diplomatic representatives and certain civil actions arising between the State and individuals.

Supreme Tribunal: Avda Baralt esq. Dos Pilatas, Foro Libertador, Caracas 1010; tel. (212) 563-9555; fax (212) 563-6506.

President: IVÁN GUILLERMO RINCÓN URDANETA.

First Vice-President: FRANKLIN ARRIECHE.

Second Vice-President: JORGE ROSELL.

Attorney-General: ISAÍAS RODRÍGUEZ.

Religion

Roman Catholicism is the religion of the majority of the population, but there is complete freedom of worship.

CHRISTIANITY

The Roman Catholic Church

For ecclesiastical purposes, Venezuela comprises nine archdioceses, 22 dioceses and four Apostolic Vicariates. There is also an apostolic exarchate for the Melkite Rite. At 31 December 1999 adherents, of whom 48,000 were of the Melkite rite, accounted for about 94% of the total population.

Latin Rite

Bishops' Conference: Conferencia Episcopal de Venezuela, Edif. Juan XXIII, 4°, Torre a Madrices, Apdo 4897, Caracas 1010; tel. (212) 442-2077; fax (212) 442-3562; f. 1985 (statutes approved 2000); Pres. Most Rev. BALTAZAR PORRAS CARDOZO, Archbishop of Mérida.

Archbishop of Barquisimeto: Most Rev. TULIO MANUEL CHIRIVELLA VARELA, Arzobispado, Calle 23, cruce con Carrera 16, Barquisimeto; tel. (251) 31-3446; fax (251) 31-3724; e-mail arquibarqui@eteron.net.

Archbishop of Calabozo: Most Rev. HELÍMENAS DE JESÚS ROJO PAREDES, Arzobispado, Calle 4, N. 11–52, Calabozo 2312; tel. (246) 71-3332; fax (246) 71-2097.

Archbishop of Caracas (Santiago de Venezuela): Cardinal IGNACIO ANTONIO VELASCO GARCÍA, Arzobispado, Plaza Bolívar, Apdo 954, Caracas 1010-A; tel. (212) 545-0212; fax (212) 545-0297.

Archbishop of Ciudad Bolívar: Most Rev. MEDARDO LUIS LUZARDO ROMERO, Arzobispado, Avda Andrés Eloy Blanco con Avda Naiguatá, Apdo 43, Ciudad Bolívar; tel. (285) 44960; fax (285) 40821; e-mail arzcb@cantv.net.ve.

Archbishop of Coro: Most Rev. ROBERTO LÜCKERT LEÓN, Arzobispado, Calle Federacion, Apdo 7342, Coro; tel. (268) 51-7024; fax (268) 51-8868; e-mail dioscoro@funflc.org.ve.

Archbishop of Cumaná: Most Rev. ALFREDO JOSÉ RODRÍGUEZ FIGUEROA, Arzobispado, Calle Catedral 34, Apdo 134, Cumaná 6101-A; tel. (293) 31-4131; fax (293) 33-3413; e-mail ajrf@telcel.net.de.

Archbishop of Maracaibo: Most Rev. UBALDO RAMÓN SANTANA SEQUERA, Arzobispado, Calle 95, entre Avdas 2 y 3, Apdo 439, Maracaibo; tel. (261) 22-5351; fax (261) 22-3258.

Archbishop of Mérida: Most Rev. BALTAZAR ENRIQUE PORRAS CARDOZO, Arzobispado, Avda 4, Plaza Bolívar, Apdo 26, Mérida 5101; tel. (274) 52-5786; fax (274) 52-1238; e-mail bepor@latimail.com.

Archbishop of Valencia en Venezuela: Most Rev. JORGE LIBERATO UROSA SAVINO, Arzobispado, Avda Urdaneta 100-54, Apdo 32, Valencia 2001-A; tel. (241) 58-5865; fax (241) 57-8061.

Melkite Rite

Apostolic Exarch: Rt. Rev. GEORGES KAHHALÉ ZOUHAÏRATY, Catedral San Jorge, Final 3a Avda de Montalban 2, Apdo 20120, Caracas 1020; tel. (212) 443-3019; fax (212) 443-0131.

The Anglican Communion

Anglicans in Venezuela are adherents of the Episcopal Church in the USA, in which the country forms a single, extra-provincial diocese attached to Province IX.

Bishop of Venezuela: Rt Rev. ORLANDO DE JESÚS GUERRERO, Avda Caroní 100, Apdo 49-143, Colinas de Bello Monte, Caracas 1042-A; tel. (212) 753-0723; fax (212) 751-3180; e-mail iglanglicanavzla@cantv.net.

Protestant Churches

Iglesia Evangélica Luterana en Venezuela: Apdo 68738, Caracas 1062-A; tel. (212) 264-1868; fax (212) 264-1363; Pres. WALTER A. ERDMANN; 4,000 mems.

The National Baptist Convention of Venezuela: Avda Santiago de Chile 12–14, Urb. Los Caobos, Caracas 1050; Apdo 61152, Chacao, Caracas 1060-A; tel. (212) 782-2308; fax (212) 781-9043; e-mail

cnbv@telcel.net.ve; f. 1951; Pres. Rev. ENRIQUE DÁMASO; Gen. Man. Rev. DANIEL RODRÍGUEZ.

BAHÁ'Í FAITH

National Spiritual Assembly of the Bahá'ís: Colinas de Bello Monte, Apdo 49133, Caracas; tel. and fax (212) 751-7669; f. 1961; mems resident in 954 localities.

The Press

DAILIES

Caracas

Así es la Noticia: Edif. El Nacional, 4°, Puente Nuevo a Puerto Escondido, Caracas; tel. (212) 408-3444; fax (212) 408-3442; f. 1996; morning; Editor IBEYISE PACHECO.

The Daily Journal: Avda Fuerzas Armadas, Crucecita a San Ramón, Apdo 1408, Caracas 1010-A; tel. (212) 562-1122; f. 1945; morning; in English; Chair. HANS NEUMANN; Editor TONY BIANCHI; circ. 18,500.

Meridiano: Edif. Bloque Dearmas, final Avda San Martín cruce con Avda La Paz, Caracas 1010; tel. (212) 406-4048; fax (212) 443-8692; e-mail meridian@ccs.internet.ve; internet www.meridiano.com.ve; f. 1969; morning; sports; Dir Dr ANDRÉS DE ARMAS; circ. 100,000.

El Mundo: Torre de la Prensa, Puente Trinidad a Panteón, Apdo 1192, Caracas; tel. (212) 596-1911; fax (212) 596-1478; f. 1958; evening; independent; Pres. VÍCTOR SIERRA; Dir LUIS OSCAR PONT; circ. 40,000.

El Nacional: Edif. El Nacional, Puente Nuevo a Puerto Escondido, El Silencio, Apdo 209, Caracas; tel. (212) 408-3111; fax (212) 481-0548; e-mail 73000.1437@compuserve.com; internet www.elnacional.com; f. 1943; morning; independent; Editor ARGENIS MÁRTINEZ; circ. 100,000.

La Razón: Avda Urdaneta, esq. de Urapal, Apdo 16362, Caracas; tel. (212) 578-3143; fax (212) 578-2397; e-mail larazon@internet.ve; internet www.razon.com; morning; independent; Dir PABLO LÓPEZ ULACIO.

Ultimas Noticias: Torre de la Prensa, Puente Trinidad a Panteón, Apdo 1192, Caracas; tel. (212) 596-1911; fax (212) 596-1433; f. 1941; morning; independent; Pres. VÍCTOR SIERRA; Editor FRANCISCO MAYORGA; circ. 100,000.

El Universal: Edif. El Universal, Avda Urdaneta esq. de Animas, Apdo 1909, Caracas; tel. (212) 561-7511; fax (212) 564-0067; e-mail mata@el-universal.com; internet www.el-universal.com; f. 1909; morning; Pres. and Editor ANDRÉS MATA OSORIO; circ. 130,000.

2001: Edif. Bloque Dearmas, 2°, final Avda San Martín, cruce con final Avda La Paz, Apdo 575, Caracas; tel. (212) 406-4111; fax (212) 443-8692; e-mail 2001@ccs.internet.ve; f. 1973; afternoon; independent; Dir ISRAEL MÁRQUEZ; circ. 100,000.

Barcelona

El Norte: Avda Intercomunal Andrés Bello, Sector Colinas del Neverí, Barcelona; tel. (281) 86-2933; fax (281) 86-8108; f. 1989; morning; Dir and Editor OMAR GONZÁLEZ MORENO.

Barquisimeto

El Impulso: Avda Los Comuneros, entre Avda República y Calle 1a, Urb. El Parque, Apdo 602, Barquisimeto; tel. (251) 50-2222; fax (251) 545-5144; f. 1904; morning; independent; Dir and Editor JUAN MANUEL CARMONA PERERA; circ. 47,000.

El Informador: Carrera 21, esq. Calle 23, Barquisimeto; tel. (251) 31-1811; fax (251) 31-0624; f. 1968; morning; Dir ALEJANDRO GÓMEZ SIGALA; circ. 45,000.

Ciudad Bolívar

El Bolivarense: Calle Igualdad 26, Apdo 91, Ciudad Bolívar; tel. (285) 24034; fax (285) 24878; f. 1957; morning; independent; Dir ALFREDO NATERA; circ. 5,000.

El Expreso: Paseo Gáspari con Calle Democracia, Ciudad Bolívar; tel. (285) 27908; fax (285) 28401; f. 1969; morning; independent; Dir J. M. GUZMÁN GÓMEZ; circ. 20,000.

Maracaibo

La Columna: Avda 6 con Calle 89, No 89–24, Apdo 420, Maracaibo; tel. (261) 22-3884; fax (261) 22-7921; f. 1924; morning; Catholic; Dir and Editor ELVY MONZART ARRAGA; circ. 20,000.

Panorama: Avda 15 No 95–60, Apdo 425, Maracaibo; tel. (261) 25-6888; fax (261) 25-6911; e-mail panorama@panodi.com; f. 1914; morning; independent; Pres. ESTEBAN PINEDA BELLOSA; Editor ROBERTO BAITTINER; circ. 135,000.

Maracay

El Aragueño: Calle 3a Oeste con Avda 1 Oeste, Urb. Ind. San Jacinto, Maracay; tel. (243) 35-9018; fax (243) 35-7866; f. 1972; morning; Editor EVERT GARCÍA; circ. 10,000.

El Siglo: Edif. 'El Siglo', Avda Bolívar Oeste 244, La Romana, Maracay; tel. (243) 54-9265; fax (243) 54-5910; e-mail elsiglo@telcel .net.ve; f. 1973; morning; independent; Editor TULIO R. CAPRILES H.; circ. 75,000.

Puerto la Cruz

El Tiempo: Avda Constitución, Paseo Miranda 39, Apdo 4733, Puerto la Cruz; tel. (281) 265-4344; fax (281) 269-9224; e-mail buzon@eltiempo.com.ve; internet www.eltiempo.com.ve; f. 1958; independent; Pres. MARÍA A. MÁRQUEZ; Editor Dr GIOCONDA DE MÁRQUEZ; circ. 75,000.

San Cristóbal

Diario Católico: Carrera 4a No 3–41, San Cristóbal; tel. (276) 43-2819; fax (276) 43-4683; f. 1924; morning; Catholic; Man. Dir Mgr NELSON ARELLANO ROA; circ. 28,000.

Diario de la Nación: Edif. La Nación, Calle 4 con Carreras 6 bis, La Concordia, Apdo 651, San Cristóbal; tel. (276) 46-2367; fax (276) 46-5178; f. 1968; morning; independent; Editor JOSÉ RAFAEL CORTEZ; circ. 31,500.

El Tigre

Antorcha: Edif. Anzoátegui, Avda Francisco de Miranda, Apdo 145, El Tigre; tel. (283) 35-2383; fax (283) 35-3923; f. 1954; morning; independent; Pres. ANTONIO BRICEÑO AMPARÁN; circ. 30,000.

Valencia

El Carabobeño: Edif. El Carabobeño, Avda Soublette 99-60, Valencia; tel. (241) 57-3533; fax (241) 57-1175; internet www .elcarabobeno.com; f. 1933; morning; Dir EDUARDO ALEMÁN PÉREZ; circ. 80,000.

PERIODICALS

Caracas

Agricultura Venezolana: Apdo 8373, Caracas 101; every 2 months; agricultural; circ. 5,000.

Alarma: Torre de la Prensa, Plaza del Panteón, Apdo 2976, Caracas 101; f. 1977; fortnightly; politics; Dir JOSÉ CAMPOS SUÁREZ; circ. 65,150.

Automóvil de Venezuela: Avda Caurimare, Qta Expo, Colinas de Bello Monte, Caracas 1050; tel. (212) 751-1355; fax (212) 751-1122; e-mail ortizauto@cantv.net; f. 1961; monthly; automotive trade; Editor ARMANDO ORTIZ P.; circ. 6,000.

Bohemia Venezolana: Edif. Bloque Dearmas, Final Avda San Martín cruce con Avda La Paz, Apdo 575, Caracas; tel. (212) 443-1066; f. 1966; weekly; general interest; Dir ROSANA ORDÓÑEZ; circ. 86,270.

Business Venezuela: Apdo 5181, Caracas 1010-A; tel. (212) 63-0833; fax (212) 32-0764; every 2 months; business and economics journal in English published by the Venezuelan-American Chamber of Commerce and Industry; Dir MICHAEL E. HEGGIE; circ. 6,000.

Caza y Pesca, Náutica: Apdo 60764, Caracas 1060-A; f. 1954; monthly; fishing, hunting and water sports; Dir HEINZ DOEBBEL; circ. 25,500.

Deportes: Torre de la Prensa, Plaza del Panteón, Apdo 2976, Caracas 101; f. 1978; fortnightly; sports review; Dir RAÚL HERNÁNDEZ; circ. 71,927.

Dominical: Torre de la Prensa, Puente Trinidad a Panteón, Apdo 1192, Caracas; tel. (212) 81-4931; fax (212) 83-8835; f. 1970; weekly; Pres. MIGUEL ANGEL CAPRILES; Dir NELSON LUIS MARTÍNEZ; circ. 352,479.

Economía Venezolana: Apdo 8373, Caracas; economics.

Elite: Torre de la Prensa, 6°, Plaza del Panteón Apdo 2976, Caracas 101; tel. (212) 81-4931; f. 1925; weekly; general interest; Dir ASDRÚBAL ZURITA; circ. 89,830.

Ellas: Edif. El Bucaré, Avda Federico Solano, Caracas 101; tel. (212) 71-2798; fortnightly; women's interest; Dir NERY RUSSO; circ. 30,000.

Gaceta Hípica: Apdo 2935, Caracas; weekly; horse racing; circ. 150,000.

Hipódromo: Torre de la Prensa, Puente Trinidad a Panteón, Apdo 1192, Caracas; tel. (212) 81-4931; fax (212) 83-8835; f. 1969; monthly; sports review; Pres. MIGUEL ANGEL CAPRILES; Dir EDUARDO HERNÁNDEZ LÓPEZ; circ. 101,548.

Kena: Edif. Humboldt, 2°, Avda Federico de Miranda, Apdo 2976, Caracas 101; tel. (212) 81-4931; f. 1964; fortnightly; women's

interest; Dirs OTTO CASALE, HORTENSIA BRACAMONTE; Editor MARÍA ELENA MATHEUS; circ. 88,750.

Momento: Torre de la Prensa, Plaza del Panteón, Apdo 2976, Caracas 101; tel. (212) 572-0322; weekly; general interest; Editor ARMANDO DE ARMAS; circ. 78,520.

Número: Apdo 75570, El Marqués, Caracas 1070; tel. (212) 283-3393; fax (212) 283-9104; f. 1980; monthly; financial, business and marketing; Editor ARTURO OBADIA BERACASA; circ. 21,000.

Páginas: Torre de la Prensa, Apdo 2976, Caracas 101; tel. (212) 81-4931; f. 1948; women's weekly; Dir NELSON ZURITA; Editor MIGUEL ANGEL CAPRILES; circ. 80,025.

El Periodista: Casa del Periodista, Avda Andrés Bello, Caracas; every 2 months; journalism.

Prensa Médica: Edif. San José, 1°, Avda Principal Maripérez, Caracas; monthly; medicine; circ. 8,000.

¿Qué Pasa?: Edif. Nuevo Central, 7°, Avda Libertador, Chacao, Caracas; tel. (212) 32-8603; fortnightly; entertainment guide; Editor MARYSABEL PAREDES; circ. 50,000.

La Semana: Apdo 60411, Chacao, Caracas 106; weekly; general interest; Dir TIBOR KORODY; circ. 40,000.

Sic: Centro Gumilla, Avda Berrizbeitia 14, Apdo 29056, Caracas; monthly; Liberal Jesuit publication.

Tribuna Médica: Apdo 50164, Caracas; weekly; medicine; circ. 7,000.

Variedades: Edif. Bloque Dearmas, final Avda San Martín cruce con Avda La Paz, Caracas 1020; tel. (212) 572-0322; women's weekly; Dir GLORIA FUENTES; Editor ARMANDO DE ARMAS; circ. 58,230.

Venezuela Gráfica: Torre de la Prensa, Plaza del Panteón, Apdo 2976, Caracas 101; tel. (212) 81-4931; f. 1951; weekly; illustrated news magazine, especially entertainment; Dir DIEGO FORTUNATO; Editor MIGUEL ANGEL CAPRILES; circ. 95,870.

Viernes: Urb. los Palos Grandes 4a Avda, Residencias Unión, Planta Baja, Local No 4, Caracas; weekly; independent; Editor MANUEL FELIPE SIERRA.

Zeta: Pinto a Santa Rosalía 44, Apdo 14067, La Candelaria, Caracas; f. 1974; weekly; politics and current affairs; Dir RAFAEL POLEO.

Zona Franca: Conda esq. Carmelitas, Caracas; monthly; literary.

Maracaibo

El Balancín: Cabimas, Maracaibo; weekly.

Maracaibo: Apdo 1308, Maracaibo; weekly.

PRESS ASSOCIATIONS

Asociación Venezolana de Periodistas: Edif. AVP, Avda Andrés Bello, Caracas; tel. (212) 782-1301.

Bloque de Prensa: Edif. El Universal, Avda Urdaneta, 5°, Caracas; tel. (212) 561-7704; fax (212) 561-9409; e-mail luichi@telcel.net; Pres. DAVID NATERA FEBRES.

Colegio Nacional de Periodistas: Casa del Periodista, Avda Andrés Bello, Caracas; tel. (212) 782-1301; Pres. GILBERTO ALCALÁ; Sec.-Gen. RUBÉN CHAPARRO.

PRESS AGENCIES

Agence France-Presse (AFP): Edif. Plaza, Of. 8–1, Avda Urdaneta, esq. La Pelota, Apdo 6254, Caracas 1010; tel. (212) 563-7212; Bureau Chief EDOUARD PONS.

Agencia EFE (Spain): Calle San Cristóbal, Quinta Altas Cumbres, Urb. Las Palmas, Caracas 1050; tel. (212) 793-7618; fax (212) 793-4920; e-mail efeven@infoline.wtfe.com; Bureau Chief FRANCISCO R. FIGUEROA.

Agenzia Nazionale Stampa Associata (ANSA) (Italy): Centro Financiero Latino, 10°, Of. 8, Animas a Plaza España, Avda Urdaneta, Caracas; tel. (212) 564-2059; fax (212) 564-2516; Correspondent KATTY SALERNO.

Associated Press (AP) (USA): Edif. El Nacional, Apto 46, Puerto Escondido a Puente Nuevo, Apdo 1015, Caracas; tel. (212) 42-7223; Chief HAROLD OLMOS.

Deutsche Presse-Agentur (dpa) (Germany): Edif. Caroata, Of. 106, Parque Central, Apdo 17018, Caracas 1080-A; tel. (212) 575-1235; fax (212) 573-6331; Correspondent ESTEBAN ENGEL.

Informatsionnoye Telegrafnoye Agentstvo Rossii—Telegrafnoye Agentstvo Suverennykh Stran (ITAR—TASS) (Russia): Edif. Fondo Común, Torre Norte, 9°, Avda Urdaneta, Caracas; Chief YEVGENIY ALEKSEYEV.

Inter Press Service (IPS) (Italy): Edif. La Línea, Of. 154-B, Avda La Libertador, Caracas 1060; tel. (212) 782-3753; fax (212) 782-0991; Correspondent ESTRELLA GUTIÉRREZ.

Prensa Latina (Cuba): Edif. Fondo Común, Torre Sur, 20°, Avda de las Fuerzas Armadas y Urdaneta, Apdo 4400, Carmelitas, Caracas; tel. (212) 561-9733; fax (212) 561-8489; Correspondent JORGE LUIS LUNA MENDOZA.

Reuters (United Kingdom): Jesuitas a Tienda Honda, Edif. Seguros Avila, 2°, Apdo 5794, Carmelitas 1010-A, Caracas; tel. (212) 83-5033; fax (212) 83-8977; Man. ANTONIO PISTOYA.

Rossiiskoye Informatsionnoye Agentstvo—Novosti (RIA—Novosti) (Russia): Edif. Magdalena, 4°, San Francisco a Sociedad, 48, Caracas; Bureau Chief AUGUSTO FIGUEROA.

United Press International (UPI) (USA): Centro Financiero Latino, 9°, Of. 5, Avda Urdaneta, Apdo 667, Caracas; tel. (212) 561-6548; Bureau Man. LUIS AZUAJE.

Xinhua (New China) News Agency (People's Republic of China): Final Calle Maracaibo, Prados del Este, Apdo 80564, Caracas; tel. (212) 40966; Bureau Chief XU YAOMING.

Publishers

Alfadil Ediciones: Edif. Alfa, Calle Los Mangos, Las Delicias de Sabana Grande, Apdo 50304, Caracas 1050-A; tel. (212) 762-3036; fax (212) 762-0210; f. 1980; general; Pres. LEONARDO MILLA A.

Armitano Editores, CA: Edif. Centro Industrial Boleíta, 4a Transversal de Boleíta, Sabana Grande, Apdo 50853, Caracas 1070; tel. (212) 234-2565; fax (212) 234-1647; e-mail armiedit@cantv.net; internet www.armitano.com; art, architecture, ecology, anthropology; Dir ERNESTO ARMITANO.

Bienes Lacónica, CA: Avda Orinoco, Quinta Praga, Las Mercedes, Apdo 69732, Caracas 1063-A; tel. (212) 752-2111; fax (212) 751-8363; f. 1977; philosophy; Gen. Man. DIEGO GIL VELUTINI.

Colegial Bolivariana, CA: Edif. COBO, 1°, Avda Diego Cisneros (Principal), Los Ruices, Apdo 70324, Caracas 1071-A; tel. (212) 239-1433; f. 1961; Dir ANTONIO JUZGADO ARIAS.

Editorial El Ateneo, CA: Complejo Cultural, Plaza Morelos, Los Caobos, Apdo 662, Caracas; tel. (212) 573-4622; f. 1931; school-books and reference; Pres. MARÍA TERESA CASTILLO; Dir ANTONIO POLO.

Ediciones Ekaré: Edif. Banco del Libro, Final Avda Luis Roche, Altamira Sur, Apdo 68284, Caracas 1062; tel. (212) 263-0091; fax (212) 263-3291; f. 1978; children's literature; Pres. CARMEN DIANA DEARDEN; Exec. Dir ELENA IRIBARREN.

Editora Ferga, CA: Torre Bazar Bolívar, 5°, Of. 501, Avda Francisco de Miranda, El Marqués, Apdo 16044, Caracas 1011-A; tel. (212) 239-1564; fax (212) 234-1008; e-mail ddex1@ibm.net; internet www.ddex.com; f. 1971; Venezuelan Exporters' Directory; Dir NELSON SÁNCHEZ MARTÍNEZ.

Fondo Editorial Común: Edif. Royal Palace, Of. 401, Avda El Bosque, Chacaíto, Apdo 50992, Caracas 1050; tel. (212) 72-3714; Pres. ALBA ILLARAMENDI; Dir PETER NEUMANN.

Fundación Biblioteca Ayacucho: Centro Financiero Latino, 12°, Of. 1, 2 y 3, Avda Urdaneta, Animas a Plaza España, Apdo 14413, Caracas 1010; tel. (212) 561-6691; fax (212) 564-5643; e-mail biblioayacucho@telcel.net.ve; f. 1974; literature; Pres. ALFREDO CHACON.

Fundarte: Edif. Tajamar, P. H., Avda Lecuna, Parque Central, Apdo 17559, Caracas 1015-A; tel. (212) 573-1719; fax (212) 574-2794; f. 1975; literature, history; Pres. ALFREDO GOSEN; Dir ROBERTO LOVERA DE SOLA.

Editorial González Porto: Sociedad a Traposos 8, Avda Universidad, Apdo 502, Caracas; Pres. Dr PABLO PERALES.

Ediciones IESA: Edif. IESA, 3°, Final Avda IESA, San Bernardino, Apdo 1640, Caracas 1010-A; tel. (212) 52-1533; fax (212) 52-4247; f. 1984; economics, business; Pres. RAMÓN PIÑANGO.

Editorial Cincel Kapelusz Venezolana, SA: Avda Cajigal, Quinta K No 29, entre Avdas Panteón y Roraima, San Bernardino, Apdo 14234, Caracas 1011-A; tel. (212) 51-7601; fax (212) 52-6281; f. 1963; school-books; Pres. DANTE TONI; Man. MAYELA MORGADO.

Ediciones La Casa Bello: Mercedes a Luneta, Apdo 134, Caracas 1010; tel. (212) 562-7100; f. 1973; literature, history; Pres. OSCAR SAMBRANO URDANETA.

Ediciones María Di Mase: 1a Avda Altamira Sur 233, Caracas 1062; tel. (212) 31-5167; f. 1979; children's books; Pres. MARÍA DI MASE; Gen. Man. ANA RODRÍGUEZ.

Monte Avila Editores Latinoamericana, CA: Avda Principal La Castellana, Quinta Cristina, Apdo 70712, Caracas 1070; tel. (212) 265-6020; fax (212) 263-8783; e-mail maelca@telcel.net.ve; f. 1968; general; Pres. MARIELA SANCHEZ URDANETA.

Ediciones Panamericanas EP, SRL: Edif. Freites, 2°, Avda Libertador cruce con Santiago de Chile, Apdo 14054, Caracas; tel. (212) 782-9891; Man. JAIME SALGADO PALACIO.

Editorial Salesiana, SA: Paradero a Salesianos 6, Apdo 369, Caracas; tel. (212) 571-6109; fax (212) 574-9451; e-mail e.salesiana@unete.com.ve; internet www.salesiana.com.ve; f. 1960; education; Man. P. CLARENCIO GARCÍA S.

Nueva Sociedad: Edif. IASA, 6°, Of. 606, Plaza La Castellana, Apdo 61712, Chacao, Caracas 1060-A; tel. (212) 265-0593; fax (212) 267-3397; e-mail nuso@nuevasoc.org.ve; f. 1972; social sciences; Dir DIETMAR DIRMOSER.

Oscar Todtmann Editores: Avda Libertador, Centro Comercial El Bosque, Local 4, Caracas 1050; tel. (212) 763-0881; fax (212) 762-5244; science, literature, photography; Dir CARSTEN TODTMANN.

Vadell Hermanos Editores, CA: Edif. Tacarigua, 6°, Calle Montes de Oca, Valencia; tel. (41) 58-4510; fax (41) 57-4152; f. 1973; science, social science; Gen. Man. MANUEL VADELL GRATEROL.

Ediciones Vega S.R.L.: Edif. Odeon, Plaza Las Tres Gracias, Los Chaguaramos, Apdo 51662, Caracas 1050-A; tel. (212) 662-2092; fax (212) 662-1397; f. 1965; educational; Man. Dir FERNANDO VEGA ALONSO.

ASSOCIATION

Cámara Venezolana del Libro: Centro Andrés Bello, Torre Oeste, 11°, Of. 112-0, Avda Andrés Bello, Apdo 51858, Caracas 1050-A; tel. (212) 793-1347; fax (212) 793-1368; f. 1969; Pres. HANS SCHNELL; Sec. ISIDORO DUARTE.

Broadcasting and Communications

TELECOMMUNICATIONS

Comisión Nacional de Telecomunicaciones (CONATEL): Ministerio de Transportes y Comunicaciones, Torre Este, 35°, Parque Central, Caracas; tel. (212) 993-5389; fax (212) 92-6033; regulatory body for telecommunications; Dir JESSE CHACON.

Compañía Anónima Nacional Teléfonos de Venezuela (CANTV): Edif. NEA, 20, Avda Libertador, Caracas 1010-A; tel. (212) 500-3016; fax (212) 500-3512; e-mail amora@cantv.com.ve; Pres. GUSTAVO ROOSEN; Gen. Man. EDUARDO MENASCÉ.

Regulatory Authorities

Cámara Venezolana de la Industria de Radiodifusión: Avda Antonio José Istúriz entre Mohedano y Country Club, La Castellana, Apdo 3955, Caracas; tel. (212) 263-2228; fax (212) 261-4783; internet www.camradio.org; Pres. MIGUEL ANGEL MARTÍNEZ.

Cámara Venezolana de la Televisión: Edif. Torre La Previsora, 7°, cruce Avda Abraham Lincoln con Las Acacias, Sabana Grande, Apdo 60423, Chacao, Caracas; tel. (212) 781-4608; regulatory body for private stations; Pres. Dr HÉCTOR PONSDOMENECH.

BROADCASTING
Radio

Radio Nacional de Venezuela: Final Calle las Marias, El Pedregal del Chapelín, POB 3979, Caracas 1050; tel. (212) 73-6022; fax (212) 731-1457; e-mail RNV2000@hotmail.com; f. 1936; state broadcasting organization; 15 stations; Dir-Gen. TERESA MANIGLIA.

There are also 20 cultural and some 500 commercial stations.

Television
Government Stations

Televisora Nacional: Apdo 3979, Caracas 1010; tel. (212) 239-9811; Dir-Gen. RICARDO TIRADO.

Venezolana de Televisión—Canal 5 y 8: Avda Montecristo, Los Ruices, Apdo 2739, Caracas; tel. (212) 239-0014; fax (212) 239-2675; 26 relay stations; Pres. Ing. FERNANDO MIRALLES.

Private Stations

Canal 10: Centro Empresarial Miranda, Avda Francisco de Miranda con Principal de los Ruices, Caracas; tel. (212) 239-8679; fax (212) 239-7757.

Canal 12—Omnivisión: Edif. Omnivisión, Calle Milan, Los Ruices Sur, Caracas; tel. (212) 256-3586; fax (212) 256-4482.

Radio Caracas Televisión (RCTV): Apdo 2057, Caracas; tel. (212) 256-3696; fax (212) 256-1812; f. 1953; commercial station; station in Caracas and 13 relay stations throughout the country; Pres. ELADIO LÁREZ; Gen. Man. CARLOS ABREU.

NCTV: Avdas 57 y Maracaibo, La Paz, Maracaibo; tel. (261) 51-2662; fax (261) 51-2729; commercial station; controls Channel 11; Dir GUSTAVO OCANDO YAMARTE.

Televisora Andina de Mérida—TAM: Avda Bolívar, Calle 23, entre Avdas 4 y 5, Mérida 5101; tel. (274) 52-5785; fax (274) 52-0098; f. 1982; controls Channel 6; Dir HUGO ANZIL Z.

Venevisión—Channel 4: Avda La Salle, Colina de los Caobos, Caracas 1050; tel. (212) 782-4444; fax (212) 781-1635; internet www.venevision.com; f. 1961; commercial; 19 relay stations; Gen. Man. M. FRAIZ-GRIJALBA.

Finance

(cap. = capital; res = reserves; dep. = deposits;
m. = million;brs = branches; amounts in bolívares unless
otherwise indicated)

BANKING

Central Bank

Banco Central de Venezuela: Avda Urdaneta esq. de las Carmelitas, Caracas 1010; tel. (212) 801-5111; fax (212) 861-0048; e-
mailmbatista@bcv.org.ve; internet www.bcv.org.ve; f. 1940; bank of
issue and clearing house for commercial banks; granted autonomy
1992; controls international reserves, interest rates and exchange
rates; cap. 10.0m., res 3,969,340.0m., dep. 4,465,022.0m. (Dec. 1998);
Chair. DIEGO LUIS CASTELLANOS ESCALONA.

Commercial Banks

Caracas

Banco del Caribe, SACA: Edif. Banco del Caribe, Dr Paúl a esq.
Salvador de León, Apdo 6704, Carmelitas, Caracas 1010; tel. (212)
505-5511; fax (212) 562-0460; e-mail producto@bancaribe.com.ve;
internet www.bancaribe.com.ve; f. 1954; cap. 8,000.0m., res
27,497.6m., dep. 340,879.6m. (Dec. 1997); Pres. EDGAR A. DAO; Vice-
Pres. and Gen. Man. Dr LUIS E. DE LLANO M.; 70 brs and agencies.

Banco de Comercio Exterior: Caracas; f. 1997 principally to
promote non-traditional exports; state-owned; cap. US $200m.

Banco de los Trabajadores de Venezuela (BTV) CA: Avda
Universidad, esq. Colón a esq. Dr Díaz, Apdo 888, Caracas; tel. (212)
541-7322; f. 1968 to channel workers' savings for the financing of
artisans and small industrial firms; came under state control in
1982; cap. and res 167.9m., dep. 8,419.9m. (Dec. 1985); Pres. JOSÉ
SÁNCHEZ PIÑA; Man. SILVERIO ANTONIO NARVÁEZ; 11 agencies.

Banco Exterior, CA, Banco Universal: Edif. Banco Exterior,
Avda Urdaneta, Urapal a Río, Apdo 14278, Caracas 1010; tel. (212)
501-0111; fax (212) 501-0612; e-mail presidenica@
bancoexterior.com; internet www.bancoexterior.com; f. 1958; cap.
45,360m., res 12,173m., dep. 356,564m. (Dec. 2000); Pres. SERGIO
SANNIA ANDREOZZI; Gen. Man. EMILIO DURAN CEBALLOS; 72 brs.

Banco Industrial de Venezuela, CA: Torre Financiera, Av Las
Delicias de Sabana Grande, Caracas 1010; tel. (212) 952-4051; fax
(212) 952-6282; e-mail webmaster@biv.com.ve; internet www.biv
.com.ve; f. 1937; state-owned; cap. 1.9m., res 110.8m., dep. 270.9m.
(Dec. 1996); Pres. BERNARDO MARTÍNEZ A.; Exec. Vice-Pres. LUIS
DELGADO; 60 brs.

Banco Internacional, CA: Edif. Banco Internacional, esq. de
Animas, Avda Urdaneta, Carmelitas, Apdo 6688, Caracas 101; tel.
(212) 506-2111; f. 1971 to take over brs. of Royal Bank of Canada,
as Banco Royal Venezolano, CA; cap. 129.3m., res 422.9m. (Dec.
1986); Pres. JOSÉ LUIS RAVENGA; Exec. Dir JAIME SILVEIRA; 9 brs.

Banco Latino, SACA: Centro Financiero Latino, Mezzanina, Avda
Urdaneta, de Animas a Plaza España, Apdo 2026, Caracas 1010-A;
tel. (212) 562-7555; fax (212) 502-5093; f. 1950; cap. 20,000m., dep.
205,194.6m. (Dec. 1995); placed under government control following
collapse in January 1994, 54% privatized in mid-1996, privatization
of remaining 46% pending; 106 brs.

Banco Mercantil, CA: Edif. Torre Mercantil, 35°, Avda Andrés
Bello 1, San Bernardino, Apdo 789, Caracas 1010-A; tel. (212) 503-
1112; fax (212) 575-1461; e-mail mercan24@bancomercantil.com;
internet www.bancomercantil.com; f. 1925; cap. 81,812.0m., res
43,821.0m., dep. 1,689,825.0m. (Dec. 1999); Chair. and CEO Dr
GUSTAVO A. MARTURET; Exec. Vice-Pres. ALFREDO RODRÍGUEZ G.; 126
brs.

Banco Metropolitano, CA: Edif. Banco Hipotecario de Crédito
Urbano, Piso 10, Avda Universidad esq. Traposos, Apdo 881, Caracas
1010-A; tel. (212) 545-6022; fax (212) 545-9574; f. 1953; cap. 118.9m.,
res 66.0m., dep. 3,379m. (Dec. 1986); Pres. J. DAVID BRILLEMBOURG;
Vice-Pres. UMBERTO PETRICCA.

Banco Provincial, SA, Banco Universal: Centro Financiero Provincial, Avda Vollmer con Avda Este O., San Bernadino, Apdo 1269,
Caracas 1011; tel. (212) 574-6611; fax (212) 574-9408; f. 1952; cap.
71,000.0m., res 155,608.2m., dep. 1,797,174.8m. (Dec. 1998); 40%
share purchased by Banco Bilbao Vizcaya (Spain) in 1997; acquired
Banco Popular, CA in Nov. 1999; Pres. JUAN CARLOS ZORRILLA HIERRO.

Banco República, CA: Edif. EDSAM, Madrices a San Jacinto No.
6, Caracas 1010-A; tel. (212) 564-8265; fax (212) 563-4090; f. 1958;
cap. 4,243m., res 482m., dep. 78,718m. (Dec. 1996); placed under
government control in 1994, scheduled for reprivatization; Pres.
OLGA FERRER DE HERNÁNDEZ; Exec. Vice-Pres. CAROLINA ALBANELL;
39 brs.

Banco Standard Chartered: Edif. Banaven, Torre D, 5°, Avda la
Estancia A, Chuao, Caracas 1060; tel. (212) 951-0149; fax (212) 951-

3397; f. 1980 as Banco Exterior de los Andes y de España, current
name adopted in 1998 following acquisition by Standard Chartered
Bank (UK); cap. US $94m., res $38.9m., dep. $943.5m. (Dec. 1996);
Chair. DAVID LORETTA; CEO FRANK D. ROBLETON.

Banco Unión, SACA: Torre Grupo Unión, Avda Universidad, esq.
El Chorro, Apdo 2044, Caracas; tel. (212) 501-7111; fax (212) 501-
7068; internet www.bancunion.com; f. 1943; 50% owned by Banco
Ganadero (Colombia); cap. 15,000.0m., res 39,239.5m., dep.
706,335.1m. (June 1998); Pres. Dr IGNACIO SALVATIERRA P.; Vice-Pres.
JOSÉ Q. SALVATIERRA; 174 brs.

Banco Venezolano de Crédito, SACA: Monjas a San Francisco,
Sur 2, No 7, Caracas 1010; tel. (212) 806-6111; fax (212) 541-2757;
e-mail jurbano@venezolano.com; internet www.venezolano.com; f.
1925; cap. 18,427.5m., res 50,643.9m., dep. 206,161.0m. (Dec. 1999);
Pres. Dr OSCAR GARCÍA MENDOZA; 57 brs.

**Banco de Venezuela, SACA, Banco Universal (Grupo San-
tander):** Torre Banco de Venezuela, Avda Universidad, esq. Sociedad a Traposos, Apdo 6268, Caracas 1010-A; tel. (212) 501-2556;
fax (212) 501-2546; internet www.bancodevenezuela.com; f. 1890;
cap. 5,000.0m., res 65,021.5m., dep. 491,274.8m. (Dec. 1996); frmly
Banco de Venezuela CA, placed under government control in 1994,
93.38% share purchased by Banco Santander (Spain) in Dec. 1996;
changed name to above in 1998; acquired Banco Caracas, CA in
Dec. 2000; Pres. JOSÉ IGNACIO RASERO; Exec. Dirs MICHEL GOGUIKIAN,
JOSÉ ANTONIO ELÓSEGUI; 202 brs and agencies.

Corp Banca, CA: Torre Corp Banca, Plaza la Castellana, Chacao,
Caracas 1060; tel. (212) 206-3333; fax (212) 206-1298; e-mail calidad
@corpbanca.com.ve; internet www.corpbanka.com.ve; f. 1969; fmrly
Banco Consolidado, current name adopted in 1997; cap. 16,633.3m.,
res 22,244.4m., dep. 560,177.0m. (Dec. 1999); Chair. RODRIGO ERRA-
ZURIZ; Exec. Pres. LAUTARO AGUILAR.

Barquisimeto, Lara

Banco de Lara: Edif. Torre Lara, Avda 20, entre Calles 27 y 28,
Apdo 545, Barquisimeto, Lara; tel. (251) 31-5211; fax (251) 31-6820;
f. 1953; cap. 4,000m., res 4,830m., dep. 87,887m. (Jan. 1996); Pres.
ARTURO GANTEAUME; Exec. Vice-Pres. CÉSAR ARISTIMUÑO; 44 agencies.

Banco Capital, CA: Carrera 17 Cruce con Calle 26, Frente a La
Plaza Bolívar, Barquisimeto, Lara; tel. (251) 31-4979; fax (251) 31-
1831; e-mail eximport@bancocapital.net; internet www
.bancocapital.net; f. 1980; cap. 1,500.0m., res 1,854.7m., dep.
60,428.3m. (Dec. 1997); Chair. and Pres. JOSÉ REINALDO FURIATI; Gen.
Man. VICENTE M. FURIATI; 13 brs.

Ciudad Guayana, Bolívar

Banco Guayana, CA: Edif. Banguayana, Prolongación Paseo Orinoco, Apdo 156, Ciudad Bolívar, Bolívar; tel. (285) 25511; f. 1955;
state-owned; cap. 80m., dep. 683.2m. (Feb. 1988); Pres. ANDRÉS E.
BELLO BILANCIERI; Gen. Man. OMAIRA UNCEIN DE NATERA.

Banco del Orinoco, SACA: Edif. Seguros Orinoco, Avda Cuchivero
con Calle Caruachí, Alta Vista, Apdo 143, Ciudad Guayana, Bolívar;
tel. (285) 61-2311; fax (285) 62-2645; f. 1980; cap. 4,800.0m., res
5,353.2m., dep. 121,862.7m. (Dec. 1997); Pres. ALFONSO TREDINIK
BRUSCO; Gen. Man. HUGO CHÁVEZ O.; 48 brs.

Coro, Falcón

Banco Federal, CA: Avda Manaure, cruce con Avda Ruiz Pineda,
Coro, Falcón; tel. (268) 51-4011; f. 1982; cap. 50m., dep. 357m. (Dec.
1986); Pres. BERNARDO PAUL; Vice-Pres. JOSÉ TOMÁS CANIELO BATALLA.

Banco de Fomento Regional Coro, CA: Avda Manaure, entre
Calles Falcón y Zamora, Coro, Falcón; tel. (268) 51-4421; f. 1950;
transferred to private ownership in 1994; cap. 20m., res 5m., dep.
353.2m. (Dec. 1985); Pres. ABRAHAM NAÍN SENIOR URBINA; Gen. Man.
DIMAS BUENO ARENAS.

Maracaibo, Zulia

Banco Occidental de Descuento, SACA: Avda 5 de Julio esq.
Avda 17, Apdo 695, Maracaibo 4001-A, Zulia; tel. (261) 59-3044; fax
(261) 59-4981; f. 1957; transferred to private ownership in 1991;
cap. 5,000.0m., res 8,743.4m., dep. 125,544.3m. (Dec. 1997); Pres.
VÍCTOR VARGAS I; Exec. Dir CÁNDIDO RODRÍGUEZ; 17 brs.

San Cristóbal, Táchira

Banco de Fomento Regional Los Andes, CA: Carrera 6, esq.
Calle 5, San Cristóbal, Táchira; tel. (276) 43-1269; f. 1951; cap. 20m.,
res 18.8m., dep. 796.2m. (Dec. 1985); Pres. EDGAR MORENO MÉNDEZ;
Exec. Vice-Pres. PEDRO ROA SÁNCHEZ.

Banco de Occidente, CA: Avda 7, entre Calles 9 y 10, Apdo 360,
San Cristóbal, Táchira; tel. (276) 43-7162; fax (276) 44-4337; f. 1944;
cap. 45m., res 55.8m., dep. 1,157.3m. (Dec. 1986); Pres. LUIS ALFREDO
JUGO RUEDA; Vice-Pres. EDGAR A. ESPEJO; 8 brs, 13 agencies.

Mortgage and Credit Institutions
Caracas

Banco Hipotecario de Crédito Urbano, CA: Edif. Banco Hipotecario de Crédito Urbano, Avda Universidad, esq. de Traposas, Caracas; tel. (212) 545-6666; f. 1958; cap. 100m., res 58.3m., dep. 268.8m. (Dec. 1986); Pres. CARLOS OBREGÓN V.

Banco Hipotecario de la Vivienda Popular, SA: Intersección Avda Roosevelt y Avda Los Ilustres, frente a la Plaza Los Símbolos, Caracas; tel. (212) 62-9971; f. 1961; cap. 100m., res 68.2m., dep. 259.3m. (Dec. 1987); Pres. HELY MALARET M.; First Vice-Pres. ALFREDO ESQUIVAR.

Banco Hipotecario Unido, SA: Edif. Banco Hipotecario Unido, Avda Este 2, No 201, Los Caobos, Apdo 1896, Caracas 1010; tel. (212) 575-1111; fax (212) 571-1075; f. 1961; cap. 230m., res 143m., dep. 8,075m. (May 1990); Pres. ARTURO J. BRILLEMBOURG; Gen. Man. ALFONSO ESPINOSA M.

Maracaibo, Zulia

Banco Hipotecario del Zulia, CA: Avda 2, El Milagro con Calle 84, Maracaibo, Zulia; tel. (261) 91-6055; f. 1963; cap. 120m., res 133.5m., dep. 671.5m. (Nov. 1986); Pres. ALBERTO LÓPEZ BRACHO.

Foreign Banks

ABN AMRO Bank NV (Netherlands): Edif. Centro Seguros Sud América, 1°, Avda Francisco de Miranda, El Rosal, Apdo 69179, Caracas 1060; tel. (212) 957-0300; fax (212) 953-5758.

Banco do Brasil SA (Brazil): Edif. Centro Lido, 5°, Avda Francisco de Miranda, El Rosal, Apdo 52023, Caracas; tel. (212) 952-2674; fax (212) 952-5251.

Citibank NA (USA): Edif. Citibank, esq. de Carmelitas a esq. de Altagracia, Apdo 1289, Caracas; tel. (212) 81-9501; fax (212) 81-6493; cap. 40m., res 203.8m., dep. 677.6m. (Dec. 1986); Pres. THOMAS J. CHARTERS; Vice-Pres. JOSÉ L. GARCÍA M.; 4 brs.

Banking Association

Asociación Bancaria de Venezuela: Torre Asociación Bancaria de Venezuela, Avda Venezuela, 1°, El Rosal, Caracas; tel. (212) 951-4711; fax (212) 951-3696; e-mail abvinfo@asobanca.com.ve; internet www.asobanca.com.ve; f. 1959; 79 mems; Pres. IGNACIO SALVATIERRA; Exec. Dir. LAURY DE CRACCO.

STOCK EXCHANGES

Bolsa de Valores de Caracas, CA: Edif. Atrium, 1°, Calle Sorocaima entre Avdas Tamanaco y Venezuela, Urbanización El Rosal, Apdo 62724-A, Caracas 1060; tel. (212) 905-5511; fax (212) 952-2640; e-mail bvc@caracasstock.com; internet www.caracasstock.com; f. 1947; 65 mems; Pres. ALEJANDRO SALCEDO THIELEN.

Bolsa de Comercio del Estado Miranda: Caracas.

Bolsa de Comercio de Valencia: Valencia.

INSURANCE
Supervisory Board

Superintendencia de Seguros: Torre Metálica, 1°–4°, Avda Francisco de Miranda, cruce con Avda Loyola, Chacao, Caracas 1061; tel. (212) 263-1344; Superintendent Dr MORELIA CORREDOR OCHOA.

Principal Insurance Companies

All companies must have at least 80% Venezuelan participation in their capital. In 1984 there were 57 insurance companies in Venezuela; the following list comprises the most important companies on the basis of revenue from premiums.

Adriática, CA de Seguros: Edif. Adriática de Seguros, Avda Andrés Bello, Apdo 1928, Caracas; tel. (212) 571-6422; fax (212) 571-5546; e-mail adriatica@adriatica; internet www.adriatica.com.ve; f. 1952; cap. 27m.; Pres. JEAN MARIE MONTEIL; Gen. Man. FRANCIS DESMAZES.

Avila, CA de Seguros: Torre Fondo Común, Avda Urdaneta Candilito a Platanal, 8°–13°, Apdo 1007, Caracas 1010; tel. (212) 507-0111; fax (212) 507-0175; f. 1936; cap. 30m.; Pres. RAMÓN RODRÍGUEZ; Vice-Pres JUAN LUIS CASAÑAS.

Carabobo, CA de Seguros: Edif. Seguros Carabobo, Calle Rondón, cruce con Avda Díaz Moreno, Apdo 138, Valencia; tel. (241) 88601; e-mail walvarez@seguroscarabobo.com; f. 1955; cap. 75m.; Pres. PAUL FRAYNO; Gen. Man. WILLIAM ALVAREZ Y.

Latinoamericana de Seguros, CA: Centro Comercial Concresa, Avda Humboldt, Nivel TD, Prados del Este, Apdo 50148, Caracas 1080; tel. (212) 979-3511; f. 1974; cap. 25m.; Pres. JOAQUÍN SILVEIRA ORTIZ; Exec. Pres. Lic. LUIS XAVIER LUJAN.

Pan American, CA de Seguros: Edif. Panavén, 1° y 4°–9°, Avda San Juan Bosco, cruce con 3 transversal, Urb. Altamira, Apdo 6166,

---

Caracas; tel. (212) 261-9655; fax (212) 261-9655; f. 1966; cap. 55m.; Pres. VICTORIA GURIDI; Vice-Pres. VICTOR MEINTJES.

Seguros Caracas, CAV: Edif. Seguros Caracas, 1°, Marrón a Cují, Apdo 981, Caracas 1010; tel. (212) 561-6122; f. 1943; cap. 600m.; Pres. Dr MOISES BENACERRAF; Exec. Vice-Pres. Dr RICARDO ECHEVERRÍA.

Seguros Catatumbo, CA: Avda 4 (Bella Vista), No 77–55, Apdo 1083, Maracaibo; tel. (261) 921-733; fax (261) 925-556; e-mail info@catatumbo.com; f. 1957; cap. 700m.; Pres. ESTEBAN R. PINEDA B.; Dir-Gen. ATENÁGORAS VERGEL RIVERA.

Seguros La Metropolitana, SA: Centro Financiero Metropolitano, Avda Andrés Bello con Avda El Parque, San Bernardino, Apdo 2197, Caracas 1011; tel. (212) 575-0033; fax (212) 576-5884; f. 1949; cap. 38m.; Pres. Dr IMANOL VALDÉS CANTOLLA; Vice-Pres. JOSÉ DÍAZ DEVESA.

Seguros Nuevo Mundo, SA: Edif. Seguros Nuevo Mundo, Avda Luis Roche con 3 transversal, Altamira, Apdo 2062, Caracas; tel. (212) 263-0333; fax (212) 263-1435; e-mail nmundo01@true.net; f. 1856; cap. 100m.; Pres. RAFAEL PEÑA ALVAREZ; Exec. Vice-Pres. RAFAEL VALENTINO.

Seguros Orinoco, CA: Esq. de Socarrás, Avda Fuerzas Armadas, Edificio Seguros Orinoco, piso 7, Caracas 1010; tel. (212) 596-4371; fax (212) 596-4070; internet www.seguros-orinoco.com; f. 1957; cap. 300m.; Pres. PAUL REIMPELL; Exec. Pres. GREGORIO SCHARIFKER.

Seguros La Seguridad, CA: Calle 3A, Frente a La Torre Express, La Urbina Sur, Apdo 473, Caracas 1010; tel. (212) 204-8737; fax (212) 204-8390; e-mail reasas@la-seguridad.com; f. 1943; cap. 5,438.5m.; Pres. ALBERTO SOSA SCHLAGETER; Vice-Pres. RAFAEL CASAS GUTIÉRREZ.

Insurance Association

Cámara de Aseguradores de Venezuela: Torre Taeca, 2°, Avda Guaicaipuro, El Rosal, Apdo 3460, Caracas 1010; tel. (212) 952-4411; fax (212) 951-3268; e-mail cavrelpublicas3@eldish.net; internet www.camaraseg.org; f. 1942; 50 mems; Pres. JUAN BLANCO URIBE.

Trade and Industry

GOVERNMENT AGENCIES

Consejo de Economía Nacional: Caracas; economic planning advisory board.

Corporación de Mercadeo Agrícola (Corpomercadeo): Edif. Torre Industrial, Calle Vargas-Boleíta, Caracas; tel. (212) 35-8044; responsible for marketing agricultural products; Pres. Dr ALBERTO SILVA GUILLÉN.

Corporación Venezolana de Guayana (CVG): Avda La Estancia 10, 13°, Apdo 7000, Caracas; f. 1960 to organize development of Guayana area, particularly its iron ore and hydroelectric resources; Pres. Gen. FRANCISCO RANGEL.

Dirección General Sectorial de Hidrocarburos: Torre Oeste, 12°, Parque Central, Caracas 1010; tel. (212) 507-6201; division of Ministry of Energy and Mines responsible for determining and implementing national policy for the exploration and exploitation of petroleum reserves and for the marketing of petroleum and its products; Dir-Gen. MANUEL ALAYETO E.

Dirección General Sectorial de Minas y Geología: Torre Oeste, 4°, Parque Central, Caracas; tel. (212) 507-5401; fax (212) 575-2497; division of Ministry of Energy and Mines responsible for formulating and implementing national policy on non-petroleum mineral reserves; Dir MIGUEL H. CANO DE LOS RÍOS.

Instituto Agrario Nacional (IAN): Quinta Barrancas, La Quebradita, Caracas; f. 1945 under Agrarian Law to assure ownership of the land to those who worked on it; now authorized to expropriate and redistribute idle or unproductive lands; Pres. Dr ANTONIO JOSÉ ALVAREZ FERNÁNDEZ.

Instituto de Crédito Agrícola y Pecuario: 40–44 Salvador de León a Socarras, Caracas; formerly the Banco Agrícola y Pecuario; administers the government crop credit scheme for small farmers; Dir-Gen. Dr ANTONIO JOSÉ ALVAREZ FERNÁNDEZ.

Instituto Nacional de la Vivienda: Edif. Banco Obrero, esq. Cruz Verde, Caracas; f. 1975; administers government housing projects; Pres. Dr LEANDRO QUINTA.

Palmavén: Edif. Palmavén, Avda Tamanaco, El Rosal, Apdo 3505, Caracas 1010-A; tel. (212) 951-4144; fax (212) 905-1324; subsidiary of PDVSA; promotes agricultural development, provides agricultural and environmental services and technical assistance to farmers; Pres. ALFREDO GRÜBER; Man. Dir EDDIE RAMÍREZ.

Superintendencia de Inversiones Extranjeras (SIEX): Edif. La Perla, Bolsa a Mercaderes, 3°, Apdo 213, Caracas 1010; tel. (212) 483-6666; fax (212) 41-4368; f. 1974; supervises foreign investment in Venezuela; Supt. Dr ANSELMO CHUECOS PÉREZ.

DEVELOPMENT ORGANIZATIONS

Corporación de Desarrollo de la Pequeña y Mediana Industria (Corpoindustria): Avda Páez, esq. Avda Las Delicias, Maracay, Aragua; tel. (243) 23459; promotes the development of small and medium-sized industries; Pres. Dr CARLOS GONZÁLEZ-LÓPEZ.

CVG Bauxita Venezolana (Bauxivén): Caracas; **f.** 1978 to develop the bauxite deposits at Los Pijiguaos; financed by the FIV and the CVG which has a majority holding; Pres. JOSÉ TOMÁS MILANO.

CHAMBERS OF COMMERCE AND INDUSTRY

Federación Venezolana de Cámaras y Asociaciones de Comercio y Producción—FEDECAMARAS: Edif. FEDECAM-ARAS, 5°, Avda El Empalme, El Bosque, Apdo 2568, Caracas; tel. (212) 731-1711; fax (212) 745-040; e-mail direje@fedecameras.org; internet www.fedecamaras.org; f. 1944; 307 mems; Pres. VICENTE BRITO.

Cámara de Comercio de Caracas: Edif. Cámara de Comercio de Caracas, Avda Andrés Eloy Blanco 215, 8°, Los Caobos, Caracas; tel. (212) 571-3222; fax (212) 571-0050; e-mail comercio@ccc.com.ve; f. 1893; 650 mems; Pres. RAFAEL ALFONZO HERNÁNDEZ.

Cámara de Industriales de Caracas: Edif. Cámara de Industriales, 3°, Avda Las Industrias esq. Pte Anauco, La Candelaria, Apdo 14255, Caracas 1011; tel. (212) 571-4224; fax (212) 571-2009; e-mail ciccs@telcel.net; internet www.cic.org.ve; f. 1939; Pres. JOSÉ ANTONIO VEGAS CHUMACEIRO; Man. Dir MARISOL FUENTES NIÑO; 550 mems.

Cámara Venezolano-Americana de Industria y Comercio: Torre Credival, 10°, Of. A, 2a Avda Campo Alegre, Apdo 5181, Caracas 1010-A; tel. (212) 263-0833; fax (212) 32-0764; f. 1950; Pres. PEDRO PALMA.

There are chambers of commerce and industry in all major provincial centres.

EMPLOYERS' ORGANIZATIONS
Caracas

Asociación Nacional de Comerciantes e Industriales: Plaza Panteón Norte 1, Apdo 33, Caracas; f. 1936; traders and industrialists; Pres. Dr HORACIO GUILLERMO VILLALOBOS; Sec. R. H. OJEDA MAZZARELLI; 500 mems.

Asociación Nacional de Industriales Metalúrgicos y de Minería de Venezuela: Edif. Cámara de Industriales, 9°, Puente Anauco a Puente República, Apdo 14139, Caracas; metallurgy and mining; Pres. JOSÉ LUIS GÓMEZ; Exec. Dir LUIS CÓRDOVA BRITO.

Asociación Textil Venezolana: Edif. Karam, 5°, Of. 503, Avda Urdaneta, Ibarras a Pelota, Apdo 6469, Caracas; tel. (212) 561-6851; fax (212) 562-8197; f. 1957; textiles; Pres. JACK LEVI; Exec. Dir AGUILES ORTÍZ; 68 mems.

Asociación Venezolana de Exportadores: Centro Comercial Coneresa, Redoma de Prados del Este 435, 2°, Prados del Este, Caracas; tel. (212) 979-0824; fax (212) 979-4542; e-mail avex@telcel .net.ve; Pres. FRANCISCO MENDOZA.

Consejo Venezolano de la Industria—Conindustria: Centro Empresarial Los Ruices, Avda Diego Cisneros 302, 3°, Caracas; tel. (212) 991-2116; fax (212) 991-7737; e-mail coindustria@ coindustria.org; internet www.coindustria.org; association of industrialists; Pres. JUAN CALVO; Dir GERARDO LUCAS.

Confederación Nacional de Asociaciones de Productores Agropecuarios—Fedeagro: Edif. Casa de Italia, Planta Baja, Avda La Industria, San Bernardino, Caracas 1010; tel. (212) 571-4035; fax (212) 573-4423; f. 1960; agricultural producers; 133 affiliated associations; Pres. FERNANDO CAMINO PEÑALVER; Exec. Sec. IVÁN LÓPEZ GONZÁLEZ.

Consejo Venezolano de la Industria: Edif. Cámara de Industriales, esq. de Puente Anauco, Caracas; industry council; Pres. GUSTAVO PÉREZ MIJARES; Co-ordinator Ing. ISRAEL DÍAZ VALLES.

Federación Nacional de Ganaderos de Venezuela: Edif. Casa de Italia, 7°, Avda La Industria, San Bernardino, Caracas; cattle owners; Dir ELÍAS CASTRO CORREAS; Sec. MIGUEL A. GRANADOS.

Unión Patronal Venezolana del Comercio: Edif. General Urdaneta, 2°, Marrón a Pelota, Apdo 6578, Caracas; trade; Sec. H. ESPINOZA BANDERS.

Other Towns

Asociación de Comerciantes e Industriales del Zulia—ACIZ: Edif. Los Cerros, 3°, Calle 77 con Avda 3C, Apdo 91, Maracaibo, Zulia; tel. (261) 91-7174; fax (261) 91-2570; f. 1941; traders and industrialists; Pres. JORGE AVILA.

Asociación Nacional de Cultivadores de Algodón (National Cotton Growers' Association): Planta Desmotadora, Carretera Guanare, Zona Industrial Acarigua; Sec. LEOPOLD BAPTISTA.

Asociación Nacional de Empresarios y Trabajadores de la Pesca: Apdo 52, Cumaná; fishermen.

Unión Nacional de Cultivadores de Tabaco: Urb. Industrial La Hamaca, Avda Hustaf Dalen, Apdo 252, Maracay; tobacco growers.

STATE HYDROCARBONS COMPANIES

Petróleos de Venezuela, SA (PDVSA): Edif. Petróleos de Venezuela, Torre Este, Avda Libertador, La Campiña, Apdo 169, Caracas 1010-A; tel. (212) 708-4111; fax (212) 708-4661; e-mail webmaster @pdvsa.com; internet www.pdvsa.com; f. 1975; holding company for national petroleum industry; responsible for petrochemical sector since 1978 and for development of coal resources in western Venezuela since 1985; Pres. Gen. GUAICAIPURO LAMEDA. The following are subsidiaries of PDVSA:

Barivén, SA: Edif. Centro Empresarial Parque del Este, Avda Francisco de Miranda, La Carlota, Apdo 893, Caracas 1010-A; tel. (212) 201-4611; fax (212) 201-4729; handles the petroleum, petrochemical and hydrocarbons industries' overseas purchases of equipment and materials; Pres. ALFREDO VISO.

Bitúmenes Orinoco, SA (BITOR): Edif. Bitúmenes Orinoco, SA, Calle Cali, Las Mercedes, Apdo 3470, Caracas 1010-A; tel. (212) 907-5111; fax (212) 908-3982; plans, develops and markets the bitumen resources of the Orinoco belt; Pres. CARLOS BORREGALES.

Carbozulia, SA: Edif. Lagovén, Calle 77 (5 de Julio) con Avda 11, Apdo 1200, Maracaibo 4001; tel. (261) 96-1600; fax (261) 96-1690; f. 1978; responsible for the commercial exploitation of the Guasare coalfields in Zulia; Pres. ATILIO OSORIO; Gen. Man. WLADIMIRO KOWALCHUK.

Corpovén, SA: Edif. Petróleos de Venezuela, Avda Libertador, La Campiña, Apdo 61373, Caracas 1060-A; tel. (212) 708-1111; fax (212) 708-1833; e-mail apti@ccinet.corpoven.pdv.com; exploration, production, refining and marketing of crude petroleum products, and gas distribution; merged with Menevén in 1986; Pres. GUILLERMO ARCHILA; Vice-Pres. RONALD PANTIN.

Intervén, SA: Edif. Centro Empresarial Parque del Este, Avda Francisco de Miranda, La Carlota, Apdo 60564, Caracas 1060-A; tel. (212) 203-1300; fax (212) 203-1300; f. 1986 to manage PDVSA's joint ventures overseas; Pres. REMIGIO FERNÁNDEZ; Vice-Pres. ARNOLDO VOLKENBORN.

INTEVEP, SA: Edif. Sede Central-Santa Rosa, Los Teques, Apdo 76343, Caracas 1010-A; tel. (212) 908-6111; fax (212) 908-6447; f. 1979; research and development branch of PDVSA; undertakes applied research and development in new products and processes and provides specialized technical services for the petroleum and petrochemical industries; Pres. GUSTAVO INCIARTE; Vice-Pres. NÉSTOR BARROETA.

Lagovén, SA: Edif. Lagovén, Avda Leonardo da Vinci, Los Chaguaramos, Apdo 889, Caracas; tel. (212) 661-1011; fax (212) 606-3637; f. 1978; state petroleum company; Pres. JULIUS TRINKUNAS; Vice-Pres. VICENTE LLATAS.

Maravén, SA: Edif. Maravén, Avda La Estancia 10, Chuao, Apdo 829, Caracas 1010-A; tel. (212) 908-2111; fax (212) 908-2885; f. 1976; state petroleum company; petroleum exploration, production, transport, refining and both domestic and international marketing; Pres. EMILIO ABOUHAMAD; Vice-Pres. GUSTAVO GABALDÓN.

Petroquímica de Venezuela, SA (Pequivén): Torre Pequivén, Avda Francisco de Miranda, Cruce Avda Mis Encantos, Chacao, Caracas; tel. (212) 201-3111; fax (212) 201-3306; f. 1956 as Instituto Venezolano de Petroquímica; became Pequivén in 1977; involved in many joint ventures with foreign and private Venezuelan interests for expanding petrochemical industry; active in regional economic integration; an affiliate of PDVSA from 1978; Pres. ARNOLD VOLKENBORN; Vice-Pres. ANTONIO ORTIZ.

Refinería Isla (Curazao), SA: POB 3843, Curaçao, Netherlands Antilles; tel. 466-2700; fax 466-2488; e-mail ndepaula@ refineriaisla.com; internet www.isla.pdv.com; f. 1985; operates a 320,000 b/d refinery and a deep-water terminal on Curaçao (Netherlands Antilles), formerly owned by the Royal Dutch-Shell group.

MAJOR COMPANIES

The following is a selection of major industrial and commercial enterprises, in terms of sales and employment, operating in Venezuela:

Metals and Mining

Aluminio del Caroní, SA (ALUCASA): Carretera Nacional Guacara, Urb. Industrial Caribe, San Joaquín, Guacara; tel. (245) 642-066; fax (245) 643-819; e-mail aluventasi@cantv.net; manufacturers of aluminium products; Pres. RAFAEL RODRÍGUEZ; 1,700 employees.

Conduven, CA: Edif. Torre Financiera, 9°, Avda Beethoven, Urb. Colinas de Bello Monte, Caracas; tel. (212) 752-4111; fax (212) 751-1542; f. 1959; manufacturers of welded pipe for use in petroleum industry, fluid conduction, electrical installations; Pres. DEZIDER WEISZ W.; 1,200 employees.

CVG Ferrominera Orinoco, CA: Vía Caracas, Edif. Administrativo I, Puerto Ordaz, Bolívar; tel. (286) 30-3336; fax (286) 22-8772;

internet www.ferrominera.com; f. 1975; subsidiary of the state-owned Corporación Venezolana de Guayana (see section on Trade and Industry—Government Agencies); iron ore mining; Pres. ROY RODRÍGUEZ; 4,100 employees.

CVG Siderúrgica del Orinoco, CA (SIDOR): Edif. General de Seguros, Avda La Estancia, Chuao, Caracas; tel. (212) 208-0860; fax (212) 993-9906; internet www.sidor.com.ve; f. 1964; formerly state-owned, privatized in 1997; steel processing; Pres. DANIEL NOVEGIL; 11,406 employees.

Siderúrgica del Turbio, SA (SIDETUR): Torre América, 14°, Avda Venezuela, Urb. Bello Monte, Caracas; tel. (212) 707-6200; fax (212) 707-6426; f. 1972; e-mail ventas@sidetur.sivensa.com; internet www.sidetur.com.ve; manufacturers of steel products including galvanized wire and steel rods; Pres. HENRIQUE MACHADO; 600 employees.

Siderúrgica Venezolana SACA (SIVENSA): Edif. Torre América, 12°, Avda Venezuela, Bello Monte, Caracas 1060; tel. (212) 708-6200; fax (212) 708-6426; www.sivensa.com; f. 1948; manufacturers of briquetted iron, steel products, wire and wire products; Chair. HENRIQUE MACHADO ZULOAGA; 10,190 employees.

Unión Industrial Venezolana, SA (UNIVENSA): Carrera 3, No 30–30 Zona Industrial Comdibar 1, Barquisimeto, Lara; tel. (251) 454-033; fax (251) 451-860; f. 1965; manufacturers of stainless steel tubing; Pres. MIGUEL GONZÁLEZ; 400 employees.

Rubber and Tobacco

Cigarrera Bigott Sucs, SA: Edif. Cigarrera Bigott, Avda Francisco de Miranda, Los Ruices, Caracas 1060; tel. (212) 203-7511; fax (212) 238-3476; f. 1968; subsidiary of Middleton Investment Co Ltd, UK; tobacco products; Pres. JOHN FULWELL; 1,000 employees.

Firestone Venezolana, CA: Carrera Valencia-Los Guayos, cruce con San Diego, Zona Industrial, Valencia, Carabobo; tel. (241) 306-011; fax (241) 332-656; subsidiary of Firestone Tire and Rubber Co (USA); rubber tyre producers; Pres. ROSENDO TORRADAS; 1,111 employees.

Tabacalera Nacional, CA: Edif. Seguros Venezuela, 2°, 3° y 4°, Avda Francisco de Miranda, Campo Alegre, Caracas 1060; tel. (212) 901-7700; fax (212) 901-7708; f. 1953; subsidiary of Phillip Morris Int. (USA); cigarette manufacturers; Pres. JOSÉ ANTONIO CORDIBO-FREYTÉS; 1,200 employees.

Food and Drink

Embotelladora Nacional, CA: Avda 66, No 255–69, Maracaibo, Zulia; tel. (261) 345-198; fax (261) 347-179; f. 1952; manufacturers of canned and bottled soft drinks; 776 employees.

Envases Venezolanas, CA: Edif. Torre Multinvest, 6°, Plaza La Castellana, Caracas 1060; tel. (212) 263-0511; fax (212) 267-6224; f. 1952; manufacturers of tin cans and metal packaging containers; Pres. FRANCISCO L. PAZ PARRA; 500 employees.

Industria Lactea Venezolana, CA (INDULAC): Apdo 1546, Caracas 1010-A; tel. (212) 257-1422; fax (212) 257-7195; f. 1966; manufacturers and distributors of dairy products; Pres. HELI RAMON HERNÁNDEZ; 2,198 employees.

Mavesa, SA: Edif. Mavesa, Avda Principal, Urb. Industrial Los Cortijos Lourdes, Caracas 1071; tel. (212) 238-1633; fax (212) 239-2503; internet www.mavesa.com.ve; f. 1949; manufacturers and distributors of consumer processed food and cleaning products; CEO ALBERTO TOVAR PHELPS; 2,827 employees.

Textiles

Rori Internacional, SA: Edif. Rori, Avda Principal Los Cortijos de Lourdes, 4ta Transversal, Caracas; tel. (212) 239-3533; fax (212) 239-3480; f. 1964; manufacturers of men's clothing; 1,200 employees.

Sudamtex de Venezuela, CA: Edif. Karam, 1° y 2°, Ibarras a Pelota, Avda Urdaneta, Caracas 1010; tel (212) 562-9222; fax (212) 562-3275; internet www.sudamtex.com; f. 1946; textile manufacturers; Pres. ALEXANDER FURTH; 2,210 employees.

Telares Los Andes, SA: Cuji a Punceres 7, Caracas 1010; tel. (212) 574-9522; fax (212) 576-2025; e-mail info@telareslosandes.com; internet www.telareslosandes.com; f. 1944; manufacturers of synthetic fabrics; Pres. JAMES VICTOR LEVY; 1,800 employees.

Chemicals

Clariant (Venezuela), SA: Edif. Torre Humboldt, Nivel TE, Of. NP 9, Avda Río Caura, Prados del Este, Caracas; tel. (212) 907-3111; fax (212) 903-3127; internet www.clariant.com; f. 1952; formerly Hoechst de Venezuela; subsidiary of Clariant Int. of Switzerland since 1997; manufacturers and distributors of chemicals, textiles, leather, paper, paint, adhesives, plastics; Gen. Man. STEVEN PILNIK; 207 employees.

Corimón, CA: Edif. Corimón, Los Cortijos de Lourdes, Calle Hans Neumann, Caracas; tel. (212) 203-5555; fax (212) 239-0002; f. 1949;

holding co. for subsidiaries producing paint, packaging and processed food; Pres. and CEO PHILIPPE ERARD; 2,655 employees.

Du Pont de Venezuela, SA: Avda Eugencio Mendoza, Zona Industrial Carabobo, Valencia; tel. (241) 407-200; fax (241) 333-425; f. 1956; manufacturers of industrial chemicals, plastics, pesticides, resins and films; Pres. JOSÉ DE ALEUCAR; 260 employees.

Pfizer, SA: Multicentro Empres del Este, Torre Libertador 1°, Avda Libertador, Caracas 1060; tel. (212) 263-3322; fax (212) 261-4566; f. 1953; subsidiary of Pfizer Inc. (USA); manufacturers of pharmaceutical products; Pres. JOSÉ CLAVIER; 250 employees.

Plastiflex, CA: Torre Phelps, 4°, Avda La Salle, Plaza Venezuela, Caracas 1050; tel. (212) 793-3133; fax (212) 793-3636; f. 1958; manufacturers of plastic sheeting and film; Man. JONA MISHAAN; 415 employees.

Procter and Gamble de Venezuela, SA: Edif. P&G, Sorokaima, Trinidad, Caracas 1080; tel. (212) 919-777; fax (212) 206-6364; subsidiary of Procter and Gamble Co (USA); manufacturers of soaps, detergents and pharmaceuticals; Pres. EMILIO E. GIRALT; 380 employees.

Electrical Equipment

Asea Brown Boveri, SA: Edif. ABB, Avda Diego Cisneros, Los Ruices, Caracas; tel. (212) 203-1920; fax (212) 237-9164; f. 1957; manufacturers of power transmission machinery and equipment; Pres. ROBERTO MUELLER; 300 employees.

General Electric de Venezuela, SA: Edif. Centro Banaven, Torre A 6°, Avda La Estancia, Caracas; tel. (212) 902-5100; fax (212) 902-5299; e-mail ana.nottaro@corporate.ge.com; internet www.ge.com/venezuela; f. 1927; subsidiary of General Electric Corpn (USA); manufacturers of television sets, radio receivers and household electrical appliances; Pres. MICHAEL NYLIN; 2,600 employees.

Miscellaneous

Cerámica Carabobo, SA: Edif. Cerámica Carabobo, Autopista del Este, Distribuidor Fábrica de Cementos, Apdo 74, Valencia; tel. (241) 256-166; fax (241) 253-855; e-mail infocc@ceramica-carabobo.com; internet www.ceramica-carabobo.com; f. 1956; manufacturers of ceramic floor and wall tiles; Pres. WILLIAM BOULTON; 1,600 employees.

Constructora Heerema, CA: Avda 28, No. 12A–95, Sector El Manzanillo, Maracaibo, Zulia; tel. (261) 613-144; fax (261) 613-008; f. 1950; civil engineering and construction, including services to petroleum and gas sectors; Pres. WILLEN DEN; 390 employees.

Ford Motors de Venezuela, SA: Avda Henry Ford Industrial Sur, Valencia, Carabobo 1041; tel. (241) 406-111 ; fax (241) 406-483; e-mail ifuentes@ford.com; internet www.ford.com.ve; subsidiary of Ford Motor Co (USA); assembly and production of motor vehicles, trucks and farm machinery; Pres. JOSÉ BISOGNO; 2,100 employees.

Nardi de Venezuela, CA: Zona Industrial Comdivar 1, Avda 3 con Calle 30, Barquisimeto, Lara; tel. (251) 454-460; fax (251) 454-942; e-mail nardivla@ven.net; f. 1971; manufacturers of agricultural subsoilers, skimmer scoops and trench diggers; 155 employees.

UTILITIES
Electricity

Electricidad de Caracas: Caracas; private utility supplying electricity to capital.

Electrificación del Caroní, CA (Edelca): state electricity co.; supplies some 70% of country's electricity.

Sistema Eléctrico de Nueva Esparta (Seneca): electricity co; privatized in October 1998.

Water

Compañía Anónima Hidrológica de la Región Capital (HIDROCAPITAL): Edif. Hidroven, Avda Augusto César Sandino con 9a Transversal, Maripérez, Caracas; tel. (212) 793-1638; fax (212) 793-6794; e-mail 73070.2174@compuserve.com; internet www.hidrocapital.com.ve; f. 1992; operates water supply in Federal District and Miranda State; Pres. JOSÉ MARÍA DE VIANA.

Instituto Nacional de Obras Sanitarias (INOS): Edif. La Paz, Caracas; autonomous government institution; administers water supply and sewerage projects; privatization plans announced in April 1990; Pres. Dr ALEXIS CARSTENS RAMOS.

TRADE UNIONS

About one-quarter of the labour force in Venezuela belongs to unions, more than one-half of which are legally recognized. In December 2000 a proposal to suspend trade-union leaders, in order to hold new elections, was approved in a referendum. The elections were scheduled for mid-2001.

Central General de Trabajadores (CGT): Communist-led.

Central Unida de Trabajadores.

Central Unitaria de Trabajadores de Venezuela (CUTV): Miseria a Velásquez, Caracas; leftist union affiliated to WFTU; 80,000 mems.

Confederación de Sindicatos Autónomos de Venezuela (CODESA): affiliated to COPEI; Pres. WILLIAM FRANCO CASALINS; Leader LAURIANO ORTIZ.

Confederación de Trabajadores de Venezuela (CTV) (Confederation of Venezuelan Workers): Edif. José Vargas, 17°, Avda Este 2, Los Caobos, Caracas; tel. (212) 575-1105; f. 1936; affiliated to Acción Democrática; Pres. FREDERICO RAMÍREZ LEON; Sec.-Gen. CÉSAR OLARTE; 1,500,000 mems from 24 regional and 16 industrial federations.

Fedenaca: peasant union.

Fedepetrol: union of petroleum workers; Pres. CARLOS ORTEGA.

Federación Campesina (FC): peasant union; CTV affiliate; Leader RUBÉN LANZ.

Fetrametal: union of metal workers; CTV affiliate; Leader JOSÉ MOLLEGAS.

Fuerza Bolivariana de Trabajadores (FBT): f. 2000; pro-government union.

Movimiento Nacional de Trabajadores para la Liberación (MONTRAL): Edif. Don Miguel, 6°, esq. Cipreses, Caracas; f. 1974; affiliated to CLAT and WFTU; Pres. LAUREANO ORTIZ BRAEAMONTE; Sec.-Gen. DAGOBERTO GONZÁLEZ; co-ordinating body for the following trade unions:

> **Central Nacional Campesina (CNC):** Pres. REINALDO VÁSQUEZ.

> **Cooperativa Nacional de Servicios Múltiples (CNTSM).**

> **Federación Nacional de Sindicatos Autónomos de Trabajadores de la Educación de Venezuela (FENASATREV):** Pres. LUIS EFRAÍN ORTA.

> **Federación de los Trabajadores de Hidrocarburos de Venezuela (FETRAHIDROCARBUROS).**

> **Frente de Trabajadores Copeyanos (FTC):** Sec.-Gen. DAGOBERTO GONZÁLEZ.

> **Movimiento Agrario Social-Cristiano (MASC):** Sec.-Gen. GUSTAVO MENDOZA.

> **Movimiento Magisterial Social-Cristiano (MMSC):** Sec.-Gen. FELIPE MONTILLA.

> **Movimiento Nacional de Trabajadores de Comunicaciones (MONTRAC).**

> **Movimiento Nacional de Trabajadores Estatales de Venezuela (MONTREV).**

Transport

RAILWAYS

In 1999 work began on lines linking Acarigua and Turén (45 km) and Morón and Riecito (100 km). Construction of the first section (Caracas–Cúa) of a line linking the capital to the existing network at Puerto Cabello (219 km in total) was also begun. Services on the underground system began in 1983 on a two-line system: east to west from Palos Verdes to Propatria; north to south from Capitolio/El Silencio to Zoológico. A southern extension from Plaza Venezuela to El Valle opened in 1995. Further extensions to the lines were under way in 1999.

CVG Ferrominera Orinoco, CA: Vía Caracas, Puerto Ordaz, Apdo 399, Bolívar; tel. (286) 30-3451; fax (286) 30-3333; e-mail 104721.2354@compuserve.com; f. 1976; state company; operates two lines San Isidro mine–Puerto Ordaz (316 km) and El Pao–Palua (55 km) for transporting iron ore; Pres. Ing. LEOPOLDO SUCRE FIGARELLA; Man. M. ARO G.

Ferrocarril de CVG Bauxilum—Operadora de Bauxita: Apdo 65038, Caracas 1065-A; tel. (212) 40-1716; fax (212) 40-1707; f. 1989; state company; operates line linking Los Pijiguaos with river Orinoco port of Gumilla (52 km) for transporting bauxite; Pres. P. MORALES.

Instituto Autónomo de Ferrocarriles del Estado (FERROCAR): Torre Este, 45° y 46°, Avda Lecuna, Parque Central, Caracas 1010; tel. (212) 309-3500; fax (212) 574-7021; e-mail planificacion@hotmail.com; state company; 336 km; Pres. JUAN CARLOS HIEDRA COBO; Vice-Pres. VITO MASTROGIACOMO PEPE.

CA Metro de Caracas: Multicentro Empresarial del Este, Edif. Miranda, Torre B, Avda Francisco de Miranda, Apdo 61036, Caracas; tel. (212) 206-7611; fax (212) 266-3346; f. 1976 to supervise the construction and use of the underground railway system; Pres. I. COMBELLAS LARES.

ROADS

In 1999 there were an estimated 96,155 km of roads, of which some 33.6% were asphalted.

Of the three great highways, the first (960 km) runs from Caracas to Ciudad Bolívar. The second, the Pan-American Highway (1,290 km), runs from Caracas to the Colombian frontier and is continued as far as Cúcuta. A branch runs from Valencia to Puerto Cabello. The third highway runs southwards from Coro to La Ceiba, on Lake Maracaibo.

A new 'marginal highway' was under construction along the western fringe of the Amazon Basin in Venezuela, Colombia, Ecuador, Peru, Bolivia and Paraguay. The Venezuelan section now runs for over 440 km and is fully paved.

INLAND WATERWAYS

Instituto Nacional de Canalizaciones: Edif. INC, Calle Caracas, Chuao, al lado de la Torre Diamen, Apdo E.61959, Caracas; f. 1952; semi-autonomous institution connected with the Ministry of Infrastructure; Pres. Rear-Adm. AGUEDO FELIPE HERNÁNDEZ; Vice-Pres. FERNANDO MARTÍ O.

Compañía Anónima La Translacustre: Maracaibo; freight and passenger service serving Lake Maracaibo, principally from Maracaibo to the road terminal from Caracas at Palmarejo.

SHIPPING

There are nine major ports, 34 petroleum and mineral ports and five fishing ports. The main port for imports is La Guaira, the port for Caracas; Puerto Cabello handles raw materials for the industrial region around Valencia. Maracaibo is the chief port for the petroleum industry. Puerto Ordaz, on the Orinoco River, was also developed to deal with the shipments of iron from Cerro Bolívar.

The Instituto Nacional de Puertos designed a programme aimed at satisfying port handling requirements up to 1995, to alleviate the long-standing problem of port congestion. A new port, Carenero, was to be built at an estimated cost of US \$139.5m., capable of handling 2m. tons of general freight and 300,000 tons of grain a year. Improvements and expansion of other ports, including five new docks at La Guaira, completed in 1979, significantly raised overall capacity.

Instituto Nacional de Puertos: Edif. Instituto Nacional de Puertos, Calle Veracruz, cruce con Cali, Las Mercedes, Caracas; tel. (212) 92-2811; f. 1976 as the sole port authority; Pres. Vice-Adm. FREDDY J. MOTA CARPIO.

Consolidada de Ferrys, CA: Torre Banhorient, 3°, Avda Las Acacias y Avda Casanova, Apdo 87, Sabana Grande, Caracas 1010-A; tel. (212) 782-8544; fax (212) 793-0739; f. 1970; Pres. RAFAEL TOVAR.

Consorcio Naviero Venezolano (Conavén): Torre Uno, 4°, Avda Orinoco, Las Mercedes, Caracas; tel. (212) 993-2922; fax (212) 993-1505; e-mail conavent@conaven.

Corpovén, SA: Edif. Petróleos de Venezuela, Avda Libertador, La Campiña, Apdo 61373, Caracas 1060-A; tel. (212) 708-1111; fax (212) 708-1833; Pres. Dr ROBERTO MANDINI; Vice-Pres. JUAN CARLOS GÓMEZ; 2 oil tankers.

Lagovén, SA: Edif. Lagovén, Avda Leonardo da Vinci, Los Chaguaramos, Apdo 889, Caracas; tel. (212) 606-3311; fax (212) 606-3637; f. 1978 as a result of the nationalization of the petroleum industry; (formerly known as the Creole Petroleum Group); transports crude petroleum and by-products between Maracaibo, Aniba and other ports in the area; Pres. B. R. NATERA; Marine Man. P. D. CAREZIS; 10 tankers.

Maravén, SA: Edif. Maravén, Avda La Estancia 10, Chuao, Apdo 829, Caracas 1010-A; tel. (212) 908-211; fax (212) 908-2885; Pres. EDUARDO LÓPEZ QUEVEDO; Vice-Pres. GUSTAVO GABALDÓN.

Marítima Aragua, SA: Centro Plaza Torre A, 15°, Avda Francisco de Miranda, Apdo 68404, Caracas 1062-A; tel. (212) 285-9770; fax (212) 285-5162; Pres. Capt. S. JUAN HUERTA.

Tacarigua Marina, CA: Torre Lincoln 7A-B, Avda Lincoln, Apdo 51107, Sabana Grande, Caracas 1050-A; tel. (212) 781-1315; Pres. R. BELLIZZI.

Transpapel, CA: Edif. Centro, 11°, Of. 111, Centro Parque Boyaca, Avda Los Dos Caminos, Apdo 61316, Caracas 1071; tel. (212) 283-8366; fax (212) 285-7749; e-mail nmaldonado@navtranspapel.com; Chair. GUILLERMO ESPINOSA F.; Man. Dir Capt. NELSON MALDONADO A.

Transporte Industrial, SA: Carretera Guanta, Km 5 Planta Vencemos, Pertigalete-Edif. Anzoátegui, Apdo 4356, Puerto la Cruz; tel. (281) 68-5607; fax (281) 68-5683; f. 1955; bulk handling and cement bulk carrier; Chair. VÍCTOR ROMO; Man. Dir RAFAEL ANEE.

Venezolana de Buques, CA: Of. 2, 19°, esq. Puente Victoria, Caracas; tel. (212) 283-9954.

Venezolana de Navegación, CA: Avda Rómulo Gallegos 8007, Sector El Samán, entre Calle El Carmen y 1a Transversal de Monte Cristo, Los Dos Caminos, Apdo 70135, Caracas 1071; tel. (212) 203-6511; fax (212) 35-7185; regular services to US ports and Germany, the Netherlands, France and Spain; associated services from Scandinavian, Baltic, Mediterranean and Japanese ports; Chair. Rear-Adm. CARLOS HERNÁNDEZ F.; Man. Dir Capt. L. E. LUGO MARÍN.

CIVIL AVIATION

There are two adjacent airports 13 km from Caracas; Maiquetía for domestic and Simón Bolívar for international services. There are 61 commercial airports, seven of which are international airports.

National Airlines

Aeropostal (Alas de Venezuela): Torre Polar II, 22°, Plaza Venezuela, Caracas 1051; tel. (212) 708-6211; fax (212) 782-6323; internet www.aeropostal.com; f. 1933; transferred to private ownership in Sept. 1996, acquired by Venezuela/US consortium Corporación Alas de Venezuela; domestic services and flights to destinations in the Caribbean, South America and the USA; Pres. and CEO NELSON RAMIZ.

Aerovías Venezolanas, SA (AVENSA): Edif. 29, 2°, Avda Universidad, esq. El Chorro, Apdo 943, Caracas 101; tel. (212) 562-3022; fax (212) 563-0225; internet www.avensa.com.ve; f. 1943; provides extensive domestic services from Caracas and international services to Europe and the USA; government-owned; Chair. ANDRÉS BOULTON; Pres. HENRY LORD BOULTON.

Air Venezuela: Aeropuerto Internacional Simón Bolívar, Maiquetía, Caracas 1161; tel. (212) 332-2259; fax (212) 761-8740; f. 1995; charter passenger services; Pres. WILLIAM E. MEDINA.

Aserca Airlines: Torre Exterior, 8°, Avda Bolivar Norte, Valencia, Carabobo 2002; tel. (241) 237-111; fax (241) 220-210; e-mail rsv@asercaairlines.com; internet www.asercaairlines.com; f. 1968; domestic services and flights to Caribbean destinations; CEO SIMEON GARCIA; Exec. Pres. JULIAN VILLALBA.

Interamericana Cargo Venezuela: Torre Bellas Artes, 9°, Avda México, Caracas; tel. (212) 572-6464; fax (212) 572-3842; f. 1982; cargo carrier; operations suspended 1994; Pres. JULIO MENDOZA; Gen. Man. FRANCISCO SALAZAR.

LASER (Línea Aérea de Servicio Ejecutivo Regional): Torre Bazar Bolívar, 8°, Avda Francisco de Miranda, El Marqués, Caracas; tel. (212) 235-6181; fax (212) 235-8359; f. 1994; scheduled and charter services to domestic and international destinations, passenger and cargo; Pres. INOCENCIO ALVAREZ.

Línea Turística Aereotuy, CA: Edif. Gran Sabana, 5°, Blvd de Sabana Grande, Apdo 2923, Carmelitas, Caracas 1050; tel. (212) 762-3009; fax (212) 761-1892; e-mail jcmarquez@ethevon.net; internet www.tuy.com; f. 1982; operates on domestic and international routes; Pres. PETER BOTTOME; Dir-Gen. JUAN C. MÁRQUEZ.

Santa Barbara Airlines: Avda 3H, No 78-51, Res. República, Local 01, Maracaibo; tel. (261) 922-090; fax (261) 927-977; f. 1995; domestic and international services; Chair. and Pres. HELI S. FERNANDEZ; CEO and Gen. Man. FRANS KRAMER.

Tourism

In 1998 Venezuela received 685,429 tourists. In 1997 tourism generated an income of US $1,086m.

Departamento de Turismo: c/o Central Information Office of the Presidency, Torre Oeste, 18°, Parque Central, Caracas; Dir Dr JESÚS FEDERICO RAVEL.

Corporación de Turismo de Venezuela (Corpoturismo): see section on The Government (Ministries—Government Agencies).

Sociedad Financiera para el Fomento del Turismo y de Recreo Público (FOMTUR): Caracas; f. 1962; government tourist development agency.

Corporación Nacional de Hoteles y Turismo (CONAHOTU): Apdo 6651, Caracas; f. 1969; government agency; Pres. ERASTO FERNÁNDEZ.

Defence

In August 2000 the Armed Forces numbered 79,000 (including the 23,000-strong National Guard and an estimated 31,000 conscripts): an Army of 34,000 (including 27,000 conscripts), a Navy of 15,000 men (including 1,000 Naval Aviation, 5,000 marines, 1,000 Coast Guard and an estimated 4,000 conscripts), and an Air Force of 7,000 men. There were an estimated 8,000 army reserves. Military service is selective and the length of service varies by region for all services.

Defence Budget: 949,000m. bolívares (US $1,404m.) in 2000.

Commander-in-Chief of the Armed Forces: Maj-Gen. MANUEL ROSENDO.

Chief of Staff of the Army: Gen. LUCAS RINCÓN ROMERO.

Chief of Staff of the Navy: Vice-Adm. JORGE MIGUEL SIERRAALTA ZAVARCE.

Chief of Staff of the Air Force: Gen. ARTURO JOSÉ GARCÍA.

Education

Primary education in Venezuela is free and compulsory between the ages of five and 15 years. Secondary education begins at the age of 15 years and lasts for a further two years. In 1993 the total enrolment of children at primary and secondary schools was equivalent to 83% of the school-age population (males 80%; females 85%). In 1996 primary enrolment was equivalent to 91% of children in the relevant age-group (males 90%; females 93%), while secondary enrolment was 40% (males 33%; females 41%). Only 50% of pupils complete their basic education, and the adult illiteracy rate was estimated to be 8.9% (males 8.2%; females 9.7%), in 1995. There were 20 state universities. Expenditure on education by the central Government was equivalent to 3.8% of GDP in 1998, compared with 7.4% of GDP in 1983.

Bibliography

For works on the region generally, see Select Bibliography (Books).

Bergquist, C. *Labor in Latin America: Comparative Essays on Chile, Argentina, Venezuela and Colombia.* Stanford, CA, Stanford University Press, 1986.

Betancourt, R. *Venezuela: Oil and Politics.* Boston, MA, Houghton Mifflin, 1979.

Blank, D. E. *Venezuela: Politics in a Petroleum Republic.* New York, NY, Praeger Publrs, 1984.

Boué, J. C. *Venezuela: The Political Economy of Oil.* Oxford, Oxford University Press (for Oxford Unit for Energy Studies), 1993.

Buxton, J. 'Venezuela', in Buxton, J., and Phillips, N. *Case Studies in Latin American Political Economy.* Manchester, Manchester University Press, 1999.

   The Failure of Political Reform in Venezuela. Hampshire, Ashgate Publishing Ltd, 2001.

Canache, D. *Venezuela: Public Opinion and Protest in a Fragile Democracy.* Boulder, CO, Lynne Rienner, 2001.

Crisp, B. F. *Democratic Institutional Design: The Powers and Incentives of Venezuelan Politicians and Interest Groups.* Stanford, CA, Stanford University Press, 2000.

Ellner, S. 'Organized Labor's Political Influence and Party Ties in Venezuela: Acción Democrática and its Labor Leadership', in *Journal of International Studies and World Affairs,* Vol. 3, 4 (Winter), 1989.

Venezuela's Movimiento al Socialismo: From Guerrilla Defeat to Innovative Politics. Durham, NC, Duke University Press, 1988.

Gil Yepes, J. A. *The Challenge of Venezuelan Democracy.* New Brunswick, NJ, Transaction Books, 1981.

Gott, R. *In the Shadow of the Liberator: The Impact of Hugo Chávez on Venezuela and Latin America.* London, Verso Books, 2000.

Hellinger, D. *Venezuela, Tarnished Democracy.* Boulder, CO, Westview Press, 1991.

Lieuwen, E. *Venezuela.* Westport, CT, Greenwood Press, 1986.

Lombardi, J. V. *Venezuela: The Search for Order, the Dream of Progress.* New York, NY, and Oxford, Oxford University Press, 1982.

   (Ed.) *Venezuelan History: A comprehensive Working Bibliography.* Boston, MA, G. K. Hall, 1977.

Martz, J. D., and Myers, D. J. (Eds). *Venezuela: The Democratic Experience.* New York, NY, Praeger Publrs, 1986.

Naim, M. *Paper Tigers and Minotaurs: The Politics of Venezuela's Economic Reforms.* Washington, DC, Carnegie Endowment for International Peace, 1993.

Salazar, J. *Oil and Development in Venezuela during the Twentieth Century.* London, Praeger Publrs, 1994.

Tulchin, J. S. *Venezuela in the Wake of Radical Reform.* Boulder, CO, Lynne Rienner, 1993.

PART THREE
Regional Information

REGIONAL ORGANIZATIONS

THE UNITED NATIONS IN SOUTH AMERICA, CENTRAL AMERICA AND THE CARIBBEAN

Address: United Nations Plaza, New York, NY 10017, USA.

Telephone: (212) 963-1234; **fax:** (212) 963-4879; **internet:** www.un.org.

The United Nations (UN) was founded on 24 October 1945. The organization, which has 189 member states, aims to maintain international peace and security and to develop international co-operation in addressing economic, social, cultural and humanitarian problems. The principal organs of the UN are the General Assembly, the Security Council, the Economic and Social Council (ECOSOC), the International Court of Justice and the Secretariat.

Secretary-General (1997–2006): Kofi Annan (Ghana).

MEMBER STATES IN SOUTH AMERICA, CENTRAL AMERICA AND THE CARIBBEAN
(with assessments for percentage contributions to UN budget for 2000, and year of admission)

Antigua and Barbuda	0.002	1981
Argentina	1.103	1945
Bahamas	0.015	1973
Barbados	0.008	1966
Belize	0.001	1981
Bolivia	0.007	1945
Brazil	1.417	1945
Chile	0.136	1945
Colombia	0.109	1945
Costa Rica	0.016	1945
Cuba	0.024	1945
Dominica	0.001	1978
Dominican Republic	0.015	1945
Ecuador	0.020	1945
El Salvador	0.012	1945
Grenada	0.001	1974
Guatemala	0.018	1945
Guyana	0.001	1966
Haiti	0.002	1945
Honduras	0.003	1945
Jamaica	0.006	1962
Mexico	0.995	1945
Nicaragua	0.001	1945
Panama	0.013	1945
Paraguay	0.014	1945
Peru	0.099	1945
Saint Christopher and Nevis	0.001	1983
Saint Lucia	0.001	1979
Saint Vincent and the Grenadines	0.001	1980
Suriname	0.004	1975
Trinidad and Tobago	0.016	1962
Uruguay	0.048	1945
Venezuela	0.160	1945

PERMANENT MISSIONS TO THE UNITED NATIONS
(with Permanent Representatives—July 2001)

Antigua and Barbuda: 610 Fifth Ave, Suite 311, New York, NY 10020; tel. (212) 541-4117; fax (212) 757-1607; e-mail antigua@un.int; internet www.un.int/antigua; Dr PATRICK ALBERT LEWIS.

Argentina: 1 United Nations Plaza, 25th Floor, New York, NY 10017; tel. (212) 688-6300; fax (212) 980-8395; e-mail argentina@un.int; internet www.un.int/argentina; ARNOLDO MANUEL LISTRE.

Bahamas: 231 East 46th St, New York, NY 10017; tel. (212) 421-6925; fax (212) 759-2135; e-mail bahamas@un.int; ANTHONY CHARLES ROLLE.

Barbados: 800 Second Ave, 2nd Floor, New York, NY 10017; tel. (212) 867-8431; fax (212) 986-1030; e-mail barbados@un.int; JUNE YVONNE CLARKE.

Belize: 800 Second Ave, Suite 400G, New York, NY 10017; tel. (212) 599-0233; fax (212) 599-3391; e-mail belize@un.int; SEWART WARREN LESLIE.

Bolivia: 211 East 43rd St, 8th Floor (Room 802), New York, NY 10017; tel. (212) 682-8132; fax (212) 682-8133; e-mail bolivia@un.int; Dr ROBERTO JORDÁN-PANDO.

Brazil: 747 Third Ave, 9th Floor, New York, NY 10017; tel. (212) 372-2600; fax (212) 371-5716; e-mail braun@delbrasonu.org; internet www.un.int/brazil; GELSON FONSECA, Jr.

Chile: 3 Dag Hammarskjöld Plaza, 305 East 47th St, 10th/11th Floor, New York, NY 10017; tel. (212) 832-3323; fax (212) 832-8714; e-mail chile@un.int; J. GABRIEL VALDÉS.

Colombia: 140 East 57th St, 5th Floor, New York, NY 10022; tel. (212) 355-7776; fax (212) 371-2813; e-mail colombia@un.int; internet www.un.int/colombia; ALFONSO VALDIVIESO.

Costa Rica: 211 East 43rd St, Room 903, New York, NY 10017; tel. (212) 986-6373; fax (212) 986-6842; e-mail costarica@un.int; BERND NIEHAUS.

Cuba: 315 Lexington Ave and 38th St, New York, NY 10016; tel. (212) 689-7215; fax (212) 779-1697; e-mail cuba@un.int; internet www.un.int/cuba; RAFAEL DAUSA CESPEDES.

Dominica: 800 Second Ave, Suite 400H, New York, NY 10017; tel. (212) 949-0853; fax (212) 808-4975; e-mail dominica@un.int; SIMON PAUL RICHARDS.

Dominican Republic: 144 East 44th St, 4th Floor, New York, NY 10017; tel. (212) 867-0833; fax (212) 986-4694; e-mail dr@un.int; PEDRO PADILLA TONOS.

Ecuador: 866 United Nations Plaza, Room 516, New York, NY 10017; tel. (212) 935-1680; fax (212) 935-1835; e-mail ecuador@un.int; internet www.un.int/ecuador; MARIO ALEMÁN.

El Salvador: 46 Park Ave, New York, NY 10016; tel. (212) 679-1616; fax (212) 725-7831; e-mail elsalvador@un.int; JOSÉ ROBERTO ANDINO-SALAZAR.

Grenada: 800 Second Ave, Suite 400K, New York, NY 10017; tel. (212) 599-0301; fax (212) 599-1540; e-mail grenada@un.int; Dr LAMUEL A. STANISLAUS.

Guatemala: 57 Park Ave, New York, NY 10016; tel. (212) 679-4760; fax (212) 685-8741; e-mail guatemala@un.int; internet www.un.int/guatemala; GERT ROSENTHAL.

Guyana: 866 United Nations Plaza, Suite 555, New York, NY 10017; tel. (212) 527-3232; fax (212) 935-7548; e-mail guyana@un.int; (vacant).

Haiti: 801 Second Ave, Room 600, New York, NY 10017; tel. (212) 370-4840; fax (212) 661-8698; e-mail haiti@un.int; PIERRE LELONG.

Honduras: 866 United Nations Plaza, Suite 417, NY 10017; tel. (212) 752-3370; fax (212) 223-0498; e-mail honduras@un.int; ANGEL EDMUNDO ORELLANA MERCADO.

Jamaica: 767 Third Ave, 9th Floor, New York, NY 10017; tel. (212) 935-7509; fax (212) 935-7607; e-mail jamaica@un.int; internet www.un.int/jamaica; M. PATRICIA DURRANT.

Mexico: 2 United Nations Plaza, 28th Floor, New York, NY 10017; tel. (212) 752-0220; fax (212) 688-8862; e-mail mexico@un.int; internet www.un.int/mexico; ROBERTA LAJOUS.

Nicaragua: 820 Second Ave, 8th Floor, New York, NY 10017; tel. (212) 490-7997; fax (212) 286-0815; e-mail nicaragua@un.int; EDUARDO J. SEVILLA SOMOZA.

Panama: 866 United Nations Plaza, Suite 4030, New York, NY 10017; tel. (212) 421-5420; fax (212) 421-2694; e-mail panama@un.int; RAMÓN A. MORALES.

Paraguay: 211 East 43rd St, Suite 400, New York, NY 10017; tel. (212) 687-3490; fax (212) 818-1282; e-mail paraguay@un.int; ELADIO LOIZAGA.

Peru: 820 Second Ave, Suite 1600, New York, NY 10017; tel. (212) 687-3336; fax (212) 972-6975; e-mail peru@un.int; JORGE LUIS VALDEZ CARRILLO.

Saint Christopher and Nevis: 414 East 75th St, 5th Floor, New York, NY 10021; tel. (212) 535-1234; fax (212) 535-6854; e-mail stkn@un.int; JOSEPH R. CHRISTMAS.

Saint Lucia: 800 Second Ave, Suite 400J, New York, NY 10017; tel. (212) 697-9360; fax (212) 697-4993; e-mail stlucia@un.int; internet www.un.int/stlucia; JULIAN ROBERT HUNTE.

Saint Vincent and the Grenadines: 801 Second Ave, 21st Floor, New York, NY 10017; tel. (212) 687-4490; fax (212) 949-5946; e-mail stvg@un.int; DENNIE M. J. WILSON.

Suriname: 866 United Nations Plaza, Suite 320, New York, NY 10017; tel. (212) 826-0660; fax (212) 980-7029; e-mail suriname@un.int; SUBHAS CHANDRA MUNGRA.

Trinidad and Tobago: 820 Second Ave, 5th Floor, New York, NY 10017; tel. (212) 697-7620; fax (212) 682-3580; e-mail tto@un.int; GEORGE W. McKENZIE.

Uruguay: 747 Third Ave, 21st Floor, New York, NY 10017; tel. (212) 752-8240; fax (212) 593-0935; e-mail uruguay@un.int; internet www.un.int/uruguay; FELIPE H. PAOLILLO.

Venezuela: 335 East 46th St, New York, NY 10017; tel. (212) 557-2055; fax (212) 557-3528; e-mail venezuela@un.int; internet www.un.int/venezuela; MILOS ALCALAY.

OBSERVERS

Caribbean Community: 97–40 62nd Drive, 15K, Rego Park, NY 11374–1336; tel. and fax (718) 896-1179; e-mail caribcomun@un.int; HAMID MOHAMMED.

Commonwealth Secretariat: 800 Second Ave, 4th Floor, New York, NY 10017; tel. (212) 599-6190; fax (212) 972-3970; e-mail chogrm@aol.com.

International Committee of the Red Cross: 801 Second Ave, 18th Floor, New York, NY 10017; tel. (212) 599-6021; fax (212) 599-6009; e-mail redcrosscommittee@un.int; Head of delegation SYLVIE JUNOD.

The following inter-governmental organizations have a standing invitation to participate as Observers, but do not maintain permanent offices at the United Nations:

African, Caribbean and Pacific Group of States.
Agency for the Prohibition of Nuclear Weapons in Latin America and the Caribbean.
Andean Community
Central American Integration System
Latin American Economic System
Latin American Parliament
Organization of American States.

Economic Commission for Latin America and the Caribbean—ECLAC

Address: Edif. Naciones Unidas, Avda Dag Hammarskjöld, Casilla 179D, Santiago, Chile.

Telephone: (2) 2102000; **fax:** (2) 2080252; **e-mail:** dpisantiago@eclac.cl; **internet:** www.eclac.org.

The UN Economic Commission for Latin America was founded in 1948 to co-ordinate policies for the promotion of economic development in the Latin American region. The current name of the Commission was adopted in 1984.

MEMBERS

Antigua and Barbuda	Costa Rica	Haiti
Argentina	Cuba	Honduras
Bahamas	Dominica	Italy
Barbados	Dominican Republic	Jamaica
Belize	Ecuador	Mexico
Bolivia	El Salvador	Netherlands
Brazil	France	Nicaragua
Canada	Grenada	Panama
Chile	Guatemala	Paraguay
Colombia	Guyana	Peru
Saint Christopher and Nevis	Spain	Portugal
	Suriname	United Kingdom
Saint Lucia	Trinidad and Tobago	USA
Saint Vincent and the Grenadines		Uruguay
		Venezuela

ASSOCIATE MEMBERS

Anguilla	Montserrat	Puerto Rico
Aruba	Netherlands Antilles	United States Virgin Islands
British Virgin Islands		

Organization

(July 2001)

COMMISSION

The Commission normally meets every two years in one of the Latin American capitals. The 28th session of the Commission was held in Mexico City in April 2000. The Commission has established the following permanent bodies:

Caribbean Development and Co-operation Committee.

Central American Development and Co-operation Committee.

Committee of High-Level Government Experts.

Committee of the Whole.

Regional Conference on the Integration of Women into the Economic and Social Development of Latin America and the Caribbean.

Regional Council for Planning.

SECRETARIAT

The Secretariat employs more than 500 staff and comprises the Office of the Executive Secretary; the Programme Planning and Operations Division; and the Office of the Secretary of the Commission. ECLAC's work programme is carried out by the following divisions: Economic Development; Social Development; International Trade and Development Finance; Production, Productivity and Management; Statistics and Economic Projections; Environment and Human Settlements; Natural Resources and Infrastructure; and Population. There is also a Woman and Development Unit, support divisions of documents and publications, and of administration, and an Economic and Social Documentation Centre (CLADES).

Executive Secretary: JOSÉ ANTONIO OCAMPO (Colombia).

Secretary of the Commission: DANIEL BLANCHARD (acting).

SUB-REGIONAL OFFICES

Caribbean: 63 Park St, Chic Bldg, 3rd Floor, POB 1113, Port of Spain, Trinidad and Tobago; tel. 623-5595; fax 623-8486; e-mail registry@eclacpos.org; internet www.searcher.eclacpos.org; f. 1956; covers non-Spanish-speaking Caribbean countries; Dir LEN ISHMAEL.

Central America and Spanish-speaking Caribbean: Avda Presidente Masaryk 29, 11570 México, DF; tel. (5) 250-1555; fax (5) 531-1151; e-mail cepal@un.org.mx; internet www.eclac.org.mx; f. 1951; covers Central America and Spanish-speaking Caribbean countries; Dir MARGARITA FLORES (acting).

There are also five national offices, in Santafé de Bogotá, Brasília, Buenos Aires, Montevideo and Washington, DC.

Activities

ECLAC collaborates with regional governments in the investigation and analysis of regional and national economic problems, and provides guidance in the formulation of development plans. Its activities include research; analysis; publication of information; provision of technical assistance; participation in seminars and conferences; training courses; and co-operation with national, regional and international organizations.

The 26th session of the Commission, which was held in San José, Costa Rica, in April 1996, considered means of strengthening the economic and social development of the region, within the framework of a document prepared by ECLAC's Secretariat, and adopted a resolution which defined ECLAC as a centre of excellence, charged with undertaking an analysis of specific aspects of the development process, in collaboration with member governments. The meeting also reviewed the impact on ECLAC of the ongoing process of reform throughout the UN system. The Commission agreed to establish an *ad hoc* working group to recommend a strategic framework for the Commission, to define priorities for a future work programme and to improve working relations between the Commission and member states. In May 1998 the 27th session of the Commission, held in Oranjestad, Aruba, approved the ongoing reform programme, and in particular efforts to enhance the effectiveness and transparency of ECLAC's activities. The main topics of debate at the meeting were public finances, fiscal management and social and economic development. The Commission adopted a Fiscal Covenant, incorporating measures to consolidate fiscal adjustment and to strengthen public management, democracy and social equity, which was to be implemented throughout the region and provide the framework for further debate at national and regional level. ECLAC's 28th session, convened in Mexico City in April 2000, debated a document prepared by the Secretariat which proposed that the pursuit of social equity, sustainable development and 'active citizenship' (with emphasis on the roles of education and employment) should form the basis of future policy-making in the region.

ECLAC works closely with other agencies within the UN system and with other regional and multinational organizations. ECLAC is co-operating with the OAS and the Inter-American Development Bank in the servicing of intergovernmental groups undertaking preparatory work for the establishment of a Free Trade Area of the Americas. In May 2001 ECLAC hosted the first meeting of the Americas Statistics Conference.

Latin American and Caribbean Institute for Economic and Social Planning—ILPES: Edif. Naciones Unidas, Avda Dag Hammarskjöld, Casilla 1567, Santiago, Chile; tel. (2) 2102506; fax (2) 2066104; e-mail pdekock@eclac.cl; f. 1962; supports regional governments through the provision of training, advisory services and research in the field of public planning policy and co-ordination. Dir FERNANDO SÁNCHEZ-ALBAVERA.

Latin American Demographic Centre—CELADE: Edif. Naciones Unidas, Avda Dag Hammarskjöld, Casilla 179D, Santiago, Chile; tel. (2) 2102002; fax (2) 2080252; e-mail djaspers@eclac.cl; internet www.eclac.org/celade; f. 1957, became an integral part of ECLAC in 1975; provides technical assistance to governments, universities and research centres in demographic analysis, population policies, integration of population factors in development planning, and data processing; conducts three-month courses on demographic analysis for development and various national and regional seminars; provides demographic estimates and projections, documentation, data processing, computer packages and training. Dir DANIEL S. BLANCHARD.

Finance

For the two-year period 2000–01 ECLAC's regular budget, an appropriation from the UN, amounted to US $78.9m. In addition, extra-budgetary activities are financed by governments, other organizations, and UN agencies, including UNDP, UNFPA and UNICEF.

Publications

Boletín del Banco de Datos del CELADE (annually).

Boletín demográfico (2 a year).

Boletín de Facilitación del Comercio y el Transporte (every 2 months).

CEPAL Review (Spanish and English, 3 a year).

CEPALINDEX (annually).

Co-operation and Development (Spanish and English, quarterly).

DOCPAL Resúmenes (population studies, 2 a year).

ECLAC Notes / Notas de la CEPAL (every 2 months).

Economic Panorama of Latin America (annually).

Economic Survey of Latin America and the Caribbean (Spanish and English, annually).

Foreign Investment in Latin America and the Caribbean.

Notas de Población (2 a year).

PLANINDEX (2 a year).

Preliminary Overview of the Economy of Latin America and the Caribbean (annually).

Social Panorama of Latin America (annually).

Statistical Yearbook for Latin America and the Caribbean (Spanish and English).

Studies, reports, bibliographical bulletins.

United Nations Development Programme—UNDP

Address: One United Nations Plaza, New York, NY 10017, USA.

Telephone: (212) 906-5315; **fax:** (212) 906-5364; **e-mail:** hq@undp.org; **internet:** www.undp.org.

The Programme was established in 1965. Its central mission is to help countries to eradicate poverty and achieve a sustainable level of human development.

Organization

(July 2001)

UNDP is responsible to the UN General Assembly, to which it reports through the UN Economic and Social Council.

EXECUTIVE BOARD

The Executive Board is responsible for providing intergovernmental support to, and supervision of, the activities of UNDP and the UN Population Fund (UNFPA, of which UNDP is the governing body). It comprises 36 members: eight from Africa, seven from Asia, four from eastern Europe, five from Latin America and the Caribbean and 12 from western Europe and other countries.

SECRETARIAT

In 2001 UNDP attempted to consolidate a process of restructuring and improving the efficiency of its administration. Offices and divisions at the Secretariat include: an Operations Support Group; the Emergency Response Division; Offices of the United Nations Development Group, the Human Development Report, Audit and Performance Review, and Communications; and Bureaux for Resources and Strategic Partnerships, Development Policy, and Management. Five regional bureaux, all at the Secretariat in New York, cover: Africa; Asia and the Pacific; the Arab states; Latin America and the Caribbean; and Europe and the Commonwealth of Independent States.

Administrator: MARK MALLOCH BROWN (United Kingdom).

Assistant Administrator and Director, Regional Bureau for Latin America and the Caribbean: ELENA MARTÍNEZ (Cuba).

REGIONAL OFFICES

Headed by Assistant Administrators, the regional bureaux share the responsibility for implementing the programme with the Administrator's office. Within certain limitations, large-scale projects may be approved and funding allocated by the Administrator, and smaller-scale projects by the Resident Representatives (see below for those in South America, Central America and the Caribbean).

COUNTRY OFFICES

In almost every country receiving UNDP assistance there is an office headed by the UNDP Resident Representative, who usually also serves as the UN Co-ordinator, responsible for the co-ordination of all UN technical assistance and operational development activities, advising the Government on formulating the country programme, ensuring that the field activities are carried out, and acting as the leader of the UN team of experts working in the country. The offices function as the primary presence of the UN in most developing countries.

OFFICES OF UNDP REPRESENTATIVES IN SOUTH AMERICA, CENTRAL AMERICA AND THE CARIBBEAN

Argentina: Casilla 2257, 1000 Capital Federal, Buenos Aires; tel. (1) 4320-8700; fax (1) 4320-8754; e-mail fo.arg@undp.org; internet www.undp.org.ar.

Barbados: POB 625C, Bridgetown; tel. 429-2521; fax 429-2448; e-mail fo.brb@undp.org; internet www.bb.undp.org (also covers Anguilla, Antigua and Barbuda, British Virgin Islands, Domnica, Grenada, Montserrat, Saint Christopher and Nevis, Saint Lucia, Saint Vincent and the Grenadines).

Bolivia: Avda Sánchez Bustamante, Casilla 9072, La Paz, Bolivia; tel. (2) 795544; fax (2) 391368; e-mail registry.bo@undp.org; internet guf.pnud.bo.

Brazil: CP 0285, 70359 Brasília, DF; tel. (61) 329-2000; fax (61) 329-0099; e-mail fo.bra@undp.org; internet www.br.undp.org.

Chile: Avda Pedro de Valdivia 0193, 7° Casilla 197D, Santiago; tel. (2) 232-4183; fax (2) 232-5804; e-mail fo.chl@undp.org.

Colombia: Apdo Aéreo 091369, Santafé de Bogotá; tel. (1) 214-2200; fax (1) 214-0110; e-mail fo.col@undp.org.

Costa Rica: Apdo Postal 4540-1000, San José; tel. 2961544; fax 2961545; e-mail fo.cr@undp.org; internet www.nu.or.cr.

Cuba: Calle 18 No. 110 (entre 1ra y 3ra), Miramar, Playa, Havana; tel. (7) 33-1512; fax (7) 33-1516; e-mail fo.cub@undp.org; internet www.undp.org/cuba.

Dominican Republic: Apdo 1424, Santo Domingo; tel. 531-3403; fax 531-3507; e-mail fo.dom@undp.org; internet www.undp.org/fodom.

Ecuador: POB 1703-4731, Quito; tel. (2) 500-553; fax (2) 500-552; e-mail fo.ecu@undp.org; internet www.pnud.org.ec.

El Salvador: POB 1114, San Salvador; tel. 2790366; fax 2791929; e-mail fo.slv@undp.org (also covers Belize).

Guatemala: Apdo Postal 23A, 01909 Guatemala City; tel. (2) 3335416; fax (2) 3370304; e-mail fo.gtm@undp.org; internet www.pnud.org.gt.

Guyana: 42 Brickdam and Boyle Place, POB 10960, Georgetown, Guyana; tel. (2) 64040; fax (2) 62942; e-mail fo.guy@undp.org; internet www.sdnp.org.gy.

Haiti: BP 557, Port-au-Prince; tel. 231400; fax 239340; e-mail fo.hti@undp.org; internet www.ht.undp.org.

Honduras: Apdo Postal 976, Tegucigalpa DC; tel. 220-1100; fax 232-8716; e-mail fo.hnd@undp.org; internet www.undp.un.hn.

Jamaica: POB 280, Kingston; tel. 9782390; fax 9268654; e-mail undpja@undp.org; internet www.undp.org/fojam (also covers Bahamas, Cayman Islands, Turks and Caicos Islands).

Mexico: Apdo Postal 105-39, 11581 México, DF; tel. (5) 250-1555; fax (5) 255-0095; e-mail fo.mex@undp.org; internet www.pnud.org.mx.

Nicaragua: Apdo Postal 3260, Managua, JR; tel. (2) 663191; fax (2) 666909; e-mail fo.nic@undp.org; internet www.undp.org.ni.

Panama: Apdo 6314, Panama 5; tel. 265-0838; fax 263-1444; e-mail registry@fopan.undp.org; internet aleph.onu.org.pa/pnud.

Paraguay: Estrella 345, Edificio Citibank, Asunción; tel. (21) 493025; fax (21) 444325; e-mail registry@undp.org.py; internet www.undp.org.py.

Peru: Apdo 27-0047, Lima 27; tel. (1) 2213636; fax (1) 4404166; e-mail fo.per@undp.org; internet www.onu.org.pe.

Trinidad and Tobago: POB 812, Port of Spain; tel. 623-7056; fax 623-1658; e-mail registry@undp.org.tt; internet www.undp.org.tt/frontsite.htm (also covers Aruba, Netherlands Antilles and Suriname).

Uruguay: J. Barrias Amorín 870, 3°, Montevideo; tel. (2) 4023357; fax (2) 4023360; e-mail onunet@undp.org.uy; internet www.onunet.org.uy/inst_pnud.htm.

Venezuela: Apdo 69005, Caracas 1062-A; tel. (2) 285-4133; fax (2) 283-7878; e-mail pnud.ven@undp.org; internet www.pnud.org.ve.

Activities

As the world's largest source of grant technical assistance in developing countries, UNDP works with more than 150 governments and 40 international agencies in order to eradicate poverty and to achieve faster economic growth and better standards of living throughout the world. Most of the work is undertaken in the field by the various United Nations agencies, or by the government of the country concerned. UNDP is committed to allocating 87% of its core resources to low-income countries with an annual income per head of less than US $750. Assistance is mostly non-monetary, comprising the provision of experts' services, consultancies, equipment, and fellowships for advanced study abroad. Most UNDP projects incorporate training for local workers. Developing countries themselves provide 50% or more of the total project costs in terms of personnel, facilities, equipment and supplies.

In June 1994 the Executive Board endorsed a proposal of the UNDP Administrator to make sustainable human development—an approach to economic growth that encompasses individual well-being and choice, equitable distribution of the benefits of development and conservation of the environment—the guiding principle of the organization. At 2001 UNDP's activities were focused on the following priority areas: democratic governance; poverty reduction; environment and sustainable energy; crisis prevention and reduction; promotion of information and communications technology; and HIV and AIDS. Two cross-cutting themes were to be incorporated into all policy areas: gender equality and South-South co-operation.

From the mid-1990s UNDP determined to assume a more active and integrative role within the UN development system. This approach has been implemented by UNDP Resident Representatives, who aim to co-ordinate UN policies to achieve sustainable human development, in consultation with other agencies. UNDP has since allocated more resources to training and skill-sharing programmes in order to promote this co-ordinating role. In late 1997 the UNDP Administrator was appointed to chair a UN Development Group, which was established as part of a series of structural reform measures initiated by the UN Secretary-General and which aimed to strengthen collaboration between some 20 UN funds, programmes and other development bodies. The Group promotes coherent policy and country level through the system of Resident Co-ordinators, country assessment mechanisms, and the UN Development Assistance Framework (UNDAF). UNDP's leading role within the process of UN reform has also been reflected in its own internal reform process, 'UNDP 2001', which focused on improving planning, managing and reporting within a results-based management framework. In 1999 Results-Oriented Annual Reports (ROARs) were compiled for the first time by country offices and regional programmes. Within the framework of the Administrator's Business Plan for 2000-03 a new Bureau for Resources and Strategic Partnerships was established to build and strengthen working partnerships with other UN bodies, donor and programme countries, international financial institutions and development banks, civil society organizations and the private sector. The Bureau was also to serve UNDP's Regional Bureaux and country offices through the exchange of information and promotion of partnership strategies.

UNDP aims to help governments to reassess their development priorities and to design initiatives for sustainable development. UNDP country officers support the formulation of national human development reports (NHDRs), which aim to facilitate activities such as policy-making, the allocation of resources and monitoring progress towards poverty eradication and sustainable development. In 1999 NHDRs were produced by 11 countries in the Latin America Caribbean region. In addition, the preparation of Advisory Notes and Country Co-operation Frameworks by UNDP officials help to highlight country-specific aspects of poverty eradication and national strategic priorities. In January 1998 the Executive Board adopted eight guiding principles relating to sustainable human development that were to be implemented by all country offices, in order to ensure a focus to UNDP activities. A network of Sub-regional Resource Facilities (SURFs) has been established to strengthen and co-ordinate UNDP's technical assistance services.

UNDP's activities to facilitate poverty eradication include support for capacity-building programmes and initiatives to generate sustainable livelihoods, for example by improving access to credit, land and technologies. In March 1996 UNDP launched the Poverty Strategies Initiative (PSI) to strengthen national capacities to assess and monitor the extent of poverty and to combat the problem. Through the PSI UNDP supported the Guatemalan Government to formulate a National Plan for the Development of Indigenous People, of whom an estimated 90% live below acceptable levels of poverty. All PSI projects were intended to involve government representatives, the private sector, social organizations and research institutions in policy debate and formulation. By 2000 30 PSI projects had been approved in the South America, Central America and Caribbean region. In September 2000 the General Assembly of the UN convened a Millennium Summit, at which governments pledged to reduce by 50% the number of people with income of less than US $1 a day and those suffering from hunger and lack of safe drinking water by 2015. Other commitments made concerned equal access to education for girls and boys, the provision of universal primary education, the reduction of maternal mortality by 75%, and the reversal of the spread of HIV/AIDS and other diseases. UNDP was to be the focus of UN efforts to achieve these Millennium Goals. In early 1997 a UNDP scheme to support private-sector and community-based initiatives to generate employment opportunities, MicroStart, became operational with some $41m. in initial funds. UNDP supports the Caribbean Project Development Facility, which is administered by the International Finance Corporation (q.v.).

Approximately one-quarter of all UNDP programme resources support national efforts to ensure efficient governance and to build effective relations between the state, the private sector and civil society, which are essential to achieving sustainable development. UNDP undertakes assessment missions to help ensure free and fair elections and works to promote human rights, an accountable and competent public sector, a competent judicial system and decentralized government and decision-making. During 1997 UNDP supported organizations responsible for monitoring elections in Mexico, and co-ordinated discussions between different groups in Panama in an attempt to establish a national consensus on the future administration of the Panama Canal. In 1998/99 UNDP assisted with the provision of new identity documentation to several hundred thousand displaced Peruvians, enabling them to participate in national elections. In July 1997 UNDP organized an International Conference on Governance for Sustainable Growth and Equity, which was held in New York, USA, and attended by more than 1,000 representatives of national and local authorities and the business and non-governmental sectors. At the Conference UNDP initiated a four-year programme to promote activities and to encourage new approaches in support of good governance.

Within UNDP's framework of urban development activities the Local Initiative Facility for Urban Environment (LIFE) undertakes small-scale environmental projects in low-income communities, in collaboration with local authorities and community-based groups. Recent schemes include public-health improvements and the environmental rehabilitation of precipitous housing areas in four Brazilian cities. Other initiatives include the Urban Management Programme and the Public-Private Partnerships Programme for the Urban Environment which aimed to generate funds, promote research and support new technologies to enhance sustainable environments in urban areas. In November 1996 UNDP initiated a process of collaboration between city authorities world-wide to promote implementation of the commitments made at the 1995 Copenhagen summit for social development (see below) and to help to combat aspects of poverty and other urban problems, such as poor housing, transport, the management of waste disposal, water supply and sanitation. The first Forum of the so-called World Alliance of Cities Against Poverty was convened in October 1998, in Lyon, France. The second Forum took place in April 2000 in Geneva, Switzerland. UNDP supports the development of national programmes that emphasize the sustainable management of natural resources, for example through its Sustainable Energy Initiative, which promotes more efficient use of energy resources and the introduction of renewable alternatives to conventional fuels. UNDP is also concerned with forest management, the aquatic environment and sustainable agriculture and food security.

UNDP jointly manages the Global Environment Facility (GEF) with the World Bank and the UN Environment Programme. The aim of the GEF, which began operations in 1991, is to support projects for reducing emissions of 'greenhouse' gases, preserving biological diversity, protecting international waters, and reducing ozone layer depletion. UNDP administers the Small Grants Programme of the GEF, which supports community-based activities by local non-governmental organizations. UNDP is also responsible for capacity building, targeted research, pre-investment activities and technical assistance under the GEF. At the 1992 UN Conference on Environment and Development UNDP initiated 'Capacity 21', a programme to support developing countries in preparing and implementing sustainable development policies through national development strategies, community based management and training programmes. During 1998 programmes funded by Capacity 21 were being undertaken in 52 countries.

In the mid-1990s UNDP expanded its role in countries in crisis and with special circumstances, working in collaboration with other UN agencies to promote relief and development efforts, in order to secure the foundations for sustainable human development and thereby increase national capabilities to prevent or pre-empt future crises. In particular, UNDP was concerned to achieve reconciliation, reintegration and reconstuction in affected countries, as well as to support emergency interventions and the management and delivery of programme aid. In the late 1990s special development initiatives undertaken included strengthening democratic institutions in Guatemala, the rehabilitation of communities for returning populations in Central America, and assistance for reconstruction following hurricanes in Costa Rica and Nicaragua. UNDP was actively involved in efforts to distribute emergency assistance throughout communities in Central America affected by 'Hurricane Mitch' in late 1998, and has subsequently undertaken assessments of the damage to infrastructure and the environment. UNDP allocated US $26m. in 1999 for 'Mitch-related' activities. In 2000 UNDP, within the framework of its disaster reduction programme, worked with the authorities in Bolivia and Peru to undertake preparation and mitigation activities to combat the impact of the El Niño weather phenomenon.

UNDP is a co-sponsor, jointly with WHO, the World Bank, UNDCP, UNICEF, UNESCO and UNFPA, of a Joint UN Programme on HIV and AIDS, which became operational on 1 January 1996. UNDP also has responsibility for co-ordinating activities following global UN conferences. In March 1995 government representatives attending the World Summit of Social Development, which was held in Copenhagen, Denmark, approved initiatives to promote the eradication of poverty, to increase and reallocate official development assistance to basic social programmes and to promote equal access to education. The Programme of Action adopted by the summit meeting advocated that UNDP support the implementation of social development programmes, co-ordinate these efforts through its field offices and organize efforts on the part of the UN system to stimulate capacity-building at local, national and regional levels. The PSI (see above) was introduced following the Summit. A Special Session of the UN General Assembly to review the implementation of the Summit's objectives was convened in June 2000. Following the UN Fourth World Conference on Women, held in Beijing, People's

Republic of China, in September 1995, UNDP led inter-agency efforts to ensure the full participation of women in all economic, political and professional activities, and assisted with further situation analysis and training activities. UNDP also created a Gender in Development Office to ensure that women participate more fully in UNDP-sponsored activities. In June 2000 a Special Session of the UN General Assembly was convened to review the conference, entitled Women 2000: Gender Equality, Development and Peace for the 21st Century (Beijing + 5). UNDP played an important role, at both national and international levels, in preparing for the second UN Conference on Human Settlements (Habitat II), which was held in Istanbul, Turkey, in June 1996. At the conference UNDP announced the establishment of a new facility, which was designed to promote private-sector investment in urban infrastructure. The facility was to be allocated initial resources of US $10m., with the aim of generating a total of $1,000m. from private sources for this sector.

Since 1990 UNDP has published an annual *Human Development Report*, incorporating a Human Development Index, which ranks countries in terms of human development, using three key indicators: life expectancy, adult literacy and basic income required for a decent standard of living. In 1997 a Human Poverty Index and a Gender-related Development Index, which assesses gender equality on the basis of life expectancy, education and income, were introduced into the Report for the first time. In 1996 UNDP implemented its first corporate communications and advocacy strategy, which aimed to generate public awareness of the activities of the UN system, to promote debate on development issues and to mobilize resources by increasing public and donor appreciation of UNDP. UNDP aims to use the developments in information technology to advance its communications strategy and to disseminate guide-lines and technical support throughout its country office network. An Information Technology for Development Programme aims to promote sustainable human development through increased use of information and communications technologies globally, while a Sustainable Development Networking Programme focuses on expanding internet connectivity in poorer countries through building national capacities and supporting local internet sites.

In October 1999 UNDP, in collaboration with an international communications company, Cisco Systems, organized NetAid, a series of international concerts that were broadcast live on the internet, with the aim of improving awareness of Third World poverty. With Cisco Systems, and other partners, UNDP has worked to establish academies of information technology to support training and capacity-building in developing countries. By June 2001 44 academies had been established in 28 countries.

Finance

UNDP is financed by the voluntary contributions of members of the United Nations and the Programme's participating agencies, as well as by cost-sharing by recipient government and third-party donors. In 2000 total voluntary contributions amounted to US $2,400m., of which $634m. was for core resources (compared with $681m. in 1999). Donor co-finance, including trust funds and cost-sharing by third parties, amounted to $571m. in 2000, while cost-sharing by programme country governments amounted to more than $900m.

Publications

Annual Report.

Choices (quarterly).

Global Public Goods: International Co-operation in the 21st Century.

Human Development Report (annually).

Poverty Report (annually).

Transitions (newsletter, every 2 months).

Associated Funds and Programmes

UNDP's associated funds and programmes, each financed separately by voluntary contributions, provide specific services through the UNDP network.

OFFICE TO COMBAT DESERTIFICATION AND DROUGHT—UNSO

The Office was established following the conclusion, in October 1994, of the UN Convention to Combat Desertification in Those Countries Experiencing Serious Drought and/or Desertification, Particularly in Africa. It replaced the former UN Sudano–Sahelian Office (UNSO), while retaining the same acronym. UNSO is responsible for UNDP's role in desertification control and dryland management. Special emphasis is given to strengthening the environmental planning and management capacities of national institutions. During 1998 UNSO, in collaboration with other international partners, supported the implementation of the UN Convention in 55 designated countries.

Director: PHILIP DOBIE.

UNITED NATIONS CAPITAL DEVELOPMENT FUND—UNCDF

The Fund was established in 1966 and became fully operational in 1974. It invests in poor communities in least-developed countries by providing economic and social infrastructure, credit for both agricultural and small-scale entrepreneurial activities, and local development funds which encourage people's participation, as well as that of local governments, in the planning and implementation of projects. UNCDF aims to promote the interests of women in community projects and to enhance their earning capacities. By 1999 56 countries had received UNCDF assistance, including three nations in the Latin America and Caribbean region. In 1998 UNCDF nominated 15 countries (including Haiti) in which to concentrate subsequent programmes. A Special Unit for Microfinance (SUM) was established in 1997 as a joint UNDP/UNCDF operation, to facilitate co-ordination between microcredit initiatives of the UN, and to support UNDP's MicroStart initiative. SUM was fully integrated into UNCDF in 1999. In May 1996 stable funding for the Fund was pledged by eight donors for a three-year period. UNCDF's annual programming budget amounts to some US $40m.

Executive Secretary: NORMAND LAUZON.

UNITED NATIONS DEVELOPMENT FUND FOR WOMEN— UNIFEM

UNIFEM is the UN's lead agency in addressing the issues relating to women in development and promoting the rights of women worldwide. The Fund provides direct financial and technical support to enable low-income women in developing countries to increase earnings, gain access to labour-saving technologies and otherwise improve the quality of their lives. It also funds activities that include women in decision-making related to mainstream development projects. In 1998 UNIFEM approved 64 new projects and continued to support some 90 ongoing programmes in more than 100 nations. UNIFEM has supported the preparation of national reports in 30 countries and used the priorities identified therein and in other regional initiatives to formulate a Women's Development Agenda for the 21st century. Through these efforts, UNIFEM played an active role in the preparation for the UN Fourth World Conference on Women, which was held in Beijing, People's Republic of China, in September 1995. In June 2000 UNIFEM participated in a Special Session of the UN General Assembly convened to review the conference, entitled Gender Equality, Development and Peace for the 21st Century (Beijing + 5). In March 2001 UNIFEM, in collaboration with International Alert, launched a Millennium Peace Prize for Women. Programme expenditure in 1999 totalled US $19.6m.

Headquarters: 304 East 45th St, New York, NY 10017, USA; tel. (212) 906-6400; fax (212) 906-6705; e-mail unifem@undp.org; internet www.unifem.undp.org.

Director: NOELEEN HEYZER (Singapore).

UNITED NATIONS VOLUNTEERS—UNV

UNV is an important source of middle-level skills for the UN development system, supplied at modest cost, particularly in the least-developed countries. Volunteers expand the scope of UNDP project activities by supplementing the work of international and host-country experts and by extending the influence of projects to local community levels. The UN Short-term Advisory Programme, which is the private-sector development branch of UNV, has increasingly focused its attention on countries in the process of economic transition. In addition to development activities, UNV has been increasingly involved in areas such as election and human-rights monitoring, peace-building and community-based progammes concerned with environmental management and protection.

Since 1994 UNV has administered UNDP's Transfer of Knowledge Through Expatriate Nationals (TOKTEN) programme, which was initiated in 1977 to enable specialists and professionals from developing countries to contribute to development efforts in their countries of origin through short-term technical assignments.

At 31 May 2001 3,067 UNVs were serving in 131 countries, of whom 12.6% were in Latin America and the Caribbean. At that time more than 30,000 had served under the initiative in some 150 countries.

Headquarters: POB 260111, 53153 Bonn, Germany; tel. (228) 8152000; fax (228) 8152001; e-mail hq@unv.org; internet www.unv.org.

Executive Co-ordinator: SHARON CAPELING-ALAKIJA.

United Nations Environment Programme—UNEP

Address: POB 30552, Nairobi, Kenya.

Telephone: (2) 621234; **fax:** (2) 622615; e-mail cpiinfo@unep.org; **internet:** www.unep.org.

The United Nations Environment Programme was established in 1972 by the UN General Assembly, following recommendations of the 1972 UN Conference on the Human Environment, in Stockholm, Sweden, to encourage international co-operation in matters relating to the human environment.

Organization

(July 2001)

GOVERNING COUNCIL

The main functions of the Governing Council, which meets every two years, are to promote international co-operation in the field of the environment and to provide general policy guide-lines for the direction and co-ordination of environmental programmes within the UN system. It comprises representatives of 58 states, elected by the UN General Assembly, for four-year terms, on a rotating basis. The Council is assisted in its work by a Committee of Permanent Representatives.

HIGH-LEVEL COMMITTEE OF MINISTERS AND OFFICIALS IN CHARGE OF THE ENVIRONMENT

The Committee was established by the Governing Council in April 1997, with a mandate to consider the international environmental agenda and to make recommendations to the Council on reform and policy issues. In addition, the Committee, comprising 36 elected members, was to provide guidance and advice to the Executive Director, to enhance UNEP's collaboration and co-operation with other multilateral bodies and to help to mobilize financial resources for UNEP.

SECRETARIAT

The Secretariat serves as a focal point for environmental action within the UN system. At October 1999 UNEP had 618 members of staff, of whom 284 were based at the organization's headquarters and 334 at regional and other offices.

Executive Director: Dr KLAUS TÖPFER (Germany).

REGIONAL OFFICE

Latin America and the Caribbean: Blvd de los Virreyes 155, Lomas Virreyes, 11000 México, DF, Mexico; tel. (5) 2027529; fax (5) 2020950; e-mail unepnet@rolac.unep.mx.

OTHER OFFICES

Convention on International Trade in Endangered Species of Wild Fauna and Flora (CITES): 15 chemin des Anémones, 1219 Châtelaine, Geneva, Switzerland; tel. (22) 9178139; fax (22) 7973417; e-mail cites@unep.ch; internet www.cites.org; Sec.-Gen. WILLEM WOUTER WIJNSTEKERS.

Global Programme of Action for the Protection of the Marine Environment from Land-based Activities: POB 16227, 2500 The Hague, Netherlands; tel. (70) 4114460; fax (70) 3456648; e-mail gpa@unep.nl; internet www.gpa.unep.org; Co-ordinator VEERLE VANDEWEERD.

Regional Co-ordinating Unit for the Caribbean Environment Programme: 14–20 Port Royal St, Kingston, Jamaica; tel. (876) 9229267; fax (876) 9229292; e-mail uneprcuja@cwjamaica.com; internet www.cep.unep.org.

Secretariat of the Basel Convention: CP 356, 15 chemin des Anémones, 1219 Châtelaine, Geneva, Switzerland; tel. (22) 9178128; fax (22) 9178218; e-mail sbc@unep.ch; internet www.basel.int; Exec. Sec. SACHIKO KUWABARA-YAMAMOTO.

Secretariat of the Convention on Biological Diversity: World Trade Centre, 393 St Jacques St West, Suite 300, Montréal, QC

H2Y 1N9, Canada; tel. (514) 288-2220; fax (514) 288-6588; e-mail secretariat@biodiv.org; internet www.biodiv.org; Exec. Sec. Dr HAMDALLAH ZEDAN.

Secretariat for the Multilateral Fund for the Implementation of the Montreal Protocol: 1800 McGill College Ave, 27th Floor, Montréal, QC H3A 3J6, Canada; tel. (514) 282-1122; fax (514) 282-0068; e-mail secretariat@unmfs.org; Chief OMAR EL-ARINI.

UNEP Chemicals: 11-13 chemin des Anémones, 1219 Châtelaine, Geneva, Switzerland; tel. (22) 9178111; fax (22) 7973460; e-mail jwillis@unep.ch; internet www.chem.unep.ch; Dir JAMES B. WILLIS.

UNEP/CMS (Convention on the Conservation of Migratory Species of Wild Animals) **Secretariat:** Martin-Luther-King-Str 8, 53175 Bonn, Germany; tel. (228) 8152401; fax (228) 8152449; e-mail cms@unep.de; internet www.wcmc.org.uk/cms; Exec. Sec. ARNULF MÜLLER-HELMBRECHT.

UNEP Division of Technology, Industry and Economics: Tour Mirabeau, 39-43 quai André Citroen, 75739 Paris Cédex 15, France; tel. 1-44-37-14-50; fax 1-44-37-14-74; e-mail uneptic@unep.fr; internet www.uneptic.org/; Dir JACQUELINE ALOISI DE LARDEREL.

UNEP International Environmental Technology Centre: 2-110 Ryokuchi koen, Tsurumi-ku, Osaka 538-0036, Japan; tel. (6) 6915-4581; fax (6) 6915-0304; e-mail ietc@unep.or.jp; Dir STEVE HALLS.

UNEP Ozone Secretariat: POB 30552, Nairobi, Kenya; tel. (2) 623885; fax (2) 623913; e-mail ozoneinfo@unep.org; internet www.unep.org/ozone/; Officer-in-Charge MICHAEL GRABER.

UNEP Secretariat for the UN Scientific Committee on the Effects of Atomic Radiation: Vienna International Centre, Wagramerstrasse 5, POB 500, 1400 Vienna, Austria; tel. (1) 26060-4330; fax (1) 26060-5902; e-mail burton.bennett@unvienna.un.or.at; Sec. BURTON G. BENNETT.

Activities

UNEP aims to maintain a constant watch on the changing state of the environment; to analyse the trends; to assess the problems using a wide range of data and techniques; and to promote projects leading to environmentally sound development. It plays a catalytic and co-ordinating role within and beyond the UN system. Many UNEP projects are implemented in co-operation with other UN agencies, particularly UNDP, the World Bank group, FAO, UNESCO and WHO. About 45 intergovernmental organizations outside the UN system and 60 international non-governmental organizations have official observer status on UNEP's Governing Council, and, through the Environment Liaison Centre in Nairobi, UNEP is linked to more than 6,000 non-governmental bodies concerned with the environment. UNEP also sponsors international conferences, programmes, plans and agreements regarding all aspects of the environment.

In February 1997 the Governing Council, at its 19th session, adopted a ministerial declaration (the Nairobi Declaration) on UNEP's future role and mandate, which recognized the organization as the principal UN body working in the field of the environment and as the leading global environmental authority, setting and overseeing the international environmental agenda. In June a Special Session of the UN General Assembly, referred to as the 'Earth Summit + 5', was convened to review the state of the environment and progress achieved in implementing the objectives of the UN Conference on Environment and Development (UNCED) in Rio de Janeiro, Brazil, in June 1992. The meeting adopted a Programme for Further Implementation of Agenda 21 (a programme of activities to promote sustainable development, adopted by UNCED) in order to intensify efforts in areas such as energy, freshwater resources and technology transfer. The meeting confirmed UNEP's essential role in advancing the Programme and as a global authority promoting a coherent legal and political approach to the environmental challenges of sustainable development. An extensive process of restructuring and realignment of functions was subsequently initiated by UNEP, and a new organizational structure reflecting the decisions of the Nairobi Declaration was implemented during 1999.

In May 2000 UNEP sponsored the first annual Global Ministerial Environment Forum, held in Malmö, Sweden, and attended by environment ministers and other government delegates from more than 130 countries. Participants reviewed policy issues in the field of the environment and addressed issues such as the impact on the environment of population growth, the depletion of the earth's natural resources, climate change and the need for fresh water supplies. The Forum issued the Malmö Declaration which identified the effective implementation of international agreements on environmental matters at national level as the most pressing challenge for policy makers. The Declaration emphasized the importance of mobilizing domestic and international resources and urged increased co-operation from civil society and the private sector in achieving sustainable development.

ENVIRONMENTAL ASSESSMENT AND EARLY WARNING

The Nairobi Declaration resolved that the strengthening of UNEP's information, monitoring and assessment capabilities was a crucial element of the organization's restructuring, in order to help establish priorities for international, national and regional action, and to ensure the efficient and accurate dissemination of emerging environmental trends and emergencies.

UNEP has developed an extensive network of collaborating centres to assist in its analysis of the state of the global environment. The outcome of its work, the first Global Environment Outlook (GEO-I), was published in January 1997. A second process of global assessment resulted in the publication of GEO-2000 in September 1999. UNEP has initiated a major Global International Waters Assessment to consider all aspects of the world's water-related issues, in particular problems of shared transboundary waters, and of future sustainable management of water resources. UNEP is also a sponsoring agency of the Joint Group of Experts on the Scientific Aspects of Marine Environmental Pollution and contributes to the preparation of reports on the state of the marine environment and on the impact of land-based activities on that environment. In November 1995 UNEP published a Global Biodiversity Assessment, which was the first comprehensive study of biological resources throughout the world.

UNEP's environmental information network includes the Global Resource Information Database (GRID), which converts collected data into information usable by decision-makers. The INFOTERRA programme facilitates the exchange of environmental information through an extensive network of national 'focal points'. At mid-2001 177 countries were participating in the network. UNEP promotes public access to environmental information, as well as participation in environmental concerns, through the INFOTERRA initiative. UNEP aims to establish in every developing region an Environment and Natural Resource Information Network (ENRIN) in order to make available technical advice and manage environmental information and data for improved decision-making and action-planning in countries most in need of assistance. UNEP aims to integrate all its information resources in order to improve access to information and to promote the international exchange of information. This was to be achieved through the design and implementation of UNEPNET, which was to operate throughout the UN system and be fully accessible through the world-wide information networks. In addition, by mid-2001, 16 so-called Mercure satellite systems were operational world-wide, linking UNEP offices and partner agencies.

UNEP's information, monitoring and assessment structures also serve to enhance early-warning capabilities and to provide accurate information during an environmental emergency.

POLICY DEVELOPMENT AND LAW

UNEP aims to promote the development of policy tools and guidelines in order to achieve the sustainable management of the world environment. At a national level it assists governments to develop and implement appropriate environmental instruments and aims to co-ordinate policy initiatives. Training workshops in various aspects of environmental law and its applications are conducted. UNEP supports the development of new legal, economic and other policy instruments to improve the effectiveness of existing environmental agreements.

UNEP was instrumental in the drafting of a Convention on Biological Diversity (CBD) to preserve the immense variety of plant and animal species, in particular those threatened with extinction. The Convention entered into force at the end of 1993; by March 2001 180 countries were parties to the CBD. UNEP supports co-operation for biodiversity assessment and management in selected developing regions and for the development of strategies for the conservation and sustainable exploitation of individual threatened species (e.g. the Global Tiger Action Plan). UNEP also provides assistance for the preparation of individual country studies and strategies to strengthen national biodiversity management and research. In 1996 an *ad hoc* working group on biosafety was established to negotiate the conclusion of a protocol to the CBD to regulate international trade in living modified organisms (including genetically modified—GM—seeds and crops and pharmaceutical derivatives), in order to reduce any potential adverse effects on biodiversity and human health. An extraordinary session of the conference of the parties to the CBD was convened in Cartagena, Colombia, in February 1999, to consider the provisional text formulated by the group and, if approved, to adopt its legally-binding provisions. The meeting, however, was suspended, owing to outstanding differences between the main producer countries and developing nations regarding the implications of the protocol on principles of free trade. An agreement on the so-called Cartagena Protocol was finally concluded at a meeting of parties to the CBD, held in Montreal, Canada, in January 2000. The Protocol permitted countries to ban imports of GM products if there were outstanding safety concerns, and provided for greater transparency in the description of products containing GM organisms, through a limited labelling system.

In October 1994 87 countries, meeting under UN auspices, signed a Convention to Combat Desertification (see UNSO, p. 815), which aimed to provide a legal framework to counter the degradation of drylands. An estimated 75% of all drylands have suffered some land degradation, affecting approximately 1,000m. people in 110 countries. A second conference of the parties to the Convention was held in Dakar, Senegal, in December 1998, a third in Recife, Brazil, in November 1999, and a fourth in Bonn, Germany, in December 2000. UNEP continues to support the implementation of the Convention, as part of its efforts to protect land resources. UNEP also aims to improve the assessment of dryland degradation and desertification in co-operation with governments and other international bodies, as well as identifying the causes of degradation and measures to overcome these.

UNEP estimates that two-thirds of the world's population will suffer chronic water shortages by 2025, owing to rising demand for drinking water as a result of growing populations, decreasing quality of water because of pollution, and increasing requirements of industries and agriculture. UNEP provides scientific, technical and administrative support to facilitate the implementation and co-ordination of regional seas conventions and plans of action. UNEP promotes international co-operation in the management of river basins and coastal areas and for the development of tools and guide-lines to achieve the sustainable management of freshwater and coastal resources. In particular, UNEP aims to control land-based activities, principally pollution, which affect freshwater resources, marine biodiversity and the coastal ecosystems of small-island developing states. In November 1995 110 governments adopted a Global Programme of Action for the Protection of the Marine Environment from Land-based Activities. UNEP aims to develop a similar global instrument to ensure the integrated management of freshwater resources, in order to address current and future needs.

In 1996 UNEP, in collaboration with FAO, began to work towards promoting and formulating a legally-binding international convention on prior informed consent (PIC) for hazardous chemicals and pesticides in international trade, extending a voluntary PIC procedure of information exchange undertaken by more than 100 governments since 1991. The Convention was adopted at a conference held in Rotterdam, Netherlands, in September 1998, and was to enter into force on being ratified by 50 signatory states. It aimed to reduce risks to human health and the environment by restricting the production, export and use of hazardous substances and enhancing information exchange procedures.

In conjunction with UNCHS (Habitat), UNDP, the World Bank and other regional organizations and institutions, UNEP promotes environmental concerns in urban planning and management through the Sustainable Cities Programme, as well as regional workshops concerned with urban pollution and the impact of transportation systems. In January 1994 UNEP inaugurated an International Environmental Technology Centre (IETC), with offices in Osaka and Shiga, Japan, in order to strengthen the capabilities of developing countries and countries with economies in transition to promote environmentally-sound management of cities and freshwater reservoirs through technology co-operation and partnerships.

UNEP has played a key role in global efforts to combat risks to the ozone layer, resultant climatic changes and atmospheric pollution. UNEP worked in collaboration with the World Meteorological Organization to formulate a Framework Convention on Climate Change, with the aim of reducing the emission of gases that have a warming effect on the atmosphere, and has remained an active participant in the ongoing process to review and enforce its implementation. UNEP was the lead agency in formulating the 1987 Montreal Protocol to the Vienna Convention for the Protection of the Ozone Layer (1985), which provided for a 50% reduction in the production of chlorofluorocarbons (CFCs) by 2000. An amendment to the Protocol was adopted in 1990, which required complete cessation of the production of CFCs by 2000 in industrialized countries and by 2010 in developing countries; these deadlines were advanced to 1996 and 2006, respectively, in November 1992. In 1997 the ninth conference of the parties (COP) to the Vienna Convention adopted a further amendment which aimed to introduce a licensing system for all controlled substances. The eleventh COP, meeting in Beijing, People's Republic of China in November/ December 1999, adopted the Beijing Amendment, which imposed tighter controls on the production and consumption of, and trade in, hydrochlorofluorocarbons. A Multilateral Fund for the Implementation of the Montreal Protocol was established in June 1990 to promote the use of suitable technologies and the transfer of technologies to developing countries. UNEP, UNDP, the World Bank and UNIDO are the sponsors of the Fund, which by 2001 had approved financing for 3,600 projects in 124 developing countries at a cost of US $1,190m. Commitments of $440m. were made to the fourth replenishment of the Fund, covering the three-year period 2000–02.

POLICY IMPLEMENTATION

UNEP's Division of Environmental Policy Implementation incorporates two main functions: technical co-operation and response to environmental emergencies.

With the UN Office for the Co-ordination of Humanitarian Assistance, UNEP has established a joint Environment Unit to mobilize and co-ordinate international assistance and expertise for countries facing environmental emergencies and natural disasters. It undertakes initial assessments of the situation, as well as post-conflict analysis, as required. During 1998 the Unit provided assistance to Chile, to combat acute river pollution. Other major environmental emergencies occurred during that year as a result of the floods and heavy rain in Mexico, and as the result of drought caused by the El Niño weather phenomenon in Brazil and Cuba.

UNEP, together with UNDP and the World Bank, is an implementing agency of the Global Environment Facility (GEF, see p. 826), which was established in 1991 as a mechanism for international co-operation in projects concerned with biological diversity, climate change, international waters and depletion of the ozone layer. UNEP services the Scientific and Technical Advisory Panel, which was established to provide expert advice on GEF programmes and operational strategies.

TECHNOLOGY, INDUSTRY AND ECONOMICS

The use of inappropriate industrial technologies and the widespread adoption of unsustainable production and consumption patterns have been identified as being inefficient in the use of renewable resources and wasteful, in particular in the use of energy and water. UNEP aims to encourage governments and the private sector to develop and adopt policies and practices that are cleaner and safer, make efficient use of natural resources, incorporate environmental costs, ensure the environmentally sound management of chemicals, and reduce pollution and risks to human health and the environment. In collaboration with other organizations and agencies UNEP works to define and formulate international guide-lines and agreements to address these issues. UNEP also promotes the transfer of appropriate technologies and organizes conferences and training workshops to provide sustainable production practices. Relevant information is disseminated through the International Cleaner Production Information Clearing House. UNEP, together with UNIDO, has established eight National Cleaner Production Centres to promote a preventive approach to industrial pollution control. In May 1999 representatives of some 33 countries signed an International Declaration on Cleaner Production, launched by UNEP in 1998, with a commitment to implement cleaner and more sustainable production methods and to monitor results.

UNEP provides institutional servicing to the Basel Convention on the Control of Transboundary Movements of Hazardous Wastes and their Disposal, which was adopted in 1989 with the aim of preventing the disposal of wastes from industrialized countries in countries that have no processing facilities. In March 1994 the second meeting of parties to the Convention agreed to ban exportation of hazardous wastes between OECD and non-OECD countries by the end of 1997. The third meeting of parties to the Convention, held in September 1995, proposed that the ban should be incorporated into the Convention as an amendment. The resulting so-called Ban Amendment required ratification by three-quarters of the 62 signatory states present at the time of its adoption before it could enter into effect; by March 2001 the Ban Amendment had been ratified by 24 states. The fourth full meeting of parties to the Convention, held in February 1998, attempted to clarify the classification and listing of hazardous wastes, which was expected to stimulate further ratifications. At July 2001 the number of parties to the Convention had increased from 30 in 1992 to 147. In December 1999 132 states adopted a Protocol to the Convention to address issues relating to liability and compensation for damages from waste exports. The governments also agreed to establish a multilateral fund to finance immediate clean-up operations following any environmental accident.

The UNEP Chemicals office was established to promote the sound management of hazardous substances, central to which was the International Register of Potentially Toxic Chemicals (IRPTC). UNEP aims to facilitate access to data on chemicals and hazardous wastes, in order to assess and control health and environmental risks, by using the IRPTC as a clearing house facility of relevant information and by publishing information and technical reports on the impact of the use of chemicals.

UNEP's OzonAction Programme works to promote information exchange, training and technological awareness. Its objective is to strengthen the capacity of governments and industry in developing countries to undertake measures towards the cost-effective phasing-out of ozone-depleting substances. UNEP also encourages the development of alternative and renewable sources of energy. To achieve this, UNEP is supporting the establishment of a network of centres to research and exchange information of environmentally-sound energy technology resources.

REGIONAL CO-OPERATION AND REPRESENTATION

UNEP maintains six regional offices throughout the world. These work to initiate and promote UNEP objectives and to ensure that all programme formulation and delivery meets the specific needs of countries and regions. They also provide a focal point for building national, sub-regional and regional partnership and enhancing local participation in UNEP initiatives. Following UNEP's reorganization a co-ordination office was established at headquarters to promote regional policy integration, to co-ordinate programme planning, and to provide necessary services to the regional offices.

UNEP provides administrative support to regional conventions, organizes conferences, workshops and seminars at national and regional levels, and may extend advisory services or technical assistance to individual governments.

CONVENTIONS

UNEP aims to develop and promote international environmental legislation in order to pursue an integrated response to global environmental issues, to enhance collaboration among existing convention secretariats, and to co-ordinate support to implement the work programmes of international instruments.

UNEP has been an active participant in the formulation of several major conventions (see above). The Division of Environmental Conventions is mandated to assist the Division of Policy Development and Law in the formulation of new agreements or protocols to existing conventions. Following the successful adoption of the Rotterdam Convention in September 1998, UNEP played a leading role in formulating a multilateral agreement to reduce and ultimately eliminate the manufacture and use of Persistent Organic Pollutants (POPs), which are considered to be a major global environmental hazard. The agreement on POPs, concluded in December 2000 at a conference sponsored by UNEP in Johannesburg, South Africa, was opened for signature in May 2001.

UNEP has been designated to provide secretariat functions to a number of global and regional environmental conventions (see above for list of offices).

COMMUNICATION AND PUBLIC INFORMATION

UNEP's public education campaigns and outreach programmes promote community involvement in environmental issues. Further communication of environmental concerns is undertaken through the media, an information centre service and special promotional events, including World Environment Day, photograph competitions and the awarding of the Sasakawa Prize to recognize distinguished service to the environment by individuals and groups. In 1996

UNEP initiated a Global Environment Citizenship Programme to promote acknowledgment of the environmental responsibilities of all sectors of society.

Finance

UNEP derives its finances from the regular budget of the United Nations and from voluntary contributions to the Environment Fund. A budget of US $120m. was authorized for the two-year period 2000–01, of which $100m. was for programme activities, $14.4m. for management and administration, and $5m. for fund programme reserves.

Publications

Annual Report.
APELL Newsletter (2 a year).
Cleaner Production Newsletter (2 a year).
Climate Change Bulletin (quarterly).
Connect (UNESCO-UNEP newsletter on environmental degradation, quarterly).
Desertification Control Bulletin (2 a year).
EarthViews (quarterly).
Environment Forum (quarterly).
Environmental Law Bulletin (2 a year).
Financial Services Initiative (2 a year).
GEF News (quarterly).
Global Environment Outlook.
GPA Newsletter.
IETC Insight (3 a year).
Industry and Environment Review (quarterly).
Leave it to Us (children's magazine, 2 a year).
Managing Hazardous Waste (2 a year).
Our Planet (quarterly).
OzonAction Newsletter (quarterly).
Tierramerica (every 2 months).
Tourism Focus (2 a year).
UNEP Chemicals Newsletter (2 a year).
UNEP Update (monthly).
World Atlas of Desertification.
Studies, reports, legal texts, technical guide-lines, etc.

United Nations High Commissioner for Refugees—UNHCR

Address: CP 2500, 1211 Geneva 2 dépôt, Switzerland.
Telephone: (22) 7398111; **fax:** (22) 7319546; **e-mail:** unhcr@unhcr.ch; **internet:** www.unhcr.ch.

The Office of the High Commissioner was established in 1951 to provide international protection for refugees and to seek durable solutions to their problems.

Organization
(July 2001)

HIGH COMMISSIONER

The High Commissioner is elected by the United Nations General Assembly on the nomination of the Secretary-General, and is responsible to the General Assembly and to the UN Economic and Social Council (ECOSOC).

High Commissioner: RUUD LUBBERS (Netherlands).
Deputy High Commissioner: MARY ANN WYRSCH (USA).

EXECUTIVE COMMITTEE

The Executive Committee of the High Commissioner's Programme, established by ECOSOC, gives the High Commissioner policy directives in respect of material assistance programmes and advice in the field of international protection. In addition, it oversees UNHCR's general policies and use of funds. The Committee, which comprises representatives of 53 states, both members and non-members of the UN, meets once a year.

ADMINISTRATION

Headquarters include the Executive Office, comprising the offices of the High Commissioner, the Deputy High Commissioner and the Assistant High Commissioner. There are separate offices for the Inspector General, the Special Envoy in the former Yugoslavia, the Director of the UNHCR liaison office in New York, and the Director of the Emergency Response Service. The other principal administrative units are the Division of Communication and Information, the Department of International Protection, the Division of Resource Management, and the Department of Operations, which is responsible for the five regional bureaux covering Africa; Asia and the Pacific; Europe; the Americas and the Caribbean; and Central Asia, South-West Asia, North Africa and the Middle East. At July 1999 there were 274 UNHCR field offices in 120 countries. At that time UNHCR employed 5,155 people, including short-term staff, of whom 4,265 (of 83%) were working in the field.

OFFICES IN SOUTH AND CENTRAL AMERICA AND THE CARIBBEAN

Regional Office for the USA and the Caribbean: 1775 K St, NW, Suite 300, Washington, DC 20006, USA; e-mail usawa@unhcr.ch.

Regional Office for Northern South America: Apdo 69045, Caracas 1062-A, Venezuela.

Regional Office for South America: Cerrito 836, 10°, Buenos Aires 1010, Argentina; e-mail argbu@unhcr.ch.

Activities

The competence of the High Commissioner extends to any person who, owing to well-founded fear of being persecuted for reasons of race, religion, nationality or political opinion, is outside the country of his or her nationality and is unable or, owing to such fear or for reasons other than personal convenience, remains unwilling to accept the protection of that country; or who, not having a nationality and being outside the country of former habitual residence, is unable or, owing to such fear or for reasons other than personal convenience, is unwilling to return to it. Refugees meeting these criteria are entitled to the protection of the Office of the High Commissioner irrespective of their geographical location. This competence may be extended by the Secretary-General or the General Assembly. Refugees who are assisted by other United Nations agencies, or who have the same rights or obligations as nationals of their country of residence, are outside the mandate of UNHCR.

In recent years there has been a significant shift in UNHCR's focus of activities. Increasingly UNHCR was called upon to support people who have been displaced within their own country (i.e. with similar needs to those of refugees but who have not crossed an international border) or those threatened with displacement as a result of armed conflict. In addition, greater support was given to refugees who had returned to their country of origin, to assist their reintegration, and to enable the local community to support the returnees. At December 2000 the refugee population world-wide provisionally totalled 12.1m. and UNHCR was concerned with an estimated further 897,000 asylum-seekers, 793,000 recently returned refugees and 7.3m. others (of whom an estimated 5.3m. were internally displaced persons—IDPs).

INTERNATIONAL PROTECTION

As laid down in the Statute of the Office, one of the two primary functions of UNHCR is to extend international protection to refugees. In the exercise of this function, UNHCR seeks to ensure that refugees and asylum-seekers are protected against *refoulement* (forcible return), that they receive asylum, and that they are treated according to internationally recognized standards. UNHCR pursues these objectives by a variety of means which include promoting the conclusion and ratification by states of international conventions for the protection of refugees. The most comprehensive instrument concerning refugees which has been elaborated at the international level is the 1951 United Nations Convention relating to the Status of Refugees, extended by a Protocol adopted in 1967. The Convention defines the rights and duties of refugees and contains provisions dealing with a variety of matters which affect their day-to-day lives. The application of the 1951 Convention and the 1967 Protocol is supervised by UNHCR. Important provisions for the treatment of refugees are also contained in a number of instruments adopted at the regional level. These include the Organization of African Unity (OAU) Convention of 1969 Governing the Specific Aspects of Refugee Problems, the European Agreement on the Abolition of Visas for Refugees, and the 1969 American Convention on Human Rights.

UNHCR actively encourages States to accede to the 1951 Convention and the 1967 Protocol: by July 2000 139 States had acceded to either or both of these basic refugee instruments. An increasing number of States have also adopted domestic legislation and/or adminstrative measures to implement the international instruments, particularly in the field of procedures for the determination of refugee status. Such measures provide an important guarantee that refugees will be accorded the standards of treatment which have been internationally established for their benefit.

UNHCR has attempted to deal with the problem of military attacks on refugee camps by formulating and encouraging the acceptance of a set of principles to ensure the safety of refugees.

ASSISTANCE ACTIVITIES

UNHCR assistance activities were formerly divided into General Programmes and Special Programmes. The latter were undertaken at the request of the UN General Assembly, the Secretary-General of the UN or member states, in response to a particular crisis. From January 2000 these were amalgamated under a single annual programme.

The first phase of an assistance operation used UNHCR's capacity of emergency preparedness and response. This enables UNHCR to address the immediate needs of refugees at short notice, for example, by employing specially-trained emergency teams and maintaining stockpiles of basic equipment, medical aid and materials. A significant proportion of UNHCR expenditure is allocated to the next phase of an operation, providing 'care and maintenance' in stable refugee circumstances. This assistance can take various forms, including the provision of food, shelter, medical care and essential supplies. Also covered in many instances are basic services, including education and counselling.

In the early 1990s UNHCR aimed to consolidate efforts to integrate certain priorities into its programme planning and implement-

ation, as a standard discipline in all phases of assistance. The considerations include awareness of specific problems confronting refugee women, the needs of refugee children, the environmental impact of refugee programmes and long-term development objectives. In an effort to improve the effectiveness of its programmes, UNHCR initiated a process of delegating authority, as well as responsibilty for operational budgets, to its regional and field representatives, in order to increase flexibility and accountability. In 1995 an Inspection and Evaluation Service (IES) was established to strengthen UNHCR's capacity to review operational effectiveness and efficiency. Responsibility for evaluation activities was transferred to a new Evaluation and Policy Analysis Unit in February 1999. Meanwhile the IES was redesignated as the Inspector General's Office.

As far as possible, assistance is geared towards the identification and implementation of durable solutions to refugee problems—this being the second statutory responsibility of UNHCR. Such solutions generally take one of three forms: voluntary repatriation, local integration or resettlement in another country. Where voluntary repatriation is feasible, the Office assists refugees to overcome obstacles preventing their return to their country of origin. This may be done through negotiations with governments involved, or by providing funds either for the physical movement of refugees or for the rehabilitation of returnees once back in their own country. When voluntary repatriation is not an option, efforts are made to assist refugees to integrate locally and to become self-supporting in their countries of asylum, for example by granting loans to refugees, or by assisting them, through vocational training or in other ways, to learn a skill and to establish themselves in gainful occupations. One major form of assistance to help refugees re-establish themselves outside camps is the provision of housing. In cases where resettlement through emigration is the only viable solution to a refugee problem, UNHCR negotiates with governments in an endeavour to obtain suitable resettlement opportunities, encourage liberalization of admission criteria and draw up special immigration schemes.

REGIONAL ASSISTANCE

In May 1989, when an International Conference on Central American Refugees (CIREFCA) was held in Guatemala, there were some 146,400 refugees receiving UNHCR assistance (both for emergency relief and for longer-term self-sufficiency programmes) in the region, as well as an estimated 1.8m. other refugees and displaced persons. UNHCR and UNDP were designated as the principal UN organizations to implement the CIREFCA plan of action for the repatriation or resettlement of refugees, alongside national co-ordinating committees. UNHCR quick-impact projects were implemented in the transport, health, agricultural production and other sectors to support returnee reintegration (of both refugees and internally displaced persons) into local communities, and to promote the self-sufficiency of the returning populations. Implementation of UNHCR's programme for the repatriation of some 45,000 Guatemalan refugees in Mexico began in January 1993 with a convoy of 2,400 people. UNHCR initiated projects to support the reintegration of Guatemalan returnees, and in 1994–95 undertook a campaign to clear undetonated explosives in forest areas where they had resettled. The CIREFCA process was formally concluded in June 1994, by which time some 118,000 refugees had voluntarily returned to their countries of origin under the auspices of the programme, while thousands of others had integrated into their host countries. In December a meeting was held, in San José, Costa Rica, to commemorate the 10th anniversary of the Cartagena Declaration, which had provided a comprehensive framework for refugee protection in the region. The meeting adopted the San José Declaration on Refugees and Displaced Persons, which aimed to harmonize legal criteria and procedures to consolidate actions for durable solutions of voluntary repatriation and local integration in the region. UNHCR's efforts in the region have subsequently emphasized legal issues and refugee protection, while assisting governments to formulate national legislation on asylum and refugees. At the end of 2000 the outstanding population of concern to UNHCR in Central America comprised an estimated 18,451, mainly Guatemalan, refugees remaining in Mexico. At that time Costa Rica was hosting a refugee population of some 5,519, of whom nearly one-half were from Nicaragua.

In 1999 the Colombian Government approved an operational plan proposed by UNHCR to address a massive population displacement that had arisen in that country in recent years (escalating from 1997), as a consequence of ongoing internal conflict and alleged human rights abuses committed by armed groups. At the end of 2000 some 525,000 IDPs were of concern to UNHCR and believed to require urgent assistance; many of these had congregated near Colombia's borders with Ecuador, Panama and Venezuela. Small influxes of Colombian refugees had entered neighbouring countries. During 2000 UNHCR monitored cross-border population movements, assisted with the implementation of an IDP registration plan, supported a pilot early warning project to forecast future population movements and provided training in emergency response to displacements. UNHCR also co-operated with UNICEF (q.v.) to improve the provision of education to displaced children. In 2001 the Office's main concerns in Colombia included supporting ongoing changes in the country's institutional framework for IDPs; enhancing the implementation at community-level of national policy on IDPs; and improving the co-ordination of concerned international agencies.

CO-OPERATION WITH OTHER ORGANIZATIONS

UNHCR works closely with other UN agencies, intergovernmental organizations and non-governmental organizations to increase the scope and effectiveness of its emergency operations. Within the UN system UNHCR co-operates, principally, with the World Food Programme in the distribution of food aid and UNICEF and the World Health Organization in the provision of family welfare and child immunization programmes. UNHCR co-operates with the UN Development Programme in development-related activities and has participated in the preparation of guide-lines for the continuum of emergency assistance to development programmes. In July 1998 UNHCR signed an agreement with the Inter-American Institute of Human Rights to undertake joint research and training and to provide other technical assistance in the fields of refugees and human rights. In 1999 UNHCR worked with 513 NGOs as 'implementing partners'.

Finance

The United Nations regular budget finances a proportion of UNHCR administrative expenditure. The majority of UNHCR expenditure (about 98%) is funded by voluntary contributions, mainly from governments. A Private Sector and Public Affairs Service, established in 2001, aims to increase funding from non-governmental donor sources, partly by developing partnerships with foundations and corporations. Prior to 2000 UNHCR's activities were designated as General Programmes and Special Programmes, with separate budgets. With effect from January 2000 these were unified under a single annual programme budget. Any further requirements identified following the approval of the annual programme budget were to be managed in the form of supplementary programmes, to be funded by separate appeals. Of the total US $831.2m. approved under the programme budget for 2001, $25.4m. (3.1%) was allocated to the Americas.

PERSONS OF CONCERN TO UNHCR IN LATIN AMERICA AND THE CARIBBEAN* (at 31 December 2000, provisional figures)

Country	Refugees	Asylum-seekers	Returnees	Others
Argentina . . .	2,396	1,274	—	—
Belize	1,250	—	—	8,567†
Brazil	2,722	543	—	—
Colombia . . .	239	12	309	525,000‡
Costa Rica . . .	5,519	1,089	—	—
Ecuador . . .	1,602	151	—	—
Mexico	18,451	11	6	—
Panama . . .	1,316	52	257	—

* Figures are provided mostly by governments, based on their own records and methods of estimation. Countries with fewer than 1,000 persons of concern to UNHCR are not listed.
† UNHCR estimates a further 20,000 undocumented displaced persons from Central America have resided in Belize since the early 1980s.
‡ Internally displaced persons.

Publications

Refugees (quarterly, in English, French, German, Italian, Japanese and Spanish).
Refugee Survey Quarterly.
The State of the World's Refugees.
UNHCR Handbook for Emergencies.

Food and Agriculture Organization—FAO

Address: Viale delle Terme di Caracalla, 00100 Rome, Italy.
Telephone: (06) 57051; **fax:** (06) 5705-3152; **e-mail:** fao-hq@fao.org; **internet:** www.fao.org.
FAO, the first specialized agency of the UN to be founded after World War II, was established in Québec, Canada, in October 1945. The Organization aims to alleviate malnutrition and hunger and serves as a co-ordinating agency for development programmes in the whole range of food and agriculture, including forestry and fisheries. It helps developing countries to promote educational and training facilities and the establishment of appropriate institutions.

Organization

(July 2001)

CONFERENCE

The governing body is the FAO Conference of member nations. It meets every two years, formulates policy, determines the Organization's programme and budget on a biennial basis, and elects new members. It also elects the Director-General of the Secretariat and the Independent Chairman of the Council. In alternate years, FAO also holds conferences in each of its five regions (the Near East, Asia and the Pacific, Africa, Latin America and the Caribbean, and Europe).

COUNCIL

The FAO Council is composed of representatives of 49 member nations, elected by the Conference for staggered three-year terms. It is the interim governing body of FAO between sessions of the Conference. The most important standing committees of the Council are: the Finance and Programme Committees, the Committee on Commodity Problems, the Committee on Fisheries, the Committee on Agriculture and the Committee on Forestry.

SECRETARIAT

The total number of staff at FAO headquarters at September 1999 was 2,278, while staff in field, regional and country offices numbered 1,865; these included 67 associate experts at headquarters and 132 in field, regional and country offices. Work is supervised by the following Departments: Administration and Finance; General Affairs and Information; Economic and Social Policy; Agriculture; Forestry; Fisheries; Sustainable Development; and Technical Co-operation.

Director-General: JACQUES DIOUF (Senegal).

REGIONAL AND SUB-REGIONAL OFFICES

Regional Office for Latin America: Avda Dag Hammarskjöld 3241, Vitacura, Casilla 10095, Santiago, Chile; tel. (2) 337-2100; fax (2) 337-2101; e-mail fao-rlc@field.fao.org; internet www.rlc.fao.org; Regional Rep. GUSTAVO GORDILLO DE ANDA.

Sub-regional Office for the Caribbean: POB 631-C, Bridgetown, Barbados; tel. 426-7110; fax 427-6075; e-mail fao-slac@field.fao.org; Sub-regional Rep. JOSEPH SYDNEY JOHNSON.

Activities

FAO aims to raise levels of nutrition and standards of living, by improving the production and distribution of food and other commodities derived from farms, fisheries and forests. FAO provides technical information, advice and assistance by disseminating information; acting as a neutral forum for discussion of food and agricultural issues; advising governments on policy and planning; and developing capacity directly in the field.

In November 1999 the FAO Conference identified the following areas of activity as FAO priorities for 2000–01: the Special Programme for Food Security; transboundary animal and plant pests and diseases; forest conservation; the Codex Alimentarius Code on food standards; and strengthening the Technical Co-operation Programme (which funds 12% of FAO's field programme expenditure). The Conference also approved a Strategic Framework for the period 2000–15, which emphasized national and international co-operation in pursuing the goals of the World Food Summit (see below). In October 1997 FAO organized its first televised fund-raising event 'TeleFood', broadcast to an estimated 500m. viewers in some 70 countries. The initiative has subsequently been repeated on an annual basis in order to raise public awareness of the problems of hunger and malnutrition. Since 1997 public donations to TeleFood have exceeded US $6m., financing more than 700 'grass-roots' projects in more than 100 countries. The projects have provided tools, seeds and other essential supplies directly to small-scale farmers, and have been especially aimed at helping women.

In November 1996 FAO hosted the World Food Summit, which was held in Rome and was attended by heads of state and senior government representatives of 186 countries. Participants approved the Rome Declaration on World Food Security and the World Food Summit Plan of Action, with the aim of halving the number of people afflicted by undernutrition, at that time estimated to total 828m. world-wide, by no later than 2015. A review conference to assess progress in achieving the goals of the summit was to be held in November 2001.

AGRICULTURE

About one-quarter of FAO's Field Programme expenditure is devoted to increasing crop production, in particular in developing countries, by a number of methods, including improved seeds and fertilizer use, soil conservation and reafforestation, better management of water resources, upgrading storage facilities, and improvements in processing and marketing. FAO places special emphasis on the cultivation of under-exploited traditional food crops, such as cassava, sweet potatoes and plantains.

FAO is concerned with the sustainable use and conservation of genetic resources, and advises governments on improving the supply of seeds and on crop protection: animal and plant gene banks are maintained. In June 1996 representatives of 150 governments attending a conference in Leipzig, Germany, organized by FAO, adopted a Global Plan of Action to conserve and improve the use of plant genetic resources, in order to enhance food security throughout the world. In particular, the Plan emphasized the importance of the production and distribution of locally-adapted plant varieties.

Plant protection, weed control, and animal health programmes form an important part of FAO's work as farming methods become more intensive, and pests more resistant to control methods. In 1985 FAO member nations approved an International Code of Conduct on the Distribution and Use of Pesticides, and in 1989 the Conference adopted an additional clause concerning 'Prior Informed Consent' (PIC), whereby international shipments of newly banned or restricted pesticides should not proceed without the agreement of importing countries. Under the clause, FAO aims to inform governments about the hazards of toxic chemicals and to urge them to take proper measures to curb trade in highly toxic agrochemicals while keeping the pesticides industry informed of control actions. In mid-1996 FAO, in collaboration with UNEP, publicized a new initiative which aimed to increase awareness of, and to promote international action on, obsolete and hazardous stocks of pesticides remaining throughout the world. In September 1998 a new legally-binding treaty on the PIC procedure for trade in hazardous chemicals and pesticides was adopted at an international conference held in Rotterdam, the Netherlands. The so-called Rotterdam Convention required that hazardous chemicals and pesticides banned or severely restricted in at least two countries should not be exported unless explicitly agreed by the importing country. It also identified certain pesticide formulations as too dangerous to be used by farmers in developing countries, and incorporated an obligation that countries halt national production of those hazardous compounds. The treaty was to enter into force on being ratified by 50 signatory states. FAO was co-operating with UNEP to provide an interim secretariat for the Convention. In July 1999 a conference on the Rotterdam Convention, held in Rome, established an Interim Chemical Review Committee with responsibility for recommending the inclusion of chemicals or pesticide formulations in the PIC procedure. By September the treaty had been signed by 60 states. As part of its continued efforts to reduce the environmental risks posed by over-reliance on pesticides, FAO is extending to other regions its Integrated Pest Management (IPM) programme in Asia and the Pacific on the adoption of safer and more effective methods of pest control. IPM reduces the need for pesticides by introducing biological control methods and natural predators, such as spiders and wasps, to avert pests. In February 2001 FAO warned that some 30% of pesticides sold in developing countries did not meet internationally accepted quality standards.

FAO's Joint Division with the international Atomic Energy Agency (IAEA), tests controlled-release formulas of pesticides and herbicides that can limit the amount of agrochemicals needed to protect crops, and is engaged in exploring biotechnologies and in developing non-toxic fertilizers (especially those that are locally available) and improved strains of food crops (especially from indigenous varieties). FAO's plant nutrition activities aim to promote nutrient management, such as the Integrated Plant Nutritions Systems (IPNS) which are based on the recycling of nutrients through crop production and the efficient use of mineral fertilizers. FAO's work on soil

conservation includes erosion control and the reclamation of degraded land, such as reafforestation after indiscriminate tree-cutting. In 1999 FAO estimated that 3m. sq km of farmland in Latin America and the Caribbean had been severely degraded and 800,000 sq km was threatened with desertification. A joint programme, with the International Fund for Agricultural Development (IFAD), was to be implemented to improve land use and productivity. FAO also assists in developing water resources and irrigation, and in preventing post-harvest losses due to inefficient storage, infestation by pests, and transport problems.

An Emergency Prevention System for Transboundary Animal and Plant Pests and Diseases (EMPRES) was established in 1994 to strengthen FAO's activities in the prevention, control and, where possible, eradication of pests, such as locusts, and of highly contagious livestock diseases (which the system categorizes as epidemic diseases of strategic importance, such as rinderpest or foot-and-mouth; diseases requiring tactical attention at international or regional level, e.g. Rift Valley fever; and emerging diseases, e.g. bovine spongiform encephalopathy—BSE).

In January 1999 the Committee on Agriculture recommended the development of a cross-sectoral programme on organic agriculture; an inter-departmental working group was subsequently formed to initiate related activities.

ENVIRONMENT

At the UN Conference on Environment and Development, held in Brazil in 1992, FAO supported the adoption of Agenda 21, a programme of activities to promote sustainable development. FAO was subsequently designated as the UN agency responsible for the chapters of Agenda 21 concerning water resources, forests, fragile mountain ecosystems and sustainable agriculture and rural development.

FISHERIES

FAO's Fisheries Department consists of a multi-disciplinary body of experts who are involved in every aspect of fisheries development from coastal surveys, improved production, processing and storage, to the compilation and analysis of statistics, development of computer databases, improvement of fishing gear, institution building and training. In November 1995 the FAO Conference adopted a Code of Conduct for Responsible Fishing, which incorporated many global fisheries and aquaculture issues (including fisheries resource conservation and development, fish catches, seafood and fish processing, commercialization, trade and research) to promote the sustainable development of the sector. In February 1999 the FAO Committee on Fisheries adopted new international measures, within the framework of the Code of Conduct, in order to reduce over-exploitation of the world's fish resources, as well as plans of action for the conservation and management of sharks and the reduction in the incidental catch of seabirds in longline fisheries. The voluntary measures were endorsed at a ministerial meeting, held in March and attended by representatives of some 126 countries, which issued a declaration to promote the implementation of the Code of Conduct and to achieve sustainable management of fisheries and aquaculture. FAO promotes aquaculture as a valuable source of animal protein, and as an income-generating activity for rural communities. In February 2000 FAO and the Network of Aquaculture Centres in Asia and the Pacific (NACA) jointly convened a Conference on Aquaculture in the Third Millennium, which was held in Bangkok, Thailand and attended by participants representing more than 200 governmental and non-governmental organizations in 66 countries. The Conference debated global trends in aquaculture and future policy measures to ensure the sustainable development of the sector.

FORESTRY

FAO focuses on the contribution of forestry to food security, on effective and responsible forest management and on maintaining a balance between the economic, ecological and social benefits of forest resources. The Organization has helped to develop national forestry programmes and to promote the sustainable development of all types of forest. FAO's Forests, Trees and People Programme promotes the sustainable management of tree and forest resources, based on local knowledge and management practices, in order to improve the livelihoods of rural people in developing countries. A Strategic Plan for Forestry was approved in March 1999; its main objectives were to maintain the environmental diversity of forests, to realise the economic potential of forests and trees within a sustainable framework, and to expand access to information on forestry.

NUTRITION

In December 1992 an International Conference on Nutrition was held in Rome, administered jointly by FAO and WHO. The Conference approved a World Declaration on Nutrition and a Plan of Action, with the aim of eliminating hunger and reducing levels of malnutrition by incorporating nutritional objectives into national development policies and government programmes. Since the conference, more than 100 countries have formulated national plans of action for nutrition, many of which were based on existing development plans such as comprehensive food security initiatives, national poverty alleviation programmes and action plans to attain the targets set by the World Summit for Children in September 1990. In October 1996 FAO, WHO and other partners jointly organized the first World Congress on Calcium and Vitamin D in Human Life, held in Rome. In January 2001 a joint team of FAO and WHO experts issued a report concerning the allergenicity of foods derived from biotechnology (i.e. genetically modified—GM foods).

PROCESSING AND MARKETING

An estimated 20% of all food harvested is lost before it can be consumed. FAO helps reduce immediate post-harvest losses, with the introduction of improved processing methods and storage systems. It also advises on the distribution and marketing of agricultural produce and on the selection and preparation of foods for optimum nutrition. Many of these activities form part of wider rural development projects. FAO evaluates new market trends and helps to develop improved plant and animal quarantine procedures. FAO continues to favour the elimination of export subsidies and related discriminatory practices, such as protectionist measures that hamper international trade in agricultural commodities. FAO has organized regional workshops and national projects in order to help member states to implement World Trade Organization regulations, in particular with regard to agricultural policy, intellectual property rights, sanitary and phytosanitary measures, technical barriers to trade and the international standards of the Codex Alimentarius. In August 1999 FAO announced the establishment of a new forum, PhAction, to promote post-harvest research and the development of effective post-harvest services and infrastructure.

FOOD SECURITY

FAO's policy on food security aims to encourage the production of adequate food supplies, to maximize stability in the flow of supplies, and to ensure access on the part of those who need them. In 1994 FAO initiated a Special Programme for Food Security (SPFS), which was designed to assist low-income countries with a food deficit to increase food production and productivity as rapidly as possible, primarily through the widespread adoption by farmers of improved production technologies, with emphasis on areas of high potential. In March 1999 FAO signed agreements with IFAD and the World Food Programme (WFP, q.v.), in order to increase co-operation under the framework of the SPFS. At April 2001 82 countries were categorized as 'low-income food-deficit', of which seven were in Latin America and the Caribbean (Bolivia, Cuba, Ecuador, Guatemala, Haiti, Honduras and Nicaragua). By June the SPFS was operational in 64 countries.

FAO's Global Information and Early Warning System (GIEWS) maintains a database on and monitors the crop and food outlook at global, regional, national and sub-national levels in order to detect emerging food supply difficulties and disasters and to ensure rapid intervention in countries experiencing food supply shortages. The GIEWS issues special alerts which describe the situation in countries or sub-regions experiencing food difficulties and recommends an appropriate international response. In 1997 the GIEWS intensified its efforts in monitoring the effects of the weather phenomenon known as El Niño on foodcrops production, particularly in Latin America and the Caribbean, and issued four special reports assessing the impact of the weather phenomenon in Latin America, Asia and Southern Africa. In late 1998 and early 1999 the GIEWS conducted missions to Honduras and Nicaragua to assess the damage to crops caused by 'Hurricane Mitch', which had struck the region in October 1998, and the implications on short- and medium-term food supply and demand. In October 1999 FAO published the first annual *State of Food Insecurity in the World*, based on data compiled by a new Food Insecurity and Vulnerability Information and Mapping Systems programme.

FAO INVESTMENT CENTRE

The Investment Centre was established in 1964 to help countries prepare viable investment projects that would attract external financing. The Centre focuses on projects concerned with the promotion of sustainable activities for land management, forestry development, environmental protection, and the alleviation of rural poverty. In 1998–99 76 projects were approved, representing a total investment of US $4,670m.

EMERGENCY RELIEF

FAO's Special Relief Operations Service provides emergency aid and attempts to rehabilitate agricultural production following nat-

ural and man-made disasters, for example through the provision of seeds, tools and technical advice. In 1997 more than 60 countries suffered the effects of heavy flooding or severe drought (occasionally, as in the case of Indonesia, folllowed by extensive forest fires), caused wholly or partially by El Niño. FAO attempted to help assess the damage to agricultural systems, to provide rehabilitation assistance and to initiate efforts to strengthen the resistance of agricultural sectors against future weather anomalies. In 1998 FAO was concerned at the possible effects of a converse climatic occurrence, 'La Niña', caused by upswelling of cold water in areas of the Pacific Ocean. Projects approved in 1999 included emergency assistance to farmers affected by 'Hurricane Georges' in Antigua and Barbuda, the Dominican Republic and St Christopher and Nevis; support to communities in Colombia following an earthquake; agricultural rehabilitation in Honduras; assistance to small-scale farmers in Chiapas, Mexico; an assessment of the effects of flooding in Venezuela; and a regional operation providing emergency assistance for the formulation of national hurricane disaster preparedness plans. Jointly with the United Nations, FAO is responsible for the WFP which provides emergency food supplies, and food aid in support of development projects.

INFORMATION

FAO functions as an information centre, collecting, analysing, interpreting and disseminating information through various media, including an extensive internet site. It issues regular statistical reports, commodity studies, and technical manuals in local languages (see list of publications below). Other materials produced by the FAO include information booklets, reference papers, reports of meetings, training manuals and audiovisuals.

FAO compiles and co-ordinates an extensive range of international databases on agriculture, fisheries, forestry, food and statistics, the most important of these being AGRIS (the International Information System for the Agricultural Sciences and Technology) and CARIS (the Current Agricultural Research Information System). Statistical databases include the GLOBEFISH databank and electronic library, FISHDAB (the Fisheries Statistical Database), FORIS (Forest Resources Information System), and GIS (the Geographic Information System). In addition, AGROSTAT PC has been designed to provide access to updated figures in six agriculture-related topics via personal computer. In 1996 FAO established a World Agricultural Information Centre (WAICENT), which offers wide access to agricultural data through the electronic media.

FAO Regional Commissions

(Based at the Rome headquarters.)

Caribbean Plant Protection Commission: f. 1967 to preserve the existing plant resources of the area.

Commission for Inland Fisheries of Latin America: f. 1976 to assist national and regional fishery and limnological surveys and programmes of research and development leading to the rational utilization of inland fishery resources.

Latin American and Caribbean Forestry Commission: f. 1948 to advise on formulation of forest policy and review and co-ordinate its implementation throughout the region; to exchange information and advise on technical problems. Mems: 31 states.

Regional Fisheries Advisory Commission for the South-west Atlantic: f. 1961 to advise FAO on fisheries in the South-west Atlantic area, to advise member countries on the administration and rational exploitation of marine and inland resources; to assist in the collection and dissemination of data, in training, and to promote liaison and co-operation. Mems: Argentina, Brazil, Uruguay.

Western Central Atlantic Fishery Commission: f. 1973 to assist international co-operation for the conservation, development and utilization of the living resources, especially shrimps, of the Western Central Atlantic.

Finance

FAO's Regular Programme, which is financed by contributions from member governments, covers the cost of the FAO's Secretariat, its Technical Co-operation Programme (TCP) and part of the cost of several special action programmes. The budget for the two years 2000–01 was maintained at US $650m., the same as for the previous biennium. Much of FAO's Field Programme is from external sources such as UNDP (which, in 1999, provided $26m., or 8.5% of total field project expenditures) and various trust funds provided by donor countries and international financing institutions (which provided $228m., or 76.5% of the total in that year). FAO's contribution to the Field Programme under the TCP amounted to $39m., or 13% of field project expenditures in 1999, while the contribution under the Special Programme for Food Security was $5m., or 2% of the total $298m.

World Food Programme

Address: Via Cesare Giulio Viola 68, Parco dei Medici, 00148 Rome, Italy.

Telephone: (06) 6513-1; **fax:** (06) 6590-632; **e-mail:** wfpinfo @wfp.org; **internet:** www.wfp.org.

WFP, which became operational in January 1963, is the principal food aid agency of the UN. It aims to eradicate chronic undernourishment by assisting social development and human growth, and to alleviate acute hunger by providing emergency relief following natural or man-made humanitarian disasters. Priority is given to vulnerable groups, such as children and pregnant women. During 2000 WFP food assistance benefited some 83m. people world-wide, of whom 22m. received aid through development projects, 25m. were refugees, returnees or internally displaced, and 36m. were victims of natural disasters. Total food deliveries amounted to 3.7m. metric tons in 83 countries.

Through its development activities WFP aims to alleviate poverty in developing countries by promoting self-reliant families and communities. Food is supplied, for example, as an incentive in labour-intensive projects which provide employment and strengthen self-help capacity. WFP supports activities that are designed to increase agricultural production, to rehabilitate and improve local infrastructure, particularly transport systems, and to encourage education, training and health programmes. Some WFP projects are intended to alleviate the effects of structural adjustment programmes (particularly programmes which involve reductions in public expenditure and in subsidies for basic foods). During 2000 WFP supported 189 development projects in 59 countries world-wide.

In the early 1990s there was a substantial shift in the balance between emergency relief and development assistance provided by WFP, owing to the growing needs of victims of drought and other natural disasters, refugees and displaced persons. WFP contingency planning for emergencies includes the maintenance of food reserves and logistical equipment at sites in Italy and Kenya and the preparation of stand-by arrangements to ensure the rapid deployment of personnel and equipment. Following a comprehensive evaluation of its activities, WFP is increasingly focused on linking its relief and development activities to provide a continuum betwen short-term relief and longer-term rehabilitation and development. In order to achieve this objective, WFP aims to integrate elements that strengthen disaster mitigation into development projects and to promote capacity-building elements within relief operations. So-called Protracted Relief and Recovery Operations (PRROs) approved in 1999 included a regional operation in Central America which was concerned with enabling communities affected by 'Hurricane Mitch' to rehabilitate farms and local infrastructures by guaranteeing household food security and promoting food-for-work initiatives, and also aimed to enhance the nutrition of schoolchildren and provide food aid to vulnerable groups; and a similar operation to support populations displaced from their homes by ongoing insecurity in Colombia. Emergency projects approved in the first half of 2001 included the provision of food aid to families in drought- and flood-affected areas of Bolivia, and to communities affected by an earthquake that occurred in January in El Salvador. In 1999 WFP expenditure on relief operations (including emergency relief and PRROs) in Latin America and the Caribbean amounted to US $67.6m.

WFP Executive Director: CATHERINE A. BERTINI (USA).

FAO Publications

Animal Health Yearbook.
Commodity Review and Outlook (annually).
Environment and Energy Bulletin.
Fertilizer Yearbook.
Food Crops and Shortages.
Food Outlook (5 a year).
Plant Protection Bulletin (quarterly).
Production Yearbook (in English, French and Spanish).
Quarterly Bulletin of Statistics.
The State of Food and Agriculture (annually).
The State of Food Insecurity in the World (annually).
The State of World Fisheries and Aquaculture (every 2 years).
The State of the World's Forests (every 2 years).
Trade Yearbook.
Unasylva (quarterly).
Yearbook of Fishery Statistics (in English, French and Spanish).
Yearbook of Forest Products (in English, French and Spanish).
World Animal Review (quarterly).
World Watch List for Domestic Animal Diversity.

International Bank for Reconstruction and Development—IBRD—and International Development Association—IDA (World Bank)

Address: 1818 H St, NW, Washington, DC 20433, USA.

Telephone: (202) 477-1234; **fax:** (202) 477-6391; **e-mail:** pic@ worldbank.org; **internet:** www.worldbank.org.

The IBRD was established in December 1945. Initially it was concerned with post-war reconstruction in Europe; since then its aim has been to assist the economic development of member nations by making loans where private capital is not available on reasonable terms to finance productive investments. Loans are made either directly to governments or to private enterprises with the guarantee of their government. The World Bank, as it is commonly known, comprises the IBRD and IDA. The affiliated group of institutions, comprising the IBRD, IDA, the International Finance Corporation (IFC, q.v.), the Multilateral Investment Guarantee Agency (MIGA, q.v.), and the International Centre for Settlement of Investment disputes (ICSID) is referred to as the World Bank Group.

Only members of the International Monetary Fund (IMF, q.v.) may be considered for membership in the Bank. Subscriptions to the capital stock of the Bank are based on each member's quota in the IMF, which is designed to reflect the country's relative economic strength. Voting rights are related to shareholdings.

Organization

(July 2001)

Officers and staff of the IBRD serve concurrently as officers and staff in the International Development Association (IDA). The Bank has offices in New York, Paris, Brussels, London and Tokyo; regional missions in Nairobi (for eastern Africa) and Abidjan (for western Africa); and resident missions in more than 70 countries.

BOARD OF GOVERNORS

The Board of Governors consists of one Governor appointed by each member nation. Typically, a Governor is the country's finance minister, central bank governor, or a minister or an official of comparable rank. The Board normally meets once a year.

EXECUTIVE DIRECTORS

The general operations of the Bank are conducted by a Board of 24 Executive Directors. Five Directors are appointed by the five members having the largest number of shares of capital stock, and the rest are elected by the Governors representing the other members. The President of the Bank is Chairman of the Board.

OFFICERS

President and Chairman of Executive Directors: JAMES D. WOLFENSOHN (USA).

Vice-President, Latin America and the Caribbean Regional Office: DAVID DE FERRANTI.

Activities

FINANCIAL OPERATIONS

The World Bank has traditionally financed capital infrastructure projects (e.g. in communications and energy). The Bank's primary objectives are the achievement of sustainable economic growth and the reduction of poverty in developing countries, and the protection of the environment. In the context of stimulating economic growth the Bank promotes both private-sector development and human resource development. The Bank's efforts to reduce poverty comprise two main elements: the compiling of country-specific assessments and the formulation of country assistance strategies (CASs) to review and guide the Bank's country programmes. Since August 1998 the Bank has published CASs, with the approval of the governments concerned. In March 1997 the Board of Executive Directors endorsed a 'Strategic Compact', providing for a programme of reforms, to be implemented over a period of 30 months, to increase the effectiveness of the Bank in achieving its central objective of poverty reduction. The reforms included greater decentralization of decision-making and investment in front-line operations, enhancing the administration of loans, and improving access to information and co-ordination of Bank activities through a knowledge-management system comprising four thematic networks: the Human Development Network; the Environmentally and Socially Sustainable Development Network; the Finance, Private Sector and Infrastructure Development Network; and the Poverty Reduction and Economic Management Network. In 1998/99 the Bank's Executive Directors endorsed a Comprehensive Development Framework (CDF) to effect a new approach to development assistance based on partnerships and country responsibility, with an emphasis on the interdependence of the social, structural, human, governmental, economic and environmental elements of development. The Framework, which aimed to enhance the overall effectiveness of development assistance, was formulated after a series of consultative meetings, organized by the Bank and attended by representatives of governments, donor agencies, financial institutions, non-governmental organizations, the private sector and academics. By May 2000 13 countries, including Bolivia and the Dominican Republic, were implementing pilot projects based on the CDF concept; in Bolivia a National Dialogue was convened, comprising representatives of government, civil society and the private sector, to formulate a five-year action plan.

IBRD loans are usually for a period of 20 years or less. Loans are made to governments, or must be guaranteed by the government concerned. IDA assistance is aimed at the poorer developing countries (i.e. mainly those with a per head GNP of less than US $885 during the financial year ending 30 June 2000 qualified for assistance in 2000/01). Under IDA lending conditions, credits can be extended to countries which, for balance of payments reasons, could not assume the burden of repayment required for IBRD loans. Terms are more favourable than those provided by the IBRD; credits are for a period of 35–40 years, with a grace period of 10 years, and carry no interest charges.

The IBRD's capital is derived from members' subscriptions to capital shares, the calculation of which is based on their quotas in the International Monetary Fund (q.v.). At 30 June 2000 the total subscribed capital of the IBRD was US $188,606m., of which the paid-in portion was $11,418m. (or 6.1%); the remainder is subject to call if required. Most of the IBRD's lendable funds come from its borrowing in world capital markets, and also from its retained earnings and the flow of repayments on its loans. Bank loans carry a variable interest rate, rather than a rate fixed at the time of borrowing.

IDA's total development resources, consisting of members' subscriptions and supplementary resources (additional subscriptions and contributions) are replenished periodically by contributions from the more affluent member countries. In November 1998 representatives of 39 donor countries agreed to provide US $11,600m. for the 12th replenishment of IDA funds, enabling total lending to amount to an estimated $20,500m. in the period July 1999–June 2002. The new IDA-12 resources were to be directed towards the following objectives: investing in people; promoting good governance; promoting broad-based growth; and protecting the environment.

During the year ending 30 June 2000 lending approved for Latin America and the Caribbean amounted to US $4,063.4m. (26.6% of

World Bank assistance in that year), of which $165.3m. was in IDA credits and the rest was in IBRD loans (see tables below). Of the total approved for the region in 1999/2000 some 32% was for projects in the finance sector, 27% for public sector management, and 16% for social protection projects.

In September 1996 the World Bank/IMF Development Committee endorsed a joint initiative to assist heavily indebted poor countries (HIPCs) to reduce their debt burden to a sustainable level, in order to make more resources available for poverty reduction and economic growth. A new Trust Fund was established by the World Bank in November to finance the initiative. The Fund, consisting of an initial allocation of US $500m. from the IBRD surplus and other contributions from multilateral creditors, was to be administered by IDA. Of the 41 HIPCs identified by the Bank, four were in Latin America and the Caribbean: Bolivia, Guyana, Honduras and Nicaragua. In order to qualify for debt relief under the initiative at the so-called 'decision point', an HIPC was required to demonstrate sound financial management for a period of three years and to produce a Poverty Reduction Strategy Paper. Having qualified, an HIPC would then implement a comprehensive programme of measures agreed with the World Bank and IMF, supported by interim assistance from those institutions and by highly-concessionary debt relief from other official (bilateral and multilateral) creditors. Subsequently 'completion point' would be reached, whereupon the World Bank and IMF were to release the remaining debt relief committed at decision point and the other official creditors would instigate a stock-of-debt reduction operation on high concessionary terms. In April 1997 the World Bank and the IMF announced that Uganda was to be the first beneficiary of the initiative. Assistance for Bolivia was approved in September which aimed to reduce the Bolivian Government's external debt by $448m., of which the Bank's share was $54m. In December 1997 the IMF and World Bank approved a debt reduction initiative for Guyana, which envisaged reducing that country's total external debt by $256m. The Bank pledged to provide some $27m. from the Trust Fund in order to purchase and cancel Guyana's debts with IDA.

In early 1999 the World Bank and IMF initiated a comprehensive review of the HIPC initiative. In June the Group of Seven industrialized nations (G-7) and Russia agreed to increase contributions to the HIPC Trust Fund and to cancel substantial amounts of outstanding debt. In September the Bank and IMF reached an agreement on an enhanced HIPC scheme which aimed to allow more countries to benefit from the initiative, to accelerate the process by which a country may qualify for assistance, and to enhance the effectiveness of debt relief. Additional revenue was to be generated through the revaluation of a percentage of IMF gold reserves. It was agreed, in order to qualify for debt relief, countries were to demonstrate an unsustainable level of debt at the 'decision point' of the process of more than 150% of the net present value (NPV) of the debt in relation to total annual exports (compared with 200%-250% under the original HIPC scheme). Other countries with a lower debt-to-export ratio were to be eligible for assistance under the initiative, providing that their export earnings were at least 30% of GDP (lowered from 40%) and government revenue at least 15% of GDP (reduced from 20%). In January 2000 Bolivia qualified for assistance totalling US $854m. in NPV terms under the enhanced initiative (conditional on assurances of co-operation from other official creditors), of which the Bank's share was $141m. A Joint IMF/World Bank Implementation Committee was established in April to co-ordinate implementation of the scheme. In June 2001 the Committee determined that Bolivia had met the targets required to reach 'completion point' of the process. Honduras reached decision point in July 2000, when debt relief totalling $556m. in NPV terms was approved, including $98m. in assistance from the Bank. Guyana reached decision point in November, at which time $329m. was approved in addition to the relief agreed under the original initiative, while Nicaragua reached decision point in December, with approved assistance of $3,267m.

TECHNICAL ASSISTANCE

The provision of technical assistance to member countries has become a major component of Bank activities. The economic sector and project analysis undertaken by the Bank in the normal course of its operations is the vehicle for considerable technical assistance. In addition, project loans and credits may include funds earmarked specifically for feasibility studies, resource surveys, management or planning advice, and training. The Economic Development Institute has become one of the most important of the Bank's activities in technical assistance. It provides training in national economic management and project analysis for government officials at the middle and upper levels of responsibility. It also runs overseas courses aiming to build up local training capability, and administers a graduate scholarship programme. The EDI helped to organize the second Annual Bank Conference of Development Economics for Latin America and the Caribbean, which was held in Santafé de Bogotá, Colombia, in July 1996, and attended by senior government officials, representatives of the private sector and academics.

In 1992 the Bank established an Institutional Development Fund (IDF); the purpose of the Fund was to provide rapid, small-scale financial assistance, to a maximum value of US $500,000, for capacity-building proposals.

ECONOMIC RESEARCH AND STUDIES

In the 1990s the World Bank's research, conducted by its own staff, was increasingly concerned with providing information to reinforce the Bank's expanding advisory role to developing countries. Consequently the principal areas of current research focus on issues such as maintaining sustainable growth while protecting the environment and the poorest sectors of society, encouraging the development of the private sector, and reducing and decentralizing government activities. The Bank chairs the Consultative Group on International Agricultural Research (CGIAR), which was formed in 1971 to raise financial support for research on improving crops and animal production in developing countries. The CGIAR supports 16 research centres.

CO-OPERATION WITH OTHER ORGANIZATIONS

The Bank co-operates closely with other UN bodies, through consultations, meetings and joint activities. It collaborates with the IMF in implementing economic adjustment programmes in developing countries. The Bank holds regular consultations with the European Union and OECD on development issues, and the Bank-NGO Committee provides an annual forum for discussion with non-governmental organizations (NGO). The Bank chairs meetings of donor governments and organizations for the co-ordination of aid to particular countries. It also conducts co-financing and aid co-ordination projects with official aid agencies, export credit institutions, and commercial banks.

The World Bank, UNDP and UNEP are implementing agencies of the Global Environment Facility (GEF), which was established in 1990, for an initial three-year pilot period, to provide concessional funding to assist developing countries to implement projects that benefit the global environment. In March 1994 countries participating in the GEF agreed to restructure and replenish it with a core fund of US $2,000m. to enable the Facility to act as the financial mechanism for the conventions on climate change and biological diversity that were signed at the UN Conference on Environment and Development in June 1992. In November 1997 36 donor countries committed themselves to a target figure of $2,750m. for the next replenishment of GEF funds. The second replenishment was approved by the Bank's Executive Board in July 1998. The GEF Secretariat is based at the World Bank's headquarters, although it functions independently of the implementing agencies.

In June 1995 the World Bank joined other international donors (including regional development banks, other UN bodies, Canada, France, the Netherlands and the USA) in establishing a Consultative Group to Assist the Poorest (CGAP), which was to channel funds to the most needy through grass-roots agencies. An initial

credit of approximately US $200m. was committed by the donors. The Bank manages the CGAP secretariat, which is responsible for the administration of external funding and for the evaluation and approval of project financing.

During 1996/97 the Bank began working with the Inter-American Development Bank and the Pan American Health Organization on a pilot programme to consider issues relating to urbanization, including youth problems, poverty, crime and violence. The Bank also collaborated with ECLAC on an initiative to improve the formulation and monitoring of poverty reduction programmes. The national statistical offices of Argentina, El Salvador, Paraguay and Peru were the first to participate in the regional project.

IBRD INSTITUTIONS

World Bank Institute—WBI: founded in March 1999 by merger of the Bank's Learning and Leadership Centre, previously responsible for internal staff training, and the Economic Development Institute (EDI), which had been established in 1955 to train government officials concerned with development programmes and policies. The new Institute aimed to emphasize the Bank's priority areas through the provision of training courses and seminars relating to poverty, crisis response, good governance and anti-corruption strategies. The WBI was also to take the lead in co-ordinating a process of consultation and dialogue with researchers and other representatives of civil society to examine poverty for the 2000/01 *World Development Report*. During 1999/2000 the WBI expanded its programmes through distance learning, global knowledge networks, and use of new technologies Under the EDI a World Links for Development programme was initiated to connect schools in developing countries with partner establishments in industrialized nations via the internet. A new initiative, Global Development Learning Network, aimed to expand access to information and learning opportunities through the internet, videoconferences and organized exchanges. Dir VINOD THOMAS (India).

International Centre for Settlement of Investment Disputes—ICSID: founded in 1966 under the Convention of the Settlement of Investment Disputes between States and Nationals of Other States. The Convention was designed to encourage the growth of private foreign investment for economic development, by creating the possibility, always subject to the consent of both parties, for a Contracting State and a foreign investor who is a national of another Contracting State to settle any legal dispute that might arise out of such an investment by conciliation and/or arbitration before an impartial, international forum. The governing body of the Centre is its Administrative Council, composed of one representative of each Contracting State, all of whom have equal voting power. The President of the World Bank is (*ex officio*) the non-voting Chairman of the Administrative Council.

At March 2001 133 states had ratified the Convention to become ICSID Contracting States. The number of cases registered with the Centre in late 2000 totalled 81, of which 35 were pending. Sec.-Gen. KO-YUNG TUNG.

WORLD BANK OPERATIONS IN LATIN AMERICA AND THE CARIBBEAN

IBRD Loans Approved, 1 July 1999–30 June 2000

Country	Purpose	Amount (US $ million)
Argentina . . .	Health Insurance for the Poor project	4.9
	Public health surveillance and disease control	52.5
Brazil	Northeast Microfinance Development project	50.0
	Administrative and fiscal reform adjustment loan	505.1
	Social security adjustment loan	505.1
	Social security technical assistance	5.1
	Ceará integrated water resource management	136.0
	Low-income sanitation technical assistance	30.3
	National environmental project	15.0
	Energy efficiency	43.4
Colombia . . .	Community works and employment	100.0
	Sierra Nevada sustainable development	5.0
	Rural education	20.0
	Earthquake recovery	225.0
	Financial sector adjustment	506.0
	Cartagena water supply, sewerage and environmental management	85.0
Costa Rica . . .	Ecomarkets projects	32.6
Dominican Republic .	Wastewater disposal in tourism centres project	5.0
	Telecommunications regulatory reform	12.3
Ecuador . . .	Financial sector technical assistance loan	10.0
	Structural adjustment	151.5
	Social Development/Health and Nutrition project	20.2
Mexico	Gender equity project	3.1
	Rural Development in Marginal Areas II project	55.0
	Bank restructuring facility adjustment loan	505.1
	Decentralization adjustment loan	606.1
Peru . . .	Indigenous and Afro-Peruvian Peoples Development project	5.0
	Health reform	80.0
	Agricultural reseach	9.6
Saint Lucia . . .	Poverty Reduction Fund project*	1.5
Uruguay . . .	OSE modernization and systems rehabilitation	27.0
	Financial sector adjustment loan	80.9
Venezuela . . .	Millennium Science Initiative project	5.0

IDA Credits approved, 1 July 1999–30 June 2000

Country	Purpose	Amount (US $ million)
Bolivia	Capacity building in hydrocarbon sector	4.8
Guyana . . .	Financial and private sector institutional development	4.8
Honduras . . .	Emergency disaster management	10.8
	Social Investment Fund IV project (supplemental credit)	22.5
Nicaragua . . .	Agricultural technology	23.6
	Basic education	39.3
	Pension and financial market reform technical assistance	8.0
	Economic management technical assistance	15.3
	Telecommunications sector reform	15.9
Saint Lucia . .	Poverty Reduction Fund project*	1.5

* Joint IBRD/IDA funded project.

Source: *World Bank Annual Report 2000.*

Publications

Abstracts of Current Studies: The World Bank Research Program (annually).

Annual Report on Operations Evaluation.

Annual Report on Portfolio Performance.

Global Commodity Markets (quarterly).

Global Development Finance (annually).

Global Economic Prospects and Developing Countries (annually).

Research News (quarterly).

Staff Working Papers.

Transition (every 2 months).

World Bank Annual Report.

World Bank Atlas (annually).

World Bank Economic Review (3 a year).

The World Bank and the Environment (annually).

World Bank Research Observer (2 a year).

World Development Indicators (annually, also on CD-Rom).

World Development Report (annually, also on CD-Rom).

International Finance Corporation—IFC

Address: 2121 Pennsylvania Ave, NW, Washington, DC 20433, USA.

Telephone: (202) 477-1234; **fax:** (202) 974-4384; **e-mail:** information@ifc.org; **internet:** www.ifc.org.

IFC was founded in 1956 as an affiliate of the World Bank to encourage the growth of productive private enterprise in its member countries, particularly in the less-developed areas.

Organization

(July 2001)

IFC is a separate legal entity in the World Bank Group. Executive Directors of the World Bank also serve as Directors of IFC. The President of the World Bank is, *ex-officio*, Chairman of the IFC Board of Directors, which has appointed him President of IFC. Subject to his overall supervision, the day-to-day operations of IFC are conducted by its staff under the direction of the Executive Vice-President.

PRINCIPAL OFFICERS

President: JAMES D. WOLFENSOHN (USA).
Executive Vice-President: PETER L. WOICKE (Germany).
Director, Latin America and the Caribbean: KARL VOLTAIRE.

REGIONAL MISSIONS AND OFFICES

Argentina: Bouchard 547, 3°, 1106 Buenos Aires: tel. (11) 4315-1666; fax (11) 4312-7184; Resident Rep. ILEANA BOZA.

Bolivia: Edif. Gundlach 73, 10°, Of. 1003, Torre Oeste, Calle Reyes Ortiz, esq. Federico Suazo, La Paz; tel. (2) 338110; fax (2) 33735; Officer JUAN-CARLOS ECHEVERRIA.

Brazil: Rua Redentor 14, Ipanema, 22421-030, Rio de Janeiro; tel. (21) 550-8990; fax (21) 550-8999; Resident Dir KARL VOLTAIRE.

Colombia: Carrera 7, 71-21, Torre A, 16°, Edif. Fiduagraria, Santafé de Bogotá, DC; tel. (1) 326-3600; fax (1) 317-4380; Resident Rep. PAOLO MARTELLI.

Dominican Republic: Calle Virgilio Diaz Ordoñez 36, esq. Gustavo Mejía Ricart, Edif. Mezzo Tempo, Suite 401, Santo Domingo; tel. 566-6815; fax 566-7746; Officer SALEM ROHANA.

Guatemala: 13 Calle 3-40, Zona 10, Edif. Atlantis, 14°, Guatemala City; tel. 367-2275; fax 366-9851; Regional Rep. for Central America YOLANDE DUHEM.

Mexico: Prado Sur 240, Col. Lomas de Chapultepec, 11000 Mexico, DF; tel. (5) 520-6191; fax (5) 520-5629; Resident Rep. MANUEL NUÑEZ.

Trinidad and Tobago: The Mutual Centre, 16 Queen's Park West, POB 751, Port of Spain; tel. 628-5074; fax 622-1003; Officer KIRK B. IFILL.

Activities

IFC provides financial support and advice for private-sector ventures and projects, and assists governments in creating conditions that stimulate the flow of domestic and foreign private savings and investment. Increasingly, IFC has worked to mobilize additional capital from other financial institutions. In all its activities IFC is guided by three major principles:

(i) The catalytic principle. IFC should seek above all to be a catalyst in helping private investors and markets to make good investments.

(ii) The business principle. IFC should function like a business in partnership with the private sector and take the same commercial risks, so that its funds, although backed by public sources, are transferred under market disciplines.

(iii) The principle of the special contribution. IFC should participate in an investment only when it makes a special contribution that supplements or complements the role of market operators.

IFC's authorized capital is US $2,450m. At 30 June 2000 paid-in capital was $2,357.6m. The World Bank is the principal source of borrowed funds, but IFC also borrows from private capital markets.

In the financial year ending 30 June 2000 project financing, approved by IFC, amounted to US $5,846m. for 259 projects, of which $3,505m. was for IFC's own account, while $2,341m. was used in loan syndications and underwriting of securities issues and investment funds. During the year IFC approved total financing of $2,724m. for 58 projects in Latin America and the Caribbean, compared with $2,449m. for 58 projects in 1998/99. IFC has identified the following as priority strategic areas for future activity in the region: expansion of private-sector participation in infrastructure and social sector activities; development of domestic capital markets; provision of resources to companies lacking access to international capital flows; and diversification of activities to less-developed national or local economies. Examples of projects supported by IFC in the region during 1999/2000 included rehabilitation of water and sewerage systems in Argentina, and the establishment of a secondary mortgage market company in that country; shrimp farming in Belize, Ecuador and Venezuela; hospital construction and improvements in Brazil, Dominican Republic and Mexico; expansion of container terminals in Brazil, Chile and Panama; development of a banana plantation in Guatemala; construction of gas-fired power plants in Mexico; and a forestry products project in Venezuela. In September 2000 IFC, with the Bank of Nova Scotia, inaugurated a new loan facility for the Caribbean to provide long-term financing, with loans in the range of $500,000 to $5m., to small and medium-sized enterprises undertaking expansion or restructuring, particularly for export-oriented projects.

IFC also provides technical assistance and advisory services to both businesses and governments, particularly in connection with privatization and corporate restructuring, private infrastructure, and the development of capital markets. Under the Technical Assistance Trust Funds Program (TATF), established in 1988, IFC manages resources contributed by various governments and agencies to provide finance for feasibility studies, project identification studies and other types of technical assistance relating to project preparation. The Foreign Investment Advisory Service (FIAS), established in 1986, is operated jointly by IFC and the IBRD: it provides advice to governments on promoting foreign investment and strengthening the country's investment framework. During 1999/2000 IFC and the World Bank combined their advisory services creating the Private Sector Advisory Services. FIAS was to operate within the framework of the new unit, alongise a Corporate Finance Services facility, which supports private-sector involvement in state-owned and -operated sectors. IFC technical assistance activities during 1999/2000 included assistance and advice relating to the restructuring of agricultural enterprises in Bolivia; restructuring of the national investment promotion agency in Colombia; a feasibility study for an initiative to support indigenous communities in Latin America and the Caribbean; studies on insurance markets in Central America; and a review of hydroelectricity production in Nicaragua.

Publications

Annual Report.
Global Agribusiness (series of industry reports).
Impact (quarterly).
Lessons of Experience (series).
Results on the Ground (series).

International Fund for Agricultural Development—IFAD

Address: Via del Serafico 107, 00142 Rome, Italy.
Telephone: (06) 54591; **fax:** (06) 5043463; **e-mail:** ifad@ifad.org; **internet:** www.ifad.org.
Following a decision by the 1974 UN World Food Conference, IFAD was established in 1977 with a mandate to combat hunger and eradicate poverty on a sustainable basis in the low-income food-deficit regions of the world. Funding operations began in January 1978.

Organization

(July 2001)

GOVERNING COUNCIL

Each member state is represented in the Governing Council by a Governor and an Alternate. Sessions are held annually, with special sessions convened as required. The Governing Council elects the President of the Fund (who also chairs the Executive Board) by a two-thirds majority for a four-year term. The President is eligible for re-election.

EXECUTIVE BOARD

The Board consists of 18 members and 18 alternates, elected by the Governing Council, one third by each category of membership. Members serve for three years. The Executive Board is responsible for the conduct and general operation of IFAD and approves loans and grants for projects; it conducts three regular sessions each year.

Following agreement on the fourth replenishment of the Fund's resources in February 1997, the governance structure of the Fund was amended. Former Category I countries (i.e. industrialized donor countries) were reclassified as List A countries and were awarded a greater share of the 1,800 votes in the Governing Council and Executive Board, in order to reflect their financial contributions to the Fund. Former Category II countries (petroleum-exporting developing donor countries) were reclassified as List B countries, while recipient developing countries, formerly Category III countries, were termed as List C countries, and divided into three regional Sub-Lists. Where previously each category was ensured equal representation on the Executive Board, the new allocation of seats was as follows: eight List A countries, four List B, and two of each Sub-List C group of countries.

President and Chairman of Executive Board: LENNART BAGE (Sweden).

Vice-President: JOHN WESTLEY (USA).

Activities

The Fund's objective is to mobilize additional resources to be made available on concessional terms for agricultural development in developing member states. IFAD provides financing primarily for projects and programmes designed to improve food production systems and to strengthen related policies and institutions. In allocating resources IFAD is guided by: the need to increase food production in the poorest food-deficit countries; the potential for increasing food production in other developing countries; and the importance of improving the nutrition, health and education of the poorest populations in developing countries i.e. small-scale farmers, artisanal fishermen, nomadic pastoralists, indigenous populations, rural women, and the rural landless. All projects emphasize the participation of beneficiaries in development initiatives, both at the local and national level.

IFAD is empowered to make both grants and loans. Grants are limited to 7.5% of the resources committed in any one financial year. Loans are available on highly concessionary, intermediate and ordinary terms. More than two-thirds of total IFAD lending is awarded on highly concessionary terms, i.e. with no interest charges, although carrying an annual service charge of 0.75%, and a repayment period of 40 years, including a 10-year grace period. To avoid duplication of work, the administration of loans, for the purposes of disbursements and supervision of project implementation, is entrusted to competent international financial institutions, with the Fund retaining an active interest. During 1999 IFAD provided financing for 57% of the costs of projects approved during that year, while the remainder was contributed by external donors, multilateral institutions and the recipient countries.

IFAD's development projects usually include a number of components, such as infrastructure (e.g. improvement of water supplies, small-scale irrigation and road construction); input supply (e.g. improved seeds, fertilizers and pesticides); institutional support (e.g. research, training and extension services); and producer incentives (e.g. pricing and marketing improvements). IFAD also attempts to enable the landless to acquire income-generating assets: by increasing the provision of credit for the rural poor, it seeks to free them from dependence on the capital maket and to generate productive activities. The Fund supports projects that are concerned with environmental conservation, in an effort to alleviate poverty that results from the deterioration of natural resources. It also extends assessment grants to review the environmental consequences of projects under preparation.

In addition to its regular efforts to identify projects and programmes, IFAD organizes special programming missions to certain selected countries to undertake a comprehensive review of the constraints affecting IFAD-type projects among the rural poor, and to help countries to design strategies for the removal of these constraints. Based on the recommendations of these missions, a number of projects have been identified or prepared. In general, these projects tend to focus on institutional improvements at the national and local level to direct inputs and services to small farmers and the landless rural poor. In Latin America and the Caribbean IFAD has aimed to formulate and implement projects that integrate the rural poor into the mainstream economy as well as local and centralized decision-making processes, enhance the productivity and market competitiveness of small-scale farmers, promote sustainable production and utilization of natural resources in environmentally fragile areas, and encourage the participation of women in rural development programmes.

During 2000 IFAD approved loans for the following projects in the Latin America and Caribbean region: management of natural resources in the Chaco and High Valley regions of Bolivia; rural development in the rubber-producing areas of Mexico; the second phase of a national smallholder support programme in Uruguay; and the development of agricultural, microenterprise and marketing activities for poor rural families in Venezuela. The projects involved total IFAD lending of approximately US $64m. At the end of 2000 the number of ongoing projects in the region amounted to 36 in 22 countries.

In November 1995 IFAD established FIDAMERICA, an electronic network which aimed to improve the efficiency and outreach of IFAD-sponsored projects in the Latin America and Caribbean region and to promote information exchange. In September 1998 the Executive Board endorsed a second phase of the project, which envisaged linking all IFAD projects in the region, specialist and technical staff, and more than 100 local organizations, working in the field.

In February 1998 IFAD inaugurated a new Trust Fund to complement the multilateral debt initiative for Heavily Indebted Poor Countries (HIPCs—see World Bank, p. 825). The Fund was intended to assist IFAD's poorest members, deemed to be eligible under the initiative, to channel resources from debt repayment to communities in need. Also in 1998 the Executive Board endorsed a policy framework for the Fund's role in providing development assistance in post-conflict situations, with the aim of achieving a continuum from emergency relief to a secure basis from which to pursue sustainable development. In 1999 IFAD was involved in a project to address problems resulting from civil conflict in Guatemala.

During the late 1990s IFAD established several partnerships within the agribusiness sector, with a view to improving performance at project level, broadening access to capital markets, and encouraging the advancement of new technologies.

Finance

IFAD's programme of work for 2000 envisaged loans and grants totalling US $441.8m. In 2001 the provisional budget for administrative expenses amounted to $53.6m.

Publications

Annual Report.

IFAD Update (2 a year).

Rural Poverty Report (annually).

Staff Working Papers (series).

Multilateral Investment Guarantee Agency—MIGA

Address: 1818 H Street, NW, Washington, DC 20433, USA.

Telephone: (202) 477-1234; **fax:** (202) 477-6391; **internet:** www.miga.org/.

MIGA was founded in 1988 as an affiliate of the World Bank, to encourage the flow of investments for productive purposes among its member countries, especially developing countries, through the provision of political risk insurance and invesment marketing services to foreign investors and host governments, respectively.

Organization

(July 2001)

MIGA is legally and financially separate from the World Bank. It is supervised by a Council of Governors (comprising one Governor and one Alternate of each member country) and an elected Board of Directors (of no less than 12 members).

President: JAMES D. WOLFENSOHN (USA).

Executive Vice-President: MOTOMICHI IKAWA (Japan).

Activities

The convention establishing MIGA took effect in April 1988. Authorized capital was US $1,082m. In April 1998 MIGA's Board of Directors approved an increase in MIGA's capital base. A grant of $150m. was transferred from the IBRD as part of the package, while the capital increase (totalling $700m. callable capital and $150m. paid-in capital) was approved by MIGA's Council of Governors in April 1999.

MIGA's purpose is to guarantee eligible investments against losses resulting from non-commercial risks, under four main categories:

(i) transfer risk resulting from host government restrictions on curency conversion and transfer;

(ii) risk of loss resulting from legislative or administrative actions of the host government;

(iii) repudiation by the host government of contracts with investors in cases in which the investor has no access to a competent forum;

(iv) the risk of armed conflict and civil unrest.

Before guaranteeing any investment MIGA must ensure that it is commercially viable, contributes to the development process and will not be harmful to the environment. During the fiscal year 1998/99 MIGA and IFC appointed the first Compliance Advisor and Ombudsman to consider the concerns of local communities directly affected by MIGA or IFC sponsored projects.

During the year to June 2000 MIGA issued 53 investment insurance contracts in 26 countries with a value of US $1,605m. The amount of direct investment associated with the contracts totalled approximately $5,450m.

MIGA also provides policy and advisory services to promote foreign investment in developing countries and transitional economies, and to disseminate information on investment opportunities. In October 1995 MIGA established a new network on investment opportunities, which connected investment promotion agencies (IPAs) throughout the world on an electronic information network. The so-called IPA*net* aimed to encourage further investments among developing countries, to provide access to comprehensive information on investment laws and conditions and to strengthen communications between governmental, business and financial associations and investors. A new version of IPA*net* was launched in 1997. In June 1998 MIGA initiated a new internet-based facility, 'PrivatizationLink', to provide information on investment opportunities resulting from the privatization of industries in emerging economies.

Publications

Annual Report.

MIGA News (quarterly).

International Monetary Fund—IMF

Address: 700 19th St, NW, Washington, DC 20431, USA.

Telephone: (202) 623-7300; **fax:** (202) 623-6278; **internet:** www.imf.org.

The IMF was established at the same time as the World Bank (IBRD) in 1945 to promote international monetary co-operation, to facilitate the expansion and balanced growth of international trade and to promote stability in foreign exchange.

Organization

(July 2001)

BOARD OF GOVERNORS

The highest authority of the Fund is exercised by the Board of Governors, on which each member country is represented by a Governor and an Alternate Governor. The Board normally meets annually. The International Monetary and Financial Committee (formerly the Interim Committee) advises and reports to the Board on matters relating to the management and adaptation of the international monetary and financial system, sudden disturbances that might threaten the system and proposals to amend the Articles of Agreement. The voting power of each country is related to its quota in the Fund.

BOARD OF EXECUTIVE DIRECTORS

The 24-member Board of Executive Directors is responsible for the day-to-day operations of the Fund. The USA, the United Kingdom, Germany, France and Japan, each appoint one Executive Director. There is also one Executive Director each from the People's Republic of China, Russia and Saudi Arabia, while the remainder are appointed by groups of member countries sharing similar interests.

OFFICERS

Managing Director: HORST KÖHLER (Germany).

First Deputy Managing Director: ANNE KRUEGER (USA).

Deputy Managing Directors: SHIGEMITSU SUGISAKI (Japan), EDUARDO ANINAT (Chile).

Director, Western Hemisphere Department: CLAUDIO M. LOSER.

Activities

The purposes of the IMF, as set out in the Articles of Agreement, are:

(i) To promote international monetary co-operation through a permanent institution which provides the machinery for consultation and collaboration on monetary problems.

(ii) To facilitate the expansion and balanced growth of international trade, and to contribute thereby to the promotion and maintenance of high levels of employment and real income and to the development of members' productive resources.

(iii) To promote exchange stability, to maintain orderly exchange arrangements among members, and to avoid competitive exchange depreciation.

(iv) To assist in the establishment of a multilateral system of payments in respect of current transactions between members and in the elimination of foreign exchange restrictions which hamper the growth of trade.

(v) To give confidence to members by making the general resources of the Fund temporarily available to them, under adequate safeguards, thus providing them with the opportunity to correct maladjustments in their balance of payments, without resorting to measures destructive of national or international prosperity.

(vi) In accordance with the above, to shorten the duration of and lessen the degree of disequilibrium in the international balances of payments of members.

In joining the Fund, each country agrees to co-operate with the above objectives, and the Fund monitors members' compliance by holding an annual consultation with each country, in order to survey the country's exchange rate policies and determine its need for assistance.

In accordance with its objective of facilitating the expansion of international trade, the IMF encourages its members to accept the obligations of Article VIII, Section two, three and four, of the IMF Articles of Agreement. Members that accept Article VIII undertake to refrain from imposing restrictions on the making of payments and transfers for current international transactions and from engaging in discriminatory currency arrangements or multiple currency practices without IMF approval. By March 2001 149 members had accepted Article VIII status.

In April 1998 the Executive Board attempted to focus discussions concerning the strengthening of the international monetary system by identifying the following fundamental approaches: reinforcing international and domestic financial systems; strengthening IMF surveillance; promoting greater availability and transparency of information regarding member countries' economic data and policies; emphasizing the central role of the IMF in crisis management; and establishing effective procedures to involve the private sector in forestalling or resolving financial crises. During 1999/2000 the Fund implemented several measures in connection with its ongoing efforts to appraise and reinforce the global financial architecture, including, in March 2000, the adoption by the Executive Board of a strengthened framework to safeguard the use of IMF resources and, in April, approval by the Board of the establishment of an independent evaluation office to complement the Fund's internal and external evaluation activities. During 2000 the Fund established the IMF Center, in Washington, DC, which aimed to promote awareness and understanding of its activities. In September the Fund's new Managing Director announced his intention to focus and streamline the principals of conditionality (which links Fund financing with the implementation of specific economic policies by the recipient countries) in order to strengthen the concept of national ownership and as part of the wider reform of the international financial system. The issue remained under discussion by the Executive Board, and was to be open to public comment.

RESOURCES

Members' subscriptions form the basic resource of the IMF. They are supplemented by borrowing. Under the General Arrangements to Borrow (GAB), established in 1962, the 'Group of Ten' industrialized nations (Belgium, Canada, France, Germany, Italy, Japan, the Netherlands, Sweden, the United Kingdom and the USA) and Switzerland (not a member of the IMF until 1992, but a full participant in the GAB from April 1984) undertake to lend the Fund up to SDR 17,000m. in their own currencies, to assist in fulfilling the balance-of-payments requirements of any member of the group, or to meet requests to the Fund from countries with balance-of-payments problems that could threaten the stability of the international monetary system. In 1983 the Fund entered into an agreement with Saudi Arabia, in association with the GAB, making available SDR 1,500m., and other borrowing arrangements were completed in 1984 with the Bank for International Settlements, the Saudi Arabian Monetary Agency, Belgium and Japan, making available a further SDR 6,000m.

In May 1996 GAB participants concluded an agreement in principle to expand the resources available for borrowing to SDR 34,000m., by securing the support of 25 countries with the financial capacity to support the international monetary system. The so-called New Arrangements to Borrow (NAB) was approved by the Executive Board in January 1997. It was to enter into force, for an initial five-year period, as soon as the five largest potential creditors participating in NAB had approved the initiative and the total credit arrangement of participants endorsing the scheme had reached at least SDR 28,900m. While the GAB credit arrangement was to remain in effect, the NAB was expected to be the first facility to be activated in the event of the Fund's requiring supplementary resources. In July 1998 the GAB was activated for the first time in more than 20 years. The NAB became effective in November, and was used for the first time as part of an extensive programme of support for Brazil, which was adopted by the IMF in early December.

DRAWING ARRANGEMENTS

Exchange transactions within the Fund take the form of members' purchases (i.e. drawings) from the Fund of the currencies of other members for the equivalent amounts of their own currencies. Fund resources are available to eligible members on an essentially short-term and revolving basis to provide members with temporary assistance to contribute to the solution of their payments problems. Before making a purchase, a member must show that its balance of payments or reserve position make the purchase necessary. Apart from this requirement, reserve-tranche purchases (i.e. purchases that do not bring the Fund's holdings of the member's currency to a level above its quota) are permitted unconditionally.

With further purchases, however, the Fund's policy of conditionality means that a member requesting assistance must agree to

adjust its economic policies, as stipulated by the IMF. All requests other than for use of the reserve tranche are examined by the Executive Board to determine whether the proposed use would be consistent with the Fund's policies, and a member must discuss its proposed adjustment programme (including fiscal, monetary, exchange and trade policies) with IMF staff. Purchases outside the reserve tranche are made in four credit tranches, each equivalent to 25% of the member's quota; a member must reverse the transaction by repurchasing its own currency (with SDRs or currencies specified by the Fund) within a specified time. A credit tranche purchase is usually made under a 'Stand-by Arrangement' with the Fund, or under the Extended Fund Facility. A Stand-by Arrangement is normally of one or two years' duration, and the amount is made available in instalments, subject to the member's observance of 'performance criteria'; repurchases must be made within three to five years. An Extended Arrangement is normally of three years' duration, and the member must submit detailed economic programmes and progress reports for each year; repurchases must be made within four to 10 years. A member whose payments imbalance is large in relation to its quota may make use of temporary facilities established by the Fund using borrowed resources, namely the 'enlarged access policy' established in 1981, which helps to finance Stand-by and Extended Arrangements for such a member, up to a limit of between 90% and 110% of the member's quota annually. In October 1994 the Executive Board agreed to increase, for three years, the annual access limit under IMF regular tranche drawings, Stand-by Arrangements and Extended Fund Facility credits from 68% to 100% of a member's quota, with the cumulative access limit remaining at 300% of quota. The arrangements were extended, on a temporary basis, in November 1997. In December 1998 the IMF approved one of its largest ever Stand-by Arrangements in support of the Brazilian economy, amounting to SDR 13,024.8m. (including some SDR 9,100m. available under the Supplemental Reserve Facility—see below). Stand-by Arrangements were approved in 1999/2000 for Argentina, amounting to SDR 5,399m., Ecuador (SDR 226.7m.) and Mexico (SDR 3,103.0m.). In January 2001 the Executive Board approved an increase in the arrangement for Argentina, which was financing an extensive economic reform programme, to SDR 10,586m. During 1999/2000 Extended Arrangements were approved for Colombia, totalling SDR 1,957m., and for Peru (SDR 383m.), although the Peruvian authorities indicated their intention not to draw under the arrangement.

In addition, special-purpose arrangements have been introduced, all of which are subject to the member's co-operation with the Fund to find an appropriate solution to its difficulties. The Compensatory and Contingency Financing Facility (CCFF) provides compensation to members whose export earnings are reduced owing to circumstances beyond their control, or who are affected by excess costs of cereal imports. In January 2000 the Executive Board resolved to eliminate the contingency component, which provided financing to help members maintain efforts at economic adjustment even when affected by a sharp increase in interest rates or other externally-derived difficulties. Repurchases must be made within three-and-a-quarter to five years. In December 1997 the Executive Board established a new Supplemental Reserve Facility (SRF) to provide short-term assistance to members experiencing exceptional balance-of-payments difficulties resulting from a sudden loss of market confidence. Repayments were to be made within one to one-and-a-half years of the purchase, unless otherwise extended by the Board. In April 1999 an additional facility was established, for a two-year period, to provide short-term financing on similar terms to the SRF in order to prevent more stable economies being affected by adverse international financial developments and to maintain investor confidence. Under the Contingent Credit Lines (CCL) member countries were to have access to up to 500% of their quota, subject to meeting various economic criteria stipulated by the Fund.

The Structural Adjustment Facility (SAF) was established in 1986 to support medium-term macroeconomic adjustment and structural reforms in low-income developing countries on concessional terms. (In November 1993 the Executive Board agreed that no new commitments would be made under the SAF.) An Enhanced Structural Adjustment Facility (ESAF) was established in 1987 to provide new resources to assist the adjustment efforts of, in particular, heavily indebted countries. Eligible members were to develop a three-year adjustment programme (with assistance given jointly by staff of the Fund and of the World Bank) to strengthen the balance-of-payments situation and foster sustainable economic growth. In February 1994 a new period of operations of the ESAF became effective, following an agreement to enlarge the ESAF Trust (the funding source for ESAF arrangements). The terms and conditions of the new facility remained the same as those of the original ESAF, but the list of countries eligible for assistance was enlarged by six to 78 (subsequently extended to 79). In September 1996 the Interim Committee of the Board of Governors endorsed measures to finance the ESAF for a further five-year (2000–2004) period, after which the facility was to become self-sustaining. The interim period of the ESAF was to be funded mainly from bilateral contributions, but drawing on the Fund's additional resources as necessary. In November 1999 the ESAF was reformulated as the Poverty Reduction and Growth Facility (PRGF) with greater emphasis on poverty reduction as a key element of growth-orientated economic strategies. Assistance under the PRGF, for which 77 countries were deemed eligible, was to be matched to specific national requirements, and based upon poverty reduction strategies, to be formulated in collaboration with non-governmental organizations, representatives of civil society, and bilateral and multilateral institutions. PRGF loans carry an interest rate of 0.5% per year and are repayable over 10 years, with a five-an-a-half-year grace period; each country is permitted to borrow up to 140% of its quotas (in exceptional circumstances the maximum access can be raised to 185%). At April 2000 PRGF arrangements were in effect with Bolivia, Guyana, Honduras, and Nicaragua.

The PRGF supports, through long-maturity loans and grants, IMF participation in a joint initiative, with the World Bank, to provide exceptional assistance to heavily indebted poor countries (HIPCs), in order to help them to achieve a sustainable level of debt management. The initiative was formally approved at the September 1996 meeting of the Interim Committee, having received the support of the 'Paris Club' of official creditors—which agreed to increase the relief on official debt from 67% to 80%. In February 1997 the Executive Board established an ESAF-HIPC Trust, through which

IMF MEMBERSHIP AND QUOTAS IN LATIN AMERICA AND THE CARIBBEAN (million SDR*)

Country	June 2001
Antigua and Barbuda	13.5
Argentina	2,117.1
Bahamas	130.3
Barbados	67.5
Belize	18.8
Bolivia	171.5
Brazil	3,036.1
Chile	856.1
Colombia	774.0
Costa Rica	164.1
Dominica	8.2
Dominican Republic	218.9
Ecuador	302.3
El Salvador	171.3
Grenada	11.7
Guatemala	210.2
Guyana	90.9
Haiti†	(81.9) 60.7
Honduras	129.5
Jamaica	273.5
Mexico	2,585.8
Nicaragua	130.0
Panama	206.6
Paraguay	99.9
Peru	638.4
Saint Christopher and Nevis	8.9
Saint Lucia	15.3
Saint Vincent and the Grenadines	8.3
Suriname	92.1
Trinidad and Tobago	335.6
Uruguay	306.5
Venezuela	2,659.1

* The Special Drawing Right (SDR) was introduced in 1970 as a substitute for gold in international payments, and was intended eventually to become the principal reserve asset in the international monetary system. Its value (which was US $1.3189 at 28 February 2001, and averaged $1.2925 in 2000) is based on the currencies of the five largest exporting countries. Each member is assigned a quota related to its national income, monetary reserves, trade balance and other economic indicators; the quota approximately determines a member's voting power and the amount of foreign exchange it may purchase from the Fund. A member's subscription is equal to its quota. In January 1998 the Board of Governors approved an increase of some 45% of total IMF resources, bringing the total value of quotas to approximately SDR 212,000m. By January 1999 member states having at least 85% of total quotas (as at December 1997) had consented to the new subscriptions enabling the increase to enter into effect. At 26 March 2001 total quotas in the Fund amounted to SDR 212,401.1m.

† At June 2001 Haiti had not yet consented to its new quota. The figure given is that determined under the Ninth General Review, while the figure in parentheses is the proposed Eleventh General Review quota.

the IMF was to channel resources for the HIPC initiative and interim ESAF operations. In all, 41 HIPCs were identified, including Bolivia, Guyana, Honduras and Nicaragua. Assistance was approved for Bolivia in September of that year, and for Guyana in December. In September 1999 the IMF Board of Governors expressed its commitment to undertaking an off-market transaction of a percentage of the Fund's gold reserves (i.e. a sale, at market prices, to central banks of member countries with repayment obligations to the Fund, which were then to be made in gold), as part of the funding arrangements of an enhanced HIPC scheme. This was undertaken during the period December 1999-April 2000. Concessional lending under the enhanced initiative was approved for Bolivia in January 2000, for Honduras in July, for Guyana in November, and for Nicaragua in December (see alsoWorld Bank).

SURVEILLANCE

Under its Articles of Agreement, the Fund is mandated to oversee the effective functioning of the international monetary system and to review the policies of individual member countries to ensure the stability of the exchange rate system. The Fund's main tools of surveillance are regular consultations with member countries conducted in accordance with Article IV of the Articles of Agreement, which cover fiscal and monetary policies, balance of payments and external debt developments, as well as policies that affect the economic performance of a country, such as the labour market, social and environmental issues, good governance and aspects of the country's capital accounts, and finance and banking sectors. In addition, World Economic Outlook discussions are held, normally twice a year, by the Executive Board to assess policy implications from a multilateral perspective and to monitor global developments. The rapid decline in the value of the Mexican peso in late 1994 and the ensuing financial crisis in that country, as well as the financial crisis in Asia, which became apparent in mid-1997, focused attention on the importance of IMF surveillance of the economies and financial policies of member states and prompted the Fund to enhance the effectiveness of its surveillance and to encourage the full and timely provision of data by member countries. In April 1996 the IMF established the Special Data Dissemination Standard, which was intended to improve access to reliable economic statistical information for member countries that have, or are seeking, access to international capital markets. In March 1999 the IMF undertook to strengthen the Standard by the introduction of a new reserves data template. By March 2001 48 countries had subscribed to the Standard. In March 1997 the Executive Board agreed to develop a General Data Dissemination System (GDDS), to encourage all member countries to improve the production and dissemination of core economic data. The operational phase of the GDDS commenced in May 2000. In April 1997, in an effort to improve the value of surveillance by means of increased transparency, the Executive Board agreed to the voluntary release of Press Information Notices, following each member's Article IV consultation with the Board. In March 2000 the Executive Board adopted a strengthened framework to safeguard the use of IMF resources. All member countries making use of Fund resources were to be required to publish annual central bank statements audited in accordance with internationally accepted standards. It was also agreed that any instance of intentional misreporting of information by a member country should be publicized. In the following month the Executive Board approved the establishment of an independent evaluation office.

TECHNICAL ASSISTANCE

Technical assistance is provided to member countries by advisory missions of IMF staff and by the Fund's various specialized departments, which advise on all aspects of economic management. Specialized technical assistance is provided by the IMF's various departments and is an increasingly important aspect of the Fund's relationship with its member countries. The IMF Institute, founded in 1964, trains officials from member countries in financial analysis and policy, balance-of-payments methodology and public finance: it also gives assistance to national and regional training centres.

In April 2001 the IMF and Brazil signed a memorandum of understanding for the establishment of a Joint Regional Training Centre for Latin America. The Centre, to be located in Brasilia, was to provide courses on macroeconomic adjustment policies, financial programming, public finance, and trade policies.

Publications

Annual Report.

Balance of Payments Statistics Yearbook.

Direction of Trade Statistics (quarterly, with yearbook).

Finance and Development (quarterly, published jointly with the World Bank).

Government Finance Statistics Yearbook.
IMF Economic Reviews (3 a year).
IMF Survey (2 a month).
International Capital Markets: Developments, Prospects and Key Policy Issues.
International Financial Statistics (annually, also on CD-Rom).

Joint BIS-IMF-OECD-World Bank Statistics on External Debt (quarterly).
Staff Papers (quarterly).
World Economic Outlook (2 a year).
Occasional papers, country reports, economic and financial surveys, pamphlets, booklets.

United Nations Educational, Scientific and Cultural Organization—UNESCO

Address: 7 place de Fontenoy, 75700 Paris, France.
Telephone: 1-45-68-10-00; **fax:** 1-45-67-16-90; **internet:** www.unesco.org.

UNESCO was established in 1946 'for the purpose of advancing, through the educational, scientific and cultural relations of the peoples of the world, the objectives of international peace and the common welfare of mankind'.

Organization

(July 2001)

GENERAL CONFERENCE

The supreme governing body of the Organization, the Conference, meets in ordinary session once in two years and is composed of representatives of the member states.

EXECUTIVE BOARD

The Board, comprising 58 members, prepares the programme to be submitted to the Conference and supervises its execution; it meets twice or sometimes three times a year.

SECRETARIAT

Director-General: KOICHIRO MATSUURA (Japan).

CO-OPERATING BODIES

In accordance with UNESCO's Constitution, national Commissions have been set up in most member states. These help to integrate work within the member states and the work of UNESCO.

REGIONAL OFFICES

Caribbean Network of Educational Innovation for Development (CARNEID): Coles Bldg, 1st Floor, Lower Bay St, St Michael, Barbados; POB 423, Bridgetown, St Michael, Barbados; tel. 4274771; fax 4360094; e-mail unesco@caribsurf.com; Head of Office R. COLLEEN WINTER-BRAITHWAITE.

International Institute for Higher Education in Latin America and the Caribbean (IESALC): Av. Los Chorros, c/c Calle Acueducto, Edif. Asovincar, Altos de Sebucán, Apdo 68394, Caracas 1062A, Venezuela; tel. (2) 283-1411; fax (2) 283-1454; e-mail caracas@unesco.org; Dir CLAUDIO RAMA VITALE.

Regional Office for Culture in Latin America and the Caribbean (ORCALC): Apdo 4158, Calzada 551, esq. a D, Vedado, Apdo 4158, Havana, Cuba; tel. 32-7741; fax 33-3144; e-mail uhlha@unesco.org; f. 1950; activities include research and programmes of cultural development and cultural tourism; maintains a documentation centre and a library of 14,500 vols; Dir FRANCISCO JOSÉ LACAYO. Publs *Oralidad* (annually), *Boletín Electrónico* (quarterly).

Regional Office for Education in Latin America and the Caribbean (OREALC): Calle Enrique Delpiano 2058, Plaza Pedro de Valdivia, Providencia, Santiago, Chile; tel. (2) 6551050; fax (2) 6551046; e-mail unesco@unesco.cl; internet www.unesco.cl; Dir ANA LUIZA MACHADO.

Regional Office for Science and Technology for Latin America and the Caribbean: Av. Brasil 2697 P.4, Casilla 859, 11300 Montevideo, Uruguay; tel. (2) 7072023; fax (2) 7072140; e-mail orcyt@unesco.org.uy; internet www.unesco.org.uy; Dir MIGUEL ANGEL ENRÍQUES BERCIANO.

Activities

UNESCO's overall work programme for 2000–01 comprised the following four major programmes: Education for All Throughout Life; the Sciences in the Service of Development; Cultural Development: Heritage and Creativity; and Communication, Information and Informatics. Education for All Throughout Life was designated as the priority programme. The work programme also incorporated a transdisciplinary project—Towards a Culture of Peace. UNESCO was responsible for co-ordinating activities relating to the International Year for the Culture of Peace, designated by the UN General Assembly to be observed in 2000. A Manifesto 2000 for a Culture of Peace and Non-violence, which was inaugurated in December 1998 at a celebration of the 50th anniversary of the Universal Declaration of Human Rights, had nearly 75m. signatories by July 2001.

EDUCATION

Since its establishment UNESCO has devoted itself to promoting education in accordance with principles based on democracy and respect for human rights.

In March 1990 UNESCO, with other UN agencies, sponsored the World Conference on Education for All. 'Education for All' was subsequently adopted as a guiding principle of UNESCO's contribution to development. The promotion of access to learning opportunities throughout an individual's life is a priority for UNESCO's 1996–2001 programme of activities: Education for All Throughout Life was a key element of the 2000–01 work programme (see above). UNESCO aims, initially, to foster basic education for all. The second part of its strategy is to renew and diversify education systems, including updating curricular programmes in secondary education, strengthening science and technology activities and ensuring equal access to education for girls and women. In December 1993 the heads of government of nine highly-populated developing countries (Bangladesh, Brazil, the People's Republic of China, Egypt, India, Indonesia, Mexico, Nigeria and Pakistan), meeting in Delhi, India, agreed to co-operate with the objective of achieving comprehensive primary education for all children and of expanding further learning opportunities for children and adults. By September 1999 all nine countries had formally signed the so-called Delhi Declaration. In November 1999 the General Conference urged for further support for new basic education projects targeting marginalized groups, including orphans, indigenous populations, refugees and the disabled. In endorsing the education programme for 2000–01 the Conference also emphasized the importance of information technologies, and the need to train teachers in the use of these, with the objective of providing educational opportunities to all. In April 2000 several UN agencies, including UNESCO and UNICEF, and other partners sponsored the World Education Forum, held in Dakar, Senegal, to assess international progress in achieving the goal of 'Education for All' and to adopt a strategy for further action, with the aim of ensuring universal basic education by 2015.

UNESCO is concerned with improving the quality, relevance and efficiency of higher education. It assists member states in reforming their national systems, organizes high-level conferences for Ministers of Education and other decision-makers and disseminates research papers. A World Conference on Higher Education was convened in October 1998 in Paris, France. The Conference adopted a World Declaration on Higher Education for the 21st Century, incorporating proposals to reform higher education, with emphasis on access to education, and educating for individual development and active participation in society. The Conference also approved a framework for Priority Action for Change and Development of Higher Education, which comprised guide-lines for governments and institutions to meet the objectives of greater accessibility, as well as improved standards and relevancy of higher education. The International Institute for Higher Education in Latin America and the Caribbean promotes regional co-operation among universities and assists member states to develop and improve national systems of higher education. As part of UNESCO's efforts to foster links between universities, an environmental studies network has been established in the Amazon region comprising 30 university departments.

Within the UN system, UNESCO is responsible for providing technical assistance and educational services in emergency situations. This includes providing education to refugees and displaced persons, as well as assistance for the rehabilitation of national education systems.

SCIENCE AND SOCIAL SCIENCES

In November 1999 the General Conference identified the following as priority areas of UNESCO science initiatives in 2000–01: combating poverty; science education; support for the integration of women in all fields of science and technology; the need for a future generations approach; environment and sustainable development; promotion of cultural diversity; the elaboration of an ethical framework for the application of scientific results; and access to scientific information. UNESCO was to continue to implement projects under the programme of the Sciences in the Service of Development, which was initiated in the previous biennium in order to foster the advancement, transfer and exchange of knowledge in the physical, natural, social and human sciences and to promote their application with the objective of improving the social and natural environment. The Conference also endorsed a Declaration on Science and the Use of Scientific Knowledge and an agenda for action, which had been adopted at the World Conference on Science, held in June/July 1999, in Budapest, Hungary.

UNESCO aims to improve the level of university teaching of the sciences through training courses, establishing national and regional networks and centres of excellence, and fostering co-operative research. In carrying out its mission, UNESCO relies on partnerships with non-governmental organizations and the world scientific communities. With the International Council of Scientific Unions and the Third World Academy of Sciences, UNESCO operates a short-term fellowship programme in the basic sciences and an exchange programme of visiting lecturers. UNESCO also sponsors several research fellowships in the social sciences and promotes the research of socio-cultural factors affecting demographic change and the study of family issues. UNESCO's engineering courses emphasize technology that is environmentally sound and/or that may offer alternative or renewable energy sources. In September 1996 UNESCO initiated a 10-year World Solar Programme, which aimed to promote the application of solar energy and to increase research, development and public awareness of all forms of ecologically-sustainable energy use.

UNESCO has over the years established various forms of intergovernmental co-operation concerned with the environmental sciences and research on natural resources, in order to support the recommendations of the UN Conference on Environment and Development, held in June 1992, and in particular, the implementation of Agenda 21 to promote sustainable development. The International Geological Correlation Programme, undertaken jointly with the International Union of Geological Sciences, aims to improve and facilitate global research of geological processes. In the context of the international Decade for Natural Disaster Reduction (declared in 1990), UNESCO has conducted scientific studies of natural hazards and means of mitigating their effects and has organized several disaster-related workshops. The International Hydrological Programme considers scientific aspects of water resources assessment and management, while an Intergovernmental Oceanographic Commission (IOC) focuses on issues relating to oceans, shorelines and marine resources, in particular the role of the ocean in climate and gobal systems. The IOC has been actively involved in the establishment of a Global Coral Reef Monitoring Network, and in activities for the 1998 International Year of the Ocean. An initiative on Environment and Development in Coastal Regions and in Small Islands is concerned with ensuring environmentally-sound and sustainable development by strengthening management of the following key areas: freshwater resources; the mitigation of coastline instability; biological diversity; coastal ecosystem productivity.

UNESCO's Man and the Biosphere Programme supports a worldwide network of biosphere reserves (comprising 393 sites in 94 countries in 2001), which aim to promote environmental conservation and research, education and training in biodiversity and problems of land use (including the fertility of tropical soils and the cultivation of sacred sites). Following the signing of the Convention to Combat Desertification in October 1994, UNESCO initiated an International Programme for Arid Land Crops, based on a network of existing institutions, to assist implementation of the Convention.

In November 1997 the UNESCO General Conference adopted a Universal Declaration on the Human Genome and Human Rights, which had been formulated by a group of specialists meeting under UNESCO auspices, the International Bioethics Committee, with the aim of providing ethical guide-lines for developments in human genetics. The Declaration identified some 100,000 hereditary genes as 'common heritage', and committed states to promoting the dissemination of relevant scientific knowledge and co-operating in genome research. The November Conference also resolved to establish a World Commission on the Ethics of Scientific Knowledge and Technology to serve as a forum for the exchange of information and ideas and to promote dialogue between scientific communities, decision-makers and the public.

UNESCO aims to assist the building and consolidation of peaceful and democratic societies. An international network of institutions and centres involved in research on conflict resolution is being established to support the promotion of peace. Other training, workshop and research activities have been undertaken in countries which have suffered conflict. The Associated Schools Project (ASPnet—comprising more than 6,700 institutions in 166 countries in 2001) has, for nearly 50 years, promoted the principles of peace, human rights, democracy and international co-operation through education. An International Youth Clearing House and Information Service (INFOYOUTH) aims to increase and consolidate the information available on the situation of young people in society, and to heighten awareness of their needs, aspirations and potential among public and private decision-makers. UNESCO's programme also focuses on the educational and cultural dimensions of physical education and sport and their capacity to preserve and improve health.

In 1994 UNESCO initiated an international social science research programme, the Management of Social Transformations (MOST), to promote capacity-building in social planning at all levels of decision-making. UNESCO sponsors several research fellowships in the social sciences. In other activities UNESCO promotes the rehabilitation of underprivileged urban areas, the research of socio-cultural factors affecting demographic change and the study of family issues.

Fundamental to UNESCO's mission is the rejection of all forms of discrimination. It disseminates scientific information aimed at combating racial prejudice, works to improve the status of women and their access to education, and promotes equality between men and women.

CULTURE

In undertaking efforts to preserve the world's cultural and natural heritage UNESCO has attempted to emphasize the link between culture and development. The 2000–01 programme Cultural Development: Heritage and Creativity was to pursue UNESCO's objectives relating to the preservation and enhancement of cultural and natural heritage and promoting living cultures, in particular through the formulation of new national and international legislation (including an instrument on underwater cultural heritage), efforts to counter the illicit trafficking of cultural property and the promotion of all forms of creativity.

UNESCO's World Heritage Programme, inaugurated in 1978, aims to protect landmarks of outstanding universal value, in accordance with the 1972 UNESCO Convention Concerning the Protection of the World Cultural and Natural Heritage, by providing financial aid for restoration, technical assistance, training and management planning. By December 2000 the 'World Heritage List' comprised 690 sites in 122 countries, including the city of Potosí (Bolivia), the Galapagos Islands (Ecuador), the Inca city of Machu Picchu in Peru, and numerous other historic sites and nature reserves in the region. UNESCO also maintains a list of World Heritage in Danger; at November 2000 this included national parks in Brazil and Ecuador, the Rio Platano Biosphere Reserve in Honduras and the Chan Chan Archaeological Zone in Peru. UNESCO supports efforts for the collection and safeguarding of humanity's non-material heritage, including oral traditions, music, dance and medicine. In co-operation with the International Council for philosophy and Humanistic Studies, the Organization is compiling a directory of endangered languages.

UNESCO encourages the translation and publication of literary works, publishes albums of art, and produces records, audiovisual programmes and travelling art exhibitions. It supports the development of book publishing and distribution, and the training of editors and managers in publishing. UNESCO is active in preparing and encouraging the enforcement of international legislation on copyright. The Regional Centre for Book Development in Latin America and the Caribbean promotes the Acuerdo de Alcance Parcial, which encourages the free flow of books, and helps countries to formulate national policies for books and reading. A self-teaching programme on the production and distribution of textbooks for the countries of Central America has been completed.

UNESCO was the leading agency for promoting the UN's World Decade for Cultural Development (1988–97). In 1992 UNESCO established a World Commission on Culture and Development to examine the links between culture and development. The first World Conference on Culture and Development was held in June 1999, in Havana, Cuba. A Mayan World project aims to safeguard the endangered Mayan culture and natural environment in Central America. In 1994 the first Congress of Maya Education was held to discuss the education of the Mayan population. The Latin America-Caribbean Project 2000 was established to foster integration, with particular emphasis on the pluralistic and dynamic nature of cultural identity.

COMMUNICATION, INFORMATION AND INFORMATICS

UNESCO's communications programme comprises three inter-related components concerned with the flow of information: a commitment to ensuring the wide dissemination of information, through the development of communications infrastructures and without impediments to freedom of expression or of the press; promotion of greater access to knowledge through international co-operation in the areas of information, libraries and archives; and efforts to harness informatics for development purposes and strengthen member states' capacities in this field. Within this framework, activities include assistance towards the development of legislation, training programmes and infrastructures for the media in countries where independent and pluralistic media are in the process of emerging; assistance, through professional organizations, in the monitoring of media independence, pluralism and diversity; promotion of exchange programmes and study tours; and improving access and opportunities for women in the media. UNESCO's fourth major work programme for 2000–01 was entitled Towards a Communication and Information Society for All.

UNESCO's International Programme for the Development of Communication (IPDC) provides support to communication and media development projects in the developing world, including the establishment of news agencies and newspapers and training editorial and technical staff. In regions affected by conflict the Programme supports efforts to establish and maintain an independent media service. In several countries in post-conflict situations UNESCO has participated in the restructuring of the media in the context of national reconciliation. In May 1994 a regional seminar on media development and democracy in Latin America and the Caribbean, organized jointly by the UN and UNESCO, was held in Santiago, Chile. The meeting adopted a declaration and plan of action designed to provide a framework for the development of pluralist media in the region.

The General Information Programme (PGI) was established in 1976 to provide a focus for UNESCO's activities in the fields of specialized information systems, documentation, libraries and archives. Under the PGI, UNESCO aims to facilitate the elaboration of information policies and plans to modernize libaries and archives services; to encourage standardization; to train information specialists; and to establish specialized information networks. The objectives of the programme are accomplished by improving access to scientific literature; the holding of national seminars on information policies; the furthering of pilot projects, and preservation and conservation efforts under the Records and Archives Management Programme (RAMP); and the training of users of library and information services. PGI's mandate extends to trends and societal impacts of information technologies. In March 1997 the first International Congress on Ethical, Legal and Societal Aspects of Digital Information ('InfoEthics') was held in Monte Carlo, Monaco. At the second 'Info-Ethics' Congress, held in October 1998, experts discussed issues concerning privacy, confidentiality and security in the electronic transfer of information. A World Commission on the Ethics of Scientific Knowledge and Technology, which had been approved by the 1997 General Conference, met for the first time in April 1999, in Oslo, Norway. UNESCO maintains an Observatory on the Information Society, which provides up-to-date information on the development of new information and communications technologies, and aims to raise awareness of related ethical, legal and societal issues. UNESCO supports the development of computer networking and the training of informatics specialists, in particular through its Intergovernmental Informatics Programme (IIP) supports training in informatics, software development and research, the modernization of public administration and informatics policies, and the development of regional computer networks. In November 1999 the General Conference resolved that PGI and IIP should merge; it was envisaged that this would be achieved in 2001.

Finance

UNESCO's activities are funded through a regular budget provided by member states and also through other sources, particularly UNDP, the World Bank, regional development banks and other bilteral Funds-in-Trust arrangements. UNESCO co-operates with many other UN agencies and international non-governmental organizations. UNESCO's total regular budget for the two years 2000–01 amounted to US \$544.4m., unchanged from the previous biennium. Extrabudgetary funds for 2000–01 were estimated at US \$250m.

Publications

(mostly in English, French and Spanish editions; Arabic, Chinese and Russian versions are also available in many cases)

Copyright Bulletin (quarterly).
International Review of Education (quarterly).
International Social Science Journal (quarterly).
Museum International (quarterly).
Nature and Resources (quarterly).
Prospects (quarterly review on education).
UNESCO Courier (monthly, in 27 languages).
UNESCO Sources (monthly).
UNESCO Statistical Yearbook.
World Communication Report.
World Educational Report (every 2 years).
World Heritage Review (quarterly).
World Information Report.
World Science Report (every 2 years).

World Health Organization—WHO

Address: Ave Appia, 1211 Geneva 27, Switzerland.
Telephone: (22) 7912111; **fax:** (22) 7913111; **e-mail:** info@who.ch; **internet:** www.who.int.

WHO was established in 1948 as the central agency directing international health work.

Organization

(July 2001)

WORLD HEALTH ASSEMBLY

The Assembly meets once a year in Geneva; it is responsible for policy making and the biennial programme and budget; it appoints the Director-General, admits new members and reviews budget contributions.

EXECUTIVE BOARD

The Board is composed of 32 health experts designated by, but not representing, their governments; they serve for three years, and the World Health Assembly elects 10 or 11 member states each year to comprise one-third of the Board. It meets at least twice a year to review the Director-General's programme, which it forwards to the Assembly with any recommendations that seem necessary. It advises on questions referred to it by the Assembly and is responsible for putting into effect the decisions and policies of the Assembly. It is also empowered to take emergency measures in case of epidemics or disasters.
Chairman: Myriam Abel (Vanuatu).

SECRETARIAT

Director-General: Gro Harlem Brundtland (Norway).
Executive Directors: Dr Anarfi Asamoah-Baah (Ghana), Maryan Baquerot, Dr David L. Heymann (USA), Ann Kern (Australia), Christopher Murray, Dr Tomris Türmen (Turkey), Dr Derek Yach (South Africa), Dr Yasuhiro Suzuki (Japan).

REGIONAL OFFICE

Regional Office for the Americas (Pan American Health Organization): Pan-American Sanitary Bureau, 525 23rd St, NW, Washington, DC 20037, USA; tel. (202) 974-3000; fax (202) 974-3000; e-mail postmaster@paho.org; internet www.paho.org; Dr Sir George Alleyne (Barbados).

Activities

WHO's objective is stated in the constitution as 'the attainment by all peoples of the highest possible level of health'.

It acts as the central authority directing international health work, and establishes relations with professional groups and government health authorities on that basis.

It supports, on request from member states, programmes to control or eradicate disease, train health workers best suited to local needs and strengthen national health systems. Aid is provided in emergencies and natural disasters.

A global programme of collaborative research and exchange of scientific information is carried out in co-operation with about 1,000 national institutions. Particular stress is laid on the widespread communicable diseases of the tropics, and the countries directly concerned are assisted in developing their research capabilities.

It keeps communicable and non-communicable diseases and other health problems under constant surveillance, promotes the exchange of prompt and accurate information and notification of outbreaks of diseases, and administers the International Health Regulations. It sets standards for the quality control of drugs, vaccines and other substances affecting health.

It collects and disseminates health data and carries out statistical analyses and comparative studies in such diseases as cancer, heart disease and mental illness.

It receives reports on drugs observed to have shown adverse reactions in any country, and transmits the information to other member states. It promotes improvements in environmental conditions, including housing, sanitation and workplaces. All available information on effects on human health of the pollutants in the environment is critically reviewed and published.

Co-operation among scientists and professional groups is encouraged, and the organization may propose international conventions and agreements. It assists in developing an informed public opinion on matters of health.

HEALTH FOR ALL

In May 1981 the 34th World Health Assembly adopted a Global Strategy in support of 'Health for all by the year 2000', which aimed to ensure the attainment by all citizens of the world of a level of health that would permit them to lead a socially and economically productive life. Primary health care was regarded as the key to 'Health for all', with the following as minimum requirements:

Safe water in the home or within 15 minutes' walking distance, and adequate sanitary facilities in the home or immediate vicinity;

Immunization against diphtheria, pertussis (whooping cough), tetanus, poliomyelitis, measles and tuberculosis;

Local health care, including availability of at least 20 essential drugs, within one hour's travel;

Trained personnel to attend childbirth, and to care for pregnant mothers and children up to at least one year old.

The Ninth General Programme of Work, for the period 1996–2001, defined a policy framework for world action on health and the management and programme development of WHO. In May 1998 the World Health Assembly agreed to the 'Health for all in the 21st century' initiative, which was to build on the primary health care approach of the 'Health for all' strategy, but which was to strengthen the emphasis on quality of life, equity in health and access to health services.

In July 1998 Dr Gro Harlem Brundtland officially took office as the new Director-General of WHO. She immediately announced an extensive reform of the organization, including restructuring the WHO technical programmes into nine groups or 'clusters', each headed by an Executive Director (see above). The groups were established within the framework of the following four main areas of activity: Combating ill health, incorporating Communicable Diseases and Non-communicable Diseases; Building healthy populations and communities, comprising the groups Health Systems and Community Health, Sustainable Development and Healthy Environments, and Social Change and Mental Health; Sustained Health, including the groups Health Technology and Pharmaceuticals, and Evidence and Information for Policy; and Internal support—reaching out, comprising External Affairs and Governing Bodies, and General Management. The impending merger of the Non-communicable Diseases and Social Change and Mental Health clusters was announced in March 2000.

COMMUNICABLE DISEASES

The Communicable Diseases group works to reduce the impact of infectious diseases world-wide through surveillance and response; prevention and contol; eradication and elimination; and research and development. The group seeks to strengthen global monitoring of important communicable disease problems and to increase the organization's capacity to provide an effective response to those problems. WHO also aims to reduce the impact of other communicable diseases through intensive, routine, prevention and control and, where possible, through the elimination or eradication of specific infections. The group advocates a functional approach to disease control, collaborating with other groups at all stages to provide an integrated response. In April 2000 WHO and several partner institutions in epidemic surveillance established a Global Outbreak Alert and Response Network.

One of WHO's major achievements was the eradication of smallpox. Following a massive international campaign of vaccination and surveillance (begun in 1958 and intensified in 1967), the last case was detected in 1977 and the eradication of the disease was declared in 1980. In 1988 the World Health Assembly declared its commitment to the similar eradication of poliomyelitis and launched the Global Polio Eradication Initiative. The last case of poliomyelitis in the Americas was reported in 1991, and in 1994 the region was declared to be 'polio free'.

WHO has collaborated with UNICEF and other international organizations to implement the Expanded Programme on Immunization (EPI), which aims to provide immunization for all children against six diseases which constitute a major cause of death and disability in the developing countries: diphtheria, pertussis (whooping cough), tetanus, poliomyelitis, measles and tuberculosis. In 1990 more than 100m. children in the developing world under the age of one had been successfully vaccinated against the targeted diseases. This achieved the objective of a rate of vaccination of 80%, which compared with a rate of vaccination of 20% in 1980. In 1992 the Assembly resolved to reach a new target of 90% immunization coverage with the six EPI vaccines; to introduce hepatitis B as a seventh vaccine; and to introduce the yellow fever vaccine in areas where it occurs endemically.

As a result of the reform of WHO implemented from mid-1998, the former Division of Control of Tropical Diseases was integrated into the Communciable Diseases group, providing member states with technical support to assist in the planning and implementation of control programmes (based on global strategies for integrated tropical disease control) at regional, sub-regional and national levels. It takes part in mobilizing resources for disease control where needed, and co-ordinating national and international participation as appropriate. The group also promotes research and training that are directly relevant to control needs, and promotes the monitoring and evaluation of control measures. WHO's Special Programme for Research and Training in Tropical Diseases, sponsored jointly by WHO, UNDP and the World Bank, comprises a world-wide network of about 5,000 scientists working on the development of vaccines, new drugs, diagnostic kits, preventive measures, and applied field research on practical community issues affecting the target diseases. The Programme aims to strengthen research institutions in developing countries, and to encourage participation by scientists and government officials from the countries most affected by tropical diseases. The Programme envisages that South American trypanosomiasis ('Chagas disease'), which causes the deaths of some 45,000 people each year and infects a further 16m.–18m., could be eliminated from the Southern Cone region of Latin America by 2010; an intergovernmental commission is implementing control programmes in the region. Chile was certified free of the transmission of Chagas disease in 1999, and in 2000 10 of the 12 Brazilian states where the disease had previously been endemic were certified free of transmission. The countries of the Andean region of Latin America initiated a plan for the elimination of transmission of Chagas disease in February 1997; a similar plan was launched by Central American governments in October. Since 1992 the Onchocerciasis Elimination Programme in the Americas has worked to control and eliminate the disease, which can cause blindness, in the following six endemic countries: Brazil, Colombia, Ecuador, Guatemala, Mexico and Venezuela. A Ministerial Conference on Malaria, organized by WHO in October 1992, adopted a global strategy setting out requirements for effective control of the disease, which kills an estimated 1m. people every year and affects a further 300m.-500m. (In 1998 there were an estimated 2.2m.-5.6m. clinical cases of malaria in Latin America and the Caribbean.) WHO assists countries where malaria is endemic to prepare national plans of action for malaria control in accordance with WHO's Global Malaria Control Strategy, which emphasized strengthening local capabilities. In July 1998 WHO declared the control of malaria a priority concern, and in October formally launched the 'Roll Back Malaria' programme, in conjunction with UNICEF, the World Bank and UNDP. Emphasis was to be placed on strengthening local health systems and on the promotion of inexpensive preventative measures, for example the use of bednets treated with insecticides. WHO, with a number of private and public partners, also supports the development of more effective antimalaria drugs and vaccines through the 'Medicines for Malaria' venture.

In July 1994 WHO, together with the Sasakawa Memorial Health Foundation, organized an international conference on the elimination of leprosy. The conference adopted a declaration on their commitment to the elimination of leprosy (the reduction of the prevalence of leprosy to less than one case per 10,000 population) by 2000 and WHO established a Special Programme devoted to this objective. The use of a combination of three drugs (known as multidrug therapy—MDT) resulted in a reduction in the number of leprosy cases world-wide from 10m.–12m. in 1988 to 680,000m. in 1999. In April 1999 WHO announced that the number of countries having more than one case of leprosy per 10,000 had declined from 122 in 1985 to 28. However, concern was expressed at the feasibility of the elimination target, in particular, given the large numbers of undetected cases of the disease. WHO reported that the continued use of MDT treatment over a period of five–10 years would result in an end to all transmission of the disease, except in India (which had about 70% of the global total of active leprosy cases in early 2000). In November 1999 WHO launched a new initiative, in collaboration with several governments and a major pharmaceutical company, to eradicate leprosy by the end of 2005. Ten countries (including Brazil) that accounted for 90% of global cases in early

2000 were to be the main focus of special efforts to achieve the eradication target.

In 1995 WHO established a Global Tuberculosis Programme to address the emerging challenges of the TB epidemic, which had been declared a global emergency by the Organization in 1993. According to WHO estimates, one-third of the world's population carries the TB bacillus and 2m.–3m. people die from the disease each year. WHO provides technical support to all member countries, with special attention being given to those with high TB prevalence, to establish effective national tuberculosis control programmes. WHO's strategy for TB control includes the use of DOTS (directly observed treatment, short-course), standardized treatment guide-lines, and result accountability through routine evaluation of treat-ment outcomes. Simultaneously, WHO is encouraging research with the aim of further disseminating DOTS, adapting DOTS for wider use, developing new tools for prevention, diagnosis and treatment, and containing new threats such as the HIV/TB co-epidemic. In March 1998 WHO identified Peru, among several countries, as achieving particularly successful results in the detection and treat-ment of the disease. In March 1999 WHO announced the launch of a new initiative, 'Stop TB', in co-operation with the World Bank, the US Government and a coalition of non-governmental organizations, which aimed to promote DOTS to ensure its use in 85% of cases by 2005, compared with some 16% in the late 1990s. However, inade-quate control of DOTS in some areas, leading to partial and inconsis-tent treatments, has resulted in the development of drug-resistant and, often, incurable strains of the disease. The incidence of so-called multidrug-resistant TB (MDR-TB) strains, that are unresponsive to the two main anti-TB drugs, has risen in recent years. In early 2001 WHO estimated that 8m. new cases of TB were occurring world-wide each year, of which the largest concentration was in south-east Asia. It envisaged a substantial increase in new cases by 2005, mainly owing to the severity of the HIV/TB co-epidemic. TB is the principal cause of death for people infected with the HIV virus.

In June 2000 WHO released a report entitled 'Overcoming Antim-icrobial Resistance', in which it warned that the misuse of antibiotics could render some common infectious illnesses unresponsive to treatment. At that time WHO issued guide-lines which aimed to mitigate the risks associated with the use of antimicrobials in livestock reared for human consumption.

NON-COMMUNICABLE DISEASES

The Non-communicable Diseases group comprises three depart-ments responsible for the surveillance, prevention and management of uninfectious diseases (such as those arising from an unhealthy diet).

'Inter-Health', a programme to combat non-communicable dis-eases, was initiated in 1990, with the particular aim of preventing an increase in the incidence of such diseases in developing countries. WHO's programmes for diabetes mellitus, chronic rheumatic dis-eases and asthma assist with the development of national pro-grammes, based upon goals and targets for the improvement of early detection, care and reduction of long-term complications. They also monitor the global epidemiological situation and co-ordinate multinational research activities concerned with the prevention and care of non-communicable diseases. In February 1999 WHO initiated a new programme, 'Vision 2020: the Right to Sight', which aimed to eliminate avoidable blindness (estimated to be as much as 80% of all cases) by 2020. Blindness was otherwise predicted to increase by as much as twofold, owing to the increased longevity of the global population.

HEALTH SYSTEMS AND COMMUNITY HEALTH

During 1998 WHO integrated its programmes relating to the health and development of children and adolescents, reproductive health and research, women's health, and health systems within the Health Systems and Community Health group. The group's aim is to improve access to sustainable health care for all by strengthening health systems and fostering individual, family and community development. Activities include newborn care; child health, including promoting and protecting the health and development of the well-child through such approaches as promotion of breast-feeding and use of the mother-baby package, as well as care of the sick child, including diarrhoeal and acute respiratory disease control and support to women and children in difficult circumstances; the promotion of safe motherhood and maternal health; adolescent health, including the promotion and development of young people and the prevention of specific health problems. Women, health and development, including addressing issues of gender, sexual violence, and harmful traditional practices; and human reproduction, including research related to contraceptive technologies and effec-tive methods. In addition, WHO aimed to provide technical leader-ship and co-ordination on reproductive health and to support countries in their efforts to ensure that people experience healthy sexual development and maturation; have the capacity for healthy equitable and responsible relationships; can achieve their reproduc-tive intentions safely and healthily; avoid illnesses, diseases and injury related to sexuality and reproduction; and receive appropriate counselling, care and rehabilitation for diseases and conditions related to sexuality and reproduction.

WHO's Division of Diarrhoeal and Acute Respiratory Disease Control encourages national programmes aimed at reducing child-hood deaths as a result of diarrhoea, particularly through the use of oral rehydration therapy, and preventive measures. The Division is also seeking to reduce deaths from pneumonia in infants through the use of a simple case-management strategy involving the recogni-tion of danger signs and treatment with an appropriate antibiotic. In September 1997 WHO, in collaboration with UNICEF, formally launched a programme advocating the Integrated Management of Childhood Illness (IMCI), following successful regional trials in more than 20 developing countries during 1996–97. IMCI recognizes that pneumonia, diarrhoea, measles, malaria and malnutrition cause some 70% of the nearly 12m. childhood deaths each year, and recommends screening sick children for all five conditions, in order to enable health workers to reach a more accurate diagnosis than may be achieved from the results of a single assessment.

In December 1995 WHO's Global Programme on AIDS (Acquired Immunodeficiency Syndrome), which began in 1987, was concluded. On 1 January 1996 a new Joint UN programme on the human immunodeficiency virus (HIV) and AIDS (UNAIDS) became opera-tional. It is sponsored jointly by WHO, the World Bank, UNDCP, UNICEF, UNDP, UNESCO and UNFPA. WHO established an Office of HIV/AIDS and Sexually-Transmitted Diseases in order to ensure continuity of its global response to the problem, which included support for national control and education plans, improving the safety of blood supplies and improving the care and support of AIDS patients. In addition, the Office was to liaise with UNAIDS, which has its secretariat at WHO headquarters, and to make available WHO's research and technical expertise. At December 2000 there were an estimated 36.1m. adults and children world-wide living with HIV/AIDS, of whom 5.3m. were estimated to have been newly infected during that year. By that time 21.8m. people, including 4.3m. children, had died of AIDS since the start of the epidemic. Some 95% of those known to be infected with HIV/AIDS live in developing countries. In May 2001 the World Health Assembly adopted a resolution urging the prompt establishment of a global fund to combat HIV/AIDS (as proposed by the UN Secretary-General and envisaged as a partnership between governments, UN bodies and other agencies, and private-sector interests), and demanding increased international co-operation to improve the availability of anti-HIV/AIDS medicines. A meeting of the Group of Seven industrialized nations and Russia (G-8), convened in Genoa, Italy, in July announced the formation of a Global AIDS and Health Fund, intended to channel resources against HIV/AIDS, malaria and TB; the Fund was expected to become operational by the end of 2001.

SUSTAINABLE DEVELOPMENT AND HEALTHY ENVIRONMENTS

The Sustainable Development and Healthy Environment group comprises four departments that concentrate on: health in sustain-able development; nutrition for health and development; protection of the human environment; and emergency and humanitarian action.

The group seeks to monitor for advantages and disadvantages for health, nutrition, environment and development arising from the process of globalization; to integrate the issue of health into poverty reduction programmes; and to promote human rights and equality. Adequate and safe food and nutrition is a priority programme area. An estimated 780m. world-wide cannot meet basic needs for energy and protein, more than 2,000m. people lack essential vitamins and minerals, and 170m. children are estimated to be malnourished.

WHO collaborates with FAO, the World Food Programme, UNICEF and other UN agencies in pursuing its objectives relating to nutrition and food safety. In December 1992 WHO and FAO held an international conference on nutrition at which a World Declaration on Nutrition was adopted to make the fight against malnutrition a development priority. Following the conference WHO promoted the elaboration and implementation of national plans of action for nutrition. WHO aims to support the enhancement of member states' capabilities in dealing with their nutrition situa-tions, and addressing scientific issues related to preventing, man-aging and monitoring protein-energy malnutrition; micronutrient malnutrition, including iodine deficiency disorders, vitamin A defic-iency, and nutritional anaemia; and diet-related non-communicable diseases such as cancer and heart disease. In collaboration with other international agencies, WHO is implementing a comprehen-sive strategy for promoting appropriate infant, young child and maternal nutrition, and for dealing effectively with nutritional emergencies in large populations. Areas of emphasis include pro-moting health-care practices that enhance successful breast-feeding; appropriate complementary feeding; refining the use and interpreta-tion of body measurements for assessing nutritional status; relevant information, education and training; and action to give effect to the

International Code of Marketing of Breast-milk Substitutes (adopted by the World Health Assembly in 1981).

WHO's Food Safety Programme aims to protect human health against risks associated with biological and chemical contaminants and additives in food. With FAO, WHO establishes food standards (through the work of the Codex Alimentarius Commission and its subsidiary committees) and evaluates food additives, pesticide residues and other contaminants and their implications for health. In January 2001 a joint team of FAO and WHO experts issued a report concerning the allergenicity of foods derived from biotechnology (i.e. genetically modified—GM foods).

WHO's Programme for the Promotion of Environmental Health undertakes a wide range of initiatives to tackle the increasing threats to health and well-being from a changing environment. They include control of air pollution, monitoring of water quality, protection against radiation, management of hazardous waste, chemical safety and housing hygiene. Some 1,200m. people world-wide have no access to clean drinking water, while a further 2,900m. people are denied suitable sanitation systems. In rural areas, the emphasis continues to be on the provision and maintenance of safe and sufficient water supplies and adequate sanitation, the health aspects of rural housing, vector control in water resource management, and the safe use of agrochemicals. In urban areas, assistance is provided to identify local environmental health priorities and to improve municipal governments' ability to deal with environmental conditions and health problems in an integrated manner; promotion of the 'Healthy City' approach is a major component of the programme. Other Programme activities include environmental health information development and management, human resources development, environmental health planning methods, research and work on problems relating to global environment change, such as UV-radiation.

Through its Division of Emergency and Humanitarian Action WHO acts as the 'health arm' of disaster relief undertaken by the UN system. In this context, WHO provides expert advice on epidemiological surveillance, control of communicable diseases, public health information and health emergency training. Its emergency preparedness activities include co-ordination, policy-making and planning, awareness-building, technical advice, training, publication of standards and guide-lines, and research. Its emergency relief activities include organizational support, the provision of emergency drugs and supplies and conducting technical emergency assessment missions. The Division's objective is to strengthen the national capacity of member states to reduce the adverse health consequences of disasters. In responding to emergency situations, WHO always tries to develop projects and activities that will assist the national authorities concerned in rebuilding or strengthening their own capacity to handle the impact of such situations.

SOCIAL CHANGE AND MENTAL HEALTH

The Social Change and Mental health group comprises four departments: Health Promotion; Disability, Injury Prevention and Rehabilitation; Mental Health; and Substance Abuse. The group works to assess the impact of injuries, violence and sensory impairments on health, and formulates guide-lines and protocols for the prevention and management of mental problems. WHO promotes decentralized and community-based health programmes and is concerned with the challenge of population ageing and encouraging healthy life-styles and self-care. Several projects have been undertaken, in collaboration between WHO regional and country offices and other relevant organizations, including: the Global School Health Initiative, to bridge the sectors of health and education and to promote the health of school-age children; the Global Strategy for Occupational Health, to promote the health of the working population and the control of occupational health risks; Community-based Rehabilitation, which aimed to provide a more enabling environment for people with disabilities; and a communication strategy to provide training and support for health communications personnel and initiatives.

The Substance Abuse department is concerned with problems of alcohol, drugs and other substance abuse. Within its Programme on Substance Abuse (PSA), which was established in 1990 in response to the global increase in substance abuse, WHO provides technical support to assist countries in formulating policies with regard to the prevention and reduction of the health and social effects of psychoactive substance abuse. PSA's sphere of activity includes epidemiological surveillance and risk assessment, advocacy and the dissemination of information, strengthening national and regional prevention and health promotion techniques and stategies, the development of cost-effective treatment and rehabilitation approaches, and also encompasses regulatory activities as required under the international drugs-control treaties in force.

The Tobacco or Health Programme, which was incorporated into the PSA in May 1994, aims to reduce the use of tobacco, by educating tobacco-users and preventing young people from adopting the habit. In 1996 WHO published its first report on the tobacco situation world-wide. According to WHO, about one-third of the world's population aged over 15 years smoke tobacco, which causes approximately 3.5m. deaths each year (through lung cancer, heart disease, chronic bronchitis and other effects). In 1998 the 'Tobacco Free Initiative', a major global anti-smoking campaign, was established. In May 1999 the World Health Assembly endorsed the formulation of a Framework Convention on Tobacco Control to help to combat the increase in tobacco use and production, and to regulate aspects of the tobacco industry.

HEALTH TECHNOLOGY AND PHARMACEUTICALS

WHO's Health Technology and Pharmaceuticals group comprises the following three departments: Essential Drugs and Other Medicines; Vaccines and Other Biologicals; and Blood Safety and Clinical Technology. Accordingly, the group promotes the development and effective use of drugs and vaccines, as well as the appropriate use of traditional medicines, the self-sufficiency of immunization programmes, and world-wide co-operation on blood safety.

In January 1999 the Executive Board adopted a resolution on WHO's Revised Drug Strategy, which placed emphasis on the inequalities of access to pharmaceuticals, and also covered specific aspects of drugs policy, quality assurance, drug promotion, drug donation, independent drug information and rational drug use. Plans of action involving co-operation with member states and other international organizations were to be developed in order to monitor and analyse the pharmaceutical and public health implications of international agreements, including trade agreements.

In September 1991 the Children's Vaccine Initative (CVI) was launched, jointly sponsored by the Rockefeller Fondation, UNDP, UNICEF, WHO and the World Bank, to facilitate the development and provision of children's vaccines. The CVI has as its ultimate goal the development of a single oral immunization shortly after birth that will protect against all major childhood diseases. In 1998 the CVI reported that 4m. children die each year of diseases for which there are existing, common vaccines. In 1999 WHO, UNICEF, the World Bank and a number of public- and private-sector partners formed the Global Alliance for Vaccines and Immunization (GAVI), which aimed to expand the provision of existing vaccines and to accelerate the development and introduction of new vaccines and technologies, with the goal of protecting children of all nationalities and from all socio-economic backgrounds against vaccine-preventable diseases.

Finance

WHO's regular budget is provided by assessment of member states and associate members. An additional fund for specific projects is provided by voluntary contributions from members and other sources, including UNDP and UNFPA. The proposed regular budget for the period 2002–03 was US $842.7m., of which $74.7m., or 8.9% of the total, was provisionally allocated for the Americas.

Publications

Bulletin of WHO (monthly).

Environmental Health Criteria.

Health Statistics from the Americas (annually).

International Digest of Health Legislation (quarterly).

International Statistical Classification of Disease and Related Health Problems, 10th Revision, 1992–94.

Weekly Epidemiological Record.

WHO Drug Information (quarterly).

World Health Report (annually).

World Health Statistics Annual.

Other UN Organizations Active in the Region

OFFICE FOR THE CO-ORDINATION OF HUMANITARIAN AFFAIRS

Address: United Nations Plaza, New York, NY 10017, USA.

Telephone: (212) 963-1234; **fax:** (212) 963-1312; **e-mail:** ochany@un.org; **internet:** www.reliefweb.int/ocha.

The Office was established in January 1998 as part of the UN Secretariat, with a mandate to co-ordinate international humanitarian assistance and to provide policy and other advice on humanitarian issues. It administers the Humanitarian Early Warning System, as well as Integrated Regional Information Networks to monitor the situation in different countries and a Disaster Response System.

Under Secretary-General for Humanitarian Affairs and Emergency Relief Co-ordinator: Kenzo Oshima (Japan).

OFFICE FOR DRUG CONTROL AND CRIME PREVENTION—ODCCP

Address: Vienna International Centre, POB 500, 1400 Vienna, Austria.

Telephone: (1) 26060-4266; **fax:** (1) 26060-5866; **e-mail:** odccp@odccp.org; **internet:** www.odccp.org.

The Office was established on 1 November 1997 to strengthen the UN's integrated approach to issues relating to drug control, crime prevention and international terrorism. It comprises two principal components: the United Nations International Drug Control Programme (UNDCP) and the Centre for International Crime Prevention (CICP), both headed by the ODCCP Executive Director.

Executive Director: Pino Arlacchi (Italy).

OFFICE OF THE UNITED NATIONS HIGH COMMISSIONER FOR HUMAN RIGHTS

Address: Palais des Nations, 1211 Geneva 10, Switzerland.

Telephone: (22) 9179353; **fax:** (22) 9179012 **e-mail:** scrt.hchr@unog.ch; **internet:** www.unhchr.ch.

The Office is a body of the UN Secretariat and is the focal point for UN human rights activities. Since September 1997 it has incorporated the Centre for Human Rights. The High Commissioner is the UN official with principal responsibility for UN human rights activities.

High Commissioner: Mary Robinson (Ireland).

UNITED NATIONS CENTRE FOR HUMAN SETTLEMENTS— UNCHS (Habitat)

Address: POB 30030, Nairobi, Kenya.

Telephone: (2) 621234; **fax:** (2) 624266; **e-mail:** habitat@unchs.org; **internet:** www.unchs.org.

The Centre was established in October 1978 to service the intergovernmental Commission on Human Settlements, and to serve as a focus for human settlements activities in the UN system.

Executive Director: Anna Kajumulo Tibaijuka (Tanzania).

Regional Offices: Edif. Teleporto, Av. President Vargas 3131/1304, 20210-030 Rio de Janeiro, Brazil; Apdo Postal 6-718, México, DF, Mexico.

UNITED NATIONS CHILDREN'S FUND—UNICEF

Address: 3 United Nations Plaza, New York, NY 10017, USA.

Telephone: (212) 326-7000; **fax:** (212) 888-7465; **e-mail:** netmaster@unicef.org; **internet:** www.unicef.org.

UNICEF was established in 1946 by the General Assembly as the UN International Children's Emergency Fund, to meet the emergency needs of children in post-war Europe and China. In 1950 its mandate was changed to emphasize programmes giving long-term benefits to children everywhere, particularly those in developing countries who are in the greatest need. UNICEF continues to provide relief and rehabilitation in emergency situations and advocates for the rights of all children.

Executive Director: Carol Bellamy (USA).

Regional Office for the Americas: Edif. 868 Albrook, 1°, Panamá 5, Panama; tel. (507) 315-0552; fax (507) 315-0554; e-mail unicef@sinfo.net; internet www.unicef.org/panama.

UNITED NATIONS CONFERENCE ON TRADE AND DEVELOPMENT—UNCTAD

Address: Palais des Nations, 1211 Geneva 10, Switzerland.

Telephone: (22) 9071234; **fax:** (22) 9070057; **e-mail:** ers@unctad.org; **internet:** www.unctad.org.

UNCTAD was established in 1964. It is the principal instrument of the UN General Assembly concerned with trade and development, and is the focal point within the UN system for integrated activities relating to trade, finance, technology, investment and sustainable development. It aims to maximize the trade and development opportunities of developing countries, in particular least-developed countries, and to assist them to adapt to the increasing globalization and liberalization of the world economy. UNCTAD undertakes consensus-building activities, research and policy analysis and technical co-operation.

Secretary-General: Rubens Ricúpero (Brazil).

UNITED NATIONS POPULATION FUND—UNFPA

Address: 220 East 42nd St, New York, NY 10017, USA.

Telephone: (212) 297-5020; **fax:** (212) 557-6416; **internet:** www.unfpa.org.

UNFPA was initially established in 1967, as the Trust Fund for Population Activities, to increase awareness of population issues and to help member states to formulate and implement population policies. The Fund became a subsidiary organ of the UN General Assembly in 1979. It adopted its current name in 1987, retaining its original acronyn.

Executive Director: Thoraya A. Obaid (Saudi Arabia).

UN Specialized Agencies

INTERNATIONAL ATOMIC ENERGY AGENCY—IAEA

Address: POB 100, Wagramerstrasse 5, 1400 Vienna, Austria.

Telephone: (1) 26000; **fax:** (1) 26007; **e-mail:** official.mail@iaea.org; **internet:** www.iaea.org/worldatom.

The Agency was founded in 1957 with the aim of enlarging the contribution of atomic energy to peace, health and prosperity throughout the world, through technical co-operation (assisting research on, and practical application of, atomic energy for peaceful uses); and safeguards (ensuring that special fissionable and other materials, services, equipment and information made available by the Agency or at its request or under its supervision are not used for any military purpose).

Director-General: Dr Mohammad el-Baradei (Egypt).

INTERNATIONAL CIVIL AVIATION ORGANIZATION— ICAO

Address: 999 University St, Montréal, QC H3C 5H7, Canada.

Telephone: (514) 954-8219; **fax:** (514) 954-6077; **e-mail:** icaohq@icao.org; **internet:** www.icao.int.

ICAO was founded in 1947 to develop the techniques of international air navigation and is responsible for establishing international standards and recommended procedures in the technical, economic and legal fields of civil aviation. It is based on the Convention on International Civil Aviation, signed in Chicago, 1944.

Secretary-General: Renato Cláudio Costa Pereira (Brazil).

Regional Office for North America, Central America and the Caribbean: Apdo Postal 5-377, CP 11590, México 5, DF, Mexico.

Regional Office for South America: Apdo 4127, Lima 100, Peru.

INTERNATIONAL LABOUR ORGANIZATION—ILO

Address: 4 route des Morillons, 1211 Geneva 22, Switzerland.

Telephone: (22) 7996111; **fax:** (22) 7998577; **internet:** www.ilo.org.

ILO was founded in 1919 to work for social justice as a basis for lasting peace. It carries out this mandate by promoting decent living standards, satisfactory conditions of work and pay and adequate employment opportunities. Methods of action include the creation of international labour standards; the provision of technical co-operation services; and research and publications on social and labour matters.

Director-General: Juan O. Somavía (Chile).

Regional Office for the Americas: Apdo Postal 3638, Lima 1, Peru.

INTERNATIONAL MARITIME ORGANIZATION—IMO

Address: 4 Albert Embankment, London, SE1 7SR, United Kingdom.

Telephone: (20) 7735-7611; **fax:** (20) 7587-3210; **e-mail:** info@imo.org; **internet:** www.imo.org.

The Inter-Governmental Maritime Consultative Organization (IMCO) began operations in 1959, as a specialized agency of the UN to facilitate co-operation among governments on technical matters affecting international shipping. Its main functions are the achievement of safe and efficient navigation, and the control of pollution caused by ships and craft operating in the marine environment. IMCO became IMO in 1982.

Secretary-General: WILLIAM A. O'NEIL (Canada).

INTERNATIONAL TELECOMMUNICATION UNION—ITU

Address: Place des Nations, 1211 Geneva 20, Switzerland.

Telephone: (22) 7305111; **fax:** (22) 7337256; **e-mail:** itumail@itu .int; **internet:** www.itu.int.

Founded in 1865, ITU became a specialized agency of the UN in 1947. It acts to encourage world co-operation in the use of telecommunication, to promote technical development, to harmonize national policies in the field, and to secure minimal costs for telecommunications products and services.

Secretary-General: YOSHIO UTSUMI (Japan).

UNITED NATIONS INDUSTRIAL DEVELOPMENT ORGANIZATION—UNIDO

Address: POB 300, 1400 Vienna, Austria.

Telephone: (1) 26026-5021; **fax:** (1) 26026-6881; **e-mail:** unido-pinfo@unido.org; **internet:** www.unido.org.

UNIDO began operations in 1967. It aims to promote sustainable and socially equitable industrial development in developing countries and in countries with economics in transition; encourages industrial partnerships between governments and the private sector and acts as a world-wide forum for industrial development; provides technical co-operation services.

Director-General: CARLOS ALFREDO MAGARIÑOS (Argentina).

UNIVERSAL POSTAL UNION—UPU

Address: Case postale, 3000 Berne 15, Switzerland.

Telephone: (31) 3503111; **fax:** (31) 3503110; **e-mail:** info@upu.int; **internet:** www.upu.int.

The General Postal Union was founded by the Treaty of Berne (1874), beginning operations in July 1875. Three years later its name was changed to the Universal Postal Union. In 1948 UPU became a Specialized Agency of the UN. It aims to develop and unify the international postal service, to study problems and to provide training.

Director-General: THOMAS E. LEAVEY (USA).

WORLD INTELLECTUAL PROPERTY ORGANIZATION—WIPO

Address: 34 chemin des Colombettes, 1211 Geneva 20, Switzerland.

Telephone: (22) 3389111; **fax:** (22) 7335428; **e-mail:** wipo.mail@ wipo.int; **internet:** www.wipo.int.

WIPO was established in 1970. It became a specialized agency of the UN in 1974 concerned with the protection of intellectual property (e.g. industrial and technical patents and literary copyrights). WIPO formulates and administers treaties embodying international norms and standards of intellectual property, establishes model laws, and facilitates applications for the protection of inventions, trademarks etc. WIPO provides legal and technical assistance to developing countries and countries with economies in transition and advises countries on obligations under the World Trade Organization's agreement on Trade-Related Aspects of Intellectual Property Rights (TRIPS).

Director-General: Dr KAMIL IDRIS (Sudan).

WORLD METEOROLOGICAL ORGANIZATION—WMO

Address: 7 bis ave de la Paix, 1211 Geneva 2, Switzerland.

Telephone: (22) 7308111; **fax:** (22) 7308181; **e-mail:** ipa@gateway .wmo.ch; **internet:** www.wmo.ch.

WMO became a specialized agency of the UN in 1951. It promotes the effective exchange and use of meteorological, climatological and hydrological information and its applications world-wide.

Secretary-General: Prof. G. O. P. OBASI (Nigeria).

United Nations Information Centres

Argentina: Junín 1940, 1°, 1113 Buenos Aires; tel. (1) 4803-7671; fax (1) 4804-7545; e-mail buenosaires@unic.org.ar; internet www.unic.org.ar (also covers Uruguay).

Bolivia: Apdo Postal 9072, Avda Mariscal Santa Cruz No. 1350, La Paz; tel. (2) 358590; fax (2) 391368; e-mail unicbol@eos.pnud.bo.

Brazil: Palácio Itamaraty, Avda Marechal Floriano 196, 20080-002 Rio de Janeiro, RJ; tel. (21) 253-2211; fax (21) 233-5753; e-mail infounic@unicrio.org.br.

Chile: Casilla 179D; Edif. Naciones Unidas, Avda Dag Hammarskjöld, Vitacura, Santiago; tel. (2) 210-2000; fax (2) 208-1946; e-mail dpisantiago@eclac.cl.

Colombia: Calle 100, No 8A-55, Of. 815, Apdo Aéreo 058964, Santafé de Bogotá 2; tel. (1) 257-6044; fax (1) 257-7936; e-mail uniccol@ mbox.unicc.org (also covers Ecuador and Venezuela).

El Salvador: Edif. Escalón, 2°, Paseo General Escalón y 87 Avda Norte, Col. Escalón, Apdo 2157, San Salvador; tel. 279-1925; fax 279-1929 (also covers Costa Rica, Guatemala and Honduras). (At mid-2001 this office was temporarily inactive.)

Mexico: Presidente Mazaryk No 29, 6°, México 11570, DF; tel. (5) 250-1364; fax (5) 203-8638; e-mail infounic@un.org.mx; internet www.cinu.org.mx (also covers Cuba and the Dominican Republic).

Nicaragua: Palacio de la Cultura, Apdo 3260, Managua; tel. (2) 664253; fax (2) 222362; e-mail cedoc@sdnnic.org.ni.

Panama: Calle Gerardo Ortega y Avda Samuel Lewis, Banco Central Hispano Bldg, Apdo 6-9083, El Dorado, Panamá; tel. 2232198; fax 2230557; e-mail cinup@sinfo.net; internet www.onu.org.pa/ cinup.

Paraguay: Casilla 1107; Estrella 354, Edif. City, 3°, Asunción; tel. (21) 493025; fax (21) 449611; e-mail unic@undp.org.py.

Peru: Apdo 14-0199; Lord Cochrane 130, San Isidro, Lima 27; tel. (1) 4418745; fax (1) 4418735; e-mail informes@uniclima.org.pe.

Trinidad and Tobago: Bretton Hall, 2nd Floor, 16 Victoria Ave, POB 130, Port of Spain; tel. 623-4813; fax 623-4332; e-mail unicpos@opus.co.tt (also covers Antigua and Barbuda, the Bahamas, Barbados, Belize, Dominica, Grenada, Guyana, Jamaica, the Netherlands Dependencies, Saint Christopher and Nevis, Saint Lucia, Saint Vincent and the Grenadines and Suriname).

ANDEAN COMMUNITY OF NATIONS
(COMUNIDAD ANDINA DE NACIONES—CAN)

Address: Avda Paseo de la República 3895, San Isidro, Lima 27; Casilla 18-1177, Lima 18, Peru.

Telephone: (1) 4111400; **fax:** (1) 2213329; **e-mail:** contacto@comunidadandina.org; **internet:** www.comunidadandina.org.

The organization was established in 1969 as the Acuerdo de Cartagena (the Cartagena Agreement), also referred to as the Grupo Andino (Andean Group) or the Pacto Andino (Andean Pact). In March 1996 member countries signed a Reform Protocol of the Cartagena Agreement, in accordance with which the Andean Group was superseded in August 1997 by the Andean Community of Nations (CAN, generally referred to as the Andean Community). The Andean Community was to promote greater economic, commercial and political integration under a new Andean Integration System (Sistema Andino de Integración), comprising the organization's bodies and institutions. The Community covers an area of 4,710,000 sq km, with some 111m. inhabitants.

MEMBERS

Bolivia Colombia Ecuador Peru Venezuela

Note: Chile withdrew from the Andean Group in 1976. Panama has observer status with the Community.

Organization
(July 2001)

ANDEAN PRESIDENTIAL COUNCIL

The presidential summits, which had been held annually since 1989, were formalized under the 1996 Reform Protocol of the Cartagena Agreement as the Andean Presidential Council. The Council provides the political leadership of the Community.

COMMISSION

The Commission consists of a plenipotentiary representative from each member country, with each country holding the presidency in turn. The Commission is the main policy-making organ of the Andean Community, and is responsible for co-ordinating Andean trade policy.

COUNCIL OF FOREIGN MINISTERS

The Council of Foreign Ministers meets annually or whenever it is considered necessary, to formulate common external policy and to co-ordinate the process of integration.

GENERAL SECRETARIAT

The General Secretariat (formerly the Junta) is the body charged with implementation of all guide-lines and decisions issued by the bodies listed above. It submits proposals to the Commission for facilitating the fulfilment of the Community's objectives. Members are appointed for a three-year term. They supervise technical officials assigned to the following Departments: External Relations, Agricultural Development, Press Office, Economic Policy, Physical Integration, Programme of Assistance to Bolivia, Industrial Development, Programme Planning, Legal Affairs, Technology. Under the reforms agreed in March 1996 the Secretary-General is elected by the Council of Foreign Ministers and has enhanced powers to adjudicate in disputes arising between member states.

Secretary-General: SEBASTIÁN ALEGRETT (Venezuela).

PARLIAMENT

Parlamento Andino: Carrera 7ª, No. 13–58, Oficina 401, Santafé de Bogotá, Colombia; tel. (1) 284-4191; fax (1) 284-3270; e-mail pandino@cable.net.co; internet www.parlamentoandino.org; f. 1979; comprises five members from each country, and meets in each capital city in turn; makes recommendations on regional policy. In April 1997 a new protocol was adopted which provided for the election of members by direct and universal voting. Sec.-Gen. Dr RUBÉN VÉLEZ NÚÑEZ.

COURT OF JUSTICE

Tribunal de Justicia de la Comunidad Andina: Calle Roca 450 y 6 de diciembre, Quito, Ecuador; tel. (2) 529998; fax (2) 565007; e-mail tjca@impsat.net.ec; internet www.altesa.net/tribunal; f. 1979, began operating in 1984; a protocol approved in May 1996 modified the Court's functions; its main responsibilities are to resolve disputes among member countries and interpret community legislation. It comprises five judges, one from each member country, appointed for a renewable period of six years. The Presidency is assumed annually by each judge in turn, by alphabetical order of country. Pres. Dr RUBEN HERDOIZA MERA (Ecuador).

Activities

In May 1979, at Cartagena, Colombia, the Presidents of the five member countries signed the 'Mandate of Cartagena', which envisaged greater economic and political co-operation, including the establishment of more sub-regional development programmes (especially in industry). In May 1989 the Group undertook to revitalize the process of Andean integration, by withdrawing measures that obstructed the programme of trade liberalization, and by complying with tariff reductions that had already been agreed upon. In May 1991, in Caracas, Venezuela, a summit meeting of the Andean Group agreed the framework for the establishment of a free-trade area on 1 January 1992 (achieved in February 1993) and for an eventual Andean common market (see below, under Trade).

In March 1996 heads of state, meeting in Trujillo, Peru, affirmed member countries' commitment to combating drugs trafficking and indirectly condemned the decision of the USA to 'decertify' the Colombian anti-narcotics campaign (and thus to suspend financial assistance to that country). At the same meeting, member countries agreed to a substantial restructuring of the Andean Group. The heads of state signed the Reform Protocol of the Cartagena Agreement, providing for the establishment of the Andean Community of Nations, which was to have more ambitious economic and political objectives than the Group. Consequently, in August 1997 the Andean Community was inaugurated, and the Group's Junta was replaced by a new General Secretariat, headed by a Secretary-General with enhanced executive and decision-making powers. The initiation of these reforms was designed to accelerate harmonization in economic matters, particularly the achievement of a common external tariff. In September 1996 the Group agreed to negotiate a free-trade agreement with the Mercado Común del Sur (Mercosur—see p. 870). (Disunity among the Andean nations had been evident in June, when Bolivia had agreed to enter into free-trade negotiations with Mercosur on a unilateral basis, thus becoming an associate member of that grouping.) In April 1997 the Peruvian Government announced its intention to withdraw from the Cartagena Agreement, owing to disagreements about the terms of Peru's full integration into the Community's trading system. Later in that month the heads of state of the four other members attended a summit meeting, in Sucre, Bolivia, and reiterated their commitment to strengthening regional integration. A high-level group of representatives was established to pursue negotiations with Peru regarding its future relationship with the Community (agreement was reached in June—see below). In April 2001 Venezuela announced that it intended to apply for membership of Mercosur (while retaining its membership of the Community).

In June 2001 the 13th presidential summit, held in Valencia, Venezuela, reiterated the objective of creating a common market and related efforts to strengthen sub-regional integration. The meeting concluded with the adoption of an Andean Co-operation Plan for the Control of Illegal Drugs and Related Offences, which was to promote a united approach to combating these problems, including through the exchange of information and experience, joint operations, control of illegal assets and preventive campaigns. An executive committee was to be established under the accord to oversee implementation of an action plan.

TRADE

Trade within the group increased by about 37% annually between 1978 and 1980. A council for customs affairs met for the first time in January 1982, aiming to harmonize national legislation within the group. In December 1984 the member states launched a new common currency, the Andean peso, aiming to reduce dependence on the US dollar and to increase regional trade. The new currency was to be backed by special contributions to the Fondo Andino de Reservas (now the Fondo Latinoamericano de Reservas) amounting to US $80m., and was to be 'pegged' to the US dollar, taking the form of financial drafts rather than notes and coins. In May 1986 a new formula for trade among member countries was agreed, in order to restrict the number of products exempted from trade liberalization measures to 40 'sensitive' products.

The 'Caracas Declaration' of May 1991 provided for the establishment of an Andean free-trade area, which entered into effect (excluding Peru—see below) in February 1993. Heads of state also agreed in May 1991 to create a common external tariff (CET), to standardize member countries' trade barriers in their dealings with the rest of the world, and envisaged the eventual creation of an Andean common market. In December heads of state defined four main levels of external tariffs (between 5% and 20%). The conclusion of negotiations, however, was subsequently delayed, notably by Ecuador's request for numerous exceptions and by a deterioration in relations between Peru and Venezuela during 1992 (following the suspension of the Peruvian Constitution in April), which halted progress completely. In August the Group approved a request by Peru for the suspension of its rights and obligations under the Pact, thereby enabling the other members to proceed with negotiations on the CET. Peru was readmitted as a full member of the Group in 1994, but participated only as an observer in the ongoing negotiations.

In November 1994 ministers of trade and integration, meeting in Quito, Ecuador, concluded a final agreement on a four-tier structure of external tariffs (although Bolivia was to retain a two-level system). The CET agreement, which came into effect in February 1995, covered 90% of the region's imports (the remainder to be incorporated by 1999, later extended to June 2000), which were to be subject to the following tariff bands: 5% for raw materials; 10%–15% for semi-manufactured goods; and 20% for finished products. In order to reach an agreement, special treatment and exemptions were granted, while Peru, initially, was to remain a 'non-active' member of the accord: Bolivia was to maintain external tariffs of 5% and 10%, Ecuador was permitted to apply the lowest rate of 5% to 990 items and was granted an initial exemption from tariffs on 400 items, while Colombia and Venezuela were granted 230 items to be subject to special treatment for four years. In June 1997 an agreement was concluded to ensure Peru's continued membership of the Community, which provided for that country's integration into the free-trade area. The Peruvian Government determined to eliminate customs duties on some 2,500 products with immediate effect, and it was agreed that the process be completed by 2005. However, negotiations were to continue with regard to the replacement of Peru's single tariff on products from outside the region with the Community's scale of external duties.

In May 1999 the Community adopted a policy on border integration and development, which aimed to prepare the border regions of member countries for the envisaged free circulation of people, goods, capital and services, and had the general objective of consolidating sub-regional security. Community heads of state, meeting in June 2000 at the 12th Andean presidential summit, approved official guide-lines for the creation of the proposed Andean common market by the end of 2005, and agreed a programme of related measures to be implemented during 2000/01. In June 2001 Andean leaders attending the annual summit meeting reaffirmed their commitment to the development of border integration zones and to the implementation of an Andean passport system, to enter into effect no later than December 2005.

EXTERNAL RELATIONS

In September 1995 heads of state of member countries identified the formulation of common positions on foreign relations as an important part of the process of relaunching the integration initiative. A Protocol Amending the Cartagena Agreement was signed in June 1997 to confirm the formulation of a common foreign policy. During 1998 the General Secretariat held consultations with government experts, academics, representatives of the private sector and other interested parties to help formulate a document on guide-lines for a common foreign policy. The guide-lines, establishing the principles, objectives and mechanisms of a common foreign policy, were approved by the Council of Foreign Ministers in 1999. The 12th Andean presidential summit, held in June 2000, expressed support for the ongoing formulation and implementation of the policy. A Council on Trade and Investment between the Andean Community and the USA has been established to strengthen the trading relations between the two parties. A co-operation agreement between the European Union and Andean Group was signed in April 1993. A Euro-Andean Forum is held periodically to promote co-operation, trade and investment between the two communities. In February 1998 the Community signed a co-operation and technical assistance agreement with the EU in order to combat drugs trafficking. In March 2000 the Community concluded an agreement to establish a political consultation and co-operation mechanism with the People's Republic of China.

In April 1998, at the 10th Andean presidential summit, an agreement was signed with Panama establishing a framework for negotiations providing for the conclusion of a free-trade accord by the end of 1998 and Panama's eventual associate membership of the Community. Also in April 1998 the Community signed a framework agreement with Mercosur on the establishment of a free-trade

accord. The process of extending trade preferences was to commence in October 1998, and the agreement was to become fully effective by January 2000. Negotiations between the two sides, however, were delayed during 1998, owing to differences regarding tariff reductions and the items to be covered by the accord. Bilateral agreements between the countries of the two groupings were extended. In January 1999 representatives of the Community and Mercosur pledged to complete the first stage of negotiations of the free-trade agreement by 31 March; this, however, was not achieved. It was agreed, in March, that the duration of bilateral trade arrangements would be extended and that the Community would initiate negotiations to conclude a free-trade area with Brazil. A preferential tariff agreement was concluded between Brazil and the Community in July; the accord entered into effect, for a period of two years, in mid-August. In August 2000 a preferential tariff agreement concluded with Argentina entered into force. The Community commenced negotiations on drafting a preferential tariff agreement with (jointly) El Salvador, Guatemala and Honduras in March of that year. In September leaders of the Community and Mercosur, meeting at a summit of Latin American heads of state, determined to relaunch negotiations, with a view to establishing a free-trade area by 1 January 2002. In July 2001 ministers of foreign affairs of the two groupings approved the establishment of a formal mechanism for political dialogue and co-ordination in order to facilitate negotiations and to enhance economic and social integration.

In March 1998 ministers of trade from 34 countries, meeting in San José, Costa Rica, concluded an agreement on the structure of negotiations for the establishment of a Free Trade Area of the Americas (FTAA). The process was formally initiated by heads of state, meeting in Santiago, Chile, in the following month. The Community negotiated as a bloc to obtain chairmanship of three of the nine negotiating groups: on market access (Colombia), on competition policy (Peru), and on intellectual property (Venezuela). The Community insisted that the final declaration issued by the meeting include recognition that the varying levels of development of the participating countries should be taken into consideration throughout the negotiating process.

In August 1999 the Secretary-General of the Community visited Guyana in order to promote bilateral trading opportunities and to strengthen relations with the Caribbean Community. The Community held a meeting on trade relations with the Caribbean Community during 2000.

INDUSTRY

Negotiations began in 1970 for the formulation of joint industrial programmes, particularly in the petrochemicals, metal-working and motor vehicle sectors, but disagreements over the allocation of different plants, and the choice of foreign manufacturers for co-operation, prevented progress and by 1984 the more ambitious schemes had been abandoned. Instead, emphasis was to be placed on assisting small and medium-sized industries, particularly in the agro-industrial and electronics sectors, in co-operation with national industrial organizations.

An Andean Agricultural Development Programme was formulated in 1976 within which 22 resolutions aimed at integrating the Andean agricultural sector were approved. In 1984 the Andean Food Security System was created to develop the agrarian sector, replace imports progressively with local produce, and improve rural living conditions. In April 1998 the Presidential Council instructed the Commission, together with ministers of agriculture, to formulate an Andean Common Agricultural Policy, including measures to harmonize trade policy instruments and legislation on animal and plant health. The 12th Andean presidential summit, held in June 2000, authorized the adoption of the concluded Policy and the enforcement of a plan of action for its implementation.

In May 1987 member countries signed the Quito Protocol, modifying the Cartagena Agreement, to amend the strict rules that had formerly been imposed on foreign investors in the region. The Protocol entered into force in May 1988. Accordingly, each government was to decide which sectors were to be closed to foreign participation, and the period within which foreign investors must transfer a majority shareholding to local investors was extended to 30 years (37 years in Bolivia and Ecuador). In March 1991 the Protocol was amended, with the aim of further liberalizing foreign investment and stimulating an inflow of foreign capital and technology. External and regional investors were to be permitted to repatriate their profits (in accordance with the laws of the country concerned) and there was no stipulation that a majority shareholding must eventually be transferred to local investors. A further directive, adopted in March, covered the formation of 'Empresas Multinacionales Andinas' (multinational enterprises) in order to ensure that at least two member countries have a shareholding of 15% or more of the capital, including the country where the enterprise was to be based. These enterprises were entitled to participate in sectors otherwise reserved for national enterprises, subject to the same conditions as national enterprises in terms of taxation and export regulations, and to gain access to the markets of all member countries.

In November 1988 member states established a bank, the Banco Intermunicipal Andino, which was to finance public works.

In May 1995 the Group initiated a programme to promote the use of cheap and efficient energy sources and greater co-operation in the energy sector. The programme planned to develop a regional electricity grid.

TRANSPORT AND COMMUNICATIONS

The Andean Community has pursued efforts to improve infrastructure throughout the region. In 1983 the Commission formulated a plan to assist land-locked Bolivia, particularly through improving roads connecting it with neighbouring countries and the Pacific Ocean. An 'open skies' agreement, giving airlines of member states equal rights to airspace and airport facilities within the grouping, was signed in May 1991. In June 1998 the Commission approved the establishment of an Andean Commission of Land Transportation Authorities, which was to oversee the operation and development of land transportation services. Similarly, an Andean Committee of Water Transportation Authorities has been established to ensure compliance with Community regulations regarding ocean transportation activities. The Community aims to facilitate the movement of goods throughout the region by the use of different modes of transport ('multimodal transport') and to guarantee operational standards. It also intends to harmonize Community transport regulations and standards with those of Mercosur countries.

In August 1996 a regulatory framework was approved for the development of a commercial Andean satellite system. In December 1997 the General Secretariat approved regulations for granting authorization for the use of the system; the Commission subsequently granted the first Community authorization to an Andean multinational enterprise (Andesat), comprising 48 companies from all five member states. The system was expected to be fully operational from mid-2002. In 1994 the Community initiated efforts to establish a digital technology infrastructure throughout the Community: the resulting Andean Digital Corridor comprises ground, under water and satellite routes providing a series of cross-border interconnections between the member countries. The Andean Internet System, which aims to provide internet protocol-based services throughout the Community, was operational in Colombia, Ecuador and Venezuela in 2000, and was to be extended to all five member countries from early 2001. In May 1999 the Andean Committee of Telecommunications Authorities agreed to remove all restrictions to free trade in telecommunications services (excluding sound broadcasting and television) by 1 January 2002. The Committee also determined to formulate provisions on interconnection and the safeguarding of free competition and principles of transparency within the sector.

Asociación de Empresas de Telecomunicaciones de la Comunidad Andina—ASETA: Calle La Pradera 510 y San Salvador, Casilla 10-1106042, Quito, Ecuador; tel. (2) 563-812; fax (2) 562-499; e-mail info@aseta.org; internet www.aseta.org.ec; f. 1974; coordinates improvements in national telecommunications services, in order to contribute to the further integration of the countries of the Andean Community. Sec.-Gen. MARCELO LÓPEZ ARJONA.

SOCIAL INTEGRATION

Several formal agreements and institutions have been established within the framework of the grouping to enhance social development and welfare (see below). The Community aims to incorporate these bodies into the process of enhanced integration and to promote greater involvement of representatives of the civil society. In May 1999 the 11th Andean presidential summit adopted a 'multidimensional social agenda' focusing on job creation and on improvements in the fields of education, health and housing throughout the Community. In June 2000 the 12th presidential summit instructed the Andean institutions to prepare individual programmes aimed at consolidating implementation of the Community's integration programme and advancing the development of the social agenda.

INSTITUTIONS

Consejo Consultivo Empresarial Andino (Andean Business Advisory Council): Paseo de la Republica 3895, Lima, Peru; tel. (1) 4111400; fax (1) 2213329; e-mail rsuarez@comunidadandina.org; first

meeting held in November 1998; a consultative institution within the framework of the Sistema Andino de Integración; comprises elected representatives of business organizations; advises Community ministers and officials on integration activities affecting the business sector.

Consejo Consultivo Laboral Andino (Andean Labour Advisory Council): Edif. José Vargas, Avda Andres Eloy Blanco, Los Caobos, Caracas, Venezuela; tel. (2) 9872501; fax (2) 9866394; a consultative institution within the framework of the Sistema Andino de Integración; comprises elected representatives of labour organizations; advises Community ministers and officers on related labour issues.

Convenio Andrés Bello (Andrés Bello Agreement): Paralela Autopista Norte, Avda 13 85–60, Santafé de Bogotá, Colombia; tel. (1) 6181701; fax (1) 6100139; e-mail ecobello@col1.telecom.com.co; internet www.cab.int.co; f. 1970, modified in 1990; aims to promote integration in the educational, technical and cultural sectors. Mems: Bolivia, Chile, Colombia, Ecuador, Panama, Peru, Spain, Venezuela.

Convenio Hipólito Unanue (Hipólito Unanue Agreement): Edif. Cartagena, Paseo de la República 3832, 3°, Lima, Peru; tel. (1) 2210074; fax (1) 4409285; e-mail postmaster@conhu.org.pe; internet www.conhu.org.pe; f. 1971 on the occasion of the first meeting of Andean ministers of health; aims to enhance the development of health services, and to promote regional co-ordination in areas such as environmental health, disaster preparedness and the prevention and control of drug abuse.

Convenio Simón Rodríguez (Simón Rodríguez Agreement): Luis Felipe Borja s/n, Edif. Géminis, 9°, Quito, Ecuador; tel. (2) 5453774; promotes a convergence of social and labour conditions throughout the Community, for example, working hours and conditions, employment and social security policies, and to promote the participation of workers and employers in the sub-regional integration process.

Corporación Andina de Fomento—CAF (Andean Development Corporation): Torre CAF, Avda Luis Roche, Altamira, Apdo 5086, Caracas, Venezuela; tel. (2) 2092111; fax (2) 2092394; e-mail sede@caf.com; internet www.caf.com; f. 1968, began operations in 1970; aims to encourage the integration of the Andean countries by specialization and an equitable distribution of investments. It conducts research to identify investment opportunities, and prepares the resulting investment projects; gives technical and financial assistance; and attracts internal and external credit. Auth. cap. US $3,000m., subscribed or underwritten by the governments of member countries, or by public, semi-public and private-sector institutions authorized by those governments. The Board of Directors comprises representatives of each country at ministerial level. Mems: the Andean Community, Brazil, Chile, Jamaica, Mexico, Panama, Paraguay, Trinidad and Tobago, and 22 private banks in the Andean region. Exec. Pres. ENRIQUE GARCÍA RODRÍGUEZ (Bolivia).

Fondo Latinoamericano de Reservas—FLAR (Latin American Reserve Fund): Edif. Banco de Occidente, Edif. Banco de Occidente, Carrera 13, No. 27–47, 10°, Santafé de Bogotá, Colombia; tel. (1) 2858511; fax (1) 2881117; e-mail agamarra@bloomberg.net; internet www.flar.net; f. 1978 as the Fondo Andino de Reservas to support the balance of payments of member countries, provide credit, guarantee loans, and contribute to the harmonization of monetary and financial policies; adopted present name in 1991, in order to allow the admission of other Latin American countries. In 1992 the Fund began extending credit lines to commercial for export financing. It is administered by an Assembly of the ministers of finance and economy of the member countries, and a Board of Directors comprising the Presidents of the central banks of the member states. In October 1995 it was agreed to expand the Fund's capital from US $800m. to $1,000m.; the increase became effective on 30 June 1997. Exec. Pres. ROBERTO GUARNIERI (Venezuela); Sec.-Gen. ANA MARÍA CARRASQUILLA (Colombia).

Universidad Andina Simón Bolívar (Simón Bolívar Andean University): Calle Real Audiencia 73, POB 608-33, Sucre, Bolivia; tel. (64) 60265; fax (64) 60833; e-mail uasb@uasb.edu.bo; internet www.uasb.edu.bo; f. 1985; institution for postgraduate study and research; promotes co-operation between other universities in the Andean region; Pres. JULIO GARRET AILLON.

Publications

Gaceta Oficial del Acuerdo de Cartagena.
Trade and Investment Guide.
Treinta Años de Integración Andina.

CARIBBEAN COMMUNITY AND COMMON MARKET—CARICOM

Address: Bank of Guyana Building, POB 10827, Georgetown, Guyana.

Telephone: (2) 69281; **fax:** (2) 67816; **e-mail:** carisec3@caricom.org; **internet:** www.caricom.org.

CARICOM was formed in 1973 by the Treaty of Chaguaramas, signed in Trinidad, as a movement towards unity in the Caribbean; it replaced the Caribbean Free Trade Association (CARIFTA), founded in 1965. A revision of the Treaty of Chaguaramas (by means of nine separate Protocols) was undertaken in the 1990s, to institute greater regional integration and to establish a single Caribbean market and economy.

MEMBERS

Anguilla*	Jamaica
Antigua and Barbuda	Montserrat
Bahamas†	Saint Christopher and Nevis
Barbados	Saint Lucia
Belize	Saint Vincent and the Grenadines
British Virgin Islands*	Suriname
Dominica	Trinidad and Tobago
Grenada	Turks and Caicos Islands*
Guyana	

* The British Virgin Islands and the Turks and Caicos Islands were granted associate membership in 1991; Anguilla's application for associate membership was approved in July 1998 and formally implemented in July 1999.

† The Bahamas is a member of the Community but not the Common Market.

Note: Haiti was accepted as a full member of the Community in July 1997, although the final terms and conditions of its accession had yet to be concluded; it was invited to participate in the deliberations of all the organs and bodies of the Community in the interim. The terms for Haiti's accession were agreed in July 1999 and required ratification by that country's parliament. Aruba, Bermuda, the Cayman Islands, Colombia, the Dominican Republic, Mexico, the Netherlands Antilles, Puerto Rico and Venezuela have observer status with the Community.

Organization

(July 2001)

HEADS OF GOVERNMENT CONFERENCE AND BUREAU

The Conference is the final authority of the Community and determines policy. It is responsible for the conclusion of treaties on behalf of the Community and for entering into relationships between the Community and international organizations and states. Decisions of the Conference are generally taken unanimously. Heads of government meet annually, although inter-sessional meetings may be convened.

At a special meeting of the Conference, held in Trinidad and Tobago in October 1992, participants decided to establish a Heads of Government Bureau, with the capacity to initiate proposals, to update consensus and to secure the implementation of CARICOM decisions. The Bureau became operational in December, comprising the Chairman of the Conference, as Chairman, as well as the incoming and outgoing Chairmen of the Conference, and the Secretary-General of the Conference, in the capacity of Chief Executive Officer.

COMMUNITY COUNCIL OF MINISTERS

In October 1992 CARICOM heads of government agreed that a Caribbean Community Council of Ministers should be established to replace the existing Common Market Council of Ministers as the second highest organ of the Community. Protocol I amending the Treaty of Chaguaramas, to restructure the organs and institutions of the Community, was formally adopted at a meeting of CARICOM heads of government in February 1997 and was signed by all member states in July. The inaugural meeting of the Community Council of Ministers was held in Nassau, the Bahamas, in February 1998. The Council consists of ministers responsible for community affairs, as well as other government ministers designated by member states, and is responsible for the development of the Community's strategic planning and co-ordination in the areas of economic integration, functional co-operation and external relations.

MINISTERIAL COUNCILS

The principal organs of the Community are assisted in their functions by the following bodies, established under Protocol I amending the Treaty of Chaguaramas: the Council for Trade and Economic Development (COTED); the Council for Foreign and Community Relations (COFCOR); the Council for Human and Social Development (COHSOD); and the Council for Finance and Planning (COFAP). The Councils are responsible for formulating policies, promoting their implementation and supervising co-operation in the relevant areas.

SECRETARIAT

The Secretariat is the main administrative body of the Caribbean Community. The functions of the Secretariat are: to service meetings of the Community and of its Committees; to take appropriate follow-up action on decisions made at such meetings; to carry out studies on questions of economic and functional co-operation relating to the region as a whole; to provide services to member states at their request in respect of matters relating to the achievement of the objectives of the Community.

Secretary-General: EDWIN W. CARRINGTON (Trinidad and Tobago).

Deputy Secretary-General: Dr CARLA BARNETT (Belize).

Activities

REGIONAL INTEGRATION

In 1989 CARICOM heads of government established the 15-member West Indian Commission to study regional political and economic integration. The Commission's final report, submitted in July 1992, recommended that CARICOM should remain a community of sovereign states (rather than a federation), but should strengthen the integration process and expand to include the wider Caribbean region. It recommended the formation of an Association of Caribbean States (ACS), to include all the countries within and surrounding the Caribbean Basin (see p. 874). In November 1997 the Secretaries-General of CARICOM and the ACS signed a Co-operation Agreement to formalize the reciprocal procedures through which the organizations work to enhance and facilitate regional integration. The Heads of Government Conference that was held in October 1992 established an Inter-Governmental Task Force, which was to undertake preparations for a reorientation of CARICOM. In February 1993 it presented a draft Charter of Civil Society for the Community, which set out principles in the areas of democracy, government, parliament, freedom of the press and human rights. The Charter was signed by Community heads of government in February 1997. Suriname was admitted to the organization in July 1995. In July 1997 the Heads of Government Conference agreed to admit Haiti as a member, although the terms and conditions of its accession to the organization had yet to be negotiated. These were finalized in July 1999. In July 2001 the CARICOM Secretary-General formally inaugurated a CARICOM Office in Haiti, which aimed to provide technical assistance in preparation of Haiti's accession to the Community.

In August 1998 CARICOM and the Dominican Republic signed a free-trade accord, covering trade in goods and services, technical barriers to trade, government procurement, and sanitary and phytosanitary measures and standards. A protocol to the agreement was signed in April 2000, following the resolution of differences concerning exempted items. The accord was ratified by the Dominican Republic in February 2001.

In July 1999 CARICOM heads of government endorsed proposals to establish a Caribbean Court of Justice, which, it was provisionally agreed, would be located in Port of Spain, Trinidad and Tobago. The Court was intended to replace the Judicial Committee of the Privy Council as the Court of Final Appeal for those countries recognizing its jurisdiction, and was also to adjudicate on trade disputes and on the interpretation of the CARICOM Treaty. An agreement establishing the Court was formally signed by 10 member countries in February 2001.

CO-ORDINATION OF FOREIGN POLICY

The co-ordination of foreign policies of member states is listed as one of the main objectives of the Community in its founding treaty. Activities include: strengthening of member states' position in international organizations; joint diplomatic action on issues of particular interest to the Caribbean; joint co-operation arrangements with third countries and organizations; and the negotiation of free-trade agreements with third countries and other regional groupings. This last area of activity has assumed increasing importance since the agreement in 1994 by almost all the governments of countries in the Americas to establish a 'Free Trade Area of the Americas' (FTAA) by 2005. In April 1997 CARICOM inaugurated a Regional Negotiating Machinery body to co-ordinate the region's external negotiations. The main focus of activities was to be the establishment of the FTAA, ACP relations with the EU, and multilateral trade negotiations under the WTO.

In 1990 a working group was established with Brazil, Colombia and Venezuela to consider ways of developing regional economic co-operation, including greater self-sufficiency in food, joint exploration for mineral resources, joint trading policies, and co-operation in communications and transport systems. In July 1991 Venezuela applied for membership of CARICOM, and offered a non-reciprocal free-trade agreement for CARICOM exports to Venezuela, over an initial five-year period. In October 1993 the newly-established Group of Three (Colombia, Mexico and Venezuela) signed joint agreements with CARICOM and Suriname on combating drugs trafficking and environmental protection. In June 1994 CARICOM and Colombia concluded an agreement on trade, economic and technical co-operation, which, *inter alia*, gives special treatment to the least-developed CARICOM countries. CARICOM has observer status in the Latin American Rio Group (see p. 876).

In 1992 Cuba applied for observer status within CARICOM, and in July 1993 a joint commission was inaugurated to establish closer ties between CARICOM and Cuba and to provide a mechanism for regular dialogue. In July 1997 the heads of government agreed to pursue consideration of a free-trade accord between the Community and Cuba. A Trade and Economic Agreement was signed by the two sides in July 2000, and a CARICOM office was established in Cuba, in February 2001. In February 1992 ministers of foreign affairs from CARICOM and Central American states met to discuss future co-operation, in view of the imminent conclusion of the North American Free Trade Agreement (NAFTA, see p. 865) between the USA, Canada and Mexico. It was agreed that a consultative forum would be established to discuss the possible formation of a Caribbean and Central American free-trade zone. In October 1993 CARICOM declared its support for NAFTA, but requested a 'grace period', during which the region's exports would have parity with Mexican products, and in March 1994 requested that it should be considered for early entry into NAFTA. In July 1996 the heads of government expressed strong concern over the complaint lodged with the World Trade Organization (WTO) by the USA, Ecuador, Guatemala and Honduras regarding the European Union's import regime on bananas, which gives preferential access to bananas from the ACP countries (see the EU, p. 860). CARICOM requested the US Government to withdraw its complaint and to negotiate a settlement. Nevertheless, WTO panel hearings on the complaint were initiated in September. Banana producers from the ACP countries were granted third-party status, at the insistence of the Eastern Caribbean ambassador to the EU, Edwin Laurent. In December a special meeting of the Heads of Government Conference was convened, in Barbados, in order to formulate a common position on relations with the USA, in particular with respect to measures to combat illegal drugs-trafficking, following reports that the US Government was planning to impose punitive measures against certain regional authorities, owing to their perceived failure to implement effective controls on illicit drugs. The Conference confirmed the need for comprehensive co-operation and technical assistance to combat the problem, but warned that any adverse measures implemented by the USA would undermine CARICOM–US relations. The Conference decided to establish a Caribbean Security Task Force to help formulate a single regional agreement on maritime interdiction, incorporating agreements already concluded by individual members.

In May 1997 CARICOM heads of government met the US President, Bill Clinton, to discuss issues of mutual concern. A partnership for prosperity and security was established at the meeting, and arrangements were instituted for annual consultations between the ministers of foreign affairs of CARICOM countries and the US Secretary of State. However, the Community failed to secure a commitment by the USA to grant the region's exports 'NAFTA-parity' status, or to guarantee concessions to the region's banana industry, following a temporary ruling of the WTO, issued in March, upholding the US trade complaint. The WTO ruling was confirmed in May and endorsed by the WTO dispute settlement body in September. The USA's opposition to a new EU banana policy (which was to terminate the import licensing system, extending import quotas to 'dollar' producers, while maintaining a limited duty-free quota for Caribbean producers) was strongly criticized by CARICOM leaders, meeting in July 1998. In March 1999 the 10th Inter-Sessional meeting of the Conference of Heads of Government, held in Paramaribo, Suriname, issued a statement condemning the imposition by the USA of sanctions against a number of EU imports, in protest at the revised EU banana regime, and the consequences of this action on Caribbean economies, and agreed to review its co-operation with the USA under the partnership for prosperity and security.

During 1998 CARICOM was particularly concerned by the movement within Nevis to secede from its federation with Saint Christopher. In July heads of government agreed to dispatch a mediation team to the country (postponed until September). The Heads of Government Conference held in March 1999 welcomed the establishment of a Constitutional Task Force by the local authorities to prepare a draft constitution, on the basis of recommendations of a previous constitutional commission and the outcome of a series of public meetings. In July 1998 heads of government expressed concern at the hostility between the Government and opposition groupings in Guyana. The two sides signed an agreement, under CARICOM auspices, and in September a CARICOM mediation mission visited Guyana to promote further dialogue. CARICOM has declared its support for Guyana in its territorial disputes with Venezuela and Suriname. In June 2000 CARICOM initiated negotiations following Suriname's removal of petroleum drilling equipment from Guyanan territorial waters. In March 2000 heads of government issued a statement supporting the territorial integrity and security of Belize in that country's ongoing border dispute with Guatemala. CARICOM subsequently urged both countries to implement the provisions of an agreement signed in November.

In July 2000 the Heads of Government meeting issued a statement strongly opposing the OECD Harmful Tax Initiative, under which punitive measures had been threatened against 35 countries, including CARICOM member states, if they failed to tighten taxation legislation. The meeting also condemned a separate list, issued by the OECD's Financial Action Task Force on Money Laundering (see p.875), which identified 15 countries, including five Caribbean states, as failing effectively to counter international money-laundering. The statement reaffirmed CARICOM's commitment to fighting financial crimes and support for any necessary reform of supervisory practices or legislation, but insisted that national taxation jurisdictions, and specifically competitive regimes designed to attract offshore business, was not a matter for OECD concern. CARICOM remained actively involved in efforts to counter the scheme, and in April 2001 presented its case to the US President.

ECONOMIC CO-OPERATION

The Caribbean Community's main field of activity is economic integration, by means of a Caribbean Common Market which replaced the former Caribbean Free Trade Association. The Secretariat and the Caribbean Development Bank undertake research on the best means of facing economic difficulties, and meetings of the Chief Executives of commercial banks and central bank officials are also held with the aim of strengthening regional co-operation. In October 1998 the CARICOM Bureau requested an urgent assessment of the impact on the region of the financial and economic instability apparent in several major economies.

During the 1980s the economic difficulties of member states hindered the development of intra-regional trade. At the annual Conference held in June/July 1987, the heads of government agreed to dismantle all obstacles to trade within CARICOM by October 1988. This was implemented as planned, but included a three-year period of protection for 17 products from the member countries of the Organisation of Eastern Caribbean States (OECS, see p. 876).

In July 1984 heads of government agreed to establish a common external tariff (CET) on certain products, in order to protect domestic industries, although implementation of the CET was considerably delayed (see below). They also urged the necessity of structural adjustment in the economies of the region, including measures to expand production and reduce imports. In 1989 the Conference of Heads of Government agreed to implement, by July 1993, a series of measures to encourage the creation of a single Caribbean market. These included the establishment of a CARICOM Industrial Programming Scheme; the inauguration of the CARICOM Enterprise Regime; abolition of passport requirements for CARICOM nationals travelling within the region; full implementation of the rules of origin and the revised scheme for the harmonization of fiscal incentives; free movement of skilled workers; removal of all remaining regional barriers to trade; establishment of a regional system of air and sea transport; and the introduction of a scheme for regional capital movement. A CARICOM Export Development Council, established in November 1989, undertook a three-year export development project to stimulate trade within CARICOM and to promote exports outside the region.

In August 1990 CARICOM heads of government mandated the governors of CARICOM members' central banks to begin a study of the means to achieve a monetary union within CARICOM; they also institutionalized meetings of CARICOM ministers of finance and senior finance officials, to take place twice a year.

The initial deadline of 1 January 1991 for the establishment of a CET was not achieved, and in July a new deadline of 1 October was set for those members which had not complied—Antigua and Barbuda, Belize, Montserrat, Saint Christopher and Nevis and Saint Lucia, whose governments feared that the tariff would cause an increase in the rate of inflation and damage domestic industries. This deadline was later (again unsuccessfully) extended to February

1992. The tariff, which imposed a maximum level of duty of 45% on imports, was also criticized by the World Bank, the IMF and the US Government as being likely to reduce the region's competitiveness. At a special meeting, held in October 1992, CARICOM heads of government agreed to reduce the maximum level of tariffs to between 30% and 35%, to be in effect by 30 June 1993 (the level was to be further lowered, to 25%–30% by 1995). The Bahamas, however, was not party to these trading arrangements (since it is a member of the Community but not of the Common Market), and Belize was granted an extension for the implementation of the new tariff levels. At the Heads of Government Conference, held in July 1995 in Guyana, Suriname was admitted as a full member of CARICOM and acceded to the treaty establishing the Common Market. It was granted until 1 January 1996 for implementation of the tariff reductions.

The 1995 Heads of Government Conference approved additional measures to promote the single market. The free movement of skilled workers (mainly graduates from recognized regional institutions) was to be permitted from 1 January 1996. At the same time an agreement on the mutual protection and provision of social security benefits was to enter into force. In July 1996 the heads of government decided that CARICOM ministers of finance, central bank governors and planning agencies should meet more frequently to address single market issues and agreed to extend the provisions of free movement to sports people, musicians and others working in the arts and media.

In July 1997 the heads of government, meeting in Montego Bay, Jamaica, agreed to accelerate economic integration, with the aim of completing a single market by 1999. At the meeting 11 member states signed Protocol II amending the Treaty of Chaguaramas, which constituted a central element of a CARICOM Single Market and Economy (CSME), providing for the right to establish enterprises, the provision of services and the free movement of capital and labour throughout participating countries. A regional collaborative network was established to promote the CSME. In November 2000 a special consultation on the single market and economy was held in Barbados, involving CARICOM and government officials, academics, and representatives of the private sector, labour organizations, the media, and other regional groupings. In February 2001 heads of government agreed to establish a new high-level sub-committee to accelerate the establishment of the CSME and to promote its objectives. The sub-committee was to be supported by a Technical Advisory Council, comprising representatives of the public and private sectors. By June all member states had signed and declared the provisional application of Protocol II, which had received two ratifications. At that time eight countries had completed the fourth phase of the CET.

In July 1998, at the meeting of heads of government, held in Saint Lucia, an agreement was signed with the Insurance Company of the West Indies to accelerate the establishment of a Caribbean Investment Fund, which was to mobilize foreign currency from extra-regional capital markets for investment in new or existing enterprises in the region. Some 60% of all funds generated were to be used by CARICOM countries and the remainder by non-CARICOM members of the ACS. The Fund was expected to become operational in 2000, with funds of US $150m.

INDUSTRY AND ENERGY

CARICOM aims to promote the development of joint ventures in exporting industries (particularly the woodwork, furniture, ceramics and foundry industries) through an agreement (reached in 1989) on an industrial programming scheme. CARICOM's Export Development Council gives training and consultancy services to regional manufacturers. Regional manufacturers' exhibitions (CARIMEX) are held every three years. The Caribbean Trade Information System (CARTIS) comprises computer databases covering country and product profiles, trade statistics, trade opportunities, institutions and bibliographical information; it links the national trade centres of CARICOM members. A protocol relating to the CARICOM Industrial Programming Scheme (CIPS), approved in 1988, is the Community's instrument for promoting the co-operative development of industry in the region. Protocol III amending the Treaty of Chaguaramas, with respect to industrial policy, was opened for signature in July 1998. At June 2001 it had been signed by 13 member states, provisionally applied by 12, and ratified by one.

The Secretariat has established a national standards bureau in each member country to harmonize technical standards, and supervises the metrication of weights and measures. In 1999 members agreed to establish a new CARICOM Regional Organization of Standards and Quality (CROSQ) to develop common regional standards and resolve disputes. CROSQ, to be located in Barbados, was scheduled to become operational in late 2001.

The CARICOM Alternative Energy Systems Project provides training, assesses energy needs and conducts energy audits. Efforts in regional energy development are directed at the collection and analysis of data for national energy policy documents.

TRANSPORT, COMMUNICATIONS AND TOURISM

A Caribbean Confederation of Shippers' Councils represents the interests of regional exporters and importers. In July 1990 the Caribbean Telecommunications Union was established to oversee developments in regional telecommunications.

In 1988 a Consultative Committee on Caribbean Regional Information Systems (CCCRIS) was established to evaluate and monitor the functioning of existing information systems and to seek to co-ordinate and advise on the establishment of new systems.

A Summit of Heads of Government on Tourism, Trade and Transportation was held in Trinidad and Tobago, in August 1995, to which all members of the ACS and regional tourism organizations were invited. In 1997 CARICOM heads of government considered a number of proposals relating to air transportation, tourism, human resource development and capital investment, which had been identified by Community ministers of tourism as critical issues in the sustainable development of the tourist industry. The heads of government requested ministers to meet regularly to develop tourism policies, and in particular to undertake an in-depth study of human resource development issues in early 1998. A new fund to help train young people from the region in aspects of the tourist industry was inaugurated in July 1997, in memory of the former Prime Minister of Jamaica, Michael Manley. A regional summit on tourism, in recognition of the importance of the industry to the economic development of the region, was scheduled to be held in The Bahamas, in October 2001.

A Multilateral Agreement Concerning the Operations of Air Services within the Caribbean Community entered into force in November 1998, providing a formal framework for the regulation of the air transport industry and enabling CARICOM-owned and – controlled airlines to operate freely within the region. In July 1999 heads of government signed Protocol VI amending the Treaty of Chaguaramas providing for a common transportation policy, with harmonized standards and practices, which was to be an integral component of the development of a single market and economy. At July 2001 Protocol VI had been signed by all states, except Montserrat.

AGRICULTURE

In 1985 the New Marketing Arrangements for Primary Agricultural Products and Livestock were instituted, with the aim of increasing the flow of agricultural commodities within the region. A computer-based Caribbean Agricultural Marketing Information System was initiated in 1987.

At the CARICOM summit meeting in July 1996 it was agreed to undertake wide-ranging measures in order to modernize the agricultural sector and to increase the international competitiveness of Caribbean agricultural produce. The CARICOM Secretariat was to support national programmes with assistance in policy formulation, human resource development and the promotion of research and technology development in the areas of productivity, marketing, agri-business and water resources management. During 1997 CARICOM Governments continued to lobby against a complaint lodged at the WTO with regard to the EU's banana import regime (offering favourable conditions to ACP producers—see above) and to generate awareness of the economic and social importance of the banana industry to the region. Protocol V amending the Treaty of Chaguaramas, which was concerned with agricultural policy, was opened for signature by heads of government in July 1998. At June 2001 it had been signed and provisionally applied by 13 member states, and ratified by one (Guyana).

HEALTH AND EDUCATION

In 1986 CARICOM and the Pan-American Health Organization launched 'Caribbean Co-operation in Health' with projects to be undertaken in six main areas: environmental protection, including the control of disease-bearing pests; development of human resources; chronic non-communicable diseases and accidents; strengthening health systems; food and nutrition; maternal and child health care; and population activities. In 2001 CARICOM was to co-ordinate a new regional partnership to reduce the spread and impact of HIV and AIDS in member countries. All countries were to prepare national strategic plans to facilitate access to funding to combat the problem. A Caribbean Environmental Health Institute (see below) aims to promote collaboration among member states in all areas of environmental management and human health. In July 2001 heads of government, meeting in the Bahamas, issued the Nassau Declaration on Health, advocating greater regional strategic co-ordination and planning in the health sector, institutional reform, and increased resources.

CARICOM educational programmes have included the improvement of reading in schools through assistance for teacher-training; and ensuring the availability of low-cost educational material throughout the region. A strategy for developing and improving technical and vocational education and training within each member state and throughout the region was completed and published in

1990. In July 1997 CARICOM heads of government adopted the recommendations of a ministerial committee, which identified priority measures for implementation in the education sector. These included the objective of achieving universal, quality secondary education and the enrolment of 15% of post-secondary students in tertiary education by 2005, as well as improved training in foreign languages and science and technology. From the late 1990s youth activities have been increasingly emphasized by the Community. These have included new programmes for disadvantaged youths, a mechanism for youth exchange and the convening of a Caribbean Youth Parliament.

EMERGENCY ASSISTANCE

A Caribbean Disaster Emergency Response Agency (CDERA) was established in 1991 to co-ordinate immediate disaster relief, primarily in the event of hurricanes. During 1997 CARICOM Governments remained actively concerned with the situation in Montserrat, which had suffered a series of massive volcanic eruptions. At the Heads of Government Conference in July, the Community pledged humanitarian, economic and technical assistance and resolved to help mobilize external assistance from regional and international donor countries and institutions. In March 1998 CARICOM heads of government agreed to establish a team, comprising representatives of the CARICOM Secretariat, CDERA and the Caribbean Development Bank, to assist the Montserrat Government in formulating programmes to provide a secure future for the island. In November the Community determined to support the countries of Central America in their reconstruction and rehabilitation efforts following the devastation caused by 'Hurricane Mitch', and to co-ordinate the provision of immediate humanitarian assistance by CARICOM member countries.

INSTITUTIONS

The following are among the institutions formally established within the framework of CARICOM.

Assembly of Caribbean Community Parliamentarians: c/o CARICOM Secretariat; an intergovernmental agreement on the establishment of a regional parliament entered into force in August 1994; inaugural meeting held in Barbados, in May 1996. Comprises up to four representatives of the parliaments of each member country, and up to two of each associate member. It aims to provide a forum for wider community involvement in the process of integration and for enhanced deliberation on CARICOM affairs; authorized to issue recommendations for the Conference of Heads of Government and to adopt resolutions on any matter arising under the Treaty of Chaguaramas.

Caribbean Agricultural Research and Development Institute—CARDI: UWI Campus, St Augustine, Trinidad and Tobago; tel. 645-1205; fax 645-1208; e-mail infocentre@cardi.org; internet www.cardi.org; f. 1975; aims to support the development of profitable and sustainable business systems and enterprises through its scientific, technological and information activities; provides training, a Caribbean agricultural information service, and technology and business advisory services. Exec. Dir HAYDEN BLADES. Publs *CARDI Update, Procicaribe News, CARDI Annual Report*, technical bulletin series.

Caribbean Centre for Development Administration—CARICAD: ICB Bldg, Roebuck St, St Michael, Barbados; tel. 4278535; fax 4361709; e-mail caricad@caribsurf.com; f. 1980; aims to assist governments in the reform of the public sector and to strengthen their managerial capacities for public administration; promotes the involvement of the private sector, non-governmental organizations and other bodies in all decision-making processes. Exec. Dir Dr P. I. GOMES.

Caribbean Disaster Emergency Response Agency—CDERA: The Garrison, St Michael, Barbados; tel. 436-9651; fax 437-7649; e-mail cdera@caribsurf.com; internet www.cdera.org; f. 1991. For activities, see Emergency Assistance above. Regional Co-ordinator JEREMY COLLYMORE.

Caribbean Environmental Health Institute—CEHI: POB 1111, The Morne, Castries, St Lucia; tel. 4522501; fax 4532721; e-mail cehi@candw.lc; internet www.cehi.org.lc; f. 1980 (began operations in 1982); provides technical and advisory services to member states in formulating environmental health policy legislation and in all areas of environmental management (for example, solid waste management, water supplies, beach and air pollution, and pesticides control); promotes, collates and disseminates relevant research; conducts courses, seminars and workshops throughout the region. Exec. Dir VINCENT SWEENEY.

Caribbean Food and Nutrition Institute: UWI Campus, St Augustine, Trinidad and Tobago; tel. 662-7025; fax 662-5511; f. 1967 to serve the governments and people of the region and to act as a catalyst among persons and organizations concerned with food and nutrition through research and field investigations, training in nutrition, dissemination of information, advisory services and production of educational material. Mems: all English-speaking Caribbean territories, including the mainland countries of Belize and Guyana. Dir Dr FITZROY HENRY. Publs *Cajanus* (quarterly), *Nyam News* (monthly), *Nutrient-Cost Tables* (quarterly), educational material.

Caribbean Food Corporation—CFC: 30 Queen's Park West, Post Office Bag 264B, Port of Spain, Trinidad and Tobago; tel. 622-5827; fax 622-4430; e-mail cfc@trinidad-net; f. 1976 (began operations in 1979); implements joint-venture projects with investors from the private and public sectors to enhance regional food self-sufficiency and reduce the need for food imports. Man. Dir E. C. CLYDE PARRIS.

Caribbean Meteorological Organization—CMO: POB 461, Port of Spain, Trinidad and Tobago; tel. 624-4481; fax 623-3634; e-mail hqcmo@tstt.net.tt; f. 1951 to co-ordinate regional activities in meteorology, operational hydrology and allied sciences; became an associate institution of CARICOM in 1983. Comprises a headquarters unit, a Council of Government Ministers, the Caribbean Meteorological Foundation and the Caribbean Institute for Meteorology and Hydrology, located in Barbados. Mems: govts of 16 countries and territories represented by the National Meteorological and Hydro-meteorological Services. Co-ordinating Dir T. W. SUTHERLAND.

ASSOCIATE INSTITUTIONS

Caribbean Development Bank: POB 408, Wildey, St Michael, Barbados; tel. 431-1600; fax 426-7269; e-mail info@caribank.org; internet www.caribank.org; f. 1969 to stimulate regional economic growth through support for agriculture, industry, transport and other infrastructure, tourism, housing and education; subscribed cap. US $687.2m. (Dec. 1999). In 1999 net approvals totalled $146.6m. for 16 projects; at the end of 1999 cumulative grant and loan disbursements totalled $1,275.0m. The Special Development Fund was replenished in 1996. Mems: CARICOM states, and Canada, Cayman Islands, the People's Republic of China, Colombia, France, Germany, Italy, Mexico, United Kingdom, Venezuela. Pres. Prof. COMPTON BOURNE.

Caribbean Law Institute: University of the West Indies, Cave Hill Campus, POB 64, Bridgetown, Barbados; tel. 417-4560; fax 417-4138.

Other Associate Institutions of CARICOM, in accordance with its constitution, are the University of Guyana and the University of the West Indies.

Publications

Annual Report.

Caribbean Trade and Investment Report.

Caribbean View (every 2 months).

Statistics — News and Views (2 a year).

CENTRAL AMERICAN INTEGRATION SYSTEM

(SISTEMA DE LA INTEGRACIÓN CENTROAMERICANA—SICA)

Address: blvd de la Orden de Malta 470, Santa Elena, Antiguo Cuscatlán, San Salvador, El Salvador.

Telephone: 289-6131; **fax:** 289-6124; **e-mail:** sgsica@sgsica.org; **internet:** www.sgsica.org.

Founded in December 1991, when the heads of state of six Central American countries signed the Protocol of Tegucigalpa to the agreement establishing the Organization of Central American States (f. 1951), creating a new framework for regional integration. A General Secretariat of the Sistema de la Integración Centroamericana (SICA) was inaugurated in February 1993 to co-ordinate the process of political, economic, social cultural and environmental integration and to promote democracy and respect for human rights throughout the region.

MEMBERS

Costa Rica	Guatemala	Nicaragua
El Salvador	Honduras	Panama

OBSERVERS

Belize	Dominican Republic	Taiwan

Organization

(July 2001)

SUMMIT MEETINGS

The meetings of heads of state of member countries serve as the supreme decision-making organ of SICA.

COUNCIL OF MINISTERS

Ministers of Foreign Affairs of member states meet regularly to provide policy direction for the process of integration.

CONSULTATIVE COMMITTEE

The Committee comprises representatives of business organizations, trade unions, academic institutions and other federations concerned with the process of integration in the region. It is an integral element of the integration system and assist the Secretary-General in determining the policies of the organization.

GENERAL SECRETARIAT

The General Secretariat of SICA was established in February 1993 to co-ordinate the process of enhanced regional integration. It comprises the following divisions: inter-institutional relations; research and co-operation; legal and political affairs; economic affairs; and communications and information.

In September 1997 Central American Common Market (CACM) heads of state, meeting in the Nicaraguan capital, signed the Managua Declaration in support of further regional integration and the establishment of a political union. A commission was to be established to consider all aspects of the policy and to formulate a timetable for the integration process. In February 1998 SICA heads of state resolved to establish a Unified General Secretariat to integrate the institutional aspects of SICA (see below) in a single office, to be located in San Salvador. The process was ongoing in 2001.

Secretary-General: Dr OSCAR ALFREDO SANTAMARÍA.

SPECIALIZED TECHNICAL SECRETARIATS

Secretaría Ejecutiva de la Comisión Centroamericana de Ambiente y Desarrollo: blvd de la Orden de Malta 470, Santa Elena, Antiguo Cuscatlán, San Salvador, El Salvador; tel. 289-6131; fax 289-6124; internet www.ccad.org.gt; f. 1989 to enhance collaboration in the promotion of sustainable development and environmental protection. Exec. Sec. MAURICIO CASTRO.

Secretaría General de la Coordinación Educativa y Cultural Centroamericana: 175m. norte de la esquina oeste del ICE, Sabana Norte, San José, Costa Rica; tel. 232-3783; fax 231-2366; f. 1982; promotes development of regional programmes in the fields of education and culture. Sec.-Gen. MARVIN HERRERA ARAYA.

Secretaría Permanente del Tratado General de Integración Económica Centroamericana—SIECA: 4A Avda 10–25, Zona 14, Apdo Postal 1237, 01901 Guatemala City, Guatemala; tel. (2) 3682319; fax (2) 3681071; e-mail sieca@pronet.net.gt; internet www.sieca.org.gt; f. 1960 to assist the process of economic integration and the establishment of a Central American Common Market (see below). Sec.-Gen. RÓGER HAROLDO RODAS MELARA.

Secretaría Técnica del Consejo de Integración Social—SISCA: blvd de la Orden de Malta 470, Santa Elena, Antiguo Cuscatlán, San Salvador, El Salvador; tel. 289-6131; fax 289-6124; e-mail hmorgado@sicanet.org.sv; Dir-Gen. Dr HUGO MORGADO.

OTHER SPECIALIZED SECRETARIATS

Secretaria de Integración Turística Centroamericana—SITCA: blvd de la Orden de Malta 470, Santa Elena, Antiguo Cuscatlán, San Salvador, El Salvador; tel. 289-6131; fax 289-6124; e-mail econtreras@sicanet.org.sv; f. 1965 to develop regional tourism activities; Sec.-Gen. EDGARDO CONTRERAS SCHNEIDER.

Secretaría del Consejo Agropecuario Centroamericano—SCAC: Sede del IICA, Apdo Postal 55-2200 Coronado, San José, Costa Rica; tel. 216-0303; fax 216-0285; e-mail rguillen@iica.ac.cr; f. 1991 to determine and co-ordinate regional policies and programmes relating to agriculture and agroindustry. Sec-Gen. RÓGER GUILLÉN BUSTOS.

Secretaría Ejecutiva del Consejo Monetario Centroamericano—CMCA (Central American Monetary Council): Ofiplaza del Este, Edif. C, 75m. oeste de la Rotonda la Bandera, San Pedro Montes de Oca, Apdo 5438, 1000 San José, Costa Rica; tel. 280-9522; fax 280-9511; e-mail secma@sol.racsa.co.cr; internet www.cmca.or.ca; f. 1964 by the presidents of Central American central banks, to co-ordinate monetary policies. Exec. Sec. MIGUEL CHORRO. Publs *Boletín Estadístico* (annually), *Informe Económico* (annually).

Secretaría Ejecutiva de la Comisión Centroamericana de Transporte Marítimo—COCATRAM: Cine Cabrera 2c. arriba y 2½ al sur, Apdo 2423, Managua, Nicaragua; tel. (2) 222754; fax (2) 222759; e-mail cocatram@ibw.com.ni; f. 1981; Exec. Sec. LIANA ZÚÑIGA DE CÁCERES.

PARLIAMENT

Address: 12A Avda 33-04, Zona 5, Guatemala City, Guatemala.

Telephone: (2) 339-0466; **fax:** (2) 334-6670; **e-mail:** cdpar@parlacen.org.gt; **internet:** www.parlacen.org.gt.

Founded 1989 within the framework of the Central American Common Market. Comprises representatives of El Salvador, Guatemala, Honduras, Nicaragua and Panama. In February 1998 heads of state of member countries resolved to limit the number of deputies to 10–15 from each country.

President: HUGO GIRAUD (Panama).

COURT OF JUSTICE

Address: Kilómetro 17½ Carretera Norte, contiguo a la TANIC, Managua, Nicaragua.

Telephone: 233-2128; **fax:** 233-2135; **e-mail:** cortecen@tmx.com.ni; **internet:** www.ccj.org.ni.

Tribunal authorized to consider disputes relating to treaties agreed within the regional integration system. In February 1998 Central American heads of state agreed to limit the number of magistrates in the Court to one per country.

AD HOC INTERGOVERNMENTAL SECRETARIATS

Comisión de Ciencia y Tecnología de Centroamérica y Panamá (Comission for Science and Technology in Central America and Panama): Col. Palmira, Avda República de Brasil 2231, Apdo Postal 4458, Tegucigalpa, Honduras; tel. and fax 232-5669; f. 1976; Pres. GERARDO ZEPEDA.

Consejo Centroamericano de Instituciones de Seguridad Social—COCISS: Caja de Seguridad Social, Panamá, Panama; tel. 261-7264; f. 1992; Pres. Dr MARIANELA MORALES.

Consejo del Istmo Centroamericano de Deportes y Recreación: 5009-1000 San José, Costa Rica; tel. 257-8770; fax 222-5003; f. 1992; Pres. HILDA GONZÁLEZ.

Secretaría Ejecutiva del Consejo Centroamericana de Vivienda y Asentamientos Humanos (Central American Council on Housing and Human Settlements): Avda la Paz 244, Tegucigalpa, Honduras; tel. 236-5804; fax 236-6560; f. 1992; Dir Dr CONCEPCIÓN RAMOS.

Secretaría Ejecutiva del Consejo de Electrificación de América Central: Apdo Postal 10032, San José, Costa Rica; tel. 220-7562; fax 220-8232; e-mail ceac@ns.ice.go.cr; f. 1985; Dir Luis Buján.

OTHER REGIONAL INSTITUTIONS

Finance

Banco Centroamericano de Integración Económica—BCIE (Central American Bank for Economic Integration): Blvd Suyapa, Contigua a Banco de Honduras, Apdo Postal 772, Tegucigalpa, Honduras; tel. 228-2243; fax 228-2185; e-mail jose_manuel_pacas@bcie.hn; f. 1961 to promote the economic integration and balanced economic development of member countries; finances public and private development projects, particularly those related to industrialization and infrastructure. By June 1993 cumulative lending amounted to US $3,217m., mainly for roads, hydroelectricity projects, housing and telecommunications. Auth. cap. $2,000m. Regional mems: Costa Rica, El Salvador, Honduras, Nicaragua; Non-regional mems: Argentina, the People's Republic of China, Colombia, Mexico. Pres. José Alejandro Arévalo. Publs *Annual Report, Revista de la Integración y el Desarrollo de Centroamérica*.

Public Administration

Centro de Coordinación para la Prevención de Desastres Naturales en América Central—CEPREDENAC: Howard, Edif. 707, Panamá, Panama; tel. 3160065; fax 3160074; e-mail secretariat @cepredenac.org; internet www.cepredenac.org; Dir Luis Rolando Durán Vargas.

Comisión Centroamericana Permanente para la Erradicación de la Producción, Tráfico, Consumo y Uso Ilícitos de Estupefacientes y Sustancias Psicotrópicas—CCP: Edif. de Comisiones, 1°, Tegucigalpa, Honduras; tel. 237-0568; fax 238-3960. Pres. Dr Carlos Sosa Coello.

Instituto Centroamericano de Administración Pública—ICAP (Central American Institute of Public Administration): POB 10025-1000, De la Heladería Pops en Curridabat 100m. sur y 50 oeste, San José, Costa Rica; tel. 234-1011; fax 225-2049; e-mail icapcr@sol.racsa.co.cr; internet www.icap.ac.cr; f. 1954 by the five Central American Republics and the United Nations, with later participation by Panama. The Institute aims to train the region's public servants, provide technical assistance and carry out research leading to reforms in public administration. Dir Dr Hugo Zelaya Cálix.

Secretaría Ejecutiva de la Comisión Regional de Recursos Hidráulicos: Blvd Rohrmoser, Pavas, Apdo Postal 21-2300, Curridabat, San José, Costa Rica; tel. 231-5791; fax 296-0047; e-mail crrhcr@sol.racsa.co.cr; f. 1966. Mems: Belize, Costa Rica, El Salvador, Guatemala, Honduras, Nicaragua, Panama; Exec. Dir Max Campos O.

Education and Health

Comité Coordinador Regional de Instituciones de Agua Potable y Saneamiento de Centro América, Panamá y República Dominicana—CAPRE: De la casa Italia, 100m. al sur y 100 al este, diagonal a farmacia Umaña, Barrio Francisco Peralta, San Pedro de Montes de OCA, San José, Costa Rica; tel. 280-4460; fax 280-4414; e-mail capregtz@sol.racsa.co.cr; f. 1979; Dir Liliana Arce Umaña.

Consejo Superior Universitario Centroamericano—CSUCA (Central American University Council): Apdo 37, Ciudad Universitaria Rodrigo Facio, 2060 San José, Costa Rica; tel. 225-2744; fax 234-0071; e-mail rsol@cariari.ucr.ac.cr; internet www.csuca.ac.cr; f. 1948 to guarantee academic, administrative and economic autonomy for universities and to encourage regional integration of higher education; maintains libraries and documentation centres; Council of 32 mems. Mems: 16 universities, in Belize, Costa Rica (four), El Salvador, Guatemala, Honduras (two), Nicaragua (four) and Panama (three). Sec.-Gen. Dr Ricardo Sol Arriaza (El Salvador). Publs *Estudios Sociales Centroamericanas* (quarterly), *Cuadernos de Investigación* (monthly), *Carta Informativa de la Secretaría General* (monthly).

Instituto de Nutrición de Centroamérica y Panamá—INCAP (Institute of Nutrition of Central America and Panama): Apdo 1188, Carretera Roosevelt, Zona 11, 01901 Guatemala City, Guatemala; tel. (2) 4723762; fax (2) 4736529; e-mail hdelgado@incap.org.gt; f. 1949 to promote the development of nutritional sciences and their application and to strengthen the technical capacity of member countries to reach food and nutrition security; provides training and technical assistance for nutrition education and planning; conducts applied research; disseminates information. Maintains library (including about 600 periodicals). Administered by the Pan American Health Organization (PAHO) and the World Health Organization. Mems: CACM mems and Belize and Panama. Dir Dr Hernán L. Delgado. Publ. *Annual Report.*

Organismo Internacional Regional de Sanidad Agropecuaria—OIRSA (International Regional Organization of Plant Protection and Animal Health): Calle Ramón Belloso, Final Pasaje Isolde, Col Escalón, Apdo Postal 61, San Salvador, El Salvador; tel. 263-1123; fax 263-1128; e-mail oirsa@ns1.oirsa.org.sv; internet www.ns1.oirsa.org.sv; f. 1953 for the prevention of the introduction of animal and plant pests and diseases unknown in the region; research, control and eradication programmes of the principal pests present in agriculture; technical assistance and advice to the ministries of agriculture and livestock of member countries; education and qualification of personnel. Mems: Belize, Costa Rica, Dominican Republic, El Salvador, Guatemala, Honduras, Mexico, Nicaragua, Panama. Exec. Dir Dr Celio Humberto Barreto.

Transport and Communications

Comisión Técnica de las Telecomunicaciones de Centroamérica—COMTELCA (Technical Commission for Telecommunications in Central America): Col. Palmira, Edif. Alpha, Avda Brasil, Apdo 1793, Tegucigalpa, Honduras; tel. 220-6666; fax 220-1197; e-mail dgeneral@comtelca.hn; internet www.comtelca.hn; f. 1966 to co-ordinate and improve the regionaltelecommunications network. Dir-Gen. Héctor Leonel Rodríguez Milla.

Corporación Centroamericana de Servicios de Navegación Aérea—COCESNA (Central American Air Navigation Service Corporation): Apdo 660, Aeropuerto de Toncontín, Tegucigalpa, Honduras; tel. 233-1143; fax 233-1219; e-mail gergral@cocesna.hn; f. 1960; offers radar air traffic control services, aeronautical telecommunications services, flight inspections and radio assistance services for air navigation; administers the Central American Aeronautical School. Gen. Man. Eduardo Marín Jimenez.

Central American Common Market—CACM (Mercado Común Centroamericano)

CACM was established by the Organization of Central American States under the General Treaty of Central American Economic Integration (Tratado General de Integración Económica Centroamericana) signed in Managua (Nicaragua) on 13 December 1960. It was ratified by all countries by September 1963. It now forms a subsystem of the Sistema de la Integración Centroamericana (SICA, see above).

MEMBERS

Costa Rica	El Salvador	Nicaragua
Guatemala	Honduras	

Organization

(April 2001)

MINISTERIAL MEETINGS

The organization's policy is formulated by regular meetings of the Council of Ministers for Economic Integration (COMIECO), meetings of other ministers, and of presidents of central banks, also play an important part.

PERMANENT SECRETARIAT

Secretaría Permanente del Tratado General de Integración Económica Centroamericana—SIECA: 4A Avda 10-25, Zona 14, Apdo 1237, 01901 Guatemala City, Guatemala; tel. 268-2151; provides institutional support for the Common Market, supervises the correct implementation of the legal instruments of economic integration, carries out relevant studies at the request of the Common Market authorities, and arranges meetings. There are departments covering the working of the Common Market; negotiations and external trade policy; external co-operation; systems and statistics; finance and administration. There is also a unit for co-operation with the private sector and finance institutions and a legal consultative committee.

Secretary-General: HAROLDO RODAS MELGAR.

Activities

The General Treaty envisaged the eventual liberalization of intraregional trade and the establishment of a free-trade area and a customs union. Economic integration in the region, however, has been hampered by ideological differences between governments, difficulties in internal supply, protectionist measures by overseas markets, external and intra-regional debts, adverse rates of exchange and high interest rates. Regular meetings of senior customs officials aim to increase co-operation, to develop a uniform terminology, and to recommend revisions of customs legislation. CACM member-countries also aim to pursue a common policy in respect of international trade agreements on commodities, raw materials and staples.

Under the Convention for Fiscal Incentives for Industrial Development, which came into operation in 1969, a wide range of tax benefits are applied to various categories of industries in the region, to encourage productivity. SIECA carries out studies on the industrial sector, compiles statistics, and provides information to member governments. It also analyses energy consumption in the region and assists governments in drawing up energy plans, aiming to reduce dependence on imported petroleum.

A co-ordinating commission supervises the marketing of four basic crops (maize, rice, beans and sorghum), recording and forecasting production figures and recommending minimum guarantee prices. Information on other crops is also compiled. A permanent commission for agricultural research and extension services monitors and co-ordinates regional projects in this field.

An agreement to establish a Central American Monetary Union was signed in 1964, with the eventual aim of establishing a common currency and aligning foreign exchange and monetary policies. The Central American Monetary Council, comprising the presidents of the member states' central banks, meets regularly to consider monetary policy and financial affairs. A Fund for Monetary Stabilization provides short-term financial assistance to members facing temporary balance-of-payments difficulties.

Trade within the region increased in value from US $33m. in 1960 to $1,129m. in 1980, but subsequently diminished every year until 1986, when it amounted to $406m. The decline was due to a number of factors: low prices for the region's main export commodities, and heavy external debts, both resulting in a severe shortage of foreign exchange, and intra-regional trade 'freezes' provoked by debts amounting to $700m. at mid-1986 (Guatemala and Costa Rica being the chief creditors, and Nicaragua and El Salvador the main debtors). In January 1986 a new CACM tariff and customs agreement came into effect, imposing standard import duties for the whole region (aimed at discouraging the import of non-essential goods from outside the region), and a uniform tariff nomenclature. Honduras, however, continued to insist on bilateral tariff agreements with other member countries. Honduras subsequently signed a temporary free-trade agreement with all the other member states. From 1987 intra-regional trade increased steadily and reached an estimated $1,840m. in 1997.

In June 1990 the presidents of the five CACM countries signed a declaration welcoming peace initiatives in El Salvador, Guatemala and Nicaragua, and appealing for a revitalization of CACM, as a means of promoting lasting peace in the region. In December the presidents committed themselves to the creation of an effective common market, proposing the opening of negotiations on a comprehensive regional customs and tariffs policy by March 1991, and the introduction of a regional 'anti-dumping' code by December 1991. They requested the support of multilateral lending institutions through investment in regional development, and the cancellation or rescheduling of member countries' debts.

In February 1993 the European Community (EC) signed a new framework co-operation agreement with the CACM member states extending the programme of economic assistance and political dialogue initiated in 1984; a further co-operation agreement with the European Union (as the EC had become) was signed in early 1996.

In October 1993 the presidents of the CACM countries and Panama signed a protocol to the 1960 General Treaty, committing themselves to full economic integration in the region (with a common external tariff of 20% for finished products and 5% for raw materials and capital goods) and creating conditions for increased free trade. The countries agreed to accelerate the removal of internal non-tariff barriers, but no deadline was set. Full implementation of the protocol was to be 'voluntary and gradual', owing to objections on the part of Costa Rica and Panama. In May 1994, however, Costa Rica committed itself to full participation in the protocol. In March 1995 a meeting of the Central American Monetary Council discussed and endorsed a reduction in the tariff levels from 20% to 15% and from 5% to 1%. However, efforts to adopt this as a common policy were hindered by the implementation of these tariff levels by El Salvador on a unilateral basis, from 1 April, and the subsequent modifications by Guatemala and Costa Rica of their external tariffs.

In May 1997 the heads of state of CACM member countries, together with the Prime Minister of Belize, conferred with the US President, Bill Clinton, in San José, Costa Rica. The leaders resolved to establish a Trade and Investment Council to promote trade relations; however, Clinton failed to endorse a request from CACM members that their products receive preferential access to US markets, on similar terms to those from Mexico agreed under the NAFTA accord. During the 1990s the Central American Governments pursued negotiations to conclude free-trade agreements with Mexico, Panama and the members of the Caribbean Community and Common Market (CARICOM). Nicaragua signed a bilateral accord with Mexico in December (Costa Rica already having done so in 1994). El Salvador, Guatemala and Honduras jointly concluded a free-trade arrangement with Mexico in May 2000; this was to enter into effect in January 2001. In November 1997, at a special summit meeting of CACM heads of state, an agreement was reached with the President of the Dominican Republic to initiate a gradual process of incorporating that country into the process of Central American integration, with the aim of promoting sustainable development throughout the region. The first sectors for increased co-operation between the two sides were to be tourism, health, investment promotion and air transport. A free-trade accord with the Dominican Republic was concluded in April 1998, and formally signed in November.

In November 1998 Central American heads of state held an emergency summit meeting to consider the devastation in the region caused by 'Hurricane Mitch'. The Presidents urged international creditors to write off the region's estimated debts of US $16,000m. to assist in the economic recovery of the countries worst-affected.

They also reiterated requests for preferential treatment for the region's exports within the NAFTA framework. In October 1999 heads of state adopted a strategic framework for the period 2000–04 to strengthen the capacity for the physical, social, economic and environmental infrastructure of Central American countries to withstand the impact of natural disasters. In particular, programmes for the integrated management and conservation of water resources, and for the prevention of forest fires were to be implemented. In June 2001 heads of state agreed to implement a plan to strengthen communications infrastructure, and to develop a single power grid throughout the region. During 2001, however, the integration process was undermined by ongoing border disputes between Guatemala and Belize, and between Honduras and Nicaragua.

Publications

Anuario Estadístico Centroamericano de Comercio Exterior.
Carta Informativa (monthly).
Cuadernos de la SIECA (2 a year).
Estadísticas Macroeconómicas de Centroamérica (annually).
Series Estadísticas Seleccionadas de Centroamérica (annually).

THE COMMONWEALTH

Address: Marlborough House, Pall Mall, London, SW1Y 5HX, United Kingdom.

Telephone: (20) 7839-3411; **fax:** (20) 7930-0827; **e-mail:** info@commonwealth.int; **internet:** www.thecommonwealth.org.

The Commonwealth is a voluntary association of 54 independent states (at mid-2001), comprising about one-quarter of the world's population. It includes the United Kingdom and most of its former dependencies, and former dependencies of Australia and New Zealand (themselves Commonwealth countries). All Commonwealth countries accept Queen Elizabeth II as the symbol of the free association of the independent member nations and as such the Head of the Commonwealth.

MEMBERS IN THE REGION

Antigua and Barbuda	Saint Vincent and the
Bahamas	Grenadines
Barbados	Trinidad and Tobago
Belize	United Kingdom Dependencies:
Dominica	Anguilla
Grenada	Bermuda
Guyana	British Virgin Islands
Jamaica	Caymen Islands
Saint Christopher and Nevis	Falkland Islands
Saint Lucia	Montserrat
	Turks and Caicos Islands

Organization

(July 2001)

The Commonwealth is not a federation: there is no central government nor are there any rigid contractual obligations such as bind members of the United Nations.

The Commonwealth has no written constitution but its members subscribe to the ideals of the Declaration of Commonwealth Principles unanimously approved by a meeting of heads of government in Singapore in 1971. Members also approved the 1977 statement on apartheid in sport (the Gleneagles Agreement); the 1979 Lusaka Declaration on Racism and Racial Prejudice; the 1981 Melbourne Declaration on relations between developed and developing countries; the 1983 New Delhi Statement on Economic Action; the 1983 Goa Declaration on International Security; the 1985 Nassau Declaration on World Order; the Commonwealth Accord on Southern Africa (1985); the 1987 Vancouver Declaration on World Trade; the Okanagan Statement and Programme of Action on Southern Africa (1987); the Langkawi Declaration on the Environment (1989); the Kuala Lumpur Statement on Southern Africa (1989); the Harare Commonwealth Declaration (1991); the Ottawa Declaration on Women and Structural Adjustment (1991); the Limassol Statement on the Uruguay Round of multilateral trade negotiations (1993); the Millbrook Commonwealth Action Programme on the Harare Declaration (1995); the Edinburgh Commonwealth Economic Declaration (1997); and the Fancourt Commonwealth Declaration on Globalization and People-centred Development (1999).

MEETINGS OF HEADS OF GOVERNMENT

Meetings are private and informal and operate not by voting but by consensus. The emphasis is on consultation and exchange of views for co-operation. A communiqué is issued at the end of every meeting. Meetings are held every two years in different capitals in the Commonwealth. The 1999 meeting was held in Durban, South Africa, in November, and the 2001 meeting was to be held in Brisbane, Australia.

OTHER CONSULTATIONS

Meetings at ministerial and official level are also held regularly. Since 1959 finance ministers have met in a Commonwealth country in the week prior to the annual meetings of the IMF and the World Bank. Meetings on education, legal, women's and youth affairs are held at ministerial level every three years. Ministers of health hold annual meetings, with major meetings every three years, and ministers of agriculture meet every two years. Ministers of trade, labour and employment, industry, science and the environment also hold periodic meetings.

Senior officials—cabinet secretaries, permanent secretaries to heads of government and others—meet regularly in the year between meetings of heads of government to provide continuity and to exchange views on various developments.

In November 1999 the heads of government meeting established a Commonwealth High Level Review Group to review the role and activities of the Commonwealth. In 2000 the Group initiated a programme of consulations to proceed with its mandate and established a working group of experts to consider the Commonwealth's role in supporting information technology capabilities in member countries.

COMMONWEALTH SECRETARIAT

The Secretariat, established by Commonwealth heads of government in 1965, operates as an international organization at the service of all Commonwealth countries. It organizes consultations between governments and runs programmes of co-operation. Meetings of heads of government, ministers and senior officials decide these programmes and provide overall direction.

The Secretariat is headed by a secretary-general (elected by heads of government), assisted by three deputy secretaries-general. One deputy is responsible for political affairs, one for economic and social affairs, and one for development co-operation (including the Commonwealth Fund for Technical Co-operation—see below). The Secretariat comprises 12 Divisions in the fields of political affairs; legal and constitutional affairs; information and public affairs; administration; economic affairs; human resource development; gender and youth affairs; science and technology; economic and legal advisory services; export and industrial development; management and training services; and general technical assistance services. It also includes a non-governmental organizations desk and a unit for strategic planning and evaluation.

Secretary-General: DONALD (DON) C. MCKINNON (New Zealand).

Deputy Secretary-General (Political): KRISHNAN SRINIVASAN (India).

Deputy Secretary-General (Economic and Social): Dame VERONICA SUTHERLAND (United Kingdom).

Deputy Secretary-General (Development Co-operation): WINSTON A. COX (Barbados).

Activities

INTERNATIONAL AFFAIRS

In October 1991 heads of government, meeting in Harare, Zimbabwe, issued the Harare Commonwealth Declaration, in which they reaffirmed their commitment to the Commonwealth Principles declared in 1971, and stressed the need to promote sustainable development and the alleviation of poverty. The Declaration placed emphasis on the promotion of democracy and respect for human rights and resolved to strengthen the Commonwealth's capacity to assist countries in entrenching democratic practices. The meeting also welcomed the political reforms introduced by the South African Government to end the system of apartheid and urged all South African political parties to commence negotiations on a new constitution as soon as possible. The meeting endorsed measures on the phased removal of punitive measures against South Africa. In December a group of six eminent Commonwealth citizens was dispatched to observe multi-party negotiations on the future of South Africa and to assist the process where possible. In October 1992, in a fresh attempt to assist the South African peace process, a Commonwealth team of 18 observers was sent to monitor political violence in the country. A second phase of the Commonwealth Mission to South Africa (COMSA) began in February 1993, comprising 10 observers with backgrounds in policing, the law, politics and public life. COMSA issued a report in May in which it urged a concerted effort to build a culture of political tolerance in South Africa. In a report on its third phase, issued in December, COMSA appealed strongly to all political parties to participate in the transitional arrangements leading to democratic elections. In October the Commonwealth heads of government, meeting in Limassol, Cyprus, agreed that a democratic and non-racial South Africa would be invited to join the organization. They endorsed the removal of all economic sanctions against South Africa, but agreed to retain the arms embargo until a post-apartheid, democratic government had been established.

In November 1995 Commonwealth heads of government, convened in New Zealand, formulated and adopted the Millbrook Commonwealth Action Programme on the Harare Declaration, to promote adherence by member countries to the fundamental principles of democracy and human rights (as proclaimed in the 1991 Declaration). The Programme incorporated a framework of measures to be pursued in support of democratic processes and institutions, and actions to be taken in response to violations of the Harare Declaration principles, in particular the unlawful removal of a democratically-elected government. A Commonwealth Ministerial Action Group on the Harare Declaration (CMAG) was to be established to implement this process and to assist the member country involved to comply with the Harare principles. On the basis of this Programme, the leaders suspended Nigeria from the Commonwealth with immediate effect, following the execution by that country's military Government of nine environmental and human rights protesters and a series of other violations of human rights. The meeting determined to expel Nigeria from the Commonwealth if no 'demonstrable progress' had been made towards the establishment of a democratic authority by the time of the next summit meeting. In addition, the Programme formulated measures to promote sustainable development in member countries, which was considered to be an important element in sustaining democracy, and to facilitate consensus-building within the international community. Earlier in the meeting a statement was issued declaring the 'overwhelming majority' of Commonwealth governments to be opposed to nuclear-testing programmes being undertaken in the South Pacific region. However, in view of events in Nigeria, the issue of nuclear testing and disagreement among member countries did not assume the significance anticipated.

In December 1995 CMAG convened for its inaugural meeting in London. The Group, comprising the ministers of foreign affairs of Canada, Ghana, Jamaica, Malaysia, New Zealand, South Africa, the United Kingdom and Zimbabwe, commenced by considering efforts to restore democratic government in the three Commonwealth countries under military regimes, i.e. The Gambia, Nigeria and Sierra Leone. At the second meeting of the Group, in April 1996, ministers commended the conduct of presidential and parliamentary elections in Sierra Leone and the announcement by The Gambia's military leaders to proceed with a transition to civilian rule. In June a three-member CMAG delegation visited The Gambia to reaffirm Commonwealth support of the transition process in that country and to identify possible areas of further Commonwealth assistance. In August the Gambian authorities issued a decree removing the ban on political activities and parties, although shortly afterwards prohibited certain parties and candidates involved in political life prior to the military take-over from contesting the elections. CMAG recommended that in such circumstances there should be no Commonwealth observers sent to either the presidential or parliamentary elections, which were held in September 1996 and January 1997 respectively. Following the restoration of a civilian Government in early 1997, CMAG requested the Commonwealth Secretary-General to extend technical assistance to The Gambia in order to consolidate the democratic transition process. In April 1996 it was noted that the human rights situation in Nigeria had continued to deteriorate. CMAG, having pursued unsuccessful efforts to initiate dialogue with the Nigerian authorities, outlined a series of punitive and restrictive measures (including visa restrictions on members of the administration, a cessation of sporting contacts and an embargo on the export of armaments) that it would recommend for collective Commonwealth action in order to exert further pressure for reform in Nigeria. Following a meeting of a high-level delegation of the Nigerian Government and CMAG in June, the Group agreed to postpone the implementation of the sanctions, pending progress on the dialogue. (Canada, however, determined, unilaterally, to impose the measures with immediate effect; the United Kingdom did so in accordance with a decision of the European Union to implement limited sanctions against Nigeria.) A proposed CMAG mission to Nigeria was postponed in August, owing to restrictions imposed by the military authorities on access to political detainees and other civilian activists in that country. In September the Group agreed to proceed with the visit and to delay further a decision on the implementation of sanction measures. CMAG, without the participation of the representative of the Canadian Government, undertook its ministerial mission in November. In July 1997 the Group reiterated the Commonwealth Secretary-General's condemnation of a military coup in Sierra Leone in May, and decided to suspend that country's participation in meetings of the Commonwealth pending the restoration of a democratic government.

In October 1997 Commonwealth heads of government, meeting in Edinburgh, the United Kingdom, endorsed CMAG's recommendation that the imposition of sanctions against Nigeria be held in abeyance pending the scheduled completion of a transition programme towards democracy by October 1998. It was also agreed that CMAG be formally constituted as a permanent organ to investigate abuses of human rights throughout the Commonwealth. Jamaica and South Africa were to be replaced as members of CMAG by Barbados and Botswana, respectively.

In March 1998 CMAG, at its ninth meeting, commended the efforts of the Economic Community of West African States in restoring the democratically-elected Government of President Ahmed Tejan Kabbah in Sierra Leone, and agreed to remove all restrictions on Sierra Leone's participation in Commonwealth activities. Later in that month, a representative mission of CMAG visited Sierra Leone to express its support for Kabbah's administration and to consider the country's needs in its process of reconstruction. At the CMAG meeting held in October members agreed that Sierra Leone should no longer be considered under the Group's mandate; however, they urged the Secretary-General to continue to assist that country in the process of national reconciliation and to facilitate negotiations with opposition forces to ensure a lasting cease-fire.

In April 1998 the Nigerian military leader, Gen. Sani Abacha, confirmed his intention to conduct a presidential election in August, but indicated that, following an agreement with other political organizations, he was to be the sole candidate. In June, however, Abacha died suddenly. His successor, Gen. Abdulsalam Abubakar, immediately released several prominent political prisoners, and in early July agreed to meet with the Secretaries-General of the UN and the Commonwealth to discuss the release of the imprisoned opposition leader, Chief Moshood Abiola. Abubakar also confirmed his intention to abide by the programme for transition to civilian rule by October. In mid-July, however, shortly before he was to have been liberated, Abiola died. The Commonwealth Secretary-General subsequently endorsed a new transition programme, which provided for the election of a civilian leader in May 1999. In October 1998 CMAG, convened for its 10th formal meeting, acknowledged Abubakar's efforts towards restoring a democratic government and recommended that member states begin to remove sanctions against Nigeria and that it resume participation in certain Commonwealth activities. The Commonwealth Secretary-General subsequently announced a programme of technical assistance to support Nigeria in the planning and conduct of democratic elections. Staff teams from the Commonwealth Secretariat observed local government, and state and governorship elections, held in December and in January 1999, respectively. A 23-member Commonwealth Observer Group was also dispatched to Nigeria to monitor preparations and conduct of legislative and presidential elections, held in late February. While the Group reported several deficiencies and irregularities in the conduct of the polling, it confirmed that, in general, the conditions had existed for free and fair elections and that the elections were a legitimate basis for the transition of power to a democratic, civilian government. In April CMAG voted to readmit Nigeria to full membership on 29 May, upon the installation of the new civilian administration.

In 1999 the Commonwealth Secretary-General appointed a Special Envoy to broker an agreement in order to end a civil dispute in Honiara, Solomon Islands. An accord was signed in late June, and it was envisaged that the Commonwealth would monitor its implementation. In October a Commonwealth Multinational Police Peace Monitoring Group was stationed in Solomon Islands; this was superseded by a Commonwealth Multinational Police Assistance Force in January 2000. Following further internal unrest, however, CMAG, in June, determined to send a new mission to Solomon Islands in order to facilitate negotiations between the opposing parties, to convey the Commonwealth's concern and to offer assistance. The Commonwealth welcomed the peace accord concluded in Solomon Islands in October, and extended its support to the International Peace Monitoring Team which was to be established to oversee implementation of the peace accords. In March 2001 CMAG urged all parties in the Solomon Islands to adhere to the timetable for parliamentary elections later in the year. In June 1999 an agreement was concluded between opposing political groups in Zanzibar, having been facilitated by the good offices of the Secretary-General; however, this was only partially implemented.

In mid-October 1999 a special meeting of CMAG was convened to consider the overthrow of the democratically-elected Government in Pakistan in a military coup. The meeting condemned the action as a violation of Commonwealth principles and urged the new authorities to declare a timetable for the return to democratic rule. CMAG also resolved to send a four-member delegation, comprising the ministers of foreign affairs of Barbados, Canada, Ghana and Malaysia, to discuss this future course of action with the military regime. Pakistan was suspended from participation in meetings of the Commonwealth with immediate effect. The suspension, pending the restoration of a democratic government, was endorsed by heads of government, meeting in November, who requested that CMAG keep the situation in Pakistan under review. At the meeting, held in Durban, South Africa, CMAG was reconstituted to comprise the ministers of foreign affairs of Australia, Bangladesh, Barbados, Botswana, Canada, Malaysia, Nigeria and the United Kingdom. It was agreed that no country would serve for more than two consecutive two-year terms. CMAG was requested to remain actively involved in the post-conflict development and rehabilitation of Sierra Leone and the process of consolidating peace. In addition, it was urged to monitor persistent violations of the Harare Declaration principles in all countries. Heads of government also agreed to establish a new ministerial group on Guyana and to reconvene a ministerial committee on Belize, in order to facilitate dialogue in ongoing territorial disputes with neighbouring countries.

In June 2000, following the overthrow in May of the Fijian Government by a group of armed civilians, and the subsequent illegal detention of members of the elected administration, CMAG suspended Fiji's participation in meetings of the Commonwealth pending the restoration of democratic rule. In September, upon the request of CMAG, the Secretary-General appointed a Special Envoy to support efforts towards political dialogue and a return to democratic rule in Fiji. The Special Envoy undertook his first visit in December.

In March 2001 CMAG resolved to send a ministerial mission to Zimbabwe, in order to relay to the government the Commonwealth's concerns at the ongoing violence and abuses of human rights in that country, as well as to discuss the conduct of parliamentary elections and extend technical assistance. The mission was rejected by the Zimbabwean Government.

Political Affairs Division: assists consultation among member governments on international and Commonwealth matters of common interest. In association with host governments, it organizes the meetings of heads of government and senior officials. The Division services committees and special groups set up by heads of government dealing with political matters. The Secretariat has observer status at the United Nations, and the Division manages a joint office in New York to enable small states, which would otherwise be unable to afford facilities there, to maintain a presence at the United Nations. The Division monitors political developments in the Commonwealth and international progress in such matters as disarmament, the concerns of small states, dismantling of apartheid and the Law of the Sea. It also undertakes research on matters of common interest to member governments, and reports back to them. The Division is involved in diplomatic training and consular co-operation.

In 1990 Commonwealth heads of government mandated the Division to support the promotion of democracy by monitoring the preparations for and conduct of parliamentary, presidential or other elections in member countries at the request of national governments. By the end of 2000 the Commonwealth had dispatched more than 30 electoral missions in accordance with this mandate. Observer groups monitored legislative elections in Zimbabwe in June 2000, in Sri Lanka during October, and in Trinidad and Tobago in December. A Commonwealth observer mission was also dispatched to Zanzibar in October to attend concurrent legislative and presidential elections, and it was agreed that Commonwealth officials would be present at local elections to be held in Pakistan over a six-month period from December. In March 2001 an observer group monitored the organization and conduct of a general election in Guyana. In the same month representatives of the Commonwealth Secretary-General were sent to Uganda and to St Vincent and the Grenadines, to be present at a presidential and general election respectively

A new expert group on good governance and the elimination of corruption in economic management convened for its first meeting in May 1998. In November 1999 Commonwealth heads of government endorsed a Framework for Principles for Promoting Good Governance and Combating Corruption, which had been drafted by the group.

LAW

Legal and Constitutional Affairs Division: promotes and facilitates co-operation and the exchange of information among member governments on legal matters. It administers, jointly with the Commonwealth of Learning, a distance training programme for legislative draftsmen and assists governments to reform national laws to meet the obligations of international conventions. The Division organizes the triennial meeting of ministers, Attorneys General and senior ministry officials concerned with the legal systems in Commonwealth countries. It has also initiated four Commonwealth schemes for co-operation on extradition, the protection of material cultural heritage, mutual assistance in criminal matters and the transfer of convicted offenders within the Commonwealth. It liaises with the Commonwealth Magistrates' and Judges' Association, the Commonwealth Legal Education Association, the Commonwealth Lawyers' Association (with which it helps to prepare the triennial Commonwealth Law Conference for the practising profession), the Commonwealth Association of Legislative Counsel, and with other international non-governmental organizations. The Division provides in-house legal advice for the Secretariat. The quarterly _Commonwealth Law Bulletin_ reports on legal developments in and beyond the Commonwealth.

The Division's Commercial Crime Unit assists member countries to combat financial and organized crime, in particular transborder criminal activities, and promotes the exchange of information regarding national and international efforts to combat serious commercial crime through a quarterly publication, _Commonwealth Legal Assistance News,_ and the _Crimewatch_ bulletin. A Human Rights Unit aims to assist governments to strengthen national institutions and other mechanisms for the protection for human rights. It also

organizes training workshops and promotes the exchange of relevant information among member countries.

ECONOMIC CO-OPERATION

In October 1997 Commonwealth heads of government, meeting in Edinburgh, the United Kingdom, signed an Economic Declaration that focused on issues relating to global trade, investment and development and committed all member countries to free-market economic principles. The Declaration also incorporated a provision for the establishment of a Trade and Investment Access Facility within the Secretariat in order to assist developing member states in the process of international trade liberalization and promote intra-Commonwealth trade.

In May 1998 the Commonwealth Secretary-General appealed to the Group of Eight industrialized nations to accelerate and expand the initiative to ease the debt burden of the most heavily indebted poor countries (HIPCs) (see World Bank and IMF). However, the Group failed to endorse the so-called 'Mauritius Mandate', adopted by Commonwealth finance ministers, meeting in Mauritius, in September 1997, which stipulated that by 2000 all eligible HIPCs should have in progress measures to reduce their external debt. In October 1998 Commonwealth finance ministers, convened in Ottawa, Canada, reiterated their appeal to international financial institutions to accelerate the HIPC initiative. The meeting also issued a Commonwealth Statement on the global economic crisis and endorsed several proposals to help to counter the difficulties experienced by several countries. These measures included a mechanism to enable countries to suspend payments on all short-term financial obligations at a time of emergency without defaulting, assistance to governments to attract private capital and to manage capital market volatility, and the development of international codes of conduct regarding financial and monetary policies and corporate governance. In March 1999 the Commonwealth Secretariat hosted a joint IMF-World Bank conference to review the HIPC scheme and initiate a process of reform. In November Commonwealth heads of government, meeting in South Africa, declared their support for measures undertaken by the World Bank and IMF to enhance the HIPC initiative. At the end of an informal retreat the leaders adopted the Fancourt Commonwealth Declaration on Globalization and People-centred Development, which emphasized the need for a more equitable spread of wealth generated by the process of globalization, and expressed a renewed commitment to the elimination of all forms of discrimination, the promotion of people-centred development and capacity-building, and efforts to ensure developing countries benefit from future multilateral trade liberalization measures.

In February 1998 the Commonwealth Secretariat hosted the first Inter-Governmental Organizations Meeting to promote co-operation between small island states and the formulation of a unified policy approach to international fora. A second meeting was convened in March 2001, where discussions focused on the forthcoming WTO ministerial meeting and the OECD's harmful tax competition initiative. In September 2000 Commonwealth finance ministers, meeting in Malta, reviewed the OECD initiative and agreed that the measures, affecting many member countries with offshore financial centres, should not be imposed on governments. The ministers mandated the involvement of the Commonwealth Secretariat in efforts to resolve the dispute; a joint working group was subsequently established by the Secretariat with the OECD.

Economic Affairs Division: organizes and services the annual meetings of Commonwealth ministers of finance and the ministerial group on small states and assists in servicing the biennial meetings of heads of government and periodic meetings of environment ministers. It engages in research and analysis on economic issues of interest to member governments and organizes seminars and conferences of government officials and experts. The Division undertook a major programme of technical assistance to enable developing Commonwealth countries to participate in the Uruguay Round of multilateral trade negotiations and has assisted the African, Caribbean and Pacific (ACP) group of countries in their trade negotiations with the European Union. It continues to help developing countries to strengthen their links with international capital markets and foreign investors. The Division also services groups of experts on economic affairs that have been commissioned by governments to report on, among other things, protectionism; obstacles to the North-South negotiating process; reform of the international financial and trading system; the debt crisis; management of technological change; the special needs of small states; the impact of change on the development process; environmental issues; women and structural adjustment; and youth unemployment. A Commonwealth Secretariat Debt Recording and Management System has been developed by the Economic and Legal Advisory Services Division, which operates the system for the benefit of member countries and concerned organizations. The Economic Affairs Division co-ordinates the Secretariat's environmental work and manages the Iwokrama International Centre for Rainforest Conservation and Development.

The Division played a catalytic role in the establishment of a Commonwealth Equity Fund, initiated in September 1990, to allow developing member countries to improve their access to private institutional investment, and promoted a Caribbean Investment Fund. The Division supported the establishment of a Commonwealth Private Investment Initiative (CPII) to mobilize capital, on a regional basis, for investment in newly-privatized companies and in small and medium-sized businesses in the private sector. The first regional fund under the CPII was launched in July 1996. The Commonwealth Africa Investment Fund (Comafin), was to be managed by the United Kingdom's official development institution, the Commonwealth Development Corporation, to assist businesses in 19 countries in sub-Saharan Africa, with initial resources of US $63.5m. In August 1997 a fund for the Pacific Islands was launched, with an initial capital of $15.0m. A $200m. South Asia Regional Fund was established at the Heads of Government Meeting in October. In October 1998 a fund for the Caribbean states was inaugurated, at a meeting of Commonwealth finance ministers.

HUMAN RESOURCES

Human Resource Development Division: consists of two departments concerned with education and health. The Division co-operates with member countries in devising strategies for human resource development.

The **Education Department** arranges specialist seminars, workshops and co-operative projects, and commissions studies in areas identified by ministers of education, whose three-yearly meetings it also services. Its present areas of emphasis include improving the quality of and access to basic education; strengthening the culture of science, technology and mathematics education in formal and non-formal areas of education; improving the quality of management in institutions of higher learning and basic education; improving the performance of teachers; strengthening examination assessment systems; and promoting the movement of students between Commonwealth countries. The Department also promotes multi-sectoral strategies to be incorporated in the development of human resources. Emphasis is placed on ensuring a gender balance, the appropriate use of technology, promoting good governance, addressing the problems of scale particular to smaller member countries, and encouraging collaboration between governments, the private sector and other non-governmental organizations.

The **Health Department** organizes ministerial, technical and expert group meetings and workshops, to promote co-operation on health matters, and the exchange of health information and expertise. The Department commissions relevant studies and provides professional and technical advice to member countries and to the Secretariat. It also supports the work of regional health organizations and promotes health for all people in Commonwealth countries.

Gender and Youth Affairs Division: consists of the Gender Affairs Department and the Commonwealth Youth Affairs Department.

The **Gender Affairs Department** is responsible for the implementation of the 1995 Commonwealth Plan of Action on Gender and Development, which was endorsed by the Heads of Government in order to achieve gender equality in the Commonwealth. The main objective of the Plan is to ensure that gender is incorporated into all policies, programmes, structures and procedures of member states and of the Commonwealth Secretariat. The Department is also addressing specific concerns such as the integration of gender issues into national budgetary processes, increasing the participation of women in politics and conflict prevention and resolution, and the promotion of human rights, including the elimination of violence against women and girls.

The **Youth Affairs Department** administers the Commonwealth Youth Programme (CYP), funded through separate voluntary contributions from governments, which seeks to promote the involvement of young people in the economic and social development of their countries. The CYP was awarded a budget of £2.1m. for 1998/99. It provides policy advice for governments and operates regional training programmes for youth workers and policy-makers through its centres in Africa, Asia, the Caribbean and the Pacific. It conducts a Youth Study Fellowship scheme, a Youth Project Fund, a Youth Exchange Programme (in the Caribbean), and a Youth Service Awards Scheme, holds conferences and seminars, carries out research and disseminates information. In May 1995 a Commonwealth Youth Credit Initiative was launched, in order to provide funds, training and advice to young entrepreneurs. In May 1998 a Commonwealth ministerial meeting, held in Kuala Lumpur, Malaysia, approved a new Plan of Action on Youth Empowerment to the Year 2005.

SCIENCE

Science and Technology Division: is partially funded and governed by the Commonwealth Science Council, consisting of 35 member governments, which aims to enhance the scientific and technological capabilities of member countries, through co-operative research, training and the exchange of information. Current priority areas of work are concerned with the promotion of sustainable development and cover biological diversity and genetic resources, water resources, and renewable energy.

TECHNICAL CO-OPERATION

Commonwealth Fund for Technical Co-operation (CFTC): f. 1971 to facilitate the exchange of skills between member countries and to promote economic and social development. It is administered by the Commonwealth Secretariat and financed by voluntary subscriptions from member governments. The CFTC responds to requests from member governments for technical assistance, such as the provision of experts for short- or medium-term projects, advice on economic or legal matters, in particular in the areas of natural resources management and public-sector reform, and training programmes. Since 1995 the CFTC has operated a volunteer scheme, the Commonwealth Service Abroad Programme, for senior professionals willing to undertake short-term assignments. The CFTC also administers the Langkawi awards for the study of environmental issues, which is funded by the Canadian Government. The CFTC budget for 1998/99 amounted to £20.5m.

CFTC activities are implemented by the following divisions:

Economic and Legal Advisory Services Division: serves as an in-house consultancy, offering advice to governments on macro-economic and financial management, capital market and private-sector development, debt management, the development of natural resources, and the negotiation of maritime boundaries and fisheries access agreements;

Export and Industrial Development Division: advises on all aspects of export marketing and the development of tourism, industry, small businesses and enterprises. Includes an Agricultural Development Unit, which provides technical assistance in agriculture and renewable resources;

General Technical Assistance Services Division: provides short- and long-term experts in all fields of development;

Management and Training Services Division: provides integrated packages of consultancy and training to enhance skills in areas such as public sector reform and the restructuring of enterprises, and arranges specific country and overseas training programmes.

The Secretariat also includes an Administration Division, a Strategic Planning and Evaluation Unit, and an Information and Public Affairs Division, which produces information publications, and radio and television programmes, about Commonwealth co-operation and consultation activities.

Finance

The Secretariat's budget for 1998/99 was £10.5m. Member governments meet the cost of the Secretariat through subscriptions on a scale related to income and population.

Publications

Commonwealth Currents (quarterly).

Commonwealth Declarations 1971–91.

Commonwealth Organisations (directory).

The Commonwealth Today.

In Common (quarterly newsletter of the Youth Programme).

International Development Policies (quarterly).

Link In to Gender and Development (2 a year).

Notes on the Commonwealth (series of reference leaflets).

Report of the Commonwealth Secretary-General (every 2 years).

The Commonwealth Yearbook.

Numerous reports, studies and papers (catalogue available).

Commonwealth Organizations

(In the United Kingdom, unless otherwise stated.)

PRINCIPAL BODIES

Commonwealth Foundation: Marlborough House, Pall Mall, London, SW1Y 5HY; tel. (20) 7930-3783; fax (20) 7839-8157; e-mail geninfo@commonwealth.int; internet www.commonwealthfoundation.com; f. 1966; intergovernmental body promoting people-to-people interaction, and collaboration within the non-governmental sector of the Commonwealth; supports non-governmental organizations, professional associations and Commonwealth arts and culture. Awards an annual Commonwealth Writers' Prize. Funds are provided by Commonwealth govts. Chair. GRACA MACHEL (Mozambique); Dir COLIN BELL (United Kingdom). Publ. *Common Path* (quarterly).

The Commonwealth of Learning (COL): 1285 West Broadway, Suite 600, Vancouver, BC V6H 3X8, Canada; tel. (604) 775-8200; fax (604) 775-8210; e-mail info@col.org; internet www.col.org; f. 1987 by Commonwealth Heads of Government to promote the devt and sharing of distance education and open learning resources, including materials, expertise and technologies, throughout the Commonwealth and in other countries; implements and assists with national and regional educational programmes; acts as consultant to international agencies and national governments; conducts seminars and studies on specific educational needs. COL is financed by Commonwealth governments on a voluntary basis; in 1999 heads of government endorsed an annual core budget for COL of US $9m. Pres. Dato' Prof. GAJARAJ DHANARAJAN (Malaysia). Publs *Connections, EdTech News.*

The following represents a selection of other Commonwealth organizations:

AGRICULTURE AND FORESTRY

Commonwealth Forestry Association: c/o Oxford Forestry Institute, South Parks Rd, Oxford, OX1 3RB; tel. (1865) 271037; fax (1865) 275074; e-mail cfa_ox@hotmail.com; f. 1921; produces, collects and circulates information relating to world forestry and promotes good management, use and conservation of forests and forest lands throughout the world. Mems: 1,000. Chair. Dr J. S. MAINI. Publs *International Forestry Review* (quarterly), *Commonwealth Forestry News* (quarterly), *Commonwealth Forestry Handbook* (irregular).

Standing Committee on Commonwealth Forestry: Forestry Commission, 231 Corstorphine Rd, Edinburgh, EH12 7AT; tel. (131) 314-6137; fax (131) 334-0442; e-mail libby.jones@forestry.gov.uk; f. 1923 to provide continuity between Confs, and to provide a forum for discussion on any forestry matters of common interest to mem. govts which may be brought to the Cttee's notice by any member country or organization; 54 mems. 1997 Conference: Victoria Falls, Zimbabwe; 2001 Conference: Perth, Australia. Sec. LIBBY JONES. Publ. *Newsletter* (quarterly).

COMMONWEALTH STUDIES

Institute of Commonwealth Studies: 28 Russell Sq., London, WC1B 5DS; tel. (20) 7862-8844; fax (20) 7862-8820; e-mail ics@sas.ac.uk; internet www.sas.ac.uk/commonwealthstudies/; f. 1949 to promote advanced study of the Commonwealth; provides a library and meeting place for postgraduate students and academic staff engaged in research in this field; offers postgraduate teaching. Dir Prof. PAT CAPLAN. Publs *Annual Report, Collected Seminar Papers, Newsletter, Theses in Progress in Commonwealth Studies.*

COMMUNICATIONS

Commonwealth Telecommunications Organization: Clareville House, 26–27 Oxendon St, London, SW1Y 4EL; tel. (20) 7930-5516; fax (20) 7930-4248; e-mail info@cto.int; internet www.cto.int; f. 1967; aims to enhance the development of telecommunications in Commonwealth countries and contribute to the communications infrastructure required for economic and social devt, through a devt and training programme. Exec. Dir Dr DAVID SOUTER. Publ. *CTO Briefing* (3 a year).

EDUCATION AND CULTURE

Association of Commonwealth Universities (ACU): John Foster House, 36 Gordon Sq., London, WC1H 0PF; tel. (20) 7380-6700; fax (20) 7387-2655; e-mail info@acu.ac.uk; internet www.acu.ac.uk; f. 1913; organizes major meetings of Commonwealth universities and their representatives; publishes factual information about Commonwealth universities and access to them; acts as a liaison office and general information centre and provides a recruitment advertising and publicity service; hosts a management consultancy service; supplies secretariats for the Commonwealth Scholarship Comm., the Marshall Aid Commemoration Comm. and the Commonwealth Universities Study Abroad Consortium; administers various other fellowship and scholarship programmes. Mems: 480 universities in 36 Commonwealth countries or regions. Sec.-Gen. Prof. MICHAEL GIBBONS. Publs include: *Commonwealth Universities Yearbook, ACU Bulletin* (5 a year), *Report of the Council of the ACU* (annually), *Awards for University Teachers and Research Workers, Awards for Postgraduate Study at Commonwealth Universities, Awards for First Degree Study at Commonwealth Universities, Awards for University Administrators and Librarians, Who's Who of Executive Heads: Vice-Chancellors, Presidents, Principals and Rectors,* Student Information Papers (study abroad series).

Commonwealth Association for Education in Journalism and Communication—CAEJC: c/o Faculty of Law, University of Western Ontario, London, ON N6A 3K7, Canada; tel. (519) 6613348; fax (519) 6613790; e-mail caejc@julian.uwo.ca; f. 1985; aims to foster high standards of journalism and communication education and research in Commonwealth countries and to promote co-operation among institutions and professions. c. 700 mems in 32 Commonwealth countries. Pres. Prof. SYED ARABI IDID (Malaysia); Sec. Prof. ROBERT MARTIN (Canada). Publ. *CAEJAC Journal* (annually).

Commonwealth Association of Science, Technology and Mathematics Educators—CASTME: c/o Education Dept, Human Resource Development Division, Commonwealth Secretariat, Marlborough House, Pall Mall, London, SW1Y 5HX; tel. (20) 7747-6282; fax (20) 7747-6287; e-mail v.goel@commonwealth.int; f. 1974; special emphasis is given to the social significance of education in these subjects. Organizes an Awards Scheme to promote effective teaching and learning in these subjects, and biennial regional seminars. Pres. Sir HERMANN BONDI; Hon. Sec. Dr VED GOEL. Publ. *CASTME Journal* (quarterly).

Commonwealth Council for Educational Administration and Management: c/o International Educational Leadership Centre, School of Management, Lincoln University Campus, Brayford Pool, Lincoln, LN6 7TS; tel. (1522) 886071; fax (1522) 886023; e-mail athody@lincoln.ac.uk; f. 1970; aims to foster quality in professional development and links among educational administrators; holds nat. and regional confs, as well as visits and seminars. Mems: 24 affiliated groups representing 3,000 persons. Pres. Prof. ANGELA THODY; Sec. GERALDINE BRISTOW. Publs *Managing Education Matters* (2 a year), *International Studies in Educational Administration* (2 a year).

Commonwealth Institute: 230 Kensington High St, London, W8 6NQ; tel. (20) 7603-4535; fax (20) 7602-7374; e-mail info@commonwealth.org.uk; internet www.commonwealth.org.uk; f. 1893 as the Imperial Institute; restructured as an independent pan-Commonwealth agency Jan. 2000; governed by a Bd of Trustees elected by the Bd of Governors; Commonwealth High Commissioners to the United Kingdom act as ex-officio Governors; the Inst. houses a Commonwealth Resource and Literature Library and a Conference and Events Centre; supplies educational resource materials and training throughout the United Kingdom; provides internet services to the Commonwealth; operates as an arts and conference centre, running a Commonwealth-based cultural programme; a new five-year strategic plan, entitled 'Commonwealth 21', was inaugurated in 1998. Chair. DAVID A. THOMPSON; Chief Exec. DAVID FRENCH. Publ. *Annual Review.*

League for the Exchange of Commonwealth Teachers: 7 Lion Yard, Tremadoc Rd, London, SW4 7NQ; tel. (20) 7498-1101; fax (20) 7720-5403; e-mail lectcom_exchange@compuserve.com; internet www.lect.org.uk; f. 1901; promotes educational exchanges between teachers in Australia, the Bahamas, Barbados, Bermuda, Canada, Guyana, India, Jamaica, Kenya, Malawi, New Zealand, Pakistan, South Africa and Trinidad and Tobago. Dir ANNA TOMLINSON. Publs *Annual Report, Exchange Teacher* (annually).

HEALTH

Commonwealth Medical Association: BMA House, Tavistock Sq., London, WC1H 9JP; tel. (20) 7272-8492; fax (20) 7272-1663; e-mail office@commat.org; internet www.commat.org; f. 1962 for the exchange of information; provision of tech. co-operation and advice; formulation and maintenance of a code of ethics; provision of continuing medical education; devt and promotion of health education programmes; and liaison with WHO and the UN on health issues; meetings of its Council are held every three years. Mems: medical asscns in Commonwealth countries. Sec. Dr J. D. J. HAVARD. Publ. *CommonHealth* (quarterly).

Commonwealth Pharmaceutical Association: 1 Lambeth High St, London, SE1 7JN; tel. (20) 7820-3399 ext. 303; fax (20) 7582-3401; e-mail eharden@rpsgb.org.uk; f. 1970 to promote the interests of pharmaceutical sciences and the profession of pharmacy in the Commonwealth; to maintain high professional standards, encourage links between members and the creation of nat. asscns; and to facilitate the dissemination of information. Holds confs (every four years) and regional meetings. Mems: 39 pharmaceutical asscns. Sec. PHILIP E. GREEN. Publ. *Quarterly Newsletter.*

Commonwealth Society for the Deaf: 34 Buckingham Palace Rd, London, SW1W 0RE; tel. (20) 7233-5700; fax (20) 7233-5800; e-mail sound.seekers@btinternet.com; internet www.sound-seekers.org.uk; promotes the health, education and general welfare of the deaf in developing Commonwealth countries; encourages and assists the development of educational facilities, the training of teachers of the deaf, and the provision of support for parents of deaf children; organizes visits by volunteer specialists to developing countries; provides audiological equipment and organizes the training of audiological maintenance technicians; conducts research into the causes and prevention of deafness. CEO Brig. J. A. DAVIS. Publ. *Annual Report*.

Sight Savers International (Royal Commonwealth Society for the Blind): Grosvenor Hall, Bolnore Rd, Haywards Heath,West Sussex, RH16 4BX; tel. (1444) 446600; fax (1444) 446688; e-mail information@sightsaversint.org.uk; internet www.sightsavers .org.uk; f. 1950 to prevent blindness and restore sight in developing countries, and to provide education and community-based training for incurably blind people; operates in collaboration with local partners, with high priority given to training local staff; Chair. DAVID THOMPSON; Dir RICHARD PORTER. Publ. *Horizons* (newsletter, 3 a year).

INFORMATION AND THE MEDIA

Commonwealth Broadcasting Association: 17 Fleet St, London, EC4Y 1AA; tel. (20) 7583-5550; fax (20) 7583-5549; e-mail cba@ cba.org.uk; internet www.oneworld.org/cba; f. 1945; gen. confs are held every two years (2002: Manchester, United Kingdom). Mems: 100 in 57 countries. Pres. BOB O'REILLY; Sec.-Gen. ELIZABETH SMITH. Publs *Commonwealth Broadcaster* (quarterly), *Commonwealth Broadcaster Directory* (annually).

Commonwealth Institute: see under Education.

Commonwealth Journalists Association: 17 Nottingham St, London, W1M 3RD; tel. (20) 7486-3844; fax (20) 7486-3822; internet www.ozemail.com.au/~pwessels/cja.html; f. 1978 to promote co-operation between journalists in Commonwealth countries, organize training facilities and confs, and foster understanding among Commonwealth peoples. Pres. MURRAY BURT; Exec. Dir IAN GILLHAM.

Commonwealth Press Union (Asscn of Commonwealth Newspapers, News Agencies and Periodicals): 17 Fleet St, London, EC4Y 1AA; tel. (20) 7583-7733; fax (20) 7583-6868; e-mail 106156.3331@compuserve.com; f. 1950; promotes the welfare of the Commonwealth press; provides training for journalists and organizes biennial confs. Mems: c. 1,000 newspapers, news agencies, periodicals in 42 Commonwealth countries. Dir ROBIN MACKICHAN. Publs *CPU News, Annual Report*.

LAW

Commonwealth Lawyers' Association: c/o The Law Society, 114 Chancery Lane, London, WC2A 1PL; tel. (20) 7320-5772; fax (20) 7831-0057; e-mail cla@lawsociety.org.uk; internet www.commonwealthlawyers.com; f. 1983 (fmrly the Commonwealth Legal Bureau); seeks to maintain and promote the rule of law throughout the Commonwealth, by ensuring that the people of the Commonwealth are served by an independent and efficient legal profession; upholds professional standards and promotes the availability of legal services; assists in organizing the triennial Commonwealth law confs. Pres. (1999–2001) CYRUS DAS; Exec. Sec. HELEN POTTS. Publs *The Commonwealth Lawyer, Clarion*.

Commonwealth Legal Advisory Service: c/o British Institute of International and Comparative Law, Charles Clore House, 17 Russell Sq., London, WC1B 5JP; tel. (20) 7862-5151; fax (20) 7862-5152; e-mail info@biicl.org; financed by the British Institute and by contributions from Commonwealth govts; provides research facilities for Commonwealth govts and law reform commissions.

Commonwealth Legal Education Association: c/o Legal and Constitutional Affairs Division, Commonwealth Secretariat, Marlborough House, Pall Mall, London, SW1Y 5HX; tel. (20) 7747-6415; fax (20) 7747-6406; e-mail clea@commonwealth.int; internet www.clea.org.uk; f. 1971 to promote contacts and exchanges and to provide information regarding legal education. Gen. Sec. JOHN HATCHARD. Publs *Commonwealth Legal Education Association Newsletter* (3 a year), *Directory of Commonwealth Law Schools* (every 2 years).

Commonwealth Magistrates' and Judges' Association: Uganda House, 58/59 Trafalgar Sq., London, WC2N 5DX; tel. (20) 7976-1007; fax (20) 7976-2395; e-mail info@cmja.org; internet www.cmja.org; f. 1970 to advance the administration of the law by promoting the independence of the judiciary, to further education in law and crime prevention and to disseminate information; confs and study tours; corporate membership for asscns of the judiciary or courts of limited jurisdiction; assoc. membership for individuals. Pres. DAVID ARMATI; Sec.-Gen. Dr KAREN BREWER. Publ. *Commonwealth Judicial Journal* (2 a year).

PARLIAMENTARY AFFAIRS

Commonwealth Parliamentary Association: Westminster House, Suite 700, 7 Millbank, London, SW1P 3JA; tel. (20) 7799-1460; fax (20) 7222-6073; e-mail hq.sec@comparlhq.org.uk; internet www.comparlhq.org.uk; f. 1911 to promote understanding and co-operation between Commonwealth parliamentarians; organization: Exec. Cttee of 32 MPs responsible to annual Gen. Assembly; 148 brs throughout the Commonwealth; holds annual Commonwealth Parliamentary Confs and seminars; also regional confs and sem-

inars; Sec.-Gen. ARTHUR DONAHOE. Publ. *The Parliamentarian* (quarterly).

PROFESSIONAL AND INDUSTRIAL RELATIONS

Commonwealth Association of Architects: 66 Portland Pl., London, W1N 4AD; tel. (20) 7490-3024; fax (20) 7253-2592; e-mail caa@gharchitects.demon.co.uk; internet www.archexchange.org; f. 1964; an asscn of 38 socs of architects in various Commonwealth countries. Objects: to facilitate the reciprocal recognition of professional qualifications; to provide a clearing house for information on architectural practice, and to encourage collaboration. Plenary confs every three years; regional confs are also held. Exec. Dir TONY GODWIN. Publs *Handbook, Objectives and Procedures: CAA Schools Visiting Boards, Architectural Education in the Commonwealth* (annotated bibliography of research), *CAA Newsnet* (2 a year), a survey and list of schools of architecture.

Commonwealth Association for Public Administration and Management—CAPAM: 1075 Bay St, Suite 402, Toronto, ON M5S 2B1, Canada; tel. (416) 920-3337; fax (416) 920-6574; e-mail capam@capam.ca; internet www.comnet.mt/capam/; f. 1994; aims to promote sound management of the public sector in Commonwealth countries and to assist those countries undergoing political or financial reforms. An international awards programme to reward innovation within the public sector was introduced in 1997, and was to be awarded every 2 years. Pres. Dr ZOLA SKWEYIYA (South Africa); Exec. Dir ART STEVENSON (Canada).

Commonwealth Trade Union Council: Congress House, 23–28 Great Russell St, London, WC1B 3LS; tel. (20) 7631-0728; fax (20) 7436-0301; e-mail info@commonwealthtuc.org; internet www.commonwealthtuc.org; f. 1979; links trade union national centres (representing more than 30m. trade union mems) throughout the Commonwealth; promotes the application of democratic principles and core labour standards, works closely with other international trade union orgs. Dir ANNIE WATSON. Publ. *Annual Report*.

SCIENCE AND TECHNOLOGY

Commonwealth Engineers' Council: c/o Institution of Civil Engineers, One Great George St, London, SW1P 3AA; tel. (20) 7222-7722; fax (20) 7222-7500; e-mail international@ice.org.uk; f. 1946; the Council meets every two years to provide an opportunity for engineering institutions of Commonwealth countries to exchange views on collaboration; there is a standing cttee on engineering education and training; organizes seminars on related topics. Sec. J. A. WHITWELL.

Commonwealth Geological Surveys Forum: c/o Commonwealth Science Council, CSC Earth Sciences Programme, Marlborough House, Pall Mall, London, SW1Y 5HX; tel. (20) 7839-3411; fax (20) 7839-6174; e-mail comsci@gn.apc.org; f. 1948 to promote collaboration in geological, geochemical, geophysical and remote sensing techniques and the exchange of information. Geological Programme Officer Dr SIYAN MALOMO.

SPORT

Commonwealth Games Federation: Walkden House, 3–10 Melton St, London, NW1 2EB; tel. (20) 7383-5596; fax (20) 7383-5506; e-mail commonwealthgamesfederation@abtinternet.com; internet www.commonwealthgames-fed.org; the Games were first held in 1930 and are now held every four years; participation is limited to competitors representing the mem. countries of the Commonwealth; to be held in Manchester, United Kingdom, in 2002. Mems: 72 affiliated bodies. Pres. HRH The Earl of WESSEX; Chair. MICHAEL FENNELL.

YOUTH

Commonwealth Youth Exchange Council: 7 Lion Yard, Tremadoc Rd, London, SW4 7NQ; tel. (20) 7498-6151; fax (20) 7720-5403; e-mail mail@cyec.demon.co.uk; f. 1970; promotes contact between groups of young people of the United Kingdom and other Commonwealth countries by means of educational exchange visits, provides information for organizers and allocates grants; 224 mem. orgs. Dir V. S. G. CRAGGS. Publs *Contact* (handbook), *Exchange* (newsletter), *Safety and Welfare* (guide-lines for Commonwealth Youth Exchange groups).

Duke of Edinburgh's Award International Association: Award House, 7-11 St Matthew St, London, SW1P 2JT; tel. (20) 7222-4242; fax (20) 7222-4141; e-mail sect@intaward.org; internet www .intaward.org; f. 1956; offers a programme of leisure activities for young people, comprising Service, Expeditions, Physical Recreation, and Skills; operates in more than 60 countries (not confined to the Commonwealth). International Sec.-Gen. PAUL ARENGO-JONES. Publs *Award World* (2 a year), *Annual Report*, handbooks and guides.

MISCELLANEOUS

British Commonwealth Ex-Services League: 48 Pall Mall, London, SW1Y 5JG; tel. (20) 7973-7263; fax (20) 7973-7308; links the ex-service orgs in the Commonwealth, assists ex-servicemen of the Crown and their dependants who are resident abroad; holds triennial confs. Grand Pres. HRH The Duke of EDINBURGH; Sec.-Gen. Lt-Col S. POPE. Publ. *Annual Report.*

Commonwealth Countries League: 14 Thistleworth Close, Isleworth, Middlesex, TW7 4QQ; tel. (20) 8737-3572; fax (20) 8568-2495; f. 1925 to secure equal opportunities and status between men and women in the Commonwealth, to act as a link between Commonwealth women's orgs, and to promote and finance secondary education of disadvantaged girls of high ability in their own countries, through the CCL Educational Fund; holds meetings with speakers and an annual Conf., organizes the annual Commonwealth Fair for fund-raising; individual mems and affiliated socs in the Commonwealth. Sec.-Gen. SHEILA O'REILLY. Publ. *CCL Newsletter* (3 a year).

Commonwealth War Graves Commission: 2 Marlow Rd, Maidenhead, Berks, SL6 7DX; tel. (1628) 634221; fax (1628) 771208; e-mail general.enq@cwgc.org; internet www.cwgc.org; f. 1917 (as Imperial War Graves Commission); responsible for the commemoration in perpetuity of the 1.7m. members of the Commonwealth Forces who died during the wars of 1914–18 and 1939–45; provides for the marking and maintenance of war graves and memorials at some 23,000 locations in 150 countries. Mems: Australia, Canada, India, New Zealand, South Africa, United Kingdom. Pres. HRH The Duke of KENT; Dir-Gen. R. KELLAWAY.

Joint Commonwealth Societies' Council: c/o Royal Commonwealth Society, 18 Northumberland Ave, London, WC2N 5BJ; tel. (20) 7930-6733; fax (20) 7930-9705; e-mail jcsc@rcsint.org; internet www.rcsint.org; f. 1947; provides a forum for the exchange of information regarding activities of mem. orgs which promote understanding among countries of the Commonwealth; co-ordinates the distribution of the Commonwealth Day message by Queen Elizabeth, organizes the observance of the Commonwealth Day and produces educational materials relating to the occasion; mems: 16 unofficial Commonwealth orgs and four official bodies. Chair. Sir PETER MARSHALL; Sec. GWENDOLYN WHITE.

Royal Commonwealth Society: 18 Northumberland Ave, London, WC2N 5BJ; tel. (20) 7930-6733; fax (20) 7930-9705; e-mail info@rcsint.org; internet www.rcsint.org; f. 1868; to promote international understanding of the Commonwealth and its people; organizes meetings and seminars on topical issues, and cultural and social events; library housed by Cambridge University Library. Chair. Sir MICHAEL McWILLIAM; Dir STUART MOLE. Publs *Annual Report, Newsletter* (3 a year), conference reports.

Royal Over-Seas League: Over-Seas House, Park Place, St James's St, London, SW1A 1LR; tel. (20) 7408-0214; fax (20) 7499-6738; f. 1910 to promote friendship and understanding in the Commonwealth; club houses in London and Edinburgh; membership is open to all British subjects and Commonwealth citizens. Chair. Sir GEOFFREY ELLERTON; Dir-Gen. ROBERT F. NEWELL. Publ. *Overseas* (quarterly).

The Victoria League for Commonwealth Friendship: 55 Leinster Sq., London, W2 4PW; tel. (20) 7243-2633; fax (20) 7229-2994; f. 1901; aims to further personal friendship among Commonwealth peoples and to provide hospitality for visitors; maintains Student House, providing accommodation for students from Commonwealth countries; has brs elsewhere in the UK and abroad. Pres. HRH Princess MARGARET, Countess of SNOWDON; Chair. COLIN WEBBER; Gen. Sec. JOHN ALLAN. Publ. *Annual Report.*

Declaration of Commonwealth Principles

(Agreed by the Commonwealth Heads of Government Meeting at Singapore, 22 January 1971.)

The Commonwealth of Nations is a voluntary association of independent sovereign states, each responsible for its own policies, consulting and co-operating in the common interests of their peoples and in the promotion of international understanding and world peace.

Members of the Commonwealth come from territories in the six continents and five oceans, include peoples of different races, languages and religions, and display every stage of economic development from poor developing nations to wealthy industrialized nations. They encompass a rich variety of cultures, traditions and institutions.

Membership of the Commonwealth is compatible with the freedom of member-governments to be non-aligned or to belong to any other grouping, association or alliance. Within this diversity all members of the Commonwealth hold certain principles in common. It is by pursuing these principles that the Commonwealth can continue to influence international society for the benefit of mankind.

We believe that international peace and order are essential to the security and prosperity of mankind; we therefore support the United Nations and seek to strengthen its influence for peace in the world, and its efforts to remove the causes of tension between nations.

We believe in the liberty of the individual, in equal rights for all citizens regardless of race, colour, creed or political belief, and in their inalienable right to participate by means of free and democratic political processes in framing the society in which they live. We therefore strive to promote in each of our countries those representative institutions and guarantees for personal freedom under the law that are our common heritage.

We recognize racial prejudice as a dangerous sickness threatening the healthy development of the human race and racial discrimination as an unmitigated evil of society. Each of us will vigorously combat this evil within our own nation.

No country will afford to regimes which practise racial discrimination assistance which in its own judgment directly contributes to the pursuit or consolidation of this evil policy. We oppose all forms of colonial domination and racial oppression and are committed to the principles of human dignity and equality.

We will therefore use all our efforts to foster human equality and dignity everywhere, and to further the principles of self-determination and non-racialism.

We believe that the wide disparities in wealth now existing between different sections of mankind are too great to be tolerated. They also create world tensions. Our aim is their progressive removal. We therefore seek to use our efforts to overcome poverty, ignorance and disease, in raising standards of life and achieving a more equitable international society.

To this end our aim is to achieve the freest possible flow of international trade on terms fair and equitable to all, taking into account the special requirements of the developing countries, and to encourage the flow of adequate resources, including governmental and private resources, to the developing countries, bearing in mind the importance of doing this in a true spirit of partnership and of establishing for this purpose in the developing countries conditions which are conducive to sustained investment and growth.

We believe that international co-operation is essential to remove the causes of war, promote tolerance, combat injustice, and secure development among the peoples of the world. We are convinced that the Commonwealth is one of the most fruitful associations for these purposes.

In pursuing these principles the members of the Commonwealth believe that they can provide a constructive example of the multi-national approach which is vital to peace and progress in the modern world. The association is based on consultation, discussion and co-operation.

In rejecting coercion as an instrument of policy they recognize that the security of each member state from external aggression is a matter of concern to all members. It provides many channels for continuing exchanges of knowledge and views on professional, cultural, economic, legal and political issues among member states.

These relationships we intend to foster and extend, for we believe that our multi-national association can expand human understanding and understanding among nations, assist in the elimination of discrimination based on differences of race, colour or creed, maintain and strengthen personal liberty, contribute to the enrichment of life for all, and provide a powerful influence for peace among nations.

The Lusaka Declaration on Racism and Racial Prejudice

The Declaration, adopted by Heads of Government in 1979, includes the following statements:

United in our desire to rid the world of the evils of racism and racial prejudice, we proclaim our faith in the inherent dignity and worth of the human person and declare that:

(i) the peoples of the Commonwealth have the right to live freely in dignity and equality, without any distinction or exclusion based on race, colour, sex, descent, or national or ethnic origin;

(ii) while everyone is free to retain diversity in his or her culture and lifestyle this diversity does not justify the perpetuation of racial prejudice or racially discriminatory practices;

(iii) everyone has the right to equality before the law and equal justice under the law; and

(iv) everyone has the right to effective remedies and protection against any form of discrimination based on the grounds of race, colour, sex, descent, or national or ethnic origin.

We reject as inhuman and intolerable all policies designed to perpetuate apartheid, racial segregation or other policies based on theories that racial groups are or may be inherently superior or inferior.

We reaffirm that it is the duty of all the peoples of the Commonwealth to work together for the total eradication of the infamous policy of apartheid which is internationally recognized as a crime against the conscience and dignity of mankind and the very existence of which is an affront to humanity.

We agree that everyone has the right to protection against acts of incitement to racial hatred and discrimination, whether committed by individuals, groups or other organizations. . . .

Inspired by the principles of freedom and equality which characterise our association, we accept the solemn duty of working together to eliminate racism and racial prejudice. This duty involves the acceptance of the principle that positive measures may be required to advance the elimination of racism, including assistance to those struggling to rid themselves and their environment of the practice.

Being aware that legislation alone cannot eliminate racism and racial prejudice, we endorse the need to initiate public information and education policies designed to promote understanding, tolerance, respect and friendship among peoples and racial groups. . . .

We note that racism and racial prejudice, wherever they occur, are significant factors contributing to tension between nations and thus inhibit peaceful progress and development. We believe that the goal of the eradication of racism stands as a critical priority for governments of the Commonwealth committed as they are to the promotion of the ideals of peaceful and happy lives for their people.

Harare Commonwealth Declaration

The following are the major points of the Declaration adopted by Heads of Government at the meeting held in Harare, Zimbabwe, in 1991:

Having reaffirmed the principles to which the Commonwealth is committed, and reviewed the problems and challenges which the world, and the Commonwealth as part of it, face, we pledge the Commonwealth and our countries to work with renewed vigour, concentrating especially in the following areas: the protection and promotion of the fundamental political values of the Commonwealth; equality for women, so that they may exercise their full and equal rights; provision of universal access to education for the population of our countries; continuing action to bring about the end of apartheid and the establishment of a free, democratic, non-racial and prosperous South Africa; the promotion of sustainable development and the alleviation of poverty in the countries of the Commonwealth; extending the benefits of development within a framework of respect for human rights; the protection of the environment through respect for the principles of sustainable development which we enunciated at Langkawi; action to combat drugs trafficking and abuse and communicable diseases; help for small Commonwealth states in tackling their particular economic and security problems; and support of the United Nations and other international institutions in the world's search for peace, disarmament and effective arms control; and in the promotion of international consensus on major global political, economic and social issues.

To give weight and effectiveness to our commitments we intend to focus and improve Commonwealth co-operation in these areas. This would include strengthening the capacity of the Commonwealth to respond to requests from members for assistance in entrenching the practices of democracy, accountable administration and the rule of law.

In reaffirming the principles of the Commonwealth and in committing ourselves to pursue them in policy and action in response to the challenges of the 1990s, in areas where we believe that the Commonwealth has a distinctive contribution to offer, we the Heads of Government express our determination to renew and enhance the value and importance of the Commonwealth as an institution which can and should strengthen and enrich the lives not only of its own members and their peoples but also of the wider community of peoples of which they are a part.

EUROPEAN UNION—REGIONAL RELATIONS

The European Community (EC) signed a non-preferential trade agreement with Uruguay in 1974 and economic and commercial co-operation agreements with Mexico in 1975 and Brazil in 1980. A five-year co-operation agreement with the members of the Central American Common Market (CACM, q.v.) and with Panama entered into force in 1987, as did a similar agreement with the member countries of the Andean Group. Priority was given to technology transfer, rural development, training, promotion of trade and investment, and co-operation in the energy sector. Co-operation agreements were signed with Argentina and Chile in 1990, and in that year tariff preferences were approved for Bolivia, Colombia, Ecuador and Peru in support of those countries' efforts to combat drugs trafficking. The first ministerial conference between the EC and the then 11 Latin American states of the Rio Group took place in April 1991; thereafter high-level joint ministerial meetings have been held on a regular basis.

In December 1991 tariff preferences were extended to Costa Rica, El Salvador, Guatemala, Honduras, Nicaragua and Panama for a three-year period. In February 1993 the EC signed a new framework co-operation agreement with the countries of the CACM; a further co-operation agreement with the countries of Central America was signed in early 1996. In April 1993 a new co-operation agreement was signed with the countries of the Andean Group (now the Andean Community, q.v.). Further trade benefits were extended to those countries in April 1997 to encourage the production of agricultural food crops in substitution of illegal drugs.

In October 1995 the EU (as the EC became in 1993) announced its intention to forge closer links with Latin America during 1996–2000, by means of strengthened political ties, an increase in economic integration and free trade, and co-operation in other areas. The first summit meeting of all EU and Latin American heads of state or government was held in Rio de Janeiro, Brazil, in June 1999.

In December 1995 a framework agreement for commercial and economic co-operation was signed with the Mercado Común del Sur (Mercosur, q.v.). The agreement also provided for formal political dialogue between the two groupings, in particular to promote regional integration and respect for democratic principles and human rights. In July 1998 the European Commission voted to commence negotiations towards an inter-regional association agreement with Mercosur and Chile, strengthening existing co-operation agreements. The first round of association negotiations began in April 2000. Progress was rapid; fourth-round negotiations were completed in March 2001 and fifth-round negotiations, on tariffs and services, were scheduled for July.

In early 1995 the EU registered a formal complaint against proposed US legislation to sanction countries and businesses trading with or investing in Cuba. The so-called 'Helms-Burton' legislation was approved by US President Clinton in March 1996, although he postponed implementation of a part of the law. In February 1997 the World Trade Organization (WTO) appointed a disputes panel, at the request of the EU, to determine whether the Helms-Burton Act contravened multilateral trade provisions; however, in April the EU agreed temporarily to withdraw its petition, and commence negotiations on a new multilateral accord on investment, while the USA was to continue to defer implementation of the law. In December 1996 the EU adopted a common position on its relations with Cuba, making any further economic co-operation contingent on that country's progress towards democracy and respect for human rights. This position has been reiterated at subsequent meetings of the European Council. In April 2000 Cuba rejected the Cotonou Agreement (see below), following criticism by some European governments of its human rights record.

In June 1996 the EU and Chile signed a framework agreement on political and economic co-operation, which provided for a process of bilateral trade liberalization, as well as co-operation in other industrial and financial areas. An EU-Chile Joint Council was established. In November 1999 the EU and Chile commenced practical negotiations on developing closer political and economic co-operation, in the framework of the proposed EU-Mercosur/Chile association agreement (see above). Fourth-round negotiations were completed in March 2001, with the succeeding round due in July. In July 1997 an economic partnership, political co-ordination and co-operation agreement was concluded by the EU and Mexico, together with an interim agreement on trade. The accords were signed in December and negotiations on a free-trade agreement were launched in July 1998. The agreement was to provide for the elimination of tariffs on industrial products by January 2007. After nine rounds, negotiations were completed in early 2000, and the main part of the interim agreement entered into effect in July. The co-operation agreement entered into force on 1 October.

During 2000 EU financial and technical co-operation assistance to countries in Latin America amounted to € 138m. Finance was provided for projects supporting peace and good governance, poverty alleviation and environmental improvements. Economic co-operation assistance in that year totalled €70m. Humanitarian aid granted to countries in the region in 2000 included €6.8m. for people affected by the flooding and landslide in December 1999 in Venezuela; €6.5m. to support displaced persons in Columbia; €2.4m. to Cuba, to assist the elderly and disabled and for disaster prevention; €1.9m. to Ecuador, for the victims of natural disasters and disease; €1.8m and €1.5m. to Nicaragua and Honduras, respectively, for communities still dependent on aid following 'Hurricane Mitch' in 1998; and €1.3m. for Peru. A four-year programme providing aid for refugees and displaced persons was launched in 2000, with funds of €15.9m. The programme focused on problems in Mexico, Nicaragua and Guatemala. The EU's Caribbean action plan under the natural disaster prevention and preparedness programme (Dipecho) provided €1.7m. in 2000. In February 2001 the European Parliament adopted a resolution opposing Plan Colombia, a US-backed initiative which aimed to combat the Colombian illegal narcotics trade through measures that included military-supported aerial crop spraying to destroy coca production; the Plan had reportedly resulted in the forced displacement of some farming communities. The Parliament urged support for the ongoing peace process in Colombia and for the adoption of structural reforms in that country as the preferred means of addressing the drugs problem. In April the EU announced an €30m. aid package designed to support the peace process. (In July the USA proposed the inauguration of a new Andean Regional Initiative, which shifted emphasis from the military-backed focus of Plan Colombia to the region-wide promotion of democracy and development.)

ACP—EU Partnership

From 1976–February 2000 the principal means of channeling Community aid to developing countries were the successive Lomé conventions, concluded by the Community and African, Caribbean and Pacific (ACP) states. The first Lomé Convention (Lomé I), which came into force on 1 April 1976, replaced the Yaoundé Conventions and the Arusha Agreement, and was designed to provide a new framework of co-operation, taking into account the varying needs of developing countries. Under Lomé I the Community committed ECU 3,052.4m. for aid and investment in developing countries, through the European Development Fund (EDF) and the European Investment Bank (EIB). Provision was made for over 99% of ACP (mainly agricultural) exports to enter the EC market duty free, while certain products that compete directly with Community agriculture were given preferential treatment but not free access: for some commodities, such as sugar, imports of fixed quantities at internal Community prices were guaranteed. The Stabex (stabilization of export earnings) scheme was designed to help developing countries withstand fluctuations in the price of their agricultural products, by paying compensation for reduced export earnings.

The second Lomé Convention (January 1981–February 1985) envisaged Community expenditure of ECU 5,530m.; it extended some of the provisions of Lomé I, and introduced new fields of co-operation. One of the most important innovations was a scheme (Sysmin), similar to Stabex, to safeguard exports of mineral products. Lomé III provided a total of ECU 8,500m. (about US $6,000m. at 30 January 1985) in assistance to the ACP states over the five years from March 1985.

The fourth Lomé Convention entered partially into force (trade provisions) on 1 March 1990, and fully into force on 1 November 1991. It covered the period 1990–February 2000. The financial protocol for 1990–95 made commitments of ECU 12,000m. (US $13,700m.), of which ECU 10,800m. was from the EDF (including ECU 1,500m. for Stabex and ECU 480m. for Sysmin) and ECU 1,200m. from the EIB. Under Lomé IV the obligation of most of the ACP states to contribute to the replenishment of Stabex resources, including the repayment of transfers made under the first three Conventions, was removed. In addition, special loans made to ACP member countries were to be cancelled, except in the case of profit-orientated businesses. Other innovations included the provision of assistance for structural adjustment programmes, measures to avoid increasing the recipient countries' indebtedness (e.g. by providing Stabex and Sysmin assistance in the form of grants, rather than loans), and increased support for the private sector, environmental protection, and control of population growth.

In September 1993 the Community announced plans to revise the Lomé Convention, with a view to establishing 'more open, equitable and transparent relations among the signatories'. In May 1994 a mid-term review of Lomé IV was initiated; however, in February 1995 a joint EU–ACP ministerial council, which was scheduled to conclude the negotiations, was adjourned, owing to significant discord among EU member states concerning reimbursement of the EDF for the period 1995–2000. In June 1995 EU heads of government reached an agreement, subsequently endorsed by an EU–ACP ministerial group, whereby ECU 14,625m. was to be allocated for the second phase of Lomé IV (ECU 12,967m. from the EDF and ECU 1,658m. from the EIB). Agreement was also reached on revision of the country-of-origin rules for manufactured goods; expansion of the preferential system of trade for ACP products; and a new protocol on the sustainable management of forest resources. At the same time, a joint declaration on support for the banana industry was issued, amid growing tension relating to the EU's banana import regime. This followed the introduction by the EC, in 1993, of an import regime designed to protect the banana industries of ACP countries (mostly in the Caribbean), which were threatened by the availability of cheaper bananas produced by countries in Latin America. Latin American countries, and later, the USA, lodged complaints against the new regime with international bodies. In April 1999, despite efforts by the EU to amend the regime, an arbitration panel of the WTO confirmed that the EU had failed to conform with WTO rules and formally authorized the USA to impose trade sanctions. In May 2000 the WTO further authorized Ecuador to impose punitive tariffs on copyrighted material from the EU, to offset losses incurred from the regime. A satisfactory accord, involving the adoption by the EU of a new system of licences and quotas to cover 2001–06, and the introduction of a tariff-only system from 2006, was eventually reached by the USA and the EU in April 2001, subject to approval by EU member states and the European Parliament. Punitive trade sanctions were subsequently suspended. The accord reduces by 100,000 tonnes the quota reserved primarily for ACP producers, adding this to the quota to be filled primarily by Latin American bananas. The Cotonou Agreement of June 2000 (see below) stated that the EU would try to ensure 'the continued viability of [ACP] banana export industries and the continuing outlet for [ACP] bananas on the Community market'.

In November 1997 the first summit of heads of state of ACP countries was held in Libreville, Gabon. The principal issues under consideration at the meeting were the strategic challenges confronting the ACP group of countries and, in particular, relations with the EU beyond 2000, when Lomé IV was scheduled to expire. The summit mandated ACP ministers of finance and of trade and industry to organize a series of regular meetings in order to strengthen co-ordination within the grouping.

Formal negotiations on the conclusion of a successor agreement to the Lomé Convention were initiated on 30 September 1998. In mid-1998 EU ministers of foreign affairs had approved a request by the Cuban Government to participate in the negotiations with observer status. (Cuba joined the ACP in December 2000, but refused to participate in the successor agreement eventually negotiated— see above.) The negotiations were concluded in February 2000, and the new partnership accord was signed by ACP and EU Heads of State and Government in June, in Cotonou, Benin. The so-called Cotonou Agreement was to enter into effect following ratification by the European Parliament and the ACP national legislatures, and was to cover the period 2000–20. It comprised the following main elements: increased political co-operation; the enhanced participation of civil society in ACP–EC partnership affairs; a strong focus on the reduction of poverty (addressing the economic and technical marginalization of developing nations was a primary concern); a reform of the existing structures for financial co-operation; and a new framework for economic and trade co-operation. Under the provisions of the new accord, the EU was to negotiate free-trade arrangements (replacing the previous non-reciprocal trade preferences) with the most developed ACP countries during 2000–08; these would be structured around a system of regional free-trade zones, and would be designed to ensure full compatibility with WTO provisions. Once in force, the agreements would be subject to revision every five years. An assessment was to be conducted in 2004 would identify those mid-ranking ACP nations also capable of entering into such free-trade deals. Meanwhile, the least-developed ACP nations were to benefit from an EU initiative to allow free access for most of their products by 2005. The preferential agreements currently in force would be retained initially (phase I), in view of a waiver granted by the WTO; thereafter ACP–EU trade was to be gradually liberalized over a period of 12–15 years (phase II). It was envisaged that Stabex and Sysmin would be eliminated gradually.

The first meeting of the ACP–EU Joint Parliamentary Assembly following the signing of the Cotonou Agreement was held in Brussels in October 2000. Resolutions were adopted on subjects including the banana dispute and AIDS. The meeting also called for increased funding for decentralized co-operation to be made available in the EU budget. In total, the EU provided € 3,612m. in financing for ACP countries in 2000; humanitarian aid to the ACP was almost € 138.1m. in that year. The EDF was allocated funds of € 13,500m. for the first five years of operation of the Cotonou Agreement.

In February 2001, under its 'everything but arms' (EBA) policy, the EU agreed to phase out trade barriers on imports of everything except military weapons from the world's 48 least developed countries, 39 of which are ACP countries. Duties on sugar, rice, bananas and some other products were to remain until 2009. There was opposition to the agreement from some Caribbean commodity exporters, who feared they would lose market share. Some sources claimed the arrangement breached the Cotonou Agreement; others, that it complemented it.

By May 2001 only 15 states had ratified the Cotonou Agreement. The ACP Council of Ministers, meeting on 11 May, appealed to all parties to accelerate the process, noting that the release of funds under the ninth EDF was contingent on the entry into force of the agreement.

SIGNATORY STATES TO THE COTONOU AGREEMENT

The European Union

Austria, Belgium, Denmark, Finland, France, Germany, Greece, Ireland, Italy, Luxembourg, Netherlands, Portugal, Spain, Sweden, United Kingdom

Caribbean ACP states

Antigua and Barbuda, Bahamas, Barbados, Belize, Dominica, Dominican Republic, Grenada, Guyana, Haiti, Jamaica, Saint Christopher and Nevis, Saint Lucia, Saint Vincent and the Grenadines, Suriname, Trinidad and Tobago

The ACP states also comprise 46 African and 14 Pacific countries.

ACP-EU INSTITUTIONS

Council of Ministers: one minister from each signatory state; one co-chairman from each of the two groups; meets annually.

Committee of Ambassadors: one ambassador from each signatory state; chairmanship alternates between the two groups; meets at least every six months.

Joint Assembly: EU and ACP are equally represented; attended by parliamentary delegates from each of the ACP countries and members of the European Parliament; one co-chairman from each group; meets twice a year.

Secretariat of the ACP-EU Council of Ministers: 175 rue de la Loi, 1048 Brussels, Belgium; tel.. (2) 285-61-11; fax (2) 285-74-58.

Centre for the Development of Industry (CDI): 52 ave Hermann Debroux, 1160 Brussels, Belgium; tel. (2) 679-18-11; fax (2) 675-19-03; e-mail director@cdi.be; internet www.cdi.be; f. 1977 to encourage investment in the ACP states by providing contacts and advice, holding promotion meetings, and helping to finance feasibility studies; Dir FERNANDO MATOS ROSA.

Technical Centre for Agricultural and Rural Co-operation: Postbus 380, 6700 AJ Wageningen, Netherlands; tel. (317) 467100; fax (317) 460067; e-mail cta@cta.nl; internet www.agricta.org; f. 1983 to provide ACP states with better access to information, research, training and innovations in agricultural development and extension; Dir CARL B. GREENIDGE.

ACP INSTITUTIONS

ACP Council of Ministers.

ACP Committee of Ambassadors.

ACP Secretariat: ACP House, 451 ave Georges Henri, 1200 Brussels, Belgium; tel. (2) 743-06-00; fax (2) 735-55-73; e-mail info@acpsec.org; internet www.acpsec.org; Sec.-Gen. JEAN-ROBERT GOULONGANA (Gabon).

INTER-AMERICAN DEVELOPMENT BANK—IDB

Address: 1300 New York Ave, NW, Washington, DC 20577, USA.
Telephone: (202) 623-1000; **fax:** (202) 623-3096; **internet:** www.iadb.org.

The Bank was founded in 1959 to promote the individual and collective development of Latin American and Caribbean countries through the financing of economic and social development projects and the provision of technical assistance. Membership was increased in 1976 and 1977 to include countries outside the region.

MEMBERS

Argentina	Ecuador	Norway
Austria	El Salvador	Panama
Bahamas	Finland	Paraguay
Barbados	France	Peru
Belgium	Germany	Portugal
Belize	Guatemala	Slovenia
Bolivia	Guyana	Spain
Brazil	Haiti	Suriname
Canada	Honduras	Sweden
Chile	Israel	Switzerland
Colombia	Italy	Trinidad and
Costa Rica	Jamaica	Tobago
Croatia	Japan	United Kingdom
Denmark	Mexico	USA
Dominican	Netherlands	Uruguay
Republic	Nicaragua	Venezuela

Organization

(July 2001)

BOARD OF GOVERNORS

All the powers of the Bank are vested in a Board of Governors, consisting of one Governor and one alternate appointed by each member country (usually ministers of finance or presidents of central banks). The Board meets annually, with special meetings when necessary. The 42nd annual meeting of the Board of Governors took place in Santiago, Chile, in March 2001.

BOARD OF EXECUTIVE DIRECTORS

The Board of Executive Directors is responsible for the operations of the Bank. It establishes the Bank's policies, approves loan and technical co-operation proposals that are submitted by the President of the Bank, and authorizes the Bank's borrowings on capital markets.

There are 12 executive directors and 12 alternates. Each Director is elected by a group of two or more countries, except the Directors representing Canada and the USA. The USA holds 30% of votes on the Board, in respect of its contribution to the Bank's capital. The Board has four standing committees, relating to: Policy and evaluation; Organization, human resources and board matters; Budget, financial policies and audit; and Programming. A steering committee was established in 1997. A new Office of Evaluation and Oversight, reporting directly to the Board, was established in 2000 as part of a reorganization of the Bank's evaluation system.

ADMINISTRATION

In 1994 the Bank reorganized its administrative structure, in order to improve management accountability and efficiency, to strengthen country focus and regional co-operation and to address the region's priorities. The Bank currently comprises three Regional Operations Departments, as well as the following departments: Finance; Legal; Research; Integration and Regional Programmes; Private Sector; External Relations; Sustainable Development; Information Technology and General Services; Strategic Planning and Budget; and Human Resources. In addition, there is an Office of the Chief Economist, an Evaluation Office, an Office of the Multilateral Investment Fund, and an External Relations Advisor. The Bank has country offices in each of its borrowing member states, and special offices in Paris, France and in Tokyo, Japan. At the end of 2000 there were 1,719 Bank staff (excluding the Board of Executive Directors and the Evaluation Office). The administrative budget for 2000 amounted to US $346.8m.

President: ENRIQUE V. IGLESIAS (Uruguay).
Executive Vice-President: K. BURKE DILLON (USA).

Activities

Loans are made to governments, and to public and private entities, for specific economic and social development projects and for sectoral reforms. These loans are repayable in the currencies lent and their terms range from 12 to 40 years. Total lending authorized by the Bank by the end of 2000 amounted to US $106,607m. During 2000 the Bank approved loans totalling $5,266m., compared with $9,486m. in 1999. Disbursements on authorized loans amounted to $7,069m. in 2000, compared with $8,387m. in the previous year.

The subscribed ordinary capital stock, including inter-regional capital, which was merged into it in 1987, totalled US $100,959.4m. at the end of 2000, of which $4,340.7m. was paid-in and $96,618.7m. was callable. The callable capital constitutes, in effect, a guarantee of the securities which the Bank issues in the capital markets in order to increase its resources available for lending. Replenishments are usually made every four years. In July 1995 the eighth general increase of the Bank's authorized capital was ratified by member countries: the Bank's resources were to be increased by $41,000m. to $102,000m.

In 2000 the Bank borrowed the equivalent of US $8,139m. on the international capital markets, bringing total borrowings outstanding to more than $41,394m. at the end of the year. During 2000 net earnings amounted to $846m. in ordinary capital resources and $135m. from the Fund for Special Operations (see below), and at the end of that year the Bank's total reserves were $8,591m.

The Fund for Special Operations enables the Bank to make concessional loans for economic and social projects where circumstances call for special treatment, such as lower interest rates and longer repayment terms than those applied to loans from the ordinary resources. The Board of Governors approved US $200m. in new contributions to the Fund in 1990, and in 1995 authorized $1,000m. in extra resources for the Fund. During 2000 the Fund made 22 loans totalling $297m., compared with loans amounting to $417m. in the previous year.

In January 1993 a Multilateral Investment Fund was established, as an autonomous fund administered by the Bank, to promote private sector development in the region. The 21 Bank members who signed the initial draft agreement in 1992 to establish the Fund pledged to contribute US $1,200m. The Fund's activities are undertaken through three separate facilities concerned with technical co-operation, human resources development and small enterprise development. In 2000 a specialist working group, established to consider MIF operations, recommended that it target its resources on the following core areas of activity: small business development; microenterprise; market functioning; and financial and capital markets. During 2000 the Fund approved $115m. for 78 projects, including $10m. to support the establishment of a special contingency fund for the rehabilitation of small businesses following natural disasters, bringing the cumulative total approved to $661m. for 386 projects since the Fund began operations.

In 1998 the Bank agreed to participate in a joint initiative by the International Monetary Fund and the World Bank to assist heavily indebted poor countries (HIPCs) to maintain a sustainable level of debt (see p. 000). Four member countries were eligible for assistance under the initiative (Bolivia, Guyana, Honduras and Nicaragua). Also in 1998, following projections of reduced resources for the Fund for Special Operations, borrowing member countries agreed to convert about US $2,400m. in local currencies held by the Bank, in order to maintain a convertible concessional Fund for poorer countries, and to help to reduce the debt-servicing payments under the HIPC initiative. In mid-2000 a committee of the Board of Governors endorsed a financial framework for the Bank's participation in an Enhanced HIPC Initiative, which aimed to broaden the eligibility criteria and accelerate the process of debt reduction. The Bank's total contribution to the initiative was estimated to be $1,100m.

In late 1998 the Board of Governors endorsed the establishment of an Emergency Loan Programme, for a one-year period, in order to help to mitigate the effects of the global financial crisis. Funds totalling US $9,000m. were to be made available under the Programme, which was to enable the bank to make large disbursements under special terms. Two emergency loans were approved in 1998, including a loan to Argentina for $2,500m., the largest amount ever approved by the Bank. In December the Bank established an emergency Consultative Group for the Reconstruction and Transformation of Central America to co-ordinate assistance to countries that had suffered extensive damage as a result of Hurricane Mitch. The Bank hosted the first meeting of the Group in the same month, which was attended by government officials, representatives of donor agencies and non-governmental organizations and academics. A total of $6,200m. was pledged in the form of emergency aid, longer-term financing and debt relief. A second meeting of the Group was held in May 1999, in Stockholm, Sweden, at which the assistance package was increased to some $9,000m., of which the

Bank and World Bank committed \$5,300m. In March 2001 the Consultative Group convened, in Madrid, Spain, to promote integration and foreign investment in Central America. The meeting, organized by the Bank, was also used to generate \$1,300m. in commitments from international donors to assist emergency relief and reconstruction efforts in El Salvador following an earthquake earlier in the year.

An increasing number of donor countries have placed funds under the Bank's administration for assistance to Latin America, outside the framework of the Ordinary Resources and the Bank's Special Operations. These trust funds, totalling some 58 in 2000, include the Social Progress Trust Fund (set up by the USA in 1961); the Venezuelan Trust Fund (set up in 1975); the Japan Special Fund (1988); and other funds administered on behalf of Austria, Belgium, Canada, Denmark, Finland, France, Israel, Italy, Japan, the Netherlands, Norway, Portugal, Spain, Sweden, Switzerland, the United Kingdom and the EU. A Program for the Development of Technical Co-operation was established in 1991, which is financed by European countries and the EU. Total cumulative lending from all these trust funds was \$1,724.4m. for loans approved by the end of 2000, of which \$1,650.4m. had been disbursed. During 2000 projects involved cofinancing by bilateral and multilateral sources amounting to \$1,888.5m., of which \$1,329.7m. was provided by the World Bank.

Following the capital increase approved in 1989, the Bank was to undertake sectoral lending for the first time, devoting up to 25% of its financing in 1990–93 to loans which would allow countries to make policy changes and improve their institutions. An environmental protection division was also formed in 1989. In December 1993 a task force presented a report on the Bank's operations to the Board of Executive Directors, which recommended greater responsibility for country offices throughout the project cycle; greater emphasis on development results, as opposed to lending targets; increased training for the personnel involved in implementing projects; and increased lending to social and poverty reduction programmes. A high-level Social Agenda Policy Group was created in 1993 to investigate the most effective means of supporting social reform in borrowing countries. In 1994 the Bank established an Independent Investigation Mechanism to assess Bank-financed projects, at the request of populations likely to be directly affected, in terms of their policy design and management. Under the eighth general increase of the Bank's resources priority areas of operation were designated as poverty reduction and social equity; modernization of state organs; and the environment. During 1995 an inter-departmental working group on poverty was established, in order to identify policies and projects likely to be effective in reducing poverty. In 1997 an inter-departmental working group was established with the aim of helping member countries to combat corruption and to promote transparency in the Bank's own lending procedures.

The Bank provides technical co-operation to help member countries to identify and prepare new projects, to improve loan execution,

Distribution of loans (US \$ million)

Sector	2000	%	1961–2000	%
Productive Sectors				
Agriculture and fisheries . .	165	3.1	11,973	11.2
Industry, mining and tourism	311	5.9	10,577	9.9
Science and technology . .	133	2.5	1,676	1.6
Physical Infrastructure				
Energy	437	8.3	16,415	15.4
Transportation and communications . .	435	8.3	12,827	12.0
Social Sectors				
Sanitation	145	2.8	9,015	8.5
Urban development . . .	685	13.0	6,655	6.2
Education	271	5.2	4,467	4.2
Social investment . . .	618	11.7	7,427	7.0
Health	10.6	0.2	2,139	2.0
Environment	142	2.7	1,493	1.4
Microenterprise . . .	0	0.0	386	0.4
Other				
Public-sector reform and modernization	1,885	35.8	17,710	16.6
Export financing	17	0.3	1,546	1.4
Other.	12	0.2	2,302	2.2
Total.	**5,266**	**100.0**	**106,607**	**100.0**

Source: *Annual Report, 2000.*

to strengthen the institutional capacity of public and private agencies, to address extreme conditions of poverty and to promote small- and micro-enterprise development. The Bank has established a special co-operation programme to facilitate the transfer of experience and technology among regional programmes. In 2000 the Bank approved 356 technical co-operation operations, totalling US \$66.7m., mainly financed by income from the Fund for Special Operations and donor trust funds. The Bank supports the efforts of the countries of the region to achieve economic integration and has provided extensive technical support for the formulation of integration strategies in the Andean, Central American and Southern Cone regions. The Bank is also supporting the initiative to establish a Free Trade Area of the Americas (FTAA) by 2005 and has provided technical assistance, developed programming strategies and produced a number of studies on relevant integration and trade issues. During the period 1998-2000 the Bank contributed an estimated \$15,000m. to projects in support of the goals of the summit meetings of the Americas, for example, strengthening democratic systems, alleviating poverty, and promoting economic integration.

INSTITUTIONS

Instituto para la Integración de América Latina y el Caribe (Institute for the Integration of Latin America and the Caribbean): Esmeralda 130, 16° and 17°, 1035 Buenos Aires, Argentina; tel. (1) 4320-1850; fax (1) 4320-1865; e-mail int/inl@iadb.org; internet www.iadb.org/intal; f. 1965 under the auspices of the Inter-American Development Bank; forms part of the Bank's Integration and Regional Programmes Department. The Institute undertakes research on all aspects of regional integration and co-operation and issues related to international trade, hemispheric integration and relations with other regions and countries of the world. Activities come under four main headings: regional and national technical co-operation projects on integration; policy fora; integration fora; and journals and information. A Documentation Center holds 100,000 documents, 12,000 books and 400 periodical titles. Dir JUAN JOSÉ TACCONE. Publs *Integración y Comercio / Integration and Trade* (3 a year), *Carta Mensual / Monthly Newsletter, Informe Mercosur / Mercosur Report* (2 a year).

Inter-American Institute for Social Development—INDES: 1300 New York Ave, NW, Washington, DC, 20057, USA; internet www.iadb.org/indes; commenced operations in 1995; aims to support the training of senior officials from public sector institutions and organizations involved with social policies and social services. INDES organizes specialized sub-regional courses and seminars and national training programmes. It produces teaching materials and also serves as a forum for the exchange of ideas on social reform. By the end of 2000 INDES had provided training for some 5,000 people.

Inter-American Investment Corporation—IIC: 1300 New York Ave, NW, Washington, DC 20057, USA; tel. (202) 623-3900; fax (202) 623-2360; e-mail iicmail@iadb.org; internet www. iadb.org/iic; f. 1986 as a legally autonomous affiliate of the Inter-American Development Bank, to promote the economic development of the region; commenced operations in 1989. The IIC's initial capital stock was US \$200m., of which 55% was contributed by developing member nations, 25.3% by the USA, and the remainder by non-regional members. In total, the IIC has 37 shareholders (26 Latin American and Caribbean countries, eight European countries, Israel, Japan and the USA). Emphasis is placed on investment in small and medium-sized enterprises without access to other suitable sources of equity or long-term loans. In 2000 the IIC approved equity investments and loans totalling \$143m. for 19 transactions. In that year the Board of Governors of the IADB agreed to increase the IIC's capital by \$500m. Gen. Man. JACQUES ROGOZINSKI. Publ. *Annual Report* (in English, French, Portuguese and Spanish).

Publications

Annual Report (in English, Spanish, Portuguese and French).

Annual Report on the Environment and Natural Resources (in English and Spanish).

Economic and Social Progress in Latin America (annually, in English and Spanish).

IDB América (monthly, English and Spanish).

IDB Projects (10 a year, in English).

Proceedings of the Annual Meeting of the Boards of Governors of the IDB and IIC (in English, Spanish, Portuguese and French).

The IDB (monthly, in English and Spanish).

Brochure series, occasional papers, working papers, reports.

LATIN AMERICAN INTEGRATION ASSOCIATION—LAIA

(ASOCIACIÓN LATINOAMERICANA DE INTEGRACIÓN—ALADI)

Address: Cebollatí 1461, Casilla 577, 11000 Montevideo, Uruguay.
Telephone: (2) 4001121; **fax:** (2) 4090649; **e-mail:** sgaladi@aladi.org; **internet:** www.aladi.org.

The Latin American Integration Association was established in August 1980 to replace the Latin American Free Trade Association, founded in February 1960.

MEMBERS

Argentina	Colombia	Paraguay
Bolivia	Cuba	Peru
Brazil	Ecuador	Uruguay
Chile	Mexico	Venezuela

Observers: People's Republic of China, Costa Rica, Dominican Republic, El Salvador, Guatemala, Honduras, Italy, Nicaragua, Panama, Portugal, Romania, Russia, Spain and Switzerland; also the UN Economic Commission for Latin America and the Caribbean (ECLAC), the UN Development Programme (UNDP), the European Union, the Inter-American Development Bank, the Organization of American States, the Andean Development Corporation, the Inter-American Institute for Co-operation on Agriculture, the Latin American Economic System, and the Pan American Health Organization.

Organization

(July 2001)

COUNCIL OF MINISTERS

The Council of Ministers of Foreign Affairs is responsible for the adoption of the Association's policies. It meets when convened by the Committee of Representatives.

EVALUATION AND CONVERGENCE CONFERENCE

The Conference, comprising plenipotentiaries of the member governments, assesses the Association's progress and encourages negotiations between members. It meets when convened by the Committee of Representatives.

COMMITTEE OF REPRESENTATIVES

The Committee, the permanent political body of the Association, comprises a permanent and a deputy representative from each member country. Permanent observers have been accredited by 15 countries and eight international organizations (see above). The Committee is the main forum for the negotiation of ALADI's initiatives and is responsible for the correct implementation of the Treaty and its supplementary regulations. There are the following auxiliary bodies:

Advisory Commission on Customs Valuation.
Advisory Commission on Financial and Monetary Affairs.
Advisory Council for Export Financing.
Advisory Council for Customs Matters.
Budget Commission.
Commission for Technical Support and Co-operation.
Council for Financial and Monetary Affairs: comprises the Presidents of member states' central banks, who examine all aspects of financial, monetary and exchange co-operation.
Council on Transport for Trade Facilitation.
Entrepreneurial Advisory Council.
Labour Advisory Council.
Meeting of Directors of National Customs Administrations.
Nomenclature Advisory Commission.
Sectoral Councils.
Tourism Council.

GENERAL SECRETARIAT

The General Secretariat is the technical body of the Association; it submits proposals for action, carries out research and evaluates activities. The Secretary-General is elected for a three-year term. There are two Assistant Secretaries-General.

Secretary-General (1999-2001): JUAN FRANCISCO ROJAS PENSO (Venezuela).

Activities

The Latin American Free Trade Association (LAFTA) was an intergovernmental organization, created by the Treaty of Montevideo in February 1960 with the object of increasing trade between the Contracting Parties and of promoting regional integration, thus contributing to the economic and social development of the member countries. The Treaty provided for the gradual establishment of a free-trade area, which would form the basis for a Latin American Common Market. Reduction of tariff and other trade barriers was to be carried out gradually until 1980.

By 1980, however, only 14% of annual trade among members could be attributed to LAFTA agreements, and it was the richest states which were receiving most benefit. In June it was decided that LAFTA should be replaced by a less ambitious and more flexible organization, the Latin American Integration Association (Asociación Latinoamericana de Integración—ALADI), established by the 1980 Montevideo Treaty, which came into force in March 1981, and was fully ratified in March 1982. Instead of across-the-board tariff cuts, the Treaty envisaged an area of economic preferences, comprising a regional tariff preference for goods originating in member states (in effect from 1 July 1984) and regional and partial scope agreements (on economic complementation, trade promotion, trade in agricultural goods, scientific and technical co-operation, the environment, tourism, and other matters), taking into account the different stages of development of the members, and with no definite timetable for the establishment of a full common market.

The members of ALADI are divided into three categories: most developed (Argentina, Brazil and Mexico); intermediate (Chile, Colombia, Peru, Uruguay and Venezuela); and least developed (Bolivia, Cuba—which joined the Association in August 1999, Ecuador and Paraguay), enjoying a special preferential system. In 2000 the value of exports within ALADI amounted to US $43,202m., compared with $34,776m. in 1999. The countries of the Southern Common Market (Mercosur) accounted for more than one-half of this total. By 2004 75% of all intra-ALADI trade was expected to be free of trade restrictions.

Certain LAFTA institutions were retained and adapted by ALADI, e.g. the Reciprocal Payments and Credits Agreement (1965, modified in 1982) and the Multilateral Credit Agreement to Alleviate Temporary Shortages of Liquidity, known as the Santo Domingo Agreement (1969, extended in 1981 to include mechanisms for counteracting global balance-of-payments difficulties and for assisting in times of natural disaster).

By August 1998 98 agreements had entered into force. Seven were 'regional agreements' (in which all 11 member countries participate). These agreements included a regional tariff preference agreement, whereby members allow imports from other member states to enter with tariffs 20% lower than those imposed on imports from other countries, and a Market Opening Lists agreement in favour of the three least developed member states, which provides for the total elimination of duties and other restrictions on imports of certain products. The remaining 91 agreements were 'partial scope agreements' (in which two or more member states participate), including: renegotiation agreements (pertaining to tariff cuts under LAFTA); trade agreements covering particular industrial sectors; the agreements establishing Mercosur (q.v.) and the Group of Three (G3); and agreements covering agriculture, gas supply, tourism, environmental protection, books, transport, sanitation and trade facilitation. A new system of tariff nomenclature, based on the 'harmonized system', was adopted from 1 January 1990 as a basis for common trade negotiations and statistics. General regimes on safeguards and rules of origin entered into force in 1987.

The Secretariat convenes meetings of entrepreneurs in various private industrial sectors, to encourage regional trade and co-operation. In early 2001 ALADI conducted a survey on small and medium-sized enterprises in order to advise the Secretary-General in formulating a programme to assist those businesses and enhance their competitiveness.

A feature of ALADI is its 'outward' projection, allowing for multilateral links or agreements with Latin American non-member countries or integration organizations, and with other developing countries or economic groups outside the continent. In February 1994 the Council of Ministers of Foreign Affairs urged that ALADI should become the co-ordinating body for the various bilateral, multilateral and regional accords (the Andean Community, Mercosur and G3 etc.), with the aim of eventually forming a region-wide common market. The General Secretariat initiated studies in preparation for a programme to undertake this co-ordinating work. At the same meeting in February there was a serious disagreement regarding the proposed adoption of a protocol to the Montevideo Treaty to enable Mexico to participate in the North American Free Trade Agreement (NAFTA), while remaining a member of ALADI. Brazil, in particular, opposed such a solution. However, in June the first Interpretative Protocol to the Montevideo Treaty was signed by the Ministers of Foreign Affairs: the Protocol allows member states to establish preferential trade agreeements with developed nations, with a temporary waiver of the most-favoured nation clause (article 44 of the Treaty), subject to the negotiation of unilateral compensation.

Mercosur (which comprises Argentina, Brazil, Paraguay and Uruguay, with Chile and Bolivia as associate members) aims to conclude free-trade agreements with the other members of ALADI. In March 2001 ALADI signed a co-operation agreement with the Andean Community to facilitate the exchange of information and consolidate regional and sub-regional integration.

Publications

Empresarios en la Integración (monthly, in Spanish).
Noticias ALADI (monthly, in Spanish).
Estadísticas y Comercio (quarterly, in Spanish).
Reports, studies, brochures, texts of agreements.

NORTH AMERICAN FREE TRADE AGREEMENT—NAFTA

Canadian section: Royal Bank Centre, 90 Sparks St, Suite 705, Ottawa, ON, K1P 5B4; **tel.:** (613) 992-9388: **fax:** (613) 992-9392.
Mexican section: Blvd Adolfo López Mateos 3025, 2°, Col Héroes de Padierna, 10700 Mexico, DF; **tel.:** (5) 629-9630; **fax:** (5) 929-9637.
US section: 14th St and Constitution Ave, NW, Room 2061, Washington, DC 20230; **tel.:** (202) 482-5438; **fax:** (202) 482-0148.
E-mail: info@nafta-sec-alena.org; **internet:** www.nafta-sec-alena.org.

The North American Free Trade Agreement (NAFTA) grew out of the free-trade agreement between the USA and Canada that was signed in January 1988 and came into effect on 1 January 1989. Negotiations on the terms of NAFTA, which includes Mexico in the free-trade area, were concluded in October 1992 and the Agreement was signed in December. The accord was ratified in November 1993 and entered into force on 1 January 1994. The NAFTA Secretariat is composed of national sections in each member country.

MEMBERS

Canada	Mexico	USA

MAIN PROVISIONS OF THE AGREEMENT

Under NAFTA almost all restrictions on trade and investment between Canada, Mexico and the USA were to be gradually removed over a 15-year period. Most tariffs were eliminated immediately on agricultural trade between the USA and Mexico, with tariffs on 6% of agricultural products (including corn, sugar, and some fruits and vegetables) to be abolished over the 15 years. Tariffs on automobiles and textiles were to be phased out over 10 years in all three countries. Mexico was to open its financial sector to US and Canadian investment, with all restrictions to be removed by 2007. Barriers to investment were removed in most sectors, with exemptions for petroleum in Mexico, culture in Canada and airlines and radio communications in the USA. Mexico was to liberalize government procurement, removing preferential treatment for domestic companies over a 10-year period. In transport, heavy goods vehicles were to have complete freedom of movement between the three countries by 2000. An interim measure, whereby transport companies could apply for special licences to travel further within the borders of each country than the existing limit of 20 miles (32 km), was postponed in December 1995, shortly before it was scheduled to come into effect. The postponement was due to concerns, on the part of the US Government, relating to the implementation of adequate safety standards by Mexican truck-drivers. The 2000 deadline for the free circulation of heavy goods vehicles was not met, owing to the persistence of these concerns. In February 2001, however, a five-member NAFTA panel of experts appointed to adjudicate on the dispute ruled that the USA was violating the Agreement. The panel demanded that the US authorities consider entry applications from Mexican-based truck companies on an individual basis. In April 1998 the fifth meeting of the three-member ministerial Free Trade Commission (see below), held in Paris, France, agreed to remove tariffs on some 600 goods, including certain chemicals, pharmaceuticals, steel and wire products, textiles, toys, and watches, from 1 August. As a result of the agreement, a number of tariffs were eliminated as much as 10 years earlier than had been originally planned.

In the case of a sudden influx of goods from one country to another that adversely affects a domestic industry, the Agreement makes provision for the imposition of short-term 'snap-back' tariffs.

Disputes are to be settled in the first instance by intergovernmental consultation. If a dispute is not resolved within 30 to 40

days, a government may call a meeting of the Free Trade Commission. In October 1994 the Commission established an Advisory Committee on Private Commercial Disputes to recommend procedures for the resolution of such disputes. If the Commission is unable to settle the issue a panel of experts in the relevant field is appointed to adjudicate. In June 1996 Canada and Mexico announced their decision to refer the newly-enacted US 'Helms-Burton' legislation on trade with Cuba to the Commission. They claimed that the legislation, which provides for punitive measures against foreign companies that engage in trade with Cuba, imposed undue restrictions on Canadian and Mexican companies and was, therefore, in contravention of NAFTA. However, at the beginning of 1997 certain controversial provisions of the Helms-Burton legislation were suspended for a period of six months by the US administration. In April these were again suspended, as part of a compromise agreement with the European Union. The relevant provisions continued to be suspended at six-monthly intervals, and remained suspended in early 2001. An Advisory Committee on Private Commercial Disputes Regarding Agricultural Goods was formed in 1998.

In December 1994 NAFTA members issued a formal invitation to Chile to seek membership of the Agreement. Formal discussions on Chile's entry began in June 1995, but were stalled in December when the US Congress failed to approve 'fast-track' negotiating authority for the US Government, which was to have allowed the latter to negotiate a trade agreement with Chile, without risk of incurring a line-by-line veto from the US Congress. In February 1996 Chile began high-level negotiations with Canada on a wide-ranging bilateral free-trade agreement. Chile, which already had extensive bilateral trade agreements with Mexico, was regarded as advancing its position with regard to NAFTA membership by means of the proposed accord with Canada. The bilateral agreement, which provided for the extensive elimination of customs duties by 2002, was signed in November 1996 and ratified by Chile in July 1997. However, in November 1997 the US Government was obliged to request the removal of the 'fast-track' proposal from the legislative agenda, owing to insufficient support within Congress.

In April 1998 heads of state of 34 countries, meeting in Santiago, Chile, agreed formally to initiate the negotiating process to establish a Free Trade Area of the Americas (FTAA). The US Government had originally proposed creating the FTAA through the gradual extension of NAFTA trading privileges on a bilateral basis. However, the framework agreed upon by ministers of trade of the 34 countries, meeting in March, provided for countries to negotiate and accept FTAA provisions on an individual basis and as part of a sub-regional economic bloc. It was envisaged that the FTAA would exist alongside the sub-regional associations, including NAFTA. The negotiating process was scheduled to be concluded in Mexico City on 31 December 2004, at which time the co-ordinating FTAA Trade Negotiations Committee was to be presided over jointly by Brazil and the USA. In April 2001 leaders of the participating countries meeting in Quebec City, Canada, agreed to conclude the FTAA by 2005 to enable it to enter into force by the end of that year.

ADDITIONAL AGREEMENTS

During 1993, as a result of domestic pressure, the new US Government negotiated two 'side agreements' with its NAFTA partners, which were to provide safeguards for workers' rights and the environment. A Commission for Labour Co-operation was established under the North American Agreement on Labour Co-operation (NAALC) to monitor implementation of labour accords and to foster co-operation in that area. The North American Commission for Environmental Co-operation (NACEC) was initiated to combat pollution, to ensure that economic development was not environmentally damaging and to monitor compliance with national and NAFTA environmental regulations. Panels of experts, with representatives from each country, were established to adjudicate in cases of alleged infringement of workers' rights or environmental damage. The panels were given the power to impose fines and trade sanctions, but only with regard to the USA and Mexico; Canada, which was opposed to such measures, was to enforce compliance with NAFTA by means of its own legal system. In 1995 the North American Fund for Environmental Co-operation (NAFEC) was established. NAFEC, which is financed by the NACEC, supports community environmental projects.

In February 1996 the NACEC consented for the first time to investigate a complaint brought by environmentalists regarding non-compliance with domestic legislation on the environment. Mexican environmentalists claimed that a company that was planning to build a pier for tourist ships (a project that was to involve damage to a coral reef) had not been required to supply adequate environmental impact studies. The NACEC was limited to presenting its findings in such a case, as it could only make a ruling in the case of complaints brought by one NAFTA government against another. The NACEC allocates the bulk of its resources to research undertaken to support compliance with legislation and agreements on the environment. However, in October 1997 the council of NAFTA ministers of the environment, meeting in Montréal, Canada, approved a new structure for the NACEC's activities. The NACEC's main objective was to be the provision of advice concerning the environmental impact of trade issues. It was also agreed that the Commission was further to promote trade in environmentally-sound products and to encourage private-sector investment in environmental trade issues.

With regard to the NAALC, National Administration Offices have been established in each of the three NAFTA countries in order to monitor labour issues and to address complaints about non-compliance with domestic labour legislation. However, punitive measures in the form of trade sanctions or fines (up to US $20m.) may only be imposed in the specific instances of contravention of national legislation regarding child labour, a minimum wage or health and safety standards. A Commission for Labour Co-operation has been established (see below) and incorporates a council of ministers of labour of the three countries.

In August 1993 the USA and Mexico agreed to establish a Border Environmental Co-operation Commission (BECC) to assist with the co-ordination of projects for the improvement of infrastructure and to monitor the environmental impact of the Agreement on the US–Mexican border area, where industrial activity was expected to intensify. The Commission is located in Ciudad Juárez, Mexico. By April 2000 the BECC had certified 44 projects, at a cost of US $949.3m. In October 1993 the USA and Mexico concluded an agreement to establish a North American Development Bank (NADB or NADBank), which was mandated to finance environmental and infrastructure projects along the US–Mexican border.

Commission for Labour Co-operation: One Dallas Center, 350 N. St Paul 2424, Dallas, TX 75201-4240, USA; tel. (214) 754-1100; fax (214) 754-1199; e-mail info@naalc.org; internet www.naalc.org; f. 1994; Exec. Dir JOHN McKENNIREY. Publ. *Annual Report*.

North American Commission for Environmental Co-operation (NACEC): 393 rue St Jacques West, Bureau 200, Montréal, QC H2Y 1N9, Canada; tel. (514) 350-4300; fax (514) 350-4314; e-mail info@ccemtl.org; internet www.cec.org; f. 1994; Exec. Dir JANINE FERRETTI; Dir of Progs GREG BLOCK. Publ. *Annual Report*.

North American Development Bank (NADB or NADBank): 203 St Mary's, Suite 300, San Antonio, TX 78205, USA; tel. (210) 231-8000; fax (210) 231-6232; internet www.nadbank.org. At April 2001 the NADB had authorized capital of US $3,000m., subscribed equally by Mexico and the USA, of which $450m. was paid-up; Man. Dir RAUL RODRIGUEZ (Mexico). Publs *Annual Report*, *NADBank News*.

ORGANIZATION OF AMERICAN STATES—OAS

(ORGANIZACIÓN DE LOS ESTADOS AMERICANOS—OEA)

Address: 17th St and Constitution Ave, NW, Washington, DC 20006, USA.

Telephone: (202) 458-3000; **fax:** (202) 458-3967; **e-mail:** pi@oas.org; **internet:** www.oas.org.

The OAS was founded at Bogotá, Colombia, in 1948 (succeeding the International Union of American Republics, founded in 1890) to foster peace, security, mutual understanding and co-operation among the nations of the Western Hemisphere.

MEMBERS

Antigua and Barbuda	Guyana
Argentina	Haiti
Bahamas	Honduras
Barbados	Jamaica
Belize	Mexico
Bolivia	Nicaragua
Brazil	Panama
Canada	Paraguay
Chile	Peru
Colombia	Saint Christopher and Nevis
Costa Rica	Saint Lucia
Cuba*	Saint Vincent and the Grenadines
Dominica	Suriname
Dominican Republic	Trinidad and Tobago
Ecuador	USA
El Salvador	Uruguay
Grenada	Venezuela
Guatemala	

* The Cuban Government was suspended from OAS activities in 1962.

Permanent Observers: Algeria, Angola, Austria, Azerbaijan, Belgium, Bosnia and Herzegovina, Bulgaria, Croatia, Cyprus, Czech Republic, Denmark, Egypt, Equatorial Guinea, Finland, France, Germany, Ghana, Greece, the Holy See, Hungary, India, Ireland, Israel, Italy, Japan, Kazakhstan, the Republic of Korea, Latvia, Lebanon, Morocco, the Netherlands, Norway, Pakistan, Philippines, Poland, Portugal, Romania, Russia, Saudi Arabia, Spain, Sri Lanka, Sweden, Switzerland, Thailand, Tunisia, Turkey, Ukraine, the United Kingdom, Yemen and the European Union.

Organization

(July 2001)

GENERAL ASSEMBLY

The Assembly meets annually and may also hold special sessions when convoked by the Permanent Council. As the supreme organ of the OAS, it decides general action and policy.

MEETINGS OF CONSULTATION OF MINISTERS OF FOREIGN AFFAIRS

Meetings are convened, at the request of any member state, to consider problems of an urgent nature and of common interest to member states, or to serve as an organ of consultation in cases of armed attack or other threats to international peace and security. The Permanent Council determines whether a meeting should be convened and acts as a provisional organ of consultation until ministers are able to assemble.

PERMANENT COUNCIL

The Council meets regularly throughout the year at OAS headquarters. It is composed of one representative of each member state with the rank of ambassador; each government may accredit alternate representatives and advisers and when necessary appoint an interim representative. The office of Chairman is held in turn by each of the representatives, following alphabetical order according to the names of the countries in Spanish. The Vice-Chairman is determined in the same way, following reverse alphabetical order. Their terms of office are three months.

The Council acts as an organ of consultation and oversees the maintenance of friendly relations between members. It supervises the work of the OAS and promotes co-operation with a variety of other international bodies including the United Nations. The official languages are English, French, Portuguese and Spanish.

INTER-AMERICAN COUNCIL FOR INTEGRAL DEVELOPMENT—CIDI

The Council was established in 1996, replacing the Inter-American Economic and Social Council and the Inter-American Council for

Education, Science and Culture. Its aim is to promote co-operation among the countries of the region, in order to accelerate economic and social development. CIDI's work focuses on eight areas: social development and education; cultural development; the generation of productive employment; economic diversification, integration and trade liberalization; strengthening democratic institutions; the exchange of scientific and technological information; the development of tourism; and sustainable environmental development. An Executive Secretary for Integral Development provides CIDI with technical and secretarial services.

Executive Secretary: RONALD SCHEMAN (USA).

Inter-American Agency for Co-operation and Development: f. November 1999 as a subsidiary body of CIDI to accelerate the development of Latin America and the Caribbean through technical co-operation and training programmes. In particular, the Agency aimed to formulate strategies for mobilizing external funds for OAS co-operation initiatives; establish criteria for the promotion and exchange of co-operation activities; prepare co-operation accords and evaluate project requests and results; and review mechanisms for promoting scholarships and professional exchange programmes. The Executive Secretary for Integral Development serves as the Agency's Director-General.

GENERAL SECRETARIAT

The Secretariat, the central and permanent organ of the Organization, performs the duties entrusted to it by the General Assembly, Meetings of Consultation of Ministers of Foreign Affairs and the Councils.

Secretary-General: CÉSAR GAVIRIA TRUJILLO (Colombia).

Assistant Secretary-General: LUIGI R. EINAUDI (USA).

INTER-AMERICAN COMMITTEES AND COMMISSIONS

Inter-American Juridical Committee: Rua Senador Vergueiro 81, Rio de Janeiro, RJ 22230-000, Brazil; tel. (21) 558-3204; fax (21) 558-4600; e-mail cjioea@trip.com.br; composed of 11 jurists, nationals of different member states, elected for a period of four years, with the possibility of re-election. The Committee's purposes are: to serve as an advisory body to the Organization on juridical matters; to promote the progressive development and codification of international law; and to study juridical problems relating to the integration of the developing countries in the hemisphere, and, in so far as may appear desirable, the possibility of attaining uniformity in legislation. Sec. MANOEL TOLOMEI MOLETTA.

Inter-American Commission on Human Rights: 1889 F St, NW, Washington, DC 20006, USA; tel. (202) 458-6002; fax (202) 458-3992; e-mail cidhoea@oas.org; internet www.cidh.oas.org; f. 1960. The Commission comprises seven members. It promotes the observance and protection of human rights in the member states of the OAS; it examines and reports on the human rights situation in member countries, and provides consultative services. During 2000 the Commission received 681 written complaints, and opened 110 new cases related to 25 member states. Exec. Sec. JORGE TAIANA.

Inter-American Court of Human Rights: Apdo Postal 6906-1000, San José, Costa Rica; tel. 234-0581; fax 234-0584; e-mail corteidh@racsa.co.cr; internet www.corteidh-oea.nu.or.cr/ci; f. 1978, as an autonomous judicial institution whose purpose is to apply and interpret the American Convention on Human Rights (which entered into force in 1978: at November 1998 the Convention had been ratified by 25 OAS member states, of which 18 had accepted the competence of the Court). The Court comprises seven jurists from OAS member states. Pres. ANTÔNIO CANÇADO TRINDADE; Sec. MANUEL E. VENTURA-ROBLES.

Inter-American Drug Abuse Control Commission—CICAD: 1889 F St, NW, Washington, DC 20006–4499, USA; tel. (202) 458-3178; fax (202) 458-3658; e-mail cicad@oas.org; internet www.cicad .oas.org; f. 1986 by the OAS to promote and facilitate multilateral co-operation in the control and prevention of the trafficking, production and use of illegal drugs, and related crimes. Mems 34 countries. Exec. Sec. DAVID R. BEALL. Publs *Statistical Survey* (annually), *Directory of Governmental Institutions Charges with the Fight Against the Illicit Production, Trafficking, Use and Abuse of Narcotic Drugs and Psychotropic Substances* (annually), *Evaluation of Progress in Drug Control* (annually).

Inter-American Telecommunication Commission: 1889 F St, NW, Washington, DC 20006, USA; tel. (202) 458-3004; fax (202) 458-6854; e-mail citel@oas.org; f. 1993; Exec. Sec. CLOVIS BAPTISTA.

Inter-American Committee on Ports: 1889 F St, NW, Washington, DC 20006, USA; tel. and fax (202) 458-3871; e-mail cgallegos@oas.org; f. 1998 to further OAS activities in the sector (previously undertaken by Inter-American port conferences); aims to develop and co-ordinate member state policies in port admin-

istration and management. The first meeting of the Committee took place in October 1999; three technical advisory groups were established to advise on port operations, port security, and navigation safety and environmental protection. An Executive Board meets annually. Sec. CARLOS GALLEGOS.

Activities

In December 1994 the first Summit of the Americas was convened in Miami, USA. The meeting endorsed the concept of a Free Trade Area of the Americas (FTAA), and also approved a Plan of Action to strengthen democracy, eradicate poverty and promote sustainable development throughout the region. The OAS subsequently embarked on an extensive process of reform and modernization to strengthen its capacity to undertake a lead role in implementing the Plan. The Organization realigned its priorities in order to respond to the mandates emerging from the Summit and developed a new institutional framework for technical assistance and co-operation, although many activities continued to be undertaken by the specialized or associated organizations of the OAS (see below). In 1998, following the second Summit of the Americas, held in April, in Santiago, Chile, the OAS established an Office of Summit Follow-Up, in order to strengthen its servicing of the meetings, and to co-ordinate tasks assigned to the Organization. The third Summit, convened in Quebec City, Canada, in April 2001, reaffirmed the central role of the OAS in implementing decisions of the summit meetings and instructed the Organization to pursue the process of reform in order to enhance its operational capabilities, in particular in the areas of human rights, combating illegal drugs, and enforcement of democratic values. The Summit declaration stated that commitment to democracy was a requirement for a country's participation in the summit process. The meeting also determined that the OAS was to be the technical secretariat for the process, assuming many of the responsibilities previously taken by the host country.

TRADE AND ECONOMIC INTEGRATION

A trade unit was established in 1995 in order to strengthen the Organization's involvement in trade issues and the process of economic integration, which became a priority area following the first Summit of the Americas. The unit was to provide technical assistance in support of the establishment of the FTAA, and to co-ordinate activities between regional and sub-regional integration organizations. In 2000 the unit was providing technical support to six of the nine FTAA negotiating groups, relating to the following areas: investment; services; dispute settlement; intellectual property rights; subsidies, anti-dumping and countervailing duties; and competition policy. In April 2001 the third Summit of the Americas requested the OAS to initiate an analysis of corporate social responsibility.

The unit operates in consultation with a Special Committee on Trade, which was established in 1993 comprising high-level officials representing each member state. The Committee studies trade issues, provides technical analyses of the economic situation in member countries and the region, and prepares reports for ministerial meetings of the FTAA. The OAS also administers an Inter-American Foreign Trade Information System which facilitates the exchange of information.

DEMOCRACY AND CIVIL SOCIETY

Two principal organs of the OAS, the Inter-American Commission on Human Rights and the Inter-American Court of Human Rights, work to secure respect for human rights in all member countries. The OAS aims to encourage more member governments to accept jurisdiction of the Court. The OAS also collaborates with member states in the strengthening of representative institutions within government and as part of a democratic civil society. The third Summit of the Americas, convened in April 2001, mandated the OAS to formulate an Inter-American Democratic Charter. A draft document was issued in June at a meeting of the General Assembly, which instructed that it be made available for public comment. Work on the Charter was scheduled to be completed by September, when a special session of the Assembly was to be held.

Through its unit for the promotion of democracy, established in 1990, the OAS provides electoral technical assistance to member states and undertakes missions to observe the conduct of elections. By late 2000 the OAS had conducted 53 electoral missions in 18 countries. In March 2001 OAS observers monitored parliamentary elections in St Vincent and the Grenadines, and in April a team of 50 experts observed the general election in Peru. The OAS also supports societies in post-conflict situations and recently-installed governments to promote democratic practices.

In June 1991 the OAS General Assembly approved a resolution on representative democracy, which authorized the Secretary-General to summon a session of the Permanent Council in cases where a democratically-elected government had been overthrown or democratic procedures abandoned in member states. The Council could then convene an *ad hoc* meeting of ministers of foreign affairs to consider the situation. The procedure was invoked following political developments in Haiti, in September 1991, and Peru, in April 1992. Ministers determined to impose trade and diplomatic sanctions against Haiti and sent missions to both countries. The resolution was incorporated into the Protocol of Washington, amending the OAS charter, which was adopted in December 1992 and entered into force in September 1997. A high-level OAS mission was dispatched to Peru in June 2000 to assist with the process of 'strengthening its institutional democratic system', following allegations that the Peruvian authorities had manipulated the re-election of that country's President in May. The mission subsequently co-ordinated negotiations between the Peruvian Government and opposition organizations. In August the OAS Secretary-General undertook the first of several high-level missions to negotiate with the authorities in Haiti in order to resolve the political crisis resulting from a disputed general election in May. (An OAS electoral monitoring team was withdrawn from Haiti in July prior to the second round of voting owing to concern at procedural irregularities.) In January 2001, following a meeting with the Haitian Prime Minister, the Assistant Secretary-General recommended that the OAS renew its efforts to establish a dialogue between the government, opposition parties and representatives of civil society in that country. In May the OAS and CARICOM undertook a joint mission to Haiti in order to assess prospects for a democratic resolution to the political uncertainties. In June the OAS General Assembly issued a resolution urging all parties in Haiti to respect democratic order. At the end of that month the OAS Secretary-General led a visit of the joint mission to Haiti, during which further progress was achieved on the establishment of a new electoral council.

An OAS Mine-Clearing Assistance Programme in Central America was established in 1992, as part of efforts to facilitate the social and economic rehabilitation of the region. By 1999 the programme had provided training for 250 de-mining experts and assisted countries in the clearance of some 28,000 anti-personnel devices. Technical support was provided by the Inter-American Defense Board (see below). In 2001 Ecuador and Peru approved OAS programmes to support national efforts to eliminate the problem of landmines. OAS activities were to include minefield surveying, civilian awareness, mine removal, the destruction of stock-piles, and victim assistance.

The OAS has formulated an Inter-American Programme of Co-operation to Combat Corruption in order to address the problem at national level and, in 1996, adopted a Convention against Corruption. The first conference of the parties to the Convention was held in Buenos Aires, Argentina, in May 2001. In June the General Assembly approved the proposed establishment of a verification mechanism, including a policy-making annual conference and an intergovernmental committee of experts. At June the Convention had been signed by 29 member states, of which 22 had ratified the treaty. A working group on transparency aims to promote accountability throughout the public sector and supports national institutions responsible for combating corruption. In 1997 the OAS organized a meeting of experts to consider measures for the prevention of crime. The meeting adopted a work programme which included commitments to undertake police training in criminology and crime investigation, to exchange legal and practical knowledge, and to measure crime and violence in member countries.

REGIONAL SECURITY

In 1991 the General Assembly established a working group to consider issues relating to the promotion of co-operation in regional security. A Special Commission on Hemispheric Security was subsequently established, while two regional conferences have been held on security and confidence-building measures. Voluntary practices agreed by member states include the holding of border meetings to co-ordinate activities, co-operation in natural disaster management, and the exchange of information on military exercises and expenditure. From 1995 meetings of ministers of defence have been convened regularly, which provide a forum for discussion of security matters. The OAS aims to address the specific security concerns of small-island states, in particular those in the Caribbean, by adopting a multidimensional approach to counter their vulnerability, for example through efforts to strengthen democracy, to combat organized crime, to mitigate the effects of natural disasters and other environmental hazards, and to address the problem of HIV/AIDS.

In June 2000 the OAS General Assembly, convened in Windsor, Canada, established a Fund for Peace in support of the peaceful settlement of territorial disputes. In 2001 the Fund was supporting efforts to resolve disputes between Belize and Guatemala and between Honduras and Nicaragua. In June an agreement was concluded to enable an OAS Civilian Verification Mission to visit Honduras and Nicaragua in order to monitor compliance with previously agreed confidence-building measures. The Mission was to be financed by the Fund for Peace.

The OAS is actively involved in efforts to combat the abuse and trafficking of illegal drugs. In 1996 members approved a Hemispheric Anti-drug Strategy, reiterating their commitment to combating the problem. In 1998 the Inter-American Drug Abuse Control Commission established a Multilateral Evaluation Mechanism (MEM) to measure aspects of the drug problem and to co-ordinate an evaluation process under which national plans of action to combat drugs trafficking were to be formulated. The first hemispheric drugs report was published by MEM in January 2001 and in February 34 national reports produced under MEM were issued together with a series of recommendations for action. A meeting to review and strengthen MEM was convened in April. Since 1996 an OAS group of experts has undertaken efforts to assist countries in reducing the demand for illegal substances. Activities include the implementation of prevention programmes for street children; the development of communication strategies; and education and community projects relating to the prevention of drug dependence.

The first Specialized Inter-American Conference on Terrorism was held in Lima, Peru, in April 1996. A Declaration and Plan of Action were adopted, according to which member states agreed to co-operate and implement measures to combat terrorism and organized crime. A second conference was held in Mar del Plata, Argentina, in 1998. Member states recommended the establishment of an Inter-American Committee against Terrorism to implement decisions relating to judicial, police and intelligence co-operation.

SOCIAL DEVELOPMENT AND EDUCATION

In June 1996 the OAS established a specialized unit for social development and education to assist governments and social institutions of member states to formulate public policies and implement initiatives relating to employment and labour issues, education development, social integration and poverty elimination. It was also to provide technical and operational support for the implementation of inter-American programmes in those sectors, and to promote the exchange of information among experts and professionals working in those fields. In June 1997 the OAS approved an Inter-American Programme to Combat Poverty. The unit serves as the technical secretariat for annual meetings on social development that were to be convened within the framework of the Programme. The unit also administers the Social Networks of Latin America and the Caribbean project, and its co-ordinating committee, which promotes sub-regional co-operation to combat poverty and discrimination. In 1999 the unit was to implement a project funded by the Inter-American Development Bank to place interns and trainees within the Social Network institutions and to promote exchanges between the institutions.

The first meeting of ministers of education of the Americas was held in Brasília, Brazil, in July 1998, based on the mandate of the second Summit of the Americas. The meeting approved an Inter-American Education Programme, formulated by the unit for social development and education, which incorporated the following six priority initiatives: education for priority social sectors; strengthening educational management and institutional development; education for work and youth development; education for citizenship and sustainability in multicultural societies; training in the use of new technologies in teaching the official languages of the OAS; and training of teachers and education administrators. Other programmes in the education sector are undertaken with international agencies and non-governmental organizations.

The OAS supports member states to formulate and implement programmes to promote productive employment and vocational training, to develop small businesses and other employment generation initiatives, and to regulate labour migration. In 1998 the OAS initiated the Labour Market Information System project, which aimed to provide reliable and up-to-date indicators of the labour situation in member countries, to determine the impact of economic policy on the labour situation, and to promote the exchange of information among relevant national and regional institutions. Labour issues were addressed by the second Summit of the Americas, and, following an Inter-American Conference of Labour Ministers, held in Viña del Mar, Chile, in October 1998, two working groups were established to consider the globalization of the economy and its social and labour dimension and the modernization of the state and labour administration.

SUSTAINABLE DEVELOPMENT AND THE ENVIRONMENT

In 1996 a summit meeting on social development adopted a plan of action, based on the objectives of the UN Conference on the

Environment and Development, which was held in Rio de Janeiro, Brazil, in June 1992. The OAS was to participate in an inter-agency group to monitor implementation of the action plan. The OAS has subsequently established new financing mechanisms and networks of experts relating to aspects of sustainable development. Technical co-operation activities include multinational basin management; a strategic plan for the Amazon; natural disaster management; and the sustainable development of border areas in Central America and South America. In December 1999 the Inter-American Council for Integral Development approved a policy framework and recommendations for action of a new Inter-American Strategy for Public Participation in Decision-making for Sustainable Development.

The following initiatives have also been undertaken: a Caribbean Disaster Mitigation Project, to help those countries to counter and manage the affects of natural disasters; a Post-Georges Disaster Mitigation initiative specifically to assist countries affected by Hurricane Georges; a Natural Hazards Project to provide a general programme of support to assess member states' vulnerability, to provide technical assistance and training to mitigate the effects of a disaster, and to assist in the planning and formulation of development and preparedness policies; the Renewable Energy in the Americas initiative to promote co-operation and strengthen renewable energy and energy efficiency; an Inter-American Water Resources Network, which aims to promote collaboration, training and the exchange of information within the sector; and a Water Level Observation Network for Central America to provide support for coastal resources management, navigation and disaster mitigation in the countries affected by Hurricane Mitch.

SCIENCE AND TECHNOLOGY

The OAS supports and develops activities to contribute to the advancement of science and technology throughout the Americas, and to promote its contribution to social and sustainable development. In particular, it promotes collaboration, dissemination of information and improved communication between experts and institutions working in the sector. Specialized bodies and projects have been established to promote activities in different fields, for example metrology; co-operation between institutions of accreditation, certification and inspection; the development of instruments of measurements and analysis of science and technology; chemistry; the development of technical standardization and related activities; and collaboration between experts and institutions involved in biotechnology and food technology. The OAS also maintains an information system to facilitate access to databases on science and technology throughout the region.

TOURISM AND CULTURE

A specialized unit for tourism was established in 1996 in order to strengthen and co-ordinate activities for the sustainable development of the tourism industry in the Americas. The unit supports regional and sub-regional conferences and workshops, as well as the Inter-American Travel Congress, which was convened for the first time in 1993 to serve as a forum to formulate region-wide tourism policies. The unit also undertakes research and analysis of the industry.

In 1998 the OAS approved an Inter-American Programme of Culture to support efforts being undertaken by member states and to promote co-operation in areas such as cultural diversity; protection of cultural heritage; training and dissemination of information; and the promotion of cultural tourism. The OAS also assists with the preparation of national and multilateral cultural projects, and co-operates with the private sector to protect and promote cultural assets and events in the region.

COMMUNICATIONS

In June 1993 the OAS General Assembly approved the establishment of an Inter-American Telecommunication Commission. The body has technical autonomy, within the statute and mandate agreed by the Assembly. It aims to facilitate and promote the development of communications in all member countries, in collaboration with the private sector and other organizations, and serves as the principal advisory body of the OAS on matters related to telecommunications.

Finance

The OAS budget for 2001, approved by the General Assembly in mid-2000, amounted to US $84.4m.

Publications

(in English and Spanish)

Américas (6 a year).
Annual Report.
Catalog of Publications (annually).
Ciencia Interamericana (quarterly).
La Educación (quarterly).
Statistical Bulletin (quarterly).
Numerous cultural, legal and scientific reports and studies.

Specialized Organizations and Associated Agencies

Inter-American Children's Institute: Avda 8 de Octubre 2904, Montevideo, Uruguay; tel. (2) 4872150; fax (2) 4873242; e-mail iinpiinfa@redfacil.com.uy; internet www.iin.org.uy; f. 1927; promotes the regional implementation of the Convention on the Rights of the Child, assists in the development of child-oriented public policies; promotes co-operation between states; and aims to develop awareness of problems affecting children and young people in the region. The Institute organizes workshops, seminars, courses, training programmes and conferences on issues relating to children, including, for example, the rights of children, children with disabilities, and the child welfare system. It also provides advisory services, statistical data and other relevant information to authorities and experts throughout the region. Dir-Gen. ALEJANDRO BONASSO. Publs *Boletín* (quarterly), *IINfancia* (2 a year).

Inter-American Commission of Women: 1889 F St, NW, Suite 880 Washington, DC 20006, USA; tel. (202) 458-6084; fax (202) 458-6094; f. 1928 for the extension of civil, political, economic, social and cultural rights for women. In 1991 a Seed Fund was established to provide financing for grass-roots projects consistent with the Commission's objectives. Pres. INDRANIE CHANDARPAL (Guyana); Exec. Sec. CARMEN LOMELLIN.

Inter-American Defense Board: 2600 16th St, NW, Washington, DC 20441, USA; tel. (202) 939-6600; works in liaison with member governments to plan and train for the common security interests of the western hemisphere; operates the Inter-American Defense College. Chair. Maj.-Gen. CARL H. FREEMAN (USA).

Inter-American Indigenous Institute: Av. de las Fuentes 106, Col. Jardines del Pedregal 01900 México, DF, Mexico; tel. (5) 595-8410; fax (5) 652-0089; f. 1940; conducts research on the situation of the indigenous peoples of America; assists the exchange of information; promotes indigenist policies in member states aimed at the elimination of poverty and development within Indian communities, and to secure their position as ethnic groups within a democratic society. Dir Dr JOSÉ MANUEL DEL VAL (Mexico); Exec. Co-ordinator EVANGELINA MENDIZABAL. Publs *América Indígena* (quarterly), *Anuario Indigenista*.

Inter-American Institute for Co-operation on Agriculture: Apdo 55–2200 Coronado, San José, Costa Rica; tel. 229-0222; fax 229-4741; f. 1942 (as the Inter-American Institute of Agricultural Sciences: new name 1980); supports the efforts of member states to improve agricultural development and rural well-being; encourages co-operation between regional organizations, and provides a forum for the exchange of experience. Dir-Gen. CARLOS AQUINO GONZÁLEZ (Dominican Republic). Publ. *Annual Report, Comuniica* (quarterly).

Pan American Development Foundation—PADF: 2600 16th St, NW, Washington, DC 20009-4202, USA; tel. (202) 458-3969; fax (202) 458-6316; f. 1962 to improve economic and social conditions in Latin America and the Caribbean through providing low-interest credit for small-scale entrepreneurs, vocational training, improved health care, agricultural development and reafforestation, and strengthening local non-governmental organizations; provides emergency disaster relief and reconstruction assistance. Mems: foundations and institutes in 35 countries. Pres. ALEXANDER WATSON; Exec. Dir JOHN SANBRAILO. Publ. *PADF Newsletter* (2 a year).

Pan American Health Organization: 525 23rd St, NW, Washington, DC 20037, USA; tel. (202) 974-3000; fax (202) 974-3663; e-mail webmaster@paho.org; internet www.paho.org; f. 1902; co-ordinates regional efforts to improve health; maintains close relations with national health organizations and serves as the Regional Office for the Americas of the World Health Organization. Dir Sir GEORGE ALLEYNE (Barbados).

Pan-American Institute of Geography and History: Ex-Arzobispado 29, 11869 México, DF, Mexico; tel. (5) 277-5888; fax (5) 271-6172; e-mail ipgh@laneta.apc.org; internet www.spin

.com.mx/~ipgh; f. 1928; co-ordinates and promotes the study of cartography, geophysics, geographyand history; it provides technical assistance, conducts training at research centres, distributes publications, and organizes technical meetings. Chair. Dr JORGE SALVADOR LARA (Ecuador); Sec.-Gen. CHESTER ZELAYA GOODMAN

(Costa Rica). Publs *Boletín Aéreo* (quarterly), *Revista Cartográfica* (2 a year), *Revista Geográfica* (2 a year), *Revista Historia de América* (2 a year), *Revista de Arqueología Americana* (2 a year), *Revista Geofísica* (2 a year), *Folklore Americano* (2 a year), *Boletín de Antropología Americana* (2 a year).

SOUTHERN COMMON MARKET— MERCOSUR/MERCOSUL

(MERCADO COMÚN DEL SUR/MERCADO COMUM DO SUL)

Address: Edif. Mercosur, Dr Luis Piera 1992, 1°, Montevideo, Uruguay.

Telephone: (2) 4029024; **fax:** (2) 4080557; **e-mail:** informatica@mercosur.org.uy; **internet:** www.mercosur.org.uy.

Mercosur (known as Mercosul in Portuguese) was established in March 1991 by the heads of state of Argentina, Brazil, Paraguay and Uruguay with the signature of the Treaty of Asunción. The primary objective of the Treaty is to achieve the economic integration of member states by means of a free flow of goods and services between member states, the establishment of a common external tariff, the adoption of common commercial policy, and the co-ordination of macroeconomic and sectoral policies. The Ouro Preto Protocol, which was signed in December 1994, conferred on Mercosur the status of an international legal entity with the authority to sign agreements with third countries, group of countries and international organizations.

MEMBERS

| Argentina | Brazil | Paraguay | Uruguay |

Chile and Bolivia are associate members.

Organization

(July 2001)

COMMON MARKET COUNCIL

The Common Market Council (Consejo Mercado Común) is the highest organ of Mercosur and is responsible for leading the integration process and for taking decisions in order to achieve the objectives of the Asunción Treaty.

COMMON MARKET GROUP

The Common Market Group (Grupo Mercado Común) is the executive body of Mercosur and is responsible for implementing concrete measures to further the integration process.

TRADE COMMISSION

The Trade Commission has competence for the area of joint commercial policy and, in particular, is responsible for monitoring the operation of the common external tariff (see below). The Brasília Protocol may be referred to for the resolution of trade disputes between member states.

JOINT PARLIAMENTARY COMMISSION

The Joint Parliamentary Commission (Comisión Parlamentaria Conjunto) is made up of parliamentarians from the member states and is charged with accelerating internal national procedures to implement Mercosur decisions, including the harmonization of country legislation.

CONSULTATIVE ECONOMIC AND SOCIAL FORUM

The Consultative Economic and Social Forum is made up of representatives from the business community and trade unions in the member countries and has a consultative role in relation to Mercosur.

ADMINISTRATIVE SECRETARIAT

Director: SANTIAGO GONZÁLEZ CRAVINO (Argentina).

Activities

Mercosur's free-trade zone entered into effect on 1 January 1995, with tariffs removed from 85% of intra-regional trade. A regime of gradual removal of duties on a list of special products was agreed, with Argentina and Brazil given four years to complete this process while Paraguay and Uruguay were allowed five years. Regimes governing intra-zonal trade in the automobile and sugar sectors remained to be negotiated. Mercosur's customs union also came into force at the start of 1995, comprising a common external tariff of 0–20%. A list of exceptions from the common external tariff was also agreed; these products were to lose their special status and be subject to the general tarification concerning foreign goods by 2006. The value of intra-Mercosur trade was estimated to have tripled during the period 1991–95 and was reported to have amounted to US $20,300m. in 1998.

In June 1995 Mercosur ministers responsible for the environment held a meeting at which they agreed to harmonize environmental legislation and to form a permanent sub-group of Mercosur. At the summit meeting held in December 1995 presidents affirmed the consolidation of free trade as Mercosur's 'permanent and most urgent goal'. To this end they agreed to prepare norms of application for Mercosur's customs code, accelerate paper procedures and increase the connections between national computerized systems. It was also agreed to increase co-operation in the areas of agriculture, industry, mining, energy, communications, transport and tourism, and finance. At this meeting Argentina and Brazil reached an accord aimed at overcoming their dispute regarding the trade in automobiles between the two countries. They agreed that cars should have a minimum of 60% domestic components and that Argentina should be allowed to complete its balance of exports of cars to Brazil, which had earlier imposed a unilateral quota on the import of Argentine cars.

In May 1996 Mercosur parliamentarians met with the aim of harmonizing legislation on patents in member countries. In December Mercosur heads of state, meeting in Fortaleza, Brazil, approved agreements on harmonizing competition practices (by 2001), on the integration of educational opportunities for postgraduates and human resources training, on the standardization of trading safeguards applied against third-country products (by 2001) and for intra-regional cultural exchanges. An Accord on Sub-regional Air Services was signed at the meeting (including by the heads of state of Bolivia and Chile) to liberalize civil transport throughout the region. In addition, the heads of state endorsed texts on consumer rights that were to be incorporated into a Mercosur Consumers' Defence Code and agreed to consider the establishment of a bank to finance the integration and development of the region.

In June 1996 the Joint Parliamentary Commission agreed that Mercosur should endorse a 'Democratic Guarantee Clause', whereby a country would be prevented from participation in Mercosur unless democratic, accountable institutions were in place. The clause was adopted by Mercosur heads of state at the summit meeting that was held in San Luis de Mendoza, Argentina, later in the month. The presidents approved the entry into Mercosur of Bolivia and Chile as associate members. An Economic Complementation Accord with Bolivia, which includes Bolivia in Mercosur's free-trade zone, but not in the customs union, was signed in December 1995 and was to come into force on 1 January 1997. In December 1996 the Accord was extended until 30 April 1997, when a free-trade zone between Bolivia and Mercosur was to become operational. Measures of the free-trade agreement, which was signed in October 1996, were to be implemented over a transitional period commencing on 28 February 1997 (revised from 1 January). Chile's Economic

Complementation Accord with Mercosur entered into effect on 1 October 1996, with duties on most products to be removed over a 10-year period (Chile's most sensitive products were given 18 years for complete tariff elimination). Chile was also to remain outside the customs union, but was to be involved in other integration projects, in particular infrastructure projects designed to give Mercosur countries access to both the Atlantic and Pacific Oceans (Chile's Pacific coast was regarded as Mercosur's potential link to the economies of the Far East).

In June 1997 the first meeting of tax administrators and customs officials of Mercosur member countries was held, with the aim of enhancing information exchange and promoting joint customs inspections. During 1997 Mercosur's efforts towards regional economic integration were threatened by Brazil's adverse external trade balance and its Government's measures to counter the deficit, which included the imposition of import duties on certain products. In November the Brazilian Government announced that it was to increase its import tariff by 3%, in a further effort to improve its external balance. The measure was endorsed by Argentina as a means of maintaining regional fiscal stability. The new external tariff, which was to remain in effect until 31 December 2000, was formally adopted by Mercosur heads of state at a meeting held in Montevideo, Uruguay, in December 1997. At the summit meeting a separate Protocol was signed providing for the liberalization of trade in services and government purchases over a 10-year period. In order to strengthen economic integration throughout the region, Mercosur leaders agreed that Chile, while still not a full member of the organization, be integrated into the Mercosur political structure, with equal voting rights. In December 1998 Mercosur heads of states agreed on the establishment of an arbitration mechanism for disputes between members, and on measures to standardize human, animal and plant health and safety regulations throughout the grouping. In March 1998 the ministers of the interior of Mercosur countries, together with representatives of the Governments of Chile and Bolivia, agreed to implement a joint security arrangement for the border region linking Argentina, Paraguay and Brazil. In particular, the initiative aimed to counter drugs trafficking, money laundering and other illegal activities in the area.

In January 1999 economic instability in Brazil, and its Government's decision effectively to devalue the national currency, the real, added pressures to relations within Mercosur. The grouping's efforts at integration were further undermined, in March, by political instability within Paraguay. As a consequence of the devaluation of its currency Brazil's important automotive industry became increasingly competitive, to the detriment of that of Argentina. In April Argentina imposed tariffs on imports of Brazilian steel and, in July, the Argentine authorities approved a decree permitting restrictions on all imports from neighbouring countries, in order to protect local industries, prompting Brazil to suspend negotiations to resolve the trading differences between the two countries. Argentina withdrew the decree a few days later, but reiterated its demand for some form of temporary safeguards on certain products as compensation for their perceived loss of competitiveness resulting from the devalued real. An extraordinary meeting of the Common Market Council was convened, at Brazil's request, in early August, in order to discuss the dispute, as well as measures to mitigate the effects of economic recession throughout the sub-region. However, little progress was achieved and the bilateral trade dispute continued to undermine Mercosur. Argentina imposed new restrictions on textiles and footwear, while, in September, Brazil withdrew all automatic import licences for Argentine products, which were consequently to be subject to the same quality control, sanitary measures and accounting checks applied to imports from non-Mercosur countries. The volume of intra-Mercosur trade shrank during 1999 as a consequence of the continuing dispute. In January 2000, however, the Argentinian and Brazilian Governments agreed to refrain from adopting potentially divisive unilateral measures and resolved to accelerate negotiations on the resolution of ongoing differences. In early March Mercosur determined to promote and monitor private accords to cover the various areas of contention, and also established a timetable for executing a convergence of regional macroeconomic policies (to which the grouping had recommitted itself at a summit meeting in December 1999). In June 2000 Argentina and Brazil signed a bilateral automobile agreement; however a new sectoral trade regime failed to be approved by the summit meeting held later in that month. The Motor Vehicle Agreement, incorporating new tariffs and a nationalization index, was endorsed by all Mercosur leaders at a meeting convened in Florianopolis, Brazil, in December. The significant outcome of that meeting was the approval of criteria, formulated by Mercosur finance ministers and central bank governors, determining monetary and fiscal targets to achieve economic convergence. Annual inflation

rates were to be no higher than 5% in 2002-2005, and reduced to 4% in 2006 and 3% from 2007 (with an exception for Paraguay). Public debt was to be reduced to 40% of GDP by 2010, and fiscal deficits were to be reduced to no more than 3% of GDP by 2002. The targets aimed to promote economic stability throughout the region, as well as to reduce competitive disparities affecting the unity of the grouping. The Florianopolis summit meeting also recommended the formulation of social indicators to facilitate achieving targets in the reduction of poverty and the elimination of child labour. Political debate surrounding the meeting, however, was dominated by the announcement of the Chilean Government that it had initiated bilateral free trade discussions with the USA, which was considered, in particular by the Brazilian authorities, to undermine Mercosur's unified position at multilateral free trade negotiations. Procedures to incorporate Chile as a full member of Mercosur were suspended.

In early 2001 Argentina imposed several emergency measures to strengthen the domestic economy, in contradiction of Mercosur's external tariffs. External commentators speculated on whether the grouping could withstand such unilateral policies. In March, however, Brazil was reported to have accepted the measures, which included an elimination of tariffs on capital goods and increase in import duties on consumer goods, as an exceptional temporary trade regime. This position was reversed by mid-2001 following Argentina's decision to exempt certain countries from import tariffs.

EXTERNAL RELATIONS

In December 1995 Mercosur and the EU signed a framework agreement for commercial and economic co-operation, which provided for co-operation in the economic, trade, industrial, scientific, institutional and cultural fields and the promotion of wider political dialogue on issues of mutual interest. In June 1997 Mercosur heads of state, convened in Asunción, Paraguay, reaffirmed the group's intention to pursue trade negotiations with the EU, Mexico and the Andean Community, as well as to negotiate as a single economic bloc in discussions with regard to the establishment of a Free Trade Area of the Americas (FTAA). Chile and Bolivia were to be incorporated into these negotiations. During 1997 negotiations to establish a free-trade accord with the Andean Community were hindered by differences regarding schedules for tariff elimination and Mercosur's insistence on a local content of 60% to qualify for rules of origin preferences. However, in April 1998 the two groupings signed an accord which committed them to the establishment of a free-trade area by January 2000. It was agreed that negotiations would commence later in 1998 on the elimination of tariffs and other restrictions to trade, measures to expand and diversify commercial activity between countries of the two groups and on the formulation of a legal and institutional framework for co-operation and economic and physical integration. In October it was reported that Mercosur was to extend existing bilateral trade agreements with the Andean Community until 31 March 1999. Negotiations in early 1999 failed to conclude an agreement on preferential tariffs between the two blocs (intended to be a basis for the establishment of a free-trade area) and the existing arrangements were again extended on a bilateral basis. At the end of March the Andean Community agreed to initiate free-trade negotiations with Brazil; a preferential tariff agreement was concluded in July. In August 2000 a similar agreement between the Community and Argentina entered into force. In September leaders of Mercosur and the Andean Community, meeting at a summit of Latin American heads of state, determined to relaunch negotiations, with a view to establishing a free-trade area by 1 January 2002. The establishment of a mechanism to support political dialogue and co-ordination between the two groupings, which aimed to enhance the integration process, was approved at the first joint meeting of ministers of foreign affairs in July 2001.

In March 1998 ministers of trade of 34 countries agreed a detailed framework for negotiations to establish the FTAA by 2005. Mercosur secured support for its request that a separate negotiating group be established to consider issues relating to agriculture, as one of nine key sectors to be discussed. The FTAA negotiating process was formally initiated by heads of state of the 34 countries meeting in Santiago, Chile in April 1998. In June Mercosur and Canada signed a Trade and Investment Co-operation Arrangement, which aimed to remove obstacles to trade and to increase economic co-operation between the two signatories. In July the European Commission proposed obtaining a mandate to commence negotiations with Mercosur and Chile towards a free-trade agreement, which, it was envisaged would provide for the elimination of tariffs over a period of 10 years. However, Mercosur requested that the EU abolish agricultural subsidies as part of any accord. Negotiations between Mercosur, Chile and the EU were initiated in April 2000. Specific discussion of tariff reductions and market access commenced at the fifth round of negotiations, held in early July 2001, at which the

EU proposed a gradual elimination of tariffs on industrial imports over a 10-year period and an extension of access quotas for agricultural products. The summit meeting held in December 2000 was attended by the President of South Africa, and it was agreed that Mercosur would initiate free trade negotiations with that country. In June 2001 Mercosur leaders agreed to pursue efforts to conclude a bilateral trade agreement with the USA, an objective previously opposed by the Brazilian authorities, while reaffirming their commitment to the FTAA process.

Finance

In December 1996 the Mercosur summit meeting approved an annual budget of US $1.2m. for the Mercosur secretariat, to be contributed by the four full member countries.

Publication

Boletín Oficial del Mercosur (quarterly).

OTHER REGIONAL ORGANIZATIONS

These organizations are arranged under the following categories:

Agriculture, Food, Forestry and Fisheries
Commodities
Development and Economic Co-operation
Economics and Finance
Education and the Arts

Government and Politics
Industrial Relations
Law
Medicine and Health
Posts and the Media

Religion and Welfare
Tourism
Trade and Industry
Transport

AGRICULTURE, FOOD, FORESTRY AND FISHERIES

CAB International—CABI: Wallingford, Oxon, OX10 8DE, United Kingdom; tel. (1491) 832111; fax (1491) 833508; e-mail cabi@cabi.org; internet www.cabi.org; f. 1929 as the Imperial Agricultural Bureaux (later Commonwealth Agricultural Bureaux); current name adopted in 1985; governmental organization which aims to improve human welfare world-wide through the generation, dissemination and application of scientific knowledge in support of sustainable development. It places particular emphasis on forestry, human health and the management of natural resources, with priority given to the needs of developing countries. CABI compiles and publishes extensive information (in a variety of print and electronic forms) on aspects of agriculture, forestry, veterinary medicine, the environment and natural resources, Third World rural development, leisure, recreation and tourism, human nutrition, and human health. Maintains regional centres in Kenya, Malaysia, Pakistan, Switzerland and Trinidad and Tobago. Mems: 40 countries. Dir-Gen. Dr DENIS BLIGHT.

CABI Bioscience: Bakeham Lane, Egham, Surrey, TW20 9TY, United Kingdom; tel. (1491) 829080; fax (1491) 829100; e-mail bioscience@cabi.org; internet www.cabi.org/bioscience; f. 1998 by integration of the capabilities and resources of the following four CABI scientific institutions: International Institute of Biological Control; International Institute of Entomology; International Institute of Parasitology; International Mycological Institute; undertakes research, consultancy, training, capacity-building and institutional development in sustainable pest management, biosystematics and molecular biology, ecological applications and environmental and industrial microbiology. There are CABI Bioscience centres in Kenya, Malaysia, Pakistan, Switzerland, Trinidad and the United Kingdom.

Inter-American Association of Agricultural Librarians, Documentalists and Information Specialists (Asociación Interamericana de Bibliotecarios, Documentalistas y Especialistas en Información Agrícolas—AIBDA): c/o IICA-CIDIA, Apdo 55-2200 Coronado, Costa Rica; tel. 216-0290; fax 216-0291; e-mail cmolesti@iica.ac.cr; internet www.iica.ac.cr; f. 1953 to promote professional improvement of its members through technical publications and meetings, and to promote improvement of library services in agricultural sciences. Mems about 400 in 29 countries and territories. Pres. MAGDA SAUDÍ; Exec. Sec. CARLOS J. MOLESTINA. Publs *Boletín Informativo* (3 a year), *Boletín Especial* (irregular), *Revista AIBDA* (2 a year), *AIBDA Actualidades* (4 or 5 a year).

Inter-American Tropical Tuna Commission—IATTC: c/o Scripps Institution of Oceanography, 8604 La Jolla Shores Drive, La Jolla, CA 92037-1508, USA; tel. (858) 546-7100; fax (858) 546-7133; e-mail rallen@iattc.org; internet www.iattc.org; f. 1950; two programmes, the Tuna-Billfish Programme and the Tuna-Dolphin programme. The Tuna-Billfish Programme investigates the biology and population dynamics of the tropical tunas of the eastern Pacific Ocean to determine the effects of fishing and natural factors on the stocks of tunas and billfish, and recommends appropriate conservation measures to maintain stocks at levels which will afford maximum sustainable catches; the Tuna-Dolphin Programme monitors dolphin levels and the number of deaths caused to dolphins by tunafishers, in order to recommend measures to maintain dolphin stocks; promotes fishing methods that avoid the needless killing of dolphins; investigates the effect of various fishing methods on different species of fish and other aquatic animals. Mems: Costa Rica, Ecuador, El Salvador, France, Guatemala, Japan, Mexico, Nicaragua, Panama, USA, Vanuatu, Venezuela. Dir ROBIN L. ALLEN. Publs *Bulletin* (irregular), *Annual Report*.

International Centre for Tropical Agriculture (Centro Internacional de Agricultura Tropical—CIAT): Apdo Aéreo 6713, Cali, Colombia; tel. (2) 445-0000; fax (2) 445-0073; e-mail ciat@cgnet.com; internet www.ciat.cgiar.org; f. 1967 to contribute to the alleviation of hunger and poverty in tropical developing countries by using new techniques in agriculture research and training focuses on production problems of the tropics concentrating on field beans, cassava, rice and tropical pastures. Dir-Gen. Dr JOACHIM VOSS. Publs

Annual Report, Growing Affinities (2 a year), *Pasturas Tropicales* (3 a year), catalogue of publications.

COMMODITIES

Association of Coffee Producing Countries (Asociación de Países Productores de Café): 7-10 Old Park Lane, 5th Floor, London W1Y 3LJ, United Kingdom; tel. (20) 7493-4790; fax (20) 7355-1690; e-mail info@acpc.org; internet www.acpc.org; f. 1993; aims to promote the co-ordination of coffee policies among its members; to seek a balance between world supply and demand, with the aim of ensuring fair and remunerative price levels; and to contribute to the development of coffee-producing countries. Mems: 29 coffee-producing countries and two international coffee orgs; Pres. RUBENS ANTÔNIO BARBOSA; Sec.-Gen. ROBÉRIO O. SILVA.

Association of Tin Producing Countries—ATPC: Menara Dayabumi, 4th Floor, Jalan Sultan Hishamuddin, 50050 Kuala Lumpur, Malaysia; tel. (3) 2747620; fax (3) 2740669; e-mail atpc@tm.net.my; f. 1983; promotes co-operation in marketing of tin, supports research, compiles and analyses data. The headquarters scheduled to be moved to Rio de Janeiro, Brazil. Mems: Bolivia, Brazil, People's Republic of China, Democratic Republic of the Congo, Malaysia, Nigeria; observers: Peru, Viet Nam. Exec. Sec. MOHAMED ZARIF MOHAMED ZAMAN (Malaysia).

Cocoa Producers' Alliance: Western House, 8–10 Broad St, POB 1718, Lagos, Nigeria; tel. (1) 2635506; fax (1) 2635684; f. 1962 to exchange technical and scientific information; to discuss problems of mutual concern to producers; to ensure adequate supplies at remunerative prices; to promote consumption. Mems: Brazil, Cameroon, Côte d'Ivoire, Dominican Republic, Ecuador, Gabon, Ghana, Malaysia, Nigeria, São Tomé and Príncipe, Togo and Trinidad and Tobago. Sec.-Gen. DJEUMO SILAS KAMGA.

Group of Latin American and Caribbean Sugar Exporting Countries (Grupo de Países Latinoamericanos y del Caribe Exportadores de Azúcar—GEPLACEA): Paseo de la Reforma 1030, Lomas de Chapultepec, México, DF 11000, Mexico; tel. (5) 20-97-11; fax (5) 20-50-89; e-mail geplacea@mail.internet.com.mx; internet www.geplacea.ipn.mx; f. 1974 to serve as a forum of consultation on the production and sale of sugar; to contribute to the adoption of agreed positions at international meetings on sugar; to exchange scientific and technical knowledge on agriculture and the sugar industry; to consider the co-ordination of the various branches of sugar processing; to co-ordinate policies of action in order to achieve fair and remunerative prices. Mems: 23 Latin American and Caribbean countries (accounting for about 45% of world sugar exports and 66% of world cane sugar production). Exec. Sec. LUIS PONCE DE LEÓN.

International Cocoa Organization—ICCO: 22 Berners St, London, W1P 3DB, United Kingdom; tel. (20) 7637-3211; fax (20) 7631-0114; e-mail exec.dir@icco.org; internet www.icco.org; f. 1973 under the International Cocoa Agreement, 1972; sees to the implementation of the agreement. The Agreement has been renewed and revised several times; the objectives of the International Cocoa Agreement, 1993 are: to promote the development and strengthening of international co-operation in all sectors of the world cocoa economy; to contribute towards stabilization of the world cocoa market; to facilitate the expansion of international trade in cocoa; to promote transparency in the workings of the world cocoa economy through dissemination of relevant data; to promote scientific research in the field; and to provide a forum for the discussion of all matters relating to the commodity. Mems: 19 exporting countries and 23 importing countries. The European Union participates as an intergovernmental organization. Chair. (2000–01) Cdr DJIKALOU SAINT-CYR (Côte d'Ivoire); Exec. Dir E. KOUAMÉ (Côte d'Ivoire). Publs *Annual Report, Quarterly Bulletin of Cocoa Statistics, The World Cocoa Directory, Cocoa Newsletter*.

International Coffee Organization: 22 Berners St, London, W1P 4DD, United Kingdom; tel. (20) 7580-8591; fax (20) 7580-6129; internet www.ico.org; f. 1963 under the International Coffee Agreement, 1962, which was renegotiated in 1968, 1976, 1983 and 1994; aims to ensure enhanced international co-operation, and to act as a centre for intergovernmental consultation and information with regard to the world coffee market; to facilitate international trade in coffee by the collection, analysis and dissemination of statistics; to act as a centre for the collection, exchange and publication of coffee information; to promote studies in the field of coffee; and to encourage an increase in coffee consumption. Mems: 44 exporting countries accounting for over 99% of world coffee exports, and 18 importing countries. Chair. of Council FERDINANDO MASSIMO (Italy); Exec. Dir CELSIUS A. LODDER (Brazil).

International Sugar Organization: 1 Canada Square, Canary Wharf, London, E14 5AA, United Kingdom; tel. (20) 7513-1144; fax (20) 7513-1146; e-mail exdir@isosugar.org; internet www.isosugar .org; administers the International Sugar Agreement negotiated in 1992 by the United Nations Sugar Conference; the agreement does not include measures for stabilizing markets; holds workshops and seminars; 58 mems. Exec. Dir Dr PETER BARON. Publs *Sugar Year Book, Monthly Statistical Bulletin, Monthly Market Report, Quarterly Market Review.*

International Tropical Timber Organization—ITTO: International Organizations Center, 5th Floor, Pacifico-Yokohama, 1-1-1 Minato-mirai, Nishi-ku, Yokohama 220, Japan; tel. (45) 223-1110; fax (45) 223-1111; e-mail itto@itto.or.jp; internet www.itto.or.jp; f. 1985 under the International Tropical Timber Agreement (1983); a new treaty, ITTA 1994, came into effect in 1997; aims to promote the conservation and wise use of tropical forest resources through sustainable management; provides forum for consultation and co-operation between producers and consumers of tropical timber, in co-operation with non-governmental organizations and timber trade associations; facilitates progress towards the 'Year 2000' objective (all trade in tropical timber to be derived from sustainably managed resources by 2000) financed by a special Bali Partnership Fund; conducts research and development in forest management, timber processing and market information. Mems: 26 producing and 26 consuming countries and the EU. Exec. Dir Dr FREEZAILAH BIN CHE YEOM (Malaysia). Publs *Annual Review, Market Information Service* (every 2 weeks), *Tropical Forest Update* (quarterly).

Sugar Association of the Caribbean (Inc.): c/o Caroni (1975) Ltd, Brechin Castle, Couva, Trinidad and Tobago; tel. 636-2449; fax 636-2847; f. 1942. Mems: national sugar cos of Barbados, Belize, Guyana, Jamaica and Trinidad and Tobago, and Sugar Asscn of Saint Christopher and Nevis and Anguilla. Chair. KARL JAMES. Sec. AZIZ MOHAMMED. Publs *SAC Handbook, SAC Annual Report, Proceedings of Meetings of WI Sugar Technologists.*

Union of Banana-Exporting Countries (Unión de Países Exportadores de Banano—UPEB): Apdo 4273, Bank of America, 7°, Panamá 5, Panama; tel. 263-6266; fax 264-8355; e-mail iicapan@ pan.gbm.net; f. 1974 as an intergovernmental agency to further the banana industry. Mems: Colombia, Costa Rica, Dominican Republic, Guatemala, Honduras, Nicaragua, Panama, Venezuela. Exec. Dir J. ENRIQUE BETANCOURT. Publs *Informe UPEB, Biblioban, Estadísticas Bananeras, Fax UPEB.*

West Indian Sea Island Cotton Association (Inc.): c/o Barbados Agricultural Development and Marketing Corporation, Fairy Valley, Christ Church, Barbados. Mems: orgs in Antigua and Barbuda, Barbados, Jamaica, Montserrat and Saint Christopher and Nevis. Pres. E. ROACH; Sec. MICHAEL I. EDGHILL.

DEVELOPMENT AND ECONOMIC CO-OPERATION

Amazonian Co-operation Council: Lima, Peru; f. 1978 by signature of the Amazon Region Co-operation Treaty; aims to promote the harmonious development of the Amazon territories of signatory countries; Lima Declaration on Sustainable Development signed by ministers of foreign affairs in December 1995. Mems: Bolivia, Brazil, Colombia, Ecuador, Guyana, Peru, Suriname, Venezuela.

Association of Caribbean States—ACS: 11–13 Victoria Ave, POB 660, Port of Spain, Trinidad and Tobago; tel. 623-2783; fax 623-2679; e-mail mail@acs-aec.org; internet www.acs-aec.org; f. July 1994 by an agreement signed by the Governments of the 13 CARICOM countries and Colombia, Costa Rica, Cuba, the Dominican Republic, El Salvador, Guatemala, Haiti, Honduras, Mexico, Nicaragua, Suriname and Venezuela. Aims to promote economic integration and co-operation in the region; to co-ordinate participation in multilateral fora; to undertake concerted action to protect the environment, particularly with regard to the Caribbean Sea; and to co-operate in the areas of science and technology, health, transport, education and culture. Policy is determined by a Ministerial Council and implemented by a Secretariat based in Port of Spain, Trinidad and Tobago. The Fourth Ordinary Meeting was held in Bridgetown, Barbados, in December 1998. In April 1999 a second Summit of Heads of State and Government was convened in Santo Domingo, Dominican Republic; a Declaration of Santo Domingo, a Plan of Action and a Declaration of the Caribbean Zone of Sustainable Tourism were signed. The Fifth Ordinary Meeting of the Council was held in Panama City, Panama, in December 1999. Mems: 25 signatory states and three associate members. Sec.-Gen. Prof. Dr NORMAN GIRVAN (Jamaica).

Council of American Development Foundations—SOLIDARIOS (Consejo de Fundaciones Americanas de Desarrollo): Calle 6 No 10, Paraíso, POB 620, Santo Domingo, Dominican Republic; tel. (809) 549-5111; fax (809) 544-0550; e-mail solidarios@codetel.net.do; f. 1972; exchanges information and experience, arranges technical assistance, raises funds to organize training programmes and workshops; administers development fund to finance programmes carried out by members; the foundations provide technical and financial assistance, including loan guarantees, to low-income groups for rural, housing and handicraft projects. Mems: 18 institutional mems in 14 Latin American and Caribbean countries. Pres. MERCEDES PIMENTEL DE CANALDA; Sec.-Gen. ISABEL CRISTINA ARANGO CALLE. Publs *Solidarios* (quarterly), *Annual Report.*

Group of Three—G3: f. 1993 by Colombia, Mexico and Venezuela to remove restrictions on trade between the three countries. The trade agreement covers market access, rules of origin, intellectual property, trade in services and government purchases and was to enter into force during the first half of 1994. Tariffs on trade between member states were to be removed on a phased basis. Co-operation was also envisaged in employment creation, the energy sector and the fight against cholera. In October 1993 the Group of three signed joint agreements with CARICOM and Suriname on combating drugs trafficking and environmental protection.

Inter-American Planning Society (Sociedad Interamericana de Planificación—SIAP): Avda Las Américas y Calle Naranjos, Edif. El Molina, 3°, Casilla 01-05-1978, Cuenca, Ecuador; tel. (7) 823860; fax (7) 823949; f. 1956 to promote development of comprehensive planning as a continuous and co-ordinated process at all levels, in order to accelerate the development of American countries. Mems: institutions and individuals in 46 countries. Pres. HERMES MARROQUÍN; Exec. Sec. LUIS E. CAMACHO (Colombia). Publs *Correo Informativo* (quarterly), *Inter-American Journal of Planning* (quarterly).

Latin American Association of Development Financing Institutions (Asociación Latinoamericana de Instituciones Financieras para el Desarrollo—ALIDE): Paseo de la República 3211, POB 3988, Lima 100, Peru; tel. (1) 442-2400; fax (1) 442-8105; e-mail sg@alide.org.pe; internet www.alide.org.pe; f. 1968 to promote co-operation among regional development financing bodies. Mems: 62 active, 8 assoc. and 8 collaborating (banks, financing institutions and development organizations in 24 countries). Sec.-Gen. ROMMEL ACEVEDO. Publs *Memoria annual, Directorio Latinoamericano de Instituciones Financieras para el Desarrollo, Boletín ALIDE* (6 a year), *ALIDE Noticias* (monthly).

Latin American Economic System (Sistema Económico Latinoamericano—SELA): Avda Francisco de Miranda, Centro Empresarial Parque del Este, 1°, La Carlota, Caracas 1017A, Venezuela; tel. (2) 202-5111; fax (2) 238-8923; e-mail difusion@sela.org; internet www.sela.org; f. 1975 by the Panama Convention; aims to accelerate the economic and social development of its members through intra-regional co-operation, and to provide a permanent system of consultation and co-ordination in economic and social matters. The Latin American Council meets annually at ministerial level; there is also a Permanent Secretariat. Associated organizations include:

> Latin American and Caribbean Trade Information and Foreign Trade Support Programme: Lima, Peru.
> Latin American Fisheries Development Organization: Lima, Peru.
> Latin American Handicraft Co-operation Programme: Caracas, Venezuela.
> Latin American Technological Information Network: Brasilia, Brazil.

Mems: 28 states; Perm. Sec. CARLOS J. MONETA (Argentina). Publs. *Capítulos del SELA* (3 a year), *SELA Newsletter* (monthly), *Strategic Issues* (monthly).

Organization of the Cooperatives of America (Organización de las Cooperativas de América): Apdo Postal 241263, Carrera 11, No 86-32, Of. 101, Santafé de Bogotá, Colombia; tel. (1) 6103296; fax (1) 6101912; f. 1963 for improving socio-economic, cultural and moral conditions through the use of the co-operatives system; works in every country of the continent; regional offices sponsor plans and activities based on the most pressing needs and special conditions of individual countries. Mems: national or local orgs in 23 countries and territories. Exec. Sec. Dr CARLOS JULIO PINEDA SUÁREZ. Publs *América Cooperativa* (monthly), *OCA News* (monthly).

ECONOMICS AND FINANCE

Centre for Latin American Monetary Studies (Centro de Estudios Monetarios Latinoamericanos): Durango 54, Col. Roma, Del. Cuauhtémoc, 06700 México, DF, Mexico; tel. and fax (5) 533-0300; e-mail cemlainf@mail.internet.com.mx; f. 1952; organizes technical training programmes on monetary policy, development finance, etc., applied research programmes on monetary and central banking policies and procedures, regional meetings of banking officials. Mems: 31 associated members (Central Banks of Latin America and the Caribbean), 28 co-operating members (development agencies, regional financial agencies and non-Latin American Central Banks).

Dir SERGIO GHIGLIAZZA. Publs *Bulletin* (every 2 months), *Monetaria* (quarterly), *Money Affairs* (2 a year).

Eastern Caribbean Central Bank: POB 89, Basseterre, St Christopher and Nevis; tel. 465-2537; fax 466-8954; e-mail eccberu@ caribsurf.com; f. 1983 by OECS governments; maintains regional currency (Eastern Caribbean dollar) and advises on the economic development of member states. Mems: Anguilla, Antigua and Barbuda, Dominica, Grenada, Montserrat, Saint Christopher and Nevis, Saint Lucia, Saint Vincent and the Grenadines. Gov. DWIGHT VENNER.

Financial Action Task Force on Money Laundering—FATF: c/o OECD Secretariat, 2 rue André-Pascal, 75775 Paris Cédex 16, France; tel. 1-45-24-82-00; fax 1-45-24-85-00; e-mail fatf.contact-@oecd.org; internet www.oecd.org/fatf; f. 1989 on the recommendation of the Group of Seven industrialized nations (G-7); secretariat headquartered at the Organization for Economic Development and Co-operation; investigates methods of money laundering, evaluates anti-money laundering mechanisms at national and international level, and formulates and promotes measures to combat money laundering; issued action plan, *The FATF Forty Recommendations: A Global Framework for Combating Money Laundering*, in 1990 (a review of the *Forty Recommendations* was ongoing in 2001); identifies non-cooperative countries in annual report; established regional task force in the Caribbean. Mems: 29 countries (including Argentina, Brazil and Mexico), the European Commission and the Gulf Co-operation Council. Exec. Sec. PATRICK MOULETTE. Publ. *Annual Report*.

Latin American Banking Federation (Federación Latinoamericana de Bancos—FELABAN): Apdo Aéreo 091959, Santafé de Bogotá, DE8, Colombia; tel. (1) 6218490; fax (1) 6218021; internet www.latinbanking.com; f. 1965 to co-ordinate efforts towards a wide and accelerated economic development in Latin American countries. Mems: 19 Latin American national banking associations. Pres. of Board MILTON AYON; Sec.-Gen. Dra MARICIELO GLEN DE TOBÓN.

EDUCATION AND THE ARTS

Association of Caribbean University and Research Institutional Libraries: Apdo Postal 23317, San Juan 00931, Puerto Rico; tel. 764-0000; fax 763-5685; e-mail vtorres@upracd.upr.clu.edu; f. 1968 to foster contact and collaboration between member universities and institutes; conferences, meetings, seminars, etc.; circulation of information through newsletters, bulletins; facilitates co-operation and the pooling of resources in research; encourages exchange of staff and students. Mems: 250. Exec. Sec. ONEIDA R. ORTIZ. Publ. *Newsletter* (2 a year).

Caribbean Council of Legal Education: Mona Campus, Kingston 7, Jamaica; tel. 92-71899; fax 92-73927; f. 1971; responsible for the training of members of the legal profession. Mems: govts of 15 countries and territories.

Caribbean Examinations Council: The Garrison, St Michael 20, Barbados; tel. 436-6261; fax 429-5421; f. 1972; develops syllabuses and conducts examinations. Mems: govts of 16 English-speaking countries and territories.

Inter-American Centre for Research and Documentation on Vocational Training (Centro Interamericano de Investigación y Documentación sobre Formación Profesional—CINTERFOR): Avda Uruguay 1238, Montevideo, Uruguay; tel. (2) 920557; fax (2) 921305; e-mail dirmvd@cinterfor.org.uy; internet www.cinterfor.org.uy; f. 1964 by the International Labour Organization (ILO) for mutual help among Latin American and Caribbean countries; a technical committee of government representatives meets every two years to consider the programme of work and budget; the Centre assists the members in planning vocational training; services are provided in documentation, research, exchange of experience; holds seminars and technical meetings. The director is appointed by the Director-General of ILO. Dir PEDRO DANIEL WEINBERG. Publs *Bulletin* (quarterly), *Documentation* (2 a year), *Bibliographical Series*, studies, monographs and technical papers.

Inter-American Confederation for Catholic Education (Confederación Interamericana de Educación Católica—CIEC): Calle 78 No 12-16, Of. 101, Apdo Aéreo 90036, Santafé de Bogotá 8, Colombia; tel. (1) 2553676; fax (1) 2550513; e-mail ciec@latino.net.co; internet www.ciec.to; f. 1945 to defend and extend the principles and rules of Catholic education, freedom of education, and human rights; organizes congress every three years. Pres. ADRIANO PACIFICO TOMASI; Sec.-Gen. MARIA CONSTANZA ARANGO A. Publ. *Educación Hoy* (quarterly).

Inter-American Music Council (Consejo Interamericano de Música—CIDEM): c/o Inter-American Music Friends, 2511 P St, NW, 230-C, Washington, DC 20007, USA; f. 1956 to promote the exchange of works, performances and information in all fields of music, to study problems relative to music education, to encourage activity in the field of musicology, to promote folklore research and music creation, to establish distribution centres for music material of the composers of the Americas, etc. Mems: national music societies of 33 American countries. Sec.-Gen. EFRAÍN PAESKY.

International Institute of Iberoamerican Literature (Instituto Internacional de Literatura Iberoamericana): 1312 CL, University of Pittsburgh, PA 15260, USA; tel. (412) 624-5246; fax (412) 624-0829; e-mail iilit@pvtt-edn; f. 1938 to advance the study of Iberoamerican literature, and intensify cultural relations among the peoples of the Americas. Mems: scholars and artists in 37 countries. Publs *Revista Iberoamericana, Memorias*.

Inter-American Organization for Higher Education—IOHE: 2954 blvd Laurier, bureau 90, Sainte-Foy, Québec, Canada G1V 4T2; tel. (418) 650-1515; fax (418) 650-1519; e-mail secretariat@ oui-iohe.qc.ca; internet www.oui-iohe.qc.ca; f. 1980 to promote co-operation among universities of the Americas and the development of higher education. Mems: 390 in 24 countries. Exec. Dir PIERRE VAN DER DONCKT.

Organization of the Catholic Universities of Latin America (Organización de Universidades Católicas de América Latina—ODUCAL): Viamonte 1856, CP 1056, Buenos Aires, Argentina; tel. (1) 813-1408; fax (1) 812-4625; f. 1953 to assist the social, economic and cultural development of Latin America through the promotion of Catholic higher education in the continent. Mems: 43 Catholic universities in Argentina, Brazil, Chile, Colombia, Dominican Republic, Ecuador, Mexico, Paraguay, Peru, Puerto Rico, Venezuela. Pres. Dr JUAN ALEJANDRO TOBÍAS (Argentina). Publs *Anuario, Sapientia, Universitas*.

Organization of Ibero-American States for Education, Science and Culture (Organización de Estados Iberoamericanos para la Educación, la Ciencia y la Cultura—OEI): Centro de Recursos Documentales e Informáticos, Calle Bravo Murillo 38, 28015 Madrid, Spain; tel. (91) 5944442; fax (91) 5943286; e-mail oeimad@oei.es; internet www.oei.es; f. 1949 (as Ibero-American Bureau of Education: name changed 1985); encourages educational, scientific and cultural co-operation in the Iberian and Latin American countries; provides technical assistance, information and documentation; promotes educational and cultural exchanges and organizes meetings and training courses; General Assembly (at ministerial level) meets every four years. Regional offices in Argentina, Colombia, Mexico and Peru; technical offices in Chile and El Salvador. Mems: 20 Ibero-American governments. Sec.-Gen. FRANCISCO JOSÉ PIÑON. Publ. *Revista Iberoamericana de Educación* (quarterly).

Union of Latin American Universities (Unión de Universidades de América Latina—UDUAL): Edif. UDUAL, Ciudad Universitaria, Apdo 70-232, Del. Coyoacán, 04510 México, DF, Mexico; tel. (5) 622-0991; fax (5) 616-1414; f. 1949 to further the improvement of university association, to organize the interchange of professors, students, research fellows and graduates and generally encourage good relations between the Latin American universities; arranges conferences, conducts statistical research; centre for university documentation. Mems: 165 universities. Pres. Dr JORGÉ BROVETO (Uruguay); Sec.-Gen. Dr ABELARDO VILLEGAS (Mexico). Publs *Universidades* (2 a year), *Gaceta UDUAL* (quarterly), *Censo* (every 2 years).

ENVIRONMENTAL CONSERVATION

Caribbean Conservation Association: Savannah Lodge, The Garrison, St Michael, Barbados; tel. 426-5373; fax 429-8483; e-mail cca@caribsurf.com; f. 1967; aims to conserve the environment and cultural heritage of the region through education, legislation, and management of museums and sites. Mems: 20 governments, 92 organizations and individuals in 33 countries and territories. Exec. Dir CALVIN HOWELL. Publ. *Caribbean Conservation News* (quarterly).

GOVERNMENT AND POLITICS

Agency for the Prohibition of Nuclear Weapons in Latin America and the Caribbean (Organismo para la Proscripción de las Armas Nucleares en la América Latina y el Caribe—OPANAL): Temístocles 78, Col. Polanco, CP 11560 México, DF, Mexico; tel. (5) 280-4923; fax (5) 280-2965; f. 1969 to administer the Treaty for the Prohibition of Nuclear Weapons in Latin America (Treaty of Tlatelolco), 1967; to ensure the absence of all nuclear weapons in the application zone of the Treaty; to provide protection against possible nuclear attacks on the zone; to contribute to the movement against proliferation of nuclear weapons; to promote general and complete disarmament; to prohibit all testing, use, manufacture, acquisition, storage, installation and any form of possession, by any means, of nuclear weapons. The organs of the Agency comprise the General Conference which meets every two years; the Council, which has a rotating membership of five countries and which meets every two months; and the secretariat. Mems: 30 states which have fully ratified the Treaty. Antigua and Barbuda, Argentina, Bahamas, Barbados, Belize, Bolivia, Brazil, Chile, Colombia, Costa Rica, Dominica, Dominican Republic, Ecuador, El Salvador, Grenada, Guatemala, Haiti, Honduras, Jamaica, Mexico, Nicaragua, Panama, Paraguay, Peru, Saint Vincent and the Grenadines, Suriname, Trinidad and Tobago, Uruguay and Venezuela. The Treaty has two additional Protocols; the first signed and ratified by France, the Netherlands, the United Kingdom and the USA; the second signed and ratified by the People's Republic of China, France, Russia, the United Kingdom and the USA. Sec.-Gen. ENRIQUE ROMÁN-MOREY (Peru).

Alliance of Small Island States—AOSIS: c/o 800 Second Ave, Suite 400D, New York, NY 10017, USA; tel. (212) 599-6196; fax (212) 599-0797; internet www.aosis.org; f. 1990 as an *ad hoc* intergovernmental grouping to focus on the special problems of small islands and low-lying coastal developing states. Mems: 43 island nations, incl. Antigua and Barbuda, the Bahamas, Barbados, Belize, Cuba, Dominica, Grenada, Guyana, Jamaica, Netherlands Antilles, Saint. Kitts and Nevis, Saint. Lucia, Saint. Vincent and the Grenadines, Suriname, Trinidad and Tobago, US Virgin Islands. Chair. TUILOMA NERONI SLADE (Samoa). Publ. *Small Islands, Big Issues.*

Comunidade dos Países de Lingua Portuguesa (Community of Portuguese-Speaking Countries): rua S. Caetano 32, 1200 Lisbon, Portugal; tel. (1) 392-8560; fax (1) 392-8588; f. 1996; aims to produce close political, economic, diplomatic and cultural links between Portuguese-speaking countries and to strengthen the influence of the Lusophone commonwealth within the international community. In May 1999 ministers of defence resolved to establish a CPLP peace-keeping force. Mems: Angola, Brazil, Cape Verde, Guinea-Bissau, Mozambique, Portugal, São Tomé e Príncipe; East Timor has observer status. Exec. Sec. Dr DULCE MARIA PEREIRA (Angola).

International Seabed Authority: 14–20 Port Royal St, Kingston, Jamaica; tel. 922-9105; fax 922-0195; internet www.isa.org.jm; f. Nov. 1994 upon the entry into force of the 1982 United Nations Convention on the Law of the Sea. The Authority is the institute through which states party to the Convention organize and control activities in the international seabed area beyond the limits of national jurisdiction, particularly with a view to administering the resources of that area. Mems: 137 (Dec. 1997). Sec.-Gen. SATYA N. NANDAN (Fiji).

Latin American Parliament (Parlamento Latinoamericano): Avda Auro Soares de Moura Andrade 564, São Paulo, Brazil; tel. (11) 3824-6325; fax (11) 3824-6324; internet www.parlatino.org; f. 1965; permanent democratic institution, representative of all existing political trends within the national legislative bodies of Latin America; aims to promote the movement towards economic, political and cultural integration of the Latin American republics, and to uphold human rights, peace and security. Mems: parliamentarians from 18 Latin American countries. Publs *Acuerdos, Resoluciones de las Asambleas Ordinarias* (annually), *Revista del Parlamento Latinoamericano* (annually).

Non-aligned Movement: c/o Permanent Representative of South Africa to the UN, 333 East 38th St, New York 10016, NY 10017, USA (no permanent secretariat); tel. (212) 213-5583; fax (212) 692-2498; f. 1961 by a meeting of 25 heads of state, aiming to link countries which refused to adhere to the main East-West military and political blocs; co-ordination bureau established in 1973; works for the establishment of a new international economic order, and especially for better terms for countries producing raw materials; maintains special funds for agricultural development, improvement of food production and the financing of buffer stocks; 'South Commission' (q.v.) promotes co-operation between developing countries; seeks changes in the United Nations to give developing countries greater decision-making power; in October 1995 member states urged the USA to lift its economic embargo against Cuba; summit conference held every three years, 12th conference of heads of state and government was held in Durban, South Africa, in 1998. Mems: 113 countries.

Organisation of Eastern Caribbean States—OECS: POB 179, The Morne, Castries, Saint Lucia; tel. 452-2537; fax 453-1628; e-mail oesec@oecs.org; internet www.oecs.org; f. 1981 by the seven states which formerly belonged to the West Indies Associated States (f. 1966). Aims to promote the harmonized development of trade and industry in member states; single market created on 1 January 1988. Principal institutions are: the Authority of Heads of Government (the supreme policy-making body), the Foreign Affairs Committee, the Defence and Security Committee, and the Economic Affairs Committee. There is also an Export Development and Agricultural Diversification Unit—EDADU (based in Dominica). Mems: Antigua and Barbuda, Dominica, Grenada, Montserrat, Saint Christopher and Nevis, Saint Lucia, Saint Vincent and the Grenadines; assoc. mem.: Anguilla, British Virgin Islands. Dir-Gen. SWINBURNE LESTRADE.

Organization of Solidarity of the Peoples of Africa, Asia and Latin America (Organización de Solidaridad de los Pueblos de Africa, Asia y América Latina—OSPAAAL): Apdos 4224 y 6130, Calle C No 670 esq. 29, Vedado, Havana 10400, Cuba; tel. 7-35136; fax 7-33985; e-mail ospaaal@ip.etecsa.cu; f. 1966 at the First Conference of Solidarity of the Peoples of Africa, Asia and Latin America, to unite, co-ordinate and encourage national liberation movements in the three continents, to oppose foreign intervention in the affairs of sovereign states, and to fight against racialism and all forms of racial discrimination. Mems: organizations and individuals in more

than 50 countries. Sec.-Gen. Dr RAMÓN PEZ FERRO. Publ. *Tricontinental* (quarterly).

Rio Group: f. 1987 (as 'Group of Eight') at a meeting in Acapulco, Mexico, of eight Latin American government leaders, who agreed to establish a 'permanent mechanism for joint political action' (other countries subsequently joined—see below). At the ninth presidential summit (Quito, Ecuador, September 1995) a declaration was adopted setting out joint political objectives, including the strengthening of democracy; combating corruption, drugs production and trafficking and 'money laundering'; and the creation of a Latin American and Caribbean free-trade area by 2005 (supporting the efforts of various regional groupings). Opposes US legislation (the 'Helms-Burton' Act), which provides for sanctions against foreign companies that trade with Cuba; also concerned with promoting sustainable development in the region, the elimination of poverty, and economic and financial stability. The Rio Group holds institutionalized ministerial conferences with the European Union (10th meeting held in Chile in March 2001; 11th meeting scheduled to be held in Greece in 2003). Mems: Argentina, Bolivia, Brazil, Chile, Colombia, Ecuador, Mexico, Panama, Paraguay, Peru, Uruguay, Venezuela.

INDUSTRIAL RELATIONS

Caribbean Congress of Labour: NUPW Bldg, Dalkeith Rd, St Michael, Barbados; tel. 429-5517; fax 427-2496; f. 1960 to fight for the recognition of trade union organizations; to build and strengthen the ties between the free trade unions of the Caribbean and the rest of the world; to support the work of the International Confederation of Free Trade Unions; to encourage the formation of national groupings and centres. Mems: 29 unions in 17 countries. Pres. LLOYD GOODLEIGH (Jamaica); Sec.-Treas. KERTIST AUGUSTUS (Dominica).

Central American Confederation of Workers (Confederación Centroamericana de Trabajadores): Apdo 226, 2200 Coronado, San José, Costa Rica; tel. 2290152; fax 2293893; e-mail icaesca@sol.racsa.co.cr; f. 1963. Mems: national confederations in seven countries. Sec.-Gen. ALSIMIRO HERRERA TORRES.

Inter-American Regional Organization of Workers (Organización Regional Interamericana de Trabajadores—ORIT): Edif. de la CTM, Vallarta No 8, 3°, 06470 México, DF, Mexico; tel. (5) 566-7024; fax (5) 592-7329; f. 1951 by the International Confederation of Free Trade Unions, to link and represent democratic labour organizations in the region; sponsors training. Mems: trade unions in 27 countries (including Canada and the USA) with over 40m. individuals. Pres. A. MADARIAGA; Gen. Sec. LUIS A. ANDERSON.

Latin American Confederation of Trade Unions (Central Latinoamericano de Trabajadores—CLAT): Apdo 6681, Caracas 1010A, Venezuela; tel. (2) 720794; fax (2) 720463; e-mail clat@telcel.net.ve; f. 1954; affiliated to the World Confederation of Labour. Mems: over 50 national and regional organizations in Latin America and the Caribbean. Sec.-Gen. JOSÉ EMILIO MASPERO.

Latin American Federation of Agricultural and Food Industry Workers (Federación Latinoamericana de Trabajadores Campesinos y de la Alimentación—FELTACA): Avda Baralt esq. Conde a Padre Cierra, Edif. Bapgel, 4°, Of. 42, Apdo 1422, Caracas 1010A, Venezuela; tel. (2) 864-6153; fax (2) 863-2447; e-mail lasso feltaca@cantv.net; f. 1961 (as Latin American Farmworkers Federation) to represent the interests of agricultural workers and workers in the food and hotel industries in Latin America. Mems: national unions in 28 countries and territories. Sec.-Gen. JOSÉ I. LASSO. Publ. *Boletín Luchemos* (quarterly).

LAW

Inter-American Bar Association (Federación Interamericana de Abogados): 1211 Connecticut Ave, NW, Suite 202,, Washington, DC 20036, USA; tel. (202) 466-5944; fax (202) 466-9546; internet www.uaba.org; f. 1940 to promote the rule of law and to establish and maintain relations between associations and organizations of lawyers in the Americas. Mems: 90 associations and 3,500 individuals in 27 countries. Pres. CAYETANO POVOLO; Sec.-Gen. LOUIS G. FERRAND. Publs *Newsletter* (quarterly), *Conference Proceedings, Membership Directory.*

International Union of Latin Notaries (Unión Internacional del Notariado Latino): Via Locatelli 5, 20124 Milan, Italy; f. 1948 to study and standardize notarial legislation and promote the progress and stability and advancement of the Latin notarial system. Mems: organizations and groups of notaries in 68 African, American, Asian and European countries. Sec. EMANUELE FERRARI. Publ. *Revista Internacional del Notariado* (quarterly).

MEDICINE AND HEALTH

Inter-American Association of Sanitary and Environmental Engineering (Asociación Interamericana de Ingeniería Sanitaria y Ambiental): Rua Nicolau Gagliardi; 354, 05429-010 São Paulo, Brazil; tel. (11) 212-4080; fax (11) 814-2441; e-mail aidis@unisys.com.br; internet www.aidis.org.br; f. 1948 to establish basic and environmental sanitation. Mems: 32 countries. Exec. Dir LUIZ AUGUSTO DE LIMA PONTES. Publs *Revista Ingeniería Sanitaria* (quarterly), *Desafio* (quarterly).

Latin American Association of National Academies of Medicine (Asociación Latinoamericana de Academias Nacionales de Medicina): Col 7 No 60-15, Santafé de Bogotá, Colombia; tel. (1) 2493122; fax (1) 2128670; f. 1967. Mems: 11 national Academies. Pres. Dr PLUTARCO NARANJO (Peru); Sec. Dr ALBERTO CÁRDENAS-ESCOVAR (Colombia).

Latin American Odontological Federation (Federación Odontológica Latinoamericana): c/o Federación Odontológica Colombiana, Calle 71 No 11-10, Of. 1101, Apdo Aéreo 52925, Santafé de Bogotá, Colombia; f. 1917; linked to International Dental Federation. Mems: national organizations in 12 countries. Sec. Dr M. E. VILLEGAS MEJIA.

Pan-American Association of Ophthalmology (Asociación Panamericana de Oftalmología): 1301 South Bowen Rd, Suite 365, Arlington, TX 76013, USA; tel. (817) 265-2831; fax (817) 275-3961; e-mail paao@flash.net; f. 1939 to promote friendship and dissemination of scientific information among the profession throughout the western hemisphere. Holds biennial congress (2001—Buenos Aires, Argentina). Mems: in 39 countries. Pres. Dr PAUL R. LICHTER (Chile); Exec. Dir FRANCISCO MARTINEZ CASTRO (Mexico). Publs *The Pan-American* (2 a year); *El Noticiero* (quarterly).

Pan-American Medical Association (Asociación Médica Panamericana): 745 Fifth Ave, New York, NY 10151, USA: tel. (212) 753-6033; f. 1925; holds inter-American congresses, conducts seminars and grants post graduate scholarships to Latin American physicians. Mems: 6,000 in 30 countries. Sec. FREDERIC C. FENIG.

POSTS AND THE MEDIA

Inter-American Press Association (Sociedad Interamericana de Prensa): Jules Dubois Bldg, 1801 SW 3rd Ave, Miami, FL 33129, USA; tel. (305) 634-2465; fax (305) 635-2272; e-mail info@sipiapa .org; internet www.sipiapa.org; f. 1942 to guard the freedom of the press in the Americas; to promote and maintain the dignity, rights and responsibilities of the profession of journalism; to foster a wider knowledge and greater interchange among the peoples of the Americas. Mems: 1,400. Exec. Dir JULIO F. MUÑOZ. Publ. *IAPA News* (monthly in English and Spanish).

Latin American Catholic Organization for the Cinema and Audiovisuals (Organización Católica Internacional del Cine y del Audiovisual): Apdo Postal 17-21-178, Quito, Ecuador; tel. (2) 548-046; fax (2) 501-658; e-mail ocic-al@seccom.ec; f. 1961 to promote and develop the work of Roman Catholic video- and film-makers. Mems: national associations of producers, video- and film-makers, cinema critics. Exec. Sec. CARLOS CORTÉS.

Latin American Catholic Press Union (Unión Católica Latinoamericana de Prensa): Apdo Postal 17-21-178, Quito, Ecuador; tel. (2) 548-046; fax (2) 501-658; f. 1959 to co-ordinate, promote and improve the Roman Catholic press in Latin America. Mems: national groups and local associations in most Latin American countries. Pres. ISMAR DE OLIVEIRA SOARES (Brazil); Exec. Sec. CARLOS EDUARDO CORTÉS (Colombia).

Latin American Catholic Radio and Television Association (Asociación Católica Latinoamericana para la Radio, la TV y los Medios Afines): Apdo Postal 17-21-178, Quito, Ecuador; tel. (2) 548-046; fax (2) 501-658; e-mail scc@seccom.ecx.ec; f. 1957 to promote activities in radio, TV and similar media in Latin America. Mems: national associations of Roman Catholic radio and TV stations, and individuals engaged in radio and TV work in 19 countries. Exec. Sec. CARLOS CORTÉS.

Postal Union of the Americas, Spain and Portugal (Unión Postal de las Américas, España y Portugal): Calle Cebollatí 1468/70, 1°, Casilla 20.042, Montevideo, Uruguay; tel. (2) 4000070; fax (2) 405046; internet www.upaepadinet.com.uy; f. 1911 to extend, facilitate and study the postal relationships of member countries. Mems: 27 countries. Sec.-Gen. MARIO FELMER KLENNER (Chile).

RELIGION AND WELFARE

Caribbean Conference of Churches: POB 616, Bridgetown, Barbados; tel. 427-2681; fax 429-2075; e-mail cccbdos@cariaccess.com; f. 1973; holds Assembly every five years; conducts study and research programmes and supports education and economic development. Mems: 34 churches in 37 countries and territories. Gen. Sec. GERARD GRANADO.

Inter-American Conference on Social Security (Conferencia Interamericana de Seguridad Social): Calle San Ramón s/n esq. Avda San Jerónimo, Unidad Independencia, Col. San Jerónimo Lídice, Deleg. Magdalena Contreras, CP 10100 México, DF, Mexico; tel. (5) 595-0177; fax (5) 683-8524; e-mail ciss@data.net.mx; internet www.ciss.org.mx; f. 1942 to facilitate and develop co-operation between social security administrations and institutions in the American states; main institutes comprise the General Assembly, the Permanent Inter-American Committee on Social Security, the

secretariat, six American Commissions of Social Security and the Inter-American Center for Social Security Studies; 17th General Assembly, 1995. Mems: governments and social security institutions in 38 countries. Pres. Dr SANTIAGO LEVY ALGAZI (Mexico); Sec.-Gen. Dr JOSÉ LUIS STEIN VELASCO (Mexico) (acting). Dir of the Interamerican Center for Social Security Studies Dr LUIS JOSÉ MARTÍNEZ VILLALBA (Uruguay). Publs *Social Security Journal / Seguridad Social* (every 2 months), monographic series, studies series.

Latin American and Caribbean Confederation of Young Men's Christian Associations (Confederación Latinoamericana y del Caribe de Asociaciones Cristianas de Jóvenes): Culpina 272, 1406 Buenos Aires, Argentina; tel. (1) 637-4727; fax (1) 637-4867; e-mail clacj@wamani.apc.org; f. 1914 to unite the Young Men's Christian Associations of the continent; to secure the more effective accomplishment of its aims, which are the moral, spiritual, intellectual, social and physical development of young men; to strengthen the work of the Associations and to sponsor the establishment of new Associations. Mems: affiliated YMCAs in 25 countries, with over 350,000 individuals. Pres. GERARDO VITUREIRA (Uruguay); Gen. Sec. NORBERTO RODRÍGUEZ (Argentina). Publs *Artículos Técnicos, Revista Trimestral, Carta Abierta, Informes Internacionales*.

Latin American Council of Churches (Consejo Latinoamericano de Iglesias—CLAI): Casilla 17-08-8522, Calle Inglaterra 943 y Mariana de Jesús, Quito, Ecuador; tel. and fax (2) 553996; e-mail israel@clai.ecuanex.net.ec; f. 1982. Mems: 147 churches in 19 countries, and nine associated organizations. Gen. Sec. Rev. ISAAEL BATISTA.

Latin American Episcopal Council (Consejo Episcopal Latinoamericano): Apdo Aéreos 5278 y 51086, Santafé de Bogotá, Colombia; tel. (1) 612-1620; fax (1) 612-1929; f. 1955 to study the problems of the Roman Catholic Church in Latin America; to co-ordinate Church activities. Mems: the Episcopal Conferences of Central and South America and the Caribbean. Pres. Archbishop OSCAR ANDRÉS RODRÍGUEZ MARADIAGA (Honduras). Publ. *CELAM* (6 a year).

TOURISM

Caribbean Tourism Organization: Sir Frank Walcott Bldg, 2nd Floor, Culloden Farm Complex, St Michael, Barbados; tel. 427-5242; fax 429-3065; e-mail ctobar@caribsurf.com; f. 1989, by merger of Caribbean Tourism Association (f. 1951) and Caribbean Tourism Research and Development Centre (f. 1974); aims to encourage and assist development in the Caribbean region through tourism; organizes annual Caribbean Tourism Conference, Sustainable Tourism Development Conference and Tourism Investment Conference; conducts training and other workshops on request. Mems: 33 Caribbean governments and 400 allied mems. Sec.-Gen. JEAN HOLDER. Publs *Caribbean Tourism Statistical News* (quarterly), *Caribbean Tourism Statistical Report* (annually).

Latin American Confederation of Tourist Organizations (Confederación de Organizaciones Turísticas de la América Latina—COTAL): Viamonte 640, 8°, 1053 Buenos Aires, Argentina; tel. (11) 4322-4003; fax (11) 4393-5696; e-mail cotal@cscom.com.ar; f. 1957 to link Latin American national associations of travel agents and their members with other tourist bodies around the world. Mems: in 21 countries. Pres. FERNANDO SOLER. Publ. *Revista COTAL* (every 2 months).

TRADE AND INDUSTRY

Cairns Group: c/o Department of Foreign Affairs and Trade, GPO Box 12, Canberra, ACT 2601, Australia; tel. (2) 6263-2222; fax (2) 6261-3111; internet www.dfat.gov.au/trade/negotiations/ cairns_group/index.html; f. 1986 by major agricultural exporting countries, aiming to bring about reforms in international agricultural trade, including reductions in export subsidies, in barriers to access and in internal support measures; represents members' interests in WTO negotiations. Mems: Argentina, Australia, Bolivia, Brazil, Canada, Chile, Colombia, Costa Rica, Fiji, Guatemala, Indonesia, Malaysia, New Zealand, Paraguay, Philippines, South Africa, Thailand, Uruguay. Chair. MARK VAILE.

Caribbean Association of Industry and Commerce: POB 442, Trinidad Hilton, Room 351, Lady Young Rd, St Ann's, Trinidad and Tobago; tel. (868) 623-4830; fax (868) 623-6116; e-mail caic@trinidad.net; internet www.trinidad.net/caic; f. 1955; aims to increase levels of employment, income, productivity and economic growth in the region. Mems: national chambers of commerce and industrial asscns in 20 countries. Exec. Dir FELIPE NAGUERA. Publs *CAIC News* (2 a month), *CAIC Speaks* (monthly), *CAIC Times* (quarterly), *Business Wave* (6 a year).

Inter-American Commercial Arbitration Commission (Comisión Interamericana de Arbitraje Comercial): OAS Administration Bldg, Room 211, 19th and Constitution Ave, NW, Washington, DC 20006, USA; tel. (202) 458-3249; fax (202) 458-3293; f. 1934 to establish an inter-American system of arbitration for the settlement of commercial disputes by means of conciliation, mediation and arbitration. Mems: national committees, commercial firms and individuals in 22 countries. Dir-Gen. ADRIANA POLANIA POLANIA.

Latin American Association of Pharmaceutical Industries (Asociación Latinoamericana de Industrias Farmaceuticas—ALIFAR): Acoyte 520, 1405 Buenos Aires, Argentina; tel. and fax (1) 4903-4440; e-mail juridico@ciifa.com.ar; f. 1980. Mems: about 400 enterprises in 15 countries. Sec.-Gen. RUBÉN ABETE; Exec. Sec. MIRTA LEVIS.

Latin American Energy Organization (Organización Latino-americana de Energía—OLADE): Edif. OLADE, Av. Mariscal Antonio José de Sucre N58-63 y Fernández Salvador, POB 17-11-6413, Quito, Ecuador; tel. (2) 598-122; fax (2) 539-684; e-mail oladel@olade.org.ec; f. 1973 to act as an instrument of co-operation in using and conserving the energy resources of the region; ministers responsible for energy of the member states meet annually to decide policy; OLADE conducts programmes aiming to integrate the energy sector into overall economic and development planning in the region; runs the Energy-Economic Information System. Mems: 26 Latin American and Caribbean countries. Exec. Sec. LUIZ A. M. DA FON-SECA. Publ. *Energy Magazine*.

Latin American Iron and Steel Institute (Instituto Latino-americano del Fierro y el Acero): Benjamin 2944, 5°, Santiago 9, Chile; tel. (2) 2330545; fax (2) 2330768; e-mail ilafa@entelchile.net; f. 1959 to help achieve the harmonious development of iron and steel production, manufacture and marketing in Latin America; conducts economic surveys on the steel sector; organizes technical conventions and meetings; disseminates industrial processes suited to regional conditions; prepares and maintains statistics on production, end uses, prices, etc., of raw materials and steel products within this area. Mems: 74; associate mems: 65; hon. mems: 27. Sec.-Gen. ANÍBAL GÓMEZ. Publs *Acero Latinoamericana* (every 2 months), *Steel Market Bulletin* (every 2 months), various technical and economic studies and reports.

Organization of the Petroleum Exporting Countries—OPEC: 1020 Vienna, Obere Donaustrasse 93, Austria; tel. (1) 211-12; fax (1) 214-98-27; e-mail prid@opec.org; internet www.opec.org; f. 1960 to unify and co-ordinate members' petroleum policies and to safe-guard their interests generally; holds regular conferences of member countries to set reference prices and production levels; conducts research in energy studies, economics and finance; provides data services and news services covering petroleum and energy issues. The OPEC Fund for International Development makes loans and grants to developing countries. Mems: Algeria, Indonesia, Iran, Iraq, Kuwait, Libya, Nigeria, Qatar, Saudi Arabia, United Arab Emirates, Venezuela. Sec.-Gen. ALI RODRÍGUEZ ARAQUE (Venezuela). Publs *OPEC Bulletin* (monthly), *OPEC Review* (quarterly), *Annual Report, Annual Statistical Bulletin*.

Regional Association of Oil and Natural Gas Companies in Latin America and the Caribbean (Asociación Regional de Empresas de Petróleo y Gas Natural en America Latina y el Caribe—ARPEL): Javier de Viana 2345, 11200 Montevideo, Uruguay; tel. (2) 400-6993; fax (2) 400-9207; e-mail arpel@adinet.com.uy; f. 1965 as the Mutual Assistance of the Latin American Oil Companies; aims to initiate and implement activities for the development of the oil and natural gas industry in Latin America and the Caribbean; promotes the expansion of business opportunities and the improvement of the competitive advantages of its members; promotes guidelines in support of competition in the sector; and supports the efficient and sustainable exploitation of hydrocarbon resources and the supply of products and services. Works in co-operation with international organizations, governments, regulatory agencies, technical institutions, universities and non-governmental organizations. Mems: enterprises in 22 countries. Sec.-Gen. ANDRÉS TIERNO ABREU. Publ. *ARPEL Comunica*.

TRANSPORT

Pan American Railway Congress Association (Asociación del Congreso Panamericano de Ferrocarriles): Avda 9 de Julio 1925, 13°, 1332 Buenos Aires, Argentina; tel. (11) 4381-4625; fax (11) 4814-1823; e-mail acpf@nat.com.ar; f. 1907; present title adopted 1941; aims to promote the development and progress of railways in the American continent; holds Congress every three years. Mems: government representatives, railway enterprises and individuals in 20 countries. Pres. JUAN CARLOS DE MARCHI (Argentina); Gen. Sec. LUIS V. DONZELLI (Argentina). Publ. *Boletín ACPF* (5 a year).

MAJOR COMMODITIES OF LATIN AMERICA

Note: For each of the commodities in this section, there are generally two statistical tables: one relating to recent levels of production, and one indicating recent trends in prices. Each production table shows estimates of output for the world and for Latin America. In addition, the table lists the main Latin American producing countries and, for comparison, the leading producers from outside the region. In most cases, the table referring to prices provides indexes of export prices, calculated in US dollars. The index for each commodity is based on specific price quotations for representative grades of that commodity in countries that are major traders (excluding countries of Eastern Europe and the former USSR).

Aluminium and Bauxite

Aluminium is the most abundant metallic element in the earth's crust, comprising about 8% of the total. However, it is much less widely used than steel, despite having about the same strength and only half of the weight. Aluminium has important applications as a metal because of its lightness, ease of fabrication and other desirable properties. Other products of alumina (aluminium oxide) are materials in refractories, abrasives, glass manufacture, other ceramic products, catalysts and absorbers. Alumina hydrates are used for the production of aluminium chemicals, fire retardant in carpet backing, and industrial fillers in plastics and related products.

The major markets for aluminium are in transportation, building and construction, electrical machinery and equipment, consumer durables and the packaging industry, which in the late 1990s accounted for about 20% of all aluminium use. Although the production of aluminium is energy-intensive, its light weight results in a net saving, particularly in the transportation industry. About one-quarter of aluminium output is consumed in the manufacture of transport equipment, particularly road motor vehicles and components, where the metal is increasingly being used as a substitute for steel. In the early 1990s steel substitution accounted for about 16% of world aluminium consumption, and it has been forecast that aluminium demand by the motor vehicle industry alone could more than double, to exceed 5.7m. tons in 2010, from around 2.4m. tons in 1990. Aluminium is of great value to the aerospace industry for its weight-saving characteristics and its low cost relative to alternative materials. Aluminium-lithium alloys command considerable potential for use in this sector, although the traditional dominance of aluminium in the aerospace sector was under challenge during the 1990s from 'composites' such as carbon-epoxy, a fusion of carbon fibres and hardened resins, whose lightness and durability can exceed that of many aluminium alloys.

World markets for finished and semi-finished aluminium products are dominated by six Western producers—Alcan (Canada), Alcoa, Reynolds, Kaiser (all USA), Pechiney (France) and algroup (Switzerland). Proposals for a merger between Alcan, algroup and Pechiney, and between Alcoa and Reynolds, were announced in August 1999. However, the proposed terms of the Pechiney-Alcan-algroup merger encountered opposition from the European Commission, on the grounds that the combined grouping could restrict market competition and adversely affect the interests of consumers. The tripartite merger plan was abandoned in April 2000, although the terms of a merger between Alcan and algroup were announced in June. The implications of the proposed amalgamation of Alcoa and Reynolds were still under consideration in mid-2000 by the European Commission and the US Government. The level of dominance of these major producers has, however, been reduced in recent years by a significant geographical shift in the location of alumina and aluminium production to areas where cheap power is available, such as Australia, Brazil, Norway, Canada and Venezuela. The Gulf states of Bahrain and Dubai, with the advantage of low energy costs, also produce primary aluminium. Since the mid-1990s Russia has also become a significant force in the world aluminium market (see below), and in April 2000 the country's three principal producers announced their intention to combine into a single group representing about 75% of Russian aluminium production and approximately 10% of world output.

Bauxite is the principal aluminium ore, but nepheline syenite, kaolin, shale, anorthosite and alunite are all potential alternative sources of alumina, although not currently economic to process. Of all bauxite mined, approximately 85% is converted to alumina (Al_2O_3) for the production of aluminium metal. The developing countries, in which 70% of known bauxite reserves are located, supply 45% of the ore required. The industry is structured in three stages: bauxite mining, alumina refining and smelting. While the high degree of 'vertical integration' (i.e., the control of successive stages of production) in the industry means that a significant proportion of trade in bauxite and alumina is in the form of intra-company transfers, and the increasing tendency to site alumina refineries near to bauxite deposits has resulted in a shrinking bauxite trade, there is a growing free market in alumina, catering for the needs of the increasing number of independent (i.e. non-integrated) smelters.

The alumina is separated from the ore by the Bayer process. After mining, bauxite is fed to process directly if mine-run material is adequate (as in Jamaica) or is crushed and beneficiated. Where the ore 'as mined' presents handling problems, or weight reduction is desirable, it may be dried prior to shipment.

Production of Bauxite (crude ore, '000 metric tons)

	1998	1999*
World total (excl. USA)	122,000	127,000
Latin America	32,433*	36,061
Latin American producers		
Brazil	11,961	12,880
Guyana†	2,600*	3,300
Jamaica†	12,646	11,688
Suriname	4,000*	4,000
Venezuela	4,826	4,193
Other leading producers		
Australia	44,553	48,416
China, People's Repub. . . .	8,200*	8,500
Guinea†	15,100	15,000
India	6,102	6,200
Kazakhstan	3,437	3,607
Russia	3,450*	3,750

* Estimated production.
† Dried equivalent of crude ore.
Source: US Geological Survey.

At the alumina plant the ore is slurried with spent-liquor directly, if the soft Caribbean type is used, or, in the case of other types, it is ball-milled to reduce it to a size which will facilitate the extraction of the alumina. The bauxite slurry is then digested with caustic soda to extract the alumina from the ore while leaving the impurities as an insoluble residue. The digest conditions depend on the aluminium minerals in the ore and the impurities. The liquor, with the dissolved alumina, is then separated from the insoluble impurities by combinations of sedimentation, decantation and filtration, and the residue is washed to minimize the soda losses. The clarified liquor is concentrated and the alumina precipitated by seeding with hydrate. The precipitated alumina is then filtered, washed and calcined to produce alumina. The ratio of bauxite to alumina is approximately 1.95:1.

The smelting of the aluminium is generally by electrolysis in molten cryolite. Because of the high consumption of electricity by the smelting process, alumina is usually smelted in areas where low-cost electricity is available. However, most of the electricity now used in primary smelting in the Western world is generated by hydroelectricity—a renewable energy source.

The recycling of aluminium is economically, as well as environmentally, desirable, as the process uses only 5% of the electricity required to produce a similar quantity of primary aluminium. Aluminium recycled from scrap currently accounts for about 40% of the total aluminium supply in the USA and for about 30% of Western European consumption. With the added impetus of environmental concerns, considerable growth world-wide in the recycling of used beverage cans (UBC) was forecast for the 1990s. In the mid-1990s, according to aluminium industry estimates, the recycling rate of UBC amounted to at least 55% world-wide.

Total world output of primary aluminium in 1999 was estimated at 23.1m. tons, of which Latin American producers accounted for about 2.1m. tons. The USA normally accounts for about one-third of total aluminium consumption (excluding communist and former communist countries). Although it is the world's principal producing country (accounting for about 16% of global output of primary aluminium in 1999), the USA does not produce a surplus of ingots, and limits production to satisfy its domestic requirements for fabrication, while importing the remainder from low-cost producers elsewhere.

In 1998 Brazil was the world's fourth largest producer of bauxite (after Australia, Guinea and Jamaica). The country possesses extensive bauxite reserves in Minas Gerais state and in the Amazon region, where deposits of some 4,600m. tons have been identified. The country's huge Albrás aluminium plant, which began operations in early 1986, achieved its installed production capacity of 150,000 tons per year in October. The plant was largely financed by Japan (which takes a share of its output). In mid-1999 work was completed on the expansion of the Pinda rolling-mill in Pindamonhangaba. The US $370m. expansion, which also included the largest recycling plant in South America, led to an increase in production from 120,000 tons per year to 280,000 tons per year. Brazil's annual output of primary aluminium was maintained at 1.2m. tons during 1992–99. However, almost all of the country's smelters (in particular, the massive Alumar plant) are the subject of expansion proposals, and production could increase rapidly during the next few years, assuming a recovery in world prices and provided that the costs of energy supplies can be contained.

Jamaica was the world's third largest producer of bauxite in 1998. A production levy on the Jamaican bauxite industry, which has operated since 1974, provides an important source of government revenue. Production capacity was increased in the second half of the 1980s in order to supply the strategic mineral stockpiles of both the USA and the USSR. However, as a result of depressed conditions in the international market (see below), sales of bauxite and alumina accounted for 51% of total export earnings in 1998, and 55% in 1999, compared with 63% in 1990. Measures to revitalize Jamaica's bauxite and alumina industry were announced in July 1998 by representatives of the Government, industry and the trade unions. Output of bauxite in 1998 was 12.7m. tons, its highest level for 25 years, but production declined to 11.7m. tons in 1999, owing to the closure of a US refinery that used Jamaican ore. Plans to expand bauxite production and improve efficiency were under discussion in 2000.

The economy of Suriname relies heavily on the mining and export of bauxite. In 1993 bauxite, alumina and aluminium accounted for 91.5% of Suriname's annual export earnings, whereas in 1978 the corresponding proportion had been 83.8%. In 1998 exports of alumina and aluminium represented an estimated 80.5% of export receipts. Guerrilla activity disrupted the industry in the 1980s and 1990s, and the sector was also affected by adverse price movements in the international market.

Venezuela's aluminium industry achieved rapid growth in the 1980s, as a result of the availability of raw materials and cheap hydroelectric power. Aluminium production, based on imported alumina, subsequently overtook iron ore to become Venezuela's main export industry after petroleum. The exploitation of bauxite reserves of 500m. tons were expected to enable Venezuela to produce 3.4m.–4.0m. tons of high-grade ore annually from mines in Bolívar State when output reached full capacity in 1992, by which time Venezuelan aluminium plants were to be supplied solely with local bauxite. According to the US Geological Survey, Venezuela's aluminium production increased from 561,000 tons in 1992 to a record 634,000 tons in 1997, but subsequently decreased, to 585,000 tons in 1998 and 570,000 tons in 1999. Aluminium's contribution to the country's export revenue was 5.2% in 1995, 3.3% in 1996 and 3.4% in 1997. In 1992 Venezuela's production of bauxite ore exceeded 1m. tons. The subsequent expansion of the bauxite sector industry has been rapid; output advanced to 2.5m. tons in 1993, and rose to 5.1m. tons per year in 1997 and 1998. In 2000 Venezuela's state-owned aluminium complex was reported to be undergoing further preparation for transfer to the private sector, following unsuccessful attempts in 1998 and 1999 to dispose of the Government's 70% holding by auction.

Guyana's nationalized bauxite production industry is a major source of the country's export revenue, providing 15.0% of total domestic exports in 1997. The state-owned Guyana Mining Enterprise Ltd (Guymine) implemented a programme of rehabilitation for the industry, which was adversely affected in the mid-1980s, and again in the early 1990s, by depressed conditions for bauxite on the world market (see below). The transfer of Guymine to the private sector commenced in 1996 and was proceeding in 2000.

In November 1998 a preliminary agreement was signed for the construction of a primary aluminium smelter, with an eventual capacity of 474,000 tons per year, at Point Lisas, Trinidad. It was envisaged that this development, with a projected cost of US $1,500m., would proceed in two stages. The first phase, with an annual capacity of 237,000 tons, was to be completed in 2002. Its metal output would, according to the proposals, be exported to Europe and North America. However, in early 1999, with international prices of aluminium at their lowest for about five years (see below), plans for the Trinidad smelter project were postponed.

Although world demand for aluminium advanced by an average of 3% annually from the late 1980s until 1994 (see below), industrial recession began, in 1990, to create conditions of over-supply. Despite the implementation of capacity reductions at an annual rate of 10% by the major Western producers, stock levels began to accumulate. The supply problem was exacerbated by a rapid rise, beginning in 1991, of exports by the USSR and its successor states, which had begun to accumulate substantial stocks of aluminium as a consequence of the collapse of the Soviet arms industry. The requirements of these countries for foreign exchange to restructure their economies led to a rapid acceleration in low-cost exports of high-grade aluminium to Western markets. These sales caused considerable dislocation of the market and involved the major Western producers in heavy financial losses. Producing members of the European Community (EC, now the European Union—EU) were particularly severely affected, and in August 1993 the EC imposed quota arrangements, under which aluminium imports from the former USSR were to be cut by 50% for an initial three-month period, while efforts were made to negotiate an agreement that would reduce the flow of low-price imports and achieve a reduction in aluminium stocks (by then estimated to total 4.5m. tons world-wide).

These negotiations, which involved the EC, the USA, Canada, Norway, Australia and Russia (but in which the minor producers, Brazil, the Gulf states, Venezuela and Ukraine were not invited to take part), began in October 1993. Initially, the negotiations made little progress, and in November the market price of high-grade aluminium ingots fell to an 11-year 'low'. Following further meetings in January 1994, however, a Memorandum of Understanding (MOU) was finalized on a plan whereby Russia was to 'restructure' its aluminium industry and reduce its output by 500,000 tons annually. By March the major Western producers had agreed to reduce annual production by about 1.2m. tons over a maximum period of two years. Additionally, Russia was to receive US $2,000m. in loan guarantees. The MOU provided for participants to monitor world aluminium supplies and prices on a regular basis. In March the EU quota was terminated. By July the world price had recovered by about 50% on the November 1993 level.

The successful operation of the MOU, combined with a strong recovery in world aluminium demand, led to the progressive reduction of stock levels and to a concurrent recovery in market prices during 1994 and 1995. Consumption in the Western industrialized countries and Japan rose by an estimated 10.3% to 17.3m. tons, representing the highest rate of annual growth since 1983. This recovery was attributed mainly to a revival in demand from the motor vehicle sector in EU countries and the USA, and to an intensified programme of public works construction in Japan. Increased levels of demand were also reported in China, and in the less industrialized countries of the South and East Asia region. Demand in the industrialized countries advanced by 11% in 1994, and by 2.2% in 1995.

Levels of world aluminium stocks were progressively reduced during 1994, and by late 1995 it was expected that the continuing fall in stock levels could enable Western smelters to resume full capacity operation during 1996. In May stock levels were reported to have fallen to their lowest level since March 1993, and exports of aluminium from Russia, totalling 2m. tons annually, were viewed as essential to the maintenance of Western supplies. Meanwhile, progress continued to be made in arrangements under the MOU for the modernization of Russian smelters and their eventual integration into the world aluminium industry. International demand for aluminium rose by 0.2% in 1995 and by 0.8% in 1996. In 1997 aluminium consumption by industrialized countries advanced by an estimated 5.4%. This growth in demand was satisfied by increased primary aluminium production, combined with sustained reductions in world levels of primary aluminium stocks. Demand in 1998, however, was adversely affected by the economic crisis in East Asia, and consumption of aluminium in established market economy countries (EMEC) rose by only 0.1%: the lowest growth in aluminium demand since 1982. However, consumption in the EMEC area increased by an estimated 3.9% in 1999, with demand for aluminium rising strongly in the USA and in much of Asia. Compared with 1998, growth in consumption was, however, reduced in Europe and Latin America. World-wide, the fastest-growing sector of aluminium demand in 1999 was the transport industry (the largest market for the metal), with consumption rising by about 9%. Demand was expected to remain strong in 2000, with sales of motor vehicles predicted to continue rising, while world aluminium output was forecast to increase, as additional smelter capacity became available. Production of primary aluminium in the first six months of 2000 was about 4% above the level for the corresponding period in 1999.

Export Price Index for Aluminium (base: 1980 = 100)

	Average	Highest month(s)	Lowest month(s)
1990	93		
1995	104		
1998	77	85 (Jan.)	72 (Dec.)
1999	77	86 (Dec.)	68 (Feb., March)
2000	88	95 (Jan., Feb.)	83 (March, April)

In November 1993 the price of high-grade aluminium (minimum purity 99.7%) on the London Metal Exchange (LME) was quoted at US $1,023.5 (£691) per metric ton, its lowest level for about eight years. In July 1994 the London price of aluminium advanced to $1,529.5 (£981) per ton, despite a steady accumulation in LME stocks of aluminium, which rose to a series of record levels , increasing from 1.9m. tons at mid-1993 to 2.7m tons in June 1994. In November 1994,

when these holdings had declined to less than 1.9m. tons, aluminium was traded at $1,987.5 (£1,269) per ton.

In January 1995 the LME aluminium price rose to US $2,149.5 (£1,346) per ton, its highest level since 1990. The price of aluminium was reduced to $1,715.5 (£1,085) per ton in May 1995, but recovered to $1,945 (£1,219) in July. It retreated to $1,609.5 (£1,021) per ton in October. Meanwhile, on 1 May the LME's holdings of aluminium were below 1m. tons for the first time since January 1992. In October 1995 these stocks stood at 523,175 tons, their lowest level for more than four years and only 19.7% of the June 1994 peak. Thereafter, stock levels moved generally higher, reaching 970,275 tons in October 1996. During that month the London price of alminium fell to $1,287 (£823) per ton, but later in the year it exceeded $1,500.

In March 1997 the London price of aluminium reached US $1,665.5 (£1,030) per ton. This was the highest aluminium price recorded in the first half of the year, despite a steady decline in LME stocks of the metal. After falling to less than $1,550 per ton, the London price of aluminium rose in August to $1,787.5 (£1,126). In that month the LME's aluminium holdings were reduced to 620,475 tons, but in October they reached 744,250 tons. Stocks subsequently decreased, but at the end of December the metal's price was $1,503.5 (£914) per ton, close to its lowest for the year. The average price of aluminium on the LME in 1997 was 72.5 US cents per lb, compared with 68.3 cents per lb in 1996 and 81.9 cents per lb in 1995.

The decline in aluminium stocks continued during the early months of 1998, but this had no major impact on prices, owing partly to forecasts of long-term oversupply. In early May the LME's holdings stood at 511,225 tons, but later that month the price of aluminium fell to less than US $1,350 per ton. In June LME stocks increased to more than 550,000 tons, and in early July the price of the metal was reduced to $1,263.5 (£768) per ton. In early September the LME's holdings decreased to about 452,000 tons (their lowest level since July 1991), and the aluminium price recovered to $1,409.5 (£840) per ton. However, the market remained depressed by a reduction in demand from some consuming countries in Asia, affected by the economic downturn, and in December 1998 the London price of aluminium declined to $1,222 (£725) per ton. For the year as a whole, the average price was 61.6 US cents per lb.

During the first quarter of 1999 the aluminium market continued to be oversupplied, and in March the London price of the metal fell to US $1,139 (£708) per ton: its lowest level, in terms of US currency, since early 1994. Later that month the LME's stocks of aluminium rose to 821,650 tons. By the end of July 1999 these holdings had been reduced to 736,950 tons, and the price of aluminium had meanwhile recovered to $1,433.5 (£902) per ton. Stock levels subsequently rose, but, following the announcement in August of proposed cost-cutting mergers among major producers (see above), the aluminium price continued to increase, reaching $1,626.5 (£1,009) per ton at the end of the year. The steady rise was also attributable to a sharp increase in the price of alumina in the second half of the year. Following an explosion at (and subsequent closure of) a US alumina refinery in July, the price of the material advanced from $160 per ton in that month to $400 per ton (its highest level for 10 years) in December. However, the average LME price of aluminium for the year (61.7 US cents per lb) was almost unchanged from the 1998 level.

With alumina remaining in short supply, prices of aluminium continued to rise during the opening weeks of 2000, and in early February the London quotation reached US $1,743.5 (£1,079) per ton: its highest level for more than two years. However, the LME's stocks of the metal also increased, reaching 868,625 tons later that month. The London price of aluminium declined to $1,413 (£891) per ton in April, but recovered to $1,599 (£1,070) in July. Throughout this period there was a steady decrease in LME holdings, which were reduced to less than 700,000 tons in April, under 600,000 tons in May and below 500,000 tons in July. At the end of July aluminium stocks were 461,975 tons: only 53% of the level reached in February.

Almost all the producers of primary aluminium outside Communist or former Communist countries are members of the International Primary Aluminium Instititute (IPAI), based in London. The IPAI's membership comprises 39 companies, operating primary aluminium smelters in 24 countries, collectively representing substantially all of the Western countries' production of primary aluminium. In 1993 the International Aluminium Committee was formed to represent most of the aluminium smelters in the former USSR.

Banana (*Musa sapientum*)

Although it is often mistakenly termed a 'tree', the banana plant is, in fact, a giant herb. It grows to a height of 3 m–9 m (10 ft–30 ft) and bears leaves which are very long and broad. The stem of the plant is formed by the overlapping bases of the leaves above. Bananas belong to the genus *Musa* but the cultivated varieties are barren hybrid forms which cannot, therefore, be assigned specific botanical names. These banana hybrids, producing edible seedless fruits, are now grown throughout the tropics, but originally diversified naturally or were developed by humans in prehistoric times from wild bananas which grow in Indo-China. The plantain hybrid has grown in central Africa for thousands of years, and traders and explorers gradually spread this and other varieties to Asia Minor and east Africa; the Spanish and Portuguese introduced them to west Africa and took them across the Atlantic to the Caribbean islands and the American continent. However, the varieties which are now most commonly traded internationally were not introduced to the New World until the 19th century.

The banana is propagated by the planting of suckers or shoots growing from the rhizome, which is left in the ground after the flowering stem, having produced its fruit, has died and been cut down. Less than one year after planting, a flowering stem begins to emerge from the tip of the plant. As it grows, the stem bends and hangs downwards. The barren male flowers which grow at the end of the stem eventually wither and fall off. The seedless banana fruits develop, without fertilization, from the clusters of female flowers further up the stem. Each stem usually bears between nine and 12 'hands' of fruit, each hand comprising 12–16 fruits. Before it is ripe, the skin of the banana fruit is green, turning yellow as it ripens. To obtain edible white flesh, the skin is peeled back. The process of fruiting and propagation can repeat itself indefinitely. In commercial cultivation the productive life of a banana field is usually limited to between five and 20 years before it is replanted, although small producers frequently allow their plants to continue fruiting for up to 60 years. Banana plantations are vulnerable to disease and to severe weather (particularly tropical storms), but the banana plant is fast-growing, and a replanted field can be ready to produce again within a year, though at a high cost.

Production of Bananas ('000 metric tons, excluding plantains)

	1999	2000
World total	62,693	64,627
Latin America	23,889	25,157
Leading Latin American producers		
Brazil	5,528	6,339
Colombia	1,570	1,570*
Costa Rica	2,700*	2,700*
Ecuador	6,392	6,816
Guatemala	733	733*
Honduras	861	453
Mexico‡	1,737	1,802
Panama	750*	807
Venezuela	1,000	1,000*
Other leading producers		
Burundi‡	1,511	1,514
China, People's Repub. . . .	4,407	4,813†
India‡	13,900†	13,900*
Indonesia	3,377	3,377*
Philippines‡	3,869	4,156
Thailand	1,720*	1,720*

* FAO estimate.
† Unofficial figure.
‡ Including plantains.

The varieties of dessert banana on which international trade is predominantly based, and which are eaten raw owing to their high sugar content (17%–19%), comprise only a few of the many varieties which are grown. Many types of sweet banana, unsuitable for export, are consumed locally. Apart from the trade in fresh, sweet bananas, the fruit has few commercial uses, although there is a small industry in dried bananas and banana flour. The numerous high-starch varieties with a lower sugar content, which are not eaten in their raw state, are used in cooking, mostly in the producing areas. Such varieties are picked when their flesh is unripe, although they are occasionally of a type which would become sweet if left to ripen. Cooking bananas, sometimes called 'plantains' (though this term is also applied to types of dessert banana in some countries), form the staple diet of millions of east Africans. Bananas can also be used for making beer, and in east Africa special varieties are cultivated for that purpose. Advances in production methods, packaging, storage and transport (containerization) have made bananas available world-wide. Although international trade is principally in the sweet dessert fruit, this type comprises less than one-fifth of total annual world banana production.

The banana was introduced into Latin America and the Caribbean by the Spanish and the Portuguese during the 16th century. The expansion of the banana industry in the small Latin American (so-called 'green' or 'banana') republics between 1880 and 1910 had a decisive effect in establishing this region as the centre of the world banana trade. Favourable soil and climatic conditions, combined with the ease of access around the Caribbean and to a major market in the USA, were major factors in the initial commercial success of the Latin American banana industry. Although advances in storage and transportation made the US market more accessible to producers in other areas, they also made available an equally important market in Europe (see below). Owing to considerably lower production costs than in other producing areas, bananas from Central and South America command the major portion of the world export market. It is there that the large multinational companies (notably United Brands, Standard Fruit and Del Monte) which dominate the world banana market are established.

Bananas are grown in most Latin American countries. Brazil is the region's leading producer of bananas, although they contribute only a small proportion of the country's total export earnings. The banana industry is of far greater economic importance in Ecuador and Honduras, where bananas are the leading cash crop, and in Colombia and Costa Rica, where they vie with coffee as the principal source of export revenue. Ecuador, the world's third largest producer of bananas (after India and Brazil), is the leading exporter, with shipments of 4.0m. metric tons (valued at US $1,070m.) in 1998. In that year bananas accounted for 25.8% of Ecuador's export earnings. Banana shipments contribute significantly to the export receipts of Honduras (providing 12.9% of the total in 1998) and Costa Rica (9% in 2000). In October 1998, however, about 70% of the Honduran crop was destroyed by 'Hurricane Mitch', necessitating extensive replanting during 1999. In that year bananas contributed only an estimated 3.0% of Honduran export revenue. Among other Latin American countries where bananas are a major export are Panama (21.1% in 1999, excluding trade of the Colón Free Zone) and Belize (16.4% in 1999). Bananas are also a useful source of foreign exchange in Colombia (where they provided 4.4% of total export earnings in 1998), Guatemala (7.5% in 1998) and Nicaragua (4.0% in 1998). The territories most dependent on bananas for export receipts are Caribbean islands, including Dominica (where bananas represented 33.4% of total exports, by value, in 1997), Guadeloupe (22.2% in 1997), Martinique (36.6% in 1997), Saint Lucia (62.5% of domestic exports in 1999) and Saint Vincent and the Grenadines (41.3% of total exports (including re-exports) in 1999).

There is no international agreement governing trade in bananas, but there are various associations—such as the Union of Banana-Exporting Countries (UPEB), comprising Colombia, Costa Rica, Guatemala, Honduras, Nicaragua, Panama and Venezuela; the Caribbean Banana Exporters' Association, comprising Jamaica, Belize, the Windward Islands and Suriname; and WIBDECO, the Windward Islands Banana Development Co—which have been formed by producer countries to protect their commercial interests. Prices vary greatly, depending on relative wages and yields in the producing countries, freight charges, and various trade agreements negotiated under the Lomé Convention between the European Community (EC, now the European Union—EU) and 71 African, Caribbean and Pacific (ACP) countries. The Lomé arrangements include a banana protocol, which ensures producers an export market, a fixed quota and certain customs duty concessions. In this connection, the prospect of a withdrawal of internal barriers to intra-EC trade, as a result of the completion of a single market with effect from January 1993, was the cause of considerable anxiety to most major banana exporters (see below).

The EU is the world's largest market for bananas, accounting, in 1996, for 3.7m. tons, representing about 40% of world banana imports. Under the market arrangements prior to the end of 1992, just over one-half of banana imports were subject to quota controls under the Lomé Convention. Approximately 20% of market supplies were imported, duty free, from former British, French and Italian colonies. The Windward Islands of Saint Lucia, Dominica and Grenada together accounted for some 90% of banana exports to the EC under the Lomé Convention's banana protocol, Jamaica and Belize also being parties to the Convention. Around 70% of bananas from the Windward Islands were exported to the United Kingdom. France maintained similar arrangements with its traditional suppliers (overseas territories such as Guadeloupe and Martinique), as did Italy (Somalia). Another 25% of EC demand was satisfied internally, mainly from Portugal (Madeira and the Azores), Spain (the Canary Islands) and Greece (Crete). The remainder of quota imports (representing 10% of overall market demand) were imported, duty free, into Germany, mainly from Latin and Central American countries. Banana consumption in Germany, at 18 kg per head annually, has been approximately twice that of other EU countries. Banana imports into the residual free market originated mainly from the same countries, but attracted a 20% import tariff.

This complex market structure, which strongly favoured the Caribbean islands, was maintained by barriers to internal trade. These prevented the re-export of imports into Germany from, for instance, Honduras or Ecuador to the United Kingdom and France. Without these restrictions, Central and Latin American exporters, enjoying the cost advantages of modern technology and large-scale production, and subject to a 20% import tariff on their EC exports, would have substantially expanded their market share, and possibly displaced Caribbean producers altogether in the longer term.

The intention of the Commission of the European Communities that the tariff-free quota system would cease after 1992 held serious implications for Caribbean producers, who, with the ACP secretariat, sought to persuade the EC to devise a new preference system to protect their existing market shares, possibly taking the form of quota allocations, which would accord with the obligations of the EC countries in relation to trade with the ACP under the terms of the Lomé Convention. These guarantee that 'no ACP state shall be placed, as regards access to its traditional markets . . . in a less favourable position than in the past or present'.

In December 1992 it was announced by the EC Commission that ACP banana producers were to retain their preferential status under the EC's single-market arrangements that were to enter into force in July 1993. These would guarantee 30% of the European banana market to ACP producers, by way of an annual duty-free quota of approximately 750,000 tons. Imports of Latin American bananas were to be limited to 2m. tons per year at a tariff of 20%, with any additional shipments to be subject to a tariff rate of 170%, equivalent to 850 European Currency Units (ECU) per ton. It was asserted that, as the proposals linked tariffs with quotas, the EC was not in contravention of the General Agreement on Tariffs and Trade (GATT) regulations on the restriction of market access.

These arrangements were opposed by Germany, Denmark, Belgium and Luxembourg, as well as by the Latin American banana producers, who forecast that their shipments to the EC, totalling approximately 2.6m. tons annually, could fall by 20%. In early 1993 the German Government unsuccessfully sought a declaration from the Court of Justice of the European Communities that the EC Commission was in violation of GATT free-trade regulations. In June the Governments of Ecuador, Guatemala, Honduras, Mexico and Panama obtained agreement by GATT to examine the validity of the EC proposals. In the mean

time, the new arrangements covering EC banana imports duly took effect on 1 July.

In February 1994 a GATT panel ruled in favour of the five Latin American producers, declaring that the EU policy on bananas unfairly favoured the ACP banana exporters and was in contravention of free-trade principles. The Latin American producers accordingly demanded that the EU increase their annual quota to 3.2m. tons and reduce the tariff level on excess shipments. The EU responded to the ruling by offering to increase the Latin American banana quota to 2.1m. tons in 1994 (with effect from 1 October) and to 2.2m. tons in 1995, and to reduce the tariff rate by one-quarter. This compromise was accepted by Colombia, Costa Rica, Nicaragua and Venezuela, but rejected by Ecuador and the other Latin American producers. The Latin American exporters assenting to the plan were each to receive specific quotas, based on their past share of the market, within the overall 2.1m.-ton quota. In October 1994 the Court of Justice of the European Communities rejected a petition by Germany seeking a quota of 2.5m. tons in that year, with subsequent annual increases of 5%.

With the accession to the EU in January 1995 of Austria, Finland and Sweden, it was anticipated that the quota for duty-free bananas would be increased by up to 350,000 tons annually to accommodate the community's enlarged membership. (This proposed level of increase, however, was viewed by Germany as inadequate.) In the same month, the US Government indicated that it was contemplating the imposition of retaliatory trade measures against both the members of the EU and those Latin American banana exporters which had agreed to the 1994 quota compromise arrangements. (Although the USA is only a marginal producer of bananas, US business interests hold substantial investments in the multinational companies operating in Central and South America.) In February 1995 the EU came under further pressure from a number of African banana-producing countries, led by Cameroon and Côte d'Ivoire, which sought further improvements in their access to EU markets under ACP arrangements. The USA, meanwhile, with the support of Germany, Belgium, the Netherlands and Finland, declared in July that renewed efforts should be made to formulate a new banana import regime that would reconcile the interests of the Latin American and ACP producers. France and the United Kingdom, however, reiterated their intention to maintain their perceived obligations towards their former Caribbean colonies, whose economies would be severely affected by the operation of a free market in bananas.

In September 1995 the USA formally instituted a complaint against the EU with the World Trade Organization (WTO), the successor organization to the GATT. Further representations to the WTO by the US Government, supported by the Governments of Ecuador, Guatemala, Honduras and Mexico, followed in February 1996. In the following month the EU, which had raised its annual duty-free banana quota to 2.35m. tons (see above), proposed a compromise reallocation of quotas, under which the Latin American producers would obtain 70.5% of the new quota (as against their existing proportion of 66.5%), while the ACP growers would receive 26% (down from 30%). An additional allowance of 90,000 tons annually was also to be extended to certain categories of bananas from Belize, Cameroon and Côte d'Ivoire. In May, however, the USA, together with Ecuador, Guatemala, Honduras and Mexico, made a concerted approach to the WTO to disallow the EU banana import regime in its entirety. Efforts by the contending groups of producers to achieve a compromise followed in July, when it was announced that ministerial meetings between the ACP and Latin American producing countries were to take place in October. In late July the EU announced that its annual quota for Latin American bananas was to be raised to 2.2m. tons to reflect increased demand from the enlarged EU membership.

An interim report issued by the WTO in March 1997 upheld the complaint instituted in 1996 by the USA and four Latin American producers, and declared the EU to be in violation of its international trade treaty obligations. Representations by the EU against the ruling were rejected by the WTO appeals committee in September 1997, and the EU was informed that it must formulate a new system for banana imports by early 1998. This ruling was accepted in principle by the EU, which in January 1998 proposed new arrangements under which it would apply a system of quotas and tariffs to both groups of producers, while retaining an import-licensing system. A quota increase to 2.5m. tons annually was to be offered to the Latin American exporters. It was also proposed to offer aid totalling ECU 450m. to the Caribbean producers to assist their banana industries towards the ability to compete efficiently in a proposed 'free' market in bananas by 2008.

In June 1998 the US Government expressed dissatisfaction with the terms of the EU plan. The EU, however, refused to agree to further consultations with the WTO appeals committee. The US position was reinforced in September when the 'Group of Seven' major industrial countries sought, without success, to persuade the EU to accept the terms of the WTO ruling. However, the EU offered a new compromise plan, whereby the Latin American banana producers would, with effect from early 1999, receive an annual quota of 2.53m. tons, at an import duty rate of US $90 per ton, with the ACP growers retaining free access for annual shipments of 857,000 tons, which the EU stated to be in compliance with the WTO decision. This was rejected in October 1998 by the USA and the Latin American petitioners (who had been joined in February by Panama), and it was announced that the US Government was to seek authorization by the WTO for a programme of trade retaliation against the EU. Following further unsuccessful negotiations, and a challenge by the EU to the legality of the proposed sanctions, the US Government published in early December a list of 16 EU exports, including cashmere clothing, biscuits, candles and electric coffee-makers, on which it intended to impose tariffs of 100% with effect from early 1999.

These measures, which were directed principally against the United Kingdom, France and Germany, and from which Denmark and the Netherlands (which had advocated acceptance of the WTO ruling) were exempted, provoked considerable anxiety internationally, on the grounds that they could lead to a wider disruption of world trade. Negotiations between representatives of the USA and the EU were resumed in January 1999, while the implementation of the proposed tariffs was suspended pending consideration by the WTO of their validity in international law. The WTO also agreed to re-examine the terms of the compromise plan put forward by the EU in the previous September.

Following sustained but unsuccessful attempts by the USA and the EU to reach a negotiated settlement, the US Government, supported by the five Latin American petitioners, announced in early March 1999 that it was to invoke the punitive tariffs. Concurrently, a number of countries in the Caribbean Community and Common Market (CARICOM) grouping announced that they were considering the abrogation of a narcotics-control agreement with the USA, which permitted US enforcement agencies to pursue suspected drugs-traffickers into their territorial waters and air space.

In April 1999 the WTO ruled that the revised EU banana import proposals represented an attempt to avoid compliance with the original WTO ruling, and formally authorized the USA to impose trade sanctions against EU goods, valued at US $191.4m. annually (compared with damages of $520m. originally claimed), to compensate for losses incurred by US companies as a consequence of the EU banana regime. (This authorization was only the second in the 51-year history of the WTO and its predecessor, GATT.) The EU announced its acceptance of the decision, although indicating that the formulation of reforms could span the period to January 2000. The USA, meanwhile, accepted the need for this period of consultation and further extended the suspension of its import tariff proposals. However, in March 2000, following a complaint by the EU, a WTO panel ruled that the sanctions against EU goods imposed by the USA were a violation of international trade rules.

In mid-2000 the European Commission proposed the possible introduction of a tariff quota system involving the distribution of licences on a 'first come, first served' basis. However, it also suggested that, if a consensus were not reached, a tariff-only solution, whereby no restrictions would be imposed on quantities but which would give ACP countries preferable rates, would be the only viable solution; the latter option was rejected by a number of EU governments as potentially damaging to EU banana-growers. Moreover, the granting of licences on a 'first come, first served' basis was subsequently rejected by representatives of Latin American banana-producing states, while the USA stated that the proposed regime did not adequately address its concerns. In July a WTO panel ruled that the sanctions against EU goods had been imposed prematurely by the USA,

some six weeks before it had received the authorization of the WTO to apply them. The European Commission indicated at this time that it would take no further action itself, but that companies affected by sanctions before the WTO authorization were free to pursue claims for compensation in the US courts. The USA, meanwhile, was reported to be planning to 'rotate' the sanctions onto a new list of goods, the US Congress having ordered a so-called 'carousel' sanctions regime under which the list would change every six months. In addition, in May, the WTO had authorized Ecuador, the world's largest banana producer, to impose sanctions of up to US $201.6m. in the form of tariffs applied on EU service providers, industrial designs and copyrights.

In October 2000 the European Commission formally approved the introduction of a tariff quota system for bananas on a 'first come, first served' basis. Such a system would retain the use of three quotas until 2006, the Commission favouring the introduction of a tariff-only regime thereafter. The third quota would permit annual imports of 850,000 and would be available to all exporters. However, ACP exporters would be granted a tariff preference of US $264 per ton, rather than $275 per ton as had previously been proposed. The proposed new tariff quota system was immediately rejected by Colombia, Costa Rica, Guatemala, Honduras, Nicaragua and Panama, which threatened renewed action with the WTO. The USA also questioned whether the new regime was 'WTO-compatible'. Shortly after the announcement of the details of the proposed new regime. EU governments declared that it provided 'a basis for settling the banana dispute'.

In March 2001 the EU announced that it would delay the introduction of the new tariff quota system for bananas in order to consider an alternative proposal, by the US fruit trading company, Chiquita Brands International, which would effectively grant quotas based on historical market share. Chiquita Brands International had, in January, initiated legal action against the European Commission in respect of losses allegedly incurred as a result of EU restrictions on banana imports. The USA had also threatened to implement new trade sanctions if the EU proceeded with the introduction of the new regime. In April the dispute over bananas appeared finally to have been resolved after the EU agreed temporarily to reallocate to Chiquita Brands International a larger share of the European banana market from 1 July 2001, the date set as a target for the introduction of the new tariff quota system. In return, the USA was reported to have agreed to suspend, from that date, the sanctions it had imposed on EU goods; and to support a waiver in the WTO that would allow a specific quota for bananas from traditional ACP exporters. Under the settlement negotiated, the EU agreed to transfer 100,000 tons of bananas from the quota reserved mainly for ACP producers to that set for Latin American producers. From 1 July most import licences to the EU would be allocated on the basis of traditional shipment levels. Some 17% of licences would be reserved for new exporters or for companies which had significantly increased their imports since a 1994–96 reference period.

Export Price Index for Bananas (base: 1980 = 100)

	Average	Highest month(s)	Lowest month(s)
1990	150		
1995	111		
1998	122	154 (Dec.)	96 (Aug.)
1999	111	130 (Dec.)	96 (Sept.)
2000	122	166 (Feb.)	90 (July)

Bananas were included by the UN Conference on Trade and Development (UNCTAD) on a list of 18 commodities in its proposed integrated programme for the regulation of international trade in primary products, based on commodity agreements backed by a common fund for financial support. The UN's Food and Agriculture Organization (FAO) and UNCTAD are seeking, through an inter-governmental group, to formulate such an international agreement on bananas, involving producers and consumers, which would ensure a proper balance of supply and demand, regulating trade in order to provide regular supplies for consumers at a price remunerative to producers. The main impediments to a trade pact are disagreements on the means by which the market would be stabilized, in particular on the definition and use of export quotas, which producers consider to be restrictive, and on the lowering of trade barriers to allow reciprocal trade, which is opposed by countries with high production costs.

The average import price at US ports of first-class bananas from Central America and Ecuador declined from 25.46 US cents per lb in 1991 to 19.91 cents per lb in 1994. The annual average rose to 20.02 cents per lb in 1995, 21.41 cents in 1996 and 22.25 cents in 1997, but eased to 21.61 cents in 1998. It fell to 19.39 cents per lb in 1999. On a monthly basis, the average price advanced from only 18.14 cents per lb in October 1998 to 24.62 cents in November (following the damage caused by 'Hurricane Mitch'), but fell to 19.66 cents in December. The monthly average increased to 23.33 cents per lb in February 1999, but was reduced to only 17.02 cents in October. Banana prices rose sharply in early 2000, and the average for February was 24.63 cents per lb.

Cocoa (*Theobroma cacao*)

This tree, up to 14 m (46 ft) tall, originated in the tropical forests of Central and South America. The first known cocoa plantations were in southern Mexico around AD 600, although the crop may have been cultivated for some centuries earlier. Cocoa first came to Europe in the 16th century, when Spanish explorers found the beans being used in Mexico as a form of primitive currency as well as the basis of a beverage. The Spanish and Portuguese introduced cocoa into West Africa at the beginning of the 19th century.

Cocoa is now widely grown in the tropics, usually at altitudes less than 300 m above sea-level, where it needs a fairly high rainfall and good soil. Cocoa trees can take up to four years from planting before producing enough fruit to merit harvesting. They may live for 80 years or more, although the fully-productive period is usually about 20 years. The tree is very vulnerable to pests and diseases, and it is highly sensitive to climatic changes. Its fruit is a large pod, about 15 cm–25 cm (6 in–10 in) long, which at maturity is yellow in some varieties and red in others. The ripe pods are cut from the tree, on which they grow directly out of the trunk and branches. When opened, cocoa pods disclose a mass of seeds (beans) surrounded by white mucilage. After harvesting, the beans and mucilage are scooped out and fermented. Fermentation lasts several days, allowing the flavour to develop. The mature fermented beans, dull red in colour, are then dried, ready to be bagged as raw cocoa which may be further processed or exported.

Cultivated cocoa trees may be broadly divided into three groups. Most cocoas belong to the Amazonian Forastero group, which now accounts for more than 80% of world cocoa production. It includes the Amelonado variety, suitable for chocolate manufacturing. Criollo cocoa is not widely grown and is used only for luxury confectionery. The third group is Trinitario, which comprises about 15% of world output and is cultivated mainly in Central America and the northern regions of South America.

Cocoa processing takes place mainly in importing countries. The processes include shelling, roasting and grinding the beans. Almost half of each bean after shelling consists of a fat called cocoa butter. In the manufacture of cocoa powder for use as a beverage, this fat is largely removed. Cocoa is a mildly stimulating drink, because of its caffeine content, and, unlike coffee and tea, is highly nutritional.

The most important use of cocoa is in the manufacture of chocolate, of which it is the main ingredient. About 90% of all cocoa produced is used in chocolate-making, for which extra cocoa butter is added, as well as other substances such as sugar—and milk in the case of milk chocolate. Proposals that were initially announced in December 1993 (and subsequently amended in November 1997) by the consumer countries of the European Union (EU), permitting chocolate-manufacturers in member states to add as much as 5% vegetable fats to cocoa solids and cocoa fats in the manufacture of chocolate products, have been perceived by producers as potentially damaging to the world cocoa trade. In 1998 it was estimated that the implementation of this plan could reduce world demand for cocoa beans by 130,000–200,000 metric tons annually. In July 1999, despite protests from Belgium, which, with France, Germany, Greece, Italy, Luxembourg, the Netherlands and Spain, prohi-

bits the manufacture or import of chocolate containing non-cocoa-butter vegetable fats, the European Commission cleared the way to the abolition of this restriction throughout the EU countries. The implementation of the new regulations took effect in May 2000.

Production of Cocoa Beans
('000 metric tons)

	1999	2000
World total	2,949	3,160
Latin America	483	540
Leading Latin American producers		
Brazil	205	210
Colombia	52	52*
Dominican Repub.	34	37
Ecuador	95	136
Mexico	37	43
Other leading producers		
Cameroon	150†	120
Côte d'Ivoire	1,153	1,300†
Ghana	398†	398†
Indonesia	344	362†
Malaysia	84	98†
Nigeria	225	225

* FAO estimates.
† Unofficial figures.

Latin America is the third most important producing area for cocoa beans after west Africa, and Asia and Oceania, providing an estimated 15.6% of the total world crop in 2000. In that year Brazil was the world's fifth largest producer of cocoa beans, after Côte d'Ivoire, Ghana, Indonesia and Nigeria. In 1998/99, when recorded world exports of cocoa beans totalled 2,118,836 metric tons, Brazil was the 15th largest exporter, after Côte d'Ivoire, Ghana, Indonesia, Nigeria, Cameroon, Ecuador, Papua New Guinea, Malaysia, the Dominican Republic, Venezuela, Guinea, Togo, Mexico, and São Tomé and Príncipe. Brazil's earnings from cocoa exports are relatively insignificant to the country's economy, compared with those from coffee. In 1998 Ecuador obtained only 1.0% of its export revenue from cocoa, compared with 3.2% in 1996 and 2.4% in 1997. The total volume of exports declined from 71,100 metric tons in 1996 to 12,135 metric tons in 1998, owing to the devastation caused to the cocoa crop as a result of El Niño (an aberrant current which periodically causes the warming of the Pacific coast of South America, disrupting usual weather patterns) in 1997–98. Cocoa exports, however, increased to 63,600 metric tons in 1999. In 1999 the Dominican Republic derived only an estimated 0.6% of its export earnings from cocoa and cocoa products (including exports from free-trade zones), compared with 2.3% in 1998. The country's cocoa crop was severely damaged by 'Hurricane Georges' in September 1998.

The principal importers of cocoa are developed countries with market economies, which account for about 80% of cocoa imports from developing countries. Recorded world imports of cocoa beans in 1998/99 were 2,142,856 tons. The principal importing countries in that year were the USA (with 428,787 tons, representing 20% of the total), the Netherlands (338,245 tons) and the United Kingdom (243,916 tons).

World prices for cocoa are highly sensitive to changes in supply and demand, making its market position volatile. Negotiations to secure international agreement on stabilizing the cocoa industry began in 1956. Full-scale cocoa conferences, under United Nations auspices, were held in 1963, 1966 and 1967, but all proved abortive. A major difficulty was the failure to agree on a fixed minimum price. In 1972 the fourth UN Cocoa Conference took place in Geneva and resulted in the first International Cocoa Agreement (ICCA), adopted by 52 countries, although the USA, the world's principal cocoa importer, did not sign. The ICCA took formal effect in October 1973. It operated for three quota years and provided for an export quota system for producing countries, a fixed price range for cocoa beans and a buffer stock to support the agreed prices. In accordance with the ICCA, the International Cocoa Organization (ICCO), based in London, was established in 1973. In December 2000 its members comprised 19 exporting countries, accounting for more than 80% of world production and exports, excluding re-exports, of cocoa beans, and 23 importing countries, accounting for around 70% of world imports of cocoa beans. The USA, a leading importer of cocoa, is not a member. Nor is Indonesia, whose production and exports of cocoa have expanded rapidly in recent years. The governing body of the ICCO is the International Cocoa Council (ICC), established to supervise implementation of the ICCA.

A second ICCA operated during 1979–81. It was followed by an extended agreement, which was in force in 1981–87. A fourth ICCA took effect in 1987. (For detailed information on these agreements, see *South America, Central America and the Caribbean 1991*.) During the period of these ICCA, the effective operation of cocoa price stabilization mechanisms was frequently impeded by a number of factors, principally by crop and stock surpluses, which continued to overshadow the cocoa market in the early 1990s. In addition, the achievement of ICCA objectives was affected by the divergent views of producers and consumers, led by Côte d'Ivoire, on one side, and by the USA, on the other, as to appropriate minimum price levels. Disagreements also developed over the allocation of members' export quotas and the conduct of price support measures by means of the buffer stock (which ceased to operate during 1983–88), and subsequently over the disposal of unspent buffer stock funds. The effectiveness of financial operations under the fourth ICCA was severely curtailed by the accumulation of arrears of individual members' levy payments, notably by Côte d'Ivoire and Brazil. The fourth ICCA was extended for a two-year period from October 1990, although the suspension of the economic clauses relating to cocoa price support operations rendered the agreement ineffective in terms of exerting any influence over cocoa market prices.

Preliminary discussions on a fifth ICCA, again held under UN auspices, ended without agreement in May 1992, when consumer members, while agreeing to extend the fourth ICCA for a further year (until October 1993), refused to accept producers' proposals for the creation of an export quota system as a means of stabilizing prices, on the grounds that such arrangements would not impose sufficient limits on total production to restore equilibrium between demand and supply. Additionally, no agreement was reached on the disposition of cocoa buffer stocks, then totalling 240,000 tons. In March 1993 ICCO delegates abandoned efforts to formulate arrangements whereby prices would be stabilized by means of a stock-withholding scheme. At a further negotiating conference in July, however, terms were finally agreed for a new ICCA, to take effect from October, subject to its ratification by at least five exporting countries (accounting for at least 80% of total world exports) and by importing countries (representing at least 60% of total imports). Unlike previous commodity agreements sponsored by the UN, the fifth ICCA aimed to achieve stable prices by regulating supplies and promoting consumption, rather than through the operation of buffer stocks and export quotas.

The fifth ICCA, operating until September 1998, entered into effect in February 1994. Under the new agreement, buffer stocks totalling 233,000 tons that had accrued from the previous ICCA were to be released on the market at the rate of 51,000 tons annually over a maximum period of 4½ years, beginning in the 1993/94 crop season. At a meeting of the ICCO, held in October 1994, it was agreed that, following the completion of the stocks reduction programme, the extent of stocks held should be limited to the equivalent of three months' consumption. ICCO members also assented to a voluntary reduction in output of 75,000 tons annually, beginning in 1993/94 and terminating in 1998/99. Further measures to achieve a closer balance of production and consumption, under which the levels of cocoa stocks would be maintained at 34% of world grindings during the 1996/97 crop year, were introduced by the ICCO in September 1996. The ICCA was subsequently extended until September 2001. In April 2000 the ICCO agreed to implement measures to remedy low levels of world prices (see below), which were to centre on the elimination of sub-grade cocoa in world trade: these cocoas were viewed by the ICCO as partly responsible for the downward trend in prices. In mid-July Côte d'Ivoire, Ghana, Nigeria and Cameroon disclosed that they had agreed to destroy a minimum of 250,000 tons of cocoa at the beginning of the 2000/01 crop season, with a view to assisting prices to recover and to 'improving the quality of cocoa' entering world markets.

A sixth ICCA was negotiated, under the auspices of the UN, in February 2001. Like its predecessor, the sixth ICCA will aim to achieve stable prices through the regulation of supplies and the promotion of consumption. The Agreement is due to take effect provisionally from 1 January 2002, subject to its ratification by at least five exporting countries (accounting for at least 80% of total world exports) and by importing countries (representing at least 60% of total imports); and definitively, subject to the same conditions, on 1 October 2003.

Export Price Index for Cocoa (base: 1980 = 100)

	Average	Highest month(s)	Lowest month(s)
1990	49		
1995	55		
1998	62	65 (May)	58 (Feb., Dec.)
1999	47	58 (Jan.)	37 (Dec.)
2000	35	38 (Jan.)	32 (Nov.)

As the above table indicates, international prices for cocoa have generally been very low in recent years. In 1992 the average of the ICCO's daily prices (based on selected quotations from the London and New York markets) was US $1,099.5 per metric ton (49.9 US cents per lb), its lowest level since 1972. The annual average price per ton subsequently rose steadily, reaching $1,456 in 1996 and $1,619 in 1997. The average rose in 1998 to $1,676 per ton, its highest level since 1987, but slumped in 1999 to $1,140 (a fall of 32.0%). In 1996 the monthly average ranged from $1,339 per ton (in March) to $1,538 (June). In 1997 it varied from $1,373 per ton (February) to $1,770 (September). The average increased in May 1998 to $1,794 per ton (its highest monthly level since February 1988), but fell in December to $1,515. In 1999 the highest monthly average was $1,455 per ton in January, and the lowest was $919 in December. The comparable figure for February 2000 was only $859 per ton: the lowest monthly average since March 1973.

On the London Commodity Exchange (LCE) the price of cocoa for short-term delivery increased from £637 (US $983) per ton in May 1993 to £1,003.5 in November, but it later retreated. In July 1994, following forecasts that the global production deficit would rise, the price reached £1,093.5 ($1,694) per ton.

In late February 1995 the London cocoa quotation for March delivery stood at £1,056.5 per ton, but in March the price was reduced to £938 (US $1,498). The downward trend continued, and in late July the LCE cocoa price was £827.5 ($1,321) per ton. Prices under short-term contracts remained below £1,000 per ton until the end of December, when the 'spot' quotation (for immediate delivery) stood at £847.5 ($1,319) per ton.

During the first quarter of 1996 London cocoa prices continued to be depressed, but in April the short-term quotation rose to more than £1,000 per ton. In May the LCE 'spot' price reached £1,104.5 (US $1,672) per ton. Cocoa prices had increased in spite of the ICCO's forecast that supply would exceed demand in 1995/96, following four consecutive years of deficits. In July 1996, however, the 'spot' quotation in London declined from £1,049 ($1,630) per ton to £924 ($1,438). In December the 'spot' price was reduced to £848.5 ($1,419) per ton.

In January and February 1997 short-term quotations for cocoa were at similarly low levels, but in March the 'spot' price on the London market rose from £894.5 (US $1,449) per ton to £1,012.5 ($1,621) in less than two weeks. On 1 July the London 'spot' price stood at £1,143 ($1,895) per ton: its highest level, in terms of sterling, for more than nine years. Three weeks later, however, the price declined to £963 ($1,615) per ton. By late August international cocoa prices had recovered strongly, in response to fears that crops would suffer storm damage, and in early September the LCE 'spot' quotation reached £1,133.5 ($1,798) per ton, while prices for longer-term contracts were at their highest for almost a decade. Thereafter, the trend in cocoa prices was generally downward. In the first half of December, however, the London price advanced from £987 ($1,663) per ton to £1,117 ($1,824).

In February 1998 the LCE price of cocoa for short-term delivery was reduced to less than £1,000 per ton. Following political unrest in Indonesia and forecasts of an increased global supply deficit, the cocoa market rallied in the first half of May, with the London 'spot' price rising from £1,072.5 (US $1,787) per ton to £1,140 ($1,857). Meanwhile, cocoa under long-term contracts was being traded at more than £1,200 per ton. However, in late June the London price of cocoa for July delivery declined to £1,002.5 per ton. During July the 'spot' price reached £1,070 ($1,752) per ton, before easing to £1,026.5 ($1,684). London cocoa prices remained above £1,000 per ton until late September, when the 'spot' quotation fell to £970 ($1,651). Later in the year there was a steady downward trend, and in late December the price of cocoa was about £860 ($1,440) per ton.

During the early weeks of 1999 the London cocoa market remained relatively stable, but in March the 'spot' price declined to £803 (US $1,307) per ton. The slump later intensified, following forecasts of plentiful crops and a weakening in consumption trends, and by late May the London price of cocoa had fallen to only £602.5 ($962) per ton. Prices subsequently rallied, and in June, with the EU failing to resolve an impasse over common rules on chocolate products (see above), the quotation for July delivery reached £819 per ton. In July, after the EU agreed to allow chocolate manufacturers to include vegetable fats, the 'spot' price of cocoa eased to £694 ($1,089) per ton, although it later recovered to £754 ($1,194). A further decline in cocoa prices ensued, and in September the 'spot' quotation fell to £601.5 ($975) per ton. After a slight recovery, the downward trend continued. In November the London cocoa price for short-term delivery was reduced to £527.5 per ton. In December the 'spot' quotation reached £570.5 ($926) per ton, but later in the month the price retreated to £530.5 ($854): its lowest level, in terms of sterling, since 1992.

Despite the coup in Côte d'Ivoire in December 1999, the cocoa market weakened further during the opening weeks of 2000, and in late February the London price for short-term delivery stood at only £590 per ton. Meanwhile, the equivalent New York price of cocoa fell in February to only US $734 per ton: its lowest level for more than 25 years. In March the London 'spot' quotation advanced to £598.5 ($940) per ton, before easing to £549 ($874). Comparable prices in May ranged from £575.5 ($880) to £606.5 ($911) per ton, and those in July were between £582 ($881) and £599 ($907). In August the LCE price of cocoa for short-term delivery fell to £564 per ton. In September, however, the London 'spot' quotation rallied, ranging between £586 ($855) and £593 ($860) in that month. In December a further downward movement occurred, the 'spot' quotation in that month ranging between £556 ($803) and £534 ($774). Early in the same month the New York second position 'futures' price declined to $707 per ton, its lowest level for 27 years.

In January 2001 the London price of cocoa for short-term delivery rose to £833 per ton, this upward movement being attributed to a steeper decline in deliveries from Côte d'Ivoire than had earlier been forecast. This recovery was sustained in February, when speculative buying and estimates of potential shortages in supply boosted the short-term price to £945. In March, however, as a result of improved forecasts of production by Côte d'Ivoire, the London 'spot' quotation declined, ranging between £799 (US $1,153) and £917 ($1,346) per ton. Comparable prices in May ranged from £745 ($1,068) to £799 ($1,136). In early May fund and speculative buying, together with renewed pessimism about the level of production in Côte d'Ivoire, boosted the price of the London July 'futures' contract to a three-week high of £815 per ton at one point. In June, however, the London price of cocoa for short-term delivery declined steadily, falling to £676 per ton late in the month. During the first two weeks of July the London 'spot' market quotation ranged between £728 ($1,024) per ton and £674 ($947) per ton.

The Cocoa Producers' Alliance (COPAL), with headquarters in Lagos, Nigeria, whose 13 members, among them Brazil, the Dominican Republic, Ecuador, Mexico and Trinidad and Tobago, include all the major producers except Indonesia, was formed in 1962 with the aim of preventing excessive price fluctuations by regulating the supply of cocoa. Members of COPAL account for about 82% of world cocoa production. COPAL has acted in concert with successive ICCA.

The principal centres for cocoa-trading in the industrialized countries are the London Cocoa Terminal Market, in the United Kingdom, and the New York Coffee, Sugar and Cocoa Exchange, in the USA.

Coffee (*Coffea*)

The coffee plant is an evergreen shrub or small tree, generally 5 m–10 m tall, indigenous to Asia and tropical Africa. Wild trees grow to 10 m, but cultivated shrubs are usually pruned to a maximum of 3 m. The dried seeds (beans) are roasted, ground and brewed in hot water to provide the most popular of the world's non-alcoholic beverages. Coffee is drunk in every country in the world, and its consumers comprise an estimated one-third of the world's adult population. Although it has little nutrient value, coffee acts as a mild stimulant, owing to the presence of caffeine, an alkaloid also present in tea and cocoa.

There are about 40 species of *Coffea*, most of which grow wild in the eastern hemisphere. The two species of chief economic importance are *C. arabica* (native to Ethiopia), which accounts for 70%–75% of world production, and *C. canephora* (the source of robusta coffee), which accounts for all but 1% of the remainder. Arabica coffee is more aromatic, but robusta, as the name implies, is a stronger plant. Coffee grows in the tropical belt, between 20°N and 20°S, and from sea-level to as much as 2,000 m above. The optimum growing conditions are found at 1,250–1,500 m above sea-level, with an average temperature of around 17°C and an average annual rainfall of 1,000–1,750 mm. Trees begin bearing fruit three to five years after planting, depending upon the variety, and give their maximum yield (up to 5 kg of fruit per year) from the sixth to the 15th year. Few shrubs remain profitable beyond 30 years.

Arabica coffee trees are grown mostly in the American tropics and supply the largest quantity and the best quality of coffee beans. In Africa and Asia arabica coffee is vulnerable in lowland areas to a serious leaf disease and consequently cultivation has been concentrated on highland areas. Some highland arabicas, such as those grown in Kenya, have a high reputation for quality.

In recent years Latin American arabica production has been inhibited by the coffee berry borer beetle, which has been described as the most damaging pest to coffee world-wide. The beetle has been estimated to cost Latin American producers US $500m. annually in lost production. Infestation has been particularly acute in Colombia, where the beetle, which cannot be effectively eliminated by pesticides, infests about 680,000 ha of the 900,000 ha under coffee. During the late 1990s experimental research, aimed at eliminating the beetle through biotechnological methods, was proceeding in Ecuador, Guatemala, Honduras, Jamaica, Mexico and India.

The robusta coffee tree, grown mainly in east and west Africa, has larger leaves than arabica, but the beans are generally smaller and of lower quality and price. However, robusta coffee has a higher yield than arabica as the trees are more resistant to disease. Robusta is also more suitable for the production of soluble ('instant') coffee. About 60% of African coffee is of the robusta variety. Soluble coffee accounts for more than one-fifth of world coffee consumption.

Each coffee berry, green at first but red when ripe, usually contains two beans (white in arabica, light brown in robusta) which are the commercial product of the plant. To produce the best quality arabica beans—known in the trade as 'mild' coffee—the berries are opened by a pulping machine and the beans fermented briefly in water before being dried and hulled into green coffee. Much of the crop is exported in green form. Robusta beans are generally prepared by dry-hulling. Roasting and grinding are usually undertaken in the importing countries, for economic reasons, and because roasted beans rapidly lose their freshness when exposed to air.

Apart from beans, coffee produces a few minor by-products. When the coffee beans have been removed from the fruit, what remains is a wet mass of pulp and, at a later stage, the dry material of the 'hull' or fibrous sleeve that protects the beans. Coffee pulp is used as cattle feed, the fermented pulp makes a good fertilizer and coffee bean oil is an ingredient in soaps, paints and polishes.

More than one-half of the world's coffee is produced on smallholdings of less than 5 ha. In most producing countries, coffee is almost entirely an export crop, for which (with the exception of Brazil, after the USA the world's second largest coffee consumer) there is little domestic demand. Green coffee accounts for some 96% of all the coffee that is exported, with soluble and roasted coffee comprising the balance. Tariffs on green/raw coffee are usually low or non-existent. The USA is the largest single importer, although its volume of coffee purchases was overtaken in 1975 by the combined imports of the (then) nine countries of the European Community (EC, now the European Union–EU).

After petroleum, coffee is the major raw material of world trade, and the single most valuable agricultural export of the tropics. Arabica coffee accounts for about two-thirds of world production. Coffee is the most important cash crop of Latin America, with a number of countries heavily dependent on it as a source of foreign exchange. Of the total world crop of coffee beans in 1998/99, Latin American countries accounted for an estimated 63.7%. During the 1990s producing countries in Asia accounted for between 16%–24% of world coffee output, while the African region supplied between 14%–19%.

Brazil and Colombia are the world's main producers of coffee beans, together consistently accounting for more than 32% of world trade in green (unroasted) coffee during the 1990s. In 1998/99 their share of the world coffee trade rose to 39%, reflecting the bumper crop from Brazil. Coffee was formerly Brazil's most important agricultural export, but its relative importance has declined in recent years. In 1991 coffee (including extracts and essences) provided 4.8% of the country's total exports, but in 1992, when prices were lower (see below), the proportion was only 3.1%. Coffee provided 4.5% of Brazil's total exports in 1996, 5.9% in 1997 and 5.1% in 1998. In terms of volume, Brazilian coffee exports reached a record level of 23.1m. bags (each of 60 kg) in 1998/99. After a devastating frost in 1975, Brazil initiated a major programme to replant coffee trees. This concentrated on the state of Minas Gerais, north of another important coffee-growing area, Paraná state, which is more prone to frost. Replanting on a smaller scale took place after the less severe frost damage which coffee plantations suffered in 1981, although efforts have continued to move the centre of production further northwards. In the late 1990s Minas Gerais accounted for about 55% of total Brazilian coffee production, its share rising to 59% in 1998/99.

The Colombian economy continues to depend heavily on coffee. 'Colombian Mild' arabica coffee beans, to which the country has given its name, are regarded as being of a superior quality to other coffee types and are grown primarily in Colombia, Kenya and Tanzania. (Colombian Milds are one of four internationally designated coffee groups, the others being Other Milds, which are produced primarily in Central America, Unwashed Arabicas, which are produced primarily in Brazil and Ethiopia, and Robustas, of which the main producers are Viet Nam, Indonesia and Brazil.) Shipments of raw coffee from Colombia accounted for 19.6% of total export earnings in 1997, and 17.4% in 1998. An earthquake in Colombia in January 1999 caused heavy damage to coffee-processing facilities, although plantations were largely unaffected. In that year raw coffee accounted for only 11.4% of total export earnings. There were fears in mid-2000 that heavy rainfall in Colombia would adversely affect that year's coffee harvest.

In the early 1990s coffee was the principal export crop in El Salvador, Guatemala, Haiti, Mexico, Nicaragua and Peru, and the second most important crop in Costa Rica, the Dominican Republic, Ecuador, Honduras and Puerto Rico. Sales of coffee contributed 33.2% of El Salvador's total export earnings in 1996, and 38.2% in 1997. Unfavourable weather, disease (rust), civil war and falling prices, however, have reduced production in recent years. In 1998 sales of coffee contributed 25.8% of El Salvador's export revenue. Sales of coffee (including soluble/instant coffee) accounted for 22.7% of Guatemala's export earnings in 1998, while sales of Nicaraguan coffee accounted for 30.2% of that country's export revenue in the same year. In Costa Rica coffee ranks second to bananas as the principal export commodity, supplying 10.8% of total export revenue in 1997. In 1998, however, coffee's contribution to Costa Rica's total export revenue declined to 7.4%, and in 1999 to only 4.3%. In 2000 coffee accounted for 4.7% of Costa Rica's total export earnings. Coffee was the principal agricultural export commodity in Honduras in 1999, contributing 20.7% of export revenue. Coffee provided 23.1% of Haiti's export earnings in 1989/90, but only 4.1% in 1997/98. The neighbouring Dominican Republic earned only 1.4% of its total export revenue from coffee (including exports from free-trade zones) in 1997. Coffee's share in Ecuador's export revenue, which was 10.8% in 1994, declined to 3.3% in 1996 and 2.2% in 1997, before rising to 2.5% in 1998. Coffee accounted for 5.1% of Peru's total export earnings in that year.

Coffee-growing areas in Central America suffered from extremely unfavourable weather conditions in 1998. Costa Rica experienced a six-month drought, and the country's coffee production in the 1998/99 season declined by about 1%. In October 1998 'Hurricane Mitch' inflicted damage to coffee crops in El Salvador, Guatemala, Honduras and Nicaragua, although it appears that the effects of the hurricane on coffee production were less severe than had originally been reported. El Salvador's coffee exports in the six months to March 1999 were 69% lower than in the corresponding period of the previous season.

Production of Green Coffee Beans ('000 metric tons)

	1999	2000
World total	6,848	7,259
Latin America	3,972	4,173
Leading Latin American producers		
Brazil	1,634	1,824
Colombia	648	630†
Costa Rica	164	164
Dominican Repub.	35	46
Ecuador	133	133
El Salvador	161	138
Guatemala	294	295
Honduras	185	196
Mexico	311	354
Nicaragua	92	82
Peru	145	155
Venezuela	67	55†
Other leading producers		
Cameroon	78†	63†
Côte d'Ivoire	365	365*
Ethiopia	232†	230†
India	265	282
Indonesia	417	430
Kenya	95	67
Philippines	117	117
Thailand	55	80
Uganda	236	205
Viet Nam	553	803

* FAO estimates.   † Unofficial figure.

Effective international attempts to stabilize coffee prices began in 1954, when a number of producing countries made a short-term agreement to fix export quotas. After three such agreements, a five-year International Coffee Agreement (ICA), covering both producers and consumers, and introducing a quota system, was signed in 1962. This led to the establishment in 1963 of the International Coffee Organization (ICO), with its headquarters in London. In January 2001 the ICO comprised 63 members (45 exporting countries, accounting for over 90% of world supplies, and 18 importing countries, accounting, until the withdrawal of the USA in 1993, for 81% of world imports). Subsequent ICAs were negotiated in 1968, 1976, 1983 and 1994 (see below), but the system of export quotas to stabilize prices was eventually abandoned in July 1989 (for detailed information on these agreements, see *South America, Central America and the Caribbean 1991*). During each successive ICA, contention arose over the allocation of members' export quotas, the operation of price support mechanisms, and, most importantly, illicit sales by some members of surplus stocks to non-members of the ICO (notably to the USSR and to countries in Eastern Europe and the Middle East). These 'leaks' of low-price coffee, often at less than one-half of the official ICA rate, also found their way to consumer members of the ICO through free ports, depressing the general market price and making it more difficult for exporters to fulfil their quotas.

The issue of coffee export quotas became further complicated in the 1980s, as consumer tastes in the main importing market, the USA, and, to a lesser extent, in the EC moved away from the robustas exported by Brazil and the main African producers and in favour of the milder arabica coffees grown in Central America. Disagreements over a new system of quota allocations, taking account of coffee by variety, had the effect of undermining efforts in 1989 to preserve the economic provisions of the ICA, pending the negotiation of a new agreement. The ensuing deadlock between consumers and producers, as well as among the producers themselves, led in July to the collapse of the quota system and the suspension of the economic provisions of the ICA. The administrative clauses of the agreement, however, continued to operate and were subsequently extended until October 1993, pending an eventual settlement of the quota issue and the entering into force of a successor ICA.

With the abandonment of the ICA quotas, coffee prices fell sharply in world markets, and were further depressed by a substantial accumulation of coffee stocks held by consumers. The response by some Latin American producers was to seek to revive prices by imposing temporary suspensions of exports; this strategy, however, merely increased losses of coffee revenue. By early 1992 there had been general agreement among the ICO exporting members that the export quota mechanism should be revived. However, disagreements persisted over the allocation of quotas, and in April 1993 it was announced that efforts to achieve a new ICA with economic provisions had collapsed. In the following month Brazil and Colombia, the two largest coffee producers, were joined by some Central American producers in a scheme to limit their annual coffee production and exports in the 1993/94 coffee year. Although world consumption of coffee exceeded the level of shipments, prices were severely depressed by surpluses of coffee stocks totalling 62m. bags, with an additional 21m. bags held in reserve by consumer countries. Prices, in real terms, stood at historic 'lows'.

In September 1993 the Latin American producers announced the formation of an Association of Coffee Producing Countries (ACPC) to implement an export-withholding, or coffee retention, plan. In the following month the 25-member Inter-African Coffee Organization (IACO) agreed to join the Latin American producers in a new plan to withhold 20% of output whenever market prices fell below an agreed limit. With the participation of Asian producers, a 28-member ACPC, with headquarters in London, was formally established in August. Its signatory member countries numbered 28 in 2001, 14 of which were ratified. Production by the 14 ratified members in 1999/2000 acounted for 61.4% of coffee output world-wide.

The ACPC coffee retention plan came into operation in October 1993 and gradually generated improved prices; by April 1994 market quotations for all grades and origins of coffee had achieved their highest levels since 1989. In June and July 1994 coffee prices escalated sharply, following reports that as much as 50% of the 1995/96 Brazilian crop had been damaged by frosts. In July 1994 both Brazil and Colombia announced a temporary suspension of coffee exports. The occurrence of drought following the Brazilian frosts further affected prospects for its 1994/95 harvest, and ensured the maintenance of a firm tone in world coffee prices during the remaining months of 1994.

The intervention of speculative activity in the coffee futures market during early 1995 led to a series of price falls, despite expectations that coffee consumption in 1995/96, at a forecast 93.4m. bags, would exceed production by about 1m. bags. In an attempt to restore prices, the ACPC announced in March 1995 that it was to modify the price ranges of the export-withholding scheme. In May the Brazilian authorities, holding coffee stocks of about 14.7m. bags, introduced new arrangements under which these stocks would be released for export only when the 20-day moving average of the ICO arabica coffee indicator rose to about US $1.90 per lb. Prices, however, continued to decline, and in July Brazil joined Colombia, Costa Rica, El Salvador and Honduras in imposing a reduction of 16% in coffee exports for a one-year period. Later in the same month the ACPC collectively agreed to limit coffee shipments to 60.4m. bags from July 1995 to June 1996. This withholding measure provided for a decrease of about 6m. bags in international coffee exports during this period. In July 1997 the ACPC announced that the withholding scheme was to be replaced by arrangements for the restriction of exports of green coffee. Total exports for 1997/98 were to be restricted to 52.75m. bags. Following the withdrawal in September 1998 of Ecuador from the export restriction scheme (and subsequently from the ACPC) and the accession of India to membership in September 1999, there were 14 ratified member countries participating in the withholding arangements. The continuing decline in world coffee prices (see below) prompted the ACPC to announce in February 2000 that it was considering the implementation of a further scheme involving the withholding of export supplies. In the following month the members indicated their intention to withdraw supplies of low-grade beans (representing about 10% of annual world exports), and on 19 May announced arrangements under which 20% of world exports would be withheld until the ICO 15-day composite price

reached 95 US cents per lb (at that time the composite price stood at 69 cents per lb). Retained stocks would only be released when the same indicator price reached 105 cents per lb. Five non-member countries, Guatemala, Honduras, Mexico, Nicaragua and Mexico, also signed a so-called London Agreement pledging to support the retention plan. Implementation of the plan, which has a duration of up to two years, was initiated by Brazil in June, with Colombia following in September. In December 2000 the ACPC identified a delay in the full implementation of the retention plan as one of the factors that had caused the average ICO composite indicator price in November to fall to its lowest level since April 1993, and the ICO robusta indicator price to its lowest level since August 1969. In May 2001 the ACPC reported that exchange prices continued to trade at historical lows. Their failure to recover, despite the implementation of the retention plan, was partly attributed to the hedging of a proportion of the 7m. bags of green coffee retained by that time. On the physical market, meanwhile, crop problems and the implementation of the retention plan had significantly increased differentials for good quality coffees, in particular those of Central America. In April 2001 the ICO daily composite indicator price averaged 47.13 cents per lb (compared with an average of 64.24 cents per lb for the whole of 2000, the lowest annual average since 1973), the lowest monthly average since September 1992.

In June 1993 the members of the ICO agreed to a further extension of the ICA, to September 1994. However, the influence of the ICO, from which the USA withdrew in October 1993, was increasingly perceived as having been eclipsed by the ACPC. In 1994 the ICO agreed provisions for a new ICA, again with primarily consultative and administrative functions, to operate for a five-year period, until September 1999. In November of that year it was agreed to extend this limited ICA until September 2001. The ICO continues to favour a resumption of quota arrangements, which it views as the most effective means of preventing sharp price fluctuations.

Export Price Index for Coffee (base: 1980 = 100)

	Average	Highest month(s)	Lowest month(s)
1990	46		
1995	83		
1998	68	89 (Feb.)	56 (Oct.)
1999	53	62 (Dec.)	44 (Sept.)
2000	44	55 (Jan.)	33 (Dec.)

International prices for coffee beans in the early 1990s were generally at very low levels, even in nominal terms (i.e., without taking inflation into account). On the London Commodity Exchange (LCE) the price of raw robusta coffee for short-term delivery fell in May 1992 to US $652.5 (£365) per metric ton, its lowest level, in terms of dollars, for more than 22 years. By December the London coffee price had recovered to $1,057.5 per ton (for delivery in January 1993). The LCE quotation eased to $837 (£542) per ton in January 1993, and remained within this range until August, when a sharp increase began. The coffee price advanced in September to $1,371 (£885) per ton, its highest level for the year. In April 1994 a further surge in prices began, and in May coffee was traded in London at more than $2,000 per ton for the first time since 1989. In late June 1994 there were reports from Brazil that frost had damaged the potential coffee harvest for future seasons, and the LCE quotation exceeded $3,000 per ton. In July, after further reports of frost damage to Brazilian coffee plantations, the London price reached $3,975 (£2,538) per ton. Market conditions then eased, but in September, as drought persisted in Brazil, the LCE price of coffee increased to $4,262.5 (£2,708) per ton: its highest level since January 1986. In December 1994, following forecasts of a rise in coffee production and a fall in consumption, the London quotation for January 1995 delivery stood at $2,481.5 per ton.

The coffee market subsequently revived, and in March 1995 the LCE price reached US $3,340 (£2,112) per ton. However, in early July coffee traded in London at $2,400 (£1,501) per ton, although later in the month, after producing countries had announced plans to limit exports, the price rose to $2,932.5 (£1,837). During September the LCE 'spot' quotation (for immediate delivery) was reduced from $2,749 (£1,770) per ton to

$2,227.5 (£1,441), but in November it advanced from $2,370 (£1,501) to $2,739.5 (£1,786). Coffee for short-term delivery was traded in December at less than $2,000 per ton, while longer-term quotations were considerably lower.

In early January 1996 the 'spot' price of coffee in London stood at US $1,798 (£1,159) per ton, but later in the month it reached $2,050 (£1,360). The corresponding quotation rose to $2,146.5 (£1,401) per ton in March, but declined to $1,844.5 (£1,220) in May. The 'spot' contract in July opened at $1,730.5 (£1,112) per ton, but within four weeks the price fell to $1,487 (£956), with the easing of concern about a threat of frost damage to Brazilian coffee plantations. In November the 'spot' quotation rose to $1,571 (£934) per ton, but slumped to $1,375.5 (£819) within a week. By the end of the year the London price of coffee (for delivery in January 1997) had been reduced to $1,259 per ton.

In early January 1997 the 'spot' price for robusta coffee stood at only US $1,237 (£734) per ton, but later in the month it reached $1,597.5 (£981). The advance in the coffee market continued in February, but in March the price per ton was reduced from $1,780 (£1,109) to $1,547.5 (£960) within two weeks. In May coffee prices rose spectacularly, in response to concerns about the scarcity of supplies and fears of frost in Brazil. The London 'spot' quotation increased from $1,595 (£986) per ton to $2,502.5 (£1,526) by the end of the month. Meanwhile, on the New York market the price of arabica coffee for short-term delivery exceeded $3 per lb for the first time since 1977. However, the rally was short-lived, and in July 1997 the London price for robusta coffee declined to $1,490 (£889) per ton. In the first half of November the coffee price rose from $1,445 (£862) per ton to $1,658 (£972). During December the price for January 1998 delivery reached $1,841 per ton, but a week later it decreased to $1,657.

The coffee market rallied in January 1998, with the London 'spot' quotation rising from US $1,746.5 (£1,066) per ton to $1,841 (£1,124). Coffee prices for the corresponding contract in March ranged from $1,609 (£977) per ton to $1,787 (£1,065). Following reports of declines in the volume of coffee exports by producing countries (owing to inadequate rainfall), the upward trend in prices continued in April, with the price of robusta for short-term delivery reaching $1,992 per ton. In the first half of May there was another surge in prices (partly as a result of political unrest in Indonesia, the main coffee-producing country in Asia), with the London quotation rising from $1,881.5 (£1,129) per ton to $2,202.5 (£1,351). Later in the month, however, the price was reduced to $1,882.5 (£1,155) per ton. Coffee prices subsequently fell further, and in late July the London 'spot' contract stood at only $1,505.5 (£909) per ton, before recovering to $1,580 (£963). The quotation per ton for September delivery reached $1,699.5 at the beginning of August, having risen by $162 in a week. In September the 'spot' price advanced from $1,640 (£974) per ton to $1,765 (£1,036) a week later. In late October a further sharp rise in coffee prices began, following storm damage in Central America, and in November the London 'spot' quotation for robusta increased from $1,872.5 (£1,123) per ton to $2,142.5 (£1,278). Meanwhile, trading in other contracts continued at less than $1,800 per ton until December, when the London price of coffee (for delivery in January 1999) rose to $1,977.

Coffee prices retreated in January 1999, with the London 'spot' quotation falling from US $1,872.5 (£1,131) per ton to $1,639 (£995). During March the price was reduced from $1,795.5 (£1,111) per ton to $1,692.5 (£1,030), but recovered to $1,795 (£1,112) within a week. As before, the market for longer-term deliveries was considerably more subdued, with coffee trading mainly within a range of $1,490–$1,590 per ton. Thereafter, a generally downward trend was evident, and in May the 'spot' price declined to $1,376.5 (£850) per ton, although it reached $1,536.5 (£962) by the end of the month. The advance was short-lived, with prices for most coffee contracts standing at less than $1,400 per ton in late June. The 'spot' price in July fell to only $1,255 (£805) per ton. In August the London quotation for September 'futures', which had been only $1,282.5 per ton in July, rose to $1,407. However, the 'spot' price in September retreated from $1,323 (£825) per ton to $1,212.5 (£754). In October the price for short-term delivery was reduced to less than $1,200 per ton. The 'spot' quotation in November advanced from $1,212 (£736) per ton to $1,399.5 (£866). Prices

strengthened further in December, with the London quotation for short-term delivery reaching $1,557 per ton. Meanwhile, the market for longer-term contracts was more stable, with prices remaining below $1,400 per ton. In that month the Brazilian Government's forecast for the country's coffee output in the year beginning April 2000 was higher than some earlier predictions, despite fears that the crop would have been damaged by the unusually dry weather there since September 1999. For 1999 as a whole, average prices of robusta coffee declined by 18.3% from the previous year's level, while arabica prices fell by 23.2%.

In January 2000 the 'spot' price of coffee in London rose strongly towards the end of the month, increasing from US $1,401.5 (£848) per ton to $1,727.5 (£1,067) within a week. However, prices of coffee 'futures' continued to be much lower: at the end of January the quotation for March delivery was $1,073.5 per ton. In February prices of robusta coffee 'futures' were below $1,000 per ton for the first time for nearly seven years. In March the 'spot' quotation eased from $993 (£628) per ton to $944 (£593). Prices continued to weaken in April, with the quotation for short-term delivery falling to less than $900 per ton. The 'spot' price in May declined to $891.5 (£602) per ton, but recovered to $941 (£639). Another downward movement ensued, and by early July the London 'spot' quotation stood at only $807 (£532) per ton. Later that month, prices briefly recovered, owing to concerns about the possible danger of frost damage to coffee crops in Brazil. The 'spot' quotation rose to $886.5 (£585) per ton, while prices of coffee 'futures' advanced to more than $1,000. However, the fear of frost was allayed, and on the next trading day the 'spot' price of coffee in London slumped to $795 (£525) per ton: its lowest level, in terms of US currency, since September 1992.

The weakness in the market was partly attributed to the abundance of supplies, particularly from Viet Nam, which has substantially increased its production and export of coffee in recent years. By mid-2000 Viet Nam had overtaken Indonesia to become the world's leading supplier of robusta coffee and was rivalling Colombia as the second-largest coffee-producing country. Viet Nam and Mexico are the most significant producers outside the ACPC, but their representatives have supported the organization's plan for a coffee retention scheme to limit exports and thus attempt to raise international prices. The plan has also been endorsed by the Organisation africaine et malgache du café (OAMCAF), a Paris-based grouping of nine African coffee-producing countries.

In the first week of September the 'spot' market quotation rallied to $829 (£577) per ton, remaining at this level until 21 September, when another downward movement occurred. Towards the end of the month the 'spot' quotation declined to $776 (£530) per ton.

At the beginning of November 2000 the London 'spot' quotation stood at only $709 (£490) per ton and was to decline steadily throughout the month, reaching $612 (£432) on 30 November. High consumer stocks and uncertainty about the size of the Brazilian crop were cited as factors responsible for the substantial decline in November, when the average ICO robusta indicator price fell to its lowest level since August 1969.

In early January the 'spot' quotation on the London market rallied, rising as high as $677 (£451) per ton. This recovery, which was attributed to concern about the lack of availability of new-crop Central American coffees and reports that producers in some countries were refusing to sell coffee for such low prices, was sustained, broadly, until March, when the downward trend resumed. On 23 March the London 'spot' quotation declined to only $570 (£399) per ton. On 17 April the London price of robusta coffee 'futures' for July delivery declined to a life-of-contract low of $560 per ton, the lowest second-month contract price ever recorded.

By May 2001 the collapse in the price of coffee had been described as the deepest crisis in a global commodity market since the 1930s, with prices at their lowest level ever in real terms. The crisis was regarded, fundamentally, as the result of an ongoing increase in world production at twice the rate of growth in consumption, this over-supply having led to an overwhelming accumulation of stocks. During May the London 'spot' quotation fell from $584 (£407) per ton to $539 (£378) per ton.

In June 2001 producers in Colombia, Mexico and Central America were reported to have agreed to destroy more than 1m. bags of low-grade coffee in a further attempt to boost prices.

The ACPC hoped that this voluntary initiative would eventually be adopted by all of its members. By this time the ACPC's retention plan was widely regarded as having failed, with only Brazil, Colombia, Costa Rica and Viet Nam having fully implemented it.

In early July 2001 the price of the robusta coffee contract for September delivery fell below $540 per ton, marking a record 30-year low. At about the same time the ICO recorded its lowest composite price ever, at 43.80 US cents per lb.

Copper

The ores containing copper are mainly copper sulphide or copper oxide. They are mined both underground and by open-cast or surface mining. After break-up of the ore body by explosives, the lumps of ore are crushed, ground and mixed with reagents and water, in the case of sulphide ores, and then subjected to a flotation process by which copper-rich minerals are extracted. The resulting concentrate, which contains about 30% copper, is then dried, smelted and cast into anode copper, which is further refined to about 99.98% purity by electrolysis (chemical decomposition by electrical action). The cathodes are then cast into convenient shapes for working or are sold as such. Oxide ores, less important than sulphides, are treated in ways rather similar to the solvent extraction process described below.

Two alternative copper extraction processes have been developed in recent years. The first of these techniques, and as yet of minor importance in the industry, is known as 'Torco' (treatment of refractory copper ores) and is used for extracting copper from silicate ores which were previously not treatable.

The second, and relatively low-cost, technique is the solvent extraction process. This is suited to the treatment of very low-grade oxidized ores and is currently being used on both new ores and waste dumps that have accumulated over previous years from conventional copper working. The copper in the ore or waste material is dissolved in acid and the copper-bearing leach solution is then mixed with a special organic-containing chemical reagent which selectively extracts the copper. After allowing the two layers to separate, the layer containing the copper is separated from the acid leach solution. The copper is extracted from the concentrated leach solution by means of electrolysis to produce refined cathodes.

Copper is ductile, resists corrosion and is an excellent conductor of heat and electricity. Its industrial uses are mainly in the electrical industry (about 60% of copper is made into wire for use in power cables, telecommunications, domestic and industrial wiring) and the building, engineering and chemical industries. Bronzes and brasses are typical copper alloys used for both industrial and decorative purposes. There are, however, substitutes for copper in almost all of its industrial uses, and in recent years aluminium has presented a challenge in the electrical and transport industries.

Since 1982, when it overtook the USA, Chile (in which, according to the US Geological Survey, about 28% of world copper reserves are located) has been the world's leading producer of copper. It is also the biggest exporter, and within the country are located the world's three largest copper mines (Chuquicamata, El Teniente and La Escondida). In 1996 La Escondida overtook Chuquicamata as the world's largest copper mine, with an annual production capacity exceeding 800,000 tons. With the opening of new, large-scale mines in the north of the country, Chilean copper production rose to 3.7m. tons in 1998 and to 4.4m. tons in 1999. The Chilean economy relies heavily on the copper industry, which accounted for an annual average of 44.1% of the country's exports in the period 1984–88, and in 1999 was the source of 37.7% of Chile's export revenue. Although the industry has been vulnerable to labour unrest in recent years, foreign investment in Chilean mining development has been rising: between 1989–95 more than one-half of all foreign investment was directed towards this sector. In 1996 the share of private mines in total copper output was 54%, while the proportion represented by the state-owned copper corporation, CODELCO, was 39%, compared with about 84% in 1980. Among the principal externally financed ventures is the Zaldivar deposit in northern Chile, believed to be one of the richest undeveloped copper ore bodies in Latin America. Chile has six refineries for processing copper, with a combined annual capacity of 1.1m. tons.

Production of Copper Ore
(copper content '000 metric tons)

	1998	1999
World total	12,200	12,600
Latin America	4,809	5,281
Leading Latin American producers		
Chile	3,687	4,383
Mexico	385	362
Peru	483	536
Other leading producers		
Australia	607	735
Canada	706	614
China, People's Repub.	486	500*
Indonesia	781	740
Poland	436	461
Russia	500	530
USA	1,860	1,600
Zambia†	315	260

* Estimated production.
† Twelve months beginning 1 April of year stated.
Source: US Geological Survey.

After Chile, the Latin American country to which the copper industry is most important is Peru. Over a decade until the mid-1990s, however, the industry was adversely affected by the country's economic instability and guerrilla attacks on the mines. The restoration of relative internal stability, however, together with the phased privatization of the state-owned mining corporation, Centromín, has stimulated foreign investment in mining exploration ventures. In June 1999 it was announced that financing had been secured for the proposed development of the Antamina copper-zinc mine in Peru. The Antamina scheme, involving Canadian interests, is the country's largest investment project, with an estimated cost of US $2,260m. The open-pit mine in the Andes mountains, due to begin operating in late 2001, was expected to yield about 270,000 tons of copper annually for 20 years. Earnings from sales of copper (mainly in the form of unwrought metal) represented 13.6% of Peru's total export revenue in 1998. The development of deposits of copper in Argentina, estimated to total 700m. tons, commenced in 1997, producing 30,000 tons in that year. Brazil, a relatively minor producer of copper in the mid-1990s, was preparing in 2000 to bring into production a new project with a forecast output of 200,000 tons of refined copper annually from 2002. In 1997 one of the world's largest undeveloped copper deposits, estimated to exceed 1,000m. tons, was identified in the Chiriqui province of western Panama. Economically exploitable deposits of copper, estimated to total 8m. tons, were identified in north-western Cuba in 1998.

The major copper-importing countries are the countries of the European Union (EU), Japan and the USA. At the close of the 1980s, demand for copper was not being satisfied in full by current production levels, which were being affected by industrial and political unrest in some producing countries, with the consequence that levels of copper stocks were declining. Production surpluses, reflecting the lower levels of industrial activity in the main importing countries, occurred in the early 1990s, but were followed by supply deficits, exacerbated by low levels of copper stocks. In 1999, according to provisional figures from the International Copper Study Group (ICSG), world-wide consumption of refined copper increased by 5.4% from its 1998 level, to reach 14,178,000 metric tons, while production, including secondary output (recovery from scrap), advanced by 2.4%, to 14,370,000 tons. There was consequently a copper surplus for the year of 192,000 tons, compared with a surplus of 586,000 tons in 1998. However, identified stocks of refined copper throughout the world increased by only 93,000 tons in 1999, to total 1,455,000 tons at the end of the year. This accumulation of copper stocks tends to depress prices (see below). Provisional data from the ICSG indicate that world-wide consumption of refined copper during January–June 2000 reached 7,657,000 tons, a rise of 8.2% on the level for the corresponding half-year in 1999. Over the same period, total production (primary and secondary) was 7,308,000 tons: 3.0% higher than in January–June 1999. As a result, there was a deficit of 349,000 tons in world copper supplies for the first six months of 2000. Identified stocks of refined copper also declined, and at the end of June they stood at 1,235,000 tons.

There is no international agreement between producers and consumers governing the stabilization of supplies and prices. Although most of the world's supply of primary and secondary copper is traded direct between producers and consumers, prices quoted on the London Metal Exchange (LME) and the New York Commodity Exchange (COMEX) provide the principal price-setting mechanism for world copper trading.

Export Price Index for Copper (base: 1980 = 100)

	Average	Highest month(s)	Lowest month(s)
1990	123		
1995	135		
1998	78	83 (March, April)	69 (Dec.)
1999	75	84 (Dec.)	65 (March)
2000	86	94 (Sept.)	80 (April)

On the LME the price of Grade 'A' copper (minimum purity 99.95%) per metric ton declined from £1,563.5 (US $2,219) in February 1993 to £1,108.5 ($1,746) in May. From 1 July 1993 the LME replaced sterling by US dollars as the basis for pricing its copper contract. In September the London copper quotation increased to $2,011.5 (£1,304) per ton, but in October, with LME stocks of copper at a 15-year 'high', the price slumped to $1,596 (£1,079). The copper price subsequently revived, with the LME quotation exceeding $1,800 per ton by the end of the year. The market remained buoyant in January 1994, although, during that month, copper stocks in LME warehouses reached 617,800 tons, their highest level since February 1978. However, stocks were quickly reduced, and the London copper price moved above $2,000 per ton in May 1994. It continued to rise, reaching $2,533.5 (£1,635) per ton in July. In December, with LME stocks of copper below 300,000 tons, the London price of the metal exceeded $3,000 per ton (a level not recorded for more than five years).

In January 1995 the London copper price reached US $3,055.5 (£1,939) per ton, but in May it fell to $2,721.5 (£1,728), although LME stocks were then less than 200,000 tons. However, in July, with copper stocks reduced to about 141,000 tons, the LME price advanced to $3,216 (£2,009) per ton, its highest level, in terms of US currency, since early 1989.

The LME's holdings of copper rose to 356,800 tons in February 1996, when the price of the metal eased to US $2,492.5 (£1,609) per ton. After increasing again, the copper price fell in April to $2,479.5 (£1,624) per ton, although in early May it recovered to $2,847.5 (£1,872). In late May and June the copper market was gravely perturbed by reports that the world's largest copper-trading company, Sumitomo Corporation of Japan, had transferred, and later dismissed, its principal trader, following revelations that he had incurred estimated losses of $1,800m. in unauthorized dealings (allegedly to maintain copper prices at artificially high levels) on international markets over a 10-year period. This news led to widespread selling of copper: in late June the LME price was reduced to $1,837.5 (£1,192) per ton, although it quickly moved above $2,000 again. In July, after LME stocks had declined to 224,100 tons, the copper price reached $2,102.5 (£1,352) per ton. The London price of copper advanced in November to $2,547.5 (£1,522) per ton, following a decline in LME stocks of the metal to 90,050 tons, their lowest level since July 1990. The copper price at the end of 1996 was $2,217 (£1,304) per ton. Meanwhile, the extent of the losses incurred in the Sumitomo scandal was revised to $2,600m.

In January 1997 the London quotation for high-grade copper reached US $2,575.5 (£1,594) per ton, despite a steady increase in LME stocks, which rose to 222,500 tons in February. In June, with copper stocks reduced to 121,550 tons, the price of the metal reached $2,709.5 (£1,644) per ton. However, LME stocks were soon replenished, rising by 82% (to about 235,000 tons) in July and exceeding 300,000 tons in September. The LME's holdings of copper increased to more than 340,000 tons in October. By the end of that month the London price of copper had fallen below $2,000 per ton, and in late December it stood at $1,696.5 (£1,015). At the end of the year the copper price, in US currency, was 23.4% lower than it had been at the beginning. For 1997 as a whole, however, the average price per ton ($2,276) was only slightly less than in the previous year ($2,294).

The copper market remained depressed in the early weeks of 1998. In February the LME's copper stocks reached 379,325 tons (their highest level since June 1994), while the London price of the metal was reduced to US $1,601.5 (£973) per ton. The copper price recovered to $1,878 (£1,122) per ton in April. LME stocks of copper decreased to less than 247,000 tons in July, and in that month the price advanced from $1,571 (£963) per ton to $1,756.5 (£1,058). London copper prices remained within this range until late October, when LME stocks exceeded 450,000 tons. At the end of November the COMEX price of high-grade copper for short-term delivery fell below 70 US cents per lb for the first time since 1987. In December 1998, with LME stocks amounting to about 550,000 tons, the London price of copper was reduced to $1,437.5 (£851) per ton. The average London copper price for the year was $1,653 per ton: 27% lower than in 1997 and, in real terms, the lowest annual price level since 1935. The decline in copper prices was attributed to a reduction in imports by some Asian countries, affected by severe financial and economic problems.

In late January 1999 the LME's stocks of copper surpassed the previous record of 645,300 tons, established in January 1978. In March 1999, with these holdings standing at more than 700,000 tons, the London price of copper fell to US $1,351.5 (£832) per ton: its lowest level, in terms of dollars, since 1987. In the same month the COMEX price slumped to only 61 cents per lb. Despite a continuing rise in stocks, the London copper quotation increased in May 1999 to $1,581.5 (£964) per ton, although later in the month, when the LME's stocks reached 776,375 tons, the price retreated to $1,354.5 (£845). Copper prices subsequently recovered, and in July, following reports of proposed reductions in refinery output, the London quotation reached $1,689.5 (£1,085) per ton. In August the LME's copper stocks increased to 795,375 tons, but in September the price exceeded $1,700 per ton. The advance in copper prices continued, and at the end of the year the London quotation was $1,854 (£1,150) per ton. For 1999 as a whole, however, the average London price of copper was $1,572 per ton: 4.9% lower than in 1998 and the lowest annual level, in real terms, for more than 60 years.

In January 2000 the LME's stocks of copper exceeded 800,000 tons for the first time. Nevertheless, on the same day, the London price of the metal rose to US $1,893.5 (£1,147) per ton: its highest level for more than two years. The accumulation of stocks continued, and in early March the LME's holdings reached a record 842,975 tons. The copper price was reduced to $1,619 (£1,021) per ton in April, but recovered to $1,859 (£1,228) in July. Throughout this period the LME's stocks of copper steadily declined, falling to less than 700,000 tons in April, under 600,000 tons in June and below 500,000 tons in July. At the end of July copper stocks were 487,750 tons: less than 58% of the level reached in March.

The ICSG, initially comprising 18 producing and importing countries, was formed in 1992 to compile and publish statistical information and to provide an intergovernmental forum on copper. In 1999 its membership comprised 24 countries, accounting for more than 80% of world trade in copper. The ICSG, which is based in Lisbon, Portugal, does not participate in trade or exercise any form of intervention in the market.

Iron Ore

The main economic iron-ore minerals are magnetite and haematite, which are used almost exclusively to produce pig-iron and direct-reduced iron (DRI). These comprise the principal raw materials for the production of crude steel. Most iron ore is processed after mining to improve its chemical and physical characteristics and is often agglomerated by pelletizing or sintering. The transformation of the ore into pig-iron is achieved through reduction by coke in blast furnaces; the proportion of ore to pig-iron yielded is usually about 1.5 or 1.6:1. Pig-iron is used to make cast iron and wrought iron products, but most of it is converted into steel by removing most of the carbon content. Particular grades of steel (e.g. stainless) are made by the addition of ferro-alloys such as chromium, nickel and manganese. In the late 1990s processing technology was being developed in the use of high-grade ore to produce DRI, which, unlike the iron used for traditional blast furnace operations, requires no melting or refining. The DRI process, which is based on the use of natural gas, has expanded rapidly in Venezuela, but, owing to technological limitations, is not expected within the foreseeable future to replace more than a small proportion of the world's traditional blast-furnace output. In 1998 Mexico overtook Venezuela as the leading producer of DRI.

Iron is, after aluminium, the second most abundant metallic element in the earth's crust, and its ore volume production is far greater than that of any other metal. Some ores contain 70% iron, while a grade of only 25% is commercially exploitable in certain areas. As the basic feedstock for the production of steel, iron ore is a major raw material in the world economy and in international trade. Because mining the ore usually involves substantial long-term investment, about 60% of trade is conducted under long-term contracts, and the mine investments are financed with some financial participation from consumers.

Iron ore is widely distributed throughout Latin America. Brazil is by far the dominant producer in the region, and its ore is of a high quality (68% iron). In terms of iron content, Brazil is the largest producer in the world, accounting for an estimated 19.2% of global output in 1999. Brazil's giant open-cast mine in the Serra do Carajás began production in 1986. The project was developed by the Companhia Vale do Rio Doce (CVRD), which also operates several other mines in the Minas Gerais state. The Carajás deposit has been stated to have 18,000m. tons of high-grade reserves (66% iron), with an estimated lifetime of 500 years at the current extraction rate of 32m. tons annually. Improved rail links have facilitated the transportation of iron ore for export from Carajás, in the country's interior. Following the construction of the Igarapava dam, in north-east Minas Gerais state, the Carajás complex was expected to become partially self-sufficient in energy. Iron ore is the main mineral export commodity in Brazil, which is the major supplier to the world market after Australia. Sales of iron ore provided 6.4% of Brazil's total export earnings in 1998. Brazil also has a major iron and steel industry, accounting for a further 9.3% of exports in 1997 and 9.2% in 1998.

Production of Iron Ore (iron content, '000 metric tons)

	1998	1999*
World total	567,531	535,427
Latin America	150,457*	140,298
Leading Latin American producers		
Brazil	124,210	114,207
Chile	6,014	5,508
Mexico	6,334	6,800
Peru	2,885	2,583
Venezuela	11,014	11,200
Other leading producers		
Australia	95,185	94,868
Canada†	24,082	21,967
China, People's Repub. . . .	74,500	63,000
India	48,000	43,500
Russia	41,700	46,900
Ukraine	28,000	26,200
USA	39,724	36,530

* Estimated production.
† Including the metal content of by-product ore.
Source: US Geological Survey.

In Venezuela, which has proven reserves of about 2,000m. tons with an iron content of more than 55%, iron ore has been overtaken by aluminium as the second most important export industry, after petroleum. Iron ore output is, however, undergoing expansion, and in the early 1990s there was installed capacity for the production of as much as 20m. tons annually. In late 1997 construction began on an iron briquette plant at Puerto Ordaz, which, following its projected completion in late 1999, was expected to raise Venezuela's annual output of iron briquettes to 6.4m. tons, with the prospect of establishing the country as the world's leading exporter of this product by 2004. Sales of iron ore provided 0.9% of Venezuela's total export earnings in 1997.

In Mexico plans for the Tehuantepec steel project, in the state of Daxaca, were at an advanced stage in 1998. The scheme, with a total projected cost of US $2,500m., involves the proposed development of the country's largest iron ore mine, with proven reserves of about 180m. tons (averaging 55% iron). It was

envisaged that the mine would have an annual output of about 6m. tons of iron ore, while the associated steel plant, using DRI technology, would produce about 4m. tons of steel per year.

Since the early 1970s world trade in iron ore has regularly exceeded 200m. metric tons (iron content) per year. In the mid-1990s the dominant exporting countries were Australia and Brazil, jointly accounting for more than 60% of world trade in iron ore. Canada, India and Ukraine are also important exporters of iron ore. The principal importers in the mid-1990s were Japan, Germany and the People's Republic of China. In 1996 almost 40% of world iron ore production was exported. World iron ore reference prices are decided annually at a series of meetings between producers and purchasers (the steel industry accounts for about 95% of all iron ore consumption). The USA and the republics of the former USSR, although major steel-producing countries, rely on domestic ore production and take little part in the price negotiations. It is generally accepted that, because of its diversity in form and quality, iron ore is ill-suited to price stabilization through an international buffer stock arrangement.

Export Price Index for Iron Ore (base: 1980 = 100)

	Average	Highest month(s)	Lowest month(s)
1990	124		
1995	140		
1998	138	147 (Oct.)	134 (Jan.–March)
1999	133	144 (Jan.)	126 (Dec.)
2000	115	126 (Jan.)	107 (Oct., Nov.)

The index of export prices for iron ore declined to 119 in April 2000. The two leading exporters of the mineral in 1990–97 were Brazil and Australia. Exports of iron ore and concentrates (excluding agglomerates) by these two countries were valued at about US $19.5 per metric ton in 1992, but the average price declined to $17.0 per ton in 1993 and to $15.5 per ton in 1994. The average per ton was $16.1 in 1995, $17.0 in 1996 and $17.2 in 1997.

The Association of Iron Ore Exporting Countries (known by its French initials as APEF) was established in 1975 to promote close co-operation among members, to safeguard their interests as iron ore exporters, to ensure the orderly growth of international trade in iron ore and to secure 'fair and remunerative' returns from its exploitation, processing and marketing. In 1995 the APEF, which also collects and disseminates information on iron ore from its secretariat in Geneva, Switzerland, had nine members, including Peru and Venezuela, but not Brazil. The UN Conference on Trade and Development (UNCTAD) compiles statistics on iron ore production and trade, and in recent years has sought to establish a permanent international forum for discussion of the industry's problems.

Maize (Indian Corn, Mealies) (*Zea mays*)

Maize is one of the world's three principal cereal crops, with wheat and rice. The principal varieties are dent maize (which has large, soft, flat grains) and flint maize (which has round, hard grains). Dent maize is the predominant type world-wide, but flint maize is widely grown in southern Africa and parts of South America. Maize may be white or yellow (there is little nutritional difference) but the former is preferred for human consumption. Native to the Americas, maize was brought to Europe by Columbus and has since been dispersed to many parts of the world. It is an annual crop, planted from seed, and matures within three to five months. It requires a warm climate and ample water supplies during the growing season. Genetically modified varieties of maize, with improved resistance to pests, are now being cultivated, particularly in the USA, and also in Argentina and China. However, further development of genetically modified maize may be slowed by consumer resistance in importing countries and doubts about its possible environmental impact.

Maize is an important food source in regions such as sub-Saharan Africa and the tropical zones of Latin America, where the climate precludes the extensive cultivation of other cereals. It is, however, inferior in nutritive value to wheat, being especially deficient in lysine, and tends to be replaced by wheat in diets, when the opportunity arises. As food for human consumption, the grain is ground into meal, or it can be made into (unleavened) corn bread and breakfast cereals. In Latin America maize meal is made into cakes, called 'tortillas'. Maize is also the source of an oil, which is used in cooking.

The high starch content of maize makes it highly suitable as a compound feed ingredient, especially for pigs and poultry. Animal feeding is the main use of maize in the USA, Europe and Japan, and large amounts are also used for feed in developing countries in Far East Asia, Latin America and, to some extent, in North Africa. Maize has a large variety of industrial uses, including the preparation of ethyl alcohol (ethanol), which may be added to petrol to produce a blended motor fuel. Maize is also a source of dextrose and fructose, which can be used as artificial sweeteners, many times as sweet as sugar. The amounts of maize used for these purposes depend, critically, on its price to the users relative to that of petroleum, sugar and other potential raw materials. Maize cobs, previously regarded as a waste product, may be used as feedstock to produce various chemicals (e.g. acetic acid and formic acid).

In recent years world production has averaged nearly 600m. metric tons annually. The USA is by far the largest producer, with annual harvests of around 240m. tons, except in years of drought or excessive heat, when output can fall significantly. In 1995, for example, the US maize crop totalled only 187m. tons. The People's Republic of China, whose maize output has been expanding rapidly, is the second largest producer; its harvest reached 133m. tons in 1998.

Maize production in Latin America grew rapidly in the early 1990s, but has subsequently not increased. The record production year was 1996, with 80m. metric tons, while the 1999 crop was estimated at 76m. tons. Three countries—Argentina, Brazil and Mexico—between them account for more than 85% of Latin America's annual maize crop. Brazil is the largest producer, with output averaging 33m. tons annually. In the north and north-east of the country, which account for about 10% of Brazil's production, maize is an important human food and is largely grown by subsistence farmers. The droughts to which these regions are prone can occasion considerable distress. Most of Brazil's maize is grown commercially for use as animal feed in the centre and south of the country. Production there varies according to the amount of government support (mostly in the form of subsidized credit) and the prices of alternative crops, especially oilseeds. Although Brazil's animal feed requirements are growing rapidly, many of the feed mills are located in the far south of the country, where maize supplies may be obtained more cheaply from Argentina than from domestic sources. Brazil's maize imports currently amount to some 1.5m. tons annually.

Mexico is Latin America's second largest maize producer in most years, with harvests averaging 18m. metric tons in the second half of the 1990s. Much of this consists of white corn rather than the yellow variety. The establishment of CIMMYT (the International Wheat and Maize Improvement Centre) at Sonora, in northern Mexico, has made that country the testing-ground for many of the technical advances in the development of different maize varieties since the 1960s. Local production, however, has been hampered by the small size of most agriculture holdings, competition for irrigated land from other crops, and the inability of small producers to afford enough fertilizers. Shortages of irrigation water commonly result in poor crops. Maize in Mexico is mainly used for human consumption, particularly in the form of tortillas. Domestic Maize is mostly reserved for this purpose, animal feed manufacturers traditionally preferring to use sorghum and, increasingly, yellow corn imported from the USA.

Recent policy changes will affect maize production and consumption trends in Mexico. The Compañía Nacional de Subsistencias Populares (CONASUPO), the parastatal food distribution company, no longer directly supports the maize market, while controls on tortilla prices have been lifted. Competition between food manufacturers for local maize will benefit the larger commercial farmers and help them finance productivity improvements, but many smaller producers will probably turn to other crops. Under the North American Free Trade Agreement, Mexico's grain market is increasingly being opened to imports from the USA: in 1998/99 Mexico became the world's third largest maize importer, with purchases of 5.5m. tons.

Argentina is Latin America's only substantial maize exporting country, and ranks second only to the USA in amounts sold.

Market liberalization in the early 1990s, particularly the abolition of export taxes, encouraged maize production. Farmers were able to plan more rationally their activities, and make longer-term investments in land improvement and up-to-date equipment. At the same time, privatization and decontrol of the ports and transport systems resulted in much greater efficiency in grain movement. However, farmers are no longer shielded from international price trends, and the low prices of the late 1990s caused many to switch from maize to oilseeds or other more profitable crops. Having reached a record 19.4m. metric tons in 1997, Argentina's maize production fell to 13.2m. tons in the following year. However, this was still 50% more than its average production in the 1980s. Commercial plantings of genetically modified maize started in 1999.

Maize is grown widely as a subsistence crop in Central America. It is one of the most important foods in El Salvador and Guatemala, where consumption per head is around 100 kg per year. In South America food use is generally declining, although it remains important in some countries, notably Bolivia, Colombia, Paraguay and Venezuela, in each of which consumption averages 40 kg–50 kg per year.

Production of Maize ('000 metric tons)

	1999	2000
World total†	605,750	590,791
Latin America†	72,930	76,353
Leading Latin American producers		
Argentina	13,500	16,200
Brazil	32,038	32,038
Chile	624	646
Colombia	975	1,010‡
Guatemala	1,109	1,109*
Mexico	18,314	18,761
Paraguay	817	900*
Peru	1,059	1,271
Venezuela	1,024	900‡
Other leading producers		
Canada	9,161	6,827
China, People's Repub.	128,287	105,231‡
France	15,656	16,395
India	10,775	11,500‡
Italy	10,016	10,207
Romania	10,935	4,200‡
USA	239,549	253,208

* Provisional.
† Including Southern Hemisphere crops seeded in the year shown, but harvested in the first half of following calendar year.
‡ Unofficial figure.

Sources: International Grains Council; FAO, *Quarterly Bulletin of Statistics*.

World trade in maize reached a record annual total of 73m. metric tons in 1989/90 (July–June), but subsequently declined, largely because of a fall in purchases by the former USSR. Although trade recovered to about 65m. tons per year in the mid-1990s, growth was again curtailed by adverse economic conditions in eastern Asia, which severely impacted on the region's meat consumption and then on its demand for animal feed. Recovery in the Asian economies, together with growing demand from Latin America and North Africa, contributed to an increase in world maize trade to 69m. tons in 1998/99.

The pre-eminent world maize exporter is the USA, which typically accounts for about three-quarters of the total. Its sales reached 60m. metric tons in 1995/96, but subsequently declined owing to increased competition from Argentina, the People's Republic of China and very low-priced supplies from a number of countries in central and eastern Europe. US exports in the late 1990s averaged 45m. tons annually.

Argentina's exports had fallen to only around 3m. metric tons per year in the late 1980s, but grew rapidly in the 1990s to peak at more than 12m. tons in 1998/99. Its main markets are in Latin America, paticularly Brazil, Chile and Peru, but it also regularly makes large sales to Japan and other importers in Asia. The world's principal maize importer is Japan. It purchased over 16m. tons annually in the early 1990s, but its trade has been slowly declining in recent years, as the domestic livestock industry has been rationalized to compete with imported meat. Rapidly increasing livestock industries elsewhere in eastern Asia have made the region the major world market for maize. Feed users in the Republic of Korea (South Korea) are willing to substitute other grains for maize, particularly feed wheat, when prices are attractive, so that maize imports are variable, averaging about 7m. tons per year. Taiwan regularly imports about 5m. tons of maize annually, but imports by other countries in the region, notably Indonesia, Malaysia and the Philippines, have been significantly affected by adverse economic conditions. In the 1980s the USSR was a major market, but the livestock industries in the successor republics of the USSR declined sharply during the 1990s, greatly reducing feed needs. From a total of 18m. tons in 1989/90, these imports declined to 4m. tons in 1993/94 and have subsequently been less than 1m. tons annually. Maize imports by Latin America have grown considerably during the 1990s. The total reached 15m. tons in 1998/99, compared with less than 6m. tons 10 years earlier. The region currently accounts for some 22% of world maize trade, compared with less than 10% in the late 1980s. Latin America's biggest importer is Mexico, whose annual purchases average more than 5m. tons, but imports by Brazil, Chile, Colombia, Peru and Venezuela all regularly exceed 1m. tons per year.

Massive levels of carry-over stocks of maize were accumulated in the USA during the mid-1980s, reaching a high point of 124m. metric tons in 1987. Government support programmes were successful in discouraging surplus production, but several poor harvests also contributed to the depletion of these stocks, which were reduced to only 11m. tons at the close of the 1995/96 marketing year. A succession of good crops in the late 1990s, and increased competition from Argentina and the People's Republic of China, led to a substantial rebuilding of US maize stocks, despite growth in domestic feed requirements, associated with the strong economy. Carry-overs reached 45m. tons at the end of 1998/99.

Export prices of maize are mainly influenced by the level of supplies in the USA, and the intensity of competition between the exporting countries. Record quotations were achieved in April 1996, when the price of US No. 2 Yellow Corn (f.o.b. Gulf Ports) reached US $210 per metric ton. Prices were very depressed in 1998 and 1999, sometimes falling below $90 per ton.

Export Price Index for Maize (base: 1980 = 100)

	Average	Highest month(s)	Lowest month(s)
1990	92		
1995	80		
1998	63	69 (Jan., March)	56 (Sept.)
1999	58	60 (Jan., Sept., Oct.)	56 (July, Dec.)
2000	54	59 (Jan., Feb., March, April)	47 (Sept.)

Petroleum

Crude oils, from which petroleum is derived, consist essentially of a wide range of hydrocarbon molecules which are separated by distillation in the refining process. Refined oil is treated in different ways to make the different varieties of fuel. More than four-fifths of total world oil supplies are used as fuel for the production of energy in the form of power or heating.

Petroleum, together with its associated mineral fuel, natural gas, is extracted both from onshore and offshore wells in many areas of the world. It is the leading raw material in international trade. World-wide demand for this commodity totalled 71.5m. barrels per day (b/d) in 1997 and 1998. The world's 'published proven' reserves of petroleum and natural gas liquids at 31 December 2000 were estimated to total 142,100m. metric tons, equivalent to about 1,037,000m. barrels (1 metric ton is equivalent to approximately 7.3 barrels, each of 42 US gallons or 34.97 imperial gallons, i.e. 159 litres). The dominant producing region is the Middle East, whose proven reserves in December 2000 accounted for 65.1% of known world deposits of crude petroleum and natural gas liquids. The Middle East accounted for 31% of world output in 2000. Latin America contained 17,600m. metric tons of proven reserves (12.4% of the world total) at the end of 2000, and accounted for 14.5% of 2000 world production.

From storage tanks at the oilfield wellhead, crude petroleum is conveyed, frequently by pumping for long distances through large pipelines, to coastal depots where it is either treated in a refinery or delivered into bulk storage tanks for subsequent shipment for refining overseas. In addition to pipeline transportation of crude petroleum and refined products, natural (petroleum) gas is, in some areas, also transported through networks of pipelines. Crude petroleum varies considerably in colour and viscosity, and these variations are a determinant both of price and of end-use after refining.

In the refining process, crude petroleum is heated until vaporized. The vapours are then separately condensed, according to their molecular properties, passed through airless steel tubes and pumped into the lower section of a high, cylindrical tower, as a hot mixture of vapours and liquid. The heavy unvaporized liquid flows out at the base of the tower as a 'residue' from which is obtained heavy fuel and bitumen. The vapours passing upwards then undergo a series of condensation processes that produce 'distillates', which form the basis of the various petroleum products.

The most important of these products is fuel oil, composed of heavy distillates and residues, which is used to produce heating and power for industrial purposes. Products in the kerosene group have a wide number of applications, ranging from heating fuels to the powering of aviation gas turbine engines. Gasoline (petrol) products fuel internal combustion engines (principally in road motor vehicles), and naphtha, a gasoline distillate, is a commercial solvent that can also be processed as a feedstock. Propane and butane, the main liquefied petroleum gases, have a wide range of industrial applications and are also used for domestic heating and cooking.

Mexico was the world's leading petroleum producer in 1921 but by 1938, when the industry was nationalized, production had fallen dramatically. The discovery of extensive deposits of petroleum in the states of Tabasco and Chiapas, and off shore in the Bay of Campeche, enabled output to increase significantly in the 1970s. Mexico's proven reserves of petroleum stood at 4,000m. metric tons at the end of 2000. Mexico was the world's fifth largest producer of petroleum in 2000 and possesses the largest petroleum refining capacity in Latin America, with a throughput estimated at about 70m. tons in 1997. Since the mid-1980s, when Mexico's petroleum revenues have been affected by lower levels of exports, together with a series of price reductions which were authorized by the Government, the commodity's contribution to the country's earnings of foreign exchange has reflected the level of prices in international petroleum markets. Mexico's sales of petroleum and its derivatives, which provided 17.2% of foreign earnings in 1992, accounted for 11.7% in 1996, 10.0% in 1997 and 5.9% in 1998. The average price of Mexican crude petroleum in 1998 was only US $6.30 per barrel: its lowest annual level for 12 years.

Brazil's proven reserves of petroleum were assessed at 657m. metric tons at the end of 1997. The state-owned petroleum company, Petróleo Brasileiro (PETROBRÁS), operates petroleum refineries with an estimated end-1997 capacity of 83.1m. tons per year, making Brazil the region's second largest petroleum refiner, after Mexico. The company's monopoly of the Brazilian petroleum sector was ended in 1997 by the adoption of legislation allowing private-sector investment in all parts of the industry. By mid-1999 foreign companies had signed 22 joint-venture contracts (with PETROBRÁS) and 12 sole-venture contracts to operate in the petroleum sector in Brazil.

The production of petroleum is the dominant economic activity in Venezuela, although the contribution of petroleum and its derivatives to the country's total export earnings, which had been more than 90% until 1986, had declined, to 77% in 1989, before recovering to 80.3% in 1991. The proportion fell to 75.2% in 1994, but rose to 81.0% in 1996. Petroleum's share of total exports in 1997 was 79.0%, and an estimated 69.8% in 1998. In 2000, when Venezuela accounted for 32.1% of Latin American production, it ranked as the world's sixth largest producer. In 1996 Venezuela was the largest single supplier of petroleum to the USA. Proven reserves were estimated at 11,100m. metric tons at the end of 2000. In 1989 the national oil company, Petróleos de Venezuela (PDVSA), planned to invest US $3,200m. in new projects, with the aim of increasing potential petroleum production to 3m. b/d by 1991. Plans to raise output capacity by a further 25% by 1996 were announced in 1991. Foreign capital was sought to assist this investment programme, and in 1992, for the first time since the industry was nationalized in 1976, foreign participation was sought for exploration and production. Further foreign participation was to be encouraged in a proposed new round of tenders for the exploration and exploitation of natural gas deposits, to take effect from 2001. In early 1998 Venezuela's petroleum output was reported to exceed 3.3m. b/d; under the expanded programme of government and foreign investment, it is intended to expand crude petroleum production to more than 5m. b/d by 2005.

Production of Crude Petroleum
('000 metric tons, including natural gas liquids)

	1999	2000
World total	3,451,800	3,589,600
Latin America	509,200	520,300
Leading Latin American producers		
Argentina	42,700	41,200
Brazil	56,400	63,500
Colombia	42,500	36,100
Ecuador	19,500	20,700
Mexico	166,100	172,100
Peru	5,800	5,300
Trinidad and Tobago	6,700	8,100
Venezuela	163,200	166,800
Other leading producers		
Canada	120,600	126,300
China, People's Repub.	160,200	162,300
Iran	175,200	186,600
Iraq	125,600	128,100
Kuwait	99,300	105,600
Nigeria	99,900	103,900
Norway	149,400	157,500
Russia	304,800	323,300
Saudi Arabia	410,300	441,200
United Arab Emirates	105,600	114,700
United Kingdom	136,600	126,200
USA	353,000	353,500

Source: BP, *Statistical Review of World Energy 2001*.

Ecuador's petroleum industry has been a significant contributor to the economy since 1972, when petroleum was exported for the first time, after the completion of the 480-km (300-mile) trans-Andean pipeline (capacity 390,000 b/d in 2000), linking the oilfields of Oriente Province with the tanker-loading port of Esmeraldas. In late 2000 bids were invited for the construction of a second pipeline, with a proposed capacity of 310,000 b/d. In 1993 Ecuador's proven reserves of petroleum were almost tripled, following discoveries in the Amazon region, and in 1994 and 1995 the Government signed contracts with numerous companies for further exploration and drilling (including rights to explore areas in the Eastern Amazon, which had previously been withheld, owing to indigenous and environmental protests). Ecuador's proven published reserves at the end of 2000 amounted to 300m. metric tons. Petroleum and its derivatives accounted for 36.3% of export revenue in 1996 but by 1998 the proportion had declined to 22.3%, reflecting lower prices.

The economy of Trinidad and Tobago has relied heavily on the petroleum industry since the 1940s. The industry received a fillip from the discovery of offshore fields in 1955, and by the 1970s petroleum accounted for about 50% of the country's gross domestic product and about 90% of its export income. Until 1998 no significant onshore discoveries had been made since the early 1970s, although there are substantial reserves of natural gas. A series of offshore discoveries in 1998–2000 were reported to constitute the largest discovery of gas and petroleum in the history of the nation, equivalent to 630m. barrels. The petroleum industry remains a vital sector of the economy, accounting, with asphalt, for an estimated 27.1% of gross domestic product in 1997. Petroleum and its derivatives accounted for 43.6% of the country's export revenue in 1997, and an estimated 42.9% in 1998.

Colombia's importance as a producer of petroleum increased dramatically in 1984, when vast reserves of petroleum were discovered at Caño-Limón, near the Venezuelan border. This deposit, the largest petroleum discovery ever made in Colombia (with proven reserves of 192m. metric tons, of which 80m.–140m. tons are recoverable), doubled the country's recoverable petrol-

eum reserves and transformed its prospects as a producer. The Caño-Limón discovery was followed in 1991 by the discovery of the Cusiana field, in the Andes foothills, with reserves estimated at 178m. tons. A further discovery, north of Cusiana at Cupiagua, with reserves estimated at 70m. tons, followed in 1992. It was anticipated that these reserves could, if fully exploitable, maintain Colombia's current export capacity into the late 1990s, when output from Caño-Limón is expected to diminish. However, naturally declining output levels, technical difficulties and political instability raised fears in 2000 that Colombia could become a net importer of petroleum by 2004. Export earnings from petroleum and its derivatives accounted for 32.5% of total foreign revenue in 1999. In December 2000 Colombia's proven reserves were estimated at 400m. tons.

Argentina had estimated proven reserves of crude petroleum totalling 400m. metric tons in December 2000. Substantial investment, however, is required in the petroleum sector before Argentina can achieve self-sufficiency in petroleum and increase production in order to generate exports. In 1993 the Government relinquished its monopoly in the petroleum sector and transferred the state corporation, Yacimientos Petrolíferos Fiscales (YPF), to private-sector ownership. Chile imports more than 50% of its petroleum requirements, but the discovery of deposits in the Strait of Magellan has encouraged the hope of satisfying domestic demand from local resources in the first few years of the 21st century; in December 1996 proven reserves amounted to 21m. tons. Peru had estimated proven petroleum reserves of up to 50m. tons in 2000, and the country is able to export petroleum that is surplus to domestic demand. Foreign participation is being sought to develop vast new deposits identified in the early 1990s at Camisea, south-east of Lima. In February 2000 a consortium comprising Pluspetrol (Argentina), Hunt Oil (USA) and SK Corp (Republic of Korea) was awarded a contract for the first stage in the development of the Camisea project. The field was expected to begin supply in 2003. Guatemala commenced petroleum exports in 1980. The level of published proven reserves was 26m. tons in December 1997. Petroleum accounted for only 2.4% of Guatemala's export earnings in 1998. Although a minor regional producer, Cuba's production of 1.7m. tons in 1998 satisfied about 22% of its domestic petroleum requirements in that year.

International petroleum prices are strongly influenced by the Organization of the Petroleum Exporting Countries (OPEC), founded in 1960 to co-ordinate the production and marketing policies of those countries whose main source of export earnings is petroleum. In mid-2001 OPEC had 11 members. Venezuela is the only Latin American participant, although Mexico, together with other non-members, has collaborated closely with OPEC in recent years.

Export Price Index for Crude Petroleum (base: 1980 = 100)

	Average	Highest month(s)	Lowest month(s)
1990	69		
1995	54		
1998	38	44 (Jan.)	30 (Dec.)
1999	54	77 (Dec.)	31 (Feb.)
2000	86	96 (Sept.)	73 (April, Dec.)

The two leading western European producers and exporters of crude petroleum are Norway and the United Kingdom. The two countries' exports of crude petroleum earned an average of US $126 per metric ton in 1993, $118 per ton in 1994, $127 per ton in 1995, $153 per ton in 1996 and $144 per ton in 1997. Prices per barrel averaged about $20 in 1992, declined to only about $14 in late 1993, but recovered to more than $18 in mid-1994. Thereafter, international petroleum prices remained relatively stable until the early months of 1995. The price per barrel reached about $20 again in April and May 1995, but eased to $17 later in the year. In April 1996 the London price of the standard grade of North Sea petroleum for short-term delivery rose to more than $23 per barrel, following reports that stocks of petroleum in Western industrialized countries were at their lowest levels for 19 years. After another fall, the price of North Sea petroleum rose in October to more than $25 per barrel, its highest level for more than five years. The price per barrel was generally in the range of $22–$24 for the remainder of the year.

Petroleum traded at US \$24–\$25 per barrel in January 1997, but the short-term quotation for the standard North Sea grade fell to less than \$17 in June. The price increased to more than \$21 per barrel in October, in response to increased tension in the Persian (Arabian) Gulf region. However, the threat of an immediate conflict in the region subsided, and petroleum prices eased. The market was also weakened by an OPEC decision, in November, to raise the upper limit on members' production quotas, and by the severe financial and economic problems affecting many countries in eastern Asia. By the end of the year the price for North Sea petroleum had again been reduced to less than \$17 per barrel.

Petroleum prices declined further in January 1998, with the standard North Sea grade trading at less than US \$15 per barrel. Later in the month the price recovered to about \$16.5 per barrel, but in March some grades of petroleum were trading at less than \$13. Later that month three of the leading exporting countries—Saudi Arabia, Venezuela and Mexico (not an OPEC member)—agreed to reduce petroleum production, in an attempt to revive prices. In response, the price of North Sea petroleum advanced to about \$15.5 per barrel. Following endorsement of the three countries' initiative by OPEC, however, there was widespread doubt that the proposals would be sufficient to have a sustained impact on prices, in view of the existence of large stocks of petroleum. Under the plan, OPEC members and five other countries (including Mexico and Norway) agreed to reduce their petroleum output between 1 April and the end of the year. The proposed reductions totalled about 1.5m. b/d (2% of world production), with Saudi Arabia making the greatest contribution (300,000 b/d). In early June, having failed to make a significant impact on international prices, the three countries that had agreed in March to restrict their production of petroleum announced further reduction in output, effective from 1 July. However, petroleum prices continued to be depressed, and in mid-June some grades sold for less than \$12 per barrel. A new agreement between OPEC and other producers, concluded later that month, envisaged further reductions in output, totalling more than 1m. b/d, but this attempt to stimulate a rise in petroleum prices had little effect. The price on world markets was generally in the range of \$12–\$14 per barrel over the period July–October. Subsequently there was further downward pressure on petroleum prices, and in December the London quotation for the standard North Sea grade was below \$10 per barrel for the first time since the introduction of the contract in 1986. For 1998 as a whole, the average price of North Sea petroleum was \$13.37 per barrel: more than 30% less than in 1997 and the lowest annual level since 1976. In real terms (i.e. taking inflation into account), international prices for crude petroleum in late 1998 were at their lowest level since the 1920s.

During the early months of 1999 there was a steady recovery in the petroleum market. In March five leading producers (including Mexico) announced plans to reduce further their combined output by about 2m. b/d. Later that month an OPEC meeting agreed reductions in members' quotas totalling 1.7m. b/d (including 585,000 b/d for Saudi Arabia), to operate for 12 months from 1 April. The new quotas represented a 7% decrease from the previous levels (applicable from July 1998). At the same time, four non-members agreed voluntary cuts in production, bringing total proposed reductions in output to about 2.1m. b/d. In May 1999 the London price of North Sea petroleum rose to about US \$17 per barrel. After easing somewhat, the price advanced again, reaching more than \$20 per barrel in August. The upward trend continued, and in late September the price of North Sea petroleum (for November delivery) was just above \$24 per barrel. After easing somewhat, prices rose again in November, when North Sea petroleum (for delivery in January 2000) was traded at more than \$25 per barrel. The surge in prices followed indications that, in contrast to 1998, the previously agreed limits on output were, to a large extent, being implemented by producers and thus having an effect on stock levels. Surveys found that the rate of compliance among the 10 OPEC countries participating in the scheme to restrict production was 87% in June and July 1999, although it fell to 83% in October.

International prices for crude petroleum rose steadily during the opening weeks of 2000, with OPEC restrictions continuing to operate and stocks declining in industrial countries. In early March the London price for North Sea petroleum exceeded US \$31.5 per barrel, but later in the month nine OPEC members agreed to restore production quotas to pre-March 1999 levels from 1 April 2000, representing a combined increase of about 1.7m. b/d. The London petroleum price fell in April to less than \$22 per barrel, but the rise in OPEC production was insufficient to increase significantly the stocks held by major consuming countries. In June the price of North Sea petroleum rose to about \$31.5 per barrel again, but later that month OPEC ministers agreed to a further rise in quotas (totalling about 700,000 b/d) from 1 July. By the end of July the North Sea petroleum price was below \$27 per barrel, but in mid-August it rose to more than \$32 for the first time since 1990 (when prices had surged in response to the Iraqi invasion of Kuwait). In New York in the same month, meanwhile, the September contract for light crude traded at a new record level of \$33 per barrel at one point. The surge in oil prices in August was attributed to continued fears regarding supply levels in coming months, especially in view of data showing US inventories to be at their lowest level for 24 years, and of indications by both Saudi Arabia and Venezuela that OPEC would not act to raise production before September. Deliberate attempts to raise the price of the expiring London September contract were an additional factor.

In early September 2000 the London price of North Sea petroleum for October delivery climbed to a new 10-year high of US \$34.55, reflecting the view that any production increase that OPEC might decide to implement would be insufficient to prevent tight supplies later in the year. In New York, meanwhile, the price of light crude for October delivery rose beyond the \$35 per barrel mark. This latest bout of price volatility reflected the imminence of an OPEC meeting, at which Saudi Arabia was expected to seek an agreement to raise the Organization's production by at least 700,000 b/d in order to stabilize the market. In the event, OPEC decided to increase production by 800,000 b/d, with effect from 1 October, causing prices in both London and New York to ease. This relaxation was short-lived, however. Just over a week after OPEC's decision was announced the price of the New York October contract for light crude closed at \$36.88 per barrel, in response to concerns over tension in the Persian (Arabian) Gulf area between Iraq and Kuwait. The same contract had at one point risen above \$37 per barrel, its highest level for 10 years. These latest increases prompted OPEC representatives to deliver assurances that production would be raised further in order to curb price levels regarded as economically damaging in the USA and other consumer countries. Towards the end of September the London price of North Sea petroleum for November delivery fell below \$30 per barrel for the first time in a month, in response to the decision of the USA to release petroleum from its strategic reserve in order to depress prices.

In the first week of October 2000, however, the price of the November contract for both North Sea petroleum traded in London and New York light crude had stabilized at around US \$30 per barrel, anxiety over political tension in the Middle East preventing the more marked decline that had been anticipated. This factor exerted stronger upward pressure during the following week, when the London price of North Sea petroleum for November delivery rose above \$35 per barrel for the first time since 1990. In early November 2000 crude oil continued to trade at more than \$30 per barrel in both London and New York, despite the announcement by OPEC of a further increase in production, this time of 500,000 b/d, and a lessening of political tension in the Middle East. Prices were volatile throughout November, with the price of both London and New York contracts for January delivery remaining in excess of \$30 per barrel at the end of the month.

During the first week of December 2000 the price of the January 'futures' contract in both London and New York declined substantially, in response, mainly, to an unresolved dispute between the UN and Iraq over the pricing of Iraqi oil. On 8 December the closing London Price of North Sea petroleum for January delivery was US \$26.56 per barrel, while the equivalent New York price for light crude was \$28.44. Trading during the second week of December was characterized by further declines, the London price of North Sea petroleum for January delivery falling below \$25 per barrel at one point. Analysts noted that prices had fallen by some 20% since mid-November, and OPEC representatives indicated that the Organization might decide to cut production in January 2001 if prices fell below its preferred trading range of $22-$28 per barrel. At $23.51 per barrel on 14 December, the price of the OPEC 'basket' of crudes was at its lowest level since May. During the third week of December the price of the OPEC 'basket' of crudes declined further, to $21.64 per barrel. Overall, during December, the price of crudes traded in both London and New York declined by some $10 per barrel, and remained subject to pressure at the end of the month.

Continued expectations that OPEC would decide to reduce production later in the month caused 'futures' prices to strengthen in the first week of January 2001. The London price of North Sea petroleum for February delivery closed at US $25.18 on 5 January, while the corresponding price for light crude traded in New York was $27.95. Prices remained firm in the second week of January, again in anticipation of a decision by OPEC to reduce production. Paradoxically, prices fell immediately after OPEC's decision to reduce production by 1.5m. b/d was announced on 17 January. However, it was widely recognized that the reduction had been factored into markets by that time.

Oil prices rose significantly at the beginning of February 2001, although the gains were attributed mainly to speculative purchases rather than to any fundamental changes in market conditions. On 2 February the London price of North Sea petroleum for March delivery closed at US $29.19 per barrel, while the corresponding price for light crude traded in New York was $31.19. On 8 February prices rose to their highest levels for two months, the London price for North Sea petroleum for March delivery exceeding $30 per barrel at one point. The upward movement came in response to a forecast, issued by the US Energy Information Administration (EIA), that the 'spot' price for West Texas Intermediate (the US 'marker' crude) would average close to $30 per barrel throughout 2001. During the remainder of the month prices in both London and New York remained largely without direction.

During the early part of March 2001 oil prices in both London and New York drifted downwards while it remained unclear whether OPEC would decide to implement a further cut in production, and what the effect of such a reduction might be. On 9 March the London price of North Sea petroleum for April delivery was US $26.33 per barrel, while the corresponding price for light crude traded in New York was $28.01 per barrel. By late March prices in both London and New York had declined further, the London price of North Sea petroleum for May delivery closing at close to $24.82 per barrel on 30 March, while the corresponding price for New York light crude was $26.35.

During the first week of April 2001 crude oil prices on both sides of the Atlantic strengthened in response to fears of a gasoline shortage in the USA later in the year. On 6 April the London price of North Sea petroleum for May delivery was US $25.17 per barrel, while New York light crude for delivery in May closed at $27.06. Strong demand for crude oil by US gasoline refiners was the strongest influence on markets throughout April as gasoline 'futures' rose markedly. Towards the end of April the price of the New York contract for gasoline for May delivery rose to the equivalent of $1.115 per gallon, higher than the previous record price recorded in August 1990.

Fears of a shortage of gasoline supplies in the USA remained the key influence on oil markets in early May 2001, with 'futures' prices rising in response to successive record prices for gasoline 'futures'. On 4 May the London price of North Sea petroleum for June delivery was US $28.19 per barrel, while that of the corresponding contract for light crude traded in New York closed at $28.36. Prices were prevented from rising further during the week ending 4 May by the report of an unexpected increase in US inventories of crude oil. A further check came in the following week, when the International Energy Agency (IEA) reduced its forecast of world growth in demand for crude oil by 300,000 b/d to 1.02m. b/d. On 18 May, however, demand for crude oil by gasoline refiners raised the price of New York crude for June delivery to its highest level for three months, while the price of the July contract rose above $30 per barrel.

The Mutual Assistance of the Latin American Oil Companies (Asistencia Recíproca Petrolera Empresarial Latinoamericana—ARPEL) exists to promote co-operation in matters of technical and economic development. ARPEL, with headquarters in Montevideo, Uruguay, has 21 members in 19 countries, including France, Norway and Spain.

Silver

Known since prehistoric times, silver is a white metal which is extremely malleable and ductile. It is one of the best metallic conductors of heat and electricity, hence its use in electrical contacts and in electroplating. Silver's most important compounds are the chloride and bromide which darken on exposure to light, the basis of photographic emulsions.

World-wide, about 77% of silver production in 1999 was generated as a by-product, or co-product, of gold, copper, lead and zinc mining operations. Methods of recovery depend upon the composition of the silver-bearing ore. The exploitation of primary sources of silver ore accounted for about 23% of silver output in 1999.

In 1999 the world-wide use of silver in fabricated products totalled 877.4m. troy ounces (a rise of 5.0% from the 1998 level). The manufacture of coins and medals absorbed 27.0m. oz (3.1% of total demand) in 1999. Of the remainder, 343.2m. oz were consumed for industrial purposes (compared with 316.7m. oz in 1998). The production of photographic materials (including X-ray film) absorbed 246.4m. oz in 1999 (compared with 244.6m. oz in 1998), while 260.8m. oz (29.7%) went into jewellery and silverware. The manufacture of electronic equipment and batteries in the major industrialized countries absorbed 148.5m. oz of silver (16.9% of world demand) in 1999. Other industrial uses for silver include the production of brazing alloys, mirrors and catalysts. In 1998, according to provisional figures, the principal user of silver in fabricated products (including coinage) was the USA, which consumed 188.8m. oz (22.5% of the world total), followed by Japan, with 112.8m. oz (13.4%), and India, with 104.3m. oz (12.4%). Other major users of silver in 1998 were Italy (57.0m. oz) and Germany (48.5m. oz).

World mine production of silver was estimated to have increased by 25% during the period 1979–85, as a result of generally higher (although widely fluctuating) prices. However, while output advanced, consumption declined, resulting in a world surplus of silver in each year during 1980–89. In 1990 this trend was reversed, and, according to the Silver Institute (an international association of miners, refiners, fabricators and manufacturers, with its headquarters in Washington, DC, USA), world demand exceeded mine and secondary (recycled and scrap silver) production, creating the first silver market supply deficit since 1978. In each of the years 1991–97 world consumption of silver outpaced mine production, which declined by 13.8% over the period 1990–94. Output recovered by 6.1% in 1995 and by 1.7% in 1996, partly as a result of new mines entering production, together with the reopening of a number of primary silver mines as a result of improved prices. A third consecutive year of increased production was achieved in 1997, when mine output rose by 8.0%, and in 1998 production advanced by a further 4.0% to a record 547.8m. oz. In 1999 the output of silver from the world's mines fell by 0.2%: the first decrease for five years. However, the most significant change in the balance between supply and demand in 1999 was an increase in net sales of silver from the official sector. In 1998 the volume of these disposals was about 40m. oz, but in 1999 the total reached 87m. oz (including estimated sales of 61m. oz, equivalent to 7% of world silver supply, by the People's Bank of China).

Mexico is the world's leading producer of silver, although the country's output declined from 91.6m. oz in 1998 to 75.2m. oz in 1999. Mexico's Proaño mine, near Fresnillo (in the state of Zacatecas), was the largest primary silver mine in the world in 1997–99. In the early 1990s Mexico's reserve base of silver ore was estimated to represent about 9.5% of the world reserve base. Peru is second to Mexico in terms of silver production, accounting for 12% of world silver output in 1998. In the same year Chile, the third most important regional producer, accounted for 7.9% of world production. Although a relatively minor producer, Argentina significantly increased its silver output in 1998 as the result of two new mines entering production. Following a positive feasibility study, development of the world's largest open-pit silver project was under way in 2000 at the San Cristóbal deposits in the Potosí department of southern Bolivia. Proven and probable reserves at San Cristóbal total 240m. metric tons of ore, containing 2.0 oz of silver per ton.

As an investment metal (an estimated 80% of the world's silver bullion stocks are speculative holdings), silver is highly sensitive to factors other than the comparative levels of supply and demand. Silver, like gold and platinum, is customarily measured in troy weight. The now obsolete troy pound contains 12 ounces (oz), each of 480 grains. One troy ounce is equal to 31.1 grams (1 kg = 32.15 troy oz), compared with the avoirdupois ounce of 28.3 grams.

Fluctuations in the price of silver bullion traditionally tended to follow trends in prices for gold and other precious metals. However, silver has come to be viewed increasingly as an industrial raw material and hence likely to decrease in price at times of economic recession. Two of the main centres for trading in silver are the London Bullion Market (LBM) and the New York Commodity Exchange (COMEX). Dealings in silver on the LBM are only on the basis of 'spot' contracts (for prompt delivery), while COMEX contracts are also for silver 'futures' (options to take delivery at specified future dates). Over a 15-day period in January 1992 the LBM price of silver per troy ounce increased from £2.06 (US $3.87) to £2.41 ($4.335), and until the middle of the year it remained within this range. Thereafter, the silver market slumped, and in August the LBM quotation was reduced to £1.83 ($3.65) per oz. In terms of sterling, the London silver price later moved sharply higher, but the trend was largely a reflection of the British currency's depreciation in relation to the US dollar. In February 1993 the LBM price reached £2.65 (then $3.77) per oz, but later in the month it stood at £2.46 (only $3.58). In March the London silver price in US currency was only $3.56 per oz: just above the 17-year 'low' of $3.55 recorded in February 1991. However, a vigorous recovery ensued, with the LBM quotation advancing to £3.66 ($5.42) per oz in August 1993, before declining to £2.55 ($3.92) in September. With demand continuing to exceed supply, another advance took the silver price to £3.45 ($5.115) per oz at the end of the year.

Silver Prices on the New York Commodity Exchange
(average 'spot' quotations, US $ per troy ounce)

	Average	Highest month(s)	Lowest month(s)
1990	4.817		
1995	5.185		
1998	5.489	6.695 (Feb.)	4.850 (Dec.)
1999	5.218	5.52 (Feb.)	5.04 (June)
2000	4.969	5.257 (Feb.)	4.631 (Dec.)

Sources: The Silver Institute; Gold Fields Mineral Services Ltd.

The recovery in the silver market continued in the early months of 1994, partly as a result of speculative activity, and by the end of March the London price had reached £3.87 (US $5.735) per oz. A week earlier, the price in US currency was $5.75 per oz. After another decline, the LBM quotation stood at £3.62 ($5.71) per oz in September. Thereafter, the price of silver moved generally downwards, declining to £2.965 ($4.64) per oz in December.

Silver prices fell further in the early months of 1995, with the metal trading in London at £2.68 (US $4.42) per oz in March. The price later rose sharply, and in May it reached £3.75 ($6.04) per oz. In August the LBM price of silver per oz stood at £3.76, then equivalent to $5.80. As on previous occasions, the surge in prices was attributed mainly to speculative investment.

Another advance took the LBM silver quotation to £3.84 (US $5.83) per oz in February 1996, but the price moved generally downward during the remainder of the year, reaching £2.81 ($4.73) in December. For the year as a whole, the average London price of silver was $5.199 per oz.

There were extreme fluctuations in the price of silver in 1997. The London price declined to £2.75 (US $4.66) per oz in January, but recovered to £3.30 ($5.26) in March. However, in early July the London quotation was reduced to £2.51 ($4.25) per oz, and a week later the price in US currency was only $4.22: its lowest level since November 1993. Prices subsequently rallied, and in December 1997, with silver in short supply after a steady decline in stocks (see below), the London quotation per oz rose to £3.76, equivalent to $6.27: a nine-year 'high' in the US currency price. Despite the strong advance in the second half of the year, the average London silver price in 1997 was $4.897 per oz, nearly

6% lower than in the previous year. The average price of gold in 1997 was 67.6 times that of silver, but by the end of the year the ratio was only 47.

During the early weeks of 1998 there was intense speculative activity, amid allegations of manipulation, in the silver market. In early February it was disclosed that one major US investor had purchased 129.7m. oz (more than 4,000 metric tons) of the metal, equivalent to about 15% of annual world demand, during the preceding six months. Three days after this report, the London silver price per oz increased to £4.76, equivalent to US $7.81: its highest level, in terms of US currency, since July 1988. Meanwhile, the price of gold (which had fallen to its lowest level for more than 18 years) was only 38.3 times that of silver: the smallest ratio since 1983. The surge in silver prices was short-lived, despite the continuing scarcity of supplies, and in May 1998, following a sharp fall in demand for the metal from India (the main importing country), the London quotation was reduced to £3.04 ($4.96) per oz. Silver prices remained fairly stable for the next few months, but they declined further in August. At the beginning of September the LBM price per oz was £2.82 ($4.73), although by the end of the month it had recovered to £3.175 ($5.385). After another fall, the price in early December stood at £2.81 ($4.69) per oz, the lowest for the year. The average London price of silver in 1998 was $5.544 per oz: 13.2% above the 1997 average and the highest annual level since 1988. The difference between the maximum and minimum prices per oz in 1998 was $3.12, equivalent to 56.3% of the annual average: the widest trading range since 1987. For 1998 as a whole, the average price of gold was 53.0 times that of silver: the lowest annual ratio since 1985.

The London silver price advanced to US $5.75 (£3.525) per oz in February 1999, but declined to $4.88 (£3.044) in June. The price recovered to $5.71 (£3.470) per oz in September and ended the year at $5.33 (£3.298). In late March 2000 the price of silver stood at $4.935 (£3.094) per oz. In terms of US currency, it was lower in early June, at $4.895 (£3.271) per oz.

Production of Silver Ore
(provisional figures, silver content, metric tons)

	1999	2000
World total	17,188	18,334
Latin America	6,558	6,959
Leading Latin American producers		
Argentina	103	99
Bolivia	424	437
Chile	1,392	1,170
Honduras	48	55
Mexico	2,338	2,744
Peru	2,231	2,438
Other leading producers		
Australia	1,720	2,060
Canada	1,166	1,174
China, People's Repub.	1,375	1,500
Poland	1,115	1,140
USSR (former)*	1,437	1,596
USA	1,950	1,970

* Estimated production. The main producers of silver among the successor states of the USSR are Russia (about 375 metric tons in 1999) and Kazakhstan (about 575 metric tons in 1999).

Sources: The Silver Institute; Gold Fields Mineral Services Ltd.

Sugar

Sugar is a sweet crystalline substance which may be derived from the juices of various plants. Chemically, the basis of sugar is sucrose, one of a group of soluble carbohydrates which are important sources of energy in the human diet. It can be obtained from trees, including the maple and certain palms, but virtually all manufactured sugar is derived from two plants, sugar beet (*Beta vulgaris*) and sugar cane, a giant perennial grass of the genus *Saccharum*.

Sugar cane, found in tropical areas, grows to a height of up to 5 m (16 ft). The plant is native to Polynesia but its distribution is now widespread. It is not necessary to plant cane every season as, if the root of the plant is left in the ground, it will grow again in the following year. This practice, known as 'ratooning', may be continued for as long as three years, when yields begin to decline. Cane is ready for cutting 12–24 months after planting, depending on local conditions. Much of the world's sugar cane is still cut by hand, but rising costs are hastening the change-over to mechanical harvesting. The cane is cut as close as possible to the ground, and the top leaves, which may be used as cattle fodder, are removed.

After cutting, the cane is loaded by hand or by machine into trucks or trailers and transported directly to a factory for processing. Sugar cane deteriorates quickly after it has been cut and should be processed as quickly as possible. At the factory the cane passes first through shredding knives or crushing rollers, which break up the hard rind and expose the inner fibre, and then to squeezing rollers, where the crushed cane is subjected to high pressure and sprayed with water. The resulting juice is heated, and lime is added for clarification and the removal of impurities. The clean juice is then concentrated in evaporators. This thickened juice is next boiled in steam-heated vacuum pans until a mixture or 'massecuite' of sugar crystals and 'mother syrup' is produced. The massecuite is then spun in centrifugal machines to separate the sugar crystals (raw cane sugar) from the residual syrup (cane molasses).

The production of beet sugar follows the same process, except that the juice is extracted by osmotic diffusion. Its manufacture produces white sugar crystals which do not require further refining. In most producing countries, it is consumed domestically, although the European Union (EU), which accounts for about 15% of total world sugar production, is a net exporter of white refined sugar. Beet sugar accounts for more than one-third of world production. Production data for sugar cane covers generally all crops harvested, except crops grown explicitly for feed. The second table covers the production of raw sugar by the centrifugal process. In the late 1990s global output of non-centrifugal sugar (i.e., produced from sugar cane which has not undergone centrifugation) was about 14m. tons per year.

Most of the raw cane sugar which is produced in the world is sent to refineries outside the country of origin, unless the sugar is for local consumption. Cuba, Thailand, Brazil and India are among the few cane-producers that export part of their output as refined sugar. The refining process further purifies the sugar crystals and eventually results in finished products of various grades, such as granulated, icing or castor sugar. The ratio of refined to raw sugar is usually about 0.9:1.

As well as providing sugar, quantities of cane are grown in some countries for seed, feed, fresh consumption, the manufacture of alcohol and other uses. Molasses may be used as cattle feed or fermented to produce alcoholic beverages for human consumption, such as rum, a distilled spirit manufactured in Caribbean countries. Sugar cane juice may be used to produce ethyl alcohol (ethanol). This chemical can be mixed with petroleum derivatives to produce fuel for motor vehicles. The steep rise in the price of petroleum after 1973 made the large-scale conversion of sugar cane into alcohol economically attractive (particularly to developing nations), especially as sugar, unlike petroleum, is a renewable source of energy. Several countries developed alcohol production by this means in order to reduce petroleum imports and to support cane growers. The blended fuel which is used in cars is known as 'gasohol', 'alcogas' or 'green petrol', as it generates fewer harmful exhaust hydrocarbons than petroleum-based fuels. The pioneer in this field was Brazil, which established the largest 'gasohol' production programme in the world. By the late 1980s ethanol accounted for about one-half of the fuel consumption of Brazilian motorists. However, the additional costs involved in adapting motor vehicle design and engineering to ethanol consumption, together with the subsequent decline in world petroleum prices, resulted in a sharp fall in Brazil's output of these vehicles during the mid-1990s. Only about 1,000 alcohol-powered cars per year were being produced in the late 1990s, compared with a record 700,000 in 1986. Moreover, Brazil had large accumulated stocks of the blended fuel (including 24% ethanol) used in such vehicles. In 1999 the Brazilian distilleries producing the sugar-based alcohol were operating considerably below their capacity. In response, the Government has adopted a series of measures intended to revive the industry. An increase in demand was

Production of Sugar Cane ('000 metric tons)

	1999	2000
World total	1,275,885	1,278,092
Latin America	550,400	542,388
Leading Latin American producers		
Argentina	16,700†	16,000†
Brazil	337,165	324,668
Colombia	36,900*	37,000*
Cuba	34,000	36,000*
Dominican Repub.	4,447	4,785
Ecuador	7,864	6,200*
Guatemala	16,350*	17,150*
Mexico	45,880	49,275
Peru	6,900*	7,750*
Venezuela	7,989	6,950†
Other leading producers		
Australia	38,534	38,343
China, People's Repub.	78,108	70,205†
India	295,700	315,100
Indonesia	23,500†	21,400†
Pakistan	55,191	46,333
Philippines	23,778	33,732
Thailand	53,494	51,210
USA	32,023	32,973

* FAO estimate.   † Unofficial figure.

Production of Centrifugal Sugar (raw value, '000 metric tons)

	1999	2000
World total	133,974	127,200
Latin America	40,847	35,034
Leading Latin American producers		
Argentina	1,578	1,530†
Brazil	21,055†	14,500†
Colombia	2,241	2,300†
Cuba	3,783	4,134†
Guatemala	1,618†	1,692†
Mexico	4,755	4,984†
Other leading producers		
Australia	5,778	5,778*
China (incl. Taiwan)	7,736†	7,800†
France	4,914	4,551†
Germany	4,300	4,550†
India	17,436	18,935
Pakistan	3,791†	2,685†
South Africa	2,536	2,646†
Thailand	5,630	5,721†
Turkey	2,400	2,374
USA	8,197	7,720*

* FAO estimate.   † Unofficial figure.

recorded in 1999, although this was widely attributed to increased petroleum prices.

After the milling of sugar, the cane has dry fibrous remnants known as bagasse, which is usually burned as fuel in sugar mills but can be pulped and used for making fibreboard, particle board and many grades of paper. As the costs of imported wood pulp have risen, cane-growing regions have turned increasingly to the manufacture of paper from bagasse. In view of rising energy costs, some countries (such as Cuba) are encouraging the use of bagasse as fuel for electricity production to save on foreign exchange from imports of petroleum. In 1979 a further possible use for sugar was demonstrated in Cuba, where an explosive made from molasses was used to fell trees. It was reported that a factory to produce the explosive, known as 'Nitromiel', was planned. Another by-product, cachaza, which had formerly been discarded, is currently being utilized as an animal feed.

In recent years sugar has encountered increased competition from other sweeteners, including maize-based products, such as isoglucose (a form of high-fructose corn syrup or HFCS), and chemical additives, such as saccharine, aspartame and xylitol. Aspartame (APM) was the most widely used high-intensity artificial sweetener in the early 1990s, although its market dominance was under challenge from sucralose, which is about 600 times as sweet as sugar (compared with 200–300 times for other intense sweeteners) and is more resistant to chemical deterioration than APM. From the late 1980s research was being conducted in the USA to formulate means of synthesizing thaumatin, a substance derived from the fruit of a west African plant, *Thaumatoccus daniellii*, which is several thousand times as sweet as sugar. If, as has been predicted, thaumatin can be commercially produced by 2000, it could obtain a substantial share of the markets for both sugar and artificial sweeteners. In 1998 the US Government approved the domestic marketing of sucralose, the only artificial sweetener made from sugar. Sucralose, which is 600 times as sweet as sugar, was stated to avoid many of the taste problems associated with other artificial sweeteners.

By its sheer geographical extent, Latin America offers a wide range of conditions for the cultivation of sugar cane and, to a limited degree, of sugar beet (in Chile and Uruguay). The sugar industries of the region operate a diversity of modern mechanized and labour-intensive cultivation and processing techniques. The highest yields in the region (and among the highest in the world) are obtained in Peru, where intensive use of fertilizers and irrigation has compensated for the natural disadvantages of light soil and aridity. Producer costs vary from country to country, according to production methods, the availability of labour and the level of wages. Central American countries export 7m.–9m. metric tons per year, making theirs the largest exporting region in the world. The sugar industry in Guatemala has been expanding rapidly in recent years; its milling capacity has been targeted to increase by 50% between 1997–2001. Colombia exports about one-third of its annual sugar output, and in 1997/98 ranked, after Brazil and Cuba, as the region's third largest sugar exporter. Venezuela, however, has become a substantial importer (about 40% of its requirements were imported in 1997), owing partly to the demands of that country's petroleum industry, which have reduced the availability of labour to other industries and necessitated the introduction of costly mechanized techniques.

South America is also a significant producer of non-centrifugal sugar, mainly from Colombia and Brazil, all of which is consumed locally. The area under sugar cultivation in the whole of Latin America has increased in an attempt to satisfy greater domestic consumption and the desire to diversify from predominant industries (e.g. coffee, cocoa) and to reduce the dependence on imported sugar.

Brazil is usually the world's largest producer of sugar cane. The area under sugar cultivation was about 3.2m. ha, or some 6% of the total cultivated area, in 1981, and has been increasing at a rate of 5%–7% per year, reflecting the importance of sugar production to the economy. Production and exports could have been expanded more if it were not for Brazil's role as a member of the International Sugar Organization (ISO, see below) in attempting to stabilize the world sugar market. Brazil is, however, a substantial exporter of raw sugar, accounting for about 10% of world sales in 1997. Its principal markets are the USA, Russia, Egypt and Algeria. An accumulation in domestic sugar stocks, resulting from a fall in demand for ethanol (see above), was expected to enhance Brazil's share of the export market in 1998. Brazilian sugar exports increased sharply in early 1999, following the devaluation of the country's currency. Subsequently, the international price of sugar fell to its lowest level for 12 years (see below). Brazil's foreign exchange earnings from sales of raw and refined sugars amounted to US $1,611.5m. (about 3.4% of total export revenue) in 1996, compared with $1,919.5m. (4.1%) in 1995.

The Cuban economy relies heavily on sales of sugar and sugar products. The share of these exports in Cuba's total earnings from trade has been as high as 90%, but low world prices in the 1980s, occasionally not even covering producers' costs, affected all sugar exporters. Sugar and sugar products accounted for 73.2% of Cuban export revenue in 1989, compared with about 43% in the late 1990s. Prior to the revolution of 1959–60, Cuba exported more than 50% of its sugar to the USA. Following the trade embargo imposed by the USA, approximately 60% of annual exports were taken by the USSR and other Eastern bloc countries, mostly under long-term

trade and barter agreements at preferential prices. (In 1990 the USSR supplied Cuba with 95% of its total petroleum requirements.) Since 1991, however, these arrangements have ceased, and the Cuban sugar trade with the successor republics of the USSR, as well as with Eastern European countries and China, is now conducted on the basis of full market prices, and Cuba has sought new markets in Canada, North Africa, and in the Middle East and Far East. However, Cuban sugar production has declined sharply since the early 1990s, owing both to adverse weather conditions and to disruptions in the procurement of fuel, fertilizers, mill equipment and other essential production inputs, as a result of the US embargoes. These factors, which resulted in the 1994/95 harvest declining to the lowest level in 50 years, necessitated over-extended harvests and the use of reserves of cane intended for future crops. These factors brought about a temporary suspension of sugar exports in 1993. Difficulties have arisen in meeting subsequent export commitments, which included an agreement to supply Russia with 1m. tons of sugar in the year to March 1996 in exchange for 3m. tons of petroleum products. Russia has remained the principal market for Cuban sugar, absorbing approximately 28% of Cuban sugar exports during 1994–96. Cuba was, however, unable to fulfil a contract to supply China with 400,000 tons of sugar during 1995. In that year the Cuban Government negotiated loans totalling US $100m. from private European sources for the purchase of fertilizers and sugar factory equipment. Additional foreign finance was obtained to assist a further recovery in the 1996/97 season, when exports of sugar were estimated to have earned $950m. in foreign exchange. A disappointing crop in 1997/98, however, was expected to generate only $432m. in export revenue.

Before the 1959 revolution, when the industry passed into state control, about 75% of Cuba's sugar cane was grown on large mill estates, and the balance was produced by private growers. The organization of areas under sugar cane, which were estimated to cover just over 1m. ha in the mid-1990s, were restructured in 1993 into units of approximately 1,000 ha, as Basic Units of Co-operative Production (UBPC). These UBPC currently comprise about 90% of state-owned sugar plantations. Few mills have been built since the 1930s (and all of these since 1980), but many of the 150 existing mills have been modernized and expanded. Cuba is recognized as a leader in the processing and marketing of sugar, but the country has failed to take adequate measures to control disease and pests, which have a deleterious effect on yields. Cuba's average yield of raw sugar stood at only 4.3 tons per ha in 1996, compared with 8.0 tons per ha in Brazil.

Mexico was a sugar exporter until 1979. The low domestic price of sugar, which the Government traditionally set below the cost of production, discouraged the purchase of modern equipment and the renovation of sugar plants. The result was stagnation in sugar production, a steady rise in domestic sugar consumption to a level among the highest in the world (45 kg per head per year), and the need to import sugar. Since 1980, as part of a plan to increase production, to slow the rate of increase in demand and to allow the Government to reduce the subsidy on sugar, domestic sugar prices have been set above the level of production costs. During the period 1980–85, as much as an additional 170,000 ha were planted to sugar cane. Under the North American Free Trade Agreement (NAFTA), which entered into operation in January 1994, Mexico could substantially increase its sugar exports to the USA and Canada after NAFTA arrangements for the duty-free access of Mexican sugar to the US market take effect in 2001. The decline in international sugar prices from 1998 had a severe effect on the Mexican sugar industry, and in 2000 the country's second largest refiner sought protection from its creditors.

The sugar sector in Colombia has undergone a major expansion since the 1960s, in an attempt to diversify the economy away from coffee. In some of the smaller Latin American countries and the Caribbean islands, sugar cultivation is the main bulwark of the economy. In Belize, sugar cane plantations occupy about 50% of the total cultivated area, while the sugar industry employs about one-quarter of the work-force. In 1996 sales of sugar and molasses accounted for an estimated 33.6% of total export earnings (excluding re-exports). Sugar cane is the principal commercial crop in the Dominican Republic, but inefficient production techniques, lack of investment and falling international sugar prices depressed the industry throughout the 1980s. The country's output of raw sugar increased from 580,000 tons in 1995 to 741,000 tons in 1996 and to 813,000 tons in 1997. However, 'Hurricane Georges' caused severe damage to cane plantations and sugar mills in September 1998. Raw sugar accounted for 12.7% of the Dominican Republic's total export revenue (excluding exports from free-trade zones) in 1995. Sugar is the principal export commodity of Barbados, and is a major export commodity in Guyana and Saint Christopher and Nevis.

The first International Sugar Agreement (ISA) was negotiated in 1958, and its economic provisions operated until 1961. A second ISA did not come into operation until 1969. It included quota arrangements and associated provisions for regulating the price of sugar traded on the open market, and established the International Sugar Organization (ISO) to administer the agreement. However, the USA and the six original members of the European Community (EC, now the EU) did not participate in the ISA, and, following its expiry in 1974, it was replaced by a purely administrative interim agreement, which remained operational until the finalization of a third ISA, which took effect in 1978. The new agreement's implementation was supervised by an International Sugar Council (ISC), which was empowered to establish price ranges for sugar-trading and to operate a system of quotas and special sugar stocks. Owing to the reluctance of the USA and EC countries (which were not a party to the agreement) to accept export controls, the ISO ultimately lost most of its power to regulate the market, and since 1984 the activities of the organization have been restricted to recording statistics and providing a forum for discussion between producers and consumers. Subsequent ISAs, without effective regulatory powers, have been in operation since 1985. (For detailed information on the successive agreements, see *South America, Central America and the Caribbean 1991*.)

Special arrangements for exports of sugar from 15 Caribbean states (including Belize and Guyana) exist in the successive Lomé Conventions, in operation since 1975, between the EU and a group of African, Caribbean and Pacific (ACP) countries, whereby a special Protocol on sugar, forming part of each Convention, requires the EU to import specified quantities of raw sugar annually from ACP countries. In June 1998 it was announced that preferential sugar prices paid by the EU to the ACP countries would fall to open-market levels within three years.

In tandem with world output of cane and beet sugars, stock levels are an important factor in determining the prices at which sugar is traded internationally. These stocks, which were at relatively low levels in the late 1980s, increased significantly in the early 1990s, owing partly to the disruptive effects of the Gulf War on demand in the Middle East (normally a major sugar-consuming area), and also as a result of substantially increased production in Mexico and the Far East. Additionally, the output of beet sugar was expected to continue rising, as a result of substantial producers' subsidies within the EU, which, together with Australia, has been increasing the areas under sugar cane and beet. World sugar stocks were reduced in the 1993/94 trading year (September–August). However, the prospect of record crops in Brazil, India and Thailand led to an increased level of sugar stocks in 1994/95. World sugar stocks continued to rise in 1995/96 and 1996/97, and advanced further in 1997/98, when world-wide consumption of raw sugar totalled about 123m. metric tons, compared with production of 126m. tons. This trend continued in 1998/99, when, according to provisional ISO data, global sugar production reached 133.2m. tons, while consumption totalled 127.8m. tons. Forecasts for 1999/2000, published in July 2000, projected another world sugar surplus, of 1.5m.–1.7m. tons.

Most of the world's sugar output is traded at fixed prices under long-term agreements. On the free market, however, sugar prices often fluctuate with extreme volatility.

Export Price Index for Sugar (base: 1980 = 100)

	Average	Highest month(s)	Lowest month(s)
1990	45		
1995	48		
1998	32	41 (Jan.)	26 (Sept.)
1999	23	29 (Jan.)	20 (April, July)
2000	28	34 (Oct.)	20 (March)

In February 1992 the import price of raw cane sugar on the London market was only US $193.0 (equivalent to £107.9 sterling) per metric ton, its lowest level, in terms of US currency, for more than four years. The London price of sugar advanced to $324.9 (£211.9) per ton in May 1993, following predictions of a world sugar deficit in 1992/93. Concurrently, sugar prices in New York were at their highest levels for three years. The London sugar price declined to $237.2 (£157.9) per ton in August 1993, but increased to $370.6 (£237.4) in December 1994.

The rise in sugar prices continued in January 1995, when the London quotation for raw sugar reached US $378.1 (£243.2) per ton, its highest level, in dollar terms, since early 1990. Meanwhile, the London price of white sugar was $426.5 (£274.4) per ton, the highest quotation for four-and-a-half years. The surge in the sugar market was partly a response to forecasts of a supply deficit in the 1994/95 season. Prices later eased, and in April 1995 raw sugar was traded in London at $326.0 (£202.1) per ton. The price recovered to $373.1 (£235.6) per ton in June, but retreated to $281.5 (£179.4) in September.

During the early months of 1996 the London price of raw sugar reached about US $330 per ton. In May the price was reduced to $262.9 (£175.3) per ton, but in July it rose to $321.4 (£206.3), despite continued forecasts of a significant sugar surplus in 1995/96. The sugar price fell to $256.3 (£156.4) per ton in December.

In January 1997 the London price of raw sugar declined to US $250.8 (£154.0) per ton, but in August it reached $288.5 (£179.1). In terms of US currency, the London sugar price advanced later in the year, standing at $298.5 (£178.3) per ton in December.

International sugar prices moved generally downward in the first half of 1998. In June, following forecasts that world output of raw sugar in 1997/98 would be significantly higher than in the previous crop year (leading to a further rise in surplus stocks), the London price was reduced to US $185.0 (£113.1) per ton. In July the quotation for raw sugar recovered to US $222.6 (£135.0) per ton, but in September, following forecasts of a higher surplus in 1998/99, the price fell to only US $168.8 (£100.2). The sugar price stayed within this range for the remainder of 1998, ending the year at $196.9 (£118.3) per ton.

In January 1999 the London price of raw sugar reached US $217.2 (£132.4) per ton, but from February the free market was affected by strong downward pressure, as sugar supplies remained plentiful. In April the London sugar price was reduced to only $127.3 (£79.0) per ton, its lowest level, in terms of US currency, since late 1986. Meanwhile, the short-term quotation in the main US sugar market declined to about 4.6 US cents per lb, also a 12 year 'low'. The slump in international sugar prices was partly a consequence of the severe economic problems affecting Russia (normally the world's leading importer of sugar) and countries in eastern Asia. The decline in demand from these areas coincided with high output, as a result of generally favourable growing conditions, in sugar-producing countries. The London price recovered to $166.2 (£105.1) per ton in June 1999, but declined to $131.4 (£84.4) in July. A renewed advance took the price to $184.3 (£111.4) per ton in October. At the end of the year the London sugar quotation stood at $162.4 (£100.8) per ton.

During the early weeks of 2000 the international sugar market was weak, and at the end of February the London price of raw sugar was reduced to US $126.5 (£80.1) per ton, its lowest level, in terms of US currency, for more than 13 years. However, there was subsequently a strong recovery in sugar prices, in response to reports of reductions in output and planting, while demand rose. At the end of July the London quotation was $264.0 (£176.3) per ton. Meanwhile, the New York price of sugar rose during that month to its highest level for more than two years.

The Group of Latin American and Caribbean Sugar Exporting Countries (GEPLACEA), with a membership of 23 Latin American and Caribbean countries, together with the Philippines, and representing about 66% of world cane production and 45% of sugar exports, complements the activities of the ISO (comprising 55 countries, including EU members, in November 1999) as a forum for co-operation and research. At the end of 1992 the USA withdrew from the ISO, following a disagreement over the formulation of members' financial contributions. The USA had previously provided about 9% of the ISO's annual budget.

Tin

The world's tin deposits, estimated by the US Geological Survey to total 8m. tons in 1998, are located mainly in the equatorial zones of Asia, in central South America and in Australia. Cassiterite is the only economically important tin-bearing mineral, and it is generally associated with tungsten, silver and tantalum minerals. There is a clear association of cassiterite with igneous rocks of granitic composition, and 'primary' cassiterite deposits occur as disseminations, or in veins and fissures in or around granites. If the primary deposits are eroded, as by rivers, cassiterite may be concentrated and deposited in 'secondary', sedimentary deposits. These secondary deposits form the bulk of the world's tin reserves. The ore is treated, generally by gravity method or flotation, to produce concentrates prior to smelting.

Tin owes its special place in industry to its unique combination of properties: low melting point, the ability to form alloys with most other metals, resistance to corrosion, non-toxicity and good appearance. Its main uses are in tinplate (about 40% of world tin consumption), in alloys (tin-lead solder, bronze, brass, pewter, bearing and type metal), and in chemical compounds (in paints, plastics, medicines, coatings and as fungicides and insecticides). In the late 1990s a number of possible new applications for tin were under study, including its use in fire-retardant chemicals, as an environmentally preferable substitute for cadmium in zinc alloy anti-corrosion coatings on steel. The possible development of a lead-free tin solder was also receiving consideration.

According to the US Geological Survey, Latin America accounted for 28.2% of world output of tin concentrates in 1997, and for 26.9% in 1998. Bolivia is the world's fifth largest producer of primary tin, and this commodity accounted for 9.3% of the country's export revenue in 1996. Since the 1970s output has been in decline, mainly as a consequence of internal economic conditions and depressed levels of world prices. In 1978 tin sales accounted for almost 60% of Bolivia's export revenues; by 1993 the comparable proportion was only 11.9%. Brazil possesses the world's largest tin mine, located at Pitinga, in Amazonas State, with identified reserves of 420,000 tons, although it was suggested in the late 1990s that the mine's total reserves could exceed 800,000 tons. As a result of adverse market conditions in the early 1990s, however, Brazilian tin output has declined, and in 1994 Peru emerged as the region's leading producer and the world's third largest source. Until recently, almost all of Peru's tin exports were in the form of ores and concentrates, which provided 1.5% of the country's total export earnings in 1996. However, Peru's first tin smelter, at Pisco, began operating in 1997, with an initial production capacity of 15,000 tons of metal per year. About 18,000 tons of tin were smelted at Pisco in 1999. In 1998 plans were announced for the resumption of tin-mining in Argentina in 2000.

Over the period 1956–85, much of the world's tin production and trade was covered by successive international agreements, administered by the International Tin Council (ITC), based in London. The aim of each successive International Tin Agreement (ITA), of which there were six, was to stabilize prices within an agreed range by using a buffer stock to regulate the supply of tin. (For detailed information on the last of these agreements, see *South America, Central America and the Caribbean 1991*.) The buffer stock was financed by producing countries, with voluntary contributions by some consuming countries. 'Floor' and 'ceiling' prices were fixed, and market operations conducted by a buffer stock manager who intervened, as necessary, to maintain prices within these agreed limits. For added protection, the ITA provided for the imposition of export controls if the 'floor' price was being threatened. The ITA was effectively terminated in October 1985, when the ITC's buffer stock manager informed the London Metal Exchange (LME) that he no longer had the funds with which to support the tin market. The factors underlying the collapse of the ITA included its limited membership (Bolivia and the USA, leading producing and consuming countries, were not signatories) and the accumulation of tin stocks which resulted from the widespread circumvention of producers' quota limits. The LME responded by suspending trading in tin, leaving the ITC owing more than £500m. to some 36 banks, tin smelters and metals traders. The crisis was eventually resolved in March 1990, when a financial settlement of £182.5m. was agreed between the ITC and its creditors. The ITC was itself dissolved in July.

These events lent new significance to the activities of the Association of Tin Producing Countries (ATPC), founded in 1983 by Malaysia, Indonesia and Thailand and later joined by Bolivia, Nigeria, Australia and Zaire (now the Democratic Republic of the Congo, DRC). Prior to the withdrawal of Australia and Thailand in 1996 (see below), members of the ATPC accounted for almost two-thirds of world production. The ATPC, which was intended to operate as a complement to the ITC and not in competition with it, introduced export quotas for tin for the year from 1 March 1987. Brazil and the People's Republic of China agreed to co-operate with the ATPC in implementing these supply restrictions, which, until their suspension in 1996 (see below), were renegotiated to cover succeeding years, with the aim of raising prices and reducing the level of surplus stocks. The ATPC membership also took stringent measures to control smuggling. Brazil and China (jointly accounting for more than one-third of world tin production) both initially held observer status at the ATPC. China became a full member in 1994, but Brazil remained as an observer, together with Peru and Viet Nam. China and Brazil agreed to participate in the export quota arrangements, for which the ATPC had no power of enforcement.

The ATPC members' combined export quota was fixed at 95,849 tons for 1991, and was reduced to 87,091 tons for 1992. However, the substantial level of world tin stocks, combined with depressed demand, led to mine closures and reductions in output, with the result that members' exports in 1991 were below quota entitlements. The progressive depletion of stock levels prompted a forecast by the ATPC, in May 1992, that export quotas would be removed in 1994 if these disposals continued at their current rate. The ATPC had previously set a target level for stocks of 20,000 tons, representing five weeks of world tin consumption. Projections that world demand for tin would remain at about 160,000 tons annually, together with continued optimism about the rate of stock disposals, led the ATPC to increase its members' 1993 export quota to 89,700 tons. The persistence, however, of high levels of annual tin exports by China (estimated to have exceeded 30,000 tons in 1993 and 1994, compared with its ATPC quota of 20,000 tons), together with sales of surplus defence stocks of tin by the US Government, necessitated a reduction of the quota to 78,000 tons for 1994. In late 1993 prices had fallen to a 20-year 'low' and world tin stocks were estimated at 38,000-40,000 tons, owing partly to the non-observance of quota limits by Brazil and China, as well as to increased production by non-ATPC members. World tin stocks resumed their rise in early 1994, reaching 48,000 tons in June. However, the effects of reduced output, from both ATPC and non-ATPC producing countries, helped to reduce stock levels to 41,000 tons at the end of December. In 1995 exports by APTC members exceeded the agreed voluntary quotas by 10%, and in May 1996, when world tin stocks were estimated to have been reduced to 31,000 tons, the ATPC suspended its quota arrangements. Shortly before the annual meeting of the ATPC was convened in September, Australia and Thailand announced their withdrawal from the organization. Although China and Indonesia indicated that they would continue to support the ATPC, together with Bolivia, Malaysia and Nigeria (Zaire had ceased to be an active producer of tin), the termination of its quota arrangements in 1996, together with the continuing recovery of the tin market, indicated that its future role would be that of a forum for tin-producers and consumers. Malaysia, Australia and Indonesia left the ATPC in 1997, and Brazil became a full member in 1998. In June 1999, when the organization's headquarters were moved from Kuala Lumpur to Rio de Janeiro, the membership comprised Brazil, Bolivia, China, the DRC and Nigeria. It was hoped that Peru would join the ATPC following its relocation to South America.

Production of Tin Concentrates (tin content, metric tons)

	1998	1999*
World total (excl. USA)	208,000	198,000
Latin America	51,662	54,903
Leading Latin American producers		
Bolivia	11,308	11,300*
Brazil	14,607	13,200
Peru	25,747	30,403
Other leading producers		
Australia	10,204	10,038
China, People's Repub.* . . .	79,000	61,700
Indonesia	40,000	47,754
Malaysia	5,756	7,340
Portugal	4,000	3,000*
Russia*	4,500	4,500
Viet Nam*	4,500	5,000

* Estimated production.
Source: US Geological Survey.

Export Price Index for Tin (base: 1980 = 100)

	Average	Highest month(s)	Lowest month(s)
1990	42		
1995	37		
1998	31	33 (May)	29 (Jan., Dec.)
1999	29	32 (Nov.)	28 (Jan., Feb., June-Aug)
2000	29	32 (Jan.)	27 (Oct.–Dec.)

Although transactions in tin contracts were resumed on the LME in 1989, the Kuala Lumpur Commodity Exchange (KLCE), in Malaysia, had become established as the main centre for international trading in the metal. In September 1993 the price of tin (ex-works) on the KLCE stood at only 10.78 Malaysian ringgits (RM) per kg, equivalent to only £2,756 (or US $4,233) per metric ton. Measured in terms of US currency, international prices for tin were at their lowest level for 20 years, without taking inflation into account. In October the Malaysian tin price recovered to RM 12.71 per kg (£3,376 or $4,990 per ton), but in November it declined to RM 11.60 per kg (£3,056 or $4,545 per ton).

The rise in tin prices continued in the early weeks of 1994, and in February the Malaysian quotation reached RM 15.15 per kg (£3,684 or US $5,449 per ton). In early March the metal's price eased to RM 14.00 per kg (£3,449 or $5,146 per ton), but later in the month it rose to RM 15.01 per kg (£3,715 or $5,515 per ton). The KLCE price was reduced in August to RM 12.99 per kg (£3,285 or $5,092 per ton), but in early November it stood at RM 16.06 per kg (then £3,896 or $6,265 per ton).

The Malaysian tin price advanced strongly in January 1995, reaching RM 16.38 per kg (£4,018 or US $6,407 per ton). However, in early March the price declined to RM 13.33 per kg (about £3,300 or $5,200 per ton). The tin market later revived, and in August the KLCE price of the metal reached RM 17.60 per kg (£4,569 or $7,060 per ton). International tin prices were then at their highest level for nearly six years. The recovery in the market was attributed partly to a continuing decline in tin stocks, resulting from a reduction in exports from China and in disposals from the USA's strategic reserves of the metal. However, the KLCE quotation was reduced to RM 15.36 per kg (£3,851 or $6,090 per ton) in October.

In the early months of 1996 there was a generally downward movement in international tin prices, and in March the Malaysian quotation fell to RM 15.28 per kg (£3,947 or US $6,015 per ton). In April the KLCE price of tin recovered to RM 16.24 per kg (£4,294 or $6,496 per ton). A further decline ensued, and in mid-December tin was traded at RM 14.31 per kg (£3,388 or $5,668 per ton).

During the first six months of 1997 the price of tin on the KLCE declined by nearly 8%. The tin market moved further downward in July, with the Malaysian price falling to RM 13.52 per kg (£3,185 or US $5,398 per ton). Later that month, after the value of the ringgit had depreciated, the equivalent of the KLCE tin price (RM 13.76 per kg) was only £3,107 ($5,199) per ton. In late August the Malaysian price stood at RM 14.70 per kg, but this was equivalent to only £3.134 ($5,061) per ton. In terms of local currency, the Malaysian tin price increased considerably in subsequent weeks, but most of the upward movement was the consequence of a decline in the ringgit's value in relation to other currencies. By the end of September the KLCE price of tin had risen to RM 18.13 per kg. This price was reportedly maintained over the first eight trading days of October, during which time the ringgit recovered some of its value. At the end of the period the Malaysian tin price was equivalent to £3,656 or $5,927 per ton. The KLCE price of tin continued to move upward in subsequent weeks, but the Malaysian currency's value declined again. At the end of the year the tin price stood at RM 20.61 per kg, equivalent to £3,218 or $5,295 per ton. During the second half of 1997 the tin price, expressed in ringgits, increased by 50.5%, but the equivalent in US dollars was 2.4% lower.

The KLCE price of tin reportedly held steady at RM 20.61 per kg for the first nine trading days of January 1998. Meanwhile, the ringgit's depreciation continued. At the currency's lowest point, the tin price was equivalent to only £2,722 or US $4,399 per ton. Later in January the tin price advanced to RM 23.43 per kg. It remained at this level for several days, as the value of the ringgit recovered, so that in early February the price was equivalent to £3,557 or $5,843 per ton. Later in February the Malaysian tin price eased to RM 19.27 per kg (£3,122 or $5,120 per ton), but in June it rose to RM 24.50 per kg. This quotation was maintained over three trading days, during which the value of the ringgit rose appreciably. As a result, the equivalent of the KLCE price increased from less than $6,000 per ton to $6,234 (£3,757). Tin prices later eased, and at the end of September the metal was traded in Malaysia at RM 20.02 per kg, equivalent to £3,100 ($5,268) per ton. Earlier that month a fixed exchange rate for the Malaysian currency (US $1 = RM 3.8) was introduced. In early November the KLCE was merged with the Malaysia Monetary Exchange to form the Commodity and Monetary Exchange of Malaysia (COMMEX Malaysia), also based in Kuala Lumpur. During the same week the Malaysian tin price rose to RM 20.65 per kg (£3,269 or $5,434 per ton), but in December it declined to RM 19.10 per kg (£2,990 or $5,026 per ton).

In January 1999, with tin stocks in plentiful supply, the COMMEX price of the metal was reduced to only RM 18.77 per kg, equivalent to £2,990 (US $4,939) per ton. However, tin prices rose steadily thereafter, and in May the Malaysian quotation reached RM 21.42 per kg (£3,500 or $5,637 per ton). After easing somewhat, the price advanced in November to RM 22.10 per kg (£3,594 or $5,816 per ton). It ended the year at RM 21.41 per kg (£3,496 or $5,634 per ton).

In January 2000 the COMMEX price of tin rose to RM 22.84 per kg, equivalent to £3,664 (US $6,011) per ton. By early June the price was reduced to RM 19.94 per kg (£3,488 or $5,247 per ton), although later in the month it recovered to RM 20.71 per kg (£3,582 or $5,450 per ton).

The success, after 1985, of the ATPC in restoring orderly conditions in tin trading (partly by the voluntary quotas and partly by working towards the reduction of tin stockpiles) unofficially established it as the effective successor to the ITC as the international co-ordinating body for tin interests. The International Tin Study Group (ITSG), comprising 36 producing and consuming countries, was established by the ATPC in 1989 to assume the informational functions of the ITC. In 1991 the secretariat of the United Nations Conference on Trade and Development (UNCTAD) assumed responsibility for the publication of statistical information on the international tin market. The International Tin Research Institute (ITRI), founded in 1932 and based in London, United Kingdom, promotes scientific research and technical development in the production and use of tin. In recent years the ITRI, whose 12 producer members supply about 60% of world tin output, has particularly sought to promote new end-uses for tin, especially in competition with aluminium.

ACKNOWLEDGEMENTS

We gratefully acknowledge the assistance of the following organizations in the preparation of this section:

Association of Coffee Producing Countries
Association of Iron Ore Exporting Countries
Association of Tin Producing Countries
Copper Development Association
Food and Agriculture Organization of the UN
Institute of Petroleum
International Cocoa Organization
International Coffee Organization
International Copper Study Group
International Grains Council
International Iron and Steel Institute
International Monetary Fund
International Primary Aluminium Institute
International Sugar Organization
International Tin Research Institute
The Silver Institute
Unión de Países Exportadores de Banano
United Nations Conference on Trade and Development
US Department of Energy
US Geological Survey, US Department of the Interior
World Bureau of Metal Statistics

Sources for Agricultural Production Tables (unless otherwise indicated): FAO, *Quarterly Bulletin of Statistics* (Rome, 2000).

Source for Export Price Indexes: UN, *Monthly Bulletin of Statistics,* issues to April 2001.

RESEARCH INSTITUTES

ASSOCIATIONS AND INSTITUTIONS STUDYING LATIN AMERICA AND THE CARIBBEAN

ARGENTINA

Centro Argentino de Datos Oceanográficos (CEADO) (Argentine Centre of Oceanographic Data): Avda Montes de Oca 2124, 1271 Buenos Aires; tel. (11) 4303-2240; fax (11) 4303-2299; e-mail postmaster@ceado.edu.ar; internet www.conae.gov.ar/~ceado; f. 1974; stores oceanographic data of national area, provides information to the scientific community, private and public enterprises and other marine users; Dir Capt. ADOLFO GIL VILLANUEVA.

Centro Argentino de Información Científica y Tecnológica (CAICYT) (Argentine Centre for Scientific and Technological Information): Saavedra 15, 1°, 1083 Buenos Aires; tel. (11) 951-6975; e-mail postmaster@caicyt.edu.ar; f. 1958; attached to Consejo Nacional de Investigaciones y Técnicas; Dir TITO SUTER.

Centro de Investigaciones Económicas (Economic Research Centre): Instituto Torcuato de Tella, Miñones 2177, 1428 Buenos Aires; tel. (11) 4783-8680; fax (11) 4783-3061; e-mail postmaster@itdtar.edu.ar; internet www.aaep.org.ar/itdt/index.html; Dir ADOLFO CANITROT; publ. *Documentos de Trabajo*.

Consejo Argentino para las Relaciones Internacionales—CARI (Argentine Council for International Relations): Uruguay 1037, 1°, 1016 Buenos Aires; tel. (1) 441-0071; fax (1) 411-1835; f. 1978; Dir CARLOS M. MUÑIZ.

Instituto Interamericano de Estadística (Inter-American Statistical Institute): Balcare 184, 2°, Of. 211, 1327 Buenos Aires; tel. (11) 4349-5772; fax (11) 4349-5776; e-mail efabb@indec.mecon.gov.ar; internet www.indec.mecon.gov.ar/iasa; f. 1940; research, seminars, technical meetings; co-ordination and co-operation with the Organization of American States; consultative status with the Economic and Social Council; Pres. RAUL P. MENTZ; Technical Sec. EVELIO O. FABBRONI: publ. *Estadística* (2 a year).

Instituto para la Integración de América Latina y el Caribe (Institute for the Integration of Latin America and the Caribbean): Esmeralda 130, 16° y 17°, 1035 Buenos Aires; tel. (1) 4320-1850; fax (1) 4320-1865; e-mail int/inl@indb.org; internet www.iadb.org/intal; f. 1965 under auspices of IDB's Integration and Regional Program Dept; research on all aspects of regional integration and co-operation; activities are channelled through four lines of action: regional and national technical projects on integration; policy forums; integration forums; journals and information; documentation centre includes 100,000 documents, 12,000 books, 400 periodicals; Dir JUAN JOSÉ TACCONE; publs *Integración y Comercio* (3 a year), *Carta Mensual* (monthly newsletter), *Informe MERCOSUR-MERCOSUL Report* (annual).

AUSTRALIA

Australian Institute of International Affairs: 32 Thesiger Court, Deakin, ACT 2600; tel. (2) 6282-2133; fax (2) 6285-2334; e-mail ceo@aiia.au; internet www.aiia.asn.au; f. 1933; 1,800 mems; brs in all States; Pres. NEAL BLEWETT; Exec. Dir ROSS COTTRILL; publ. *The Australian Journal of International Affairs* (3 a year), *Australia in World Affairs* (every 5 years).

AUSTRIA

Österreichische Forschungsstiftung für Entwicklungshilfe (Austrian Foundation for Development Research): 1090 Vienna, Bergasse 7; tel (222) 317-40-10; fax (222) 317-40-15; e-mail office@oefse.at; internet www.oefse.at; f. 1967; documentation and information on development aid, developing countries and international development, particularly relating to Austria; library of 35,000 vols, 250 periodicals; Pres. Prof. K. ZAPOTOCZKY; publs *Ausgewählte Neue Literatur zur Entwicklungspolitik* (3 a year), *Österreichische Entwicklungspolitik* (annually), Länderprofile.

Österreichische Gesellschaft für Aussenpolitik und Internationale Beziehungen (Austrian Society for Foreign Policy and International Relations): 1010 Vienna, Hofburg, Schweizertor, Brunnenstiege; f. 1958; lectures, discussions; approx. 500 mems; Pres. Dr WOLFGANG SCHALLENBERG; publ. *Österreichisches Jahrbuch für Internationale Politik* (annually).

Österreichisches Institut für Entwicklungshilfe und technische Zusammenarbeit mit den Entwicklungsländern (Austrian Institute for Development Aid and Technical Co-operation with the Developing Countries): 1010 Vienna, Wipplingerstr. 35; tel. (1) 42-65-04; f. 1963; projects for training of industrial staff; Pres Dr HANS IGLER, ERICH HOFSTETTER.

Österreichisches Lateinamerika Institut (Austrian Latin American Institute): 1090 Vienna, Schlickgasse 1; tel. (1) 310-74-65; fax (1) 310-74-68-21; e-mail office@lai.at; internet www.lai.at; f. 1967; Dir Dr SIEGFRIED HITTMAIR; publs *Jahrbuch des Österreichischen Lateinamerika Instituts* (annually), *Diálogo Austria-América Latina* (annually).

BELGIUM

Académie Royale des Sciences d'Outre-Mer/Koninklijke Academie voor Overzeese Wetenschappen (Royal Academy of Overseas Sciences): 1 rue Defacqz b. 3, 1000 Brussels; tel. (2) 538-02-11; fax (2) 539-23-53; e-mail kaowarsom@skynet.be; f. 1928; the promotion of scientific knowledge of overseas areas, especially those with particular development problems; 66 hon. mems, 50 mems; Perm. Sec. Prof. Y. VERHASSELT; publs *Bulletin des Séances / Mededelingen der Zittingen, Mémoires / Verhandelingen, Recueils d'Etudes Historiques / Historische bijdragen, Biographie belge d'Outre-Mer / Belgische Overzeese Biographie, Actes Symposiums Annuels / Acta Jaarlijkse Symposia*.

Institut d'Etudes du Développement (Institute for Developing Studies): Université Catholique de Louvain, 7 place des Doyens, 1348 Louvain-La-Neuve; tel. (2) 047-39-35; fax (2) 047-28-05; e-mail vandenbossche@dvlp.ucl.ac.be; f. 1961; Pres. J. PH. PEEMANS.

Institut Royal des Relations Internationales: 13 rue de la Charité, 1210 Brussels; tel. (2) 223-41-14; fax (2) 223-41-16; e-mail irri.kiib@euronest.be; f. 1947; research in international relations, international economics, international law and international politics; specialized library containing 16,500 vols and 600 periodicals; archives; lectures and conferences are held; Dir-Gen. ÉMILE MASSA; publs *Studia Diplomatica* (6 a year), *Internationale Spectator* (monthly).

Institute of Development Policy and Management: Middelheimlaan 1, 2020 Antwerp; tel. (3) 218-06-60; fax (3) 218-06-66; e-mail wiwa@maze.ruca.ua.ac.be; f. 1965; attached to the Antwerp University Centre; courses in development studies; library of 8,500 vols, 300 periodicals, 700 theses; Pres. Prof. Dr D. VAN DEN BULCKE.

BRAZIL

Centro de Estatística e Informações (Statistics and Information Centre): Centro Administrativo da Bahia, 4a Avda 435, 41750-300 Salvador, BA; tel. (71) 371-9665; fax (71) 371-9664; f. 1938; statistics, natural resources, economic indicators; library of 15,448 vols; Dir. RENATA PROSERPIO; publ. *Bahia Análise e Dados* (every four months).

Instituto Brasileiro de Economia (Brazilian Institute of Economics): Getúlio Vargas Foundation, CP 62591, 22257-970 Rio de Janeiro, RJ; tel. (21) 536-9219; fax (21) 551-3549; e-mail abrandao@fgvrj.br; f. 1951; Dir A. SALAZAR BRANDÃO; publs *National Accounts* (annually), *Conjuntura Econômica* (monthly), *Agroanalysis* (monthly).

Instituto Brasileiro de Relações Internacionais (Brazilian Institute of International Relations): Multiuso 1, Bloco B, Campus Universitário, CP 4602, 70910-900 Brasília, DF; tel. (61) 348-2590; fax (61) 274-1448; f. 1954; 1,000 vols; Exec. Dir JOSÉ CARLOS B. ALEIXO; Sec. ALCIDES COSTA VAZ; publ. *Revista Brasileira de Política Internacional* (quarterly).

Instituto Nacional de Pesquisas Da Amazônia (INPA) (National Institute for Amazonian Research): Avda André Araújo 2936, Petrópolis, CEP 69083-000, Manaus, AZ, Apdo 478; tel. (92) 643-3300; fax (92) 643-3095; e-mail wmaster@inpa.gov.br; internet www.inpa.gov.br; f. 1952; research on Amazonian rain forest; runs postgraduate programme in tropical biology and natural resources; Co-ordinator CHARLES ROLAND CLEMENT.

Instituto de Relações Internacionais (Institute of International Relations): Pontifícia Universidade Católica do Rio de Janeiro, rua Marquês de São Vicente 225, Gávea, 22453-900 Rio de Janeiro, RJ; tel. (21) 529-9494; fax (21) 274-1296; e-mail iripuc@rdc.puc-rio.br; Dir JOSÉ MARIA GÓMEZ.

CANADA

Canadian Association of Latin American Studies/Association Canadienne des Etudes Latino-Américaines: c/o Prof. ANTONIO

URRELLO, Dept of French, Hispanic and Italian Studies, University of British Columbia, Vancouver, BC V6T 1W5; f. 1969; 200 mems; Pres. J. C. M. OGELSBY; Vice-Pres. CLAUDE MORIN; publs *North South / Nord Sud / Norte Sur, Canadian Journal of Latin American Studies* (2 a year), *Newsletter* (quarterly), *Directory of Canadian Scholars and Universities interested in Latin American Studies.*

Canadian Council for International Co-operation/Conseil canadien pour la coopération internationale: 1 Nicholas St, Suite 300, Ottawa, ON K1N 7B7; tel. (613) 241-7007; 236-4547; fax (613) 241-5302; f. 1968 (formerly Overseas Institute of Canada, f. 1961); co-ordination centre for voluntary agencies working in international development; 115 mems; Pres. and CEO BETTY PLEWES; Chair. CAMERON CHARLEROIS; publs *Newsletter* (6 a year), *Directory of Canadian NGOs.*

Canadian Institute of International Affairs: Glendon Hall, 2275 Bayview Ave, Toronto, ON M4N 3M6; tel. (416) 487-6830; fax (416) 487-6831; e-mail mailbox@ciia.org; internet www.ciia.org; f. 1928; 2,100 mems in 23 brs; library of 8,000 vols; Pres. and CEO BARBARA McDOUGALL; Chair. ALAN BROADBENT; publs *Behind the Headlines, International Journal, Annual Report.*

Canadian Institute of Island Studies: University of Prince Edward Island, 550 University Ave, Charlottetown, PE C1A 4P3; tel. (902) 566-0439; fax (902) 566-0420; e-mail iis@upei.ca; internet www.upei.ca/~iis/.

Centre for Research in Latin America and the Caribbean (CERLAC): York University, 240 York Lanes, 4700 Keele St, North York, ON M3J 1P3; tel. (416) 736-5237; fax (416) 736-5737; e-mail cerlac@yorku.ca; internet www.yorku.ca/cerlac/; f. 1978; interdisciplinary research organization; seeks to build academic and cultural links with the region; research findings made available through publs, lectures, seminars etc.; Dir RICARDO GRINSPUN.

CHILE

Centro Latinoamericano de Documentación Económica y Social (CLADES) (Latin American Centre for Economic and Social Documentation): Avda Dag Hammarskjöld, Casilla 179-D, Santiago; tel. (2) 2102427; fax (2) 2102422; f. 1971; part of UN Economic Commission for Latin America; aids the development of documentation centres; aims to establish easy access to economic and social information; undertakes research, technical assistance, etc.; library of 2,500 vols, 100 periodicals, 3,500 micro-films; Dir CLAUDIONOR EVANGELISTA; publs *PLANINDEX, INFOPLAN, INFOPLAN: Temas Especiales del Desarrollo, Terminology Newsletter.*

Corporación de Investigaciones Económicas para Latinoamérica: MacIver 125, 5°, Casilla 16496, Correo 9, Santiago; tel. (2) 6333836; fax (2) 6334411; e-mail cieplan@lascar.puc.cl; f. 1976; economic research; Dir JOAQUIN VIAL.

Facultad Latinoamericana de Ciencias Sociales (FLACSO) — Programa Santiago: Casilla 3213, Correo Central, Santiago; tel. (2) 2256955; fax (2) 2741004; e-mail flacso@flacso.cl; internet www.flacso.cl; f. 1957; research in sociology, education, political science, international affairs; library of 18,000 vols, 592 periodicals; Dir FRANCISCO ROIAS ARAVENA; publs *Nueva Serie, Serie Libros FLASCO.*

Instituto Antártico Chileno: Luis Thayer Ojeda 814, Casilla 16521, Correo 9, Santiago; tel. (2) 2310105; fax (2) 2320440; e-mail inach@inach.cl; internet www.inach.cl; f. 1963; a centre for technological and scientific development on matters relating to the Antarctic; 43 mems; library of 2,550 vols and 400 periodicals; Dir OSCAR PINOCHET DE LA BARRA; publs *Serie Científica* (annually), *Boletín Antártico Chileno* (2 a year).

Instituto de Estudios Internacionales: Universidad de Chile, Condell 249, Casilla 14187, Suc. 21, Santiago; tel. (2) 2745377; fax (2) 2740155; e-mail inesint@abello.dic.uchile.cl; f. 1966; research and teaching institute for international relations, political science, international law, economics and studies on Pacific Basin; Dir RODRIGO DIAZ-ALBÓNICO; publ. *Estudios Internacionales* (quarterly).

Instituto Latinoamericano y del Caribe de Planificación Económica y Social (ILPES) (Latin American and Caribbean Institute for Economic and Social Planning): Edif. Naciones Unidas, Avda Dag Hammarskjöld, Casilla 1567, Santiago; tel. (2) 2102506; fax (2) 2066104; e-mail pdekock@eclac.cl; f. 1962 by UN Economic Commission for Latin America; provides technical assistance, training for govt officials and research on planning techniques; acts as technical Secretariat of the Regional Council for Planning (CRP), the meetings of the Presiding Officers of the CRP and the System of Co-operation among Planning Bodies of Latin American and the Caribbean; Dir ARTURO NÚÑEZ DEL PRADO; publs *Cuadernos del ILPES, ILPES Bulletin.*

PEOPLE'S REPUBLIC OF CHINA

Centre for International Studies: 22 Xianmen Da Jie, POB 1744, Beijing; tel (10) 3097083; fax (10) 3095802; f. 1982; special agency

of the State Council (cabinet); advisory research org.; 30 staff; Dir-Gen. LI LUYE.

China Institute of Contemporary International Relations: 2A Wanshousi, Haidian, Beijing 100081; tel. (10) 8418640; fax (10) 8418641; f. 1980; Pres. SHEN RURONG.

Institute of Latin American Studies, Chinese Academy of Social Sciences: POB 1113, Beijing; tel (10) 64014011; e-mail latinlat@public.bta.net.cn; f. 1961; 60 mems; library of 40,000 vols; Dir LI MINGDE; publ. *Latin-American Studies.*

Institute of World Economics and Politics, Chinese Academy of Social Sciences: 5 Jianguomen Nei Da Jie, Beijing 100732; tel. (10) 5137744; fax (10) 5126105; e-mail guyy@sun.ihep.ic.cn; Dir PU SHAN.

COLOMBIA

Centro de Estudios sobre Desarrollo Económico (CEDE) (Centre for Economic Development Studies): Carrera 1E, No 18A-10, Apdo Aéro 4976, Santafé de Bogotá; tel. (1) 3412240; fax (1) 2815771; e-mail cede@uniandes.edu.co; f. 1948; research in all aspects of economic development; 40 research staff; library of 40,000 vols; Dir JOSÉ LEIBOVICH; publs *Desarrollo y Sociedad* (quarterly), *Cuadernos CEDE,* documents series.

Centro de Información y Documentación Biblioteca Fernández de Madrid: Universidad de Cartagena, Centro Carrera 6, No 36-100, Cartagena; tel. (95) 6646182; fax (95) 6697778; e-mail unicart@cartagena.cetcol.net.co; f. 1827; Librarian LUIS EDUARDO ESPINAL A.

Centro Regional para el Fomento del Libro en América Latina y el Caribe (CERLALC) (Regional Centre for the Promotion of Books in Latin America and the Caribbean): Calle 70, No 9-52, Apdo Aereo 57348, Santafé de Bogotá; tel. (1) 3217501; fax (1) 3217503; e-mail libro@cerlalc.com; internet www.cerlalc.com; f. 1972 by UNESCO and Colombian Govt; promotes production and circulation of books and development of libraries; provides training; promotes protection of copyright; 21 mem. countries; Dir ALMA BYINGTON DE ARBOLEDA; publs *El Libro en America Latina y el Caribe* (quarterly), *Boletín Informativo CERLALC* (quarterly).

Latin American Centre: Pontifícia Universidad Javeriana, Carrera 10, No 65-48, Of. 424, Santafé de Bogotá; tel. (1) 5421660; fax (1) 6401759; e-mail dl-clam@javercol.javeriana.edu.co; Dir E. CRISTINA MONTAÑA.

COSTA RICA

Centro Agronómico Tropical de Investigación y Enseñanza (CATIE) (Tropical Agricultural Research and Higher Education Center): Apdo 65, 7170 Turrialba; tel. 556-2426; fax 556-1533; e-mail cnavarro@catie.ac.cr; internet www.catie.ac.cr; f. 1973; applied research, graduate and short-term training; mems: Inter-American Institute for Co-operation on Agriculture–IICA, Belize, Brazil, Colombia, Costa Rica, Dominican Republic, Ecuador, El Salvador, Guatemala, Honduras, Mexico, Nicaragua, Panama, Venezuela; library of 80,000 vols; Dir Dr RUBÉN GUEVARA-MONCADA; publs *Boletín de Semillas Forestales, Revista MIP, Revista Forestal Centroamericana, Revista Agroforestería — las Américas, Noticias de Turrialba* (quarterly), *Informe Anual.*

Instituto Centroamericano de Administración Pública (ICAP) (Central American Institute of Public Administration): Apdo 10025-1000, San José; tel. 234-1011; fax 225-2049; e-mail icapcr@sol.racsa.co.cr; internet www.icap.ac.cr; f. 1954; technical assistance from UNDP; public administration, economic development and integration; library of 30,800 vols; Dir Dr HUGO ZELAYA CALIX; publ. *Revista.*

Instituto de Estudios Centroamericanos (Institute of Central American Studies): Apdo 1524, 2050 San Pedro; tel. 253-3195; fax 234-7682; e-mail mesoamer@sal.sacsa.co.cr; f. 1981; Exec. Dir LINDA J. HOLLAND; publ. *Mesoamérica* (monthly).

Inter-American Institute for Co-operation on Agriculture: Apdo 55, 2200 Coronado, San José; tel. 290222; fax 294741; f. 1942; agricultural development and rural well-being; mems: 32 countries of the Americas and Caribbean; library of 75,000 vols; Dir-Gen. Dr MARTÍN E. PIÑEIRO; publ. *Turrialba* (quarterly).

Latin American Demographic Centre (CELADE-San José): De la Iglesia de San Pedro 300 Mts Sur y 125 Este, Apdo 833-2050, San José; tel. 253166; f. 1957; analysis of demographic trends, population and development research, teaching and training, and diverse information on population; library of 9,600 vols; Dir ANTONIO ORTEGA.

CUBA

Centro de Estudios Sobre América (CEA) (Centre for Studies on the Americas): Calle 18, No 316E, entre 3ra y Sta, Playa, Havana 13; tel. (7) 33-2716; fax (7) 33-1490; e-mail cea@tinored.cu; f. 1978; Dir LUIS SUÁREZ SALAZAR.

Centro de Información Bancaria y Económica, Banco Central de Cuba (Banking and Economic Information Centre, Central Bank of Cuba): Cuba 410, Havana 10100; tel. (7) 62-8318; fax (7) 66-6661; f. 1950; library of 32,000 vols; Man. Nuadis Planas Garcia; Library Dept Chief Jorge Fernández Pérez; publs *Cuba: Half Yearly Economic Report* (1 a year), *Journal of the Central Bank of Cuba*.

Instituto de Política Internacional (Institute of International Politics): Ministerio de Relaciones Exteriores, Calzada 360, Vedado, Havana; tel. (7) 32-3279; f. 1962; 11 mems; Dir René Alvárez Ríos.

CZECH REPUBLIC

Ústav mezinárodních vztahů (Institute of International Relations): 118 50 Prague 1, Nerudova 3; tel. (2) 51108111; fax (2) 51108222; e-mail umv@iir.cz; internet www.czechia.com/iir; f. 1957; research on international relations and foreign and security policy of the Czech Republic, publishing, training, education; Dir Jiří Šedivý; Deputy Dir Kristina Larischová; publs include *International Relations* (quarterly), *International Politics* (monthly) in Czech, and *Perspectives—Review of Central European Affairs* (2 a year) in English.

DENMARK

Center for Udviklingsforskning (Centre for Development Research): Gammel Kongevej 5, 1610 Copenhagen V; tel. 33-85-46-00; fax 33-25-81-10; e-mail cdr@cdr.dk; internet www.cdr.dk; f. 1969; library of 45,000 vols; promotes and undertakes research in the economic and social development of developing countries and in relations between industrialized and developing countries; Chair. Prof. Mogens N. Pederson; publs *Den Ny Verden* (quarterly), *Researching Development,* (quarterly), *CDR Working Papers, CDR Library Papers, Annual Report* (English).

Udenrigspolitiske Selskab (Foreign Policy Society): Amaliegade 40A, 1256 Copenhagen K; tel. 33-14-88-86; fax 33-14-85-20; f. 1946; studies, debates, courses and conferences on international affairs; library of 150 periodicals and publs from UN, OECD, WTO, EU; Dir Klaus Carsten Pedersen; Chair. Erling Olsen; publs *Udenrigs, Udenrigspolitiske Skrifter*.

DOMINICAN REPUBLIC

Centro de Investigación Económica para el Caribe—CIECA (Economic Research Centre for the Caribbean): Apdo Postal 3117, Santo Domingo, DN; tel. 686-8696; fax 686-8687; e-mail cieca@codetel.net.do; internet www.serex.gov.do/cieca; f. 1987; Exec. Dir Jefrey R. Lizardo.

ECUADOR

Centro Internacional de Estudios Superiores de Comunicación para América Latina: Diego de Almagro 2155 y Andrade Marín, Apdo 584, Quito; tel. (2) 548-011; fax (2) 524-177; f. 1959; research in communications and training of communicators; library of 16,500 documents, 2,000 vols; Dir-Gen. Dr Asdrúbal de la Torre; publ. *Chasqui* (quarterly).

Instituto Latinoamericano de Investigaciones Sociales (ILDIS) (Latin American Social Sciences Research Institute): Casilla 17-03-367, Quito; tel. (2) 562-103; fax (2) 504-337; f. 1974; research in economics, sociology, political science and education; library of 15,000 vols; Dir Dr Reinhart Wettmann.

FRANCE

Académie du Monde Latin: 217 blvd Saint-Germain, 75007 Paris; aims to encourage contact between leading personalities of countries whose language, culture and civilization are of Latin origin; 100 co-opted mems; Pres. Paulo de Berredo Carneiro (Brazil).

Association d'Etudes et d'Informations Politiques Internationales: 86 blvd Haussmann, 75008 Paris; f. 1949; Dir G. Albertini; publs *Est & Ouest* (Paris, 2 a month), *Documenti sul Comunismo* (Rome), *Este y Oeste* (Caracas).

Centre de Coopération Internationale en Recherche Agronomique pour le Developpement–Cultures Pérennes (CIRAD–CP): blvd de la Lironde, BP 5053, 34032 Montpellier Cédex 1; tel. 4-67-61-58-00; fax 4-67-61-56-59; internet www.cirad.fr; f. 1992; scientific and technical research; experimental stations, industrial plantations; technical assistance in 30 tropical countries; Dir Denis Despréaux; publ. *Plantations Recherche Développement* (every 2 months).

Centre d'Etudes Prospectives et d'Informations Internationales: 9 rue Georges Pitard, 75015 Paris; tel. 1-53-68-55-00; fax 1-53-68-55-03; e-mail postmaster@cepii.fr; internet www.cepii.fr; f. 1978; study of international economic development prospects; 50 mems; library of 20,000 vols, 400 periodicals; Dir L. Fontagné; Gen. Sec. A.-M. Boudard; publs *Economie Internationale* (quarterly), *La Lettre du CEPII, CEPII Newsletter for foreign correspondents* (2 a year), books.

Département des Productions Fruitières et Horticoles (CIRAD-FLHOR): Ave Agropolis, 34398 Montpellier, Cédex 5; tel. 4-67-61-58-00; fax 4-67-61-59-86; internet www.cirad.fr; f. 1945; brs in Martinique, Guadeloupe, several African countries and Corsica; Dir Jean-Pierre Gaillard; publ. *Fruits* (6 a year).

Ecole des Hautes Etudes Internationales: 4 place Saint-Germain des Prés, 77553 Paris Cédex II; tel. 1-42-22-68-06; f. 1904; Pres. M. Schumann; Dir P. Chaigneau.

Ibero-American Centre for Study and Research: Institut Catholique de Paris, 21 rue d'Assas, Paris Cédex 06; Dirs J. Descola, J. Pingle.

Institut d'Etudes Ibériques et Ibéroaméricaines: Université de Bordeaux III, Esplanade des Antilles, Domaine Universitaire, 33405 Talence Cédex; tel. 5-56-84-52-89; fax 5-56-84-51-86; e-mail berton@montaigne.u_bordeaux.fr; f. 1943; teaching and research; 30 staff; library of 51,000 vols; Dir J. M. Desvois.

Institut Européen des Hautes Etudes Internationales (I EHEI): 10 ave des Fleurs, 06000 Nice; tel. 4-93-97-93-70; fax 4-93-97-93-71; e-mail iehei@wanadoo.fr; internet www.cife.org; f. 1964; library of 4,000 vols; Dir Claude Nigoul.

Institut de Recherche pour le Développement (IRD): 213 rue La Fayette, 75010 Paris; tel. 1-48-03-77-77; fax 1-48-03-08-29; internet www.ird.fr; f. 1943; a public corporation charged to aid developing countries by means of research, with special application to human environment problems and food production; library and documentation centre; Pres. Philipee Lazar: Dir-Gen. Jean-Pierre Muller.

Institut de Recherches Agronomiques Tropicales et des Cultures Vivrières (IRAT): 110 rue de l'Université, 75340 Paris Cédex; tel. 1-45-50-32-10; fax 1-93-37-79-39; f. 1960; works in numerous stations in Africa, the Antilles, French Guiana, Brazil; research into general agronomy, the cultivation of food crops, sugar cane, forages, spices, etc.; 220 research workers and technicians; library of 28,000 vols; Dir F. Bour; publ. *L'Agronomie Tropicale* (quarterly).

Institut des Hautes Etudes de l'Amérique Latine: 28 rue Saint-Guillaume, 75007 Paris; tel. 1-44-39-86-00; internet www.iheal.univ-paris3.fr; teaching and research unit of Université de Paris III Sorbonne Nouvelle; Dir Jean-Michel Blanquer; publs *Cahiers des Amériques Latines* (3 a year), *Alizés, REDIAL, Travaux et Mémoires*.

Institut Français des Relations Internationales: 27 rue de la Procession, 75740 Paris Cédex 15; tel. 1-40-61-60-00; fax 1-40-61-60-60; f. 1979; studies foreign policy, economy, defence and strategy; 500 mems; library of 30,000 vols; Dir Thierry de Montbrial; publs *Politique Etrangère* (quarterly), *Lettre d'Information* (every 2 months), *Travaux et recherches, Les Cahiers de l'IFRI, Rapport Annuel sur le Système Economique et les Stratégies—RAMSES.*

Institut Pluridisciplinaire d'Etudes sur l'Amérique Latine de Toulouse: Maison de la Recherche, Université de Toulouse Le Mirail, 5 allées Antonio Machado, 31058 Toulouse Cédex; tel. 5-61-50-43-93; fax 5-61-50-36-25; f. 1985; specialized research; economic documentation centre; 31 staff; Dir J. Gilard; publs *Caravelle, L'Ordinaire Mexique-Amérique Centrale, Les Ateliers de Caravelle.*

Laboratoire Interdisciplinaire de Recherche sur Les Amériques (LIRA): Université de Rennes II, 6 ave Gaston Berger, 35043 Rennes Cédex; tel. 2-99-14-16-06; e-mail jean-pierre.sanchez@uhb.fr; f. 1966; general and musical studies on region; Dir Jean-Pierre Sanchez.

Musée de l'Homme: Palais de Chaillot, place du Trocadéro, 75116 Paris; tel. 1-44-05-72-72; fax 1-44-05-72-91; f. 1878; library of 250,000 vols, 5,000 periodicals; ethnography, anthropology, prehistory; attached to the Muséum National d'Histoire Naturelle; also a research and education centre; Profs Bernard Dupzigne, André Langaney, Henry de Lumley; publ. *Objets et mondes* (quarterly).

Societé des Américanistes: Musée de l'Homme, 17 place du Trocadéro, 75116 Paris; tel. 1-47-04-63-11; f. 1896; 500 mems; Pres. C. Baudez; Gen. Sec. D. Michelet; publ. *Journal.*

GERMANY

Deutsche Gesellschaft für Auswärtige Politik eV (German Society for Foreign Affairs): 10787 Berlin, Rauchstr. 17-18; tel. and fax (30) 254231; e-mail info@dgap.org; internet www.dgap.org; f. 1955; 1,600 mems; discusses and promotes research on problems of international politics; research library of 52,500 vols; Pres. Dr Ulrich Cartellieri; Exec. Vice-Pres. Dr Immo Stabreit; Dir Research Institute Prof. Dr Karl Kaiser; publs *Die Internationale Politik* (yearbook), *Internationale Politik* (monthly).

Deutsches Übersee Institut (German Overseas Institute): 20354 Hamburg 36, Neuer Jungfernstieg 21; tel. (40) 42834593; fax (40) 42834547; e-mail duei@uni-hamburg.de; internet www.rrz.uni-hamburg.de/duei/; f. 1966; incl. a section on Latin America; Head Dr Werner Draguhn.

Ibero-Amerikanisches Institut Preussischer Kulturbesitz: 10722 Berlin, Potsdamer Str. 37, Postfach 1247; tel. (30) 2662502; fax (30) 2662503; f. 1930; library and research institute; 800,000 vols; Dir Dr GUENTHER MAIHOLD; publs *Ibero-Amerikanisches Archiv, Indiana* (reviews), *Iberoamericana, Monumenta Americana, Quellenwerke, Bibliotheca Ibero-Americana, Miscellanea* (monograph series).

Institute of Latin American Studies: Universität Rostock, 18055 Rostock, Universitätsplatz 1; f. 1964; teaching in economics, law, sociology, history, literature, anthropology and geography of Latin America; publ. *Lateinamerika* (2 a year).

Lateinamerika-Institut der Freien Universität Berlin: 14197 Berlin, Rüdesheimer Str. 54–56; tel. (30) 8383072; e-mail lai@zedat.fu-berlin.de; f. 1970; teaching and research; Dir Prof. Dr MANFRED NITSCH.

Stiftung Wissenschaft und Politik—SWP, Forschungsinstitut für Internationale Politik und Sicherheit (Foundation for Science and Politics, Research Institute for International Politics and Security): 82067 Ebenhausen, Zeller Weg 27; tel. (8178) 700; fax (8178) 70312; internet www.lrz-muenchen.de; f. 1962; Dir Dr CHRISTOPH BERTRAM.

GUADELOUPE

Caribbean Research Centre: Université des Antilles et de la Guyane, 97159 Pointe-à-Pitre Cédex; tel. 938640; fax 938639; Dir ALAIN YACOU.

GUATEMALA

Instituto Centroamericano de Investigación y Tecnología Industrial (ICAITI) (Central American Research Institute for Industry): Avda La Reforma 4–47, Zona 10, Apdo 1552, Guatemala City; tel. 331-0631; fax 331-7470; e-mail general@icaiti.org.gt; f. 1956; research on marketing, development of new industries and manufacturing techniques, microbiology, geology and energy research projects, establishment of Central American standards, information services to industry, and professional advice; library of 36,000 vols; Dir Ing. LUIS FIDEL CIFUENTES E. (acting).

Instituto de Nutrición de Centroamérica y Panamá (INCAP) (Institute of Nutrition of Central America and Panama): Carretera Roosevelt, Zona 11, 01901 Guatemala City; tel. 472-3762; fax 473-6529; e-mail webmaster@incap.org.gt; internet www.incap.org.gt; f. 1949; represents the following countries: Belize, Costa Rica, El Salvador, Guatemala, Honduras, Nicaragua, Panama; administered by Pan American Health Organization (PAHO)/World Health Organization (WHO); Programmes of Agricultural and Food Sciences, Nutrition and Health, Food and Nutrition Education, Technical Co-operation; postgraduate course in food and nutrition and allied fields; library of 70,500 vols; Dir Dr HERNÁN L. DELGADO; publs various documents.

Instituto de Relaciones Internacionales y de Investigaciones para la Paz (International Relations and Peace Research Institute): 1A Calle 9-52, Zona 1, 01001 Guatemala City; tel. 28260; fax 531; Dir Dr L. A. PADILLA.

GUYANA

Guyana Institute of International Affairs: POB 101176, Georgetown; tel. (2) 77768; fax (2) 29542; f. 1965; 175 mems; library of 5,000 vols; Pres. DONALD A. B. TROTMAN; publs *Annual Journal of International Affairs,* occasional papers.

INDIA

Indian Council of World Affairs: Sapru House, Barakhamba Rd, New Delhi 110 001; tel. (11) 3317246; fax (11) 331208; f. 1943; non-governmental institution for the study of Indian and international questions; 2,625 mems; library of 124,122 vols; Pres. HARCHARAN SINGH JOSH; Hon. Sec.-Gen. S. C. PARASHER; publs *India Quarterly, Foreign Affairs Reports* (monthly).

INDONESIA

Centre for Strategic and International Studies: Jalan Tanah Abang III/23–27, Jakarta 10160; tel. (21) 3865532; fax (21) 375317; internet www.csis.or.id; f. 1971; library of 25,000 vols; Exec. Dir Dr HADI SOESASTRO; publs *The Indonesian Quarterly, Analisis* (6 a year).

ISRAEL

International Institute for Development, Labour and Co-operative Studies (Afro-Asian Institute of the Histradut): 7 Nehardea St, POB 16201, Tel Aviv 64235; tel. and fax (3) 5229195; f. 1958; seminars and courses for leadership of trade unions, co-operative and development institutions, community organizations, women's and youth groups, etc., in African, Asian, Caribbean and Pacific regions; library of 15,000 vols; Dir and Principal Dr Y. PAZ.

ITALY

Istituto Affari Internazionali: Palazzo Rondinini, Via Angelo Brunetti 9, 00186 Rome; tel (06) 3224360; fax (06) 3224363; e-mail iai@iai.it; internet www.iai.it; f. 1965; library of 13,000 vols; Pres. CESARE MERLINI; Dir GIANNI BONVICINI; publs *The International Spectator* (quarterly in English), *L'Italia nella Politica Internazionale* (annually).

Istituto Italo–Latino Americano: Palazzo Santacroce, Pasolini Piazza Benedetto Cairoli 3, 00186 Rome; tel. (06) 684921; fax (06) 6872834; e-mail info@iila.org; internet www.iila.org; f. 1966 by 20 Latin American states and Italy; cultural activities, commercial exchanges, economic and sociological, scientific and technical research, etc.; awards student grants; library of 90,000 vols; Sec.-Gen. MARIO MAGLIANO.

Istituto per gli Studi di Politica Internazionale (ISPI): Palazzo Clerici, Via Clerici 5, 20121 Milan; tel. (02) 8633131; fax (02) 8692055; e-mail ispi.eventi@tiscalinet.it; internet www.ispinet.it; f. 1933 for the promotion of the study and knowledge of all problems concerning international relations; seminars at postgraduate level; library of 100,000 vols; Pres. BORIS BIANCHERI; Man. Dir Dr GIOVANNI ROGGERO FOSSATI; publs *Relazioni Internazionali* (6 a year), *Papers* (20 a year).

Istituto per le relazioni fra l'Italia e i paesi dell'Africa, America Latina e Medio Oriente (IPALMO) (Institute for Relations between Italy and the Countries of Africa, Latin America and the Middle East): Via del Tritone 62B, 00187 Rome; tel. (06) 6792734; fax (06) 6797849; e-mail ipalmo@ipalmo.com; internet www.ipalmo.com; f. 1971; Pres. GILBERTO BONALUMI; publ. *Politica Internazionale* (every 2 months).

JAMAICA

Caribbean Food and Nutrition Institute: University of the West Indies, POB 140, Mona, Kingston 7; tel. 927-1540; fax 927-2657; internet www.cfni.paho.org; f. 1967; research and field investigations, training in nutrition, dissemination of information, advisory services, production of educational material; mems: all English-speaking Caribbean territories, Belize, Guyana and Suriname; library of 4,500 vols; Dir Dr ADELINE WYNANTE PATTERSON; publs *Cajanus* (quarterly), *Nyam News Nutrient-Cost Tables* (quarterly).

Institute of Social and Economic Research: University of the West Indies, Mona Campus, Mona, Kingston 7; tel. 927-0233; fax 927-2409; f. 1948; applied research and graduate teaching programme relating to the Caribbean; brs in Barbados and Trinidad and Tobago; Dir NORMAN P. GIRVAN.

JAPAN

Ajia Keizai Kenkyusho (Institute of Developing Economies): 42 Ichigaya-Hommura-cho, Shinjuku-ku, Tokyo 162; tel. (3) 3353-4231; fax (3) 3226-8475; e-mail apec@ide.go.ip; internet www.ide.go.ip; f. 1960; merged with Japan External Trade Organization in 1998; researches industrial devt and political change in Latin America; library of 335,840 vols; Chair. YOTARO IIDA; Pres. KATSUHISA YAMADA; publ. *Developing Economies* (quarterly).

Centre for Latin American Studies: Nanzan University, 18 Yamazato-cho, Showa-ku, Nagoya 466; e-mail cfls@ic.nanzan-u.ac.jp; internet www.nanzan-u.ac.jp; f. 1983; an institute specializing in the study of contemporary Latin America (social sciences).

Tokyo University of Foreign Studies: 3-11-1, Asahi-cho, Fuchu-shi, Tokyo 183; tel. (3) 3917-6111; e-mail w3@is.tufs.ac.jp; internet www.tufs.ac.jp; f. 1899; programmes of study into world languages, cultures and international relations; Pres. Dr MINEO NAKAJIMA.

REPUBLIC OF KOREA

Institute of Brazilian Studies: Kyung Hee University, 1 Hoiki Dong, Dongdaemun-ku, Seoul 131; tel. (2) 965-8000; f. 1978.

Institute of Latin American Studies: Hankuk University of Foreign Studies, 270 Ly Moon Dong, Dongdaemun-ku, Seoul; tel. (2) 961-4159; fax (2) 959-7738; Dir Prof. CHUNG KYU HO.

MEXICO

Centro Coordinador y Difusor Estudios Latinoamericanos: Torre I de Humanidades 1°, City University, 04510 Mexico, DF; tel. (5) 6221009; fax (5) 6221910; f. 1978; attached to Universidad Nacional de México; study of Latin America and the Caribbean in all disciplines (history, literature, philosophy, etc.); library of 11,898 monographs, 8,700 magazines, 3,000 pamphlets, 160 theses, 150 records; Dir Dr IGNACIO DÍAZ RUIZ; publs *Anuario Estudios Latinoamericanos, Serie Nuestra América* (3 a year).

Centro de Cooperación Regional para la Educación de Adultos en América Latina y el Caribe (CREFAL) (Regional Co-operation Centre for Adult Education in Latin America and the Caribbean): Avda Lázaro Cardenas s/n, Col. Revolución, 61609

Patzcuaro, Michoacán; tel. 43420005; fax 43420092; e-mail crefal@ yreri.crefal.edu.mx; internet www.crefal.edu.mx; f. 1951 by UNESCO and OAS; admin. by Board of Directors from mem. countries; regional technical assistance, specialist training in literary and adult education, research; library of 42,799 vols; Dir JUAN F. MILLIAN; publs *Revista Interamericana de Educación de Adultos* (quarterly), *Circular Informativa* (quarterly). *Boletín de Resúmenes Analíticos* (2 a year).

Centro de Estudios Educativos, AC (Education Studies Centre): Avda Revolución 1291, Col. Tlacopoa, San Angel, 01040 México, DF; tel (5) 5935719; fax (5) 6642728; e-mail ceemexico@compuserve .com.mx; f. 1963; scientific research into the problems of education in Mexico and Latin America; 16 researchers; library of 30,000 vols and 400 periodicals; Dir-Gen. LUIS MORFÍN LÓPEZ; publ. *Revista Latinoamericana de Estudios Educativos* (quarterly).

Centro de Estudios Internacionales (Centre for International Studies): Colegio de México, Camino al Ajusco 20, Col. Pedregal de Santa Teresa, 01000 México, DF; tel. (5) 449-3000; fax (5) 645-0464; e-mail ancova@colmex.mx; internet www.colmex.mx; f. 1960; research and teaching in international relations and public administration; Dir MARÍA CELIA TORO.

Centro de Estudios Monetarios Latinoamericanos (Centre for Latin American Monetary Studies): Durango 54, Col. Roma, Del. Cuauhtémoc, 06700 México, DF; tel (5) 5330300; fax (5) 2077024; f. 1952; organizes technical training programmes on monetary policy, development finance, etc; applied research programmes, regional meetings of banking officials; 65 mems; Dir SERGIO GHIGLIAZZA; Deputy Dir LUIS A. GIORGIO; publs *Bulletin* (every 2 months), *Monetaria* (quarterly), *Money Affairs* (2 a year), *Supervisory and Fiscalization Bulletin* (3 a year).

Centro de Relaciones Internacionales (CRI) (Centre for International Relations): Ciudad Universitaria, FCPM, 04510 México, DF; tel. (5) 6551344; attached to the Faculty of Political and Social Sciences of the Universidad Nacional Autónoma de México; f. 1970; co-ordinates and promotes research in all aspects of international relations and Mexico's foreign policy, as well as the training of researchers in different fields: Disciplinary construction problems, Co-operation and International Law, Developing nations, Actual problems in world society, Africa, Asia, Peace Research; 30 full mems; library of 16,000 vols; Dir Lic. ILEANA CID CAPETILLO; publs *Relaciones Internacionales* (quarterly), *Cuadernos, Boletín Informativo del CRI*.

Consejo Latinamericano de Investigación para la Paz (CLAIP) (Latin American Peace Research Council): Calle Magnolia 39, Col. San Jeronimo Lidice, 10200 México, DF; internet www .copri.dk/ipra/claip.html; f. 1978; holds conferences; Sec.-Gen. PAULA PIRES DE NIELSON; publ. *Boletín Informativo CLAIP*.

Pan American Institute of Geography and History: Ex-Arzobispado 29, Col. Observatorio, 11860 México, DF; tel. (5) 2775888; fax (5) 2716172; e-mail ipgh@laneta.apc.org; f. 1928; promotion of professional improvement and application of modern methodology in cartography, geography, geophysics, history, anthropology and archaeology in the Western Hemisphere; mems: nations of the Organization of American States; library of 300,000 vols; Sec.-Gen. CARLOS CARVALLO YÁÑEZ (Chile); publs *Revista Cartográfica, Revista Geográfica, Revista de Historia de América, Revista Geofísica, Boletín de Antropología Americana, Folklore Americano, Revista de Arqueologia Americana, Boletín Aéreo* (quarterly), 400 books and monographs.

THE NETHERLANDS

Institute of Social Studies: POB 29776, 2502 LT The Hague; tel. (70) 426-0460; fax (70) 426-0799; e-mail promotions@iss.nl; internet www.iss.nl; f. 1952; postgraduate courses in development studies and international relations; Pres. Prof. L. F. W. DE KLERK; publs *Development and Change* (quarterly), *Working Papers* (several sub-series; irregular), *Occasional Papers* (irregular).

NICARAGUA

Coordinadora Regional de Investigaciones Económicas y Sociales (CRIES) (Regional Co-ordinating Committee of Economic and Social Research): De Iglesia El Carmen 1c. al Largo, Apdo 3516, Managua; tel. (2) 22-5137; fax (2) 22-6180; research into economic development and other socio-economic and socio-political issues in Central America and the Caribbean; Pres. XAVIER GOROS-TIAGA; publs *Cuadernos de Pensamiento Propio, Revista Pensamiento Propio* (monthly), *Servicios Especiales* (2 a month).

Instituto Histórico Centroamericano (IHCA) (Central American Historical Institute): Universidad Centroamericana, Apdo A-194, Managua; tel. (2) 78-2557; fax (2) 77-2583; e-mail envio@ns.uca .rain.ni; Dir JOSÉ IDIÁQUEZ.

PAKISTAN

Area Study Centre for Africa, North and South America: Quaid-i-Azam University, Islamabad; tel. (51) 230834; fax (51)

230833; f. 1978; teaching and research; library of 10,000 vols, microfilm/microfiche collection; Dir Dr RASUL BAKHSH RAIS; publ. *Pakistan Journal of American Studies* (2 a year).

PANAMA

Centro de Estudios Latinamericanos 'Justo Arosamena' (Justo Arosamena Centre for Latin American Studies): Apdo 63093, El Dorado, Panamá; tel. 23-0028; fax 69-2032; f. 1977 for the analysis and dissemination of international agreements and intervention and other foreign-affairs issues; Exec. Sec. M. A. GANDÁSEGUI.

PARAGUAY

Servicio Técnico Interamericano de Cooperación Agrícola (Inter-American Technical Service for Agricultural Co-operation): Casilla de Correo 819, Asunción; f. 1943; 10,000 vols; Lib. LUCILA M. I. CARDUS.

PERU

Centro de Investigaciones Económicas y Sociales (CIESUL) (Economic and Social Research Centre): Universidad de Lima, Lima; internet www.ulima.edu.pe.

Centro Peruano de Estudios Internacionales (CEPEI) (Peruvian Centre for International Studies): San Ignacio de Loyola 554, Miraflores 8, Lima 18; tel. (1) 4457225; fax (1) 4451094; f. 1983; external relations, incl. Peru's border relations; Exec. Pres. Dr EDUARDO FERRERO COSTA; publ. *Cronología de Las Relaciones Internacionales del Peru* (quarterly).

Instituto de Economía de Libre Mercado (IELM) (Institute of Free Market Economics): Universidad San Ignacio de Loyola, Calle San Ignacio de Loyola 150, La Molina; tel. 3490016; e-mail jsardon@ amauta.rcp.net.pe; f. 1993; studies economic, political and social history of the area; Dir JOSÉ LUIS SARDON.

POLAND

Centre for Latin American Studies: University of Warsaw, Szturmowa 4, 02-678 Warsaw; tel. (22) 5534209; fax (22) 5534210; e-mail cesla@plearn.edu.pl; f. 1988; documentation service; Dir Prof. ANDRZEJ DEMBICZ; publ. *CESLA 'Estudios y Memorias' Series*.

Polski Instytut Spraw Międzynarodowych (Polish Institute for International Affairs): 00-950 Warsaw, Warecka 1a; tel. (22) 8263021; fax (22) 8272454; f. 1947; international relations; library of 125,000 vols; Dir Dr HENRYK SZLAJFER; publs *Sprawy Miedzynarodowe* (quarterly), *Zbiór Dokumentów* (monthly, in various languages).

PUERTO RICO

Association of Caribbean Universities and Research Institutes: POB 11532, Caparra Heights Station, San Juan, PR 00922; f. 1968 to foster contact and collaboration between member universities and institutes; conferences, meetings, seminars, etc.; circulation of information; facilitates co-operation and the pooling of resources in research; encourages exchanges of staff and students; mems: 50 institutions; Pres. Dr ORVILLE KEAN; Sec.-Gen. GERARD LATORTUE; publ. *Caribbean Educational Bulletin* (quarterly).

Association of Caribbean Universities, Research and Library Institutes: Apdo 23317, San Juan, PR 00931; tel. 764-0000; fax 763-5685; f. 1969 to facilitate devt and use of libraries, archives and information services; identification, collection and preservation of information resources; c. 200 mems; Pres. WILLIMAE JOHNSON; Exec. Sec. ONEIDA R. ORITZ; publs *ACURIL Newsletter*, Conference Proceedings.

Institute of Caribbean Studies: POB 23361, University Station, Río Piedras, PR 00931; tel. 764-0000; fax 764-3099; f. 1959; research and publishing; 10 mems; library of 150 vols; Dir Dr PEDRO J. RIVERA GUZMÁN; publ. *Caribbean Studies*.

RUSSIA

Institute of Latin America: 113035 Moscow, B. Ordynka 21; tel. (095) 951-53-23; fax (095) 953-40-70; e-mail ilaran@pol.ru; internet www.plugcom.ru/~ilaran/; concerned with the economic, social, political and cultural development of Latin American countries; Dir Dr V. M. DAVYDOV.

Institute of World Economics and International Relations: 117859 Moscow, Profsoyuznaya 23; tel. (095) 120-43-32; fax (095) 310-70-27; e-mail imemoran@glasnet.ru; f. 1956; Dir V. A. MARTYNOV (acting).

SENEGAL

Centre des Hautes Etudes Afro-Ibéro-Américaines: Université Cheikh Anta Diop de Dakar, Dakar-Fann, Dakar; tel. 22-05-30; concerned with all matters relating to Africa and Latin America in the fields of law, science and the arts.

SPAIN

Escuela de Estudios Hispanoamericanos: Alfonso XII 16, 41002 Seville; tel. (95) 4500972; fax (95) 4224331; e-mail bibescu@cica.es; f. 1943; studies history of the Americas; Dir Library ISABEL REAL DÍAZ.

Instituto de Cooperación Iberoamericana (Institute for Ibero-American Co-operation): Avda de los Reyes Católicos 4, Ciudad Universitaria, 28040 Madrid; tel. (91) 5838100; fax (91) 5838310; f. 1946; promotes cultural understanding between Spain and America by organizing conferences, exhibitions and exchanges, scholarships; finances programmes of cultural, scientific, economic and technical co-operation; information department; Centre for Advanced Hispanic Studies; organizes programmes to diffuse the Spanish language and culture in the USA and Europe; library of 510,000 vols and 7,000 periodicals; Pres. FERNANDO VILLALONGA; Sec.-Gen. LUIS ESPINOSA; publs include *Cuadernos Hispanoamericanos* (monthly), *Pensamiento Iberoamericano* (2 a year).

Instituto de Cuestiones Internacionales y Política Exterior (INCIPE) (Institute of International Affairs and Foreign Policy): Rafael Calvo 42, 28010 Madrid; tel. (91) 3086882; fax (91) 3191584; e-mail incipe@mad.servicom.es; internet www.incipe-ceri.org; f. 1988; Dir ALONSO ALVAREZ DE TOLEDO; publ. *La Opinión Pública Española y la Política Exterior* (2 a year).

Instituto de Relaciones Europeo-Latinoamericanas (IRELA) (Institute for European-Latin American Relations): Calle Pedro de Valdivia 10, Apdo 2600, 28028 Madrid; tel. (91) 5617200; fax (91) 5626499; e-mail info@ivcla.org; f. 1984; research, conferences, etc.; Pres. ROLF LINKOHR; Dir WOLF GRABENDORFF; publs *Dossiers* (8 a year), *Working Papers* (6 a year).

Real Academia Hispano-Americana (Royal Spanish-American Academy): Calle Almirante Vienna 14, Apdo 16, 11009 Cádiz; f. 1910; 29 mems; Dir ANTONIO OROZCO ACUAVIVA; publs *Anuario, Boletín*.

SWEDEN

Ibero-American Institute: University of Göteborg, POB 200, 405 30 Göteborg; tel (31) 773-18-07; fax (31) 773-18-04; f. 1939; information, research, courses; library of 50,000 vols; Dir Dr ROLAND ANRUP; publ. *Anales*, regular cultural series, monographs.

Latinamerika-Institutet i Stockholm (Institute of Latin American Studies, Stockholm University): 106 91 Stockholm; tel. (8) 16-28-82; fax (8) 15-65-82; e-mail lai@lai.su.se; internet www.lai.su.se; f. 1951; research on economic, political and social development in the region; library of 50,000 vols; Dir WEINE KARLSSON; Lib. BRITT JOHANSSON; publ. *Nordic Journal of Latin American Studies (Ibero Americana).*

SWITZERLAND

Institut Universitaire d'Etudes du Développement (University Institute of Development Studies): 24 rue Rothschild, 1202 Geneva; tel. (22) 9065940; fax (22) 9065947; e-mail iued@unige.ch; internet www.unige.ch/iued/; f. 1961; African history, Middle Eastern and Latin American studies, international relations, Switzerland–Third World economic relations; Dir J. L. MAURER.

Institut Universitaire des Hautes Etudes Internationales (Graduate Institute of International Studies): 132 rue de Lausanne, 1202 Geneva 21; tel. (22) 9085700; fax (22) 9085710; e-mail info@hei.unige.ch; internet www.unige.ch/hei/; f. 1927; a research and teaching institution studying international questions from the juridical, political and economic viewpoints; Dir Prof. PETER TSCHOPP.

Schweizerisches Institut für Auslandforschung (Swiss Institute of International Studies): Seilergraben 49, 8001 Zürich; tel (1) 6326362; fax (1) 6321947; e-mail siafum@pw.unizh.ch; internet www.siaf.ch; f. 1943; Dir Prof. Dr DIETER RULOFF; publ. *Sozialwissenschaftliche Studien* (annually).

Zentrum für Internationale Studien (Centre for International Studies): Seilergraben 45–49, 8001 Zurich; tel. (1) 6327968; fax (1) 6321941; e-mail cispostmaster@sipo.gess.ethz.ch; internet www.cis.ethz.ch; f. 1997; international relations, security studies and conflict research; Man. Dir Prof. KURT R. SPILLMAN.

TRINIDAD AND TOBAGO

Caribbean Agricultural Research and Development Institute (CARDI): University of the West Indies, St Augustine Campus, St Augustine; tel. 645-1205; fax 645-1208; e-mail itservices@cardi.org; internet www.cardi.org; f. 1975; mems: CARICOM countries (see Part Three, Regional Organizations); provides technical assistance, technology devt and transfer in agriculture and animal sciences; library of 3,000 vols; Exec. Dir Dr SAMSUNDAR PARASRAM; publs *Annual Reports, Research Reports and Papers, Fact-sheets, Technical Bulletins and Papers, Agricultural Profiles.*

Caribbean Food and Nutrition Institute (CFNI): University of the West Indies, POB 140, St Augustine; tel. 663-1544; fax 663-1544; e-mail cfni@cablenett.net; internet www.cfni.paho.org.

Institute of International Relations: University of the West Indies, St Augustine Campus, St Augustine; tel. 662-2002; f. 1966; diplomatic training and postgraduate teaching and research; Dir FRANK BARSOTTI (acting).

Institute of Social and Economic Research (ISER): Faculty of Social Sciences, University of the West Indies, St Augustine; tel 662-2002; fax 662-6295; e-mail fssuwisa@carib-link.net; internet www.uwi.tt/8082/iser/iser.htm; f. 1950; researches social, political and economic systems of the Caribbean region; provides social, political, economic and demographic information.

UNITED KINGDOM

Centre for Caribbean Studies: University of Warwick, Coventry CV4 7AL; tel. (24) 7652-3443; fax (24) 7652-3473; e-mail m.davies@warwick.ac.uk; f. 1984; MA and PhD programme, conferences and symposia, lectures, publishing; Dir. Dr D. DABYDEEN; publs *Warwick Series in Caribbean Studies, Working Paper Series.*

Centre for Latin American Studies: University of Cambridge, History Faculty Bldg, West Road, Cambridge CB3 9EF; tel. (1223) 335390; fax (1223) 335397; internet www.latin-american.cam.ac.uk; f. 1969; research and graduate teaching, mainly in comparative history, state formation, Mexican history, Caribbean studies, religion, social change, politics and economics; Dir Dr C. A. JONES; publs *Cambridge Latin American Miniatures, Working Paper Series.*

Commonwealth Institute: Kensington High St, London W8 6NQ; tel. (20) 7603-4535; fax (20) 7602-7374; e-mail info@commonwealth.org; internet www.commonwealth.org.uk; aims to promote and celebrate the Commonwealth by engaging Commonwealth peoples in business, cultural, educational and public affairs programmes to contribute to the progress and prosperity of Commonwealth countries; permanent exhibitions of Commonwealth countries including the Caribbean, open to the public with special provision for visiting parties; CEO DAVID FRENCH.

David Livingstone Institute of Overseas Development Studies: University of Strathclyde, Livingstone Tower, 26 Richmond St, Glasgow, G1 1LH; tel. (141) 552-4400; fax (141) 522-0775; e-mail g.zawdle@strath.ac.uk; f. 1973; economic, scientific and technological research; Dir Dr JAMES PICKETT.

Hispanic and Luso-Brazilian Council: Canning House, 2 Belgrave Square, London SW1X 8PJ; tel. (20) 7235-2303; fax (20) 7235-3587; e-mail enquiries@canninghouse.com; internet www.canninghouse.com; f. 1943; cultural, educational and economic links with Latin America, Spain and Portugal; 250 corporate mems; library of 55,000 vols; Dir-Gen. PHILIP A. MCLEAN; publ. *British Bulletin of Publications on Latin America, the Caribbean, Portugal and Spain* (2 a year).

Institute of Commonwealth Studies: 28 Russell Square, London WC1B 5DS; tel. (20) 7862-8844; fax (20) 7862-8820; f. 1949; attached to University of London; for postgraduate research in social sciences and recent history relating to the Commonwealth; library of 160,000 vols, includes library of West India Committee; Dir Prof. A. P. CAPLAN.

Institute of Development Studies: University of Sussex, Falmer, Brighton, Sussex BN1 9RE; tel. (1273) 606261; fax (1273) 621202; e-mail ids@ids.ac.uk; internet www.ids.ac.uk; f. 1966; research, training, graduate teaching, advisory work, information services; Dir Dr KEITH BEZANSON; publs *IDS Bulletin* (quarterly), *Research Reports, Discussion Papers* (monthly), *Policy Briefing Papers, Annual Report, Publications Catalogue.*

Institute of Latin American Studies: University of Liverpool, Liverpool L69 3BX; tel. (151) 794-3079; fax (151) 794-3080; e-mail fisher@liverpool.ac.uk; f. 1966; university centre for the development of teaching and research on Latin America; 11 faculty mems; library of 50,000 vols; Dir Prof. JOHN R. FISHER; publs monographs, research papers.

Institute of Latin American Studies: 31 Tavistock Square, London WC1H 9HA; tel. (20) 7862-8870; fax (20) 7862-8886; f. 1965; graduate study centre within the School of Advanced Study of the University of London; co-ordinates national information on Latin American studies in the United Kingdom; library of bibliographies, guides and research aids; Dir Prof. JAMES DUNKERLEY; publs monographs, research papers and miscellaneous material.

International Development Centre: Queen Elizabeth House, 21 St Giles, Oxford; tel. (1865) 273600; fax (1865) 273607; e-mail qeh@qeh.ox.ac.uk; internet www.qeh.ox.ac.uk; f. 1986; attached to the University of Oxford; specializes in Development Studies; Dir Prof. F. STEWART.

Latin American Centre: St Antony's College, Oxford OX2 6JF; tel. (1865) 274486; fax (1865) 274489; e-mail enquiries@lac.ox.ac.uk; internet www.lac.ox.ac.uk; Dir Dr A. KNIGHT.

Overseas Development Institute: Portland Huse, Stag Pl., London SW1E 5DP; tel. (20) 7922-0300; fax (20) 7922-0399; e-mail odi@odi.org.uk; internet www.odi.org.uk; f. 1960 to act as a research and information centre on overseas development issues and problems; library of 20,000 vols; Dir SIMON MAXWELL; publs *Development Policy Review* (quarterly), *Index to Development Literature* (6 a year), books, pamphlets, briefing papers.

Royal Commonwealth Society: 18 Northumberland Ave, London WC2N 5BJ; tel. (20) 7930-6733; fax (20) 7930-7905; e-mail info@rcsint.org; internet www.rcsint.org; f. 1868; organizes public affairs programme; Chair. of Central Council Sir MICHAEL MCWILLIAM; Dir PETER LUFF; publs *Newsletter* (3 a year), *Conference Reports*.

Royal Institute of International Affairs: Chatham House, 10 St James's Square, London SW1Y 4LE; tel. (20) 7957-5700; fax (20) 7957-5710; e-mail contact@riia.org; internet www.riia.org; f. 1920; an independent body which aims to promote the study and understanding of international affairs; over 400 corporate mems and many individual mems; library of 160,000 vols, 650 periodicals; Dir Prof. VICTOR BULMER-THOMAS; publs *The World Today* (monthly), *International Affairs* (quarterly).

USA

Border Research Institute: New Mexico State University, 4200 Research Drive, POB 30001, Dept 3BR1, Las Cruces, NM 88003-8001; tel. (505) 646-3524; fax (505) 646-5474; e-mail bri@nmsu.edu; internet www.nmsu.edu~bri; f. 1978; research and analysis of internatonal border issues, including the US–Mexico border, economic development and NAFTA; library of 3,200 vols.

Brookings Institution: 1775 Massachusetts Ave, NW, Washington, DC 20036; tel. (202) 797-6000; fax (202) 797-6004; e-mail eapublic@brook.edu; internet www.brook.edu; f. 1916; 61 professional mems; research, education and publishing in the fields of economics, government and foreign policy; library of 80,000 vols; Pres. MICHAEL H. ARMACOST; publs *The Brookings Review* (quarterly), *Brookings Papers on Economic Activity* (3 a year).

Center for Economic Research: Florida International University, University Park, DM 319-B, Miami, FL 33199; tel. (305) 348-3283; fax (305) 348-3605; e-mail salazar@fin.edu; f. 1982 to conduct economic research, with emphasis on the Caribbean basin and Cuba; Dir Prof. SALAZAR; publ. *Caribbean Basin Country Projections*.

Center for International Policy (CIP): 1755 Massachusetts Ave NW, Suite 55, Washington, DC 20036; tel. (202) 232-3317; fax (202) 232-3440; e-mail cip@ciponline.org; internet www.ciponline.org; f. 1975; promotes international co-operation and demilitarization; Pres. ROBERT E. WHITE; publ. *International Policy Report*.

Center for International Studies: Massachusetts Institute of Technology, Cambridge, MA 02139; tel. (617) 253-8093; internet web.mit.edu/cis/www/index.html; f. 1952; development, migration, defence and arms control studies, environment, trade, political economy; MIT–Japan Program; Dir MICHAEL ROTHSCHILD.

Center for Latin American Studies: University of Florida, POB 115530, 319 GRI, Gainesville, FL 32611-5530; tel. (352) 392-0375; fax (352) 392-7682; e-mail www@latam.ufl.edu; internet www .latam.ufl.edu; f. 1931; graduate teaching and research; tropical resources and development, population and social change, culture and the state, Haitian Creole language programmes; extensive Latin American collection in library; Dir C. WOOD; publ. *The Latin-americanist* (2 a year).

Center of International Studies: 116 Bendheim Hall, Princeton University, Princeton, NJ 08544; tel. (609) 452-4851; internet www.wws.princeton.edu/~cis; f. 1951; an academic research institute of Princeton University; international relations; 40 faculty mems; Dir MICHAEL DOYLE; publs *World Politics* (quarterly), books, occasional papers.

Council on Foreign Relations, Inc.: 58 East 68th St, New York, NY 10021; tel. (212) 434-9400; fax (212) 861-2504; e-mail communications@cfr.org; internet www.cfr.org; f. 1921; 3,420 mems; Foreign Relations Library of 18,000 vols, 300 periodicals; Pres. LESLIE H. GELB; Chair. PETER PETERSON; publs *Foreign Affairs* (6 a year), and books on major issues of US foreign policy.

Council on Hemispheric Affairs: Suite 401, 724 Ninth St, NW, Washington, DC 20001; tel. (202) 393-3322; fax (202) 393-3423; e-mail coha@dettal.org; internet www.coha.org; f. 1975; conducts research into relations between North and South America; Chair. Dr PETER BOURNE; Dir LAURENCE BIRNS; publ. *News and Analysis* (2 a week).

Helen Kellogg Institute for International Studies: University of Notre Dame, 216 Hesburgh Center for International Studies, Notre Dame, IN 46556-5677; tel. (219) 631-6580; fax (219) 631-6717; internet www.nd.edu/~kellogg; f. 1982; international research, particularly focused upon Latin America; Dir SCOTT MAINWARING; publs *Working Paper Series, Newsletter* (2 a year).

Hispanic Society of America: 613 West 155th St, New York, NY 10032; tel. (212) 926-2234; e-mail info@hispanicsociety.org; internet www.hispanicsociety.org; f. 1904; maintains a public museum, rare book room, research staff, publishing section; 400 hon. mems; library

of 300,000 vols and 250,000 manuscripts; Dir MITCHELL A. CODDING, Jr.

Institute for Latin American Studies: Sid Richardson Hall 1.310, University of Texas at Austin, Austin, TX 78712; tel. (512) 471-5551; fax (512) 471-3090; e-mail ilas@uts.cc.utexas.edu; internet www.lanic.utexas.edu/ilas; Dir Dr NICOLAS SHUMWAY.

Institute of Latin American and Iberian Studies: Columbia University, 420 West 118th St, Rm 830, New York, NY 10027; tel. (212) 854-4643; internet www.columbia.edu/cu/ilas; f. 1961; co-ordinates events, lectures and seminars on subjects relating to Latin America and Spain; Dir Prof. DOUGLAS A. CHALMERS.

Inter-American Dialogue: 1211 Connecticut Ave, Suite 510, Washington, DC 20036; tel. (202) 822-9002; fax (202) 822-9553; e-mail iad@thedialogue.org; internet www.iadialog.org; f. 1982; centre for policy analysis, communication and exchange on Western affairs; 100 mems; Pres. PETER HAKIM.

Latin American and Caribbean Center: Florida International University, University Park, Miami, FL 33199; tel. (305) 348-2000; internet lacc.fin.edu; f. 1979; university research institute; Dir EDUARDO A. GAMARRA; publ. *Hemisphere* (3 a year).

Latin American Center: University of California, Los Angeles (UCLA), Los Angeles, CA 90095-1447; tel. (310) 825-4571; e-mail latinamctr@isop.ucla.edu; internet www.isop.ucla.edu/lac; Dir CARLOS ALBERTO TORRES.

Latin American and Iberian Institute: University of New Mexico, Albuquerque, NM 87131; tel. (505) 277-2961; e-mail laiinfo@ unm.edu; internet www.unm.edu/%7Elaiinfo/index.html; Dir GILBERT W. MERKX; publ. *Latin American Research Review*.

Library of International Relations: 565 W Adams, Chicago, IL 60661; tel (312) 906-5600; fax (312) 906-5685; internet www.lir.org; f. 1932; aims to stimulate interest and research in international problems; conducts seminars, etc.; library of over 200,000 books, documents and periodicals; Pres. HOKEN SEKI.

Middle American Research Institute: Tulane University, New Orleans, LA 70118; tel. (504) 865-5110; e-mail mari@tulane.edu; internet tulane.edu/~mari; f. 1924; publs on archaeology in Mesoamerica and related subjects; Dir E. WYLLYS ANDREWS V.; publs books, miscellaneous papers.

North-South Center: University of Miami, POB 248205, Coral Gables, FL 33124; tel. (305) 284-6868; fax (305) 284-6370; e-mail nscenter@miami.edu; internet www.miami.edu/usc; f. 1984; research on contemporary intra-American relations; Dir AMBLER J. MOSS, Jr; publ. *Journal of Interamerican Studies and World Affairs* (every 3 months).

Paul H. Nitze School of Advanced International Studies: Johns Hopkins University, 1740 Massachusetts Ave, Washington, DC 20036; tel. (202) 663-5600; fax (202) 663-5656; internet www.sais-jhu.edu; Dean STEPHEN SZABO.

Pre-Columbian Studies, Dumbarton Oaks: 1703 32nd St, NW, Washington, DC 20007; tel. (202) 339-6440; fax (202) 625-0284; e-mail pre-columbian@doaks.org; internet www.doaks.org/ Pre-Columbian.html; f. 1962; residential fellowships, annual symposia, seminars, etc.; Pre-Columbian art collection; library of 24,000 vols on Pre-Columbian history; Dir of Studies JEFFREY QUILTER; publs annual symposia vols and occasional monographs.

School of International and Public Affairs: Columbia University, 420 West 118th St, Rm 1414, New York, NY 10027; tel. (212) 854-4604; internet www.sipa.columbia.edu; Dean LISA ANDERSON.

Woodrow Wilson Center—Latin American Program: 1000 Jefferson Drive, SW, Washington, DC 20560; tel. (202) 691-4030; fax (202) 357-4439; e-mail lap@wwic.siedu; f. 1968; residential fellowship programme: inter-American dialogue, inter-American economic issues, conferences, history and culture of Latin America, administration of social policy and governance, resolution of civil conflict; Dir JOSEPH S. TULCHIN; publ. *Working Paper Series*.

URUGUAY

Asociación Sudamericana de Estudios Geopolíticos e Internacionales (South American Association of Geopolitical and International Studies): Quiebrayugos 4814, Casilla Correo 18.11z, 11400 Montevideo; tel. (2) 6192953; fax (2) 9161923; f. 1979; research into inter-American issues, including that of economic integration in the Southern Cone; Sec.-Gen. Prof. BERNARDO QUAGLIOTTI DE BELLIS; publ. *Geosur* (6 a year).

Centro de Estadísticas Nacionales y Comercio Internacional del Uruguay (CENCI Uruguay) (Centre for National Statistics and International Trade): Misiones 1361, 2°, Montevideo; tel. (2) 9154578; e-mail cenci@adinet.com.uy; f. 1957; economic and statistical information on all Latin American countries; mem. of ALADI and CEPAL; library of 1,500 vols; Dirs CHRISTINA VERTESI, KENNETH BRUNNER; publs *Manual Práctico del Importador, Manual Práctico del Exportador, Manual Práctico Aduanero, Manual Práctico del Contribuyente, Valor en Aduana, Análisis Estadístico de Importa-*

ción-Exportación del Uruguay, Indice Alfabético del Sistema Armonizado, etc.

Centro Latinoamericano de Economía Humana (CLAEH) (Latin American Centre for Human Economy): Zelmar Michelini 1220, 11100 Montevideo; tel. (2) 919252; fax (2) 921127; e-mail claeh@chasque.apc.org; internet www.claeh.org.uy; f. 1958 to conduct research into economics and other social sciences; Dir ÁLVARO ARROYO; publ. *Cuadernos del CLAEH* (3 a year).

VENEZUELA

Centro de Estudios del Desarrollo (CENDES) (Centre for Development Studies): Universidad Central de Venezuela, Edif. FUNDAVAC, Avda Neverí, Colinas de Bello Monte, Apdo 47604, Caracas 1041-A; tel. (2) 753-3475; fax (2) 751-2691; e-mail cendes@reacciun.ve; internet www.ucv.ve/cendes/main.html; f. 1961; research on all aspects of development in Venezuela and Latin America; library of 30,000 vols; Dir Prof. LUIS GOMEZ CALCAÑO; publs *Anuario de Estudios del Desarrollo, CENDES Newsletter* (3 a year), *Cuadernos del CENDES* (3 a year).

Centro Experimental de Estudios Latinoamericanos (CEELA) (Experimental Centre for Latin American Studies): Universidad del Zulia, Apdo de Correos 526, Maracaibo 4011, Edo Zulia; tel. (61) 518430; research in socio-economic development especially the Andean Pact model, inflation and crises in Latin America; conferences and seminars; Dir Dr GASTON PARRA LUZARDO; publ. *Cuadernos Latinoamericanos*.

Centro de Historia del Estado Carabobo: Valencia, Edo de Carabobo; f. 1979 to conduct research in national and regional history, preserve and improve regional archives, conserve monuments, encourage and publicize celebrations of national historic events, and establish cultural relations with similar Venezuelan and foreign organizations; 24 mems; Pres. LUIS CUBILLÁN; Sec Dr MARCO TULIO MÉRIDA; publ. *Boletín*.

Instituto de Altos Estudios de América Latina (Institute for Advanced Latin American Studies): Apdo 17271, El Conde, Caracas 101; tel. (2) 573-8824; f. 1975; research, seminars, publs, on Latin America; attached to Universidad Simón Bolívar; library of 3,000 vols; Dir MIGUEL ANGEL BURELLI RIVAS; publs *Mundo Nuevo: Revista de Estudios Latinoamericanos* (quarterly), working papers, books.

Instituto de Investigaciones Económicas y Sociales (IIES) (Institute of Economic and Social Research): Universidad Católica Andrés Bello, Caracas; e-mail lespana@ucab.edu.ve; studies labour and demographic economics; Dir LUIS PEDRO ESPAÑA; internet www.ucab.edu.ve/investigacion/iies/.

Instituto Latinoamericano de Investigaciones Sociales (ILDIS) (Latin American Institute for Social Research): Edif. Parsa, 1°, Plaza la Castellana, 61712 CLACO, Caracas 1060; tel. (2) 33-3741; f. 1974; conducts research in the social sciences, particularly economics, education, politics, and sociology.

Instituto Venezolano de Estudios Sociales y Politicos (INVESP) (Venezuelan Institute of Social and Political Studies): Edif. Centro Parque Caraboo, Torre B, 21°, Of. 2115, Avda Universidad, Caracas; tel. and fax (2) 574-6549; f. 1986; affiliated to the South American Commission on Peace, Regional Security and Democracy in Chile; research on foreign policy, including relations with the Caribbean and Latin America; Dir Dr ANDRÉS SERBÍN.

YUGOSLAVIA

Institute of International Politics and Economics: 11000 Belgrade, POB 750, Makedonska 25; tel. (11) 3225611; fax (11) 3224013; e-mail iipe@diplomacy.bg.ac.yu; internet www.diplomacy.bg.ac.yu; f. 1947; international relations, world economy, international law, social, economic and political development in all countries; library of 250,000 vols; Dir Prof. VATROSLAV VEKARIĆ.

SELECT BIBLIOGRAPHY
(PERIODICALS)

Al Día. Latin American Newsletters, 61 Old St, London, EC1V 9HW, United Kingdom; tel. (20) 7251-0012; fax (20) 7253-8193; f. 1987; current affairs in Latin America; Spanish; Editor Miguel Ángel Diez; monthly.

Amazonía Peruana. Gonzales Prada 626, Magdalena, Apdo 14-0166, Lima 14, Peru; tel. (1) 4615223; f. 1976; Amazon anthropology, ethnology and linguistics, community development, bilingual education; Spanish, but with abstracts in English, French and German; Dir Pierre Guérig; 2 a year.

AméricaEconomía. Nanbie Ltd, Galvarino Gallardo 1576, Santiago, Chile; tel. (2) 223-7913; fax (2) 223-1903; f. 1986; Latin American business, economics and finance; Spanish; monthly.

AméricaEconomía 500. 420 Lexington Ave, 25th Floor, New York, NY 10170, USA; tel. (212) 808-7215; f. 1989; business and finance; annual.

América Indígena. Avda Insurgentes Sur 1690, Col. Florida, 01030 México, DF, Mexico; tel. (5) 6600007; fax (5) 5348090; f. 1940; anthropology, rural development, Indians of the Americas, ethnology; Spanish and Portuguese, with abstracts in English; Editor Dir Dr José Matos Mar (Instituto Indigenista Interamericano); quarterly.

América Latina. Institute of Latin America of the Russian Academy of Sciences, B. Ordynka 21, 113035 Moscow, Russia; tel. (095) 951-53-23; fax (095) 953-40-70; cultural, economic, political and social development of Latin American countries; Spanish; Editor Vladimir M. Davydov; quarterly.

América Latina Internacional. Latin American Faculty of Social Science, Argentina—FLACSO, Ayacucho 551, 1026 Buenos Aires, Argentina; tel. (11) 4375-2438; fax (11) 4375-1373; e-mail postmaster@flacso.cci.org.ar; f. 1993; Latin American international relations, international trade and finances, regional integration and Mercosur; Spanish; Editor S.R.L. Miño y Davila; 2 a year.

Américas Magazine. Organization of American States, Suite 300, 19th and Constitution Ave, NW, Washington, DC 20006, USA; tel. (202) 458-6218; fax (202) 458-6217; f. 1949; culture, history, literature, travel, art, music, book reviews, Inter-American System; English and Spanish editions; Editor James Patrick Kiernan; 6 a year.

Americas Review. Walden Publishing Ltd, 2 Market St, Saffron Walden CB10 1HZ, United Kingdom; tel. (1799) 521150; fax (1799) 524805; e-mail waldenpub@easynet.co.uk; internet www.worldinformation.com; f. 1979; business, economic and political issues concerning North, South and Central America and the Caribbean; English; Editor David Heslam; annual.

Americas Update. 427 Bloor St W, Toronto, MSS 1X7, Canada; tel. (416) 967-5562; fax (416) 922-8587; e-mail amupdate@web.net; f. 1979; politics and socio-economic development of Latin America and the Caribbean, with emphasis on Canada's relations with the region; English; quarterly.

Anales de Investigación Histórica. Departamento de Historia, Universidad de Puerto Rico, Río Piedras 00931, Puerto Rico; tel. 760-0000; f. 1974; historical research on the Caribbean, especially Puerto Rico; Spanish; Editors Gervasio García, Fernando Pico, Andrés Ramos; annual.

Análisis Semanal. Elizade 119, 10°, Casilla 4925, Guayaquil, Ecuador; fax (4) 326-842; analysis of economy of Ecuador; Spanish; weekly.

Andean Report. Andean Air Mail and Peruvian Times SA, Floor B, Suite 6, Pasaje Los Pinos 156, Casilla 531, Miraflores, Lima 100, Peru; tel. (1) 4472552; fax (1) 4467888; f. 1975; commerce, development, economics and politics of Peru, including mining and petroleum; English; Editor Nicholas Asheshov; monthly.

Andes: Revista Interamerican. Casilla 4171, La Paz, Bolivia; f. 1967; politics and government in Latin America; Spanish.

Anuário Estatístico do Brasil. Fundação Instituto Brasileiro de Geografia e Estatística, Centro de Documentaçao e Disseminaçao de Informações, rua General Canabarro 706, 2° andar, Maracanã 20.271-201, Rio de Janeiro, Brazil; tel. (21) 264-5424; fax (21) 284-1109; internet www.ibge.gov.br; f. 1936; statistical data on physical environment, population, economic affairs, national accounts, etc.; Portuguese; annual.

Anuario de Estudios Americanos. Escuela de Estudios Hispanoamericanos, Alfonso XII, Sevilla 16, Spain; tel. (95) 4222843; f. 1944; humanities and social sciences of the Americas; Spanish, Portuguese, English and French; Dir Rosario Sevilla Soler; 2 a year.

Anuario de Estudios Centroamericanos. Instituto de Investigaciones Sociales, 2060 Universidad de Costa Rica, Costa Rica; tel. 533721; f. 1974; history, society, politics and economics relating to Central America; Spanish; Editor Oscar Fernández; 2 a year.

Anuario Indigenista. Calle Nubes 232, Col. Pedregal de San Angel, 01900 México, DF, Mexico; tel. (5) 5680819; fax (5) 6521274; f. 1962; Indians of the Americas, policies, anthropology, government, minorities; Spanish, Portuguese; Dir José Matos Mar (Instituto Indigenista Interamericano); annual.

Apuntes del CENES. Centre for Economic Studies—CENES, Pedagogic and Technological University of Colombia, Faculty of Economics, Apdo Aéreo 1234, Carretera Central del Norte, Tunja, Boyacá, Colombia; tel. (87) 42-2174; fax (87) 42-5237; f. 1983; national economic and development studies, politics and culture; Spanish; Editor Luis E. Vallejo Zamudio; 2 a year.

Archivo Ibero Americano. Joaquín Costa 36, 28002 Madrid, Spain; tel. (91) 5619900; f. 1914; history of Spain and Hispanic America, mainly relating to the Franciscan Order; quarterly.

¡Basta!. Chicago Religious Task Force on Central America, Suite 1400, 59 East Van Buren, Chicago, IL 60605, USA; tel. (312) 663-4398; fax (312) 427-4171; f. 1984; analysis of social and political events in Central America: theological debate, news and information; English; 3 a year.

Boletín de la Academia Nacional de la Historia. Balcarce 139, 1064 Buenos Aires, Argentina; tel. (1) 4343-4416; fax (11) 4331-4633; e-mail postmaster@anh.edu.ar; f. 1924; history of Argentina and America, principally as review of activities of the Academia Nacional de la Historia; Spanish; annual.

Boletín Americanista. Universidad de Barcelona, Facultad de Geografía e Historia, Barcelona, Spain; tel. (93) 3333466; fax (93) 4498510; f. 1959; anthropology, economics, geography, history of America; Spanish, English and French; Editor Dr Miquel Izard; annual.

Boletín del Instituto Latinoamericano y del Caribe de Planificación Económica y Social. Edif. Naciones Unidas, Av. Dag Hammarskjöld s/n, Vitacura, Casilla 1567, Santiago, Chile; tel (2) 210-2617; fax (2) 206-6104; e-mail pdekock@eclac.cl; f. 1976, publication suspended 1982, refounded 1996; economics; Spanish and English; Editor PAUL DEKOCK; 2 a year.

Borderlines. Interhemispheric Resource Center, POB 4505, Albuquerque, NM 87196, USA; tel. (505) 842-8288; fax (505) 246-1601; e-mail resourcectr@igc.apc.org; f. 1993; information on the US—Mexican border region and US—Mexican relations; international business and organizations; English; Editor George Kouros; 11 a year.

Brasilinform. CP 38079, Gávea, 22.451 Rio de Janeiro, RJ, Brazil; political, economic and general news; English; weekly.

Brazil. Fundação Visconde de Cabo Frio, SIG, Q 4 Lote 217, 70.610 Brasília, DF, Brazil; tel. (61) 223-5180; deals with trade and industry of Brazil and is published by Fundação Visconde de Cabo Frio under the auspices of the Trade Promotion Department of the Ministry of Foreign Affairs and of the Vice-Presidency of Resources and Operations of the Banco do Brasil; Editor Fernando Luz; Portuguese, German and French editions (quarterly), English and Spanish editions (monthly).

Brazil Country Report. Orbis Publications, LLC, 3201 New Mexico Ave, NW, Suite 249, Washington, DC, USA; tel. (202) 237-0155; fax (202) 237-0596; economy, politics, business environment, market development and future prospects of Brazil; annual.

Brazil News Update. Brazilian Chamber of Commerce in Great Britain, 32 Green St, London, W1Y 3FD, United Kingdom; tel. (20) 7499-0186; fax (20) 7493-5105; f. 1989; commerce and industry in Brazil; English; 6 a year.

Brazil Service. International Reports, 11300 Rockville Pike, Rockville, MD 20852-3030, USA; tel. (301) 816-8950; Brazilian business and investment; English; Editor-in-Chief Robert G. Taylor; 2 a month.

Brazil Watch. Orbis Publications, LLC, 3201 New Mexico Ave, NW, Suite 329, Washington, DC, USA; tel. (202) 237-0155; fax (202) 237-0596; politics, economics and business of Brazil; English; Editor Richard Foster; fortnightly.

Bulletin of Hispanic Studies. Department of Hispanic Studies, The University, Liverpool L69 3BX, United Kingdom; tel. and fax (151) 794-2773; e-mail d.s.severin@liv.ac.uk; f. 1923; language, literature and civilization of Spain, Portugal and Latin America; mainly English and Spanish, occasionally Portuguese, Catalan and French; Editor Prof. Dorothy Sherman Severin; quarterly.

Bulletin de l'Institut Français d'Etudes Andines. IFEA, Casilla 18-1217, Lima 18, Peru; tel. (1) 4476070; fax (1) 4457650; e-mail postmaster@ifea.org.pe; f. 1972; geology and human and social sciences in the Andes; French, Spanish and English; Editor Anne-Marie Brougère; 3 a year.

Bulletin of Latin American Research. Blackwell Publishers, 108 Cowley Rd, Oxford, OX4 1JF, United Kingdom; tel. (1865) 791100; fax (1865) 791347; internet www.blackwellpublishers.co.uk; on behalf of The Society of Latin American Studies; current interest research in social sciences and humanities; English; Editor Paul Garner; 4 a year.

Business Latin America. Business International Corpn, 1 Dag Hammarskjöld Plaza, New York, NY 10017, USA; tel. (212) 750-6300; English; Editor Jan Rovira Burch; weekly.

Cahiers des Amériques Latines. Institut des Hautes Etudes de l'Amérique Latine, 28 rue Saint-Guillaume, 75007 Paris, France; tel. 1-44-39-86-00; fax 1-45-48-79-53; e-mail iheal.edition@univ-paris3.fr; f. 1968; political science, economy, urbanism, geography, history, sociology, ethnology, etc.; mainly French, but also Spanish and English; 3 a year.

Canadian Journal of Latin American and Caribbean Studies / Revue canadienne des études latino-américaines et caraïbes. Canadian Association of Latin American and Caribbean Studies, Dept of Sociology, University of Western Ontario, London, Ontario N6A 5CZ, Canada; tel. (519) 661-3606; fax (519) 661-3200; e-mail hewitt@julian.uwo.ca; f. 1969; political, economic, cultural, etc.; English, French, Portuguese and Spanish; Editor W. E. Hewitt; 2 a year.

Caribbean Affairs. 93 Frederick St, Port of Spain, Trinidad and Tobago; tel. 624-2477; fax 627-3013; f. 1988; business, political and social affairs of the Caribbean; English; Editor Owen Baptiste; quarterly.

Caribbean Business. 1700 Fernández Juncos Ave, San Juan, PR 00909, Puerto Rico; tel. 728-3000; fax 728-7325; f. 1973; business and finance; English; Man. Editor Manuel A. Casiano, Jr; weekly.

Caribbean Handbook. FT Caribbean (European Agent), Suite 53, Omnibus Business Centre, 39–41 North Rd, London N7 9DP, United Kingdom; tel. (20) 7607-3430; fax (20) 7700-0429; f. 1983; business, economic and political information on the Caribbean region, including country profiles; English; Editor Lindsay Maxwell; annual.

Caribbean Insight. Suite 18, Westminster Palace Gardens, 1–7 Artillery Row, London SW1P 1RR, United Kingdom; tel. (20) 7799-1521; fax (20) 7340-1050; e-mail insight@caribbean-council.com; business, political and social; English; Editor Rod Prince; weekly.

Caribbean Newsletter. Friends for Jamaica Collective, Park West Station, POB 20392, New York, NY 10025, USA; f. 1981; analysis of events in the Caribbean; Caribbean–American issues; English; quarterly.

Caribbean Quarterly. POB 1, Kingston 7, Jamaica; tel. 977-1689; fax 927-1920; f. 1949; general; English; Editor Rex Nettleford; quarterly.

Caribbean Review. 9700 SW 67th Ave, Miami, FL 33156-3272, USA; tel. (305) 284-8466; fax (305) 284-1019; f. 1969; all subjects relating to the Caribbean, Latin America and their emigrant groups; Editor Barry B. Levine; quarterly.

Caribbean Studies. Institute of Caribbean Studies, Box 23361, University Station, Río Piedras, PR 00931-3361, Puerto Rico; tel. (787) 764-2943; fax (787) 764-3099; Caribbean affairs; English; Editor (vacant); 2 a year.

Caribbean Update. 52 Maple Ave, Maplewood, NJ 07040, USA; tel. (973) 762-1565; fax (201) 762-9585; e-mail mexcarib@compuserve.com; f. 1985; business, economics and politics in the Caribbean region; English; Editor and Publisher Kal Wagenheim; monthly.

The Caribbean Yearbook of International Relations. Institute of International Relations, University of the West Indies, St Augustine Campus, St Augustine, Trinidad and Tobago; tel. 662-2002; international politics and relations; English; annual.

El Caribe Contemporáneo. Centro de Estudios Latinoamericanos, Facultad de Ciencias Políticas y Sociales, Universidad Nacional Autónoma de México, 04510 México, DF, Mexico; tel. (5) 6551344; f. 1980; political organization and government; Spanish; Dir Dr Pablo A. Maríñez A.; 2 a year.

Carta Internacional. International Relations Research Programme, University of São Paulo, Rua do Anfiteatro 181, Colméia, Cidade Universitária, 05508-900 São Paulo, SP, Brazil; tel. (11) 818-3061; fax (11) 210-4154; e-mail guilhon@usp.br; internet www.usp.br/melint; Brazilian foreign and economic policy, regional integration, NAFTA and Mercosur; English, Portuguese and Spanish; Dir J. A. Guilhon Albuquerque; monthly.

Central America Report. Inforpress Centroamericana, 9 Calle 'A' 3-56, Zona 1, Guatemala City, Guatemala; tel. 229-432; f. 1972; review of economics and politics of Central America; English; Dir Richard Wilson-Grau; weekly.

Centroamerica Internacional. Latin American Faculty of Social Sciences, Costa Rica—FLACSO, General Secretariat, Apdo 5429, 1000 San José, Costa Rica; tel. 257-0533; fax 221-5671; f. 1989; Central American, South American and Caribbean international relations, regional integration; Spanish; 2 a month.

CEPAL Review / Revista de la CEPAL. Casilla 179-D, Santiago, Chile; tel. (2) 2102000; fax (2) 2080252; f. 1976; a publication of the UN Economic Commission for Latin America dealing with socio-economic topics; English and Spanish; Editor Oscar Altimir; 3 a year.

Chile Ahora. Ministry of Foreign Affairs, Palacio de la Moneda, Santiago, Chile; all aspects of life in Chile; Spanish; Editor M. Angelica Huidobro G. H.; monthly.

Chronicle of Latin American Economic Affairs. Latin American Institute, Latin American Data Base, 801 Yale NE, Albuquerque, NM 87131-1016, USA; tel. (505) 277-6839; fax (505) 277-5989; internet www.ladb.unm.edu/; f. 1986; economic and political conditions in Latin America; accessible via the internet and CD-ROM; English; weekly.

Colombia Internacional. Centre for International Studies, University of the Andes, Calle 19, No. 1-46, Apdo 4976, Santafé de Bogotá, Colombia; tel. (1) 286-7504; fax (1) 284-1890; international co-operation, Latin American integration, drugs-trafficking controls: Spanish: quarterly

Colonial Latin American Review. Carfax Publishing, Taylor & Francis Group, 11 New Fetter Lane, London EC4P 4EE, United Kingdom; tel. (20) 7583-9855; fax (20) 7842-2298; internet www.tandf.co.uk/journals/carfax; f. 1992; colonial period in Latin America; English, with articles in Portuguese and Spanish; Editor Raquel Chang-Rodríguez; 2 a year.

Comercio Exterior. Banco Nacional de Comercio Exterior, SA, Cerrada de Malintzin 28, Col. del Carmen, Coyoacán, 04100 México, DF, Mexico; tel. (5) 6880688; f. 1951; international trade, analysis of Latin America's economics, general economics; Spanish; monthly.

Cono Sur. Latin American Faculty of Social Science, Chile—FLACSO, Leopoldo Urrutia 1950, Ñuñoa, Santiago, Chile; tel. (2) 225-9938; fax (2) 274-1004; e-mail flacso@flacso.cl; internet www.flacso.cl; f. 1982; international relations, particularly concerning Argentina, Chile and Uruguay; Spanish; 2 a month.

Contexto Internacional. Institute of International Relations, Pontifical Catholic University of Rio de Janeiro, Rua Marquês de São Vicente 225, Gávea, 22453-900 Rio de Janeiro, RJ, Brazil; tel. (21) 529-9494; fax (21) 274-1296; e-mail iripuc@rdc.puc-rio.br; international relations, Brazilian foreign policy, Latin American and European integration, US–Latin American relations; Portuguese; Editor Sonia de Camargo; 2 a year.

The Courier ACP-European Union. European Commission, 200 rue de la Loi, 1049 Brussels, Belgium; tel. (2) 299-11-11; fax (2) 299-30-02; internet www.europa.eu.int/comm/development/publicat/courier/index_en.htm; affairs of the African, Caribbean and Pacific countries and the European Union; English and French editions; Editor Simon Horner; 6 a year.

Cronología de las Relaciones Internacionales del Peru. Peruvian Centre for International Studies, San Ignacio de Loyola 554, Miraflores 8, Lima 18, Peru; tel. (1) 4457225; fax (1) 4451094; economic and political international relations of Peru; Spanish; quarterly.

Cuadernos de Economía. Casilla 76, Correo 17, Santiago, Chile; tel. (2) 6864314; fax (2) 5521310; e-mail echamorr@volcan.facea.puc.cl; f. 1963; applied economies as contribution to economic policy, with special emphasis in Latin America; Spanish, with English abstracts; Editor Rolf Lüders; 3 a year.

Cuadernos Hispanoamericanos. Avda de los Reyes Católicos 4, 28040 Madrid, Spain; tel. (91) 5838399; f. 1948; humanities, particularly relating to Hispanic America; Spanish; Editor Blas Matamoro; monthly.

Cuba Internacional. Calle 21, No. 406, Vedado, Havana 4; Apdo B603, Havana 3, Cuba; tel. (7) 329-3531; f. 1959; politics and foreign affairs; Spanish and Russian; monthly.

Cuba Update. Center for Cuban Studies, 124 West 23rd St, New York, NY 10011, USA; tel. (212) 242-0559; f. 1977; Cuban foreign affairs, culture and development; English; Editor Sandra Levinson; quarterly.

The Developing Economies. Ajia Keizai Kenkyusho (Institute of Developing Economies), 42 Ichigaya-Hommura-cho, Shinjuku-ku, Tokyo 162-8442, Japan; f. 1962; English; quarterly.

Development Policy Review. Overseas Development Institute, Regent's College, Inner Circle, Regent's Park, London NW1 4NS, United Kingdom; tel. (20) 7487-7413; fax (20) 7487-7590; f. 1982; Editor David Booth; 4 a year.

Economia Brasileira e Suas Perspectivas. Associação Promotora de Estudos de Economia, rua Sorocaya 295, Botafogo, Rio de Janeiro, RJ, Brazil; fax (21) 266-3597; f 1962; Brazilian economic issues, published by the Association for the Promotion of Economic Studies; Portuguese and English; Editor Basílio Martins; annual.

Economía Mexicana Nueva Época. Centre for the Research and Teaching of Economics—CIDE, Carretera México–Toluca 3655 (km 16.5), Col. Lomas de Santa Fe, Del. Alvaro Obregón, 01210 México, DF, Mexico; tel. (5) 727-9839; fax (5) 727-9878; e-mail ecomex@dis1.cide.mx; f. 1992; economic problems in Mexico and Latin America; Spanish and English; Editor Francisco Alejandro Villagómez; 2 a year.

Economic Development and Cultural Change. University of Chicago, 1130 East 59th St, Chicago, IL 60637, USA; tel. (312) 702-7951; f. 1952; various aspects of economic development and cultural change; English; Editor D. Gale Johnson; quarterly.

Economic and Social Progress in Latin America. Inter-American Development Bank, 1300 New York Ave, NW, Washington, DC 20577, USA; tel. (202) 623-1403; f. 1961; socio-economic conditions and development; individual country reports; French, Portuguese and Spanish; annual.

Enlace: Política y Derechos Humanos en las Americas. Washington Office on Latin America, 400 C St, NE, Washington, DC 20002, USA; tel. (202) 544-8045; fax (202) 546-5288; e-mail wola@igc.apc.org; f. 1991; US foreign-policy implications for human rights and democratization in Latin America; Spanish; Editor Rachel Neild; quarterly.

Environment Watch: Latin America. Cutter Information Corporation, Suite 1, 37 Broadway, Arlington, MA 02174-5552, USA; tel. (617) 641-5125; fax (617) 648-1950; e-mail jstoub@igc.apc.org; f. 1991; environmental policy, law and corporate initiaties in Latin America; English; Editor Jeffrey Stoub; monthly.

Estadística y Economía. Instituto Nacional de Estadísticas, Avda Presidente Bulnes 418, Casilla 498, Correo 3, Santiago, Chile; tel. (2) 366-7777; fax (2) 671-2169; f. 1843; commerce and economics; Spanish; 2 a year.

Estudios de Coyuntura. Universidad del Zulia, Facultad de Ciencias Ecónomicas y Sociales, Apdo 526, Maracaibo 4011, Estado Zulia, Venezuela; tel. (61) 51-7697; fax (61) 51-2525; f. 1989; business and economics; Editor Hernan Pardo; Spanish; 2 a year.

Estudios de Cultura Maya. Centro de Estudios Mayas, Instituto de Investigaciones Filológicas, Circuito Mario de la Cueva, Ciudad Universitaria, 04510 México, DF, Mexico; tel. (5) 6227490; fax (5) 6657874; f. 1961; anthropology, archaeology, history, epigraphy and linguistics of the Mayan groups; Spanish, English and French; Editor Ana Luisa Izquierdo; irregular.

Estudios Económicos. Universidad Nacional del Sur, Departamento de Economía, 12 de Octubre y San Juan, 8000 Bahía Blanca, Argentina; tel. and fax (91) 25432; f. 1962; Spanish; Editor Ricardo Bara; annual.

Estudios de Historia Moderna y Contemporánea de México. Instituto de Investigaciones Históricas, Circuito Mario de la Cueva, Ciudad Universitaria, 04510 México, DF, Mexico; tel. (5) 6651344; f. 1967; history of Mexico from independence war (1810) to present; Spanish; Editor Alvaro Matute; irregular.

Estudios Internacionales. Institute of International Studies, University of Chile, Avda Condell 249, Providencia, Casilla 14187, Santiago 9, Chile; tel. (2) 274-5377; fax (2) 274-0155; e-mail inesint@abello.dic.uchile.cl; f. 1966; contemporary international relations, particularly concerning Latin America; Spanish; Editor Pilar Alamos; quarterly.

Estudios Internacionales. International Relations and Peace Research Institute, 1A Calle 9–52, Zona 1, 01001 Guatemala City, Guatemala; tel. 228-260; international relations; Spanish, 2 a year.

Estudios Paraguayos. Universidad Católica, Casilla 1718, Asunción, Paraguay; tel. (21) 446251; fax (21) 445245; f. 1973; philosophy, politics, law, history, linguistics, economics, literature; Spanish; 2 a year.

Estudios Políticos. Facultad de Ciencias Políticas y Sociales, Universidad Nacional Autónoma de México, Ciudad Universitaria, Apdo 70–266, 04510 México, DF, Mexico; tel. (5) 665-1233; fax (5) 666-8334; e-mail igarza@sociolan.politicas.unam.mx; f. 1975; politics of government, political science; Spanish; quarterly.

Estudios Públicos. Centro de Estudios Públicos, Monseñor Sótero Sanz 175, Santiago, Chile; tel. (2) 2315324; fax: (2) 2335253; e-mail dparra@cepchile.cl; f. 1980; forum of ideas and commentary on economic development and public policy in Latin America; English, Spanish; 4 a year.

Estudios Sociales. Miguel Claro 1460, Santiago, Chile; tel. (2) 2043418; fax (2) 2741828; f. 1973; sociology, history, anthropology, economics, political science, education, philosophy, social psychology, law; Spanish; Editor Antonio Cruz; quarterly.

FIDE, Coyuntura y Desarrollo. Development Research Foundation—FIDE, Sánchez de Loria 1338, 1241 Buenos Aires, Argentina; tel. and fax (11) 4931-9257; national and international socio-economic analysis and economic theory; Spanish; monthly.

Foro Internacional. Colegio de México, Camino al Ajusco 20, Col. Pedregal de Santa Teresa, 01000 México, DF, Mexico; tel. (5) 645-5955; fax (5) 645-0464; f. 1960; political and economic articles on Latin America; Mexican foreign policy and relations with the USA; Spanish; Editor Francisco Gil-Villegas; quarterly.

Global Studies: Latin America. Dushkin Publishing Group Inc, Sluice Dock, Guilford, CT 06437-9989, USA; tel. (203) 453-4351; fax (203) 453-6000; f. 1991; articles on Mexico, Central America, South America and the Caribbean; English; Editor Paul Goodwin; every 2 years.

Hemisphere. Latin American and Caribbean Center, Florida International University, University Park, Miami, FL 33199, USA; tel. (305) 348-2894; fax (305) 349-3593; e-mail newmana@fiv.edu; f. 1988; Latin American and Caribbean Affairs; English; Editors Eduardo A. Gamarra, Alisa Newman; 3 a year.

Hispanic American Historical Review (HAHR). Duke University Press, 905 W. Main St, Suite 18B, Durham, NC 27701, USA; tel. (919) 687-3600; fax (919) 688-4574; e-mail subscriptions@dukeupress.edu; internet www.dukeupress.edu; f. 1918; Editors Gilbert M. Joseph, Stuart B. Schwartz; annual.

Historia. Casilla 6277, Santiago 22, Chile; tel. (2) 2048666; f. 1961; history of Chile and related subjects; Spanish; Editor Nicolás Cruz; annual.

Historia Mexicana. Colegio de México, Camino al Ajusco 20, Pedregal de Santa Teresa 10740, México, DF, Mexico; tel. (5) 6455955; fax (5) 6450464; f. 1951; history of Mexico; Spanish; Editor Solange Alberro; quarterly.

Historiografía y Bibliografía Americanista. Escuela de Estudios H. A. Alfonso XII, Sevilla 16, Spain; tel. (95) 4222843; f. 1963; history, bibliography and general information on the Americas, published by the Escuela de Estudios Hispanoamericanos; Spanish, English, French and Portuguese; Dir Rosario Sevilla Soler; 2 a year.

Ibero-Amerikanisches Archiv. Zeitschrift fur Sozialwissenschaften und Geschichte. 60318 Frankfurt am Main, Wielandstrasse 40, Verlag Klaus Dieter Vervuert, Germany; tel (69) 5974617; fax (69) 5978743; f. 1975; politics, sociology, history in Spain, Latin America and Portugal; English, German, Spanish and Portuguese; Editors Walter L. Bernecker, Reinhard Liehr, Herbert J. Nickel, Dieter Nohlen, Günter Vollmer, Peter Waldmann; quarterly.

Iberoamericana. 60318 Frankfurt am Main, Wielandstrasse 40, Verlag Klaus Dieter Vervuert, Germany; tel. (69) 5974617; fax (69) 5978743; f. 1977; Latin American language, literature and cultural affairs; Spanish and German; Editors Dietrich Brìesemeister, Frauke Gewecke, Inke Gunia, Helmut C. Jacobs, Georg A. Kaiser, Jürgen M. Meisel, Klaus Meyer-Minnemann, Dieter Reichardt, Klaus Zimmermann; quarterly.

Iberoamericana: Nordic Journal of Latin American and Caribbean Studies. Institute of Latin American Studies, Stockholm University, 106 91 Stockholm, Sweden; tel. (8) 16-29-04; fax (8) 15-65-82; e-mail lai@lai.su.se; articles on economic, political and local developments in Latin America and the Caribbean; English, Portuguese, Spanish.

Indicadores Económicos. Contraloría General de la República, Dirección de Estadística y Censo, Apdo 5213, Panamá 5, Panama; tel. 206-4800; fax 206-4801; f. 1996; economic indicators for Panama; Spanish; 2 a year.

Industri-Noticias. Publi-News Latinoamericano, SACV, Colina 436, México, DF, Mexico; f. 1966; business, economics and industry; Spanish; Editor Roberto J. Márquez; monthly.

Industria. Sindicato de Industriales de Panamá, Apdo 6-4798, El Dorado, Panamá, Panama; tel. 30-0169; fax 30-0805; f. 1953; economics and industry in Panama; Spanish; Editor Flor Ortega; quarterly.

Industria Venezolana. Editorial Guía Industrial, Apdo 60772, Chacao, Caracas 101, Venezuela; f. 1971; economics and industry in Venezuela; Spanish; Editor Jose Precedo; 6 a year.

Informe Latinoamericano. Latin American Newsletters, 61 Old St, London, EC1V 9HW, United Kingdom; tel. (20) 7251-0012; fax (20) 7253-8193; f. 1982; Latin American News; book reviews; Spanish; Editor Eduardo Crawley; weekly.

Información Sistemática. Valencia 84, Insurgentes Mixcoac, Del. Benito Juárez, 03920 México, DF, Mexico; tel. (5) 5986043;

fax (5) 5986325; f. 1976; clippings archive since 1976; electronic database since 1988; daily summary of 11 newspapers; Spanish; Dirs Bernarda Avalos, Lupita Flores; customized frequency.

Information Services Latin America. 464 19th St, Oakland, CA 94612, USA; tel. (510) 835-0678; fax (510) 835-3017; e-mail datacenter@datacenter.org; reprinted articles from nine major daily news sources; English; monthly.

Integración Financiera—pasado, presente y futuro de las finanzas en Colombia y el mundo. Medios and Medios Publicidad Cía Ltda, No. 11-45, Of. 802, Calle 63, Apdo 036943, Santafé de Bogotá, DC, Colombia; tel. (1) 255-0992; fax (1) 249-4696; f. 1984; financial-sector development in Colombia and the rest of Latin America; Spanish; Editor Raúl Rodríguez Puerto; 6 a year.

Integración y Comercio. Institute for the Integration of Latin America and the Caribbean, Esmeralda 130, 16° y 17°, 1035 Buenos Aires, Argentina; tel. (11) 4320-1850; fax (11) 4320-1865; e-mail int/inl@iadb.org; internet www.iabd.org/intal; f. 1965; Latin American integration; Spanish; 3 a year.

Investigaciones y Ensayos. Balcarce 139, 1064 Buenos Aires, Argentina; tel. (11) 4343-4416; fax (11) 4331-4633; e-mail postmaster@anh.edu.ar; f. 1966; history of Argentina and America; Spanish; published by the Academia Nacional de la Historia; 2 a year.

Jahrbuch für Geschichte Lateinamerikas. 20146 Hamburg, Von-Melle-Park 6, Universität Hamburg Historisches Seminar, Germany; published by Böhlau-Verlag, Cologne and Vienna; tel. (40) 428384839; fax (40) 428383955; f. 1964; political, economic, social and cultural history of Latin America from colonial period to present; articles in Spanish, English, French, German and Portuguese; Dir Prof. Dr Horst Pietschmann; annual.

Journal of Development Studies. Frank Cass, Newbury House, 900 Eastern Ave, Newbury Park, Ilford, Essex IG2 7HH, United Kingdom; tel. (20) 8599-8866; fax (20) 8599-0984; e-mail jnlsubs@frankcass.com; internet www.frankcass.com; f. 1964; Editors David Booth, Christopher Colclough, John Harriss, Chris Miller, James Putzel; 6 a year.

Journal of Iberian and Latin American Studies. Carfax Publishing, Taylor & Francis Group, 11 New Fetter Lane, London EC4P 4EE, United Kingdom; tel. (20) 7583-9855; fax (2) 7842-2298; internet www.tandf.co.uk/journals/carfax; fmrly known as *Tesserae*; language, literature, history and culture of Latin America and Iberian peninsula; Editors Jordi Larios, Montserrat Lunati; English, with articles in Catalan and Spanish; 2 a year.

Journal of Interamerican Studies and World Affairs. University of Miami, POB 248123, Coral Gables, FL 33124C, USA; tel. (1305) 284-5554; fax (305) 284-4406; f. 1959; Latin American–US relations and Latin America's international relations; English; Editor William Smith; quarterly.

Journal of Latin American Cultural Studies. Carfax Publishing, Taylor & Francis Group, 11 New Fetter Lane, London EC4P 4EE, United Kingdom; tel. (20) 7583-9855; fax (20) 7842-2298; internet www.tandf.co.uk/journals/carfax; history and analysis of Latin American culture; English; Editors Catherine Boyle, John Kraniauskas, Julio Ramos, Nicolau Sevcenko, David Treece; 3 a year.

Journal of Latin American Studies. Cambridge University Press, The Edinburgh Building, Shaftesbury Rd, Cambridge, CB2 2RU, United Kingdom; tel. (1223) 312393; sponsored by Centres or Insts of Latin American Studies at Univs of Cambridge, Exeter, Glasgow, Liverpool, London and Oxford; Editors Prof. James Dunkerley, Laurence Whitehead; 3 a year.

Journal de la Société des Américanistes. Musée de l'Homme, 17 place du Trocadéro, 75116 Paris, France; tel. 1-47-04-63-11; f. 1896; archaeology, ethnology, ethnohistory and linguistics of the American continent; French, Spanish, English and Portuguese; Editor Dominique Michelet; annual.

Journal of Supreme Court History. Blackwell Publrs, 108 Cowley Rd, Oxford, OX4 1JF, United Kingdom; tel. (1865) 791100; fax (1865) 791347; f. 1975; on behalf of the Supreme Court Historical Society; collects and preserves the history of the Supreme Court of the USA; English; Editor Melvin I. Uroffky; 3 a year.

Kañina. Facultad de Letras, Ciudad Universitaria Rodrigo Facio, Universidad de Costa Rica, San Pedro, San José, Costa

Rica; tel. 207-5107; fax 207-5089; e-mail kanina@cariari .ucr.ac.cr; f. 1976; arts and literature; mainly Spanish but also French, English and Italian; Editor Victor Sánchez Corrales; 3 a year.

Lagniappe Letter / Quarterly Monitor. 159 West 53rd St, 28th Floor, New York, NY 10019, USA; tel. (212) 765-5520; fax (212) 765-2927; internet www.lais.com; Latin American business; English; Editor Rosemary Werrett; fortnightly/quarterly.

Lagniappe Monthly on Latin American Projects and Finance. 159 West 53rd St, 28th Floor, New York, NY, USA; tel. (212) 765-5520; fax (212) 765-2927; internet www.lais.com; Latin American business; Editor Rosemary Werrett; monthly.

LARF Report. Latin America Reserve Fund—LARF, Apdo 24153, Santafé de Bogotá, DC, Colombia; tel. (1) 285-8511; fax (1) 288-1117; f. 1979; economic summary of Bolivia, Colombia, Ecuador, Peru and Venezuela; Spanish and English; annual.

Lateinamerika: Analysen-Daten-Dokumentation. Institut für Iberoamerika-Kunde, 20354 Hamburg, Alsterglacis 8, Germany; tel. (40) 41478201; fax (40) 41478241; e-mail iikhh@rr2.uni hamburg.de; internet www.rr2.uni-hamburg.de; political, economic and social development, regional integration and international relations of Latin America; German, Spanish and Portuguese.

Lateinamerika Anders Panorama. Informationsgruppe Lateinamerika, 1060 Vienna, Münzwardeingasse 2, Austria; f. 1976; news and analysis of Latin American affairs; German; Editors Werner Hörner, Hermann Klosius; 2 a month.

Lateinamerika Jahrbuch. Institut für Iberoamerika-Kunde, 20354 Hamburg, Alsterglacis 8, Germany; tel. (40) 41478201; fax (40) 41478241; political, business and social review; annual.

Latin America and Caribbean Contemporary Record. Holmes and Meier Publishers Inc, 160 Broadway East Wing, New York, NY 10038, USA; tel. (212) 374-0100; fax (212) 374-1313; f. 1981; analysis of events and trends in Latin America and the Caribbean; English; Editors James Malloy, Eduardo Gamarra; annual.

Latin American Economy and Business. Latin American Newsletters, 61 Old St, London EC1V 9HW, United Kingdom; tel. (20) 7251-0012; fax (20) 7253-8193; e-mail subs@latinnews.com; economic data and indicators; English; Editor Will Ollard; monthly.

Latin American Index. Welt Publishing LLC, 1413 K St, NW, Suite 1400, Washington, DC 20005, USA; tel. (202) 371-0555; fax (202) 408-9369; political, economic and social affairs of Latin America, and US–Latin American relations; English; Editor William Knepper; 23 a year.

Latin American Monitor. 370 Old York Rd, London SW18 1SP, United Kingdom; tel. (181) 870-9748; fax (181) 870-9740; publishes 5 regional reports: (i) Mexico and Brazil; (ii) Central America; (iii) Andean Group; (iv) Southern Cone; (v) Caribbean; English; 10 a year (also five annual reports on Argentina, Brazil, Chile, Mexico and Venezuela).

Latin American Perspectives. University of California, POB 5703, Riverside, CA 92517-5703, USA; tel. (909) 787-5037; fax (909) 787-5685; e-mail laps@ucrac1.ucr.edu; internet wizard.ucr.edu/lap/lap.html; economics, political science, international relations, philosophy, history, sociology, geography, anthropology and literature; English; Editor Ronald H. Chilcote; 6 a year.

Latin American Regional Reports. Latin American Newsletters, 61 Old St, London EC1V 9HW, United Kingdom; tel. (20) 7251-0012; fax (20) 7253-8193; e-mail subs@latinnews.com; internet www.latinnews.com; regional reports on: Andean Group; Brazil; Mexico and NAFTA; Southern Cone; Caribbean and Central America; English; Editors Colin Harding, Will Ollard; every 5 weeks.

Latin American Research Review (LARR). Latin American Studies Association, Latin American and Iberian Institute, 801 Yale NE, University of New Mexico, Albuquerque, NM 87131-1016, USA; tel. (505) 277-5985; fax (505) 277-5989; e-mail editor@larr.unm.edu; internet larr.unm.edu; f. 1965; articles, research notes and essays dealing with contemporary issues; Editor Gilbert W. Merkx; 3 a year.

Latin American Special Reports. Latin American Newsletters, 61 Old St, London EC1V 9HW, United Kingdom; tel. (20) 7251-0012; fax (20) 7253-8193; e-mail subs@latinnews.com; internet www.latinnews.com; each edition provides detailed information on and analysis of one specific subject; English and Spanish; Editor Eduardo Crawley; 6 a year.

Latin American Studies in Asia. K. K. Roy (Pvt) Ltd, 55 Gariahat Rd, POB 10210, Calcutta 700 019, India; tel. (33) 4754872; f. 1991; Latin American and Caribbean affairs; English; Editor Dr K. K. Roy; quarterly.

Latin American Weekly Report. Latin American Newsletters, 61 Old St, London EC1V 9HW, United Kingdom; tel. (20) 7251-0012; fax (20) 7253-8193; e-mail subs@latinnews.com; internet www.latinnews.com; political, economic and general news; English and Spanish; Editor Eduardo Crawley; weekly.

Latinskaya Amerika. Institute of Latin American Studies, Russian Academy of Sciences, 119034 Moscow, per. Kropotkinskii 24, Russia; tel. (095) 201-54-84; fax (095) 201-23-52; f. 1969; politics, economic development, history and culture of Latin American countries; Russian; Editor Vladimir N. Krestyaninov; monthly.

Latin Studies Journal. Center for Latino Research, Northeastern University, Dept of Sociology and Anthropology, 521 Holmes Hall, Boston, MA 02115, USA; tel. (617) 373-2000; f. 1990; Latin American affairs; Latin American-North American relations; Editor Felix Padilla; 3 a year.

Lecturas de Economía. Centre for Economic Research, University of Antioquia, Apdo Aéreo 1226, Ciudad Universitaria, Medellín, Antioquia, Colombia; tel. (4) 210-5841; fax (4) 263-8282; f. 1980; economic issues; Spanish; Editor Jorge Lotero Contreras; 2 a year.

Luso-Brazilian Review. University of Wisconsin Press, 1018 Van Hise Hall, 1220 Linden Dr., Madison, WI 53706, USA; tel. (608) 265-8296; fax (608) 262-9671; e-mail lusobraz@ vms2.macc.wisc.edu; f. 1961; history, social sciences and literature; Editors Robert M Levine, Ellen W. Sapega, Severino J. Albuquerque; 2 a year.

Mesoamérica. Centro de Investigaciones Regionales de Mesoamérica (CIRMA)/Plumsock Mesoamerican Studies, POB 38, South Woodstock, VT 05071, USA; tel. (802) 457-1199; fax (802) 457-2212; e-mail pmsvt@aol.com; f. 1980; anthropology, history, archaeology, linguistics and social sciences of southern Mexico and Central America; Spanish; Editors Armando J. Alfonzo U., W. George Lovell; 2 a year.

Mexico Service. International Reports, 11300 Rockville Pike, Rockville, MD 20852-3030, USA; tel. (301) 816-8950; f. 1980; business and finance in Brazil; English; Editor-in-Chief Robert G. Taylor; Editor Andrew Vogel; every 2 weeks.

Mexico Watch. Orbis Publications Ltd, 3201 New Mexico Ave, NW, Suite 249, Washington, DC, USA; tel. (202) 237-0155; fax (202) 237-0596; politics, economics and business of Brazil; English; monthly.

Mundo Nuevo. Revista de Estudios Latinoamericanos. Apdo 17271, Caracas 1015-A, Venezuela; tel. (2) 573-8824; f. 1975; international relations, politics, economy of Latin America; Spanish, but some articles are published in their original languages, English, French and Portuguese; published by the Instituto de Altos Estudios de América Latina, University Simón Bolívar; quarterly.

Mundus. Wissenschaftliche Verlagsgesellschaft GmbH, Birkenwaldstr. 44, 70191 Stuttgart, Germany; tel. (711) 25820; fax (711) 2582290; f. 1965; review of German research on Latin America, Asia and Africa; English; Editor Jürgen Hohnholz (Institute for Scientific Co-operation); quarterly.

NACLA Report on the Americas. 475 Riverside Drive, Suite 454, New York, NY 10015, USA; tel. (212) 870-3146; fax (212) 870-3305; e-mail nacla@igv.apc.org; f. 1966; publication of North American Congress on Latin America covering US foreign policy towards Latin America and the Caribbean, and domestic developments in the region; English; Editor Jo Marie Burt; 6 a year.

Negobancos–Negocios y Bancos. Bolívar 8-103, Apdo 1907, 06000 México, DF, Mexico; tel. (5) 510-1884; fax (5) 512-9411; f. 1951; business and economics; Spanish; Dir Alfredo Farrugia Reed; every 2 weeks.

Nordeste: Análise Conjuntural. Banco do Nordeste do Brasil, Escritório Técnico de Estudos Econômicos do Nordeste, Praça Murilo Borges, No. 1, CP 628, Fortaleza, CE, Brazil; f. 1972 as Análise Conjuntural de Economia Nordestina; adopted existing name in 1974; Brazilian economy, including statistics; Portuguese; Editor João de Aquino Limaverde.

Noti Cen. University of New Mexico, Latin American Institute, Latin American Data Base, 801 Yale, Albuquerque, NM 87131-1016, USA; tel. (505) 277-6839; e-mail info@ladb.unm.net; internet ladb.unm.edu; sustainable development, economic and political affairs in Central America and the Caribbean; weekly.

Noticias Indigenistas de América / Indian News of the Americas. Instituto Indigenista Interamericano, Avda Insurgentes Sur 1690, Col. Florida, 01030 México, DF, Mexico; tel. (5) 6600007; fax (5) 5348090; f. 1978; news of the Indians of the Americas, government policies, anthropology; Spanish and English editions; Editor Dr José Matos Mar; 3 a year.

Noticias de Latino América Documentos. 41 rue de Suède, 1060 Brussels, Belgium; tel. (2) 538-78-81; extracts from Latin American press; Spanish; Editor Kristin Minne; every two months.

Notisur. University of New Mexico, Latin American Institute, Latin American Data Base, 801 Yale, NE, Albuquerque, NM 87131-1016, USA; tel. (505) 277-6389; fax (505) 277-5989; e-mail info@ladb.unm.edu; internet www.ladb.unm.edu; provides alternative viewpoints on political and economic affairs in South America, particularly on human rights and peace issues and sustainable development; Spanish; Editor Patricia Hynds; weekly.

Opciones. Territorial esq. Gen Suárez, Plaza de la Revolución, Havana, Cuba; economics and politics; Spanish; weekly.

Panorama Económico. Bancomer, SA, Grupo Investigaciones Económicas, Centro Bancomer, Avda Universidad 1200, 03339 México, DF, Mexico; tel. (5) 534-0034; fax (5) 621-3230; f. 1966; Mexican economy, in particular the automobile and textiles industries; Spanish and English; Editor Eduardo Millan Lozano; 6 a year.

Panorama Económico Latinoamericano (PEL). Ediciones Cubanas, Obispo 527, Apdo 605, Havana, Cuba; f. 1960; book reviews and statistics; available on micro-film; Spanish; Editor José Bodes Gómez; 2 a month

Panorama Latinoamericano. Moscow, Zubovskii bul. 4, Russia; tel. (095) 201-55-79; review of economic, political, cultural, and social life of Latin America drawn from Russian Press and published by Novosti Press Agency; Spanish; fortnightly.

Paz. South American Commission for Peace, Regional Security and Democracy, Callao 3461, Las Condes, Casilla 16637, Correo 9, Santiago, Chile; tel. (2) 232-8329; fax (2) 233-3502; Spanish; 2 a year.

Pesquisa e Planejamento Econômico. Av. Antônio Carlos 51, 16° andar, CP 2672, 20.020-010 Rio de Janeiro, RJ, Brazil; tel. (21) 220-769; fax (21) 240-0756; e-mail webmaster@alpha.ipea.gov.br; internet www.ipea.gov.br; f. 1970; economics and planning; Portuguese and English; Editors Laura Ramos, Claudio Considera; quarterly.

Política Externa. International Relations Research Programme, University of São Paulo, Rua do Anfiteatro 181, Colméia, favo 14, Cidade Universitária, 05508-900 São Paulo, SP, Brazil; tel. (11) 818-3061; fax (11) 814-7342; e-mail guilhon@usp.br; Brazilian foreign and economic policy, regional integration, NAFTA and Mercosur; Portuguese.

Problemas del Desarrollo—revista latinoamericana de economía. Instituto de Investigaciones Económicas de la Universidad Nacional Autónoma de México, Ciudad Universitaria, Del. Coyoacán, 04510, México, DF, Mexico; tel. (5) 623-0105; fax (5) 623-0097; e-mail revprode@servidor.unam.mx; f. 1969; economic, political and social affairs of Mexico, Latin America and the Third World; Spanish, with English and French abstracts; quarterly.

Puerto Rico Business Review / Puerto Rico Economic Indicators. Government Development Bank for Puerto Rico, POB 42001, San Juan, PR 00940-2001, Puerto Rico; tel. 722-2525; fax 268-5496; f. 1976; English; Editor María Nevares; quarterly.

Quarterly Economic Report. Central Statistical Office, 35–41 Queen St, POB 98, Port of Spain, Trinidad and Tobago; tel. 623-6495; f. 1950; English.

Quarterly Statistical Digest. Central Bank of the Bahamas, Research Dept, Frederick St, POB N-4868, Nassau, Bahamas; tel. 322-2193; fax 356-4324; Bahamian economy statistics; English; quarterly.

Quehacer. Centro de Estudios y Promoción del Desarrollo—DESCO, León de la Fuente 110, Magdalena del Mar, Lima 17, Peru; tel. (1) 2641316; fax (1) 2640128; e-mail qh@desco.org.pe; internet www.desco.org.pe; f. 1979; business development and research; Spanish; Editor Juan Larco Guichard; 6 a year.

Relaciones Internacionales. Facultad de Ciencias Políticas y Sociales, Universidad Nacional Autónoma de México, Apdo 70–266, 04510 México, DF, Mexico; tel. (5) 622-9412; f. 1973; international relations; Spanish; Editor Roberto Domínguez; Dir Consuelo Dávila; 3 a year.

Review: Latin American Literature and Arts. 680 Park Ave, New York, NY 10021, USA; tel. (212) 249-8950; f. 1967; Latin American literature in translation, articles on visual arts, theatre, music, cinema, book reviews; English, but poetry is, in addition, published in the vernacular; Editors Alfred MacAdam, Daniel Shapiro; 2 a year.

Revista Análisis. Revistas Interamericanos SA, Apdo 8038, Panama 7, Panama; tel. 26-0073; fax 26-3758; f. 1979; economic and political analysis; academic; Spanish; Editor Mario A. Rognoni; monthly.

Revista Argentina de Estudios Estratégicos. Argentine Centre of Strategic Studies, Viamonte 494, 3°, Of. 11, 1053 Buenos Aires, Argentina; tel. (11) 4312-1605; fax (11) 4312-5802; the armed forces; Spanish; quarterly.

Revista de Biología Tropical. Universidad de Costa Rica, Ciudad Universitaria, San José, Costa Rica; tel. 2535223; fax 2075550; e-mail julianm@cariari.ucr.ac.cr; f. 1953; biology, ecology, taxonomy, etc. of Neotropics and African tropics; Spanish and English; Editor Julián Monge-Nájera; quarterly, with supplements.

Revista Brasileira de Economia. Praia de Botafogo 190, Rm 1125, 22.253-900 Rio de Janeiro, RJ, Brazil; tel. (21) 536-9250; f. 1947; economic theory, economic policy and econometrics; Portuguese and English; Editor João Victor Issler; quarterly.

Revista Brasileira de Estatística. Fundação Instituto Brasileiro de Geografia e Estatística, Avda Chile 500, 10° andar, 20.031-170 Rio de Janeiro, RJ, Brazil; tel. (21) 514-0470; fax (21) 514-4785; f. 1940; statistical subjects by means of articles, analysis, etc.; Portuguese; 2 a year.

Revista Brasileira de Estudos Políticos. Av. Alvares Cabral 211, salá 1206, CP 1301, 30170-000 Belo Horizonte, MG, Brazil; tel. (31) 224-8507; f. 1956; public law, political science, economics, history; Portuguese; published by Universidade Federal de Minas Gerais; Dirs Prof. Orlando M. Carvalho, Prof. Raul Machado Horta; 2 a year.

Revista Brasileira de Geografia. Fundação Instituto Brasileiro de Geografia e Estatística, Directoria de Geociências, Av. Brasil 15.671, bloco 3-B, térreo, Parada de Lucas, 21.241-051 Rio de Janeiro, RJ, Brazil; tel. (21) 391-1420; fax (21) 391-770; f. 1939; advanced geographic, socio-economic and scientific articles, also news and translations; Portuguese, with English summaries; 2 a year.

Revista Chilena de Historia y Geografía. Sociedad Chilena de Historia y Geografía, Londres 65, Casilla 1386, Santiago, Chile; tel. (2) 38249; f. 1911; history, geography, anthropology, archaeology, genealogy, numismatics; Spanish; Dir José Rafael Reyes; annual.

Revista de Ciencias Sociales. POB 23345, San Juan, PR 00931-3345, Puerto Rico; tel. (787) 764-0000; fax (787) 764-3625; f. 1957; sociology, anthropology, history, economics, geography, political sciences, psychology; Spanish; Editor Jorge Duany; 2 a year.

Revista de Ciencias Sociales de la Universidad de Costa Rica. Instituto de Investigaciones Sociales Dirección, Apdo 498, Montes de Oca 2050, Costa Rica; tel. 2073050; fax 2075569; e-mail ceciliaa@cariari.ucr.ac.cr; f. 1956; sociology, anthropology, geography, history, etc., with special reference to Costa Rica and Central America; Spanish; Editor Cecilia Arguedas; Dir Daniel Camacho; quarterly.

Revista Ecuador Debate. Centro Andino de Acción Popular—CAAP, Utreras 733 y Selva Alegre, Quito, Ecuador; tel. (2) 522-

763; fax (2) 568-452; e-mail caapl@caap.org.ec; f. 1983; economic conditions and agriculture; Spanish; Editor Freddy Rivera Vélez; 3 a year.

Revista Educación. Facultad de Educación, Ciudad Universitaria Rodrigo Facio, San José, Costa Rica; tel. 207-5635; f. 1977; education; Spanish; Dir Marta Rojas Porras; Editor María Elena Camacho; 2 a year.

Revista Estudios Sociales Centroamericanos. CSUCA, Apdo 37 Ciudad Universitaria Rodrigo Facio, San José, Costa Rica; tel. 252744; f. 1972; socio-economic and political aspects of Central America; Spanish; Editor Mario Lungo Uclés; 3 a year.

Revista Europea de Estudios Latinoamericanos y del Caribe / European Review of Latin American and Caribbean Studies. Centre for Latin American Research and Documentation (CEDLA), Keizersgracht 395–397, 1016 EK Amsterdam, Netherlands; tel. (20) 525-34-98; fax (20) 625-51-27; e-mail secretariat@cedla.uva.nl; internet www.cedla.uva.nl; f. 1989; social scientific research on Latin America and the Caribbean (anthropology, economics, geography, history, politics, sociology, etc.); English and Spanish; Editor K. Willingham; 2 a year.

Revista Geológica de América Central. Escuela Centroamericana de Geología, Apdo 35, 2060 Universidad de Costa Rica, San José, Costa Rica; tel. 2257941; fax 2342347; e-mail skussmau@cariari.ucr.ac.cr; f. 1984; geology and geophysics of Central America; Spanish, with abstracts in English and English, with abstracts in Spanish; annual.

Revista do Instituto Histórico e Geográfico Brasileiro. Av. Augusto Severo 8, 10° andar, 20.021-040 Rio de Janeiro, RJ, Brazil; tel. (21) 232-1312; fax (21) 252-4430; f. 1838; history and geography; Portuguese; quarterly.

Revista Latinoamericana de Estudios Urbanos y Regionales. Instituto de Estudios Urbanos, Univ. Católica de Chile, Casilla 16002, Correo 9, Santiago, Chile; tel. (2) 2325057; fax (2) 2328805; f. 1970; urban and regional development in Latin America; Spanish, with English abstracts; Editor Gloria Jénez; quarterly.

Revista do Mercado Comum do Sul — Mercosul / Revista del Mercado Común del Sur — Mercosur. Editora Terceiro Mundo, Rua da Gloria 122, 105–106, 20241 Rio de Janeiro, RJ, Brazil; tel. (21) 242-0763; fax (21) 252-8455; f. 1992; Latin American integration; Portuguese and Spanish; monthly.

Revista Mexicana de Ciencias Políticas y Sociales. Facultad de Ciencias Políticas y Sociales, Universidad Autónoma de México, 04510 México, DF, Mexico; tel. (5) 6229433; fax (5) 6651786; f. 1955; political and social sciences; Spanish; Assoc. Dir Judit Bokser Misses; quarterly.

Revista Mexicana de Política Exterior. Matias Romero Institute for Diplomatic Studies, Reforma Norte 707, esq. Avda Peralvillo, Col. Morales, 06200 México, DF, Mexico; tel. (5) 529-9514; fax (5) 327-3031; Spanish; Editor Dulce María Méndez; quarterly.

Revista 'Repertorio Americano'. Instituto de Estudios Latinoamericanos, Universidad Nacional, Apdo 86, Heredia, Costa Rica; tel. and fax 277-3430; e-mail idela@una.ac.cr; f. 1919; Latin American and Spanish culture; Spanish; 2 a year.

Revista Venezolana de Análisis de Coyuntura. Research Institute of the Faculty of Economic and Social Sciences, Central University of Venezuela, Oficina de Publicaciones, Apdo Postal 54057, Caracas 1051-A, Venezuela; tel. and fax (2) 605-2523; f. 1980 as Boletín de Indicadores Socio-económicos; adopted existing name in 1995; socio-economic issues; Spanish; 2 a year.

Revista Venezolana de Economía y Ciencias Sociales. Research Institute of the Faculty of Economic and Social Sciences, Central University of Venezuela, Oficina de Publicaciones, Apdo Postal 54057, Caracas 1051-A, Venezuela; tel. and fax (2) 605-2523; f. 1958 as Economía y Ciencias Sociales; changed name as above in 1995; Spanish; Editor Dick Parker; 3 a year.

Semana Económica. Apdo 671, Lima, Peru; tel. (1) 4455237; fax (1) 4455946; f. 1985; economic affairs; Spanish; Editor Augusto Alvare-Rodrich; weekly.

Síntesis Económica. Calle 70A, No. 10–52, Apdo Aéreo 34284, Santafé de Bogotá, DC, Colombia; tel. (1) 212-5121; fax (1) 212-8365; f. 1975; Spanish; Dir Félix Lafaurie Rivera; weekly.

Sourcemex. University of New Mexico, Latin American Institute, Latin American Data Base, 801 Yale, NE, Albuquerque, NM 87131-1016, USA; tel. (505) 277-6389; fax (505) 277-5989; e-mail info@ladb.unm.net; internet www.ladb.unm.edu; economic news and analysis in Mexico; weekly.

Spiegel der lateinamerikanischen Presse / Boletín de Prensa Latinoamericana. Institut für Iberoamerika Kunde, 20354 Hamburg, Alsterglacis 8, Germany; tel. (40) 41478201; fax (40) 41478241; political, business and social extracts from Latin American press; Spanish and Portuguese; 3 a year.

Summary of World Broadcasts Part 5: Africa, Latin America and the Caribbean Weekly Economic Reports. BBC Monitoring Caversham Park, Reading, RG4 8TZ, United Kingdom; tel. (1734) 469289; fax (1734) 463823; e-mail 100431.2524@compuserve.com; f. 1939; economic information; English.

Suplemento Antropológico. Centro de Estudios Antropológicos de la Universidad Católica, Casilla 1718, Asunción, Paraguay; tel. (21) 446251; fax (21) 445245; f. 1965; practical and theoretical problems of the indigenous peoples of the River Plate basin (Bolivia, Brazil, Uruguay, Argentina and Paraguay); Spanish; 2 a year.

Terra Ameriga. Salita Santa Maria della Sanità 43, 16122 Genoa, Italy; tel. (010) 814737; f. 1964; archaeology, anthropology, ethnology, history, linguistics, literature, etc. of ancient America, published by Associazione Italiana Studi Americanistici; annual.

Third World Quarterly. 188 Copse Hill, London SW20 0SP, United Kingdom; tel. and fax (20) 8947-1243; Editor Shahid Qadir.

Tricontinental. Organization of Solidarity of the Peoples of Asia, Africa and Latin America, Calle C, No. 668, esq. 29, Vedado, Apdo 4224, Havana, Cuba; tel. (7) 30-4941; fax (7) 33-3985; f. 1967; analysis of cultural, political and social developments in Cuba and other developing countries; Spanish, French and English; Editor Ana María Pellón Sáez; quarterly.

El Trimestre Económico. Fondo de Cultura Económica, SA, Carretera Picacho Ajusco 227, Col. Bosques del Pedregal, Del. Tlaplan, 14200 México, DF, Mexico; tel. (5) 227-4672; fax (5) 227-4673; f. 1934; economic development and economic theory, employment and investment policy; Spanish; Editor Rodolfo de la Torre; quarterly.

Uruguay Económico. Ministerio de Economía y Finanzas, Asesoría Economico-Financiera, Col. 1013, 8°, Montevideo, Uruguay; f. 1978; economy of Uruguay; published by the Economic and Financial Advisory Office of the Uruguayan Ministry of Economy and Finance; Spanish; 2 a year.

Uruguay Síntesis Económico. Banco Central del Uruguay, Departamento de Estadísticas Económicas, Paysando y Florida, Casilla 1467, Montevideo, Uruguay; tel. (2) 917117; fax (2) 921634; economic conditions in Uruguay; publication of the Economic Statistics Department of the Central Bank of Uruguay; Spanish; 2 a year.

Visión (La Revista Latinoamericana Visión). Arguímedes 199, 6° y 7°, Col. Polanco, 11570 México, DF, Mexico; tel. (5) 203-6091; f. 1950; news and analysis of Latin America; Spanish Gen. Man. Roberto Bello; 2 a month.

Washington Letter on Latin America. 1117 North 19th St, Arlington, VA 22209, USA; tel. (703) 247-3433; political and economic; English; Editor Barbara Annis; 24 a year.

Zeitschrift für Lateinamerika Wien. 100 Vienna, Schlickgasse 1, Austria; tel. (1) 310-74-65; fax (1) 310-74-65-21; e-mail office@lai.at; internet www.lai.at; f. 1965; social sciences and foreign policy; German and Spanish; Editor Gerhard Drekonja; annual.

SELECT BIBLIOGRAPHY
(BOOKS)

South America

Adelman, J. 'Reflections on Argentine Labour and the Rise of Perón', in *Bulletin of Latin American Research*, Vol. 11, No. 3, (Sept.). 1992.

Adler, E. *The Power of Ideology: The Quest for Technological Autonomy in Argentina and Brazil*. Berkeley and Los Angeles, CA, University of California Press, 1987.

Allison, G. T. *Essence of Decision: Explaining the Cuban Missile Crisis*. Boston, MA, Little Brown, 1971.

Almond, G. A., and Verba, S. *The Civic Culture: Political Attitudes and Democracy in Five Nations*, 2nd edn. Newbury Park, CA, Sage Publications, 1989.

Angell, A. et al. *Decentralizing Development: The Political Economy of Institutional Change in Colombia and Chile*. Oxford, Oxford University Press, 2001.

Anglade, C., and Fortín, C. *The State and Capital Accumulation in Latin America*. London, Macmillan, 1985.

Archetti, E. P., Cammack. P., and Roberts, B. (Eds). *Sociology of 'Developing Societies': Latin America*. Basingstoke, Macmillan, 1987.

Aviel, J. F. 'Political Participation of Women in Latin America', in *Western Political Quarterly*, Vol. 34. 1981.

Baloyra, E. A. (Ed.). *Comparing New Democracies, Transition and Consolidation in Mediterranean Europe and the Southern Cone*. Boulder, CO, Westview Press, 1987.

Bethell, L., and Roxborough, I. (Eds). *Latin America between the Second World War and the Cold War, 1944–1948*. Cambridge, Cambridge University Press, 1993.

Black, J. K. 'Elections and Other Trivial Pursuits: Latin America and the New World Order', in *Third World Quarterly*, Vol. 14, No. 3. 1993.

Latin America: Its Problems and Its Promise, 3rd edn. Boulder, CO, Westview Press, 1998.

Bouvier, V. *Alliance or Compliance, Implications of the Chilean Experience for the Catholic Church in Latin America*. Syracuse, NY, Syracuse University Press, 1983.

Bruneau, T. C. *The Political Transformation of the Brazilian Catholic Church*. Cambridge, Cambridge University Press, 1974.

Bulmer-Thomas, V. *The Economic History of Latin America Since Independence*. Cambridge, Cambridge University Press, 1994.

The New Economic Model in Latin America and its Impact on Income Distribution and Poverty. Basingstoke, Macmillan, 1996.

Calvert, P. *A Study of Revolution*. Oxford, Clarendon Press, 1970.

'Latin America: Laboratory of Revolution', in *Revolutionary Theory and Political Reality*, edited by Noel O'Sullivan. Brighton, Harvester Press, 1983.

'Demilitarisation in Latin America', in *Third World Quarterly*, Vol. 7. 1985.

(Ed.). *Political and Economic Encyclopedia of South America and the Caribbean*. Harlow, Essex, Longman, 1991.

The International Politics of Latin America. Manchester, Manchester University Press, 1994.

Calvert, P., and Calvert, S. *Latin America in the Twentieth Century*, 2nd edn. Basingstoke, Macmillan, 1993.

Calvert, P., and Milbank, S. *The Ebb and Flow of Military Government in South America*, (Conflict Studies No. 198). London, Institute for the Study of Conflict, 1987.

Camp, R. A. *Democracy in Latin America: Patterns and Cycles*. Wilmington, DE, SR Books, 1996.

Castañeda, J. G. *Utopia Unarmed: The Latin American Left after the Cold War*. New York, NY, Vintage Books, 1994.

Castro, D. (Ed.). *Revolution and Revolutionaries, Guerrilla Movements in Latin America*. Scholarly Review Books, 1999.

Clapham, C., and Philip, G. (Eds). *The Political Dilemmas of Military Regimes*. London, Croom Helm, 1985.

Clissold, S. *Soviet Relations with Latin America, 1918–1968: A Documentary Survey*. London, Oxford University Press for Royal Institute of International Affairs, 1969.

Collier, D. (Ed.). *The New Authoritarianism in Latin America*. Princeton, NJ, Princeton University Press, 1979.

Collinson, H. (Ed.). *Green Guerrillas: Environmental Conflicts and Initiatives in Latin America*. London, Latin American Bureau, 1996.

Conniff, M. L. *Latin American Populism in Comparative Perspective*. Albuquerque, NM, University of New Mexico Press, 1982.

Cubitt, T. *Latin American Society*, 2nd edn. Harlow, Longman, 1995.

De Janvry, A. *The Agrarian Question and Reformism in Latin America*. Baltimore, MD, Johns Hopkins University Press, 1981.

Desch, M. C. *When the Third World Matters: Latin America and United States Grand Strategy*. Baltimore, MD, Johns Hopkins University Press, 1993.

De Soto, H. *The Other Path: The Invisible Revolution in the Third World*. New York, NY, Harper Row, 1989.

Di Tella, T. S. *Latin American Politics: A Theoretical Framework*. Austin, TX, University of Texas Press, 1990.

Dix, R. H. 'The Breakdown of Authoritarian Regimes', in *Western Political Quarterly*, Vol. 35. 1982.

'Populism: Authoritarian and Democratic', in *Latin American Research Review*, Vol. 20. 1985.

Domínguez, F. (Ed.). *Identity and Discursive Practices: Spain and Latin America*. Bern, Peter Lang AG, 2000.

Duran, E. *European Interests in Latin America*. London, Royal Institute of International Affairs, 1985.

Eckstein, S. E. *Back from the Future: Cuba under Castro*. Princeton, NJ, Princeton University Press, 1994.

(Ed.). *Power and Popular Protest: Latin American Social Movements*. Berkeley, CA, University of California Press, 1989.

Feinberg, R. E. *The Intemperate Zone: The Third World Challenge to US Foreign Policy*. New York, NY, W. W. Norton, 1983.

Ferrell, R. H. *Latin American Diplomacy: The Twentieth Century*. New York, NY, W. W. Norton, 1988.

Finer, S. E. *The Man on Horseback: The Role of the Military in Politics*, 2nd revised edn. Harmondsworth, Penguin, 1976.

Fisher, J. *Out of the Shadows: Women, Resistance and Politics in South America*. London, Latin American Bureau, 1993.

Foders, F., and Feldsieper, M. *The Transformation of Latin America: Economic Development in the Early 1990s*. Northampton, MA, Edward Elgar Publishing, 2000.

Foweraker, J. *Theorizing Social Movements*. London, Pluto Press, 1995.

Gilbert, A. *Latin America*. London, Routledge, 1990.

   The Latin American City, revised edn. London, Latin American Bureau, 1998.

Gillespie, R. *Soldiers of Perón: Argentina's Montoneros*. Oxford, Clarendon Press, 1982.

Gleijeses, P. *The Dominican Crisis: The 1965 Constitutional Revolt and American Intervention*. Baltimore, MD, Johns Hopkins University Press, 1979.

Graham-Yooll, A. *A State of Fear: Memories of Argentina's Nightmare*. London, Eland, 1986.

Green, D. *Silent Revolution: The Rise of Market Economics in Latin America*. London, Cassell/Latin American Bureau, 1995.

Guillermoprieto, A. *Looking for History: Dispatches from Latin America*. New York, NY, Pantheon Books, 2001.

Gutierrez, G. *A Theology of Liberation*. London, SLM Press, 1973.

Gwynne, R. N., and Kay, C. (Eds). *Latin America Transformed: Globalization and Modernity*. London, Arnold, 1999.

Harrison, L. E. *Underdevelopment is a State of Mind: The Latin American Case*. Lanham, MD, University Press of America, 1985.

Hinds, H. E., Jr, and Tatum, C. M. (Eds). *Handbook of Latin American Popular Culture*. Westport, CT, Greenwood Press, 1985.

Jones, G. A., and Varley, A. 'The Contest for the City Centre: Street Traders versus Buildings', in *Bulletin of Latin American Research*, Vol. 13, No. 1 (Jan.). 1994.

Keegan, J. (Ed.). *World Armies*. London, Macmillan, 1983.

Kennedy, J. J. *Catholicism, Nationalism and Democracy in Argentina*. South Bend, IN, University of Notre Dame Press, 1958.

Kirk, J. 'John Paul II and the Exorcism of Liberation Theology...', in *Bulletin of Latin American Research*, Vol. 4, No. 1. 1985.

Lehmann, D. *Democracy and Development in Latin America*. Cambridge, Polity Press, 1990.

LeoGrande, W. 'Enemies Evermore: US Policy Towards Cuba After Helms-Burton', in *Journal of Latin American Studies*, Vol. 29. 1997.

Levine, D. H. (Ed.). *Churches and Politics in Latin America*. Beverley Hills, CA, Sage Publications, 1979.

Linz, J. J., and Stepan, A. (Eds). *The Breakdown of Democratic Regimes: Latin America*. Baltimore, MD, Johns Hopkins University Press, 1978.

Lipset, S. M., and Solari, A. (Eds). *Elites in Latin America*. New York, NY, Oxford University Press, 1967.

Lockhart, J., and Schwartz, S. B. *Early Latin America: A History of Colonial Spanish America and Brazil*. New York, NY, Cambridge University Press, 1983.

Loveman, B., and Davies, T. M. (Eds). *The Politics of Antipolitics: The Military in Latin America*. Lincoln, NE, University of Nebraska Press, 1978.

Loveman, B. *The Constitution of Tyranny: Regimes of Exception in Latin America*. Pittsburgh, PA, University of Pittsburgh Press, 1994.

Lowenthal, A. F. (Ed.). *Armies and Politics in Latin America*. New York, NY, Holmes and Meier, 1976.

Lynch, J. *Argentine Dictator: Juan Manuel de Rosas, 1829–1852*. Oxford, Clarendon Press, 1981.

MacDonald, S. B., and Fauriol, G. A. *Fast Forward: Latin America on the Edge of the 21st Century*. New Brunswick, NJ, and London, Transaction Publishers, 1997.

Maier, J., and Weatherhead, R. W. (Eds). *The Latin American University*. Albuquerque, NM, University of New Mexico Press, 1979.

Mainwaring, S., O'Donnell, G., and Valenzuela, J. S. (Eds). *Issues in Democratic Consolidation: The New South American Democracies in Comparative Perspective*. South Bend, IN, University of Notre Dame Press, 1992.

Malloy, J. M. (Ed.). *Authoritarianism and Corporatism in Latin America*. Pittsburgh, PA, University of Pittsburgh Press, 1977.

Malloy, J. M., and Seligson, M. A. (Eds). *Authoritarians and Democrats: Regime Transition in Latin America*. Pittsburgh, PA, University of Pittsburgh Press, 1987.

Martz, J. D. (Ed.). *United States Policy in Latin America: A Quarter Century of Crisis and Challenge, 1961–1986*. Lincoln, NE, University of Nebraska Press, 1988.

Martz, J. D., and Schoultz, L. (Eds). *Latin America, the United States and the Inter-American System*. Boulder, CO, Westview Press, 1980.

Meso-Lago, C. *Market, Socialist, and Mixed Economies: Comparative Policy and Performance in Chile, Cuba, and Costa Rica*. Baltimore, MD, Johns Hopkins University Press, 2000.

Morris, M. A., and Millán, V. *Controlling Latin American Conflicts: Ten Approaches*. Boulder, CO, Westview Press, 1983.

Mouzelis, N. P. *Politics in the Semi-Periphery: Early Parliamentarism and Late Industrialization in The Balkans and Latin America*. Basingstoke, Macmillan, 1986.

Munck, R. *Politics and Dependency in the Third World: The Case of Latin America*. London, Zed Books, 1984.

Muñoz, H., and Tulchin, J. S. (Eds). *Latin American Nations in World Politics*. Boulder, CO, Westview Press, 1984.

Nunn, F. M. *The Time of the Generals: Latin American Professional Militarism in World Perspective*. Lincoln, NE, University of Nebraska Press, 1992.

   Yesterday's Soliders: European Military Professionalism in South America, 1890–1940. Lincoln, NE, University of Nebraska Press, 1983.

O'Brien, P., and Cammack, P. (Eds). *Generals in Retreat: The Crisis of Military Rule in Latin America*. Manchester, Manchester University Press, 1985.

O'Donnell, G. *Delegative Democracy*. South Bend, IN, University of Notre Dame Press, 1992.

   Counterpoints: Selected Essays on Authoritarianism and Democratization. Notre Dame, IN, University of Notre Dame, 2000.

O'Donnell, G., Schmitter, P., and Whitehead, L. (Eds). *Transitions from Authoritarian Rule*. Baltimore, MD, Johns Hopkins University Press, 1986.

Painter, M., and Durham, W. H. *The Social Causes of Environmental Destruction in Latin America*. Ann Arbor, MI, University of Michigan Press, 1995.

Parkinson, F. *Latin America, the Cold War and the World Powers, 1945–1973*. Beverley Hills, CA, Sage Publications, 1974.

Pastor, R. A. *Condemned to Repetition: The United States and Nicaragua*. Princeton, NJ, Princeton University Press, 1987.

Pearce, J. (Ed.). *The European Challenge: Europe's New Role in Latin America*. London, Latin American Bureau, 1982.

Perkins, D. *A History of the Monroe Doctrine*. London, Longman, 1960.

Petras, J., and Morley, M. *Latin America in the Time of Cholera: Electoral Politics, Market Economy, and Permanent Crisis*. New York, NY, Routledge, 1992.

Philip, G. *Oil and Politics in Latin America: Nationalist Movements and State Companies*. Cambridge, Cambridge University Press, 1982.

   The Military and South American Politics. London, Croom Helm, 1985.

   'The New Economic Liberalism in Latin America: Friends or Enemies?', in *Third World Quarterly*, Vol. 14, No. 3. 1993.

Pike, F. B. 'The Catholic Church and Modernization in Peru and Chile', in *Journal of Inter-American Affairs*, Vol. 20, No. 272. 1966.

   The United States and Latin America: Myths and Stereotypes of Civilization and Nature. Austin, TX, University of Texas Press, 1992.

Poppino, R. *International Communism in Latin America: A History of the Movement, 1917–1963*. New York, NY, The Free Press, 1964.

Portes, A. 'Latin American Urbanization During the Years of the Crisis', in *Latin American Research Review*, Vol. 24, No. 3. 1989.

Przeworski, A., and Wallerstein, M. 'Structural Dependence on the State for Capital', in *American Political Science Review*, Vol. 82, (March). 1988.

Rakowski, C. A. (Ed.). *Contrapunto: The Informal Sector Debate in Latin America*. Albany, NY, State University of New York Press, 1994.

Randall, L. 'Lies, Damn Lies and Argentine GDP', in *Latin American Research Review*, Vol. 11. 1974.

Ritter, A. R. M., and Kirk, J. M. *Cuba in the International System: Normalization and Intergration*. London, Macmillan, 1995.

Roberts, B. R. *The Making of Citizens: Cities of Peasants Revisited*. London, Arnold, 1995.

Roberts, K. M. *Deepening Democracy? The Modern Left and Social Movements in Chile and Peru*. Stanford, CA, Stanford University Press, 2000.

Rouquié, A. *The Military and the State in Latin America*. Berkeley, CA, University of California Press, 1987.

Ruhl, M. 'Social Mobilisation, Military Tradition and Current Patterns of Civil–Military Relations in Latin America', in *Western Political Quarterly*, Vol. 35. 1982.

Sarmiento, D. F. *Life in the Argentine Republic in the Days of the Tyrants (or Civilization and Barbarism)*. New York, NY, Collier Books, 1961.

Schmitter, P. C. (Ed.). *Military Rule in Latin America: Function, Consequences and Perspectives*. Beverly Hills, CA, Sage Publications, 1973.

Scranton, M. E. *The Noriega Years: US–Panamanian Relations, 1981–1990*. Boulder, CO, Lynne Rienner, 1991.

Seckinger, R. 'The Central American Militaries: A Survey of the Literature', in *Latin American Research Review*, Vol. 16. 1981.

Shafer, D. M. *Deadly Paradigms: The Failure of US Counterinsurgency Policy*. Princeton, NJ, Princeton University Press, 1988.

Sheahan, J. *Patterns of Development in Latin America: Poverty, Repression and Economic Strategy*. Princeton, NJ, Princeton University Press, 1987.

Sherman, J. W. *Latin America in Crisis*. Boulder, CO, Westview Press, 2000.

Sigmund, P. E. *The United States and Democracy in Chile*. Baltimore, MD, Johns Hopkins for Twentieth Century Fund, 1993.

Silvert, K. H. *The Conflict Society: Reaction and Revolution in Latin America*. New York, NY, American Universities Field Staff Inc., 1966.

Skidmore, T. E., and Smith, P. H. *Modern Latin America*. Oxford, Oxford University Press, 2000.

Smith, B. *The Church and Politics in Chile, Challenges to Modern Catholicism*. Princeton, NJ, Princeton University Press, 1982.

Spalding, H. A. *Organised Labor in Latin America: Historical Case Studies of Urban Workers in Dependent Societies*. New York, NY, Harper and Row, 1977.

Sunkel, O. (Ed.). *Development from Within: Towards a Neostructuralist Approach for Latin America*. Boulder, CO, and London, Lynne Rienner, 1993.

Tamarin, D. *The Argentine Labor Movement, 1930–1945: A Study in the Origins of Peronism*. Albuquerque, NM, University of New Mexico Press, 1985.

Thomas, J. R. *Bibliographical Dictionary of Latin American Historians and Historiography*. Westport, CT, Greenwood Press, 1984.

Thorp, R. (Ed.). *Latin America in the 1930s: The Role of the Periphery in World Crisis*. Basingstoke, Macmillan, 1984.

Thorp, R., and Whitehead, L. (Eds). *Latin American Debt and the Adjustment Crisis*. Basingstoke, Macmillan, 1987.

Tiano, S. 'Authoritarianism and Political Culture in Argentina and Chile in the mid 1960s', in *Latin American Research Review*, Vol. 31. 1986.

Timerman, J. *Prisoner without a Name, Cell without a Number*. Harmondsworth, Penguin, 1982.

Tokman, V. E., and Klein, E. *Regulation and the Informal Economy: Microenterprises in Chile, Ecuador, and Jamaica*. Boulder, CO, Lynne Rienner Publrs, 1995.

Trubowitz, P. *Defining the National Interest: Conflict and Change in American Foreign Policy*. Chicago, IL, University of Chicago Press, 1998.

Tulchin, J. S., and Garland, A. M. (Eds). *Social Development in Latin America*. Boulder, CO, Lynne Rienner, 2000.

Tulchin, J. S., and Espach, R. H. *Latin America in the New International System*. Boulder, CO, Lynne Rienner Publrs, 2000.

Turner, B. (Ed.). *Latin America Profiled: Essential Facts on Society, Business and Politics in Latin America (Syb Factbook)*. New York, NY, St Martin's Press, 2000.

Wesson, R. (Ed.). *The Latin American Military Institution*. New York, NY, Praeger Publrs, 1986.

Wilgus, A. C. (Ed.). *South American Dictators During the First Century of Independence*. New York, NY, Russell and Russell, 1963.

Wilkie, J. W., and Perkal, A. (Eds). *Statistical Abstract of Latin America*. Los Angeles, CA, University of California (Los Angeles) Latin American Center, annual.

Wood, B. *The Dismantling of the Good Neighbor Policy*. Austin, TX, University of Texas Press, 1985.

Wright, T. C. *Latin America in the Era of the Cuban Revolution*. New York, NY, Praeger Publrs, 2000.

Central America

Adelman, A., and Reading, R. (Eds). *Confrontation in the Caribbean Basin: International Perspectives on Security, Sovereignty and Survival*. Pittsburgh, PA, Centre for Latin American Studies, 1984.

Aguilera, G. *El fusil y el olivo: la cuestión militar en Centroamérica*. USA, FLACSO/DEI, 1988.

Anderson, T. P. *Politics in Central America: Guatemala, El Salvador, Honduras and Nicaragua*. New York, NY, Praeger Publrs, 1988.

Barry, T. *Roots of Rebellion: Land and Hunger in Central America*. USA, South End Press, 1987.

Blachman, M., *et al. Confronting Revolution: Security through Diplomacy in Central America*. New York, NY, Pantheon, 1986.

Blakemore, H. *Central American Crisis: Challenge to US Diplomacy*. London, Institute for the Study of Conflict, 1984.

Booth, J. A., and Walker, T. W. *Understanding Central America*, 3rd edn. Boulder, CO, Westview Press, 1999.

Booth, J., and Seligson, M. *Elections and Democracy in Central America*. Chapel Hill, NC, University of North Carolina Press, 1989.

Bulmer-Thomas, V. *Studies in the Economics of Central America*. London, Macmillan, 1989.

Chomsky, A., and Lauria-Santiago, A. (Eds). *Identity and Struggle at the Margins of the Nation-State: The Laboring Peoples of Central America and the Hispanic Caribbean*. Durham, NC, Duke University Press, 1998.

Dunkerley, J. *Power in the Isthmus: A Political History of Modern Central America*. London: Verso, 1988.

The Pacification of Central America. London and New York, NY, Verso, 1994.

Flora, J., and Torres-Rivas, E. (Eds). *Central America*. Austin, TX, Central America Resource Center, 1989.

Goodman, L. W., Leogrande, W. M., and Mendelson Forman, J. (Eds). *Political Parties and Democracy in Central America*. Boulder, CO, Westview Press, 1992.

Holland, S., and Anderson, D. *Kissinger's Kingdom? A Counterreport on Central America*. Nottingham, Spokesman, 1984.

Karnes, T. L. *The Failure of Union in Central America, 1824–1960*. Chapel Hill, NC, University of North Carolina Press.

Kirk, J. M., and Schuyler, G. V. (Eds). *Central America: Democracy, Development and Change*. New York, NY, Praeger Publrs, 1989.

Krenn, M. L. *The Chains of Interdependence: US Policy toward Central America, 1945–1954*. M. E. Sharpe, 1996.

LaFeber, W. *Inevitable Revolutions: The United States in Central America*. London, W. W. Norton, 1983.

Leiken, R. S. (Ed.). *Central America: Anatomy of Conflict*. New York, NY, Pergamon Press, 1984.

Parker, F. D. *Central American Republics*. New York, NY, and London, Greenwood Press, 1981.

Pérez-Brignoli, H. *A Brief History of Central America*. Berkeley, CA, University of California Press, 1989.

Pearce, J. *Under the Eagle: US Intervention in Central America and the Caribbean*, 2nd edn. London, Latin America Bureau, 1982.

The Report of the President's National Bipartisan Commission on Central America. London, Collier Macmillan, 1984.

Schooley, H. *Conflict in Central America*. Harlow, Keesing's International—Longman, 1987.

Schulz, D. E., and Graham, D. H. (Eds). *Revolution and Counter-revolution in Central America and the Caribbean*. Boulder, CO, Westview Press, 1984.

Sieder, R. (Ed.). *Central America: Fragile Transition*. London and Basingstoke, Macmillan with Institute of Latin American Studies Series, 1996.

Vilas, C. *Between Earthquakes and Volcanoes, Market, State, and the Revolutions in Central America*. New York, NY, Monthly Review Press, 1995.

Torres-Rivas, E. *Repression and Resistance: The Struggle for Democracy in Central America*. Boulder, CO, Westview Press, 1989.

Wiarda, H. J. (Ed.). *US Policy in Central America: Consultant Papers for the Kissinger Commission*. Washington, DC, American Enterprise Institute for Public Policy Research, 1984.

Woodward, R. L. *Central America: Historical Perspectives on the Contemporary Crises*. London, Greenwood, 1988.

The Caribbean

Adelman, A., and Reading, R. (Eds). *Confrontation in the Caribbean Basin: International Perspectives on Security, Sovereignty and Survival*. Pittsburgh, PA, Center for Latin American Studies, 1984.

Ahmed, B., and Afroz, S. *The Political Economy of Food and Agriculture in the Caribbean*. Kingston, Ian Randle Publrs, 1996.

Anderson, T. D. *Geopolitics of the Caribbean: Ministates in a Wider World*. New York, NY, Praeger Publrs, 1985.

Annual Report of the Secretary-General of the Caribbean Community. Georgetown, Caribbean Community Secretariat, 1981–.

Ayala, C. J. *American Sugar Kingdom: The Plantation Economy of the Spanish Caribbean 1898–1934*. Chapel Hill, NC, University of North Carolina Press, 1999.

Birbalsingh, F. (Ed.). *Indo-Caribbean Resistance*. Toronto, TSAR, 1993.

Buxton, J., and Phillips, N. *Case Studies in Latin American Political Economy*. Manchester, Manchester University Press, 1999.

Chamberlain, M. (Ed.). *Caribbean Migration: Globalised Identities*. London, Routledge, 1998.

Desch, M. C., Domínguez, J. I., Serbin, A. (Eds). *From Pirates to Druglords, the Post-Cold War Caribbean Security Environment*. Oxford, Heinemann, 1998.

Domínguez, J. I. *Democratic Politics in Latin America and the Caribbean*. Baltimore, MD, Johns Hopkins University Press, 1998.

Dunn, H. S. (Ed.). *Globalization, Communications and Caribbean Identity*. Kingston, Ian Randle Publrs, 1995.

Ferguson, J. *Far From Paradise: An Introduction to Caribbean Development*. London, Latin America Bureau, 1990.

Gaspar, D. B., and Geggus, D. P. (Eds). *A Turbulent Time: The French Revolution and the Greater Caribbean*. Bloomington, IN, Indiana University Press, 1997.

Graham, N. A., and Edwards, K. L. *The Caribbean Basin to the Year 2000: Demographic, Economic and Resource-use Trends in Seventeen Countries: A Compendium of Statistics and Projections*. Boulder, CO, Westview Press, 1984.

Griffith, I. L., and Sedoc-Dahlberg, B. N. (Eds). *Democracy and Human Rights in the Caribbean*. Boulder, CO, Westview Press, 1997.

Grossman, L. S. *The Political Ecology of Bananas, Contract Farming, Peasants and Agrarian Change in the Eastern Caribbean*. Chapel Hill, NC, University of North Carolina Press, 1998.

Hall, K., and Benn, D. (Eds). *Contending with Destiny: The Caribbean in the 21st Century*. Kingston, Ian Randle Publrs, 2000.

Hennessy, A. (Ed.). *Intellectuals in the Twentieth Century Caribbean—Unity in Variety*, Vol. II: *The Hispanic and Francophone Caribbean*. Basingstoke, Macmillan, 1992.

Hodge, A. *The Caribbean*. Hove, East Sussex, Macdonald Young, 1998.

Holme, P. *Colonial Encounters: Europe and the Native Caribbean 1492–1797*. London, Methuen, 1986.

Hope, K. *Urbanization in the Commonwealth Caribbean*. Boulder, CO, Westview Press, 1986.

Hope, K. R. *Economic Development in the Caribbean*. New York, NY, Praeger Publrs, 1986.

Development Finance and the Development Process: A Case Study of Selected Caribbean Countries. London, Greenwood, 1987.

Klak, T. *Globalization and Neoliberalism: The Caribbean Context*. Lanham, MD, Rowman & Littlefield Publrs, 1998.

Klein, H. S. *African Slavery in Latin America and the Caribbean*. New York, NY, Oxford University Press, 1986.

Maingot, A. P. *US Power and Caribbean Security: Geopolitics in a Sphere of Influence*. London, Lynne Rienner, 1989.

Mandle, J. R. *Persistent Underdevelopment: Change and Economic Modernization in the West Indies*. Newark, NJ, Gordon & Breach, 1996.

Marshall, D. D. *Caribbean Political Economy at the Crossroads: NAFTA and Regional Developmentalism*. Basingstoke, Macmillan, 1998.

Mintz, S. *Caribbean Transformations*. Baltimore, MD, Johns Hopkins University Press, 1974.

Munro, D. G. *Intervention and Dollar Diplomacy in the Caribbean, 1900–1921*. Princeton, NJ, Princeton University Press, 1964.

The United States and the Caribbean Republics. Princeton, NJ, Princeton University Press, 1974.

Olwig, K. F. (Ed.). *Small Islands, Large Questions: Society, Culture and Resistance in the Post-Emancipation Caribbean*. London, Frank Cass, 1995.

Palmer, R. W. (Ed.). *US–Caribbean Relations, Their Impact on Peoples and Culture*. Westport, CT, Greenwood Press, 1998.

Pattullo, P. *Fire from the Mountain: The Story of the Montserrat Volcano*. London, Constable and Co Ltd, 2000.

Payne, A., and Sutton, P. (Eds). *Modern Caribbean Politics*. Baltimore, MD, Johns Hopkins University Press, 1993.

Randall, S. J., and Mount, G. S. *The Caribbean Basin: An International History*. London, Routledge, 1998.

Richardson, B. C. *The Caribbean in the Wider World, 1492–1992: A Regional Geography*. Cambridge, Cambridge University Press, 1992.

Sutton, P. *Dual Legacies in the Contemporary Caribbean: Continuing Aspects of British and French Domination*. London, Frank Cass, 1986.

Thomas, C. Y. *The Poor and the Powerless: Economic Policy and Change in the Caribbean*. New York, NY, Monthly Review Press, 1989.

Thomas-Hope, E. M. (Ed.). *Perspectives on Caribbean Regional Identity*. Liverpool, Centre for Latin American Studies, 1984.

Explanation in Caribbean Migration, Perception and the Image: Jamaica, Barbados, Saint Vincent. London, Macmillan, 1992.

Thompson, A. O. *The Haunting Past: Politics, Economics and Race in Caribbean Life.* Oxford, James Curry Publrs, 1997.

Williams, E. E. *From Columbus to Castro: The History of the Caribbean 1492–1969.* London, André Deutsch, 1970.

Worrell, D. *Small Island Economies; Structure and Performance in the English-Speaking Caribbean since 1970.* New York, NY, Praeger Publrs, 1987.

Wucker, M. *Why the Cocks Fight: Dominicans, Haitians, and the Struggle for Hispaniola.* New York, NY, Hill & Wang Publishing, 2000.

Young, A. H., and Phillips, D. E. *Militarization in the Non-Hispanic Caribbean.* London, Lynne Rienner, 1986.

INDEX OF REGIONAL ORGANIZATIONS

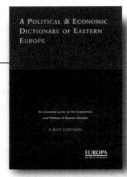

Europa's Regional Surveys of the World

A unique series of regularly revised reference titles aimed at businesses, libraries, universities, government departments, embassies, newspapers and international organizations

'Europa's Regional Surveys of the World are justly renowned for their exceptionally high levels of production, content and accuracy.' Reference Reviews

South America, Central America and the Caribbean

- An incomparable source of factual and statistical information for this vast region
- Reflects the very latest political and economic developments
- Includes contributions from over 30 leading authorities on Latin American and Caribbean affairs
- Provides a systematic survey of each country
- Enlightened commentary on topical issues, such as international trade and the banana war, the environment and the drug crisis

Africa South of the Sahara

- A one-volume library of essential data on all the countries of Sub-Saharan Africa
- Over 1,200 pages of economic and demographic statistics, wide-ranging directory material and authoritative articles
- Contributions from 50 leading experts on African affairs
- Incisive analysis and the latest available information
- Includes details of international organizations active in the region

Central and South Eastern Europe

- This title is one of the two new successor volumes to Europa's award-winning Eastern Europe and the Commonwealth of Independent States
- Includes country-by-country surveys, political, economic and social information
- Detailed articles by acknowledged experts cover issues of regional importance such as integration with the West, social policy and religion, the Macedonian Question
- Coverage of regional organizations, research institutes and periodicals
- A select bibliography and a political profile section

Western Europe

- Over 660 pages of statistics, directory and analytical information
- Introductory essays on the region cover political, economic and social issues ranging from the impact of the European Union to Western Europe's environmental politics and its relations with the wider world
- Acknowledged authorities write on regional and country-specific topics
- Chronologies detailing the history of each country

Eastern Europe, Russia and Central Asia

- This title is one of the two successor volumes to the award-winning Eastern Europe and the Commonwealth of Independent States
- Includes country-by-country surveys, political, economic and social information
- Articles by acknowledged authorities covering regional issues such as the politics of energy and the environment
- Coverage of regional organizations, institutes and periodicals
- A select bibliography and a political profile section

The Middle East and North Africa

- Covers the Middle Eastern world from Algeria to Yemen
- Draws together the events of the past twelve months
- Provides comprehensive information on the United Nations and all major international organizations operating in the area
- A detailed calendar of events, expert articles, up to date statistics and directory information
- An invaluable reference source in business matters relating to the area

The Far East and Australasia

- A systematic survey of all the countries of East Asia, South Asia, South-East Asia, Australasia and the Pacific Islands
- Essential for anyone with a professional interest in this part of the world, the book keeps you up to date with current economic and political developments
- Presents over 1,400 pages of statistics, directory information and expert analysis
- Provides details of all major international organizations active in the region

The USA and Canada

- Invaluable reference guide to the political, economic and social affairs of these two powerful North American nations
- Contributions from over 30 acknowledged authorities
- Specially commissioned articles cover issues such as the USA and the United Nations, Aboriginal Peoples in North America, the Canadian Economy
- Includes wide-ranging statistics and directory information
- Provides geographical and historical introductions to each state/province, data on the economies, and a comprehensive governmental and legislative directory section

For further information on any of the above titles contact our marketing department on:

tel. + 44 (0) 20 7842 2110   fax. + 44 (0) 20 7842 2249

e-mail info.europa@tandf.co.uk   www.europapublications.co.uk

Other Titles from Europa

Political Chronologies of the World Series

- Each of the six volumes profiles the major events in the histories of the region
- Includes an individual chronology for each country
- The chronologies provide concise details of events from early history to the mid-twentieth century and present greater detail on more recent events
- Available individually or as a six-volume set

A Political Chronology of Europe
A Political Chronology of Central, South and East Asia
A Political Chronology of the Middle East
A Political Chronology of Africa
A Political Chronology of South-East Asia and Oceania
A Political Chronology of the Americas

The International Who's Who of Women

- Over 5,500 detailed biographies of the most talented and distinguished women in the world today
- Includes women from all occupations, from Heads of State to supermodels
- Over 500 new entries for this edition
- Includes an extensive index by profession
- A must for libraries and press offices

Gutteridge and Megrah's Law of Bankers' Commerical Credits

- Presents a systematic study of the law of bankers' commercial credits
- Includes a table of cases and statutes relevant to bankers' commercial credits
- Provides information on the types of credit, mechanism and operation
- Discusses the legal aspects; relationship between buyer and seller; bankers' security

A Dictionary of Modern Politics

By David Robertson

- A thorough guide to the complex terminology and ideology which surrounds the world of politics
- Over 500 definitions/mini essays
- Defines political theories, ideas and "isms"
- Explains highly specialized terms
- Invaluable for anyone concerned with politics and current affairs

The International Directory of Government

- The definitive guide to people in power world-wide
- Details over 17,500 government ministries, departments, agencies, corporations and their connected bodies and people who work within them
- Also includes an outline of the each country's legislature and governmental system
- Explains the constitutional position of the head of state
- Entries contain: name and title of principal officials, postal and e-mail address, telephone, telex and fax numbers, and an outline of each organization's activities

International Relations Research Directory

- Directory information on every major research institute concerned with international relations throughout the world
- Provides details of institutes names, address, telephone, fax and e-mail, principal officers, date of foundation, activities and publications
- Lists periodicals and journals in the field of international relations with details of name, address, telephone, fax and e-mail, editor, publisher, date of foundation, subject of coverage, frequency and circulation

Who's Who in International Affairs

- Provides up-to-date biographical information on more than 7,000 principal figures in the fields of international politics, economics, legal, medical, cultural and scientific affairs
- Fully indexed by organization and nationality, it is a useful directory of international organizations as well as an invaluable A-Z guide of leading personalities
- Each entry contains, where available, name, nationality, date of birth, family details, education, career details, publications, contact address, telephone, fax numbers, e-mail addresses and leisure interests

Profiles of People in Power: the World's Government Leaders

- Individual country sections explain the types of government; the respective roles of the head of state, the head of government and the legislature
- Lists the most recent heads of state and head of goverment, with dates of office
- Biographical profiles of the current head of state and head of government and other significant past leaders who remain an active political presence
- Photographic section of many of the world's political leaders

For further information on any of the above titles contact our marketing department on:

tel. + 44 (0) 20 7842 2110   fax. + 44 (0) 20 7842 2249

e-mail info.europa@tandf.co.uk   www.europapublications.co.uk

EUROPA PUBLICATIONS · Taylor & Francis Group